Encyclopedia of Business Information Sources

ISSN 0071-0210

Encyclopedia of Business Information Sources

A Bibliographic Guide to More Than 34,000 Citations Covering Over 1,100 Subjects of Interest to Business Personnel

Includes: Abstracts and Indexes, Almanacs and Yearbooks, Bibliographies, Biographical Sources, CD-ROM Databases, Directories, Encyclopedias and Dictionaries, Financial Ratios, Handbooks and Manuals, Internet Databases, Online Databases, Periodicals and Newsletters, Price Sources, Research Centers and Institutes, Statistics Sources, Trade and Professional Societies, and Other Sources of Information on Each Topic

16th EDITION

James Woy,
Editor

GALE GROUP
THOMSON LEARNING
Detroit • New York • San Diego • San Francisco
Boston • New Haven, Conn. • Waterville, Maine
London • Munich

Editor: James Woy
Editorial Assistants: Jewel D. Phelps-Guinn, Elizabeth K. Secor

Gale Group Staff

Coordinating Editor: Linda D. Hall
Technical Training Specialist: Michael Weaver
Managing Editor: Keith Jones

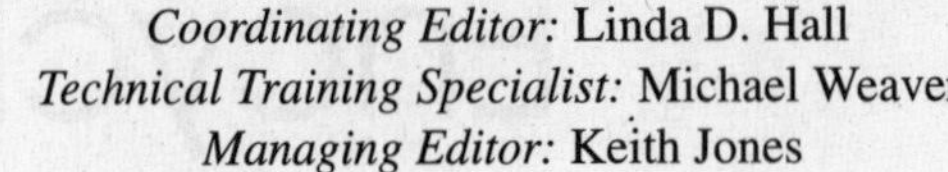

Theresa A. Rocklin, *Manager, Systems and Programming*
Charles Beaumont, *Programmer/Analyst*

Mary Beth Trimper, *Production Director*
Evi Seoud, *Assistant Production Manager*
Nekita McKee, *Production Assistant*

Manager of Data Capture Services: Ron Montgomery
Data Capture Coordinators: Gwen Tucker, Frances Monroe, Nekkita Bankston, Cynthia Jones

Graphic Services Manager: Barbara Yarrow
Product Design Manager: Cynthia Baldwin

ISBN 0-7876-3494-8
ISSN 0071-0210

Printed in the United States of America

Contents

Highlights of This Edition vii

Introduction ix

User's Guide xi

Outline of Contents xiii

Business Information Sources 1

Sources Cited 911

Highlights of This Edition

- ➤ 34,000 Citations
- ➤ Useful Web Sites Described
- ➤ E-mail Addresses Included
- ➤ Alphabetic "Sources Cited" Section

The *Encyclopedia of Business Information Sources (EBIS)* now includes more than 34,000 citations, dealing with more than 1,100 business, financial, and industrial topics. The subjects cover a variety of business-related concerns. These include, for example:

- ◆ Business functions—Accounting; Administration; Personnel Management
- ◆ Computer-related subjects—Computer Graphics; Computer Software Industry; Local Area Networks
- ◆ Foreign trade— International Marketing; Latin American Markets; North American Free Trade Agreement (NAFTA)
- ◆ Information industry topics—Electronic Publishing; Internet; Multimedia

Easy to Use

A convenient and accessible grouping of information sources is provided for each business topic, designed to reduce the time spent by busy librarians and business people in the search for key sources of information on specific subjects. An extensive Outline of Contents makes the exact heading for any subject easy to locate. Many cross-references provide additional assistance in finding needed information.

"Sources Cited" Section

For users with a specific title, organization, or service in mind, an alphabetic list of sources follows the main text. This Sources Cited section repeats all entries from the main text, sorting them alphabetically by publication title or organization name. The Sources Cited section also includes complete contact information.

Introduction

As the information needs of business managers and information professionals continue to increase, timely and convenient access becomes more valuable. The *Encyclopedia of Business Information Sources (EBIS)* is designed to assist these individuals in locating material relevant to today's rapidly-changing business environment.

The *Encyclopedia of Business Information Sources*, now in its 16th edition, is a primary place to look for information on business topics. Because business activity occurs in many different areas of human endeavor, the range of subjects in *EBIS* is very broad. A search can be initiated here for information sources on such general business topics as Accounting or Finance for sources on the business aspects of high-technology subjects, such as Electronics or Fiber Optics, or for sources on community-related topics—for example, Business Ethics or Social Responsibility. Users of EBIS have more 1,100 specific topics from which to choose.

EBIS simplifies the information-gathering process by making knowledge of important sources readily available, with the sources conveniently grouped according to specific subjects. Within these topics, there is the additional convenience of type-of-material categories: directories, periodicals, handbooks, and so forth.

EBIS thus serves two kinds of information needs—for a quick survey of publications and organizations relating to a particular topic, and for reference to a specific source that will provide a single fact or statistic.

Extensive Updating

Thousands of changes and additions were required to update this edition. Information was verified through reliable sources and independent research of the editorial staff. Current editions of *Gale's Encyclopedia of Associations* and *Research Centers Directory* were used to update nonprint sources in the categories of "Trade Associations and Professional Societies" and "Research Centers and Institutes."

Standard business or economic compilations, such as the annual *Economic Report of the President* and Robert Morris Associates' *Annual Statement Studies*, have been carefully examined and entered under topics for which these publications contain significant data.

Many out-of-print and discontinued items have been deleted from this edition of *EBIS,* although a few titles considered to be unique or of particular interest have been retained. Should it be desirable to consult these works, they may be available at local libraries.

New material for this edition has been collected in various ways. These include examining publishers' catalogs or brochures, reviewing material in business libraries, scanning lists of recommended titles, and discussing publications with business librarians. Publishers' Internet Web pages have also been useful.

Online Database Vendors

With regard to online databases included in *EBIS,* it should be noted that many of them are available through the following widely-used online information services:

DataStar
The Dialog Corporation
11000 Regency Parkway, Suite 10
Cary, NC 27511
(800)332-2564 or (919)462-8600
Fax: (919)468-9890
http://www.dialog.com

DIALOG
The Dialog Corporation
11000 Regency Parkway, Suite 10
Cary, NC 27511
(800)334-2564 or (919)462-8600
Fax: (919)468-9890
http://www.dialog.com

InfoTrac
Gale Group, Inc
27500 Drake Road
Farmington Hills, MI 48331-3535
(800)877-4253 or (248) 699-4253
Fax: (800) 414-5043 or (248)699-8096
http://www.gale.com/gale/infotrac

LEXIS-NEXIS
Reed-Elsevier Inc.
P. O. Box 933
Dayton, OH 45401-0933
(800)227-4908 or (937)865-6800
Fax: (937)865-6909
http://www.lexisnexis.com

OCLC FirstSearch
OCLC Online Computer Library Center, Inc.
6565 Frantz Rd.
Dublin, OH 43017-3395
(800)848-5878 or (614)764-6000
Fax: (614)764-6096
http://www.oclc.org

Ovid Technologies, Inc.
333 Seventh Ave., Fourth Floor
New York, NY 10001
(800)950-2035 or (646)674-6300
Fax: (212)563-3784
http://www.ovid.com

Questel-Orbit, Inc.
8000 Westpark Drive
McLean, VA 22102
(800)456-7248 or (703)442-0900
Fax: (703)893-4632
http://www.questel.orbit.com

WESTLAW
West Group
620 Opperman Drive
Eagan, MN 55123
(800)328-4880 or (651)687-7000
Fax: (612)687-5827
http://www.westlaw.com

Available in Electronic Format

EBIS is available for licensing on magnetic tape or diskette in a fielded format. Either the complete database or a custom selection of entries may be ordered. The database is available for internal data processing and nonpublishing purposes only. For more information, call 800-877-4253.

Suggestions Are Welcome

Although considerable attention that has been directed toward keeping errors and inconsistencies to a minimum, some have no doubt occurred. Corrections or suggestions for improvement of future editions are greatly appreciated. Please send to:

Editor
Encyclopedia of Business Information Sources
The Gale Group
27500 Drake Road
Farmington Hills, MI 48331-3535
Phone: 800-877-4253

User's Guide

◆ Main Section ◆

Arrangement of the Entries

In the main section of the *Encyclopedia of Business Information Sources (EBIS),* entries are arranged alphabetically by ❶ topic, and further subdivided by ❷ type of source and ❸ publication title or organization name. For example:

❶ CORPORATE FINANCE

❷ DIRECTORIES

❸ *America's Corporate Finance Directory.* National Register Publishing Co., Reed Elsevier Inc. Annual. $730.00. A directory of financial information, covering 5,000 major U. S. corporations.

❸ *Corporate Finance Sourcebook.* National Register Publishing Co., Reed Elsevier Inc. Annual. $650.00. Lists more than 3,700 organizations providing corporate capital.

❷ ONLINE DATABASES

❸ *ABI/INFORM.* Proquest Co. Provides online indexing to business-related material occurring in more than 1,000 periodicals from 1971 to the present. Inquire as to online cost and availability.

❷ RESEARCH CENTERS AND INSTITUTES

❸ Bendheim Center for Finance. Princeton University, Dept. of Economics, Princeton, NJ 08544. Phone: (609)258-4023. Fax: (609)258-6419.

Locate Topics in the Outline of Contents Section

EBIS covers more than 1,100 topics. The efficient way to locate a particular topic is to scan the Outline of Contents section which follows this User's Guide. The Outline of Contents lists the topics alphabetically.

Users can determine at a glance the specific form of the subject term that has been employed. Numerous cross-references provide assistance where necessary. If the term being sought—for example, Cellular Telephones—has not been used as a subject heading, the Outline of Contents will refer to the term actually used. In this case, sources about Cellular Telephones will be found under Mobile Telephone Industry.

18 Kinds of Sources

Material under each topic is grouped according to the type of source or form in which the information is provided. A user can look under the topic of interest (Corporate Finance, for example) to find key information sources arranged as follows:

- General Works
- Abstracts and Indexing Services
- Almanacs and Yearbooks
- Bibliographies
- Biographical Sources
- CD-ROM Databases
- Directories
- Encyclopedias and Dictionaries
- Financial Ratios
- Handbooks and Manuals
- Internet Databases
- Online Databases
- Periodicals and Newsletters
- Price Sources
- Research Centers and Institutes
- Statistics Sources
- Trade/Professional Associations
- Other Sources

Content of the Entries

The content of the entries is described here and illustrated in the sample entries that appear on the previous page.

- Entries for publications and online databases list the title of the work, the name of the author (where applicable), the name of the publisher or provider, frequency or year of publication, and price. Brief descriptive notes are often added to clarify listings. Entries included in the "Internet Databases" category provide the name of the Web site, the name of the provider or host, telephone/fax numbers, E-mail address, the URL address, and information on content and cost (most are free).

- Entries for trade associations and research centers provide the organization name, address, telephone/fax numbers, and Internet information where available. Many of these entries include a brief description of the organization.

◆ Sources Cited Section ◆

Arrangement of the Entries

In this section the entries are arranged alphabetically by publication title, database title, or organization name. The Sources Cited section repeats all of the entries from the main section of *EBIS*.

Contact Information

The Sources Cited section is where contact information will be found for print publishers and for publishers or providers of online databases. Generally supplies are postal addresses, telephone/fax numbers, and Internet addresses for Web sites and e-mail.

Outline of Contents

Abbreviations 1
Abrasives Industry 1
Absenteeism 1
Academic Degrees 1
Academic Dissertations—*See:* Dissertations
Accident Insurance 2
Accidents 2
Accountability, Social—*See:* Social Responsibility
Accountants—*See:* Certified Public Accountants
Accounting 3
Accounting, Bank—*See:* Bank Accounting
Accounting, Computers in—*See:* Computers in Accounting
Accounting, Cost—*See:* Cost Accounting
Accounting, Government—*See:* Government Accounting
Accounting Research 5
Acid Rain 6
Acoustical Engineering—*See:* Noise Control
Acquisitions and Mergers—*See:* Mergers and Acquisitions
Actuarial Science 6
Additives and Flavorings 6
Adhesives 7
Administration 8
Administrative Decision Making—*See:* Decision-Making
Administrative Law and Regulation 10
Adult Education 10
Advertising 11
Advertising Agencies 12
Advertising Art—*See:* Commercial Art
Advertising, Cooperative—*See:* Cooperative Advertising
Advertising Copy 13
Advertising, Industrial—*See:* Industrial Advertising
Advertising Law and Regulation 13
Advertising Media 14
Advertising, Point-of-Sale—*See:* Point-of-Purchase Advertising
Advertising Research 15
Advertising Specialties 15
Advisory Services—*See:* Investment Advisory Services
Aerosol Industry—*See:* Pressure Packaging
Aerospace Industry 16
Affirmative Action Programs 17
Affluent Market 17
After-Dinner Speaking—*See:* Public Speaking
Age and Employment—*See:* Employment of Older Workers
Aging—*See:* Retirement
Agreements—*See:* Contracts
Agribusiness 18
Agricultural Chemicals 19
Agricultural Credit 20
Agricultural Economics 20
Agricultural Extension Work 21
Agricultural Foreign Trade—*See:* Foreign Agriculture
Agricultural Labor—*See:* Farmers; Labor
Agricultural Machinery 21
Agricultural Market—*See:* Farm Markets
Agricultural Products—*See:* Farm Produce
Agricultural Statistics 22
Agricultural Surpluses—*See:* Farm Produce
Agriculture 22
Agronomy—*See:* Agriculture
AIDS Policy 24
Air Bases—*See:* Air Force
Air Cargo—*See:* Air Freight
Air Conditioning Industry 25
Air Force 26
Air Freight 26
Air Pilots 27
Air Pollution 28
Air Traffic—*See:* Air Travel
Air Transportation—*See:* Air Freight; Air Travel; Airline Industry
Air Travel 29
Aircraft Industry—*See:* Airplane Industry
Aircraft Owners and Pilots—*See:* Air Pilots; Business Aviation
Airline Industry 30
Airlines Time Tables—*See:* Timetables
Airplane Electronics—*See:* Avionics
Airplane Industry 32
Airplanes, Business—*See:* Business Aviation
Airports 33
Alarms—*See:* Electronic Security Systems
Alcohol as Fuel—*See:* Fuel
Alcoholic Beverages—*See:* Distilling Industry
Alcoholism 34
Alkali Industry 34
Alloys—*See:* Metal Industry
Aluminum Foil—*See:* Aluminum Industry

Aluminum Industry 35
American Stock Exchange—*See:* Stock Exchanges
Amusement Industry 36
Amusement Parks—*See:* Amusement Industry
Animal Industry—*See:* Livestock Industry
Animation, Computer—*See:* Computer Animation
Anniversaries and Holidays 36
Annual Reports of Corporations—*See:* Corporation Reports
Annual Wage Plans—*See:* Wages and Salaries
Annuities 37
Annuity Tables—*See:* Interest
Answering Service—*See:* Telephone Answering Service
Anthracite Coal—*See:* Coal Industry
Antimony Industry—*See:* Metal Industry
Antiques as an Investment 38
Antitrust Actions 38
Anxiety—*See:* Stress (Anxiety)
Apartment Houses 38
Apparatus, Scientific—*See:* Scientific Apparatus and Instrument Industries
Apparel, Children's—*See:* Children's Apparel Industry
Apparel Industry—*See:* Clothing Industry
Apparel, Men's—*See:* Men's Clothing Industry
Apparel, Women's—*See:* Women's Apparel
Apple Industry 39
Appliances—*See:* Electric Appliance Industry
Applications for Positions—*See:* Job Resumes
Appraisal (All Property)—*See:* Valuation
Appraisal of Real Estate—*See:* Real Property Valuation
Aquaculture 40
Arbitration 40
Architecture 41
Archives Management—*See:* Records Management
Area Development—*See:* Industrial Development
Armament and Defense—*See:* Defense Industries
Armaments Market—*See:* Military Market
Army 42
Art as an Investment 42
Art Business 43
Art, Commercial—*See:* Commercial Art
Art Dealers—*See:* Art Business
Art in Industry 44
Artificial Intelligence 44
Artificial Limbs—*See:* Prosthetics Industry
Arts Management 46
Asbestos Industry 47
Asian Markets 47
Asphalt Industry 50
Associations 50
Associations, International—*See:* International Agencies
Astronautics—*See:* Rocket Industry
Athletic Goods—*See:* Sporting Goods Industry
Atlases—*See:* Maps
Atomic Power—*See:* Nuclear Energy
Attorneys—*See:* Lawyers
Auctions 52
Audience Research—*See:* Advertising Media; Market Research
Audio Equipment Industry—*See:* High Fidelity/Stereo
Audiovisual Aids in Education 52
Audiovisual Aids in Industry 52
Audiovisual Equipment Industry 53
Auditing 53
Auditing, Internal—*See:* Internal Auditing
Authorities—*See:* Consultants
Authors—*See:* Writers and Writing
Automated Teller Machines (ATM)—*See:* Bank Automation
Automatic Control Equipment—*See:* Scientific Apparatus and Instrument Industries
Automatic Data Systems—*See:* Automation; Computers; Systems in Management
Automatic Identification Systems 54
Automatic Translating—*See:* Machine Translating
Automation 55
Automation, Bank—*See:* Bank Automation
Automation, Library—*See:* Library Automation
Automation, Office—*See:* Office Automation
Automation, Retail—*See:* Point-of-Sale Systems (POS)
Automatons—*See:* Robots
Automobile Accessories Industry—*See:* Automobile Equipment Industry
Automobile Accidents—*See:* Traffic Accidents and Traffic Safety
Automobile Batteries—*See:* Battery Industry
Automobile Dealers 56
Automobile Equipment Industry 56
Automobile Industry—*See:* Automotive Industry
Automobile Insurance 57
Automobile Laws—*See:* Motor Vehicle Law and Regulation
Automobile Lease and Rental Services 57
Automobile Licenses—*See:* Motor Vehicle Law and Regulation
Automobile Parts Industry—*See:* Automobile Equipment Industry
Automobile Rental Services—*See:* Automobile Lease and Rental Services
Automobile Repair Industry 58
Automobile Road Guides—*See:* Maps
Automobile Service Stations—*See:* Gasoline Service Stations
Automobile Telephones—*See:* Mobile Telephone Industry
Automobiles 58
Automobiles, Used—*See:* Used Car Industry
Automotive Industry 59
AV Equipment Industry—*See:* Audiovisual Equipment Industry
Aviation, Business—*See:* Business Aviation
Aviation Electronics—*See:* Avionics
Aviation Industry 61
Avionics 62
Awards—*See:* Contests, Prizes, and Awards
Baby Clothes—*See:* Children's Apparel Industry
Baby Sitting 63

Bag Industry—*See:* Paper Bag Industry
Baking Industry . . . 63
Balance of Payments . . . 64
Balance of Trade—*See:* Balance of Payments; Foreign Trade
Ball Bearings—*See:* Bearings and Ball Bearings
Ball Point Pens—*See:* Writing Instruments
Banana Industry . . . 65
Bank Accounting . . . 65
Bank Automation . . . 65
Bank Credit—*See:* Bank Loans
Bank Deposits . . . 66
Bank Failures . . . 66
Bank Finance—*See:* Bank Loans
Bank Law—*See:* Banking Law and Regulation
Bank Loans . . . 67
Bank Management . . . 69
Bank Marketing . . . 69
Bank Reserves . . . 70
Bank Technology—*See:* Bank Automation
Bank Teller Machines—*See:* Bank Automation
Banking Law and Regulation . . . 70
Bankruptcy . . . 71
Banks and Banking . . . 72
Bar Codes—*See:* Automatic Identification Systems; Point-of-Sale Systems (POS)
Barber and Beauty Shops . . . 75
Barley Industry—*See:* Agriculture
Barrels—*See:* Cooperage Industry
Barter and Countertrade . . . 76
Battery Industry . . . 76
Bauxite—*See:* Mines and Mineral Resources
Bazaars—*See:* Fairs
Bean Industry—*See:* Agriculture; Canned Food Industry
Bearings and Ball Bearings . . . 77
Beauty Industry—*See:* Barber and Beauty Shops; Cosmetics Industry
Beauty Shops and Barber Shops—*See:* Barber and Beauty Shops
Bedding Industry—*See:* Furniture Industry
Bee Industry—*See:* Honey Industry
Beef Industry—*See:* Cattle Industry
Beer Industry—*See:* Brewing Industry
Beets and Beet Sugar Industry—*See:* Sugar Industry
Behavioral Sciences—*See:* Human Relations; Industrial Psychology
Benefits, Employee—*See:* Employee Benefit Plans
Bequests—*See:* Wills
Beryllium Industry—*See:* Metal Industry
Better Business Bureaus . . . 77
Beverage Industry . . . 77
Bibliography . . . 78
Bicycle Industry . . . 79
Billboards—*See:* Outdoor Advertising
Binding of Books—*See:* Bookbinding
Bioengineering—*See:* Biotechnology
Biography . . . 79
Biotechnology . . . 80
Birth Certificates—*See:* Vital Statistics
Births and Deaths—*See:* Vital Statistics
Bituminous Coal—*See:* Coal Industry
Black Business—*See:* Minority Business
Black Consumers—*See:* Minority Markets
Black Newspapers—*See:* Minority Newspapers
Blood Pressure—*See:* Hypertension
Blue Collar Theft—*See:* Crime and Criminals; Fraud and Embezzlement
Blue Collar Workers—*See:* Labor
Blue Sky Law—*See:* Securities Law and Regulation
Boarding Schools—*See:* Private Schools
Boards of Directors—*See:* Corporate Directors and Officers
Boards of Trade—*See:* Chambers of Commerce
Boat Industry . . . 83
Boilers—*See:* Heating and Ventilation
Bonds . . . 83
Bonds, Government—*See:* Government Bonds
Bonds, Junk—*See:* Junk Bond Financing
Bonds, Municipal—*See:* Municipal Bonds
Book Catalogs . . . 85
Book Collecting . . . 86
Book Industry . . . 86
Book Reviews . . . 87
Book Stores—*See:* Bookselling
Bookbinding . . . 87
Bookkeeping—*See:* Accounting
Bookseller's Catalogs—*See:* Book Catalogs
Bookselling . . . 88
Boots and Shoes—*See:* Shoe Industry
Boring Machinery—*See:* Machinery
Botany, Economic—*See:* Economic Botany
Bottle Industry—*See:* Container Industry; Glass Container Industry
Bottled Water Industry—*See:* Water Supply
Box Industry . . . 89
Boxes, Paper—*See:* Paper Box and Paper Container Industries
Boy's Clothing—*See:* Children's Apparel Industry; Men's Clothing Industry
Brainstorming—*See:* Creativity
Branch Stores—*See:* Chain Stores
Brand Awareness Studies—*See:* Market Research
Brand Names—*See:* Trademarks and Trade Names
Bread Industry—*See:* Baking Industry
Brewing Industry . . . 89
Bribes and Payoffs—*See:* Business Ethics
Brick Industry—*See:* Clay Industry; Refractories
Broadcasting—*See:* Radio Broadcasting Industry; Television Broadcasting Industry
Brokers, Stock—*See:* Stock Brokers
Budget, Federal—*See:* Federal Budget
Budgeting, Business . . . 90
Budgeting, Personal—*See:* Personal Finance

Building and Loan Associations—*See:* Savings and Loan Associations
Building Contracts 90
Building Equipment—*See:* Construction Equipment
Building Estimating—*See:* Estimating
Building Industry 91
Building Loans—*See:* Mortgages
Building Maintenance—*See:* Maintenance of Buildings
Building Management—*See:* Property Management
Building Materials Industry 93
Building Repair and Reconstruction—*See:* Home Improvement Industry
Building Research 94
Building Stone—*See:* Quarrying
Building Supply Industry—*See:* Building Materials Industry
Buildings, Prefabricated—*See:* Prefabricated House Industry
Buildings, Residential—*See:* Housing
Bullion—*See:* Money
Bureaucracy 94
Bureaus of Business Research 95
Burglar Alarms—*See:* Electronic Security Systems
Burlap Industry 95
Bus Line Time Tables—*See:* Timetables
Buses—*See:* Motor Buses
Business 96
Business Administration—*See:* Administration
Business Airplanes—*See:* Business Aviation
Business and Government—*See:* Regulation of Industry
Business and Professional Women—*See:* Employment of Women
Business and Society—*See:* Social Responsibility
Business Appraisal—*See:* Valuation
Business Archives—*See:* Records Management
Business Aviation 99
Business Brokers—*See:* Business Enterprises, Sale of
Business Budgeting—*See:* Budgeting, Business
Business Choice—*See:* Occupations
Business Colleges—*See:* Business Education; Colleges and Universities
Business Communication—*See:* Business Correspondence; Communication
Business Conditions 100
Business Consolidation—*See:* Mergers and Acquisitions
Business Consultants—*See:* Consultants; Management Consultants
Business Correspondence 102
Business Cycles 102
Business Depressions—*See:* Business Cycles
Business Directories—*See:* Catalogs and Directories
Business Economics 103
Business Education 104
Business Enterprises, Sale of 105
Business Ethics 105
Business Etiquette—*See:* Etiquette
Business Failures 106
Business Fiction—*See:* Business in Fiction
Business Films—*See:* Audiovisual Aids in Industry
Business Finance—*See:* Finance; Financial Analysis
Business Flying—*See:* Air Travel; Airline Industry; Business Aviation
Business Forecasting 106
Business Forms—*See:* Forms and Blanks
Business Gifts—*See:* Gift Business
Business History 108
Business in Fiction 109
Business Indicators—*See:* Economic Indicators
Business Information Sources—*See:* Information Sources
Business Innovation 109
Business Intelligence—*See:* Competitive Intelligence
Business, International—*See:* International Business
Business Interruption Insurance 109
Business Journalism 110
Business Law 110
Business Letters—*See:* Business Correspondence
Business Libraries—*See:* Special Libraries
Business Literature 111
Business Loans—*See:* Bank Loans
Business Machines—*See:* Office Equipment and Supplies
Business Management—*See:* Administration; Industrial Management
Business Marketing—*See:* Industrial Marketing
Business Mathematics 112
Business Mergers—*See:* Mergers and Acquisitions
Business Morale—*See:* Human Relations
Business Organization and Administration—*See:* Industrial Management
Business Periodicals—*See:* Trade Journals
Business Planning—*See:* Business Start-Up Plans and Proposals; Planning
Business Proposals—*See:* Business Start-Up Plans and Proposals
Business Psychology—*See:* Industrial Psychology
Business Ratios—*See:* Financial Ratios
Business Records Management—*See:* Records Management
Business Reports—*See:* Corporation Reports; Report Writing
Business Research 113
Business Responsibility—*See:* Social Responsibility
Business Schools—*See:* Business Education
Business, Small—*See:* Small Business
Business Start-Up Plans and Proposals 114
Business Statistics 115
Business Strategy 117
Business to Business Marketing—*See:* Industrial Marketing
Business Travel 117
Business Trends—*See:* Business Cycles; Business Forecasting
Business Valuation—*See:* Valuation
Business Writing—*See:* Business Correspondence; Report Writing; Writers and Writing
Businessmen in Fiction—*See:* Business in Fiction
Butane—*See:* Propane and Butane Gas Industry
Butcher Shops—*See:* Meat Industry

Butter Industry—*See:* Dairy Industry
Buying—*See:* Purchasing
Buying a Business—*See:* Business Enterprises, Sale of
Buying Power—*See:* Purchasing Power
Buyouts, Leveraged—*See:* Leveraged Buyouts
By-Products—*See:* Waste Products
Cable Addresses 121
Cable Television Industry 121
CAD/CAM—*See:* Computer-Aided Design and Manufacturing (CAD/CAM)
Cafeterias—*See:* Restaurants, Lunchrooms, Etc.
Cafeterias, Employee—*See:* Employee Lunchrooms and Cafeterias
Calendar—*See:* Chronology
Camcorders—*See:* Video Recording Industry
Camera Industry 122
Camper Industry—*See:* Recreational Vehicle Industry
Camping Industry—*See:* Recreation Industry
Canadian Markets 123
Candy Industry 125
Canned Beverages—*See:* Beverage Industry
Canned Food Industry 126
Canvassing—*See:* Direct Marketing
Capital Equipment—*See:* Industrial Equipment Industry
Capital Gains Tax 126
Capital, Venture—*See:* Venture Capital
Car Phones—*See:* Mobile Telephone Industry
Carbonated Beverages—*See:* Beverage Industry
Cards, Greeting—*See:* Greeting Card Industry
Career Planning—*See:* Vocational Guidance
Careers—*See:* Job Hunting; Occupations
Caribbean Area—*See:* Latin American Markets
Carpentry 127
Carpet Cleaning Industry—*See:* Cleaning Industry
Carpet Industry—*See:* Floor Coverings; Oriental Rug Industry
Carriers—*See:* Automobiles; Freight Transport
Cartography—*See:* Maps
Carwash Industry 127
Case Studies 127
Cash Flow and Cash Management 128
Casinos—*See:* Gambling Industry
Casks—*See:* Cooperage Industry
Cassette Recording—*See:* Sound Recorders and Recording; Video Recording Industry
Casting—*See:* Foundries
Castor Bean Industry—*See:* Oil and Fats Industry
Casualty Insurance 128
Catalogs and Directories 129
Caterers and Catering 130
Cattle Industry 130
CATV—*See:* Cable Television Industry
CD-ROM Devices—*See:* Multimedia; Optical Disk Storage Devices
Cellular Telephones—*See:* Mobile Telephone Industry
Cement Industry 131
Cemeteries—*See:* Funeral Homes and Directors
Census Reports 132
Central America—*See:* Latin American Markets
Ceramic Tile Industry—*See:* Tile Industry
Ceramics Industry 133
Cereal Industry—*See:* Grain Industry
Certified Public Accountants 134
Chain Stores 135
Chambers of Commerce 136
Charitable Trusts—*See:* Foundations
Charity—*See:* Philanthropy
Charts—*See:* Graphs and Charts
Charts, Stock Market—*See:* Technical Analysis (Finance)
Checkless Banking—*See:* Electronic Funds Transfer Systems (EFTS)
Cheese Industry 136
Chemical Engineering 137
Chemical Industries 138
Chemical Laboratories—*See:* Laboratories
Chemical Marketing 140
Child Care—*See:* Day Care Centers
Child Labor 140
Child Market—*See:* Youth Market
Children's Apparel Industry 140
China—*See:* Asian Markets
Chinaware—*See:* Tableware
Chlorine Industry—*See:* Chemical Industries
Chocolate Industry 141
Christmas Cards—*See:* Greeting Card Industry
Chromium Industry—*See:* Metal Industry
Chronology 141
Cigar and Cigarette Industry 142
Cigarette Industry—*See:* Cigar and Cigarette Industry
Cinema—*See:* Motion Picture Theaters
Cinematography—*See:* Motion Picture Photography
Circulation Management (Publishing) 142
Cities and Towns 143
Citizenship 145
Citrus Fruit Industry 145
City Attorneys—*See:* Municipal Government
City Clerks—*See:* Municipal Government
City Finance—*See:* Municipal Finance
City Government—*See:* Municipal Government
City Planning 146
Civil Engineering 147
Civil Rights 147
Civil Service 148
Clay Industry 149
Cleaning Compositions—*See:* Cleaning Products Industry
Cleaning Industry 150
Cleaning Products Industry 150
Climate 151
Clinical Laboratory Industry 152
Clipping Services 152
Clock and Watch Industry 152
Closed-end Funds 153

Closely Held Corporations 153
Clothing, Children's—*See:* Children's Apparel Industry
Clothing Industry 154
Clothing, Men's—*See:* Men's Clothing Industry
Clothing, Women's—*See:* Women's Apparel
Clubs 155
Clubs, Women's—*See:* Women's Clubs
Coal Gasification—*See:* Energy Sources
Coal Industry 155
Coal Mining Industry—*See:* Coal Industry
Coal Tar Products—*See:* Chemical Industries
Coast Guard 157
Coatings, Industrial—*See:* Industrial Coatings
Cobalt Industry—*See:* Metal Industry
Cocoa Industry 157
Coconut Oil Industry—*See:* Oil and Fats Industry
Coding, Product—*See:* Point-of-Sale Systems (POS)
Coffee Industry 157
Cogeneration of Energy 158
Coin Machines—*See:* Vending Machines
Coins as an Investment 159
Coke Industry 159
Cold Storage Warehouses—*See:* Refrigeration Industry; Warehouses
Collectibles—*See:* Antiques as an Investment; Art as an Investment; Coins as an Investment; Hobby Industry
Collecting of Accounts 159
Collective Bargaining 160
College and School Newspapers 160
College and University Libraries 161
College Degrees—*See:* Academic Degrees
College Enrollment 161
College Entrance Requirements 162
College Faculties 162
College Instructors and Professors—*See:* College Faculties
College Libraries—*See:* College and University Libraries
College Newspapers—*See:* College and School Newspapers
College Placement Bureaus 163
College Presidents 163
College Publishers—*See:* University Presses
College Stores 163
College Teachers—*See:* College Faculties
Colleges and Universities 163
Color in Industry 165
Color Photography—*See:* Photographic Industry
Color Television—*See:* Television Apparatus Industry
Columnists—*See:* Writers and Writing
Commercial Art 166
Commercial Aviation—*See:* Business Aviation
Commercial Code—*See:* Business Law
Commercial Correspondence—*See:* Business Correspondence
Commercial Credit—*See:* Commercial Lending
Commercial Education—*See:* Business Education
Commercial Finance Companies—*See:* Finance Companies
Commercial Law and Regulation—*See:* Business Law
Commercial Lending 166
Commercial Photography 167
Commercial Real Estate—*See:* Industrial Real Estate
Commercial Statistics—*See:* Business Statistics
Commodities 167
Commodity Exchanges—*See:* Commodity Futures Trading
Commodity Futures Trading 168
Common Market—*See:* European Markets
Communication 170
Communication, Computer—*See:* Computer Communications
Communication Equipment Industry—*See:* Telecommunications; Telephone Industry
Communication, Mass—*See:* Mass Media
Communication Systems 171
Communications Satellites 172
Community Antenna Television—*See:* Cable Television Industry
Community Chests—*See:* Community Funds
Community Colleges—*See:* Junior Colleges
Community Development 173
Community Funds 174
Community Planning—*See:* City Planning
Community Relations 174
Community Shopping Centers—*See:* Shopping Centers
Commuter Airlines—*See:* Airline Industry
Compact Discs—*See:* Optical Disk Storage Devices
Companies—*See:* Corporations; Industry; Private Companies
Company Anniversaries—*See:* Anniversaries and Holidays
Company Histories—*See:* Business History
Compensation of Employees—*See:* Wages and Salaries
Compensation of Executives—*See:* Executive Compensation
Competitive Intelligence 175
Composite Materials 176
Compressors—*See:* Pumps and Compressors
Comptrollers—*See:* Corporate Directors and Officers
Computer Accessories—*See:* Computer Peripherals and Accessories
Computer-Aided Design and Manufacturing (CAD/CAM) 178
Computer Animation 178
Computer Bulletin Boards—*See:* Computer Communications
Computer Communications 179
Computer Crime and Security 182
Computer Dealers—*See:* Computer Retailing
Computer Graphics 183
Computer Imaging—*See:* Document Imaging
Computer Industry—*See:* Computers; Microcomputers and Minicomputers
Computer Integrated Manufacturing (CIM)—*See:* Computer-Aided Design and Manufacturing (CAD/CAM); Systems Integration
Computer Law 184
Computer Networks—*See:* Computer Communications; Local Area Networks
Computer Output Microfilm (COM)—*See:* Microforms

Computer Peripherals and Accessories 185
Computer Programming—*See:* Computer Software Industry
Computer Resellers—*See:* Computer Retailing
Computer Retailing 187
Computer Security—*See:* Computer Crime and Security
Computer Software Industry 187
Computer Stores—*See:* Computer Retailing
Computer Viruses—*See:* Computer Crime and Security
Computer Vision—*See:* Machine Vision
Computerized Translation—*See:* Machine Translating
Computers 189
Computers, Home—*See:* Microcomputers and Minicomputers
Computers in Accounting 192
Computers in Banking—*See:* Bank Automation; Computers in Finance
Computers in Education 193
Computers in Finance 194
Computers in Government 194
Computers in Investing—*See:* Computers in Finance
Computers in Libraries—*See:* Library Automation; Online Information Systems
Computers, Personal—*See:* Microcomputers and Minicomputers
Computers, Portable—*See:* Portable Computers
Concessions 195
Conciliation, Industrial—*See:* Arbitration
Concrete Industry 195
Condiments Industry—*See:* Spice Industry
Condominiums 196
Confectionery Industry—*See:* Candy Industry
Conference Management—*See:* Meeting Management
Conferences, Workshops, and Seminars 196
Conflict Management—*See:* Arbitration; Negotiation
Conglomerates—*See:* Corporations
Congress—*See:* United States Congress
Conservation—*See:* Natural Resources
Construction Contracts—*See:* Building Contracts
Construction, Electrical—*See:* Electrical Construction Industry
Construction Equipment 197
Construction Estimating—*See:* Estimating
Construction Industries, Electrical—*See:* Electrical Construction Industry
Construction Industry—*See:* Building Industry
Consular Service—*See:* Diplomatic and Consular Service
Consultants 197
Consultants, Engineering—*See:* Engineering Consultants
Consultants, Management—*See:* Management Consultants
Consumer Affairs 198
Consumer Credit 199
Consumer Economics 200
Consumer Education 201
Consumer Electronics 201
Consumer Finance Companies—*See:* Finance Companies
Consumer Loans—*See:* Consumer Credit
Consumer Price Indexes 202
Consumer Research—*See:* Consumer Economics
Consumer Surveys 203
Consumers' Cooperative Societies—*See:* Cooperatives
Consumers' Leagues—*See:* Cooperatives
Consumers, Mature—*See:* Mature Consumer Market
Consumers' Products Research—*See:* Quality of Products
Contact Lens and Intraocular Lens Industries 204
Container Industry 204
Contests, Prizes, and Awards 205
Contractions—*See:* Abbreviations
Contractors—*See:* Building Contracts; Building Industry
Contractors, Electrical—*See:* Electrical Construction Industry
Contracts 205
Contracts, Government—*See:* Government Contracts
Control Equipment Industry 206
Controllers—*See:* Corporate Directors and Officers
Convenience Stores 207
Convention Management—*See:* Meeting Management
Conventions 208
Convertibility of Currency—*See:* Foreign Exchange
Convertible Securities 208
Conveying Machinery 209
Cookie Industry—*See:* Baking Industry; Snack Food Industry
Cooking Utensils—*See:* Housewares Industry
Cookware—*See:* Housewares Industry
Cooperage Industry 209
Cooperative Advertising 209
Cooperative Agriculture—*See:* Cooperatives
Cooperative Housing—*See:* Condominiums; Cooperatives
Cooperative Movement—*See:* Cooperatives
Cooperatives 210
Copiers—*See:* Copying Machine Industry
Copper Industry 210
Copying Machine Industry 211
Copyright 211
Copywriting—*See:* Advertising Copy
Cordage Industry—*See:* Rope and Twine Industry
Corn Industry 212
Corporate Acquisitions and Mergers—*See:* Mergers and Acquisitions
Corporate Culture 213
Corporate Directors and Officers 213
Corporate Finance 214
Corporate Formation—*See:* Incorporation
Corporate Giving—*See:* Philanthropy
Corporate Histories—*See:* Business History
Corporate Image 217
Corporate Income Tax 217
Corporate Planning—*See:* Planning
Corporate Real Estate—*See:* Industrial Real Estate
Corporate Responsibility—*See:* Social Responsibility
Corporation Law and Regulation 218
Corporation Reports 219
Corporations 220

Corporations, Closely Held—*See:* Closely Held Corporations; Private Companies
Corporations, Multinational—*See:* Multinational Corporations
Corporations, Professional—*See:* Professional Corporations
Correctional Institutions—*See:* Law Enforcement Industries
Correspondence—*See:* Business Correspondence
Correspondence Schools and Courses 223
Corrosion Control Industry 223
Corrugated Paperboard—*See:* Paperboard and Paperboard Packaging Industries
Cosmetics Industry 224
Cost Accounting 225
Cost Control 225
Cost of Living Indexes—*See:* Consumer Price Indexes
Costume Jewelry—*See:* Jewelry Business
Cotton Industry 226
Cotton Textile Industry—*See:* Textile Industry
Cottonseed Oil Industry—*See:* Oil and Fats Industry
Council Manager Plan—*See:* Municipal Government
Counseling 227
Counterfeiting 227
Countertrade—*See:* Barter and Countertrade
Country Clubs—*See:* Clubs
County Finance 228
County Government 228
County Officials—*See:* County Government
County Planning—*See:* Regional Planning
Coupons and Refunds 228
Courts 228
Cracker Industry—*See:* Baking Industry; Snack Food Industry
Crafts—*See:* Gift Business; Hobby Industry
Creativity 229
Credit 230
Credit, Bank—*See:* Bank Loans
Credit Card Industry 231
Credit, Consumer—*See:* Consumer Credit
Credit Insurance 232
Credit Management 232
Credit Unions 232
Crime and Criminals 233
Crime, Computer—*See:* Computer Crime and Security
Critical Path Method/PERT (Program Evaluation and Review Technique) 235
Crops—*See:* Farm Produce
Cruise Lines—*See:* Steamship Lines
Cryogenics 235
Culture, Corporate—*See:* Corporate Culture
Currency—*See:* Money
Currency Convertibility—*See:* Foreign Exchange
Currency Exchange Rates 236
Current Events 236
Curtain Industry—*See:* Window Covering Industry
Customer Service 237
Customs Brokers 238
Customs House, U.S. Customs Service 238
Customs Tax—*See:* Tariff
Cycles, Business—*See:* Business Cycles
Dairy Industry 239
Dairy Products 239
Dangerous Materials—*See:* Hazardous Materials
Data Bases, Online—*See:* Online Information Systems
Data Communications—*See:* Computer Communications
Data Identification Systems, Automatic—*See:* Automatic Identification Systems
Data Systems—*See:* Systems in Management
Dates (Chronology)—*See:* Chronology
Day Care Centers 240
DDT—*See:* Pesticide Industry
Death Tax—*See:* Inheritance Tax
Deaths and Births—*See:* Vital Statistics
Debates and Debating 240
Debentures—*See:* Bonds
Debt Collection—*See:* Collecting of Accounts
Debt, National—*See:* National Debt
Deceptive Advertising—*See:* Advertising Law and Regulation
Decision-Making 241
Decoration, Interior—*See:* Interior Decoration
Deductions (Income Tax)—*See:* Income Tax
Defense Contracts—*See:* Government Contracts
Defense Industries 241
Defense Market—*See:* Military Market
Deficit, Federal—*See:* National Debt
Dehydrated Foods—*See:* Food Industry
Demography—*See:* Market Statistics; Population; Vital Statistics
Dental Supply Industry 242
Department Stores 243
Depreciation 243
Depression—*See:* Mental Health
Depressions, Business—*See:* Business Cycles
Derivative Securities 243
Desalination Industry 245
Design and Manufacturing, Computer-Aided—*See:* Computer-Aided Design and Manufacturing (CAD/CAM)
Design in Industry 246
Desktop Publishing 246
Detergents—*See:* Cleaning Products Industry
Developing Areas 248
Development, Community—*See:* Community Development
Development Credit Corporations—*See:* Credit
Development, Industrial—*See:* Industrial Development
Development, Urban—*See:* Urban Development
Diamond Industry 249
Diamonds, Industrial—*See:* Industrial Diamonds
Dictating Machines—*See:* Office Equipment and Supplies
Die Casting—*See:* Tool Industry
Diesel Engines—*See:* Engines
Diet 249

Digital Computers—*See:* Computers
Digital Media—*See:* Electronic Publishing; Multimedia; Online Information Systems; Optical Disk Storage Devices
Diners—*See:* Restaurants, Lunchrooms, Etc.
Dinnerware—*See:* Tableware
Diplomatic and Consular Service 250
Direct Costing—*See:* Cost Accounting
Direct Debit Systems—*See:* Point-of-Sale Systems (POS)
Direct Mail Advertising 251
Direct Marketing 251
Direct Selling—*See:* Direct Marketing
Directories—*See:* Catalogs and Directories
Directors—*See:* Corporate Directors and Officers
Disability Insurance 252
Disabled—*See:* Handicapped Workers
Discharged Servicemen—*See:* Veterans
Discipline of Employees—*See:* Employee Discipline
Discount Houses 253
Discoveries, Scientific and Technological—*See:* Inventions; Patents
Discrimination in Employment—*See:* Affirmative Action Programs
Dishware—*See:* Tableware
Disinfection and Disinfectant—*See:* Sanitation Industry
Disk Storage Devices, Optical—*See:* Optical Disk Storage Devices
Dismissal of Employees 253
Display of Merchandise 254
Disposable Fabrics—*See:* Nonwoven Fabrics Industry
Disputes, Labor—*See:* Arbitration; Strikes and Lockouts
Dissertations 255
Distilling Industry 255
Distribution 256
Dividends 256
Divorce 257
Do-It-Yourself—*See:* Home Improvement Industry
Docks—*See:* Ports
Doctors' Degrees—*See:* Academic Degrees
Document Imaging 258
Documentation (Information Retrieval)—*See:* Online Information Systems
Documents—*See:* Government Publications
Dog Food—*See:* Pet Industry
Domestic Appliances—*See:* Electric Appliance Industry
Donations, Charitable—*See:* Philanthropy
Door Industry 259
Door-to-Door Selling—*See:* Direct Marketing
Douglas Fir—*See:* Lumber Industry
Dow Theory 260
Downsizing—*See:* Dismissal of Employees
Drafting, Mechanical—*See:* Mechanical Drawing
Drapery Industry—*See:* Window Covering Industry
Dried Foods—*See:* Food Industry
Drilling and Boring Machinery—*See:* Machinery
Drinking and Traffic Accidents—*See:* Traffic Accidents and Traffic Safety
Drive-in and Curb Services 260
Drug Abuse and Traffic 260
Drug Industry—*See:* Pharmaceutical Industry
Drug Stores 261
Drugs—*See:* Drug Abuse and Traffic; Narcotics; Pharmaceutical Industry
Drugs, Generic—*See:* Generic Drug Industry
Drugs, Nonprescription—*See:* Nonprescription Drug Industry
Drunkenness—*See:* Alcoholism
Dry Cleaning Industry—*See:* Cleaning Industry
Duplicating Machines—*See:* Copying Machine Industry
Duties—*See:* Tariff; Taxation
Dyes and Dyeing 262
E-commerce—*See:* Electronic Commerce
Eating Facilities, Employees—*See:* Employee Lunchrooms and Cafeterias
Eating Places—*See:* Restaurants, Lunchrooms, Etc.
Ecology—*See:* Environment
Econometrics 263
Economic Botany 263
Economic Conditions—*See:* Business Conditions
Economic Cycles—*See:* Business Cycles
Economic Development 264
Economic Entomology 265
Economic Forecasting—*See:* Business Forecasting
Economic Geology 266
Economic History—*See:* Business History
Economic Indicators 266
Economic Planning—*See:* Economic Policy
Economic Policy 267
Economic Research 268
Economic Responsibility—*See:* Social Responsibility
Economic Statistics 269
Economics 271
Economics, Business—*See:* Business Economics
Economics, Mathematical—*See:* Econometrics
Editors and Editing 272
Education—*See:* Schools
Education, Business—*See:* Business Education
Education, Computers in—*See:* Computers in Education
Education, Employee—*See:* Training of Employees
Education, Executive—*See:* Executive Training and Development
Education, Federal Aid—*See:* Federal Aid
Education, Higher—*See:* Colleges and Universities
Education, Technical—*See:* Technical Education
Education, Vocational—*See:* Vocational Education
Educational Films—*See:* Audiovisual Aids in Education
Efficiency, Industrial—*See:* Time and Motion Study
EFTPOS (Electronic Funds Transfer Point-of-Sale Systems)—*See:* Point-of-Sale Systems (POS)
EFTS—*See:* Electronic Funds Transfer Systems (EFTS)
Egg Industry—*See:* Poultry Industry
Electric Apparatus—*See:* Electrical Equipment Industry

Electric Appliance Industry 273
Electric Contractors—*See:* Electrical Construction Industry
Electric Lamps—*See:* Lighting
Electric Lighting—*See:* Lighting
Electric Motor Industry—*See:* Electrical Equipment Industry
Electric Power—*See:* Electric Utilities
Electric Power Cogeneration—*See:* Cogeneration of Energy
Electric Power Plants 274
Electric Power, Rural—*See:* Rural Electrification
Electric Rates 275
Electric Signs—*See:* Signs and Sign Boards
Electric Utilities 275
Electric Wire—*See:* Wire Industry
Electrical Construction Industry 276
Electrical Engineering 277
Electrical Equipment Industry 277
Electronic Commerce 278
Electronic Components—*See:* Electronics Industry; Semiconductor Industry
Electronic Funds Transfer Point-of-Sale Systems (EFTPOS)—*See:* Point-of-Sale Systems (POS)
Electronic Funds Transfer Systems (EFTS) 280
Electronic Mail—*See:* Computer Communications
Electronic Media—*See:* Interactive Media; Multimedia
Electronic Optics—*See:* Optoelectronics
Electronic Publishing 280
Electronic Security Systems 282
Electronics, Aviation—*See:* Avionics
Electronics, Consumer—*See:* Consumer Economics
Electronics Industry 282
Electronics, Medical—*See:* Medical Electronics
Electroplating—*See:* Metal Finishing
Elevators 284
Embassies—*See:* Diplomatic and Consular Service
Embezzlement—*See:* Fraud and Embezzlement
Emerging Markets—*See:* Developing Areas
Emigration—*See:* Immigration and Emigration
Employee Benefit Plans 284
Employee Counseling—*See:* Counseling
Employee Discipline 286
Employee Dismissal—*See:* Dismissal of Employees
Employee Education—*See:* Training of Employees
Employee Efficiency—*See:* Time and Motion Study
Employee Health Programs—*See:* Employee Wellness Programs
Employee Lunchrooms and Cafeterias 286
Employee Magazines—*See:* House Organs
Employee Manuals—*See:* Procedure Manuals
Employee Motivation—*See:* Motivation (Psychology)
Employee Pamphlets—*See:* Pamphlets
Employee Participation—*See:* Participative Management
Employee Rating—*See:* Rating of Employees
Employee Relocation—*See:* Relocation of Employees
Employee Representation in Management 286
Employee Selection—*See:* Recruitment of Personnel
Employee Stock Ownership Plans 287
Employee Suggestions—*See:* Suggestion Systems
Employee Theft—*See:* Crime and Criminals; Fraud and Embezzlement
Employee Training—*See:* Training of Employees
Employee Wellness Programs 287
Employees, Temporary—*See:* Temporary Employees
Employment 288
Employment Agencies and Services 290
Employment in Foreign Countries 291
Employment Interviewing—*See:* Interviewing; Job Hunting
Employment Management—*See:* Personnel Management
Employment of Older Workers 291
Employment of the Handicapped—*See:* Handicapped Workers
Employment of Women 291
Employment Resumes—*See:* Job Resumes
Employment Security—*See:* Unemployment Insurance
Employment Tests—*See:* Psychological Testing
Endowments—*See:* Foundations
Energy Cogeneration—*See:* Cogeneration of Energy
Energy, Geothermal—*See:* Geothermal Energy
Energy, Nuclear—*See:* Nuclear Energy
Energy, Solar—*See:* Solar Energy
Energy Sources 292
Engineering Consultants 294
Engines 294
Entertainment Industry—*See:* Amusement Industry; Show Business
Entomology, Economic—*See:* Economic Entomology
Entrance Requirements—*See:* College Entrance Requirements
Entrepreneurial Capital—*See:* Venture Capital
Entrepreneurial History—*See:* Business History
Entrepreneurs and Intrapreneurs 295
Environment 296
Environmental Control—*See:* Air Pollution; Land Utilization; Water Pollution
Environmental Law 299
Environmental Pollution—*See:* Air Pollution; Water Pollution
Equal Employment Opportunity 300
Equipment Leasing 300
Ergonomics—*See:* Human Engineering
Essential Oils—*See:* Additives and Flavorings; Perfume Industry
Estate Planning 301
Estate Tax—*See:* Inheritance Tax
Estimating 302
Ethical Drug Industry—*See:* Pharmaceutical Industry
Ethics—*See:* Business Ethics; Social Responsibility
Etiquette 303
Eurocurrency 303
Eurodollars—*See:* Eurocurrency
European Consumer Market 303
European Economic Community—*See:* European Markets
European Markets 305

European Union—See: European Markets
Evaluation of Performance—See: Rating of Employees
Event Planning—See: Special Event Planning
Exchange, Foreign—See: Foreign Exchange
Exchange Rates—See: Currency Exchange Rates
Exchanges, Commodity—See: Commodity Futures Trading
Exchanges, Stock—See: Stock Exchanges
Excise Tax 307
Executive Compensation 307
Executive Education—See: Executive Training and Development
Executive Rating—See: Rating of Employees
Executive Recruiting—See: Recruitment of Personnel
Executive Salaries—See: Executive Compensation
Executive Search Services—See: Employment Agencies and Services; Recruitment of Personnel
Executive Secretaries—See: Office Practice
Executive Stress—See: Stress (Anxiety)
Executive Training and Development 308
Executives 309
Executives, Women—See: Women Executives
Exercise Equipment Industry—See: Fitness Industry
Exhibits—See: Display of Merchandise; Trade Shows
Expense Control—See: Cost Control
Expert Systems—See: Artificial Intelligence
Explosives Industry 310
Export-Import Trade 311
Expositions—See: Conventions; Fairs
Eyecare Industry—See: Contact Lens and Intraocular Lens Industries; Ophthalmic Industry
Fabrics, Industrial—See: Industrial Fabrics Industry
Fabrics, Nonwoven—See: Nonwoven Fabrics Industry
Facilities Management—See: Factory Management
Facsimile Systems 313
Factory Location—See: Location of Industry
Factory Maintenance—See: Maintenance of Buildings
Factory Management 313
Factory Security—See: Industrial Security Programs
Failures, Bank—See: Bank Failures
Failures, Business—See: Business Failures
Fair Employment Practices—See: Equal Employment Opportunity; Labor
Fair Trade—See: Prices and Pricing
Fairs 314
Family Corporations—See: Closely Held Corporations
Family Law 314
Farm Business—See: Agribusiness
Farm Credit—See: Agricultural Credit
Farm Equipment Industry—See: Agricultural Machinery
Farm Implements—See: Agricultural Machinery
Farm Income—See: Agricultural Statistics
Farm Journals 315
Farm Labor—See: Farmers; Labor
Farm Machinery—See: Agricultural Machinery
Farm Management 315
Farm Markets 315
Farm Produce 316
Farmers 317
Farms—See: Agriculture
Fashion Industry 317
Fast Food Industry 317
Fastener Industry 318
Fats—See: Oil and Fats Industry
FAX—See: Facsimile Systems
Federal Aid 318
Federal Aid for Education—See: Federal Aid
Federal Aid to Research—See: Federal Aid
Federal Budget 319
Federal Employees—See: Bureaucracy; Government Employees
Federal Government 319
Federal Insurance Contributions Act (FICA)—See: Social Security
Federal Regulation—See: Regulation of Industry
Federal Reserve System 321
Federal Statistics—See: Government Statistics
Feed and Feedstuffs Industry 322
Fertilizer Industry 322
Festivals—See: Anniversaries and Holidays; Fairs
Fiber Industry 323
Fiber Optics Industry 324
Fiction, Business—See: Business in Fiction
Files and Filing (Documents) 325
Films, Motion Picture—See: Motion Picture Industry
Filmstrips—See: Audiovisual Aids in Education; Audiovisual Aids in Industry
Filter Industry 325
Finance 326
Finance, Bank—See: Bank Loans
Finance Companies 328
Finance, Computers in—See: Computers in Finance
Finance, Corporate—See: Corporate Finance
Finance, International—See: International Finance
Finance, Personal—See: Personal Finance
Finance, Public—See: Public Finance
Financial Analysis 329
Financial Futures Trading 330
Financial Management 331
Financial Planning 333
Financial Ratios 334
Financial Services—See: Investment Advisory Services
Financial Statements—See: Corporation Reports; Financial Analysis
Fire Alarms—See: Electronic Security Systems
Fire Insurance 335
Fire Prevention 335
Fire Protection 336
Firearms Industry 336
Firing of Employees—See: Dismissal of Employees
Fish Culture—See: Aquaculture
Fish Industry 336
Fitness Industry 337

Fixed Income Securities—*See:* Bonds
Flavorings—*See:* Additives and Flavorings
Floor Coverings 338
Florist Shops 339
Flour Industry 339
Fluidics Industry 340
Fluorescent Lighting—*See:* Lighting
Flying—*See:* Air Pilots; Air Travel; Airline Industry; Business Aviation
FM Broadcasting—*See:* Radio Broadcasting Industry
Focus Groups—*See:* Market Research; Survey Methods
Food Additives—*See:* Additives and Flavorings
Food Equipment and Machinery 341
Food Industry 342
Food Machinery—*See:* Food Equipment and Machinery
Food Packaging—*See:* Packaging
Food, Processed—*See:* Processed Food Industry
Food Processing—*See:* Food Industry; Processed Food Industry
Food Service Industry 344
Food Service, Institutional—*See:* Food Service Industry
Food, Snack—*See:* Snack Food Industry
Food, Specialty—*See:* Specialty Food Industry
Footwear—*See:* Shoe Industry
Forecasting—*See:* Business Forecasting; Futuristics
Foreign Agriculture 345
Foreign Automobiles 345
Foreign Business—*See:* International Business
Foreign Commerce—*See:* Foreign Trade
Foreign Credit 345
Foreign Employment—*See:* Employment in Foreign Countries
Foreign Exchange 346
Foreign Investments 347
Foreign Language Press and Newspapers 347
Foreign Law—*See:* International Law and Regulation
Foreign Markets—*See:* Foreign Trade
Foreign Operations—*See:* International Business
Foreign Radio and Television 348
Foreign Service—*See:* Diplomatic and Consular Service
Foreign Study—*See:* Study Abroad
Foreign Trade 348
Foremen—*See:* Factory Management
Forest Products 350
Forgeries 351
Forges—*See:* Foundries
Forms and Blanks 351
Forms of Address—*See:* Etiquette
Forwarding Companies—*See:* Freight Transport
Forwarding Freight—*See:* Freight Transport
Foundations 352
Foundries 353
Fountain Pens—*See:* Writing Instruments
401(k) Retirement Plans 353
Fragrance Industry—*See:* Perfume Industry
Franchises 355
Fraud and Embezzlement 355
Fraud, Computer—*See:* Computer Crime and Security
Freedom of Information 356
Freight, Air—*See:* Air Freight
Freight Forwarders—*See:* Freight Transport
Freight Rates 356
Freight Ships—*See:* Ships, Shipping and Shipbuilding
Freight Transport 356
Fringe Areas—*See:* City Planning; Urban Development
Fringe Benefits 357
Frozen Food Industry 358
Fruit Industry 358
Fruit Juice Industry—*See:* Beverage Industry; Citrus Fruit Industry
Fuel 359
Fuel Cells—*See:* Battery Industry
Fuel Oil Industry 360
Fuel, Synthetic—*See:* Synthetic Fuels
Fund-Raising 360
Funds, Community—*See:* Community Funds
Funds, Mutual—*See:* Investment Companies
Funeral Homes and Directors 361
Fur Industry 362
Furnishings (Men's Clothing)—*See:* Men's Clothing Industry
Furniture Industry 362
Futures, Financial—*See:* Financial Futures Trading
Futures Trading—*See:* Commodity Futures Trading
Futuristics 363
Gambling Industry 365
Games—*See:* Toy Industry
Games, Management—*See:* Management Games
Garages—*See:* Gasoline Service Stations
Garbage Disposal—*See:* Sanitation Industry
Garden Supply Industry 365
Garment Industry—*See:* Clothing Industry
Gas and Oil Engines—*See:* Engines
Gas Appliances 365
Gas Companies—*See:* Public Utilities
Gas Engines—*See:* Engines
Gas Industry 366
Gas, Liquefied Petroleum—*See:* Propane and Butane Gas Industry
Gas, Natural—*See:* Natural Gas
Gas Pipelines—*See:* Pipeline Industry
Gas Rates—*See:* Gas Industry
Gasohol—*See:* Fuel
Gasoline Engines—*See:* Engines
Gasoline Industry 367
Gasoline Service Stations 367
GATT—*See:* General Agreement on Tariffs and Trade (GATT)
Gauges—*See:* Tool Industry
Gear Industry 368
Gems and Gemstones 368
General Agreement on Tariffs and Trade (GATT) 369

General Aviation—*See:* Business Aviation
Generators, Electric—*See:* Electrical Equipment Industry
Generic Drug Industry 369
Generic Products—*See:* Private Label Products
Genetic Engineering 370
Geothermal Energy 371
Gift Business 372
Gift Tax 372
Girls' Clothing—*See:* Children's Apparel Industry
Glass Container Industry 373
Glass Industry 373
Glassware Industry 374
Glove Industry 374
Glue Industry—*See:* Adhesives
Going Public—*See:* New Issues (Finance)
Gold 374
Golf Industry 375
Gourmet Foods—*See:* Specialty Food Industry
Government Accounting 376
Government Administration—*See:* Public Administration
Government Agencies—*See:* Federal Government; Municipal Government; State Government
Government Aid—*See:* Federal Aid
Government and Business—*See:* Regulation of Industry
Government Bonds 377
Government Budget—*See:* Federal Budget
Government, Computers in—*See:* Computers in Government
Government Contracts 378
Government Documents—*See:* Government Publications
Government Employees 378
Government Expenditures—*See:* Federal Budget
Government Finance—*See:* Public Finance
Government Housing Projects—*See:* Housing
Government Investigations 380
Government Officials—*See:* Bureaucracy; Government Employees
Government Procurement—*See:* Government Purchasing
Government Publications 381
Government Purchasing 382
Government Regulation of Industry—*See:* Regulation of Industry
Government Regulation of Railroads—*See:* Interstate Commerce
Government Research 382
Government Research Support—*See:* Federal Aid
Government Service—*See:* Civil Service
Government, State—*See:* State Government
Government Statistics 383
Government Surplus—*See:* Surplus Products
Graduate Work in Universities 383
Graft (Politics)—*See:* Crime and Criminals
Grain Dealers—*See:* Grain Industry
Grain Elevators—*See:* Grain Industry
Grain Industry 385
Granite—*See:* Quarrying
Grants-in-Aid 386
Grape Industry—*See:* Fruit Industry
Graphic Arts Industry 387
Graphics, Computer—*See:* Computer Graphics
Graphs and Charts 387
Graphite—*See:* Mines and Mineral Resources
Gravel Industry—*See:* Quarrying
Grease—*See:* Lubrication and Lubricants
Greeting Card Industry 388
Grinding and Polishing—*See:* Abrasives Industry
Grocery Business 388
Gross National Product 389
Group Insurance—*See:* Health Insurance
Group Medical Practice 389
Growth Stocks—*See:* Stocks
Guaranteed Wages—*See:* Wages and Salaries
Guidance—*See:* Counseling; Vocational Guidance
Guided Missiles—*See:* Rocket Industry
Gums and Resins—*See:* Naval Stores
Guns—*See:* Firearms Industry
Haberdashery—*See:* Men's Clothing Industry
Hair Care Products—*See:* Cosmetics Industry
Hairdressers—*See:* Barber and Beauty Shops
Half-Tone Process—*See:* Photoengraving
Handicapped Workers 391
Handicrafts—*See:* Gift Business; Hobby Industry
Handling of Materials—*See:* Materials Handling
Harassment, Sexual—*See:* Sexual Harassment in the Workplace
Harbors—*See:* Ports
Hard Fibers Industry—*See:* Fiber Industry
Hardware Industry 391
Hardwood Industry 392
Harvesting Machinery—*See:* Agricultural Machinery
Hat Industry—*See:* Men's Clothing Industry; Millinery Industry
Hay Industry—*See:* Feed and Feedstuffs Industry
Hazardous Materials 393
Health Care Industry 395
Health Club Industry—*See:* Fitness Industry
Health Food Industry 399
Health, Industrial—*See:* Industrial Hygiene
Health Insurance 400
Health Maintenance Organizations 402
Health of Employees—*See:* Employee Wellness Programs
Heating and Ventilation 403
Helicopters 404
Hens—*See:* Poultry Industry
Herbs 404
Hide Industry—*See:* Cattle Industry
High Blood Pressure—*See:* Hypertension
High Fidelity/Stereo 405
High Technology—*See:* Technology
High Yield Bonds—*See:* Junk Bond Financing
Higher Education—*See:* Colleges and Universities
Highway Accidents—*See:* Traffic Accidents and Traffic Safety

Highways—*See:* Roads and Highways
Hire Purchase Plan—*See:* Installment Plan Purchasing
Hispanic Markets—*See:* Minority Markets
History, Business—*See:* Business History
HMOs—*See:* Health Maintenance Organizations
Hobby Industry 405
Hog Industry—*See:* Livestock Industry; Swine Industry
Hoisting Machinery—*See:* Conveying Machinery; Elevators
Holidays—*See:* Anniversaries and Holidays
Home Appliances—*See:* Electric Appliance Industry
Home-Based Businesses—*See:* Self-Employment
Home Building Industry—*See:* Building Industry
Home Computers—*See:* Microcomputers and Minicomputers
Home Decoration—*See:* Interior Decoration
Home Education—*See:* Correspondence Schools and Courses
Home Freezers—*See:* Frozen Food Industry
Home Furnishings—*See:* Floor Coverings; Furniture Industry; Interior Decoration
Home Furniture Industry—*See:* Furniture Industry
Home Health Care Industry 406
Home Improvement Industry 407
Home Ownership 407
Home Textiles—*See:* Linen Industry
Homes for the Aged—*See:* Nursing Homes
Honey Industry 408
Hong Kong—*See:* Asian Markets
Honorary Degrees—*See:* Academic Degrees
Hops—*See:* Brewing Industry
Horology—*See:* Clock and Watch Industry
Horticulture—*See:* Nurseries (Horticultural)
Hosiery Industry 409
Hospital Administration 409
Hospital Equipment 410
Hospitality Industry—*See:* Hotel and Motel Industry; Restaurants, Lunchrooms, Etc.; Travel Industry
Hospitals—*See:* Hospital Administration
Hotel and Motel Industry 411
House Buying and Selling—*See:* Home Ownership
House Decoration—*See:* Interior Decoration
House of Representatives—*See:* United States Congress
House Organs 413
House-to-House Selling—*See:* Direct Marketing
Household Appliances—*See:* Electric Appliance Industry
Household Furnishings—*See:* Furniture Industry
Household Products Industry—*See:* Cleaning Products Industry
Houses, Prefabricated—*See:* Prefabricated House Industry
Housewares Industry 413
Housing 413
Housing Management—*See:* Property Management
Human Engineering 415
Human Motivation—*See:* Motivation (Psychology)
Human Relations 415
Human Resources Management—*See:* Personnel Management
Human Rights—*See:* Civil Rights
Humor and Jokes 416
Hydraulic Engineering and Machinery 416
Hydrocarbons—*See:* Petroleum Industry
Hydroelectric Industry 417
Hygiene—*See:* Industrial Hygiene
Hypertension 417
Ice Cream Industry 419
Identification Systems, Automatic—*See:* Automatic Identification Systems
Illegal Aliens—*See:* Immigration and Emigration
Image, Corporate—*See:* Corporate Image
Immigration and Emigration 419
Import Trade—*See:* Export-Import Trade
Incandescent Lamps—*See:* Lighting
Incentive—*See:* Motivation (Psychology)
Incentive Merchandising—*See:* Premiums
Income 420
Income Tax 422
Income Tax, State—*See:* State Taxes
Incorporation 424
Independent Schools—*See:* Private Schools
Index Trading—*See:* Stock Index Trading
Indexing 425
Indicators, Economic—*See:* Economic Indicators
Individual Retirement Accounts 425
Industrial Advertising 426
Industrial Arbitration—*See:* Arbitration; Industrial Relations
Industrial Coatings 426
Industrial Controls—*See:* Control Equipment Industry
Industrial Counseling—*See:* Personnel Management; Vocational Guidance
Industrial Design—*See:* Design in Industry
Industrial Development 428
Industrial Diamonds 428
Industrial Directories—*See:* Catalogs and Directories
Industrial Disputes—*See:* Arbitration; Strikes and Lockouts
Industrial Distribution—*See:* Distribution
Industrial Efficiency—*See:* Time and Motion Study
Industrial Engineering 428
Industrial Equipment Industry 429
Industrial Equipment Leasing—*See:* Rental Services
Industrial Fabrics Industry 430
Industrial Fasteners—*See:* Fastener Industry
Industrial Hygiene 430
Industrial Journalism—*See:* Business Journalism
Industrial Location—*See:* Location of Industry
Industrial Management 431
Industrial Marketing 432
Industrial Medicine 433
Industrial Morale—*See:* Human Relations
Industrial Parks—*See:* Industrial Development
Industrial Photography—*See:* Commercial Photography
Industrial Productivity—*See:* Productivity
Industrial Psychology 433
Industrial Purchasing—*See:* Purchasing

Industrial Real Estate 434
Industrial Recreation 434
Industrial Relations 435
Industrial Research 435
Industrial Robots—*See:* Robots
Industrial Safety 436
Industrial Security Programs 437
Industrial Statistics—*See:* Business Statistics; Statistical Methods
Industrial Toxicology—*See:* Industrial Hygiene
Industrial Welfare—*See:* Employee Benefit Plans
Industry 437
Industry, Regulation of—*See:* Regulation of Industry
Infants Wear—*See:* Children's Apparel Industry
Inflation 441
Information Brokers—*See:* Information Industry
Information, Freedom of—*See:* Freedom of Information
Information Industry 442
Information Management Systems—*See:* Management Information Systems
Information Retrieval (Documentation)—*See:* Online Information Systems
Information Sources 446
Information Systems, Management—*See:* Management Information Systems
Information Systems, Online—*See:* Online Information Systems
Inheritance Tax 448
Initial Public Offerings—*See:* New Issues (Finance)
Injuries—*See:* Accidents
Ink—*See:* Printing Ink Industry
Inland Marine Insurance—*See:* Marine Insurance
Inland Waterways—*See:* Waterways
Innovation, Business—*See:* Business Innovation
Innovation in Products—*See:* New Products
Insecticides—*See:* Pesticide Industry
Insects—*See:* Economic Entomology
Inservice Training—*See:* Training of Employees
Insider Trading 449
Insolvency—*See:* Bankruptcy
Installment Plan Purchasing 450
Institutional Food Service—*See:* Food Service Industry
Institutional Investments 450
Instruction of Employees—*See:* Training of Employees
Instruction, Programmed—*See:* Programmed Learning
Instruments, Musical—*See:* Musical Instruments Industry
Instruments, Scientific—*See:* Scientific Apparatus and Instrument Industries
Instruments, Surgical—*See:* Surgical Instruments Industry
Insulation 454
Insurance 454
Insurance, Accident—*See:* Accident Insurance
Insurance Actuaries—*See:* Actuarial Science
Insurance Agents 457
Insurance, Automobile—*See:* Automobile Insurance
Insurance, Business Interruption—*See:* Business Interruption Insurance
Insurance, Casualty—*See:* Casualty Insurance
Insurance, Disability—*See:* Disability Insurance
Insurance, Fire—*See:* Fire Insurance
Insurance, Health—*See:* Health Insurance
Insurance Law and Regulation 457
Insurance, Liability—*See:* Property and Liability Insurance
Insurance, Life—*See:* Life Insurance
Insurance, Long-Term Care—*See:* Long-Term Care Insurance
Insurance, Marine—*See:* Marine Insurance
Insurance, Property—*See:* Property and Liability Insurance
Insurance, Social—*See:* Social Security
Insurance, Title—*See:* Title Insurance
Insurance Underwriters 458
Insurance, Unemployment—*See:* Unemployment Insurance
Integrated Circuits—*See:* Semiconductor Industry
Integrated Systems—*See:* Systems Integration
Intellectual Property 458
Intelligence, Artificial—*See:* Artificial Intelligence
Interactive Media 459
Interactive Television—*See:* Interactive Media; Videotex/Teletext
Interest 461
Interior Decoration 463
Internal Auditing 463
Internal Publications—*See:* House Organs
Internal Revenue Service—*See:* Income Tax
International Agencies 464
International Associations—*See:* International Agencies
International Business 465
International Corporations—*See:* Multinational Corporations
International Development—*See:* Developing Areas
International Economics 468
International Finance 470
International Institutions—*See:* International Agencies
International Investments—*See:* Foreign Investments
International Law and Regulation 472
International Marketing 473
International Monetary Fund (IMF) 475
International Organizations—*See:* International Agencies
International Taxation 475
International Trade—*See:* Foreign Trade
Internet 476
Internet Commerce—*See:* Electronic Commerce
Internship Programs 483
Interpersonal Relations—*See:* Human Relations
Interstate Commerce 483
Interviewing 483
Intranets (Computer Networks) 484
Intraocular Lens Industry—*See:* Contact Lens and Intraocular Lens Industries
Intrapreneurs—*See:* Entrepreneurs and Intrapreneurs
Inventions 484
Inventory Control 485

Investment Advisory Services 485
Investment Analysis—*See:* Financial Analysis
Investment Banking 485
Investment Clubs 486
Investment Companies 486
Investment Companies, Closed-end—*See:* Closed-end Funds
Investment Dealers—*See:* Stock Brokers
Investment Services—*See:* Investment Advisory Services
Investment Trusts—*See:* Investment Companies
Investments 488
Investments, Institutional—*See:* Institutional Investments
Investments, Real Estate—*See:* Real Estate Investments
IRAs—*See:* Individual Retirement Accounts
Iron and Steel Industry 492
Iron and Steel Scrap Metal Industry 493
Iron Foundries—*See:* Foundries
Irrigation 493
ISO 9000 Standards—*See:* Total Quality Management (TQM)
Isotopes 493
Janitorial Services—*See:* Maintenance of Buildings
Japan—*See:* Asian Markets
Java (Computer Program Language) 495
Jet Propulsion—*See:* Rocket Industry
Jewelry Business 495
Job Descriptions 496
Job Hunting 496
Job Interviews—*See:* Interviewing
Job Performance—*See:* Rating of Employees
Job Resumes 497
Job Searching—*See:* Job Hunting
Job Training—*See:* Training of Employees
Jobbers—*See:* Rack Jobbers; Wholesale Trade
Jobbers, Rack—*See:* Rack Jobbers
Jobless Compensation—*See:* Unemployment Insurance
Jobs in Foreign Countries—*See:* Employment in Foreign Countries
Jokes—*See:* Humor and Jokes
Journalism 497
Journalism, Business—*See:* Business Journalism
Journals, Trade—*See:* Trade Journals
Judiciary—*See:* Courts
Juice Industry—*See:* Beverage Industry; Citrus Fruit Industry
Juke Boxes—*See:* Vending Machines
Junior Colleges 498
Junk—*See:* Waste Products
Junk Bond Financing 498
Juries—*See:* Trials and Juries
Jurists—*See:* Lawyers
Jurors—*See:* Courts
Jute Industry 499
Juveniles—*See:* Youth Market
Keogh Plans 501
Keyless Data Entry—*See:* Automatic Identification Systems
Keys—*See:* Locks and Keys
Kitchens 501
Knit Goods Industry 501
Kosher Foods Industry 502
Labels and Labeling 503
Labor 503
Labor Arbitration—*See:* Arbitration
Labor Discipline—*See:* Employee Discipline
Labor Disputes—*See:* Arbitration; Strikes and Lockouts
Labor Force—*See:* Labor Supply
Labor Law and Regulation 504
Labor Market—*See:* Labor Supply
Labor Organization—*See:* Labor Unions
Labor Productivity—*See:* Productivity
Labor Relations—*See:* Industrial Relations; Labor
Labor Supply 505
Labor Unions 506
Laboratories 506
Laboratories, Clinical—*See:* Clinical Laboratory Industry
Laboratory Equipment—*See:* Scientific Apparatus and Instrument Industries
Lace Industry 507
Lacquer and Lacquering—*See:* Paint and Painting
Lamb Industry—*See:* Sheep Industry
Lamps—*See:* Lighting
Land Companies—*See:* Real Estate Business
Land Utilization 507
Landlord and Tenant—*See:* Apartment Houses; Property Management; Real Estate Business
Landscape Architecture 507
LAN—*See:* Local Area Networks
Laptop Computers—*See:* Portable Computers
Lard Industry—*See:* Oil and Fats Industry
Laserdisks—*See:* Optical Disk Storage Devices
Lasers 508
Lathing—*See:* Plaster and Plastering
Latin American Markets 508
Laundry Industry 511
Law 511
Law, Business—*See:* Business Law
Law, Computer—*See:* Computer Law
Law Enforcement Industries 513
Law, Environmental—*See:* Environmental Law
Law, Family—*See:* Family Law
Law Firms—*See:* Lawyers
Law, State—*See:* State Law
Lawn Care Industry 514
Laws 514
Laws, Advertising—*See:* Advertising Law and Regulation
Laws, Banking—*See:* Banking Law and Regulation
Lawyers 515
Layoffs—*See:* Dismissal of Employees
Lead Industry 517
Leadership 517
Leading Indicators—*See:* Economic Indicators
Learning, Programmed—*See:* Programmed Learning
Leasing Services—*See:* Automobile Lease and Rental Services; Equipment Leasing; Rental Services

Leather Industry 518
Legal Forms—*See:* Forms and Blanks
Legal Holidays—*See:* Anniversaries and Holidays
Legal Profession—*See:* Lawyers
Legal Rights—*See:* Civil Rights
Legations—*See:* Diplomatic and Consular Service
Legislation—*See:* Laws
Legislative Investigations—*See:* Government Investigations
Legislative Procedure 518
Legislatures 519
Leisure Industry—*See:* Amusement Industry; Recreation Industry; Show Business; Sports Business
Lemons—*See:* Citrus Fruit Industry
Lenses, Contact—*See:* Contact Lens and Intraocular Lens Industries
Lenses, Intraocular—*See:* Contact Lens and Intraocular Lens Industries
Letter Writing—*See:* Business Correspondence
Leveraged Buyouts 519
Liability Insurance—*See:* Property and Liability Insurance; Professional Liability
Liability, Product—*See:* Product Safety and Liability
Liability, Professional—*See:* Professional Liability
Librarians 520
Libraries 521
Libraries, College and University—*See:* College and University Libraries
Libraries, Public—*See:* Libraries
Libraries, Special—*See:* Special Libraries
Library Automation 522
Library Management 524
Library Research 526
License Plates—*See:* Motor Vehicle Law and Regulation
Licenses 527
Licensing Agreements 527
Life Insurance 528
Lift Trucks—*See:* Materials Handling
Lighting 529
Limestone Industry 530
Limited Partnerships—*See:* Partnership
Linear Programming 530
Linen Industry 530
Lingerie Industry—*See:* Underwear Industry
Liquefied Petroleum Gas—*See:* Propane and Butane Gas Industry
Liquor Industry—*See:* Distilling Industry
Liquor Law and Regulation 530
Liquor Stores 531
Literary Agents—*See:* Writers and Writing
Literary Property—*See:* Copyright
Literature Searching, Online—*See:* Online Information Systems
Lithography 531
Livestock Industry 531
Loan Companies—*See:* Finance Companies; Savings and Loan Associations
Loans—*See:* Bank Loans; Consumer Credit; Credit
Loans, Bank—*See:* Bank Loans
Loans, Commercial—*See:* Commercial Lending
Loans, Student—*See:* Scholarships and Student Aid
Lobbying—*See:* Pressure Groups
Lobster Industry 532
Local Area Networks 532
Local Government—*See:* County Government; Municipal Government; State Government
Location of Industry 533
Lockouts—*See:* Strikes and Lockouts
Locks and Keys 534
Locomotives—*See:* Railroads
Logging—*See:* Lumber Industry
Logistic Research—*See:* Operations Research
Logos—*See:* Corporate Image; Trademarks and Trade Names
Long-Term Care Insurance 534
Long-Term Health Care Industry—*See:* Health Care Industry; Nursing Homes
Low Temperature Technology—*See:* Cryogenics
Lubrication and Lubricants 535
Luggage Industry 535
Lumber Industry 535
Lunchrooms—*See:* Restaurants, Lunchrooms, Etc.
Lunchrooms, Employee—*See:* Employee Lunchrooms and Cafeterias
Macaroni 537
Machine Design 537
Machine Shops 537
Machine Tool Industry 537
Machine Translating 538
Machine Vision 538
Machinery 539
Machinery, Used—*See:* Surplus Products
Magazine Circulation—*See:* Circulation Management (Publishing)
Magazines—*See:* Periodicals
Magnesium Industry 540
Magnetic Records and Recordings—*See:* Sound Recorders and Recording
Mail Order Business 540
Mail Service—*See:* Postal Services
Mailing Lists 541
Maintenance of Buildings 541
Malls, Shopping—*See:* Shopping Centers
Malpractice—*See:* Professional Liability
Managed Care—*See:* Health Insurance; Health Maintenance Organizations
Management—*See:* Administration; Factory Management; Financial Management; Industrial Management; Management Theory; Office Management; Public Administration; Sales Management
Management, Bank—*See:* Bank Management
Management by Objectives—*See:* Industrial Management
Management Consultants 542

Management Development—*See:* Executive Training and Development
Management, Financial—*See:* Financial Management
Management Games 543
Management Information Systems 543
Management of Factories—*See:* Factory Management
Management, Operations—*See:* Operations Management
Management, Participative—*See:* Participative Management
Management, Production—*See:* Operations Management
Management, Scientific—*See:* Time and Motion Study
Management Systems—*See:* Systems in Management
Management Theory 545
Manpower—*See:* Labor Supply
Manuals, Procedure—*See:* Procedure Manuals
Manufactured Housing—*See:* Prefabricated House Industry
Manufacturers—*See:* Corporations; Industry; Private Companies
Manufacturers' Agents 546
Manufacturing—*See:* Industry
Manufacturing, Computer-Aided—*See:* Computer-Aided Design and Manufacturing (CAD/CAM)
Maps 546
Marble 546
Margarine Industry 547
Marinas 547
Marine Engineering 547
Marine Insurance 548
Marine Law—*See:* Maritime Law and Regulation
Maritime Industry—*See:* Ships, Shipping and Shipbuilding
Maritime Law and Regulation 548
Market Research 549
Market Statistics 551
Market Surveys—*See:* Consumer Surveys; Market Research; Survey Methods
Market Testing of New Products—*See:* Consumer Surveys; Market Research
Marketing 553
Marketing, Bank—*See:* Bank Marketing
Marketing, Chemical—*See:* Chemical Marketing
Marketing, Direct—*See:* Direct Marketing
Marketing, Industrial—*See:* Industrial Marketing
Marketing, International—*See:* International Marketing
Marketing, Multilevel—*See:* Multilevel Marketing
Marking Machines 555
Masonry 555
Mass Media 555
Mass Transportation—*See:* Public Transportation; Transportation Industry
Materials 557
Materials, Building—*See:* Building Materials Industry
Materials, Composite—*See:* Composite Materials
Materials Handling 558
Materials, Hazardous—*See:* Hazardous Materials
Mathematical Statistics—*See:* Statistical Methods
Mathematics, Business—*See:* Business Mathematics
Mature Consumer Market 559
Measures—*See:* Weights and Measures
Meat Industry 559
Meat Packing Industry—*See:* Meat Industry
Mechanical Drawing 561
Mechanical Engineering 561
Mechanical Power Transmission—*See:* Power (Mechanical)
Media, Interactive—*See:* Interactive Media
Media Law—*See:* Advertising Law and Regulation; Mass Media
Media, Mass—*See:* Mass Media
Media Research 561
Mediation—*See:* Arbitration
Medical Care Industry—*See:* Health Care Industry
Medical Economics (Practice Management) 562
Medical Electronics 563
Medical Equipment—*See:* Hospital Equipment; Surgical Instruments Industry
Medical Insurance—*See:* Health Insurance
Medical Laboratories—*See:* Clinical Laboratory Industry
Medical Liability—*See:* Professional Liability
Medical Service, Industrial—*See:* Industrial Medicine
Medical Technology 564
Medicare 565
Medicine, Industrial—*See:* Industrial Medicine
Meeting Management 567
Meetings—*See:* Conferences, Workshops, and Seminars
Meetings, Sales—*See:* Sales Conventions
Men's Clothing Industry 568
Mental Health 569
Mental Institutions 569
Merchandising—*See:* Marketing; Retail Trade
Merchant Marine—*See:* Ships, Shipping and Shipbuilding
Merchants—*See:* Retail Trade
Mergers and Acquisitions 570
Merit Rating—*See:* Rating of Employees
Metal Finishing 571
Metal Industry 571
Metal Industry, Nonferrous—*See:* Nonferrous Metal Industry
Metal Plating—*See:* Metal Finishing
Metal Powders—*See:* Powder Metallurgy Industry
Metal Working Industry 572
Metallurgy 573
Metals, Precious—*See:* Gold; Metal Industry; Platinum Industry; Silver Industry
Metals, Rare Earth—*See:* Rare Earth Metals
Meteorology—*See:* Weather and Weather Forecasting
Metric System—*See:* Weights and Measures
Metropolitan Areas—*See:* Cities and Towns; City Planning; Market Statistics; Urban Development
Mexico—*See:* Latin American Markets
Microcomputers and Minicomputers 574
Microfiche—*See:* Microforms
Microfilm—*See:* Microforms
Microforms 576
Micrographics—*See:* Microforms
Microphotography—*See:* Microforms

Microprocessors—*See:* Microcomputers and Minicomputers
Microsoft Windows—*See:* Windows (Software)
Microwaves 577
Migration—*See:* Immigration and Emigration
Migration of Industry—*See:* Location of Industry
Military Commissaries—*See:* Post Exchanges
Military Market 577
Milk Industry—*See:* Dairy Industry
Millers and Milling—*See:* Flour Industry
Millinery Industry 578
Millwork—*See:* Woodworking Industries
Mineralogy 578
Mines and Mineral Resources 578
Minicomputers—*See:* Microcomputers and Minicomputers
Mining—*See:* Mines and Mineral Resources
Ministers of State—*See:* Diplomatic and Consular Service
Minority Business 579
Minority Markets 580
Minority Newspapers 580
Missile Industry—*See:* Rocket Industry
Mobile Home Industry 580
Mobile Telephone Industry 581
Modems—*See:* Computer Communications
Modular Construction—*See:* Prefabricated House Industry
Molasses Industry 581
Monetary Policy—*See:* Economic Policy; Money
Money 582
Money Market—*See:* Money
Money Market Funds—*See:* Investment Companies
Money Raising—*See:* Business Start-Up Plans and Proposals; Fund-Raising; Venture Capital
Money Rates—*See:* Interest
Monopolies—*See:* Antitrust Actions
Morale, Industrial—*See:* Human Relations
Mortality—*See:* Vital Statistics
Mortgage Banks 584
Mortgages 584
Motel Industry—*See:* Hotel and Motel Industry
Motion Picture Cameras—*See:* Camera Industry
Motion Picture Industry 586
Motion Picture Photography 587
Motion Picture Theaters 587
Motion Pictures in Education—*See:* Audiovisual Aids in Education
Motion Pictures in Industry—*See:* Audiovisual Aids in Industry
Motion Study—*See:* Time and Motion Study
Motivation (Psychology) 588
Motivation Pamphlets—*See:* Pamphlets
Motivation Posters—*See:* Posters
Motor Bus Lines Time Tables—*See:* Timetables
Motor Buses 588
Motor Cars—*See:* Automobiles
Motor Home Industry—*See:* Mobile Home Industry; Recreational Vehicle Industry
Motor Transport—*See:* Trucking Industry
Motor Truck Industry—*See:* Trucking Industry
Motor Truck Trailers—*See:* Truck Trailers
Motor Trucks—*See:* Trucks (Manufacturing)
Motor Vehicle Equipment Industry—*See:* Automobile Equipment Industry
Motor Vehicle Law and Regulation 588
Motor Vehicle Licenses—*See:* Motor Vehicle Law and Regulation
Motor Vehicle Parking—*See:* Parking
Motor Vehicle Parts Industry—*See:* Automobile Equipment Industry
Motor Vehicles—*See:* Automobiles; Motor Buses; Trucks (Manufacturing)
Motor Vehicles, Foreign—*See:* Foreign Automobiles
Motor Vehicles, Used—*See:* Used Car Industry
Motorcycles 589
Motors—*See:* Engines
Moving of Employees—*See:* Relocation of Employees
Moving Picture Industry—*See:* Motion Picture Industry
Multifamily Housing—*See:* Apartment Houses; Condominiums
Multilevel Marketing 589
Multimedia 589
Multinational Corporations 592
Multiple Dwellings—*See:* Apartment Houses; Condominiums
Municipal Bonds 595
Municipal Employees—*See:* Civil Service; Municipal Government
Municipal Finance 596
Municipal Government 596
Mushroom Industry 597
Music Industry 597
Musical Instruments Industry 599
Mutual Funds—*See:* Investment Companies
Mutual Savings Banks—*See:* Savings Banks
NAFTA—*See:* North American Free Trade Agreement
Narcotics 601
National Accounting 601
National Brands—*See:* Trademarks and Trade Names
National Debt 602
National Holidays—*See:* Anniversaries and Holidays
National Income—*See:* Income; National Accounting
National Planning—*See:* Economic Policy
National Product—*See:* Gross National Product
Nations, Law of—*See:* International Law and Regulation
Natural Gas 603
Natural Resources 604
Naval Law—*See:* Maritime Law and Regulation
Naval Stores 604
Navy 604
Negotiation 605
Networks, Computer—*See:* Computer Communications; Local Area Networks
New Issues (Finance) 606
New Products 606

New York Stock Exchange—*See:* Stock Exchanges
Newsletters 607
Newspaper Clippings—*See:* Clipping Services
Newspaper Market Research 608
Newspaper Work—*See:* Journalism
Newspapers 608
Newspapers, School—*See:* College and School Newspapers
Newsprint Paper Industry—*See:* Paper Industry
Nickel Industry—*See:* Metal Industry
Noise Control 610
Nonferrous Metal Industry 610
Non-Foods Merchandisers—*See:* Rack Jobbers
Nonprescription Drug Industry 611
Nonprofit Corporations 612
Non-Wage Payments—*See:* Employee Benefit Plans; Fringe Benefits
Nonwoven Fabrics Industry 613
North American Free Trade Agreement 614
Notaries 615
Notebook Computers—*See:* Portable Computers
Notions—*See:* Gift Business
Nuclear Energy 615
Numerical Control of Machinery (NC))—*See:* Computer-Aided Design and Manufacturing (CAD/CAM)
Numismatics—*See:* Coins as an Investment
Nurseries (Horticultural) 616
Nursery Schools—*See:* Day Care Centers
Nursing Homes 617
Nut Industry 618
Nutrition—*See:* Diet
Nylon—*See:* Synthetic Textile Fiber Industry
Oats Industry—*See:* Feed and Feedstuffs Industry; Grain Industry
Obsolete Securities 619
Occupational Health—*See:* Industrial Hygiene
Occupational Safety—*See:* Industrial Safety
Occupational Therapy 619
Occupations 619
Ocean Liners—*See:* Steamship Lines
Oceanographic Industries 620
OECD—*See:* Organization for Economic Cooperation and Development
Off-Price Retailers—*See:* Discount Houses
Office Appliances—*See:* Office Equipment and Supplies
Office Automation 621
Office Buildings 621
Office Design 622
Office Equipment and Supplies 622
Office Forms—*See:* Forms and Blanks
Office Furniture Industry 623
Office in the Home—*See:* Self-Employment
Office Machines—*See:* Office Equipment and Supplies
Office Management 623
Office Practice 624
Office Supplies—*See:* Office Equipment and Supplies
Office Systems—*See:* Systems in Management; Word Processing
Official Publications—*See:* Government Publications
Officials and Employees—*See:* Government Employees
Offset Printing—*See:* Graphic Arts Industry; Printing and Printing Equipment Industries
Offshore Petroleum Industry 624
Oil—*See:* Oil and Fats Industry; Petroleum Industry
Oil and Fats Industry 624
Oil Burner Industry—*See:* Fuel Oil Industry
Oil Field Machinery—*See:* Petroleum Equipment Industry
Oil Fuel Industry—*See:* Fuel Oil Industry
Oil Industry—*See:* Petroleum Industry
Oil Marketing—*See:* Petroleum Marketing
Oil Tankers—*See:* Tank Ships
Oilseed Industry—*See:* Oil and Fats Industry
Old Age—*See:* Retirement
Old Age and Survivors Insurance—*See:* Social Security
Old Age Homes—*See:* Nursing Homes
Older Consumers—*See:* Mature Consumer Market
Older Workers—*See:* Employment of Older Workers
Oleomargarine Industry—*See:* Margarine Industry
Olive Oil Industry 625
On-the-Job Training—*See:* Training of Employees
Onion Industry 626
Online Commerce—*See:* Electronic Commerce
Online Information Systems 626
Operating Ratios—*See:* Financial Ratios
Operations Management 631
Operations Research 631
Ophthalmic Industry 631
Opiates—*See:* Narcotics
Opinion Polls—*See:* Public Opinion
Optical Disk Storage Devices 632
Optical Engineering—*See:* Optics Industry
Optical Fibers—*See:* Fiber Optics Industry
Optical Publishing Systems—*See:* Optical Disk Storage Devices
Optics Industry 634
Options (Puts and Calls)—*See:* Stock Option Contracts
Optoelectronics 635
Optometric Industry—*See:* Ophthalmic Industry
Orange Industry—*See:* Citrus Fruit Industry
Ordnance Market—*See:* Military Market
Organization—*See:* Industrial Management
Organization for Economic Cooperation and Development 636
Organization for European Economic Cooperation—*See:* Organization for Economic Cooperation and Development
Organization Theory—*See:* Management Theory
Organizations—*See:* Associations
Organized Labor—*See:* Labor Unions
Oriental Rug Industry 636
Orthopedic Appliance Industry—*See:* Prosthetics Industry
Outdoor Advertising 636

Outdoor Amusements—*See:* Amusement Industry
Outplacement Consultants—*See:* Employment Agencies and Services
Over-the-Counter Drugs—*See:* Nonprescription Drug Industry
Over-the-Counter Securities Industry 636
Overseas Employment—*See:* Employment in Foreign Countries
Oxyacetylene Welding—*See:* Welding
Oyster Industry 637
Packaging 639
Packaging Labels—*See:* Labels and Labeling
Packaging Machinery 639
Packaging, Pressure—*See:* Pressure Packaging
Packing Industry—*See:* Meat Industry
Paint and Painting 640
Pamphlets 640
Paper Bag Industry 641
Paper Board Industry—*See:* Paperboard and Paperboard Packaging Industries
Paper Box and Paper Container Industries 641
Paper Containers—*See:* Paper Box and Paper Container Industries
Paper Industry 641
Paper Money 642
Paperback Books—*See:* Paperbound Book Industry
Paperboard and Paperboard Packaging Industries 642
Paperbound Book Industry 643
Paperwork Management—*See:* Office Management; Records Management
Parking 643
Parks 643
Parliamentary Procedure 644
Participative Management 644
Part-Time Employees—*See:* Temporary Employees
Partnership 644
Party Plan Selling—*See:* Direct Marketing
Passports 645
Pasta Industry 645
Patents 645
Pay Planning—*See:* Executive Compensation; Wages and Salaries
Payroll Administration—*See:* Wages and Salaries
Peach Industry 647
Peanut and Peanut Oil Industries 647
Pear Industry 647
Pecan Industry 648
Pencils—*See:* Writing Instruments
Penny Stocks—*See:* Over-the-Counter Securities Industry
Pens—*See:* Writing Instruments
Pensions 648
Pepper Industry—*See:* Spice Industry
Performance Evaluation—*See:* Rating of Employees
Performing Arts—*See:* Show Business
Perfume Industry 650
Periodical Circulation—*See:* Circulation Management (Publishing)
Periodicals 651
Periodicals, Business—*See:* Trade Journals
Personal Care Products—*See:* Cosmetics Industry
Personal Computers—*See:* Microcomputers and Minicomputers; Portable Computers
Personal Finance 653
Personal Finance Companies—*See:* Finance Companies
Personnel Interviewing—*See:* Interviewing
Personnel Management 655
Personnel Manuals—*See:* Procedure Manuals
Personnel Recruitment—*See:* Recruitment of Personnel
Personnel Testing—*See:* Psychological Testing; Rating of Employees
PERT (Program Evaluation and Review Technique)—*See:* Critical Path Method/PERT (Program Evaluation and Review Technique)
Pest Control Industry 657
Pesticide Industry 658
Pet Food—*See:* Pet Industry
Pet Industry 658
Petrochemical Industry 659
Petroleum Equipment Industry 659
Petroleum Industry 660
Petroleum Industry, Offshore—*See:* Offshore Petroleum Industry
Petroleum Marketing 662
Pharmaceutical Industry 662
Pharmacies—*See:* Drug Stores
Philanthropy 665
Philately—*See:* Stamps as an Investment
Phonograph and Phonograph Record Industries 667
Photocopying Industry—*See:* Copying Machine Industry
Photoengraving 667
Photographic Industry 667
Photography, Commercial—*See:* Commercial Photography
Photography, Industrial—*See:* Commercial Photography
Photomechanical Processes—*See:* Graphic Arts Industry
Photonics 668
Physical Distribution—*See:* Distribution
Physical Fitness Industry—*See:* Fitness Industry
Picketing—*See:* Strikes and Lockouts
Piers—*See:* Ports
Pig Industry—*See:* Swine Industry
Piggyback Transport—*See:* Truck Trailers
Pilots—*See:* Air Pilots
Pineapple Industry 669
Pipe 669
Pipeline Industry 669
Pipes (Smoking)—*See:* Tobacco and Tobacco Industry
Pistols—*See:* Firearms Industry
Placement Bureaus—*See:* College Placement Bureaus
Planned Economy—*See:* Economic Policy
Planning 670

Plans, Business—*See:* Business Start-Up Plans and Proposals; Planning
Plant Engineering—*See:* Factory Management
Plant Location—*See:* Location of Industry
Plant Maintenance—*See:* Maintenance of Buildings
Plant Management—*See:* Factory Management
Plant Protection—*See:* Industrial Security Programs
Plant Sites—*See:* Location of Industry
Plaster and Plastering 671
Plastic Containers—*See:* Container Industry
Plastics Industry 671
Plating—*See:* Metal Finishing
Platinum Industry 673
Plumbing Industry 673
Plywood Industry 673
Point-of-Purchase Advertising 674
Point-of-Sale Systems (POS) 674
Police Equipment—*See:* Law Enforcement Industries
Policy Manuals—*See:* Procedure Manuals
Political Economy—*See:* Economics
Polls, Opinion—*See:* Public Opinion
Pollution of Air—*See:* Air Pollution
Pollution of Water—*See:* Water Pollution
Polymers—*See:* Chemical Industries; Plastics Industry
Popcorn Industry—*See:* Snack Food Industry
Population 674
Porcelain Industry—*See:* Pottery Industry
Pork—*See:* Swine Industry
Port Authorities—*See:* Ports
Portable Computers 677
Portable Databases—*See:* Optical Disk Storage Devices
Portfolio Management—*See:* Institutional Investments
Portland Cement—*See:* Cement Industry
Ports 678
Positions—*See:* Occupations
Post Exchanges 679
Postal Services 679
Posters 679
Potash Industry 679
Potato Chip Industry—*See:* Potato Industry; Snack Food Industry
Potato Industry 680
Potatoes, Sweet—*See:* Sweet Potato Industry
Pottery Industry 680
Poultry Industry 680
Poverty—*See:* Public Welfare
Powder Metallurgy Industry 681
Power Companies—*See:* Electric Utilities
Power (Mechanical) 682
Power Plants, Electric—*See:* Electric Power Plants
Power Tool Industry 682
Power Transmission (Mechanical)—*See:* Power (Mechanical)
Practice Management—*See:* Medical Economics (Practice Management)
Precious Metals—*See:* Gold; Metal Industry; Platinum Industry; Silver Industry
Precious Stones—*See:* Gems and Gemstones
Prefabricated House Industry 683
Premiums 683
Prepaid Medical Care—*See:* Health Insurance; Health Maintenance Organizations
Prepared Foods—*See:* Processed Food Industry
Presidents of Companies—*See:* Executives
Press Clippings—*See:* Clipping Services
Pressure Groups 683
Pressure Packaging 683
Pressure Sensitive Tape Industry—*See:* Adhesives
Pretzel Industry—*See:* Snack Food Industry
Price Coding, Electronic—*See:* Point-of-Sale Systems (POS)
Prices and Pricing 684
Prime Rate—*See:* Interest
Printing and Printing Equipment Industries 684
Printing Ink Industry 685
Printing Style Manuals 685
Prisons—*See:* Law Enforcement Industries
Private Companies 686
Private Label Products 687
Private Schools 687
Privatization 688
Prizes—*See:* Contests, Prizes, and Awards
Procedure Manuals 688
Process Control Equipment—*See:* Control Equipment Industry
Processed Food Industry 688
Procurement, Government—*See:* Government Purchasing
Produce Industry—*See:* Vegetable Industry
Product Coding—*See:* Point-of-Sale Systems (POS)
Product Design—*See:* Design in Industry
Product Development—*See:* New Products
Product Liability—*See:* Product Safety and Liability
Product Management—*See:* Marketing
Product Quality—*See:* Quality of Products
Product Rating Research—*See:* Quality of Products
Product Safety and Liability 689
Product Testing—*See:* Quality of Products
Production Control 690
Production Engineering—*See:* Industrial Engineering
Production Management—*See:* Operations Management
Productivity 690
Products, New—*See:* New Products
Products, Quality of—*See:* Quality of Products
Professional Associations—*See:* Associations
Professional Corporations 691
Professional Liability 691
Professional Practice Management, Medical—*See:* Medical Economics (Practice Management)
Professions—*See:* Occupations
Professors and Instructors—*See:* College Faculties
Profit Sharing 692

Program Evaluation and Review Technique—*See:* Critical Path Method/PERT (Program Evaluation and Review Technique)
Programmed Learning ... 693
Programming, Computer—*See:* Computer Software Industry
Programming, Linear—*See:* Linear Programming
Programs, Television—*See:* Television Programs
Project Management ... 693
Promotion—*See:* Sales Promotion
Promotional Merchandise—*See:* Premiums
Proofreading—*See:* Printing Style Manuals
Propane and Butane Gas Industry ... 694
Property and Liability Insurance ... 694
Property Management ... 695
Property Tax ... 696
Proposals, Business—*See:* Business Start-Up Plans and Proposals
Prosthetics Industry ... 696
Protective Services—*See:* Industrial Security Programs
Psychological Testing ... 696
Psychology—*See:* Human Relations; Mental Health; Motivation (Psychology)
Psychology, Industrial—*See:* Industrial Psychology
Public Accountants—*See:* Certified Public Accountants
Public Administration ... 697
Public Assistance—*See:* Public Welfare
Public Documents—*See:* Government Publications
Public Finance ... 698
Public Housing—*See:* Housing
Public Libraries—*See:* Libraries
Public Opinion ... 699
Public Relations and Publicity ... 700
Public Service Corporations—*See:* Public Utilities
Public Speaking ... 701
Public Transportation ... 701
Public Utilities ... 702
Public Welfare ... 703
Public Works ... 704
Publicity—*See:* Public Relations and Publicity
Publishers, College—*See:* University Presses
Publishing, Desktop—*See:* Desktop Publishing
Publishing, Electronic—*See:* Electronic Publishing
Publishing Industry ... 705
Pulpwood Industry—*See:* Woodpulp Industry
Pumps and Compressors ... 707
Purchasing ... 708
Purchasing Agents—*See:* Purchasing
Purchasing Power ... 708
Puts and Calls—*See:* Stock Option Contracts
Quality Control ... 711
Quality of Products ... 711
Quarrying ... 711
Rack Jobbers ... 713
Radio and Television Advertising ... 713
Radio and Television Repair Industry ... 713
Radio Broadcasting Industry ... 714
Radio Equipment Industry ... 715
Radio Stations—*See:* Radio Broadcasting Industry
Radioisotopes—*See:* Isotopes
Radiological Equipment—*See:* X-Ray Equipment Industry
Radios—*See:* Radio Equipment Industry
Railroad Equipment Industry ... 715
Railroad Time Tables—*See:* Timetables
Railroads ... 716
Raisin Industry ... 716
Rare Books—*See:* Book Collecting
Rare Earth Metals ... 716
Rating of Employees ... 717
Ratio Analysis—*See:* Financial Ratios
Real Estate Appraisal—*See:* Real Property Valuation
Real Estate Business ... 717
Real Estate, Industrial—*See:* Industrial Real Estate
Real Estate Investment Trusts ... 718
Real Estate Investments ... 718
Real Estate Management—*See:* Property Management
Real Estate Taxes—*See:* Property Tax; Tax Shelters; Taxation
Real Property Valuation ... 719
Recessions—*See:* Business Cycles
Recording Industry—*See:* Sound Recorders and Recording; Video Recording Industry
Records Management ... 720
Records, Phonograph—*See:* Phonograph and Phonograph Record Industries
Recreation, Industrial—*See:* Industrial Recreation
Recreation Industry ... 720
Recreational Vehicle Industry ... 721
Recruitment of Personnel ... 721
Recycling ... 722
Redevelopment, Urban—*See:* Urban Development
Reference Sources—*See:* Information Sources
Refineries—*See:* Petroleum Industry
Refractories ... 722
Refrigeration Industry ... 723
Refuse Disposal—*See:* Sanitation Industry
Regional Airlines—*See:* Airline Industry
Regional Planning ... 723
Registration of Trademarks—*See:* Trademarks and Trade Names
Regulation of Industry ... 724
Regulation of Securities—*See:* Securities Law and Regulation
Regulations—*See:* Laws; Regulation of Industry
Rehabilitation, Vocational—*See:* Vocational Rehabilitation
REIT's—*See:* Real Estate Investment Trusts
Relocation of Employees ... 725
Remodeling—*See:* Home Improvement Industry
Rental, Equipment—*See:* Equipment Leasing
Rental Housing—*See:* Apartment Houses; Real Estate Investments
Rental Services ... 726

Rental Services, Automobile—*See:* Automobile Lease and Rental Services
Report Writing 726
Reports—*See:* Corporation Reports; Report Writing
Research, Advertising—*See:* Advertising Research
Research and Development 727
Research, Business—*See:* Business Research
Research, Economic—*See:* Economic Research
Research, Industrial—*See:* Industrial Research
Research, Library—*See:* Library Research
Research, Marketing—*See:* Market Research
Resellers, Computer—*See:* Computer Retailing
Resins—*See:* Naval Stores; Plastics Industry
Resources—*See:* Natural Resources
Restaurants, Lunchrooms, Etc. 728
Restraint of Trade—*See:* Antitrust Actions
Resumes—*See:* Job Resumes
Retail Automation—*See:* Point-of-Sale Systems (POS)
Retail Security—*See:* Shoplifting
Retail Selling—*See:* Salesmen and Salesmanship
Retail Trade 729
Retailers, Computer—*See:* Computer Retailing
Retailers, Off-Price—*See:* Discount Houses
Retiree Market—*See:* Mature Consumer Market
Retirement 731
Retirement Age—*See:* Employment of Older Workers
Retirement Communities 732
Retirement Income Plans—*See:* 401(k) Retirement Plans; Individual Retirement Accounts
Reviews—*See:* Book Reviews
Rice Industry 734
Rifles—*See:* Firearms Industry
Risk Management 734
Road Maps—*See:* Maps
Road Materials—*See:* Asphalt Industry; Concrete Industry
Road Signs—*See:* Signs and Sign Boards
Roads and Highways 736
Roads, Toll—*See:* Toll Roads
Robots 737
Rock Products—*See:* Quarrying
Rocket Industry 738
Roller Bearings—*See:* Bearings and Ball Bearings
Roofing Industry 738
Rope and Twine Industry 739
Rubber and Rubber Goods Industries 739
Rug Industry—*See:* Floor Coverings
Rugs, Oriental—*See:* Oriental Rug Industry
Rules of Order—*See:* Parliamentary Procedure
Rum Industry—*See:* Distilling Industry
Rural Community Development—*See:* Community Development
Rural Credit—*See:* Agricultural Credit
Rural Electrification 739
Rye Industry 740
Safe Deposits (Banking) 741
Safety 741
Safety Appliances—*See:* Industrial Safety
Safety Education—*See:* Safety
Safety, Industrial—*See:* Industrial Safety
Safety, Product—*See:* Product Safety and Liability
Salad Oil Industry—*See:* Oil and Fats Industry
Salaries—*See:* Executive Compensation; Wages and Salaries
Sale of Business Enterprises—*See:* Business Enterprises, Sale of
Sales Auction—*See:* Auctions
Sales Contests—*See:* Sales Promotion
Sales Conventions 742
Sales Finance Companies—*See:* Finance Companies
Sales Management 742
Sales Meetings—*See:* Meeting Management; Sales Conventions
Sales Promotion 742
Sales Representatives—*See:* Manufacturers' Agents
Sales Tax 743
Salesmen and Salesmanship 743
Salmon Industry 744
Salt Industry 744
Sand and Gravel Industry—*See:* Quarrying
Sanitation Industry 744
Satellite Communications—*See:* Communications Satellites
Savings and Loan Associations 745
Savings Banks 746
Savings Bonds—*See:* Government Bonds
Saw Industry 746
Sawmills—*See:* Lumber Industry
Schedules, Transportation—*See:* Timetables
Scholarships and Student Aid 746
School Computers—*See:* Computers in Education
School Journalism—*See:* College and School Newspapers
Schools 747
Schools, Private—*See:* Private Schools
Scientific Apparatus and Instrument Industries 748
Scientific Laboratories—*See:* Laboratories
Scientific Research—*See:* Research and Development
Scrap—*See:* Waste Products
Scrap Metal—*See:* Iron and Steel Scrap Metal Industry
Screw Machine Industry—*See:* Machine Tool Industry
Seafood Industry 749
Sealants—*See:* Adhesives
Seaports—*See:* Ports
Secretarial Practice—*See:* Office Practice
Secretaries—*See:* Office Practice
Securities 750
Securities and Exchange Commission—*See:* Securities Law and Regulation
Securities, Convertible—*See:* Convertible Securities
Securities, Derivative—*See:* Derivative Securities
Securities Law and Regulation 752
Securities, Obsolete—*See:* Obsolete Securities
Securities, Tax Exempt—*See:* Municipal Bonds
Security Analysis—*See:* Financial Analysis
Security, Computer—*See:* Computer Crime and Security

Security Dealers—*See:* Stock Brokers
Security, Industrial—*See:* Industrial Security Programs
Security Systems, Electronic—*See:* Electronic Security Systems
Seed Industry 754
Selenium Industry 755
Self-Employment 755
Selling—*See:* Salesmen and Salesmanship
Selling a Business—*See:* Business Enterprises, Sale of
Selling by Telephone—*See:* Telephone Selling
Semiconductor Industry 756
Seminars—*See:* Conferences, Workshops, and Seminars
Senate—*See:* United States Congress
Senior Citizens—*See:* Employment of Older Workers; Mature Consumer Market; Retirement
Sensors, Industrial—*See:* Control Equipment Industry
Serial Publications—*See:* Periodicals
Service, Customer—*See:* Customer Service
Service Industries 757
Service Industry, Food—*See:* Food Service Industry
Service Men, Discharged—*See:* Veterans
Service Merchandisers—*See:* Rack Jobbers
Service Stations—*See:* Gasoline Service Stations
Severance Pay—*See:* Wages and Salaries
Sewage Disposal—*See:* Sanitation Industry
Sewing Machine Industry 758
Sexual Harassment in the Workplace 758
Shareholders—*See:* Stockholders
Shares of Stock—*See:* Stocks
Sheep Industry 760
Sheet Metal Industry 760
Shellfish Industry 761
Shelters, Tax—*See:* Tax Shelters
Shipbuilding—*See:* Ships, Shipping and Shipbuilding
Shipment of Goods—*See:* Freight Transport; Packaging; Postal Services; Traffic Management (Industrial); Trucking Industry
Shipping—*See:* Ships, Shipping and Shipbuilding
Ships, Shipping and Shipbuilding 761
Shoe Industry 763
Shop Practice—*See:* Machine Shops
Shoplifting 763
Shopping—*See:* Consumer Economics; Consumer Education
Shopping Centers 763
Shorthand 764
Shorthand Reporting 764
Show Business 764
Show Windows—*See:* Display of Merchandise
Sickness Insurance—*See:* Health Insurance
Signs and Sign Boards 765
Silk Industry 765
Silver Industry 765
Silverware—*See:* Tableware
Skip Tracers—*See:* Collecting of Accounts
Slot Machines—*See:* Vending Machines
Small Arms—*See:* Firearms Industry
Small Business 766
Small Business Investment Companies 768
Small Loan Companies—*See:* Finance Companies
Smoking Policy 768
Snack Food Industry 768
Snuff—*See:* Tobacco and Tobacco Industry
Soaps and Detergents—*See:* Cleaning Products Industry
Social Accounting—*See:* National Accounting
Social Responsibility 769
Social Security 770
Social Welfare—*See:* Public Welfare
Society and Business—*See:* Social Responsibility
Sodium Chloride Industry—*See:* Salt Industry
Soft Drink Industry 771
Software Industry, Computer—*See:* Computer Software Industry
Softwood Industry—*See:* Forest Products; Lumber Industry
Solar Energy 772
Sole Proprietorship—*See:* Self-Employment
Solid State Devices—*See:* Semiconductor Industry
Solid Waste Treatment—*See:* Sanitation Industry
Sound Recorders and Recording 773
South America—*See:* Latin American Markets
Soybean Industry 774
Space Industry—*See:* Aerospace Industry; Rocket Industry
Special Days and Weeks—*See:* Anniversaries and Holidays
Special Event Planning 775
Special Libraries 775
Specialists—*See:* Consultants
Specialty Food Industry 777
Speculation 778
Speech Recognition—*See:* Voice Recognition
Speeches—*See:* Public Speaking
Spice Industry 779
Sporting Goods Industry 779
Sports Business 780
Sportswear—*See:* Clothing Industry; Women's Apparel
Spot Radio Advertising—*See:* Radio and Television Advertising
Spot Welding—*See:* Welding
Staff Magazines—*See:* House Organs
Stainless Steel—*See:* Iron and Steel Industry
Stamps as an Investment 781
Standard Industrial Classification—*See:* Industry
Standard Metropolitan Statistical Areas—*See:* Cities and Towns; City Planning; Urban Development
Standardization 781
Start-Up Plans—*See:* Business Start-Up Plans and Proposals
State Employees—*See:* Government Employees
State Finance—*See:* Public Finance
State Government 781
State Income Tax—*See:* State Taxes
State Law 783
State Legislatures—*See:* Legislatures; State Government
State Taxes 783
Stationery Industry—*See:* Office Equipment and Supplies

Statistical Methods 784
Statistics, Business—*See:* Business Statistics
Statistics, Mathematical—*See:* Statistical Methods
Statistics Sources 785
Statistics, Vital—*See:* Vital Statistics
Statutes—*See:* Laws
Steam Heating—*See:* Heating and Ventilation
Steamship Lines 787
Steel Foundries—*See:* Foundries
Steel Industry—*See:* Iron and Steel Industry
Stenographers—*See:* Office Practice
Stenography—*See:* Shorthand
Stereophonic Sound—*See:* High Fidelity/Stereo
Stock and Stock Breeding—*See:* Livestock Industry
Stock Brokers 788
Stock Dividends—*See:* Dividends
Stock Exchanges 790
Stock Index Trading 791
Stock Market—*See:* Stock Exchanges
Stock Market Charts—*See:* Technical Analysis (Finance)
Stock Offerings, Initial—*See:* New Issues (Finance)
Stock Option Contracts 792
Stock Ownership Plans—*See:* Employee Benefit Plans; Employee Stock Ownership Plans; Executive Compensation
Stockbrokers—*See:* Stock Brokers
Stockholders 792
Stockings—*See:* Hosiery Industry
Stocks 793
Stockyards—*See:* Livestock Industry; Meat Industry
Stone Industry—*See:* Quarrying
Storage—*See:* Warehouses
Store Displays—*See:* Display of Merchandise
Stores, Convenience—*See:* Convenience Stores
Stores, Department—*See:* Department Stores
Stores (Retail Trade)—*See:* Retail Trade
Strategic Planning—*See:* Planning
Strategy, Business—*See:* Business Strategy
Street Lighting—*See:* Lighting
Street Maps—*See:* Maps
Stress (Anxiety) 797
Strikes and Lockouts 798
Structural Materials—*See:* Building Materials Industry
Student Aid—*See:* Scholarships and Student Aid
Study Abroad 798
Style Manuals—*See:* Printing Style Manuals
Subchapter "S" Corporations—*See:* Corporations; Professional Corporations
Subject Headings—*See:* Indexing
Subliminal Advertising—*See:* Advertising
Substance Abuse—*See:* Alcoholism; Drug Abuse and Traffic
Suburban Shopping Centers—*See:* Shopping Centers
Sugar Industry 799
Suggestion Systems 800
Sulphur Industry 800
Sulphuric Acid—*See:* Sulphur Industry
Sun, Energy From—*See:* Solar Energy
Superconductors 800
Supermarkets 801
Supervision—*See:* Administration; Factory Management; Industrial Management
Supply Management—*See:* Inventory Control; Purchasing
Surgical Instruments Industry 801
Surplus Farm Produce—*See:* Farm Produce
Surplus Products 802
Survey Methods 803
Surveys, Consumer—*See:* Consumer Surveys
Sweet Potato Industry 803
Sweetener Industry—*See:* Sugar Industry
Swimming Pool Industry 804
Swindlers and Swindling—*See:* Crime and Criminals; Fraud and Embezzlement
Swine Industry 804
Synthetic Fuels 804
Synthetic Textile Fiber Industry 805
Syrup Industry—*See:* Molasses Industry; Sugar Industry
Systems Engineering—*See:* Industrial Engineering
Systems in Management 805
Systems Integration 806
Tableware 809
Tailoring 809
Tall Oil Industry 809
Tank Ships 809
Tank Trucks—*See:* Trucking Industry
Tankers—*See:* Tank Ships
Tanning Industry 810
Tape Recording—*See:* Sound Recorders and Recording; Video Recording Industry
Tariff 810
Tax Administration 810
Tax, Estate—*See:* Inheritance Tax
Tax, Excise—*See:* Excise Tax
Tax Exempt Securities—*See:* Municipal Bonds
Tax, Gift—*See:* Gift Tax
Tax, Income—*See:* Income Tax
Tax, Inheritance—*See:* Inheritance Tax
Tax Law and Regulation 810
Tax Management—*See:* Taxation
Tax Planning 812
Tax, Property—*See:* Property Tax
Tax, Sales—*See:* Sales Tax; State Taxes; Taxation
Tax Shelters 813
Taxation 814
Taxation, International—*See:* International Taxation
Taxes, State—*See:* State Taxes
Taxicabs 816
Taylor System of Shop Management—*See:* Time and Motion Study
Tea Industry 816
Tea Rooms—*See:* Restaurants, Lunchrooms, Etc.
Technical Analysis (Finance) 817
Technical Assistance 818

Technical Books—*See:* Technology
Technical Education 818
Technical Literature—*See:* Technology
Technical Societies—*See:* Associations
Technical Writing 818
Technological Unemployment—*See:* Unemployment
Technology 819
Technology Transfer 821
Teenage Market—*See:* Youth Market
Telecommunications 822
Telecommuting 824
Telegraph 825
Telemarketing 825
Telemetering 826
Telephone Answering Service 826
Telephone Equipment Industry 826
Telephone Industry 827
Telephone Selling 828
Telephones—*See:* Telephone Equipment Industry
Telephones, Mobile—*See:* Mobile Telephone Industry
Telescopes 828
Teletext—*See:* Videotex/Teletext
Television Advertising—*See:* Radio and Television Advertising
Television Apparatus Industry 828
Television Broadcasting Industry 829
Television, Cable—*See:* Cable Television Industry
Television Engineering 831
Television, Foreign—*See:* Foreign Radio and Television
Television Programs 832
Television Recording—*See:* Video Recording Industry
Television Repair Industry—*See:* Radio and Television Repair Industry
Television, Satellite—*See:* Communications Satellites
Television Stations—*See:* Television Broadcasting Industry
Teller Machines—*See:* Bank Automation
Temperature (Climate)—*See:* Climate; Weather and Weather Forecasting
Temporary Employees 832
Tennis Industry 832
Termination of Employment—*See:* Dismissal of Employees
Testing of Materials—*See:* Materials; Standardization
Testing of Personnel—*See:* Psychological Testing; Rating of Employees
Testing of Products—*See:* Quality of Products
Textbooks—*See:* Book Industry; Publishing Industry
Textile Design 833
Textile Fibers—*See:* Fiber Industry; Synthetic Textile Fiber Industry
Textile Fibers, Synthetic—*See:* Synthetic Textile Fiber Industry
Textile Industry 833
Textile Machinery 834
Textile Mills—*See:* Textile Industry
Textiles, Home—*See:* Linen Industry
Textiles, Industrial—*See:* Industrial Fabrics Industry
Textiles, Nonwoven—*See:* Nonwoven Fabrics Industry
Theater Management 834
Theaters, Motion Picture—*See:* Motion Picture Theaters
Theft—*See:* Crime and Criminals; Shoplifting
Theses—*See:* Dissertations
Third World Nations—*See:* Developing Areas
Tile Industry 835
Timber Industry—*See:* Lumber Industry
Time and Motion Study 835
Timetables 836
Tin Industry 836
Tire Industry 836
Titanium Industry 837
Title Insurance 837
Titles of Degrees—*See:* Academic Degrees
Toasts 837
Tobacco and Tobacco Industry 838
Toiletries—*See:* Cosmetics Industry; Perfume Industry
Toll Roads 839
Tomato Industry 839
Tool Industry 839
Tools, Power—*See:* Power Tool Industry
Total Quality Management (TQM) 840
Tourist Industry—*See:* Travel Industry
Town Government—*See:* Municipal Government
Town Planning—*See:* City Planning
Towns and Cities—*See:* Cities and Towns
Toxic Substances—*See:* Hazardous Materials
Toxicology, Industrial—*See:* Industrial Hygiene
Toy Industry 841
Tractors—*See:* Agricultural Machinery
Trade—*See:* Business; Foreign Trade
Trade Associations—*See:* Associations
Trade, Boards of—*See:* Chambers of Commerce
Trade Catalogs—*See:* Catalogs and Directories
Trade Directories—*See:* Catalogs and Directories
Trade Exhibits—*See:* Conventions; Fairs; Trade Shows
Trade Fairs—*See:* Conventions; Fairs; Trade Shows
Trade Journals 841
Trade Names—*See:* Trademarks and Trade Names
Trade Secrets 843
Trade Shows 843
Trade Unions—*See:* Labor Unions
Trademarks and Trade Names 844
Trades—*See:* Occupations
Trading—*See:* Barter and Countertrade
Traffic Accidents and Traffic Safety 846
Traffic Engineering 846
Traffic Management (Industrial) 846
Traffic Management (Streets and Highways) 847
Trailers—*See:* Mobile Home Industry; Recreational Vehicle Industry; Truck Trailers
Training of Employees 847
Trains—*See:* Railroads
Transducers, Industrial—*See:* Control Equipment Industry
Transistors—*See:* Semiconductor Industry

Translating Machines—*See:* Machine Translating
Translations and Translators 848
Transportation Equipment Industry 848
Transportation Industry 848
Transportation, Public—*See:* Public Transportation
Transportation Time Tables—*See:* Timetables
Travel Agencies 850
Travel, Air—*See:* Air Travel
Travel, Business—*See:* Business Travel
Travel Industry 851
Travel Trailers—*See:* Recreational Vehicle Industry
Treasurers—*See:* Corporate Directors and Officers
Treasury Bonds—*See:* Government Bonds
Trees—*See:* Forest Products; Lumber Industry
Trends, Business—*See:* Business Cycles; Business Forecasting
Trials and Juries 852
Truck Trailers 852
Trucking Industry 853
Trucks (Manufacturing) 853
Trust Companies—*See:* Banks and Banking; Trusts and Trustees
Trusts and Trustees 854
Trusts, Investment—*See:* Investment Companies
Tuna Fish Industry 855
Turkey Industry 855
Turnpikes—*See:* Toll Roads
Turpentines and Resins—*See:* Naval Stores
Twine Industry—*See:* Rope and Twine Industry
Two-Income Families—*See:* Employment of Women; Women in the Work Force
Type and Type Founding 856
Typesetting 856
Typewriter Industry—*See:* Office Equipment and Supplies; Word Processing
Typography—*See:* Printing and Printing Equipment Industries; Typesetting
Ultrasonics 857
Underdeveloped Areas and Countries—*See:* Developing Areas; Economic Development; Technical Assistance
Undertakers and Undertaking—*See:* Funeral Homes and Directors
Underwear Industry 857
Underwriters—*See:* Insurance Underwriters
Unemployment 857
Unemployment Insurance 858
Uniform Commercial Code—*See:* Business Law
Uniforms 858
Unions—*See:* Labor Unions
United Funds—*See:* Community Funds
United Nations 859
United States Congress 859
United States Customs Service—*See:* Customs House, U.S. Customs Service
United States Government Bonds—*See:* Government Bonds
United States Government Publications—*See:* Government Publications
Universal Product Code (UPC)—*See:* Point-of-Sale Systems (POS)
Universities—*See:* Colleges and Universities
University Degrees—*See:* Academic Degrees
University Libraries—*See:* College and University Libraries
University Presses 860
Unix 860
Unlisted Securities—*See:* Over-the-Counter Securities Industry
Upholstery 861
Uranium Industry 861
Urban Areas—*See:* Cities and Towns
Urban Development 862
Urban Management—*See:* Municipal Government
Urban Planning—*See:* City Planning
Urban Transportation—*See:* Public Transportation; Transportation Industry
Used Car Industry 863
Used Products—*See:* Surplus Products
Utensils, Cooking—*See:* Housewares Industry
Utilities, Public—*See:* Public Utilities
Vacuum Cleaners 865
Valuation 865
Valves 865
Variable Annuities—*See:* Annuities
Variety Stores 866
Varnish and Varnishing 866
VCR—*See:* Video Recording Industry
Vegetable Industry 866
Vegetable Oil Industry—*See:* Oil and Fats Industry
Vending Machines 867
Veneers and Veneering 867
Venture Capital 868
Veterans 868
Veterinary Products 869
Vice—*See:* Crime and Criminals
Video Cameras—*See:* Video Recording Industry
Video Recording Industry 869
Videocassettes—*See:* Video Recording Industry
Videodiscs—*See:* Video Recording Industry
Videotape—*See:* Video Recording Industry
Videotex/Teletext 871
Viewtext—*See:* Videotex/Teletext
Virtual Reality 872
Viruses, Computer—*See:* Computer Crime and Security
Visual Education—*See:* Audiovisual Aids in Education
Vital Statistics 873
Vitamins 874
Vocabulary 875
Vocational Education 875
Vocational Guidance 875
Vocational Rehabilitation 876
Vocations—*See:* Occupations
Voice Recognition 876

Volume Feeding—*See:* Food Service Industry
Wage Differentials—*See:* Wages and Salaries
Wage Incentives—*See:* Wages and Salaries
Wage Negotiations—*See:* Collective Bargaining
Wages and Salaries 879
Wallpaper Industry 881
Warehouses 881
Warm Air Heating—*See:* Heating and Ventilation
Washing Machine Industry—*See:* Electric Appliance Industry
Waste Disposal—*See:* Sanitation Industry
Waste Management 881
Waste Products 882
Watch Industry—*See:* Clock and Watch Industry
Water Pollution 882
Water Power—*See:* Hydroelectric Industry
Water Supply 884
Waterfronts—*See:* Ports
Waterways 884
Waterworks—*See:* Water Supply
Wealthy Consumers—*See:* Affluent Market
Weapons Market—*See:* Defense Industries; Military Market
Weather and Weather Forecasting 885
Weaving 885
Weekly Newspapers—*See:* Newspapers
Weight Control—*See:* Diet
Weights and Measures 885
Welding 886
Welfare, Public—*See:* Public Welfare
Wellness Programs—*See:* Employee Wellness Programs
Wharves—*See:* Ports
Wheat Industry 886
Whiskey Industry—*See:* Distilling Industry
White Collar Crime—*See:* Crime and Criminals; Fraud and Embezzlement
Wholesale Trade 887
Wills 888
Wind Energy—*See:* Cogeneration of Energy
Window Covering Industry 888
Window Displays—*See:* Display of Merchandise
Windows (Software) 889
Wine Industry 890
Wire Industry 891
Wiring, Electric—*See:* Electrical Construction Industry
Women Accountants 892
Women Engineers 892
Women Executives 892
Women in Industry—*See:* Employment of Women; Women in the Work Force
Women in the Work Force 893
Women Lawyers 894
Women Managers—*See:* Women Executives
Women Physicians 894
Women's Apparel 894
Women's Clubs 895
Wood—*See:* Forest Products; Lumber Industry
Wood Finishing—*See:* Woodworking Industries
Woodpulp Industry 895
Woodworking Industries 896
Wool and Worsted Industry 896
Word Processing 897
Words—*See:* Vocabulary
Work Clothes—*See:* Uniforms
Work Force—*See:* Labor Supply
Work Measurement—*See:* Time and Motion Study
Work Schedules—*See:* Factory Management; Industrial Management
Work Simplification—*See:* Time and Motion Study
Work Stoppages—*See:* Strikes and Lockouts
Work Study—*See:* Time and Motion Study
Workers' Compensation 898
Working Class—*See:* Labor
Working Mothers—*See:* Employment of Women; Women in the Work Force
Working Women—*See:* Employment of Women; Women in the Work Force
Workmen's Compensation—*See:* Workers' Compensation
Workshops—*See:* Conferences, Workshops, and Seminars
World Banking—*See:* International Finance
World Law—*See:* International Law and Regulation
World Trade—*See:* Foreign Trade
World Wide Web—*See:* Internet
Worsted Industry—*See:* Wool and Worsted Industry
Worthless Securities—*See:* Obsolete Securities
Writers and Writing 899
Writing, Business—*See:* Business Correspondence; Report Writing; Writers and Writing
Writing Instruments 901
Writing, Technical—*See:* Technical Writing
X-Ray Equipment Industry 903
Yachts—*See:* Boat Industry
Yarn 905
Youth Market 905
Zero-Base Budgeting—*See:* Budgeting, Business
Zero Defects—*See:* Quality Control
Zinc Industry 907
Zip Code—*See:* Postal Services
Zoning 907

A

ABBREVIATIONS

ENCYCLOPEDIAS AND DICTIONARIES

Acronyms, Initialisms, and Abbreviations Dictionary. The Gale Group. • Annual. $650.00. Three volumes. Provides more than 586,000 definitions in all subject areas.

International Acronyms, Initialisms, and Abbreviations Dictionary. The Gale Group. • 2000. $465.00. Fifth edition. Two volumes. Contains over 210,000 English and non-English entries used internationally and in specific countries.

Periodical Title Abbreviations. The Gale Group. • 2000. $735.00. 13th edition. Two volumes. $245.00 per volume Vol. 1 *By Abbreviation*; vol. 2 *By Title.* Lists more than 145,000 different abbreviations.

Reverse Acronyms, Initialisms, and Abbreviations Dictionary. The Gale Group. • 1998. $375.00. In three parts.

World Guide to Abbreviations of Organizations. Available from The Gale Group. • 1987. $125.00. 11th edition. Published by Chapman and Hall.

ABRASIVES INDUSTRY

GENERAL WORKS

Abrasive Ages. William G. Pinkstone. Sutter House. • 1975. $16.95.

ABSTRACTS AND INDEXES

Alloys Index. Cambridge Information Group. • Monthly. $445.00 per year. Annual cumulation, $760.00 per year. Auxiliary publication to *Metals Abstracts* and *Metals Abstracts Index.*

Chemical Abstracts. Chemical Abstracts Service. • Weekly. $22,600.00 per year.

Metals Abstracts. Cambridge Information Group. • Monthly. $2,305.00 per year.

FINANCIAL RATIOS

Annual Statement Studies. Robert Morris Associates: The Association of Lending and Credit Risk Professiona. • Annual. Free to members; non-members, $140.00. Median and quartile financial ratios are given for over 400 kinds of manufacturing, wholesale, retail, construction, and consumer finance establishments. Data is sorted by both asset size and sales volume. Includes a clearly written "Definition of Ratios" and an alphabetical industry index.

HANDBOOKS AND MANUALS

AGA Publications. Abrasive Grain Association. • Series of booklets on uses of abrasive grains.

ONLINE DATABASES

F & S Index. The Gale Group. • Contains about four million citations to worldwide business, financial, and industrial or consumer product literature appearing from 1972 to date. Weekly updates. Inquire as to online cost and availability.

METADEX. Cambridge Scientific Abstracts. • Covers the worldwide literature of metals, metallurgy, and materials science, 1966 to date. Includes detailed alloys indexing from 1974. Biweekly updating. Inquire as to online cost and availability. (Formerly produced by ASM International.).

PERIODICALS AND NEWSLETTERS

Abrasives Magazine. Abrasive Magazine, Inc. • Eight times a year. $27.00 per year.

Grits and Grinds. Norton Co. • Quarterly. Free.

PRICE SOURCES

Chemical and Engineering News: The Newsmagazine of the Chemical World. American Chemical Society. • Weekly. Institutions, $181.00 per year; others, price on application.

STATISTICS SOURCES

Mineral Commodity Summaries. Available from U. S. Government Printing Office. • Annual. Published by the U. S. Geological Survey, Department of the Interior (http://www.usgs.gov). Contains detailed, five-year data for about 90 nonfuel minerals. Covers a wide range of statistics, including production, imports, exports, consumption, reserves, prices, tariff information, and industry employment. (Two pages are devoted to each mineral.).

Minerals Yearbook. Available from U.S. Government Printing Office. • Annual. Three volumes.

United States Census of Mineral Industries. Bureau of the Census, U.S. Department of Commerce. Available from U.S. Government Printing Office. • Quinquennial.

TRADE/PROFESSIONAL ASSOCIATIONS

Abrasive Engineering Society. P.O. Box 3157, Butler, PA 16003-3157. Phone: (724)282-6210 E-mail: grind@nauticom.net • URL: http://www.nauticom.net/www/grind.

Unified Abrasives Manufacturers Association - Bonoded Division. 30200 Detroit Ave., Cleveland, OH 44145-1967. Phone: (440)899-0010 Fax: (440)892-1404 E-mail: djh@wherryassoc.com • URL: http://www.gwi.corp.

United Abrasives Manufacturers Association - Coated Division. 30200 Detroit Rd., Cleveland, OH 44145-1967. Phone: (440)899-0010 Fax: (440)892-1404 E-mail: djh@wherryassoc.com.

OTHER SOURCES

Abrasive Engineering Society Conference Proceedings. Abrasive Engineering Society. • Annual. Price varies.

ABSENTEEISM

ABSTRACTS AND INDEXES

Business Periodicals Index. H. W. Wilson Co. • Monthly, except August, with quarterly and annual cumulations. Service basis for print edition; CD-ROM edition, $1,495.00 per year.

Personnel Management Abstracts. • Quarterly. $190.00 per year. Includes annual cumulation.

DIRECTORIES

Business Organizations, Agencies, and Publications Directory. The Gale Group. • 1999. $425.00. 12th edition. Over 40,000 entries describing 39 types of business information sources. Classified by type of organization, publication, or serviceIncludes state, national, and international agencies and organizations. Master index to names and keywords. Also includes e-mail addresses and web site URL's.

ONLINE DATABASES

Wilson Business Abstracts Online. H. W. Wilson Co. • Indexes and abstracts 600 major business periodicals, plus the *Wall Street Journal* and the business section of the *New York Times*. Indexing is from 1982, abstracting from 1990, with the two newspapers included from 1993. Updated weekly. Inquire as to online cost and availability. (*Business Periodicals Index* without abstracts is also available online.).

PERIODICALS AND NEWSLETTERS

HR Magazine (Human Resources): Strategies and Solutions for Human Resource Professionals. Society for Human Resource Management. • Monthly. Free to members; non-members, $125.00 per year. Formerly *Personnel Administrator.*

TRADE/PROFESSIONAL ASSOCIATIONS

American Management Association. 1601 Broadway, New York, NY 10019-7420. Phone: 800-262-9699 or (212)586-8100 Fax: (212)903-8168 • URL: http://www.amanet.org.

Society for Human Resource Management. 1800 Duke St., Alexandria, VA 22314-3499. Phone: 800-283-7476 or (703)548-3440 Fax: (703)535-6490 E-mail: shrm@shrm.org • URL: http://www.shrm.org.

ACADEMIC DEGREES

See also: COLLEGES AND UNIVERSITIES

ABSTRACTS AND INDEXES

Current Index to Journals in Education (CIJE). Oryx Press. • Monthly. $245.00 per year. Semiannual cumulations, $475.00.

Education Index. H.W. Wilson Co. • 10 times a year. Service basis.

ONLINE DATABASES

Education Index Online. H. W. Wilson Co. • Indexes a wide variety of periodicals related to schools, colleges, and education, 1984 to date. Monthly updates. Inquire as to online cost and availability.

PERIODICALS AND NEWSLETTERS

Resources in Education. Educational Resources Information Center. Available from U.S. Government Printing Office. • Monthly. $102.00 per year. Reports on educational research.

STATISTICS SOURCES

Digest of Education Statistics. Available from U. S. Government Printing Office. • Annual. $44.00. Covers all areas of education from kindergarten through graduate school. Includes data from both government and private sources. Compiled by National Center for Education Statistics, U. S. Department of Education.

Occupational Projections and Training Data. Available from U. S. Government Printing Office. • Biennial. $7.00. Issued by Bureau of Labor Statistics, U. S. Department of Labor. Contains projections of employment change and job openings over the next 15 years for about 500 specific occupations. Also includes the number of associate, bachelor's, master's, doctoral, and professional degrees awarded in a recent year for about 900 specific fields of study.

ACADEMIC DISSERTATIONS

See: DISSERTATIONS

ACCIDENT INSURANCE

See also: AUTOMOBILE INSURANCE; CASUALTY INSURANCE; INSURANCE

GENERAL WORKS

Modern Accident Investigation and Analysis: An Executive Guide to Accident Investigation. Ted S. Ferry. John Wiley and Sons, Inc. • 1988. $140.00. Second edition.

Property and Liability Insurance. Solomon S. Huebner and others. Prentice Hall. • 1995. $96.00.

ALMANACS AND YEARBOOKS

Insurance Almanac: Who, What, When and Where in Insurance. Underwriter Printing and Publishing Co. • Annual. $145.00. Lists insurance agencies and brokerage firms; U.S. and Canadian insurance companies, adjusters, appraisers, auditors, investigators, insurance officials and insurance organizations.

CD-ROM DATABASES

U. S. Insurance: Life, Accident, and Health. Sheshunoff Information Services, Inc. • Monthly. Price on application. CD-ROM provides detailed, current information on the financial characteristics of more than 2,300 life, accident, and health insurance companies.

DIRECTORIES

Best's Directory of Recommended Insurance Attorneys and Adjusters. A. M. Best Co. • Annual. $1130.00. Two volumes. More than 5,000 American, Canadian, and foreign insurance defense law firms; lists 1,200 national and international insurance adjusting firms. Formerly *Best's Directory of Recommended Insurance Adjusters.*

ENCYCLOPEDIAS AND DICTIONARIES

Dictionary of Insurance. Lewis E. Davids. Rowman and Littlefield Publishers, Inc. • 1990. $17.95. Seventh revised edition.

Dictionary of Insurance Terms. Harvey W. Rubin. Barron's Educational Series, Inc. • 2000. $12.95. Fourth edition. Defines terms in a wide variety of insurance fields. Price on application.

Insurance Words and Their Meanings: A Dictionary of Insurance Terms. Diana Kowatch. The Rough Notes Co., Inc. • 1998. $38.50. 16th revised edition.

Rupp's Insurance and Risk Management Glossary. Richard V. Rupp. Available from CCH, Inc. • 1996. $35.00. Second edition. Published by NILS Publishing Co. Provides definitions of 6,400 insurance words and phrases. Includes a guide to acronyms and abbreviations.

FINANCIAL RATIOS

Best's Key Rating Guide. A.M. Best Co. • Annual. $95.00. Financial information and ratings on over 2,000 property/casualty insurers.

HANDBOOKS AND MANUALS

Life and Health Insurance Law. William F. Meyer. West Group. • 1972. $125.00. Covers the legal aspects of life, health, and accident insurance.

ONLINE DATABASES

ABI/INFORM. Bell & Howell Information and Learning. • Provides online indexing to business-related material occurring in over 1,000 periodicals from 1971 to the present. Inquire as to online cost and availability.

Best's Company Reports. A. M. Best Co. • Provides full financial data online for U. S. insurance companies (life, health, property, casualty), including balance sheet data, income statements, expenses, premium income, losses, and investments. Includes *Best's Company Reports, Best's Insurance News,* and Best's ratings of insuarance companies. Inquire as to online cost and availability.

I.I.I. Data Base Search. Insurance Information Institute. • Provides online citations and abstracts of insurance-related literature in magazines, newspapers, trade journals, and books. Emphasis is on property and casualty insurance issues, including highway safety, product safety, and environmental liability. Inquire as to online cost and availability.

PERIODICALS AND NEWSLETTERS

Journal of Risk and Insurance. American Risk and Insurance Association. • Quarterly. $90.00 per year.

PRICE SOURCES

Policy Statistics Service. The National Underwriter Co.

STATISTICS SOURCES

Accident Facts. National Safety Council. • Annual. $37.95.

TRADE/PROFESSIONAL ASSOCIATIONS

American Insurance Association. 1130 Connecticut Ave., N.W., Suite 1000, Washington, DC 20036. Phone: 800-242-2302 or (202)828-7100 or (202)828-7183 Fax: (202)293-1219.

Insurance Information Institute. 110 William St., New York, NY 10038. Phone: 800-331-9146 Fax: (212)791-1807 E-mail: info@iii.org • URL: http://www.iii.org.

National Association of Insurance Brokers. 701 Pennsylvania Ave., N.W., Ste. 750, Washington, DC 20004-2661. Phone: (202)783-4400 Fax: (202)628-6707.

OTHER SOURCES

Life, Health, and Accident Insurance Law Reports. CCH, Inc. • $835.00 per year. Looseleaf service. Monthly updates.

ACCIDENTS

See also: ACCIDENT INSURANCE; SAFETY; TRAFFIC ACCIDENTS AND TRAFFIC SAFETY

GENERAL WORKS

Safety. Alton, L. ThyGerson. Jones and Bartlett Publishing, Inc. • 1992. $33.75. Second edition.

ABSTRACTS AND INDEXES

Health and Safety Science Abstracts. Institute of Safety and Systems Management. Cambridge Information Group. • Quarterly. $775.00 per year. Formerly *Safety Science Abstracts Journal.*

Safety and Health at Work. International Labour Office. • Bimonthly. $240.00 per year. Formerly *Occupational Safety and Health Abstracts.*

CD-ROM DATABASES

OSH-ROM: Occupational Safety and Health Information on CD-ROM. Available from SilverPlatter Information, Inc. • Price and frequency on application. Produced in Geneva by the International Occupational Safety and Health Information Centre, International Labour Organization (http://www.ilo.org). Provides about two million citations and abstracts to the worldwide literature of industrial safety, industrial hygiene, hazardous materials, and accident prevention. Material is included from journals, technical reports, books, government publications, and other sources. Time span varies.

ENCYCLOPEDIAS AND DICTIONARIES

Encyclopedia of Occupational Health and Safety 1983. International Labour Office. • 1991. $270.00. Third revised edition. Two volumes.

INTERNET DATABASES

National Center for Health Statistics: Monitoring the Nation's Health. National Center for Health Statistics, Centers for Disease Control and Preventio. Phone: (301)458-4636 E-mail: nchsquery@cdc.gov • URL: http://www.cdc.gov/nchswww • Web site provides detailed data on diseases, vital statistics, and health care in the U. S. Includes a search facility and links to many other health-related Web sites. "Fastats A to Z" offers quick data on hundreds of topics from Accidents to Work-Loss Days, with links to Comprehensive Data and related sources. Frequent updates. Fees: Free.

ONLINE DATABASES

American Statistics Index: A Comprehensive Guide and Index to the Statistical Publications of the United States Government [Online]. Congressional Information Service, Inc. • Indexes and abstracts, 1973 to date. Inquire as to online cost and availability.

Embase. Elsevier Science, Inc. • Worldwide medical literature, 1974 to present. Weekly updates. Inquire as to online cost and availability.

Information Bank Abstracts. New York Times Index Dept. • Provides indexing and abstracting of current affairs, primarily from the final late edition of *The New York Times* and the Eastern edition of *The Wall Street Journal.* Time period is 1969 to present, with daily updates. Inquire as to online cost and availability.

Labordoc. International Labour Office. • Indexing of labor literature and the publications of the International Labour Organization, 1965 to present. Monthly updates. Inquire as to online cost and availability.

PERIODICALS AND NEWSLETTERS

Accident Analysis and Prevention. Elsevier Science. • Bimonthly. $1123.00 per year.

Accident Prevention. Flight Safety Foundation, Inc. • Monthly. Memebers, $120.00 per year; non-members, $240.00 per year. Covers airline safety. Formerly *Accident Prevention Bulletin.*

BNA's Safetynet. Bureau of National Affairs, Inc. • Biweekly. $680.00 per year. Looseleaf. Formerly *Job Safety and Health.*

Hazard Prevention. System Safety Society, Inc. • Quarterly. Free to members; non-members, $45.00 per year.

Human Factors and Aviation Medicine. Flight Safety Foundation. • Bimonthly. Members, $120.00 per year; non-members, $240.00 per year.

Occupational Hazards: Magazine of Health and Environment. Penton Media Inc. • Monthly. $50.00 per year. Industrial safety and security management.

Product Safety News. National Safety Council. • Monthly. Members, $21.00 per year; non-members, $25.00 per year.

Safety and Health: The International Safety Health and Environment Magazine. National Safety Council. • Monthly. Members, $80.00 per year; non-members, $91.00 per year. Formerly *National Safety and Health News.*

Traffic Safety: The Magazine for Traffic Safety Professionals. National Safety Council. • Bimonthly. Members, $33.00 per year; non-members, $44.00 per year.

STATISTICS SOURCES

Accident Facts. National Safety Council. • Annual. $37.95.

Health and Environment in America's Top-Rated Cities: A Statistical Profile. Grey House Publishing. • Biennial. $195.00. Covers 75 U. S. cities. Includes statistical and other data on a wide variety of topics, such as air quality, water quality, recycling, hospitals, physicians, health care costs, death rates, infant mortality, accidents, and suicides.

Metropolitan Life Insurance Co. Statistical Bulletin SB. Metropolitan Life Insurance Co. • Quarterly. Individuals, $50.00 per year. Covers a wide range of social, economic and demographic health concerns.

Occupational Injuries and Illnesses by Industry. Bureau of Labor Statistics, U.S. Department of Labor. Available from U.S. Government Printing Office. • Annual.

Report on the American Workforce. Available from U. S. Government Printing Office. • Annual. $15.00. Issued by the U. S. Department of Labor (http://www.dol.gov). Appendix contains tabular statistics, including employment, unemployment, price indexes, consumer expenditures, employee benefits (retirement, insurance, vacation, etc.), wages, productivity, hours of work, and occupational injuries. Annual figures are shown for up to 50 years.

Vital Statistics of the United States. Public Health Service, U.S. Dept. of Health and Human Services. Available from U.S. Government Printing Office. • Annual. Two volumes.

TRADE/PROFESSIONAL ASSOCIATIONS

International Association of Industrial Accident Boards and Commissions. 1201 Wakarusa Dr., Lawrence, KS 66049. Phone: (785)840-9103 Fax: (785)840-9107 E-mail: workcomp@iaiabc.org • URL: http://www.iaiabc.org • Members are government agencies, insurance companies, lawyers, unions, self-insurers, and others with an interest in industrial safety and the administration of workers' compensation laws.

National Safety Council. 1121 Spring Lake Dr., Itasca, IL 60143-3201. Phone: 800-621-7615 or (630)285-1121 Fax: (630)285-1315 • URL: http://www.nsc.org.

OTHER SOURCES

Employment Safety and Health Guide. CCH, Inc. • Weekly. $1,095.00 per year. Four looseleaf volumes.

ACCOUNTABILITY, SOCIAL

See: SOCIAL RESPONSIBILITY

ACCOUNTANTS

See: CERTIFIED PUBLIC ACCOUNTANTS

ACCOUNTING

See also: AUDITING; CERTIFIED PUBLIC ACCOUNTANTS; COMPUTERS IN ACCOUNTING; COST ACCOUNTING; GOVERNMENT ACCOUNTING; WOMEN ACCOUNTANTS

GENERAL WORKS

Accounting and Finance for Non-Specialists. Peter Atrill and Eddie McLaney. Prentice Hall. • 2000. Third edition. Price on application. Includes the measurement and reporting of financial performance and cash flow.

Accounting: The Basis for Business Decisions. Robert F. Meigs and Mary A. Meigs. McGraw-Hill. • 1995. $68.75. 10th edition.

Accounting Theory. Ahmed Riahi-Belkaoui. Thomson Learning. • 2000. $77.99. Fourth edition. (ITBP Textbook Series.).

Advanced Accounting. Debra Jeter and others. John Wiley and Sons, Inc. • 2000. $107.95. Seventh edition. Reflects recent pronouncements of the Financial Accounting Standards Board (FASB) and the Governmental Accounting Standards Board (GASB).

Basic Accounting for the Small Business: Simple, Foolproof Techniques for Keeping Your Books Straight and Staying Out of Trouble. Clive C. Cornish. Self-Counsel Press, Inc. • 1993. $8.95. Ninth revised edition. (Business Series).

Financial Reporting: An Accounting Revolution. William H. Beaver. Prentice Hall. • 1997. $52.00. Third edition. (Contemporary Topics in Accounting Series).

Fundamental Accounting Principles. Kermit D. Larson and Paul B. Miller. McGraw-Hill Higher Education. • 1995. $72.00. 14th edition.

Fundamentals of Financial and Managerial Accounting. Kermit D. Larson and others. McGraw-Hill Higher Education. • 1993. $72.00.

Management Accounting. Don R. Hansen. South-Western College Publishing. • 1999. $98.95. Fifth edition. (SWC-Accounting).

Managerial Accounting. Harold M. Sollenberger and Arnold Schneider. South-Western Publishing Co. • 1996. $80.95. Ninth edition. (SWC-Accounting).

ABSTRACTS AND INDEXES

Accounting and Tax Index. UMI. • Quarterly. Price on application. Includes annual cumulative bound volume. Indexes accounting, auditing, and taxation literature appearing in journals, books, pamphlets, conference proceedings, and newsletters. (UMI is University Microfilms International, a Bell & Howell Co.).

Accounting Articles. CCH, Inc. • Monthly. $594.00 per year. Looseleaf service.

Business Periodicals Index. H. W. Wilson Co. • Monthly, except August, with quarterly and annual cumulations. Service basis for print edition; CD-ROM edition, $1,495.00 per year.

ALMANACS AND YEARBOOKS

Yearbook. Association of Government Accountants. • Annual.

BIBLIOGRAPHIES

Business Information Sources. Lorna M. Daniells. California Princeton Fulfillment Services. • 1993. $42.50. Third revised edition. Basic business sources, with discussion and full annotations.

CD-ROM DATABASES

Business Source Plus. EBSCO Information Services. • Monthly. $1,495.00 per year. Provides CD-ROM citations and abstracts to articles in about 650 business periodicals and newspapers, including *The Wall Street Journal.* Full text is provided from 200 selected periodicals. Covers accounting, communications, economics, finance, management, marketing, and other business subjects.

WILSONDISC: Wilson Business Abstracts. H. W. Wilson Co. • Monthly. $2,495.00 per year, including unlimited online access to *Wilson Business Abstracts* through WILSONLINE. Provides CD-ROM "cover-to-cover" abstracting and indexing of over 600 prominent business periodicals. Indexing is from 1982, abstracting from 1990. (*Business Periodicals Index* without abstracts is available on CD-ROM at $1,495 per year.).

DIRECTORIES

Business and Finance Career Directory. Visible Ink Press. • 1992. $17.95.

Emerson's Directory of Leading U.S. Accounting Firms. Available from Hoover's, Inc. • Biennial. $195.00. Published by the Emerson Company (http://www.emersoncompany.com). Provides information on 500 major CPA firms.

National Society of Public Accountants - Yearbook. National Society of Accountants. • Annual. Free to members, government agencies and libraries; not available to others.

Who Audits America: A Directory of Publicly Held Corporations and the Accounting Firms Who Audit Them. Data Financial Press. • Semiannual. $125.00. 8,500 publicly held corporations that report to the Securities and Exchange Commission, and their accounting firms.

ENCYCLOPEDIAS AND DICTIONARIES

Blackwell Encyclopedic Dictionary of Accounting. Rashad Abdel-khalik. Blackwell Publishers. • 1997. $105.95. The editor is associated with the University of Florida. Contains definitions of key terms combined with longer articles written by various U. S. and foreign business educators. Includes bibliographies and index. (Blackwell Encyclopedia of Management Series).

Dictionary of Accounting. Ralph Estes. MIT Press. • 1985. $11.95. Second edition.

Dictionary of Accounting Terms. Joel G. Siegel and Jae K. Shim. Barron's Educational Series, Inc. • 1995. $11.95. Second edition.

Encyclopedia of Accounting Systems. Tom M. Plank and Lois R. Plank. Prentice Hall. • 1994. $110.00. Three volumes.

Encyclopedia of Business. The Gale Group. • 2000. $425.00. Second edition. Two volumes. Contains more than 700 signed articles covering major business disciplines and concepts. International in scope.

Encyclopedia of Business and Finance. Burton Kaliski, editor. Available from The Gale Group. • 2001. $240.00. Two volumes. Published by Macmillan Reference USA. Contains articles by various contributors on accounting, business administration, banking, finance, management information systems, and marketing.

The History of Accounting: An Encyclopedia. Michael Chatfield and Richard Vangermeersch, editors. Garland Publishing, Inc. • 1996. $100.00. Contains more than 400 alphabetical entries by various contributors, covering the history of accounting from 750 B.C. to the modern era. Includes a bibliography for each entry and an index. (Reference Library of the Humanities Series, Vol. 1573).

International Dictionary of Accounting Acronyms. Thomas W. Morris, editor. Fitzroy Dearborn Publishers. • 1999. $45.00. Defines 2,000 acronyms used in worldwide accounting and finance.

FINANCIAL RATIOS

Income and Fees of Accountants in Public Practice. National Society of Accountants. • Triennial. Members, $35.00; non-members, $50.00.

HANDBOOKS AND MANUALS

Accountants' Handbook. Douglas R. Carmichael and others, editors. John Wiley and Sons, Inc. • 1999. $135.00. Ninth edition. Chapters are written by various accounting and auditing specialists.

Accountant's Handbook of Fraud and Commercial Crime. G. Jack Bologna and others. John Wiley and Sons, Inc. • 1992. $155.00. *1996 Supplement,* $65.00.

Accounting and Budgeting in Public and Non-profit Organizations: A Manager's Guide. C. William Garner. Jossey-Bass, Inc. Publishers. • Date not set. $39.95. An accounting primer for non-profit executives with no formal training in accounting. Includes an explanation of Generally Accepted Accounting Principles (GAAP) as applied to non-profit organizations. (Public Administration-Non Profit Sector Series).

Accounting and Recordkeeping for the Self-Employed. Jack Fox. John Wiley and Sons, Inc. • 1994. Price on application.

Accounting Deskbook: The Accountant's Everyday Instant Answer Book. Douglas L. Blensly and Tom M. Plank. Prentice Hall. • 1995. $69.95. 10th edition. 2000 *Supplement*, $39.95. Covers more than 230 accounting topics with examples, checklists, worksheets, and tables.

Accounting for Libraries and Other Not-for-Profit Organizations. G. Stevenson Smith. American Library Association. • 1999. $82.00. Second edition. Covers accounting fundamentals for nonprofit organizations. Includes a glossary.

Accounting Trends and Techniques in Published Corporate Annual Reports. American Institute of Certified Public Accountants. • Annual. $50.00.

AICPA Audit and Accounting Manual. American Institute of Certified Public Accountants. • 1999. $99.00. Covers working papers, internal control, audit approach, etc.

AICPA Codification of Statements on Auditing Standards. American Institute of Certified Public Accountants. • 1999. $81.25. Includes *Auditing Interpretations* and *International Auditing Guidelines*.

AICPA Codification of Statements on Standards for New Accounting and Review Services. American Institute of Certified Public Accountants. • 1998. $19.00.

AICPA Professional Standards, U. S. Auditing Standards, Accounting and Review Services, Ethics, Bylaws, International Accounting, International Auditing, Management Advisory Services, Quality Control, and Tax Practice. American Institute of Certified Public Accountants. • Annual. $180.00. Two volumes. Updates. Looseleaf. Three parts: Accounting, Ethics, Auditing.

AICPA Technical Practice Aids. American Institute of Certified Public Accountants. • $180.00 per year. Looseleaf service. Periodic supplementation. Advisory opinions, statements of position, and other material.

Applying GAAP and GAAS. Matthew Bender & Co., Inc. • Two looseleaf volumes. Periodic supplementation. Price on application. In-depth explanations of generally accepted accounting principles (GAAP) and generally accepted auditing standards (GAAS).

Bookkeeping Service. Entrepreneur Media, Inc. • Looseleaf. $59.50. A practical guide to starting a computer-oriented bookkeeping business. Covers profit potential, start-up costs, market size evaluation, pricing, accounting, advertising, promotion, etc. (Start-Up Business Guide No. E2335.).

FASB Accounting Standards. McGraw-Hill Professional. • Annual. Five volumes (prices vary). Includes *Financial Accounting Concepts, General Standards, Industry Standards*, and two volumes of *Original Pronouncements*. An appendix lists titles of American Institute of Certified Public Accountants (AICPA) and Financial Accounting Standards Board (FASB) documents.

Financial Accounting Standards: Explanation and Analysis. CCH, Inc. • Annual.

Financial Shenanigans: How to Detect Accounting Gimmicks and Fraud in Financial Reports. Howard M. Schilit. McGraw-Hill. • 1993. $22.95. Tells how to interpret the footnotes and fine print in corporate annual and other reports.

GAAP for Governments: Interpretation and Application of Generally Accepted Accounting Principles for State and Local Governments. John Wiley and Sons, Inc. • Annual. $134.00. (Includes CD-ROM.).

Guide to Financial Reporting and Analysis. Eugene E. Comiskey and Charles W. Mulford. John Wiley and Sons, Inc. • 2000. $75.00. Provides financial statement examples to illustrate the application of generally accepted accounting principles.

IAS: Interpretation and Application of International Accounting Standards. John Wiley and Sons, Inc. • Annual. $65.00. (Also available on CD-ROM.).

Marketing for CPAs, Accountants, and Tax Professionals. William J. Winston. Haworth Press, Inc. • 1995. $49.95.

Miller GAAP Guide: A Comprehensive Restatement of All Current Promulgated Generally Accepted Accounting Principles. Harcourt Brace Professional Publishing. • Annual. $69.00. Monthly updates. Includes all current Financial Accounting Standards Board (FASB) statements, interpretations, and technical bulletins.

Miller Governmental GAAP Guide: A Comprehensive Interpretation of All Current Promulgated Governmental Generally Accepted Accounting Principles for State and Local and Local Governments. Larry P. Bailey. Harcourt Brace Professional Publishing. • Annual. $79.00. Includes reporting standards for hospitals, colleges, and other non-profit organizations. Provides a model comprehensive annual financial report.

Not-for-Profit GAAP: Interpretation and Application of Generally Accepted Accounting Principles for Not-for-Profit Organizations. John Wiley and Sons, Inc. • Annual. $65.00. (Also available on CD-ROM.).

Practitioner's Guide to GAAS. John Wiley and Sons, Inc. • Annual. $131.00. Covers GAAS: Generally Accepted Auditing Standards, promulgated by the American Institute of Certified Public Accountants. (Includes CD-ROM.).

SEC Accounting Rules, with Financial Reporting Releases, Codification of Financial Reporting Policies, Accounting and Auditing Enforcement Releases, and Staff Accounting Bulletins. CCH, Inc. • Looseleaf. $448.00.

Simplified Small Business Accounting. Daniel Sitarz. National Book Network. • 1998. $19.95. Second edition. Includes basic forms and instructions for small business accounting and bookkeeping. (Small Business Library Series).

Transnational Accounting. Dieter Ordelheide and others, editors. Groves Dictionaries. • 2000. $650.00. Three volumes. Published by Macmillan (UK). Provides detailed descriptions of financial accounting principles and practices in 14 major countries (10 European, plus the U. S., Canada, Australia, and Japan). Includes tables, exhibits, index, and a glossary of 244 accounting terms in eight languages.

U. S. Master Accounting Guide. CCH, Inc. • Annual. $65.95. Summarizes key accounting, business, and financial information from various sources. Includes digests, tables, charts, formulas, ratios, examples, and explanatory text.

U. S. Master GAAP Guide. CCH, Inc. • Annual. $69.00. Covers the generally accepted accounting principles (GAAP) contained in the professional pronouncements of the Accounting Principles Board (APB) or the Financial Accounting Standards Board (FASB). Includes general discussions, flow charts, and detailed examples. Arranged by topic.

INTERNET DATABASES

Rutgers Accounting Web (RAW). Rutgers University Accounting Research Center. Phone: (201)648-5172 Fax: (201)648-1233 • URL: http://www.rutgers.edu/accounting • RAW Web site provides extensive links to sources of national and international accounting information, such as the Big Six accounting firms, the Financial Accounting Standards Board (FASB), SEC filings (EDGAR), journals, publishers, software, the International Accounting Network, and "Internet's largest list of accounting firms in USA." Searching is offered. Fees: Free.

ONLINE DATABASES

Accounting and Tax Database. Bell & Howell Information and Learning. • Provides indexing and abstracting of the literature of accounting, taxation, and financial management, 1971 to date. Updating is weekly. Especially covers accounting, auditing, banking, bankruptcy, employee compensation and benefits, cash management, financial planning, and credit. Inquire as to online cost and availability.

Management Contents. The Gale Group. • Covers a wide range of management, financial, marketing, personnel, and administrative topics. About 150 leading business journals are indexed and abstracted from 1974 to date, with monthly updating. Inquire as to online cost and availability.

Wilson Business Abstracts Online. H. W. Wilson Co. • Indexes and abstracts 600 major business periodicals, plus the *Wall Street Journal* and the business section of the *New York Times*. Indexing is from 1982, abstracting from 1990, with the two newspapers included from 1993. Updated weekly. Inquire as to online cost and availability. (*Business Periodicals Index* without abstracts is also available online.).

PERIODICALS AND NEWSLETTERS

Accounting Review. American Accounting Association. • Quarterly. Free to members; non-members, $125.00 per year.

Accounting Today: The Newspaper for the Accounting Professional. Faulkner & Gray, Inc. • Biweekly. $84.00 per year. Provides news of accounting and taxes.

Bowman's Accounting Report. Hudson Sawyer Professional Services Marketing, Inc. • Monthly. $275.00 per year. Newsletter. Provides information and news relating to the accounting profession, with emphasis on certified public accounting firms.

Government Accountants Journal. Association of Government Accountants. • Quarterly. $60.00 per year.

Journal of Accountancy. American Institute of Certified Public Accountants. • Monthly. $59.00 per year.

Journal of Accounting Research. Institute of Professional Accounting. • Semiannual. Students, $80.00 per year; others, $90.00 per year. Includes annual supplement. Accepts for review unpublished research in the fields of empirical and experimental accounting.

Journal of Corporate Accounting and Finance. John Wiley and Sons, Inc., Subscription Dept. • Bimonthly. $263.00 per year. Topics include government regulation, corporate taxation, financial risk, business valuation, and strategic planning.

National Public Accountant. National Society of Accountants. • Monthly. Free to members; non-members, $18.00 per year. For accounting and tax practitioners.

NSPA Washington Reporter. National Society of Accountants. • Monthly. Membership.

The Practical Accountant: Accounting and Taxes in Everyday Practice. Faulkner and Gray, Inc. • Monthly. $60.00 per year. Covers tax planning, financial planning, practice management, client relationships, and related topics.

Public Accounting Report. Strafford Publications, Inc. • 23 times a year. $297.00 per year. Newsletter. Presents news and trends affecting the accounting profession.

RESEARCH CENTERS AND INSTITUTES

Accounting Research Program. University of California, John E. Anderson Graduate School of Management, Los Angeles, CA 90095-1481. Phone: (310)206-6462 Fax: (310)267-2163 E-mail: pat.hughes@anderson.ucla.edu.

Center for International Education and Research in Accounting. University of Illinois at Urbana-Champaign. 1206 S. Sixth St., 320 Commerce West Bldg., Champaign, IL 61820. Phone: (217)333-4545 Fax: (217)244-6565 E-mail: b-smith@uiuc.edu • URL: http://www.cba.uiuc.edu/ciera.

TRADE/PROFESSIONAL ASSOCIATIONS

American Accounting Association. 5717 Bessie Dr., Sarasota, FL 34233-2399. Phone: (941)921-7747 Fax: (941)923-4093 E-mail: aaahq@packet.net • URL: http://www.rutgers.edu/accounting/raw/aaa.

American Institute of Certified Public Accountants. 1211 Ave. of the Americas, New York, NY 10036-8775. Phone: 800-862-4272 or (212)596-6200 Fax: (212)596-6213 • URL: http://www.aicpa.org.

Association for Accounting Administration. 136 S. Keowee St., Dayton, OH 45402. Phone: (937)222-0030 Fax: (937)222-5794 E-mail: aaainfo@cpaadmin.org • URL: http://www.cpaadmin.org • Members are accounting and office systems executives. Includes an Information Management Committee.

Association of Government Accountants. 2208 Mount Vernon Ave., Alexandria, VA 22301-1314. Phone: 800-242-7211 or (703)684-6931 Fax: (703)548-9367 • URL: http://www.agacgfm.org • Members are employed by federal, state, county, and city government agencies. Includes accountants, auditors, budget officers, and other government finance administrators and officials.

Financial Accounting Foundation. P.O. Box 5116, Norwalk, CT 06856. Phone: (203)847-0700 Fax: (203)849-9714 E-mail: webmaster@fasb.org • URL: http://www.gasb.org.

Financial Executives Institute. P.O. Box 1938, Morristown, NJ 07962-1938. Phone: (973)898-4600 Fax: (973)898-4649.

Institute of Internal Auditors. 249 Maitland Ave., Altamonte Springs, FL 32701-4201. Phone: (407)830-7600 Fax: (407)831-5171 E-mail: iia@theiia.org • URL: http://www.theiia.org.

Institute of Management Accountants. 10 Paragon Dr., Montvale, NJ 07645. Phone: 800-638-4427 or (201)573-9000 Fax: (201)573-8483 E-mail: info@imanet.org • URL: http://www.imanet.org.

National Society of Public Accountants. 1010 N. Fairfax St., Alexandria, VA 22314-1574. Phone: 800-966-6679 or (703)549-6400 Fax: (703)549-2984 E-mail: nsa@wizard.net • URL: http://www.nsa.org.

OTHER SOURCES

Accounting Research Studies. American Institute of Certified Public Accountants. • Irregular.

FASB Accounting Standards Current Text. Financial Accounting Standards Board. • Looseleaf.

FASB Accounting Standards Current Text: General Standards. Financial Accounting Standards Board. • Irregular. Price on application.

FASB Accounting Standards Current Text: Industries Standards. Financial Accounting Standards Board. • Irregular. Price on application.

FASB Accounting Standards Current Text: Professional Standards. Financial Accounting Standards Board. • Irregular. Price on application.

FASB Accounting Standards Current Text: Technical Practice Aids. Financial Accounting Standards Board. • Irregular. Price on application.

FASB Original Pronouncements. Financial Accounting Standards Board. • Irregular. Price on application.

Financial Accounting Series. Financial Accounting Standards Board. • Price on application.

Forensic Accounting and Financial Fraud. American Management Association Extension Institute. • Looseleaf. $130.00. Self-study course. Emphasis is on practical explanations, examples, and problem solving. Quizzes and a case study are included.

Fundamentals of Finance and Accounting for Nonfinancial Managers. American Management Association Extension Institute. • Looseleaf. $110.00. Self-study course. Emphasis is on practical explanations, examples, and problem solving. Quizzes and a case study are included.

Keeping the Books: Basic Recordkeeping and Accounting for the Successful Small Business. Linda Pinson. Dearborn Financial Publishing. • 2000. $22.95. Fifth edition. Covers bookkeeping systems, financial statements, and IRS tax record requirements. Includes illustrations, worksheets, and forms.

Management Advisory Services Guideline Series. American Institute of Certified Public Accountants. • Irregular. Price varies.

Movie Money: Understanding Hollywood's Creative Accounting Practices. Bill Daniels and others. Silman-James Press. • 1998. $19.95. Explains the numerous amd mysterious accounting methods used by the film industry to arrive at gross and net profit figures. The authors also discuss profit participation, audits, claims, and negotiating.

Statements of Financial Accounting Standards: Original Pronouncements. John Wiley and Sons, Inc. • 1996. Price on application.

ACCOUNTING, BANK

See: BANK ACCOUNTING

ACCOUNTING, COMPUTERS IN

See: COMPUTERS IN ACCOUNTING

ACCOUNTING, COST

See: COST ACCOUNTING

ACCOUNTING, GOVERNMENT

See: GOVERNMENT ACCOUNTING

ACCOUNTING RESEARCH

ABSTRACTS AND INDEXES

Business Periodicals Index. H. W. Wilson Co. • Monthly, except August, with quarterly and annual cumulations. Service basis for print edition; CD-ROM edition, $1,495.00 per year.

ALMANACS AND YEARBOOKS

Research in Accounting Regulation. JAI Press, Inc. • Irregular. $78.50.

BIBLIOGRAPHIES

Accounting Research Directory. John C. Gardner and others, editors. Markus Wiener Publishing, Inc. • Irregular. $69.95. Contains lists and evaluations of all publications in seven leading accounting, journals.

DIRECTORIES

Business Organizations, Agencies, and Publications Directory. The Gale Group. • 1999. $425.00. 12th edition. Over 40,000 entries describing 39 types of business information sources. Classified by type of organization, publication, or serviceIncludes state, national, and international agencies and organizations. Master index to names and keywords. Also includes e-mail addresses and web site URL's.

ENCYCLOPEDIAS AND DICTIONARIES

Blackwell Encyclopedic Dictionary of Accounting. Rashad Abdel-khalik. Blackwell Publishers. • 1997. $105.95. The editor is associated with the University of Florida. Contains definitions of key terms combined with longer articles written by various U. S. and foreign business educators. Includes bibliographies and index. (Blackwell Encyclopedia of Management Series).

INTERNET DATABASES

Rutgers Accounting Web (RAW). Rutgers University Accounting Research Center. Phone: (201)648-5172 Fax: (201)648-1233 • URL: http://www.rutgers.edu/accounting • RAW Web site provides extensive links to sources of national and international accounting information, such as the Big Six accounting firms, the Financial Accounting Standards Board (FASB), SEC filings (EDGAR), journals, publishers, software, the International Accounting Network, and "Internet's largest list of accounting firms in USA." Searching is offered. Fees: Free.

ONLINE DATABASES

EconLit. American Economic Association. • Covers the worldwide literature of economics as contained in selected monographs and about 550 journals. Subjects include microeconomics, macroeconomics, economic history, inflation, money, credit, finance, accounting theory, trade, natural resource economics, and regional economics. Time period is 1969 to present, with monthly updates. Inquire as to online cost and availability.

Wilson Business Abstracts Online. H. W. Wilson Co. • Indexes and abstracts 600 major business periodicals, plus the *Wall Street Journal* and the business section of the *New York Times.* Indexing is from 1982, abstracting from 1990, with the two newspapers included from 1993. Updated weekly. Inquire as to online cost and availability. (*Business Periodicals Index* without abstracts is also available online.).

PERIODICALS AND NEWSLETTERS

CPA Technology Advisor (Certified Public Accountant): Profitable Strategies and Practical Solutions for Managing. Harcourt Brace Professional Publishing. • Monthly. $237.00 per year. Newsletter. Describes hardware and software products and makes recommendations. Formerly *C P A Technology Report.*

Journal of Accounting Research. Institute of Professional Accounting. • Semiannual. Students, $80.00 per year; others, $90.00 per year. Includes annual supplement. Accepts for review unpublished research in the fields of empirical and experimental accounting.

RESEARCH CENTERS AND INSTITUTES

Accounting Research Program. University of California, John E. Anderson Graduate School of Management, Los Angeles, CA 90095-1481. Phone: (310)206-6462 Fax: (310)267-2163 E-mail: pat.hughes@anderson.ucla.edu.

Bureau of Economic and Business Research. University of Illinois at Urbana-Champaign, 1206 S. Sixth St., Champaign, IL 61820. Phone: (217)333-2330 Fax: (217)244-7410 E-mail: g-oldman@uiuc.edu • URL: http://www.cba.uiuc.edu/research.

Ira B. McGladrey Institute of Accounting Research. University of Iowa, W262 PBAB, Iowa City, IA 52242. Phone: (319)335-0919 Fax: (319)335-1956 E-mail: morton-pincus@uiowa.edu • URL: http://www.biz.uiowa.edu/acct/outreach/mcglad.html.

TRADE/PROFESSIONAL ASSOCIATIONS

American Accounting Association. 5717 Bessie Dr., Sarasota, FL 34233-2399. Phone: (941)921-7747 Fax: (941)923-4093 E-mail: aaahq@packet.net • URL: http://www.rutgers.edu/accounting/raw/aaa.

American Woman's Society of Certified Public Accountants. 401 N. Michigan Ave., Chicago, IL 60611. Phone: 800-297-2721 or (312)644-6610 Fax: (312)321-6869 E-mail: awscpa__hq@sba.com.

Financial Accounting Foundation. P.O. Box 5116, Norwalk, CT 06856. Phone: (203)847-0700 Fax: (203)849-9714 E-mail: webmaster@fasb.org • URL: http://www.gasb.org.

ACID RAIN

See also: ENVIRONMENT

ABSTRACTS AND INDEXES

Environment Abstracts. Congressional Information Service. • Monthly. Price varies. Provides multidisciplinary coverage of the world's environmental literature. Incorporates *Acid Rain Abstracts.*

Environment Abstracts Annual: A Guide to the Key Environmental Literature of the Year. Congressional Information Service. • Annual. $495.00. A yearly cumulation of *Environment Abstracts.*

Environmental Periodicals Bibliography: A Current Awareness Bibliography Featuring Citations of Scientific and Popular Articles in Serial Publications in the Area of the Environment. Environmental Studies Institute. International Academy at Santa Barbara. • Monthly. Price varies. An index to current environmental literature.

Pollution Abstracts. Cambridge Information Group. • Monthly. $895.00 per year; with index, $985.00 per year.

CD-ROM DATABASES

Environment Abstracts on CD-ROM. Congressional Information Service, Inc. • Quarterly. $1,295.00 per year. Contains the following CD-ROM databases: *Environment Abstracts, Energy Abstracts,* and *Acid Rain Abstracts.* Length of coverage varies.

DIRECTORIES

Gale Environmental Sourcebook: A Guide to Organizations, Agencies, and Publications. The Gale Group. • 1993. $95.00. Second edition. A directory of print and non-print information sources on a wide variety of environmental topics.

ENCYCLOPEDIAS AND DICTIONARIES

Wiley Encyclopedia of Energy and the Environment. Frederick John Francis. John Wiley and Sons, Inc. • 1999. $1,500.00. Four volumes. Second edition. Covers a wide variety of energy and environmental topics, including legal and policy issues.

ONLINE DATABASES

Enviroline. Congressional Information Service, Inc. • Provides online indexing and abstracting of worldwide environmental and natural resource literature from 1975 to date. Updated monthly. Inquire as to online cost and availability.

PAIS International. Public Affairs Information Service, Inc. • Corresponds to the former printed publications, *PAIS Bulletin* (1976-90) and *PAIS Foreign Language Index* (1972-90), and to the current *PAIS International in Print* (1991 to date). Covers economic, political, and sociological material appearing in periodicals, books, government documents, and other publications. Updating is monthly. Inquire as to online cost and availability.

Pollution Abstracts [online]. Cambridge Scientific Abstracts. • Provides indexing and abstracting of international, environmentally related literature, 1970 to date. Monthly updates. Inquire as to online cost and availability.

STATISTICS SOURCES

Statistical Record of the Environment. The Gale Group. • 1996. $120.00. Third edition. Provides over 875 charts, tables, and graphs of major environmental statistics, arranged by subject. Covers population growth, hazardous waste, nuclear energy, acid rain, pesticides, and other subjects related to the environment. A keyword index is included.

TRADE/PROFESSIONAL ASSOCIATIONS

Izaak Walton League of America. IWLA Conservation Center, 707 Conversation Lane, Gaithersburg, MD 20878. Phone: 800-453-5463 or (301)548-0150 Fax: (301)548-0146 E-mail: general@iwla.org • URL: http://www.iwla.org • Sponsors the Acid Rain Project, an environmental protection program.

OTHER SOURCES

Environment Reporter. Bureau of National Affairs, Inc. • Weekly. $2,844.00 per year. 18 volumes. Looseleaf. Covers legal aspects of wide variety of environmental concerns.

ACOUSTICAL ENGINEERING

See: NOISE CONTROL

ACQUISITIONS AND MERGERS

See: MERGERS AND ACQUISITIONS

ACTUARIAL SCIENCE

ALMANACS AND YEARBOOKS

American Academy of Actuaries Yearbook. American Academy of Actuaries. • Annual. $25.00.

Casualty Actuarial Society Yearbook. Casualty Actuarial Society. • Annual. $40.00. Approximately 2,500 actuaries working in insurance other than life insurance.

Society of Actuaries Yearbook. Society of Actuaries. • Annual. $25.00. Includes alphabetical list of actuaries.

PERIODICALS AND NEWSLETTERS

The Actuary. Society of Actuaries. • 10 times a year. $25.00 per year.

Contingencies: The Magazine of the Actuarial Profession. American Academy of Actuaries. • Bimonthly. $30.00 per year. Provides non-technical articles on the actuarial aspects of insurance, employee benefits, and pensions.

STATISTICS SOURCES

Vital Statistics of the United States: Life Tables. Available from U. S. Government Printing Office. • Annual. $2.25. Produced by the National Center for Health Statistics, Public Health Service, U. S. Department of Health and Human Services. Provides detailed data on expectation of life by age, race, and sex. Historical data is shown annually from the year 1900. (Vital Statistics, volume 2, section 6.).

TRADE/PROFESSIONAL ASSOCIATIONS

American Academy of Actuaries. 1100 17th St., N.W., 7th Fl., Washington, DC 20036. Phone: (202)223-8196 Fax: (202)872-1948 • URL: http://www.actuary.org.

Casualty Actuarial Society. 1100 N. Glebe Rd., Suite 600, Arlington, VA 22201. Phone: (703)276-3100 Fax: (703)276-3108 E-mail: office@casact.org • URL: http://www.casact.org.

Conference of Consulting Actuaries. 1110 W. Lake Cook Rd., Suite. 235, Buffalo Grove, IL 60089-1968. Phone: (847)419-9090 Fax: (847)419-9091 E-mail: cca@ccactuaries.org • URL: http://www.ccactuaries.org.

Society of Actuaries. 475 N. Martingale Rd., Suite 800, Schaumburg, IL 60173-2226. Phone: (847)706-3500 Fax: (847)706-3599 • URL: http://www.soa.org.

ADDITIVES AND FLAVORINGS

GENERAL WORKS

Spices: Flavor Chemistry and Antioxidant Properties. Sara J. Risch and Chi-Tang Ho, editors. American Chemical Society. • 1997. $105.00. A review of spice chemistry "from both practical and historical perspectives." Covers antixidant properties of specific spices and potential health benefits. (ACS Symposium Series, No. 660.).

ABSTRACTS AND INDEXES

Applied Science and Technology Index. H. W. Wilson Co. • 11 times a year. Quarterly and annual cumulations. Service basis for print edition; CD-ROM edition, $1,495.00 per year. Indexes a wide variety of English language technical, industrial, and engineering periodicals.

Current Contents: Engineering, Computing and Technology. Institute for Scientific Information. • Weekly. $730.00 per year. Reproductions of contents pages of technical journals. Includes *Author Index, Address Directory, Current Book Contents* and *Title Word Index.* Formerly *Current Contents: Engineering, Technology and Applied Sciences.*

Food Science and Technology Abstracts. International Food Information Service Publishing.

• Monthly. $1,780.00 per year. Provides worldwide coverage of the literature of food technology and food production.

Foods Adlibra: Key to the World's Food Literature. Foods Adlibra Publications. • Semimonthly.Provides journal citations and abstracts to the literature of food technology and packaging.

ALMANACS AND YEARBOOKS

Feed Additive Compendium. Miller Publishing Co. • Annual. $225.00. Eleven supplements. Covers the use of drugs as additives to livestock and poultry feed.

CD-ROM DATABASES

Food Science and Technology Abstracts [CD-ROM]. Available from SilverPlatter Information, Inc. • Quarterly. $3,700 per year. Produced by International Food Information Service (home page is http://www.ifis.org). Provides worldwide coverage on CD-ROM of the literature of food technology and production. Various types of publications are indexed, with abstracts, including about 1,800 periodicals. Time period is 1969 to date.

DIRECTORIES

Food Processing Guide and Directory. Putman Publishing Co. • Annual. $75.00. Lists over 5,390 food ingredient and equipment manufacturers.

Prepared Foods Food Industry Sourcebook. Cahners Business Information. • Annual. $35.00. Provides information on more than 3,000 manufacturers and suppliers of products, ingredients, supplies, and equipment for the food processing industry.

Specialty Food Industry Directory. Phoenix Media Network, Inc. • Annual. Included in subscription to Food Distribution Magazine. Lists manufacturers and suppliers of specialty foods, and services and equipment for the specialty food industry. Featured food products include legumes, sauces, spices, upscale cheese, specialty beverages, snack foods, baked goods, ethnic foods, and specialty meats.

ENCYCLOPEDIAS AND DICTIONARIES

Dictionary of Food and Ingredients. Robert S. Igoe and Y.H. Hui. Aspen Publishers, Inc. • 1995. $30.00. Third edition.

Foods and Nutrition Encyclopedia. Audrey H. Ensminger and others. CRC Press, Inc. • 1993. $382.00. Second edition. Two volumes.

HANDBOOKS AND MANUALS

Food and Beverage Market Place: Suppliers Guide. Grey House Publishing. • 2000. $225.00. Second editon. Contains details on companies providing the food industry with a wide variety of supplies, ingredients, packaging, equipment, machinery, instrumentation, chemicals, etc.

ONLINE DATABASES

Applied Science and Technology Index Online. H. W. Wilson Co. • Provides online indexing of 400 major scientific, technical, industrial, and engineering periodicals. Time period is 1983 to date. Monthly updates. Inquire as to online cost and availability.

Food Science and Technology Abstracts [online]. IFIS North American Desk. • Produced by International Food Information Service. Provides about 500,000 online citations, with abstracts, to the international literature of food science, technology, commodities, engineering, and processing. Approximately 2,000 periodicals are covered. Time period is 1969 to date, with monthly updates. Inquire as to online cost and availability.

FOODS ADLIBRA. General Mills, Inc. • Contains online citations, with abstracts, to the technical and business literature of food processing and packaging. New products and new ingredients are featured. Covers about 250 trade journals and 500 research journals from 1974 to date, with monthly updates. Inquire as to online cost and availability.

PROMT: Predicasts Overview of Markets and Technology. The Gale Group. • Companies, products, applied technologies and markets. U.S. and international literature coverage, 1972 to date. Inquire as to online cost and availability. Provides abstracts from more than 1,600 publications. Weekly updates.

PERIODICALS AND NEWSLETTERS

Flavour and Fragrance Journal. John Wiley and Sons, Inc., Journals Div. • Bimonthly. Institutions, $905.00 per year.

Food Additives and Contaminants: Analysis, Surveillance, Evaluation, Control. Taylor and Francis, Inc. • Eight times a year. $1,598.00 per year.

Food Chemical News. Food Chemical News, Inc. • Weekly. $1,187.00 per year. Newsletter.

Food Distribution Magazine. Phoenix Media Network, Inc. • Monthly. $49.00 per year. Edited for marketers and buyers of domestic and imported, specialty or gourmet food products, including ethnic foods, seasonings, and bakery items.

Food Processing. Putman Publishing Co. • Monthly. Free to qualified personnel; others, $98.00 per year. Edited for executive and operating personnel in the food processing industry.

The Monell Connection: From the Monell Chemical Senses Center, a Nonprofit Scientific Institute Devoted to Research on Taste and Smell. Monell Chemical Senses Center. • Three times a year. Free. Newsletter. Includes brief summaries of selected papers describing ongoing work of Monell scientists.

Perfumer and Flavorist. Allured Publishing Corp. • Bimonthly. $135.00 per year. Provides information on the art and technology of flavors and fragrances, including essential oils, aroma chemicals, and spices.

RESEARCH CENTERS AND INSTITUTES

Food Research Institute. University of Wisconsin-Madison, Dept. of Food Microbiology and Toxicology, 1925 Willow Dr., Madison, WI 53706. Phone: (608)263-7777 Fax: (608)263-1114 E-mail: mwpariza@facstaff.wisc.edu • URL: http://www.wisc.edu/fri/.

Institute of Food Science. Cornell University, 114 Stocking Hall, Ithaca, NY 14853. Phone: (607)255-7915 Fax: (607)254-4868 E-mail: mrm1@cornell.edu • URL: http://www.nysaes.cornell.edu/cifs/ • Research areas include the chemistry and processing of food commodities, food processing engineering, food packaging, and nutrition.

Monell Chemical Senses Center. 3500 Market St., Philadelphia, PA 19104-3308. Phone: (215)898-8878 Fax: (215)898-2084 E-mail: beauchamp@monell.org • URL: http://www.monell.org • Does multidisciplinary research relating to taste and smell (the chemical senses), including investigation of the sensory qualities of food.

TRADE/PROFESSIONAL ASSOCIATIONS

Chemical Sources Association. P.O. Box 3189, Secaucus, NJ 07096-3189. Phone: (201)392-8900 Fax: (201)348-3877 E-mail: chemsources@nilegalink.com • URL: http://www.chemsources.org • Rare chemicals and oils for flavors.

Flavor and Extract Manufacturers Association of the United States. 1620 Eye St., N.W. Suite 925, Washington, DC 20006. Phone: (202)293-5800 Fax: (202)463-8998.

International Food Additives Council. 5775 Peachtree-Dunwoody Rd., Suite 500-G, Atlanta, GA 30342. Phone: (404)252-3663 Fax: (404)252-0774 E-mail: ifac@assnhq.com • Manufacturers of additives.

National Association of Fruits, Flavors and Syrups. P.O. Box 545, Matawan, NJ 07747. Phone: (732)583-8272 Fax: (732)583-0798 E-mail: naffs@naffs.org • URL: http://www.naffs.org • Manufacturers of fruit and syrup toppings, flavors and stabilizers for the food industry.

Society of Flavor Chemists. c/o Mike Fasano, Bush Boake Allen, Inc., 2711 W. Irving Park Rd., Chicago, IL 60618. Phone: (773)463-7600 Fax: (773)463-6731.

OTHER SOURCES

Food and Beverage Additives. Available from MarketResearch.com. • 1998. $3,200.00. Published by the Freedonia Group. Market data with forecasts to 2002 and 2007 on coloring agents, flavors, preservatives, stabilizers, etc.

Major Food and Drink Companies of the World. Available from The Gale Group. • 2001. $855.00. Fourth edition. Two volumes. Published by Graham & Whiteside. Contains profiles and trade names for more than 9,000 important food and beverage companies in various countries. In addition to foods, includes both alcoholic and nonalcoholic drink products.

Thomas Food and Beverage Market Place. Grey House Publishing. • Annual. $295.00. Three volumes. Contains more than 40,000 entries covering food companies, beverages, food equipment, warehouse companies, food brokers, wholesalers, importers, and exporters. Formerly *Thomas Food Industry Register.*

ADHESIVES

GENERAL WORKS

Adhesion Science. J. Comyn. American Chemical Society. • 1997. Published by The Royal Society of Chemistry. Provides basic scientific and technical information on "common adhesives." (RSC Paperback Series).

ABSTRACTS AND INDEXES

Applied Science and Technology Index. H. W. Wilson Co. • 11 times a year. Quarterly and annual cumulations. Service basis for print edition; CD-ROM edition, $1,495.00 per year. Indexes a wide variety of English language technical, industrial, and engineering periodicals.

Chemical Abstracts. Chemical Abstracts Service. • Weekly. $22,600.00 per year.

CPI Digest: Key to World Literature Serving the Coatings, Plastics, Fibers, Adhesives, and Related Industries (Chemical Process Industries). CPI Information Services. • Monthly. $397.00 per year. Abstracts of business and technical articles for polymer-based, chemical process industries. Includes a monthly list of relevant U. S. patents. International coverage.

NTIS Alerts: Materials Sciences. National Technical Information Service. • Semimonthly. $220.00 per year. Provides descriptions of government-sponsored research reports and software, with ordering information. Covers ceramics, glass, coatings, composite materials, alloys, plastics, wood, paper, adhesives, fibers, lubricants, and related subjects. Formerly *Abstract Newsletter.*

DIRECTORIES

Adhesives Age Directory. Intertec Publishing Corp. • Annual. $59.95. Formerly *Adhesives Red Book.*

Adhesives Technology Handbook. Arthur H. Landrock. Noyes Data Corp. • 1986. $64.00.

U. S. Glass, Metal, and Glazing: Buyers Guide. Key Communications, Inc. • Annual. $20.00. A directory of supplies and equipment for the glass fabrication and installation industry.

ENCYCLOPEDIAS AND DICTIONARIES

ASM Materials Engineering Dictionary. Joseph R. Davis, editor. ASM International. • 1992. $146.00. Contains 10,000 entries, 700 illustrations, and 150 tables relating to metals, plastics, ceramics, composites, and adhesives. Includes "Technical Briefs" on 64 key material groups.

FINANCIAL RATIOS

Annual Statement Studies. Robert Morris Associates: The Association of Lending and Credit Risk Professiona. • Annual. Free to members; non-members, $140.00. Median and quartile financial ratios are given for over 400 kinds of manufacturing, wholesale, retail, construction, and consumer finance establishments. Data is sorted by both asset size and sales volume. Includes a clearly written "Definition of Ratios" and an alphabetical industry index.

HANDBOOKS AND MANUALS

Assembly Buyer's Guide. Cahners Business Information. • Annual. $25.00. Lists manufacturers and suppliers of equipment relating to assembly automation, fasteners, adhesives, robotics, and power tools.

Construction Sealants and Adhesives. Julian R. Panek and John P. Cook. John Wiley and Sons, Inc. • 1991. $120.00. Third edition. (Practical Construction Guides Series).

Handbook of Adhesives. Irving Skeist. Chapman and Hall. • 1989. $105.00. Third edition.

Handbook of Pressure Sensitive Adhesive Technology. Donatas Satas. Satas and Associates. • 1999. $150.00. Third revised edition.

ONLINE DATABASES

CA Search. Chemical Abstracts Service. • Guide to chemical literature, 1967 to present. Inquire as to online cost and availability.

PaperChem Database. Information Services Div. • Worldwide coverage of the scientific and technical paper industry chemical literature, including patents, 1967 to present. Weekly updates. Inquire as to online cost and availability.

World Surface Coatings Abstracts [Online]. Paint Research Association of Great Britain. • Indexing and abstracting of the literature of paint and surface coatings, 1976 to present. Monthly updates. Inquire as to online cost and availability.

PERIODICALS AND NEWSLETTERS

Adhesives Age. Chemical Week Associates. • Monthly. $60.00 per year. Includes annual *Directory.*

The Composites and Adhesives Newsletter. T-C Press. • Quarterly. $190.00. Presents news of the composite materials and adhesives industries, with particular coverage of new products and applications.

International Journal of Adhesion and Adhesives. Elsevier Science. • Six times a year. $797.00 per year. Published in England.

Journal of Adhesion. Gordon and Breach Publishing Group. • 16 times a year. Four volumes. Academic institutions, $3,954.00 per year; corporations, $6,510.00 per year.

U. S. Glass, Metal, and Glazing. Key Communications, Inc. • Monthly. $39.00 per year. Edited for glass fabricators, glaziers, distributors, and retailers. Special feature issues are devoted to architectural glass, mirror glass, windows, storefronts, hardware, machinery, sealants, and adhesives. Regular topics include automobile glass and fenestration (window design and placement).

RESEARCH CENTERS AND INSTITUTES

ORTECH Corporation. 2395 Speakman Dr., Mississauga, ON, Canada L5K 1B3. Phone: (905)822-4111 E-mail: mail@dieselnet.com • URL: http://www.dieselnet.com/com/xf005.html.

STATISTICS SOURCES

Annual Survey of Manufactures. Available from U. S. Government Printing Office. • Annual. Prices vary. Issued by the U. S. Census Bureau as an interim update to the *Census of Manufactures.* Includes data on number of manufacturing establishments in various industries, employment, labor costs, value of shipments, capital expenditures, inventories, energy costs, and assets. (See also Census Bureau home page, http://www.census.gov/.).

U. S. Industry and Trade Outlook: The McGraw-Hill Companies and the U.S. Department of Commerce/International Trade Administration. Datapso Research Corp. • Annual. $69.95. Produced by the International Trade Administration, U. S. Department of Commerce, in a "public-private" partnership with DRI/McGraw-Hill and Standard & Poor's. Provides basic data, outlook for the current year, and "Long-Term Prospects" (five-year projections) for a wide variety of products and services. Includes high technology industries. Formerly *U. S. Industrial Outlook.*

TRADE/PROFESSIONAL ASSOCIATIONS

Adhesive and Sealant Council. 7979 Old Georgetown Rd., Bethesda, MD 20814. Phone: (301)986-9700 Fax: (301)986-9795 • URL: http://www.ascouncil.org.

Adhesives Manufacturers Association. 401 N. Michigan Ave., 24th Fl., Chicago, IL 60611-4267. Phone: (312)644-6610 Fax: (312)321-6869 E-mail: ama@sba.com • URL: http://www.adhesives.org/ama.

OTHER SOURCES

Adhesives and Sealants. ASM International. • 1990. $186.00. Volume three. (Engineered Materials Handbook Series).

Assembly. Cahners Business Information. • Monthly. $68.00 per year. Covers assembly, fastening, and joining systems. Includes information on automation and robotics.

ADMINISTRATION

See also: BUSINESS; EXECUTIVES; INDUSTRIAL MANAGEMENT; PUBLIC ADMINISTRATION

GENERAL WORKS

Business and Administrative Communication. Kitty O. Locker. McGraw-Hill. • 2000. Fifth edition. Price on application.

Creative Management. Jane Henry. Sage Publications, Inc. • 1991. $60.00.

The Functions of the Executive. Chester I. Barnard. Harvard University Press. • 1971. $18.95.

Fundamentals of Management. James H. Donnelly. McGraw-Hill. • 1997. 10th edition. Price on application.

The Human Side of Enterprise. Douglas McGregor. McGraw-Hill. • 1985. $40.00.

The Leader of the Future: New Essays by World-Class Leaders and Thinkers. Jossey-Bass, Inc., Publishers. • 1996. $25.00. Contains 32 articles on leadership by "executives, consultants, and commentators." (Management Series).

Management. John Schermerhorn. John Wiley and Sons, Inc. • 1998. $97.95. Sixth edition.

Management: Concepts, Practice, and Skills. Premeaux Mondy. South-Western College Publishing. • 1999. $39.95. Eighth edition. (SWC-General Business Series).

Management: Skills and Application. Leslie W. Rue and Lloyd L. Byars. McGraw-Hill. • 1999. $59.65. Ninth edition. An introductory text covering the principles of successful management. Arranged according to the following "Skills:" Planning, Organizing, Staffing, Directing, and Controlling. Includes a glossary of key terms and three indexes. (Irwin Professional Publishing.).

The One-Minute Manager: Putting the One-Minute Manager to Work. Kenneth Blanchard. Berkley Publishing Group. • 1993. $21.90. Two volumes.

Reengineering Management: The Mandate for New Leadership. James Champy. DIANE Publishing Co. • 1998. $25.00.

Reengineering the Corporation: A Manifesto for Business Revolution. Michael Hammer and James Champy. HarperCollins Publishers, Inc. • 1999. $16.00. Revised edition.

The Witch Doctors: Making Sense of the Management Gurus. John Micklethwait and Adrian Wooldridge. Crown Publishing Group, Inc. • 1996. $25.00. A critical, iconoclastic, and practical view of consultants, business school professors, and modern management theory, written by two members of the editorial staff of *The Economist.*

ABSTRACTS AND INDEXES

Business Periodicals Index. H. W. Wilson Co. • Monthly, except August, with quarterly and annual cumulations. Service basis for print edition; CD-ROM edition, $1,495.00 per year.

BIBLIOGRAPHIES

Business Information Sources. Lorna M. Daniells. California Princeton Fulfillment Services. • 1993. $42.50. Third revised edition. Basic business sources, with discussion and full annotations.

CD-ROM DATABASES

Business Source Plus. EBSCO Information Services. • Monthly. $1,495.00 per year. Provides CD-ROM citations and abstracts to articles in about 650 business periodicals and newspapers, including *The Wall Street Journal.* Full text is provided from 200 selected periodicals. Covers accounting, communications, economics, finance, management, marketing, and other business subjects.

Profiles in Business and Management: An International Directory of Scholars and Their Research [CD-ROM]. Harvard Business School Publishing. • Annual. $595.00 per year. Fully searchable CD-ROM version of two-volume printed directory. Contains bibliographic and biographical information for over 5600 business and management experts active in 21 subject areas. Formerly *International Directory of Business and Management Scholars.*

WILSONDISC: Wilson Business Abstracts. H. W. Wilson Co. • Monthly. $2,495.00 per year, including unlimited online access to *Wilson Business Abstracts* through WILSONLINE. Provides CD-ROM "cover-to-cover" abstracting and indexing of over 600 prominent business periodicals. Indexing is from 1982, abstracting from 1990. (*Business Periodicals Index* without abstracts is available on CD-ROM at $1,495 per year.).

DIRECTORIES

Profiles in Business and Management: An International Directory of Scholars and Their Research Version 2.0. Claudia Bruce, editor. Harvard Business School Press. • 1996. $495.00. Two volumes. Provides backgrounds, publications, and current research projects of more than 5,600 business and management experts.

Reference Book of Corporate Managements. Dun and Bradstreet Information Services. • Annual. Libraries, $650.00 per year; others, $795.00 per year. Lease basis. Management executives at over 12,000 leading United States companies.

Standard and Poor's Register of Corporations, Directors and Executives. Standard and Poor's. • Annual. $675.00. Periodic supplementation. Over 55,000 public and privately held corporations in the U.S. Three volumes. Three supplements.

ENCYCLOPEDIAS AND DICTIONARIES

Blackwell Encyclopedic Dictionary of Strategic Management. Derek F. Channon, editor. Blackwell Publishers. • 1997. $110.00. The editor is associated with Imperial College, London. Contains definitions of key terms combined with longer articles written by various U. S. and foreign business educators. Includes bibliographies and index. (Blackwell Encyclopedia of Management Series.).

Dictionary of Business and Management. Jerry M. Rosenberg. John Wiley and Sons, Inc. • 1992. $14.95. Third edition. (Business Dictionary Series).

Every Manager's Guide to Business Processes: A Glossary of Key Terms and Concepts for Today's Business Leader. Peter G. W. Keen. Harvard Business School Press. • 1995. $14.95. Provides definitions of contemporary business terms, such as "outsourcing," "benchmarking," and "groupware.".

Field Guide to Business Terms: A Glossary of Essential Tools and Concepts for Today's Manager. Alistair D. Williamson, editor. Harvard Business School Press. • 1993. $16.95. Defines fundamental terms. (Harvard Business Economist Reference Series).

International Encyclopedia of Business and Management. Malcolm Warner, editor. Routledge, Inc. • 1996. $1,319.95. Six volumes. Contains more than 500 articles on global management issues. Includes extensive bibliographies, cross references, and an index of key words and phrases.

International Encyclopedia of Public Policy and Administration. Jay M. Shafritz, editor. HarperCollins Publishers. • 1997. $550.00. Four volumes. Covers 20 major areas, such as public administration, government budgeting, industrial policy, nonprofit management, organizational theory, public finance, labor relations, and taxation. Includes a brief bibliography for each major entry and a comprehensive index.

HANDBOOKS AND MANUALS

AMA Management Handbook. John J. Hampton, editor. AMACOM. • 1994. $110.00. Third edition. Provides 200 chapters in 16 major subject areas. Covers a wide variety of business and industrial management topics.

Developing E-Business Architectures: A Manager's Guide. Paul Harmon and others. Academic Press. • 2000. $34.95.

Management: Skills and Application. Leslie W. Rue. McGraw-Hill Higher Education. • 1996. $39.95. Eighth edition.

Organization Charts: Structures of More Than 200 Businesses and Non-Profit Organizations. The Gale Group. • 1999. $165.00. Third edition. Includes an introductory discussion of the history and use of such charts.

Professional's Guide to Successful Management: The Eight Essentials for Running Your Firm, Practice, or Partnership. Carol A. O'Connor. McGraw-Hill. • 1994. Price on application.

Reengineering Revolution: A Handbook. Michael Hammer and Steven Stanton. HarperInformation. • 1995. $16.00.

INTERNET DATABASES

EBSCO Information Services. Ebsco Publishing. Phone: 800-871-8508 or (508)356-6500 Fax: (508)356-5640 E-mail: ep@epnet.com • URL: http://www.epnet.com • Fee-based Web site providing Internet access to a wide variety of databases, including business-related material. Full text is available for many periodical titles, with daily updates. Fees: Apply.

ProQuest Direct. Bell & Howell Information and Learning. Phone: 800-521-0600 or (313)761-4700 Fax: (313)973-9145 • URL: http://www.umi.com/proquest • Fee-based Web site providing Internet access to more than 3,000 periodicals, newspapers, and other publications. Many items are available full-text, with daily updates. Includes extensive corporate and financial information from Disclosure, Inc. Fees: Apply.

ONLINE DATABASES

ABI/INFORM. Bell & Howell Information and Learning. • Provides online indexing to business-related material occurring in over 1,000 periodicals from 1971 to the present. Inquire as to online cost and availability.

Business and Management Practices. Responsive Database Services, Inc. • Provides fulltext of management articles appearing in more than 350 relevant publications. Emphasis is on "the processes, methods, and strategies of managing a business." Time span is 1995 to date. Inquire as to online cost and availability. (Also available in a CD-ROM version.).

Management Contents. The Gale Group. • Covers a wide range of management, financial, marketing, personnel, and administrative topics. About 150 leading business journals are indexed and abstracted from 1974 to date, with monthly updating. Inquire as to online cost and availability.

Wilson Business Abstracts Online. H. W. Wilson Co. • Indexes and abstracts 600 major business periodicals, plus the *Wall Street Journal* and the business section of the *New York Times*. Indexing is from 1982, abstracting from 1990, with the two newspapers included from 1993. Updated weekly. Inquire as to online cost and availability. (*Business Periodicals Index* without abstracts is also available online.).

PERIODICALS AND NEWSLETTERS

The Academy of Management Executive. Oxford University Press, Journals. • Quarterly. $135.00 per year. Contains articles relating to the practical application of management principles and theory.

Academy of Management Journal. Academy of Management. • Bimonthly. $95.00 per year. Presents research papers on management-related topics.

Administrative Science Quarterly. Cornell University Press, Johnson Graduate School of Management. • Individuals: $55.00 per year; institutions, $100.00 per year.

California Management Review. University of California at Berkeley. • Quarterly. Individuals, $50.00 per year; institutions, $65.00 per year; students, $24.00 per year.

Forbes. Forbes, Inc. • Biweekly. $59.95 per year. Includes supplements: *Forbes ASAP* and *Forbes FYI*.

Fortune Magazine. Time Inc., Business Information Group. • Biweekly. $59.95 per year. Edited for top executives and upper-level managers.

Leader to Leader. Peter F. Drucker Foundation for Nonprofit Management. Jossey-Bass Publishers. • Quarterly. Individuals, $149.00 per year; institutions, $149.00 per year. Contains articles on "management, leadership, and strategy" written by "leading executives, thinkers, and consultants." Covers both business and nonprofit issues.

Management International Review: Journal of International Business. Betriebswirtschaftlicher Verlag Dr. Th. Gabler Gmbh. • Quarterly.

Management Review. American Management Association. • Membership.

Management Science. Institute for Operations Research and the Management Sciences. • Monthly. Individuals, $143.00 per year; institutions, $327.00 per year. Provides an interchange of information between management and management scientists in industry, academia, the military and government.

Management Update. Harvard Business School Publishing. • Monthly. $99.00 per year. Newsletter. Covers "ideas, trends, and solutions" for middle management.

Sam Advanced Management Journal. Society for the Advancement of Management. Texas A & M University - Corpus Christi, College of Business. • Quarterly. $49.00. Provides information on leading business topics for practicing managers.

Women as Managers: Strategies for Success. Economics Press, Inc. • Biweekly. $69.00 per year. Newsletter. Covers management skills and techniques leading to higher career levels. Discusses problems women face on the job.

RESEARCH CENTERS AND INSTITUTES

Board of Research. Babson College, Babson Park, MA 02457. Phone: (718)239-5339 Fax: (718)239-6416 • URL: http://www.babson.edu/bor • Research areas include management, entrepreneurial characteristics, and multi-product inventory analysis.

Conference Board, Inc. 845 Third Ave., New York, NY 10022. Phone: (212)759-0900 Fax: (212)980-7014 E-mail: richard.cavanaugh@conference-board.org • URL: http://www.conference-board.org.

Financial Executives Research Foundation. P.O. Box 1938, Morristown, NJ 07962-1938. Phone: (973)898-4608 Fax: (973)898-6636 E-mail: rcolson@fei.org • URL: http://www.ferf.org.

TRADE/PROFESSIONAL ASSOCIATIONS

Academy of Management. P.O. Box 3020, Briarcliff Manor, NY 10510-3020. Phone: (914)923-2607 Fax: (914)923-2615 E-mail: aom@academy.pace.edu • URL: http://www.aom.pace.edu • Members are university professors of management and selected business executives.

American Management Association. 1601 Broadway, New York, NY 10019-7420. Phone: 800-262-9699 or (212)586-8100 Fax: (212)903-8168 • URL: http://www.amanet.org.

National Association of Professional Organizers. 1033 La Posada Drive, Suite 220, Austin, TX 78752. Phone: (512)454-8626 Fax: (512)454-3036 E-mail: napo@assnmgmt.com • URL: http://www.napo.net • Members are concerned with time management, productivity, and the efficient organization of documents and activities.

Society for Advancement of Management. Texas A&M University-Corpus Christi, College of Business, 6300 Ocean Dr., Corpus Christi, TX 78412. Phone: 888-827-6077 or (361)825-6045 or (361)825-5574 Fax: (361)825-2725 E-mail: moustafa@falcon.tamucc.edu • URL: http://www.enterprise.tamucc.edu/sam/.

OTHER SOURCES

Dynamic E-Business Implementation Management: How to Effectively Manage E-Business Implementation. Bennet P. Lientz and Kathryn P. Rea. Academic Press. • 2000. $44.95.

How to Manage Conflict in the Organization. American Management Association Extension Institute. • Looseleaf. $110.00. Self-study course. Emphasis is on practical explanations, examples, and problem solving. Quizzes and a case study are included.

InSite 2. Intelligence Data/Thomson Financial. • Fee-based Web site consolidates information in a "Base Pack" consisting of Business InSite, Market InSite, and Company InSite. Optional databases are Consumer InSite, Health and Wellness InSite, Newsletter InSite, and Computer InSite. Includes fulltext content from more than 2,500 trade publications, journals, newsletters, newspapers, analyst reports, and other sources. Continuous updating. Formerly produced by The Gale Group.

ADMINISTRATIVE DECISION MAKING

See: DECISION-MAKING

ADMINISTRATIVE LAW AND REGULATION

See also: BUSINESS LAW; CORPORATION LAW AND REGULATION; LABOR LAW AND REGULATION; LAW; LAWS; LAWYERS

GENERAL WORKS

Administrative Law. Steven J. Cann. Sage Publications, Inc. • 1998. $55.00. Second edition.

ABSTRACTS AND INDEXES

Current Law Index: Multiple Access to Legal Periodicals. The Gale Group. • Monthly. $650.00 per year. Produced in cooperation with the American Association of Law Libraries. Indexes more than 900 law journals, legal newspapers, and specialty publications from the U.S., Canada, U.K., Ireland, Australia, and New Zealand.

Index to Legal Periodicals and Books. H. W. Wilson Co. • Monthly. Quarterly and annual cumulations. $270.00 per year. CD-ROM version available at $1,495.00 per year.

BIBLIOGRAPHIES

Current Publications in Legal and Related Fields. American Association of Law Libraries. Fred B. Rothman and Co. • Nine times a year. $185.00 per year. Annual cumulation.

Law Books Published. Glanville Publishers, Inc. • Two times a year. $160.00 per year. Supplement to *Law Books in Print.*

CD-ROM DATABASES

WILSONDISC: Index to Legal Periodicals and Books. H. W. Wilson Co. • Monthly. Including unlimited online access to *Index to Legal Periodicals* through WILSONLINE. Contains CD-ROM indexing of more than 800 English language legal periodicals from 1981 to date and 2,500 books.

ENCYCLOPEDIAS AND DICTIONARIES

Communicating with Legal Databases: Terms and Abbreviations for the Legal Researcher. Anne L. McDonald. Neal-Schuman Publishers, Inc. • 1987. $82.50.

HANDBOOKS AND MANUALS

Code of Federal Regulations. Office of the Federal Register, U.S. General Services Administration. Available from U.S. Government Printing Office. • $1,094.00 per year. Complete service.

ONLINE DATABASES

Index to Legal Periodicals and Books (Online). H. W. Wilson Co. • Broad coverage of law journals and books 1981 to date. Monthly updates. Inquire as to online cost and availability.

LEXIS. LEXIS-NEXIS. • The various LEXIS databases provide full text and indexing for a wide variety of legal cases, statutes, orders, and opinions.

PERIODICALS AND NEWSLETTERS

Administrative Law Review. American University, Washington College of Law. • Quarterly. Members; $35.00 per year; non-members, $40.00 per year. Scholarly legal journal on developments in the field of administrative law.

Federal Register. Office of the Federal Register. Available from U.S. Government Printing Office. • Daily except Saturday and Sunday. $697.00 per year. Publishes regulations and legal notices issued by federal agencies, including executive orders and presidential proclamations. Issued by the National Archives and Records Administration (http://www.nara.gov).

RESEARCH CENTERS AND INSTITUTES

Lexis.com Research System. Lexis-Nexis Group. Phone: 800-227-9597 or (937)865-6800 Fax: (937)865-6909 E-mail: webmaster@prod.lexis-nexis.com • URL: http://www.lexis.com • Fee-based Web site offers extensive searching of a wide variety of legal sources. Additional features include Daily Opinion Service, lexis.com Bookstore, Career Center, CLE Center, Law Schools, and Practice Pages ("Pages specific to areas of specialty").

TRADE/PROFESSIONAL ASSOCIATIONS

American Bar Association. 750 N. Lake Shore Dr., Chicago, IL 60611. Phone: 800-285-2221 or (312)988-5000 Fax: (312)988-5528 E-mail: info@abanet.org • URL: http://www.abanet.org.

Federal Administrative Law Judges Conference. 2000 Pennsylvania Ave., N.W., Ste. PMB 260, Washington, DC 20006-1846. Phone: (202)219-2539 Fax: (202)219-3289 • URL: http://www.faljc.org.

OTHER SOURCES

Administrative Law. Matthew Bender & Co., Inc. • $1,200.00 per year. Six looseleaf volumes. Periodic supplementation. Covers investigations, adjudications, hearings, licenses, judicial review, and so forth.

ADULT EDUCATION

See also: CORRESPONDENCE SCHOOLS AND COURSES; GRADUATE WORK IN UNIVERSITIES; TRAINING OF EMPLOYEES; VOCATIONAL EDUCATION

GENERAL WORKS

Administering Successful Programs for Adults: Promoting Excellence in Adult, Community, and Continuing Education. Michael W. Galbraith and others. Krieger Publishing Co. • 1996. $24.50. Provides practical advice on the "day-to-day duties and responsibilities of organizing and administering successful programs in adult, community, and continuing education settings." (Professional Practices in Adult Education and Human Resource Development Series).

Adults as Learners: Increasing Participation and Facilities Learning. Kathryn P. Cross. Jossey-Bass Inc., Publishers. • 1981. $28.95. (Classic Series).

ABSTRACTS AND INDEXES

Current Index to Journals in Education (CIJE). Oryx Press. • Monthly. $245.00 per year. Semiannual cumulations, $475.00.

Education Index. H.W. Wilson Co. • 10 times a year. Service basis.

ALMANACS AND YEARBOOKS

Research and Investigation in Adult Education: Annual Register. Americ[illegible] and Continuing Edu[illegible]

BIBLIOGRAPHIES

Education for Older Adult Learning: A Selected, Annotated Bibliography. Reva M. Greenberg. Greenwood Publishing Group, Inc. • 1993. $75.00. Describes more than 700 books, articles, and other items relating to formal and informal education for older adults. (Bibliographies and Indexes in Gerontology Series, No. 20).

CD-ROM DATABASES

ERIC on SilverPlatter. Available from SilverPlatter Information, Inc. • Quarterly. $700.00 per year. Produced by the Office of Educational Research and Improvement, U. S. Dept. of Education. Provides CD-ROM indexing and abstracting of a wide variety of literature relating to education. Archival discs are available from 1966.

DIRECTORIES

American Association for Adult and Continuing Education: Membership Directory. American Association for Adult and Continuing Education. • Irregular.

Peterson's Guide to Distance Learning. Peterson's. • 1996. $24.95. Provides detailed information on accredited college and university programs available through television, radio, computer, videocassette, and audiocassette resources. Covers 700 U. S. and Canadian institutions. Formerly *The Electronic University.*

ONLINE DATABASES

Education Index Online. H. W. Wilson Co. • Indexes a wide variety of periodicals related to schools, colleges, and education, 1984 to date. Monthly updates. Inquire as to online cost and availability.

ERIC. Educational Resources Information Center. • Broad range of educational literature, 1966 to present. Monthly updates. Inquire as to online cost and availability.

Information Bank Abstracts. New York Times Index Dept. • Provides indexing and abstracting of current affairs, primarily from the final late edition of *The New York Times* and the Eastern edition of *The Wall Street Journal.* Time period is 1969 to present, with daily updates. Inquire as to online cost and availability.

PERIODICALS AND NEWSLETTERS

Adult and Continuing Education Today. Learning Resources Network. • BiWeekly. $95.00 per year.

Adult Education Quarterly. American Association for Adult and Continuing Education. • Quarterly. $50.00 per year.

Adult Learning. American Association for Adult and Continuing Education. • 10 times a year. $58.00 per year.

Resources in Education. Educational Resources Information Center. Available from U.S. Government Printing Office. • Monthly. $102.00 per year. Reports on educational research.

RESEARCH CENTERS AND INSTITUTES

Center for Adult Education. Columbia University. Teachers College, 525 W. 120th St., New York, NY 10027. Phone: (212)678-3816 Fax: (212)678-3957 E-mail: vjm5@columbia.edu.

ERIC Clearinghouse on Adult, Career and Vocational Education. Ohio State University. Center on Education and Training for Employment, 1900 Kenny Rd., Columbus, OH 43210-1090. Phone: 800-848-4815 or (614)292-7069 Fax: (614)292-1260 E-mail: ericacve@postbox.acs.ohio-state.edu • URL: http://www.ericacve/org.

National Institute for Work and Learning. Academy for Educational Development, 1875 Connecticut Ave., N.W., Washington, DC 20009. Phone: (202)884-8187 Fax: (202)884-8422 E-mail: ich[illegible]er@aed.org • URL: http://www.niwl.org •

Research areas include adult education, training, unemployment insurance, and career development.

STATISTICS SOURCES

Digest of Education Statistics. Available from U. S. Government Printing Office. • Annual. $44.00. Covers all areas of education from kindergarten through graduate school. Includes data from both government and private sources. Compiled by National Center for Education Statistics, U. S. Department of Education.

TRADE/PROFESSIONAL ASSOCIATIONS

American Association for Adult and Continuing Education. 1200 19th St., N.W., Suite 300, Washington, DC 20036. Phone: (202)429-5131 Fax: (202)223-4579 • URL: http://www.albany.edu/aaace.

Association for Continuing Higher Education. c/o Dr. Wayne Whelan, Trident Technical College, P.O. Box 118067 CE-M, Charleston, SC 29423-8067. Phone: 800-807-2343 or (803)574-6658 Fax: (803)574-6470 E-mail: zpbarrineaui@trident.tec.sc.us • URL: http://www.charleston.net/org/ache.

University Continuing Education Association. One Dupont Circle, N.W., Suite 615, Washington, DC 20036. Phone: (202)659-3130 Fax: (202)785-0374 E-mail: postmaster@nucea.edu • URL: http://www.nucea.edu.

ADVERTISING

See also: ADVERTISING AGENCIES; ADVERTISING MEDIA; ADVERTISING SPECIALTIES; DIRECT MAIL ADVERTISING; INDUSTRIAL ADVERTISING; MARKETING; OUTDOOR ADVERTISING; PUBLIC RELATIONS AND PUBLICITY; RADIO AND TELEVISION ADVERTISING

GENERAL WORKS

Advertising. Ray Wright. Trans-Atlantic Publications, Inc. • 2000. $49.50.

The Advertising Business: Operations, Creativity, Media Planning, Integrated Communications. John P. Jones, editor. Sage Publications, Inc. • 1999. $85.00. Contains articles by professionals in various fields of advertising.

Advertising Management. Rajeev Batra. Prentice Hall. • 1995. $99.00. Fifth edition.

Advertising: Principles and Practice. William Wells and John Burnett. Prentice Hall. • 2000. Fifth edition. Price on application.

Breaking Up America: Advertisers and the New Media World. Joseph Turow. University of Chicago Press. • 1997. $22.50. A social criticism of target marketing, market segmentation, and customized media.

Cases in Advertising Communication Management. Stephen A. Greyser. Prentice Hall. • 1991. $30.00. Third edition.

Contemporary Advertising. William F. Arens. McGraw-Hill. • 1998. $83.13. Seventh edition.

Creative Strategy in Advertising; What the Copywriter Should Know About the Creative Side of the Business. A. Jerome Jewler. Wadsworth Publishing. • 2000. $52.00. Seventh edition. (Mass Communication Series).

The Design of Advertising. Roy Paul Nelson. Brown and Benchmark. • 1996. Seventh edition. Price on application.

How to Promote, Publicize, and Advertise Your Growing Business: Getting the Word Out Without Spending a Fortune. Kim Baker and Sunny Baker. John Wiley and Sons, Inc. • 1992. $107.50.

International Advertising: Realities and Myths. John P. Jones, editor. Sage Publications, Inc. • 1999. $76.00. Includes articles by advertising professionals in 10 different countries.

Introduction to Advertising and Promotion: An Integrated Marketing Communications Perspective. George E. Belch and Michael A. Belch. McGraw-Hill Higher Education. • 1994. $69.94. Third edition.

Kleppner's Advertising Procedure. Prentice Hall. • 1995. $230.00. 13th edition. (Prentice Hall College Title Series).

ABSTRACTS AND INDEXES

Business Periodicals Index. H. W. Wilson Co. • Monthly, except August, with quarterly and annual cumulations. Service basis for print edition; CD-ROM edition, $1,495.00 per year.

Communication Abstracts. Sage Publications, Inc. • Bimonthly. Individuals, $185.00 per year; institutions, $805.00 per year. Provides broad coverage of the literature of communications, including broadcasting and advertising.

What's New in Advertising and Marketing. Special Libraries Association, Advertising and Marketing Div. • Quarterly. Non-profit organizations, $20.00 per year; corporations, $30.00 per year. Lists and briefly describes a wide variety of free or inexpensive material relating to advertising, marketing, and media.

ALMANACS AND YEARBOOKS

Advertisers Annual. Hollis Directories Ltd. • Annual. $420.00. About 2,700 advertising and media agencies in the United Kingdom, Ireland and abroad, relevant to all forms of advertising.

BIBLIOGRAPHIES

Information Sources in Advertising History. Richard W. Pollay, editor. Greenwood Publishing Group, Inc. • 1979. $65.00.

Topicator: Classified Guide to Articles in the Advertising/Communications/Marketing Periodical Press. • Bimonthly. $110.00 per year. An index of major articles appearing in 20 leading magazines in the advertising, communications, and marketing fields.

BIOGRAPHICAL SOURCES

The Ad Men and Women: A Biographical Dictionary of Advertising. Edd Applegate, editor. Greenwood Publishing Group, Inc. • 1994. $85.00. Provides extended biographical profiles of "54 men and women who have shaped advertising from the nineteenth century to the present." Includes bibliographies.

CD-ROM DATABASES

Advertiser and Agency Red Books Plus. National Register Publishing, Reed Reference Publishing. • Quarterly. $1,295.00 per year. The CD-ROM version of *Standard Directory of Advertisers, Standard Directory of Advertising Agencies*, and *Standard Directory of International Advertisers and Agencies*.

Business Source Plus. EBSCO Information Services. • Monthly. $1,495.00 per year. Provides CD-ROM citations and abstracts to articles in about 650 business periodicals and newspapers, including *The Wall Street Journal*. Full text is provided from 200 selected periodicals. Covers accounting, communications, economics, finance, management, marketing, and other business subjects.

WILSONDISC: Wilson Business Abstracts. H. W. Wilson Co. • Monthly. $2,495.00 per year, including unlimited online access to *Wilson Business Abstracts* through WILSONLINE. Provides CD-ROM "cover-to-cover" abstracting and indexing of over 600 prominent business periodicals. Indexing is from 1982, abstracting from 1990. (*Business Periodicals Index* without abstracts is available on CD-ROM at $1,495 per year.).

DIRECTORIES

Advertising Age-Leading National Advertisers. Crain Communications, Inc. • Annual. $5.00. List of the 100 leading advertisers in terms of the amount spent in national advertising and below-the-line forms of spending.

Advertising Organizations and Publications: A Resource Guide. John P. Jones, editor. Sage Publications, Inc. • 2000. $70.00. Describes advertising associations, books, periodicals, etc.

International Advertising Association Membership Directory. International Advertising Association. • Annual. Membership. Over 3,600 advertisers, advertising agencies, media, and other firms involved in advertising.

Standard Directory of Advertisers: Business Classifications Edition. National Register Publishing. • Annual $659.00; with supplements, $759.00. Arranged by product or service. Provides information on the advertising programs of over 20,000 companies, including advertising/marketing personnel and the names of advertising agencies used.

Standard Directory of Advertisers: Geographic Edition. National Register Publishing. • Annual $659.00; with supplements, $759.00. Arranged geographically by state. Provides information on the advertising programs of over 10,000 companies, including advertising/marketing personnel and the names of advertising agencies used. Includes *Advertiser/Agency* supplement.

ENCYCLOPEDIAS AND DICTIONARIES

Blackwell Encyclopedic Dictionary of Marketing. Barbara R. Lewis and Dale Littler, editors. Blackwell Publishers. • 1996. $105.95. The editors are associated with the Manchester School of Management. Contains definitions of key terms combined with longer articles written by various U. S. and foreign business educators. Includes bibliographies and index. (Blackwell Encyclopedia of Management series.).

Complete Multilingual Dictionary of Advertising, Marketing, and Communications. Hans W. Paetzel, editor. NTC/Contemporary Publishing. • 1994. $49.95. Provides translations of about 8,000 technical and general terms. English, French and German terms.

Dictionary of Marketing and Advertising. Jerry M. Rosenberg. John Wiley and Sons, Inc. • 1995. $79.95. (Business Dictionary Series).

HANDBOOKS AND MANUALS

Advertising Manager's Handbook. Robert W. Bly. Prentice Hall. • 1998. $79.95. Second edition.

Advertising: What It Is and How to Do It. Roderick White. McGraw-Hill. • 1993. $16.95. Third edition.

Dartnell's Advertising Manager's Handbook. David Bushko, editor. Dartnell Corp. • 1997. $69.95. Fourth revised edition.

Do-It-Yourself Advertising: How to Produce Great Ads, Brochures, Catalogs, Direct Mail, and Much More!. Fred E. Hahn and Kenneth G. Mangun. John Wiley and Sons, Inc. • 1997. $45.00. Second edition. Covers magazines, newspapers, flyers, brochures, catalogs, direct mail, telemarketing, trade shows, and radio/TV promotions. Includes checklists. (Small Business Series).

Logo Power: How to Create Effective Company Logos. William Haig and Laurel Harper. John Wiley & Sons, Inc. • 1997. $39.95. Explains how to plan, develop, evaluate, and implement a company logo system.

Marketing Without Advertising. Michael Phillips and Salli Rasberry. Nolo.com. • 1996. $19.00. Second revised edition. How to market a small business economically.

ONLINE DATABASES

Management Contents. The Gale Group. • Covers a wide range of management, financial, marketing, personnel, and administrative topics. About 150 leading business journals are indexed and abstracted from 1974 to date, with monthly updating. Inquire as to online cost and availability.

Marketing and Advertising Reference Service (MARS). The Gale Group. • Provides abstracts of literature relating to consumer marketing and advertising, including all forms of advertising media. Time period is 1984 to date. Daily updates. Inquire as to online cost and availability.

Simmons Study of Media and Markets. Simmons Market Research Bureau. • Market and media survey data relating to the American consumer. Inquire as to online cost and availability.

Wilson Business Abstracts Online. H. W. Wilson Co. • Indexes and abstracts 600 major business periodicals, plus the *Wall Street Journal* and the business section of the *New York Times*. Indexing is from 1982, abstracting from 1990, with the two newspapers included from 1993. Updated weekly. Inquire as to online cost and availability. (*Business Periodicals Index* without abstracts is also available online.).

PERIODICALS AND NEWSLETTERS

Advertising Age: The International Newspaper of Marketing. Crain Communications, Inc. • Weekly. $109.00 per year. Includes supplement *Creativity*.

Advertising Age's Euromarketing. Crain Communications, Inc. • Weekly. $295.00 per year. Newsletter on European advertising and marketing.

ADWEEK. BPI Communications, Inc. • Weekly. Price varies. Covers local, national, and international advertising news and trends. Includes critiques of advertising campaigns.

IAA World News. International Advertising Association. • Quarterly. $80.00 per year. Formerly *International Advertiser*.

International Journal of Advertising: The Quarterly Review of Marketing Communications. Advertising Association. NTC Publications, Ltd. • Quarterly. Price on application.

Journal of Advertising Research. Advertising Research Foundation. • Bimonthly. $100.00 per year.

Journal of Promotion Management: Innovations in Planning and Applied Research for Advertising, Sales Promotion, Personal Selling, Public Relations, and Re-Seller Support. Haworth Press, Inc. • Semiannual. Individuals, $40.00 per year; institutions, $65.00 per year; libraries, $95.00 per year.

The Licensing Letter. EPM Communications, Inc. • Monthly. $447.00 per year. Newsletter. Covers all aspects of licensed merchandising (compensation of a person or an organization for being associated with a product or service).

Med Ad News. Engel Publishing Partners. • Monthly. $150.00 per year. Covers the field of pharmaceutical advertising and marketing.

Media Industry Newsletter. Phillips Business Information, Inc. • Weekly. $595.00 per year. News of advertising, broadcasting, and publishing. Reports on the number of advertising pages in major magazines.

STATISTICS SOURCES

Advertising Age: National Expenditures in Newspapers. Crain Communications, Inc. • Annual.

U. S. Industry and Trade Outlook: The McGraw-Hill Companies and the U.S. Department of Commerce/ International Trade Administration. Datapso Research Corp. • Annual. $69.95. Produced by the International Trade Administration, U. S. Department of Commerce, in a "public-private" partnership with DRI/McGraw-Hill and Standard & Poor's. Provides basic data, outlook for the current year, and "Long-Term Prospects" (five-year projections) for a wide variety of products and services. Includes high technology industries. Formerly *U. S. Industrial Outlook.*

TRADE/PROFESSIONAL ASSOCIATIONS

Advertising and Marketing International Network. c/o B. Vaughn Sink, 12323 Nantucket, Wichita, KS 67235. Phone: (316)722-7535 Fax: (316)722-8353 E-mail: vaughn-sink@shscom.com • URL: http://www.aminworldwide.com.

Advertising Council. 261 Madison Ave., 11th Fl., New York, NY 10016-2303. Phone: 800-933-7727 or (212)922-1500 Fax: (212)922-1676 • URL: http://www.adcouncil.org.

Advertising Research Foundation. 641 Lexington Ave., New York, NY 10022. Phone: (212)751-5656 Fax: (212)319-5265 E-mail: email@arfsite.org • URL: http://www.arfsite.org.

American Advertising Federation. 1101 Vermont Ave., N.W., Suite 500, Washington, DC 20005. Phone: (202)898-0089 Fax: (202)898-0159 E-mail: aaf@aaf.org • URL: http://www.aaf.org.

Association of National Advertisers. 708 Third Ave., New York, NY 10017-4270. Phone: (212)697-5950 Fax: (212)661-8057 • URL: http://www.ana.net.

Direct Marketing Association. 1120 Ave. of the Americas, New York, NY 10036-6700. Phone: (212)768-7277 Fax: (212)302-6714 E-mail: webmaster@the-dma.org • URL: http://www.the-dma.org.

International Advertising Association. 521 Fifth Ave., Suite 1807, New York, NY 10175. Phone: (212)557-1133 Fax: (212)983-0455 E-mail: iaaglobal@iaaglobal.org • URL: http://www.iaaglobal.org.

National Advertising Review Board. 845 Third Ave., New York, NY 10022. Phone: (212)754-1320 Fax: (212)308-4743 E-mail: ehaueter@narb.bbb.org • URL: http://www.bbb.org.

ADVERTISING AGENCIES

See also: ADVERTISING

GENERAL WORKS

Where the Suckers Moon: The Life and Death of an Advertising Campaign. Randall Rothenberg. Random House, Inc. • 1995. $16.00. Presents the story of an advertising agency's failed automobile campaign.

CD-ROM DATABASES

Advertiser and Agency Red Books Plus. National Register Publishing, Reed Reference Publishing. • Quarterly. $1,295.00 per year. The CD-ROM version of *Standard Directory of Advertisers, Standard Directory of Advertising Agencies*, and *Standard Directory of International Advertisers and Agencies.*

DIRECTORIES

Standard Directory of Advertising Agencies: The Agency Red Book. National Register Publishing. • Semiannual $659.00. With sup[illegible] information on nearl[illegible]

agencies and branch offices. Includes annual billings by media and names of clients. Includes *Advertiser/ Agency* supplement.

Standard Directory of International Advertisers and Agencies: The International Red Book. R. R. Bowker. • Annual. $569.00. Includes about 8,000 foreign companies and their advertising agencies. Geographic, company name, personal name, and trade name indexes are provided.

FINANCIAL RATIOS

Almanac of Business and Industrial Financial Ratios. Leo Troy. Prentice Hall. • Annual. $99.95. Contains financial ratios derived from federal tax returns. Ratios for each of about 200 industries are arranged according to company asset size.

Annual Statement Studies. Robert Morris Associates: The Association of Lending and Credit Risk Professiona. • Annual. Free to members; non-members, $140.00. Median and quartile financial ratios are given for over 400 kinds of manufacturing, wholesale, retail, construction, and consumer finance establishments. Data is sorted by both asset size and sales volume. Includes a clearly written "Definition of Ratios" and an alphabetical industry index.

HANDBOOKS AND MANUALS

Advertising Agency. Entrepreneur Media, Inc. • Looseleaf. $59.50. A practical guide to starting a small advertising agency. Covers profit potential, start-up costs, market size evaluation, pricing, accounting, advertising, promotion, etc. (Start-Up Business Guide No. E1223.).

ONLINE DATABASES

ABI/INFORM. Bell & Howell Information and Learning. • Provides online indexing to business-related material occurring in over 1,000 periodicals from 1971 to the present. Inquire as to online cost and availability.

Information Bank Abstracts. New York Times Index Dept. • Provides indexing and abstracting of current affairs, primarily from the final late edition of *The New York Times* and the Eastern edition of *The Wall Street Journal*. Time period is 1969 to present, with daily updates. Inquire as to online cost and availability.

Management Contents. The Gale Group. • Covers a wide range of management, financial, marketing, personnel, and administrative topics. About 150 leading business journals are indexed and abstracted from 1974 to date, with monthly updating. Inquire as to online cost and availability.

PERIODICALS AND NEWSLETTERS

American Advertising. American Advertising Federation. • Quarterly. Membership.

TRADE/PROFESSIONAL ASSOCIATIONS

American Association of Advertising Agencies. 405 Lexington Ave., 18th Fl., New York, NY 10174-1801. Phone: (212)682-2500 Fax: (212)682-8391 E-mail: http://www.aaaa.org.

International Advertising Association. 521 Fifth Ave., Ste. 1807, New York, NY 10175. Phone: (212)557-1133 Fax: (212)983-0455 E-mail: iaa@iaaglobal.org • URL: http://www.iaaglobal.org.

International Communications Agency Network. P.O. Box 490, Rollinsville, CO 80474-0490. Phone: (303)258-9511 Fax: (303)258-3090 E-mail: hq@icomagencies.com • URL: http://www.icomagencies.com.

League of Advertising Agencies. 65 Reade St., Suite 3A, New York, NY 10007. Phone: (212)528-0364 Fax: (212)766-1181 • URL: http://www.adaagencies.com.

North American Advertising Agency Network. 234 [illegible] Delaware Ave., Pennington, NJ 08534-1603.

Western States Advertising Agencies Association. 6404 Wilshire Blvd., Suite 1111, Los Angeles, CA 90048. Phone: (323)655-1951 Fax: (323)655-8627.

ADVERTISING ART

See: COMMERCIAL ART

ADVERTISING, COOPERATIVE

See: COOPERATIVE ADVERTISING

ADVERTISING COPY

GENERAL WORKS

Advertising Copywriting. Philip W. Burton. NTC/Contemporary Publishing. • 1996. $44.95. Seventh edition. (NTC Business Book Series).

ABSTRACTS AND INDEXES

Business Periodicals Index. H. W. Wilson Co. • Monthly, except August, with quarterly and annual cumulations. Service basis for print edition; CD-ROM edition, $1,495.00 per year.

DIRECTORIES

ADWEEK Agency Directory. BPI Communications, Inc. • Annual. $340.00. Over 5,200 advertising agencies, public relations firms, and media buying services, and related organizations in the U.S. Supplement to *Client-Brand Directory* and *Major Media Directory.*

HANDBOOKS AND MANUALS

Copywriter's Handbook. Robert W. Bly. Henry Holt & Co., LLC. • 1995. $13.95.

Copywriting Secrets and Tactics: How to Put More Sell into All Your Copy. Herschell G. Lewis. Dartnell Corp. • $91.50. Looseleaf service.

How to Produce Creative Advertising: Traditional Techniques and Computer Applications. Thomas Bivins and Ann Keding. NTC/Contemporary Publishing. • 1993. $37.95. Covers copywriting, advertising design, and the use of desktop publishing techniques in advertising. (NTC Business Book Series).

ONLINE DATABASES

Wilson Business Abstracts Online. H. W. Wilson Co. • Indexes and abstracts 600 major business periodicals, plus the *Wall Street Journal* and the business section of the *New York Times.* Indexing is from 1982, abstracting from 1990, with the two newspapers included from 1993. Updated weekly. Inquire as to online cost and availability. (*Business Periodicals Index* without abstracts is also available online.).

PERIODICALS AND NEWSLETTERS

Computer Publishing and Advertising Report: The Biweekly Newsletter for Publishing and Advertising Executives in the Computer Field. SIMBA Information, Inc. • Biweekly. $549.00 per year. Newsletter. Covers computer book publishing and computer-related advertising in periodicals and other media. Provides data on computer book sales and advertising in computer magazines.

Print: America's Graphic Design Magazine. RC Publications, Inc. • Bimonthly. $53.00 per year. Emphasizes creative trends.

TRADE/PROFESSIONAL ASSOCIATIONS

Advertising Research Foundation. 641 Lexington Ave., New York, NY 10022. Phone: (212)751-5656 Fax: (212)319-5265 E-mail: email@arfsite.org • URL: http://www.arfsite.org.

OTHER SOURCES

How to Write Successful Promotional Copy. American Management Association Extension Institute. • Looseleaf. $98.00. Self-study course. Emphasis is on practical explanations, examples, and problem solving. Quizzes are included.

Teach Yourself Copywriting. J. Jonathan Gabay. NTC/Contemporary Publishing Group. • 2001. $14.95. Second edition. Includes material on copywriting for e-commerce websites.

ADVERTISING, INDUSTRIAL

See: INDUSTRIAL ADVERTISING

ADVERTISING LAW AND REGULATION

See also: BUSINESS LAW

GENERAL WORKS

Impact of Advertising Law on Business and Public Policy. Ross D. Petty. Greenwood Publishing Group, Inc. • 1992. $55.00. Analyzes cases under the Federal Trade Commission and Lanham Acts.

ABSTRACTS AND INDEXES

Business Periodicals Index. H. W. Wilson Co. • Monthly, except August, with quarterly and annual cumulations. Service basis for print edition; CD-ROM edition, $1,495.00 per year.

Current Law Index: Multiple Access to Legal Periodicals. The Gale Group. • Monthly. $650.00 per year. Produced in cooperation with the American Association of Law Libraries. Indexes more than 900 law journals, legal newspapers, and specialty publications from the U.S., Canada, U.K., Ireland, Australia, and New Zealand.

Index to Legal Periodicals and Books. H. W. Wilson Co. • Monthly. Quarterly and annual cumulations. $270.00 per year. CD-ROM version available at $1,495.00 per year.

ALMANACS AND YEARBOOKS

Advertising Law: Year in Review. CCH, Inc. • Annual. $85.00. Summarizes the year's significant legal and regulatory developments.

BIBLIOGRAPHIES

Bowker's Law Books and Serials in Print: A Multimedia Sourcebook. R. R. Bowker. • Annual $725.00. Three volumes. Includes supplement.

Law Books in Print: Law Books in English Published Throughout the World. Glanville Publishers, Inc. • Triennial. $750.00. Supplement available, *Law Books Publisher.*

Legal Looseleafs in Print. Arlene L. Eis, editor. Infosources Publishing. • Annual. $106.00. Lists over 3,800 titles by more than 300 publishers.

DIRECTORIES

Lawyer's Register International by Specialties and Fields of Law Including a Directory of Corporate Counsel. Lawyer's Register Publishing Co. • Annual. $329.00. Three volumes. Referral source for law firms.

HANDBOOKS AND MANUALS

Rights and Liabilities of Publishers, Broadcasters, and Reporters. Slade R. Metcalf and Robin Bierstedt. Shepard's. • 1982. $200.00. Two volumes. A legal manual for the media.

ONLINE DATABASES

ABI/INFORM. Bell & Howell Information and Learning. • Provides online indexing to business-related material occurring in over 1,000 periodicals from 1971 to the present. Inquire as to online cost and availability.

Legal Resource Index. The Gale Group. • Broad coverage of law literature appearing in legal, business, and other periodicals, 1980 to date. Monthly updates. Inquire as to online cost and availability.

LEXIS. LEXIS-NEXIS. • The various LEXIS databases provide full text and indexing for a wide variety of legal cases, statutes, orders, and opinions.

Management Contents. The Gale Group. • Covers a wide range of management, financial, marketing, personnel, and administrative topics. About 150 leading business journals are indexed and abstracted from 1974 to date, with monthly updating. Inquire as to online cost and availability.

PAIS International. Public Affairs Information Service, Inc. • Corresponds to the former printed publications, *PAIS Bulletin* (1976-90) and *PAIS Foreign Language Index* (1972-90), and to the current *PAIS International in Print* (1991 to date). Covers economic, political, and sociological material appearing in periodicals, books, government documents, and other publications. Updating is monthly. Inquire as to online cost and availability.

Trade & Industry Index. The Gale Group. • Provides indexing of business periodicals, January 1981 to date. Daily updates. (Full text articles from some periodicals are available online, 1983 to date, in the companion database, *Trade & Industry ASAP.*) Inquire as to online cost and availability.

PERIODICALS AND NEWSLETTERS

Media and the Law. SIMBA Information. • Semimonthly. $327.00 per year. Newsletter.

RESEARCH CENTERS AND INSTITUTES

Center for Study of Responsive Law. P.O. Box 19367, Washington, DC 20036. Phone: (202)387-8030 Fax: (202)234-5176 E-mail: csrl@csrl.org • URL: http://www.csrl.org • A consumer-oriented research group.

Lexis.com Research System. Lexis-Nexis Group. Phone: 800-227-9597 or (937)865-6800 Fax: (937)865-6909 E-mail: webmaster@prod.lexis-nexis.com • URL: http://www.lexis.com • Fee-based Web site offers extensive searching of a wide variety of legal sources. Additional features include Daily Opinion Service, lexis.com Bookstore, Career Center, CLE Center, Law Schools, and Practice Pages ("Pages specific to areas of specialty").

TRADE/PROFESSIONAL ASSOCIATIONS

National Advertising Review Board. 845 Third Ave., New York, NY 10022. Phone: (212)754-1320 Fax: (212)308-4743 E-mail: ehaueter@narb.bbb.org • URL: http://www.bbb.org.

National Consumer Law Center. 18 Tremont St., Suite 400, Boston, MA 02108. Phone: (617)523-8010 or (617)523-8089 Fax: (617)523-7398 E-mail: consumerlaw@nclc.org • URL: http://www.consumerlaw.org.

OTHER SOURCES

Advertising Compliance Service Newsletter. John Lichtenberger. • Bimonthly. $495.00 per year.

Lindey on Entertainment, Publishing and the Arts: Agreements and the Law. Alexander Lindey, editor. West Group. • $673.00 per year. Looseleaf service. Periodic supplementation. Provides basic forms, applicable law, and guidance. (Entertainment and Communication Law Series).

ADVERTISING MEDIA

See also: ADVERTISING; MASS MEDIA; RADIO AND TELEVISION ADVERTISING

GENERAL WORKS

Advertising Media Planning. Jack Z. Sissors. NTC/ Contemporary Publishing. • 1995. $52.95. Fifth edition. Introduction to media planning.

Breaking Up America: Advertisers and the New Media World. Joseph Turow. University of Chicago Press. • 1997. $22.50. A social criticism of target marketing, market segmentation, and customized media.

Electronic Media Ratings. Karen Buzzard. Butterworth-Heinemann. • 1992. $22.95. Provides basic information about TV and radio audience-rating techniques. Includes glossary and bibliography. (Electronic Media Guide Series).

Essentials of Media Planning: A Marketing Viewpoint. Arnold M. Barban and others. NTC/ Contemporary Publishing. • 1993. $29.95. Third edition. Practical guide to media analysis. (NTC Business Book Series).

BIBLIOGRAPHIES

Topicator: Classified Guide to Articles in the Advertising/Communications/Marketing Periodical Press. • Bimonthly. $110.00 per year. An index of major articles appearing in 20 leading magazines in the advertising, communications, and marketing fields.

DIRECTORIES

Business Publication Advertising Source. SRDS. • Monthly. $682.00 per year. Issued in three parts: (1) U. S. Business Publications, (2) U. S. Healthcare Publications, and (3) International Publications. Provides detailed advertising rates, profiles of editorial content, management names, "Multiple Publications Publishers," circulation data, and other trade journal information. Formerly *Business Publication Rates and Data.*

CARD The Media Information Network (Canadian Advertising Rates and Data). Available from SRDS. • Biennial. $225.00 per issue. Published by Maclean Hunter Publishing Ltd. (Toronto). Provides advertising rates and other information relating to Canadian media: daily newspapers, weekly community newspapers, consumer magazines, business publications, school publications, religious publications, radio, and television.

Community Publication Advertising Source. SRDS. • Semiannual. $161.00 per issue. Provides advertising rates for weekly community newspapers, shopping guides, and religious newspapers, with circulation data and other information. Formerly *Community Publication Rates and Data.*

Consumer Magazine and Advertising Source. SRDS. • Monthly. $661.00 per year. Contains advertising rates and other data for U. S. consumer magazines and agricultural publications. Also provides consumer market data for population, households, income, and retail sales. Formerly *Consumer Magazine and Agri-Media Source.*

Direct Marketing List Source. SRDS. • Bimonthly. $542.00 per year. Provides detailed information and rates for business, farm, and consumer mailing lists (U. S., Canadian, and international). Includes current postal information and directories of list brokers, compilers, and managers. Formerly *Direct Mail List Rates and Data.*

Hispanic Media and Market Source. SRDS. • Quarterly. $271.00 per year. Provides detailed information on the following Hispanic advertising media in the U. S.: TV, radio, newspapers, magazines, direct mail, outdoor, and special events. Formerly *Hispanic Media and Markets.*

Interactive Advertising Source. SRDS. • Quarterly. $561.00 per year. Provides descriptive profiles, rates, audience, personnel, etc., for producers of various forms of interactive or multimedia advertising: online/Internet, CD-ROM, interactive TV, interactive cable, interactive telephone, interactive kiosk, and others. Includes online supplement *SRDS' URlink.*

International Media Guide: Business Professional Publications: Asia Pacific/Middle East/Africa. International Media Guides, Inc. • Annual. $285.00. Provides information on 3,000 trade journals "from Africa to the Pacific Rim," including advertising rates and circulation data.

International Media Guide: Business Professional Publications: Europe. International Media Guides, Inc. • Annual. $285.00. Describes 6,000 trade journals from Eastern and Western Europe, with advertising rates and circulation data.

International Media Guide: Business/Professional Publications: The Americas. International Media Guides, Inc. • Annual. $285.00. Describes trade journals from North, South, and Central America, with advertising rates and circulation data.

International Media Guide: Consumer Magazines Worldwide. International Media Guides, Inc. • Annual. $285.00. Contains descriptions of 4,500 consumer magazines in 24 subject categories in 200 countries, including U. S. Provides details of advertising rates and circulation.

International Media Guide: Newspapers Worldwide. International Media Guides, Inc. • Annual. $285.00. Provides advertising rates, circulation, and other details relating to newspapers in major cities of the world (covers 200 countries, including U. S.).

Marketer's Guide to Media. BPI Communications, Inc. • Quarterly. $105.00. Presents cost, circulation, and audience statistics for various mass media segments, including television, radio, magazines, newspapers, telephone yellow pages, and cinema. Formerly *Mediaweek's Guide to Media.*

Newspaper Advertising Source. SRDS. • Monthly. $662.00 per year. Lists newspapers geographically, with detailed information on advertising rates, special features, personnel, circulation, etc. Includes a section on college newspapers. Also provides consumer market data for population, households, income, and retail sales. Formerly *Newspaper Rates and Data.*

Out-of-Home Advertising Source. SRDS. • Annual. $299.00. Provides detailed information on non-traditional or "out-of-home" advertising media: outdoor, aerial, airport, mass transit, bus benches, school, hotel, in-flight, in-store, theater, stadium, taxi, truckstop, kiosk, shopping malls, and others.

Print Media Production Source. SRDS. • Quarterly. $401.00 per year. Contains details of printing and mechanical production requirements for advertising in specific trade journals, consumer magazines, and newspapers. Formerly *Print Media Production Data.*

Radio Advertising Source. SRDS. • Quarterly. $490.00 per year. Contains detailed information on U. S. radio stations, networks, and corporate owners, with maps of market areas. Includes key personnel.

The SHOOT Directory for Commercial Production and Postproduction. BPI Communications. • Annual. $79.00. Lists production companies, advertising agencies, and sources of professional television, motion picture, and audio equipment.

Technology Media Source. SRDS. • Annual. $291.00. Contains detailed information on business publications, consumer magazines, and direct mail lists that may be of interest to "technology marketers." Emphasis is on aviation and telecommunications.

TV and Cable Source. SRDS. • Quarterly. $464.00 per year. Provides detailed information on U. S. television stations, cable systems, networks, and group owners, with maps and market data. Includes key personnel.

ENCYCLOPEDIAS AND DICTIONARIES

Broadcast Communications Dictionary. Lincoln Diamant. Greenwood Publishing Group Inc. • 1989. $57.95. Third revised edition.

NTC's Mass Media Dictionary. R. Terry Ellmore. NTC/Contemporary Publishing. • 1993. $24.95. Covers television, radio, newspapers, magazines, film, graphic arts, books, billboards, public relations, and advertising. Terms are related to production, research, audience measurement, audio-video engineering, printing, publishing, and other areas.

HANDBOOKS AND MANUALS

Click Here! Internet Advertising: How the Pros Attract, Design, Price, Place, and Measure Ads Online. Eugene Marlow. John Wiley and Sons, Inc. • 1997. $29.95. Covers pricing, effectiveness, Web site selection, content, and other aspects of Internet advertising. (Business Technology Series).

Media Math: Basic Techniques for Media Evaluation. Robert W. Hall. NTC/Contemporary Publishing. • 1994. $19.95. Second edition. (NTC Business Book Series).

Newspaper Association of America: Newspaper Advertising Planbook. Newspaper Association of America. • Annual. Price on application. Formerly *Newspaper Advertising Bureau. Newspaper Advertising Planbook.*

Online Marketing Handbook: How to Promote, Advertise and Sell, Your Products and Services on the Internet. Daniel S. Janal. John Wiley and Sons, Inc. • 1998. $29.95. Revised edition. Provides step-by-step instructions for utilizing online publicity, advertising, and sales promotion. Contains chapters on interactive marketing, online crisis communication, and Web home page promotion, with numerous examples and checklists.

ONLINE DATABASES

Arbitron Radio County Coverage. Arbitron Co. • Ratings of radio and TV stations plus audience measurement data, updated frequently. Inquire as to online cost and availability.

Management Contents. The Gale Group. • Covers a wide range of management, financial, marketing, personnel, and administrative topics. About 150 leading business journals are indexed and abstracted from 1974 to date, with monthly updating. Inquire as to online cost and availability.

Nielsen Station Index. Nielsen Media Research. • Measures local television station audiences in about 220 U. S. geographic areas. Includes current and some historical data. Inquire as to online cost and availability.

Nielsen Television Index. Nielsen Media Research. • Measures national television program audiences by sampling approximately 4,000 U. S. households. Time period is 1970 to date, with weekly updates.

PERIODICALS AND NEWSLETTERS

Advertising Age: The International Newspaper of Marketing. Crain Communications, Inc. • Weekly. $109.00 per year. Includes supplement *Creativity.*

Advertising Age's B to B: News Monthly Concerning the How-To Strategic and Tact ical Marketing, Sales and Advertising of Business-to-Business Products and Services. Crain Communications, Inc. • Monthly. $49.00 per year. Formerly Business Marketing.

Broadcasting and Cable. Cahners Business Information, Broadcasting and Cable's International Group. • 51 times a year. $149.00 per year. Formerly *Broadcasting.*

Interactive Marketing and P R News: News and Practical Advice on Using Interactive Advertising and Marketing to Sell Your Products. Phillips Business Information, Inc. • Biweekly. $495.00 per year. Newsletter. Provides information and guidance on merchandising via CD-ROM ("multimedia catalogs"), the Internet, and interactive TV. Topics include "cybermoney", addresses for e-mail marketing, "virtual malls," and other interactive subjects. Formerly *Interactive Marketing News.*

Internet Business Report: Software, Tools and Platforms. Jupiter Media Metrix. • Semimonthly. $695.00 per year; with electronic software, $795.00 per year. Newsletter. Covers Internet advertising, fee collection, and attempts in general to make the Internet/World Wide Web profitable. Includes news of how businesses are using the Internet for sales promotion and public relations.

The Marketing Pulse: The Exclusive Insight Provider to the Entertainment, Marketing, Advertising and Media Industries. Unlimited Positive Communications, Inc. • Monthly. $300.00 per year. Newsletter concerned with advertising media forecasts and analyses. Emphasis is on TV and radio.

Medical Marketing and Media. CPS Communications, Inc. • Monthly. Individuals, $75.00 per year; institutions, $100.00 per person. Contains articles on marketing, direct marketing, advertising media, and sales personnel for the healthcare and pharmaceutical industries.

SHOOT: The Leading Newsweekly for Commercial Production and Postproduction. BPI Communications. • Weekly. $115.00 per year. Covers animation, music, sound design, computer graphics, visual effects, cinematography, and other aspects of television and motion picture production, with emphasis on TV commercials.

STATISTICS SOURCES

Circulation [year]. SRDS. • Annual. $256.00. Contains detailed statistical analysis of newspaper circulation by metropolitan area or county and data on television viewing by area. Includes maps.

DMA Statistical Fact Book. Direct Marketing Association, Inc. • Annual. $165.95 to non-members; $105.95 to members. Provides data in five sections covering direct response advertising, media, mailing lists, market applications, and "Practical Management Information." Includes material on interactive/online marketing. (Cover title: *Direct Marketing Association's Statistical Fact Book.*).

TRADE/PROFESSIONAL ASSOCIATIONS

Association of Free Community Papers. P.O. Box 2020, Idaho Springs, CO 80452. Phone: 877-203-2327 or (303)567-0355 Fax: (303)567-0520 E-mail: afcp@aspobox.com • URL: http://www.afcp.org.

Magazine Publishers of America. 919 Third Ave., 22nd Fl., New York, NY 10022. Phone: (212)872-3700 Fax: (212)888-4217 E-mail: infocenter@magazine.org • URL: http://www.magazine.org • Members are publishers of consumer and other periodicals.

Newsletter Publishers Association. 1501 Wilson Blvd., Suite 509, Arlington, VA 22209-2403. Phone: 800-356-9302 or (703)527-2333 Fax: (703)841-0629 E-mail: npa@newsletter.org.

Radio Advertising Bureau. 261 Madison Ave., 23rd Fl., New York, NY 10016. Phone: 800-232-3131 or (212)681-7200 Fax: (212)681-7223 • URL: http://www.rab.com.

Television Bureau of Advertising. Three E. 54th St., New York, NY 10022. Phone: (212)486-1111 Fax: (212)935-5631 E-mail: info@tvb.org • URL: http://www.tvb.org.

OTHER SOURCES

eMarketer's eAdvertising Report. Available from MarketResearch.com. • 1999. $795.00. Market research data published by eMarketer. Covers the growth of the Internet online advertising market. Includes future trends and Internet users' attitudes.

Online Advertising Report. Jupiter Media Metrix. • Annual. $750.00. Market research report. Provides five-year forecasts of Internet advertising and subscription revenue. Contains analysis of online advertising trends and practices, with company profiles.

ADVERTISING, POINT-OF-SALE

See: POINT-OF-PURCHASE ADVERTISING

ADVERTISING RESEARCH

See also: MARKET RESEARCH; MEDIA RESEARCH

ABSTRACTS AND INDEXES

Business Periodicals Index. H. W. Wilson Co. • Monthly, except August, with quarterly and annual cumulations. Service basis for print edition; CD-ROM edition, $1,495.00 per year.

HANDBOOKS AND MANUALS

How Advertising Works: The Role of Research. John P. Jones, editor. Sage Publications, Inc. • 1998. $74.00. Includes sections entitled "Research Before the Advertising Runs" and "Research After the Advertising Has Run.".

Successful Advertising Research Methods. Jack B. Haskins and Alice Gagnard-Kendrick. NTC/Contemporary Publishing. • 1994. $49.95. (NTC Business Book Series).

ONLINE DATABASES

ABI/INFORM. Bell & Howell Information and Learning. • Provides online indexing to business-related material occurring in over 1,000 periodicals from 1971 to the present. Inquire as to online cost and availability.

Management Contents. The Gale Group. • Covers a wide range of management, financial, marketing, personnel, and administrative topics. About 150 leading business journals are indexed and abstracted from 1974 to date, with monthly updating. Inquire as to online cost and availability.

Trade & Industry Index. The Gale Group. • Provides indexing of business periodicals, January 1981 to date. Daily updates. (Full text articles from some periodicals are available online, 1983 to date, in the companion database, *Trade & Industry ASAP.*) Inquire as to online cost and availability.

PERIODICALS AND NEWSLETTERS

Journal of Advertising Research. Advertising Research Foundation. • Bimonthly. $100.00 per year.

Mediaweek: Incorporating Marketing and Media Decisions. BPI Communications, Inc. • 47 times a year. $145.00 per year. Published for advertising media buyers and managers.

TRADE/PROFESSIONAL ASSOCIATIONS

Advertising Research Foundation. 641 Lexington Ave., New York, NY 10022. Phone: (212)751-5656 Fax: (212)319-5265 E-mail: email@arfsite.org • URL: http://www.arfsite.org.

American Academy of Advertising. c/o Dr. Robert L. King, University of Richmond, School of Business, Richmond, VA 23173. Phone: (804)289-8902 Fax: (804)289-8878 E-mail: rking@richmond.edu.

OTHER SOURCES

MarketingClick Network: American Demographics. Intertec Publishing, a Primedia Co. • Web site provides full-text articles from *American Demographics, Marketing Tools,* and *Forecast,* with keyword searching. The *Marketing Tools Directory* can also be searched online, listing suppliers of products, information, and services for advertising, market research, and marketing. Fees: Free.

ADVERTISING SPECIALTIES

See also: ADVERTISING

DIRECTORIES

Creative's Illustrated Guide to P-O-P Exhibits and Promotion. Magazines Creative, Inc. • Annual. $25.00. Lists sources of point-of-purchase displays, signs, and exhibits and sources of other promotional materials and equipment. Available online.

Incentive-Merchandise and Travel Directory. Bill Communications, Inc. • Annual. $5.00. A special issue of *Incentive* magazine.

PROMO Magazine's SourceBook: The Only Guide to the $70 Billion Promotion Industry. Intertec Publishing. • Annual. $49.95. Lists service and supply companies for the promotion industry. Includes annual salary survey and award winning campaigns.

FINANCIAL RATIOS

Annual Statement Studies. Robert Morris Associates: The Association of Lending and Credit Risk Professiona. • Annual. Free to members; non-members, $140.00. Median and quartile financial ratios are given for over 400 kinds of manufacturing, wholesale, retail, construction, and consumer finance establishments. Data is sorted by both asset size and sales volume. Includes a clearly written "Definition of Ratios" and an alphabetical industry index.

HANDBOOKS AND MANUALS

Specialty Advertising. Entrepreneur Media, Inc. • Looseleaf. $59.50. A practical guide to starting a business dealing in advertising specialties. Covers profit potential, market size evaluation, start-up costs, pricing, accounting, advertising, promotion, etc. (Start-Up Business Guide No. E1292.).

ONLINE DATABASES

ABI/INFORM. Bell & Howell Information and Learning. • Provides online indexing to business-related material occurring in over 1,000 periodicals from 1971 to the present. Inquire as to online cost and availability.

Management Contents. The Gale Group. • Covers a wide range of management, financial, marketing, personnel, and administrative topics. About 150 leading business journals are indexed and abstracted from 1974 to date, with monthly updating. Inquire as to online cost and availability.

PERIODICALS AND NEWSLETTERS

Creative: The Magazine of Promotion and Marketing. Magazines Creative, Inc. • Bimonthly. $30.00 per year. Covers promotional materials, including exhibits, incentives, point-of-purchase advertising, premiums, and specialty advertising.

Incentive: Managing and Marketing Through Motivation. Bill Communications, Inc. • Monthly. $55.00 per year.

Retail Ad World. Visual Reference Publications, Inc. • Semimonthly. $399.00 per year. Weekly report on outstanding advertising by department stores, specialty stores and shopping centers with reprints of current advertising. Formerly *Retail Rd Week.*

STATISTICS SOURCES

Incentive-State of the Industry and Annual Facts Review. Bill Communications, Inc. • Annual. $5.00. A special issue of *Incentive* magazine.

TRADE/PROFESSIONAL ASSOCIATIONS

Promotional Products Association International. 3125 Skyway Circle, N., Irving, TX 75038-3526. Phone: 888-492-6891 Fax: (972)258-3004 E-mail: rayf@ppa.org • URL: http://www.ppa.org.

ADVISORY SERVICES

See: INVESTMENT ADVISORY SERVICES

AEROSOL INDUSTRY

See: PRESSURE PACKAGING

AEROSPACE INDUSTRY

See also: AIRPLANE INDUSTRY; AVIATION INDUSTRY; DEFENSE INDUSTRIES; ROCKET INDUSTRY

ABSTRACTS AND INDEXES

Air University Library Index to Military Periodicals. U.S. Air Force. • Quarterly. Free to qualified personnel. Annual cumulation.

Applied Science and Technology Index. H. W. Wilson Co. • 11 times a year. Quarterly and annual cumulations. Service basis for print edition; CD-ROM edition, $1,495.00 per year. Indexes a wide variety of English language technical, industrial, and engineering periodicals.

Engineering Index Monthly: Abstracting and Indexing Services Covering Sources of the World's Engineering Literature. Engineering Information, Inc. • Monthly. $2,300.00 per year. Provides indexing and abstracting of the world's engineering and technical literature.

International Aerospace Abstracts. American Institute of Aeronautics and Astronautics, Inc. • Monthly. $1,625.00 per year.

ALMANACS AND YEARBOOKS

Progress in Aerospace Sciences: An International Journal. Elsevier Science. • Bimonthly. $1,257.00 per year. Text in English, French and German.

CD-ROM DATABASES

COMPENDEX PLUS [CD-ROM]. Engineering Information, Inc. • Quarterly. $3,450.00 per year. Provides CD-ROM indexing and abstracting of the world's engineering and technical information appearing in journals, reports, books, and proceedings, 1985 to date.

DIRECTORIES

International ABC Aerospace Directory. Janes's Information Group. • 1998. $500.00. 28,000 aviation aerospace manufacturers, airlines, associations, government agencies, etc. Formerly *Interavia ABC Aerospace Directory.*

World Aviation Directory. McGraw-Hill Aviation Week Group. • Semiannual. $225.00 per year. Two volumes. Lists aviation, aerospace, and missile manufacturers. Includes *World Aviation Directory Buyer's Guide.*

ENCYCLOPEDIAS AND DICTIONARIES

Dictionary of Aviation. R. J. Hall and R. D. Campbell. Available from St. James Press. • 1991. $50.00. Published by Blackwell Scientific. Includes aeronautical words, phrases, acronyms, and abbreviations.

Macmillan Encyclopedia of Transportation. Available from The Gale Group. • 2000. $375.00. Six volumes. Published by Macmillan Reference USA. Covers the business, technology, and history of transportation on land, on water, in the air, and in space. Includes definitions, cross-references, and 200 color illustrations.

INTERNET DATABASES

Fedstats. Federal Interagency Council on Statistical Policy. Phone: (202)395-7254 • URL: http://www.fedstats.gov • Web site features an efficient search facility for full-text statistics produced by more than 70 federal agencies, including the Census Bureau, the Bureau of Economic Analysis, and the Bureau of Labor Statistics. Boolean searches can be made within one agency or for all agencies combined. Links are offered to international statistical bureaus, including the UN, IMF, OECD, UNESCO, Eurostat, and 20 individual countries. Fees: Free.

ONLINE DATABASES

Aerospace/Defense Markets and Technology. The Gale Group. • Abstracts of commerical aerospace/defense related literature, 1982 to date. Also includes information about major defense contracts awarded by the U. S. Department of Defense. International coverage. Inquire as to online cost and availability.

COMPENDEX PLUS. Engineering Information, Inc. • Provides online indexing and abstracting of the world's engineering and technical information appearing in journals, reports, books, and proceedings. Time period is 1970 to date, with weekly updates. Inquire as to online cost and availability.

DRI U.S. Central Database. Data Products Division. • Provides more than 23,000 business, financial, demographic, economic, foreign trade, and industry-related time series for the U.S. Includes national income, population, retail-wholesale trade, price indexes, labor data, housing, industrial production, banking, interest rates, money supply, etc. Time period is generally 1947 to date (some data back to 1929). Updating varies. Inquire as to online cost and availability.

F & S Index. The Gale Group. • Contains about four million citations to worldwide business, financial, and industrial or consumer product literature appearing from 1972 to date. Weekly updates. Inquire as to online cost and availability.

PERIODICALS AND NEWSLETTERS

Advanced Composites Monthly. Composite Market Reports, Inc. • Monthly. $2,325.00 per year. Newsletter. Quarterly calenders and updates. Emphasizes aerospace applications of advanced composite materials throughout the world. Includes industry news, research news, and case histories of applications. Supplement available *GraFiber.*

Aerospace Daily. Aviation Week Newsletter. McGraw-Hill. • Five times per week. $1,595.00 per year.

Air Force Journal of Logistics. Available from U. S. Government Printing Office. • Quarterly. $15.00 per year. Issued by the Air Force Logistics Management Center, Air Force Department, Defense Department. Presents research and information of interest to professional Air Force logisticians.

Aviation Week and Space Technology. McGraw-Hill Aviation Week Group. • Monthly. $89.00 per year.

Defense Daily: The Daily of Aerospace and Defense. Phillips Business Information, Inc. • Daily (five times a week). $1,697.00 per year. Newsletter.

Flying Safety. U.S. Air Force. Available from U.S. Government Printing Office. • Monthly. $46.00 per year. Published in the interest of safer flying. Articles cover many fields of flight, aircraft engineering, training and safety measures in the air and on the ground.

Space Business News. Phillips Business Information, Inc. • Biweekly. $797.00 per year. Newsletter. Covers business applications in space, including remote sensing and satellites.

Space Times. American Astronautical Society. • Bimonthly. Institutions, $80.00 per year. Covers current developments in astronautics.

RESEARCH CENTERS AND INSTITUTES

Center for Space Research. Massachusetts Institute of Technology. 77 Massachusetts Ave., Cambridge, MA 02139. Phone: (617)253-7501 Fax: (617)253-8061 • URL: http://www.space.mit.edu.

Earth Data Analysis. University of New Mexico. Bandelier West, Albuquerque, NM 87131-6031. Phone: (505)277-3622 Fax: (505)277-3614 E-mail: edac@spock.unm.edu • URL: http://www.edac.unm.edu.

Graduate Aeronautical Laboratories. California Institute of Technology. Mail Code 105-50, Pasadena, CA 91125. Phone: (626)395-4751 Fax: (818)449-2677 E-mail: http://www.galcit.caltech.edu/.

Jet Propulsion Laboratory. 4800 Oak Grove Dr., Bldg. 180, Room 904, Pasadena, CA 91109. Phone: (818)354-3405 Fax: (818)393-4218.

Joint Institute for Advancement of Flight Sciences. George Washington University, NASA Langley Research Center, Mail Stop 269, Hampton, VA 23681-2199. Phone: (757)864-1982 Fax: (757)864-5894 E-mail: jiafs@seas.gwu.edu • URL: http://www.seas.gwu.edu/seas/jiafs • Conducts research in aeronautics, astronautics, and acoustics (flight-produced noise).

Ohio Aerospace Institute. 22800 Cedar Point Rd., Cleveland, OH 44142. Phone: (440)962-3000 Fax: (440)962-3120 E-mail: michaelsalkind@oai.org • URL: http://www.oai.org • Aerospace-related research, education, and technology transfers.

Physical Science Laboratory. New Mexico State University. P.O. Box 30002, Las Cruces, NM 88003-0002. Phone: (505)522-9100 Fax: (505)522-9434 E-mail: dbirx@psl.nmsu.edu • URL: http://www.psl.nmsu.edu.

Space Institute. University of Tennessee. BH Goethert Parkway, Tullahoma, TN 37388-8897. Phone: (931)393-7213 Fax: (931)393-7211 E-mail: egleason@utsi.edu • URL: http://www.utsi.edu.

STATISTICS SOURCES

Aerospace Facts and Figures. Aerospace Industries Association of America. • Annual. $35.00. Includes financial data for the aerospace industries.

Annual Survey of Manufactures. Available from U. S. Government Printing Office. • Annual. Prices vary. Issued by the U. S. Census Bureau as an interim update to the *Census of Manufactures.* Includes data on number of manufacturing establishments in various industries, employment, labor costs, value of shipments, capital expenditures, inventories, energy costs, and assets. (See also Census Bureau home page, http://www.census.gov/.).

Business Statistics of the United States. Courtenay M. Slater, editor. Bernan Associates. • 1999. $74.00. Fifth edition. Based on *Business Statistics*, formerly issue by the Bureau of Economic Analysis, U. S. Department of Commerce. Provides basic data for a wide variety of U. S. industries, services, and economic indicators. Most statistics are shown annually for 29 years and monthly for the most recent four years.

Manufacturing Profiles. Available from U. S. Government Printing Office. • Annual. Issued by the U. S. Census Bureau. A printed consolidation of the entire *Current Industrial Report* series, presenting "all the data compiled." Contains statistics on production, shipments, inventories, consumption, exports, imports, and orders for a wide variety of manufactured products. (See also Census Bureau home page, http://www.census.gov/.).

Standard & Poor's Industry Surveys. Standard & Poor's. • Semiannual. $1,800.00. Two looseleaf volumes. Includes monthly supplements. Provides detailed, individual surveys of 52 major industry groups. Each survey is revised on a semiannual basis. Also includes "Monthly Investment Review" (industry group investment analysis) and monthly "Trends & Projections" (economic analysis).

Statistical Handbook on Technology. Paula Berinstein, editor. Oryx Press. • 1999. $65.00. Provides statistical data on such items as the Internet, online services, computer technology, recycling, patents, prescription drug sales, telecommunications, and aerospace. Includes charts, tables, and graphs. Edited for the general reader. (Statistical Handbook Series).

Survey of Current Business. Available from U. S. Government Printing Office. • Monthly. $49.00 per year. Issued by Bureau of Economic Analysis, U. S. Department of Commerce. Presents a wide variety of business and economic data.

TRADE/PROFESSIONAL ASSOCIATIONS

Aerospace Education Foundation. 1501 Lee Highway, Arlington, VA 22209-1198. Phone: 800-727-3337 or (703)247-5839 Fax: (703)247-5853 E-mail: aefstaff@aef.org • URL: http://www.aef.org.

Aerospace Electrical Society. 18231 Fernando Circle, Villa Park, CA 92861. Phone: (714)538-1002.

Aerospace Industries Association of America. 1250 Eye St., N.W., Washington, DC 20005. Phone: (202)371-8400 Fax: (202)371-8470 E-mail: aia@aia-aerospace.org • URL: http://www.aia-aerospace.org.

ASM International. 9639 Kinsman Rd., Materials Park, OH 44073. Phone: 800-336-5152 or (216)338-5151 Fax: (216)338-4634 E-mail: memserv@po.asm-intl.org • URL: http://www.asm-intl.org • Members are materials engineers, metallurgists, industry executives, educators, and others concerned with a wide range of materials and metals. Divisions include Aerospace, Composites, Electronic Materials and Processing, Energy, Highway/Off-Highway Vehicle, Joining, Materials Testing and Quality Control, Society of Carbide and Tool Engineers, and Surface Engineering.

Society for the Advancement of Material and Process Engineering. P.O. Box 2459, Covina, CA 91722-8459. Phone: 800-562-7360 or (626)331-0616 Fax: (626)332-8929 E-mail: sampeibo@aol.com • URL: http://www.sampe.org.

OTHER SOURCES

Aerospace America [online]. American Institute of Aeronautics and Astronautics. • Provides complete text of the periodical, *Aerospace America*, 1984 to date, with monthly updates. Also includes news from the *AIAA Bulletin.* Inquire as to online cost and availability.

Aerospace Database. American Institute of Aeronautics and Astronautics. • Contains abstracts of literature covering all aspects of the aerospace and aircraft in series 1983 to date. Semimonthly updates. Inquire as to online cost and availability.

AFFIRMATIVE ACTION PROGRAMS

See also: EQUAL EMPLOYMENT OPPORTUNITY

GENERAL WORKS

Affirmative Action. Lynne Eisaguirre. ABC-CLIO, Inc. • 1999. $45.00. Provides an impartial survey and analysis of affirmative action controversies, including historical background and statistical data. (Contemporary World Issues.).

Equal Opportunity Law. David P. Twomey. South-Western Publishing Co. • 1996. $31.50. Third edition.

HANDBOOKS AND MANUALS

Equal Employment Opportunity Compliance Manual: Procedures, Forms, Affirmative Action Programs, Laws, Regulations. Prentice Hall. • Two looseleaf volumes. Periodic supplementation. Price on application.

Equality in the Workplace: An Equal Opportunities Handbook for Trainers. Helen Collins. Blackwell Publishers. • 1995. $43.95. (Human Resource Management in Action Series).

ONLINE DATABASES

ABI/INFORM. Bell & Howell Information and Learning. • Provides online indexing to business-related material occurring in over 1,000 periodicals from 1971 to the present. Inquire as to online cost and availability.

Information Bank Abstracts. New York Times Index Dept. • Provides indexing and abstracting of current affairs, primarily from the final late edition of *The New York Times* and the Eastern edition of *The Wall Street Journal*. Time period is 1969 to present, with daily updates. Inquire as to online cost and availability.

Management Contents. The Gale Group. • Covers a wide range of management, financial, marketing, personnel, and administrative topics. About 150 leading business journals are indexed and abstracted from 1974 to date, with monthly updating. Inquire as to online cost and availability.

PERIODICALS AND NEWSLETTERS

Affirmative Action Register: The E E O Recruitment Publication. Affirmative Action, Inc. • Monthly. Free to qualified personnel; others, $15.00 per year. "The *Affirmative Action Register* is the only nationwide publication that provides for systematic distribution to mandated minorities, females, handicapped, veterans, and Native Americans." Each issue consists of recruitment advertisements placed by equal opportunity employers (institutions and companies).

Civil Rights: State Capitals. Wakeman-Walworth, Inc. • Weekly. $245.00 per year. Newsletter. Includes coverage of state affirmative action programs. Formerly *From the State Capitals: Civil Rights.*

MBI: The National Report on Minority, Women-Owned, and Disadvantaged Businesses. Community Development Services, Inc. CD Publications. • Semimonthly. $372.00 per year. Newsletter. Provides news of affirmative action, government contracts, minority business employment, and education/training for minorities in business. Formerly *Minorities in Business.*

School Law News: The Independent Biweekly News Service on Legal Developments in Education. Aspen Publishers, Inc. • Biweekly. $305.00 per year.

RESEARCH CENTERS AND INSTITUTES

Industrial Relations Section. Massachusetts Institute of Technology. Sloan School of Management, 50 Memorial Dr., E 52-586, 77 Massachusetts Ave., Cambridge, MA 02139-4037. Phone: (617)253-2671 Fax: (617)253-7696.

TRADE/PROFESSIONAL ASSOCIATIONS

American Association for Affirmative Action. 5530 Wisconsin Ave., Ste. 1110, Chevy Chase, MD 20815-4330. Phone: 800-252-8952 Fax: (301)656-9008 E-mail: lsshaw@aol.com • URL: http://www.affirmativeaction.org.

National Association for Equal Opportunity in Higher Education. 8701 Georgia Ave., Ste 200, Silver Spring, MD 20910. Phone: (301)650-2440 Fax: (301)495-3306 E-mail: hponder@nafeo.org • URL: http://www.nafeo.org.

OTHER SOURCES

Affirmative Action Compliance Manual for Federal Contractors. Bureau of National Affairs, Inc. • Two looseleaf volumes. $410.00 per year. Monthly updates.

BNA Fair Employment Practice Service. Bureau of National Affairs, Inc. • Weekly. $501.00 per year. Three volumes. Looseleaf.

Employment Discrimination. Matthew Bender & Co., Inc. • $1,260.00. Nine looseleaf volumes. Periodic supplementation, $849.00. Treatise on both substantive and procedural law governing employment discrimination based on sex, age, race, religion, national origin, etc.

AFFLUENT MARKET

GENERAL WORKS

Marketing to the Affluent. Thomas J. Stanley. McGraw-Hill Professional. • 1988. $55.00. Discusses demographics, psychographics, and buying habits.

ABSTRACTS AND INDEXES

Business Periodicals Index. H. W. Wilson Co. • Monthly, except August, with quarterly and annual cumulations. Service basis for print edition; CD-ROM edition, $1,495.00 per year.

DIRECTORIES

Business Organizations, Agencies, and Publications Directory. The Gale Group. • 1999. $425.00. 12th edition. Over 40,000 entries describing 39 types of business information sources. Classified by type of organization, publication, or serviceIncludes state, national, and international agencies and organizations. Master index to names and keywords. Also includes e-mail addresses and web site URL's.

Guide to Private Fortunes. Available from The Gale Group. • 1994. $255.00. Third edition. Published by The Taft Group. Provides biographical information and philanthropic histories for 1,250 individuals with a net worth of over $25 million or who have demonstrated a pattern of substantial charitable giving. Formerly *Fund Raiser's Guide to Private Fortunes*, and before that, *America's Wealthiest People.*

Wealth Ranking Annual. Mark W. Scott. The Taft Group. • 1997. $95.00. Contains reprints of wealth rankings and compensation lists appearing in periodicals and newspapers. Includes about 600 lists naming more than 6,000 individuals.

Who's Wealthy in America: A Directory of the 109,100 Richest People in the United States. The Taft Group. • Annual. $445.00. Two volumes. Includes Company Name Index (indicates insider stock holdings), Geographic Index, Political Contribution Index, and Alma Mater Index.

HANDBOOKS AND MANUALS

Networking with the Affluent and Their Advisers. Thomas J. Stanley. McGraw-Hill Professional. • 1993. $17.95. Discusses specific methods of prospecting for wealthy clients, with examples.

Selling to the Affluent: The Professional's Guide to Closing the Sales That Count. Thomas Stanley. McGraw-Hill Professional. • 1990. $55.00.

ONLINE DATABASES

Marketing and Advertising Reference Service (MARS). The Gale Group. • Provides abstracts of literature relating to consumer marketing and advertising, including all forms of advertising media. Time period is 1984 to date. Daily updates. Inquire as to online cost and availability.

PROMT: Predicasts Overview of Markets and Technology. The Gale Group. • Companies, products, applied technologies and markets. U.S. and international literature coverage, 1972 to date. Inquire as to online cost and availability. Provides abstracts from more than 1,600 publications. Weekly updates.

Wilson Business Abstracts Online. H. W. Wilson Co. • Indexes and abstracts 600 major business periodicals, plus the *Wall Street Journal* and the business section of the *New York Times*. Indexing is from 1982, abstracting from 1990, with the two newspapers included from 1993. Updated weekly. Inquire as to online cost and availability. (*Business Periodicals Index* without abstracts is also available online.).

PERIODICALS AND NEWSLETTERS

Asset Management. Dow Jones Financial Publishing Corp. • Bimonthly. $345.00 per year. Covers the management of the assets of affluent, high net worth investors. Provides information on various financial products and services.

Bloomberg Personal Finance. Bloomberg L.P. • Monthly. $24.95 per year. Provides advice on personal finance, investments, travel, real estate, and maintaining an "upscale life style." Formerly *Bloomberg Personal.*

The Boomer Report: The Insights You Need to Reach America's Most Influential Consumer Group. Age Wave Communications Corp. • Monthly. $195.00 per year. Newsletter. Presents market research relating to the "baby boomers," an age group generally defined as having been born between 1950 and 1970.

City & Country Club Life: The Social Magazine for South Florida. Club Publications, Inc. • Bimonthly. $15.00 per year.

Fortune Magazine. Time Inc., Business Information Group. • Biweekly. $59.95 per year. Edited for top executives and upper-level managers.

Journal of Private Portfolio Management. Institutional Investor. • Quarterly. $280.00 per year. Edited for managers of wealthy individuals' investment portfolios.

Money. Time Inc. • Monthly. $39.95 per year. Covers all aspects of family finance; investments, careers, shopping, taxes, insurance, consumerism, etc.

Palm Beach Illustrated: The Best of Boca Raton to Vero Beach. Palm Beach Media Group. • 10 times a year. $30.00 per year. Includes *Palm Beach Social Observer*. Formerly *Illustrated.*

Private Asset Management. Institutional Investor. • Biweekly. $2,105.00 per year. Newsletter. Edited for managers investing the private assets of wealthy ("high-net-worth") individuals. Includes marketing, taxation, regulation, and fee topics.

Profit Investor Portfolio: The International Magazine of Money and Style. Profit Publications, Inc. • Bimonthly. $29.95 per year. A glossy consumer magazine featuring specific investment recommendations and articles on upscale travel and shopping.

Robb Report: The Magazine for the Luxury Lifestyle. Robb Report, Inc. • Monthly. $65.00 per year. Consumer magazine featuring advertisements for expensive items-antique automobiles, boats, airplanes, large houses, etc.

Town and Country. Hearst Corp. • Monthly. $24.00 per year.

Travel and Leisure. American Express Publishing Corp. • Monthly. $39.00 per year. In three regional editions and one demographic edition.

Vanity Fair. Conde Nast Publications, Inc.,. • Monthly. $20.00 per year.

Worth: Financial Intelligence. Worth Media. • 10 times a year. $18.00 per year. Contains articles for affluent consumers on personal financial management, including investments, estate planning, and taxes.

STATISTICS SOURCES

Lifestyle Market Analyst. SRDS. • Annual. $391.00. Published in conjunction with NDL (National Demographics & Lifestyles). Provides extensive lifestyle data on interests, activities, and hobbies within specific geographic and demographic markets.

Social Statistics of the United States. Mark S. Littman, editor. Bernan Press. • 2000. $65.00. Includes statistical data on population growth, labor force, occupations, environmental trends, leisure time use, income, poverty, taxes, and other economic or demographic topics.

Statistical Handbook on Consumption and Wealth in the United States. Chandrika Kaul and Valerie Tomaselli-Moschovitis. Oryx Press. • 1999. $65.00. Provides more than 400 graphs, tables, and charts dealing with basic income levels, income inequalities, spending patterns, taxation, subsidies, etc. (Statistical Handbook Series).

A Statistical Portrait of the United States: Social Conditions and Trends. Mark S. Littman, editor. Bernan Press. • 1998. $89.00. Covers "social, economic, and environmental trends in the United States over the past 25 years." Includes statistical tables, graphs, and analysis relating to such topics as population, income, poverty, wealth, labor, housing, education, healthcare, air/water quality, and government.

OTHER SOURCES

The Affluent Market. MarketResearch.com. • 1998. $2,250.00 Consumer market data. Includes demographics of affluent house holds and the expenditures of the affluent on 250 types of products.

AFTER-DINNER SPEAKING

See: PUBLIC SPEAKING

AGE AND EMPLOYMENT

See: EMPLOYMENT OF OLDER WORKERS

AGING

See: RETIREMENT

AGREEMENTS

See: CONTRACTS

AGRIBUSINESS

GENERAL WORKS

Cases in Agribusiness Management. George J. Seperich and others. Holcomb Hathaway, Inc. • 1995. $27.95. Second edition.

ABSTRACTS AND INDEXES

World Agricultural Economics and Rural Sociology Abstracts: Abstracts of World Literature. Available from CABI Publishing. • Monthly. $1095.00 per year. Published in England by CABI Publishing. Provides worldwide coverage of the literature.

ALMANACS AND YEARBOOKS

Research in Domestic and International Agribusiness Management. JAI Press, Inc. • Irregular. $73.25.

DIRECTORIES

Agri Marketing: Marketing Services Guide. Doane Agricultural Services. • Annual. $30.00. Wide range of listings related to agricultural marketing.

Agricultural Guide to Washington: Whom to Contact and Where. Dow Elunco. • Biennial. Free. Heads of congressional committees and subcommittees in Washington, D.C. that deal with agricultural matters, and members of federal agencies and trade associations concerned with agribusiness.

BioScan: The Worldwide Biotech Industry Reporting Service. American Health Consultants, Inc. • Bimonthly. $1,395.00 per year. Looseleaf. Provides detailed information on over 900 U. S. and foreign companies broadly classified as biotechnological. In addition to medical technology and advanced pharmaceutical firms, includes firms doing research in food processing, waste management, agriculture, and veterinary science.

HANDBOOKS AND MANUALS

Agricultural Finance. Warren F. Lee and others. Iowa State University Press. • 1988. $44.95. Eighth revised edition.

INTERNET DATABASES

Fedstats. Federal Interagency Council on Statistical Policy. Phone: (202)395-7254 • URL: http://www.fedstats.gov • Web site features an efficient search facility for full-text statistics produced by more than 70 federal agencies, including the Census Bureau, the Bureau of Economic Analysis, and the Bureau of Labor Statistics. Boolean searches can be made within one agency or for all agencies combined. Links are offered to international statistical bureaus, including the UN, IMF, OECD, UNESCO, Eurostat, and 20 individual countries. Fees: Free.

ONLINE DATABASES

Business and Industry. Responsive Database Services, Inc. • Contains online citations, abstracts, and selected fulltext from more than 1,000 trade journals, newspapers, and other publications. Provides general coverage of both manufacturing and service industries, including marketing, production, industry trends, key events, and information on specific companies. Time span is 1994 to date. Daily updates. Inquire as to online cost and availability. (Also available in a CD-ROM version.).

DRI U.S. Central Database. Data Products Division. • Provides more than 23,000 business, financial, demographic, economic, foreign trade, and industry-related time series for the U.S. Includes national income, population, retail-wholesale trade, price indexes, labor data, housing, industrial production, banking, interest rates, money supply, etc. Time period is generally 1947 to date (some data back to 1929). Updating varies. Inquire as to online cost and availability.

PROMT: Predicasts Overview of Markets and Technology. The Gale Group. • Companies,

products, applied technologies and markets. U.S. and international literature coverage, 1972 to date. Inquire as to online cost and availability. Provides abstracts from more than 1,600 publications. Weekly updates.

Tablebase. Responsive Database Services, Inc. • Provides online numerical tabular data from a wide variety of business, organization, and government sources, including 900 trade journals. Includes industry and individual company statistics relating to products, market share, sales forecasts, production, exports, market trends, etc. Time span is 1997 to date. Weekly updates. Inquire as to online cost and availability. (Also available in a CD-ROM version.).

PERIODICALS AND NEWSLETTERS

Ag Executive. Ag Executive, Inc. • Monthly. $84.00 per year. Newsletter. Topics include farm taxes, accounting, real estate, and financial planning.

Ag Lender. Doane Agricultural Services. • Nine times a year. Price on application. Formerly *Agri Finance.*

AgExporter. Available from U. S. Government Printing Office. • Monthly. $44.00 per year. Issued by the Foreign Agricultural Service, U. S. Department of Agriculture. Edited for U. S. exporters of farm products. Provides practical information on exporting, including overseas trade opportunities.

Agri Marketing: The Magazine for Professionals Selling to the Farm Market. Doane Agricultural Services. • 11 times a year. $30.00 per year.

Agribusiness: An International Journal. John Wiley and Sons, Inc., Journals Div. • Bimonthly. Institutions, $845.00 per year.

Agribusiness Fieldman. Western Agricultural Publishing Co., Inc. • Monthly. $19.95 per year.

Agricultural Outlook. Available from U. S. Government Printing Office. • Monthly. $60.00 per year. Issued by the Economic Research Service of the U. S. Department of Agriculture. Provides analysis of agriculture and the economy.

Doane's Agricultural Report. Doane Agricultural Services. • Weekly. $98.00 per year. Edited for "high volume document printing" professionals. Covers imaging, printing, and mailing.

Farm Industry News. Intertec Publishing Co., Agribusiness Div. • 12 times a year. $25.00 per year. Includes new products for farm use.

Journal of International Food and Agribusiness Marketing. Haworth Press, Inc. • Quarterly. Individuals, $60.00 per year; institutions, $75.00 per year; libraries, $175.00 per year.

Kiplinger Agriculture Letter. Kiplinger Washington Editors, Inc. • Biweekly. $56.00 per year. Newsletter.

Outlook for United States Agricultural Trade. Available from U. S. Government Printing Office. • Quarterly. $10.00 per year. Issued by the Economic Research Service, U. S. Department of Agriculture. (Situation and Outlook Reports.).

Washington Agricultural Record. • Weekly. $65.00 per year. Newsletter.

RESEARCH CENTERS AND INSTITUTES

Giannini Foundation of Agricultural Economics. University of California. 248 Giannini Hall, No. 3310, Berkeley, CA 94720-3310. Phone: (510)642-7121 Fax: (510)643-8911 E-mail: dote@are.berkeley.edu • URL: http://www.are.berkeley.edu/library.

STATISTICS SOURCES

Business Statistics of the United States. Courtenay M. Slater, editor. Bernan Associates. • 1999. $74.00. Fifth edition. Based on *Business Statistics*, formerly issue by the Bureau of Economic Analysis, U. S. Department of Commerce. Provides basic data for a wide variety of U. S. industries, services, and economic indicators. Most statistics are shown annually for 29 years and monthly for the most recent four years.

Encyclopedia of American Industries. The Gale Group. • 1998. $560.00. Second edition. Two volumes. $280.00 per volume. Volume one is *Manufacturing Industries* and volume two is *Service and Non-Manufacturing Industries.* Provides the history, development, and recent status of approximately 1,000 industries. Includes statistical graphs, with industry and general indexes.

OECD Agricultural Outlook. Organization for Economic Cooperation and Development. • Annual. $31.00. Provides a five-year outlook for agricultural markets in various countries of the world, including the U. S., other OECD countries, and selected non-OECD nations.

Standard & Poor's Industry Surveys. Standard & Poor's. • Semiannual. $1,800.00. Two looseleaf volumes. Includes monthly supplements. Provides detailed, individual surveys of 52 major industry groups. Each survey is revised on a semiannual basis. Also includes "Monthly Investment Review" (industry group investment analysis) and monthly "Trends & Projections" (economic analysis).

Survey of Current Business. Available from U. S. Government Printing Office. • Monthly. $49.00 per year. Issued by Bureau of Economic Analysis, U. S. Department of Commerce. Presents a wide variety of business and economic data.

TRADE/PROFESSIONAL ASSOCIATIONS

Agribusiness Council. 1312 18th St., N.W., Suite 300, Washington, DC 20036. Phone: (202)296-4563 or (202)887-0238 Fax: (202)887-9178 E-mail: agenergy@aol.com.

Agriculture Council of America. 11020 King St., Suite 205, Overland, KS 66210. Phone: 888-982-4329 or (913)491-1895 Fax: (913)491-6502 E-mail: info@agday.org • URL: http://www.agday.org.

American Society of Agricultural Consultants. 950 S. Cherry St., Suite 508, Denver, CO 80222-2664. Phone: (303)759-5091 Fax: (303)758-0190 E-mail: asac@agri-associations.org • URL: http://www.agri-associations.org/asac.

International Trade Council. 3114 Circle Hill Rd., Alexandria, VA 22305-1606. Phone: (703)548-1234 Fax: (703)548-6126 E-mail: wisdom@itctrade.com • Promotes free trade for agricultural products.

National Agri-Marketing Association. 11020 King St., Suite 205, Overland Park, KS 66210. Phone: (913)491-6500 Fax: (913)491-6502 E-mail: agrimktg@nama.org • URL: http://www.nama.org • Agricultural advertisers and marketers.

National Council of Agricultural Employers. 1112 16th St., N.W. Suite 920, Washington, DC 20036. Phone: (202)728-0300 Fax: (202)728-0303 E-mail: ncae@erols.com.

OTHER SOURCES

Infrastructure Industries USA. The Gale Group. • 2001. $240.00. Replaces *Agriculture, Forestry, Fishing, Mining, and Construction USA* and *Transportation and Public Utilities USA.* Presents statistics and projections relating to economic activity in a wide variety of natural resource and construction industries.

AGRICULTURAL CHEMICALS

See also: CHEMICAL INDUSTRIES; FERTILIZER INDUSTRY; POTASH INDUSTRY

GENERAL WORKS

Textbook of Soil Chemical Analysis. P.R. Hesse. Chemical Publishing Co., Inc. • 1972. $85.00.

ABSTRACTS AND INDEXES

Biological and Agricultural Index. H.W. Wilson Co. • 11 times a year. Annual and quarterly cumulations. Service basis.

ENCYCLOPEDIAS AND DICTIONARIES

Kirk-Othmer Encyclopedia of Chemical Technology. John Wiley and Sons, Inc. • 1991-97. $7,350.00, prepaid. 21 volumes. Fourth edition. Four volumes are scheduled to be published each year, with individual volumes available at $350.00.

FINANCIAL RATIOS

Industry Norms and Key Business Ratios. Desk Top Edition. Dun and Bradstreet Corp., Business Information Services. • Annual. Five volumes. $475.00 per volume. $1,890.00 per set. Covers over 800 kinds of businesses, arranged by Standard Industrial Classification number. More detailed editions covering longer periods of time are also available.

HANDBOOKS AND MANUALS

Crop Protection Chemicals Reference. Chemical and Pharmaceutical Press, Inc. • 1994. $130.00. 10th edition. Contains the complete text of product labels. Indexed by manufacturer, product category, pest use, crop use, chemical name, and brand name.

Farm Chemicals Handbook. Meister Publishing Co. • Annual. $92.00. Manufacturers and suppliers of fertilizers, pesticides, and related equipment used in agribusiness.

ONLINE DATABASES

Agricola. U.S. National Agricultural Library. • Covers worldwide agricultural literature. Over 2.8 million citations, 1970 to present, with monthly updates. Inquire as to online cost and availability.

CA Search. Chemical Abstracts Service. • Guide to chemical literature, 1967 to present. Inquire as to online cost and availability.

Derwent Crop Protection File. Derwent, Inc. • Provides citations to the international journal literature of agricultural chemicals and pesticides from 1968 to date, with updating eight times per year. Formerly *PESTDOC.* Inquire as to online cost and availability.

PERIODICALS AND NEWSLETTERS

AOAC International Journal. AOAC International. • Bimonthly. Members $176.00 per year; non-members, $242.00 per year; institutions, $262.00 per year. Formerly *Association of Official Analytical Chemist Journal.*

Dealer Progress: How Smart Agribusiness is Growing. Clear Window, Inc. • Bimonthly. $40.00 per year. Published in association with the Fertilizer Institute. Includes information on fertilizers and agricultural chemicals, including farm pesticides. Formerly *Progress.*

Farm Chemicals. Meister Publishing Co. • Monthly. $47.00 per year.

Soil Science: An Interdisciplinary Approach to Soils Research. Williams and Wilkins Co. • Monthly. Individuals, $131.00 per year; institutions, $236.00 per year.

WACA News. Western Agricultural Chemicals Association. • Quarterly. Free.

PRICE SOURCES

Chemical Market Reporter. Schnell Publishing Co., Inc. • Weekly. $139.00 per year. Quotes current prices for a wide range of chemicals. Formerly *Chemical Marketing Reporter.*

RESEARCH CENTERS AND INSTITUTES

Laboratory for Pest Control Application Technology. Ohio State University, Ohio Agricultural Research and Development Center, Wooster, OH 44691. Phone: (330)263-3726 Fax: (330)263-3686 E-mail: hall.1@osu.edu • URL: http://www.oardc.ohio-state.edu/lpcat/ • Conducts pest control research in cooperation with the U. S. Department of Agriculture.

Mount Vernon Research and Extension Unit. Washington State University. 16650 Memorial Highway, Mount Vernon, WA 98273. Phone: (360)848-6120 Fax: (360)848-6159.

Office of the Texas State Chemist. Texas A & M University. P.O. Box 3160, College Station, TX 77841-3160. Phone: (409)845-1121 Fax: (409)845-1389 E-mail: g-latimer@tamu.edu • URL: http://www.otscweb.tamu.edu.

Soil Testing Laboratory. University of Massachusetts at Amherst. West Experiment Station, Amherst, MA 01003-8020. Phone: (413)545-2311 Fax: (413)545-1931 • URL: http://www.umass.edu/t/soils/soiltest.

Tennessee Agricultural Experiment Station. University of Tennessee, Knoxville. P.O. Box 1071, Knoxville, TN 37901-1071. Phone: (865)974-7121 Fax: (865)974-6479 E-mail: drichard@utk.edu • URL: http://www.funnelweb.utcc.utk.edu/~taescomm/default.html.

STATISTICS SOURCES

U. S. Industry and Trade Outlook: The McGraw-Hill Companies and the U.S. Department of Commerce/International Trade Administration. Datapso Research Corp. • Annual. $69.95. Produced by the International Trade Administration, U. S. Department of Commerce, in a "public-private" partnership with DRI/McGraw-Hill and Standard & Poor's. Provides basic data, outlook for the current year, and "Long-Term Prospects" (five-year projections) for a wide variety of products and services. Includes high technology industries. Formerly *U. S. Industrial Outlook.*

WEFA Industrial Monitor. John Wiley and Sons, Inc. • Annual. $65.00. Prepared by industry analysts at WEFA, an economic forecasting and consulting firm (originally Wharton Econometric Forecasting Associates). Contains discussions of the outlook for major U. S. industries, with many 10-year forecasts (WEFA Web site is http://www.wefa.com).

TRADE/PROFESSIONAL ASSOCIATIONS

American Crop Protection Association. 1156 15th St., N.W., Suite 400, Washington, DC 20005. Phone: (202)296-1585 Fax: (202)463-0474 • URL: http://www.acpa.org.

AOAC International. 481 N. Frederick Ave., No. 500, Gaithersburg, MD 20877-2504. Phone: (301)924-7077 Fax: (301)924-7089 E-mail: aoac@aoac.org • URL: http://www.aoac.org.

The Fertilizer Institute. 501 Second St., N.E., Washington, DC 20002. Phone: (202)675-8250 Fax: (202)544-8123 • URL: http://www.tfi.org.

Western Crop Protection Association. 3835 N. Freeway Blvd., Suite 140, Sacramento, CA 95834. Phone: (916)568-3660 Fax: (916)565-0113.

OTHER SOURCES

Agrochemical Companies Fact File. Theta Reports/PJB Medical Publications, Inc. • Annual. $1,460.00. Provides detailed profiles of more than 360 crop protection companies worldwide, including manufacturers of agrochemicals and biopesticides. Coverage includes finances, products, and joint ventures. Major agrochemical trading companies are also profiled. (Theta Report No. DS190E.).

Major Chemical and Petrochemical Companies of the World. Available from The Gale Group. • 2001. $855.00. Third edition. Two volumes. Published by Graham & Whiteside. Contains profiles of more than 7,000 important chemical and petrochemical companies in various countries. Subject areas include general chemicals, specialty chemicals, agricultural chemicals, petrochemicals, industrial gases, and fertilizers.

World Agrochemical Markets. Theta Reports/PJB Medical Publications, Inc. • 2000. $1,040.00. Market research data. Covers the demand for crop protection products in 11 countries having major markets and 20 countries having minor markets. (Theta Report No. DS196E.).

AGRICULTURAL CREDIT

See also: AGRICULTURAL ECONOMICS; CREDIT

GENERAL WORKS

Financial Management in Agriculture. Peter Barry and others. Interstate Publishers, Inc. • 2000. $66.25. Sixth edition.

ABSTRACTS AND INDEXES

Biological and Agricultural Index. H.W. Wilson Co. • 11 times a year. Annual and quarterly cumulations. Service basis.

ALMANACS AND YEARBOOKS

Agricultural Credit and Related Data. American Bankers Association. • Annual.

Farm Mortgage Debt. U.S. Department of Agriculture, Economic Research Service. • Annual.

HANDBOOKS AND MANUALS

Agricultural Finance. Warren F. Lee and others. Iowa State University Press. • 1988. $44.95. Eighth revised edition.

INTERNET DATABASES

USDA. United States Department of Agriculture. Phone: (202)720-2791 E-mail: agsec@usda.gov • URL: http://www.usda.gov • The USDA home page has six sections: News and Information; What's New; About USDA; Agencies; Opportunities; Search and Help. Keyword searching is offered from the USDA home page and from various individual agency home pages. Agencies are the Economic Research Service, Agricultural Marketing Service, National Agricultural Statistics Service, National Agricultural Library, and about 12 others. Updating varies. Fees: Free.

ONLINE DATABASES

Agricola. U.S. National Agricultural Library. • Covers worldwide agricultural literature. Over 2.8 million citations, 1970 to present, with monthly updates. Inquire as to online cost and availability.

EconLit. American Economic Association. • Covers the worldwide literature of economics as contained in selected monographs and about 550 journals. Subjects include microeconomics, macroeconomics, economic history, inflation, money, credit, finance, accounting theory, trade, natural resource economics, and regional economics. Time period is 1969 to present, with monthly updates. Inquire as to online cost and availability.

PERIODICALS AND NEWSLETTERS

ABA Bankers News. American Bankers Association. • Biweekly. Members, $48.00 per year; non-members, $96.00 per year. Formerly *ABA Banker News Weekly.* Incorporating *Agricultural Banker.*

Ag Lender. Doane Agricultural Services. • Nine times a year. Price on application. Formerly *Agri Finance.*

RESEARCH CENTERS AND INSTITUTES

Giannini Foundation of Agricultural Economics. University of California. 248 Giannini Hall, No. 3310, Berkeley, CA 94720-3310. Phone: (510)642-7121 Fax: (510)643-8911 E-mail: dote@are.berkeley.edu • URL: http://www.are.berkeley.edu/library.

STATISTICS SOURCES

Agricultural Finance Databook. U. S. Federal Reserve System. • Quarterly. $5.00 per year. (Federal Reserve Statistical Release, E.15.).

Agricultural Statistics. Available from U. S. Government Printing Office. • Annual. Produced by the National Agricultural Statistics Service, U. S. Department of Agriculture. Provides a wide variety of statistical data relating to agricultural production, supplies, consumption, prices/price-supports, foreign trade, costs, and returns, as well as farm labor, loans, income, and population. In many cases, historical data is shown annually for 10 years. In addition to farm data, includes detailed fishery statistics.

TRADE/PROFESSIONAL ASSOCIATIONS

Agribusiness Council. 1312 18th St., N.W., Suite 300, Washington, DC 20036. Phone: (202)296-4563 or (202)887-0238 Fax: (202)887-9178 E-mail: agenergy@aol.com.

AGRICULTURAL ECONOMICS

GENERAL WORKS

Agricultural Economics and Agribusiness. Gail L. Cramer and others. John Wiley and Sons, Inc. • 2000. Eighth edition. Price on application.

Agriculture, Economics and Resource Management. Milton M. Snodgrass and Luther T. Wallace. Prentice Hall. • 1980. $48.20. Second edition.

ABSTRACTS AND INDEXES

NTIS Alerts: Agriculture & Food. National Technical Information Service. • Semimonthly. $195.00 per year. Provides descriptions of government-sponsored research reports and software, with ordering information. Covers agricultural economics, horticulture, fisheries, veterinary medicine, food technology, and related subjects. Formerly *Abstract Newsletter.*

World Agricultural Economics and Rural Sociology Abstracts: Abstracts of World Literature. Available from CABI Publishing. • Monthly. $1095.00 per year. Published in England by CABI Publishing. Provides worldwide coverage of the literature.

ALMANACS AND YEARBOOKS

Agricultural Policies, Markets, and Trade: Monitoring and Evaluation. Organization for Economic Cooperation and Development. Available from OECD Publications and Information Center. • Annual. $62.00. A yearly report on agricultural and trade policy developments in OECD member countries.

CD-ROM DATABASES

AGRICOLA on SilverPlatter. Available from SilverPlatter Information, Inc. • Quarterly. $825.00 per year. Produced by the National Agricultural Library. Provides about three million citations on CD-ROM to the literature of agriculture, agricultural economics, animal sciences, entomology, fertilizer, food, forestry, nutrition, pesticides, plant science, water resources, and other topics. Each quarterly disc covers the past ten years, with archival discs available from 1970.

EconLit. Available from SilverPlatter Information, Inc. • Monthly. Single-user, $1,600.00 per year. Multi-user, $2,400.00 per year. Provides CD-ROM citations, with abstracts, to articles from more than 500 economics journals. Time period is 1969 to date. Produced by the American Economic Association.

ENCYCLOPEDIAS AND DICTIONARIES

Dictionary of Agriculture: From Abaca to Zoonosis. Kathryn L. Lipton. Lynne Rienner Publishers, Inc. • 1995. $75.00. Emphasis is on agricultural economics.

Encyclopedia of Agriculture Science. Charles J. Arntzen and Ellen M. Ritter, editors. Academic Press, Inc. • 1994. $625.00. Four volumes.

INTERNET DATABASES

USDA. United States Department of Agriculture. Phone: (202)720-2791 E-mail: agsec@usda.gov • URL: http://www.usda.gov • The USDA home page has six sections: News and Information; What's New; About USDA; Agencies; Opportunities; Search and Help. Keyword searching is offered from the USDA home page and from various individual agency home pages. Agencies are the Economic Research Service, Agricultural Marketing Service, National Agricultural Statistics Service, National Agricultural Library, and about 12 others. Updating varies. Fees: Free.

ONLINE DATABASES

CAB Abstracts. CAB International North America. • Contains 46 specialized abstract collections covering over 10,000 journals and monographs in the areas of agriculture, horticulture, forest products, farm products, nutrition, dairy science, poultry, grains, animal health, entomology, etc. Time period is 1972 to date, with monthly updates. Inquire as to online cost and availability. *CAB Abstracts on CD-ROM* also available, with annual updating.

EconLit. American Economic Association. • Covers the worldwide literature of economics as contained in selected monographs and about 550 journals. Subjects include microeconomics, macroeconomics, economic history, inflation, money, credit, finance, accounting theory, trade, natural resource economics, and regional economics. Time period is 1969 to present, with monthly updates. Inquire as to online cost and availability.

PERIODICALS AND NEWSLETTERS

Agricultural Outlook. Available from U. S. Government Printing Office. • Monthly. $60.00 per year. Issued by the Economic Research Service of the U. S. Department of Agriculture. Provides analysis of agriculture and the economy.

American Journal of Agricultural Economics. American Agricultural Economics Association Blackwell Publishers, Inc. • Five times a year. $123.00 per year. Provides a forum for creative and scholarly work in agriculture economics.

Doane's Agricultural Report. Doane Agricultural Services. • Weekly. $98.00 per year. Edited for "high volume document printing" professionals. Covers imaging, printing, and mailing.

Land Economics: A Quarterly Journal Devoted to the Study of Economic and Social Institutions. University of Wisconsin at Madison, Land Tenure Center. University of Wisconsin Press, Journals Div. • Quarterly. Individuals, $47.00 per year; institutions, $127.00 per year.

STATISTICS SOURCES

Agricultural Statistics. Available from U. S. Government Printing Office. • Annual. Produced by the National Agricultural Statistics Service, U. S. Department of Agriculture. Provides a wide variety of statistical data relating to agricultural production, supplies, consumption, prices/price-supports, foreign trade, costs, and returns, as well as farm labor, loans, income, and population. In many cases, historical data is shown annually for 10 years. In addition to farm data, includes detailed fishery statistics.

Agriculture Fact Book. Available from U. S. Government Printing Office. • Annual. Issued by the Office of Communications, U. S. Department of Agriculture. Includes data on U. S. agriculture, farmers, food, nutrition, and rural America. Programs of the Department of Agriculture in six areas are described: rural economic development, foreign trade, nutrition, the environment, inspection, and education.

Economic Accounts for Agriculture. Organization for Economic Cooperation and Development. Available from OECD Publications and Information Center. • Annual. $51.00. Provides data for 14 years on agricultural output and its components, intermediate consumption, and gross value added to net income and capital formation. Relates to various commodities produced by OECD member countries.

TRADE/PROFESSIONAL ASSOCIATIONS

American Agricultural Economics Association. 415 S. Duff Ave., No. C, Ames, IA 50010-6600. Phone: (515)233-3202 Fax: (515)233-3101 E-mail: info@aaea.org • URL: http://www.aaea.org.

International Association of Agricultural Economists. 1211 W. 22nd St., Suite 216, Oak Brook, IL 60521. Phone: (630)571-9393 Fax: (630)571-9580 E-mail: iaae@farmfoundation.org • URL: http://www.ag.iastate.edu/journals/agecon.

OTHER SOURCES

Agricultural Law. Matthew Bender & Co., Inc. • $2,120.00 per year. 15 looseleaf volumes. Periodic supplementation. Covers all aspects of state and federal law relating to farms, ranches and other agricultural interests. Includes five volumes dealing with agricultural estate, tax and business planning.

AGRICULTURAL EXTENSION WORK

DIRECTORIES

County Agents Directory: The Reference Book for Agricultural Extension Workers. Doane Agricultural Services. • Biennial. $23.95. About 17,000 county agents and university agricultural extension workers.

ONLINE DATABASES

Agricola. U.S. National Agricultural Library. • Covers worldwide agricultural literature. Over 2.8 million citations, 1970 to present, with monthly updates. Inquire as to online cost and availability.

AGRICULTURAL FOREIGN TRADE

See: FOREIGN AGRICULTURE

AGRICULTURAL LABOR

See: FARMERS; LABOR

AGRICULTURAL MACHINERY

GENERAL WORKS

Farm Power and Machinery Management. Donnell Hunt. Iowa State University Press. • 1995. $56.95. Ninth edition.

ABSTRACTS AND INDEXES

Agricultural Engineering Abstracts. Available from CABI Publishing North America. • Monthly. $735.00 per year. Published in England by CABI Publishing.

DIRECTORIES

Farm Equipment Wholesalers Association Membership Directory. Farm Equipment Wholesalers Association. • Annual. $50.00. Lists approximately 100 members.

Implement and Tractor Product File. Intertec Publishing. • Annual. $25.00.

NAEDA Equipment Dealer Buyer's Guide. North American Equipment Dealers Association. • Annual. $28.00. List of manufacturers and suppliers of agricultural, lawn and garden, and light industrial machinery.

Thomas Register of American Manufacturers and Thomas Register Catalog File. Thomas Publishing Co., Inc. • Annual. $149.00. 34 volumes. A three-part system offering information on a wide variety of industrial equipment and supplies.

FINANCIAL RATIOS

Almanac of Business and Industrial Financial Ratios. Leo Troy. Prentice Hall. • Annual. $99.95. Contains financial ratios derived from federal tax returns. Ratios for each of about 200 industries are arranged according to company asset size.

Annual Statement Studies. Robert Morris Associates: The Association of Lending and Credit Risk Professiona. • Annual. Free to members; non-members, $140.00. Median and quartile financial ratios are given for over 400 kinds of manufacturing, wholesale, retail, construction, and consumer finance establishments. Data is sorted by both asset size and sales volume. Includes a clearly written "Definition of Ratios" and an alphabetical industry index.

Cost of Doing Business: Farm and Power Equipment Dealers, Industrial Dealers, and Outdoor Power Equipment Dealers. North American Equipment Dealers Association. • Annual. $50.00. Provides data on sales, profit margins, expenses, assets, and employee productivity.

Industry Norms and Key Business Ratios. Desk Top Edition. Dun and Bradstreet Corp., Business Information Services. • Annual. Five volumes. $475.00 per volume. $1,890.00 per set. Covers over 800 kinds of businesses, arranged by Standard Industrial Classification number. More detailed editions covering longer periods of time are also available.

HANDBOOKS AND MANUALS

Official Industrial Equipment Guide. North American Equipment Dealers Association. • Semiannual. Price varies.

Regional Official Guides: Tractors and Farm Equipment. North American Equipment Dealers Association. • Quarterly. Membership.

ONLINE DATABASES

Agricola. U.S. National Agricultural Library. • Covers worldwide agricultural literature. Over 2.8 million citations, 1970 to present, with monthly updates. Inquire as to online cost and availability.

F & S Index. The Gale Group. • Contains about four million citations to worldwide business, financial, and industrial or consumer product literature appearing from 1972 to date. Weekly updates. Inquire as to online cost and availability.

Thomas Register Online. Thomas Publishing Co., Inc. • Provides concise information on approximately 194,000 U. S. companies, mainly manufacturers, with over 50,000 product classifications. Indexes over 115,000 trade names. Information is updated semiannually. Inquire as to online cost and availability.

PERIODICALS AND NEWSLETTERS

Farm Equipment. Cygnus Publishing, Inc. • Bimonthly. $48.00 per year. Includes annual*Product* issue.

Implement and Tractor: The Business Magazine of the Farm and Industrial Equipment Industry. Freiburg Publishing Co., Inc. • Seven times a year.

$25.00 per year. Includes annuals *Product File* and *Red Book.*

NAEDA Equipment Dealer. North American Equipment Dealers Association. • Monthly. $40.00 per year. Covers power equipment for farm, outdoor, and industrial use. Formerly *Farm and Power Equipment Dealer.*

PRICE SOURCES

PPI Detailed Report. Bureau of Labor Statistics, U.S. Department of Labor. Available from U.S. Government Printing Office. • Monthly. $55.00 per year. Formerly *Producer Price Indexes.*

RESEARCH CENTERS AND INSTITUTES

Agricultural Engineering Research Center. Texas A & M University, Scoats Hall, College Station, TX 77843-2117. Phone: (409)845-3903 Fax: (409)862-3442 E-mail: gilly@tamu.edu • URL: http://www.tamu.edu.

Idaho Agricultural Experiment Station. University of Idaho. Agricultural Science Bldg., Moscow, ID 83844-2337. Phone: (208)885-7173 Fax: (208)885-6654 E-mail: agres@uidaho.edu.

Milan Experiment Station. University of Tennessee, Knoxville. 6205 Ellington Dr., Milan, TN 38358. Phone: (901)686-7362 Fax: (901)686-3558 E-mail: utmilan@usit.net • URL: http://www.utk.edu/~minnotil.

National Soil Dynamics Laboratory-U.S. Dept. of Agriculture Agricultural Research Service. P.O. Box 3439, Auburn, AL 36831-3439. Phone: (334)887-4741 Fax: (334)887-8597 E-mail: derbach@eng.auburn.edu • URL: http://www.msa.ars.usda.gov/area/mis-bio/sdr/mssdr/htm.

Tennessee Agricultural Experiment Station. University of Tennessee, Knoxville. P.O. Box 1071, Knoxville, TN 37901-1071. Phone: (865)974-7121 Fax: (865)974-6479 E-mail: drichard@utk.edu • URL: http://www.funnelweb.utcc.utk.edu/~taescomm/default.html.

STATISTICS SOURCES

Annual Survey of Manufactures. Available from U. S. Government Printing Office. • Annual. Prices vary. Issued by the U. S. Census Bureau as an interim update to the *Census of Manufactures.* Includes data on number of manufacturing establishments in various industries, employment, labor costs, value of shipments, capital expenditures, inventories, energy costs, and assets. (See also Census Bureau home page, http://www.census.gov/.).

Manufacturing Profiles. Available from U. S. Government Printing Office. • Annual. Issued by the U. S. Census Bureau. A printed consolidation of the entire *Current Industrial Report* series, presenting "all the data compiled." Contains statistics on production, shipments, inventories, consumption, exports, imports, and orders for a wide variety of manufactured products. (See also Census Bureau home page, http://www.census.gov/.).

U. S. Industry and Trade Outlook: The McGraw-Hill Companies and the U.S. Department of Commerce/International Trade Administration. Datapso Research Corp. • Annual. $69.95. Produced by the International Trade Administration, U. S. Department of Commerce, in a "public-private" partnership with DRI/McGraw-Hill and Standard & Poor's. Provides basic data, outlook for the current year, and "Long-Term Prospects" (five-year projections) for a wide variety of products and services. Includes high technology industries. Formerly *U. S. Industrial Outlook.*

United States Census of Manufactures. U.S. Bureau of the Census. • Quinquennial. Results presented in reports, tape, CD-ROM, and Diskette files.

TRADE/PROFESSIONAL ASSOCIATIONS

Farm Equipment Manufacturers Association. 1000 Executive Parkway, Suite 100, St. Louis, MO 63141-6369. Phone: (314)878-2304 Fax: (314)878-1742 E-mail: femashort@aol.com • URL: http://www.farmequip.org.

Farm Equipment Wholesalers Association. P.O. Box 1347, Iowa City, IA 52244. Phone: (319)354-5156 Fax: (319)354-5157 E-mail: info@fewa.org • URL: http://www.fewa.org.

North American Equipment Dealers Association. 1195 Smizer Mill Rd., Fenton, MO 63026-3480. Phone: (636)349-5000 Fax: (314)821-0674 E-mail: naeda@naeda.com • URL: http://www.naeda.com.

AGRICULTURAL MARKET

See: FARM MARKETS

AGRICULTURAL PRODUCTS

See: FARM PRODUCE

AGRICULTURAL STATISTICS

See also: BUSINESS STATISTICS

INTERNET DATABASES

USDA. United States Department of Agriculture. Phone: (202)720-2791 E-mail: agsec@usda.gov • URL: http://www.usda.gov • The USDA home page has six sections: News and Information; What's New; About USDA; Agencies; Opportunities; Search and Help. Keyword searching is offered from the USDA home page and from various individual agency home pages. Agencies are the Economic Research Service, Agricultural Marketing Service, National Agricultural Statistics Service, National Agricultural Library, and about 12 others. Updating varies. Fees: Free.

ONLINE DATABASES

American Statistics Index: A Comprehensive Guide and Index to the Statistical Publications of the United States Government [Online]. Congressional Information Service, Inc. • Indexes and abstracts, 1973 to date. Inquire as to online cost and availability.

STATISTICS SOURCES

Agricultural Statistics. Available from U. S. Government Printing Office. • Annual. Produced by the National Agricultural Statistics Service, U. S. Department of Agriculture. Provides a wide variety of statistical data relating to agricultural production, supplies, consumption, prices/price-supports, foreign trade, costs, and returns, as well as farm labor, loans, income, and population. In many cases, historical data is shown annually for 10 years. In addition to farm data, includes detailed fishery statistics.

Agriculture Fact Book. Available from U. S. Government Printing Office. • Annual. Issued by the Office of Communications, U. S. Department of Agriculture. Includes data on U. S. agriculture, farmers, food, nutrition, and rural America. Programs of the Department of Agriculture in six areas are described: rural economic development, foreign trade, nutrition, the environment, inspection, and education.

FAO Quarterly Bulletin of Statistics. Food and Agriculture Organization of the United Nations. Available from UNIPUB. • Quarterly. $20.00 per year. Provides international data on agricultural production, trade, and prices, covering the major commodities of many countries. Text in English, French, and Spanish. Formerly *FAO Monthly Bulletin of Statistics.*

Foreign Agricultural Trade of the United States. Available from U. S. Government Printing Office. • Monthly. $50.00 per year. Issued by the Economic Research Service of the U. S. Department of Agriculture. Provides data on U. S. exports and imports of agricultural commodities.

United States Census of Agriculture. U.S. Bureau of the Census. • Quinquennial. Results presented in reports, tape, CD-ROM, and Diskette files.

World Agricultural Supply and Demand Estimates. Available from U. S. Government Printing Office. • Monthly. $38.00 per year. Issued by the Economics and Statistics Service and the Foreign Agricultural Service of the U. S. Department of Agriculture. Consists mainly of statistical data and tables.

AGRICULTURAL SURPLUSES

See: FARM PRODUCE

AGRICULTURE

See also: COOPERATIVES; FOREIGN AGRICULTURE

GENERAL WORKS

Agribusiness Management. David Downey and Steven Erickson. McGraw-Hill. • 1987. $81.56. Second edition.

ABSTRACTS AND INDEXES

Agrindex: International Information System for the Agricultural Sciences and Technology. Food and Agriculture Organization of the United Nations. UNIPUB. • Monthly. $500.00 per year. Text in English, French, and Spanish.

Biological and Agricultural Index. H.W. Wilson Co. • 11 times a year. Annual and quarterly cumulations. Service basis.

ALMANACS AND YEARBOOKS

Advances in Agronomy. Academic Press, Inc., Journal Div. • Annual. Prices vary.

FAO Yearbook: Trade. Available from Bernan Associates. • Annual. Published by the Food and Agriculture Organization of the United Nations (FAO). A compliation of international trade statistics for agricultural, fishery, and forest products. Text in English, French, and Spanish.

The State of Food and Agriculture. Available from Bernan Associates. • Annual. Published by the Food and Agriculture Organization of the United Nations (FAO). A yearly review of world and regional agricultural and food activities. Includes tables and graphs. Text in English.

Yearbook of Agriculture. U.S. Department of Agriculture. Available from U.S. Government Printing Office. • Annual.

BIBLIOGRAPHIES

Bibliography of Agriculture. U.S. National Agricultural Libary, Technical Information Systems. Oryx Press. • Monthly. $695.00. Annual cumulation.

CD-ROM DATABASES

AGRICOLA on SilverPlatter. Available from SilverPlatter Information, Inc. • Quarterly. $825.00 per year. Produced by the National Agricultural Library. Provides about three million citations on CD-ROM to the literature of agriculture, agricultural economics, animal sciences, entomology, fertilizer, food, forestry, nutrition, pesticides, plant science, water resources, and other topics. Each quarterly disc covers the past ten years, with archival discs available from 1970.

WILSONDISC: Biological and Agricultural Index. H. W. Wilson Co. • Monthly. $1,495.00 per year, including unlimited online access to *Biological and Agricultural Index* through WILSONLINE. Provides CD-ROM indexing of over 250 periodicals covering agriculture, agricultural chemicals, biochemistry, biotechnology, entomology, horticulture, and related topics.

DIRECTORIES

International Directory of Agricultural Engineering Institutions. Food and Agriculture Organization of the United Nations. Available from Bernan Associates. • 1995. Free for institutions and development agencies.

Internet Tools of the Profession: A Guide for Information Professionals. Hope N. Tillman, editor. Special Libraries Association. • 1997. $49.00. Second edition. Consists of 14 sections by various authors or compilers. After two introductory articles on searching the Internet, there are 12 annotated lists of useful Web sites, covering the SLA, business and finance, chemistry, education, food and agriculture, information technology, insurance and employee benefits, law, library management, metals and materials, pharmaceuticals, and telecommunications. An index is provided.

ENCYCLOPEDIAS AND DICTIONARIES

Dictionary of Agriculture: From Abaca to Zoonosis. Kathryn L. Lipton. Lynne Rienner Publishers, Inc. • 1995. $75.00. Emphasis is on agricultural economics.

Encyclopedia of Agriculture Science. Charles J. Arntzen and Ellen M. Ritter, editors. Academic Press, Inc. • 1994. $625.00. Four volumes.

FINANCIAL RATIOS

Almanac of Business and Industrial Financial Ratios. Leo Troy. Prentice Hall. • Annual. $99.95. Contains financial ratios derived from federal tax returns. Ratios for each of about 200 industries are arranged according to company asset size.

HANDBOOKS AND MANUALS

Dun & Bradstreet/Gale Group Industry Handbooks. The Gale Group. • 2000. $630.00. Five volumes. $145.00 per volume. Each volume covers two or more major industries: 1. *Entertainment and Hospitality*; 2. *Construction and Agriculture*; 3. *Chemicals and Pharmaceuticals*; 4. *Computers & Software and Broadcasting & Telecommunications*; 5. *Insurance and Health & Medical Services.* The following are included for each industry: overview, statistics, financial ratios, rankings, merger information, company directory, directory of associations, and consultants directory.

INTERNET DATABASES

Internet Tools of the Profession. Special Libraries Association. Phone: (202)234-4700 Fax: (202)265-9317 E-mail: hope@tiac.net • URL: http://www.sla.org/pubs/itotp • Web site is designed to update the printed *Internet Tools of the Profession.* Provides links to a wide range of useful databases in business, finance, industry, information technology, insurance, law, library management, telecommunications, and other subject areas. Fees: Free.

USDA. United States Department of Agriculture. Phone: (202)720-2791 E-mail: agsec@usda.gov • URL: http://www.usda.gov • The USDA home page has six sections: News and Information; What's New; About USDA; Agencies; Opportunities; Search and Help. Keyword searching is offered from the USDA home page and from various individual agency home pages. Agencies are the Economic Research Service, Agricultural Marketing Service, National Agricultural Statistics Service, National Agricultural Library, and about 12 others. Updating varies. Fees: Free.

WilsonWeb Periodicals Databases. H. W. Wilson. Phone: 800-367-6770 or (718)588-8400 Fax: 800-590-1617 or (718)992-8003 E-mail: custserv@hwwilson.com • URL: http://www.hwwilson.com/ • Web sites provide fee-based access to *Wilson Business Full Text, Applied Science & Technology Full Text, Biological & Agricultural Index, Library Literature & Information Science Full Text,* and *Readers' Guide Full Text, Mega Edition.* Daily updates.

ONLINE DATABASES

Agricola. U.S. National Agricultural Library. • Covers worldwide agricultural literature. Over 2.8 million citations, 1970 to present, with monthly updates. Inquire as to online cost and availability.

Biological and Agricultural Index Online. H. W. Wilson Co. • Indexes a wide variety of agricultural and biological periodicals, 1983 to date. Monthly updates. Inquire as to online cost and availability.

CAB Abstracts. CAB International North America. • Contains 46 specialized abstract collections covering over 10,000 journals and monographs in the areas of agriculture, horticulture, forest products, farm products, nutrition, dairy science, poultry, grains, animal health, entomology, etc. Time period is 1972 to date, with monthly updates. Inquire as to online cost and availability. *CAB Abstracts on CD-ROM* also available, with annual updating.

Information Bank Abstracts. New York Times Index Dept. • Provides indexing and abstracting of current affairs, primarily from the final late edition of *The New York Times* and the Eastern edition of *The Wall Street Journal.* Time period is 1969 to present, with daily updates. Inquire as to online cost and availability.

PERIODICALS AND NEWSLETTERS

Agricultural Outlook. Available from U. S. Government Printing Office. • Monthly. $60.00 per year. Issued by the Economic Research Service of the U. S. Department of Agriculture. Provides analysis of agriculture and the economy.

Agricultural Research. Available from U. S. Government Printing Office. • Monthly. $45.00 per year. Issued by the Agricultural Research Service of the U. S. Department of Agriculture. Presents results of research projects related to a wide variety of farm crops and products.

Agronomy Journal. American Society of Agronomy, Inc. • Bimonthly. Free to members; non-members, $171.00 per year.

Crop Science - Soil Science - Agronomy News. American Society of Agronomy, Inc. • Monthly. Free to members; non-members, $12.00 per year. Formerly *Agronomy News.*

Journal of Agricultural and Food Information. Haworth Press, Inc. • Quarterly. Individuals, $45.00 per year; libraries and other institutions, $85.00 per year. A journal for librarians and others concerned with the acquisition of information on food and agriculture.

Journal of Sustainable Agriculture: Innovations for the Long-Term and Lasting Maintenance and Enhancement of Agricultural Resources, Production and Environmental Quality. Haworth Press, Inc. • Quarterly. Individuals, $50.00 per year; institutions, $75.00 per year; libraries, $185.00 per year. Two volumes. An academic and practical journal concerned with resource depletion and environmental misuse.

Kiplinger Agriculture Letter. Kiplinger Washington Editors, Inc. • Biweekly. $56.00 per year. Newsletter.

News for Family Farmers and Rural Americans. Farmers Educational and Cooperative Union of America. • Monthly. $10.00 per year. Formerly *National Farmers Union Washington Newsletter.*

Washington Agricultural Record. • Weekly. $65.00 per year. Newsletter.

RESEARCH CENTERS AND INSTITUTES

Agricultural Experiment Station. Cornell University. 245 Roberts Hall, Ithaca, NY 14853-5905. Phone: (607)255-2552 Fax: (607)255-9499 E-mail: wrc2@cornell.edu • URL: http://www.cals.cornell.edu/ofr.

California Agricultural Experiment Station. University of California at Berkeley. 1111 Franklin St., 6th Fl., Oakland, CA 94607-5200. Phone: (510)987-0060 Fax: (510)451-2317 E-mail: wr.gomes@ucop.edu • URL: http://www.ucop.edu/anrhome/danr.html.

Florida Agricultural Experiment Station. University of Florida. Institute of Food and Agricultural Science, P.O. Box 110200, Gainesville, FL 32611-0200. Phone: (352)392-1784 Fax: (352)392-4965 E-mail: rlj@gnv.ifas.ufl.edu • URL: http://www.research.ifas.ufl.edu.

Michigan Agricultural Experiment Station. Michigan State University. 109 Agricultural Hall, East Lansing, MI 48224-1039. Phone: (517)355-0123 Fax: (517)355-5406 E-mail: gray@pilot.msu.edu • URL: http://www.msu.edu.

Ohio Agricultural Research and Development Center. Ohio State University. 1680 Madison Ave., Wooster, OH 44691-4096. Phone: (330)263-3701 Fax: (330)263-3688 E-mail: oardc@osu.edu • URL: http://www.oardc.ohio-state.edu.

Tennessee Agricultural Experiment Station. University of Tennessee, Knoxville. P.O. Box 1071, Knoxville, TN 37901-1071. Phone: (865)974-7121 Fax: (865)974-6479 E-mail: drichard@utk.edu • URL: http://www.funnelweb.utcc.utk.edu/~taescomm/default.html.

Wisconsin Agricultural Experiment Station. University of Wisconsin - Madison. 140 Agricultural Hall, 1450 Linden Dr., Madison, WI 53706. Phone: (608)262-4930 Fax: (608)262-4556 E-mail: elton.aberle@ccmail.adp.wisc.edu • URL: http://www.cals.wisc.edu.

STATISTICS SOURCES

Agricultural Statistics. Available from U. S. Government Printing Office. • Annual. Produced by the National Agricultural Statistics Service, U. S. Department of Agriculture. Provides a wide variety of statistical data relating to agricultural production, supplies, consumption, prices/price-supports, foreign trade, costs, and returns, as well as farm labor, loans, income, and population. In many cases, historical data is shown annually for 10 years. In addition to farm data, includes detailed fishery statistics.

Agriculture Fact Book. Available from U. S. Government Printing Office. • Annual. Issued by the Office of Communications, U. S. Department of Agriculture. Includes data on U. S. agriculture, farmers, food, nutrition, and rural America. Programs of the Department of Agriculture in six areas are described: rural economic development, foreign trade, nutrition, the environment, inspection, and education.

FAO Quarterly Bulletin of Statistics. Food and Agriculture Organization of the United Nations. Available from UNIPUB. • Quarterly. $20.00 per year. Provides international data on agricultural production, trade, and prices, covering the major commodities of many countries. Text in English, French, and Spanish. Formerly *FAO Monthly Bulletin of Statistics.*

Monthly Bulletin of Statistics. United Nations Publications. • Monthly. $295.00 per year. Provides current data for about 200 countries on a wide variety of economic, industrial, and demographic subjects. Compiled by United Nations Statistical Office.

OECD Agricultural Outlook. Organization for Economic Cooperation and Development. • Annual. $31.00. Provides a five-year outlook for agricultural markets in various countries of the world, including the U. S., other OECD countries, and selected non-OECD nations.

Statistical Yearbook. United Nations Publications. • Annual. $125.00. Contains statistics for about 200 countries on a wide variety of economic, industrial, and demographic topics. Compiled by United Nations Statistical Office.

United States Census of Agriculture. U.S. Bureau of the Census. • Quinquennial. Results presented in reports, tape, CD-ROM, and Diskette files.

World Statistics Pocketbook. United Nations Publications. • Annual. $10.00. Presents basic economic, social, and environmental indicators for about 200 countries and areas. Covers more than 50 items relating to population, economic activity, labor force, agriculture, industry, energy, trade, transportation, communication, education, tourism, and the environment. Statistical sources are noted.

TRADE/PROFESSIONAL ASSOCIATIONS

Agricultural Research Institute. 9650 Rockville Pike, Bethesda, MD 20814-3998. Phone: (301)530-7122 Fax: (301)530-7007 E-mail: ari@nalusda.gov • URL: http://www.ia-usa.org/a0026.htm.

Agriculture Council of America. 11020 King St., Suite 205, Overland, KS 66210. Phone: 888-982-4329 or (913)491-1895 Fax: (913)491-6502 E-mail: info@agday.org • URL: http://www.agday.org.

American Farm Bureau Federation. 225 Touhy Ave., Park Ridge, IL 60068. Phone: (847)685-8600 Fax: (847)685-8896 • URL: http://www.fb.com.

American Society of Agricultural Engineers. 2950 Niles Rd., St. Joseph, MI 49085-9659. Phone: (616)429-0300 Fax: (616)429-3852 E-mail: hq@asae.org • URL: http://www.asae.org.

American Society of Agronomy. 677 S. Segoe Rd., Madison, WI 53711. Phone: (608)273-8080 Fax: (608)273-2021 E-mail: headquarters@agronomy.org • URL: http://www.agronomy.org.

National Association of State Departments of Agriculture. 1156 15th St., N.W., Suite 1020, Washington, DC 20005. Phone: (202)296-9680 Fax: (202)296-9686 E-mail: nasda@patriot.net • URL: http://www.nasda-hq.org.

National Grange. 1616 H St., N.W., Washington, DC 20006. Phone: 888-447-2643 or (202)628-3507 Fax: (202)347-1091 • URL: http:// www.nationalgrange.org.

OTHER SOURCES

Agricultural Law. Matthew Bender & Co., Inc. • $2,120.00 per year. 15 looseleaf volumes. Periodic supplementation. Covers all aspects of state and federal law relating to farms, ranches and other agricultural interests. Includes five volumes dealing with agricultural estate, tax and business planning.

FedWorld: A Program of the United States Department of Commerce. National Technical Information Service. • Web site offers "a comprehensive central access point for searching, locating, ordering, and acquiring government and business information." Emphasis is on searching the Web pages, databases, and government reports of a wide variety of federal agencies. Fees: Free.

FirstGov: Your First Click to the U. S. Government. General Services Administration. • Free Web site provides extensive links to federal agencies covering a wide variety of topics, such as agriculture, business, consumer safety, education, the environment, government jobs, grants, health, social security, statistics sources, taxes, technology, travel, and world affairs. Also provides links to federal forms, including IRS tax forms. Searching is offered, both keyword and advanced.

Infrastructure Industries USA. The Gale Group. • 2001. $240.00. Replaces *Agriculture, Forestry, Fishing, Mining, and Construction USA* and *Transportation and Public Utilities USA.* Presents statistics and projections relating to economic activity in a wide variety of natural resource and construction industries.

AGRONOMY

See: AGRICULTURE

AIDS POLICY

GENERAL WORKS

AIDS and Drug Abuse in the Workplace: Resolving the Thorny Legal-Medical Issues. Charles G. Bakaly and Saul G. Kramer. Harcourt Brace and Co. • 1991. $40.00.

Women, Men, the Family and HIV/AIDS: A Sociological Perspective on the Epidemic in America. Carole A. Campbell. Cambridge University Press. • 1999. $49.95.

ABSTRACTS AND INDEXES

AIDS: Abstracts of the Psychological and Behavioral Literature, 1983-1991. John Anderson and others, editors. American Psychological Association. • 1991. $19.95. Third edition. (Bibliographies in Psychology Series: No.6).

Business Periodicals Index. H. W. Wilson Co. • Monthly, except August, with quarterly and annual cumulations. Service basis for print edition; CD-ROM edition, $1,495.00 per year.

Current Law Index: Multiple Access to Legal Periodicals. The Gale Group. • Monthly. $650.00 per year. Produced in cooperation with the American Association of Law Libraries. Indexes more than 900 law journals, legal newspapers, and specialty publications from the U.S., Canada, U.K., Ireland, Australia, and New Zealand.

Readers' Guide to Periodical Literature. H. W. Wilson Co. • Monthly. $220.00 per year. CD-ROM edition, $1,495 per year, including annual cumulation. Indexes about 250 peridicals of general interest.

Social Sciences Index. H. W. Wilson Co. • Quarterly, with annual cumulation. Service basis for print edition; CD-ROM edition, $1,495 per year. Indexes more than 400 periodicals covering economics, environmental policy, government, insurance, labor, health care policy, plannning, public administration, public welfare, urban studies, women's issues, criminology, and related topics.

BIBLIOGRAPHIES

AIDS Literature and Law Review. University Publishing Group, Inc. • Monthly. $225.00 per year. Contains abstracts of journal and newspaper articles. Formerly *AIDS Literature and News Review.*

How to Find Information About AIDS. Jeffrey T. Huber, editor. Haworth Press, Inc. • 1992. $49.95. Second edition. Includes print, electronic, and organizational sources of information. Local and national hotlines are listed.

CD-ROM DATABASES

AGRICOLA on SilverPlatter. Available from SilverPlatter Information, Inc. • Quarterly. $825.00 per year. Produced by the National Agricultural Library. Provides about three million citations on CD-ROM to the literature of agriculture, agricultural economics, animal sciences, entomology, fertilizer, food, forestry, nutrition, pesticides, plant science, water resources, and other topics. Each quarterly disc covers the past ten years, with archival discs available from 1970.

AIDSLINE CD-ROM. Available from SilverPlatter Information, Inc. • Quarterly. $595.00 per year. Produced by the National Library of Medicine (http://www.nlm.nih.gov). In addition to medical citations, CD-ROM database includes references to social, behavioral, and health policy issues. Time period is 1980 to date.

Social Science Source. EBSCO Publishing. • Monthly. $1,495.00 per year. Provides CD-ROM citations and abstracts to social science articles in more than 600 periodicals, with full text from 125 periodicals. Covers economics, political science, public policy, international relations, psychology, and other topics. Time period is most recent five years.

Social Sciences Citation Index: Compact Disc Edition with Abstracts. Institute for Scientific Information. • Quarterly. Provides CD-ROM indexing and abstracting of "significant articles" from 1,400 social science journals worldwide, with additional selections from 3,200 other journals, 1986 to date. Includes economics, business, finance, management, communications, demographics, information and library science, political science, sociology, and many other subjects.

WILSONDISC: Wilson Social Sciences Abstracts. H. W. Wilson Co. • Monthly. Including unlimited online access to *Social Sciences Index* through WILSONLINE. Provides CD-ROM indexing from 1983 and abstracting from 1994 of more than 400 periodicals covering economics, area studies, community health, public administration, public welfare, urban studies, and many other topics related to the social sciences.

ENCYCLOPEDIAS AND DICTIONARIES

Encyclopedia of AIDS: A Social, Political, Cultural, and Scientific Record of the HIV Epidemic. Raymond A. Smith, editor. Fitzroy Dearborn Publishers. • 1998. $125.00. Emphasis is historical, covering the years 1981 to 1996. Includes information on AIDS law, policy, and activism.

HANDBOOKS AND MANUALS

AIDS and the Law. David W. Webber, editor. John Wiley and Sons, Inc. • 1997. $150.00. Third edition. (Civil Rights Library Series).

AIDS Benefits Handbook: Everything You Need to Know to Get Social Security, Welfare, Medicaid, Medicare, Food Stamps, Housing, Drugs, and Other Benefits. Thomas P. McCormack. Yale University Press. • 1990. $37.50.

AIDS Issues in the Workplace: A Response Model for Human Resource Management. Dale A. Masi. Greenwood Publishing Group, Inc. • 1990. $59.95.

AIDS Law. Margaret C. Jasper. Oceana Publications, Inc. • 1996. $22.50. (Legal Almanac Series).

AIDS Law Today: A New Guide for the Public. Yale AIDS Law Project Staff. Yale University Press. • 1993. $52.00. Second edition.

AIDS Reference Guide: A Sourcebook for Planners and Decision Makers. Atlantic Information Services, Inc. • $335.00 Looseleaf. Two volumes. Includes twelve updates and twelve newsletters. Covers a wide range of AIDS topics, including "Employment Policies and Issues," "Legal Issues," "Financing Issues," "Impact on Healthcare Providers," "Global Issues," and "Legislative, Regulatory, and Governance Issues.".

Legal Aspects of AIDS. Donald H. Hermann and William P. Schurgin. West Group. • $130.00 per year. Looseleaf Service. Periodic supplementation. Includes issue employment discrimination, housing discrimination, and insurance. This work also "traces the historical progression of the disease and its spread." (Civil Rights Series).

ONLINE DATABASES

AIDSLINE. U. S. National Library of Medicine, MEDLARS Management Section. • Provides about 200,000 online citations (some abstracts) to the worldwide literature of Acquired Immune Deficiency Syndrome, compiled from MEDLINE and Health Planning and Administration databases. Coverage includes social and health policy issues. Time span is 1980 to date, with weekly updates. Inquire as to online cost and availability.

Index to Legal Periodicals and Books (Online). H. W. Wilson Co. • Broad coverage of law journals and books 1981 to date. Monthly updates. Inquire as to online cost and availability.

Newspaper and Periodical Abstracts. Bell & Howell Information and Learning. • Provides online coverage (citations and abstracts) of 25 major newspapers, 1,600 perodicals, and 70 TV programs. Covers business, economics, current affairs, health, fitness, sports, education, technology, government, consumer affairs, psychology, the arts, and the social sciences. Time period is 1986 to date, with daily updates. Inquire as to online cost and availability.

Readers' Guide Abstracts Online. H. W. Wilson Co. • Indexes and abstracts general interest periodicals, 1983 to date. Weekly updates. Inquire as to online cost and availability.

Wilson Business Abstracts Online. H. W. Wilson Co. • Indexes and abstracts 600 major business periodicals, plus the *Wall Street Journal* and the business section of the *New York Times*. Indexing is from 1982, abstracting from 1990, with the two newspapers included from 1993. Updated weekly. Inquire as to online cost and availability. (*Business Periodicals Index* without abstracts is also available online.).

Wilson Social Sciences Abstracts Online. H. W. Wilson Co. • Provides online abstracting and indexing of more than 415 periodicals covering area studies, community health, public administration, public welfare, urban studies, and many other social science topics. Time period is 1994 to date for abstracts and 1983 to date for indexing, with updates monthly. Inquire as to online cost and availability.

PERIODICALS AND NEWSLETTERS

AIDS and Public Policy Journal. Andrews Publications. • Quarterly. Individuals, $59.00 per year; institutions, $115.00 per year.

AIDS Policy and Law: The Biweekly Newsletter on Legislation, Regulation, and Litigation Concerning AIDS. LRP Publications. • Biweekly. $487.00 per year. Newsletter for personnel managers, lawyers, and others.

RESEARCH CENTERS AND INSTITUTES

Center for Women Policy Studies. 1211 Connecticut Ave., N.W. Suite 312, Washington, DC 20036. Phone: (202)872-1770 Fax: (202)296-8962 E-mail: cwps@centerwomenpolicy.org • URL: http://www.centerwomenpolicy.org • Conducts research on the policy issues that affect the legal, economic, educational, and social status of women, including sexual harassment in the workplace, and women and AIDS.

Lexis.com Research System. Lexis-Nexis Group. Phone: 800-227-9597 or (937)865-6800 Fax: (937)865-6909 E-mail: webmaster@prod.lexis-nexis.com • URL: http://www.lexis.com • Fee-based Web site offers extensive searching of a wide variety of legal sources. Additional features include Daily Opinion Service, lexis.com Bookstore, Career Center, CLE Center, Law Schools, and Practice Pages ("Pages specific to areas of specialty").

TRADE/PROFESSIONAL ASSOCIATIONS

AIDS Action Council. 1875 Connecticut Ave., N.W., Suite 700, Washington, DC 20009. Phone: 800-644-2437 or (202)986-1300 Fax: (202)986-1345 E-mail: aidsaction@aidsaction.org • URL: http://www.aidsaction.org • Political action organization.

American Foundation for AIDS Research. 120 Wall St., 13th Fl., New York, NY 10005. Phone: 800-392-6327 or (212)806-1600 Fax: (212)806-1601 E-mail: donors@amfar.org • URL: http://www.amfar.org • Purpose is to raise funds to support AIDS research.

OTHER SOURCES

AIDS Law and Litigation Reporter: The National Journal of Record of AIDS-Related Litigation. Andrews Publications. • Semimonthly. $2,975.00 per year.

AIDS Litigation Reporter (Acquired Immune Deficiency Syndrome): The National Journal of Record of AIDS-Related Litigation. Andrews Publications. • Semimonthly. $775.00 per year. Provides reports on a wide variety of legal cases in which AIDS is a factor.

AIR BASES

See: AIR FORCE

AIR CARGO

See: AIR FREIGHT

AIR CONDITIONING INDUSTRY

See also: HEATING AND VENTILATION; REFRIGERATION INDUSTRY

GENERAL WORKS

Modern Refrigeration and Air Conditioning. Andrew D. Althouse and others. Goodheart-Willcox Publishers. • 1996. $55.96.

Refrigeration and Air Conditioning. A.R. Trott and T. Welch. Butterworth-Heinemann. • 2000. $59.95. Third edition.

ABSTRACTS AND INDEXES

Applied Science and Technology Index. H. W. Wilson Co. • 11 times a year. Quarterly and annual cumulations. Service basis for print edition; CD-ROM edition, $1,495.00 per year. Indexes a wide variety of English language technical, industrial, and engineering periodicals.

NTIS Alerts: Energy. National Technical Information Service. • Semimonthly. $245.00 per year. Provides descriptions of government-sponsored research reports and software, with ordering information. Covers electric power, batteries, fuels, geothermal energy, heating/cooling systems, nuclear technology, solar energy, energy policy, and related subjects. Formerly *Abstract Newsletter.*

DIRECTORIES

Air Conditioning, Heating, and Refrigeration News-Directory. Business News Publishing Co. • Annual. $235.00.

AMCA Directory of Licensed Products. Air Movement and Control Association. • Annual. Free. Lists member manufacturers of equipment and supplies for the air and movement control industry.

ASHRAE Handbook. American Society of Heating, Refrigerating, and Air Conditioning Engineers, Inc. • Annual. Members, $98.00; non-members, $248.00. Four volumes.

The Wholesaler "Wholesaling 100". TMB Publishing, Inc. • Annual. $25.00. Provides information on the 100 leading wholesalers of plumbing, piping, heating, and air conditioning equipment.

ENCYCLOPEDIAS AND DICTIONARIES

Macmillan Encyclopedia of Energy. Available from The Gale Group. • 2001. $350.00. Three volumes. Published by Macmillan Reference USA. Covers the business, technology, and history of a wide variety of energy sources.

FINANCIAL RATIOS

American Supply Association Operating Performance Report. American Supply Association. • Annual. Members, $45.00; non-members, $150.00.

Annual Statement Studies. Robert Morris Associates: The Association of Lending and Credit Risk Professiona. • Annual. Free to members; non-members, $140.00. Median and quartile financial ratios are given for over 400 kinds of manufacturing, wholesale, retail, construction, and consumer finance establishments. Data is sorted by both asset size and sales volume. Includes a clearly written "Definition of Ratios" and an alphabetical industry index.

Industry Norms and Key Business Ratios. Desk Top Edition. Dun and Bradstreet Corp., Business Information Services. • Annual. Five volumes. $475.00 per volume. $1,890.00 per set. Covers over 800 kinds of businesses, arranged by Standard Industrial Classification number. More detailed editions covering longer periods of time are also available.

HANDBOOKS AND MANUALS

Air Conditioning Testing-Adjusting-Balancing: A Field Practice Manual. John Gladstone. Engineers Press. • 1991. $44.95. Second edition.

Guide to Energy Efficient Commercial Equipment. Margaret Suozzo and others. American Council for an Energy Efficient Economy. • 1997. $25.00. Provides information on specifying and purchasing energy-saving systems for buildings (heating, air conditioning, lighting, and motors).

No-Regrets Remodeling: Creating a Comfortable, Healthy Home That Saves Energy. Available from American Council for an Energy-Efficient Economy. • 1997. $19.95. Edited by *Home Energy* magazine. Serves as a home remodeling guide to efficient heating, cooling, ventilation, water heating, insulation, lighting, and windows.

ONLINE DATABASES

F & S Index. The Gale Group. • Contains about four million citations to worldwide business, financial, and industrial or consumer product literature appearing from 1972 to date. Weekly updates. Inquire as to online cost and availability.

Management Contents. The Gale Group. • Covers a wide range of management, financial, marketing, personnel, and administrative topics. About 150 leading business journals are indexed and abstracted from 1974 to date, with monthly updating. Inquire as to online cost and availability.

PERIODICALS AND NEWSLETTERS

Air Conditioning, Heating, and Refrigeration News. Business News Publishing Co. • Weekly. $87.00 per year. Includes *Annual Directory* and *Statistical Summary.*

ASHRAE Journal: Heating, Refrigeration, Air Conditioning, Ventilation. American Society of Heating, Refrigerating and Air Conditioning

Engineers, Inc. • Monthly. Free to members; non-members, $59.00 per year.

Dealerscope Consumer Electronics Marketplace: For CE,PC and Major Appliance Retailers. North American Publishing Co. • Monthly. Free to qualified personnel; others, $79.00 per year. Formerly *Dealerscope Merchandising.*

Heating/Piping/Air Conditioning Engineering: The Magazine of Mechanical Systems Engineering. Penton Media Inc. • Monthly. Free to qualified personnel; others, $65.00 per year. Covers design, specification, installation, operation, and maintenance for systems in industrial, commercial, and institutional buildings. Formerly Heating, Piping and Air Conditioning.

Koldfax. Air-Conditioning and Refrigeration Institute. • Monthly. Membership. Newsletter.

Shop Talk. Paul Allen. International Mobile Air Conditioning Association. • Monthly. Free to members; non-members, $50.00 per year. News and features relating to motor vehicle air conditioning and installed accessory industry.

The Wholesaler. TMB Publishing, Inc. • Monthly. $75.00 per year. Edited for wholesalers and distributors of plumbing, piping, heating, and air conditioning equipment.

RESEARCH CENTERS AND INSTITUTES

Energy Systems Laboratory. Texas A & M University. College Station, TX 77843. Phone: (409)845-6402 Fax: (409)845-6334 E-mail: doneal@mengr.tamu.edu • URL: http://www-esl.tamu.edu.

Institute for Environmental Research. Kansas State University. Seaton Hall, Manhattan, KS 66506. Phone: (785)532-5620 Fax: (785)532-6642 E-mail: hosni@ksu.edu • URL: http://www.engg.ksu.edu/ier.

Mechanical and Nuclear Engineering Research Laboratories. Kansas State University. Rathbone Hall, Room 302, Manhattan, KS 66506. Phone: (913)532-5610 Fax: (913)532-7057 • URL: http://www.mne.ksu.edu/home/html.

Ray W. Herrick Laboratories. Purdue University, School of Mechanical Engineering, West Lafayette, IN 47907-1077. Phone: (765)494-2132 Fax: (765)494-0787 E-mail: rhlab@ecn.purdue.edu.

STATISTICS SOURCES

Annual Survey of Manufactures. Available from U. S. Government Printing Office. • Annual. Prices vary. Issued by the U. S. Census Bureau as an interim update to the *Census of Manufactures.* Includes data on number of manufacturing establishments in various industries, employment, labor costs, value of shipments, capital expenditures, inventories, energy costs, and assets. (See also Census Bureau home page, http://www.census.gov/.).

Major Home Appliance Industry Fact Book: A Comprehensive Reference on the United States Major Home Appliance Industry. Association of Home Appliance Manufacturers. • Biennial. $35.00. Includes statistical data on manufacturing, industry shipments, distribution, and ownership.

Manufacturing Profiles. Available from U. S. Government Printing Office. • Annual. Issued by the U. S. Census Bureau. A printed consolidation of the entire *Current Industrial Report* series, presenting "all the data compiled." Contains statistics on production, shipments, inventories, consumption, exports, imports, and orders for a wide variety of manufactured products. (See also Census Bureau home page, http://www.census.gov/.).

Refrigeration, Air Conditioning, and Warm Air Heating Equipment. U. S. Bureau of the Census. • Annual. Provides data on quantity and value of shipments by manufacturers. Formerly *Air Conditioning and Refrigeration Equipment.* (Current Industrial Reports, MA-35M.).

U. S. Industry and Trade Outlook: The McGraw-Hill Companies and the U.S. Department of Commerce/International Trade Administration. Datapso Research Corp. • Annual. $69.95. Produced by the International Trade Administration, U. S. Department of Commerce, in a "public-private" partnership with DRI/McGraw-Hill and Standard & Poor's. Provides basic data, outlook for the current year, and "Long-Term Prospects" (five-year projections) for a wide variety of products and services. Includes high technology industries. Formerly *U. S. Industrial Outlook.*

TRADE/PROFESSIONAL ASSOCIATIONS

Air-Conditioning and Refrigeration Institute. 4301 N. Fairfax Dr., Suite 425, Arlington, VA 22203. Phone: (703)524-8800 Fax: (703)528-3816 E-mail: ari@ari.org • URL: http://www.ari.org.

Air Conditioning Contractors of America. 1712 New Hampshire Ave., N.W., Washington, DC 20009. Phone: (202)483-9370 Fax: (202)588-1217 E-mail: comm@acca.org • URL: http://www.acca.org.

American Society of Heating, Refrigerating and Air Conditioning Engineers. 1791 Tullie Circle, N.E., Atlanta, GA 30329. Phone: 800-527-4723 or (404)636-8400 Fax: (404)321-5478 E-mail: ashrae@ashrae.org • URL: http://www.ashrae.org.

International Mobile Air Conditioning Association. P.O. Box 9000, Fort Worth, TX 76147-2000. Phone: (817)732-4600 or (817)732-6348 Fax: (817)732-9610 E-mail: info@imaca.org • URL: http://www.imaca.org • Serves the automotive, boat, and aircraft air conditioning industries.

Sheet Metal and Air Conditioning Contractors' National Association. 4201 Lafayette Center Dr., Chantilly, VA 20151-1209. Phone: (703)803-2980 Fax: (703)803-3732 E-mail: info@smacna.org • URL: http://www.smacna.org.

OTHER SOURCES

ASHRAE Transactions. American Society of Heating, Refrigerating, and Air Conditioning Engineers, Inc. • Semiannual. Members, $126.00 per year; non-members, $187.00 per year.

Major Energy Companies of the World. Available from The Gale Group. • 2001. $855.00. Fourth edition. Published by Graham & Whiteside. Contains detailed information on more than 3,300 important energy companies in various countries. Industries include electricity generation, coal, natural gas, nuclear energy, petroleum, fuel distribution, and equipment for energy production.

AIR FORCE

ABSTRACTS AND INDEXES

Air University Library Index to Military Periodicals. U.S. Air Force. • Quarterly. Free to qualified personnel. Annual cumulation.

DIRECTORIES

Department of Defense Telephone Directory. Available from U. S. Government Printing Office. • Three times a year. $44.00 per year. An alphabetical directory of U. S. Department of Defense personnel, including Departments of the Army, Navy, and Air Force.

Directory of U.S. Military Bases Worldwide. William R. Evinger, editor. Oryx Press. • 1998. $125.00. Third edition.

ONLINE DATABASES

American Statistics Index: A Comprehensive Guide and Index to the Statistical Publications of the United States Government [Online]. Congressional Information Service, Inc. • Indexes and abstracts, 1973 to date. Inquire as to online cost and availability.

Information Bank Abstracts. New York Times Index Dept. • Provides indexing and abstracting of current affairs, primarily from the final late edition of *The New York Times* and the Eastern edition of *The Wall Street Journal.* Time period is 1969 to present, with daily updates. Inquire as to online cost and availability.

PERIODICALS AND NEWSLETTERS

Aerospace Journal. Available from U.S. Government Printing Office. • Quarterly. $29.00 per year. Published to stimulate professional thought concerning aerospace doctrines, strategy, tactics and related techniques. Formerly *Air University Review.*

Air Force Magazine: The Force Behind the Force. Air Force Association. • Monthly. $30.00 per year.

Air Force Times. Army Times Publishing Co. • Weekly. $52.00 per year. In two editions: Domestic and International.

Airman: Official Magazine of the U.S. Air Force. Available from U.S. Government Printing Office. • Monthly. $41.00 per year.

STATISTICS SOURCES

Annual Report of the Secretary of Defense. U.S. Department of Defense, Office of the Secretary. • Annual.

Budget of the United States Government. U.S. Office of Management and Budget. Available from U.S. Government Printing Office. • Annual.

Military Prime Contract Awards and Subcontract Payments. U.S. Department of Defense, Office of the Secretary. • Annual.

TRADE/PROFESSIONAL ASSOCIATIONS

Air Force Aid Society. 1745 Jefferson Davis Highway, No. 202, Arlington, VA 22202. Phone: (703)607-3134 Fax: (703)607-3022.

Air Force Association. 1501 Lee Highway, Arlington, VA 22209. Phone: 800-727-3337 or (703)247-5800 Fax: (703)247-5853 E-mail: polcom@afa.org • URL: http://www.afa.org.

Air Force Historical Foundation. c/o Lieutenant Colonel Maynard Y. Binge, Bldg. 1535, Suite A-122, Andrews AFB, MD 20762-7002. Phone: (301)736-1959 or (301)981-2139 Fax: (301)981-3574 E-mail: bingem@andrews.af.mil • URL: http://www.andrews.af.mil/tenants/historic/historic.htm.

Air Force Sergeants Association. P.O. Box 50, Temple Hills, MD 20757. Phone: (301)899-3500 Fax: (301)899-8136.

OTHER SOURCES

Carroll's Defense Organization Charts. Carroll Publishing. • Quarterly. $1,470.00 per year. Provides more than 200 large, fold-out paper charts showing personnel relationships in 2,400 U. S. military offices. Charts are also available online and on CD-ROM.

AIR FREIGHT

See also: FREIGHT TRANSPORT

ABSTRACTS AND INDEXES

Business Periodicals Index. H. W. Wilson Co. • Monthly, except August, with quarterly and annual cumulations. Service basis for print edition; CD-ROM edition, $1,495.00 per year.

Current Literature in Traffic and Transportation. Northwestern University, Transportation Library. • Quarterly. $25.00 per year.

DIRECTORIES

Air Freight Directory. Air Cargo, Inc. • Bimonthly. $84.00 per year. Air freight motor carriers.

National Customs Brokers and Forwarders Association of America: Membership Directory. National Customs Brokers and Forwarders Association of America, Inc. • Annual. $25.00. Lists about 600 customs brokers, international air cargo agents, and freight forwarders in the U.S.

OAG Air Cargo Guide. OAG Worldwide. • Monthly. $239.00 per year. Shows current domestic and international air freight schedules. Diskette edition, $449.00 per year.

Quick Caller Area Air Cargo Directories. Fourth Seacoast Publishing Co., Inc. • Annual. $16.00 for each regional edition. Six regionals. Reference source for the air cargo industry.

World Aviation Directory. McGraw-Hill Aviation Week Group. • Semiannual. $225.00 per year. Two volumes. Lists aviation, aerospace, and missile manufacturers. Includes *World Aviation Directory Buyer's Guide.*

ENCYCLOPEDIAS AND DICTIONARIES

Macmillan Encyclopedia of Transportation. Available from The Gale Group. • 2000. $375.00. Six volumes. Published by Macmillan Reference USA. Covers the business, technology, and history of transportation on land, on water, in the air, and in space. Includes definitions, cross-references, and 200 color illustrations.

ONLINE DATABASES

ABI/INFORM. Bell & Howell Information and Learning. • Provides online indexing to business-related material occurring in over 1,000 periodicals from 1971 to the present. Inquire as to online cost and availability.

Management Contents. The Gale Group. • Covers a wide range of management, financial, marketing, personnel, and administrative topics. About 150 leading business journals are indexed and abstracted from 1974 to date, with monthly updating. Inquire as to online cost and availability.

PROMT: Predicasts Overview of Markets and Technology. The Gale Group. • Companies, products, applied technologies and markets. U.S. and international literature coverage, 1972 to date. Inquire as to online cost and availability. Provides abstracts from more than 1,600 publications. Weekly updates.

Trade & Industry Index. The Gale Group. • Provides indexing of business periodicals, January 1981 to date. Daily updates. (Full text articles from some periodicals are available online, 1983 to date, in the companion database, *Trade & Industry ASAP.*) Inquire as to online cost and availability.

TRIS: Transportation Research Information Service. National Research Council. • Contains abstracts and citations to a wide range of transportation literature, 1968 to present, with monthly updates. Includes references to the literature of air transportation, highways, ships and shipping, railroads, trucking, and urban mass transportation. Formerly *TRIS-ON-LINE.* Inquire as to online cost and availability.

PERIODICALS AND NEWSLETTERS

Air Cargo News. Air Cargo News, Inc. • Monthly. $36.00 per year.

Air Cargo World. Intertec Publishing Corp. • Monthly. $58.00 per year.

Air Transport World. Penton Media Inc. • Monthly. Free to qualified personnel, others, $55.00 per year. Includes supplement *World Airline Reports.*

Aviation Week and Space Technology. McGraw-Hill Aviation Week Group. • Monthly. $89.00 per year.

Cargo Facts. • Monthly. $345.00 per year. Newsletter. Provides analysis of developments in the air freight and express industry.

Jet Cargo News: For Air Shipping Decision Makers. Hagall Publishing Co. • Monthly. $30.00 per year. Covers development of air cargo related technologies, containerization, regulation and documentation, market opportunities, routing, rates, trends and interviews with transportation industry executives worldwide.

RESEARCH CENTERS AND INSTITUTES

Transportation Center. Northwestern University, 600 Foster, Evanston, IL 60208-4055. Phone: (847)491-7287 Fax: (847)491-3090 E-mail: a-gellman@northwestern.edu • URL: http://www.nutcweb.tpc.nwu.edu.

STATISTICS SOURCES

Air Transport. Air Transport Association of America. • Annual. $20.00.

FAA Aviation Forecasts. Federal Aviation Administration. Available from U. S. Government Printing Office. • Annual. $15.00.

FAA Statistical Handbook of Aviation. Federal Aviation Administration. Available from U. S. Government Printing Office. • Annual.

TRADE/PROFESSIONAL ASSOCIATIONS

Air and Expedited Motor Carriers Conference. 2200 Mill Rd., Alexandria, VA 22314. Phone: (703)838-7978 Fax: (703)519-1866.

Air Transport Association of America. 1301 Pennsylvania Ave., Suite 1100, Washington, DC 20004-7017. Phone: (202)626-4000 Fax: (202)626-4166 E-mail: ata@air-transport.org • URL: http://www.air-transport.org.

Cargo Airline Association. 1220 19th St., N.W., Suite 400, Washington, DC 20036. Phone: (202)293-1030 Fax: (202)293-4377 E-mail: cargoair@aol.com.

International Federation of Freight Forwarders Associations. P.O. Box 8493, CH-8050 Zurich, Switzerland. Phone: 41 1 3116511 Fax: 41 1 3119044 E-mail: info@fita.com • URL: http://www.fiata.com.

Regional Airline Association. 1200 19th St., N.W., Suite 300, Washington, DC 20036-2422. Phone: (202)857-1170 Fax: (202)429-5113 E-mail: raa@dc.sba.com • URL: http://www.raa.org • Scheduled commuter air carriers.

OTHER SOURCES

Aviation Law Reports. CCH, Inc. • $2,419.00 per year. Four looseleaf volumes. Semimonthly updates.

AIR PILOTS

BIBLIOGRAPHIES

Aviation. Available from U. S. Government Printing Office. • Annual. Free. Lists government publications. (GPO Subject Bibliography Number 18).

DIRECTORIES

Airport/Facility Directory. U. S. National Ocean Service. • Bimonthly. $140.00 per year, complete. Issued in seven regional volumes (single region, $20.00 per year). Provides detailed non-military airport information for pilots, including control center and navigational data.

Airports USA. Aircraft Owners and Pilots Association. • Annual. $24.95. Primarily for pilots.

Jet and Propjet: Corporate Directory. AvCom International. • Annual. $21.95. Owners of business jet and turboprop aircraft. Formerly *Propjet.*

List of Certificated Pilot Schools. Federal Aviation Administration. Available from U. S. Government Printing Office. • Annual.

Professional Pilot-FBO Directory. Queensmith Communications Corp. • Annual. $8.00. Includes information for about 1,500 airports and fixed-base operators.

HANDBOOKS AND MANUALS

An Invitation to Fly: Basics for the Private Pilot. Dennis Glaeser. Wadsworth Publishing. • 1998. $69.95. Sixth edition. Prepares beginning pilots for FAA written test. (Aviation Series).

PERIODICALS AND NEWSLETTERS

Air Line Pilot; The Magazine of Professional Flight Deck Crews. Air Line Pilots Association. • Monthly. $26.00 per year.

AOPA Pilot. Aircraft Owners and Pilots Association. • Monthly. Membership.

FAA Aviation News. Federal Aviation Administration. Available from U. S. Government Printing Office. • Bimonthly. $28.00. per year. Designed to help airmen become safer pilots. Includes updates on major rule changes and proposals.

Flight International. Reed Business Information. • Weekly. $170.00 per year. Technical aerospace coverage.

Flying. Hachette Filipacchi Magazines, Inc. • Monthly. $26.00 per year.

Plane and Pilot. Werner Publishing Corp. • Monthly. $16.95 per year.

Professional Pilot Magazine. Queensmith Communications Corp. • Monthly. $36.00 per year. Edited for career pilots in all areas of aviation: airline, corporate, charter, and military. Includes flying technique, avionics, navigation, accident analysis, career planning, corporate profiles, and business aviation news.

RESEARCH CENTERS AND INSTITUTES

Institute of Aviation Research Laboratory. University of Illinois. One Airport Rd., Bldg. Q5, Savoy, IL 61874. Phone: (217)244-8617 Fax: (217)244-8647 E-mail: cwickens@uiuc.edu • URL: http://www.aviation.uiuc.edu.

STATISTICS SOURCES

FAA Statistical Handbook of Aviation. Federal Aviation Administration. Available from U. S. Government Printing Office. • Annual.

TRADE/PROFESSIONAL ASSOCIATIONS

Air Line Pilots Association International. 535 Herndon Parkway, Herndon, VA 20170. Phone: (703)689-2270 Fax: (703)689-4370 • URL: http://www.alpa.org.

Aircraft Owners and Pilots Association. 421 Aviation Way, Frederick, MD 21701. Phone: 800-872-2672 or (301)695-2000 Fax: (301)695-2375 E-mail: aopahq@aopa.org • URL: http://www.aopa.org.

Allied Pilots Association. 14600 Trinity Blvd., No. 500, Fort Worth, TX 76155-2512. Phone: 800-323-1470 or (972)988-3188 Fax: (972)606-5668.

International Council of Aircraft Owner and Pilot Associations. 421 Aviation Way, Frederick, MD 21701. Phone: (301)695-2220 Fax: (301)695-2375 E-mail: ruth.moser@aopa.org • URL: http://www.iaopa.org.

Lawyer-Pilots Bar Association. P.O. Box 685, Poolesville, MD 20837. Phone: (301)972-7700 Fax: (301)972-7727.

National Association of Flight Instructors. c/o Ohio State University Airport, 20 North St., Dublin, OH 43017. Phone: (614)889-6148 Fax: (614)889-2610.

Ninety-Nines, International Organization of Women Pilots. 501 Third St., N.W., 2nd Fl., Washington, DC. E-mail: lgildersleeve@cwa-union.org • URL: http://www.newsguild.org • Licensed women pilots.

Pilots International Association. P.O. Box 907, Minneapolis, MN 55440. Phone: 800-328-3323 or (612)588-5175 Fax: (612)520-6760.

Society of Experimental Test Pilots. P.O. Box 986, Lancaster, CA 93584-0986. Phone: (805)942-9574 Fax: (805)940-0398 E-mail: setp@netport.com • URL: http://www.netport.com/setp/.

Whirly-Girls (International Women Helicopter Pilots). P.O. Box 7446, Menlo Park, CA 94026. Phone: (415)462-1441 Fax: (415)323-3840 E-mail: whirlygrls@aol.com.

AIR POLLUTION

See also: ENVIRONMENT

GENERAL WORKS

Pollution: Causes, Effects, and Control. R. M. Harrison, editor. American Chemical Society. • 1996. $71.00. Third edition. Published by The Royal Society of Chemistry. A basic introduction to pollution of air, water, and land. Includes discussions of pollution control technologies.

ABSTRACTS AND INDEXES

Environment Abstracts. Congressional Information Service. • Monthly. Price varies. Provides multidisciplinary coverage of the world's environmental literature. Incorporates *Acid Rain Abstracts*.

Environment Abstracts Annual: A Guide to the Key Environmental Literature of the Year. Congressional Information Service. • Annual. $495.00. A yearly cumulation of *Environment Abstracts*.

Environmental Periodicals Bibliography: A Current Awareness Bibliography Featuring Citations of Scientific and Popular Articles in Serial Publications in the Area of the Environment. Environmental Studies Institute. International Academy at Santa Barbara. • Monthly. Price varies. An index to current environmental literature.

Excerpta Medica: Environmental Health and Pollution Control. Elsevier Science. • 16 times a year. 2,506.00 per year. Section 46 of *Excerpta Medica*. Covers air, water, and land pollution and noise control.

NTIS Alerts: Environmental Pollution & Control. National Technical Information Service. • Semimonthly. $245.00 per year. Provides descriptions of government-sponsored research reports and software, with ordering information. Covers the following categories of environmental pollution: air, water, solid wastes, radiation, pesticides, and noise. Formerly *Abstract Newsletter*.

Pollution Abstracts. Cambridge Information Group. • Monthly. $895.00 per year; with index, $985.00 per year.

ALMANACS AND YEARBOOKS

Environmental Viewpoints. The Gale Group. • 1993. $195.00. Three volumes. $65.00 per volume. A compendium of excerpts of about 200 articles on a wide variety of environmental topics, selected from both popular and professional periodicals. Arranged alphabetically by topic, with a subject/keyword index.

Gale Environmental Almanac. The Gale Group. • 1994. $110.00. Contains 15 chapters, each on a broad topic related to the environment, such as "Waste and Recycling." Each chapter has a topical overview, charts, statistics, and illustrations. Includes a glossary of environmental terms and a bibliography.

CD-ROM DATABASES

Environment Abstracts on CD-ROM. Congressional Information Service, Inc. • Quarterly. $1,295.00 per year. Contains the following CD-ROM databases: *Environment Abstracts, Energy Abstracts*, and *Acid Rain Abstracts*. Length of coverage varies.

DIRECTORIES

Environmental Career Directory. Visible Ink Press. • 1993. $17.95. Includes career information relating to workers in conservation, recycling, wildlife management, pollution control, and other areas. Provides advice from "insiders," resume suggestions, a directory of companies that may offer entry-level positions, and a directory of career information sources. (Career Advisor Series.).

Gale Environmental Sourcebook: A Guide to Organizations, Agencies, and Publications. The Gale Group. • 1993. $95.00. Second edition. A directory of print and non-print information sources on a wide variety of environmental topics.

Pollution Engineering-Product/Service Locator. Cahners Business Information. • Annual. $24.95. Supplement to *Pollution Engineering*. Formerly *Pollution Engineering Locator*.

Pollution Equipment News Buyer's Guide. Rimbach Publishing, Inc. • Annual. $100.00. Over 3,000 manufacturers of pollution control equipment and products.

ENCYCLOPEDIAS AND DICTIONARIES

Encyclopedia of Environmental Science. John Mongillo and Linda Zierdt-Warshaw. Oryx Press. • 2000. $95.00. Provides information on more than 1,000 topics relating to the environment. Includes graphs, tables, maps, illustrations, and 400 Web site addresses.

Environmental Encyclopedia. The Gale Group. • 1998. $235.00. Second edition. Provides over 1,300 articles on all aspects of the environment. Written in non-technical style.

Wiley Encyclopedia of Energy and the Environment. Frederick John Francis. John Wiley and Sons, Inc. • 1999. $1,500.00. Four volumes. Second edition. Covers a wide variety of energy and environmental topics, including legal and policy issues.

HANDBOOKS AND MANUALS

Air Pollution. O. Hutzinger, editor. Springer-Verlag New York, Inc. • 1989. $154.95. Two volumes. Vol. 4, Part B, $190.95; Vol. 4, Part C, $154.95. (Handbook of Environmental Chemistry Series).

Air Pollution: Federal Law and Analysis. David P. Currie. West Group. • $110.00. Periodic supplementation. Explains Clean Air Act and related laws, rules and regulations.

Industrial Pollution Prevention Handbook. Harry M. Freeman. McGraw-Hill. • 1992. $115.00.

Statistics for the Environment: Statistical Aspects of Health and the Environment. Vic Barnett and K. Feridun Turkman, editors. John Wiley and Sons, Inc. • 1999. $180.00. Contains articles on the statistical analysis and interpretation of environmental monitoring and sampling data. Areas covered include meteorology, pollution of the environment, and forest resources.

ONLINE DATABASES

Enviroline. Congressional Information Service, Inc. • Provides online indexing and abstracting of worldwide environmental and natural resource literature from 1975 to date. Updated monthly. Inquire as to online cost and availability.

Pollution Abstracts [online]. Cambridge Scientific Abstracts. • Provides indexing and abstracting of international, environmentally related literature, 1970 to date. Monthly updates. Inquire as to online cost and availability.

PERIODICALS AND NEWSLETTERS

Air and Waste Management Association Journal. Association Journal. • Monthly. Individuals, $110.00 per year; nonprofit institutions, $130.00 per year; others, $240.00 per year. Includes annual *Directory of Governmental Air Pollution Agencies*.

Air Pollution Control. Bureau of National Affairs. • Biweekly. $798.00 per year. Newsletter.

Air-Water Pollution Report: The Weekly Report on Environmental Executives. Business Publishers, Inc. • Weekly. $667.00 per year. Newsletter covering legislation, regulation, business news, research news, etc. Formed by merger of *Environment Week* and *Air-Water Pollution Report*.

Atmospheric Environment. Elsevier Science. • 36 times a year. $4,402.00 per year. Text in English, French and German.

Ecology USA. Business Publishers, Inc. • Biweekly. $135.00 per year.

Environmental Business Journal: Strategic Information for a Changing Industry. Environmental Business Publishing Co. • Monthly. $495.00 per year. Newsletter. Includes both industrial and financial information relating to individual companies and to the environmental industry in general. Covers air pollution, wat es, U. S. Department of Health and Human Services. Provides conference, workshop, and symposium proceedings, as well as extensive reviews of environmental prospects.

Environmental Regulation: State Capitals. Wakeman-Walworth, Inc. • Weekly. $245.00 per year. Newsletter. Formerly *From the State Capitals: Environmental Regulation*.

World Wastes: The Independent Voice of the Industry. Intertec Publishing Corp. • Monthly. $52.00 per year. Includes annual catalog. Formerly *Management of World Wastes: The Independent Voice of the Industry*.

RESEARCH CENTERS AND INSTITUTES

Air Pollution Research Center. University of California, Riverside. 211 Fawcett Laboratory, Riverside, CA 92521. Phone: (909)787-5124 Fax: (909)787-5004 E-mail: ratkins@mail.ucr.edu • URL: http://www.cnas.ucr.edu/~saprc/saprc.html.

Air Pollution Research Laboratory. University of Florida. 408 Black Hall, Gainesville, FL 32611. Phone: (352)392-0845 Fax: (352)392-3076.

Center for Energy and Environmental Studies. Carnegie Mellon University Department of Engineering and Public Policy. Baker Hall 128-A, Pittsburgh, PA 15213. Phone: (412)268-5897 Fax: (412)268-3757.

Environmental Health Sciences Research Laboratory. Tulane University. F. Edward Hebert Research Center, New Orleans, LA 70112. Phone: (504)588-5374 Fax: (504)584-1726 • URL: http://www.sph.tulane.edu.

Environmental Resources Research Institute. Pennsylvania State University. 100 Land and Water Resource Bldg., University Park, PA 16802. Phone: (814)863-0291 Fax: (814)865-3378 E-mail: ajm2@psu.edu • URL: http://www.erri.psu.edu.

STATISTICS SOURCES

Air Quality Data. U.S. Environmental Protection Agency. • Annual.

Annual Survey of Manufactures. Available from U. S. Government Printing Office. • Annual. Prices vary. Issued by the U. S. Census Bureau as an interim update to the *Census of Manufactures*.

Includes data on number of manufacturing establishments in various industries, employment, labor costs, value of shipments, capital expenditures, inventories, energy costs, and assets. (See also Census Bureau home page, http://www.census.gov/.).

Health and Environment in America's Top-Rated Cities: A Statistical Profile. Grey House Publishing. • Biennial. $195.00. Covers 75 U. S. cities. Includes statistical and other data on a wide variety of topics, such as air quality, water quality, recycling, hospitals, physicians, health care costs, death rates, infant mortality, accidents, and suicides.

Manufacturing Profiles. Available from U. S. Government Printing Office. • Annual. Issued by the U. S. Census Bureau. A printed consolidation of the entire *Current Industrial Report* series, presenting "all the data compiled." Contains statistics on production, shipments, inventories, consumption, exports, imports, and orders for a wide variety of manufactured products. (See also Census Bureau home page, http://www.census.gov/.).

Standard & Poor's Industry Surveys. Standard & Poor's. • Semiannual. $1,800.00. Two looseleaf volumes. Includes monthly supplements. Provides detailed, individual surveys of 52 major industry groups. Each survey is revised on a semiannual basis. Also includes "Monthly Investment Review" (industry group investment analysis) and monthly "Trends & Projections" (economic analysis).

Statistical Record of the Environment. The Gale Group. • 1996. $120.00. Third edition. Provides over 875 charts, tables, and graphs of major environmental statistics, arranged by subject. Covers population growth, hazardous waste, nuclear energy, acid rain, pesticides, and other subjects related to the environment. A keyword index is included.

U. S. Industry and Trade Outlook: The McGraw-Hill Companies and the U.S. Department of Commerce/International Trade Administration. Datapso Research Corp. • Annual. $69.95. Produced by the International Trade Administration, U. S. Department of Commerce, in a "public-private" partnership with DRI/McGraw-Hill and Standard & Poor's. Provides basic data, outlook for the current year, and "Long-Term Prospects" (five-year projections) for a wide variety of products and services. Includes high technology industries. Formerly *U. S. Industrial Outlook.*

TRADE/PROFESSIONAL ASSOCIATIONS

Air and Waste Management Association. One Gateway Center, 3rd Fl., Pittsburgh, PA 15222. Phone: 800-270-3444 or (412)232-3444 Fax: (412)232-3450 E-mail: info@awma.org • URL: http://www.awma.org.

Association of Local Air Pollution Control Officials. 444 N. Capitol St., N. W., Suite 307, Washington, DC 20001. Phone: (202)624-7864 Fax: (202)624-7863.

OTHER SOURCES

Environment Reporter. Bureau of National Affairs, Inc. • Weekly. $2,844.00 per year. 18 volumes. Looseleaf. Covers legal aspects of wide variety of environmental concerns.

AIR TRAFFIC

See: AIR TRAVEL

AIR TRANSPORTATION

See: AIR FREIGHT; AIR TRAVEL; AIRLINE INDUSTRY

AIR TRAVEL

See also: AIRLINE INDUSTRY

GENERAL WORKS

Just in Case; A Passenger's Guide to Airplane Safety and Survival. Daniel A. Johnson. Perseus Publishing. • 1984. $19.95.

Safe Trip Abroad. Available from U. S. Government Printing Office. • 1996. $1.25. Issued by the Bureau of Consular Affairs, U. S. State Department (http://www.state.gov). Provides practical advice for international travel.

ABSTRACTS AND INDEXES

Business Periodicals Index. H. W. Wilson Co. • Monthly, except August, with quarterly and annual cumulations. Service basis for print edition; CD-ROM edition, $1,495.00 per year.

Current Literature in Traffic and Transportation. Northwestern University, Transportation Library. • Quarterly. $25.00 per year.

BIBLIOGRAPHIES

Travel and Tourism. Available from U. S. Government Printing Office. • Annual. Free. Issued by the Superintendent of Documents. A list of government publications on the travel industry and tourism. Formerly *Mass Transit, Travel and Tourism.* (Subject Bibliography No. 302.).

DIRECTORIES

ASU Travel Guide: The Airline Employee's Discount Directory. Christopher Gil, editor. A S U Travel Guide, Inc. • Quarterly. $34.95. Lists air travel discounts available to airline employees.

OAG Desktop Flight Guide, North American Edition. OAG Worldwide. • Biweekly. $285.00 per year. Provides detailed airline travel schedules for the U. S., Canada, Mexico, and the Caribbean. Includes aircraft seat charts and airport diagrams. Formerly *Official Airline Guide, North American Edition.*

OAG Flight Guide. OAG Worldwide. • Monthly. $399.00 per year. Provides detailed airline schedules for international travel (travel within North America not included).

HANDBOOKS AND MANUALS

Fly-Rights: A Consumer Guide to Air Travel. Available from U. S. Government Printing Office. • 1994. $2.00. 10th edition. Issued by the U. S. Department of Transportation. Explains the rights and responsibilities of air travelers.

Health Information for International Travel. Available from U. S. Government Printing Office. • Annual. Issued by Centers for Disease Control, U. S. Department of Health and Human Services. Discusses potential health risks of international travel and specifies vaccinations required by different countries.

ONLINE DATABASES

ABI/INFORM. Bell & Howell Information and Learning. • Provides online indexing to business-related material occurring in over 1,000 periodicals from 1971 to the present. Inquire as to online cost and availability.

Management Contents. The Gale Group. • Covers a wide range of management, financial, marketing, personnel, and administrative topics. About 150 leading business journals are indexed and abstracted from 1974 to date, with monthly updating. Inquire as to online cost and availability.

Newspaper and Periodical Abstracts. Bell & Howell Information and Learning. • Provides online coverage (citations and abstracts) of 25 major newspapers, 1,600 perodicals, and 70 TV programs. Covers business, economics, current affairs, health, fitness, sports, education, technology, government, consumer affairs, psychology, the arts, and the social sciences. Time period is 1986 to date, with daily updates. Inquire as to online cost and availability.

OAG Electronic Edition Travel Service. Official Airline Guides, Inc. • Current airline flight schedules and fare information. Inquire as to online cost and availability.

Trade & Industry Index. The Gale Group. • Provides indexing of business periodicals, January 1981 to date. Daily updates. (Full text articles from some periodicals are available online, 1983 to date, in the companion database, *Trade & Industry ASAP.*) Inquire as to online cost and availability.

United States International Air Travel Statistics. U. S. Department of Transportation, Center for Transportation Information. • Provides detailed statistics on air passenger travel between the U. S. and foreign countries for both scheduled and charter flights. Time period is 1975 to date, with monthly updates. Inquire as to online cost and availability.

PERIODICALS AND NEWSLETTERS

Aviation Week and Space Technology. McGraw-Hill Aviation Week Group. • Monthly. $89.00 per year.

Consumer Reports Travel Letter. Consumers Union of the United States, Inc. • Monthly. $39.00 per year. Newsletter with information on air fares, travel discounts, special hotel rates, etc.

Frequent Flyer: For Business People Who Must Travel. OAG Worldwide. • Monthly. $89.00 per year to individuals. Also known as *OAG Frequent Flyer.* Edited for business travelers. Contains news of frequent flyer programs, airport developments, airline services, and business travel trends. Available only with *OAG Flight Guide.*

Front Row Advisor: Business and First Class Air Travel and the Alluring World of Free Upgrades. Diversified Specialties, Inc. • Bimonthly. $145.00 per year. Newsletter. Contains information on opportunities provided by airlines to upgrade coach seats to business class, including frequent flyer upgrades.

Inside Flyer. Frequent Flyer Services. • Monthly. $75.00 per year. Newsletter. Provides information relating to frequent flyer awards and air travel.

Interline Adventures. Grand Adventures Tour and Travel Publishing Corp. • Bimonthly. $18.95 per year. Contains information on air travel for airline personnel. Formerly *Airfair and Airfare Interline.*

Jax Fax Travel Marketing Magazine: The Official Leisure Travel Booking Magazine. Jet Airtransport Exchange, Inc. • Monthly. $15.00 per year. Trade magazine for travel agents.

Newsline: Research News from the U. S. Travel Data Center. Travel Industry Association of America. • Monthly. $55.00 per year. Newsletter. Covers trends in the U. S. travel industry.

Summary of Health Information for International Travel. U. S. Department of Health and Human Services. • Biweekly. Formerly *Weekly Summary of Health Information for International Travel.*

Travel Smart: Pay Less, Enjoy More. Communications House, Inc. • Monthly. $44.00 per year. Newsletter. Provides information and recommendations for travelers. Emphasis is on travel value and opportunities for bargains.

RESEARCH CENTERS AND INSTITUTES

Travel Industry Association of America. Research Dept., 1100 New York Ave., N.W., No. 450, Washington, DC 20005. Phone: (202)408-8422 Fax: (202)408-1255 E-mail: scook@tia.org • URL: http://www.tia.org • Conducts economic, statistical, and market research relating to the U. S. travel industry.

Affiliated with the Travel Industry Association of America.

STATISTICS SOURCES

Air Carrier Traffic Statistics Monthly. U. S. Department of Transportation. • Monthly. Provides passenger traffic data for large airlines.

Air Transport. Air Transport Association of America. • Annual. $20.00.

Economic Review of Travel in America. Travel Industry Association of America. • Annual. Members, $75.00; non-members, $125.00. Presents a statistical summary of travel in the U.S., including travel expenditures, travel industry employment, tax data, international visitors, etc.

FAA Aviation Forecasts. Federal Aviation Administration. Available from U. S. Government Printing Office. • Annual. $15.00.

FAA Statistical Handbook of Aviation. Federal Aviation Administration. Available from U. S. Government Printing Office. • Annual.

Outlook for Travel and Tourism. Travel Industry Association of America. • Annual. Members, $100.00; non-members, $175.00. Contains forecasts of the performance of the U. S. travel industry, including air travel, business travel, recreation (attractions), and accomodations.

Summary of International Travel to the United States. International Trade Administration, Tourism Industries. U.S. Dept. of Commerce. • Monthly. Quarterly and annual versions available. Provides statistics on air travel to the U.S. from each of 90 countries. Formerly *Summary and Analysis of International Travel to the United States.*

World Air Transport Statistics. International Air Transport Association. • Annual. $180.00.

TRADE/PROFESSIONAL ASSOCIATIONS

Air Traffic Control Association. 2300 Clarendon Blvd., Suite 711, Arlington, VA 22201. Phone: (703)522-5717 Fax: (703)527-7251 E-mail: atca@worldnet.att.net • URL: http://www.atca.org.

Air Transport Association of America. 1301 Pennsylvania Ave., Suite 1100, Washington, DC 20004-7017. Phone: (202)626-4000 Fax: (202)626-4166 E-mail: ata@air-transport.org • URL: http://www.air-transport.org.

Aviation Consumer Action Project. 2001 S St., N.W., Suite 410, Washington, DC 20009. Phone: (202)638-4000 Fax: (202)638-0746 E-mail: acap71@erols.org.

Aviation Safety Institute. 6797 N. High St., Suite 316, Worthington, OH 43085. Phone: (614)885-4242 Fax: (614)885-5891 • URL: http://www.asionline.org.

Flight Safety Foundation. 601 Madison St., Suite 300, Alexandria, VA 22314. Phone: (703)739-6700 Fax: (703)739-6708 • URL: http://www.flightsafety.org.

International Air Transport Association. P.O. Box 113, Montreal, QC, Canada H42 1M1. Phone: (514)874-0202 Fax: (514)874-9632 • URL: http://www.iata.org.

International Airline Passengers Association. P.O. Box 700188, Dallas, TX 75370. Phone: 800-821-4272 or (904)404-9980 Fax: (972)233-5348 E-mail: iapa@iapauia.com • URL: http://www.iapa.com.

National Air Carrier Association. 1730 M St., N.W., Suite 806, Washington, DC 20036. Phone: (202)833-8200 Fax: (202)659-9479 • Charter airlines.

AIRCRAFT INDUSTRY

See: AIRPLANE INDUSTRY

AIRCRAFT OWNERS AND PILOTS

See: AIR PILOTS; BUSINESS AVIATION

AIRLINE INDUSTRY

See also: AIR TRAVEL

GENERAL WORKS

Air Transportation: A Management Perspective. Alexander Wells. Wadsworth Publishing. • 1998. $69.95. Fourth edition.

Commuter Airlines. Alexander T. Wells and Franklin D. Richey. Krieger Publishing Co. • 1996. $46.50. Provides an overview of the commuter airline industry, including operating and management functions.

FAA Historical Chronology: Civil Aviation and the Federal Government, 1926-1996. Edmund Preston, editor. Available from U. S. Government Printing Office. • 1998. $29.00. Third edition. Issued by the Federal Aviation Administration, U. S. Department of Transportation (http://www.dot.gov). Provides a compilation of historical information about the FAA and the earlier Civil Aeronautics Board (CAB). Chronological arrangement.

Opportunities in Airline Careers. Adrian A. Paradis. NTC/Contemporary Publishing. • 1989. $14.95. Covers the full scope of careers with commercial airlines. (Opportunities in... Series).

Pricing and Capacity Determination in International Air Transport. Peter P. C. Haanappel. Kluwer Law International. • 1984. $66.00.

ABSTRACTS AND INDEXES

Business Periodicals Index. H. W. Wilson Co. • Monthly, except August, with quarterly and annual cumulations. Service basis for print edition; CD-ROM edition, $1,495.00 per year.

Current Literature in Traffic and Transportation. Northwestern University, Transportation Library. • Quarterly. $25.00 per year.

NTIS Alerts: Transportation. National Technical Information Service. • Semimonthly. $210.00 per year. Provides descriptions of government-sponsored research reports and software, with ordering information. Covers air, marine, highway, inland waterway, pipeline, and railroad transportation. Formerly *Abstract Newsletter.*

BIBLIOGRAPHIES

Federal Aviation Regulations. Available from U. S. Government Printing Office. • Annual. Free. Lists government publications. GPO Subject Bibliography Number 12.

DIRECTORIES

Airline Handbook. AeroTravel Research. • Annual. $16.00. Directory of commercial airlines, both scheduled and chartered.

Annual Report of the Commuter Regional Airline Industry. Regional Airline Association. • Annual. $75.00. Lists commuter and regional airlines and gives statistical information.

ASU Travel Guide: The Airline Employee's Discount Directory. Christopher Gil, editor. A S U Travel Guide, Inc. • Quarterly. $34.95. Lists air travel discounts available to airline employees.

International ABC Aerospace Directory. Janes's Information Group. • 1998. $500.00. 28,000 aviation aerospace manufacturers, airlines, associations, government agencies, etc. Formerly *Interavia ABC Aerospace Directory.*

Jane's World Airlines. Jane's Information Group. • $892.00. Looseleaf. Quarterly updates. CD-Rom edition, $1,475.00. Provides detailed financial and operating data for 500 airlines throughout the world.

National Air Transportation Association Official Membership Directory. National Air Transportation Association. • Annual. $95.00. List more than 1,000 regular, associate, and affliate members; regular members include airport service organizations, air taxi operators, and commuter airlines.

OAG Desktop Flight Guide, North American Edition. OAG Worldwide. • Biweekly. $285.00 per year. Provides detailed airline travel schedules for the U. S., Canada, Mexico, and the Caribbean. Includes aircraft seat charts and airport diagrams. Formerly *Official Airline Guide, North American Edition.*

OAG Flight Guide. OAG Worldwide. • Monthly. $399.00 per year. Provides detailed airline schedules for international travel (travel within North America not included).

World Aviation Directory. McGraw-Hill Aviation Week Group. • Semiannual. $225.00 per year. Two volumes. Lists aviation, aerospace, and missile manufacturers. Includes *World Aviation Directory Buyer's Guide.*

ENCYCLOPEDIAS AND DICTIONARIES

Macmillan Encyclopedia of Transportation. Available from The Gale Group. • 2000. $375.00. Six volumes. Published by Macmillan Reference USA. Covers the business, technology, and history of transportation on land, on water, in the air, and in space. Includes definitions, cross-references, and 200 color illustrations.

FINANCIAL RATIOS

Almanac of Business and Industrial Financial Ratios. Leo Troy. Prentice Hall. • Annual. $99.95. Contains financial ratios derived from federal tax returns. Ratios for each of about 200 industries are arranged according to company asset size.

Annual Statement Studies. Robert Morris Associates: The Association of Lending and Credit Risk Professiona. • Annual. Free to members; non-members, $140.00. Median and quartile financial ratios are given for over 400 kinds of manufacturing, wholesale, retail, construction, and consumer finance establishments. Data is sorted by both asset size and sales volume. Includes a clearly written "Definition of Ratios" and an alphabetical industry index.

Industry Norms and Key Business Ratios. Desk Top Edition. Dun and Bradstreet Corp., Business Information Services. • Annual. Five volumes. $475.00 per volume. $1,890.00 per set. Covers over 800 kinds of businesses, arranged by Standard Industrial Classification number. More detailed editions covering longer periods of time are also available.

INTERNET DATABASES

Fedstats. Federal Interagency Council on Statistical Policy. Phone: (202)395-7254 • URL: http://www.fedstats.gov • Web site features an efficient search facility for full-text statistics produced by more than 70 federal agencies, including the Census Bureau, the Bureau of Economic Analysis, and the Bureau of Labor Statistics. Boolean searches can be made within one agency or for all agencies combined. Links are offered to international statistical bureaus, including the UN, IMF, OECD, UNESCO, Eurostat, and 20 individual countries. Fees: Free.

ONLINE DATABASES

ABI/INFORM. Bell & Howell Information and Learning. • Provides online indexing to business-related material occurring in over 1,000 periodicals from 1971 to the present. Inquire as to online cost and availability.

DRI U.S. Central Database. Data Products Division. • Provides more than 23,000 business, financial, demographic, economic, foreign trade, and industry-related time series for the U.S. Includes national income, population, retail-wholesale trade, price indexes, labor data, housing, industrial production, banking, interest rates, money supply, etc. Time period is generally 1947 to date (some data back to 1929). Updating varies. Inquire as to online cost and availability.

Globalbase. The Gale Group. • Provides more than one million online summaries of business, industrial, and economic news reports from more than 1,000 publications worldwide. Covers a wide range of material appearing in international trade journals, professional magazines, and newspapers. Time period is 1984 to date, with weekly updates. Inquire as to online cost and availability.

Management Contents. The Gale Group. • Covers a wide range of management, financial, marketing, personnel, and administrative topics. About 150 leading business journals are indexed and abstracted from 1974 to date, with monthly updating. Inquire as to online cost and availability.

OAG Electronic Edition Travel Service. Official Airline Guides, Inc. • Current airline flight schedules and fare information. Inquire as to online cost and availability.

PAIS International. Public Affairs Information Service, Inc. • Corresponds to the former printed publications, *PAIS Bulletin* (1976-90) and *PAIS Foreign Language Index* (1972-90), and to the current *PAIS International in Print* (1991 to date). Covers economic, political, and sociological material appearing in periodicals, books, government documents, and other publications. Updating is monthly. Inquire as to online cost and availability.

PROMT: Predicasts Overview of Markets and Technology. The Gale Group. • Companies, products, applied technologies and markets. U.S. and international literature coverage, 1972 to date. Inquire as to online cost and availability. Provides abstracts from more than 1,600 publications. Weekly updates.

Trade & Industry Index. The Gale Group. • Provides indexing of business periodicals, January 1981 to date. Daily updates. (Full text articles from some periodicals are available online, 1983 to date, in the companion database, *Trade & Industry ASAP.*) Inquire as to online cost and availability.

TRIS: Transportation Research Information Service. National Research Council. • Contains abstracts and citations to a wide range of transportation literature, 1968 to present, with monthly updates. Includes references to the literature of air transportation, highways, ships and shipping, railroads, trucking, and urban mass transportation. Formerly *TRIS-ON-LINE.* Inquire as to online cost and availability.

PERIODICALS AND NEWSLETTERS

Air Transport World. Penton Media Inc. • Monthly. Free to qualified personnel, others, $55.00 per year. Includes supplement *World Airline Reports.*

Airline Financial News. Phillips Business Information, Inc. • Weekly. $697.00 per year. Newsletter on the financial situation of airlines.

Aviation Daily. Aviation Week Newsletter. McGraw-Hill. • Daily. $1,595.00 per year. Newsletter. Covers current developments in air transportation and aviation manufacturing.

Aviation Week and Space Technology. McGraw-Hill Aviation Week Group. • Monthly. $89.00 per year.

Frequent Flyer: For Business People Who Must Travel. OAG Worldwide. • Monthly. $89.00 per year to individuals. Also known as *OAG Frequent Flyer.* Edited for business travelers. Contains news of frequent flyer programs, airport developments, airline services, and business travel trends. Available only with *OAG Flight Guide.*

Interline Adventures. Grand Adventures Tour and Travel Publishing Corp. • Bimonthly. $18.95 per year. Contains information on air travel for airline personnel. Formerly *Airfair and Airfare Interline.*

Professional Pilot Magazine. Queensmith Communications Corp. • Monthly. $36.00 per year. Edited for career pilots in all areas of aviation: airline, corporate, charter, and military. Includes flying technique, avionics, navigation, accident analysis, career planning, corporate profiles, and business aviation news.

World Airline News. Phillips Business Information, Inc. • Weekly. $697.00 per year. Newsletter. Covers the international airline industry.

RESEARCH CENTERS AND INSTITUTES

Center for Transportation Studies. Massachusetts Institute of Technology. 77 Massachusetts Ave. Room 1-235, Cambridge, MA 02139. Phone: (617)253-5320 Fax: (617)253-4560 E-mail: ctsmail@mit.edu • URL: http://www.web.mit.edu/cts/www/.

Transportation Center. Northwestern University, 600 Foster, Evanston, IL 60208-4055. Phone: (847)491-7287 Fax: (847)491-3090 E-mail: a-gellman@northwestern.edu • URL: http://www.nutcweb.tpc.nwu.edu.

STATISTICS SOURCES

Air Carrier Financial Statistics. U. S. Department of Transportation. • Quarterly. Contains profit and loss and asset information for specific airlines.

Air Carrier Industry Scheduled Service Traffic Statistics. U. S. Department of Transportation. • Quarterly. Includes data for commuter airlines.

Air Carrier Traffic Statistics Monthly. U. S. Department of Transportation. • Monthly. Provides passenger traffic data for large airlines.

Air Transport. Air Transport Association of America. • Annual. $20.00.

Airport Activity Statistics of Certificated Route Air Carriers. U. S. Department of Transportation. Available from U. S. Government Printing Office. • Annual $47.00.

Business Statistics of the United States. Courtenay M. Slater, editor. Bernan Associates. • 1999. $74.00. Fifth edition. Based on *Business Statistics*, formerly issue by the Bureau of Economic Analysis, U. S. Department of Commerce. Provides basic data for a wide variety of U. S. industries, services, and economic indicators. Most statistics are shown annually for 29 years and monthly for the most recent four years.

FAA Aviation Forecasts. Federal Aviation Administration. Available from U. S. Government Printing Office. • Annual. $15.00.

FAA Statistical Handbook of Aviation. Federal Aviation Administration. Available from U. S. Government Printing Office. • Annual.

Standard & Poor's Industry Surveys. Standard & Poor's. • Semiannual. $1,800.00. Two looseleaf volumes. Includes monthly supplements. Provides detailed, individual surveys of 52 major industry groups. Each survey is revised on a semiannual basis. Also includes "Monthly Investment Review" (industry group investment analysis) and monthly "Trends & Projections" (economic analysis).

Standard & Poor's Statistical Service. Current Statistics. Standard & Poor's. • Monthly. $688.00 per year. Includes 10 *Basic Statistics* sections, *Current Statistics Supplements* and *Annual Security Price Index Record.*

Survey of Current Business. Available from U. S. Government Printing Office. • Monthly. $49.00 per year. Issued by Bureau of Economic Analysis, U. S. Department of Commerce. Presents a wide variety of business and economic data.

Transportation Statistics Annual Report. Available from U. S. Government Printing Office. • Annual. $21.00. Issued by Bureau of Transportation Statistics, U. S. Department of Transportation. Provides data on operating revenues, expenses, employees, passenger miles (where applicable), and other factors for airlines, automobiles, buses, local transit, pipelines, railroads, ships, and trucks.

WEFA Industrial Monitor. John Wiley and Sons, Inc. • Annual. $65.00. Prepared by industry analysts at WEFA, an economic forecasting and consulting firm (originally Wharton Econometric Forecasting Associates). Contains discussions of the outlook for major U. S. industries, with many 10-year forecasts (WEFA Web site is http://www.wefa.com).

World Air Transport Statistics. International Air Transport Association. • Annual. $180.00.

TRADE/PROFESSIONAL ASSOCIATIONS

Aeronautical Repair Station Association. 121 N. Henry St., Alexandria, VA 22314. Phone: (703)739-9543 Fax: (703)739-9488 E-mail: arsa@arsa.org • URL: http://www.arsa.org.

Air Line Pilots Association International. 535 Herndon Parkway, Herndon, VA 20170. Phone: (703)689-2270 Fax: (703)689-4370 • URL: http://www.alpa.org.

Air Transport Association of America. 1301 Pennsylvania Ave., Suite 1100, Washington, DC 20004-7017. Phone: (202)626-4000 Fax: (202)626-4166 E-mail: ata@air-transport.org • URL: http://www.air-transport.org.

International Air Transport Association. P.O. Box 113, Montreal, QC, Canada H42 1M1. Phone: (514)874-0202 Fax: (514)874-9632 • URL: http://www.iata.org.

International Airline Passengers Association. P.O. Box 700188, Dallas, TX 75370. Phone: 800-821-4272 or (904)404-9980 Fax: (972)233-5348 E-mail: iapa@iapauia.com • URL: http://www.iapa.com.

National Air Carrier Association. 1730 M St., N.W., Suite 806, Washington, DC 20036. Phone: (202)833-8200 Fax: (202)659-9479 • Charter airlines.

National Air Transportation Association. 4226 King St., Alexandria, VA 22302. Phone: 800-808-6282 or (703)845-9000 Fax: (703)845-8176 • URL: http://www.nata-online.org.

Regional Airline Association. 1200 19th St., N.W., Suite 300, Washington, DC 20036-2422. Phone: (202)857-1170 Fax: (202)429-5113 E-mail: raa@dc.sba.com • URL: http://www.raa.org • Scheduled commuter air carriers.

OTHER SOURCES

Aviation Law Reports. CCH, Inc. • $2,419.00 per year. Four looseleaf volumes. Semimonthly updates.

AIRLINES TIME TABLES

See: TIMETABLES

AIRPLANE ELECTRONICS

See: AVIONICS

AIRPLANE INDUSTRY

See also: AEROSPACE INDUSTRY; AVIATION INDUSTRY

ABSTRACTS AND INDEXES

Applied Science and Technology Index. H. W. Wilson Co. • 11 times a year. Quarterly and annual cumulations. Service basis for print edition; CD-ROM edition, $1,495.00 per year. Indexes a wide variety of English language technical, industrial, and engineering periodicals.

Business Periodicals Index. H. W. Wilson Co. • Monthly, except August, with quarterly and annual cumulations. Service basis for print edition; CD-ROM edition, $1,495.00 per year.

Science Citation Index. Institute for Scientific Information. • Bimonthly. $15,020.00 per year. Annual cumulation. Includes *Source Index, Citation Index, Permuterm Subject Index,* and *Corporate Index.*

DIRECTORIES

Aviation Buyer's Directory. Air Service Directory, Inc. • Quarterly. $45.00 per year. Lists aircraft for sale and sources of parts and supplies.

International ABC Aerospace Directory. Janes's Information Group. • 1998. $500.00. 28,000 aviation aerospace manufacturers, airlines, associations, government agencies, etc. Formerly *Interavia ABC Aerospace Directory.*

World Aviation Directory. McGraw-Hill Aviation Week Group. • Semiannual. $225.00 per year. Two volumes. Lists aviation, aerospace, and missile manufacturers. Includes *World Aviation Directory Buyer's Guide.*

ENCYCLOPEDIAS AND DICTIONARIES

Dictionary of Aviation. R. J. Hall and R. D. Campbell. Available from St. James Press. • 1991. $50.00. Published by Blackwell Scientific. Includes aeronautical words, phrases, acronyms, and abbreviations.

FINANCIAL RATIOS

Almanac of Business and Industrial Financial Ratios. Leo Troy. Prentice Hall. • Annual. $99.95. Contains financial ratios derived from federal tax returns. Ratios for each of about 200 industries are arranged according to company asset size.

Annual Statement Studies. Robert Morris Associates: The Association of Lending and Credit Risk Professiona. • Annual. Free to members; non-members, $140.00. Median and quartile financial ratios are given for over 400 kinds of manufacturing, wholesale, retail, construction, and consumer finance establishments. Data is sorted by both asset size and sales volume. Includes a clearly written "Definition of Ratios" and an alphabetical industry index.

Industry Norms and Key Business Ratios. Desk Top Edition. Dun and Bradstreet Corp., Business Information Services. • Annual. Five volumes. $475.00 per volume. $1,890.00 per set. Covers over 800 kinds of businesses, arranged by Standard Industrial Classification number. More detailed editions covering longer periods of time are also available.

HANDBOOKS AND MANUALS

A Field Guide to Airplanes of North America. M. R. Montgomery. Houghton Mifflin Co. • 1992. $12.95. Looseleaf service.

INTERNET DATABASES

Fedstats. Federal Interagency Council on Statistical Policy. Phone: (202)395-7254 • URL: http://www.fedstats.gov • Web site features an efficient search facility for full-text statistics produced by more than 70 federal agencies, including the Census Bureau, the Bureau of Economic Analysis, and the Bureau of Labor Statistics. Boolean searches can be made within one agency or for all agencies combined. Links are offered to international statistical bureaus, including the UN, IMF, OECD, UNESCO, Eurostat, and 20 individual countries. Fees: Free.

ONLINE DATABASES

ABI/INFORM. Bell & Howell Information and Learning. • Provides online indexing to business-related material occurring in over 1,000 periodicals from 1971 to the present. Inquire as to online cost and availability.

Aerospace/Defense Markets and Technology. The Gale Group. • Abstracts of commerical aerospace/defense related literature, 1982 to date. Also includes information about major defense contracts awarded by the U. S. Department of Defense. International coverage. Inquire as to online cost and availability.

DRI U.S. Central Database. Data Products Division. • Provides more than 23,000 business, financial, demographic, economic, foreign trade, and industry-related time series for the U.S. Includes national income, population, retail-wholesale trade, price indexes, labor data, housing, industrial production, banking, interest rates, money supply, etc. Time period is generally 1947 to date (some data back to 1929). Updating varies. Inquire as to online cost and availability.

Globalbase. The Gale Group. • Provides more than one million online summaries of business, industrial, and economic news reports from more than 1,000 publications worldwide. Covers a wide range of material appearing in international trade journals, professional magazines, and newspapers. Time period is 1984 to date, with weekly updates. Inquire as to online cost and availability.

Management Contents. The Gale Group. • Covers a wide range of management, financial, marketing, personnel, and administrative topics. About 150 leading business journals are indexed and abstracted from 1974 to date, with monthly updating. Inquire as to online cost and availability.

PROMT: Predicasts Overview of Markets and Technology. The Gale Group. • Companies, products, applied technologies and markets. U.S. and international literature coverage, 1972 to date. Inquire as to online cost and availability. Provides abstracts from more than 1,600 publications. Weekly updates.

Scisearch. Institute for Scientific Information. • Broad, multidisciplinary index to the literature of science and technology, 1974 to present. Inquire as to online cost and availability. Coverage of literature is worldwide, with weekly updates.

Trade & Industry Index. The Gale Group. • Provides indexing of business periodicals, January 1981 to date. Daily updates. (Full text articles from some periodicals are available online, 1983 to date, in the companion database, *Trade & Industry ASAP.*) Inquire as to online cost and availability.

PERIODICALS AND NEWSLETTERS

A/C Flyer: Best Read Resale Magazine Worldwide. McGraw-Hill. • Monthly. $28.00 per year. Lists used airplanes for sale by dealers, brokers, and private owners. Provides news and trends relating to the aircraft resale industry. Special issues include "Product & Service Buyer's Guide" and "Dealer/Broker Directory.".

Aerospace America. American Institute of Aeronautics and Astronautics, Inc. • Monthly. Free to members; non-members, $75.00 per year. Provides coverage of key issues affecting the aerospace field.

Aerospace Engineering Magazine. Society of Automotive Engineers. • Monthly. $66.00 per year. Provides technical information that can be used in the design of new and improved aerospace systems.

Air Market News. General Publications Co. • Bimonthly. Free to qualified personnel. Subject matter is news of aircraft products and services.

Aviation Maintenance. Phillips Business Information, Inc. • Monthly. Free to qualified personnel. Formerly *Aviation Equipment Maintenance.*

Aviation Week and Space Technology. McGraw-Hill Aviation Week Group. • Monthly. $89.00 per year.

Flight International. Reed Business Information. • Weekly. $170.00 per year. Technical aerospace coverage.

Flying. Hachette Filipacchi Magazines, Inc. • Monthly. $26.00 per year.

Journal of Aircraft: Devoted to Aeronautical Science and Technology. American Institute of Aeronautics and Astronautics, Inc. • Bimonthly. Members, $50.00 per year; non-members, $175.00 per year; institutions, $350.00 per year.

Trade-a-Plane. • 36 times a year. $98.00 per year. Subject matter is aircraft for sale or trade.

RESEARCH CENTERS AND INSTITUTES

Center for Aeromechanics Research. University of Texas at Austin. Aerospace Engineering & Engineering Mechanics, WRW Room 220, Austin, TX 78712-1085. Phone: (512)471-5962 Fax: (512)471-3788 E-mail: varghese@mail.utexas.edu • URL: http://www.ae.utexas.edu/research/car/.

Ohio Aerospace Institute. 22800 Cedar Point Rd., Cleveland, OH 44142. Phone: (440)962-3000 Fax: (440)962-3120 E-mail: michaelsalkind@oai.org • URL: http://www.oai.org • Aerospace-related research, education, and technology transfers.

STATISTICS SOURCES

Aerospace Facts and Figures. Aerospace Industries Association of America. • Annual. $35.00. Includes financial data for the aerospace industries.

Annual Survey of Manufactures. Available from U. S. Government Printing Office. • Annual. Prices vary. Issued by the U. S. Census Bureau as an interim update to the *Census of Manufactures.* Includes data on number of manufacturing establishments in various industries, employment, labor costs, value of shipments, capital expenditures, inventories, energy costs, and assets. (See also Census Bureau home page, http://www.census.gov/.).

Business Statistics of the United States. Courtenay M. Slater, editor. Bernan Associates. • 1999. $74.00. Fifth edition. Based on *Business Statistics,* formerly issue by the Bureau of Economic Analysis, U. S. Department of Commerce. Provides basic data for a wide variety of U. S. industries, services, and economic indicators. Most statistics are shown annually for 29 years and monthly for the most recent four years.

FAA Statistical Handbook of Aviation. Federal Aviation Administration. Available from U. S. Government Printing Office. • Annual.

Manufacturing Profiles. Available from U. S. Government Printing Office. • Annual. Issued by the U. S. Census Bureau. A printed consolidation of the entire *Current Industrial Report* series, presenting "all the data compiled." Contains statistics on production, shipments, inventories, consumption, exports, imports, and orders for a wide variety of manufactured products. (See also Census Bureau home page, http://www.census.gov/.).

Standard & Poor's Statistical Service. Current Statistics. Standard & Poor's. • Monthly. $688.00 per year. Includes 10 *Basic Statistics* sections, *Current Statistics Supplements* and *Annual Security Price Index Record.*

Survey of Current Business. Available from U. S. Government Printing Office. • Monthly. $49.00 per year. Issued by Bureau of Economic Analysis, U. S. Department of Commerce. Presents a wide variety of business and economic data.

WEFA Industrial Monitor. John Wiley and Sons, Inc. • Annual. $65.00. Prepared by industry analysts at WEFA, an economic forecasting and consulting firm (originally Wharton Econometric Forecasting Associates). Contains discussions of the outlook for major U. S. industries, with many 10-year forecasts (WEFA Web site is http://www.wefa.com).

TRADE/PROFESSIONAL ASSOCIATIONS

Aeronautical Repair Station Association. 121 N. Henry St., Alexandria, VA 22314. Phone: (703)739-9543 Fax: (703)739-9488 E-mail: arsa@arsa.org • URL: http://www.arsa.org.

Aerospace Industries Association of America. 1250 Eye St., N.W., Washington, DC 20005. Phone: (202)371-8400 Fax: (202)371-8470 E-mail: aia@aia-aerospace.org • URL: http://www.aia-aerospace.org.

American Institute of Aeronautics and Astronautics. 1801 Alexander Bell Dr., Suite 500, c/o Michael Lewis, Reston, VA 20191-4344. Phone: 800-639-2422 or (703)264-7500 Fax: (703)264-7551 E-mail: customerserv@aiaa.org • URL: http://www.aiaa.org.

Flight Safety Foundation. 601 Madison St., Suite 300, Alexandria, VA 22314. Phone: (703)739-6700 Fax: (703)739-6708 • URL: http://www.flightsafety.org.

General Aviation Manufacturers Association. 1400 K St., N.W., Suite 801, Washington, DC 20005. Phone: (202)393-1500 Fax: (202)842-4063 • URL: http://www.generalaviation.org.

National Business Aviation Association. 1200 18th St., N.W., Suite 400, Washington, DC 20036. Phone: (202)783-9000 Fax: (202)331-8364 E-mail: info@nba.org • URL: http://www.nbaa.org.

OTHER SOURCES

Aerospace America [online]. American Institute of Aeronautics and Astronautics. • Provides complete text of the periodical, *Aerospace America*, 1984 to date, with monthly updates. Also includes news from the *AIAA Bulletin*. Inquire as to online cost and availability.

Aerospace Database. American Institute of Aeronautics and Astronautics. • Contains abstracts of literature covering all aspects of the aerospace and aircraft in series 1983 to date. Semimonthly updates. Inquire as to online cost and availability.

Aviation Law Reports. CCH, Inc. • $2,419.00 per year. Four looseleaf volumes. Semimonthly updates.

Jane's All the World's Aircraft. Jane's Information Group, Inc. • Annual. $300.00; CD-Rom edition, $425.00.

AIRPLANES, BUSINESS

See: BUSINESS AVIATION

AIRPORTS

ABSTRACTS AND INDEXES

Business Periodicals Index. H. W. Wilson Co. • Monthly, except August, with quarterly and annual cumulations. Service basis for print edition; CD-ROM edition, $1,495.00 per year.

Current Literature in Traffic and Transportation. Northwestern University, Transportation Library. • Quarterly. $25.00 per year.

DIRECTORIES

Airport/Facility Directory. U. S. National Ocean Service. • Bimonthly. $140.00 per year, complete. Issued in seven regional volumes (single region, $20.00 per year). Provides detailed non-military airport information for pilots, including control center and navigational data.

Airports USA. Aircraft Owners and Pilots Association. • Annual. $24.95. Primarily for pilots.

Jane's Air Traffic Control. Jane's Information Group. • Annual. $350.00; CD-Rom edition, $650.00. International coverage of equipment and supplies for both civil and military airports. Formerly *Jane's Airport and ATC Equipment.*

OAG Business Travel Planner: North America. Cahners Travel Group. • Quarterly. $149.00 per year. Arranged according to more than 14,700 destinations in the U. S., Canada, Mexico, and the Caribbean. Lists more than 32,000 hotels, with AAA ratings where available. Provides information on airports, ground transportation, coming events, and climate.

OAG Travel Planner: Asia Pacific. Cahners Travel Group. • Quarterly. $130.00 per year. Arranged according to more than 5,000 destinations throughout Asia and the Pacific. Lists about 5,000 hotels, with information on airports, ground transportation, coming events, and climate.

OAG Travel Planner: Europe. Cahners Travel Group. • Quarterly. $130.00 per year. Arranged according to more than 13,850 destinations in Europe. Lists more than 14,700 hotels, with information on airports, ground transportation, coming events, and climate.

Professional Pilot-FBO Directory. Queensmith Communications Corp. • Annual. $8.00. Includes information for about 1,500 airports and fixed-base operators.

World Aviation Directory. McGraw-Hill Aviation Week Group. • Semiannual. $225.00 per year. Two volumes. Lists aviation, aerospace, and missile manufacturers. Includes *World Aviation Directory Buyer's Guide.*

FINANCIAL RATIOS

Annual Statement Studies. Robert Morris Associates: The Association of Lending and Credit Risk Professiona. • Annual. Free to members; non-members, $140.00. Median and quartile financial ratios are given for over 400 kinds of manufacturing, wholesale, retail, construction, and consumer finance establishments. Data is sorted by both asset size and sales volume. Includes a clearly written "Definition of Ratios" and an alphabetical industry index.

ONLINE DATABASES

ABI/INFORM. Bell & Howell Information and Learning. • Provides online indexing to business-related material occurring in over 1,000 periodicals from 1971 to the present. Inquire as to online cost and availability.

Management Contents. The Gale Group. • Covers a wide range of management, financial, marketing, personnel, and administrative topics. About 150 leading business journals are indexed and abstracted from 1974 to date, with monthly updating. Inquire as to online cost and availability.

PAIS International. Public Affairs Information Service, Inc. • Corresponds to the former printed publications, *PAIS Bulletin* (1976-90) and *PAIS Foreign Language Index* (1972-90), and to the current *PAIS International in Print* (1991 to date). Covers economic, political, and sociological material appearing in periodicals, books, government documents, and other publications. Updating is monthly. Inquire as to online cost and availability.

Trade & Industry Index. The Gale Group. • Provides indexing of business periodicals, January 1981 to date. Daily updates. (Full text articles from some periodicals are available online, 1983 to date, in the companion database, *Trade & Industry ASAP.*) Inquire as to online cost and availability.

PERIODICALS AND NEWSLETTERS

Airport Business. Cygnus Publishing, Inc., Johnson Hill Press. • Nine times a year. $54.00 per year.

Airport Press. • Monthly. $32.00 per year.

Aviation Week and Space Technology. McGraw-Hill Aviation Week Group. • Monthly. $89.00 per year.

Jane's Airport Review: The Global Airport Business Magazine. Jane's Information Group, Inc. • 10 times a year. $170.00 per year. CD-Rom edition, $1,075.00 per year. Edited for airport managers. Covers all aspects of airport operations.

STATISTICS SOURCES

Airport Activity Statistics of Certificated Route Air Carriers. U. S. Department of Transportation. Available from U. S. Government Printing Office. • Annual $47.00.

FAA Aviation Forecasts. Federal Aviation Administration. Available from U. S. Government Printing Office. • Annual. $15.00.

FAA Statistical Handbook of Aviation. Federal Aviation Administration. Available from U. S. Government Printing Office. • Annual.

TRADE/PROFESSIONAL ASSOCIATIONS

Air Transport Association of America. 1301 Pennsylvania Ave., Suite 1100, Washington, DC 20004-7017. Phone: (202)626-4000 Fax: (202)626-4166 E-mail: ata@air-transport.org • URL: http://www.air-transport.org.

Airports Council International - North America. 1775 K St., N.W., No. 500, Washington, DC 20006. Phone: (202)293-8500 Fax: (202)331-1362 • URL: http://www.aci-na.org.

American Association of Airport Executives. 601 Madison St., Alexandria, VA 22314. Phone: (703)824-0500 Fax: (703)820-1395 E-mail: member.services@airportnet.org • URL: http://www.airportnet.org.

International Air Transport Association. P.O. Box 113, Montreal, QC, Canada H42 1M1. Phone: (514)874-0202 Fax: (514)874-9632 • URL: http://www.iata.org.

National Air Transportation Association. 4226 King St., Alexandria, VA 22302. Phone: 800-808-6282 or (703)845-9000 Fax: (703)845-8176 • URL: http://www.nata-online.org.

ALARMS

See: ELECTRONIC SECURITY SYSTEMS

ALCOHOL AS FUEL

See: FUEL

ALCOHOLIC BEVERAGES

See: DISTILLING INDUSTRY

ALCOHOLISM

See also: DRUG ABUSE AND TRAFFIC

GENERAL WORKS

Alcoholism: Causes, Effect and Treatment. Joseph F. Perez. Accelerated Development. • 1992. $23.95. Third edition.

The Facts About Drug Use: Coping with Drugs and Alcohol in Your Family, at Work, in Your Community. Barry Stimmel, editor. The Haworth Press, Inc. • 1992. $14.95. A comprehensive overview of drug dependence, including alcoholism.

ABSTRACTS AND INDEXES

Alcoholism Digest Annual. Information Planning Associates, Inc. • Annual. Price on application.

Excerpta Medica: Drug Dependence, Alcohol Abuse, and Alcoholism. Elsevier Science. • Bimonthly. $1,079.00 per year. Section 40 of *Excerpta Medica.*

Psychological Abstracts. American Psychological Association. • Monthly. Members, $799.00 per year; individuals and institutions, $1,075.00 per year. Covers the international literature of psychology and the behavioral sciences. Includes journals, technical reports, dissertations, and other sources.

BIBLIOGRAPHIES

Alcohol Education Materials: An Annotated Bibliography. Gail Gleason Milgram. Rutgers Center of Alcohol Studies Publications. • 1981. $70.00. Five volumes, 1950-1981. Volumes 1 and 2, $20.00 per volume; volumes 3, 4, and 5, $10.00 per volume. Price on application.

International Bibliography of Studies on Alcohol. Sarah S. Jordy, compiler. Rutgers Center of Alcohol Studies Publications. • 1966-1974. $250.00. Three volumes. Volume one, *References*, 1901-1950; volume two, *Indexes.* 1901-1980; volume three, *References* and *Indexes*, 1951-1960.

Social and Behavioral Aspects of Female Alcoholism: An Annotated Bibliography. H. Paul Chalfant and Brent S. Roper, compliers. Greenwood Publishing Group, Inc. • 1980. $55.00.

CD-ROM DATABASES

Health Reference Center. The Gale Group. • Monthly. Provides CD-ROM citations, abstracts, and selected full-text articles on many health-related subjects. Includes references to medical journals, general periodicals, newsletters, newspapers, pamphlets, and medical reference books.

Magazine Index Plus. The Gale Group. • Monthly. $4,000.00 per year (includes InfoTrac workstation). Provides full text on CD-ROM for about 100 popular, general interest magazines and indexing for 300 others. Includes special indexing of reviews and product evaluations. Time period is 1980 to date.

DIRECTORIES

National Directory of Drug Abuse and Alcoholism Treatment Programs. Substance Abuse and Mental Health Services Administration. • Annual. Free. Lists 10,000 federal, state, local, and privately funded agencies administering or providing drug abuse and alcoholism treatment services.

ENCYCLOPEDIAS AND DICTIONARIES

Encyclopedia of Drugs, Alcohol, and Addictive Behavior. Available from The Gale Group. • 2001. $425.00. Second edition. Four volumes. Published by Macmillan Reference USA. Covers the social, economic, political, and medical aspects of addiction.

HANDBOOKS AND MANUALS

Drug Abuse Handbook. Steven B. Karch, editor. CRC Press, Inc. • 1997. $99.95. Provides comprehensive coverage of drug abuse issues and trends. Edited for healthcare professionals.

Handbook of Drug and Alcohol Abuse. F. Hofman and others. Oxford University Press, Inc. • 1992. $27.95. Third edition.

Substance Abuse: A Comprehensive Textbook. Joyce H. Lowinson and others. Lippincott Williams & Wilkins. • 1997. $155.00. Third edition. Covers the medical, psychological, socioeconomic, and public health aspects of drug and alcohol abuse.

ONLINE DATABASES

Embase. Elsevier Science, Inc. • Worldwide medical literature, 1974 to present. Weekly updates. Inquire as to online cost and availability.

Information Bank Abstracts. New York Times Index Dept. • Provides indexing and abstracting of current affairs, primarily from the final late edition of *The New York Times* and the Eastern edition of *The Wall Street Journal.* Time period is 1969 to present, with daily updates. Inquire as to online cost and availability.

Mental Health Abstracts. IFI/Plenum Data Corp. • Provides indexing and abstracting of mental health and mental illness literature appearing in more than 1,200 journals and other sources from 1969 to date. Monthly updates. Inquire as to online cost and availability.

PsycINFO. American Psychological Association. • Provides indexing and abstracting of the worldwide literature of psychology and the behavioral sciences. Time period is 1967 to date, with monthly updates. Inquire as to online cost and availability.

PERIODICALS AND NEWSLETTERS

Addiction Research Foundation Journal: Addiction News for Professionals. Addiction Research Foundation of Ontario, Subscription-Marketing Dept. • Six times a year. $19.00 per year. News and opinions from the drug and alcohol field around th world. Formerly *Alcoholism and Drug Addiction Research Foundation Journal.*

Alcohol Research and Health. Available from U. S. Government Printing Office. • Quarterly. $22.00 per year. Issued by the National Institute on Alcohol Abuse and Alcoholism. Presents alcohol-related research findings and descriptions of alcoholism prevention and treatment programs.

Alcoholism: Clinical and Experimental Research. Research Society on Alcoholism. Williams & Wilkins Co. • Monthly. Individuals, $251.00 per year; institutions, $484.00 per year.

Alcoholism Treatment Quarterly: The Practitioner's Quarterly for Individual, Group, and Family Therapy. Haworth Press, Inc. • Quarterly. Individuals, $50.00 per year; institutions, $120.00 per year; libraries, $350.00 per year. Edited for professionals working with alcoholics and their families. Formerly *Alcoholism Counseling and Treatment.*

American Journal of Drug and Alcohol Abuse. Marcel Dekker Journals. • Quarterly. $750.00 per year.

Drug and Alcohol Abuse Education. Editorial Resources, Inc. • Monthly. $84.00 per year. Newsletter covering education, prevention, and treatment relating to abuse of drugs and alcohol.

Drugs and Society: A Journal of Contemporary Issues. Haworth Press, Inc. • Quarterly. Individuals, $42.00 per year; institutions, $90.00 per year;libraries, $200.00 per year. Edited for researchers and practitioners. Covers various areas of susbstance abuse, including alcoholism.

Employee Assistance Quarterly. Haworth Press, Inc. • Quarterly. Individuals, $40.00 per year; institutions. $80.00 per year; libraries, $375.00 per year. An academic and practical journal focusing on employee alcoholism and mental health problems. Formerly *Labor-Management Alcoholism Journal.*

Journal of Studies on Alcohol. Rutgers Center of Alcohol Studies. Alcohol Research Documentation, Inc. • Bimonthly. Individuals, $140.00 per year; institutions, $175.00 per year.

Professional Counselor Magazine: Serving the Mental Health and Addictions Fields. Health Communications, Inc. • Bimonthly. $26.00 per year. Covers both clinical and societal aspects of substance abuse.

Workplace Substance Abuse Advisor. LRP Publications. • Biweekly. $377.00 per year. Newsletter. Covers federal and local laws relating to alcohol and drug use and testing. Provides information on employee assistance plans. Formerly *National Report on Substance Abuse.*

RESEARCH CENTERS AND INSTITUTES

Mental Sciences Institute. University of Texas Houston Health Science Center. 1300 Moursund Ave., Houston, TX 77030. Phone: (713)500-2500 Fax: (713)500-2553 E-mail: robert.w.guynn@uth.tmc.edu • URL: http://www.msi.uth.tmc.edu.

Research Institute on Addictions. State University of New York at Buffalo, 1021 Main St., Buffalo, NY 14203-1016. Phone: (716)887-2566 Fax: (716)887-2252 E-mail: connors@ria.org • URL: http://www.ria.org/.

STATISTICS SOURCES

Statistics on Alcohol, Drug, and Tobacco Use: A Selection of Statistical Charts, Graphs and Tables about Alcohol, Drug and Tobacco Use from a Variety of Published Sources with Explanatory Comments. The Gale Group. • 1995. $65.00. Includes graphs, charts, and tables arranged within subject chapters. Citations to data sources are provided.

TRADE/PROFESSIONAL ASSOCIATIONS

Al-Anon Family Group Headquarters, World Service Office. 1600 Corporate Landing Pkwy., Virginia Beach, VA 23454-5617. Phone: 888-425-2666 or (757)563-1600 Fax: (757)563-1655 E-mail: wso@al-anon.org • URL: http://www.al-anon.alateen.org.

Alcoholics Anonymous World Services. Grand Central Station, P.O. Box 459, New York, NY 10163. Phone: (212)870-3400 Fax: (212)870-3003 E-mail: http://www.aa.org.

American Council on Alcohol Problems. 2376 Lakeside Dr., Birmingham, AL 35244. Phone: (205)985-9062 Fax: (205)985-9015.

International Health and Temperance Association. 12501 Old Columbia Pike, Silver Spring, MD 20904. Phone: (301)680-6719 Fax: (301)680-6707 E-mail: 74617.2242@compuserve.com.

National Council on Alcoholism and Drug Dependence. 12 W. 21st St., New York, NY 10010. Phone: 800-622-2255 or (212)206-6770 Fax: (212)645-1690 E-mail: national@ncadd.org • URL: http://www.ncadd.org.

ALKALI INDUSTRY

See also: POTASH INDUSTRY

DIRECTORIES

OPD Chemical Buyers Directory. Schnell Publishing Co., Inc. • Annual. $129.00. Included in subscription to *Chemical Marketing Reporter.* About 1,500 suppliers of chemical process materials and more than 300 companies which transport and store chemicals in the U.S.

ONLINE DATABASES

CA Search. Chemical Abstracts Service. • Guide to chemical literature, 1967 to present. Inquire as to online cost and availability.

F & S Index. The Gale Group. • Contains about four million citations to worldwide business, financial, and industrial or consumer product literature appearing from 1972 to date. Weekly updates. Inquire as to online cost and availability.

PERIODICALS AND NEWSLETTERS

Better Crops With Plant Food. Potash and Phosphate Institute. • Quarterly. $8.00.

PRICE SOURCES

Chemical Market Reporter. Schnell Publishing Co., Inc. • Weekly. $139.00 per year. Quotes current prices for a wide range of chemicals. Formerly *Chemical Marketing Reporter.*

STATISTICS SOURCES

Minerals Yearbook. Available from U.S. Government Printing Office. • Annual. Three volumes.

TRADE/PROFESSIONAL ASSOCIATIONS

Potash and Phosphate Institute. 655 Engineering Dr., No. 110, Norcross, GA 30092. Phone: (770)447-0335 Fax: (770)448-0439 E-mail: ppi@ppi-far.org • URL: http://www.ppi-far.org.

ALLOYS

See: METAL INDUSTRY

ALUMINUM FOIL

See: ALUMINUM INDUSTRY

ALUMINUM INDUSTRY

ABSTRACTS AND INDEXES

Aluminum Industry Abstracts: A Monthly Review of the World's Technical Literature on Aluminum. Aluminum Association. • Monthly. $595.00 per year. Formerly*World Aluminum Abstracts.*

Nonferrous Metals Alert. Cambridge Information Group. • Monthly. $340.00 per year. Provides citations to the business and industrial literature of nonferrous metals. (Materials Business Information Series).

ALMANACS AND YEARBOOKS

CRB Commodity Yearbook. Commodity Research Bureau. CRB. • Annual. $99.95.

CD-ROM DATABASES

METADEX Materials Collection: Metals-Polymers-Ceramics. Cambridge Scientific Abstracts. • Quarterly. $6,950.00 per year. Provides CD-ROM citations to the worldwide literature of materials science and metallurgy. Corresponds to *Metals Abstracts, Alloys Index, Steels Alert, Nonferrous Alert, Polymers/Ceramics/Composites Alert,* and *Engineered Materials Abstracts.* (Formerly produced by ASM International.).

DIRECTORIES

Dun's Industrial Guide: The Metalworking Directory. Dun and Bradstreet Information Services Dun & Bradstreet Corp. • Annual. Libraries, $485; commercial institutions, $795.00. Lease basis. Three volumes. Lists about 65,000 U. S. manufacturing plants using metal and suppliers of metalworking equipment and materials. Includes names and titles of key personnel. Products, purchases, and processes are indicated.

ONLINE DATABASES

F & S Index. The Gale Group. • Contains about four million citations to worldwide business, financial, and industrial or consumer product literature appearing from 1972 to date. Weekly updates. Inquire as to online cost and availability.

Materials Business File. Cambridge Scientific Abstracts. • Provides online abstracts and citations to worldwide materials literature, covering the business and industrial aspects of metals, plastics, ceramics, and composites. Corresponds to *Steels Alert, Nonferrous Metals Alert,* and *Polymers/Ceramics/Composites Alert.* Time period is 1985 to date, with monthly updates. (Formerly produced by ASM International.) Inquire as to online cost and availability.

METADEX. Cambridge Scientific Abstracts. • Covers the worldwide literature of metals, metallurgy, and materials science, 1966 to date. Includes detailed alloys indexing from 1974. Biweekly updating. Inquire as to online cost and availability. (Formerly produced by ASM International.).

PERIODICALS AND NEWSLETTERS

Engineering and Mining Journal (E&MJ). Intertec Publishing Corp. • Monthly. $69.00 per year.

Light Metal Age. Fellom Publishing Co. • Bimonthly. $40.00 per year. Edited for production and engineering executives of the aluminum industry and other nonferrous light metal industries.

Metal Center News. Hitchcock Publishing. • 13 times a year. $89.00 per year.

New Steel: Mini and Integrated Mill Management and Technologies. Cahners Business Information. • Monthly. $89.00 per year. Covers the primary metals industry, both ferrous and nonferrous. Includes technical, marketing, and product development articles. Formerly *Iron Age.*

33 Metalproducing: For Primary Producers of Steel, Aluminum, and Copper-Base Alloys. Penton Media, Inc. • Monthly. $65.00 per year. Covers metal production technology and methods and industry news. Includes a bimonthly *Nonferrous Supplement.*

PRICE SOURCES

Chemical and Engineering News: The Newsmagazine of the Chemical World. American Chemical Society. • Weekly. Institutions, $181.00 per year; others, price on application.

Chemical Market Reporter. Schnell Publishing Co., Inc. • Weekly. $139.00 per year. Quotes current prices for a wide range of chemicals. Formerly *Chemical Marketing Reporter.*

Metals Week. McGraw-Hill Commodity Services Group. • Weekly. $770.00 per year.

STATISTICS SOURCES

Aluminum Standards and Data. Aluminum Association Inc. • Biennial. $25.00.

Aluminum Statistical Review. Aluminum Association Inc. • Annual. $50.00.

Annual Survey of Manufactures. Available from U. S. Government Printing Office. • Annual. Prices vary. Issued by the U. S. Census Bureau as an interim update to the *Census of Manufactures.* Includes data on number of manufacturing establishments in various industries, employment, labor costs, value of shipments, capital expenditures, inventories, energy costs, and assets. (See also Census Bureau home page, http://www.census.gov/.).

Manufacturing Profiles. Available from U. S. Government Printing Office. • Annual. Issued by the U. S. Census Bureau. A printed consolidation of the entire *Current Industrial Report* series, presenting "all the data compiled." Contains statistics on production, shipments, inventories, consumption, exports, imports, and orders for a wide variety of manufactured products. (See also Census Bureau home page, http://www.census.gov/.).

Metal Statistics. Cahners Business Information. • Annual. $250.00. Provides statistical data on a wide variety of metals, metal products, ores, alloys, and scrap metal. Includes data on prices, production, consumption, shipments, imports, and exports.

Mineral Commodity Summaries. Available from U. S. Government Printing Office. • Annual. Published by the U. S. Geological Survey, Department of the Interior (http://www.usgs.gov). Contains detailed, five-year data for about 90 nonfuel minerals. Covers a wide range of statistics, including production, imports, exports, consumption, reserves, prices, tariff information, and industry employment. (Two pages are devoted to each mineral.).

Minerals Yearbook. Available from U.S. Government Printing Office. • Annual. Three volumes.

Standard & Poor's Industry Surveys. Standard & Poor's. • Semiannual. $1,800.00. Two looseleaf volumes. Includes monthly supplements. Provides detailed, individual surveys of 52 major industry groups. Each survey is revised on a semiannual basis. Also includes "Monthly Investment Review" (industry group investment analysis) and monthly "Trends & Projections" (economic analysis).

U. S. Industry and Trade Outlook: The McGraw-Hill Companies and the U.S. Department of Commerce/International Trade Administration. Datapso Research Corp. • Annual. $69.95. Produced by the International Trade Administration, U. S. Department of Commerce, in a "public-private" partnership with DRI/McGraw-Hill and Standard & Poor's. Provides basic data, outlook for the current year, and "Long-Term Prospects" (five-year projections) for a wide variety of products and services. Includes high technology industries. Formerly *U. S. Industrial Outlook.*

United States Census of Mineral Industries. Bureau of the Census, U.S. Department of Commerce. Available from U.S. Government Printing Office. • Quinquennial.

WEFA Industrial Monitor. John Wiley and Sons, Inc. • Annual. $65.00. Prepared by industry analysts at WEFA, an economic forecasting and consulting firm (originally Wharton Econometric Forecasting Associates). Contains discussions of the outlook for major U. S. industries, with many 10-year forecasts (WEFA Web site is http://www.wefa.com).

TRADE/PROFESSIONAL ASSOCIATIONS

Aluminum Association. 900 19th St., N.W., Suite 300, Washington, DC 20006. Phone: (202)862-5100 Fax: (202)862-5164 • URL: http://www.aluminum.org.

Aluminum Extruders Council. 1000 N. Rand Rd., Suite 214, Wauconda, IL 60084. Phone: (847)526-2010 Fax: (847)526-3993 E-mail: mail@aec.org • URL: http://www.aec.org.

American Architectural Manufacturers Association. 1827 Walden Office Square, Suite 104, Schamburg, IL 60173. Phone: (847)303-5664 Fax: (847)303-5774 E-mail: webmaster@aamanet.org • URL: http://www.aamanet.org • Members are manufacturers of a wide variety of architectural products. Includes a Residential/Commercial Window and Door Committee.

National Association of Aluminum Distributors. 1900 Arch St., Philadelphia, PA 19103-1498. Phone: (215)564-3484 Fax: (215)963-9784 E-mail: naad@fernley.com • URL: http://www.naad.org.

AMERICAN STOCK EXCHANGE

See: STOCK EXCHANGES

AMUSEMENT INDUSTRY

See also: CONCESSIONS; FAIRS; MOTION PICTURE INDUSTRY; RADIO BROADCASTING INDUSTRY; RECREATION INDUSTRY; SHOW BUSINESS; TELEVISION BROADCASTING INDUSTRY

ABSTRACTS AND INDEXES

IMM Abstracts and Index: A Survey of World Literature on the Economic Geology and Mining of All Minerals (Except Coal), Mineral Processing, and Nonferrous Extraction Metallurgy. Institution of Mining and Metallurgy. • Bimonthly. Members, $142.00 per year; non-members, $215.00 per year. Provides international coverage of the literature of mining and nonferrous metallurgy. Includes mineral economics, tunnelling, and rock mechanics.

BIBLIOGRAPHIES

The Influence of Disney Entertainment Parks on Architecture and Development. Stephen J. Rebori. Sage Publications, Inc. • 1995. $10.00. (CPL-Bibliographies Series, vol. 321).

DIRECTORIES

Cavalcade of Acts and Attractions. BPI Communications, Amusement Business Div. • Annual. $92.00. Directory of personal appearance artists, touring shows and other specialized entertainment. Lists promoters, producers, managers and booking agents.

Directory of Funparks and Attractions: International Guide to Amusement Parks, Family Entertainment Centers, Waterparks, and Attractions. BPI Communications, Amusement Business Div. • Annual. $60.00. Over 2,100, amusement parks, theme parks, family entertainment centers, water parks, zoos, kiddielands and other tourist attractions in U.S., Canada and overseas. Formerly *Amusement Business Directory of Funparks and Attractions.*

Directory of North American Fairs, Festivals and Expositions. BPI Communications, Amusement Business Div. • Annual. $65.00. Lists over 5,000 fairs, festivals and expositions in the U.S. and Canada which run three days or more. Formerly *Calvacade and Directory of Fairs.*

Grey House Performing Arts Directory. Grey House Publishing. • 2001. $220.00. Contains more than 7,700 entries covering dance, instrumental music, vocal music, theatre, performance series, festivals, performance facilities, and media sources.

International Amusement Industry Buyers Guide. Amusement Business. • Annual. $60.00. Manufacturers, importers and suppliers of all types of rides, games and merchandise as well as food and drink equipment and supplies. Formerly *Amusement Industry Buyers Guide.*

International Association of Amusement Parks and Attractions International Directory and Buyers Guide. International Association of Amusement Parks and Attractions. • Annual. $83.00. Over 1,800 member amusement parks, attractions and industry suppliers.

Music Address Book: How to Reach Anyone Who's Anyone in the Music Business. Michael Levine. HarperCollins Publishers. • 1994. $16.00. Second editon.

Resorts and Parks Purchasing Guide. Klevens Publications, Inc. • Annual. $60.00. Lists suppliers of products and services for resorts and parks, including national parks, amusement parks, dude ranches, golf resorts, ski areas, and national monument areas.

FINANCIAL RATIOS

Almanac of Business and Industrial Financial Ratios. Leo Troy. Prentice Hall. • Annual. $99.95. Contains financial ratios derived from federal tax returns. Ratios for each of about 200 industries are arranged according to company asset size.

Annual Statement Studies. Robert Morris Associates: The Association of Lending and Credit Risk Professiona. • Annual. Free to members; non-members, $140.00. Median and quartile financial ratios are given for over 400 kinds of manufacturing, wholesale, retail, construction, and consumer finance establishments. Data is sorted by both asset size and sales volume. Includes a clearly written "Definition of Ratios" and an alphabetical industry index.

HANDBOOKS AND MANUALS

Complete Guide to Special Event Management: Business Insights, Financial Advice and Successful Strategies from Ernst and Young, Consultants to the Olympics, the Emmy Awards and the PGA Tour. Ernst and Young Staff. John Wiley and Sons, Inc. • 1992. $29.95. Covers the marketing, financing, and general management of special events in the fields of art, entertainment, and sports.

Dun & Bradstreet/Gale Group Industry Handbooks. The Gale Group. • 2000. $630.00. Five volumes. $145.00 per volume. Each volume covers two or more major industries: 1. *Entertainment and Hospitality*; 2. *Construction and Agriculture*; 3. *Chemicals and Pharmaceuticals*; 4. *Computers & Software and Broadcasting & Telecommunications*; 5. *Insurance and Health & Medical Services.* The following are included for each industry: overview, statistics, financial ratios, rankings, merger information, company directory, directory of associations, and consultants directory.

Entertainment Law. Robert Fremlin. West Group. • $560.00. Looseleaf service. Includes updates. (Entertainment and Communicat Law Series).

Entertainment, Publishing, and the Arts Handbook. Robert Thorne and John D. Viera, editors. West Group. • Annual. $152.00. Presents recent legal cases, issues, developments, and trends.

ONLINE DATABASES

ABI/INFORM. Bell & Howell Information and Learning. • Provides online indexing to business-related material occurring in over 1,000 periodicals from 1971 to the present. Inquire as to online cost and availability.

F & S Index. The Gale Group. • Contains about four million citations to worldwide business, financial, and industrial or consumer product literature appearing from 1972 to date. Weekly updates. Inquire as to online cost and availability.

Information Bank Abstracts. New York Times Index Dept. • Provides indexing and abstracting of current affairs, primarily from the final late edition of *The New York Times* and the Eastern edition of *The Wall Street Journal.* Time period is 1969 to present, with daily updates. Inquire as to online cost and availability.

Management Contents. The Gale Group. • Covers a wide range of management, financial, marketing, personnel, and administrative topics. About 150 leading business journals are indexed and abstracted from 1974 to date, with monthly updating. Inquire as to online cost and availability.

PERIODICALS AND NEWSLETTERS

Amusement Business: International Live Entertainment and Amusement Industry Newsletter. BPI Communications, Inc. • Weekly. $159.00 per year.

Funworld. International Association of Amusement Parks and Attractions. • 11 times a year. Members, $22.00 per year; non-members, $40.00 per year. Analysis and statistics of the international amusement park industry. Text in English; sections in French, German, Japanese and Spanish.

IEG's Sponsorship Report: The International Newsletter of Event Sponsorship and Lifestyle Marketing. International Events Group, Inc. • Biweekly. $415.00 per year. Newsletter reporting on corporate sponsorship of special events: sports, music, festivals, and the arts. Edited for event producers, directors, and marketing personnel.

TRADE/PROFESSIONAL ASSOCIATIONS

Amusement Industry Manufacturers and Suppliers International. P.O. Box 49947, Sarasota, FL 34320-6947. Phone: (941)954-3101 Fax: (941)954-3201 E-mail: aimsinterl@aol.com • URL: http://www.aimsintl.org.

International Association of Amusement Parks and Attractions. 1448 Duke St., Alexandria, VA 22314. Phone: (703)836-4800 Fax: (703)836-4801 E-mail: iaapa@iaapa.org • URL: http://www.iaapa.org.

Outdoor Amusement Business Association. 1035 S. Semoran Blvd., 1045 A, Winter Park, FL 32792. Phone: 800-517-6222 or (407)681-9444 Fax: (407)681-9445 E-mail: oaba@aol.com • URL: http://www.oaba.org.

OTHER SOURCES

Lindey on Entertainment, Publishing and the Arts: Agreements and the Law. Alexander Lindey, editor. West Group. • $673.00 per year. Looseleaf service. Periodic supplementation. Provides basic forms, applicable law, and guidance. (Entertainment and Communication Law Series).

Sports and Entertainment Litigation Reporter: National Journal of Record Covering Crititcal Issues in Entertainment Law Field. Andrews Publications. • Monthly. $775.00 per year. Provides reports on lawsuits involving films, TV, cable broadcasting, stage productions, radio, and other areas of the entertainment business.Formerly *Entertainment Litigation Reporter.*

AMUSEMENT PARKS

See: AMUSEMENT INDUSTRY

ANIMAL INDUSTRY

See: LIVESTOCK INDUSTRY

ANIMATION, COMPUTER

See: COMPUTER ANIMATION

ANNIVERSARIES AND HOLIDAYS

See also: CHRONOLOGY; SPECIAL EVENT PLANNING

GENERAL WORKS

The Folklore of American Holidays. The Gale Group. • 1999. $125.00. Third edition. Festivals, rituals, beliefs, superstitions, etc., arranged according to holiday.

The Folklore of World Holidays. The Gale Group. • 1999. $125.00. Second edition. Contains descriptions of the important holidays in more than 150 countries.

ABSTRACTS AND INDEXES

Holidays and Festivals Index. Helene Henderson and Barry Puckett, editors. Omnigraphics, Inc. • 1995. $84.00. Serves as an index to more than 3,000 holidays, festivals, celebrations, and other observances found in 27 standard reference works.

DIRECTORIES

Chase's Calendar of Events: The Day-by-Day Directory. NTC/Contemporary Publishing. • Annual. $59.95. Provides information for over 10,000 special days and special events throughout the world. Chronological arrangement with an alphbetical index. Formerly *Chase's Annual Events.*

ENCYCLOPEDIAS AND DICTIONARIES

Holidays, Festivals, and Celebrations of the World Dictionary: Detailing More Than 2,000 Observances from All 50 States and More Than 100 Nations. Sue Ellen Thompson, editor. Omnigraphics, Inc. • 1997. $84.00. Second edition.

The World Almanac Dictionary of Dates. Laurence Urdang, editor. Allyn and Bacon/Longman. • 1982. $31.95.

HANDBOOKS AND MANUALS

Anniversaries and Holidays. Bernard Trawicky. American Library Association. • 1997. $45.00. Fifth edition. Provides information on 3,500 holidays and anniversaries.

Holidays and Anniversaries of the World. The Gale Group. • 1998. $120.00. Third edition.

TRADE/PROFESSIONAL ASSOCIATIONS

Holiday Institute of Yonkers. c/o William Bickel, P.O. Box 2, Kenvil, NJ 07847-0002. E-mail: bbickel@cris.com.

ANNUAL REPORTS OF CORPORATIONS

See: CORPORATION REPORTS

ANNUAL WAGE PLANS

See: WAGES AND SALARIES

ANNUITIES

GENERAL WORKS

Investing During Retirement: The Vanguard Guide to Managing Your Retirement Assets. Vanguard Group. McGraw-Hill Professional. • 1996. $17.95. A basic, general guide to investing after retirement. Covers pension plans, basic principles of investing, types of mutual funds, asset allocation, retirement income planning, social security, estate planning, and contingencies. Includes glossary and worksheets for net worth, budget, and income.

Life Insurance in Estate Planning. James C. Munch, Jr. Aspen Books. • 1981. $80.00. Includes current supplement.

Your Life Insurance Options. Alan Lavine. John Wiley and Sons, Inc. • 1993. $12.95. Tells how to buy life insurance, including the selection of a company and agent. Describes term life, whole life, variable life, universal life, and annuities. Includes a glossary of insurance terms and jargon. (ICFP Personal Wealth Building Guide Series).

ALMANACS AND YEARBOOKS

Investment Companies Yearbook. Securities Data Publishing. • Annual. $310.00. Provides an "entire history of recent events in the mutual funds industry," with emphasis on changes during the past year. About 100 pages are devoted to general information and advice for fund investors. Includes 600 full-page profiles of popular mutual funds, with brief descriptions of 10,000 others, plus 7,000 variable annuities and 500 closed-end funds. Contains a glossary of technical terms, a Web site index, and an overall book index. Also known as *Wiesenberger Investment Companies Yearbook.* (Securities Data Publishing is a unit of Thomson Financial.).

DIRECTORIES

S & P's Insurance Book. Standard & Poor's Ratings Group, Insurance Rating Services. • Quarterly. Price on application. Contains detailed financial analyses and ratings of various kinds of insurance companies.

S & P's Insurance Digest: Life Insurance Edition. Standard & Poor's Ratings Group, Insurance Rating Services. • Quarterly. Contains concise financial analyses and ratings of life insurance companies.

ENCYCLOPEDIAS AND DICTIONARIES

Dictionary of Finance and Investment Terms. John Downes and Jordan E. Goodman. Barron's Educational Series, Inc. • 1998. $12.95. Fifth revised edition. Provides clear explanations of more than 5,000 business, banking, financial, investment, and tax terms. Includes a separate list of financial abbreviations and acronyms.

Rupp's Insurance and Risk Management Glossary. Richard V. Rupp. Available from CCH, Inc. • 1996. $35.00. Second edition. Published by NILS Publishing Co. Provides definitions of 6,400 insurance words and phrases. Includes a guide to acronyms and abbreviations.

HANDBOOKS AND MANUALS

Charitable Planning Primer. Ralph G. Miller and Adam Smalley. CCH, Inc. • 1999. $99.00. Covers the legal and tax aspects of charitable giving and planned gifts. Includes annuity documents, tax forms, tables, and examples.

The Complete Book of Insurance: The Consumer's Guide to Insuring Your Life, Health, Property, and Income. Ben G. Baldwin. McGraw-Hill Professional. • 1996. $24.95. Revised edition. Provides basic information and advice on various kinds of insurance: life, health, property (fire), disability, long-term care, automobile, liability, and annuities.

Federal Tax Course: General Edition. CCH, Inc. • Annual. $123.00. Provides basic reference and training for various forms of federal taxation: individual, business, corporate, partnership, estate, gift, etc. Includes *Federal Taxation Study Manual.*

Federal Tax Manual. CCH, Inc. • Looseleaf. $175.00 per year. Covers "basic federal tax rules and forms affecting individuals and businesses." Includes a copy of *Annuity, Depreciation, and Withholding Tables.*

Financial Planning Applications. William J. Ruckstuhl. Maple-Vail Book, The Manufacturing Group. • 2000. $68.00. 16th edition. Emphasis on annuities and life insurance. (Huebner School Series.).

How to Build Wealth with Tax-Sheltered Investments. Kerry Anne Lynch. American Institute for Economic Research. • 2000. $6.00. Provides practical information on conservative tax shelters, including defined-contribution pension plans, individual retirement accounts, Keogh plans, U. S. savings bonds, municipal bonds, and various kinds of annuities: deferred, variable-rate, immediate, and foreign-currency. (Economic Education Bulletin.).

An Insurance Guide for Seniors. Insurance Forum, Inc. • 1997. $15.00. Provides concise advice and information on Medicare, Medicare supplement insurance, HMOs, long-term care insurance, automobile insurance, life insurance, annuities, and pensions. An appendix lists "Financially Strong Insurance Companies." (*The Insurance Forum*, vol. 24, no. 4.).

McGill's Life Insurance. Edward E. Graves, editor. The American College. • 1998. $71.00. Second edition. Contains chapters by various authors on diverse kinds of life insurance, as well as annuities, disability insurance, long-term care insurance, risk management, reinsurance, and other insurance topics. Originally by Dan M. McGill.

Working with Tax-Sheltered Annuities. CCH, Inc. • 1997. $69.00. Emphasis is on legal aspects of tax-deferred annuities.

INTERNET DATABASES

InsWeb. InsWeb Corp. Phone: (650)372-2129 E-mail: info@insweb.com • URL: http://www.insweb.com • Web site offers a wide variety of advice and information on automobile, life, health, and "other" insurance. Includes glossaries of insurance terms, Standard & Poor's ratings of individual insurance companies, and "Financial Needs Estimators." Searching is available. Fees: Free.

PERIODICALS AND NEWSLETTERS

Annuity and Life Insurance Shopper. United States Annuities. • Quarterly. $65.00 per year. Provides information on rates and performance for fixed annuities, variable annuities, and term life policies issued by more than 250 insurance companies.

Annuity Market News. Securities Data Publishing. • Monthly. $625.00 per year. Newsletter. Edited for investment and insurance professionals. Covers the marketing, management, and servicing of variable and fixed annuity products. (Securities Data Publishing is a unit of Thomson Financial.).

Best's Review: Inurance Issues and Analysis. A.M. Best Co. • Monthly. $25.00 per year. Editorial coverage of significant industry trends, developments, and important events. Formerly Best's Review: Property-Casualty Insurance.

Broker World. Insurance Publications, Inc. • Monthly. $6.00 per year. Edited for independent insurance agents and brokers. Special feature issue topics include annuities, disability insurance, estate planning, and life insurance.

Financial Planning: The Magazine for Financial Service Professionals. Securities Data Publishing. • Monthly. $79.00 per year. Edited for independent financial planners and insurance agents. Covers retirement planning, estate planning, tax planning, and insurance, including long-term healthcare considerations. Special features include a Retirement Planning Issue, Mutual Fund Performance Survey, and Variable Life and Annuity Survey. (Securities Data Publishing is a unit of Thomson Financial.).

Guide to Life, Health, and Annuity Insurers: A Quarterly Compilation of Insurance Company Ratings and Analysis. Weiss Ratings, Inc. • Quarterly. $438.00 per year. Emphasis is on rating of financial safety and relative risk. Includes annual summary.

National Underwriter. The National Underwriter Co. • Weekly. Two editions: *Life* or *Health.* $83.00 per year, each edition.

On Wall Street. Securities Data Publishing. • Monthly. $96.00 per year. Edited for securities dealers. Includes articles on financial planning, retirement planning, variable annuities, and money management, with special coverage of 401(k) plans and IRAs. (Securities Data Publishing is a unit of Thomson Financial.).

STATISTICS SOURCES

Morningstar Variable Annuity Performance Report. Morningstar, Inc. • Monthly. $125.00 per year.

Provides detailed statistics and ratings for more than 2,000 variable annuities and variable-life products.

TRADE/PROFESSIONAL ASSOCIATIONS

Association for Advanced Life Underwriting. 1922 F St., N. W., Washington, DC 20006. Phone: (202)331-6081 Fax: (202)331-2164.

ANNUITY TABLES

See: INTEREST

ANSWERING SERVICE

See: TELEPHONE ANSWERING SERVICE

ANTHRACITE COAL

See: COAL INDUSTRY

ANTIMONY INDUSTRY

See: METAL INDUSTRY

ANTIQUES AS AN INVESTMENT

See also: ART AS AN INVESTMENT

DIRECTORIES

Antique Shop Guide-Central Edition. Mayhill Publications. • Annual. $3.50. Covers 10 midwestern states, western Pennsylvania, and West Virginia.

National Antique and Art Dealers Association of America Membership Directory. National Antique and Art Dealers Association of America. • Annual. $5.00. Provides a list of 46 members and their areas of specialization in the decorative arts.

HANDBOOKS AND MANUALS

Collectibles Broker. Entrepreneur Media, Inc. • Looseleaf. $59.50. A practical guide to starting a brokerage service for collectibles. Covers profit potential, start-up costs, market size evaluation, owner's time required, pricing, accounting, advertising, promotion, etc. (Start-Up Business Guide No. E1360.).

PERIODICALS AND NEWSLETTERS

Antique Dealer and Collector's Guide. Statuscourt Ltd. • Monthly. $66.00 per year. Incorporates *Art and Antiques.*

Art and Antiques. Trans World Publishing Co. • 11 times a year. $36.00 per year. Formerly *Antique Monthly.*

The Magazine Antiques. Brant Publications, Inc. • Monthly. Individuals, $39.95 per year; libraries, $34.95 per year. Emphasizes antique furniture, but also covers paintings, architecture, glass and textiles. Formerly *Antiques.*

PRICE SOURCES

Kovels' Antiques and Collectibles. Ralph and Terry Kovel. Crown Publishers Group, Inc. • Annual. $19.95.

Miller's Antiques Price Guide. Judith Miller, compiler and editor. Antique Collectors' Club. • Annual. $35.00.

Pictorial Price Guide to American Antiques: 2000-2001. Dorothy Hammond. Viking Penguin. • 1999. $19.95. 21st edition.

Warman's Antiques and Collectibles Price Guide. Krause Publications, Inc. • Annual. $16.95. Manufacturer profiles, key events, current status, collector's clubs, museums, resources available for Americana and collectibles.

TRADE/PROFESSIONAL ASSOCIATIONS

Antique Appraisal Association of America. 11361 Garden Grove Blvd., Garden Grove, CA 92643. Phone: (714)530-7090.

Art and Antique Dealers League of America. 1040 Madison Ave., New York, NY 10021-0111. Phone: (212)879-7558.

Mid-Am Antique Appraisers Association. P.O. Box MPO 9681, Springfield, MO 65801. Phone: (417)865-7269 Fax: (417)865-7269 • URL: http://www.idfa.org.

The Questers. 210 S. Quince St., Philadelphia, PA 19107. Phone: (215)923-5183 • For the study and appreciation of antiques.

World Antique Dealers Association. c/o Don McLaughlin, 818 Marion Ave., Mansfield, OH 44906. Phone: (419)756-4374 Fax: (419)756-4979 E-mail: drjm@richnet.net.

ANTITRUST ACTIONS

GENERAL WORKS

American Industry-Structure, Conduct, Performance. Richard E. Caves. Prentice Hall. • 1992. $51.93. Seventh edition.

Antitrust Adviser. Shepard's. • 1985. $105.00. Third edition. General overview of the Sherman Act, the Clayton Act, the Robinson-Patman Act, and the Federal Trade Commission Act.

Monopolies in America: Empire Builders and Their Enemies from Jay Gould to Bill Gates. Charles R. Geisst. Oxford University Press, Inc. • 2000. $30.00. Provides a panoramic, historical view of U. S. trusts, monopolies, and antitrust activities.

ABSTRACTS AND INDEXES

Current Law Index: Multiple Access to Legal Periodicals. The Gale Group. • Monthly. $650.00 per year. Produced in cooperation with the American Association of Law Libraries. Indexes more than 900 law journals, legal newspapers, and specialty publications from the U.S., Canada, U.K., Ireland, Australia, and New Zealand.

HANDBOOKS AND MANUALS

Antitrust Division Manual. Available from U. S. Government Printing Office. • Looseleaf. $60.00. Includes basic manual, with supplementary material for an indeterminate period. Serves as a guide to the operating policies and procedures of the Antitrust Division of the U. S. Department of Justice (http://www.usdoj.gov). Covers suggested methods of conducting investigations and litigation.

Antitrust Law and Practice. West Publishing Co., College and School Div. • Periodic supplementation. Price on application.

Antitrust Law Handbook, 1993. William C. Holmes. West Group. • 1991. $85.00 (Antitrust Series).

Antitrust Laws and Trade Regulation: Desk Edition. Matthew Bender & Co., Inc. • $600.00. Two looseleaf volumes. Periodic supplementation. The history and organization of the antitrust laws.

Corporate Counsellor's Deskbook. Dennis J. Block and Michael A. Epstein, editors. Panel Publishing. • 1999. $220.00. Fifth edition. Looseleaf. Annual supplementation. Covers a wide variety of corporate legal issues, including internal investigations, indemnification, insider trading, intellectual property, executive compensation, antitrust, export-import, real estate, environmental law, government contracts, and bankruptcy.

PERIODICALS AND NEWSLETTERS

The Antitrust Bulletin. Federal Legal Publications, Inc. • Quarterly. Institutions, $85.00 per year.

Antitrust Law and Economics Review. Charles E. Mueller, editor. Antitrust Law and Economics Review, Inc. • Quarterly. $129.50 per year.

Antitrust Law Journal. American Bar Association, Antitrust Law Section. • Three times a year. Free to members; non-members, $40.00 per year.

RESEARCH CENTERS AND INSTITUTES

Lexis.com Research System. Lexis-Nexis Group. Phone: 800-227-9597 or (937)865-6800 Fax: (937)865-6909 E-mail: webmaster@prod.lexis-nexis.com • URL: http://www.lexis.com • Fee-based Web site offers extensive searching of a wide variety of legal sources. Additional features include Daily Opinion Service, lexis.com Bookstore, Career Center, CLE Center, Law Schools, and Practice Pages ("Pages specific to areas of specialty").

OTHER SOURCES

Antitrust and Trade Regulation Report. Bureau of National Affairs, Inc. • Weekly. $1,277.00 per year. Looseleaf service.

Antitrust Counseling and Litigation Techniques. Matthew Bender & Co., Inc. • Five looseleaf volumes. Annual supplement. Price on application.

Antitrust Laws and Trade Regulation. Matthew Bender & Co., Inc. • 16 looseleaf volumes. $1,650.00. Periodic supplementation. Covers provisions and applications of the Sherman, Clayton, Robinson-Patman, and Federal Trade Commission Acts. Also covers state antitrust laws. Issued with *Antitrust Laws and Trade Regulation Newsletter.*

Antitrust Litigation Reporter: The National Journal of Record on Antitrust Litigation. Andrews Publications. • Monthly. $775.00 per year. Provides reports on federal and state antitrust statutes.

Callmann Unfair Competition, Trademarks & Monopolies: 1981-1989. Rudolf Callmann and Louis Altman. West Group. • Nine looseleaf volumes. $1,195.00. Periodic supplementation. Covers various aspects of anti-competitive behavior.

Intellectual Property and Antitrust Law. William C. Holmes. West Group. • Looseleaf. $145.00. Periodic supplementation. Includes patent, trademark, and copyright practices.

ANXIETY

See: STRESS (ANXIETY)

APARTMENT HOUSES

See also: BUILDING INDUSTRY; CONDOMINIUMS; REAL ESTATE BUSINESS

GENERAL WORKS

Real Estate Finance and Investments. William B. Brueggeman and Jeffrey Fisher. McGraw-Hill. • 1996. $68.25. 10th edition. Covers mortgage loans, financing, risk analysis, income properties, land development, real estate investment trusts, and related topics.

Rethinking Rental Housing. John I. Gilderbloom and Richard P. Applebaum. Temple University Press. • 1987. $44.95. Emphasis on social and political factors.

CD-ROM DATABASES

Sourcebooks America CD-ROM. CACI Marketing Systems. • Annual. $1,250.00. Provides the CD-ROM version of *The Sourcebook of ZIP Code Demographics: Census Edition* and *The Sourcebook of County Demographics: Census Edition.*

HANDBOOKS AND MANUALS

Every Landlord's Legal Guide. Marcia Stewart. Nolo.com. • 2000. $44.95. Fourth edition.

Every Tenant's Legal Guide. Janet Portman and Marcia Stewart. Nolo.com. • 1999. $26.95. Second edition.

Real Estate Finance and Investment Manual. Jack Cummings. Prentice Hall. • 1997. $34.95. Second edition.

Tenants' Rights. Myron Moskovitz and Ralph Warner. Nolo.com. • 1999. $21.95. 14th edition.

ONLINE DATABASES

American Statistics Index: A Comprehensive Guide and Index to the Statistical Publications of the United States Government [Online]. Congressional Information Service, Inc. • Indexes and abstracts, 1973 to date. Inquire as to online cost and availability.

Information Bank Abstracts. New York Times Index Dept. • Provides indexing and abstracting of current affairs, primarily from the final late edition of *The New York Times* and the Eastern edition of *The Wall Street Journal*. Time period is 1969 to present, with daily updates. Inquire as to online cost and availability.

PERIODICALS AND NEWSLETTERS

Affordable Housing Finance. Alexander & Edwards Publishing. • Ten times a year. $119.00 per year. Provides advice and information on obtaining financing for lower-cost housing. Covers both government and private sources.

AOMA Newsletter: Profile of the Multi-Family Housing Industry. Apartment Owners and Managers Association of America. • Monthly. Free to members; non-members, $125.00 per year.

Apartment Finance Today. Alexander & Edwards Publishing. • Bimonthly. $29.00 per year. Covers mortgages and financial services for apartment developers, builders, and owners.

Apartment Management Magazine. Apartment News Publications, Inc. • Monthly. $24.00 per year. In four Los Angeles area editions.

Apartment Management Newsletter: Wealth Building Techniques for Apartment Owners and Their Managers. Apartment Management Publishing Co., Inc. • Monthly. $95.00 per year.

Apartment Management Report: For Managers of Apartments. Apartment Owners and Managers Association of America. • Monthly. $85.00 per year.

Buildings: The Facilities Construction and Management Journal. Stamats Communications, Inc. • Monthly. $70.00 per year. Serves professional building ownership/management organizations.

Housing the Elderly Report. Community Development Services, Inc. CD Publications. • Monthly. $197.00 per year. Newsletter. Edited for retirement communities, apartment projects, and nursing homes. Covers news relative to business and property management issues.

Ledger Quarterly: A Financial Review for Community Association Practitioners. Community Associations Institute. • Quarterly. Members, $40.00 per year; non-members, $67.00 per year. Newsletter. Provides current information on issues affecting the finances of condominium, cooperative, homeowner, apartment, and other community housing associations.

Managing Housing Letter. Community Development Services, Inc. CD Publications. • Monthly. $225.00 per year. Newsletter for housing professionals. Provides property management advice and news relating to private and publicly-funded rental housing.

Marketscore. CB Richard Ellis. • Quarterly. Price on application. Newsletter. Provides proprietary forecasts of commercial real estate performance in metropolitan areas.

Metropolitan Home: Style for Our Generation. Hachette Filipacchi Magazines, Inc. • Bimonthly. $17.94 per year.

Multi-Housing News (MHN). Miller Freeman, Inc. • Six times a year. $30.00 per year. Individuals and firms primarily engaged in the development, construction, planning and management of multi-housing.

Quarterly Market Report. CB Richard Ellis. • Quarterly. Price on application. Newsletter. Reviews current prices, rents, capitalization rates, and occupancy trends for commercial real estate.

PRICE SOURCES

National Real Estate Index. CB Richard Ellis. • Price and frequency on application. Provides reports on commercial real estate prices, rents, capitalization rates, and trends in more than 65 metropolitan areas. Time span is 12 years. Includes urban office buildings, suburban offices, warehouses, retail properties, and apartments.

STATISTICS SOURCES

American Housing Survey for the United States in [year]. Available from U. S. Government Printing Office. • Biennial. Issued by the U. S. Census Bureau (http://www.census.gov). Covers both owner-occupied and renter-occupied housing. Includes data on such factors as condition of building, type of mortgage, utility costs, and housing occupied by minorities. (Current Housing Reports, H150.).

Characteristics of Apartments Completed. U.S. Bureau of the Census. Available from U.S. Government Printing Office. • Annual.

Housing Starts. U.S. Bureau of the Census. Available from U.S. Government Printing Office. • Monthly. $39.00 per year. Construction Reports: C-20.

Housing Statistics of the United States. Patrick A. Simmons, editor. Bernan Press. • 2000. $74.00. Third edition. (Bernan Press U.S. Data Book Series).

Market Absorption of Apartments. U.S. Bureau of the Census. Available from U.S. Government Printing Office. • Quarterly and annual. $16.00 per year. Current Housing Report H-130.

U. S. Housing Markets. Hanley-Wood, Inc. • Monthly. $345.00 per year. Includes eight interim reports. Provides data on residential building permits, apartment building completions, rental vacancy rates, sales of existing homes, average home prices, housing affordability, etc. All major U. S. cities and areas are covered.

Value of New Construction Put in Place. U.S. Bureau of the Census. Available from U.S. Government Printing Office. • Monthly. $42.00 per year.

TRADE/PROFESSIONAL ASSOCIATIONS

Community Associations Institute. 1630 Duke St., Alexandria, VA 22314. Phone: (703)548-8600 Fax: (703)684-1581 • URL: http://www.caionline.org • Members are condominium associations, homeowners associations, builders, property managers, developers, and others concerned with the common facilities and services in condominiums, townhouses, planned unit developments, and other planned communities.

OTHER SOURCES

Apartment Building Income-Expense Analysis. Institute of Real Estate Management. • Annual.

APPARATUS, SCIENTIFIC

See: SCIENTIFIC APPARATUS AND INSTRUMENT INDUSTRIES

APPAREL, CHILDREN'S

See: CHILDREN'S APPAREL INDUSTRY

APPAREL INDUSTRY

See: CLOTHING INDUSTRY

APPAREL, MEN'S

See: MEN'S CLOTHING INDUSTRY

APPAREL, WOMEN'S

See: WOMEN'S APPAREL

APPLE INDUSTRY

See also: FRUIT INDUSTRY

GENERAL WORKS

North American Apples Varieties, Rootstocks, Outlook. R.F. Carlson and others. Michigan State University Press. • 1970. $15.00.

ALMANACS AND YEARBOOKS

CRB Commodity Yearbook. Commodity Research Bureau. CRB. • Annual. $99.95.

CD-ROM DATABASES

Food Science and Technology Abstracts [CD-ROM]. Available from SilverPlatter Information, Inc. • Quarterly. $3,700 per year. Produced by International Food Information Service (home page is http://www.ifis.org). Provides worldwide coverage on CD-ROM of the literature of food technology and production. Various types of publications are indexed, with abstracts, including about 1,800 periodicals. Time period is 1969 to date.

FINANCIAL RATIOS

Industry Norms and Key Business Ratios. Desk Top Edition. Dun and Bradstreet Corp., Business Information Services. • Annual. Five volumes. $475.00 per volume. $1,890.00 per set. Covers over 800 kinds of businesses, arranged by Standard Industrial Classification number. More detailed editions covering longer periods of time are also available.

INTERNET DATABASES

USDA. United States Department of Agriculture. Phone: (202)720-2791 E-mail: agsec@usda.gov • URL: http://www.usda.gov • The USDA home page has six sections: News and Information; What's New; About USDA; Agencies; Opportunities; Search and Help. Keyword searching is offered from the USDA home page and from various individual agency home pages. Agencies are the Economic Research Service, Agricultural Marketing Service, National Agricultural Statistics Service, National Agricultural Library, and about 12 others. Updating varies. Fees: Free.

ONLINE DATABASES

Agricola. U.S. National Agricultural Library. • Covers worldwide agricultural literature. Over 2.8 million citations, 1970 to present, with monthly updates. Inquire as to online cost and availability.

Biological and Agricultural Index Online. H. W. Wilson Co. • Indexes a wide variety of agricultural and biological periodicals, 1983 to date. Monthly updates. Inquire as to online cost and availability.

CAB Abstracts. CAB International North America. • Contains 46 specialized abstract collections covering over 10,000 journals and monographs in the areas of agriculture, horticulture, forest products, farm products, nutrition, dairy science, poultry, grains, animal health, entomology, etc. Time period is 1972 to date, with monthly updates. Inquire as to online cost and availability. *CAB Abstracts on CD-ROM* also available, with annual updating.

Food Science and Technology Abstracts [online]. IFIS North American Desk. • Produced by International Food Information Service. Provides about 500,000 online citations, with abstracts, to the international literature of food science, technology, commodities, engineering, and processing. Approximately 2,000 periodicals are covered. Time period is 1969 to date, with monthly updates. Inquire as to online cost and availability.

PERIODICALS AND NEWSLETTERS

American Fruit Grower. Meister Publishing Co. • Monthly. $27.47 per year.

Apple News. International Apple Institute. • Biweekly. Newsletter. Price on application.

Good Fruit Grower. Fruit Commission. • Semimonthly. $30.00 per year.

Journal of Tree Fruit Production. Haworth Press, Inc. • Semiannual. Individuals, $45.00 per year; institutions, $75.00 per year; libraries, $85.00 per year. A research journal for tree fruit growers.

PRICE SOURCES

PPI Detailed Report. Bureau of Labor Statistics, U.S. Department of Labor. Available from U.S. Government Printing Office. • Monthly. $55.00 per year. Formerly *Producer Price Indexes.*

RESEARCH CENTERS AND INSTITUTES

Fruit Research and Extension Center. Pennsylvania State University. P.O. Box 300, Biglerville, PA 17307-0300. Phone: (717)677-6116 Fax: (717)677-4112 E-mail: lah4@psu.edu • URL: http://www.frec.cas.psu.edu.

Peninsular Agricultural Research Station. University of Wisconsin - Madison. 4312 Highway 42, Sturgeon Bay, WI 54235. Phone: (414)743-5406 Fax: (414)743-1080 E-mail: rweidman@facstaff.wisc.edu • URL: http://www.wisc.edu/.

Rutgers Agricultural Research and Extension Center. Rutgers University. 121 Northville Rd., Bridgeton, NJ 08302-9452. Phone: (609)455-3100 Fax: (609)455-3133 E-mail: ball@aesop.rutgers.edu.

Sandhills Research Station. North Carolina Dept. of Agriculture. 2664 Windblow Rd., Jackson Springs, NC 27281. Phone: (910)974-4673 Fax: (910)974-4462.

Tree Fruit Research and Education Center. West Virginia University. P.O. Box 609, Kearneysville, WV 25430. Phone: (304)876-6353 Fax: (304)876-6034 E-mail: hhogmire@wvu.edu • URL: http://www.caf.wvu.edu/kearneysville/wvufarm1.html.

STATISTICS SOURCES

Agricultural Statistics. Available from U. S. Government Printing Office. • Annual. Produced by the National Agricultural Statistics Service, U. S. Department of Agriculture. Provides a wide variety of statistical data relating to agricultural production, supplies, consumption, prices/price-supports, foreign trade, costs, and returns, as well as farm labor, loans, income, and population. In many cases, historical data is shown annually for 10 years. In addition to farm data, includes detailed fishery statistics.

United States Census of Agriculture. U.S. Bureau of the Census. • Quinquennial. Results presented in reports, tape, CD-ROM, and Diskette files.

TRADE/PROFESSIONAL ASSOCIATIONS

Processed Apples Institute. 5775 Peachtree-Dunwoody Rd., Suite 500-G, Atlanta, GA 30342. Phone: (404)252-3663 Fax: (404)252-0774 E-mail: pai@assnhq.com • URL: http://www.appleproducts.org.

U.S. Apple Association. 6707 Old Dominion Dr., Suite 320, McLean, VA 22101. Phone: (703)442-8850 Fax: (703)790-0845 • URL: http://www.usapple.org.

OTHER SOURCES

Major Food and Drink Companies of the World. Available from The Gale Group. • 2001. $855.00. Fourth edition. Two volumes. Published by Graham & Whiteside. Contains profiles and trade names for more than 9,000 important food and beverage companies in various countries. In addition to foods, includes both alcoholic and nonalcoholic drink products.

Thomas Food and Beverage Market Place. Grey House Publishing. • Annual. $295.00. Three volumes. Contains more than 40,000 entries covering food companies, beverages, food equipment, warehouse companies, food brokers, wholesalers, importers, and exporters. Formerly *Thomas Food Industry Register.*

APPLIANCES

See: ELECTRIC APPLIANCE INDUSTRY

APPLICATIONS FOR POSITIONS

See: JOB RESUMES

APPRAISAL (ALL PROPERTY)

See: VALUATION

APPRAISAL OF REAL ESTATE

See: REAL PROPERTY VALUATION

AQUACULTURE

ABSTRACTS AND INDEXES

Aquatic Sciences and Fisheries Abstracts. Food and Agriculture Organization of the United Nations. Cambridge Information Group. • Monthly. Part one, $1,045.00 per year; part two, $815.00 per year.

DIRECTORIES

Aquaculture-Buyers Guide. Achill River Corp. • Annual. $20.00. Lists about 1,400 sources of supplies and services.

ONLINE DATABASES

ASFA Aquaculture Abstracts [Online]. Cambridge Scientific Abstracts. • Indexing and abstracting of the literature of marine life, 1984 to present. Inquire as to online cost and availability.

PERIODICALS AND NEWSLETTERS

Aquaculture; An International Journal Devoted to Fundamental Aquatic Food Resources. Elsevier Science. • 44 times a year. $2,704.00 per year. Text in English.

Aquaculture Magazine. Achill River Corp. • Bimonthly. $15.00 per year.

Journal of Aquatic Food Product Technology: An International Journal Devoted to Foods from Marine and Inland Waters of the World. Haworth Press, Inc. • Quarterly. Individuals, $60.00 per year; institutions, $95.00 per year; libraries, $225.00 per year.

RESEARCH CENTERS AND INSTITUTES

Aquacultural Research and Teaching Facility. Texas A & M University, Wildlife and Fisheries Sciences, College Station, TX 77843. Phone: (409)272-3422 Fax: (409)845-3786 E-mail: d-gatlin@tamu.edu.

Department of Fisheries and Allied Aquacultures. Auburn University - Alabama Agricultural Experiment Station, Auburn, AL 36849-5419. Phone: (334)844-4786 Fax: (334)844-9208 E-mail: jjensen@acesag.auburn.edu • URL: http://www.ag.auburn.edu/dept/faa/.

TRADE/PROFESSIONAL ASSOCIATIONS

American Fisheries Society. 5410 Grosvenor Lane, Suite 110, Bethesda, MD 20814. Phone: (301)897-8616 Fax: (301)897-8096 E-mail: main@fisheries.org • URL: http://www.fisheries.org.

Aquatic Research Institute. 2242 Davis Court, Hayward, CA 94545. Phone: (510)785-2216 Fax: (510)784-0945 E-mail: rofen@prado.com.

ARBITRATION

GENERAL WORKS

Labor Relations. Arthur A. Sloan and Fred Witney. Prentice Hall. • 1996. $91.00. Ninth edition. Emphasizes collective bargaining and arbitration.

When Talk Works: Profiles of Mediators. Deborah M. Kolb. Jossey-Bass, Inc., Publishers. • 1997. $25.95. Provides interview-based profiles of expert mediators in labor, business, education, family matters, community relations, foreign affairs, and other fields. (Management Series).

BIBLIOGRAPHIES

Labor Arbitration: An Annotated Bibliography, 1991-1996. Charles J. Coleman and others, editors. Cornell Universtiy Press. • 1997. $25.00. (ILR Bibliography Series, No. 18).

DIRECTORIES

Martindale-Hubbell Dispute Resolution Directory. Martindale-Hubbell. • Annual. Produced in cooperation with the American Arbitration Association. Over 45,000 judges, attorneys, law firms, and other neutral experts that specialize in dispute resolution and arbitration.

HANDBOOKS AND MANUALS

Business Arbitration-What You Need to Know. Robert Coulson. American Arbitration Association. • 1991. $10.00 Fourth edition. Alternatives to the courts in settling business disputes.

Construction Arbitration Handbook. James Acret. Shepard's. • 1985. $110.00. Explains the arbitration of disputes involving builders.

Domke on Commercial Arbitration; The Law and Practice of Commercial Arbitration. Gabriel Wilner and Rudolphe DeSeife. West Group. • 1992. $225.00. Two volumes. Revised edition.

ONLINE DATABASES

Instant Computer Arbitration Search. LRP Publications. • Provides citations to U. S. labor arbitration cases and a detailed directory of about 2,500 public and private labor arbitrators. Weekly updates. Cases date from 1970. Inquire as to online cost and availability.

PERIODICALS AND NEWSLETTERS

Dispute Resolution Journal. American Arbitration Association. • Quarterly. $55.00 per year. Formerly *Arbitration Journal.*

Labor Relations Bulletin. Bureau of Business Practice, Inc. • Monthly. $99.84 per year. Labor arbitration case analysis. Formerly *Discipline and Grievances.*

Securities Arbitration Commentator: Covering Significant Issues and Events in Securities/ Commodities Arbitration. Richard P. Ryder. • Monthly. $348.00 per year. Newsletter. Edited for attorneys and other professionals concerned with securities arbitration.

Summary of Labor Arbitration Awards. American Arbitration Association, Inc. • Monthly. $120.00 per year.

Weekly Summary of the National Labor Relations Board Cases. Available from U. S. Government Printing Office. • Weekly. $174.00 per year. Issued by the Division of Information, National Labor Relations Board.

TRADE/PROFESSIONAL ASSOCIATIONS

American Arbitration Association. 355 Madison Ave., New York, NY 10017-4605. Phone: 800-778-7879 or (212)716-5800 Fax: (212)716-5905 • URL: http://www.adr.org.

National Academy of Arbitrators. Auburn University, College of Business, 403 Lawler Bldg., Auburn, AL 36849-5260. Phone: (334)844-2817 Fax: (334)844-1498 E-mail: naa@naarb.org • URL: http://www.naarb.org.

OTHER SOURCES

Labor Arbitration Awards. CCH, Inc. • Weekly. $1,099.00 per year. Looseleaf service.

Labor Arbitration Reports. Bureau of National Affairs, Inc. • Weekly. $797 per year. Looseleaf.

ARCHITECTURE

See also: BUILDING INDUSTRY

ABSTRACTS AND INDEXES

Architectural Publications Index. British Architectural Library. RIBA Publications Ltd. • Quarterly. Individuals, $270.00 per year. Formerly *Architectural Periodicals Index.*

Art Index. H. W. Wilson Co. • Quarterly. Annual cumulations. Service basis for print edition; CD-ROM edition, $1,495.00 per year. Subject and author index to periodicals in art, architecture, industrial design, city planning, photography, and various related topics.

Avery Index to Architectural Periodicals. Columbia University, Avery Architectural Library. Available from G.K. Hall Co., Macmillan Library Reference. • Annual. $995.00.

NTIS Alerts: Building Industry Technology. National Technical Information Service. • Semimonthly. $210.00 per year. Provides descriptions of government-sponsored research reports and software, with ordering information. Covers architecture, construction management, building materials, maintenance, furnishings, and related subjects. Formerly *Abstract Newsletter.*

BIOGRAPHICAL SOURCES

Contemporary Architects. Available from The Gale Group. • 1994. $175.00. Third edition. Published by St. James Press. Living architects of the world and influential architects of earlier times.

DIRECTORIES

Accredited Programs in Architecture; And Professional Degrees Conferred on Completion of Their Curricula in Architecture. National Architectural Accrediting Board. • Annual. Free.

Guide to Architecture Schools. Association of Collegiate Schools of Architecture. • Irregular. $19.95. Descriptions of 120 accredited degree programs and related organizations in architecture. Formerly *Guide to Architecture Schools in North America.*

ENCYCLOPEDIAS AND DICTIONARIES

A Dictionary of Architecture. Henry Saylor. John Wiley and Sons, Inc. • 1994. $39.95.

Dictionary of Architecture and Construction. Cyril M. Harris. McGraw-Hill Professional. • 2000. $69.95. Third edition.

Encyclopedia of Architecture: Design, Engineering and Construction. Joseph A. Wilkes and R. T. Packard, editors. John Wiley and Sons, Inc. • 1990. $1,440.00. Five volumes.

Illustrated Dictionary of Historic Architecture. Cyril M. Harris, editor. Dover Publications, Inc. • 1983. $16.95.

International Dictionary of Architects and Architecture. Randall Van Vynckt. St. James Press. • 1993. $260.00. Two volumes. Volume one: *Architects.* Volume two: *Architecture.*

Penguin Dictionary of Architecture and Landscape Architecture. Nicolas Pevsner and others. Viking Penguin. • 2000. $16.95. Fifth edition.

FINANCIAL RATIOS

Almanac of Business and Industrial Financial Ratios. Leo Troy. Prentice Hall. • Annual. $99.95. Contains financial ratios derived from federal tax returns. Ratios for each of about 200 industries are arranged according to company asset size.

Annual Statement Studies. Robert Morris Associates: The Association of Lending and Credit Risk Professiona. • Annual. Free to members; non-members, $140.00. Median and quartile financial ratios are given for over 400 kinds of manufacturing, wholesale, retail, construction, and consumer finance establishments. Data is sorted by both asset size and sales volume. Includes a clearly written "Definition of Ratios" and an alphabetical industry index.

HANDBOOKS AND MANUALS

Architects and Engineers: Their Professional Responsibilities. James Acret. McGraw-Hill. • 1977. $95.00. Second edition. Covers legal responsibilities, liabilities, and malpractice.

Architects Handbook of Professional Practice. David Haviland. American Institute of Architects Press. • 1994. $225.00. 12th edition.

Architectural Graphic Standards. C.G. Ramsey and others. John Wiley and Sons, Inc. • 2000. $600.00. Tenth edition.

New Uses for Obsolete Buildings. Urban Land Institute. • 1996. $64.95. Covers various aspects of redevelopment: zoning, building codes, environment, economics, financing, and marketing. Includes eight case studies and 75 descriptions of completed "adaptive use projects.".

ONLINE DATABASES

Art Index Online. H. W. Wilson Co. • Indexes a wide variety of art-related periodicals, 1984 to date. Monthly updates. Inquire as to online cost and availability.

ARTbibliographies Modern. ABC-CLIO, Inc. • Covers the literature of contemporary art and related subjects from 1974 to date, including art collecting, exhibitions, galleries, graphic design, photography, etc. Inquire as to online cost and availability.

Avery Architecture Index. Avery Architectural and Fine Arts Library. • Indexes a wide range of periodicals related to architecture and design. Subjects include building design, building materials, interior design, housing, land use, and city planning. Time span: 1977 to date. *bul* URL: http://www-rlg.stanford.edu/cit-ave.html.

PERIODICALS AND NEWSLETTERS

Architectural Record. American Institute of Architects. McGraw-Hill Construction Information Group. • Monthly $59.00 per year. Includes supplements *Record Interiors.* and *Record Houses.*

Architectural Review. Fenner, Reed and Jackson. • Monthly. Individuals, $100.00 per year; students, $60.00 per year. Visits innovative buildings around the world.

Architecture. BPI Communications, Inc. • Monthly. $55.00 per year. Incorporates *Building Renovation.*

Design Cost Data: The Cost Estimating Magazine for Architects, Builders and Specifiers. L. M. Rector Corp. • Bimonthly. $64.80 per year. Provides a preliminary cost estimating system for architects, contractors, builders, and developers, utilizing historical data. Includes case studies of actual costs. Formerly *Design Cost and Data.*

Journal of Architectural Education. Association of Collegiate Schools of Architecture. MIT Press. • Quarterly. Individuals, $50.00 per year; institutions, $175.00 per year. Articles on architectural education, theory and practice.

PRICE SOURCES

Building Construction Cost Data. R.S. Means Co., Inc. • Annual. $76.95. Lists over 20,000 entries for estimating.

RESEARCH CENTERS AND INSTITUTES

Center for Environmental Design Research. University of California at Berkeley. 390 Wurster Hall, No. 1839, Berkeley, CA 94720-1839. Phone: (510)642-2896 Fax: (510)643-5571 E-mail: cedr@ced.berkley.edu • URL: http://www.ced.berkley.edu/cedr.

TRADE/PROFESSIONAL ASSOCIATIONS

American Institute of Architects. 1735 New York Ave., N.W., Washington, DC 20006. Phone: (202)626-7300 Fax: (202)626-7421 E-mail: jhoke@aia.org • URL: http://www.aiaonline.com.

National Architectural Accrediting Board. 1735 New York Ave., N.W., Washington, DC 20006. Phone: (202)783-2007 Fax: (202)783-2822 E-mail: info@naab.org • URL: http://www.naab.org.

Society of American Registered Architects. 305 E. 46th St., New York, NY 10017. Phone: (212)486-1549 E-mail: bertolini@aol.com • URL: http://www.sara.national.org.

OTHER SOURCES

Forms and Agreements for Architects, Engineers and Contractors. Albert Dib. West Group. • Four looseleaf volumes. $495.00. Periodic supplementation. Covers evaluation of construction documents and alternative clauses. Includes pleadings for litigation and resolving of claims. (Real Property-Zoning Series).

ARCHIVES MANAGEMENT

See: RECORDS MANAGEMENT

AREA DEVELOPMENT

See: INDUSTRIAL DEVELOPMENT

ARMAMENT AND DEFENSE

See: DEFENSE INDUSTRIES

ARMAMENTS MARKET

See: MILITARY MARKET

ARMY

CD-ROM DATABASES

Leadership Library on CD-ROM: Who's Who in the Leadership of the United States. Leadership Directories, Inc. • Quarterly. $2,641.00 per year, including access to Internet version (weekly updates). Contains all 14 *Yellow Book* personnel directories on CD-ROM, providing contact and brief biographical information for about 400,000 individuals. Covers business, government, financial institutions, news media, law firms, associations, foreign representatives, and nonprofit organizations. Includes photographs.

DIRECTORIES

Carroll's Federal & Federal Regional Directory: CD-ROM Edition. Carroll Publishing. • Bimonthly. $800.00 per year. Provides CD-ROM listings of more than 120,000 (55,000 high-level and 65,000 mid-level) U. S. government officials in Washington and throughout the country, including in military installations. Also available online.

Carroll's Federal Regional Directory. Carroll Publishing. • Semiannual. $255.00 per year. Lists more than 28,000 non-Washington based federal executives in administrative agencies, the courts, and military bases. Arranged in four sections: Alphabetical (last names), Organizational, Geographical, and Keyword. Includes maps.

Department of Defense Telephone Directory. Available from U. S. Government Printing Office. • Three times a year. $44.00 per year. An alphabetical directory of U. S. Department of Defense personnel, including Departments of the Army, Navy, and Air Force.

Directory of U.S. Military Bases Worldwide. William R. Evinger, editor. Oryx Press. • 1998. $125.00. Third edition.

Federal Regional Yellow Book: Who's Who in the Federal Government's Departments, Agencies, Military Installations, and Service Academies Outside of Washington, DC. Leadership Directories, Inc. • Semiannual. $235.00 per year. Lists over 36,000 federal officials and support staff at 8,000 regional offices.

HANDBOOKS AND MANUALS

The Army Officer's Guide. Keith E. Bonn. Stackpole Books. • 1999. $22.95. 48th edition.

The NCO Guide. Robert L. Rush. Stackpole Books, Inc. • 1999. $18.95. edition.

ONLINE DATABASES

American Statistics Index: A Comprehensive Guide and Index to the Statistical Publications of the United States Government [Online]. Congressional Information Service, Inc. • Indexes and abstracts, 1973 to date. Inquire as to online cost and availability.

PERIODICALS AND NEWSLETTERS

Armed Forces Comptroller. American Society of Military Comptrollers. • Quarterly. $15.00 per year.

Armed Forces Journal International. Armed Forces Journal International, Inc. • Monthly. $45.00 per year. A defense magazine for career military officers and industry executives. Covers defense events, plans, policies, budgets, and innovations.

Army Logistician: The Professional Bulletin of United States Army Logistics. United States Army Logistics Management College. Available from U.S. Government Printing Office. • Bimonthly. $21.00 per year.

Army Reserve Magazine. Available from U. S. Government Printing Office. • Quarterly. $14.00 per year. Issued by the Army Reserve, U. S. Department of Defense.

Army Times. Army Times Publishing Co. • Weekly. $52.00 per year. In two editions: Domestic and International.

Soldiers. Available from U. S. Government Printing Office. • Monthly. $28.00 per year. Provides information on the policies, plans, operations, and technical developments of the U.S. Department of the Army (http://www.army.mil).

STATISTICS SOURCES

Annual Report of the Secretary of Defense. U.S. Department of Defense, Office of the Secretary. • Annual.

Budget of the United States Government. U.S. Office of Management and Budget. Available from U.S. Government Printing Office. • Annual.

Labour Force Statistics, 1977/1997: 1998 Edition. Organization for Economic Cooperation and Development. Available from OECD Publications and Information Center. • 1999. $98.00. Provides 21 years of data for OECD member countries on population, employment, unemployment, civilian labor force, armed forces, and other labor factors.

Military Prime Contract Awards and Subcontract Payments. U.S. Department of Defense, Office of the Secretary. • Annual.

Population Projections of the United States by Age, Sex, Race, and Hispanic Origin: 1995 to 2050. Available from U. S. Government Printing Office. • 1996. $8.50. Issued by the U. S. Bureau of the Census (http://www.census.gov). Contains charts and tables. Appendixes include detailed data on fertility rates by age, life expectancy, immigration, and armed forces population. (Current Population Reports, P25-1130.).

Quarterly Labour Force Statistics. Organization for Economic Cooperation and Development. Available from OECD Publications and Information Center. • Quarterly. $60.00 per year. Provides current data for OECD member countries on population, employment, unemployment, civilian labor force, armed forces, and other labor factors.

TRADE/PROFESSIONAL ASSOCIATIONS

Army and Air Force Mutual Aid Association. 102 Sheridan Ave., Fort Myer, VA 22211-1110. Phone: 800-336-4538 or (703)522-3060 Fax: (703)522-1336 E-mail: info@aafmaa.com • URL: http://www.aafmaa.com.

Army Aviation Association of America. 49 Richmondville Ave., Westport, CT 06880-2000. Phone: (203)226-8184 Fax: (203)222-9863 E-mail: aaaa@quad-a.org • URL: http://www.quad-a.org.

Army Emergency Relief. 200 Stovall St., Alexandria, VA 22332. Phone: (703)428-0000 Fax: (703)325-7183 E-mail: aer@aerhq.org • URL: http://www.aerhq.org.

Association of the United States Army. 2425 Wilson Blvd., Arlington, VA 22201-3385. Phone: 800-336-4570 or (703)841-4300 Fax: (703)525-9039 E-mail: ausainfo@ausa.org • URL: http://www.ausa.org.

OTHER SOURCES

Army AL&T: Acquisitions, Logistics, and Technology Bulletin. Available from U. S. Government Printing Office. • Bimonthly. $20.00 per year. Produced by the U. S. Army Materiel Command (http://www.amc.army.mil). Reports on Army research, development, and acquisition. Formerly *Army RD&A.*

Carroll's Defense Organization Charts. Carroll Publishing. • Quarterly. $1,470.00 per year. Provides more than 200 large, fold-out paper charts showing personnel relationships in 2,400 U. S. military offices. Charts are also available online and on CD-ROM.

ART AS AN INVESTMENT

See also: ANTIQUES AS AN INVESTMENT

ABSTRACTS AND INDEXES

Art Index. H. W. Wilson Co. • Quarterly. Annual cumulations. Service basis for print edition; CD-ROM edition, $1,495.00 per year. Subject and author index to periodicals in art, architecture, industrial design, city planning, photography, and various related topics.

BIOGRAPHICAL SOURCES

Contemporary Artists. Available from The Gale Group. • 1996. $170.00. Fourth edition. Published by St. James Press. International coverage.

Who's Who in American Art. Available from Reed Elsevier. • Biennial. $210.00. Lists about 11,800 people active in visual arts. Published by Marquis Who's Who.

Who's Who in Art. Available from The Gale Group. • 2000. $135.00. 29th edition. Contains about 3,000 brief biographies of artists, designers, curators, critics, and other art-related individuals. International coverage, with British emphasis. Published by Art Trade Press.

DIRECTORIES

American Art Directory. National Register Publishing Co. • Biennial. $165.00. About 7,000 museums, art libraries and art organizations; also includes, 1,700 art schools.

Art Now Gallery Guides. Art Now, Inc. • 10 times a year. In eight regional editions. International coverage. Prices vary.Lists current exhibitions in over 1,800 art galleries and museums.

Classified Directory of Artists' Signatures, Symbols, and Monograms. H. H. Caplan, editor. Dealer's Choice Books, Inc. • 1982. $125.00. Second edition. American artists.

International Directory of Arts. Available from The Gale Group. • Biennial. $295.00. Three volumes. A guide to 150,000 art sources and markets in 175 countries. Includes artists, collectors, dealers, galleries, museums, art schools, auctioneers, restorers, publishers, libraries, and associations. Published by K. G. Saur.

National Antique and Art Dealers Association of America Membership Directory. National Antique and Art Dealers Association of America. • Annual. $5.00. Provides a list of 46 members and their areas of specialization in the decorative arts.

HANDBOOKS AND MANUALS

How to Invest in Your First Works of Art: A Guide for the New Collector. John Carlin. Yarrow Press. • 1990. $11.95.

ONLINE DATABASES

Art Index Online. H. W. Wilson Co. • Indexes a wide variety of art-related periodicals, 1984 to date. Monthly updates. Inquire as to online cost and availability.

PERIODICALS AND NEWSLETTERS

Antique Dealer and Collector's Guide. Statuscourt Ltd. • Monthly. $66.00 per year. Incorporates *Art and Antiques.*

Art and Auction. Auction Guild. • 11 times a year. $42.00 per year.

Art in America. Brant Publications, Inc. • Monthly. $39.95 per year. Comprehensive reviews of U.S. and worldwide exhibits.

ARTnews. Artnews LLC. • 11 times a year. $39.95 per year.

PRICE SOURCES

International Auction Records: Engravings, Drawings, Watercolors, Paintings, Sculpture.

Archer Fields, Inc. • 1993. $179.00. Back volumes available for most years.

Leonard's Annual Price Index of Art Auctions. Auction Index, Inc. • Annual. $245.00. List 19 major auction houses.

TRADE/PROFESSIONAL ASSOCIATIONS

Allied Artists of America. 15 Gramercy Park, S., New York, NY 10003. Phone: (212)582-6411.

American Artists Professional League. 47 Fifth Ave., New York, NY 10003. Phone: (212)645-1345 Fax: (212)645-1345.

Art and Antique Dealers League of America. 1040 Madison Ave., New York, NY 10021-0111. Phone: (212)879-7558.

Art Dealers Association of America. 575 Madison Ave., New York, NY 10022. Phone: (212)940-8590 Fax: (212)940-7013 E-mail: artdeal@rosenman.com • URL: http://www.artdealers.org.

Art Information Center. 55 Mercer St., 3rd Fl., New York, NY 10013. Phone: (212)966-3443 • For contemporary art.

Association of Artist-Run Galleries. 591 Broadway, Suite 2A, New York, NY 10012. Phone: (212)924-6520.

International Confederation of Art Dealers. 32 rue Ernest Allard, B-1000 Brussels (Belgium),. Phone: 32 2 5116777 E-mail: walterfeilchenfeldt@compuserve.com • URL: http://www.cinoa.org.

National Association of Women Artists. 41 Union Square, W., 906, New York, NY 10003-3278. Phone: (212)675-1616 Fax: (212)675-1616 E-mail: nawomen@msn.com • URL: http://www.anny.org.

ART BUSINESS

See also: ARTS MANAGEMENT

GENERAL WORKS

Economic Impact of the Arts: A Sourcebook. Anthony Radich. National Conference of State Legislatures. • 1987. $15.00. A collection of writings and studies on the economic impact of the arts.

ABSTRACTS AND INDEXES

Art Index. H. W. Wilson Co. • Quarterly. Annual cumulations. Service basis for print edition; CD-ROM edition, $1,495.00 per year. Subject and author index to periodicals in art, architecture, industrial design, city planning, photography, and various related topics.

BIBLIOGRAPHIES

Subject Bibliography: Art and Artists. Available from U. S. Government Printing Office. • Annual. Free. Lists books, pamphlets, periodicals, and other government publications on art-related topics. (Subject Bibliography No. SB-107.).

BIOGRAPHICAL SOURCES

Who's Who in American Art. Available from Reed Elsevier. • Biennial. $210.00. Lists about 11,800 people active in visual arts. Published by Marquis Who's Who.

Who's Who in Art. Available from The Gale Group. • 2000. $135.00. 29th edition. Contains about 3,000 brief biographies of artists, designers, curators, critics, and other art-related individuals. International coverage, with British emphasis. Published by Art Trade Press.

CD-ROM DATABASES

WILSONDISC: Art Index. H. W. Wilson Co. • Monthly. $1,495.00 per year. Provides CD-ROM indexing of art-related literature from 1982 to date. Price includes online service.

DIRECTORIES

American Art Directory. National Register Publishing Co. • Biennial. $165.00. About 7,000 museums, art libraries and art organizations; also includes, 1,700 art schools.

Art Business News Buyer's Guide. Advanstar Communications, Inc. • Annual. $25.00. Lists companies furnishing supplies and services to art dealers and framers. Includes art by subject and media.

Art Marketing Sourcebook. ArtNetwork Press. • Biennial. $23.95. Over 2,000 representatives, consultants, galleries, critics, architects, interior designers, corporations, museum curators, and art organizations. Formerly *Directory of Art Associations and Exhibition Space.*

Art Now Gallery Guides. Art Now, Inc. • 10 times a year. In eight regional editions. International coverage. Prices vary.Lists current exhibitions in over 1,800 art galleries and museums.

Art Sources Directory. Art Marketing Institute. • Irregular. $95.00. Lists buyers and suppliers of art and art materials. Includes artists' grants, competitions, shows, associations, and publications.

Artist's and Graphic Designer's Market: 2,500 Places to Sell Your Art and Design. F and W. Publications, Inc. • Annual. $24.99. Lists art galleries, advertising agencies, TV producers, publishers, and other buyers of free-lance art work. Formerly *Artist's Market.*

Artist's Resource Handbook. Daniel Grant. Allworth Press. • 1997. $18.95. Second revised edition. A directory of organizations and services that may be helpful to artists. Published in cooperation with the American Council for the Arts.

International Directory of Arts. Available from The Gale Group. • Biennial. $295.00. Three volumes. A guide to 150,000 art sources and markets in 175 countries. Includes artists, collectors, dealers, galleries, museums, art schools, auctioneers, restorers, publishers, libraries, and associations. Published by K. G. Saur.

Who's Who in Art Materials. National Art Materials Trade Association. • Annual. Free to members; non-members, $110.00 per year. Lists retailers and manufacturers of artists' supplies.

ENCYCLOPEDIAS AND DICTIONARIES

Art Business Encyclopedia. Leonard DuBoff. Allworth Press. • 1994. $18.95. Defines words, phrases, and concepts relating to the business of art, with emphasis on legal matters. Includes relevant statutes, arranged by state. Published in cooperation with the American Council for the Arts.

HANDBOOKS AND MANUALS

Art Law: The Guide for Collectors, Investors, Dealers, and Artists. Ralph E. Lerner and Judith Bresler. Practising Law Institute. • 1997. $125.00. Two volumes. Second edition. Covers artist/dealer relationships, artists' rights, appraisals, museum law, tax aspects, estate planning issues, and other legal topics relating to visual art. There are six main headings: Dealers, Artwork Transactions, Artists' Rights, Collectors, Taxes and Estate Planning, and Museums and Multimedia.

Entertainment, Publishing, and the Arts Handbook. Robert Thorne and John D. Viera, editors. West Group. • Annual. $152.00. Presents recent legal cases, issues, developments, and trends.

ONLINE DATABASES

Art Index Online. H. W. Wilson Co. • Indexes a wide variety of art-related periodicals, 1984 to date. Monthly updates. Inquire as to online cost and availability.

ARTbibliographies Modern. ABC-CLIO, Inc. • Covers the literature of contemporary art and related subjects from 1974 to date, including art collecting, exhibitions, galleries, graphic design, photography, etc. Inquire as to online cost and availability.

Newspaper and Periodical Abstracts. Bell & Howell Information and Learning. • Provides online coverage (citations and abstracts) of 25 major newspapers, 1,600 perodicals, and 70 TV programs. Covers business, economics, current affairs, health, fitness, sports, education, technology, government, consumer affairs, psychology, the arts, and the social sciences. Time period is 1986 to date, with daily updates. Inquire as to online cost and availability.

PERIODICALS AND NEWSLETTERS

Art Business News. Advanstar Communications, Inc. • Monthly. $43.00 per year.

The ARTnewsletter: The International Biweekly Business Report on the Art Market. ARTnews LLC. • Biweekly. $249.00 per year. Newsletter on forthcoming auctions, price trends, ownership squabbles, criminal cases, etc.

Picture Framing Magazine. Hobby Publications, Inc. • Monthly. $20.00 per year. Published for retailers, wholesalers, and manufacturers of picture frames.

RESEARCH CENTERS AND INSTITUTES

International Foundation for Art Research, Inc. 500 Fifth Ave., Suite 1234, New York, NY 10110. Phone: (212)391-6234 Fax: (212)391-8794 E-mail: kferg@ifar.org • URL: http://www.ifar.org • Research fields are art theft and the authenticity of art objects. Maintains an information archive on stolen art and operates an authentication service.

STATISTICS SOURCES

United States Census of Service Industries. U.S. Bureau of the Census. • Quinquennial. Various reports available.

TRADE/PROFESSIONAL ASSOCIATIONS

Americans for the Arts. 1000 Vermont Ave., N.W., 12th Fl., Washington, DC 20005. Phone: 800-321-4510 or (202)371-2830 Fax: (202)371-0424 • URL: http://www.artsusa.org • Members are arts organizations and interested individuals. Conducts research and provides information and clearinghouse services relating to the visual arts.

Art and Antique Dealers League of America. 1040 Madison Ave., New York, NY 10021-0111. Phone: (212)879-7558.

Art and Creative Materials Institute. 100 Boylston St., Suite 1050, Boston, MA 02116. Phone: (781)293-4100 Fax: (781)293-0808 E-mail: acmi@fanningnet.com • URL: http://www.creative-industries.com/acmi • Members are manufacturers of school and professional art and craft materials.

Art Dealers Association of America. 575 Madison Ave., New York, NY 10022. Phone: (212)940-8590 Fax: (212)940-7013 E-mail: artdeal@rosenman.com • URL: http://www.artdealers.org.

Art Information Center. 55 Mercer St., 3rd Fl., New York, NY 10013. Phone: (212)966-3443 • For contemporary art.

National Antique and Art Dealers Association of America. 220 E. 57th St., New York, NY 10022. Phone: (212)826-9707 Fax: (212)832-9493 • URL: http://www.dir-dd.com/naadaa.html/.

OTHER SOURCES

Opportunities in Visual Arts Careers. Mark Salmon. NTC/Contemporary Publishing Group. • 2001. $15.95. Edited for students and job seekers. Includes education requirements and salary data. (VGM Career Books.).

ART, COMMERCIAL

See: COMMERCIAL ART

ART DEALERS

See: ART BUSINESS

ART IN INDUSTRY

See also: ARCHITECTURE; COMMERCIAL ART; DESIGN IN INDUSTRY; GRAPHIC ARTS INDUSTRY

ABSTRACTS AND INDEXES

Art Index. H. W. Wilson Co. • Quarterly. Annual cumulations. Service basis for print edition; CD-ROM edition, $1,495.00 per year. Subject and author index to periodicals in art, architecture, industrial design, city planning, photography, and various related topics.

BIBLIOGRAPHIES

The Arts and the World of Business: A Selected Bibliography. Charlotte Georgi. Scarecrow Press, Inc. • 1979. $24.00. Second edition.

CD-ROM DATABASES

WILSONDISC: Art Index. H. W. Wilson Co. • Monthly. $1,495.00 per year. Provides CD-ROM indexing of art-related literature from 1982 to date. Price includes online service.

DIRECTORIES

International Directory of Corporate Art Collections. ARTnews. • Biennial. $109.95. Contains information on about 1,300 corporate art collections maintained or sponsored in the U. S., Canada, Europe, and Japan.

ONLINE DATABASES

ABI/INFORM. Bell & Howell Information and Learning. • Provides online indexing to business-related material occurring in over 1,000 periodicals from 1971 to the present. Inquire as to online cost and availability.

Art Index Online. H. W. Wilson Co. • Indexes a wide variety of art-related periodicals, 1984 to date. Monthly updates. Inquire as to online cost and availability.

ARTbibliographies Modern. ABC-CLIO, Inc. • Covers the literature of contemporary art and related subjects from 1974 to date, including art collecting, exhibitions, galleries, graphic design, photography, etc. Inquire as to online cost and availability.

TRADE/PROFESSIONAL ASSOCIATIONS

American Institute of Graphic Arts. 164 Fifth Ave., New York, NY 10010. Phone: 800-548-1634 or (212)807-1990 Fax: (212)807-1799 • URL: http://www.aiga.org.

Society of Illustrators. 128 E. 63rd St., New York, NY 10021. Phone: (212)838-2560 Fax: (212)838-2561 E-mail: society@societyillustrators.org • URL: http://www.societyillustrator.org.

OTHER SOURCES

Arts Management. Radius Group Inc. • Five times a year. $22.00 per year. National news service for those who finance, manage and communicate the arts.

ARTIFICIAL INTELLIGENCE

See also: MICROCOMPUTERS AND MINICOMPUTERS; ROBOTS

GENERAL WORKS

The Age of Spiritual Machines: When Computers Exceed Human Intelligence. Ray Kurzweil. Viking Penguin. • 1999. $25.95. Provides speculation on the future of artificial intelligence and "computer consciousness.".

Artificial Intelligence. P. Henry. Addison-Wesley Longman, Inc. • 2001. Fourth edition. Price on application.

Artificial Intelligence in Perspective. Daniel G. Bobrow, editor. MIT Press. • 1994. $42.50. (Artificial Intelligence Series).

Artificial Intelligence: Its Role in the Information Industry. Peter Davies. Information Today, Inc. • 1991. $39.50.

Artificial Intelligence: Its Scope and Limits. Kluwer Academic Publishers. • 1990. $137.50.

Fluid Concepts and Creative Analogies: Computer Models of the Fundamental Mechanisms of Thought. Douglas Hofstadter. Available from Harpercollisn Publishing. • 1995. $22.00. A readable description of progress in artificial intelligence at the Fluid Analogies Research Group of Indiana University.

ABSTRACTS AND INDEXES

Applied Science and Technology Index. H. W. Wilson Co. • 11 times a year. Quarterly and annual cumulations. Service basis for print edition; CD-ROM edition, $1,495.00 per year. Indexes a wide variety of English language technical, industrial, and engineering periodicals.

Business Periodicals Index. H. W. Wilson Co. • Monthly, except August, with quarterly and annual cumulations. Service basis for print edition; CD-ROM edition, $1,495.00 per year.

Computer and Control Abstracts. Available from INSPEC, Inc. • Monthly. $2,160.00 per year. Section C of *Science Abstracts.*

Computer and Information Systems Abstracts Journal: An Abstract Journal Pertaining to the Theory, Design, Fabrication and Application of Computer and Information Systems. Cambridge Information Group. • Monthly. $1,045 per year.

Computer Literature Index: A Subject/Author Index to Computer and Data Processing Literature. Applied Computer Research, Inc. • Quarterly, with annual cumulation. $245.00 per year. Contains brief abstracts of book and periodical literature covering all phases of computing, including approximately 70 specific application areas.

Current Contents: Engineering, Computing and Technology. Institute for Scientific Information. • Weekly. $730.00 per year. Reproductions of contents pages of technical journals. Includes *Author Index, Address Directory, Current Book Contents* and *Title Word Index.* Formerly *Current Contents: Engineering, Technology and Applied Sciences.*

Key Abstracts: Artificial Intelligence. Available from INSPEC, Inc. • Monthly. $240.00 per year. Provides international coverage of journal and proceedings literature, including material on expert systems and knowledge engineering. Published in England by the Institution of Electrical Engineers (IEE).

Microcomputer Abstracts. Information Today, Inc. • Quarterly. $225.00 per year. Provides abstracts covering a wide variety of personal and business microcomputer literature. Formerly *Microcomputer Index.*

NTIS Alerts: Biomedical Technology & Human Factors Engineering. National Technical Information Service. • Semimonthly. $210.00 per year. Provides descriptions of government-sponsored research reports and software, with ordering information. Covers biotechnology, ergonomics, bionics, artificial intelligence, prosthetics, and related subjects. Formerly *Abstract Newsletter.*

Science Citation Index. Institute for Scientific Information. • Bimonthly. $15,020.00 per year. Annual cumulation. Includes *Source Index, Citation Index, Permuterm Subject Index,* and *Corporate Index.*

BIBLIOGRAPHIES

Computer Book Review. • Quarterly. $30.00 per year. Includes annual index. Reviews new computer books. Back issues available.

CD-ROM DATABASES

Science Citation Index: Compact Disc Edition. Institute for Scientific Information. • Quarterly. Provides CD-ROM indexing of the world's scientific and technical literature. Corresponds to online *Scisearch* and printed *Science Citation Index.*

DIRECTORIES

Business Organizations, Agencies, and Publications Directory. The Gale Group. • 1999. $425.00. 12th edition. Over 40,000 entries describing 39 types of business information sources. Classified by type of organization, publication, or serviceIncludes state, national, and international agencies and organizations. Master index to names and keywords. Also includes e-mail addresses and web site URL's.

Corptech Directory of Technology Companies. Corporate Technology Information Services, Inc. c/o Eileen Kennedy. • Annual. $795.00. Four volumes. Profiles of more than 45,000 manufacturers and developers of high technology products. Includes private companies, publicly-held corporations, and subsidiaries. Formerly *Corporate Technology Directory.*

Faulkner Information Service. Faulkner Information Services, Inc. • Looseleaf. Monthly updates. Many titles and volumes, covering virtually all aspects of computer software and hardware. Gives descriptions and technical data for specific products, including producers' names and addresses. Prices and details on request. Formerly (The Auerbach Series).

Information Sources: The Annual Directory of the Information Industry Association. Software and Information Industry Association. • Annual. Members, $75.00; non-members, $125.00.

MicroLeads Vendor Directory on Disk (Personal Computer Industry). Chromatic Communications Enterprises, Inc. • Annual. $495.00. Includes computer hardware manufacturers, software producers, book-periodical publishers, and franchised or company-owned chains of personal computer equipment retailers, support services and accessory manufacturers. Formerly *MicroLeads U.S. Vender Directory.*

The Software Encyclopedia: A Guide for Personal, Professional, and Business Users. R. R. Bowker. • Annual. $255.00. Two volumes. Volume one lists software programs by title and producer. Volume two provides information on programs according to application and operating system. Includes prices and requirements for hardware and memory.

ENCYCLOPEDIAS AND DICTIONARIES

Artificial Intelligence Dictionary: A Dictionary Specifically for Artificial Intelligence Users and Specialists. Ellen Thro. Slawson Communications, Inc. • 1991. $24.95. Includes common lay words that lead to correct medical terms. (Lance A. Leventhal Microtrend Series).

Dictionary of Computing. Valerie Illingworth, editor. Oxford University Press, Inc. • 1996. $49.95. Fourth edition.

Dictionary of Information Technology and Computer Science. Tony Gunton. Blackwell Publishers. • 1994. $50.95. Second edition. Covers key words, phrases, abbreviations, and acronyms used in computing and data communications.

HANDBOOKS AND MANUALS

Artificial Intelligence and Software Engineering. Darek Partridge. Fitzroy Dearborn Publishers, Inc. • 1998. $55.00. Includes applications of artificial intelligence software to banking and financial services.

Artificial Intelligence: Concepts and Applications. A.R. Mirzai, editor. MIT Press. • 1990. $42.00. (Artificial Intelligence Series).

Artificial Intelligence in the Capital Markets: State-of-the-Art Applications. Roy A Freedman and Robert A. Klein. McGraw-Hill Professional. • 1994. $85.00.

Expert Systems for Business: Concepts and Applications. D. V. Pigford. Course Technology, Inc. • 1995. $42.95. Second edition.

Handbook of Artificial Intelligence. Avron Barr and others. Addison-Wesley Longman, Inc. • 1989. $27.95.

Managing Expert Systems. Efraim Tuban and Jay Liebowitz. Idea Group Publishing. • 1992. $53.50.

ONLINE DATABASES

Applied Science and Technology Index Online. H. W. Wilson Co. • Provides online indexing of 400 major scientific, technical, industrial, and engineering periodicals. Time period is 1983 to date. Monthly updates. Inquire as to online cost and availability.

Computer Database. The Gale Group. • Provides online citations with abstracts to material appearing in about 150 trade journals and newsletters in the subject areas of computers, telecommunications, and electronics. Time period is 1983 to date, with weekly updates. Inquire as to online cost and availability.

Globalbase. The Gale Group. • Provides more than one million online summaries of business, industrial, and economic news reports from more than 1,000 publications worldwide. Covers a wide range of material appearing in international trade journals, professional magazines, and newspapers. Time period is 1984 to date, with weekly updates. Inquire as to online cost and availability.

Internet and Personal Computing Abstracts. Information Today, Inc. • Contains abstracts covering a wide variety of personal and business microcomputer literature appearing in more than 100 journals and popular magazines. Time period is 1981 to date, with monthly updates. Formerly *Microcomputer Index.* Inquire as to online cost and availability.

PROMT: Predicasts Overview of Markets and Technology. The Gale Group. • Companies, products, applied technologies and markets. U.S. and international literature coverage, 1972 to date. Inquire as to online cost and availability. Provides abstracts from more than 1,600 publications. Weekly updates.

Scisearch. Institute for Scientific Information. • Broad, multidisciplinary index to the literature of science and technology, 1974 to present. Inquire as to online cost and availability. Coverage of literature is worldwide, with weekly updates.

Wilson Business Abstracts Online. H. W. Wilson Co. • Indexes and abstracts 600 major business periodicals, plus the *Wall Street Journal* and the business section of the *New York Times.* Indexing is from 1982, abstracting from 1990, with the two newspapers included from 1993. Updated weekly. Inquire as to online cost and availability. (*Business Periodicals Index* without abstracts is also available online.).

PERIODICALS AND NEWSLETTERS

AI Magazine (Artificial Intelligence). American Association for Artificial Intelligence. AAAI Press. • Quarterly. $50.00 per year. Information on artificial intelligence research and innovative applications of the science.

AI Trends: Newsletter. Relayer Group. • Monthly. $295.00 per year.

Computer Industry Report. International Data Corp. • Semimonthly. $495.00 per year. Newsletter. Annual supplement. Also known as "The Gray Sheet." Formerly *EDP Industry Report and Market Review.*

Computer Languages. Elsevier Science. • Quarterly. $778.00 per year.

Computers in Human Behavior. Elsevier Science. • Bimonthly. $902.00 per year.

EDP Weekly: The Leading Weekly Computer News Summary. Computer Age and E D P News Services. • Weekly. $495.00 per year. Newsletter. Summarizes news from all areas of the computer and microcomputer industries.

Industrial Computing. ISA Services, Inc. • Monthly. $50.00 per year. Published by the Instrument Society of America. Edited for engineering managers and systems integrators. Subject matter includes industrial software, programmable controllers, artificial intelligence systems, and industrial computer networking systems.

Intelligent Systems Report (ISR). Lionheart Publishing, Inc. • Monthly. $299.00 per year. Newsletter. Formed by merger of*Neural Network News*and *AI Week.*

International Journal of Intelligent Systems. John Wiley and Sons, Inc. • Monthly. Institutions, $1,549.00 per year.

Release 1.0: Esther Dyson's Monthly Report. EDventure Holdings, Computer Publications Div. • 15 times a year. $695.00 per year. Newsletter.

Report. Louis G. Robinson and Associates. • Monthly. $295.00 per year. Newsletter. Articles cover the artificial intelligence field. Formerly *Artificial Intelligence Report.*

Telematics and Informatics: An International Journal. Elsevier Science. • Quarterly. $713.00 per year.

RESEARCH CENTERS AND INSTITUTES

Artificial Intelligence and Computer Vision Laboratory. University of Cincinnati, Dept. of Electrical, Computer Engineering and Computer Scien, 802 Rhodes Hall, Cincinnati, OH 45221-0030. Phone: (513)556-4778 Fax: (513)556-7326 E-mail: william.wee@uc.edu • Fields of research include computer vision, computer graphics, and artificial intelligence.

Artificial Intelligence Laboratory. University of Texas at Austin, Taylor Hall 2.124, Austin, TX 78712-1188. Phone: (512)471-9569 Fax: (512)471-8885 E-mail: novak@cs.utexas.edu • URL: http://www.cs.utexas.edu/users/ai-lab.

Carnegie Mellon Research Institute. Carnegie Mellon University, 700 Technology Dr., Pittsburgh, PA 15219. Phone: (412)268-3190 Fax: (412)268-3101 E-mail: twillke@emu.edu • Multidisciplinary research activities include expert systems applications, minicomputer and microcomputer systems design, genetic engineering, and transportation systems analysis.

Center for Artificial Intelligence. University of Pennsylvania, Computer and Information Science Dept., Moore School of Electrical Engineering, 200 S. 33rd St., Philadelphia, PA 19104-6389. Phone: (215)898-3191 Fax: (215)898-0587 E-mail: joshi@linc.cis.upenn.edu.

Center for Intelligent Machines and Robotics. University of Florida, 300 MEB, Gainesville, FL 32611. Phone: (352)392-0814 Fax: (352)392-1071 E-mail: cimar@cimar.me.ufl.edu • URL: http://ww.me.ufl.edu/cimar/.

Center for Research in Computing Technology. Harvard University, Pierce Hall, 29 Oxford St., Cambridge, MA 02138. Phone: (617)495-2832 Fax: (617)495-9837 E-mail: cheatham@das.harvard.edu • URL: http://www.das.harvard.edu/cs.grafs.html • Conducts research in computer vision, robotics, artificial intelligence, systems programming, programming languages, operating systems, networks, graphics, database management systems, and telecommunications.

Collaboratory for Research on Electronic Work. University of Michigan, 1075 Beal Ave., Ann Arbor, MI 48109-2112. Phone: (734)647-4948 Fax: (734)936-3168 E-mail: finholt@umich.edu • URL: http://crew.umich.edu/ • Concerned with the design and use of computer-based tools for thinking and planning in the professional office.

Digital Image Analysis Laboratory. University of Arizona, Dept. of Electrical and Computer Engineering, Tucson, AZ 85721. Phone: (520)621-4554 Fax: (520)621-8076 E-mail: schowengerdt@ece.arizona.edu • URL: http://www.ece.arizona.edu/~dial • Research fields include image processing, computer vision, and artificial intelligence.

Imaging and Computer Vision Center-Computer Vision Center for Vertebrate Brain Mapping. Drexel University, 32nd and Market Sts., Room 110-7, Philadelphia, PA 19104. Phone: (215)895-2279 Fax: (215)895-4987 • URL: http://www.drexel.icvc.com • Fields of research include computer vision, robot vision, and expert systems.

Institute for Systems Research. University of Maryland, A. V. Williams Bldg., No. 115, College Park, MD 20742-3311. Phone: (301)405-6602 Fax: (301)314-9220 E-mail: isr@isr.umd.edu • URL: http://www.isr.umd.edu/ • A National Science Foundation Engineering Research Center. Areas of research include communication systems, manufacturing systems, chemical process systems, artificial intelligence, and systems integration.

Institute of Advanced Manufacturing Sciences, Inc. 1111 Edison Dr., Cincinnati, OH 45216. Phone: (513)948-2000 Fax: (513)948-2109 E-mail: conley@iams.org • URL: http://www.iams.org • Fields of research include quality improvement, computer-aided design, artificial intelligence, and employee training.

Intelligent Computer Systems Research Institute. University of Miami, P.O. Box 248235, Coral Gables, FL 33124-8235. Phone: (305)284-5195 E-mail: dhertz@umiami.ir.miami.edu.

Laboratory for Computer Science. Massachusetts Institute of Technology, 545 Technology Square, Bldg. NE43, Cambridge, MA 02139. Phone: (617)253-5851 Fax: (617)258-8682 E-mail: mld@hq.lcs.mit.edu • URL: http://www.lcs.mit.edu/ • Research is in four areas: Intelligent Systems; Parallel Systems; Systems, Languages, and Networks; and Theory. Emphasis is on the application of online computing.

McGill Centre for Intelligent Machines. McGill University, 3480 University St., Room 410, Montreal, QC, Canada H3A 2A7. Phone: (514)398-6319 Fax: (514)398-7348 E-mail: cim@cim.mcgill.ca • URL: http://www.cim.mcgill.ca.

Robot Vision Laboratory. Purdue University, School of Electrical and Computer Engineering, West

Lafayette, IN 47907-1285. Phone: (765)494-3456 Fax: (765)494-6440 E-mail: kak@ecn.purdue.edu • URL: http://www.ecn.purdue.edu.

Studio for Creative Inquiry. Carnegie Mellon University, College of Fine Arts, Pittsburgh, PA 15213-3890. Phone: (412)268-3454 Fax: (412)268-2829 E-mail: mmbm@andrew.cmu.edu/ • URL: http://www.cmu.edu/studio/ • Research areas include artificial intelligence, virtual reality, hypermedia, multimedia, and telecommunications, in relation to the arts.

STATISTICS SOURCES

U. S. Industry and Trade Outlook: The McGraw-Hill Companies and the U.S. Department of Commerce/ International Trade Administration. Datapso Research Corp. • Annual. $69.95. Produced by the International Trade Administration, U. S. Department of Commerce, in a "public-private" partnership with DRI/McGraw-Hill and Standard & Poor's. Provides basic data, outlook for the current year, and "Long-Term Prospects" (five-year projections) for a wide variety of products and services. Includes high technology industries. Formerly *U. S. Industrial Outlook.*

TRADE/PROFESSIONAL ASSOCIATIONS

American Association for Artificial Intelligence. 445 Burgess Dr., Menlo Park, CA 94025-3442. Phone: (650)328-3123 Fax: (650)321-4457 E-mail: info@aaai.org • URL: http://www.aaai.org.

Cognitive Science Society. c/o Patty Homan, 5618 Ann Arbor Saline Rd., Saline, MI 48176. Phone: (734)429-9248 Fax: (734)429-9248 E-mail: cogsci@umich.edu • URL: http://www.umich.edu/~cogsci/.

Instrument Society of America (ISA). P.O. Box 12277, Research Triangle Park, NC 27709. Phone: (919)549-8411 Fax: (919)549-8288 E-mail: info@isa.org • URL: http://www.isa.org • Members are engineers and others concerned with industrial instrumentation, systems, computers, and automation.

Society for Computer Simulation International. P.O. Box 17900, San Diego, CA 92177-1810. Phone: (858)277-3888 Fax: (858)277-3930 E-mail: info@scs.org • URL: http://www.scs.org.

Special Interest Group on Artificial Intelligence. Association for Computing Machinery, 1515 Broadway, New York, NY 10036-5701. Phone: (212)626-7440 Fax: (212)302-5826 E-mail: acmhelp@acm.org • URL: http://www.acm.org/sigart/.

OTHER SOURCES

Artificial Intelligence: Reality or Fantasy?. Leslie Chase and Robert Landers, editors. Software and Information Industry Association. • 1984. $59.95. General information and market considerations.

DataWorld. Faulkner Information Services, Inc. • Four looseleaf volumes, with monthly supplements. $1,395.00 per year. Describes and evaluates both hardware and software relating to midrange, micro, and mainframe computers. Available on CD-ROM.

James Martin Productivity Series, Volume Seven. Digital Consulting Associates. • 1989. $50.00. Covers intelligent desktop workstations, expert systems (artificial intelligence), computer-aided software engineering (CASE), advanced development methodologies, and other high technology computer topics.

World of Computer Science. The Gale Group. • 2001. $150.00. Alphabetical arrangement. Contains 650 entries covering discoveries, theories, concepts, issues, ethics, and people in the broad area of computer science and technology.

ARTIFICIAL LIMBS

See: PROSTHETICS INDUSTRY

ARTS MANAGEMENT

See also: ART BUSINESS; FOUNDATIONS; FUND-RAISING; GRANTS-IN-AID

GENERAL WORKS

Arts Management Reader. Alvin H. Reiss. Marcel Dekker, Inc. • 1979. $55.00.

Management Control in Nonprofit Organizations. Robert N. Anthony and David W. Young. McGraw-Hill Higher Education. • 1998. $89.06. Sixth edition.

Marketing for Non-profit Organizations. David L. Rados. Greenwood Publishing Group, Inc. • 1996. $59.95. Second edition.

Marketing the Arts: Praeger Series in Public and Nonprofit Sector Marketing. Michael P. Mokwa and others. Greenwood Publishing Group Inc. • 1980. $59.95. (Praeger Special Studies Series).

Theatre Management and Production in America: Commercial, Stock, Resident, College, Community and Presenting Organizations. Stephen Langley. Quite Specific Media Group, Ltd. • 1990. $37.50. Revised edition.

This Business of Art. Lee E. Caplin. Prentice Hall. • 1997. $24.95. Third edition.

ABSTRACTS AND INDEXES

Art Index. H. W. Wilson Co. • Quarterly. Annual cumulations. Service basis for print edition; CD-ROM edition, $1,495.00 per year. Subject and author index to periodicals in art, architecture, industrial design, city planning, photography, and various related topics.

BIBLIOGRAPHIES

The Arts and the World of Business: A Selected Bibliography. Charlotte Georgi. Scarecrow Press, Inc. • 1979. $24.00. Second edition.

DIRECTORIES

Gale's Guide to the Arts: A Gale Ready Reference Handbook. The Gale Group. • 2000. $125.00. Contains descriptions of information sources of interest to nonprofit art groups, including publications, online databases, museums, government agencies, and associations. Three indexes and a glossary are provided.

Guide to Arts Administration Training and Research. Americans for the Arts. • Biennial. $12.95. Lists 33 institutions. Formerly *Survey of Arts Administration Training.*

HANDBOOKS AND MANUALS

Art Law: The Guide for Collectors, Investors, Dealers, and Artists. Ralph E. Lerner and Judith Bresler. Practising Law Institute. • 1997. $125.00. Two volumes. Second edition. Covers artist/dealer relationships, artists' rights, appraisals, museum law, tax aspects, estate planning issues, and other legal topics relating to visual art. There are six main headings: Dealers, Artwork Transactions, Artists' Rights, Collectors, Taxes and Estate Planning, and Museums and Multimedia.

Art Marketing Handbook: Marketing Art in the Nineties. Calvin J. Goodman. Gee Tee Bee. • 1991. $60.00. Sixth revised edition. A complete guide to all aspects of the art market.

Arts Management: A Guide to Finding Funds and Winning Audiences. Alvin H. Reiss. Fund Raising Institute. • 1992. $45.00.

The Community Orchestra: A Handbook for Conductors, Managers and Boards. James Van Horn. Greenwood Publishing Group Inc. • 1979. $49.95.

Complete Guide to Special Event Management: Business Insights, Financial Advice and Successful Strategies from Ernst and Young, Consultants to the Olympics, the Emmy Awards and the PGA Tour. Ernst and Young Staff. John Wiley and Sons, Inc. • 1992. $29.95. Covers the marketing, financing, and general management of special events in the fields of art, entertainment, and sports.

Presenting Performances: A Handbook for Sponsors. Thomas Wolf. Americans for the Arts. • 1991. $16.95. Revised edition.

ONLINE DATABASES

ABI/INFORM. Bell & Howell Information and Learning. • Provides online indexing to business-related material occurring in over 1,000 periodicals from 1971 to the present. Inquire as to online cost and availability.

Art Index Online. H. W. Wilson Co. • Indexes a wide variety of art-related periodicals, 1984 to date. Monthly updates. Inquire as to online cost and availability.

PERIODICALS AND NEWSLETTERS

Art Business News. Advanstar Communications, Inc. • Monthly. $43.00 per year.

Art Reference Services Quarterly. Haworth Press, Inc. • Quarterly. Individuals, $38.00 per year; libraries and other institutions, $75.00 per year. A journal for art librarians.

Journal of Arts Management, Law, and Society. Helen Dwight Reid Educational Foundation. Helderf Publications. • Quarterly. Individuals, $50.00 per year; institutions, $100.00 per year. Addresses current and ongoing issues in arts policy, management, low and governance from a range of philosophical and national perspectives encompassing diverse disciplinary viewpoints. Formerly *Journal of Arts Management and Law.*

Variety: The International Entertainment Weekly. Cahners Business Information, Broadcasting and Cable's International Group. • Weekly. $219.00 per year. Contains national and international news of show business, with emphasis on motion pictures and television.

Washington International Arts Letter. Allied Business Consultants, Inc. Allied Business Consultants, Inc. • Quarterly. 124.00 per year.

RESEARCH CENTERS AND INSTITUTES

Center for Arts Administration Program. Florida State University. 123 Carothers Hall, Tallahassee, FL 32306-4408. Phone: (850)644-2158 Fax: (850)644-5067 E-mail: cdorn@mailer.fsu.edu • URL: http://www.fsu.edu/~svad/artedpages.

Foundation Center. 79 Fifth Ave., New York, NY 10003-3076. Phone: 800-424-9836 or (212)807-3690 Fax: (212)807-3691 • URL: http://www.fdncenter.org.

TRADE/PROFESSIONAL ASSOCIATIONS

Americans for the Arts. 1000 Vermont Ave., N.W., 12th Fl., Washington, DC 20005. Phone: 800-321-4510 or (202)371-2830 Fax: (202)371-0424 • URL: http://www.artsusa.org • Members are arts organizations and interested individuals. Conducts research and provides information and clearinghouse services relating to the visual arts.

Association of Performing Arts Presenters. 1112 16th St., N.W., No. 400, Washington, DC 20036. Phone: (202)833-2787 Fax: (202)833-1543 E-mail: artspres@artspresenters.org • URL: http://www.artspresenter.org.

Business Committee for the Arts. 1775 Broadway, Suite 510, New York, NY 10019-1942. Phone:

(212)664-0600 Fax: (212)956-5980 E-mail: info@bcainc.org • URL: http://www.bcainc.org.

International Society for the Performing Arts. P.O. Box 909, Rye, NY 10580-0909. Phone: (914)921-1550 Fax: (914)921-1593 E-mail: info@ispa.org • URL: http://www.ispa.org.

Professional Arts Management Institute. 110 Riverside Dr. No. 4E, New York, NY 10024. Phone: (212)579-2039 or (212)787-1194 Fax: (212)579-2049.

OTHER SOURCES

Arts Management. Radius Group Inc. • Five times a year. $22.00 per year. National news service for those who finance, manage and communicate the arts.

Financial Management Strategies for Arts Organization. Robert P. Gallo and Frederick J. Turk. Americans for the Arts. • 1984. $16.95.

Lindey on Entertainment, Publishing and the Arts: Agreements and the Law. Alexander Lindey, editor. West Group. • $673.00 per year. Looseleaf service. Periodic supplementation. Provides basic forms, applicable law, and guidance. (Entertainment and Communication Law Series).

ASBESTOS INDUSTRY

ABSTRACTS AND INDEXES

Environment Abstracts. Congressional Information Service. • Monthly. Price varies. Provides multidisciplinary coverage of the world's environmental literature. Incorporates *Acid Rain Abstracts.*

Environment Abstracts Annual: A Guide to the Key Environmental Literature of the Year. Congressional Information Service. • Annual. $495.00. A yearly cumulation of *Environment Abstracts.*

Pollution Abstracts. Cambridge Information Group. • Monthly. $895.00 per year; with index, $985.00 per year.

CD-ROM DATABASES

Environment Abstracts on CD-ROM. Congressional Information Service, Inc. • Quarterly. $1,295.00 per year. Contains the following CD-ROM databases: *Environment Abstracts, Energy Abstracts,* and *Acid Rain Abstracts.* Length of coverage varies.

DIRECTORIES

OPD Chemical Buyers Directory. Schnell Publishing Co., Inc. • Annual. $129.00. Included in subscription to *Chemical Marketing Reporter.* About 1,500 suppliers of chemical process materials and more than 300 companies which transport and store chemicals in the U.S.

ONLINE DATABASES

CA Search. Chemical Abstracts Service. • Guide to chemical literature, 1967 to present. Inquire as to online cost and availability.

Enviroline. Congressional Information Service, Inc. • Provides online indexing and abstracting of worldwide environmental and natural resource literature from 1975 to date. Updated monthly. Inquire as to online cost and availability.

F & S Index. The Gale Group. • Contains about four million citations to worldwide business, financial, and industrial or consumer product literature appearing from 1972 to date. Weekly updates. Inquire as to online cost and availability.

Toxline. National Library of Medicine. • Abstracting service covering human and animal toxicity studies, 1965 to present (older studies available in *Toxback* file). Monthly updates. Inquire as to online cost and availability.

PERIODICALS AND NEWSLETTERS

Asbestos and Lead Abatement Report: Inspection, Analysis, Removal, Maintenance, Alternatives. Business Publishers, Inc. • Biweekly. $357.00 per year. Newsletter on legal issues relating to the removal or containment of asbestos and lead. Includes news of research activities.

Engineering and Mining Journal (E&MJ). Intertec Publishing Corp. • Monthly. $69.00 per year.

PRICE SOURCES

Chemical and Engineering News: The Newsmagazine of the Chemical World. American Chemical Society. • Weekly. Institutions, $181.00 per year; others, price on application.

Chemical Market Reporter. Schnell Publishing Co., Inc. • Weekly. $139.00 per year. Quotes current prices for a wide range of chemicals. Formerly *Chemical Marketing Reporter.*

RESEARCH CENTERS AND INSTITUTES

Asbestos Institute. 1200 McGill College, Suite 1640, Montreal, QC, Canada H3B 4G7. Phone: (514)877-9797 Fax: (514)844-9717 E-mail: ai@asbestos-institute.ca • URL: http://www.asbestos-institute.ca/main.html.

STATISTICS SOURCES

Mineral Commodity Summaries. Available from U. S. Government Printing Office. • Annual. Published by the U. S. Geological Survey, Department of the Interior (http://www.usgs.gov). Contains detailed, five-year data for about 90 nonfuel minerals. Covers a wide range of statistics, including production, imports, exports, consumption, reserves, prices, tariff information, and industry employment. (Two pages are devoted to each mineral.).

Minerals Yearbook. Available from U.S. Government Printing Office. • Annual. Three volumes.

TRADE/PROFESSIONAL ASSOCIATIONS

Asbestos Information Association/North America. 1745 Jefferson Davis Highway, Suite 406, Arlington, VA 22202. Phone: (703)412-1150 Fax: (703)412-1152 E-mail: aiabjpigg@aol.com.

OTHER SOURCES

Asbestos Litigation Reporter: The National Journal of Record of Asbestos Litigation. Andrews Publications. • Semimonthly. $995.00 per year. Provides reports on legal cases involving asbestos as a health hazard.

ASIAN MARKETS

GENERAL WORKS

China: Foreign Trade Reform. World Bank, The Office of the Publisher. • 1994. $30.00. Makes recommendations for trade liberalization and the reduction of export-import bureaucracy in China. (World Bank Country Study.).

Doing Business in China: The Last Great Market. Geoffrey Murray. St. Martin's Press. • 1994. $80.00.

Trade Policy Review - Japan. Bernan Press. • 1998. $50.00. Co-published by Bernan Press and the World Trade Organization. Available in English, French, or Spanish versions. Provides WTO analysis of Japan's overall economic environment, trade policy objectives, and "policy developments affecting trade and investment.".

ABSTRACTS AND INDEXES

F & S Index: International. The Gale Group. • Monthly. $1,295.00 per year, including quarterly and annual cumulations. Provides annotated citations to marketing, business, financial, and industrial literature. Coverage of international business activity includes trade journals, financial magazines, business newspapers, and special reports. Areas included are Asia, Latin America, Africa, the Middle East, Oceania, and Canada. Formerly *Predicasts F & S Index: International.*

PAIS International in Print. Public Affairs Information Service, Inc. • Monthly. $650.00 per year; cumulations three times a year. Provides topical citations to the worldwide literature of public affairs, economics, demographics, sociology, and trade. Text in English; indexed materials in English, French, German, Italian, Portuguese and Spanish.

ALMANACS AND YEARBOOKS

Emerging Markets Analyst. • Monthly. $895.00 per year. Provides an annual overview of the emerging financial markets in 24 countries of Latin America, Asia, and Europe. Includes data on international mutual funds and closed-end funds.

Japan Economic Almanac: An Annual In-Depth Report on the State of the Japanese Economy. Nihon Keizai Shimbun America, Inc. Japan Economic Almanac. • Annual. $59.50. Lists of Japanese government agencies, and professional and trade organizations. Text in English.

People's Republic of China Year Book. International Publications Service. • Annual. $146.00. Published by China Year Book Publishing House. Serves as the official yearbook of the People's Republic of China. Covers developments in various aspects of life in China, including the economy, industry, transportation, telecommunications, agriculture, technology, demographics, the legal system, health, and foreign relations. Includes many statistical tables and photographs. Text in Chinese.

BIBLIOGRAPHIES

Japanese Automobile Industry: An Annotated Bibliography. Sheu-Yueh J. Chao, compiler. Greenwood Publishing Group, Inc. • 1994. $75.00. Describes about 600 books, articles, papers, and documents written in English. Emphasis is on material published since 1980. (Bibliographies and Indexes in Economics and Economic History Series, No. 157).

CD-ROM DATABASES

Asia Pacific Kompass on Disc. Available from Kompass USA, Inc. • Annual. $2,190.00. CD-ROM provides information on more than 280,000 companies in Australia, China, Hong Kong, India, Korea, Malaysia, New Zealand, Philippines, Singapore, Thailand, and Taiwan. Classification system covers approximately 50,000 products and services.

F & S Index Plus Text. The Gale Group. • Monthly. $7,575.00 per year. Provides CD-ROM citations to worldwide business, marketing, and industrial material appearing in a large assortment of trade journals, newspapers, and other publications. Time period is four years.

Hoover's Company Capsules on CD-ROM. Hoover's, Inc. • Quarterly. $349.95 per year (single-user). Provides the CD-ROM version of *Hoover's Handbook of American Business, Hoover's Handbook of Emerging Companies, Hoover's Handbook of World Business, Hoover's Guide to Computer Companies, Hoover's Guide to Media Companies, Hoover's Handbook of Private Companies,* and various regional guides. Includes more than 11,000 profiles of companies.

Japan 250,000 CD-ROM. Available from Dun & Bradstreet, Inc. • Annual. Price on application. Produced by Tokyo Shoko Research, Ltd. CD-ROM contains basic information on 250,000 Japanese companies.

Kompass CD-ROM Editions. Available from Kompass USA, Inc. • Annual. Prices vary. CD-ROM versions of Kompass international trade directories are available for each of 30 major countries and eight world regions. Searching is provided for 50,000 product/service items and many company details.

PAIS on CD-ROM. Public Affairs Information Service, Inc. • Quarterly. $1,995.00 per year. Provides a CD-ROM version of the online service, *PAIS International*. Contains over 400,000 citations to the literature of contemporary social, political, and economic issues.

World Consumer Markets. The Gale Group. • Annual. $2,500.00. Pblished by Euromonitor. Provides five- year historical data, current data, and forecasts, on CD-ROM for 330 consumer products in 55 countries. Market data is presented in a standardized format for each country.

World Database of Consumer Brands and Their Owners on CD-ROM. The Gale Group. • Annual. $3,190.00. Produced by Euromonitor. Provides detailed information on CD-ROM for about 10,000 companies and 80,000 brands around the world. Covers 1,000 product sectors.

World Marketing Forecasts on CD-ROM. The Gale Group. • Annual. $2,500.00. Produced by Euromonitor. Provides detailed forecast data for the years to 2012 on CD-ROM for 54 countries in all parts of the world. Covers a wide range of social, demographic, economic, and market factors. Includes specific forecasts for many kinds of consumer products.

DIRECTORIES

Asia: A Directory and Sourcebook. Available from The Gale Group. • Irregular. $430.00. Published by Euromonitor. Lists official and unofficial sources of information for Hong Kong, China, Singapore, Taiwan, India, Indonesia, Malaysia, Pakistan, the Philippines, South Korea, Sri Lanka, and Thailand. Includes profiles of leading companies and assessments of consumer markets.

Asia Pacific Securities Handbook. Available from Hoover's, Inc. • Annual. $99.95. Published in Hong Kong. Provides detailed descriptions of stock exchanges in 17 Asia Pacific countries, including Australia, China, Hong Kong, India, Japan, and Singapore. Lists largest public companies and most active stock issues.

Asian Pacific Markets: A Guide to Company and Industry Information Sources. Washington Researchers Ltd. • Irregular. $335.00. A directory of government offices, "experts," publications, and databases related to Asian markets and companies. Includes individual chapters on "the 11 most important nations in Asia." Formerly *Asian Markets.*

Asia's 7,500 Largest Companies. Dun & Bradstreet Information Services. • Annual. $250.00. Published in London by ELC Publishing Ltd. Provides information on the top 7,500 companies in Hong Kong, Indonesia, Japan, South Korea, Malaysia, the Philippines, Singapore, Taiwan, Thailand, and China.

Business Directory of Hong Kong. Available from Estrin & Diamond Publications. • Annual. $160.00. Published in Hong Kong by Current Publications Ltd. Provides information on more than 12,300 Hong Kong businesses in various fields, including manufacturing, finance, services, construction, transportation, and foreign trade.

China: A Directory and Sourcebook. Available from The Gale Group. • 1998. $590.00. Second edition. Published by Euromonitor. Describes about 800 companies in both China and Hong Kong. Sourcebook section provides 500 information sources.

Directory of Consumer Brands and Their Owners: Asia Pacific. Available from The Gale Group. • 1998. $990.00. Published by Euromonitor. Provides information about brands available from major Asia Pacific companies. Descriptions of companies are also included.

Directory of Japanese-Affiliated Companies in the USA and Canada. Available from The Gale Group. • Annual. $375.00. Published by the Japanese External Trade Organization (JETRO). Provides data on more than 5,000 Japanese-affiliated companies located in the U. S. and Canada. (CD-ROM version included with printed directory.).

Dun's Asia Pacific Key Business Enterprises. Dun and Bradstreet Information Services. • Annual. Price on application. Provides information on 30,000 companies in 14 Pacific Rim countries. Firms have sales of ten million dollars or over, or have 500 or more employees.

Dun's Key Decision-Makers in Hong Kong Business. Dun and Bradstreet Information Services. • Annual. $380.00. Provides information on over 8,000 major Hong Kong companies.

Euromonitor Directory of Asian Companies. Gale Group, Inc. • 1997. $550.00. Provides detailed profiles of 5,000 major companies in Southeast Asia. Countries are China, Hong Kong, India, Indonesia, Korea, Malaysia, Pakistan, Phillippines, Singapore, Sri Lanka, Taiwan, Thailand, and Vietnam.

Hoover's Handbook of World Business: Profiles of Major European, Asian, Latin American, and Canadian Companies. Hoover's, Inc. • Annual. $99.95. Contains detailed profiles of more than 300 large foreign companies. Includes indexes by industry, location, executive name, company name, and brand name.

International Directory of Consumer Brands and Their Owners. Available from The Gale Group. • 1997. $450.00. Published by Euromonitor. Contains detailed information on more than 38,000 consumer product brands and their companies in 62 countries of the world, excluding Europe.

International Media Guide: Business Professional Publications: Asia Pacific/Middle East/Africa. International Media Guides, Inc. • Annual. $285.00. Provides information on 3,000 trade journals "from Africa to the Pacific Rim," including advertising rates and circulation data.

Japan Trade Directory 2000-2001. Available from The Gale Group. • 2000. $350.00. 18th edition. Published by the Japan External Trade Organization (JETRO). Provides information on about 2,800 Japanese companies currently active in exporting or importing.

Kompass International Trade Directories. Available from MarketResearch.com. • Annual. Prices and volumes vary. Kompass directories are published internationally for each of more than 70 countries, from Algeria to Yugoslavia. The Kompass classification system covers 50,000 individual product and service categories. Most directories include a tradename index and company profiles.

Major Companies of South West Asia 2001. Available from The Gale Group. • 2001. $550.00. Fifth edition. Published by Graham and Whiteside. Provides information on 3,600 leading businesses in India and 2,500 in Turkey, Pakistan, Iran, and other countries of the region.

Major Companies of the Far East and Australasia 2001. Available from The Gale Group. • 2001. $1,475.00. 17th edition. Three volumes. Published in London by Graham & Whiteside, Provides information on about 13,000 major companies. Volume one ($575.00): *South East Asia.* Volume two ($575.00): *East Asia.* Volume three *Australia, New Zealand, and Papua New Guinea.*($390.00).

Major Market Share Companies: Asia Pacific. Available from The Gale Group. • 2000. $900.00. Published by Euromonitor (http://www.euromonitor.com). Provides consumer market share data and rankings for multinational and regional companies. Covers leading firms in Japan, China, Australia, South Korea, Indonesia, Malaysia, Philippines, and Thailand.

Who Owns Whom: Australasia & Asia, Middle East and Africa. Dun & Bradstreet Information Services. • Annual. $500.00. Two volumes. Published in England by Dun & Bradstreet Ltd. Provides information on 5,500 parent companies and their foreign and domestic subsidiaries. Parent companies are located in Singapore, Hong Kong, Japan, the Philippines, South Korea, Taiwan, Thailand, New Guinea, Malaysia, Indonesia, New Zealand, and Australia. Formerly *Who Owns Whom: Australasia and Far East.*

ENCYCLOPEDIAS AND DICTIONARIES

Encyclopedia of Business. The Gale Group. • 2000. $425.00. Second edition. Two volumes. Contains more than 700 signed articles covering major business disciplines and concepts. International in scope.

HANDBOOKS AND MANUALS

Asian Company Handbook. Available from Hoover's, Inc. • 1998. $79.95. Published by Toyo Keizai, Japan. Text in English. Provides detailed profiles of 1,060 publicly-traded companies listed on stock exchanges in Hong Kong, Indonesia, Malaysia, the Republic of Korea, Singapore, Taiwan, and Thailand.

Business Guide to Modern China. Jon P. Alston and Yongxin He. Michigan State University Press. • 1996. $29.95. (International Business Series).

China Business: The Portable Encyclopedia for Doing Business with China. Christine Genzberger and others. World Trade Press. • 1994. $24.95. Covers economic data, import/export possibilities, basic tax and trade laws, travel information, and other useful facts for doing business with the People's Republic of China. (Country Business Guides Series).

Hong Kong Business: The Portable Encyclopedia for Doing Business with Hong Kong. World Trade Press. • 1994. $24.95. Covers economic data, import/export possibilities, basic tax and trade laws, travel information, and other useful facts for doing business with Hong Kong. (Country Business Guides Series).

Japan Business: The Portable Encyclopedia for Doing Business with Japan. Christine Genzberger and others. World Trade Press. • 1944. $24.95. (Country Business Guide Series).

Japan Company Handbook. Available from Hoover's, Inc. • Quarterly. $444.00 per year. Two volumes (current quarterly two-volume edition available at $120.00). Published by Toyo Keizai, Japan. Text in English. Contains profiles of 2,500 Japanese companies. First volume covers larger publicly-held companies; second volume provides information on smaller publicly-held firms.

Singapore Business: The Portable Encyclopedia for Doing Business with Singapore. World Trade Press. • 1994. $24.95. Covers economic data, import/export possibilities, basic tax and trade laws, travel information, and other useful facts for doing business with Singapore. (Country Business Guides Series).

Taiwan Business: The Portable Encyclopedia for Doing Business with Taiwan. World Trade Press. • 1994. $24.95. Covers economic data, import/export possibilities, basic tax and trade laws, travel information, and other useful facts for doing business with Taiwan. (Country Business Guides).

INTERNET DATABASES

Asia, Inc. Online. Manager Media Group, Hong Kong. Phone: (852)581-8088 Fax: (852)851-0962 E-mail: marketing@manager.com • URL: http://www.asia-inc.com • Web site provides Asian business news and information. Includes "Today's Financial News" (commentary and Asian stock prices), "This Week's Special Items," "Feature Stories," "Net Resources," "Archive," and other contents. Includes a search facility. Fees: Free.

ONLINE DATABASES

Euromonitor Market Research. Euromonitor International. • Provides the complete text online of Euromonitor market analysis reports. Covers consumer goods market research data for all major countries, with emphasis on specific product categories. Time period is current. Continuous updating. Inquire as to online cost and availability.

F & S Index. The Gale Group. • Contains about four million citations to worldwide business, financial, and industrial or consumer product literature appearing from 1972 to date. Weekly updates. Inquire as to online cost and availability.

Globalbase. The Gale Group. • Provides more than one million online summaries of business, industrial, and economic news reports from more than 1,000 publications worldwide. Covers a wide range of material appearing in international trade journals, professional magazines, and newspapers. Time period is 1984 to date, with weekly updates. Inquire as to online cost and availability.

Japan Economic Newswire Plus. Kyodo News International, Inc. • Provides full text in English of news items relating to business, economics, industry, trade, and finance in Japan and the Pacific Rim countries. Time period is 1982 to date, with daily updates. Inquire as to online cost and availability.

PAIS International. Public Affairs Information Service, Inc. • Corresponds to the former printed publications, *PAIS Bulletin* (1976-90) and *PAIS Foreign Language Index* (1972-90), and to the current *PAIS International in Print* (1991 to date). Covers economic, political, and sociological material appearing in periodicals, books, government documents, and other publications. Updating is monthly. Inquire as to online cost and availability.

PROMT: Predicasts Overview of Markets and Technology. The Gale Group. • Companies, products, applied technologies and markets. U.S. and international literature coverage, 1972 to date. Inquire as to online cost and availability. Provides abstracts from more than 1,600 publications. Weekly updates.

PERIODICALS AND NEWSLETTERS

ADWEEK Asia. BPI Communications, Inc. • Bimonthly. $99.00 per year. Covers advertising and marketing across the Asia-Pacific area. Published in Hong Kong.

Asia Inc.: The Region's Business Magazine. Asia, Inc., Ltd. • Monthly. $79.00 per year. Contains business, financial, and other news and commentary from various countries in Asia. Main sections are "At Work," "Asia Abroad: A World of Business," and "After Hours: Travel and Leisure." Text in English.

Asia Pacific Economic Review: Bridging Pacific Rim Business and Society. Zencore, Inc. • Monthly. $35.00 per year. Includes special issues on individual countries: Taiwan, Malayasia, China/ Hong Kong, Japan, and Korea.

Asia Times: The Voice of Asia. Available from Asia Times Circulation Dept. • Daily. $392.00 per year. Published in Thailand by Asia Network Publication Co. Ltd. A business newspaper presenting trade, financial, and general news from most Asian countries. Includes 100 high volume, large capitalization stock price quotes from each of nine markets: Tokyo, Hong Kong, Seoul, Taipei, Bangkok, Manila, Kuala Lumpur, Singapore, and Jakarta. (A Manager Media Group publication.).

The Asian Wall Street Journal. Dow Jones & Co., Inc. • Daily. $610.00 per year (air mail). Published in Hong Kong. Also available in a weekly edition at $259.00 per year: *Asian Wall Street Journal Weekly.*

Business Week China. Ministry of Foreign Economic Relations and Trade, Institute of International Tra. McGraw-Hill. • Bimonthly. Price on application. Edited for business and government officials in the People's Republic of China. Selected Chinese translation of *Business Week.*

Business Week International: The World's Only International Newsweekly of Business. McGraw-Hill. • Weekly. $105.00 per year.

China Business and Trade. Welt Publishing, LLC. • Semimonthly. Institutions, $367.20 per year; corporations, $459.00 per year. Newsletter. Covers business and trade developments in the People's Republic of China.

China Business Review. United States-China Business Council. • Bimonthly. $99.00 per year. Covers trends and issues affecting U. S. investment and trade with China and Hong Kong.

East Asian Executive Reports. International Executive Reports Ltd. • Monthly. $455.00 per year. Newsletter. Covers the legal, financial, and practical aspects of doing business in East Asia, including importing, joint ventures, and licensing.

Emerging Markets Quarterly. Institutional Investor. • Quarterly. $325.00 per year. Newsletter on financial markets in developing areas, such as Africa, Latin America, Southeast Asia, and Eastern Europe. Topics include institutional investment opportunities and regulatory matters. Formerly *Emerging Markets Weekly.*

Far Eastern Economic Review. Dow Jones International Marketing Service. • Weekly. $205.00 per year (air mail). Published in Hong Kong by Review Publishing Co., a Dow Jones subsidiary (GPO Box 160, Hong Kong). Covers Asian business, economics, politics, and international relations. Includes reports on individual countries and companies, business trends, and stock price quotations.

Hong Kong Week. Dow Jones & Co. • Weekly. $260.00 per year (air mail). A guide to investing in Hong Kong and China. Provides stock prices, market analysis, and commentary. Edited and published in Hong Kong by the *Asian Wall Street Journal.*

Institutional Investor International Edition: The Magazine for International Finance and Investment. Institutional Investor. • Monthly. $415.00 per year. Covers the international aspects of professional investing and finance. Emphasis is on Europe, the Far East, and Latin America.

The Japan Times: Weekly International Edition. JTUSA, Inc. • Weekly. $140.00 per year. Provides news and commentary on Japan's economy, trade policies, and Japanese life in general. Regular features include "Business Briefs," "Market Reports," "Lifestyle," and "Issue Analysis." Supplement available *The Japan Times Weekly.* Text in English.

Journal of Asia-Pacific Business. Haworth Press, Inc. • Quarterly. Individuals, $60.00 per year; institutions, $100.00 per year; libraries, $125.00 per year. An academic and practical journal concerned with marketing, finance, and other aspects of doing business in Asia.

Journal of Asian Business. Southeast Asia Business Program. University of Michigan. • Quarterly. Individuals, $25.00 per year; institutions, $40.00 per year. An international academic journal covering business in all parts of Asia.

Journal of East-West Business. Haworth Press, Inc. • Quarterly. Individuals, $60.00 per year; institutions, $120.00 per year; libraries, $174.00 per year. An academic and practical journal focusing on business in the developing regions of Asia and Eastern Europe.

Journal of the Asia Pacific Economy. Routledge Journals. • Three times a year. Individuals, $64.00 per year; institutions, $292.00 per year. Covers economic, political, social, cultural, and historical factors affecting Asian commerce and trade.

Market: Asia Pacific. Available from MarketResearch.com. • Monthly. $397.00 per year. Newsletter. Published by Market Newsletters. Provides market trends and demographic data for countries of the Asia Pacific region.

Market Research International. Euromonitor International. • Monthly. $1,130.00 per year. Emphasis is on international consumer market research. Includes International Market Review, Global Market Trends and Developments, USA Market Report, Japan Market Report, Emerging Markets, and Market Focus (concise country reports).

The Nikkei Weekly: Japan's Leading Business Newspaper. Nikkei America, Inc. • Weekly. $108.00 per year. A newspaper in English "dedicated to all aspects of Japanese business and its influence on people, markets and political trends around the world." Includes English versions of articles appearing in leading Japanese business newspapers, such as *Nihon Keizai Shimbun, Nikkei Marketing Journal*, and *Nikkei Financial Daily.*

RESEARCH CENTERS AND INSTITUTES

Center on Japanese Economy and Business. Columbia University, 521 Uris Hall, 3022 Broadway, New York, NY 10027-6902. Phone: (212)854-3976 Fax: (212)678-6958 E-mail: hpatrick@claven.gsb.colombia.edu • URL: http://www.gsb.columbia.edu/japan/ • Research areas include Pacific Basin trade policy.

Industrial Research Institute for Pacific Nations. California State Polytechnic University, Pomona, School of Business Administration, 3801 W. Temple Ave., Bldg. 66, Room 217, Pomona, CA 91768. Phone: (909)869-2399 Fax: (909)869-6799 • URL: http://www.hkjinacsu.edu • Conducts research on the Pacific nations marketplace.

STATISTICS SOURCES

China Marketing Data and Statistics. Available from The Gale Group. • 2000. $430.00. Second edition. Two volumes. Published by Euromonitor. In addition to national statistics, includes data for 30 cities and 400 administrative areas. Major source is the Chinese State Statistical Bureau.

Consumer Asia 2001. Available from The Gale Group. • 2001. $970.00. Eighth edition. Published by Euromonitor. Provides statistical andanalytical surveys of factors affecting Asian consumer markets: energy, labor, population, finance, debt, tourism, consumer expenditures, household characteristics, etc. Emphasis is on Hong Kong, Singapore, Taiwan, South Korea, Indonesia, and Malaysia.

Consumer China 2001. Available from The Gale Group. • 2001. $970.00. Seventh edition. Published by Euromonitor. Provides demographic and consumer market data for China.

Consumer International 2000/2001. Available from The Gale Group. • 1998. $1,190.00. Seventh edition. Published by Euromonitor. Contains extensive consumer market, economic, and demographic data for 27 major, non-European countries, including the U. S. and Canada. Includes consumer market size (volume and value) for 150 product types in 14 categories (food, clothing, automobiles, cosmetics, appliances, etc.).

Emerging Stock Markets Factbook. International Finance Corporation, Capital Market Dept. • Annual. $100.00. Published by the International Finance Corporation (IFC). Provides statistical profiles of more than 26 emerging stock markets in various countries of the world. Includes regional, composite, and industry indexes.

The Far East and Australasia 2000. Taylor and Francis, Inc. • Annual. $480.00. Published by Europa. Includes country statistical surveys of demographics, finance, trade, and agriculture. (Regional Surveys of the World.).

Gale Country and World Rankings Reporter. The Gale Group. • 1997. $135.00. Second edition. Provides about 3,000 statistical ranking tables and charts covering more than 235 nations. Sources include the United Nations and various government publications.

International Marketing Forecasts 2001. Available from The Gale Group. • 2000. $1,090.00. Third edition. Published by Euromonitor. Contains demographic, economic, and market forecasts to the year 2010 for major, non-European countries, including the U. S. and Canada. Forecasts include market-size data for 15 consumer product sectors, such as food, clothing, and automobiles.

Retail Trade International. The Gale Group. • 2000. $1,990.00. Second edition. Six volumes. Presents comprehensive data on retail trends in 51 countries. Includes textual analysis and profiles of major retailers. Covers Europe, Asia, the Middle East, Africa and the Americas.

Statistical Indicators for Asia and the Pacific. United Nations Publications. • Quarterly. $80.00 per year. Provides data on economic and demographic trends in the region. Text in English.

Statistical Yearbook for Asia and the Pacific. United Nations Publications. • Annual. $90.00. Includes 56 countries of the region. Contains data on national accounts, trade, industry, banking, wages, consumption, population, and other economic and demographic subjects. Text in English and French.

TRADE/PROFESSIONAL ASSOCIATIONS

American Indonesian Chamber of Commerce. 711 Third Ave., 17th Fl., New York, NY 10017. Phone: (212)687-4505 Fax: (212)867-9882.

Chinese American Association of Commerce. 778 Clay St., Suite C, San Francisco, CA 94108. Phone: (415)362-4306 Fax: (415)362-1478 • Members are individuals interested in improving trade between the U. S. and the People's Republic of China.

Japan Economic Institute of America. 1000 Connecticut Ave., N. W., Suite 211, Washington, DC 20036. Phone: (202)296-5633 Fax: (202)296-8333 E-mail: jei@jei.org • URL: http://www.jei@.org • Provides current information on U. S.-Japan economic and trade relations. Funded by the Japanese Foreign Ministry.

Japan External Trade Organization. 1221 Ave. of the Americas, New York, NY 10020. Phone: (212)997-0400 Fax: (212)997-0464 • URL: http://www.jetro.org • Encourages American companies to export goods to Japan. Makes information available on Japanese marketing and distribution systems.

Korea Trade Promotion Center. 460 Park Ave., Room 402, New York, NY 10022. Phone: 800-568-7248 or (212)826-0900 Fax: (212)888-4930 • Provides information about Korean products and promotes trade between the U. S. and Korea.

OTHER SOURCES

Asian Business. TPL Corp Ltd. • Monthly. $105.00 per year. Covers Asian business, investment, and franchise opportunities, especially in Hong Kong, Singapore, and Taiwan.

Japanese Company Factfinder: Teikoku Databank. Teikoku Databank America, Inc. • Quarterly. $1,920.00 per year to academic and public libraries. $3,200 per year to businesses. CD-ROM provides detailed financial and descriptive information on more than 186,000 Japanese companies doing business overseas.

The Market for Consumer Products in Southeast Asia. MarketResearch.com. • 1997. $2,500.00. Market research report. Covers Asian consumer markets for food, cosmetics, pharmaceuticals, medical devices, and building materials. Market projections are provided to the year 2001.

ASPHALT INDUSTRY

BIBLIOGRAPHIES

Catalog of Asphalt Institute Publications. Asphalt Institute. • Annual. Free.

DIRECTORIES

OPD Chemical Buyers Directory. Schnell Publishing Co., Inc. • Annual. $129.00. Included in subscription to *Chemical Marketing Reporter*. About 1,500 suppliers of chemical process materials and more than 300 companies which transport and store chemicals in the U.S.

ONLINE DATABASES

F & S Index. The Gale Group. • Contains about four million citations to worldwide business, financial, and industrial or consumer product literature appearing from 1972 to date. Weekly updates. Inquire as to online cost and availability.

PERIODICALS AND NEWSLETTERS

Asphalt. Asphalt Institute. • Three times a year. Free.

HMAT (Hot Mix Asphalt Technology). National Asphalt Pavement Association. • Quarterly. Free to qualified personnel. Formerly *HMAT*.

Oil Daily: Daily Newspaper of the Petroleum Industry. Energy Intelligence Group. • Daily. $1,145.00 per year. Newspaper for the petroleum industry.

PRICE SOURCES

Chemical Market Reporter. Schnell Publishing Co., Inc. • Weekly. $139.00 per year. Quotes current prices for a wide range of chemicals. Formerly *Chemical Marketing Reporter*.

PPI Detailed Report. Bureau of Labor Statistics, U.S. Department of Labor. Available from U.S. Government Printing Office. • Monthly. $55.00 per year. Formerly *Producer Price Indexes*.

RESEARCH CENTERS AND INSTITUTES

Bituminous Research Laboratory. Iowa State University of Science and Technology. Dept. of Civil and Construction Engineering, Ames, IA 50011. Phone: (515)294-7439 Fax: (515)294-8216 E-mail: dyl@iastate.edu • URL: http://www.iastate.edu.

Engineering Experiment Station. Ohio State University. 2070 Neil Ave., Columbus, OH 43210-1275. Phone: (614)292-2411 Fax: (614)292-9615 E-mail: fortner.1@osu.edu • URL: http://www.osu.edu.

Texas Transportation Institute, Systems Planning Division. Texas A & M University. College Station, TX 77843-3135. Phone: (979)845-8552 Fax: (979)945-9356 E-mail: h.richardson@tamu.edu • URL: http://www.tti.tamu.edu.

STATISTICS SOURCES

Minerals Yearbook. Available from U.S. Government Printing Office. • Annual. Three volumes.

TRADE/PROFESSIONAL ASSOCIATIONS

Asphalt Emulsion Manufacturers Association. Three Church Circle, PMB 250, Annapolis, MD 21401. Phone: (410)267-0023 E-mail: krissorf@compuserve.com • URL: http://www.aema.org.

Asphalt Institute. P.O. Box 14052, Lexington, KY 40512-4052. Phone: (606)288-4960 Fax: (606)288-4999 • URL: http://www.asphaltinstitute.org.

Association of Asphalt Paving Technologists. 400 Selby Ave., Suite 1, St. Paul, MN 55102. Phone: (651)293-9188 Fax: (651)293-9193 E-mail: asphalttechnology@worldnet.att.net.

National Asphalt Pavement Association. NAPA Bldg., 5100 Forbes Blvd., Lanham, MD 20706-4413. Phone: 888-468-6499 or (301)731-4748 Fax: (301)731-4621 E-mail: napa@hotmix.org • URL: http://www.hotmix.org.

OTHER SOURCES

Asphalt Products and Markets. Available from MarketResearch.com. • 1998. $3,200.00. Published by the Freedonia Group. Market data with forecasts to 2002 and 2007. Includes information on paving, coating, and roofing asphalt products.

ASSOCIATIONS

See also: CLUBS; WOMEN'S CLUBS

ALMANACS AND YEARBOOKS

Association Meeting Trends. American Society of Association Executives. • 1999. $90.00.

BIOGRAPHICAL SOURCES

Who's Who in Association Management. American Society of Association Executives. • Annual. $160.00. Lists paid executives who are members of the association and suppliers of products and services to the association.

CD-ROM DATABASES

Associations Unlimited. The Gale Group. • Semiannual. Includes all information on CD-ROM from all of the Gale *Encyclopedia of Associations* directories, plus association materials from about 2,500 of the associations-full-text documents and membership applications.

Encyclopedia of Associations CD-ROM. The Gale Group. • Semiannual. $1,095.00 per year, single user; $1,895.00 per year, network. Available for IBM or MAC. Provides detailed CD-ROM information on over 160,000 international, national, regional, state, and local organizations. Corresponds to the various volumes and supplements that make up the Gale *Encyclopedia of Associations* series.

World Database of Business Information Sources on CD-ROM. The Gale Group. • Annual. Produced by Euromonitor. Presents Euromonitor's entire information source database on CD-ROM. Contains a worldwide total of about 35,000 publications, organizations, libraries, trade fairs, and online databases.

Yearbook of International Organizations PLUS. R. R. Bowker. • Annual. $1,500.00. Compiled by the Union of International Organizations, Brussels. Includes the *Yearbook of International Organizations* and *Who's Who in International Organizations*.

DIRECTORIES

Associations Canada: The Directory of Associations in Canada. Micromedia. • Annual. $299.00. Provides detailed information in English and French on 20,000 active Canadian associations. Includes subject, keyword, personal name, and other indexes. Formerly *Directory of Associations in Canada.*

Associations Yellow Book: Who's Who at the Leading U. S. Trade and Professional Associations. Leadership Directories, Inc. • Semiannual. $235.00 per year. Gives the names and titles of over 43,000 staff members in about 1,100 major associations. Six indexes are included: association name, individual name, industry, budget, acronym, and political action committee (PAC).

Directory of Association Meeting Planners' and Conference/Convention Directors. Salesman's Guide. • Annual. $259.95. Lists about 13,600 planners of meetings for over 8,100 national associations. Provides past and future convention locations, dates held, number of attendees, exhibit space required, and other convention information. Formerly *Association Meeting Planners.*

Directory of British Associations and Associations in Ireland. CBD Research Research Ltd. • Biennial. $320.00. Lists about 7,000 national organizations of England Wales, Scotland, Northern Ireland, and the Irish Republic. Published by CBD Research.

The Directory of Business Information Resources: Associations, Newsletters, Magazine Trade Shows. Grey House Publishing, Inc. • Annual. $195.00. Provides concise information on associations, newsletters, magazines, and trade shows for each of 90 major industry groups. An "Entry & Company Index" serves as a guide to titles, publishers, and organizations.

Directory of Trade and Professional Associations in the European Union. Euroconfidentiel S. A. • Annual. $160.00. Includes more than 9,000 EU-related associations.

Encyclopedia of Associations. The Gale Group. • Annual. $1,425.00. Three volumes. Volume 1, National Organizations, $545.00; Volume 2, Geographic and Executive Indexes, $425.00; Volume 3, supplement, $455.00.

Encyclopedia of Associations: International Organizations. The Gale Group. • Annual. $615.00. Two volumes. Includes detailed information on more than 20,600 international nonprofit membership organizations.

Encyclopedia of Associations: Regional, State, and Local Organizations. The Gale Group. • Annual. $600.00. Five volumes. $140.00 per volume. Each volume covers a particular region of the U. S.

National Directory of Nonprofit Organizations 2002. Available from The Gale Group. • 2001. $535.00. 13th edition. Two volumes. Volume one, $370.00; volume two, $240.00. Contains over 250,000 listings of nonprofit organizations, indexed by 260 areas of activity. Indicates income range and IRS tax filing status for each organization.

National Trade and Professional Associations of the United States. Columbia Books, Inc. • Annual. $99.00. Provides key facts on approximately 7,500 trade associations, labor and professional organizations. Formerly *National Trade and Professional Association of the United States and Labor Unions.*

Public Interest Profiles, 1998-1999. Available from Congressional Quarterly, Inc. • 1996. $175.00. Published by Foundation for Public Affairs. Provides detailed information on more than 250 influential public interest and public policy organizations (lobbyists) in the U.S. Includes e-mail addresses and Web sites where available.

State and Regional Associations of the United States. Columbia Books, Inc. • Annual. $79.00. Provides information on over 7,500 state and regional business associations, professional societies, and labor unions.

Washington Information Directory. Congressional Quarterly, Inc. • Annual. $119.00. Published by Congressional Quarterly, Inc. Lists names, addresses, phone numbers, fax numbers, and some Internet addresses for Congress, federal agencies, and nonprofit organizations in Washington, DC. Includes brief descriptions of each group and a subject index.

World Directory of Marketing Information Sources. Available from The Gale Group. • 2001. $590.00. Third edition. Published by Euromonitor. Provides details on more than 6,000 sources of marketing information, including publications, libraries, associations, market research companies, online databases, and governmental organizations. Coverage is worldwide.

World Directory of Trade and Business Associations. Available from The Gale Group. • 2000. $595.00. Third edition. Published by Euromonitor. Provides detailed information on approximately 5,000 trade associations in various countries of the world. Includes subject and geographic indexes.

Yearbook of International Organizations. Available from The Gale Group. • Annual. $1,300.00. Four volumes: (1) *Organization Descriptions and Index* (32,000 organizations in 225 countries); (2) *International Organization Participation* (geographic arrangement); (3) *Global Action Networks* (a subject directory with 4,300 categories); (4) *Internationa Organization Bibliography and Resources.* Published by K. G. Saur.

ENCYCLOPEDIAS AND DICTIONARIES

World Guide to Abbreviations of Organizations. Available from The Gale Group. • 1987. $125.00. 11th edition. Published by Chapman and Hall.

FINANCIAL RATIOS

Association Operating Ratio Report. American Society of Association Executives. • 1997. $165.00. Contains comparison data from associations.

HANDBOOKS AND MANUALS

Law of Associations: An Operating Legal Manual for Executives and Counsel. George D. Webster, editor. Matthew Bender & Co., Inc. • $255.00. Looseleaf service. Periodic supplementation. Coverage of all legal and tax aspects of non-profit associations.

Principles of Association Management. Henry Ernstthal and Bob Jones. American Society of Association Executives. • 1996. $43.95. Third edition.

Professional Corporations and Associations. Berrien C. Eaton. Matthew Bender & Co., Inc. • $1,140.00. Six looseleaf volumes. Periodic supplementation. Detailed information on forming, operating and changing a professional corporation or association.

INTERNET DATABASES

GaleNet: Your Information Community. The Gale Group. Phone: 800-877-GALE or (248)699-GALE Fax: 800-414-5043 or (248)699-8069 E-mail: galenet@gale.com • URL: http://www.galenet.com • Web site provides a wide variety of full-text information from Gale databases, Taft, and other sources. Covers associations, biography, business directories, education, the information industry, literature, publishing, and science. Fee-based subscriptions are available for individual databases (free demonstration). Includes Boolean search features and the BRS/Search user interface.

ONLINE DATABASES

Encyclopedia of Associations [Online]. The Gale Group. • Provides detailed information on about 160,000 U. S. and International non-profit organizations. Semiannual updates. Inquire as to online cost and availability.

Industry Insider. Thomson Financial Securities Data. • Contains full-text online industry research reports from more than 200 leading trade associations, covering 50 specific industries. Reports include extensive statistics and market research data. Inquire as to online cost and availability.

PERIODICALS AND NEWSLETTERS

Association Management. American Society of Association Executives. • Monthly. $30.00.

Association Trends. Martineau Corporation. • Weekly. $95.00 per year. For staff executives of national, local, regional trade and professional associations. Contains news and information on association management and related issues.

Don Kramer's Nonprofit Issues. Don Kramer Publisher. • Monthly. $129.00 per year. Newsletter with legal emphasis. Covers the laws, rules, regulations, and taxes affecting nonprofit organizations.

STATISTICS SOURCES

Association Executive Compensation Study. American Society of Association Executives. • 1999. $150.00. A salary survey.

TRADE/PROFESSIONAL ASSOCIATIONS

American Society of Association Executives. 1575 Eye St., N.W., Washington, DC 20005-1168. Phone: (202)626-2723 or (202)626-2742 Fax: (202)371-8825 E-mail: feedback@asaenet.org • URL: http://www.asaenet.org.

International Association of Association Management Companies. 414 Plaza Dr., Suite 209, Westmont, IL 60559. Phone: (630)655-1669 Fax: (630)655-0391 E-mail: info@iaamc.org • URL: http://www.iaamc.org.

Trade Associations amd Professional Bodies of the Continental European Union. Available from The Gale Group. 27500 Drake Rd., Farmington Hills, MI 48331-3535. Phone: 800-877-GALE or (248)699-GALE Fax: 800-414-5043 or (248)699-8069 E-mail: galeord@galegroup.com • URL: http://www.galegroup.com • 2000. $280.00. Published by Graham & Whiteside. Provides detailed information on more than 3,600 business and professional organizations in Europe.

OTHER SOURCES

Washington [year]. Columbia Books, Inc. • Annual. $129.00. Provides information on about 5,000 Washington, DC key businesses, government offices, non-profit organizations, and cultural institutions, with the names of about 25,000 principal executives. Includes Washington media, law offices, foundations, labor unions, international organizations, clubs, etc.

ASSOCIATIONS, INTERNATIONAL

See: INTERNATIONAL AGENCIES

ASTRONAUTICS

See: ROCKET INDUSTRY

ATHLETIC GOODS

See: SPORTING GOODS INDUSTRY

ATLASES

See: MAPS

ATOMIC POWER

See: NUCLEAR ENERGY

ATTORNEYS

See: LAWYERS

AUCTIONS

PERIODICALS AND NEWSLETTERS

The Auctioneer. National Auctioneers Association. • Monthly. Membership. News of interest to auctioneers.

PRICE SOURCES

Book Auction Records. Dawson UK Ltd. • Annual. $200.00.

TRADE/PROFESSIONAL ASSOCIATIONS

Burley Auction Warehouse Association. 620 S. Broadway St., Lexington, KY 40508-3126. Phone: (606)255-4504 Fax: (606)255-4534 E-mail: bawa@gte.net.

Livestock Marketing Association. 7509 Tiffany Springs Parkway, Kansas City, MO 64153-2315. Phone: 800-821-2048 or (816)891-0502 Fax: (816)891-0552.

National Auctioneers Association. 8880 Ballentine, Overland Park, KS 66214. Phone: (913)541-8084 Fax: (913)894-5281 E-mail: naahq@aol.com • URL: http://www.auctioneers.org.

NAtional Auto Auction Association. 5320-D Spectrum Dr., Frederick, MD 21703-7337. Phone: (301)696-0400 Fax: (301)631-1359 E-mail: naaa@earthlink.net • URL: http://www.naaa.com.

AUDIENCE RESEARCH

See: ADVERTISING MEDIA; MARKET RESEARCH

AUDIO EQUIPMENT INDUSTRY

See: HIGH FIDELITY/STEREO

AUDIOVISUAL AIDS IN EDUCATION

See also: AUDIOVISUAL AIDS IN INDUSTRY

ALMANACS AND YEARBOOKS

Educational Media and Technology Yearbook. Libraries Unlimited, Inc. • Annual. $65.00.

BIBLIOGRAPHIES

Films and Audiovisual Information. Available from U. S. Government Printing Office. • Annual. Free. Issued by the Superintendent of Documents. A list of government publications on motion picture and audiovisual topics. Formerly *Motion Pictures, Films and Audiovisual Information.* (Subject Bibliography No. 73.).

CD-ROM DATABASES

A-V Online (CD-ROM). Access Innovations, Inc. • Annual. $795.00 per year. Provides CD-ROM descriptions of all types of non-print educational materials, covering all learning levels.

ERIC on SilverPlatter. Available from SilverPlatter Information, Inc. • Quarterly. $700.00 per year. Produced by the Office of Educational Research and Improvement, U. S. Dept. of Education. Provides CD-ROM indexing and abstracting of a wide variety of literature relating to education. Archival discs are available from 1966.

DIRECTORIES

Directory of Video, Computer, and Audio-Visual Products. International Communications Industries Association. • Annual. $65.00. Contains detailed descriptions and photographs of specific items of equipment. Includes video cameras, overhead projectors, LCD panels, computer projection systems, film recording equipment, etc. A "Glossary of Terms" is also provided.

Film and Video Finder. National Information Center for Educational Media. Plexus Publishing, Inc. • Biennial. $295.00. Contains 92,000 listings of film and video educational, technical and vocational children's programs and literary materials.

Filmstrip and Slide Set Finder, 1990: A Comprehensive Index to 35mm Educational Filmstrips and Slide Sets. Plexus Publishing, Inc. • 1990. $225.00. Three volumes.

Index to AV Producers and Distributors (Educational Audiovisual Materials). National Information Center for Educational Media. c/o Plexus Publishing, Inc. • Biennial. $89.00. A directory listing about 23,300 producers and distributors of all types of audiovisual educational materials.

Peterson's Guide to Distance Learning. Peterson's. • 1996. $24.95. Provides detailed information on accredited college and university programs available through television, radio, computer, videocassette, and audiocassette resources. Covers 700 U. S. and Canadian institutions. Formerly *The Electronic University.*

The Video Source Book. The Gale Group. • 2000. $345.00. 26th edition. Two volumes. Describes 160,000 video programs currently available on tape and disc. Includes Subject Category Index, Videodisc Index, Captioned Index (for hearing impaired), and Credits Index (actors, directors, etc.).

HANDBOOKS AND MANUALS

Educators Guide to Free Films, Filmstrips and Slides. Educators Progress Service, Inc. • Annual. $34.95. Lists more than 978 educational and recreational films in all subject areas for free use by teachers and other educators. Formerly *Educators Guide to Free Filmstrips and Slides.*

Educators Guide to Free Videotapes. James Berger, editor. Educators Progress Service, Inc. • Annual. $34.95. Lists free-loan audiotapes, videotapes and records. Formerly *Educators Guide to Free Audio and Video Materials.*

Handbook of Educational Technology: Practical Guide for Teachers. Fred Percival and others. Nichols Publishing Co. • 1993. $39.95. Third edition.

ONLINE DATABASES

A-V Online. Access Innovations, Inc. • Provides online descriptions of non-print educational materials for all levels, kindergarten to graduate school. Includes all types of audio, film, and video media. Updated quarterly. Inquire as to online cost and availability.

ERIC. Educational Resources Information Center. • Broad range of educational literature, 1966 to present. Monthly updates. Inquire as to online cost and availability.

PERIODICALS AND NEWSLETTERS

Communications Industries Report. International Communications Industries Association. • Monthly. Free.

Educational Marketer: The Educational Publishing Industry's Voice of Authority Since 1968. SIMBA Information. • Three times a month. $479.00 per year. Newsletter. Edited for suppliers of educational materials to schools and colleges at all levels. Covers print and electronic publishing, software, audiovisual items, and multimedia. Includes corporate news and educational statistics.

Educational Technology Research and Development. Association for Educational Communications and Technology. • Quarterly. $55.00 per year.

Multimedia Schools: A Practical Journal of Multimedia, CD-Rom, Online and Internet in K-12. Information Today, Inc. • Five times a year. $39.95 per year. Edited for school librarians, media center directors, computer coordinators, and others concerned with educational multimedia. Coverage includes the use of CD-ROM sources, the Internet, online services, and library technology.

TechTrends: For Leaders in Education and Training. Association for Educational Communications and Technology. • Bimonthly. $40.00 per year.

RESEARCH CENTERS AND INSTITUTES

Division of Educational Research and Service. Louisiana Tech University. Tech Station, P.O. Box 3163, Ruston, LA 71272. Phone: (318)257-3712 Fax: (318)257-2379 E-mail: jdauzat@latech.edu • URL: http://www.latech.edu.

Instructional Media Development Center. University of Wisconsin - Madison. 1025 W. Johnson St., Madison, WI 53706. Phone: (608)262-3330 Fax: (608)263-6447 E-mail: livingston@facstaff.wisc.edu • URL: http://www.imdc.soemadison.wisc.edu.

TRADE/PROFESSIONAL ASSOCIATIONS

Association for Educational Communications and Technology. 1800 N. Stonelake Dr., Ste. 2, Bloomington, IN 47404. Phone: (812)335-7675 Fax: (812)335-7678 E-mail: aect@aect.org • URL: http://www.aect.org.

International Communications Industries Association. 11242 Waples Mill Rd., Suite 200, Fairfax, VA 22030-6079. Phone: 800-659-7469 or (703)273-2700 Fax: (703)278-8082 E-mail: icia@icia.org • Members are manufacturers and suppliers of audio-visual, video, and computer graphics equipment and materials.

AUDIOVISUAL AIDS IN INDUSTRY

See also: AUDIOVISUAL AIDS IN EDUCATION

BIBLIOGRAPHIES

Films and Audiovisual Information. Available from U. S. Government Printing Office. • Annual. Free. Issued by the Superintendent of Documents. A list of government publications on motion picture and audiovisual topics. Formerly *Motion Pictures, Films and Audiovisual Information.* (Subject Bibliography No. 73.).

DIRECTORIES

The Video Source Book. The Gale Group. • 2000. $345.00. 26th edition. Two volumes. Describes 160,000 video programs currently available on tape and disc. Includes Subject Category Index, Videodisc Index, Captioned Index (for hearing impaired), and Credits Index (actors, directors, etc.).

HANDBOOKS AND MANUALS

Power Pitches: How to Produce Winning Presentations Using Charts, Slides, Video, and Multimedia. Alan L. Brown. McGraw-Hill Professional. • 1997. $39.95. Includes "Ten Rules of Power Pitching.".

ONLINE DATABASES

ERIC. Educational Resources Information Center. • Broad range of educational literature, 1966 to present. Monthly updates. Inquire as to online cost and availability.

PERIODICALS AND NEWSLETTERS

Harvard Management Communication Letter. Harvard Business School Press. • Monthly. $79.00 per year. Newsletter. Provides practical advice on both electronic and conventional business communication: e-mail, telephone, cell phones, memos, letters, written reports, speeches, meetings, and visual presentations (slides, flipcharts, easels, etc.). Also covers face-to-face communication, discussion, listening, and negotiation.

Presentations: Technology and Techniques for Effective Communication. Lakewood Publications, Inc. • Monthly. $50.00 per year. Covers the use of presentation hardware and software, including audiovisual equipment and computerized display systems. Includes an annual *"Buyers Guide to Presentation Products."*.

TRADE/PROFESSIONAL ASSOCIATIONS

Communications Media Management Association. P.O. Box 227, Wheaton, IL 60189. Phone: (630)653-2772 Fax: (630)653-2882 E-mail: cmma@cmma.net • URL: http://www.cmma.net.

AUDIOVISUAL EQUIPMENT INDUSTRY

BIBLIOGRAPHIES

Films and Audiovisual Information. Available from U. S. Government Printing Office. • Annual. Free. Issued by the Superintendent of Documents. A list of government publications on motion picture and audiovisual topics. Formerly *Motion Pictures, Films and Audiovisual Information.* (Subject Bibliography No. 73.).

DIRECTORIES

AV Market Place: The Complete Business Directory of: Audio, Audio Visual, Computer Systems, Film, Video, Programming - with industry yellow pages. R. R. Bowker. • Annual. $165.00. Lists over 7,000 producers and distributors of a wide variety of audiovisual and video equipment, computer systems, films, and tapes. Includes many application-specific listings.

AV Presentation Buyer's Guide. Cygnus Business Media. • Annual. $6.00. Lists of film and slide laboratory services and manufacturers of media production and presentation equipment and audiovisual supplies. Formerly *Audio Visual Communications Buyer's Guide.*

Directory of Video, Computer, and Audio-Visual Products. International Communications Industries Association. • Annual. $65.00. Contains detailed descriptions and photographs of specific items of equipment. Includes video cameras, overhead projectors, LCD panels, computer projection systems, film recording equipment, etc. A "Glossary of Terms" is also provided.

ENCYCLOPEDIAS AND DICTIONARIES

Multimedia and the Web from A to Z. Patrick M. Dillon and David C. Leonard. Oryx Press. • 1998. $39.95. Second enlarged revised edition. Defines more than 1,500 terms relating to software and hardware in the areas of computing, online technology, telecommunications, audio, video, motion pictures, CD-ROM, and the Internet. Includes acronyms and an annotated bibliography. Formerly *Multimedia Technology from A to Z* (1994).

PERIODICALS AND NEWSLETTERS

AV Guide: The Learning Media Newsletter. Educational Screen, Inc. • Monthly. $15.00 per year. Provides information on audiovisual aids. Formerly *AV Guide Newsletter.*

Media and Methods: Educational Products, Technologies and Programs for Schools and Universities. American Society of Educators. • Five times a year. $33.50 per year.

Presentations: Technology and Techniques for Effective Communication. Lakewood Publications, Inc. • Monthly. $50.00 per year. Covers the use of presentation hardware and software, including audiovisual equipment and computerized display systems. Includes an annual *"Buyers Guide to Presentation Products."*.

TRADE/PROFESSIONAL ASSOCIATIONS

International Communications Industries Association. 11242 Waples Mill Rd., Suite 200, Fairfax, VA 22030-6079. Phone: 800-659-7469 or (703)273-2700 Fax: (703)278-8082 E-mail: icia@icia.org • Members are manufacturers and suppliers of audio-visual, video, and computer graphics equipment and materials.

International Recording Media Association. 182 Nassau St., Suite 204, Princeton, NJ 08542. Phone: (609)279-1700 Fax: (609)279-1999 E-mail: info@recordingmedia.org • URL: http://www.recordingmedia.org • Members are manufacturers and distributors of audiotape, videotape, and associated equipment.

AUDITING

See also: ACCOUNTING; CERTIFIED PUBLIC ACCOUNTANTS; COST ACCOUNTING; INTERNAL AUDITING

GENERAL WORKS

Auditing. Jack C. Robertson and Timothy J. Louwers. McGraw-Hill. • 1998. $91.43. Ninth edition.

Auditing: Integrated Approach. Alvin A. Arens. Simon and Schuster Trade Prentice Hall. • 1999. $98.00. Eighth edition.

Principles of Auditing. O. Ray Whittington and Kurt Pany. McGraw-Hill Higher Education. • 2000. $90.31. 13th edition.

ABSTRACTS AND INDEXES

Accounting and Tax Index. UMI. • Quarterly. Price on application. Includes annual cumulative bound volume. Indexes accounting, auditing, and taxation literature appearing in journals, books, pamphlets, conference proceedings, and newsletters. (UMI is University Microfilms International, a Bell & Howell Co.).

Accounting Articles. CCH, Inc. • Monthly. $594.00 per year. Looseleaf service.

DIRECTORIES

America's Corporate Finance Directory. National Register Publishing. • Annual. $699.00. A directory of financial executives employed at over 5,000 U. S. corporations. Includes a listing of the outside financial services (banks, pension managers, insurance firms, auditors) used by each corporation.

Who Audits America: A Directory of Publicly Held Corporations and the Accounting Firms Who Audit Them. Data Financial Press. • Semiannual. $125.00. 8,500 publicly held corporations that report to the Securities and Exchange Commission, and their accounting firms.

ENCYCLOPEDIAS AND DICTIONARIES

Blackwell Encyclopedic Dictionary of Accounting. Rashad Abdel-khalik. Blackwell Publishers. • 1997. $105.95. The editor is associated with the University of Florida. Contains definitions of key terms combined with longer articles written by various U. S. and foreign business educators. Includes bibliographies and index. (Blackwell Encyclopedia of Management Series).

Dictionary of Accounting Terms. Joel G. Siegel and Jae K. Shim. Barron's Educational Series, Inc. • 1995. $11.95. Second edition.

International Dictionary of Accounting Acronyms. Thomas W. Morris, editor. Fitzroy Dearborn Publishers. • 1999. $45.00. Defines 2,000 acronyms used in worldwide accounting and finance.

HANDBOOKS AND MANUALS

Accountants' Handbook. Douglas R. Carmichael and others, editors. John Wiley and Sons, Inc. • 1999. $135.00. Ninth edition. Chapters are written by various accounting and auditing specialists.

Accountant's Handbook of Fraud and Commercial Crime. G. Jack Bologna and others. John Wiley and Sons, Inc. • 1992. $155.00. *1996 Supplement,* $65.00.

AICPA Audit and Accounting Manual. American Institute of Certified Public Accountants. • 1999. $99.00. Covers working papers, internal control, audit approach, etc.

AICPA Codification of Statements on Auditing Standards. American Institute of Certified Public Accountants. • 1999. $81.25. Includes *Auditing Interpretations* and *International Auditing Guidelines.*

AICPA Codification of Statements on Standards for New Accounting and Review Services. American Institute of Certified Public Accountants. • 1998. $19.00.

AICPA Professional Standards, U. S. Auditing Standards, Accounting and Review Services, Ethics, Bylaws, International Accounting, International Auditing, Management Advisory Services, Quality Control, and Tax Practice. American Institute of Certified Public Accountants. • Annual. $180.00. Two volumes. Updates. Looseleaf. Three parts: Accounting, Ethics, Auditing.

AICPA Technical Practice Aids. American Institute of Certified Public Accountants. • $180.00 per year. Looseleaf service. Periodic supplementation. Advisory opinions, statements of position, and other material.

Applying GAAP and GAAS. Matthew Bender & Co., Inc. • Two looseleaf volumes. Periodic supplementation. Price on application. In-depth explanations of generally accepted accounting principles (GAAP) and generally accepted auditing standards (GAAS).

Financial Accounting Standards: Explanation and Analysis. CCH, Inc. • Annual.

Government Auditing Standards. Available from U. S. Government Printing Office. • 1994. $6.50. Revised edition. Issued by the U. S. General Accounting Office (http://www.gao.gov). Contains standards for CPA firms to follow in financial and performance audits of federal government agencies and programs. Also known as the "Yellow Book.".

Handbook of Accounting and Auditing. John C. Burton and others. Warren, Gorham, and Lamont/ RIA Group. • Looseleaf service. $160.00. Updated annually.

Miller GAAS Guide: A Comprehensive Restatement of Generally Accepted Auditing Standards for Auditing, Attestation, Compilation and Review and the Code of Professional Conduct. Larry P. Bailey. Harcourt Brace Professional Publishing. • Annual. $69.00. Monthly updates. Includes industry audit guides and a model audit program.

Modern Auditing. William C. Boynton and Walter G. Kell. John Wiley and Sons, Inc. • 2000. Seventh edition. Price on application.

Practitioner's Guide to GAAS. John Wiley and Sons, Inc. • Annual. $131.00. Covers GAAS: Generally Accepted Auditing Standards, promulgated by the American Institute of Certified Public Accountants. (Includes CD-ROM.).

SEC Accounting Rules, with Financial Reporting Releases, Codification of Financial Reporting Policies, Accounting and Auditing Enforcement Releases, and Staff Accounting Bulletins. CCH, Inc. • Looseleaf. $448.00.

U. S. Master Auditing Guide. CCH, Inc. • Annual. $65.00. Covers such topics as auditing standards, audit management, compliance, consulting, governmental audits, forensic auditing, and fraud. Includes checklists, charts, graphs, and sample reports.

U. S. Master GAAP Guide. CCH, Inc. • Annual. $69.00. Covers the generally accepted accounting principles (GAAP) contained in the professional pronouncements of the Accounting Principles Board (APB) or the Financial Accounting Standards Board (FASB). Includes general discussions, flow charts, and detailed examples. Arranged by topic.

ONLINE DATABASES

Accounting and Tax Database. Bell & Howell Information and Learning. • Provides indexing and abstracting of the literature of accounting, taxation, and financial management, 1971 to date. Updating is weekly. Especially covers accounting, auditing, banking, bankruptcy, employee compensation and benefits, cash management, financial planning, and credit. Inquire as to online cost and availability.

PERIODICALS AND NEWSLETTERS

Internal Auditor. Institute of Internal Auditors, Inc. • Bimonthly. $60.00 per year.

Journal of Accounting, Auditing and Finance. New York University Vincent C. Ross Institute of Accounting Research. Greenwood Publishing Group Inc., Subscription Publications. • Quarterly. $135.00 per year.

TRADE/PROFESSIONAL ASSOCIATIONS

American Institute of Certified Public Accountants. 1211 Ave. of the Americas, New York, NY 10036-8775. Phone: 800-862-4272 or (212)596-6200 Fax: (212)596-6213 • URL: http://www.aicpa.org.

Information Systems Audit and Control Association. 3701 Algonquin Rd., Suite 1010, Rolling Meadows, IL 60008. Phone: (847)253-1545 Fax: (847)253-1443 E-mail: webmaster@isaca.org • URL: http://www.isaca.org.

Institute of Internal Auditors. 249 Maitland Ave., Altamonte Springs, FL 32701-4201. Phone: (407)830-7600 Fax: (407)831-5171 E-mail: iia@theiia.org • URL: http://www.theiia.org.

OTHER SOURCES

Auditing Research Monographs. American Institute of Certified Public Accountants. • Irregular. Price varies.

FASB Accounting Standards Current Text. Financial Accounting Standards Board. • Looseleaf.

FASB Accounting Standards Current Text: General Standards. Financial Accounting Standards Board. • Irregular. Price on application.

FASB Accounting Standards Current Text: Industries Standards. Financial Accounting Standards Board. • Irregular. Price on application.

FASB Accounting Standards Current Text: Professional Standards. Financial Accounting Standards Board. • Irregular. Price on application.

FASB Accounting Standards Current Text: Technical Practice Aids. Financial Accounting Standards Board. • Irregular. Price on application.

FASB Original Pronouncements. Financial Accounting Standards Board. • Irregular. Price on application.

Financial Accounting Series. Financial Accounting Standards Board. • Price on application.

Internal Revenue Manual: Audit and Administration. CCH, Inc. • Irregular $1,156.00. Reproduces IRS audit provisions and procedures.

Statements of Financial Accounting Standards: Original Pronouncements. John Wiley and Sons, Inc. • 1996. Price on application.

AUDITING, INTERNAL

See: INTERNAL AUDITING

AUTHORITIES

See: CONSULTANTS

AUTHORS

See: WRITERS AND WRITING

AUTOMATED TELLER MACHINES (ATM)

See: BANK AUTOMATION

AUTOMATIC CONTROL EQUIPMENT

See: SCIENTIFIC APPARATUS AND INSTRUMENT INDUSTRIES

AUTOMATIC DATA SYSTEMS

See: AUTOMATION; COMPUTERS; SYSTEMS IN MANAGEMENT

AUTOMATIC IDENTIFICATION SYSTEMS

See also: POINT-OF-SALE SYSTEMS (POS)

ABSTRACTS AND INDEXES

Applied Science and Technology Index. H. W. Wilson Co. • 11 times a year. Quarterly and annual cumulations. Service basis for print edition; CD-ROM edition, $1,495.00 per year. Indexes a wide variety of English language technical, industrial, and engineering periodicals.

CompuMath Citation Index. Institute for Scientific Information. • Three times a year. $1,090.00 per year. Provides citations to the worldwide literature of computer science and mathematics.

Computer and Information Systems Abstracts Journal: An Abstract Journal Pertaining to the Theory, Design, Fabrication and Application of Computer and Information Systems. Cambridge Information Group. • Monthly. $1,045 per year.

Computer Literature Index: A Subject/Author Index to Computer and Data Processing Literature. Applied Computer Research, Inc. • Quarterly, with annual cumulation. $245.00 per year. Contains brief abstracts of book and periodical literature covering all phases of computing, including approximately 70 specific application areas.

NTIS Alerts: Computers, Control & Information Theory. National Technical Information Service. • Semimonthly. $235.00 per year. Provides descriptions of government-sponsored research reports and software, with ordering information. Covers computer hardware, software, control systems, pattern recognition, image processing, and related subjects. Formerly *Abstract Newsletter*.

CD-ROM DATABASES

WILSONDISC: Applied Science and Technology Abstracts. H. W. Wilson Co. • Monthly. $1,495.00 per year, including unlimited access to the online version of *Applied Science and Technology Abstracts* through WILSONLINE. Provides CD-ROM indexing and abstracting of 400 prominent scientific, technical, engineering, and industrial periodicals. Indexing coverage is provided from 1983 to date and abstracting from 1993 to date.

DIRECTORIES

Frontline Solutions Buyer's Guide. Advanstar Communications, Inc. • Annual. $34.95. Provides information on manufacturers and suppliers of bar code, magnetic stripe, machine vision, optical character recognition, voice data, smart card, radio frequency, and other automatic identification systems. Formerly (Automatic I.D. News Buyer's Guide).

ID Systems Buyers Guide. Helmers Publishing, Inc. • Annual. Price on application. Provides information on over 750 companies manufacturing automatic identification equipment, including scanners, data collection terminals, and bar code systems.

Manufacturing Systems: Buyers Guide. Cahners Business Information. • Annual. Price on application. Contains information on companies manufacturing or supplying materials handling systems, CAD/CAM systems, specialized software for manufacturing, programmable controllers, machine vision systems, and automatic identification systems.

Sensors Buyers Guide. Advanstar Communications. • Annual. Price on application. Provides information on over 1,400 manufacturers of high technology sensors.

ONLINE DATABASES

Applied Science and Technology Index Online. H. W. Wilson Co. • Provides online indexing of 400 major scientific, technical, industrial, and engineering periodicals. Time period is 1983 to date. Monthly updates. Inquire as to online cost and availability.

Computer Database. The Gale Group. • Provides online citations with abstracts to material appearing in about 150 trade journals and newsletters in the subject areas of computers, telecommunications, and electronics. Time period is 1983 to date, with weekly updates. Inquire as to online cost and availability.

Hard Sciences. Cambridge Scientific Abstracts. • Provides the online version of *Computer and Information Systems Abstracts, Electronics and*

Communications Abstracts, Health and Safety Science Abstracts, ISMEC: Mechanical Engineering Abstracts (Information Service in Mechanical Engineering) and *Solid State and Superconductivity Abstracts*. Time period is 1981 to date, with monthly updates. Inquire as to online cost and availability.

PROMT: Predicasts Overview of Markets and Technology. The Gale Group. • Companies, products, applied technologies and markets. U.S. and international literature coverage, 1972 to date. Inquire as to online cost and availability. Provides abstracts from more than 1,600 publications. Weekly updates.

PERIODICALS AND NEWSLETTERS

Card Technology. Faulkner & Gray, Inc. • Monthly. $79.00 per year. Covers advanced technology for credit, debit, and other cards. Topics include smart cards, optical recognition, and card design.

Frontline Solutions. Advanstar Communications, Inc. • Monthly. $41.00 per year. Provides news and information about the applications and technology of automated data capture systems. Formerly (Automatic I.D. News).

ID Systems: Integrating Data Capture Across the Supply Chain. Helmers Publishing, Inc. • Monthly. $55.00 per year. Covers trends in automatic identification technology and management.

ID World: The Magazine of Personal Identification and Biometrics. Faulkner & Gray, Inc. • Bimonthly. Controlled circulation. Covers personal identification systems, including smart cards and finger prints. Includes articles on legal, regulatory, and privacy issues.

Item Processing Report. Phillips Business Information, Inc. • Biweekly. $695.00 per year. Newsletter for banks on check processing, document imaging, and optical character recognition.

Manufacturing Computer Solutions. Hitchcock Publishing. • Monthly. Free to qualified personnel; others; $75.00 per year. Edited for managers of factory automation, emphasizing the integration of systems in manufacturing. Subjects include materials handling, CAD/CAM, specialized software for manufacturing, programmable controllers, machine vision, and automatic identification systems. Formerly *Manufacturing Systems*.

Sensors: The Journal of Applied Sensing Technology. Advanstar Communications. • Monthly. $62.00 per year. Edited for design, production, and manufacturing engineers involved with sensing systems. Emphasis is on emerging technology.

TRADE/PROFESSIONAL ASSOCIATIONS

AIM U.S.A. 634 Alpha Dr., Pittsburgh, PA 15238-2802. Phone: 800-338-0206 or (412)963-8588 Fax: (412)963-8753 E-mail: info@aimglobal.org • URL: http://www.aimusa.org • Members are companies concerned with automatic identification and data capture, including bar code systems, magnetic stripes, machine vision, voice technology, optical character recognition, and systems integration technology.

Automatic Identification Manufacturers International. 623 Alpha Dr., Pittsburgh, PA 15238. Phone: (412)936-8009 Fax: (412)963-8753 • Members are automatic identification manufacturers and suppliers. Systems may utilize bar codes, magnetic stripes, radio frequencies, machine vision, voice technology, optical character recognition, or systems integration.

Uniform Code Council. 7887 Washington Village Dr., Ste. 300, Dayton, OH 45459-8605. Phone: (937)435-3870 Fax: (937)435-7317 E-mail: info@uc-council.org • URL: http://www.uc-council.org • Concerned with developing a universal product coding system to assign a unique identification number to every product sold in the United States.

AUTOMATIC TRANSLATING

See: MACHINE TRANSLATING

AUTOMATION

See also: COMPUTERS; CONTROL EQUIPMENT INDUSTRY; LINEAR PROGRAMMING; MACHINE VISION; ONLINE INFORMATION SYSTEMS; OPERATIONS RESEARCH; ROBOTS

GENERAL WORKS

Automatic Control Systems. Benjamin C. Kuo. Simon and Schuster Trade. • 1999. $95.00. Seventh edition.

ABSTRACTS AND INDEXES

Applied Science and Technology Index. H. W. Wilson Co. • 11 times a year. Quarterly and annual cumulations. Service basis for print edition; CD-ROM edition, $1,495.00 per year. Indexes a wide variety of English language technical, industrial, and engineering periodicals.

Key Abstracts: Factory Automation. Available from INSPEC, Inc. • Monthly. $240.00 per year. Provides international coverage of journal and proceedings literature, including publications on CAD/CAM, materials handling, robotics, and factory management. Published in England by the Institution of Electrical Engineers (IEE).

NTIS Alerts: Manufacturing Technology. National Technical Information Service. • Semimonthly. $265.00 per year. Provides descriptions of government-sponsored research reports and software, with ordering information. Covers computer-aided design and manufacturing (CAD/CAM), engineering materials, quality control, machine tools, robots, lasers, productivity, and related subjects. Formerly *Abstract Newsletter*.

BIBLIOGRAPHIES

Automation. Available from U. S. Government Printing Office. • Annual. Free. Issued by the Superintendent of Documents. A list of government publications on automation, computers, and related topics. Formerly *Computers and Data Processing*. (Subject Bibliography No. 51.).

CD-ROM DATABASES

Computer Select. The Gale Group. • Monthly. $1,250.00 per year. Provides one year of full-text on CD-ROM for 120 leading computer-related publications. Also includes 70,000 product specifications and brief profiles of 13,000 computer product vendors and manufacturers.

DIRECTORIES

Control Engineering Buyers Guide. Cahners Business Information. • Annual. Free to qualified personnel. Contains specifications, prices, and manufacturers' listings for computer software, as related to control engineering.

Data Sources: The Comprehensive Guide to the Data Processing Industry Hardware, Data Communications Products, Software, Company Profiles. The Gale Group. • Semiannual. $495.00 per year. Two volumes. Describes hardware and software for all computer operating sysems, including prices and technical details. Lists about 75,000 products from 14,000 suppliers. Industry-specific software applications are described.

Sensors Buyers Guide. Advanstar Communications. • Annual. Price on application. Provides information on over 1,400 manufacturers of high technology sensors.

HANDBOOKS AND MANUALS

Assembly Buyer's Guide. Cahners Business Information. • Annual. $25.00. Lists manufacturers and suppliers of equipment relating to assembly automation, fasteners, adhesives, robotics, and power tools.

ONLINE DATABASES

INSPEC. Institute of Electrical and Electronics Engineers (IEEE). • Provides indexing and abstracting of the worldwide literature of electrical engineering, electronics, physics, computer technology, information technology, and industrial controls. Time period is 1970 to date, with weekly updates. Inquire as to online cost and availability. (INSPEC is Information Services for the Physics and Engineering Communities.).

PERIODICALS AND NEWSLETTERS

Advanced Manufacturing Technology: Monthly Report. Technical Insights. • Monthly. $695.00 per year. Newsletter. Covers technological developments relating to robotics, computer graphics, automation, computer-integrated manufacturing, and machining.

Automatica. Elsevier Science. • Bimonthly. $1,792.00 per year. Text in English, French, German, and Russian.

Industrial Computing. ISA Services, Inc. • Monthly. $50.00 per year. Published by the Instrument Society of America. Edited for engineering managers and systems integrators. Subject matter includes industrial software, programmable controllers, artificial intelligence systems, and industrial computer networking systems.

Information Week: For Business and Technology Managers. CMP Publications, Inc. • Weekly. $149.00 per year. The magazine for information systems management.

Managing Automation. Thomas Publishing Co. • Monthly. Free to qualified personnel. Coverage includes software for manufacturing, systems planning, integration in process industry automation, computer integrated manufacturing (CIM), computer networks for manufacturing, management problems, industry news, and new products.

Sensors: The Journal of Applied Sensing Technology. Advanstar Communications. • Monthly. $62.00 per year. Edited for design, production, and manufacturing engineers involved with sensing systems. Emphasis is on emerging technology.

RESEARCH CENTERS AND INSTITUTES

Coordinated Science Laboratory. University of Illinois at Urbana-Champaign. 1308 W. Main St,. Room 202, Urbana, IL 61801-2307. Phone: (217)333-2511 Fax: (217)244-1764 E-mail: vwinckle@uiuc.edu • URL: http://www.csl.uiuc.edu.

Division of Engineering Research. Michigan State University. B-100 Engineering Research Complex, East Lansing, MI 48824. Phone: (517)355-5104 Fax: (517)353-5547 E-mail: wadem@egr.msu.edu • URL: http://www.egr.msu.edu/der.

Industrial Relations Research Institute. University of Wisconsin-Madison, 4226 Social Science Bldg., Madison, WI 53706. Phone: (608)262-1882 Fax: (608)265-4591 • URL: http://www.polyglot.lss.wisc.edu/irr/irr.html.

Institute of Labor and Industrial Relations. University of Illinois at Urbana-Champaign. 504 E. Armory Ave., Champaign, IL 61820. Phone: (217)333-1480 Fax: (217)244-9290 E-mail: feuille@uiuc.edu • URL: http://www.ilir.uiuc.edu.

Stanford Integrated Manufacturing Association. Stanford University, Bldg. 02-530, Stanford, CA 94305-3036. Phone: (650)723-9038 Fax: (650)723-5034 E-mail: susan.hansen@stanford.edu • URL: http://www.sima.stanford.edu/ • Consists of four research centers: Center for Automation and Manufacturing Science, Center for Design Research, Center for Materials Formability and Processing Science, and Center for Teaching and Research in Integrated Manufacturing Systems. Research fields include automation, robotics, intelligent systems, computer vision, design in manufacturing, materials science, composite materials, and ceramics.

TRADE/PROFESSIONAL ASSOCIATIONS

Computer and Automated Systems Association of Society of Manufacturing Engineers. P.O. Box 930, Dearborn, MI 48121-0930. Phone: (313)271-1500 Fax: (313)271-2861 • URL: http://www.sme.org/casa • Sponsored by the Society of Manufacturing Engineers.

Instrument Society of America (ISA). P.O. Box 12277, Research Triangle Park, NC 27709. Phone: (919)549-8411 Fax: (919)549-8288 E-mail: info@isa.org • URL: http://www.isa.org • Members are engineers and others concerned with industrial instrumentation, systems, computers, and automation.

Special Interest Group for Design Automation. Association for Computing Machinery, 1515 Broadway, New York, NY 10036-5701. Phone: (212)869-7440 Fax: (212)302-5826 E-mail: sigs@acm.org • URL: http://www.acm.org.

OTHER SOURCES

Annual Reviews in Control. Elsevier Science. • Annual. $329.00 per year. Formerly*Annual Review in Automatic Programming.*

Assembly. Cahners Business Information. • Monthly. $68.00 per year. Covers assembly, fastening, and joining systems. Includes information on automation and robotics.

AUTOMATION, BANK

See: BANK AUTOMATION

AUTOMATION, LIBRARY

See: LIBRARY AUTOMATION

AUTOMATION, OFFICE

See: OFFICE AUTOMATION

AUTOMATION, RETAIL

See: POINT-OF-SALE SYSTEMS (POS)

AUTOMATONS

See: ROBOTS

AUTOMOBILE ACCESSORIES INDUSTRY

See: AUTOMOBILE EQUIPMENT INDUSTRY

AUTOMOBILE ACCIDENTS

See: TRAFFIC ACCIDENTS AND TRAFFIC SAFETY

AUTOMOBILE BATTERIES

See: BATTERY INDUSTRY

AUTOMOBILE DEALERS

See also: AUTOMOTIVE INDUSTRY; USED CAR INDUSTRY

GENERAL WORKS

Car Ownership Forecasting. E.W. Allanson, editor. Gordon and Breach Publishing Group. • 1982. $173.00. Volume one.

What Your Car Really Costs: How to Keep a Financially Safe Driving Record. American Institute for Economic Research. • 1999. $6.00. Contains "Should You Buy or Lease?," "Should You Buy New or Used?," "Dealer Trade-in or Private Sale?," "Lemon Laws," and other car buying information. Includes rankings of specific models for resale value, 1992 to 1998. (Economic Education Bulletin.).

DIRECTORIES

NAFA Annual Reference Book. National Association of Fleet Administrators. • Annual. $45.00. Automobile manufacturers' sales and leasing representatives throughout the country.

Supplier's Source Directory. Intertec Publishing Corp. • Annual. $10.00. Lists companies that furnish services and equipment for new car dealers. Formerly *Auto Age Buyer's Guide.*

FINANCIAL RATIOS

Almanac of Business and Industrial Financial Ratios. Leo Troy. Prentice Hall. • Annual. $99.95. Contains financial ratios derived from federal tax returns. Ratios for each of about 200 industries are arranged according to company asset size.

Annual Statement Studies. Robert Morris Associates: The Association of Lending and Credit Risk Professiona. • Annual. Free to members; non-members, $140.00. Median and quartile financial ratios are given for over 400 kinds of manufacturing, wholesale, retail, construction, and consumer finance establishments. Data is sorted by both asset size and sales volume. Includes a clearly written "Definition of Ratios" and an alphabetical industry index.

Industry Norms and Key Business Ratios. Desk Top Edition. Dun and Bradstreet Corp., Business Information Services. • Annual. Five volumes. $475.00 per volume. $1,890.00 per set. Covers over 800 kinds of businesses, arranged by Standard Industrial Classification number. More detailed editions covering longer periods of time are also available.

HANDBOOKS AND MANUALS

Used Car Sales. Entrepreneur Media, Inc. • Looseleaf. $59.50. A practical guide to getting started in the business of selling used cars. Covers profit potential, start-up costs, market size evaluation, owner's time required, site selection, lease negotiation, pricing, accounting, advertising, etc. (Start-Up Business Guide No. E2330.).

PERIODICALS AND NEWSLETTERS

Automotive News: Engineering, Financial, Manufacturing, Sales, Marketing, Servicing. Crain Communications, Inc. • Weekly. $114.00 per year. Business news coverage of the automobile industry at the retail, wholesale, and manufacturing levels. Includes statistics.

Car Dealer Insider. United Communications Group. • Weekly. $275.00. per year. Newsletter covering management trends and industry news.

Chilton's Automotive Marketing: A Monthly Publication for the Retail Jobber and Distributor of Automotive Aftermarket. Cahners Business Information. • Monthly. Free to qualified personnel; others, $48.00 per year. Includes marketing of automobile batteries. Formerly *Automotive Aftermarket News.*

Dealer Business. Ward's Communications. • Monthly. $36.00 per year. Formerly *Auto Age.*

NADA'S Automotive Executive. National Automobile Dealers Association. • Monthly. $24.00 per year.

Used Car Dealer. National Independent Automobile Dealers Association. • Monthly. Members, $36.00 per year; non-members, $120.00 per year.

STATISTICS SOURCES

U. S. Industry and Trade Outlook: The McGraw-Hill Companies and the U.S. Department of Commerce/ International Trade Administration. Datapso Research Corp. • Annual. $69.95. Produced by the International Trade Administration, U. S. Department of Commerce, in a "public-private" partnership with DRI/McGraw-Hill and Standard & Poor's. Provides basic data, outlook for the current year, and "Long-Term Prospects" (five-year projections) for a wide variety of products and services. Includes high technology industries. Formerly *U. S. Industrial Outlook.*

TRADE/PROFESSIONAL ASSOCIATIONS

National Automobile Dealers Association. 8400 Westpark Dr., McLean, VA 22102. Phone: (703)821-7000 Fax: (703)821-7075 E-mail: nada@nada.org • URL: http://www.nada.org.

National Independent Automobile Dealers Association. 2521 Brown Blvd., Arlington, TX 76006-5203. Phone: (817)640-3838 Fax: (817)649-5866 E-mail: rb@niada.com • URL: http://www.niada.com.

OTHER SOURCES

Car Dealer Insider: Profit Making Secrets for the Competitive Dealer. United Communications Group (UCG). • Weekly. $295.00 per year. Newsletter. Provides automotive industry news, with ideas and advice for car dealers on advertising, marketing, and management. Formerly *Car and Truck Dealer Insider Newsletter.*

AUTOMOBILE EQUIPMENT INDUSTRY

See also: AUTOMOBILE DEALERS; AUTOMOTIVE INDUSTRY

DIRECTORIES

Directory of Automotive Aftermarket Suppliers. Chain Store Guide. • Annual. $300.00. Covers auto supply store chains. Includes distributors.

FINANCIAL RATIOS

Industry Norms and Key Business Ratios. Desk Top Edition. Dun and Bradstreet Corp., Business Information Services. • Annual. Five volumes. $475.00 per volume. $1,890.00 per set. Covers over 800 kinds of businesses, arranged by Standard Industrial Classification number. More detailed editions covering longer periods of time are also available.

ONLINE DATABASES

Ward's AutoInfoBank. Ward's Communications, Inc. • Provides weekly, monthly, quarterly, and annual statistical data drom 1965 to date for U. S. and imported cars and trucks. Covers production, shipments, sales, inventories, optional equipment, etc. Updating varies by series. Inquire as to online cost and availability.

PERIODICALS AND NEWSLETTERS

Automotive Recycling. Automotive Recyclers Association. • Bimonthly. Free to members; non-members, $40.00 per year. Foremrly *Dismantl ers Digest.*

Brake and Frontend: The Complete Car Undercar Service Magazine. Babcox Publications. • Monthly. $64.00 per year.

Chilton's Automotive Marketing: A Monthly Publication for the Retail Jobber and Distributor of Automotive Aftermarket. Cahners Business Information. • Monthly. Free to qualified personnel; others, $48.00 per year. Includes marketing of automobile batteries. Formerly *Automotive Aftermarket News.*

SEMA News. Specialty Equipment Marketing Association. • Monthly. 24.95 per year.

PRICE SOURCES

Orion Car Stereo Blue Book. Orion Research Corp. • Annual. $144.00. Quotes retail and wholesale prices of used stereo sound equipment for automobiles. Original list prices and years of manufacture are also shown.

STATISTICS SOURCES

Annual Survey of Manufactures. Available from U. S. Government Printing Office. • Annual. Prices vary. Issued by the U. S. Census Bureau as an interim update to the *Census of Manufactures.* Includes data on number of manufacturing establishments in various industries, employment, labor costs, value of shipments, capital expenditures, inventories, energy costs, and assets. (See also Census Bureau home page, http://www.census.gov/.).

Standard & Poor's Industry Surveys. Standard & Poor's. • Semiannual. $1,800.00. Two looseleaf volumes. Includes monthly supplements. Provides detailed, individual surveys of 52 major industry groups. Each survey is revised on a semiannual basis. Also includes "Monthly Investment Review" (industry group investment analysis) and monthly "Trends & Projections" (economic analysis).

U. S. Industry and Trade Outlook: The McGraw-Hill Companies and the U.S. Department of Commerce/ International Trade Administration. Datapso Research Corp. • Annual. $69.95. Produced by the International Trade Administration, U. S. Department of Commerce, in a "public-private" partnership with DRI/McGraw-Hill and Standard & Poor's. Provides basic data, outlook for the current year, and "Long-Term Prospects" (five-year projections) for a wide variety of products and services. Includes high technology industries. Formerly *U. S. Industrial Outlook.*

TRADE/PROFESSIONAL ASSOCIATIONS

Automotive Service Industry Association. 25 Northwest Point, Elk Grove Village, IL 60007-1035. Phone: (847)228-1310 Fax: (847)228-1510 • Members are distributors and manufacturers of automotive replacement parts.

International Mobile Air Conditioning Association. P.O. Box 9000, Fort Worth, TX 76147-2000. Phone: (817)732-4600 or (817)732-6348 Fax: (817)732-9610 E-mail: info@imaca.org • URL: http://www.imaca.org • Serves the automotive, boat, and aircraft air conditioning industries.

Motor and Equipment Manufacturers Association. P.O. Box 13966, Research Triangle Park, NC 27709-3966. Phone: (919)549-4800 Fax: (919)549-4824 • URL: http://www.mema.com.

AUTOMOBILE INDUSTRY

See: AUTOMOTIVE INDUSTRY

AUTOMOBILE INSURANCE

See also: ACCIDENT INSURANCE; CASUALTY INSURANCE; INSURANCE

GENERAL WORKS

Smarter Insurance Solutions. Janet Bamford. Bloomberg Press. • 1996. $19.95. Provides practical advice to consumers, with separate chapters on the following kinds of insurance: automobile, homeowners, health, disability, and life. (Bloomberg Personal Bookshelf Series).

ABSTRACTS AND INDEXES

Insurance Periodicals Index. Specials Libraries Association, Insurance and Employees Benefits Div. CCH/NILS Publishing Co. • Annual. $250.00. Compiled by the Insurance and Employee Benefits Div., Special Libraries Association. A yearly index of over 15,000 articles from about 35 insurance periodicals. Arrangement is by subject, with an index to authors.

BIBLIOGRAPHIES

Insurance and Employee Benefits Literature. Special Libraries Association, Insurance and Employee Benefits Div. • Bimonthly. $15.00 per year.

CD-ROM DATABASES

U. S. Insurance: Property and Casualty. Sheshunoff Information Services, Inc. • Monthly. Price on application. CD-ROM provides detailed, current financial information on more than 3,200 property and casualty insurance companies.

ENCYCLOPEDIAS AND DICTIONARIES

Dictionary of Insurance. Lewis E. Davids. Rowman and Littlefield Publishers, Inc. • 1990. $17.95. Seventh revised edition.

Dictionary of Insurance Terms. Harvey W. Rubin. Barron's Educational Series, Inc. • 2000. $12.95. Fourth edition. Defines terms in a wide variety of insurance fields. Price on application.

Insurance Words and Their Meanings: A Dictionary of Insurance Terms. Diana Kowatch. The Rough Notes Co., Inc. • 1998. $38.50. 16th revised edition.

Rupp's Insurance and Risk Management Glossary. Richard V. Rupp. Available from CCH, Inc. • 1996. $35.00. Second edition. Published by NILS Publishing Co. Provides definitions of 6,400 insurance words and phrases. Includes a guide to acronyms and abbreviations.

HANDBOOKS AND MANUALS

Best's Casualty Loss Reserve Development. A.M. Best Co. • Annual. $600.00. Looseleaf. Provides ten years of reserving patterns for the largest companies in the major casualty line.

The Complete Book of Insurance: The Consumer's Guide to Insuring Your Life, Health, Property, and Income. Ben G. Baldwin. McGraw-Hill Professional. • 1996. $24.95. Revised edition. Provides basic information and advice on various kinds of insurance: life, health, property (fire), disability, long-term care, automobile, liability, and annuities.

An Insurance Guide for Seniors. Insurance Forum, Inc. • 1997. $15.00. Provides concise advice and information on Medicare, Medicare supplement insurance, HMOs, long-term care insurance, automobile insurance, life insurance, annuities, and pensions. An appendix lists "Financially Strong Insurance Companies." (*The Insurance Forum,* vol. 24, no. 4.).

Insurance Smart: How to Buy the Right Insurance at the Right Price. Jeffrey P. O'Donnell. John Wiley and Sons, Inc. • 1991. $12.95. Advice for insurance buyers on automobile, homeowner, business, farm, health, and life coverage.

No-Fault and Uninsured Motorist Auto Insurance. Matthew Bender & Co., Inc. • $880.00. Four looseleaf volumes. Periodic supplementation. For both plaintiff's and defendant's counsel.

INTERNET DATABASES

InsWeb. InsWeb Corp. Phone: (650)372-2129 E-mail: info@insweb.com • URL: http://www.insweb.com • Web site offers a wide variety of advice and information on automobile, life, health, and "other" insurance. Includes glossaries of insurance terms, Standard & Poor's ratings of individual insurance companies, and "Financial Needs Estimators." Searching is available. Fees: Free.

ONLINE DATABASES

Best's Company Reports. A. M. Best Co. • Provides full financial data online for U. S. insurance companies (life, health, property, casualty), including balance sheet data, income statements, expenses, premium income, losses, and investments. Includes *Best's Company Reports, Best's Insurance News,* and Best's ratings of insurance companies. Inquire as to online cost and availability.

I.I.I. Data Base Search. Insurance Information Institute. • Provides online citations and abstracts of insurance-related literature in magazines, newspapers, trade journals, and books. Emphasis is on property and casualty insurance issues, including highway safety, product safety, and environmental liability. Inquire as to online cost and availability.

PERIODICALS AND NEWSLETTERS

Automobile Insurance Losses, Collision Coverages, Variations by Make and Series. Highway Loss Data Institute. • Semiannual. Membership.

New York No-Fault Arbitration Reports. American Arbitration Association. • Monthly. $90.00 per year. Looseleaf. Clear and concise summaries of cases dealing with important issues in the field. Back issues available.

STATISTICS SOURCES

Property-Casualty Insurance Facts. Insurance Information Institute. • Annual. $22.50. Formerly *Insurance Facts.*

TRADE/PROFESSIONAL ASSOCIATIONS

American Insurers Highway Safety Alliance. 3025 Highland Parkway, No. 800, Downers Grove, IL 60515-1260. Phone: (847)330-8560 Fax: (847)330-8602.

Insurance Services Office. Seven World Trade Center, New York, NY 10048. Phone: (212)898-6000 Fax: (212)898-5525.

OTHER SOURCES

Automobile Liability Insurance. Irvin E. Schermer. West Group. • Three looseleaf volumes. $395.00. Periodic supplementation.

The Law of Liability Insurance. Matthew Bender & Co., Inc. • $1,230.00. Five looseleaf volumes. Periodic supplementation. Explains the terms and phases essential for a general understanding of liability insurance, and discusses injuries to both persons and property.

AUTOMOBILE LAWS

See: MOTOR VEHICLE LAW AND REGULATION

AUTOMOBILE LEASE AND RENTAL SERVICES

GENERAL WORKS

What Your Car Really Costs: How to Keep a Financially Safe Driving Record. American Institute for Economic Research. • 1999. $6.00. Contains "Should You Buy or Lease?," "Should You Buy New or Used?," "Dealer Trade-in or Private Sale?," "Lemon Laws," and other car buying information. Includes rankings of specific models for resale value, 1992 to 1998. (Economic Education Bulletin.).

DIRECTORIES

Avis Licensee Directory. Avis Licensee Association. • Irregular. Membership.

FINANCIAL RATIOS

Annual Statement Studies. Robert Morris Associates: The Association of Lending and Credit Risk Professiona. • Annual. Free to members; non-members, $140.00. Median and quartile financial ratios are given for over 400 kinds of manufacturing, wholesale, retail, construction, and consumer finance establishments. Data is sorted by both asset size and sales volume. Includes a clearly written "Definition of Ratios" and an alphabetical industry index.

HANDBOOKS AND MANUALS

CCH Guide to Car, Travel, Entertainment, and Home Office Deductions. CCH, Inc. • Annual. $42.00. Explains how to claim maximum tax deductions for common business expenses. Includes automobile depreciation tables, lease value tables, worksheets, and examples of filled-in tax forms.

Limousine Service. Entrepreneur Media, Inc. • Looseleaf. $59.50. A practical guide to starting a limousine service. Covers profit potential, start-up costs, market size evaluation, owner's time required, site selection, lease negotiation, pricing, accounting, advertising, promotion, etc. (Start-Up Business Guide No. E1224.).

Used-Car Rental Agency. Entrepreneur Media, Inc. • Looseleaf. $59.50. A practical guide to starting a used-car rental business. Covers profit potential, start-up costs, market size evaluation, owner's time required, site selection, lease negotiation pricing, accounting, advertising, promotion, etc. (Start-Up Business Guide No. E1108.).

Vehicle Leasing. Entrepreneur Media, Inc. • Looseleaf. $59.50. A practical guide to starting an automobile leasing business. Covers profit potential, start-up costs, market size evaluation, owner's time required, site selection, lease negotiation, pricing, accounting, advertising, promotion, etc. (Start-Up Business Guide No. E2329.).

TRADE/PROFESSIONAL ASSOCIATIONS

American Automotive Leasing Association. 700 13th St. N.W., Suite 950, Washington, DC 20005. Phone: (202)393-7292 Fax: (202)393-7293 E-mail: amautolsg@aol.com.

American Car Rental Association. 11250 Roger Bacon Dr., No. 8, Reston, VA 20190-5202. Phone: (703)234-4148 Fax: (703)435-4390 E-mail: ghogan@asdrohanmgmt.com • URL: http://www.acra.org.

OTHER SOURCES

Car Rental Insider. United Communications Group (UCG). • Biweekly. $235.00 per year. Newsletter. Contains news of the automobile leasing and renting industry, including information on legislation, insurance, consumer trends, and rental management.

AUTOMOBILE LICENSES

See: MOTOR VEHICLE LAW AND REGULATION

AUTOMOBILE PARTS INDUSTRY

See: AUTOMOBILE EQUIPMENT INDUSTRY

AUTOMOBILE RENTAL SERVICES

See: AUTOMOBILE LEASE AND RENTAL SERVICES

AUTOMOBILE REPAIR INDUSTRY

ABSTRACTS AND INDEXES

Business Periodicals Index. H. W. Wilson Co. • Monthly, except August, with quarterly and annual cumulations. Service basis for print edition; CD-ROM edition, $1,495.00 per year.

CD-ROM DATABASES

ABI/INFORM Global. Bell & Howell Information and Learning. • Monthly. $6,500.00 per year. Provides CD-ROM indexing and abstracting of worldwide business literature appearing in over 1,200 periodicals for the most recent five years. Archival discs are available from 1971. Formerly *ABI/INFORM OnDisc.*

F & S Index Plus Text. The Gale Group. • Monthly. $7,575.00 per year. Provides CD-ROM citations to worldwide business, marketing, and industrial material appearing in a large assortment of trade journals, newspapers, and other publications. Time period is four years.

WILSONDISC: Wilson Business Abstracts. H. W. Wilson Co. • Monthly. $2,495.00 per year, including unlimited online access to *Wilson Business Abstracts* through WILSONLINE. Provides CD-ROM "cover-to-cover" abstracting and indexing of over 600 prominent business periodicals. Indexing is from 1982, abstracting from 1990. (*Business Periodicals Index* without abstracts is available on CD-ROM at $1,495 per year.).

DIRECTORIES

Fleet Owner Specs and Buyers' Directory. Intertec Publishing Corp. • Annual. $5.00. Lists of manufacturers of equipment and materials used in the operation, management, and maintenance of truck and bus fleets.

FINANCIAL RATIOS

Almanac of Business and Industrial Financial Ratios. Leo Troy. Prentice Hall. • Annual. $99.95. Contains financial ratios derived from federal tax returns. Ratios for each of about 200 industries are arranged according to company asset size.

ONLINE DATABASES

ABI/INFORM. Bell & Howell Information and Learning. • Provides online indexing to business-related material occurring in over 1,000 periodicals from 1971 to the present. Inquire as to online cost and availability.

F & S Index. The Gale Group. • Contains about four million citations to worldwide business, financial, and industrial or consumer product literature appearing from 1972 to date. Weekly updates. Inquire as to online cost and availability.

PROMT: Predicasts Overview of Markets and Technology. The Gale Group. • Companies, products, applied technologies and markets. U.S. and international literature coverage, 1972 to date. Inquire as to online cost and availability. Provides abstracts from more than 1,600 publications. Weekly updates.

Trade & Industry Index. The Gale Group. • Provides indexing of business periodicals, January 1981 to date. Daily updates. (Full text articles from some periodicals are available online, 1983 to date, in the companion database, *Trade & Industry ASAP.*) Inquire as to online cost and availability.

Wilson Business Abstracts Online. H. W. Wilson Co. • Indexes and abstracts 600 major business periodicals, plus the *Wall Street Journal* and the business section of the *New York Times.* Indexing is from 1982, abstracting from 1990, with the two newspapers included from 1993. Updated weekly. Inquire as to online cost and availability. (*Business Periodicals Index* without abstracts is also available online.).

PERIODICALS AND NEWSLETTERS

Fleet Owner. Intertec Publishing Corp. • Monthly. $45.00 per year.

Motor Age: For the Professional Automotive Import and Domestic Service Industry. Cahners Business Information. • Monthly. $49.00 per year. Published for independent automotive repair shops and gasoline service stations.

MOTOR: Covering the World of Automotive Service. Hearst Business Publishing. • Monthly. $48.00 per year. Edited for professional automobile and light-truck mechanics. Includes industry news and market trends.

TRADE/PROFESSIONAL ASSOCIATIONS

Automotive Service Association. P.O. Box 929, Bedford, TX 76095-0929. Phone: 800-272-7467 or (817)283-6205 Fax: (817)685-0225 E-mail: asainfo@asashop.org • URL: http://www.asashop.org • Members are body, paint, radiator, transmission, brake, and other shops or garages doing automotive repair work.

Automotive Service Industry Association. 25 Northwest Point, Elk Grove Village, IL 60007-1035. Phone: (847)228-1310 Fax: (847)228-1510 • Members are distributors and manufacturers of automotive replacement parts.

Gasoline and Automotive Service Dealers Association. 9520 Seaview Ave., Brooklyn, NY 11236. Phone: (718)241-1111 Fax: (718)763-6589 • Members are owners and operators of automobile service stations and repair shops.

National Institute for Automotive Service Excellence. 13505 Dulles Technology Dr., Suite 2, Herndon, VA 20171-3421. Phone: 877-273-8324 or (703)713-3800 Fax: (703)713-0727 • URL: http://www.asecert.org • A public interest organization which promotes high standards in automotive service and repair. Encourages effective training programs for automobile mechanics/technicians.

AUTOMOBILE ROAD GUIDES

See: MAPS

AUTOMOBILE SERVICE STATIONS

See: GASOLINE SERVICE STATIONS

AUTOMOBILE TELEPHONES

See: MOBILE TELEPHONE INDUSTRY

AUTOMOBILES

See also: AUTOMOTIVE INDUSTRY; FOREIGN AUTOMOBILES; USED CAR INDUSTRY

GENERAL WORKS

What Your Car Really Costs: How to Keep a Financially Safe Driving Record. American Institute for Economic Research. • 1999. $6.00. Contains

"Should You Buy or Lease?," "Should You Buy New or Used?," "Dealer Trade-in or Private Sale?," "Lemon Laws," and other car buying information. Includes rankings of specific models for resale value, 1992 to 1998. (Economic Education Bulletin.).

CD-ROM DATABASES

Magazine Index Plus. The Gale Group. • Monthly. $4,000.00 per year (includes InfoTrac workstation). Provides full text on CD-ROM for about 100 popular, general interest magazines and indexing for 300 others. Includes special indexing of reviews and product evaluations. Time period is 1980 to date.

Sourcebooks America CD-ROM. CACI Marketing Systems. • Annual. $1,250.00. Provides the CD-ROM version of *The Sourcebook of ZIP Code Demographics: Census Edition* and *The Sourcebook of County Demographics: Census Edition.*

DIRECTORIES

A.A.A. Offices to Serve You-Names and Addresses of Affiliated Motor Clubs and Associations. American Automobile Association. • Annual.

ENCYCLOPEDIAS AND DICTIONARIES

Elsevier's Dictionary of Automotive Engineering. A. Schellings. Elsevier Science. • 1998. Price on application.

Macmillan Encyclopedia of Transportation. Available from The Gale Group. • 2000. $375.00. Six volumes. Published by Macmillan Reference USA. Covers the business, technology, and history of transportation on land, on water, in the air, and in space. Includes definitions, cross-references, and 200 color illustrations.

HANDBOOKS AND MANUALS

CCH Guide to Car, Travel, Entertainment, and Home Office Deductions. CCH, Inc. • Annual. $42.00. Explains how to claim maximum tax deductions for common business expenses. Includes automobile depreciation tables, lease value tables, worksheets, and examples of filled-in tax forms.

INTERNET DATABASES

Fedstats. Federal Interagency Council on Statistical Policy. Phone: (202)395-7254 • URL: http://www.fedstats.gov • Web site features an efficient search facility for full-text statistics produced by more than 70 federal agencies, including the Census Bureau, the Bureau of Economic Analysis, and the Bureau of Labor Statistics. Boolean searches can be made within one agency or for all agencies combined. Links are offered to international statistical bureaus, including the UN, IMF, OECD, UNESCO, Eurostat, and 20 individual countries. Fees: Free.

ONLINE DATABASES

American Statistics Index: A Comprehensive Guide and Index to the Statistical Publications of the United States Government [Online]. Congressional Information Service, Inc. • Indexes and abstracts, 1973 to date. Inquire as to online cost and availability.

DRI U.S. Central Database. Data Products Division. • Provides more than 23,000 business, financial, demographic, economic, foreign trade, and industry-related time series for the U.S. Includes national income, population, retail-wholesale trade, price indexes, labor data, housing, industrial production, banking, interest rates, money supply, etc. Time period is generally 1947 to date (some data back to 1929). Updating varies. Inquire as to online cost and availability.

Ward's AutoInfoBank. Ward's Communications, Inc. • Provides weekly, monthly, quarterly, and annual statistical data drom 1965 to date for U. S. and imported cars and trucks. Covers production, shipments, sales, inventories, optional equipment, etc. Updating varies by series. Inquire as to online cost and availability.

PERIODICALS AND NEWSLETTERS

Antique Automobile. Antique Automobile Club of America. • Membership.

Automobile Quarterly: The Connoisseur's Magazine of Motoring Today, Yesterday and Tomorrow. Automobile Quarterly, Inc. • Five times a year. $89.95 per year.

Car and Driver. Hachette Filipacchi Magazines, Inc. • Monthly. $21.94 per year.

Motor Trend. EMAP USA. • Monthly.$17.94. per year.

Special Interest Autos. Watering Inc., Special Interest Publications. • Bimonthly. $19.95 per year.

PRICE SOURCES

Edmunds New Car Prices-Domestic and Import. Edmund Publications Corp. • Three times a year. $15.00 per year. Wholesale and retail prices for all American and import models and accessories. Includes federal crash reports, leasing facts, and accident report forms. Formerly *Edmund's New Car Prices.* Incorporates *Edmund's Foreign Car Prices.*

NADA Appraisal Guides. National Automobile Dealers Association. • Prices and frequencies vary. Guides to prices of used cars, old used cars, motorcycles, mobile homes, recreational vehicles, and mopeds.

RESEARCH CENTERS AND INSTITUTES

Engineering Experiment Station. Ohio State University. 2070 Neil Ave., Columbus, OH 43210-1275. Phone: (614)292-2411 Fax: (614)292-9615 E-mail: fortner.1@osu.edu • URL: http://www.osu.edu.

Southwest Research Institute. P.O. Box 28510, San Antonio, TX 78228-0510. Phone: (210)684-5111 Fax: (210)522-3496 E-mail: jkittle@swri.org • URL: http://www.swri.org.

STATISTICS SOURCES

Business Statistics of the United States. Courtenay M. Slater, editor. Bernan Associates. • 1999. $74.00. Fifth edition. Based on *Business Statistics*, formerly issue by the Bureau of Economic Analysis, U. S. Department of Commerce. Provides basic data for a wide variety of U. S. industries, services, and economic indicators. Most statistics are shown annually for 29 years and monthly for the most recent four years.

Highway Statistics. Federal Highway Administration, U.S. Department of Transportation. Available from U.S. Government Printing Office. • Annual. $26.00.

Survey of Current Business. Available from U. S. Government Printing Office. • Monthly. $49.00 per year. Issued by Bureau of Economic Analysis, U. S. Department of Commerce. Presents a wide variety of business and economic data.

Transportation Statistics Annual Report. Available from U. S. Government Printing Office. • Annual. $21.00. Issued by Bureau of Transportation Statistics, U. S. Department of Transportation. Provides data on operating revenues, expenses, employees, passenger miles (where applicable), and other factors for airlines, automobiles, buses, local transit, pipelines, railroads, ships, and trucks.

TRADE/PROFESSIONAL ASSOCIATIONS

American Automobile Association. 1000 AAA Dr., No. 28, Heathrow, FL 32746. Phone: (407)444-4240 Fax: (407)444-7380 • URL: http://www.aaa.com.

AUTOMOBILES, USED

See: USED CAR INDUSTRY

AUTOMOTIVE INDUSTRY

See also: AUTOMOBILES; FOREIGN AUTOMOBILES; USED CAR INDUSTRY

GENERAL WORKS

The Machine That Changed the World. James P. Womack and others. Available from Gale Group. • 1990. $24.95. Based on a five-year study of the future of the automobile industry by the International Motor Vehicle Program at Massachusetts Institute of Technology.

ABSTRACTS AND INDEXES

Engineering Index Monthly: Abstracting and Indexing Services Covering Sources of the World's Engineering Literature. Engineering Information, Inc. • Monthly. $2,300.00 per year. Provides indexing and abstracting of the world's engineering and technical literature.

ALMANACS AND YEARBOOKS

Automotive News Market Data Book. Crain Communications, Inc. • Annual. $19.95. Directory of automotive vendors and worldwide vehicle manufacturing. Formerly *Automotive News Almanac.*

Ward's Automotive Yearbook. Ward's Communications, Inc. • Annual. $385.00. Comprehensive statistical information on automotive production, sales, truck data and suppliers. Included with subscription to *Ward's Automotive Reports.*

BIBLIOGRAPHIES

Japanese Automobile Industry: An Annotated Bibliography. Sheu-Yueh J. Chao, compiler. Greenwood Publishing Group, Inc. • 1994. $75.00. Describes about 600 books, articles, papers, and documents written in English. Emphasis is on material published since 1980. (Bibliographies and Indexes in Economics and Economic History Series, No. 157).

CD-ROM DATABASES

COMPENDEX PLUS [CD-ROM]. Engineering Information, Inc. • Quarterly. $3,450.00 per year. Provides CD-ROM indexing and abstracting of the world's engineering and technical information appearing in journals, reports, books, and proceedings, 1985 to date.

World Marketing Forecasts on CD-ROM. The Gale Group. • Annual. $2,500.00. Produced by Euromonitor. Provides detailed forecast data for the years to 2012 on CD-ROM for 54 countries in all parts of the world. Covers a wide range of social, demographic, economic, and market factors. Includes specific forecasts for many kinds of consumer products.

DIRECTORIES

Automotive Warehouse Distributors Association-Membership Directory. Automotive Warehouse Distributors Association. • Annual. $100.00. Over 500 automotive parts distributors, 200 manufacturers of automotive parts, and 8 marketing associations,17 manufacturer representatives, and 15 affiliate members.

ENCYCLOPEDIAS AND DICTIONARIES

Automotive Troubleshooting: Glossary. William Carroll. Coda Publication. • 1973. $5.00.

Macmillan Encyclopedia of Transportation. Available from The Gale Group. • 2000. $375.00. Six volumes. Published by Macmillan Reference USA. Covers the business, technology, and history of transportation on land, on water, in the air, and in space. Includes definitions, cross-references, and 200 color illustrations.

FINANCIAL RATIOS

Almanac of Business and Industrial Financial Ratios. Leo Troy. Prentice Hall. • Annual. $99.95.

Contains financial ratios derived from federal tax returns. Ratios for each of about 200 industries are arranged according to company asset size.

Annual Statement Studies. Robert Morris Associates: The Association of Lending and Credit Risk Professiona. • Annual. Free to members; non-members, $140.00. Median and quartile financial ratios are given for over 400 kinds of manufacturing, wholesale, retail, construction, and consumer finance establishments. Data is sorted by both asset size and sales volume. Includes a clearly written "Definition of Ratios" and an alphabetical industry index.

Industry Norms and Key Business Ratios. Desk Top Edition. Dun and Bradstreet Corp., Business Information Services. • Annual. Five volumes. $475.00 per volume. $1,890.00 per set. Covers over 800 kinds of businesses, arranged by Standard Industrial Classification number. More detailed editions covering longer periods of time are also available.

HANDBOOKS AND MANUALS

SAE Handbook. Society of Automotive Engineers. • Annual. $425.00. Three volumes. Contains standards, recommended practices and information reports on ground vehicle design, manufacturing, testing and performance.

INTERNET DATABASES

Fedstats. Federal Interagency Council on Statistical Policy. Phone: (202)395-7254 • URL: http://www.fedstats.gov • Web site features an efficient search facility for full-text statistics produced by more than 70 federal agencies, including the Census Bureau, the Bureau of Economic Analysis, and the Bureau of Labor Statistics. Boolean searches can be made within one agency or for all agencies combined. Links are offered to international statistical bureaus, including the UN, IMF, OECD, UNESCO, Eurostat, and 20 individual countries. Fees: Free.

ONLINE DATABASES

Business and Industry. Responsive Database Services, Inc. • Contains online citations, abstracts, and selected fulltext from more than 1,000 trade journals, newspapers, and other publications. Provides general coverage of both manufacturing and service industries, including marketing, production, industry trends, key events, and information on specific companies. Time span is 1994 to date. Daily updates. Inquire as to online cost and availability. (Also available in a CD-ROM version.).

COMPENDEX PLUS. Engineering Information, Inc. • Provides online indexing and abstracting of the world's engineering and technical information appearing in journals, reports, books, and proceedings. Time period is 1970 to date, with weekly updates. Inquire as to online cost and availability.

DRI U.S. Central Database. Data Products Division. • Provides more than 23,000 business, financial, demographic, economic, foreign trade, and industry-related time series for the U.S. Includes national income, population, retail-wholesale trade, price indexes, labor data, housing, industrial production, banking, interest rates, money supply, etc. Time period is generally 1947 to date (some data back to 1929). Updating varies. Inquire as to online cost and availability.

Euromonitor Market Research. Euromonitor International. • Provides the complete text online of Euromonitor market analysis reports. Covers consumer goods market research data for all major countries, with emphasis on specific product categories. Time period is current. Continuous updating. Inquire as to online cost and availability.

F & S Index. The Gale Group. • Contains about four million citations to worldwide business, financial, and industrial or consumer product literature appearing from 1972 to date. Weekly updates. Inquire as to online cost and availability.

Tablebase. Responsive Database Services, Inc. • Provides online numerical tabular data from a wide variety of business, organization, and government sources, including 900 trade journals. Includes industry and individual company statistics relating to products, market share, sales forecasts, production, exports, market trends, etc. Time span is 1997 to date. Weekly updates. Inquire as to online cost and availability. (Also available in a CD-ROM version.).

Ward's AutoInfoBank. Ward's Communications, Inc. • Provides weekly, monthly, quarterly, and annual statistical data drom 1965 to date for U. S. and imported cars and trucks. Covers production, shipments, sales, inventories, optional equipment, etc. Updating varies by series. Inquire as to online cost and availability.

PERIODICALS AND NEWSLETTERS

Autocar. Haymarket Publishing, Ltd. • Monthly. $230.00 per year. Formerly *Autocar and Motor.*

Automotive Engineering Magazine. Society of Automotive Engineers. • Monthly. $96.00 per year. Provides 86,000 automotive product planners and engineers with state-of-the-art technology that can be applied to the development of new and improved vehicles. Supplement available *Off-Highway Engineering.*

Automotive Industries. Cahners Business Information. • Monthly. $74.00 per year.

Automotive News: Engineering, Financial, Manufacturing, Sales, Marketing, Servicing. Crain Communications, Inc. • Weekly. $114.00 per year. Business news coverage of the automobile industry at the retail, wholesale, and manufacturing levels. Includes statistics.

Car Dealer Insider. United Communications Group. • Weekly. $275.00. per year. Newsletter covering management trends and industry news.

NADA'S Automotive Executive. National Automobile Dealers Association. • Monthly. $24.00 per year.

Road and Track. Hachette Filipacchi Magazines, Inc. • Monthly. $21.94 per year.

Ward's Auto World. • Monthly. Free to members; non-members, $55.00 per year. In-depth news and analysis of the automotive industry.

Ward's Automotive Reports. Ward's Communications. • Weekly. $1,195.00. per year. Vital statistical information on production, sales and inventory. Exclusive news of critical interest to the automotive industry. *Ward's Automotive Yearbook* included with subscription.

PRICE SOURCES

Automotive Market Report. Automotive Auction Publishing, Inc. • Biweekly. $130.00 Per Year. Current wholesale values of used vehicles.

STATISTICS SOURCES

American Trucking Trends. American Trucking Associations. Trucking Information Services, Inc. • Annual. $45.00.

Annual Survey of Manufactures. Available from U. S. Government Printing Office. • Annual. Prices vary. Issued by the U. S. Census Bureau as an interim update to the *Census of Manufactures.* Includes data on number of manufacturing establishments in various industries, employment, labor costs, value of shipments, capital expenditures, inventories, energy costs, and assets. (See also Census Bureau home page, http://www.census.gov/.).

Business Statistics of the United States. Courtenay M. Slater, editor. Bernan Associates. • 1999. $74.00. Fifth edition. Based on *Business Statistics*, formerly issue by the Bureau of Economic Analysis, U. S. Department of Commerce. Provides basic data for a wide variety of U. S. industries, services, and economic indicators. Most statistics are shown annually for 29 years and monthly for the most recent four years.

Consumer Canada 1996. Available from The Gale Group. • 1996. $750.00. Published by Euromonitor. Provides consumer market, socioeconomic, and demographic data for Canada. Includes consumer market size (volume and value) for many specific kinds of products.

Consumer International 2000/2001. Available from The Gale Group. • 1998. $1,190.00. Seventh edition. Published by Euromonitor. Contains extensive consumer market, economic, and demographic data for 27 major, non-European countries, including the U. S. and Canada. Includes consumer market size (volume and value) for 150 product types in 14 categories (food, clothing, automobiles, cosmetics, appliances, etc.).

Encyclopedia of American Industries. The Gale Group. • 1998. $560.00. Second edition. Two volumes. $280.00 per volume. Volume one is *Manufacturing Industries* and volume two is *Service and Non-Manufacturing Industries.* Provides the history, development, and recent status of approximately 1,000 industries. Includes statistical graphs, with industry and general indexes.

European Marketing Forecasts 2001. Available from The Gale Group. • 2000. $1,190.00. Third edition. Published by Euromonitor. Contains demographic, economic, and market forecasts for the countries of Europe to the year 2010. Forecasts include market-size data for 15 consumer product sectors (food, clothing, automobiles, consumer electronics, etc.).

International Marketing Forecasts 2001. Available from The Gale Group. • 2000. $1,090.00. Third edition. Published by Euromonitor. Contains demographic, economic, and market forecasts to the year 2010 for major, non-European countries, including the U. S. and Canada. Forecasts include market-size data for 15 consumer product sectors, such as food, clothing, and automobiles.

Standard & Poor's Industry Surveys. Standard & Poor's. • Semiannual. $1,800.00. Two looseleaf volumes. Includes monthly supplements. Provides detailed, individual surveys of 52 major industry groups. Each survey is revised on a semiannual basis. Also includes "Monthly Investment Review" (industry group investment analysis) and monthly "Trends & Projections" (economic analysis).

Statistics of Income: Corporation Income Tax Returns. U.S. Internal Revenue Service. Available from U.S. Government Printing Office. • Annual. $26.00.

Survey of Current Business. Available from U. S. Government Printing Office. • Monthly. $49.00 per year. Issued by Bureau of Economic Analysis, U. S. Department of Commerce. Presents a wide variety of business and economic data.

United States Census of Manufactures. U.S. Bureau of the Census. • Quinquennial. Results presented in reports, tape, CD-ROM, and Diskette files.

TRADE/PROFESSIONAL ASSOCIATIONS

ASM International. 9639 Kinsman Rd., Materials Park, OH 44073. Phone: 800-336-5152 or (216)338-5151 Fax: (216)338-4634 E-mail: memserv@

po.asm-intl.org • URL: http://www.asm-intl.org • Members are materials engineers, metallurgists, industry executives, educators, and others concerned with a wide range of materials and metals. Divisions include Aerospace, Composites, Electronic Materials and Processing, Energy, Highway/Off-Highway Vehicle, Joining, Materials Testing and Quality Control, Society of Carbide and Tool Engineers, and Surface Engineering.

Automotive Engine Rebuilders Association. 330 Lexington Dr., Buffalo Grove, IL 60089-6998. Phone: (847)541-6550 Fax: (847)541-5808 E-mail: info@aera.com • URL: http://www.aera.org.

Automotive Market Research Council. P.O. Box 13966, Research Triangle Park, NC 27709-3966. Phone: (919)549-4800 Fax: (919)549-4824.

Automotive Service Industry Association. 25 Northwest Point, Elk Grove Village, IL 60007-1035. Phone: (847)228-1310 Fax: (847)228-1510 • Members are distributors and manufacturers of automotive replacement parts.

Automotive Trade Association Executives. 8400 Westpark Dr., McLean, VA 22102. Phone: (703)821-7072 Fax: (703)556-8581.

Automotive Warehouse Distributors Association. 9140 Ward Parkway, Kansas City, MO 64114. Phone: (816)444-3500 Fax: (816)444-0330 • URL: http://www.awda.org.

SAE International. 400 Commonwealth Dr., Warrendale, PA 15096-0001. Phone: (724)776-4841 Fax: (724)776-5760 E-mail: swiss@sae.org • URL: http://www.sae.org.

OTHER SOURCES

Business & Company Resource Center. The Gale Group. • Fee-based Web site provides a wide range of business, industry, and specific company information. Access is offered to trade journal articles, market research data, insider trading activity, major shareholder data, corporate histories, emerging technology reports, corporate earnings estimates, press releases, and other sources. Provides detailed company profiles, industry overviews, and rankings. Offers integration of Predicasts PROMT, Newsletters ASAP, Investext Plus, Business Index ASAP, Brands and Their Companies, and other databases (many have full text).

AV EQUIPMENT INDUSTRY

See: AUDIOVISUAL EQUIPMENT INDUSTRY

AVIATION, BUSINESS

See: BUSINESS AVIATION

AVIATION ELECTRONICS

See: AVIONICS

AVIATION INDUSTRY

See also: AEROSPACE INDUSTRY; AIRLINE INDUSTRY; AIRPLANE INDUSTRY; BUSINESS AVIATION

GENERAL WORKS

ATP-FAR 135, Airline Transport Pilot: A Comprehensive Text and Workbook for the en Exam. K.T. Boyd. Iowa State University Press. • 1994. $29.95. Third edition.

FAA Historical Chronology: Civil Aviation and the Federal Government, 1926-1996. Edmund Preston, editor. Available from U. S. Government Printing Office. • 1998. $29.00. Third edition. Issued by the Federal Aviation Administration, U. S. Department of Transportation (http://www.dot.gov). Provides a compilation of historical information about the FAA and the earlier Civil Aeronautics Board (CAB). Chronological arrangement.

BIBLIOGRAPHIES

Aviation. Available from U. S. Government Printing Office. • Annual. Free. Lists government publications. (GPO Subject Bibliography Number 18).

DIRECTORIES

Air Freight Directory. Air Cargo, Inc. • Bimonthly. $84.00 per year. Air freight motor carriers.

World Aviation Directory. McGraw-Hill Aviation Week Group. • Semiannual. $225.00 per year. Two volumes. Lists aviation, aerospace, and missile manufacturers. Includes *World Aviation Directory Buyer's Guide.*

ENCYCLOPEDIAS AND DICTIONARIES

Dictionary of Aviation. R. J. Hall and R. D. Campbell. Available from St. James Press. • 1991. $50.00. Published by Blackwell Scientific. Includes aeronautical words, phrases, acronyms, and abbreviations.

Macmillan Encyclopedia of Transportation. Available from The Gale Group. • 2000. $375.00. Six volumes. Published by Macmillan Reference USA. Covers the business, technology, and history of transportation on land, on water, in the air, and in space. Includes definitions, cross-references, and 200 color illustrations.

FINANCIAL RATIOS

Industry Norms and Key Business Ratios. Desk Top Edition. Dun and Bradstreet Corp., Business Information Services. • Annual. Five volumes. $475.00 per volume. $1,890.00 per set. Covers over 800 kinds of businesses, arranged by Standard Industrial Classification number. More detailed editions covering longer periods of time are also available.

ONLINE DATABASES

F & S Index. The Gale Group. • Contains about four million citations to worldwide business, financial, and industrial or consumer product literature appearing from 1972 to date. Weekly updates. Inquire as to online cost and availability.

PERIODICALS AND NEWSLETTERS

AIAA Journal: Devoted to Aerospace Research and Development. American Institute of Aeronautics and Astronautics, Inc. • Monthly. Members, $65.00 per year; non-members, $185.00 per year; institutions, $645.00 per year.

Air Transport World. Penton Media Inc. • Monthly. Free to qualified personnel, others, $55.00 per year. Includes supplement *World Airline Reports.*

Aviation Daily. Aviation Week Newsletter. McGraw-Hill. • Daily. $1,595.00 per year. Newsletter. Covers current developments in air transportation and aviation manufacturing.

Aviation Week and Space Technology. McGraw-Hill Aviation Week Group. • Monthly. $89.00 per year.

Human Factors and Aviation Medicine. Flight Safety Foundation. • Bimonthly. Members, $120.00 per year; non-members, $240.00 per year.

The ICAO Journal. International Civil Aviation Organization c/o Document Sales Unit. • Ten times a year. $25.00 per year. Editions in English, French and Spanish.

Weekly of Business Aviation. Aviation Week Newsletter. McGraw-Hill. • Weekly. $540.00 per year.

RESEARCH CENTERS AND INSTITUTES

Avionics Engineering Center. Ohio University. 239 Stocker Center, Athens, OH 45701. Phone: (740)593-1534 Fax: (740)593-1604 E-mail: rankinj@ohiou.edu • URL: http://www.ent.ohiou.edu/avn/.

Flight Mechanics Laboratory. Texas A & M University, College Station, TX 77843-3141. Phone: (409)845-1732 Fax: (409)845-6051 E-mail: ward@aero.tamu.edu.

Flight Research Laboratory. University of Kansas. 138 Nichols Hall, Lawrence, KS 66045-2969. Phone: (785)864-3999 Fax: (785)864-7789 E-mail: mewing@aerospace.ae.ukans.edu • URL: http://www.ukans.edu.

Institute of Aviation Research Laboratory. University of Illinois. One Airport Rd., Bldg. Q5, Savoy, IL 61874. Phone: (217)244-8617 Fax: (217)244-8647 E-mail: cwickens@uiuc.edu • URL: http://www.aviation.uiuc.edu.

Joint Institute for Advancement of Flight Sciences. George Washington University, NASA Langley Research Center, Mail Stop 269, Hampton, VA 23681-2199. Phone: (757)864-1982 Fax: (757)864-5894 E-mail: jiafs@seas.gwu.edu • URL: http://www.seas.gwu.edu/seas/jiafs • Conducts research in aeronautics, astronautics, and acoustics (flight-produced noise).

STATISTICS SOURCES

Aerospace Facts and Figures. Aerospace Industries Association of America. • Annual. $35.00. Includes financial data for the aerospace industries.

Air Transport. Air Transport Association of America. • Annual. $20.00.

FAA Statistical Handbook of Aviation. Federal Aviation Administration. Available from U. S. Government Printing Office. • Annual.

Handbook of Airline Statistics. National Aeronautics and Space Administration. • Biennial.

International Civil Aviation Organization Digests of Statistics. International Civil Aviation Organization c/o Document Sales Unit. • Irregular. $54.00. Contains financial data and traffic data for international airports. Text in English, French, Russian and Spanish.

TRADE/PROFESSIONAL ASSOCIATIONS

Air Transport Association of America. 1301 Pennsylvania Ave., Suite 1100, Washington, DC 20004-7017. Phone: (202)626-4000 Fax: (202)626-4166 E-mail: ata@air-transport.org • URL: http://www.air-transport.org.

Aviation Development Council. 141-07 20th Ave., Suite 404, Whitestone, NY 11357. Phone: (718)746-0212 Fax: (718)746-1006.

Aviation Distributors and Manufacturers Association International. 1900 Arch St., Philadelphia, PA 19103-1498. Phone: (215)564-3484 Fax: (215)564-2175 E-mail: assnhqt@netaxc.com.

General Aviation Manufacturers Association. 1400 K St., N.W., Suite 801, Washington, DC 20005. Phone: (202)393-1500 Fax: (202)842-4063 • URL: http://www.generalaviation.org.

International Air Transport Association. P.O. Box 113, Montreal, QC, Canada H42 1M1. Phone: (514)874-0202 Fax: (514)874-9632 • URL: http://www.iata.org.

National Aeronautic Association of the U.S.A. 1815 N. Fort Myer Dr., Suite 700, Arlington, VA 22209-1805. Phone: 800-644-9777 or (703)527-0226 Fax: (703)527-0229 E-mail: naa@naa-usa.org • URL: http://www.naa.ycg.org.

National Air Transportation Association. 4226 King St., Alexandria, VA 22302. Phone: 800-808-6282 or (703)845-9000 Fax: (703)845-8176 • URL: http://www.nata-online.org.

National Association of State Aviation Officials. 8401 Colesville Rd., Suite 505, Silver Spring, MD 20910. Phone: (301)588-0587 Fax: (301)588-1803 • URL: http://www.nasao.org.

National Aviation Club. 1815 N. Fort Myer Dr., No. 500, Arlington, VA 22209. Phone: (703)527-0226 Fax: (703)527-0229.

University Aviation Association. 3410 Skyway Dr., Auburn, AL 36830. Phone: (334)844-2434 Fax: (334)844-2432 E-mail: uaa@auburn.edu • URL: http://www.uaa.auburn.edu.

OTHER SOURCES

Aviation Law Reports. CCH, Inc. • $2,419.00 per year. Four looseleaf volumes. Semimonthly updates.

Jane's All the World's Aircraft. Jane's Information Group, Inc. • Annual. $300.00; CD-Rom edition, $425.00.

AVIONICS

See also: ELECTRONICS INDUSTRY

GENERAL WORKS

Advances in Optotronics and Avionics Technologies. M. Garcia, editor. John Wiley and Sons, Inc. • 1996. $90.00.

ABSTRACTS AND INDEXES

Applied Science and Technology Index. H. W. Wilson Co. • 11 times a year. Quarterly and annual cumulations. Service basis for print edition; CD-ROM edition, $1,495.00 per year. Indexes a wide variety of English language technical, industrial, and engineering periodicals.

Science Citation Index. Institute for Scientific Information. • Bimonthly. $15,020.00 per year. Annual cumulation. Includes *Source Index*, *Citation Index*, *Permuterm Subject Index*, and *Corporate Index*.

CD-ROM DATABASES

Science Citation Index: Compact Disc Edition. Institute for Scientific Information. • Quarterly. Provides CD-ROM indexing of the world's scientific and technical literature. Corresponds to online *Scisearch* and printed *Science Citation Index*.

DIRECTORIES

ECN's Electronic Industry Telephone Directory. Cahners Business Information. • Annual. $55.00. Information on 30,000 electronic manufacturers, distributors, and representatives. Formerly *Electronic Industry Telephone Directory*.

International ABC Aerospace Directory. Janes's Information Group. • 1998. $500.00. 28,000 aviation aerospace manufacturers, airlines, associations, government agencies, etc. Formerly *Interavia ABC Aerospace Directory*.

Jane's Avionics. • Annual. $350.00. Civil/military airborne equipment. International coverage.

World Aviation Directory. McGraw-Hill Aviation Week Group. • Semiannual. $225.00 per year. Two volumes. Lists aviation, aerospace, and missile manufacturers. Includes *World Aviation Directory Buyer's Guide*.

ENCYCLOPEDIAS AND DICTIONARIES

Wiley Encyclopedia of Electrical and Electronics Engineering. John G. Webster, editor. John Wiley and Sons, Inc. • 1999. $6,495.00. 24 volumes. Contains about 1,400 articles, each with bibliography. Arrangement is according to 64 categories.

HANDBOOKS AND MANUALS

Modern Aviation Electronics. Albert D. Helfrick. Prentice Hall. • 1994. $67.60. Second edition.

ONLINE DATABASES

Aerospace/Defense Markets and Technology. The Gale Group. • Abstracts of commerical aerospace/defense related literature, 1982 to date. Also includes information about major defense contracts awarded by the U. S. Department of Defense. International coverage. Inquire as to online cost and availability.

Globalbase. The Gale Group. • Provides more than one million online summaries of business, industrial, and economic news reports from more than 1,000 publications worldwide. Covers a wide range of material appearing in international trade journals, professional magazines, and newspapers. Time period is 1984 to date, with weekly updates. Inquire as to online cost and availability.

Scisearch. Institute for Scientific Information. • Broad, multidisciplinary index to the literature of science and technology, 1974 to present. Inquire as to online cost and availability. Coverage of literature is worldwide, with weekly updates.

PERIODICALS AND NEWSLETTERS

Aerospace America. American Institute of Aeronautics and Astronautics, Inc. • Monthly. Free to members; non-members, $75.00 per year. Provides coverage of key issues affecting the aerospace field.

Aerospace and Defense Science. Aerospace and Defense Science, Inc. • Quarterly. $24.00 per year. Provides executive overviews and insights into defense and aerospace technologies and future applications.

Aerospace Engineering Magazine. Society of Automotive Engineers. • Monthly. $66.00 per year. Provides technical information that can be used in the design of new and improved aerospace systems.

Aviation Week and Space Technology. McGraw-Hill Aviation Week Group. • Monthly. $89.00 per year.

Avionics.

Defense Electronics. Intertec Publishing Corp. • Monthly. $52.00 per year.

Flight International. Reed Business Information. • Weekly. $170.00 per year. Technical aerospace coverage.

Journal of Electronic Defense. Association of Old Crows. Horizon-House Publications, Inc. • Monthly. Free to members; non-members, $120.00 per year.

Professional Pilot Magazine. Queensmith Communications Corp. • Monthly. $36.00 per year. Edited for career pilots in all areas of aviation: airline, corporate, charter, and military. Includes flying technique, avionics, navigation, accident analysis, career planning, corporate profiles, and business aviation news.

RESEARCH CENTERS AND INSTITUTES

Avionics Engineering Center. Ohio University. 239 Stocker Center, Athens, OH 45701. Phone: (740)593-1534 Fax: (740)593-1604 E-mail: rankinj@ohiou.edu • URL: http://www.ent.ohiou.edu/avn/.

TRADE/PROFESSIONAL ASSOCIATIONS

Aeronautical Repair Station Association. 121 N. Henry St., Alexandria, VA 22314. Phone: (703)739-9543 Fax: (703)739-9488 E-mail: arsa@arsa.org • URL: http://www.arsa.org.

Aerospace Electrical Society. 18231 Fernando Circle, Villa Park, CA 92861. Phone: (714)538-1002.

Aircraft Electronics Association. 4217 S. Hocker, Independence, MO 64055-0963. Phone: (816)373-6565 Fax: (816)478-3100 • URL: http://www.aeaavnews.org.

American Institute of Aeronautics and Astronautics. 1801 Alexander Bell Dr., Suite 500, c/o Michael Lewis, Reston, VA 20191-4344. Phone: 800-639-2422 or (703)264-7500 Fax: (703)264-7551 E-mail: customerserv@aiaa.org • URL: http://www.aiaa.org.

Aviation Distributors and Manufacturers Association International. 1900 Arch St., Philadelphia, PA 19103-1498. Phone: (215)564-3484 Fax: (215)564-2175 E-mail: assnhqt@netaxc.com.

Avionics Maintenance Conference. c/o Aeronautical Radio, Inc., 2551 Riva Rd., Annapolis, MD 21401. Phone: (410)266-4116 Fax: (410)266-2047.

Institute of Electrical and Electronics Engineers; Aerospace and Electronic Systems Society. Three Park Ave., 17th Fl., New York, NY 10016-5997. Phone: (212)419-7900 Fax: (212)752-4929 • URL: http://www.ieee.org.

Instrument Society of America: Aerospace Division. P.O. Box 12277, Research Triangle Park, NC 27709. Phone: (919)549-8411 Fax: (919)549-8288 E-mail: info@isa.org • URL: http://www.isa.org.

RTCA. 1140 Connecticut Ave. N.W., Suite 1020, Washington, DC 20036. Phone: (202)833-9339 Fax: (202)833-9434 E-mail: info@rtca.org • URL: http://www.rtca.org.

OTHER SOURCES

Aerospace America [online]. American Institute of Aeronautics and Astronautics. • Provides complete text of the periodical, *Aerospace America*, 1984 to date, with monthly updates. Also includes news from the *AIAA Bulletin*. Inquire as to online cost and availability.

Aerospace Database. American Institute of Aeronautics and Astronautics. • Contains abstracts of literature covering all aspects of the aerospace and aircraft in series 1983 to date. Semimonthly updates. Inquire as to online cost and availability.

AWARDS

See: CONTESTS, PRIZES, AND AWARDS

B

BABY CLOTHES

See: CHILDREN'S APPAREL INDUSTRY

BABY SITTING

See also: DAY CARE CENTERS

GENERAL WORKS

How to Organize a Babysitting Cooperative and Get Some Free Time Away From the Kids. Carole T. Meyers. Carousel Press. • 1976. $6.95.

HANDBOOKS AND MANUALS

The Babysitter's Handbook. Dorling Kindersley Publishing, Inc. • 1995. $12.95.

ONLINE DATABASES

ERIC. Educational Resources Information Center. • Broad range of educational literature, 1966 to present. Monthly updates. Inquire as to online cost and availability.

BAG INDUSTRY

See: PAPER BAG INDUSTRY

BAKING INDUSTRY

See also: FOOD INDUSTRY; SNACK FOOD INDUSTRY

ABSTRACTS AND INDEXES

Flour Milling and Baking Research Association Abstracts. Flour Milling and Baking Research Association. • Bimonthly. Membership.

Food Science and Technology Abstracts. International Food Information Service Publishing. • Monthly. $1,780.00 per year. Provides worldwide coverage of the literature of food technology and food production.

Foods Adlibra: Key to the World's Food Literature. Foods Adlibra Publications. • Semimonthly.Provides journal citations and abstracts to the literature of food technology and packaging.

CD-ROM DATABASES

Food Science and Technology Abstracts [CD-ROM]. Available from SilverPlatter Information, Inc. • Quarterly. $3,700 per year. Produced by International Food Information Service (home page is http://www.ifis.org). Provides worldwide coverage on CD-ROM of the literature of food technology and production. Various types of publications are indexed, with abstracts, including about 1,800 periodicals. Time period is 1969 to date.

DIRECTORIES

Directory of Delicatessen Products. Pacific Rim Publishing Co. • Annual. Included with February issue of *Deli News.* Lists suppliers of cheeses, lunch meats, packaged fresh meats, kosher foods, gourmet-specialty items, and bakery products.

Specialty Food Industry Directory. Phoenix Media Network, Inc. • Annual. Included in subscription to Food Distribution Magazine. Lists manufacturers and suppliers of specialty foods, and services and equipment for the specialty food industry. Featured food products include legumes, sauces, spices, upscale cheese, specialty beverages, snack foods, baked goods, ethnic foods, and specialty meats.

World Food Marketing Directory. Available from The Gale Group. • 2001. $1,090.00. Second edition. Three volumes. Published by Euromonitor. Provides detailed information on the major food companies of the world, including specific brand data.

FINANCIAL RATIOS

Almanac of Business and Industrial Financial Ratios. Leo Troy. Prentice Hall. • Annual. $99.95. Contains financial ratios derived from federal tax returns. Ratios for each of about 200 industries are arranged according to company asset size.

Annual Statement Studies. Robert Morris Associates: The Association of Lending and Credit Risk Professiona. • Annual. Free to members; non-members, $140.00. Median and quartile financial ratios are given for over 400 kinds of manufacturing, wholesale, retail, construction, and consumer finance establishments. Data is sorted by both asset size and sales volume. Includes a clearly written "Definition of Ratios" and an alphabetical industry index.

Industry Norms and Key Business Ratios. Desk Top Edition. Dun and Bradstreet Corp., Business Information Services. • Annual. Five volumes. $475.00 per volume. $1,890.00 per set. Covers over 800 kinds of businesses, arranged by Standard Industrial Classification number. More detailed editions covering longer periods of time are also available.

HANDBOOKS AND MANUALS

Baker's Manual. Joseph Amendola. John Wiley and Sons, Inc. • 1993. $32.95. Fourth edition.

Bakery. Entrepreneur Media, Inc. • Looseleaf. $59.50. A practical guide to starting a retail bakery. Covers profit potential, start-up costs, market size evaluation, owner's time required, site selection, lease negotiation, pricing, accounting, advertising, promotion, etc. (Start-Up Business Guide No. E1158.).

Donut Shop. Entrepreneur Media, Inc. • Looseleaf. $59.50. A practical guide to starting a doughnut shop. Covers profit potential, start-up costs, market size evaluation, owner's time required, site selection, lease negotiation, pricing, accounting, advertising, promotion, etc. (Start-Up Business Guide No. E1126.).

How to Make Money in Cake Decorating: Owning and Operating a Successful Business in Your Home. Del Carnes. Deco-Press Publishing Co. • 1987. $10.99 Revised edition. (How to Profit Series: volume one).

Pizzeria. Entrepreneur Media, Inc. • Looseleaf. $59.50. A practical guide to starting a pizza shop. Covers profit potential, start-up costs, market size evaluation, owner's time required, site selection, lease negotiation, pricing, accounting, advertising, promotion, etc. (Start-Up Business Guide No. E1006.).

Practical Baking. William J. Sultan. John Wiley and Sons, Inc. • 1990. $55.95. Fifth edition.

ONLINE DATABASES

F & S Index. The Gale Group. • Contains about four million citations to worldwide business, financial, and industrial or consumer product literature appearing from 1972 to date. Weekly updates. Inquire as to online cost and availability.

Food Science and Technology Abstracts [online]. IFIS North American Desk. • Produced by International Food Information Service. Provides about 500,000 online citations, with abstracts, to the international literature of food science, technology, commodities, engineering, and processing. Approximately 2,000 periodicals are covered. Time period is 1969 to date, with monthly updates. Inquire as to online cost and availability.

FOODS ADLIBRA. General Mills, Inc. • Contains online citations, with abstracts, to the technical and business literature of food processing and packaging. New products and new ingredients are featured. Covers about 250 trade journals and 500 research journals from 1974 to date, with monthly updates. Inquire as to online cost and availability.

PERIODICALS AND NEWSLETTERS

Baking and Snack. Sosland Publishing Co. • Monthly. Free to qualified personnel; others, $30.00 per year. Covers manufacturing systems and ingredients for baked goods and snack foods.

Deli News. Delicatessen Council of Southern California, Inc. Pacific Rim Publishing Co. • Monthly. $25.00 per year. Includes product news and comment related to cheeses, lunch meats, packaged fresh meats, kosher foods, gourmet-specialty items, and bakery products.

Fancy Food. Talcott Communications Corp. • Monthly. $34.00 per year. Emphasizes new specialty food products and the business management aspects of the specialty food and confection industries. Includes special issues on wine, cheese, candy, "upscale" cookware, and gifts.

Food Distribution Magazine. Phoenix Media Network, Inc. • Monthly. $49.00 per year. Edited for marketers and buyers of domestic and imported, specialty or gourmet food products, including ethnic foods, seasonings, and bakery items.

Gourmet Retailer. Bill Communications, Business Communications Group. • Monthly. $24.00 per year. Covers upscale food and housewares, including confectionery items, bakery operations, and coffee.

Reference Source. Sosland Publishing Co. • Annual. $45.00 per year. A statistical reference manual and specification guide for wholesale baking. Formerly *Bakers Digest.*

Snack Food and Wholesale Bakery: The Magazine That Defines the Snack Food Industry. Stagnito Publishing Co. • Monthly. Free to qualified personnel; others, $65.00 per year. Provides news and information for producers of pretzels, potato chips, cookies, crackers, nuts, and other snack foods. Includes *Annual Buyers Guide* and *State of Industry Report.*

Specialty Baker's Voice. Specialty Bakery Owners of America. • Monthly. $25.00 per year.

PRICE SOURCES

PPI Detailed Report. Bureau of Labor Statistics, U.S. Department of Labor. Available from U.S. Government Printing Office. • Monthly. $55.00 per year. Formerly *Producer Price Indexes.*

RESEARCH CENTERS AND INSTITUTES

Food and Feed Grain Institute. Kansas State University. Waters Hall, Room 105, Manhattan, KS 66506-4030. Phone: (785)532-4057 Fax: (785)532-5861 E-mail: reb@ksu.edu • URL: http://www.ksu.edu.

Quality Bakers of America Cooperative Laboratory. 70 Riverdale Ave., Greenwich, CT 06831. Phone: (203)531-7100 Fax: (203)531-5978 • URL: http://www.qba.com.

STATISTICS SOURCES

Annual Survey of Manufactures. Available from U. S. Government Printing Office. • Annual. Prices vary. Issued by the U. S. Census Bureau as an interim update to the *Census of Manufactures.* Includes data on number of manufacturing establishments in various industries, employment, labor costs, value of shipments, capital expenditures, inventories, energy costs, and assets. (See also Census Bureau home page, http://www.census.gov/.).

U. S. Industry and Trade Outlook: The McGraw-Hill Companies and the U.S. Department of Commerce/ International Trade Administration. Datapso Research Corp. • Annual. $69.95. Produced by the International Trade Administration, U. S. Department of Commerce, in a "public-private" partnership with DRI/McGraw-Hill and Standard & Poor's. Provides basic data, outlook for the current year, and "Long-Term Prospects" (five-year projections) for a wide variety of products and services. Includes high technology industries. Formerly *U. S. Industrial Outlook.*

United States Census of Manufactures. U.S. Bureau of the Census. • Quinquennial. Results presented in reports, tape, CD-ROM, and Diskette files.

TRADE/PROFESSIONAL ASSOCIATIONS

Allied Trades of the Baking Industry. 4510 W. 89th St., Suite 110, Shawnee Mission, KS 66207. Phone: (913)341-0765 Fax: (913)341-3625.

American Bakers Association. 1350 Eye St., N.W., Suite 1290, Washington, DC 20005-3005. Phone: (202)789-0300 Fax: (202)898-1164 E-mail: info@americanbakers.org • URL: http://www.americanbakers.org.

American Institute of Baking. P.O. Box 3999, Manhattan, KS 66502-3999. Phone: (785)537-4750 Fax: (785)537-1493 E-mail: mailbox@aibonline.org • URL: http://www.aibonline.org.

American Society of Baking. Two N. Riverside Plaza, Room 1733, Chicago, IL 60606. Phone: (312)332-2246 Fax: (312)332-6560 E-mail: asbe@asbe.org • URL: http://www.asbe.org.

Baking Industry Sanitation Standards Committee. c/o Barbara Chalik, 1400 W. Devon Ave., Ste. 4200, Chicago, IL 60660. Phone: (773)761-4100 E-mail: bakesan@aol.com • URL: http://www.bakingsanitation.com.

BEMA (Bakery Equipment Manufacturers Association). 401 N. Michigan Ave., Chicago, IL 60611. Phone: (312)644-6610 Fax: (312)527-6640 E-mail: bema@sba.com • URL: http://www.bema.org.

Retailer's Bakery Association. c/o Peggy Hoffman, 14239 Park Center Dr., Laurel, MD 20707. Phone: 800-638-0924 or (301)725-2149 Fax: (301)725-2187 E-mail: rba@rbanet.com • URL: http://www.rbanet.com.

OTHER SOURCES

American Society of Baking. American Society of Bakery Engineers. • Annual. Free to members.

The Bread Market. Available from MarketResearch.com. • 2000. $3,250.00. Published by Packaged Facts. Provides market data on a wide variety of packaged, frozen, and fresh- baked bread products.

Major Food and Drink Companies of the World. Available from The Gale Group. • 2001. $855.00. Fourth edition. Two volumes. Published by Graham & Whiteside. Contains profiles and trade names for more than 9,000 important food and beverage companies in various countries. In addition to foods, includes both alcoholic and nonalcoholic drink products.

The Market for Sweet Baked Goods. MarketResearch.com. • 2000. $2,750.00. Market research data. Covers both fresh and frozen, bakery products.

Thomas Food and Beverage Market Place. Grey House Publishing. • Annual. $295.00. Three volumes. Contains more than 40,000 entries covering food companies, beverages, food equipment, warehouse companies, food brokers, wholesalers, importers, and exporters. Formerly *Thomas Food Industry Register.*

BALANCE OF PAYMENTS

See also: FOREIGN TRADE

GENERAL WORKS

The Balance of Payments in a Monetary Economy. John F. Kyle. Books on Demand. • 1976. $64.50. (Irving Fisher Award Series).

CD-ROM DATABASES

EconLit. Available from SilverPlatter Information, Inc. • Monthly. Single-user, $1,600.00 per year. Multi-user, $2,400.00 per year. Provides CD-ROM citations, with abstracts, to articles from more than 500 economics journals. Time period is 1969 to date. Produced by the American Economic Association.

World Trade Atlas CD-ROM. Global Trade Information Services, Inc. • Monthly. $4,920.00 per year. ($3,650.00 per year with quarterly updates.) Provides government statistics on trade between the U. S. and each of more than 200 countries. Includes import-export data, trade balances, product information, market share, price data, etc. Time period is the most recent three years.

INTERNET DATABASES

Fedstats. Federal Interagency Council on Statistical Policy. Phone: (202)395-7254 • URL: http://www.fedstats.gov • Web site features an efficient search facility for full-text statistics produced by more than 70 federal agencies, including the Census Bureau, the Bureau of Economic Analysis, and the Bureau of Labor Statistics. Boolean searches can be made within one agency or for all agencies combined. Links are offered to international statistical bureaus, including the UN, IMF, OECD, UNESCO, Eurostat, and 20 individual countries. Fees: Free.

ONLINE DATABASES

American Statistics Index: A Comprehensive Guide and Index to the Statistical Publications of the United States Government [Online]. Congressional Information Service, Inc. • Indexes and abstracts, 1973 to date. Inquire as to online cost and availability.

Balance of Payments Statistics. International Monetary Fund. • Time series compiled by IMF, mid-1960's to present. Inquire as to online cost and availability.

DRI U.S. Central Database. Data Products Division. • Provides more than 23,000 business, financial, demographic, economic, foreign trade, and industry-related time series for the U.S. Includes national income, population, retail-wholesale trade, price indexes, labor data, housing, industrial production, banking, interest rates, money supply, etc. Time period is generally 1947 to date (some data back to 1929). Updating varies. Inquire as to online cost and availability.

EconLit. American Economic Association. • Covers the worldwide literature of economics as contained in selected monographs and about 550 journals. Subjects include microeconomics, macroeconomics, economic history, inflation, money, credit, finance, accounting theory, trade, natural resource economics, and regional economics. Time period is 1969 to present, with monthly updates. Inquire as to online cost and availability.

OECD Main Economic Indicators. Organization for Economic Cooperation and Development. • International statistics provided by OECD, 1960 to date. Monthly updates. Inquire as to online cost and availability.

PERIODICALS AND NEWSLETTERS

IMF Survey. International Monetary Fund, Publication Services. • 23 times a year. $79.00 per year. Newsletter. Covers IMF activities in international finance, trade, commodities, and foreign exchange. Editions in English, French, and Spanish.

International Monetary Fund Staff Papers. International Monetary Fund, Publication Services. • Quarterly. Individuals, $56.00 per year; students, $28.00 per year. Contains studies by IMF staff members on balance of payments, foreign exchange, fiscal policy, and related topics.

STATISTICS SOURCES

Business Statistics of the United States. Courtenay M. Slater, editor. Bernan Associates. • 1999. $74.00. Fifth edition. Based on *Business Statistics*, formerly issue by the Bureau of Economic Analysis, U. S. Department of Commerce. Provides basic data for a wide variety of U. S. industries, services, and economic indicators. Most statistics are shown annually for 29 years and monthly for the most recent four years.

International Financial Statistics. International Monetary Fund, Publications Services. • Monthly. Individuals, $246.00 per year; libraries, $123.00 per year. Includes a wide variety of current data for individual countries in Europe and elsewhere. Annual issue available. Editions available in French and Spanish.

Monthly Bulletin of Statistics. United Nations Publications. • Monthly. $295.00 per year. Provides current data for about 200 countries on a wide variety of economic, industrial, and demographic subjects. Compiled by United Nations Statistical Office.

Statistical Yearbook. United Nations Publications. • Annual. $125.00. Contains statistics for about 200 countries on a wide variety of economic, industrial, and demographic topics. Compiled by United Nations Statistical Office.

Survey of Current Business. Available from U. S. Government Printing Office. • Monthly. $49.00 per year. Issued by Bureau of Economic Analysis, U. S. Department of Commerce. Presents a wide variety of business and economic data.

BALANCE OF TRADE

See: BALANCE OF PAYMENTS; FOREIGN TRADE

BALL BEARINGS

See: BEARINGS AND BALL BEARINGS

BALL POINT PENS

See: WRITING INSTRUMENTS

BANANA INDUSTRY

See also: FRUIT INDUSTRY

GENERAL WORKS

The Banana: Its History, and Cultivation. Philip Keep Reynolds. Gordon Press Publishers. • 1981. $250.00. Reprint of 1977 edition.

CD-ROM DATABASES

Food Science and Technology Abstracts [CD-ROM]. Available from SilverPlatter Information, Inc. • Quarterly. $3,700 per year. Produced by International Food Information Service (home page is http://www.ifis.org). Provides worldwide coverage on CD-ROM of the literature of food technology and production. Various types of publications are indexed, with abstracts, including about 1,800 periodicals. Time period is 1969 to date.

INTERNET DATABASES

USDA. United States Department of Agriculture. Phone: (202)720-2791 E-mail: agsec@usda.gov • URL: http://www.usda.gov • The USDA home page has six sections: News and Information; What's New; About USDA; Agencies; Opportunities; Search and Help. Keyword searching is offered from the USDA home page and from various individual agency home pages. Agencies are the Economic Research Service, Agricultural Marketing Service, National Agricultural Statistics Service, National Agricultural Library, and about 12 others. Updating varies. Fees: Free.

ONLINE DATABASES

Abstracts on Tropical Agriculture. Koninklijk Instituut voor de Tropen/Royal Tropical Institute. • Abstracts of journals, articles, monographs, conferences, reports, 1975 to present. Inquire as to online cost and availability.

Agricola. U.S. National Agricultural Library. • Covers worldwide agricultural literature. Over 2.8 million citations, 1970 to present, with monthly updates. Inquire as to online cost and availability.

Food Science and Technology Abstracts [online]. IFIS North American Desk. • Produced by International Food Information Service. Provides about 500,000 online citations, with abstracts, to the international literature of food science, technology, commodities, engineering, and processing. Approximately 2,000 periodicals are covered. Time period is 1969 to date, with monthly updates. Inquire as to online cost and availability.

PERIODICALS AND NEWSLETTERS

BGF Bulletin. Banana Growers Federation Co-Operative Ltd. • Monthly. $35.00 per year. Formerly *Banana Bulletin.*

PRICE SOURCES

PPI Detailed Report. Bureau of Labor Statistics, U.S. Department of Labor. Available from U.S. Government Printing Office. • Monthly. $55.00 per year. Formerly *Producer Price Indexes.*

RESEARCH CENTERS AND INSTITUTES

Food Technology Laboratory. University of Puerto Rico. Agricultural Experiment Station, P.O. Box 21360, San Juan, PR 00928. Phone: (787)767-8281 Fax: (787)763-0096.

Hawaii Institute of Tropical Agriculture and Human Resources. University of Hawaii at Manoa, Honolulu, HI 96822. Phone: (808)956-8131 Fax: (808)956-9105 E-mail: tadean2@avax.ctahr.hawaii.edu • URL: http://www.ctahr.hawaii.edu • Concerned with the production and marketing of tropical food and ornamental plant products, including pineapples, bananas, coffee, and macadamia nuts.

Kauai Agricultural Station. University of Hawaii at Manoa. 7370 Kuamoo Rd., Kapaa, HI 96746. Phone: (808)822-4984 Fax: (808)822-2190.

STATISTICS SOURCES

Agricultural Statistics. Available from U. S. Government Printing Office. • Annual. Produced by the National Agricultural Statistics Service, U. S. Department of Agriculture. Provides a wide variety of statistical data relating to agricultural production, supplies, consumption, prices/price-supports, foreign trade, costs, and returns, as well as farm labor, loans, income, and population. In many cases, historical data is shown annually for 10 years. In addition to farm data, includes detailed fishery statistics.

OTHER SOURCES

Major Food and Drink Companies of the World. Available from The Gale Group. • 2001. $855.00. Fourth edition. Two volumes. Published by Graham & Whiteside. Contains profiles and trade names for more than 9,000 important food and beverage companies in various countries. In addition to foods, includes both alcoholic and nonalcoholic drink products.

Thomas Food and Beverage Market Place. Grey House Publishing. • Annual. $295.00. Three volumes. Contains more than 40,000 entries covering food companies, beverages, food equipment, warehouse companies, food brokers, wholesalers, importers, and exporters. Formerly *Thomas Food Industry Register.*

BANK ACCOUNTING

HANDBOOKS AND MANUALS

Handbook of Bank Accounting: Understanding and Applying Standards and Regulations. Charles J. Woelfel. McGraw-Hill Professional. • 1992. $65.00. "Written to meet the practical needs of senior- and middle-level bank accountants.." Covers managerial accounting, the theory and practice of bank accounting, financial statement analysis, bank examinations, audits, and related topics.

INTERNET DATABASES

Rutgers Accounting Web (RAW). Rutgers University Accounting Research Center. Phone: (201)648-5172 Fax: (201)648-1233 • URL: http://www.rutgers.edu/accounting • RAW Web site provides extensive links to sources of national and international accounting information, such as the Big Six accounting firms, the Financial Accounting Standards Board (FASB), SEC filings (EDGAR), journals, publishers, software, the International Accounting Network, and "Internet's largest list of accounting firms in USA." Searching is offered. Fees: Free.

PERIODICALS AND NEWSLETTERS

Bank Accounting and Finance. Institutional Investor. • Quarterly. $250.00 per year. Emphasis is on the practical aspects of bank accounting and bank financial management.

Bank Auditing and Accounting Report. Warren, Gorham and Lamont/RIA Group. • Monthly. $199.00 per year. Newsletter covering bank regulations, accounting techniques, and audit controls.

Journal of Bank Cost and Management Accounting. Association for Management Information in Financial Services. • Three times a year. $100.00 per year.

TRADE/PROFESSIONAL ASSOCIATIONS

Association for Management Information in Financial Services. 7950 E. La Junta Rd., Scottsdale, AZ 85255-2798. Phone: (602)515-2160 Fax: (602)515-2101 E-mail: ami@amifs.org • URL: http://www.amifs.org • Members are financial institution employees interested in management accounting and cost analysis.

Bank Administration Institute. One N. Franklin St., Suite 1000, Chicago, IL 60606. Phone: 800-224-9889 or (312)653-2464 Fax: (312)683-2373 E-mail: info@bai.org • URL: http://www.bai.org • Provides educational and advisory services to bank managers. Includes Audit Commission and Accounting and Finance Commission.

BANK AUTOMATION

ABSTRACTS AND INDEXES

Business Periodicals Index. H. W. Wilson Co. • Monthly, except August, with quarterly and annual cumulations. Service basis for print edition; CD-ROM edition, $1,495.00 per year.

DIRECTORIES

Bank Systems and Technology-Directory and Buyer's Guide. Miller Freeman, Inc. • Annual. $25.00. List of more than 1,800 manufacturers, distributors, and other suppliers of equipment and materials to the banking industry.

HANDBOOKS AND MANUALS

Bank Systems Management: The Project Management Guide to Planning and Implementing Systems. Kent S. Belasco. McGraw-Hill Professional. • 1993. $62.50.

Bank Technology Review: A Bank Manager's Guide to New Technology Products, Systems, and Applications. Tom Groenfeldt. McGraw-Hill Professional. • 1995. $37.50.

ONLINE DATABASES

ABI/INFORM. Bell & Howell Information and Learning. • Provides online indexing to business-related material occurring in over 1,000 periodicals from 1971 to the present. Inquire as to online cost and availability.

Computer Database. The Gale Group. • Provides online citations with abstracts to material appearing in about 150 trade journals and newsletters in the subject areas of computers, telecommunications, and electronics. Time period is 1983 to date, with weekly updates. Inquire as to online cost and availability.

Management Contents. The Gale Group. • Covers a wide range of management, financial, marketing, personnel, and administrative topics. About 150 leading business journals are indexed and abstracted from 1974 to date, with monthly updating. Inquire as to online cost and availability.

Trade & Industry Index. The Gale Group. • Provides indexing of business periodicals, January 1981 to date. Daily updates. (Full text articles from some periodicals are available online, 1983 to date, in the companion database, *Trade & Industry ASAP.*) Inquire as to online cost and availability.

PERIODICALS AND NEWSLETTERS

Bank Automation News. • Biweekly. $595.00 per year. Newsletter.

Bank Letter: Newsletter of Commercial and Institutional Banking. Institutional Investor, Newsletters Div. • Weekly. $2,220.00 per year. Newsletter. Covers retail banking, commercial lending, foreign loans, bank technology, government regulations, and other topics related to banking.

Bank Network News; News and Analysis of Shared EFT Networks. Faulkner & Gray, Inc. • Semimonthly. $395.00 per year. Newsletter.

Bank Systems and Technology: For Senior-Level Executives in Operations and Technology. Miller Freeman, Inc. • 13 times a year. $65.00 per year. Focuses on strategic planning for banking executives. Formerly *Bank Systems and Equipment.*

Bank Technology News: Banking's Information Source for Systems Purchasing. Faulkner & Gray, Inc. • Monthly. $48.00 per year.

Card Technology. Faulkner & Gray, Inc. • Monthly. $79.00 per year. Covers advanced technology for credit, debit, and other cards. Topics include smart cards, optical recognition, and card design.

Corporate EFT Report (Electronic Funds Tranfer). Phillips Business Information, Inc. • Biweekly. $595.00 per year. Newsletter on subject of electronic funds transfer.

EFT Report (Electronic Funds Transfer). Phillips Business Information, Inc. • Biweekly. $695.00 per year. Newsletter on subject of electronic funds transfer.

Financial Service Online. Faulkner & Gray, Inc. • Monthly. $95.00 per year. Covers the operation and management of interactive financial services to consumers in their homes for banking, investments, and bill-paying.

Future Banker: The Vision of Leadership in an Electronic Age. American Banker. • Monthly. $79.00 per year. Covers technology innovation for the banking industry, including online banking.

Item Processing Report. Phillips Business Information, Inc. • Biweekly. $695.00 per year. Newsletter for banks on check processing, document imaging, and optical character recognition.

WebFinance. Securities Data Publishing. • Semimonthly. $995.00 per year. Newsletter (also available online at www.webfinance.net). Covers the Internet-based provision of online financial services by banks, online brokers, mutual funds, and insurance companies. Provides news stories, analysis, and descriptions of useful resources. (Securities Data Publishing is a unit of Thomson Financial.).

STATISTICS SOURCES

Statistical Information on the Financial Services Industry. American Bankers Association. • Annual. Members, $150.00; non-members, $275.00. Presents a wide variety of data relating to banking and financial services, including consumer economics, personal finance, credit, government loans, capital markets, and international banking.

TRADE/PROFESSIONAL ASSOCIATIONS

Association for Financial Technology. Blendonview Office Park, 5008-2 Pine Creek Dr., Westerville, OH 43081-4899. Phone: (614)895-1208 Fax: (614)895-3466 E-mail: aft@fitech.org • URL: http://www.fitech.org • Concerned with bank computer technology.

Bank Administration Institute; Operations and Technology Commission. One N. Franklin St., Suite 1000, Chicago, IL 60606. Phone: 800-224-9889 or (312)653-2464 Fax: (312)683-2373 E-mail: info@bai.org • URL: http://www.bai.org.

Electronic Funds Transfer Association. 950 Herndon Parkway, Suite 390, Herndon, VA 22170. Phone: (703)435-9800 Fax: (703)435-7157 E-mail: efta@aol.com • URL: http://www.efta.org.

NACHA: The Electronic Payments Association. 13665 Dulles Technology Dr., Ste. 300, Herndon, VA 20171. Phone: 800-487-9180 or (703)561-1100 Fax: (703)787-0996 • URL: http://www.nacha.org.

National Independent Bank Equipment and Systems Association. 1411 Peterson, Suite 101, Park Ridge, IL 60068. Phone: 800-843-6082 or (847)825-8419 Fax: (847)825-8445 E-mail: nibesa@nibesa.com • URL: http://www.nibesa.com.

OTHER SOURCES

Endpoint Express. United Communications Group (UCG). • Biweekly. $355.00 per year. Newsletter. Covers bank payment systems, including checks, electronic funds transfer (EFT), point-of-sale (POS), and automated teller machine (ATM) operations. Formerly *Bank Office Bulletin.*

Online Banking. MarketResearch.com. • 2000. $3,450.00. Market research report. Includes demographics relating to the users and nonusers of online banking services. Provides market forecasts.

The U. S. Market for Plastic Payment Cards. Available from MarketResearch.com. • 1998. $2,500.00. Market research report published by Packaged Facts. Covers credit cards, charge cards, debit cards, and smart cards. Provides profiles of Visa, Mastercard, American Express, Discover, Diners Club, and others.

BANK CREDIT

See: BANK LOANS

BANK DEPOSITS

See also: BANKS AND BANKING; ELECTRONIC FUNDS TRANSFER SYSTEMS (EFTS)

GENERAL WORKS

Consumer Reports Money Book: How to Get It, Save It, and Spend It Wisely. Janet Bamford and others. Consumers Union of the United States, Inc. • 1997. $29.95. Revised edition. Covers budgeting, retirement planning, bank accounts, insurance, and other personal finance topics.

ABSTRACTS AND INDEXES

Accounting and Tax Index. UMI. • Quarterly. Price on application. Includes annual cumulative bound volume. Indexes accounting, auditing, and taxation literature appearing in journals, books, pamphlets, conference proceedings, and newsletters. (UMI is University Microfilms International, a Bell & Howell Co.).

HANDBOOKS AND MANUALS

Deposit Account Operations. Institute of Financial Education. • 1997. $49.95.

Deposit Accounts Regulation Manual. Kenneth F. Hall. West Group. • 1993. $135.00. Provides yearly coverage of federal laws and regulations governing bank deposit accounts, including Truth-in-Savings, Federal Deposit Insurance, Electronic Funds Transfers, fee disclosure, privacy issues, and reserve requirements. (Commercial Law Series).

Deposit Operations. David H. Friedman. American Bankers Association. • 1992. Price on application.

Insurance of Accounts Handbook: A Practical Guide to the FDIC Regulations. Institute of Financial Education. • 1993. $25.00. Second edition. A guide for bankers to the regulations of the Federal Deposit Insurance Corporation.

ONLINE DATABASES

American Statistics Index: A Comprehensive Guide and Index to the Statistical Publications of the United States Government [Online]. Congressional Information Service, Inc. • Indexes and abstracts, 1973 to date. Inquire as to online cost and availability.

EconLit. American Economic Association. • Covers the worldwide literature of economics as contained in selected monographs and about 550 journals. Subjects include microeconomics, macroeconomics, economic history, inflation, money, credit, finance, accounting theory, trade, natural resource economics, and regional economics. Time period is 1969 to present, with monthly updates. Inquire as to online cost and availability.

PERIODICALS AND NEWSLETTERS

Jumbo Rate News. Bauer Financial Newsletters, Inc. • Weekly. $445.00 per year. Newsletter. Lists more than 1,100 of the highest interest rates available for "jumbo" certificates of deposit ($100,000 or more).

STATISTICS SOURCES

Aggregate Reserves of Depository Institutions and the Monetary Base. U.S. Federal Reserve System. • Weekly.

Assets and Liabilities of Commercial Banks in the United States. U. S. Federal Reserve System. • Weekly. $30.00 per year. (Federal Reserve Statistical Release, H.8.).

Debits and Deposit Turnover at Commercial Banks. Board of Governors. • Monthly. $5.00 per year.

Economic Indicators. Council of Economic Advisors, Executive Office of the President. Available from U.S. Government Printing Office. • Monthly. $55.00 per year.

Federal Reserve Bulletin. U.S. Federal Reserve System. • Monthly. $25.00 per year. Provides statistics on banking and the economy, including interest rates, money supply, and the Federal Reserve Board indexes of industrial production.

Statistical Information on the Financial Services Industry. American Bankers Association. • Annual. Members, $150.00; non-members, $275.00. Presents a wide variety of data relating to banking and financial services, including consumer economics, personal finance, credit, government loans, capital markets, and international banking.

BANK FAILURES

GENERAL WORKS

Does Financial Deregulation Work? A Critique of Free Market Approaches. Bruce Coggins. Edward Elgar Publishing, Inc. • 1998. $85.00. Provides a critique of bank deregulation in the United States. Includes suggestions for more effective financial regulation. (New Directions in Modern Economics Series).

Financial Institutions and Markets. Robert W. Kolb and Ricardo J. Rodriguez. Blackwell Publishers. • 1996. $77.95. Contains 40 articles (chapters) by various authors on U. S. financial markets and other topics. Includes separate chapters on the International Monetary Fund, inflation, monetary policy, the national debt, bank failures, derivatives, stock prices, initial public offerings, government bonds, pensions, foreign exchange, international markets, and other subjects.

The Greatest Ever Bank Robbery: The Collapse of the Savings and Loan Industry. Martin Mayer. Pearson Education and Technology. • 1992. $12.95. Reprint edition.

Preventing Bank Crises: Lessons from Recent Global Bank Failures. Gerard Caprio and others, editors. The World Bank, Office of the Publisher. • 1998. $40.00. Examines worldwide problems with bank regulation, bank infrastructure, public accountability, and political influence.

Transnational Bank Behavior and the International Debt Crisis. United Nations Publications. • 1990.

ABSTRACTS AND INDEXES

Banking Information Index. U M I Banking Information Index. • Monthly. Price on application. Covers a wide variety of banking, business, and financial subjects in periodicals. Formerly *Banking Literature Index.*

Business Periodicals Index. H. W. Wilson Co. • Monthly, except August, with quarterly and annual cumulations. Service basis for print edition; CD-ROM edition, $1,495.00 per year.

BIBLIOGRAPHIES

The Savings and Loan Crisis: An Annotated Bibliography. Pat L. Talley, compiler. Greenwood Publishing Group, Inc. • 1993. $65.00. Includes 360 scholarly and popular titles (books and research papers). (Bibliographies and Indexes in Economic History, No. 14).

CD-ROM DATABASES

ABI/INFORM Global. Bell & Howell Information and Learning. • Monthly. $6,500.00 per year. Provides CD-ROM indexing and abstracting of worldwide business literature appearing in over 1,200 periodicals for the most recent five years. Archival discs are available from 1971. Formerly *ABI/INFORM OnDisc.*

PAIS on CD-ROM. Public Affairs Information Service, Inc. • Quarterly. $1,995.00 per year. Provides a CD-ROM version of the online service, *PAIS International.* Contains over 400,000 citations to the literature of contemporary social, political, and economic issues.

WILSONDISC: Business Periodicals Index. H. W. Wilson Co. • Monthly. $1,495.00 per year. Provides CD-ROM indexing of business periodicals from 1982 to date. Price includes online service.

DIRECTORIES

Banksearch. Thomas Financial Media. • Quarterly. $275.00 per year. Rates banks as to loan exposure, capital adequacy, asset quality, liquidity, and other factors. Arranged geographically. Formerly *Sheshunoff Bank Quarterly Ratings and Analysis.*

HANDBOOKS AND MANUALS

Analyzing Banking Risk: A Framework for Assessing Corporate Governance and Financial Risk Management. Hennie van Greuning and Sonja Brajovic Bratanovic. The World Bank, Office of the Publisher. • 1999. $100.00. Provides a guide to the analysis of banking risk for bank executives, bank supervisors, and risk analysts. Includes a CD-ROM with spreadsheet-based tables to assist in the interpretation and analysis of a bank's financial risk.

ONLINE DATABASES

ABI/INFORM. Bell & Howell Information and Learning. • Provides online indexing to business-related material occurring in over 1,000 periodicals from 1971 to the present. Inquire as to online cost and availability.

American Banker Full Text. American Banker-Bond Buyer, Database Services. • Provides complete text online of the daily *American Banker.* Inquire as to online cost and availability.

Banking Information Source. Bell & Howell Information and Learning. • Provides indexing and abstracting of periodical and other literature from 1982 to date, with weekly updates. Covers the financial services industry: banks, savings institutions, investment houses, credit unions, insurance companies, and real estate organizations. Emphasis is on marketing and management. Inquire as to online cost and availability. (Formerly *FINIS: Financial Industry Information Service.*).

F & S Index. The Gale Group. • Contains about four million citations to worldwide business, financial, and industrial or consumer product literature appearing from 1972 to date. Weekly updates. Inquire as to online cost and availability.

LEXIS Banking Library. LEXIS-NEXIS. • Provides legal decisions and regulatory material relating to the banking industry, as well as full text of banking journals. Time period varies. Inquire as to online cost and availability.

PAIS International. Public Affairs Information Service, Inc. • Corresponds to the former printed publications, *PAIS Bulletin* (1976-90) and *PAIS Foreign Language Index* (1972-90), and to the current *PAIS International in Print* (1991 to date). Covers economic, political, and sociological material appearing in periodicals, books, government documents, and other publications. Updating is monthly. Inquire as to online cost and availability.

Trade & Industry Index. The Gale Group. • Provides indexing of business periodicals, January 1981 to date. Daily updates. (Full text articles from some periodicals are available online, 1983 to date, in the companion database, *Trade & Industry ASAP.*) Inquire as to online cost and availability.

Wilson Business Abstracts Online. H. W. Wilson Co. • Indexes and abstracts 600 major business periodicals, plus the *Wall Street Journal* and the business section of the *New York Times.* Indexing is from 1982, abstracting from 1990, with the two newspapers included from 1993. Updated weekly. Inquire as to online cost and availability. (*Business Periodicals Index* without abstracts is also available online.).

PERIODICALS AND NEWSLETTERS

Bank Mergers & Acquisitions: The Authoritative Newsletter Providing In-Depth Analysis of the Restructuring of American Banking. SNL Securities. • Monthly. $795.00 per year. Newsletter. Includes information on transactions assisted by the Federal Deposit Insurance Corporation (FDIC) for commercial banks or by the Resolution Trust Corporation (RTC) for savings and loan institutions.

Troubled and Problematic Bank and Thrift Report. Bauer Communications, Inc. • Quarterly. $225.00 per year. Newsletter provides information on seriously undercapitalized ("Troubled") banks and savings institutions, as defined by a federal Prompt Corrective Action Rule. "Problematic" banks and thrifts are those meeting regulatory capital levels, but showing negative trends.

RESEARCH CENTERS AND INSTITUTES

Banking Research Center. Northwestern University, 401 Anderson Hall, 2001 Sheridan Rd., Evanston, IL 60208. Phone: (847)491-3562 Fax: (847)491-5719 E-mail: m-fishman@nwu.edu • Does research in the management and public regulation of financial institutions. A unit of the J. L. Kellogg Graduate School of Management.

Catalyst Institute. 33 N. LaSalle St., Suite 1900, Chicago, IL 60602-2604. Phone: (312)541-5400 Fax: (312)541-5401 E-mail: postmaster@catalystinstitute.org • URL: http://www.dstcatalyst.com • Investigates the financial services industry, including bank failures and the domino effect, the liability crisis, and regulations designed to prevent bank failures.

Financial Institutions Center. University of Florida, College of Business Administration, 327 Business Bldg., Gainesville, FL 32611. Phone: (352)392-2610 • Studies monetary policy and the regulation of financial institutions.

Morin Center for Banking and Financial Law. Boston University, School of Law, 765 Commonwealth Ave., Boston, MA 02215. Phone: (617)353-3023 Fax: (617)353-2444 E-mail: banklaw@bu.edu • URL: http://www.web.bu.edu/law • Research fields include banking law, regulation of depository institutions, and deposit insurance.

Salomon Center. New York University. Stern School of Business, 44 W. Fourth St., New York, NY 10012-1126. Phone: (212)998-0707 Fax: (212)995-4220 E-mail: iwalter@stern.nyu.edu • URL: http://www.stern.nyu.edu/salmon/.

TRADE/PROFESSIONAL ASSOCIATIONS

American Council of State Savings Supervisors. P.O. Box 34175, Washington, DC 20043-4175. Phone: (202)922-5153 Fax: (202)922-6237 • Members are state savings and loan supervisors. Includes a Joint Committee on Examinations and Education.

Conference of State Bank Supervisors. 1015 18th St., N. W., Suite 1100, Washington, DC 20036-5275. Phone: 800-886-2727 or (202)296-2840 Fax: (202)296-1928 E-mail: nmilner@csbsdc.org • URL: http://www.csbsdc.org/index.html • Members are state officials responsible for supervision of state-chartered banking institutions.

OTHER SOURCES

Bank and Lender Litigation Reporter: The Nationwide Litigation Report of Failed National and State Banks and Savings and Loan Associations, including FDIC and FSLIC Complaints and Related Actions Among Shareholders, Officers, Directors, Ins. Andrews Publications. • Semimonthly. $875.00 per year. Provides summaries of significant litigation and regulatory agency complaints. Formerly *Lender Liability Litigation Reporter.*

Bank and Thrift Case Digest. West Group. • Three looseleaf volumes. Periodic supplementation. Provides court decisions involving claims against failed banks and savings institutions or on behalf of insured banks and savings institutions.

BANK FINANCE

See: BANK LOANS

BANK LAW

See: BANKING LAW AND REGULATION

BANK LOANS

See also: COMMERCIAL LENDING; CONSUMER CREDIT; CREDIT

GENERAL WORKS

The New Face of Credit Risk Management: Balancing Growth and Credit Quality in an Integrated Risk Management Environment. Charles B. Wendel. Robert Morris Associates. • 1999. $65.00. Contains "In-depth interviews with senior credit officers from five major financial institutions." Coverage includes modeling, scoring, and other technology related to the management of credit risk.

Spilled Milk: A Special Collection from The Journal of Commercial Bank Lending on Loans that Went Sour. Robert Morris Associates. • 1985. $33.50. Two volumes.

ABSTRACTS AND INDEXES

Business Periodicals Index. H. W. Wilson Co. • Monthly, except August, with quarterly and annual cumulations. Service basis for print edition; CD-ROM edition, $1,495.00 per year.

DIRECTORIES

Business Capital Sources. Tyler G. Hicks. International Wealth Success, Inc. • 2000. $15.00. 11th edition. Lists about 1,500 banks, insurance and mortgage companies, commerical finance, leasing and venture capital firms that lend money for business investment.

Corporate Finance Sourcebook: The Guide to Major Capital Investment Source and Related Financial Services. R. R. Bowker. • Annual. $625.00. Lists more than 3,550 sources of corporate capital: investment bankers, securities firms, pension management companies, trust companies, insurance companies, and private lenders. Includes the names of over 13,000 key personnel.

ENCYCLOPEDIAS AND DICTIONARIES

Credit and Lending Dictionary. Daphne Smith and Shelley W. Geehr, editors. Robert Morris Associates. • 1994. $25.00.

FINANCIAL RATIOS

Money of the Mind: Borrowing and Lending in America from the Civil War to Michael Milken. James Grant. Farrar, Straus, and Giroux, LLC. • 1992. $16.00. A critical anlysis by the editor of *Grant's Interest Rate Observer.*

HANDBOOKS AND MANUALS

Preparing Loan Proposals. John C. Wisdom. John Wiley and Sons, Inc. • 1997. $150.00. Second editon. 1998 Supplement, $55.00.

Problem Loan Strategies; A Decision Process for Commercial Bankers. John E. McKinley and others. Robert Morris Associates. • 1998. $53.00. Revised edition.

SBA Loan Guide. Entrepreneur Meida, Inc. • Looseleaf. $59.50. A practical guide to obtaining loans through the Small Business Administration. (Start-Up Business Guide No. E1315.).

Structuring Commercial Loan Agreements. Rodger Tighe. Warren, Gorham & Lamont/RIA Group. • Looseleaf. $115.00. Biennial supplementation. An aid to structuring commercial loan agreements.

Truth in Lending Manual. Warren, Gorham & Lamont/RIA Group. • 1991. $175.00. Semiannual updates.

Where to Go When the Bank Says No: Alternatives to Financing Your Business. David R. Evanson. Bloomberg Press. • 1998. $24.95. Emphasis is on obtaining business financing in the $250,000 to $15,000,000 range. Business plans are discussed. (Bloomberg Small Business Series).

INTERNET DATABASES

BanxQuote Banking, Mortgage, and Finance Center. BanxQuote, Inc. Phone: 800-765-3000 or (212)643-8000 Fax: (212)643-0020 E-mail: info@banx.com • URL: http://www.banx.com • Web site quotes interest rates paid by banks around the country on various savings products, as well as rates paid by consumers for automobile loans, mortgages, credit cards, home equity loans, and personal loans. Also provided: stock quotes, indexes, stock options, futures trading data, economic indicators, and links to many other financial sites. Daily updates. Fees: Free.

Fedstats. Federal Interagency Council on Statistical Policy. Phone: (202)395-7254 • URL: http://www.fedstats.gov • Web site features an efficient search facility for full-text statistics produced by more than 70 federal agencies, including the Census Bureau, the Bureau of Economic Analysis, and the Bureau of Labor Statistics. Boolean searches can be made within one agency or for all agencies combined. Links are offered to international statistical bureaus, including the UN, IMF, OECD, UNESCO, Eurostat, and 20 individual countries. Fees: Free.

ONLINE DATABASES

ABI/INFORM. Bell & Howell Information and Learning. • Provides online indexing to business-related material occurring in over 1,000 periodicals from 1971 to the present. Inquire as to online cost and availability.

DRI U.S. Central Database. Data Products Division. • Provides more than 23,000 business, financial, demographic, economic, foreign trade, and industry-related time series for the U.S. Includes national income, population, retail-wholesale trade, price indexes, labor data, housing, industrial production, banking, interest rates, money supply, etc. Time period is generally 1947 to date (some data back to 1929). Updating varies. Inquire as to online cost and availability.

Management Contents. The Gale Group. • Covers a wide range of management, financial, marketing, personnel, and administrative topics. About 150 leading business journals are indexed and abstracted from 1974 to date, with monthly updating. Inquire as to online cost and availability.

Trade & Industry Index. The Gale Group. • Provides indexing of business periodicals, January 1981 to date. Daily updates. (Full text articles from some periodicals are available online, 1983 to date, in the companion database, *Trade & Industry ASAP.*) Inquire as to online cost and availability.

PERIODICALS AND NEWSLETTERS

Bank Credit Analyst. BCA Publications Ltd. • Monthly. $695.00 per year. "The independent monthly forecast and analysis of trends in business conditions and major investment markets based on a continuous appraisal of money and credit flows." Includes many charts and graphs relating to money, credit, and securities in the U. S.

Bank Loan Report. Securities Data Publishing. • Weekly. $3,600.00 per year. Newsletter. Covers the syndicated loan marketplace for corporate finance professionals. (Securities Data Publishing is a unit of Thomson Financial.).

Commercial Lending Litigation News. LRP Publications. • Biweekly. $597.00 per year. Newsletter on court decisions, settlements, significant new cases, legislation, regulation, and industry trends. Formerly *Lender Liability News.*

Consumer Credit and Truth-in-Lending Compliance Report. Warren, Gorham and Lamont/RIA Group. • Monthly. $183.75 per year. Newsletter. Focuses on the latest regulatory rulings and findings involving consumer lending and credit activity. Formerly *Bank Installment Lending Newsletter.*

Consumer Finance Newsletter. Financial Publishing Co. • Monthly. $24.50 per year. Covers changes in state and federal consumer lending regulations.

Grant's Interest Rate Observer. James Grant, editor. Interest Rate Publishing Corp. • Biweekly. $495.00 per year. Newsletter containing detailed analysis of money-related topics, including interest rate trends, global credit markets, fixed-income investments, bank loan policies, and international money markets.

International Bank Credit Analyst. BCA Publications Ltd. • Monthly. $795.00 per year. "A monthly forecast and analysis of currency movements, interest rates, and stock market developments in the principal countries, based on a continuous appraisal of money and credit trends worldwide." Includes many charts and graphs providing international coverage of money, credit, and securities.

Journal of Lending and Credit Risk Management. Robert Morris Associates. • 10 times a year. Members, $35.00 per year; non-members, $85.00 per year. Formerly *Journal of Commercial Bank Lending.*

Lender Liability Law Report. Warren, Gorham & Lamont/RIA Group. • Monthly. $183.00 per year. Newsletter on cases and legislation affecting lenders.

RESEARCH CENTERS AND INSTITUTES

Credit Research Center. Georgetown University. 3240 Prospect St., N.W., Suite 300, Washington, DC 20007. Phone: (202)625-0103 Fax: (202)625-0104 E-mail: msb-crc@msb.edu • URL: http://www.msb.edu/prog/crc.

STATISTICS SOURCES

Business Statistics of the United States. Courtenay M. Slater, editor. Bernan Associates. • 1999. $74.00. Fifth edition. Based on *Business Statistics*, formerly issue by the Bureau of Economic Analysis, U. S. Department of Commerce. Provides basic data for a wide variety of U. S. industries, services, and economic indicators. Most statistics are shown annually for 29 years and monthly for the most recent four years.

Global Development Finance: External Public Debt of Developing Countries. World Bank, The Office of the Publisher. • Irregular. Prices vary. Includes supplements. Contains detailed data from the International Bank for Reconstruction and Development (World Bank) on the external debt load of over 100 developing countries.

Statistical Information on the Financial Services Industry. American Bankers Association. • Annual. Members, $150.00; non-members, $275.00. Presents a wide variety of data relating to banking and financial services, including consumer economics, personal finance, credit, government loans, capital markets, and international banking.

Survey of Current Business. Available from U. S. Government Printing Office. • Monthly. $49.00 per year. Issued by Bureau of Economic Analysis, U. S. Department of Commerce. Presents a wide variety of business and economic data.

TRADE/PROFESSIONAL ASSOCIATIONS

Credit Research Foundation. 8815 Center Park Dr., Columbia, MD 21045. Phone: (410)740-5499 Fax: (410)740-4620.

National Association of Credit Management. 8840 Columbia, 100 Parkway, Columbia, MD 21045-2158. Phone: 800-955-8815 or (410)740-5560 Fax: (410)740-5574 E-mail: nacminfo@nacm.org • URL: http://www.nacm.org.

Robert Morris Associates- Association of Lending and Credit Risk Professionals. One Liberty Place, 1650 Market St., Suite 2300, Philadelphia, PA 19103-7398. Phone: (215)446-4000 Fax: (215)446-4101 • URL: http://www.rmahq.org.

OTHER SOURCES

Bank and Lender Litigation Reporter: The Nationwide Litigation Report of Failed National and State Banks and Savings and Loan Associations, including FDIC and FSLIC Complaints and Related Actions Among Shareholders, Officers, Directors, Ins. Andrews Publications. • Semimonthly. $875.00 per year. Provides summaries of significant litigation and regulatory agency complaints. Formerly *Lender Liability Litigation Reporter.*

Consumer and Commercial Credit: Installment Sales. Prentice Hall. • Three looseleaf volumes. Periodic supplementation. Price on application. Covers secured transactions under the Uniform Commercial Code and the Uniform Consumer Credit Code. Includes retail installment sales, home improvement loans, higher education loans, and other kinds of installment loans.

Country Finance. Economist Intelligence Unit. • Semiannual (quarterly for "fast-changing countries"). $395.00 per year for each country. Discusses banking and financial conditions in each of 47 countries. Includes foreign exchange regulations, the currency outlook, sources of capital, financing techniques, and tax considerations. Formerly Financing Foreign Operations.

BANK MANAGEMENT

See also: BANKS AND BANKING

GENERAL WORKS

Bank Management: Text and Cases. George H. Hempel and Donald G. Simonson. John Wiley and Sons, Inc. • 1998. $106.95. Fifth edition.

Reengineering the Bank: A Blueprint for Survival and Success. Paul H. Allen. McGraw-Hill Professional. • 1994. $40.00.

ABSTRACTS AND INDEXES

Banking Information Index. U M I Banking Information Index. • Monthly. Price on application. Covers a wide variety of banking, business, and financial subjects in periodicals. Formerly *Banking Literature Index.*

Business Periodicals Index. H. W. Wilson Co. • Monthly, except August, with quarterly and annual cumulations. Service basis for print edition; CD-ROM edition, $1,495.00 per year.

BIBLIOGRAPHIES

Financial Institutions. Available from U. S. Government Printing Office. • Annual. Free. Lists government publications. Formerly *Banks and Banking.* GPO Subject Bibliography No. 128.

BIOGRAPHICAL SOURCES

Who's Who in Finance and Industry. Marquis Who's Who. • Biennial. $295.00. Provides over 22,400 concise biographies of business leaders in all fields.

Who's Who in International Banking. Bowker-Saur. • Irregular. $400.00. Contains biographical sketches of about 4,000 bankers. Worldwide coverage.

DIRECTORIES

Business and Finance Career Directory. Visible Ink Press. • 1992. $17.95.

Planning Resource Directory. American Bankers Association. • Annual. $45.00. Describes consulting firms and other organizations that assist banks in strategic planning.

HANDBOOKS AND MANUALS

Bank Investments and Funds Management. Gerald O. Hatler. American Bankers Association. • 1991. $49.00. Second edition. Focuses on portfolio management, risk analysis, and investment strategy.

Bank Systems Management: The Project Management Guide to Planning and Implementing Systems. Kent S. Belasco. McGraw-Hill Professional. • 1993. $62.50.

Banking Crimes: Fraud, Money Laundering, Embezzlement. John K. Villa. West Group. • Annual. $125.00. Covers fraud and embezzlement. Looseleaf.

Commercial Bank Management: Producing and Selling Financial Services. Peter S. Rose. McGraw-Hill. • 1998. $88.44. Fourth edition.

Handbook of Bank Accounting: Understanding and Applying Standards and Regulations. Charles J. Woelfel. McGraw-Hill Professional. • 1992. $65.00. "Written to meet the practical needs of senior- and middle-level bank accountants.." Covers managerial accounting, the theory and practice of bank accounting, financial statement analysis, bank examinations, audits, and related topics.

Strategic Management for Bankers. Richard W. Sapp and Roger W. Smith. Strategic Leadership Forum. • 1984. $23.00.

Trust Department Administration and Operations. Matthew Bender & Co., Inc. • $305.00. Two looseleaf volumes. Periodic supplementation. A procedural manual, training guide and idea source.

ONLINE DATABASES

ABI/INFORM. Bell & Howell Information and Learning. • Provides online indexing to business-related material occurring in over 1,000 periodicals from 1971 to the present. Inquire as to online cost and availability.

American Banker Full Text. American Banker-Bond Buyer, Database Services. • Provides complete text online of the daily *American Banker.* Inquire as to online cost and availability.

Banking Information Source. Bell & Howell Information and Learning. • Provides indexing and abstracting of periodical and other literature from 1982 to date, with weekly updates. Covers the financial services industry: banks, savings institutions, investment houses, credit unions, insurance companies, and real estate organizations. Emphasis is on marketing and management. Inquire as to online cost and availability. (Formerly *FINIS: Financial Industry Information Service.*).

Management Contents. The Gale Group. • Covers a wide range of management, financial, marketing, personnel, and administrative topics. About 150 leading business journals are indexed and abstracted from 1974 to date, with monthly updating. Inquire as to online cost and availability.

Trade & Industry Index. The Gale Group. • Provides indexing of business periodicals, January 1981 to date. Daily updates. (Full text articles from some periodicals are available online, 1983 to date, in the companion database, *Trade & Industry ASAP.*) Inquire as to online cost and availability.

PERIODICALS AND NEWSLETTERS

ABA Banking Journal. American Bankers Association, Member Communications. Simmons-Boardman Publishing Corp. • Monthly. Free to qualified personnel; others, $25.00 per year.

American Banker. Thomson Financial Media. • Daily. $825.00 per year. Includes*Future Banker.*

Bank Asset/Liability Management. Warren, Gorham & Lamont/RIA Group. • Monthly. $193.75 per year. Newsletter. For bankers concerned with balancing an asset and liability portfolio.

Bank Strategies. Bank Administration Institute. • Monthly. $59.00 per year. Formerly *Bank Management.*

Bank Systems and Technology: For Senior-Level Executives in Operations and Technology. Miller Freeman, Inc. • 13 times a year. $65.00 per year. Focuses on strategic planning for banking executives. Formerly *Bank Systems and Equipment.*

The Community Bank President. Siefer Consultants, Inc. • Monthly. $329.00 per year.

Fee Income Growth Strategies. Siefer Consultants, Inc. • Monthly. $329.00 per year. Newsletter. Covers operations management for banks and other financial institutions. Formerly *Noninterest Income Growth Strategies.*

Future Banker: The Vision of Leadership in an Electronic Age. American Banker. • Monthly. $79.00 per year. Covers technology innovation for the banking industry, including online banking.

Journal of Banking and Financial Services. Warren, Gorham and Lamont, Inc. • Bimonthly. $115.00. per year. Enables bankers to obtain a more generalized view of the industry. Contains articles for bankers, by bankers and top consultants in the field. Formerly*Bankers' Magazine.*

Operations Alert. America's Community Bankers. • Biweekly. Free to members; non-members, $200.00 per year. Newsletter reporting on regulatory and new product developments that affect community banking operations.

RESEARCH CENTERS AND INSTITUTES

Banking Research Center. Northwestern University, 401 Anderson Hall, 2001 Sheridan Rd., Evanston, IL 60208. Phone: (847)491-3562 Fax: (847)491-5719 E-mail: m-fishman@nwu.edu • Does research in the management and public regulation of financial institutions. A unit of the J. L. Kellogg Graduate School of Management.

STATISTICS SOURCES

Bank Operating Statistics. Federal Deposit Insurance Corp. • Annual. Price on application. Based on Reports of Condition and Reports of Income.

TRADE/PROFESSIONAL ASSOCIATIONS

American Bankers Association. 1120 Connecticut Ave., N.W., Washington, DC 20036. Phone: 800-226-5377 or (202)663-5000 Fax: (202)663-7543 • URL: http://www.aba.com.

Bank Administration Institute. One N. Franklin St., Suite 1000, Chicago, IL 60606. Phone: 800-224-9889 or (312)653-2464 Fax: (312)683-2373 E-mail: info@bai.org • URL: http://www.bai.org • Provides educational and advisory services to bank managers. Includes Audit Commission and Accounting and Finance Commission.

Financial Women International. 200 N. Glebe Rd., Ste. 820, Arlington, VA 22203-3728. Phone: (703)807-2007 Fax: (703)807-0111 E-mail: info@fwi.org • URL: http://www.fwi.org.

Independent Community Bankers of America. One Thomas Circle, N.W., Suite 400, Washington, DC 20005. Phone: 800-422-8439 or (202)659-8111 Fax: (202)659-9216 E-mail: info@icba.org • URL: http://www.icba.org.

National Bankers Association. 1513 P St., N.W., Washington, DC 20005. Phone: (202)588-5432 Fax: (202)588-5443 • Minority bankers.

OTHER SOURCES

Control of Banking. Prentice Hall. • Two looseleaf volumes. $465.00 per year. Periodic supplementation. Banking rules and regulations affecting day-to-day operations and financial practices of banks.

BANK MARKETING

GENERAL WORKS

Bank Marketing for the 90's: New Ideas from 55 of the Best Marketers in Banking. Don Wright. John Wiley and Sons, Inc. • 1991. $99.95.

Bankers in the Selling Role: A Consultative Guide to Cross Selling Financial Services. Linda Richardson. John Wiley and Sons, Inc. • 1992. $22.50. Second edition.

ABSTRACTS AND INDEXES

Banking Information Index. U M I Banking Information Index. • Monthly. Price on application. Covers a wide variety of banking, business, and financial subjects in periodicals. Formerly *Banking Literature Index*.

Business Periodicals Index. H. W. Wilson Co. • Monthly, except August, with quarterly and annual cumulations. Service basis for print edition; CD-ROM edition, $1,495.00 per year.

DIRECTORIES

Bank Marketing Annual Buyer's Guide. Bank Marketing Association. • Annual. $20.00.

ONLINE DATABASES

ABI/INFORM. Bell & Howell Information and Learning. • Provides online indexing to business-related material occurring in over 1,000 periodicals from 1971 to the present. Inquire as to online cost and availability.

Banking Information Source. Bell & Howell Information and Learning. • Provides indexing and abstracting of periodical and other literature from 1982 to date, with weekly updates. Covers the financial services industry: banks, savings institutions, investment houses, credit unions, insurance companies, and real estate organizations. Emphasis is on marketing and management. Inquire as to online cost and availability. (Formerly *FINIS: Financial Industry Information Service*.).

Management Contents. The Gale Group. • Covers a wide range of management, financial, marketing, personnel, and administrative topics. About 150 leading business journals are indexed and abstracted from 1974 to date, with monthly updating. Inquire as to online cost and availability.

Trade & Industry Index. The Gale Group. • Provides indexing of business periodicals, January 1981 to date. Daily updates. (Full text articles from some periodicals are available online, 1983 to date, in the companion database, *Trade & Industry ASAP*.) Inquire as to online cost and availability.

PERIODICALS AND NEWSLETTERS

Bank Investment Product News. Institutional Investor, Newsletters Div. • Weekly. $1,195.00 per year. Newsletter. Edited for bank executives. Covers the marketing and regulation of financial products sold through banks, such as mutual funds, stock brokerage services, and insurance.

Bank Marketing. Bank Marketing Association. • Monthly. Members, $80.00 per year; non-members, $120.00 per year. Includes a Buyer's Guide.

Financial Services Marketing: Finding, Keeping, and Profiting From the Right Customers. American Banker. • Bimonthly. Price on application. Covers marketing for a variety of financial institutions, including banks, investment companies, securities dealers, and credit unions.

International Journal of Bank Marketing. MCB University Press Ltd. • Seven times a year. $10,899.00 per year.

TRADE/PROFESSIONAL ASSOCIATIONS

American Bankers Association. 1120 Connecticut Ave., N.W., Washington, DC 20036. Phone: 800-226-5377 or (202)663-5000 Fax: (202)663-7543 • URL: http://www.aba.com.

Bank Marketing Association. 1120 Connecticut Ave., N.W., Washington, DC 20036. Phone: 800-433-9013 or (202)663-5268 Fax: (202)828-4540 • URL: http://www.bmanet.org.

OTHER SOURCES

Home Banking Report. Jupiter Media Metrix. • Annual. $695.00. Market research report. Covers banking from home by phone or online, with projections of growth in future years.

BANK RESERVES

See also: BANKS AND BANKING

HANDBOOKS AND MANUALS

Deposit Accounts Regulation Manual. Kenneth F. Hall. West Group. • 1993. $135.00. Provides yearly coverage of federal laws and regulations governing bank deposit accounts, including Truth-in-Savings, Federal Deposit Insurance, Electronic Funds Transfers, fee disclosure, privacy issues, and reserve requirements. (Commercial Law Series).

ONLINE DATABASES

American Statistics Index: A Comprehensive Guide and Index to the Statistical Publications of the United States Government [Online]. Congressional Information Service, Inc. • Indexes and abstracts, 1973 to date. Inquire as to online cost and availability.

DRI Financial and Credit Statistics. Data Products Division. • Contains U. S. and international statistical data relating to money markets, interest rates, foreign exchange, banking, and stock and bond indexes. Time period is 1973 to date, with continuous updating. Inquire as to online cost and availability.

STATISTICS SOURCES

Assets and Liabilities of Commercial Banks in the United States. U. S. Federal Reserve System. • Weekly. $30.00 per year. (Federal Reserve Statistical Release, H.8.).

Federal Reserve Bulletin. U.S. Federal Reserve System. • Monthly. $25.00 per year. Provides statistics on banking and the economy, including interest rates, money supply, and the Federal Reserve Board indexes of industrial production.

Statistical Information on the Financial Services Industry. American Bankers Association. • Annual. Members, $150.00; non-members, $275.00. Presents a wide variety of data relating to banking and financial services, including consumer economics, personal finance, credit, government loans, capital markets, and international banking.

BANK TECHNOLOGY

See: BANK AUTOMATION

BANK TELLER MACHINES

See: BANK AUTOMATION

BANKING LAW AND REGULATION

GENERAL WORKS

Does Financial Deregulation Work? A Critique of Free Market Approaches. Bruce Coggins. Edward Elgar Publishing, Inc. • 1998. $85.00. Provides a critique of bank deregulation in the United States. Includes suggestions for more effective financial regulation. (New Directions in Modern Economics Series).

Improving Access to Bank Information for Tax Purposes. Organization for Economic Cooperation and Development. • 2000. $66.00. Discusses ways to improve the international exchange of bank account information for tax determinations.

Law and Banking Principles. James C. Conboy. American Bankers Association. • 1996. $60.00. Sixth edition. Discusses legal issues facing the banking industry.

Preventing Bank Crises: Lessons from Recent Global Bank Failures. Gerard Caprio and others, editors. The World Bank, Office of the Publisher. • 1998. $40.00. Examines worldwide problems with bank regulation, bank infrastructure, public accountability, and political influence.

Reforming the Bank Regulatory Structure. Andrew S. Carron. Brookings Institution Press. • 1985. $8.95.

ABSTRACTS AND INDEXES

Business Periodicals Index. H. W. Wilson Co. • Monthly, except August, with quarterly and annual cumulations. Service basis for print edition; CD-ROM edition, $1,495.00 per year.

Index to Legal Periodicals and Books. H. W. Wilson Co. • Monthly. Quarterly and annual cumulations. $270.00 per year. CD-ROM version available at $1,495.00 per year.

ALMANACS AND YEARBOOKS

Securities, Commodities, and Banking: Year in Review. CCH, Inc. • Annual. $55.00. Summarizes the year's significant legal and regulatory developments.

BIBLIOGRAPHIES

Financial Institutions. Available from U. S. Government Printing Office. • Annual. Free. Lists government publications. Formerly *Banks and Banking*. GPO Subject Bibliography No. 128.

Law Books in Print: Law Books in English Published Throughout the World. Glanville Publishers, Inc. • Triennial. $750.00. Supplement available, *Law Books Publisher*.

Legal Looseleafs in Print. Arlene L. Eis, editor. Infosources Publishing. • Annual. $106.00. Lists over 3,800 titles by more than 300 publishers.

DIRECTORIES

Lawyer's Register International by Specialties and Fields of Law Including a Directory of Corporate Counsel. Lawyer's Register Publishing Co. • Annual. $329.00. Three volumes. Referral source for law firms.

HANDBOOKS AND MANUALS

Bank Tax Guide. CCH, Inc. • Annual. $195.00. Summarizes and explains federal tax rules affecting financial institutions.

Banking Law. Matthew Bender & Co., Inc. • $1,970.00. 20 volumes. Periodic supplementation. Operational guidance for bank officers, with analysis of statutory law and agency regulations. Includes *Checks*, *Drafts* and *Notes* as volumes 7, 7a, 8, 8a.

Banking Law Manual: Legal Guide to Commercial Banks, Thrift Institutions, and Credit Unions. Matthew Bender & Co., Inc. • $215.00. Looseleaf service. Periodic supplementation. Desk reference, procedural guide, or training and management tool for the banking professional.

Law and Banking: Applications. Craig W. Smith. American Bankers Association. • 1996. $60.00. Covers laws pertaining to collections, secured transactions, letters of credit, check processing, collateral, fraud, and default.

ONLINE DATABASES

ABI/INFORM. Bell & Howell Information and Learning. • Provides online indexing to business-related material occurring in over 1,000 periodicals from 1971 to the present. Inquire as to online cost and availability.

Legal Resource Index. The Gale Group. • Broad coverage of law literature appearing in legal, business, and other periodicals, 1980 to date. Monthly updates. Inquire as to online cost and availability.

LEXIS. LEXIS-NEXIS. • The various LEXIS databases provide full text and indexing for a wide variety of legal cases, statutes, orders, and opinions.

LEXIS Banking Library. LEXIS-NEXIS. • Provides legal decisions and regulatory material relating to the banking industry, as well as full text of banking journals. Time period varies. Inquire as to online cost and availability.

Management Contents. The Gale Group. • Covers a wide range of management, financial, marketing, personnel, and administrative topics. About 150 leading business journals are indexed and abstracted from 1974 to date, with monthly updating. Inquire as to online cost and availability.

PAIS International. Public Affairs Information Service, Inc. • Corresponds to the former printed publications, *PAIS Bulletin* (1976-90) and *PAIS Foreign Language Index* (1972-90), and to the current *PAIS International in Print* (1991 to date). Covers economic, political, and sociological material appearing in periodicals, books, government documents, and other publications. Updating is monthly. Inquire as to online cost and availability.

Trade & Industry Index. The Gale Group. • Provides indexing of business periodicals, January 1981 to date. Daily updates. (Full text articles from some periodicals are available online, 1983 to date, in the companion database, *Trade & Industry ASAP.*) Inquire as to online cost and availability.

PERIODICALS AND NEWSLETTERS

Banking Law Journal. Warren, Gorham and Lamont, Inc/RIA Group. • Monthly. $135.98 per year. Latest developments in banking law.

International Financial Law Review. American Educational Systems. • Monthly. $695.00 per year.

RESEARCH CENTERS AND INSTITUTES

Banking Research Center. Northwestern University, 401 Anderson Hall, 2001 Sheridan Rd., Evanston, IL 60208. Phone: (847)491-3562 Fax: (847)491-5719 E-mail: m-fishman@nwu.edu • Does research in the management and public regulation of financial institutions. A unit of the J. L. Kellogg Graduate School of Management.

Center for Study of Responsive Law. P.O. Box 19367, Washington, DC 20036. Phone: (202)387-8030 Fax: (202)234-5176 E-mail: csrl@csrl.org • URL: http://www.csrl.org • A consumer-oriented research group.

Lexis.com Research System. Lexis-Nexis Group. Phone: 800-227-9597 or (937)865-6800 Fax: (937)865-6909 E-mail: webmaster@prod.lexis-nexis.com • URL: http://www.lexis.com • Fee-based Web site offers extensive searching of a wide variety of legal sources. Additional features include Daily Opinion Service, lexis.com Bookstore, Career Center, CLE Center, Law Schools, and Practice Pages ("Pages specific to areas of specialty").

Morin Center for Banking and Financial Law. Boston University, School of Law, 765 Commonwealth Ave., Boston, MA 02215. Phone: (617)353-3023 Fax: (617)353-2444 E-mail: banklaw@bu.edu • URL: http://www.web.bu.edu/law • Research fields include banking law, regulation of depository institutions, and deposit insurance.

Rodney L. White Center for Financial Research. University of Pennsylvania, 3254 Steinberg Hall-Dietrich Hall, Philadelphia, PA 19104. Phone: (215)898-7616 Fax: (215)573-8084 E-mail: rlwtcr@finance.wharton.upenn.edu • URL: http://www.finance.wharton.upenn.edu/~rlwctr • Research areas include financial management, money markets, real estate finance, and international finance.

TRADE/PROFESSIONAL ASSOCIATIONS

BANKPAC. c/o Heather Harrell, American Bankers Association, 1120 Connecticut Ave., N.W., Washington, DC 20036. Phone: (202)663-5117 or (202)663-5113 Fax: (202)663-7544 • Serves as the political action committee of the American Bankers Association.

Conference of State Bank Supervisors. 1015 18th St., N. W., Suite 1100, Washington, DC 20036-5275. Phone: 800-886-2727 or (202)296-2840 Fax: (202)296-1928 E-mail: nmilner@csbsdc.org • URL: http://www.csbsdc.org/index.html • Members are state officials responsible for supervision of state-chartered banking institutions.

Independent Community Bankers of America. One Thomas Circle, N.W., Suite 400, Washington, DC 20005. Phone: 800-422-8439 or (202)659-8111 Fax: (202)659-9216 E-mail: info@icba.org • URL: http://www.icba.org.

OTHER SOURCES

Bank and Thrift Case Digest. West Group. • Three looseleaf volumes. Periodic supplementation. Provides court decisions involving claims against failed banks and savings institutions or on behalf of insured banks and savings institutions.

Control of Banking. Prentice Hall. • Two looseleaf volumes. $465.00 per year. Periodic supplementation. Banking rules and regulations affecting day-to-day operations and financial practices of banks.

Federal Banking Law Reports. CCH, Inc. • Weekly. $1,402.00 per year. Looseleaf service.

BANKRUPTCY

See also: BUSINESS FAILURES; BUSINESS LAW; LAW

GENERAL WORKS

Bankruptcy Law Fundamentals. Richard I. Aaron. West Group. • Looseleaf. $145.00. Periodic supplementation.

How to Use Credit Wisely. American Institute for Economic Research. • 1996. $6.00. Provides succinct coverage of various consumer debt topics, including credit cards, credit scoring systems, credit history, credit reports, and bankruptcy. Relevant federal legislation is briefly described, including the Fair Credit Reporting Act (FCRA) and the Fair Credit Billing Act (FCBA). (Economic Education Bulletin.).

Mergers, Acquisitions, and Corporate Restructurings. Patrick A. Gaughan. John Wiley and Sons, Inc. • 1999. $75.00. Second edition. Covers mergers, acquisitions, divestitures, internal reorganizations, joint ventures, leveraged buyouts, bankruptcy workouts, and recapitalizations.

ABSTRACTS AND INDEXES

Accounting and Tax Index. UMI. • Quarterly. Price on application. Includes annual cumulative bound volume. Indexes accounting, auditing, and taxation literature appearing in journals, books, pamphlets, conference proceedings, and newsletters. (UMI is University Microfilms International, a Bell & Howell Co.).

Current Law Index: Multiple Access to Legal Periodicals. The Gale Group. • Monthly. $650.00 per year. Produced in cooperation with the American Association of Law Libraries. Indexes more than 900 law journals, legal newspapers, and specialty publications from the U.S., Canada, U.K., Ireland, Australia, and New Zealand.

Index to Legal Periodicals and Books. H. W. Wilson Co. • Monthly. Quarterly and annual cumulations. $270.00 per year. CD-ROM version available at $1,495.00 per year.

ALMANACS AND YEARBOOKS

American Law Yearbook. The Gale Group. • Annual. $155.00. Serves as a yearly supplement to *West's Encyclopedia of American Law.* Describes new legal developments in many subject areas.

Annual Survey of Bankruptcy. William L. Norton, Jr. and others. West Group. • 1979. $145.00.

Bankruptcy Yearbook and Almanac. New Generation Research, Inc. • Annual. Price on application.

CD-ROM DATABASES

WILSONDISC: Index to Legal Periodicals and Books. H. W. Wilson Co. • Monthly. Including unlimited online access to *Index to Legal Periodicals* through WILSONLINE. Contains CD-ROM indexing of more than 800 English language legal periodicals from 1981 to date and 2,500 books.

DIRECTORIES

National Directory of Corporate Distress Specialists: A Comprehensive Guide to Firms and Professionals Providing Services in Bankruptcies, Workouts, Turnarounds, and Distressed Investments. Joel W. Lustig, editor. Lustig Data Research, Inc. • Annual. $245.00. Provides information on 1,400 specialist firms in 17 subject areas-attorneys, accountants, financial advisors, investors, valuation consultants, turnaround managers, liquidators, etc. Nine indexes are included.

ENCYCLOPEDIAS AND DICTIONARIES

West's Encyclopedia of American Law. Available from The Gale Group. • 1997. $995.00. Second edition. 12 volumes. Published by West Group. Covers a wide variety of legal topics for the general reader. Formerly *Guide to American Law: Everyone's Legal Encyclopedia* (1985).

HANDBOOKS AND MANUALS

Bankruptcy and Insolvency Accounting. Grant Newton. John Wiley and Sons, Inc. • 2000. $330.00. Three volumes.

Bankruptcy and Insolvency Taxation. Grant W. Newton and Gilbert D. Bloom. John Wiley and Sons, Inc. • 1993. $180.00. Second edition. 2000 cumulative supplement, $85.00.

Bankruptcy Basics. Available from U. S. Government Printing Office. • 1998. $3.50. Second edition. Issued by the Bankruptcy Judges Division, Administrative Office of the United States Courts. Provides concise explanation of five Chapters of the U.S. Bankruptcy Code: Chapter 7 (Liquidation), Chapter 9 (Municipal), Chapter 11 (Reorganization), Chapter 12 (Family Farmer), and Chapter 13 (Debt Adjustment). Includes a seven-page glossary, "Bankruptcy Terminology.". (Public Information Series.).

Bankruptcy Concepts: A Desk Reference for Lenders. Bonnie K. Donahue. Robert Morris Associates. • 1994. $55.00. Designed to help loan officers deal with the intricacies of bankruptcy law. Chapters include a brief history of bankruptcy law, basic bankruptcy principles, and "Adjustments of Debts.".

Bankruptcy Law Manual. Benjamin Weintraub and Alan N. Resnick. West Group. • $210.00. Looseleaf service. Periodic supplementation. Complete, practical to modern bankruptcy practice and procedure.

Bankruptcy Practice Handbook. Rosemary E. Williams. West Group. • Looseleaf. $145.00. Periodic supplementation.

Bankruptcy Reorganization. Martin J. Bienenstock. Practising Law Institute. • 1987. $108.00.

Chapter 11: Reorganizations. Shepard's. • 1983. $105.00. Annual supplementation.

Chapter 13: Practice and Procedure. William Drake and Jeffrey W. Morris. Shepard's. • Looseleaf service. $105.00. Annual supplementation.

Collier Bankruptcy Practice Guide. Matthew Bender & Co., Inc. • $1,180.00. Six looseleaf volumes. Periodic supplementation. Strategic and procedural guide for all cases instituted under the code.

Consumer Bankruptcy. Allyn Buzzell, editor. American Bankers Association. • 1991. $39.00. Second edition. Includes a step-by-step guide for banks on responding to a consumer bankruptcy filing.

Corporate Counsellor's Deskbook. Dennis J. Block and Michael A. Epstein, editors. Panel Publishing. • 1999. $220.00. Fifth edition. Looseleaf. Annual supplementation. Covers a wide variety of corporate legal issues, including internal investigations, indemnification, insider trading, intellectual property, executive compensation, antitrust, export-import, real estate, environmental law, government contracts, and bankruptcy.

Corporate Financial Distress and Bankruptcy: A Complete Guide to Predicting and Avoiding Distress and Profiting from Bankruptcy. Edward I. Altman. John Wiley and Sons, Inc. • 1993. $99.95. Second edition. Provides practical advice on analyzing the financial position of a corporation, with case studies. Includes a discussion of the junk bond market.

Cowans Bankruptcy Law and Practice. West Publishing Co., College and School Div. • 1986. $180.00.

Debt Free: The National Bankruptcy Kit. Daniel Sitarz. National Book Network. • 1998. $19.95. Second edition. Includes basic forms and instructions for use in uncomplicated personal bankruptcy situations. (Small Business Library Series).

Herzog's Bankruptcy Forms and Practice. Asa S. Herzog and others. West Group. • Two looseleaf volumes. $250.00. Periodic supplementation.

Taxation of Financially Distressed Businesses. David B. Newman. West Group. • 1993. $120.00. Covers bankruptcy, foreclosure, abandonment, legal reporting requirements, and other tax-related subjects. (Tax Series).

ONLINE DATABASES

Accounting and Tax Database. Bell & Howell Information and Learning. • Provides indexing and abstracting of the literature of accounting, taxation, and financial management, 1971 to date. Updating is weekly. Especially covers accounting, auditing, banking, bankruptcy, employee compensation and benefits, cash management, financial planning, and credit. Inquire as to online cost and availability.

American Statistics Index: A Comprehensive Guide and Index to the Statistical Publications of the United States Government [Online]. Congressional Information Service, Inc. • Indexes and abstracts, 1973 to date. Inquire as to online cost and availability.

Index to Legal Periodicals and Books (Online). H. W. Wilson Co. • Broad coverage of law journals and books 1981 to date. Monthly updates. Inquire as to online cost and availability.

LEXIS. LEXIS-NEXIS. • The various LEXIS databases provide full text and indexing for a wide variety of legal cases, statutes, orders, and opinions.

PERIODICALS AND NEWSLETTERS

American Bankruptcy Law Journal. National Conference of Bankruptcy Judges. • Quarterly. $65.00.

Chapter 11 Update: Monitors All Major Developments in Today's Corporate Bankruptcies and Examines Pertinent Court Decisions Related to Chapter 11 Filings. Andrews Publications. • Semimonthly. $500.00 per year. Newsletter on corporate Chapter 11 bankruptcy filings.

Collections and Credit Risk: The Monthly Magazine for Collections and Credit Policy Professionals. Faulkner & Gray, Inc. • Monthly. $95.00 per year. Contains articles on the technology and business management of credit and collection functions. Includes coverage of bad debts, bankruptcy, and credit risk management.

Credit Risk Management. Phillips Business Information, Inc. • Biweekly. $695.00 per year. Newsletter on consumer credit, including delinquency aspects.

Insolvency Law & Practice. Tolley Publishing Co. Ltd. • Bimonthly. $250.00 per year. United Kingdom emphasis.

Journal of Bankruptcy Law and Practice. Warren, Gorham & Lamont/RIA Group. • Bimonthly. $228.00 per year. Provides guidance in bankruptcy law practice, including analysis of recent developments in case law.

Norton Bankruptcy Law Adviser. William L. Norton, Jr. West Group. • Monthly. $310.00 per year. Newsletter.

RESEARCH CENTERS AND INSTITUTES

Lexis.com Research System. Lexis-Nexis Group. Phone: 800-227-9597 or (937)865-6800 Fax: (937)865-6909 E-mail: webmaster@prod.lexis-nexis.com • URL: http://www.lexis.com • Fee-based Web site offers extensive searching of a wide variety of legal sources. Additional features include Daily Opinion Service, lexis.com Bookstore, Career Center, CLE Center, Law Schools, and Practice Pages ("Pages specific to areas of specialty").

STATISTICS SOURCES

Weekly Business Failures. Dun & Bradstreet, Economic Analysis Dept. • Weekly. $450.00 per year.

TRADE/PROFESSIONAL ASSOCIATIONS

American Bankruptcy Institute. 44 Canal Center Plaza, Suite 404, Alexandria, VA 22314. Phone: (703)739-0800 Fax: (703)739-1060 E-mail: info@abiworld.org • URL: http://www.abiworld.org • Members are accountants, lawyers, bankers, and other interested individuals. Promotes the exchange of information on bankruptcy and insolvency issues and compiles statistics.

Association of Insolvency Accountants. 132 W. Main, Suite 200, Medford, OR 97501. Phone: (541)858-1665 or (541)848-9362 Fax: (541)858-9187 E-mail: aira@ccountry.net.

National Conference of Bankruptcy Judges. c/o Christine J. Molick, 235 Secret Cove Dr., Lexington, SC 29072. Phone: (803)957-6225.

OTHER SOURCES

Bankruptcy Law Reports. CCH, Inc. • Biweekly. $1,208.00 per year. Three looseleaf volumes.

Collier on Bankruptcy. Lawrence P. King and others. Matthew Bender & Co., Inc. • $2,570.00. 16 looseleaf volumes. Periodic supplementation. Detailed discussion, by the leading bankruptcy authorities, of the Bankruptcy Code as amended.

The Fragile Middle Class: Americans in Debt. Teresa A. Sullivan and others. Yale University Press. • 2000. $32.50. Provides an analysis of a 1991 survey of personal bankruptcies in five states of the U. S. Serves as a sequel to the authors' *As We Forgive Our Debtors* (1989), an analysis of 1981 bankruptcies.

BANKS AND BANKING

See also: ELECTRONIC FUNDS TRANSFER SYSTEMS (EFTS)

GENERAL WORKS

Bankers in the Selling Role: A Consultative Guide to Cross Selling Financial Services. Linda Richardson. John Wiley and Sons, Inc. • 1992. $22.50. Second edition.

The Bankers: The Next Generation: The New Worlds of Money, Credit, and Banking in an Electronic Age. Martin Mayer. NAL-Dutton. • 1998. $16.95. A popularly written discussion of the future of banks, bankers, and banking.

The Business of Banking for Bank Directors. George K. Darling and James F. Chaston. Robert Morris Associates. • 1995. $33.00. Presents basic banking concepts and issues for new directors of financial institutions. Emphasis is on the specific duties of directors.

The Death of the Banker: The Decline and Fall of the Great Financial Dynasties and the Triumph of the Small Investor. Ron Chernow. Vintage Books. • 1997. $12.00. Contains three essays: "J. Pierpont Morgan," "The Warburgs," and "The Death of the Banker" (discusses the decline of banks in personal finance and the rise of mutual funds and stock brokers).

The Economics of Money, Banking and Financial Markets. Frederic S. Miskin. Addison Wesley Longman, Inc. • 1999. $98.00. Fifth edition. (Economics Series).

Michie on Banks on Banking. LEXIS Publishing. • 13 volumes. Price on application.

Money, Banking, and Financial Markets. Lloyd Thomas. McGraw-Hill. • 1996. $82.50.

Money, Banking and the Economy. Thomas Mayer and others. W. W. Norton & Co., Inc. • 1996. $85.50. Sixth edition.

Money: Its Origins, Development, Debasement, and Prospects. John H. Wood. American Institute for Economic Research. • 1999. $10.00. A politically conservative view of monetary history, the gold standard, banking systems, and inflation. Includes a list of references. (Economic Education Bulletin.).

Principles of Banking. American Bankers Association. • 1998. Price on application.

Principles of Money, Banking and Financial Markets. Lawrence S. Ritter, editor. Addison Wesley Educational Publications, Inc. • 1999. $26.00 10th edition.

ABSTRACTS AND INDEXES

Banking Information Index. U M I Banking Information Index. • Monthly. Price on application. Covers a wide variety of banking, business, and financial subjects in periodicals. Formerly *Banking Literature Index.*

Business Periodicals Index. H. W. Wilson Co. • Monthly, except August, with quarterly and annual cumulations. Service basis for print edition; CD-ROM edition, $1,495.00 per year.

NTIS Alerts: Business & Economics. National Technical Information Service.

World Banking Abstracts: The International Journal of the Financial Services Industry. Basil Blackwell, Inc. • Bimonthly. $866.00 per year. Provides worldwide coverage of articles appearing in over 400 financial publications.

ALMANACS AND YEARBOOKS

The Bankers' Almanac. Reed Business Information. • Semiannual. $730.00. Six volumes. Lists more than 4,500 banks; international coverage. Lists more than

4,500 banks; international coverage. Formerly *Bankers' Almanac and Yearbook.*

BIBLIOGRAPHIES

Banking in the U. S.: An Annotated Bibliography. Jean Deuss. Scarecrow Press, Inc. • 1990. $26.50.

Business Information Sources. Lorna M. Daniells. California Princeton Fulfillment Services. • 1993. $42.50. Third revised edition. Basic business sources, with discussion and full annotations.

The FED in Print: Economics and Banking Topics. Federal Reserve Bank of Philadelphia. • Semiannual. Free. Business and banking topics.

Information Sources in Finance and Banking. R. G. Lester, editor. Bowker-Saur. • 1995. $125.00. Published by K. G. Saur. International coverage.

BIOGRAPHICAL SOURCES

Who's Who in Finance and Industry. Marquis Who's Who. • Biennial. $295.00. Provides over 22,400 concise biographies of business leaders in all fields.

Who's Who in International Banking. Bowker-Saur. • Irregular. $400.00. Contains biographical sketches of about 4,000 bankers. Worldwide coverage.

CD-ROM DATABASES

WILSONDISC: Wilson Business Abstracts. H. W. Wilson Co. • Monthly. $2,495.00 per year, including unlimited online access to *Wilson Business Abstracts* through WILSONLINE. Provides CD-ROM "cover-to-cover" abstracting and indexing of over 600 prominent business periodicals. Indexing is from 1982, abstracting from 1990. (*Business Periodicals Index* without abstracts is available on CD-ROM at $1,495 per year.).

DIRECTORIES

American Bankers Association Key to Routing Numbers. Thomas Financial Information. • Semiannual. $125.00. per year. Lists over 30,000 finanical institutions in the U.S. and their routing members.

America's Corporate Finance Directory. National Register Publishing. • Annual. $699.00. A directory of financial executives employed at over 5,000 U. S. corporations. Includes a listing of the outside financial services (banks, pension managers, insurance firms, auditors) used by each corporation.

Central Banking Directory. Available from European Business Publications, Inc. • Biennial. Published in England by Central Banking Publications. Provides detailed information on over 160 central banks around the world. A full page is devoted to each country included. Included in subscription to *Central Banking.*

Directory of Trust Banking. Thomson Financial Publishing. • Annual. $315.00. Contains profiles of bank affiliated trust companies, independent trust companies, trust investment advisors, and trust fund managers. Provides contact information for professional personnel at more than 3,000 banking and other financial institutions.

Financial Yellow Book: Who's Who at the Leading U. S. Financial Institutions. Leadership Directories, Inc. • Semiannual. $235.00. Gives the names and titles of over 31,000 key executives in financial institutions. Includes the areas of banking, investment, money management, and insurance. Five indexes are provided: institution, executive name, geographic by state, financial service segment, and parent company.

Institutional Buyers of Bank and Thrift Stocks: A Targeted Directory. Investment Data Corp. • Annual. $645.00. Provides detailed profiles of about 600 institutional buyers of bank and savings and loan stocks. Includes names of financial analysts and portfolio managers.

Major Financial Institutions of Europe. European Business Publications, Inc. • Annual. $495.00. Contains profiles of over 7,000 financial institutions in Europe such as banks, investment companies, and insurance companies. Formerly *Major Financial Institutions of Continental Europe.*

McFadden American Financial Directory. Thomson Financial Publishing. • Semiannual. $415.00 per year. Five volumes. Contains information on more than 23,000 banks, savings institutions, and credit unions in the U. S., Canada, and Mexico. Includes names of officers for key departments, financial statistics, hours of operation, branch information, and other data.

Plunkett's Financial Services Industry Almanac: The Leading Firms in Investments, Banking, and Financial Information. Available from Plunkett Research, Ltd. • Annual. $245.00. Discusses important trends in various sectors of the financial industry. Five hundred major banking, credit card, investment, and financial services companies are profiled.

Polk Financial Institutions Directory. Thomson Financial Publishing. • Semiannual. $330.00 per semiannual volume. Provides detailed information on "virtually every bank, savings and loan, and major credit union in North America, including banks and branches in Canada, Mexico, the Caribbean, and Central America." Supersedes *Polk's Bank Directory.*

Polk World Bank Directory. Thomson Financial Publishing. • Annual. $330.00. Contains detailed listings of banks around the world, including the top 1,000 U. S. banks. Includes performance ratios for the three most recent fiscal years (return on assets, return on equity, etc.).

Polk World Banking Profiles: 2,000 Major Banks of the World. Thomson Financial Publishing. • Annual. $319.00. Provides extensive, three-year financial data for 2,000 U. S. and foreign banks. Includes analysis of 12 financial ratios and credit ratings from five leading bank rating agencies.

Thomson Bank Directory. Thomson Financial Publishing. • Semiannual. $395.00 per year. Four volumes. Provides detailed information on head offices and branches of banks in the United States and foreign countries.

The Top 5,000 European Companies 2000/2001. Available from The Gale Group. • 2001. $630.00. Second edition. Published by Graham & Whiteside. In addition to about 5,000 manufacturing and service companies, includes the 500 largest banks in Europe and the 100 largest insurance companies.

The Top 5,000 Global Companies 2000/2001. Available from The Gale Group. • Published by Graham & Whiteside. Includes about 5,000 manufacturing and service companies worldwide, plus the world's 500 largest banks and 100 largest insurance companies.

Vickers Directory of Institutional Investors. Vickers Stock Research Corp. • Semiannual. $195.00 per year. Detailed alphabetical listing of more than 4,000 U. S., Canadian, and foreign institutional investors. Includes insurance companies, banks, endowment funds, and investment companies. Formerly *Directory of Institutional Investors.*

ENCYCLOPEDIAS AND DICTIONARIES

The A-Z Vocabulary for Investors. American Institute for Economic Research. • 1997. $7.00. Second half of book is a "General Glossary" of about 400 financial terms "most-commonly used" in investing. First half contains lengthier descriptions of types of banking institutions (commercial banks, thrift institutions, credit unions), followed by succinct explanations of various forms of investment: stocks, bonds, options, futures, commodities, and "Other Investments" (collectibles, currencies, mortgages, precious metals, real estate, charitable trusts). (Economic Education Bulletin.).

Blackwell Encyclopedic Dictionary of Finance. Dean Paxson and Douglas Wood, editors. Blackwell Publishers. • 1997. $110.00. The editors are associated with the University of Manchester. Contains definitions of key terms combined with longer articles written by various U. S. and foreign business educators. Includes bibliographies and index. (Blackwell Encyclopedia of Management Series).

Dictionary of Banking. Jerry M. Rosenberg. John Wiley and Sons, Inc. • 1992. $19.95. Third edition. (Business Dictionary Series).

Dictionary of Banking and Finance Terms: 'AAA to Zloty'. John Clark. State Mutual Book and Periodical Services Ltd. • 1998. $60.00.

Dictionary of Banking: Over 4,000 Terms Defined and Explained. Charles J. Woelfel. McGraw-Hill Professional. • 1994. $24.95. Contains brief definitions of more than 4,000 banking terms.

Dictionary of Banking Terms. Thomas P. Fitch. Barron's Educational Series, Inc. • 2000. Fifth edition. Price on application.

Dictionary of Finance and Investment Terms. John Downes and Jordan E. Goodman. Barron's Educational Series, Inc. • 1998. $12.95. Fifth revised edition. Provides clear explanations of more than 5,000 business, banking, financial, investment, and tax terms. Includes a separate list of financial abbreviations and acronyms.

Encyclopedia of Banking and Finance. Charles J. Woelfel. McGraw-Hill Professional. • 1996. $50.00. 10th revised edition.

Encyclopedia of Business. The Gale Group. • 2000. $425.00. Second edition. Two volumes. Contains more than 700 signed articles covering major business disciplines and concepts. International in scope.

Encyclopedia of Business and Finance. Burton Kaliski, editor. Available from The Gale Group. • 2001. $240.00. Two volumes. Published by Macmillan Reference USA. Contains articles by various contributors on accounting, business administration, banking, finance, management information systems, and marketing.

The Language of Banking: Terms and Phrases Used in the Financial Industry. Michael G. Hales. McFarland & Co., Inc., Publishers. • 1994. $32.50. Provides detailed explanations of about 1,200 banking and finance terms.

The New Palgrave Dictionary of Money and Finance. Peter Newman and others, editors. Groves Dictionaries. • 1998. $550.00. Three volumes. Consists of signed essays on over 1,000 financial topics, each with a bibliography. Covers a wide variety of financial, monetary, and investment areas. A detailed subject index is provided.

The Thorndike Encyclopedia of Banking and Financial Tables. David Thorndike. Warren, Gorham and Lamont/RIA Group. • 1991. $79.00.

FINANCIAL RATIOS

Almanac of Business and Industrial Financial Ratios. Leo Troy. Prentice Hall. • Annual. $99.95. Contains financial ratios derived from federal tax returns. Ratios for each of about 200 industries are arranged according to company asset size.

The Financial Elite: Database of Financial Services Companies. Donnelley Marketing. • Quarterly. Price on application. Formerly compiled by Database America. Provides current information on CD-ROM for 500,000 major U. S. companies offering financial services. Data for each firm includes year started, type of financial service, annual revenues, name of top executive, and number of employees.

Major Financial Institutions of the World. Available from The Gale Group. • 2001. $855.00. Fourth edition. Two volumes. Published by Graham & Whiteside. Contains detailed information on more than 7,500 important financial institutions in various countries. Includes banks, investment companies, and insurance companies.

Resumes for Banking and Financial Careers, With Sample Cover Letters. NTC/Contemporary Publishing Group. • 2001. $10.95. Second edition. Contains 100 sample resumes and 20 cover letters. (VGM Professional Resumes Series.).

HANDBOOKS AND MANUALS

The Bank Director's Handbook. Edwin B Cox and others. Greenwood Publishing Group, Inc. • 1986. $65.00. Second edition.

Banking and Finance on the Internet. Mary J. Cronin, editor. John Wiley and Sons, Inc. • 1997. $45.00. Contains articles on Internet services, written by bankers, money mangers, investment analysts, and stockbrokers. Emphasis is on operations management. (Communications Series).

How to Charter a Commercial Bank. Douglas V. Austin and others. CCH, Inc. • 1999. $350.00. Provides detailed information on how to start a commercial bank, including both technical and practical requirements.

International Banking. Peter K. Oppenheim. American Bankers Association. • 1991. $51.00. Sixth edition. Covers letters of credit, money transfers, collections, and other aspects of global banking.

Moody's Bank and Finance Manual. Moody's Investor Service. • Annual. $995.00 per year. Four volumes. Includes biweekly supplements in *Moody's Bank and Finance News Report.*

INTERNET DATABASES

The Bauer Group: Reporting On and Analyzing the Performance of U. S. Banks, Thrifts, and Credit Unions. Bauer Financial Reports, Inc. Phone: 800-388-6686 or (305)445-9500 Fax: 800-230-9569 or (305)445-6775 • URL: http://www.bauerfinancial.com • Web site provides ratings (0 to 5 stars) of individual banks and credit unions, based on capital ratios and other financial criteria. Online searching for bank or credit union names is offered. Fees: Free.

Europa: The European Union's Server. European Union 352 4301 35 349. E-mail: pressoffice@eurostat.cec.be • URL: http://www.europa.eu.int • Web site provides access to a wide variety of EU information, including statistics (Eurostat), news, policies, publications, key issues, and official exchange rates for the euro. Includes links to the European Central Bank, the European Investment Bank, and other institutions. Fees: Free.

Fedstats. Federal Interagency Council on Statistical Policy. Phone: (202)395-7254 • URL: http://www.fedstats.gov • Web site features an efficient search facility for full-text statistics produced by more than 70 federal agencies, including the Census Bureau, the Bureau of Economic Analysis, and the Bureau of Labor Statistics. Boolean searches can be made within one agency or for all agencies combined. Links are offered to international statistical bureaus, including the UN, IMF, OECD, UNESCO, Eurostat, and 20 individual countries. Fees: Free.

ONLINE DATABASES

American Banker Full Text. American Banker-Bond Buyer, Database Services. • Provides complete text online of the daily *American Banker.* Inquire as to online cost and availability.

Banking Information Source. Bell & Howell Information and Learning. • Provides indexing and abstracting of periodical and other literature from 1982 to date, with weekly updates. Covers the financial services industry: banks, savings institutions, investment houses, credit unions, insurance companies, and real estate organizations. Emphasis is on marketing and management. Inquire as to online cost and availability. (Formerly *FINIS: Financial Industry Information Service.*).

DRI Financial and Credit Statistics. Data Products Division. • Contains U. S. and international statistical data relating to money markets, interest rates, foreign exchange, banking, and stock and bond indexes. Time period is 1973 to date, with continuous updating. Inquire as to online cost and availability.

DRI U.S. Central Database. Data Products Division. • Provides more than 23,000 business, financial, demographic, economic, foreign trade, and industry-related time series for the U.S. Includes national income, population, retail-wholesale trade, price indexes, labor data, housing, industrial production, banking, interest rates, money supply, etc. Time period is generally 1947 to date (some data back to 1929). Updating varies. Inquire as to online cost and availability.

LEXIS Banking Library. LEXIS-NEXIS. • Provides legal decisions and regulatory material relating to the banking industry, as well as full text of banking journals. Time period varies. Inquire as to online cost and availability.

Wilson Business Abstracts Online. H. W. Wilson Co. • Indexes and abstracts 600 major business periodicals, plus the *Wall Street Journal* and the business section of the *New York Times.* Indexing is from 1982, abstracting from 1990, with the two newspapers included from 1993. Updated weekly. Inquire as to online cost and availability. (*Business Periodicals Index* without abstracts is also available online.).

PERIODICALS AND NEWSLETTERS

ABA Bankers News. American Bankers Association. • Biweekly. Members, $48.00 per year; non-members, $96.00 per year. Formerly *ABA Banker News Weekly.* Incorporating *Agricultural Banker.*

ABA Banking Journal. American Bankers Association, Member Communications. Simmons-Boardman Publishing Corp. • Monthly. Free to qualified personnel; others, $25.00 per year.

American Banker. Thomson Financial Media. • Daily. $825.00 per year. Includes*Future Banker.*

Applied Financial Economics. Routledge Journals. • Bimonthly. Individuals, $648.00 per year; institutions, $1,053.00 per year. Covers practical aspects of financial economics, banking, and monetary economics. Supplement to *Applied Economics.*

Bank Letter: Newsletter of Commercial and Institutional Banking. Institutional Investor, Newsletters Div. • Weekly. $2,220.00 per year. Newsletter. Covers retail banking, commercial lending, foreign loans, bank technology, government regulations, and other topics related to banking.

Bank Marketing. Bank Marketing Association. • Monthly. Members, $80.00 per year; non-members, $120.00 per year. Includes a Buyer's Guide.

Bank Rate Monitor: The Weekly Financial Rate Reporter. Advertising News Service, Inc. • Weekly. $895.00 per year. Newsletter. Includes online addition and monthly supplement. Provides detailed information on interest rates currently paid by U. S. banks and savings institutions.

Bank Strategies. Bank Administration Institute. • Monthly. $59.00 per year. Formerly *Bank Management.*

The Banker. Financial Times. • Monthly. $197.00 per year. Includes supplement. Published in England.

Banking Law Journal. Warren, Gorham and Lamont, Inc/RIA Group. • Monthly. $135.98 per year. Latest developments in banking law.

Central Banking: Policy, Markets, Supervision. Available from European Business Publications, Inc. • Quarterly. $350.00 per year, including annual *Central Banking Directory.* Published in England by Central Banking Publications. Reports and comments on the activities of central banks around the world. Also provides discussions of the International Monetary Fund (IMF), the Organization for Economic Cooperation and Development (OECD), the Bank for International Settlements (BIS), and the World Bank.

Financial Markets, Institutions, and Instruments. New York University, Salomon Center. Blackwell Publishers. • Five times a year. $219.00 per year. Edited to "bridge the gap between the academic and professional finance communities." Special fifth issue each year provides surveys of developments in four areas: money and banking, derivative securities, corporate finance, and fixed-income securities.

Guide to Banks and Thrifts: A Quarterly Compilation of Financial Institutions Ratings and Analysis. Weiss Ratings, Inc. • Quarterly. $438.00 per year. Emphasis is on rating of financial safety and relative risk. Includes annual summary.

Journal of Banking and Financial Services. Warren, Gorham and Lamont, Inc. • Bimonthly. $115.00. per year. Enables bankers to obtain a more generalized view of the industry. Contains articles for bankers, by bankers and top consultants in the field. Formerly*Bankers' Magazine.*

Journal of Lending and Credit Risk Management. Robert Morris Associates. • 10 times a year. Members, $35.00 per year; non-members, $85.00 per year. Formerly *Journal of Commercial Bank Lending.*

Journal of Money, Credit and Banking. Paul D. Evans, editor. Ohio State University Press. • Quarterly. Individuals $48.00 per year; institutions, $135.00 per year. Reports major findings in the study of financial markets, monetary and fiscal policy credit markets, money and banking, portfolio management and related subjects.

Jumbo Rate News. Bauer Financial Newsletters, Inc. • Weekly. $445.00 per year. Newsletter. Lists more than 1,100 of the highest interest rates available for "jumbo" certificates of deposit ($100,000 or more).

Letters of Credit Report: Bank Guaranties and Acceptance. Aspen Law and Business. • Bimonthly. $299.00 per year. Newsletter. Covers letters of credit, bank acceptances, and bank guarantees.

One Hundred Highest Yields Among Federally-Insured Banks and Savings Institutions. Advertising News Service, Inc. • Weekly. $124.00 per year. Newsletter.

Recommended Bank and Thrift Report. Bauer Communications, Inc. • Quarterly. $585.00 per year. Newsletter provides information on "safe, financially sound" commercial banks, savings banks, and savings and loan institutions. Various factors are considered, including tangible capital ratios and total risk-based capital ratios. (Six regional editions are also available at $150.00 per edition per year.).

The Safe Money Report. Weiss Ratings, Inc. • Monthly. $148.00 per year. Newsletter. Provides financial advice and current safety ratings of various banks, savings and loan companies, insurance companies, and securities dealers.

Treasury Manager's Report: Strategic Information for the Financial Executive. Phillips Business Information, Inc. • Biweekly. $595.00. Newsletter reporting on legal developments affecting the operations of banks, savings institutions, and other financial service organizations. Formerly *Financial Services Law Report.*

Troubled and Problematic Bank and Thrift Report. Bauer Communications, Inc. • Quarterly. $225.00 per year. Newsletter provides information on seriously undercapitalized ("Troubled") banks and savings institutions, as defined by a federal Prompt Corrective Action Rule. "Problematic" banks and thrifts are those meeting regulatory capital levels, but showing negative trends.

U. S. Banker. Faulkner & Gray, Inc. • Monthly. $52.00 per year. Covers a wide variety of current banking topics.

RESEARCH CENTERS AND INSTITUTES

American Institute for Economic Research. P.O. Box 1000, Great Barrington, MA 01230. Phone: (413)528-1216 Fax: (413)528-0103 E-mail: info@aier.org • URL: http://www.aier.org.

National Bureau of Economic Research, Inc. 1050 Massachusetts Ave., Cambridge, MA 02138-5398. Phone: (617)868-3900 Fax: (617)868-2742 E-mail: msfeldst@nber.org • URL: http://www.nber.org.

National Opinion Research Center. 1155 E. 60th St., Chicago, IL 60637. Phone: (773)753-7500 Fax: (773)753-7886 E-mail: cloud.patricia@norcmail.uchicago.edu • URL: http://www.norc.uchicago.edu.

STATISTICS SOURCES

Assets and Liabilities of Commercial Banks in the United States. U. S. Federal Reserve System. • Weekly. $30.00 per year. (Federal Reserve Statistical Release, H.8.).

Bank Operating Statistics. Federal Deposit Insurance Corp. • Annual. Price on application. Based on Reports of Condition and Reports of Income.

Bank Profitability: Financial Statements of Banks. Organization for Economic Cooperation and Development. Available from OECD Publications and Information Center. • Annual. $60.00. Presents data for 10 years on bank profitability in OECD member countries.

Business Statistics of the United States. Courtenay M. Slater, editor. Bernan Associates. • 1999. $74.00. Fifth edition. Based on *Business Statistics*, formerly issue by the Bureau of Economic Analysis, U. S. Department of Commerce. Provides basic data for a wide variety of U. S. industries, services, and economic indicators. Most statistics are shown annually for 29 years and monthly for the most recent four years.

Economic Indicators. Council of Economic Advisors, Executive Office of the President. Available from U.S. Government Printing Office. • Monthly. $55.00 per year.

Federal Reserve Bulletin. U.S. Federal Reserve System. • Monthly. $25.00 per year. Provides statistics on banking and the economy, including interest rates, money supply, and the Federal Reserve Board indexes of industrial production.

Financial Market Trends. Organization for Economic Cooperation and Development. • Three times a year. $100.00 per year. Provides analysis of developments and trends in international and national capital markets. Includes charts and graphs on interest rates, exchange rates, stock market indexes, bank stock indexes, trading volumes, and loans outstanding. Data from OECD countries includes international direct investment, bank profitability, institutional investment, and privatization.

Ranking the Banks. American Banker. • Annual. Price on application. Ranks domestic and foreign banks by 75 financial parameters.

Standard & Poor's Industry Surveys. Standard & Poor's. • Semiannual. $1,800.00. Two looseleaf volumes. Includes monthly supplements. Provides detailed, individual surveys of 52 major industry groups. Each survey is revised on a semiannual basis. Also includes "Monthly Investment Review" (industry group investment analysis) and monthly "Trends & Projections" (economic analysis).

Statistical Information on the Financial Services Industry. American Bankers Association. • Annual. Members, $150.00; non-members, $275.00. Presents a wide variety of data relating to banking and financial services, including consumer economics, personal finance, credit, government loans, capital markets, and international banking.

Survey of Current Business. Available from U. S. Government Printing Office. • Monthly. $49.00 per year. Issued by Bureau of Economic Analysis, U. S. Department of Commerce. Presents a wide variety of business and economic data.

TRADE/PROFESSIONAL ASSOCIATIONS

American Bankers Association. 1120 Connecticut Ave., N.W., Washington, DC 20036. Phone: 800-226-5377 or (202)663-5000 Fax: (202)663-7543 • URL: http://www.aba.com.

Bankers' Association for Foreign Trade. 2121 K. St. N.W., Suite 701, Washington, DC 20037. Phone: (202)452-0952 Fax: (202)452-0959 E-mail: baft@baft.org • URL: http://www.baft.org.

Bretton Woods Committee. 1990 M St., N.W., Suite 450, Washington, DC 20036. Phone: (202)331-1616 Fax: (202)785-9423 E-mail: info@brettonwoods.org • URL: http://www.brettonwoods.org • Members are corporate executives, government officials, college administrators, bankers, and other "National Leaders." Seeks to inform and educate the public as to the activities of the International Monetary Fund, the World Bank, and other multinational development banking organizations. Promotes U. S. participation in multinational banking.

Consumer Bankers Association. 1000 Wilson Blvd., Suite 3012, Arlington, VA 22209-3908. Phone: (703)276-1750 Fax: (703)528-1290 E-mail: cba@cbanet.org • URL: http://www.cbanet.org.

Financial Services Round Table. 805 15th St., N.W., Suite 600, Washington, DC 20005. Phone: (202)289-4322 Fax: (202)289-1903 E-mail: info@bankersound.org.

Independent Community Bankers of America. One Thomas Circle, N.W., Suite 400, Washington, DC 20005. Phone: 800-422-8439 or (202)659-8111 Fax: (202)659-9216 E-mail: info@icba.org • URL: http://www.icba.org.

Mortgage Bankers Association of America. c/o Janice Stango, 1125 15th St., N.W., Washington, DC 20005. Phone: (202)861-6500 Fax: (202)785-2967.

World Bank. 1818 H St., N. W., Washington, DC 20433. Phone: (202)477-1234 Fax: (202)477-6391 • URL: http://www.worldbank.org • Comprises the International Bank for Reconstruction and Development and the International Development Association, with over 130 member countries.

OTHER SOURCES

BNA's Banking Report: Legal and Regulatory Developments in the Financial Services Industry. Bureau of National Affairs, Inc. • Weekly. $1,221.00 per year. Two volumes. Looseleaf. Emphasis on federal regulations.

Factiva. Dow Jones Reuters Business Interactive, LLC. • Fee-based Web site provides "global news and business information through Web sites and content integration solutions." Includes Dow Jones and Reuters newswires, The Wall Street Journal, and more than 7,000 other sources of current news, historical articles, market research reports, and investment analysis. Content includes 96 major U. S. newspapers, 900 non-English sources, trade publications, media transcripts, country profiles, news photos, etc.

Federal Banking Law Reports. CCH, Inc. • Weekly. $1,402.00 per year. Looseleaf service.

Information, Finance, and Services USA. The Gale Group. • 2001. $240.00. Replaces *Service Industries USA* and *Finance, Insurance, and Real Estate USA.* Presents statistics and projections relating to economic activity in a wide variety of non-manufacturing areas.

Nexis.com. Lexis-Nexis Group. • Fee-based Web site offers searching of about 2.8 billion documents in some 30,000 news, business, and legal information sources. Features include a subject directory covering 1,200 topics in 34 categories and a Company Dossier containing information on more than 500,000 public and private companies. Boolean searching is offered.

Online Banking. MarketResearch.com. • 2000. $3,450.00. Market research report. Includes demographics relating to the users and nonusers of online banking services. Provides market forecasts.

BAR CODES

See: AUTOMATIC IDENTIFICATION SYSTEMS; POINT-OF-SALE SYSTEMS (POS)

BARBER AND BEAUTY SHOPS

See also: COSMETICS INDUSTRY

GENERAL WORKS

Cosmetology. Jack Rudman. National Learning Corp. • $43.95. (Occupational Competency Examination Series: OCE-13).

The Professional Cosmetologist. John Dalton. West Publishing Co., College and School Div. • 1992. $42.50. Fourth edition.

FINANCIAL RATIOS

Annual Statement Studies. Robert Morris Associates: The Association of Lending and Credit Risk Professiona. • Annual. Free to members; non-members, $140.00. Median and quartile financial ratios are given for over 400 kinds of manufacturing, wholesale, retail, construction, and consumer finance establishments. Data is sorted by both asset size and sales volume. Includes a clearly written "Definition of Ratios" and an alphabetical industry index.

Dealer Operating Analysis. Beauty and Barber Supply Institute. • Annual.

HANDBOOKS AND MANUALS

Beauty Supply Store. Entrepreneur Media, Inc. • Looseleaf. $59.50. A practical guide to starting a store for professional beauty supplies. Covers profit potential, start-up costs, market size evaluation, owner's time required, site selection, lease negotiation, pricing, accounting, advertising, promotion, etc. (Start-Up Business Guide No. E1277.).

Van Dean Manual. Milady Staff Editors. Milady Publishing Co. • 1990. $36.95. Revised edition.

ONLINE DATABASES

F & S Index. The Gale Group. • Contains about four million citations to worldwide business, financial, and industrial or consumer product literature appearing from 1972 to date. Weekly updates. Inquire as to online cost and availability.

PERIODICALS AND NEWSLETTERS

American Salon. National Hairdressers and Cosmetologists Association. Advanstar Communications, Inc. • Monthly. $24.00 per year. Supplement available*American Salon Distributor-Manufacturer News.*

Hairdressers' Journal International. Reed Business Information. • Weekly. $112.00 per year.

Modern Salon Magazine. Vance Publishing Corp. • Monthly. $20.00 per year.

STATISTICS SOURCES

United States Census of Service Industries. U.S. Bureau of the Census. • Quinquennial. Various reports available.

TRADE/PROFESSIONAL ASSOCIATIONS

Beauty and Barber Supply Institute. 15825 N. 71st St., Ste. 100, Scottsdale, AZ 85254-2187. Phone: 800-468-2274 Fax: (480)905-0708 E-mail: spano@bbsi.org • URL: http://www.bbsi.org.

Hair International/Associated Masters Barbers and Beauticians of America. P.O. Box 273, Palmyra, PA 17078-1712. Phone: (717)838-0795 Fax: (717)838-0796 E-mail: hairint@nbn.net • URL: http://www.hairinternational.com.

National Cosmetology Association. 401 N. Michigan Ave., Chicago, IL 60611-4255. Phone: 800-527-1683 E-mail: ncal@sba.com • URL: http://www.nca-now.com.

Textile Processors, Service Trades, Health Care, Professional and Technical Employees International Union. 303 E. Wacker Dr., Suite 1109, Chicago, IL 60601. Phone: (312)946-0450 Fax: (312)964-0453.

OTHER SOURCES

Beauty Salons. Available from MarketResearch.com. • 1997. $995.00. Market research report published by Specialists in Business Information. Covers beauty salon revenues, as well as sales of supplies and equipment for beauty salons and barber shops.

BARLEY INDUSTRY

See: AGRICULTURE

BARRELS

See: COOPERAGE INDUSTRY

BARTER AND COUNTERTRADE

HANDBOOKS AND MANUALS

Personal and Business Bartering. James Stout. McGraw-Hill Professional. • 1985. $14.95.

PERIODICALS AND NEWSLETTERS

Barter Communique. Full Circle Marketing Corp. • Quarterly. $30.00 per year. Lists barter businesses and publications.

Barter Update. Ed A. Doyle, editor. Update Publicare Co. c/o Prosperity and Profits Unlimited, Distribution Services. • Annual. $4.00 per year.

Countertrade and Offset: Weekly Intelligence on Unconventional and Reciprocal International Trade. CTO Data Services. • 24 times a year. $688.00 per year. Newsletter. Intelligence on reciprocal international trade and unconventional trade finance. Covers developments and trends in the directory publishing industry, including publisher profiles, start-ups, corporate acquisitions, and business opportunities. Includes *Directory of Countertrade Services.* Formerly *Countertrade Outlook.* itions, and business opportunities. Formerly *Cowles-Simba Report on Directory Publishing.*

Trade Channel. Trade Channel Organization. • Monthly. $88.00 per year. Features export "offers" and import "wants." Worldwide coverage. Technical products and consumer products. Each edition $88.00 per year. Formerly *Export Channel.*

TRADE/PROFESSIONAL ASSOCIATIONS

International Reciprocal Trade Association. 175 W. Jackson, Blvd., Suite 625, Chicago, IL 60604. Phone: (312)461-0236 Fax: (312)461-0474 E-mail: admin1@irta.net • URL: http://www.irta.net • Promotes commercial barter industry.

OTHER SOURCES

International Counterpurchase Contracts. United Nations Publications. • 1990. Trade agreements.

BATTERY INDUSTRY

ABSTRACTS AND INDEXES

Applied Science and Technology Index. H. W. Wilson Co. • 11 times a year. Quarterly and annual cumulations. Service basis for print edition; CD-ROM edition, $1,495.00 per year. Indexes a wide variety of English language technical, industrial, and engineering periodicals.

Current Contents: Engineering, Computing and Technology. Institute for Scientific Information. • Weekly. $730.00 per year. Reproductions of contents pages of technical journals. Includes *Author Index, Address Directory, Current Book Contents* and *Title Word Index.* Formerly *Current Contents: Engineering, Technology and Applied Sciences.*

NTIS Alerts: Energy. National Technical Information Service. • Semimonthly. $245.00 per year. Provides descriptions of government-sponsored research reports and software, with ordering information. Covers electric power, batteries, fuels, geothermal energy, heating/cooling systems, nuclear technology, solar energy, energy policy, and related subjects. Formerly *Abstract Newsletter.*

DIRECTORIES

Macrae's Blue Book: Serving the Original Equipment Market. MacRae's Blue Book, Inc. • Annual. $170.00. Two volumes. Lists about 50,000 manufacturers of a wide variety of industrial equipment and supplies.

SLIG Buyers' Guide: Starting, Lighting, Ignition, Generating Systems. Independent Battery Manufacturers Association. • Biennial. $25.00 per year. Over 1,900 manufacturers and rebuilders of heavy-duty storage batteries.

Thomas Register of American Manufacturers and Thomas Register Catalog File. Thomas Publishing Co., Inc. • Annual. $149.00. 34 volumes. A three-part system offering information on a wide variety of industrial equipment and supplies.

ENCYCLOPEDIAS AND DICTIONARIES

Macmillan Encyclopedia of Energy. Available from The Gale Group. • 2001. $350.00. Three volumes. Published by Macmillan Reference USA. Covers the business, technology, and history of a wide variety of energy sources.

HANDBOOKS AND MANUALS

Handbook of Batteries. David Linden. McGraw-Hill. • 1995. $125.00. Second edition.

ONLINE DATABASES

Applied Science and Technology Index Online. H. W. Wilson Co. • Provides online indexing of 400 major scientific, technical, industrial, and engineering periodicals. Time period is 1983 to date. Monthly updates. Inquire as to online cost and availability.

PROMT: Predicasts Overview of Markets and Technology. The Gale Group. • Companies, products, applied technologies and markets. U.S. and international literature coverage, 1972 to date. Inquire as to online cost and availability. Provides abstracts from more than 1,600 publications. Weekly updates.

Thomas Register Online. Thomas Publishing Co., Inc. • Provides concise information on approximately 194,000 U. S. companies, mainly manufacturers, with over 50,000 product classifications. Indexes over 115,000 trade names. Information is updated semiannually. Inquire as to online cost and availability.

PERIODICALS AND NEWSLETTERS

Advanced Battery Technology. Seven Mountains Scientific, Inc. • Monthly. $165.00 per year. Newsletter. Provides technical and marketing information for the international battery industry.

Aftermarket Business. Advanstar Communications, Inc. • Monthly. $45.00 per year. Automobile aftermarket, including batteries.

Battery and EV Technology News. Business Communications Co., Inc. • Monthly. $450.00 per year. Newsletter. Technical and economic studies of electric vehicles and battery technology.

The Battery Man: International Journal for Starting, Lighting, Ignition and Generating Systems. Independent Battery Manufacturers Association. • Monthly. $22.00 per year.

Chilton's Automotive Marketing: A Monthly Publication for the Retail Jobber and Distributor of Automotive Aftermarket. Cahners Business Information. • Monthly. Free to qualified personnel; others, $48.00 per year. Includes marketing of automobile batteries. Formerly *Automotive Aftermarket News.*

Industrial Equipment News. Thomas Publishing Co. • Monthly. $95.00 per year. Free. What's new in equipment, parts and materials.

New Equipment Digest Market. Penton Media Inc. • Monthly. Free to qualified personnel; others, $55.00 per year. Formerly *Material Handling Engineering.*

New Equipment Reporter: New Products Industrial News. De Roche Publications. • Monthly. Controlled circulation.

RESEARCH CENTERS AND INSTITUTES

Electrochemical Analysis and Diagnostic Laboratory. Argonne National Laboratory, Chemical Technology Div., Bldg. 205, 9800 S. Cass Ave., Argonne, IL 60439. Phone: (630)252-4516 Fax: (630)252-4176 E-mail: bloom@cmt.anl.gov.

STATISTICS SOURCES

Annual Survey of Manufactures. Available from U. S. Government Printing Office. • Annual. Prices vary. Issued by the U. S. Census Bureau as an interim update to the *Census of Manufactures.* Includes data on number of manufacturing establishments in various industries, employment, labor costs, value of shipments, capital expenditures, inventories, energy costs, and assets. (See also Census Bureau home page, http://www.census.gov/.).

TRADE/PROFESSIONAL ASSOCIATIONS

Automotive Aftermarket Industry Association. 4600 East-West Highway, Suite 300, Bethesda, MD 20814-3415. Phone: (301)654-6664 Fax: (301)654-3299 E-mail: aia@aftermarket.org • URL: http://www.aftermarket.org • Retailers, distributors, and manufacturers.

Battery Council International. 401 N. Michigan Ave., Chicago, IL 60611. Phone: (312)644-6610 Fax: (312)321-6869 E-mail: info@batterycouncil.org • URL: http://www.batterycouncil.org • Manufacturers of lead-acid storage batteries.

Independent Battery Manufacturers Association. 100 Larchwood Dr., Largo, FL 34640. Phone: (727)586-1408 • Manufacturers of lead-acid storage batteries.

OTHER SOURCES

Major Energy Companies of the World. Available from The Gale Group. • 2001. $855.00. Fourth edition. Published by Graham & Whiteside. Contains detailed information on more than 3,300 important energy companies in various countries. Industries include electricity generation, coal, natural gas, nuclear energy, petroleum, fuel distribution, and equipment for energy production.

BAUXITE

See: MINES AND MINERAL RESOURCES

BAZAARS

See: FAIRS

BEAN INDUSTRY

See: AGRICULTURE; CANNED FOOD INDUSTRY

BEARINGS AND BALL BEARINGS

See also: ENGINES

ABSTRACTS AND INDEXES

Applied Science and Technology Index. H. W. Wilson Co. • 11 times a year. Quarterly and annual cumulations. Service basis for print edition; CD-ROM edition, $1,495.00 per year. Indexes a wide variety of English language technical, industrial, and engineering periodicals.

DIRECTORIES

Dun's Industrial Guide: The Metalworking Directory. Dun and Bradstreet Information Services Dun & Bradstreet Corp. • Annual. Libraries, $485; commercial institutions, $795.00. Lease basis. Three volumes. Lists about 65,000 U. S. manufacturing plants using metal and suppliers of metalworking equipment and materials. Includes names and titles of key personnel. Products, purchases, and processes are indicated.

HANDBOOKS AND MANUALS

International Bearing Interchange (IBI Guide). Interchange, Inc. • Biennial. $195.00. Two volumes. Cross-references for ball bearing, straight and curved roller bearings, tappered cones and cups, pillow blocks and flange units; from the latest back to 1918.

ONLINE DATABASES

Applied Science and Technology Index Online. H. W. Wilson Co. • Provides online indexing of 400 major scientific, technical, industrial, and engineering periodicals. Time period is 1983 to date. Monthly updates. Inquire as to online cost and availability.

METADEX. Cambridge Scientific Abstracts. • Covers the worldwide literature of metals, metallurgy, and materials science, 1966 to date. Includes detailed alloys indexing from 1974. Biweekly updating. Inquire as to online cost and availability. (Formerly produced by ASM International.).

STATISTICS SOURCES

Annual Survey of Manufactures. Available from U. S. Government Printing Office. • Annual. Prices vary. Issued by the U. S. Census Bureau as an interim update to the *Census of Manufactures.* Includes data on number of manufacturing establishments in various industries, employment, labor costs, value of shipments, capital expenditures, inventories, energy costs, and assets. (See also Census Bureau home page, http://www.census.gov/.).

Anti-Friction Bearings. U.S. Bureau of the Census. • Annual.

Manufacturing Profiles. Available from U. S. Government Printing Office. • Annual. Issued by the U. S. Census Bureau. A printed consolidation of the entire *Current Industrial Report* series, presenting "all the data compiled." Contains statistics on production, shipments, inventories, consumption, exports, imports, and orders for a wide variety of manufactured products. (See also Census Bureau home page, http://www.census.gov/.).

U. S. Industry and Trade Outlook: The McGraw-Hill Companies and the U.S. Department of Commerce/International Trade Administration. Datapso Research Corp. • Annual. $69.95. Produced by the International Trade Administration, U. S. Department of Commerce, in a "public-private" partnership with DRI/McGraw-Hill and Standard & Poor's. Provides basic data, outlook for the current year, and "Long-Term Prospects" (five-year projections) for a wide variety of products and services. Includes high technology industries. Formerly *U. S. Industrial Outlook.*

TRADE/PROFESSIONAL ASSOCIATIONS

American Bearing Manufacturers Association. 1200 19th St., N.W., Suite 300, Washington, DC 20036-2422. Phone: (202)429-5155 Fax: (202)857-1115 E-mail: abma@dc.sba.com • URL: http://www.abma-dc.org.

Bearing Specialists Association. 800 Roosevelt Rd.., Bldg. C, Suite 20, Glen Ellyn, IL 60137. Phone: (630)858-3838 Fax: (630)790-3095 E-mail: info@bsahame.org • URL: http://www.bsahame.org.

BEAUTY INDUSTRY

See: BARBER AND BEAUTY SHOPS; COSMETICS INDUSTRY

BEAUTY SHOPS AND BARBER SHOPS

See: BARBER AND BEAUTY SHOPS

BEDDING INDUSTRY

See: FURNITURE INDUSTRY

BEE INDUSTRY

See: HONEY INDUSTRY

BEEF INDUSTRY

See: CATTLE INDUSTRY

BEER INDUSTRY

See: BREWING INDUSTRY

BEETS AND BEET SUGAR INDUSTRY

See: SUGAR INDUSTRY

BEHAVIORAL SCIENCES

See: HUMAN RELATIONS; INDUSTRIAL PSYCHOLOGY

BENEFITS, EMPLOYEE

See: EMPLOYEE BENEFIT PLANS

BEQUESTS

See: WILLS

BERYLLIUM INDUSTRY

See: METAL INDUSTRY

BETTER BUSINESS BUREAUS

See also: CONSUMER EDUCATION

DIRECTORIES

Directory of Better Business Bureaus. Council of Better Business Bureaus, Inc. • Annual. Free. Send stamped, self-addressed envelope. Lists about 185 Better Business Bureaus in the United States and Canada.

TRADE/PROFESSIONAL ASSOCIATIONS

Council of Better Business Bureaus. 4200 Wilson Blvd., Suite 800, Arlington, VA 22203-1838. Phone: (703)276-0100 Fax: (703)525-8277 E-mail: bbb@bbb.org • URL: http://www.bbb.org.

BEVERAGE INDUSTRY

See also: BREWING INDUSTRY; DISTILLING INDUSTRY; SOFT DRINK INDUSTRY

ABSTRACTS AND INDEXES

Food Science and Technology Abstracts. International Food Information Service Publishing. • Monthly. $1,780.00 per year. Provides worldwide coverage of the literature of food technology and food production.

Foods Adlibra: Key to the World's Food Literature. Foods Adlibra Publications. • Semimonthly.Provides journal citations and abstracts to the literature of food technology and packaging.

CD-ROM DATABASES

Food Science and Technology Abstracts [CD-ROM]. Available from SilverPlatter Information, Inc. • Quarterly. $3,700 per year. Produced by International Food Information Service (home page is http://www.ifis.org). Provides worldwide coverage on CD-ROM of the literature of food technology and production. Various types of publications are indexed, with abstracts, including about 1,800 periodicals. Time period is 1969 to date.

World Marketing Forecasts on CD-ROM. The Gale Group. • Annual. $2,500.00. Produced by Euromonitor. Provides detailed forecast data for the years to 2012 on CD-ROM for 54 countries in all parts of the world. Covers a wide range of social, demographic, economic, and market factors. Includes specific forecasts for many kinds of consumer products.

DIRECTORIES

Beverage Industry - Annual Manual. Stagnito Communications, Inc. • Annual. $55.00. Provides statistical information on multiple beverage markets. Includes an industry directory. Supplement to *Beverage Industry.*

The Beverage Marketing Directory. Beverage Marketing Corp. • Annual. $845.00. Provides information for approximately 11,000 beverage companies and suppliers to beverage companies. Includes sales volume and brand names. Formerly *National Beverage Marketing Directory.*

Food Chemicals News Directory. Food Chemical News. CRC Press, Inc. • Semiannual. $497.00. Over 2,000 subsidiaries belonging to nearly 250 corporate parents plus an additional 3,000 independent processors. Formerly *Hereld's 1,500.*

Specialty Food Industry Directory. Phoenix Media Network, Inc. • Annual. Included in subscription to Food Distribution Magazine. Lists manufacturers and suppliers of specialty foods, and services and equipment for the specialty food industry. Featured food products include legumes, sauces, spices, upscale cheese, specialty beverages, snack foods, baked goods, ethnic foods, and specialty meats.

World Drinks Marketing Directory. Available from The Gale Group. • 2001. $1,090.00. Second edition. Published by Euromonitor. Provides detailed infromation on the leading beverage companies of the world, including specifi brand data.

FINANCIAL RATIOS

Industry Norms and Key Business Ratios. Desk Top Edition. Dun and Bradstreet Corp., Business Information Services. • Annual. Five volumes. $475.00 per volume. $1,890.00 per set. Covers over 800 kinds of businesses, arranged by Standard Industrial Classification number. More detailed editions covering longer periods of time are also available.

ONLINE DATABASES

Euromonitor Market Research. Euromonitor International. • Provides the complete text online of Euromonitor market analysis reports. Covers consumer goods market research data for all major countries, with emphasis on specific product categories. Time period is current. Continuous updating. Inquire as to online cost and availability.

Food Science and Technology Abstracts [online]. IFIS North American Desk. • Produced by International Food Information Service. Provides about 500,000 online citations, with abstracts, to the international literature of food science, technology, commodities, engineering, and processing. Approximately 2,000 periodicals are covered. Time period is 1969 to date, with monthly updates. Inquire as to online cost and availability.

FOODS ADLIBRA. General Mills, Inc. • Contains online citations, with abstracts, to the technical and business literature of food processing and packaging. New products and new ingredients are featured. Covers about 250 trade journals and 500 research journals from 1974 to date, with monthly updates. Inquire as to online cost and availability.

PERIODICALS AND NEWSLETTERS

Advertising Age: The International Newspaper of Marketing. Crain Communications, Inc. • Weekly. $109.00 per year. Includes supplement *Creativity.*

Beverage World: Magazine of the Beverage Industry. Bill Communications, Inc. • Monthly. $55.00 per year.

Food Distribution Magazine. Phoenix Media Network, Inc. • Monthly. $49.00 per year. Edited for marketers and buyers of domestic and imported, specialty or gourmet food products, including ethnic foods, seasonings, and bakery items.

Soft Drink Letter. Whitaker Newsletter, Inc. • Biweekly. $299.00 per year. For owners and managers of bottling operations. Covers soft drinks, juices. Formerly *Leisure Beverage Insider Newsletter.*

PRICE SOURCES

Beverage Industry News. BIN Publications. • Monthly. $49.00 per year. Incorporates *Beverage Industry News Merchandiser.*

Beverage Media. Beverage Media, Ltd. • Monthly. $78.00 per year. Wholesale prices.

PPI Detailed Report. Bureau of Labor Statistics, U.S. Department of Labor. Available from U.S. Government Printing Office. • Monthly. $55.00 per year. Formerly *Producer Price Indexes.*

STATISTICS SOURCES

Consumer Canada 1996. Available from The Gale Group. • 1996. $750.00. Published by Euromonitor. Provides consumer market, socioeconomic, and demographic data for Canada. Includes consumer market size (volume and value) for many specific kinds of products.

Consumer International 2000/2001. Available from The Gale Group. • 1998. $1,190.00. Seventh edition. Published by Euromonitor. Contains extensive consumer market, economic, and demographic data for 27 major, non-European countries, including the U. S. and Canada. Includes consumer market size (volume and value) for 150 product types in 14 categories (food, clothing, automobiles, cosmetics, appliances, etc.).

European Marketing Forecasts 2001. Available from The Gale Group. • 2000. $1,190.00. Third edition. Published by Euromonitor. Contains demographic, economic, and market forecasts for the countries of Europe to the year 2010. Forecasts include market-size data for 15 consumer product sectors (food, clothing, automobiles, consumer electronics, etc.).

Impact Beverage Trends in America. M. Shanken Communications, Inc. • Annual. $695.00. Detailed compilations of data for various segments of the liquor, beer, and soft drink industries.

International Marketing Forecasts 2001. Available from The Gale Group. • 2000. $1,090.00. Third edition. Published by Euromonitor. Contains demographic, economic, and market forecasts to the year 2010 for major, non-European countries, including the U. S. and Canada. Forecasts include market-size data for 15 consumer product sectors, such as food, clothing, and automobiles.

Standard & Poor's Industry Surveys. Standard & Poor's. • Semiannual. $1,800.00. Two looseleaf volumes. Includes monthly supplements. Provides detailed, individual surveys of 52 major industry groups. Each survey is revised on a semiannual basis. Also includes "Monthly Investment Review" (industry group investment analysis) and monthly "Trends & Projections" (economic analysis).

U. S. Industry and Trade Outlook: The McGraw-Hill Companies and the U.S. Department of Commerce/ International Trade Administration. Datapso Research Corp. • Annual. $69.95. Produced by the International Trade Administration, U. S. Department of Commerce, in a "public-private" partnership with DRI/McGraw-Hill and Standard & Poor's. Provides basic data, outlook for the current year, and "Long-Term Prospects" (five-year projections) for a wide variety of products and services. Includes high technology industries. Formerly *U. S. Industrial Outlook.*

United States Census of Manufactures. U.S. Bureau of the Census. • Quinquennial. Results presented in reports, tape, CD-ROM, and Diskette files.

TRADE/PROFESSIONAL ASSOCIATIONS

International Bottled Water Association. 1700 Diagonal Rd., Suite 650, Alexandria, VA 22314. Phone: (703)683-5213 Fax: (703)683-4074 • URL: http://www.bottledwater.org.

National Beverage Packaging Association. c/o Gary Lile, No. 1 Busch Place, OSC-2N, St. Louis, MO 63118. Phone: (314)577-2443 Fax: (314)577-2972 E-mail: gary.lileoanheuser-busch.com • Members are concerned with the packaging of soft drinks, beer, and juices.

National Soft Drink Association. 1101 16th St., N.W., Washington, DC 20036. Phone: (202)463-6732 Fax: (202)463-8178 E-mail: info@nsda.org • URL: http://www.nsda.org.

OTHER SOURCES

Fruit Juices. Available from MarketResearch.com. • 1998. $5,900.00. Published by Euromonitor Publications Ltd. Provides consumer market data and forecasts to 2002 for the United States, the United Kingdom, Germany, France, and Italy. Includes fresh, frozen, bottled, and canned fruit and vegetable juices.

Major Food and Drink Companies of the World. Available from The Gale Group. • 2001. $855.00. Fourth edition. Two volumes. Published by Graham & Whiteside. Contains profiles and trade names for more than 9,000 important food and beverage companies in various countries. In addition to foods, includes both alcoholic and nonalcoholic drink products.

Thomas Food and Beverage Market Place. Grey House Publishing. • Annual. $295.00. Three volumes. Contains more than 40,000 entries covering food companies, beverages, food equipment, warehouse companies, food brokers, wholesalers, importers, and exporters. Formerly *Thomas Food Industry Register.*

BIBLIOGRAPHY

See also: BOOK CATALOGS; BUSINESS LITERATURE

GENERAL WORKS

Bibliography Without Footnotes. Herbert H. Hoffman. Headway Publications. • 1978. $4.00. Second edition.

Elements of Bibliography: A Guide to Information Sources and Practical Applications. Robert B. Harmon. Scarecrow Press, Inc. • 1998. $49.50. Third edition.

Elements of Bibliography: A Simplified Approach. Robert B. Harmon. Scarecrow Press, Inc. • 1989. $37.00. Revised edition.

Introduction to the Study of Bibliography. H. Horne. Gordon Press Publishers. • 1976. $59.95.

New Introduction to Bibliography. Philip Gaskell. Oak Knoll Press. • 1996. $29.95.

Some Aspects of Bibliography. J. Ferguson. Gordon Press Publishers. • 1976. $59.95.

ABSTRACTS AND INDEXES

Bibliographic Index: A Subject List of Bibliographies in English and Foreign Languages.

H.W. Wilson Co. • Three issues a year. Third issues cumulates all three issues. Service basis.

CD-ROM DATABASES

Books in Print On Disc: The Complete Books in Print System on Compact Laser Disc. Bowker Electronic Publishing. • Monthly. $1195.00 per year. The CD-ROM version of *Books in Print, Forthcoming Books*, and other Bowker bibliographic publications: lists the books of over 50,000 U.S. publishers. Includes books recently declared out-of-print. Also available with full text book reviews.

CDMARC: Bibliographic. U. S. Library of Congress. • Quarterly. $1,340.00 per year. Provides bibliographic records on CD-ROM for over five million books cataloged by the Library of Congress since 1968. (MARC is Machine Readable Cataloging.).

LISA Plus: Library and Information Science Abstracts. Bowker-Saur, Reed Reference Publishing. • Quarterly. $1,450.00 per year. Provides CD-ROM abstracting and indexing of the world's library and information science literature. Covers a wide variety of topics.

World Database of Business Information Sources on CD-ROM. The Gale Group. • Annual. Produced by Euromonitor. Presents Euromonitor's entire information source database on CD-ROM. Contains a worldwide total of about 35,000 publications, organizations, libraries, trade fairs, and online databases.

ENCYCLOPEDIAS AND DICTIONARIES

Dictionary of Bibliometrics. Virgil Diodato. Haworth Press, Inc. • 1994. $39.95. Contains detailed explanations of 225 terms, with references. (Bibliometrics is "the application of mathematical and statistical techniques to the study of publishing and professional communication.").

HANDBOOKS AND MANUALS

The Chicago Manual of Style: The Essential Guide for Authors, Editors, and Publishers. University of Chicago Press. • 1993. $40.00. 14th edition.

A Manual of Bibliography. Walter T. Rogers. Gordon Press Publishers. • 1977. $75.00.

INTERNET DATABASES

Amazon.com. Amazon.com, Inc. Phone: 800-201-7575 or (206)346-2992 Fax: (206)346-2950 E-mail: info@amazon.com • URL: http://www.amazon.com • "Welcome to Earth's Biggest Bookstore." Amazon.com claims to have more than 2.5 million titles that can be ordered online, but only through the Web site - no orders by mail, telephone, fax, or E-mail. Discounts are generally 30% for hardcovers and 20% for paperbacks. Efficient search facilities, including Boolean, make this Web site useful for reference (many titles have online reviews). Fees: Free.

ONLINE DATABASES

Books in Print Online. Bowker Electronic Publishing. • The online version of *Books in Print, Forthcoming Books, Paperbound Books in Print*, and other Bowker bibliographic publications: lists the books of over 50,000 U. S. publishers. Includes books recently declared out-of-print. Updated monthly. Inquire as to online cost and availability.

LC MARC: Books. U. S. Library of Congress. • Contains online bibliographic records for over five million books cataloged by the Library of Congress since 1968. Updating is weekly or monthly. Inquire as to online cost and availability. (MARC is machine readable cataloging.).

LISA Online: Library and Information Science Abstracts. Bowker-Saur, Reed Reference Publishing. • Provides abstracting and indexing of the world's library and information science literature from 1969 to the present. Covers a wide variety of topics in over 550 journals from 60 countries, with biweekly updates. Inquire as to online cost and availability.

PERIODICALS AND NEWSLETTERS

Bulletin of Bibliography. Greenwood Publishing Group, Inc. • Quarterly. $115.00 per year.

Research Strategies: A Journal of Library Concepts and Instruction. JAI Press, Inc. • Quarterly. $135.00 per year. Edited for librarians involved in bibliographic or library instruction.

TRADE/PROFESSIONAL ASSOCIATIONS

Bibliographical Society of America. Lenox Hill Station, P.O. Box 1537, New York, NY 10021. Phone: (212)452-2710 Fax: (212)452-2710 E-mail: bsa@bibsocamer.org • URL: http://www.bibsocamer.org.

Bibliographical Society of the University of Virginia. c/o Penelope Weiss, University of Virginia, Alderman Library, Charlottesville, VA 22903. Phone: (804)924-7013 or (804)924-7951 Fax: (804)924-1431 E-mail: bibsoc@virginia.edu.

BICYCLE INDUSTRY

DIRECTORIES

Bicycle Dealer Showcase Buyers Guide. Skies America Publishing Co. • Annual. Free to qualified personnel.

Interbike Directory. Miller Freeman, Inc. • Annual. $75.00. Provides information on approximately 1,850 worldwide manufacturers and distributors of bicycles, parts, and accessories.

PERIODICALS AND NEWSLETTERS

American Bicyclist. Willow Publishing Co. • Monthly. Free to qualified personnel; others, $35.00 per year. Trade journal edited for bicycle retailers and wholesalers. Includes product reviews.

Bicycling. Rodale Press, Inc. • 11 times a year. $19.97 per year. Information on buying and repairing bicycles.

Outspokin'. National Bicycle Dealers Association. • Monthly. $100.00 per year. Association membership newsletter for bicycle retailers.

RESEARCH CENTERS AND INSTITUTES

Human Power, Biochemechanics, and Robotics Laboratory. Cornell University, Dept. of Theoretical and Applied Mechanics, 306 Kimball Hall, Ithaca, NY 14853. Phone: (607)255-7108 Fax: (607)255-2011 E-mail: ruina@cornell.edu • URL: http://www.tam.cornell.edu/~ruina • Conducts research relating to human muscle-powered machines, such as bicycles and rowers.

STATISTICS SOURCES

U. S. Industry and Trade Outlook: The McGraw-Hill Companies and the U.S. Department of Commerce/International Trade Administration. Datapso Research Corp. • Annual. $69.95. Produced by the International Trade Administration, U. S. Department of Commerce, in a "public-private" partnership with DRI/McGraw-Hill and Standard & Poor's. Provides basic data, outlook for the current year, and "Long-Term Prospects" (five-year projections) for a wide variety of products and services. Includes high technology industries. Formerly *U. S. Industrial Outlook.*

United States Census of Manufactures. U.S. Bureau of the Census. • Quinquennial. Results presented in reports, tape, CD-ROM, and Diskette files.

TRADE/PROFESSIONAL ASSOCIATIONS

Bicycle Product Suppliers Association. 1900 Arch St., Philadelphia, PA 19103-1498. Phone: (215)564-3484 Fax: (215)963-9785 E-mail: assnhqt@netaxs.com • URL: http://www.bpsa.org.

National Bicycle Dealers Association. 777 W. 19th St., Ste. 0, Costa Mesa, CA 92627. Phone: (949)722-6909 Fax: (949)722-1747 E-mail: bikeshops@aol.com • URL: http://www.nbda.com • Members are independent bicycle retailers.

OTHER SOURCES

Bicycles. Available from MarketResearch.com. • 1999. $1,295.00 Published by Specialists in Business Information, Inc. ProvidesU.S. and international market data for bicycles and bicycle parts. Gives profiles of major manufacturers.

BILLBOARDS

See: OUTDOOR ADVERTISING

BINDING OF BOOKS

See: BOOKBINDING

BIOENGINEERING

See: BIOTECHNOLOGY

BIOGRAPHY

ABSTRACTS AND INDEXES

Abridged Biography and Genealogy Master Index. The Gale Group. • 1995. $475.00. Second edition. Three volumes. Indexes 266 widely held biographical reference sources, with approximately 2.2 million citations. Based on the larger *Biography and Genealogy Master Index.*

Author Biographies Master Index. The Gale Group. • 1997. $290.00. Fith edition. Two volumes. Contains over 1,140,000 references tobiographies of 550,000 different authors.

Bio-Base: A Master Index on Microfiche to Biographical Sketches Found in Current and Retrospective Biographical Dictionaries. The Gale Group. • Annual. $1,095.00; update, $295.00. Indexes more than 12 million biographical sketches.

Biography and Genealogy Master Index. The Gale Group. • Annual. $270.00. Three volumes. Previous editions available.

Biography Index. H.W. Wilson Co. • Quarterly. $215.00 per year. Annual and biennial cumulations.

Index to Marquis Who's Who Publications. Marquis Who's Who. • Annual. $115.00. A combined index to current editions of most Marquis Who's Who publications. Contains over 320,000 entries.

BIOGRAPHICAL SOURCES

Almanac of Famous People. The Gale Group. • 2001. $140.00. Two volumes. Seventh edition. Contains about 30,000 short biographies, with bibliographic citations. Chronological, geographic, and occupational indexes. Formerly *Biography Almanac.*

American Men and Women of Science A Biographical Directory of Today's Leaders in Physical, Biological and Related Sciences. R. R. Bowker. • 1995. $900.00. Eight volumes. Over 119,600 United States and Canadian scientists active in the physical, biological, mathematical, computer science and engineering fields.

Canadian Who's Who. University of Toronto Press, Reverence Div. • Annual. $165.00. Provides concise biographical information in English and French on 15,000 prominent Canadians.

Celebrity Register. The Gale Group. • 1989. $99.00. Fifth edition. Compiled by Celebrity Services

International (Earl Blackwell). Contains profiles of 1,300 famous individuals in the performing arts, sports, politics, business, and other fields.

Contemporary Entrepreneurs: Profiles of Entrepreneurs and the Businesses They Started, Representing 74 Companies in 30 Industries. Craig E. Aronoff and John L. Ward, editors. Omnigraphics, Inc. • 1992. $95.00.

Current Biography. H. W. Wilson Co. • Monthly, except December. $78.00 per year. Includes profiles of business people and economists who have been prominent in the news.

Current Biography Yearbook. H. W. Wilson Co. • Annual. $69.00. The yearly cumulation of *Current Biography*.

Directory of American Scholars. The Gale Group. • 1999. $495.00. Ninth edition. Five volumes. Provides biographical information and publication history for more than 24,000 scholars in the humanities. Previously published (1942-1982) by R. R. Bowker.

Encyclopedia of World Biography. The Gale Group. • 1998. $995.00. Second edition. 17 volumes. Provides biographies of about 7,000 "internationally renowned" individuals from all eras and subject fields. Includes illustrations, bibliographies, and index. Formerly *McGraw-Hill Encyclopedia of World Biography* (1973).

Financial Post Directory of Directors. Financial Post Datagroup. • Annual. $159.95. Provides brief biographical information on 16,000 directors and key officers of Canadian companies who are also Canadian residents.

International Who's Who. The Gale Group. • Annual. $365.00. Provides up-to-date biographical information on important individuals in international affairs, government, diplomacy, the liberal professions, and all branches of the arts and sports. Published by Europa.

International Who's Who of Women. Available from Taylor and Francis, Inc. • 1997. $390.00. Second edition. Published by Europa. Contains biographical profiles of more than 5,000 eminent women from all countries.

Newsmakers. The Gale Group. • Annual. $145.00. Three softbound issues and one hardbound annual. Biographical information on individuals currently in the news. Includes photographs. Formerly *Contemporary Newsmakers*.

Who Knows Who: Networking Through Corporate Boards. Who Know Who Publishing. • 1994. $150.00. Fifth edition. Shows the connections between the board members of major U. S. corporations and major foundations and nonprofit organizations.

Who's Who Among African Americans. The Gale Group. • 2000. $175.00. 13th edition. Includes many business leaders.

Who's Who: An Annual Biographical Dictionary. St. Martin's Press, Inc. • Annual. $110.00. Over 29,000 prominent individuals worldwide, but with emphasis on the United Kingdom.

Who's Who in America. Marquis Who's Who. • Annual. Libraries, $575.00. Three volumes. Contains over 105,000 concise biographies, with a Geographic/Professional Index.

Who's Who in Canadian Business. Who's Who Publications. • Annual. $179.95. Contains brief biographies of 5,000 individuals prominent in Canadian business.

Who's Who in Finance and Industry. Marquis Who's Who. • Biennial. $295.00. Provides over 22,400 concise biographies of business leaders in all fields.

Who's Who in Science and Engineering. Marquis Who's Who. • Biennial. $269.00. Provides concise biographical information on 26,000 prominent engineers and scientists. International coverage, with geographical and professional indexes.

Who's Who in the World. Marquis Who's Who. • Annual. $379.95. Provides biographical profiles of about 40,000 prominent individuals. International coverage.

Who's Who of American Women. Marquis Who's Who. • Biennial. $259.00. Provides over 27,000 biographical profiles of important women, including individuals prominent in business, finance, and industry.

CD-ROM DATABASES

Complete Marquis Who's Who. Marquis Who's Who, Reed Reference Publishing. • Frequency and price on application. Contains CD-ROM biographical profiles of over 800,000 notable individuals. Includes *Who's Who in America, Who Was Who in America*, and 14 regional and professonal directories.

Current Biography on WILSONDISC. H. W. Wilson Co. • Annual. $189.00 ($129.00 renewal). Provides the most recent 12 years of *Current Biography* on CD-ROM.

WILSONDISC: Biography Index. H. W. Wilson Co. • Quarterly. $1,095.00 per year, including unlimited online access to *Biography Index* through WILSONLINE. Provides CD-ROM indexing of biographical information appearing in books, critical studies, fiction, periodicals, obituaries, and other printed sources. Time period is 1984 to date. Corresponds to the printed and online *Biography Index*.

DIRECTORIES

Cyberhound's Guide to People on the Internet. The Gale Group. • 1997. $79.00. Second edition. Provides descriptions of about 5,500 Internet databases maintained by or for prominent individuals in business, the professions, entertainment, and sports. Indexed by name, subject, and keyword (master index).

ENCYCLOPEDIAS AND DICTIONARIES

Dictionary of International Biography. Taylor & Francis, Inc. • 1996. $199.00. 24th edition.

Knowledge Exchange Business Encyclopedia: Your Complete Business Advisor. Lorraine Spurge, editor. Knowledge Exchange LLC. • 1997. $45.00. Provides definitions of business terms and financial expressions, profiles of leading industries, tables of economic statistics, biographies of business leaders, and other business information. Includes "A Chronology of Business from 3000 B.C. Through 1995." Contains illustrations and three indexes.

INTERNET DATABASES

GaleNet: Your Information Community. The Gale Group. Phone: 800-877-GALE or (248)699-GALE Fax: 800-414-5043 or (248)699-8069 E-mail: galenet@gale.com • URL: http://www.galenet.com • Web site provides a wide variety of full-text information from Gale databases, Taft, and other sources. Covers associations, biography, business directories, education, the information industry, literature, publishing, and science. Fee-based subscriptions are available for individual databases (free demonstration). Includes Boolean search features and the BRS/Search user interface.

ONLINE DATABASES

Biography Index Online. H. W. Wilson Co. • An index to biographies appearing in periodicals, newspapers, current books, and other sources. Covers 1984 to date. Inquire as to online cost and availability.

Biography Master Index [Online]. The Gale Group. • An index to biographies appearing in hundreds of biographical reference volumes, both historical and current. Inquire as to online cost and availability.

Gale Biographies. The Gale Group. • Provides online biographical profiles (text) of more than 140,000 prominent individuals, past and present, from all fields of activity. Corresponds to various Gale print sources. Quarterly updates. Inquire as to online cost and availability.

Marquis Who's Who Online. Marquis Who's Who, Reed Reference Publishing. • Contains information on over 825,000 prominent individuals, present and past. Semiannual updates. Inquire as to online cost and availability.

The New York Times Biographical File. New York Times Online Services. • Makes available online the full text of more than 15,000 biographies that have appeared in *The New York Times* from 1980 to the present. Updating is weekly. Inquire as to online cost and availability.

Standard & Poor's Register: Biographical. Standard & Poor's Corp. • Contains brief biographies of approximately 70,000 business executives and directors. Corresponds to the biographical volume of *Standard & Poor's Register of Corporations, Directors, and Executives*. Updated twice a year. Inquire as to online cost and availability.

PERIODICALS AND NEWSLETTERS

Biography: An Interdisciplinary Quarterly. Biographical Research Center. University of Hawaii Press Journals Dept. • Quarterly. Individuals, $28.00 per year; institutions, $40.00 per year.

The New York Times Biographical Service. UMI. • Monthly. Price on application.

TRADE/PROFESSIONAL ASSOCIATIONS

New York Genealogical and Biographical Society. 122 E. 58th St., New York, NY 10022-1939. Phone: (212)755-8532 Fax: (212)754-4218 • URL: http://www.nygbs.org.

OTHER SOURCES

American Business Leaders: From Colonial Times to the Present. Neil A. Hamilton. ABC-CLIO, Inc. • 1999. $150.00. Two volumes. Contains biographies of 413 notable business figures. Historical coverage is from the 17th century to the 1990s.

net.people: The Personalities and Passions Behind the Web Sites. Eric C. Steinert and Thomas E. Bleier. Information Today, Inc. • 2000. $19.95. Presents the personal stories of 36 Web "entrepreneurs and visionaries." (CyberAge Books.).

BIOTECHNOLOGY

See also: GENETIC ENGINEERING

GENERAL WORKS

Biotechnology. John E. Smith. Cambridge University Press. • 1996. $59.95. Third edition. Provides discussions of biotechnology in relation to medicine, agriculture, food, the environment, biological fuel generation, genetics, ethics, safety, etc. Includes a glossary and bibliography. (Studies in Biology Series).

Introduction to Biotechnology: Demystifying the Concepts. David B. Bourgaize. Addison-Wesley Longman, Inc. • 1999. $63.00.

ABSTRACTS AND INDEXES

Agricultural and Environmental Biotechnology Abstracts. Cambridge Information Group. • Bimonthly. $345.00 per year. Formerly *Biotechnology Research Abstracts*.

Applied Science and Technology Index. H. W. Wilson Co. • 11 times a year. Quarterly and annual cumulations. Service basis for print edition; CD-ROM edition, $1,495.00 per year. Indexes a wide variety of English language technical, industrial, and engineering periodicals.

BioCommerce Abstracts. Biocommerce Data, Ltd. • Semimonthly. $2,715 per year. Quarterly cumulation. Includes CD-Rom. Emphasis is on commercial biotechnology.

Current Biotechnology. The Royal Society of Chemistry. Publications Expediting, Inc. • Monthly. $1,229.00 per year. Reports on the latest scientific, technical and commercial advances in the field of technology. Formerly *Current Biotechnology Abstracts.*

Current Contents: Engineering, Computing and Technology. Institute for Scientific Information. • Weekly. $730.00 per year. Reproductions of contents pages of technical journals. Includes *Author Index, Address Directory, Current Book Contents* and *Title Word Index.* Formerly *Current Contents: Engineering, Technology and Applied Sciences.*

Excerpta Medica: Biophysics, Bioengineering, and Medical Instrumentation. Elsevier Science. • 16 times a year. $2,207.00 per year. Section 27 of *Excerpta Medica.*

Index Medicus. National Library of Medicine. Available from U. S. Government Printing Office. • Monthly. $522.00 per year. Bibliographic listing of references to current articles from approximately 3,000 of the world's biomedical journals.

NTIS Alerts: Biomedical Technology & Human Factors Engineering. National Technical Information Service. • Semimonthly. $210.00 per year. Provides descriptions of government-sponsored research reports and software, with ordering information. Covers biotechnology, ergonomics, bionics, artificial intelligence, prosthetics, and related subjects. Formerly *Abstract Newsletter.*

Science Citation Index. Institute for Scientific Information. • Bimonthly. $15,020.00 per year. Annual cumulation. Includes *Source Index, Citation Index, Permuterm Subject Index,* and *Corporate Index.*

ALMANACS AND YEARBOOKS

Annual Review of Biophysics and Biomolecular Structure. Annual Reviews, Inc. • Annual. $70.00. Formerly *Annual Review of Biophysics and Bioengineering.*

Plunkett's Biotech and Genetics Industry Almanac. Plunkett Research, Ltd. • Annual. $199.99. Provides detailed profiles of 400 leading biotech corporations. Includes information on current trends and research in the field of biotechnology/genetics.

BIBLIOGRAPHIES

Aslib Book Guide: A Monthly List of Recommended Scientific and Technical Books. Available from Information Today, Inc. • Monthly. Members, $164.00 per year; non-members, $204.00 per year. Published in London by Aslib: The Association for Information Management. Formerly *Aslib Book List.*

Information Sources in the Life Sciences. H. V. Wyatt, editor. Bowker-Saur. • 1997. $95.00. Fourth edition. Includes an evaluation of biotechnology information sources. (Guides to Information Sources Series).

BIOGRAPHICAL SOURCES

Dictionary of American Medical Biography. Martin Kaufman and others. Greenwood Publishing Group Inc. • 1984. $195.00. Two volumes. Vol. one, $100.00; vol. two, $100.00.

Who's Who in Science and Engineering. Marquis Who's Who. • Biennial. $269.00. Provides concise biographical information on 26,000 prominent engineers and scientists. International coverage, with geographical and professional indexes.

CD-ROM DATABASES

BioMed Strategies. Thomson Financial Securities Data. • Monthly. $2,995.00 per year. CD-ROM contains full text of investment analysts' reports on companies operating in the following fields: biotechnology, pharmaceuticals, medical products, and health care.

Biotechnology Abstracts on CD-ROM. Derwent, Inc. • Quarterly. Price on application. Provides CD-ROM indexing and abstracting of the world's biotechnology journal literature since 1982, including genetic engineering topics.

CSA Life Sciences Collection [CD-ROM]. Cambridge Scientific Abstracts. • Quarterly. Includes CD-ROM versions of *Biotechnology Research Abstracts, Entomology Abstracts, Genetics Abstracts,* and about 20 other abstract collections.

Science Citation Index: Compact Disc Edition. Institute for Scientific Information. • Quarterly. Provides CD-ROM indexing of the world's scientific and technical literature. Corresponds to online *Scisearch* and printed *Science Citation Index.*

WILSONDISC: Biological and Agricultural Index. H. W. Wilson Co. • Monthly. $1,495.00 per year, including unlimited online access to *Biological and Agricultural Index* through WILSONLINE. Provides CD-ROM indexing of over 250 periodicals covering agriculture, agricultural chemicals, biochemistry, biotechnology, entomology, horticulture, and related topics.

DIRECTORIES

BioScan: The Worldwide Biotech Industry Reporting Service. American Health Consultants, Inc. • Bimonthly. $1,395.00 per year. Looseleaf. Provides detailed information on over 900 U. S. and foreign companies broadly classified as biotechnological. In addition to medical technology and advanced pharmaceutical firms, includes firms doing research in food processing, waste management, agriculture, and veterinary science.

Biotechnology Directory. Grove's Dictionaries Inc. • Annual. $295.00. Provides information on more than 10,000 biotechnology-related companies and organizations. Geographical arrangement, with name and product indexes.

Genetic Engineering and Biotechnology Firms Worldwide Directory. Mega-Type Publishing. • Annual. $299.00. About 6,000 firms, including major firms with biotechnology divisions as well as small independent firms.

International Instrumentation and Controls Buyers Guide. Keller International Publishing, LLC. • Annual. Controlled circulation. Lists over 310 suppliers of precision instrument products and services.

Medical and Health Information Directory. The Gale Group. • 1999. $630.00. Three volumes. 12th edition. Vol. one covers medical organizations, agencies, and institutions; vol. two includes bibliographic, library, and database information; vol. three is a guide to services available for various medical and health problems.

Medical Research Centres: A World Directory of Organizations and Programmes. Allyn and Bacon/ Longman. • Irregular. $535.00. Two volumes. Contains profiles of about 7,000 medical research facilities around the world. Includes medical, dental, nursing, pharmaceutical, psychiatric, and surgical research centers.

ENCYCLOPEDIAS AND DICTIONARIES

Biotechnology from A to Z. William Bains. Oxford University Press, Inc. • 1998. $27.95. Second edition. Covers the terminology of biotechnology for non-specialists.

INTERNET DATABASES

National Library of Medicine (NLM). National Institutes of Health (NIH). Phone: 888-346-3656 or (301)496-1131 Fax: (301)480-3537 E-mail: access@nlm.nih.gov • URL: http://www.nlm.nih.gov • NLM Web site offers free access through MEDLINE ("PubMed") to about nine million references to articles appearing in some 3,800 biomedical journals, with abstracts. Search interfaces range from "simple keywords to advanced Boolean expressions." The NLM site offers many links to other sources of biomedical and technical information (the National Center for Biotechnology Information, for example). Fees: Free.

ONLINE DATABASES

Applied Science and Technology Index Online. H. W. Wilson Co. • Provides online indexing of 400 major scientific, technical, industrial, and engineering periodicals. Time period is 1983 to date. Monthly updates. Inquire as to online cost and availability.

CSA Life Sciences Collection. Cambridge Scientific Abstracts. • Includes online versions of *Biotechnology Research Abstracts, Entomology Abstracts, Genetics Abstracts,* and about 20 other abstract collections. Time period is 1978 to date, with monthly updates. Inquire as to online cost and availability.

Derwent Biotechnology Abstracts. Derwent, Inc. • Provides indexing and abstracting of the world's biotechnology journal literature since 1982, including genetic engineering topics. Monthly updates. Inquire as to online cost and availability.

F-D-C Reports. FDC Reports, Inc. • An online version of "The Gray Sheet" (medical devices), "The Pink Sheet" (pharmaceuticals), "The Rose Sheet" (cosmetics), "The Blue Sheet" (biomedical), and "The Tan Sheet" (nonprescription). Contains full-text information on legal, technical, corporate, financial, and marketing developments from 1987 to date, with weekly updates. Inquire as to online cost and availability.

Globalbase. The Gale Group. • Provides more than one million online summaries of business, industrial, and economic news reports from more than 1,000 publications worldwide. Covers a wide range of material appearing in international trade journals, professional magazines, and newspapers. Time period is 1984 to date, with weekly updates. Inquire as to online cost and availability.

PROMT: Predicasts Overview of Markets and Technology. The Gale Group. • Companies, products, applied technologies and markets. U.S. and international literature coverage, 1972 to date. Inquire as to online cost and availability. Provides abstracts from more than 1,600 publications. Weekly updates.

Scisearch. Institute for Scientific Information. • Broad, multidisciplinary index to the literature of science and technology, 1974 to present. Inquire as to online cost and availability. Coverage of literature is worldwide, with weekly updates.

PERIODICALS AND NEWSLETTERS

Applied Genetics News. Business Communications Co., Inc. • Monthly. $415.00 per year. Newsletter on research developments.

Biomedical Instrumentation and Technology. Association for the Advancement of Medical Instrumentation. Hanley and Belfus, Inc. • Bimonthly. Individuals, $106.00 per year; institutions, $136.00 per year.

Biomedical Products. Cahners Business Information, New Product Information. • Monthly. $43.90 per year. Features new products and services.

Bioscience. American Institute of Biological Sciences. • Monthly. Members, $70.00 per year; institutions, $190.00 per year.

BioTechniques: The Journal of Laboratory Technology for Bioresearch. Eaton Publishing. • 12 times a year. $110.00 per year.

BioWorld Today: The Daily Biotechnology Newspaper. American Health Consultants, Inc., BioWorld Publishing Group. • Daily. $1,897.00 per year. Covers news of the biotechnology and genetic engineering industries, with emphasis on finance, investments, and marketing.

BioWorld Week: The Weekly Biotechnology Report. American Health Consultants, Inc., BioWorld Publishing Group. • Weekly. $747.00 per year. Provides a weekly summary of business and financial news relating to the biotechnology and genetic engineering industries.

Changing Medical Markets: The Monthly Newsletter for Executives in the Healthcare and Biotechnology Industries. Theta Reports/PJB Medical Publications, Inc. • Monthly. $295.00 per year. Newsletter. Covers developments in medical technology, new products, corporate trends, medical market research, mergers, personnel, and other healthcare topics.

Genetic Engineering News: The Information Source of the Biotechnology Industry. Mary Ann Liebert, Inc. • Biweekly. Institutions, $397.00 per year. Newsletter. Business and financial coverage.

Genetic Technology News. Technical Insights. • 51 times a year. $885.00 per year. Reports on genetic engineering and its uses in the chemical, pharmaceutical, food processing and energy industries as well as in agriculture, animal breeding and medicine. Includes three supplements: *Patent Update*, *Strategic Partners Reports*, and *Market Forecasts*.

Health News Daily. F-D-C Reports, Inc. • Daily. $1,350.00 per year. Newsletter providing broad coverage of the healthcare business, including government policy, regulation, research, finance, and insurance. Contains news of pharmaceuticals, medical devices, biotechnology, and healthcare delivery in general.

Health Policy and Biomedical Research: The Blue Sheet. F-D-C Reports, Inc. • 51 Times a year. $619.00 per year. Newsletter. Emphasis is on news of medical research agencies and institutions, especially the National Institutes of Health (NIH).

IEEE Engineering in Medicine and Biology Magazine. Institute of Electrical and Electronics Engineers, Inc. • Bimonthly. $176.00 per year. Published for biomedical engineers.

Journal of Biotechnology. Elsevier Science. • 25 times a year. $2,758.00 per year. Text and summaries in English.

Journal of Chemical Technology and Biotechnology. John Wiley and Sons, Inc. Journals Div. • Monthly. Institutions, $1,275.00 per year.

McGraw-Hill's Biotechnology Newswatch. McGraw-Hill Chemical Engineering Div. • Semimonthly. $825.00 per year. Newsletter.

Prescription Pharmaceuticals and Biotechnology: The Pink Sheet. F-D-C Reports, Inc. • Weekly. $1,170 per year. Newsletter covering business and regulatory developments affecting the pharmaceutical and biotechnology industries. Provides information on generic drug approvals and includes a drug sector stock index.

RESEARCH CENTERS AND INSTITUTES

Biotechnology Process Engineering Center. Massachusetts Institute of Technology, 77 Massachusetts Ave., Room 16-429, Cambridge, MA 02139-4307. Phone: (617)253-0805 Fax: (617)253-2400 E-mail: childs@mit.edu • URL: http://www.web.mit.edu/bpec/ • Includes an Industrial Advisory Board and a Biotechnology Industrial Consortium.

Laboratory of Electronics. Rockefeller University, 1230 York Ave., New York, NY 10021. Phone: (212)327-8613 Fax: (212)327-7613 E-mail: ros@rockvax.rockefeller.edu • Studies the application of computer engineering and electronics to biomedicine.

Laser Biomedical Research Center. Massachusetts Institute of Technology, 77 Massachusetts Ave., Cambridge, MA 02139. Phone: (617)253-7700 Fax: (617)253-4513 E-mail: msfeld@mit.edu • URL: http://www.web.mit.edu/spectroscopy/www/staff/msfeld.html • Concerned with the medical use of lasers.

Mayo Biomedical Imaging Resource. Mayo Clinic, 200 First St., S. W., Rochester, MN 55902. Phone: (507)284-4937 Fax: (507)284-1632 E-mail: rar@mayo.edu • URL: http://www.mayo.edu/bir • Develops three-dimensional medical imaging systems and software.

Molecular Biology Institute. University of California, Los Angeles, 405 Hilgard Ave., Los Angeles, CA 90024-1570. Phone: (310)825-1018 Fax: (310)206-7286 E-mail: berk@.mbi.ucla.edu • URL: http://www.mbi.ucla.edu.

Salk Institute for Biological Studies. P.O. Box 85800, San Diego, CA 92186-5800. Phone: (858)453-4100 Fax: (858)552-8285 E-mail: pollard@salk.edu • URL: http://www.salk.edu.

STATISTICS SOURCES

Standard & Poor's Industry Surveys. Standard & Poor's. • Semiannual. $1,800.00. Two looseleaf volumes. Includes monthly supplements. Provides detailed, individual surveys of 52 major industry groups. Each survey is revised on a semiannual basis. Also includes "Monthly Investment Review" (industry group investment analysis) and monthly "Trends & Projections" (economic analysis).

TRADE/PROFESSIONAL ASSOCIATIONS

American Institute for Medical and Biological Engineering. 1901 Pennsylvania Ave., N.W., Suite 401, Washington, DC 20006. Phone: (202)496-9660 Fax: (202)466-8489.

American Institute of Biological Sciences. 1444 Eye St., N.W., Suite 200, Washington, DC 20005-2210. Phone: (202)628-1500 Fax: (202)628-1509 E-mail: jkolber@aibs.org • URL: http://www.aibs.org.

Biomedical Engineering Society. 8401 Corporate Dr., Ste. 110, Landover, MD 20785-2224. Phone: (301)459-1999 Fax: (301)459-2444 E-mail: bmes@netcom.com • URL: http://www.bmes.org.

Biotechnology Industry Organization. 1625 K St., N.W., Suite 1100, Washington, DC 20006. Phone: 800-255-3304 or (202)857-0244 Fax: (202)857-0237 E-mail: info@bio.org • URL: http://wwww.bio.org.

Institute of Electrical and Electronics Engineers; Engineering in Medicine and Biology Society. Three Park Ave., 17th Fl., New York, NY 10016-5997. Phone: (212)419-7900 Fax: (212)752-4929 • URL: http://www.ieee.org.

Special Interest Group on Biomedical Computing. Association for Computing Machinery, 1515 Broadway, New York, NY 10036. Phone: (212)869-7440 Fax: (212)302-5826 E-mail: sigs@acm.org • URL: http://www.acm.org/sigbio • Concerned with medical informatics, molecular databases, medical multimedia, and computerization in general as related to the health and biological sciences.

OTHER SOURCES

Biotechnology and the Law. Iver P. Cooper. West Group. • Two looseleaf volumes. $260.00. per year. Periodic supplementation.

Biotechnology Instrumentation Markets. Theta Reports/PJB Medical Publications, Inc. • 1999. $1,495.00. Contains market research data, with projections through the year 2002. Covers such products as specialized analytical instruments, filters/membranes, and mass spectrometers. (Theta Report No. 960.).

Global Seed Markets. Theta Reports/PJB Medical Publications, Inc. • 2000. $1,040.00. Market research data. Covers the major seed sectors, including cereal crops, legumes, oilseed crops, fibre crops, and beet crops. Provides analysis of biotechnology developments. (Theta Report No. DS208E.).

New and Breaking Technologies in the Pharmaceutical and Medical Device Industries. Theta Reports/PJB Medical Publications, Inc. • 1999. $1,695.00. Market research data. Includes forecasts of medical technology and drug developments to 2005-2010.

BIRTH CERTIFICATES

See: VITAL STATISTICS

BIRTHS AND DEATHS

See: VITAL STATISTICS

BITUMINOUS COAL

See: COAL INDUSTRY

BLACK BUSINESS

See: MINORITY BUSINESS

BLACK CONSUMERS

See: MINORITY MARKETS

BLACK NEWSPAPERS

See: MINORITY NEWSPAPERS

BLOOD PRESSURE

See: HYPERTENSION

BLUE COLLAR THEFT

See: CRIME AND CRIMINALS; FRAUD AND EMBEZZLEMENT

BLUE COLLAR WORKERS

See: LABOR

BLUE SKY LAW

See: SECURITIES LAW AND REGULATION

BOARDING SCHOOLS

See: PRIVATE SCHOOLS

BOARDS OF DIRECTORS

See: CORPORATE DIRECTORS AND OFFICERS

BOARDS OF TRADE

See: CHAMBERS OF COMMERCE

BOAT INDUSTRY

See also: MARINAS; SHIPS, SHIPPING AND SHIPBUILDING

ALMANACS AND YEARBOOKS

Pacific Boating Almanac. ProStar Publications, Inc. • Annual. $24.95 per volume. Three volumes. Volume one, *Pacific Northwest*; volume two, *Northern California and the Delta*; volume three *Southern California and Mexico.* Lists over 3,000 marine facilities serving recreational boating.

DIRECTORIES

National Marine Representatives Association-Directory. National Marine Representatives Association. • Annual. Membership. Approximately 400 independent representatives selling pleasure craft and other small boats, motors, and marine accessories.

Sailboat Buyers Guide. Commonwealth Business Media. • Annual. $5.95. Over 2,000 Sailboat and equipment manufacturers. Formerly *Sailboat and Equipment and Shipbuilding.*

FINANCIAL RATIOS

Almanac of Business and Industrial Financial Ratios. Leo Troy. Prentice Hall. • Annual. $99.95. Contains financial ratios derived from federal tax returns. Ratios for each of about 200 industries are arranged according to company asset size.

Annual Statement Studies. Robert Morris Associates: The Association of Lending and Credit Risk Professiona. • Annual. Free to members; non-members, $140.00. Median and quartile financial ratios are given for over 400 kinds of manufacturing, wholesale, retail, construction, and consumer finance establishments. Data is sorted by both asset size and sales volume. Includes a clearly written "Definition of Ratios" and an alphabetical industry index.

ONLINE DATABASES

Magazine Index. The Gale Group. • General magazine indexing (popular literature), 1973 to present. Daily updates. Inquire as to online cost and availability.

PERIODICALS AND NEWSLETTERS

America's Western Boating Magazine. Sailing Co. • 10 times a year. $28.00 per year. Covers the thirteen Western United States; British Columbia, Canada, and the West Coast of Mexico.

Boat and Motor Dealer. Preston Publications, Inc. • Monthly. $48.00. Boat retailing.

Boating. Hachette Filipacchi Magazines, Inc. • Monthly. $28.00 per year.

Boating Industry: The Management Magazine of the Boating Industry. Intertec Publishing Corp. • Monthly. $38.00 per year. Supplement available: *Boating Industry Marine Buyer's Guide.*

Lookout. National Boating Federation. • Bimonthly. Membership.

Vapor Trail's Boating News and International Yachting and Cruiser and Manufacturers Report. Gemini Productions, Ltd. • Monthly. $24.00 per year.

PRICE SOURCES

NADA Marine Appraisal Guide. National Automobile Dealers Association. N.A.D.A. Appraisal Guides. • Three times a year. $100.00 per year. Formerly *NADA Small Boat Appraisal Guide.*

Used Boat Price Guide. BUC International Corp. • Semiannual. Three volumes. Formerly *Older Boat Price Guide.*

STATISTICS SOURCES

Annual Survey of Manufactures. Available from U. S. Government Printing Office. • Annual. Prices vary. Issued by the U. S. Census Bureau as an interim update to the *Census of Manufactures.* Includes data on number of manufacturing establishments in various industries, employment, labor costs, value of shipments, capital expenditures, inventories, energy costs, and assets. (See also Census Bureau home page, http://www.census.gov/.).

U. S. Industry and Trade Outlook: The McGraw-Hill Companies and the U.S. Department of Commerce/International Trade Administration. Datapso Research Corp. • Annual. $69.95. Produced by the International Trade Administration, U. S. Department of Commerce, in a "public-private" partnership with DRI/McGraw-Hill and Standard & Poor's. Provides basic data, outlook for the current year, and "Long-Term Prospects" (five-year projections) for a wide variety of products and services. Includes high technology industries. Formerly *U. S. Industrial Outlook.*

TRADE/PROFESSIONAL ASSOCIATIONS

American Boat and Yacht Council. 3069 Solomons Island Rd., Edgewater, MD 21037-1416. Phone: (410)956-1050 Fax: (410)956-2737 E-mail: info@abycinc.org.

American Boat Builders and Repairers Association. 425 E. 79th St., No. 11B, New York, NY 10021-1006. Phone: (212)396-4246 Fax: (212)396-4243 E-mail: abbra2@aol.com • URL: http://www.abbrayacht.com.

Association of Marine Engine Manufacturers. c/o David Broome, 1819 L St., N. W., Ste. 700, Washington, DC 20036-3830. Phone: (202)861-1180 Fax: (202)861-1181.

Boat Owners Association of the United States. 880 S. Pickett St., Alexandria, VA 22304. Phone: 800-937-9307 or (703)823-9550 Fax: (703)461-2847 • URL: http://www.boatus.com.

National Marine Manufacturers Association. 200 E. Randolph Dr., Suite 5100, Chicago, IL 60601. Phone: (312)946-6200 Fax: (312)946-0388 • URL: http://www.nmma.org.

National Marine Representatives Association. P.O. Box 360, Gurnee, IL 60031. Phone: (847)662-3167 Fax: (847)336-7126.

OTHER SOURCES

Pleasure Boats. Available from MarketResearch.com. • 1997. $1,495.00. Market research report published by Specialists in Business Information. Covers inboard, outboard, sterndrive, sail, inflatable, personal watercraft, and canoes.

BOILERS

See: HEATING AND VENTILATION

BONDS

See also: GOVERNMENT BONDS; MUNICIPAL BONDS

GENERAL WORKS

AAA Rated: Unscrambling the Bond Market. Lydia LaFaro. Reference & User Services Association (RUSA). • 1997. $20.00. Provides basic information on various kinds of bonds and their ratings. Includes a "comprehensive glossary of terms related to the bond market." (RUSA Occasional Papers Series, No. 22.).

Fixed-Income Investment: Recent Research. Thomas S. Ho, editor. McGraw-Hill Professional. • 1994. $65.00. Discusses bond portfolio management, the yield curve, bond pricing methods, and related subjects.

Investing During Retirement: The Vanguard Guide to Managing Your Retirement Assets. Vanguard Group. McGraw-Hill Professional. • 1996. $17.95. A basic, general guide to investing after retirement. Covers pension plans, basic principles of investing, types of mutual funds, asset allocation, retirement income planning, social security, estate planning, and contingencies. Includes glossary and worksheets for net worth, budget, and income.

Investing in the Over-the-Counter Markets: Stocks, Bonds, IPOs. Alvin D. Hall. John Wiley and Sons, Inc. • 1995. $29.95. Provides advice and information on investing in "unlisted" or NASDAQ (National Association of Securities Dealers Automated Quotation System) stocks, bonds, and initial public offerings (IPOs).

Understanding Corporate Bonds. Harold Kerzner. McGraw-Hill Professional. • 1990. $24.95. A general introduction to investing in corporate bonds. Includes a discussion of high-risk (junk) bonds.

ABSTRACTS AND INDEXES

Investment Statistics Locator. Linda H. Bentley and Jennifer J. Kiesl, editors. Oryx Press. • 1994. $69.95. Expanded revised edition. Provides detailed subject indexing of more than 50 of the most-used sources of financial and investment data. Includes an annotated bibliography.

ALMANACS AND YEARBOOKS

Fixed Income Almanac: The Bond Investor's Compendium of Key Market, Product, and Performance Data. Livingston G. Douglas. McGraw-Hill Professional. • 1993. $75.00. Presents 20 years of data in 350 graphs and charts. Covers bond market volatility, yield spreads, high-yield (junk) corporate bonds, default rates, and other items, such as Federal Reserve policy.

DIRECTORIES

Corporate Bond Desk Reference: U. S. Buyside and Sellside Profiles. Capital Access International. • Annual. $395.00. Provides "detailed buyside and sellside profiles and contacts" for the the corporate bond market. (Desk Reference Series, volume one.).

Moody's Municipal and Government Manual. Financial Information Services. • Annual. $2,495.00 per year. Updated biweekly in *News Reports.*

Mortgage & Asset-Based Desk Reference: U. S. Buyside and Sellside Profiles. Capital Access International. • Annual. $395.00. Provides "detailed buyside and sellside profiles and contacts" for the mortgage and asset-based securities market.

Standard and Poor's Corporate Registered Bond Interest Record. Standard and Poor's. • Annual. $2,600.00 per year. Weekly updates.

Standard and Poor's Directory of Bond Agents. Standard and Poor's. • Bimonthly. $1,075.00 per year.

Value Line Options: the All-in-One Service for Listed Options. Value Line, Inc. • Weekly. $445.00 per year. Formerly *Value Line Option and Convertible Survey.*

ENCYCLOPEDIAS AND DICTIONARIES

The A-Z Vocabulary for Investors. American Institute for Economic Research. • 1997. $7.00. Second half of book is a "General Glossary" of about 400 financial terms "most-commonly used" in investing. First half contains lengthier descriptions of types of banking institutions (commercial banks, thrift institutions, credit unions), followed by succinct explanations of various forms of investment: stocks, bonds, options, futures, commodities, and "Other Investments" (collectibles, currencies, mortgages, precious metals, real estate, charitable trusts). (Economic Education Bulletin.).

Blackwell Encyclopedic Dictionary of Finance. Dean Paxson and Douglas Wood, editors. Blackwell Publishers. • 1997. $110.00. The editors are associated with the University of Manchester. Contains definitions of key terms combined with longer articles written by various U. S. and foreign business educators. Includes bibliographies and index. (Blackwell Encyclopedia of Management Series).

Dictionary of Finance and Investment Terms. John Downes and Jordan E. Goodman. Barron's Educational Series, Inc. • 1998. $12.95. Fifth revised edition. Provides clear explanations of more than 5,000 business, banking, financial, investment, and tax terms. Includes a separate list of financial abbreviations and acronyms.

HANDBOOKS AND MANUALS

Convertible Securities: The Latest Instruments, Portfolio Strategies, and Valuation Analysis. John P. Calamos. McGraw-Hill Professional. • 1998. $65.00. Second edition.

Dynamic Asset Allocation: Strategies for the Stock, Bond, and Money Markets. David A. Hammer. John Wiley and Sons, Inc. • 1991. $49.95. A practical guide to the distribution of investment portfolio funds among various kinds of assets. (Finance Editions Series).

Fixed Income Analytics: State-of-the-Art Analysis and Valuation Modeling. Ravi E. Dattatreya, editor. McGraw-Hill Professional. • 1991. $69.95. Discusses the yield curve, structure and value in corporate bonds, mortgage-backed securities, and other topics.

Fixed Income Mathematics: Analytical and Statistical Techniques. Frank J. Fabozzi. McGraw-Hill Professional. • 1996. $60.00. Third edition. Covers the basics of fixed income analysis, as well as more advanced techniques used for complex securities.

Handbook of Fixed Income Securities. Frank J. Fabozzi. McGraw-Hill Higher Education. • 2000. $99.95. Sixth edition. Topics include risk measurement, valuation techniques, and portfolio strategy.

Introduction to Option-Adjusted Spread Analysis. Tom Windas. Bloomberg Press. • 1996. $40.00. Discusses the limitations of traditional, yield-based, risk and return analysis of bonds. (Bloomberg Professional Library.).

Kiss Your Stockbroker Goodbye: A Guide to Independent Investing. John G. Wells. St. Martin's Press. • 1997. $25.95. The author believes that the small investor is throwing money away by using full-commission brokers when discount brokers and many sources of information are easily available. Contains separate chapters on stocks, bonds, mutual funds, asset allocation, financial planners, and related topics. Wells is a securities analyst (CFA) and portfolio manager.

Municipal Bonds: The Comprehensive Review of Municipal Securities and Public Finance. Robert Lamb and Stephen Rappaport. McGraw-Hill. • 1987. $34.95.

INTERNET DATABASES

DBC Online: America's Leading Provider of Real-Time Market Data to the Individual Investor. Data Broadcasting Corp. Phone: (415)571-1800 E-mail: dbcinfo@dbc.com • URL: http://www.dbc.com • Web site provides a wide variety of real-time securities market prices, data, and charts. Covers bonds ("BondVu"), stocks, commodities, options, mutual funds, major indexes, industry indexes, international markets, etc. Also includes news, SEC documents ("Smart-Edgar"), and various other features. Fees: Both free and fee-based, depending on level of information.

Fedstats. Federal Interagency Council on Statistical Policy. Phone: (202)395-7254 • URL: http://www.fedstats.gov • Web site features an efficient search facility for full-text statistics produced by more than 70 federal agencies, including the Census Bureau, the Bureau of Economic Analysis, and the Bureau of Labor Statistics. Boolean searches can be made within one agency or for all agencies combined. Links are offered to international statistical bureaus, including the UN, IMF, OECD, UNESCO, Eurostat, and 20 individual countries. Fees: Free.

Thomson Investors Network. Thomson Financial. Phone: (212)807-3800 • URL: http://thomsoninvest.net • Web site provides detailed data on insider trading, institutional portfolios, and "First Call" earnings estimates. Includes a stock screening (filtering) application, a search facility, and price quotes on stocks, bonds, and mutual funds. Continuous updating. Fees: $34.95 per year for general service. First Call earnings service is $19.95 per month or $199.00 per year.

Thomson Real Time Quotes: Real Fast...Real Free...Real Quotes...Real Time. Thomson Financial. Phone: (212)807-3800 • URL: http://www.thomsonfn.com/ • Web site provides continuous updating of prices for stocks, bonds, mutual funds, and options. Includes headline business news and market analysis. Fees: Free.

U. S. Securities and Exchange Commission. Phone: 800-732-0330 or (202)942-7040 Fax: (202)942-9634 E-mail: webmaster@sec.gov • URL: http://www.sec.gov • SEC Web site offers free access through EDGAR to text of official corporate filings, such as annual reports (10-K), quarterly reports (10-Q), and proxies. (EDGAR is "Electronic Data Gathering, Analysis, and Retrieval System.") An example is given of how to obtain executive compensation data from proxies. Text of the daily *SEC News Digest* is offered, as are links to other government sites, non-government market regulators, and U. S. stock exchanges. Search facilities are extensive. Fees: Free.

Wall Street Journal Interactive Edition. Dow Jones & Co., Inc. Phone: 800-369-2834 or (212)416-2000 Fax: (212)416-2658 E-mail: inquiries@interactive.wsj.com • URL: http://www.wsj.com • Fee-based Web site providing online searching of worldwide information from the *The Wall Street Journal.* Includes "Company Snapshots," "The Journal's Greatest Hits," "Index to Market Data," "14-Day Searchable Archive," "Journal Links," etc. Financial price quotes are available. Fees: $49.00 per year; $29.00 per year to print subscribers.

Web Finance: Covering the Electronic Evolution of Finance. Securities Data Publishing. Phone: (212)765-5311 or 800-455-5844 Fax: (212)321-2336 E-mail: webfinance@tfn.com • URL: http://www.webfinance.net • Bi-weekly print and daily web-site publication of financial services on the Web, including financial links, archives, brokerage stocks, deal financing, and other financial and investment news and information.

ONLINE DATABASES

Disclosure SEC Database. Disclosure, Inc. • Provides information from records filed with the Securities and Exchange Commission by publicly owned corporations, 1977 to present. Weekly updates. Inquire as to online cost and availability.

DRI U.S. Central Database. Data Products Division. • Provides more than 23,000 business, financial, demographic, economic, foreign trade, and industry-related time series for the U.S. Includes national income, population, retail-wholesale trade, price indexes, labor data, housing, industrial production, banking, interest rates, money supply, etc. Time period is generally 1947 to date (some data back to 1929). Updating varies. Inquire as to online cost and availability.

Fitch IBCA Ratings Delivery Service. Fitch IBCA, Inc. • Provides online delivery of Fitch financial ratings in three sectors: "Corporate Finance" (corporate bonds, insurance companies), "Structured Finance" (asset-backed securities), and "U.S. Public Finance" (municipal bonds). Daily updates. Inquire as to online cost and availability.

Value Line Convertible Data Base. Value Line Publishing, Inc. • Provides online data for about 600 convertible bonds and other convertible securities: price, yield, premium, issue size, liquidity, and maturity. Information is current, with weekly updates. Inquire as to online cost and availability.

PERIODICALS AND NEWSLETTERS

Barron's: The Dow Jones Business and Financial Weekly. Dow Jones and Co., Inc. • Weekly. $145.00 per year.

The Bond Buyer. American Banker Newsletter, Thomson Financial Media. • Daily edition, $1,897 per year. Weekly edition, $525.00 per year. Reports on new municipal bond issues.

Bondweek: The Newsweekly of Fixed Income and Credit Markets. Institutional Investor. • Weekly. $2,220.00 per year. Newsletter. Covers taxable, fixed-income securities for professional investors, including corporate, government, foreign, mortgage, and high-yield.

CreditWeek. Standard and Poor's. • Weekly. $1,695.00 per year.

Emerging Markets Debt Report. Securities Data Publishing. • Weekly. $895.00 per year. Newsletter. Provides information on new and prospective sovereign and corporate bond issues from developing countries. Includes an emerging market bond index and pricing data. (Securities Data Publishing is a unit of Thomson Financial.).

Financial Markets, Institutions, and Instruments. New York University, Salomon Center. Blackwell Publishers. • Five times a year. $219.00 per year. Edited to "bridge the gap between the academic and professional finance communities." Special fifth issue each year provides surveys of developments in four areas: money and banking, derivative securities, corporate finance, and fixed-income securities.

The Financial Post: Canadian's Business Voice. Financial Post Datagroup. • Daily. $234.00 per year. Provides Canadian business, economic, financial, and investment news. Features extensive price quotes from all major Canadian markets: stocks, bonds, mutual funds, commodities, and currencies. Supplement available: *Financial Post 500.* Includes annual supplement.

Financial Times [London]. Available from FT Publications, Inc. • Daily, except Sunday. $184.00 per year. An international business and financial newspaper, featuring news from London, Paris, Frankfurt, New York, and Tokyo. Includes worldwide stock and bond market data, commodity market data, and monetary/currency exchange information.

Financial Trader. Miller Freeman, Inc. • 11 times a year. $160.00 per year. Edited for professional traders. Covers fixed income securities, emerging markets, derivatives, options, futures, and equities.

Grant's Interest Rate Observer. James Grant, editor. Interest Rate Publishing Corp. • Biweekly. $495.00 per year. Newsletter containing detailed analysis of money-related topics, including interest rate trends, global credit markets, fixed-income investments, bank loan policies, and international money markets.

Income Fund Outlook. Institute for Econometric Research. • Monthly. $100.00 per year. Newsletter. Contains tabular data on money market funds, certificates of deposit, bond funds, and tax-free bond funds. Includes specific recommendations, fund news, and commentary on interest rates.

Investor's Business Daily. Investor's Business Daily, Inc. • Daily. $169.00 per year. Newspaper.

Journal of Fixed Income. Institutional Investor. • Quarterly. $325.00 per year. Covers a wide range of fixed-income investments for institutions, including bonds, interest-rate options, high-yield securities, and mortgages.

Journal of Investing. Institutional Investor. • Quarterly. $310.00 per year. Edited for professional investors. Topics include equities, fixed-income securities, derivatives, asset allocation, and other institutional investment subjects.

Moody's Bond Record and Annual Bond Record Service. Information Services. • Monthly. $425.00 per year. Formerly *Moody's Bond Record.*

Moody's Bond Survey. Financial Information Services. • Weekly. $1,350.00 per year. Newsletter.

MuniStatements. American Banker Newsletter, Thomson Financial Services Co. • Microfiche. Monthly shipments of Official Statements of municipal bond offerings. Back files available. Price on application.

Richard C. Young's Intelligence Report. Phillips Publishing International, Inc. • Monthly. $99.00 per year. Newsletter. Provides conservative advice for investing in stocks, fixed-income securities, and mutual funds.

Standard and Poor's Bond Guide. Standard and Poor's. • Monthly. $239.00 per year.

Standard and Poor's Ratings Handbook. Standard & Poor's. • Monthly. $275.00 per year. Newsletter. Provides news and analysis of international credit markets, including information on new bond issues. Formerly *Credit Week International Ratings.*

Standard and Poor's Semiweekly Called Bond Record. Standard & Poor's. • Semiweekly. $1,175.00 per year.

The Wall Street Journal. Dow Jones & Co., Inc. • Daily. $175.00 per year. Covers news and trends relating to business, industry, finance, the economy, and international commerce. Provides extensive price and other data for the securities, commodity, options, futures, foreign exchange, and money markets.

PRICE SOURCES

National Bond Summary. National Quotation Bureau, Inc. • Monthly. $420.00 per year. Semiannual cumulations. Includes price quotes for both active and inactive issues.

STATISTICS SOURCES

Business Statistics of the United States. Courtenay M. Slater, editor. Bernan Associates. • 1999. $74.00. Fifth edition. Based on *Business Statistics*, formerly issue by the Bureau of Economic Analysis, U. S. Department of Commerce. Provides basic data for a wide variety of U. S. industries, services, and economic indicators. Most statistics are shown annually for 29 years and monthly for the most recent four years.

International Guide to Securities Market Indices. Henry Shilling, editor. Fitzroy Dearborn Publishers. • 1996. $140.00. Describes 400 stock market, bond market, and other financial price indexes maintained in various countries of the world (300 of the indexes are described in detail, including graphs and 10-year data).

SBBI Monthly Market Reports. Ibbotson Associates. • Monthly. $995.00 per year. These reports provide current updating of stocks, bonds, bills, and inflation (SBBI) data. Each issue contains the most recent month's investment returns and index values for various kinds of securities, as well as monthly statistics for the past year. Analysis is included.

SBBI Quarterly Market Reports. Ibbotson Associates. • Quarterly. $495.00 per year. Each quarterly volume contains detailed updates to stocks, bonds, bills, and inflation (SBBI) data. Includes total and sector returns for the broad stock market, small company stocks, intermediate and long-term government bonds, long-term corporate bonds, and U. S. Treasury Bills. Analyses, tables, graphs, and market consensus forecasts are provided.

Stocks, Bonds, Bills, and Inflation Yearbook. Ibbotson Associates. • Annual. $92.00. Provides detailed data from 1926 to the present on inflation and the returns from various kinds of financial investments, such as small-cap stocks and long-term government bonds.

Survey of Current Business. Available from U. S. Government Printing Office. • Monthly. $49.00 per year. Issued by Bureau of Economic Analysis, U. S. Department of Commerce. Presents a wide variety of business and economic data.

OTHER SOURCES

Factiva. Dow Jones Reuters Business Interactive, LLC. • Fee-based Web site provides "global news and business information through Web sites and content integration solutions." Includes Dow Jones and Reuters newswires, The Wall Street Journal, and more than 7,000 other sources of current news, historical articles, market research reports, and investment analysis. Content includes 96 major U. S. newspapers, 900 non-English sources, trade publications, media transcripts, country profiles, news photos, etc.

Fitch Insights. Fitch Investors Service, Inc. • Biweekly. $1,040.00 per year. Includes bond rating actions and explanation of actions. Provides commentary and Fitch's view of the financial markets.

Nexis.com. Lexis-Nexis Group. • Fee-based Web site offers searching of about 2.8 billion documents in some 30,000 news, business, and legal information sources. Features include a subject directory covering 1,200 topics in 34 categories and a Company Dossier containing information on more than 500,000 public and private companies. Boolean searching is offered.

BONDS, GOVERNMENT

See: GOVERNMENT BONDS

BONDS, JUNK

See: JUNK BOND FINANCING

BONDS, MUNICIPAL

See: MUNICIPAL BONDS

BOOK CATALOGS

See also: BIBLIOGRAPHY; BUSINESS LITERATURE

BIBLIOGRAPHIES

American Book Publishing Record: Arranged by Dewey Decimal Classification and Indexed by Author, Title, and Subject. R. R. Bowker. • Monthly. $299.00. per year. Includes annual cumulation.

American Reference Books Annual. Bohdan S. Wynar others, editors. Libraries Unlimited, Inc. • Annual. $110.00.

Books in Print. R. R. Bowker. • Annual. $595.00. Nine volumes. Annual supplement, $250.00 (three volumes).

Forthcoming Books. R. R. Bowker. • Bimonthly. $289.00 per year. Supplement to *Books in Print.*

Subject Guide to Books in Print. R. R. Bowker. • Annual. $339.00. Seven volumes.

CD-ROM DATABASES

Bowker/Whitaker Global Books in Print On Disc. R. R. Bowker. • Monthly. $2,055.00 per year. Provides CD-ROM listing of English language books published throughout the world, including U. S., U. K., Canada, and Australia. Combines data from R. R. Bowker's *Books in Print Plus* and J. Whitaker & Sons Ltd.'s *Bookbank.* Includes more than two million titles.

CDMARC: Bibliographic. U. S. Library of Congress. • Quarterly. $1,340.00 per year. Provides bibliographic records on CD-ROM for over five million books cataloged by the Library of Congress since 1968. (MARC is Machine Readable Cataloging.).

LISA Plus: Library and Information Science Abstracts. Bowker-Saur, Reed Reference Publishing. • Quarterly. $1,450.00 per year. Provides CD-ROM abstracting and indexing of the world's library and information science literature. Covers a wide variety of topics.

DIRECTORIES

Publishers' Trade List Annual: A Buying and Reference Guide to Books and Related Products. R. R. Bowker. • Annual. $315.00. Three volumes. About 1,000 publishers in the United States, with their catalogs.

INTERNET DATABASES

Publishers' Catalogues Home Page. Northern Lights Internet Solutions Ltd. Phone: (306)931-0020 Fax: (306)931-7667 E-mail: info@lights.com • URL: http://www.lights.com/publisher • Provides links to the Web home pages of about 1,700 U. S. publishers (including about 80 University presses) and publishers in 48 foreign countries. "International/Multinational Publishers" are included, such as the International Monetary Fund, the World Bank, and the World Trade Organization. Publishers are arranged in convenient alphabetical lists. Searching is offered. Fees: Free.

ONLINE DATABASES

Book Review Index [Online]. The Gale Group. • Cites reviews of books and periodicals in journals, 1969 to present. Inquire as to online cost and availability.

LC MARC: Books. U. S. Library of Congress. • Contains online bibliographic records for over five million books cataloged by the Library of Congress since 1968. Updating is weekly or monthly. Inquire as to online cost and availability. (MARC is machine readable cataloging.).

LISA Online: Library and Information Science Abstracts. Bowker-Saur, Reed Reference Publishing. • Provides abstracting and indexing of the world's library and information science literature from 1969 to the present. Covers a wide variety of topics in over 550 journals from 60 countries, with biweekly updates. Inquire as to online cost and availability.

PERIODICALS AND NEWSLETTERS

Publishers Weekly: The International News Magazine of Book Publishing. Cahners Business Information, Broadcasting and Cables International Group. • Weekly. $189.00 per year. The international news magazine of book publishing.

BOOK COLLECTING

See also: BIBLIOGRAPHY

ALMANACS AND YEARBOOKS

AB Bookman's Yearbook: Specialist Book Trade Annual (Antiquarian Bookman). • Annual.

DIRECTORIES

American Book Trade Directory. R. R. Bowker. • Annual. $255.00 More than 30,000 bookstores and other book outlets in the U.S. and Canada; 1,500 U.S. and Canadian book wholesalers and paperback distributors.

Antiquarian, Specialty, and Used Book Sellers: A Subject Guide and Directory. James M. Ethridge and Karen Ethridge, editors. Omnigraphics, Inc. • 1997. $85.00. Second edition. Provides information on more than 3,000 specialized book dealers. Indexed by store name, store owner, and subject specialty.

International Directory of Book Collectors. Oak Knoll Press. • Irregular. $50.00. Over 1,500 listings. Published in England by Trigon Press.

Sheppard's Bookdealers in Europe: A Directory of Dealers in Secondhand and Antiquarian Books on the Continent of Europe. Richard Joseph Publishers, Ltd. • Biennial. $54.00. 1,746 dealers in antiquarian and secondhand books in 24 European countries.

HANDBOOKS AND MANUALS

Book Collecting: A Comprehensive Guide. Allen Ahearn and Patricia Ahearn. Penguin Putnam Book for Young Readers. • 2000. $45.00.

PERIODICALS AND NEWSLETTERS

AB Bookman's Weekly: For the Specialist Book World (Antiquarian Bookman). • Weekly. $125.00 per year. Includes *A B Bookman's Yearbook.*

Book Collector. Nicolas J. Barker. Collector Ltd. • Quarterly. $62.00 per year. Subscription.

PRICE SOURCES

American Book-Prices Current. Bancroft-Parkman, Inc. • Annual. $109.95.

Bookman's Price Index. The Gale Group. • Annual. 65 volumes. $320.00 per volume. Price guide to out more than 17,000 out-of-print and rare books.

TRADE/PROFESSIONAL ASSOCIATIONS

Antiquarian Booksellers Association of America. 20 W. 44th St., 4th Fl., New York, NY 10036-6604. Phone: (212)944-8291 Fax: (212)944-8293 • URL: http://www.abaa.org.

Bibliographical Society of America. Lenox Hill Station, P.O. Box 1537, New York, NY 10021. Phone: (212)452-2710 Fax: (212)452-2710 E-mail: bsa@bibsocamer.org • URL: http://www.bibsocamer.org.

Grolier Club. 47 E. 60th St., New York, NY 10022. Phone: (212)838-6690 Fax: (212)838-2445 E-mail: ejh@grolierclub.org • URL: http://www.grolierclub.org.

BOOK INDUSTRY

See also: BIBLIOGRAPHY; BOOK COLLECTING; BOOKSELLING; PAPERBOUND BOOK INDUSTRY; PUBLISHING INDUSTRY

ALMANACS AND YEARBOOKS

Bowker Annual: Library and Book Trade Almanac. R. R. Bowker. • Annual. $175.00. Lists of accredited library schools; scholarships for education in library science; library organizations; major libraries; publishing and book sellers organizations. Includes statistics and news of the book business.

Trade Book Publishing: Review, Forecast, and Segment Analysis. SIMBA Information. • 1999. $1,495.00. Reviews current conditions in the book publishing industry, including analysis of market segments, retailing aspects, and profiles of major publishers.

BIBLIOGRAPHIES

American Book Publishing Record: Arranged by Dewey Decimal Classification and Indexed by Author, Title, and Subject. R. R. Bowker. • Monthly. $299.00. per year. Includes annual cumulation.

Managing the Publishing Process: An Annotated Bibliography. Bruce W. Speck. Greenwood Publishing Group, Inc. • 1995. $75.00. (Bibliographies and Indexes in Mass Media and Communications Series, No. 9).

CD-ROM DATABASES

LISA Plus: Library and Information Science Abstracts. Bowker-Saur, Reed Reference Publishing. • Quarterly. $1,450.00 per year. Provides CD-ROM abstracting and indexing of the world's library and information science literature. Covers a wide variety of topics.

DIRECTORIES

American Book Trade Directory. R. R. Bowker. • Annual. $255.00 More than 30,000 bookstores and other book outlets in the U.S. and Canada; 1,500 U.S. and Canadian book wholesalers and paperback distributors.

International Literary Market Place: The Directory of the International Book Publishing Industry. R. R. Bowker. • Annual. $189.95. More than 10,370 publishers in over 180 countries outside the U.S.and Canada and about 1,150 trade and professional organizations related to publishing abroad.

Literary Market Place: The Directory of the American Book Publishing Industry. R. R. Bowker. • Annual. $199.95. Two volumes. Over 16,000 firms or organizations offering services related to the publishing industry.

Plunkett's Entertainment and Media Industry Almanac. Available from Plunkett Research, Ltd. • Biennial. $149.99. Provides profiles of leading firms in online information, films, radio, television, cable, multimedia, magazines, and book publishing. Includes World Wide Web sites, where available, plus information on careers and industry trends.

Publishers Directory: A Guide to New and Established Private and Special-Interest, Avant-Garde and Alternative, Organizational Association, Government and Institution Presses. The Gale Group. • 2000. $400.00. 23rd edition. Contains detailed information on more than 20,000 U.S. and Canadian publishers as well as small, independent presses.

Publishers, Distributors, and Wholesalers of the United States: A Directory of Publishers, Distributors, Associations, Wholesalers, Software Producers and Manufactureres Listing Editorial and Ordering Addresses, and and ISBN Publisher Prefi. R. R. Bowker. • Annual. $229.00. Two volumes. Lists more than 101,000 publishers, book distributors, and wholesalers. Includes museum and association imprints, inactive publishers, and publishers' fields of activity.

Publishers' International ISBN Directory. Available from The Gale Group. • Annual. $425.00. Three volumes. Compiled by the International ISBN Agency and published by K. G. Saur. Provides names and addresses of over 426,000 publishers in the United States and 210 other countries. Three sections: alphabetical, geographic, and ISBN number. Formerly *International ISBN Publishers' Directory.* Published by K. G. Saur.

Publishers' Trade List Annual: A Buying and Reference Guide to Books and Related Products. R. R. Bowker. • Annual. $315.00. Three volumes. About 1,000 publishers in the United States, with their catalogs.

Sheppard's Bookdealers in North America. Richard Joseph Publishers, Ltd. • Biennial. $54.00. Over 3,364 dealers in antiquarian and secondhand books in the U.S. and Canada.

Writer's Guide to Book Editors, Publishers, and Literary Agents, 2000-2001: Who They Are, What They Want, and How to Win Them Over. Jeff Herman. Prima Publishing. • Annual. $27.95; with CD-ROM, $49.95. Directory for authors includes information on publishers' response times and pay rates.

ENCYCLOPEDIAS AND DICTIONARIES

NTC's Mass Media Dictionary. R. Terry Ellmore. NTC/Contemporary Publishing. • 1993. $24.95. Covers television, radio, newspapers, magazines, film, graphic arts, books, billboards, public relations, and advertising. Terms are related to production, research, audience measurement, audio-video engineering, printing, publishing, and other areas.

FINANCIAL RATIOS

Annual Statement Studies. Robert Morris Associates: The Association of Lending and Credit Risk Professiona. • Annual. Free to members; non-members, $140.00. Median and quartile financial ratios are given for over 400 kinds of manufacturing, wholesale, retail, construction, and consumer finance establishments. Data is sorted by both asset size and sales volume. Includes a clearly written "Definition of Ratios" and an alphabetical industry index.

HANDBOOKS AND MANUALS

ABA Book Buyer's Handbook. American Booksellers Association. • Annual. Membership. Trade policies. Formerly *Book Buyer's Handbook.*

Buying Books: A How-To-Do-It Manual for Librarians. Audrey Eaglen. Neal-Schuman Publishers, Inc. • 2000. $45.00. Second edition. Discusses vendor selection and book ordering in the age of electronic commerce. Covers both print and electronic bibliographic sources. (How-to-Do-It Manual for Librarians Series).

Getting Your Book Published. Christine S. Smedley and Mitchell Allen. Sage Publications, Inc. • 1993. $37.00. A practical guide for academic and professional authors. Covers the initial book prospectus, contract negotiation, production procedures, and marketing. (Survival Skills for Scholars, vol. 10).

INTERNET DATABASES

Amazon.com. Amazon.com, Inc. Phone: 800-201-7575 or (206)346-2992 Fax: (206)346-2950 E-mail:

info@amazon.com • URL: http://www.amazon.com • "Welcome to Earth's Biggest Bookstore." Amazon.com claims to have more than 2.5 million titles that can be ordered online, but only through the Web site - no orders by mail, telephone, fax, or E-mail. Discounts are generally 30% for hardcovers and 20% for paperbacks. Efficient search facilities, including Boolean, make this Web site useful for reference (many titles have online reviews). Fees: Free.

Publishers' Catalogues Home Page. Northern Lights Internet Solutions Ltd. Phone: (306)931-0020 Fax: (306)931-7667 E-mail: info@lights.com • URL: http://www.lights.com/publisher • Provides links to the Web home pages of about 1,700 U. S. publishers (including about 80 University presses) and publishers in 48 foreign countries. "International/Multinational Publishers" are included, such as the International Monetary Fund, the World Bank, and the World Trade Organization. Publishers are arranged in convenient alphabetical lists. Searching is offered. Fees: Free.

ONLINE DATABASES

LISA Online: Library and Information Science Abstracts. Bowker-Saur, Reed Reference Publishing. • Provides abstracting and indexing of the world's library and information science literature from 1969 to the present. Covers a wide variety of topics in over 550 journals from 60 countries, with biweekly updates. Inquire as to online cost and availability.

Wilson Publishers Directory Online. H. W. Wilson Co. • Provides names and addresses of more than 34,000 English-language book publishers and distributors appearing in *Cumulative Book Index* and other H. W. Wilson databases. Updated three times a week. Inquire as to online cost and availability.

PERIODICALS AND NEWSLETTERS

Advertising Age: The International Newspaper of Marketing. Crain Communications, Inc. • Weekly. $109.00 per year. Includes supplement *Creativity.*

Book Marketing Update. Open Horizons Publishing. • Monthly. $60.00 per year. Newsletter for book publishers.

Book Publishing Report: Weekly News and Analysis of Events Shaping the Book Industry. SIMBA Information. • Weekly. $525.00 per year. Newsletter. Covers book publishing mergers, marketing, finance, personnel, and trends in general. Formerly *BP Report on the Business of Book Publishing.*

Computer Publishing and Advertising Report: The Biweekly Newsletter for Publishing and Advertising Executives in the Computer Field. SIMBA Information, Inc. • Biweekly. $549.00 per year. Newsletter. Covers computer book publishing and computer-related advertising in periodicals and other media. Provides data on computer book sales and advertising in computer magazines.

Publishers Weekly: The International News Magazine of Book Publishing. Cahners Business Information, Broadcasting and Cables International Group. • Weekly. $189.00 per year. The international news magazine of book publishing.

PRICE SOURCES

American Book-Prices Current. Bancroft-Parkman, Inc. • Annual. $109.95.

STATISTICS SOURCES

Annual Survey of Manufactures. Available from U. S. Government Printing Office. • Annual. Prices vary. Issued by the U. S. Census Bureau as an interim update to the *Census of Manufactures.* Includes data on number of manufacturing establishments in various industries, employment, labor costs, value of shipments, capital expenditures, inventories, energy costs, and assets. (See also Census Bureau home page, http://www.census.gov/.).

Book Industry Trends. Book Industry Study Group, Inc. • Annual. $650.00.

U. S. Industry and Trade Outlook: The McGraw-Hill Companies and the U.S. Department of Commerce/International Trade Administration. Datapso Research Corp. • Annual. $69.95. Produced by the International Trade Administration, U. S. Department of Commerce, in a "public-private" partnership with DRI/McGraw-Hill and Standard & Poor's. Provides basic data, outlook for the current year, and "Long-Term Prospects" (five-year projections) for a wide variety of products and services. Includes high technology industries. Formerly *U. S. Industrial Outlook.*

TRADE/PROFESSIONAL ASSOCIATIONS

Association of American Publishers. 71 Fifth Ave., New York, NY 10003-3004. Phone: (212)255-0200 Fax: (212)255-7007 • URL: http://www.publishers.org.

Book Industry Study Group. 160 Fifth Ave., New York, NY 10010. Phone: (212)929-1393 Fax: (212)989-7542 E-mail: sandy@booksinfo.org • URL: http://www.bisg.org.

Book Manufacturers Institute. 65 William St., Suite 300, Wellesley, MA 02181. Phone: (781)239-0103 Fax: (781)239-0106.

Women's National Book Association. 160 Fifth Ave., Room 604, New York, NY 10010. Phone: (212)675-7805 Fax: (212)989-7542 E-mail: skpassoc@cwismail.com • URL: http://www.bookbuzz.com/wnba.htm.

BOOK REVIEWS

ABSTRACTS AND INDEXES

Book Review Digest: An Index to Reviews of Current Books. H.W. Wilson Co. • 10 times a year. Quarterly and annual cumulation. Service basis.

Book Review Index. The Gale Group. • Annual. $295.00. Three yearly issues. An index to reviews appearing in hundreds of periodicals. Back volumes available.

Children's Book Review Index. The Gale Group. • Annual. $155.00. Back volumes available. Contains more than 25,000 review citations.

BIBLIOGRAPHIES

American Reference Books Annual. Bohdan S. Wynar others, editors. Libraries Unlimited, Inc. • Annual. $110.00.

Booklist. American Library Association. • 22 times a year. $74.50. Reviews library materials for school and public libraries. Incorporates *Reference Books Bulletin.*

Reference Books Bulletin: A Compilation of Evaluations. Mary Ellen Quinn, editor. American Library Association. • Annual. $28.50. Contains reference book reviews that appeared during the year in *Booklist.*

CD-ROM DATABASES

Books in Print with Book Reviews On Disc. Bowker Electronic Publishing. • Monthly. $1,755.00 per year. The CD-ROM version of *Books in Print, Forthcoming Books,*and other Bowker bibliographic publications, with the addition of full text book reviews from *Publishers Weekly, Library Journal, Booklist, Choice,* and other periodicals.

INTERNET DATABASES

Amazon.com. Amazon.com, Inc. Phone: 800-201-7575 or (206)346-2992 Fax: (206)346-2950 E-mail: info@amazon.com • URL: http://www.amazon.com • "Welcome to Earth's Biggest Bookstore." Amazon.com claims to have more than 2.5 million titles that can be ordered online, but only through the Web site - no orders by mail, telephone, fax, or E-mail. Discounts are generally 30% for hardcovers and 20% for paperbacks. Efficient search facilities, including Boolean, make this Web site useful for reference (many titles have online reviews). Fees: Free.

ONLINE DATABASES

Book Review Index [Online]. The Gale Group. • Cites reviews of books and periodicals in journals, 1969 to present. Inquire as to online cost and availability.

PERIODICALS AND NEWSLETTERS

Children's Book Review Service. Ann L. Kalkhoff, editor. Children's Book Review Service Inc. • Monthly. $40.00 per year. Includes two Supplements.

Choice: Current Reviews for Academic Libraries. Association of College Research Libraries. Choice. • 11 times a year. $200.00 per year. A publication of the Association of College and Research Libraries. Contains book reviews, primarily for college and university libraries.

Library Journal. Cahners Business Information, Broadcasting and Cable's International Group. • 20 times a year. $109.00 per year.

New York Times Book Review. New York Times Co. • Weekly. $54.60 per year. Supplement to *New York Times.*

Reference and User Services Quarterly. American Library Association. • Quarterly. $50.00 per year. Official publication of the Reference and User Services Association (RUSA), a division of the American Library Association. In addition to articles, includes reviews of databases, reference books, and library professional material. Formerly *RQ.*

BOOK STORES

See: BOOKSELLING

BOOKBINDING

GENERAL WORKS

Books for the Millions: A History of the Men Whose Methods and Machines Packaged the Printed Word. Frank E. Comparato. Labyrinthos. • 1971. $12.50.

BIBLIOGRAPHIES

Conservation of Library Materials: A Manual and Bibliography on the Care, Repair and Restoration of Library Materials. George M. Cunha and Dorothy G. Cunha. Scarecrow Press, Inc. • 1972. Two volumes. Volume one, $47.50; volume two, $50.00.

CD-ROM DATABASES

LISA Plus: Library and Information Science Abstracts. Bowker-Saur, Reed Reference Publishing. • Quarterly. $1,450.00 per year. Provides CD-ROM abstracting and indexing of the world's library and information science literature. Covers a wide variety of topics.

DIRECTORIES

Guild of Book Workers-Membership List. Guild of Book Workers. • Annual. $40.00. About 800 amateur and professional workers in the handbook crafts of bookbinding, calligraphy, illuminating, and decorative papermaking.

Opportunities for Study in Hand Bookbinding and Calligraphy. Guild of Book Workers, Inc. • Free. About 150 teachers, schools, and centers offering hand bookbinding and calligraphic services; international coverage.

FINANCIAL RATIOS

Annual Statement Studies. Robert Morris Associates: The Association of Lending and Credit Risk Professiona. • Annual. Free to members; non-members, $140.00. Median and quartile financial ratios are given for over 400 kinds of manufacturing, wholesale, retail, construction, and consumer finance establishments. Data is sorted by both asset size and sales volume. Includes a clearly written "Definition of Ratios" and an alphabetical industry index.

HANDBOOKS AND MANUALS

Binding of Books. Herbert P. Horne. M.S.G. Haskell House. • 1969. $75.00. Reprint of 1894 edition. (Reference Series No. 44).

Book Repair: A How-To-Do-It Manual for Librarians. Kenneth Lavender and Scott Stockton. Neal-Schuman Publishers, Inc. • 1992. $45.00. Covers basic book repair and conservation techniques.

Books: Their Care and Repair. H. W. Wilson Co. • 1984. $42.00. Covers the repair of books, maps, and documents and the various kinds of pamphlet binding.

ONLINE DATABASES

LISA Online: Library and Information Science Abstracts. Bowker-Saur, Reed Reference Publishing. • Provides abstracting and indexing of the world's library and information science literature from 1969 to the present. Covers a wide variety of topics in over 550 journals from 60 countries, with biweekly updates. Inquire as to online cost and availability.

PIRA. Technical Centre for the Paper and Board, Printing and Packaging Industries. • Citations and abstracts pertaining to bookbinding and other pulp, paper, and packaging industries, 1975 to present. Weekly updates. Inquire as to online cost and availability.

PERIODICALS AND NEWSLETTERS

The New Library Scene. Library Binding Institute. • Quarterly. $24.00 per year.

TRADE/PROFESSIONAL ASSOCIATIONS

Binding Industries of America. 70 E. Lake St., Chicago, IL 60601. Phone: (312)372-7606 or (312)704-5000 Fax: (312)709-5025 E-mail: bial@ix.netcom.com • URL: http://www.bindingindustries.org.

Guild of Book Workers. 521 Fifth Ave., 17th Fl., New York, NY 10175. Phone: (212)292-4444.

Library Binding Institute. 5241 Lincoln Dr., Suite 321, Edina, MN 55436-2703. Phone: (612)939-0165 Fax: (612)939-0213 E-mail: 71035.sallymoyer@libibinders.org.

OTHER SOURCES

Early American Bookbindings from the Collection of Michael Papantonio. Michael Papantonio. Oak Knoll Press. • 1985. $27.50. Second edition.

BOOKKEEPING

See: ACCOUNTING

BOOKSELLER'S CATALOGS

See: BOOK CATALOGS

BOOKSELLING

See also: BIBLIOGRAPHY; BOOK COLLECTING; BOOK INDUSTRY

GENERAL WORKS

The Book Market: How to Write, Publish, and Market Your Book. Aron M. Mathieu. Andover Press. • 1981. $19.95.

The Business of Publishing: How to Survive and Prosper in the Publishing and Bookselling Industry. Leonard Shatzkin. McGraw-Hill. • 1995. $24.95.

ALMANACS AND YEARBOOKS

Bowker Annual: Library and Book Trade Almanac. R. R. Bowker. • Annual. $175.00. Lists of accredited library schools; scholarships for education in library science; library organizations; major libraries; publishing and book sellers organizations. Includes statistics and news of the book business.

BIBLIOGRAPHIES

American Book Publishing Record: Arranged by Dewey Decimal Classification and Indexed by Author, Title, and Subject. R. R. Bowker. • Monthly. $299.00. per year. Includes annual cumulation.

DIRECTORIES

American Book Trade Directory. R. R. Bowker. • Annual. $255.00 More than 30,000 bookstores and other book outlets in the U.S. and Canada; 1,500 U.S. and Canadian book wholesalers and paperback distributors.

Antiquarian Booksellers' Association of America-Membership List. Antiquarian Booksellers' Association of America. • Annual. Free. Lists about 470 rare book dealers. Send self-addressed business-size envelope with $1.43 postage.

Antiquarian, Specialty, and Used Book Sellers: A Subject Guide and Directory. James M. Ethridge and Karen Ethridge, editors. Omnigraphics, Inc. • 1997. $85.00. Second edition. Provides information on more than 3,000 specialized book dealers. Indexed by store name, store owner, and subject specialty.

International Literary Market Place: The Directory of the International Book Publishing Industry. R. R. Bowker. • Annual. $189.95. More than 10,370 publishers in over 180 countries outside the U.S.and Canada and about 1,150 trade and professional organizations related to publishing abroad.

Literary Market Place: The Directory of the American Book Publishing Industry. R. R. Bowker. • Annual. $199.95. Two volumes. Over 16,000 firms or organizations offering services related to the publishing industry.

Sheppard's Bookdealers in Europe: A Directory of Dealers in Secondhand and Antiquarian Books on the Continent of Europe. Richard Joseph Publishers, Ltd. • Biennial. $54.00. 1,746 dealers in antiquarian and secondhand books in 24 European countries.

Sheppard's Bookdealers in North America. Richard Joseph Publishers, Ltd. • Biennial. $54.00. Over 3,364 dealers in antiquarian and secondhand books in the U.S. and Canada.

FINANCIAL RATIOS

Annual Statement Studies. Robert Morris Associates: The Association of Lending and Credit Risk Professiona. • Annual. Free to members; non-members, $140.00. Median and quartile financial ratios are given for over 400 kinds of manufacturing, wholesale, retail, construction, and consumer finance establishments. Data is sorted by both asset size and sales volume. Includes a clearly written "Definition of Ratios" and an alphabetical industry index.

HANDBOOKS AND MANUALS

ABA Book Buyer's Handbook. American Booksellers Association. • Annual. Membership. Trade policies. Formerly *Book Buyer's Handbook.*

Book Marketing Handbook: Tips and Techniques for the Sale and Promotion of Scientific, Technical, Professional, and Scholarly Books and Journals. Nat G. Bodian. R. R. Bowker. • Two volumes. $64.95 per volume. Volume one, 1980; volume two, 1983.

Children's Bookstore. Entrepreneur Media, Inc. • Looseleaf. $59.50. A practical guide to starting a children's bookstore. Covers profit potential, start-up costs, market size evaluation, owner's time required, site selection, lease negotiation, pricing, accounting, advertising, promotion, etc. (Start-Up Business Guide No. E1293.).

Used Book Store. Entrepreneur Media, Inc. • Looseleaf. $59.50. A practical guide to starting a used book store. Covers profit potential, start-up costs, market size evaluation, owner's time required, site selection, lease negotiation, pricing, accounting, advertising, promotion, etc. (Start-Up Business Guide No. E1117.).

INTERNET DATABASES

Amazon.com. Amazon.com, Inc. Phone: 800-201-7575 or (206)346-2992 Fax: (206)346-2950 E-mail: info@amazon.com • URL: http://www.amazon.com • "Welcome to Earth's Biggest Bookstore." Amazon.com claims to have more than 2.5 million titles that can be ordered online, but only through the Web site - no orders by mail, telephone, fax, or E-mail. Discounts are generally 30% for hardcovers and 20% for paperbacks. Efficient search facilities, including Boolean, make this Web site useful for reference (many titles have online reviews). Fees: Free.

BookWeb. American Booksellers Association. Phone: 800-637-0037 or (914)591-2665 Fax: (914)591-2720 E-mail: info@bookweb.org • URL: http://www.bookweb.org/bookstores • Web site provides descriptions of more than 4,500 independent bookstores, searchable by name, specialty, or zip code. Fees: Free.

PERIODICALS AND NEWSLETTERS

The Bookseller: The Organ of the Book Trade. J. Whitaker and Sons, Ltd. • Weekly. $178.00 per year. Provides international book trade news.

Bookselling This Week. American Booksellers Association. • Weekly. Members, $30.00 per year; non-members, $60.00 per year. Newsletter. Formerly *ABA Newswire.*

Bookstore Journal. Christian Booksellers Association. C B A Service Corp. • Monthly. $45.00 per year. Edited for religious book stores.

The Library Bookseller; Books Wanted by College and University Libraries. Danna D'Esopo Jackson, editor. • Monthly. $50.00 per year.

Publishers Weekly: The International News Magazine of Book Publishing. Cahners Business Information, Broadcasting and Cables International Group. • Weekly. $189.00 per year. The international news magazine of book publishing.

PRICE SOURCES

American Book-Prices Current. Bancroft-Parkman, Inc. • Annual. $109.95.

Bookman's Price Index. The Gale Group. • Annual. 65 volumes. $320.00 per volume. Price guide to out more than 17,000 out-of-print and rare books.

STATISTICS SOURCES

United States Census of Retail Trade. U.S. Bureau of the Census. • Quinquennial.

TRADE/PROFESSIONAL ASSOCIATIONS

American Booksellers Association. 828 S. Broadway, Tarrytown, NY 10591. Phone: 800-637-

0037 or (914)591-2665 Fax: (914)591-2720 E-mail: info@bookweb.org • URL: http://www.bookweb.org/.

Antiquarian Booksellers Association of America, 20 W. 44th St., 4th Fl., New York, NY 10036-6604. Phone: (212)944-8291 Fax: (212)944-8293 • URL: http://www.abaa.org.

CBA-Christian Booksellers Association. P.O. Box 200, Colorado Springs, CO 80901. Phone: 800-252-1950 or (719)576-7880 Fax: (719)576-9240 E-mail: info@cba-intl.org • URL: http://www.cbaonline.org.

International Booksellers Federation. Rue du Grande Hoslice 34A, B-1000 Brussels, Belgium. Phone: 32 2 2234940 Fax: 32 20 2234941 E-mail: eurobooks@skynet.be.

BOOTS AND SHOES

See: SHOE INDUSTRY

BORING MACHINERY

See: MACHINERY

BOTANY, ECONOMIC

See: ECONOMIC BOTANY

BOTTLE INDUSTRY

See: CONTAINER INDUSTRY; GLASS CONTAINER INDUSTRY

BOTTLED WATER INDUSTRY

See: WATER SUPPLY

BOX INDUSTRY

See also: PAPER BOX AND PAPER CONTAINER INDUSTRIES

DIRECTORIES

National Paperbox Association Membership Directory. National Paperbox Association. • Annual. $125.00.

FINANCIAL RATIOS

Annual Statement Studies. Robert Morris Associates: The Association of Lending and Credit Risk Professiona. • Annual. Free to members; non-members, $140.00. Median and quartile financial ratios are given for over 400 kinds of manufacturing, wholesale, retail, construction, and consumer finance establishments. Data is sorted by both asset size and sales volume. Includes a clearly written "Definition of Ratios" and an alphabetical industry index.

ONLINE DATABASES

PIRA. Technical Centre for the Paper and Board, Printing and Packaging Industries. • Citations and abstracts pertaining to bookbinding and other pulp, paper, and packaging industries, 1975 to present. Weekly updates. Inquire as to online cost and availability.

PERIODICALS AND NEWSLETTERS

Boxboard Containers International. Intertec Publishing Corp. • Monthly. $28.00 per year. Formerly *Boxboard Containers.*

Paperboard Packaging Worldwide. Advanstar Communications, Inc. • Monthly. $39.00 per year.

PRICE SOURCES

PPI Detailed Report. Bureau of Labor Statistics, U.S. Department of Labor. Available from U.S. Government Printing Office. • Monthly. $55.00 per year. Formerly *Producer Price Indexes.*

STATISTICS SOURCES

Fibre Box Industry Statistical Report. Fibre Box Association. • Annual.

United States Census of Manufactures. U.S. Bureau of the Census. • Quinquennial. Results presented in reports, tape, CD-ROM, and Diskette files.

TRADE/PROFESSIONAL ASSOCIATIONS

Fibre Box Association. 2850 Golf Rd., Rolling Meadows, IL 60008. Phone: (847)364-9600 Fax: (847)364-9639 • URL: http://www.fibrebox.org.

National Paperbox Association. 801 N. Fairfax St., Suite 211, Alexandria, VA 22314-1757. Phone: (703)684-2212 Fax: (703)683-6920 E-mail: boxmaker@paperbox.org • URL: http://www.paperbox.org.

Pacific Coast Paper Box Manufacturers' Association. P.O. Box 60957, Los Angeles, CA 90060-0957. Phone: (323)581-1183 Fax: (213)581-1183 E-mail: ed_mozley@msn.com.

Wirebound Box Manufacturers Association. 3623 Sprucewood Lane, Wilmette, IL 60091. Phone: (847)251-5575 Fax: (847)251-5898.

BOXES, PAPER

See: PAPER BOX AND PAPER CONTAINER INDUSTRIES

BOY'S CLOTHING

See: CHILDREN'S APPAREL INDUSTRY; MEN'S CLOTHING INDUSTRY

BRAINSTORMING

See: CREATIVITY

BRANCH STORES

See: CHAIN STORES

BRAND AWARENESS STUDIES

See: MARKET RESEARCH

BRAND NAMES

See: TRADEMARKS AND TRADE NAMES

BREAD INDUSTRY

See: BAKING INDUSTRY

BREWING INDUSTRY

See also: BEVERAGE INDUSTRY; DISTILLING INDUSTRY

ALMANACS AND YEARBOOKS

Brewers Almanac. Beer Institute. • Annual. $170.00.

The U.S. Beer Market: Impact Databank Review and Forecast. M. Shanken Communications, Inc. • Annual. $845.00. Includes industry commentary and statistics.

DIRECTORIES

Brewers Digest Annual Buyers Guide and Brewery Directory. Siebel Publishing Co., Inc. • Annual. $50.00. Lists breweries throughout the western hemisphere.

Modern Brewery Age Blue Book. Business Journals, Inc. • Annual. $265.00. Over 3,000 breweries, beer wholesalers, importers, trade associations, regulatory agencies, and suppliers to malt beverage industry; international coverage. Supplement to *Modern Brewery Age.*

National Licensed Beverage Association-Members Directory. National Licensed Beverage Association. • Annual. $40.00.

ENCYCLOPEDIAS AND DICTIONARIES

Dictionary of the History of the American Brewing and Distilling Industries. William L. Downard. Greenwood Publishing Group Inc. • 1980. $69.50.

INTERNET DATABASES

Fedstats. Federal Interagency Council on Statistical Policy. Phone: (202)395-7254 • URL: http://www.fedstats.gov • Web site features an efficient search facility for full-text statistics produced by more than 70 federal agencies, including the Census Bureau, the Bureau of Economic Analysis, and the Bureau of Labor Statistics. Boolean searches can be made within one agency or for all agencies combined. Links are offered to international statistical bureaus, including the UN, IMF, OECD, UNESCO, Eurostat, and 20 individual countries. Fees: Free.

ONLINE DATABASES

DRI U.S. Central Database. Data Products Division. • Provides more than 23,000 business, financial, demographic, economic, foreign trade, and industry-related time series for the U.S. Includes national income, population, retail-wholesale trade, price indexes, labor data, housing, industrial production, banking, interest rates, money supply, etc. Time period is generally 1947 to date (some data back to 1929). Updating varies. Inquire as to online cost and availability.

PERIODICALS AND NEWSLETTERS

American Society of Brewing Chemists Journal. American Society of Brewing Chemists. • Quarterly. Members, $95.00 per year; non-members, $137.00 per year; corporate members, $195.00 per year; student members, $25.00 per year.

ASBC Newsletter. American Society of Brewing Chemists. • Quarterly. Members, $95.00 per year; non-members, $130.00 per year; corporate members, $195.00 per year; student members, $26.00 per year.

Beer Marketer's Insights. Beer Marketer's Insights, Inc. • 23 times a year. $435.00 per year. Newsletter for brewers and wholesalers.

Brewers Digest. Siebel Publishing Co., Inc. • Monthly. $25.00 per year. Covers all aspects of brewing. Annual *Buyers' Guide* and *Directory* available.

Brewing and Distilling International. Brewery Traders Publications, Ltd. • Monthly. $160.00 per year.

Impact: U.S. News and Research for the Wine, Spirits, and Beer Industries. M. Shanken Communications, Inc. • Biweekly. $375.00 per year. Newsletter covering the marketing, economic, and financial aspects of alcoholic beverages.

Kane's Beverage Week: The Newsletter of Beverage Marketing. Whitaker Newsletters, Inc. • Weekly. $449.00 per year. Newsletter. Covers news relating to the alcoholic beverage industries, including social, health, and legal issues.

Malt Advocate. Malt Advocate, Inc. • Quarterly. $16.00 per year. Provides information for consumers of upscale whiskey and beer.

MBAA Technical Quarterly. Master Brewers Association of the Americas. • Quarterly. $100.00 per year. Includes membership.

Modern Brewery Age. Business Journals, Inc. • Bimonthly. $85.00 per year. Annual supplement available *Blue Book.*

PRICE SOURCES

Beverage Media. Beverage Media, Ltd. • Monthly. $78.00 per year. Wholesale prices.

Feedstuffs: The Weekly Newspaper for Agribusiness. ABC, Inc. • Weekly. $109.00 per year.

RESEARCH CENTERS AND INSTITUTES

Cereal Crops Research Unit U.S. Department of Agricultural Research Service. 501 N. Walnut St., Madison, WI 53705. Phone: (608)262-3355 Fax: (608)264-5528 E-mail: dmpeter4@facstaff.wisc.edu.

STATISTICS SOURCES

Annual Survey of Manufactures. Available from U. S. Government Printing Office. • Annual. Prices vary. Issued by the U. S. Census Bureau as an interim update to the *Census of Manufactures.* Includes data on number of manufacturing establishments in various industries, employment, labor costs, value of shipments, capital expenditures, inventories, energy costs, and assets. (See also Census Bureau home page, http://www.census.gov/.).

Beer Statistics News. Beer Marketer's Insights, Inc. • 24 times a year. $360.00 per year. Market share and shipments by region and brewer.

Business Statistics of the United States. Courtenay M. Slater, editor. Bernan Associates. • 1999. $74.00. Fifth edition. Based on *Business Statistics*, formerly issue by the Bureau of Economic Analysis, U. S. Department of Commerce. Provides basic data for a wide variety of U. S. industries, services, and economic indicators. Most statistics are shown annually for 29 years and monthly for the most recent four years.

Impact Beverage Trends in America. M. Shanken Communications, Inc. • Annual. $695.00. Detailed compilations of data for various segments of the liquor, beer, and soft drink industries.

Monthly Statistical Release: Beer. U. S. Bureau of Alcohol, Tobacco, and Firearms. • Monthly.

Standard & Poor's Industry Surveys. Standard & Poor's. • Semiannual. $1,800.00. Two looseleaf volumes. Includes monthly supplements. Provides detailed, individual surveys of 52 major industry groups. Each survey is revised on a semiannual basis. Also includes "Monthly Investment Review" (industry group investment analysis) and monthly "Trends & Projections" (economic analysis).

Survey of Current Business. Available from U. S. Government Printing Office. • Monthly. $49.00 per year. Issued by Bureau of Economic Analysis, U. S. Department of Commerce. Presents a wide variety of business and economic data.

TRADE/PROFESSIONAL ASSOCIATIONS

American Society of Brewing Chemists. 3340 Pilot Knob Rd., Saint Paul, MN 55121-2097. Phone: (612)454-7250 Fax: (612)454-0766 E-mail: asbc@scisoc.org • URL: http://www.scisoc.org/asbc.

Beer Institute. 122 C. St., N.W., No. 750, Washington, DC 20001-2109. Phone: 800-379-2739 or (202)737-2337 Fax: (202)737-7004 E-mail: beer@mnsinc.com • URL: http://www.beerinst.org.

Brewers' Association of America. 2627 Marion Ave., Durham, NC 27705. Phone: (919)493-1829 Fax: (919)490-0865.

Brewery and Soft Drink Workers Conference-U.S.A. and Canada. 25 Louisiana Ave., N.W., Washington, DC 20001. Phone: (202)624-6922 Fax: (202)624-6925.

Master Brewers Association of the Americas. 2421 N. Mayfair Rd., Ste. 310, Wauwatosa, WI 53226-1407. Phone: (414)774-8558 E-mail: mbaa@mbaa.com • URL: http://www.mbaa.com.

National Beer Wholesalers' Association. 1100 S. Washington St., Alexandria, VA 22314. Phone: 800-300-6417 or (703)683-4300 Fax: (703)683-8965 • URL: http://www.nbwa.org.

World Association of Alcohol Beverage Industries. 1131 Rockingham Ln., No. 122, Richardson, TX 75080. Phone: 800-466-6920 or (972)664-9021 Fax: (972)664-9024 • URL: http://www.waabi.org.

OTHER SOURCES

Liquor Control Law Reports: Federal and All States. CCH, Inc. • $3,338.00 per year. Nine looseleaf volumes. Biweekly updates. Federal and state regulation and taxation of alcoholic beverages.

Major Food and Drink Companies of the World. Available from The Gale Group. • 2001. $855.00. Fourth edition. Two volumes. Published by Graham & Whiteside. Contains profiles and trade names for more than 9,000 important food and beverage companies in various countries. In addition to foods, includes both alcoholic and nonalcoholic drink products.

The Market for Craft and Specialty Beer. MarketResearch.com. • 1997. $595.00. Market research report with projections to the year 2001. Includes brewing company profiles.

Thomas Food and Beverage Market Place. Grey House Publishing. • Annual. $295.00. Three volumes. Contains more than 40,000 entries covering food companies, beverages, food equipment, warehouse companies, food brokers, wholesalers, importers, and exporters. Formerly *Thomas Food Industry Register.*

BRIBES AND PAYOFFS

See: BUSINESS ETHICS

BRICK INDUSTRY

See: CLAY INDUSTRY; REFRACTORIES

BROADCASTING

See: RADIO BROADCASTING INDUSTRY; TELEVISION BROADCASTING INDUSTRY

BROKERS, STOCK

See: STOCK BROKERS

BUDGET, FEDERAL

See: FEDERAL BUDGET

BUDGETING, BUSINESS

GENERAL WORKS

Basics of Budgeting. Robert G. Finney. AMACOM. • 1993. $19.95.

ABSTRACTS AND INDEXES

Accounting and Tax Index. UMI. • Quarterly. Price on application. Includes annual cumulative bound volume. Indexes accounting, auditing, and taxation literature appearing in journals, books, pamphlets, conference proceedings, and newsletters. (UMI is University Microfilms International, a Bell & Howell Co.).

HANDBOOKS AND MANUALS

Budgeting: A How-to-Do-it Manual for Librarians. Alice S. Warner. Neal-Schuman Publishers, Inc. • 1998. $49.95. Explains six forms of budgeting suitable for various kinds of libraries. Includes a bibliography. (How-to-Do-It Series).

Handbook of Budgeting. Robert Rachlin and H. W. Sweeny. John Wiley and Sons, Inc. • 1998. $160.00. Fourth edition. 2000 Supplement, $60.00.

Little Black Book of Budgets and Forecasts. Michael C. Thomsett. AMACOM. • 1988. $14.95. A concise guide to business budgeting and forecasting. (Little Black Book Series).

Total Business Budgeting: A Step-by-Step Guide with Forms. Robert Rachlin. John Wiley and Sons, Inc. • 1999. $69.95. Second edition.

PERIODICALS AND NEWSLETTERS

Cost Control Strategies for Managers, Controllers and Finance Executives. Siefer Consultants, Inc. • Monthly. $259.00 per year. Newsletter. Provides a variety of ideas on business budgeting and controlling company expenses. Formerly *Cost Control Strategies for Financial Institutions.*

Journal of Cost Management. Warren, Gorham and Lamont/RIA Group. • Bimonthly. $123.98 per year. Includes articles on business budgeting.

Strategic Finance. Institute of Management Accountants. • Monthly. $140.00 per year; non-profit institutions, $70.00 per year. Provides articles on corporate finance, cost control, cash flow, budgeting, corporate taxes, and other financial management topics.

TRADE/PROFESSIONAL ASSOCIATIONS

National Association of State Budget Officers. Hall of States, 444 N. Capitol St., N.W., Ste. 642, Washington, DC 20001. Phone: (202)624-5382 Fax: (202)624-7745 • URL: http://www.nasbo.org.

BUDGETING, PERSONAL

See: PERSONAL FINANCE

BUILDING AND LOAN ASSOCIATIONS

See: SAVINGS AND LOAN ASSOCIATIONS

BUILDING CONTRACTS

See also: BUILDING INDUSTRY; CONTRACTS

GENERAL WORKS

Construction Contracting. Richard H. Clough and Glenn A. Sears. John Wiley and Sons, Inc. • 1994. $99.00. Sixth edition.

ABSTRACTS AND INDEXES

Current Law Index: Multiple Access to Legal Periodicals. The Gale Group. • Monthly. $650.00 per year. Produced in cooperation with the American Association of Law Libraries. Indexes more than 900 law journals, legal newspapers, and specialty publications from the U.S., Canada, U.K., Ireland, Australia, and New Zealand.

DIRECTORIES

ABC Today-Associated Builders and Contractors National Membership Directory. Associated Builders and Contractors, Inc. ABC Publications. • Annual. $150.00. List of approximately 19,000 member construction contractors and suppliers. Formerly *Builder and Contractor-Associated Builders and Contractors Membership Directory.*

Blue Book of Building and Construction. Blue Book of Building and Construction. • Annual. Controlled circulation. 11 regional editions. Lists architects, contractors, subcontractors, manufacturers and suppliers of constructions materials and equipment.

ENR Top 400 Construction Contractors (Engineering News-Record). McGraw-Hill. • Annual. $10.00. Lists 400 United States contractors receiving largest dollar volume of contracts in preceding calendar year.

ONLINE DATABASES

American Statistics Index: A Comprehensive Guide and Index to the Statistical Publications of the United States Government [Online]. Congressional Information Service, Inc. • Indexes and abstracts, 1973 to date. Inquire as to online cost and availability.

PERIODICALS AND NEWSLETTERS

Construction Law Adviser: Monthly Practical Advice for Lawyers and Construction Professionals. West Group. • Monthly. $295.00 per year. Newsletter.

Constructor: The Management Magazine of the Construction Industry. Associated General Contractors of America. AGC Information, Inc. • Monthly. Free to members; non-members, $250.00 per year. Includes *Directory*.

Government Contractor. Federal Publications, Inc. • Weekly. $1,032.00 per year.

The Subcontractor. American Subcontractors Association. • Monthly. $40.00 per year.

RESEARCH CENTERS AND INSTITUTES

Lexis.com Research System. Lexis-Nexis Group. Phone: 800-227-9597 or (937)865-6800 Fax: (937)865-6909 E-mail: webmaster@prod.lexis-nexis.com • URL: http://www.lexis.com • Fee-based Web site offers extensive searching of a wide variety of legal sources. Additional features include Daily Opinion Service, lexis.com Bookstore, Career Center, CLE Center, Law Schools, and Practice Pages ("Pages specific to areas of specialty").

TRADE/PROFESSIONAL ASSOCIATIONS

American Institute of Constructors. 466 94th Ave., N., Saint Petersburg, FL 33702. Phone: (727)578-0317 Fax: (727)578-9982 E-mail: aicnatl@aol.com • URL: http://www.aicnet.org.

American Subcontractors Association. 1004 Duke St., Alexandria, VA 22314. Phone: (703)684-3450 Fax: (703)836-3482 E-mail: asaoffice-hq@aol.com • URL: http://www.asaonline.com.

Associated Builders and Contractors. 1300 N. 17th St., Arlington, VA 22209. Phone: (703)812-2000 Fax: (703)812-8200 E-mail: bakum@abc.org • URL: http://www.abc.org.

Associated General Contractors of America. 333 John Carlyle St., Ste. 200, Alexandria, VA 22314. Phone: (703)548-3118 Fax: (703)548-3119 E-mail: info@agc.org • URL: http://www.agc.org.

Associated Specialty Contractors. Three Bethesda Metro Center, Suite 1100, Bethesda, MD 20814. Phone: (301)657-3110 Fax: (301)215-4500.

OTHER SOURCES

Forms and Agreements for Architects, Engineers and Contractors. Albert Dib. West Group. • Four looseleaf volumes. $495.00. Periodic supplementation. Covers evaluation of construction documents and alternative clauses. Includes pleadings for litigation and resolving of claims. (Real Property-Zoning Series).

Government Contracts Reports. CCH, Inc. • $2,249.00 per year. 10 looseleaf volumes. Weekly updates. Laws and regulations affecting government contracts.

BUILDING EQUIPMENT

See: CONSTRUCTION EQUIPMENT

BUILDING ESTIMATING

See: ESTIMATING

BUILDING INDUSTRY

See also: APARTMENT HOUSES; ARCHITECTURE; BUILDING MATERIALS INDUSTRY; CONSTRUCTION EQUIPMENT; DOOR INDUSTRY; ELECTRICAL CONSTRUCTION INDUSTRY; ESTIMATING; HOME IMPROVEMENT INDUSTRY; OFFICE BUILDINGS; PREFABRICATED HOUSE INDUSTRY

GENERAL WORKS

Fundamentals of Construction Estimating and Cost Accounting. Keith Collier. Prentice Hall. • 2000. Third edition. Price on application.

ABSTRACTS AND INDEXES

Applied Science and Technology Index. H. W. Wilson Co. • 11 times a year. Quarterly and annual cumulations. Service basis for print edition; CD-ROM edition, $1,495.00 per year. Indexes a wide variety of English language technical, industrial, and engineering periodicals.

NTIS Alerts: Building Industry Technology. National Technical Information Service. • Semimonthly. $210.00 per year. Provides descriptions of government-sponsored research reports and software, with ordering information. Covers architecture, construction management, building materials, maintenance, furnishings, and related subjects. Formerly *Abstract Newsletter*.

BIBLIOGRAPHIES

Carpenters and Builders Library. John E. Ball. Pearson Education and Technology. • 1991. Four volumes. $21.95 per volume. Sixth edition.

DIRECTORIES

ABC Today-Associated Builders and Contractors National Membership Directory. Associated Builders and Contractors, Inc. ABC Publications. • Annual. $150.00. List of approximately 19,000 member construction contractors and suppliers. Formerly *Builder and Contractor-Associated Builders and Contractors Membership Directory.*

Aberdeen's Concrete Construction Buyers' Guide. The Aberdeen Group. • Annual. $5.00. Lists sources of products and services related to building with concrete.

Builder: Buyer's Guide. Hanley-Wood, LLC. • Annual. $10.00. A directory of products and services for the home building and remodeling industry.

Building Officials and Code Administrators International-Membership Directory. Building Officials and Code Administrators International BOCA. • Annual. $16.00. Approximately 14,000 construction code officials, architects, engineers, trade associations, and manufacturers.

Construction Specifier - Member Directory. Construction Specifications Institute. • Annual. $30.00. Roster of construction specifers by the institute, and 17,200 members.

Magazine of Masonry Construction Buyers' Guide. The Aberdeen Group. • Annual. $3.00. Lists manufacturers or suppliers of products and services related to masonry construction.

ProSales Buyer's Guide. Hanley-Wood, LLC. • Annual. $5.00. A directory of equipment for professional builders.

ENCYCLOPEDIAS AND DICTIONARIES

Dictionary of Architecture and Construction. Cyril M. Harris. McGraw-Hill Professional. • 2000. $69.95. Third edition.

Dictionary of Building. Randall McMullan. G P Courseware. • 1991. $59.50.

Encyclopedia of Architecture: Design, Engineering and Construction. Joseph A. Wilkes and R. T. Packard, editors. John Wiley and Sons, Inc. • 1990. $1,440.00. Five volumes.

FINANCIAL RATIOS

Almanac of Business and Industrial Financial Ratios. Leo Troy. Prentice Hall. • Annual. $99.95. Contains financial ratios derived from federal tax returns. Ratios for each of about 200 industries are arranged according to company asset size.

Construction Industry Annual Financial Survey. Construction Financial Management Association. • Annual. $149.00. Contains key financial ratios for various kinds and sizes of construction contractors.

HANDBOOKS AND MANUALS

Building Construction Handbook. Ray Chudley. Butterworth-Heinemann. • 1998. $34.95. Third edition.

Construction Arbitration Handbook. James Acret. Shepard's. • 1985. $110.00. Explains the arbitration of disputes involving builders.

Dun & Bradstreet/Gale Group Industry Handbooks. The Gale Group. • 2000. $630.00. Five volumes. $145.00 per volume. Each volume covers two or more major industries: 1. *Entertainment and Hospitality*; 2. *Construction and Agriculture*; 3. *Chemicals and Pharmaceuticals*; 4. *Computers & Software and Broadcasting & Telecommunications*; 5. *Insurance and Health & Medical Services*. The following are included for each industry: overview, statistics, financial ratios, rankings, merger information, company directory, directory of associations, and consultants directory.

Guide to Energy Efficient Commercial Equipment. Margaret Suozzo and others. American Council for an Energy Efficient Economy. • 1997. $25.00. Provides information on specifying and purchasing energy-saving systems for buildings (heating, air conditioning, lighting, and motors).

New Uses for Obsolete Buildings. Urban Land Institute. • 1996. $64.95. Covers various aspects of redevelopment: zoning, building codes, environment, economics, financing, and marketing. Includes eight case studies and 75 descriptions of completed "adaptive use projects.".

Standard Handbook of Structural Details for Building Construction. Morton Newman. McGraw-Hill. • 1993. $99.95. Second edition.

INTERNET DATABASES

Fedstats. Federal Interagency Council on Statistical Policy. Phone: (202)395-7254 • URL: http://www.fedstats.gov • Web site features an efficient search facility for full-text statistics produced by more than 70 federal agencies, including the Census Bureau, the Bureau of Economic Analysis, and the Bureau of Labor Statistics. Boolean searches can be made within one agency or for all agencies combined. Links are offered to international statistical bureaus, including the UN, IMF, OECD, UNESCO, Eurostat, and 20 individual countries. Fees: Free.

ONLINE DATABASES

Business and Industry. Responsive Database Services, Inc. • Contains online citations, abstracts, and selected fulltext from more than 1,000 trade journals, newspapers, and other publications. Provides general coverage of both manufacturing and service industries, including marketing, production, industry trends, key events, and information on specific companies. Time span is 1994 to date. Daily updates. Inquire as to online cost and availability. (Also available in a CD-ROM version.).

DRI U.S. Central Database. Data Products Division. • Provides more than 23,000 business, financial, demographic, economic, foreign trade, and industry-related time series for the U.S. Includes national income, population, retail-wholesale trade, price indexes, labor data, housing, industrial production, banking, interest rates, money supply, etc. Time period is generally 1947 to date (some data back to 1929). Updating varies. Inquire as to online cost and availability.

Tablebase. Responsive Database Services, Inc. • Provides online numerical tabular data from a wide variety of business, organization, and government sources, including 900 trade journals. Includes industry and individual company statistics relating to products, market share, sales forecasts, production, exports, market trends, etc. Time span is 1997 to date. Weekly updates. Inquire as to online cost and availability. (Also available in a CD-ROM version.).

PERIODICALS AND NEWSLETTERS

The Aberdeen's Concrete Construction. Aberdeen Group. • Monthly. $30.00 per year. Covers methods of building with precast, prestressed, and other forms of concrete. Emphasis is on technology and new products or construction procedures.

The Aberdeen's Magazine of Masonry Construction. Aberdeen Group. • Monthly. $30.00 per year. Covers the business, production, and marketing aspects of various kind of masonry construction: brick, concrete block, glass block, etc.

Builder: Official Publication of the National Association of Home Builders. National Association of Home Builders of the United States. Hanley-Wood, LLC. • Monthly. $29.95 per year. Covers the home building and remodeling industry in general, including design, construction, and marketing.

Building Design and Construction. Cahners Publishing Inc. • Monthly. $108.90 per year. For non-residential building owners, contractors, engineers and architects.

Buildings: The Facilities Construction and Management Journal. Stamats Communications, Inc. • Monthly. $70.00 per year. Serves professional building ownership/management organizations.

CFMA Building Profits. Construction Financial Management Association. • Bimonthly. Controlled circulation. Covers the financial side of the construction industry.

Commercial Building: Tranforming Plans into Buildings. Stamats Communications. • Bimonthly. $48.00 per year. Edited for building contractors, engineers, and architects. Includes special features on new products, climate control, plumbing, and vertical transportation.

Construction Law Adviser: Monthly Practical Advice for Lawyers and Construction Professionals. West Group. • Monthly. $295.00 per year. Newsletter.

Construction Specifier: For Commercial and Industrial Construction. Construction Specifications Institute. • Monthly. Free to members; non-members, $36.00 per year; universities, $30.00 per year. Technical aspects of the construction industry.

Design Cost Data: The Cost Estimating Magazine for Architects, Builders and Specifiers. L. M. Rector Corp. • Bimonthly. $64.80 per year. Provides a preliminary cost estimating system for architects, contractors, builders, and developers, utilizing historical data. Includes case studies of actual costs. Formerly *Design Cost and Data.*

ENR Connecting the Industry Worldwide (Engineering News-Record). McGraw-Hill. • Weekly. $74.00 per year.

Professional Builder. Cahners Business Information. • Monthly. $99.90 per year. Provides price and market forecasts on industrial products, components and materials. Office products, business systems and transportation. Includes supplement *Luxury Homes.* Formerly *Professional Builder and Remodeler.*

ProSales: For Dealers and Distributors Serving the Professional Contractor. Hanley-Wood, LLC. • Monthly. $36.00 per year. Includes special feature issues on selling, credit, financing, and the marketing of power tools.

PRICE SOURCES

Building Construction Cost Data. R.S. Means Co., Inc. • Annual. $76.95. Lists over 20,000 entries for estimating.

Means Construction Cost Indexes. R.S. Means Co., Inc. • Quarterly. $198.00 per year.

Means Labor Rates for the Construction Industry. R. S. Means Co., Inc. • Annual. $174.95. Formerly *Labor Rates for the Construction Industry.*

RESEARCH CENTERS AND INSTITUTES

Building Technology Center. Stevens Institute of Technology, Castle Point on the Hudson, Hoboken, NJ 07030. Phone: (201)420-5100 Fax: (201)420-5593.

Construction Industry Institute. University of Texas at Austin, 3208 Red River, Suite 300, Austin, TX 78705-2697. Phone: (512)232-3000 Fax: (512)499-8101 E-mail: k.eickman@mail.utexas.edu • URL: http://www.construction-institution.org • Research activities are related to the management, planning, and design aspects of construction project execution.

Construction Research Center. Georgia Institute of Technology, Atlanta, GA 30332-0245. Phone: (404)894-3013 Fax: (404)894-9140 E-mail: steve.johnson@mse.gatech.edu • URL: http://www.arch.gatech.edu/crc/ • Conducts interdisciplinary research in all aspects of construction, including planning, design, cost estimating, and management.

STATISTICS SOURCES

Business Statistics of the United States. Courtenay M. Slater, editor. Bernan Associates. • 1999. $74.00. Fifth edition. Based on *Business Statistics*, formerly issue by the Bureau of Economic Analysis, U. S. Department of Commerce. Provides basic data for a wide variety of U. S. industries, services, and economic indicators. Most statistics are shown annually for 29 years and monthly for the most recent four years.

Encyclopedia of American Industries. The Gale Group. • 1998. $560.00. Second edition. Two volumes. $280.00 per volume. Volume one is *Manufacturing Industries* and volume two is *Service and Non-Manufacturing Industries.* Provides the history, development, and recent status of approximately 1,000 industries. Includes statistical graphs, with industry and general indexes.

Expenditures for Residential Improvements and Repairs. Available from U. S. Government Printing Office. • Quarterly. $14.00 per year. Bureau of the Census Construction Report, C50. Provides estimates of spending for housing maintenance, repairs, additions, alterations, and major replacements.

Standard & Poor's Industry Surveys. Standard & Poor's. • Semiannual. $1,800.00. Two looseleaf volumes. Includes monthly supplements. Provides detailed, individual surveys of 52 major industry groups. Each survey is revised on a semiannual basis. Also includes "Monthly Investment Review" (industry group investment analysis) and monthly "Trends & Projections" (economic analysis).

Survey of Current Business. Available from U. S. Government Printing Office. • Monthly. $49.00 per year. Issued by Bureau of Economic Analysis, U. S. Department of Commerce. Presents a wide variety of business and economic data.

U. S. Industry Profiles: The Leading 100. The Gale Group. • 1998. $120.00. Second edition. Contains detailed profiles, with statistics, of 100 industries in the areas of manufacturing, construction, transportation, wholesale trade, retail trade, and entertainment.

United States Census of Construction Industries. U.S. Bureau of the Census. • Quinquennial. Results presented in reports, tape, and CD-ROM files.

Value of New Construction Put in Place. U.S. Bureau of the Census. Available from U.S. Government Printing Office. • Monthly. $42.00 per year.

WEFA Industrial Monitor. John Wiley and Sons, Inc. • Annual. $65.00. Prepared by industry analysts at WEFA, an economic forecasting and consulting firm (originally Wharton Econometric Forecasting Associates). Contains discussions of the outlook for major U. S. industries, with many 10-year forecasts (WEFA Web site is http://www.wefa.com).

TRADE/PROFESSIONAL ASSOCIATIONS

Building and Construction Trades Department - AFL-CIO. 1155 15th St., N.W., 4th Fl., Washington, DC 20005. Phone: (202)347-1461 Fax: (202)628-0724 • URL: http://www.buildingtrades.org.

Building Officials and Code Administrators International. 4051 W. Flossmoor Rd., Country Club Hills, IL 60478. Phone: (708)799-2300 Fax: (708)799-4981 E-mail: member@bocai.org • URL: http://www.bocai.org.

Construction Financial Management Association. 29 Emmons Dr., Suite F-50, Princeton, NJ 08540. Phone: (609)452-8000 Fax: (609)452-0474 E-mail: info@cfma.org • URL: http://www.cfma.org • Members are accountants and other financial managers in the construction industry.

Construction Industry Manufacturers Association. 111 E. Wisconsin Ave., Suite 1000, Milwaukee, WI 53202. Phone: (414)272-0943 Fax: (414)277-1170 E-mail: cima@cimanet.com • URL: http://www.cimanet.com.

National Association of Home Builders of the United States. 17120 N. Dallas Pkwy., Ste. 175, Dallas, TX 75248. Phone: 800-252-9001 or (972)732-0090 Fax: (972)732-6067 • URL: http://www.nahb.com.

National Association of the Remodeling Industry. 4900 Seminary Rd., Suite 320, Alexandria, VA 22311. Phone: (703)575-1100 Fax: (703)575-1121 E-mail: info@nari.org • URL: http://www.nari.org.

National Association of Women In Construction. 327 S. Adams St., Fort Worth, TX 76104. Phone: 800-552-3506 or (817)877-5551 Fax: (817)877-

0324 E-mail: nawic@onramp.net • URL: http://www.nawic.org.

National Constructors Association. 1730 M St., N.W., Suite 503, Washington, DC 20036. Phone: (202)466-8880 Fax: (202)466-7512.

OTHER SOURCES

Construction Labor Report. Bureau of National Affairs, Inc. • Weekly. $1,039.00 per year. Two volumes. Looseleaf.

Dodge Reports. F. W. Dodge Group. • Daily. Price on application. Individual reports on new construction jobs.

Dodge/SCAN. F. W. Dodge Group. • Price on application. Provides plans and specifications of new construction jobs.

Door Hardware. Available from MarketResearch.com. • 1997. $495.00. Market research report published by Specialists in Business Information. Covers locks, closers, doorknobs, security devices, and other door hardware. Presents market data relative to demographics, sales growth, shipments, exports, imports, price trends, and end-use. Includes company profiles.

Doors. Available from MarketResearch.com. • 1999. $2,250.00. Market research report published by Specialists in Business Information. Covers residential doors, including garage doors. Presents market data relative to demographics, sales growth, shipments, exports, imports, price trends, and end-use. Includes company profiles.

Forms and Agreements for Architects, Engineers and Contractors. Albert Dib. West Group. • Four looseleaf volumes. $495.00. Periodic supplementation. Covers evaluation of construction documents and alternative clauses. Includes pleadings for litigation and resolving of claims. (Real Property-Zoning Series).

Infrastructure Industries USA. The Gale Group. • 2001. $240.00. Replaces *Agriculture, Forestry, Fishing, Mining, and Construction USA* and *Transportation and Public Utilities USA*. Presents statistics and projections relating to economic activity in a wide variety of natural resource and construction industries.

International Conference of Building Officials. Uniform Building Code. International Conference of Building Officials. • Members, $144.55; non-members, $180.70.

Windows. Available from MarketResearch.com. • 1999. $2,250.00. Market research report published by Specialists in Business Information. Covers metal, wood, and vinyl windows. Presents market data relative to demographics, sales growth, shipments, exports, imports, price trends, and end-use. Includes company profiles.

BUILDING LOANS

See: MORTGAGES

BUILDING MAINTENANCE

See: MAINTENANCE OF BUILDINGS

BUILDING MANAGEMENT

See: PROPERTY MANAGEMENT

BUILDING MATERIALS INDUSTRY

GENERAL WORKS

Basic Construction Material. Charles Herubin and Theodore Marotta. Prentice-Hall. • 1996. $77.00. Fifth edition.

Construction Materials and Processes. Donald A. Watson. McGraw-Hill. • 1986. $83.34. Third edition.

Materials of Construction. Ronald C. Smith. McGraw-Hill. • 1987. $53.85. Fourth edition.

DIRECTORIES

Builder: Buyer's Guide. Hanley-Wood, LLC. • Annual. $10.00. A directory of products and services for the home building and remodeling industry.

Construction Equipment Buyers' Guide. Cahners Business Information. • Annual. Included in subscription to *Construction Equipment.*

Directory of Building Products and Hardlines Distributors. Chain Store Guide. • Annual. $280.00. Includes hardware, houseware, and building supply distributors. Formerly *Directory of Hardline Distributors.*

Directory of Home Center Operators and Hardware Chains. Chain Store Age. • Annual. $300.00. Nearly 5,400 home center operators, paint and home decorating chains, and lumber and building materials companies.

International Conference of Building Officials - Membership Directory. International Conference of Building Officials. • Annual. Price on application.

North American Building Material Distribution Association-Membership. North American Building Material Distribution Association. • Annual. $895.00, About 200 wholesale distributors of building products who are members, and 150 manufacturers in that field who are associate members and over 600 of their locations. Formerly *National Building Material Distributors Association Membership and Product Directory.*

North American Wholesale Lumber Association - Distribution Directory. North American Wholesale Lumber Association. • Annual. $50.00. Over 600 wholesalers and manufacturers of lumber and related forest products.

Remodeling Product Guide. Hanley-Wood, LLC. • Annual. $10.00. A directory of products and services for the home remodeling industry. Formerly *Remodeling-Guide to Manufacturers.*

U. S. Glass, Metal, and Glazing: Buyers Guide. Key Communications, Inc. • Annual. $20.00. A directory of supplies and equipment for the glass fabrication and installation industry.

ENCYCLOPEDIAS AND DICTIONARIES

Dictionary of Architecture, Building, Construction and Materials. Herbert Bucksch. French and European Publishers, Inc. • 1983. Second edition. Two volumes. $295.00 per volume. Text in English and German.

Encyclopedia of Materials: Science and Technology. K.H.J. Buschow and others, editors. Pergamon Press/Elsevier Science. • 2001. $6,875.00. Eleven volumes. Provides extensive technical information on a wide variety of materials, including metals, ceramics, plastics, optical materials, and building materials. Includes more than 2,000 articles and 5,000 illustrations.

Illustrated Dictionary of Building Materials and Techniques: An Invaluable Sourcebook to the Tools, Terms, Materials, and Techniques Used by Building Professionals. Paul Bianchina. John Wiley and Sons, Inc. • 1993. $49.95. Contains 4,000 definitions of building and building materials terms, with 500 illustrations. Includes materials grades, measurements, and specifications.

FINANCIAL RATIOS

Almanac of Business and Industrial Financial Ratios. Leo Troy. Prentice Hall. • Annual. $99.95. Contains financial ratios derived from federal tax returns. Ratios for each of about 200 industries are arranged according to company asset size.

Annual Statement Studies. Robert Morris Associates: The Association of Lending and Credit Risk Professiona. • Annual. Free to members; non-members, $140.00. Median and quartile financial ratios are given for over 400 kinds of manufacturing, wholesale, retail, construction, and consumer finance establishments. Data is sorted by both asset size and sales volume. Includes a clearly written "Definition of Ratios" and an alphabetical industry index.

Cost of Doing Business and Financial Position Survey of the Retail Lumber and Building Material Dealers of the Northeastern States. Northeastern Retail Lumber Association. • Annual. Free to members; non-members, $300.00. Includes sales figures, profit margins, pricing methods, rates of return, and other financial data for retailers of lumber and building supplies in the Northeast.

HANDBOOKS AND MANUALS

Construction Materials: Types, Uses, and Applications. Caleb Hornbostel. John Wiley and Sons, Inc. • 1991. $225.00. Second edition. (Practical Construction Guides Series).

Materials Handbook. George S. Brady and others. McGraw-Hill. • 1996. $99.00. 14th edition.

INTERNET DATABASES

Fedstats. Federal Interagency Council on Statistical Policy. Phone: (202)395-7254 • URL: http://www.fedstats.gov • Web site features an efficient search facility for full-text statistics produced by more than 70 federal agencies, including the Census Bureau, the Bureau of Economic Analysis, and the Bureau of Labor Statistics. Boolean searches can be made within one agency or for all agencies combined. Links are offered to international statistical bureaus, including the UN, IMF, OECD, UNESCO, Eurostat, and 20 individual countries. Fees: Free.

ONLINE DATABASES

American Statistics Index: A Comprehensive Guide and Index to the Statistical Publications of the United States Government [Online]. Congressional Information Service, Inc. • Indexes and abstracts, 1973 to date. Inquire as to online cost and availability.

DRI U.S. Central Database. Data Products Division. • Provides more than 23,000 business, financial, demographic, economic, foreign trade, and industry-related time series for the U.S. Includes national income, population, retail-wholesale trade, price indexes, labor data, housing, industrial production, banking, interest rates, money supply, etc. Time period is generally 1947 to date (some data back to 1929). Updating varies. Inquire as to online cost and availability.

PERIODICALS AND NEWSLETTERS

Building Material Retailer. National Lumber and Building Material Dealers Association. • Monthly. $25.00 per year. Includes special feature issues on hand and power tools, lumber, roofing, kitchens, flooring, windows and doors, and insulation.

National Home Center News: News and Analysis for the Home Improvement, Building, Material Industry. Lebhar-Friedman, Inc. • 22 times a year. $99.00 per year. Includes special feature issues on hardware and tools, building materials, millwork, electrical supplies, lighting, and kitchens.

U. S. Glass, Metal, and Glazing. Key Communications, Inc. • Monthly. $39.00 per year. Edited for glass fabricators, glaziers, distributors, and retailers. Special feature issues are devoted to architectural glass, mirror glass, windows, storefronts, hardware, machinery, sealants, and adhesives. Regular topics include automobile glass and fenestration (window design and placement).

PRICE SOURCES

PPI Detailed Report. Bureau of Labor Statistics, U.S. Department of Labor. Available from U.S. Government Printing Office. • Monthly. $55.00 per year. Formerly *Producer Price Indexes.*

RESEARCH CENTERS AND INSTITUTES

NAHB Research Center. 400 Prince George's Blvd., Upper Marlboro, MD 20772. Phone: 800-638-8556 or (301)249-4000 Fax: (301)430-6180 E-mail: lbowles@nahbrc.org • URL: http://www.nahbrc.com.

School of Architecture-Building Research Council. University of Illinois at Urbana-Champaign. One E. Saint Mary's Rd., Champaign, IL 61820. Phone: 800-336-0616 or (217)333-1801 Fax: (217)244-2204 E-mail: kgallghr@cso.uiuc.edu • URL: http://www.arch.uiuc.edu/brc.

STATISTICS SOURCES

Business Statistics of the United States. Courtenay M. Slater, editor. Bernan Associates. • 1999. $74.00. Fifth edition. Based on *Business Statistics*, formerly issue by the Bureau of Economic Analysis, U. S. Department of Commerce. Provides basic data for a wide variety of U. S. industries, services, and economic indicators. Most statistics are shown annually for 29 years and monthly for the most recent four years.

Survey of Current Business. Available from U. S. Government Printing Office. • Monthly. $49.00 per year. Issued by Bureau of Economic Analysis, U. S. Department of Commerce. Presents a wide variety of business and economic data.

TRADE/PROFESSIONAL ASSOCIATIONS

International Conference of Building Officials. 5360 Workman Mill Rd., Whittier, CA 90601-2298. Phone: 800-284-4406 or (562)699-0541 Fax: (562)695-4694 • URL: http://www.icbo.org.

National Lumber and Building Materials Dealers Association. 40 Ivy St., S.E., Washington, DC 20003. Phone: 800-634-8695 or (202)547-2230 Fax: (202)547-8645.

North American Building Material Distribution Association. 401 N. Michigan Ave., Chicago, IL 60611. Phone: 888-747-7862 or (312)321-6845 Fax: (312)644-0310 E-mail: nbmda@sba.com • URL: http://www.nbmda.org.

OTHER SOURCES

The Home Improvement Market. Available from MarketResearch.com. • 1999. $2,750.00. Market research report published by Packaged Facts. Covers the market for lumber, finishing materials, tools, hardware, etc.

BUILDING REPAIR AND RECONSTRUCTION

See: HOME IMPROVEMENT INDUSTRY

BUILDING RESEARCH

See also: ARCHITECTURE; BUILDING INDUSTRY; BUSINESS RESEARCH

PERIODICALS AND NEWSLETTERS

Building Research. Building Research Publications Board. • Membership.

RESEARCH CENTERS AND INSTITUTES

Centre for Building Science. University of Toronto Department of Engineering. 35 Saint George St., Toronto, ON, Canada M5S 1A4. Phone: (416)978-3096 Fax: (416)978-5054 E-mail: pressna@civ.utoronto.ca • URL: http://www.civ.utoronto.ca.

NAHB Research Center. 400 Prince George's Blvd., Upper Marlboro, MD 20772. Phone: 800-638-8556 or (301)249-4000 Fax: (301)430-6180 E-mail: lbowles@nahbrc.org • URL: http://www.nahbrc.com.

School of Architecture-Building Research Council. University of Illinois at Urbana-Champaign. One E. Saint Mary's Rd., Champaign, IL 61820. Phone: 800-336-0616 or (217)333-1801 Fax: (217)244-2204 E-mail: kgallghr@cso.uiuc.edu • URL: http://www.arch.uiuc.edu/brc.

TRADE/PROFESSIONAL ASSOCIATIONS

Building Officials and Code Administrators International. 4051 W. Flossmoor Rd., Country Club Hills, IL 60478. Phone: (708)799-2300 Fax: (708)799-4981 E-mail: member@bocai.org • URL: http://www.bocai.org.

BUILDING STONE

See: QUARRYING

BUILDING SUPPLY INDUSTRY

See: BUILDING MATERIALS INDUSTRY

BUILDINGS, PREFABRICATED

See: PREFABRICATED HOUSE INDUSTRY

BUILDINGS, RESIDENTIAL

See: HOUSING

BULLION

See: MONEY

BUREAUCRACY

See also: GOVERNMENT EMPLOYEES

GENERAL WORKS

Bureaucracy: What Government Agencies Do and Why They Do It. James Q. Wilson. Basic Books. • 1991. $23.00.

Improving Public Productivity: Concepts and Practice. Ellen D. Rosen. Sage Publications, Inc. • 1993. $52.00. A discussion of strategies for improving service quality and client satisfaction in public agencies at the local, state, and national level. Methods for measuring public sector productivity are included.

The Logic of Organizations. Bengt Abrahamsson. Sage Publications, Inc. • 1993. $42.00. Consists of two major sections: "The Emergence of Bureaucracy.." and "Administration Theory..".

ABSTRACTS AND INDEXES

Business Periodicals Index. H. W. Wilson Co. • Monthly, except August, with quarterly and annual cumulations. Service basis for print edition; CD-ROM edition, $1,495.00 per year.

BIBLIOGRAPHIES

Census of Governments: Subject Bibliography No. 156. Available from U. S. Government Printing Office. • Annual. Free. Lists government publications.

Intergovernmental Relations. Available from U. S. Government Printing Office. • Annual. Free. Lists government publications. (Subject Bibliography 211.).

CD-ROM DATABASES

Leadership Library on CD-ROM: Who's Who in the Leadership of the United States. Leadership Directories, Inc. • Quarterly. $2,641.00 per year, including access to Internet version (weekly updates). Contains all 14 *Yellow Book* personnel directories on CD-ROM, providing contact and brief biographical information for about 400,000 individuals. Covers business, government, financial institutions, news media, law firms, associations, foreign representatives, and nonprofit organizations. Includes photographs.

National Newspaper Index CD-ROM. The Gale Group. • Monthly. Provides comprehensive CD-ROM indexing of all material appearing in the late edition of the *New York Times*, the final edition of the *Washington Post*, the national edition of the *Christian Science Monitor*, the home edition of the *Los Angeles Times*, and the *Wall Street Journal*. Time period is four years. Also available online.

The New York Times Ondisc. New York Times Online Services. • Monthly. $2,650.00 per year. CD-ROM discs contain the full text of *The New York Times*, final edition. Inquire as to time period covered and availability of backfiles.

Newspaper Abstracts Ondisc. Bell & Howell Information and Learning. • Monthly. $2,950.00 per year (covers 1989 to date; archival discs are available for 1985-88). Provides cover-to-cover CD-ROM indexing and abstracting of 19 major newspapers, including the *New York Times, Wall Street Journal, Washington Post, Chicago Tribune,* and *Los Angeles Times.*

Staff Directories on CD-ROM. CQ Staff Directories, Inc. • Three times a year. $495.00 per year. Provides the contents on CD-ROM of *Congressional Staff Directory, Federal Staff Directory*, and *Judicial Staff Directory.* Includes photographs and maps.

DIRECTORIES

The Almanac of the Executive Branch. Maximov Publications. • Annual. $149.00. Provides detailed information on more than 830 key staff memebers of the executive branch of the federal government. Includes educational background, previous employment, job responsibilities, etc.

Almanac of the Unelected: Staff of the U. S. Congress. Bernan Press. • Annual. $275.00. Provides detailed information on key staff members of the legislative branch of the federal government. Includes educational background, previous employment, job responsibilities, etc.

Carroll's Federal & Federal Regional Directory: CD-ROM Edition. Carroll Publishing. • Bimonthly. $800.00 per year. Provides CD-ROM listings of more than 120,000 (55,000 high-level and 65,000 mid-level) U. S. government officials in Washington and throughout the country, including in military installations. Also available online.

Carroll's Federal Directory. Carroll Publishing. • Bimonthly. $325.00 per year. Lists 40,000 key U. S.

officials, including members of Congress, Cabinet members, federal judges, Executive Office of the President personnel, and a wide variety of administrators.

Carroll's Federal Regional Directory. Carroll Publishing. • Semiannual. $255.00 per year. Lists more than 28,000 non-Washington based federal executives in administrative agencies, the courts, and military bases. Arranged in four sections: Alphabetical (last names), Organizational, Geographical, and Keyword. Includes maps.

Congressional Yellow Book: Who's Who in Congress, Including Committees and Key Staff. Leadership Directories, Inc. • Quarterly. $305.00 per year. Looseleaf. A directory of members of congress, including their committees and their key aides.

Federal Regional Yellow Book: Who's Who in the Federal Government's Departments, Agencies, Military Installations, and Service Academies Outside of Washington, DC. Leadership Directories, Inc. • Semiannual. $235.00 per year. Lists over 36,000 federal officials and support staff at 8,000 regional offices.

Federal Staff Directory: With Biographical Information on Executive Staff Personnel. CQ Staff Directories, Inc. • Three times a year. $227.00 per year. Single copies, $89.00. Lists 40,000 staff members of federal departments and agencies, with biographies of 2,600 key executives. Includes keyword and name indexes.

Federal Yellow Book: Who's Who in the Federal Departments and Agencies. Leadership Directories, Inc. • Quarterly. $305.00 per year. White House, Executive Office of the President and departments and agencies of the executive branch nationwide, plus 38,000 other personnel.

Government Phone Book USA: Your Comprehensive Guide to Federal, State, County, and Local Government Offices in the United States. Omnigraphics, Inc. • Annual. $230.00. Contains more than 168,500 listings of federal, state, county, and local government offices and personnel, including legislatures. Formerly *Government Directory of Addresses and Phone Numbers.*

United States Government Manual. National Archives and Records Administration. Available from U.S. Government Printing Office. • Annual. $46.00.

ENCYCLOPEDIAS AND DICTIONARIES

International Encyclopedia of Public Policy and Administration. Jay M. Shafritz, editor. HarperCollins Publishers. • 1997. $550.00. Four volumes. Covers 20 major areas, such as public administration, government budgeting, industrial policy, nonprofit management, organizational theory, public finance, labor relations, and taxation. Includes a brief bibliography for each major entry and a comprehensive index.

ONLINE DATABASES

ABI/INFORM. Bell & Howell Information and Learning. • Provides online indexing to business-related material occurring in over 1,000 periodicals from 1971 to the present. Inquire as to online cost and availability.

Information Bank Abstracts. New York Times Index Dept. • Provides indexing and abstracting of current affairs, primarily from the final late edition of *The New York Times* and the Eastern edition of *The Wall Street Journal.* Time period is 1969 to present, with daily updates. Inquire as to online cost and availability.

Management Contents. The Gale Group. • Covers a wide range of management, financial, marketing, personnel, and administrative topics. About 150 leading business journals are indexed and abstracted from 1974 to date, with monthly updating. Inquire as to online cost and availability.

PAIS International. Public Affairs Information Service, Inc. • Corresponds to the former printed publications, *PAIS Bulletin* (1976-90) and *PAIS Foreign Language Index* (1972-90), and to the current *PAIS International in Print* (1991 to date). Covers economic, political, and sociological material appearing in periodicals, books, government documents, and other publications. Updating is monthly. Inquire as to online cost and availability.

Trade & Industry Index. The Gale Group. • Provides indexing of business periodicals, January 1981 to date. Daily updates. (Full text articles from some periodicals are available online, 1983 to date, in the companion database, *Trade & Industry ASAP.*) Inquire as to online cost and availability.

PERIODICALS AND NEWSLETTERS

Administration and Society. Sage Publications, Inc. • Bimonthly. Individuals, $85.00 per year; institutions, $420.00 per year. Scholarly journal concerned with public administration and the effects of bureaucracy.

Federal Manager. Federal Managers' Association. • Quarterly. $24.00 per year. Formerly *Federal Managers Quarterly.*

Government Computer News: The Newspaper Serving Computer Users Throughout the Federal Government. Cahners Business Information. • 32 times a year. Free to qualified personnel.

Government Executive: Federal Government's Business Magazine. National Journal Group, Inc. • Monthly. $48.00 per year. Includes management of computerized information systems in the federal government.

Public Administration Review. American Society for Public Administration. • Bimonthly. $80.00 per year.

The Public Manager: The Journal for Practitioners. Bureaucrat, Inc. • Quarterly. Individuals, $30.00 per year; institutions, $55.00 per year. Formerly *Bureaucrat.*

TRADE/PROFESSIONAL ASSOCIATIONS

American Society for Public Administration. 1120 G St., N.W., Suite 700, Washington, DC 20005-3885. Phone: (202)393-7878 Fax: (202)638-4952 E-mail: info@aspanet.org • URL: http://www.aspanet.org.

Federal Managers Association. 1641 Prince St., Alexandria, VA 22314-2818. Phone: (703)683-8700 Fax: (703)683-8707 E-mail: fma@ix.netcom.com • URL: http://www.fpmj.com.

Freedom of Information Clearinghouse. 1600 20th St., N.W., Washington, DC 20009. Phone: (202)588-1000 Fax: (202)588-7790 • Promotes citizen access to government-held information.

Fund for Constitutional Government. 122 Maryland Ave., N.E., 3rd Fl., Washington, DC 20002. Phone: (202)546-3732 Fax: (202)543-3156 • Provides legal and strategic counsel for government "whistleblowers.".

International Association of Professional Bureaucrats. c/o Dr. James H. Boren, One Plaza S., Suite 129, Tahlequah, OK 74464. Phone: (918)456-1357 Fax: (918)458-0124 E-mail: mumbles@www.jimboren.com • URL: http://www.jimboren.com • Motto of Association: "When in doubt, mumble.".

OTHER SOURCES

Government Employee Relations Report. Bureau of National Affairs, Inc. • Weekly. $999.00 per year. Three volumes. Looseleaf. Concerned with labor relations in the public sector.

BUREAUS OF BUSINESS RESEARCH

See also: BUSINESS RESEARCH; ECONOMIC RESEARCH

CD-ROM DATABASES

Profiles in Business and Management: An International Directory of Scholars and Their Research [CD-ROM]. Harvard Business School Publishing. • Annual. $595.00 per year. Fully searchable CD-ROM version of two-volume printed directory. Contains bibliographic and biographical information for over 5600 business and management experts active in 21 subject areas. Formerly *International Directory of Business and Management Scholars.*

DIRECTORIES

Profiles in Business and Management: An International Directory of Scholars and Their Research Version 2.0. Claudia Bruce, editor. Harvard Business School Press. • 1996. $495.00. Two volumes. Provides backgrounds, publications, and current research projects of more than 5,600 business and management experts.

ONLINE DATABASES

EconLit. American Economic Association. • Covers the worldwide literature of economics as contained in selected monographs and about 550 journals. Subjects include microeconomics, macroeconomics, economic history, inflation, money, credit, finance, accounting theory, trade, natural resource economics, and regional economics. Time period is 1969 to present, with monthly updates. Inquire as to online cost and availability.

RESEARCH CENTERS AND INSTITUTES

Bureau of Economic and Business Research. University of Florida. P.O. Box 117145, Gainesville, FL 32611-7145. Phone: (352)392-0171 Fax: (352)392-4739 E-mail: bebr@bebr.cba.ufl.edu • URL: http://www.bebr.ufl.edu.

National Bureau of Economic Research, Inc. 1050 Massachusetts Ave., Cambridge, MA 02138-5398. Phone: (617)868-3900 Fax: (617)868-2742 E-mail: msfeldst@nber.org • URL: http://www.nber.org.

BURGLAR ALARMS

See: ELECTRONIC SECURITY SYSTEMS

BURLAP INDUSTRY

See also: JUTE INDUSTRY

ABSTRACTS AND INDEXES

Textile Technology Digest. Institute of Textile Technology. • Monthly. $535.00 per year. Provides indexing and abstracting of a wide variety of textile technology literature.

ALMANACS AND YEARBOOKS

CRB Commodity Yearbook. Commodity Research Bureau. CRB. • Annual. $99.95.

CD-ROM DATABASES

Textile Technology Digest [CD-ROM]. Textile Information Center, Institute of Textile Technology. • Quarterly. $1,700.00 per year. Provides CD-ROM indexing and abstracting of worldwide journals and monographs in various areas of textile technology, production, and management. Covers 1978 to date.

ENCYCLOPEDIAS AND DICTIONARIES

Encyclopedia of Textiles. French and European Publications, Inc. • 1980. $39.95. Third edition.

Textile Terms and Definitions. J.E. McIntyre and Paul N. Daniels, editors. Available from State

Mutual Book and Periodical Service Ltd., Trade Order Dept. • 1995. $110.00. 10th edition. Published by the Textile Insitute (UK). Includes more than 1,000 definitions of textile processes, fiber types, and end products. Illustrated.

ONLINE DATABASES

Agricola. U.S. National Agricultural Library. • Covers worldwide agricultural literature. Over 2.8 million citations, 1970 to present, with monthly updates. Inquire as to online cost and availability.

Textile Technology Digest [online]. Textile Information Center, Institute of Textile Technology. • Contains indexing and abstracting of more than 300 worldwide journals and monographs in various areas of textile technology, production, and management. Time period is 1978 to date, with monthly updating. Inquire as to online cost and availability.

Textiles Information Treatment Users' Service (TITUS). Institut Textile de France. • Citations and abstracts of the worldwide literature on textiles, 1968 to present. Monthly updates. Inquire as to online cost and availability.

World Textiles. Elsevier Science, Inc. • Provides abstracting and indexing from 1970 of worldwide textile literature (periodicals, books, pamphlets, and reports). Includes U. S., European, and British patent information. Updating is monthly. Inquire as to online cost and availability.

PRICE SOURCES

PPI Detailed Report. Bureau of Labor Statistics, U.S. Department of Labor. Available from U.S. Government Printing Office. • Monthly. $55.00 per year. Formerly *Producer Price Indexes.*

STATISTICS SOURCES

FAO Quarterly Bulletin of Statistics. Food and Agriculture Organization of the United Nations. Available from UNIPUB. • Quarterly. $20.00 per year. Provides international data on agricultural production, trade, and prices, covering the major commodities of many countries. Text in English, French, and Spanish. Formerly *FAO Monthly Bulletin of Statistics.*

TRADE/PROFESSIONAL ASSOCIATIONS

Burlap and Jute Association. c/o Susan Spiegel, Drawer 8, Dayton, OH 45401. Phone: (973)476-8272 Fax: (973)258-0029 E-mail: tbpa@aol.com.

Textile Bag and Packing Association. Drawer 8, Dayton, OH 45401. Phone: 800-543-3400 or (973)476-8272 Fax: (973)258-0029 E-mail: tbpa@aol.com.

Textile Institute. Saint James Bldgs., 4th Fl., Oxford St., Manchester M1 6FQ, England. Phone: 44 161 2371188 Fax: 44 161 2361991 E-mail: tiihq@textileinst.org.uk • URL: http://www.texi.org • Members in 100 countries involved with textile industry management, marketing, science, and technology.

OTHER SOURCES

Textile Business Outlook. Statistikon Corp. • Quarterly. $985.00 per year. Analyzes current business, marketing, and financial conditions for the worldwide textile industry (fibers and fabrics). Includes statistical forecasts.

BUS LINE TIME TABLES

See: TIMETABLES

BUSES

See: MOTOR BUSES

BUSINESS

See also: ADMINISTRATION; CORPORATIONS; ECONOMICS; EXECUTIVES; INDUSTRY; INTERNATIONAL BUSINESS

GENERAL WORKS

Business Essentials. Prentice Hall. • 2000. Third edition. Price on application.

Reengineering Management: The Mandate for New Leadership. James Champy. DIANE Publishing Co. • 1998. $25.00.

Reengineering the Corporation: A Manifesto for Business Revolution. Michael Hammer and James Champy. HarperCollins Publishers, Inc. • 1999. $16.00. Revised edition.

The Shape of Things to Come: Seven Imperatives for Winning in the New World of Business. Richard W. Oliver. McGraw-Hill. • 1998. $24.95. Contains predictions relating to the influence of information technology on 21st century business. (Business Week Books.).

Understanding Business. William G. Nickels and others. McGraw-Hill Professional. • 2001. $56.25. Sixth edition.

ABSTRACTS AND INDEXES

Business Periodicals Index. H. W. Wilson Co. • Monthly, except August, with quarterly and annual cumulations. Service basis for print edition; CD-ROM edition, $1,495.00 per year.

NTIS Alerts: Business & Economics. National Technical Information Service.

Social Sciences Citation Index. Institute for Scientific Information. • Three times a year. $6,900 per year. Annual cumulation. Includes *Source Index, Citation Index, Permuterm Subject Index,* and *Corporate Index.*

ALMANACS AND YEARBOOKS

Information Please Business Almanac. Information Please LLC. • Annual. $21.95.

Irwin Business and Investment Almanac, 1996. Summer N. Levine and Caroline Levine. McGraw-Hill Professional. • 1995. $75.00. A review of last year's business activity. Covers a wide variety of business and economic data: stock market statistics, industrial information, commodity futures information, art market trends, comparative living costs for U. S. metropolitan areas, foreign stock market data, etc. Formerly *Business One Irwin Business and Investment Almanac.*

BIBLIOGRAPHIES

The Basic Business Library: Core Resources. Bernard S. Schlessinger and June H. Schlessinger. Oryx Press. • 1994. $43.50. Third edition. Consists of three parts: (1) "Core List of Printed Business Reference Sources," (2) "The Literature of Business Reference and Business Libraries: 1976-1994," and (3) "Business Reference Sources and Services: Essays." Part one lists 200 basic titles, with annotations and evaluations.

Bibliographic Guide to Business and Economics. Available from The Gale Group. • Annual. $795.00. Three volumes. Published by G. K. Hall & Co. Lists business and economics publications cataloged by the New York Public Library and the Library of Congress.

Bibliographic Guide to Conference Publications. Available from The Gale Group. • Annual. $545.00. Two volumes. Published by G. K. Hall & Co., Lists a wide range of conference publications cataloged by the New York Public Library and the Library of Congress.

Business Information Sources. Lorna M. Daniells. California Princeton Fulfillment Services. • 1993. $42.50. Third revised edition. Basic business sources, with discussion and full annotations.

BIOGRAPHICAL SOURCES

Who's Who in Finance and Industry. Marquis Who's Who. • Biennial. $295.00. Provides over 22,400 concise biographies of business leaders in all fields.

CD-ROM DATABASES

ABI/INFORM Global. Bell & Howell Information and Learning. • Monthly. $6,500.00 per year. Provides CD-ROM indexing and abstracting of worldwide business literature appearing in over 1,200 periodicals for the most recent five years. Archival discs are available from 1971. Formerly *ABI/INFORM OnDisc.*

Business Source Plus. EBSCO Information Services. • Monthly. $1,495.00 per year. Provides CD-ROM citations and abstracts to articles in about 650 business periodicals and newspapers, including *The Wall Street Journal.* Full text is provided from 200 selected periodicals. Covers accounting, communications, economics, finance, management, marketing, and other business subjects.

F & S Index Plus Text. The Gale Group. • Monthly. $7,575.00 per year. Provides CD-ROM citations to worldwide business, marketing, and industrial material appearing in a large assortment of trade journals, newspapers, and other publications. Time period is four years.

Hoover's Company Capsules on CD-ROM. Hoover's, Inc. • Quarterly. $349.95 per year (single-user). Provides the CD-ROM version of *Hoover's Handbook of American Business, Hoover's Handbook of Emerging Companies, Hoover's Handbook of World Business, Hoover's Guide to Computer Companies, Hoover's Guide to Media Companies, Hoover's Handbook of Private Companies,* and various regional guides. Includes more than 11,000 profiles of companies.

16 Million Businesses Phone Directory. Info USA. • Annual. $29.95. Provides more than 16 million yellow pages telephone directory listings on CD-ROM for all ZIP Code areas of the U. S.

Social Sciences Citation Index: Compact Disc Edition. Institute for Scientific Information. • Quarterly. Provides CD-ROM indexing of the world's social sciences literature, including economics, business, finance, management, communications, demographics, information and library science, political science, sociology, etc. Corresponds to online *Social Scisearch* and printed *Social Sciences Citation Index.*

Social Sciences Citation Index: Compact Disc Edition with Abstracts. Institute for Scientific Information. • Quarterly. Provides CD-ROM indexing and abstracting of "significant articles" from 1,400 social science journals worldwide, with additional selections from 3,200 other journals, 1986 to date. Includes economics, business, finance, management, communications, demographics, information and library science, political science, sociology, and many other subjects.

WILSONDISC: Wilson Business Abstracts. H. W. Wilson Co. • Monthly. $2,495.00 per year, including unlimited online access to *Wilson Business Abstracts* through WILSONLINE. Provides CD-ROM "cover-to-cover" abstracting and indexing of over 600 prominent business periodicals. Indexing is from 1982, abstracting from 1990. (*Business Periodicals Index* without abstracts is available on CD-ROM at $1,495 per year.).

DIRECTORIES

American Big Businesses Directory. American Business Directories. • Annual. $595.00. Lists

177,000 public and private U. S. companies in all fields having 100 or more employees. Includes sales volume, number of employees, and name of chief executive. Formerly *Big Businesses Directory*.

American Business Locations Directory. The Gale Group. • 1999. $575.00. Second edition. (Four U. S. regional volumes and index volume). Provides 150,000 specific site locations for the 1,000 largest industiral and service companies in the U. S. Entries include the following for each location: address, senior officer, number of employees, sales volume, Standard Industrial Classification (SIC) codes, and name of parent company.

American Manufacturers Directory. American Business Directories. • Annual. $595.00. Lists more than 150,000 public and private U. S. manufacturers having 20 or more employees. Includes sales volume, number of employees, and name of chief executive or owner.

America's Corporate Families and International Affliates. Dun and Bradstreet Information Services. • Annual. Libraries, $895.00; corporations, $1,020.00. Lease basis. Three Volumes U.S. parent companies with foreign affiliates and foreign parent companies with U.S. affiliates.

Business and Finance Career Directory. Visible Ink Press. • 1992. $17.95.

Business Organizations, Agencies, and Publications Directory. The Gale Group. • 1999. $425.00. 12th edition. Over 40,000 entries describing 39 types of business information sources. Classified by type of organization, publication, or serviceIncludes state, national, and international agencies and organizations. Master index to names and keywords. Also includes e-mail addresses and web site URL's.

The Corporate Directory of U.S. Public Companies. Walker's Western Research. • Annual. $360.00. Two volumes. Contains information on more than 10,000 publicly-traded companies, including names of executives and major subsidiaries. Includes financial and stock data.

Cyberhound's Guide to Companies on the Internet. The Gale Group. • 1996. $79.00. Presents critical descriptions and ratings of more than 2,000 company or corporate Internet databases. Includes a glossary of Internet terms, a bibliography, and indexes.

CyberTools for Business: Practical Web Sites that will Save You Time and Money. Wayne Harris. Hoover's, Inc. • 1997. $19.95. Describes 100 World Wide Web sites that are useful for business, investing, and job hunting. Also lists Web addresses for about 4,500 public and private companies.

D and B Million Dollar Directory. Dun and Bradstreet Information Services. • Annual. Commercial institutions, $1,395.00; libraries, $1,275.00. Lease basis.

Directory of Companies Required to File Annual Reports with the Securities and Exchange Commission. Securities and Exchange Commission. Available from U.S. Government Printing Office. • Annual. $46.00.

Guide to American Directories. Bernard Klein. B. Klein Publications. • Biennial. $95.00. Provides 8,000 listings with descriptions, prices, etc.

Hoover's Masterlist of Major U. S. Companies. Hoover's, Inc. • Biennial. $99.95. Provides brief information, including annual sales, number of employees, and chief executive, for about 5,100 U. S. companies, both public and private.

Internet Tools of the Profession: A Guide for Information Professionals. Hope N. Tillman, editor. Special Libraries Association. • 1997. $49.00. Second edition. Consists of 14 sections by various authors or compilers. After two introductory articles on searching the Internet, there are 12 annotated lists of useful Web sites, covering the SLA, business and finance, chemistry, education, food and agriculture, information technology, insurance and employee benefits, law, library management, metals and materials, pharmaceuticals, and telecommunications. An index is provided.

Kompass USA. Kompass USA, Inc. • Annual. $375.00. Four volumes. Includes information on about 125,000 U.S. companies. Classification system covers approximately 50,000 products and services. Product and tradename indexes are provided.

Peterson's Job Opportunities for Business Majors. Peterson's. • Annual. $21.95. Provides career information for the 2,000 largest U. S. employers in various industries.

Principal International Businesses: The World Marketing Directory. Dun and Bradstreet Information Services. • Annual. $5000. Provides information about 50,000 major businesses located in over 140 countries. Geographic arrangement with company name and product indexes.

Standard and Poor's Register of Corporations, Directors and Executives. Standard and Poor's. • Annual. $675.00. Periodic supplementation. Over 55,000 public and privately held corporations in the U.S. Three volumes. Three supplements.

Thomas Register of American Manufacturers and Thomas Register Catalog File. Thomas Publishing Co., Inc. • Annual. $149.00. 34 volumes. A three-part system offering information on a wide variety of industrial equipment and supplies.

Ward's Business Directory of U. S. Private and Public Companies. The Gale Group. • 2000. $2,590.00. Eight volumes. *Ward's* contains basic information on about 120,000 business firms, of which 90 percent are private companies. Includes mid-year *Supplement*. Volumes available individually. Prices vary.

ENCYCLOPEDIAS AND DICTIONARIES

Dictionary of Business and Management. Jerry M. Rosenberg. John Wiley and Sons, Inc. • 1992. $14.95. Third edition. (Business Dictionary Series).

Encyclopedia of Business. The Gale Group. • 2000. $425.00. Second edition. Two volumes. Contains more than 700 signed articles covering major business disciplines and concepts. International in scope.

Encyclopedia of Business and Finance. Burton Kaliski, editor. Available from The Gale Group. • 2001. $240.00. Two volumes. Published by Macmillan Reference USA. Contains articles by various contributors on accounting, business administration, banking, finance, management information systems, and marketing.

Every Manager's Guide to Business Processes: A Glossary of Key Terms and Concepts for Today's Business Leader. Peter G. W. Keen. Harvard Business School Press. • 1995. $14.95. Provides definitions of contemporary business terms, such as "outsourcing," "benchmarking," and "groupware.".

Field Guide to Business Terms: A Glossary of Essential Tools and Concepts for Today's Manager. Alistair D. Williamson, editor. Harvard Business School Press. • 1993. $16.95. Defines fundamental terms. (Harvard Business Economist Reference Series).

International Encyclopedia of Business and Management. Malcolm Warner, editor. Routledge, Inc. • 1996. $1,319.95. Six volumes. Contains more than 500 articles on global management issues. Includes extensive bibliographies, cross references, and an index of key words and phrases.

Knowledge Exchange Business Encyclopedia: Your Complete Business Advisor. Lorraine Spurge, editor. Knowledge Exchange LLC. • 1997. $45.00. Provides definitions of business terms and financial expressions, profiles of leading industries, tables of economic statistics, biographies of business leaders, and other business information. Includes "A Chronology of Business from 3000 B.C. Through 1995." Contains illustrations and three indexes.

HANDBOOKS AND MANUALS

Doing Business in the United States: Legal Opportunities and Pitfalls. Lawrence B. Landman. John Wiley and Sons, Inc. • 1997. $35.00.

Industry and Product Classification Manual (SIC Basis). Available from National Technical Information Service. • 1992. Issued by U. S. Bureau of the Census. Contains extended Standard Industrial Classification (SIC) numbers used by the Census Bureau to allow a more detailed classification of industry, services, and agriculture.

North American Industry Classification System (NAICS). Available from Bernan Press. • 1998. $32.50. Issued by the Executive Office of the President, Office of Management and Budget (OMB). The 1997 NAICS six-digit classification scheme replaces the 1987 Standard Industrial Classification (SIC) four-digit system. Detailed information on NAICS is available at http://www.census.gov/epcd/www/naics.html.

Organization Charts: Structures of More Than 200 Businesses and Non-Profit Organizations. The Gale Group. • 1999. $165.00. Third edition. Includes an introductory discussion of the history and use of such charts.

Organizing Corporate and Other Business Enterprises. Matthew Bender & Co., Inc. • $240.00. Looseleaf service. Periodic supplementation. A guide to and tax factors to be considered in selecting a form of business organization for the attorney advising proposed or existing small businesses.

Reengineering Revolution: A Handbook. Michael Hammer and Steven Stanton. HarperInformation. • 1995. $16.00.

Standard Industrial Classification Manual. U.S. Department of Commerce, Bureau of the Census. Available from U.S. Government Printing Office. • 1987. $36.00.

INTERNET DATABASES

Bureau of Economic Analysis (BEA). U. S. Department of Commerce, Bureau of Economic Analysis. Phone: (202)606-9900 Fax: (202)606-5310 E-mail: webmaster@bea.doc.gov • URL: http://www.bea.doc.gov • Web site includes "News Release Information" covering national, regional, and international economic estimates from the BEA. Highlights of releases appear online the same day, complete text and tables appear the next day. "Recent News Releases" section provides titles for past nine months, with links. "BEA Data and Methodology" includes "Frequently Requested NIPA Data" (national income and product accounts, such as gross domestic product and personal income). Other statistics are available. Fees: Free.

Business Week Online. McGraw-Hill. Phone: (212)512-2762 Fax: (212)512-6590 • URL: http://www.businessweek.com • Web site provides complete contents of current issue of *Business Week* plus "BW Daily" with additonal business news, financial market quotes, and corporate information from Standard & Poor's. Includes various features, such as "Banking Center" with mortgage and interest data, and "Interactive Computer Buying Guide." The "Business Week Archive" is fully searchable back to 1991. Fees: Mostly free, but full-text archive articles are $2.00 each.

Fedstats. Federal Interagency Council on Statistical Policy. Phone: (202)395-7254 • URL: http://www.fedstats.gov • Web site features an efficient search facility for full-text statistics produced by more than 70 federal agencies, including the Census Bureau, the Bureau of Economic Analysis, and the Bureau of Labor Statistics. Boolean searches can be made within one agency or for all agencies combined. Links are offered to international statistical bureaus, including the UN, IMF, OECD, UNESCO, Eurostat, and 20 individual countries. Fees: Free.

GaleNet: Your Information Community. The Gale Group. Phone: 800-877-GALE or (248)699-GALE Fax: 800-414-5043 or (248)699-8069 E-mail: galenet@gale.com • URL: http://www.galenet.com • Web site provides a wide variety of full-text information from Gale databases, Taft, and other sources. Covers associations, biography, business directories, education, the information industry, literature, publishing, and science. Fee-based subscriptions are available for individual databases (free demonstration). Includes Boolean search features and the BRS/Search user interface.

Internet Tools of the Profession. Special Libraries Association. Phone: (202)234-4700 Fax: (202)265-9317 E-mail: hope@tiac.net • URL: http://www.sla.org/pubs/itotp • Web site is designed to update the printed *Internet Tools of the Profession.* Provides links to a wide range of useful databases in business, finance, industry, information technology, insurance, law, library management, telecommunications, and other subject areas. Fees: Free.

1997 NAICS and 1987 SIC Correspondence Tables. U. S. Census Bureau. Phone: (301)457-4100 Fax: (301)457-1296 E-mail: naics@census.gov • URL: http://www.census.gov/epcd/www/naicstab.htm • Web site provides detailed tables for converting four-digit Standard Industrial Classification (SIC) numbers to the six-digit North American Industrial Classification System (NAICS) or vice versa: "1987 SIC Matched to 1997 NAICS" or "1997 NAICS Matched to 1987 SIC." Fees: Free.

Switchboard. Switchboard, Inc. Phone: (508)898-1000 Fax: (508)898-1755 E-mail: webmaster@switchboard.com • URL: http://www.switchboard.com • Web site provides telephone numbers and street addresses for more than 100 million business locations and residences in the U. S. Broad industry categories are available. Fees: Free.

Wall Street Journal Interactive Edition. Dow Jones & Co., Inc. Phone: 800-369-2834 or (212)416-2000 Fax: (212)416-2658 E-mail: inquiries@interactive.wsj.com • URL: http://www.wsj.com • Fee-based Web site providing online searching of worldwide information from the *The Wall Street Journal.* Includes "Company Snapshots," "The Journal's Greatest Hits," "Index to Market Data," "14-Day Searchable Archive," "Journal Links," etc. Financial price quotes are available. Fees: $49.00 per year; $29.00 per year to print subscribers.

WilsonWeb Periodicals Databases. H. W. Wilson. Phone: 800-367-6770 or (718)588-8400 Fax: 800-590-1617 or (718)992-8003 E-mail: custserv@hwwilson.com • URL: http://www.hwwilson.com/ • Web sites provide fee-based access to *Wilson Business Full Text, Applied Science & Technology Full Text, Biological & Agricultural Index, Library Literature & Information Science Full Text,* and *Readers' Guide Full Text, Mega Edition.* Daily updates.

ONLINE DATABASES

ABI/INFORM. Bell & Howell Information and Learning. • Provides online indexing to business-related material occurring in over 1,000 periodicals from 1971 to the present. Inquire as to online cost and availability.

Business and Industry. Responsive Database Services, Inc. • Contains online citations, abstracts, and selected fulltext from more than 1,000 trade journals, newspapers, and other publications. Provides general coverage of both manufacturing and service industries, including marketing, production, industry trends, key events, and information on specific companies. Time span is 1994 to date. Daily updates. Inquire as to online cost and availability. (Also available in a CD-ROM version.).

Disclosure SEC Database. Disclosure, Inc. • Provides information from records filed with the Securities and Exchange Commission by publicly owned corporations, 1977 to present. Weekly updates. Inquire as to online cost and availability.

Dow Jones Text Library. Dow Jones and Co., Inc. • Full text and edited news stories and articles on business affairs; 1984 to date. Inquire as to online cost and availability.

DRI U.S. Central Database. Data Products Division. • Provides more than 23,000 business, financial, demographic, economic, foreign trade, and industry-related time series for the U.S. Includes national income, population, retail-wholesale trade, price indexes, labor data, housing, industrial production, banking, interest rates, money supply, etc. Time period is generally 1947 to date (some data back to 1929). Updating varies. Inquire as to online cost and availability.

F & S Index. The Gale Group. • Contains about four million citations to worldwide business, financial, and industrial or consumer product literature appearing from 1972 to date. Weekly updates. Inquire as to online cost and availability.

PROMT: Predicasts Overview of Markets and Technology. The Gale Group. • Companies, products, applied technologies and markets. U.S. and international literature coverage, 1972 to date. Inquire as to online cost and availability. Provides abstracts from more than 1,600 publications. Weekly updates.

Social Scisearch. Institute for Scientific Information. • Broad, multidisciplinary index to the literature of the social sciences, 1972 to present. Weekly updates. Worldwide coverage. Inquire as to online cost and availability.

Thomas Register Online. Thomas Publishing Co., Inc. • Provides concise information on approximately 194,000 U. S. companies, mainly manufacturers, with over 50,000 product classifications. Indexes over 115,000 trade names. Information is updated semiannually. Inquire as to online cost and availability.

Trade & Industry Index. The Gale Group. • Provides indexing of business periodicals, January 1981 to date. Daily updates. (Full text articles from some periodicals are available online, 1983 to date, in the companion database, *Trade & Industry ASAP.*) Inquire as to online cost and availability.

Wilson Business Abstracts Online. H. W. Wilson Co. • Indexes and abstracts 600 major business periodicals, plus the *Wall Street Journal* and the business section of the *New York Times.* Indexing is from 1982, abstracting from 1990, with the two newspapers included from 1993. Updated weekly. Inquire as to online cost and availability. (*Business Periodicals Index* without abstracts is also available online.).

PERIODICALS AND NEWSLETTERS

Barron's: The Dow Jones Business and Financial Weekly. Dow Jones and Co., Inc. • Weekly. $145.00 per year.

Business Strategies Bulletin. CCH, Inc. • Monthly. $166.00 per year. Newsletter.

Business 2.0. Imagine Media, Inc. • Monthly. $12.00 per year. General business magazine emphasizing ideas and innovation.

Business Week. McGraw-Hill. • Weekly. $54.95 per year. Last volume is a double issue.

Canadian Business. Canadian Business Media. • 21 times a year. $34.70 per year. Edited for corporate managers and executives, this is a major periodical in Canada covering a variety of business, economic, and financial topics. Emphasis is on the top 500 Canadian corporations.

Commerce Business Daily. Industry and Trade Administration, U.S. Department of Commerce. Available from U.S. Government Printing Office. • Daily. Priority, $324.00 per year; non-priority, $275.00 per year. Synopsis of *U.S. Government Proposed Procurement, Sales and Contract Awards.*

Commercial and Financial Chronicle. William B. Dana Co. • Weekly. $140.00. per year.

CONTEXT: Business in a World Being Transformed by Technology. Diamond Technology Partners, Inc. • Quarterly. Price on application. Covers developments and trends in business and information technology for non-technical senior executives.

Daily Report for Executives. Bureau of National Affairs, Inc. • Daily. $6,927.00 per year. Newsletter. Covers legal, regulatory, economic, and tax developments affecting corporations.

Fast Company: How Smart Business Works. Fast Company Inc. • Monthly. $23.95 per year. Covers business management, with emphasis on creativity, leadership, innovation, career advancement, teamwork, the global economy, and the "new workplace.".

Forbes. Forbes, Inc. • Biweekly. $59.95 per year. Includes supplements: *Forbes ASAP* and *Forbes FYI.*

Fortune Magazine. Time Inc., Business Information Group. • Biweekly. $59.95 per year. Edited for top executives and upper-level managers.

Harvard Business Review. Harvard University, Graduate School of Business Administration. Harvard Businss School Publishing. • Bimonthly. $95.00 per year.

Industry Week: The Industry Management Magazine. Penton Media, Inc. • 18 times a year. Free to qualified personnel; others, $65.00 per year. Edited for industrial and business managers. Covers organizational and technological developments affecting industrial management.

The Journal of Business. University of Chicago Press, Journals Div. • Quarterly. Individuals, $27.00 per year; institutions, $65.00 per year; students, $17.00 per year.

Journal of World Business. Columbia University, Trustees of Columbia University. JAI Press, Inc. • Quarterly. $258.00 per year.

Kiplinger Washington Letter. Kiplinger Washington Editors, Inc. • Weekly. $76.00 per year.

Smart Business for the New Economy. Ziff-Davis. • Monthly. $12.00 per year. Provides practical advice for doing business in an economy dominated by technology and electronic commerce.

The Wall Street Journal. Dow Jones & Co., Inc. • Daily. $175.00 per year. Covers news and trends relating to business, industry, finance, the economy, and international commerce. Provides extensive price and other data for the securities, commodity, options, futures, foreign exchange, and money markets.

RESEARCH CENTERS AND INSTITUTES

Board of Research. Babson College, Babson Park, MA 02457. Phone: (718)239-5339 Fax: (718)239-6416 • URL: http://www.babson.edu/bor • Research areas include management, entrepreneurial characteristics, and multi-product inventory analysis.

Conference Board, Inc. 845 Third Ave., New York, NY 10022. Phone: (212)759-0900 Fax: (212)980-7014 E-mail: richard.cavanaugh@conference-board.org • URL: http://www.conference-board.org.

National Bureau of Economic Research, Inc. 1050 Massachusetts Ave., Cambridge, MA 02138-5398. Phone: (617)868-3900 Fax: (617)868-2742 E-mail: msfeldst@nber.org • URL: http://www.nber.org.

STATISTICS SOURCES

American Business Climate and Economic Profiles. The Gale Group. • 1993. $135.00. Provides business, industrial, demographic, and economic figures for all states and 300 metropolitan areas. Includes production, taxation, population, growth rates, labor force data, incomes, total sales, etc.

Business Statistics of the United States. Courtenay M. Slater, editor. Bernan Associates. • 1999. $74.00. Fifth edition. Based on *Business Statistics*, formerly issue by the Bureau of Economic Analysis, U. S. Department of Commerce. Provides basic data for a wide variety of U. S. industries, services, and economic indicators. Most statistics are shown annually for 29 years and monthly for the most recent four years.

County Business Patterns. Available from U. S. Government Printing Office. • Irregular. 52 issues containing annual data for each state, the District of Columbia, and a U. S. Summary. Produced by U.S. Bureau of the Census (http://www.census.gov). Provides local establishment and employment statistics by industry.

Economic Indicators. Council of Economic Advisors, Executive Office of the President. Available from U.S. Government Printing Office. • Monthly. $55.00 per year.

Gale Book of Averages. The Gale Group. • 1994. $70.00. Contains 1,100-1,200 statistical averages on a variety of topics, with references to published sources. Subjects include business, labor, consumption, crime, and other areas of contemporary society.

Statistical Abstract of the United States. Available from U. S. Government Printing Office. • Annual. $51.00. Issued by the U. S. Bureau of the Census.

Survey of Current Business. Available from U. S. Government Printing Office. • Monthly. $49.00 per year. Issued by Bureau of Economic Analysis, U. S. Department of Commerce. Presents a wide variety of business and economic data.

TRADE/PROFESSIONAL ASSOCIATIONS

American Management Association. 1601 Broadway, New York, NY 10019-7420. Phone: 800-262-9699 or (212)586-8100 Fax: (212)903-8168 • URL: http://www.amanet.org.

Business Council. 888 17th St., N.W., No. 506, Washington, DC 20006. Phone: (202)298-7650 Fax: (202)785-0296.

OTHER SOURCES

Business & Company Resource Center. The Gale Group. • Fee-based Web site provides a wide range of business, industry, and specific company information. Access is offered to trade journal articles, market research data, insider trading activity, major shareholder data, corporate histories, emerging technology reports, corporate earnings estimates, press releases, and other sources. Provides detailed company profiles, industry overviews, and rankings. Offers integration of Predicasts PROMT, Newsletters ASAP, Investext Plus, Business Index ASAP, Brands and Their Companies, and other databases (many have full text).

The Business Elite: Database of Corporate America. Donnelley Marketing. • Quarterly. $795.00. Formerly compiled by Database America. Provides current information on CD-ROM for about 850,000 businesses, comprising all U. S. private and public companies having more than 20 employees or sales of more than $1 million. Data for each firm includes detailed industry classification, year started, annual sales, name of top executive, and number of employees.

Business Organizations with Tax Planning. Zolman Cavitch. Matthew Bender & Co., Inc. • $2,570.00. 16 looseleaf volumes. Periodic supplementation. In-depth analytical coverage of corporation law and all relevant aspects of federal corporation taxation.

Business Rankings Annual. The Gale Group. • Annual. $305.00.Two volumes. Compiled by the Business Library Staff of the Brooklyn Public Library. This is a guide to lists and rankings appearing in major business publications. The top ten names are listed in each case.

Business Strategies. CCH, Inc. • Semimonthly. $819.00 per year. Four looseleaf volumes. Semimonthly updates. Legal, tax, and accounting aspects of business planning and decision-making. Provides information on start-ups, forms of ownership (partnerships, corporations), failing businesses, reorganizations, acquisitions, and so forth. Includes *Business Strategies Bulletin,* a monthly newsletter.

D & B Business Locator. Dun & Bradstreet, Inc. • Quarterly. $2,495.00 per year. CD-ROM provides concise information on more than 10 million U. S. companies or businesses. Includes data on number of employees.

Dun's Middle Market Disc. Dun & Bradstreet, Inc. • Quarterly. Price on application. CD-ROM provides information on more than 150,000 middle market U. S. private companies and their executives.

Dun's Million Dollar Disc. Dun & Bradstreet, Inc. • Quarterly. $3,800.00 per year to libraries; $5,500.00 per year to businesses. CD-ROM provides information on more than 240,000 public and private U. S. companies having sales volume of $5 million or more or 100 employees or more. Includes biographical data on more than 640,000 company executives.

Factiva. Dow Jones Reuters Business Interactive, LLC. • Fee-based Web site provides "global news and business information through Web sites and content integration solutions." Includes Dow Jones and Reuters newswires, The Wall Street Journal, and more than 7,000 other sources of current news, historical articles, market research reports, and investment analysis. Content includes 96 major U. S. newspapers, 900 non-English sources, trade publications, media transcripts, country profiles, news photos, etc.

InSite 2. Intelligence Data/Thomson Financial. • Fee-based Web site consolidates information in a "Base Pack" consisting of Business InSite, Market InSite, and Company InSite. Optional databases are Consumer InSite, Health and Wellness InSite, Newsletter InSite, and Computer InSite. Includes fulltext content from more than 2,500 trade publications, journals, newsletters, newspapers, analyst reports, and other sources. Continuous updating. Formerly produced by The Gale Group.

Manufacturing and Distribution USA. The Gale Group. • 2000. $375.00. Three volumes. Replaces *Manufacturing USA* and *Wholesale and Retail Trade USA*. Presents statistics and projections relating to economic activity in more than 500 business classifications.

Nexis.com. Lexis-Nexis Group. • Fee-based Web site offers searching of about 2.8 billion documents in some 30,000 news, business, and legal information sources. Features include a subject directory covering 1,200 topics in 34 categories and a Company Dossier containing information on more than 500,000 public and private companies. Boolean searching is offered.

U. S. Business Advisor. Small Business Administration. • Web site provides "a one-stop electronic link to all the information and services government provides for the business community." Covers about 60 federal agencies that exist to assist or regulate business. Detailed information is provided on financial assistance, workplace issues, taxes, regulations, international trade, and other business topics. Searching is offered. Fees: Free.

World Business Rankings Annual. The Gale Group. • 1998. $189.00. Provides 2,500 ranked lists of international companies, compiled from a variety of published sources. Each list shows the "top ten" in a particular category. Keyword indexing, a country index, and citations are provided.

BUSINESS ADMINISTRATION

See: ADMINISTRATION

BUSINESS AIRPLANES

See: BUSINESS AVIATION

BUSINESS AND GOVERNMENT

See: REGULATION OF INDUSTRY

BUSINESS AND PROFESSIONAL WOMEN

See: EMPLOYMENT OF WOMEN

BUSINESS AND SOCIETY

See: SOCIAL RESPONSIBILITY

BUSINESS APPRAISAL

See: VALUATION

BUSINESS ARCHIVES

See: RECORDS MANAGEMENT

BUSINESS AVIATION

See also: AVIATION INDUSTRY

ABSTRACTS AND INDEXES

Business Periodicals Index. H. W. Wilson Co. • Monthly, except August, with quarterly and annual cumulations. Service basis for print edition; CD-ROM edition, $1,495.00 per year.

Current Literature in Traffic and Transportation. Northwestern University, Transportation Library. • Quarterly. $25.00 per year.

BIBLIOGRAPHIES

Aviation. Available from U. S. Government Printing Office. • Annual. Free. Lists government publications. (GPO Subject Bibliography Number 18).

DIRECTORIES

Airport/Facility Directory. U. S. National Ocean Service. • Bimonthly. $140.00 per year, complete. Issued in seven regional volumes (single region, $20.00 per year). Provides detailed non-military airport information for pilots, including control center and navigational data.

Aviation Buyer's Directory. Air Service Directory, Inc. • Quarterly. $45.00 per year. Lists aircraft for sale and sources of parts and supplies.

Jet and Propjet: Corporate Directory. AvCom International. • Annual. $21.95. Owners of business jet and turboprop aircraft. Formerly *Propjet.*

Professional Pilot-FBO Directory. Queensmith Communications Corp. • Annual. $8.00. Includes information for about 1,500 airports and fixed-base operators.

World Aviation Directory. McGraw-Hill Aviation Week Group. • Semiannual. $225.00 per year. Two volumes. Lists aviation, aerospace, and missile manufacturers. Includes *World Aviation Directory Buyer's Guide.*

ONLINE DATABASES

ABI/INFORM. Bell & Howell Information and Learning. • Provides online indexing to business-related material occurring in over 1,000 periodicals from 1971 to the present. Inquire as to online cost and availability.

Management Contents. The Gale Group. • Covers a wide range of management, financial, marketing, personnel, and administrative topics. About 150 leading business journals are indexed and abstracted from 1974 to date, with monthly updating. Inquire as to online cost and availability.

PROMT: Predicasts Overview of Markets and Technology. The Gale Group. • Companies, products, applied technologies and markets. U.S. and international literature coverage, 1972 to date. Inquire as to online cost and availability. Provides abstracts from more than 1,600 publications. Weekly updates.

Trade & Industry Index. The Gale Group. • Provides indexing of business periodicals, January 1981 to date. Daily updates. (Full text articles from some periodicals are available online, 1983 to date, in the companion database, *Trade & Industry ASAP.*) Inquire as to online cost and availability.

PERIODICALS AND NEWSLETTERS

A/C Flyer: Best Read Resale Magazine Worldwide. McGraw-Hill. • Monthly. $28.00 per year. Lists used airplanes for sale by dealers, brokers, and private owners. Provides news and trends relating to the aircraft resale industry. Special issues include "Product & Service Buyer's Guide" and "Dealer/ Broker Directory.".

AOPA Pilot. Aircraft Owners and Pilots Association. • Monthly. Membership.

Aviation Week and Space Technology. McGraw-Hill Aviation Week Group. • Monthly. $89.00 per year.

Business and Commercial Aviation. McGraw-Hill, Aviation Week Group. • Monthly. $52.00 per year. Supplement available: *Annual Planning Purchasing Handbook.*

FAA Aviation News. Federal Aviation Administration. Available from U. S. Government Printing Office. • Bimonthly. $28.00. per year. Designed to help airmen become safer pilots. Includes updates on major rule changes and proposals.

Flyer. Flyer Media, Inc. • Biweekly. $29.00 per year. Formerly *General Aviation News and Flyer.*

Flying. Hachette Filipacchi Magazines, Inc. • Monthly. $26.00 per year.

Professional Pilot Magazine. Queensmith Communications Corp. • Monthly. $36.00 per year. Edited for career pilots in all areas of aviation: airline, corporate, charter, and military. Includes flying technique, avionics, navigation, accident analysis, career planning, corporate profiles, and business aviation news.

Trade-a-Plane. • 36 times a year. $98.00 per year. Subject matter is aircraft for sale or trade.

Weekly of Business Aviation. Aviation Week Newsletter. McGraw-Hill. • Weekly. $540.00 per year.

RESEARCH CENTERS AND INSTITUTES

Ohio Aerospace Institute. 22800 Cedar Point Rd., Cleveland, OH 44142. Phone: (440)962-3000 Fax: (440)962-3120 E-mail: michaelsalkind@oai.org • URL: http://www.oai.org • Aerospace-related research, education, and technology transfers.

STATISTICS SOURCES

Air Transport. Air Transport Association of America. • Annual. $20.00.

TRADE/PROFESSIONAL ASSOCIATIONS

Aircraft Owners and Pilots Association. 421 Aviation Way, Frederick, MD 21701. Phone: 800-872-2672 or (301)695-2000 Fax: (301)695-2375 E-mail: aopahq@aopa.org • URL: http://www.aopa.org.

General Aviation Manufacturers Association. 1400 K St., N.W., Suite 801, Washington, DC 20005. Phone: (202)393-1500 Fax: (202)842-4063 • URL: http://www.generalaviation.org.

International Council of Aircraft Owner and Pilot Associations. 421 Aviation Way, Frederick, MD 21701. Phone: (301)695-2220 Fax: (301)695-2375 E-mail: ruth.moser@aopa.org • URL: http://www.iaopa.org.

National Business Aviation Association. 1200 18th St., N.W., Suite 400, Washington, DC 20036. Phone: (202)783-9000 Fax: (202)331-8364 E-mail: info@nba.org • URL: http://www.nbaa.org.

OTHER SOURCES

Aviation Law Reports. CCH, Inc. • $2,419.00 per year. Four looseleaf volumes. Semimonthly updates.

BUSINESS BROKERS

See: BUSINESS ENTERPRISES, SALE OF

BUSINESS BUDGETING

See: BUDGETING, BUSINESS

BUSINESS CHOICE

See: OCCUPATIONS

BUSINESS COLLEGES

See: BUSINESS EDUCATION; COLLEGES AND UNIVERSITIES

BUSINESS COMMUNICATION

See: BUSINESS CORRESPONDENCE; COMMUNICATION

BUSINESS CONDITIONS

See also: BANKRUPTCY; BUSINESS CYCLES; BUSINESS FORECASTING

GENERAL WORKS

Dow 40,000: Strategies for Profiting from the Greatest Bull Market in History. David Elias and Charles V. Moore. McGraw-Hill. • 1999. $24.95. Predicts continuing strong growth in the U. S. economy, low interest rates, and low inflation, resulting in a level of 40,000 for the Dow Jones Industrial Average in the year 2016.

Trends 2000: How to Prepare For and Profit From the Changes of the 21st Century. Gerald Celente. Little, Brown and Co. • 1998. $14.99. Emphasis is on economic, social, and political trends.

ALMANACS AND YEARBOOKS

Political Risk Yearbook. The P R S Group. • Annual. $1,200.00. Eight regional volumes. Each volume covers a separate region of the world and assesses economic and political conditions as they relate to the risk of doing business.

CD-ROM DATABASES

Magazine Index Plus. The Gale Group. • Monthly. $4,000.00 per year (includes InfoTrac workstation). Provides full text on CD-ROM for about 100 popular, general interest magazines and indexing for 300 others. Includes special indexing of reviews and product evaluations. Time period is 1980 to date.

National Newspaper Index CD-ROM. The Gale Group. • Monthly. Provides comprehensive CD-ROM indexing of all material appearing in the late edition of the *New York Times*, the final edition of the *Washington Post*, the national edition of the *Christian Science Monitor*, the home edition of the *Los Angeles Times*, and the *Wall Street Journal.* Time period is four years. Also available online.

The New York Times Ondisc. New York Times Online Services. • Monthly. $2,650.00 per year. CD-ROM discs contain the full text of *The New York Times*, final edition. Inquire as to time period covered and availability of backfiles.

Newspaper Abstracts Ondisc. Bell & Howell Information and Learning. • Monthly. $2,950.00 per year (covers 1989 to date; archival discs are available for 1985-88). Provides cover-to-cover CD-ROM indexing and abstracting of 19 major newspapers, including the *New York Times, Wall Street Journal, Washington Post, Chicago Tribune,* and *Los Angeles Times.*

HANDBOOKS AND MANUALS

Nations of the World: A Political, Economic, and Business Handbook. Grey House Publishing. • 2000. $135.00. Includes descriptive data on economic characteristics, population, gross domestic product (GDP), banking, inflation, agriculture, tourism, and other factors. Covers "all the nations of the world.".

INTERNET DATABASES

Fedstats. Federal Interagency Council on Statistical Policy. Phone: (202)395-7254 • URL: http://www.fedstats.gov • Web site features an efficient search facility for full-text statistics produced by more than 70 federal agencies, including the Census Bureau, the Bureau of Economic Analysis, and the Bureau of Labor Statistics. Boolean searches can be made within one agency or for all agencies combined. Links are offered to international statistical bureaus, including the UN, IMF, OECD,

UNESCO, Eurostat, and 20 individual countries. Fees: Free.

ONLINE DATABASES

Country Report Services. The PRS Group. • Provides full text of reports describing the business risks and opportunities currently existing in more than 150 countries of the world. Contains a wide variety of statistics and forecasts relating to economics political and social conditions. Also includes demographics, tax, and currency information. Updated monthly. Inquire as to online cost and availability.

DRI U.S. Central Database. Data Products Division. • Provides more than 23,000 business, financial, demographic, economic, foreign trade, and industry-related time series for the U.S. Includes national income, population, retail-wholesale trade, price indexes, labor data, housing, industrial production, banking, interest rates, money supply, etc. Time period is generally 1947 to date (some data back to 1929). Updating varies. Inquire as to online cost and availability.

EconBase: Time Series and Forecasts. WEFA, Inc. • Presents online econometric data for business conditions, economics, demographics, industry, finance, employment, household income, interest rates, prices, etc. Includes two-year forecasts for a wide range of economic indicators. Time span is 1948 to date, with monthly updates. Inquire as to online cost and availability.

Information Bank Abstracts. New York Times Index Dept. • Provides indexing and abstracting of current affairs, primarily from the final late edition of *The New York Times* and the Eastern edition of *The Wall Street Journal.* Time period is 1969 to present, with daily updates. Inquire as to online cost and availability.

Newspaper and Periodical Abstracts. Bell & Howell Information and Learning. • Provides online coverage (citations and abstracts) of 25 major newspapers, 1,600 perodicals, and 70 TV programs. Covers business, economics, current affairs, health, fitness, sports, education, technology, government, consumer affairs, psychology, the arts, and the social sciences. Time period is 1986 to date, with daily updates. Inquire as to online cost and availability.

OECD Main Economic Indicators. Organization for Economic Cooperation and Development. • International statistics provided by OECD, 1960 to date. Monthly updates. Inquire as to online cost and availability.

PERIODICALS AND NEWSLETTERS

Economic Perspectives (Chicago). Federal Reserve Bank of Chicago. • Quarterly. Free.

Federal Reserve Bank of Atlanta: Economic Review. Federal Reserve Bank of Atlanta. • Quarterly. Free.

Federal Reserve Bank of Dallas: Economic Review. Federal Reserve Bank of Dallas. • Quarterly. Free.

Federal Reserve Bank of Kansas City: Economic Review. Federal Reserve Bank of Kansas City. • Quarterly.Free.

Federal Reserve Bank of Minneapolis: Quarterly Review. Federal Reserve Bank of Minneapolis, Research Dept. • Quarterly. Free.

Federal Reserve Bank of New York: Economic Policy Review. Federal Reserve Bank of New York Public Information Office. • Quarterly. Free.

Federal Reserve Bank of Philadelphia: Business Review. Federal Reserve Bank of Philadelphia, Research Dept. • Bimonthly. Free. Contains articles on current topics in economics, finance, and banking. The Bank also maintains a world wide web site at http://www.libertynet.org/~fedrsrv/fedpage.html.

Federal Reserve Bank of Richmond: Economic Quarterly. Federal Reserve Bank of Richmond, Research Dept. • Bimonthly. Free. Formerly *Federal Reserve Bank of Richmond: Economic Review.*

Federal Reserve Bank of Saint Louis: Review. Federal Reserve Bank of Saint Louis. • Bimonthly. Free.

Federal Reserve Bank of San Francisco Economic Letter. Federal Reserve Bank of San Francisco. Economic Letter. • 38 times a year. Free. Formerly *Federal Reserve Bank of San Francisco: Weekly Letter.*

Federal Reserve Bank of San Francisco: Economic Review. Federal Reserve Bank of San Francisco. • Three times a year. Free.

The Levy Institute Forecast. Bard College, Jerome Levy Economics Institute. • 12 times a year. $295.00 per year. Looseleaf service. Includes quarterly supplement. Formerly *Industry Forecast.*

Ragan's Annual Report Review. Lawence Ragan Communications, Inc. • Monthly. $287.00 per year. Newsletter on business trends and tactics as reflected in corporate annual reports. Formerly *Corporate Annual Report.*

Research Reports. American Institute for Economic Research. • Semimonthly. $59.00 per year. Newsletter. Alternate issues include charts of "Primary Leading Indicators," "Primary Roughly Coincident Indicators," and "Primary Lagging Indicators," as issued by The Conference Board (formerly provided by the U. S. Department of Commerce).

STATISTICS SOURCES

Business Statistics of the United States. Courtenay M. Slater, editor. Bernan Associates. • 1999. $74.00. Fifth edition. Based on *Business Statistics*, formerly issue by the Bureau of Economic Analysis, U. S. Department of Commerce. Provides basic data for a wide variety of U. S. industries, services, and economic indicators. Most statistics are shown annually for 29 years and monthly for the most recent four years.

Economic Indicators. Council of Economic Advisors, Executive Office of the President. Available from U.S. Government Printing Office. • Monthly. $55.00 per year.

Economic Indicators Handbook: Time Series, Conversions, Documentation. The Gale Group. • 2000. $195.00. Sixth edition. Provides data for about 175 U. S. economic indicators, such as the consumer price index (CPI), gross national product (GNP), and the rate of inflation. Values for series are given since inception, in both original form and adjusted for inflation. A bibliography of sources is included.

Main Economic Indicators. OECD Publication and Information Center. • Monthly. $450.00 per year. "The essential source of timely statistics for OECD member countries." Includes a wide variety of business, economic, and industrial data for the 29 OECD nations.

Main Economic Indicators: Historical Statistics. OECD Publications and Information Center. • Annual. $50.00.

OECD Economic Outlook. OECD Publications and Information Center. • Semiannual. $95.00 per year. Contains a wide range of economic and monetary data relating to the member countries of the Organization for Economic Cooperation and Development. Includes about 100 statistical tables and graphs, with 24-month forecasts for each of the OECD countries. Provides extensive review and analysis of recent economic trends.

OECD Economic Survey of the United States. OECD Publications and Information Center. • Annual. $30.00.

OECD Economic Surveys. OECD Publications and Information Center. • Annual. $30.00 each. These are separate, yearly reviews for each of the economies of the industrialized nations that comprise the OECD. Each edition includes forecasts, analyses, and detailed statistical tables for the country being surveyed. (The combined series, one annual volume for each nation, is available at $485.00.).

Standard & Poor's Industry Surveys. Standard & Poor's. • Semiannual. $1,800.00. Two looseleaf volumes. Includes monthly supplements. Provides detailed, individual surveys of 52 major industry groups. Each survey is revised on a semiannual basis. Also includes "Monthly Investment Review" (industry group investment analysis) and monthly "Trends & Projections" (economic analysis).

Survey of Current Business. Available from U. S. Government Printing Office. • Monthly. $49.00 per year. Issued by Bureau of Economic Analysis, U. S. Department of Commerce. Presents a wide variety of business and economic data.

The World Economic Factbook. Available from The Gale Group. • 2000. $450.00. Seventh edition. Published by Euromonitor. Presents key economic facts and figures for each of 200 countries, including details of chief industries, export-import trade, currency, political risk, household expenditures, and the economic situation in general.

World Economic Outlook: A Survey by the Staff of the International Monetary Fund. International Monetary Fund, Publications Services. • Semiannual. $62.00 per year. Presents international statistics combined with forecasts and analyses of the world economy. Editions available in Arabic, English, French and Spanish.

World Economic Prospects: A Planner's Guide to International Market Conditions. Available from The Gale Group. • 2000. $450.00. Second edition. Published by Euromonitor. Ranks 78 countries by specific economic characteristics, such as gross domestic product (GDP) per capita and short term growth prospects. Discusses the economic situation, prospects, and market potential of each of the countries.

OTHER SOURCES

Consensus Forecasts: A Digest of International Economic Forecasts. Consensus Economics Inc. • Monthly. $565.00 per year. Provides a survey of more than 200 "prominent" financial and economic forecasters, covering 20 major countries. Two-year forecasts for each country include future growth, inflation, interest rates, and exchange rates. Each issue contains analysis of business conditions in various countries.

Factiva. Dow Jones Reuters Business Interactive, LLC. • Fee-based Web site provides "global news and business information through Web sites and content integration solutions." Includes Dow Jones and Reuters newswires, The Wall Street Journal, and more than 7,000 other sources of current news, historical articles, market research reports, and investment analysis. Content includes 96 major U. S. newspapers, 900 non-English sources, trade publications, media transcripts, country profiles, news photos, etc.

Nexis.com. Lexis-Nexis Group. • Fee-based Web site offers searching of about 2.8 billion documents in some 30,000 news, business, and legal information sources. Features include a subject directory covering 1,200 topics in 34 categories and a Company Dossier containing information on more than 500,000 public and private companies. Boolean searching is offered.

Working Americans, 1880-1999, Volume One: The Working Class. Grey House Publishing. • 2000. $135.00. Provides detailed information on the lifestyles and economic life of working class families in the 12 decades from 1880 to 1999. Includes such items as selected consumer prices, income, family finances, budgets, life at home, jobs, and working conditions. (Universal Reference Publications.).

Working Americans, 1880-1999, Volume Two: The Middle Class. Grey House Publishing. • 2000. $135.00. Furnishes details of the social and economic lives of middle class Americans during the years 1880 to 1999. Describes such items as selected consumer prices, income, family finances, budgets, life at home, jobs, and working conditions. (Universal Reference Publications.).

World Economic and Social Survey: Trends and Policies in the World Economy. United Nations Publications. • Annual. $55.00. Includes discussion and "an extensive statistical annex of economic, trade, and financial indicators, incorporating current data and forecasts.".

World Economic Situation and Prospects. United Nations Publications. • Annual. $15.00. Serves as a supplement and update to the UN *World Economic and Social Survey.*

BUSINESS CONSOLIDATION

See: MERGERS AND ACQUISITIONS

BUSINESS CONSULTANTS

See: CONSULTANTS; MANAGEMENT CONSULTANTS

BUSINESS CORRESPONDENCE

See also: COMMUNICATION; REPORT WRITING

GENERAL WORKS

Business English. Mary E. Guffey. South-Western College Publishing. • 2001. $47.00. Seventh edition. (South-Western College-Busines Communications Series).

Improving Writing Skills: Memos, Letters, Reports, and Proposals. Arthur A. Berger. Sage Publications, Inc. • 1993. $37.00. Emphasis is on the business correspondence required of university professors and other academic personnel. (Survival Skills for Scholars, vol. 9).

Writing Business Letters and Reports. Carmella E. Mansfield and Margaret Hilton Bahniuk. Pearson Education and Technology. • 1981. $24.61.

Writing That Works: How to Write Effective E-Mails, Letters, Resumes, Presentations, Plans, Reports and Other Business Communications. Kenneth Roman. HarperCollins Publishers, Inc. • 2000. $13.00. Enlarged revised edition.

ENCYCLOPEDIAS AND DICTIONARIES

Lifetime Encyclopedia of Letters. Harold E. Meyer. Prentice Hall. • 1999. $35.00. Third revised expanded edition. Contains about 800 model letters and 400 alternative opening and closing sentences. Model letters are for sales, collection, complaints, apology, congratulations, fund raising, resignation, termination, etc.

HANDBOOKS AND MANUALS

AMA Handbook of Business Letters. Jeffrey L. Seglin. AMACOM. • 1996. $69.95. Second edition. Contains 300 sample letters, with advice on business correspondence.

Business Letter Writing. Sheryl Lindsell-Roberts. Pearson Education and Technology. • 1994. $12.00.

Business Letters for Busy People: More Than 200 Timesaving, Ready-to-Use Business Letters for Any Occasion. Jim Dugger. Career Press, Inc. • 1995. $15.99. Third edition.

Business Writing the Modular Way: How to Research, Organize and Compose Effective Memo Letters, Articles, Reports, Proposals, Manuals, Specifications and Books. Harley Bjelland. Books on Demand. • 1992. $80.70. Covers research and organization for various kinds of business writing, from simple to complex.

Complete Book of Model Business Letters. Jack Griffin. Prentice Hall. • 1997. $34.95.

Handbook for Business Writing. L. Sue Baugh. NTC/Contemporary Publishing. • 1993. $24.95. Second edition. Covers reports, letters, memos, and proposals. (Handbook for... Series).

Handbook for Memo Writing. L. Sue Baugh. NTC/ Contemporary Publishing. • 1995. $32.95. (NTC Business Book Series).

Handbook for Practical Letter Writing. L. Sue Baugh. NTC/Contemporary Publishing. • 1993. $29.95.

Katharine Gibbs Handbook of Business English. Pearson Education and Technology. • 1987. $5.95.

Little Black Book of Business Letters. Michael C. Thomsett. AMACOM. • 1988. $14.95. Includes examples of various kinds of business correspondence. (Little Black Book Series).

Logo Power: How to Create Effective Company Logos. William Haig and Laurel Harper. John Wiley & Sons, Inc. • 1997. $39.95. Explains how to plan, develop, evaluate, and implement a company logo system.

McGraw-Hill Handbook of Business Letters. Roy W. Poe. McGraw-Hill. • 1993. $59.50. Third edition. Contains about 200 model business letters in 13 categories. Writing style, organization, objective, and underlying psychology are discussed for each example.

175 High-Impact Cover Letters. Richard H. Beatty. John Wiley and Sons, Inc. • 1996. $10.95. Second edition. Provides samples of cover letters for resumes.

PERIODICALS AND NEWSLETTERS

Harvard Management Communication Letter. Harvard Business School Press. • Monthly. $79.00 per year. Newsletter. Provides practical advice on both electronic and conventional business communication: e-mail, telephone, cell phones, memos, letters, written reports, speeches, meetings, and visual presentations (slides, flipcharts, easels, etc.). Also covers face-to-face communication, discussion, listening, and negotiation.

BUSINESS CYCLES

See also: BUSINESS CONDITIONS; BUSINESS FORECASTING; BUSINESS RESEARCH

GENERAL WORKS

Business Cycles: A Theoretical, Historical and Statistical Analysis of the Capitalist Process. Joseph A. Schumpeter. Porcupine Press, Inc. • 1989. $24.95.

Business Cycles and Forecasting. Howard J. Sherman and David X. Kolk. Addison-Wesley Educational Publications, Inc. • 1997. $101.00.

Business Cycles: Theory, History, Indicators, and Forecasting. Victor Zarnowitz. University of Chicago Press. • 1992. $77.00.

Forecasting Business Trends. American Institute for Economic Research. • 2000. $6.00. Summarizes methods of economic forecasting, statistical indicators, methods of analyzing business cycles, and use of leading, coincident, and lagging indicators. Includes charts, tables, and a glossary of terms. (Economic Education Bulletin.).

Great Inflations of the 20th Century: Theories, Policies, and Evidence. Pierre L. Siklos, editor. Edward Elgar Publishing, Inc. • 1995. $95.00. Contains reprints of papers on the history and economic analysis of major inflations.

It was a Very Good Year: Extraordinary Moments in Stock Market History. Martin S. Fridson. John Wiley and Sons, Inc. • 1997. $29.95. Provides details on what happened during each of the ten best years for the stock market since 1900.

Prosperity and Depression: A Theoretical Analysis of Cyclical Movements. Gottfried Haberler. Harvard University Press. • 1964. $35.00. Fourth edition. (Economic Studies No. 105).

A Short History of Financial Euphoria. John Kenneth Galbraith. Viking Penguin. • 1994. $10.95. An analysis of speculative euphoria and subsequent crashes, from the Holland tulip mania in 1637 to the 1987 unpleasantness in the U. S. stock market.

Stock Market Crashes and Speculative Manias. Eugene N. White, editor. Edward Elgar Publishing, Inc. • 1996. $230.00. Contains reprints of 23 articles dating from 1905 to 1994. (International Library of Macroeconomic and Financial History Series: No. 13).

What Will the Next Recession Mean to You?. C. Edgar Murray, editor. American Institute for Economic Research. • 2001. $6.00. Revised edition. Provides historical background of U.S. recessions and gives conservative advice on "Coping with a Recession." (Economic Education Bulletin Series).

ABSTRACTS AND INDEXES

Abstract of Previous Meetings. Society for the Investigation of Recurring Events. • Monthly. Price on application.

ENCYCLOPEDIAS AND DICTIONARIES

Business Cycles and Depressions: An Encyclopedia. David Glasner, editor. Garland Publishing, Inc. • 1997. $100.00. Contains 327 alphabetical entries by various contributors. Defines and reviews all significant depressions, recessions, and financial crises in the U. S. and Europe since 1790. Includes chronologies, bibliographies, and indexes.

HANDBOOKS AND MANUALS

Fibonacci Applications and Strategies for Traders. Robert Fischer. John Wiley and Sons, Inc. • 1993. $49.95. Provides a new look at the Elliott Wave Theory and Fibonacci numbers as applied to commodity prices, business cycles, and interest rate movements. (Traders Library).

Investor's Guide to Economic Indicators. Charles R. Nelson. John Wiley and Sons, Inc. • 1989. $17.95.

INTERNET DATABASES

Fedstats. Federal Interagency Council on Statistical Policy. Phone: (202)395-7254 • URL: http://www.fedstats.gov • Web site features an efficient search facility for full-text statistics produced by more than 70 federal agencies, including the Census Bureau, the Bureau of Economic Analysis, and the Bureau of Labor Statistics. Boolean searches can be made within one agency or for all agencies combined. Links are offered to international statistical bureaus, including the UN, IMF, OECD, UNESCO, Eurostat, and 20 individual countries. Fees: Free.

ONLINE DATABASES

DRI U.S. Central Database. Data Products Division. • Provides more than 23,000 business, financial, demographic, economic, foreign trade, and industry-related time series for the U.S. Includes national income, population, retail-wholesale trade, price indexes, labor data, housing, industrial production, banking, interest rates, money supply, etc. Time period is generally 1947 to date (some data back to 1929). Updating varies. Inquire as to online cost and availability.

EconLit. American Economic Association. • Covers the worldwide literature of economics as contained in selected monographs and about 550 journals. Subjects include microeconomics, macroeconomics, economic history, inflation, money, credit, finance, accounting theory, trade, natural resource economics, and regional economics. Time period is 1969 to present, with monthly updates. Inquire as to online cost and availability.

PERIODICALS AND NEWSLETTERS

Crawford Perspectives. Arch Crawford. • Monthly. $250.00 per year.

Cycle Projections. Foundation for the Study of Cycles. • Monthly. $125.00 per year. Newsletter includes trend projections for stocks, commodities, real estate, and the economy. Short, intermediate, and long-term cycles are covered.

Cycles. Foundation for the Study of Cycles. • Bimonthly. Membership. Provides information on cycle research in economic and other areas.

Trading Cycles. R.E. Andrews, editor. Andrews Publications, Inc. • Monthly. $97.99 per year. Technical investment newsletter. Formerly *Andrews Trading Cycles.*

RESEARCH CENTERS AND INSTITUTES

Bureau of Economic and Business Research. University of Florida. P.O. Box 117145, Gainesville, FL 32611-7145. Phone: (352)392-0171 Fax: (352)392-4739 E-mail: bebr@bebr.cba.ufl.edu • URL: http://www.bebr.ufl.edu.

Conference Board, Inc. 845 Third Ave., New York, NY 10022. Phone: (212)759-0900 Fax: (212)980-7014 E-mail: richard.cavanaugh@conference-board.org • URL: http://www.conference-board.org.

National Bureau of Economic Research, Inc. 1050 Massachusetts Ave., Cambridge, MA 02138-5398. Phone: (617)868-3900 Fax: (617)868-2742 E-mail: msfeldst@nber.org • URL: http://www.nber.org.

STATISTICS SOURCES

The AIER Chart Book. AIER Research Staff. American Institute for Economic Research. • Annual. $3.00. A compact compilation of long-range charts ("Purchasing Power of the Dollar," for example, goes back to 1780) covering various aspects of the U. S. economy. Includes inflation, interest rates, debt, gold, taxation, stock prices, etc. (Economic Education Bulletin.).

Business Cycle Indicators. Conference Board, Inc. • Monthly. $120.00 per year. Contains detailed business and economic statistics in tables that were formerly published by the U. S. Department of Commerce in *Survey of Current Business*, and before that, in the discontinued *Business Conditions Digest*. Includes composite indexes of leading economic indicators, coincident indicators, and lagging indicators.

Business Statistics of the United States. Courtenay M. Slater, editor. Bernan Associates. • 1999. $74.00. Fifth edition. Based on *Business Statistics*, formerly issue by the Bureau of Economic Analysis, U. S. Department of Commerce. Provides basic data for a wide variety of U. S. industries, services, and economic indicators. Most statistics are shown annually for 29 years and monthly for the most recent four years.

Leading Economic Indicators and Related Composite Indexes. Conference Board, Inc. • Monthly. $24.00 per year. Shows monthly changes in the composite indexes of leading, coincident, and lagging economic indicators, formerly computed by the U. S. Department of Commerce. Tables present monthly data for up to 10 years, with a one-page line chart covering 18 years. (The Conference Board News.).

Survey of Current Business. Available from U. S. Government Printing Office. • Monthly. $49.00 per year. Issued by Bureau of Economic Analysis, U. S. Department of Commerce. Presents a wide variety of business and economic data.

TRADE/PROFESSIONAL ASSOCIATIONS

Foundation for the Study of Cycles. 214 Carnegie Center, Suite 204, Princeton, NJ 08540-6237. Phone: (609)987-1401 Fax: (609)987-0726 E-mail: cycles@cycles.org • URL: http://www.cycles.org • Members are individuals interested in economic, financial, natural, and social cycles.

Society for the Investigation of Recurring Events. c/o Jon Wood, P.O. Box 1020, Downington, PA 19335. Phone: (610)269-5900 Fax: (610)269-5901 E-mail: sirecycles@aol.com.

BUSINESS DEPRESSIONS

See: BUSINESS CYCLES

BUSINESS DIRECTORIES

See: CATALOGS AND DIRECTORIES

BUSINESS ECONOMICS

GENERAL WORKS

Managerial Economics. Mark Hirschey. Harcourt Trade Publications. • 1995. $31.25. Eighth edition.

Managerial Economics: Analysis, Problems, Cases. Dale Truett and Lila Truett. South-Western College Publishing. • 1995. $75.25. Fifth edition. (Principles of Economics Series).

Managerial Economics: Applied Microeconomics for Decision Making. Charles S. Maurice and Christopher R. Thomas. McGraw-Hill Higher Education. • 1994. $69.75. Fifth edition.

ABSTRACTS AND INDEXES

Business Periodicals Index. H. W. Wilson Co. • Monthly, except August, with quarterly and annual cumulations. Service basis for print edition; CD-ROM edition, $1,495.00 per year.

BIBLIOGRAPHIES

Business Library Review: An International Journal. International Publishers Distributor. • Quarterly. Academic institutions, $318.00 per year;corporations, $501.00 per year.Incorporates *The Wall Street Review of Books* and *Economics and Business: An Annotated Bibliography.* Publishes scholarly reviews of books on a wide variety of topics in business, economics, and finance. Text in French.

CD-ROM DATABASES

Business Source Plus. EBSCO Information Services. • Monthly. $1,495.00 per year. Provides CD-ROM citations and abstracts to articles in about 650 business periodicals and newspapers, including *The Wall Street Journal*. Full text is provided from 200 selected periodicals. Covers accounting, communications, economics, finance, management, marketing, and other business subjects.

EconLit. Available from SilverPlatter Information, Inc. • Monthly. Single-user, $1,600.00 per year. Multi-user, $2,400.00 per year. Provides CD-ROM citations, with abstracts, to articles from more than 500 economics journals. Time period is 1969 to date. Produced by the American Economic Association.

DIRECTORIES

Business Organizations, Agencies, and Publications Directory. The Gale Group. • 1999. $425.00. 12th edition. Over 40,000 entries describing 39 types of business information sources. Classified by type of organization, publication, or serviceIncludes state, national, and international agencies and organizations. Master index to names and keywords. Also includes e-mail addresses and web site URL's.

National Association for Business Economists: Membership Directory. National Association for Business Economists. • Annual. Membership.

ENCYCLOPEDIAS AND DICTIONARIES

Blackwell Encyclopedic Dictionary of Managerial Economics. Robert McAuliffe, editor. Blackwell Publishers. • 1997. $105.95. The editor is associated with Boston College. Contains definitions of key terms combined with longer articles written by various U. S. and foreign business educators. Includes bibliographies and index. *Blackwell Encyclopedia of Management Series.*

Dictionary of Economics. Jae K. Shim and Joel G. Siegel. John Wiley and Sons, Inc. • 1995. $79.95. Contains 2,200 definitions of economic terms. Includes graphs, charts, tables, and economic formulas. (Business Dictionary Series).

INTERNET DATABASES

The Dismal Scientist. Dismal Sciences, Inc. Phone: (610)241-1000 Fax: (610)696-3836 E-mail: webmaster@dismal.com • URL: http://www.dismal.com • Web site contains a wide variety of economic data and rankings. A search feature provides detailed economic profiles of local areas by ZIP code. Major divisions of the site are Economy, Data, Thoughts, Forecasts, and Toolkit, with many specially written articles and currrent analysis by "recognized economists." Fees: Free.

ONLINE DATABASES

Wilson Business Abstracts Online. H. W. Wilson Co. • Indexes and abstracts 600 major business periodicals, plus the *Wall Street Journal* and the business section of the *New York Times*. Indexing is from 1982, abstracting from 1990, with the two newspapers included from 1993. Updated weekly. Inquire as to online cost and availability. (*Business Periodicals Index* without abstracts is also available online.).

PERIODICALS AND NEWSLETTERS

Applied Economics Letters. Routledge Journals. • Monthly. $554.00 per year. Provides short accounts of new, original research in practical economics. Supplement to *Applied Economics.*

Applied Financial Economics. Routledge Journals. • Bimonthly. Individuals, $648.00 per year; institutions, $1,053.00 per year. Covers practical aspects of financial economics, banking, and monetary economics. Supplement to *Applied Economics.*

Business Economics: Designed to Serve the Needs of People Who Use Economics in Their Work. National Association for Business Economics. • Quarterly. Individuals, $60.00 per year; institution, $54.00 per year. Features articles on applied economics.

Challenge: The Magazine of Economic Affairs. M. E. Sharpe, Inc. • Bimonthly. Individuals, $45.00 per year; institutions, $146.00 per year. A nontechnical journal on current economic policy and economic trends.

The Economist. Economist Intelligence Unit. • 51 times a year. Individuals, $130.00 per year; institutions, $125.00 per year.

Fortune Magazine. Time Inc., Business Information Group. • Biweekly. $59.95 per year. Edited for top executives and upper-level managers.

Harvard Business Review. Harvard University, Graduate School of Business Administration. Harvard Businss School Publishing. • Bimonthly. $95.00 per year.

Horizons. Indiana University School of Business. JAI Press Inc. • Bimonthly. Individuals, $105.00 per year; institutions, $225.00 per year. Presents articles on issues of interest to business executives.

The Journal of Business. University of Chicago Press, Journals Div. • Quarterly. Individuals, $27.00 per year; institutions, $65.00 per year; students, $17.00 per year.

Managerial and Decision Economics: The International Journal of Research and Progress in Management Economics. Available from John Wiley and Sons, Inc., Journals Div. • Eight times a year. $905.00 per year. Deals with economic problems in the field of managerial and decision economics. International coverage. Published in England by John Wiley and Sons Ltd.

NABE News. National Association for Business Economics. • Bimonthly. $95.00 per year. Membership newsletter. Contains feature articles, news of local chapters and roundtables, reviews of seminars and meetings, personal notes and advertisements of interest to the business economist.

Quarterly Journal of Business and Economics. University of Nebraska at Lincoln, College of Business Administration. • Quarterly. Individuals, $16.00 per year; institutions, $30.00 per year.

The Quarterly Review of Economics and Finance. University of Illinois at Urbana-Champaign, Bureau of Economics and Business Res. Available from JAI Press, Inc. • Five times a year. $349.00 per year. Includes annual supplement. Formerly *Quarterly Review of Economics and Business.*

Sloan Management Review. Sloan Management Review Association. Massachusetts Institute of Technology, Sloan School of Management. • Quarterly. $89.00 per year.

TRADE/PROFESSIONAL ASSOCIATIONS

National Association for Business Economics. 1233 20th St., N.W., Suite 505, Washington, DC 20036. Phone: (202)463-6223 Fax: (202)463-6239 E-mail: nabe@nabe.com • URL: http://www.nabe.com.

Society of American Business Editors and Writers. c/o University of Missouri,, School of Journalism, 76 Gannet Hall, Columbia, MO 65211. Phone: (573)882-7862 or (573)882-8985 Fax: (573)884-1372 E-mail: carolyn-guniss@jmail.jour.missouri.edu • URL: http://www.sabew.org.

BUSINESS EDUCATION

See also: ADULT EDUCATION; COLLEGES AND UNIVERSITIES; GRADUATE WORK IN UNIVERSITIES; VOCATIONAL EDUCATION

GENERAL WORKS

Can Ethics Be Taught? Perspectives, Challenges, and Approaches at the Harvard Business School. Thomas R. Piper and others. Harvard Business School Press. • 1993. $24.95.

Gravy Training: Inside the Business of Business Schools. Stuart Crainer and Des Dearlove. Jossey-Bass, Inc., Publishers. • 1999. $25.00. Provides a critical look at major American business schools.

Mastering Management Education: Innovations in Teaching Effectiveness. Charles M. Vance, editor. Sage Publications, Inc. • 1993. $52.00. A collection of articles from the *Journal of Management Education.* Chapters cover lecture and discussion methods, case-study teaching, group-learning skills, and other business education topics.

Principles and Trends in Business Education. Louis C. Nanassy. Pearson Education and Technology. • 1977. Price on application.

Teaching Business Studies. David Needham and others. McGraw-Hill. • 1992. $15.99.

Trends and Developments in Business Administration Programs. Donald L. Joyal. Greenwood Publishing Group, Inc. • 1982. $35.00.

The Witch Doctors: Making Sense of the Management Gurus. John Micklethwait and Adrian Wooldridge. Crown Publishing Group, Inc. • 1996. $25.00. A critical, iconoclastic, and practical view of consultants, business school professors, and modern management theory, written by two members of the editorial staff of *The Economist.*

ABSTRACTS AND INDEXES

Business Education Index of Business Education Articles, Research Studies and Textbooks Compiled from a Selected List of Periodicals, Publishers and Yearbooks Published During the Calendar Year. Delta Pi Epsilon Graduate Business Education Society, National Office. • Annual. $25.00.

Current Index to Journals in Education (CIJE). Oryx Press. • Monthly. $245.00 per year. Semiannual cumulations, $475.00.

Education Index. H.W. Wilson Co. • 10 times a year. Service basis.

Educational Administration Abstracts. Corwin Press, Inc. • Quarterly. Indivduals, $110.00 per year; institutions, $475.00 per year.

ALMANACS AND YEARBOOKS

National Business Education Yearbook. National Business Education Association. • Annual. $15.00.

BIOGRAPHICAL SOURCES

Who's Who in American Education. Marquis Who's Who. • Biennial. $159.95. Contains over 27,000 concise biographies of teachers, administrators, and other individuals involved in all levels of American education.

CD-ROM DATABASES

College Blue Book CD-ROM. Available from The Gale Group. • Annual. $250.00. Produced by Macmillan Reference USA. Serves as electronic version of printed *College Blue Book.* Provides detailed information on programs, degrees, and financial aid sources in the U.S. and Canada.

ERIC on SilverPlatter. Available from SilverPlatter Information, Inc. • Quarterly. $700.00 per year. Produced by the Office of Educational Research and Improvement, U. S. Dept. of Education. Provides CD-ROM indexing and abstracting of a wide variety of literature relating to education. Archival discs are available from 1966.

WILSONDISC: Education Index. H. W. Wilson Co. • Monthly. $1,295.00 per year. Provides CD-ROM indexing of education-related literature from 1983 to date. Price includes online service.

DIRECTORIES

Business Week's Guide to the Best Business Schools. John A. Byrne. McGraw-Hill. • 1997. $16.95. Fifth edition. Includes the best regional business schools.

Faculty White Pages. The Gale Group. • 1991. $135.00. "Telephone book" classified arrangement of over 537,000 U. S. college faculty members in 41 subject sections. A roster of institutions is included.

Insider's Guide to the Top Ten Business Schools. Tom Fischgrund, editor. Little, Brown and Co. • 1990. $10.95. Fourth edition.

Peterson's Graduate and Professional Programs: Business, Education, Health, Information Studies, Law, and Social Work. Peterson's Magazine Group. • Annual. $27.95. Provides details of graduate and professional programs in business, law, information, and other fields at colleges and universities. Formerly *Peterson's Guide to Graduate Programs in Business, Education, Health, Information Studies, Law and Social Work.*

Peterson's Guide to MBA Programs: The Most Comprehensive Guide to U. S., Canadian, and International Business Schools. Peterson's. • 1996. $21.95. Provides detailed information on about 850 graduate programs in business at 700 colleges and universities in the U. S., Canada, and other countries.

Profiles in Business and Management: An International Directory of Scholars and Their Research Version 2.0. Claudia Bruce, editor. Harvard Business School Press. • 1996. $495.00. Two volumes. Provides backgrounds, publications, and current research projects of more than 5,600 business and management experts.

HANDBOOKS AND MANUALS

Financing Graduate School: How to Get Money for Your Master's or Ph.D. Patricia McWade. Peterson's. • 1996. $16.95. Second revised edition. Discusses the practical aspects of various types of financial aid for graduate students. Includes bibliographic and directory information.

Official Guide for GMAT Review (Graduate Management Admission Test). Graduate Management Admissions Council. Educational Testing Service. • Biennial. $11.95. Provides sample tests, answers, and explanations for the Graduate Management Admission Test (GMAT).

Training and Development Handbook: A Guide to Human Resource Development. Robert L. Craig. McGraw-Hill. • 1996. $89.50. Fourth edition.

ONLINE DATABASES

ERIC. Educational Resources Information Center. • Broad range of educational literature, 1966 to present. Monthly updates. Inquire as to online cost and availability.

PERIODICALS AND NEWSLETTERS

Business Education Forum. National Business Education Association. • Four times a year. Libraries, $70.00 per year. Includes *Yearbook* and *Keying In,* a newsletter.

International Review for Business Education. • Semiannual. $36.00 per year. Text in English, French, German, Italian, and Spanish.

Journal of Education for Business. Helen Dwight Reid Educational Foundation. Heldref Publications. • Bimonthly. Individuals, $38.00 per year; institutions, $64.00 per year. Features basic and applied research-based articles on business fundamentals, career education, consumer economics, distributive education, management, and trends in communications, information systems, and knowledge systems in business.

Journal of Management Education. Organizational Behavior Teaching Society. Sage Publications, Inc. • Quarterly. Individuals, $65.00 per year; institutions, $270.00 per year. A scholarly journal dealing with the teaching and training of business students and managers.

Journal of Teaching in International Business. Haworth Press, Inc. • Quarterly. Individuals, $50.00 per year; institutions, $75.00 per year; libraries, $185.00 per year.

Resources in Education. Educational Resources Information Center. Available from U.S. Government Printing Office. • Monthly. $102.00 per year. Reports on educational research.

STATISTICS SOURCES

Degrees and Other Awards Conferred by Institutions of Higher Education. Available from U. S. Government Printing Office. • Annual. Issued by the National Center for Education Statistics, U. S. Department of Education. Provides data on the number of degrees awarded at the associate's, bachelor's, master's, and doctor's levels. Includes fields of study and racial-ethnic-sex data by major field or discipline.

Occupational Projections and Training Data. Available from U. S. Government Printing Office. • Biennial. $7.00. Issued by Bureau of Labor Statistics, U. S. Department of Labor. Contains projections of employment change and job openings over the next 15 years for about 500 specific occupations. Also includes the number of associate, bachelor's, master's, doctoral, and professional degrees awarded in a recent year for about 900 specific fields of study.

TRADE/PROFESSIONAL ASSOCIATIONS

Delta Pi Epsilon. P.O. Box 4340, Little Rock, AR 72214. Phone: (501)562-1233 Fax: (501)562-1293 E-mail: dpe@ipa.net • URL: http://www.dpe.org • A professional society for teachers of business subjects.

Delta Sigma Pi. P.O. 230, Oxford, OH 45056-0230. Phone: (513)523-1907 Fax: (513)523-7292 E-mail: centraloffice@dspnet.org • URL: http://www.dspnet.org • A professional fraternity related to education in business administration.

Graduate Management Admission Council. 1750 Tysons Blvd., No. 1100, McLean, VA 22102-4220. Phone: (703)749-0131 Fax: (703)749-0169 E-mail: gmat@ets.org • URL: http://www.gmat.org • Members are graduate schools of business administration and management.

International Society for Business Education-United States Chapter. 1914 Association Dr., Reston, VA 20191. Phone: (703)860-8300 Fax: (703)620-4483 E-mail: nbea@nbea.org • URL: http://www.nbea.org/nbea.html.

National Business Education Association. 1914 Association Dr., Reston, VA 22091-1596. Phone: (703)860-8300 Fax: (703)860-4483 E-mail: nbea@nbea.org • URL: http://www.nbea.org/nbea.html.

OTHER SOURCES

American Universities and Colleges. Walter de Gruyter, Inc. • 2001. $249.50. 16th edition. Two volumes. Produced in collaboration with the American Council on Education. Provides full descriptions of more than 1,900 institutions of higher learning, including details of graduate and professional programs.

Educational Rankings Annual: A Compilation of Approximately 3,500 Published Rankings and Lists on Every Aspect of Education. The Gale Group. • 2000. $220.00. Provides national, regional, local, and international rankings of a wide variety of educational institutions, including business and professional schools.

BUSINESS ENTERPRISES, SALE OF

See also: SMALL BUSINESS

GENERAL WORKS

Buying and Selling a Business. Ralph Warner, editor. Nolo.com. • 1998. Price on application.

Buying and Selling a Small Business: A Complete Guide to a Successful Deal. Ernest J. Honigmann. CCH, Inc. • 1999. $91.95.

How to Sell Your Business for More Money. Gary Schine. Consultants Press. • 1991. $29.95.

ABSTRACTS AND INDEXES

Business Periodicals Index. H. W. Wilson Co. • Monthly, except August, with quarterly and annual cumulations. Service basis for print edition; CD-ROM edition, $1,495.00 per year.

Index to Legal Periodicals and Books. H. W. Wilson Co. • Monthly. Quarterly and annual cumulations. $270.00 per year. CD-ROM version available at $1,495.00 per year.

CD-ROM DATABASES

ABI/INFORM Global. Bell & Howell Information and Learning. • Monthly. $6,500.00 per year. Provides CD-ROM indexing and abstracting of worldwide business literature appearing in over 1,200 periodicals for the most recent five years. Archival discs are available from 1971. Formerly *ABI/INFORM OnDisc.*

WILSONDISC: Index to Legal Periodicals and Books. H. W. Wilson Co. • Monthly. Including unlimited online access to *Index to Legal Periodicals* through WILSONLINE. Contains CD-ROM indexing of more than 800 English language legal periodicals from 1981 to date and 2,500 books.

WILSONDISC: Wilson Business Abstracts. H. W. Wilson Co. • Monthly. $2,495.00 per year, including unlimited online access to *Wilson Business Abstracts* through WILSONLINE. Provides CD-ROM "cover-to-cover" abstracting and indexing of over 600 prominent business periodicals. Indexing is from 1982, abstracting from 1990. (*Business Periodicals Index* without abstracts is available on CD-ROM at $1,495 per year.).

DIRECTORIES

Business Brokers Directory. American Business Directories. • Annual. Price on application. Lists about 3,383 U. S. business brokers. Information is derived from telephone yellow page directories.

HANDBOOKS AND MANUALS

Acquiring or Selling the Privately Held Company. Practising Law Institute. • 1995. $149.00. Two volumes. (Corporate Law and Practice Series).

Business Brokerage. Entrepreneur Media, Inc. • Looseleaf. $59.50. A practical guide to starting a brokerage service for the sale and purchase of small businesses. Covers profit potential, start-up costs, market size evaluation, owner's time required, pricing, accounting, advertising, promotion, etc. (Start-Up Business Guide No. E1317.).

CCH Guide to Business Valuation. CCH, Inc. • Looseleaf. $295.00 per year, including quarterly newsletter. Covers latest developments and trends in the evaluation of businesses.

Corporate Valuation: Tools for Effective Appraisal and Decision Making. Randolph W. Westerfield and others. McGraw-Hill Professional. • 1993. $65.00. Discusses the four most widely-used corporate appraisal methods.

ONLINE DATABASES

ABI/INFORM. Bell & Howell Information and Learning. • Provides online indexing to business-related material occurring in over 1,000 periodicals from 1971 to the present. Inquire as to online cost and availability.

Index to Legal Periodicals and Books (Online). H. W. Wilson Co. • Broad coverage of law journals and books 1981 to date. Monthly updates. Inquire as to online cost and availability.

Management Contents. The Gale Group. • Covers a wide range of management, financial, marketing, personnel, and administrative topics. About 150 leading business journals are indexed and abstracted from 1974 to date, with monthly updating. Inquire as to online cost and availability.

Trade & Industry Index. The Gale Group. • Provides indexing of business periodicals, January 1981 to date. Daily updates. (Full text articles from some periodicals are available online, 1983 to date, in the companion database, *Trade & Industry ASAP.*) Inquire as to online cost and availability.

Wilson Business Abstracts Online. H. W. Wilson Co. • Indexes and abstracts 600 major business periodicals, plus the *Wall Street Journal* and the business section of the *New York Times.* Indexing is from 1982, abstracting from 1990, with the two newspapers included from 1993. Updated weekly. Inquire as to online cost and availability. (*Business Periodicals Index* without abstracts is also available online.).

BUSINESS ETHICS

See also: SOCIAL RESPONSIBILITY

GENERAL WORKS

American Business Values. Gerald F. Cavanaugh. Prentice Hall. • 1997. $38.60. Fourth edition.

Business Ethics. J. Michael Hoffman. McGraw-Hill. • 2000. $39.25. Fourth edition.

Business Ethics: Roles and Responsibilities. Joseph Badaracco. McGraw-Hill Higher Education. • 1994. $63.50.

Business, Government, and Society: A Managerial Perspective: Text and Cases. George A. Steiner and John F. Steiner. McGraw-Hill. • 1999. $82.19. Ninth edition. (Management Series).

Business, Government, and Society: Managing Competitiveness, Ethics, and Social Issues. Newman S. Perry. Prentice Hall. • 1994. $54.80.

Can Ethics Be Taught? Perspectives, Challenges, and Approaches at the Harvard Business School. Thomas R. Piper and others. Harvard Business School Press. • 1993. $24.95.

Case Studies in Business Ethics. Thomas Donaldson and Al Gini, editors. Prentice-Hall. • 1995. $36.20. Fourth edition.

Case Studies in Business, Society, and Ethics. Thomas L. Beauchamp, editor. Prentice Hall. • 1997. $31.80. Fourth edition.

Corporate Social Challenge: Cases and Commentaries. James E. Stacey and Frederick D. Sturdivant, editors. McGraw-Hill Professional. • 1994. $41.95. Fifth edition.

The Ethics of Management. LaRue T. Hosmer. McGraw-Hill Professional. • 1995. $33.50. Third edition.

The Moral Foundations of Professional Ethics. Alan H. Goldman. Rowman and Littlefield Publishing Inc. • 1980. $25.50. (Philosophy and Society Series).

BIBLIOGRAPHIES

A Bibliography of Business Ethics, 1981-1985: University of Virginia. Donald G. Jones and Patricia Bennett, editors. The Edwin Mellen Press. • 1986.

$99.95. (Mellen Studies in Business Series: volume two).

ENCYCLOPEDIAS AND DICTIONARIES

Blackwell Encyclopedic Dictionary of Business Ethics. Patricia H. Werhane and R. Edward Freeman, editors. Blackwell Publishers. • 1997. $105.95. The editors are associated with the University of Virginia. Contains definitions of key terms combined with longer articles written by various U. S. and foreign business educators. Includes bibliographies and index. (Blackwell Encyclopedia of Management Series).

HANDBOOKS AND MANUALS

ABA/BNA Lawyer's Manual on Professional Conduct. American Bar Association. Bureau of National Affairs, Inc. • Biweekly. $845.00 per year. Looseleaf. Covers American Bar Association's model rules governing ethical practice of law.

Codes of Professional Responsibility: Ethic Standards in Business, Health and Law. Rena Gorlin, editor. Bureau of National Affairs, Inc. • 1998. $95.00. Fourth edition. Contains full text or substantial excerpts of the official codes of ethics of major professional groups in the fields of law, business, and health care.

Managing Business Ethics: Straight Talk About How to Do It Right. Linda K. Trevino and Katherine A. Nelson. John Wiley and Sons, Inc. • 1999. $49.95. Second edition. Includes "Ethics and the Individual," "Ethics and the Manager," and "Ethics and the Organization.".

PERIODICALS AND NEWSLETTERS

Business and Society: A Journal of Interdisciplinary Exploration. International Association for Business and Society Research Committee. Sage Publications, Inc. • Quarterly. Individuals, $65.00 per year; institutions, $265.00 per year.

Journal of Business Ethics. Kluwer Academic Publishers. • 20 times a year. Institutions, $1,202.40 per year.

Positive Leadership: Improving Performance Through Value-Centered Management. Lawence Ragan Communications, Inc. • Monthly. $119.00 per year. Newsletter. Emphasis is on employee motivation, family issues, ethics, and community relations.

RESEARCH CENTERS AND INSTITUTES

Business, Government, and Society Research Institute. University of Pittsburgh. School of Business, Mervis Hall, Pittsburgh, PA 15260. Phone: (412)648-1555 Fax: (412)648-1693 E-mail: mitnick@pitt.edu.

Olsson Center for Applied Ethics. University of Virginia. Darden School, P.O. Box 6550, Charlottesville, VA 22906. Phone: (804)924-0935 Fax: (804)924-6378 E-mail: ref8d@virginia.edu • URL: http://www.darden.virginia.edu.

BUSINESS ETIQUETTE

See: ETIQUETTE

BUSINESS FAILURES

See also: BANK FAILURES; BANKRUPTCY

GENERAL WORKS

Predictability of Corporate Failure. R. A. I. Van Frederikslust. Kluwer Academic Publishers. • 1978. $77.50.

Why Entrepreneurs Fail: Avoid the 20 Fatal Pitfalls of Running Your Own Business. James W. Halloran. McGraw-Hill Professional. • 1991. $14.95.

ABSTRACTS AND INDEXES

Business Periodicals Index. H. W. Wilson Co. • Monthly, except August, with quarterly and annual cumulations. Service basis for print edition; CD-ROM edition, $1,495.00 per year.

DIRECTORIES

National Directory of Corporate Distress Specialists: A Comprehensive Guide to Firms and Professionals Providing Services in Bankruptcies, Workouts, Turnarounds, and Distressed Investments. Joel W. Lustig, editor. Lustig Data Research, Inc. • Annual. $245.00. Provides information on 1,400 specialist firms in 17 subject areas-attorneys, accountants, financial advisors, investors, valuation consultants, turnaround managers, liquidators, etc. Nine indexes are included.

HANDBOOKS AND MANUALS

Taxation of Financially Distressed Businesses. David B. Newman. West Group. • 1993. $120.00. Covers bankruptcy, foreclosure, abandonment, legal reporting requirements, and other tax-related subjects. (Tax Series).

INTERNET DATABASES

Fedstats. Federal Interagency Council on Statistical Policy. Phone: (202)395-7254 • URL: http://www.fedstats.gov • Web site features an efficient search facility for full-text statistics produced by more than 70 federal agencies, including the Census Bureau, the Bureau of Economic Analysis, and the Bureau of Labor Statistics. Boolean searches can be made within one agency or for all agencies combined. Links are offered to international statistical bureaus, including the UN, IMF, OECD, UNESCO, Eurostat, and 20 individual countries. Fees: Free.

ONLINE DATABASES

ABI/INFORM. Bell & Howell Information and Learning. • Provides online indexing to business-related material occurring in over 1,000 periodicals from 1971 to the present. Inquire as to online cost and availability.

DRI U.S. Central Database. Data Products Division. • Provides more than 23,000 business, financial, demographic, economic, foreign trade, and industry-related time series for the U.S. Includes national income, population, retail-wholesale trade, price indexes, labor data, housing, industrial production, banking, interest rates, money supply, etc. Time period is generally 1947 to date (some data back to 1929). Updating varies. Inquire as to online cost and availability.

Trade & Industry Index. The Gale Group. • Provides indexing of business periodicals, January 1981 to date. Daily updates. (Full text articles from some periodicals are available online, 1983 to date, in the companion database, *Trade & Industry ASAP.*) Inquire as to online cost and availability.

PERIODICALS AND NEWSLETTERS

Business Strategies Bulletin. CCH, Inc. • Monthly. $166.00 per year. Newsletter.

Insolvency Law & Practice. Tolley Publishing Co. Ltd. • Bimonthly. $250.00 per year. United Kingdom emphasis.

STATISTICS SOURCES

Business Failure Record. Dun & Bradstreet, Economic Analysis Dept. • Annual. Free upon request. Provides historical business failure data.

Business Statistics of the United States. Courtenay M. Slater, editor. Bernan Associates. • 1999. $74.00. Fifth edition. Based on *Business Statistics*, formerly issue by the Bureau of Economic Analysis, U. S. Department of Commerce. Provides basic data for a wide variety of U. S. industries, services, and economic indicators. Most statistics are shown annually for 29 years and monthly for the most recent four years.

FAA Statistical Handbook of Aviation. Federal Aviation Administration. Available from U. S. Government Printing Office. • Annual.

Monthly Business Failures. Dun & Bradstreet, Economic Analysis Dept. • Monthly. $30.00 per year. Provides number of failures and liabilities in over 100 lines of business.

Quarterly Analysis of Failures. Dun & Bradstreet, Economic Analysis Dept. • Quarterly. $20.00.

Standard & Poor's Statistical Service. Current Statistics. Standard & Poor's. • Monthly. $688.00 per year. Includes 10 *Basic Statistics* sections, *Current Statistics Supplements* and *Annual Security Price Index Record.*

Survey of Current Business. Available from U. S. Government Printing Office. • Monthly. $49.00 per year. Issued by Bureau of Economic Analysis, U. S. Department of Commerce. Presents a wide variety of business and economic data.

Weekly Business Failures. Dun & Bradstreet, Economic Analysis Dept. • Weekly. $450.00 per year.

OTHER SOURCES

Business Strategies. CCH, Inc. • Semimonthly. $819.00 per year. Four looseleaf volumes. Semimonthly updates. Legal, tax, and accounting aspects of business planning and decision-making. Provides information on start-ups, forms of ownership (partnerships, corporations), failing businesses, reorganizations, acquisitions, and so forth. Includes *Business Strategies Bulletin,* a monthly newsletter.

BUSINESS FICTION

See: BUSINESS IN FICTION

BUSINESS FILMS

See: AUDIOVISUAL AIDS IN INDUSTRY

BUSINESS FINANCE

See: FINANCE; FINANCIAL ANALYSIS

BUSINESS FLYING

See: AIR TRAVEL; AIRLINE INDUSTRY; BUSINESS AVIATION

BUSINESS FORECASTING

See also: BUSINESS CYCLES; BUSINESS STATISTICS; ECONOMIC POLICY

GENERAL WORKS

The Art of the Long View: Planning for the Future in an Uncertain World. Peter Schwartz. Doubleday. • 1991. $15.95. Covers strategic planning for corporations and smaller firms. Includes "The World in 2005: Three Scenarios.".

Business Cycles and Forecasting. Howard J. Sherman and David X. Kolk. Addison-Wesley Educational Publications, Inc. • 1997. $101.00.

Business Cycles: Theory, History, Indicators, and Forecasting. Victor Zarnowitz. University of Chicago Press. • 1992. $77.00.

Business Forecasting. Holton J. Wilson. McGraw-Hill Professional. • 2001. $67.50. Fourth edition.

Business Forecasting for Management. Branko Pecar. McGraw-Hill. • 1994. $14.95.

Decision Making and Forecasting: With Emphasis on Model Building and Policy Analysis. Kneale T. Marshall and Robert M. Oliver. McGraw-Hill. • 1995. $86.88.

Econometric Models and Economic Forecasts. Robert S. Pindyck and Daniel L. Rubinfield. McGraw-Hill. • 1997. $86.88. Fourth edition.

The 500 Year Delta: What Happens After What Comes Next. Jim Taylor and others. HarperCollins Publishers. • 1998. $14.00. Provides analysis of major corporate and political trends.

Forecasting Business Trends. American Institute for Economic Research. • 2000. $6.00. Summarizes methods of economic forecasting, statistical indicators, methods of analyzing business cycles, and use of leading, coincident, and lagging indicators. Includes charts, tables, and a glossary of terms. (Economic Education Bulletin.).

The Fortune Sellers: The Big Business of Buying and Selling Predictions. William A. Sherden. John Wiley and Sons, Inc. • 1997. $29.95. The author states that predictions are notoriously unreliable in any field, including the stock market, the economy, and the weather. (Forecasters in all areas don't have to be right; they just have to be interesting.).

The Shape of Things to Come: Seven Imperatives for Winning in the New World of Business. Richard W. Oliver. McGraw-Hill. • 1998. $24.95. Contains predictions relating to the influence of information technology on 21st century business. (Business Week Books.).

The Witch Doctor of Wall Street: A Noted Financial Expert Guides You Through Today's Voodoo Economics. Robert H. Parks. Prometheus Books. • 1996. $25.95. The author, a professor of finance at Pace University, discusses "Practice and Malpractice" in relation to the following: business forecasting, economic theory, interest rates, monetary policy, the stock market, and corporate finance. Includes "A Short Primer on Derivatives," as an appendix.

BIBLIOGRAPHIES

Future Survey Annual: A Guide to the Recent Literature of Trends, Forecasts, and Policy Proposals. World Future Society. • Annual. $35.00.

CD-ROM DATABASES

World Marketing Forecasts on CD-ROM. The Gale Group. • Annual. $2,500.00. Produced by Euromonitor. Provides detailed forecast data for the years to 2012 on CD-ROM for 54 countries in all parts of the world. Covers a wide range of social, demographic, economic, and market factors. Includes specific forecasts for many kinds of consumer products.

DIRECTORIES

Strategic Leadership Forum Membership Directory. Strategic Leadership Forum. • Annual. About 4,000 strategic management executives, consultants and academics. Membership.

HANDBOOKS AND MANUALS

Guide to Everyday Economic Statistics. Gary E. Clayton and Martin G. Giesbrecht. McGraw-Hill. • 1997. $14.38. Fourth edition. Contains clear explanations of the commonly used economic indicators.

Using Econometrics: A Practical Guide. A. H. Studenmund. Addison-Wesley Longman, Inc. • 2001. Fourth edition. Price on application.

ONLINE DATABASES

EconBase: Time Series and Forecasts. WEFA, Inc. • Presents online econometric data for business conditions, economics, demographics, industry, finance, employment, household income, interest rates, prices, etc. Includes two-year forecasts for a wide range of economic indicators. Time span is 1948 to date, with monthly updates. Inquire as to online cost and availability.

EconLit. American Economic Association. • Covers the worldwide literature of economics as contained in selected monographs and about 550 journals. Subjects include microeconomics, macroeconomics, economic history, inflation, money, credit, finance, accounting theory, trade, natural resource economics, and regional economics. Time period is 1969 to present, with monthly updates. Inquire as to online cost and availability.

Euromonitor Market Research. Euromonitor International. • Provides the complete text online of Euromonitor market analysis reports. Covers consumer goods market research data for all major countries, with emphasis on specific product categories. Time period is current. Continuous updating. Inquire as to online cost and availability.

Globalbase. The Gale Group. • Provides more than one million online summaries of business, industrial, and economic news reports from more than 1,000 publications worldwide. Covers a wide range of material appearing in international trade journals, professional magazines, and newspapers. Time period is 1984 to date, with weekly updates. Inquire as to online cost and availability.

MarkIntel. Thomson Financial Securities Data. • Provides the current full text online of more than 45,000 market research reports covering 54 industries, from 43 leading research firms worldwide. Reports include extensive forecasts and market analysis. Inquire as to online cost and availability.

PERIODICALS AND NEWSLETTERS

Barometer of Business. Harris Trust and Savings Bank. • Bimonthly. Free.

Blue Chip Economic Indicators: What Top Economists Are Saying About the U.S. Outlook for the Year Ahead. Aspen Publishers, Inc. • Monthly. $654.00 per year. Newsletter containing U. S. economic consensus forecasts.

Blue Chip Financial Forecasts: What Top Analysts are Saying About U. S. and Foreign Interest Rates, Monetary Policy, Inflation, and Economic Growth. Aspen Publishers, Inc. • Monthly. $654.00 per year. Newsletter. Gives forecasts about a year in advance for interest rates, inflation, currency exchange rates, monetary policy, and economic growth rates.

Journal of Business Forecasting Methods and Systems. Graceway Publishing Co. • Quarterly. $70.00 per year. Includes articles on forecasting methods and provides actual business and economic forecasts.

Journal of Forecasting. Available from John Wiley and Sons, Inc., Journals Div. • Seven times a year. Institutions, $760.00 per year. A centralized focus on recent development in the art and science of forecasting International coverage. Published in England by John Wiley and Sons Ltd.

Long Range Planning. Strategic Planning Society. Elsevier Science. • Bimonthly. $1,104.00 per year.

Technological Forecasting and Social Change. Elsevier Science. • Nine times a year. $688.00 per year. Three volumes.

The Trends Journal: The Authority on Trends Management. Gerald Celente, editor. Trends Research Institute. • Quarterly. $185.00 per year. Newsletter. Provides forecasts on a wide variety of economic, social, and political topics. Includes "Hot Trends to Watch.".

RESEARCH CENTERS AND INSTITUTES

Bureau of Economic and Business Research. University of Florida. P.O. Box 117145, Gainesville, FL 32611-7145. Phone: (352)392-0171 Fax: (352)392-4739 E-mail: bebr@bebr.cba.ufl.edu • URL: http://www.bebr.ufl.edu.

Business Forecasting Project. University of California, Los Angeles. 110 Westwood Plaza, Gold Hall B302, Los Angeles, CA 90095. Phone: (310)825-1623 Fax: (310)206-9440 E-mail: business.forecast@anderson.edu • URL: http://www.anderson.ucla.edu/research/forecast.

Economic Forecasting Center. Georgia State University, College of Business Administration, University Plaza, 35 Broad St., Atlanta, GA 30303-3083. Phone: (404)651-3282 Fax: (404)651-3299 E-mail: efcdon@langate.gsu.edu • URL: http://www-ecfor.gsu.edu • Concerned with national and regional economic analysis and forecasting.

National Bureau of Economic Research, Inc. 1050 Massachusetts Ave., Cambridge, MA 02138-5398. Phone: (617)868-3900 Fax: (617)868-2742 E-mail: msfeldst@nber.org • URL: http://www.nber.org.

STATISTICS SOURCES

The Book of European Forecasts. Available from The Gale Group. • 1996. $320.00. Second edition. Published by Euromonitor. Presents economic, commercial, demographic, and social forecasts for Europe, with statistical data and commentary.

Consumer Canada 1996. Available from The Gale Group. • 1996. $750.00. Published by Euromonitor. Provides consumer market, socioeconomic, and demographic data for Canada. Includes consumer market size (volume and value) for many specific kinds of products.

Consumer International 2000/2001. Available from The Gale Group. • 1998. $1,190.00. Seventh edition. Published by Euromonitor. Contains extensive consumer market, economic, and demographic data for 27 major, non-European countries, including the U. S. and Canada. Includes consumer market size (volume and value) for 150 product types in 14 categories (food, clothing, automobiles, cosmetics, appliances, etc.).

Country Data Forecasts. Bank of America, World Information Services, Dept. 3015. • Looseleaf, with semiannual updates. $495.00 per year. Provides detailed statistical tables for 80 countries, showing historical data and five-year forecasts of 23 key economic series. Includes population, inflation figures, debt, per capita income, foreign trade, exchange rates, and other data.

Economic Indicators. Council of Economic Advisors, Executive Office of the President. Available from U.S. Government Printing Office. • Monthly. $55.00 per year.

Economic Outlook. Available from Basil Blackwell, Inc. • Quarterly. $658.00 per year. Published by the London Business School. Includes country and global forecasts of over 170 economic and business variables. Actual data is shown for two years, with forecasts up to ten years.

European Marketing Forecasts 2001. Available from The Gale Group. • 2000. $1,190.00. Third edition. Published by Euromonitor. Contains demographic, economic, and market forecasts for the countries of Europe to the year 2010. Forecasts include market-size data for 15 consumer product sectors (food, clothing, automobiles, consumer electronics, etc.).

International Marketing Forecasts 2001. Available from The Gale Group. • 2000. $1,090.00. Third edition. Published by Euromonitor. Contains demographic, economic, and market forecasts to the year 2010 for major, non-European countries, including the U. S. and Canada. Forecasts include market-size data for 15 consumer product sectors, such as food, clothing, and automobiles.

International Survey of Business Expectations. Dun & Bradstreet Corp., Economic Analysis Dept. • Quarterly. $40.00 per year. A survey of international business executives regarding their quarterly expectations for sales, profits, prices, inventories, employment, and new orders. Results are given for each of 14 major foreign countries and the U. S.

Statistical Forecasts of the United States. The Gale Group. • 1995. $99.00. Second edition. Provides both long-term and short-term statistical forecasts relating to basic items in the U. S.: population, employment, labor, crime, education, and health care. Data in the form of charts, graphs, and tables has been taken from a wide variety of government and private sources. Includes a subject index and an "Index of Forecast by Year.".

U. S. Market Trends and Forecasts. The Gale Group. • 2000. $315.00. Second edition. Provides graphic representation of market statistics by means of pie charts and tables for each of 30 major industries and 400 market segments. Includes market forecasts and historical overviews.

U. S. Survey of Business Expectations. Dun & Bradstreet Corp., Economic Analysis Dept. • Quarterly. 40.00 per year. A survey of 3,000 U. S. business executives as to their expectations for next quarter's sales, profits, prices, inventories, employment, exports, and new orders.

TRADE/PROFESSIONAL ASSOCIATIONS

Hudson Institute. Herman Kahn Center, 5395 Emerson Way, Indianapolis, IN 46226. Phone: 800-483-7660 or (317)545-1000 Fax: (317)545-9639 E-mail: info@hudson.org • URL: http://www.hudson.org.

Institute for the Future. 2744 Sand Hill Rd., Menlo Park, CA 94025-7020. Phone: (650)854-6322 Fax: (650)854-7850 • URL: http://www.iftf.org.

National Policy Association. 1424 16th St., N.W., Suite 700, Washington, DC 20036. Phone: (202)265-7685 Fax: (202)797-5516 E-mail: npa@npa1.org • URL: http://www.npa1.org.

Renewable Natural Resources Foundation. 5430 Grosvenor Lane, Bethesda, MD 20814. Phone: (301)493-9101 Fax: (301)493-6148 E-mail: rnrf@aol.com • URL: http://www.rnrf.org.

World Future Society. 7910 Woodmont Ave., Suite 450, Bethesda, MD 20814. Phone: 800-989-8274 or (301)656-8274 Fax: (301)951-0394 E-mail: info@wfs.org • URL: http://www.wfs.org • Members are individuals concerned with forecasts and ideas about the future.

OTHER SOURCES

Consensus Forecasts: A Digest of International Economic Forecasts. Consensus Economics Inc. • Monthly. $565.00 per year. Provides a survey of more than 200 "prominent" financial and economic forecasters, covering 20 major countries. Two-year forecasts for each country include future growth, inflation, interest rates, and exchange rates. Each issue contains analysis of business conditions in various countries.

MarketingClick Network: American Demographics. Intertec Publishing, a Primedia Co. • Web site provides full-text articles from *American Demographics*, *Marketing Tools*, and *Forecast*, with keyword searching. The *Marketing Tools Directory* can also be searched online, listing suppliers of products, information, and services for advertising, market research, and marketing. Fees: Free.

Sales Forecasting. American Management Association Extension Institute. • Looseleaf. $110.00. Self-study course. Emphasis is on practical explanations, examples, and problem solving. Quizzes and a case study are included.

BUSINESS FORMS

See: FORMS AND BLANKS

BUSINESS GIFTS

See: GIFT BUSINESS

BUSINESS HISTORY

GENERAL WORKS

Age of Giant Corporations: A Microeconomic History of American Business, 1914-1984. Robert Sobel. Greenwood Publishing Group Inc. • 1993. $55.00. Third edition. (Contributions in Economics and Economic History Series, No.46).

American Decades. The Gale Group. • 1996. $890.00. $99.00 per volume. Consists of 10 volumes, each covering a decade during the period 1900-1989. "Each volume begins with an overview and chronology covering the entire decade. Subject chapters follow, each including an overview, subject-specific timeline and alphabetically arranged entries..".

Business History of the World: A Chronology. Richard B. Robinson, compiler. Greenwood Publishing Group, Inc. • 1993. $79.50. Provides "a basic chronology of the business world outside the United States from prehistory through the 1980s.".

Crystal Fire: The Birth of the Information Age. Michael Riordan and Lillian Hoddeson. W. W. Norton & Co., Inc. • 1997. $27.50. A history of the transistor, from early electronic experiments to practical development at the former Bell Telephone Laboratories.

The Death of the Banker: The Decline and Fall of the Great Financial Dynasties and the Triumph of the Small Investor. Ron Chernow. Vintage Books. • 1997. $12.00. Contains three essays: "J. Pierpont Morgan," "The Warburgs," and "The Death of the Banker" (discusses the decline of banks in personal finance and the rise of mutual funds and stock brokers).

Devil Take the Hindmost: A History of Financial Speculation. Edward Chancellor. Farrar, Straus & Giroux, LLC. • 1999. $25.00. Covers such events as the Dutch tulip mania of 1637, the South Sea bubble of 1720, and the Japanese real estate and stock market boom of the 1980's.

FAA Historical Chronology: Civil Aviation and the Federal Government, 1926-1996. Edmund Preston, editor. Available from U. S. Government Printing Office. • 1998. $29.00. Third edition. Issued by the Federal Aviation Administration, U. S. Department of Transportation (http://www.dot.gov). Provides a compilation of historical information about the FAA and the earlier Civil Aeronautics Board (CAB). Chronological arrangement.

Great Inflations of the 20th Century: Theories, Policies, and Evidence. Pierre L. Siklos, editor. Edward Elgar Publishing, Inc. • 1995. $95.00. Contains reprints of papers on the history and economic analysis of major inflations.

History of Black Business in America: Capitalism, Race, Entrepreneurship. Juliet E. K. Walker. Available from The Gale Group. • 1998. $45.00. Published by Twayne Publishers. Includes profiles of African American business pioneers. (Evolution of Modern Business Series.).

It was a Very Good Year: Extraordinary Moments in Stock Market History. Martin S. Fridson. John Wiley and Sons, Inc. • 1997. $29.95. Provides details on what happened during each of the ten best years for the stock market since 1900.

Stock Market Crashes and Speculative Manias. Eugene N. White, editor. Edward Elgar Publishing, Inc. • 1996. $230.00. Contains reprints of 23 articles dating from 1905 to 1994. (International Library of Macroeconomic and Financial History Series: No. 13).

United States Business History, 1602-1988: A Chronology. Richard B. Robinson. Greenwood Publishing Group, Inc. • 1990. $75.00.

DIRECTORIES

International Directory of Company Histories. St. James Press. • 1989-2000. 33 volumes. Prices vary. Provides detailed histories of about 2,200 major corporations. Cumulative indexing is provided for company names, personal names, and industries.

Notable Corporate Chronologies. The Gale Group. • 1998. $390.00. Second edition. Two volumes. Contains about 1,150 chronological profiles of major corporations, showing events that were important in each company's development. Volume four is a *Master Index*.

ENCYCLOPEDIAS AND DICTIONARIES

Business Cycles and Depressions: An Encyclopedia. David Glasner, editor. Garland Publishing, Inc. • 1997. $100.00. Contains 327 alphabetical entries by various contributors. Defines and reviews all significant depressions, recessions, and financial crises in the U. S. and Europe since 1790. Includes chronologies, bibliographies, and indexes.

Encyclopedia of American Economic History. Glenn Porter. Available from Gale Group. • 1980. $350.00. Three volumes. Individual volumes, $120.00.

Gale Encyclopedia of U.S. Economic History. The Gale Group. • 2000. $205.00. Two volumes. Contains about 1,000 alphabetically arranged entries. Includes industry profiles, biographies, social issue profiles, geographic profiles, and chronological tables.

The History of Accounting: An Encyclopedia. Michael Chatfield and Richard Vangermeersch, editors. Garland Publishing, Inc. • 1996. $100.00. Contains more than 400 alphabetical entries by various contributors, covering the history of accounting from 750 B.C. to the modern era. Includes a bibliography for each entry and an index. (Reference Library of the Humanities Series, Vol. 1573).

PERIODICALS AND NEWSLETTERS

Business History. ISBS. • Quarterly. Individuals, $58.00 per year; institutions, $265.00 per year.

Business History Review. Harvard Business School Publishing. • Quarterly. Individuals, $35.00 per year; institutions, $75.00 per year; students, $20.00 per year.

Explorations in Economic History. Academic Press, Inc., Journal Div. • Quarterly. $360.00 per year.

Financial History: Chronicling the History of America's Capital Markets. Museum of American Financial History. • Quarterly. Membership. Contains articles on early stock and bond markets and trading in the U. S., with photographs and other illustrations. Current trading in rare and unusual, obsolete stock and bond certificates is featured. Formerly *Friends or Financial History*.

Front and Center: The Newsletter of the John W. Hartman Center for Sales, Advertising, and

Marketing History. John W. Hartman Center for Sales, Advertising, and Marketing History. • Semiannual. Free.

Journal of Economic History. Economic History Association. Cambridge University Press, Journals Dept. • Quarterly. $115.00 per year.

RESEARCH CENTERS AND INSTITUTES

John W. Hartman Center for Sales, Advertising, and Marketing History. Special Collections Library, Duke University, P.O. Box 90185, Durham, NC 27708-0185. Phone: (919)660-5827 Fax: (919)660-5934 E-mail: hartman-center@duke.edu • URL: http://www.scriptorium.lib.duke.edu/hartman/ • Concerned with the study of the roles of sales, advertising, and marketing in society.

STATISTICS SOURCES

Encyclopedia of American Industries. The Gale Group. • 1998. $560.00. Second edition. Two volumes. $280.00 per volume. Volume one is *Manufacturing Industries* and volume two is *Service and Non-Manufacturing Industries.* Provides the history, development, and recent status of approximately 1,000 industries. Includes statistical graphs, with industry and general indexes.

TRADE/PROFESSIONAL ASSOCIATIONS

Business History Conference. c/o Roger Horowitz, Hagley Museum and Library, P.O. Box 3630, Wilmington, DE 19807-0630. Phone: (302)658-2400 Fax: (302)655-3188 E-mail: rh@hdel.edu • URL: http://www.eh.net/~bhc/.

Economic History Association. University of Kansas, Department of Economics, 213 Summerfield Hall, Lawrence, KS 66045. Phone: (785)864-3501 or (785)864-2847 Fax: (785)864-5270 E-mail: eha@falcon.cc.ukans.edu • URL: http://www.eh.net/eha • Members are teachers and students of economic history.

Newcomen Society of the United States. 412 Newcomen Rd., Exton, PA 19341. Phone: (610)363-6600 Fax: (610)363-0612 E-mail: newcomen@libertynet.org • URL: http://www.libertynet.org/newcomen.

OTHER SOURCES

American Business Leaders: From Colonial Times to the Present. Neil A. Hamilton. ABC-CLIO, Inc. • 1999. $150.00. Two volumes. Contains biographies of 413 notable business figures. Historical coverage is from the 17th century to the 1990s.

Business & Company Resource Center. The Gale Group. • Fee-based Web site provides a wide range of business, industry, and specific company information. Access is offered to trade journal articles, market research data, insider trading activity, major shareholder data, corporate histories, emerging technology reports, corporate earnings estimates, press releases, and other sources. Provides detailed company profiles, industry overviews, and rankings. Offers integration of Predicasts PROMT, Newsletters ASAP, Investext Plus, Business Index ASAP, Brands and Their Companies, and other databases (many have full text).

Goldsmiths' Kress Library of Economic Literature: A Consolidated Guide to the Microfilm Collection, 1976-1983. Primary Source Media. • $2,100.00. Seven volumes. Individual volumes, $250.00. An estimated 60,000 titles on 1,500 reels of microfilm (or fiche).

The Great Game: The Emergence of Wall Street as a World Power, 1653-2000. John S. Gordon. Scribner. • 1999. $25.00. Provides a history of U. S. financial markets, featuring such key figures as Alexander Hamilton, Commodore Vanderbilt, J. P. Morgan, Charles Merrill, and Michael Milken.

100 Years of Wall Street. Charles R. Geisst. McGraw-Hill. • 1999. $29.95. A popularly written, illustrated history of the American stock market. About 200 photographs, charts, cartoons, and reproductions of stock certificates are included.

The Power of Gold: The History of an Obsession. Peter L. Bernstein. John Wiley and Sons, Inc. • 2000. $27.95. Covers the economic and financial history of gold from ancient times to the present.

Wall Street: A History. Charles R. Geisst. Oxford University Press. • 1997. $35.00. Presents the history of the U. S. stock market according to four distinct eras: 1790 to the Civil War, the Civil War to 1929, 1929 to 1954, and from 1954 to recent years.

The World Economy: A Millennial Perspective. Angus Maddison. Organization for Economic Cooperation and Development. • 2001. $63.00. "...covers the development of the entire world economy over the past 2000 years," including data on world population and gross domestic product (GDP) since the year 1000, and exports since 1820. Focuses primarily on the disparity in economic performance among nations over the very long term. More than 200 statistical tables and figures are provided (detailed information available at http://www.theworldeconomy.org).

BUSINESS IN FICTION

ONLINE DATABASES

Magazine Index. The Gale Group. • General magazine indexing (popular literature), 1973 to present. Daily updates. Inquire as to online cost and availability.

BUSINESS INDICATORS

See: ECONOMIC INDICATORS

BUSINESS INFORMATION SOURCES

See: INFORMATION SOURCES

BUSINESS INNOVATION

See also: BUSINESS START-UP PLANS AND PROPOSALS; NEW PRODUCTS; RESEARCH AND DEVELOPMENT

GENERAL WORKS

Cases in Corporate Innovation. The Gale Group. • 1999. $295.00. Reviews and analyzes about 300 cases to illustrate both successful and failed management of innovation.

Innovation: Leadership Strategies for the Competitive Edge. Thomas D. Kuczmarski. NTC/Contemporary Publishing. • 1995. $37.95. (NTC Business Book Series).

The Innovator's Dilemma: When New Technologies Cause Great Firms to Fail. Clayton M. Christensen. Harvard Business School Press. • 1997. $27.50. Discusses management myths relating to innovation, change, and research and development. (Mangement of Innovation and Change Series).

ABSTRACTS AND INDEXES

Business Periodicals Index. H. W. Wilson Co. • Monthly, except August, with quarterly and annual cumulations. Service basis for print edition; CD-ROM edition, $1,495.00 per year.

DIRECTORIES

IVCI Directory of Business Incubators in United States and Canada. Baxter Associates, Inc. International Venture Capital Institute, Inc. • $49.95. Lists approximately 700 start-up services (office space, accounting, legal, financial advice, research, etc.). Formerly *IVCI Directory of Business Incubators and University Research and Science Parks.*

ONLINE DATABASES

Wilson Business Abstracts Online. H. W. Wilson Co. • Indexes and abstracts 600 major business periodicals, plus the *Wall Street Journal* and the business section of the *New York Times.* Indexing is from 1982, abstracting from 1990, with the two newspapers included from 1993. Updated weekly. Inquire as to online cost and availability. (*Business Periodicals Index* without abstracts is also available online.).

PERIODICALS AND NEWSLETTERS

Business 2.0. Imagine Media, Inc. • Monthly. $12.00 per year. General business magazine emphasizing ideas and innovation.

Fast Company: How Smart Business Works. Fast Company Inc. • Monthly. $23.95 per year. Covers business management, with emphasis on creativity, leadership, innovation, career advancement, teamwork, the global economy, and the "new workplace.".

Journal of Product Innovation Management: An International Publication of the Product Development and Management Association. Product Development and Management Association. Elsevier Science. • Bimonthly. $425.00 per year. Covers new product planning and development.

Technology Business: The Magazine of Strategies for Innovation, Management, and Marketing. Technology Business LLC. • Bimonthly. Price on application. Edited for executives and managers of high technology firms.

RESEARCH CENTERS AND INSTITUTES

Huntsman Center for Global Competition and Innovation. University of Pennsylvania, 3620 Locust Walk, Suite 1400, Philadelphia, PA 19104. Phone: (215)898-2104 Fax: (215)573-2129 E-mail: dayg@wharton.upenn.edu • URL: http://www.fourps.wharton.upenn.edu/ • Conducts research related to international business.

BUSINESS INTELLIGENCE

See: COMPETITIVE INTELLIGENCE

BUSINESS, INTERNATIONAL

See: INTERNATIONAL BUSINESS

BUSINESS INTERRUPTION INSURANCE

See also: INSURANCE

HANDBOOKS AND MANUALS

Business Insurance Guide: How to Purchase the Best and Most Affordable Insurance. Jamie McLeroy. Summers Press, Inc. • Looseleaf service. $96.50.

Business Interruption Coverage. American Bar Association. • 1987. $29.95. Produced by ABA Tort and Insurance Practice Section. Covers legal aspects of business interruption insurance.

Insuring Your Business: What You Need to Know to Get the Best Insurance Coverage for Your Business. Sean Mooney. Insurance Information Institute. • 1992. $22.50.

PERIODICALS AND NEWSLETTERS

Business Insurance: News Magazine for Corporate Risk, Employee Benefit and Financial Executives.

Crain Communications, Inc. • Weekly. $89.00 per year. Covers a wide variety of business insurance topics, including risk management, employee benefits, workers compensation, marine insurance, and casualty insurance.

Jounal of Finacial Services Professionals. American Society of CLU and Ch F C. • Bimonthly. $38.00 per year. Provides information on life insurance and financial planning, including estate planning, retirement, tax planning, trusts, business insurance, long-term care insurance, disability insurance, and employee benefits. Formerly (American Society of CLU and Ch F C Journal).

BUSINESS JOURNALISM

See also: FARM JOURNALS; HOUSE ORGANS; TRADE JOURNALS

GENERAL WORKS

The Art of Editing. Floyd K. Baskette and Jack Z. Sissors. Allyn and Bacon, Inc. • 2000. 7th edition. Price on applications.

DIRECTORIES

Cabell's Directory of Publishing Opportunities in Economics, and Finance. Cabell Publishing Co. • 1997. $89.95. Provides editorial policies of commercial and scholarly periodicals in the areas of business and economics. Formerly *Cabell's Directory of Publishing Opportunities in Accounting, Economics, and Finance.*

Editor and Publisher Market Guide. Editor and Publisher Co., Inc. • Annual. $125.00. More than 1,700 newspaper markets in the Unite States and Canada.

Magazines Careers Directory: A Practical One-Stop Guide to Getting a Job in Publc Relations. Visible Ink Press. • 1993. $17.95. Fifth edition. Includes information on magazine publishing careers in art, editing, sales, and business management. Provides advice from "insiders," resume suggestions, a directory of companies that may offer entry-level positions, and a directory of career information sources. *Career Advisor Series.*

Professional Freelance Writers Directory. The National Writers Association. • Annual. $15.00. About 200 professional members selected from the club's membership on the basis of significant articles or books, or production of plays or movies.

Writer's Market: 8000 Editors Who Buy What You Write. F & W Publications, Inc. • Annual. $27.99. More than 4,000 buyers of books, articles, short stories, plays, gags, verses, fillers, and other original written material. Includes book and periodical publishers, greeting card publishers, play producers and publishers, audiovisual material producers, syndicates, and contests, and awards. Formerly *Writer's Market: Where and How to Sell What You Write.*

ONLINE DATABASES

Super Searchers in the News: The Online Secrets of Journalists and News Researchers. Paula J. Hane and Reva Basch. Information Today, Inc. • 2000. $24.95. Contains online searching advice from 10 professional news researchers and fact checkers. (CyberAge Books.).

PERIODICALS AND NEWSLETTERS

Freelance Writer's Report. Dana K. Cassell, editor. CNW Publishing. • Monthly. $39.00 per year. Newsletter. Provides marketing tips and information on new markets for freelance writers. Includes interviews with editors and advice on taxation and legalities.

Journal of Technical Writing and Communication. Baywood Publishing Co., Inc. • Quarterly. $170.00 per year.

A S B P E Editor's Notes. American Society of Business Press Editors. • Bimonthly. Membership. Newsletter. Formerly (American Society of Business Press Editors).

RESEARCH CENTERS AND INSTITUTES

Knight Center for Specialized Journalism. University of Maryland, 290 University College, College Park, MD 20742-1645. Phone: (301)985-7279 Fax: (301)985-7840 E-mail: knight@umail.umd.edu • URL: http://www.inform.umd.edu/knight • Research area is media coverage of complex subjects, such as economics, law, science, and medicine.

TRADE/PROFESSIONAL ASSOCIATIONS

American Society of Business Press Editors. 107 W. Ogden Ave., LaGrange, IL 60525-2022. Phone: (708)352-6950 Fax: (708)352-3780 E-mail: 7114.34@compuserve.com • URL: http://www.asbpe.com.

International Association of Business Communicators. One Hallidie Plaza, Suite 600, San Francisco, CA 94102. Phone: (415)544-4700 Fax: (415)544-4747 E-mail: leader-centre@iabc.com • URL: http://www.iabc.com.

Society of Publication Designers. 60 E. 42nd St., Suite 721, New York, NY 10165. Phone: (212)983-8585 Fax: (212)983-6043 • URL: http://www.spd.org.

BUSINESS LAW

GENERAL WORKS

Business Law. S.B. Marsh and J. Soulsby. Trans-Atlantic Publications, Inc. • 1999. Seventh. $48.00. Seventh edition.

Business Law and the Regulatory Environment: Concepts and Cases. Jane Mallor and A. James Barnes. McGraw-Hill Higher Education. • 1997. $101.25. 10th edition.

Business Law Made Simple. Stephen G. Christianson. Doubleday. • 1995. $12.00.

Business Law: Principles and Cases in the Legal Environment. Daniel V. Davidson and Brenda E. Knowles. South-Western Publishing Co. • 1997. $107.95. Sixth edition. (Miscellaneous/Catalogs Series).

Business Law: Principles and Practices. Arnold J. Goldman. Houghton Mifflin Co. • 2000. $60.45. Fifth edition.

Business Law: The Legal, Ethical, and International Environment. Henry R. Cheesman. Prentice Hall. • 1997. $105.00. Third edition.

Contemporary Business: Alternate Study Guide. Louis E. Boone. Dryden Press. • 1998. $88.50. Ninth edition.

Contemporary Business Law and the Legal Environment: Principles and Cases. J. David Reitzel and others. McGraw-Hill. • 1994. $72.74. Fifth revised edition.

Law for Business. John E. Adamson. South-Western Publishing Co. • 1992. $49.95. 14th edition. (LA-Business Law Series).

Modern Business Law. Thomas W. Dunfee and others. McGraw-Hill. • 1995. $90.94. Third edition.

West's Business Law: Text and Cases, Legal, Ethical, Regulatory and International Environment. Kenneth Clarkson. South-Western College Publishing. • 2000. $109.95. Eighth edition.

ABSTRACTS AND INDEXES

Current Law Index: Multiple Access to Legal Periodicals. The Gale Group. • Monthly. $650.00 per year. Produced in cooperation with the American Association of Law Libraries. Indexes more than 900 law journals, legal newspapers, and specialty publications from the U.S., Canada, U.K., Ireland, Australia, and New Zealand.

Index to Legal Periodicals and Books. H. W. Wilson Co. • Monthly. Quarterly and annual cumulations. $270.00 per year. CD-ROM version available at $1,495.00 per year.

ALMANACS AND YEARBOOKS

American Law Yearbook. The Gale Group. • Annual. $155.00. Serves as a yearly supplement to *West's Encyclopedia of American Law.* Describes new legal developments in many subject areas.

BIBLIOGRAPHIES

Encyclopedia of Legal Information Sources. The Gale Group. • 1992. $180.00. Second edition. Lists more than 23,000 law-related information sources, including print, nonprint, and organizational.

International Legal Books in Print. Bowker-Saur. • Irregular. $375.00. Two volumes. Covers English-language law books published or distributed within the United Kingdom, Europe, and current or former British Commonwealth countries.

Legal Information: How to Find It, How to Use It. Kent Olson. Oryx Press. • 1998. $59.95. Recommends sources for various kinds of legal information.

CD-ROM DATABASES

WILSONDISC: Index to Legal Periodicals and Books. H. W. Wilson Co. • Monthly. Including unlimited online access to *Index to Legal Periodicals* through WILSONLINE. Contains CD-ROM indexing of more than 800 English language legal periodicals from 1981 to date and 2,500 books.

DIRECTORIES

Law and Legal Information Directory. The Gale Group. • 2000. $405.00. 11th edition. Two volumes. Contains a wide range of sources of legal information, such as associations, law schools, courts, federal agencies, referral services, libraries, publishers, and research centers. There is a separate chapter for each of 23 types of information source or service.

ENCYCLOPEDIAS AND DICTIONARIES

Communicating with Legal Databases: Terms and Abbreviations for the Legal Researcher. Anne L. McDonald. Neal-Schuman Publishers, Inc. • 1987. $82.50.

Dictionary of Commercial, Financial and Legal Terms in Two Languages. R. Herbst. Adlers Foreign Books, Inc. • Two volumes. Vol. A, $179.50; vol. B $179.50. Text in English and German.

The Dictionary of Practical Law. Charles F. Hemphill, Jr. and Phyllis Hemphill. Pearson Eduation and Technology. • 1979. $12.95.

HANDBOOKS AND MANUALS

Digest of Commercial Laws of the World. Paul E. Comeau and N. Stephan Kinsella. Oceana Publications, Inc. • Looseleaf service. $295.00.

The Law in (Plain English) for Small Businesses. Leonard D. DuBoff. Allworth Press. • 1998. $19.95. Third revised edition. Discusses and explains legal issues relating to the organization, financing, and operation of a small business.

Manual of Credit and Commercial Laws. National Association of Credit Management. • Annual. Free to members; non-members, $125.00. Formerly *Credit Manual of Commercial Laws.*

Small Business Legal Smarts. Deborah L. Jacobs. Bloomberg Press. • 1998. $16.95. Discusses common legal problems encountered by small business owners. (Small Business Series Personal Bookshelf.).

Uniform Commercial Code. James White and Robert S. Summers. West Publishing Co., College and School Div. • 1995. Fourth edition. Four volumes. Price on application. (Practitioner Treatise Series).

Uniform Commercial Code in a Nutshell. Bradford Stone. West Publishing Co. • 1995. $23.50. Fourth edition. (Nutshell Series).

Warren's Forms of Agreements. Matthew Bender & Co., Inc. • $940.00. Seven looseleaf volumes. Periodic supplementation. A compact source of forms that business transaction lawyers are most frequently asked to document.

ONLINE DATABASES

Index to Legal Periodicals and Books (Online). H. W. Wilson Co. • Broad coverage of law journals and books 1981 to date. Monthly updates. Inquire as to online cost and availability.

Law of the Super Searchers: The Online Secrets of Top Legal Researchers. T. R. Halvorson and Reva Basch. Information Today, Inc. • 1999. $24.95. Eight law researchers explain how to find useful legal information online. (CyberAge Books.).

Legal Resource Index. The Gale Group. • Broad coverage of law literature appearing in legal, business, and other periodicals, 1980 to date. Monthly updates. Inquire as to online cost and availability.

LEXIS. LEXIS-NEXIS. • The various LEXIS databases provide full text and indexing for a wide variety of legal cases, statutes, orders, and opinions.

PERIODICALS AND NEWSLETTERS

Business Lawyer. American Bar Association. • Quarterly. Memebers $99.00 per year; non-memebers, $149.00 per year.

Commercial Law Journal. Commercial Law League of America. • 10 times a year. $99.00 per year.

Federal Register. Office of the Federal Register. Available from U.S. Government Printing Office. • Daily except Saturday and Sunday. $697.00 per year. Publishes regulations and legal notices issued by federal agencies, including executive orders and presidential proclamations. Issued by the National Archives and Records Administration (http://www.nara.gov).

Uniform Commercial Code Bulletin. West Group. • Monthly. $200.00 per year. Newsletter. Includes case summaries of recent UCC decisions.

RESEARCH CENTERS AND INSTITUTES

Alabama Law Institute. University of Alabama. P.O. Box 861425, Tuscaloosa, AL 35486-0013. Phone: (205)348-7411 Fax: (205)348-8411 E-mail: mccurle@law.ua.edu • URL: http://www.law.ua.edu/ali.

Lexis.com Research System. Lexis-Nexis Group. Phone: 800-227-9597 or (937)865-6800 Fax: (937)865-6909 E-mail: webmaster@prod.lexis-nexis.com • URL: http://www.lexis.com • Fee-based Web site offers extensive searching of a wide variety of legal sources. Additional features include Daily Opinion Service, lexis.com Bookstore, Career Center, CLE Center, Law Schools, and Practice Pages ("Pages specific to areas of specialty").

TRADE/PROFESSIONAL ASSOCIATIONS

Commercial Law League of America. 150 N. Michigan Ave., No. 600, Chicago, IL 60601. Phone: 800-978-2552 or (312)781-2000 Fax: (312)781-2010 E-mail: clla@clla.org • URL: http://www.clla.org.

OTHER SOURCES

Basic Legal Forms with Commentary. Marvin Hyman. Warren, Gorham and Lamont/RIA Group. • Looseleaf. $105.00. Periodic supplementation. Forms for any type of legal transaction. Includes commentary.

Business Law Monographs. Matthew Bender & Co., Inc. • $1,450.00. 36 looseleaf volumes. Quarterly updates. Intended for in-house and outside corporate counsel. Each monograph concentrates on a particular subject.

Computer Law: Evidence and Procedures. David Bender. Matthew Bender & Co., Inc. • $580.00. Three looseleaf volumes. Periodic supplementation. Covers the concepts and techniques of evidence and discovery procedures as they apply to computer-based information, and to the protection of computer software under intellectual property.

Current Legal Forms with Tax Analysis. Matthew Bender and Co., Inc. • Quarterly. $730.00 per year. 23 looseleaf volumes. Periodic supplementation, $1,685.00.

Documents of Title Under the Uniform Commercial Code. American Law Institute-American Bar Association. • 1990. $90.00. Second edition.

Factiva. Dow Jones Reuters Business Interactive, LLC. • Fee-based Web site provides "global news and business information through Web sites and content integration solutions." Includes Dow Jones and Reuters newswires, The Wall Street Journal, and more than 7,000 other sources of current news, historical articles, market research reports, and investment analysis. Content includes 96 major U. S. newspapers, 900 non-English sources, trade publications, media transcripts, country profiles, news photos, etc.

Forms of Business Agreements and Resolutions-Annotated, Tax Tested. Prentice Hall. • Three looseleaf volumes. Periodic supplementation. Price on application.

Nexis.com. Lexis-Nexis Group. • Fee-based Web site offers searching of about 2.8 billion documents in some 30,000 news, business, and legal information sources. Features include a subject directory covering 1,200 topics in 34 categories and a Company Dossier containing information on more than 500,000 public and private companies. Boolean searching is offered.

BUSINESS LETTERS

See: BUSINESS CORRESPONDENCE

BUSINESS LIBRARIES

See: SPECIAL LIBRARIES

BUSINESS LITERATURE

See also: BUSINESS; BUSINESS HISTORY; BUSINESS RESEARCH; ECONOMIC RESEARCH; GOVERNMENT PUBLICATIONS

ABSTRACTS AND INDEXES

Business Periodicals Index. H. W. Wilson Co. • Monthly, except August, with quarterly and annual cumulations. Service basis for print edition; CD-ROM edition, $1,495.00 per year.

Index of Economic Articles in Journals and Collective Volumes. American Economic Association. • Irregular. $160.00.

BIBLIOGRAPHIES

The Basic Business Library: Core Resources. Bernard S. Schlessinger and June H. Schlessinger. Oryx Press. • 1994. $43.50. Third edition. Consists of three parts: (1) "Core List of Printed Business Reference Sources," (2) "The Literature of Business Reference and Business Libraries: 1976-1994," and (3) "Business Reference Sources and Services: Essays." Part one lists 200 basic titles, with annotations and evaluations.

Bibliographic Guide to Business and Economics. Available from The Gale Group. • Annual. $795.00. Three volumes. Published by G. K. Hall & Co. Lists business and economics publications cataloged by the New York Public Library and the Library of Congress.

Bibliographic Guide to Conference Publications. Available from The Gale Group. • Annual. $545.00. Two volumes. Published by G. K. Hall & Co., Lists a wide range of conference publications cataloged by the New York Public Library and the Library of Congress.

Business Information Sources. Lorna M. Daniells. California Princeton Fulfillment Services. • 1993. $42.50. Third revised edition. Basic business sources, with discussion and full annotations.

Business Library Review: An International Journal. International Publishers Distributor. • Quarterly. Academic institutions, $318.00 per year;corporations, $501.00 per year.Incorporates *The Wall Street Review of Books* and *Economics and Business: An Annotated Bibliography.* Publishes scholarly reviews of books on a wide variety of topics in business, economics, and finance. Text in French.

Guide to Special Issues and Indexes of Periodicals. Miriam Uhlan and Doris B. Katz, editors. Special Libraries Association. • 1994. $59.00. Fourth edition. A listing, with prices, of the special issues of over 1700 U. S. and Canadian periodicals in business, industry, technology, science, and the arts. Includes a comprehensive subject index.

U. S. Government Information for Business. U. S. Government Printing Office. • Annual. Free. A selected list of currently available publications, periodicals, and electronic products on business, trade, labor, federal regulations, economics, and other topics. Also known as *Business Catalog.*

DIRECTORIES

Cabell's Directory of Publishing Opportunities in Economics, and Finance. Cabell Publishing Co. • 1997. $89.95. Provides editorial policies of commercial and scholarly periodicals in the areas of business and economics. Formerly *Cabell's Directory of Publishing Opportunities in Accounting, Economics, and Finance.*

Cabell's Directory of Publishing Opportunities in Management. Cabell Publishing Co. • 1997. $89.95. Provides editorial policies of more than 300 management periodicals. Emphasis is on publishing opportunities for college faculty members. Formerly *Cabell's Directory of Publishing Opportunities Business and Economics.*

ENCYCLOPEDIAS AND DICTIONARIES

Words That Mean Business: Three Thousand Terms for Access to Business Information. Warner-Eddison Associates. Neal-Schuman Publishers, Inc. • 1981. $60.00.

INTERNET DATABASES

Amazon.com. Amazon.com, Inc. Phone: 800-201-7575 or (206)346-2992 Fax: (206)346-2950 E-mail: info@amazon.com • URL: http://www.amazon.com • "Welcome to Earth's Biggest Bookstore." Amazon.com claims to have more than 2.5 million titles that can be ordered online, but only through the

Web site - no orders by mail, telephone, fax, or E-mail. Discounts are generally 30% for hardcovers and 20% for paperbacks. Efficient search facilities, including Boolean, make this Web site useful for reference (many titles have online reviews). Fees: Free.

EBSCO Information Services. Ebsco Publishing. Phone: 800-871-8508 or (508)356-6500 Fax: (508)356-5640 E-mail: ep@epnet.com • URL: http://www.epnet.com • Fee-based Web site providing Internet access to a wide variety of databases, including business-related material. Full text is available for many periodical titles, with daily updates. Fees: Apply.

ProQuest Direct. Bell & Howell Information and Learning. Phone: 800-521-0600 or (313)761-4700 Fax: (313)973-9145 • URL: http://www.umi.com/proquest • Fee-based Web site providing Internet access to more than 3,000 periodicals, newspapers, and other publications. Many items are available full-text, with daily updates. Includes extensive corporate and financial information from Disclosure, Inc. Fees: Apply.

ONLINE DATABASES

ABI/INFORM. Bell & Howell Information and Learning. • Provides online indexing to business-related material occurring in over 1,000 periodicals from 1971 to the present. Inquire as to online cost and availability.

EconLit. American Economic Association. • Covers the worldwide literature of economics as contained in selected monographs and about 550 journals. Subjects include microeconomics, macroeconomics, economic history, inflation, money, credit, finance, accounting theory, trade, natural resource economics, and regional economics. Time period is 1969 to present, with monthly updates. Inquire as to online cost and availability.

Newsletter Database. The Gale Group. • Contains the full text of about 600 U. S. and international newsletters covering a wide range of business and industrial topics. Time period is 1988 to date, with daily updates. Inquire as to online cost and availability.

Trade & Industry Index. The Gale Group. • Provides indexing of business periodicals, January 1981 to date. Daily updates. (Full text articles from some periodicals are available online, 1983 to date, in the companion database, *Trade & Industry ASAP.*) Inquire as to online cost and availability.

PERIODICALS AND NEWSLETTERS

Business and Finance Division Bulletin. Special Libraries Association, Business and Finance Div. • Quarterly. $12.00 per year.

Business Information Alert: Sources, Strategies and Signposts for Information Professionals. Donna T. Heroy, editor. Alert Publications, Inc. • 10 times per year. $152.00 per year. Newsletter for business librarians and information specialists.

INFO. Tulsa City-County Library, Business & Technology Dept. • Bimonthly. Free. Newsletter listing selected new books in business, economics, and technology.

The Information Report. Washington Researchers Ltd. • Monthly. $160.00 per year. Newsletter listing private and government sources of information, mainly on business or economics.

Journal of Economic Literature. American Economic Association. • Quarterly. $135.00 per year. Includes *American Economic Review* and *Journal of Economic Perspectives.*

SI: Special Issues. Trip Wyckoff, editor. Hoover's, Inc. • Bimonthly. $149.95 per year. Newsletter. Serves as a supplement to *Directory of Business Periodical Special Issues.* Provides current information on trade journal special issues and editorial calendars.

OTHER SOURCES

InSite 2. Intelligence Data/Thomson Financial. • Fee-based Web site consolidates information in a "Base Pack" consisting of Business InSite, Market InSite, and Company InSite. Optional databases are Consumer InSite, Health and Wellness InSite, Newsletter InSite, and Computer InSite. Includes fulltext content from more than 2,500 trade publications, journals, newsletters, newspapers, analyst reports, and other sources. Continuous updating. Formerly produced by The Gale Group.

BUSINESS LOANS

See: BANK LOANS

BUSINESS MACHINES

See: OFFICE EQUIPMENT AND SUPPLIES

BUSINESS MANAGEMENT

See: ADMINISTRATION; INDUSTRIAL MANAGEMENT

BUSINESS MARKETING

See: INDUSTRIAL MARKETING

BUSINESS MATHEMATICS

See also: STATISTICAL METHODS

GENERAL WORKS

Business Math: Practical Applications. Cheryl Cleaves and others. Prentice Hall. • 1993. Third annotated edition. Price on application.

Business Mathematics. Charles D. Miller and others. Addison Wesley Educational Publications, Inc. • 1999. $78.00. Eighth edition.

Business Mathematics for Colleges. James Dietz. South-Western Publishing Co. • 1995. $59.95. 11th edition. (MB-Business/Vocational Math Series).

Contemporary Business Mathematics. John Webber. McGraw-Hill Higher Education. • 1994. $61.50.

Mathematics with Applications in Management and Economics. Gordon D. Prichett and John C. Saber. McGRaw-Hill Higher Education. • 1993. $72.75. Seventh revised edition.

ABSTRACTS AND INDEXES

CompuMath Citation Index. Institute for Scientific Information. • Three times a year. $1,090.00 per year. Provides citations to the worldwide literature of computer science and mathematics.

CD-ROM DATABASES

MathSci Disc. American Mathematical Society. • Semiannual. Price on application. Provides CD-ROM citations, with abstracts, to the literature of mathematics, statistics, and computer science, 1940 to date.

HANDBOOKS AND MANUALS

Fixed Income Mathematics: Analytical and Statistical Techniques. Frank J. Fabozzi. McGraw-Hill Professional. • 1996. $60.00. Third edition. Covers the basics of fixed income analysis, as well as more advanced techniques used for complex securities.

An Introduction to the Mathematics of Financial Derivatives. Salih N. Neftci. Academic Press, Inc. • 2000. $59.95. Second edition. Covers the mathematical models underlying the pricing of derivatives. Includes explanations of basic financial calculus for students, derivatives traders, risk managers, and others concerned with derivatives.

ONLINE DATABASES

MathSci. American Mathematical Society. • Provides online citations, with abstracts, to the literature of mathematics, statistics, and computer science. Time period is 1940 to date, with monthly updates. Inquire as to online cost and availability.

PERIODICALS AND NEWSLETTERS

Mathematical Finance: An International Journal of Mathematics, Statistics, and Financial Economics. Blackwell Publishers. • Quarterly. $342.00 per year. Covers the use of sophisticated mathematical tools in financial research and practice.

RESEARCH CENTERS AND INSTITUTES

Center for Mathematical Studies in Economics and Management Sciences. Northwestern University, Leverone Hall, Room 317, 2001 Sheridan Rd., Evanston, IL 60208-2014. Phone: (847)491-3527 Fax: (847)491-2530 E-mail: sreiter@casbah.acns.nwu.edu • URL: http://www.kellogg.nwu.edu/research/math.

Institute for Mathematics and Its Applications. University of Minnesota, 514 Vincent Hall, 206 Church St., S. E., Minneapolis, MN 55455-0436. Phone: (612)624-6066 Fax: (612)626-7370 E-mail: staff@ima.umn.edu • URL: http://www.ima.umn.edu • Research areas include various topics connected with industrial and applied mathematics.

TRADE/PROFESSIONAL ASSOCIATIONS

Industrial Mathematics Society. P.O. Box 159, Roseville, MI 48066. Phone: (810)771-0403 • Areas of interest include applied mathematics, computers, statistics, and operations analysis.

Society for Industrial and Applied Mathematics. 3600 University City Science Center, Philadelphia, PA 19104-2688. Phone: 800-447-7426 or (215)382-9800 Fax: (215)386-7999 E-mail: siam@siam.org • URL: http://www/siam.org.

OTHER SOURCES

How to Use Math as a Business Tool. American Management Association Extension Institute. • Looseleaf. $89.95. Self-study course. Emphasis is on practical explanations, examples, and problem solving. Quizzes are included.

BUSINESS MERGERS

See: MERGERS AND ACQUISITIONS

BUSINESS MORALE

See: HUMAN RELATIONS

BUSINESS ORGANIZATION AND ADMINISTRATION

See: INDUSTRIAL MANAGEMENT

BUSINESS PERIODICALS

See: TRADE JOURNALS

BUSINESS PLANNING

See: BUSINESS START-UP PLANS AND PROPOSALS; PLANNING

BUSINESS PROPOSALS

See: BUSINESS START-UP PLANS AND PROPOSALS

BUSINESS PSYCHOLOGY

See: INDUSTRIAL PSYCHOLOGY

BUSINESS RATIOS

See: FINANCIAL RATIOS

BUSINESS RECORDS MANAGEMENT

See: RECORDS MANAGEMENT

BUSINESS REPORTS

See: CORPORATION REPORTS; REPORT WRITING

BUSINESS RESEARCH

See also: BUSINESS LITERATURE; BUREAUS OF BUSINESS RESEARCH; COMPETITIVE INTELLIGENCE; ECONOMIC RESEARCH

GENERAL WORKS

Business Research for Decision Making. Duane Davis. Wadsworth Publishing Co. • 1999. $62.00. Fifth edition. (Business Statistics Series).

Super Searchers Do Business: The Online Secrets of Top Business Researchers. Mary E.Bates and Reva Basch. Information Today, Inc. • 1999. $24.95. Presents the results of interviews with "11 leading researchers who use the Internet and online services to find critical business information." (CyberAge Books.).

BIBLIOGRAPHIES

Analyzing Your Competition: Simple, Low-Cost Techniques for Intelligence Gathering. Michael Strenges. MarketResearch.com. • 1997. $95.00. Third edition. Mainly an annotated listing of specific, business information sources, but also contains concise discussions of information-gathering techniques. Indexed by publisher and title.

Bibliographic Guide to Business and Economics. Available from The Gale Group. • Annual. $795.00. Three volumes. Published by G. K. Hall & Co. Lists business and economics publications cataloged by the New York Public Library and the Library of Congress.

Bibliographic Guide to Conference Publications. Available from The Gale Group. • Annual. $545.00. Two volumes. Published by G. K. Hall & Co., Lists a wide range of conference publications cataloged by the New York Public Library and the Library of Congress.

Business Information: How to Find It, How to Use It. Michael R. Lavin. Oryx Press. • 2001. $61.00. Third edition. Combines discussions of business research techniques with detailed descriptions of major business publications and databases. Includes title and subject indexes.

Business Information Sources. Lorna M. Daniells. California Princeton Fulfillment Services. • 1993. $42.50. Third revised edition. Basic business sources, with discussion and full annotations.

Business Research Handbook: Methods and Sources for Lawyers and Business Professionals. Kathy E. Shimpock. Aspen Law and Business. • $145.00. Looseleaf. Periodic supplementation. Provides detailed advice on how to find business information. Describes a wide variety of data sources, both private and government.

International Business Information: How to Find It, How to Use It. Ruth Pagell and Michael Halperin. Oryx Press. • 1997. $84.50. Second revised edition.

CD-ROM DATABASES

Profiles in Business and Management: An International Directory of Scholars and Their Research [CD-ROM]. Harvard Business School Publishing. • Annual. $595.00 per year. Fully searchable CD-ROM version of two-volume printed directory. Contains bibliographic and biographical information for over 5600 business and management experts active in 21 subject areas. Formerly *International Directory of Business and Management Scholars.*

World Database of Business Information Sources on CD-ROM. The Gale Group. • Annual. Produced by Euromonitor. Presents Euromonitor's entire information source database on CD-ROM. Contains a worldwide total of about 35,000 publications, organizations, libraries, trade fairs, and online databases.

DIRECTORIES

Association for University Business and Economic Research Membership Directory. Association for University Business and Economic Research. • Annual. $10.00. Member institutions in the United States and abroad with centers, bureaus, departments, etc., concerned with business and economic research.

Business Organizations, Agencies, and Publications Directory. The Gale Group. • 1999. $425.00. 12th edition. Over 40,000 entries describing 39 types of business information sources. Classified by type of organization, publication, or serviceIncludes state, national, and international agencies and organizations. Master index to names and keywords. Also includes e-mail addresses and web site URL's.

Directory of Special Libraries and Information Centers. The Gale Group. • 1999. $845.00. 25th edition. Three volumes. Two available separately: volume one,*Directory of Special Libraries and Information Centers,*' $610.00; volume two *Geographic and Personnel Indexes,* $510.00. Contains 24,000 entries from the U.S., Canada, and 80 other countries. A detailed subject index is included in volume one.

Finding Business Research on the Web: A Guide to the Web's Most Valuable Sites. MarketResearch.com. • Looseleaf. $175.00. Includes detailed rating charts. Contains profiles of the "100 best web sites.".

Profiles in Business and Management: An International Directory of Scholars and Their Research Version 2.0. Claudia Bruce, editor. Harvard Business School Press. • 1996. $495.00. Two volumes. Provides backgrounds, publications, and current research projects of more than 5,600 business and management experts.

Research Centers Directory. The Gale Group. • Annual. $575.00. Two volumes. Lists more than 14,200 centers.

Subject Directory of Special Libraries and Information Centers. The Gale Group. • Annual. $845.00. Three volumes, available separately: volume one, *Business, Government, and Law Libraries,* $595.00; volume two, *Computer, Engineering, and Law Libraries,* $595.00; volume three, *Health Sciences Libraries,* $340.00. Altogether, 14,000 entries from the *Directory of Special Libraries and Information Centers* are arranged in 14 subject chapters.

World Directory of Business Information Web Sites. Available from The Gale Group. • 2001. $650.00. Fourth edition. Published by Euromonitor. Provides detailed descriptions of a wide variety of business-related Web sites. More than 1,500 sites are included from around the world. Covers statistics sources, market research, company information, rankings, surveys, economic data, etc.

ENCYCLOPEDIAS AND DICTIONARIES

Words That Mean Business: Three Thousand Terms for Access to Business Information. Warner-Eddison Associates. Neal-Schuman Publishers, Inc. • 1981. $60.00.

HANDBOOKS AND MANUALS

The Business Library and How to Use It: A Guide to Sources and Research Strategies for Information on Business and Management. Ernest L. Maier and others, editors. Omnigraphics, Inc. • 1996. $56.00. Explains library research methods and describes specific sources of business information. A revision of *How to Use the Business Library,* by H. Webster Johnson and others (fifth edition, 1984).

Find It Online: The Complete Guide to Online Research. Alan M. Schlein and others. National Book Network. • 1998. $19.95. Presents the general principles of online searching for information about people, phone numbers, public records, news, business, investments, etc. Covers both free and fee-based sources. (BRB Publications.).

Finding Market Research on the Web: Best Practices of Professional Researchers. Robert I. Berkman. MarketResearch.com. • 1999. $235.00. Provides tips and techniques for locating useful market research data through the Internet.

How To Find Information About Companies: The Corporate Intelligence Source Book. Washington Researchers. • Annual. $885.00. In three parts. $395.00 per volume. In part one, over 9,000 sources of corporate intelligence, including federal, state and local repositories of company filings, individual industry experts, published sources, databases, CD-Rom products, and corporate research services. Parts two and three provide guidelines for company research.

International Business Information on the Web: Searcher Magazine's Guide to Sites and Strategies for Global Business Research. Sheri R. Lanza and Barbara Quint. Information Today, Inc. • 2001. $29.95. (CyberAge Books.).

A New Archetype for Competitive Intelligence. John J. McGonagle and Carolyn M. Vella. Greenwood Publishing Group, Inc. • 1996. $59.95. Covers competitive intelligence, strategic intelligence, market intelligence, defensive intelligence, and cyber-intelligence. Includes an overview of sources and techniques for data gathering. A bibliography, glossary, and index are provided.

Recruiter's Research Blue Book: A How-To Guide for Researchers, Search Consultants, Corporate Recruiters, Small Business Owners, Venture Capitalists, and Line Executives. Andrea A. Jupina. Kennedy Information. • 2000. $179.00. Second edition. Provides detailed coverage of the role that research plays in executive recruiting. Includes such practical items as "Telephone Interview Guide," "Legal Issues in Executive Search," and "How to Create an Execuive Search Library." Covers both person-to-person research and research using printed and online business information sources. Includes an extensive directory of recommended sources. Formerly *Handbook of Executive Search Research.*

INTERNET DATABASES

Internet Business Intelligence: How to Build a Big Company System on a Small Company Budget. David Vine. Information Today, Inc. 143 Old Marlton Pike, Medford, NJ 08055-8750. Phone: 800-300-9868 or (609)654-6266 Fax: (609)654-4309 E-mail: custserv@infotoday.com • URL: http://www.infotoday.com • 2000. $29.95. Covers the obtaining of valuable business intelligence data through use of the Internet.

ONLINE DATABASES

EconLit. American Economic Association. • Covers the worldwide literature of economics as contained in selected monographs and about 550 journals. Subjects include microeconomics, macroeconomics, economic history, inflation, money, credit, finance, accounting theory, trade, natural resource economics, and regional economics. Time period is 1969 to present, with monthly updates. Inquire as to online cost and availability.

NTIS Bibliographic Data Base. National Technical Information Service. • Contains citations and abstracts to unrestricted reports of government-sponsored research, 1964 to date. Covers a wide range of technical, engineering, business, and social science topics. Monthly updates. Inquire as to online cost and availability.

Super Searchers Cover the World: The Online Secrets of International Business Researchers. Mary E. Bates and Reva Basch. Information Today, Inc. • 2001. $24.95. Presents interviews with 15 experts in the area of online searching for international business information. (CyberAge Books.).

Super Searchers on Mergers & Acquisitions: The Online Secrets of Top Corporate Researchers and M & A Pros. Jan Tudor and Reva Basch. Information Today, Inc. • 2001. $24.95. Presents the results of interviews with 13 "top M & A information pros." Covers the finding, evaluating, and delivering of relevant data on companies and industries. (CyberAge Books.).

Super Searchers on Wall Street: Top Investment Professionals Share Their Online Research Secrets. Amelia Kassel and Reva Basch. Information Today, Inc. • 2000. $24.95. Gives the results of interviews with "10 leading financial industry research experts." Explains how online information is used by stock brokers, investment bankers, and individual investors. Includes relevant Web sites and other sources. (CyberAge Books.).

PERIODICALS AND NEWSLETTERS

BiblioData's Price Watcher: The Researcher's Guide to Online Prices. BiblioData. • Semimonthly. Individuals $129.00 per year; institutions, $169.00 per year; nonprofit organizations, $129.00 per year. Newsletter. Provides detailed analysis and reviews of pricing schemes used by Internet and other online information providers.

Corporate Library Update: News for Information Managers and Special Librarians. Cahners Business Information. • Biweekly. $95.00 per year. Newsletter. Covers information technology, management techniques, new products, trends, etc.

The CyberSkeptic's Guide to Internet Research. BiblioData. • 10 times a year. $104.00 per year; nonprofit organizations, $159.00 per year. Newsletter. Presents critical reviews of World Wide Web sites and databases, written by information professionals. Includes "Late Breaking News" of Web sites.

The Information Advisor: Tips and Techniques for Smart Information Users. MarketResearch.com. • Monthly. $149.00 per year. Newsletter. Evaluates and discusses online, CD-ROM, and published sources of business, financial, and market research information.

Internet Search Advantage: Professional's Guide to Internet Searching. Z-D Journals. • Monthly. $199.00 per year. Newsletter. Covers Internet research, utilities, agents, configurations, subject searches, search theory, etc. Emphasis is on the efficient use of various kinds of search engines. Includes E-mail alert service.

Journal of Business and Finance Librarianship. Haworth Press, Inc. • Quarterly. Individuals, $40.00 per year; institutions, $85.00 per year; libraries, $85.00 per year.

Journal of Business Research. Elsevier Science. • Nine times a year. $1,128.00 per year. Covers theoretical and empirical advances in marketing, finance, international business, risk management, and other business topics.

Society of Research Administrators Journal. Society of Research Administrators, Inc. • Quarterly. Members, $35.00 per year; non-members, $45.00 per year.

RESEARCH CENTERS AND INSTITUTES

Bureau of Economic and Business Research. University of Illinois at Urbana-Champaign, 1206 S. Sixth St., Champaign, IL 61820. Phone: (217)333-2330 Fax: (217)244-7410 E-mail: g-oldman@uiuc.edu • URL: http://www.cba.uiuc.edu/research.

Conference Board, Inc. 845 Third Ave., New York, NY 10022. Phone: (212)759-0900 Fax: (212)980-7014 E-mail: richard.cavanaugh@conference-board.org • URL: http://www.conference-board.org.

Institute of Business and Economic Research. University of California at Berkeley, School of Business, F502 Haas, Berkeley, CA 94720-1922. Phone: (510)642-1922 Fax: (510)642-5018 E-mail: barde@uclink4.berkeley.edu • URL: http://www.haas.berkeley.edu/groups/iber • Research fields are business administration, economics, finance, real estate, and international development.

National Bureau of Economic Research, Inc. 1050 Massachusetts Ave., Cambridge, MA 02138-5398. Phone: (617)868-3900 Fax: (617)868-2742 E-mail: msfeldst@nber.org • URL: http://www.nber.org.

TRADE/PROFESSIONAL ASSOCIATIONS

Industrial Research Institute. 1550 M St., N.W., Suite 1100, Washington, DC 20005-1712. Phone: (202)296-8811 Fax: (202)776-0756.

National Association for Business Economics. 1233 20th St., N.W., Suite 505, Washington, DC 20036. Phone: (202)463-6223 Fax: (202)463-6239 E-mail: nabe@nabe.com • URL: http://www.nabe.com.

Society of Research Administrators. 1200 19th St., N.W., Ste. 300, Washington, DC 20036-2422. Phone: (202)857-1141 Fax: (202)828-6049 E-mail: sra@dc.sba.com • URL: http://www.sra.rams.com.

OTHER SOURCES

Business Information Desk Reference: Where to Find Answers to Your Business Questions. Melvyn N. Freed and Virgil P. Diodato. Prentice Hall. • 1992. $20.00. Offers a unique, question and answer approach to business information sources. Covers print sources, online databases, trade associations, and government agencies.

FedWorld: A Program of the United States Department of Commerce. National Technical Information Service. • Web site offers "a comprehensive central access point for searching, locating, ordering, and acquiring government and business information." Emphasis is on searching the Web pages, databases, and government reports of a wide variety of federal agencies. Fees: Free.

FirstGov: Your First Click to the U. S. Government. General Services Administration. • Free Web site provides extensive links to federal agencies covering a wide variety of topics, such as agriculture, business, consumer safety, education, the environment, government jobs, grants, health, social security, statistics sources, taxes, technology, travel, and world affairs. Also provides links to federal forms, including IRS tax forms. Searching is offered, both keyword and advanced.

The Information Catalog. MarketResearch.com. • Quarterly. Free. Mainly a catalog of market research reports from various publishers, but also includes business and marketing reference sources. Includes keyword title index. Formerly *The Information Catalog: Marketing Intelligence Studies, Competitor Reports, Business and Marketing Sources.*

BUSINESS RESPONSIBILITY

See: SOCIAL RESPONSIBILITY

BUSINESS SCHOOLS

See: BUSINESS EDUCATION

BUSINESS, SMALL

See: SMALL BUSINESS

BUSINESS START-UP PLANS AND PROPOSALS

See also: BUSINESS INNOVATION; VENTURE CAPITAL

GENERAL WORKS

Business Plan: Planning for the Small Business. Alan West. Nichols Publishing Co. • 1988. $21.95.

ABSTRACTS AND INDEXES

Business Periodicals Index. H. W. Wilson Co. • Monthly, except August, with quarterly and annual cumulations. Service basis for print edition; CD-ROM edition, $1,495.00 per year.

DIRECTORIES

IVCI Directory of Business Incubators in United States and Canada. Baxter Associates, Inc. International Venture Capital Institute, Inc. • $49.95. Lists approximately 700 start-up services (office space, accounting, legal, financial advice, research, etc.). Formerly *IVCI Directory of Business Incubators and University Research and Science Parks.*

ENCYCLOPEDIAS AND DICTIONARIES

Encyclopedia of Small Business. The Gale Group. • 1998. $395.00. Two volumes. Contains about 500 informative entries on a wide variety of topics affecting small business. Arrangement is alphabetical.

HANDBOOKS AND MANUALS

Anatomy of a Business Plan: A Step-by-Step Guide to Start Smart, Building the Business and Securing Your Companies Future. Linda J. Pinson. Dearborn, A Kaplan Professional Co. • 1999. $21.95. Fourth edition.

Business Plans Handbook. The Gale Group. • 2001. $135.00. Contains examples of detailed plans for starting or developing various kinds of businesses. Categories within plans include statement of purpose, market description, personnel requirements, financial needs, etc.

How to Write Proposals that Produce. Joel P. Bowman and Bernadine P. Branchaw. Oryx Press. •

1992. $23.50. An extensive guide to effective proposal writing for both nonprofit organizations and businesses. Covers writing style, intended audience, format, use of graphs, charts, and tables, documentation, evaluation, oral presentation, and related topics.

McGraw-Hill Guide to Starting Your Own Business: A Step-By-Step Blueprint for the First-Time Entrepreneur. Stephen C. Harper. McGraw-Hill. • 1992. $12.95. Places emphasis on the construction of an effective, realistic business plan.

New Venture Creation: Entrepreneurship for the 21st Century. Jeffrey A. Timmons and others. McGraw-Hill Professional. • 1998. Fifth edition. Price on application.

Preparing a Successful Business Plan: How to Plan to Succeed and Secure Financial Banking. Matthew Record. Trans-Atlantic Publications, Inc. • 2000. $19.95. Thirdd edition. (Business and Management Series).

Preparing Loan Proposals. John C. Wisdom. John Wiley and Sons, Inc. • 1997. $150.00. Second editon. 1998 Supplement, $55.00.

Proposal Development: How to Respond and Win the Bid. Bud Porter-Roth. PSI Research. • 1998. $21.95. Third revised edition. A step-by-step guide to the practical details of preparing, printing, and submitting business proposals of various kinds. (Successful Business Library Series).

Proposal Planning and Writing. Lynn E. Miner and others. Oryx Press. • 1998. $34.50. Second edition. Discusses the steps necessary to locate and obtain funding from the federal government, foundations, and corporations.

Proposal Preparation. Rodney D. Stewart and Ann L. Stewart. John Wiley and Sons, Inc. • 1992. $125.00. Second edition. Covers proposals of various kinds.

Restaurant Start-Up Guide: A 12-Month Plan for Successfully Starting a Restaurant. Peter Rainsford and David H. Bangs. Dearborn Financial Publishing. • 2000. $22.95. Second edition. Emphasizes the importance of advance planning for restaurant startups.

Start Right in E-Business: A Step-by-Step Guide to Successful E-Business Implementation. Bennet P. Lientz and Kathryn P. Rea. Academic Press. • 2000. $44.95.

Start-Up Business Guides. Entrepreneur Media, Inc. • Looseleaf. $59.50 each. Practical guides to starting a wide variety of small businesses.

Starting on a Shoestring: Building a Business Without a Bankroll. Arnold S. Goldstein. John Wiley and Sons, Inc. • 1995. $29.95. Third edition. Includes chapters on venture capital and Small Business Administration (SBA) loans.

Startup: An Entrepreneur's Guide to Launching and Managing a New Business. William J. Stolze. Rock Beach Press. • 1989. $24.95.

Successful Business Plan: Secrets and Strategies. Rhonda M. Abrams. Rhonda, Inc. • 1999. $27.95. Third edition. (Successful Business Library Series).

The Total Business Plan: How to Write, Rewrite, and Revise. Patrick D. O'Hara. John Wiley and Sons, Inc. • 1994. $49.95. Second edition. Covers concept, strategy, research, writing, revising, and presentation. Includes a disk.

Ultimate Guide to Raising Money for Growing Companies. Michael C. Thomsett. McGraw-Hill Professional. • 1990. $45.00. Discusses the preparation of a practical business plan, how to manage cash flow, and debt vs. equity decisions.

Where to Go When the Bank Says No: Alternatives to Financing Your Business. David R. Evanson. Bloomberg Press. • 1998. $24.95. Emphasis is on obtaining business financing in the $250,000 to $15,000,000 range. Business plans are discussed. (Bloomberg Small Business Series).

Writing Effective Business Plans. Entrepreneur Media, Inc. • Looseleaf. $49.50. A step-by-step guide. Includes a sample business plan.

ONLINE DATABASES

Wilson Business Abstracts Online. H. W. Wilson Co. • Indexes and abstracts 600 major business periodicals, plus the *Wall Street Journal* and the business section of the *New York Times.* Indexing is from 1982, abstracting from 1990, with the two newspapers included from 1993. Updated weekly. Inquire as to online cost and availability. (*Business Periodicals Index* without abstracts is also available online.).

PERIODICALS AND NEWSLETTERS

Business Start-Ups: Smart Ideas for Your Small Business. Entrepreneur Media, Inc. • Monthly. $14.97 per year. Provides advice for starting a small business. Includes business trends, new technology, E-commerce, and case histories ("real-life stories").

Small Business Advisory. Financial News Associates. • Monthly. $120.00 per year. Newsletter.

Small Business Opportunities. Harris Publications, Inc. • Bimonthly. $9.97.

Success: For the Innovative Entrepreneur. Success Holdings LLC. • Monthly. $19.97 per year. Provides information to help individuals advance in business.

RESEARCH CENTERS AND INSTITUTES

Berkley Center for Entrepreneurial Studies. New York University, Management Education Center, Stern School of Business, 44 W. Fourth St., Suite 8-165 B, New York, NY 10012. Phone: (212)998-0070 Fax: (212)995-4211 E-mail: lpoole@stern.nyu.edu • URL: http://www.stern.nyu.edu/bces.

TRADE/PROFESSIONAL ASSOCIATIONS

National Business Incubation Association. 20 E. Circle Dr., Suite 190, Athens, OH 45701. Phone: (740)593-4331 Fax: (740)593-1996 E-mail: info@nbia.org • URL: http://www.nbia.org • Members are business assistance professionals concerned with business startups, entrepreneurship, and effective small business management.

OTHER SOURCES

Cyberfinance: Raising Capital for the E-Business. Martin B. Robins. CCH, Inc. • 2001. $79.00. Covers the taxation, financial, and legal aspects of raising money for new Internet-based ("dot.com") companies, including the three stages of startup, growth, and initial public offering.

Entrepreneurship.com. Tim Burns. Dearborn Financial Publishing. • 2000. $19.95. Provides basic advice and information on the topic of dot.com startups, including business plan creation and financing.

How to Write a Business Plan. American Management Association Extension Institute. • Looseleaf. $130.00. Self-study course. Emphasis is on practical explanations, examples, and problem solving. Quizzes and a case study are included.

U. S. Business Advisor. Small Business Administration. • Web site provides "a one-stop electronic link to all the information and services government provides for the business community." Covers about 60 federal agencies that exist to assist or regulate business. Detailed information is provided on financial assistance, workplace issues, taxes, regulations, international trade, and other business topics. Searching is offered. Fees: Free.

BUSINESS STATISTICS

See also: ECONOMIC STATISTICS; MARKET STATISTICS; STATISTICAL METHODS

GENERAL WORKS

Business Statistics: A Decision-Making Approach. David F. Groebner and Patrick W. Shannon. Prentice Hall. • 1993. $72.80. Fourth edition.

Business Statistics: Contemporary Decision Making. Ken Black. South-Western Publishing Co. • 2000. $65.00. Third edition.

Business Statistics for Management and Economics. Wayne W. Daniel and James C. Terrell. Houghton Mifflin Co. • 2000. $19.47. Seventh edition.

Business Statistics for Quality and Productivity. John M. Levine. Prentice Hall. • 1994. $94.07. (Prentice Hall College Title Series).

Business Statistics Practice. Bruce L. Bowerman. McGraw-Hill. • 2000. $68.00. Second edition.

Complete Business Statistics. Amir D. Aczel. McGraw-Hill. • 1998. $90.95. Fourth edition. (Irwin/McGraw-Hill Operations and Decision Sciences Series).

Statistics for Management. Richard Levin and David S. Rubin. Prentice Hall. • 1997. $99.00. Seventh edition.

Understanding Business Statistics. John E. Hanke and Arthur G. Reitsch. McGraw-Hill Higher Education. • 1993. $71.25. Second edition.

ABSTRACTS AND INDEXES

Current Index to Statistics: Applications, Methods, and Theory. American Statistical Association. • Annual. Price on application. An index to journal articles on statistical applications and methodology.

Statistical Reference Index: A Selective Guide to American Statistical Publications from Sources Other than the United States Government. Congressional Information Service, Inc. • Monthly. Quarterly and annual cumulations. Price varies. Service basis.

ALMANACS AND YEARBOOKS

National Accounts Statistics: Main Aggregates and Detailed Tables. United Nations Publications. • Annual. $160.00.

BIBLIOGRAPHIES

Statistics Sources: A Subject Guide to Data on Industrial, Business, Social, Educational, Financial and Other Topics for the U. S. and Selected Foreign Countries. The Gale Group. • 2000. $475.00. 25th edition. Two volumes. Lists sources of statistical information for more than 20,000 topics.

World Directory of Non-Official Statistical Sources. Gale Group, Inc. • 2001. $590.00. Provides detailed descriptions of more than 4,000 regularly published, non-governmental statistics sources. Includes surveys, studies, market research reports, trade journals, databank compilations, and other print sources. Coverage is international, with four indexes.

CD-ROM DATABASES

Statistical Abstract of the United States on CD-ROM. Hoover's, Inc. • Annual. $49.95. Provides all statistics from official print version, plus expanded historical data, greater detail, and keyword searching features.

Statistical Masterfile. Congressional Information Service. • Quarterly. Price varies. Provides CD-ROM versions of *American Statistics Index, Index to International Statistics,* and *Statistical Reference Index.* Contains indexing and abstracting of a wide variety of published statistics sources, both governmental and private.

DIRECTORIES

Directory of Statisticians. American Statistical Association. • Triennial. Free to members; non-members, $125.00. List more than 25,000 memebers.

ENCYCLOPEDIAS AND DICTIONARIES

A Dictionary of Statistical Terms. F.H. Marriott. Allyn and Bacon/Longman. • 1990. $76.65. Fifth edition.

HANDBOOKS AND MANUALS

Business Statistics by Example. Terry Sincich. Prentice Hall. • 1995. $86.00. Fifth edition. Includes disk.

Dun & Bradstreet/Gale Group Industry Handbooks. The Gale Group. • 2000. $630.00. Five volumes. $145.00 per volume. Each volume covers two or more major industries: 1. *Entertainment and Hospitality*; 2. *Construction and Agriculture*; 3. *Chemicals and Pharmaceuticals*; 4. *Computers & Software and Broadcasting & Telecommunications*; 5. *Insurance and Health & Medical Services.* The following are included for each industry: overview, statistics, financial ratios, rankings, merger information, company directory, directory of associations, and consultants directory.

Finding Statistics Online: How to Locate the Elusive Numbers You Need. Paula Berinstein. Information Today, Inc. • 1998. $29.95. Provides advice on efficient searching when looking for statistical data on the World Wide Web or from commercial online services and database producers. (CyberAge Books.).

Little Black Book of Business Statistics. Michael C. Thomsett. AMACOM. • 1990. $14.95. A practical guide to the effective use and interpretation of statistics by business managers. (Little Black Book Series).

INTERNET DATABASES

Fedstats. Federal Interagency Council on Statistical Policy. Phone: (202)395-7254 • URL: http://www.fedstats.gov • Web site features an efficient search facility for full-text statistics produced by more than 70 federal agencies, including the Census Bureau, the Bureau of Economic Analysis, and the Bureau of Labor Statistics. Boolean searches can be made within one agency or for all agencies combined. Links are offered to international statistical bureaus, including the UN, IMF, OECD, UNESCO, Eurostat, and 20 individual countries. Fees: Free.

U. S. Census Bureau: The Official Statistics. U. S. Bureau of the Census. Phone: (301)763-4100 Fax: (301)763-4794 • URL: http://www.census.gov • Web site is "Your Source for Social, Demographic, and Economic Information." Contains "Current U. S. Population Count," "Current Economic Indicators," and a wide variety of data under "Other Official Statistics." Keyword searching is provided. Fees: Free.

ONLINE DATABASES

American Statistics Index: A Comprehensive Guide and Index to the Statistical Publications of the United States Government [Online]. Congressional Information Service, Inc. • Indexes and abstracts, 1973 to date. Inquire as to online cost and availability.

DRI U.S. Central Database. Data Products Division. • Provides more than 23,000 business, financial, demographic, economic, foreign trade, and industry-related time series for the U.S. Includes national income, population, retail-wholesale trade, price indexes, labor data, housing, industrial production, banking, interest rates, money supply, etc. Time period is generally 1947 to date (some data back to 1929). Updating varies. Inquire as to online cost and availability.

Industry Insider. Thomson Financial Securities Data. • Contains full-text online industry research reports from more than 200 leading trade associations, covering 50 specific industries. Reports include extensive statistics and market research data. Inquire as to online cost and availability.

OECD Main Economic Indicators. Organization for Economic Cooperation and Development. • International statistics provided by OECD, 1960 to date. Monthly updates. Inquire as to online cost and availability.

Tablebase. Responsive Database Services, Inc. • Provides online numerical tabular data from a wide variety of business, organization, and government sources, including 900 trade journals. Includes industry and individual company statistics relating to products, market share, sales forecasts, production, exports, market trends, etc. Time span is 1997 to date. Weekly updates. Inquire as to online cost and availability. (Also available in a CD-ROM version.).

PERIODICALS AND NEWSLETTERS

American Statistician. American Statistical Association. • Quarterly. Individuals, $15.00 per year; libraries, $75.00 per year.

JASA (Journal of the American Statistical Association). American Statistical Association. • Quarterly. Members, $39.00 per year; non-members, $310.00 per year. Formerly *Amercan Statistical Association Journal.*

Journal of Business and Economic Statistics. American Statistical Association. • Quarterly. Libraries, $90.00 per year. Emphasis is on statistical measurement and applications for business and economics.

STATISTICS SOURCES

Business Statistics of the United States. Courtenay M. Slater, editor. Bernan Associates. • 1999. $74.00. Fifth edition. Based on *Business Statistics*, formerly issue by the Bureau of Economic Analysis, U. S. Department of Commerce. Provides basic data for a wide variety of U. S. industries, services, and economic indicators. Most statistics are shown annually for 29 years and monthly for the most recent four years.

County Business Patterns. Available from U. S. Government Printing Office. • Irregular. 52 issues containing annual data for each state, the District of Columbia, and a U. S. Summary. Produced by U.S. Bureau of the Census (http://www.census.gov). Provides local establishment and employment statistics by industry.

Economic Indicators. Council of Economic Advisors, Executive Office of the President. Available from U.S. Government Printing Office. • Monthly. $55.00 per year.

Economic Report of the President: Together with the Annual Report of the Council of Economic Advisors. Available from U. S. Government Printing Office. • Annual. $29.00. Includes about 130 pages of "Statistical Tables Relating to Income, Employment, and Production." Tables cover national income, employment, wages, productivity, manufacturing, prices, credit, finance (public and private), corporate profits, and foreign trade.

Industrial Commodity Statistics Yearbook. United Nations Dept. of Economic and Social Affairs. United Nations Publications. • Annual.

International Trade Statistics Yearbook. United Nations Statistical Office. United Nations Publications. • Annual. $135.00. Two volumes.

Main Economic Indicators. OECD Publication and Information Center. • Monthly. $450.00 per year. "The essential source of timely statistics for OECD member countries." Includes a wide variety of business, economic, and industrial data for the 29 OECD nations.

Manufacturers' Shipments, Inventories, and Orders. Available from U. S. Government Printing Office. • Monthly. $70.00 per year. Issued by Bureau of the Census, U. S. Department of Commerce. Includes monthly *Advance Report on Durable Goods.* Provides data on production, value, shipments, and consumption for a wide variety of manufactured products. (Current Industrial Reports, M3-1.).

Metropolitan Life Insurance Co. Statistical Bulletin SB. Metropolitan Life Insurance Co. • Quarterly. Individuals, $50.00 per year. Covers a wide range of social, economic and demographic health concerns.

Statistical Abstract of the United States. Available from U. S. Government Printing Office. • Annual. $51.00. Issued by the U. S. Bureau of the Census.

Survey of Current Business. Available from U. S. Government Printing Office. • Monthly. $49.00 per year. Issued by Bureau of Economic Analysis, U. S. Department of Commerce. Presents a wide variety of business and economic data.

TRADE/PROFESSIONAL ASSOCIATIONS

American Statistical Association. 1429 Duke St., Alexandria, VA 22314-3402. Phone: (703)684-1221 Fax: (703)684-2037 E-mail: asainfo@amstat.org • URL: http://www.amstat.org • A professional society concerned with statistical theory, methodology, and applications. Sections include Survey Research Methods, Government Statistics, and Business and Economic Statistics.

Econometric Society. Northwestern University, Dept. of Economics, Evanston, IL 60208-2600. Phone: (708)491-3615 • URL: http://www.econometricsociety.org.es.

International Statistical Institute. P.O. Box 950, NL-2270 AZ Voorburg, Netherlands. E-mail: isi@cbs.vu.nl • URL: http://www.cbs.nl/isi.

OTHER SOURCES

Business Rankings Annual. The Gale Group. • Annual. $305.00.Two volumes. Compiled by the Business Library Staff of the Brooklyn Public Library. This is a guide to lists and rankings appearing in major business publications. The top ten names are listed in each case.

FedWorld: A Program of the United States Department of Commerce. National Technical Information Service. • Web site offers "a comprehensive central access point for searching, locating, ordering, and acquiring government and business information." Emphasis is on searching the Web pages, databases, and government reports of a wide variety of federal agencies. Fees: Free.

FirstGov: Your First Click to the U. S. Government. General Services Administration. • Free Web site provides extensive links to federal agencies covering a wide variety of topics, such as agriculture, business, consumer safety, education, the environment, government jobs, grants, health, social security, statistics sources, taxes, technology, travel, and world affairs. Also provides links to federal forms, including IRS tax forms. Searching is offered, both keyword and advanced.

InSite 2. Intelligence Data/Thomson Financial. • Fee-based Web site consolidates information in a "Base Pack" consisting of Business InSite, Market InSite, and Company InSite. Optional databases are Consumer InSite, Health and Wellness InSite, Newsletter InSite, and Computer InSite. Includes fulltext content from more than 2,500 trade publications, journals, newsletters, newspapers, analyst reports, and other sources. Continuous updating. Formerly produced by The Gale Group.

Major Performance Rankings. Available from The Gale Group. • 2001. $1,100.00. Published by Euromonitor. Ranks 2,500 leading consumer product companies worldwide by various kinds of business and financial data, such as sales, profit, and market share. Includes international, regional, and country rankings.

World Consumer Income and Expenditure Patterns. Available from The Gale Group. • 2001. $990.00. Second edition. Two volumes. Published by Euromonitor. Provides data for 52 countries on consumer income, earning power, spending patterns, and savings. Expenditures are detailed for 75 product or service categories.

BUSINESS STRATEGY

See also: PLANNING

GENERAL WORKS

The Art of the Long View: Planning for the Future in an Uncertain World. Peter Schwartz. Doubleday. • 1991. $15.95. Covers strategic planning for corporations and smaller firms. Includes "The World in 2005: Three Scenarios.".

Business Policy: Managing Strategic Processes. Joseph L. Bower and others. McGraw-Hill Higher Education. • 1995. $72.75. Eighth edition.

Business Strategy and Policy. Danny R. Arnold and others. Houghton Mifflin Software, School and College Div. • 1991. Third edition. Three volumes. Price on application.

Cases in Strategic Management. A.J. Strickland. McGraw-Hill. • 2000. $41.25. 12th edition.

Cases in Strategic Marketing: An Integrated Approach. William J. McDonald. Pearson Education and Technology. • 1997. $53.00. Second edition.

Corporate Internet Planning Guide: Aligning Internet Strategy with Business Goals. Richard J. Gascoyne and Koray Ozcubucku. John Wiley and Sons, Inc. • 1996. $34.95. Provides administrative advice on planning, developing, and managing corporate Internet or intranet functions. Emphasis is on strategic planning. (Business, Commerce, Management Series).

Developing Business Strategies. David A. Adler. John Wiley and Sons, Inc. • 1998. $39.95. Fifth edition.

If Your Strategy is So Terrific, How Come It Doesn't Work?. William S. Birnbaum. Books on Demand. • 1990. $77.50. Introduces the strategic matrix for business analysis and planning.

The Leader of the Future: New Essays by World-Class Leaders and Thinkers. Jossey-Bass, Inc., Publishers. • 1996. $25.00. Contains 32 articles on leadership by "executives, consultants, and commentators." (Management Series).

Marketing Strategy. Orville C. Walker and others. McGraw Hill. • 1998. $61.56. Third edition.

Marketing Strategy: Relationships, Offerings, Timing, and Resource Allocations. Devanathan Sudharshan. Prentice Hall. • 1995. $98.00.

Strategic Management. David Hunger and Thomas L. Wheelen. Prentice Hall. • 1999. $51.00. Seventh edition.

Strategic Management: Formulation, Implementation, and Control. John A. Pearce and Richard B. Robinson. McGraw-Hill Higher Education. • 1996. $72.75. Sixth edition.

Strategic Marketing. David W. Cravens. McGraw-Hill Professional. • 2000. Sixth edition. Price on application.

Strategic Planning Plus: An Organizational Guide. Roger Kaufman. Sage Publications, Inc. • 1992. $48.00.

Web Visions: An Inside Look at Successful Business Strategies on the Net. Eugene Marlow. John Wiley and Sons, Inc. • 1996. $30.95. The author explains the techniques that have been used by various corporations for success on the World Wide Web.

ABSTRACTS AND INDEXES

Business Periodicals Index. H. W. Wilson Co. • Monthly, except August, with quarterly and annual cumulations. Service basis for print edition; CD-ROM edition, $1,495.00 per year.

DIRECTORIES

Business Organizations, Agencies, and Publications Directory. The Gale Group. • 1999. $425.00. 12th edition. Over 40,000 entries describing 39 types of business information sources. Classified by type of organization, publication, or serviceIncludes state, national, and international agencies and organizations. Master index to names and keywords. Also includes e-mail addresses and web site URL's.

ENCYCLOPEDIAS AND DICTIONARIES

Blackwell Encyclopedic Dictionary of Strategic Management. Derek F. Channon, editor. Blackwell Publishers. • 1997. $110.00. The editor is associated with Imperial College, London. Contains definitions of key terms combined with longer articles written by various U. S. and foreign business educators. Includes bibliographies and index. (Blackwell Encyclopedia of Management Series.).

Field Guide to Strategy: A Glossary to Essential Tools and Concepts for Today's Manager. McGraw-Hill. • 1993. $29.95. Defines fundamental terms.

HANDBOOKS AND MANUALS

Manager's Guide to Financial Statement Analysis. Stephen F. Jablonsky and Noah P. Barsky. John Wiley and Sons, Inc. • 1998. $67.95. The two main sections are "Financial Statements and Business Strategy" and "Market Valuation and Business Strategy.".

Strategic Planning: A Practical Guide. Peter Rea and Harold Kerzner. John Wiley and Sons, Inc. • 1997. $69.95. Covers strategic planning for manufacturing firms, small businesses, and large corporations. (Industrial Engineering Series).

INTERNET DATABASES

Intelligence Data. Thomson Financial. Phone: 800-654-0393 or (212)806-8023 Fax: (212)806-8004 • URL: http://www.intelligencedata.com • Fee-based Web site provides a wide variety of information relating to competitive intelligence, strategic planning, business development, mergers, acquisitions, sales, and marketing. "Intelliscope" feature offers searching of other Thomson units, such as Investext, MarkIntel, InSite 2, and Industry Insider. Weekly updating.

ONLINE DATABASES

Business and Management Practices. Responsive Database Services, Inc. • Provides fulltext of management articles appearing in more than 350 relevant publications. Emphasis is on "the processes, methods, and strategies of managing a business." Time span is 1995 to date. Inquire as to online cost and availability. (Also available in a CD-ROM version.).

Wilson Business Abstracts Online. H. W. Wilson Co. • Indexes and abstracts 600 major business periodicals, plus the *Wall Street Journal* and the business section of the *New York Times.* Indexing is from 1982, abstracting from 1990, with the two newspapers included from 1993. Updated weekly. Inquire as to online cost and availability. (*Business Periodicals Index* without abstracts is also available online.).

PERIODICALS AND NEWSLETTERS

Daily Report for Executives. Bureau of National Affairs, Inc. • Daily. $6,927.00 per year. Newsletter. Covers legal, regulatory, economic, and tax developments affecting corporations.

Journal of Business Strategy. Faulkner and Gray, Inc. • Bimonthly. $84.00 per year. Devoted to the theory and practice of strategy, planning, implementation and competitive analysis. Covers every aspect of business from advertising to systems design. Incorporates*Journal of European Business.*

Journal of Economics and Management Strategy. MIT Press. • Quarterly. Individuals, $45.00 per year; institutions, $135.00 per year. Covers "theoretical and empirical industrial organization, applied game theory, and management strategy.".

Leader to Leader. Peter F. Drucker Foundation for Nonprofit Management. Jossey-Bass Publishers. • Quarterly. Individuals, $149.00 per year; institutions, $149.00 per year. Contains articles on "management, leadership, and strategy" written by "leading executives, thinkers, and consultants." Covers both business and nonprofit issues.

Manager's Intelligence Report: Insider's Fast Track to Better Management. Lawence Ragan Communications, Inc. • Monthly. $129.00 per year. Newsletter on various aspects of management, including strategy, employee morale, and time management.

Strategic Management Journal. Available from John Wiley and Sons, Inc., Journals Div. • Monthly. Insitutions, $145.00 per year. Original refereed material concerned with all aspects of strategic management. Devoted to the development and improvement of both theory and practice. Provides international coverage. Published in England by John Wiley and Sons Ltd.

Strategy and Business. Booz-Allen & Hamilton. • Quarterly. $38.00 per year.

RESEARCH CENTERS AND INSTITUTES

Hubert H. Humphrey Institute of Public Affairs. University of Minnesota, 300 Hubert Center, 301 19th Ave., S., Minneapolis, MN 55455. Phone: (612)625-0669 Fax: (612)625-6351 E-mail: jbrandl@hhh.umn.edu • URL: http://www.hhh.umn.edu • Studies strategic management in both the private and the public sectors.

Strategic Planning Institute. P.O. Box 447, Newton Center, MA 02459-0004. Phone: (617)491-9200 Fax: (617)491-1634 • Conducts research in business information and strategy.

BUSINESS TO BUSINESS MARKETING

See: INDUSTRIAL MARKETING

BUSINESS TRAVEL

See also: AIR TRAVEL; TRAVEL INDUSTRY

GENERAL WORKS

Safe Trip Abroad. Available from U. S. Government Printing Office. • 1996. $1.25. Issued by the Bureau of Consular Affairs, U. S. State Department (http://www.state.gov). Provides practical advice for international travel.

Unofficial Business Traveler's Pocket Guide: 249 Tips Even the Best Business Travelers May Not Know. Christopher J. McGinnis. McGraw-Hill. • 1998. $10.95. Arranged by subject categories, such as airports, frequent traveler programs, eating, and staying well.

ABSTRACTS AND INDEXES

Business Periodicals Index. H. W. Wilson Co. • Monthly, except August, with quarterly and annual cumulations. Service basis for print edition; CD-ROM edition, $1,495.00 per year.

Leisure, Recreation, and Tourism Abstracts. Available from CABI Publishing North America. • Quarterly. $470.00 per year. Published in England by CABI Publishing. Provides coverage of the worldwide literature of travel, recreation, sports, and the hospitality industry. Emphasis is on research.

Readers' Guide to Periodical Literature. H. W. Wilson Co. • Monthly. $220.00 per year. CD-ROM edition, $1,495 per year, including annual cumulation. Indexes about 250 peridicals of general interest.

BIBLIOGRAPHIES

Travel and Tourism. Available from U. S. Government Printing Office. • Annual. Free. Issued by the Superintendent of Documents. A list of government publications on the travel industry and tourism. Formerly *Mass Transit, Travel and Tourism.* (Subject Bibliography No. 302.).

DIRECTORIES

City Profiles USA: A Traveler's Guide to Major U. S. and Canadian Cities. Darren L. Smith, editor. Omnigraphics, Inc. • Annual. $110.00. A directory of information useful to business and other travelers in major cities. Includes services, facilities, attractions, and events. Arranged by city.

Corporate Travel's Blackbook. Miller Freeman Books. • Annual. $15.00. Included with subscription to *Corporate Travel.* Gives sources of corporate travel packages. Formerly *Corporate Travel-Directory "Blackbook".*

Craighead's International Business, Travel, and Relocation Guide to 81 Countries. Available from The Gale Group. • 2000. $725.00. Tenth edition. Four volumes. Compiled by Craighead Publications, Inc. Provides a wide range of business travel and relocation information for 78 different countries, including details on currency, customs regulations, visas, passports, healthcare, transportation, shopping, insurance, travel safety, etc. Formerly *International Business Travel and RelocatDirectory.*

Internet Resources and Services for International Business: A Global Guide. Lewis-Guodo Liu. Oryx Press. • 1998. $49.95. Describes more than 2,500 business-related Web sites from 176 countries. Includes five major categories: general information, economics, business and trade, business travel, and contacts. Indexed by Web site name, country, and subject.

OAG Business Travel Planner: North America. Cahners Travel Group. • Quarterly. $149.00 per year. Arranged according to more than 14,700 destinations in the U. S., Canada, Mexico, and the Caribbean. Lists more than 32,000 hotels, with AAA ratings where available. Provides information on airports, ground transportation, coming events, and climate.

OAG Travel Planner: Asia Pacific. Cahners Travel Group. • Quarterly. $130.00 per year. Arranged according to more than 5,000 destinations throughout Asia and the Pacific. Lists about 5,000 hotels, with information on airports, ground transportation, coming events, and climate.

OAG Travel Planner: Europe. Cahners Travel Group. • Quarterly. $130.00 per year. Arranged according to more than 13,850 destinations in Europe. Lists more than 14,700 hotels, with information on airports, ground transportation, coming events, and climate.

HANDBOOKS AND MANUALS

CCH Guide to Car, Travel, Entertainment, and Home Office Deductions. CCH, Inc. • Annual. $42.00. Explains how to claim maximum tax deductions for common business expenses. Includes automobile depreciation tables, lease value tables, worksheets, and examples of filled-in tax forms.

Fodor's World Weather Guide. E. A. Pearce and C. G. Smith. Random House, Inc. • 1998. $17.95. Written for travelers. Describes the weather at 2,000 locations in 200 countries. Includes temperature/rainfall charts, climate discomfort factors, a glossary of weather terms, and maps.

Health Information for International Travel. Available from U. S. Government Printing Office. • Annual. Issued by Centers for Disease Control, U. S. Department of Health and Human Services. Discusses potential health risks of international travel and specifies vaccinations required by different countries.

ONLINE DATABASES

Readers' Guide Abstracts Online. H. W. Wilson Co. • Indexes and abstracts general interest periodicals, 1983 to date. Weekly updates. Inquire as to online cost and availability.

Wilson Business Abstracts Online. H. W. Wilson Co. • Indexes and abstracts 600 major business periodicals, plus the *Wall Street Journal* and the business section of the *New York Times.* Indexing is from 1982, abstracting from 1990, with the two newspapers included from 1993. Updated weekly. Inquire as to online cost and availability. (*Business Periodicals Index* without abstracts is also available online.).

PERIODICALS AND NEWSLETTERS

Business Travel News: News and Ideas for Business Travel Management. Miller Freeman, Inc. • 29 times a year. $115.00 per year. Includes annual directory of travel sources. Formerly *Corporate Travel.*

Frequent Flyer: For Business People Who Must Travel. OAG Worldwide. • Monthly. $89.00 per year to individuals. Also known as *OAG Frequent Flyer.* Edited for business travelers. Contains news of frequent flyer programs, airport developments, airline services, and business travel trends. Available only with *OAG Flight Guide.*

Front Row Advisor: Business and First Class Air Travel and the Alluring World of Free Upgrades. Diversified Specialties, Inc. • Bimonthly. $145.00 per year. Newsletter. Contains information on opportunities provided by airlines to upgrade coach seats to business class, including frequent flyer upgrades.

Inside Flyer. Frequent Flyer Services. • Monthly. $75.00 per year. Newsletter. Provides information relating to frequent flyer awards and air travel.

Newsline: Research News from the U. S. Travel Data Center. Travel Industry Association of America. • Monthly. $55.00 per year. Newsletter. Covers trends in the U. S. travel industry.

Runzheimer Reports on Travel Management. Runzheimer International. • Monthly. $354.00 per year. Newsletter on the control of business travel costs.

Summary of Health Information for International Travel. U. S. Department of Health and Human Services. • Biweekly. Formerly *Weekly Summary of Health Information for International Travel.*

Travel Manager's Executive Briefing. American Business Publishing. • Semimonthly. $437.00 per year. Newsletter on travel expense cost control. Formerly *Travel Expense Management.*

Travel Weekly. Cahners Travel Group. • Weekly. $220.00 per year. Includes cruise guides, a weekly "Business Travel Update," and special issues devoted to particular destinations and areas. Edited mainly for travel agents and tour operators.

RESEARCH CENTERS AND INSTITUTES

American Hotel Foundation. 1201 New York Ave., N.W., Suite 600, Washington, DC 20005-3931. Phone: (202)289-3180 Fax: (202)289-3199 E-mail: dviehland@ahma.com • URL: http://www.ahma.com/ahf.htm.

STATISTICS SOURCES

Economic Review of Travel in America. Travel Industry Association of America. • Annual. Members, $75.00; non-members, $125.00. Presents a statistical summary of travel in the U.S., including travel expenditures, travel industry employment, tax data, international visitors, etc.

Outlook for Travel and Tourism. Travel Industry Association of America. • Annual. Members, $100.00; non-members, $175.00. Contains forecasts of the performance of the U. S. travel industry, including air travel, business travel, recreation (attractions), and accomodations.

Summary of International Travel to the United States. International Trade Administration, Tourism Industries. U.S. Dept. of Commerce. • Monthly. Quarterly and annual versions available. Provides statistics on air travel to the U.S. from each of 90 countries. Formerly *Summary and Analysis of International Travel to the United States.*

Survey of Business Travelers. Travel Industry Association of America. • Biennial. Members, $100.00 per year; non-members, $175.00 per year.

TRADE/PROFESSIONAL ASSOCIATIONS

International Airline Passengers Association. P.O. Box 700188, Dallas, TX 75370. Phone: 800-821-4272 or (904)404-9980 Fax: (972)233-5348 E-mail: iapa@iapauia.com • URL: http://www.iapa.com.

National Association of Business Travel Agents. 3699 Wilshire Blvd.,, Ste. 700, Los Angeles, CA 90010-2726. Phone: (213)382-3335 Fax: (213)480-7712 E-mail: sjfaber@earthlink.net • Members specialize in corporate and business travel services.

Society of Incentive and Travel Executives. 21 W. 38th St., 10th Fl., New York, NY 10018. Phone: (212)575-0910 Fax: (212)575-1838 E-mail: hq@site-intl.org • URL: http://www.site-intl.org • Members include both users and suppliers of incentive travel.

BUSINESS TRENDS

See: BUSINESS CYCLES; BUSINESS FORECASTING

BUSINESS VALUATION

See: VALUATION

BUSINESS WRITING

See: BUSINESS CORRESPONDENCE; REPORT WRITING; WRITERS AND WRITING

BUSINESSMEN IN FICTION

See: BUSINESS IN FICTION

BUTANE

See: PROPANE AND BUTANE GAS INDUSTRY

BUTCHER SHOPS

See: MEAT INDUSTRY

BUTTER INDUSTRY

See: DAIRY INDUSTRY

BUYING

See: PURCHASING

BUYING A BUSINESS

See: BUSINESS ENTERPRISES, SALE OF

BUYING POWER

See: PURCHASING POWER

BUYOUTS, LEVERAGED

See: LEVERAGED BUYOUTS

BY-PRODUCTS

See: WASTE PRODUCTS

C

CABLE ADDRESSES

DIRECTORIES

Marconi's International Register: Linking Buyers and Sellers Worldwide Through Fax and Business Listings. Telegraphic Cable and Radio Registrations, Inc. • Annual. $150.00. Lists more than 45,000 firms throughout the world in all lines of business. In four sections.

Thomas Register of American Manufacturers and Thomas Register Catalog File. Thomas Publishing Co., Inc. • Annual. $149.00. 34 volumes. A three-part system offering information on a wide variety of industrial equipment and supplies.

CABLE TELEVISION INDUSTRY

See also: TELEVISION BROADCASTING INDUSTRY

ABSTRACTS AND INDEXES

Business Periodicals Index. H. W. Wilson Co. • Monthly, except August, with quarterly and annual cumulations. Service basis for print edition; CD-ROM edition, $1,495.00 per year.

BIOGRAPHICAL SOURCES

The Highwaymen: Warriors on the Information Superhighway. Ken Auletta. Harcourt Trade Publications. • 1998. $13.00. Revised expanded edition. Contains critical articles about Ted Turner, Rupert Murdoch, Barry Diller, Michael Eisner, and other key figures in electronic communications, entertainment, and information.

CD-ROM DATABASES

Hoover's Company Capsules on CD-ROM. Hoover's, Inc. • Quarterly. $349.95 per year (single-user). Provides the CD-ROM version of *Hoover's Handbook of American Business, Hoover's Handbook of Emerging Companies, Hoover's Handbook of World Business, Hoover's Guide to Computer Companies, Hoover's Guide to Media Companies, Hoover's Handbook of Private Companies,* and various regional guides. Includes more than 11,000 profiles of companies.

Telecom Strategies. Thomson Financial Securities Data. • Monthly. $2,995.00 per year. CD-ROM contains full text of investment analysts' reports on companies operating in the following fields: telecommunications, broadcasting, and cable communications.

DIRECTORIES

Bacon's Radio and TV Cable Directories. Bacon's Publishing Co. • Annual. $295.00. Two volumes. Includes educational and public broadcasters. Covers all United States broadcast media. Formerly *Bacon's Radio - TV Directory.*

Broadcasting and Cable Yearbook. R. R Bowker. • Annual. $179.95. Two volumes. Published in conjunction with *Broadcasting* magazine. Provides information on U. S. and Canadian TV stations, radio stations, cable TV companies, and radio-TV services of various kinds.

Burrelle's Media Directory: Broadcast Media. Burrelle's Information Services. • Annual. $275.00. Two volumes. *Radio* volume lists more than 12,000 radio stations in the U. S. and Canada. *Television and Cable* volume lists more than 1,700 television stations and cable systems. Provides detailed descriptions, including programming and key personnel.

Cable Communications-Products Directory and Buyers' Guide. Udo Salewsky, editor. Ter-Sat Media Publications, Ltd. • Annual. $20.00. Lists about 300 manufacturers and distributors of cable television-specific equipment and services; primarily covers United States and Canada.

Cable TV Financial Databook: Sourcebook for All Key Financial Data on Cable TV. Paul Kagan Associates, Inc. • Annual. $495.00. Includes analysis of operating results of private and public cable television companies, historical data and projections.

Gale Directory of Publications and Broadcast Media. The Gale Group. • Annual. $650.00. Five volumes. A guide to publications and broadcasting stations in the U. S. and Canada, including newspapers, magazines, journals, radio stations, television stations, and cable systems. Geographic arrangement. Volume three consists of statistical tables, maps, subject indexes, and title index. Formerly *Ayer Directory of Publications.*

Interactive Advertising Source. SRDS. • Quarterly. $561.00 per year. Provides descriptive profiles, rates, audience, personnel, etc., for producers of various forms of interactive or multimedia advertising: online/Internet, CD-ROM, interactive TV, interactive cable, interactive telephone, interactive kiosk, and others. Includes online supplement *SRDS' URlink.*

International Television and Video Almanac: Reference Tool of the Television and Home Video Industries. Quigley Publishing Co., Inc. • Annual. $119.00.

Plunkett's Entertainment and Media Industry Almanac. Available from Plunkett Research, Ltd. • Biennial. $149.99. Provides profiles of leading firms in online information, films, radio, television, cable, multimedia, magazines, and book publishing. Includes World Wide Web sites, where available, plus information on careers and industry trends.

TV and Cable Source. SRDS. • Quarterly. $464.00 per year. Provides detailed information on U. S. television stations, cable systems, networks, and group owners, with maps and market data. Includes key personnel.

ENCYCLOPEDIAS AND DICTIONARIES

Jones Dictionary of Cable Television Terminology: Including Related Computer and Satellite Definitions. Glenn R. Jones. Jones Twenty-First Century Ltd. • 1996. $14.95.

HANDBOOKS AND MANUALS

Cable and Station Coverage Atlas. Warren Publishing Inc. • Annual. $474.00.

ONLINE DATABASES

ABI/INFORM. Bell & Howell Information and Learning. • Provides online indexing to business-related material occurring in over 1,000 periodicals from 1971 to the present. Inquire as to online cost and availability.

ERIC. Educational Resources Information Center. • Broad range of educational literature, 1966 to present. Monthly updates. Inquire as to online cost and availability.

Gale Database of Publications and Broadcast Media. The Gale Group. • An online directory containing detailed information on over 67,000 periodicals, newspapers, broadcast stations, cable systems, directories, and newsletters. Corresponds to the following print sources: *Gale Directory of Publications and Broadcast Media; Directories in Print; City and State Directories in Print; Newsletters in Print.* Semiannual updates. Inquire as to online cost and availability.

Magazine Index. The Gale Group. • General magazine indexing (popular literature), 1973 to present. Daily updates. Inquire as to online cost and availability.

Management Contents. The Gale Group. • Covers a wide range of management, financial, marketing, personnel, and administrative topics. About 150 leading business journals are indexed and abstracted from 1974 to date, with monthly updating. Inquire as to online cost and availability.

PROMT: Predicasts Overview of Markets and Technology. The Gale Group. • Companies, products, applied technologies and markets. U.S. and international literature coverage, 1972 to date. Inquire as to online cost and availability. Provides abstracts from more than 1,600 publications. Weekly updates.

Trade & Industry Index. The Gale Group. • Provides indexing of business periodicals, January 1981 to date. Daily updates. (Full text articles from some periodicals are available online, 1983 to date, in the companion database, *Trade & Industry ASAP.*) Inquire as to online cost and availability.

PERIODICALS AND NEWSLETTERS

Broadcasting and Cable. Cahners Business Information, Broadcasting and Cable's International Group. • 51 times a year. $149.00 per year. Formerly *Broadcasting.*

Cable TV Investor: Newsletter on Investments in Cable TV Systems and Publicly Held Cable TV Stocks. Paul Kagan Associates, Inc. • Monthly. $895.00 per year.

Cable TV Programming: Newsletter on Programs for Pay Cable TV and Analysis of Basic Cable Networks. Paul Kagan Associates, Inc. • Monthly. $745.00 per year.

Cable TV Technology: Newsletter on Technical Advances, Construction of New Systems and Rebuild of Existing Systems. Paul Kagan Associates, Inc. • Monthly. $695.00 per year. Newsletter. Contains news of cable TV technical advances.

Cablevision: The Analysis and Features Bi-Weekly of the Cable Television Industry. Cahners Business Information, Broadcasting and Cable's International Group. • Semimonthly. $65.00 per year.

Communications Daily: The Authoritative News Service of Electronic Communications. Warren Publishing Inc. • Daily. $3,006.00 per year. Newsletter. Covers telecommunications, including the telephone industry, broadcasting, cable TV, satellites, data communications, and electronic publishing. Features corporate and industry news.

Electronic Media. Crain Communications, Inc. • Weekly. $119.00 per year.

The Hollywood Reporter. • Daily. $219.00 per year. Covers the latest news in film, TV, cable, multimedia, music, and theatre. Includes box office grosses and entertainment industry financial data.

Multichannel News. Cahners Business Information. • Weekly. $119.00 per year. Covers the business, programming, marketing, and technology concerns of cable television operators and their suppliers.

Tele.com: Business and Technology for Public Network Service Providers. CMP Publications, Inc. • 14 times a year. $125.00 per year. Edited for executives and managers at both traditional telephone companies and wireless communications companies. Also provides news and information for Internet services providers and cable TV operators.

Telecom Business: Opportunities for Network Service Providers, Resellers, and Suppliers in the Competitive Telecom Industry. MultiMedia Publishing Corp. • Monthly. $56.95 per year. Provides business and technical information for telecommunications executives in various fields.

Television Digest with Consumer Electronics. Warren Communication News. • Weekly. $944.00 per year. Newsletter featuring new consumer entertainment products utilizing electronics. Also covers the television broadcasting and cable TV industries, with corporate and industry news.

Warren's Cable Regulation Monitor: The Authoritative Weekly News Service Covering Federal, State, and Local Cable Activities and Trends. Warren Publishing Inc. • Weekly. $594.00 per year. Newsletter. Emphasis is on Federal Communications Commission regulations affecting cable television systems. Covers rate increases made by local systems and cable subscriber complaints filed with the FCC.

STATISTICS SOURCES

Cable Television Revenues. U.S. Federal Communications Commission. • Annual.

Cable TV Facts. Cabletelevision Advertising Bureau. • Annual. Free to members; non-members, $10.00. Provides statistics on cable TV and cable TV advertising in the U. S.

Standard & Poor's Industry Surveys. Standard & Poor's. • Semiannual. $1,800.00. Two looseleaf volumes. Includes monthly supplements. Provides detailed, individual surveys of 52 major industry groups. Each survey is revised on a semiannual basis. Also includes "Monthly Investment Review" (industry group investment analysis) and monthly "Trends & Projections" (economic analysis).

Television and Cable Factbook. Warren Publishing Inc. • Annual. $495.00. Three volumes. Commercial and noncommercial television stations and networks.

U. S. Industry and Trade Outlook: The McGraw-Hill Companies and the U.S. Department of Commerce/ International Trade Administration. Datapso Research Corp. • Annual. $69.95. Produced by the International Trade Administration, U. S. Department of Commerce, in a "public-private" partnership with DRI/McGraw-Hill and Standard & Poor's. Provides basic data, outlook for the current year, and "Long-Term Prospects" (five-year projections) for a wide variety of products and services. Includes high technology industries. Formerly *U. S. Industrial Outlook.*

TRADE/PROFESSIONAL ASSOCIATIONS

Alliance for Community Media. 666 11th St., N.W., Suite 806, Washington, DC 20001. Phone: (202)393-2650 Fax: (202)393-2653 E-mail: alliancecm@aol.com • URL: http://www.alliancecm.org.

Cabletelevision Advertising Bureau. 830 Third Ave., New York, NY 10017. Phone: (212)508-1200 Fax: (212)832-3268 • URL: http://www.cabletvadbureau.com.

CTMA, The Marketing Society for the Cable and Telecommunications Industry. 201 N. Union, Suite 440, Alexandria, VA 23314. Phone: (703)549-4200 Fax: (703)684-1167 E-mail: ctam@ctam.com • URL: http://www.ctam.com.

Institute of Electrical and Electronics Engineers; Consumer Electronics Society. Three Park Ave., 17th Fl., New York, NY 10016-5997. Phone: (212)419-7900 Fax: (212)752-4929 • URL: http://www.ieee.org.

National Cable Television Association. 1724 Massachusetts Ave., N.W., Washington, DC 20036. Phone: (202)775-3550 Fax: (202)775-3675.

National Cable Television Institute. 801 W. Mineral Ave., Littleton, CO 80120-4501. Phone: (303)797-9393 Fax: (303)797-9394 • URL: http://www.ncti.com.

Society of Cable Telecommunications Engineers. 140 Philips Rd., Exton, PA 19341-1318. Phone: 800-542-5040 or (610)363-6888 Fax: (610)363-5898 E-mail: info@scte.org • URL: http://www.scte.org.

Women in Cable and Telecommunications. 230 W. Monroe St., Ste. 2630, Chicago, IL 60606-4702. Phone: (312)634-2330 Fax: (312)634-2345 E-mail: information@wict.org • URL: http://www.wict.org.

OTHER SOURCES

Cable Television and Other Nonbroadcast Media: Law and Policy. Daniel J. Brenner and others. West Group. • $145.00 per year. Looseleaf service. Periodic supplementation. (Entertainment and Communications Law Series).

Infrastructure Industries USA. The Gale Group. • 2001. $240.00. Replaces *Agriculture, Forestry, Fishing, Mining, and Construction USA* and *Transportation and Public Utilities USA.* Presents statistics and projections relating to economic activity in a wide variety of natural resource and construction industries.

Telecommunications Regulation: Cable, Broadcasting, Satellite, and the Internet. Matthew Bender & Co., Inc. • Looseleaf. $700.00. Four volumes. Semiannual updates. Covers local, state, and federal regulation, with emphasis on the Telecommunications Act of 1996. Includes regulation of television, telephone, cable, satellite, computer communication, and online services. Formerly *Cable Television Law.*

CAD/CAM

See: COMPUTER-AIDED DESIGN AND MANUFACTURING (CAD/CAM)

CAFETERIAS

See: RESTAURANTS, LUNCHROOMS, ETC.

CAFETERIAS, EMPLOYEE

See: EMPLOYEE LUNCHROOMS AND CAFETERIAS

CALENDAR

See: CHRONOLOGY

CAMCORDERS

See: VIDEO RECORDING INDUSTRY

CAMERA INDUSTRY

See also: PHOTOGRAPHIC INDUSTRY

GENERAL WORKS

A Century of Cameras. Eaton S. Lothrop. Morgan and Morgan, Inc. • 1982. $24.00. Revised edition.

Photography in Focus. Mark Jacobs and Ken Kokrda. NTC/Contemporary Publishing. • 1996. $27.95. Fifth revised edition.

DIRECTORIES

Photographer's Market: 2000 Places to Sell Your Photographs. F & W Publications, Inc. • Annual. $23.99. Lists 2,000 companies and publications that purchase original photographs.

Who's Who in Professional Imaging. Professional Photographers of America, Inc. • Annual. $110.00. Lists over 18,000 members. Formerly *Buyers Guide to Qualified Photographers.*

ENCYCLOPEDIAS AND DICTIONARIES

Focal Encyclopedia of Photography. Leslie Stroebel and Richard D. Zakia, editors. Butterworth-Heinemann. • 1993. $56.95. Third edition.

FINANCIAL RATIOS

Almanac of Business and Industrial Financial Ratios. Leo Troy. Prentice Hall. • Annual. $99.95. Contains financial ratios derived from federal tax returns. Ratios for each of about 200 industries are arranged according to company asset size.

Annual Statement Studies. Robert Morris Associates: The Association of Lending and Credit Risk Professiona. • Annual. Free to members; non-members, $140.00. Median and quartile financial ratios are given for over 400 kinds of manufacturing, wholesale, retail, construction, and consumer finance establishments. Data is sorted by both asset size and sales volume. Includes a clearly written "Definition of Ratios" and an alphabetical industry index.

Cost of Doing Business Survey. Photo Marketing Association International. • Biennial. $225.00. Emphasis is on photographic retailing.

HANDBOOKS AND MANUALS

Black and White Photography: A Basic Manual. Henry Horenstein. Little, Brown and Co. • 1983. $24.95. Revised edition.

PERIODICALS AND NEWSLETTERS

Japan Camera Trade News: Monthly Information on Photographic Products, Optical Instruments and Accessories. K. Eda, editor. Genyosha Publications, Inc. • Monthly. $75.00 per year. Information on the photographic industry worldwide. Text in English.

PRICE SOURCES

Orion Camera Blue Book. Orion Research Corp. • Annual. $144.00. Published by Orion Research

Corporation. Quotes retail and wholesale prices of used cameras and equipment. Original list prices and years of manufacture are also shown.

STATISTICS SOURCES

U. S. Industry and Trade Outlook: The McGraw-Hill Companies and the U.S. Department of Commerce/ International Trade Administration. Datapso Research Corp. • Annual. $69.95. Produced by the International Trade Administration, U. S. Department of Commerce, in a "public-private" partnership with DRI/McGraw-Hill and Standard & Poor's. Provides basic data, outlook for the current year, and "Long-Term Prospects" (five-year projections) for a wide variety of products and services. Includes high technology industries. Formerly *U. S. Industrial Outlook.*

United States Census of Manufactures. U.S. Bureau of the Census. • Quinquennial. Results presented in reports, tape, CD-ROM, and Diskette files.

TRADE/PROFESSIONAL ASSOCIATIONS

National Association of Photo Equipment Technicians. 3000 Picture Place, Jackson, MI 49201. Phone: (517)788-8100 Fax: (517)788-8371.

Photographic and Imaging Manufacturers Association. 550 Mamaroneck Ave., Ste. 307, Harrison, NY 10528-1612. Phone: (914)698-7603 Fax: (914)698-7609 E-mail: pima@pima.net • URL: http://www.pima.net.

Photoimaging Manufacturers and Distributors Association. 109 White Oak Lane, Ste. 72F, Old Bridge, NJ 08857. Phone: (732)679-3460 Fax: (732)679-2294 E-mail: bclarkpmda@aol.com.

CAMPER INDUSTRY

See: RECREATIONAL VEHICLE INDUSTRY

CAMPING INDUSTRY

See: RECREATION INDUSTRY

CANADIAN MARKETS

ABSTRACTS AND INDEXES

Canadian Index. Micromedia Ltd. • Monthly, with annual cumulation. Price varies. Indexes approximately 500 Canadian periodicals of all kinds, including business magazines and trade journals. Ten daily Canadian newspapers are also indexed.

Canadian Periodical Index. The Gale Group. • Monthly. $515.00 per year. Annual cumulation. Indexes more than 400 English and French language periodicals.

F & S Index: International. The Gale Group. • Monthly. $1,295.00 per year, including quarterly and annual cumulations. Provides annotated citations to marketing, business, financial, and industrial literature. Coverage of international business activity includes trade journals, financial magazines, business newspapers, and special reports. Areas included are Asia, Latin America, Africa, the Middle East, Oceania, and Canada. Formerly *Predicasts F & S Index: International.*

ALMANACS AND YEARBOOKS

Canadian Almanac and Directory. Available from The Gale Group. • Annual. $259.00. Published by Micromedia. Contains general information and statistical data relating to Canada and provides information on about 60,000 Canadian agencies, associations, institutions, museums, libraries, etc.

BIOGRAPHICAL SOURCES

Canadian Who's Who. University of Toronto Press, Reverence Div. • Annual. $165.00. Provides concise biographical information in English and French on 15,000 prominent Canadians.

Financial Post Directory of Directors. Financial Post Datagroup. • Annual. $159.95. Provides brief biographical information on 16,000 directors and key officers of Canadian companies who are also Canadian residents.

Who's Who in Canadian Business. Who's Who Publications. • Annual. $179.95. Contains brief biographies of 5,000 individuals prominent in Canadian business.

CD-ROM DATABASES

Canada Year Book on CD-ROM. Statistics Canada, Publications Division. • Annual. $90.00. CD-ROM in English and French provides basic statistical and other information on Canada. Contains multimedia features and search capabilities.

CanCorp Plus Canadian Financial Database. Micromedia Ltd. • Monthly. $3,600.00 per year. Also available quarterly at $2,975.00 per year. Provides comprehensive information on CD-ROM for more than 11,000 public and private Canadian corporations. Emphasis is on detailed financial data for up to seven years.

CPI.Q: The Canadian Periodical Index Full-Text on CD-ROM. The Gale Group. • Bimonthly. Provides CD-ROM citations from 1988 to date for more than 400 English and French language periodicals. Contains full-text coverage from 1995 to date for 150 periodicals.

Hoover's Company Capsules on CD-ROM. Hoover's, Inc. • Quarterly. $349.95 per year (single-user). Provides the CD-ROM version of *Hoover's Handbook of American Business, Hoover's Handbook of Emerging Companies, Hoover's Handbook of World Business, Hoover's Guide to Computer Companies, Hoover's Guide to Media Companies, Hoover's Handbook of Private Companies,* and various regional guides. Includes more than 11,000 profiles of companies.

World Database of Consumer Brands and Their Owners on CD-ROM. The Gale Group. • Annual. $3,190.00. Produced by Euromonitor. Provides detailed information on CD-ROM for about 10,000 companies and 80,000 brands around the world. Covers 1,000 product sectors.

World Marketing Forecasts on CD-ROM. The Gale Group. • Annual. $2,500.00. Produced by Euromonitor. Provides detailed forecast data for the years to 2012 on CD-ROM for 54 countries in all parts of the world. Covers a wide range of social, demographic, economic, and market factors. Includes specific forecasts for many kinds of consumer products.

DIRECTORIES

Associations Canada: The Directory of Associations in Canada. Micromedia. • Annual. $299.00. Provides detailed information in English and French on 20,000 active Canadian associations. Includes subject, keyword, personal name, and other indexes. Formerly *Directory of Associations in Canada.*

Canada Company Handbook: The Globe and Mail Report on Business. Globe Information Services. • Annual. $49.95. Provides information on 400 Canadian companies. Detailed fianncial data and rankings are presented for firms listed on the Toronto Stock Exchange.

Canadian Directory of Shopping Centres. Maclean Hunter Business Publications. • Annual. $400.00. Two volumes (Eastern Canada and Western Canada). Describes about 1,700 shopping centers and malls, including those under development.

Canadian Key Business Directory. Available from Dun & Bradstreet Information Services. • Annual. $450.00. Published by Dun & Bradstreet Canada Ltd. Provides information in English and French on 20,000 leading Canadian business firms.

Canadian Trade Index. Alliance of Manufacturers Exporters and Importers Canada. • Annual. $190.00. Provides information on about 15,000 manufacturers in Canada, including key personnel. Indexed by trade name, product, and location.

CARD The Media Information Network (Canadian Advertising Rates and Data). Available from SRDS. • Biennial. $225.00 per issue. Published by Maclean Hunter Publishing Ltd. (Toronto). Provides advertising rates and other information relating to Canadian media: daily newspapers, weekly community newspapers, consumer magazines, business publications, school publications, religious publications, radio, and television.

Directory of Canadian Trademarks. Thomson & Thomson. • Annual. Price on application. Provides owner, registration, and classification information for Canadian trademarks registered with the Canadian Intellectual Property Office (CIPO).

Directory of Retail Chains in Canada. Maclean Hunter Business Publications. • Annual. $340.00. Provides detailed information on approximately 1,600 retail chains of all sizes in Canada.

Fraser's Canadian Trade Directory. Fraser's Trade Directories. • Annual. $200.00. A product classified listing of more than 42,000 Canadian manufacturers and distributors and 14,000 foreign companies having Canadian representation. Includes trade name index.

Hoover's Handbook of World Business: Profiles of Major European, Asian, Latin American, and Canadian Companies. Hoover's, Inc. • Annual. $99.95. Contains detailed profiles of more than 300 large foreign companies. Includes indexes by industry, location, executive name, company name, and brand name.

International Directory of Consumer Brands and Their Owners. Available from The Gale Group. • 1997. $450.00. Published by Euromonitor. Contains detailed information on more than 38,000 consumer product brands and their companies in 62 countries of the world, excluding Europe.

International Media Guide: Business/Professional Publications: The Americas. International Media Guides, Inc. • Annual. $285.00. Describes trade journals from North, South, and Central America, with advertising rates and circulation data.

Major Market Share Companies: The Americas. Available from The Gale Group. • 2000. $900.00. Published by Euromonitor (http://www.euromonitor.com). Provides consumer market share data and rankings for multinational and regional companies. Covers leading firms in the U.S., Canada, Mexico, Brazil, Argentina, Venezuela, and Chile.

Survey of Industrials. Financial Post Datagroup. • Annual. $119.95 Contains detailed information on more than 2,200 publicly owned Canadian manufacturing, retailing, and service corporations. Includes the "Financial Post 500," a ranking of the largest Canadian companies.

INTERNET DATABASES

Canadian American Trade Site: Promoting Trade Between Canada and the Southeastern United States. Small Business Development Center of South Carolina. Phone: 800-243-7232 or (803)777-4909 Fax: (803)777-4403 E-mail: canamtr@darla.badm.sc.edu • URL: http://canamtrade.badm.sc.edu • Web site provides information about trade between the U. S. and

Canada. Includes links to other trade-related Web sites. Fees: Free.

CANOE: Canadian Online Explorer. Canoe Limited Partnership. Phone: (416)947-2027 Fax: (416)947-2209 • URL: http://www.canoe.ca • Web site provides a wide variety of Canadian news and information, including business and financial data. Includes "Money," "Your Investment," "Technology," and "Stock Quotes." Allows keyword searching, with links to many other sites. Daily updating. Fees: Free.

The Financial Post (Web site). National Post Online (Hollinger/CanWest). Phone: (244)383-2300 Fax: (416)383-2443 • URL: http://www.nationalpost.com/financialpost/ • Provides a broad range of Canadian business news online, with daily updates. Includes news, opinion, and special reports, as well as "Investing," "Money Rates," "Market Watch," and "Daily Mutual Funds." Allows advanced searching (Boolean operators), with links to various other sites. Fees: Free.

GLOBEnet: Canada's National Web Site. The Globe and Mail Co. Phone: 800-268-9128 or (416)585-5250 Fax: (416)585-5249 • URL: http://www.globeandmail.ca • Web site provides access to selected sections of *The Globe and Mail: Canada's National Newspaper*. Includes current news, national issues, career information, "Report on Business," and other topics. Keyword searching is offered for "a seven-day archive of the portion of the *Globe and Mail* that we publish online" (refers to the Web site). Daily updates. Fees: free.

Statistics Canada!. Statistics Canada. Phone: 800-267-6677 or (613)951-7277 Fax: 800-899-9734 or (613)951-1582 • URL: http://www.statcan.ca • Web site in English and French provides basic statistical information relating to economic and social conditions in Canada: "The Land," "The People," "The Economy," "The State." Includes daily news, latest indicators, products and services, and links to other sites. Keyword searching is provided. Fees: Free.

TAXNET. Carswell/Thomas Professional Publishing. Phone: 800-387-5164 or (416)609-3800 Fax: (416)298-5082 • URL: http://www.carswell.com/taxnet.htm • Fee-based Web site provides complete coverage of Canadian tax law and regulation, including income tax, provincial taxes, accounting, and payrolls. Daily updates. Base price varies according to product.

ONLINE DATABASES

Canada NewsWire. Canada NewsWire Ltd. • Provides the complete online text of currrent press releases from more than 5,000 Canadian companies, institutions, and government agencies, including stock exchanges and the Ontario Securities Commission. Emphasis is on mining, petroleum, technology, and pharmaceuticals. Time span is 1996 to date, with daily updates. Inquire as to online cost and availability.

Canadian Business and Current Affairs Fulltext. Micromedia Ltd. • Provides full-text of eight Canadian daily newspapers and more than 100 Canadian business magazines and trade journals. Indexing is 1982 to date, with selected full text from 1993. Updates are twice a month. Inquire as to online cost and availability.

Canadian Dun's Enhanced Market Identifiers. Dun & Bradstreet Canada. • Contains descriptive and sales information for more than 900,000 Canadian companies and branch offices. Quarterly updates. Inquire as to online cost and availability.

CanCorp Plus Canadian Financial Database. Micromedia Ltd. • Provides detailed information, including descriptive, marketing, personnel, and financial data, for more than 11,000 public and private Canadian corporations. Weekly updates. Inquire as to online cost and availability.

CANSIM Time Series Database. Statistics Canada, Statistical Reference Center. • CANSIM is the Canadian Socio-Economic Information Management System. Contains more than 700,000 statistical time series relating to Canadian business, industry, trade, economics, finance, labor, health, welfare, and demographics. Time period is mainly 1946 to date, with daily updating. Inquire as to online cost and availability.

Euromonitor Market Research. Euromonitor International. • Provides the complete text online of Euromonitor market analysis reports. Covers consumer goods market research data for all major countries, with emphasis on specific product categories. Time period is current. Continuous updating. Inquire as to online cost and availability.

The Globe and Mail Online. The Globe and Mail Co. • Contains full text of more than 1.1 million news stories and articles that have appeared daily in *The Globe and Mail: Canada's National Newspaper*, including "Report on Business." Time span is 1977 to date. Daily updates of the complete newspaper are provided. Inquire as to online cost and availability.

PERIODICALS AND NEWSLETTERS

Canada-U. S. Trade. Carswell. • Monthly. $185.00 per year. Newsletter on all current aspects of trade between the U. S. and Canada.

Canadian Business. Canadian Business Media. • 21 times a year. $34.70 per year. Edited for corporate managers and executives, this is a major periodical in Canada covering a variety of business, economic, and financial topics. Emphasis is on the top 500 Canadian corporations.

The Canadian Employer. Carswell. • Monthly. $185.00 per year. Newsletter. Provides current information on Canadian employment and labor laws.

The Canadian Taxpayer. Carswell. • Semimonthly. $330.00 per year. Newsletter. Covers tax trends and policies in Canada.

The Financial Post: Canadian's Business Voice. Financial Post Datagroup. • Daily. $234.00 per year. Provides Canadian business, economic, financial, and investment news. Features extensive price quotes from all major Canadian markets: stocks, bonds, mutual funds, commodities, and currencies. Supplement available: *Financial Post 500*. Includes annual supplement.

Globe and Mail Report on Business. Globe and Mail Publishing. • Monthly. Controlled circulation. Provides general coverage of business activity in Canada, with emphasis on the economy, foreign trade, technology, and personal finance.

Marketing Magazine. Maclean Hunter Business Publications. • Weekly. $60.00 per year. "Canada's national weekly publication dedicated to the businesses of marketing, advertising, and media." Includes annual Marketing Awards, quarterly Digital Marketing (emerging technology), Promo Marketing, and PR Quarterly (special issues on public relations).

RESEARCH CENTERS AND INSTITUTES

Canadian-American Center. University of Maine - Canada House, 154 College Ave., Orono, ME 04473. Phone: (207)581-4220 Fax: (207)581-4223 E-mail: hornsby@maine.edu • URL: http://www.ume.maine.edu/canam • Research areas include Canadian-American business, economics, and trade.

Canadian Studies Program. University of Vermont, 589 Main St., Burlington, VT 05401. Phone: (802)656-3062 Fax: (802)656-8518 E-mail: canada@zoo.uvm.edu • URL: http://www.uvm.edu/~canada • Research areas include Canadian corporate strategies, telecommunications, and natural resources.

Center for Canadian-American Studies. Western Washington University, Canada House, Room 201, Bellingham, WA 98225-9110. Phone: (360)650-3728 Fax: (360)650-3995 E-mail: canam@cc.edu • URL: http://www.wwu.edu/~canam • Research areas include Canadian business and economics.

Conference Board of Canada. 255 Smyth Rd., Ottawa, ON, Canada K1H 8M7. Phone: 800-267-0666 or (613)526-3280 Fax: (613)526-4857 • URL: http://www.conferenceboard.ca • Research areas include economics, finance, international business, and consumer buying intentions.

Statistics Canada. Ottawa, ON, Canada K1A OT6. Phone: 800-267-6677 or (613)951-7277 Fax: 800-899-9734 or (613)951-1582 • URL: http://www.statcan.ca • Issues compilations of census data and other facts relating to Canadian business, finance, industry, economics, and society in general. Statistics Canada is the country's national statistical agency, required to collect data according to the Statistics Act.

STATISTICS SOURCES

Canada Year Book. Statistics Canada, Operations and Integration Div., Circulation Management. • Annual. $66.00. Contains "sixteen chapters on the social, economic, demographic and cultural life of Canada," with more than 300 tables, charts and graphs.

Canadian Market Outlook. DRI Canck. • Quarterly. Price on application. Presents detailed forecasts of Canadian business and economic data.

Consumer Canada 1996. Available from The Gale Group. • 1996. $750.00. Published by Euromonitor. Provides consumer market, socioeconomic, and demographic data for Canada. Includes consumer market size (volume and value) for many specific kinds of products.

Consumer International 2000/2001. Available from The Gale Group. • 1998. $1,190.00. Seventh edition. Published by Euromonitor. Contains extensive consumer market, economic, and demographic data for 27 major, non-European countries, including the U. S. and Canada. Includes consumer market size (volume and value) for 150 product types in 14 categories (food, clothing, automobiles, cosmetics, appliances, etc.).

Financial Post Markets Canadian Demographics: Complete Demographics for Canadian Urban Markets. Financial Post Datagroup. • Annual. $145.00 Provides demographic and economic profiles of Canadian urban consumer regions with populations of 10,000 or more. Includes current data and projections for population, retail sales, personal income, and other market characteristics. CD-ROM available. Formerly *Canadian Markets*.

Handbook of North American Industry: NAFTA and the Economies of its Member Nations. John E. Cremeans, editor. Bernan Press. • 1999. $89.00. Second edition. Provides detailed industry statistics for the U.S., Canada, and Mexico.

International Marketing Forecasts 2001. Available from The Gale Group. • 2000. $1,090.00. Third edition. Published by Euromonitor. Contains demographic, economic, and market forecasts to the year 2010 for major, non-European countries, including the U. S. and Canada. Forecasts include market-size data for 15 consumer product sectors, such as food, clothing, and automobiles.

Market Research Handbook. Statistics Canada, Publications Div. • Annual. $132.00. Contains a wide variety of demographic and other data relevant to Canadian markets.

Provincial Outlook. Conference Board of Canada. • Quarterly. Free to members; non-members, $3,000.00 per year. Contains detailed forecasts of economic conditions in each of the Canadian provinces.

TRADE/PROFESSIONAL ASSOCIATIONS

Alliance of Manufacturers and Exporters of Canada. 5995 Azebury Rd., Ste. 900, Mississauga, ON, Canada L5R 3PQ. Phone: (905)568-8300 Fax: (905)568-8300 E-mail: national@the-alliance.com • URL: http://www.the-alliance.org.

Canada-United States Business Association. 600 Renaissance Center, Suite 1100, Detroit, MI 48243. Phone: (313)567-2208 Fax: (313)567-2164 • Promotes business and trade between the U. S. and Canada.

Canadian-American Business Council. 1629 K St., N. W., Suite 1100, Washington, DC 20006. Phone: (202)785-6717 Fax: (202)331-4212 E-mail: canambusco@aol.com • Promotes trade between Canada and the United States.

OTHER SOURCES

Bizlink. Rogers Media. • Web site provides news and information from 30 Canadian business and industrial publications issued by Rogers Media (formerly Maclean Hunter). Keyword searching is available for "all of the Bizlink archive" or for each of seven areas: Industry, Financial, Construction, Retailing, Marketing, Media, and Agriculture. Updates are daily. Fees: Free.

FP Corporate Connection. Available from Hoover's, Inc. • Annual. $675.00. CD-ROM from the Financial Post DataGroup provides detailed information on Canada's top 4,000 public and private companies. 16,000 executives are listed.

CANDY INDUSTRY

See also: CHOCOLATE INDUSTRY; COCOA INDUSTRY

ABSTRACTS AND INDEXES

Food Science and Technology Abstracts. International Food Information Service Publishing. • Monthly. $1,780.00 per year. Provides worldwide coverage of the literature of food technology and food production.

Foods Adlibra: Key to the World's Food Literature. Foods Adlibra Publications. • Semimonthly.Provides journal citations and abstracts to the literature of food technology and packaging.

CD-ROM DATABASES

Food Science and Technology Abstracts [CD-ROM]. Available from SilverPlatter Information, Inc. • Quarterly. $3,700 per year. Produced by International Food Information Service (home page is http://www.ifis.org). Provides worldwide coverage on CD-ROM of the literature of food technology and production. Various types of publications are indexed, with abstracts, including about 1,800 periodicals. Time period is 1969 to date.

DIRECTORIES

Candy Buyers' Directory. Manufacturing Confectioner Publishing Co. • Annual. $65.00. Lists confectionary and snack manufacturers by category and brand name. Includes *Directory of Candy Brokers.*

Candy Industry Buying Guide. Stagnito Publishing Co. • Annual. $25.00. List of approximately 600 suppliers of ingredients, equipment, services, and supplies to the candy industry.

Food Chemicals News Directory. Food Chemical News. CRC Press, Inc. • Semiannual. $497.00. Over 2,000 subsidiaries belonging to nearly 250 corporate parents plus an additional 3,000 independent processors. Formerly *Hereld's 1,500.*

FINANCIAL RATIOS

Annual Statement Studies. Robert Morris Associates: The Association of Lending and Credit Risk Professiona. • Annual. Free to members; non-members, $140.00. Median and quartile financial ratios are given for over 400 kinds of manufacturing, wholesale, retail, construction, and consumer finance establishments. Data is sorted by both asset size and sales volume. Includes a clearly written "Definition of Ratios" and an alphabetical industry index.

ONLINE DATABASES

F & S Index. The Gale Group. • Contains about four million citations to worldwide business, financial, and industrial or consumer product literature appearing from 1972 to date. Weekly updates. Inquire as to online cost and availability.

Food Science and Technology Abstracts [online]. IFIS North American Desk. • Produced by International Food Information Service. Provides about 500,000 online citations, with abstracts, to the international literature of food science, technology, commodities, engineering, and processing. Approximately 2,000 periodicals are covered. Time period is 1969 to date, with monthly updates. Inquire as to online cost and availability.

FOODS ADLIBRA. General Mills, Inc. • Contains online citations, with abstracts, to the technical and business literature of food processing and packaging. New products and new ingredients are featured. Covers about 250 trade journals and 500 research journals from 1974 to date, with monthly updates. Inquire as to online cost and availability.

PERIODICALS AND NEWSLETTERS

Candy Industry: The Global Magazine of Chocolate and Confectionary. Stagnito Publishing Co. • Monthly $39.00 per year.

Confectioner: Where Confectionery The Magazine. Stagnito Communcations, Inc. • Bimonthly. $30.00 per year. Covers a wide variety of topics relating to the distribution and retailing of candy and snacks.

Distribution Channels: The Magazine for Candy, Tobacco, Grocery and General Merchandise Distributors. American Wholesalers Marketers Association. • 10 times a year. $46.00 per year. Formerly *Candy Wholesaler.*

Fancy Food. Talcott Communications Corp. • Monthly. $34.00 per year. Emphasizes new specialty food products and the business management aspects of the specialty food and confection industries. Includes special issues on wine, cheese, candy, "upscale" cookware, and gifts.

Gourmet Retailer. Bill Communications, Business Communications Group. • Monthly. $24.00 per year. Covers upscale food and housewares, including confectionery items, bakery operations, and coffee.

Manufacturing Confectioner. Manufacturing Confectioner Publishing Co. • Monthly. $35.00 per year. Buying guide available *Purchasing Executives' Number.*

The Spotlight. Cordite Fidelity, Inc. • Weekly. $59.00 per year.

PRICE SOURCES

PPI Detailed Report. Bureau of Labor Statistics, U.S. Department of Labor. Available from U.S. Government Printing Office. • Monthly. $55.00 per year. Formerly *Producer Price Indexes.*

STATISTICS SOURCES

Annual Survey of Manufactures. Available from U. S. Government Printing Office. • Annual. Prices vary. Issued by the U. S. Census Bureau as an interim update to the *Census of Manufactures.* Includes data on number of manufacturing establishments in various industries, employment, labor costs, value of shipments, capital expenditures, inventories, energy costs, and assets. (See also Census Bureau home page, http://www.census.gov/.).

Manufacturing Profiles. Available from U. S. Government Printing Office. • Annual. Issued by the U. S. Census Bureau. A printed consolidation of the entire *Current Industrial Report* series, presenting "all the data compiled." Contains statistics on production, shipments, inventories, consumption, exports, imports, and orders for a wide variety of manufactured products. (See also Census Bureau home page, http://www.census.gov/.).

U. S. Industry and Trade Outlook: The McGraw-Hill Companies and the U.S. Department of Commerce/ International Trade Administration. Datapso Research Corp. • Annual. $69.95. Produced by the International Trade Administration, U. S. Department of Commerce, in a "public-private" partnership with DRI/McGraw-Hill and Standard & Poor's. Provides basic data, outlook for the current year, and "Long-Term Prospects" (five-year projections) for a wide variety of products and services. Includes high technology industries. Formerly *U. S. Industrial Outlook.*

United States Census of Manufactures. U.S. Bureau of the Census. • Quinquennial. Results presented in reports, tape, CD-ROM, and Diskette files.

TRADE/PROFESSIONAL ASSOCIATIONS

American Wholesale Marketers Association. 1128 16th St., Washington, DC 20036. Phone: 800-482-2962 or (202)463-2124 Fax: (202)463-6456 E-mail: davids@awmanet.org • URL: http://www.awmanet.org.

Bakery, Confectionery and Tobacco Workers International Union. 10401 Connecticut Ave., Room 400, Kensington, MD 20895. Phone: (301)933-8600 Fax: (301)946-8452.

National Candy Brokers Association. 710 East Ogden Ave., Suite 600, Naperville, IL 60563-8603. Phone: (630)369-2406 Fax: (630)369-2488 E-mail: ncba@b-online.com • URL: http://www.candynet.com • Members are manufacturers' and importers' brokers specializing in the marketing of candy and related products.

National Confectioners Association of the U.S. 7900 Westpark Dr., Suite A-320, McLean, VA 22102. Phone: (703)790-5750 Fax: (703)790-5752 E-mail: smith@candyusa.org • URL: http://www.candyusa.org.

National Confectionery Sales Association. 10225 Berea Rd., Suite B, Cleveland, OH 44102. Phone: (216)631-8200 Fax: (216)631-8210 • URL: http://www.candyhlloffame.com.

Retail Confectioners International. 1807 Glenview Rd., Glenview, IL 60025. Phone: 800-545-5381 or (847)724-6120 Fax: (847)724-2719 E-mail: rciinfo@retconint.org • URL: http://www.retconint.org.

OTHER SOURCES

The Candy Dish. National Candy Brokers Association. • Quarterly. Apply. Provides industry news and event information for candy brokers and distributors.

The Candy Market. Available from MarketResearch.com. • 1998. $2,500.00. Published by Packaged Facts. Provides market data on chocolate and non-chocolate candy, with sales projections to 2002.

Major Food and Drink Companies of the World. Available from The Gale Group. • 2001. $855.00. Fourth edition. Two volumes. Published by Graham & Whiteside. Contains profiles and trade names for more than 9,000 important food and beverage companies in various countries. In addition to foods, includes both alcoholic and nonalcoholic drink products.

NCBA Membership Roster. National Candy Brokers Association. • Annual. $25.00. Lists broker, manufacturer, and distributor members of the National Candy Brokers Association.

Thomas Food and Beverage Market Place. Grey House Publishing. • Annual. $295.00. Three volumes. Contains more than 40,000 entries covering food companies, beverages, food equipment, warehouse companies, food brokers, wholesalers, importers, and exporters. Formerly *Thomas Food Industry Register.*

CANNED BEVERAGES

See: BEVERAGE INDUSTRY

CANNED FOOD INDUSTRY

See also: FISH INDUSTRY; FOOD INDUSTRY; FROZEN FOOD INDUSTRY

ABSTRACTS AND INDEXES

Food Science and Technology Abstracts. International Food Information Service Publishing. • Monthly. $1,780.00 per year. Provides worldwide coverage of the literature of food technology and food production.

Foods Adlibra: Key to the World's Food Literature. Foods Adlibra Publications. • Semimonthly.Provides journal citations and abstracts to the literature of food technology and packaging.

ALMANACS AND YEARBOOKS

Almanac of the Canning, Freezing, Preserving Industries, Vol. Two. Edward E. Judge and Sons, Inc. • Annual. $71.00. Contains U. S. food laws and regulations and detailed production statistics.

CD-ROM DATABASES

Food Science and Technology Abstracts [CD-ROM]. Available from SilverPlatter Information, Inc. • Quarterly. $3,700 per year. Produced by International Food Information Service (home page is http://www.ifis.org). Provides worldwide coverage on CD-ROM of the literature of food technology and production. Various types of publications are indexed, with abstracts, including about 1,800 periodicals. Time period is 1969 to date.

DIRECTORIES

Directory of the Canning, Freezing, Preserving Industries. Edward E. Judge and Sons, Inc. • Biennial. $175.00. Provides information on about 2,950 packers of a wide variety of food products.

Prepared Foods Food Industry Sourcebook. Cahners Business Information. • Annual. $35.00. Provides information on more than 3,000 manufacturers and suppliers of products, ingredients, supplies, and equipment for the food processing industry.

World Food Marketing Directory. Available from The Gale Group. • 2001. $1,090.00. Second edition. Three volumes. Published by Euromonitor. Provides detailed information on the major food companies of the world, including specific brand data.

ENCYCLOPEDIAS AND DICTIONARIES

Encyclopedia of Food Science, Food Technology, and Nutrition. Robert Macrae and others, editors. Academic Press, Inc. • 1993. Eight volumes. $2,414.00.

INTERNET DATABASES

USDA. United States Department of Agriculture. Phone: (202)720-2791 E-mail: agsec@usda.gov • URL: http://www.usda.gov • The USDA home page has six sections: News and Information; What's New; About USDA; Agencies; Opportunities; Search and Help. Keyword searching is offered from the USDA home page and from various individual agency home pages. Agencies are the Economic Research Service, Agricultural Marketing Service, National Agricultural Statistics Service, National Agricultural Library, and about 12 others. Updating varies. Fees: Free.

ONLINE DATABASES

F & S Index. The Gale Group. • Contains about four million citations to worldwide business, financial, and industrial or consumer product literature appearing from 1972 to date. Weekly updates. Inquire as to online cost and availability.

Food Science and Technology Abstracts [online]. IFIS North American Desk. • Produced by International Food Information Service. Provides about 500,000 online citations, with abstracts, to the international literature of food science, technology, commodities, engineering, and processing. Approximately 2,000 periodicals are covered. Time period is 1969 to date, with monthly updates. Inquire as to online cost and availability.

FOODS ADLIBRA. General Mills, Inc. • Contains online citations, with abstracts, to the technical and business literature of food processing and packaging. New products and new ingredients are featured. Covers about 250 trade journals and 500 research journals from 1974 to date, with monthly updates. Inquire as to online cost and availability.

PERIODICALS AND NEWSLETTERS

Food Production/Management: Monthly Publication of the Canning, Glass-Packing Aseptic, and Frozen Food Industry. Arthur Judge, editor. CTI Publications, Inc. • Monthly. $35.00 per year.

Prepared Foods. Cahners Business Information. • Monthly. $99.90 per year. Edited for food manufacturing management, marketing, and operations personnel.

PRICE SOURCES

Supermarket News: The Industry's Weekly Newspaper. Fairchild Publications. • Weekly. Individuals, $68.00 per year; instututions, $44.50 per year; corporations, $89.00 per year.

STATISTICS SOURCES

Agricultural Statistics. Available from U. S. Government Printing Office. • Annual. Produced by the National Agricultural Statistics Service, U. S. Department of Agriculture. Provides a wide variety of statistical data relating to agricultural production, supplies, consumption, prices/price-supports, foreign trade, costs, and returns, as well as farm labor, loans, income, and population. In many cases, historical data is shown annually for 10 years. In addition to farm data, includes detailed fishery statistics.

Annual Survey of Manufactures. Available from U. S. Government Printing Office. • Annual. Prices vary. Issued by the U. S. Census Bureau as an interim update to the *Census of Manufactures.* Includes data on number of manufacturing establishments in various industries, employment, labor costs, value of shipments, capital expenditures, inventories, energy costs, and assets. (See also Census Bureau home page, http://www.census.gov/.).

United States Census of Manufactures. U.S. Bureau of the Census. • Quinquennial. Results presented in reports, tape, CD-ROM, and Diskette files.

TRADE/PROFESSIONAL ASSOCIATIONS

Food Processing Machinery and Supplies Association. 200 Daingerfield Rd., Alexandria, VA 22314-2800. Phone: 800-331-8816 or (703)684-1080 Fax: (703)548-6563 E-mail: info@fpmsa.org • URL: http://www.fpmsa.org.

National Food Processors Association. 1301 Eye St., N.W., Ste. 300, Washington, DC 20005. Phone: (202)639-5900 Fax: (202)639-5932 E-mail: nfpa@nfpa-food.org • URL: http://www.nfpa-food.org.

National Meat Canners Association. 1700 N. Moore St., Suite 1600, Arlington, VA 22209. Phone: (703)841-3680 Fax: (703)527-0938 E-mail: ami@intercamp.com • URL: http://www.meatami.com.

OTHER SOURCES

Major Food and Drink Companies of the World. Available from The Gale Group. • 2001. $855.00. Fourth edition. Two volumes. Published by Graham & Whiteside. Contains profiles and trade names for more than 9,000 important food and beverage companies in various countries. In addition to foods, includes both alcoholic and nonalcoholic drink products.

Thomas Food and Beverage Market Place. Grey House Publishing. • Annual. $295.00. Three volumes. Contains more than 40,000 entries covering food companies, beverages, food equipment, warehouse companies, food brokers, wholesalers, importers, and exporters. Formerly *Thomas Food Industry Register.*

CANVASSING

See: DIRECT MARKETING

CAPITAL EQUIPMENT

See: INDUSTRIAL EQUIPMENT INDUSTRY

CAPITAL GAINS TAX

See also: TAXATION

ABSTRACTS AND INDEXES

Accounting and Tax Index. UMI. • Quarterly. Price on application. Includes annual cumulative bound volume. Indexes accounting, auditing, and taxation literature appearing in journals, books, pamphlets, conference proceedings, and newsletters. (UMI is University Microfilms International, a Bell & Howell Co.).

INTERNET DATABASES

The Digital Daily. Internal Revenue Service. Phone: (202)622-5000 Fax: (202)622-5844 • URL: http://www.irs.ustreas.gov • Web site provides a wide variety of tax information, including IRS forms and publications. Includes "Highlights of New Tax Law." Searching is available. Fees: Free.

ONLINE DATABASES

Accounting and Tax Database. Bell & Howell Information and Learning. • Provides indexing and abstracting of the literature of accounting, taxation, and financial management, 1971 to date. Updating is weekly. Especially covers accounting, auditing, banking, bankruptcy, employee compensation and benefits, cash management, financial planning, and credit. Inquire as to online cost and availability.

EconLit. American Economic Association. • Covers the worldwide literature of economics as contained in selected monographs and about 550 journals.

Subjects include microeconomics, macroeconomics, economic history, inflation, money, credit, finance, accounting theory, trade, natural resource economics, and regional economics. Time period is 1969 to present, with monthly updates. Inquire as to online cost and availability.

PERIODICALS AND NEWSLETTERS

National Tax Journal. National Tax Association - Tax Institute of America. • Quarterly. Members, $85.00 per year; membership libraries, $100.00 per year; membership corporations, $130.00 per year. Topics of current interest in the field of taxation and public finance in the U.S. and foreign countries.

RESEARCH CENTERS AND INSTITUTES

Institute for Tax Administration. Academy for International Training. 900 Wilshire Blvd., Suite 624, Los Angeles, CA 90017. Phone: (213)623-1103 Fax: (213)623-7012.

International Tax Program. Harvard University, Pound Hall, Room 400, Cambridge, MA 02138. Phone: (617)495-4406 Fax: (617)495-0423 • URL: http://www.law.harvard.edu/programs/itp • Studies the worldwide problems of taxation, including tax law and tax administration.

STATISTICS SOURCES

Statistics of Income Bulletin. Available from U.S. Government Printing Office. • Quarterly. $35.00 per year. Current data compiled from tax returns relating to income, assets, and expenses of individuals and businesses. (U. S. Internal Revenue Service.).

TRADE/PROFESSIONAL ASSOCIATIONS

Citizens for a Sound Economy. 1250 H St., N.W., Suite 700, Washington, DC 20005-3908. Phone: 888-564-6273 or (202)783-3870 Fax: (202)783-4687 E-mail: cse@cse.org • URL: http://www.cse.org.

Federation of Tax Administrators. 444 N. Capitol St., Suite 348, Washington, DC 20001. Phone: (202)624-5890 Fax: (202)624-7888 • URL: http://www.taxadmin.org.

Tax Executives Institute. 1200 G St., N.W., No. 300, Washington, DC 20005-3814. Phone: (202)638-5601 Fax: (202)638-5607 E-mail: askter@tei.org • URL: http://www.tei.org.

OTHER SOURCES

Taxation of Securities Transactions. Matthew Bender & Co., Inc. • $260.00. Looseleaf service.Periodic supplementation. Covers taxation of a wide variety of securities transactions, including those involving stocks, bonds, options, short sales, new issues, mutual funds, dividend distributions, foreign securities, and annuities.

CAPITAL, VENTURE

See: VENTURE CAPITAL

CAR PHONES

See: MOBILE TELEPHONE INDUSTRY

CARBONATED BEVERAGES

See: BEVERAGE INDUSTRY

CARDS, GREETING

See: GREETING CARD INDUSTRY

CAREER PLANNING

See: VOCATIONAL GUIDANCE

CAREERS

See: JOB HUNTING; OCCUPATIONS

CARIBBEAN AREA

See: LATIN AMERICAN MARKETS

CARPENTRY

See also: HOME IMPROVEMENT INDUSTRY; WOODWORKING INDUSTRIES

GENERAL WORKS

Carpentry and Building Construction. John Feirer and Gilbert Hutchings. Glencoe/McGraw-Hill. • 1999. $53.25. Fifth edition.

Modern Carpentry: Building Construction Details in Easy-To-Understand Form. Willis H. Wagner and Howard S. Smith. Goodheart-Willcox Publishers. • 2000. $49.28.

BIBLIOGRAPHIES

Carpenters and Builders Library. John E. Ball. Pearson Education and Technology. • 1991. Four volumes. $21.95 per volume. Sixth edition.

DIRECTORIES

Wood Digest Showcase. Cygnus Publishing, Inc., Johnson Hill Press, Inc. • Annual. Controlled circulation. Formerly *Furniture Wood/Digest-Showcase.*

ENCYCLOPEDIAS AND DICTIONARIES

Illustrated Dictionary of Building Materials and Techniques: An Invaluable Sourcebook to the Tools, Terms, Materials, and Techniques Used by Building Professionals. Paul Bianchina. John Wiley and Sons, Inc. • 1993. $49.95. Contains 4,000 definitions of building and building materials terms, with 500 illustrations. Includes materials grades, measurements, and specifications.

FINANCIAL RATIOS

Annual Statement Studies. Robert Morris Associates: The Association of Lending and Credit Risk Professiona. • Annual. Free to members; non-members, $140.00. Median and quartile financial ratios are given for over 400 kinds of manufacturing, wholesale, retail, construction, and consumer finance establishments. Data is sorted by both asset size and sales volume. Includes a clearly written "Definition of Ratios" and an alphabetical industry index.

ONLINE DATABASES

Magazine Index. The Gale Group. • General magazine indexing (popular literature), 1973 to present. Daily updates. Inquire as to online cost and availability.

PERIODICALS AND NEWSLETTERS

The Carpenter. United Brotherhood of Carpenters and Joiners of America. • Bimonthly. Free to members; non-members, $10.00 per year.

TRADE/PROFESSIONAL ASSOCIATIONS

International Association of Machinists and Aerospace Workers. 9000 Machinists Place, Upper Marlboro, MD 20772-2687. Phone: (301)967-4500 Fax: (301)967-4595 • URL: http://www.iamaw.org/.

United Brotherhood of Carpenters and Joiners of America. 101 Constitution Ave., N.W., Washington, DC 20001. Phone: (202)546-6206 Fax: (202)543-5724.

CARPET CLEANING INDUSTRY

See: CLEANING INDUSTRY

CARPET INDUSTRY

See: FLOOR COVERINGS; ORIENTAL RUG INDUSTRY

CARRIERS

See: AUTOMOBILES; FREIGHT TRANSPORT

CARTOGRAPHY

See: MAPS

CARWASH INDUSTRY

ONLINE DATABASES

Trade & Industry Index. The Gale Group. • Provides indexing of business periodicals, January 1981 to date. Daily updates. (Full text articles from some periodicals are available online, 1983 to date, in the companion database, *Trade & Industry ASAP.*) Inquire as to online cost and availability.

PERIODICALS AND NEWSLETTERS

American Clean Car. Crain Communications, Inc. • Bimonthly. $35.00 per year. Provides articles on new products and management for the carwash industry.

Auto Laundry News: The Voice of the Car Care Industry. E.W. Williams Publications Co. • Monthly. $48.00 per year. Covers management, technical information, trends, and marketing for the vehicle cleaning industry. Edited for owners, operators, managers, and investors.

Professional Carwashing and Detailing. National Trade Publications, Inc. • Monthly. $49.00 per year. Edited for owners, operators, and managers of automatic carwashes, custom hand carwash facilities, detail shops, and coin-operated, self-service carwashes.

TRADE/PROFESSIONAL ASSOCIATIONS

Car Wash Owners and Suppliers Association. 1822 South St., Racine, WI 53404. Phone: (414)639-4393.

CASE STUDIES

GENERAL WORKS

Case Studies in Business Ethics. Thomas Donaldson and Al Gini, editors. Prentice-Hall. • 1995. $36.20. Fourth edition.

Case Studies in Business, Society, and Ethics. Thomas L. Beauchamp, editor. Prentice Hall. • 1997. $31.80. Fourth edition.

Case Studies in Finance: Managing for Corporate Value Creation. Robert Bruner. McGraw-Hill Professional. • 1998. Third edition. Price on application.

Case Studies in Financial Decision Making. Diana R. Harrington and Kenneth M. Eades. Dryden Press. • 1993. $63.50. Third edition.

Cases in Advertising Communication Management. Stephen A. Greyser. Prentice Hall. • 1991. $30.00. Third edition.

Cases in Corporate Acquisitions, Buyouts, Mergers, and Takeovers. The Gale Group. • 1999. $310.00. Reviews and analyzes about 300 cases of both success and failure in corporate acquisitiveness.

Cases in Corporate Innovation. The Gale Group. • 1999. $295.00. Reviews and analyzes about 300 cases to illustrate both successful and failed management of innovation.

Cases in Financial Mangement: Directed Versions. Eugene Brigham and Louis Gapenski. Dryden Press. • 1993. $32.00.

Cases in Financial Statement Reporting and Analysis. Leopold A. Bernstein and Mostafa M. Maksy. McGraw-Hill Higher Education. • 1985. $36.95. Second edition.

Cases in International Finance. Gunter Duffey. Addison-Wesley Longman, Inc. • 2001. Price on application.

Cases in Marketing Management. Kenneth L. Bernhardt and Thomas C. Kinnear. McGraw-Hill Higher Education. • 1997. Ninth edition. Price on application.

Cases in Portfolio Management. John A. Quelch. McGraw-Hill Higher Education. • 1994. $52.99.

Cases in Strategic Management. A.J. Strickland. McGraw-Hill. • 2000. $41.25. 12th edition.

Cases in Strategic Marketing: An Integrated Approach. William J. McDonald. Pearson Education and Technology. • 1997. $53.00. Second edition.

Cases in Total Quality Management. Jay H. Heizer. Course Technology, Inc. • 1997. $45.95. (GC Principles in Management Series.).

Corporate Social Challenge: Cases and Commentaries. James E. Stacey and Frederick D. Sturdivant, editors. McGraw-Hill Professional. • 1994. $41.95. Fifth edition.

Dirty Business: Exploring Corporate Misconduct: Analysis and Cases. Maurice Punch. Sage Publications, Inc. • 1996. $79.95. Covers organizational misbehavior and white-collar crime. Includes "Ten Cases of Corporate Deviance.".

Managing Quality in America's Most Admired Companies. Jay W. Spechler. Engineering and Management Press. • 1993. $49.95. Part one provides "Guidelines for Implementing Quality Management," including detailed information on the Malcolm Baldridge National Quality Award. Part two contains 30 "Case Studies of Quality Management in Leading Companies.".

Marketing Management: Text and Cases. Douglas J. Dalrymple and Leonard J. Parsons. John Wiley and Sons, Inc. • 1994. $92.95. Sixth edition.

PR News Casebook. The Gale Group. • 1993. $99.00. A collection of about 1,000 case studies covering major public relations campaigns and events, taken from the pages of *PR News.* Covers such issues as boycotts, new products, anniversaries, plant closings, downsizing, and stockholder relations.

Project Management Casebook. David I. Cleland and others, editors. Project Management Institute. • 1998. $69.95. Provides 50 case studies in various areas of project management.

Public Relations Practices: Managerial Case Studies and Problems. Allen H. Center. Prentice Hall. • 2000. $46.67. Sixth edition.

Strategic Marketing Problems: Cases and Comments. Roger A. Kerin and Robert A. Peterson. Prentice Hall. • 2000. $91.33. Ninth edition.

CASH FLOW AND CASH MANAGEMENT

GENERAL WORKS

Accounting and Finance for Non-Specialists. Peter Atrill and Eddie McLaney. Prentice Hall. • 2000. Third edition. Price on application. Includes the measurement and reporting of financial performance and cash flow.

Operational Cash Flow Management and Control. Morris A. Nunes. Prentice Hall. • 1982. $34.95.

ABSTRACTS AND INDEXES

Accounting and Tax Index. UMI. • Quarterly. Price on application. Includes annual cumulative bound volume. Indexes accounting, auditing, and taxation literature appearing in journals, books, pamphlets, conference proceedings, and newsletters. (UMI is University Microfilms International, a Bell & Howell Co.).

DIRECTORIES

TMA Membership Directory. Treasury Management Association. • Annual. Membership. Formerly *NCCMA Membership Directory.*

ENCYCLOPEDIAS AND DICTIONARIES

Blackwell Encyclopedic Dictionary of Accounting. Rashad Abdel-khalik. Blackwell Publishers. • 1997. $105.95. The editor is associated with the University of Florida. Contains definitions of key terms combined with longer articles written by various U. S. and foreign business educators. Includes bibliographies and index. (Blackwell Encyclopedia of Management Series).

HANDBOOKS AND MANUALS

Analysis and Use of Financial Statements. Gerald I. White and others. John Wiley and Sons, Inc. • 1997. $112.95. Second edition. Includes analysis of financial ratios, cash flow, inventories, assets, debt, etc. Also covered are employee benefits, corporate investments, multinational operations, financial derivatives, and hedging activities.

Corporate Liquidity: Management and Measurement. Kenneth L. Parkinson and Jarl G. Kallberg. McGraw-Hill Higher Education. • 1992. $67.95. Topics include cash management and risk.

Cost Management Handbook. Barry J. Brinker. John Wiley and Sons, Inc. • 2000. $140.00.

Essentials of Cash Management. Peter S. Adam and Wiliam Harrison, editors. Treasury Management Association. • 1998. $95.50. Sixth edition.

How to Manage Corporate Cash Effectively. Joseph E. Finnerty. AMACOM. • 1991. $59.95. A practical approach to cash flow problems.

Small Business Survival Guide: How to Manage Your Cash, Profits and Taxes. Robert E. Fleury. Sourcebooks, Inc. • 1995. $17.95. Third revised edition.

Ultimate Guide to Raising Money for Growing Companies. Michael C. Thomsett. McGraw-Hill Professional. • 1990. $45.00. Discusses the preparation of a practical business plan, how to manage cash flow, and debt vs. equity decisions.

ONLINE DATABASES

Accounting and Tax Database. Bell & Howell Information and Learning. • Provides indexing and abstracting of the literature of accounting, taxation, and financial management, 1971 to date. Updating is weekly. Especially covers accounting, auditing, banking, bankruptcy, employee compensation and benefits, cash management, financial planning, and credit. Inquire as to online cost and availability.

PERIODICALS AND NEWSLETTERS

Corporate Cashflow: The Magazine of Treasury Management. Intertec Publishing Corp. • Monthly. $78.00 per year. Published for chief financial officers of corporations. Includes annual *Directory.*

Cost Control Strategies for Managers, Controllers and Finance Executives. Siefer Consultants, Inc. • Monthly. $259.00 per year. Newsletter. Provides a variety of ideas on business budgeting and controlling company expenses. Formerly *Cost Control Strategies for Financial Institutions.*

Strategic Finance. Institute of Management Accountants. • Monthly. $140.00 per year; non-profit institutions, $70.00 per year. Provides articles on corporate finance, cost control, cash flow, budgeting, corporate taxes, and other financial management topics.

TMA News. Treasury Management Association. • Monthly. Membership.

TRADE/PROFESSIONAL ASSOCIATIONS

Association for Financial Professionals. 7315 Wisconsin Ave., Suite 600-W, Bethesda, MD 20814-3211. Phone: (301)907-2862 Fax: (301)907-2864 E-mail: afp@afponline.org • URL: http://www.afponline.org • Members are corporate treasurers and other managers of business finance. Formerly Treasury Management Association.

Independent Cash Register Dealers Association. 1900 CrossBeam Dr., Charlotte, NC 28217. Phone: (704)357-3124 Fax: (704)357-3127 E-mail: info@icrda.org • URL: http://www.icrda.org.

OTHER SOURCES

How to Manage Corporate Cash. American Management Association Extension Institute. • Looseleaf. $110.00. Self-study course. Emphasis is on practical explanations, examples, and problem solving. Quizzes and a case study are included.

Managing Credit and Collections to Improve Cash Flow. American Management Association Extension Institute. • Looseleaf. $130.00. Self-study course. Emphasis is on practical explanations, examples, and problem solving. Quizzes and a case study are included.

Planning Cash Flow. American Management Association Extension Institute. • Looseleaf. $110.00. Self-study course. Emphasis is on practical explanations, examples, and problem solving. Quizzes and a case study are included.

CASINOS

See: GAMBLING INDUSTRY

CASKS

See: COOPERAGE INDUSTRY

CASSETTE RECORDING

See: SOUND RECORDERS AND RECORDING; VIDEO RECORDING INDUSTRY

CASTING

See: FOUNDRIES

CASTOR BEAN INDUSTRY

See: OIL AND FATS INDUSTRY

CASUALTY INSURANCE

See also: ACCIDENT INSURANCE; INSURANCE

ABSTRACTS AND INDEXES

Insurance Periodicals Index. Specials Libraries Association, Insurance and Employees Benefits Div. CCH/NILS Publishing Co. • Annual. $250.00. Compiled by the Insurance and Employee Benefits Div., Special Libraries Association. A yearly index of over 15,000 articles from about 35 insurance periodicals. Arrangement is by subject, with an index to authors.

ALMANACS AND YEARBOOKS

Casualty Actuarial Society Yearbook. Casualty Actuarial Society. • Annual. $40.00. Approximately

2,500 actuaries working in insurance other than life insurance.

Insurance Law Review. Pat Magarick. West Group. • 1990. $125.00. Provides review of legal topics within the casualty insurance area, including professional liability, product liability, and environmental issues.

Property and Casualty Insurance: Year in Review. CCH, Inc. • Annual. $75.00. Summarizes the year's significant legal and regulatory developments.

CD-ROM DATABASES

U. S. Insurance: Property and Casualty. Sheshunoff Information Services, Inc. • Monthly. Price on application. CD-ROM provides detailed, current financial information on more than 3,200 property and casualty insurance companies.

DIRECTORIES

S & P's Insurance Book. Standard & Poor's Ratings Group, Insurance Rating Services. • Quarterly. Price on application. Contains detailed financial analyses and ratings of various kinds of insurance companies.

S & P's Insurance Digest: Property-Casualty and Reinsurance Edition. Standard & Poor's Ratings Group, Insurance Rating Services. • Quarterly. Contains concise financial analyses and ratings of property-casualty insurance companies.

ENCYCLOPEDIAS AND DICTIONARIES

Dictionary of Insurance. Lewis E. Davids. Rowman and Littlefield Publishers, Inc. • 1990. $17.95. Seventh revised edition.

Dictionary of Insurance Terms. Harvey W. Rubin. Barron's Educational Series, Inc. • 2000. $12.95. Fourth edition. Defines terms in a wide variety of insurance fields. Price on application.

Insurance Words and Their Meanings: A Dictionary of Insurance Terms. Diana Kowatch. The Rough Notes Co., Inc. • 1998. $38.50. 16th revised edition.

Rupp's Insurance and Risk Management Glossary. Richard V. Rupp. Available from CCH, Inc. • 1996. $35.00. Second edition. Published by NILS Publishing Co. Provides definitions of 6,400 insurance words and phrases. Includes a guide to acronyms and abbreviations.

ONLINE DATABASES

Best's Company Reports. A. M. Best Co. • Provides full financial data online for U. S. insurance companies (life, health, property, casualty), including balance sheet data, income statements, expenses, premium income, losses, and investments. Includes *Best's Company Reports*, *Best's Insurance News*, and Best's ratings of insuarance companies. Inquire as to online cost and availability.

I.I.I. Data Base Search. Insurance Information Institute. • Provides online citations and abstracts of insurance-related literature in magazines, newspapers, trade journals, and books. Emphasis is on property and casualty insurance issues, including highway safety, product safety, and environmental liability. Inquire as to online cost and availability.

PERIODICALS AND NEWSLETTERS

Best's Review: Inurance Issues and Analysis. A.M. Best Co. • Monthly. $25.00 per year. Editorial coverage of significant industry trends, developments, and important events. Formerly Best's Review: Property-Casualty Insurance.

Business Insurance: News Magazine for Corporate Risk, Employee Benefit and Financial Executives. Crain Communications, Inc. • Weekly. $89.00 per year. Covers a wide variety of business insurance topics, including risk management, employee benefits, workers compensation, marine insurance, and casualty insurance.

CPCU Journal. Chartered Property and Casualty Underwriters Society. • Quarterly. $25.00 per year. Published by the Chartered Property and Casualty Underwriters Society (CPCU). Edited for professional insurance underwriters and agents.

Fire, Casualty and Surety Bulletin. The National Underwriter Co. • Monthly. $420.00 per year. Five base volumes. Monthly updates.

Guide to Property and Casualty Insurers: A Quarterly Compilation of Insurance Company Ratings and Analysis. Weiss Ratings, Inc. • Quarterly. $438.00 per year. Emphasis is on rating of financial safety and relative risk. Includes annual summary.

Insurance and Technology. Miller Freeman. • Monthly. $65.00 per year. Covers information technology and systems management as applied to the operation of life, health, casualty, and property insurance companies.

Journal of Risk and Insurance. American Risk and Insurance Association. • Quarterly. $90.00 per year.

National Underwriter, Property and Casualty Edition. The National Underwriter Co. • Weekly. $88.00 per year.

Professional Agent. National Association of Professional Insurance Agents. • Monthly. Members, $12,00 per year; non-members, $24.00 per year. Provides sales and marketing advice for independent agents in various fields of insurance, including life, health, property, and casualty.

Risk Management. Risk and Insurance Management Society. Risk Management Society Publishing, Inc. • Monthly. $54.00 per year.

RESEARCH CENTERS AND INSTITUTES

S. S. Huebner Foundation. University of Pennsylvania, Vance Hall, Room 430, Philadelphia, PA 19104-6301. Phone: (215)898-9631 Fax: (215)573-2218 E-mail: cummins@wharton.upenn.edu • URL: http://www.rider.wharton.upenn.edu/~sshuebne/ • Awards grants for research in various areas of insurance.

STATISTICS SOURCES

Best's Aggregates and Averages: Property-Casualty. A.M. Best Co. • Annual. $335.00. Statistical summary of composite property casualty business. 400 pages of historical data, underwriting expenses and underwriting experience by line.

Property-Casualty Insurance Facts. Insurance Information Institute. • Annual. $22.50. Formerly *Insurance Facts.*

Standard & Poor's Industry Surveys. Standard & Poor's. • Semiannual. $1,800.00. Two looseleaf volumes. Includes monthly supplements. Provides detailed, individual surveys of 52 major industry groups. Each survey is revised on a semiannual basis. Also includes "Monthly Investment Review" (industry group investment analysis) and monthly "Trends & Projections" (economic analysis).

TRADE/PROFESSIONAL ASSOCIATIONS

American Insurance Association. 1130 Connecticut Ave., N.W., Suite 1000, Washington, DC 20036. Phone: 800-242-2302 or (202)828-7100 or (202)828-7183 Fax: (202)293-1219.

Casualty Actuarial Society. 1100 N. Glebe Rd., Suite 600, Arlington, VA 22201. Phone: (703)276-3100 Fax: (703)276-3108 E-mail: office@casact.org • URL: http://www.casact.org.

Conference of Casualty Insurance Companies. P.O. Box 68700, Indianapolis, IN 46268. Phone: (317)875-5250 Fax: (317)879-8408 • URL: http://www.namic.org.

Council of Insurance Agents and Brokers. 701 Pennsylvania Ave., N.W., Suite 750, Washington, DC 20004-2608. Phone: (202)783-4400 Fax: (202)783-4410 E-mail: ciab@ciab.com • URL: http://www.ciab.com.

CPCU Society. 720 Providence Rd., Malvern, PA 19355-0709. Phone: 800-932-2728 E-mail: cpcu@ansiweb.com • URL: http://www.cpcusociety.org.

National Association of Professional Insurance Agents. 400 N. Washington St., Alexandria, VA 22314. Phone: (703)836-9340 Fax: (703)836-1279 E-mail: piaweb@pianet.org • URL: http://www.pianet.com • Members are independent agents in various fields of insurance.

OTHER SOURCES

Best's Insurance Reports: Property-Casualty. A.M. Best Co. • Annual. $745.00. Guide to over 1,750 major property/casualty companies.

BestWeek: Property-Casualty. A.M. Best Co. • Weekly. $495.00 per year. Newsletter. Focuses on key areas of the insurance industry. Formerly *Best's Insurance Management Reports: Property-Casualty.*

Casualty Insurance Claims: Coverage-Investigation-Law. Pat Magarick. West Group. • Two looseleaf volumes. $215.00. Annual supplementation.

Fire and Casualty Insurance Law Reports. CCH, Inc. • $870.00 per year. Looseleaf service. Semimonthly updates.

Insurance Day. Available from Informa Publishing Group Ltd. • Three times a week. $440.00 per year. Published in the UK by Lloyd's List (http://www.lloydslist.com). A newspaper providing international coverage of property/casualty/liability insurance, reinsurance, and risk, with an emphasis on marine insurance.

CATALOGS AND DIRECTORIES

See also: ASSOCIATIONS; BOOK CATALOGS

BIBLIOGRAPHIES

Books in Print. R. R. Bowker. • Annual. $595.00. Nine volumes. Annual supplement, $250.00 (three volumes).

Guide to Special Issues and Indexes of Periodicals. Miriam Uhlan and Doris B. Katz, editors. Special Libraries Association. • 1994. $59.00. Fourth edition. A listing, with prices, of the special issues of over 1700 U. S. and Canadian periodicals in business, industry, technology, science, and the arts. Includes a comprehensive subject index.

Serials for Libraries; An Annotated Guide to Continuations, Annuals, Yearbooks, Almanacs, Transactions, Proceedings, Directories, Services. Diane Sciattara. Neal-Schuman Publishers, Inc. • 1985. $85.00. Second edition.

CD-ROM DATABASES

MediaFinder CD-ROM: Oxbridge Directories of Print Media and Catalogs. Oxbridge Communications, Inc. • Quarterly. $1,695.00 per year. CD-ROM includes about 100,000 listings from *Standard Periodical Directory, National Directory of Catalogs, National Directory of British Mail Order Catalogs, National Directory of German Mail Order Catalogs, Oxbridge Directory of Newsletters, National Directory of Mailing Lists, College Media Directory*, and *National Directory of Magazines.*

DIRECTORIES

Catalog Age/Direct Sourcebook. Intertec Publishing Co. • Annual. $35.00. Lists of approximately 300 suppliers of products and services for direct marketing, especially catalog marketing.

Catalog of Catalogs: The Complete Mail-Order Directory. Edward L. Palder. Woodbine House. •

Biennial. $25.95. Provides information on more than 14,000 U. S. and Canadian companies that issue catalogs and sell through the mail. Arrangement is by product, with an index to company names.

Directories in Print. The Gale Group. • Annual. $530.00. Three volumes. Includes interedition *Supplement*. An annotated guide to approximately 15,500 business, industrial, professional, and scientific directories. Formerly *Directory of Directories*.

Grey House Directory of Special Issues: A Guide to Business Magazines' Buyer's Guides & Directory Issues. Grey House Publishing. • 2001. $105.00. Provides information on more than 4,000 specialized directories issued by trade journals, arranged according to 90 industry groups.

Guide to American Directories. Bernard Klein. B. Klein Publications. • Biennial. $95.00. Provides 8,000 listings with descriptions, prices, etc.

Library Journal: Reference [year]: Print, CD-ROM, Online. Cahners Business Information. • Annual. Issued in November as supplement to *Library Journal*. Lists new and updated reference material, including general and trade print titles, directories, annuals, CD-ROM titles, and online sources. Includes material from more than 150 publishers, arranged by company name, with an index by subject. Addresses include e-mail and World Wide Web information, where available.

The National Directory of Catalogs. Oxbridge Communications. • Annual. $595.00. Describes over 7,000 catalogs within 78 subject areas. Includes CD-ROM.

Trade Directories of the World. Croner Publications, Inc. • Annual. 100.00.Looseleaf. Monthly supplements. Lists over 3,300 publications.

HANDBOOKS AND MANUALS

Directory Publishing: A Practical Guide. SIMBA Information. • 1996. $44.95. Fourth edition. Provides an overall review of the directory publishing industry, including types of directories, research, sales estimates, expenses, advertising, sales promotion, editorial content, and legal considerations.

Do-It-Yourself Advertising: How to Produce Great Ads, Brochures, Catalogs, Direct Mail, and Much More!. Fred E. Hahn and Kenneth G. Mangun. John Wiley and Sons, Inc. • 1997. $45.00. Second edition. Covers magazines, newspapers, flyers, brochures, catalogs, direct mail, telemarketing, trade shows, and radio/TV promotions. Includes checklists. (Small Business Series).

The Perfect Sales Piece: A Complete Do-It-Yourself Guide to Creating Brochures, Catalogs, Fliers, and Pamphlets. Robert W. Bly. John Wiley and Sons, Inc. • 1994. $49.95. A guide to the use of various forms of printed literature for direct selling, sales promotion, and marketing. (Small Business Editions Series).

INTERNET DATABASES

dNET. dNET Online Services, Inc. Phone: 800-378-3638 or (215)569-0100 Fax: (215)569-0101 E-mail: booksales@d-net.com • URL: http://www.d-net.com • "Where the World Goes for Directory Information." Web site provides ordering information for more than 3,200 U. S. and foreign directories, with brief descriptions of content. Searching is by keyword, title, topic, or publisher. There is also an extensive listing of products and services for directory publishers. Fees: Free. Frequent updates.

ONLINE DATABASES

Books in Print Online. Bowker Electronic Publishing. • The online version of *Books in Print, Forthcoming Books, Paperbound Books in Print,* and other Bowker bibliographic publications: lists the books of over 50,000 U. S. publishers. Includes books recently declared out-of-print. Updated monthly. Inquire as to online cost and availability.

Gale Database of Publications and Broadcast Media. The Gale Group. • An online directory containing detailed information on over 67,000 periodicals, newspapers, broadcast stations, cable systems, directories, and newsletters. Corresponds to the following print sources: *Gale Directory of Publications and Broadcast Media; Directories in Print; City and State Directories in Print; Newsletters in Print.* Semiannual updates. Inquire as to online cost and availability.

PERIODICALS AND NEWSLETTERS

Catalog Age. Cowles Business Media, Inc. • Monthly. $72.00 per year. Edited for catalog marketing and management personnel.

CSM. CSM Marketing, Inc. • Monthly. $30.00 per year. Formerly *Catalog Showroom Merchandiser*.

DM News: The Newspaper of Direct Marketing. DM News Corp. • Weekly. $75.00 per year. Includes special feature issues on catalog marketing, telephone marketing, database marketing, and fundraising. Includes monthly supplements. *DM News International, DRTV News,* and *TeleServices*.

The SIMBA Report on Directory Publishing. SIMBA Information. • Monthly. $59.00 per year. Newsletter.

Yellow Pages and Directory Report: The Newsletter for the Yellow Page and Directory Publishing Industry. SIMBA Information. • 22 times a year. $579.00 per year. Newsletter. Covers the yellow pages publishing industry, including electronic directory publishing, directory advertising, and special interest directories.

STATISTICS SOURCES

DMA State of the Catalog Industry Report. Direct Marketing Association, Inc. • Annual. $495.00. Provides merchandising, operating, and financial statistics on consumer and business-to-business marketing through both print and electronic (interactive) catalogs. (Produced in association with W. A. Dean & Associates.).

TRADE/PROFESSIONAL ASSOCIATIONS

Association of Directory Publishers. 230 E. Ohio St., 4th Fl., Chicago, IL 60611-3268. Phone: (312)644-6810 Fax: (312)644-8557 E-mail: adp@bostrom.com • URL: http://www.adp.org.

National Association of Catalog Showroom Merchandisers. 186 Birch Hill Rd., Locust Valley, NY 11560-1832. Phone: 800-334-4711.

National Catalog Managers Association. c/o Judy Shaffer, 735 Tollgate Rd., Elgin, IL 60123-9332. Phone: 800-323-8024 or (314)453-0905 Fax: (314)453-0472 E-mail: jks1@swbell.net.

OTHER SOURCES

DMA Direct and Interactive Marketing Buying Practices Study. Direct Marketing Association, Inc. • 2000. $1,295.00. Provides marketing research data relating to consumer purchasing from catalogs. "Incidence and profile of Internet buying" is also included. (Research conducted by Elrick & Lavidge.).

The U. S. Market for Catalog Shopping. Available from MarketResearch.com. • 1997. $2,250.00. Market research report published by Packaged Facts. Includes analysis of catalog shopping market by age, ethnic groups, and income.

CATERERS AND CATERING

See also: HOTEL AND MOTEL INDUSTRY; RESTAURANTS, LUNCHROOMS, ETC.

GENERAL WORKS

Fundamentals of Professional Food Preparation: A Laboratory Text-Workbook. Donald V. Laconi. John Wiley and Sons, Inc. • 1995. $54.95.

Successful Catering. William Reynolds and Michael Roman. John Wiley & Sons, Inc. • 1991. $59.95. Third edition.

HANDBOOKS AND MANUALS

Catering Handbook. Hal Weiss and Edith Weiss. John Wiley and Sons, Inc. • 1990. $42.95.

Catering Service. Entrepreneur Media, Inc. • Looseleaf. $59.50. A practical guide to starting a food and beverage catering business. Covers profit potential, start-up costs, market size evaluation, owner's time required, site selection, pricing, accounting, advertising, promotion, etc. (Start-Up Business Guide No. E1215.).

Club Manager's Guide to Private Parties and Club Functions. Joe Perdue and others. John Wiley and Sons, Inc. • 1998. $49.95. Covers on-premises catering at clubs, including member relations, meal functions, beverage functions, room setup, staffing, etc.

How to Manage a Successful Catering Business. Manfred Ketterer. John Wiley and Sons, Inc. • 1990. $54.95. Second edition.

Start and Run a Profitable Catering Business: From Thyme to Timing: Your Step-by-Step Business Plan. George Erdosh. Self-Counsel Press, Inc. • 1994. $14.95. Provides information on contracts, equipment, licenses, staff, planning, organizing catered events, and other aspects of catering.

PERIODICALS AND NEWSLETTERS

Catering Industry Employee. Hotel Employees and Restaurant Employees International Union, AFL0-CIO. • Bimonthly. $5.00.

Catering Magazine: The Magazine for Off-Premise Caterers. MiniCo., Inc. • Bimonthly. Price on application. Covers the marketing and management aspects of the catering business.

Chef. Talcott Communications Corp. • Monthly. $24.00 per year. Edited for executive chefs, food and beverage directors, caterers, banquet and club managers, and others responsible for food buying and food service. Special coverage of regional foods is provided.

TRADE/PROFESSIONAL ASSOCIATIONS

International Food Service Executive's Association. 3739 Mykonos Court, Boca Raton, FL 33498-1282. Phone: (561)998-7758 Fax: (561)998-3878 E-mail: hq@ifsea.org • URL: http://www.ifsea.org.

Mobile Industrial Caterers' Association. 1240 N. Jefferson St., Suite G, Anaheim, CA 92807. Phone: (714)632-6800 Fax: (714)632-5405.

CATTLE INDUSTRY

See also: DAIRY INDUSTRY; LIVESTOCK INDUSTRY

FINANCIAL RATIOS

Annual Statement Studies. Robert Morris Associates: The Association of Lending and Credit Risk Professiona. • Annual. Free to members; non-members, $140.00. Median and quartile financial ratios are given for over 400 kinds of manufacturing, wholesale, retail, construction, and consumer finance establishments. Data is sorted by both asset size and sales volume. Includes a clearly written

"Definition of Ratios" and an alphabetical industry index.

INTERNET DATABASES

BEEF. National Cattlemen's Beef Association. Phone: (303)694-0305 Fax: (303)694-2851 E-mail: cows@beef.org • URL: http://www.beef.org • Web site provides detailed information from the "Cattle and Beef Handbook," including "Beef Economics" (production, sales, consumption, retail value, foreign competition, etc.). Text of monthly newsletter is also available: "The Beef Brief-Issues & Trends in the Cattle Industry." Keyword searching is offered. Fees: Free.

Fedstats. Federal Interagency Council on Statistical Policy. Phone: (202)395-7254 • URL: http://www.fedstats.gov • Web site features an efficient search facility for full-text statistics produced by more than 70 federal agencies, including the Census Bureau, the Bureau of Economic Analysis, and the Bureau of Labor Statistics. Boolean searches can be made within one agency or for all agencies combined. Links are offered to international statistical bureaus, including the UN, IMF, OECD, UNESCO, Eurostat, and 20 individual countries. Fees: Free.

USDA. United States Department of Agriculture. Phone: (202)720-2791 E-mail: agsec@usda.gov • URL: http://www.usda.gov • The USDA home page has six sections: News and Information; What's New; About USDA; Agencies; Opportunities; Search and Help. Keyword searching is offered from the USDA home page and from various individual agency home pages. Agencies are the Economic Research Service, Agricultural Marketing Service, National Agricultural Statistics Service, National Agricultural Library, and about 12 others. Updating varies. Fees: Free.

ONLINE DATABASES

DRI U.S. Central Database. Data Products Division. • Provides more than 23,000 business, financial, demographic, economic, foreign trade, and industry-related time series for the U.S. Includes national income, population, retail-wholesale trade, price indexes, labor data, housing, industrial production, banking, interest rates, money supply, etc. Time period is generally 1947 to date (some data back to 1929). Updating varies. Inquire as to online cost and availability.

PERIODICALS AND NEWSLETTERS

Beef. Intertec Publishing Co., Agribusiness Div. • 13 times a year. $35.00 per year.

Cattleman. Texas and Southwestern Cattle Raisers Association, Inc. • Monthly. $40.00 per year.

Livestock Market Digest. Livestock Market Digest, Inc. • Weekly. $20.00 per year.

Livestock Weekly. Southwest Publishing, Inc. • Weekly. $25.00 per year.

PRICE SOURCES

The National Provisioner: Serving Meat, Poultry, and Seafood Processors. Stagnito Communications, Inc. • Monthly. Free to qualified personnel; others, $65.00 per year. Annual *Buyer's Guide* available. Meat, poultry and seafood newsletter.

RESEARCH CENTERS AND INSTITUTES

Beef Cattle and Sheep Research Center. Pennsylvania State University. 324 Henning Bldg., University Park, PA 16802. Phone: (814)865-5893 Fax: (814)863-6042 E-mail: rswope@das.psu.edu • URL: http://www.das.cas.psu.edu/.

Cottonwood Range and Livestock Research Station. South Dakota State University. HCR 1, P.O. Box 66, Philip, SD 57567. Phone: (605)386-4445 Fax: (605)386-4505 E-mail: sdsuctwd@gwtc.net • URL: http://www.abs.sdstate.edu/ars/cotton.htm.

Iberia Research Station. Louisiana State University. P.O. Box 466, Jeanerette, LA 70544. Phone: (318)276-5527 Fax: (318)276-9088 E-mail: sviator@ctr.lsu.edu.

U.S. Department of Agricultural Research Service Fort Keogh Livestock and Range Research Laboratory. Montana Agricultural Experiment Station. P.O. Box 2021, Miles City, MT 59301. Phone: (406)232-4970 Fax: (406)232-8209 E-mail: rod@larrl.ars.usda.gov • URL: http://larrl.ars.usda.gov/.

STATISTICS SOURCES

Agricultural Statistics. Available from U. S. Government Printing Office. • Annual. Produced by the National Agricultural Statistics Service, U. S. Department of Agriculture. Provides a wide variety of statistical data relating to agricultural production, supplies, consumption, prices/price-supports, foreign trade, costs, and returns, as well as farm labor, loans, income, and population. In many cases, historical data is shown annually for 10 years. In addition to farm data, includes detailed fishery statistics.

Business Statistics of the United States. Courtenay M. Slater, editor. Bernan Associates. • 1999. $74.00. Fifth edition. Based on *Business Statistics*, formerly issue by the Bureau of Economic Analysis, U. S. Department of Commerce. Provides basic data for a wide variety of U. S. industries, services, and economic indicators. Most statistics are shown annually for 29 years and monthly for the most recent four years.

Survey of Current Business. Available from U. S. Government Printing Office. • Monthly. $49.00 per year. Issued by Bureau of Economic Analysis, U. S. Department of Commerce. Presents a wide variety of business and economic data.

TRADE/PROFESSIONAL ASSOCIATIONS

Interstate Producers Livestock Association. 1705 W. Luthy Dr., Peoria, IL 61615. Phone: (309)691-5360 Fax: (309)691-3891.

Livestock Marketing Association. 7509 Tiffany Springs Parkway, Kansas City, MO 64153-2315. Phone: 800-821-2048 or (816)891-0502 Fax: (816)891-0552.

National Cattlemen's Beef Association. P.O. Box 3469, Englewood, CO 80155. Phone: (312)467-5520 Fax: (312)467-9767 E-mail: cattle@beef.org • URL: http://www.beef.org/ncba.htm.

Society for Range Management. 445 Union Blvd., Ste. 230, Lakewood, CO 80228. Phone: (303)355-7070 Fax: (303)355-5059 E-mail: srmden@ix.netcom.com • URL: http://www.srm.org.

Texas Longhorn Breeders Association of America. 2315 N. Main St., Suite 402, Fort Worth, TX 76106. Phone: (817)625-6241 Fax: (817)625-1388 E-mail: btlbaa@tlbaa.com.

U.S. Hide, Skin and Leather Association. 1700 N. Moore St., Suite 1600, Arlington, VA 22209. Phone: (703)841-5485 Fax: (703)841-9656 E-mail: lcandon@ushsla.org • URL: http://www.mratami.org.

CATV

See: CABLE TELEVISION INDUSTRY

CD-ROM DEVICES

See: MULTIMEDIA; OPTICAL DISK STORAGE DEVICES

CELLULAR TELEPHONES

See: MOBILE TELEPHONE INDUSTRY

CEMENT INDUSTRY

See also: CONCRETE INDUSTRY

DIRECTORIES

American Cement Directory: Directory of Cement Companies and Personnel. Bradley Pulverizer Co. • Annual. $71.00. About 200 cement manufacturing plants in the United States, Canada,Mexico, Central and South America.

Pit and Quarry Buyers' Guide. Advanstar Communications, Inc. • Annual. $25.00. Lists approximately 1,000 manufacturers and other suppliers of equipment products and services to the nonmetallic mining and quarrying industry. Absorbed: *Ready-Mix-Reference Manual.*

FINANCIAL RATIOS

Almanac of Business and Industrial Financial Ratios. Leo Troy. Prentice Hall. • Annual. $99.95. Contains financial ratios derived from federal tax returns. Ratios for each of about 200 industries are arranged according to company asset size.

HANDBOOKS AND MANUALS

Cement Data Book: International Process Engineering in the Cement Industry. Walter H. Duda. French and European Publications, Inc. • 1985. $950.00. Third edition. Three volumes. Vol.1, $375.00; vol.2, $325.00; vol.3, $250.00. Text in English and German.

INTERNET DATABASES

Fedstats. Federal Interagency Council on Statistical Policy. Phone: (202)395-7254 • URL: http://www.fedstats.gov • Web site features an efficient search facility for full-text statistics produced by more than 70 federal agencies, including the Census Bureau, the Bureau of Economic Analysis, and the Bureau of Labor Statistics. Boolean searches can be made within one agency or for all agencies combined. Links are offered to international statistical bureaus, including the UN, IMF, OECD, UNESCO, Eurostat, and 20 individual countries. Fees: Free.

ONLINE DATABASES

DRI U.S. Central Database. Data Products Division. • Provides more than 23,000 business, financial, demographic, economic, foreign trade, and industry-related time series for the U.S. Includes national income, population, retail-wholesale trade, price indexes, labor data, housing, industrial production, banking, interest rates, money supply, etc. Time period is generally 1947 to date (some data back to 1929). Updating varies. Inquire as to online cost and availability.

F & S Index. The Gale Group. • Contains about four million citations to worldwide business, financial, and industrial or consumer product literature appearing from 1972 to date. Weekly updates. Inquire as to online cost and availability.

PERIODICALS AND NEWSLETTERS

Cement and Concrete Research. Elsevier Science. • Monthly. $1,761.00 per year. Text in English, French, German and Russian.

Cement, Quarry and Mineral Aggregates Newsletter. National Safety Council. • Bimonthly. Members, $15.00 per year; non-members, $19.00 per year.

Pit and Quarry. Advanstar Communications, Inc. • Monthly. $49.00 per year. Covers crushed stone, sand and gravel, etc.

Quarry Management: The Monthly Journal for the Quarrying, Asphalt, Concrete and Recycling

Industries. Institute of Quarrying. QMJ Publishing Ltd. • Monthly. $60.00 per year.

Rock Products: Industry's Recognized Authority. Intertec Publishing Corp. • Monthly. Price on application.

RESEARCH CENTERS AND INSTITUTES

Center for Cement Composite Materials. University of Illinois at Urbana-Champaign. 204 Ceramics Bldg., 105 S. Goodwin Ave., Urbana, IL 61801. Phone: (217)244-6210 Fax: (217)244-6917 E-mail: lstruble@uiuc.edu.

STATISTICS SOURCES

Annual Survey of Manufactures. Available from U. S. Government Printing Office. • Annual. Prices vary. Issued by the U. S. Census Bureau as an interim update to the *Census of Manufactures.* Includes data on number of manufacturing establishments in various industries, employment, labor costs, value of shipments, capital expenditures, inventories, energy costs, and assets. (See also Census Bureau home page, http://www.census.gov/.).

Business Statistics of the United States. Courtenay M. Slater, editor. Bernan Associates. • 1999. $74.00. Fifth edition. Based on *Business Statistics*, formerly issue by the Bureau of Economic Analysis, U. S. Department of Commerce. Provides basic data for a wide variety of U. S. industries, services, and economic indicators. Most statistics are shown annually for 29 years and monthly for the most recent four years.

Mineral Commodity Summaries. Available from U. S. Government Printing Office. • Annual. Published by the U. S. Geological Survey, Department of the Interior (http://www.usgs.gov). Contains detailed, five-year data for about 90 nonfuel minerals. Covers a wide range of statistics, including production, imports, exports, consumption, reserves, prices, tariff information, and industry employment. (Two pages are devoted to each mineral.).

Minerals Yearbook. Available from U.S. Government Printing Office. • Annual. Three volumes.

Survey of Current Business. Available from U. S. Government Printing Office. • Monthly. $49.00 per year. Issued by Bureau of Economic Analysis, U. S. Department of Commerce. Presents a wide variety of business and economic data.

United States Census of Manufactures. U.S. Bureau of the Census. • Quinquennial. Results presented in reports, tape, CD-ROM, and Diskette files.

WEFA Industrial Monitor. John Wiley and Sons, Inc. • Annual. $65.00. Prepared by industry analysts at WEFA, an economic forecasting and consulting firm (originally Wharton Econometric Forecasting Associates). Contains discussions of the outlook for major U. S. industries, with many 10-year forecasts (WEFA Web site is http://www.wefa.com).

TRADE/PROFESSIONAL ASSOCIATIONS

Cement Employers Association. 122 E. Broad St., 2nd Fl., Bethlehem, PA 18018. Phone: (215)868-8060.

Cement, Lime, Gypsum, and Allied Workers Division. New Brotherhood Bldg., Suite 570, 753 State Ave., Kansas City, MO 66101. Phone: (913)371-2640 Fax: (913)281-8106.

Operative Plasterers and Cement Masons International Association of U.S. and Canada. 14405 Laurel Place, Suite 300, Laurel, MD 20707. Phone: (301)470-4200 Fax: (301)470-2502 E-mail: opcmiaintl@opcmia.org • URL: http://www.opcmia.org.

Portland Cement Association. 5420 Old Orchard Rd., Skokie, IL 60077-1083. Phone: (847)966-6200 Fax: (847)966-9781 • URL: http://www.portcement.org.

CEMETERIES

See: FUNERAL HOMES AND DIRECTORS

CENSUS REPORTS

See also: GOVERNMENT PUBLICATIONS; POPULATION

GENERAL WORKS

Moving Power and Money: The Politics of Census Taking. Barbara E. Bryant and William Dunn. New Strategist Publications, Inc. • 1995. $24.95. Barbara Everitt Bryant was Director of the U. S. Census Bureau from 1989 to 1993. She provides a plan for reducing the costs of census taking, improving accuracy, and overcoming public resistance to the census.

ABSTRACTS AND INDEXES

Population Abstract of the U. S. The Gale Group. • 2000. $185.00. Historical emphasis. Includes a "breakdown of urban and rural population from the earliest census to the present.".

BIBLIOGRAPHIES

Census Catalog and Guide. U. S. Government Printing Office. • Annual. Lists publications and electronic media products currently available from the U. S. Bureau of the Census, along with some out of print items. Includes comprehensive title and subject indexes. Formerly *Bureau of the Census Catalog.*

Monthly Product Announcement. U. S. Bureau of the Census, Customer Services. • Monthly. Lists Census Bureau publications and products that became available during the previous month.

CD-ROM DATABASES

Sourcebooks America CD-ROM. CACI Marketing Systems. • Annual. $1,250.00. Provides the CD-ROM version of *The Sourcebook of ZIP Code Demographics: Census Edition* and *The Sourcebook of County Demographics: Census Edition.*

HANDBOOKS AND MANUALS

Industry and Product Classification Manual (SIC Basis). Available from National Technical Information Service. • 1992. Issued by U. S. Bureau of the Census. Contains extended Standard Industrial Classification (SIC) numbers used by the Census Bureau to allow a more detailed classification of industry, services, and agriculture.

North American Industry Classification System (NAICS). Available from Bernan Press. • 1998. $32.50. Issued by the Executive Office of the President, Office of Management and Budget (OMB). The 1997 NAICS six-digit classification scheme replaces the 1987 Standard Industrial Classification (SIC) four-digit system. Detailed information on NAICS is available at http://www.census.gov/epcd/www/naics.html.

Understanding the Census: A Guide for Marketers, Planners, Grant Writers, and Other Data Users. Michael R. Lavin. Epoch Books, Inc. • 1996. $49.95. Contains basic explanations of U. S. Census "concepts, methods, terminology, and data sources." Includes practical advice for locating and using Census data.

INTERNET DATABASES

Fedstats. Federal Interagency Council on Statistical Policy. Phone: (202)395-7254 • URL: http://www.fedstats.gov • Web site features an efficient search facility for full-text statistics produced by more than 70 federal agencies, including the Census Bureau, the Bureau of Economic Analysis, and the Bureau of Labor Statistics. Boolean searches can be made within one agency or for all agencies combined. Links are offered to international statistical bureaus, including the UN, IMF, OECD, UNESCO, Eurostat, and 20 individual countries. Fees: Free.

1997 NAICS and 1987 SIC Correspondence Tables. U. S. Census Bureau. Phone: (301)457-4100 Fax: (301)457-1296 E-mail: naics@census.gov • URL: http://www.census.gov/epcd/www/naicstab.htm • Web site provides detailed tables for converting four-digit Standard Industrial Classification (SIC) numbers to the six-digit North American Industrial Classification System (NAICS) or vice versa: "1987 SIC Matched to 1997 NAICS" or "1997 NAICS Matched to 1987 SIC." Fees: Free.

ONLINE DATABASES

American Statistics Index: A Comprehensive Guide and Index to the Statistical Publications of the United States Government [Online]. Congressional Information Service, Inc. • Indexes and abstracts, 1973 to date. Inquire as to online cost and availability.

PERIODICALS AND NEWSLETTERS

Population and Development Review. Population Council. • Quarterly. $36.00 per year. *Supplements* available. Text in English, summaries in English, French and Spanish.

Population Bulletin. Population Reference Bureau, Inc. • Quarterly. $7.00 per issue.

RESEARCH CENTERS AND INSTITUTES

Alabama State Data Center. University of Alabama. P.O. Box 870221, Tuscaloosa, AL 35487. Phone: (205)348-6191 Fax: (205)348-2951 E-mail: awatters@cba.ua.edu • URL: http://www.cber.cba.ua.edu.

Institute for Public Policy and Business Research. University of Kansas Survey Research Center. 607 Blake Hall, Lawrence, KS 66045. Phone: (785)864-3701 Fax: (785)864-3683 E-mail: ippbr-src@ukans.edu • URL: http://www.ukans.edu/cwis/units/ippbr.

STATISTICS SOURCES

County and City Extra: Annual Metro, City and County Data Book. Mark Littman and Deirdre A. Gaquin. Bernan Press. • 1999. $109.00. Updates and augments data published irregularly in print form by the U. S. Census Bureau in *County and City Data Book.* Covers "every state, county, metropolitan area, and congressional district in the United States, as well as all U. S. cities with a 1990 population of 25,000 or more." Contains a wide range tic maps.

County Business Patterns. Available from U. S. Government Printing Office. • Irregular. 52 issues containing annual data for each state, the District of Columbia, and a U. S. Summary. Produced by U.S. Bureau of the Census (http://www.census.gov). Provides local establishment and employment statistics by industry.

Current Population Reports: Household Economic Studies, Series P-70. Available from U. S. Government Printing Office. • Irregular. $16.00 per year. Issued by the U.S. Bureau of the Census (http://www.census.gov). Each issue covers a special topic relating to household socioeconomic characteristics.

Current Population Reports: Population Characteristics, Special Studies, and Consumer Income, Series P-20, P-23, and P-60. Available from U. S. Government Printing Office. • Irregular. $39.00 per year. Issued by the U.S. Bureau of the Census (http://www.census.gov). Each issue covers a special topic relating to population or income. Series P-20, *Population Characteristics*, provides statistical studies on such items as mobility, fertility, education, and marital status. Series P-23, *Special Studies*, consists of occasional reports on methodology. Series P-60, *Consumer Income*, publishes reports on income in relation to age, sex, education, occupation, family size, etc.

Current Population Reports: Population Estimates and Projections, Series P-25. Available from U. S. Government Printing Office. • Irregular. $14.00 per year. Issued by the U.S. Bureau of the Census (http://www.census.gov). Provides monthly, mid-year, and annual population estimates, including data for states and Standard Metropolitan Statistical Areas. Projections are given for the U.S. population in future years.

Historical Statistics of the United States, Colonial Times to 1970: A Statistical Abstract Supplement. U.S. Bureau of the Census. Available from U.S. Government Printing Office. • 1975. $79.00. Two volumes.

Places, Towns, and Townships, 1998. Deirdre A. Gaquin and Richard W. Dodge, editors. Bernan Press. • 1997. $89.00. Second edition. Presents demographic and economic statistics from the U. S. Census Bureau and other government sources for places, cities, towns, villages, census designated places, and minor civil divisions. Contains more than 60 data categories.

Population of States and Counties of the United States: 1790-1990. Available from National Technical Information Service. • 1996. $35.00. Issued by the U. S. Census Bureau (http://www.census.gov). Provides data on the number of inhabitants of the U. S., states, territories, and counties according to 21 decennial censuses from 1790 to 1990. Includes descriptions of county origins and lists prior county names, where applicable.

Population Projections of the United States by Age, Sex, Race, and Hispanic Origin: 1995 to 2050. Available from U. S. Government Printing Office. • 1996. $8.50. Issued by the U. S. Bureau of the Census (http://www.census.gov). Contains charts and tables. Appendixes include detailed data on fertility rates by age, life expectancy, immigration, and armed forces population. (Current Population Reports, P25-1130.).

The Sourcebook of ZIP Code Demographics. Available from The Gale Group. • 2000. $495.00. 15th edition. Published by CACI Marketing Systems. Presents detailed statistical profiles of every ZIP code in America, based on the 1990 census. Each profile contains data on more than 70 variables.

State and Metropolitan Area Data Book. Available from U. S. Government Printing Office. • 1998. $31.00. Issued by the U. S. Bureau of the Census. Presents a wide variety of statistical data for U. S. regions, states, counties, metropolitan areas, and central cities, with ranking tables. Time period is 1970 to 1990.

Statistical Abstract of the United States. Available from U. S. Government Printing Office. • Annual. $51.00. Issued by the U. S. Bureau of the Census.

United States Census of Agriculture. U.S. Bureau of the Census. • Quinquennial. Results presented in reports, tape, CD-ROM, and Diskette files.

United States Census of Construction Industries. U.S. Bureau of the Census. • Quinquennial. Results presented in reports, tape, and CD-ROM files.

United States Census of Governments. Bureau of the Census, U.S. Department of Commerce. Available from U.S. Government Printing Office. • Quinquennial.

United States Census of Manufactures. U.S. Bureau of the Census. • Quinquennial. Results presented in reports, tape, CD-ROM, and Diskette files.

United States Census of Mineral Industries. Bureau of the Census, U.S. Department of Commerce. Available from U.S. Government Printing Office. • Quinquennial.

United States Census of Population. Bureau of the Census, U.S. Department of Commerce. Available from U.S. Government Printing Office. • Quinquennial.

United States Census of Retail Trade. U.S. Bureau of the Census. • Quinquennial.

United States Census of Service Industries. U.S. Bureau of the Census. • Quinquennial. Various reports available.

United States Census of Transportation. Bureau of the Census, U.S. Department of Commerce. Available from U.S. Government Printing Office. • Quinquennial.

United States Census of Wholesale Trade. Bureau of the Census, U.S. Department of Commerce. Available from U.S. Government Printing Office. • Quinquennial.

TRADE/PROFESSIONAL ASSOCIATIONS

Population Association of America. 721 Ellsworth Dr., Suite 303, Silver Spring, MD 20910. Phone: (301)565-6710 Fax: (301)565-7850 E-mail: info@popassoc.org • URL: http://www.popassoc.org.

Population Council. One Dag Hammerskjold Plaza, New York, NY 10017. Phone: (212)339-0500 Fax: (212)755-6052 E-mail: pubinfo@popcouncil.org • URL: http://www.popcouncil.org.

Population Reference Bureau. 1875 Connecticut Ave., N.W., Suite 520, Washington, DC 20009. Phone: 800-877-9881 or (202)483-1100 Fax: (202)328-3937 E-mail: popref@prb.org • URL: http://www.prb.org.

CENTRAL AMERICA

See: LATIN AMERICAN MARKETS

CERAMIC TILE INDUSTRY

See: TILE INDUSTRY

CERAMICS INDUSTRY

See also: CLAY INDUSTRY; POTTERY INDUSTRY

GENERAL WORKS

Introduction to Ceramics. W. David Kingery and others. John Wiley and Sons, Inc. • 1976. $175.00. Second edition. (Science and Technology of Materials Series).

ABSTRACTS AND INDEXES

Applied Science and Technology Index. H. W. Wilson Co. • 11 times a year. Quarterly and annual cumulations. Service basis for print edition; CD-ROM edition, $1,495.00 per year. Indexes a wide variety of English language technical, industrial, and engineering periodicals.

Engineered Materials Abstracts. Cambridge Information Group. • Monthly. $995.00 per year. Provides citations to the technical and engineering literature of plastic, ceramic, and composite materials.

NTIS Alerts: Materials Sciences. National Technical Information Service. • Semimonthly. $220.00 per year. Provides descriptions of government-sponsored research reports and software, with ordering information. Covers ceramics, glass, coatings, composite materials, alloys, plastics, wood, paper, adhesives, fibers, lubricants, and related subjects. Formerly *Abstract Newsletter*.

Polymers/Ceramics/Composites Alert. Cambridge Information Group. • Monthly. $340.00 per year. Provides citations to the business and industrial literature of plastic, ceramic, and composite materials. (Materials Business Information Series).

World Ceramics Abstracts. British Ceramic Research Ltd. Ceram Research. • Monthly. $710.00 per year. Formerly *British Ceramic Abstracts*.

CD-ROM DATABASES

METADEX Materials Collection: Metals-Polymers-Ceramics. Cambridge Scientific Abstracts. • Quarterly. $6,950.00 per year. Provides CD-ROM citations to the worldwide literature of materials science and metallurgy. Corresponds to *Metals Abstracts, Alloys Index, Steels Alert, Nonferrous Alert, Polymers/Ceramics/Composites Alert,* and *Engineered Materials Abstracts.* (Formerly produced by ASM International.).

ENCYCLOPEDIAS AND DICTIONARIES

ASM Materials Engineering Dictionary. Joseph R. Davis, editor. ASM International. • 1992. $146.00. Contains 10,000 entries, 700 illustrations, and 150 tables relating to metals, plastics, ceramics, composites, and adhesives. Includes "Technical Briefs" on 64 key material groups.

Encyclopedia of Advanced Materials. David Bloor and others. Elsevier Science. • 1994. $1,811.25. Four volumes.

Encyclopedia of Materials: Science and Technology. K.H.J. Buschow and others, editors. Pergamon Press/Elsevier Science. • 2001. $6,875.00. Eleven volumes. Provides extensive technical information on a wide variety of materials, including metals, ceramics, plastics, optical materials, and building materials. Includes more than 2,000 articles and 5,000 illustrations.

HANDBOOKS AND MANUALS

ASM Engineered Materials Reference Book. Michael L. Bauccio. ASM International. • 1994. $139.00. Second edition. Provides information on a wide range of materials, with special sections on ceramics, industrial glass products, and plastics.

Ceramics: A Potter's Handbook. Glenn C. Nelson. Harcourt Brace College Publishers. • 1998. $42.50. Sixth edition.

ONLINE DATABASES

Applied Science and Technology Index Online. H. W. Wilson Co. • Provides online indexing of 400 major scientific, technical, industrial, and engineering periodicals. Time period is 1983 to date. Monthly updates. Inquire as to online cost and availability.

Engineered Materials Abstracts [online]. Cambridge Scientific Abstracts. • Provides online citations to the technical and engineering literature of plastic, ceramic, and composite materials. Time period is 1986 to date, with monthly updates. (Formerly produced by ASM International.) Inquire as to online cost and availability.

F & S Index. The Gale Group. • Contains about four million citations to worldwide business, financial, and industrial or consumer product literature appearing from 1972 to date. Weekly updates. Inquire as to online cost and availability.

Materials Business File. Cambridge Scientific Abstracts. • Provides online abstracts and citations to worldwide materials literature, covering the business and industrial aspects of metals, plastics, ceramics, and composites. Corresponds to *Steels Alert, Nonferrous Metals Alert,* and *Polymers/Ceramics/ Composites Alert.* Time period is 1985 to date, with monthly updates. (Formerly produced by ASM International.) Inquire as to online cost and availability.

METADEX. Cambridge Scientific Abstracts. • Covers the worldwide literature of metals, metallurgy, and materials science, 1966 to date. Includes detailed alloys indexing from 1974. Biweekly updating. Inquire as to online cost and availability. (Formerly produced by ASM International.).

PERIODICALS AND NEWSLETTERS

American Ceramic Society Bulletin. American Ceramic Society. • Monthly. Free to members; non-members, $50.00 per year.

American Ceramic Society Journal. American Ceramic Society. • Monthly. Members, $125.00 per year; non-members, $625.00 per year. Includes subscription to *Ceramic Bulletin and Abstracts.*

Ceramic Industries International. Turret RAI plc. • Bimonthly. $115.00. per year.

Ceramic Industry: The Magazine for Refractories, Traditional and Advanced Ceramic Manufacturers. Business News Publishing Co. • 13 times a year. $65.00 per year. Includes *Data Buyers Guide, Materials Handbook, Economic Forecast,* and *Giants in Ceramic.*

Ceramics Monthly. American Ceramic Society. • 10 times a year. $28.00 per year.

High-Tech Materials Alert: Advanced Materials-Their Uses and Manufacture. Technical Insights. • Monthly. $695.00 per year. Newsletter on technical developments relating to high-performance materials, including metals and ceramics. Includes market forecasts.

RESEARCH CENTERS AND INSTITUTES

Edward Orton, Jr. Ceramic Foundation. 6991 Old 3C Highway, Westerville, OH 43086. Phone: (614)895-2663 Fax: (614)895-5610 E-mail: schorr@ortonceramic.com • URL: http://www.ortonceramic.com.

Edward Orton Jr. Ceramic Foundation-Refractories Testing and Research Center. 6991 Old 3C Highway, Westerville, OH 43082. Phone: (614)895-2663 Fax: (614)895-5610 E-mail: homeny@ortonceramic.com • URL: http://www.ortonceramic.com.

Materials Processing Center. Massachusetts Institute of Technology, 77 Massachusetts Ave., Room 12-007, Cambridge, MA 02139-4307. Phone: (617)253-5179 Fax: (617)258-6900 E-mail: fmpage@.mit.edu • URL: http://www.web.mit.edu/mpc/www/ • Conducts processing, engineering, and economic research in ferrous and nonferrous metals, ceramics, polymers, photonic materials, superconductors, welding, composite materials, and other materials.

Stanford Integrated Manufacturing Association. Stanford University, Bldg. 02-530, Stanford, CA 94305-3036. Phone: (650)723-9038 Fax: (650)723-5034 E-mail: susan.hansen@stanford.edu • URL: http://www.sima.stanford.edu/ • Consists of four research centers: Center for Automation and Manufacturing Science, Center for Design Research, Center for Materials Formability and Processing Science, and Center for Teaching and Research in Integrated Manufacturing Systems. Research fields include automation, robotics, intelligent systems, computer vision, design in manufacturing, materials science, composite materials, and ceramics.

STATISTICS SOURCES

Ceramic Industry Data Book Buyer's Guide. Business News Publishing Co. • Annual. $25.00. Included with subscription to *Ceramic Industry.* Formerly *Ceramic Data Book.*

Refractories. U. S. Bureau of the Census. • Annual. Provides data on value of manufacturers' shipments, quantity, exports, imports, etc. (Current Industrial Reports, MA-32C.).

TRADE/PROFESSIONAL ASSOCIATIONS

ABG Division United Steel Worker. 3362 Hollenberg Dr., Bridgeton, MO 63044. Phone: (314)739-6142 Fax: (314)739-1216.

American Ceramic Society. P.O.Box 6136, Westerville, OH 43086-6136. Phone: (614)890-4700 Fax: (614)899-6109 E-mail: info@acers.org • URL: http://www.acers.org.

Associated Glass and Pottery Manufacturers. c/o Custom Deco, 1343 Miami St., Toledo, OH 43605. Phone: (419)698-2900 Fax: (419)698-9928.

Glass Molders, Pottery, Plastics and Allied Workers International Union. P.O. Box 607, Media, PA 19063. Phone: (610)565-5051 Fax: (610)565-0983.

Hobby Industry Association of America. 319 E. 54th St., Elmwood Park, NJ 07407. Phone: (201)794-1133 Fax: (201)797-0657 E-mail: hia@ix.netcom.com.

International Ceramic Association. P.O. Box 39, Glen Burnie, MD 21061. Phone: (410)923-3425.

National Institute of Ceramic Engineers. c/o D. C. Folz, University of Florida, Department of Materials Science and, Engineering, P.O. Box 116400, Gainesville, FL 32611-6400. Phone: (352)392-3163 Fax: (352)846-2033 E-mail: dfolz@mse.ufl.edu • URL: http://www.acers.org.

CEREAL INDUSTRY

See: GRAIN INDUSTRY

CERTIFIED PUBLIC ACCOUNTANTS

See also: ACCOUNTING; WOMEN ACCOUNTANTS

ABSTRACTS AND INDEXES

Accounting and Tax Index. UMI. • Quarterly. Price on application. Includes annual cumulative bound volume. Indexes accounting, auditing, and taxation literature appearing in journals, books, pamphlets, conference proceedings, and newsletters. (UMI is University Microfilms International, a Bell & Howell Co.).

Accounting Articles. CCH, Inc. • Monthly. $594.00 per year. Looseleaf service.

CD-ROM DATABASES

The Tax Directory [CD-ROM]. Tax Analysts. • Quarterly. Provides *The Tax Directory* listings on CD-ROM, covering federal, state, and international tax officials, tax practitioners, and corporate tax executives.

DIRECTORIES

Emerson's Directory of Leading U.S. Accounting Firms. Available from Hoover's, Inc. • Biennial. $195.00. Published by the Emerson Company (http://www.emersoncompany.com). Provides information on 500 major CPA firms.

The Tax Directory. Tax Analysts. • Annual. $299.00. ($399.00 with quarterly CD-ROM updates.) Four volumes: *Government Officials Worldwide* (lists 15,000 state, federal, and international tax officials, with basic corporate and individual income tax rates for 100 countries); *Private Sector Professionals Worldwide* (lists 25,000 U.S. and foreign tax practitioners: accountants, lawyers, enrolled agents, and actuarial firms); *Corporate Tax Managers Worldwide* (lists 10,000 tax managers employed by U.S. and foreign companies).

ENCYCLOPEDIAS AND DICTIONARIES

Encyclopedia of Accounting Systems. Tom M. Plank and Lois R. Plank. Prentice Hall. • 1994. $110.00. Three volumes.

HANDBOOKS AND MANUALS

Accountants' Liability. Practising Law Institute. • Looseleaf. $135.00. Annual revisions. Covers all aspects of accountants' professional liability issues, including depositions and court cases.

AICPA Audit and Accounting Manual. American Institute of Certified Public Accountants. • 1999. $99.00. Covers working papers, internal control, audit approach, etc.

AICPA Technical Practice Aids. American Institute of Certified Public Accountants. • $180.00 per year. Looseleaf service. Periodic supplementation. Advisory opinions, statements of position, and other material.

Best Practices for Financial Advisors. Mary Rowland. • 1997. $40.00. Provides advice for professional financial advisors on practice management, ethics, marketing, and legal concerns. (Bloomberg Professional Library.).

CPA Examination Review Business Law and Professional Responibilities. Patrick R. Delaney. John Wiley and Sons, Inc. • 1996. $109.00.

Getting Started in Investment Planning Services. James E. Grant. CCH, Inc. • 1999. $85.00. Second edition. Provides advice and information for lawyers and accountants who are planning to initiate fee-based investment services.

Marketing for CPAs, Accountants, and Tax Professionals. William J. Winston. Haworth Press, Inc. • 1995. $49.95.

Professional Resumes for Tax and Accounting Occupations. David H. Noble. CCH, Inc. • 1999. $49.95. Written for accounting, tax, law, and finance professionals. In addition to advice, provides 335 sample resumes and 22 cover letters.

Valuing Professional Practices: A Practitioner's Guide. Robert Reilly and Robert Schweihs. CCH, Inc. • 1997. $99.00. Provides a basic introduction to estimating the dollar value of practices in various professional fields.

INTERNET DATABASES

Rutgers Accounting Web (RAW). Rutgers University Accounting Research Center. Phone: (201)648-5172 Fax: (201)648-1233 • URL: http://www.rutgers.edu/accounting • RAW Web site provides extensive links to sources of national and international accounting information, such as the Big Six accounting firms, the Financial Accounting Standards Board (FASB), SEC filings (EDGAR), journals, publishers, software, the International Accounting Network, and "Internet's largest list of accounting firms in USA." Searching is offered. Fees: Free.

PERIODICALS AND NEWSLETTERS

Bowman's Accounting Report. Hudson Sawyer Professional Services Marketing, Inc. • Monthly. $275.00 per year. Newsletter. Provides information and news relating to the accounting profession, with emphasis on certified public accounting firms.

The CPA Journal. New York State Society of Certified Public Accountants. • Monthly. $42.00 per year.

The CPA Letter: A News Report to Members. American Institute of Certified Public Accountants - Communications. • 8 times a year. Free to members; non-members, $40.00 per year.

CPA Managing Partner Report: Management News for Accounting Executives. Strafford Publications, Inc. • Monthly. $297.00 per year. Newsletter. Covers practice management and professional relationships.

CPA Marketing Report. Strafford Publications, Inc. • Monthly. $287.00 per year. Newsletter. Contains strategies for practice development.

CPA Personnel Report. Strafford Publications, Inc. • Monthly. $287.00 per year. Newsletter. Provides advice on human relations and personnel procedures for accounting firms.

Journal of Accountancy. American Institute of Certified Public Accountants. • Monthly. $59.00 per year.

National Public Accountant. National Society of Accountants. • Monthly. Free to members; non-members, $18.00 per year. For accounting and tax practitioners.

The Practical Accountant: Accounting and Taxes in Everyday Practice. Faulkner and Gray, Inc. • Monthly. $60.00 per year. Covers tax planning, financial planning, practice management, client relationships, and related topics.

Public Accounting Report. Strafford Publications, Inc. • 23 times a year. $297.00 per year. Newsletter. Presents news and trends affecting the accounting profession.

Tax Practice. Tax Analysts. • Weekly. $199.00 per year. Newsletter. Covers news affecting tax practitioners and litigators, with emphasis on federal court decisions, rules and regulations, and tax petitions. Provides a guide to Internal Revenue Service audit issues.

Taxation for Accountants. Warren, Gorham & Lamont/RIA Group. • Monthly. $125.00. per year. Emphasis is on current tax developments as they affect accountants and their clients. Includes advice on tax software and computers.

RESEARCH CENTERS AND INSTITUTES

Accounting Research Program. University of California, John E. Anderson Graduate School of Management, Los Angeles, CA 90095-1481. Phone: (310)206-6462 Fax: (310)267-2163 E-mail: pat.hughes@anderson.ucla.edu.

STATISTICS SOURCES

U. S. Industry and Trade Outlook: The McGraw-Hill Companies and the U.S. Department of Commerce/International Trade Administration. Datapso Research Corp. • Annual. $69.95. Produced by the International Trade Administration, U. S. Department of Commerce, in a "public-private" partnership with DRI/McGraw-Hill and Standard & Poor's. Provides basic data, outlook for the current year, and "Long-Term Prospects" (five-year projections) for a wide variety of products and services. Includes high technology industries. Formerly *U. S. Industrial Outlook.*

TRADE/PROFESSIONAL ASSOCIATIONS

American Institute of Certified Public Accountants. 1211 Ave. of the Americas, New York, NY 10036-8775. Phone: 800-862-4272 or (212)596-6200 Fax: (212)596-6213 • URL: http://www.aicpa.org.

American Woman's Society of Certified Public Accountants. 401 N. Michigan Ave., Chicago, IL 60611. Phone: 800-297-2721 or (312)644-6610 Fax: (312)321-6869 E-mail: awscpa__hq@sba.com.

National Association of State Boards of Accountancy. 150 Fourth Ave., N., Ste. 00, Nashville, TN 37219-2415. Phone: (615)880-4200 Fax: (615)880-4290 E-mail: communications@nasba.org • URL: http://www.nasba.org.

National Society of Public Accountants. 1010 N. Fairfax St., Alexandria, VA 22314-1574. Phone: 800-966-6679 or (703)549-6400 Fax: (703)549-2984 E-mail: nsa@wizard.net • URL: http://www.nsa.org.

Tax Analysts. 6830 N. Fairfax Dr., Arlington, VA 22213. Phone: 800-955-3444 or (703)533-4400 Fax: (703)533-4444 E-mail: webmaster@tax.org • URL: http://www.tax.org • An advocacy group reviewing U. S. and foreign income tax developments. Includes a Tax Policy Advisory Board.

OTHER SOURCES

Andrews' Professional Liability Litigation Reporter. Andrews Publications. • Monthly. $550.00 per year. Provides reports on lawsuits against attorneys, accountants, and investment professionals.

Avoiding Tax Malpractice. Robert Feinschreiber and Margaret Kent. CCH, Inc. • 2000. $75.00. Covers malpractice considerations for professional tax practitioners.

CHAIN STORES

See also: DISCOUNT HOUSES; DRUG STORES; FRANCHISES; RETAIL TRADE

DIRECTORIES

Directory of Automotive Aftermarket Suppliers. Chain Store Guide. • Annual. $300.00. Covers auto supply store chains. Includes distributors.

Directory of Chain Restaurant Operators. Chain Store Guide. • Annual. $300.00. Includes fast food establishments, and leading chain hotel copanies operating foodservice unit.

Directory of Discount and General Merchandise Stores. Chain Store Guide. • Annual. $300.00. Includes retailers and wholesalers of housewares, giftwares, novelties, toys, hobby materials, crafts, and stationery. Formerly *Directory of Discount Stores Catalog Showrooms.*

Directory of Home Center Operators and Hardware Chains. Chain Store Age. • Annual. $300.00. Nearly 5,400 home center operators, paint and home decorating chains, and lumber and building materials companies.

Directory of Retail Chains in Canada. Maclean Hunter Business Publications. • Annual. $340.00. Provides detailed information on approximately 1,600 retail chains of all sizes in Canada.

Directory of Supermarket, Grocery, and Convenience Store Chains. Chain Store Guide. • Annual. $300.00. Provides information on about 2,200 food store chains operating 30,000 individual stores. Store locations are given.

Discount Store News - Top Chains. Chain Store Guide. • Annual. $79.00.

European Directory of Retailers and Wholesalers. Available from The Gale Group. • 1997. $790.00. Second edition. Published by Euromonitor. Provides detailed information on more than 4,000 major retail and wholesale businesses in 17 countries of Western Europe. Contains 26 categories, such as supermarkets, superstores, department stores, discount stores, franchise operators, mail order, etc. Includes company, product, and geographic indexes.

National Association of Chain Drug Stores - Communications Directory. National Association of Chain Drug Stores. • Annual. Membership. About 150 chain drug retailers and their 31,000 individual pharmacies; 900 supplier companies; state boards of pharmacy, pharmaceutical and retail associations, colleges of pharmacy; drug trade associations.

Plunkett's Retail Industry Almanac: Complete Profiles on the Retail 500-The Leading Firms in Retail Stores, Services, Catalogs, and On-Line Sales. Available from Plunkett Research, Ltd. • Annual. $179.99. Provides detailed profiles of 500 major U. S. retailers. Industry trends are discussed.

INTERNET DATABASES

Fedstats. Federal Interagency Council on Statistical Policy. Phone: (202)395-7254 • URL: http://www.fedstats.gov • Web site features an efficient search facility for full-text statistics produced by more than 70 federal agencies, including the Census Bureau, the Bureau of Economic Analysis, and the Bureau of Labor Statistics. Boolean searches can be made within one agency or for all agencies combined. Links are offered to international statistical bureaus, including the UN, IMF, OECD, UNESCO, Eurostat, and 20 individual countries. Fees: Free.

ONLINE DATABASES

DRI U.S. Central Database. Data Products Division. • Provides more than 23,000 business, financial, demographic, economic, foreign trade, and industry-related time series for the U.S. Includes national income, population, retail-wholesale trade, price indexes, labor data, housing, industrial production, banking, interest rates, money supply, etc. Time period is generally 1947 to date (some data back to 1929). Updating varies. Inquire as to online cost and availability.

F & S Index. The Gale Group. • Contains about four million citations to worldwide business, financial, and industrial or consumer product literature appearing from 1972 to date. Weekly updates. Inquire as to online cost and availability.

PERIODICALS AND NEWSLETTERS

Chain Drug Review: The Reporter for the Chain Drug Store Industry. Racher Press, Inc. • Biweekly. $136.00 per year. Covers news and trends of concern to the chain drug store industry. Includes special articles on OTC (over-the-counter) drugs.

Chain Store Age: The Newsmagazine for Retail Executives. Lebhar-Friedman, Inc. • Monthly. $105.00 per year. Formerly *Chain Store Age Executive with Shopping Center Age.*

Drug Topics. Medical Economics Co., Inc. • 23 times a year. $61.00 per year. Edited for retail pharmacists, hospital pharmacists, pharmacy chain store executives, wholesalers, buyers, and others concerned with drug dispensing and drug store management. Provides information on new products, including personal care items and cosmetics.

DSN Retailing Today (Discount Store News). Lebhar-Friedman, Inc. • Biweekly. $119.00 per year. Includes supplement *Apparel Merchandising.* Formerly Discount Store News.

Franchising World. International Franchise Association. • Bimonthly. $18.00 per year. Formerly *Franchising Opportunities.*

Retail Monitor International. Euromonitor International. • Monthly. $1,050.00 per year. Covers many aspects of international retailing, with emphasis on market research data. Includes profiles of leading retail groups, country profiles, retail news, trends, consumer credit information, and "Retail Factfile" (statistics).

Retail Pharmacy News. McMahon Publishing Group. • Monthly. $70.00 per year. Featues include product news for pharmacists and financial news for chain store executives.

Stores. National Retail Federation. N R F Enterprises, Inc. • Monthly. $49.00 per year.

Value Retail News: The Journal of Outlet and Off-Price Retail and Development. Off-Price Specialists, Inc. Value Retail News. • Monthly. Members $99.00 per year; non-members, $144.00 per year. Provides news of the off-price and outlet store industry. Emphasis is on real estate for outlet store centers.

RESEARCH CENTERS AND INSTITUTES

Center for Retail Management. J. L. Kellogg Graduate School of Management, Northwestern University, Evanston, IL 60208. Phone: (847)467-3600 Fax: (847)467-3620 • URL: http://www.retailing-network.com • Conducts research related to retail marketing and management.

Center for Retailing Studies. Texas A & M University, Department of Marketing, 4112 Tamus, College Station, TX 77843-4112. Phone: (979)845-0325 Fax: (979)845-5230 E-mail: berryle@tamu.edu • URL: http://www.crstamu.org • Research areas include retailing issues and consumer economics.

STATISTICS SOURCES

Business Statistics of the United States. Courtenay M. Slater, editor. Bernan Associates. • 1999. $74.00. Fifth edition. Based on *Business Statistics*, formerly issue by the Bureau of Economic Analysis, U. S. Department of Commerce. Provides basic data for a wide variety of U. S. industries, services, and economic indicators. Most statistics are shown annually for 29 years and monthly for the most recent four years.

Survey of Current Business. Available from U. S. Government Printing Office. • Monthly. $49.00 per year. Issued by Bureau of Economic Analysis, U. S. Department of Commerce. Presents a wide variety of business and economic data.

TRADE/PROFESSIONAL ASSOCIATIONS

CIES: Food Business Forum. 8445 Colesville Rd., Ste. 710, Silver Spring, MD 20910. E-mail: usoffice@ciesnet.com • URL: http://www.ciesnet.com.

International Mass Retail Association. 1700 N. Moore St., Suite 2250, Arlington, VA 22209. Phone: (703)841-2300 Fax: (703)841-1184 • URL: http://www.imra.org.

National Association of Chain Drug Stores. c/o Ronald L. Ziegler, P.O. Box 1417-D49, Alexandria, VA 22313-1480. Phone: (703)549-3001 Fax: (703)836-4869 E-mail: homepage_info@nacds.org • URL: http://www.nacds.org.

CHAMBERS OF COMMERCE

DIRECTORIES

World Chamber of Commerce Directory. • Annual. $35.00.

PERIODICALS AND NEWSLETTERS

Business Counsel: A Quarterly Update of the Litigation Activities of the U.S. Chambers of Commerce. National Chamber Litigation Center (NCLC). • Quarterly. Free to members; non-member legal libraries, $15.00 per year.

Chamber Executive. American Chamber of Commerce Executives. • Monthly. $187.00 per year. Edited for local chamber of commerce managers.

TRADE/PROFESSIONAL ASSOCIATIONS

American Chamber of Commerce Executives. P.O. Box 2966, Alexandria, VA 22902. Phone: (804)973-3987 Fax: (804)978-7449 E-mail: info@acce.org • URL: http://www.acce.org.

Council of State Chambers of Commerce. 20 Wacker Dr., Ste. 1950, Chicago, IL 60606. Phone: (312)236-1361 Fax: (312)853-6165.

United States Council for International Business. 1212 Ave. of the Americas, 21st Fl., New York, NY 10036-1689. Phone: (212)354-4480 Fax: (212)575-0327 E-mail: info@uscib.org • URL: http://www.uscib.org.

CHARITABLE TRUSTS

See: FOUNDATIONS

CHARITY

See: PHILANTHROPY

CHARTS

See: GRAPHS AND CHARTS

CHARTS, STOCK MARKET

See: TECHNICAL ANALYSIS (FINANCE)

CHECKLESS BANKING

See: ELECTRONIC FUNDS TRANSFER SYSTEMS (EFTS)

CHEESE INDUSTRY

See also: DAIRY INDUSTRY

ABSTRACTS AND INDEXES

Food Science and Technology Abstracts. International Food Information Service Publishing. • Monthly. $1,780.00 per year. Provides worldwide coverage of the literature of food technology and food production.

Foods Adlibra: Key to the World's Food Literature. Foods Adlibra Publications. • Semimonthly.Provides journal citations and abstracts to the literature of food technology and packaging.

ALMANACS AND YEARBOOKS

CRB Commodity Yearbook. Commodity Research Bureau. CRB. • Annual. $99.95.

CD-ROM DATABASES

Food Science and Technology Abstracts [CD-ROM]. Available from SilverPlatter Information, Inc. • Quarterly. $3,700 per year. Produced by International Food Information Service (home page is http://www.ifis.org). Provides worldwide coverage on CD-ROM of the literature of food technology and production. Various types of publications are indexed, with abstracts, including about 1,800 periodicals. Time period is 1969 to date.

DIRECTORIES

Cheese Market News Market Directory. Quarne Publishing LLC. • Annual. $40.00. Lists suppliers of equipment, services, and ingredients for the cheese industry.

Dairy Foods Market Directory. Cahners Business Information. • Annual. $99.90. Lists a wide variety of suppliers to the dairy industry.

Directory of Delicatessen Products. Pacific Rim Publishing Co. • Annual. Included with February issue of *Deli News*. Lists suppliers of cheeses, lunch meats, packaged fresh meats, kosher foods, gourmet-specialty items, and bakery products.

Specialty Food Industry Directory. Phoenix Media Network, Inc. • Annual. Included in subscription to Food Distribution Magazine. Lists manufacturers and suppliers of specialty foods, and services and equipment for the specialty food industry. Featured food products include legumes, sauces, spices, upscale cheese, specialty beverages, snack foods, baked goods, ethnic foods, and specialty meats.

HANDBOOKS AND MANUALS

The Cheese Handbook: A Guide to the World's Best Cheese. T.A. Layton. Dover Publications, Inc. • 1973. $4.50. Revised edition.

INTERNET DATABASES

USDA. United States Department of Agriculture. Phone: (202)720-2791 E-mail: agsec@usda.gov • URL: http://www.usda.gov • The USDA home page has six sections: News and Information; What's New; About USDA; Agencies; Opportunities; Search and Help. Keyword searching is offered from the USDA home page and from various individual agency home pages. Agencies are the Economic Research Service, Agricultural Marketing Service, National Agricultural Statistics Service, National Agricultural Library, and about 12 others. Updating varies. Fees: Free.

ONLINE DATABASES

F & S Index. The Gale Group. • Contains about four million citations to worldwide business, financial, and industrial or consumer product literature appearing from 1972 to date. Weekly updates. Inquire as to online cost and availability.

Food Science and Technology Abstracts [online]. IFIS North American Desk. • Produced by International Food Information Service. Provides about 500,000 online citations, with abstracts, to the international literature of food science, technology, commodities, engineering, and processing. Approximately 2,000 periodicals are covered. Time period is 1969 to date, with monthly updates. Inquire as to online cost and availability.

FOODS ADLIBRA. General Mills, Inc. • Contains online citations, with abstracts, to the technical and business literature of food processing and packaging. New products and new ingredients are featured. Covers about 250 trade journals and 500 research journals from 1974 to date, with monthly updates. Inquire as to online cost and availability.

PERIODICALS AND NEWSLETTERS

Cheese Importers Association of America Bulletin. Cheese Importer Association of America. • Irregular. Membership.

Cheese Market News. Quarne Publishing L.L.C. • Weekly. $85.00 per year. Covers market trends, legislation, and new products.

Cheese Reporter. Richard Groves, editor. Cheese Reporter Publishing Co., Inc. • Weekly. $80.00 per year. Reports technology, production, sales, merchandising, promotion, research and general industry news of and pertaining to the manufacture and marketing of cheese.

Dairy Foods: Innovative Ideas and Technologies for Dairy Processors. Cahners Business Information. • Monthly. $99.90 per year. Provides broad coverage of new developments in the dairy industry, including cheese and ice cream products. Includes an annual *Supplement*.

Deli News. Delicatessen Council of Southern California, Inc. Pacific Rim Publishing Co. • Monthly. $25.00 per year. Includes product news and comment related to cheeses, lunch meats, packaged fresh meats, kosher foods, gourmet-specialty items, and bakery products.

Fancy Food. Talcott Communications Corp. • Monthly. $34.00 per year. Emphasizes new specialty food products and the business management aspects of the specialty food and confection industries. Includes special issues on wine, cheese, candy, "upscale" cookware, and gifts.

Food Distribution Magazine. Phoenix Media Network, Inc. • Monthly. $49.00 per year. Edited for marketers and buyers of domestic and imported, specialty or gourmet food products, including ethnic foods, seasonings, and bakery items.

PRICE SOURCES

Dairy Market Statistics. U.S. Department of Agriculture, Agricultural Marketing Service. • Annual.

STATISTICS SOURCES

Agricultural Statistics. Available from U. S. Government Printing Office. • Annual. Produced by the National Agricultural Statistics Service, U. S. Department of Agriculture. Provides a wide variety of statistical data relating to agricultural production, supplies, consumption, prices/price-supports, foreign trade, costs, and returns, as well as farm labor, loans, income, and population. In many cases, historical data is shown annually for 10 years. In addition to farm data, includes detailed fishery statistics.

Annual Survey of Manufactures. Available from U. S. Government Printing Office. • Annual. Prices vary. Issued by the U. S. Census Bureau as an interim update to the *Census of Manufactures.* Includes data on number of manufacturing establishments in various industries, employment, labor costs, value of shipments, capital expenditures, inventories, energy costs, and assets. (See also Census Bureau home page, http://www.census.gov/.).

TRADE/PROFESSIONAL ASSOCIATIONS

Cheese Importers Association of America. 460 Park Ave., 11th Fl., New York, NY 10022. Phone: (212)753-7500 Fax: (212)688-2870.

National Cheese Institute. 1250 H St., N.W., Suite 900, Washington, DC 20005. Phone: (202)737-4332 Fax: (202)331-7820 • URL: http://www.idfa.org.

Wisconsin Cheese Makers' Association. Three S. Pinckney, Suite 620, Madison, WI 53703. Phone: (608)255-2027 Fax: (608)255-4434.

OTHER SOURCES

Major Food and Drink Companies of the World. Available from The Gale Group. • 2001. $855.00. Fourth edition. Two volumes. Published by Graham & Whiteside. Contains profiles and trade names for more than 9,000 important food and beverage companies in various countries. In addition to foods, includes both alcoholic and nonalcoholic drink products.

Thomas Food and Beverage Market Place. Grey House Publishing. • Annual. $295.00. Three volumes. Contains more than 40,000 entries covering food companies, beverages, food equipment, warehouse companies, food brokers, wholesalers, importers, and exporters. Formerly *Thomas Food Industry Register.*

U. S. Cheese Market. Available from MarketResearch.com. • 1999. $2,750.00. Market research data published by Packaged Facts. Includes projections to 2003.

CHEMICAL ENGINEERING

See also: CHEMICAL INDUSTRIES

GENERAL WORKS

Chemical Engineering for Chemists. Richard G. Griskey. American Chemical Society. • 1997. $130.00. Provides basic knowledge of chemical engineering and engineering economics.

ABSTRACTS AND INDEXES

Applied Science and Technology Index. H. W. Wilson Co. • 11 times a year. Quarterly and annual cumulations. Service basis for print edition; CD-ROM edition, $1,495.00 per year. Indexes a wide variety of English language technical, industrial, and engineering periodicals.

Chemical Abstracts. Chemical Abstracts Service. • Weekly. $22,600.00 per year.

Chemical Industry Notes. Chemical Abstracts Service. • Weekly. $1,135.00 per year.

Engineering Index Monthly: Abstracting and Indexing Services Covering Sources of the World's Engineering Literature. Engineering Information, Inc. • Monthly. $2,300.00 per year. Provides indexing and abstracting of the world's engineering and technical literature.

Process Engineering Suppliers Guide. Information Handling Services. • Semiannual. Price on application. Manufacturers and suppliers of materials, components and equipment for process engineering in the United Kingdom; includes foreign firms represented in the United Kingdom. Formerly *Process Engineering Index.*

ALMANACS AND YEARBOOKS

Advances in Chemical Engineering. Academic Press, Inc., Journal Div. • Annual. Prices vary.

BIBLIOGRAPHIES

Encyclopedia of Physical Science and Engineering Information. The Gale Group. • 1996. $160.00. Second edition. Includes print, electronic, and other information sources for a wide range of scientific, technical, and engineering topics.

BIOGRAPHICAL SOURCES

Who's Who in Science and Engineering. Marquis Who's Who. • Biennial. $269.00. Provides concise biographical information on 26,000 prominent engineers and scientists. International coverage, with geographical and professional indexes.

CD-ROM DATABASES

COMPENDEX PLUS [CD-ROM]. Engineering Information, Inc. • Quarterly. $3,450.00 per year. Provides CD-ROM indexing and abstracting of the world's engineering and technical information appearing in journals, reports, books, and proceedings, 1985 to date.

DIRECTORIES

Chemical and Engineering News-Career Opportunities Issue. American Chemical Society. • Annual. $9.00.

Chemical Engineering-Buyer's Guide. McGraw-Hill Chemical Week Associates. • Annual. Included with subscripiton to Chemical Engineering. Over 4,000 firms supplying equipment and machinery to the chemical processing industry. Formerly *Chemical Engineering-Equipment Buyer's Guide.*

Consulting Services. Association of Consulting Chemists and Chemical Engineers, Inc. • Biennial. $30.00. Directory containing one-page "scope sheet" for each member and an extensive classified directory.

Peterson's Graduate and Professional Programs: Engineering and Applied Sciences. Peterson's. • Annual. $37.95. Provides details of more than 3,400 graduate and professional programs in engineering and related fields at colleges and universities. Formerly *Peterson's Guide to Graduate Programs in Engineering and Professional Sciences.*

Plunkett's Engineering and Research Industry Almanac. Plunkett Research, Ltd. • Annual. $179.99. Contains detailed profiles of major engineering and technology corporations. Includes CD-ROM.

ENCYCLOPEDIAS AND DICTIONARIES

Dictionary of Chemical Terminology. Dobromila Kryt. Elsevier Science. • 1980. $190.75. Text in English, French, German, Polish, and Russian.

HANDBOOKS AND MANUALS

Handbook of Chemical Engineering Calculations. Nicholas P. Chopey and Tyler G. Hicks, editors. McGraw-Hill. • 1992. $89.95. Second edition.

ONLINE DATABASES

Applied Science and Technology Index Online. H. W. Wilson Co. • Provides online indexing of 400 major scientific, technical, industrial, and engineering periodicals. Time period is 1983 to date. Monthly updates. Inquire as to online cost and availability.

CA Search. Chemical Abstracts Service. • Guide to chemical literature, 1967 to present. Inquire as to online cost and availability.

COMPENDEX PLUS. Engineering Information, Inc. • Provides online indexing and abstracting of the world's engineering and technical information appearing in journals, reports, books, and proceedings. Time period is 1970 to date, with weekly updates. Inquire as to online cost and availability.

Current Contents Connect. Institute for Scientific Information. • Provides online abstracts of articles listed in the tables of contents of about 7,500 journals. Coverage is very broad, including science, social science, life science, technology, engineering, industry, agriculture, the environment, economics, and arts and humanities. Time period is two years, with weekly updates. Inquire as to online cost and availability.

NTIS Bibliographic Data Base. National Technical Information Service. • Contains citations and abstracts to unrestricted reports of government-sponsored research, 1964 to date. Covers a wide range of technical, engineering, business, and social science topics. Monthly updates. Inquire as to online cost and availability.

Who's Who in Technology [Online]. The Gale Group. • Provides online biographical profiles of over 25,000 American scientists, engineers, and others in technology-related occupations. Inquire as to online cost and availability.

PERIODICALS AND NEWSLETTERS

AICHE Journal. American Institute of Chemical Engineers. • Monthly. Members, $95.00 per year; non-members, $765.00 per year; students, $35.00 per year. Devoted to research and technological developments in chemical engineering and allied fields. Available online.

CEC Communications (Chemical Engineering Communications). IPD (International Publishers Distributors). • Bimonthly. Institutions, $87.00 per year; corporations, $135.00 per year. Formerly *Chemical Engineering Communications.*

Chemical Engineering. McGraw-Hill Chemical Week Associates. • Monthly. $29.50 per year. Includes annual *Chemical Engineering Buyers Guide.*

Chemical Engineering Progress. American Institute of Chemical Engineers. • Monthly. $85.00 per year. Covers current advances and trends in the chemical process and related industries. Supplement available *AICh Extra.*

Chemical Equipment. Cahners Business Information, New Product Information Unit. • Monthly. $39.95 per year. Covers the design, building, and operation of chemical process plants. Includes end-of-year *Chemical Equipment Literature Review.*

Industrial and Engineering Chemistry Research. American Chemical Society. • Monthly. Institutions, $1,343 per year; others, price on application. Available on line . Fromerly *Industrial and Engineering Chemistry Product Research and Development.*

Journal of Chemical and Engineering Data. American Chemical Society. • Bimonthly. Institutions, $659.00 per year; others, price on application.

PRICE SOURCES

Chemical and Engineering News: The Newsmagazine of the Chemical World. American Chemical Society. • Weekly. Institutions, $181.00 per year; others, price on application.

RESEARCH CENTERS AND INSTITUTES

Alberta Research Council. 250 Karl Clark Rd., Edmonton, AB, Canada T6N 1E4. Phone: (780)450-5111 Fax: (780)450-5333 E-mail: referral@arc.ab.ca • URL: http://www.arc.ab.ca.

Division of Engineering Research. Michigan State University. B-100 Engineering Research Complex, East Lansing, MI 48824. Phone: (517)355-5104 Fax: (517)353-5547 E-mail: wadem@egr.msu.edu • URL: http://www.egr.msu.edu/der.

Institute for Systems Research. University of Maryland, A. V. Williams Bldg., No. 115, College Park, MD 20742-3311. Phone: (301)405-6602 Fax: (301)314-9220 E-mail: isr@isr.umd.edu • URL: http://www.isr.umd.edu/ • A National Science Foundation Engineering Research Center. Areas of research include communication systems, manufacturing systems, chemical process systems, artificial intelligence, and systems integration.

STATISTICS SOURCES

Chemical and Engineering News: Facts and Figures. American Chemical Society, Microforms and Back Issues Office. • Annual. $20.00. List of 100 largest chemical producers by total chemical sales.

TRADE/PROFESSIONAL ASSOCIATIONS

American Chemical Society. 1155 16th St., N.W., Washington, DC 20036. Phone: 800-227-5558 or (202)872-4600 Fax: (202)872-4615 E-mail: meminfo@acs.org • URL: http://www.acs.org.

American Institute of Chemical Engineers. Three Park Ave., New York, NY 10016-5991. Phone: 800-242-4363 or (212)591-7338 Fax: (212)591-8897 E-mail: xpress@aiche.org • URL: http://www.aiche.org.

Association of Consulting Chemists and Chemical Engineers. P.O. Box 297, Sparta, NJ 07871. Phone: (973)729-6671 Fax: (973)729-7088 E-mail: info@chemconsult.org • URL: http://www.chemconsult.org.

CHEMICAL INDUSTRIES

See also: AGRICULTURAL CHEMICALS; FERTILIZER INDUSTRY; PLASTICS INDUSTRY

GENERAL WORKS

Chemistry Today and Tomorrow: The Central, Useful, and Creative Science. Ronald Breslow. American Chemical Society. • 1996. $19.95. Written in nontechnical language for the general reader. Discusses the various disciplines of chemistry, such as medicinal, environmental, and industrial.

Understanding Toxicology: Chemicals, Their Benefits and Uses. H. Bruno Schiefer and others. CRC Press, Inc. • 1997. $34.95. Provides a basic introduction to chemical interactions and toxicology for the general reader.

ABSTRACTS AND INDEXES

Applied Science and Technology Index. H. W. Wilson Co. • 11 times a year. Quarterly and annual cumulations. Service basis for print edition; CD-ROM edition, $1,495.00 per year. Indexes a wide variety of English language technical, industrial, and engineering periodicals.

Chemical Abstracts. Chemical Abstracts Service. • Weekly. $22,600.00 per year.

BIBLIOGRAPHIES

How to Find Chemical Information: A Guide for Practicing Chemists, Educators, and Students. Robert E. Maizell. John Wiley and Sons, Inc. • 1998. $69.95. Third edition.

Information Sources in Chemistry. Fy Hon Rowland and Peter Rhodes, editors. Bowker-Saur. • 2000. $100.00. Fifth edition. Evaluates information sources on a wide range of chemical topics. (Guides to Information Sources Series).

CD-ROM DATABASES

Chem-Bank. SilverPlatter Information, Inc. • Quarterly. $1,595.00 per year. Provides CD-ROM information on hazardous substances, including 140,000 chemicals in the *Registry of Toxic Effects of Chemical Substances* and 60,000 materials covered by the *Toxic Substances Control Act Initial Inventory*.

Chemical Strategies. Thomson Financial Securities Data. • Monthly. $2,995.00 per year. CD-ROM contains full text of investment analysts' reports on companies active in the chemical industries.

DIRECTORIES

CEC Chemical Equipment Catalog: Equipment for the Process Industries. Cahners Business Information. • Annual. $60.00. Provides catalog descriptions of chemical processing equipment in 12 major product or service categories.

Chem Sources International. Chemical Sources International, Inc. • Semiannual. $875.00. List of 2,500 chemical producers and distributors in 80 countries;lists agents and representatives of 7,400 industry firms.

Chem Sources USA. Chemical Sources International, Inc. • Annual. $395.00. List of 100 chemical producers and distributors in the U. S.

Chemcyclopedia. American Chemical Society. • Annual. $60.00. Lists 10,000 chemicals in 12 product groups, produced by 900 manufacturers. Includes chemical characteristics, trade names, and indexes.

Chemical Industry Europe. State Mutual Book and Periodical Service, Ltd. • Annual. $150.00. About 10,500 companies within the chemical industry. Available in English, French, German, Italian and Spanish. Formerly *Chemical Industry Directory.*

Chemical Week-Buyers Guide. Chemical Week Associates. • Annual. $115.00. Included in subscription to *Chemical Week.*

Directory of Chemical Producers - United States. SRI Consulting. • Annual. $2,030.00. Information on over 1,200 United States basic chemical producers, manufacturing nearly 8,000 chemicals in commercial quantities at 3,500 plant locations.

Internet Tools of the Profession: A Guide for Information Professionals. Hope N. Tillman, editor. Special Libraries Association. • 1997. $49.00. Second edition. Consists of 14 sections by various authors or compilers. After two introductory articles on searching the Internet, there are 12 annotated lists of useful Web sites, covering the SLA, business and finance, chemistry, education, food and agriculture, information technology, insurance and employee benefits, law, library management, metals and materials, pharmaceuticals, and telecommunications. An index is provided.

Major Chemical and Petrochemical Companies of Europe. Kluwer Law International. • Annual. $315.00. Published by Graham & Whiteside Ltd., London. Includes financial, personnel, and product information for chemical companies in Western Europe.

McCutcheon's: Emulsifiers and Detergents. Publishing Co., McCutcheon's Div. • Annual. $180.00. Two volumes. $275.00 per volume. North American volume contains detailed information on surface active agents produced in North America. Company names, addresses and telephone numbers are included. International volume contains detailed information on surface active agents produced in Europe and Asia or in any country outside North America. Company names, addresses and telephone numbers are included.

McCutcheon's Functional Materials: North American Edition. Publishing Co., McCutcheon Div. • Annual. $170.00. Two volumes. North American edition contains detailed information on surfactant-related products produced in North America. Examples are enzymes, lubricants, waxes, and corrosion inhibitors. Company names, addresses and telephone numbers are included. International edition contains detailed information on surfactant-related products produced in Europe and Asia. Examples are enzymes, lubricants, waxes, and corrosion inhibitors. Company names, addresses, and telephone numbers are included.

OPD Chemical Buyers Directory. Schnell Publishing Co., Inc. • Annual. $129.00. Included in subscription to *Chemical Marketing Reporter.* About 1,500 suppliers of chemical process materials and more than 300 companies which transport and store chemicals in the U.S.

Purchasing/CPI Chemicals Yellow Pages. Cahners Publishing Co. • Annual. $85.00. Manufacturers and distributors of 10,000 chemicals and raw materials, containers and packaging, transportation services and storage facilities; includes environmental servicer companies. Formerly *CPI Purchasing-Chemicals Directory.*

ENCYCLOPEDIAS AND DICTIONARIES

Kirk-Othmer Encyclopedia of Chemical Technology. John Wiley and Sons, Inc. • 1991-97. $7,350.00, prepaid. 21 volumes. Fourth edition. Four volumes are scheduled to be published each year, with individual volumes available at $350.00.

McGraw-Hill Encyclopedia of Science & Technology. McGraw-Hill. • 1997. $1,995.00. Eighth edition. 20 volumes.

FINANCIAL RATIOS

Almanac of Business and Industrial Financial Ratios. Leo Troy. Prentice Hall. • Annual. $99.95. Contains financial ratios derived from federal tax returns. Ratios for each of about 200 industries are arranged according to company asset size.

Annual Statement Studies. Robert Morris Associates: The Association of Lending and Credit Risk Professiona. • Annual. Free to members; non-members, $140.00. Median and quartile financial ratios are given for over 400 kinds of manufacturing, wholesale, retail, construction, and consumer finance establishments. Data is sorted by both asset size and sales volume. Includes a clearly written "Definition of Ratios" and an alphabetical industry index.

Quarterly Financial Report for Manufacturing, Mining, and Trade Corporations. U.S. Federal Trade Commission and U.S. Securities and Exchange Commission. Available from U.S. Government Printing Office. • Quarterly. $39.00 per year.

HANDBOOKS AND MANUALS

Comprehensive Guide to the Hazardous Properties of Chemical Substances. Pradyot Patnaik. John Wiley and Sons, Inc. • 1998. $130.00. Second edition.

Dun & Bradstreet/Gale Group Industry Handbooks. The Gale Group. • 2000. $630.00. Five volumes. $145.00 per volume. Each volume covers two or more major industries: 1. *Entertainment and Hospitality*; 2. *Construction and Agriculture*; 3. *Chemicals and Pharmaceuticals*; 4. *Computers & Software and Broadcasting & Telecommunications*; 5. *Insurance and Health & Medical Services.* The following are included for each industry: overview, statistics, financial ratios, rankings, merger information, company directory, directory of associations, and consultants directory.

INTERNET DATABASES

Fedstats. Federal Interagency Council on Statistical Policy. Phone: (202)395-7254 • URL: http://www.fedstats.gov • Web site features an efficient search facility for full-text statistics produced by more than 70 federal agencies, including the Census Bureau, the Bureau of Economic Analysis, and the Bureau of Labor Statistics. Boolean searches can be made within one agency or for all agencies combined. Links are offered to international statistical bureaus, including the UN, IMF, OECD, UNESCO, Eurostat, and 20 individual countries. Fees: Free.

Internet Tools of the Profession. Special Libraries Association. Phone: (202)234-4700 Fax: (202)265-9317 E-mail: hope@tiac.net • URL: http://www.sla.org/pubs/itotp • Web site is designed to update the printed *Internet Tools of the Profession.* Provides links to a wide range of useful databases in business, finance, industry, information technology, insurance, law, library management, telecommunications, and other subject areas. Fees: Free.

ONLINE DATABASES

Business and Industry. Responsive Database Services, Inc. • Contains online citations, abstracts, and selected fulltext from more than 1,000 trade journals, newspapers, and other publications. Provides general coverage of both manufacturing and service industries, including marketing, production, industry trends, key events, and information on specific companies. Time span is 1994 to date. Daily updates. Inquire as to online cost and availability. (Also available in a CD-ROM version.).

CA Search. Chemical Abstracts Service. • Guide to chemical literature, 1967 to present. Inquire as to online cost and availability.

DRI U.S. Central Database. Data Products Division. • Provides more than 23,000 business, financial, demographic, economic, foreign trade, and industry-related time series for the U.S. Includes national income, population, retail-wholesale trade, price indexes, labor data, housing, industrial production, banking, interest rates, money supply, etc. Time period is generally 1947 to date (some data back to 1929). Updating varies. Inquire as to online cost and availability.

F & S Index. The Gale Group. • Contains about four million citations to worldwide business, financial, and industrial or consumer product literature appearing from 1972 to date. Weekly updates. Inquire as to online cost and availability.

Tablebase. Responsive Database Services, Inc. • Provides online numerical tabular data from a wide variety of business, organization, and government sources, including 900 trade journals. Includes industry and individual company statistics relating to products, market share, sales forecasts, production, exports, market trends, etc. Time span is 1997 to date. Weekly updates. Inquire as to online cost and availability. (Also available in a CD-ROM version.).

PERIODICALS AND NEWSLETTERS

American Oil Chemists' Society Journal. American Oil Chemists' Society. AOCS Press. • Monthly. Individuals, $145.00 per year; institutions, $195.00 per year. Includes *INFORM: International News on Fats, Oils and Related Materials.*

Chemical Equipment. Cahners Business Information, New Product Information Unit. • Monthly. $39.95 per year. Covers the design, building, and operation of chemical process plants. Includes end-of-year *Chemical Equipment Literature Review.*

Chemical Processing. Putman Media. • Monthly. Free to qualified personnel; others, $67.00 per year.

Chemical Week. Chemical Week Associates. • 49 times a year. $139.00 per year. Includes annual *Buyers' Guide.*

Journal of Chemical Information and Computer Sciences. American Chemical Society. • Bimonthly. Institutions, $454.00 per year; others, price on application.

PetroChemical News: A Weekly News Service in English Devoted to the Worldwide Petrochemical Industry. William F. Bland Co. • Weekly. $739.00 per year. Report of current and significant news about the petrochemical business worldwide.

Today's Chemist at Work. American Chemical Society. • Monthly. Institutions, $160.00 per year; others, price on application. Provide pracrtical information for chemists on day-to-day operations. Product coverage includes chemicals, equipment, apparatus, instruments, and supplies.

PRICE SOURCES

Chemical and Engineering News: The Newsmagazine of the Chemical World. American Chemical Society. • Weekly. Institutions, $181.00 per year; others, price on application.

Chemical Market Reporter. Schnell Publishing Co., Inc. • Weekly. $139.00 per year. Quotes current prices for a wide range of chemicals. Formerly *Chemical Marketing Reporter.*

RESEARCH CENTERS AND INSTITUTES

ORTECH Corporation. 2395 Speakman Dr., Mississauga, ON, Canada L5K 1B3. Phone: (905)822-4111 E-mail: mail@dieselnet.com • URL: http://www.dieselnet.com/com/xf005.html.

STATISTICS SOURCES

Annual Review of the Chemical Industry. United Nations Publications. • Annual. $100.00.

Annual Survey of Manufactures. Available from U. S. Government Printing Office. • Annual. Prices vary. Issued by the U. S. Census Bureau as an interim update to the *Census of Manufactures.* Includes data on number of manufacturing establishments in various industries, employment, labor costs, value of shipments, capital expenditures, inventories, energy costs, and assets. (See also Census Bureau home page, http://www.census.gov/.).

Business Statistics of the United States. Courtenay M. Slater, editor. Bernan Associates. • 1999. $74.00. Fifth edition. Based on *Business Statistics*, formerly issue by the Bureau of Economic Analysis, U. S. Department of Commerce. Provides basic data for a wide variety of U. S. industries, services, and economic indicators. Most statistics are shown annually for 29 years and monthly for the most recent four years.

Encyclopedia of American Industries. The Gale Group. • 1998. $560.00. Second edition. Two volumes. $280.00 per volume. Volume one is *Manufacturing Industries* and volume two is *Service and Non-Manufacturing Industries.* Provides the history, development, and recent status of approximately 1,000 industries. Includes statistical graphs, with industry and general indexes.

Manufacturing Profiles. Available from U. S. Government Printing Office. • Annual. Issued by the U. S. Census Bureau. A printed consolidation of the entire *Current Industrial Report* series, presenting "all the data compiled." Contains statistics on production, shipments, inventories, consumption, exports, imports, and orders for a wide variety of manufactured products. (See also Census Bureau home page, http://www.census.gov/.).

Standard & Poor's Industry Surveys. Standard & Poor's. • Semiannual. $1,800.00. Two looseleaf volumes. Includes monthly supplements. Provides detailed, individual surveys of 52 major industry groups. Each survey is revised on a semiannual basis. Also includes "Monthly Investment Review" (industry group investment analysis) and monthly "Trends & Projections" (economic analysis).

Survey of Current Business. Available from U. S. Government Printing Office. • Monthly. $49.00 per year. Issued by Bureau of Economic Analysis, U. S. Department of Commerce. Presents a wide variety of business and economic data.

Synthetic Organic Chemicals: United States Production and Sales. International Trade Commission. Available from U.S. Government Printing Office. • Annual.

United States Census of Manufactures. U.S. Bureau of the Census. • Quinquennial. Results presented in reports, tape, CD-ROM, and Diskette files.

WEFA Industrial Monitor. John Wiley and Sons, Inc. • Annual. $65.00. Prepared by industry analysts at WEFA, an economic forecasting and consulting firm (originally Wharton Econometric Forecasting Associates). Contains discussions of the outlook for major U. S. industries, with many 10-year forecasts (WEFA Web site is http://www.wefa.com).

TRADE/PROFESSIONAL ASSOCIATIONS

American Chemical Society. 1155 16th St., N.W., Washington, DC 20036. Phone: 800-227-5558 or (202)872-4600 Fax: (202)872-4615 E-mail: meminfo@acs.org • URL: http://www.acs.org.

Association of Consulting Chemists and Chemical Engineers. P.O. Box 297, Sparta, NJ 07871. Phone: (973)729-6671 Fax: (973)729-7088 E-mail: info@chemconsult.org • URL: http://www.chemconsult.org.

Chemical Management and Resources Association. 60 Bay St., Suite 702, Staten Island, NY 10301. Phone: (718)876-8800 • Members are individuals engaged in chemical market research.

Chemical Manufacturers Association. 1300 Wilson Blvd., Arlington, VA 22209. Phone: (703)741-5000 Fax: (703)741-6000 • URL: http://www.cmahq.com.

Chemical Specialties Manufacturers Association. 1913 Eye St., N.W., Washington, DC 20006. Phone: (202)872-8110 Fax: (202)872-8114 E-mail: info@csma.org.

Commercial Development and Marketing Association. 1850 M St., N.W., Suite 700, Washington, DC 20036. Phone: (202)721-4110 Fax: (202)296-8120 E-mail: info@commercialdevelopment.com • URL: http://www.cdmaonline.com.

Council of Chemical Association Executives. c/o CMA, 1300 Wilson Blvd., Arlington, VA 22209. Phone: (703)741-5120 Fax: (703)741-6000 • URL: http://www.cmahq.com.

International Chemical Workers Union. 1655 W. Market St., Akron, OH 44313. Phone: (330)867-2444 Fax: (330)867-0544.

National Association of Chemical Distributors. 1525 Wilson Blvd., Suite 1250, Arlington, VA 22209. Phone: (703)527-6223 Fax: (703)527-7747 • URL: http://www.nacd.com.

Sales Association of the Chemical Industry. 66 Morris Ave., Suite 2-A, Springfield, NJ 07081. Phone: (973)379-1100 Fax: (973)379-6507 • Members are chemical sales personnel, including sales managers and executives.

OTHER SOURCES

Business & Company Resource Center. The Gale Group. • Fee-based Web site provides a wide range of business, industry, and specific company information. Access is offered to trade journal articles, market research data, insider trading activity, major shareholder data, corporate histories, emerging technology reports, corporate earnings estimates, press releases, and other sources. Provides detailed company profiles, industry overviews, and rankings. Offers integration of Predicasts PROMT, Newsletters ASAP, Investext Plus, Business Index ASAP, Brands and Their Companies, and other databases (many have full text).

Chemical Regulation Reporter: A Weekly Review of Affecting Chemical Users and Manufacturers. Bureau of National Affairs, Inc. • Weekly. Price varies. Irregular supplements.

Major Chemical and Petrochemical Companies of the World. Available from The Gale Group. • 2001. $855.00. Third edition. Two volumes. Published by Graham & Whiteside. Contains profiles of more than 7,000 important chemical and petrochemical companies in various countries. Subject areas include general chemicals, specialty chemicals, agricultural chemicals, petrochemicals, industrial gases, and fertilizers.

CHEMICAL LABORATORIES

See: LABORATORIES

CHEMICAL MARKETING

ABSTRACTS AND INDEXES

Business Periodicals Index. H. W. Wilson Co. • Monthly, except August, with quarterly and annual cumulations. Service basis for print edition; CD-ROM edition, $1,495.00 per year.

DIRECTORIES

Chem Sources International. Chemical Sources International, Inc. • Semiannual. $875.00. List of 2,500 chemical producers and distributors in 80 countries;lists agents and representatives of 7,400 industry firms.

Chem Sources USA. Chemical Sources International, Inc. • Annual. $395.00. List of 100 chemical producers and distributors in the U. S.

Chemical Wholesalers Directory. American Business Directories. • Annual. Price on application. Lists 8,082 United States wholesalers and 1,199 Canadian wholesalers. Compiled from telephone company yellow pages.

OPD Chemical Buyers Directory. Schnell Publishing Co., Inc. • Annual. $129.00. Included in subscription to *Chemical Marketing Reporter.* About 1,500 suppliers of chemical process materials and more than 300 companies which transport and store chemicals in the U.S.

ONLINE DATABASES

PROMT: Predicasts Overview of Markets and Technology. The Gale Group. • Companies, products, applied technologies and markets. U.S. and international literature coverage, 1972 to date. Inquire as to online cost and availability. Provides abstracts from more than 1,600 publications. Weekly updates.

Wilson Business Abstracts Online. H. W. Wilson Co. • Indexes and abstracts 600 major business periodicals, plus the *Wall Street Journal* and the business section of the *New York Times.* Indexing is from 1982, abstracting from 1990, with the two newspapers included from 1993. Updated weekly. Inquire as to online cost and availability. (*Business Periodicals Index* without abstracts is also available online.).

PERIODICALS AND NEWSLETTERS

Chemical Week. Chemical Week Associates. • 49 times a year. $139.00 per year. Includes annual *Buyers' Guide.*

PRICE SOURCES

Chemical Market Reporter. Schnell Publishing Co., Inc. • Weekly. $139.00 per year. Quotes current prices for a wide range of chemicals. Formerly *Chemical Marketing Reporter.*

STATISTICS SOURCES

Annual Bulletin of Trade in Chemical Products. Economic Commission for Europe. United Nations Publications. • Annual. $47.00.

Chemical and Engineering News: Facts and Figures. American Chemical Society, Microforms and Back Issues Office. • Annual. $20.00. List of 100 largest chemical producers by total chemical sales.

Chemical Week: Financial Survey of the 300 Largest Companies in the U. S. Chemical Process Industries. Chemical Week Associates. • Annual. $8.00. Supersedes *Chemical Week-Chemical Week 300.*

Synthetic Organic Chemicals: United States Production and Sales. International Trade Commission. Available from U.S. Government Printing Office. • Annual.

TRADE/PROFESSIONAL ASSOCIATIONS

American Chemical Society. 1155 16th St., N.W., Washington, DC 20036. Phone: 800-227-5558 or (202)872-4600 Fax: (202)872-4615 E-mail: meminfo@acs.org • URL: http://www.acs.org.

Chemical Management and Resources Association. 60 Bay St., Suite 702, Staten Island, NY 10301. Phone: (718)876-8800 • Members are individuals engaged in chemical market research.

Chemical Manufacturers Association. 1300 Wilson Blvd., Arlington, VA 22209. Phone: (703)741-5000 Fax: (703)741-6000 • URL: http://www.cmahq.com.

National Association of Chemical Distributors. 1525 Wilson Blvd., Suite 1250, Arlington, VA 22209. Phone: (703)527-6223 Fax: (703)527-7747 • URL: http://www.nacd.com.

Sales Association of the Chemical Industry. 66 Morris Ave., Suite 2-A, Springfield, NJ 07081. Phone: (973)379-1100 Fax: (973)379-6507 • Members are chemical sales personnel, including sales managers and executives.

CHILD CARE

See: DAY CARE CENTERS

CHILD LABOR

See also: LABOR; LABOR LAW AND REGULATION

ONLINE DATABASES

American Statistics Index: A Comprehensive Guide and Index to the Statistical Publications of the United States Government [Online]. Congressional Information Service, Inc. • Indexes and abstracts, 1973 to date. Inquire as to online cost and availability.

Labordoc. International Labour Office. • Indexing of labor literature and the publications of the International Labour Organization, 1965 to present. Monthly updates. Inquire as to online cost and availability.

LEXIS. LEXIS-NEXIS. • The various LEXIS databases provide full text and indexing for a wide variety of legal cases, statutes, orders, and opinions.

TRADE/PROFESSIONAL ASSOCIATIONS

National Child Labor Committee. 1501 Broadway, Suite 1111, New York, NY 10036. Phone: (212)840-1801 Fax: (212)768-0963 E-mail: nclckapow@aol.com.

National Youth Employment Coalition. 1836 Jefferson Place., N.W., Washington, DC 20036. Phone: (202)659-1064 Fax: (202)659-0339 E-mail: nyec@nyec.org • URL: http://www.nyec.org.

CHILD MARKET

See: YOUTH MARKET

CHILDREN'S APPAREL INDUSTRY

See also: CLOTHING INDUSTRY

DIRECTORIES

Buyer's Guide to the New York Market. Earnshaw Publications, Inc. • Annual. Included with *Earnshaw's Magazine.*

Directory of Apparel Specialty Stores. Chain Store Age. • Annual. $260.00. Over 5,000 companies that own over 55,500 women's and 474 children's apparel specialty companies operating over 2,200 stores. Generally includes product lines, sales volume, year founded, key personnel, and related information.

Garment Manufacturer's Index. Klevens Publications, Inc. • Annual. $60.00. A directory of about 8,000 manufacturers and suppliers of products and services used in the making of men's, women's, and children's clothing. Includes fabrics, trimmings, factory equipment, and other supplies.

Nationwide Directory of Women's and Children's Wear Buyers. Salesman's Guide. • Annual. $229.00. About 7,200 retail stores selling women's dresses, coats, sportswear, intimate apparel, and women's accessories, infants' to teens wear, and accessories; coverage does not include New York metropolitan area.

FINANCIAL RATIOS

Annual Statement Studies. Robert Morris Associates: The Association of Lending and Credit Risk Professiona. • Annual. Free to members; non-members, $140.00. Median and quartile financial ratios are given for over 400 kinds of manufacturing, wholesale, retail, construction, and consumer finance establishments. Data is sorted by both asset size and sales volume. Includes a clearly written "Definition of Ratios" and an alphabetical industry index.

HANDBOOKS AND MANUALS

Children's Clothing Store. Entrepreneur Media, Inc. • Looseleaf. $59.50. A practical guide to starting a children's clothing shop. Covers profit potential, start-up costs, market size evaluation, owner's time required, site selection, lease negotiation, pricing, accounting, advertising, promotion, etc. (Start-Up Business Guide No. E1161.).

ONLINE DATABASES

F & S Index. The Gale Group. • Contains about four million citations to worldwide business, financial, and industrial or consumer product literature appearing from 1972 to date. Weekly updates. Inquire as to online cost and availability.

PERIODICALS AND NEWSLETTERS

Baby and Junior: International Trade Magazine for Children's and Youth Fashions and Supplies. Meisenbach GmbH. • 10 times a year. 60.00 per year. Text in German.

Earnshaw's Infants, Girls and Boys Wear Review. Earnshaw Publications, Inc. • Annual. $24.00.

STATISTICS SOURCES

Annual Survey of Manufactures. Available from U. S. Government Printing Office. • Annual. Prices vary. Issued by the U. S. Census Bureau as an interim update to the *Census of Manufactures.* Includes data on number of manufacturing establishments in various industries, employment, labor costs, value of shipments, capital expenditures, inventories, energy costs, and assets. (See also Census Bureau home page, http://www.census.gov/.).

Manufacturing Profiles. Available from U. S. Government Printing Office. • Annual. Issued by the U. S. Census Bureau. A printed consolidation of the entire *Current Industrial Report* series, presenting "all the data compiled." Contains statistics on production, shipments, inventories, consumption, exports, imports, and orders for a wide variety of manufactured products. (See also Census Bureau home page, http://www.census.gov/.).

TRADE/PROFESSIONAL ASSOCIATIONS

Bureau of Wholesale Sales Representatives. 1100 Spring St. N.W., Suite 700, Atlanta, GA 30309. Phone: 800-877-1808 or (404)870-7600 Fax: (404)870-7601 E-mail: repline@aol.com • URL: http://www.bwsr.com.

Industrial Association of Juvenile Apparel Manufacturers. 1430 Broadway, Suite 1603, New York, NY 10018. Phone: (212)244-2953 Fax: (212)221-3540.

Infant and Juvenile Manufacturers Association. One Penn Plaza, Suite 4401, New York, NY 10119-4499. Phone: (212)695-8100 Fax: (212)629-4013 E-mail: inj@ferster.com.

United Infants' and Children's Wear Association. 1430 Broadway, Rm. 1603, New York, NY 10018-3308. Phone: (212)244-2953 Fax: (212)221-3540.

CHINA

See: ASIAN MARKETS

CHINAWARE

See: TABLEWARE

CHLORINE INDUSTRY

See: CHEMICAL INDUSTRIES

CHOCOLATE INDUSTRY

See also: CANDY INDUSTRY; COCOA INDUSTRY

GENERAL WORKS

Chocolate Fads, Folklore, and Fantasies: 1,000 Chunks of Chocolate Information. Linda K. Fuller. The Haworth Press, Inc. • 1994. $49.95. Includes "Choco-Marketing-Mania Survey," "Media Citations: Chocolate 1979-1992," "Choco-References," and addresses of chocolate companies. (Original Book Series).

ABSTRACTS AND INDEXES

Food Science and Technology Abstracts. International Food Information Service Publishing. • Monthly. $1,780.00 per year. Provides worldwide coverage of the literature of food technology and food production.

Foods Adlibra: Key to the World's Food Literature. Foods Adlibra Publications. • Semimonthly.Provides journal citations and abstracts to the literature of food technology and packaging.

CD-ROM DATABASES

Food Science and Technology Abstracts [CD-ROM]. Available from SilverPlatter Information, Inc. • Quarterly. $3,700 per year. Produced by International Food Information Service (home page is http://www.ifis.org). Provides worldwide coverage on CD-ROM of the literature of food technology and production. Various types of publications are indexed, with abstracts, including about 1,800 periodicals. Time period is 1969 to date.

ONLINE DATABASES

Food Science and Technology Abstracts [online]. IFIS North American Desk. • Produced by International Food Information Service. Provides about 500,000 online citations, with abstracts, to the international literature of food science, technology, commodities, engineering, and processing. Approximately 2,000 periodicals are covered. Time period is 1969 to date, with monthly updates. Inquire as to online cost and availability.

FOODS ADLIBRA. General Mills, Inc. • Contains online citations, with abstracts, to the technical and business literature of food processing and packaging. New products and new ingredients are featured. Covers about 250 trade journals and 500 research journals from 1974 to date, with monthly updates. Inquire as to online cost and availability.

STATISTICS SOURCES

Statistical Bulletin of the International Office of Cocoa, Chocolate and Sugar Confectionary. International Office of Cocoa, Chocolate and Sugar Confectionary. • Annual.

TRADE/PROFESSIONAL ASSOCIATIONS

American Cocoa Research Institute. 7900 Westpark Dr., Suite A-320, McLean, VA 22102. Phone: (703)790-5011 Fax: (703)790-5752 E-mail: info@candyusa.org.

Chocolate Manufacturers Association of the U.S.A. 7900 Westpark Dr., Suite A-320, McLean, VA 22102. Phone: (703)790-5011 Fax: (703)790-5752 E-mail: info@candyusa.org • URL: http://www.candyusa.org.

Cocoa Merchants' Association of America. 26 Broadway, Suite 707, New York, NY 10004. Phone: (212)363-7334 Fax: (212)363-7678.

OTHER SOURCES

The Candy Market. Available from MarketResearch.com. • 1998. $2,500.00. Published by Packaged Facts. Provides market data on chocolate and non-chocolate candy, with sales projections to 2002.

Major Food and Drink Companies of the World. Available from The Gale Group. • 2001. $855.00. Fourth edition. Two volumes. Published by Graham & Whiteside. Contains profiles and trade names for more than 9,000 important food and beverage companies in various countries. In addition to foods, includes both alcoholic and nonalcoholic drink products.

Thomas Food and Beverage Market Place. Grey House Publishing. • Annual. $295.00. Three volumes. Contains more than 40,000 entries covering food companies, beverages, food equipment, warehouse companies, food brokers, wholesalers, importers, and exporters. Formerly *Thomas Food Industry Register.*

CHRISTMAS CARDS

See: GREETING CARD INDUSTRY

CHROMIUM INDUSTRY

See: METAL INDUSTRY

CHRONOLOGY

See also: ANNIVERSARIES AND HOLIDAYS

GENERAL WORKS

American Decades. The Gale Group. • 1996. $890.00. $99.00 per volume. Consists of 10 volumes, each covering a decade during the period 1900-1989. "Each volume begins with an overview and chronology covering the entire decade. Subject chapters follow, each including an overview, subject-specific timeline and alphabetically arranged entries..".

Business History of the World: A Chronology. Richard B. Robinson, compiler. Greenwood Publishing Group, Inc. • 1993. $79.50. Provides "a basic chronology of the business world outside the United States from prehistory through the 1980s.".

FAA Historical Chronology: Civil Aviation and the Federal Government, 1926-1996. Edmund Preston, editor. Available from U. S. Government Printing Office. • 1998. $29.00. Third edition. Issued by the Federal Aviation Administration, U. S. Department of Transportation (http://www.dot.gov). Provides a compilation of historical information about the FAA and the earlier Civil Aeronautics Board (CAB). Chronological arrangement.

It was a Very Good Year: Extraordinary Moments in Stock Market History. Martin S. Fridson. John Wiley and Sons, Inc. • 1997. $29.95. Provides details on what happened during each of the ten best years for the stock market since 1900.

United States Business History, 1602-1988: A Chronology. Richard B. Robinson. Greenwood Publishing Group, Inc. • 1990. $75.00.

ALMANACS AND YEARBOOKS

The Annual Register: A Record of World Events. Keesing's Worldwide, LLC. • Annual. $185.00. Published by Keesings Worldwide. Lists major economic, social, and cultural events of the past year. International coverage.

DIRECTORIES

Chase's Calendar of Events: The Day-by-Day Directory. NTC/Contemporary Publishing. • Annual. $59.95. Provides information for over 10,000 special days and special events throughout the world. Chronological arrangement with an alphbetical index. Formerly *Chase's Annual Events.*

ENCYCLOPEDIAS AND DICTIONARIES

Encyclopedia of American Facts and Dates. Gorton Carruth. HarperCollins Publishers. • 1997. $45.00. 10th edition.

Gale Encyclopedia of U.S. Economic History. The Gale Group. • 2000. $205.00. Two volumes. Contains about 1,000 alphabetically arranged entries. Includes industry profiles, biographies, social issue profiles, geographic profiles, and chronological tables.

Knowledge Exchange Business Encyclopedia: Your Complete Business Advisor. Lorraine Spurge, editor. Knowledge Exchange LLC. • 1997. $45.00. Provides definitions of business terms and financial expressions, profiles of leading industries, tables of economic statistics, biographies of business leaders, and other business information. Includes "A Chronology of Business from 3000 B.C. Through 1995." Contains illustrations and three indexes.

HANDBOOKS AND MANUALS

New York Public Library Book of Chronologies. Bruce Wetterau. Pearson Education and Technology. • 1994. $16.00.

CIGAR AND CIGARETTE INDUSTRY

See also: SMOKING POLICY; TOBACCO AND TOBACCO INDUSTRY

GENERAL WORKS

Rise and Fall of the Cigarette: A Social and Cultural History of Smoking in the U. S. Allan Brandt. Basic Books. • 1997. $25.00.

Smoking and Politics: Policy Making and the Federal Bureaucracy. A. Lee Fritschler and James M. Hoepler. Prentice Hall. • 1995. $33.00. Fifth edition.

ALMANACS AND YEARBOOKS

Tobacco Retailers Almanac. Retail Tobacco Dealers of America. • Annual. Price on application.

DIRECTORIES

Perelman's Pocket Cyclopedia of Cigars. Perelman, Pioneer and Co. • Annual. $12.95. Contains profiles of more than 1,000 brands of cigars marketed in the U. S.

Tobacco International Buyers' Guide and Directory. Lockwood Trade Journal Co., Inc. • Annual. $40.00. Formerly*Tobacco Internatonal Directory and Buyers' Guide.*

United States Distribution Journal-Source Book. Bill Communications. • Annual. $95.00. Formerly *United States Distribution Journal Buyers Guide.*

INTERNET DATABASES

Fedstats. Federal Interagency Council on Statistical Policy. Phone: (202)395-7254 • URL: http://www.fedstats.gov • Web site features an efficient search facility for full-text statistics produced by more than 70 federal agencies, including the Census Bureau, the Bureau of Economic Analysis, and the Bureau of Labor Statistics. Boolean searches can be made within one agency or for all agencies combined. Links are offered to international statistical bureaus, including the UN, IMF, OECD, UNESCO, Eurostat, and 20 individual countries. Fees: Free.

ONLINE DATABASES

Agricola. U.S. National Agricultural Library. • Covers worldwide agricultural literature. Over 2.8 million citations, 1970 to present, with monthly updates. Inquire as to online cost and availability.

DRI U.S. Central Database. Data Products Division. • Provides more than 23,000 business, financial, demographic, economic, foreign trade, and industry-related time series for the U.S. Includes national income, population, retail-wholesale trade, price indexes, labor data, housing, industrial production, banking, interest rates, money supply, etc. Time period is generally 1947 to date (some data back to 1929). Updating varies. Inquire as to online cost and availability.

PERIODICALS AND NEWSLETTERS

Smokeshop. Lockwood Publications. • Bimonthly. $32.00 per year.

TMA Guide to Tobacco Taxes: Summaries of Key Provisions of Tobacco Tax Laws, All Tobacco Products, All States. Tobacco Merchant's Association of the United States, Inc. • Looseleaf service. Members, $495.00 per year; non-members, $895.00 per year. Quarterly updates.

Tobacco Barometer: Cigars, Cigarettes. Tobacco Merchants Association of the United States, Inc. • Monthly. Free. Guide to manufactured production, taxable removals, and tax-exempt removals for cigarettes, large cigars, little cigars, chewing tobacco, snuff, and pipe tobacco.

Tobacco-Cigarette News. International Press Cutting Service. • Weekly. $75.00 per year. Text in English. Formerly *Tobacco News.*

PRICE SOURCES

Tobacco Market Review. U.S. Department of Agriculture, Agricultural Marketing Service. • Annual.

RESEARCH CENTERS AND INSTITUTES

Border Belt Tobacco Research Station. North Carolina Dept. of Agriculture, 86 Border Belt Dr., Whiteville, NC 28472-6828. Phone: (910)648-4703 Fax: (910)648-4858 E-mail: borderbelt.resst@ncmail.net.

Lower Coastal Plain Research Station/Cunningham Research Station. 200 Cunningham Rd., Kinston, NC 28501. Phone: (252)527-3579 Fax: (252)527-2036 E-mail: lowercoastal.resst@ncmail.net • URL: http://www.agr.state.nc.us/research/lcptrs.htm.

Oxford Tobacco Research Station. North Carolina Department of Agriculture. P.O. Box 1555, Oxford, NC 27565. Phone: (919)693-2483 Fax: (919)693-6747.

Tobacco and Health Research Institute. University of Kentucky. Cooper and University Drives, Lexington, KY 40546. Phone: (606)257-5798 Fax: (606)323-1077 E-mail: mdavies@pop.uky.edu • URL: http://www.uky.edu/~thri/homeweb.html.

STATISTICS SOURCES

Annual Survey of Manufactures. Available from U. S. Government Printing Office. • Annual. Prices vary. Issued by the U. S. Census Bureau as an interim update to the *Census of Manufactures.* Includes data on number of manufacturing establishments in various industries, employment, labor costs, value of shipments, capital expenditures, inventories, energy costs, and assets. (See also Census Bureau home page, http://www.census.gov/.).

Business Statistics of the United States. Courtenay M. Slater, editor. Bernan Associates. • 1999. $74.00. Fifth edition. Based on *Business Statistics,* formerly issue by the Bureau of Economic Analysis, U. S. Department of Commerce. Provides basic data for a wide variety of U. S. industries, services, and economic indicators. Most statistics are shown annually for 29 years and monthly for the most recent four years.

Monthly Statistical Bulletin. Cigar Association of America. • Monthly. Membership.

Standard & Poor's Industry Surveys. Standard & Poor's. • Semiannual. $1,800.00. Two looseleaf volumes. Includes monthly supplements. Provides detailed, individual surveys of 52 major industry groups. Each survey is revised on a semiannual basis. Also includes "Monthly Investment Review" (industry group investment analysis) and monthly "Trends & Projections" (economic analysis).

Survey of Current Business. Available from U. S. Government Printing Office. • Monthly. $49.00 per year. Issued by Bureau of Economic Analysis, U. S. Department of Commerce. Presents a wide variety of business and economic data.

Tobacco Situation and Outlook. Available from U. S. Government Printing Office. • Three times per year. $11.00 per year. Issued by the Economic Research Service of the U. S. Department of Agriculture. Provides current statistical information on supply, demand, and prices.

TRADE/PROFESSIONAL ASSOCIATIONS

American Wholesale Marketers Association. 1128 16th St., Washington, DC 20036. Phone: 800-482-2962 or (202)463-2124 Fax: (202)463-6456 E-mail: davids@awmanet.org • URL: http://www.awmanet.org.

Cigar Association of America. 1707 H St., N.W., Ste. 800, Washington, DC 20006. Phone: (202)223-8204 Fax: (202)833-0379.

Retail Tobacco Dealers of America. 12 Galloway Ave., Ste. 1B, Cockeysville, MD 21030. Phone: (410)628-1674 Fax: (410)628-1679 E-mail: rtda@msn.com • URL: http://www.rtda.org.

Retail, Wholesale and Department Store Union. 30 E. 29th St., New York, NY 10016. Phone: (212)684-5300 Fax: (212)779-2809 E-mail: rwdsu@aol.com.

Tobacconists' Association of America. Eastland Mall, Suite 121, Evansville, IN 47715. Phone: (812)479-8070 Fax: (812)479-5939.

OTHER SOURCES

The Cigar Market. Available from MarketResearch.com. • 1997. $1,230.00. Market research report published by Packaged Facts. Who smokes cigars? Why are they smoking? Are they likely to continue? Sales projections are provided to the year 2001.

Cigarettes: Anatomy of an Industry, from Seed to Smoke. Available from W. W. Norton & Co., Inc. • 2001. $24.95. Published by The New Press. Covers the history, economic ramifications, marketing strategies, and legal problems of the cigarette industry. Popularly written.

Tobacco Industry Litigation Reporter: The National Journal of Record of Litigation Affecting the Tobacco Industry. Andrews Publications. • Monthly. $725.00 per year. Reports on major lawsuits brought against tobacco companies.

CIGARETTE INDUSTRY

See: CIGAR AND CIGARETTE INDUSTRY

CINEMA

See: MOTION PICTURE THEATERS

CINEMATOGRAPHY

See: MOTION PICTURE PHOTOGRAPHY

CIRCULATION MANAGEMENT (PUBLISHING)

See also: PERIODICALS

ONLINE DATABASES

Management Contents. The Gale Group. • Covers a wide range of management, financial, marketing, personnel, and administrative topics. About 150 leading business journals are indexed and abstracted from 1974 to date, with monthly updating. Inquire as to online cost and availability.

Trade & Industry Index. The Gale Group. • Provides indexing of business periodicals, January 1981 to date. Daily updates. (Full text articles from some periodicals are available online, 1983 to date, in the companion database, *Trade & Industry ASAP.*) Inquire as to online cost and availability.

PERIODICALS AND NEWSLETTERS

Circulation Management. Intertec Publishing Co. • Monthly. $39.00 per year. Edited for circulation professionals in the magazine and newsletter publishing industry. Covers marketing, planning, promotion, management, budgeting, and related topics.

STATISTICS SOURCES

Circulation [year]. SRDS. • Annual. $256.00. Contains detailed statistical analysis of newspaper circulation by metropolitan area or county and data on television viewing by area. Includes maps.

TRADE/PROFESSIONAL ASSOCIATIONS

American Business Press. 675 Third Ave., Suite 415, New York, NY 10017. Phone: (212)661-6360 Fax: (212)370-0736 E-mail: abp@abp2.com • URL: http://www.americanbusinesspress.com • Members are publishers of business and technical periodicals with audited circulation. Includes a Publishing Management Committee.

Audit Bureau of Circulations. 900 N. Meacham Rd., Schaumburg, IL 60173-4968. Phone: (847)605-0909 Fax: (847)605-0483 • URL: http://www.accessabvs.com • Verifies newspaper and periodical circulation statements. Includes a Business Publications Industry Committee and a Magazine Directors Advisory Committee.

BPA International. 270 Madison Ave., New York, NY 10016-0699. Phone: (212)779-3200 Fax: (212)779-3615 • URL: http://www.bpai.com • Verifies business and consumer periodical circulation statements. Includes a Circulation Managers Committee. *Formerly Business Publications Audit of Circulation.*

Circulation Council of DMA. 1120 Ave. of the Americas, New York, NY 10036. Phone: (212)768-7277 Fax: (212)768-4546 • URL: http://www.the-dma.org • A division of the Direct Marketing Association. Members include publishers and circulation directors.

Fulfillment Management Association (FMA). 60 E. 42nd St., Suite 1146, New York, NY 10165. Phone: (212)277-1530 Fax: (212)277-1597 • URL: http://www.com/fma • Members includes publishing circulation executives. Includes a Training and Education Committee and a Career Guidance Committee.

Magazine Publishers of America. 919 Third Ave., 22nd Fl., New York, NY 10022. Phone: (212)872-3700 Fax: (212)888-4217 E-mail: infocenter@magazine.org • URL: http://www.magazine.org • Members are publishers of consumer and other periodicals.

OTHER SOURCES

Grossman on Circulation. Gordon W. Grossman. Intertec Publishing. • 2000. $99.95. Produced by *Circulation Management* magazine. Covers magazine circulation management and marketing, with emphasis on circulaton incentives, such as free-issue offers, sweepstakes, premiums, "freemiums," and professional courtesy offers. Includes examples of promotions used at 500 consumer and trade publications.

CITIES AND TOWNS

See also: MUNICIPAL GOVERNMENT; URBAN DEVELOPMENT

GENERAL WORKS

Cities for the 21st Century. OECD Publications and Information Center. • 1994. $39.00. Contains discussions of the economic, social, and environmental problems of today's cities.

Twentieth-Century American City. Jon C. Teaford. Johns Hopkins University Press. • 1993. $38.95. Second edition. (American Moment Series).

ABSTRACTS AND INDEXES

PAIS International in Print. Public Affairs Information Service, Inc. • Monthly. $650.00 per year; cumulations three times a year. Provides topical citations to the worldwide literature of public affairs, economics, demographics, sociology, and trade. Text in English; indexed materials in English, French, German, Italian, Portuguese and Spanish.

Population Abstract of the U. S. The Gale Group. • 2000. $185.00. Historical emphasis. Includes a "breakdown of urban and rural population from the earliest census to the present.".

Readers' Guide to Periodical Literature. H. W. Wilson Co. • Monthly. $220.00 per year. CD-ROM edition, $1,495 per year, including annual cumulation. Indexes about 250 peridicals of general interest.

Sage Public Administration Abstracts. Sage Publications, Inc. • Quarterly. Individuals, $150.00 per year; institutions, $575.00 per year.

Sage Urban Studies Abstracts. Sage Publications, Inc. • Quarterly. Individuals, $150.00 per year; institutions, $560.00 per year.

Social Sciences Index. H. W. Wilson Co. • Quarterly, with annual cumulation. Service basis for print edition; CD-ROM edition, $1,495 per year. Indexes more than 400 periodicals covering economics, environmental policy, government, insurance, labor, health care policy, plannning, public administration, public welfare, urban studies, women's issues, criminology, and related topics.

ALMANACS AND YEARBOOKS

Municipal Year Book. International City/County Management Association. • Annual. $84.95. An authoritative resume of activities and statistical data of American cities.

CD-ROM DATABASES

National Newspaper Index CD-ROM. The Gale Group. • Monthly. Provides comprehensive CD-ROM indexing of all material appearing in the late edition of the *New York Times*, the final edition of the *Washington Post*, the national edition of the *Christian Science Monitor*, the home edition of the *Los Angeles Times*, and the *Wall Street Journal.* Time period is four years. Also available online.

The New York Times Ondisc. New York Times Online Services. • Monthly. $2,650.00 per year. CD-ROM discs contain the full text of *The New York Times*, final edition. Inquire as to time period covered and availability of backfiles.

Newspaper Abstracts Ondisc. Bell & Howell Information and Learning. • Monthly. $2,950.00 per year (covers 1989 to date; archival discs are available for 1985-88). Provides cover-to-cover CD-ROM indexing and abstracting of 19 major newspapers, including the *New York Times, Wall Street Journal, Washington Post, Chicago Tribune,* and *Los Angeles Times.*

PAIS on CD-ROM. Public Affairs Information Service, Inc. • Quarterly. $1,995.00 per year. Provides a CD-ROM version of the online service, *PAIS International.* Contains over 400,000 citations to the literature of contemporary social, political, and economic issues.

Social Science Source. EBSCO Publishing. • Monthly. $1,495.00 per year. Provides CD-ROM citations and abstracts to social science articles in more than 600 periodicals, with full text from 125 periodicals. Covers economics, political science, public policy, international relations, psychology, and other topics. Time period is most recent five years.

Social Sciences Citation Index: Compact Disc Edition with Abstracts. Institute for Scientific Information. • Quarterly. Provides CD-ROM indexing and abstracting of "significant articles" from 1,400 social science journals worldwide, with additional selections from 3,200 other journals, 1986 to date. Includes economics, business, finance, management, communications, demographics, information and library science, political science, sociology, and many other subjects.

Sourcebooks America CD-ROM. CACI Marketing Systems. • Annual. $1,250.00. Provides the CD-ROM version of *The Sourcebook of ZIP Code Demographics: Census Edition* and *The Sourcebook of County Demographics: Census Edition.*

WILSONDISC: Readers' Guide to Periodical Literature. H. W. Wilson Co. • Monthly. $1,095.00 per year, including unlimited online access to *Readers' Guide to Periodical Literature* through WILSONLINE. Provides CD-ROM indexing of about 250 general interest periodicals. Covers 1983 to date. (*Readers' Guide Abstracts* also available on CD-ROM at $1,995 per year.).

WILSONDISC: Wilson Social Sciences Abstracts. H. W. Wilson Co. • Monthly. Including unlimited online access to *Social Sciences Index* through WILSONLINE. Provides CD-ROM indexing from 1983 and abstracting from 1994 of more than 400 periodicals covering economics, area studies, community health, public administration, public welfare, urban studies, and many other topics related to the social sciences.

DIRECTORIES

American City and County Municipal Index: Purchasing Guide for City, Township, County Officials and Consulting Engineers. Intertec Publishing Corp. • Annual. $61.95. Includes a directory of city and county governments with populations of 10,000 or more. Names and telephone numbers of municipal purchasing officials are listed. Also includes a directory of manufacturers and suppliers of materials, equipment, and services for municipalities.

Carroll's Municipal/County Directory: CD-ROM Edition. Carroll Publishing. • Semiannual. $750.00 per year. Provides CD-ROM listings of about 99,000 city, town, and county officials in the U. S. Also available online.

Carroll's Municipal Directory. Carroll Publishing. • Semiannual. $255.00 per year. Lists about 50,000 officials in 7,900 U. S. towns and cities, with expanded listings for cities having a population of over 25,000. Top 100 cities are ranked by population and size.

City Profiles USA: A Traveler's Guide to Major U. S. and Canadian Cities. Darren L. Smith, editor. Omnigraphics, Inc. • Annual. $110.00. A directory of information useful to business and other travelers in major cities. Includes services, facilities, attractions, and events. Arranged by city.

Encyclopedia of Associations: Regional, State, and Local Organizations. The Gale Group. • Annual. $600.00. Five volumes. $140.00 per volume. Each volume covers a particular region of the U. S.

Municipal Yellow Book: Who's Who in the Leading City and County Governments and Local Authorities. Leadership Directories, Inc. • Semiannual. $235.00 per year. Lists approximately 32,000 key personnel in city and county departments, agencies, subdivisions, and branches.

HANDBOOKS AND MANUALS

Comparative Guide to American Suburbs. Grey House Publishing. • 2001. $130.00. Second edition. Contains detailed profiles of 1,800 suburban communities having a population of 10,000 or more and located within the 50 largest metropolitan areas. Includes ranking tables for income, unemployment, new housing permits, home prices, and crime, as well as information on school districts. (Universal Reference Publications.).

INTERNET DATABASES

The Dismal Scientist. Dismal Sciences, Inc. Phone: (610)241-1000 Fax: (610)696-3836 E-mail: webmaster@dismal.com • URL: http://www.dismal.com • Web site contains a wide variety of economic data and rankings. A search feature provides detailed economic profiles of local areas by ZIP code. Major divisions of the site are Economy, Data, Thoughts, Forecasts, and Toolkit, with many specially written articles and currrent analysis by "recognized economists." Fees: Free.

U. S. Census Bureau: The Official Statistics. U. S. Bureau of the Census. Phone: (301)763-4100 Fax: (301)763-4794 • URL: http://www.census.gov • Web site is "Your Source for Social, Demographic, and Economic Information." Contains "Current U. S. Population Count," "Current Economic Indicators," and a wide variety of data under "Other Official Statistics." Keyword searching is provided. Fees: Free.

ONLINE DATABASES

Newspaper and Periodical Abstracts. Bell & Howell Information and Learning. • Provides online coverage (citations and abstracts) of 25 major newspapers, 1,600 perodicals, and 70 TV programs. Covers business, economics, current affairs, health, fitness, sports, education, technology, government, consumer affairs, psychology, the arts, and the social sciences. Time period is 1986 to date, with daily updates. Inquire as to online cost and availability.

PAIS International. Public Affairs Information Service, Inc. • Corresponds to the former printed publications, *PAIS Bulletin* (1976-90) and *PAIS Foreign Language Index* (1972-90), and to the current *PAIS International in Print* (1991 to date). Covers economic, political, and sociological material appearing in periodicals, books, government documents, and other publications. Updating is monthly. Inquire as to online cost and availability.

Readers' Guide Abstracts Online. H. W. Wilson Co. • Indexes and abstracts general interest periodicals, 1983 to date. Weekly updates. Inquire as to online cost and availability.

Wilson Social Sciences Abstracts Online. H. W. Wilson Co. • Provides online abstracting and indexing of more than 415 periodicals covering area studies, community health, public administration, public welfare, urban studies, and many other social science topics. Time period is 1994 to date for abstracts and 1983 to date for indexing, with updates monthly. Inquire as to online cost and availability.

PERIODICALS AND NEWSLETTERS

American City and County: Administration, Engineering and Operations in Relation to Local Government. Intertec Publishing Corp. • Monthly. $58.00 per year. Edited for mayors, city managers, and other local officials. Emphasis is on equipment and basic services.

Downtown Idea Exchange: Essential Information for Downtown Research and Development Center. Downtown Research and Development Center. Alexander Communications Group, Inc. • Semimonthly. $157.00 per year. Newsletter for those concerned with central business districts. Provides news and other information on planning, development, parking, mass transit, traffic, funding, and other topics.

Downtown Promotion Reporter. Downtown Research and Development Center. Alexander Communications Group, Inc. • Monthly. $157.00 per year. Newsletter. Provides information on public relations, market research, advertising, budgeting, etc. Edited for promoters of downtown areas in cities and towns.

ICMA Newsletter. International City/County Management Association. • Biweekly. $175.00 per year. Covers news of developments in local government, professional municipal management, and federal regulation applied to municipalities.

Nation's Cities Weekly. National League of Cities. • Weekly. $96.00 per year. Topics covered by special issues include city budgets, surface transportation, water supply, economic development, finances, telecommunications, and computers.

RESEARCH CENTERS AND INSTITUTES

Institute of Urban and Regional Development. University of California at Berkeley, 316 Wurster Hall, Berkeley, CA 94720-1870. Phone: (510)642-4874 Fax: (510)643-9576 E-mail: iurd@uclink.berkeley.edu • URL: http://www.ced.berkeley.edu/iurd • Research topics include the effects of changing economic trends in urban areas.

Urban Institute. 2100 M St., N. W., Washington, DC 20037. Phone: (202)833-7200 Fax: (202)728-0232 E-mail: paffairs@ui.urban.org • URL: http://www.urban.org • Research activities include the study of urban economic affairs, development, housing, productivity, and municipal finance.

Urban Land Institute. 1025 Thomas Jefferson Ave. N.W., Suite 500W, Washington, DC 20004. Phone: (202)624-7000 Fax: (202)624-7140 E-mail: rlevitt@uli.org • URL: http://www.uli.org • Studies urban land planning and the growth and development of urbanized areas, including central city problems, industrial development, community development, residential development, taxation, shopping centers, and the effects of development on the environment.

STATISTICS SOURCES

American Business Climate and Economic Profiles. The Gale Group. • 1993. $135.00. Provides business, industrial, demographic, and economic figures for all states and 300 metropolitan areas. Includes production, taxation, population, growth rates, labor force data, incomes, total sales, etc.

American Cost of Living Survey. The Gale Group. • 1995. $160.00. Second edition. Cost of living data is provided for 455 U.S. cities and metroploitan areas.

American Places Dictionary: A Guide to 45,000 Populated Places, Natural Features, and Other United States Places. Frank R. Abate, editor. Omnigraphics, Inc. • 1994. $400.00. Four regional volumes: Northeast, South, Midwest, and West. Provides statistical data and other information on 45,000 U. S. cities, towns, townships, boroughs, and villages. Includes detailed state profiles, county profiles, and more than 10,000 name origins. Arranged by state, then by county. (Individual regional volumes are available at $100.00.).

America's Top Rated Cities: A Statistical Handbook. Grey House Publishing. • Annual. $195.00. Four volumes. Each volume covers major cities in a region of the U. S.: Northeastern, Eastern, Southern, Central, and Western. Volumes are available individually at $49.00. City statistics cover the "Business Environment" (finances, employment, taxes, utilities, etc.) and the "Living Environment" (cost of living, housing, education, health care, climate, etc.).

America's Top-Rated Smaller Cities: A Statistical Handbook. Grey House Publishing. • Biennial. $125.00. Provides detailed profiles of 60 U. S. cities ranging in population from 25,000 to 100,000. Includes data on cost of living, employment, income, taxes, climate, media, and many other factors.

Cities of the United States. The Gale Group. • 2001. $425.00. Fourth edition. Four regional volumes. $125.00 per volume. Detailed information is provided on 164 U. S. cities. Includes economic data, climate, geography, government, and history, with maps and photographs.

Cities of the World. The Gale Group. • 1998. $350.00. Fifth edition. Four regional volumes. $99.00 per volume. Detailed information is provided for more than 3,407 cities in 177 countries (excluding U.S.) Includes maps and photographs. Based in U.S. State Department reports.

County and City Data Book, a Statistical Abstract Supplement. U.S. Bureau of the Census. Available from U.S. Government Printing Office. • 1994. $60.00.

County and City Extra: Annual Metro, City and County Data Book. Mark Littman and Deirdre A. Gaquin. Bernan Press. • 1999. $109.00. Updates and augments data published irregularly in print form by the U. S. Census Bureau in *County and City Data Book.* Covers "every state, county, metropolitan area, and congressional district in the United States, as well as all U. S. cities with a 1990 population of 25,000 or more." Contains a wide range tic maps.

Crime in America's Top-Rated Cities: A Statistical Profile. Grey House Publishing. • Biennial. $125.00. Contains 20-year data for major crime categories in 75 cities, suburbs, metropolitan areas, and the U. S. Also includes statistics on correctional facilities, inmates, hate crimes, illegal drugs, and other crime-related matters.

Current Population Reports: Population Estimates and Projections, Series P-25. Available from U. S. Government Printing Office. • Irregular. $14.00 per year. Issued by the U.S. Bureau of the Census (http://www.census.gov). Provides monthly, mid-year, and annual population estimates, including data for states and Standard Metropolitan Statistical Areas. Projections are given for the U.S. population in future years.

Ernst & Young Almanac and Guide to U. S. Business Cities: 65 Leading Places to Do Business. John Wiley and Sons, Inc. • 1994. $16.95. Provides demographic, business, economic, and site selection data for 65 major U. S. cities.

Facts About the Cities. Allan Carpenter and Carl Provorse. H. W. Wilson Co. • 1996. $65.00. Second edition. Contains a wide variety of information on 300 American cities, including cities in Puerto Rico, Guam, and the U. S. Virgin Islands. Data is provided on the workplace, taxes, revenues, cost of living, population, climate, housing, transportation, etc.

Gale City and Metro Rankings Reporter. The Gale Group. • 1996. $134.00. Second edition. Provides about 3,000 statistical ranking tables covering more than 1,500 U. S. cities and Metropolitan Statistical Areas. Covers economic, demographic, social, governmental, and cultural factors. Sources are private studies and government data.

Geographic Reference Report: Annual Report of Costs, Wages, salaries, and Human Resource Statistics for the United States and Canada. ERI. • Annual. $389.00. Provides demographic and other data for each of 298 North American metropolian areas, including local salaries, wage differentials, cost-of-living, housing costs, income taxation, employment, unemployment, population, major employers, crime rates, weather, etc.

Health and Environment in America's Top-Rated Cities: A Statistical Profile. Grey House Publishing. • Biennial. $195.00. Covers 75 U. S. cities. Includes statistical and other data on a wide variety of topics, such as air quality, water quality, recycling, hospitals, physicians, health care costs, death rates, infant mortality, accidents, and suicides.

Markets of the United States for Business Planners: Historical and Current Profiles of 183 U. S. Urban Economies by Major Section and Industry, with Maps, Graphics, and Commentary. Thomas F. Conroy, editor. Omnigraphics, Inc. • 1995. $240.00. Second edition. Two volumes. Based on statistics from the Personal Income and Earnings Database of the Bureau of Economic Analysis, U. S. Dept. of Commerce. Provides extensive personal income data for all urban market areas of the U. S.

Moving and Relocation Sourcebook and Directory: Reference Guide to the 100 Largest Metropolitan Areas in the United States. Kay Gill, editor. Omnigraphics, Inc. • 1998. $185.00. Second edition. Provides extensive statistical and other descriptive data for the 100 largest metropolitan areas in the U. S. Includes maps and a discussion of factors to be considered when relocating.

Places, Towns, and Townships, 1998. Deirdre A. Gaquin and Richard W. Dodge, editors. Bernan Press. • 1997. $89.00. Second edition. Presents demographic and economic statistics from the U. S. Census Bureau and other government sources for places, cities, towns, villages, census designated places, and minor civil divisions. Contains more than 60 data categories.

Social Statistics of the United States. Mark S. Littman, editor. Bernan Press. • 2000. $65.00. Includes statistical data on population growth, labor force, occupations, environmental trends, leisure time use, income, poverty, taxes, and other economic or demographic topics.

State and Metropolitan Area Data Book. Available from U. S. Government Printing Office. • 1998. $31.00. Issued by the U. S. Bureau of the Census. Presents a wide variety of statistical data for U. S. regions, states, counties, metropolitan areas, and central cities, with ranking tables. Time period is 1970 to 1990.

Statistical Abstract of the United States. Available from U. S. Government Printing Office. • Annual. $51.00. Issued by the U. S. Bureau of the Census.

A Statistical Portrait of the United States: Social Conditions and Trends. Mark S. Littman, editor. Bernan Press. • 1998. $89.00. Covers "social, economic, and environmental trends in the United States over the past 25 years." Includes statistical tables, graphs, and analysis relating to such topics as population, income, poverty, wealth, labor, housing, education, healthcare, air/water quality, and government.

ULI Market Profiles: North America. Urban Land Institute. • Annual. Members, $249.95; non-members, $299.95. Provides real estate marketing data for residential, retail, office, and industrial sectors. Covers 76 U. S. metropolitan areas and 13 major foreign metropolitan areas.

TRADE/PROFESSIONAL ASSOCIATIONS

International City/County Management Association. 777 N. Capitol St., N. E., Suite 500, Washington, DC 20002-4201. Phone: (202)289-4262 Fax: (202)962-3500 • URL: http://www.icma.org • Members are administrators and assistant administrators of cities, counties, and regions. Formerly known as the International City Managers' Association (ICMA).

National Association of Towns and Townships. 444 N. Capitol St., N.W. Suite 208, Washington, DC 20001. Phone: (202)624-3550 Fax: (202)625-3554 • Provides technical and other assistance to officials of small communities.

National League of Cities. 1301 Pennsylvania Ave., N.W., Washington, DC 20004-1763. Phone: (202)626-3000 Fax: (202)626-3043 E-mail: pa@nlc.org • URL: http://www.nlc.org.

United States Conference of Mayors. 1620 Eye St., N. W., Washington, DC 20006. Phone: (202)293-7330 Fax: (202)293-2352 E-mail: info@usmayors.org • URL: http://www.usmayors.org • Promotes improved municipal government, with emphasis on federal cooperation.

OTHER SOURCES

Commercial Atlas and Marketing Guide. Rand McNally. • Annual. $395.00. Includes maps and marketing data: population, transportation, communication, and local area business statistics. Provides information on more than 128,000 U.S. locations.

Omni Gazetteer of the United States of America: A Guide to 1,500,000 Place Names in the United States and Territories. Frank R. Abate, editor. Omnigraphics, Inc. • 1991. $3,025.00. 11 volumes. Comprehensive listing of cities, towns, suburbs, villages, boroughs, structures, facilities, locales, historic places, and named geographic features. Population is shown where applicable. Individual regional volumes are available at $275.00.

Township Atlas of the United States. The Gale Group. • 2000. $85.00. Fourth edition. Covers the 48 contiguous states. Includes state maps, county maps, townships, subdivisions, and indexes.

Zip Code Mapbook of Metropolitan Areas. CACI Marketing Systems. • 1992. $195.00. Second edition. Contains Zip Code two-color maps of 326 metropolitan areas. Includes summary statistical profiles of each area: population characteristics, employment, housing, and income.

CITIZENSHIP

See also: CIVIL RIGHTS

HANDBOOKS AND MANUALS

Complete Guide to Becoming a U. S. Citizen. Eve P. Steinberg. Pearson Education and Technology. • 1994. $11.95.

ONLINE DATABASES

Magazine Index. The Gale Group. • General magazine indexing (popular literature), 1973 to present. Daily updates. Inquire as to online cost and availability.

PERIODICALS AND NEWSLETTERS

Presidential Studies Quarterly. Center for the Study of the Presidency. • Quarterly. Individuals, $120.00 per year; institutions, $195.00 per year.

TRADE/PROFESSIONAL ASSOCIATIONS

Center for the Study of the Presidency. 1020 19th St., N.W., Ste. 250, Washington, DC 20036. Phone: (202)872-9800 Fax: (202)872-9811 E-mail: thecsp@aol.com.

Ethics Resource Center. 1747 Pennsylvania Ave., N.W., Suite 400, Washington, DC 20006. Phone: 800-777-1285 or (202)737-2258 Fax: (202)737-2227 E-mail: ethics@ethics.org • URL: http://www.ethics.org.

National Conference on Citizenship. 4770 Biscayne Blvd., Suite 1150, Miami, FL 33137. Phone: (305)576-4310 Fax: (305)576-7412.

National Immigration Forum. 220 Eye St., N.E., Suite 220, Washington, DC 20002. Phone: (202)544-0004 Fax: (202)544-1905 • URL: http://www.immigrationforum.org.

CITRUS FRUIT INDUSTRY

ABSTRACTS AND INDEXES

Food Science and Technology Abstracts. International Food Information Service Publishing. • Monthly. $1,780.00 per year. Provides worldwide coverage of the literature of food technology and food production.

Foods Adlibra: Key to the World's Food Literature. Foods Adlibra Publications. • Semimonthly.Provides journal citations and abstracts to the literature of food technology and packaging.

CD-ROM DATABASES

Food Science and Technology Abstracts [CD-ROM]. Available from SilverPlatter Information, Inc. • Quarterly. $3,700 per year. Produced by International Food Information Service (home page is http://www.ifis.org). Provides worldwide coverage on CD-ROM of the literature of food technology and production. Various types of publications are indexed, with abstracts, including about 1,800 periodicals. Time period is 1969 to date.

DIRECTORIES

American Fruit Grower Source Book. Meister Publishing Co. • Annual. $5.00.

FINANCIAL RATIOS

Annual Statement Studies. Robert Morris Associates: The Association of Lending and Credit Risk Professiona. • Annual. Free to members; non-members, $140.00. Median and quartile financial ratios are given for over 400 kinds of manufacturing, wholesale, retail, construction, and consumer finance establishments. Data is sorted by both asset size and sales volume. Includes a clearly written "Definition of Ratios" and an alphabetical industry index.

INTERNET DATABASES

USDA. United States Department of Agriculture. Phone: (202)720-2791 E-mail: agsec@usda.gov • URL: http://www.usda.gov • The USDA home page has six sections: News and Information; What's New; About USDA; Agencies; Opportunities; Search and Help. Keyword searching is offered from the USDA home page and from various individual agency home pages. Agencies are the Economic Research Service, Agricultural Marketing Service, National Agricultural Statistics Service, National Agricultural Library, and about 12 others. Updating varies. Fees: Free.

ONLINE DATABASES

Agricola. U.S. National Agricultural Library. • Covers worldwide agricultural literature. Over 2.8 million citations, 1970 to present, with monthly updates. Inquire as to online cost and availability.

Food Science and Technology Abstracts [online]. IFIS North American Desk. • Produced by International Food Information Service. Provides about 500,000 online citations, with abstracts, to the international literature of food science, technology, commodities, engineering, and processing. Approximately 2,000 periodicals are covered. Time period is 1969 to date, with monthly updates. Inquire as to online cost and availability.

FOODS ADLIBRA. General Mills, Inc. • Contains online citations, with abstracts, to the technical and business literature of food processing and packaging. New products and new ingredients are featured. Covers about 250 trade journals and 500 research journals from 1974 to date, with monthly updates. Inquire as to online cost and availability.

PERIODICALS AND NEWSLETTERS

Agricultural Research and Extension Center at Uvalde. Texas A & M University.

Citrograph: Magazine of the Citrus Industry. Western Agricultural Publishing Co., Inc. • Monthly. $19.95 per year. Gives produce growing tips.

Citrus Industry Magazine. Association Publications Corp. • Monthly. $20.00 per year. Gives food growing tips.

Triangle. Florida Citrus Mutual. • Weekly. Membership.

PRICE SOURCES

California Farmer: The Business Magazine for Commercial Agriculture. Farm Progress Cos. • 15 times a year. $21.95 per year. Three editions: Northern, Southern and Central Valley.

Supermarket News: The Industry's Weekly Newspaper. Fairchild Publications. • Weekly. Individuals, $68.00 per year; instututions, $44.50 per year; corporations, $89.00 per year.

RESEARCH CENTERS AND INSTITUTES

Citrus Center. Texas A & M University at Kingsville. P.O. Box 1150, Weslaco, TX 78599. Phone: (956)968-2132 Fax: (956)969-0649 E-mail: j-dagraca@tamu.edu • URL: http://www.primera.tamu.edu/kcchome.

Citrus Research and Education Center, Lake Alfred. University of Florida. 700 Experiment Station Rd., Lake Alfred, FL 33850. Phone: (863)956-1151 Fax: (863)956-4631 E-mail: hwbr@lal.ufl.edu • URL: http://www.lal.ufl.edu.

Citrus Research Center and Agricultural Experiment Station. University of California. 202 College Bldg. North, Riverside, CA 92521. Phone: (909)787-7291 Fax: (909)787-4190 E-mail: philip.roberts@ucr.edu • URL: http://www.cnas.ucr.edu.

Lindcove Research and Extension Center. University of California. 22963 Carson Ave., Exeter, CA 93221. Phone: (209)592-2408 Fax: (209)592-5947 E-mail: uclrec@ucdavis.edu.

STATISTICS SOURCES

Agricultural Statistics. Available from U. S. Government Printing Office. • Annual. Produced by the National Agricultural Statistics Service, U. S. Department of Agriculture. Provides a wide variety of statistical data relating to agricultural production, supplies, consumption, prices/price-supports, foreign trade, costs, and returns, as well as farm labor, loans, income, and population. In many cases, historical data is shown annually for 10 years. In addition to farm data, includes detailed fishery statistics.

Fruit and Tree Nuts Situation and Outlook Report. Available from U. S. Government Printing Office. • Three times a year. $13.00 per year. (Economic Research Service, U. S. Department of Agriculture.).

United States Census of Agriculture. U.S. Bureau of the Census. • Quinquennial. Results presented in reports, tape, CD-ROM, and Diskette files.

TRADE/PROFESSIONAL ASSOCIATIONS

Florida Citrus Mutual. Citrus Mutual Bldg., P.O. Box 89, Lakeland, FL 33801. Phone: (813)682-1111 Fax: (813)682-1074 • URL: http://www.fl-citrus-mutual.com.

Florida Department of Citrus. P.O. Box 148, Lakeland, FL 33802-0148. Phone: (863)499-2500 Fax: (863)499-4300 • URL: http://www.floridajuice.com.

Florida Gift Fruit Shippers Association. 521 N. Kirkman Rd., Orlando, FL 32808. Phone: 800-432-8607 or (407)295-1491 Fax: (407)290-0918 • URL: http://www.fgfsa.com.

Sunkist Growers. P.O. Box 7888, Van Nuys, CA 91409-7888. Phone: (818)986-4800 Fax: (818)379-7511.

OTHER SOURCES

Major Food and Drink Companies of the World. Available from The Gale Group. • 2001. $855.00. Fourth edition. Two volumes. Published by Graham & Whiteside. Contains profiles and trade names for more than 9,000 important food and beverage companies in various countries. In addition to foods, includes both alcoholic and nonalcoholic drink products.

Thomas Food and Beverage Market Place. Grey House Publishing. • Annual. $295.00. Three volumes. Contains more than 40,000 entries covering food companies, beverages, food equipment, warehouse companies, food brokers, wholesalers, importers, and exporters. Formerly *Thomas Food Industry Register.*

CITY ATTORNEYS

See: MUNICIPAL GOVERNMENT

CITY CLERKS

See: MUNICIPAL GOVERNMENT

CITY FINANCE

See: MUNICIPAL FINANCE

CITY GOVERNMENT

See: MUNICIPAL GOVERNMENT

CITY PLANNING

See also: REGIONAL PLANNING; URBAN DEVELOPMENT; ZONING

GENERAL WORKS

City Planning in America: Between Promise and Despair. Mary E. Hommann. Greenwood Publishing Group, Inc. • 1993. $49.95.

The Practice of Local Government Planning. Frank S. So and Judith Getzels. International City/County Management Association. • 2000. Third edition. Price on application. (Municipal Management Series).

ABSTRACTS AND INDEXES

Art Index. H. W. Wilson Co. • Quarterly. Annual cumulations. Service basis for print edition; CD-ROM edition, $1,495.00 per year. Subject and author index to periodicals in art, architecture, industrial design, city planning, photography, and various related topics.

Journal of Planning Literature. Ohio State University, Dept. of City and Regional Planning. Sage Publications, Inc. • Quarterly. Individuals, $75.00 per year; institutions, $525.00 per year. Provides reviews and abstracts of city and regional planning lierature.

Social Sciences Index. H. W. Wilson Co. • Quarterly, with annual cumulation. Service basis for print edition; CD-ROM edition, $1,495 per year. Indexes more than 400 periodicals covering economics, environmental policy, government, insurance, labor, health care policy, plannning, public administration, public welfare, urban studies, women's issues, criminology, and related topics.

ALMANACS AND YEARBOOKS

Institute on Planning, Zoning and Eminent Domain, Southwestern Legal Foundation:Proceedings, 1971-1994. William S. Hein & Co., Inc. • 1971. $2,887.00. 24 volumes.

CD-ROM DATABASES

Social Science Source. EBSCO Publishing. • Monthly. $1,495.00 per year. Provides CD-ROM citations and abstracts to social science articles in more than 600 periodicals, with full text from 125 periodicals. Covers economics, political science, public policy, international relations, psychology, and other topics. Time period is most recent five years.

Social Sciences Citation Index: Compact Disc Edition with Abstracts. Institute for Scientific Information. • Quarterly. Provides CD-ROM indexing and abstracting of "significant articles" from 1,400 social science journals worldwide, with additional selections from 3,200 other journals, 1986 to date. Includes economics, business, finance, management, communications, demographics, information and library science, political science, sociology, and many other subjects.

WILSONDISC: Wilson Social Sciences Abstracts. H. W. Wilson Co. • Monthly. Including unlimited online access to *Social Sciences Index* through WILSONLINE. Provides CD-ROM indexing from 1983 and abstracting from 1994 of more than 400 periodicals covering economics, area studies, community health, public administration, public welfare, urban studies, and many other topics related to the social sciences.

ENCYCLOPEDIAS AND DICTIONARIES

Encyclopedia of Urban Planning. Arnold Whittick, editor. Krieger Publishing Co. • 1980. $79.50.

HANDBOOKS AND MANUALS

Progress in Planning. Donald R. Diamond and J.B. McLoughlin, editors. Elsevier Science. • Eight times a year. $619.00 per year.

Urban Parks and Open Space. Gayle L. Berens and others. Urban Land Institute. • 1997. Price on application. Covers financing, design, management, and public-private partnerships relative to the development of open space for new urban parks. Includes color illustrations and the history of urban parks.

Zoning and Planning Deskbook. Douglas W. Kmiec. West Group. • $145.00. Looseleaf service. Periodic supplementation. Emphasis is on legal issues.

Zoning and Planning Law Handbook. West Group. • 1996. Price on application. (Real Property-Zoning Series).

ONLINE DATABASES

Art Index Online. H. W. Wilson Co. • Indexes a wide variety of art-related periodicals, 1984 to date. Monthly updates. Inquire as to online cost and availability.

Wilson Social Sciences Abstracts Online. H. W. Wilson Co. • Provides online abstracting and indexing of more than 415 periodicals covering area studies, community health, public administration, public welfare, urban studies, and many other social science topics. Time period is 1994 to date for abstracts and 1983 to date for indexing, with updates monthly. Inquire as to online cost and availability.

PERIODICALS AND NEWSLETTERS

American Planning Association Journal. American Planning Association. • Quarterly. Members, $33.00 per year; non-members $65.00 per year.

Journal of Housing and Community Development. National Association of Housing and Redevelopment Officials (NAHRO). • Bimonthly. $24.00 per year. Formerly *Journal of Housing.*

Land Use Law and Zoning Digest. American Planning Association. • Monthly. $275.00 per year. Covers judicial decisions and state laws affecting zoning and land use. Edited for city planners and lawyers. Monthly supplement available *Zoning News.*

Planning. American Planning Association. • Monthly. Free to members; non-members, $60.00 per year.

Planning and Zoning News. Planning and Zoning Center, Inc. • Monthly. $175.00 per year. Newsletter on planning and zoning issues in the United States.

Urban Land: News and Trends in Land Development. Urban Land Institute. • Monthly. Membership.

Zoning and Planning Law Report. West Group. • 11 times a year. $283.00 per year. Newsletter.

RESEARCH CENTERS AND INSTITUTES

Center for Urban and Regional Studies. University of North Carolina at Chapel Hill. Hickerson House, Campus Box 3410, Chapel Hill, NC 27599-3410. Phone: (919)962-3074 Fax: (919)962-2518 E-mail: brohe.@unc.edu • URL: http://www.unc.edu/depts/curs.

Program on International Studies in Planning. Cornell University, 200 W. Sibley Hall, Ithaca, NY 14853. Phone: (607)255-2186 Fax: (607)255-6681 E-mail: bdl5@cornell.edu • URL: http://www.inet.crp.cornell.edu/organizations/isp/default.htm • Research activities are related to international urban and regional planning, with emphasis on developing areas.

STATISTICS SOURCES

Facts About the Cities. Allan Carpenter and Carl Provorse. H. W. Wilson Co. • 1996. $65.00. Second edition. Contains a wide variety of information on 300 American cities, including cities in Puerto Rico, Guam, and the U. S. Virgin Islands. Data is provided on the workplace, taxes, revenues, cost of living, population, climate, housing, transportation, etc.

TRADE/PROFESSIONAL ASSOCIATIONS

American Planning Association. 122 S. Michigan Ave., Suite. 1600, Chicago, IL 60603-6107. Phone: (312)431-9100 Fax: (312)431-9985 E-mail: research@planning.org • URL: http://www.planning.org.

Council for Urban Economic Development. 1730 K St., N.W., Suite 700, Washington, DC 20006. Phone: (202)223-4735 Fax: (202)223-4745 E-mail: mail@urbandevelopment.com • URL: http://www.cued.org.

National Association of Housing and Redevelopment Officials. 630 Eye St., N.W., Washington, DC 20001. Phone: (202)289-3500 Fax: (202)289-8181 E-mail: nahro@nahro.org • URL: http://www.nahro.org.

National Community Development Association. 522 21st St., N.W., Suite 120, Washington, DC 20006. Phone: (202)293-7587 Fax: (202)887-5546.

OTHER SOURCES

American Land Planning Law. Norman Williams, and John Taylor. West Group. • $750.00. Eight volumes. Periodic supplementation. (Real Property and Zoning Series).

CIVIL ENGINEERING

ABSTRACTS AND INDEXES

Applied Science and Technology Index. H. W. Wilson Co. • 11 times a year. Quarterly and annual cumulations. Service basis for print edition; CD-ROM edition, $1,495.00 per year. Indexes a wide variety of English language technical, industrial, and engineering periodicals.

Engineering Index Monthly: Abstracting and Indexing Services Covering Sources of the World's Engineering Literature. Engineering Information, Inc. • Monthly. $2,300.00 per year. Provides indexing and abstracting of the world's engineering and technical literature.

Fluid Abstracts: Civil Engineering. Elsevier Science. • Monthly. $1,319.00 per year. Annual cumulation. Includes the literature of coastal structures.Published in England by Elsevier Science Publishing Ltd. Formerly *Civil Engineering Hydraulics Abstracts.*

BIBLIOGRAPHIES

Encyclopedia of Physical Science and Engineering Information. The Gale Group. • 1996. $160.00. Second edition. Includes print, electronic, and other information sources for a wide range of scientific, technical, and engineering topics.

BIOGRAPHICAL SOURCES

Who's Who in Engineering. American Association of Engineering Societies. • Triennial. Members, $149.00; non-members, $242.00. Lists about 15,000 engineers who have received professional recognition for outstanding achievement.

CD-ROM DATABASES

COMPENDEX PLUS [CD-ROM]. Engineering Information, Inc. • Quarterly. $3,450.00 per year. Provides CD-ROM indexing and abstracting of the world's engineering and technical information appearing in journals, reports, books, and proceedings, 1985 to date.

DIRECTORIES

American Society of Civil Engineers-Official Register. American Society of Civil Engineers. • Annual. Free.

Peterson's Graduate and Professional Programs: Engineering and Applied Sciences. Peterson's. • Annual. $37.95. Provides details of more than 3,400 graduate and professional programs in engineering and related fields at colleges and universities. Formerly *Peterson's Guide to Graduate Programs in Engineering and Professional Sciences.*

HANDBOOKS AND MANUALS

Architects and Engineers: Their Professional Responsibilities. James Acret. McGraw-Hill. • 1977. $95.00. Second edition. Covers legal responsibilities, liabilities, and malpractice.

Civil Engineering Practice: Engineering Success By Analysis of Failure. David D. Piesold. McGraw-Hill. • 1991. $52.00.

Standard Handbook for Civil Engineers. Frederick S. Merritt and others. McGraw-Hill. • 1995. $150.00. Fourth edition.

ONLINE DATABASES

Applied Science and Technology Index Online. H. W. Wilson Co. • Provides online indexing of 400 major scientific, technical, industrial, and engineering periodicals. Time period is 1983 to date. Monthly updates. Inquire as to online cost and availability.

Civil Engineering Database (CEDB). American Society of Civil Engineers. • Provides abstracts of the U. S. and international literature of civil engineering, 1975 to date. Inquire as to online cost and availability.

COMPENDEX PLUS. Engineering Information, Inc. • Provides online indexing and abstracting of the world's engineering and technical information appearing in journals, reports, books, and proceedings. Time period is 1970 to date, with weekly updates. Inquire as to online cost and availability.

NTIS Bibliographic Data Base. National Technical Information Service. • Contains citations and abstracts to unrestricted reports of government-sponsored research, 1964 to date. Covers a wide range of technical, engineering, business, and social science topics. Monthly updates. Inquire as to online cost and availability.

TRIS: Transportation Research Information Service. National Research Council. • Contains abstracts and citations to a wide range of transportation literature, 1968 to present, with monthly updates. Includes references to the literature of air transportation, highways, ships and shipping, railroads, trucking, and urban mass transportation. Formerly *TRIS-ON-LINE.* Inquire as to online cost and availability.

PERIODICALS AND NEWSLETTERS

American Society of Civil Engineers. Proceedings. American Society of Civil Engineers. • Monthly. $2,289.00 per year. Consists of the Journals of the various Divisions of the Society.

ASCE News. American Society of Civil Engineers. • Monthly. $42.00 per year. Newsletter.

Civil Engineering: Engineered Design and Construction. American Society of Civil Engineers. • Monthly. $125.00 per year.

ENR Connecting the Industry Worldwide (Engineering News-Record). McGraw-Hill. • Weekly. $74.00 per year.

RESEARCH CENTERS AND INSTITUTES

Engineering Dean's Office. University of California at Berkeley, 308 Mclaughin Hall, No. 1702, Berkeley, CA 94720-1706. Phone: (510)642-7594 Fax: (510)643-8653 E-mail: dma@coe.berkeley.edu • Research fields include civil, electrical, industrial, mechanical, and other types of engineering.

New Mexico Engineering Research Institute. University of New Mexico. 901 University Blvd., S.E., Albuquerque, NM 87106-4339. Phone: (505)272-7200 Fax: (505)272-7203 E-mail: oneil@nmeri.umm.edu • URL: http://www.nmeri.umn.edu.

TRADE/PROFESSIONAL ASSOCIATIONS

American Society of Civil Engineers. 1801 Alexander Bell Dr., Reston, VA 20191-4400. Phone: 800-548-2723 or (703)295-6000 Fax: (703)295-6222 E-mail: webmaster@asce.org • URL: http://www.asce.org.

OTHER SOURCES

American Society of Civil Engineers: Transactions. American Society of Civil Engineers. • Annual. $230.00.

Forms and Agreements for Architects, Engineers and Contractors. Albert Dib. West Group. • Four looseleaf volumes. $495.00. Periodic supplementation. Covers evaluation of construction documents and alternative clauses. Includes pleadings for litigation and resolving of claims. (Real Property-Zoning Series).

CIVIL RIGHTS

See also: CITIZENSHIP; HUMAN RELATIONS

GENERAL WORKS

Civil Liberties Under the Constitution. M. Glenn Abernathy and A. Perry Barbara. University of South Carolina Press. • 1993. $34.95. Sixth edition.

The Limits of Liberty: Between Anarchy and Leviathan. James M. Buchanan. University of Chicago Press. • 2000. $20.00. (Collected Works of James M. Buchanan: Vol. 7).

Taking Rights Seriously. Ronald Dworkin. Harvard University Press. • 1977. $40.50.

ABSTRACTS AND INDEXES

Current Law Index: Multiple Access to Legal Periodicals. The Gale Group. • Monthly. $650.00 per year. Produced in cooperation with the American Association of Law Libraries. Indexes more than 900 law journals, legal newspapers, and specialty publications from the U.S., Canada, U.K., Ireland, Australia, and New Zealand.

Social Sciences Index. H. W. Wilson Co. • Quarterly, with annual cumulation. Service basis for print edition; CD-ROM edition, $1,495 per year. Indexes more than 400 periodicals covering economics, environmental policy, government, insurance, labor, health care policy, plannning, public administration, public welfare, urban studies, women's issues, criminology, and related topics.

ALMANACS AND YEARBOOKS

World Labour Report. International Labour Office. • Irregular. Price varies. Volume eight. International coverage. Reviews significant recent events and labor policy developments in the following areas: employment, human rights, labor relations, and working conditions.

CD-ROM DATABASES

Social Science Source. EBSCO Publishing. • Monthly. $1,495.00 per year. Provides CD-ROM citations and abstracts to social science articles in more than 600 periodicals, with full text from 125 periodicals. Covers economics, political science, public policy, international relations, psychology, and other topics. Time period is most recent five years.

Social Sciences Citation Index: Compact Disc Edition with Abstracts. Institute for Scientific Information. • Quarterly. Provides CD-ROM indexing and abstracting of "significant articles" from 1,400 social science journals worldwide, with additional selections from 3,200 other journals, 1986 to date. Includes economics, business, finance, management, communications, demographics, information and library science, political science, sociology, and many other subjects.

WILSONDISC: Wilson Social Sciences Abstracts. H. W. Wilson Co. • Monthly. Including unlimited online access to *Social Sciences Index* through WILSONLINE. Provides CD-ROM indexing from 1983 and abstracting from 1994 of more than 400 periodicals covering economics, area studies, community health, public administration, public welfare, urban studies, and many other topics related to the social sciences.

DIRECTORIES

Human Rights Organizations and Periodicals Directory. Meiklejohn Civil Liberties Institute. • Biennial. Individuals, $70.00 per year; libraries and institutions, $76.00 per year. Over 1,100 United States organiations and periodicals dedicated to improving human rights.

ENCYCLOPEDIAS AND DICTIONARIES

Encyclopedia of Crime and Justice. Available from The Gale Group. • 2001. $425.00. Second edition. Four volumes. Published by Macmillan Reference USA. Contains extensive information on a wide variety of topics pertaining to crime, criminology, social issues, and the courts. (A revision of 1982 edition.).

HANDBOOKS AND MANUALS

Federal Civil Rights Acts. Rodney A. Smolla. West Group. • Two looseleaf volumes. $245.00. Covers current legislation relating to a wide range of civil rights issues, including discrimination in employment, housing, property rights, and voting. (Civil Right Series).

Legal Aspects of AIDS. Donald H. Hermann and William P. Schurgin. West Group. • $130.00 per year. Looseleaf Service. Periodic supplementation. Includes issue employment discrimination, housing discrimination, and insurance. This work also "traces the historical progression of the disease and its spread." (Civil Rights Series).

Manual on Employment Discrimination Law and Civil Rights Action in the Federal Courts. Charles R. Richey. West Group. • $100.00. Looseleaf service. Periodic supplementation.

Women and the Law. Carol H. Lefcourt, editor. West Group. • $140.00. Looseleaf service. Periodic supplementation. Covers such topics as employment discrimination, pay equity (comparable worth), sexual harassment in the workplace, property rights, and child custody issues. (Civil Rights Series).

ONLINE DATABASES

Legal Resource Index. The Gale Group. • Broad coverage of law literature appearing in legal, business, and other periodicals, 1980 to date. Monthly updates. Inquire as to online cost and availability.

Wilson Social Sciences Abstracts Online. H. W. Wilson Co. • Provides online abstracting and indexing of more than 415 periodicals covering area studies, community health, public administration, public welfare, urban studies, and many other social science topics. Time period is 1994 to date for abstracts and 1983 to date for indexing, with updates monthly. Inquire as to online cost and availability.

PERIODICALS AND NEWSLETTERS

Civil Liberties. American Civil Liberties Union. • Annual. Membership.

Civil Rights: State Capitals. Wakeman-Walworth, Inc. • Weekly. $245.00 per year. Newsletter. Includes coverage of state affirmative action programs. Formerly *From the State Capitals: Civil Rights.*

CORE Magazine. Congress of Racial Equality. CORE Publications. • Quarterly. $10.00 per year.

Police Misconduct and Civil Rights Law Report. National Lawyers Guild Civil Liberties Committee. West Group. • Bimonthly. $194.00 per year. Newsletter.

RESEARCH CENTERS AND INSTITUTES

Center for National Policy. One Massachusetts Ave., N.W., Suite 333, Washington, DC 20001-1401. Phone: (202)682-1800 Fax: (202)682-1818 E-mail: mostein@cnponline.org • URL: http://www.cnponline.org.

Earl Warren Legal Institute. University of California at Berkeley. Boalt Hall, Berkeley, CA 94720. Phone: (510)642-5125 Fax: (510)643-2698 E-mail: zimring@mail.law.berkeley.edu.

Lexis.com Research System. Lexis-Nexis Group. Phone: 800-227-9597 or (937)865-6800 Fax: (937)865-6909 E-mail: webmaster@prod.lexis-nexis.com • URL: http://www.lexis.com • Fee-based Web site offers extensive searching of a wide variety of legal sources. Additional features include Daily Opinion Service, lexis.com Bookstore, Career Center, CLE Center, Law Schools, and Practice Pages ("Pages specific to areas of specialty").

TRADE/PROFESSIONAL ASSOCIATIONS

American Civil Liberties Union. 125 S. Broad St., 18th Fl., New York, NY 10004-2400. Phone: (212)549-2500 Fax: (212)549-2646 E-mail: aclu@aclu.org • URL: http://www.aclu.org/.

Leadership Conference on Civil Rights. 1629 K St., N.W., Suite 1010, Washington, DC 20006. Phone: (202)466-3311 Fax: (202)466-3435.

National Association for the Advancement of Colored People. 4805 Mount Hope Dr., Baltimore, MD 21215. Phone: (410)358-8900 Fax: (410)358-3818 • URL: http://www.naacp.org/.

National Urban League. 120 Wall St., New York, NY 10021. Phone: (212)558-5300 Fax: (212)344-5332 E-mail: info@nul.org • URL: http://www.nul.org.

Southern Christian Leadership Conference. 334 Auburn Ave., N.E., Atlanta, GA 30303. Phone: (404)522-1420 Fax: (404)659-7390.

OTHER SOURCES

Age Discrimination. Shepard's. • Three looseleaf volumes. $300.00. Annual supplementation. Emphasis on the Age Discrimination Act, the Age Discrimination in Employment Act, and the Equal Credit Opportunity Act.

Civil Rights Actions. Matthew Bender & Co., Inc. • $980.00. Seven looseleaf volumes. Semiannual updates, $661.00. Contains legal analysis of civil rights activities.

Employment Discrimination. Matthew Bender & Co., Inc. • $1,260.00. Nine looseleaf volumes. Periodic supplementation, $849.00. Treatise on both substantive and procedural law governing employment discrimination based on sex, age, race, religion, national origin, etc.

Employment Discrimination: Law and Litigation. Merrick T. Rossein. West Group. • $220.00 per year. Looseleaf service. Periodic supplementation. Covers employment provisions of the Civil Rights Act, the Equal Pay Act, and related topics.

Fair Housing: Discrimination in Real Estate, Community Development and Revitalization. James A. Kushner. Shepard's. • 1983. $140.00. Second edition. (Individual Rights Series).

Government Discrimination: Equal Protection Law and Litigation. James A. Kushner. West Group. • $140.00 per year. Looseleaf service. Periodic supplementation. Covers discrimination in employment, housing, and other areas by local, state, and federal offices or agencies. (Civil Rights Series).

Housing Discrimination: Law and Litigation. Robert G. Schwemm. West Group. • Looseleaf. $130.00. Periodic supplementation. Covers provisions of the Fair Housing Act and related topics. (Civil Rights Series).

World of Criminal Justice. The Gale Group. • 2001. $150.00. Two volumes. Contains both topical and biographical entries relating to the criminal justice system and criminology.

CIVIL SERVICE

See also: GOVERNMENT EMPLOYEES

GENERAL WORKS

Improving Public Productivity: Concepts and Practice. Ellen D. Rosen. Sage Publications, Inc. • 1993. $52.00. A discussion of strategies for improving service quality and client satisfaction in public agencies at the local, state, and national level. Methods for measuring public sector productivity are included.

Public Personnel Administration: Policies and Procedures for Personnel. Prentice Hall. • Looseleaf service. Price on application.

ABSTRACTS AND INDEXES

Social Sciences Index. H. W. Wilson Co. • Quarterly, with annual cumulation. Service basis for print edition; CD-ROM edition, $1,495 per year. Indexes more than 400 periodicals covering economics, environmental policy, government, insurance, labor, health care policy, plannning, public administration, public welfare, urban studies, women's issues, criminology, and related topics.

ALMANACS AND YEARBOOKS

Federal Employees Almanac. Federal Employees New Digest, Inc. • Annual. $11.95. Comprehensive guide for federal employees.

CD-ROM DATABASES

Social Science Source. EBSCO Publishing. • Monthly. $1,495.00 per year. Provides CD-ROM citations and abstracts to social science articles in more than 600 periodicals, with full text from 125

For publishers addresses, refer to SOURCES CITED section at the back of the book.

periodicals. Covers economics, political science, public policy, international relations, psychology, and other topics. Time period is most recent five years.

Social Sciences Citation Index: Compact Disc Edition with Abstracts. Institute for Scientific Information. • Quarterly. Provides CD-ROM indexing and abstracting of "significant articles" from 1,400 social science journals worldwide, with additional selections from 3,200 other journals, 1986 to date. Includes economics, business, finance, management, communications, demographics, information and library science, political science, sociology, and many other subjects.

WILSONDISC: Wilson Social Sciences Abstracts. H. W. Wilson Co. • Monthly. Including unlimited online access to *Social Sciences Index* through WILSONLINE. Provides CD-ROM indexing from 1983 and abstracting from 1994 of more than 400 periodicals covering economics, area studies, community health, public administration, public welfare, urban studies, and many other topics related to the social sciences.

ENCYCLOPEDIAS AND DICTIONARIES

International Encyclopedia of Public Policy and Administration. Jay M. Shafritz, editor. HarperCollins Publishers. • 1997. $550.00. Four volumes. Covers 20 major areas, such as public administration, government budgeting, industrial policy, nonprofit management, organizational theory, public finance, labor relations, and taxation. Includes a brief bibliography for each major entry and a comprehensive index.

HANDBOOKS AND MANUALS

Civil Service Handbook: How to Get a Civil Service Job. Pearson Education and Technology. • 1999. $12.95. 14th edition. (Arco Civil Service Series).

The Federal Manager's Handbook: A Guide to Rehabilitating or Removing the Problem Employee. G. Jerry Shaw and William L. Bransford. FPMI Communications, Inc. • 1997. $24.95. Third revised edition.

Federal Personnel Manual. U.S. Office of Personnel Management. Available from U.S. Government Printing Office. • Looseleaf service. Periodic supplementation. Available in parts.

Office of Personnel Management Operating Manuals. Available from U. S. Government Printing Office. • Four looseleaf manuals at various prices ($25.00 to $190.00). Price of each manual includes updates for an indeterminate period. Manuals provides details of the federal wage system, the federal wage system "Nonappropriated Fund", personnel recordkeeping, personnel actions, qualification standards, and data reporting.

ONLINE DATABASES

Magazine Index. The Gale Group. • General magazine indexing (popular literature), 1973 to present. Daily updates. Inquire as to online cost and availability.

Wilson Social Sciences Abstracts Online. H. W. Wilson Co. • Provides online abstracting and indexing of more than 415 periodicals covering area studies, community health, public administration, public welfare, urban studies, and many other social science topics. Time period is 1994 to date for abstracts and 1983 to date for indexing, with updates monthly. Inquire as to online cost and availability.

PERIODICALS AND NEWSLETTERS

Federal Employee. National Federation of Federal Employees. • Monthly. $15.00 per year.

Federal Human Resources Week. LRP Publications. • 48 times a year. $325.00 per year. Newsletter. Covers federal personnel issues, including legislation, benefits, budgets, and downsizing.

Federal Jobs Digest. Breakthrough Publications, Inc. • Biweekly. Individuals, $125.00 per year; libraries, $112.50 per year. Lists 15,000 immediate job openings within the federal government in each issue.

Federal Times. Army Times Publishing Co. • Weekly. $52.00 per year.

Public Personnel Management. International Personnel Management Association. • Quarterly. $50.00 per year.

TRADE/PROFESSIONAL ASSOCIATIONS

Federation of International Civil Servants' Associations. Palais des Nations, Rm. BOC 74, CH-1211 Geneva 10, Switzerland. E-mail: ficsa@ficsa.org • URL: http://www.ficsa.org.

International Personnel Management Association. 1617 Duke St., Alexandria, VA 22314. Phone: (703)549-7100 Fax: (703)684-0948 E-mail: ipma@impa-hr.org • URL: http://www.ipma-hr.org.

OTHER SOURCES

Carroll's Federal Organization Charts. Carroll Publishing. • Quarterly. $950.00 per year. Provides 200 large, fold-out paper charts showing personnel relationships in 2,100 federal departments and agencies. Charts are also available online and on CD-ROM.

Opportunities in Government Careers. Neale J. Baxter. NTC/Contemporary Publishing Group. • 2001. $15.95. Edited for students and job seekers. Includes education requirements and salary data. (VGM Career Books.).

CLAY INDUSTRY

See also: CERAMICS INDUSTRY; POTTERY INDUSTRY

GENERAL WORKS

An Introduction to Clay Colloid Chemistry: For Clay Technologists, Geologists and Soil Scientists. H. Van Olphen. Krieger Publishing Co. • 1991. $69.50. Second edition.

Structural Clay Products. W.E. Brownell. Springer-Verlag New York, Inc. • 1977. $91.95. (Applied Mineralogy Series: Vol. 9).

HANDBOOKS AND MANUALS

Clay Mineralogy. M. J. Wilson. John Wiley and Sons, Inc. • 1992. $105.00.

INTERNET DATABASES

Fedstats. Federal Interagency Council on Statistical Policy. Phone: (202)395-7254 • URL: http://www.fedstats.gov • Web site features an efficient search facility for full-text statistics produced by more than 70 federal agencies, including the Census Bureau, the Bureau of Economic Analysis, and the Bureau of Labor Statistics. Boolean searches can be made within one agency or for all agencies combined. Links are offered to international statistical bureaus, including the UN, IMF, OECD, UNESCO, Eurostat, and 20 individual countries. Fees: Free.

ONLINE DATABASES

DRI U.S. Central Database. Data Products Division. • Provides more than 23,000 business, financial, demographic, economic, foreign trade, and industry-related time series for the U.S. Includes national income, population, retail-wholesale trade, price indexes, labor data, housing, industrial production, banking, interest rates, money supply, etc. Time period is generally 1947 to date (some data back to 1929). Updating varies. Inquire as to online cost and availability.

PERIODICALS AND NEWSLETTERS

Clays and Clay Minerals. Clay Minerals Society. • Bimonthly. $195.00 per year.

PRICE SOURCES

Chemical Market Reporter. Schnell Publishing Co., Inc. • Weekly. $139.00 per year. Quotes current prices for a wide range of chemicals. Formerly *Chemical Marketing Reporter.*

RESEARCH CENTERS AND INSTITUTES

Geotechnical/Civil Engineering Materials Research Laboratories. Iowa State University of Science and Technology. 481 Town Engineering, Ames, IA 50011. Phone: (515)294-9470 Fax: (515)294-8216 E-mail: bergeson@çcelab.iastate.edu • URL: http://www.cce.iastate.edu/research/geo-mat.

STATISTICS SOURCES

Annual Survey of Manufactures. Available from U. S. Government Printing Office. • Annual. Prices vary. Issued by the U. S. Census Bureau as an interim update to the *Census of Manufactures.* Includes data on number of manufacturing establishments in various industries, employment, labor costs, value of shipments, capital expenditures, inventories, energy costs, and assets. (See also Census Bureau home page, http://www.census.gov/.).

Business Statistics of the United States. Courtenay M. Slater, editor. Bernan Associates. • 1999. $74.00. Fifth edition. Based on *Business Statistics*, formerly issue by the Bureau of Economic Analysis, U. S. Department of Commerce. Provides basic data for a wide variety of U. S. industries, services, and economic indicators. Most statistics are shown annually for 29 years and monthly for the most recent four years.

Manufacturing Profiles. Available from U. S. Government Printing Office. • Annual. Issued by the U. S. Census Bureau. A printed consolidation of the entire *Current Industrial Report* series, presenting "all the data compiled." Contains statistics on production, shipments, inventories, consumption, exports, imports, and orders for a wide variety of manufactured products. (See also Census Bureau home page, http://www.census.gov/.).

Mineral Commodity Summaries. Available from U. S. Government Printing Office. • Annual. Published by the U. S. Geological Survey, Department of the Interior (http://www.usgs.gov). Contains detailed, five-year data for about 90 nonfuel minerals. Covers a wide range of statistics, including production, imports, exports, consumption, reserves, prices, tariff information, and industry employment. (Two pages are devoted to each mineral.).

Minerals Yearbook. Available from U.S. Government Printing Office. • Annual. Three volumes.

Survey of Current Business. Available from U. S. Government Printing Office. • Monthly. $49.00 per year. Issued by Bureau of Economic Analysis, U. S. Department of Commerce. Presents a wide variety of business and economic data.

United States Census of Mineral Industries. Bureau of the Census, U.S. Department of Commerce. Available from U.S. Government Printing Office. • Quinquennial.

TRADE/PROFESSIONAL ASSOCIATIONS

ABG Division United Steel Worker. 3362 Hollenberg Dr., Bridgeton, MO 63044. Phone: (314)739-6142 Fax: (314)739-1216.

Brick Industry Association. 11490 Commerce Park Dr., Reston, VA 20191. Phone: (703)620-0010 Fax: (703)620-3928 E-mail: brickinfo@bia.org • URL: http://www.bia.org.

Clay Minerals Society. P.O. Box 4416, Boulder, CO 80306. Phone: (303)444-6405 Fax: (303)444-2260 E-mail: peberl@clays.org.

Expanded Shale Clay and Slate Institute. 2225 E. Murray Holladay Rd., Suite 102, Salt Lake City, UT 84117. Phone: (801)272-7070 Fax: (801)272-3377 • URL: http://www.escsi.org.

CLEANING COMPOSITIONS

See: CLEANING PRODUCTS INDUSTRY

CLEANING INDUSTRY

See also: LAUNDRY INDUSTRY

ABSTRACTS AND INDEXES

Textile Technology Digest. Institute of Textile Technology. • Monthly. $535.00 per year. Provides indexing and abstracting of a wide variety of textile technology literature.

CD-ROM DATABASES

Textile Technology Digest [CD-ROM]. Textile Information Center, Institute of Textile Technology. • Quarterly. $1,700.00 per year. Provides CD-ROM indexing and abstracting of worldwide journals and monographs in various areas of textile technology, production, and management. Covers 1978 to date.

DIRECTORIES

National Association of Institutional Linen Management Survey. National Association of Institutional Laundry Management. • Biennial. $100.00. Lists managers of in-house laundries for institutions, hotels, schools, etc.

ENCYCLOPEDIAS AND DICTIONARIES

Encyclopedia of Textiles. French and European Publications, Inc. • 1980. $39.95. Third edition.

Textile Terms and Definitions. J.E. McIntyre and Paul N. Daniels, editors. Available from State Mutual Book and Periodical Service Ltd., Trade Order Dept. • 1995. $110.00. 10th edition. Published by the Textile Insitute (UK). Includes more than 1,000 definitions of textile processes, fiber types, and end products. Illustrated.

FINANCIAL RATIOS

Annual Statement Studies. Robert Morris Associates: The Association of Lending and Credit Risk Professiona. • Annual. Free to members; non-members, $140.00. Median and quartile financial ratios are given for over 400 kinds of manufacturing, wholesale, retail, construction, and consumer finance establishments. Data is sorted by both asset size and sales volume. Includes a clearly written "Definition of Ratios" and an alphabetical industry index.

HANDBOOKS AND MANUALS

Carpet Cleaning Service. Entrepreneur Media, Inc. • Looseleaf. $59.50. A practical guide to starting a carpet cleaning business. Covers profit potential, start-up costs, market size evaluation, owner's time required, pricing, accounting, advertising, promotion, etc. (Start-Up Business Guide No. E1053.).

Dry Cleaning Shop. Entrepreneur Media, Inc. • Looseleaf. $59.50. A practical guide to starting a dry cleaning business. Covers profit potential, start-up costs, market size evaluation, owner's time required, site selection, lease negotiation, pricing, accounting, advertising, promotion, etc. (Start-Up Business Guide No. E1037.).

Everything You Need to Know to Start a House Cleaning Service. Mary P. Johnson. Cleaning Consultant Services, Inc. • 1999. $38.00 Revised edition.

ONLINE DATABASES

Textile Technology Digest [online]. Textile Information Center, Institute of Textile Technology. • Contains indexing and abstracting of more than 300 worldwide journals and monographs in various areas of textile technology, production, and management. Time period is 1978 to date, with monthly updating. Inquire as to online cost and availability.

Textiles Information Treatment Users' Service (TITUS). Institut Textile de France. • Citations and abstracts of the worldwide literature on textiles, 1968 to present. Monthly updates. Inquire as to online cost and availability.

PERIODICALS AND NEWSLETTERS

American Coin-Op: The Magazine for Coin-Operated Laundry and Drycleaning Businessmen. Crain Communications, Inc. • Monthly. $35.00 per year.

American Drycleaner. Crain Communications, Inc. • Monthly. $35.00 per year.

Cleaning Business: Published Monthly for the Self-Employed Cleaning and Maintenance Professionals. William R. Griffin, Publisher. • Monthly. $20.00 per year. Formerly *Service Business.*

Coin Launderer and Cleaner. Sheidko Corp. • Monthly. $25.00 per year.

Drycleaners News. Zackin Publications, Inc. • Monthly. $36.00.

Industrial Launderer. Institute of Industrial Launderers. • Monthly. $100.00 per year.

STATISTICS SOURCES

Annual Survey of Manufactures. Available from U. S. Government Printing Office. • Annual. Prices vary. Issued by the U. S. Census Bureau as an interim update to the *Census of Manufactures.* Includes data on number of manufacturing establishments in various industries, employment, labor costs, value of shipments, capital expenditures, inventories, energy costs, and assets. (See also Census Bureau home page, http://www.census.gov/.).

United States Census of Service Industries. U.S. Bureau of the Census. • Quinquennial. Various reports available.

TRADE/PROFESSIONAL ASSOCIATIONS

Coin Laundry Association. 1315 Butterfield Rd., Suite 212, Downers Grove, IL 60515. Phone: (630)963-5547 Fax: (630)963-5864 E-mail: info@coinlaundry.org • URL: http://www.coinlaundry.org.

International Fabricare Institute. 12251 Tech Rd., Silver Spring, MD 20904. Phone: 800-638-2627 or (301)622-1900 Fax: (301)236-9320 E-mail: wecare@ifi.org • URL: http://www.ifi.org.

Multi-Housing Laundry Association. 4101 Lake Boone Trail, Suite 201, Raleigh, NC 27607. Phone: (919)787-5181 Fax: (919)787-4916.

National Association of Institutional Linen Management. 2130 Lexington Rd., Suite H, Richmond, KY 40475. Phone: (606)624-0177 Fax: (606)624-3580 E-mail: nailm@iclub.org • URL: http://www.nailm.com.

Neighborhood Cleaners Association International. 252 West 29th St., 2nd Fl., New York, NY 10001-5201. Phone: (212)967-3002 Fax: (212)967-2242 • Members are dry cleaning establishments.

Textile Care Allied Trades Association. 271 U.S. Highway 46, No. 203-D, Fairfield, NJ 07004-2458. Phone: (973)244-1790 Fax: (973)244-4455 E-mail: tcata@ix.netcom.com.

Textile Institute. Saint James Bldgs., 4th Fl., Oxford St., Manchester M1 6FQ, England. Phone: 44 161 2371188 Fax: 44 161 2361991 E-mail: tiihq@textileinst.org.uk • URL: http://www.texi.org • Members in 100 countries involved with textile industry management, marketing, science, and technology.

Textile Processors, Service Trades, Health Care, Professional and Technical Employees International Union. 303 E. Wacker Dr., Suite 1109, Chicago, IL 60601. Phone: (312)946-0450 Fax: (312)964-0453.

OTHER SOURCES

Textile Business Outlook. Statistikon Corp. • Quarterly. $985.00 per year. Analyzes current business, marketing, and financial conditions for the worldwide textile industry (fibers and fabrics). Includes statistical forecasts.

CLEANING PRODUCTS INDUSTRY

ABSTRACTS AND INDEXES

Applied Science and Technology Index. H. W. Wilson Co. • 11 times a year. Quarterly and annual cumulations. Service basis for print edition; CD-ROM edition, $1,495.00 per year. Indexes a wide variety of English language technical, industrial, and engineering periodicals.

CD-ROM DATABASES

World Marketing Forecasts on CD-ROM. The Gale Group. • Annual. $2,500.00. Produced by Euromonitor. Provides detailed forecast data for the years to 2012 on CD-ROM for 54 countries in all parts of the world. Covers a wide range of social, demographic, economic, and market factors. Includes specific forecasts for many kinds of consumer products.

DIRECTORIES

Household and Personal Products Industry - Buyers Guide. Rodman Publications. • Annual. $12.00. Lists of suppliers to manufacturers of cosmetics, toiletries, soaps, detergents, and related household and personal products.

Household and Personal Products Industry Contract Packaging and Private Label Directory. Rodman Publications. • Annual. $12.00. Provides information on about 450 companies offering private label or contract packaged household and personal care products, such as detergents, cosmetics, polishes, insecticides, and various aerosol items.

McCutcheon's: Emulsifiers and Detergents. Publishing Co., McCutcheon's Div. • Annual. $180.00. Two volumes. $275.00 per volume. North American volume contains detailed information on surface active agents produced in North America. Company names, addresses and telephone numbers are included. International volume contains detailed information on surface active agents produced in Europe and Asia or in any country outside North America. Company names, addresses and telephone numbers are included.

McCutcheon's Functional Materials: North American Edition. Publishing Co., McCutcheon Div. • Annual. $170.00. Two volumes. North American edition contains detailed information on surfactant-related products produced in North America. Examples are enzymes, lubricants, waxes, and corrosion inhibitors. Company names, addresses and telephone numbers are included. International edition contains detailed information on surfactant-related products produced in Europe and Asia. Examples are enzymes, lubricants, waxes, and corrosion inhibitors. Company names, addresses, and telephone numbers are included.

OPD Chemical Buyers Directory. Schnell Publishing Co., Inc. • Annual. $129.00. Included in subscription to *Chemical Marketing Reporter.* About 1,500 suppliers of chemical process materials and more than 300 companies which transport and store chemicals in the U.S.

Soap/Cosmetics/Chemical Specialties Blue Book. Cygnus Business Media. • Annual. $15.00. Sources of raw materials, equipment and services for the soap, cosmetic and chemical specialities. Formerly Soap/Cosetics/Chemical Special.

FINANCIAL RATIOS

Annual Statement Studies. Robert Morris Associates: The Association of Lending and Credit Risk Professiona. • Annual. Free to members; non-members, $140.00. Median and quartile financial ratios are given for over 400 kinds of manufacturing, wholesale, retail, construction, and consumer finance establishments. Data is sorted by both asset size and sales volume. Includes a clearly written "Definition of Ratios" and an alphabetical industry index.

ONLINE DATABASES

CA Search. Chemical Abstracts Service. • Guide to chemical literature, 1967 to present. Inquire as to online cost and availability.

Euromonitor Market Research. Euromonitor International. • Provides the complete text online of Euromonitor market analysis reports. Covers consumer goods market research data for all major countries, with emphasis on specific product categories. Time period is current. Continuous updating. Inquire as to online cost and availability.

PROMT: Predicasts Overview of Markets and Technology. The Gale Group. • Companies, products, applied technologies and markets. U.S. and international literature coverage, 1972 to date. Inquire as to online cost and availability. Provides abstracts from more than 1,600 publications. Weekly updates.

PERIODICALS AND NEWSLETTERS

Household and Personal Products Industry: The Magazine for the Detergent, Soap, Cosmetic and Toiletry, Wax, Polish and Aerosol Industries. Rodman Publications. • Monthly. $48.00 per year. Covers marketing, packaging, production, technical innovations, private label developments, and aerosol packaging for soap, detergents, cosmetics, insecticides, and a variety of other household products.

ISSA Today. International Sanitary Supply Association, Inc. • Monthly. $75.00 per year.

Soap and Cosmetics. Cygnus Business Media. • Monthly. $60.00 per year. Formerly *Soap, Cosmetics, Chemical Specialities.*

PRICE SOURCES

Chemical and Engineering News: The Newsmagazine of the Chemical World. American Chemical Society. • Weekly. Institutions, $181.00 per year; others, price on application.

Chemical Market Reporter. Schnell Publishing Co., Inc. • Weekly. $139.00 per year. Quotes current prices for a wide range of chemicals. Formerly *Chemical Marketing Reporter.*

STATISTICS SOURCES

Consumer Canada 1996. Available from The Gale Group. • 1996. $750.00. Published by Euromonitor. Provides consumer market, socioeconomic, and demographic data for Canada. Includes consumer market size (volume and value) for many specific kinds of products.

Consumer International 2000/2001. Available from The Gale Group. • 1998. $1,190.00. Seventh edition. Published by Euromonitor. Contains extensive consumer market, economic, and demographic data for 27 major, non-European countries, including the U. S. and Canada. Includes consumer market size (volume and value) for 150 product types in 14 categories (food, clothing, automobiles, cosmetics, appliances, etc.).

European Marketing Forecasts 2001. Available from The Gale Group. • 2000. $1,190.00. Third edition. Published by Euromonitor. Contains demographic, economic, and market forecasts for the countries of Europe to the year 2010. Forecasts include market-size data for 15 consumer product sectors (food, clothing, automobiles, consumer electronics, etc.).

International Marketing Forecasts 2001. Available from The Gale Group. • 2000. $1,090.00. Third edition. Published by Euromonitor. Contains demographic, economic, and market forecasts to the year 2010 for major, non-European countries, including the U. S. and Canada. Forecasts include market-size data for 15 consumer product sectors, such as food, clothing, and automobiles.

U. S. Industry and Trade Outlook: The McGraw-Hill Companies and the U.S. Department of Commerce/ International Trade Administration. Datapso Research Corp. • Annual. $69.95. Produced by the International Trade Administration, U. S. Department of Commerce, in a "public-private" partnership with DRI/McGraw-Hill and Standard & Poor's. Provides basic data, outlook for the current year, and "Long-Term Prospects" (five-year projections) for a wide variety of products and services. Includes high technology industries. Formerly *U. S. Industrial Outlook.*

TRADE/PROFESSIONAL ASSOCIATIONS

National Housewares Manufacturers Association. 6400 Shafer Court, Suite 650, Rosemont, IL 60018. Phone: 800-843-6462 or (847)292-4200 Fax: (847)292-4211 • URL: http://www.housewares.org • Members are manufacturers of housewares and small appliances.

Soap and Detergent Association. 1500 K St., N.W., Washington, DC 20005.

OTHER SOURCES

Household Cleaning Agents. Available from MarketResearch.com. • 1998. $5,900.00. Published by Euromonitor Publications Ltd. Provides consumer market data and forecasts to 2002 for the United States, the United Kingdom, Germany, France, and Italy. Covers dishwashing detergents, floor cleaning products, scourers, polishes, bleaching products, etc.

CLIMATE

See also: TRAVEL INDUSTRY; WEATHER AND WEATHER FORECASTING

ABSTRACTS AND INDEXES

Meteorological and Geoastrophysical Abstracts. American Meteorological Society. • Monthly. $1.120.00 per year.

ALMANACS AND YEARBOOKS

The Weather Almanac: A Reference Guide to Weather, Climate, and Air Quality in the United States and Its Key Cities, Comprising Statistics, Principles, and Terminology. The Gale Group. • 1999. $145.00. Ninth edition. Weather reports for 108 major U.S. cities and a climatic overview of the country.

CD-ROM DATABASES

World WeatherDisc. WeatherDisc Associates,Inc. • Annual. $195.00. Provides climatological and meteorological data on CD-ROM from as far back as the 18th century to recent months and years. Coverage is international, including weather observations from over 5,700 airports around the world and about 1,900 U. S. weather stations.

DIRECTORIES

Compendium of Education and Training Facilities for Meteorology and Operational Hydrology. American Meteorological Society. • 1996. $50.00. Approximately 233 training institutions for meteorology and operational hydrology in nearly 100 countries. Formerly *Compendium of Training Facilities for Meteorology and Operational Hydrology.*

Curricula in the Atmospheric Oceanic, Hydrologic and Related Sciences. American Meteorological Society. • Biennial. $40.00. Formerly *Curricula in the Atmospheric and Oceanographic Sciences-Colleges and Universities in the U.S. and Canada.*

HANDBOOKS AND MANUALS

Climates of the States. The Gale Group. • 1998. $245.00. Fourth edition. Two volumes. State-by-state summaries of climatebased on first order weather reporting stations.

Fodor's World Weather Guide. E. A. Pearce and C. G. Smith. Random House, Inc. • 1998. $17.95. Written for travelers. Describes the weather at 2,000 locations in 200 countries. Includes temperature/ rainfall charts, climate discomfort factors, a glossary of weather terms, and maps.

Statistics for the Environment: Statistical Aspects of Health and the Environment. Vic Barnett and K. Feridun Turkman, editors. John Wiley and Sons, Inc. • 1999. $180.00. Contains articles on the statistical analysis and interpretation of environmental monitoring and sampling data. Areas covered include meteorology, pollution of the environment, and forest resources.

USA Today Weather Book. Jack Williams. Random House, Inc. • 1997. $20.00. Contains a state-by-state guide to U. S. climate, with color illustrations. Author (weather editor of *USA Today*) includes discussions of weather patterns and computerized forecasting.

Weather of U.S. Cities. The Gale Group. • 1996. $225.00. Fifth edition.

PERIODICALS AND NEWSLETTERS

International Journal of Climatology. Royal Meteorological Society. Available from John Wiley and Sons, Inc., Journals Div. • 15 time a year. Institutions, $1,730.00 per year. Published in England by John Wiley and Sons Ltd.

Journal of the Atmospheric Sciences. American Meteorological Society. • Semimonthly. $495.00 per year.

Weather and Climate Report. Nautilus Press, Inc. • Monthly. $95.00 per year.

Weatherwise: The Magazine About the Weather. Helen Dwight Reid Educational Foundation. Heldref Publications. • Bimonthly. Individuals, $29.00 per year; institutions, $62.00 per year. Popular magazine devoted to weather.

RESEARCH CENTERS AND INSTITUTES

Atmospheric Sciences Research Center. University of Albany, State University of New York. 251 Fuller Rd., Albany, NY 12203-3640. Phone: (518)437-8701 Fax: (518)437-8711 E-mail: kld@asrc.cestm.albany.edu • URL: http://www.asrc.cestm.albany.edu.

Center for Climatic Research. University of Wisconsin - Madison. 1139 Atmospheric, Oceanic and Space Science Bldg., 1225 W. Dayton St., Madison, WI 53706. Phone: (608)262-2839 Fax: (608)263-4190 E-mail: jek@facstaff.wisc.edu • URL: http://www.plum.meteor.wisc.edu.

Institute of Atmospheric Physics. University of Arizona. P.O. Box 210081, Tucson, AZ 85721. Phone: (520)621-6831 Fax: (520)621-6833 E-mail: asdept@atmo.atmo.arizona.edu • URL: http://www.atmo.arizona.edu.

Office of Climatology. Arizona State University. Tempe, AZ 85287-1508. Phone: (602)965-6265 Fax: (602)965-1473 E-mail: robert.balling@asu.edu.

STATISTICS SOURCES

Local Climatological Data. U.S. National Climatic Data Center. • Monthly.

TRADE/PROFESSIONAL ASSOCIATIONS

American Institute of Biomedical Climatology. 1050 Eagle Rd., Newtown, NJ 18940-2500. URL: http://www.pollen.com/aibc.html.

American Meteorological Society. 45 Beacon St., Boston, MA 02108-3693. Phone: (617)227-2425 Fax: (617)742-8718 E-mail: webadmin@ametsoc.org • URL: http://www.ametsoc.org/ams.

International Association of Meteorology and Atmospheric Sciences. University of Toronto, Dept. of Physics, c/o Professor R. List, Toronto, ON, Canada M5S 1A7. Phone: (416)978-2982 or (416)494-3621 Fax: (416)978-8905 E-mail: list@atmosp.physics.utoronto.ca • URL: http://www.iamas.org.

World Meteorological Organization. Seven bis avenue de la Paix, CH-1211 Geneva 2, Switzerland. Phone: 41 22 7308111 Fax: 41 22 7308181 • URL: http://www.wmo.ch.

CLINICAL LABORATORY INDUSTRY

BIBLIOGRAPHIES

Encyclopedia of Health Information Sources. The Gale Group. • 1993. $180.00. Second edition. Both print and nonprint sources of information are listed for 450 health-related topics.

DIRECTORIES

CLR (Clinical Laboratory Reference). Medical Laboratory Observer. Medical Economics Co., Inc. • Annual. $32.00. Describes diagnostic reagents, test systems, instruments, equipment, and services for medical laboratories. Includes "Directory of Diagnostic Marketers" and "Index of Tests, Equipment, and Services.".

Encyclopedia of Medical Organizations and Agencies. The Gale Group. • 2000. $285.00. 11th edition. Information on over 14,000 public and private organizations in medicine and related fields.

Health Devices Sourcebook. ECRI (Emergency Care Research Institute). • Annual. Lists over 6,000 manufacturers of a wide variety of medical equipment and supplies, including clinical laboratory equipment, testing instruments, surgical instruments, patient care equipment, etc.

Health Industry Buyers Guide. Spring House. • Annual. $195.00. About 4,000 manufacturers of hospital and physician's supplies and equipment. Formerly *Surgical Trade Buyers Guide.*

Laboratories Medical Directory. InfoUSA. • Annual. Price on application. Lists over 8,234 laboratories. Compiled from telephone company yellow pages.

Major Non-Hospital Clinical Laboratories. SMG Marketing Group, Inc. • Annual. $525.00.

FINANCIAL RATIOS

Almanac of Business and Industrial Financial Ratios. Leo Troy. Prentice Hall. • Annual. $99.95. Contains financial ratios derived from federal tax returns. Ratios for each of about 200 industries are arranged according to company asset size.

Annual Statement Studies. Robert Morris Associates: The Association of Lending and Credit Risk Professiona. • Annual. Free to members; non-members, $140.00. Median and quartile financial ratios are given for over 400 kinds of manufacturing, wholesale, retail, construction, and consumer finance establishments. Data is sorted by both asset size and sales volume. Includes a clearly written "Definition of Ratios" and an alphabetical industry index.

Industry Norms and Key Business Ratios. Desk Top Edition. Dun and Bradstreet Corp., Business Information Services. • Annual. Five volumes. $475.00 per volume. $1,890.00 per set. Covers over 800 kinds of businesses, arranged by Standard Industrial Classification number. More detailed editions covering longer periods of time are also available.

PERIODICALS AND NEWSLETTERS

Clinical Lab Letter. Lippincott Williams and Wilkins, Publishers. • 22 times a year. Individuals, $327.00 per year; institutions, $409.00 per year. Newsletter on clinical laboratory management, safety, and technology.

Clinical Laboratory Management Review. Clinical Laboratory Management Association. Williams & Wilkins. • Bimonthly. Individuals, $106.00 per year; institutions, $143.00 per year.

Journal of Clinical Laboratory Analysis. John Wiley and Sons, Inc., Journals Div. • Bimonthly. Institutions, $935.00 per year. Original articles on newly developing assays.

MLO (Medical Laboratory Observer). Medical Economics Publishing Co., Inc. • Monthly. $70.00 per year. Covers management, regulatory, and technical topics for clinical laboratory administrators.

TRADE/PROFESSIONAL ASSOCIATIONS

American Association of Bioanalysts. 917 Locust St., Suite 1100, St. Louis, MO 63101-1413. Phone: (314)241-1445 Fax: (314)241-1449 E-mail: aab1445@primary.net • URL: http://www.aab.org • Members are owners and managers of bioanalytical clinical laboratories.

American Clinical Laboratory Association. 1250 H St., N. W., Suite 880, Washington, DC 20005. Phone: (202)637-9466 Fax: (202)637-2050 E-mail: acla@erols.com • Members are owners of clinical laboratories operating for a profit.

American Medical Technologists. 710 Higgins Rd., Park Ridge, IL 60068. Phone: 800-275-1268 or (847)823-5169 Fax: (847)823-0458 E-mail: amtmail@aol.com • National professional registry of medical laboratory technicians and medical assistants.

American Society for Clinical Laboratory Science. 7910 Woodmont Ave., Suite 530, Bethedsa, MD 20814. Phone: (301)657-2768 Fax: (301)657-2909 E-mail: ascls@ascls.org • URL: http://www.ascls.org • Seeks to promote high standards in clincal laboratory methods.

Clinical Laboratory Management Association. 989 Old Eagle School Rd., Suite 815, Wayne, PA 19087. Phone: (610)995-9580 Fax: (610)995-9568 • URL: http://www.clma.org • Members are individuals who manage or supervise clinical laboratories.

National Committee for Clinical Laboratory Studies. 940 W. Valley Rd., Suite 1400, Wayne, PA 19087-1898. Phone: (610)688-0100 Fax: (610)688-0700 E-mail: exoffice@nccls.org • URL: http://www.nccls.org • Promotes the development of national standards for clinical laboratory testing.

CLIPPING SERVICES

See also: NEWSPAPERS; PERIODICALS

ABSTRACTS AND INDEXES

Vertical File Index: Guide to Pamphlets and References to Current Topics. H.W. Wilson Co. • 11 times a year. $50.00 per year. A subject and title index to selected pamphlet material.

ALMANACS AND YEARBOOKS

Editor and Publisher International Yearbook: Encyclopedia of the Newspaper Industry. Editor and Publisher Co., Inc. • Annual. $125.00. Daily and Sunday newspapers in the United States and Canada.

DIRECTORIES

Literary Market Place: The Directory of the American Book Publishing Industry. R. R. Bowker. • Annual. $199.95. Two volumes. Over 16,000 firms or organizations offering services related to the publishing industry.

ONLINE DATABASES

National Newspaper Index. The Gale Group. • Citations to news items in five major newspapers, 1970 to present. Weekly updates. Inquire as to online cost and availability.

TRADE/PROFESSIONAL ASSOCIATIONS

International Federation of Press Cutting Agencies. Streulistrasse 19, CH-8030 Zurich, Switzerland. Phone: 41 1 3888200 Fax: 41 1 3888201.

OTHER SOURCES

Bacon's Newspaper/Magazine Directories. Bacon's Publishing Co. • Annual. $295.00 per year. Quarterly update. Two volumes: Magazines and Newspapers. Covers print media in the United States and Canada. Formerly *Bacon's Publicity Checker.*

CLOCK AND WATCH INDUSTRY

See also: JEWELRY BUSINESS

GENERAL WORKS

From Sundials to Atomic Clocks: Understanding Time and Frequency. James Jespersen. Dover Publications, Inc. • 1999. $12.95. Second revised edition.

HANDBOOKS AND MANUALS

The Watch Repairer's Manual. Henry B. Fried. American Watchmakers Institute. • $35.00. Fourth revised edition.

PERIODICALS AND NEWSLETTERS

Journal Suisse d'Horlogerie et de Bijouterie Internationale. Editions Scriptar S.A. • Six times a year. $95.00. Text in English, French and German. Formery J S H- Journal Suisse d'Horlogerie e+ de Bijouterie Internationale.

Modern Jeweler. Cygnus Business Media. • Monthly. $60.00 per year. Edited for retail jewelers. Covers the merchandising of jewelry, gems, and watches. Supersedes in part *Modern Jeweler.*

National Jeweler. Miller Freeman, Inc. • 24 times a year. $100.00 per year. For jewelry retailers.

Watch and Clock Review. Golden Bell Press Inc. • 10 times a year. $19.50 per year. Formerly *American Horologist and Jeweler.*

STATISTICS SOURCES

Annual Survey of Manufactures. Available from U. S. Government Printing Office. • Annual. Prices vary. Issued by the U. S. Census Bureau as an interim update to the *Census of Manufactures.* Includes data on number of manufacturing establishments in various industries, employment, labor costs, value of shipments, capital expenditures, inventories, energy costs, and assets. (See also Census Bureau home page, http://www.census.gov/.).

TRADE/PROFESSIONAL ASSOCIATIONS

American Watch Association. P.O. Box 464, Washington, DC 20044. Phone: (703)759-3377.

American Watchmakers Institute. 701 Enterprise Dr., Harrison, OH 45030. Phone: (513)367-9800 Fax: (513)367-1414 E-mail: jlubic@awi-net.org • URL: http://www.awi-net.org.

Watchmakers of Switzerland Information Center. 201 W. Passaic St., Suite 103, Rochelle Park, NJ 07662-3126. Phone: (201)291-8811 Fax: (201)291-7966 E-mail: info@swisswatch.org • URL: http://www.fhusa.com.

CLOSED-END FUNDS

See also: INVESTMENT COMPANIES

ALMANACS AND YEARBOOKS

Emerging Markets Analyst. • Monthly. $895.00 per year. Provides an annual overview of the emerging financial markets in 24 countries of Latin America, Asia, and Europe. Includes data on international mutual funds and closed-end funds.

Investment Companies Yearbook. Securities Data Publishing. • Annual. $310.00. Provides an "entire history of recent events in the mutual funds industry," with emphasis on changes during the past year. About 100 pages are devoted to general information and advice for fund investors. Includes 600 full-page profiles of popular mutual funds, with brief descriptions of 10,000 others, plus 7,000 variable annuities and 500 closed-end funds. Contains a glossary of technical terms, a Web site index, and an overall book index. Also known as *Wiesenberger Investment Companies Yearbook.* (Securities Data Publishing is a unit of Thomson Financial.).

DIRECTORIES

Morningstar Closed-End Fund 250. Morningstar Staff. McGraw-Hill Professional. • 1996. $35.00. Provides detailed information on 50 actively traded closed-end investment companies. Past data is included for up to 12 years, depending on life of the fund.

HANDBOOKS AND MANUALS

Herzfeld's Guide to Closed-End Funds. Thomas J. Herzsfeld. McGraw-Hill. • 1992. $22.95. Provides advice and information on investing in closed-end investment companies.

INTERNET DATABASES

DBC Online: America's Leading Provider of Real-Time Market Data to the Individual Investor. Data Broadcasting Corp. Phone: (415)571-1800 E-mail: dbcinfo@dbc.com • URL: http://www.dbc.com • Web site provides a wide variety of real-time securities market prices, data, and charts. Covers bonds ("BondVu"), stocks, commodities, options, mutual funds, major indexes, industry indexes, international markets, etc. Also includes news, SEC documents ("Smart-Edgar"), and various other features. Fees: Both free and fee-based, depending on level of information.

U. S. Securities and Exchange Commission. Phone: 800-732-0330 or (202)942-7040 Fax: (202)942-9634 E-mail: webmaster@sec.gov • URL: http://www.sec.gov • SEC Web site offers free access through EDGAR to text of official corporate filings, such as annual reports (10-K), quarterly reports (10-Q), and proxies. (EDGAR is "Electronic Data Gathering, Analysis, and Retrieval System.") An example is given of how to obtain executive compensation data from proxies. Text of the daily *SEC News Digest* is offered, as are links to other government sites, non-government market regulators, and U. S. stock exchanges. Search facilities are extensive. Fees: Free.

Wall Street Journal Interactive Edition. Dow Jones & Co., Inc. Phone: 800-369-2834 or (212)416-2000 Fax: (212)416-2658 E-mail: inquiries@interactive.wsj.com • URL: http://www.wsj.com • Fee-based Web site providing online searching of worldwide information from the *The Wall Street Journal.* Includes "Company Snapshots," "The Journal's Greatest Hits," "Index to Market Data," "14-Day Searchable Archive," "Journal Links," etc. Financial price quotes are available. Fees: $49.00 per year; $29.00 per year to print subscribers.

Web Finance: Covering the Electronic Evolution of Finance. Securities Data Publishing. Phone: (212)765-5311 or 800-455-5844 Fax: (212)321-2336 E-mail: webfinance@tfn.com • URL: http://www.webfinance.net • Bi-weekly print and daily web-site publication of financial services on the Web, including financial links, archives, brokerage stocks, deal financing, and other financial and investment news and information.

PERIODICALS AND NEWSLETTERS

Closed-End Fund Digest. Morningstar, Inc. • Monthly. $195.00 per year. Newsletter. Provides news and statistical information for approximately 500 closed-end investment funds. Includes recommendations of specific funds.

Financial Trader. Miller Freeman, Inc. • 11 times a year. $160.00 per year. Edited for professional traders. Covers fixed income securities, emerging markets, derivatives, options, futures, and equities.

Investor's Guide to Closed-End Funds. Thomas J. Herzfeld Advisors, Inc. • Monthly. $475.00 per year. Looseleaf. Provides detailed information on closed-end investment funds, including charts and recommendations.

Mutual Funds Update. Securities Data Publishing. • Monthly. $325.00 per year. Provides recent performance information and statistics for approximately 10,000 mutual funds, as compiled from the CDA/Wiesenberger database. Includes commentary and analysis relating to the mutual fund industry. Information is provided on new funds, name changes, mergers, and liquidations. (Securities Data Publishing is a unit of Thomson Financial.).

The Wall Street Journal. Dow Jones & Co., Inc. • Daily. $175.00 per year. Covers news and trends relating to business, industry, finance, the economy, and international commerce. Provides extensive price and other data for the securities, commodity, options, futures, foreign exchange, and money markets.

TRADE/PROFESSIONAL ASSOCIATIONS

Investment Company Institute. 1401 H St., N. W., 12th Fl., Washington, DC 20005-2148. Phone: (202)326-5800 Fax: (202)326-8309 E-mail: info@ici.com • URL: http://www.ici.com • Members are investment companies offering mutual funds (open-end) and closed-end funds. Includes a Closed-End Investment Company Division.

OTHER SOURCES

Factiva. Dow Jones Reuters Business Interactive, LLC. • Fee-based Web site provides "global news and business information through Web sites and content integration solutions." Includes Dow Jones and Reuters newswires, The Wall Street Journal, and more than 7,000 other sources of current news, historical articles, market research reports, and investment analysis. Content includes 96 major U. S. newspapers, 900 non-English sources, trade publications, media transcripts, country profiles, news photos, etc.

Nexis.com. Lexis-Nexis Group. • Fee-based Web site offers searching of about 2.8 billion documents in some 30,000 news, business, and legal information sources. Features include a subject directory covering 1,200 topics in 34 categories and a Company Dossier containing information on more than 500,000 public and private companies. Boolean searching is offered.

CLOSELY HELD CORPORATIONS

See also: PRIVATE COMPANIES

GENERAL WORKS

Corporate and Tax Aspects of Closely Held Corporations. William H. Painter. Aspen Books. • 1981. $80.00. Second edition.

ABSTRACTS AND INDEXES

Business Periodicals Index. H. W. Wilson Co. • Monthly, except August, with quarterly and annual cumulations. Service basis for print edition; CD-ROM edition, $1,495.00 per year.

DIRECTORIES

Business Organizations, Agencies, and Publications Directory. The Gale Group. • 1999. $425.00. 12th edition. Over 40,000 entries describing 39 types of business information sources. Classified by type of organization, publication, or serviceIncludes state, national, and international agencies and organizations. Master index to names and keywords. Also includes e-mail addresses and web site URL's.

Directory of Corporate Affiliations. National Register Publishing. • Annual. $1,159.00. Five volumes. Volumes one and two: Master Index; volume three: U.S. Public Companies; volume four: U.S. Private Companies; volume five: International Public and Private Companies.

HANDBOOKS AND MANUALS

Managing and Operating a Closely-Held Corporation. Michael Diamond. John Wiley and Sons, Inc. • 1991. $135.00.

Valuing a Business: Analysis and Appraisal of Closely Held Companies. Shannon P. Pratt and others. McGraw-Hill. • 2000. $95.00. Fourth edition. Includes information on how to appraise partial interests and how to write a valuation report.

ONLINE DATABASES

Wilson Business Abstracts Online. H. W. Wilson Co. • Indexes and abstracts 600 major business periodicals, plus the *Wall Street Journal* and the business section of the *New York Times.* Indexing is from 1982, abstracting from 1990, with the two newspapers included from 1993. Updated weekly. Inquire as to online cost and availability. (*Business Periodicals Index* without abstracts is also available online.).

PERIODICALS AND NEWSLETTERS

Inc.: The Magazine for Growing Companies. Goldhirsh Group, Inc. • 18 times a year. $19.00 per year. Edited for small office and office-in-the-home businesses with from one to 25 employees. Covers management, office technology, and lifestyle. Incorporates *Self-Employed Professional.*

RESEARCH CENTERS AND INSTITUTES

Lexis.com Research System. Lexis-Nexis Group. Phone: 800-227-9597 or (937)865-6800 Fax: (937)865-6909 E-mail: webmaster@prod.lexis-nexis.com • URL: http://www.lexis.com • Fee-based Web site offers extensive searching of a wide variety of legal sources. Additional features include Daily Opinion Service, lexis.com Bookstore, Career Center, CLE Center, Law Schools, and Practice Pages ("Pages specific to areas of specialty").

OTHER SOURCES

Close Corporations: Law and Practice. Little, Brown and Co. • $350.00. Two volumes. Volume one $175.00; volume two, $175.00. Periodic supplementation. Covers family and other closely held corporations.

CLOTHING, CHILDREN'S

See: CHILDREN'S APPAREL INDUSTRY

CLOTHING INDUSTRY

See also: CHILDREN'S APPAREL INDUSTRY; FASHION INDUSTRY; MEN'S CLOTHING INDUSTRY; TAILORING; WOMEN'S APPAREL

GENERAL WORKS

Fashion Merchandising: An Introduction. Elaine Stone. McGraw-Hill. • 1989. $45.72. Fifth edition. (Marketing Series).

Fashion Merchandising and Marketing. Marian H. Jernigan and Cynthia R. Easterling. Prentice Hall. • 1990. $47.20.

ABSTRACTS AND INDEXES

Textile Technology Digest. Institute of Textile Technology. • Monthly. $535.00 per year. Provides indexing and abstracting of a wide variety of textile technology literature.

ALMANACS AND YEARBOOKS

International Association of Clothing Designers Convention Yearbook. International Association of Clothing Designers. • Annual. Price on application.

CD-ROM DATABASES

Textile Technology Digest [CD-ROM]. Textile Information Center, Institute of Textile Technology. • Quarterly. $1,700.00 per year. Provides CD-ROM indexing and abstracting of worldwide journals and monographs in various areas of textile technology, production, and management. Covers 1978 to date.

World Marketing Forecasts on CD-ROM. The Gale Group. • Annual. $2,500.00. Produced by Euromonitor. Provides detailed forecast data for the years to 2012 on CD-ROM for 54 countries in all parts of the world. Covers a wide range of social, demographic, economic, and market factors. Includes specific forecasts for many kinds of consumer products.

DIRECTORIES

American Apparel Manufacturers Association Directory of Members and Associate Members. American Apparel Manufacturers Association. • Annual. $100.00. Lists 900 clothing manufacturers and suppliers of goods and services to apparel manufacturers.

Directory of Apparel Specialty Stores. Chain Store Guide. • Annual. $260.00. Lists over 5,000 women's, men's, family and sporting goods retailers.

Garment Manufacturer's Index. Klevens Publications, Inc. • Annual. $60.00. A directory of about 8,000 manufacturers and suppliers of products and services used in the making of men's, women's, and children's clothing. Includes fabrics, trimmings, factory equipment, and other supplies.

Nationwide Directory of Major Mass Market Merchandisers. Salesman's Guide. • Annual. $179.95. Lists buyers of clothing for major retailers. (Does not include the metropolitan New York City area.).

ENCYCLOPEDIAS AND DICTIONARIES

Encyclopedia of Textiles. French and European Publications, Inc. • 1980. $39.95. Third edition.

Textile Terms and Definitions. J.E. McIntyre and Paul N. Daniels, editors. Available from State Mutual Book and Periodical Service Ltd., Trade Order Dept. • 1995. $110.00. 10th edition. Published by the Textile Insitute (UK). Includes more than 1,000 definitions of textile processes, fiber types, and end products. Illustrated.

FINANCIAL RATIOS

Almanac of Business and Industrial Financial Ratios. Leo Troy. Prentice Hall. • Annual. $99.95. Contains financial ratios derived from federal tax returns. Ratios for each of about 200 industries are arranged according to company asset size.

Special Statistical Report on Profit, Production and Sales Trends in the Men's and Boy's Tailored Clothing Industry. Clothing Manufacturers Association of the U.S.A. • 1983. $15.00.

INTERNET DATABASES

Fedstats. Federal Interagency Council on Statistical Policy. Phone: (202)395-7254 • URL: http://www.fedstats.gov • Web site features an efficient search facility for full-text statistics produced by more than 70 federal agencies, including the Census Bureau, the Bureau of Economic Analysis, and the Bureau of Labor Statistics. Boolean searches can be made within one agency or for all agencies combined. Links are offered to international statistical bureaus, including the UN, IMF, OECD, UNESCO, Eurostat, and 20 individual countries. Fees: Free.

ONLINE DATABASES

DRI U.S. Central Database. Data Products Division. • Provides more than 23,000 business, financial, demographic, economic, foreign trade, and industry-related time series for the U.S. Includes national income, population, retail-wholesale trade, price indexes, labor data, housing, industrial production, banking, interest rates, money supply, etc. Time period is generally 1947 to date (some data back to 1929). Updating varies. Inquire as to online cost and availability.

Euromonitor Market Research. Euromonitor International. • Provides the complete text online of Euromonitor market analysis reports. Covers consumer goods market research data for all major countries, with emphasis on specific product categories. Time period is current. Continuous updating. Inquire as to online cost and availability.

Textile Technology Digest [online]. Textile Information Center, Institute of Textile Technology. • Contains indexing and abstracting of more than 300 worldwide journals and monographs in various areas of textile technology, production, and management. Time period is 1978 to date, with monthly updating. Inquire as to online cost and availability.

World Textiles. Elsevier Science, Inc. • Provides abstracting and indexing from 1970 of worldwide textile literature (periodicals, books, pamphlets, and reports). Includes U. S., European, and British patent information. Updating is monthly. Inquire as to online cost and availability.

PERIODICALS AND NEWSLETTERS

Apparel Industry Magazine. Shore-Varrone, Inc. • Monthly. $65.00 per year.

Sportstyle. Fairchild Merchandising Group. • Monthly. $35.00 per year.

Textile Hi-Lights. American Textile Manufacturers Institute, Inc. • Quarterly. $125.00 per year. Monthly supplements.

Textile World. Intertec Publishing Corp., Textile Publications. • Monthly. Price on application.

WWD (Women's Wear Daily): The Retailer's Daily Newspaper. Fairchild Publications. • Daily. Institutions, $75.00 per year; corporations $195.00 per year.

RESEARCH CENTERS AND INSTITUTES

International Textile Center. Texas Tech University. P.O. Box 45019, Lubbock, TX 79409-5019. Phone: (806)747-3790 Fax: (806)747-3796 E-mail: itc@ttu.edu • URL: http://www.itc.ttu.edu.

Textiles and Materials. Philadelphia University, Schoolhouse Lane and Henry Ave., Philadelphia, PA 19144. Phone: (215)951-2751 Fax: (215)951-2651 E-mail: brooksteind@philaau.edu • URL: http://www.philaau.edu • Many research areas, including industrial and nonwoven textiles.

STATISTICS SOURCES

Annual Survey of Manufactures. Available from U. S. Government Printing Office. • Annual. Prices vary. Issued by the U. S. Census Bureau as an interim update to the *Census of Manufactures.* Includes data on number of manufacturing establishments in various industries, employment, labor costs, value of shipments, capital expenditures, inventories, energy costs, and assets. (See also Census Bureau home page, http://www.census.gov/.).

Business Statistics of the United States. Courtenay M. Slater, editor. Bernan Associates. • 1999. $74.00. Fifth edition. Based on *Business Statistics,* formerly issue by the Bureau of Economic Analysis, U. S. Department of Commerce. Provides basic data for a wide variety of U. S. industries, services, and economic indicators. Most statistics are shown annually for 29 years and monthly for the most recent four years.

Consumer Canada 1996. Available from The Gale Group. • 1996. $750.00. Published by Euromonitor. Provides consumer market, socioeconomic, and demographic data for Canada. Includes consumer market size (volume and value) for many specific kinds of products.

Consumer International 2000/2001. Available from The Gale Group. • 1998. $1,190.00. Seventh edition. Published by Euromonitor. Contains extensive consumer market, economic, and demographic data for 27 major, non-European countries, including the U. S. and Canada. Includes consumer market size (volume and value) for 150 product types in 14 categories (food, clothing, automobiles, cosmetics, appliances, etc.).

European Marketing Forecasts 2001. Available from The Gale Group. • 2000. $1,190.00. Third edition. Published by Euromonitor. Contains demographic, economic, and market forecasts for the countries of Europe to the year 2010. Forecasts include market-size data for 15 consumer product sectors (food, clothing, automobiles, consumer electronics, etc.).

International Marketing Forecasts 2001. Available from The Gale Group. • 2000. $1,090.00. Third edition. Published by Euromonitor. Contains demographic, economic, and market forecasts to the year 2010 for major, non-European countries, including the U. S. and Canada. Forecasts include market-size data for 15 consumer product sectors, such as food, clothing, and automobiles.

Manufacturing Profiles. Available from U. S. Government Printing Office. • Annual. Issued by the U. S. Census Bureau. A printed consolidation of the entire *Current Industrial Report* series, presenting "all the data compiled." Contains statistics on production, shipments, inventories, consumption, exports, imports, and orders for a wide variety of manufactured products. (See also Census Bureau home page, http://www.census.gov/.).

Standard & Poor's Industry Surveys. Standard & Poor's. • Semiannual. $1,800.00. Two looseleaf volumes. Includes monthly supplements. Provides detailed, individual surveys of 52 major industry groups. Each survey is revised on a semiannual basis. Also includes "Monthly Investment Review" (industry group investment analysis) and monthly "Trends & Projections" (economic analysis).

Survey of Current Business. Available from U. S. Government Printing Office. • Monthly. $49.00 per year. Issued by Bureau of Economic Analysis, U. S. Department of Commerce. Presents a wide variety of business and economic data.

WEFA Industrial Monitor. John Wiley and Sons, Inc. • Annual. $65.00. Prepared by industry analysts at WEFA, an economic forecasting and consulting firm (originally Wharton Econometric Forecasting Associates). Contains discussions of the outlook for major U. S. industries, with many 10-year forecasts (WEFA Web site is http://www.wefa.com).

TRADE/PROFESSIONAL ASSOCIATIONS

Amalgamated Clothing and Textile Workers Union. 1710 Broadway, New York, NY 10019. Phone: (212)265-7000 Fax: (212)265-3415.

American Apparel Manufacturers Association. 2500 Wilson Blvd., Suite 301, Arlington, VA 22201. Phone: 800-520-2262 or (703)524-1864 Fax: (703)522-6741 • URL: http://www.americanapparel.org.

Chamber of Commerce of the Apparel Industry. 570 Seventh Ave., 10th Fl., New York, NY 10018. Phone: (212)354-0907 Fax: (212)768-4732.

Clothing Manufacturers of the U.S.A. 730 Broadway, 9th Fl., New York, NY 10003. Phone: (212)529-0823 Fax: (212)529-1443.

International Association of Clothing Designers and Executives. 475 Park Ave., S., 17th Fl., New York, NY 10016. Phone: (212)685-6602 Fax: (212)545-1709.

Textile Institute. Saint James Bldgs., 4th Fl., Oxford St., Manchester M1 6FQ, England. Phone: 44 161 2371188 Fax: 44 161 2361991 E-mail: tiihq@textileinst.org.uk • URL: http://www.texi.org • Members in 100 countries involved with textile industry management, marketing, science, and technology.

Union of Needletrades, Industrial and Textile Employees. 1710 Broadway, New York, NY 10019. Phone: (212)265-7000 Fax: (212)315-3803 • URL: http://www.uniteunion.org.

United Food and Commercial Workers International Union. 1775 K. St., N.W., Washington, DC 20006. Phone: (202)223-3111 Fax: (202)466-1562 • URL: http://www.ufcw.org.

OTHER SOURCES

Textile Business Outlook. Statistikon Corp. • Quarterly. $985.00 per year. Analyzes current business, marketing, and financial conditions for the worldwide textile industry (fibers and fabrics). Includes statistical forecasts.

CLOTHING, MEN'S

See: MEN'S CLOTHING INDUSTRY

CLOTHING, WOMEN'S

See: WOMEN'S APPAREL

CLUBS

See also: ASSOCIATIONS; WOMEN'S CLUBS

GENERAL WORKS

The American Country Club: Its Origins and Development. James M. Mayo. Rutgers University Press. • 1998. $25.00.

ALMANACS AND YEARBOOKS

CMAA Yearbook. Club Managers Association of America. • Annual. Membership directory.

DIRECTORIES

Club Industry: Buyers Guide. Intertec Publishing Corp. • Annual. $25.00. A directory of over 1,000 companies furnishing equipment, supplies, and services to health and fitness clubs.

FINANCIAL RATIOS

Annual Statement Studies. Robert Morris Associates: The Association of Lending and Credit Risk Professiona. • Annual. Free to members; non-members, $140.00. Median and quartile financial ratios are given for over 400 kinds of manufacturing, wholesale, retail, construction, and consumer finance establishments. Data is sorted by both asset size and sales volume. Includes a clearly written "Definition of Ratios" and an alphabetical industry index.

HANDBOOKS AND MANUALS

Club Manager's Guide to Private Parties and Club Functions. Joe Perdue and others. John Wiley and Sons, Inc. • 1998. $49.95. Covers on-premises catering at clubs, including member relations, meal functions, beverage functions, room setup, staffing, etc.

Club, Recreation, and Sport Management. Tom Sawyer and Owen Smith. Sagamore Publishing, Inc. • 1998. $44.95.

Robert's Rules of Order. Henry M. Roberts and William J. Evans, editors. HarperCollins Publishers. • 2000. $17.00. 10th edition.

ONLINE DATABASES

Magazine Index. The Gale Group. • General magazine indexing (popular literature), 1973 to present. Daily updates. Inquire as to online cost and availability.

PERIODICALS AND NEWSLETTERS

The Bottomline. International Association of Hospitality Accountants. • Bimonthly. Free to members, educational institutions and libraries; others, $50.00 per year. Contains articles on accounting, finance, information technology, and management for hotels, resorts, casinos, clubs, and other hospitality businesses.

Club Director. National Club Association. • Six times a year. $18.00 per year. Magazine for directors, owners and managers of private clubs.

Club Management: The Resource for Successful Club Operations. Club Managers Association of America. Finan Publishing Co. • Bimonthly. $21.95 per year.

GFWC Clubwoman. General Federation of Women's Clubs. • Bimonthly. $6.00 per year.

Hospitality Technology: Infosystems for Foodservice and Lodging. Edgell Communications, Inc. • Monthly. $36.00 per year. Covers information technology, computer communications, and software for foodservice and lodging enterprises.

STATISTICS SOURCES

Clubs in Town and Country. Pannell Kerr Forster. • Annual. $50.00. Provides financial statistics and other information relating to city clubs and country clubs of different sizes in various areas of the U. S.

Profiles of Success. International Health, Racquet, and Sportsclub Association. • Annual. Members, $125.00; non-members, $500.00. Provides detailed financial statistics for commercial health clubs, sports clubs, and gyms.

TRADE/PROFESSIONAL ASSOCIATIONS

Club Managers Association of America. 1733 King St., Alexandria, VA 22314-2720. Phone: (703)739-9500 Fax: (703)739-0124 E-mail: cmaa@cmaa.org • URL: http://www.cmaa.org.

Hospitality Financial and Technology Professionals. 11709 Boulder Lane, Suite 110, Austin, TX 78726. Phone: 800-646-4387 or (512)249-5333 Fax: (512)249-1533 E-mail: hftp@hftp.org • URL: http://www.hitecshow • Members are accounting and finance officers in the hotel, motel, casino, club, and other areas of the hospitality industry.

International Health, Racquet and Sportsclub Association. 263 Summer St., Boston, MA 02210. Phone: 800-228-4772 or (617)951-0055 Fax: (617)951-0056 E-mail: info@ihrsa.org • URL: http://www.ihrsa.org • Members are for-profit health clubs, sports clubs, and gyms.

International Military Community Executives Association. 1125 Duke St., Alexandria, VA 22314-3513. Phone: (703)548-0093 Fax: (703)548-0095 E-mail: dpavlik@erols.com.

National Club Association. One Lafayette Center, 1120 20th St., N.W., Suite 725, Washington, DC 20036-3406. Phone: (202)822-9822 Fax: (202)822-9808.

OTHER SOURCES

Washington [year]. Columbia Books, Inc. • Annual. $129.00. Provides information on about 5,000 Washington, DC key businesses, government offices, non-profit organizations, and cultural institutions, with the names of about 25,000 principal executives. Includes Washington media, law offices, foundations, labor unions, international organizations, clubs, etc.

CLUBS, WOMEN'S

See: WOMEN'S CLUBS

COAL GASIFICATION

See: ENERGY SOURCES

COAL INDUSTRY

See also: COKE INDUSTRY; ENERGY SOURCES

GENERAL WORKS

Coal and Modern Coal Processing: An Introduction. G.J. Pitt and G.R. Milward, editors. Academic Press, Inc. • 1979. $73.00.

Coal Liquefaction Fundamentals. Darrell Duayne Whitehurst, editor. American Chemical Society. • 1980. $49.95. (ACS Symposium Series: No. 139).

ALMANACS AND YEARBOOKS

Coal Information. OECD Publications and Information Center. • Annual. $200.00. A yearly report on world coal market trends and prospects.

CRB Commodity Yearbook. Commodity Research Bureau. CRB. • Annual. $99.95.

BIBLIOGRAPHIES

The Coal Industry in America: Bibliography and Guide to Studies. Robert F. Munn. West Virginia University Press. • 1977. $12.50. Second edition.

DIRECTORIES

Financial Times Energy Yearbook: Mining 2000. Available from The Gale Group. • Annual. $320.00.

Published by Financial Times Energy. Provides production and financial details for more than 800 major mining companies worldwide. Includes coverage of reserves, operations, properties, and growth rates. Formerly *Financial Times International Yearbook: Mining.*

Keystone Coal Industry Manual. Intertec Publishing Corp. • Annual. $275.00.

ENCYCLOPEDIAS AND DICTIONARIES

Wiley Encyclopedia of Energy and the Environment. Frederick John Francis. John Wiley and Sons, Inc. • 1999. $1,500.00. Four volumes. Second edition. Covers a wide variety of energy and environmental topics, including legal and policy issues.

FINANCIAL RATIOS

Almanac of Business and Industrial Financial Ratios. Leo Troy. Prentice Hall. • Annual. $99.95. Contains financial ratios derived from federal tax returns. Ratios for each of about 200 industries are arranged according to company asset size.

Annual Statement Studies. Robert Morris Associates: The Association of Lending and Credit Risk Professiona. • Annual. Free to members; non-members, $140.00. Median and quartile financial ratios are given for over 400 kinds of manufacturing, wholesale, retail, construction, and consumer finance establishments. Data is sorted by both asset size and sales volume. Includes a clearly written "Definition of Ratios" and an alphabetical industry index.

HANDBOOKS AND MANUALS

Coal Facts. National Mining Association. • Annual. $15.00.

INTERNET DATABASES

Fedstats. Federal Interagency Council on Statistical Policy. Phone: (202)395-7254 • URL: http://www.fedstats.gov • Web site features an efficient search facility for full-text statistics produced by more than 70 federal agencies, including the Census Bureau, the Bureau of Economic Analysis, and the Bureau of Labor Statistics. Boolean searches can be made within one agency or for all agencies combined. Links are offered to international statistical bureaus, including the UN, IMF, OECD, UNESCO, Eurostat, and 20 individual countries. Fees: Free.

NMA. National Mining Association. Phone: (202)463-2625 Fax: (202)463-6152 • URL: http://www.nma.org • Web site provides information on the U. S. coal and mineral industries. Includes "Salient Statistics of the Mining Industry," showing a wide variety of annual data (six years) for coal and non-fuel minerals. Publications of the National Mining Association are described and links are provided to other sites. (National Mining Association formerly known as National Coal Association.) Fees: Free.

ONLINE DATABASES

DRI U.S. Central Database. Data Products Division. • Provides more than 23,000 business, financial, demographic, economic, foreign trade, and industry-related time series for the U.S. Includes national income, population, retail-wholesale trade, price indexes, labor data, housing, industrial production, banking, interest rates, money supply, etc. Time period is generally 1947 to date (some data back to 1929). Updating varies. Inquire as to online cost and availability.

Energyline. Congressional Information Service, Inc. • Provides online citations and abstracts to the literature of all forms of energy: petroleum, natural gas, coal, nuclear power, solar energy, etc. Time period is 1971 to 1993 (closed file). Inquire as to online cost and availability.

PERIODICALS AND NEWSLETTERS

Black Diamond. Black Diamond Co., Inc. • Monthly. $36.00 per year.

Coal Age. Intertec Publishing Corp. • Monthly. Free to qualified personnel; others, $36.00 per year. Formerly *Coal.*

The Coal Leader: Dedicated to Public Awareness and Understanding in the Mine Industry. National Independent Coal Operators Association. • Monthly. $18.00 per year. Formerly *National Coal Leader.*

Coal Outlook. Pasha Publishing. • Weekly. $1,097.00 per year.

Coal Week. McGraw-Hill Energy and Business Newsletter. • Weekly. $912.00 per year. Newsletter. Edited as "a weekly intelligence report for executives in the coal industry and peripheral operations." Covers prices, markets, politics, and coal economics.

Coal Week International. McGraw-Hill, Chemical Engineering Div. • Weekly. $1,186.00 per year. Newsletter. Covers international trade in various types of coal, including prices, production, markets, regulation, research, and synthetic fuels. (Energy and Business Newsletters.).

Energy and Fuels. American Chemical Society. • Bimonthly. Institutions, $728.00 per year; others, price on application. an interdisciplinary technical journal covering non-nuclear energy sources: petroleum, gas, synthetic fuels, etc.

Mining Voice. National Mining Association. • Bimonthly. $36.00 per year. Covers U. S. mining issues and trends, with emphasis on coal. Formerly *Coal Voice.*

Mining Week. National Mining Association. • Weekly. Free to members; non-members, $100.00 per year. Newsletter. Covers legislative, business, research, and other developments of interest to the mining industry.

Power Generation. Pasha Publishing. • Weekly. $790.00 per year. Newsletter. Formerly *Coals and Synfuels Technology.*

PRICE SOURCES

International Energy Agency. Energy Prices and Taxes. OECD Publications and Information Center. • Quarterly. $350.00 per year. Compiled by the International Energy Agency. Provides data on prices and taxation of petroleum products, natural gas, coal, and electricity. Diskette edition, $800.00. (Published in Paris).

RESEARCH CENTERS AND INSTITUTES

Canadian Energy Research Institute. 3512 33rd St., N. W., Suite 150, Calgary, AB, Canada T2L 2A6. Phone: (403)282-1231 Fax: (403)284-4181 E-mail: ceri@ceri.ca • URL: http://www.ceri.ca • Conducts research on the economic aspects of various forms of energy, including petroleum, natural gas, coal, nuclear, and water power (hydroelectric).

Center for Applied Energy Research. University of Kentucky, 2540 Research Dr., Lexington, KY 40511-8410. Phone: (606)257-0305 Fax: (606)257-0220 E-mail: mcalister@caer.uky.edu • URL: http://www.caer.uky.edu.

Coal Research Center. Southern Illinois University at Carbondale. Mail Code 4623, Carbondale, IL 62901. Phone: (618)536-5521 Fax: (618)453-7346 E-mail: jmead@siu.edu • URL: http://www.siu.edu.

Energy and Environmental Research Center. University of North Dakota. P.O. Box 9018, Grand Forks, ND 58202-9018. Phone: (701)777-5000 Fax: (701)777-5181 E-mail: ghg@eerc.und.nodak.edu.

Energy Institute. Pennsylvania State University. C211 Coal Utilization Laboratory, University Park, PA 16802. Phone: (814)863-1337 Fax: (814)863-7432 E-mail: schobert@ems.psu.edu • URL: http://www.energyinstitute.psu.edu/.

Viking Systems International. 2070 William Pitt Way, Pittsburgh, PA 15238. Phone: (412)826-3355 Fax: (412)826-3353.

STATISTICS SOURCES

Annual Energy Outlook [year], with Projections to [year]. Available from U. S. Government Printing Office. • Annual. Issued by the Energy Information Administration, U. S. Department of Energy (http://www.eia.doe.gov). Contains detailed statistics and 20-year projections for electricity, oil, natural gas, coal, and renewable energy. Text provides extensive discussion of energy issues and "Market Trends.".

Annual Energy Review. Available from U. S. Government Printing Office. • Annual Issued by the Energy Information Administration, Office of Energy Markets and End Use, U. S. Department of Energy. Presents long-term historical as well as recent data on production, consumption, stocks, imports, exports, and prices of the principal energy commodities in the U. S.

Business Statistics of the United States. Courtenay M. Slater, editor. Bernan Associates. • 1999. $74.00. Fifth edition. Based on *Business Statistics*, formerly issue by the Bureau of Economic Analysis, U. S. Department of Commerce. Provides basic data for a wide variety of U. S. industries, services, and economic indicators. Most statistics are shown annually for 29 years and monthly for the most recent four years.

Coal Transportation Statistics. National Mining Association. • Annual. Non-profit organizations, $25.00; others, $35.00. Formerly *Coal Traffic Annual.*

Energy Balances of OECD Countries. Organization for Economic Cooperation and Development. Available from OECD Publications and Information Center. • Irregular. $110.00. Presents two-year data on the supply and consumption of solid fuels, oil, gas, and electricity, expressed in oil equivalency terms. Historical tables are also provided. Relates to OECD member countries.

Minerals Yearbook. Available from U.S. Government Printing Office. • Annual. Three volumes.

Monthly Energy Review. Available from U. S. Government Printing Office. • Monthly. $98.00 per year. Issued by the Energy Information Administration, Office of Energy Markets and End Use, U. S. Department of Energy. Contains current and historical statistics on U. S. production, storage, imports, and consumption of petroleum, natural gas, and coal.

Quarterly Coal Report. Energy Information Administration, U.S. Department of Energy. Available from U.S. Government Printing Office. • Quarterly. $30.00 per year. Annual summary.

Quarterly Mining Review. National Mining Association. • Quarterly. $300.00 per year. Contains detailed data on production, shipments, consumption, stockpiles, and trade for coal and various minerals. (Publisher formerly National Coal Association.).

Steam Electric Market Analysis. National Mining Association. • Monthly. $300.00 per year. Covers 400 major electric power plants, with detailed data on coal consumption and stockpiles. Shows percent of power generated by fuel type. (Publisher formerly National Coal Association.).

Survey of Current Business. Available from U. S. Government Printing Office. • Monthly. $49.00 per year. Issued by Bureau of Economic Analysis, U. S.

For publishers addresses, refer to SOURCES CITED section at the back of the book.

Department of Commerce. Presents a wide variety of business and economic data.

United States Census of Mineral Industries. Bureau of the Census, U.S. Department of Commerce. Available from U.S. Government Printing Office. • Quinquennial.

Weekly Statistical Summary. National Mining Association. • Weekly. $100.00 per year. A detailed report on coal production and consumption.

WEFA Industrial Monitor. John Wiley and Sons, Inc. • Annual. $65.00. Prepared by industry analysts at WEFA, an economic forecasting and consulting firm (originally Wharton Econometric Forecasting Associates). Contains discussions of the outlook for major U. S. industries, with many 10-year forecasts (WEFA Web site is http://www.wefa.com).

TRADE/PROFESSIONAL ASSOCIATIONS

International Union United Mine Workers of America. 900 15th St., N.W., Washington, DC 20005. Phone: (202)842-7200 Fax: (202)842-7227 • URL: http://www.umwa.org.

National Mining Association. 1130 17th St., N.W., Washington, DC 20036-4677. Phone: (202)463-2625 Fax: (202)857-6152 E-mail: rlawson@nma.org • URL: http://www.nma.org.

Rocky Mountain Coal Mining Institute. 3000 Youngfield, No. 324, Lakewood, CO 80215-6553. Phone: (303)238-9099 Fax: (303)238-0509 E-mail: rmcoalmine@aol.com.

COAL MINING INDUSTRY

See: COAL INDUSTRY

COAL TAR PRODUCTS

See: CHEMICAL INDUSTRIES

COAST GUARD

DIRECTORIES

Register of Officers [United States Coast Guard]. U.S. Coast Guard. • Annual.

HANDBOOKS AND MANUALS

Coast Guardsman's Manual. George E. Krietmeyer. Naval Institute Press. • 2000. $21.95. Ninth edition.

ONLINE DATABASES

American Statistics Index: A Comprehensive Guide and Index to the Statistical Publications of the United States Government [Online]. Congressional Information Service, Inc. • Indexes and abstracts, 1973 to date. Inquire as to online cost and availability.

PERIODICALS AND NEWSLETTERS

Coast Guard Reservist. Commandant, U.S. Coast Guard. • Monthly. Free.

Ocean Navigator: Marine Navigation and Ocean Voyaging. Navigator Publishing LLC. • Eight times a year. $26.00 per year.

TRADE/PROFESSIONAL ASSOCIATIONS

United States Coast Guard Auxiliary. Commandant, U.S. Coast Guard HQ (G-OCX), 2100 Second St., S.W., Room 3001, Washington, DC 20593. Phone: (202)267-1010 or (202)267-1001 Fax: (202)267-4460 • URL: http://www.cgaux.org.

United States Coast Guard Chief Petty Officer Association. 5520G Hempstead Way, Springfield, VA 22151. Phone: (703)941-0395 Fax: (703)941-0397 E-mail: cgcpoa@aol.com.

COATINGS, INDUSTRIAL

See: INDUSTRIAL COATINGS

COBALT INDUSTRY

See: METAL INDUSTRY

COCOA INDUSTRY

See also: CHOCOLATE INDUSTRY

ALMANACS AND YEARBOOKS

CRB Commodity Yearbook. Commodity Research Bureau. CRB. • Annual. $99.95.

CD-ROM DATABASES

Food Science and Technology Abstracts [CD-ROM]. Available from SilverPlatter Information, Inc. • Quarterly. $3,700 per year. Produced by International Food Information Service (home page is http://www.ifis.org). Provides worldwide coverage on CD-ROM of the literature of food technology and production. Various types of publications are indexed, with abstracts, including about 1,800 periodicals. Time period is 1969 to date.

DIRECTORIES

OPD Chemical Buyers Directory. Schnell Publishing Co., Inc. • Annual. $129.00. Included in subscription to *Chemical Marketing Reporter.* About 1,500 suppliers of chemical process materials and more than 300 companies which transport and store chemicals in the U.S.

ONLINE DATABASES

Food Science and Technology Abstracts [online]. IFIS North American Desk. • Produced by International Food Information Service. Provides about 500,000 online citations, with abstracts, to the international literature of food science, technology, commodities, engineering, and processing. Approximately 2,000 periodicals are covered. Time period is 1969 to date, with monthly updates. Inquire as to online cost and availability.

PERIODICALS AND NEWSLETTERS

Barron's: The Dow Jones Business and Financial Weekly. Dow Jones and Co., Inc. • Weekly. $145.00 per year.

Coffee and Cocoa International. DMG Business Media Ltd. International Trade Publications Ltd. • Seven times a year. $185.00 per year.

Daily Market Report. Coffee, Sugar and Coca Exchange, Inc. • Daily except Saturday and Sunday. $110.00 per year.

PRICE SOURCES

The New York Times. New York Times Co. • Daily. $374.40 per year. Supplements available: *New York Times Book Review, New York Times Magazine, Sophisticated Traveler* and *Fashions of the Times.*

STATISTICS SOURCES

FAO Quarterly Bulletin of Statistics. Food and Agriculture Organization of the United Nations. Available from UNIPUB. • Quarterly. $20.00 per year. Provides international data on agricultural production, trade, and prices, covering the major commodities of many countries. Text in English, French, and Spanish. Formerly *FAO Monthly Bulletin of Statistics.*

TRADE/PROFESSIONAL ASSOCIATIONS

American Cocoa Research Institute. 7900 Westpark Dr., Suite A-320, McLean, VA 22102. Phone: (703)790-5011 Fax: (703)790-5752 E-mail: info@candyusa.org.

Cocoa Merchants' Association of America. 26 Broadway, Suite 707, New York, NY 10004. Phone: (212)363-7334 Fax: (212)363-7678.

OTHER SOURCES

Major Food and Drink Companies of the World. Available from The Gale Group. • 2001. $855.00. Fourth edition. Two volumes. Published by Graham & Whiteside. Contains profiles and trade names for more than 9,000 important food and beverage companies in various countries. In addition to foods, includes both alcoholic and nonalcoholic drink products.

Thomas Food and Beverage Market Place. Grey House Publishing. • Annual. $295.00. Three volumes. Contains more than 40,000 entries covering food companies, beverages, food equipment, warehouse companies, food brokers, wholesalers, importers, and exporters. Formerly *Thomas Food Industry Register.*

COCONUT OIL INDUSTRY

See: OIL AND FATS INDUSTRY

CODING, PRODUCT

See: POINT-OF-SALE SYSTEMS (POS)

COFFEE INDUSTRY

See also: TEA INDUSTRY

GENERAL WORKS

The Book of Coffee and Tea: A Guide to the Appreciation of Fine Coffees, Teas and Herbal Beverages. Joel Schapira and others. St. Martin's Press. • 1996. $14.95. Second edition.

ALMANACS AND YEARBOOKS

CRB Commodity Yearbook. Commodity Research Bureau. CRB. • Annual. $99.95.

DIRECTORIES

World Coffee and Tea OCS Buyer's Guide. GCI Publishing Co., Inc. • Annual. $5.00. Directory of manufacturers and suppliers of equipment and products for the office coffee service industry. Formerly *World Coffee and Tea-Office Coffee Service Red Book Directory.*

HANDBOOKS AND MANUALS

Coffee and Tea Store. Entrepreneur Media, Inc. • Looseleaf. $59.50. A practical guide to starting a coffee and tea store. Covers profit potential, start-up costs, market size evaluation, owner's time required, site selection, lease negotiation, pricing, accounting, advertising, promotion, etc. (Start-Up Business Guide No. E1202.).

INTERNET DATABASES

USDA. United States Department of Agriculture. Phone: (202)720-2791 E-mail: agsec@usda.gov • URL: http://www.usda.gov • The USDA home page has six sections: News and Information; What's New; About USDA; Agencies; Opportunities; Search and Help. Keyword searching is offered from the USDA home page and from various individual agency home pages. Agencies are the Economic Research Service, Agricultural Marketing Service, National Agricultural Statistics Service, National Agricultural Library, and about 12 others. Updating varies. Fees: Free.

PERIODICALS AND NEWSLETTERS

Barron's: The Dow Jones Business and Financial Weekly. Dow Jones and Co., Inc. • Weekly. $145.00 per year.

Coffee and Cocoa International. DMG Business Media Ltd. International Trade Publications Ltd. • Seven times a year. $185.00 per year.

Coffee Intelligence. Coffee Publications. • Monthly. $95.00 per year. Provides trade information for the coffee industry.

The Coffee Reporter. National Coffee Association of U.S.A Inc. • Weekly. $65.00 per year.

Daily Market Report. Coffee, Sugar and Coca Exchange, Inc. • Daily except Saturday and Sunday. $110.00 per year.

Fancy Food. Talcott Communications Corp. • Monthly. $34.00 per year. Emphasizes new specialty food products and the business management aspects of the specialty food and confection industries. Includes special issues on wine, cheese, candy, "upscale" cookware, and gifts.

Gourmet Retailer. Bill Communications, Business Communications Group. • Monthly. $24.00 per year. Covers upscale food and housewares, including confectionery items, bakery operations, and coffee.

Tea and Coffee Trade Journal. Lockwood Trade Journal Co., Inc. • Monthly. $30.00 per year. Current trends in coffee roasting and tea packing industry.

World Coffee and Tea. GCI Publishing Co., Inc. • Monthly. $24.00.

PRICE SOURCES

Supermarket News: The Industry's Weekly Newspaper. Fairchild Publications. • Weekly. Individuals, $68.00 per year; instututions, $44.50 per year; corporations, $89.00 per year.

RESEARCH CENTERS AND INSTITUTES

Adjuntas Substation. University of Puerto Rico. HC-01 Box 4508, Adjuntas, Puerto Rico 00601-9717. Phone: (787)829-3614 Fax: (787)829-4714.

Hawaii Institute of Tropical Agriculture and Human Resources. University of Hawaii at Manoa, Honolulu, HI 96822. Phone: (808)956-8131 Fax: (808)956-9105 E-mail: tadean2@avax.ctahr.hawaii.edu • URL: http://www.ctahr.hawaii.edu • Concerned with the production and marketing of tropical food and ornamental plant products, including pineapples, bananas, coffee, and macadamia nuts.

STATISTICS SOURCES

Agricultural Statistics. Available from U. S. Government Printing Office. • Annual. Produced by the National Agricultural Statistics Service, U. S. Department of Agriculture. Provides a wide variety of statistical data relating to agricultural production, supplies, consumption, prices/price-supports, foreign trade, costs, and returns, as well as farm labor, loans, income, and population. In many cases, historical data is shown annually for 10 years. In addition to farm data, includes detailed fishery statistics.

Annual Survey of Manufactures. Available from U. S. Government Printing Office. • Annual. Prices vary. Issued by the U. S. Census Bureau as an interim update to the *Census of Manufactures.* Includes data on number of manufacturing establishments in various industries, employment, labor costs, value of shipments, capital expenditures, inventories, energy costs, and assets. (See also Census Bureau home page, http://www.census.gov/.).

FAO Quarterly Bulletin of Statistics. Food and Agriculture Organization of the United Nations. Available from UNIPUB. • Quarterly. $20.00 per year. Provides international data on agricultural production, trade, and prices, covering the major commodities of many countries. Text in English, French, and Spanish. Formerly *FAO Monthly Bulletin of Statistics.*

TRADE/PROFESSIONAL ASSOCIATIONS

Coffee, Sugar and Cocoa Exchange. Four World Trade Center, New York, NY 10048. Phone: 800-433-4348 or (212)742-6000 Fax: (212)748-4321 E-mail: webmaster@csce.com • URL: http://www.csce.com.

International Coffee Organization. 22 Berners St., London W1P 4DD, England. Phone: 44 171 5808591 Fax: 44 171 5806129 E-mail: info@ico.org • URL: http://www.ico.org.

National Coffee Association of the U.S.A. 15 Maiden Lane, Ste. 1405, New York, NY 10038-4003. Phone: (212)344-5596 Fax: (212)425-7059 E-mail: info@coffeescience.org • URL: http://www.coffeescience.org.

OTHER SOURCES

Coffee and Tea Market. MarketResearch.com. • 1999. $2,750.00. Market data with forecasts to 2004. Covers many types of coffee and tea.

COGENERATION OF ENERGY

GENERAL WORKS

Renewable Energy: Power for a Sustainable Future. Godfrey Boyle, editor. Available from Taylor & Francis. • 1996. $39.95. Published by Open University Press. Contains ten chapters, each on a particular renewable energy source, including solar, biomass, hydropower, wind, and geothermal.

BIOGRAPHICAL SOURCES

Energy and Nuclear Sciences International Who's Who. Allyn and Bacon/Longman. • 1990. $310.00. Third edition.

CD-ROM DATABASES

Environment Abstracts on CD-ROM. Congressional Information Service, Inc. • Quarterly. $1,295.00 per year. Contains the following CD-ROM databases: *Environment Abstracts, Energy Abstracts,* and *Acid Rain Abstracts.* Length of coverage varies.

DIRECTORIES

Energy User News: Energy Technology Buyers Guide. Cahners Business Information. • Annual. $10.00. List of about 400 manufacturers, manufacturers' representatives, dealers, and distributors of energy management equipment. *Annual Review* and *Forecast* issue.

The International Competitive Power Industry Directory. PennWell Corp. • Annual. $75.00. Lists suppliers of services, products, and equipment for the hydro, geothermal, solar, and wind power industries.

Plunkett's Energy Industry Almanac: Complete Profiles on the Energy Industry 500 Companies. Plunkett Research Ltd. • Annual. $149.99. Includes major oil companies, utilities, pipelines, alternative energy companies, etc. Provides information on industry trends.

SYNERJY: A Directory of Renewable Energy. Synerjy. • Semiannual. Individuals, $30.00 per year; others, $62.00 per year. Includes organizations, publishers, and other resources. Lists articles, patents, government publications, research groups and facilities.

ENCYCLOPEDIAS AND DICTIONARIES

Wiley Encyclopedia of Energy and the Environment. Frederick John Francis. John Wiley and Sons, Inc. • 1999. $1,500.00. Four volumes. Second edition. Covers a wide variety of energy and environmental topics, including legal and policy issues.

ONLINE DATABASES

Energyline. Congressional Information Service, Inc. • Provides online citations and abstracts to the literature of all forms of energy: petroleum, natural gas, coal, nuclear power, solar energy, etc. Time period is 1971 to 1993 (closed file). Inquire as to online cost and availability.

PROMT: Predicasts Overview of Markets and Technology. The Gale Group. • Companies, products, applied technologies and markets. U.S. and international literature coverage, 1972 to date. Inquire as to online cost and availability. Provides abstracts from more than 1,600 publications. Weekly updates.

PERIODICALS AND NEWSLETTERS

Alternative Energy Retailer. Zackin Publications, Inc. • Monthly. $32.00 per year.

Energy Conversion and Management. Elsevier Science. • 18 times a year. $2,835.00 per year. Presents a scholarly approach to alternative or renewable energy sources. Text in English, French and German.

Energy: The International Journal. Elsevier Science. • Monthly. $1,608.00 per year.

Energy Today. Trends Publishing, Inc. • Monthly. $795.00 per year. Newsletter. Provides direct access to U.S. and international policies, plans, programs, projects and events in energy development, research, management and conservation.

Independent Energy: The Power Industry's Business Magazine. PennWell Corp., Industrial Div. • 10 times a year. $127.00 per year. Covers non-utility electric power plants (cogeneration) and other alternative sources of electric energy.

Independent Power Report: An Exclusive Biweekly Covering the Cogeneration and Small Power Market. McGraw-Hill, Energy and Business Newsletter. • Biweekly. $815.00 per year. Newsletter. Covers industry trends, new projects, new contracts, rate changes, and regulations, with emphasis on the Federal Energy Regulatory Commission (FERC). Formerly *Cogeneration Report.*

National Energy Journal. c/o J. P. Dunlavey. National Wood Stove and Fireplace Journal, Inc. • Monthly. $21.00 per year.

Power. McGraw-Hill. • Monthly. Free to qualified personnel; others, $55.00 per year.

Private Power Executive. Pequot Publishing, Inc. • Bimonthly. $90.00 per year. Covers private power (non-utility) enterprises, including cogeneration projects and industrial self-generation.

Renewable Energy News Digest. Sun Words. • Monthly. $60.00 per year. Newsletter. Covers geothermal, solar, wind, cogenerated, and other energy sources.

World Cogeneration: A Power Source for Partnering in the 90's. Dick Flanagan. • Five times a year. $36.00 per year. Edited for managers and executives of independent and cogeneration electric power plants. Provides analysis of industry trends.

RESEARCH CENTERS AND INSTITUTES

Energy Laboratory. Massachusetts Institute of Technology. Bldg. E40-455, Cambridge, MA 02139-4307. Phone: (617)253-3401 Fax: (617)253-8013 E-mail: testerel@mit.edu • URL: http://www.web.mit.edu/energylab/www/.

Hawaii Natural Energy Institute. University of Hawaii at Manoa, 2540 Dole St., Holmes Hall 246, Honolulu, HI 96822. Phone: (808)956-8890 Fax: (808)956-2336 E-mail: hnei@hawaii.edu • URL: http://www.soest.hawaii.edu • Research areas include geothermal, wind, solar, hydroelectric, and other energy sources.

STATISTICS SOURCES

Annual Energy Outlook [year], with Projections to [year]. Available from U. S. Government Printing Office. • Annual. Issued by the Energy Information Administration, U. S. Department of Energy (http://www.eia.doe.gov). Contains detailed statistics and

20-year projections for electricity, oil, natural gas, coal, and renewable energy. Text provides extensive discussion of energy issues and "Market Trends.".

International Energy Annual. Available from U. S. Government Printing Office. • Annual. $34.00. Issued by the Energy Information Administration, U. S. Department of Energy. Provides production, consumption, import, and export data for primary energy commodities in more than 200 countries and areas. In addition to petroleum products and alcohol, renewable energy sources are covered (hydroelectric, geothermal, solar, and wind).

TRADE/PROFESSIONAL ASSOCIATIONS

American Wind Energy Association. 122 C St., N.W., 4th Fl., Washington, DC 20001. Phone: (202)383-2500 Fax: (202)383-2505 E-mail: windmail@awea.org • URL: http://www.econet.org/awea/.

Association of Energy Engineers. 4025 Pleasantdale Rd., Suite 420, Atlanta, GA 30340. Phone: (770)447-5083 Fax: (770)446-3969 E-mail: info@aeecenter.org • URL: http://www.aeecenter.org • Members are engineers and other professionals concerned with energy management and cogeneration.

Electric Power Supply Association. 1401 H St., N. W., Suite 760, Washington, DC 20005. Phone: (202)789-7200 Fax: (202)789-7201 • URL: http://www.epsa.org • Members are independent power producers.

COIN MACHINES

See: VENDING MACHINES

COINS AS AN INVESTMENT

ALMANACS AND YEARBOOKS

Coin Yearbook. Numismatic Publishing Co. • Annual. Price on application.

DIRECTORIES

Stamp Exchangers Annual Directory. Levine Publications. • Annual. $18.00. Lists over 500 people worldwide who are interested in exchanging stamps, coins, and other collectibles with Americans.

PERIODICALS AND NEWSLETTERS

Coin Dealer Newsletter. • Weekly. $98.00 per year. Newsletter for dealers and investors covering U. S. coins from 1793 to the present. Provides current prices, information, and market analysis.

Coin World. Amos Press, Inc. • Weekly. $29.95 per year.

Coinage. Miller Magazines, Inc. • Monthly. $23.00 per year.

Coins. Krause Publications, Inc. • Monthly. $25.98 per year.

Numismatic News. Krause Publications, Inc. • Weekly. $32.00 per year.

PRICE SOURCES

Coin Prices. Krause Publications, Inc. • Bimonthly. $18.95 per year. Gives current values of U. S. coins.

TRADE/PROFESSIONAL ASSOCIATIONS

American Numismatic Association. 818 N. Cascade Ave., Colorado Springs, CO 80903-3279. Phone: (719)632-2646 Fax: (719)634-4085 E-mail: ana@money.org • URL: http://www.money.org.

American Numismatic Society. Broadway at 155th St., New York, NY 10032. Phone: (212)234-3130 Fax: (212)234-3381 E-mail: info@amnumsoc.org • URL: http://www.amnumsoc2.org.

International Numismatic Society Authentication Bureau. P.O. Box 2091, Aston, PA 19014-0091. Phone: (610)494-2880 Fax: (610)494-2270.

Numismatics International. P.O. Box 670013, Dallas, TX 75367-0013. Phone: (214)361-7543 Fax: (972)547-6610 E-mail: johnvan@ix.netcom.com • URL: http://www.numis.org.

Professional Numismatists Guild. c/o Robert Brueggeman, 3950 Concordia Lane, Fallbrook, CA 92028. Phone: (760)728-1300 Fax: (760)728-8507 E-mail: info@pngdealers.com • URL: http://www.pngdealers.com.

Society for International Numismatics. P.O. Box 943, Santa Monica, CA 90406. Phone: (310)399-1085.

Society of Philatelists and Numismatists. 1929 Millis St., Montebello, CA 90640-4533. 1929 Millis St.,.

COKE INDUSTRY

See also: COAL INDUSTRY

ALMANACS AND YEARBOOKS

CRB Commodity Yearbook. Commodity Research Bureau. CRB. • Annual. $99.95.

PERIODICALS AND NEWSLETTERS

Gas World International. American Educational Systems. • Monthly. $240.00 per year. Formerly *Gas World.*

RESEARCH CENTERS AND INSTITUTES

Energy and Environmental Research Center. University of North Dakota. P.O. Box 9018, Grand Forks, ND 58202-9018. Phone: (701)777-5000 Fax: (701)777-5181 E-mail: ghg@eerc.und.nodak.edu.

Energy Institute. Pennsylvania State University. C211 Coal Utilization Laboratory, University Park, PA 16802. Phone: (814)863-1337 Fax: (814)863-7432 E-mail: schobert@ems.psu.edu • URL: http://www.energyinstitute.psu.edu/.

Engineering Experiment Station. Ohio State University. 2070 Neil Ave., Columbus, OH 43210-1275. Phone: (614)292-2411 Fax: (614)292-9615 E-mail: fortner.1@osu.edu • URL: http://www.osu.edu.

STATISTICS SOURCES

American Iron and Steel Annual Statistical Report. American Iron and Steel Institute. • Annual. $100.00 per year.

Minerals Yearbook. Available from U.S. Government Printing Office. • Annual. Three volumes.

Quarterly Coal Report. Energy Information Administration, U.S. Department of Energy. Available from U.S. Government Printing Office. • Quarterly. $30.00 per year. Annual summary.

TRADE/PROFESSIONAL ASSOCIATIONS

American Coke and Coal Chemicals Institute. 1255 23rd St., N.W., Washington, DC 20037. Phone: (202)452-1140 Fax: (202)833-3636.

COLD STORAGE WAREHOUSES

See: REFRIGERATION INDUSTRY; WAREHOUSES

COLLECTIBLES

See: ANTIQUES AS AN INVESTMENT; ART AS AN INVESTMENT; COINS AS AN INVESTMENT; HOBBY INDUSTRY

COLLECTING OF ACCOUNTS

See also: CREDIT

DIRECTORIES

American Collectors Association - Membership Roster. American Collectors Association, Inc. • Annual. Membership.

Blue Book of Commercial Collection. International Association Commercial Collectors. • Annual. $25.00.

Regency International Directory of Private Investigators, Private Detectives, Security Guards, and Security Equipment Suppliers. Available from Thomas Publications. • Annual. $60.00. Over 5,000 detective agencies, firms specializing in security. bailiffs, and trade protection societies; worldwide coverage. Published in England by Regency International Directory.

Skipmaster: Collection Reference Manual. Skipmaster, Inc. • Annual. Price on application. Lists sources of information useful for debt collecting and skip tracing, such as city clerks and tax assesors.

FINANCIAL RATIOS

Annual Statement Studies. Robert Morris Associates: The Association of Lending and Credit Risk Professiona. • Annual. Free to members; non-members, $140.00. Median and quartile financial ratios are given for over 400 kinds of manufacturing, wholesale, retail, construction, and consumer finance establishments. Data is sorted by both asset size and sales volume. Includes a clearly written "Definition of Ratios" and an alphabetical industry index.

HANDBOOKS AND MANUALS

The Check is Not in the Mail: How to Get Paid More, in Full, on Time, at Less Cost, and Without Losing Valued Customers. Leonard Sklar. Baroque Publishing. • 1995. $19.95. Explains how to establish the right collection cycle, what is harassment, choosing a collection agency, and collection procedures in general.

Collection Agency. Entrepreneur Media, Inc. • Looseleaf. $59.50. A practical guide to starting a collection agency. Covers profit potential, start-up costs, market size evaluation, owner's time required, pricing, accounting, advertising, promotion, etc. (Start-Up Business Guide No. E1207.).

IRS Tax Collection Procedures. CCH, Inc. • Looseleaf. $189.00. Supplementation available. Covers IRS collection personnel, payment arrangements, penalties, abatements, summons, liens, etc.

Practical Guide to Credit and Collection. George O. Bancroft. AMACOM. • 1989. $29.95.

PERIODICALS AND NEWSLETTERS

Collections and Credit Risk: The Monthly Magazine for Collections and Credit Policy Professionals. Faulkner & Gray, Inc. • Monthly. $95.00 per year. Contains articles on the technology and business management of credit and collection functions. Includes coverage of bad debts, bankruptcy, and credit risk management.

Collector. American Collectors Association, Inc. • Monthly. Members, $30.00 per year; non-members, $60.00 per year. Provides news and education in the field of credit and collections.

Credit & Collections News. Faulkner & Gray, Inc. • Weekly. $425.00 per year. Newsletter. Covers trends and new developments in credit and collections, including technology.

TRADE/PROFESSIONAL ASSOCIATIONS

American Collectors Association. ACA Center, 4040 E. 70th St., Minneapolis, MN 55435-4199.

Phone: (612)926-6547 Fax: (612)926-1624 E-mail: aca@collector.com • URL: http://www.collector.com.

International Association of Commercial Collectors. 4040 W. 70th St., Minneapolis, MN 55435. Phone: (612)925-0760 Fax: (612)926-1624 E-mail: smitht@collector.com • URL: http://www.commercialcollector.com • Collection agencies specializing in the recovery of commercial accounts receivable.

OTHER SOURCES

Consumer and Commercial Credit: Installment Sales. Prentice Hall. • Three looseleaf volumes. Periodic supplementation. Price on application. Covers secured transactions under the Uniform Commercial Code and the Uniform Consumer Credit Code. Includes retail installment sales, home improvement loans, higher education loans, and other kinds of installment loans.

Debtor-Creditor Law. Matthew Bender & Co., Inc. • $1,595.00. 10 looseleaf volumes. Periodic supplementation. Covers all aspects of the creation and enforcement of the debtor-creditor relationship.

Managing Credit and Collections to Improve Cash Flow. American Management Association Extension Institute. • Looseleaf. $130.00. Self-study course. Emphasis is on practical explanations, examples, and problem solving. Quizzes and a case study are included.

U. S. Credit Bureaus and Collection Agencies: An Industry Analysis. Available from MarketResearch.com. • 1999. $1,395.00. Market research report published by Marketdata Enterprises. Includes forecasts of industry growth to the year 2002 and provides profiles of Dun & Bradstreet, Equifax, Experion, and TransUnion.

COLLECTIVE BARGAINING

See also: ARBITRATION; LABOR UNIONS

GENERAL WORKS

Collective Bargaining and Labor. Terry L. Leap. Prentice Hall. • 1994. $90.00. Second edition.

Collective Bargaining and Labor Relations. E. Edward Herman. Prentice Hall. • 1997. $87.00. Fourth edition.

Collective Bargaining by Objectives: A Positive Approach. Reed C. Richardson. Prentice Hall. • 1977. $18.95. Second edition.

Labor Relations. Arthur A. Sloan and Fred Witney. Prentice Hall. • 1996. $91.00. Ninth edition. Emphasizes collective bargaining and arbitration.

Labor Relations: Development, Structure, Process. John A. Fossum. McGraw-Hill Professional. • 1999. Seventh edition. Price on application.

ALMANACS AND YEARBOOKS

Employment Outlook. OECD Publications and Information Center. • Annual. $50.00. Outlines the employment prospects for the coming year in OECD countries. Also discusses labor force growth, job creation, labor standards, and collective bargaining.

DIRECTORIES

International Centre for Settlement of Investment Disputes - Annual Report. International Centre for Settlement of Investment Disputes. • Annual. Free. Editions available in French and Spanish.

IRRA-Membership Directory. Industrial Relations Research Association. • Quadrennial. $25.00. About 4,200 business people, union leaders, government officials, lawyers, arbitrators, academics, consultants, and others interested in labor relations.

Profiles of American Labor Unions. The Gale Group. • 1998. $305.00. Second edition. Provides detailed information on more than 280 national labor unions. Includes descriptions of about 800 bargaining agreements and biographies of more than 170 union officials. Local unions are also listed. Four indexes. Formerly *American Directory of Organized Labor* (1992).

ONLINE DATABASES

Labordoc. International Labour Office. • Indexing of labor literature and the publications of the International Labour Organization, 1965 to present. Monthly updates. Inquire as to online cost and availability.

LEXIS. LEXIS-NEXIS. • The various LEXIS databases provide full text and indexing for a wide variety of legal cases, statutes, orders, and opinions.

PERIODICALS AND NEWSLETTERS

Dispute Resolution Journal. American Arbitration Association. • Quarterly. $55.00 per year. Formerly *Arbitration Journal.*

Labor Relations Bulletin. Bureau of Business Practice, Inc. • Monthly. $99.84 per year. Labor arbitration case analysis. Formerly *Discipline and Grievances.*

Summary of Labor Arbitration Awards. American Arbitration Association, Inc. • Monthly. $120.00 per year.

Union Labor Report. Bureau of National Affairs, Inc. • Biweekly. $848.00 per year.

RESEARCH CENTERS AND INSTITUTES

Center for Labor Education and Research. University of Alabama at Birmingham. 1044 11th St., S., Birmingham, AL 35294-4500. Phone: (205)934-2101 Fax: (205)975-5087 E-mail: rjohnson@uab.edu • URL: http://www.uab.edu.

Institute of Industrial Relations. University of California, Los Angeles. Public Policy Bldg., Los Angeles, CA 90095. Phone: (310)825-4390 Fax: (310)794-6410 • URL: http://www.sppsr.ucla.edu/resctrs/industri.htm.

TRADE/PROFESSIONAL ASSOCIATIONS

American Arbitration Association. 355 Madison Ave., New York, NY 10017-4605. Phone: 800-778-7879 or (212)716-5800 Fax: (212)716-5905 • URL: http://www.adr.org.

Institute of Collective Bargaining and Group Relations. c/o Professor Harry Katz, Cornell University, School of Industrial and Labor Relations, Ives Hall, Room 293, Ithaca, NY 14853. Phone: (607)255-3230 Fax: (607)255-6840.

National Academy of Arbitrators. Auburn University, College of Business, 403 Lawler Bldg., Auburn, AL 36849-5260. Phone: (334)844-2817 Fax: (334)844-1498 E-mail: naa@naarb.org • URL: http://www.naarb.org.

OTHER SOURCES

Collective Bargaining Negotiations and Contracts. Bureau of National Affairs, Inc. • Biweekly. $1,056.00. Two volumes. Looseleaf.

Labor Arbitration Reports. Bureau of National Affairs, Inc. • Weekly. $797 per year. Looseleaf.

COLLEGE AND SCHOOL NEWSPAPERS

See also: NEWSPAPERS

GENERAL WORKS

The Mass Media and the School Newspaper. De Witt C. Reddick. West Publishing Co., College and School Div. • 1986. $24.75. Second edition. (Mass Communication Series).

Scholastic Journalism. Earl E. English and others. Iowa State University Press. • 1996. $32.95. Ninth edition.

Writing and Editing School News: A Basic Project Text in Scholastic Journalism. William Harwood. Clark Publishing, Inc. • 1996. $33.33. Fourth revised edition.

CD-ROM DATABASES

MediaFinder CD-ROM: Oxbridge Directories of Print Media and Catalogs. Oxbridge Communications, Inc. • Quarterly. $1,695.00 per year. CD-ROM includes about 100,000 listings from *Standard Periodical Directory, National Directory of Catalogs, National Directory of British Mail Order Catalogs, National Directory of German Mail Order Catalogs, Oxbridge Directory of Newsletters, National Directory of Mailing Lists, College Media Directory*, and *National Directory of Magazines.*

DIRECTORIES

Burrelle's Media Directory: Newspapers and Related Media. Burrelle's Information Services. • Annual. $275.00. Two volumes. *Daily Newspapers* volume lists more than 2,000 daily publications in the U. S., Canada, and Mexico. *Non-Daily Newspapers* volume lists more than 10,000 items published no more than three times a week. Provides detailed descriptions, including key personnel.

College Media Directory. Oxbridge Communications, Inc. • 1997. $245.00. Lists more than 6,000 publications from about 3,500 colleges and universities.

Newspaper Advertising Source. SRDS. • Monthly. $662.00 per year. Lists newspapers geographically, with detailed information on advertising rates, special features, personnel, circulation, etc. Includes a section on college newspapers. Also provides consumer market data for population, households, income, and retail sales. Formerly *Newspaper Rates and Data.*

ONLINE DATABASES

Magazine Index. The Gale Group. • General magazine indexing (popular literature), 1973 to present. Daily updates. Inquire as to online cost and availability.

PERIODICALS AND NEWSLETTERS

College Media Review. College Media Advisors. University of Memphis. • Quarterly. Free to members; non-members, $15.00 per year.

Columbia Journalism Review. Columbia University, Graduate School of Journalism. • Bimonthly. $19.95 per year. Critical review of news media.

Quill and Scroll. International Honorary Society for High School Journalists. Quill and Scroll Society. • Quarterly. $13.00 per year. Devoted exclusively to the field of high school publications.

TRADE/PROFESSIONAL ASSOCIATIONS

Associated Collegiate Press. University of Minnesota. 2221 University Ave., S.E., Suite 121, Minneapolis, MN 55414. Phone: (612)625-8335 Fax: (612)626-0720 E-mail: info@studentpress.org • URL: http://www.studentpress.org.

College Media Advisors. University of Memphis. MJ-300, Memphis, TN 38152-6661. Phone: (901)678-2403 Fax: (901)678-4798 E-mail: nsplbrgr@cc.memphis.edu • URL: http://www.spub.ksu-edu/~cma.

College Press Service. c/o Carol Monaghan, 435 N. Michigan Ave., Suite 1400, Chicago, IL 60611. Phone: 800-245-6536 or (312)222-4444 Fax: (312)222-3459.

Columbia Scholastic Press Advisors Association. Columbia University. Mail Code 5711, New York, NY 10027-6902. Phone: (212)854-9400 Fax:

(212)854-9401 E-mail: cspa@columbia.edu • URL: http://www.cloumbia.edu/cu/cspa.

National Scholastic Press Association. University of Minnesota. 2221 University Ave., S.E., Suite 121, Minneapolis, MN 55414. Phone: (612)625-8335 Fax: (612)626-0720 E-mail: info@studentpress.org • URL: http://www.studentpress.org.

Quill and Scroll Society. School of Journalism. University of Iowa. Iowa City, IA 52242. Phone: (319)335-5795 E-mail: quill-scroll@uiowa.edu • URL: http://www.uiowa.edu/~quill-sc.

COLLEGE AND UNIVERSITY LIBRARIES

GENERAL WORKS

The Academic Library in Transition: Planning for the 1990s. Beverly P. Lynch, editor. Neal-Schuman Publishers, Inc. • 1989. $49.95.

Participative Management in Academic Libraries. Maurice P. Marchant. Greenwood Publishing Group, Inc. • 1977. $45.00. (Contributions in Librarianship and Information Science Series, No. 16).

ABSTRACTS AND INDEXES

Library Literature and Information Science: An Index to Library and Information Science Publications. H. W. Wilson Co. • Bimonthly. Annual cumulation. Service basis. Formerly *Library Literature.*

ALMANACS AND YEARBOOKS

Bowker Annual: Library and Book Trade Almanac. R. R. Bowker. • Annual. $175.00. Lists of accredited library schools; scholarships for education in library science; library organizations; major libraries; publishing and book sellers organizations. Includes statistics and news of the book business.

CD-ROM DATABASES

ERIC on SilverPlatter. Available from SilverPlatter Information, Inc. • Quarterly. $700.00 per year. Produced by the Office of Educational Research and Improvement, U. S. Dept. of Education. Provides CD-ROM indexing and abstracting of a wide variety of literature relating to education. Archival discs are available from 1966.

LISA Plus: Library and Information Science Abstracts. Bowker-Saur, Reed Reference Publishing. • Quarterly. $1,450.00 per year. Provides CD-ROM abstracting and indexing of the world's library and information science literature. Covers a wide variety of topics.

WILSONDISC: Library Literature and Information Science Index. H. W. Wilson Co. • Quarterly. Including unlimited access to the online version of *Library Literature*. Provides CD-ROM indexing of about 300 periodicals, covering a wide range of topics having to do with libraries, library management, and the information industry.

DIRECTORIES

American Library Directory. R. R. Bowker. • Annual. $269.95. Two volumes. Includes *Library Resource Guide*. Information on more than 36,000 public, academic, special and government libraries and library-related organizations in the U.S., Canada, and Mexico.

Cyberhound's Guide to Internet Libraries. The Gale Group. • 1996. 79.00. Presents critical descriptions and ratings of more than 2,000 library Internet databases. Includes a glossary of Internet terms, a bibliography, and indexes.

Gale Directory of Learning Worldwide: A Guide to Faculty and Institutions of Higher Education, Research, and Culture. The Gale Group. • 2000. $410.00. Two volumes. Describes about 26,000 colleges, universities, research institutes, libraries, museums, scholarly associations, academies, and archives around the world. Arranged by country.

World Guide to Libraries. Available from The Gale Group. • Biennial. $450.00. Two volumes. Provides information on more than 44,000 academic, government, and public libraries in 196 countries. Published by K. G. Saur.

ENCYCLOPEDIAS AND DICTIONARIES

World Encyclopedia of Library and Information Services. Robert Wedgeworth, editor. American Library Association. • 1993. $200.00. Third edition. Contains about 340 articles from various contributors.

HANDBOOKS AND MANUALS

Raising Money for Academic and Research Libraries: A How-To- Do-It Manual for Librarians. Barbara I. Dewey, editor. Neal-Schuman Publishers, Inc. • 1991. $45.00. (How-to-Do-It Series).

Strategic Management for Academic Libraries: A Handbook. Robert M. Hayes. Greenwood Publishing Group, Inc. • 1993. $65.00. (Library Management Collection).

Working with Faculty to Design Undergraduate Information Literacy Programs: A How-To-Do-It Manual for Librarians. Rosemary M. Young and Stephana Harmony. Neal-Schuman Publishers, Inc. • 1999. $45.00. Includes sample forms, surveys, evaluations, and assignments for credit courses or single sessions.

ONLINE DATABASES

American Library Directory Online. R. R. Bowker. • Provides information on over 37,000 U. S. and Canadian libraries, including college, special, and public. Annual updates. Inquire as to online cost and availability.

ERIC. Educational Resources Information Center. • Broad range of educational literature, 1966 to present. Monthly updates. Inquire as to online cost and availability.

Library Literature Online. H. W. Wilson Co. • Contains online indexing of a wide variety of library and information science literature from 1984 to date, with updating quarterly. Inquire as to online cost and availability.

LISA Online: Library and Information Science Abstracts. Bowker-Saur, Reed Reference Publishing. • Provides abstracting and indexing of the world's library and information science literature from 1969 to the present. Covers a wide variety of topics in over 550 journals from 60 countries, with biweekly updates. Inquire as to online cost and availability.

PERIODICALS AND NEWSLETTERS

American Libraries. American Library Association. • 11 times a year. Institutions and libraries only, $60.00 per year. Current news and information concerning the library industry.

ARL: A Bimonthly Newsletter of Research Library Issues and Actions. Association of Research Libraries. • Bimonthly. Members, $25.00; non-members, $50.00 per year.

Choice: Current Reviews for Academic Libraries. Association of College Research Libraries. Choice. • 11 times a year. $200.00 per year. A publication of the Association of College and Research Libraries. Contains book reviews, primarily for college and university libraries.

College and Research Libraries (CRL). Association of College and Research Libraries. American Library Association. • Bimonthly. $60.00 per year. Supplement available *C and R L News.*

College and Research Libraries News. Association of College and Research Libraries. American Library Association. • 11 times per year. Free to members; non-members, $35.00 per year. Supplement to *College and Research Libraries.*

College and Undergraduate Libraries. Haworth Press, Inc. • Semiannual. Individuals, $30.00 per year; libraries and other institutions, $90.00 per year. A practical journal dealing with everyday library problems.

Community and Junior College Libraries: The Journal for Learning Resources Centers. Haworth Press, Inc. • Semiannual. Individuals, $34.00 per year; institutions, $60.00 per year.

Focus: On the Center for Research Libraries. Center for Research Libraries. • Bimonthly. Free. Newsletter. Provides news of Center activites.

The Journal of Academic Librarianship: Articles, Features, and Book Reviews for the Academic Librarian Professional. Jai Press, Inc. • Bimonthly. $208.00 per year.

STATISTICS SOURCES

ALA Survey of Librarian Salaries. American Library Association. • Annual. $55.00. Provides data on salaries paid to librarians in academic and public libraries. Position categories range from beginning librarian to director.

ARL Annual Salary Survey. Association of Research Libraries. • Annual. Members, $39.00; non-members, $79.00. Statistics on salaries by institution, region, position, sex/race and other data for the 119 research libraries in ARL.

ARL Statistics. Association of Research Libraries. • Annual. Members, $39.00; non-members, $79.00. Presents a variety of statistics for about 120 university and other major research libraries.

TRADE/PROFESSIONAL ASSOCIATIONS

Association of College and Research Libraries. 50 E. Huron St., Chicago, IL 60611-2795. Phone: 800-545-2433 or (312)280-2521 Fax: (312)280-2520 E-mail: acrl@ala.org • URL: http://www.ala.org/acrl.html.

Association of Research Libraries. 21 Dupont Circle N.W., Suite 800, Washington, DC 20036. Phone: (202)296-2296 Fax: (202)872-0884 E-mail: arlhq@arl.org • URL: http://www.arl.org.

International Association of Technological University Libraries. c/o Dr. S. Koskial, Helsinki University of Technology, Otaniementie 9, SF 02150 Espoo, Finland. Phone: 358 9 4514112 Fax: 358 9 4514132 E-mail: john@lib.chalmers.se.

Research Libraries Group. 1200 Villa St., Mountain View, CA 94041-1100. Phone: 800-537-7546 or (650)962-9951 Fax: (650)964-0943 E-mail: bl.ric@rlg.bitnet.

COLLEGE DEGREES

See: ACADEMIC DEGREES

COLLEGE ENROLLMENT

See also: COLLEGE ENTRANCE REQUIREMENTS; COLLEGES AND UNIVERSITIES

DIRECTORIES

College Blue Book. Pearson Education and Technology. • Biennial. $625.00. Five volumes. Covers 3,000 two and four year colleges and universities, professional schools in medicine, law, etc.; over 7,500 trade technical, and business schools, and community colleges; over 2,000 public and private sources of financial aid; coverage includes Canada.

ONLINE DATABASES

American Statistics Index: A Comprehensive Guide and Index to the Statistical Publications of the United States Government [Online]. Congressional Information Service, Inc. • Indexes and abstracts, 1973 to date. Inquire as to online cost and availability.

ERIC. Educational Resources Information Center. • Broad range of educational literature, 1966 to present. Monthly updates. Inquire as to online cost and availability.

RESEARCH CENTERS AND INSTITUTES

ERIC Clearinghouse on Adult, Career and Vocational Education. Ohio State University. Center on Education and Training for Employment, 1900 Kenny Rd., Columbus, OH 43210-1090. Phone: 800-848-4815 or (614)292-7069 Fax: (614)292-1260 E-mail: ericacve@postbox.acs.ohio-state.edu • URL: http://www.ericacve/org.

Institutional Research Office. University of the Pacific. 3601 Pacific Ave., Stockton, CA 95211. Phone: (209)946-3190 Fax: (209)946-2063 E-mail: rbrodnick@upo.edu.

STATISTICS SOURCES

College Facts Chart. National Beta Club. • Annual. $7.00. Reference guide to American colleges and universities. Charts locate tuition and fee costs, telephone numbers and school size.

Digest of Education Statistics. Available from U. S. Government Printing Office. • Annual. $44.00. Covers all areas of education from kindergarten through graduate school. Includes data from both government and private sources. Compiled by National Center for Education Statistics, U. S. Department of Education.

Ethnic Enrollment Data From Institutions of Higher Education. U.S. Dept. of Health and Human Services, Office for Civil Rights. • Annual.

Occupational Projections and Training Data. Available from U. S. Government Printing Office. • Biennial. $7.00. Issued by Bureau of Labor Statistics, U. S. Department of Labor. Contains projections of employment change and job openings over the next 15 years for about 500 specific occupations. Also includes the number of associate, bachelor's, master's, doctoral, and professional degrees awarded in a recent year for about 900 specific fields of study.

OTHER SOURCES

American Universities and Colleges. Walter de Gruyter, Inc. • 2001. $249.50. 16th edition. Two volumes. Produced in collaboration with the American Council on Education. Provides full descriptions of more than 1,900 institutions of higher learning, including details of graduate and professional programs.

COLLEGE ENTRANCE REQUIREMENTS

See also: COLLEGE ENROLLMENT; COLLEGES AND UNIVERSITIES; GRADUATE WORK IN UNIVERSITIES

BIBLIOGRAPHIES

College Admissions: A Selected Annotated Bibliography. Linda Sparks, compiler. Greenwood Publishing Group, Inc. • 1993. $55.00. Describes about 1,000 professional or academic items relating to undergraduate college admissions in the United States. Topics include marketing and recruitment. (Popular guides are not included.) (Bibliographic and Indexes in Education Series, No.11).

DIRECTORIES

College Admissions Data Handbook. Riverside Publishing. • Annual. $195.00. Four volumes. Gives detailed admissions data for approximately $1,650.00 four year accredited colleges in the U.S. Four volumes. Looseleaf service. Single regional books are available.

College Blue Book. Pearson Education and Technology. • Biennial. $625.00. Five volumes. Covers 3,000 two and four year colleges and universities, professional schools in medicine, law, etc.; over 7,500 trade technical, and business schools, and community colleges; over 2,000 public and private sources of financial aid; coverage includes Canada.

Lovejoy's College Guide. Pearson Education and Technology. • Semiannual. $45.00. 2,500 American colleges, universities, and technical institutes and selected foreign colleges accredited by U.S. regional accrediting associations.

ONLINE DATABASES

ERIC. Educational Resources Information Center. • Broad range of educational literature, 1966 to present. Monthly updates. Inquire as to online cost and availability.

PERIODICALS AND NEWSLETTERS

College Board Review. College Board Publications. • Quarterly. $25.00 per year.

NACAC Bulletin. National Association for College Admission Counseling. • 10 times a year. Members, $30.00 per year; non-members, $40.00 per year. Provides news of counseling and admission trends, tools and strategies in admission counseling to 4,500 member association.

TRADE/PROFESSIONAL ASSOCIATIONS

ACT-American College Testing. P.O. Box 168, Iowa City, IA 52243. Phone: (319)337-1000 Fax: (319)337-3021 E-mail: mediarelations@act.org • URL: http://www.act.org.

American Association of Collegiate Registrars and Admissions Officers. One Dupont Circle, N.W., Suite 520, Washington, DC 20036. Phone: (202)293-9161 Fax: (202)872-8857 E-mail: info@aacrao.edu • URL: http://www.aacrao.org.

The College Board. 45 Columbus Ave., New York, NY 10017. Phone: (212)713-8000 E-mail: mro@collegeboard.org • URL: http://www.collegeboard.org.

Educational Testing Service. Rosedale Rd., Princeton, NJ 08541. Phone: (609)921-9000 Fax: (609)734-5410 E-mail: etsinfo@ets.org • URL: http://www.ets.org.

Graduate Management Admission Council. 1750 Tysons Blvd., No. 1100, McLean, VA 22102-4220. Phone: (703)749-0131 Fax: (703)749-0169 E-mail: gmat@ets.org • URL: http://www.gmat.org • Members are graduate schools of business administration and management.

National Association for College Admission Counseling. 1631 Prince St., Alexandria, VA 22314-2818. Phone: (703)836-2222 Fax: (703)836-8015 • URL: http://www.nacac.com.

COLLEGE FACULTIES

GENERAL WORKS

Improving Writing Skills: Memos, Letters, Reports, and Proposals. Arthur A. Berger. Sage Publications, Inc. • 1993. $37.00. Emphasis is on the business correspondence required of university professors and other academic personnel. (Survival Skills for Scholars, vol. 9).

Rhythms of Academic Life: Personal Accounts of Careers in Academia. Peter J. Frost and M. Susan Taylor, editors. Sage Publications, Inc. • 1996. $62.00. Contains articles by various authors on college teaching, research, publishing, tenure, and related topics. Contributions are described as "sometimes poignant and often humorous." (Foundations for Organizational Science and Series).

The Scope of Faculty Collective Bargaining: An Analysis of Faculty Union Agreements at Four-Year Institutions of Higher Education. Ronald L. Johnstone, editor. Greenwood Publishing Group, Inc. • 1981. $52.95.(Contributions to the Study of Education Series, No. 2).

Technology and Teaching. Les Lloyd, editor. Information Today, Inc. • 1997. $42.50. Contains multimedia computer application case studies relating to college level curricula and teaching.

BIOGRAPHICAL SOURCES

Directory of American Scholars. The Gale Group. • 1999. $495.00. Ninth edition. Five volumes. Provides biographical information and publication history for more than 24,000 scholars in the humanities. Previously published (1942-1982) by R. R. Bowker.

Who's Who in American Education. Marquis Who's Who. • Biennial. $159.95. Contains over 27,000 concise biographies of teachers, administrators, and other individuals involved in all levels of American education.

CD-ROM DATABASES

Profiles in Business and Management: An International Directory of Scholars and Their Research [CD-ROM]. Harvard Business School Publishing. • Annual. $595.00 per year. Fully searchable CD-ROM version of two-volume printed directory. Contains bibliographic and biographical information for over 5600 business and management experts active in 21 subject areas. Formerly *International Directory of Business and Management Scholars.*

DIRECTORIES

Faculty White Pages. The Gale Group. • 1991. $135.00. "Telephone book" classified arrangement of over 537,000 U. S. college faculty members in 41 subject sections. A roster of institutions is included.

Fulbright Scholar Program: Grants for Faculty and Professionals. Council for International Exchange of Scholars. • Annual. Free. Formerly *Fulbright Scholar Program-Faculty Grants, Research and Lecturing Awards.*

Gale Directory of Learning Worldwide: A Guide to Faculty and Institutions of Higher Education, Research, and Culture. The Gale Group. • 2000. $410.00. Two volumes. Describes about 26,000 colleges, universities, research institutes, libraries, museums, scholarly associations, academies, and archives around the world. Arranged by country.

National Faculty Directory. Available from The Gale Group. • 2001. $770.00. 32nd edition. Four volumes. 2001 supplement, $325.00. Complied by CMG Information Services.

Profiles in Business and Management: An International Directory of Scholars and Their Research Version 2.0. Claudia Bruce, editor. Harvard Business School Press. • 1996. $495.00. Two volumes. Provides backgrounds, publications, and current research projects of more than 5,600 business and management experts.

HANDBOOKS AND MANUALS

Developing a Consulting Practice. Robert O. Metzger. Sage Publications, Inc. • 1993. $37.00. Aimed at university professors and other academic personnel who wish to go into the consulting business. Contains practical advice on identifying skills, finding clients, making proposals, and management details. (Survival Skills for Scholars, vol. 3).

Getting Your Book Published. Christine S. Smedley and Mitchell Allen. Sage Publications, Inc. • 1993. $37.00. A practical guide for academic and professional authors. Covers the initial book prospectus, contract negotiation, production procedures, and marketing. (Survival Skills for Scholars, vol. 10).

ONLINE DATABASES

ERIC. Educational Resources Information Center. • Broad range of educational literature, 1966 to present. Monthly updates. Inquire as to online cost and availability.

PERIODICALS AND NEWSLETTERS

ACADEME. American Association of University Professors. • Bimonthly. $62.00 per year.

College Teaching: International Quarterly Journal. Helen Dwight Reid Educational Foundation. Heldref Publications. • Quarterly. Individuals, $36.00 per year; institutions, $66.00 per year. Practical ideas, successful methods, and new programs for faculty development.

Journal of Higher Education. Ohio State University Press. • Bimonthly. Individuals, $42.00 per year; institutions, $90.00 per year. Issues important to faculty administrators and program managers in higher education.

RESEARCH CENTERS AND INSTITUTES

ERIC Clearinghouse for Community Colleges. University of California, Los Angeles. P.O. Box 951521, Los Angeles, CA 90095-1521. Phone: 800-832-8256 or (310)825-3931 Fax: (310)206-8095 E-mail: ericc@ucla.edu • URL: http://www.gseis.ucla.edu/eric/eric.html.

ERIC Clearinghouse on Higher Education. George Washington University. Graduate School of Education and Human Development, One Dupont Circle, Suite 630, Washington, DC 20036. Phone: 800-773-3742 or (202)296-2597 Fax: (202)452-1844 E-mail: akezar@eric-he.edu • URL: http://www.eriche.org.

STATISTICS SOURCES

The Annual Report on the Economic Status of the Profession. American Association of University Professors. • Special annual issue of *ACADEME.*

Biennial Survey of Education in the United States. U.S. Department of Education. • Biennial.

Digest of Education Statistics. Available from U. S. Government Printing Office. • Annual. $44.00. Covers all areas of education from kindergarten through graduate school. Includes data from both government and private sources. Compiled by National Center for Education Statistics, U. S. Department of Education.

TRADE/PROFESSIONAL ASSOCIATIONS

American Association of University Professors. 1012 14th St., N.W., 5th Fl., Washington, DC 20005. Phone: 800-424-2973 or (202)737-5900 Fax: (202)737-5526 • URL: http://www.aaup.org.

University Professors for Academic Order. 724 Walnut Ave., Redlands, CA 92373. Phone: (909)792-1264.

COLLEGE INSTRUCTORS AND PROFESSORS

See: COLLEGE FACULTIES

COLLEGE LIBRARIES

See: COLLEGE AND UNIVERSITY LIBRARIES

COLLEGE NEWSPAPERS

See: COLLEGE AND SCHOOL NEWSPAPERS

COLLEGE PLACEMENT BUREAUS

DIRECTORIES

NACE National Directory: Who's Who in Career Planning, Placement, and Recruitment. National Association of Colleges and Employers. • Annual. Members, $32.95; non-members, $47.95. Lists over 2,200 college placement offices and about 2,000 companies interested in recruiting college graduates. Gives names of placement and recruitment personnel. Formerly *CPC National Dierctory.*

PERIODICALS AND NEWSLETTERS

Journal of Career Planning and Employment: The International Magazine of Placement and Recruitment. National Association of Colleges and Employers. • Quarterly. Free to members; non-members, $72.00 per year. Includes *Spotlight* newsletter. Formerly *Journal of College Placement.*

STATISTICS SOURCES

NACE Salary Survey: A Study of Beginning Salary Offers. National Association of Colleges and Employers. • Four times a year. Free to members; non-members, $220.00 per year. Formerly *PC Salary Survey.* Formerly College Placement Council, Inc.

TRADE/PROFESSIONAL ASSOCIATIONS

Association of Master of Business Administration Executives. c/o AMBA Center, Five Summit Place, Branford, CT 06405. Phone: (203)315-5221 Fax: (203)483-6186.

National Student Employment Association. c/o Jane Adams, P.O. Box 23606, Eugene, OR 97402. Phone: (541)484-6935 Fax: (541)484-6935 E-mail: janie.barnett@aacrao.nche.edu.

COLLEGE PRESIDENTS

See also: COLLEGES AND UNIVERSITIES

BIOGRAPHICAL SOURCES

Who's Who in American Education. Marquis Who's Who. • Biennial. $159.95. Contains over 27,000 concise biographies of teachers, administrators, and other individuals involved in all levels of American education.

PERIODICALS AND NEWSLETTERS

For Your Information. Western New York Library Resources Council. • Bimonthly. Free.

STATISTICS SOURCES

Digest of Education Statistics. Available from U. S. Government Printing Office. • Annual. $44.00. Covers all areas of education from kindergarten through graduate school. Includes data from both government and private sources. Compiled by National Center for Education Statistics, U. S. Department of Education.

TRADE/PROFESSIONAL ASSOCIATIONS

American Association of University Administrators. 17103 Preston Rd., No. 250, Dallas, TX 75248-1332. Phone: (205)463-2682 Fax: (205)463-1129 E-mail: allanw@allianceedu.org.

Association of American Universities. 1200 New York Ave., Suite 550, Washington, DC 20005. Phone: (202)408-7500 Fax: (202)408-8184 • URL: http://www.tulane.edu/~aau/.

Center for Leadership Development. c/o American Council on Education. One Dupont Circle, N.W., 8th Fl., Washington, DC 20036. Phone: (202)939-9418 Fax: (202)785-8056.

National Council of Administrative Women in Education. One Potbelly Beach Rd., Aptos, CA 95003-3579. One Potbelly Beach Rd.,.

COLLEGE PUBLISHERS

See: UNIVERSITY PRESSES

COLLEGE STORES

See also: BOOKSELLING; DEPARTMENT STORES; RETAIL TRADE

DIRECTORIES

Directory of College Stores. B. Klein Publications, Inc. • Irregular. $75.00. Covers about 4,400 stores selling books, stationery, personal care items, gifts, etc., which serve primarily a college student population.

PERIODICALS AND NEWSLETTERS

The College Store. National Association of College Stores. • Six times a year. Members, $54.00 per year; non-members, $64.00 per year. Formerly *College Store Journal.*

College Store Executive. Executive Business Media, Inc. • 10 times a year. $40.00 per year.

TRADE/PROFESSIONAL ASSOCIATIONS

National Association of College Auxiliary Services. P.O. Box 5546, Charlottesville, VA 22905. Phone: (804)245-8425 Fax: (804)245-8453 • URL: http://www.nacas.org.

National Association of College Stores. 500 E. Lorain St., Oberlin, OH 44074-1298. Phone: 800-622-7498 or (440)775-7777 Fax: (216)775-4769 E-mail: info@nacs.org • URL: http://www.nacs.org.

COLLEGE TEACHERS

See: COLLEGE FACULTIES

COLLEGES AND UNIVERSITIES

See also: COLLEGE ENROLLMENT; COLLEGE ENTRANCE REQUIREMENTS; COLLEGE FACULTIES; COLLEGE PRESIDENTS; GRADUATE WORK IN UNIVERSITIES; SCHOLARSHIPS AND STUDENT AID

GENERAL WORKS

Higher Education in American Society. Phillip G. Altbach and others, editors. Prometheus Books. • 1994. $24.95. Third edition. (Frontiers of Education Series).

Public Policy and College Management: Title III of the Higher Education Act. Edward P. Saint John. Greenwood Publishing Group, Inc. • 1981. $55.00.

ABSTRACTS AND INDEXES

Current Index to Journals in Education (CIJE). Oryx Press. • Monthly. $245.00 per year. Semiannual cumulations, $475.00.

Education Index. H.W. Wilson Co. • 10 times a year. Service basis.

Educational Administration Abstracts. Corwin Press, Inc. • Quarterly. Indivduals, $110.00 per year; institutions, $475.00 per year.

Index of Majors. The College Board Publications. • Annual. $17.95.

BIBLIOGRAPHIES

A Bibliographic Guide to American Colleges and Universities from Colonial Times to the Present. Mark Beach. Greenwood Publishing Group Inc. • 1975. $55.00.

Index to Anthologies on Postsecondary Education, 1960-1978. Richard H. Quay, compiler. Greenwood Publishing Group, Inc. • 1980. $55.00.

CD-ROM DATABASES

College Blue Book CD-ROM. Available from The Gale Group. • Annual. $250.00. Produced by Macmillan Reference USA. Serves as electronic version of printed *College Blue Book.* Provides detailed information on programs, degrees, and financial aid sources in the U.S. and Canada.

ERIC on SilverPlatter. Available from SilverPlatter Information, Inc. • Quarterly. $700.00 per year. Produced by the Office of Educational Research and Improvement, U. S. Dept. of Education. Provides CD-ROM indexing and abstracting of a wide variety of literature relating to education. Archival discs are available from 1966.

Leadership Library on CD-ROM: Who's Who in the Leadership of the United States. Leadership Directories, Inc. • Quarterly. $2,641.00 per year, including access to Internet version (weekly updates). Contains all 14 *Yellow Book* personnel directories on CD-ROM, providing contact and brief biographical information for about 400,000 individuals. Covers business, government, financial institutions, news media, law firms, associations, foreign representatives, and nonprofit organizations. Includes photographs.

WILSONDISC: Education Index. H. W. Wilson Co. • Monthly. $1,295.00 per year. Provides CD-ROM indexing of education-related literature from 1983 to date. Price includes online service.

DIRECTORIES

Accredited Institutions of Postsecondary Education. Allison Anaya, editor. Oryx Press. • Annual. $39.95. Lists more than 5,500 accredited institutions and programs.

Chronicle Four-Year College Databook, 1996-97. Chronicle Guidance Publications, Inc. • 1996. $24.99. Revised edition. More than 790 baccalaureate, master's, doctoral, and first professional programs offered by more than 2,130 colleges and universities in the United States. Formerly *Chronicle Buide to Four-Year College Majors.*

College Blue Book. Pearson Education and Technology. • Biennial. $625.00. Five volumes. Covers 3,000 two and four year colleges and universities, professional schools in medicine, law, etc.; over 7,500 trade technical, and business schools, and community colleges; over 2,000 public and private sources of financial aid; coverage includes Canada.

Faculty White Pages. The Gale Group. • 1991. $135.00. "Telephone book" classified arrangement of over 537,000 U. S. college faculty members in 41 subject sections. A roster of institutions is included.

Gale Directory of Learning Worldwide: A Guide to Faculty and Institutions of Higher Education, Research, and Culture. The Gale Group. • 2000. $410.00. Two volumes. Describes about 26,000 colleges, universities, research institutes, libraries, museums, scholarly associations, academies, and archives around the world. Arranged by country.

Guide to Federal Funding for Education. Education Funding Research Council. • Quarterly. $297.00 per year. Describes approximately 407 federal education programs that award grants and contracts. Includes semimonthly supplement: *Grant Updates.*

Lovejoy's College Guide. Pearson Education and Technology. • Semiannual. $45.00. 2,500 American colleges, universities, and technical institutes and selected foreign colleges accredited by U.S. regional accrediting associations.

National Faculty Directory. Available from The Gale Group. • 2001. $770.00. 32nd edition. Four volumes. 2001 supplement, $325.00. Complied by CMG Information Services.

New Riders' Official World Wide Web Yellow Pages. Pearson Education and Technology. • 1997. $34.99. A broadly classified listing of Web sites, with brief descriptions of sites and a subject index to narrower topics. Includes a guide to using the Internet and a separate, alphabetical listing of more than 1,500 college and university Web sites, both U. S. and foreign. Includes CD-ROM.

Nonprofit Sector Yellow Book: Who's Who in the Management of the Leading Foundations, Universities, Museums, and Other Nonprofit Organizations. Leadership Directories, Inc. • Semiannual. $235.00 per year. Covers management personnel and board members of about 1,000 prominent, nonprofit organizations: foundations, colleges, museums, performing arts groups, medical institutions, libraries, private preparatory schools, and charitable service organizations.

Patterson's Schools Classified. Educational Directories, Inc. • Annual. $15.00. Lists more than 7,000 accredited colleges, universities, junior colleges, and vocational schools. Includes brief descriptions. Classified arrangement, with index to name of school. Included in *Patterson's American Education.*

Peterson's Guide to Distance Learning. Peterson's. • 1996. $24.95. Provides detailed information on accredited college and university programs available through television, radio, computer, videocassette, and audiocassette resources. Covers 700 U. S. and Canadian institutions. Formerly *The Electronic University.*

Peterson's Guide to Four-Year Colleges. Peterson's. • Annual. $19.95. Provides information on more than 2,000 accredited degree-granting colleges and universities in the U. S. and Canada.

Peterson's Guide to Graduate and Professional Programs: An Overview. Peterson's. • Annual. $27.95. Six volumes provide details of more than 31,000 graduate programs at 1,600 colleges and universities: 1. An Overview; 2. Humanities, Arts, and Social Sciences; 3. MBA; 4. Visual and Performing Arts; 5. Engineering and Applied Sciences; 6. Business, Education, Health, Information Studies, Law, and Social Work. (Volumes are available individually.).

Peterson's Register of Higher Education. Peterson's. • Annual. $49.95. Provides concise information on 3,700 colleges and other postsecondary educational institutions in the U. S.

The World of Learning. Available from The Gale Group. • $712.50. 50th edition. Covers about 26,000 colleges, libraries, museums, learned societies, academies, and research institutions throughout the world. Published by Europa Publications.

HANDBOOKS AND MANUALS

The College Handbook. The College Board Publications. • Annual. $25.95. Over 3,200 undergraduate schools.

Office Procedures and Technology for Colleges. Patsy J. Fulton. South-Western Publishing Co. • 1998. $39.95. 11th edition. (KF-Office Education Series).

Peterson's Guide to Colleges for Careers in Computing: The Only Combined Career and College Guide for Future Computer Professionals. Peterson's. • 1996. $14.95. Describes career possibilities in various fields related to computers.

INTERNET DATABASES

U. S. Census Bureau: The Official Statistics. U. S. Bureau of the Census. Phone: (301)763-4100 Fax: (301)763-4794 • URL: http://www.census.gov • Web site is "Your Source for Social, Demographic, and Economic Information." Contains "Current U. S. Population Count," "Current Economic Indicators," and a wide variety of data under "Other Official Statistics." Keyword searching is provided. Fees: Free.

ONLINE DATABASES

Education Index Online. H. W. Wilson Co. • Indexes a wide variety of periodicals related to schools, colleges, and education, 1984 to date. Monthly updates. Inquire as to online cost and availability.

ERIC. Educational Resources Information Center. • Broad range of educational literature, 1966 to present. Monthly updates. Inquire as to online cost and availability.

PERIODICALS AND NEWSLETTERS

American School and University: Facilities, Purchasing, and Business Administration. Intertec Publishing Corp. • Monthly. Free to qualified personnel; others, $65.00 per year.

Athletic Management. Momentum Media. • Bimonthly. $24.00 per year. Formerly *College Athletic Management.*

Change: The Magazine of Higher Learning. American Association of Higher Education. Helderf Publications. • Bimonthly. Individuals, $40.00 per year; institutions, $82.00 per year.

The Chronicle of Higher Education. Chronicle of Higher Education, Inc. • 49 times a year. $75.00 per year. Includes *Almanac.* Provides news, book reviews and job listings for college professors and administrators. Suplement available: *Chronicle of Higher Education Almanac.*

College and University. American Association of Collegiate Registrars and Admissions Officers. • Quarterly. Free to members; non-members, $50.00 per year. Addresses issues in higher education; looks at new procedures, policies, technology; reviews new publications.

Community College Journal. American Association of Community and Junior Colleges. • Bimonthly. $28.00 per year. Formerly *Community, Technical and Junior College Journal.*

Community College Week: The Independent Voice Serving Community, Technical and Junior Colleges. Cox, Matthews & Associates. • Biweekly. $40.00 per year. Covers a wide variety of current topics relating to the administration and operation of community colleges.

Higher Education and National Affairs. American Council on Education. • Biweekly. $60.00 per year.

Journal of Higher Education. Ohio State University Press. • Bimonthly. Individuals, $42.00 per year; institutions, $90.00 per year. Issues important to faculty administrators and program managers in higher education.

Journal of Marketing for Higher Education. Haworth Press, Inc. • Quarterly. Individuals, $60.00 per year; institutions, $120.00 per year; libraries, $225.00 per year.

New Directions for Higher Education. Jossey-Bass. • Quarterly. Institutions, $114.00 per year. Sample issue free to librarians.

The Presidency: The Magazine for Higher Education Leaders. American Council on Education. • Three times a year. Members, $27.00 per year; non-members, $30.00 per year. Formerly *Educational Record.*

Resources in Education. Educational Resources Information Center. Available from U.S. Government Printing Office. • Monthly. $102.00 per year. Reports on educational research.

University Business: Solutions for Today's Higher Education. University Business, LLC. • Bimonthly. $49.00 per year. Edited for college administrators, including managers of business services, finance, computing, and telecommunications. Includes information on relevant technological advances.

RESEARCH CENTERS AND INSTITUTES

Center for the Study of Higher Education. Pennsylvania State University. 403 S. Allen St., Suite 104, University Park, PA 16801-5252. Phone: (814)865-6346 Fax: (814)865-3638 E-mail: fxc2@psu.edu • URL: http://www.ed.psu.edu/cshe.

ERIC Clearinghouse for Community Colleges. University of California, Los Angeles. P.O. Box 951521, Los Angeles, CA 90095-1521. Phone: 800-832-8256 or (310)825-3931 Fax: (310)206-8095 E-mail: ericc@ucla.edu • URL: http://www.gseis.ucla.edu/eric/eric.html.

ERIC Clearinghouse on Adult, Career and Vocational Education. Ohio State University. Center on Education and Training for Employment, 1900 Kenny Rd., Columbus, OH 43210-1090. Phone: 800-848-4815 or (614)292-7069 Fax: (614)292-1260 E-mail: ericacve@postbox.acs.ohio-state.edu • URL: http://www.ericacve/org.

STATISTICS SOURCES

Degrees and Other Awards Conferred by Institutions of Higher Education. Available from U. S. Government Printing Office. • Annual. Issued by the National Center for Education Statistics, U. S. Department of Education. Provides data on the number of degrees awarded at the associate's, bachelor's, master's, and doctor's levels. Includes fields of study and racial-ethnic-sex data by major field or discipline.

Digest of Education Statistics. Available from U. S. Government Printing Office. • Annual. $44.00. Covers all areas of education from kindergarten through graduate school. Includes data from both government and private sources. Compiled by National Center for Education Statistics, U. S. Department of Education.

Fact Book on Higher Education, 1989-1990. Charles J. Andersen and others. Pearsono Education and Technology. • 1989. $41.95. Published in conjunction with the American Council on Education. (Ace-Macmillan Higher Education Series).

School Enrollment, Social and Economic Characteristics of Students. Available from U. S. Government Printing Office. • Annual. Issued by the U. S. Bureau of the Census. Presents detailed tabulations of data on school enrollment of the civilian noninstitutional population three years old and over. Covers nursery school, kindergarten, elementary school, high school, college, and graduate school. Information is provided on age, race, sex, family income, marital status, employment, and other characteristics.

Social Statistics of the United States. Mark S. Littman, editor. Bernan Press. • 2000. $65.00. Includes statistical data on population growth, labor force, occupations, environmental trends, leisure time use, income, poverty, taxes, and other economic or demographic topics.

Statistical Abstract of the United States. Available from U. S. Government Printing Office. • Annual. $51.00. Issued by the U. S. Bureau of the Census.

A Statistical Portrait of the United States: Social Conditions and Trends. Mark S. Littman, editor. Bernan Press. • 1998. $89.00. Covers "social, economic, and environmental trends in the United States over the past 25 years." Includes statistical tables, graphs, and analysis relating to such topics as population, income, poverty, wealth, labor, housing, education, healthcare, air/water quality, and government.

UNESCO Statistical Yearbook. Bernan Press. • Annual. $95.00. Co-published by Bernan Press and the United Nations Educational, Scientific, and Cultural Organization (http://www.unesco.org). Presents statistical data from more than 200 countries on education, technology, research, broadcasting, cinema, book publishing, newspapers, libraries, museums, and population. Includes charts, maps, and graphs.

TRADE/PROFESSIONAL ASSOCIATIONS

Academy for Educational Development. 1875 Connecticut Ave., N.W., Washington, DC 20009-5721. Phone: (202)884-8000 Fax: (202)884-8400 E-mail: admin@aeda.org • URL: http://www.aed.org.

American Council on Education. One Dupont Circle, N.W., Suite 800, Washington, DC 20036. Phone: (202)939-9300 Fax: (202)833-4760 E-mail: web@ace.nche.edu • URL: http://www.acenet.edu.

Association of American Colleges and Universities. 1818 R St., N.W., Washington, DC 20009. Phone: (202)387-3760 Fax: (202)265-9532 E-mail: info@aacu.nw.dc.us • URL: http://www.aacu-edu.org.

Association of American Universities. 1200 New York Ave., Suite 550, Washington, DC 20005. Phone: (202)408-7500 Fax: (202)408-8184 • URL: http://www.tulane.edu/~aau/.

Association of American University Presses. 71 W. 23rd St., Suite 901, New York, NY 10010-4102. Phone: (212)989-1010 Fax: (212)989-0275 E-mail: aaupny@aol.com • URL: http://www.aaupnet.org.

Association of Governing Boards of Universities and Colleges. One Dupont Circle, N.W., Suite 400, Washington, DC 20036. Phone: 800-356-6317 or (202)296-8400 Fax: (202)223-7053 • URL: http://www.agb.org.

Association of Graduate Schools in the Association of American Universities. 1200 New York Ave., Suite 550, Washington, DC 20005. Phone: (202)408-7500 Fax: (202)408-8184.

The College Board. 45 Columbus Ave., New York, NY 10017. Phone: (212)713-8000 E-mail: mro@collegeboard.org • URL: http://www.collegeboard.org.

Council for Advancement and Support of Education. 1307 New York Ave. N.W., Suite 1000, Washington, DC 20005. Phone: (202)328-5900 Fax: (202)387-4973.

Council of Graduate Schools. One Dupont Circle, N.W., Suite 430, Washington, DC 20036-1173. Phone: (202)223-3791 Fax: (202)331-7157 E-mail: ngaffney@cgs.nche.edu • URL: http://www.cgsnet.org.

OTHER SOURCES

American Universities and Colleges. Walter de Gruyter, Inc. • 2001. $249.50. 16th edition. Two volumes. Produced in collaboration with the American Council on Education. Provides full descriptions of more than 1,900 institutions of higher learning, including details of graduate and professional programs.

Educational Rankings Annual: A Compilation of Approximately 3,500 Published Rankings and Lists on Every Aspect of Education. The Gale Group. • 2000. $220.00. Provides national, regional, local, and international rankings of a wide variety of educational institutions, including business and professional schools.

COLOR IN INDUSTRY

See also: ART IN INDUSTRY

GENERAL WORKS

Color in Business, Science, and Industry. Deane B. Judd and Gunter Wyszecki. John Wiley and Sons, Inc. • 1975. $195.00. Third edition. (Pure and Applied Optics Series).

Color in the Office: Design Trends from 1950 to 1990 and Beyond. Sara O. Marberry. John Wiley & Sons, Inc. • 1993. $75.00. Presents past, present, and future color trends in corporate office design. Features color photographs of traditional, postmodern, and neoclassical office designs. (Architecture Series).

Industrial Color Technology. Ruth M. Johnston and Max Saltzman, editors. American Chemical Society. • 1972. $21.95. (Advances in Chemistry Series: No. 107).

HANDBOOKS AND MANUALS

Color Science: Concepts and Methods, Quantitative Data and Formulae. Gunter Wyszecki and W.S. Stiles. John Wiley and Sons, Inc. • 1982. $270.00. Second edition. (Pure and Applied Optics Series).

Industrial Color Testing: Fundamentals and Techniques. Hans G. Volz. John Wiley and Sons, Inc. • 1995. $195.00.

The Physics and Chemistry of Color: [The Fifteen Causes of Color]. Kurt Nassau. John Wiley and Sons, Inc. • 1983. $170.00. (Pure and Applied Optics Series).

ONLINE DATABASES

CA Search. Chemical Abstracts Service. • Guide to chemical literature, 1967 to present. Inquire as to online cost and availability.

PERIODICALS AND NEWSLETTERS

Chromatographia: An International Journal for Rapid Communication in Chromatography and Associated Techniques. Elsevier Science. • 24 times a year. $1,245.00 per year. Text in English; summaries in English, French and German.

Color Publishing. PennWell Corp., Advanced Technology Div. • Bimonthly. $29.70 per year.

Color Research and Application. John Wiley and Sons, Inc. • Bimonthly. Institutions, $645 per year. International coverage.

PRICE SOURCES

Chemical Market Reporter. Schnell Publishing Co., Inc. • Weekly. $139.00 per year. Quotes current prices for a wide range of chemicals. Formerly *Chemical Marketing Reporter.*

RESEARCH CENTERS AND INSTITUTES

Center for Imaging Science. Rochester Institute of Technology, 54 Lomb Memorial Dr., Rochester, NY 14623. Phone: (716)475-5994 Fax: (716)475-5988 E-mail: gatley@cis.rit.edu • URL: http://www.cis.rit.edu • Activities include research in color science and digital image processing.

Chemistry Laboratories. Rensselaer Polytechnic Institute. Cogswell Laboratory, Troy, NY 12180-3590. Phone: (518)276-6344 Fax: (518)276-4887 E-mail: applet@rpi.edu.

TRADE/PROFESSIONAL ASSOCIATIONS

American Association of Textile Chemists and Colorists. P.O. Box 12215, Research Triangle Park, NC 27709-2215. Phone: (919)549-8141 Fax: (919)549-8933 • URL: http://www.aatcc.org.

Color Association of the United States. 589 Eighth Ave., 12th Fl., New York, NY 10018-3005. Phone: (212)372-8600 Fax: (212)290-1175 E-mail: caus@colorassociation.com • URL: http://www.colorassociation.com.

Color Marketing Group. 5904 Richmond Highway, No. 408, Alexandria, VA 22303. Phone: (703)329-8500 Fax: (703)329-0155 E-mail: cmg@colormarketing.org • URL: http://www.colormarketing.org.

Color Pigments Manufacturers Association. P.O. Box 20839, Alexandria, VA 22320. Phone: (703)684-4044 Fax: (703)684-1795 E-mail: cpma@cpma.com.

Optical Society of America. 2010 Massachusetts Ave., N.W., Washington, DC 20036-1023. Phone: (202)223-8130 Fax: (202)223-1096 • URL: http://www.osa.org.

COLOR PHOTOGRAPHY

See: PHOTOGRAPHIC INDUSTRY

COLOR TELEVISION

See: TELEVISION APPARATUS INDUSTRY

COLUMNISTS

See: WRITERS AND WRITING

COMMERCIAL ART

See also: ART IN INDUSTRY; CREATIVITY; DESIGN IN INDUSTRY; GRAPHIC ARTS INDUSTRY

ABSTRACTS AND INDEXES

Art Index. H. W. Wilson Co. • Quarterly. Annual cumulations. Service basis for print edition; CD-ROM edition, $1,495.00 per year. Subject and author index to periodicals in art, architecture, industrial design, city planning, photography, and various related topics.

ALMANACS AND YEARBOOKS

Art Directors Annual. Art Directors Club Inc. Rotovision, S.A. • Annual. $70.00. Formerly *Annual of Advertising, Editorial and Television Art and Design with the Annual Copy Awards.*

Graphis Design: International Annual of Design and Illustration. Watson-Guptill Publications. • Annual. $69.00. Text in English, French, and German. Formerly *Graphis Annual.*

CD-ROM DATABASES

WILSONDISC: Art Index. H. W. Wilson Co. • Monthly. $1,495.00 per year. Provides CD-ROM indexing of art-related literature from 1982 to date. Price includes online service.

DIRECTORIES

Graphic Arts Blue Book. A. F. Lewis and Co. Inc. • Auuual. $85.00. Eight regional editions. Printing plants, bookbinders, imagesetters, platemakers, paper merchants, paper manufacturers, printing machine manufacturers and dealers, and others serving the printing industry.

Magazines Careers Directory: A Practical One-Stop Guide to Getting a Job in Publc Relations. Visible Ink Press. • 1993. $17.95. Fifth edition. Includes information on magazine publishing careers in art, editing, sales, and business management. Provides advice from "insiders," resume suggestions, a directory of companies that may offer entry-level positions, and a directory of career information sources. *Career Advisor Series.*

Peterson's Professional Degree Programs in the Visual and Performing Arts. Peterson's. • Annual. $24.95. A directory of more than 900 degree programs in art, music, theater, and dance at 600 colleges and professional schools.

ONLINE DATABASES

Art Index Online. H. W. Wilson Co. • Indexes a wide variety of art-related periodicals, 1984 to date. Monthly updates. Inquire as to online cost and availability.

ARTbibliographies Modern. ABC-CLIO, Inc. • Covers the literature of contemporary art and related subjects from 1974 to date, including art collecting, exhibitions, galleries, graphic design, photography, etc. Inquire as to online cost and availability.

PERIODICALS AND NEWSLETTERS

Art Direction: The Magazine of Visual Communication. Advertising Trade Publications, Inc. • Monthly. $29.97 per year. Current advertising in art, photography, design, type, etc.

Graphic Design: U.S.A. Kaye Publishing Corp. • Monthly. $60.00.

Graphis: International Journal of Visual Communication. Graphis Inc. • Bimonthly. $90.00 per year. Text in English, French and German.

RESEARCH CENTERS AND INSTITUTES

Technical and Educational Center of the Graphic Arts and Imaging. Rochester Institute of Technology, 67 Lomb Memorial Dr., Rochester, NY 14623-5603. Phone: 800-724-2536 or (716)475-2680 Fax: (716)475-7000 E-mail: webmail@rit.edu • URL: http://www.rit.edu/cime/te.

TRADE/PROFESSIONAL ASSOCIATIONS

Art Directors Club. 101 W. 29th St., New York, NY 10001. Phone: (212)643-1440 Fax: (212)643-4266 E-mail: adcny@interport.net • URL: http://www.adcny.org.

Graphic Artists Guild. 90 John St., Suite 403, New York, NY 10038-3202. Phone: 800-500-2627 or (212)791-3400 Fax: (212)791-0333 E-mail: pr@gag.com • URL: http://www.gag.org/.

Society of American Graphic Artists. 32 Union Square, Room 1214, New York, NY 10003. Phone: (212)260-5706.

OTHER SOURCES

Opportunities in Visual Arts Careers. Mark Salmon. NTC/Contemporary Publishing Group. • 2001. $15.95. Edited for students and job seekers. Includes education requirements and salary data. (VGM Career Books.).

COMMERCIAL AVIATION

See: BUSINESS AVIATION

COMMERCIAL CODE

See: BUSINESS LAW

COMMERCIAL CORRESPONDENCE

See: BUSINESS CORRESPONDENCE

COMMERCIAL CREDIT

See: COMMERCIAL LENDING

COMMERCIAL EDUCATION

See: BUSINESS EDUCATION

COMMERCIAL FINANCE COMPANIES

See: FINANCE COMPANIES

COMMERCIAL LAW AND REGULATION

See: BUSINESS LAW

COMMERCIAL LENDING

See also: BANK LOANS

GENERAL WORKS

The Art of Commercial Lending. Edward Morsman. Robert Morris Associates. • 1997. $64.00. Describes the diverse skills required for success as a commercial lender. Covers both personal and institutional aspects.

The New Face of Credit Risk Management: Balancing Growth and Credit Quality in an Integrated Risk Management Environment. Charles B. Wendel. Robert Morris Associates. • 1999. $65.00. Contains "In-depth interviews with senior credit officers from five major financial institutions." Coverage includes modeling, scoring, and other technology related to the management of credit risk.

ABSTRACTS AND INDEXES

Business Periodicals Index. H. W. Wilson Co. • Monthly, except August, with quarterly and annual cumulations. Service basis for print edition; CD-ROM edition, $1,495.00 per year.

DIRECTORIES

Business Organizations, Agencies, and Publications Directory. The Gale Group. • 1999. $425.00. 12th edition. Over 40,000 entries describing 39 types of business information sources. Classified by type of organization, publication, or serviceIncludes state, national, and international agencies and organizations. Master index to names and keywords. Also includes e-mail addresses and web site URL's.

Corporate Finance Sourcebook: The Guide to Major Capital Investment Source and Related Financial Services. R. R. Bowker. • Annual. $625.00. Lists more than 3,550 sources of corporate capital: investment bankers, securities firms, pension management companies, trust companies, insurance companies, and private lenders. Includes the names of over 13,000 key personnel.

ENCYCLOPEDIAS AND DICTIONARIES

Credit and Lending Dictionary. Daphne Smith and Shelley W. Geehr, editors. Robert Morris Associates. • 1994. $25.00.

HANDBOOKS AND MANUALS

Commercial Lending. George E. Ruth. American Bankers Association. • 1990. $57.00. Second edition. Discusses the practical aspects of commercial lending.

How to Charter a Commercial Bank. Douglas V. Austin and others. CCH, Inc. • 1999. $350.00. Provides detailed information on how to start a commercial bank, including both technical and practical requirements.

Manual of Credit and Commercial Laws. National Association of Credit Management. John Wiley and Sons, Inc. • Annual. $125.00. Formerly *Credit Manual of Commercial Laws.*

ONLINE DATABASES

TRW Business Credit Profiles. TRW Inc., Business Credit Services Division. • Provides credit history (trade payments, payment trends, payment totals, payment history, etc.) for public and private U. S. companies. Key facts and banking information are also given. Updates are weekly. Inquire as to online cost and availability.

Wilson Business Abstracts Online. H. W. Wilson Co. • Indexes and abstracts 600 major business periodicals, plus the *Wall Street Journal* and the business section of the *New York Times*. Indexing is from 1982, abstracting from 1990, with the two newspapers included from 1993. Updated weekly. Inquire as to online cost and availability. (*Business Periodicals Index* without abstracts is also available online.).

PERIODICALS AND NEWSLETTERS

Bank Letter: Newsletter of Commercial and Institutional Banking. Institutional Investor, Newsletters Div. • Weekly. $2,220.00 per year. Newsletter. Covers retail banking, commercial lending, foreign loans, bank technology, government regulations, and other topics related to banking.

Commercial Lending Litigation News. LRP Publications. • Biweekly. $597.00 per year. Newsletter on court decisions, settlements, significant new cases, legislation, regulation, and industry trends. Formerly *Lender Liability News.*

Commercial Lending Review. Institutional Investor. • Quarterly. $195.00 per year. Edited for senior-level lending officers. Includes specialized lending techniques, management issues, legal developments, and reviews of specific industries.

Journal of Lending and Credit Risk Management. Robert Morris Associates. • 10 times a year. Members, $35.00 per year; non-members, $85.00 per year. Formerly *Journal of Commercial Bank Lending.*

Lender Liability Law Report. Warren, Gorham & Lamont/RIA Group. • Monthly. $183.00 per year. Newsletter on cases and legislation affecting lenders.

TRADE/PROFESSIONAL ASSOCIATIONS

International Association of Commercial Collectors. 4040 W. 70th St., Minneapolis, MN 55435. Phone: (612)925-0760 Fax: (612)926-1624 E-mail: smitht@collector.com • URL: http://www.commercialcollector.com • Collection agencies specializing in the recovery of commercial accounts receivable.

National Association of Credit Management. 8840 Columbia, 100 Parkway, Columbia, MD 21045-2158. Phone: 800-955-8815 or (410)740-5560 Fax: (410)740-5574 E-mail: nacminfo@nacm.org • URL: http://www.nacm.org.

Robert Morris Associates- Association of Lending and Credit Risk Professionals. One Liberty Place, 1650 Market St., Suite 2300, Philadelphia, PA 19103-7398. Phone: (215)446-4000 Fax: (215)446-4101 • URL: http://www.rmahq.org.

OTHER SOURCES

Bank and Lender Litigation Reporter: The Nationwide Litigation Report of Failed National and State Banks and Savings and Loan Associations, including FDIC and FSLIC Complaints and Related Actions Among Shareholders, Officers, Directors, Ins. Andrews Publications. • Semimonthly. $875.00 per year. Provides summaries of significant litigation and regulatory agency complaints. Formerly *Lender Liability Litigation Reporter.*

COMMERCIAL PHOTOGRAPHY

See also: PHOTOGRAPHIC INDUSTRY

ABSTRACTS AND INDEXES

Art Index. H. W. Wilson Co. • Quarterly. Annual cumulations. Service basis for print edition; CD-ROM edition, $1,495.00 per year. Subject and author index to periodicals in art, architecture, industrial design, city planning, photography, and various related topics.

BIOGRAPHICAL SOURCES

Contemporary Photographers. Available from The Gale Group. • 1995. $175.00. Provides biographical and critical information on more than 850 international photographers.

DIRECTORIES

American Society of Photographers - Membership Directory. American Society of Photographers, Inc. • Annual. Price on application.

Photographer's Market: 2000 Places to Sell Your Photographs. F & W Publications, Inc. • Annual. $23.99. Lists 2,000 companies and publications that purchase original photographs.

Who's Who in Professional Imaging. Professional Photographers of America, Inc. • Annual. $110.00. Lists over 18,000 members. Formerly *Buyers Guide to Qualified Photographers.*

ENCYCLOPEDIAS AND DICTIONARIES

Focal Encyclopedia of Photography. Leslie Stroebel and Richard D. Zakia, editors. Butterworth-Heinemann. • 1993. $56.95. Third edition.

FINANCIAL RATIOS

Annual Statement Studies. Robert Morris Associates: The Association of Lending and Credit Risk Professiona. • Annual. Free to members; non-members, $140.00. Median and quartile financial ratios are given for over 400 kinds of manufacturing, wholesale, retail, construction, and consumer finance establishments. Data is sorted by both asset size and sales volume. Includes a clearly written "Definition of Ratios" and an alphabetical industry index.

HANDBOOKS AND MANUALS

Photographic Evidence. Charles C. Scott. West Publishing Co., College and School Div. • Second edition. Three volumes. Price on application. Includes current supplement. Supplement edition available. Photography from a technical-legal standpoint.

ONLINE DATABASES

Art Index Online. H. W. Wilson Co. • Indexes a wide variety of art-related periodicals, 1984 to date. Monthly updates. Inquire as to online cost and availability.

Magazine Index. The Gale Group. • General magazine indexing (popular literature), 1973 to present. Daily updates. Inquire as to online cost and availability.

PERIODICALS AND NEWSLETTERS

News Photographer: Dedicated to the Service and Advancement of News Photography. National Press Photographers Association, Inc. • Monthly. $38.00 per year.

Professional Photographer. Professional Photographers of America. PPA Publications and Events, Inc. • Monthly. $27.00 per year.

Studio Photography and Design. Cygnus Business Media. • Monthly. $60.00 per year. Incorporates *Comercial Image.*

TRADE/PROFESSIONAL ASSOCIATIONS

American Society of Media Photographers. 150 N. Second St., Philadelphia, PA 19106. Phone: (215)451-2767 E-mail: info@asmp.org • URL: http://www.asmp.org.

National Press Photographers Association. 3200 Croasdaile Dr., Suite 306, Durham, NC 27705. Phone: (919)383-7246 Fax: (919)383-7261 E-mail: nppa@mindspring.com • URL: http://www.nppa.org.

Professional Photographers of America. 229 Peachtree St., N.E., Suite 2200, Atlanta, GA 30303. Phone: 800-786-6277 or (404)522-8600 Fax: (404)614-6404 E-mail: dmmahon@ppa.com • URL: http://www.ppa.com.

COMMERCIAL REAL ESTATE

See: INDUSTRIAL REAL ESTATE

COMMERCIAL STATISTICS

See: BUSINESS STATISTICS

COMMODITIES

See also: COMMODITY FUTURES TRADING

ALMANACS AND YEARBOOKS

Commodity Review and Outlook: 1993-94. Available from Bernan Associates. • Annual. Published by the Food and Agriculture Organization of the United Nations (FAO). Reviews the global outlook for over 20 commodity groups.

CRB Commodity Yearbook. Commodity Research Bureau. CRB. • Annual. $99.95.

Securities, Commodities, and Banking: Year in Review. CCH, Inc. • Annual. $55.00. Summarizes the year's significant legal and regulatory developments.

UNCTAD Commodity Yearbook. United Nations Conference on Trade and Development. United Nations Publications. • Annual.

CD-ROM DATABASES

World Trade Database. Statistics Canada, International Trade Division. • Annual. $3,500.00. CD-ROM provides 13 years of export-import data for 600 commodities traded by the 160 member countries of the United Nations.

ENCYCLOPEDIAS AND DICTIONARIES

Dictionary of Agriculture: From Abaca to Zoonosis. Kathryn L. Lipton. Lynne Rienner Publishers, Inc. • 1995. $75.00. Emphasis is on agricultural economics.

INTERNET DATABASES

USDA. United States Department of Agriculture. Phone: (202)720-2791 E-mail: agsec@usda.gov • URL: http://www.usda.gov • The USDA home page has six sections: News and Information; What's New; About USDA; Agencies; Opportunities; Search and Help. Keyword searching is offered from the USDA home page and from various individual agency home pages. Agencies are the Economic Research Service, Agricultural Marketing Service, National Agricultural Statistics Service, National Agricultural Library, and about 12 others. Updating varies. Fees: Free.

ONLINE DATABASES

American Statistics Index: A Comprehensive Guide and Index to the Statistical Publications of the United States Government [Online]. Congressional Information Service, Inc. • Indexes and abstracts, 1973 to date. Inquire as to online cost and availability.

CAB Abstracts. CAB International North America. • Contains 46 specialized abstract collections covering over 10,000 journals and monographs in the areas of agriculture, horticulture, forest products, farm products, nutrition, dairy science, poultry, grains, animal health, entomology, etc. Time period is 1972 to date, with monthly updates. Inquire as to online cost and availability. *CAB Abstracts on CD-ROM* also available, with annual updating.

EconLit. American Economic Association. • Covers the worldwide literature of economics as contained in selected monographs and about 550 journals. Subjects include microeconomics, macroeconomics, economic history, inflation, money, credit, finance, accounting theory, trade, natural resource economics, and regional economics. Time period is 1969 to present, with monthly updates. Inquire as to online cost and availability.

PERIODICALS AND NEWSLETTERS

CRB Futures Chart Service. Bridge Publishing. • Weekly. $425.00 per year. Formerly *CRB Futures Chart Service.*

Financial Times [London]. Available from FT Publications, Inc. • Daily, except Sunday. $184.00 per year. An international business and financial newspaper, featuring news from London, Paris, Frankfurt, New York, and Tokyo. Includes worldwide stock and bond market data, commodity market data, and monetary/currency exchange information.

Global Commodity Markets. The World Bank, Office of the Publisher. • Quarterly. $645.00 per year. Covers international trends in the production, consumption, and trade patterns of primary commodities, including food, metals, minerals, energy, and fertilizers. Includes electronic monthly updates and electronic access to the quarterly.

The Journal of Futures Markets. John Wiley and Sons, Inc., Journals Div. • Eight times a year. $1,140.00 per year.

Kimball Letter. Kimball Associates. • Biweekly. $60.00 per year. Provides information on large trader positions in commodity futures.

PRICE SOURCES

CRB Commodity Index Report. Commodity Research Bureau. Bridge-CRB. • Weekly. $295.00 per year. Quotes the CRB Futures Price Index and the CRB Spot Market Index for the last five business days, plus the previous week, month, and year. Includes tables and graphs.

Monthly Commodity Price Bulletin. United Nations Publications. • Monthly. $125.00 per year. Provides monthly average prices for the previous 12 months for a wide variety of commodities traded internationally.

PPI Detailed Report. Bureau of Labor Statistics, U.S. Department of Labor. Available from U.S. Government Printing Office. • Monthly. $55.00 per year. Formerly *Producer Price Indexes.*

Wholesale Commodity Report. Financial Times. • Weekly. $144.00 to $165.00 per year depending on postal rates.

STATISTICS SOURCES

Agricultural Statistics. Available from U. S. Government Printing Office. • Annual. Produced by the National Agricultural Statistics Service, U. S. Department of Agriculture. Provides a wide variety of statistical data relating to agricultural production, supplies, consumption, prices/price-supports, foreign trade, costs, and returns, as well as farm labor, loans, income, and population. In many cases, historical data is shown annually for 10 years. In addition to farm data, includes detailed fishery statistics.

Economic Accounts for Agriculture. Organization for Economic Cooperation and Development. Available from OECD Publications and Information Center. • Annual. $51.00. Provides data for 14 years on agricultural output and its components, intermediate consumption, and gross value added to net income and capital formation. Relates to various commodities produced by OECD member countries.

FAO Quarterly Bulletin of Statistics. Food and Agriculture Organization of the United Nations. Available from UNIPUB. • Quarterly. $20.00 per year. Provides international data on agricultural production, trade, and prices, covering the major commodities of many countries. Text in English, French, and Spanish. Formerly *FAO Monthly Bulletin of Statistics.*

Foreign Trade by Commodities (Series C). OECD Publications and Information Center. • Annual. $625.00. Five volumes. Presents detailed five-year export-import data for specific commodities in OECD member countries.

Industrial Commodity Statistics Yearbook. United Nations Dept. of Economic and Social Affairs. United Nations Publications. • Annual.

Monthly Bulletin of Statistics. United Nations Publications. • Monthly. $295.00 per year. Provides current data for about 200 countries on a wide variety of economic, industrial, and demographic subjects. Compiled by United Nations Statistical Office.

Statistical Yearbook. United Nations Publications. • Annual. $125.00. Contains statistics for about 200 countries on a wide variety of economic, industrial, and demographic topics. Compiled by United Nations Statistical Office.

TRADE/PROFESSIONAL ASSOCIATIONS

Futures Industry Association. 2001 Pennsylvania, N.W., Suite 600, Washington, DC 20006-1807. Phone: (202)466-5460 Fax: (202)296-3184 E-mail: info@fiafii.org • URL: http://www.fiafii.org.

New York Mercantile Exchange. World Financial Center, One North End Ave., New York, NY 10282-1101. Phone: (212)299-2000 or (212)748-5265 Fax: (212)301-4700 • URL: http://www.nymex.com.

COMMODITY EXCHANGES

See: COMMODITY FUTURES TRADING

COMMODITY FUTURES TRADING

GENERAL WORKS

Education of a Speculator. Victor Niederhoffer. John Wiley and Sons, Inc. • 1997. $29.95. An autobiography providing basic advice on speculation, investment, and the commodity futures market.

Futures Markets. A. G. Malliaris, editor. Edward Elgar Publishing, Inc. • 1997. $450.00. Three volumes. Consists of reprints of 70 articles dating from 1959 to 1993, on futures market volatility, speculation, hedging, stock indexes, portfolio insurance, interest rates, and foreign currencies. (International Library of Critical Writings in Financial Economics.).

Getting Started in Futures. Todd Lofton. John Wiley and Sons, Inc. • 1997. $18.95. Third edition. A general introduction to commodity and financial futures trading. Includes case studies and a glossary. (All About Series).

Inside the Financial Futures Markets. Mark Powers and Mark Castelino. John Wiley and Sons, Inc. • 1991. $55.00. Third edition.

Trading to Win: The Psychology of Mastering the Markets. Ari Kiev. John Wiley and Sons, Inc. • 1998. $34.95. A mental health guide for stock, bond, and commodity traders. Tells how to keep speculative emotions in check, overcome self-doubt, and focus on a winning strategy. (Trading Advantage Series).

ALMANACS AND YEARBOOKS

CRB Commodity Yearbook. Commodity Research Bureau. CRB. • Annual. $99.95.

Irwin Business and Investment Almanac, 1996. Summer N. Levine and Caroline Levine. McGraw-Hill Professional. • 1995. $75.00. A review of last year's business activity. Covers a wide variety of business and economic data: stock market statistics, industrial information, commodity futures information, art market trends, comparative living costs for U. S. metropolitan areas, foreign stock market data, etc. Formerly *Business One Irwin Business and Investment Almanac.*

Supertrader's Almanac-Reference Manual: Reference Guide and Analytical Techniques for Investors. Market Movements, Inc. • 1991. $55.00. Explains technical methods for the trading of commodity futures, and includes data on seasonality, cycles, trends, contract characteristics, highs and lows, etc.

DIRECTORIES

Futures Guide to Computerized Trading. Futures Magazine, Inc. • Annual. $10.00. "A directory of products and services for the computerized trader." Provides information on computer software applications for commodity traders and money managers, including trading methods and technical analysis.

Futures Magazine SourceBook: The Most Complete List of Exchanges, Companies, Regulators, Organizations, etc., Offering Products and Services to the Futures and Options Industry. Futures Magazine, Inc. • Annual. $19.50. Provides information on commodity futures brokers, trading method services, publications, and other items of interest to futures traders and money managers.

Handbook of World Stock and Commodity Exchanges. Blackwell Publishers. • Annual. $265.00. Provides detailed information on over 200 stock and commodity exchanges in more than 50 countries.

St. James World Directory of Futures and Options. St. James Press. • 1991. $95.00. Contains information on approximately 50 commodity futures exchanges located in various countries. Over 350 futures and options trading contracts are described.

ENCYCLOPEDIAS AND DICTIONARIES

Encyclopedia of Chart Patterns. Thomas N. Bulkowski. John Wiley and Sons, Inc. • 2000. $79.95. Provides explanations of the predictive value of various chart patterns formed by stock and commodity price movements.

International Encyclopedia of Futures and Options. Michael R. Ryder, editor. Fitzroy Dearborn Publishers. • 2000. $275.00. Two volumes. Covers terminology, concepts, events, individuals, and markets.

HANDBOOKS AND MANUALS

Agricultural Options: Trading, Risk Management, and Hedging. Christopher A. Bobin. John Wiley and Sons, Inc. • 1990. $49.95. Practical advice on trading commodity futures options (puts and calls).

Commodity Trading Manual. Patrick J. Catania and others. Chicago Board of Trade. • 1993. $45.95. Revised edition. Textbook and reference manual.

Derivatives: A Comprehensive Resource for Options, Futures, Interest Rate Swaps, and Mortgage Securities. Fred D. Arditti. Harvard

Business School Press. • 1996. $60.00. Published by Harvard Business School Press. Provides detailed explanations of various kinds of financial derivatives (options, futures, swaps, etc.) and their trading tactics, uses, and risks. (Financial Management Association Survey and Synthesis Series).

Fibonacci Applications and Strategies for Traders. Robert Fischer. John Wiley and Sons, Inc. • 1993. $49.95. Provides a new look at the Elliott Wave Theory and Fibonacci numbers as applied to commodity prices, business cycles, and interest rate movements. (Traders Library).

Money Management Strategies for Futures Traders. Nauzer J. Balsara. John Wiley and Sons, Inc. • 1992. $69.95. How to limit risk and avoid catastrophic losses. (Financial Editions Series).

National Futures Association Manual. National Futures Association. • Quarterly. Looseleaf. Price on application. Rules and regulations concerning commodity futures trading.

Options: The International Guide to Valuation and Trading Strategies. Gordon Gemmill. McGraw-Hill. • 1993. $37.95. Covers valuation techniques for American, European, and Asian options. Trading strategies are discussed for options on currencies, stock indexes, interest rates, and commodities.

Regulation of the Commodities Futures and Options Markets. Bob McKinney. Shepard's. • 1995. Second revised edition. Price on application.

Trading for a Living: Psychology, Trading Tactics, Money Management. Alexander Elder. John Wiley and Sons, Inc. • 1993. $59.95. Covers technical and chart methods of trading in commodity and financial futures, options, and stocks. Includes Elliott Wave Theory, oscillators, moving averages, point-and-figure, and other technical approaches. (Finance Editions Series).

INTERNET DATABASES

BanxQuote Banking, Mortgage, and Finance Center. BanxQuote, Inc. Phone: 800-765-3000 or (212)643-8000 Fax: (212)643-0020 E-mail: info@banx.com • URL: http://www.banx.com • Web site quotes interest rates paid by banks around the country on various savings products, as well as rates paid by consumers for automobile loans, mortgages, credit cards, home equity loans, and personal loans. Also provided: stock quotes, indexes, stock options, futures trading data, economic indicators, and links to many other financial sites. Daily updates. Fees: Free.

Chicago Board of Trade: The World's Leading Futures Exchange. Chicago Board of Trade. Phone: (312)345-3500 Fax: (312)341-3027 E-mail: comments@cbot.com • URL: http://www.cbot.com • Web site provides a wide variety of statistics, commentary, charts, and news relating to both agricultural and financial futures trading. For example, Web page "MarketPlex: Information MarketPlace to the World" offers prices & volume, contract specifications & margins, government reports, etc. The CBOT *Statistical Annual*, in book form for 109 years, is now offered online. Searching is available, with daily updates for current data. Fees: Mostly free (some specialized services are fee-based).

Futures Online. Oster Communications, Inc. Phone: 800-601-8907 or (319)277-1278 Fax: (319)277-7982 • URL: http://www.futuresmag.com • Web site presents updates of *Futures* magazine and links to other futures-related sites. Includes "Futures Industry News," "Technical Talk," "Today's Hot Markets," "Futures Talk" (forums), "Futures Library" (archives, 1993 to date), and other features. Keyword searching is available. Updating: daily. Fees: Free.

Wall Street Journal Interactive Edition. Dow Jones & Co., Inc. Phone: 800-369-2834 or (212)416-2000 Fax: (212)416-2658 E-mail: inquiries@interactive.wsj.com • URL: http://www.wsj.com • Fee-based Web site providing online searching of worldwide information from the *The Wall Street Journal*. Includes "Company Snapshots," "The Journal's Greatest Hits," "Index to Market Data," "14-Day Searchable Archive," "Journal Links," etc. Financial price quotes are available. Fees: $49.00 per year; $29.00 per year to print subscribers.

PERIODICALS AND NEWSLETTERS

Consensus: National Futures and Financial Weekly. Consensus, Inc. • Weekly. $365.00 per year. Newspaper. Contains news, statistics, and special reports relating to agricultural, industrial, and financial futures markets. Features daily basis price charts, reprints of market advice, and "The Consensus Index of Bullish Market Opinion" (charts show percent bullish of advisors for various futures).

CRB Futures Chart Service. Bridge Publishing. • Weekly. $425.00 per year. Formerly *CRB Futures Chart Service.*

The Financial Post: Canadian's Business Voice. Financial Post Datagroup. • Daily. $234.00 per year. Provides Canadian business, economic, financial, and investment news. Features extensive price quotes from all major Canadian markets: stocks, bonds, mutual funds, commodities, and currencies. Supplement available: *Financial Post 500.* Includes annual supplement.

Futures Market Service. Commodity Research Bureau. • Weekly. $155.00 per year.

Futures: News, Analysis, and Strategies for Futures, Options, and Derivatives Traders. Futures Magazine, Inc. • Monthly. $39.00 per year. Edited for institutional money managers and traders, brokers, risk managers, and individual investors or speculators. Includes special feature issues on interest rates, technical indicators, currencies, charts, precious metals, hedge funds, and derivatives. Supplements available.

The Journal of Futures Markets. John Wiley and Sons, Inc., Journals Div. • Eight times a year. $1,140.00 per year.

Managed Account Reports: The Clearing House for Commodity Money Management. Managed Account Reports, Inc. • Monthly. $425.00 per year. Newsletter. Reviews the performance and other characteristics of commodity trading advisors and their commodity futures funds or managed accounts. Includes tables and graphs.

The Wall Street Journal. Dow Jones & Co., Inc. • Daily. $175.00 per year. Covers news and trends relating to business, industry, finance, the economy, and international commerce. Provides extensive price and other data for the securities, commodity, options, futures, foreign exchange, and money markets.

PRICE SOURCES

CRB Commodity Index Report. Commodity Research Bureau. Bridge-CRB. • Weekly. $295.00 per year. Quotes the CRB Futures Price Index and the CRB Spot Market Index for the last five business days, plus the previous week, month, and year. Includes tables and graphs.

STATISTICS SOURCES

Statistical Annual: Grains, Options on Agricultural Futures. Chicago Board of Trade. • Annual. Includes historical data on Wheat Futures, Options on Wheat Futures, Corn Futures, Options on Corn Futures, Oats Futures, Soybean Futures, Options on Soybean Futures, Soybean Oil Futures, Soybean Meal Futures.

Statistical Annual: Interest Rates, Metals, Stock Indices, Options on Financial Futures, Options on Metals Futures. Chicago Board of Trade. • Annual. Includes historical data on GNMA CDR Futures, Cash-Settled GNMA Futures, U. S. Treasury Bond Futures, U. S. Treasury Note Futures, Options on Treasury Note Futures, NASDAQ-100 Futures, Major Market Index Futures, Major Market Index MAXI Futures, Municipal Bond Index Futures, 1,000-Ounce Silver Futures, Options on Silver Futures, and Kilo Gold Futures.

TRADE/PROFESSIONAL ASSOCIATIONS

National Futures Association. 200 W. Madison St., Chicago, IL 60606-3447. Phone: 800-621-3570 or (312)781-1410 Fax: (312)781-1467 E-mail: public__affairs@nfa.futures.org • URL: http://www.nfa.futures.org.

New York Mercantile Exchange. World Financial Center, One North End Ave., New York, NY 10282-1101. Phone: (212)299-2000 or (212)748-5265 Fax: (212)301-4700 • URL: http://www.nymex.com.

OTHER SOURCES

Commodity Futures Law Reports. CCH, Inc. • Semimonthly. $995.00 per year. Looseleaf service. Periodic supplementation. Includes legal aspects of financial futures and stock options trading.

Factiva. Dow Jones Reuters Business Interactive, LLC. • Fee-based Web site provides "global news and business information through Web sites and content integration solutions." Includes Dow Jones and Reuters newswires, The Wall Street Journal, and more than 7,000 other sources of current news, historical articles, market research reports, and investment analysis. Content includes 96 major U. S. newspapers, 900 non-English sources, trade publications, media transcripts, country profiles, news photos, etc.

Information, Finance, and Services USA. The Gale Group. • 2001. $240.00. Replaces *Service Industries USA* and *Finance, Insurance, and Real Estate USA.* Presents statistics and projections relating to economic activity in a wide variety of non-manufacturing areas.

Nexis.com. Lexis-Nexis Group. • Fee-based Web site offers searching of about 2.8 billion documents in some 30,000 news, business, and legal information sources. Features include a subject directory covering 1,200 topics in 34 categories and a Company Dossier containing information on more than 500,000 public and private companies. Boolean searching is offered.

Securities Litigation and Regulation Reporter: The National Journal of Record ofCommodities Litigation. Andrews Publications. • Semimonthly. $1,294.00 per year. Provides reports on litigation involving the rules and decisions of the Commodity Futures Trading Commission. Formerly *Securities and Commodities Litigation Reporter.*

COMMON MARKET

See: EUROPEAN MARKETS

COMMUNICATION

See also: BUSINESS CORRESPONDENCE; BUSINESS JOURNALISM; COMMUNICATION SYSTEMS; COMMUNICATIONS SATELLITES; COMPUTER COMMUNICATIONS; CORPORATION REPORTS; TELECOMMUNICATIONS

GENERAL WORKS

Business and Administrative Communication. Kitty O. Locker. McGraw-Hill. • 2000. Fifth edition. Price on application.

Business Communication. John M. Penrose and James M. Lahiff. Prentice Hall. • 1996. $70.00. Fifth edition.

Business Communications. Carol M. Lehman and others. South-Western Publishing Co. • 1995. $67.95. 11th edition.

Business Communications Made Simple. Butterworth-Heinemann. • Date not set. $19.95.

Business English. Mary E. Guffey. South-Western College Publishing. • 2001. $47.00. Seventh edition. (South-Western College-Busines Communications Series).

Contemporary Business Communication. Louis E. Boone and others. Prentice Hall. • 1996. $80.00. Second edition.

Crisis Response: Inside Stories on Managing Image Under Siege. The Gale Group. • 1993. $60.00. Presents first-hand accounts by media relations professionals of major business crises and how they were handled. Topics include the following kinds of crises: environmental, governmental, corporate image, communications, and product.

Human Communication: An Interpersonal Introduction. Thomas Steinfatt. Pearson Education and Technology. • 1977. Price on application.

I'll Get Back to You: 156 Ways to Get People to Return Your Calls and Other Helpful Sales Tips. Robert L. Shook and Eric Yaverbaum. McGraw-Hill. • 1996. $9.95. Presents advice from business executives, celebrities, and others on how to make telephone calls seem important.

Interface Culture: How New Technology Transforms the Way We Create and Communicate. Steven Johnson. HarperCollins Publishers. • 1997. $24.00. A discussion of how computer interfaces and online technology ("cyberspace") affect society in general.

Introduction to Mass Communications. Phillip H. Agee. Addison-Wesley Educational Publications, Inc. • 2000. 13th edition. Price on application.

ABSTRACTS AND INDEXES

Communication Abstracts. Sage Publications, Inc. • Bimonthly. Individuals, $185.00 per year; institutions, $805.00 per year. Provides broad coverage of the literature of communications, including broadcasting and advertising.

Psychological Abstracts. American Psychological Association. • Monthly. Members, $799.00 per year; individuals and institutions, $1,075.00 per year. Covers the international literature of psychology and the behavioral sciences. Includes journals, technical reports, dissertations, and other sources.

Social Sciences Citation Index. Institute for Scientific Information. • Three times a year. $6,900 per year. Annual cumulation. Includes *Source Index, Citation Index, Permuterm Subject Index*, and *Corporate Index.*

Social Sciences Index. H. W. Wilson Co. • Quarterly, with annual cumulation. Service basis for print edition; CD-ROM edition, $1,495 per year. Indexes more than 400 periodicals covering economics, environmental policy, government, insurance, labor, health care policy, plannning, public administration, public welfare, urban studies, women's issues, criminology, and related topics.

ALMANACS AND YEARBOOKS

Communication Yearbook. International Communication Association. • Annual. $49.95.

Sage Series in Written Communication: An International Survey of Research and Theory. Sage Publications, Inc. • Irregular. $22.95.

BIBLIOGRAPHIES

Business and Technical Writing: An Annotated Bibliography of Books 1880-1980. Gerald J. Alred and others. Scarecrow Press, Inc. • 1981. $21.00.

CD-ROM DATABASES

Business Source Plus. EBSCO Information Services. • Monthly. $1,495.00 per year. Provides CD-ROM citations and abstracts to articles in about 650 business periodicals and newspapers, including *The Wall Street Journal.* Full text is provided from 200 selected periodicals. Covers accounting, communications, economics, finance, management, marketing, and other business subjects.

Social Science Source. EBSCO Publishing. • Monthly. $1,495.00 per year. Provides CD-ROM citations and abstracts to social science articles in more than 600 periodicals, with full text from 125 periodicals. Covers economics, political science, public policy, international relations, psychology, and other topics. Time period is most recent five years.

Social Sciences Citation Index: Compact Disc Edition. Institute for Scientific Information. • Quarterly. Provides CD-ROM indexing of the world's social sciences literature, including economics, business, finance, management, communications, demographics, information and library science, political science, sociology, etc. Corresponds to online *Social Scisearch* and printed *Social Sciences Citation Index.*

Social Sciences Citation Index: Compact Disc Edition with Abstracts. Institute for Scientific Information. • Quarterly. Provides CD-ROM indexing and abstracting of "significant articles" from 1,400 social science journals worldwide, with additional selections from 3,200 other journals, 1986 to date. Includes economics, business, finance, management, communications, demographics, information and library science, political science, sociology, and many other subjects.

WILSONDISC: Wilson Business Abstracts. H. W. Wilson Co. • Monthly. $2,495.00 per year, including unlimited online access to *Wilson Business Abstracts* through WILSONLINE. Provides CD-ROM "cover-to-cover" abstracting and indexing of over 600 prominent business periodicals. Indexing is from 1982, abstracting from 1990. (*Business Periodicals Index* without abstracts is available on CD-ROM at $1,495 per year.).

WILSONDISC: Wilson Social Sciences Abstracts. H. W. Wilson Co. • Monthly. Including unlimited online access to *Social Sciences Index* through WILSONLINE. Provides CD-ROM indexing from 1983 and abstracting from 1994 of more than 400 periodicals covering economics, area studies, community health, public administration, public welfare, urban studies, and many other topics related to the social sciences.

DIRECTORIES

World Book of IABC Communicators. International Association of Business Communicators. • Annual. Membership. About 13,000 association members involved with organizational, corporate, and public relations and other communications fields. Formerly *Directory of Business and Organizational Communicators.*

ENCYCLOPEDIAS AND DICTIONARIES

Blackwell Encyclopedic Dictionary of Organizational Behavior. Nigel Nicholson, editor. Blackwell Publishers. • 1995. $105.95. The editor is associated with the London Business School. Contains definitions of key terms combined with longer articles written by various U. S. and foreign business educators. Includes bibliographies and index. *Blackwell Encyclopedia of Management Series.*

Complete Multilingual Dictionary of Advertising, Marketing, and Communications. Hans W. Paetzel, editor. NTC/Contemporary Publishing. • 1994. $49.95. Provides translations of about 8,000 technical and general terms. English, French and German terms.

Dictionary of Bibliometrics. Virgil Diodato. Haworth Press, Inc. • 1994. $39.95. Contains detailed explanations of 225 terms, with references. (Bibliometrics is "the application of mathematical and statistical techniques to the study of publishing and professional communication.").

Encyclopedia of Communication and Information. Available from The Gale Group. • 2001. $325.00. Three volumes. Published by Macmillan Reference USA.

HANDBOOKS AND MANUALS

Gower Handbook of Internal Communication. Eileen Scholes, editor. Ashgate Publishing Co. • 1997. $113.95. Consists of 38 chapters written by various authors, with case studies. Covers more than 45 communication techniques, "from team meetings to web sites." Published by Gower in England.

Lesly's Handbook of Public Relations and Communications. Philip Lesly. NTC/Contemporary Publishing. • 1997. $100.00. Fifth edition.

Personnel Management: Communications. Prentice Hall. • Looseleaf. Periodic supplementation. Price on application. Includes how to write effectively and how to prepare employee publications.

ONLINE DATABASES

PsycINFO. American Psychological Association. • Provides indexing and abstracting of the worldwide literature of psychology and the behavioral sciences. Time period is 1967 to date, with monthly updates. Inquire as to online cost and availability.

Social Scisearch. Institute for Scientific Information. • Broad, multidisciplinary index to the literature of the social sciences, 1972 to present. Weekly updates. Worldwide coverage. Inquire as to online cost and availability.

Wilson Business Abstracts Online. H. W. Wilson Co. • Indexes and abstracts 600 major business periodicals, plus the *Wall Street Journal* and the business section of the *New York Times.* Indexing is from 1982, abstracting from 1990, with the two newspapers included from 1993. Updated weekly. Inquire as to online cost and availability. (*Business Periodicals Index* without abstracts is also available online.).

Wilson Social Sciences Abstracts Online. H. W. Wilson Co. • Provides online abstracting and indexing of more than 415 periodicals covering area studies, community health, public administration, public welfare, urban studies, and many other social science topics. Time period is 1994 to date for abstracts and 1983 to date for indexing, with updates monthly. Inquire as to online cost and availability.

PERIODICALS AND NEWSLETTERS

Business Communication Quarterly. Association for Business Communication. • Quarterly. Memebers, $65.00 per year; non-memebers, $150.00 per year.

Features articles about teaching and writing course outlines. Description of training programs, problems, soutions, etc. Includes *Journal of Business Communcation*.

Business Communications Review. BCR Enterprises, Inc. • Bimonthly. $45.00 per year. Edited for communications managers in large end-user companies and institutions. Includes special feature issues on intranets and network management.

Communication Briefings: A Monthly Idea Source for Decision Makers. Briefings Publishing Group. • Monthly. $100.00 per year. Newsletter. Presents useful ideas for communication, public relations, customer service, human resources, and employee training.

Communication Research. Sage Publications, Inc. • Bimonthly. Individuals, $85.00 per year; institutions, $450.00 per year.

Communication World: The Magazine for Communication Professionals. International Association of Business Communicators. • 10 times a year. Libraries, $95.00 per year. Emphasis is on public relations, media relations, corporate communication, and writing.

Communications News. American Society of Association Executives Communications Section. • Monthly. Membership.

Communications News: Solutions for Today's Networking Decision Managers. Nelson Publishing, Inc. • Monthly. Free to qualified personnel; others, $79.00 per year. Includes coverage of "Internetworking" and "Intrenetworking." Emphasis is on emerging telecommunications technologies.

The Customer Communicator. Alexander Communications Group, Inc. • Monthly. $167.00 per year. Newsletter. Contains news and advice for business firms on how to improve customer relations and communications.

Harvard Management Communication Letter. Harvard Business School Press. • Monthly. $79.00 per year. Newsletter. Provides practical advice on both electronic and conventional business communication: e-mail, telephone, cell phones, memos, letters, written reports, speeches, meetings, and visual presentations (slides, flipcharts, easels, etc.). Also covers face-to-face communication, discussion, listening, and negotiation.

Human Communication Research. International Communication Association. Oxford University Press, Journals. • Quarterly. Individuals, $74.00 per year; institutions, $243.00 per year. A scholarly journal of interpersonal communication.

Journal of Business and Technical Communication. Sage Publications, Inc. • Individuals, $65.00 per year; institutions, $340.00 per year.

Journal of Business Communication. Association for Business Communication. • Individuals, $65.00 per year; Insititutions, $150.00 per year. Includes *Association for Business Communiation Bulletin*.

Management Communication Quarterly: An International Journal. Sage Publications, Inc. • Quarterly. Individuals, $65.00; institutions, $310.00 per year. A scholarly journal on managerial and organizational communication effectiveness.

9-1-1 Magazine: Public Safety Communications and Response. Official Publications, Inc. • Bimonthly. $31.95 per year. Covers technical information and applications for public safety communications personnel.

Presentations: Technology and Techniques for Effective Communication. Lakewood Publications, Inc. • Monthly. $50.00 per year. Covers the use of presentation hardware and software, including audiovisual equipment and computerized display systems. Includes an annual *"Buyers Guide to Presentation Products."*.

The Successful Benefits Communicator. Lawence Ragan Communications, Inc. • Monthly. $117.00 per year. Newsletter on techniques for providing useful information to employees about benefits. Formerly *Techniques for the Benefits Communicator*.

Teleconference Magazine: The Magazine on Interactive Mulitmedia. Advanstar Communications, Inc. • Monthly. $60.00 per. year. Provides articles on new technology and the practical use of teleconferencing in business communications.

Written Communication: A Quarterly Journal of Research, Theory, and Application. Sage Publications, Inc. • Quarterly. Individuals, $70.00 per year; institutions, $320.00 per year.

RESEARCH CENTERS AND INSTITUTES

East-West Center. 1601 East-West Rd., Honolulu, HI 96848-1601. Phone: (808)944-7111 Fax: (808)944-7376 E-mail: ewcinfo@ewc.hawaii.edu • URL: http://www.ewc.hawaii.edu.

STATISTICS SOURCES

AM/FM Broadcast Financial Data/TV Broadcast Financial Data. U.S. Federal Communications Commission. • Annual. Free.

World Factbook. U.S. National Technical Information Service. • Annual. $83.00. Prepared by the Central Intelligence Agency. For all countries of the world, provides current economic, demographic, geographic, communications, government, defense force, and illicit drug trade information (where applicable).

World Statistics Pocketbook. United Nations Publications. • Annual. $10.00. Presents basic economic, social, and environmental indicators for about 200 countries and areas. Covers more than 50 items relating to population, economic activity, labor force, agriculture, industry, energy, trade, transportation, communication, education, tourism, and the environment. Statistical sources are noted.

TRADE/PROFESSIONAL ASSOCIATIONS

Association for Business Communication. Baruch College, 17 Lexington Ave., New York, NY 10010. Phone: (212)387-1340 Fax: (212)387-1655 E-mail: myersabc@compuserve.com • URL: http://www.theabc.org.

International Association of Business Communicators. One Hallidie Plaza, Suite 600, San Francisco, CA 94102. Phone: (415)544-4700 Fax: (415)544-4747 E-mail: leader-centre@iabc.com • URL: http://www.iabc.com.

International Communications Association. 3530 Forest Ln., Ste. 200, Dallas, TX 75234. Phone: 800-422-4636 or (214)902-3632 Fax: 877-902-6521 E-mail: information@icanet.com • URL: http://www.icahdq.org.

International Institute of Communications. Wescott House, 3rd Fl. 35 Portland Place, London W1N 3AG, England. Phone: 44 207 3239622 Fax: 44 207 3239623 E-mail: enquiries@iicom.org • URL: http://www. iicom.org.

Society for Technical Communication. 901 N. Stuart St., Suite 904, Arlington, VA 22203-1854. Phone: (703)522-4114 Fax: (703)522-2075 E-mail: stc@stc-va.org • URL: http://www.stc-va.org.

OTHER SOURCES

Commodities Regulation: Fraud, Manipulation, and Other Claims. Jerry W. Markham. West Group. • Two looseleaf volumes. $250.00. Periodic supplementation. Covers the commodity futures trading prohibitions of the Commodity Exchange Act.

COMMUNICATION, COMPUTER

See: COMPUTER COMMUNICATIONS

COMMUNICATION EQUIPMENT INDUSTRY

See: TELECOMMUNICATIONS; TELEPHONE INDUSTRY

COMMUNICATION, MASS

See: MASS MEDIA

COMMUNICATION SYSTEMS

See also: COMPUTERS; TELECOMMUNICATIONS

GENERAL WORKS

Analog and Digital Communications. Hwei P. Hsu. McGraw-Hill. • 1997. $15.95.

Corporate Internet Planning Guide: Aligning Internet Strategy with Business Goals. Richard J. Gascoyne and Koray Ozcubucku. John Wiley and Sons, Inc. • 1996. $34.95. Provides administrative advice on planning, developing, and managing corporate Internet or intranet functions. Emphasis is on strategic planning. (Business, Commerce, Management Series).

ABSTRACTS AND INDEXES

Electronics and Communications Abstracts Journal: Comprehensive Coverage of Essential Scientific Literature. Cambridge Information Group. • Monthly. $1,045.00 per year.

ALMANACS AND YEARBOOKS

Communications Outlook. OECD Publications and Information Center. • Annual. $65.00. Provides international coverage of yearly telecommunications activity. Includes charts, graphs, and maps.

CD-ROM DATABASES

Datapro on CD-ROM: Communications Analyst. Gartner Group, Inc. • Monthly. Price on application. Provides detailed information on products and services for communications systems, including local area networks and voice systems.

DIRECTORIES

Plunkett's E-Commerce and Internet Business Almanac. Plunkett Research, Ltd. • Annual. $199.99. Contains detailed profiles of 250 large companies engaged in various areas of Internet commerce, including e-business Web sites, communications equipment manufacturers, and Internet service providers. Includes CD-ROM.

Telecommunications Directory. The Gale Group. • 2000. $595.00. 12th edition. National and international voice, data, facsimile, and video communications services. Formerly *Telecommunications Systems and Services Directory*.

Telehealth Buyer's Guide. Miller Freeman. • Annual. $10.00. Lists sources of telecommunications and information technology products and services for the health care industry.

HANDBOOKS AND MANUALS

Business Multimedia Explained: A Manager's Guide to Key Terms and Concepts. Peter G. W. Keen. Harvard Business School Press. • 1997. $39.95.

Digital Cellular Telecommunications Systems. Douglas A. Kerr. McGraw-Hill. • 1997. $50.00.

INTERNET DATABASES

Interactive Week: The Internet's Newspaper. Ziff Davis Media, Inc. 28 E. 28th St., New York, NY 10016. Phone: (212)503-3500 Fax: (212)503-5680 E-mail: iweekinfo@zd.com • URL: http://www.zd.com • Weekly. $99.00 per year. Covers news and trends relating to Internet commerce, computer communications, and telecommunications.

PERIODICALS AND NEWSLETTERS

C E D: The Premier Magazine of Broadband Communications. Cahners Business Information. • Monthly. $75.00 per year. Formerly *Communications Engineering and Design.*

Call Center Magazine. Miller Freeman. • Monthly. $14.00 per year. Covers telephone and online customer service, help desk, and marketing operations. Includes articles on communications technology.

CC News: The Business Newspaper for Call Center and Customer Care Professionals. United Publications, Inc. • Eight times a year. Price on application. Includes news of call center technical developments.

IEEE Transactions on Communications. Institute of Electrical and Electronics Engineers, Inc. • Monthly. Individuals, $150.00 per year; institutions, $215.00 per year.

Internet Telephony Magazine: The Authority on Voice, Video, Fax, and Data Convergence. Technology Marketing Corp. • Monthly. $29.00 per year. Covers the business and technology of telephone and other communications service via the Internet.

PCS Systems and Technology: Personal Communications Services Technology of the Digital Wireless Age. Cahners Business Information. • Nine times a year. Price on application. Covers network management and other technical topics.

Poptronics. Gernsback Publications, Inc. • Monthly. $19.99 per year. Incorporates *Electronics Now.*

RCR (Radio Communications Report): The Newspaper for the Wireless Communications Industry. RCR Publications/Crain Communications. • Weekly. $39.00 per year. Covers news of the wireless communications industry, including business and financial developments.

Tele.com: Business and Technology for Public Network Service Providers. CMP Publications, Inc. • 14 times a year. $125.00 per year. Edited for executives and managers at both traditional telephone companies and wireless communications companies. Also provides news and information for Internet services providers and cable TV operators.

Telecom Business: Opportunities for Network Service Providers, Resellers, and Suppliers in the Competitive Telecom Industry. MultiMedia Publishing Corp. • Monthly. $56.95 per year. Provides business and technical information for telecommunications executives in various fields.

Telecommunications Reports. Telecommunications Reports International, Inc. • Weekly. Institutions, $1,695.00 per year. Includes *TR Daily.* Regulatory newsletter.

Telecons. Applied Business Telecommunications. • Bimonthly. $30.00 per year. Topics include teleconferencing, videoconferencing, distance learning, telemedicine, and telecommuting.

Telehealth Magazine. Miller Freeman. • Bimonthly. $50.00 per year. Covers Internet, wireless, and other telecommunications technologies for health care professionals.

Wireless Integration: Solutions for Enterprise Decision Makers. PennWell Corp., Advanced Technology Div. • Bimonthly. $48.00 per year. Edited for networking and communications managers. Special issues cover the wireless office, wireless intranet/Internet, mobile wireless, telemetry, and buyer's guide directory information.

Wireless Review: Intelligence for Competitive Providers. Intertec Publishing Corp. • Semimonthly. $48.00 per year. Covers business and technology developments for wireless service providers. Includes special issues on a wide variety of wireless topics. Formed by merger of *Cellular Business* and *Wireless World.*

RESEARCH CENTERS AND INSTITUTES

Communications and Signal Processing Laboratory. University of Michigan. EECS Bldg. 4240, North Campus, Ann Arbor, MI 48109-2122. Phone: (734)763-0564 Fax: (734)763-8041 E-mail: hero@eecsumich.edu • URL: http://www.eecs.umich.edu/systems/homecspl.com.

Institute for Systems Research. University of Maryland, A. V. Williams Bldg., No. 115, College Park, MD 20742-3311. Phone: (301)405-6602 Fax: (301)314-9220 E-mail: isr@isr.umd.edu • URL: http://www.isr.umd.edu/ • A National Science Foundation Engineering Research Center. Areas of research include communication systems, manufacturing systems, chemical process systems, artificial intelligence, and systems integration.

Laboratory for Information and Decision Systems. Massachusetts Institute of Technology, Bldg. 35, Room 308, Cambridge, MA 02139-4307. Phone: (617)253-2141 Fax: (617)253-3578 E-mail: chan@mit.edu • URL: http://www.justice.mit.edu • Research areas include data communication networks and fiber optic networks.

Space, Telecommunications, and Radioscience Laboratory. Stanford University. David Packard Electrical and Engineering Bldg., Room 355, Stanford, CA 94305-9515. Phone: (650)723-8121 Fax: (650)723-9251 E-mail: inan@nova.stanford.edu • URL: http://www.star.stanford.edu.

STATISTICS SOURCES

Communication Equipment, and Other Electronic Systems and Equipment. U. S. Bureau of the Census. • Annual. Provides data on shipments: value, quantity, imports, and exports. (Current Industrial Reports, MA-36P.).

Electronic Market Data Book. Electronic Industries Association, Marketing Services Dept. • Annual. Members, $75.00; non-members, $125.00.

OECD Information Technology Outlook 2000: ICTs, E-Commerce and the Information Economy. Organization for Economic Cooperation and Development. • 2000. $72.00. Provides data on information and communications technology (ICT) and electronic commerce in 11 OECD nations (includes U. S.). Coverage includes network infrastructure, electronic payment systems, financial transaction technologies, intelligent agents, global navigation systems, and portable flat panel display technologies.

TRADE/PROFESSIONAL ASSOCIATIONS

Armed Forces Communications and Electronics Association. 4400 Fair Lakes Court, Fairfax, VA 22033. Phone: 800-336-4583 or (703)631-6100 Fax: (703)631-4693 • URL: http://www.afcea.org.

International Communications Association. 3530 Forest Ln., Ste. 200, Dallas, TX 75234. Phone: 800-422-4636 or (214)902-3632 Fax: 877-902-6521 E-mail: information@icanet.com • URL: http://www.icahdq.org.

International Teleconferencing Association. P.O. Box 906, Syosset, NY 11791-0079. Phone: (516)941-2020 Fax: (516)941-2015 E-mail: staff@itca.org • URL: http://www.itca.org • Members are vendors and users of teleconferencing equipment. Special Interest Groups include Telecommuting.

TCA-The Information Technology and Telecommunications Association. 74 New Montgomery St., Suite 230, San Francisco, CA 94105-3419. Phone: (415)777-4647 Fax: (415)777-5295.

OTHER SOURCES

Faulkner's Enterprise Networking. Faulkner Information Services, Inc. • Three looseleaf volumes, with monthly updates. $1,275.00 per year. Contains product reports and management articles relating to computer communications and networking. Available on CD-ROM. Quarterly updates. Formerly *Data Communications Reports.*

Faulkner's Telecommunications World. Faulkner Information Services, Inc. • Three looseleaf volumes, with monthly updates. $1,260.00 per year. Contains product reports, technology overviews and management articles relating to all aspects of voice and data communications.

Major Information Technology Companies of the World. Available from The Gale Group. • 2001. $885.00. Third edition. Published by Graham & Whiteside. Contains profiles of more than 2,600 leading information technology companies in various countries.

COMMUNICATIONS SATELLITES

See also: TELECOMMUNICATIONS

GENERAL WORKS

Future Trends in Telecommunications. R. J. Horrocks and R.W. Scarr. John Wiley and Sons, Inc. • 1993. $235.00. Includes fiber optics technology, local area networks, and satellite communications. Discusses the future of telecommunications for the consumer and for industry. *Communication and Distributed Systems Series.*

Global Telecommunications: The Technology, Administration, and Policies. Raymond Akwule. Butterworth-Heinemann. • 1992. $46.95. Provides basic information on networks, satellite systems, socioeconomic impact, tariffs, government regulation, etc.

Principles of Communications Satellites. Gary D, Gordon and Walter L. Morgan. John Wiley and Sons, Inc. • 1993. $99.00.

Satellite Communications: The First Quarter Century of Service. David W. Rees. John Wiley and Sons, Inc. • 1990. $123.00. A survey of the history of communications satellites, emphasizing business applications.

ABSTRACTS AND INDEXES

NTIS Alerts: Communication. National Technical Information Service. • Semimonthly. $210.00 per year. . Provides descriptions of government-sponsored research reports and software, with ordering information. Covers common carriers, satellites, radio/TV equipment, telecommunication regulations, and related subjects.

ALMANACS AND YEARBOOKS

Communication Technology Update. Butterworth-Heinemann. • Annual. $36.95. Reviews technological developments and statistical trends in five key areas: mass media, computers, consumer electronics, communications satellites, and telephony. Includes television, cellular phones, and the Internet. (Focal Press.).

DIRECTORIES

International Satellite Directory: A Complete Guide to the Satellite Communications Industry. Design Publishers, Inc. • Annual. $275.00. Lists satellite operators, common carriers, earth stations, manufacturers, associations, etc.

Phillips World Satellite Almanac. Phillips Business Information, Inc. • Annual. $267.00. All commercial satellite systems and operators (operational and planned), booking contracts, PTT decision makers, and transportation brokers. Incorporates *Satellite Systems Handbook* and *World Satellite Annual.*

Satellite Communications - Satellite Industry Directory. Phillips Business Information, Inc. • Annual. $275.00. Provides information on about 2,000 providers of equipment and services for the satellite communications industry.

ENCYCLOPEDIAS AND DICTIONARIES

Jones Dictionary of Cable Television Terminology: Including Related Computer and Satellite Definitions. Glenn R. Jones. Jones Twenty-First Century Ltd. • 1996. $14.95.

Telecom Lingo Guide. Warren Communication News. • 1996. $60.00. Eighth edition. Defines more than 1,000 words, phrases, and acronyms frequently used in the telecommunications industry.

HANDBOOKS AND MANUALS

Satellite-Based Cellular Communications. Bruno Pattan. McGraw-Hill. • 1997. $69.00. (Telecommunications Series).

Satellite Broadcasting: The Politics and Implications of the New Media. Ralph M. Negrine, editor. Routledge. • 1988. $65.00. Second edition.

PERIODICALS AND NEWSLETTERS

Communications Daily: The Authoritative News Service of Electronic Communications. Warren Publishing Inc. • Daily. $3,006.00 per year. Newsletter. Covers telecommunications, including the telephone industry, broadcasting, cable TV, satellites, data communications, and electronic publishing. Features corporate and industry news.

Satellite Communications. Intertec Publishing Corp. • Monthly. $42.00 per year.

Satellite News: The Monthly Newsletter Covering Management, Marketing Technology, and Regulation. Phillips Business Information, Inc. • 50 times a year. $997.00 per year.

Satellite Week: The Authoritative News Service for Satellite Communications and Allied Fields. Warren Publishing Inc. • Weekly. $964.00 per year. Newsletter. Covers satellite broadcasting, telecommunications, and the industrialization of space.

Space Business News. Phillips Business Information, Inc. • Biweekly. $797.00 per year. Newsletter. Covers business applications in space, including remote sensing and satellites.

Via Satellite. Phillips Business Information, Inc. • Monthly. $49.00 per year. Covers the communications satellite industry.

Wireless Week. Cahners Business Information. • 51 times a year. $59.00 per year. Covers news of cellular telephones, mobile radios, communications satellites, microwave transmission, and the wireless industry in general.

RESEARCH CENTERS AND INSTITUTES

Applied Research Laboratories. University of Texas at Austin. University Station, P.O. Box 8029, Austin, TX 78713-8029. Phone: (512)835-3200 Fax: (512)835-3529 E-mail: penrod@arlut.utexas.edu • URL: http://www.arlut.utexas.edu.

Center for Space Research. Massachusetts Institute of Technology. 77 Massachusetts Ave., Cambridge, MA 02139. Phone: (617)253-7501 Fax: (617)253-8061 • URL: http://www.space.mit.edu.

Engineering Experiment Station. Ohio State University. 2070 Neil Ave., Columbus, OH 43210-1275. Phone: (614)292-2411 Fax: (614)292-9615 E-mail: fortner.1@osu.edu • URL: http://www.osu.edu.

Space Institute. University of Tennessee. BH Goethert Parkway, Tullahoma, TN 37388-8897. Phone: (931)393-7213 Fax: (931)393-7211 E-mail: egleason@utsi.edu • URL: http://www.utsi.edu.

Space, Telecommunications, and Radioscience Laboratory. Stanford University. David Packard Electrical and Engineering Bldg., Room 355, Stanford, CA 94305-9515. Phone: (650)723-8121 Fax: (650)723-9251 E-mail: inan@nova.stanford.edu • URL: http://www.star.stanford.edu.

STATISTICS SOURCES

U. S. Industry and Trade Outlook: The McGraw-Hill Companies and the U.S. Department of Commerce/International Trade Administration. Datapso Research Corp. • Annual. $69.95. Produced by the International Trade Administration, U. S. Department of Commerce, in a "public-private" partnership with DRI/McGraw-Hill and Standard & Poor's. Provides basic data, outlook for the current year, and "Long-Term Prospects" (five-year projections) for a wide variety of products and services. Includes high technology industries. Formerly *U. S. Industrial Outlook.*

TRADE/PROFESSIONAL ASSOCIATIONS

International Telecommunications Satellite Organization. 3400 International Dr., N.W., Washington, DC 20008-3098. Phone: (202)944-6800 Fax: (202)944-7898 • URL: http://www.intelsat.int.

OTHER SOURCES

Major Telecommunications Companies of the World. Available from The Gale Group. • 2001. $855.00. Fourth edition. Published by Graham & Whiteside. Contains detailed information and trade names for more than 4,000 important telecommunications companies in various countries.

Telecommunications Regulation: Cable, Broadcasting, Satellite, and the Internet. Matthew Bender & Co., Inc. • Looseleaf. $700.00. Four volumes. Semiannual updates. Covers local, state, and federal regulation, with emphasis on the Telecommunications Act of 1996. Includes regulation of television, telephone, cable, satellite, computer communication, and online services. Formerly *Cable Television Law*.

Wireless Data Networks. Warren Publishing Inc. • 1998. $1,995.00. Fourth edition. Presents market research information relating to cellular data networks, paging networks, packet radio networks, satellite systems, and other areas of wireless communication. Contains "summaries of recent developments and trends in wireless markets.".

COMMUNITY ANTENNA TELEVISION

See: CABLE TELEVISION INDUSTRY

COMMUNITY CHESTS

See: COMMUNITY FUNDS

COMMUNITY COLLEGES

See: JUNIOR COLLEGES

COMMUNITY DEVELOPMENT

See also: PLANNING; URBAN DEVELOPMENT

GENERAL WORKS

Placemaking: The Art and Practice of Building Communities. Lynda H. Schneekloth and Robert G. Shibley. John Wiley and Sons, Inc. • 1995. $59.95.

ABSTRACTS AND INDEXES

Social Sciences Index. H. W. Wilson Co. • Quarterly, with annual cumulation. Service basis for print edition; CD-ROM edition, $1,495 per year. Indexes more than 400 periodicals covering economics, environmental policy, government, insurance, labor, health care policy, plannning, public administration, public welfare, urban studies, women's issues, criminology, and related topics.

CD-ROM DATABASES

Social Science Source. EBSCO Publishing. • Monthly. $1,495.00 per year. Provides CD-ROM citations and abstracts to social science articles in more than 600 periodicals, with full text from 125 periodicals. Covers economics, political science, public policy, international relations, psychology, and other topics. Time period is most recent five years.

Social Sciences Citation Index: Compact Disc Edition with Abstracts. Institute for Scientific Information. • Quarterly. Provides CD-ROM indexing and abstracting of "significant articles" from 1,400 social science journals worldwide, with additional selections from 3,200 other journals, 1986 to date. Includes economics, business, finance, management, communications, demographics, information and library science, political science, sociology, and many other subjects.

WILSONDISC: Wilson Social Sciences Abstracts. H. W. Wilson Co. • Monthly. Including unlimited online access to *Social Sciences Index* through WILSONLINE. Provides CD-ROM indexing from 1983 and abstracting from 1994 of more than 400 periodicals covering economics, area studies, community health, public administration, public welfare, urban studies, and many other topics related to the social sciences.

DIRECTORIES

Funding Sources for Community and Economic Development: A Guide to Current Sources for Local Programs and Projects. Oryx Press. • 2000. $64.95. Sixth edition. Provides information on 2,600 funding sources. Includes "A Guide to Proposal Planning.".

HANDBOOKS AND MANUALS

New Uses for Obsolete Buildings. Urban Land Institute. • 1996. $64.95. Covers various aspects of redevelopment: zoning, building codes, environment, economics, financing, and marketing. Includes eight case studies and 75 descriptions of completed "adaptive use projects.".

Zoning and Planning Law Handbook. West Group. • 1996. Price on application. (Real Property-Zoning Series).

ONLINE DATABASES

Magazine Index. The Gale Group. • General magazine indexing (popular literature), 1973 to present. Daily updates. Inquire as to online cost and availability.

Wilson Social Sciences Abstracts Online. H. W. Wilson Co. • Provides online abstracting and indexing of more than 415 periodicals covering area studies, community health, public administration, public welfare, urban studies, and many other social science topics. Time period is 1994 to date for abstracts and 1983 to date for indexing, with updates monthly. Inquire as to online cost and availability.

PERIODICALS AND NEWSLETTERS

Community Development Digest: Semimonthly Development, Planning, Infrastructure, Financing. Community Services Development, Inc. C D Publications. • Semimonthly. $423.00 per year. Newsletter.

Community Journal. Community Service, Inc. • Quarterly. $25.00 per year.

International Society for Community Development Newsletter. • Semiannual. Membership.

Ledger Quarterly: A Financial Review for Community Association Practitioners. Community Associations Institute. • Quarterly. Members, $40.00 per year; non-members, $67.00 per year. Newsletter. Provides current information on issues affecting the finances of condominium, cooperative, homeowner, apartment, and other community housing associations.

Zoning and Planning Law Report. West Group. • 11 times a year. $283.00 per year. Newsletter.

RESEARCH CENTERS AND INSTITUTES

Institute of Cultural Affairs. c/o ICA Counterpoints, 4750 N. Sheridan Rd., Chicago, IL 60640. Phone: (773)769-6363 Fax: (773)769-1144 E-mail: dmcicac@igc.apc.org.

Midwest Research Institute. 425 Volker Blvd., Kansas City, MO 64110-2299. Phone: (816)753-7600 Fax: (816)753-8420 E-mail: bmaidment@mriresearch.org • URL: http://www.mriresearch.org.

Regional Developement Services. East Carolina University. Willis Bldg., 300 E. First St., Greenville, NC 27858-4353. Phone: (252)328-6650 Fax: (252)328-4356 E-mail: deliaa@mail.ecu.edu • URL: http://ecuvax.cis.ecu.edu/ia/rds/rds.htm.

Urban Land Institute. 1025 Thomas Jefferson Ave. N.W., Suite 500W, Washington, DC 20004. Phone: (202)624-7000 Fax: (202)624-7140 E-mail: rlevitt@uli.org • URL: http://www.uli.org • Studies urban land planning and the growth and development of urbanized areas, including central city problems, industrial development, community development, residential development, taxation, shopping centers, and the effects of development on the environment.

STATISTICS SOURCES

Agriculture Fact Book. Available from U. S. Government Printing Office. • Annual. Issued by the Office of Communications, U. S. Department of Agriculture. Includes data on U. S. agriculture, farmers, food, nutrition, and rural America. Programs of the Department of Agriculture in six areas are described: rural economic development, foreign trade, nutrition, the environment, inspection, and education.

Budget of the United States Government. U.S. Office of Management and Budget. Available from U.S. Government Printing Office. • Annual.

TRADE/PROFESSIONAL ASSOCIATIONS

Community Associations Institute. 1630 Duke St., Alexandria, VA 22314. Phone: (703)548-8600 Fax: (703)684-1581 • URL: http://www.caionline.org • Members are condominium associations, homeowners associations, builders, property managers, developers, and others concerned with the common facilities and services in condominiums, townhouses, planned unit developments, and other planned communities.

Community Development Society. 1123 N. Water St., Milwaukee, WI 53202. Phone: (414)276-7106 Fax: (414)276-7704 E-mail: cole@svinicki.com • URL: http://www.comm-dev.org.

Community Service. P.O. Box 243, Yellow Springs, OH 45387. Phone: (937)767-2161 Fax: (937)767-2826 E-mail: communityservice@usa.net.

Small Towns Institute. P.O. Box 517, Ellensburg, WA 98926. Phone: (509)925-1830 Fax: (509)963-1753.

OTHER SOURCES

American Land Planning Law. Norman Williams, and John Taylor. West Group. • $750.00. Eight volumes. Periodic supplementation. (Real Property and Zoning Series).

Fair Housing: Discrimination in Real Estate, Community Development and Revitalization. James A. Kushner. Shepard's. • 1983. $140.00. Second edition. (Individual Rights Series).

COMMUNITY FUNDS

See also: FUND-RAISING

DIRECTORIES

Funding Sources for Community and Economic Development: A Guide to Current Sources for Local Programs and Projects. Oryx Press. • 2000. $64.95. Sixth edition. Provides information on 2,600 funding sources. Includes "A Guide to Proposal Planning.".

STATISTICS SOURCES

Giving U.S.A: The Annual Compilation of Total Philanthropic Giving Estimates. American Association of Fund-Raising Counsel. AAFRC Trust for Philanthropy. • Annual. $49.95.

United Way Annual Report. United Way of America. • Annual. Price on application.

TRADE/PROFESSIONAL ASSOCIATIONS

National Society of Fund Raising Executives. 1101 King St., Suite 700, Alexandria, VA 22314. Phone: 800-666-5863 or (703)684-0410 Fax: (703)684-0540 E-mail: nsfre@nsfre.org • URL: http://www.nsfre.org.

United Way of America. 701 N. Fairfax St., Alexandria, VA 22314. Phone: (703)836-7100 Fax: (703)683-7840 E-mail: betty.beene@uwi.unitedway.org • URL: http://www.unitedway.org.

COMMUNITY PLANNING

See: CITY PLANNING

COMMUNITY RELATIONS

See also: SOCIAL RESPONSIBILITY

ABSTRACTS AND INDEXES

Business Periodicals Index. H. W. Wilson Co. • Monthly, except August, with quarterly and annual cumulations. Service basis for print edition; CD-ROM edition, $1,495.00 per year.

Readers' Guide to Periodical Literature. H. W. Wilson Co. • Monthly. $220.00 per year. CD-ROM edition, $1,495 per year, including annual cumulation. Indexes about 250 peridicals of general interest.

Social Sciences Index. H. W. Wilson Co. • Quarterly, with annual cumulation. Service basis for print edition; CD-ROM edition, $1,495 per year. Indexes more than 400 periodicals covering economics, environmental policy, government, insurance, labor, health care policy, plannning, public administration, public welfare, urban studies, women's issues, criminology, and related topics.

CD-ROM DATABASES

National Newspaper Index CD-ROM. The Gale Group. • Monthly. Provides comprehensive CD-ROM indexing of all material appearing in the late edition of the *New York Times*, the final edition of the *Washington Post*, the national edition of the *Christian Science Monitor*, the home edition of the *Los Angeles Times*, and the *Wall Street Journal*. Time period is four years. Also available online.

The New York Times Ondisc. New York Times Online Services. • Monthly. $2,650.00 per year. CD-ROM discs contain the full text of *The New York Times*, final edition. Inquire as to time period covered and availability of backfiles.

Newspaper Abstracts Ondisc. Bell & Howell Information and Learning. • Monthly. $2,950.00 per year (covers 1989 to date; archival discs are available for 1985-88). Provides cover-to-cover CD-ROM indexing and abstracting of 19 major newspapers, including the *New York Times, Wall Street Journal, Washington Post, Chicago Tribune,* and *Los Angeles Times*.

Social Science Source. EBSCO Publishing. • Monthly. $1,495.00 per year. Provides CD-ROM citations and abstracts to social science articles in more than 600 periodicals, with full text from 125 periodicals. Covers economics, political science, public policy, international relations, psychology, and other topics. Time period is most recent five years.

Social Sciences Citation Index: Compact Disc Edition with Abstracts. Institute for Scientific Information. • Quarterly. Provides CD-ROM indexing and abstracting of "significant articles" from 1,400 social science journals worldwide, with additional selections from 3,200 other journals, 1986 to date. Includes economics, business, finance, management, communications, demographics, information and library science, political science, sociology, and many other subjects.

WILSONDISC: Wilson Social Sciences Abstracts. H. W. Wilson Co. • Monthly. Including unlimited online access to *Social Sciences Index* through WILSONLINE. Provides CD-ROM indexing from 1983 and abstracting from 1994 of more than 400 periodicals covering economics, area studies, community health, public administration, public welfare, urban studies, and many other topics related to the social sciences.

DIRECTORIES

Business Organizations, Agencies, and Publications Directory. The Gale Group. • 1999. $425.00. 12th edition. Over 40,000 entries describing 39 types of business information sources. Classified by type of organization, publication, or serviceIncludes state, national, and international agencies and organizations. Master index to names and keywords. Also includes e-mail addresses and web site URL's.

National Directory of Corporate Public Affairs. Columbia Books, Inc. • Annual. $109.00. Lists about 2,000 corporations that have foundations or other public affairs activities.

Shopping for a Better World: A Quick and Easy Guide to Socially Responsible Supermarket Shopping. Council on Economic Priorities. • Annual. $14.00. Rates 186 major corporations according to 10 social criteria: advancement of minorities, advancement of women, environmental concerns, South African investments, charity, community outreach, nuclear power, animal testing, military contracts, and social disclosure. Includes American, Japanese and British firms.

ENCYCLOPEDIAS AND DICTIONARIES

Blackwell Encyclopedic Dictionary of Business Ethics. Patricia H. Werhane and R. Edward Freeman, editors. Blackwell Publishers. • 1997. $105.95. The editors are associated with the University of Virginia. Contains definitions of key terms combined with longer articles written by various U. S. and foreign business educators.

Includes bibliographies and index. (Blackwell Encyclopedia of Management Series).

ONLINE DATABASES

Information Bank Abstracts. New York Times Index Dept. • Provides indexing and abstracting of current affairs, primarily from the final late edition of *The New York Times* and the Eastern edition of *The Wall Street Journal*. Time period is 1969 to present, with daily updates. Inquire as to online cost and availability.

Readers' Guide Abstracts Online. H. W. Wilson Co. • Indexes and abstracts general interest periodicals, 1983 to date. Weekly updates. Inquire as to online cost and availability.

Wilson Business Abstracts Online. H. W. Wilson Co. • Indexes and abstracts 600 major business periodicals, plus the *Wall Street Journal* and the business section of the *New York Times*. Indexing is from 1982, abstracting from 1990, with the two newspapers included from 1993. Updated weekly. Inquire as to online cost and availability. (*Business Periodicals Index* without abstracts is also available online.).

Wilson Social Sciences Abstracts Online. H. W. Wilson Co. • Provides online abstracting and indexing of more than 415 periodicals covering area studies, community health, public administration, public welfare, urban studies, and many other social science topics. Time period is 1994 to date for abstracts and 1983 to date for indexing, with updates monthly. Inquire as to online cost and availability.

PERIODICALS AND NEWSLETTERS

Community Relations Report. Joe Williams Communications. • Monthly. $160.00 per year. Newsletter on corporate community relations.

Corporate Public Issues and Their Management: The Executive Systems Approach to Public Policy Formation. Issue Action Publications, Inc. • Semimonthly. $195.00 per year. Newsletter.

Positive Leadership: Improving Performance Through Value-Centered Management. Lawence Ragan Communications, Inc. • Monthly. $119.00 per year. Newsletter. Emphasis is on employee motivation, family issues, ethics, and community relations.

RESEARCH CENTERS AND INSTITUTES

Center for Corporate Community Relations. Boston College, 55 Lee Rd., Chestnut Hill, MA 02467. Phone: (617)552-4545 Fax: (617)552-8499 E-mail: cccr@bc.edu • URL: http://www.bc.edu/cccr • Areas of study include corporate images within local communities, corporate community relations, social vision, and philanthropy.

Center for Public-Private Sector Cooperation. University of Colorado-Denver, 1445 Market St., Suite 380, Denver, CO 80202-1727. Phone: (303)820-5650 Fax: (303)820-5656 E-mail: lcarlson@carbon.cudenver.edu.

TRADE/PROFESSIONAL ASSOCIATIONS

National Association for Community Leadership. 200 S. Meridian St., Suite 250, Indianapolis, IN 46225. Phone: (317)637-7408 Fax: (317)637-7413 E-mail: commlead@indy.net • Affiliated with American Chamber of Commerce Executives.

COMMUNITY SHOPPING CENTERS

See: SHOPPING CENTERS

COMMUTER AIRLINES

See: AIRLINE INDUSTRY

COMPACT DISCS

See: OPTICAL DISK STORAGE DEVICES

COMPANIES

See: CORPORATIONS; INDUSTRY; PRIVATE COMPANIES

COMPANY ANNIVERSARIES

See: ANNIVERSARIES AND HOLIDAYS

COMPANY HISTORIES

See: BUSINESS HISTORY

COMPENSATION OF EMPLOYEES

See: WAGES AND SALARIES

COMPENSATION OF EXECUTIVES

See: EXECUTIVE COMPENSATION

COMPETITIVE INTELLIGENCE

See also: BUSINESS RESEARCH

GENERAL WORKS

Information Management for the Intelligent Organization: The Art of Scanning the Environment. Chun Wei Choo. Information Today, Inc. • 1998. $39.50. Second edition. Published on behalf of the American Society for Information Science (ASIS). Covers the general principles of acquiring, creating, organizing, and using information within organizations.

Knowledge Management for the Information Professional. T. Kanti Srikantaiah and Michael Koenig, editors. Information Today, Inc. • 2000. $44.50. Contains articles by 26 contributors on the concept of "knowledge management.".

Millennium Intelligence: Understanding and Conducting Competitive Intelligence in the Digital Age. Jerry Miller, editor. Information Today, Inc. • 1999. $29.95. Contains essays by various authors on competitive intelligence information sources, legal aspects, intelligence skills, corporate security, and other topics. (CyberAge Books.).

Online Competitive Intelligence: Increase Your Profits Using Cyber-Intelligence. Helen P. Burwell. Facts on Demand Press. • 1999. $25.95. Covers the selection and use of online sources for competitive intelligence. Includes descriptions of many Internet Web sites, classified by subject.

BIBLIOGRAPHIES

Analyzing Your Competition: Simple, Low-Cost Techniques for Intelligence Gathering. Michael Strenges. MarketResearch.com. • 1997. $95.00. Third edition. Mainly an annotated listing of specific, business information sources, but also contains concise discussions of information-gathering techniques. Indexed by publisher and title.

DIRECTORIES

KMWorld Buyer's Guide. Knowledge Asset Media. • Semiannual. Controlled circulation as part of *KMWorld*. Contains corporate and product profiles related to various aspects of knowledge management and information systems. (Knowledge Asset Media is a an affiliate of Information Today, Inc.).

HANDBOOKS AND MANUALS

Competitive Intelligence From Black Ops to Boardrooms: How Businesses Gather, Analyze, and Use Information to Succeed in the Global Marketplace. Larry Kahaner. Simon & Schuster Trade. • 1996. $24.00. Emphasizes corporate espionage as opposed to more traditional information gathering (the author is a former licensed private investigator). Includes a "Glossary of Competitive Intelligence.".

Intelligence Essentials for Everyone. Available from U. S. Government Printing Office. • 1999. $6.50. Issued by the Joint Military Intelligence College, Defense Intelligence Agency, U. S. Department of Defense (http://www.dia.mil/). Written for "businesses worldwide." Explains how to collect, process, analyze, and manage business intelligence information.

A New Archetype for Competitive Intelligence. John J. McGonagle and Carolyn M. Vella. Greenwood Publishing Group, Inc. • 1996. $59.95. Covers competitive intelligence, strategic intelligence, market intelligence, defensive intelligence, and cyber-intelligence. Includes an overview of sources and techniques for data gathering. A bibliography, glossary, and index are provided.

New Competitor Intelligence: The Complete Resource for Finding, Analyzing, and Using Information About Your Competitors. Leonard M. Fuld. John Wiley and Sons, Inc. • 1994. $80.50. Second edition. Topics include data sources, strategy, analysis of competition, and how to establish a competitive intelligence system.

INTERNET DATABASES

Competitive Intelligence Guide. Fuld & Co. Phone: (617)492-5900 Fax: (617)492-7108 E-mail: info@fuld.com • URL: http://www.fuld.com • Web site includes "Intelligence Index" (links to Internet sites), "Strategic Intelligence Organizer" (game-board format), "Intelligence Pyramid" (graphics), "Thoughtleaders" (expert commentary), "Intelligence System Evaluator" (interactive questionnaire), and "Reference Resource" (book excerpts from *New Competitor Intelligence*). Fees: information provided by Web site is free, but Fuld & Co. offers fee-based research and consulting services.

EBSCO Information Services. Ebsco Publishing. Phone: 800-871-8508 or (508)356-6500 Fax: (508)356-5640 E-mail: ep@epnet.com • URL: http://www.epnet.com • Fee-based Web site providing Internet access to a wide variety of databases, including business-related material. Full text is available for many periodical titles, with daily updates. Fees: Apply.

Ebusiness Forum: Global Business Intelligence for the Digital Age. Economist Intelligence Unit (EIU), Economist Group. Phone: 800-938-4685 or (212)554-0600 Fax: (212)586-0248 E-mail: newyork@eiu.com • URL: http://www.ebusinessforum.com • Web site provides information relating to multinational business, with an emphasis on activities in specific countries. Includes rankings of countries for "e-business readiness," additional data on the political, economic, and business environment in 180 nations ("Doing Business in.."), and "Today's News Analysis." Fees: Free, but registration is required for access to all content. Daily updates.

Intelligence Data. Thomson Financial. Phone: 800-654-0393 or (212)806-8023 Fax: (212)806-8004 • URL: http://www.intelligencedata.com • Fee-based

Web site provides a wide variety of information relating to competitive intelligence, strategic planning, business development, mergers, acquisitions, sales, and marketing. "Intelliscope" feature offers searching of other Thomson units, such as Investext, MarkIntel, InSite 2, and Industry Insider. Weekly updating.

Internet Business Intelligence: How to Build a Big Company System on a Small Company Budget. David Vine. Information Today, Inc. 143 Old Marlton Pike, Medford, NJ 08055-8750. Phone: 800-300-9868 or (609)654-6266 Fax: (609)654-4309 E-mail: custserv@infotoday.com • URL: http://www.infotoday.com • 2000. $29.95. Covers the obtaining of valuable business intelligence data through use of the Internet.

ProQuest Direct. Bell & Howell Information and Learning. Phone: 800-521-0600 or (313)761-4700 Fax: (313)973-9145 • URL: http://www.umi.com/proquest • Fee-based Web site providing Internet access to more than 3,000 periodicals, newspapers, and other publications. Many items are available full-text, with daily updates. Includes extensive corporate and financial information from Disclosure, Inc. Fees: Apply.

ONLINE DATABASES

Super Searchers on Mergers & Acquisitions: The Online Secrets of Top Corporate Researchers and M & A Pros. Jan Tudor and Reva Basch. Information Today, Inc. • 2001. $24.95. Presents the results of interviews with 13 "top M & A information pros." Covers the finding, evaluating, and delivering of relevant data on companies and industries. (CyberAge Books.).

PERIODICALS AND NEWSLETTERS

KMWorld: Creating and Managing the Knowledge-Based Enterprise. Knowledge Asset Media. • Monthly. Controlled circulation. Provides articles on knowledge management, including business intelligence, multimedia content management, document management, e-business, and intellectual property. Emphasis is on business-to-business information technology. (Knowledge Asset Media is a an affiliate of Information Today, Inc.).

Knowledge Management. CurtCo Freedom Group. • Monthly. Controlled circulation. Covers applications of information technology and knowledge management strategy.

Ragan's Journal of Business Intelligence. Lawence Ragan Communications, Inc. • Bimonthly. $199.00 per year. Includes articles on competitive intelligence, knowledge management, legalities, ethics, and counterintelligence.

Strategy and Business. Booz-Allen & Hamilton. • Quarterly. $38.00 per year.

RESEARCH CENTERS AND INSTITUTES

Super Searchers Go to the Source: The Interviewing and Hands-On Information Strategies of Top Primary Researchers - Online, On the Phone, and In Person. Risa Sacks and Reva Basch. Information Today, Inc. 143 Old Marlton Pike, Medford, NJ 08055-8750. Phone: 800-300-9868 or (609)654-6266 Fax: (609)654-4309 E-mail: custserv@infotoday.com • URL: http://www.infotoday.com • 2001. $24.95. Explains how information-search experts use various print, electronic, and live sources for competitive intelligence and other purposes. (CyberAge Books.).

TRADE/PROFESSIONAL ASSOCIATIONS

Society of Competitive Intelligence Professionals. 1700 Diagonal Rd., Suite 600, Alexandria, VA 22314. Phone: (703)739-0696 Fax: (703)739-2524 E-mail: info@scip.org • URL: http://www.scip.org • Members are professionals involved in competitor intelligence and analysis.

OTHER SOURCES

Factiva. Dow Jones Reuters Business Interactive, LLC. • Fee-based Web site provides "global news and business information through Web sites and content integration solutions." Includes Dow Jones and Reuters newswires, The Wall Street Journal, and more than 7,000 other sources of current news, historical articles, market research reports, and investment analysis. Content includes 96 major U. S. newspapers, 900 non-English sources, trade publications, media transcripts, country profiles, news photos, etc.

InSite 2. Intelligence Data/Thomson Financial. • Fee-based Web site consolidates information in a "Base Pack" consisting of Business InSite, Market InSite, and Company InSite. Optional databases are Consumer InSite, Health and Wellness InSite, Newsletter InSite, and Computer InSite. Includes fulltext content from more than 2,500 trade publications, journals, newsletters, newspapers, analyst reports, and other sources. Continuous updating. Formerly produced by The Gale Group.

Nexis.com. Lexis-Nexis Group. • Fee-based Web site offers searching of about 2.8 billion documents in some 30,000 news, business, and legal information sources. Features include a subject directory covering 1,200 topics in 34 categories and a Company Dossier containing information on more than 500,000 public and private companies. Boolean searching is offered.

COMPOSITE MATERIALS

See also: MATERIALS

ABSTRACTS AND INDEXES

Applied Science and Technology Index. H. W. Wilson Co. • 11 times a year. Quarterly and annual cumulations. Service basis for print edition; CD-ROM edition, $1,495.00 per year. Indexes a wide variety of English language technical, industrial, and engineering periodicals.

Engineered Materials Abstracts. Cambridge Information Group. • Monthly. $995.00 per year. Provides citations to the technical and engineering literature of plastic, ceramic, and composite materials.

Engineering Index Monthly: Abstracting and Indexing Services Covering Sources of the World's Engineering Literature. Engineering Information, Inc. • Monthly. $2,300.00 per year. Provides indexing and abstracting of the world's engineering and technical literature.

Key Abstracts: Advanced Materials. Available from INSPEC, Inc. • Monthly. $240.00 per year. Provides international coverage of journal and proceedings literature, including publications on ceramics and composite materials. Published in England by the Institution of Electrical Engineers (IEE).

NTIS Alerts: Manufacturing Technology. National Technical Information Service. • Semimonthly. $265.00 per year. Provides descriptions of government-sponsored research reports and software, with ordering information. Covers computer-aided design and manufacturing (CAD/CAM), engineering materials, quality control, machine tools, robots, lasers, productivity, and related subjects. Formerly *Abstract Newsletter.*

NTIS Alerts: Materials Sciences. National Technical Information Service. • Semimonthly. $220.00 per year. Provides descriptions of government-sponsored research reports and software, with ordering information. Covers ceramics, glass, coatings, composite materials, alloys, plastics, wood, paper, adhesives, fibers, lubricants, and related subjects. Formerly *Abstract Newsletter.*

Polymers/Ceramics/Composites Alert. Cambridge Information Group. • Monthly. $340.00 per year. Provides citations to the business and industrial literature of plastic, ceramic, and composite materials. (Materials Business Information Series).

CD-ROM DATABASES

COMPENDEX PLUS [CD-ROM]. Engineering Information, Inc. • Quarterly. $3,450.00 per year. Provides CD-ROM indexing and abstracting of the world's engineering and technical information appearing in journals, reports, books, and proceedings, 1985 to date.

Materials Science Citation Index. Institute for Scientific Information. • Bimonthly. Contains current, CD-ROM citations and abstracts, providing international coverage of materials science journals.

METADEX Materials Collection: Metals-Polymers-Ceramics. Cambridge Scientific Abstracts. • Quarterly. $6,950.00 per year. Provides CD-ROM citations to the worldwide literature of materials science and metallurgy. Corresponds to *Metals Abstracts, Alloys Index, Steels Alert, Nonferrous Alert, Polymers/Ceramics/Composites Alert,* and *Engineered Materials Abstracts.* (Formerly produced by ASM International.).

WILSONDISC: Applied Science and Technology Abstracts. H. W. Wilson Co. • Monthly. $1,495.00 per year, including unlimited access to the online version of *Applied Science and Technology Abstracts* through WILSONLINE. Provides CD-ROM indexing and abstracting of 400 prominent scientific, technical, engineering, and industrial periodicals. Indexing coverage is provided from 1983 to date and abstracting from 1993 to date.

DIRECTORIES

Directory of Composites Manufacturers, Suppliers, and Services. Society of Manufacturing Engineers. • Biennial. $25.00 per year. Provides information for more than 500 firms involved in the production of composite materials: composite manufacturers, material suppliers, service companies, consultants, etc.

Engineering Plastics and Composites. William A. Woishnis and others, editors. ASM International. • 1993. $149.00. Second edition. In four sections: (1) Trade names of plastics, reinforced plastics, and resin composites; (2) Index to materials, with suppliers and other information; (3) Suppliers alphabetically, with trade names; (4) Supplier contact information. (Materials Data Series).

ENCYCLOPEDIAS AND DICTIONARIES

ASM Materials Engineering Dictionary. Joseph R. Davis, editor. ASM International. • 1992. $146.00. Contains 10,000 entries, 700 illustrations, and 150 tables relating to metals, plastics, ceramics, composites, and adhesives. Includes "Technical Briefs" on 64 key material groups.

Comprehensive Composite Materials. Anthony Kelly and Carl Zweben, editors-in-chief. Elsevier Science. • 2000. $3,250.00. Six volumes. Provides detailed information on a wide variety of materials used in composites, including metals, polymers, cements, concrete, carbon, ceramics, and fibers. (Pergamon Press.).

Encyclopedia of Advanced Materials. David Bloor and others. Elsevier Science. • 1994. $1,811.25. Four volumes.

Encyclopedia of Materials: Science and Technology. K.H.J. Buschow and others, editors. Pergamon Press/Elsevier Science. • 2001. $6,875.00. Eleven volumes. Provides extensive technical information on a wide variety of materials, including metals, ceramics, plastics, optical materials, and building materials. Includes more than 2,000 articles and 5,000 illustrations.

Materials Science and Technology: A Comprehensive Treatment. R. W. Cahn and others, editors. John Wiley and Sons, Inc. • 1997. $7,349.00. 18 volumes. Each volume covers a particular area of high-performance materials technology.

HANDBOOKS AND MANUALS

Advanced Polymer Composites: Principles and Applications. Bor Z. Jang. ASM International. • 1994. $93.00.

Joining of Composite Matrix Materials. Mel M. Schwartz. ASM International. • 1994. $59.00.

Machining of Composite Materials No. 2: Proceedings of ASM 1993 Materials Congress, Materials Week' 93, October 17-21, 1993. Held in Pittsburgh, PA. T. S. Srivatsan and others, editors. Books on Demand. • 1994. $58.00.

ONLINE DATABASES

Applied Science and Technology Index Online. H. W. Wilson Co. • Provides online indexing of 400 major scientific, technical, industrial, and engineering periodicals. Time period is 1983 to date. Monthly updates. Inquire as to online cost and availability.

COMPENDEX PLUS. Engineering Information, Inc. • Provides online indexing and abstracting of the world's engineering and technical information appearing in journals, reports, books, and proceedings. Time period is 1970 to date, with weekly updates. Inquire as to online cost and availability.

Current Contents Connect. Institute for Scientific Information. • Provides online abstracts of articles listed in the tables of contents of about 7,500 journals. Coverage is very broad, including science, social science, life science, technology, engineering, industry, agriculture, the environment, economics, and arts and humanities. Time period is two years, with weekly updates. Inquire as to online cost and availability.

Engineered Materials Abstracts [online]. Cambridge Scientific Abstracts. • Provides online citations to the technical and engineering literature of plastic, ceramic, and composite materials. Time period is 1986 to date, with monthly updates. (Formerly produced by ASM International.) Inquire as to online cost and availability.

Materials Business File. Cambridge Scientific Abstracts. • Provides online abstracts and citations to worldwide materials literature, covering the business and industrial aspects of metals, plastics, ceramics, and composites. Corresponds to *Steels Alert, Nonferrous Metals Alert,* and *Polymers/Ceramics/ Composites Alert.* Time period is 1985 to date, with monthly updates. (Formerly produced by ASM International.) Inquire as to online cost and availability.

METADEX. Cambridge Scientific Abstracts. • Covers the worldwide literature of metals, metallurgy, and materials science, 1966 to date. Includes detailed alloys indexing from 1974. Biweekly updating. Inquire as to online cost and availability. (Formerly produced by ASM International.).

PROMT: Predicasts Overview of Markets and Technology. The Gale Group. • Companies, products, applied technologies and markets. U.S. and international literature coverage, 1972 to date. Inquire as to online cost and availability. Provides abstracts from more than 1,600 publications. Weekly updates.

PERIODICALS AND NEWSLETTERS

Advanced Composites Monthly. Composite Market Reports, Inc. • Monthly. $2,325.00 per year. Newsletter. Quarterly calenders and updates. Emphasizes aerospace applications of advanced composite materials throughout the world. Includes industry news, research news, and case histories of applications. Supplement available *GraFiber.*

The Composites and Adhesives Newsletter. T-C Press. • Quarterly. $190.00. Presents news of the composite materials and adhesives industries, with particular coverage of new products and applications.

Composites Industry Monthly. Composite Market Reports, Inc. • Monthly. $1,495.00 per year. Newsletter. Supplement to *ACM Monthly.* Emphasizes non-aerospace applications of composite materials. Includes quarterly calendars, meetings and other periodic supplements and indexes.

High-Tech Materials Alert: Advanced Materials-Their Uses and Manufacture. Technical Insights. • Monthly. $695.00 per year. Newsletter on technical developments relating to high-performance materials, including metals and ceramics. Includes market forecasts.

International Materials Review. ASM International, Materials Information. • Bimonthly. Members, $305.00 per year; non-members, $734.00 per year. Provides technical and research coverage of metals, alloys, and advanced materials. Formerly *International Metals Review.*

Journal of Advanced Materials. Society for the Advancement of Material and Process Engineering. • Quarterly. Members $20.00 per year; non-members, $60.00 per year. Contains technical and research articles. Formerly *SAMPE Quarterly.*

Journal of Materials Research. Materials Research Society. • Monthly. Members, $80.00 per year; non-members, $750.00 per year. Covers the preparation, properties, and processing of advanced materials.

SAMPE Journal. Society for the Advancement of Material and Process Engineering. • Bimonthly. $65.00 per year. Provides technical information.

RESEARCH CENTERS AND INSTITUTES

Center for Composite Materials. University of Delaware, Newark, DE 19716-3144. Phone: (302)831-8149 Fax: (302)831-8525 E-mail: info@ccm.udel.edu • URL: http://www.ccm.udel.edu.

Center for Composite Materials and Structures. Virginia Polytechnic Institute and State University, 201 Hancock Hall, MC 0257, Blacksburg, VA 24061-0257. Phone: (540)231-4969 Fax: (540)231-9452 E-mail: dbaird@vt.edu • URL: http://www.g3.net/ccms/.

Composite Materials and Structures Center. Michigan State University, College of Engineering, 2100 Engineering Bldg., East Lansing, MI 48824-1226. Phone: (517)353-5466 Fax: (517)432-1634 E-mail: cmsc@engr.smsu.edu • URL: http://www.cmscsun.egr.msu.edu/index/html • Studies polymer, metal, and ceramic based composites.

Composite Materials Research Group. University of Wyoming, Department of Mechanical Engineering, University Station, P.O. Box 3295, Laramie, WY 82071. Phone: (307)766-2371 Fax: (307)766-4444 • URL: http://www.eng.uwyo.edu/cmrg.

Materials Processing Center. Massachusetts Institute of Technology, 77 Massachusetts Ave., Room 12-007, Cambridge, MA 02139-4307. Phone: (617)253-5179 Fax: (617)258-6900 E-mail: fmpage@.mit.edu • URL: http://www.web.mit.edu/mpc/www/ • Conducts processing, engineering, and economic research in ferrous and nonferrous metals, ceramics, polymers, photonic materials, superconductors, welding, composite materials, and other materials.

Stanford Integrated Manufacturing Association. Stanford University, Bldg. 02-530, Stanford, CA 94305-3036. Phone: (650)723-9038 Fax: (650)723-5034 E-mail: susan.hansen@stanford.edu • URL: http://www.sima.stanford.edu/ • Consists of four research centers: Center for Automation and Manufacturing Science, Center for Design Research, Center for Materials Formability and Processing Science, and Center for Teaching and Research in Integrated Manufacturing Systems. Research fields include automation, robotics, intelligent systems, computer vision, design in manufacturing, materials science, composite materials, and ceramics.

TRADE/PROFESSIONAL ASSOCIATIONS

ASM International. 9639 Kinsman Rd., Materials Park, OH 44073. Phone: 800-336-5152 or (216)338-5151 Fax: (216)338-4634 E-mail: memserv@po.asm-intl.org • URL: http://www.asm-intl.org • Members are materials engineers, metallurgists, industry executives, educators, and others concerned with a wide range of materials and metals. Divisions include Aerospace, Composites, Electronic Materials and Processing, Energy, Highway/Off-Highway Vehicle, Joining, Materials Testing and Quality Control, Society of Carbide and Tool Engineers, and Surface Engineering.

Composites Manufacturing Association of the Society of Manufacturing Engineers. P.O. Box 930, Dearborn, MI 48121-0930. Phone: 800-733-4763 or (313)271-1500 Fax: (313)271-2861 • URL: http://www.sme.org • Members are composites manufacturing professionals and students.

Materials Research Society. 506 Keystone Dr., Warrendale, PA 15086-7537. Phone: (724)779-3003 Fax: (724)779-8313 E-mail: info@mrs.org • URL: http://www.mrs.org • Members are individuals concerned with multidisciplinary research in the technology of advanced materials.

SPI Composites Institute. 1801 K St., N.W., Suite 600K, Washington, DC 20006-1301. E-mail: ci@socplas.org • URL: http://www.socplas.org/businessunits/index/ci.html • A division of the Society of the Plastics Industry. Members are molders and fabricators of reinforced plastics.

Suppliers of Advanced Composite Materials Association. 1600 Wilson Blvd., Suite 901, Arlington, VA 22209. Phone: (703)841-1556 Fax: (703)841-1559 E-mail: staff@sacma.org • URL: http://www.sacma.org • Members are manufacturers and suppliers of fiber-reinforced advanced composite finished products.

OTHER SOURCES

Business & Company Resource Center. The Gale Group. • Fee-based Web site provides a wide range of business, industry, and specific company information. Access is offered to trade journal articles, market research data, insider trading activity, major shareholder data, corporate histories, emerging technology reports, corporate earnings estimates, press releases, and other sources. Provides detailed company profiles, industry overviews, and rankings. Offers integration of Predicasts PROMT, Newsletters ASAP, Investext Plus, Business Index ASAP, Brands and Their Companies, and other databases (many have full text).

COMPRESSORS

See: PUMPS AND COMPRESSORS

COMPTROLLERS

See: CORPORATE DIRECTORS AND OFFICERS

COMPUTER ACCESSORIES

See: COMPUTER PERIPHERALS AND ACCESSORIES

COMPUTER-AIDED DESIGN AND MANUFACTURING (CAD/CAM)

See also: COMPUTER GRAPHICS

GENERAL WORKS

Computer Aided Design. Robert Becker and Carmo J. Pereira, editors. Marcel Dekker, Inc. • 1993. $235.00.

Systems Approach to Computer-Integrated Design and Manufacturing. Nanua Singh. John Wiley and Sons, Inc. • 1995. $99.95.

ABSTRACTS AND INDEXES

Applied Science and Technology Index. H. W. Wilson Co. • 11 times a year. Quarterly and annual cumulations. Service basis for print edition; CD-ROM edition, $1,495.00 per year. Indexes a wide variety of English language technical, industrial, and engineering periodicals.

Key Abstracts: Factory Automation. Available from INSPEC, Inc. • Monthly. $240.00 per year. Provides international coverage of journal and proceedings literature, including publications on CAD/CAM, materials handling, robotics, and factory management. Published in England by the Institution of Electrical Engineers (IEE).

NTIS Alerts: Manufacturing Technology. National Technical Information Service. • Semimonthly. $265.00 per year. Provides descriptions of government-sponsored research reports and software, with ordering information. Covers computer-aided design and manufacturing (CAD/CAM), engineering materials, quality control, machine tools, robots, lasers, productivity, and related subjects. Formerly *Abstract Newsletter.*

Science Citation Index. Institute for Scientific Information. • Bimonthly. $15,020.00 per year. Annual cumulation. Includes *Source Index, Citation Index, Permuterm Subject Index,* and *Corporate Index.*

DIRECTORIES

CAD/CAM,CAE: Survey, Review and Buyers' Guide. Daratech, Inc. • $972.00 per year. Looseleaf service. Includes computer-aided engineering (CAE). (Daratech Series in CAD-CAM, CAE).

Manufacturing Systems: Buyers Guide. Cahners Business Information. • Annual. Price on application. Contains information on companies manufacturing or supplying materials handling systems, CAD/CAM systems, specialized software for manufacturing, programmable controllers, machine vision systems, and automatic identification systems.

Modern Machine Shop Material Working Technology Guide. Gardner Publications, Inc. • Annual. $15.00. Lists products and services for the metalworking industry. Formerly *Modern Machine Shop CNC and Software Guide.*

S. Klein Directory of Computer Suppliers: Hardware, Software, Systems and Services. Technology and Business Communications, Inc. • 1987. $73.00.

HANDBOOKS AND MANUALS

Mechanical Engineer's Reference Book. E. H. Smith, editor. Society of Automotive Engineers, Inc. • 1994. $135.00. 12th edition. Covers mechanical engineering principles, computer integrated engineering systems, design standards, materials, power transmission, and many other engineering topics. (Authored Royalty Series).

ONLINE DATABASES

Computer Database. The Gale Group. • Provides online citations with abstracts to material appearing in about 150 trade journals and newsletters in the subject areas of computers, telecommunications, and electronics. Time period is 1983 to date, with weekly updates. Inquire as to online cost and availability.

Globalbase. The Gale Group. • Provides more than one million online summaries of business, industrial, and economic news reports from more than 1,000 publications worldwide. Covers a wide range of material appearing in international trade journals, professional magazines, and newspapers. Time period is 1984 to date, with weekly updates. Inquire as to online cost and availability.

Scisearch. Institute for Scientific Information. • Broad, multidisciplinary index to the literature of science and technology, 1974 to present. Inquire as to online cost and availability. Coverage of literature is worldwide, with weekly updates.

PERIODICALS AND NEWSLETTERS

ACM Transactions on Graphics. Association for Computing Machinery. • Semiannual. Free to members; non-members, $110.00 per year.

Commline. Numeridex, Inc. • Bimonthly. Free to qualified personnel; others, $20.00 per year. Emphasizes NC/CNC (numerically controlled and computer numerically controlled machinery).

Computer-Aided Engineering; Data Base Applications in Design and Manufacturing. Penton Media Inc. • Monthly. $55.00 per year.

IEEE Computer Graphics and Applications. Insityte of Electrical and Electronics Engineers, Inc. • Bimonthly. Free to members; non-members, $485.00 per year.

IEEE Transactions on Visualization and Computer Graphics. Institute of Electrical and Electronics Engineers. • Quarterly. $490.00 per year. Topics include computer vision, computer graphics, image processing, signal processing, computer-aided design, animation, and virtual reality.

Manufacturing Computer Solutions. Hitchcock Publishing. • Monthly. Free to qualified personnel; others; $75.00 per year. Edited for managers of factory automation, emphasizing the integration of systems in manufacturing. Subjects include materials handling, CAD/CAM, specialized software for manufacturing, programmable controllers, machine vision, and automatic identification systems. Formerly *Manufacturing Systems.*

Robotics and Computer-Integrated Manufacturing: An International Journal. Elsevier Science. • Bimonthly. $900.00 per year.

RESEARCH CENTERS AND INSTITUTES

Advanced Manufacturing Engineering Institute. University of Hartford, United Technologies Hall, Room 215, West Hartford, CT 06117. Phone: 800-678-4844 or (860)768-4615 Fax: (860)768-5073 E-mail: shetty@mail.hartford.edu • URL: http://www.uharay.hartford.edu/eau.

Computer Network Center. Purdue University at Indianapolis, 799 W. Michigan St., Room 142, Indianapolis, IN 46202-2144. Phone: (317)274-2938 Fax: (317)274-8470 E-mail: greg@engr.iupui.edu • URL: http://www.engr.iupui.edu.

Institute of Advanced Manufacturing Sciences, Inc. 1111 Edison Dr., Cincinnati, OH 45216. Phone: (513)948-2000 Fax: (513)948-2109 E-mail: conley@iams.org • URL: http://www.iams.org • Fields of research include quality improvement, computer-aided design, artificial intelligence, and employee training.

Laboratory for Manufacturing and Productivity. Massachusetts Institute of Technology, 77 Massachusetts Ave., Bldg. 35, Room 234, Cambridge, MA 02139. Phone: (617)253-2113 Fax: (617)253-1556 E-mail: gutowski@mit.edu • URL: http://www.mit.edu/lmp/.

STATISTICS SOURCES

U. S. Industry and Trade Outlook: The McGraw-Hill Companies and the U.S. Department of Commerce/International Trade Administration. Datapso Research Corp. • Annual. $69.95. Produced by the International Trade Administration, U. S. Department of Commerce, in a "public-private" partnership with DRI/McGraw-Hill and Standard & Poor's. Provides basic data, outlook for the current year, and "Long-Term Prospects" (five-year projections) for a wide variety of products and services. Includes high technology industries. Formerly *U. S. Industrial Outlook.*

TRADE/PROFESSIONAL ASSOCIATIONS

American Automatic Control Council. Dept. of EECS, Northwestern University, 2145 Sheridan Rd., Evanston, IL 60208-3118. Phone: (847)491-8175 Fax: (847)491-4455 E-mail: acc@ece.nwu.edu.

Computer Aided Manufacturing International. 3301 Airport Freeway, No. 324, Bedford, TX 76021-6032. Phone: (817)860-1654 Fax: (817)275-6450.

Computer and Automated Systems Association of Society of Manufacturing Engineers. P.O. Box 930, Dearborn, MI 48121-0930. Phone: (313)271-1500 Fax: (313)271-2861 • URL: http://www.sme.org/casa • Sponsored by the Society of Manufacturing Engineers.

IEEE Computer Society. 1730 Massachusetts Ave., N. W., Washington, DC 20036. Phone: (202)371-0101 Fax: (202)728-9614 E-mail: csinfo@computer.org • URL: http://www.computer.org • A society of the Institute of Electrical and Electronics Engineers. Said to be the world's largest organization of computer professionals. Some of the specific committees are: Computer Communications; Computer Graphics; Computers in Education; Design Automation; Office Automation; Personal Computing; Robotics; Security and Privacy; Software Engineering.

Special Interest Group on Design Automation. Association for Computing Machinery, 1515 Broadway, New York, NY 10036. Phone: (212)869-7440 Fax: (212)302-5826 E-mail: sigs@acm.org • URL: http://www.acm.org/sigda • Concerned with computer-aided design systems and software. Publishes the semiannual *SIGDA Newsletter.*

COMPUTER ANIMATION

See also: VIRTUAL REALITY

ALMANACS AND YEARBOOKS

Computer Animation [year]. Institute of Electrical and Electronic Engineers. • Annual. $110.00.

CD-ROM DATABASES

Computer Select. The Gale Group. • Monthly. $1,250.00 per year. Provides one year of full-text on CD-ROM for 120 leading computer-related publications. Also includes 70,000 product specifications and brief profiles of 13,000 computer product vendors and manufacturers.

DIRECTORIES

Data Sources: The Comprehensive Guide to the Data Processing Industry Hardware, Data Communications Products, Software, Company Profiles. The Gale Group. • Semiannual. $495.00 per year. Two volumes. Describes hardware and software for all computer operating sysems, including prices and technical details. Lists about 75,000 products from 14,000 suppliers. Industry-specific software applications are described.

Information Marketplace Directory. SIMBA Information. • 1996. $295.00. Second edition. Lists computer-based information processing and multimedia companies, including those engaged in animation, audio, video, and interactive video.

The SHOOT Directory for Commercial Production and Postproduction. BPI Communications. • Annual. $79.00. Lists production companies, advertising agencies, and sources of professional television, motion picture, and audio equipment.

ENCYCLOPEDIAS AND DICTIONARIES

Cyberspeak: An Online Dictionary. Andy Ihnatko. Random House, Inc. • 1996. $12.95. An informal guide to the language of computers, multimedia, and the Internet.

New Hacker's Dictionary. Eric S. Raymond. MIT Press. • 1996. $39.00. Third edition. Includes three classifications of hacker communication: slang, jargon, and "techspeak.".

HANDBOOKS AND MANUALS

The Art of 3-D Computer Animation and Imaging. Isaac V. Kerlow. John Wiley and Sons, Inc. • 2000. $59.95. Second edition. Covers special effects, hypermedia formats, video output, the post-production process, etc. Includes full-color illustrations and step-by-step examples. (Design and Graphic Design Series).

Computer Animation Techniques. Pearson Education and Technology. • 1996. $50.00.

Interactive Computer Animation. Nadia M. Thalmann and Daniel Thalmann, editors. Prentice Hall. • 1996. $55.00. Contains 11 chapters by various authors. Includes such items as "Warp Generation and Transition Control in Image Morphing" and "Sculpting, Clothing and Hairdressing Our Virtual Humans.".

INTERNET DATABASES

Wired News. Wired Digital, Inc. Phone: (415)276-8400 Fax: (415)276-8499 E-mail: newsfeedback@wired.com • URL: http://www.wired.com • Provides summaries and full-text of "Top Stories" relating to the Internet, computers, multimedia, telecommunications, and the electronic information industry in general. These news stories are placed in the broad categories of Politics, Business, Culture, and Technology. Affiliated with *Wired* magazine. Fees: Free.

PERIODICALS AND NEWSLETTERS

DV: Digital Video. Miller Freeman, Inc. • Monthly. $29.97 per year. Edited for producers and creators of digital media. Includes topics relating to video, audio, animation, multimedia, interactive design, and special effects. Covers both hardware and software, with product reviews. Formerly *Digital Video Magazine*.

Interactivity: Tools and Techniques for Interactive Media Developers. Miller Freeman, Inc. • Monthly. $59.95 per year. Edited for professional interactive media developers. Includes a special issue on computer animation.

NewMedia: The Magazine for Creators of the Digital Future. HyperMedia Communications, Inc. • Monthly. $29.95 per year. Edited for multimedia professionals, with emphasis on digital video and Internet graphics, including animation. Contains reviews of new products. Formerly *NewMedia Age*.

SHOOT: The Leading Newsweekly for Commercial Production and Postproduction. BPI Communications. • Weekly. $115.00 per year. Covers animation, music, sound design, computer graphics, visual effects, cinematography, and other aspects of television and motion picture production, with emphasis on TV commercials.

3D Design. Miller Freeman, Inc. • Monthly. $50.00 per year. Edited for computer graphics and multimedia professionals. Special features include "Animation Mania" and "Interactive 3D.".

RESEARCH CENTERS AND INSTITUTES

Computer Graphics Laboratory. New York Institute of Technology, Fine Arts, Old Westbury, NY 11568. Phone: (516)686-7542 Fax: (516)686-7428 E-mail: pvoci@nyit.edu • Research areas include computer graphics, computer animation, and digital sound.

Graphics, Visualization, and Usability Center. Georgia Institute of Technology, Mail Code 0280, Atlanta, GA 30332-0280. Phone: (404)894-4488 Fax: (404)894-0673 E-mail: jarek@cc.gatech.edu • URL: http://www.cc.gatech.edu/gvu/ • Research areas include computer graphics, multimedia, image recognition, interactive graphics systems, animation, and virtual realities.

Inter-Arts Center. San Francisco State University, School of Creative Arts, 1600 Holloway Ave., San Francisco, CA 94132. Phone: (415)338-1478 Fax: (415)338-6159 E-mail: jimdavis@sfsu.edu • URL: http://www.sfsu.edu/~iac • Research areas include multimedia, computerized experimental arts processes, and digital sound.

UCLA Film and Television Archive-Research and Study Center. University of California, Los Angeles, 405 Hhilgard Ave., 45 Powell Library, Los Angeles, CA 90095-1517. Phone: (310)206-5388 Fax: (310)206-5392 E-mail: arsc@ucla.edu • URL: http://www.cinema.ucla.edu/ • Research areas include animation.

TRADE/PROFESSIONAL ASSOCIATIONS

International Animated Film Society, ASIFA-Hollywood. 725 S. Victory Blvd., Burbank, CA 91502. Phone: (818)842-8330 Fax: (818)842-5645 E-mail: info@asita.hollywood.org • URL: http://www.home.earthlink.net/~asifa • Members are professional animation artists, fans, and students. Promotes advancements in the art of animation.

Special Interest Group on Computer Graphics and Interactive Techniques. Association for Computing Machinery, 1515 Broadway, New York, NY 10036. Phone: (212)869-7440 Fax: (212)302-5826 E-mail: sigs@acm.org • URL: http://www.acm.org/siggraph • Concerned with research, technology, and applications for the technical, academic, business, and art communities. Publishes the quarterly newsletter *Computer Graphics*.

COMPUTER BULLETIN BOARDS

See: COMPUTER COMMUNICATIONS

COMPUTER COMMUNICATIONS

See also: INTERNET; LOCAL AREA NETWORKS; MICROCOMPUTERS AND MINICOMPUTERS; ONLINE INFORMATION SYSTEMS; TELECOMMUNICATIONS; TELECOMMUTING

GENERAL WORKS

Analog and Digital Communications. Hwei P. Hsu. McGraw-Hill. • 1997. $15.95.

Computer Networks. Andrew S. Tanenbaum. Prentice Hall. • 1996. $85.00. Third edition.

Data Smog: Surviving the Information Glut. David Shenk. HarperCollins Publishers. • 1997. $24.00. A critical view of both the electronic and print information industries. Emphasis is on information overload.

Digital Literacy: Personal Preparation for the Internet Age. Paul Gilster. John Wiley and Sons, Inc. • 1997. $22.95. Provides practical advice for the online consumer on how to evaluate various aspects of the Internet ("digital literacy" is required, as well as "print literacy").

Interface Culture: How New Technology Transforms the Way We Create and Communicate. Steven Johnson. HarperCollins Publishers. • 1997. $24.00. A discussion of how computer interfaces and online technology ("cyberspace") affect society in general.

Internet for Everyone: A Guide for Users and Providers. Richard Wiggins. McGraw-Hill. • 1994. $29.95.

What Will Be: How the New World of Information Will Change Our Lives. Michael L. Dertouzos. HarperSan Francisco. • 1997. $25.00. A discussion of the "information market place" of the future, including telecommuting, virtual reality, and computer recognition of speech. The author is director of the MIT Laboratory for Computer Science.

Wired Neighborhood. Stephen Doheny-Farina. Yale University Press. • 1996. $32.00. The author examines both the hazards and the advantages of "making the computer the center of our public and private lives," as exemplified by the Internet and telecommuting.

ABSTRACTS AND INDEXES

Applied Science and Technology Index. H. W. Wilson Co. • 11 times a year. Quarterly and annual cumulations. Service basis for print edition; CD-ROM edition, $1,495.00 per year. Indexes a wide variety of English language technical, industrial, and engineering periodicals.

Business Periodicals Index. H. W. Wilson Co. • Monthly, except August, with quarterly and annual cumulations. Service basis for print edition; CD-ROM edition, $1,495.00 per year.

Communication Abstracts. Sage Publications, Inc. • Bimonthly. Individuals, $185.00 per year; institutions, $805.00 per year. Provides broad coverage of the literature of communications, including broadcasting and advertising.

Computer and Control Abstracts. Available from INSPEC, Inc. • Monthly. $2,160.00 per year. Section C of *Science Abstracts*.

Computer and Information Systems Abstracts Journal: An Abstract Journal Pertaining to the Theory, Design, Fabrication and Application of Computer and Information Systems. Cambridge Information Group. • Monthly. $1,045 per year.

Computer Literature Index: A Subject/Author Index to Computer and Data Processing Literature. Applied Computer Research, Inc. • Quarterly, with annual cumulation. $245.00 per year. Contains brief abstracts of book and periodical literature covering all phases of computing, including approximately 70 specific application areas.

Current Contents: Engineering, Computing and Technology. Institute for Scientific Information. • Weekly. $730.00 per year. Reproductions of contents pages of technical journals. Includes *Author Index, Address Directory, Current Book Contents* and *Title Word Index*. Formerly *Current Contents: Engineering, Technology and Applied Sciences*.

Electronics and Communications Abstracts Journal: Comprehensive Coverage of Essential Scientific Literature. Cambridge Information Group. • Monthly. $1,045.00 per year.

Key Abstracts: Computer Communications and Storage. Available from INSPEC, Inc. • Monthly. $240.00 per year. Provides international coverage of journal and proceedings literature, including material on optical disks and networks. Published in England by the Institution of Electrical Engineers (IEE).

LAMP (Literature Analysis of Microcomputer Publications). Soft Images. • Bimonthly. $89.95 per year. Annual cumulation.

Science Citation Index. Institute for Scientific Information. • Bimonthly. $15,020.00 per year. Annual cumulation. Includes *Source Index*, *Citation Index*, *Permuterm Subject Index*, and *Corporate Index*.

ALMANACS AND YEARBOOKS

Communication Technology Update. Focal Press. • Annual. $32.95. A yearly review of developments in electronic media, telecommunications, and the Internet.

BIBLIOGRAPHIES

Computer Book Review. • Quarterly. $30.00 per year. Includes annual index. Reviews new computer books. Back issues available.

DIRECTORIES

Boardwatch Magazine Directory of Internet Service Providers. Penton Media Inc. • Monthly. $36.00 per year. Lists thousands of Internet service providers by state and telephone area code, with monthly fees, ISDN availability, and other information. Includes a "Glossary of Internet Terms" and detailed technical articles on accessing the Internet.

Business Organizations, Agencies, and Publications Directory. The Gale Group. • 1999. $425.00. 12th edition. Over 40,000 entries describing 39 types of business information sources. Classified by type of organization, publication, or serviceIncludes state, national, and international agencies and organizations. Master index to names and keywords. Also includes e-mail addresses and web site URL's.

Computer Review. • Semiannual. $425.00 per year; renewal subscription, $355.00 per year. A complete reference to the global internet market. Covers top 1,000 information technology companies.

Cyberhound's Guide to International Discussion Groups. Visible Ink Press. • 1996. $79.00 Second edition. Presents critical descriptions and ratings of more tha 4,400 Internet discussion groups (newsgroups) covering a wide variety of topics.

Data Communications Production Selection Guide. McGraw-Hill. • Semiannual. $25.00. List of networking vendors. Formerly *Data Communications Buyer's Guide.*

Dial Up! Gale's Bulletin Board Locator. The Gale Group. • 1996. $49.00. Contains access and other information for 10,000 computer bulletin boards in the U. S. Arranged geographically, with indexes to bulletin board names, organizations, and topics.

Directory of Top Computer Executives. Applied Computer Research, Inc. • Semiannual. Price varies. Two volumes. Lists large companies and government agencies, with names of their data and systems executives.

Information Sources: The Annual Directory of the Information Industry Association. Software and Information Industry Association. • Annual. Members, $75.00; non-members, $125.00.

MicroLeads Vendor Directory on Disk (Personal Computer Industry). Chromatic Communications Enterprises, Inc. • Annual. $495.00. Includes computer hardware manufacturers, software producers, book-periodical publishers, and franchised or company-owned chains of personal computer equipment retailers, support services and accessory manufacturers. Formerly *MicroLeads U.S. Vender Directory.*

Network Buyers Guide. Miller Freeman. • Annual. $5.00. Lists suppliers of products for local and wide area computer networks. Formerly *LAN Buyers Guide Issue.*

Plunkett's E-Commerce and Internet Business Almanac. Plunkett Research, Ltd. • Annual. $199.99. Contains detailed profiles of 250 large companies engaged in various areas of Internet commerce, including e-business Web sites, communications equipment manufacturers, and Internet service providers. Includes CD-ROM.

Plunkett's InfoTech Industry Almanac: Complete Profiles on the InfoTech 500-the Leading Firms in the Movement and Management of Voice, Data, and Video. Available from Plunkett Research, Ltd. • Annual. $149.99. Five hundred major information companies are profiled, with corporate culture aspects. Discusses major trends in various sectors of the computer and information industry, including data on careers and job growth. Includes several indexes.

Telecommunications Directory. The Gale Group. • 2000. $595.00. 12th edition. National and international voice, data, facsimile, and video communications services. Formerly *Telecommunications Systems and Services Directory.*

ENCYCLOPEDIAS AND DICTIONARIES

CyberDictionary: Your Guide to the Wired World. Knowledge Exchange LLC. • 1996. $17.95. Includes many illustrations.

Dictionary of Computing. Valerie Illingworth, editor. Oxford University Press, Inc. • 1996. $49.95. Fourth edition.

Dictionary of Information Technology and Computer Science. Tony Gunton. Blackwell Publishers. • 1994. $50.95. Second edition. Covers key words, phrases, abbreviations, and acronyms used in computing and data communications.

Dictionary of PC Hardware and Data Communications Terms. Mitchell Shnier. Thomson Learning. • 1996. $19.95. (Online updates to print version available at http://www.ora.com/reference/dictionary.).

Encyclopedia of Communication and Information. Available from The Gale Group. • 2001. $325.00. Three volumes. Published by Macmillan Reference USA.

Every Manager's Guide to Information Technology: A Glossary of Key Terms and Concepts for Today's Business Leader. Peter G. W. Keen. Harvard Business School Press. • 1995. $18.95. Second edition. Provides definitions of terms related to computers, data communications, and information network systems. (Harvard Business Economist Reference Series).

HANDBOOKS AND MANUALS

Compuserve Internet Tour Guide. Richard Wagner. Ventana Communications Group, Inc. • 1996. $34.95. A detailed guide to accessing various features of the Internet by way of the Compuserve online service.

The Cybrarian's Manual. Pat Ensor, editor. American Library Association. • 1996. $35.00. Provides information for librarians concerning the Internet, expert systems, computer networks, client/server architecture, Web pages, multimedia, information industry careers, and other "cyberspace" topics.

The Essential Guide to Bulletin Board Systems. Patrick R. Dewey. Information Today, Inc. • 1998. $39.50. Provides details on the setup and operation of online bulletin board systems. Covers both hardware and software.

The Modem Reference: The Complete Guide to PC Communications. Michael A. Banks. Information Today, Inc. • 2000. $29.95. Fourth edition. Covers personal computer data communications technology, including fax transmissions, computer networks, modems, and the Internet. Popularly written.

The Official America Online Internet Guide. David Peal. Ventana Communications Group, Inc. • 1999. $24.95. Provides a detailed explanation of the various features of versio of America Online, including electronic mail procedures and "Using the Internet.".

INTERNET DATABASES

InfoTech Trends. Data Analysis Group. Phone: (707)894-9100 Fax: (707)486-5618 E-mail: support@infotechtrends.com • URL: http://www.infotechtrends.com • Web site provides both free and fee-based market research data on the information technology industry, including computers, peripherals, telecommunications, the Internet, software, CD-ROM/DVD, e-commerce, and workstations. Fees: Free for current (most recent year) data; more extensive information has various fee structures. Formerly *Computer Industry Forecasts.*

Interactive Week: The Internet's Newspaper. Ziff Davis Media, Inc. 28 E. 28th St., New York, NY 10016. Phone: (212)503-3500 Fax: (212)503-5680 E-mail: iweekinfo@zd.com • URL: http://www.zd.com • Weekly. $99.00 per year. Covers news and trends relating to Internet commerce, computer communications, and telecommunications.

ONLINE DATABASES

ABI/INFORM. Bell & Howell Information and Learning. • Provides online indexing to business-related material occurring in over 1,000 periodicals from 1971 to the present. Inquire as to online cost and availability.

Applied Science and Technology Index Online. H. W. Wilson Co. • Provides online indexing of 400 major scientific, technical, industrial, and engineering periodicals. Time period is 1983 to date. Monthly updates. Inquire as to online cost and availability.

Computer Database. The Gale Group. • Provides online citations with abstracts to material appearing in about 150 trade journals and newsletters in the subject areas of computers, telecommunications, and electronics. Time period is 1983 to date, with weekly updates. Inquire as to online cost and availability.

Globalbase. The Gale Group. • Provides more than one million online summaries of business, industrial, and economic news reports from more than 1,000 publications worldwide. Covers a wide range of material appearing in international trade journals, professional magazines, and newspapers. Time period is 1984 to date, with weekly updates. Inquire as to online cost and availability.

Internet and Personal Computing Abstracts. Information Today, Inc. • Contains abstracts covering a wide variety of personal and business microcomputer literature appearing in more than 100 journals and popular magazines. Time period is 1981 to date, with monthly updates. Formerly *Microcomputer Index.* Inquire as to online cost and availability.

Management Contents. The Gale Group. • Covers a wide range of management, financial, marketing, personnel, and administrative topics. About 150 leading business journals are indexed and abstracted from 1974 to date, with monthly updating. Inquire as to online cost and availability.

PROMT: Predicasts Overview of Markets and Technology. The Gale Group. • Companies, products, applied technologies and markets. U.S. and international literature coverage, 1972 to date. Inquire as to online cost and availability. Provides abstracts from more than 1,600 publications. Weekly updates.

Scisearch. Institute for Scientific Information. • Broad, multidisciplinary index to the literature of science and technology, 1974 to present. Inquire as to online cost and availability. Coverage of literature is worldwide, with weekly updates.

Trade & Industry Index. The Gale Group. • Provides indexing of business periodicals, January 1981 to date. Daily updates. (Full text articles from some periodicals are available online, 1983 to date, in the companion database, *Trade & Industry ASAP.*) Inquire as to online cost and availability.

Wilson Business Abstracts Online. H. W. Wilson Co. • Indexes and abstracts 600 major business periodicals, plus the *Wall Street Journal* and the business section of the *New York Times*. Indexing is from 1982, abstracting from 1990, with the two newspapers included from 1993. Updated weekly. Inquire as to online cost and availability. (*Business Periodicals Index* without abstracts is also available online.).

PERIODICALS AND NEWSLETTERS

Boardwatch Magazine: Guide to the Internet, World Wide Web, and BBS. Penton Media Inc. • Monthly. $72.00 per year. Covers World Wide Web publishing, Internet technology, educational aspects of online communication, Internet legalities, and other computer communication topics.

Business Communications Review. BCR Enterprises, Inc. • Bimonthly. $45.00 per year. Edited for communications managers in large end-user companies and institutions. Includes special feature issues on intranets and network management.

CIO: The Magazine for Information Executives. CIO Communications. • Semimonthly. $89.00 per year. Edited for chief information officers. Includes a monthly "Web Business" section (incorporates the former *WebMaster* periodical) and a monthly "Enterprise" section for company executives other than CIOs.

Communications News. American Society of Association Executives Communications Section. • Monthly. Membership.

Communications News: Solutions for Today's Networking Decision Managers. Nelson Publishing, Inc. • Monthly. Free to qualified personnel; others, $79.00 per year. Includes coverage of "Internetworking" and "Intrenetworking." Emphasis is on emerging telecommunications technologies.

Computer Communications Review. Association for Computing Machinery, Special Interest Group on Data Communicatio. • Quarterly. $37.00 per year.

Computer Industry Report. International Data Corp. • Semimonthly. $495.00 per year. Newsletter. Annual supplement. Also known as "The Gray Sheet." Formerly *EDP Industry Report and Market Review.*

Computerworld: Newsweekly for Information Technology Leaders. Computerworld, Inc. • Weekly. $39.95 per year.

Data Communications. CMP Media, Inc. • 18 times a year. $125.00 per year.

Electronic Messaging News: Strategies, Applications, and Standards. Phillips Business Information, Inc. • Biweekly. $597.00 per year. Newsletter.

IEEE Communications Magazine. Institute of Electrical and Electronics Engineers. • Monthly. $190.00 per year.

Information Processing and Management: An International Journal. Elsevier Science. • Bimonthly. $981.00 per year. Text in English, French, German and Italian.

Information Today: The Newspaper for Users and Producers of Electronic Information Services. Information Today, Inc. • 11 times a year. $57.95 per year.

Insurance Networking: Strategies and Solutions for Electronic Commerce. Faulkner & Gray, Inc. • 10 times a year. $63.95 per year. Covers information technology for the insurance industry, with emphasis on computer communications and the Internet.

Interactive Marketing and P R News: News and Practical Advice on Using Interactive Advertising and Marketing to Sell Your Products. Phillips Business Information, Inc. • Biweekly. $495.00 per year. Newsletter. Provides information and guidance on merchandising via CD-ROM ("multimedia catalogs"), the Internet, and interactive TV. Topics include "cybermoney", addresses for e-mail marketing, "virtual malls," and other interactive subjects. Formerly *Interactive Marketing News.*

International Journal of Communication Systems. Available from John Wiley and Sons, Inc., Journals Div. • Bimonthly. Institutions, $995.00 per year. Published in England by John Wiley and Sons Ltd. Formerly *International Journal of Digital and Analog Communication Systems.*

Internet Business Journal: Commercial Opportunities in the Networking Age. Strangelove Internet Enterprises, Inc. • Monthly. $149.00 per year. $75.00 per year to individuals and nonprofit libraries. Emphasis is on commercial opportunities presented by the Internet.

Interoperability. Miller Freeman, Inc. • Quarterly. Price on application. Covers the operation of wide-area networks, including UNIX systems.

Link-Up: The Newsmagazine for Users of Online Services, CD-Rom, and the Internet. Information Today, Inc. • Bimonthly. $29.95 per year.

Network Computing: Computing in a Network Environment. CMP Publications, Inc. • Semimonthly. $95.00 per year.

Network: Strategies and Solutions for the Network Professional. Miller Freeman. • Monthly. $29.95 per year. Covers network products and peripherals for computer professionals. Includes annual network managers salary survey and annual directory issue. Formerly *LAN: The Network Solutions Magazine.*

Network World: The Newsweekly of Enterprise Network Computing. Network World Inc. • Weekly. $129.00 per year. Includes special feature issues on enterprise Internets, network operating systems, network management, high-speed modems, LAN management systems, and Internet access providers.

Online: The Leading Magazine for Information Professionals. Online, Inc. • Bimonthly. $110.00 per year. General coverage of the online information industry.

PCS Systems and Technology: Personal Communications Services Technology of the Digital Wireless Age. Cahners Business Information. • Nine times a year. Price on application. Covers network management and other technical topics.

Silicon Alley Reporter. Rising Tide Studios. • Monthly. $29.95 per year. Covers the latest trends in e-commerce, multimedia, and the Internet.

Tele.com: Business and Technology for Public Network Service Providers. CMP Publications, Inc. • 14 times a year. $125.00 per year. Edited for executives and managers at both traditional telephone companies and wireless communications companies. Also provides news and information for Internet services providers and cable TV operators.

Telecom Business: Opportunities for Network Service Providers, Resellers, and Suppliers in the Competitive Telecom Industry. MultiMedia Publishing Corp. • Monthly. $56.95 per year. Provides business and technical information for telecommunications executives in various fields.

Telematics and Informatics: An International Journal. Elsevier Science. • Quarterly. $713.00 per year.

Wired. Wired Ventures Ltd. • Monthly. $24.00 per year. Edited for creators and managers in various areas of electronic information and entertainment, including multimedia, the Internet, and video. Often considered to be the primary publication of the "digital generation.".

Wireless Data News. Phillips Business Information, Inc. • 25 times a year. $797.00 per year. Newsletter. Covers the wireless data communications industry, including wireless LANs.

Wireless Integration: Solutions for Enterprise Decision Makers. PennWell Corp., Advanced Technology Div. • Bimonthly. $48.00 per year. Edited for networking and communications managers. Special issues cover the wireless office, wireless intranet/Internet, mobile wireless, telemetry, and buyer's guide directory information.

Wireless Review: Intelligence for Competitive Providers. Intertec Publishing Corp. • Semimonthly. $48.00 per year. Covers business and technology developments for wireless service providers. Includes special issues on a wide variety of wireless topics. Formed by merger of *Cellular Business* and *Wireless World.*

RESEARCH CENTERS AND INSTITUTES

Center for Research in Computing Technology. Harvard University, Pierce Hall, 29 Oxford St., Cambridge, MA 02138. Phone: (617)495-2832 Fax: (617)495-9837 E-mail: cheatham@das.harvard.edu • URL: http://www.das.harvard.edu/cs.grafs.html • Conducts research in computer vision, robotics, artificial intelligence, systems programming, programming languages, operating systems, networks, graphics, database management systems, and telecommunications.

Concord Consortium, Inc. 37 Thoreau St., Concord, MA 01742. Phone: (978)369-4367 Fax: (978)371-0696 E-mail: shea@concord.org • URL: http://www.concord.org • Research areas include educational applications of computers and computer networks.

Information Sciences Institute. University of Southern California, 4676 Admiralty Way, Suite 1001, Marina del Rey, CA 90292. Phone: (310)822-1511 Fax: (310)823-6714 • URL: http://www.isi.edu • Research fields include online information and computer science, with emphasis on the World Wide Web.

Laboratory for Information and Decision Systems. Massachusetts Institute of Technology, Bldg. 35, Room 308, Cambridge, MA 02139-4307. Phone: (617)253-2141 Fax: (617)253-3578 E-mail: chan@mit.edu • URL: http://www.justice.mit.edu • Research areas include data communication networks and fiber optic networks.

STATISTICS SOURCES

Communication Equipment, and Other Electronic Systems and Equipment. U. S. Bureau of the Census. • Annual. Provides data on shipments: value, quantity, imports, and exports. (Current Industrial Reports, MA-36P.).

OECD Information Technology Outlook 2000: ICTs, E-Commerce and the Information Economy. Organization for Economic Cooperation and Development. • 2000. $72.00. Provides data on information and communications technology (ICT) and electronic commerce in 11 OECD nations (includes U. S.). Coverage includes network infrastructure, electronic payment systems, financial transaction technologies, intelligent agents, global navigation systems, and portable flat panel display technologies.

Standard & Poor's Industry Surveys. Standard & Poor's. • Semiannual. $1,800.00. Two looseleaf volumes. Includes monthly supplements. Provides detailed, individual surveys of 52 major industry groups. Each survey is revised on a semiannual basis. Also includes "Monthly Investment Review" (industry group investment analysis) and monthly "Trends & Projections" (economic analysis).

TRADE/PROFESSIONAL ASSOCIATIONS

Association for Interactive Media. 1301 Connecticut Ave. N.W., 5th Fl., Washington, DC 20036-5105. Phone: (202)408-0008 Fax: (202)408-0111 E-mail: info@interactivehg.org • URL: http://www.interactivehg.org • Members are companies engaged in various interactive enterprises, utilizing the Internet, interactive television, computer communications, and multimedia.

Computer and Communications Industry Association. 666 11th St., N.W., Suite 600, Washington, DC 20001. Phone: (202)783-0070 Fax: (202)783-0534 E-mail: ccianet@aol.com • URL: http://www.ccianet.org.

Electronic Frontier Foundation. 1550 Bryant St., Suite 725, San Francisco, CA 94103. Phone: (415)436-9333 Fax: (415)436-9993 E-mail: info@eff.org • URL: http://www.eff.org • Members are individuals with an interest in computer-based communications. Promotes electronic communication civil liberties and First Amendment rights.

IEEE Computer Society. 1730 Massachusetts Ave., N. W., Washington, DC 20036. Phone: (202)371-0101 Fax: (202)728-9614 E-mail: csinfo@computer.org • URL: http://www.computer.org • A society of the Institute of Electrical and Electronics Engineers. Said to be the world's largest organization of computer professionals. Some of the specific committees are: Computer Communications; Computer Graphics; Computers in Education; Design Automation; Office Automation; Personal Computing; Robotics; Security and Privacy; Software Engineering.

International Council for Computer Communication. P.O. Box 9745, Washington, DC 20016-9745. Phone: (703)836-7787 Fax: (703)836-7787 E-mail: iccc@icccgovernors.org • URL: http://www.icccgovernors.org.

International Interactive Communications Society. 4840 McKnight Rd., Suite A, Pittsburgh, PA 15237. Phone: (412)734-1928 Fax: (412)369-3507 E-mail: worldhq@iics.org • URL: http://www.iics.org • Members are interactive media professionals concerned with intetractive arts and technologies.

Special Interest Group on Data Communication. Association for Computing Machinery, 1515 Broadway, New York, NY 10036. Phone: (212)869-7440 Fax: (212)302-5826 E-mail: sigs@acm.org • URL: http://www.acm.org/sigcomm • Focuses on network architecture, protocols, and distributed systems. Publishes a quarterly newsletter *Computer Communication Review*.

Special Interest Group on Management of Data. Association for Computing Machinery, 1515 Broadway, New York, NY 10036. Phone: (212)869-7440 Fax: (212)302-5826 E-mail: sigs@acm.org • URL: http://www.acm.org/sigmod • Concerned with database management systems. Publishes the quarterly newsletter *SIGMOD Record*.

Special Interest Group on Supporting Group Work. Association for Computing, 1515 Broadway, 17th Fl., New York, NY 10036. Phone: (212)869-7440 Fax: (212)302-5826 E-mail: rivkin@acm.org • URL: http://www.acm.org/siggroup/ • Concerned with office automation and computer communications.

OTHER SOURCES

Faulkner's Enterprise Networking. Faulkner Information Services, Inc. • Three looseleaf volumes, with monthly updates. $1,275.00 per year. Contains product reports and management articles relating to computer communications and networking. Available on CD-ROM. Quarterly updates. Formerly *Data Communications Reports*.

Major Information Technology Companies of the World. Available from The Gale Group. • 2001. $885.00. Third edition. Published by Graham & Whiteside. Contains profiles of more than 2,600 leading information technology companies in various countries.

Major Telecommunications Companies of the World. Available from The Gale Group. • 2001. $855.00. Fourth edition. Published by Graham & Whiteside. Contains detailed information and trade names for more than 4,000 important telecommunications companies in various countries.

Wireless Data Networks. Warren Publishing Inc. • 1998. $1,995.00. Fourth edition. Presents market research information relating to cellular data networks, paging networks, packet radio networks, satellite systems, and other areas of wireless communication. Contains "summaries of recent developments and trends in wireless markets.".

COMPUTER CRIME AND SECURITY

GENERAL WORKS

Computer Virus Crisis. Philip E. Fites and others. DIANE Publishing Co. • 1999. $15.00. Second reprint edition.

ABSTRACTS AND INDEXES

Applied Science and Technology Index. H. W. Wilson Co. • 11 times a year. Quarterly and annual cumulations. Service basis for print edition; CD-ROM edition, $1,495.00 per year. Indexes a wide variety of English language technical, industrial, and engineering periodicals.

Business Periodicals Index. H. W. Wilson Co. • Monthly, except August, with quarterly and annual cumulations. Service basis for print edition; CD-ROM edition, $1,495.00 per year.

Computer and Control Abstracts. Available from INSPEC, Inc. • Monthly. $2,160.00 per year. Section C of *Science Abstracts*.

Computer and Information Systems Abstracts Journal: An Abstract Journal Pertaining to the Theory, Design, Fabrication and Application of Computer and Information Systems. Cambridge Information Group. • Monthly. $1,045 per year.

Computer Literature Index: A Subject/Author Index to Computer and Data Processing Literature. Applied Computer Research, Inc. • Quarterly, with annual cumulation. $245.00 per year. Contains brief abstracts of book and periodical literature covering all phases of computing, including approximately 70 specific application areas.

Current Contents: Engineering, Computing and Technology. Institute for Scientific Information. • Weekly. $730.00 per year. Reproductions of contents pages of technical journals. Includes *Author Index, Address Directory, Current Book Contents* and *Title Word Index*. Formerly *Current Contents: Engineering, Technology and Applied Sciences*.

Microcomputer Abstracts. Information Today, Inc. • Quarterly. $225.00 per year. Provides abstracts covering a wide variety of personal and business microcomputer literature. Formerly *Microcomputer Index*.

DIRECTORIES

Business Organizations, Agencies, and Publications Directory. The Gale Group. • 1999. $425.00. 12th edition. Over 40,000 entries describing 39 types of business information sources. Classified by type of organization, publication, or serviceIncludes state, national, and international agencies and organizations. Master index to names and keywords. Also includes e-mail addresses and web site URL's.

Computer Security Buyer's Guide. Computer Security Institute. • Annual. $95.00. About 650 suppliers and consultants of computer security products.

Faulkner Information Service. Faulkner Information Services, Inc. • Looseleaf. Monthly updates. Many titles and volumes, covering virtually all aspects of computer software and hardware. Gives descriptions and technical data for specific products, including producers' names and addresses. Prices and details on request. Formerly (The Auerbach Series).

Security: Product Service Suppliers Guide. Cahners Business Information. • Annual. $50.00 Includes computer and information protection products. Formerly *Security - World Product Directory*.

ENCYCLOPEDIAS AND DICTIONARIES

Dictionary of Computing. Valerie Illingworth, editor. Oxford University Press, Inc. • 1996. $49.95. Fourth edition.

HANDBOOKS AND MANUALS

Computer Crime Law. Jay J. Bloombecker. West Group. • $125.00 per year. Looseleaf service. Provides analysis of recent case law and emerging trends in computer-related crime. Includes current information on the technical aspects of computer crime.

Computer Security Basics. Deborah F. Russell and G. T. Gangemi. Thomson Learning. • 1991. $29.95. (Computer Science Series).

Corporate Fraud. Michael J. Comer. Available from Ashgate Publishing Co. • 1997. $113.95. Third edition. Examines new risks of corporate fraud related to "electronic commerce, derivatives, computerization, empowerment, downsizing, and other recent developments." Covers fraud detection, prevention, and internal control systems. Published by Gower in England.

Guidelines for Consumer Protection in the Context of Electronic Commerce. Organization for Economic Cooperation and Development. • 2000. $20.00. Provides a guide to effective consumer protection in online business-to-consumer transactions.

Halting the Hacker: A Guide to Computer Security. Donald A. Pipkin. Prentice Hall. • 1996. $44.95.

Short Course on Computer Viruses. Frederick B. Cohen. John Wiley and Sons, Inc. • 1994. $44.95. Second edition.

Trade Secret Protection in an Information Age. Gale R. Peterson. Glasser Legalworks. • Looseleaf. $149.00, including sample forms on disk. Periodic supplementation available. Covers trade secret law relating to computer software, online databases, and multimedia products. Explanations are based on more than 1,000 legal cases. Sample forms on disk include work-for-hire examples and covenants not to compete.

ONLINE DATABASES

Applied Science and Technology Index Online. H. W. Wilson Co. • Provides online indexing of 400 major scientific, technical, industrial, and engineering periodicals. Time period is 1983 to date. Monthly updates. Inquire as to online cost and availability.

Computer Database. The Gale Group. • Provides online citations with abstracts to material appearing in about 150 trade journals and newsletters in the subject areas of computers, telecommunications, and electronics. Time period is 1983 to date, with weekly updates. Inquire as to online cost and availability.

Internet and Personal Computing Abstracts. Information Today, Inc. • Contains abstracts covering a wide variety of personal and business microcomputer literature appearing in more than 100 journals and popular magazines. Time period is 1981 to date, with monthly updates. Formerly *Microcomputer Index.* Inquire as to online cost and availability.

PROMT: Predicasts Overview of Markets and Technology. The Gale Group. • Companies, products, applied technologies and markets. U.S. and international literature coverage, 1972 to date. Inquire as to online cost and availability. Provides abstracts from more than 1,600 publications. Weekly updates.

Wilson Business Abstracts Online. H. W. Wilson Co. • Indexes and abstracts 600 major business periodicals, plus the *Wall Street Journal* and the business section of the *New York Times.* Indexing is from 1982, abstracting from 1990, with the two newspapers included from 1993. Updated weekly. Inquire as to online cost and availability. (*Business Periodicals Index* without abstracts is also available online.).

PERIODICALS AND NEWSLETTERS

Computer Fraud and Security. Elsevier Science. • Monthly. $710.00 per year. Newsletter. Formerly *Computer Fraud and Security Bulletin.*

Computer Industry Report. International Data Corp. • Semimonthly. $495.00 per year. Newsletter. Annual supplement. Also known as "The Gray Sheet." Formerly *EDP Industry Report and Market Review.*

Computer-Law Journal: International Journal of Computer, Communication and Information Law. Center for Computer Law. • Quarterly. $97.50 per year.

Computer Security Digest. Jack Bologna. Computer Protection Systems, Inc. • Monthly. $125.00 per year. Newsletter. Abstracts of news events that involve computer crimes and security.

Computer Security Journal. Computer Security Institute. Miller Freeman, Inc. • Semiannual. $100.00 per year.

Computers and Security: The International Journal Devoted to the Study of the Technical and Financial Aspects of Computer Security. International Federation for Information Processing on Computer Security. Elsevier Science. • Eight times a year. $648.00 per year.

EDP Weekly: The Leading Weekly Computer News Summary. Computer Age and E D P News Services. • Weekly. $495.00 per year. Newsletter. Summarizes news from all areas of the computer and microcomputer industries.

FBI Law Enforcement Bulletin. Available from U. S. Government Printing Office. • Monthly. $36.00 per year. Issued by Federal Bureau of Investigation, U. S. Department of Justice. Contains articles on a wide variety of law enforcement and crime topics, including computer-related crime.

Information Systems Security. Auerbach Publications. • Quarterly. $175.00 per year. Formerly *Journal of Information Systems Security.*

Responsible Computing. National Center for Computer Crime Data. • Semiannual. $54.00 per year. Newsletter.

Security Management. American Society for Industrial Security. • Monthly. Free to members; non-members, $48.00 per year. Articles cover the protection of corporate assets, including personnel property and information security.

Security: The Magazine for Buyers of Security Products, Systems and Service. Cahners Business Information. • Monthly. $82.90 per year.

Software Law Journal. Center for Computer Law. • Quarterly. $97.50 per year.

White-Collar Crime Reporter: Information and Analyses Concerning White-Collar Practice. Andrews Publications. • 10 times a year. $550.00 per year. Newsletter. Provides information on trends in white collar crime.

TRADE/PROFESSIONAL ASSOCIATIONS

ASIS International (American Society for Industrial Security). 1625 Prince St., Alexandria, VA 22314-2818. Phone: (703)519-6200 Fax: (703)519-6299 • URL: http://www.asisonline.org.

Computer Security Institute. 600 Harrison St., San Francisco, CA 94107. Phone: (415)905-2626 Fax: (415)905-2218 E-mail: csi@mfi.com • URL: http://www.gocsi.com.

IEEE Computer Society. 1730 Massachusetts Ave., N. W., Washington, DC 20036. Phone: (202)371-0101 Fax: (202)728-9614 E-mail: csinfo@computer.org • URL: http://www.computer.org • A society of the Institute of Electrical and Electronics Engineers. Said to be the world's largest organization of computer professionals. Some of the specific committees are: Computer Communications; Computer Graphics; Computers in Education; Design Automation; Office Automation; Personal Computing; Robotics; Security and Privacy; Software Engineering.

National Center for Computer Crime Data. 1222 17th Ave., Suite B, Santa Cruz, CA 95062. Phone: (408)475-4457 Fax: (408)475-5336 E-mail: nudnic@ix.netcom.com • Conducts research, compiles statistics, provides case studies and other information.

Special Interest Group on Security, Audit, and Control. c/o Association for Computing Machinery, 1515 Broadway, 17th Fl., New York, NY 10036. Phone: (212)869-7440 Fax: (212)302-5826 E-mail: acmhelp@acm.org • URL: http://www.acm.org/sig_hp/sigsac.html.

OTHER SOURCES

DataWorld. Faulkner Information Services, Inc. • Four looseleaf volumes, with monthly supplements. $1,395.00 per year. Describes and evaluates both hardware and software relating to midrange, micro, and mainframe computers. Available on CD-ROM.

Faulkner's Local Area Networking. Faulkner Information Services, Inc. • Looseleaf, with monthly updates. $715.00 per year. Contains product reports and other information relating to PC networking, including security, gateways/bridges, and emerging standards. Formerly *Microcomputer Communications.*

COMPUTER DEALERS

See: COMPUTER RETAILING

COMPUTER GRAPHICS

See also: COMPUTER-AIDED DESIGN AND MANUFACTURING (CAD/CAM); COMPUTER ANIMATION

GENERAL WORKS

Computer Graphics. Donald Hearn and M. Pauline Baker. Prentice Hall. • 2000. Price on application.

ABSTRACTS AND INDEXES

Computer Literature Index: A Subject/Author Index to Computer and Data Processing Literature. Applied Computer Research, Inc. • Quarterly, with annual cumulation. $245.00 per year. Contains brief abstracts of book and periodical literature covering all phases of computing, including approximately 70 specific application areas.

LAMP (Literature Analysis of Microcomputer Publications). Soft Images. • Bimonthly. $89.95 per year. Annual cumulation.

ALMANACS AND YEARBOOKS

Advances in Computer Vision and Image Processing. JAI Press, Inc. • Dates vary. $270.75. Three volumes. Volume one, $90.25; volume two, $90.25; volume three,$90.25.

BIBLIOGRAPHIES

Computer Book Review. • Quarterly. $30.00 per year. Includes annual index. Reviews new computer books. Back issues available.

DIRECTORIES

Directory of Video, Computer, and Audio-Visual Products. International Communications Industries Association. • Annual. $65.00. Contains detailed descriptions and photographs of specific items of equipment. Includes video cameras, overhead projectors, LCD panels, computer projection systems, film recording equipment, etc. A "Glossary of Terms" is also provided.

S. Klein Directory of Computer Suppliers: Hardware, Software, Systems and Services. Technology and Business Communications, Inc. • 1987. $73.00.

The SHOOT Directory for Commercial Production and Postproduction. BPI Communications. • Annual. $79.00. Lists production companies, advertising agencies, and sources of professional television, motion picture, and audio equipment.

ENCYCLOPEDIAS AND DICTIONARIES

Dictionary of Computer Graphics Technology and Application. Roy Lanham. Springer-Verlag New York, Inc. • 1995. $21.95. Second edition.

Graphically Speaking: An Illustrated Guide to the Working Language of Design and Publishing. Mark Beach. Coast to Coast Books. • 1992. $29.50. Provides practical definitions of 2,800 terms used in printing, graphic design, publishing, and desktop publishing. Over 300 illustrations are included, about 40 in color.

HANDBOOKS AND MANUALS

Designing Infographics. Eric K. Meyer. Hayden. • 1997. $39.99. A basic handbook on the design and presentation of computer-generated charts, graphs, tables, maps, diagrams, etc.

An Interactive Guide to Multimedia. Que Education and Training. • 1996. $85.00, including CD-ROM. Explains multimedia production and application, including graphics, text, video, sound, editing, etc.

Learning Web Design: A Beginner's Guide to HTML, Graphics, and Beyond. Jennifer Niederst. O'Reilly & Associates, Inc. • 2001. $34.95. Written for beginners who have no previous knowledge of how Web design works.

Web Style Guide: Basic Design Principles for Creating Web Sites. Patrick J. Lynch and Sarah

Horton. Yale University Press. • 1999. $35.00. Covers design of content, interface, page layout, graphics, and multimedia aspects.

ONLINE DATABASES

Computer Database. The Gale Group. • Provides online citations with abstracts to material appearing in about 150 trade journals and newsletters in the subject areas of computers, telecommunications, and electronics. Time period is 1983 to date, with weekly updates. Inquire as to online cost and availability.

Internet and Personal Computing Abstracts. Information Today, Inc. • Contains abstracts covering a wide variety of personal and business microcomputer literature appearing in more than 100 journals and popular magazines. Time period is 1981 to date, with monthly updates. Formerly *Microcomputer Index.* Inquire as to online cost and availability.

PROMT: Predicasts Overview of Markets and Technology. The Gale Group. • Companies, products, applied technologies and markets. U.S. and international literature coverage, 1972 to date. Inquire as to online cost and availability. Provides abstracts from more than 1,600 publications. Weekly updates.

PERIODICALS AND NEWSLETTERS

ACM Transactions on Graphics. Association for Computing Machinery. • Semiannual. Free to members; non-members, $110.00 per year.

Advanced Manufacturing Technology: Monthly Report. Technical Insights. • Monthly. $695.00 per year. Newsletter. Covers technological developments relating to robotics, computer graphics, automation, computer-integrated manufacturing, and machining.

Computer Graphics. Special Interest Group on Computer Graphics. • Quarterly. Members, $59.00 per year; non-members, $95.00 per year; students, $50.00 per year.

Computer Graphics World. PennWell Corp., Advanced Technology Div. • Monthly. $55.00 per year.

Computers and Graphics: International Journal of Systems Applications in Computer Graphic. Elsevier Science. • Bimonthly. $1,444.00 per year.

Desktop Publishers Journal. Business Media Group LLC. • Ten times a year. $49.00 per year. Edited for professional publishers, graphic designers, and industry service providers. Covers new products and emerging technologies for the electronic publishing industry.

Engineering Design Graphics Journal. American Society for Engineering Education. • Three times a year. Members, $6.00 per year; non-members, $20.00 per year;institutions, $10.00 per year. Concerned with engineering graphics, computer graphics, geometric modeling, computer-aided drafting, etc.

IEEE Computer Graphics and Applications. Insityte of Electrical and Electronics Engineers, Inc. • Bimonthly. Free to members; non-members, $485.00 per year.

IEEE Transactions on Visualization and Computer Graphics. Institute of Electrical and Electronics Engineers. • Quarterly. $490.00 per year. Topics include computer vision, computer graphics, image processing, signal processing, computer-aided design, animation, and virtual reality.

IMAGES. IMAGE Society. • Semiannual. $25.00 per year. Provides news of virtual reality developments and the IMAGE Society.

The Journal of Visualization and Computer Animation. Available from John Wiley and Sons, Inc., Journals Div. • Quarterly. Institutions, $760.00 per year. Research papers on the technological developments (both hardware and software) that will make animation tools more accessible to end-users. International coverage. Published in England by John Wiley and Sons Ltd.

SHOOT: The Leading Newsweekly for Commercial Production and Postproduction. BPI Communications. • Weekly. $115.00 per year. Covers animation, music, sound design, computer graphics, visual effects, cinematography, and other aspects of television and motion picture production, with emphasis on TV commercials.

Step-By-Step Electronic Design: The How-To Newsletter for Electronic Designers. Dynamic Graphics, Inc. • Monthly. $48.00 per year;with*Step-by-Step Graphics*,$90.00 per year.

Step-By-Step Graphics: The How-To Reference Magazine for Visual Communicators. Dynamic Graphics, Inc. • Bimonthly. $42.00 per year; with *Step-by-Step Electronic Design*, $90.00 per year.

RESEARCH CENTERS AND INSTITUTES

Artificial Intelligence and Computer Vision Laboratory. University of Cincinnati, Dept. of Electrical, Computer Engineering and Computer Scien, 802 Rhodes Hall, Cincinnati, OH 45221-0030. Phone: (513)556-4778 Fax: (513)556-7326 E-mail: william.wee@uc.edu • Fields of research include computer vision, computer graphics, and artificial intelligence.

Computer Graphics Laboratory. New York Institute of Technology, Fine Arts, Old Westbury, NY 11568. Phone: (516)686-7542 Fax: (516)686-7428 E-mail: pvoci@nyit.edu • Research areas include computer graphics, computer animation, and digital sound.

Computer Vision Laboratory. University of Maryland, Center for Automation Research, College Park, MD 20742-3275. Phone: (301)405-4526 Fax: (301)314-9115 E-mail: yiannis@cfar.umd.edu • URL: http://www.cfar.umd.edu/cvl/.

Electronic Visualization Laboratory. University of Illinois at Chicago, Engineering Research Facility, 842 W. Taylor St., Room 2032, Chicago, IL 60607-7053. Phone: (312)996-3002 Fax: (312)413-7585 E-mail: tom@eecs.uic.edu • URL: http://www.evl.uic.edu • Research areas include computer graphics, virtual reality, multimedia, and interactive techniques.

Graphics, Visualization, and Usability Center. Georgia Institute of Technology, Mail Code 0280, Atlanta, GA 30332-0280. Phone: (404)894-4488 Fax: (404)894-0673 E-mail: jarek@cc.gatech.edu • URL: http://www.cc.gatech.edu/gvu/ • Research areas include computer graphics, multimedia, image recognition, interactive graphics systems, animation, and virtual realities.

Image Science Research Group. Worcester Polytechnic Institute, Computer Science Department, 100 Institute Rd., Worcester, MA 01609. Phone: (508)831-5671 Fax: (508)831-5776 E-mail: isrg@cs.wpi.edu • URL: http://www.cs.wpi.edu/research/ • Areas of research include image processing, computer graphics, and computational vision.

Institute for Information Science and Technology. George Washington University, 801 22nd St., N. W., 6th Fl., Washington, DC 20052. Phone: (202)994-6208 Fax: (202)994-0227 E-mail: helgert@seas.gwu.edu • Research areas include computer graphics and image processing.

TRADE/PROFESSIONAL ASSOCIATIONS

IEEE Computer Society. 1730 Massachusetts Ave., N. W., Washington, DC 20036. Phone: (202)371-0101 Fax: (202)728-9614 E-mail: csinfo@computer.org • URL: http://www.computer.org • A society of the Institute of Electrical and Electronics Engineers. Said to be the world's largest organization of computer professionals. Some of the specific committees are: Computer Communications; Computer Graphics; Computers in Education; Design Automation; Office Automation; Personal Computing; Robotics; Security and Privacy; Software Engineering.

IMAGE Society. P.O. Box 6221, Chandler, AZ 85246-6221. Phone: (602)839-8709 E-mail: image@asu.edu • URL: http://www.public.asu.edu/~image • Promotes the technical advancement and application of real-time visual simulation. Special Interest Groups include Computer Image Generation, Virtual Reality Ancillary Technologies, and Virtual Reality in Education and Training.

International Communications Industries Association. 11242 Waples Mill Rd., Suite 200, Fairfax, VA 22030-6079. Phone: 800-659-7469 or (703)273-2700 Fax: (703)278-8082 E-mail: icia@icia.org • Members are manufacturers and suppliers of audio-visual, video, and computer graphics equipment and materials.

Special Interest Group on Computer Graphics and Interactive Techniques. Association for Computing Machinery, 1515 Broadway, New York, NY 10036. Phone: (212)869-7440 Fax: (212)302-5826 E-mail: sigs@acm.org • URL: http://www.acm.org/siggraph • Concerned with research, technology, and applications for the technical, academic, business, and art communities. Publishes the quarterly newsletter *Computer Graphics*.

Special Interest Group on Design Automation. Association for Computing Machinery, 1515 Broadway, New York, NY 10036. Phone: (212)869-7440 Fax: (212)302-5826 E-mail: sigs@acm.org • URL: http://www.acm.org/sigda • Concerned with computer-aided design systems and software. Publishes the semiannual *SIGDA Newsletter*.

World Computer Graphics Association. 16006 Philmont Ln., Bowie, MD.

COMPUTER IMAGING

See: DOCUMENT IMAGING

COMPUTER INDUSTRY

See: COMPUTERS; MICROCOMPUTERS AND MINICOMPUTERS

COMPUTER INTEGRATED MANUFACTURING (CIM)

See: COMPUTER-AIDED DESIGN AND MANUFACTURING (CAD/CAM); SYSTEMS INTEGRATION

COMPUTER LAW

ABSTRACTS AND INDEXES

Computer Literature Index: A Subject/Author Index to Computer and Data Processing Literature. Applied Computer Research, Inc. • Quarterly, with annual cumulation. $245.00 per year. Contains brief abstracts of book and periodical literature covering all phases of computing, including approximately 70 specific application areas.

Current Law Index: Multiple Access to Legal Periodicals. The Gale Group. • Monthly. $650.00 per year. Produced in cooperation with the American Association of Law Libraries. Indexes more than 900

law journals, legal newspapers, and specialty publications from the U.S., Canada, U.K., Ireland, Australia, and New Zealand.

Index to Legal Periodicals and Books. H. W. Wilson Co. • Monthly. Quarterly and annual cumulations. $270.00 per year. CD-ROM version available at $1,495.00 per year.

BIBLIOGRAPHIES

Encyclopedia of Legal Information Sources. The Gale Group. • 1992. $180.00. Second edition. Lists more than 23,000 law-related information sources, including print, nonprint, and organizational.

CD-ROM DATABASES

LegalTrac. The Gale Group. • Monthly. $5,000.00 per year. Price includes workstation. Provides CD-ROM indexing of periodical literature relating to legal matters from 1980 to date. Corresponds to online *Legal Resource Index.*

WILSONDISC: Index to Legal Periodicals and Books. H. W. Wilson Co. • Monthly. Including unlimited online access to *Index to Legal Periodicals* through WILSONLINE. Contains CD-ROM indexing of more than 800 English language legal periodicals from 1981 to date and 2,500 books.

DIRECTORIES

Law and Legal Information Directory. The Gale Group. • 2000. $405.00. 11th edition. Two volumes. Contains a wide range of sources of legal information, such as associations, law schools, courts, federal agencies, referral services, libraries, publishers, and research centers. There is a separate chapter for each of 23 types of information source or service.

Lawyer's Register International by Specialties and Fields of Law Including a Directory of Corporate Counsel. Lawyer's Register Publishing Co. • Annual. $329.00. Three volumes. Referral source for law firms.

HANDBOOKS AND MANUALS

Computer Law: Cases, Comments, Questions. Peter B. Maggs and others. West Publishing Co., College and School Div. • 1992. Price on application. (Amrican Casebook Series).

Computer Law Forms Handbook: A Legal Guide to Drafting and Negotiating. Laurens R. Schwartz. West Group. • Annual. $162.00.

Fundamentals of Computer-High Technology Law. James V. Vergari and Virginia V. Shue. American Law Institute-American Bar Association. • 1991. $29.00.

ONLINE DATABASES

Computer Database. The Gale Group. • Provides online citations with abstracts to material appearing in about 150 trade journals and newsletters in the subject areas of computers, telecommunications, and electronics. Time period is 1983 to date, with weekly updates. Inquire as to online cost and availability.

Index to Legal Periodicals and Books (Online). H. W. Wilson Co. • Broad coverage of law journals and books 1981 to date. Monthly updates. Inquire as to online cost and availability.

Law of the Super Searchers: The Online Secrets of Top Legal Researchers. T. R. Halvorson and Reva Basch. Information Today, Inc. • 1999. $24.95. Eight law researchers explain how to find useful legal information online. (CyberAge Books.).

Legal Resource Index. The Gale Group. • Broad coverage of law literature appearing in legal, business, and other periodicals, 1980 to date. Monthly updates. Inquire as to online cost and availability.

PERIODICALS AND NEWSLETTERS

Computer Law and Tax Report: Monthly Newsletter Covering Computer-Related Law and Tax Issues. Roditti Reports Corp. • Monthly. $297.00 per year. Newsletter.

Computer-Law Journal: International Journal of Computer, Communication and Information Law. Center for Computer Law. • Quarterly. $97.50 per year.

Computer Law Reporter: A Monthly Journal of Computer Law and Practice, Intellectual Property, Copyright and Trademark Law. Computer Law Reporter, Inc. • Monthly. $1,650.00 per year.

Computer Law Strategist. American Lawyer Media, L.P. • Monthly. $265.00 per year.

Software Law Journal. Center for Computer Law. • Quarterly. $97.50 per year.

RESEARCH CENTERS AND INSTITUTES

Center for the Study of Law, Science, and Technology. Arizona State University, College of Law, P.O. Box 877906, Tempe, AZ 85287-7906. Phone: (602)965-2554 Fax: (602)965-2427 E-mail: daniel.strouse@asu.edu • URL: http://www.law.asu.edu • Studies the legal problems created by technological advances.

Lexis.com Research System. Lexis-Nexis Group. Phone: 800-227-9597 or (937)865-6800 Fax: (937)865-6909 E-mail: webmaster@prod.lexis-nexis.com • URL: http://www.lexis.com • Fee-based Web site offers extensive searching of a wide variety of legal sources. Additional features include Daily Opinion Service, lexis.com Bookstore, Career Center, CLE Center, Law Schools, and Practice Pages ("Pages specific to areas of specialty").

TRADE/PROFESSIONAL ASSOCIATIONS

Computer Law Association. 3028 Javier Rd., Suite 402, Fairfax, VA 22031. Phone: (703)560-7747 Fax: (703)207-7028 E-mail: clanet@aol.com • URL: http://www.cla.org • Members are lawyers and others concerned with the legal problems affecting computer-telecommunications technology.

OTHER SOURCES

Computer and Online Industry Litigation Reporter: The National Journal of Record of Computer Online Industry. Andrews Publications, Inc. • Semimonthly. $875.00 per year. Provides complete text of key decisions relating to copyright, patents, trademarks, breach of contract, etc. Formerly *Computer Industry Litigation Reporter.*

Computer Software: Protection, Liability, Forms. L. J. Kutten. West Group. • Three looseleaf volumes. $350.00. Periodic supplementation. Covers copyright law, patents, trade secrets, licensing, publishing contracts, and other legal topics related to computer software.

Guide to Computer Law. CCH, Inc. • $551.00 per year. Two looseleaf volumes, updated semimonthly.

COMPUTER NETWORKS

See: COMPUTER COMMUNICATIONS; LOCAL AREA NETWORKS

COMPUTER OUTPUT MICROFILM (COM)

See: MICROFORMS

COMPUTER PERIPHERALS AND ACCESSORIES

See also: MICROCOMPUTERS AND MINICOMPUTERS

ABSTRACTS AND INDEXES

Applied Science and Technology Index. H. W. Wilson Co. • 11 times a year. Quarterly and annual cumulations. Service basis for print edition; CD-ROM edition, $1,495.00 per year. Indexes a wide variety of English language technical, industrial, and engineering periodicals.

Business Periodicals Index. H. W. Wilson Co. • Monthly, except August, with quarterly and annual cumulations. Service basis for print edition; CD-ROM edition, $1,495.00 per year.

Computer and Control Abstracts. Available from INSPEC, Inc. • Monthly. $2,160.00 per year. Section C of *Science Abstracts.*

Computer and Information Systems Abstracts Journal: An Abstract Journal Pertaining to the Theory, Design, Fabrication and Application of Computer and Information Systems. Cambridge Information Group. • Monthly. $1,045 per year.

Computer Literature Index: A Subject/Author Index to Computer and Data Processing Literature. Applied Computer Research, Inc. • Quarterly, with annual cumulation. $245.00 per year. Contains brief abstracts of book and periodical literature covering all phases of computing, including approximately 70 specific application areas.

Microcomputer Abstracts. Information Today, Inc. • Quarterly. $225.00 per year. Provides abstracts covering a wide variety of personal and business microcomputer literature. Formerly *Microcomputer Index.*

CD-ROM DATABASES

Datapro on CD-ROM: Computer Systems Hardware and Software. Gartner Group, Inc. • Monthly. Price on application. CD-ROM provides product specifications, product reports, user surveys, and market forecasts for a wide range of computer hardware and software.

DIRECTORIES

Better Buys for Business: The Independent Consumer Guide to Office Equipment. What to Buy for Business, Inc. • 10 times a year. $134.00 per year. Each issue is on a particular office product, with detailed evaluation of specific models: 1. Low-Volume Copier Guide, 2. Mid-Volume Copier Guide, 3. High-Volume Copier Guide, 4. Plain Paper Fax and Low-Volume Multifunctional Guide, 5. Mid/High-Volume Multifunctional Guide, 6. Laser Printer Guide, 7. Color Printer and Color Copier Guide, 8. Scan-to-File Guide, 9. Business Phone Systems Guide, 10. Postage Meter Guide, with a Short Guide to Shredders.

Computer Parts and Supplies Directory. American Business Directories. • Annual. Price on application. Lists 8,347 companies. Compiled from telephone company yellow pages.

Control Engineering Buyers Guide. Cahners Business Information. • Annual. Free to qualified personnel. Contains specifications, prices, and manufacturers' listings for computer software, as related to control engineering.

Corptech Directory of Technology Companies. Corporate Technology Information Services, Inc. c/o Eileen Kennedy. • Annual. $795.00. Four volumes. Profiles of more than 45,000 manufacturers and developers of high technology products. Includes private companies, publicly-held corporations, and subsidiaries. Formerly *Corporate Technology Directory.*

Directory of Computer V A R's and System Integrators. Chain Store Guide. • Annual. $290.00. Provides information on computer companies that modify, enhance, or customize hardware or software. Includes systems houses, systems integrators, turnkey systems specialists, original equipment manufacturers, and value added retailers. Formerly *Directory of Value Added Resellers.*

Essential Business Buyer's Guide, from Cellular Services and Overnight Mail to Internet Access Providers, 401(k) Plans, and Desktop Computers: The Ultimate Guide to Buying Office Equipment, Products, and Services. Sourcebooks, Inc. • 1996. $18.95. Compiled by the staff of *Business Consumer Guide.* Lists recommended brands of office equipment.

Faulkner Information Service. Faulkner Information Services, Inc. • Looseleaf. Monthly updates. Many titles and volumes, covering virtually all aspects of computer software and hardware. Gives descriptions and technical data for specific products, including producers' names and addresses. Prices and details on request. Formerly (The Auerbach Series).

Interactive Multimedia Association Membership Directory. Interactive Multimedia Association. • Annual. $60.00. Includes membership listing and a *Buyer's Guide.*

Laptop Buyer's Guide and Handbook. Bedford Communications, Inc. • Monthly. $18.00 per year. Contains informative articles and critical reviews of laptop, notebook, subnotebook, and handheld computers. Includes portable peripheral equipment, such as printers and scanners. Directory information includes company profiles (major manufacturers), product comparison charts, street price guide, list of manufacturers, and list of dealers.

Network Buyers Guide. Miller Freeman. • Annual. $5.00. Lists suppliers of products for local and wide area computer networks. Formerly *LAN Buyers Guide Issue.*

ENCYCLOPEDIAS AND DICTIONARIES

Dictionary of Computer Terms. Brian Phaffenberger. Pearson Education and Technology. • 1997. $10.95. Sixth edition.

Dictionary of PC Hardware and Data Communications Terms. Mitchell Shnier. Thomson Learning. • 1996. $19.95. (Online updates to print version available at http://www.ora.com/reference/dictionary.).

FINANCIAL RATIOS

Industry Norms and Key Business Ratios. Desk Top Edition. Dun and Bradstreet Corp., Business Information Services. • Annual. Five volumes. $475.00 per volume. $1,890.00 per set. Covers over 800 kinds of businesses, arranged by Standard Industrial Classification number. More detailed editions covering longer periods of time are also available.

HANDBOOKS AND MANUALS

Guide to Energy Efficient Office Equipment. Loretta A. Smith and others. American Council for an Energy Efficient Economy. • 1996. $12.00. Second edition. Provides information on selecting, purchasing, and using energy-saving computers, monitors, printers, copiers, and other office devices.

The Modem Reference: The Complete Guide to PC Communications. Michael A. Banks. Information Today, Inc. • 2000. $29.95. Fourth edition. Covers personal computer data communications technology, including fax transmissions, computer networks, modems, and the Internet. Popularly written.

INTERNET DATABASES

InfoTech Trends. Data Analysis Group. Phone: (707)894-9100 Fax: (707)486-5618 E-mail: support@infotechtrends.com • URL: http://www.infotechtrends.com • Web site provides both free and fee-based market research data on the information technology industry, including computers, peripherals, telecommunications, the Internet, software, CD-ROM/DVD, e-commerce, and workstations. Fees: Free for current (most recent year) data; more extensive information has various fee structures. Formerly *Computer Industry Forecasts.*

ONLINE DATABASES

Applied Science and Technology Index Online. H. W. Wilson Co. • Provides online indexing of 400 major scientific, technical, industrial, and engineering periodicals. Time period is 1983 to date. Monthly updates. Inquire as to online cost and availability.

Internet and Personal Computing Abstracts. Information Today, Inc. • Contains abstracts covering a wide variety of personal and business microcomputer literature appearing in more than 100 journals and popular magazines. Time period is 1981 to date, with monthly updates. Formerly *Microcomputer Index.* Inquire as to online cost and availability.

PROMT: Predicasts Overview of Markets and Technology. The Gale Group. • Companies, products, applied technologies and markets. U.S. and international literature coverage, 1972 to date. Inquire as to online cost and availability. Provides abstracts from more than 1,600 publications. Weekly updates.

Wilson Business Abstracts Online. H. W. Wilson Co. • Indexes and abstracts 600 major business periodicals, plus the *Wall Street Journal* and the business section of the *New York Times.* Indexing is from 1982, abstracting from 1990, with the two newspapers included from 1993. Updated weekly. Inquire as to online cost and availability. (*Business Periodicals Index* without abstracts is also available online.).

PERIODICALS AND NEWSLETTERS

EDP Weekly: The Leading Weekly Computer News Summary. Computer Age and E D P News Services. • Weekly. $495.00 per year. Newsletter. Summarizes news from all areas of the computer and microcomputer industries.

Interactive Home: Consumer Technology Monthly. Jupiter Media Metrix. • Monthly. $625.00 per year. Newsletter on devices to bring the Internet into the average American home. Covers TV set-top boxes, game devices, telephones with display screens, handheld computer communication devices, the usual PCs, etc.

Network: Strategies and Solutions for the Network Professional. Miller Freeman. • Monthly. $29.95 per year. Covers network products and peripherals for computer professionals. Includes annual network managers salary survey and annual directory issue. Formerly *LAN: The Network Solutions Magazine.*

PC Letter: The Insider's Guide to the Personal Computer Industry. David Coursey, editor. Stewart Alsop. • 22 times a year. $495.00 per year. Newsletter. Includes reviews of new PC hardware and software.

Presentations: Technology and Techniques for Effective Communication. Lakewood Publications, Inc. • Monthly. $50.00 per year. Covers the use of presentation hardware and software, including audiovisual equipment and computerized display systems. Includes an annual *"Buyers Guide to Presentation Products."*.

PRICE SOURCES

Orion Computer Blue Book. Orion Research Corp. • Quarterly. $516.00 per year. $129.00 per issue. Quotes retail and wholesale prices of used computers and equipment. Original list prices and years of manufacture are also shown.

RESEARCH CENTERS AND INSTITUTES

Battelle Memorial Institute. 505 King Ave., Columbus, OH 43201-2693. Phone: 800-201-2011 or (614)424-6424 Fax: (614)424-3260 • URL: http://www.battelle.org • Multidisciplinary research facilities at various locations include: Microcomputer Applications and Technology Center; Battelle Industrial Technology Center; Technology and Society Research Center; Office of Transportation Systems and Planning; Office of Waste Technology Development; Materials Information Center; Office of Nuclear Waste Isolation.

Carnegie Mellon Research Institute. Carnegie Mellon University, 700 Technology Dr., Pittsburgh, PA 15219. Phone: (412)268-3190 Fax: (412)268-3101 E-mail: twillke@emu.edu • Multidisciplinary research activities include expert systems applications, minicomputer and microcomputer systems design, genetic engineering, and transportation systems analysis.

Center for Advanced Technology in Computers and Information Systems. Columbia University, 161 Fort Washington Ave., AP1310, New York, NY 10032. Phone: (212)305-2944 Fax: (212)305-0196 E-mail: d1330@columbia.edu • URL: http://www.cpmc.columbia.edu/catc/.

STATISTICS SOURCES

Computers and Office and Accounting Machines. U. S. Bureau of the Census. • Annual. Provides data on shipments: value, quantity, imports, and exports. (Current Industrial Reports, MA-35R.).

Standard & Poor's Industry Surveys. Standard & Poor's. • Semiannual. $1,800.00. Two looseleaf volumes. Includes monthly supplements. Provides detailed, individual surveys of 52 major industry groups. Each survey is revised on a semiannual basis. Also includes "Monthly Investment Review" (industry group investment analysis) and monthly "Trends & Projections" (economic analysis).

TRADE/PROFESSIONAL ASSOCIATIONS

CDLA, The Computer Leasing and Remarketing Association. 11921 Freedom Dr., Suite 550, Reston, VA 20190-5608. Phone: (703)904-4337 Fax: (703)904-4339 E-mail: info@itra.net • URL: http://www.itra.net.

Computing Technology Industry Association. 450 E. 22nd St., Suite 230, Lombard, IL 60148-6158. Phone: (630)268-1818 Fax: (630)268-1384 E-mail: info@comptia.org • URL: http://www.comptia.org • Members are resellers of various kinds of microcomputers and computer equipment.

OTHER SOURCES

DataWorld. Faulkner Information Services, Inc. • Four looseleaf volumes, with monthly supplements. $1,395.00 per year. Describes and evaluates both hardware and software relating to midrange, micro, and mainframe computers. Available on CD-ROM.

COMPUTER PROGRAMMING

See: COMPUTER SOFTWARE INDUSTRY

COMPUTER RESELLERS

See: COMPUTER RETAILING

COMPUTER RETAILING

DIRECTORIES

Computer Dealers Directory. American Business Directories. • Annual. Price on application. Lists over 30,847 computer dealers. Brand names are indicated. Compiled from telephone company yellow pages. Regional editions and franchise editions available.

Directory of Computer Consumer Electronics Retailers. Chain Store Guide. • Annual. $290.00. Detailed information about companies operating computer and/or computer software stores. Formerly *Directory of Computer Dealers and Distributors Retailers.*

Directory of Computer V A R's and System Integrators. Chain Store Guide. • Annual. $290.00. Provides information on computer companies that modify, enhance, or customize hardware or software. Includes systems houses, systems integrators, turnkey systems specialists, original equipment manufacturers, and value added retailers. Formerly *Directory of Value Added Resellers.*

MicroLeads Vendor Directory on Disk (Personal Computer Industry). Chromatic Communications Enterprises, Inc. • Annual. $495.00. Includes computer hardware manufacturers, software producers, book-periodical publishers, and franchised or company-owned chains of personal computer equipment retailers, support services and accessory manufacturers. Formerly *MicroLeads U.S. Vender Directory.*

FINANCIAL RATIOS

Annual Statement Studies. Robert Morris Associates: The Association of Lending and Credit Risk Professiona. • Annual. Free to members; non-members, $140.00. Median and quartile financial ratios are given for over 400 kinds of manufacturing, wholesale, retail, construction, and consumer finance establishments. Data is sorted by both asset size and sales volume. Includes a clearly written "Definition of Ratios" and an alphabetical industry index.

HANDBOOKS AND MANUALS

Software Store. Entrepreneur Media, Inc. • Looseleaf. $59.50. A practical guide to opening a computer software retail establishment. Covers profit potential, start-up costs, market size evaluation, owner's time required, site selection, lease negotiation, pricing, accounting, advertising, promotion, etc. (Start-Up Business Guide No. E1261.).

PERIODICALS AND NEWSLETTERS

Computer Reseller News: The Newspaper for Microcomputer Reselling. CMP Publications, Inc. • Weekly. $209.00 per year. Includes bimonthly supplement. Incorporates *Computer Reseller Sources and Macintosh News.* Formerly *Computer Retailer News.*

Computer Shopper: The Computer Magazine for Direct Buyers. Ziff-Davis Publishing Co. • Monthly. $24.97 per year. Nationwide marketplace for computer equipment.

TRADE/PROFESSIONAL ASSOCIATIONS

CDLA, The Computer Leasing and Remarketing Association. 11921 Freedom Dr., Suite 550, Reston, VA 20190-5608. Phone: (703)904-4337 Fax: (703)904-4339 E-mail: info@itra.net • URL: http://www.itra.net.

Computing Technology Industry Association. 450 E. 22nd St., Suite 230, Lombard, IL 60148-6158. Phone: (630)268-1818 Fax: (630)268-1384 E-mail: info@comptia.org • URL: http://www.comptia.org • Members are resellers of various kinds of microcomputers and computer equipment.

COMPUTER SECURITY

See: COMPUTER CRIME AND SECURITY

COMPUTER SOFTWARE INDUSTRY

See also: COMPUTERS; MICROCOMPUTERS AND MINICOMPUTERS; UNIX; WINDOWS (SOFTWARE)

GENERAL WORKS

Managing Software Development Projects: Formula for Success. Neal Whitten. John Wiley and Sons, Inc. • 1995. $54.99. Second edition.

Microsoft Secrets: How the World's Most Powerful Software Company Creates Technology, Shapes Markets, and Manages People. Michael A. Cusumano and Richard W. Selby. Free Press. • 1995. $29.50. Describes the internal workings of the Microsoft Corporation, including marketing, technical innovation, and human relations.

ABSTRACTS AND INDEXES

Computer Literature Index: A Subject/Author Index to Computer and Data Processing Literature. Applied Computer Research, Inc. • Quarterly, with annual cumulation. $245.00 per year. Contains brief abstracts of book and periodical literature covering all phases of computing, including approximately 70 specific application areas.

Key Abstracts: Software Engineering. Available from INSPEC, Inc. • Monthly. $240.00 per year. Provides international coverage of journal and proceedings literature. Published in England by the Institution of Electrical Engineers (IEE).

LAMP (Literature Analysis of Microcomputer Publications). Soft Images. • Bimonthly. $89.95 per year. Annual cumulation.

Microcomputer Abstracts. Information Today, Inc. • Quarterly. $225.00 per year. Provides abstracts covering a wide variety of personal and business microcomputer literature. Formerly *Microcomputer Index.*

ALMANACS AND YEARBOOKS

Computer Industry Almanac. Egil Juliussen and Karen Petska. Computer Industry Almanac, Inc. • Annual. $63.00. Analyzes recent trends in various segments of the computer industry, with forecasts, employment data and industry salary information. Includes directories of computer companies, industry organizations, and publications.

BIBLIOGRAPHIES

Computer Book Review. • Quarterly. $30.00 per year. Includes annual index. Reviews new computer books. Back issues available.

BIOGRAPHICAL SOURCES

Gates: How Microsoft's Mogul Reinvented an Industry and Made Himself the Richest Man in America. Stephen Manes and Paul Andrews. Simon & Schuster Trade. • 1994. $14.00.

Hard Drive: Bill Gates and the Making of the Microsoft Empire. James Wallace and Jim Erickson. John Wiley and Sons, Inc. • 1992. $22.95. A biography of William H. Gates, chief executive of the Microsoft Corporation.

CD-ROM DATABASES

Computer Select. The Gale Group. • Monthly. $1,250.00 per year. Provides one year of full-text on CD-ROM for 120 leading computer-related publications. Also includes 70,000 product specifications and brief profiles of 13,000 computer product vendors and manufacturers.

Datapro on CD-ROM: Computer Systems Hardware and Software. Gartner Group, Inc. • Monthly. Price on application. CD-ROM provides product specifications, product reports, user surveys, and market forecasts for a wide range of computer hardware and software.

Hoover's Company Capsules on CD-ROM. Hoover's, Inc. • Quarterly. $349.95 per year (single-user). Provides the CD-ROM version of *Hoover's Handbook of American Business, Hoover's Handbook of Emerging Companies, Hoover's Handbook of World Business, Hoover's Guide to Computer Companies, Hoover's Guide to Media Companies, Hoover's Handbook of Private Companies,* and various regional guides. Includes more than 11,000 profiles of companies.

DIRECTORIES

Computing and Software Career Directory. The Gale Group. • 1993. $39.00. Includes career information relating to programmers, software engineers, technical writers, systems experts, and other computer specialists. Provides advice from "insiders," resume suggestions, a directory of companies that may offer entry-level positions, and a directory of career information sources. (Career Advisor Series.).

Data Sources: The Comprehensive Guide to the Data Processing Industry Hardware, Data Communications Products, Software, Company Profiles. The Gale Group. • Semiannual. $495.00 per year. Two volumes. Describes hardware and software for all computer operating sysems, including prices and technical details. Lists about 75,000 products from 14,000 suppliers. Industry-specific software applications are described.

Directory of Computer Consumer Electronics Retailers. Chain Store Guide. • Annual. $290.00. Detailed information about companies operating computer and/or computer software stores. Formerly *Directory of Computer Dealers and Distributors Retailers.*

MicroLeads Vendor Directory on Disk (Personal Computer Industry). Chromatic Communications Enterprises, Inc. • Annual. $495.00. Includes computer hardware manufacturers, software producers, book-periodical publishers, and franchised or company-owned chains of personal computer equipment retailers, support services and accessory manufacturers. Formerly *MicroLeads U.S. Vender Directory.*

The Software Encyclopedia: A Guide for Personal, Professional, and Business Users. R. R. Bowker. • Annual. $255.00. Two volumes. Volume one lists software programs by title and producer. Volume two provides information on programs according to application and operating system. Includes prices and requirements for hardware and memory.

303 Software Programs to Use in Your Library: Descriptions, Evaluations, and Practical Advice. Patrick R. Dewey. American Library Association. • 1997. $36.00. Contains profiles of a wide variety of software (21 categories) that may be useful in libraries. Includes prices, company addresses, glossary, bibliography, and an index.

ENCYCLOPEDIAS AND DICTIONARIES

Cyberspeak: An Online Dictionary. Andy Ihnatko. Random House, Inc. • 1996. $12.95. An informal guide to the language of computers, multimedia, and the Internet.

Dictionary of Information Technology and Computer Science. Tony Gunton. Blackwell Publishers. • 1994. $50.95. Second edition. Covers key words, phrases, abbreviations, and acronyms used in computing and data communications.

New Hacker's Dictionary. Eric S. Raymond. MIT Press. • 1996. $39.00. Third edition. Includes three classifications of hacker communication: slang, jargon, and "techspeak.".

HANDBOOKS AND MANUALS

Artificial Intelligence and Software Engineering. Darek Partridge. Fitzroy Dearborn Publishers, Inc. • 1998. $55.00. Includes applications of artificial intelligence software to banking and financial services.

Dun & Bradstreet/Gale Group Industry Handbooks. The Gale Group. • 2000. $630.00. Five volumes. $145.00 per volume. Each volume covers two or more major industries: 1. *Entertainment and Hospitality*; 2. *Construction and Agriculture*; 3. *Chemicals and Pharmaceuticals*; 4. *Computers & Software and Broadcasting & Telecommunications*; 5. *Insurance and Health & Medical Services.* The following are included for each industry: overview, statistics, financial ratios, rankings, merger information, company directory, directory of associations, and consultants directory.

Music Technology Buyer's Guide. United Entertainment Media, Inc. • $7.95. Annual. Lists more than 4,000 hardware and software music production products from 350 manufacturers. Includes synthesizers, MIDI hardware and software, mixers, microphones, music notation software, etc. Produced by the editorial staffs of *Keyboard* and *EQ* magazines.

Software Engineering. Ian Sommerville. Addison Wesley Longman, Inc. • 2000. $80.00. Sixth edition. (International Computer Science Series).

Software Reviews and Audits Handbook. Charles P. Hollocker. John Wiley and Sons, Inc. • 1990. $79.99. Includes document samples, forms, and checklists. (Industrial Software Engineering Practice Series).

INTERNET DATABASES

InfoTech Trends. Data Analysis Group. Phone: (707)894-9100 Fax: (707)486-5618 E-mail: support@infotechtrends.com • URL: http://www.infotechtrends.com • Web site provides both free and fee-based market research data on the information technology industry, including computers, peripherals, telecommunications, the Internet, software, CD-ROM/DVD, e-commerce, and workstations. Fees: Free for current (most recent year) data; more extensive information has various fee structures. Formerly *Computer Industry Forecasts.*

Wired News. Wired Digital, Inc. Phone: (415)276-8400 Fax: (415)276-8499 E-mail: newsfeedback@wired.com • URL: http://www.wired.com • Provides summaries and full-text of "Top Stories" relating to the Internet, computers, multimedia, telecommunications, and the electronic information industry in general. These news stories are placed in the broad categories of Politics, Business, Culture, and Technology. Affiliated with *Wired* magazine. Fees: Free.

ONLINE DATABASES

Computer Database. The Gale Group. • Provides online citations with abstracts to material appearing in about 150 trade journals and newsletters in the subject areas of computers, telecommunications, and electronics. Time period is 1983 to date, with weekly updates. Inquire as to online cost and availability.

Internet and Personal Computing Abstracts. Information Today, Inc. • Contains abstracts covering a wide variety of personal and business microcomputer literature appearing in more than 100 journals and popular magazines. Time period is 1981 to date, with monthly updates. Formerly *Microcomputer Index.* Inquire as to online cost and availability.

Microcomputer Software Guide Online. R. R. Bowker. • Provides information on more than 30,000 microcomputer software applications from more than 4,000 producers. Corresponds to printed *Software Encyclopedia*, but with monthly updates. Inquire as to online cost and availability.

PROMT: Predicasts Overview of Markets and Technology. The Gale Group. • Companies, products, applied technologies and markets. U.S. and international literature coverage, 1972 to date. Inquire as to online cost and availability. Provides abstracts from more than 1,600 publications. Weekly updates.

SoftBase: Reviews, Companies, and Products. Information Sources, Inc. • Describes and reviews business software packages. Inquire as to online cost and availability.

PERIODICALS AND NEWSLETTERS

Computer Languages. Elsevier Science. • Quarterly. $778.00 per year.

Computerworld: Newsweekly for Information Technology Leaders. Computerworld, Inc. • Weekly. $39.95 per year.

Dr. Dobb's Journal: Software Tools for the Professional Programmer. • Monthly. $34.95 per year. A technical publication covering software development, languages, operating systems, and applications.

EC Software News. Faulkner & Gray, Inc. • Monthly. $59.95 per year. Newsletter. Covers the latest developments in e-commerce software, both business-to-business and business-to-consumer.

IEEE Software. Insutitute of Electrical and Electronic Engineers, Inc. • Bimonthly. Free to members; non-members, $495.00 per year. Covers software engineering, technology, and development. Affiliated with the Institute of Electrical and Electronics Engineers.

Industrial Computing. ISA Services, Inc. • Monthly. $50.00 per year. Published by the Instrument Society of America. Edited for engineering managers and systems integrators. Subject matter includes industrial software, programmable controllers, artificial intelligence systems, and industrial computer networking systems.

InfoWorld: Defining Technology for Business. InfoWorld Publishing. • Weekly. $160.00 per year. For personal computing professionals.

Insurance and Technology. Miller Freeman. • Monthly. $65.00 per year. Covers information technology and systems management as applied to the operation of life, health, casualty, and property insurance companies.

Journal of Software Maintenance and Evolution Research and Practice. Available from John Wiley and Sons, Inc., Journals Div. • Bimonthly. Institutions, $1,145.00 per year. Published in England by John Wiley and Sons Ltd. Provides international coverage of subject matter.

Managing Automation. Thomas Publishing Co. • Monthly. Free to qualified personnel. Coverage includes software for manufacturing, systems planning, integration in process industry automation, computer integrated manufacturing (CIM), computer networks for manufacturing, management problems, industry news, and new products.

MSDN Magazine (Microsoft Systems for Developers). • Monthly. $84.95 per year. Produced for professional software developers using Windows, MS-DOS, Visual Basic, and other Microsoft Corporation products. Incorporates *Microsoft Systems Journal.*

Network Computing: Computing in a Network Environment. CMP Publications, Inc. • Semimonthly. $95.00 per year.

PC Letter: The Insider's Guide to the Personal Computer Industry. David Coursey, editor. Stewart Alsop. • 22 times a year. $495.00 per year. Newsletter. Includes reviews of new PC hardware and software.

Soft.Letter: Trends and Strategies in Software Publishing. Mercury Group,Inc. • Semimonthly. $395.00 per year. Newsletter on the software industry, including new technology and financial aspects.

Software Digest: The Independent Comparative Ratings Report for PC and LAN Software. National Software Testing Laboratories, Inc. • 12 times a year. $450.00 per year. Critical evaluations of personal computer software.

Software Economics Letter: Maximizing Your Return on Corporate Software. Computer Economics, Inc. • Monthly. $395.00 per year. Newsletter for information systems managers. Contains data on business software trends, vendor licensing policies, and other corporate software management issues.

Software Law Journal. Center for Computer Law. • Quarterly. $97.50 per year.

Software Magazine. Wiesner Publishing, Inc. • Monthly. $42.00 per year.

Telematics and Informatics: An International Journal. Elsevier Science. • Quarterly. $713.00 per year.

Upgrade. Software and Information Industry Association. • Monthly. $75.00 per year. Covers news and trends relating to the software, information, and Internet industries. Formerly *SPA News* from Software Publisers Association.

STATISTICS SOURCES

Standard & Poor's Industry Surveys. Standard & Poor's. • Semiannual. $1,800.00. Two looseleaf volumes. Includes monthly supplements. Provides detailed, individual surveys of 52 major industry groups. Each survey is revised on a semiannual basis. Also includes "Monthly Investment Review" (industry group investment analysis) and monthly "Trends & Projections" (economic analysis).

U. S. Industry and Trade Outlook: The McGraw-Hill Companies and the U.S. Department of Commerce/ International Trade Administration. Datapso Research Corp. • Annual. $69.95. Produced by the International Trade Administration, U. S. Department of Commerce, in a "public-private" partnership with DRI/McGraw-Hill and Standard & Poor's. Provides basic data, outlook for the current year, and "Long-Term Prospects" (five-year projections) for a wide variety of products and services. Includes high technology industries. Formerly *U. S. Industrial Outlook.*

TRADE/PROFESSIONAL ASSOCIATIONS

IEEE Computer Society. 1730 Massachusetts Ave., N. W., Washington, DC 20036. Phone: (202)371-0101 Fax: (202)728-9614 E-mail: csinfo@computer.org • URL: http://www.computer.org • A society of the Institute of Electrical and Electronics Engineers. Said to be the world's largest organization of computer professionals. Some of the specific committees are: Computer Communications; Computer Graphics; Computers in Education; Design Automation; Office Automation; Personal Computing; Robotics; Security and Privacy; Software Engineering.

Information Technology Association of America. c/o ITAA, 1616 N. Fort Myer Dr., Suite 1300, Arlington, VA 22209-9998. Phone: (703)522-5055 Fax: (703)525-2279 • Members are computer software and services companies. Maintains an Information Systems Integration Services Section.

Instrument Society of America (ISA). P.O. Box 12277, Research Triangle Park, NC 27709. Phone: (919)549-8411 Fax: (919)549-8288 E-mail: info@isa.org • URL: http://www.isa.org • Members are engineers and others concerned with industrial instrumentation, systems, computers, and automation.

Interactive Digital Software Association. 1775 Eye St., N.W., Ste. 420, Washington, DC 20005. E-mail: info@idsa.com • URL: http://www.e3expo.com • Members are interactive entertainment software publishers concerned with rating systems, software piracy, government relations, and other industry issues.

Software and Information Industry Association. 1730 M St., N. W., Suite 700, Washington, DC 20036-4510. Phone: (202)452-1600 Fax: (202)223-8756 • URL: http://www.siia.net • A trade association for the software and digital content industry. Divisions are Content, Education, Enterprise, Financial Information Services, Global, and Internet. Includes an Online Content Committee. Formerly Software Publishers Association.

Special Interest Group on Programming Languages. c/o Association for Computing Machinery, 1515 Broadway, 17th Fl., New York, NY 10036. Phone: (212)869-7440 Fax: (212)302-5826 E-mail: acmhelp@acm.org • URL: http://www.acm.org/sigplan/.

Special Interest Group on Software Engineering. Association for Computing Machinery, 1515 Broadway, New York, NY 10036. Phone: (212)869-7440 Fax: (212)302-5826 E-mail: sigs@acm.org • URL: http://www.acm.org/sigsoft • Concerned with all aspects of software development and maintenance. Publishes *Software Engineering Notes*, a bimonthly newsletter.

OTHER SOURCES

Computer Software: Protection, Liability, Forms. L. J. Kutten. West Group. • Three looseleaf volumes. $350.00. Periodic supplementation. Covers copyright law, patents, trade secrets, licensing, publishing contracts, and other legal topics related to computer software.

Consumer Internet Economy. Jupiter Media Metrix. • 1999. $3,495.00. Market research report. Provides data and forecasts relating to various hardware and software elements of the Internet, including browsers, provision of service, telephone line modems, cable modems, wireless access devices, online advertising, programming languages, and Internet chips. Includes company profiles.

Datapro Software Finder. Gartner Group, Inc. • Quarterly. $1,770.00 per year. CD-ROM provides detailed information on more than 18,000 software products for a wide variety of computers, personal to mainframe. Covers software for 130 types of business, finance, and industry. (Editions limited to either microcomputer or mainframe software are available at $995.00 per year.).

DataWorld. Faulkner Information Services, Inc. • Four looseleaf volumes, with monthly supplements. $1,395.00 per year. Describes and evaluates both hardware and software relating to midrange, micro, and mainframe computers. Available on CD-ROM.

EQ: The Project Recording and Sound Magazine. United Entertainment Media, Inc. • Monthly. $36.00 per year. Provides advice on professional music recording equipment and technique.

James Martin Productivity Series, Volume Seven. Digital Consulting Associates. • 1989. $50.00. Covers intelligent desktop workstations, expert systems (artificial intelligence), computer-aided software engineering (CASE), advanced development methodologies, and other high technology computer topics.

Keyboard: Making Music with Technology. United Entertainment Media, Inc. • Monthly. $36.00 per year. Emphasis is on recording systems, keyboard technique, and computer-assisted music (MIDI) systems.

World of Computer Science. The Gale Group. • 2001. $150.00. Alphabetical arrangement. Contains 650 entries covering discoveries, theories, concepts, issues, ethics, and people in the broad area of computer science and technology.

COMPUTER STORES

See: COMPUTER RETAILING

COMPUTER VIRUSES

See: COMPUTER CRIME AND SECURITY

COMPUTER VISION

See: MACHINE VISION

COMPUTERIZED TRANSLATION

See: MACHINE TRANSLATING

COMPUTERS

See also: AUTOMATION; COMMUNICATION SYSTEMS; COMPUTER SOFTWARE INDUSTRY; LINEAR PROGRAMMING; MICROCOMPUTERS AND MINICOMPUTERS; OPERATIONS RESEARCH; PORTABLE COMPUTERS

GENERAL WORKS

The Age of Spiritual Machines: When Computers Exceed Human Intelligence. Ray Kurzweil. Viking Penguin. • 1999. $25.95. Provides speculation on the future of artificial intelligence and "computer consciousness.".

Basic Computer Concepts. Que Staff. Que Education & Training, Macmillan Computer Publishing. • 1997. $16.99.

Being Digital. Nicholas Negroponte. Vintage Books. • 1995. $28.00. A kind of history of multimedia, with visions of future technology and public participation. Predicts how computers will affect society in years to come.

Computers. Timothy Trainor and Diane Krasnewich. McGraw-Hill. • 1996. $52.50. Fifth edition.

Computers and Information Processing. South-Western Publishing Co. • 1998. $29.95. Seventh edition.

Computers: The User Perspective. Sarah E. Hutchinson and Stacey C. Sawyer. McGraw-Hill Higher Education. • 1991. $41.95. Third edition.

Designing the User Interface: Strategies for Effective Human-Computer Interaction. Ben Shneiderman. Addison Wesley Longman, Inc. • 1997. $44.95. Third edition. Provides an introduction to computer user-interface design. Covers usability testing, dialog boxes, menus, command languages, interaction devices, tutorials, printed user manuals, and related subjects.

Introducing Computers: Concepts, Systems, and Applications with Getting Started Set, 1990-1991. Robert H. Blissmer. John Wiley and Sons, Inc. • 1995. $20.95.

Introduction to Computer Theory. Daniel I. Cohen. John Wiley and Sons, Inc. • 1996. $92.95. Second edition.

Probable Tomorrows: How Science and Technology Will Transform Our Lives in the Next Twenty Years. Marvin J. Cetron and Owen L. Davies. St. Martin's Press. • 1997. $24.95. Predicts the developments in technological products, services, and "everyday conveniences" by the year 2017. Covers such items as personal computers, artificial intelligence, telecommunications, highspeed railroads, and healthcare.

Recent Advances and Issues in Computers. Martin K. Gay. Oryx Press. • 2000. $44.95. Includes recent developments in computer science, computer engineering, and commercial software applications. (Oryx Frontiers of Science Series.).

The Trouble with Computers: Usefulness, Useability, and Productivity. Thomas K. Landauer. MIT Press. • 1995. $30.00. A critical view of computers and how they are being used.

ABSTRACTS AND INDEXES

Applied Science and Technology Index. H. W. Wilson Co. • 11 times a year. Quarterly and annual cumulations. Service basis for print edition; CD-ROM edition, $1,495.00 per year. Indexes a wide variety of English language technical, industrial, and engineering periodicals.

CompuMath Citation Index. Institute for Scientific Information. • Three times a year. $1,090.00 per year. Provides citations to the worldwide literature of computer science and mathematics.

Computer Abstracts. Anbar Electronic Intelligence. MCB University Press Ltd. • Bimonthly. $3,799.00 per year.

Computer and Information Systems Abstracts Journal: An Abstract Journal Pertaining to the Theory, Design, Fabrication and Application of Computer and Information Systems. Cambridge Information Group. • Monthly. $1,045 per year.

Computer Literature Index: A Subject/Author Index to Computer and Data Processing Literature. Applied Computer Research, Inc. • Quarterly, with annual cumulation. $245.00 per year. Contains brief abstracts of book and periodical literature covering all phases of computing, including approximately 70 specific application areas.

Computing Reviews. Association for Computing Machinery. • Monthly. Free to members; non-members, $130.00 per year.

NTIS Alerts: Computers, Control & Information Theory. National Technical Information Service. • Semimonthly. $235.00 per year. Provides descriptions of government-sponsored research reports and software, with ordering information. Covers computer hardware, software, control systems, pattern recognition, image processing, and related subjects. Formerly *Abstract Newsletter.*

ALMANACS AND YEARBOOKS

Advances in Computers. Academic Press, Inc., Journal Div. • Annual. Prices vary.

Communication Technology Update. Butterworth-Heinemann. • Annual. $36.95. Reviews technological developments and statistical trends in five key areas: mass media, computers, consumer electronics, communications satellites, and telephony. Includes television, cellular phones, and the Internet. (Focal Press.).

Computer Industry Almanac. Egil Juliussen and Karen Petska. Computer Industry Almanac, Inc. • Annual. $63.00. Analyzes recent trends in various segments of the computer industry, with forecasts, employment data and industry salary information. Includes directories of computer companies, industry organizations, and publications.

Information Technology Outlook. OECD Publications and Information Center. • Biennial. $72.00. A review of recent developments in international markets for computer hardware, software, and services. Also examines current legal provisions for information systems security and privacy in OECD countries.

BIBLIOGRAPHIES

ACM Electronic Guide to Computing Literature: Bibliographic Listing, Author IndeIndex, Category Index, Proper Noun Subject Index, Reviewer Index, Source Index. Association for Computing Machinery. • Quarterly. Members, $175.00; non-members, $499.00 per year. A comprehensive guide to each year's computer literature (books, proceedings, journals, etc.), with an emphasis on technical material. Indexed by author, keyword, category, proper noun, reviewer, and source. Formerly *ACM Guide to Computing Literature*.

Aslib Book Guide: A Monthly List of Recommended Scientific and Technical Books. Available from Information Today, Inc. • Monthly. Members, $164.00 per year; non-members, $204.00 per year. Published in London by Aslib: The Association for Information Management. Formerly *Aslib Book List*.

Automation. Available from U. S. Government Printing Office. • Annual. Free. Issued by the Superintendent of Documents. A list of government publications on automation, computers, and related topics. Formerly *Computers and Data Processing*. (Subject Bibliography No. 51.).

Computing Information Directory: Comprehensive Guide to the Computing and Computer Engineering Literature. Peter A. Hildebrandt, Inc. • Annual. $229.95. Describes computer journals, newsletters, handbooks, dictionaries, indexing services, review resources, directories, and other computer information sources. Includes a directory of publishers and a master subject index.

IEEE Publications Bulletin. Institute of Electrical and Electronics Engineers. • Quarterly. Free. Provides information on all IEEE journals, proceedings, and other publications.

BIOGRAPHICAL SOURCES

Who's Who in Science and Engineering. Marquis Who's Who. • Biennial. $269.00. Provides concise biographical information on 26,000 prominent engineers and scientists. International coverage, with geographical and professional indexes.

CD-ROM DATABASES

Computer Select. The Gale Group. • Monthly. $1,250.00 per year. Provides one year of full-text on CD-ROM for 120 leading computer-related publications. Also includes 70,000 product specifications and brief profiles of 13,000 computer product vendors and manufacturers.

Datapro on CD-ROM: Computer Systems Hardware and Software. Gartner Group, Inc. • Monthly. Price on application. CD-ROM provides product specifications, product reports, user surveys, and market forecasts for a wide range of computer hardware and software.

Electronic Strategies. Thomson Financial Securities Data. • Monthly. $2,995.00 per year. CD-ROM contains full text of investment analysts' reports on companies operating in the following fields: electronics, computers, semiconductors, and office products.

Hoover's Company Capsules on CD-ROM. Hoover's, Inc. • Quarterly. $349.95 per year (single-user). Provides the CD-ROM version of *Hoover's Handbook of American Business, Hoover's Handbook of Emerging Companies, Hoover's Handbook of World Business, Hoover's Guide to Computer Companies, Hoover's Guide to Media Companies, Hoover's Handbook of Private Companies,* and various regional guides. Includes more than 11,000 profiles of companies.

MathSci Disc. American Mathematical Society. • Semiannual. Price on application. Provides CD-ROM citations, with abstracts, to the literature of mathematics, statistics, and computer science, 1940 to date.

WILSONDISC: Wilson Business Abstracts. H. W. Wilson Co. • Monthly. $2,495.00 per year, including unlimited online access to *Wilson Business Abstracts* through WILSONLINE. Provides CD-ROM "cover-to-cover" abstracting and indexing of over 600 prominent business periodicals. Indexing is from 1982, abstracting from 1990. (*Business Periodicals Index* without abstracts is available on CD-ROM at $1,495 per year.).

DIRECTORIES

Data Communications Production Selection Guide. McGraw-Hill. • Semiannual. $25.00. List of networking vendors. Formerly *Data Communications Buyer's Guide*.

Data Sources: The Comprehensive Guide to the Data Processing Industry Hardware, Data Communications Products, Software, Company Profiles. The Gale Group. • Semiannual. $495.00 per year. Two volumes. Describes hardware and software for all computer operating sysems, including prices and technical details. Lists about 75,000 products from 14,000 suppliers. Industry-specific software applications are described.

Directory of Computer V A R's and System Integrators. Chain Store Guide. • Annual. $290.00. Provides information on computer companies that modify, enhance, or customize hardware or software. Includes systems houses, systems integrators, turnkey systems specialists, original equipment manufacturers, and value added retailers. Formerly *Directory of Value Added Resellers*.

Open Systems Products Directory. UniForum. • Annual. $50.00. A guide to Unix and open systems products from about 2,100 vendors. Lists software, hardware, systems, tools, peripherals, services, and publications.

Peterson's Computer Science and Electrical Engineering Programs. Peterson's. • 1996. $24.95. A guide to 900 accredited graduate degree programs related to computers or electrical engineering at colleges and universities in the U. S. and Canada.

Plunkett's InfoTech Industry Almanac: Complete Profiles on the InfoTech 500-the Leading Firms in the Movement and Management of Voice, Data, and Video. Available from Plunkett Research, Ltd. • Annual. $149.99. Five hundred major information companies are profiled, with corporate culture aspects. Discusses major trends in various sectors of the computer and information industry, including data on careers and job growth. Includes several indexes.

ENCYCLOPEDIAS AND DICTIONARIES

Business Dictionary of Computers. Jerry M. Rosenberg. John Wiley and Sons, Inc. • 1993. $14.95. Third edition. Provides concise definitions of over 7,500 computer terms, including slang terms, abbreviations, acronyms, and technical jargon. (Business Dictionary Series).

Computer Dictionary. Donald D. Spencer. Camelot Publishing Co. • 1993. $24.95. Fourth edition.

Computer Glossary: The Complete Illustrated Desk Reference. Alan Freedman. AMACOM. • 1998. $29.95. Eighth edition.

Cyberspeak: An Online Dictionary. Andy Ihnatko. Random House, Inc. • 1996. $12.95. An informal guide to the language of computers, multimedia, and the Internet.

Dictionary of Information Technology and Computer Science. Tony Gunton. Blackwell Publishers. • 1994. $50.95. Second edition. Covers key words, phrases, abbreviations, and acronyms used in computing and data communications.

Encyclopedia of Computer Science and Technology. Marcel Dekker, Inc. • Dates vary. 39 volumes. $7,605.00. $195.00 per volume. Contains scholarly articles written by computer experts. Includes bibliographies.

New Hacker's Dictionary. Eric S. Raymond. MIT Press. • 1996. $39.00. Third edition. Includes three classifications of hacker communication: slang, jargon, and "techspeak.".

HANDBOOKS AND MANUALS

Computer Repair Service. Entrepreneur Media, Inc. • Looseleaf. $59.50. A practical guide to starting a computer repair service. Covers profit potential, start-up costs, market size evaluation, owner's time required, site selection, lease negotiation, pricing, accounting, advertising, promotion, etc. (Start-Up Business Guide No. E1256.).

Dun & Bradstreet/Gale Group Industry Handbooks. The Gale Group. • 2000. $630.00. Five volumes. $145.00 per volume. Each volume covers two or more major industries: 1. *Entertainment and Hospitality*; 2. *Construction and Agriculture*; 3. *Chemicals and Pharmaceuticals*; 4. *Computers & Software and Broadcasting & Telecommunications*; 5. *Insurance and Health & Medical Services*. The following are included for each industry: overview, statistics, financial ratios, rankings, merger information, company directory, directory of associations, and consultants directory.

Guide to Energy Efficient Office Equipment. Loretta A. Smith and others. American Council for an Energy Efficient Economy. • 1996. $12.00. Second edition. Provides information on selecting, purchasing, and using energy-saving computers, monitors, printers, copiers, and other office devices.

Peterson's Guide to Colleges for Careers in Computing: The Only Combined Career and College Guide for Future Computer Professionals. Peterson's. • 1996. $14.95. Describes career possibilities in various fields related to computers.

INTERNET DATABASES

InfoTech Trends. Data Analysis Group. Phone: (707)894-9100 Fax: (707)486-5618 E-mail: support@infotechtrends.com • URL: http://www.infotechtrends.com • Web site provides both free and fee-based market research data on the information technology industry, including computers, peripherals, telecommunications, the Internet, software, CD-ROM/DVD, e-commerce, and workstations. Fees: Free for current (most recent year) data; more extensive information has various fee structures. Formerly *Computer Industry Forecasts*.

Wired News. Wired Digital, Inc. Phone: (415)276-8400 Fax: (415)276-8499 E-mail: newsfeedback@wired.com • URL: http://www.wired.com • Provides summaries and full-text of "Top Stories" relating to the Internet, computers, multimedia, telecommunications, and the electronic information industry in general. These news stories are placed in the broad categories of Politics, Business, Culture, and Technology. Affiliated with *Wired* magazine. Fees: Free.

ONLINE DATABASES

Applied Science and Technology Index Online. H. W. Wilson Co. • Provides online indexing of 400 major scientific, technical, industrial, and engineering periodicals. Time period is 1983 to date. Monthly updates. Inquire as to online cost and availability.

Computer Database. The Gale Group. • Provides online citations with abstracts to material appearing in about 150 trade journals and newsletters in the subject areas of computers, telecommunications, and electronics. Time period is 1983 to date, with weekly updates. Inquire as to online cost and availability.

Hard Sciences. Cambridge Scientific Abstracts. • Provides the online version of *Computer and Information Systems Abstracts, Electronics and Communications Abstracts, Health and Safety Science Abstracts, ISMEC: Mechanical Engineering Abstracts (Information Service in Mechanical Engineering)* and *Solid State and Superconductivity Abstracts.* Time period is 1981 to date, with monthly updates. Inquire as to online cost and availability.

INSPEC. Institute of Electrical and Electronics Engineers (IEEE). • Provides indexing and abstracting of the worldwide literature of electrical engineering, electronics, physics, computer technology, information technology, and industrial controls. Time period is 1970 to date, with weekly updates. Inquire as to online cost and availability. (INSPEC is Information Services for the Physics and Engineering Communities.).

MathSci. American Mathematical Society. • Provides online citations, with abstracts, to the literature of mathematics, statistics, and computer science. Time period is 1940 to date, with monthly updates. Inquire as to online cost and availability.

Wilson Business Abstracts Online. H. W. Wilson Co. • Indexes and abstracts 600 major business periodicals, plus the *Wall Street Journal* and the business section of the *New York Times.* Indexing is from 1982, abstracting from 1990, with the two newspapers included from 1993. Updated weekly. Inquire as to online cost and availability. (*Business Periodicals Index* without abstracts is also available online.).

PERIODICALS AND NEWSLETTERS

ACM Computing Surveys: The Survey and Tutorial Journal of the ACM. Association for Computing Machinery. • Quarterly. Free to members; non-members, $100.00 per year.

Association for Computing Machinery Communications. Association for Computing Machinery. • Monthly. Free to members; non-members, $114.00 per year.

Association for Computing Machinery Journal. Association for Computing Machinery. • Quarterly. Members, $45.00 per year; non-members, $200.00 per year.

CIO: The Magazine for Information Executives. CIO Communications. • Semimonthly. $89.00 per year. Edited for chief information officers. Includes a monthly "Web Business" section (incorporates the former *WebMaster* periodical) and a monthly "Enterprise" section for company executives other than CIOs.

Computer. Institute of Electrical and Electronic Engineers. • Monthly. $760.00 per year. Edited for computer technology professionals.

Computer Economics Report: The Financial Advisor of Data Processing Users. Computer Economics, Inc. • Monthly. $595.00 per year. Newsletter on lease/purchase decisions, prices, discounts, residual value forecasts, personnel allocation, cost control, and other corporate computer topics. Edited for information technology (IT) executives.

Computer Letter: Business Issues in Technology. Technologic Partners, Inc. • 40 times a year. $595.00 per year. Computer industry newsletter with emphasis on information for investors.

Computer Publishing and Advertising Report: The Biweekly Newsletter for Publishing and Advertising Executives in the Computer Field. SIMBA Information, Inc. • Biweekly. $549.00 per year. Newsletter. Covers computer book publishing and computer-related advertising in periodicals and other media. Provides data on computer book sales and advertising in computer magazines.

Computer Reseller News: The Newspaper for Microcomputer Reselling. CMP Publications, Inc. • Weekly. $209.00 per year. Includes bimonthly supplement. Incorporates *Computer Reseller Sources and Macintosh News.* Formerly *Computer Retailer News.*

Computer Shopper: The Computer Magazine for Direct Buyers. Ziff-Davis Publishing Co. • Monthly. $24.97 per year. Nationwide marketplace for computer equipment.

Computerworld: Newsweekly for Information Technology Leaders. Computerworld, Inc. • Weekly. $39.95 per year.

IBM Journal of Research and Development. International Business Machines Corp. • Bimonthly. $180.00 per year.

Industrial Computing. ISA Services, Inc. • Monthly. $50.00 per year. Published by the Instrument Society of America. Edited for engineering managers and systems integrators. Subject matter includes industrial software, programmable controllers, artificial intelligence systems, and industrial computer networking systems.

Information Processing and Management: An International Journal. Elsevier Science. • Bimonthly. $981.00 per year. Text in English, French, German and Italian.

Information Retrieval and Library Automation. Lomond Publications, Inc. • Monthly. $75.00 per year. Summarizes research events and literature worldwide.

Intranet and Networking Strategies Report: Advising IT Decision Makers on Best Practices and Current Trends. Computer Economics, Inc. • Monthly. $395.00 per year. Newsletter. Edited for information technology managers. Covers news and trends relating to a variety of corporate computer network and management information systems topics. Emphasis is on costs.

IT Cost Management Strategies: The Planning Assistant for IT Directors. Computer Economics, Inc. • Monthly. $495.00 per year. Newsletter for information technology professionals. Covers data processing costs, budgeting, financial management, and related topics.

Library Computing. Sage Publications, Inc. • Quarterly. Individuals, $65.00 per year; institutions, $255.00 per year. Formerly *Library Software Review.*

Network Computing: Computing in a Network Environment. CMP Publications, Inc. • Semimonthly. $95.00 per year.

The Red Herring: The Business of Technology. Herring Communications, Inc. • Monthly. $49.00 per year. Contains ars on investing in high technology, especially within the computer, communications, and information industries. Initial public offerings (IPOs) are emphasized. Includes technology stock listings and the Red Herring "Tech 250" stock index.

PRICE SOURCES

Computer Price Guide: The Blue Book of Used IBM Computer Prices. Computer Economics, Inc. • Quarterly. $140.00 per year. Provides average prices of used IBM computer equipment, including "complete lists of obsolete IBM equipment." Includes a newsletter on trends in the used computer market. Edited for dealers, leasing firms, and business computer buyers.

RESEARCH CENTERS AND INSTITUTES

Center for Integrated Systems. Stanford University, 420 Vis Palou Mall, Stanford, CA 94305-4070. Phone: (650)725-3621 Fax: (650)725-0991 E-mail: rdasher@cis.stanford.edu • URL: http://www.cis.stanford.edu • Research programs include manufacturing science, design science, computer architecture, semiconductor technology, and telecommunications.

Center for Research in Computing Technology. Harvard University, Pierce Hall, 29 Oxford St., Cambridge, MA 02138. Phone: (617)495-2832 Fax: (617)495-9837 E-mail: cheatham@das.harvard.edu • URL: http://www.das.harvard.edu/cs.grafs.html • Conducts research in computer vision, robotics, artificial intelligence, systems programming, programming languages, operating systems, networks, graphics, database management systems, and telecommunications.

Computation Center. University of Texas at Austin. Austin, TX 78712. Phone: (512)471-3241 Fax: (512)475-9282 E-mail: t.edgar@cc.utexas.edu • URL: http://www.utexas.edu/acits.

Engineering Systems Research Center. University of California at Berkeley. 3115 Etcheverry Hall, No. 1750, Berkeley, CA 94720-1750. Phone: (510)642-4994 Fax: (510)643-8982 E-mail: esrc@esrc.berkeley.edu • URL: http://www.esrc.berkeley.edu/esrc/.

International Data Corp. (IDC). Five Speen St., Framingham, MA 01701. Phone: (508)935-4389 Fax: (508)935-4789 • URL: http://www.idcresearch.com • Private research firm specializing in market research related to computers, multimedia, and telecommunications.

Laboratory for Computer Science. Massachusetts Institute of Technology, 545 Technology Square, Bldg. NE43, Cambridge, MA 02139. Phone: (617)253-5851 Fax: (617)258-8682 E-mail: mld@hq.lcs.mit.edu • URL: http://www.lcs.mit.edu/ • Research is in four areas: Intelligent Systems; Parallel Systems; Systems, Languages, and Networks; and Theory. Emphasis is on the application of online computing.

RAND. P.O. Box 2138, Santa Monica, CA 90407-2138. Phone: (310)393-0411 Fax: (310)393-4818 E-mail: correspondence@rand.org • URL: http://www.rand.org.

SRI International. 333 Ravenswood Ave., Menlo Park, CA 94025-3493. Phone: (650)859-2000 Fax: (650)326-5512 E-mail: inquiryline@sri.com • URL: http://www.sri.com • Private research firm specializing in market research in high technology areas.

STATISTICS SOURCES

Annual Survey of Manufactures. Available from U. S. Government Printing Office. • Annual. Prices vary. Issued by the U. S. Census Bureau as an interim update to the *Census of Manufactures.* Includes data on number of manufacturing establishments in various industries, employment, labor costs, value of shipments, capital expenditures, inventories, energy costs, and assets. (See also Census Bureau home page, http://www.census.gov/.).

Computer Publishing Market Forecast. SIMBA Information. • Annual. $1,995.00. Provides market data on computer-related books, magazines, newsletters, and other publications. Includes profiles of major publishers of computer-related material.

Computers and Office and Accounting Machines. U. S. Bureau of the Census. • Annual. Provides data on shipments: value, quantity, imports, and exports. (Current Industrial Reports, MA-35R.).

Information Systems Spending: An Analysis of Trends and Strategies. Computer Economics, Inc. • Annual. $1,595.00. Three volumes. Based on "in-depth surveys of public and private companies amd government organizations." Provides detailed data on management information systems spending, budgeting, and benchmarks. Includes charts, graphs, and analysis.

Manufacturing Profiles. Available from U. S. Government Printing Office. • Annual. Issued by the U. S. Census Bureau. A printed consolidation of the entire *Current Industrial Report* series, presenting "all the data compiled." Contains statistics on production, shipments, inventories, consumption, exports, imports, and orders for a wide variety of manufactured products. (See also Census Bureau home page, http://www.census.gov/.).

Standard & Poor's Industry Surveys. Standard & Poor's. • Semiannual. $1,800.00. Two looseleaf volumes. Includes monthly supplements. Provides detailed, individual surveys of 52 major industry groups. Each survey is revised on a semiannual basis. Also includes "Monthly Investment Review" (industry group investment analysis) and monthly "Trends & Projections" (economic analysis).

Statistical Handbook on Technology. Paula Berinstein, editor. Oryx Press. • 1999. $65.00. Provides statistical data on such items as the Internet, online services, computer technology, recycling, patents, prescription drug sales, telecommunications, and aerospace. Includes charts, tables, and graphs. Edited for the general reader. (Statistical Handbook Series).

U. S. Industry and Trade Outlook: The McGraw-Hill Companies and the U.S. Department of Commerce/ International Trade Administration. Datapso Research Corp. • Annual. $69.95. Produced by the International Trade Administration, U. S. Department of Commerce, in a "public-private" partnership with DRI/McGraw-Hill and Standard & Poor's. Provides basic data, outlook for the current year, and "Long-Term Prospects" (five-year projections) for a wide variety of products and services. Includes high technology industries. Formerly *U. S. Industrial Outlook.*

WEFA Industrial Monitor. John Wiley and Sons, Inc. • Annual. $65.00. Prepared by industry analysts at WEFA, an economic forecasting and consulting firm (originally Wharton Econometric Forecasting Associates). Contains discussions of the outlook for major U. S. industries, with many 10-year forecasts (WEFA Web site is http://www.wefa.com).

TRADE/PROFESSIONAL ASSOCIATIONS

Association for Computing Machinery. 1515 Broadway, 17th Fl., New York, NY 10036. Phone: (212)626-0500 Fax: (212)944-1318 E-mail: acmhelp@acm.org • URL: http://www.acm.org • Includes many Special Interest Groups.

Association for Data Center, Networking and Enterprise Systems. 742 E. Chapman Ave., Orange, CA 92666. Phone: (714)997-7966 Fax: (714)997-9743 E-mail: afcom@afcom.com • URL: http://www.afcom.com • Members are data processing operations management professionals.

Association of Information Technology Professionals. 315 S. Northwest Highway, Suite 200, Park Ridge, IL 60068-4278. Phone: 800-224-9371 or (847)825-8124 Fax: (847)825-1693 E-mail: aitp_hq@aitp.org • URL: http://www.aitp.org.

Computer and Automated Systems Association of Society of Manufacturing Engineers. P.O. Box 930, Dearborn, MI 48121-0930. Phone: (313)271-1500 Fax: (313)271-2861 • URL: http://www.sme.org/casa • Sponsored by the Society of Manufacturing Engineers.

Information Technology Association of America. c/o ITAA, 1616 N. Fort Myer Dr., Suite 1300, Arlington, VA 22209-9998. Phone: (703)522-5055 Fax: (703)525-2279 • Members are computer software and services companies. Maintains an Information Systems Integration Services Section.

Institute of Electrical and Electronics Engineers. Three Park Ave., 17th Fl., New York, NY 10016-5997. Phone: (212)419-7900 Fax: (212)752-4929 • URL: http://www.ieee.org.

Instrument Society of America (ISA). P.O. Box 12277, Research Triangle Park, NC 27709. Phone: (919)549-8411 Fax: (919)549-8288 E-mail: info@isa.org • URL: http://www.isa.org • Members are engineers and others concerned with industrial instrumentation, systems, computers, and automation.

Special Interest Group on Applied Computing. Association for Computing Machinery, 1515 Broadway, New York, NY 10036-5701. Phone: (212)869-7440 Fax: (212)302-5826 E-mail: sigs@acm.org • URL: http://www.acm.org/sigapp • Concerned with "innovative applications, technology transfer, experimental computing, strategic research, and the management of computing." Publishes a semiannual newsletter, *Applied Computing Review.*

OTHER SOURCES

Business & Company Resource Center. The Gale Group. • Fee-based Web site provides a wide range of business, industry, and specific company information. Access is offered to trade journal articles, market research data, insider trading activity, major shareholder data, corporate histories, emerging technology reports, corporate earnings estimates, press releases, and other sources. Provides detailed company profiles, industry overviews, and rankings. Offers integration of Predicasts PROMT, Newsletters ASAP, Investext Plus, Business Index ASAP, Brands and Their Companies, and other databases (many have full text).

DataWorld. Faulkner Information Services, Inc. • Four looseleaf volumes, with monthly supplements. $1,395.00 per year. Describes and evaluates both hardware and software relating to midrange, micro, and mainframe computers. Available on CD-ROM.

Survey of Advanced Technology. Computer Economics, Inc. • Annual. $795.00. Surveys the corporate use (or neglect) of advanced computer technology. Topics include major technology trends and emerging technologies.

World of Computer Science. The Gale Group. • 2001. $150.00. Alphabetical arrangement. Contains 650 entries covering discoveries, theories, concepts, issues, ethics, and people in the broad area of computer science and technology.

COMPUTERS, HOME

See: MICROCOMPUTERS AND MINICOMPUTERS

COMPUTERS IN ACCOUNTING

ABSTRACTS AND INDEXES

Accounting and Tax Index. UMI. • Quarterly. Price on application. Includes annual cumulative bound volume. Indexes accounting, auditing, and taxation literature appearing in journals, books, pamphlets, conference proceedings, and newsletters. (UMI is University Microfilms International, a Bell & Howell Co.).

Accounting Articles. CCH, Inc. • Monthly. $594.00 per year. Looseleaf service.

Business Periodicals Index. H. W. Wilson Co. • Monthly, except August, with quarterly and annual cumulations. Service basis for print edition; CD-ROM edition, $1,495.00 per year.

Computer Literature Index: A Subject/Author Index to Computer and Data Processing Literature. Applied Computer Research, Inc. • Quarterly, with annual cumulation. $245.00 per year. Contains brief abstracts of book and periodical literature covering all phases of computing, including approximately 70 specific application areas.

Key Abstracts: Business Automation. Available from INSPEC, Inc. • Monthly. $240.00 per year. Provides international coverage of journal and proceedings literature. Published in England by the Institution of Electrical Engineers (IEE).

CD-ROM DATABASES

ABI/INFORM Global. Bell & Howell Information and Learning. • Monthly. $6,500.00 per year. Provides CD-ROM indexing and abstracting of worldwide business literature appearing in over 1,200 periodicals for the most recent five years. Archival discs are available from 1971. Formerly *ABI/INFORM OnDisc.*

WILSONDISC: Business Periodicals Index. H. W. Wilson Co. • Monthly. $1,495.00 per year. Provides CD-ROM indexing of business periodicals from 1982 to date. Price includes online service.

DIRECTORIES

Accounting Software Guide. Anderson McLean, Inc. • Annual. $29.95. Lists accounting software by type of application and by name of dealer or producer.

ENCYCLOPEDIAS AND DICTIONARIES

Blackwell Encyclopedic Dictionary of Accounting. Rashad Abdel-khalik. Blackwell Publishers. • 1997. $105.95. The editor is associated with the University of Florida. Contains definitions of key terms combined with longer articles written by various U. S. and foreign business educators. Includes bibliographies and index. (Blackwell Encyclopedia of Management Series).

HANDBOOKS AND MANUALS

Accountant's Handbook of Information Technology. G. Jack Bologna and Anthony M. Walsh. John Wiley and Sons, Inc. • 1997. $125.00.

INTERNET DATABASES

Rutgers Accounting Web (RAW). Rutgers University Accounting Research Center. Phone: (201)648-5172 Fax: (201)648-1233 • URL: http://www.rutgers.edu/accounting • RAW Web site provides extensive links to sources of national and international accounting information, such as the Big Six accounting firms, the Financial Accounting Standards Board (FASB), SEC filings (EDGAR), journals, publishers, software, the International Accounting Network, and "Internet's largest list of accounting firms in USA." Searching is offered. Fees: Free.

ONLINE DATABASES

ABI/INFORM. Bell & Howell Information and Learning. • Provides online indexing to business-related material occurring in over 1,000 periodicals from 1971 to the present. Inquire as to online cost and availability.

Computer Database. The Gale Group. • Provides online citations with abstracts to material appearing in about 150 trade journals and newsletters in the subject areas of computers, telecommunications, and electronics. Time period is 1983 to date, with weekly updates. Inquire as to online cost and availability.

Wilson Business Abstracts Online. H. W. Wilson Co. • Indexes and abstracts 600 major business periodicals, plus the *Wall Street Journal* and the business section of the *New York Times.* Indexing is from 1982, abstracting from 1990, with the two newspapers included from 1993. Updated weekly. Inquire as to online cost and availability. (*Business Periodicals Index* without abstracts is also available online.).

PERIODICALS AND NEWSLETTERS

Accounting Technology. Faulkner & Gray, Inc. • Nine times a year. $58.00 per year. Provides advice and information on computers and software for accountants. Formerly *Computers in Accounting.*

CPA Software News. Cygnus Business Media. • Eight times a year. $39.95 per year. Provides articles and reviews relating to computer technology and software for accountants.

CPA Technology Advisor (Certified Public Accountant): Profitable Strategies and Practical Solutions for Managing. Harcourt Brace Professional Publishing. • Monthly. $237.00 per year. Newsletter. Describes hardware and software products and makes recommendations. Formerly *C P A Technology Report.*

Quantum PC Report for CPAs. Quantum Professional Publishing. • Monthly. $235.00 per year. Newsletter on personal computer software and hardware for the accounting profession.

RESEARCH CENTERS AND INSTITUTES

Accounting Research Program. University of California, John E. Anderson Graduate School of Management, Los Angeles, CA 90095-1481. Phone: (310)206-6462 Fax: (310)267-2163 E-mail: pat.hughes@anderson.ucla.edu.

TRADE/PROFESSIONAL ASSOCIATIONS

American Institute of Certified Public Accountants. 1211 Ave. of the Americas, New York, NY 10036-8775. Phone: 800-862-4272 or (212)596-6200 Fax: (212)596-6213 • URL: http://www.aicpa.org.

Association for Accounting Administration. 136 S. Keowee St., Dayton, OH 45402. Phone: (937)222-0030 Fax: (937)222-5794 E-mail: aaainfo@cpaadmin.org • URL: http://www.cpaadmin.org • Members are accounting and office systems executives. Includes an Information Management Committee.

Institute of Internal Auditors. 249 Maitland Ave., Altamonte Springs, FL 32701-4201. Phone: (407)830-7600 Fax: (407)831-5171 E-mail: iia@theiia.org • URL: http://www.theiia.org.

COMPUTERS IN BANKING

See: BANK AUTOMATION; COMPUTERS IN FINANCE

COMPUTERS IN EDUCATION

See also: MICROCOMPUTERS AND MINICOMPUTERS

GENERAL WORKS

Computer Studies: Computers in Education. John Hirschbuhl and Loretta Wilkinson. McGraw-Hill. • 1997. $11.64. Eighth edition.

Computers in Education. Paul F. Merrill and others. Allyn and Bacon, Inc. • 1995. $59.00. Third edition.

The Evolving Virtual Library: Practical and Philosophical Perspectives. Laverna M. Saunders, editor. Information Today, Inc. • 1999. $39.50. Second edition. Various authors cover trends in library and school use of the Internet, intranets, extranets, and electronic databases.

Net Curriculum: An Educator's Guide to Using the Internet. Linda Joseph. Information Today, Inc. • 1999. $29.95. Covers various educational aspects of the Internet. Written for K-12 teachers, librarians, and media specialists by a columnist for *Multimedia Schools.* (CyberAge Books.).

Technology and Teaching. Les Lloyd, editor. Information Today, Inc. • 1997. $42.50. Contains multimedia computer application case studies relating to college level curricula and teaching.

ABSTRACTS AND INDEXES

Computer Literature Index: A Subject/Author Index to Computer and Data Processing Literature. Applied Computer Research, Inc. • Quarterly, with annual cumulation. $245.00 per year. Contains brief abstracts of book and periodical literature covering all phases of computing, including approximately 70 specific application areas.

ALMANACS AND YEARBOOKS

Educational Media and Technology Yearbook. Libraries Unlimited, Inc. • Annual. $65.00.

CD-ROM DATABASES

Multimedia Schools: A Practical Journal of Multimedia, CD-ROM, Online, and Internet in K-12. Information Today, Inc. • Bimonthly. $39.95 per year. Provides purchasing recommendations and technical advice relating to the use of high-tech multimedia products in schools.

DIRECTORIES

TESS: (The Educational Software Selector). Educational Products Information Exchange. EPIE Institute. • Semiannual. $79.95 per year. Lists over 900 suppliers of educational software for Mackintosh, Apple II, MS-DOS and Windows compatible computers and videodisc players. Formerly *The Latest and Best of TESS: The Educational Software Selector.*

ENCYCLOPEDIAS AND DICTIONARIES

Dictionary of Computing. Valerie Illingworth, editor. Oxford University Press, Inc. • 1996. $49.95. Fourth edition.

HANDBOOKS AND MANUALS

Handbook of Educational Technology: Practical Guide for Teachers. Fred Percival and others. Nichols Publishing Co. • 1993. $39.95. Third edition.

ONLINE DATABASES

Computer Database. The Gale Group. • Provides online citations with abstracts to material appearing in about 150 trade journals and newsletters in the subject areas of computers, telecommunications, and electronics. Time period is 1983 to date, with weekly updates. Inquire as to online cost and availability.

Education Index Online. H. W. Wilson Co. • Indexes a wide variety of periodicals related to schools, colleges, and education, 1984 to date. Monthly updates. Inquire as to online cost and availability.

PERIODICALS AND NEWSLETTERS

Boardwatch Magazine: Guide to the Internet, World Wide Web, and BBS. Penton Media Inc. • Monthly. $72.00 per year. Covers World Wide Web publishing, Internet technology, educational aspects of online communication, Internet legalities, and other computer communication topics.

Computer Industry Report. International Data Corp. • Semimonthly. $495.00 per year. Newsletter. Annual supplement. Also known as "The Gray Sheet." Formerly *EDP Industry Report and Market Review.*

Computers in the Schools: The Interdisciplinary Journal of Practice, Theory, and Applied Research. Haworth Press, Inc. • Quarterly. Individuals, $60.00 per year; institutions, $90.00 per year; libraries, $300.00 per year.

Educational Technology News. Business Publishers, Inc. • Biweekly. $318.00 per year. Newsletter. Formerly *Education Computer News.*

Electronic Learning in Your Classroom. Scholastic, Inc. • Four times a year. $19.95 per year. Includes classroom applications for computers. For teachers of grades K-12. Formerly *Electronic Learning.*

Home Office Computing: Building Better Businesses with Technology. Freedom Technology Media Group. • Monthly. $16.97 per year. Office automation for the self-employed and small businesses. Formerly *Family and Home Office Computing.*

Mathematics and Computer Education. George M. Miller, editor. MATYC Journal, Inc. • Three times a year. Individuals, $29.00 per year; institutions, $70.00 per year. Articles for high school and college teachers.

Multimedia Schools: A Practical Journal of Multimedia, CD-Rom, Online and Internet in K-12. Information Today, Inc. • Five times a year. $39.95 per year. Edited for school librarians, media center directors, computer coordinators, and others concerned with educational multimedia. Coverage includes the use of CD-ROM sources, the Internet, online services, and library technology.

T H E Journal (Technological Horizons in Education). Ed Warnshius Ltd. • 11 times a year. $29.00 per year. For educators of all levels.

Technology and Learning: The Leading Magazine of Electronic Education. Miller Freeman, Inc. • Eight times a year. $29.95 per year. Covers all levels of computer/electronic education-elementary to college. Formerly *Classroom Computer Learning.*

University Business: Solutions for Today's Higher Education. University Business, LLC. • Bimonthly. $49.00 per year. Edited for college administrators, including managers of business services, finance, computing, and telecommunications. Includes information on relevant technological advances.

RESEARCH CENTERS AND INSTITUTES

Computer-Based Education and Instructional Design Project. Temple University. Psychological Studies Dept., Broad and Montgomery, Ritter Annex, Room 217, Philadelphia, PA 19122. Phone: (215)204-6109 Fax: (215)204-6103 E-mail: snelbeck@vm.temple.edu.

Concord Consortium, Inc. 37 Thoreau St., Concord, MA 01742. Phone: (978)369-4367 Fax: (978)371-0696 E-mail: shea@concord.org • URL: http://www.concord.org • Research areas include educational applications of computers and computer networks.

Instructional Technology Center. University of Delaware, College of Education, 305 Willard Hall, Wilmington, DE 19716. Phone: (302)831-8164 Fax: (302)831-4110 E-mail: fth@udel.edu • URL: http://www.udel.edu.

TRADE/PROFESSIONAL ASSOCIATIONS

IEEE Computer Society. 1730 Massachusetts Ave., N. W., Washington, DC 20036. Phone: (202)371-0101 Fax: (202)728-9614 E-mail: csinfo@computer.org • URL: http://www.computer.org • A society of the Institute of Electrical and Electronics Engineers. Said to be the world's largest organization of computer professionals. Some of the specific committees are: Computer Communications; Computer Graphics; Computers in Education; Design Automation; Office Automation;

Personal Computing; Robotics; Security and Privacy; Software Engineering.

International Society for Technology in Education. 480 Chamelton St., Eugene, OR 97401-2626. Phone: 800-336-5191 or (541)302-3777 Fax: (541)302-3778 E-mail: custsvc@iste.org • URL: http://www.iste.org.

Special Interest Group for Computer Science Education. c/o Association for Computing Machinery, 1515 Broadway, New York, NY 10036-5701. Phone: (212)869-7440 Fax: (212)302-5826 E-mail: sigs@acm.org • URL: http://www.acm.org • Concerned with education relating to computer science and technology on various levels, ranging from secondary school to graduate degree programs.

Special Interest Group for Computer Uses in Education. c/o Association for Computing Machinery, 1515 Broadway, New York, NY 10036-5701. Phone: (212)869-7440 Fax: (212)302-5826 E-mail: sigs@acm.org • URL: http://www.acm.org • Concerned with the use of the computer as a teaching device.

OTHER SOURCES

NetSavvy: Building Information Literacy in the Classroom. Ian Jukes and others. Phi Delta Kappa International. • 2000. $27.95. Second edition. Provides practical advice on the teaching of computer, Internet, and technological literacy. Includes sample lesson plans and grade-level objectives.

Using Technology to Increase Student Learning. Linda E. Reksten. Phi Delta Kappa International. • 2000. $34.95. Emphasis is on the use of computer technology in schools.

COMPUTERS IN FINANCE

ABSTRACTS AND INDEXES

Banking Information Index. U M I Banking Information Index. • Monthly: Price on application. Covers a wide variety of banking, business, and financial subjects in periodicals. Formerly *Banking Literature Index.*

Business Periodicals Index. H. W. Wilson Co. • Monthly, except August, with quarterly and annual cumulations. Service basis for print edition; CD-ROM edition, $1,495.00 per year.

Computer Literature Index: A Subject/Author Index to Computer and Data Processing Literature. Applied Computer Research, Inc. • Quarterly, with annual cumulation. $245.00 per year. Contains brief abstracts of book and periodical literature covering all phases of computing, including approximately 70 specific application areas.

CD-ROM DATABASES

ABI/INFORM Global. Bell & Howell Information and Learning. • Monthly. $6,500.00 per year. Provides CD-ROM indexing and abstracting of worldwide business literature appearing in over 1,200 periodicals for the most recent five years. Archival discs are available from 1971. Formerly *ABI/INFORM OnDisc.*

WILSONDISC: Business Periodicals Index. H. W. Wilson Co. • Monthly. $1,495.00 per year. Provides CD-ROM indexing of business periodicals from 1982 to date. Price includes online service.

DIRECTORIES

Futures Guide to Computerized Trading. Futures Magazine, Inc. • Annual. $10.00. "A directory of products and services for the computerized trader." Provides information on computer software applications for commodity traders and money managers, including trading methods and technical analysis.

Futures Magazine SourceBook: The Most Complete List of Exchanges, Companies, Regulators, Organizations, etc., Offering Products and Services to the Futures and Options Industry. Futures Magazine, Inc. • Annual. $19.50. Provides information on commodity futures brokers, trading method services, publications, and other items of interest to futures traders and money managers.

Microbanker Software Buyer's Guide. Microbanker, Inc. • Annual. $245.00 per year. Includes suppliers of over 1,550 financial application programs for microcomputers.

HANDBOOKS AND MANUALS

Artificial Intelligence and Software Engineering. Darek Partridge. Fitzroy Dearborn Publishers, Inc. • 1998. $55.00. Includes applications of artificial intelligence software to banking and financial services.

Artificial Intelligence in the Capital Markets: State-of-the-Art Applications. Roy A Freedman and Robert A. Klein. McGraw-Hill Professional. • 1994. $85.00.

INTERNET DATABASES

Futures Online. Oster Communications, Inc. Phone: 800-601-8907 or (319)277-1278 Fax: (319)277-7982 • URL: http://www.futuresmag.com • Web site presents updates of *Futures* magazine and links to other futures-related sites. Includes "Futures Industry News," "Technical Talk," "Today's Hot Markets," "Futures Talk" (forums), "Futures Library" (archives, 1993 to date), and other features. Keyword searching is available. Updating: daily. Fees: Free.

ONLINE DATABASES

ABI/INFORM. Bell & Howell Information and Learning. • Provides online indexing to business-related material occurring in over 1,000 periodicals from 1971 to the present. Inquire as to online cost and availability.

Banking Information Source. Bell & Howell Information and Learning. • Provides indexing and abstracting of periodical and other literature from 1982 to date, with weekly updates. Covers the financial services industry: banks, savings institutions, investment houses, credit unions, insurance companies, and real estate organizations. Emphasis is on marketing and management. Inquire as to online cost and availability. (Formerly *FINIS: Financial Industry Information Service.*).

Computer Database. The Gale Group. • Provides online citations with abstracts to material appearing in about 150 trade journals and newsletters in the subject areas of computers, telecommunications, and electronics. Time period is 1983 to date, with weekly updates. Inquire as to online cost and availability.

Mastering Online Investing: How to Use the Internet to Become a More Successful Investor. Michael C. Thomsett. Dearborn Financial Publishing. • 2001. $19.95. Emphasis is on the Internet as an information source for intelligent investing, avoiding "speculation and fads.".

Super Searchers on Wall Street: Top Investment Professionals Share Their Online Research Secrets. Amelia Kassel and Reva Basch. Information Today, Inc. • 2000. $24.95. Gives the results of interviews with "10 leading financial industry research experts." Explains how online information is used by stock brokers, investment bankers, and individual investors. Includes relevant Web sites and other sources. (CyberAge Books.).

Wilson Business Abstracts Online. H. W. Wilson Co. • Indexes and abstracts 600 major business periodicals, plus the *Wall Street Journal* and the business section of the *New York Times.* Indexing is from 1982, abstracting from 1990, with the two newspapers included from 1993. Updated weekly. Inquire as to online cost and availability. (*Business Periodicals Index* without abstracts is also available online.).

PERIODICALS AND NEWSLETTERS

Computerized Investing. American Association of Individual Investors. • Bimonthly. $40.00 per year. Newsletter on computer-aided investment analysis. Includes reviews of software.

Financial Service Online. Faulkner & Gray, Inc. • Monthly. $95.00 per year. Covers the operation and management of interactive financial services to consumers in their homes for banking, investments, and bill-paying.

Future Banker: The Vision of Leadership in an Electronic Age. American Banker. • Monthly. $79.00 per year. Covers technology innovation for the banking industry, including online banking.

Online Investor: Personal Investing for the Digital Age. Stock Trends, Inc. • Monthly. $24.95 per year. Provides advice and Web site reviews for online traders.

Securities Industry News. American Banker. • Weekly. $275.00 per year. Covers securities dealing and processing, including regulatory compliance, shareholder services, human resources, transaction clearing, and technology.

Wall Street and Technology: For Senior-Level Executives in Technology and Information Management in Securities and Invesment Firms. Miller Freeman, Inc. • Monthly. $99.00 per year. Includes material on the use of computers in technical investment strategies. Formerly *Wall Computer Review.*

WebFinance. Securities Data Publishing. • Semimonthly. $995.00 per year. Newsletter (also available online at www.webfinance.net). Covers the Internet-based provision of online financial services by banks, online brokers, mutual funds, and insurance companies. Provides news stories, analysis, and descriptions of useful resources. (Securities Data Publishing is a unit of Thomson Financial.).

RESEARCH CENTERS AND INSTITUTES

Institute for Quantitative Research in Finance. Church Street Station, P.O. Box 6194, New York, NY 10249-6194. Phone: (212)744-6825 Fax: (212)517-2259 E-mail: daleberman@compuserve • Financial research areas include quantitative methods, securities analysis, and the financial structure of industries. Also known as the "Q Group.".

OTHER SOURCES

The Options Workbook: Proven Strategies from a Market Wizard. Anthony J. Saliba. Dearborn Financial Publishing. • 2001. $40.00. Emphasis is on computerized trading on the Chicago Board Options Exchange. Includes information on specific trading strategies.

COMPUTERS IN GOVERNMENT

ABSTRACTS AND INDEXES

Computer Literature Index: A Subject/Author Index to Computer and Data Processing Literature. Applied Computer Research, Inc. • Quarterly, with annual cumulation. $245.00 per year. Contains brief abstracts of book and periodical literature covering all phases of computing, including approximately 70 specific application areas.

Sage Public Administration Abstracts. Sage Publications, Inc. • Quarterly. Individuals, $150.00 per year; institutions, $575.00 per year.

CD-ROM DATABASES

NTIS on SilverPlatter. Available from SilverPlatter Information, Inc. • Quarterly. $2,850.00 per year. Produced by the National Technical Information Service. Provides a CD-ROM guide to over 500,000 government reports on a wide variety of technical, industrial, and business topics.

PAIS on CD-ROM. Public Affairs Information Service, Inc. • Quarterly. $1,995.00 per year. Provides a CD-ROM version of the online service, *PAIS International.* Contains over 400,000 citations to the literature of contemporary social, political, and economic issues.

ONLINE DATABASES

Computer Database. The Gale Group. • Provides online citations with abstracts to material appearing in about 150 trade journals and newsletters in the subject areas of computers, telecommunications, and electronics. Time period is 1983 to date, with weekly updates. Inquire as to online cost and availability.

NTIS Bibliographic Data Base. National Technical Information Service. • Contains citations and abstracts to unrestricted reports of government-sponsored research, 1964 to date. Covers a wide range of technical, engineering, business, and social science topics. Monthly updates. Inquire as to online cost and availability.

PAIS International. Public Affairs Information Service, Inc. • Corresponds to the former printed publications, *PAIS Bulletin* (1976-90) and *PAIS Foreign Language Index* (1972-90), and to the current *PAIS International in Print* (1991 to date). Covers economic, political, and sociological material appearing in periodicals, books, government documents, and other publications. Updating is monthly. Inquire as to online cost and availability.

PERIODICALS AND NEWSLETTERS

Federal Computer Week: The Newspaper for the Government Systems Community. FCW Government Technology Group. • 41 times a year. $95.00 per year.

Governing: The States and Localities. • Monthly. $39.95 per year. Edited for state and local government officials. Covers finance, office management, computers, telecommunications, environmental concerns, etc.

Government Computer News: The Newspaper Serving Computer Users Throughout the Federal Government. Cahners Business Information. • 32 times a year. Free to qualified personnel.

Government Executive: Federal Government's Business Magazine. National Journal Group, Inc. • Monthly. $48.00 per year. Includes management of computerized information systems in the federal government.

Government Technology: Solutions for State and Local Government in the Information Age. • Monthly. Free to qualified personnel.

RESEARCH CENTERS AND INSTITUTES

Government Finance Officers Center Association Research Center. 180 N. Michigan Ave., Suite 800, Chicago, IL 60601. Phone: (312)977-9700 Fax: (312)977-4806 E-mail: rmiranda@gfoa.org • URL: http://www.gfoa.org • Provides consulting and research services in state and local finance. Designs and produces microcomputer software packages for use in government finance functions.

COMPUTERS IN INVESTING

See: COMPUTERS IN FINANCE

COMPUTERS IN LIBRARIES

See: LIBRARY AUTOMATION; ONLINE INFORMATION SYSTEMS

COMPUTERS, PERSONAL

See: MICROCOMPUTERS AND MINICOMPUTERS

COMPUTERS, PORTABLE

See: PORTABLE COMPUTERS

CONCESSIONS

See also: FAIRS; FRANCHISES

DIRECTORIES

Concession Profession. National Association of Concessionaires. • Biennial. Membership. Advertising vehicle serving the concession industry. Formerly *Insite.*

TRADE/PROFESSIONAL ASSOCIATIONS

National Association of Concessionaires. 35 E. Wacker Dr., Suite 1816, Chicago, IL 60601. Phone: (312)236-3858 Fax: (312)236-7809 E-mail: smcross@earthlink.net • URL: http://www.naconline.org.

National Park Hospitality Association. 1275 New York Ave., N.W., Suite 450, Washington, DC 20005. Phone: (202)682-9507 Fax: (202)682-9509 E-mail: npha@erols.com.

CONCILIATION, INDUSTRIAL

See: ARBITRATION

CONCRETE INDUSTRY

See also: BUILDING INDUSTRY; CEMENT INDUSTRY

GENERAL WORKS

Design of Concrete Structures. Arthur H. Nilson and David Darwin. McGraw-Hill. • 1997. $95.31. 12th edition. (Construction Engineering and Project Management Series).

Reinforced Concrete Fundamentals. Phil M. Ferguson and others. John Wiley and Sons, Inc. • 1988. $117.95. Fifth edition.

ALMANACS AND YEARBOOKS

The Concrete Yearbook. EMAP Construction. • Annual. $115.00.

DIRECTORIES

Aberdeen's Concrete Construction Buyers' Guide. The Aberdeen Group. • Annual. $5.00. Lists sources of products and services related to building with concrete.

Concrete Journal Buyers' Guide. The Aberdeen Group. • Annual. $3.00. Lists manufacturers or suppliers of concrete-related products and services.

Concrete Repair Digest Buyers' Guide. The Aberdeen Group. • Annual. $3.00. Lists sources of products and services for concrete repair and maintenance specialists.

Magazine of Masonry Construction Buyers' Guide. The Aberdeen Group. • Annual. $3.00. Lists manufacturers or suppliers of products and services related to masonry construction.

ENCYCLOPEDIAS AND DICTIONARIES

Cement and Concrete Terminology. American Concrete Institute. • 1990. $54.50.

FINANCIAL RATIOS

Annual Statement Studies. Robert Morris Associates: The Association of Lending and Credit Risk Professiona. • Annual. Free to members; non-members, $140.00. Median and quartile financial ratios are given for over 400 kinds of manufacturing, wholesale, retail, construction, and consumer finance establishments. Data is sorted by both asset size and sales volume. Includes a clearly written "Definition of Ratios" and an alphabetical industry index.

HANDBOOKS AND MANUALS

ACI Manual of Concrete Practice. American Concrete Institute. • Free to members; non-members, $595.00 per set. Five volumes.

PERIODICALS AND NEWSLETTERS

The Aberdeen's Concrete Construction. Aberdeen Group. • Monthly. $30.00 per year. Covers methods of building with precast, prestressed, and other forms of concrete. Emphasis is on technology and new products or construction procedures.

The Aberdeen's Magazine of Masonry Construction. Aberdeen Group. • Monthly. $30.00 per year. Covers the business, production, and marketing aspects of various kind of masonry construction: brick, concrete block, glass block, etc.

Concrete International. American Concrete Institute. • Monthly. $122.00 per year. Covers practical technology, industry news, and business management relating to the concrete construction industry.

The Concrete Producer. The Aberdeen Group. • Monthly. $27.00 per year. Covers the production and marketing of various concrete products, including precast and prestressed concrete. Formerly *Aberdeen's Concrete Journal.*

Concrete Products. Intertec Publishing Corp. • Monthly. $36.00 per year.

RESEARCH CENTERS AND INSTITUTES

Center for Cement Composite Materials. University of Illinois at Urbana-Champaign. 204 Ceramics Bldg., 105 S. Goodwin Ave., Urbana, IL 61801. Phone: (217)244-6210 Fax: (217)244-6917 E-mail: lstruble@uiuc.edu.

ORTECH Corporation. 2395 Speakman Dr., Mississauga, ON, Canada L5K 1B3. Phone: (905)822-4111 E-mail: mail@dieselnet.com • URL: http://www.dieselnet.com/com/xf005.html.

STATISTICS SOURCES

Annual Survey of Manufactures. Available from U. S. Government Printing Office. • Annual. Prices vary. Issued by the U. S. Census Bureau as an interim update to the *Census of Manufactures.* Includes data on number of manufacturing establishments in various industries, employment, labor costs, value of shipments, capital expenditures, inventories, energy costs, and assets. (See also Census Bureau home page, http://www.census.gov/.).

TRADE/PROFESSIONAL ASSOCIATIONS

American Concrete Institute. P.O. Box 9094, Farmington Hills, MI 48333-9094. Phone: (248)848-3700 Fax: (248)848-3701 E-mail: teching@aci-int.org • URL: http://www.aci-int.org.

National Concrete Masonry Association. 2302 Horse Pen Rd., Herndon, VA 20171-3499. Phone: (703)713-1900 Fax: (703)713-1910 E-mail: ncma@ncma.org • URL: http://www.ncma.org.

National Ready Mixed Concrete Association. 900 Spring St., Silver Spring, MD 20910. Phone: 888-846-7622 or (301)587-1400 Fax: (301)585-4219 E-mail: bgarbini@nrmca.org • URL: http://www.nrmc.org.

CONDIMENTS INDUSTRY

See: SPICE INDUSTRY

CONDOMINIUMS

See also: APARTMENT HOUSES; HOUSING; REAL ESTATE BUSINESS

GENERAL WORKS

Condominiums, The Effects of Conversion on a Community. John R. Dinkelspiel and others. Greenwood Publishing Group, Inc. • 1981. $55.00.

CD-ROM DATABASES

Sourcebooks America CD-ROM. CACI Marketing Systems. • Annual. $1,250.00. Provides the CD-ROM version of *The Sourcebook of ZIP Code Demographics: Census Edition* and *The Sourcebook of County Demographics: Census Edition.*

FINANCIAL RATIOS

Almanac of Business and Industrial Financial Ratios. Leo Troy. Prentice Hall. • Annual. $99.95. Contains financial ratios derived from federal tax returns. Ratios for each of about 200 industries are arranged according to company asset size.

HANDBOOKS AND MANUALS

How to Buy a House, Condo, or Co-op. Jean C. Thomsett. Consumers Union of the United States, Inc. • 1996. $84.75. Fifth edition.

Your Dream Home: A Comprehensive Guide to Buying a House, Condo, or Co-op. Marguerite Smith. Available from Little, Brown & Co. • 1997. $10.99. Published by Warner Books.

ONLINE DATABASES

American Statistics Index: A Comprehensive Guide and Index to the Statistical Publications of the United States Government [Online]. Congressional Information Service, Inc. • Indexes and abstracts, 1973 to date. Inquire as to online cost and availability.

PERIODICALS AND NEWSLETTERS

Condo Business. Shelter Pubications. • Monthly. $65.00 per year. Covers condominum development and administration industries.

Ledger Quarterly: A Financial Review for Community Association Practitioners. Community Associations Institute. • Quarterly. Members, $40.00 per year; non-members, $67.00 per year. Newsletter. Provides current information on issues affecting the finances of condominium, cooperative, homeowner, apartment, and other community housing associations.

Mortgage and Real Estate Executives Report. Warren, Gorham and Lamont/RIA Group. • Semimonthly. $159.75 per year. Newsletter. Source of ideas and new updates. Covers the latest opportunities and developments.

STATISTICS SOURCES

American Housing Survey for the United States in [year]. Available from U. S. Government Printing Office. • Biennial. Issued by the U. S. Census Bureau (http://www.census.gov). Covers both owner-occupied and renter-occupied housing. Includes data on such factors as condition of building, type of mortgage, utility costs, and housing occupied by minorities. (Current Housing Reports, H150.).

Housing Statistics of the United States. Patrick A. Simmons, editor. Bernan Press. • 2000. $74.00. Third edition. (Bernan Press U.S. Data Book Series).

TRADE/PROFESSIONAL ASSOCIATIONS

Community Associations Institute. 1630 Duke St., Alexandria, VA 22314. Phone: (703)548-8600 Fax: (703)684-1581 • URL: http://www.caionline.org • Members are condominium associations, homeowners associations, builders, property managers, developers, and others concerned with the common facilities and services in condominiums, townhouses, planned unit developments, and other planned communities.

Institute of Real Estate Management. 430 N. Michigan Ave., Chicago, IL 60611-4090. Phone: 800-837-0706 or (312)329-6000 Fax: (312)410-7960 E-mail: rvukas@irem.org • URL: http://www.irem.org.

National Association of Realtors. 430 N. Michigan Ave., Chicago, IL 60611. Phone: 800-874-6500 Fax: (312)329-5962 • URL: http://www.realtor.com.

OTHER SOURCES

Condominium Law and Practice Forms. Patrick J. Rohan and Melvin A. Reskin. Matthew Bender & Co., Inc. • $1,400.00. Eight looseleaf volumes. Periodic supplementation. Guide for handling condominium transactions. (Real Estate Transaction Series).

CONFECTIONERY INDUSTRY

See: CANDY INDUSTRY

CONFERENCE MANAGEMENT

See: MEETING MANAGEMENT

CONFERENCES, WORKSHOPS, AND SEMINARS

See also: CONVENTIONS; SALES CONVENTIONS

BIBLIOGRAPHIES

Bibliographic Guide to Conference Publications. Available from The Gale Group. • Annual. $545.00. Two volumes. Published by G. K. Hall & Co., Lists a wide range of conference publications cataloged by the New York Public Library and the Library of Congress.

DIRECTORIES

Directory of Corporate Meeting Planners. Salesman's Guide. • Annual. $385.00. Lists about 18,000 planners of off-site meetings for over 11,000 U. S. and Canadian corporations. Provides information on number of attendees and professional speaker usage.

Forthcoming International Scientific and Technical Conferences. Information Today, Inc. • Quarterly. Members, $164.00 per year; non-members, $204.00 per year.

International Congress Calendar. Union of International Associations. • Quarterly. $375.00 per year. Over 7,000 international meetings scheduled up to 12 to 15 months.

Trade Shows Worldwide: An International Directory of Events, Facilities and Suppliers. The Gale Group. • 2000. $299.00. 16th edition. Provides detailed information from over 75 countries on more than 8,400 trade shows and exhibitions. Separate sections are provided for trade shows/exhibitions, for sponsors/organizers, and for services, facilities, and information sources. Indexing is by date, location, subject, name, and keyword.

ENCYCLOPEDIAS AND DICTIONARIES

Conference Terminology in English, Spanish, Russian, Italian, German and Hungarian. J. Herbert. Elsevier Science. • 1976. $130.25. Second revised edition.

HANDBOOKS AND MANUALS

How to Develop and Promote Successful Seminars and Workshops: A Definitive Guide to Creating and Marketing Seminars, Workshops, Classes, and Conferences. Howard L. Shenson. John Wiley and Sons, Inc. • 1990. $99.50.

How to Make it Big in the Seminar Business. Paul Karasik. McGraw-Hill. • 1995. $15.95. Covers the organizing and marketing of seminars or workshops, including fee determination, promotion, scheduling, and evaluation.

Seminar Promoting. Entrepreneur Media, Inc. • Looseleaf. $59.50. A practical guide to starting a seminar promotion business. Covers profit potential, start-up costs, market size evaluation, owner's time required, site selection, pricing, accounting, advertising, promotion, etc. (Start-Up Business Guide No. E1071.).

Workshops: Designing and Facilitating Experiential Learning. Jeff E. Brooks-Harris and Susan R. Stock-Ward. Sage Publications, Inc. • 1999. $55.00. Presents a practical approach to designing, running, and evaluating workshops in business, adult education, and other areas. Includes references.

INTERNET DATABASES

Trade Show Central: The Internet's Leading Trade Show Information Resource!. Trade Show Central. Phone: (781)235-8095 Fax: (781)416-4500 • URL: http://www.tscentral.com • Web site provides information on "more than 30,000 Trade Shows, Conferences, and Seminars, 5,000 service providers, and 5,000 venues and facilities around the world." Searching is offered by trade show name, industry category, date, and location. Results may be sorted by event name, city, country, or date. Includes a "Career Center" for trade show personnel. Continuous updating. Fees: Free.

PERIODICALS AND NEWSLETTERS

The Meeting Professional. Meeting Professionals International. • Monthly. $50.00 per year. Published for professionals in the meeting and convention industry. Contains news, features, and how-to's for domestic and international meetings management. Formerly *Meeting Manager.*

Scientific Meetings. Scientific Meetings Publications. • Quarterly. $85.00 per year. Provides information on forthcoming scientific, technical, medical, health, engineering and management meetings held throughout the world.

World Meetings: Outside United States and Canada. Available from Gale Group. • Quarterly. $195.00 per year.

World Meetings: United States and Canada. Available from Gale Group. • Quarterly. $195.00 per year.

TRADE/PROFESSIONAL ASSOCIATIONS

International Association of Conference Translators. 15, route des Morillons, CH-1218 Grand-Saconnex, Switzerland. Phone: 41 22 7910666 Fax: 41 22 7885644 E-mail: aitc@atge.automail.com.

CONFLICT MANAGEMENT

See: ARBITRATION; NEGOTIATION

CONGLOMERATES

See: CORPORATIONS

CONGRESS

See: UNITED STATES CONGRESS

CONSERVATION

See: NATURAL RESOURCES

CONSTRUCTION CONTRACTS

See: BUILDING CONTRACTS

CONSTRUCTION, ELECTRICAL

See: ELECTRICAL CONSTRUCTION INDUSTRY

CONSTRUCTION EQUIPMENT

See also: BUILDING INDUSTRY; CIVIL ENGINEERING; HOUSING

GENERAL WORKS

Construction Contracting. Richard H. Clough and Glenn A. Sears. John Wiley and Sons, Inc. • 1994. $99.00. Sixth edition.

DIRECTORIES

Builder: Buyer's Guide. Hanley-Wood, LLC. • Annual. $10.00. A directory of products and services for the home building and remodeling industry.

Construction Equipment Buyers' Guide. Cahners Business Information. • Annual. Included in subscription to *Construction Equipment.*

Construction Equipment Distribution-Directory. Associated Equipment Distributors. • Annual. $100.00 per year. Lists about 1,300 members of the association.

ProSales Buyer's Guide. Hanley-Wood, LLC. • Annual. $5.00. A directory of equipment for professional builders.

ENCYCLOPEDIAS AND DICTIONARIES

Dictionary of Civil Engineering and Construction Machinery and Equipment. Herbert Bucksch. French and European Publishers, Inc. • 1976. $275.00. Two volumes. Vol. 1, $225.00; vol. 2, $225.00. Text in English and French.

FINANCIAL RATIOS

Almanac of Business and Industrial Financial Ratios. Leo Troy. Prentice Hall. • Annual. $99.95. Contains financial ratios derived from federal tax returns. Ratios for each of about 200 industries are arranged according to company asset size.

Annual Statement Studies. Robert Morris Associates: The Association of Lending and Credit Risk Professiona. • Annual. Free to members; non-members, $140.00. Median and quartile financial ratios are given for over 400 kinds of manufacturing, wholesale, retail, construction, and consumer finance establishments. Data is sorted by both asset size and sales volume. Includes a clearly written "Definition of Ratios" and an alphabetical industry index.

HANDBOOKS AND MANUALS

Complete Building Equipment Maintenance Desk Book. Sheldon J. Fuchs, editor. Prentice Hall. • 1992. $69.95. Second edition.

PERIODICALS AND NEWSLETTERS

Construction Equipment Distribution. Associated Equipment Distributors. • Monthly. Members, $20.00 per year; non-members, $40.00 per year.

Construction Equipment Operation and Maintenance. Construction Publications Inc. • Bimonthly. $12.00 per year. Information for users of construction equipment and industry news.

Equipment Today. Cygnus Publishing, Inc. • Monthly. $65.00 per year. Includes annual *Product* issue Formerly *Equipment Guide News.*

STATISTICS SOURCES

Annual Survey of Manufactures. Available from U. S. Government Printing Office. • Annual. Prices vary. Issued by the U. S. Census Bureau as an interim update to the *Census of Manufactures.* Includes data on number of manufacturing establishments in various industries, employment, labor costs, value of shipments, capital expenditures, inventories, energy costs, and assets. (See also Census Bureau home page, http://www.census.gov/.).

Manufacturing Profiles. Available from U. S. Government Printing Office. • Annual. Issued by the U. S. Census Bureau. A printed consolidation of the entire *Current Industrial Report* series, presenting "all the data compiled." Contains statistics on production, shipments, inventories, consumption, exports, imports, and orders for a wide variety of manufactured products. (See also Census Bureau home page, http://www.census.gov/.).

U. S. Industry and Trade Outlook: The McGraw-Hill Companies and the U.S. Department of Commerce/ International Trade Administration. Datapso Research Corp. • Annual. $69.95. Produced by the International Trade Administration, U. S. Department of Commerce, in a "public-private" partnership with DRI/McGraw-Hill and Standard & Poor's. Provides basic data, outlook for the current year, and "Long-Term Prospects" (five-year projections) for a wide variety of products and services. Includes high technology industries. Formerly *U. S. Industrial Outlook.*

TRADE/PROFESSIONAL ASSOCIATIONS

Associated Equipment Distributors. 615 W. 22nd St., Oak Brook, IL 60521. Phone: 800-388-0650 or (630)574-0650 Fax: (630)574-0132 E-mail: info@aednet.org.

CIMA Marketing Communications Council. 111 E. Wisconsin Ave., Suite 1000, Milwaukee, WI 53202. Phone: (414)272-0943 Fax: (414)272-1170.

Construction Industry Manufacturers Association. 111 E. Wisconsin Ave., Suite 1000, Milwaukee, WI 53202. Phone: (414)272-0943 Fax: (414)277-1170 E-mail: cima@cimanet.com • URL: http://www.cimanet.com.

CONSTRUCTION ESTIMATING

See: ESTIMATING

CONSTRUCTION INDUSTRIES, ELECTRICAL

See: ELECTRICAL CONSTRUCTION INDUSTRY

CONSTRUCTION INDUSTRY

See: BUILDING INDUSTRY

CONSULAR SERVICE

See: DIPLOMATIC AND CONSULAR SERVICE

CONSULTANTS

See also: ENGINEERING CONSULTANTS; MANAGEMENT CONSULTANTS

GENERAL WORKS

Dangerous Company: The Secret Story of the Consulting Powerhouses and the Corporations They Save and Ruin. James O'Shea and Charles Madigan. Random House, Inc. • 1997. $27.50. A critical view of the major consulting firms in the U. S. and how they influence large corporations.

Is It Too Late to Run Away and Join the Circus? Finding the Life You Really Want. Marti Smye. Simon and Schuster Trade. • 1998. $14.95. Provides philosophical and inspirational advice on leaving corporate life and becoming self-employed as a consultant or whatever. Central theme is dealing with major changes in life style and career objectives. (Macmillan Business Book.).

The Witch Doctors: Making Sense of the Management Gurus. John Micklethwait and Adrian Wooldridge. Crown Publishing Group, Inc. • 1996. $25.00. A critical, iconoclastic, and practical view of consultants, business school professors, and modern management theory, written by two members of the editorial staff of *The Economist.*

DIRECTORIES

AMA International Member and Marketing Services Guide. American Marketing Association. • Annual. $150.00. Lists professional members of the American Marketing Association. Also contains information on providers of marketing support services and products, including software, communications, direct marketing, promotion, research, and consulting companies. Includes geographical and alphabetical indexes. Formerly *Marketing Yellow Pages and AMA International Membership Directory.*

Consultants and Consulting Organizations Directory. The Gale Group. • 2001. $795.00. 23rd edition. Three volumes. Includes mid-year *Supplement.*

Directory of Executive Compensation Consultants. Kennedy Information, LLC. • 1993. $47.50. Includes over 250 office locations maintained by about 65 executive compensation consulting firms.

Directory of Management Consultants. Kennedy Information, LLC. • Annual. $149.00. Contains profiles of more than 1,800 general and specialty management consulting firms in the U. S., Canada, and Mexico.

Dun's Consultants Directory. Dun and Bradstreet Information Services. • 1996. $425.00. Lease basis. Lists about 25,000 top consulting firms in more than 200 fields.

Emerson's Directory of Leading U.S. Technology Consulting Firms. Available from Hoover's, Inc. • Biennial. $195.00. Published by the Emerson Company (http://www.emersoncompany.com). Provides information on 500 major consulting firms specializing in technology.

Nelson's Directory of Pension Fund Consultants. Wiesenberger/Thomson Financial. • Annual. $350.00. Covers the pension plan sponsor industry. More than 325 worldwide consulting firms are described.

HANDBOOKS AND MANUALS

Business Plan Guide for Independent Consultants. Herman Holtz. John Wiley and Sons, Inc. • 1994. $115.00.

The Consultant's Proposal, Fee, and Contract Problem-Solver. Ronald Tepper. John Wiley and Sons, Inc. • 1993. $24.95. Provides advice for consultants on fees, contracts, proposals, and client communications. Includes case histories in 10 specific fields, such as finance, marketing, engineering, and management.

Consulting Business. Entrepreneur Media, Inc. • Looseleaf. $59.50. A practical guide to becoming a business consultant. Covers profit potential, start-up costs, market size evaluation, pricing, accounting, advertising, promotion, etc. (Start-Up Business Guide No. E1151.).

The Contract and Fee-Setting Guide for Consultants and Professionals. Howard L. Shenson. John Wiley and Sons, Inc. • 1990. $108.95.

Developing a Consulting Practice. Robert O. Metzger. Sage Publications, Inc. • 1993. $37.00. Aimed at university professors and other academic personnel who wish to go into the consulting business. Contains practical advice on identifying skills, finding clients, making proposals, and management details. (Survival Skills for Scholars, vol. 3).

Flawless Consulting: A Guide to Getting Your Expertise Used. Peter Block. Jossey-Bass, Inc., Publishers. • 1999. $39.95. Second edition.

How to Make It Big as a Consultant. William A. Cohen. AMACOM. • 2001. $17.95. Third edition. Step-by-step instructions for finding clients, writing proposals, pricing services, etc.

How to Succeed as an Independent Consultant. Herman Holtz. John Wiley and Sons, Inc. • 1993. $34.95. Third edition. Covers a wide variety of marketing, financial, professional, and ethical issues for consultants. Includes bibliographic and organizational information.

INTERNET DATABASES

FindLaw: Internet Legal Resources. FindLaw, Inc. Phone: (650)322-8430 E-mail: info@findlaw.com • URL: http://www.findlaw.com • Web site provides a wide variety of information and links relating to laws, law schools, professional development, lawyers, the U. S. Supreme Court, consultants (experts), law reviews, legal news, etc. Online searching is provided. Fees: Free.

PERIODICALS AND NEWSLETTERS

Consultants News. Kennedy Information, LLC. • Monthly. $229.00 per year. Newsletter. News and ideas for management consultants.

STATISTICS SOURCES

An Analysis of Outplacement Consulting in North America. Kennedy Information, LLC. • 1995. $35.00. Fourth edition. Includes ranking of leading outplacement consulting firms and estimates of market share and total revenue.

TRADE/PROFESSIONAL ASSOCIATIONS

American Consultants League. 30466 Prince William St., Prince Anne, MD 21853. Phone: (410)651-4869 • Members are part-time and full-time consultants in various fields. Offers marketing and legal advice.

Society for Advancement of Management. Texas A&M University-Corpus Christi, College of Business, 6300 Ocean Dr., Corpus Christi, TX 78412. Phone: 888-827-6077 or (361)825-6045 or (361)825-5574 Fax: (361)825-2725 E-mail: moustafa@falcon.tamucc.edu • URL: http://www.enterprise.tamucc.edu/sam/.

CONSULTANTS, ENGINEERING

See: ENGINEERING CONSULTANTS

CONSULTANTS, MANAGEMENT

See: MANAGEMENT CONSULTANTS

CONSUMER AFFAIRS

ABSTRACTS AND INDEXES

Business Periodicals Index. H. W. Wilson Co. • Monthly, except August, with quarterly and annual cumulations. Service basis for print edition; CD-ROM edition, $1,495.00 per year.

NTIS Alerts: Business & Economics. National Technical Information Service.

Readers' Guide to Periodical Literature. H. W. Wilson Co. • Monthly. $220.00 per year. CD-ROM edition, $1,495 per year, including annual cumulation. Indexes about 250 peridicals of general interest.

CD-ROM DATABASES

Magazine Index Plus. The Gale Group. • Monthly. $4,000.00 per year (includes InfoTrac workstation). Provides full text on CD-ROM for about 100 popular, general interest magazines and indexing for 300 others. Includes special indexing of reviews and product evaluations. Time period is 1980 to date.

National Newspaper Index CD-ROM. The Gale Group. • Monthly. Provides comprehensive CD-ROM indexing of all material appearing in the late edition of the *New York Times*, the final edition of the *Washington Post*, the national edition of the *Christian Science Monitor*, the home edition of the *Los Angeles Times*, and the *Wall Street Journal*. Time period is four years. Also available online.

The New York Times Ondisc. New York Times Online Services. • Monthly. $2,650.00 per year. CD-ROM discs contain the full text of *The New York Times*, final edition. Inquire as to time period covered and availability of backfiles.

Newspaper Abstracts Ondisc. Bell & Howell Information and Learning. • Monthly. $2,950.00 per year (covers 1989 to date; archival discs are available for 1985-88). Provides cover-to-cover CD-ROM indexing and abstracting of 19 major newspapers, including the *New York Times, Wall Street Journal, Washington Post, Chicago Tribune,* and *Los Angeles Times*.

WILSONDISC: Readers' Guide to Periodical Literature. H. W. Wilson Co. • Monthly. $1,095.00 per year, including unlimited online access to *Readers' Guide to Periodical Literature* through WILSONLINE. Provides CD-ROM indexing of about 250 general interest periodicals. Covers 1983 to date. (*Readers' Guide Abstracts* also available on CD-ROM at $1,995 per year.).

DIRECTORIES

Business Organizations, Agencies, and Publications Directory. The Gale Group. • 1999. $425.00. 12th edition. Over 40,000 entries describing 39 types of business information sources. Classified by type of organization, publication, or serviceIncludes state, national, and international agencies and organizations. Master index to names and keywords. Also includes e-mail addresses and web site URL's.

Consumer Sourcebook: A Directory and Guide. The Gale Group. • 2001. $290.00. 14th edition. Consumer-oriented agencies, associations, institutes, centers, etc.

ONLINE DATABASES

Information Bank Abstracts. New York Times Index Dept. • Provides indexing and abstracting of current affairs, primarily from the final late edition of *The New York Times* and the Eastern edition of *The Wall Street Journal*. Time period is 1969 to present, with daily updates. Inquire as to online cost and availability.

Newspaper and Periodical Abstracts. Bell & Howell Information and Learning. • Provides online coverage (citations and abstracts) of 25 major newspapers, 1,600 perodicals, and 70 TV programs. Covers business, economics, current affairs, health, fitness, sports, education, technology, government, consumer affairs, psychology, the arts, and the social sciences. Time period is 1986 to date, with daily updates. Inquire as to online cost and availability.

Readers' Guide Abstracts Online. H. W. Wilson Co. • Indexes and abstracts general interest periodicals, 1983 to date. Weekly updates. Inquire as to online cost and availability.

Wilson Business Abstracts Online. H. W. Wilson Co. • Indexes and abstracts 600 major business periodicals, plus the *Wall Street Journal* and the business section of the *New York Times*. Indexing is from 1982, abstracting from 1990, with the two newspapers included from 1993. Updated weekly. Inquire as to online cost and availability. (*Business Periodicals Index* without abstracts is also available online.).

PERIODICALS AND NEWSLETTERS

Consumer Affairs Letter: Monthly Report to Management on Issue Activities, Strategies, etc. of Consumer Groups. George Idelson. • Monthly. Non-profit institutions, $125.00 per year; corporations, $247.00 per year.

Journal of Consumer Affairs. American Council on Consumer Interests. • Semiannual. Individuals, $80.00 per year; institutions, $205.00 per year. Includes *Consumer News and Reviews*, *Advancing the Consumer Interest* and *Consumer Interest Annual*.

RESEARCH CENTERS AND INSTITUTES

American Council on Consumer Awareness, Inc. P.O. Box 17291, St. Paul, MN 55117-4263. Phone: (612)489-2835 Fax: (612)489-5650 E-mail: acca@pioneerplanet.infi.net.

Center for Consumer Research. University of Florida, P.O. Box 117160, Gainesville, FL 32611-7160. Phone: (352)392-0161 Fax: (352)846-0457 E-mail: cohenj@dale.cba.ufl.edu • URL: http://www.cba.ufl.edu/centers.consumer.htm.

Consumer Education Research Center. 1980 Springfield Ave., Maplewood, NJ 07040-3438. Phone: 800-872-0121 or (973)275-3955 Fax: (973)275-3980 E-mail: cerc@planet.net • URL: http://www.planet.net/cerc.

Consumer Research Center. The Conference Board, Inc., 845 Third Ave., New York, NY 10022. Phone: (212)759-0900 Fax: (212)980-7014 E-mail: franco@conference-board.org • URL: http://www.crc-conquest.org • Conducts research on the consumer market, including elderly and working women segments.

TRADE/PROFESSIONAL ASSOCIATIONS

American Consumers Association. 2633 Flossmoor Rd., Flossmoor, IL 60422. Phone: (708)957-2900 E-mail: tuetall@aol.com • Promotes the interests and well-being of consumers.

American Council on Consumer Interests. 240 Stanley Hall, Columbia, MO 65211. Phone: (573)882-3817 Fax: (573)884-6571 E-mail: acci@missouri.edu • URL: http://www.consusmerinterests.org.

Consumer Federation of America. 1424 16th St., N. W., Suite 604, Washington, DC 20036. Phone: (202)387-6121 • Members are national, regional, state, and local consumer groups.

Consumer Information Center. 18th and F St., N.W., Room G-142, Washington, DC 20405. Phone: 888-

878-3256 Fax: (202)501-4281 E-mail: cic.info@pueblo.gsa.gov • URL: http://www.pueblo.gsa.gov • Develops, promotes, and distributes information of interest to consumers.

National Consumers League. 1701 K. St. N.W., No. 1200, Washington, DC 20006. Phone: (202)835-3323 Fax: (202)835-0747 E-mail: ncl@nclnet.org • URL: http://www.fraud.org/ • Promotes consumer affairs.

People's Medical Society. 462 Walnut St., Allentown, PA 18102. Phone: 800-624-8773 or (610)770-1670 Fax: (610)770-0607 E-mail: mad1@peoplesmed.org • URL: http://www.peoplesmed.org • A consumer affairs society concerned with the cost, quality, and management of the American health care system.

Public Citizen. 1600 20th St., N.W., Washington, DC 20009. Phone: (202)588-1000 Fax: (202)588-7798 E-mail: pcmail@citizen.org • URL: http://www.citizen.org • Founded by Ralph Nader. Promotes citizen advocacy of consumer rights.

Society of Consumer Affairs Professionals in Business. 801 N. Fairfax St., Suite 404, Alexandria, VA 22314. Phone: (703)519-3700 Fax: (703)549-4886 E-mail: socap@socap.com • URL: http://www.socap.org • Members are managers of consumer affairs departments of business firms.

OTHER SOURCES

Consumer Protection and the Law. Dee Pridgen. West Group. • Looseleaf. $135.00. Periodic supplementation. Covers advertising, sales practices, unfair trade practices, consumer fraud, and product warranties.

CONSUMER CREDIT

See also: CREDIT; INSTALLMENT PLAN PURCHASING

GENERAL WORKS

Consumer and Commercial Credit Management. Robert H. Cole and Lon Mishler. McGraw-Hill Professional. • 1997. 11th edition. Price on application.

How to Use Credit Wisely. American Institute for Economic Research. • 1996. $6.00. Provides succinct coverage of various consumer debt topics, including credit cards, credit scoring systems, credit history, credit reports, and bankruptcy. Relevant federal legislation is briefly described, including the Fair Credit Reporting Act (FCRA) and the Fair Credit Billing Act (FCBA). (Economic Education Bulletin.).

The Lifetime Book of Money Management. Grace W. Weinstein. Visible Ink Press. • 1993. $15.95. Third edition. Gives popularly-written advice on investments, life and health insurance, owning a home, credit, retirement, estate planning, and other personal finance topics.

ABSTRACTS AND INDEXES

Banking Information Index. U M I Banking Information Index. • Monthly. Price on application. Covers a wide variety of banking, business, and financial subjects in periodicals. Formerly *Banking Literature Index.*

FINANCIAL RATIOS

Annual Statement Studies. Robert Morris Associates: The Association of Lending and Credit Risk Professiona. • Annual. Free to members; non-members, $140.00. Median and quartile financial ratios are given for over 400 kinds of manufacturing, wholesale, retail, construction, and consumer finance establishments. Data is sorted by both asset size and sales volume. Includes a clearly written "Definition of Ratios" and an alphabetical industry index.

HANDBOOKS AND MANUALS

Consumer Credit Compliance Manual. John R. Fonseca. West Group. • 1984. $135.00. Second edition. Interprets current consumer credit laws and regulations.

Cost of Personal Borrowing in the United States. Financial Publishing Co. • Annual. $175.00.

Credit Consulting. Entrepreneur Media, Inc. • Looseleaf. $59.50. A practical guide to starting a consumer credit and debt counseling and consulting service. Covers profit potential, start-up costs, market size evaluation, owner's time required, pricing, accounting, advertising, promotion, etc. (Start-Up Business Guide No. E1321.).

INTERNET DATABASES

BanxQuote Banking, Mortgage, and Finance Center. BanxQuote, Inc. Phone: 800-765-3000 or (212)643-8000 Fax: (212)643-0020 E-mail: info@banx.com • URL: http://www.banx.com • Web site quotes interest rates paid by banks around the country on various savings products, as well as rates paid by consumers for automobile loans, mortgages, credit cards, home equity loans, and personal loans. Also provided: stock quotes, indexes, stock options, futures trading data, economic indicators, and links to many other financial sites. Daily updates. Fees: Free.

Fedstats. Federal Interagency Council on Statistical Policy. Phone: (202)395-7254 • URL: http://www.fedstats.gov • Web site features an efficient search facility for full-text statistics produced by more than 70 federal agencies, including the Census Bureau, the Bureau of Economic Analysis, and the Bureau of Labor Statistics. Boolean searches can be made within one agency or for all agencies combined. Links are offered to international statistical bureaus, including the UN, IMF, OECD, UNESCO, Eurostat, and 20 individual countries. Fees: Free.

ONLINE DATABASES

Banking Information Source. Bell & Howell Information and Learning. • Provides indexing and abstracting of periodical and other literature from 1982 to date, with weekly updates. Covers the financial services industry: banks, savings institutions, investment houses, credit unions, insurance companies, and real estate organizations. Emphasis is on marketing and management. Inquire as to online cost and availability. (Formerly *FINIS: Financial Industry Information Service.*).

DRI U.S. Central Database. Data Products Division. • Provides more than 23,000 business, financial, demographic, economic, foreign trade, and industry-related time series for the U.S. Includes national income, population, retail-wholesale trade, price indexes, labor data, housing, industrial production, banking, interest rates, money supply, etc. Time period is generally 1947 to date (some data back to 1929). Updating varies. Inquire as to online cost and availability.

PERIODICALS AND NEWSLETTERS

Bank Letter: Newsletter of Commercial and Institutional Banking. Institutional Investor, Newsletters Div. • Weekly. $2,220.00 per year. Newsletter. Covers retail banking, commercial lending, foreign loans, bank technology, government regulations, and other topics related to banking.

Business Credit. National Association of Credit Management. • Monthly. $34.00 per year. Formerly *Credit and Financial Management.*

Consumer Credit and Truth-in-Lending Compliance Report. Warren, Gorham and Lamont/RIA Group. • Monthly. $183.75 per year. Newsletter. Focuses on the latest regulatory rulings and findings involving consumer lending and credit activity. Formerly *Bank Installment Lending Newsletter.*

Consumer Finance Bulletin. American Financial Services Association. • Monthly. $126.00 per year.

Consumer Finance Newsletter. Financial Publishing Co. • Monthly. $24.50 per year. Covers changes in state and federal consumer lending regulations.

Consumer Trends: An Independent Newsletter on Credit Issues and Financial Affairs. International Credit Association. • Monthly. $100.00 per year.

Credit. American Financial Services Association. • Bimonthly. Members, $12.00 per year; non-members, $22.00 per year.

Credit Risk Management. Phillips Business Information, Inc. • Biweekly. $695.00 per year. Newsletter on consumer credit, including delinquency aspects.

Credit World. International Credit Association. • Bimonthly. Free to members; non-members, $60.00 per year.

STATISTICS SOURCES

Business Statistics of the United States. Courtenay M. Slater, editor. Bernan Associates. • 1999. $74.00. Fifth edition. Based on *Business Statistics*, formerly issue by the Bureau of Economic Analysis, U. S. Department of Commerce. Provides basic data for a wide variety of U. S. industries, services, and economic indicators. Most statistics are shown annually for 29 years and monthly for the most recent four years.

Consumer Credit. U. S. Federal Reserve System. • Monthly. $5.00 per year. (Federal Reserve Statistical Release, G.19.).

Statistical Information on the Financial Services Industry. American Bankers Association. • Annual. Members, $150.00; non-members, $275.00. Presents a wide variety of data relating to banking and financial services, including consumer economics, personal finance, credit, government loans, capital markets, and international banking.

Survey of Current Business. Available from U. S. Government Printing Office. • Monthly. $49.00 per year. Issued by Bureau of Economic Analysis, U. S. Department of Commerce. Presents a wide variety of business and economic data.

TRADE/PROFESSIONAL ASSOCIATIONS

American Financial Services Association. 919 18th St., N.W., Washington, DC 20006. Phone: (202)296-5544 Fax: (202)223-0321 E-mail: afsa@afsamail.com • URL: http://www.americanfinsvcs.org.

Consumer Credit Insurance Association. 542 S. Dearborn St., No. 400, Chicago, IL 60605. Phone: (312)939-2242 Fax: (312)939-8287 E-mail: bburfeind@cciaonline.

International Credit Association. P.O. Box 15945-314, Lenexa, KS 66285-5945. Phone: (913)307-9432 Fax: (913)541-0156 E-mail: ica@ica-credit.org • URL: http://www.ica-credit.org.

National Association of Consumer Credit Administrators. P.O. Box 10709, Raleigh, NC 27605-0709. Phone: (919)733-3016 Fax: (919)733-6918.

National Foundation for Consumer Credit. 8611 Second Ave., Suite 100, Silver Spring, MD 20910-3372. Phone: 800-388-2227 or (301)589-5600 Fax: (301)495-5623 • URL: http://www.nfcc.org.

OTHER SOURCES

Consumer and Commercial Credit: Installment Sales. Prentice Hall. • Three looseleaf volumes. Periodic supplementation. Price on application.

Covers secured transactions under the Uniform Commercial Code and the Uniform Consumer Credit Code. Includes retail installment sales, home improvement loans, higher education loans, and other kinds of installment loans.

Consumer Credit and Compliance Guide with Annual Percentage Rate Tables. David Thorndike. Warren, Gorham and Lamont/RIA Group. • $88.00. Periodic supplementation.

Consumer Credit and the Law. Dee Pridgen. West Group. • Looseleaf. $135.00.

Consumer Credit Guide. CCH, Inc. • Biweekly. $1,206.00 per year. Looseleaf service.

Consumer Credit Laws: Transaction and Forms. Matthew Bender & Co., Inc. • $720.00. Four looseleaf volumes. Periodic supplementation. Detailed treatment of the law with practical step-by-step guidance for every stage of a consumer credit transaction.

The Fragile Middle Class: Americans in Debt. Teresa A. Sullivan and others. Yale University Press. • 2000. $32.50. Provides an analysis of a 1991 survey of personal bankruptcies in five states of the U. S. Serves as a sequel to the authors' *As We Forgive Our Debtors* (1989), an analysis of 1981 bankruptcies.

U. S. Credit Bureaus and Collection Agencies: An Industry Analysis. Available from MarketResearch.com. • 1999. $1,395.00. Market research report published by Marketdata Enterprises. Includes forecasts of industry growth to the year 2002 and provides profiles of Dun & Bradstreet, Equifax, Experion, and TransUnion.

CONSUMER ECONOMICS

See also: CONSUMER EDUCATION; ECONOMIC RESEARCH; MARKET RESEARCH

GENERAL WORKS

Consumer Behavior. Robert D. Blackwell and others. Dryden Press. • 1994. $102.50. Eighth edition.

Money: Who Has How Much and Why. Andrew Hacker. Available from Simon & Schuster Trade. • 1998. $13.00. Published by Scribner's Reference. A discourse on the distribution of wealth in America, with emphasis on the gap between rich and poor.

CD-ROM DATABASES

EconLit. Available from SilverPlatter Information, Inc. • Monthly. Single-user, $1,600.00 per year. Multi-user, $2,400.00 per year. Provides CD-ROM citations, with abstracts, to articles from more than 500 economics journals. Time period is 1969 to date. Produced by the American Economic Association.

Sourcebook America. The Gale Group. • Annual. $995.00. Produced by CACI Marketing Systems. A combination on CD-ROM of *The Sourcebook of ZIP Code Demographics* and *The Sourcebook of County Demographics.* Provides detailed population and socio-economic data (about 75 items) for each of 3,141 U. S. counties and approximately 30,000 ZIP codes, plus states, metropolitan areas, and media market areas. Includes forecasts to the year 2004.

World Marketing Forecasts on CD-ROM, The Gale Group. • Annual. $2,500.00. Produced by Euromonitor. Provides detailed forecast data for the years to 2012 on CD-ROM for 54 countries in all parts of the world. Covers a wide range of social, demographic, economic, and market factors. Includes specific forecasts for many kinds of consumer products.

HANDBOOKS AND MANUALS

Hispanic Market Handbook. The Gale Group. • 1995. $85.00. Provides advice on marketing consumer items to Hispanic Americans. Includes case studies and demographic profiles.

INTERNET DATABASES

Bureau of Economic Analysis (BEA). U. S. Department of Commerce, Bureau of Economic Analysis. Phone: (202)606-9900 Fax: (202)606-5310 E-mail: webmaster@bea.doc.gov • URL: http://www.bea.doc.gov • Web site includes "News Release Information" covering national, regional, and international economic estimates from the BEA. Highlights of releases appear online the same day, complete text and tables appear the next day. "Recent News Releases" section provides titles for past nine months, with links. "BEA Data and Methodology" includes "Frequently Requested NIPA Data" (national income and product accounts, such as gross domestic product and personal income). Other statistics are available. Fees: Free.

Bureau of Labor Statistics (BLS). U. S. Department of Labor, Bureau of Labor Statistics. Phone: (202)523-1092 E-mail: labstat.helpdesk@bls.gov • URL: http://www.bls.gov • Web site provides a great variety of employment, wage, price, and economic data. Some links are "Data," "Economy at a Glance," "Keyword Search of BLS Web Pages," "Regional Information," and "Other Statistical Sites." Fees: Free.

Fedstats. Federal Interagency Council on Statistical Policy. Phone: (202)395-7254 • URL: http://www.fedstats.gov • Web site features an efficient search facility for full-text statistics produced by more than 70 federal agencies, including the Census Bureau, the Bureau of Economic Analysis, and the Bureau of Labor Statistics. Boolean searches can be made within one agency or for all agencies combined. Links are offered to international statistical bureaus, including the UN, IMF, OECD, UNESCO, Eurostat, and 20 individual countries. Fees: Free.

ONLINE DATABASES

EconLit. American Economic Association. • Covers the worldwide literature of economics as contained in selected monographs and about 550 journals. Subjects include microeconomics, macroeconomics, economic history, inflation, money, credit, finance, accounting theory, trade, natural resource economics, and regional economics. Time period is 1969 to present, with monthly updates. Inquire as to online cost and availability.

Euromonitor Market Research. Euromonitor International. • Provides the complete text online of Euromonitor market analysis reports. Covers consumer goods market research data for all major countries, with emphasis on specific product categories. Time period is current. Continuous updating. Inquire as to online cost and availability.

PERIODICALS AND NEWSLETTERS

American Demographics: Consumer Trends for Business Leaders. Intertec Publishing Co. • Monthly. $69.00 per year.

Family Economics and Nutrition Review. Available from U. S. Government Printing Office. • Quarterly. $19.00 per year. Issued by the Consumer and Food Economics Institute, U. S. Department of Agriculture. Provides articles on consumer expenditures and budgeting for food, clothing, housing, energy, education, etc.

Journal of Consumer Research; An Interdisciplinary Quarterly. University of Chicago Press, Journals Div. • Quarterly. Members, $45.00 per year; institutions, $99.00 per year; students, $25.00. Covers various aspects of consumer behavior.

RESEARCH CENTERS AND INSTITUTES

National Bureau of Economic Research, Inc. 1050 Massachusetts Ave., Cambridge, MA 02138-5398. Phone: (617)868-3900 Fax: (617)868-2742 E-mail: msfeldst@nber.org • URL: http://www.nber.org.

STATISTICS SOURCES

Business Statistics of the United States. Courtenay M. Slater, editor. Bernan Associates. • 1999. $74.00. Fifth edition. Based on *Business Statistics,* formerly issue by the Bureau of Economic Analysis, U. S. Department of Commerce. Provides basic data for a wide variety of U. S. industries, services, and economic indicators. Most statistics are shown annually for 29 years and monthly for the most recent four years.

Consumer Canada 1996. Available from The Gale Group. • 1996. $750.00. Published by Euromonitor. Provides consumer market, socioeconomic, and demographic data for Canada. Includes consumer market size (volume and value) for many specific kinds of products.

Consumer Expenditure Survey. Available from U. S. Government Printing Office. • Biennial. Issued by the Bureau of Labor Statistics, U. S. Department of Labor (http://www.bls.gov). Contains data on various kinds of consumer spending, according to household income, education, etc. (Bureau of Labor Statistics Bulletin.).

Consumer International 2000/2001. Available from The Gale Group. • 1998. $1,190.00. Seventh edition. Published by Euromonitor. Contains extensive consumer market, economic, and demographic data for 27 major, non-European countries, including the U. S. and Canada. Includes consumer market size (volume and value) for 150 product types in 14 categories (food, clothing, automobiles, cosmetics, appliances, etc.).

Consumer Power: How Americans Spend. Margaret Ambry. McGraw-Hill Professional. • 1992. $27.50. Contains detailed statistics on consumer income and spending. Nine major categories of products and services are covered, with spending data and dollar size of market for each item.

Consumer USA 2000. Available from The Gale Group. • 2000. $900.00. Fifth edition. Published by Euromonitor. Provides demographic and consumer market data for the United States. Forecasts to the year 2005.

Current Population Reports: Household Economic Studies, Series P-70. Available from U. S. Government Printing Office. • Irregular. $16.00 per year. Issued by the U.S. Bureau of the Census (http://www.census.gov). Each issue covers a special topic relating to household socioeconomic characteristics.

Current Population Reports: Population Characteristics, Special Studies, and Consumer Income, Series P-20, P-23, and P-60. Available from U. S. Government Printing Office. • Irregular. $39.00 per year. Issued by the U.S. Bureau of the Census (http://www.census.gov). Each issue covers a special topic relating to population or income. Series P-20, *Population Characteristics,* provides statistical studies on such items as mobility, fertility, education, and marital status. Series P-23, *Special Studies,* consists of occasional reports on methodology. Series P-60, *Consumer Income,* publishes reports on income in relation to age, sex, education, occupation, family size, etc.

Demographics USA: County Edition. Market Statistics. • Annual. $435.00. Contains 200 statistical series for each of 3,000 counties. Includes population, household income, employment, retail sales, and consumer expenditures. Also provides Effective Buying Income, Buying Power Index, and data summaries by Metro Market, Media Market, and State. (CD-ROM version is available.).

Demographics USA: ZIP Edition. Market Statistics. • Annual. $435.00. Contains 50 statistical series for each of 40,000 ZIP codes. Includes population, household income, employment, retail sales, and consumer expenditures. Also provides Effective Buying Income, Business Characteristics, and data summaries by state, region, and the first three digits of ZIP codes. (CD-ROM version is available.).

European Marketing Forecasts 2001. Available from The Gale Group. • 2000. $1,190.00. Third edition. Published by Euromonitor. Contains demographic, economic, and market forecasts for the countries of Europe to the year 2010. Forecasts include market-size data for 15 consumer product sectors (food, clothing, automobiles, consumer electronics, etc.).

Gale Book of Averages. The Gale Group. • 1994. $70.00. Contains 1,100-1,200 statistical averages on a variety of topics, with references to published sources. Subjects include business, labor, consumption, crime, and other areas of contemporary society.

Handbook of U. S. Labor Statistics: Employment, Earnings, Prices, Productivity, and Other Labor Data. Eva E. Jacobs, editor. Bernan Associates. • 1999. $74.00. Based on *Handbook of Labor Statistics*, formerly issued by the Bureau of Labor Statistics, U. S. Department of Labor. Includes the Bureau's projections of employment in the U. S. by industry and occupation. Provides a wide variety of data on the work force, prices, fringe benefits, and consumer expenditures.

Household Spending: Who Spends How Much On What. Hoai Tran. New Strategist Publications, Inc. • 1999. $94.95. Fifth edition. Gives facts about the buying habits of U. S. consumers according to income, age, household type, and household size. Includes spending data for about 1,000 products and services.

International Marketing Forecasts 2001. Available from The Gale Group. • 2000. $1,090.00. Third edition. Published by Euromonitor. Contains demographic, economic, and market forecasts to the year 2010 for major, non-European countries, including the U. S. and Canada. Forecasts include market-size data for 15 consumer product sectors, such as food, clothing, and automobiles.

Money Income in the United States. Available from U. S. Government Printing Office. • Annual. $19.00. Issued by the U. S. Bureau of the Census. Presents data on consumer income in current and constant dollars, both totals and averages (means, medians, distributions). Includes figures for a wide variety of demographic and occupational characteristics. (Current Population Reports, P60-209.).

Sourcebook of Zip Code Demographics. CACI Marketing Systems. • 2000. $495.00. 15th revised edition. Published by CACI, Inc. Provides data on 75 demographic and socio-economic characteristics for each ZIP code in the U. S.

Statistical Handbook on Consumption and Wealth in the United States. Chandrika Kaul and Valerie Tomaselli-Moschovitis. Oryx Press. • 1999. $65.00. Provides more than 400 graphs, tables, and charts dealing with basic income levels, income inequalities, spending patterns, taxation, subsidies, etc. (Statistical Handbook Series).

Statistical Handbook on the American Family. Bruce A. Chadwick and Tim B. Heaton, editors. Oryx Press. • 1998. $65.00. Includes data on education, health, politics, employment, expenditures, social characteristics, the elderly, and women in the labor force. Historical statistics on marriage, birth, and divorce are shown from 1900 on. A list of sources and a subject index are provided. (Statistical Handbook Series).

Statistical Information on the Financial Services Industry. American Bankers Association. • Annual. Members, $150.00; non-members, $275.00. Presents a wide variety of data relating to banking and financial services, including consumer economics, personal finance, credit, government loans, capital markets, and international banking.

World Consumer Income and Expenditure Patterns. Available from The Gale Group. • 2001. $650.00. Published by Euromonitor (http://www.euromonitor.com). Provides data on consumer income, earning power, and expenditures for 52 countries around the world.

OTHER SOURCES

The Value of a Dollar: Millennium Edition, 1860-1999. Grey House Publishing. • 1999. $135.00. Second edition. Shows the actual prices of thousands of items available to consumers from the Civil War era to recent years. Includes selected data on consumer expenditures, investments, income, and jobs. (Universal Reference Publications.).

Working Americans, 1880-1999, Volume One: The Working Class. Grey House Publishing. • 2000. $135.00. Provides detailed information on the lifestyles and economic life of working class families in the 12 decades from 1880 to 1999. Includes such items as selected consumer prices, income, family finances, budgets, life at home, jobs, and working conditions. (Universal Reference Publications.).

Working Americans, 1880-1999, Volume Two: The Middle Class. Grey House Publishing. • 2000. $135.00. Furnishes details of the social and economic lives of middle class Americans during the years 1880 to 1999. Describes such items as selected consumer prices, income, family finances, budgets, life at home, jobs, and working conditions. (Universal Reference Publications.).

World Consumer Income and Expenditure Patterns. Available from The Gale Group. • 2001. $990.00. Second edition. Two volumes. Published by Euromonitor. Provides data for 52 countries on consumer income, earning power, spending patterns, and savings. Expenditures are detailed for 75 product or service categories.

CONSUMER EDUCATION

See also: BETTER BUSINESS BUREAUS; CONSUMER ECONOMICS

CD-ROM DATABASES

Consumers Reference Disc. National Information Services Corp. • Quarterly. Provides the CD-ROM version of *Consumer Health and Nutrition Index* from Oryx Press and *Consumers Index to Product Evaluations and Information Sources* from Pierian Press. Contains citations to consumer health articles and consumer product evaluations, tests, warnings, and recalls.

DIRECTORIES

Consumer Sourcebook: A Directory and Guide. The Gale Group. • 2001. $290.00. 14th edition. Consumer-oriented agencies, associations, institutes, centers, etc.

HANDBOOKS AND MANUALS

The Consumer Health Information Source Book. Alan Rees, editor. Oryx Press. • 2000. $59.50. Sixth edition. Bibliography of current literature and guide to organizations.

PERIODICALS AND NEWSLETTERS

Bottom Line-Personal. Bottom Line Information, Inc. • Semimonthly. $29.95 per year. Provides information to help sophisticated people lead more productive lives.

Consumer Reports. Consumers Union of the United States, Inc. • Semimonthly. $24.00 per year. Includes *Annual Buying Guide.*

Consumers Digest: Best Buys, Best Prices, Best Reports for People Who Demand Value. Consumers Digest Inc. • Bimonthly. $15.97.

Consumer's Research Magazine: Analyzing Consumer Issues. Consumers' Research Inc. • Monthly. $24.00 per year.

eShopper. Ziff-Davis. • Bimonthly. $9.97 per year. A consumer magazine providing advice and information for "shopping on the Web.".

FDA Consumer. Available from U. S. Government Printing Office. • Bimonthly. $23.00 per year. Issued by the U. S. Food and Drug Administration. Provides consumer information about FDA regulations and product safety.

Journal of Consumer Affairs. American Council on Consumer Interests. • Semiannual. Individuals, $80.00 per year; institutions, $205.00 per year. Includes *Consumer News and Reviews, Advancing the Consumer Interest* and *Consumer Interest Annual.*

RESEARCH CENTERS AND INSTITUTES

Consumer Education Research Center. 1980 Springfield Ave., Maplewood, NJ 07040-3438. Phone: 800-872-0121 or (973)275-3955 Fax: (973)275-3980 E-mail: cerc@planet.net • URL: http://www.planet.net/cerc.

Consumers' Research. 800 Maryland Ave., N.E., Washington, DC 20002. Phone: (202)546-1713 Fax: (202)546-1638 E-mail: crmag@aol.com.

TRADE/PROFESSIONAL ASSOCIATIONS

American Council on Consumer Interests. 240 Stanley Hall, Columbia, MO 65211. Phone: (573)882-3817 Fax: (573)884-6571 E-mail: acci@missouri.edu • URL: http://www.consusmerinterests.org.

Consumer Federation of America. 1424 16th St., N. W., Suite 604, Washington, DC 20036. Phone: (202)387-6121 • Members are national, regional, state, and local consumer groups.

Consumers Education and Protective Association International. 6048 Ogontz Ave., Philadelphia, PA 19141-1347. Phone: (215)424-1441 Fax: (215)424-8045.

National Consumers League. 1701 K. St. N.W., No. 1200, Washington, DC 20006. Phone: (202)835-3323 Fax: (202)835-0747 E-mail: ncl@nclnet.org • URL: http://www.fraud.org/ • Promotes consumer affairs.

CONSUMER ELECTRONICS

See also: ELECTRIC APPLIANCE INDUSTRY

GENERAL WORKS

The Consumer Electronics Industry and the Future of American Manufacturing: How the U. S. Lost the Lead and Why We Must Get Back in the Game. Susan W. Sanderson. Economic Policy Institute. • 1990. $12.00.

ABSTRACTS AND INDEXES

Readers' Guide to Periodical Literature. H. W. Wilson Co. • Monthly. $220.00 per year. CD-ROM edition, $1,495 per year, including annual cumulation. Indexes about 250 peridicals of general interest.

ALMANACS AND YEARBOOKS

Communication Technology Update. Butterworth-Heinemann. • Annual. $36.95. Reviews technological developments and statistical trends in five key areas: mass media, computers, consumer electronics, communications satellites, and telephony. Includes television, cellular phones, and the Internet. (Focal Press.).

CD-ROM DATABASES

World Marketing Forecasts on CD-ROM. The Gale Group. • Annual. $2,500.00. Produced by Euromonitor. Provides detailed forecast data for the years to 2012 on CD-ROM for 54 countries in all parts of the world. Covers a wide range of social, demographic, economic, and market factors. Includes specific forecasts for many kinds of consumer products.

DIRECTORIES

Directory of Computer and Consumer Electronics. Chain Store Age. • Annual. $290.00. Includes 2,900 "leading" retailers and over 200 "top" distributors. Formerly *Directory of Consumer Electronics Retails and Distributors*.

FINANCIAL RATIOS

Industry Norms and Key Business Ratios. Desk Top Edition. Dun and Bradstreet Corp., Business Information Services. • Annual. Five volumes. $475.00 per volume. $1,890.00 per set. Covers over 800 kinds of businesses, arranged by Standard Industrial Classification number. More detailed editions covering longer periods of time are also available.

ONLINE DATABASES

Euromonitor Market Research. Euromonitor International. • Provides the complete text online of Euromonitor market analysis reports. Covers consumer goods market research data for all major countries, with emphasis on specific product categories. Time period is current. Continuous updating. Inquire as to online cost and availability.

Readers' Guide Abstracts Online. H. W. Wilson Co. • Indexes and abstracts general interest periodicals, 1983 to date. Weekly updates. Inquire as to online cost and availability.

PERIODICALS AND NEWSLETTERS

Audio Week: The Authoritative News Service of the Audio Consumer Electronics Industry. • Weekly. $617.00. Newsletter. Provdies audio industry news, company news, and new product information.

Dealerscope Consumer Electronics Marketplace: For CE,PC and Major Appliance Retailers. North American Publishing Co. • Monthly. Free to qualified personnel; others, $79.00 per year. Formerly *Dealerscope Merchandising*.

Television Digest with Consumer Electronics. Warren Communication News. • Weekly. $944.00 per year. Newsletter featuring new consumer entertainment products utilizing electronics. Also covers the television broadcasting and cable TV industries, with corporate and industry news.

TWICE: This Week in Consumer Electronics. Cahners Business Information, Broadcasting and Cable's International Group. • 29 times a year. Free to qualified personnel; others, $99.90 per year. Contains marketing and manufacturing news relating to a wide variety of consumer electronic products, including video, audio, telephone, and home office equipment.

PRICE SOURCES

Orion Audio Blue Book. Orion Research Corp. • Annual. $179.00. Quotes retail and wholesale prices of used audio equipment. Original list prices and years of manufacture are also shown.

Orion Video and Television Blue Book. Orion Research Corp. • Annual. $144.00. Quotes retail and wholesale prices of used video and TV equipment. Original list prices and years of manufacture are also shown.

STATISTICS SOURCES

Annual Survey of Manufactures. Available from U. S. Government Printing Office. • Annual. Prices vary. Issued by the U. S. Census Bureau as an interim update to the *Census of Manufactures.* Includes data on number of manufacturing establishments in various industries, employment, labor costs, value of shipments, capital expenditures, inventories, energy costs, and assets. (See also Census Bureau home page, http://www.census.gov/.).

Consumer Canada 1996. Available from The Gale Group. • 1996. $750.00. Published by Euromonitor. Provides consumer market, socioeconomic, and demographic data for Canada. Includes consumer market size (volume and value) for many specific kinds of products.

Consumer International 2000/2001. Available from The Gale Group. • 1998. $1,190.00. Seventh edition. Published by Euromonitor. Contains extensive consumer market, economic, and demographic data for 27 major, non-European countries, including the U. S. and Canada. Includes consumer market size (volume and value) for 150 product types in 14 categories (food, clothing, automobiles, cosmetics, appliances, etc.).

European Marketing Forecasts 2001. Available from The Gale Group. • 2000. $1,190.00. Third edition. Published by Euromonitor. Contains demographic, economic, and market forecasts for the countries of Europe to the year 2010. Forecasts include market-size data for 15 consumer product sectors (food, clothing, automobiles, consumer electronics, etc.).

International Marketing Forecasts 2001. Available from The Gale Group. • 2000. $1,090.00. Third edition. Published by Euromonitor. Contains demographic, economic, and market forecasts to the year 2010 for major, non-European countries, including the U. S. and Canada. Forecasts include market-size data for 15 consumer product sectors, such as food, clothing, and automobiles.

Manufacturing Profiles. Available from U. S. Government Printing Office. • Annual. Issued by the U. S. Census Bureau. A printed consolidation of the entire *Current Industrial Report* series, presenting "all the data compiled." Contains statistics on production, shipments, inventories, consumption, exports, imports, and orders for a wide variety of manufactured products. (See also Census Bureau home page, http://www.census.gov/.).

Standard & Poor's Industry Surveys. Standard & Poor's. • Semiannual. $1,800.00. Two looseleaf volumes. Includes monthly supplements. Provides detailed, individual surveys of 52 major industry groups. Each survey is revised on a semiannual basis. Also includes "Monthly Investment Review" (industry group investment analysis) and monthly "Trends & Projections" (economic analysis).

U. S. Industry and Trade Outlook: The McGraw-Hill Companies and the U.S. Department of Commerce/ International Trade Administration. Datapso Research Corp. • Annual. $69.95. Produced by the International Trade Administration, U. S. Department of Commerce, in a "public-private" partnership with DRI/McGraw-Hill and Standard & Poor's. Provides basic data, outlook for the current year, and "Long-Term Prospects" (five-year projections) for a wide variety of products and services. Includes high technology industries. Formerly *U. S. Industrial Outlook*.

TRADE/PROFESSIONAL ASSOCIATIONS

Electronic Industries Association. 2500 Wilson Blvd., Arlington, VA 22201. Phone: (703)907-7500 Fax: (703)907-7501 • URL: http://www.eia.org • Includes a Solid State Products Committee.

Electronics Representatives Association. 444 N. Michigan Ave., Suite 1960, Chicago, IL 60611. Phone: 800-776-7377 or (312)527-3050 Fax: (312)527-3783 E-mail: info@era.org • URL: http://www.era.org • Includes a Consumer Products Division. Members are manufacturers' representatives.

IEEE Consumer Electronics Society. c/o IEEE Corporate Office, 445 Hoes Lane, Piscataway, NJ 08855-1331. Phone: (212)419-7900 Fax: (212)419-7570 • URL: http://www.ieee.org • Affiliated with the Institute of Electrical and Electronics Engineers. Concerned with design and manufacture.

Professional Audiovideo Retailers Association. 10 E. 22nd St., Suite 310, Lombard, IL 60148. Phone: (630)268-1500 Fax: (630)953-8957 E-mail: parahdq@aol.com • URL: http://www.paralink.org • Members are retailers of high quality equipment.

OTHER SOURCES

U. S. Home Theater Market. Available from MarketResearch.com. • 1997. $2,,500.00. Market research report published by Packaged Facts. Covers big-screen TV, high definition TV, audio equipment, and video sources. Market projections are provided to the year 2001.

CONSUMER FINANCE COMPANIES

See: FINANCE COMPANIES

CONSUMER LOANS

See: CONSUMER CREDIT

CONSUMER PRICE INDEXES

INTERNET DATABASES

Fedstats. Federal Interagency Council on Statistical Policy. Phone: (202)395-7254 • URL: http://www.fedstats.gov • Web site features an efficient search facility for full-text statistics produced by more than 70 federal agencies, including the Census Bureau, the Bureau of Economic Analysis, and the Bureau of Labor Statistics. Boolean searches can be made within one agency or for all agencies combined. Links are offered to international statistical bureaus, including the UN, IMF, OECD, UNESCO, Eurostat, and 20 individual countries. Fees: Free.

ONLINE DATABASES

DRI U.S. Central Database. Data Products Division. • Provides more than 23,000 business, financial, demographic, economic, foreign trade, and industry-related time series for the U.S. Includes national income, population, retail-wholesale trade, price indexes, labor data, housing, industrial production, banking, interest rates, money supply, etc. Time period is generally 1947 to date (some data back to 1929). Updating varies. Inquire as to online cost and availability.

PRICE SOURCES

CPI Detailed Report: Consumer Price Index. Available from U.S. Government Printing Office. • Monthly. $45.00 per year. Cost of living data.

STATISTICS SOURCES

ACCRA Cost of Living Index (Association for Applied Community Reseach). ACCRA. • Quarterly.

$130.00 per year. Compares price levels for 280-310 U.S. cities.

American Cost of Living Survey. The Gale Group. • 1995. $160.00. Second edition. Cost of living data is provided for 455 U.S. cities and metroploitan areas.

Bulletin of Labour Statistics: Supplementing the Annual Data Presented in the Year Book of Labour Statistics. International Labour Ofice. ILO Publications Center. • Quarterly. $84.00 per year. Includes five *Supplements.* A supplement to *Yearbook of Labour Statistics.* Provides current labor and price index statistics for over 130 countries. Generally includes data for the most recent four years. Text in English, French and Spanish.

Business Statistics of the United States. Courtenay M. Slater, editor. Bernan Associates. • 1999. $74.00. Fifth edition. Based on *Business Statistics*, formerly issue by the Bureau of Economic Analysis, U. S. Department of Commerce. Provides basic data for a wide variety of U. S. industries, services, and economic indicators. Most statistics are shown annually for 29 years and monthly for the most recent four years.

Economic Indicators. Council of Economic Advisors, Executive Office of the President. Available from U.S. Government Printing Office. • Monthly. $55.00 per year.

Economic Indicators Handbook: Time Series, Conversions, Documentation. The Gale Group. • 2000. $195.00. Sixth edition. Provides data for about 175 U. S. economic indicators, such as the consumer price index (CPI), gross national product (GNP), and the rate of inflation. Values for series are given since inception, in both original form and adjusted for inflation. A bibliography of sources is included.

Geographic Reference Report: Annual Report of Costs, Wages, salaries, and Human Resource Statistics for the United States and Canada. ERI. • Annual. $389.00. Provides demographic and other data for each of 298 North American metropolian areas, including local salaries, wage differentials, cost-of-living, housing costs, income taxation, employment, unemployment, population, major employers, crime rates, weather, etc.

Monthly Labor Review. Available from U. S. Government Printing Office. • Monthly. $43.00 per year. Issued by the Bureau of Labor Statistics, U. S. Department of Labor. Contains data on the labor force, wages, work stoppages, price indexes, productivity, economic growth, and occupational injuries and illnesses.

Prices and Earnings Around the Globe. Union Bank of Switzerland. • Irregular. Free. Published in Zurich. Compares prices and purchasing power in 48 major cities of the world. Wages and hours are also compared. Text in English, French, German, and Italian.

Report on the American Workforce. Available from U. S. Government Printing Office. • Annual. $15.00. Issued by the U. S. Department of Labor (http://www.dol.gov). Appendix contains tabular statistics, including employment, unemployment, price indexes, consumer expenditures, employee benefits (retirement, insurance, vacation, etc.), wages, productivity, hours of work, and occupational injuries. Annual figures are shown for up to 50 years.

Survey of Current Business. Available from U. S. Government Printing Office. • Monthly. $49.00 per year. Issued by Bureau of Economic Analysis, U. S. Department of Commerce. Presents a wide variety of business and economic data.

United States Department of State Indexes of Living Costs Abroad, Quarters Allowances, and Hardship Differentials. Available from U. S. Government Printing Office. • Quarterly. $10.00 per year. Provides data on the difference in living costs between Washington, DC and each of 160 foreign cities.

The Value of a Dollar. Grey House Publishing, Inc. • 1999. $125.00.

World Cost of Living Survey. The Gale Group. • 1999. $255.00. Second edition. Arranged by country and then by city within each country. Provides cost of living data for many products and services. Includes indexes and an annotated bibliography.

Year Book of Labour Statistics. International Labour Office. • Annual. $168.00. Presents a wide range of labor and price data for most countries of the world. Supplement available *Sources and Methods. Labour Statistics.*

OTHER SOURCES

The Value of a Dollar: Millennium Edition, 1860-1999. Grey House Publishing. • 1999. $135.00. Second edition. Shows the actual prices of thousands of items available to consumers from the Civil War era to recent years. Includes selected data on consumer expenditures, investments, income, and jobs. (Universal Reference Publications.).

Working Americans, 1880-1999, Volume One: The Working Class. Grey House Publishing. • 2000. $135.00. Provides detailed information on the lifestyles and economic life of working class families in the 12 decades from 1880 to 1999. Includes such items as selected consumer prices, income, family finances, budgets, life at home, jobs, and working conditions. (Universal Reference Publications.).

Working Americans, 1880-1999, Volume Two: The Middle Class. Grey House Publishing. • 2000. $135.00. Furnishes details of the social and economic lives of middle class Americans during the years 1880 to 1999. Describes such items as selected consumer prices, income, family finances, budgets, life at home, jobs, and working conditions. (Universal Reference Publications.).

CONSUMER RESEARCH

See: CONSUMER ECONOMICS

CONSUMER SURVEYS

See also: MARKET RESEARCH

GENERAL WORKS

Consumer Behavior. Robert D. Blackwell and others. Dryden Press. • 1994. $102.50. Eighth edition.

Interbrand Choice, Strategy and Bilateral Market Power. Michael E. Porter. Harvard University Press. • 1976. $16.50. (Economic Studies No. 146).

ALMANACS AND YEARBOOKS

Research Alert Yearbook: Vital Facts on Consumer Behavior and Attitudes. EPM Communications, Inc. • Annual. $295.00. Provides summaries of consumer market research from the newsletters *Research Alert, Youth Markets Alert, and Minority Markets Alert.* Includes tables, charts, graphs, and textual summaries for 41 subject categories. Sources include reports, studies, polls, and focus groups.

DIRECTORIES

Bradford's International Directory of Marketing Research Agencies n the United States and the World. Business Research Services, Inc. • Annual. $90.00. Over 1,800 marketing research agencies and management consultants in market research. Formerly *Bradford's Directory of Marketing Research Agencies and Management Consultants.*

Findex: The Worldwide Directory of Market Research Reports, Studies, and Surveys. MarketResearch.com. • Annual. $400.00. Provides brief annotations of market research reports and related publications from about 1,000 publishers, arranged by topic. Back of book includes Report Titles by Publisher, Publishers/Distributors Directory, Subject Index, Geography Index, and Company Index. (Formerly published by Cambridge Information Group.).

Focus Group Directory: International Directory of Focus Group Companies and Services. New York AMA-Green Book. • Annual. $80.00. Contains information on companies offering focus group facilities, including recruiting, moderating, and transcription services.

GreenBook: Worldwide Directory of Marketing Research Companies and Services. New York Ama-Green Book. • Annual. $145.00. Contains information in 300 categories on more than 2,500 market research companies, consultants, field services, computer services, survey research companies, etc. Indexed by specialty, industry, company, computer program, and personnel. Formerly (Greenbook Worldwide International Directory of Marketing Research Companies and Services).

Marketing Know-How: Your Guide to the Best Marketing Tools and Sources. Intertec Publishing. • 1996. $49.95. Describes more than 700 public and private sources of consumer marketing data. Also discusses market trends and provides information on such marketing techniques as cluster analysis, focus groups, and geodemographic analysis.

MRA Blue Book Research Services Directory. Marketing Research Association. • Annual. $169.95. Lists more than 1,200 international marketing research companies and survey services. Formerly *Directory of Research Services Provided by Members of the Marketing Research Association.*

HANDBOOKS AND MANUALS

An American Profile: Attitudes and Behaviors of the American People, 1972-1989. The Gale Group. • 1990. $89.50. A summary of responses to about 300 questions in the General Social Survey conducted annually by the National Opinion Research Center, covering family characteristics, social behavior, religion, political opinions, etc. Includes a chronology of significant world events from 1972 to 1989 and a subject-keyword index.

Constructing Effective Questionnaires. Robert A. Peterson. Sage Publications, Inc. • 1999. $70.00. Covers the construction and wording of questionnaires for survey research.

Focus Group Kit. David L. Morgan and Richard A. Krueger, editors. Sage Publications, Inc. • 1997. $99.95. Six volumes. Various authors cover the basics of focus group research, including planning, developing questions, moderating, and analyzing results.

Handbook for Focus Group Research. Thomas L. Greenbaum. Sage Publications, Inc. • 1997. $49.95. Second edition. Includes glossary and index.

ONLINE DATABASES

FINDEX. Kalorama Information. • Provides online annotations of market research reports and related publications from about 1,000 publishers. Time period is 1972 to date, with quarterly updates. (Formerly produced by Cambridge Information Group.) Inquire as to online cost and availability.

Simmons Study of Media and Markets. Simmons Market Research Bureau. • Market and media survey data relating to the American consumer. Inquire as to online cost and availability.

PERIODICALS AND NEWSLETTERS

The Boomer Report: The Insights You Need to Reach America's Most Influential Consumer Group. Age Wave Communications Corp. • Monthly. $195.00 per year. Newsletter. Presents market research relating to the "baby boomers," an age group generally defined as having been born between 1950 and 1970.

Consumer Confidence Survey. Conference Board, Inc. • Monthly. Members, $95.00 per year; non-members, $195.00 per year. Attitudes toward business conditions and employment, plans to buy major durable goods, and intended vacations. Formerly *Consumer Attitudes and Buying Plans.*

Consumer Trends: An Independent Newsletter on Credit Issues and Financial Affairs. International Credit Association. • Monthly. $100.00 per year.

Public Pulse: Roper's Authoritative Report on What Americans are Thinking, D oing, and Buying. Roper Starch Worldwide. • Monthly. $297.00. Newsletter. Contains news of surveys of American attitudes, values, and behavior. Each issue includes a research supplement giving "complete facts and figures behind each survey question.".

Research Alert: A Bi-Weekly Report of Consumer Marketing Studies. EPM Communications, Inc. • Semimonthly. $369.00 per year. Newsletter. Provides descriptions (abstracts) of new, consumer market research reports from private, government, and academic sources. Includes sample charts and tables.

RESEARCH CENTERS AND INSTITUTES

Conference Board, Inc. 845 Third Ave., New York, NY 10022. Phone: (212)759-0900 Fax: (212)980-7014 E-mail: richard.cavanaugh@conference-board.org • URL: http://www.conference-board.org.

STATISTICS SOURCES

Consumer Expenditure Survey. Available from U. S. Government Printing Office. • Biennial. Issued by the Bureau of Labor Statistics, U. S. Department of Labor (http://www.bls.gov). Contains data on various kinds of consumer spending, according to household income, education, etc. (Bureau of Labor Statistics Bulletin.).

Lifestyle Market Analyst. SRDS. • Annual. $391.00. Published in conjunction with NDL (National Demographics & Lifestyles). Provides extensive lifestyle data on interests, activities, and hobbies within specific geographic and demographic markets.

TRADE/PROFESSIONAL ASSOCIATIONS

National Council on Public Polls. 1375 Kings Highway East, Suite 300, Fairfield, CT 06430. Phone: 800-239-0909 Fax: (203)331-1750 • Members are public opinion polling organizations.

OTHER SOURCES

MarketingClick Network: American Demographics. Intertec Publishing, a Primedia Co. • Web site provides full-text articles from *American Demographics*, *Marketing Tools*, and *Forecast*, with keyword searching. The *Marketing Tools Directory* can also be searched online, listing suppliers of products, information, and services for advertising, market research, and marketing. Fees: Free.

CONSUMERS' COOPERATIVE SOCIETIES

See: COOPERATIVES

CONSUMERS' LEAGUES

See: COOPERATIVES

CONSUMERS, MATURE

See: MATURE CONSUMER MARKET

CONSUMERS' PRODUCTS RESEARCH

See: QUALITY OF PRODUCTS

CONTACT LENS AND INTRAOCULAR LENS INDUSTRIES

See also: OPHTHALMIC INDUSTRY

ABSTRACTS AND INDEXES

Index Medicus. National Library of Medicine. Available from U. S. Government Printing Office. • Monthly. $522.00 per year. Bibliographic listing of references to current articles from approximately 3,000 of the world's biomedical journals.

BIBLIOGRAPHIES

Medical and Health Care Books and Serials in Print: An Index to Literature in Health Sciences. R. R. Bowker. • Annual. $265.95. Two volumes.

DIRECTORIES

Contact Lens Manufacturers Association: Directory of Members. Contact Lens Manufacturers Association. • Annual. Membership.

Medical and Health Information Directory. The Gale Group. • 1999. $630.00. Three volumes. 12th edition. Vol. one covers medical organizations, agencies, and institutions; vol. two includes bibliographic, library, and database information; vol. three is a guide to services available for various medical and health problems.

HANDBOOKS AND MANUALS

Physicians' Desk Reference for Ophthalmology. Medical Economics Publishing Co., Inc. • Irregular. $49.95. Provides detailed descriptions of ophthalmological instrumentation, equipment, supplies, lenses, and prescription drugs. Indexed by manufacturer, product name, product category, active drug ingredient, and instrumentation. Editorial discussion is included.

ONLINE DATABASES

Embase. Elsevier Science, Inc. • Worldwide medical literature, 1974 to present. Weekly updates. Inquire as to online cost and availability.

Medline. Medlars Management Section. • Provides indexing and abstracting of worldwide medical literature, 1966 to date. Weekly updates. Inquire as to online cost and availability.

PERIODICALS AND NEWSLETTERS

CLAO Journal. Contact Lens Association of Ophthalmologists. Kellner/McCaffery Associates, Inc. • Quarterly. $76.00 per year. Formerly *Contact and Intraocular Lens Medical Journal.* Provides scientific reports on contact lenses and cornea.

Contact Lens Spectrum. Boucher Communications, Inc. • 20 times a year. $43.00 per year. Provides news and information on clinical issues and the contact lens industry. Incorporates *Contact Lens Forum.*

International Contact Lens Clinic. Elsevier Science. • Bimonthly. $272.00 per year.

Ocular Surgery News. Slack, Inc. • Biweekly. Individuals, $295.00 per year; institutions, $315.00 per year. Formerly *IOL & Ocular Surgery News.*

TRADE/PROFESSIONAL ASSOCIATIONS

American Optometric Association; Contact Lens Section. 243 N. Lindbergh Blvd., St. Louis, MO 63141. Phone: (314)991-4100 Fax: (314)991-4101 • URL: http://www.aoanet.org.

American Society of Cataract and Refractive Surgery. 4000 Legato Rd., No. 850, Fairfax, VA 22033. Phone: 800-451-1339 or (703)591-2220 Fax: (703)591-0614 E-mail: ascrs@ascrs.org • URL: http://www.ascrs.org.

Contact Lens Association of Ophthalmologists. c/o John S. Massare, 721 Papworth Ave., Suites 205 and 206, Metairie, LA 70005. Phone: (504)835-3937 Fax: (504)833-5884 E-mail: jmassare@clao.org • URL: http://www.clao.org.

Contact Lens Manufacturers Association. 4400 East-West Highway, Suite 33, Bethesda, MD 20814. Phone: (301)654-2229 Fax: (301)654-1611.

Contact Lens Society of America. 441 Carlisle Dr., Herndon, VA 20170-4837. Phone: (703)437-5100 Fax: (703)437-0727.

OTHER SOURCES

Health Care Products and Remedies. Available from MarketResearch.com. • 1997. $600.00 each. Consists of market reports published by Simmons Market Research Bureau on each of about 25 health care product categories. Examples are cold remedies, contraceptives, hearing aids, bandages, headache remedies, eyeglasses, contact lenses, and vitamins. Each report covers buying patterns and demographics.

New Ophthalmology: Treatments and Technologies. Theta Reports/PJB Medical Publications, Inc. • 2000. $1,695. Provides market research data relating to eye surgery, including LASIK, cataract surgery, and associated technology. (Theta Report No. 911.).

World Contact and Intraocular Lenses and Ophthalmic Devices Markets. Available from MarketResearch.com. • 1996. $995.00. Published by Theta Corporation. Provides market data on soft contact lenses, hard lenses, and lens care products, with forecasts to 2000.

CONTAINER INDUSTRY

See also: COOPERAGE INDUSTRY; GLASS CONTAINER INDUSTRY; PAPER BAG INDUSTRY; PAPER BOX AND PAPER CONTAINER INDUSTRIES

DIRECTORIES

Official Container Directory. Advanstar Communications, Inc. • Semiannual. $75.00. About 3,000 manufacturers of corrugated and solid fiber containers, folding cartons, rigid boxes, fiber cans and tubes, and fiber drums. Includes a buying guide.

Packaging Digest Machinery/Materials Guide. Cahners Business Information. • Annual. $46.00. List of more than 3,100 manufacturers of machinery and materials for the packaging industry, and about 260 contract packagers.

ENCYCLOPEDIAS AND DICTIONARIES

Wiley Encyclopedia of Packaging Technology. Aaron Brody and Kenneth Marsh, editors. John Wiley and Sons, Inc. • 1997. $190.00. Second edition.

FINANCIAL RATIOS

Annual Statement Studies. Robert Morris Associates: The Association of Lending and Credit Risk Professiona. • Annual. Free to members; non-members, $140.00. Median and quartile financial ratios are given for over 400 kinds of manufacturing, wholesale, retail, construction, and consumer finance establishments. Data is sorted by both asset size and sales volume. Includes a clearly written "Definition of Ratios" and an alphabetical industry index.

INTERNET DATABASES

Fedstats. Federal Interagency Council on Statistical Policy. Phone: (202)395-7254 • URL: http://www.fedstats.gov • Web site features an efficient search facility for full-text statistics produced by more than 70 federal agencies, including the Census Bureau, the Bureau of Economic Analysis, and the Bureau of Labor Statistics. Boolean searches can be made within one agency or for all agencies combined. Links are offered to international statistical bureaus, including the UN, IMF, OECD, UNESCO, Eurostat, and 20 individual countries. Fees: Free.

ONLINE DATABASES

DRI U.S. Central Database. Data Products Division. • Provides more than 23,000 business, financial, demographic, economic, foreign trade, and industry-related time series for the U.S. Includes national income, population, retail-wholesale trade, price indexes, labor data, housing, industrial production, banking, interest rates, money supply, etc. Time period is generally 1947 to date (some data back to 1929). Updating varies. Inquire as to online cost and availability.

PERIODICALS AND NEWSLETTERS

Cantech International. Trend Publishing. • Bimonthly. $70.00 per year. Covers metal can manufacturing, tooling, and decorating.

Packaging Digest. Cahners Business Information. • 13 times a year. $92.90 per year.

PRICE SOURCES

Official Board Markets: "The Yellow Sheet". Mark Arzoumanian. Advanstar Communications, Inc. • Weekly. $150.00 per year. Covers the corrugated container, folding carton, rigid box and waste paper industries.

STATISTICS SOURCES

American Iron and Steel Annual Statistical Report. American Iron and Steel Institute. • Annual. $100.00 per year.

Annual Survey of Manufactures. Available from U. S. Government Printing Office. • Annual. Prices vary. Issued by the U. S. Census Bureau as an interim update to the *Census of Manufactures.* Includes data on number of manufacturing establishments in various industries, employment, labor costs, value of shipments, capital expenditures, inventories, energy costs, and assets. (See also Census Bureau home page, http://www.census.gov/.).

Business Statistics of the United States. Courtenay M. Slater, editor. Bernan Associates. • 1999. $74.00. Fifth edition. Based on *Business Statistics*, formerly issue by the Bureau of Economic Analysis, U. S. Department of Commerce. Provides basic data for a wide variety of U. S. industries, services, and economic indicators. Most statistics are shown annually for 29 years and monthly for the most recent four years.

Manufacturing Profiles. Available from U. S. Government Printing Office. • Annual. Issued by the U. S. Census Bureau. A printed consolidation of the entire *Current Industrial Report* series, presenting "all the data compiled." Contains statistics on production, shipments, inventories, consumption, exports, imports, and orders for a wide variety of manufactured products. (See also Census Bureau home page, http://www.census.gov/.).

Survey of Current Business. Available from U. S. Government Printing Office. • Monthly. $49.00 per year. Issued by Bureau of Economic Analysis, U. S. Department of Commerce. Presents a wide variety of business and economic data.

TRADE/PROFESSIONAL ASSOCIATIONS

Associated Cooperage Industries of America. 2100 Gardiner Lane, Suite 100-E, Louisville, KY 40205-2947. Phone: (502)459-6113 Fax: (502)459-6113.

Can Manufacturers Institute. 1625 Massachusetts Ave., N.W., Suite 500, Washington, DC 20036. Phone: (202)232-4677 Fax: (202)232-5756 E-mail: clee@cancentral.com • URL: http://www.cancentral.com.

Containerization and Intermodal Institute. 195 Fairfield Ave., Suite 2D, West Caldwell, NJ 07006. Phone: (973)226-0160 Fax: (973)364-1212 E-mail: cII@bsya.com.

National Beverage Packaging Association. c/o Gary Lile, No. 1 Busch Place, OSC-2N, St. Louis, MO 63118. Phone: (314)577-2443 Fax: (314)577-2972 E-mail: gary.lileoanheuser-busch.com • Members are concerned with the packaging of soft drinks, beer, and juices.

Steel Shipping Container Institute. 1100 14th St., N.W., Suite 1020, Washington, DC 20005. Phone: (202)408-1900 Fax: (202)408-1972 E-mail: ssci@steelcontainers.com • URL: http://www.steelcontainers.com.

CONTESTS, PRIZES, AND AWARDS

DIRECTORIES

Awards, Honors, and Prizes. The Gale Group. • 2001. 18th edition. Two volumes. Domestic volume, $245.00. International volume, $275.00.

Contests for Students: All You Need to Know to Enter and Win 600 Contests. The Gale Group. • 1999. $45.00. Second edition. details 600 regional, national, and international contests for elementary, junior high, and high school students.

Peterson's Scholarships, Grants, and Prizes: Your Complete Guide to College Aid from Private Sources. Peterson's. • 1998. $26.95. Second edition.

The PROMO 100 Promotion Agency Ranking. Intertec Publishing Co. • Annual. $9.95. Provides information on 100 leading product promotion agencies.

R and I Blue Book (Recognition and Identification). Engravers Journal, Inc. • Price on application. Annual. Over 200 manufacturers and suppliers of trophies, plaques, engraving and marking equipment and supplies to the recognition and identification (R&I) industry. Formerly *Awards Specialist Directory.*

World of Winners: A Current and Historical Perspective on Awards and Their Winners. The Gale Group. • 1991. $80.00 Second edition. Lists 100,000 recipients of 2,500 awards, honors, and prizes in 12 subject categories. Indexed by organization, recipient, and award. Covers all years for each award.

ONLINE DATABASES

Marketing and Advertising Reference Service (MARS). The Gale Group. • Provides abstracts of literature relating to consumer marketing and advertising, including all forms of advertising media. Time period is 1984 to date. Daily updates. Inquire as to online cost and availability.

PERIODICALS AND NEWSLETTERS

Potentials: Ideas and Products that Motivate. Lakewood Publications, Inc. • 10 times a year. $24.00 per year. Covers incentives, premiums, awards, and gifts as related to promotional activities. Formerly *Potentials in Marketing.*

PROMO: Promotion Marketing Worldwide. Simba Information Inc. • Monthly. $65.00 per year. Edited for companies and agencies that utilize couponing, point-of-purchase advertising, special events, games, contests, premiums, product samples, and other unique promotional items.

TRADE/PROFESSIONAL ASSOCIATIONS

Awards and Recognition Association. 4700 W. Lake Ave., Glenview, IL 60025. Phone: 800-344-2148 or (847)375-4800 Fax: (847)375-6309 • URL: http://www.ara.org.

CONTRACTIONS

See: ABBREVIATIONS

CONTRACTORS

See: BUILDING CONTRACTS; BUILDING INDUSTRY

CONTRACTORS, ELECTRICAL

See: ELECTRICAL CONSTRUCTION INDUSTRY

CONTRACTS

See also: BUILDING CONTRACTS; GOVERNMENT CONTRACTS

GENERAL WORKS

An Introduction to the Law of Contract. Patrick S. Atiyah. Oxford University Press, Inc. • 1995. $80.00. Fifth edition. (Claredon Law Series).

ABSTRACTS AND INDEXES

Current Law Index: Multiple Access to Legal Periodicals. The Gale Group. • Monthly. $650.00 per year. Produced in cooperation with the American Association of Law Libraries. Indexes more than 900 law journals, legal newspapers, and specialty publications from the U.S., Canada, U.K., Ireland, Australia, and New Zealand.

Index to Legal Periodicals and Books. H. W. Wilson Co. • Monthly. Quarterly and annual cumulations. $270.00 per year. CD-ROM version available at $1,495.00 per year.

ALMANACS AND YEARBOOKS

American Law Yearbook. The Gale Group. • Annual. $155.00. Serves as a yearly supplement to *West's Encyclopedia of American Law.* Describes new legal developments in many subject areas.

CD-ROM DATABASES

WILSONDISC: Index to Legal Periodicals and Books. H. W. Wilson Co. • Monthly. Including unlimited online access to *Index to Legal Periodicals* through WILSONLINE. Contains CD-ROM indexing of more than 800 English language legal periodicals from 1981 to date and 2,500 books.

ENCYCLOPEDIAS AND DICTIONARIES

West's Encyclopedia of American Law. Available from The Gale Group. • 1997. $995.00. Second edition. 12 volumes. Published by West Group. Covers a wide variety of legal topics for the general reader. Formerly *Guide to American Law: Everyone's Legal Encyclopedia* (1985).

HANDBOOKS AND MANUALS

Contracts for the Film and Television Industry. Mark Litwak. Silman-James Press. • 1999. $35.95. Second expanded edition. Contains a wide variety of sample entertainment contracts. Includes material on rights, employment, joint ventures, music, financing, production, distribution, merchandising, and the retaining of attorneys.

Corbin on Contracts. Arthur L. Corbin. West Publishing Co., College and School Div. • 14 volumes. Price on application.

Legal Guide to Independent Contractor Status. Robert W. Wood. Panel Publishers. • 1999. $165.00. Third edition. A guide to the legal and tax-related differences between employers and independent contractors. Includes examples of both "safe" and "troublesome" independent contractor designations. Penalties and fines are discussed.

Williston on Contracts. Richard A. Lord. West Group. • 1990. $507.00. 28 volumes. Encyclopedic coverage of contract law.

ONLINE DATABASES

Index to Legal Periodicals and Books (Online). H. W. Wilson Co. • Broad coverage of law journals and books 1981 to date. Monthly updates. Inquire as to online cost and availability.

LEXIS. LEXIS-NEXIS. • The various LEXIS databases provide full text and indexing for a wide variety of legal cases, statutes, orders, and opinions.

PERIODICALS AND NEWSLETTERS

Contract Management. National Contract Management Association. • Monthly. $72.00 per year.

RESEARCH CENTERS AND INSTITUTES

Lexis.com Research System. Lexis-Nexis Group. Phone: 800-227-9597 or (937)865-6800 Fax: (937)865-6909 E-mail: webmaster@prod.lexis-nexis.com • URL: http://www.lexis.com • Fee-based Web site offers extensive searching of a wide variety of legal sources. Additional features include Daily Opinion Service, lexis.com Bookstore, Career Center, CLE Center, Law Schools, and Practice Pages ("Pages specific to areas of specialty").

TRADE/PROFESSIONAL ASSOCIATIONS

National Contract Management Association. 1912 Woodford Rd., Vienna, VA 22182. Phone: 800-344-8096 or (703)448-9231 Fax: (703)448-0939 • URL: http://www.ncmahq.org.

OTHER SOURCES

Government Contracts Reports. CCH, Inc. • $2,249.00 per year. 10 looseleaf volumes. Weekly updates. Laws and regulations affecting government contracts.

CONTRACTS, GOVERNMENT

See: GOVERNMENT CONTRACTS

CONTROL EQUIPMENT INDUSTRY

See also: AUTOMATION; FLUIDICS INDUSTRY

ABSTRACTS AND INDEXES

Applied Science and Technology Index. H. W. Wilson Co. • 11 times a year. Quarterly and annual cumulations. Service basis for print edition; CD-ROM edition, $1,495.00 per year. Indexes a wide variety of English language technical, industrial, and engineering periodicals.

Engineering Index Monthly: Abstracting and Indexing Services Covering Sources of the World's Engineering Literature. Engineering Information, Inc. • Monthly. $2,300.00 per year. Provides indexing and abstracting of the world's engineering and technical literature.

Key Abstracts: Machine Vision. Available from INSPEC, Inc. • Monthly. $240.00 per year. Provides international coverage of journal and proceedings literature on optical noncontact sensing. Published in England by the Institution of Electrical Engineers (IEE).

Key Abstracts: Robotics and Control. Available from INSPEC, Inc. • Monthly. $240.00 per year. Provides international coverage of journal and proceedings literature. Published in England by the Institution of Electrical Engineers (IEE).

NTIS Alerts: Computers, Control & Information Theory. National Technical Information Service. • Semimonthly. $235.00 per year. Provides descriptions of government-sponsored research reports and software, with ordering information. Covers computer hardware, software, control systems, pattern recognition, image processing, and related subjects. Formerly *Abstract Newsletter*.

Science Citation Index. Institute for Scientific Information. • Bimonthly. $15,020.00 per year. Annual cumulation. Includes *Source Index*, *Citation Index*, *Permuterm Subject Index*, and *Corporate Index*.

CD-ROM DATABASES

COMPENDEX PLUS [CD-ROM]. Engineering Information, Inc. • Quarterly. $3,450.00 per year. Provides CD-ROM indexing and abstracting of the world's engineering and technical information appearing in journals, reports, books, and proceedings, 1985 to date.

DIRECTORIES

CEC Chemical Equipment Catalog: Equipment for the Process Industries. Cahners Business Information. • Annual. $60.00. Provides catalog descriptions of chemical processing equipment in 12 major product or service categories.

Control Engineering Buyers Guide. Cahners Business Information. • Annual. Free to qualified personnel. Contains specifications, prices, and manufacturers' listings for computer software, as related to control engineering.

ID Systems Buyers Guide. Helmers Publishing, Inc. • Annual. Price on application. Provides information on over 750 companies manufacturing automatic identification equipment, including scanners, data collection terminals, and bar code systems.

International Instrumentation and Controls Buyers Guide. Keller International Publishing, LLC. • Annual. Controlled circulation. Lists over 310 suppliers of precision instrument products and services.

ISA Directory of Instrumentation. Instrument Society of America. • Annual. $100.00. Over 2,400 manufacturers of control and instrumentation equipment, over 1,000 manufacturers' representatives, and several hundred service companies; coverage includes Canada.

Macrae's Blue Book: Serving the Original Equipment Market. MacRae's Blue Book, Inc. • Annual. $170.00. Two volumes. Lists about 50,000 manufacturers of a wide variety of industrial equipment and supplies.

Manufacturing Systems: Buyers Guide. Cahners Business Information. • Annual. Price on application. Contains information on companies manufacturing or supplying materials handling systems, CAD/CAM systems, specialized software for manufacturing, programmable controllers, machine vision systems, and automatic identification systems.

Sensors Buyers Guide. Advanstar Communications. • Annual. Price on application. Provides information on over 1,400 manufacturers of high technology sensors.

Test and Measurement World Annual Buyer's Guide. Cahners Business Information, Global Electronics Div. • Annual. Free to qualified personnel; others, $32.95. List of over 1,500 suppliers of test, measurement, inspection, and monitoring products and services.

Thomas Register of American Manufacturers and Thomas Register Catalog File. Thomas Publishing Co., Inc. • Annual. $149.00. 34 volumes. A three-part system offering information on a wide variety of industrial equipment and supplies.

FINANCIAL RATIOS

Industry Norms and Key Business Ratios. Desk Top Edition. Dun and Bradstreet Corp., Business Information Services. • Annual. Five volumes. $475.00 per volume. $1,890.00 per set. Covers over 800 kinds of businesses, arranged by Standard Industrial Classification number. More detailed editions covering longer periods of time are also available.

HANDBOOKS AND MANUALS

Control Handbook. William S. Levine, editor. CRC Press, Inc. • 1996. $159.95. Contains about 140 articles by various authors on automatic control, control theory, and control engineering. (Electrical Engineering Handbook Series).

ONLINE DATABASES

COMPENDEX PLUS. Engineering Information, Inc. • Provides online indexing and abstracting of the world's engineering and technical information appearing in journals, reports, books, and proceedings. Time period is 1970 to date, with weekly updates. Inquire as to online cost and availability.

FLUIDEX. Available from Elsevier Science, Inc., Secondary Publishing Division. • Produced in the Netherlands by Elsevier Science B.V. Provides indexing and abstracting of the international literature of fluid engineering and technology, 1973 to date, with monthly updates. Also known as *Fluid Engineering Abstracts*. Inquire as to online cost and availability.

Globalbase. The Gale Group. • Provides more than one million online summaries of business, industrial, and economic news reports from more than 1,000 publications worldwide. Covers a wide range of material appearing in international trade journals, professional magazines, and newspapers. Time period is 1984 to date, with weekly updates. Inquire as to online cost and availability.

INSPEC. Institute of Electrical and Electronics Engineers (IEEE). • Provides indexing and abstracting of the worldwide literature of electrical engineering, electronics, physics, computer technology, information technology, and industrial controls. Time period is 1970 to date, with weekly updates. Inquire as to online cost and availability. (INSPEC is Information Services for the Physics and Engineering Communities.).

Scisearch. Institute for Scientific Information. • Broad, multidisciplinary index to the literature of science and technology, 1974 to present. Inquire as to online cost and availability. Coverage of literature is worldwide, with weekly updates.

Thomas Register Online. Thomas Publishing Co., Inc. • Provides concise information on approximately 194,000 U. S. companies, mainly manufacturers, with over 50,000 product classifications. Indexes over 115,000 trade names. Information is updated semiannually. Inquire as to online cost and availability.

PERIODICALS AND NEWSLETTERS

Control Engineering: Covering Control, Instrumentation and Automation Systems Worldwide. Cahners Business Information. • Monthly. $99.90 per year.

IEEE Industry Applications Magazine. Institute of Electrical and Electronics Engineers. • Bimonthly. $190.00 per year. Covers new industrial applications of power conversion, drives, lighting, and control. Emphasis is on the petroleum, chemical, rubber, plastics, textile, and mining industries.

Industrial Computing. ISA Services, Inc. • Monthly. $50.00 per year. Published by the Instrument Society of America. Edited for engineering managers and systems integrators. Subject matter includes industrial software, programmable controllers, artificial intelligence systems, and industrial computer networking systems.

Instrumentation and Automation News: Instruments, Controls, Manufacturing Software, Electronics and Mechanical Components. Cahners Business Information. • Monthly. Price on application.

INTECH: The International Journal of Instrumentation and Control. ISA Services, Inc. • Monthly. $85.00 per year.

Manufacturing Computer Solutions. Hitchcock Publishing. • Monthly. Free to qualified personnel; others; $75.00 per year. Edited for managers of factory automation, emphasizing the integration of systems in manufacturing. Subjects include materials handling, CAD/CAM, specialized software for manufacturing, programmable controllers, machine vision, and automatic identification systems. Formerly *Manufacturing Systems.*

Measurement and Control. Measurements and Data Corp. • 10 times a year. $22.00 per year. Supplement available: *M & C: Measurement and Control News.*

Processing. Putman Media. • 14 times a year. $54.00 per year. Emphasis is on descriptions of new products for all areas of industrial processing, including valves, controls, filters, pumps, compressors, fluidics, and instrumentation.

Sensor Technology: A Monthly Intgelligence Service. Technical Insights. • Monthly. $685.00 per year. Newsletter on technological developments relating to industrial sensors and process control.

Sensors: The Journal of Applied Sensing Technology. Advanstar Communications. • Monthly. $62.00 per year. Edited for design, production, and manufacturing engineers involved with sensing systems. Emphasis is on emerging technology.

Test and Measurement World: The Magazine for Quality in Electronics. Cahners Business Information, Global Electronics Div. • 15 times a year. $77.90 per year.

RESEARCH CENTERS AND INSTITUTES

Instrumentation and Control Laboratory. Princeton University. Department of MAE, Engineering Quadrangle, Princeton, NJ 08544. Phone: (609)452-5154 Fax: (609)452-6109 E-mail: enoch@princeton.edu.

STATISTICS SOURCES

Annual Survey of Manufactures. Available from U. S. Government Printing Office. • Annual. Prices vary. Issued by the U. S. Census Bureau as an interim update to the *Census of Manufactures.* Includes data on number of manufacturing establishments in various industries, employment, labor costs, value of shipments, capital expenditures, inventories, energy costs, and assets. (See also Census Bureau home page, http://www.census.gov/.).

Manufacturing Profiles. Available from U. S. Government Printing Office. • Annual. Issued by the U. S. Census Bureau. A printed consolidation of the entire *Current Industrial Report* series, presenting "all the data compiled." Contains statistics on production, shipments, inventories, consumption, exports, imports, and orders for a wide variety of manufactured products. (See also Census Bureau home page, http://www.census.gov/.).

U. S. Industry and Trade Outlook: The McGraw-Hill Companies and the U.S. Department of Commerce/ International Trade Administration. Datapso Research Corp. • Annual. $69.95. Produced by the International Trade Administration, U. S. Department of Commerce, in a "public-private" partnership with DRI/McGraw-Hill and Standard & Poor's. Provides basic data, outlook for the current year, and "Long-Term Prospects" (five-year projections) for a wide variety of products and services. Includes high technology industries. Formerly *U. S. Industrial Outlook.*

TRADE/PROFESSIONAL ASSOCIATIONS

American Automatic Control Council. Dept. of EECS, Northwestern University, 2145 Sheridan Rd., Evanston, IL 60208-3118. Phone: (847)491-8175 Fax: (847)491-4455 E-mail: acc@ece.nwu.edu.

Fluid Controls Institute. 1330 Sumner Ave., Cleveland, OH 44115. Phone: (216)241-7333 Fax: (216)241-0105 E-mail: fci@fluidcontrolsinstitute.org • URL: http://www.fluidcontrolsinstitute.org.

Institute of Electrical and Electronics Engineers; Control Systems Society. Three Park Ave., 17th Fl., New York, NY 10016-5997. Phone: (212)419-7900 Fax: (212)752-4929 • URL: http://www.ieee.org.

Instrument Society of America: Automatic Control Systems Division. P.O. Box 12277, Durham, NC 27709. Phone: (919)549-8411 Fax: (919)549-8288 E-mail: info@isa.org • URL: http://www.isa.org.

Instrument Society of America (ISA). P.O. Box 12277, Research Triangle Park, NC 27709. Phone: (919)549-8411 Fax: (919)549-8288 E-mail: info@isa.org • URL: http://www.isa.org • Members are engineers and others concerned with industrial instrumentation, systems, computers, and automation.

Process Equipment Manufacturers Association. 111 Park Place, Falls Church, VA 22046. Phone: (703)538-1796 Fax: (703)241-5603 E-mail: info@pemanet.org • URL: http://www.pemanet.org.

SAMA Group of Associations. 225 Reinekers Ln., Ste. 625, Alexandria, VA 23314. Phone: (703)836-1360 Fax: (703)836-6644.

OTHER SOURCES

Industrial Controls. Available from MarketResearch.com. • 1998. $3,400.00. Published by the Freedonia Group. Market data with forecasts to 2002 and 2006. Includes computerized controls and conventional controls.

CONTROLLERS

See: CORPORATE DIRECTORS AND OFFICERS

CONVENIENCE STORES

ABSTRACTS AND INDEXES

Business Periodicals Index. H. W. Wilson Co. • Monthly, except August, with quarterly and annual cumulations. Service basis for print edition; CD-ROM edition, $1,495.00 per year.

CD-ROM DATABASES

ABI/INFORM Global. Bell & Howell Information and Learning. • Monthly. $6,500.00 per year. Provides CD-ROM indexing and abstracting of worldwide business literature appearing in over 1,200 periodicals for the most recent five years. Archival discs are available from 1971. Formerly *ABI/INFORM OnDisc.*

F & S Index Plus Text. The Gale Group. • Monthly. $7,575.00 per year. Provides CD-ROM citations to worldwide business, marketing, and industrial material appearing in a large assortment of trade journals, newspapers, and other publications. Time period is four years.

WILSONDISC: Wilson Business Abstracts. H. W. Wilson Co. • Monthly. $2,495.00 per year, including unlimited online access to *Wilson Business Abstracts* through WILSONLINE. Provides CD-ROM "cover-to-cover" abstracting and indexing of over 600 prominent business periodicals. Indexing is from 1982, abstracting from 1990. (*Business Periodicals Index* without abstracts is available on CD-ROM at $1,495 per year.).

DIRECTORIES

Convenience Store News Buyers Guide. Bill Communications. • Annual. $200.00. Provides information on convenience store chains, including service station stores, and suppliers of products, equipment, and services to convenience stores.

Directory of Supermarket, Grocery, and Convenience Store Chains. Chain Store Guide. • Annual. $300.00. Provides information on about 2,200 food store chains operating 30,000 individual stores. Store locations are given.

European Directory of Retailers and Wholesalers. Available from The Gale Group. • 1997. $790.00. Second edition. Published by Euromonitor. Provides detailed information on more than 4,000 major retail and wholesale businesses in 17 countries of Western Europe. Contains 26 categories, such as supermarkets, superstores, department stores, discount stores, franchise operators, mail order, etc. Includes company, product, and geographic indexes.

Trade Dimensions' Directory of Convenience Stores. Trade Dimensions. • Annual. $245.00. Provides information on over 1,300 convenience store chains having four or more convenience stores. Formerly *Directory of Convenience Stores.*

HANDBOOKS AND MANUALS

Convenience Food Store. Entrepreneur Media, Inc. • Looseleaf. $59.50. A practical guide to starting a convenience food store. Covers profit potential, start-up costs, market size evaluation, owner's time required, site selection, lease negotiation, pricing, accounting, advertising, promotion, etc. (Start-Up Business Guide No. E1173.).

ONLINE DATABASES

ABI/INFORM. Bell & Howell Information and Learning. • Provides online indexing to business-related material occurring in over 1,000 periodicals from 1971 to the present. Inquire as to online cost and availability.

F & S Index. The Gale Group. • Contains about four million citations to worldwide business, financial, and industrial or consumer product literature appearing from 1972 to date. Weekly updates. Inquire as to online cost and availability.

PROMT: Predicasts Overview of Markets and Technology. The Gale Group. • Companies, products, applied technologies and markets. U.S. and international literature coverage, 1972 to date. Inquire as to online cost and availability. Provides abstracts from more than 1,600 publications. Weekly updates.

Trade & Industry Index. The Gale Group. • Provides indexing of business periodicals, January 1981 to date. Daily updates. (Full text articles from some periodicals are available online, 1983 to date, in the companion database, *Trade & Industry ASAP.*) Inquire as to online cost and availability.

Wilson Business Abstracts Online. H. W. Wilson Co. • Indexes and abstracts 600 major business periodicals, plus the *Wall Street Journal* and the business section of the *New York Times.* Indexing is from 1982, abstracting from 1990, with the two newspapers included from 1993. Updated weekly. Inquire as to online cost and availability. (*Business Periodicals Index* without abstracts is also available online.).

PERIODICALS AND NEWSLETTERS

Convenience Store Decisions. Meehan Publishing Co. • Monthly. $60.00 per year. Edited for headquarters and regional management personnel of convenience store chains.

Convenience Store News: The Information Source for the Industry. Bill Communications, Business Communications Group. • 15 times a year. Free to qualified personnel; others, $85.00 per year. Contains news of industry trends and merchandising techniques.

CSP: The Magazine for C-Store People. CSP Information Group. • Monthly. $48.00 per year. Emphasizes the influence of people (both store personnel and consumers) on the C-store industry.

Oil Express: Inside Report on Trends in Petroleum Marketing Without the Influ nce of Advertising. Aspen Publishers, Inc. • Weekly. $337.00 per year. Newsletter. Provides news of trends in petroleum marketing and convenience store operations. Includes *U. S. Oil Week's Price Monitor* (petroleum product prices) and *C-Store Digest* (news concerning convenience stores operated by the major oil companies) and *Fuel Oil Update.* Formerly (U.S. Oil Week).

RESEARCH CENTERS AND INSTITUTES

Center for Retail Management. J. L. Kellogg Graduate School of Management, Northwestern University, Evanston, IL 60208. Phone: (847)467-3600 Fax: (847)467-3620 • URL: http://www.retailing-network.com • Conducts research related to retail marketing and management.

Center for Retailing Studies. Texas A & M University, Department of Marketing, 4112 Tamus, College Station, TX 77843-4112. Phone: (979)845-0325 Fax: (979)845-5230 E-mail: berryle@tamu.edu • URL: http://www.crstamu.org • Research areas include retailing issues and consumer economics.

TRADE/PROFESSIONAL ASSOCIATIONS

National Association of Convenience Stores. 1605 King St., Alexandria, VA 22314-2792. Phone: (703)684-3600 Fax: (703)836-4564 E-mail: nacs@cstorecentral.com • URL: http://www.cstorecentral.com • Members are small retail stores that sell a variety of food and nonfood items and that usually have extended hours of opening.

OTHER SOURCES

Business & Company Resource Center. The Gale Group. • Fee-based Web site provides a wide range of business, industry, and specific company information. Access is offered to trade journal articles, market research data, insider trading activity, major shareholder data, corporate histories, emerging technology reports, corporate earnings estimates, press releases, and other sources. Provides detailed company profiles, industry overviews, and rankings. Offers integration of Predicasts PROMT, Newsletters ASAP, Investext Plus, Business Index ASAP, Brands and Their Companies, and other databases (many have full text).

CONVENTION MANAGEMENT

See: MEETING MANAGEMENT

CONVENTIONS

See also: CONFERENCES, WORKSHOPS, AND SEMINARS; SALES CONVENTIONS; TRADE SHOWS

DIRECTORIES

AudArena Stadium International Guide and Facility Buyers Guide. BPI Communications, Amusement Business Div. • Annual. $95.00. More than 4,400 arenas, auditoriums, stadiums, exhibit halls, and coliseums in U.S., Canada and in less depth, Europe and South America. Formerly *Audarena Stadium International Guide.*

Directory of Association Meeting Planners and Conference/Convention Directors. Salesman's Guide. • Annual. $259.95. Lists about 13,600 planners of meetings for over 8,100 national associations. Provides past and future convention locations, dates held, number of attendees, exhibit space required, and other convention information. Formerly *Association Meeting Planners.*

Directory of Conventions Regional Editions. Bill Communications. • Annual. $155.00 per volume. Four volumes. Set $285.00. Over 14,000 meetings of North American national, regional, and state and local organizations.

The HCEA: A Directory of Health Care Meetings and Conventions. Healthcare Convention and Healthcare Exhibitors Association. • Semiannual. Free to members; non-members, $245.00 per year. Lists more than 2,400 health care meetings, most of which have an exhibit program. Formerly *Handbook-A Directory of Health Care Meetings and Conventions.*

Trade Shows Worldwide: An International Directory of Events, Facilities and Suppliers. The Gale Group. • 2000. $299.00. 16th edition. Provides detailed information from over 75 countries on more than 8,400 trade shows and exhibitions. Separate sections are provided for trade shows/exhibitions, for sponsors/organizers, and for services, facilities, and information sources. Indexing is by date, location, subject, name, and keyword.

TradeShow and Convention Guide. BPI Communications. • Annual. $115.00. Dates and data for convention and trade shows for the next five years; local companies that supply services such as photograpy, exhibit design etc.; halls and hotels catering to conventions and shows.

HANDBOOKS AND MANUALS

Sports, Convention, and Entertainment Facilities. David C. Petersen. Urban Land Institute. • 1996. $59.95. Provides advice and information on developing, financing, and operating amphitheaters, arenas, convention centers, and stadiums. Includes case studies of 70 projects.

INTERNET DATABASES

Trade Show Central: The Internet's Leading Trade Show Information Resource!. Trade Show Central. Phone: (781)235-8095 Fax: (781)416-4500 • URL: http://www.tscentral.com • Web site provides information on "more than 30,000 Trade Shows, Conferences, and Seminars, 5,000 service providers, and 5,000 venues and facilities around the world." Searching is offered by trade show name, industry category, date, and location. Results may be sorted by event name, city, country, or date. Includes a "Career Center" for trade show personnel. Continuous updating. Fees: Free.

ONLINE DATABASES

Conference Papers Index. Cambridge Scientific Abstracts. • Citations to scientific and technical papers presented at meetings, 1973 to present. Inquire as to online cost and availability.

PERIODICALS AND NEWSLETTERS

Journal of Convention and Exhibition Management. Haworth Press, Inc. • Quarterly. Individuals $50.00 per year; institutions, $85.00 per year; libraries, $95.00 per year.

Scientific Meetings. Scientific Meetings Publications. • Quarterly. $85.00 per year. Provides information on forthcoming scientific, technical, medical, health, engineering and management meetings held throughout the world.

Successful Meetings: The Authority on Meetings and Incentive Travel Management. Bill Communications, Inc. • Monthly. $65.00 per year.

World Meetings: United States and Canada. Available from Gale Group. • Quarterly. $195.00 per year.

TRADE/PROFESSIONAL ASSOCIATIONS

International Association of Convention and Visitor Bureaus. 2000 L St., N.W., Suite 702, Washington, DC 20036. Phone: (202)296-7888 Fax: (202)296-7889 E-mail: info@iacvb.org • URL: http://www.iacvb.org.

International Association of Exposition Management. 5001 LBJ Freeway, Suite 350, Dallas, TX 75244-6120. Phone: (972)458-8002 Fax: (972)458-8119 • URL: http://www.iaem.org.

Meeting Professionals International. 4455 LBJ Freeway, Suite 1200, Dallas, TX 75244-5903. Phone: (972)702-3000 Fax: (972)702-3070 • URL: http://www.mpiweb.org • Members are fee-based meeting planners, meeting consultants, and providers of meeting services.

Professional Convention Management Association. 100 Vestavia Office Parkway, Suite 220, Birmingham, AL 35216. Phone: (205)823-7262 Fax: (205)822-3891 • URL: http://www.pcma.org.

Religious Conference Management Association. One RCA Dome, Suite 120, Indianapolis, IN 46225. Phone: (317)632-1888 Fax: (317)632-7909 • URL: http://www.rcmaweb.org.

CONVERTIBILITY OF CURRENCY

See: FOREIGN EXCHANGE

CONVERTIBLE SECURITIES

See also: SECURITIES

HANDBOOKS AND MANUALS

Convertible Securities: The Latest Instruments, Portfolio Strategies, and Valuation Analysis. John P. Calamos. McGraw-Hill Professional. • 1998. $65.00. Second edition.

Handbook of Derivative Instruments: Investment Research, Analysis, and Portfolio Applications. Atsuo Konishi and Ravi E. Dattatreya, editors. McGraw-Hill Professional. • 1996. $80.00. Second revised edition. Contains 41 chapters by various authors on all aspects of derivative securities, including such esoterica as "Inverse Floaters," "Positive Convexity," "Exotic Options," and "How to Use the Holes in Black-Scholes.".

Handbook of Equity Derivatives. Jack C. Francis and others, editors. John Wiley and Sons, Inc. • 1999. $95.00. Contains 27 chapters by various authors.

Covers options (puts and calls), stock index futures, warrants, convertibles, over-the-counter options, swaps, legal issues, taxation, etc. (Financial Engineering Series).

International Handbook of Convertible Securities. Thomas C. Noddings and others. AMACOM. • 1998. $75.00. Includes new structures for convertible securities and advanced hedging strategies.

INTERNET DATABASES

DBC Online: America's Leading Provider of Real-Time Market Data to the Individual Investor. Data Broadcasting Corp. Phone: (415)571-1800 E-mail: dbcinfo@dbc.com • URL: http://www.dbc.com • Web site provides a wide variety of real-time securities market prices, data, and charts. Covers bonds ("BondVu"), stocks, commodities, options, mutual funds, major indexes, industry indexes, international markets, etc. Also includes news, SEC documents ("Smart-Edgar"), and various other features. Fees: Both free and fee-based, depending on level of information.

U. S. Securities and Exchange Commission. Phone: 800-732-0330 or (202)942-7040 Fax: (202)942-9634 E-mail: webmaster@sec.gov • URL: http://www.sec.gov • SEC Web site offers free access through EDGAR to text of official corporate filings, such as annual reports (10-K), quarterly reports (10-Q), and proxies. (EDGAR is "Electronic Data Gathering, Analysis, and Retrieval System.") An example is given of how to obtain executive compensation data from proxies. Text of the daily *SEC News Digest* is offered, as are links to other government sites, non-government market regulators, and U. S. stock exchanges. Search facilities are extensive. Fees: Free.

Wall Street Journal Interactive Edition. Dow Jones & Co., Inc. Phone: 800-369-2834 or (212)416-2000 Fax: (212)416-2658 E-mail: inquiries@interactive.wsj.com • URL: http://www.wsj.com • Fee-based Web site providing online searching of worldwide information from the *The Wall Street Journal*. Includes "Company Snapshots," "The Journal's Greatest Hits," "Index to Market Data," "14-Day Searchable Archive," "Journal Links," etc. Financial price quotes are available. Fees: $49.00 per year; $29.00 per year to print subscribers.

Web Finance: Covering the Electronic Evolution of Finance. Securities Data Publishing. Phone: (212)765-5311 or 800-455-5844 Fax: (212)321-2336 E-mail: webfinance@tfn.com • URL: http://www.webfinance.net • Bi-weekly print and daily web-site publication of financial services on the Web, including financial links, archives, brokerage stocks, deal financing, and other financial and investment news and information.

ONLINE DATABASES

Value Line Convertible Data Base. Value Line Publishing, Inc. • Provides online data for about 600 convertible bonds and other convertible securities: price, yield, premium, issue size, liquidity, and maturity. Information is current, with weekly updates. Inquire as to online cost and availability.

PERIODICALS AND NEWSLETTERS

Bondweek: The Newsweekly of Fixed Income and Credit Markets. Institutional Investor. • Weekly. $2,220.00 per year. Newsletter. Covers taxable, fixed-income securities for professional investors, including corporate, government, foreign, mortgage, and high-yield.

Financial Trader. Miller Freeman, Inc. • 11 times a year. $160.00 per year. Edited for professional traders. Covers fixed income securities, emerging markets, derivatives, options, futures, and equities.

The Wall Street Journal. Dow Jones & Co., Inc. • Daily. $175.00 per year. Covers news and trends relating to business, industry, finance, the economy, and international commerce. Provides extensive price and other data for the securities, commodity, options, futures, foreign exchange, and money markets.

OTHER SOURCES

Factiva. Dow Jones Reuters Business Interactive, LLC. • Fee-based Web site provides "global news and business information through Web sites and content integration solutions." Includes Dow Jones and Reuters newswires, The Wall Street Journal, and more than 7,000 other sources of current news, historical articles, market research reports, and investment analysis. Content includes 96 major U. S. newspapers, 900 non-English sources, trade publications, media transcripts, country profiles, news photos, etc.

Nexis.com. Lexis-Nexis Group. • Fee-based Web site offers searching of about 2.8 billion documents in some 30,000 news, business, and legal information sources. Features include a subject directory covering 1,200 topics in 34 categories and a Company Dossier containing information on more than 500,000 public and private companies. Boolean searching is offered.

CONVEYING MACHINERY

See also: MACHINERY; MATERIALS HANDLING

DIRECTORIES

Modern Materials Handling Casebook Directory. Cahners Business Information. • Annual. $25.00. Lists about 2,300 manufacturers of equipment and supplies in the materials handling industry. Supplement to *Modern Materials Handling*.

PERIODICALS AND NEWSLETTERS

CEMA Bulletin. Conveyor Equipment Manufacturers Association. • Quarterly. Controlled circulation.

Material Handling Management: Educating Industry on Product Handling, Flow Strategies, and Automation Technology. Penton Media Inc. • 13 times a year. Free to qualified personnel; other, $50.00 per year. Formerly *Material Handling Engineering*.

Modern Materials Handling. Cahners Publishing Co., Inc. • 14 times a year. $92.90 per year. For managers and engineers who buy or specify equipment used to move, store, control and protect products throughout the manufacturing and warehousing cycles. Includes *Casebook Directory* and *Planning Guide*. Also includes *ADC News and Solutions*.

On the Mhove. Material Handling Institute. • Quarterly. Free. Formerly *MHI News*.

PHL Bulletin (Packaging, Handling, Logistics). National Institute of Packaging, Handling, and Logistics Engineers. • Monthly. $50.00 per year.

TRADE/PROFESSIONAL ASSOCIATIONS

Association of Professional Material Handling Consultants. 8720 Red Oak Blvd., Suite 201, Charlotte, NC 28217. Phone: (704)676-1184 Fax: (704)676-1199 E-mail: 102512.1772@compuserve.com • URL: http://www.mhia.org/apmhc.

Conveyor Equipment Manufacturers Association. 6724 Lone Oak Blvd., Naples, FL 34109. Phone: (941)514-5441 Fax: (914)514-3470 E-mail: cema@cemanet.org • URL: http://www.cemanet.org.

Material Handling Equipment Distributors Association. 201 Route 45, Vernon Hills, IL 60061. Phone: (847)680-3500 Fax: (847)362-6989 E-mail: connect@mheda.org • URL: http://www.mheda.com.

Material Handling Industry. 8720 Red Oak Blvd., Suite 201, Charlotte, NC 28217. Phone: 800-345-1815 or (704)676-1190 Fax: (704)676-1199 E-mail: vwheller@mhia.org • URL: http://www.mhia.org.

COOKIE INDUSTRY

See: BAKING INDUSTRY; SNACK FOOD INDUSTRY

COOKING UTENSILS

See: HOUSEWARES INDUSTRY

COOKWARE

See: HOUSEWARES INDUSTRY

COOPERAGE INDUSTRY

See also: CONTAINER INDUSTRY

DIRECTORIES

Association of Container Reconditioners-Membership and Industrial Supply Directory. Association of Container Reconditioners. • Annual. $30.00. Lists approximately 215 container reconditioners and dealers, worldwide. Also lists suppliers of machinery and accessories.

TRADE/PROFESSIONAL ASSOCIATIONS

Associated Cooperage Industries of America. 2100 Gardiner Lane, Suite 100-E, Louisville, KY 40205-2947. Phone: (502)459-6113 Fax: (502)459-6113.

COOPERATIVE ADVERTISING

ABSTRACTS AND INDEXES

Business Periodicals Index. H. W. Wilson Co. • Monthly, except August, with quarterly and annual cumulations. Service basis for print edition; CD-ROM edition, $1,495.00 per year.

DIRECTORIES

Business Organizations, Agencies, and Publications Directory. The Gale Group. • 1999. $425.00. 12th edition. Over 40,000 entries describing 39 types of business information sources. Classified by type of organization, publication, or serviceIncludes state, national, and international agencies and organizations. Master index to names and keywords. Also includes e-mail addresses and web site URL's.

Co-op Advertising Programs Sourcebook. R. R. Bowker. • Semiannual. $499.00 per year. Lists 5,000 cooperative advertising programs offered by manufacturers. Formerly *Co-op Source Directory*.

Radio Co-op Directory. Radio Advertising Bureau. • Annual. $199.00. Lists over 5,000 manufacturers providing cooperative allowances for radio advertising.

ONLINE DATABASES

Marketing and Advertising Reference Service (MARS). The Gale Group. • Provides abstracts of literature relating to consumer marketing and advertising, including all forms of advertising media. Time period is 1984 to date. Daily updates. Inquire as to online cost and availability.

Wilson Business Abstracts Online. H. W. Wilson Co. • Indexes and abstracts 600 major business periodicals, plus the *Wall Street Journal* and the business section of the *New York Times*. Indexing is from 1982, abstracting from 1990, with the two newspapers included from 1993. Updated weekly. Inquire as to online cost and availability. (*Business Periodicals Index* without abstracts is also available online.).

STATISTICS SOURCES

Radio Facts. Radio Advertising Bureau. • Annual. $50.00.

TRADE/PROFESSIONAL ASSOCIATIONS

Newsletter Publishers Association. 1501 Wilson Blvd., Suite 509, Arlington, VA 22209-2403. Phone: 800-356-9302 or (703)527-2333 Fax: (703)841-0629 E-mail: npa@newsletter.org.

Radio Advertising Bureau. 261 Madison Ave., 23rd Fl., New York, NY 10016. Phone: 800-232-3131 or (212)681-7200 Fax: (212)681-7223 • URL: http://www.rab.com.

COOPERATIVE AGRICULTURE

See: COOPERATIVES

COOPERATIVE HOUSING

See: CONDOMINIUMS; COOPERATIVES

COOPERATIVE MOVEMENT

See: COOPERATIVES

COOPERATIVES

GENERAL WORKS

History of Work Cooperation in America: Cooperatives, Cooperative Movements, Collectivity, and Communalism From Early America to the Present. John Curl. Homeward Press. • 1980. $8.00.

DIRECTORIES

Directory of Wholesale Grocers: Service Merchandisers. Chain Store Age. • Annual. $300.00. Profiles over 2,000 cooperatives, voluntaries, non-sponsoring wholesalers, cash and carry warehouses, and nearly 220 service merchandisers. Formerly *Directory of Cooperatives, Voluntaries, and Wholesale Grocers.*

HANDBOOKS AND MANUALS

How to Buy a House, Condo, or Co-op. Jean C. Thomsett. Consumers Union of the United States, Inc. • 1996. $84.75. Fifth edition.

Your Dream Home: A Comprehensive Guide to Buying a House, Condo, or Co-op. Marguerite Smith. Available from Little, Brown & Co. • 1997. $10.99. Published by Warner Books.

PERIODICALS AND NEWSLETTERS

CHF Newsbriefs. Cooperative Housing Foundation. • Quarterly. Single issue free.

Communities: Journal of Cooperative Living. Fellowship for International Communities. • Monthly. $18.00 per year.

Cooperative Housing Bulletin. National Association of Housing Cooperatives. • Bimonthly. $50.00 per year. Includes *Cooperative Housing Journal.*

Rural Cooperatives. Available from U. S. Government Printing Office. • Bimonthly. $15.00 per year. Issued by the U. S. Department of Agriculture. Contains articles on cooperatives in rural America. Formerly *Farmer Cooperatives.*

TRADE/PROFESSIONAL ASSOCIATIONS

International Co-operative Alliance. 15, route des Morillons, CH-1218 Grand-Saconnex, Switzerland. E-mail: ica@coop.org • URL: http://www.coop.org.

National Cooperative Business Association. 1401 New York Ave., N.W., Suite 1100, Washington, DC 20005. Phone: (202)638-6222 Fax: (202)638-1374 E-mail: ncba@ncba.org • URL: http://www.cooperative.org.

Universal Cooperatives. P.O. Box 460, Minneapolis, MN 55440-0460. Phone: (612)854-0800 Fax: (612)854-5744.

OTHER SOURCES

Cooperative Housing Law and Practice-Forms. Patrick J. Rohan and Melvin A. Reskin. Matthew Bender & Co., Inc. • $860.00. Six looseleaf volumes. Periodic supplementation. Covers every aspect of the creation, financing, operation, sale and tax consequences of cooperatives. (Real Estate Transaction Series).

COPIERS

See: COPYING MACHINE INDUSTRY

COPPER INDUSTRY

See also: METAL INDUSTRY; MINES AND MINERAL RESOURCES

ABSTRACTS AND INDEXES

IMM Abstracts and Index: A Survey of World Literature on the Economic Geology and Mining of All Minerals (Except Coal), Mineral Processing, and Nonferrous Extraction Metallurgy. Institution of Mining and Metallurgy. • Bimonthly. Members, $142.00 per year; non-members, $215.00 per year. Provides international coverage of the literature of mining and nonferrous metallurgy. Includes mineral economics, tunnelling, and rock mechanics.

Nonferrous Metals Alert. Cambridge Information Group. • Monthly. $340.00 per year. Provides citations to the business and industrial literature of nonferrous metals. (Materials Business Information Series).

ALMANACS AND YEARBOOKS

CRB Commodity Yearbook. Commodity Research Bureau. CRB. • Annual. $99.95.

CD-ROM DATABASES

METADEX Materials Collection: Metals-Polymers-Ceramics. Cambridge Scientific Abstracts. • Quarterly. $6,950.00 per year. Provides CD-ROM citations to the worldwide literature of materials science and metallurgy. Corresponds to *Metals Abstracts, Alloys Index, Steels Alert, Nonferrous Alert, Polymers/Ceramics/Composites Alert,* and *Engineered Materials Abstracts.* (Formerly produced by ASM International.).

ONLINE DATABASES

Materials Business File. Cambridge Scientific Abstracts. • Provides online abstracts and citations to worldwide materials literature, covering the business and industrial aspects of metals, plastics, ceramics, and composites. Corresponds to *Steels Alert, Nonferrous Metals Alert,* and *Polymers/Ceramics/Composites Alert.* Time period is 1985 to date, with monthly updates. (Formerly produced by ASM International.) Inquire as to online cost and availability.

METADEX. Cambridge Scientific Abstracts. • Covers the worldwide literature of metals, metallurgy, and materials science, 1966 to date. Includes detailed alloys indexing from 1974. Biweekly updating. Inquire as to online cost and availability. (Formerly produced by ASM International.).

PERIODICALS AND NEWSLETTERS

Barron's: The Dow Jones Business and Financial Weekly. Dow Jones and Co., Inc. • Weekly. $145.00 per year.

New Steel: Mini and Integrated Mill Management and Technologies. Cahners Business Information. • Monthly. $89.00 per year. Covers the primary metals industry, both ferrous and nonferrous. Includes technical, marketing, and product development articles. Formerly *Iron Age.*

Oil Daily: Daily Newspaper of the Petroleum Industry. Energy Intelligence Group. • Daily. $1,145.00 per year. Newspaper for the petroleum industry.

33 Metalproducing: For Primary Producers of Steel, Aluminum, and Copper-Base Alloys. Penton Media, Inc. • Monthly. $65.00 per year. Covers metal production technology and methods and industry news. Includes a bimonthly *Nonferrous Supplement.*

PRICE SOURCES

Chemical and Engineering News: The Newsmagazine of the Chemical World. American Chemical Society. • Weekly. Institutions, $181.00 per year; others, price on application.

Metals Week. McGraw-Hill Commodity Services Group. • Weekly. $770.00 per year.

The New York Times. New York Times Co. • Daily. $374.40 per year. Supplements available: *New York Times Book Review, New York Times Magazine, Sophisticated Traveler* and *Fashions of the Times.*

STATISTICS SOURCES

Annual Survey of Manufactures. Available from U. S. Government Printing Office. • Annual. Prices vary. Issued by the U. S. Census Bureau as an interim update to the *Census of Manufactures.* Includes data on number of manufacturing establishments in various industries, employment, labor costs, value of shipments, capital expenditures, inventories, energy costs, and assets. (See also Census Bureau home page, http://www.census.gov/.).

Mineral Commodity Summaries. Available from U. S. Government Printing Office. • Annual. Published by the U. S. Geological Survey, Department of the Interior (http://www.usgs.gov). Contains detailed, five-year data for about 90 nonfuel minerals. Covers a wide range of statistics, including production, imports, exports, consumption, reserves, prices, tariff information, and industry employment. (Two pages are devoted to each mineral.).

Minerals Yearbook. Available from U.S. Government Printing Office. • Annual. Three volumes.

Non-Ferrous Metal Data Yearbook. American Bureau of Metal Statistics. • Annual. $395.00. Provides about 200 statistical tables covering many nonferrous metals. Includes production, consumption, inventories, exports, imports, and other data.

Standard & Poor's Industry Surveys. Standard & Poor's. • Semiannual. $1,800.00. Two looseleaf volumes. Includes monthly supplements. Provides detailed, individual surveys of 52 major industry groups. Each survey is revised on a semiannual basis. Also includes "Monthly Investment Review" (industry group investment analysis) and monthly "Trends & Projections" (economic analysis).

U. S. Industry and Trade Outlook: The McGraw-Hill Companies and the U.S. Department of Commerce/International Trade Administration. Datapso Research Corp. • Annual. $69.95. Produced by the International Trade Administration, U. S. Department of Commerce, in a "public-private" partnership with DRI/McGraw-Hill and Standard &

Poor's. Provides basic data, outlook for the current year, and "Long-Term Prospects" (five-year projections) for a wide variety of products and services. Includes high technology industries. Formerly *U. S. Industrial Outlook.*

United States Census of Mineral Industries. Bureau of the Census, U.S. Department of Commerce. Available from U.S. Government Printing Office. • Quinquennial.

WEFA Industrial Monitor. John Wiley and Sons, Inc. • Annual. $65.00. Prepared by industry analysts at WEFA, an economic forecasting and consulting firm (originally Wharton Econometric Forecasting Associates). Contains discussions of the outlook for major U. S. industries, with many 10-year forecasts (WEFA Web site is http://www.wefa.com).

TRADE/PROFESSIONAL ASSOCIATIONS

American Bureau of Metal Statistics. P.O. Box 805, Chatham, NJ 07928. Phone: (973)701-2299 Fax: (973)701-2152 E-mail: info@abms.com • URL: http://www.abms.com • Members are metal companies. Compiles and publishes detailed statistical data on a wide variety of nonferrous metals: aluminum, copper, gold, lead, nickel, platinum, silver, tin, titanium, uranium, zinc, and others.

Copper and Brass Fabricators Council. 1050 17th St., N.W., Suite 440, Washington, DC 20036. Phone: (202)833-8575 Fax: (202)331-8267 E-mail: copbrass@aol.com.

Copper and Brass Servicenter Association. 994 Old Eagle School Rd., Suite 1019, Wayne, PA 19087-1802. Phone: (610)971-4850 Fax: (610)971-4859 E-mail: fbrown@cbsa.copper-brass.org.

Copper Development Association. 260 Madison Ave., New York, NY 10016. Phone: 800-232-3282 or (212)251-7200 Fax: (212)251-7234 E-mail: staff@cda.copper.org • URL: http://www.copper.org.

International Copper Association. 260 Madison Ave., New York, NY 10016. Phone: (212)251-7240 Fax: (212)251-7245 E-mail: ica@copper.org • URL: http://www.copper.org.

Non-Ferrous Metals Producers Committee. c/o Kenneth Button, Economic Consulting Service, 2030 M. St., N.W., Suite 800, Washington, DC 20036. Phone: (202)466-7720 Fax: (202)466-2710 • Members are copper, lead, and zinc producers. Promotes the copper, lead, and zinc mining and metal industries.

COPYING MACHINE INDUSTRY

DIRECTORIES

Better Buys for Business: The Independent Consumer Guide to Office Equipment. What to Buy for Business, Inc. • 10 times a year. $134.00 per year. Each issue is on a particular office product, with detailed evaluation of specific models: 1. Low-Volume Copier Guide, 2. Mid-Volume Copier Guide, 3. High-Volume Copier Guide, 4. Plain Paper Fax and Low-Volume Multifunctional Guide, 5. Mid/High-Volume Multifunctional Guide, 6. Laser Printer Guide, 7. Color Printer and Color Copier Guide, 8. Scan-to-File Guide, 9. Business Phone Systems Guide, 10. Postage Meter Guide, with a Short Guide to Shredders.

Essential Business Buyer's Guide, from Cellular Services and Overnight Mail to Internet Access Providers, 401(k) Plans, and Desktop Computers: The Ultimate Guide to Buying Office Equipment, Products, and Services. Sourcebooks, Inc. • 1996. $18.95. Compiled by the staff of *Business Consumer Guide.* Lists recommended brands of office equipment.

HANDBOOKS AND MANUALS

Guide to Energy Efficient Office Equipment. Loretta A. Smith and others. American Council for an Energy Efficient Economy. • 1996. $12.00. Second edition. Provides information on selecting, purchasing, and using energy-saving computers, monitors, printers, copiers, and other office devices.

PERIODICALS AND NEWSLETTERS

Digital Information Network. Buyers Laboratory, Inc. • Monthly. $725.00 per year. Newsletter. Information on the copier industry, including test reports on individual machines. Formerly *Digital Information Network.*

TRADE/PROFESSIONAL ASSOCIATIONS

International Reprographic Association. 800 Enterprise Dr., Suite 202, Oak Brook, IL 60523. Phone: 800-833-4742 or (630)571-4685 Fax: (630)571-4731 • URL: http://www.irga.com.

COPYRIGHT

GENERAL WORKS

Copyright for the Nineties: 1997 Supplement and Appendix. Robert A. Gorman and Jane C. Ginsburg. LEXIS Publishing. • 1998. $52.00.

Copyright, Patent, Trademark and Related State Doctrines; Cases and Materials on the Law of Intellectual Property. Paul Goldstein. Foundation Press, Inc. • 1999. $43.50. Fourth edition.

ABSTRACTS AND INDEXES

Current Law Index: Multiple Access to Legal Periodicals. The Gale Group. • Monthly. $650.00 per year. Produced in cooperation with the American Association of Law Libraries. Indexes more than 900 law journals, legal newspapers, and specialty publications from the U.S., Canada, U.K., Ireland, Australia, and New Zealand.

Library Literature and Information Science: An Index to Library and Information Science Publications. H. W. Wilson Co. • Bimonthly. Annual cumulation. Service basis. Formerly *Library Literature.*

ALMANACS AND YEARBOOKS

Intellectual Property Law Review. W. Bryan Forney, editor. West Group. • 1992. $115.00. Patent, trademark, and copyright practices.

CD-ROM DATABASES

WILSONDISC: Library Literature and Information Science Index. H. W. Wilson Co. • Quarterly. Including unlimited access to the online version of *Library Literature.* Provides CD-ROM indexing of about 300 periodicals, covering a wide range of topics having to do with libraries, library management, and the information industry.

DIRECTORIES

Directory of Intellectual Property Attorneys. Aspen Law and Business. • Annual. Price on application.

ENCYCLOPEDIAS AND DICTIONARIES

McCarthy's Desk Encyclopedia of Intellectual Property. J. Thomas McCarthy. BNA Books. • 1995. $75.00.Second edition. Defines legal terms relating to patents, trademarks, copyrights, trade secrets, entertainment, and the computer industry.

HANDBOOKS AND MANUALS

Clearance and Copyright: Everything the Independent Filmmaker Needs to Know. Michael C. Donaldson. Silman-James Press. • 1996. $26.95. Covers film rights problems in pre-production, production, post-production, and final release. Includes sample contracts and forms.

The Copyright Book: A Practical Guide. William S. Strong. MIT Press. • 1999. $34.95. Fifth edition.

Copyright Handbook: How to Protect and Use Written Words. Stephen Fishman. Nolo.com. • 1997. $24.95. Fourth revised edition. Includes sample forms and copyright agreements.

Copyright Handbook: How to Protect and Use Written Works. Stephen Fishman. Nolo.com. • 1999. $34.95. Fifth edition.

Copyright Law '99 and Beyond Handbook. Glasser Legalworks. • 1999. $95.00. Examines current trends in copyright litigation. Based on a 1999 seminar held in cooperation with the U. S. Copyright Office.

Copyright Law of the United States of America. Available from U. S. Government Printing Office. • Annual. $4.75. Issued by U. S. Copyright Office, Library of Congress. Provides the text of copyright law contained in Title 17 of the U. S. Code.

Copyright Primer for Librarians and Educators. Janis H. Bruwelheide. American Library Association. • 1995. $25.00. Second edition.

Copyright Principles, Law, and Practice. Paul Goldstein. Aspen Books. • 1989. $375.00. Three volumes.

Copyrights, Patents, and Trademarks: Protect Your Rights Worldwide. Hoyt L. Barber. McGraw-Hill. • 1996. $32.95. Second edition.

Coyle's Information Highway Handbook: A Practical File on the New Information Order. Karen Coyle. American Library Association. • 1997. $30.00. Provides useful "essays on copyright, access, privacy, censorship, and the information marketplace.".

The Fair Use Privilege in Copyright Law. Bureau of National Affairs, Inc. • 1995. $115.00. Second edition. A comprehensive analysis of fair use.

How to Register Copyrights and Protect Them. Robert B. Chickering and Susan Hartman. Available from Gale Group. • 1981. $12.95.

Intellectual Property Infringement Damages: A Litigation Support Handbook. Russell L. Parr. John Wiley and Sons, Inc. • 1999. $145.00. Annual supplement, $60.00. Describes how to calculate damages for patent, trademark, and copyright infringement. (Intellectual Property Series).

Libraries and Copyright: A Guide to Copyright Law in the Nineties. Laura N. Gasaway and Sarah K. Wiant. Special Libraries Association. • 1994. $59.00. Provides practical explanations of copyright law. Includes an extensive bibliography.

Nimmer on Copyright. Melville B. Nimmer. Matthew Bender & Co., Inc. • $1,116.00. Six looseleaf volumes. Periodic supplementation. Analytical and practical guide on the law of literary, musical, and artistic proprerty.

Patent, Copyright, and Trademark: A Desk Reference to Intellectual Property Law. Stephen Elias. Nolo.com. • 1999. $24.95. Third revised edition. Contains practical explanations of the legalities of patents, copyrights, trademarks, and trade secrets. Includes examples of relevant legal forms. A 1985 version was called *Nolo's Intellectual Property Law Dictionary.* (Nolo Press Self-Help Law Series).

Patent, Trademark, and Copyright Laws, 2000. Jeffrey Samuels. BNA Books. • $95.00. Date not set. Contains text of "all pertinent intellectual property legislation to date.".

Protecting Trade Secrets, Patents, Copyrights, and Trademarks. Robert C. Dorr and Christopher H. Munch. Panel Publishers. • Looseleaf service. $165.00.

ONLINE DATABASES

LEXIS. LEXIS-NEXIS. • The various LEXIS databases provide full text and indexing for a wide variety of legal cases, statutes, orders, and opinions.

Library Literature Online. H. W. Wilson Co. • Contains online indexing of a wide variety of library and information science literature from 1984 to date, with updating quarterly. Inquire as to online cost and availability.

U. S. Copyrights. Available from DIALOG. • Provides access to registration details for all active copyright registrations on file at the U. S. Copyright Office since 1978. Contains information on initial registration, renewal, assignments, and ownership status. Weekly updates. Inquire as to online cost and availability.

PERIODICALS AND NEWSLETTERS

BNA's Patent, Trademark and Copyright Journal. Bureau of National Affairs, Inc. • Weekly. $1,366.00 per year.

Copyright Bulletin: Quarterly Review. Available from Bernan Associates. • Quarterly. $30.00 per year.

Copyright Society of the United States of America Journal. Copyright Society of the U.S.A. • Quarterly. Individuals, $125.00 per year; nonprofit organizations, $50.00 per year; corporations, $500.00 per year.

Information Outlook: The Monthly Magazine of the Special Libraries Association. Special Libraries Association. • Monthly. $65.00 per year. Topics include information technology, the Internet, copyright, research techniques, library management, and professional development. Replaces *Special Libraries* and *SpeciaList*.

Intellectual Property Today. Omega Communications. • Monthly. $48.00 per year. Covers legal developments in copyright, patents, trademarks, and licensing. Emphasizes the effect of new technology on intellectual property. Formerly *Law Works*.

RESEARCH CENTERS AND INSTITUTES

Lexis.com Research System. Lexis-Nexis Group. Phone: 800-227-9597 or (937)865-6800 Fax: (937)865-6909 E-mail: webmaster@prod.lexis-nexis.com • URL: http://www.lexis.com • Fee-based Web site offers extensive searching of a wide variety of legal sources. Additional features include Daily Opinion Service, lexis.com Bookstore, Career Center, CLE Center, Law Schools, and Practice Pages ("Pages specific to areas of specialty").

PTC Research Foundation. Franklin Pierce Law Center. Two White St., Concord, NH 03301. Phone: (603)228-1541 Fax: (603)224-3342 E-mail: cblank@fplc.edu.

TRADE/PROFESSIONAL ASSOCIATIONS

Copyright Clearance Center. 222 Rosewood Dr., Danvers, MA 01923. Phone: (978)750-8400 Fax: (508)750-4744.

Copyright Society of the U.S.A. 1133 Ave. of the Americas, New York, NY 10036. Phone: (212)354-6401 E-mail: barpan@interport.com • URL: http://www.csusa.org.

International Copyright Information Center. c/o Association of American Publishers, 50 F St., N.W., 4th Fl., Washington, DC 20001. Phone: (202)347-3375 Fax: (202)347-3690 • URL: http://www.publishers.org.

OTHER SOURCES

Catalog of Copyright Entries. U.S. Library of Congress, Copyright Office. Available from U.S. Government Printing Office. • Frequency and prices vary.

Copyright Law in Business and Practice. John W. Hazard. West Group. • 1998. $160.00.

Copyright Law Reports. CCH, Inc. • $703.00 per year. Two looseleaf volumes. Monthly updates.

Copyright Laws and Treaties of the World. Bureau of National Affairs, Inc. • Looseleaf. $695.00. Three volumes. Periodic supplementation.

Forms and Agreements on Intellectual Property and International Licensing. Leslie W. Melville. West Group. • $375.00. Three looseleaf volumes. Periodic supplementation.

Intellectual Property and Antitrust Law. William C. Holmes. West Group. • Looseleaf. $145.00. Periodic supplementation. Includes patent, trademark, and copyright practices.

Lindey on Entertainment, Publishing and the Arts: Agreements and the Law. Alexander Lindey, editor. West Group. • $673.00 per year. Looseleaf service. Periodic supplementation. Provides basic forms, applicable law, and guidance. (Entertainment and Communication Law Series).

COPYWRITING

See: ADVERTISING COPY

CORDAGE INDUSTRY

See: ROPE AND TWINE INDUSTRY

CORN INDUSTRY

See also: FEED AND FEEDSTUFFS INDUSTRY

ABSTRACTS AND INDEXES

Field Crop Abstracts: Monthly Abstract Journal on World Annual Cereal, Legume, Root, Oilseed and Fibre Crops. Available from CABI Publishing North America. • Monthly. $1,465.00 per year. Published in England by CABI Publishing, formerly Commonwealth Agricultural Bureaux. Provides worldwide coverage of the literature.

Maize Abstracts. Available from CABI Publishing North America. • Bimonthly. $795.00 per year. Published in England by CABI Publishing. Provides worldwide coverage of the literature.

ALMANACS AND YEARBOOKS

Corn Annual. Corn Refiners Association, Inc. • Annual. Single copies free.

CRB Commodity Yearbook. Commodity Research Bureau. CRB. • Annual. $99.95.

CD-ROM DATABASES

Food Science and Technology Abstracts [CD-ROM]. Available from SilverPlatter Information, Inc. • Quarterly. $3,700 per year. Produced by International Food Information Service (home page is http://www.ifis.org). Provides worldwide coverage on CD-ROM of the literature of food technology and production. Various types of publications are indexed, with abstracts, including about 1,800 periodicals. Time period is 1969 to date.

DIRECTORIES

American Vegetable Grower Source Book. Meister Publishing Co. • Annual. $2.75. Formerly *American Vegetable Grower Buyers' Guide*.

INTERNET DATABASES

Fedstats. Federal Interagency Council on Statistical Policy. Phone: (202)395-7254 • URL: http://www.fedstats.gov • Web site features an efficient search facility for full-text statistics produced by more than 70 federal agencies, including the Census Bureau, the Bureau of Economic Analysis, and the Bureau of Labor Statistics. Boolean searches can be made within one agency or for all agencies combined. Links are offered to international statistical bureaus, including the UN, IMF, OECD, UNESCO, Eurostat, and 20 individual countries. Fees: Free.

USDA. United States Department of Agriculture. Phone: (202)720-2791 E-mail: agsec@usda.gov • URL: http://www.usda.gov • The USDA home page has six sections: News and Information; What's New; About USDA; Agencies; Opportunities; Search and Help. Keyword searching is offered from the USDA home page and from various individual agency home pages. Agencies are the Economic Research Service, Agricultural Marketing Service, National Agricultural Statistics Service, National Agricultural Library, and about 12 others. Updating varies. Fees: Free.

ONLINE DATABASES

Biological and Agricultural Index Online. H. W. Wilson Co. • Indexes a wide variety of agricultural and biological periodicals, 1983 to date. Monthly updates. Inquire as to online cost and availability.

CAB Abstracts. CAB International North America. • Contains 46 specialized abstract collections covering over 10,000 journals and monographs in the areas of agriculture, horticulture, forest products, farm products, nutrition, dairy science, poultry, grains, animal health, entomology, etc. Time period is 1972 to date, with monthly updates. Inquire as to online cost and availability. *CAB Abstracts on CD-ROM* also available, with annual updating.

DRI U.S. Central Database. Data Products Division. • Provides more than 23,000 business, financial, demographic, economic, foreign trade, and industry-related time series for the U.S. Includes national income, population, retail-wholesale trade, price indexes, labor data, housing, industrial production, banking, interest rates, money supply, etc. Time period is generally 1947 to date (some data back to 1929). Updating varies. Inquire as to online cost and availability.

Food Science and Technology Abstracts [online]. IFIS North American Desk. • Produced by International Food Information Service. Provides about 500,000 online citations, with abstracts, to the international literature of food science, technology, commodities, engineering, and processing. Approximately 2,000 periodicals are covered. Time period is 1969 to date, with monthly updates. Inquire as to online cost and availability.

PERIODICALS AND NEWSLETTERS

Barron's: The Dow Jones Business and Financial Weekly. Dow Jones and Co., Inc. • Weekly. $145.00 per year.

PRICE SOURCES

Agricultural Letter. Federal Reserve Bank of Chicago. • Quarterly. Free.

The New York Times. New York Times Co. • Daily. $374.40 per year. Supplements available: *New York Times Book Review*, *New York Times Magazine*, *Sophisticated Traveler* and *Fashions of the Times*.

RESEARCH CENTERS AND INSTITUTES

Agricultural Research Division. University of Nebraska - Lincoln. 207 Agricultural Hall, Lincoln, NE 68583-0704. Phone: (402)472-2045 Fax: (402)472-9071 E-mail: dnelson@.unl.edu • URL: http://ianrwww.unl.edu/ianr/ard/index.htm.

California Agricultural Experiment Station. University of California at Berkeley. 1111 Franklin St., 6th Fl., Oakland, CA 94607-5200. Phone: (510)987-0060 Fax: (510)451-2317 E-mail: wr.gomes@ucop.edu • URL: http://www.ucop.edu/anrhome/danr.html.

New Mexico Agricultural Experiment Station. New Mexico State University. P.O. Box 30003, Dept. 3BF, Las Cruces, NM 88003. Phone: (505)646-3125 Fax: (505)646-5975 E-mail: garyc@nmsu.edu • URL: http://www.cahe.nmsu.edu/cahe/aes/.

New York State Agricultural Experiment Station. Cornell University. 630 W. North St., Geneva, NY 14456. Phone: (315)787-2211 Fax: (315)787-2276 E-mail: jeh3@cornell.edu • URL: http://www.nyseas.cornell.edu/.

STATISTICS SOURCES

Agricultural Statistics. Available from U. S. Government Printing Office. • Annual. Produced by the National Agricultural Statistics Service, U. S. Department of Agriculture. Provides a wide variety of statistical data relating to agricultural production, supplies, consumption, prices/price-supports, foreign trade, costs, and returns, as well as farm labor, loans, income, and population. In many cases, historical data is shown annually for 10 years. In addition to farm data, includes detailed fishery statistics.

Business Statistics of the United States. Courtenay M. Slater, editor. Bernan Associates. • 1999. $74.00. Fifth edition. Based on *Business Statistics*, formerly issue by the Bureau of Economic Analysis, U. S. Department of Commerce. Provides basic data for a wide variety of U. S. industries, services, and economic indicators. Most statistics are shown annually for 29 years and monthly for the most recent four years.

Statistical Annual: Grains, Options on Agricultural Futures. Chicago Board of Trade. • Annual. Includes historical data on Wheat Futures, Options on Wheat Futures, Corn Futures, Options on Corn Futures, Oats Futures, Soybean Futures, Options on Soybean Futures, Soybean Oil Futures, Soybean Meal Futures.

Survey of Current Business. Available from U. S. Government Printing Office. • Monthly. $49.00 per year. Issued by Bureau of Economic Analysis, U. S. Department of Commerce. Presents a wide variety of business and economic data.

United States Census of Agriculture. U.S. Bureau of the Census. • Quinquennial. Results presented in reports, tape, CD-ROM, and Diskette files.

WEFA Industrial Monitor. John Wiley and Sons, Inc. • Annual. $65.00. Prepared by industry analysts at WEFA, an economic forecasting and consulting firm (originally Wharton Econometric Forecasting Associates). Contains discussions of the outlook for major U. S. industries, with many 10-year forecasts (WEFA Web site is http://www.wefa.com).

TRADE/PROFESSIONAL ASSOCIATIONS

American Corn Millers' Federation. 600 Maryland Ave., S.W., Suite 305 W, Washington, DC 20024. Phone: (202)554-1614 Fax: (202)554-1616 E-mail: cornmiller@aol.com.

Corn Refiners Association. 1701 Pennsylvania Ave., N.W., Suite 950, Washington, DC 20006. Phone: (202)331-1634 Fax: (202)331-2054 E-mail: details@corn.org • URL: http://www.corn.org.

National Corn Growers Association. 1000 Executive Parkway, Suite 105, St. Louis, MO 63141-6397. Phone: (314)275-9915 Fax: (314)275-7061 E-mail: corninfo@ncga.com • URL: http://www.ncga.com/.

OTHER SOURCES

Corn: Origin, History, Technology, and Production. C. Wayne Smith and others, editors. John Wiley and Sons, Inc. • 2002. $250.00. (Wiley Series in Crop Science.).

Major Food and Drink Companies of the World. Available from The Gale Group. • 2001. $855.00. Fourth edition. Two volumes. Published by Graham & Whiteside. Contains profiles and trade names for more than 9,000 important food and beverage companies in various countries. In addition to foods, includes both alcoholic and nonalcoholic drink products.

Thomas Food and Beverage Market Place. Grey House Publishing. • Annual. $295.00. Three volumes. Contains more than 40,000 entries covering food companies, beverages, food equipment, warehouse companies, food brokers, wholesalers, importers, and exporters. Formerly *Thomas Food Industry Register.*

CORPORATE ACQUISITIONS AND MERGERS

See: MERGERS AND ACQUISITIONS

CORPORATE CULTURE

GENERAL WORKS

The Character of a Corporation: How Your Company's Culture Can Make or Break Your Business. Rob Goffee and Gareth Jones. HarperCollins Publishers, Inc. • 1998. $25.00. Provides advice on establishing a positive business environment.

Corporate Culture and Organizational Effectiveness. Daniel R. Denison. Aviat, Inc. • 1990. Includes five case studies. Price on application.

Corporate Cultures: The Rites and Rituals of Corporate Life. Terrance E. Deal and Allan Kennedy. Perseus Publishing. • 1982. $15.00.

The Web of Inclusion: Building an Organization for Everyone. Sally Helgesen. Doubleday. • 1995. $25.95.

ABSTRACTS AND INDEXES

Business Periodicals Index. H. W. Wilson Co. • Monthly, except August, with quarterly and annual cumulations. Service basis for print edition; CD-ROM edition, $1,495.00 per year.

DIRECTORIES

Business Organizations, Agencies, and Publications Directory. The Gale Group. • 1999. $425.00. 12th edition. Over 40,000 entries describing 39 types of business information sources. Classified by type of organization, publication, or serviceIncludes state, national, and international agencies and organizations. Master index to names and keywords. Also includes e-mail addresses and web site URL's.

ENCYCLOPEDIAS AND DICTIONARIES

International Encyclopedia of Business and Management. Malcolm Warner, editor. Routledge, Inc. • 1996. $1,319.95. Six volumes. Contains more than 500 articles on global management issues. Includes extensive bibliographies, cross references, and an index of key words and phrases.

HANDBOOKS AND MANUALS

Gaining Control of the Corporate Culture. Ralph H. Kilmann and others. Jossey-Bass, Inc., Publishers. • 1985. $43.95. (Management Series).

ONLINE DATABASES

Wilson Business Abstracts Online. H. W. Wilson Co. • Indexes and abstracts 600 major business periodicals, plus the *Wall Street Journal* and the business section of the *New York Times*. Indexing is from 1982, abstracting from 1990, with the two newspapers included from 1993. Updated weekly. Inquire as to online cost and availability. (*Business Periodicals Index* without abstracts is also available online.).

PERIODICALS AND NEWSLETTERS

Chief Executive Magazine. Chief Executive Group, Inc. • 10 times a year. $95.00 per year.

Corporate Public Issues and Their Management: The Executive Systems Approach to Public Policy Formation. Issue Action Publications, Inc. • Semimonthly. $195.00 per year. Newsletter.

Fortune Magazine. Time Inc., Business Information Group. • Biweekly. $59.95 per year. Edited for top executives and upper-level managers.

Harvard Business Review. Harvard University, Graduate School of Business Administration. Harvard Businss School Publishing. • Bimonthly. $95.00 per year.

Journal of Business Strategy. Faulkner and Gray, Inc. • Bimonthly. $84.00 per year. Devoted to the theory and practice of strategy, planning, implementation and competitive analysis. Covers every aspect of business from advertising to systems design. Incorporates*Journal of European Business.*

RESEARCH CENTERS AND INSTITUTES

Business, Government, and Society Research Institute. University of Pittsburgh. School of Business, Mervis Hall, Pittsburgh, PA 15260. Phone: (412)648-1555 Fax: (412)648-1693 E-mail: mitnick@pitt.edu.

OTHER SOURCES

Creating a Culture of Competence. Michael Zwell. John Wiley and Sons, Inc. • 2000. $35.95. Emphasizes employee participation to arrive at a desired change in organizational culture.

CORPORATE DIRECTORS AND OFFICERS

See also: EXECUTIVES

GENERAL WORKS

The Business of Banking for Bank Directors. George K. Darling and James F. Chaston. Robert Morris Associates. • 1995. $33.00. Presents basic banking concepts and issues for new directors of financial institutions. Emphasis is on the specific duties of directors.

BIOGRAPHICAL SOURCES

Newsmakers. The Gale Group. • Annual. $145.00. Three softbound issues and one hardbound annual. Biographical information on individuals currently in the news. Includes photographs. Formerly *Contemporary Newsmakers.*

Who Knows Who: Networking Through Corporate Boards. Who Know Who Publishing. • 1994. $150.00. Fifth edition. Shows the connections between the board members of major U. S. corporations and major foundations and nonprofit organizations.

Who's Who in Finance and Industry. Marquis Who's Who. • Biennial. $295.00. Provides over 22,400 concise biographies of business leaders in all fields.

DIRECTORIES

Reference Book of Corporate Managements. Dun and Bradstreet Information Services. • Annual. Libraries, $650.00 per year; others, $795.00 per year. Lease basis. Management executives at over 12,000 leading United States companies.

Standard and Poor's Register of Corporations, Directors and Executives. Standard and Poor's. • Annual. $675.00. Periodic supplementation. Over 55,000 public and privately held corporations in the U.S. Three volumes. Three supplements.

ENCYCLOPEDIAS AND DICTIONARIES

Encyclopedia of Corporate Meetings, Minutes and Resolutions. William Sardell, editor. Prentice Hall. • 1985. $125.00. Third edition. Two volumes.

HANDBOOKS AND MANUALS

Corporate Controller. Paul J. Wendell. Warren, Gorham and Lamont/RIA Group. • Bimonthly.

$130.00. Covers every aspect of a controller's responsibilities.

Directors' and Officers' Liability. Practising Law Institute. • Looseleaf. $125.00. Annual revisions. Covers all aspects of liability issues for corporate directors and executives. Indemnification, insurance, and dispute resolution are included as topics.

Directors' and Officers' Liability Insurance. Practising Law Institute. • 1992. $70.00. Legal handbook. (Commercial Law and Practice Course Handbook Series).

Law of Corporate Officers and Directors: Indemnification and Insurance. Joseph W. Bishop, Jr. West Group. • 1990. $130.00. Practical guidance for developing corporate policy, drafting agreements and litigation.

Law of Corporate Officers and Directors: Rights, Duties, and Liabilities. Edward Brodsky and M. Patricia Adamski. West Group. • 1990. $130.00. Defines accountability for making policy.

Organization Charts: Structures of More Than 200 Businesses and Non-Profit Organizations. The Gale Group. • 1999. $165.00. Third edition. Includes an introductory discussion of the history and use of such charts.

Principles of Corporate Governance: Analysis and Recommendations. Mike Greenwald, editor. American Law Institute-American Bar Association. • 1994. $135.00. Two volumes. An examination of the duties and responsibilities of directors and officers of business corporations. Seven parts cover (1) definitions, (2) objectives and conduct, (3) corporate structure and oversight committees, (4) business judgment, (5) fair dealing, (6) tender offers, and (7) legal remedies.

Responsibilities of Corporate Officers and Directors Under Federal Securities Law. CCH, Inc. • Annual. $55.00. Includes discussions of indemnification, "D & O" insurance, corporate governance, and insider liability.

Responsibilities of Corporate Officers and Directors Under Federal Securities Laws. CCH, Inc. • 2000. $65.00.

ONLINE DATABASES

Standard & Poor's Register: Biographical. Standard & Poor's Corp. • Contains brief biographies of approximately 70,000 business executives and directors. Corresponds to the biographical volume of *Standard & Poor's Register of Corporations, Directors, and Executives.* Updated twice a year. Inquire as to online cost and availability.

PERIODICALS AND NEWSLETTERS

Corporate Controller. Faulkner and Gray, Inc. • Bimonthly. $115.00 per year.

Director's Monthly. National Association of Corporate Directors. • Monthly. $350.00 per year. Newsletter.

Forbes. Forbes, Inc. • Biweekly. $59.95 per year. Includes supplements: *Forbes ASAP* and *Forbes FYI.*

Fortune Magazine. Time Inc., Business Information Group. • Biweekly. $59.95 per year. Edited for top executives and upper-level managers.

RESEARCH CENTERS AND INSTITUTES

Financial Executives Research Foundation. P.O. Box 1938, Morristown, NJ 07962-1938. Phone: (973)898-4608 Fax: (973)898-6636 E-mail: rcolson@fei.org • URL: http://www.ferf.org.

TRADE/PROFESSIONAL ASSOCIATIONS

American Management Association. 1601 Broadway, New York, NY 10019-7420. Phone: 800-262-9699 or (212)586-8100 Fax: (212)903-8168 • URL: http://www.amanet.org.

American Society of Corporate Secretaries. 521 Fifth Ave., New York, NY 10175-0003. Phone: (212)681-2000 Fax: (212)681-2005 • URL: http://www.ascs.org.

International Management Council of the YMCA. 430 S. 20th St., Suite 3, Omaha, NE 68102-2506. Phone: 800-688-9622 or (402)345-1904 Fax: (402)345-4480 E-mail: imcoffice@msn.com • URL: http://www.imc-ymca.org.

National Association of Corporate Directors. 1701 L St., N.W., Suite 560, Washington, DC 20036. Phone: (202)775-0509 Fax: (202)775-4857 E-mail: info@nacdoline.org • URL: http://www.nacdonline.org.

Professional Services Management Association. 4101 Lake Boone Trail, Ste. 201, Raleigh, NC 27607. Phone: (919)571-2562 Fax: (919)787-4916.

OTHER SOURCES

Corporate Directors' Compensation. Conference Board, Inc. • Irregular.

Corporate Officers and Directors Liability Litigation Reporter: The Twice Monthly National Journal of Record of Litigation Based on Fiduciary Responsibility. Andrews Publications. • Semimonthly. $890.00 per year. Provides reports on lawsuits in the area of corporate officers' fiduciary responsibility.

Corporate Secretary's Guide. CCH, Inc. • Monthly. $590.00 per year. Includes newsletter and semimonthly updates. Published in consultation with the American Society of Corporate Secretaries. Covers the duties of corporate secretaries, especially as related to taxation and securities.

Corporation Forms. Prentice Hall. • Looseleaf. Periodic supplementation. Price on application.

Standard & Poor's Corporations. Available from Dialog OnDisc. • Monthly. Price on application. Produced by Standard & Poor's. Contains three CD-ROM files: Executives, Private Companies, and Public Companies, providing detailed information on more than 70,000 business executives, 55,000 private companies, and 12,000 publicly-traded corporations.

CORPORATE FINANCE

See also: FINANCE; FINANCIAL MANAGEMENT

GENERAL WORKS

Accounting and Finance for Non-Specialists. Peter Atrill and Eddie McLaney. Prentice Hall. • 2000. Third edition. Price on application. Includes the measurement and reporting of financial performance and cash flow.

Case Studies in Finance: Managing for Corporate Value Creation. Robert Bruner. McGraw-Hill Professional. • 1998. Third edition. Price on application.

Corporate Finance. Stephen A. Ross and others. McGraw-Hill Professional. • 1998. Fifth edition. Price on application. *Irwin-McGraw Hill Finance, Insurance and Real Estate Series.*

Corporate Finance and the Securities Laws. Charles J. Johnson and Joseph McLaughlin. Panel Publishers. • 1997. $170.00. Second edition.

Corporate Financial Reporting: Text and Cases. E. Richard Brownlee and others. McGraw-Hill Professional. • 1997. Third edition. Price on application.

Mergers, Acquisitions, and Corporate Restructurings. Patrick A. Gaughan. John Wiley and Sons, Inc. • 1999. $75.00. Second edition. Covers mergers, acquisitions, divestitures, internal reorganizations, joint ventures, leveraged buyouts, bankruptcy workouts, and recapitalizations.

Theory of Corporate Finance. Michael J. Brennan, editor. Edward Elgar Publishing, Inc. • 1996. $440.00. Two volumes. Consists of reprints of 46 articles dating from 1976 to 1994. (International Library of Critical Writings in Financial Economics Series: volume one).

The Witch Doctor of Wall Street: A Noted Financial Expert Guides You Through Today's Voodoo Economics. Robert H. Parks. Prometheus Books. • 1996. $25.95. The author, a professor of finance at Pace University, discusses "Practice and Malpractice" in relation to the following: business forecasting, economic theory, interest rates, monetary policy, the stock market, and corporate finance. Includes "A Short Primer on Derivatives," as an appendix.

ABSTRACTS AND INDEXES

Banking Information Index. U M I Banking Information Index. • Monthly. Price on application. Covers a wide variety of banking, business, and financial subjects in periodicals. Formerly *Banking Literature Index.*

Business Periodicals Index. H. W. Wilson Co. • Monthly, except August, with quarterly and annual cumulations. Service basis for print edition; CD-ROM edition, $1,495.00 per year.

BIBLIOGRAPHIES

Business Information Sources. Lorna M. Daniells. California Princeton Fulfillment Services. • 1993. $42.50. Third revised edition. Basic business sources, with discussion and full annotations.

CD-ROM DATABASES

ABI/INFORM Global. Bell & Howell Information and Learning. • Monthly. $6,500.00 per year. Provides CD-ROM indexing and abstracting of worldwide business literature appearing in over 1,200 periodicals for the most recent five years. Archival discs are available from 1971. Formerly *ABI/INFORM OnDisc.*

Business Source Plus. EBSCO Information Services. • Monthly. $1,495.00 per year. Provides CD-ROM citations and abstracts to articles in about 650 business periodicals and newspapers, including *The Wall Street Journal.* Full text is provided from 200 selected periodicals. Covers accounting, communications, economics, finance, management, marketing, and other business subjects.

Buyout Financing Sources/M & A Intermediaries. Securities Data Publishing. • Annual. $895.00. Provides the CD-ROM combination of *Directory of Buyout Financing Sources* and *Directory of M & A Intermediaries.* Contains information on more than 1,000 financing sources (banks, insurance companies, venture capital firms, etc.) and 850 intermediaries (corporate acquirers, valuation firms, lawyers, accountants, etc.). Also includes back issues of *Buyouts Newsletter* and *Mergers & Acquisitions Report.* Fully searchable. (Securities Data Publishing is a unit of Thomson Financial.).

Compact D/SEC. Disclosure, Inc. • Monthly. Contains three CD-ROM files. (1) Disclosure: Provides Securities and Exchange Commission filings for over 12,500 publicly held corporations. (2) Disclosure/Spectrum Ownership Profiles: Provides detailed corporate descriptions and complete ownership information for over 6,000 public companies. (3) Zacks Earnings Estimates: Provides earnings per share forecasts for about 4,000 U. S. corporations.

Corporate Affiliations Plus. National Register Publishing, Reed Reference Publishing. • Quarterly. $1,995.00 per year. Provides CD-ROM discs corresponding to *Directory of Corporate Affiliations* and *Corporate Finance Bluebook.* Contains corporate financial services information and worldwide data on subsidiaries and affiliates.

WILSONDISC: Business Periodicals Index. H. W. Wilson Co. • Monthly. $1,495.00 per year. Provides CD-ROM indexing of business periodicals from 1982 to date. Price includes online service.

DIRECTORIES

America's Corporate Finance Directory. National Register Publishing. • Annual. $699.00. A directory of financial executives employed at over 5,000 U. S. corporations. Includes a listing of the outside financial services (banks, pension managers, insurance firms, auditors) used by each corporation.

Corporate Bond Desk Reference: U. S. Buyside and Sellside Profiles. Capital Access International. • Annual. $395.00. Provides "detailed buyside and sellside profiles and contacts" for the the corporate bond market. (Desk Reference Series, volume one.).

Corporate Finance Sourcebook: The Guide to Major Capital Investment Source and Related Financial Services. R. R. Bowker. • Annual. $625.00. Lists more than 3,550 sources of corporate capital: investment bankers, securities firms, pension management companies, trust companies, insurance companies, and private lenders. Includes the names of over 13,000 key personnel.

Directory of Buyout Financing Sources. Securities Data Publishing. • Annual. $395.00. Describes more than 1,000 U. S. and foreign sources of financing for buyout deals. Indexed by personnel, company, industry, and location. (Securities Data Publishing is a unit of Thomson Financial.).

Zacks Analyst Directory: Listed by Broker. Zacks Investment Research. • Quarterly. $395.00 per year. Lists stockbroker investment analysts and gives the names of major U. S. corporations covered by those analysts.

Zacks Analyst Directory: Listed by Company. Zacks Investment Research. • Quarterly. $395.00 per year. Lists major U. S. corporations and gives the names of stockbroker investment analysts covering those companies.

Zacks EPS Calendar. Zacks Investment Research. • Biweekly. $1,250.00 per year. (Also available monthly at $895.00 per year.) Lists anticipated reporting dates of earnings per share for major U. S. corporations.

ENCYCLOPEDIAS AND DICTIONARIES

Blackwell Encyclopedic Dictionary of Finance. Dean Paxson and Douglas Wood, editors. Blackwell Publishers. • 1997. $110.00. The editors are associated with the University of Manchester. Contains definitions of key terms combined with longer articles written by various U. S. and foreign business educators. Includes bibliographies and index. (Blackwell Encyclopedia of Management Series).

Dictionary of Finance and Investment Terms. John Downes and Jordan E. Goodman. Barron's Educational Series, Inc. • 1998. $12.95. Fifth revised edition. Provides clear explanations of more than 5,000 business, banking, financial, investment, and tax terms. Includes a separate list of financial abbreviations and acronyms.

The New Palgrave Dictionary of Money and Finance. Peter Newman and others, editors. Groves Dictionaries. • 1998. $550.00. Three volumes. Consists of signed essays on over 1,000 financial topics, each with a bibliography. Covers a wide variety of financial, monetary, and investment areas. A detailed subject index is provided.

FINANCIAL RATIOS

Major Financial Institutions of the World. Available from The Gale Group. • 2001. $855.00. Fourth edition. Two volumes. Published by Graham & Whiteside. Contains detailed information on more than 7,500 important financial institutions in various countries. Includes banks, investment companies, and insurance companies.

HANDBOOKS AND MANUALS

Analysis and Use of Financial Statements. Gerald I. White and others. John Wiley and Sons, Inc. • 1997. $112.95. Second edition. Includes analysis of financial ratios, cash flow, inventories, assets, debt, etc. Also covered are employee benefits, corporate investments, multinational operations, financial derivatives, and hedging activities.

Corporate Financial Analysis: Decisions in a Global Environment. Diana R. Harrington and Brent D. Wilson. McGraw-Hill Professional. • 1993. $50.00. Fourth edition.

Corporate Financial Distress and Bankruptcy: A Complete Guide to Predicting and Avoiding Distress and Profiting from Bankruptcy. Edward I. Altman. John Wiley and Sons, Inc. • 1993. $99.95. Second edition. Provides practical advice on analyzing the financial position of a corporation, with case studies. Includes a discussion of the junk bond market.

Corporate Liquidity: Management and Measurement. Kenneth L. Parkinson and Jarl G. Kallberg. McGraw-Hill Higher Education. • 1992. $67.95. Topics include cash management and risk.

Financing the Corporation. Richard A. Booth. West Group. • $110.00. Looseleaf service. Periodic supplementation. Covers a wide variety of corporate finance legal topics, from initial capital structure to public sale of securities.

Fundamentals of Corporate Finance. Stephen Ross and Randy Westerfield. McGraw-Hill. • 1998. $69.25. Fifth edition.

SEC Handbook: Rules and Forms for Financial Statements and Related Disclosures. CCH, Inc. • Annual. $54.00. Contains full text of rules and requirements set by the Securities and Exchange Commisssion for preparation of corporate financial statements.

Swap Literacy. Elizabeth Ungar. Bloomberg Press. • 1996. $40.00. Written for corporate finance officers. Provides basic information on arbitrage, hedging, and speculation, involving interest rate, currency, and other types of financial swaps. (Bloomberg Professional Library.).

INTERNET DATABASES

DBC Online: America's Leading Provider of Real-Time Market Data to the Individual Investor. Data Broadcasting Corp. Phone: (415)571-1800 E-mail: dbcinfo@dbc.com • URL: http://www.dbc.com • Web site provides a wide variety of real-time securities market prices, data, and charts. Covers bonds ("BondVu"), stocks, commodities, options, mutual funds, major indexes, industry indexes, international markets, etc. Also includes news, SEC documents ("Smart-Edgar"), and various other features. Fees: Both free and fee-based, depending on level of information.

FIS Online: The Preferred Source for Global Business and Financial Information. Mergent. Phone: 800-342-5647 or (212)413-7601 Fax: (212)413-7777 E-mail: fis@fisonline.com • URL: http://www.fisonline.com • Fee-based Web site provides detailed information on more than 10,000 publicly-owned corporations listed on the New York Stock Exchange, American Stock Exchange, NASDAQ, and U. S. regional exchanges. Searching is offered on eight financial variables and six text fields. Weekly updating. Fees: Rates on application. (Mergent is publisher of Moody's Manuals.).

Thomson Investors Network. Thomson Financial. Phone: (212)807-3800 • URL: http://thomsoninvest.net • Web site provides detailed data on insider trading, institutional portfolios, and "First Call" earnings estimates. Includes a stock screening (filtering) application, a search facility, and price quotes on stocks, bonds, and mutual funds. Continuous updating. Fees: $34.95 per year for general service. First Call earnings service is $19.95 per month or $199.00 per year.

U. S. Securities and Exchange Commission. Phone: 800-732-0330 or (202)942-7040 Fax: (202)942-9634 E-mail: webmaster@sec.gov • URL: http://www.sec.gov • SEC Web site offers free access through EDGAR to text of official corporate filings, such as annual reports (10-K), quarterly reports (10-Q), and proxies. (EDGAR is "Electronic Data Gathering, Analysis, and Retrieval System.") An example is given of how to obtain executive compensation data from proxies. Text of the daily *SEC News Digest* is offered, as are links to other government sites, non-government market regulators, and U. S. stock exchanges. Search facilities are extensive. Fees: Free.

Web Finance: Covering the Electronic Evolution of Finance. Securities Data Publishing. Phone: (212)765-5311 or 800-455-5844 Fax: (212)321-2336 E-mail: webfinance@tfn.com • URL: http://www.webfinance.net • Bi-weekly print and daily web-site publication of financial services on the Web, including financial links, archives, brokerage stocks, deal financing, and other financial and investment news and information.

ONLINE DATABASES

ABI/INFORM. Bell & Howell Information and Learning. • Provides online indexing to business-related material occurring in over 1,000 periodicals from 1971 to the present. Inquire as to online cost and availability.

Banking Information Source. Bell & Howell Information and Learning. • Provides indexing and abstracting of periodical and other literature from 1982 to date, with weekly updates. Covers the financial services industry: banks, savings institutions, investment houses, credit unions, insurance companies, and real estate organizations. Emphasis is on marketing and management. Inquire as to online cost and availability. (Formerly *FINIS: Financial Industry Information Service.*).

Fitch IBCA Ratings Delivery Service. Fitch IBCA, Inc. • Provides online delivery of Fitch financial ratings in three sectors: "Corporate Finance" (corporate bonds, insurance companies), "Structured Finance" (asset-backed securities), and "U.S. Public Finance" (municipal bonds). Daily updates. Inquire as to online cost and availability.

LEXIS Financial Information Service. LEXIS-NEXIS. • Includes many business and financial files, including the full text of *SEC News Digest*, *Zacks Earnings Forecaster*, SEC filings, and brokerage house research reports. Various time spans and updating frequencies. Inquire as to online cost and availability.

Management Contents. The Gale Group. • Covers a wide range of management, financial, marketing, personnel, and administrative topics. About 150 leading business journals are indexed and abstracted from 1974 to date, with monthly updating. Inquire as to online cost and availability.

Trade & Industry Index. The Gale Group. • Provides indexing of business periodicals, January 1981 to date. Daily updates. (Full text articles from some periodicals are available online, 1983 to date, in the companion database, *Trade & Industry ASAP*.) Inquire as to online cost and availability.

Wilson Business Abstracts Online. H. W. Wilson Co. • Indexes and abstracts 600 major business periodicals, plus the *Wall Street Journal* and the business section of the *New York Times*. Indexing is from 1982, abstracting from 1990, with the two newspapers included from 1993. Updated weekly. Inquire as to online cost and availability. (*Business Periodicals Index* without abstracts is also available online.).

Zacks Earnings Estimates. Zacks Investment Research. • Provides online earnings projections for about 6,000 U. S. corporations, based on investment analysts' reports. Data is mainly from 200 major brokerage firms. Time span varies according to online provider, with daily or weekly updates. Inquire as to online cost and availability.

PERIODICALS AND NEWSLETTERS

Bank Loan Report. Securities Data Publishing. • Weekly. $3,600.00 per year. Newsletter. Covers the syndicated loan marketplace for corporate finance professionals. (Securities Data Publishing is a unit of Thomson Financial.).

Business Finance. Duke Communications International. • Monthly. $59.00 per year. Covers trends in finance, technology, and economics for corporate financial executives.

CFO: The Magazine for Senior Financial Executives. CFO Publishing Corp., The Economist Group. • Monthly. Free to qualified subscribers; others, $50.00 per year.

Corporate Cashflow: The Magazine of Treasury Management. Intertec Publishing Corp. • Monthly. $78.00 per year. Published for chief financial officers of corporations. Includes annual *Directory*.

Corporate Financing Week: The Newsweekly of Corporate Finance, Investment Banking and M and A. Institutional Investor. • Weekly. $2,550.00 per year. Newsletter for corporate finance officers. Emphasis is on debt and equity financing, mergers, leveraged buyouts, investment banking, and venture capital.

F W's Corporate Finance: The Magazine fo the Financing Strategist. Financial World Partners. • Quarterly. $50.00 per year. Edited for financial executives of U. S. corporations. Covers leveraged buyouts, mergers, insurance, pensions, risk management, and other corporate topics. Includes case studies. Formerly *Corporate Finance*.

Financial Markets, Institutions, and Instruments. New York University, Salomon Center. Blackwell Publishers. • Five times a year. $219.00 per year. Edited to "bridge the gap between the academic and professional finance communities." Special fifth issue each year provides surveys of developments in four areas: money and banking, derivative securities, corporate finance, and fixed-income securities.

Global Finance. Global Finance Media, Inc. • Monthly. $300.00 per year. Edited for corporate financial executives and money managers responsible for "cross-border" financial transactions.

Journal of Corporate Accounting and Finance. John Wiley and Sons, Inc., Subscription Dept. • Bimonthly. $263.00 per year. Topics include government regulation, corporate taxation, financial risk, business valuation, and strategic planning.

Strategic Finance. Institute of Management Accountants. • Monthly. $140.00 per year; non-profit institutions, $70.00 per year. Provides articles on corporate finance, cost control, cash flow, budgeting, corporate taxes, and other financial management topics.

Zacks Analyst Watch. Zacks Investment Research. • Biweekly. $250.00 per year. Provides the results of research by stockbroker investment analysts on major U. S. corporations.

Zacks Earnings Forecaster. Zacks Investment Research. • Biweekly. $495.00 per year. (Also available monthly at $375.00 per year.) Provides estimates by stockbroker investment analysts of earnings per share of individual U. S. companies.

Zacks Profit Guide. Zacks Investment Research. • Quarterly. $375.00 per year. Provides analysis of total return and stock price performance of major U. S. companies.

RESEARCH CENTERS AND INSTITUTES

Center for Finance and Real Estate. University of California, Los Angeles, John E. Anderson Graduate School of Management, P.O. Box 951481, Los Angeles, CA 90095-1481. Phone: (310)825-1953 Fax: (310)206-5455 E-mail: wtorous@anderson.ucla.edu • URL: http://www.agsm.ucla.edu/acadunit/finance/realestate.

STATISTICS SOURCES

Economic Report of the President: Together with the Annual Report of the Council of Economic Advisors. Available from U. S. Government Printing Office. • Annual. $29.00. Includes about 130 pages of "Statistical Tables Relating to Income, Employment, and Production." Tables cover national income, employment, wages, productivity, manufacturing, prices, credit, finance (public and private), corporate profits, and foreign trade.

Standard & Poor's Stock Reports: American Stock Exchange. Standard & Poor's. • Irregular. $1,035.00 per year. Looseleaf service. Provides two pages of financial details and other information for each corporation listed on the American Stock Exchange.

Standard & Poor's Stock Reports: NASDAQ and Regional Exchanges. Standard & Poor's. • Irregular. $1,100.00 per year. Looseleaf service. Provides two pages of financial details and other information for each corporation included.

Standard & Poor's Stock Reports: New York Stock Exchange. Standard & Poor's. • Irregular. $1,295.00 per year. Looseleaf service. Provides two pages of financial details and other information for each corporation with stock listed on the N. Y. Stock Exchange.

TRADE/PROFESSIONAL ASSOCIATIONS

Association for Financial Professionals. 7315 Wisconsin Ave., Suite 600-W, Bethesda, MD 20814-3211. Phone: (301)907-2862 Fax: (301)907-2864 E-mail: afp@afponline.org • URL: http://www.afponline.org • Members are corporate treasurers and other managers of business finance. Formerly Treasury Management Association.

Financial Executives Institute. P.O. Box 1938, Morristown, NJ 07962-1938. Phone: (973)898-4600 Fax: (973)898-4649.

Financial Management Association International. College of Business Administration, University of South Florida, Tampa, FL 33620-5500. Phone: (813)974-2084 Fax: (813)974-3318 E-mail: fma@coba.usf.edu • URL: http://www.fma.org • Members are corporate financial officers and professors of financial management.

National Association of Corporate Treasurers. 11250 Roger Bacon Dr., Suite 8, Reston, VA 20190. Phone: (703)318-4227 Fax: (703)435-4390 E-mail: nact@nact.org • URL: http://www.nact.org • Members are corporate financial executives.

OTHER SOURCES

Business & Company Resource Center. The Gale Group. • Fee-based Web site provides a wide range of business, industry, and specific company information. Access is offered to trade journal articles, market research data, insider trading activity, major shareholder data, corporate histories, emerging technology reports, corporate earnings estimates, press releases, and other sources. Provides detailed company profiles, industry overviews, and rankings. Offers integration of Predicasts PROMT, Newsletters ASAP, Investext Plus, Business Index ASAP, Brands and Their Companies, and other databases (many have full text).

Corporate Dividends and Stock Repurchases. Barbara Black. West Group. • $130.00. Looseleaf service. Periodic supplementation. Covers the law relating to dividends in general, illegal dividends, stock splits, stock dividends, corporate repurchases, and other dividend topics.

Cyberfinance: Raising Capital for the E-Business. Martin B. Robins. CCH, Inc. • 2001. $79.00. Covers the taxation, financial, and legal aspects of raising money for new Internet-based ("dot.com") companies, including the three stages of startup, growth, and initial public offering.

FASB Accounting Standards Current Text. Financial Accounting Standards Board. • Looseleaf.

FASB Accounting Standards Current Text: General Standards. Financial Accounting Standards Board. • Irregular. Price on application.

FASB Accounting Standards Current Text: Industries Standards. Financial Accounting Standards Board. • Irregular. Price on application.

FASB Accounting Standards Current Text: Professional Standards. Financial Accounting Standards Board. • Irregular. Price on application.

FASB Accounting Standards Current Text: Technical Practice Aids. Financial Accounting Standards Board. • Irregular. Price on application.

FASB Original Pronouncements. Financial Accounting Standards Board. • Irregular. Price on application.

Financial Accounting Series. Financial Accounting Standards Board. • Price on application.

Fundamentals of Finance and Accounting for Nonfinancial Managers. American Management Association Extension Institute. • Looseleaf. $110.00. Self-study course. Emphasis is on practical explanations, examples, and problem solving. Quizzes and a case study are included.

How to Manage Corporate Cash. American Management Association Extension Institute. • Looseleaf. $110.00. Self-study course. Emphasis is on practical explanations, examples, and problem solving. Quizzes and a case study are included.

Managing Financial Risk with Forwards, Futures, Options, and Swaps. American Management Association Extension Institute. • Looseleaf. $130.00. Self-study course. Emphasis is on practical explanations, examples, and problem solving. Quizzes and a case study are included.

Statements of Financial Accounting Standards: Original Pronouncements. John Wiley and Sons, Inc. • 1996. Price on application.

CORPORATE FORMATION

See: INCORPORATION

CORPORATE GIVING

See: PHILANTHROPY

CORPORATE HISTORIES

See: BUSINESS HISTORY

CORPORATE IMAGE

GENERAL WORKS

Corporate Identity: Making Business Strategy Visible Through Design. Wally Olins. McGraw-Hill. • 1990. $50.00.

Crisis Response: Inside Stories on Managing Image Under Siege. The Gale Group. • 1993. $60.00. Presents first-hand accounts by media relations professionals of major business crises and how they were handled. Topics include the following kinds of crises: environmental, governmental, corporate image, communications, and product.

Living Logos: How U. S. Corporations Revitalize Their Trademarks. David E. Carter, editor. Art Direction Book Co. • 1993. $22.95. Traces the history and evolution of 70 famous U. S. company logos.

Shaping the Corporate Image: An Analytical Guide for Executive Decision Makers. Marion G. Sobol and others. Greenwood Publishing Group, Inc. • 1992. $49.95.

The 22 Immutable Laws of Branding: How to Build a Product or Service Into a World-Class Brand. Al Ries and Laura Ries. HarperInformation. • 1999. $23.00. Provides advice on attaining positive brand recognition.

ABSTRACTS AND INDEXES

Business Periodicals Index. H. W. Wilson Co. • Monthly, except August, with quarterly and annual cumulations. Service basis for print edition; CD-ROM edition, $1,495.00 per year.

PAIS International in Print. Public Affairs Information Service, Inc. • Monthly. $650.00 per year; cumulations three times a year. Provides topical citations to the worldwide literature of public affairs, economics, demographics, sociology, and trade. Text in English; indexed materials in English, French, German, Italian, Portuguese and Spanish.

CD-ROM DATABASES

ABI/INFORM Global. Bell & Howell Information and Learning. • Monthly. $6,500.00 per year. Provides CD-ROM indexing and abstracting of worldwide business literature appearing in over 1,200 periodicals for the most recent five years. Archival discs are available from 1971. Formerly *ABI/INFORM OnDisc.*

PAIS on CD-ROM. Public Affairs Information Service, Inc. • Quarterly. $1,995.00 per year. Provides a CD-ROM version of the online service, *PAIS International.* Contains over 400,000 citations to the literature of contemporary social, political, and economic issues.

WILSONDISC: Wilson Business Abstracts. H. W. Wilson Co. • Monthly. $2,495.00 per year, including unlimited online access to *Wilson Business Abstracts* through WILSONLINE. Provides CD-ROM "cover-to-cover" abstracting and indexing of over 600 prominent business periodicals. Indexing is from 1982, abstracting from 1990. (*Business Periodicals Index* without abstracts is available on CD-ROM at $1,495 per year.).

HANDBOOKS AND MANUALS

Corporate Image: A Practical Guide to the Implementation of a Corporate Identity Program. Nicholas Ind. Beekman Publishers, Inc. • 1990. $44.95.

Corporate Image: Communicating Visions and Values. Allyson LaBorde, editor. Conference Board, Inc. • 1993. $100.00.

Logo Power: How to Create Effective Company Logos. William Haig and Laurel Harper. John Wiley & Sons, Inc. • 1997. $39.95. Explains how to plan, develop, evaluate, and implement a company logo system.

The New Guide to Identity: How to Create and Sustain Change Through Managing Identity. Wally Olins. Ashgate Publishing Co. • 1996. $22.95. A guide to corporate identity through the effective use of industrial design and graphics. Includes color illustrations.

ONLINE DATABASES

ABI/INFORM. Bell & Howell Information and Learning. • Provides online indexing to business-related material occurring in over 1,000 periodicals from 1971 to the present. Inquire as to online cost and availability.

Management Contents. The Gale Group. • Covers a wide range of management, financial, marketing, personnel, and administrative topics. About 150 leading business journals are indexed and abstracted from 1974 to date, with monthly updating. Inquire as to online cost and availability.

PAIS International. Public Affairs Information Service, Inc. • Corresponds to the former printed publications, *PAIS Bulletin* (1976-90) and *PAIS Foreign Language Index* (1972-90), and to the current *PAIS International in Print* (1991 to date). Covers economic, political, and sociological material appearing in periodicals, books, government documents, and other publications. Updating is monthly. Inquire as to online cost and availability.

Trade & Industry Index. The Gale Group. • Provides indexing of business periodicals, January 1981 to date. Daily updates. (Full text articles from some periodicals are available online, 1983 to date, in the companion database, *Trade & Industry ASAP.*) Inquire as to online cost and availability.

Wilson Business Abstracts Online. H. W. Wilson Co. • Indexes and abstracts 600 major business periodicals, plus the *Wall Street Journal* and the business section of the *New York Times*. Indexing is from 1982, abstracting from 1990, with the two newspapers included from 1993. Updated weekly. Inquire as to online cost and availability. (*Business Periodicals Index* without abstracts is also available online.).

PERIODICALS AND NEWSLETTERS

Directors & Boards. • Quarterly. $295.00 per year. Edited for corporate board members and senior executive officers.

RESEARCH CENTERS AND INSTITUTES

Center for Corporate Community Relations. Boston College, 55 Lee Rd., Chestnut Hill, MA 02467. Phone: (617)552-4545 Fax: (617)552-8499 E-mail: cccr@bc.edu • URL: http://www.bc.edu/cccr • Areas of study include corporate images within local communities, corporate community relations, social vision, and philanthropy.

TRADE/PROFESSIONAL ASSOCIATIONS

Public Relations Society of America. 33 Irving Place, 3rd Fl., New York, NY 10003-2376. Phone: 800-937-7772 or (212)995-2230 Fax: (212)995-0757 E-mail: hq@prsa.org • URL: http://www.prsa.org.

CORPORATE INCOME TAX

See also: TAXATION

GENERAL WORKS

Corporate and Tax Aspects of Closely Held Corporations. William H. Painter. Aspen Books. • 1981. $80.00. Second edition.

Taxation of the Closely Held Corporation. Theodore Ness and Eugene L. Vogel. Warren, Gorham and Lamont/RIA Group. • Looseleaf service. $160.00 per year. Periodic supplementation.

ABSTRACTS AND INDEXES

Accounting and Tax Index. UMI. • Quarterly. Price on application. Includes annual cumulative bound volume. Indexes accounting, auditing, and taxation literature appearing in journals, books, pamphlets, conference proceedings, and newsletters. (UMI is University Microfilms International, a Bell & Howell Co.).

CD-ROM DATABASES

Federal Tax Products. Available from U. S. Government Printing Office. • Annual. $20.00. CD-ROM issued by the Internal Revenue Service (http://www.irs.treas.gov/forms_pubs/). Provides current tax forms, instructions, and publications. Also includes older tax forms beginning with 1991.

The Tax Directory [CD-ROM]. Tax Analysts. • Quarterly. Provides *The Tax Directory* listings on CD-ROM, covering federal, state, and international tax officials, tax practitioners, and corporate tax executives.

DIRECTORIES

The Tax Directory. Tax Analysts. • Annual. $299.00. ($399.00 with quarterly CD-ROM updates.) Four volumes: *Government Officials Worldwide* (lists 15,000 state, federal, and international tax officials, with basic corporate and individual income tax rates for 100 countries); *Private Sector Professionals Worldwide* (lists 25,000 U.S. and foreign tax practitioners: accountants, lawyers, enrolled agents, and actuarial firms); *Corporate Tax Managers Worldwide* (lists 10,000 tax managers employed by U.S. and foreign companies).

HANDBOOKS AND MANUALS

Corporate, Partnership, Estate, and Gift Taxation 1997. James W. Pratt and William Kulsrud, editors. McGraw-Hill Higher Education. • 1996. $71.25. 10th edition.

Corporate Taxes: Worldwide Summaries. Price Waterhouse Coopers. John Wiley and Sons, Inc. • 1999. $95.00. Summarizes the corporate tax regulations of more than 125 countries. Provides information useful for international tax planning and foreign investments.

Corporation and Partnership Tax Return Guide. Research Institute of America Inc. • 2000. $16.50. Revised edition.

Corporation-Partnership-Fiduciary Filled-in Tax Return Forms, 1999. CCH, Inc. • 1999. $21.50.

Federal Income Taxation of Corporations and Shareholders. Boris I. Bittker and James S. Eustice. Warren, Gorham and Lamont/RIA Group. • Looseleaf service. $235.00. Two volumes. Periodic supplementation. Provides details concerning best methods for structuring various corporation transactions. Actual forms used by top tax specialists covering a diverse range of tax situations are shown.

Federal Tax Course: General Edition. CCH, Inc. • Annual. $123.00. Provides basic reference and training for various forms of federal taxation: individual, business, corporate, partnership, estate, gift, etc. Includes *Federal Taxation Study Manual.*

Federal Tax Manual. CCH, Inc. • Looseleaf. $175.00 per year. Covers "basic federal tax rules and forms affecting individuals and businesses." Includes a copy of *Annuity, Depreciation, and Withholding Tables.*

Tax Planning for Corporations and Shareholders: Forms. Matthew Bender & Co., Inc. • $200.00. Looseleaf service. Periodic supplementation.

U. S. Master Multistate Corporate Tax Guide. CCH, Inc. • Annual. $67.00. Provides corporate income tax information for 47 states, New York City, and the District of Columbia.

INTERNET DATABASES

CCH Essentials: An Internet Tax Research and Primary Source Library. CCH, Inc. Phone: 800-248-3248 or (773)866-6000 Fax: 800-224-8299 or (773)866-3608 E-mail: cust_serv@cch.com • URL: http://tax.cch.com/essentials • Fee-based Web site provides full-text coverage of federal tax law and regulations, including rulings, procedures, tax court decisions, and IRS publications, announcements, notices, and penalties. Includes explanation, analysis, tax planning guides, and a daily tax news service. Searching is offered, including citation search. Fee: $495.00 per year.

The Digital Daily. Internal Revenue Service. Phone: (202)622-5000 Fax: (202)622-5844 • URL: http://www.irs.ustreas.gov • Web site provides a wide variety of tax information, including IRS forms and publications. Includes "Highlights of New Tax Law." Searching is available. Fees: Free.

Fedstats. Federal Interagency Council on Statistical Policy. Phone: (202)395-7254 • URL: http://www.fedstats.gov • Web site features an efficient search facility for full-text statistics produced by more than 70 federal agencies, including the Census Bureau, the Bureau of Economic Analysis, and the Bureau of Labor Statistics. Boolean searches can be made within one agency or for all agencies combined. Links are offered to international statistical bureaus, including the UN, IMF, OECD, UNESCO, Eurostat, and 20 individual countries. Fees: Free.

Rutgers Accounting Web (RAW). Rutgers University Accounting Research Center. Phone: (201)648-5172 Fax: (201)648-1233 • URL: http://www.rutgers.edu/accounting • RAW Web site provides extensive links to sources of national and international accounting information, such as the Big Six accounting firms, the Financial Accounting Standards Board (FASB), SEC filings (EDGAR), journals, publishers, software, the International Accounting Network, and "Internet's largest list of accounting firms in USA." Searching is offered. Fees: Free.

Tax Analysts [Web site]. Tax Analysts. Phone: 800-955-3444 or (703)533-4400 Fax: (703)533-4444 • URL: http://www.tax.org • The three main sections of Tax Analysts home page are "Tax News" (Today's Tax News, Feature of the Week, Tax Snapshots, Tax Calendar); "Products & Services" (Product Catalog, Press Releases); and "Public Interest" (Discussion Groups, Tax Clinic, Tax History Project). Fees: Free for coverage of current tax events; fee-based for comprehensive information. Daily updating.

ONLINE DATABASES

Accounting and Tax Database. Bell & Howell Information and Learning. • Provides indexing and abstracting of the literature of accounting, taxation, and financial management, 1971 to date. Updating is weekly. Especially covers accounting, auditing, banking, bankruptcy, employee compensation and benefits, cash management, financial planning, and credit. Inquire as to online cost and availability.

DRI U.S. Central Database. Data Products Division. • Provides more than 23,000 business, financial, demographic, economic, foreign trade, and industry-related time series for the U.S. Includes national income, population, retail-wholesale trade, price indexes, labor data, housing, industrial production, banking, interest rates, money supply, etc. Time period is generally 1947 to date (some data back to 1929). Updating varies. Inquire as to online cost and availability.

PERIODICALS AND NEWSLETTERS

Highlights and Documents. Tax Analysts. • Daily. $2,249.00 per year, including monthly indexes. Newsletter. Provides daily coverage of IRS, congressional, judicial, state, and international tax developments. Includes abstracts and citations for "all tax documents released within the previous 24 to 48 hours." Annual compilation available *Highlights and Documents on Microfiche.*

Journal of Corporate Taxation. Warren, Gorham, and Lamont/RIA Group. • Looseleaf service. $195.00 per year. Quarterly updates. Analysis and guidance for practitioners. Provides ongoing coverage of currently proposed tax reform bills.

Strategic Finance. Institute of Management Accountants. • Monthly. $140.00 per year; non-profit institutions, $70.00 per year. Provides articles on corporate finance, cost control, cash flow, budgeting, corporate taxes, and other financial management topics.

Tax Notes: The Weekly Tax Service. Tax Analysts. • Weekly. $1,699.00 per year. Includes an *Annual* and 1985-1996 compliations on CD-ROM. Newsletter. Covers "tax news from all federal sources," including congressional committees, tax courts, and the Internal Revenue Service. Each issue contains "summaries of every document that pertains to federal tax law," with citations. Commentary is provided.

Tax Practice. Tax Analysts. • Weekly. $199.00 per year. Newsletter. Covers news affecting tax practitioners and litigators, with emphasis on federal court decisions, rules and regulations, and tax petitions. Provides a guide to Internal Revenue Service audit issues.

STATISTICS SOURCES

Business Statistics of the United States. Courtenay M. Slater, editor. Bernan Associates. • 1999. $74.00. Fifth edition. Based on *Business Statistics*, formerly issue by the Bureau of Economic Analysis, U. S. Department of Commerce. Provides basic data for a wide variety of U. S. industries, services, and economic indicators. Most statistics are shown annually for 29 years and monthly for the most recent four years.

Statistics of Income Bulletin. Available from U.S. Government Printing Office. • Quarterly. $35.00 per year. Current data compiled from tax returns relating to income, assets, and expenses of individuals and businesses. (U. S. Internal Revenue Service.).

Statistics of Income: Corporation Income Tax Returns. U.S. Internal Revenue Service. Available from U.S. Government Printing Office. • Annual. $26.00.

Survey of Current Business. Available from U. S. Government Printing Office. • Monthly. $49.00 per year. Issued by Bureau of Economic Analysis, U. S. Department of Commerce. Presents a wide variety of business and economic data.

TRADE/PROFESSIONAL ASSOCIATIONS

Tax Analysts. 6830 N. Fairfax Dr., Arlington, VA 22213. Phone: 800-955-3444 or (703)533-4400 Fax: (703)533-4444 E-mail: webmaster@tax.org • URL: http://www.tax.org • An advocacy group reviewing U. S. and foreign income tax developments. Includes a Tax Policy Advisory Board.

Tax Executives Institute. 1200 G St., N.W., No. 300, Washington, DC 20005-3814. Phone: (202)638-5601 Fax: (202)638-5607 E-mail: askter@tei.org • URL: http://www.tei.org.

OTHER SOURCES

Business Transactions: Tax Analysis. Research Institute of America. • Three looseleaf volumes. Biweekly updates. Price on application. Analyzes the tax consequences of various business decisions for sole proprietorships, partnerships, S corporations, and other corporations.

Business Transactions: Tax Planning. Research Institute of America, Inc. • Four looseleaf volumes. Monthly updates. Price on application. Covers the tax planning aspects of business decisions for sole proprietorships, partnerships, S corporations, and other corporations.

Capital Changes Reports. CCH, Inc. • Weekly. $1,310.00. Six looseleaf volumes. Arranged alphabetically by company. This service presents a chronological capital history that includes reorganizations, mergers and consolidations. Recent actions are found in Volume One - "New Matters.".

Corporation Forms. Prentice Hall. • Looseleaf. Periodic supplementation. Price on application.

Factiva. Dow Jones Reuters Business Interactive, LLC. • Fee-based Web site provides "global news and business information through Web sites and content integration solutions." Includes Dow Jones and Reuters newswires, The Wall Street Journal, and more than 7,000 other sources of current news, historical articles, market research reports, and investment analysis. Content includes 96 major U. S. newspapers, 900 non-English sources, trade publications, media transcripts, country profiles, news photos, etc.

Federal Income Taxation of Corporations Filing Consolidated Returns. Herbert J. Lerner and Richard S. Antes. Matthew Bender & Co., Inc. • $650.00. Four looseleaf volumes. Periodic supplementation.

Manufacturers' Tax Alert. CCH, Inc. • Monthly. $297.00 per year. Newsletter. Covers the major tax issues affecting manufacturing companies. Includes current developments in various kind of federal, state, and international taxes: sales, use, franchise, property, and corporate income.

Nexis.com. Lexis-Nexis Group. • Fee-based Web site offers searching of about 2.8 billion documents in some 30,000 news, business, and legal information sources. Features include a subject directory covering 1,200 topics in 34 categories and a Company Dossier containing information on more than 500,000 public and private companies. Boolean searching is offered.

CORPORATE PLANNING

See: PLANNING

CORPORATE REAL ESTATE

See: INDUSTRIAL REAL ESTATE

CORPORATE RESPONSIBILITY

See: SOCIAL RESPONSIBILITY

CORPORATION LAW AND REGULATION

See also: ADMINISTRATIVE LAW AND REGULATION; BUSINESS LAW; INCORPORATION; LAW

GENERAL WORKS

Economics of Corporation Law and Securities Regulation. Richard A. Posner and Kenneth E. Scott, editors. Aspen Books. • 1981. $20.95.

ABSTRACTS AND INDEXES

Current Law Index: Multiple Access to Legal Periodicals. The Gale Group. • Monthly. $650.00

per year. Produced in cooperation with the American Association of Law Libraries. Indexes more than 900 law journals, legal newspapers, and specialty publications from the U.S., Canada, U.K., Ireland, Australia, and New Zealand.

Index to Legal Periodicals and Books. H. W. Wilson Co. • Monthly. Quarterly and annual cumulations. $270.00 per year. CD-ROM version available at $1,495.00 per year.

ALMANACS AND YEARBOOKS

American Law Yearbook. The Gale Group. • Annual. $155.00. Serves as a yearly supplement to *West's Encyclopedia of American Law.* Describes new legal developments in many subject areas.

BIBLIOGRAPHIES

Encyclopedia of Legal Information Sources. The Gale Group. • 1992. $180.00. Second edition. Lists more than 23,000 law-related information sources, including print, nonprint, and organizational.

International Legal Books in Print. Bowker-Saur. • Irregular. $375.00. Two volumes. Covers English-language law books published or distributed within the United Kingdom, Europe, and current or former British Commonwealth countries.

Legal Information: How to Find It, How to Use It. Kent Olson. Oryx Press. • 1998. $59.95. Recommends sources for various kinds of legal information.

CD-ROM DATABASES

WILSONDISC: Index to Legal Periodicals and Books. H. W. Wilson Co. • Monthly. Including unlimited online access to *Index to Legal Periodicals* through WILSONLINE. Contains CD-ROM indexing of more than 800 English language legal periodicals from 1981 to date and 2,500 books.

DIRECTORIES

Law and Legal Information Directory. The Gale Group. • 2000. $405.00. 11th edition. Two volumes. Contains a wide range of sources of legal information, such as associations, law schools, courts, federal agencies, referral services, libraries, publishers, and research centers. There is a separate chapter for each of 23 types of information source or service.

ENCYCLOPEDIAS AND DICTIONARIES

Communicating with Legal Databases: Terms and Abbreviations for the Legal Researcher. Anne L. McDonald. Neal-Schuman Publishers, Inc. • 1987. $82.50.

West's Encyclopedia of American Law. Available from The Gale Group. • 1997. $995.00. Second edition. 12 volumes. Published by West Group. Covers a wide variety of legal topics for the general reader. Formerly *Guide to American Law: Everyone's Legal Encyclopedia* (1985).

HANDBOOKS AND MANUALS

Corporate Counsellor's Deskbook. Dennis J. Block and Michael A. Epstein, editors. Panel Publishing. • 1999. $220.00. Fifth edition. Looseleaf. Annual supplementation. Covers a wide variety of corporate legal issues, including internal investigations, indemnification, insider trading, intellectual property, executive compensation, antitrust, export-import, real estate, environmental law, government contracts, and bankruptcy.

Law of Corporate Officers and Directors: Indemnification and Insurance. Joseph W. Bishop, Jr. West Group. • 1990. $130.00. Practical guidance for developing corporate policy, drafting agreements and litigation.

Law of Corporate Officers and Directors: Rights, Duties, and Liabilities. Edward Brodsky and M. Patricia Adamski. West Group. • 1990. $130.00. Defines accountability for making policy.

Model Business Corporation Act Annotated. American Bar Association Business Law Staff. Prentice Hall. • 1985. Third edition. Four volumes. Price on application.

Organizing Corporate and Other Business Enterprises. Matthew Bender & Co., Inc. • $240.00. Looseleaf service. Periodic supplementation. A guide to and tax factors to be considered in selecting a form of business organization for the attorney advising proposed or existing small businesses.

Publicly Traded Corporations: Governance, Operation, and Regulation. John H. Matheson. West Group. • 1993. $130.00. Covers a wide range of corporate legal problems and issues, including shareholder communications and "tender offers and change of control transactions." (Corporate Law Series).

ONLINE DATABASES

Index to Legal Periodicals and Books (Online). H. W. Wilson Co. • Broad coverage of law journals and books 1981 to date. Monthly updates. Inquire as to online cost and availability.

Legal Resource Index. The Gale Group. • Broad coverage of law literature appearing in legal, business, and other periodicals, 1980 to date. Monthly updates. Inquire as to online cost and availability.

LEXIS. LEXIS-NEXIS. • The various LEXIS databases provide full text and indexing for a wide variety of legal cases, statutes, orders, and opinions.

PERIODICALS AND NEWSLETTERS

Daily Report for Executives. Bureau of National Affairs, Inc. • Daily. $6,927.00 per year. Newsletter. Covers legal, regulatory, economic, and tax developments affecting corporations.

Federal Register. Office of the Federal Register. Available from U.S. Government Printing Office. • Daily except Saturday and Sunday. $697.00 per year. Publishes regulations and legal notices issued by federal agencies, including executive orders and presidential proclamations. Issued by the National Archives and Records Administration (http://www.nara.gov).

Fletcher Corporation Law Adviser. West Group. • Monthly. $250.00 per year. Newsletter.

Securities and Federal Corporate Law Report. West Group. • 11 times a year. $308.00 per year. Newsletter.

Securities Regulation and Law Report. Bureau of National Affairs. • Weekly. $1,294.00 per year. Two volumes. Looseleaf.

RESEARCH CENTERS AND INSTITUTES

Lexis.com Research System. Lexis-Nexis Group. Phone: 800-227-9597 or (937)865-6800 Fax: (937)865-6909 E-mail: webmaster@prod.lexis-nexis.com • URL: http://www.lexis.com • Fee-based Web site offers extensive searching of a wide variety of legal sources. Additional features include Daily Opinion Service, lexis.com Bookstore, Career Center, CLE Center, Law Schools, and Practice Pages ("Pages specific to areas of specialty").

TRADE/PROFESSIONAL ASSOCIATIONS

Academy of Legal Studies in Business. Dept. of Finance, 120 Upham Hall, Miami University, Oxford, OH 45056. Phone: 800-831-2903 or (513)529-2945 Fax: (513)529-6992 • URL: http://www.alsb.org.

OTHER SOURCES

Business Law Monographs. Matthew Bender & Co., Inc. • $1,450.00. 36 looseleaf volumes. Quarterly updates. Intended for in-house and outside corporate counsel. Each monograph concentrates on a particular subject.

Close Corporations: Law and Practice. Little, Brown and Co. • $350.00. Two volumes. Volume one $175.00; volume two, $175.00. Periodic supplementation. Covers family and other closely held corporations.

Corporate Compliance Series. West Group. • Eleven looseleaf volumes, with periodic supplementation. $990.00. Covers criminal and civil liability problems for corporations. Includes employee safety, product liability, pension requirements, securities violations, equal employment opportunity issues, intellectual property, employee hiring and firing, and other corporate compliance topics.

Corporate Criminal Liability. Kathleen F. Brickley. West Group. • $335.00 per year. Three looseleaf volumes. Periodic supplementation. Discusses how the general principles of criminal law apply to the corporate world. Provides a detailed analysis of liability under major federal crime statutes.

Corporate Practice Series. Bureau of National Affairs, Inc. • Weekly. $795.00 per year. Series of about 30 "portfolios" on various aspects of corporate law. Includes BNA's *Corporate Counsel Weekly.*

Corporation Forms. Prentice Hall. • Looseleaf. Periodic supplementation. Price on application.

Fletcher Corporation Forms Annotated, 1980-1990. West Group. • $995.00. 12th edition. 21 volumes.

How to Form Your Own Corporation Without a Lawyer for Under $75.00. Ted Nicholas and Sean P. Melvin. Dearborn Financial Publishing. • 1999. $19.95. 26th edition.

CORPORATION REPORTS

See also: BUSINESS JOURNALISM; COMMUNICATION

GENERAL WORKS

Cases in Financial Statement Reporting and Analysis. Leopold A. Bernstein and Mostafa M. Maksy. McGraw-Hill Higher Education. • 1985. $36.95. Second edition.

Corporate Financial Reporting: Text and Cases. E. Richard Brownlee and others. McGraw-Hill Professional. • 1997. Third edition. Price on application.

Financial Statement Analysis: Theory, Application and Interpretation. Leopold A. Bernstein and John J Wild. McGraw-Hill. • 1997. $62.36. Sixth edition.

Understanding Financial Statements. Adlyn M. Fraser and Aileen Orminston. Prentice Hall. • 2000. Sixth edition. Price on application. Emphasis is on the evaluation and interpretation of financial statements.

CD-ROM DATABASES

SEC Online on SilverPlatter. Available from SilverPlatter Information, Inc. • Quarterly. $3,950.00 per year to nonprofit organizations; $6,950.00 per year to businesses. Produced by Disclosure, Inc. Provides complete text on CD-ROM of documents filed with the Securities and Exchange Commission by over 5,000 publicly held corporations, including 10K forms (annual), 10Q forms (quarterly), and proxies. Also includes annual reports to stockholders.

FINANCIAL RATIOS

Reliable Financial Reporting and Internal Control: A Global Implementation Guide. Dmitris N. Chorafas. John Wiley and Sons, Inc. • 2000. $65.00. Discusses financial reporting and control as related to doing business internationally.

HANDBOOKS AND MANUALS

Accounting Trends and Techniques in Published Corporate Annual Reports. American Institute of Certified Public Accountants. • Annual. $50.00.

Analysis and Use of Financial Statements. Gerald I. White and others. John Wiley and Sons, Inc. • 1997. $112.95. Second edition. Includes analysis of financial ratios, cash flow, inventories, assets, debt, etc. Also covered are employee benefits, corporate investments, multinational operations, financial derivatives, and hedging activities.

Environmental Accounting: Current Issues, Abstracts, and Bibliography. United Nations Publications. • 1992. Provides guidelines for environmental disclosure in corporate annual reports.

Financial Shenanigans: How to Detect Accounting Gimmicks and Fraud in Financial Reports. Howard M. Schilit. McGraw-Hill. • 1993. $22.95. Tells how to interpret the footnotes and fine print in corporate annual and other reports.

Financial Statement Analysis: A Practitioner's Guide. McGraw-Hill. • 1998. $60.00. Sixth edition.

Financial Statement Analysis: The Investor's Self Study Guide to Interpreting and Analyzing. Charles J. Woelfel. McGraw-Hill Professional. • 1993. $22.95. Revised edition.

Guide to Financial Reporting and Analysis. Eugene E. Comiskey and Charles W. Mulford. John Wiley and Sons, Inc. • 2000. $75.00. Provides financial statement examples to illustrate the application of generally accepted accounting principles.

Guide to Preparing Financial Statements. John R. Clay and others. Practitioners Publishing Co. • 1998. Three looseleaf volumes. Price on application.

How to Produce Creative Advertising: Traditional Techniques and Computer Applications. Thomas Bivins and Ann Keding. NTC/Contemporary Publishing. • 1993. $37.95. Covers copywriting, advertising design, and the use of desktop publishing techniques in advertising. (NTC Business Book Series).

How to Produce Creative Publications: Traditional Techniques and Computer Applications. Thomas Bivins and William E. Ryan. NTC/Contemporary Publishing. • 1994. $32.95. A practical guide to the writing, designing, and production of magazines, annual reports, brochures, and newsletters by traditional methods and by desktop publishing.

How to Read a Financial Report: Wringing Cash Flow and Other Vital Signs Out of the Numbers. John A. Tracy. John Wiley and Sons, Inc. • 1999. $29.95. Fifth edition.

Manager's Guide to Financial Statement Analysis. Stephen F. Jablonsky and Noah P. Barsky. John Wiley and Sons, Inc. • 1998. $67.95. The two main sections are "Financial Statements and Business Strategy" and "Market Valuation and Business Strategy.".

SEC Financial Reporting: Annual Reports to Shareholders, Form 10-K, and Quarterly Financial Reporting. Matthew Bender & Co., Inc. • $215.00. Looseleaf service. Periodic supplementation. Coverage of aspects of financial reporting and disclosure under Regulations S-X and S-K, with step-by-step procedures for preparing information for Form 10-K and annual shareholders reports.

SEC Handbook: Rules and Forms for Financial Statements and Related Disclosures. CCH, Inc. • Annual. $54.00. Contains full text of rules and requirements set by the Securities and Exchange Commisssion for preparation of corporate financial statements.

INTERNET DATABASES

Wall Street Journal Interactive Edition. Dow Jones & Co., Inc. Phone: 800-369-2834 or (212)416-2000 Fax: (212)416-2658 E-mail: inquiries@interactive.wsj.com • URL: http://www.wsj.com • Fee-based Web site providing online searching of worldwide information from the *The Wall Street Journal.* Includes "Company Snapshots," "The Journal's Greatest Hits," "Index to Market Data," "14-Day Searchable Archive," "Journal Links," etc. Financial price quotes are available. Fees: $49.00 per year; $29.00 per year to print subscribers.

ONLINE DATABASES

Compustat. Standard and Poor's. • Financial data on publicly held U.S. and some foreign corporations; data held for 20 years. Inquire as to online cost and availability.

Disclosure SEC Database. Disclosure, Inc. • Provides information from records filed with the Securities and Exchange Commission by publicly owned corporations, 1977 to present. Weekly updates. Inquire as to online cost and availability.

EDGAR Plus. Disclosure, Inc. • Provides SEC corporate filings full-text, plus other information, such as Fortune and Forbes rankings. Time period is 1968 to date, with continuous updating. Inquire as to online cost and availability. (EDGAR is the SEC's Electronic Data Gathering, Analysis, and Retrieval system.).

F & S Index. The Gale Group. • Contains about four million citations to worldwide business, financial, and industrial or consumer product literature appearing from 1972 to date. Weekly updates. Inquire as to online cost and availability.

SEC Online. Disclosure, Inc. • Provides complete text online of reports filed by over 5,000 public corporations with the U. S. Securities and Exchange Commission. Includes 10-K (official annual reports), 10-Q (quarterly), proxy statements, annual reports for stockholders, and other documents. Covers 1987 to date, with updates two or three times a week. Inquire as to online cost and availability.

PERIODICALS AND NEWSLETTERS

Journal of Financial Statement Analysis. Institutional Investor. • Quarterly. $280.00 per year. Covers the practical analysis and interpretation of corporate financial reports.

Ragan's Annual Report Review. Lawence Ragan Communications, Inc. • Monthly. $287.00 per year. Newsletter on business trends and tactics as reflected in corporate annual reports. Formerly *Corporate Annual Report.*

The Wall Street Journal. Dow Jones & Co., Inc. • Daily. $175.00 per year. Covers news and trends relating to business, industry, finance, the economy, and international commerce. Provides extensive price and other data for the securities, commodity, options, futures, foreign exchange, and money markets.

RESEARCH CENTERS AND INSTITUTES

Design Research Unit. Massachusetts College of Art, 621 Huntington Ave., Boston, MA 02115. Phone: (617)232-1492 Fax: (617)566-4034 • Conducts research related to the design of printed matter, including annual reports, letterheads, posters, and brochures.

STATISTICS SOURCES

Standard & Poor's Stock Reports: American Stock Exchange. Standard & Poor's. • Irregular. $1,035.00 per year. Looseleaf service. Provides two pages of financial details and other information for each corporation listed on the American Stock Exchange.

Standard & Poor's Stock Reports: NASDAQ and Regional Exchanges. Standard & Poor's. • Irregular. $1,100.00 per year. Looseleaf service. Provides two pages of financial details and other information for each corporation included.

Standard & Poor's Stock Reports: New York Stock Exchange. Standard & Poor's. • Irregular. $1,295.00 per year. Looseleaf service. Provides two pages of financial details and other information for each corporation with stock listed on the N. Y. Stock Exchange.

TRADE/PROFESSIONAL ASSOCIATIONS

Financial Accounting Foundation. P.O. Box 5116, Norwalk, CT 06856. Phone: (203)847-0700 Fax: (203)849-9714 E-mail: webmaster@fasb.org • URL: http://www.gasb.org.

Financial Executives Institute. P.O. Box 1938, Morristown, NJ 07962-1938. Phone: (973)898-4600 Fax: (973)898-4649.

Financial Management Association International. College of Business Administration, University of South Florida, Tampa, FL 33620-5500. Phone: (813)974-2084 Fax: (813)974-3318 E-mail: fma@coba.usf.edu • URL: http://www.fma.org • Members are corporate financial officers and professors of financial management.

OTHER SOURCES

Corporation Forms. Prentice Hall. • Looseleaf. Periodic supplementation. Price on application.

Factiva. Dow Jones Reuters Business Interactive, LLC. • Fee-based Web site provides "global news and business information through Web sites and content integration solutions." Includes Dow Jones and Reuters newswires, The Wall Street Journal, and more than 7,000 other sources of current news, historical articles, market research reports, and investment analysis. Content includes 96 major U. S. newspapers, 900 non-English sources, trade publications, media transcripts, country profiles, news photos, etc.

Nexis.com. Lexis-Nexis Group. • Fee-based Web site offers searching of about 2.8 billion documents in some 30,000 news, business, and legal information sources. Features include a subject directory covering 1,200 topics in 34 categories and a Company Dossier containing information on more than 500,000 public and private companies. Boolean searching is offered.

CORPORATIONS

See also: MULTINATIONAL CORPORATIONS

GENERAL WORKS

Cases and Materials on Corporations-Including Partnerships and Limited Partnerships. Robert W. Hamilton. West Publishing Co., College and School Div. • 1998. $68.50. Sixth edition. American Case book Series.

Cases in Corporate Acquisitions, Buyouts, Mergers, and Takeovers. The Gale Group. • 1999. $310.00. Reviews and analyzes about 300 cases of both success and failure in corporate acquisitiveness.

Cases in Corporate Innovation. The Gale Group. • 1999. $295.00. Reviews and analyzes about 300 cases to illustrate both successful and failed management of innovation.

Corporate Cultures: The Rites and Rituals of Corporate Life. Terrance E. Deal and Allan Kennedy. Perseus Publishing. • 1982. $15.00.

Dangerous Company: The Secret Story of the Consulting Powerhouses and the Corporations They Save and Ruin. James O'Shea and Charles Madigan. Random House, Inc. • 1997. $27.50. A critical view of the major consulting firms in the U. S. and how they influence large corporations.

Dirty Business: Exploring Corporate Misconduct: Analysis and Cases. Maurice Punch. Sage Publications, Inc. • 1996. $79.95. Covers organizational misbehavior and white-collar crime. Includes "Ten Cases of Corporate Deviance.".

The ERC Closely-Held Corporation Guide. Harvey Frank. Prentice Hall. • 1983. $59.95. Second edition.

Reengineering Management: The Mandate for New Leadership. James Champy. DIANE Publishing Co. • 1998. $25.00.

Reengineering the Corporation: A Manifesto for Business Revolution. Michael Hammer and James Champy. HarperCollins Publishers, Inc. • 1999. $16.00. Revised edition.

Up Against the Corporate Wall: Cases in Business and Society. S. Prakash Sethi and Paul Steidlmeier. Prentice Hall. • 1996. $57.00. Sixth edition.

CD-ROM DATABASES

CanCorp Plus Canadian Financial Database. Micromedia Ltd. • Monthly. $3,600.00 per year. Also available quarterly at $2,975.00 per year. Provides comprehensive information on CD-ROM for more than 11,000 public and private Canadian corporations. Emphasis is on detailed financial data for up to seven years.

Corporate Affiliations Plus. National Register Publishing, Reed Reference Publishing. • Quarterly. $1,995.00 per year. Provides CD-ROM discs corresponding to *Directory of Corporate Affiliations* and *Corporate Finance Bluebook.* Contains corporate financial services information and worldwide data on subsidiaries and affiliates.

Hoover's Company Capsules on CD-ROM. Hoover's, Inc. • Quarterly. $349.95 per year (single-user). Provides the CD-ROM version of *Hoover's Handbook of American Business, Hoover's Handbook of Emerging Companies, Hoover's Handbook of World Business, Hoover's Guide to Computer Companies, Hoover's Guide to Media Companies, Hoover's Handbook of Private Companies,* and various regional guides. Includes more than 11,000 profiles of companies.

InvesText [CD-ROM]. Thomson Financial Securities Data. • Monthly. $5,000.00 per year. Contains full text on CD-ROM of investment research reports from about 250 sources, including leading brokers and investment bankers. Reports are available on both U. S. and international publicly traded corporations. Separate industry reports cover more than 50 industries. Time span is 1982 to date.

WILSONDISC: Wilson Business Abstracts. H. W. Wilson Co. • Monthly. $2,495.00 per year, including unlimited online access to *Wilson Business Abstracts* through WILSONLINE. Provides CD-ROM "cover-to-cover" abstracting and indexing of over 600 prominent business periodicals. Indexing is from 1982, abstracting from 1990. (*Business Periodicals Index* without abstracts is available on CD-ROM at $1,495 per year.).

DIRECTORIES

The Almanac of American Employers: The Only Complete Guide to the Hottest, Fastest-Growing Major Corporations. Plunkett Research, Ltd. • Annual. $149.99. Provides descriptions of 500 large corporations, including salaries/benefits ratings, corporate culture profiles, types of employment, and other company information for job-seekers. Includes four indexes.

American Big Businesses Directory. American Business Directories. • Annual. $595.00. Lists 177,000 public and private U. S. companies in all fields having 100 or more employees. Includes sales volume, number of employees, and name of chief executive. Formerly *Big Businesses Directory.*

American Business Locations Directory. The Gale Group. • 1999. $575.00. Second edition. (Four U. S. regional volumes and index volume). Provides 150,000 specific site locations for the 1,000 largest industrial and service companies in the U. S. Entries include the following for each location: address, senior officer, number of employees, sales volume, Standard Industrial Classification (SIC) codes, and name of parent company.

American Manufacturers Directory. American Business Directories. • Annual. $595.00. Lists more than 150,000 public and private U. S. manufacturers having 20 or more employees. Includes sales volume, number of employees, and name of chief executive or owner.

The Corporate Directory of U.S. Public Companies. Walker's Western Research. • Annual. $360.00. Two volumes. Contains information on more than 10,000 publicly-traded companies, including names of executives and major subsidiaries. Includes financial and stock data.

Corporate Yellow Book: Who's Who at the Leading U.S. Companies. Leadership Directions, Inc. • Quarterly. $305.00 per year. Lists names and titles of over 51,000 key executives in major U. S. corporations. Includes four indexes: industry, personnel, geographic by state, and company/subsidiary. Companion volume to *Financial Yellow Book.*

Cyberhound's Guide to Companies on the Internet. The Gale Group. • 1996. $79.00. Presents critical descriptions and ratings of more than 2,000 company or corporate Internet databases. Includes a glossary of Internet terms, a bibliography, and indexes.

CyberTools for Business: Practical Web Sites that will Save You Time and Money. Wayne Harris. Hoover's, Inc. • 1997. $19.95. Describes 100 World Wide Web sites that are useful for business, investing, and job hunting. Also lists Web addresses for about 4,500 public and private companies.

D and B Million Dollar Directory. Dun and Bradstreet Information Services. • Annual. Commercial institutions, $1,395.00; libraries, $1,275.00. Lease basis.

Directory of Companies Required to File Annual Reports with the Securities and Exchange Commission. Securities and Exchange Commission. Available from U.S. Government Printing Office. • Annual. $46.00.

Directory of Corporate Affiliations. National Register Publishing. • Annual. $1,159.00. Five volumes. Volumes one and two: Master Index; volume three: U.S. Public Companies; volume four: U.S. Private Companies; volume five: International Public and Private Companies.

Hoover's Handbook of American Business: Profiles of Major U. S. Companies. Hoover's, Inc. • $149.95. 10th revised edition. Two volumes. Provides detailed profiles of more than 700 large public and private companies, including history, executives, brand names, key competitors, and up to 10 years of financial data. Includes indexes by industry, location, executive name, company name, and brand name.

Hoover's Handbook of Emerging Companies: Profiles of America's Most Exciting Growth Enterprises. Hoover's, Inc. • 2000. $89.95. Contains detailed profiles of 300 rapidly growing corporations. Includes indexes by industry, location, executive name, company name, and brand name.

Hoover's Masterlist of Major U. S. Companies. Hoover's, Inc. • Biennial. $99.95. Provides brief information, including annual sales, number of employees, and chief executive, for about 5,100 U. S. companies, both public and private.

International Directory of Company Histories. St. James Press. • 1989-2000. 33 volumes. Prices vary. Provides detailed histories of about 2,200 major corporations. Cumulative indexing is provided for company names, personal names, and industries.

Job Seeker's Guide to Private and Public Companies. The Gale Group. • 1995. $365.00. Third edition. Four regional volumes: *The West, The Midwest, The Northeast,* and *The South.* Covers about 15,000 companies, providing information on personnel department contacts, corporate officials, company benefits, application procedures, etc. Regional volumes are available separately at $99.00.

Kompass USA. Kompass USA, Inc. • Annual. $375.00. Four volumes. Includes information on about 125,000 U.S. companies. Classification system covers approximately 50,000 products and services. Product and tradename indexes are provided.

Peterson's Job Opportunities for Business Majors. Peterson's. • Annual. $21.95. Provides career information for the 2,000 largest U. S. employers in various industries.

Plunkett's Companion to the Almanac of American Employers: Mid-Size Firms. Plunkett Research, Ltd. • Annual. $149.99. Provides job-seekers with detailed information about fast-growing, medium-size corporations. Includes diskette.

Reference Book of Corporate Managements. Dun and Bradstreet Information Services. • Annual. Libraries, $650.00 per year; others, $795.00 per year. Lease basis. Management executives at over 12,000 leading United States companies.

Standard & Poor's 500 Guide. McGraw-Hill. • Annual. $24.95. Contains detailed profiles of the companies included in Standard & Poor's 500 Index of stock prices. Includes income and balance sheet data for up to 10 years, with growth and stability rankings for 500 major corporations.

Standard & Poor's MidCap 400 Guide. McGraw-Hill. • Annual. $24.95. Contains detailed profiles of the companies included in Standard & Poor's MidCap 400 Index of stock prices. Includes income and balance sheet data for up to 10 years, with growth and stability rankings for 400 midsized corporations.

Standard and Poor's Register of Corporations, Directors and Executives. Standard and Poor's. • Annual. $675.00. Periodic supplementation. Over 55,000 public and privately held corporations in the U.S. Three volumes. Three supplements.

Standard & Poor's SmallCap 600 Guide. McGraw-Hill. • Annual. $24.95. Contains detailed profiles of the companies included in Standard & Poor's SmallCap 600 Index of stock prices. Includes income and balance sheet data for up to 10 years, with growth and stability rankings for 600 small capitalization corporations.

Survey of Industrials. Financial Post Datagroup. • Annual. $119.95 Contains detailed information on more than 2,200 publicly owned Canadian manufacturing, retailing, and service corporations. Includes the "Financial Post 500," a ranking of the largest Canadian companies.

Ward's Business Directory of U. S. Private and Public Companies. The Gale Group. • 2000. $2,590.00. Eight volumes. *Ward's* contains basic information on about 120,000 business firms, of which 90 percent are private companies. Includes mid-year *Supplement.* Volumes available individually. Prices vary.

FINANCIAL RATIOS

Quarterly Financial Report for Manufacturing, Mining, and Trade Corporations. U.S. Federal Trade Commission and U.S. Securities and Exchange Commission. Available from U.S. Government Printing Office. • Quarterly. $39.00 per year.

HANDBOOKS AND MANUALS

Analysis of Financial Statements. Leopold A. Bernstein and John J. Wild. McGraw-Hill. • 1999. $60.00. Fifth edition. Includes practical examples of analysis.

Corporate Valuation: Tools for Effective Appraisal and Decision Making. Randolph W. Westerfield and others. McGraw-Hill Professional. • 1993. $65.00. Discusses the four most widely-used corporate appraisal methods.

Dun & Bradstreet/Gale Group Industry Handbooks. The Gale Group. • 2000. $630.00. Five volumes. $145.00 per volume. Each volume covers two or more major industries: 1. *Entertainment and Hospitality*; 2. *Construction and Agriculture*; 3. *Chemicals and Pharmaceuticals*; 4. *Computers & Software and Broadcasting & Telecommunications*; 5. *Insurance and Health & Medical Services.* The following are included for each industry: overview, statistics, financial ratios, rankings, merger information, company directory, directory of associations, and consultants directory.

Incorporating Your Business: The Complete Guide That Tells All You Should Know About Establishing and Operating a Small Corporation. Professional Report Editors and John Kirk. NTC/Contemporary Publishing. • 1986. $14.95.

Incorporation Kit. Entrepreneur Media, Inc. • Looseleaf. $59.50. A practical guide to incorporating a small business. Includes sample forms and information on how to construct bylaws and articles of incorporation. (Start-Up Business Guide No. E7100.).

Organizing Corporate and Other Business Enterprises. Matthew Bender & Co., Inc. • $240.00. Looseleaf service. Periodic supplementation. A guide to and tax factors to be considered in selecting a form of business organization for the attorney advising proposed or existing small businesses.

Reengineering Revolution: A Handbook. Michael Hammer and Steven Stanton. HarperInformation. • 1995. $16.00.

Subchapter S Manual. P. L. Faber and Martin E. Holbrook. Prentice Hall. • Annual. Price on application.

INTERNET DATABASES

Business Week Online. McGraw-Hill. Phone: (212)512-2762 Fax: (212)512-6590 • URL: http://www.businessweek.com • Web site provides complete contents of current issue of *Business Week* plus "BW Daily" with additonal business news, financial market quotes, and corporate information from Standard & Poor's. Includes various features, such as "Banking Center" with mortgage and interest data, and "Interactive Computer Buying Guide." The "Business Week Archive" is fully searchable back to 1991. Fees: Mostly free, but full-text archive articles are $2.00 each.

EBSCO Information Services. Ebsco Publishing. Phone: 800-871-8508 or (508)356-6500 Fax: (508)356-5640 E-mail: ep@epnet.com • URL: http://www.epnet.com • Fee-based Web site providing Internet access to a wide variety of databases, including business-related material. Full text is available for many periodical titles, with daily updates. Fees: Apply.

FIS Online: The Preferred Source for Global Business and Financial Information. Mergent. Phone: 800-342-5647 or (212)413-7601 Fax: (212)413-7777 E-mail: fis@fisonline.com • URL: http://www.fisonline.com • Fee-based Web site provides detailed information on more than 10,000 publicly-owned corporations listed on the New York Stock Exchange, American Stock Exchange, NASDAQ, and U. S. regional exchanges. Searching is offered on eight financial variables and six text fields. Weekly updating. Fees: Rates on application. (Mergent is publisher of Moody's Manuals.).

GaleNet: Your Information Community. The Gale Group. Phone: 800-877-GALE or (248)699-GALE Fax: 800-414-5043 or (248)699-8069 E-mail: galenet@gale.com • URL: http://www.galenet.com • Web site provides a wide variety of full-text information from Gale databases, Taft, and other sources. Covers associations, biography, business directories, education, the information industry, literature, publishing, and science. Fee-based subscriptions are available for individual databases (free demonstration). Includes Boolean search features and the BRS/Search user interface.

Hoover's Online. Hoover's, Inc. Phone: 800-486-8666 or (512)374-4500 Fax: (512)374-4501 • URL: http://www.hoovers.com • Web site provides stock quotes, lists of companies, and a variety of business information at no charge. In-depth company profiles are available at $29.95 per month.

ProQuest Direct. Bell & Howell Information and Learning. Phone: 800-521-0600 or (313)761-4700 Fax: (313)973-9145 • URL: http://www.umi.com/proquest • Fee-based Web site providing Internet access to more than 3,000 periodicals, newspapers, and other publications. Many items are available full-text, with daily updates. Includes extensive corporate and financial information from Disclosure, Inc. Fees: Apply.

Switchboard. Switchboard, Inc. Phone: (508)898-1000 Fax: (508)898-1755 E-mail: webmaster@switchboard.com • URL: http://www.switchboard.com • Web site provides telephone numbers and street addresses for more than 100 million business locations and residences in the U. S. Broad industry categories are available. Fees: Free.

ONLINE DATABASES

Business and Industry. Responsive Database Services, Inc. • Contains online citations, abstracts, and selected fulltext from more than 1,000 trade journals, newspapers, and other publications. Provides general coverage of both manufacturing and service industries, including marketing, production, industry trends, key events, and information on specific companies. Time span is 1994 to date. Daily updates. Inquire as to online cost and availability. (Also available in a CD-ROM version.).

CanCorp Plus Canadian Financial Database. Micromedia Ltd. • Provides detailed information, including descriptive, marketing, personnel, and financial data, for more than 11,000 public and private Canadian corporations. Weekly updates. Inquire as to online cost and availability.

Disclosure SEC Database. Disclosure, Inc. • Provides information from records filed with the Securities and Exchange Commission by publicly owned corporations, 1977 to present. Weekly updates. Inquire as to online cost and availability.

Dow Jones Text Library. Dow Jones and Co., Inc. • Full text and edited news stories and articles on business affairs; 1984 to date. Inquire as to online cost and availability.

InvesText. Thomson Financial Securities Data. • Provides full text online of investment research reports from more than 300 sources, including leading brokers and investment bankers. Reports are available on approximately 50,000 U. S. and international corporations. Separate industry reports cover 54 industries. Time span is 1982 to date, with daily updates. Inquire as to online cost and availability.

Moody's Corporate News: International. Moody's Investors Service, Inc. • Provides financial and other business news relating to over 5,000 corporations in 100 countries, excluding the U. S. Time period is 1983 to date, with weekly updates. Inquire as to online cost and availability.

Standard & Poor's Corporate Descriptions. Standard & Poor's Corp. • Provides current, detailed financial and other information on approximately 12,000 publicly held U. S. and foreign corporations. Corresponds to the printed *Standard & Poor's Corporation Records.* Updating is twice a month. Inquire as to online cost and availability.

Standard and Poor's Daily News Online. Standard and Poor's Corp. • Full text of business news and other information, 1984 to present. Inquire as to online cost and availability.

Standard & Poor's Register: Corporate. Standard & Poor's Corp. • Contains brief descriptions, with names of key executives, of about 55,000 public and private U. S. companies. Corresponds to the corporate volume of *Standard & Poor's Register of Corporations, Directors, and Executives.* Updated quarterly. Inquire as to online cost and availability.

Tablebase. Responsive Database Services, Inc. • Provides online numerical tabular data from a wide variety of business, organization, and government sources, including 900 trade journals. Includes industry and individual company statistics relating to products, market share, sales forecasts, production, exports, market trends, etc. Time span is 1997 to date. Weekly updates. Inquire as to online cost and availability. (Also available in a CD-ROM version.).

Wilson Business Abstracts Online. H. W. Wilson Co. • Indexes and abstracts 600 major business periodicals, plus the *Wall Street Journal* and the business section of the *New York Times.* Indexing is from 1982, abstracting from 1990, with the two newspapers included from 1993. Updated weekly. Inquire as to online cost and availability. (*Business Periodicals Index* without abstracts is also available online.).

PERIODICALS AND NEWSLETTERS

Business Strategies Bulletin. CCH, Inc. • Monthly. $166.00 per year. Newsletter.

Corporate Jobs Outlook!. Plunkett Research, Ltd. • Bimonthly. $179.99 per year. Newsletter. Presents data on job possibilities at fast-growing, mid-sized corporations. Supplement available *Almanac of American Employers.*

Corporate Secretary. American Society of Corporate Secretaries. • Quarterly. Free to members; non-members, $95.00 per year.

Forbes. Forbes, Inc. • Biweekly. $59.95 per year. Includes supplements: *Forbes ASAP* and *Forbes FYI.*

Fortune Magazine. Time Inc., Business Information Group. • Biweekly. $59.95 per year. Edited for top executives and upper-level managers.

RESEARCH CENTERS AND INSTITUTES

Business, Government, and Society Research Institute. University of Pittsburgh. School of Business, Mervis Hall, Pittsburgh, PA 15260. Phone: (412)648-1555 Fax: (412)648-1693 E-mail: mitnick@pitt.edu.

Olsson Center for Applied Ethics. University of Virginia. Darden School, P.O. Box 6550, Charlottesville, VA 22906. Phone: (804)924-0935

For publishers addresses, refer to SOURCES CITED section at the back of the book.

Fax: (804)924-6378 E-mail: ref8d@virginia.edu • URL: http://www.darden.virginia.edu.

STATISTICS SOURCES

New Business Incorporations. Dun & Bradstreet, Economic Analysis Dept. • Monthly. $25.00 per year. Gives the number of new business incorporations in each of the 50 states. Includes commentary.

Statistics of Income: Corporation Income Tax Returns. U.S. Internal Revenue Service. Available from U.S. Government Printing Office. • Annual. $26.00.

TRADE/PROFESSIONAL ASSOCIATIONS

American Society of Corporate Secretaries. 521 Fifth Ave., New York, NY 10175-0003. Phone: (212)681-2000 Fax: (212)681-2005 • URL: http://www.ascs.org.

Association for Corporate Growth. 1926 Waukegan Rd., Suite 1, Glenview, IL 60025-1770. Phone: 800-699-1331 or (847)657-6730 Fax: (847)657-6819 E-mail: acghq@tcag.com • URL: http://www.acg.org.

Strategic Leadership Forum. 435 N. Michigan Ave., Suite 1717, Chicago, IL 60611-4067. Phone: 800-873-5995 or (312)644-0829 Fax: (312)644-8557 • URL: http://www.slfnet.org.

OTHER SOURCES

Business & Company Resource Center. The Gale Group. • Fee-based Web site provides a wide range of business, industry, and specific company information. Access is offered to trade journal articles, market research data, insider trading activity, major shareholder data, corporate histories, emerging technology reports, corporate earnings estimates, press releases, and other sources. Provides detailed company profiles, industry overviews, and rankings. Offers integration of Predicasts PROMT, Newsletters ASAP, Investext Plus, Business Index ASAP, Brands and Their Companies, and other databases (many have full text).

The Business Elite: Database of Corporate America. Donnelley Marketing. • Quarterly. $795.00. Formerly compiled by Database America. Provides current information on CD-ROM for about 850,000 businesses, comprising all U. S. private and public companies having more than 20 employees or sales of more than $1 million. Data for each firm includes detailed industry classification, year started, annual sales, name of top executive, and number of employees.

Business Organizations with Tax Planning. Zolman Cavitch. Matthew Bender & Co., Inc. • $2,570.00. 16 looseleaf volumes. Periodic supplementation. In-depth analytical coverage of corporation law and all relevant aspects of federal corporation taxation.

Business Rankings Annual. The Gale Group. • Annual. $305.00.Two volumes. Compiled by the Business Library Staff of the Brooklyn Public Library. This is a guide to lists and rankings appearing in major business publications. The top ten names are listed in each case.

Business Strategies. CCH, Inc. • Semimonthly. $819.00 per year. Four looseleaf volumes. Semimonthly updates. Legal, tax, and accounting aspects of business planning and decision-making. Provides information on start-ups, forms of ownership (partnerships, corporations), failing businesses, reorganizations, acquisitions, and so forth. Includes *Business Strategies Bulletin,* a monthly newsletter.

Close Corporations: Law and Practice. Little, Brown and Co. • $350.00. Two volumes. Volume one $175.00; volume two, $175.00. Periodic supplementation. Covers family and other closely held corporations.

Corporation Forms. Prentice Hall. • Looseleaf. Periodic supplementation. Price on application.

Dun's Million Dollar Disc. Dun & Bradstreet, Inc. • Quarterly. $3,800.00 per year to libraries; $5,500.00 per year to businesses. CD-ROM provides information on more than 240,000 public and private U. S. companies having sales volume of $5 million or more or 100 employees or more. Includes biographical data on more than 640,000 company executives.

Factiva. Dow Jones Reuters Business Interactive, LLC. • Fee-based Web site provides "global news and business information through Web sites and content integration solutions." Includes Dow Jones and Reuters newswires, The Wall Street Journal, and more than 7,000 other sources of current news, historical articles, market research reports, and investment analysis. Content includes 96 major U. S. newspapers, 900 non-English sources, trade publications, media transcripts, country profiles, news photos, etc.

Infogate. Infogate, Inc. • Web site provides current news and information on seven "channels": News, Fun, Sports, Info, Finance, Shop, and Travel. Among the content partners are Business Wire, CBS MarketWatch, CNN, Morningstar, Standard & Poor's, and Thomson Investors Network. Fees: Free, but downloading of Infogate software is required (includes personalized news feature). Updating is continuous. Formerly Pointcast Network.

InSite 2. Intelligence Data/Thomson Financial. • Fee-based Web site consolidates information in a "Base Pack" consisting of Business InSite, Market InSite, and Company InSite. Optional databases are Consumer InSite, Health and Wellness InSite, Newsletter InSite, and Computer InSite. Includes fulltext content from more than 2,500 trade publications, journals, newsletters, newspapers, analyst reports, and other sources. Continuous updating. Formerly produced by The Gale Group.

Major Performance Rankings. Available from The Gale Group. • 2001. $1,100.00. Published by Euromonitor. Ranks 2,500 leading consumer product companies worldwide by various kinds of business and financial data, such as sales, profit, and market share. Includes international, regional, and country rankings.

Mergent Company Data. Mergent FIS, Inc. • Monthly. Price on application. CD-ROM provides detailed financial statement information for more than 10,000 New York Stock Exchange, American Stock Exchange, and NASDAQ corporations. Includes balance sheets, income statements, dividend history, annual price ranges, stock splits, Moody's debt ratings, etc. Formerly *Moody's Company Data.*

Nexis.com. Lexis-Nexis Group. • Fee-based Web site offers searching of about 2.8 billion documents in some 30,000 news, business, and legal information sources. Features include a subject directory covering 1,200 topics in 34 categories and a Company Dossier containing information on more than 500,000 public and private companies. Boolean searching is offered.

Standard & Poor's Corporations. Available from Dialog OnDisc. • Monthly. Price on application. Produced by Standard & Poor's. Contains three CD-ROM files: Executives, Private Companies, and Public Companies, providing detailed information on more than 70,000 business executives, 55,000 private companies, and 12,000 publicly-traded corporations.

World Business Rankings Annual. The Gale Group. • 1998. $189.00. Provides 2,500 ranked lists of international companies, compiled from a variety of published sources. Each list shows the "top ten" in a particular category. Keyword indexing, a country index, and citations are provided.

CORPORATIONS, CLOSELY HELD

See: CLOSELY HELD CORPORATIONS; PRIVATE COMPANIES

CORPORATIONS, MULTINATIONAL

See: MULTINATIONAL CORPORATIONS

CORPORATIONS, PROFESSIONAL

See: PROFESSIONAL CORPORATIONS

CORRECTIONAL INSTITUTIONS

See: LAW ENFORCEMENT INDUSTRIES

CORRESPONDENCE

See: BUSINESS CORRESPONDENCE

CORRESPONDENCE SCHOOLS AND COURSES

See also: ADULT EDUCATION

DIRECTORIES

Directory of Accredited Home Study Schools. National Home Study. • Annual. Free. Lists more than 70 accredited home study schools and the subjects they offer.

PERIODICALS AND NEWSLETTERS

DETC News. Distance Education and Training Council. • Semiannual. Free. Items of interest to correspondence educators. Formerly *NHSC News.*

RESEARCH CENTERS AND INSTITUTES

ERIC Clearinghouse on Adult, Career and Vocational Education. Ohio State University. Center on Education and Training for Employment, 1900 Kenny Rd., Columbus, OH 43210-1090. Phone: 800-848-4815 or (614)292-7069 Fax: (614)292-1260 E-mail: ericacve@postbox.acs.ohio-state.edu • URL: http://www.ericacve/org.

TRADE/PROFESSIONAL ASSOCIATIONS

Distance Education and Training Council. 1601 18th St., N.W., Washington, DC 20009. Phone: (202)234-5100 Fax: (202)332-1386 • URL: http://www.detc.org.

University Continuing Education Association. One Dupont Circle, N.W., Suite 615, Washington, DC 20036. Phone: (202)659-3130 Fax: (202)785-0374 E-mail: postmaster@nucea.edu • URL: http://www.nucea.edu.

CORROSION CONTROL INDUSTRY

See also: INDUSTRIAL COATINGS

ABSTRACTS AND INDEXES

Corrosion Abstracts: Abstracts of the World's Literature on Corrosion and Corrosion Mitigation.

National Association of Corrosion Engineers. Cambridge Information Group. • Bimonthly. Members, $215.00 per year; non-members, $250.00 per year. Provides abstracts of the worldwide literature of corrosion and corrosion control. Also available on CD-ROM.

DIRECTORIES

Coatings-Protective Directory. American Business Directories. • Annual. Price on application. Lists about 3,095 sources of corrosion control protective coatings. Includes number of employees and name of manager or owner.

HANDBOOKS AND MANUALS

Corrosion Control. Samuel A. Bradford. Chapman and Hall. • 1992. $80.50. Discusses basic corrosion theory, corrosion causes, coatings, plastics, metals, and many other highly detailed, technical topics. (Chapman & Hall.).

Corrosion of Stainless Steels. A. John Sedriks. John Wiley and Sons, Inc. • 1996. $86.50. Second edition. Covers the corrosion and corrosion control of stainless steels used in a variety of applications. (Corrosion Monograph Series).

Maintenance Engineering Handbook. Lindley R. Higgins. McGraw-Hill. • 1994. $125.00. Fifth edition. Contains about 60 chapters by various authors in 12 major sections covering all elements of industrial and plant maintenance.

PERIODICALS AND NEWSLETTERS

Corrosion: Journal of Science and Engineering. National Association of Corrosion Engineers. NACE International. • Monthly. Members, $95.00 per year; non-members, $160.00 per year. Covers corrosion control science, theory, engineering, and practice.

Materials Performance: Articles on Corrosion Science and Engineering Solutions for Corrosion Problems. National Association of Corrosion Engineers. NACE International. • Monthly. $100.00 per year. Covers the protection and performance of materials in corrosive environments. Includes information on new materials and industrial coatings.

RESEARCH CENTERS AND INSTITUTES

Center for Applied Thermodynamics. University of Idaho, College of Engineering, Moscow, ID 83843. Phone: (208)885-6107 Fax: (208)885-6007 E-mail: lindar@uidaho.edu • URL: http://www.calvin.engr.uidaho.edu/~cats/cats.html.

Corrosion Engineering Laboratory. Texas A & M University, Mechanical Engineering Dept. 3123, College Station, TX 77843. Phone: (409)845-9779 Fax: (409)862-2418 E-mail: rgriffin@mengr.tamu.edu • URL: http://www.mengr.tamu.edu/researchgroups/corrosion.html • Research areas include various types of corrosion, including atmospheric, seawater, and stress-related.

Corrosion Research Center. University of Minnesota, 221 Church St., S. E., Minneapolis, MN 55455. Phone: (612)625-4048 Fax: (612)626-7246 E-mail: dshores@maroon.tc.umn.edu • URL: http://www.cems.umn.edu • Research areas include the effect of corrosion on high technology materials and devices.

Fontana Corrosion Center. Ohio State University, 477 Watts, 2041 College Rd., Columbus, OH 43210. Phone: (614)688-4128 Fax: (614)292-9857 E-mail: frankel.10@osu.edu • URL: http://www.erbs1.eng.ohio-state.edu/~frankel • Research areas include metal coatings and corrosion of alloys.

TRADE/PROFESSIONAL ASSOCIATIONS

NACE International: The Corrosion Society. P.O. Box 218340, Houston, TX 77218-8340. Phone: (281)228-6223 Fax: (281)228-6300 E-mail: msd@mail.nace.org • URL: http://www.nace.org • Members are engineers, scientists, and technicians concerned with corrosion control and prevention.

National Association of Metal Finishers. 112 J Elden St., Herndon, VA 20170. Phone: (703)709-8299 Fax: (703)709-1036 E-mail: namf@erols.com • URL: http://www.namf.org • Members are management personnel of metal and plastic finishing companies. Finishing includes plating, coating, polishing, rustproofing, and other processes.

CORRUGATED PAPERBOARD

See: PAPERBOARD AND PAPERBOARD PACKAGING INDUSTRIES

COSMETICS INDUSTRY

See also: BARBER AND BEAUTY SHOPS; PERFUME INDUSTRY

GENERAL WORKS

Cosmetics: Science and Technology. M.S. Balsam and Edward Sagarin, editors. Krieger Publishing Co. • 1992. $375.00. Second edition. Three volumes. Vol. one, $135.00; vol. two, $143.50; vol. three, $163.50.

West's Textbook of Cosmetology. Jerry J. Ahern. West Publishing Co., College and School Div. • 1986. $37.00. Second edition.

CD-ROM DATABASES

World Marketing Forecasts on CD-ROM. The Gale Group. • Annual. $2,500.00. Produced by Euromonitor. Provides detailed forecast data for the years to 2012 on CD-ROM for 54 countries in all parts of the world. Covers a wide range of social, demographic, economic, and market factors. Includes specific forecasts for many kinds of consumer products.

DIRECTORIES

Household and Personal Products Industry - Buyers Guide. Rodman Publications. • Annual. $12.00. Lists of suppliers to manufacturers of cosmetics, toiletries, soaps, detergents, and related household and personal products.

Household and Personal Products Industry Contract Packaging and Private Label Directory. Rodman Publications. • Annual. $12.00. Provides information on about 450 companies offering private label or contract packaged household and personal care products, such as detergents, cosmetics, polishes, insecticides, and various aerosol items.

Who's Who: The CTFA Membership Directory (Cosmetics Industry). Cosmetic, Toiletry, and Fragrance Association. • Annual. $100.00. Lists about 1,000 member companies, with key personnel, products, and services.

World Cosmetics and Toiletries Directory. Available from The Gale Group. • 2001. $1,90.00. Second edition. Three volumes. Published by Euromonitor. Provides detailed descriptions of the world's cosmetics and toiletries companies. Includes consumers market research data.

ENCYCLOPEDIAS AND DICTIONARIES

The Consumer's Dictionary of Cosmetic Ingredients. Ruth Winter. Crown Publishers Group, Inc. • 1999. $16.00. Fifth edition.

FINANCIAL RATIOS

Annual Statement Studies. Robert Morris Associates: The Association of Lending and Credit Risk Professiona. • Annual. Free to members; non-members, $140.00. Median and quartile financial ratios are given for over 400 kinds of manufacturing, wholesale, retail, construction, and consumer finance establishments. Data is sorted by both asset size and sales volume. Includes a clearly written "Definition of Ratios" and an alphabetical industry index.

HANDBOOKS AND MANUALS

Beauty Supply Store. Entrepreneur Media, Inc. • Looseleaf. $59.50. A practical guide to starting a store for professional beauty supplies. Covers profit potential, start-up costs, market size evaluation, owner's time required, site selection, lease negotiation, pricing, accounting, advertising, promotion, etc. (Start-Up Business Guide No. E1277.).

Formulary of Cosmetic Preparations. Anthony L. Hunting, editor. Micelle Press, Inc. • 1991. $135.00. Two volumes. Volume one, *Decorative Cosmetics* $60.00; volume two *Creams, Lotions and Milks* $95.00.

Handbook of Over-the-Counter Drugs. Max Leber and others. Celestial Arts Publishing Co. • 1992. $22.95. Provides detailed, consumer information on the ingredients of nonprescription drugs and popular cosmetics.

Standard Textbook of Cosmetology: A Practical Course on the Scientific Fundamentals of Beauty Culture for Students and Practicing Cosmetologists. Constance V. Kibbe. Milady Publishing Co. • 1992. $51.95. Ninth edition. (Standard Texts of Cosmetology).

ONLINE DATABASES

Euromonitor Market Research. Euromonitor International. • Provides the complete text online of Euromonitor market analysis reports. Covers consumer goods market research data for all major countries, with emphasis on specific product categories. Time period is current. Continuous updating. Inquire as to online cost and availability.

F & S Index. The Gale Group. • Contains about four million citations to worldwide business, financial, and industrial or consumer product literature appearing from 1972 to date. Weekly updates. Inquire as to online cost and availability.

PERIODICALS AND NEWSLETTERS

Cosmetic World News: The International News Magazine of the Perfumery, Cosemetics and Toiletries Industry. World News Publications. • Bimonthly. $192.00 per year.

Cosmetics and Toiletries: The International Journal of Cosmetic Technology. Allured Publishing Corp. • Monthly. $98.00 per year.

CTFA News. Cosmetic, Toiletry, and Fragrance Association. • Bimonthly. Newsletter.

Drug Topics. Medical Economics Co., Inc. • 23 times a year. $61.00 per year. Edited for retail pharmacists, hospital pharmacists, pharmacy chain store executives, wholesalers, buyers, and others concerned with drug dispensing and drug store management. Provides information on new products, including personal care items and cosmetics.

Household and Personal Products Industry: The Magazine for the Detergent, Soap, Cosmetic and Toiletry, Wax, Polish and Aerosol Industries. Rodman Publications. • Monthly. $48.00 per year. Covers marketing, packaging, production, technical innovations, private label developments, and aerosol packaging for soap, detergents, cosmetics, insecticides, and a variety of other household products.

Soap and Cosmetics. Cygnus Business Media. • Monthly. $60.00 per year. Formerly *Soap, Cosmetics, Chemical Specialities.*

Toiletries, Fragrances, and Skin Care: The Rose Sheet. F-D-C Reports, Inc. • Weekly. $710.00 per year. Newsletter. Provides industry news, regulatory news, market data, and a "Weekly Trademark Review" for the cosmetics industry.

STATISTICS SOURCES

Consumer Canada 1996. Available from The Gale Group. • 1996. $750.00. Published by Euromonitor. Provides consumer market, socioeconomic, and demographic data for Canada. Includes consumer market size (volume and value) for many specific kinds of products.

Consumer International 2000/2001. Available from The Gale Group. • 1998. $1,190.00. Seventh edition. Published by Euromonitor. Contains extensive consumer market, economic, and demographic data for 27 major, non-European countries, including the U. S. and Canada. Includes consumer market size (volume and value) for 150 product types in 14 categories (food, clothing, automobiles, cosmetics, appliances, etc.).

European Marketing Forecasts 2001. Available from The Gale Group. • 2000. $1,190.00. Third edition. Published by Euromonitor. Contains demographic, economic, and market forecasts for the countries of Europe to the year 2010. Forecasts include market-size data for 15 consumer product sectors (food, clothing, automobiles, consumer electronics, etc.).

International Marketing Forecasts 2001. Available from The Gale Group. • 2000. $1,090.00. Third edition. Published by Euromonitor. Contains demographic, economic, and market forecasts to the year 2010 for major, non-European countries, including the U. S. and Canada. Forecasts include market-size data for 15 consumer product sectors, such as food, clothing, and automobiles.

U. S. Industry and Trade Outlook: The McGraw-Hill Companies and the U.S. Department of Commerce/ International Trade Administration. Datapso Research Corp. • Annual. $69.95. Produced by the International Trade Administration, U. S. Department of Commerce, in a "public-private" partnership with DRI/McGraw-Hill and Standard & Poor's. Provides basic data, outlook for the current year, and "Long-Term Prospects" (five-year projections) for a wide variety of products and services. Includes high technology industries. Formerly *U. S. Industrial Outlook.*

WEFA Industrial Monitor. John Wiley and Sons, Inc. • Annual. $65.00. Prepared by industry analysts at WEFA, an economic forecasting and consulting firm (originally Wharton Econometric Forecasting Associates). Contains discussions of the outlook for major U. S. industries, with many 10-year forecasts (WEFA Web site is http://www.wefa.com).

TRADE/PROFESSIONAL ASSOCIATIONS

American Association of Cosmetology Schools/ Cosmetology Educators of America. 11811 N. Tatum Blvd., Ste. 1085, Phoenix, AZ 85028-1633. Phone: 800-831-1086 or (602)788-1170 Fax: (602)404-8900 E-mail: jim@beautyschools.org • URL: http://www.beautyschools.org.

Cosmetic, Toiletry and Fragrance Association. 1101 17th St., N.W., Suite 300, Washington, DC 20036. Phone: (202)331-1770 Fax: (202)331-1969 • URL: http://www.ctfa.org/.

National Beauty Culturists' League. 25 Logan Circle, N.W., Washington, DC 20005. Phone: (202)332-2695 Fax: (202)332-0940.

National Cosmetology Association. 401 N. Michigan Ave., Chicago, IL 60611-4255. Phone: 800-527-1683 E-mail: ncal@sba.com • URL: http:// www.nca-now.com.

National Interstate Council of State Boards of Cosmetology. Capitol Station, P.O. Box 11390, Columbia, SC 29211. Phone: (803)799-9800 Fax: (803)376-2277.

Society of Cosmetic Chemists. 120 Wall St., Suite 2400, New York, NY 10005. Phone: (212)668-1500 Fax: (212)668-1504.

OTHER SOURCES

Food Law Reports. CCH, Inc. • Weekly. $1,349.00 per year. Six looseleaf volumes. Covers regulation of adulteration, packaging, labeling, and additives. Formerly *Food Drug Cosmetic Law Reports.*

The Suncare Products Market. Available from MarketResearch.com. • 1996. $1,230.00. Published by Packaged Facts. Provides market data on sun screen lotions, after-sun products, and sunless tanning cosmetics, with sales projections.

The U.S. Skincare Market. Available from MarketResearch.com. • 1999. $2,750.00. Published by Packaged Facts. Provides market data on skincare products such as moisturizers, cleansers, and toners, with sales projections to 2003.

COST ACCOUNTING

See also: ACCOUNTING; COST CONTROL

GENERAL WORKS

Cost Accounting. Prentice Hall. • 1999. $105.00. 10th edition.

Cost Accounting: Managerial Emphasis. Prentice Hall. • 2000. 10th edition. Price on application.

ABSTRACTS AND INDEXES

Accounting Articles. CCH, Inc. • Monthly. $594.00 per year. Looseleaf service.

Business Periodicals Index. H. W. Wilson Co. • Monthly, except August, with quarterly and annual cumulations. Service basis for print edition; CD-ROM edition, $1,495.00 per year.

ENCYCLOPEDIAS AND DICTIONARIES

Blackwell Encyclopedic Dictionary of Accounting. Rashad Abdel-khalik. Blackwell Publishers. • 1997. $105.95. The editor is associated with the University of Florida. Contains definitions of key terms combined with longer articles written by various U. S. and foreign business educators. Includes bibliographies and index. (Blackwell Encyclopedia of Management Series).

Dictionary of Accounting Terms. Joel G. Siegel and Jae K. Shim. Barron's Educational Series, Inc. • 1995. $11.95. Second edition.

International Dictionary of Accounting Acronyms. Thomas W. Morris, editor. Fitzroy Dearborn Publishers. • 1999. $45.00. Defines 2,000 acronyms used in worldwide accounting and finance.

FINANCIAL RATIOS

Income and Fees of Accountants in Public Practice. National Society of Accountants. • Triennial. Members, $35.00; non-members, $50.00.

HANDBOOKS AND MANUALS

Accountants' Handbook. Douglas R. Carmichael and others, editors. John Wiley and Sons, Inc. • 1999. $135.00. Ninth edition. Chapters are written by various accounting and auditing specialists.

Cost Accounting Standards Board Regulations. CCH, Inc. • 1999. $24.00. Covers Federal Acquisition Regulation (FAR) cost accounting standards for both defense and civilian government contracts. Provides the rules for estimating and reporting costs for contracts of more than $500,000.

Handbook of Cost Accounting. Sidney Davidson and Roman L. Weil. Simon and Schuster Trade. • 1999. $79.95.

Handbook of Cost Accounting Theory and Techniques. Ahmed Righi-Belkaoui. Greenwood Publishing Group, Inc. • 1991. $89.50.

INTERNET DATABASES

Rutgers Accounting Web (RAW). Rutgers University Accounting Research Center. Phone: (201)648-5172 Fax: (201)648-1233 • URL: http://www.rutgers.edu/ accounting • RAW Web site provides extensive links to sources of national and international accounting information, such as the Big Six accounting firms, the Financial Accounting Standards Board (FASB), SEC filings (EDGAR), journals, publishers, software, the International Accounting Network, and "Internet's largest list of accounting firms in USA." Searching is offered. Fees: Free.

ONLINE DATABASES

ABI/INFORM. Bell & Howell Information and Learning. • Provides online indexing to business-related material occurring in over 1,000 periodicals from 1971 to the present. Inquire as to online cost and availability.

Wilson Business Abstracts Online. H. W. Wilson Co. • Indexes and abstracts 600 major business periodicals, plus the *Wall Street Journal* and the business section of the *New York Times.* Indexing is from 1982, abstracting from 1990, with the two newspapers included from 1993. Updated weekly. Inquire as to online cost and availability. (*Business Periodicals Index* without abstracts is also available online.).

PERIODICALS AND NEWSLETTERS

Journal of Bank Cost and Management Accounting. Association for Management Information in Financial Services. • Three times a year. $100.00 per year.

Management for Strategic Business Ideas. Society of Management Accountants of Canada. • 10 times a year. $60.00 per year. Text in English and French.

TRADE/PROFESSIONAL ASSOCIATIONS

American Institute of Certified Public Accountants. 1211 Ave. of the Americas, New York, NY 10036-8775. Phone: 800-862-4272 or (212)596-6200 Fax: (212)596-6213 • URL: http://www.aicpa.org.

Association for Management Information in Financial Services. 7950 E. La Junta Rd., Scottsdale, AZ 85255-2798. Phone: (602)515-2160 Fax: (602)515-2101 E-mail: ami@amifs.org • URL: http:/ /www.amifs.org • Members are financial institution employees interested in management accounting and cost analysis.

Institute of Internal Auditors. 249 Maitland Ave., Altamonte Springs, FL 32701-4201. Phone: (407)830-7600 Fax: (407)831-5171 E-mail: iia@ theiia.org • URL: http://www.theiia.org.

Institute of Management Accountants. 10 Paragon Dr., Montvale, NJ 07645. Phone: 800-638-4427 or (201)573-9000 Fax: (201)573-8483 E-mail: info@ imanet.org • URL: http://www.imanet.org.

OTHER SOURCES

Cost Accounting Standards Guide. CCH, Inc. • Monthly. $350.00 per year. Looseleaf serivce. Periodic supplementation.

COST CONTROL

See also: COST ACCOUNTING

GENERAL WORKS

Controllership: The Work of the Managerial Accountant. James D. Wilson and others. John Wiley and Sons, Inc. • 1999. $170.00. Sixth edition. 2000 Supplement, $60.00.

Cost Estimating. Rodney D. Stewart. John Wiley and Sons, Inc. • 1991. $130.00. Second edition. Discusses high technology engineering cost forecasting, including the estimation of software costs.

DIRECTORIES

AACE International-Directory of Members. AACE International. • Annual. $10.00 per year. 6,000 cost engineers, estimators, and cost management professionals worldwide.

ENCYCLOPEDIAS AND DICTIONARIES

Blackwell Encyclopedic Dictionary of Operations Management. Nigel Slack, editor. Blackwell Publishers. • 1997. $105.95. The editor is associated with the University of Warwick, England. Contains definitions of key terms combined with longer articles written by various U. S. and foreign business educators. Includes bibliographies and index. (Blackwell Encyclopedia of Management Series.).

HANDBOOKS AND MANUALS

Cost Control Handbook. R. M. Wilson. Ashgate Publishing Co. • 1983. $102.95. Second edition.

Cost Management Handbook. Barry J. Brinker. John Wiley and Sons, Inc. • 2000. $140.00.

PERIODICALS AND NEWSLETTERS

Cost Control Strategies for Managers, Controllers and Finance Executives. Siefer Consultants, Inc. • Monthly. $259.00 per year. Newsletter. Provides a variety of ideas on business budgeting and controlling company expenses. Formerly *Cost Control Strategies for Financial Institutions.*

Cost Engineering: The Journal of Cost Estimating, Cost Control, and Project Management. American Association of Cost Engineers. • Monthly. $57.00 per year. Subjects include cost estimation and cost control.

IT Cost Management Strategies: The Planning Assistant for IT Directors. Computer Economics, Inc. • Monthly. $495.00 per year. Newsletter for information technology professionals. Covers data processing costs, budgeting, financial management, and related topics.

Journal of Cost Management. Warren, Gorham and Lamont/RIA Group. • Bimonthly. $123.98 per year. Includes articles on business budgeting.

Strategic Finance. Institute of Management Accountants. • Monthly. $140.00 per year; non-profit institutions, $70.00 per year. Provides articles on corporate finance, cost control, cash flow, budgeting, corporate taxes, and other financial management topics.

OTHER SOURCES

AACE International. Transactions of the Annual Meetings. American Association of Cost Engineers. AACE International. • Annual. Price varies. Contains texts of papers presented at AACE meetings.

COST OF LIVING INDEXES

See: CONSUMER PRICE INDEXES

COSTUME JEWELRY

See: JEWELRY BUSINESS

COTTON INDUSTRY

See also: TEXTILE INDUSTRY

GENERAL WORKS

Cotton Production Prospects for the Decade to 2002: A Global Review. Hamdy M. Eisa and others. World Bank, The Office of the Publisher. • 1994. $22.00. Provides information on cotton's key technologies, marketing, consumption, production trends, and price prospects. (Technical Paper Series, No. 231).

ABSTRACTS AND INDEXES

Textile Technology Digest. Institute of Textile Technology. • Monthly. $535.00 per year. Provides indexing and abstracting of a wide variety of textile technology literature.

CD-ROM DATABASES

Textile Technology Digest [CD-ROM]. Textile Information Center, Institute of Textile Technology. • Quarterly. $1,700.00 per year. Provides CD-ROM indexing and abstracting of worldwide journals and monographs in various areas of textile technology, production, and management. Covers 1978 to date.

DIRECTORIES

Cotton International. Meister Publishing Co. • Annual. $30.00.

Davison's Textile Blue Book. Davison Publishing Co. • Annual. $165.00. Over 8,400 companies in the textile industry in the United States, Canada, and Mexico, including about 4,400 textile plants.

ENCYCLOPEDIAS AND DICTIONARIES

Encyclopedia of Textiles. French and European Publications, Inc. • 1980. $39.95. Third edition.

Textile Terms and Definitions. J.E. McIntyre and Paul N. Daniels, editors. Available from State Mutual Book and Periodical Service Ltd., Trade Order Dept. • 1995. $110.00. 10th edition. Published by the Textile Insitute (UK). Includes more than 1,000 definitions of textile processes, fiber types, and end products. Illustrated.

INTERNET DATABASES

Fedstats. Federal Interagency Council on Statistical Policy. Phone: (202)395-7254 • URL: http://www.fedstats.gov • Web site features an efficient search facility for full-text statistics produced by more than 70 federal agencies, including the Census Bureau, the Bureau of Economic Analysis, and the Bureau of Labor Statistics. Boolean searches can be made within one agency or for all agencies combined. Links are offered to international statistical bureaus, including the UN, IMF, OECD, UNESCO, Eurostat, and 20 individual countries. Fees: Free.

USDA. United States Department of Agriculture. Phone: (202)720-2791 E-mail: agsec@usda.gov • URL: http://www.usda.gov • The USDA home page has six sections: News and Information; What's New; About USDA; Agencies; Opportunities; Search and Help. Keyword searching is offered from the USDA home page and from various individual agency home pages. Agencies are the Economic Research Service, Agricultural Marketing Service, National Agricultural Statistics Service, National Agricultural Library, and about 12 others. Updating varies. Fees: Free.

ONLINE DATABASES

DRI U.S. Central Database. Data Products Division. • Provides more than 23,000 business, financial, demographic, economic, foreign trade, and industry-related time series for the U.S. Includes national income, population, retail-wholesale trade, price indexes, labor data, housing, industrial production, banking, interest rates, money supply, etc. Time period is generally 1947 to date (some data back to 1929). Updating varies. Inquire as to online cost and availability.

Textile Technology Digest [online]. Textile Information Center, Institute of Textile Technology. • Contains indexing and abstracting of more than 300 worldwide journals and monographs in various areas of textile technology, production, and management. Time period is 1978 to date, with monthly updating. Inquire as to online cost and availability.

World Textiles. Elsevier Science, Inc. • Provides abstracting and indexing from 1970 of worldwide textile literature (periodicals, books, pamphlets, and reports). Includes U. S., European, and British patent information. Updating is monthly. Inquire as to online cost and availability.

PERIODICALS AND NEWSLETTERS

Barron's: The Dow Jones Business and Financial Weekly. Dow Jones and Co., Inc. • Weekly. $145.00 per year.

Cotton Digest International. Cotton Digest Co., Inc. • Monthly. $40.00 per year. Formerly *Cotton Digest.*

Cotton Farming. Vance Publishing Corp. • Nine times a year. $35.00 per year.

Cotton Grower. Meister Publishing Co. • 10 times a year. $32.10 per year.

Cotton: Review of the World Situation. International Cotton Advisory Committee. • Bimonthly. $135.00 per year. Monthly updates available by fax. Editions in English, French, and Spanish.

Cotton's Week. National Cotton Council of America. • Weekly. Free to members; non-members, $250.00 per year. Newsletter.

PRICE SOURCES

Cotton Price Statistics. U.S. Department of Agriculture. • Monthly.

The New York Times. New York Times Co. • Daily. $374.40 per year. Supplements available: *New York Times Book Review, New York Times Magazine, Sophisticated Traveler* and *Fashions of the Times.*

Weekly Cotton Trade Report. New York Cotton Exchange. • Weekly. $100.00 per year.

RESEARCH CENTERS AND INSTITUTES

Institute of Textile Technology. 2551 Ivy Rd., Charlottesville, VA 22903-4614. Phone: (804)296-5511 Fax: (804)296-2957 E-mail: library@itt.edu • URL: http://www.itt.edu.

Tropical Research and Education Center. University of Florida, 18905 S.W. 280th St., Homestead, FL 33031. Phone: (305)246-6340 Fax: (305)246-7003 E-mail: hom@gnv.ifas.ufl.edu • URL: http://www.ifas.ufl.edu/~trecweb.

STATISTICS SOURCES

Agricultural Statistics. Available from U. S. Government Printing Office. • Annual. Produced by the National Agricultural Statistics Service, U. S. Department of Agriculture. Provides a wide variety of statistical data relating to agricultural production, supplies, consumption, prices/price-supports, foreign trade, costs, and returns, as well as farm labor, loans, income, and population. In many cases, historical data is shown annually for 10 years. In addition to farm data, includes detailed fishery statistics.

Annual Survey of Manufactures. Available from U. S. Government Printing Office. • Annual. Prices vary. Issued by the U. S. Census Bureau as an interim update to the *Census of Manufactures.* Includes data on number of manufacturing establishments in various industries, employment, labor costs, value of shipments, capital expenditures, inventories, energy costs, and assets. (See also Census Bureau home page, http://www.census.gov/.).

Business Statistics of the United States. Courtenay M. Slater, editor. Bernan Associates. • 1999. $74.00. Fifth edition. Based on *Business Statistics*, formerly issue by the Bureau of Economic Analysis, U. S. Department of Commerce. Provides basic data for a wide variety of U. S. industries, services, and economic indicators. Most statistics are shown annually for 29 years and monthly for the most recent four years.

International Textile Machinery Shipment Statistics. International Textile Manufacturers Federation. •

Annual. 250 Swiss francs. Formerly *International Cotton Industry Statistics*.

Manufacturing Profiles. Available from U. S. Government Printing Office. • Annual. Issued by the U. S. Census Bureau. A printed consolidation of the entire *Current Industrial Report* series, presenting "all the data compiled." Contains statistics on production, shipments, inventories, consumption, exports, imports, and orders for a wide variety of manufactured products. (See also Census Bureau home page, http://www.census.gov/.).

Quality of Cotton Report. Agricultural Marketing Service. U.S. Department of Agriculture. • Weekly.

Survey of Current Business. Available from U. S. Government Printing Office. • Monthly. $49.00 per year. Issued by Bureau of Economic Analysis, U. S. Department of Commerce. Presents a wide variety of business and economic data.

United States Census of Agriculture. U.S. Bureau of the Census. • Quinquennial. Results presented in reports, tape, CD-ROM, and Diskette files.

WEFA Industrial Monitor. John Wiley and Sons, Inc. • Annual. $65.00. Prepared by industry analysts at WEFA, an economic forecasting and consulting firm (originally Wharton Econometric Forecasting Associates). Contains discussions of the outlook for major U. S. industries, with many 10-year forecasts (WEFA Web site is http://www.wefa.com).

TRADE/PROFESSIONAL ASSOCIATIONS

American Cotton Shippers Association. P.O. Box 3366, Memphis, TN 38173. Phone: (901)525-2272 Fax: (901)527-8303 • URL: http://www.acsa-cotton.org.

American Textile Manufacturers Institute. 1130 Connecticut Ave., N.W., Ste. 1200, Washington, DC 20036. Phone: (202)862-0500 Fax: (202)862-0570 • URL: http://www.atmi.org.

Cotton Council International. 1521 New Hampshire Ave., N.W., Washington, DC 20036. Phone: (202)745-7805 Fax: (202)483-4040 E-mail: cottonusa@cotton.org • URL: http://www.cottonusa.org.

Cotton Incorporated. 1370 Ave. of the Americas, 34th Fl., New York, NY 10019. Phone: (212)586-1070 Fax: (212)265-5386.

National Cotton Council of America. P.O. Box 820285, Memphis, TN 38182-0285. Phone: (901)274-9030 Fax: (901)725-0510 E-mail: info@cotton.org • URL: http://www.cotton.org/ncc.

Textile Institute. Saint James Bldgs., 4th Fl., Oxford St., Manchester M1 6FQ, England. Phone: 44 161 2371188 Fax: 44 161 2361991 E-mail: tiihq@textileinst.org.uk • URL: http://www.texi.org • Members in 100 countries involved with textile industry management, marketing, science, and technology.

OTHER SOURCES

Cotton: Origin, History, Technology, and Production. C. Wayne Smith and J. Tom Cothren, editors. John Wiley and Sons, Inc. • 1999. $250.00. (Wiley Series in Crop Science.).

Textile Business Outlook. Statistikon Corp. • Quarterly. $985.00 per year. Analyzes current business, marketing, and financial conditions for the worldwide textile industry (fibers and fabrics). Includes statistical forecasts.

COTTON TEXTILE INDUSTRY

See: TEXTILE INDUSTRY

COTTONSEED OIL INDUSTRY

See: OIL AND FATS INDUSTRY

COUNCIL MANAGER PLAN

See: MUNICIPAL GOVERNMENT

COUNSELING

See also: PERSONNEL MANAGEMENT; VOCATIONAL GUIDANCE

GENERAL WORKS

The Helping Relationship: Process and Skills. Lawrence M. Brammer and Ginger A. MacDonald. Allyn and Bacon, Inc. • 1998. $46.00. Seventh edition.

Is It Too Late to Run Away and Join the Circus? Finding the Life You Really Want. Marti Smye. Simon and Schuster Trade. • 1998. $14.95. Provides philosophical and inspirational advice on leaving corporate life and becoming self-employed as a consultant or whatever. Central theme is dealing with major changes in life style and career objectives. (Macmillan Business Book.).

ABSTRACTS AND INDEXES

Psychological Abstracts. American Psychological Association. • Monthly. Members, $799.00 per year; individuals and institutions, $1,075.00 per year. Covers the international literature of psychology and the behavioral sciences. Includes journals, technical reports, dissertations, and other sources.

DIRECTORIES

Directory of Counseling Services. International Association of Counseling Services. • Annual. $50.00. About 200 accredited services in the United States and Canada concerned with psychological educational, and vocational counseling, including those at colleges and universities and public and private agencies.

ENCYCLOPEDIAS AND DICTIONARIES

Blackwell Encyclopedic Dictionary of Human Resource Management. Lawrence H. Peters and Charles R. Greer, editors. Blackwell Publishers. • 1996. $105.95. The editors are associated with Texas Christian University. Contains definitions of key terms combined with longer articles written by various U. S. and foreign business educators. Includes bibliographies and index. (Blackwell Encyclopedia of Management Series).

HANDBOOKS AND MANUALS

Introduction to the Counseling Profession. Dave Capuzzi and Douglas Gross. Allyn and Bacon, Inc. • 2000. $73.00. Third edition.

On Becoming a Counselor: A Basic Guide for Non-Professional Counselors. Eugene Kennedy and Sara Charles. Crossroad Publishing Co. • 1989. $19.95.

Sexual Orientation in the Workplace: Gays, Lesbians, Bisexuals and Heterosexuals Working Together. Amy J. Zuckerman and George F. Simons. Sage Publications, Inc. • 1996. $18.95. A workbook containing "a variety of simple tools and exercises" to provide skills for "working realistically and effectively with diverse colleagues.".

ONLINE DATABASES

PsycINFO. American Psychological Association. • Provides indexing and abstracting of the worldwide literature of psychology and the behavioral sciences. Time period is 1967 to date, with monthly updates. Inquire as to online cost and availability.

PERIODICALS AND NEWSLETTERS

Counseling and Values. Association for Religious and Value Issues in Counseling. American Counseling Association. • Three times a year. Individuals, $18.00 per year; institutions, $29.00 per year.

The Counseling Psychologist. American Psychological Association. Sage Publications, Inc. • Bimonthly. Individuals, $75.00 per year; institutions, $395.00 per year.

Counseling Services: IACS Newsletter. International Association of Counseling Services. • Three times a year. Membership.

Employee Assistance Quarterly. Haworth Press, Inc. • Quarterly. Individuals, $40.00 per year; institutions. $80.00 per year; libraries, $375.00 per year. An academic and practical journal focusing on employee alcoholism and mental health problems. Formerly *Labor-Management Alcoholism Journal*.

Journal of Counseling Psychology. American Psychological Association. • Quarterly. Members, $38.00 per year; non-members, $76.00 per year; institutions, $164.00 per year.

Journal of Mental Health Counseling. American Counseling Association. • Quarterly.$131.00 per year. The official journal of the American Mental Health Counselors Association.

Professional Counselor Magazine: Serving the Mental Health and Addictions Fields. Health Communications, Inc. • Bimonthly. $26.00 per year. Covers both clinical and societal aspects of substance abuse.

RESEARCH CENTERS AND INSTITUTES

Bureau of Educational Research and Evaluation. Mississippi State University. P.O. Box 9710, Mississippi State, MS 39762. Phone: (662)325-3717 Fax: (662)325-8784 E-mail: jmw50@ra.msstate.edu • URL: http://www.msstate.edu.

TRADE/PROFESSIONAL ASSOCIATIONS

American Counseling Association. 5999 Stevenson Ave., Alexandria, VA 22304-3300. Phone: 800-347-6647 or (703)823-9800 Fax: (703)823-0252 • URL: http://www.counseling.org.

American Mental Health Counselors Association. 801 N. Fairfax St. Suite 304, Alexandria, VA 22314. Phone: 800-326-2642 or (703)548-6002 Fax: (703)548-5233 • URL: http://www.amhca.org.

American Rehabilitation Counseling Association. c/o American Counseling Association, 5999 Stevenson Ave., Alexandria, VA 22304. Phone: 800-347-6647 or (703)823-9800 Fax: (703)823-0252.

Association of Career Management Consulting Firms International. 204 E. St., N.E., Washington, DC 20002. Phone: (202)857-1185 Fax: (202)547-6348 • URL: http://www.aocfi.org • Promotes professional standards of competence, objectivity, and integrity in the service of clients.

International Association of Counseling Services. 101 S. Whiting St., Suite 211, Alexandria, VA 22304. Phone: (703)823-9840 Fax: (703)823-9843 E-mail: iacs@gmu.edu.

National Institute of Management Counsellors. P.O. Box 193, Great Neck, NY 11022. Phone: (516)482-5683.

COUNTERFEITING

See also: CRIME AND CRIMINALS; FORGERIES

GENERAL WORKS

Becker the Counterfeiter. G. F. Hill. Obol International. • 1979. $20.00.

HANDBOOKS AND MANUALS
Counterfeiting and Forgery: A Practical Guide to the Law. Roland Rowell. LEXIS Publishing. • 1986. $100.00.

COUNTERTRADE

See: BARTER AND COUNTERTRADE

COUNTRY CLUBS

See: CLUBS

COUNTY FINANCE

See also: PUBLIC FINANCE

DIRECTORIES
Moody's Municipal and Government Manual. Financial Information Services. • Annual. $2,495.00 per year. Updated biweekly in *News Reports.*

RESEARCH CENTERS AND INSTITUTES
Institute for Tax Administration. Academy for International Training. 900 Wilshire Blvd., Suite 624, Los Angeles, CA 90017. Phone: (213)623-1103 Fax: (213)623-7012.

STATISTICS SOURCES
Facts and Figures on Government Finance. Tax Foundation, Inc. • Annual. $60.00.

United States Census of Governments. Bureau of the Census, U.S. Department of Commerce. Available from U.S. Government Printing Office. • Quinquennial.

TRADE/PROFESSIONAL ASSOCIATIONS
Association of Government Accountants. 2208 Mount Vernon Ave., Alexandria, VA 22301-1314. Phone: 800-242-7211 or (703)684-6931 Fax: (703)548-9367 • URL: http://www.agacgfm.org • Members are employed by federal, state, county, and city government agencies. Includes accountants, auditors, budget officers, and other government finance administrators and officials.

National Association of County Treasurers and Finance Officers. c/o National Association of Counties, 440 First St., N.W., 8th Fl., Washington, DC 20001. Phone: (202)393-6226 Fax: (202)393-2630.

COUNTY GOVERNMENT

See also: MUNICIPAL GOVERNMENT

BIOGRAPHICAL SOURCES
Who's Who in American Politics. Marquis Who's Who. • Biennial. $275.00. Two volumes. Contains about 27,000 biographical sketches of local, state, and national elected or appointed individuals.

DIRECTORIES
Carroll's County Directory. Carroll Publishing. • Semiannual. $255.00 per year. Lists about 42,000 officials in 3,100 U. S. counties, with expanded listings for counties having a population of over 50,000. Includes state maps.

Carroll's Municipal/County Directory: CD-ROM Edition. Carroll Publishing. • Semiannual. $750.00 per year. Provides CD-ROM listings of about 99,000 city, town, and county officials in the U. S. Also available online.

Directory of Regional Councils. National Association of Regional Councils. • Annual. $100.00. Lists about 535 regional councils within U.S., including contacts and counties they serve. Formerly *National Association of Regional Councils-Directory of Regional Councils.*

Government Phone Book USA: Your Comprehensive Guide to Federal, State, County, and Local Government Offices in the United States. Omnigraphics, Inc. • Annual. $230.00. Contains more than 168,500 listings of federal, state, county, and local government offices and personnel, including legislatures. Formerly *Government Directory of Addresses and Phone Numbers.*

Municipal Yellow Book: Who's Who in the Leading City and County Governments and Local Authorities. Leadership Directories, Inc. • Semiannual. $235.00 per year. Lists approximately 32,000 key personnel in city and county departments, agencies, subdivisions, and branches.

PERIODICALS AND NEWSLETTERS
County News. National Association of Counties.

Governing: The States and Localities. • Monthly. $39.95 per year. Edited for state and local government officials. Covers finance, office management, computers, telecommunications, environmental concerns, etc.

Public Risk. Public Risk Management Association. • 10 times a year. $125.00 per year. Covers risk management for state and local governments, including various kinds of liabilities.

RESEARCH CENTERS AND INSTITUTES
Citizens League Research Institute. 50 Public Square, Terminal Tower, No. 843, Cleveland, OH 44113-2284. Phone: (216)241-5340 Fax: (216)736-7626 E-mail: staff@citizensleague.org • URL: http://www.citizensleague.org.

Urban Institute. 2100 M St., N. W., Washington, DC 20037. Phone: (202)833-7200 Fax: (202)728-0232 E-mail: paffairs@ui.urban.org • URL: http://www.urban.org • Research activities include the study of urban economic affairs, development, housing, productivity, and municipal finance.

STATISTICS SOURCES
County and City Data Book, a Statistical Abstract Supplement. U.S. Bureau of the Census. Available from U.S. Government Printing Office. • 1994. $60.00.

United States Census of Governments. Bureau of the Census, U.S. Department of Commerce. Available from U.S. Government Printing Office. • Quinquennial.

TRADE/PROFESSIONAL ASSOCIATIONS
National Association of Counties. 440 First St., N.W., 8th Fl., Washington, DC 20001. Phone: (202)393-6226 Fax: (202)393-2630.

National Association of County Administrators. P.O. Box 34435, Bethesda, MD 20827. Phone: (301)469-7460 Fax: (301)365-0598 E-mail: nacaexec@aol.com • URL: http://ww.naco.org.

National Association of County Planners. c/o National Association of Counties, 440 First St., N.W., 8th Fl., Washington, DC 20001. Phone: (202)393-6226 Fax: (202)393-2630.

Public Risk Management Association. 1815 N. Fort Meyer Dr., Ste. 1020, Arlington, VA 22209-1805. Phone: (703)528-7701 Fax: (703)528-7966 E-mail: info@primacentral.org • URL: http://www.primacentral.org • Members are state and local government officials concerned with risk management and public liabilities.

OTHER SOURCES
Local Government Law. Chester J. Antieau. Matthew Bender & Co., Inc. • $1,070.00. Seven looseleaf volumes. Periodic supplementation. States the principle of law for all types of local governments, and backs those principles with case citations from all jurisdictions. Examines the laws and their impact in three primary cases.

COUNTY OFFICIALS

See: COUNTY GOVERNMENT

COUNTY PLANNING

See: REGIONAL PLANNING

COUPONS AND REFUNDS

ABSTRACTS AND INDEXES
Business Periodicals Index. H. W. Wilson Co. • Monthly, except August, with quarterly and annual cumulations. Service basis for print edition; CD-ROM edition, $1,495.00 per year.

CD-ROM DATABASES
WILSONDISC: Wilson Business Abstracts. H. W. Wilson Co. • Monthly. $2,495.00 per year, including unlimited online access to *Wilson Business Abstracts* through WILSONLINE. Provides CD-ROM "cover-to-cover" abstracting and indexing of over 600 prominent business periodicals. Indexing is from 1982, abstracting from 1990. (*Business Periodicals Index* without abstracts is available on CD-ROM at $1,495 per year.).

DIRECTORIES
The PROMO 100 Promotion Agency Ranking. Intertec Publishing Co. • Annual. $9.95. Provides information on 100 leading product promotion agencies.

HANDBOOKS AND MANUALS
Coupon Mailer Service. Entrepreneur Media, Inc. • Looseleaf. $59.50. A practical guide to starting a service for mailing business promotion discount coupons to consumers. Covers profit potential, start-up costs, market size evaluation, owner's time required, pricing, accounting, advertising, promotion, etc. (Start-Up Business Guide No. E1232.).

ONLINE DATABASES
Wilson Business Abstracts Online. H. W. Wilson Co. • Indexes and abstracts 600 major business periodicals, plus the *Wall Street Journal* and the business section of the *New York Times.* Indexing is from 1982, abstracting from 1990, with the two newspapers included from 1993. Updated weekly. Inquire as to online cost and availability. (*Business Periodicals Index* without abstracts is also available online.).

PERIODICALS AND NEWSLETTERS
Moneytalk. Moneytalk, Inc. • Monthly. $22.00 per year. Newsletter for consumers on how to save money through the use of manufacturers' coupons and refund offers.

PROMO: Promotion Marketing Worldwide. Simba Information Inc. • Monthly. $65.00 per year. Edited for companies and agencies that utilize couponing, point-of-purchase advertising, special events, games, contests, premiums, product samples, and other unique promotional items.

Refundable Bundle. • Bimonthly. $10.00 per year. Newsletter for grocery shoppers. Each issue provides details of new coupon and refund offers.

COURTS

See also: LAW; LAWS; LAWYERS

GENERAL WORKS
Courts, Judges and Politics: An Introduction to the Judicial Process. Walter Murphy and Charles H. Pritchett. McGraw-Hill. • 1986. $56.88. Fourth edition.

Government by Judiciary: The Transformation of the Fourteenth Amendment. Raoul Berger. Liberty Fund, Inc. • 1997. $19.50. Second revised edition.

ABSTRACTS AND INDEXES

Current Law Index: Multiple Access to Legal Periodicals. The Gale Group. • Monthly. $650.00 per year. Produced in cooperation with the American Association of Law Libraries. Indexes more than 900 law journals, legal newspapers, and specialty publications from the U.S., Canada, U.K., Ireland, Australia, and New Zealand.

Index to Legal Periodicals and Books. H. W. Wilson Co. • Monthly. Quarterly and annual cumulations. $270.00 per year. CD-ROM version available at $1,495.00 per year.

ALMANACS AND YEARBOOKS

American Law Yearbook. The Gale Group. • Annual. $155.00. Serves as a yearly supplement to *West's Encyclopedia of American Law.* Describes new legal developments in many subject areas.

BIBLIOGRAPHIES

Criminal Justice Information: How to Find It, How to Use It. Dennis C. Benamati and others. Oryx Press. • 1997. $59.95. A guide to print, electronic, and online criminal justice information resources. Includes statistical reports, directories, periodicals, monographs, databases, and other sources.

BIOGRAPHICAL SOURCES

Who's Who in American Law. Marquis Who's Who. • Biennial. $285.00. Contains over 22,000 concise biographies of American lawyers, judges, and others in the legal field.

CD-ROM DATABASES

Leadership Library on CD-ROM: Who's Who in the Leadership of the United States. Leadership Directories, Inc. • Quarterly. $2,641.00 per year, including access to Internet version (weekly updates). Contains all 14 *Yellow Book* personnel directories on CD-ROM, providing contact and brief biographical information for about 400,000 individuals. Covers business, government, financial institutions, news media, law firms, associations, foreign representatives, and nonprofit organizations. Includes photographs.

Staff Directories on CD-ROM. CQ Staff Directories, Inc. • Three times a year. $495.00 per year. Provides the contents on CD-ROM of *Congressional Staff Directory, Federal Staff Directory,* and *Judicial Staff Directory.* Includes photographs and maps.

WILSONDISC: Index to Legal Periodicals and Books. H. W. Wilson Co. • Monthly. Including unlimited online access to *Index to Legal Periodicals* through WILSONLINE. Contains CD-ROM indexing of more than 800 English language legal periodicals from 1981 to date and 2,500 books.

DIRECTORIES

Almanac of the Federal Judiciary. Publishers, Inc. • Annual. $295.00 per set. Two volumes. Volume one provides information on federal district judges; volume two relates to federal circuit judges.

American Bench: Judges of the Nation. Forster-Long, Inc. • Annual. $360.00. Features biographies of 18,000 members of the U.S. Judiciary at federal, state and local levels.

Carroll's Federal & Federal Regional Directory: CD-ROM Edition. Carroll Publishing. • Bimonthly. $800.00 per year. Provides CD-ROM listings of more than 120,000 (55,000 high-level and 65,000 mid-level) U. S. government officials in Washington and throughout the country, including in military installations. Also available online.

Carroll's Federal Directory. Carroll Publishing. • Bimonthly. $325.00 per year. Lists 40,000 key U. S. officials, including members of Congress, Cabinet members, federal judges, Executive Office of the President personnel, and a wide variety of administrators.

Judicial Staff Directory: With Biographical Information on Judges and Key Court Staff. CQ Staff Directories, Inc. • Annual. $89.00 per no. Lists 16,000 federal court personnel, including 1,300 federal judges and their staffs, with biographies of judges and key executives. Includes maps of court jurisdictions.

Judicial Yellow Book: Who's Who in Federal and State Courts. Leadership Directories, Inc. • Semiannual. $235.00 per year. Lists more than 3,200 judges and staffs in various federal courts and 1,200 judges and staffs in state courts. Includes biographical profiles of judges.

Want's Federal-State Court Directory. Want Publishing Co. • Annual. $35.00. All federal court judges and clerks of court, and United States attorneys and magistrates, judges; state supreme court justices and State court administrators; Supreme Court Chief Justices of Canada and other nations.

ENCYCLOPEDIAS AND DICTIONARIES

Encyclopedia of Crime and Justice. Available from The Gale Group. • 2001. $425.00. Second edition. Four volumes. Published by Macmillan Reference USA. Contains extensive information on a wide variety of topics pertaining to crime, criminology, social issues, and the courts. (A revision of 1982 edition.).

West's Encyclopedia of American Law. Available from The Gale Group. • 1997. $995.00. Second edition. 12 volumes. Published by West Group. Covers a wide variety of legal topics for the general reader. Formerly *Guide to American Law: Everyone's Legal Encyclopedia* (1985).

ONLINE DATABASES

Auto-Cite. West Group. • Provides information concerning federal and state case law, administrative decisions, and taxation. Daily updates. Inquire as to online cost and availability.

Index to Legal Periodicals and Books (Online). H. W. Wilson Co. • Broad coverage of law journals and books 1981 to date. Monthly updates. Inquire as to online cost and availability.

LEXIS. LEXIS-NEXIS. • The various LEXIS databases provide full text and indexing for a wide variety of legal cases, statutes, orders, and opinions.

PERIODICALS AND NEWSLETTERS

Center Court. National Center for State Courts. • Quarterly. Free. Formerly *State Court Report.*

Court Review. American Judges Association. National Center for State Courts. • Quarterly. Free to members; non-members, $25.00 per year.

Family Court Review. Association of Family and Conciliation Courts. Sage Publications, Inc. • Quarterly. $230.00 per year.

Judges' Journal. American Bar Association, Judicial Administration Div. • Quarterly. Free to members; non-members, $25.00 per year. Focuses on the court.

U. S. Supreme Court Bulletin. CCH, Inc. • Monthly and on each decision day while the Court is in session.

United States Law Week: A National Survey of Current Law. Bureau of National Affairs, Inc. • Weekly. $989.00 per year. Covers U.S. Supreme Court proceedings and gives full text of decisions. Also provides detailed reports on important legislative and regulatory actions.

RESEARCH CENTERS AND INSTITUTES

Lexis.com Research System. Lexis-Nexis Group. Phone: 800-227-9597 or (937)865-6800 Fax: (937)865-6909 E-mail: webmaster@prod.lexis-nexis.com • URL: http://www.lexis.com • Fee-based Web site offers extensive searching of a wide variety of legal sources. Additional features include Daily Opinion Service, lexis.com Bookstore, Career Center, CLE Center, Law Schools, and Practice Pages ("Pages specific to areas of specialty").

STATISTICS SOURCES

Annual Report of the Director. Administrative Office of the United States Courts. • Annual.

State Court Caseload Statistics. National Center for State Courts. • Annual. Price on application.

Statistics on Crime, Justice, and Punishment. The Gale Group. • 1996. $65.00. Volume three. Includes graphs, charts, and tables arranged within subject chapters. Citations to data sources are provided.

TRADE/PROFESSIONAL ASSOCIATIONS

Fund for Modern Courts. 19 W. 44th St., Room 1200, New York, NY 10036. Phone: (212)575-1577 Fax: (212)869-1133 E-mail: justice@moderncourts.org.

National Association for Court Management. P.O. Box 8798, Williamsburg, VA 23187-8798. Phone: 800-616-6165 or (757)259-1841 or (757)253-2000 Fax: (757)259-1520 • URL: http://www.ncsc.dni.us/nacm/nacm.htm.

National Center for State Courts. 300 Newport Ave., Williamsburg, VA 23185. Phone: (757)253-2000 Fax: (757)220-0449.

National Council of Juvenile and Family Court Judges. 1041 N. Virginia St., Reno, NV 89557. Phone: (775)784-6012 Fax: (775)784-6628 • URL: http://www.ncjfcj.unr.edu.

OTHER SOURCES

World of Criminal Justice. The Gale Group. • 2001. $150.00. Two volumes. Contains both topical and biographical entries relating to the criminal justice system and criminology.

CRACKER INDUSTRY

See: BAKING INDUSTRY; SNACK FOOD INDUSTRY

CRAFTS

See: GIFT BUSINESS; HOBBY INDUSTRY

CREATIVITY

GENERAL WORKS

Corporate Creativity: How Innovation and Improvement Actually Happen. Alan G. Robinson and Sam Stern. Berrett-Koehler Pulishers, Inc. • 1997. $29.95. Describes the six "essential elements" of business creativity.

Creative Management. Jane Henry. Sage Publications, Inc. • 1991. $60.00.

Imaginization: The Art of Creative Management. Gareth Morgan. Sage Publications, Inc. • 1993. $45.00.

Interface Culture: How New Technology Transforms the Way We Create and Communicate. Steven Johnson. HarperCollins Publishers. • 1997. $24.00. A discussion of how computer interfaces and online technology ("cyberspace") affect society in general.

Lateral Thinking: Creativity Step by Step. Edward de Bono. HarperTrade. • 1990. $15.00.

ABSTRACTS AND INDEXES

Psychological Abstracts. American Psychological Association. • Monthly. Members, $799.00 per year;

individuals and institutions, $1,075.00 per year. Covers the international literature of psychology and the behavioral sciences. Includes journals, technical reports, dissertations, and other sources.

ALMANACS AND YEARBOOKS

Creativity. Art Direction Magazine. Art Directon Book Co., Inc. • Annual. $62.95.

ONLINE DATABASES

PsycINFO. American Psychological Association. • Provides indexing and abstracting of the worldwide literature of psychology and the behavioral sciences. Time period is 1967 to date, with monthly updates. Inquire as to online cost and availability.

PERIODICALS AND NEWSLETTERS

Business 2.0. Imagine Media, Inc. • Monthly. $12.00 per year. General business magazine emphasizing ideas and innovation.

Fast Company: How Smart Business Works. Fast Company Inc. • Monthly. $23.95 per year. Covers business management, with emphasis on creativity, leadership, innovation, career advancement, teamwork, the global economy, and the "new workplace.".

Journal of Creative Behavior. Creative Education Foundation, Inc. • Quarterly. Individulas, $70.00 per year; institutions, $85.00 per year.

RESEARCH CENTERS AND INSTITUTES

Center for Studies in Creativity. State University of New York College at Buffalo. 244 Chase Hall, 1300 Elmwood Ave., Buffalo, NY 14222-1095. Phone: (716)878-6223 Fax: (716)878-4040 E-mail: pucciogj@buffalostate.edu • URL: http://www.buffalostate.edu/~creatcnt/.

Institute of Personality and Social Research. University of California at Berkeley. 4143 Tolman Hall, Berkeley, CA 94720. Phone: (510)642-5050 Fax: (510)643-9334 • URL: http://www.ls.berkeley.edu/dept/ipsr.

TRADE/PROFESSIONAL ASSOCIATIONS

National Association for Creative Children and Adults. 8080 Springvalley Dr., Cincinnati, OH 45236. Phone: (513)631-1777.

CREDIT

See also: AGRICULTURAL CREDIT; CONSUMER CREDIT; CREDIT INSURANCE; CREDIT MANAGEMENT; FOREIGN CREDIT

GENERAL WORKS

The New Face of Credit Risk Management: Balancing Growth and Credit Quality in an Integrated Risk Management Environment. Charles B. Wendel. Robert Morris Associates. • 1999. $65.00. Contains "In-depth interviews with senior credit officers from five major financial institutions." Coverage includes modeling, scoring, and other technology related to the management of credit risk.

ABSTRACTS AND INDEXES

Banking Information Index. U M I Banking Information Index. • Monthly. Price on application. Covers a wide variety of banking, business, and financial subjects in periodicals. Formerly *Banking Literature Index.*

CD-ROM DATABASES

EconLit. Available from SilverPlatter Information, Inc. • Monthly. Single-user, $1,600.00 per year. Multi-user, $2,400.00 per year. Provides CD-ROM citations, with abstracts, to articles from more than 500 economics journals. Time period is 1969 to date. Produced by the American Economic Association.

WILSONDISC: Wilson Business Abstracts. H. W. Wilson Co. • Monthly. $2,495.00 per year, including unlimited online access to *Wilson Business Abstracts* through WILSONLINE. Provides CD-ROM "cover-to-cover" abstracting and indexing of over 600 prominent business periodicals. Indexing is from 1982, abstracting from 1990. (*Business Periodicals Index* without abstracts is available on CD-ROM at $1,495 per year.).

ENCYCLOPEDIAS AND DICTIONARIES

Blackwell Encyclopedic Dictionary of Finance. Dean Paxson and Douglas Wood, editors. Blackwell Publishers. • 1997. $110.00. The editors are associated with the University of Manchester. Contains definitions of key terms combined with longer articles written by various U. S. and foreign business educators. Includes bibliographies and index. (Blackwell Encyclopedia of Management Series).

Credit and Lending Dictionary. Daphne Smith and Shelley W. Geehr, editors. Robert Morris Associates. • 1994. $25.00.

Encyclopedia of Banking and Finance. Charles J. Woelfel. McGraw-Hill Professional. • 1996. $50.00. 10th revised edition.

FINANCIAL RATIOS

Money of the Mind: Borrowing and Lending in America from the Civil War to Michael Milken. James Grant. Farrar, Straus, and Giroux, LLC. • 1992. $16.00. A critical anlysis by the editor of *Grant's Interest Rate Observer.*

HANDBOOKS AND MANUALS

Manual of Credit and Commercial Laws. National Association of Credit Management. • Annual. Free to members; non-members, $125.00. Formerly *Credit Manual of Commercial Laws.*

Practical Guide to Credit and Collection. George O. Bancroft. AMACOM. • 1989. $29.95.

INTERNET DATABASES

EBSCO Information Services. Ebsco Publishing. Phone: 800-871-8508 or (508)356-6500 Fax: (508)356-5640 E-mail: ep@epnet.com • URL: http://www.epnet.com • Fee-based Web site providing Internet access to a wide variety of databases, including business-related material. Full text is available for many periodical titles, with daily updates. Fees: Apply.

Fedstats. Federal Interagency Council on Statistical Policy. Phone: (202)395-7254 • URL: http://www.fedstats.gov • Web site features an efficient search facility for full-text statistics produced by more than 70 federal agencies, including the Census Bureau, the Bureau of Economic Analysis, and the Bureau of Labor Statistics. Boolean searches can be made within one agency or for all agencies combined. Links are offered to international statistical bureaus, including the UN, IMF, OECD, UNESCO, Eurostat, and 20 individual countries. Fees: Free.

ProQuest Direct. Bell & Howell Information and Learning. Phone: 800-521-0600 or (313)761-4700 Fax: (313)973-9145 • URL: http://www.umi.com/proquest • Fee-based Web site providing Internet access to more than 3,000 periodicals, newspapers, and other publications. Many items are available full-text, with daily updates. Includes extensive corporate and financial information from Disclosure, Inc. Fees: Apply.

ONLINE DATABASES

Accounting and Tax Database. Bell & Howell Information and Learning. • Provides indexing and abstracting of the literature of accounting, taxation, and financial management, 1971 to date. Updating is weekly. Especially covers accounting, auditing, banking, bankruptcy, employee compensation and benefits, cash management, financial planning, and credit. Inquire as to online cost and availability.

Banking Information Source. Bell & Howell Information and Learning. • Provides indexing and abstracting of periodical and other literature from 1982 to date, with weekly updates. Covers the financial services industry: banks, savings institutions, investment houses, credit unions, insurance companies, and real estate organizations. Emphasis is on marketing and management. Inquire as to online cost and availability. (Formerly *FINIS: Financial Industry Information Service.*).

DRI Financial and Credit Statistics. Data Products Division. • Contains U. S. and international statistical data relating to money markets, interest rates, foreign exchange, banking, and stock and bond indexes. Time period is 1973 to date, with continuous updating. Inquire as to online cost and availability.

DRI U.S. Central Database. Data Products Division. • Provides more than 23,000 business, financial, demographic, economic, foreign trade, and industry-related time series for the U.S. Includes national income, population, retail-wholesale trade, price indexes, labor data, housing, industrial production, banking, interest rates, money supply, etc. Time period is generally 1947 to date (some data back to 1929). Updating varies. Inquire as to online cost and availability.

EconLit. American Economic Association. • Covers the worldwide literature of economics as contained in selected monographs and about 550 journals. Subjects include microeconomics, macroeconomics, economic history, inflation, money, credit, finance, accounting theory, trade, natural resource economics, and regional economics. Time period is 1969 to present, with monthly updates. Inquire as to online cost and availability.

TRW Business Credit Profiles. TRW Inc., Business Credit Services Division. • Provides credit history (trade payments, payment trends, payment totals, payment history, etc.) for public and private U. S. companies. Key facts and banking information are also given. Updates are weekly. Inquire as to online cost and availability.

Wilson Business Abstracts Online. H. W. Wilson Co. • Indexes and abstracts 600 major business periodicals, plus the *Wall Street Journal* and the business section of the *New York Times.* Indexing is from 1982, abstracting from 1990, with the two newspapers included from 1993. Updated weekly. Inquire as to online cost and availability. (*Business Periodicals Index* without abstracts is also available online.).

PERIODICALS AND NEWSLETTERS

Bank Credit Analyst. BCA Publications Ltd. • Monthly. $695.00 per year. "The independent monthly forecast and analysis of trends in business conditions and major investment markets based on a continuous appraisal of money and credit flows." Includes many charts and graphs relating to money, credit, and securities in the U. S.

Bondweek: The Newsweekly of Fixed Income and Credit Markets. Institutional Investor. • Weekly. $2,220.00 per year. Newsletter. Covers taxable, fixed-income securities for professional investors, including corporate, government, foreign, mortgage, and high-yield.

Credit. American Financial Services Association. • Bimonthly. Members, $12.00 per year; non-members, $22.00 per year.

Credit & Collections News. Faulkner & Gray, Inc. • Weekly. $425.00 per year. Newsletter. Covers trends and new developments in credit and collections, including technology.

Grant's Interest Rate Observer. James Grant, editor. Interest Rate Publishing Corp. • Biweekly. $495.00

per year. Newsletter containing detailed analysis of money-related topics, including interest rate trends, global credit markets, fixed-income investments, bank loan policies, and international money markets.

International Bank Credit Analyst. BCA Publications Ltd. • Monthly. $795.00 per year. "A monthly forecast and analysis of currency movements, interest rates, and stock market developments in the principal countries, based on a continuous appraisal of money and credit trends worldwide." Includes many charts and graphs providing international coverage of money, credit, and securities.

STATISTICS SOURCES

Business Statistics of the United States. Courtenay M. Slater, editor. Bernan Associates. • 1999. $74.00. Fifth edition. Based on *Business Statistics*, formerly issue by the Bureau of Economic Analysis, U. S. Department of Commerce. Provides basic data for a wide variety of U. S. industries, services, and economic indicators. Most statistics are shown annually for 29 years and monthly for the most recent four years.

Economic Report of the President: Together with the Annual Report of the Council of Economic Advisors. Available from U. S. Government Printing Office. • Annual. $29.00. Includes about 130 pages of "Statistical Tables Relating to Income, Employment, and Production." Tables cover national income, employment, wages, productivity, manufacturing, prices, credit, finance (public and private), corporate profits, and foreign trade.

Statistical Information on the Financial Services Industry. American Bankers Association. • Annual. Members, $150.00; non-members, $275.00. Presents a wide variety of data relating to banking and financial services, including consumer economics, personal finance, credit, government loans, capital markets, and international banking.

Survey of Current Business. Available from U. S. Government Printing Office. • Monthly. $49.00 per year. Issued by Bureau of Economic Analysis, U. S. Department of Commerce. Presents a wide variety of business and economic data.

TRADE/PROFESSIONAL ASSOCIATIONS

National Association of Credit Management. 8840 Columbia, 100 Parkway, Columbia, MD 21045-2158. Phone: 800-955-8815 or (410)740-5560 Fax: (410)740-5574 E-mail: nacminfo@nacm.org • URL: http://www.nacm.org.

National Institute of Credit. Credit Research Foundation of the NACM, 8815 Centre Park Dr., Suite 200, Columbia, MD 21045. Phone: (410)740-5560 Fax: (410)740-5574 • URL: http://www.nacm.org.

OTHER SOURCES

Age Discrimination. Shepard's. • Three looseleaf volumes. $300.00. Annual supplementation. Emphasis on the Age Discrimination Act, the Age Discrimination in Employment Act, and the Equal Credit Opportunity Act.

Consumer and Commercial Credit: Installment Sales. Prentice Hall. • Three looseleaf volumes. Periodic supplementation. Price on application. Covers secured transactions under the Uniform Commercial Code and the Uniform Consumer Credit Code. Includes retail installment sales, home improvement loans, higher education loans, and other kinds of installment loans.

Debtor-Creditor Law. Matthew Bender & Co., Inc. • $1,595.00. 10 looseleaf volumes. Periodic supplementation. Covers all aspects of the creation and enforcement of the debtor-creditor relationship.

InSite 2. Intelligence Data/Thomson Financial. • Fee-based Web site consolidates information in a "Base Pack" consisting of Business InSite, Market InSite, and Company InSite. Optional databases are Consumer InSite, Health and Wellness InSite, Newsletter InSite, and Computer InSite. Includes fulltext content from more than 2,500 trade publications, journals, newsletters, newspapers, analyst reports, and other sources. Continuous updating. Formerly produced by The Gale Group.

Managing Credit and Collections to Improve Cash Flow. American Management Association Extension Institute. • Looseleaf. $130.00. Self-study course. Emphasis is on practical explanations, examples, and problem solving. Quizzes and a case study are included.

CREDIT, BANK

See: BANK LOANS

CREDIT CARD INDUSTRY

GENERAL WORKS

How to Use Credit Wisely. American Institute for Economic Research. • 1996. $6.00. Provides succinct coverage of various consumer debt topics, including credit cards, credit scoring systems, credit history, credit reports, and bankruptcy. Relevant federal legislation is briefly described, including the Fair Credit Reporting Act (FCRA) and the Fair Credit Billing Act (FCBA). (Economic Education Bulletin.).

ABSTRACTS AND INDEXES

Business Periodicals Index. H. W. Wilson Co. • Monthly, except August, with quarterly and annual cumulations. Service basis for print edition; CD-ROM edition, $1,495.00 per year.

DIRECTORIES

BIN Number Directory of all Visa and Mastercard Issuing Banks. Fraud and Theft Information Bureau. • Annual. $1,175.00. Base edition. Semiannual updates, $360.00 per year. Numerical arrangement of about 30,000 banks worldwide. BIN numbers (also called ISO or prefix numbers) identify a credit card holder's issuing bank.

Business Organizations, Agencies, and Publications Directory. The Gale Group. • 1999. $425.00. 12th edition. Over 40,000 entries describing 39 types of business information sources. Classified by type of organization, publication, or serviceIncludes state, national, and international agencies and organizations. Master index to names and keywords. Also includes e-mail addresses and web site URL's.

Card Industry Directory. Faulkner & Gray, Inc. • Annual. $425.00.

Card Marketing Buyer's Guide. Faulkner & Gray, Inc. • Annual. Price on application. Lists companies concerned with the marketing of credit cards and other forms of payment cards.

Credit Card Management Buyer's Guide. Faulkner & Gray, Inc. • Annual. Free. Lists companies related to the management of credit cards and debit cards.

Credit Card Marketing Sourcebook. Faulkner & Gray, Inc. • Annual. Price on application.

International Association of Financial Crimes Investigators: Membership Directory. International Association of Financial Crimes Investigators. • Annual. Membership. About 3,500 firms and individuals engaged in investigation of fraudulent use of credit cards. Formerly *International Association of Credit Card Investigators-Membership Directory.* Formerly International Association of Credit Card Investigators.

Low Rate and No Fee List. Bankcard Holders of America. • Quarterly. $4.00 per copy. Lists about 50 banks offering relatively low interest rates and/or no annual fee for credit card accounts. Formerly *Low Interest Rate.*

Plunkett's Financial Services Industry Almanac: The Leading Firms in Investments, Banking, and Financial Information. Available from Plunkett Research, Ltd. • Annual. $245.00. Discusses important trends in various sectors of the financial industry. Five hundred major banking, credit card, investment, and financial services companies are profiled.

INTERNET DATABASES

BanxQuote Banking, Mortgage, and Finance Center. BanxQuote, Inc. Phone: 800-765-3000 or (212)643-8000 Fax: (212)643-0020 E-mail: info@banx.com • URL: http://www.banx.com • Web site quotes interest rates paid by banks around the country on various savings products, as well as rates paid by consumers for automobile loans, mortgages, credit cards, home equity loans, and personal loans. Also provided: stock quotes, indexes, stock options, futures trading data, economic indicators, and links to many other financial sites. Daily updates. Fees: Free.

ONLINE DATABASES

Marketing and Advertising Reference Service (MARS). The Gale Group. • Provides abstracts of literature relating to consumer marketing and advertising, including all forms of advertising media. Time period is 1984 to date. Daily updates. Inquire as to online cost and availability.

Wilson Business Abstracts Online. H. W. Wilson Co. • Indexes and abstracts 600 major business periodicals, plus the *Wall Street Journal* and the business section of the *New York Times.* Indexing is from 1982, abstracting from 1990, with the two newspapers included from 1993. Updated weekly. Inquire as to online cost and availability. (*Business Periodicals Index* without abstracts is also available online.).

PERIODICALS AND NEWSLETTERS

Bankcard Consumer News. Bankcard Holders of America. • Bimonthly. $24.00 per year. Newsletter for consumers.

Card Marketing. Faulkner & Gray, Inc. • Monthly. $73.95. Edited for payment card marketing executives: credit cards, debit cards, phone cards, "loyalty" cards, and smart cards.

Card News: The Executive Report on the Transaction Card Marketplace. Phillips Business Information, Inc. • Biweekly. $695.00 per year. Newsletter on transaction cards, debit and credit cards, automatic teller machines, etc.

Card Technology. Faulkner & Gray, Inc. • Monthly. $79.00 per year. Covers advanced technology for credit, debit, and other cards. Topics include smart cards, optical recognition, and card design.

Credit. American Financial Services Association. • Bimonthly. Members, $12.00 per year; non-members, $22.00 per year.

Credit Card Management. Faulkner & Gray, Inc. • Monthly. $98.00 per year. Edited for bankers and other credit card managers. Supplements available: *Card Technology Review* and *Debit Card Directory.*

Credit Card News. Faulkner & Gray, Inc. • Semimonthly. $465.00 per year. Newsletter. Covers the latest trends in credit card marketing. Includes the effects of government regulation and court decisions.

Credit Risk Management. Phillips Business Information, Inc. • Biweekly. $695.00 per year. Newsletter on consumer credit, including delinquency aspects.

Credit World. International Credit Association. • Bimonthly. Free to members; non-members, $60.00 per year.

The Nilson Report. HSN Consultants, Inc. • Semimonthly. $695.00 per year. Newsletter. Provides market and other data on the credit card industry.

Online Marketplace. Jupiter Media Metrix. • Monthly. $695.00 per year. Newsletter on the collection of electronic payments ("e-money") for goods and services offered through the Internet. Covers trends in retailing, banking, travel, and other areas.

RESEARCH CENTERS AND INSTITUTES

Credit Research Center. Georgetown University. 3240 Prospect St., N.W., Suite 300, Washington, DC 20007. Phone: (202)625-0103 Fax: (202)625-0104 E-mail: msb-crc@msb.edu • URL: http://www.msb.edu/prog/crc.

STATISTICS SOURCES

Statistical Information on the Financial Services Industry. American Bankers Association. • Annual. Members, $150.00; non-members, $275.00. Presents a wide variety of data relating to banking and financial services, including consumer economics, personal finance, credit, government loans, capital markets, and international banking.

TRADE/PROFESSIONAL ASSOCIATIONS

American Financial Services Association. 919 18th St., N.W., Washington, DC 20006. Phone: (202)296-5544 Fax: (202)223-0321 E-mail: afsa@afsamail.com • URL: http://www.americanfinsvcs.org.

Bankcard Holders of America. 333 Maple Ave. E., No. 2005, Vienna, VA 22180-4717. 333 Maple Ave. E., No. 2005, • Promotes the "wise and careful" use of credit cards. A consumer organization.

Credit Card Users of America. P.O. Box 7100, Beverly Hills, CA 90212. Phone: (818)343-4434 • Supports the rights of credit card users.

International Association of Financial Crimes. 385 Bel Marin Keys Blvd., Ste. H, Novato, CA 94949-5636. Phone: (415)897-8800 Fax: (415)898-0798 • Members are officials who investigate criminal violations of credit card laws.

International Credit Association. P.O. Box 15945-314, Lenexa, KS 66285-5945. Phone: (913)307-9432 Fax: (913)541-0156 E-mail: ica@ica-credit.org • URL: http://www.ica-credit.org.

MasterCard International. 2000 Purchase St., Purchase, NY 10577. Phone: (914)249-2000 Fax: (914)249-5510 • Members are banks and financial institutions issuing the MasterCard credit card. MasterCard International is the licensor.

National Foundation for Consumer Credit. 8611 Second Ave., Suite 100, Silver Spring, MD 20910-3372. Phone: 800-388-2227 or (301)589-5600 Fax: (301)495-5623 • URL: http://www.nfcc.org.

OTHER SOURCES

Internet Payments Report. Jupiter Media Metrix. • Annual. $1,095.00. Market research report. Provides data, comment, and forecasts on the collection of electronic payments ("e-money") for goods and services offered through the Internet.

The U. S. Market for Plastic Payment Cards. Available from MarketResearch.com. • 1998. $2,500.00. Market research report published by Packaged Facts. Covers credit cards, charge cards, debit cards, and smart cards. Provides profiles of Visa, Mastercard, American Express, Discover, Diners Club, and others.

CREDIT, CONSUMER

See: CONSUMER CREDIT

CREDIT INSURANCE

See also: INSURANCE

BIOGRAPHICAL SOURCES

Who's Who in Insurance. Underwriter Printing and Publishing Co. • Annual. $130.00. Contains over 5,000 biographies of insurance officials, leading agents and brokers, and high-ranking company officials.

ONLINE DATABASES

Best's Company Reports. A. M. Best Co. • Provides full financial data online for U. S. insurance companies (life, health, property, casualty), including balance sheet data, income statements, expenses, premium income, losses, and investments. Includes *Best's Company Reports*, *Best's Insurance News*, and Best's ratings of insuarance companies. Inquire as to online cost and availability.

PERIODICALS AND NEWSLETTERS

CCIA Newsletter. Consumer Credit Insurance Association. • Monthly. Membership.

TRADE/PROFESSIONAL ASSOCIATIONS

Consumer Credit Insurance Association. 542 S. Dearborn St., No. 400, Chicago, IL 60605. Phone: (312)939-2242 Fax: (312)939-8287 E-mail: bburfeind@cciaonline.

Foreign Credit Insurance Association. 40 Rector St., 11th Fl., New York, NY 10006. Phone: (212)306-5000 Fax: (212)513-4704.

CREDIT MANAGEMENT

See also: CREDIT

HANDBOOKS AND MANUALS

Credit Department Management. D. Laurence Blackstone. Robert Morris Associates. • 1992. $65.00. Second edition.

Credit Management Handbook. Burt Edwards and others. Ashgate Publishing Co. • 1997. $96.95. Fourth edition. Published by Gower in England.

Credit Risk Management: A Guide to Sound Business Decisions. H. A. Schaeffer. John Wiley and Sons, Inc. • 2000. $69.95. Covers corporate credit policies, credit authorization procedures, and analysis of business credit applications. Includes 12 "real-life" case studies.

PERIODICALS AND NEWSLETTERS

Business Credit. National Association of Credit Management. • Monthly. $34.00 per year. Formerly *Credit and Financial Management*.

Collections and Credit Risk: The Monthly Magazine for Collections and Credit Policy Professionals. Faulkner & Gray, Inc. • Monthly. $95.00 per year. Contains articles on the technology and business management of credit and collection functions. Includes coverage of bad debts, bankruptcy, and credit risk management.

The Credit Memo. New York Credit and Financial Management Association. • Bimonthly. Membership. Formerly *Credit Executive*.

Letters of Credit Report: Bank Guaranties and Acceptance. Aspen Law and Business. • Bimonthly. $299.00 per year. Newsletter. Covers letters of credit, bank acceptances, and bank guarantees.

TRADE/PROFESSIONAL ASSOCIATIONS

Credit Research Foundation. 8815 Center Park Dr., Columbia, MD 21045. Phone: (410)740-5499 Fax: (410)740-4620.

National Association of Consumer Credit Administrators. P.O. Box 10709, Raleigh, NC 27605-0709. Phone: (919)733-3016 Fax: (919)733-6918.

National Association of Credit Management. 8840 Columbia, 100 Parkway, Columbia, MD 21045-2158. Phone: 800-955-8815 or (410)740-5560 Fax: (410)740-5574 E-mail: nacminfo@nacm.org • URL: http://www.nacm.org.

Society of Certified Credit Executives. P.O. Box 15945-314, Lenexa, KS 66285-5945. Phone: (913)541-0156 E-mail: ica@ica-credit.org • URL: http://www.ica-credit.org.

OTHER SOURCES

Consumer and Commercial Credit: Installment Sales. Prentice Hall. • Three looseleaf volumes. Periodic supplementation. Price on application. Covers secured transactions under the Uniform Commercial Code and the Uniform Consumer Credit Code. Includes retail installment sales, home improvement loans, higher education loans, and other kinds of installment loans.

CREDIT UNIONS

See also: SAVINGS AND LOAN ASSOCIATIONS

ABSTRACTS AND INDEXES

Banking Information Index. U M I Banking Information Index. • Monthly. Price on application. Covers a wide variety of banking, business, and financial subjects in periodicals. Formerly *Banking Literature Index*.

ALMANACS AND YEARBOOKS

Credit Union Report. Credit Union National Association. • Annual. $25.00. Credit union leagues, associations, for each of the 50 states and the District of Columbia.

DIRECTORIES

Callahan's Credit Union Directory. Callahan & Associates, Inc. • Annual. $135.00. Covers 11,843 state, federal, and United States credit unions; regulators, organizations, and leagues.Includes financial data.

McFadden American Financial Directory. Thomson Financial Publishing. • Semiannual. $415.00 per year. Five volumes. Contains information on more than 23,000 banks, savings institutions, and credit unions in the U. S., Canada, and Mexico. Includes names of officers for key departments, financial statistics, hours of operation, branch information, and other data.

Polk Financial Institutions Directory. Thomson Financial Publishing. • Semiannual. $330.00 per semiannual volume. Provides detailed information on "virtually every bank, savings and loan, and major credit union in North America, including banks and branches in Canada, Mexico, the Caribbean, and Central America." Supersedes *Polk's Bank Directory*.

Thomson Credit Union Directory. Thomson Financial Publishing. • Semiannual. $145.00 per year. Provides information on all U. S. credit unions, including branch offices. Includes national statistics and ranking of 300 top credit unions.

HANDBOOKS AND MANUALS

National Credit Union Administration Rules and Regulations. Available from U. S. Government Printing Office. • Looseleaf. $130.00 for basic manual, including updates for an indeterminate period. Incorporates all amendments and revisions.

INTERNET DATABASES

The Bauer Group: Reporting On and Analyzing the Performance of U. S. Banks, Thrifts, and Credit

Unions. Bauer Financial Reports, Inc. Phone: 800-388-6686 or (305)445-9500 Fax: 800-230-9569 or (305)445-6775 • URL: http://www.bauerfinancial.com • Web site provides ratings (0 to 5 stars) of individual banks and credit unions, based on capital ratios and other financial criteria. Online searching for bank or credit union names is offered. Fees: Free.

ONLINE DATABASES

Banking Information Source. Bell & Howell Information and Learning. • Provides indexing and abstracting of periodical and other literature from 1982 to date, with weekly updates. Covers the financial services industry: banks, savings institutions, investment houses, credit unions, insurance companies, and real estate organizations. Emphasis is on marketing and management. Inquire as to online cost and availability. (Formerly *FINIS: Financial Industry Information Service.*).

PERIODICALS AND NEWSLETTERS

Credit Union Executive Journal: For Active Leaders and Managers of Credit Unions. Credit Union National Association, Communications Div. CUNA Publications. • Bimonthly. $99.00 per year. A management journal for credit union CEOs and senior executives.

Credit Union Magazine: For Credit Union Elected Officials, Managers and Employees. Credit Union National Association, Communications Div. CUNA Publications. • Monthly. $38.00 per year. News analysis and operational information for credit union management, staff, directors, and committee executives.

CUIS (Credit Union Information Service). United Communications Group. • Biweekly. $277.00 per year. Newsletter. Supplement available *CUIS Special Reoprt.*

Financial Services Marketing: Finding, Keeping, and Profiting From the Right Customers. American Banker. • Bimonthly. Price on application. Covers marketing for a variety of financial institutions, including banks, investment companies, securities dealers, and credit unions.

United States National Credit Union Administration NCUA Quarterly. National Credit Union Administration.

STATISTICS SOURCES

Statistical Information on the Financial Services Industry. American Bankers Association. • Annual. Members, $150.00; non-members, $275.00. Presents a wide variety of data relating to banking and financial services, including consumer economics, personal finance, credit, government loans, capital markets, and international banking.

U. S. Industry and Trade Outlook: The McGraw-Hill Companies and the U.S. Department of Commerce/ International Trade Administration. Datapso Research Corp. • Annual. $69.95. Produced by the International Trade Administration, U. S. Department of Commerce, in a "public-private" partnership with DRI/McGraw-Hill and Standard & Poor's. Provides basic data, outlook for the current year, and "Long-Term Prospects" (five-year projections) for a wide variety of products and services. Includes high technology industries. Formerly *U. S. Industrial Outlook.*

TRADE/PROFESSIONAL ASSOCIATIONS

Credit Union Executives Society. 6410 Enterprise Lane, Suite 300, Madison, WI 53719-1145. Phone: 800-252-2664 or (608)271-2664 Fax: (608)271-2303 E-mail: cues@cues.org • URL: http://www.cues.org.

Credit Union National Association. P.O. Box 431, Madison, WI 53701. Phone: 800-356-9655 or (608)231-4000 • URL: http://www.cuna.org.

Defense Credit Union Council. 805 15th St., N.W., Suite 300, Washington, DC 20005-2207. Phone: 800-356-9655 or (202)682-5993 Fax: (202)654-7000 E-mail: dcucl@cuna.com • URL: http://www.dcuc.org.

National Association of Federal Credit Unions. P.O. Box 3769, Washington, DC 20007. Phone: 800-336-4644 or (703)522-4770 Fax: (703)524-1082 • URL: http://www.nafcunet.org.

National Credit Union Management Association. c/o J.K. Anchors, 4989 Rebel Trial, N.W., Atlanta, GA 30327. Phone: (404)255-6828 Fax: (404)851-1752 • URL: http://www.nacuso.org • Members are large credit unions.

World Council of Credit Unions. P.O. Box 2982, Madison, WI 53701. Phone: (608)231-7130 Fax: (608)238-8020 E-mail: mail@woccu.org • URL: http://www.woccu.org.

OTHER SOURCES

The CEO Report. United Communications Group (UCG). • Biweekly. $287.00 per year. Newsletter for credit union executives. Formerly *Credit Union Information Service.*

Credit Union Guide. Credit Union National Association. Prentice Hall. • Four looseleaf volumes. Periodic supplementation. Price on application. Laws, regulations, and developments affecting credit unions.

CRIME AND CRIMINALS

See also: COMPUTER CRIME AND SECURITY; COUNTERFEITING; FORGERIES; FRAUD AND EMBEZZLEMENT; SHOPLIFTING

GENERAL WORKS

Crime, Criminals, and Corrections. Donal E. Macnamara and Lloyd McCorkle. John Jay Press. • 1982. $17.00.

Crimes Against Business: A Practical Guide to the Prevention and Detection of Business Crime. Jules B. Kroll, editor. Ayer Co. Publishers, Inc. • 1980. $102.95 per volume. Two volumes.

Dirty Business: Exploring Corporate Misconduct: Analysis and Cases. Maurice Punch. Sage Publications, Inc. • 1996. $79.95. Covers organizational misbehavior and white-collar crime. Includes "Ten Cases of Corporate Deviance.".

Introduction to Security. Robert J. Fishcher and Gion Green. Butterworth-Heinemann. • 1998. $39.95. Sixth edition.

ABSTRACTS AND INDEXES

Current Law Index: Multiple Access to Legal Periodicals. The Gale Group. • Monthly. $650.00 per year. Produced in cooperation with the American Association of Law Libraries. Indexes more than 900 law journals, legal newspapers, and specialty publications from the U.S., Canada, U.K., Ireland, Australia, and New Zealand.

Index to Legal Periodicals and Books. H. W. Wilson Co. • Monthly. Quarterly and annual cumulations. $270.00 per year. CD-ROM version available at $1,495.00 per year.

Social Sciences Index. H. W. Wilson Co. • Quarterly, with annual cumulation. Service basis for print edition; CD-ROM edition, $1,495 per year. Indexes more than 400 periodicals covering economics, environmental policy, government, insurance, labor, health care policy, plannning, public administration, public welfare, urban studies, women's issues, criminology, and related topics.

ALMANACS AND YEARBOOKS

American Law Yearbook. The Gale Group. • Annual. $155.00. Serves as a yearly supplement to *West's Encyclopedia of American Law.* Describes new legal developments in many subject areas.

BIBLIOGRAPHIES

Criminal Justice Information: How to Find It, How to Use It. Dennis C. Benamati and others. Oryx Press. • 1997. $59.95. A guide to print, electronic, and online criminal justice information resources. Includes statistical reports, directories, periodicals, monographs, databases, and other sources.

CD-ROM DATABASES

National Newspaper Index CD-ROM. The Gale Group. • Monthly. Provides comprehensive CD-ROM indexing of all material appearing in the late edition of the *New York Times*, the final edition of the *Washington Post*, the national edition of the *Christian Science Monitor*, the home edition of the *Los Angeles Times*, and the *Wall Street Journal.* Time period is four years. Also available online.

The New York Times Ondisc. New York Times Online Services. • Monthly. $2,650.00 per year. CD-ROM discs contain the full text of *The New York Times*, final edition. Inquire as to time period covered and availability of backfiles.

Newspaper Abstracts Ondisc. Bell & Howell Information and Learning. • Monthly. $2,950.00 per year (covers 1989 to date; archival discs are available for 1985-88). Provides cover-to-cover CD-ROM indexing and abstracting of 19 major newspapers, including the *New York Times, Wall Street Journal, Washington Post, Chicago Tribune,* and *Los Angeles Times.*

Social Science Source. EBSCO Publishing. • Monthly. $1,495.00 per year. Provides CD-ROM citations and abstracts to social science articles in more than 600 periodicals, with full text from 125 periodicals. Covers economics, political science, public policy, international relations, psychology, and other topics. Time period is most recent five years.

Social Sciences Citation Index: Compact Disc Edition with Abstracts. Institute for Scientific Information. • Quarterly. Provides CD-ROM indexing and abstracting of "significant articles" from 1,400 social science journals worldwide, with additional selections from 3,200 other journals, 1986 to date. Includes economics, business, finance, management, communications, demographics, information and library science, political science, sociology, and many other subjects.

WILSONDISC: Index to Legal Periodicals and Books. H. W. Wilson Co. • Monthly. Including unlimited online access to *Index to Legal Periodicals* through WILSONLINE. Contains CD-ROM indexing of more than 800 English language legal periodicals from 1981 to date and 2,500 books.

WILSONDISC: Wilson Social Sciences Abstracts. H. W. Wilson Co. • Monthly. Including unlimited online access to *Social Sciences Index* through WILSONLINE. Provides CD-ROM indexing from 1983 and abstracting from 1994 of more than 400 periodicals covering economics, area studies, community health, public administration, public welfare, urban studies, and many other topics related to the social sciences.

ENCYCLOPEDIAS AND DICTIONARIES

Encyclopedia of Crime and Justice. Available from The Gale Group. • 2001. $425.00. Second edition. Four volumes. Published by Macmillan Reference USA. Contains extensive information on a wide variety of topics pertaining to crime, criminology, social issues, and the courts. (A revision of 1982 edition.).

West's Encyclopedia of American Law. Available from The Gale Group. • 1997. $995.00. Second edition. 12 volumes. Published by West Group.

Covers a wide variety of legal topics for the general reader. Formerly *Guide to American Law: Everyone's Legal Encyclopedia* (1985).

HANDBOOKS AND MANUALS

Accountant's Handbook of Fraud and Commercial Crime. G. Jack Bologna and others. John Wiley and Sons, Inc. • 1992. $155.00. *1996 Supplement*, $65.00.

Banking Crimes: Fraud, Money Laundering, Embezzlement. John K. Villa. West Group. • Annual. $125.00. Covers fraud and embezzlement. Looseleaf.

Burglar Alarm Sales and Installation. Entrepreneur Media, Inc. • Looseleaf. $59.50. A practical guide to starting a burglar alarm service. Covers profit potential, start-up costs, market size evaluation, owner's time required, pricing, accounting, advertising, promotion, etc. (Start-Up Business Guide No. E1091.).

Criminal Law Deskbook. Patrick McCloskey and Ronald Schoenberg. Matthew Bender and Co., Inc. • Irregular. $205.00. Discussions of the basic principles of criminal procedure, substantive law, and criminal trial strategy and tactics.

Criminal Procedure Handbook. Tertius Geldenhuys and J.J. Joubert, editors. Gaunt, Inc. • 1999. $42.50. Fourth edition.

Private Investigator. Entrepreneur Media, Inc. • Looseleaf. $59.50. A practical guide to starting a private investigation agency. Covers profit potential, start-up costs, market size evaluation, pricing, accounting, advertising, promotion, etc. (Start-Up Business Guide No. E1320.).

Securities Crimes. Marvin Pickholz. West Group. • $145.00. Looseleaf service. Periodic supplementation. Analyzes the enfo of federal securities laws from the viewpoint of the defendant. Discusses Securities and Exchange Commission (SEC) investigations and federal sentencing guidelines.

Security Applications in Industry and Institutions. Lawrence J. Fennelly, editor. Butterworth-Heinemann. • 1992. $46.95. Contains 19 chapters written by various security professionals in the U. S. Covers bank security, hotel security, shoplifting, college campus crime prevention, security in office buildings, hospitals, museums, libraries, etc.

INTERNET DATABASES

U. S. Census Bureau: The Official Statistics. U. S. Bureau of the Census. Phone: (301)763-4100 Fax: (301)763-4794 • URL: http://www.census.gov • Web site is "Your Source for Social, Demographic, and Economic Information." Contains "Current U. S. Population Count," "Current Economic Indicators," and a wide variety of data under "Other Official Statistics." Keyword searching is provided. Fees: Free.

ONLINE DATABASES

Index to Legal Periodicals and Books (Online). H. W. Wilson Co. • Broad coverage of law journals and books 1981 to date. Monthly updates. Inquire as to online cost and availability.

Information Bank Abstracts. New York Times Index Dept. • Provides indexing and abstracting of current affairs, primarily from the final late edition of *The New York Times* and the Eastern edition of *The Wall Street Journal.* Time period is 1969 to present, with daily updates. Inquire as to online cost and availability.

LEXIS. LEXIS-NEXIS. • The various LEXIS databases provide full text and indexing for a wide variety of legal cases, statutes, orders, and opinions.

NCJRS: National Criminal Justice Reference Service. U.S. Department of Justice. • References print and non-print information on law enforcement and criminal justice, 1972 to present. Monthly updates. Inquire as to online cost and availability.

Newspaper and Periodical Abstracts. Bell & Howell Information and Learning. • Provides online coverage (citations and abstracts) of 25 major newspapers, 1,600 perodicals, and 70 TV programs. Covers business, economics, current affairs, health, fitness, sports, education, technology, government, consumer affairs, psychology, the arts, and the social sciences. Time period is 1986 to date, with daily updates. Inquire as to online cost and availability.

Wilson Social Sciences Abstracts Online. H. W. Wilson Co. • Provides online abstracting and indexing of more than 415 periodicals covering area studies, community health, public administration, public welfare, urban studies, and many other social science topics. Time period is 1994 to date for abstracts and 1983 to date for indexing, with updates monthly. Inquire as to online cost and availability.

PERIODICALS AND NEWSLETTERS

Criminal Law Advocacy Reporter. Matthew Bender and Co., Inc. • Monthly. $310.00 per year. Analysis of the latest cases and trends in criminal law and procedure.

Criminology; An Interdisciplinary Journal. American Society of Criminology. • Quarterly. Individuals, $50.00 per year; institutions, $90.00 per year.

FBI Law Enforcement Bulletin. Available from U. S. Government Printing Office. • Monthly. $36.00 per year. Issued by Federal Bureau of Investigation, U. S. Department of Justice. Contains articles on a wide variety of law enforcement and crime topics, including computer-related crime.

International Police Review. Jane's Information Group, Inc. • Bimonthy. Institutions, $215.00 per year. Covers "every aspect" of policing and security throughout the world, including organized crime, money laundering, drugs, illegal immigration, forensic science, and police technology.

Security: The Magazine for Buyers of Security Products, Systems and Service. Cahners Business Information. • Monthly. $82.90 per year.

White-Collar Crime Reporter: Information and Analyses Concerning White-Collar Practice. Andrews Publications. • 10 times a year. $550.00 per year. Newsletter. Provides information on trends in white collar crime.

RESEARCH CENTERS AND INSTITUTES

Academy for State and Local Government. 444 N. Capitol St., N.W., Suite 345, Washington, DC 20001. Phone: (202)434-4850 Fax: (202)434-4851.

Lexis.com Research System. Lexis-Nexis Group. Phone: 800-227-9597 or (937)865-6800 Fax: (937)865-6909 E-mail: webmaster@prod.lexis-nexis.com • URL: http://www.lexis.com • Fee-based Web site offers extensive searching of a wide variety of legal sources. Additional features include Daily Opinion Service, lexis.com Bookstore, Career Center, CLE Center, Law Schools, and Practice Pages ("Pages specific to areas of specialty").

National Council on Crime and Delinquency. 1970 Broadway, Suite 500, Oakland, CA 94612. Phone: (510)208-0500 Fax: (510)208-0511 E-mail: pthumasosf.nccd-crc.org • URL: http://www.nccd-crc.com.

STATISTICS SOURCES

Crime in America's Top-Rated Cities: A Statistical Profile. Grey House Publishing. • Biennial. $125.00. Contains 20-year data for major crime categories in 75 cities, suburbs, metropolitan areas, and the U. S. Also includes statistics on correctional facilities, inmates, hate crimes, illegal drugs, and other crime-related matters.

Gale Book of Averages. The Gale Group. • 1994. $70.00. Contains 1,100-1,200 statistical averages on a variety of topics, with references to published sources. Subjects include business, labor, consumption, crime, and other areas of contemporary society.

Gale City and Metro Rankings Reporter. The Gale Group. • 1996. $134.00. Second edition. Provides about 3,000 statistical ranking tables covering more than 1,500 U. S. cities and Metropolitan Statistical Areas. Covers economic, demographic, social, governmental, and cultural factors. Sources are private studies and government data.

Gale Country and World Rankings Reporter. The Gale Group. • 1997. $135.00. Second edition. Provides about 3,000 statistical ranking tables and charts covering more than 235 nations. Sources include the United Nations and various government publications.

Gale State Rankings Reporter. The Gale Group. • 1996. $110.00. Second edition Provides 3,000 ranked lists of states under 35 subject headings. Sources are newspapers, periodicals, books, research institute publications, and government publications.

Prisoners in State and Federal Institutions. Bureau of Justice Statistics, U.S. Department of Justice. Available from U.S. Government Printing Office. • Annual.

Social Statistics of the United States. Mark S. Littman, editor. Bernan Press. • 2000. $65.00. Includes statistical data on population growth, labor force, occupations, environmental trends, leisure time use, income, poverty, taxes, and other economic or demographic topics.

Sourcebook of Criminal Justice Statistics. Available from U. S. Government Printing Office. • Annual. $56.00. Issued by the Bureau of Justice Statistics, U. S. Department of Justice (http://www.usdoj.gov/bjs). Contains both crime data and corrections statistics.

Statistical Abstract of the United States. Available from U. S. Government Printing Office. • Annual. $51.00. Issued by the U. S. Bureau of the Census.

Statistical Abstract of the World. The Gale Group. • 1997. $80.00. Third edition. Provides data on a wide variety of economic, social, and political topics for about 200 countries. Arranged by country.

Statistical Forecasts of the United States. The Gale Group. • 1995. $99.00. Second edition. Provides both long-term and short-term statistical forecasts relating to basic items in the U. S.: population, employment, labor, crime, education, and health care. Data in the form of charts, graphs, and tables has been taken from a wide variety of government and private sources. Includes a subject index and an "Index of Forecast by Year.".

A Statistical Portrait of the United States: Social Conditions and Trends. Mark S. Littman, editor. Bernan Press. • 1998. $89.00. Covers "social, economic, and environmental trends in the United States over the past 25 years." Includes statistical tables, graphs, and analysis relating to such topics as population, income, poverty, wealth, labor, housing, education, healthcare, air/water quality, and government.

Statistics on Crime, Justice, and Punishment. The Gale Group. • 1996. $65.00. Volume three. Includes graphs, charts, and tables arranged within subject chapters. Citations to data sources are provided.

Statistics on Weapons and Violence: A Selection of Statistical Charts, Graphs and Tables about Weapons and Violence from a Variety of Published Sources with Explanatory Comments. The Gale

Group. • 1995. $65.00. Includes graphs, charts, and tables arranged within subject chapters. Citations to data sources are provided. (Statistics for Students Series).

Uniform Crime Reports for the United States. Federal Bureau of Investigation, U.S. Department of Justice. Available from U.S. Government Printing Office. • Annual. Price varies.

Vital Statistics of the United States. Public Health Service, U.S. Dept. of Health and Human Services. Available from U.S. Government Printing Office. • Annual. Two volumes.

World Statistics Pocketbook. United Nations Publications. • Annual. $10.00. Presents basic economic, social, and environmental indicators for about 200 countries and areas. Covers more than 50 items relating to population, economic activity, labor force, agriculture, industry, energy, trade, transportation, communication, education, tourism, and the environment. Statistical sources are noted.

TRADE/PROFESSIONAL ASSOCIATIONS

American Society of Criminology. 1314 Kinnear Rd., Suite 212, Columbus, OH 43212. Phone: (614)292-9207 Fax: (614)292-6767.

OTHER SOURCES

Business Crime: Criminal Liability of the Business Community. Matthew Bender & Co., Inc. • $1,380.00. Seven looseleaf volumes. Periodic supplementation. Guide to the many criminal problems that can arise in modern business practice. Provides how-to guidance.

Corporate Criminal Liability. Kathleen F. Brickley. West Group. • $335.00 per year. Three looseleaf volumes. Periodic supplementation. Discusses how the general principles of criminal law apply to the corporate world. Provides a detailed analysis of liability under major federal crime statutes.

Criminal Defense Technique. Matthew Bender & Co., Inc. • $1,900.00. 10 looseleaf volumes. Periodic supplementation.

Criminal Law Reporter. Bureau of National Affairs, Inc. • Weekly. $519.00 per year. Includes full text of U. S. Supreme Court criminal law decisions.

World of Criminal Justice. The Gale Group. • 2001. $150.00. Two volumes. Contains both topical and biographical entries relating to the criminal justice system and criminology.

CRIME, COMPUTER

See: COMPUTER CRIME AND SECURITY

CRITICAL PATH METHOD/ PERT (PROGRAM EVALUATION AND REVIEW TECHNIQUE)

GENERAL WORKS

Critical Path Methods in Construction Practice. James M. Antill and Ronald Woodhead. John Wiley and Sons, Inc. • 1990. $120.00. Fourth edition.

Project Management with CPM, Pert and Precedence Diagramming. Joseph J. Moder and others. Blitz Publishing Co. • 1995. $40.00. Third edition.

PERIODICALS AND NEWSLETTERS

Project Management Journal. Project Management Institute. • Quarterly. $100.00 per year. Contains technical articles dealing with the interests of the field of project management.

TRADE/PROFESSIONAL ASSOCIATIONS

Project Management Institute. Four Campus Blvd., Newton Square, PA 19073-3200. Phone: (610)356-4600 Fax: (610)356-4647 E-mail: pmihq@pmi.org • URL: http://www.pmi.org.

CROPS

See: FARM PRODUCE

CRUISE LINES

See: STEAMSHIP LINES

CRYOGENICS

GENERAL WORKS

Progress in Low Temperature Physics. D. F. Brewer, editor. Elsevier Science. • 1996. $244.00. Volume 14.

Recent Advances in Cryogenic Engineering. J. P. Kelley and J. Goodman, editors. American Society of Mechanical Engineers. • 1993. $30.00.

ABSTRACTS AND INDEXES

Applied Science and Technology Index. H. W. Wilson Co. • 11 times a year. Quarterly and annual cumulations. Service basis for print edition; CD-ROM edition, $1,495.00 per year. Indexes a wide variety of English language technical, industrial, and engineering periodicals.

Current Contents: Engineering, Computing and Technology. Institute for Scientific Information. • Weekly. $730.00 per year. Reproductions of contents pages of technical journals. Includes *Author Index, Address Directory, Current Book Contents* and *Title Word Index.* Formerly *Current Contents: Engineering, Technology and Applied Sciences.*

ALMANACS AND YEARBOOKS

Advances in Cryogenic Engineering. Plenum Publishing Corp. • Irregular. Price varies. Represents *Cryogenic Engineering Conference Proceedings.*

BIBLIOGRAPHIES

Encyclopedia of Physical Science and Engineering Information. The Gale Group. • 1996. $160.00. Second edition. Includes print, electronic, and other information sources for a wide range of scientific, technical, and engineering topics.

CD-ROM DATABASES

COMPENDEX PLUS [CD-ROM]. Engineering Information, Inc. • Quarterly. $3,450.00 per year. Provides CD-ROM indexing and abstracting of the world's engineering and technical information appearing in journals, reports, books, and proceedings, 1985 to date.

Science Citation Index: Compact Disc Edition. Institute for Scientific Information. • Quarterly. Provides CD-ROM indexing of the world's scientific and technical literature. Corresponds to online *Scisearch* and printed *Science Citation Index.*

WILSONDISC: Applied Science and Technology Abstracts. H. W. Wilson Co. • Monthly. $1,495.00 per year, including unlimited access to the online version of *Applied Science and Technology Abstracts* through WILSONLINE. Provides CD-ROM indexing and abstracting of 400 prominent scientific, technical, engineering, and industrial periodicals. Indexing coverage is provided from 1983 to date and abstracting from 1993 to date.

ONLINE DATABASES

Applied Science and Technology Index Online. H. W. Wilson Co. • Provides online indexing of 400 major scientific, technical, industrial, and engineering periodicals. Time period is 1983 to date. Monthly updates. Inquire as to online cost and availability.

F & S Index. The Gale Group. • Contains about four million citations to worldwide business, financial, and industrial or consumer product literature appearing from 1972 to date. Weekly updates. Inquire as to online cost and availability.

Globalbase. The Gale Group. • Provides more than one million online summaries of business, industrial, and economic news reports from more than 1,000 publications worldwide. Covers a wide range of material appearing in international trade journals, professional magazines, and newspapers. Time period is 1984 to date, with weekly updates. Inquire as to online cost and availability.

PROMT: Predicasts Overview of Markets and Technology. The Gale Group. • Companies, products, applied technologies and markets. U.S. and international literature coverage, 1972 to date. Inquire as to online cost and availability. Provides abstracts from more than 1,600 publications. Weekly updates.

Scisearch. Institute for Scientific Information. • Broad, multidisciplinary index to the literature of science and technology, 1974 to present. Inquire as to online cost and availability. Coverage of literature is worldwide, with weekly updates.

PERIODICALS AND NEWSLETTERS

CryoGas International: The Source of Timely and Relevant Information for the Industrial Gas and Cyrogenics Industries. J. R. Campbell & Associates, Inc. • 11 times a year. $150.00 per year. Reports developments in technology market development and new products for the industrial gases and cryogenic equipment industries. Formerly *Cryogenic Information Report.*

Cryogenics: The International Journal of Low Temperature Engineering and Research. Elsevier Science. • Monthly. $1,779.00 per year.

Journal of Low Temperature Physics. Plenum Publishing Corp. • Semimonthly. $1,350.00 per year. Covers the science of cryogenics.

RESEARCH CENTERS AND INSTITUTES

Edward L. Ginzton Laboratory. Stanford University, 450 Via Palou, Stanford, CA 94305-4085. Phone: (650)023-0111 Fax: (650)725-9355 E-mail: dabm@ee.stanford.edu • URL: http://www.stanford.edu/group/ginzton • Research fields include low-temperature physics and superconducting electronics.

Kurata Thermodynamics Laboratory. University of Kansas, Dept. of Chemical and Petroleum Engineering, Lawrence, KS 66045. Phone: (913)864-3860 Fax: (913)864-4967 E-mail: cshowat@ukans.edu • URL: http://www.engr.ukans.edu/~ktl • Investigates the behavior of various materials over a wide range of temperatures.

Laboratory for Electromagnetic and Electronic Systems. Massachusetts Institute of Technology, 77 Massachusetts Ave., Bldg. 10, Room 172, Cambridge, MA 02139. Phone: (617)253-4631 Fax: (617)258-6774 E-mail: jgk@mit.edu • URL: http://power.mit.edu/index.html • Research areas include heat transfer and cryogenics.

Microkelvin Laboratory. Cornell University, Clark Hall, H Corridor, Ithaca, NY 14853. Phone: (607)255-6059 Fax: (607)255-6428 • Focuses on electronic behavior changes in metals, insulators, and semiconductors at ultra-low temperatures.

Thermophysical Properties Research Laboratory. 2595 Yeager Rd., West Lafayette, IN 47906. Phone: (765)463-1581 Fax: (765)463-5235 E-mail: rtaylor@tprl.com • URL: http://www.tprl.com •

Studies the thermophysical properties of materials from cryogenic to very high temperatures.

W. W. Hansen Experimental Physics Laboratory. Stanford University, 445 Via Palou St., Stanford, CA 94305-4085. Phone: (650)723-0280 Fax: (650)725-8311 • Conducts large-scale cryogenic research.

TRADE/PROFESSIONAL ASSOCIATIONS

Cryogenic Engineering Conference. c/o Dr. J. Theilacker, P.O. Box 500, Batavia, IL 60510. Phone: (630)840-3238 Fax: (630)840-4989 • Members are researchers and managers concerned with the science and technology of extreme cold. Subjects of interest include superconductivity, liquefied gases, and cryobiology.

Cryogenic Society of America. c/o Laurie Huget, Huget Advertising, 1033 South Blvd., Oak Park, IL 60302. Phone: (708)383-6220 Fax: (708)383-9337 E-mail: csa@huget.com • URL: http://www.-csa.fnal.gov • Seeks to encourage the dissemination of information on low temperature industrial technology.

OTHER SOURCES

Superconductor Week. WestTech. • Weekly. $397.00 per year. Newsletter. Covers applications of superconductivity and cryogenics, including new markets and products.

CULTURE, CORPORATE

See: CORPORATE CULTURE

CURRENCY

See: MONEY

CURRENCY CONVERTIBILITY

See: FOREIGN EXCHANGE

CURRENCY EXCHANGE RATES

See also: FOREIGN EXCHANGE

ALMANACS AND YEARBOOKS

World Currrency Yearbook. International Currency Analysis, Inc. • Annual. $250.00. Directory of more than 110 central banks worldwide.

HANDBOOKS AND MANUALS

International Guide to Foreign Currency Management. Gary Shoup, editor. Fitzroy Dearborn Publishers. • 1998. $65.00. Written for corporate financial managers. Covers the market for currencies, price forecasting, exposure of various kinds, and risk management.

Strategic Trading in the Foreign Exchange Markets. Gary Klopfenstein. Fitzroy Dearborn Publishers. • 1999. $65.00. Describes the tactics of successful foreign exchange traders.

INTERNET DATABASES

Europa: The European Union's Server. European Union 352 4301 35 349. E-mail: pressoffice@eurostat.cec.be • URL: http://www.europa.eu.int • Web site provides access to a wide variety of EU information, including statistics (Eurostat), news, policies, publications, key issues, and official exchange rates for the euro. Includes links to the European Central Bank, the European Investment Bank, and other institutions. Fees: Free.

The Financial Post (Web site). National Post Online (Hollinger/CanWest). Phone: (244)383-2300 Fax: (416)383-2443 • URL: http://www.nationalpost.com/financialpost/ • Provides a broad range of Canadian business news online, with daily updates. Includes news, opinion, and special reports, as well as "Investing," "Money Rates," "Market Watch," and "Daily Mutual Funds." Allows advanced searching (Boolean operators), with links to various other sites. Fees: Free.

Financial Times: Where Information Becomes Intelligence. FT Group. Phone: (212)752-4500 Fax: (212)688-8229 • URL: http://www.ft.com • Web site provides extensive data and information relating to international business and finance, with daily updates. Includes Markets Today, Company News, Economic Indicators, Equities, Currencies, Capital Markets, Euro Prices, etc. Fees: Free (registration required).

PERIODICALS AND NEWSLETTERS

Blue Chip Financial Forecasts: What Top Analysts are Saying About U. S. and Foreign Interest Rates, Monetary Policy, Inflation, and Economic Growth. Aspen Publishers, Inc. • Monthly. $654.00 per year. Newsletter. Gives forecasts about a year in advance for interest rates, inflation, currency exchange rates, monetary policy, and economic growth rates.

The Financial Post: Canadian's Business Voice. Financial Post Datagroup. • Daily. $234.00 per year. Provides Canadian business, economic, financial, and investment news. Features extensive price quotes from all major Canadian markets: stocks, bonds, mutual funds, commodities, and currencies. Supplement available: *Financial Post 500.* Includes annual supplement.

Financial Times Currency Forecaster: Consensus Forecasts of the Worldwide Currency and Economic Outlook. Capitol Publications, Inc. • Monthly. $695.00 per year. Newsletter. Provides forecasts of foreign currency exchange rates and economic conditions. Supplement available: *Mid-Month Global Financial Report.*

Financial Times [London]. Available from FT Publications, Inc. • Daily, except Sunday. $184.00 per year. An international business and financial newspaper, featuring news from London, Paris, Frankfurt, New York, and Tokyo. Includes worldwide stock and bond market data, commodity market data, and monetary/currency exchange information.

International Market Alert. International Reports, Inc. • Daily. Prices varies. Newsletter. Covers activities of central banks, foreign exchange markets, and New York bond and money markets. Gives specific hedging advice for major currencies. Available online.

Rundt's World Business Intelligence. S. J. Rundt and Associates, Inc. • Weekly. $695.00 per year. Formerly *Rundt's Weekly Intelligence.*

RESEARCH CENTERS AND INSTITUTES

Institute for International Economics. 11 Dupont Circle, N. W., Suite 620, Washington, DC 20036. Phone: (202)328-9000 Fax: (202)328-5432 • URL: http://www.iie.com • Research fields include a wide range of international economic issues, including foreign exchange rates.

STATISTICS SOURCES

Foreign Exchange Currency Rates. Dow Jones & Co., Inc. • Annual. $50.00. Contains a compilation for the year of daily foreign exchange rate tables. These daily tables from *The Wall Street Journal* are also available on a monthly basis at $15.00 per month.

International Financial Statistics. International Monetary Fund, Publications Services. • Monthly. Individuals, $246.00 per year; libraries, $123.00 per year. Includes a wide variety of current data for individual countries in Europe and elsewhere. Annual issue available. Editions available in French and Spanish.

CURRENT EVENTS

See also: CLIPPING SERVICES; NEWSPAPERS; PERIODICALS

ALMANACS AND YEARBOOKS

The Annual Register: A Record of World Events. Keesing's Worldwide, LLC. • Annual. $185.00. Published by Keesings Worldwide. Lists major economic, social, and cultural events of the past year. International coverage.

Facts-on-File Yearbook. Facts on File, Inc. • Annual. $100.00.

World Almanac and Book of Facts. World Almanac Education Group, Inc. • Annual. $10.95.

Worldmark Yearbook. The Gale Group. • Annual. $305.00. Three volumes. Covers economic, social, and political events in about 230 countries. Includes statistical data, directories, and a bibliography.

BIOGRAPHICAL SOURCES

Newsmakers. The Gale Group. • Annual. $145.00. Three softbound issues and one hardbound annual. Biographical information on individuals currently in the news. Includes photographs. Formerly *Contemporary Newsmakers.*

CD-ROM DATABASES

National Newspaper Index CD-ROM. The Gale Group. • Monthly. Provides comprehensive CD-ROM indexing of all material appearing in the late edition of the *New York Times*, the final edition of the *Washington Post*, the national edition of the *Christian Science Monitor*, the home edition of the *Los Angeles Times*, and the *Wall Street Journal.* Time period is four years. Also available online.

The New York Times Ondisc. New York Times Online Services. • Monthly. $2,650.00 per year. CD-ROM discs contain the full text of *The New York Times*, final edition. Inquire as to time period covered and availability of backfiles.

Newspaper Abstracts Ondisc. Bell & Howell Information and Learning. • Monthly. $2,950.00 per year (covers 1989 to date; archival discs are available for 1985-88). Provides cover-to-cover CD-ROM indexing and abstracting of 19 major newspapers, including the *New York Times, Wall Street Journal, Washington Post, Chicago Tribune,* and *Los Angeles Times.*

DIRECTORIES

Cyberhound's Guide to People on the Internet. The Gale Group. • 1997. $79.00. Second edition. Provides descriptions of about 5,500 Internet databases maintained by or for prominent individuals in business, the professions, entertainment, and sports. Indexed by name, subject, and keyword (master index).

ENCYCLOPEDIAS AND DICTIONARIES

Americana Annual. Grolier Inc. • Annual. $29.95.

BBC World Glossary of Current Affairs. Available from St. James Press. • 1991. $85.00. Published by Longman Group Ltd. Provides definitions of 7,000 terms used in world affairs. Arranged by country, with an alphabetical index.

INTERNET DATABASES

GLOBEnet: Canada's National Web Site. The Globe and Mail Co. Phone: 800-268-9128 or (416)585-5250 Fax: (416)585-5249 • URL: http://www.globeandmail.ca • Web site provides access to selected sections of *The Globe and Mail: Canada's National Newspaper.* Includes current news, national issues, career information, "Report on Business," and other topics. Keyword searching is offered for "a seven-day archive of the portion of the *Globe and Mail* that we publish online" (refers to the Web site). Daily updates. Fees: free.

ONLINE DATABASES

The Globe and Mail Online. The Globe and Mail Co. • Contains full text of more than 1.1 million news stories and articles that have appeared daily in *The Globe and Mail: Canada's National Newspaper*, including "Report on Business." Time span is 1977 to date. Daily updates of the complete newspaper are provided. Inquire as to online cost and availability.

Information Bank Abstracts. New York Times Index Dept. • Provides indexing and abstracting of current affairs, primarily from the final late edition of *The New York Times* and the Eastern edition of *The Wall Street Journal*. Time period is 1969 to present, with daily updates. Inquire as to online cost and availability.

Newspaper and Periodical Abstracts. Bell & Howell Information and Learning. • Provides online coverage (citations and abstracts) of 25 major newspapers, 1,600 perodicals, and 70 TV programs. Covers business, economics, current affairs, health, fitness, sports, education, technology, government, consumer affairs, psychology, the arts, and the social sciences. Time period is 1986 to date, with daily updates. Inquire as to online cost and availability.

Super Searchers in the News: The Online Secrets of Journalists and News Researchers. Paula J. Hane and Reva Basch. Information Today, Inc. • 2000. $24.95. Contains online searching advice from 10 professional news researchers and fact checkers. (CyberAge Books.).

PERIODICALS AND NEWSLETTERS

Canadian News Facts: The Indexed Digest of Canadian Current Events. MPL Communication, Inc. • Bimonthly. $200.00 per year. Monthly and quarterly indexes. A summary of current events in Canada.

Facts-on-File World News Digest With Index. Facts on File, Inc. • Weekly. $725.00 per year. Looseleaf service.

Intelligence Digest: A Review of World Affairs; International Political, Economic and Strategic Intelligence. Intelligence International, Ltd. • 46 times a year. $227.00 per year. Provides political, strategic and economic information. Gives warnings on political trends and current affairs.

Keesing's Record of World Events. Keesing's Worldwide,LLC. • Monthly. $357.00 per year.

OTHER SOURCES

Infogate. Infogate, Inc. • Web site provides current news and information on seven "channels": News, Fun, Sports, Info, Finance, Shop, and Travel. Among the content partners are Business Wire, CBS MarketWatch, CNN, Morningstar, Standard & Poor's, and Thomson Investors Network. Fees: Free, but downloading of Infogate software is required (includes personalized news feature). Updating is continuous. Formerly Pointcast Network.

CURTAIN INDUSTRY

See: WINDOW COVERING INDUSTRY

CUSTOMER SERVICE

GENERAL WORKS

Keeping Customers for Life. Joan K. Cannie and Donald Caplin. AMACOM. • 1990. $14.95. A guide to keeping customers satisfied by providing quality service.

Keeping Customers Happy: Strategies for Success. Jacqueline Dunckel. Self-Counsel Press, Inc. • 1994. $9.95. Third edition.

Total Customer Service-The Ultimate Weapon: A Six Point Plan for Giving Your Business the Competitive Edge in the 1990's. William H. Davidow and Bro Uttal. Harper Trade. • 1990. $13.00.

ABSTRACTS AND INDEXES

Business Periodicals Index. H. W. Wilson Co. • Monthly, except August, with quarterly and annual cumulations. Service basis for print edition; CD-ROM edition, $1,495.00 per year.

Readers' Guide to Periodical Literature. H. W. Wilson Co. • Monthly. $220.00 per year. CD-ROM edition, $1,495 per year, including annual cumulation. Indexes about 250 peridicals of general interest.

HANDBOOKS AND MANUALS

Assessing Service Quality: Satisfying the Expectations of Library Customers. Peter Hernon and Ellen Altman. American Library Association. • 1998. $40.00. Discusses surveys, focus groups, and other data collection methods for measuring the quality of library service. Includes sample forms and an annotated bibliography.

Customer Service: A Practical Approach. Elaine K. Harris. Prentice Hall. • 1995. $43.33. Covers various topics in relation to providing good customer service: problem solving; strategy; planning; communication; coping with difficult customers; motivation; leadership. Glossary, information sources, and index are included.

Customer Service Excellence: A Concise Guide for Librarians. Darlene E. Weingand. American Library Association. • 1997. $30.00. Includes information on quality of service benchmarks, teamwork, patron-librarian conflict management, "customer service language," and other library service topics.

Customer Service Operations: The Complete Guide. Warren Blanding. AMACOM. • 1991. $75.00. Covers standards, procedures, customer satisfaction, complaint policies, and other customer service topics.

Gower Handbook of Customer Service. Peter Murley, editor. Ashgate Publishing Co. • 1996. $113.95. Consists of 40 articles (chapters) written by various authors. Among the topics covered are benchmarking, customer surveys, focus groups, control groups, employee selection, incentives, training, teamwork, and telephone techniques. Published by Gower in England.

Marketing Manager's Handbook. Sidney J. Levy and others. Prentice Hall. • 2000. Price on application. Contains 71 chapters by various authors on a wide variety of marketing topics, including market segmentation, market research, international marketing, industrial marketing, survey methods, customer service, advertising, pricing, planning, strategy, and ethics.

Service Quality Handbook. Eberhard E. Scheuing and William F. Christopher, editors. AMACOM. • 1993. $75.00. Contains articles by various authors on the management of service to customers.

ONLINE DATABASES

Readers' Guide Abstracts Online. H. W. Wilson Co. • Indexes and abstracts general interest periodicals, 1983 to date. Weekly updates. Inquire as to online cost and availability.

Wilson Business Abstracts Online. H. W. Wilson Co. • Indexes and abstracts 600 major business periodicals, plus the *Wall Street Journal* and the business section of the *New York Times*. Indexing is from 1982, abstracting from 1990, with the two newspapers included from 1993. Updated weekly. Inquire as to online cost and availability. (*Business Periodicals Index* without abstracts is also available online.).

PERIODICALS AND NEWSLETTERS

Call Center Magazine. Miller Freeman. • Monthly. $14.00 per year. Covers telephone and online customer service, help desk, and marketing operations. Includes articles on communications technology.

CC News: The Business Newspaper for Call Center and Customer Care Professionals. United Publications, Inc. • Eight times a year. Price on application. Includes news of call center technical developments.

Call Center CMR Solutions: The Authority on Teleservices, Sales, and Support Since 1982. Technology Marketing Corp. • Monthly. $49.00 per year. Emphasis is on telemarketing, selling, and customer service. Formerly *Call Center Solutions*.

Communication Briefings: A Monthly Idea Source for Decision Makers. Briefings Publishing Group. • Monthly. $100.00 per year. Newsletter. Presents useful ideas for communication, public relations, customer service, human resources, and employee training.

The Customer Communicator. Alexander Communications Group, Inc. • Monthly. $167.00 per year. Newsletter. Contains news and advice for business firms on how to improve customer relations and communications.

Customer Service Newsletter. Alexander Communications Group, Inc. • Monthly. $167.00 per year. Newsletter. Contains news and ideas for customer service managers.

Journal of Relationship Marketing: Innovations for Service, Quality and Value. Haworth Press, Inc. • Quarterly. Individuals, $50.00 per year; institutions, $75.00 per year; libraries, $200.00 per year.

RESEARCH CENTERS AND INSTITUTES

Center for the Study of Services. 733 15th St., N.W., Suite 820, Washington, DC 20005. Phone: 800-475-7283 or (202)347-9612 Fax: (202)347-4000 E-mail: editors@checkbook.org • URL: http://www.checkbook.org • Evaluates consumer services.

Marketing Science Institute. 1000 Massachusetts Ave., Cambridge, MA 02138. Phone: (617)491-2060 Fax: (617)491-2065 • URL: http://www.msi.org.

TRADE/PROFESSIONAL ASSOCIATIONS

International Customer Service Association. 401 N. Michigan Ave., Chicago, IL 60611-4267. Phone: 800-360-4272 or (312)321-6800 Fax: (312)245-1084 E-mail: icsa@sba.com • URL: http://www.icsa.com • Members are customer service professionals in business and government.

National Retail Federation. 325 Seventh St., N.W., Suite 1000, Washington, DC 20004-2802. Phone: 800-673-4692 or (202)783-7971 Fax: (202)737-2849 E-mail: nrf@nrf.com • URL: http://www.nrf.com.

OTHER SOURCES

Achieving the Competitive Edge with Customer Service. American Management Association Extension Institute. • Looseleaf. $110.00. Self-study course. Emphasis is on practical explanations, examples, and problem solving. Quizzes and a case study are included.

CUSTOMS BROKERS

See also: CUSTOMS HOUSE, U.S. CUSTOMS SERVICE; EXPORT-IMPORT TRADE; FOREIGN TRADE

DIRECTORIES

American Export Register. Available from Thomas Publishing Co., International Div. • Annual. $120.00. Two volumes. Supplement available *American Export Products.* Lists over 44,000 American firms with exporting programs. Includes *American Export Products.* Formerly *American Register of Exporters and Importers.*

National Customs Brokers and Forwarders Association of America: Membership Directory. National Customs Brokers and Forwarders Association of America, Inc. • Annual. $25.00. Lists about 600 customs brokers, international air cargo agents, and freight forwarders in the U.S.

PERIODICALS AND NEWSLETTERS

International Trade Reporter Export Reference Manual. Bureau of National Affairs, Inc. • Weekly. $874.00 per year. Looseleaf. Formerly *Export Shipping Manual.*

TRADE/PROFESSIONAL ASSOCIATIONS

National Customs Brokers and Forwarders Association of America. 1200 18th St., N.W., Suite 901, Washington, DC 20036. Phone: (202)466-0222 Fax: (202)466-0226 E-mail: staff@ncbfaa.org • URL: http://www.ncbfaa.org.

CUSTOMS HOUSE, U.S. CUSTOMS SERVICE

GENERAL WORKS

Customs Law and Administration: Including Treaties and International Agreements and Customs Law and Administration Statutes. Oceana Publications, Inc. • Looseleaf service. $400.00. Two volumes.

CD-ROM DATABASES

U. S. Exports of Merchandise on CD-ROM. U. S. Bureau of the Census, Foreign Trade Div.,. • Monthly. $1,200 per year. Provides export data in the most extensive detail available, including product, quantity, value, shipping weight, country of destination, customs district of exportation, etc.

U. S. Imports of Merchandise (CD-ROM). U. S. Bureau of the Census, Foreign Trade Division. • Monthly. $1,200 per year. Provides import data in the most extensive detail available, including product, quantity, value, shipping weight, country of origin, customs district of entry, rate provision, etc.

DIRECTORIES

U.S. Custom House Guide. Commonwealth Business Media. • Annual. $475.00. Quarterly supplements. List of ports having custom facilities, customs officials, port authorities, chambers of commerce, embassies and consulates, foreign trade zones, and other organizations; related trade services.

HANDBOOKS AND MANUALS

Importers Manual U. S. A.: The Single Source Reference for Importing to the United States. Edward G. Hinkelman. World Trade Press. • 1997. $87.00. Second edition. Published by World Trade Press. Covers U. S. customs regulations, letters of credit, contracts, shipping, insurance, and other items relating to importing. Includes 60 essays on practical aspects of importing.

NAFTA: The North American Free Trade Agreement, A Guide to Customs Procedures. Available from U. S. Government Printing Office. • 1994. $7.00. Revised edition. Issued by the Customs Service, U. S. Treasury Department. Provides a summary of NAFTA customs requirements and benefits. (Customs Publication No. 571.).

PERIODICALS AND NEWSLETTERS

Customs Bulletin and Decisions. Available from U. S. Government Printing Office. • Weekly. $220.00 per year. Issued by U. S. Customs Service, Department of the Treasury. Contains regulations, rulings, decisions, and notices relating to customs laws.

TRADE/PROFESSIONAL ASSOCIATIONS

National Treasury Employees Union. 901 E St., N.W., Suite 600, Washington, DC 20004. Phone: (202)783-4085 Fax: (202)783-4085.

OTHER SOURCES

Customs Regulations of the United States. Available from U. S. Government Printing Office. • Looseleaf. $123.00. Issued by U. S. Customs Service, Department of the Treasury. Reprint of regulations published to carry out customs laws of the U. S. Includes supplementary material for an indeterminate period.

FedWorld: A Program of the United States Department of Commerce. National Technical Information Service. • Web site offers "a comprehensive central access point for searching, locating, ordering, and acquiring government and business information." Emphasis is on searching the Web pages, databases, and government reports of a wide variety of federal agencies. Fees: Free.

CUSTOMS TAX

See: TARIFF

CYCLES, BUSINESS

See: BUSINESS CYCLES

D

DAIRY INDUSTRY

See also: CHEESE INDUSTRY; DAIRY PRODUCTS

ABSTRACTS AND INDEXES

Biological and Agricultural Index. H.W. Wilson Co. • 11 times a year. Annual and quarterly cumulations. Service basis.

Dairy Science Abstracts. Available from CABI Publishing North America. • Monthly. $1095.00 per year. Published in England by CABI Publishing. Provides worldwide coverage of the literature.

DIRECTORIES

Dairy Foods Market Directory. Cahners Business Information. • Annual. $99.90. Lists a wide variety of suppliers to the dairy industry.

ONLINE DATABASES

Biological and Agricultural Index Online. H. W. Wilson Co. • Indexes a wide variety of agricultural and biological periodicals, 1983 to date. Monthly updates. Inquire as to online cost and availability.

CAB Abstracts. CAB International North America. • Contains 46 specialized abstract collections covering over 10,000 journals and monographs in the areas of agriculture, horticulture, forest products, farm products, nutrition, dairy science, poultry, grains, animal health, entomology, etc. Time period is 1972 to date, with monthly updates. Inquire as to online cost and availability. *CAB Abstracts on CD-ROM* also available, with annual updating.

PERIODICALS AND NEWSLETTERS

Dairy Foods: Innovative Ideas and Technologies for Dairy Processors. Cahners Business Information. • Monthly. $99.90 per year. Provides broad coverage of new developments in the dairy industry, including cheese and ice cream products. Includes an annual *Supplement.*

DFISA Reporter. Dairy and Food Industries Supply Association, Inc. • Monthly. Free. Provides industry and association news to manufacturers of equipment products and services to the dairy and food industry.

International Association of Food Industry Supliers Reporter. International Association on Food Industry Suppliers. • Monthly. Free.

Journal of Dairy Research. Cambridge University Press, Journals Dept. • Quarterly. $395.00 per year.

RESEARCH CENTERS AND INSTITUTES

Caine Dairy Center. Utah State University. 4300 S. Highway 89-91, Wellsville, UT 84339. Phone: (435)245-6067 Fax: (435)245-7680.

Quebec Dairy Herd Analyses Service. 555 des Anciens Combattans, Saint-Anne de Bellevue, QC, Canada H9X 3R4. Phone: (514)398-7880 Fax: (514)398-7963 E-mail: bertrand@mail.patlq.mcgill.ca • URL: http://www.patlq.mcgill.ca.

STATISTICS SOURCES

United States Census of Agriculture. U.S. Bureau of the Census. • Quinquennial. Results presented in reports, tape, CD-ROM, and Diskette files.

TRADE/PROFESSIONAL ASSOCIATIONS

American Dairy Science Association. c/o Molly Kelley, 1111 N. Dunlap Ave., Savoy, IL 61874. Phone: (217)356-3182 Fax: (217)398-4119 E-mail: adsa@assochq.org • URL: http://www.adsa.uiuc.edu/.

Dairy Industry Committee. 1451 Dolley Madison Blvd., Mc Lean, VA 22101-3850. Phone: (703)761-2600 Fax: (703)761-4334 • URL: http://www.iafis.org.

Dairy Society International. 7185 Ruritan Dr., Chambersburg, PA 17201. Phone: (717)375-4392.

International Association of Food Industry Suppliers. 1451 Dolley Madison Blvd., Mc Lean, VA 22101-3850. Phone: (703)761-2600 Fax: (703)761-4334 E-mail: info@iafis.org • URL: http://www.iafis.org.

National Dairy Council. 10255 W. Higgins Rd., Suite 900, Rosemont, IL 60018-5616. Phone: (847)803-2000 Fax: (847)803-2077 • URL: http://www.dairyinfo.com.

United Dairy Industry Association. O'Hare International Center, 10255 Higgins Rd., Suite 900, Rosemont, IL 60018. Phone: (847)803-2000 Fax: (847)803-2077.

DAIRY PRODUCTS

See also: DAIRY INDUSTRY

GENERAL WORKS

Engineering for Dairy and Food Products. Arthur W. Farrall. Krieger Publishing Co. • 1980. $46.50. Revised edition.

ABSTRACTS AND INDEXES

Food Science and Technology Abstracts. International Food Information Service Publishing. • Monthly. $1,780.00 per year. Provides worldwide coverage of the literature of food technology and food production.

Foods Adlibra: Key to the World's Food Literature. Foods Adlibra Publications. • Semimonthly.Provides journal citations and abstracts to the literature of food technology and packaging.

CD-ROM DATABASES

Food Science and Technology Abstracts [CD-ROM]. Available from SilverPlatter Information, Inc. • Quarterly. $3,700 per year. Produced by International Food Information Service (home page is http://www.ifis.org). Provides worldwide coverage on CD-ROM of the literature of food technology and production. Various types of publications are indexed, with abstracts, including about 1,800 periodicals. Time period is 1969 to date.

DIRECTORIES

Dairy Field Buyer's Guide. Stagnito Publishing Co. • Annual. $55.00. Lists more than 500 suppliers of equipment and services and distributors for the dairy processing industry.

ENCYCLOPEDIAS AND DICTIONARIES

Foods and Nutrition Encyclopedia. Audrey H. Ensminger and others. CRC Press, Inc. • 1993. $382.00. Second edition. Two volumes.

FINANCIAL RATIOS

Almanac of Business and Industrial Financial Ratios. Leo Troy. Prentice Hall. • Annual. $99.95. Contains financial ratios derived from federal tax returns. Ratios for each of about 200 industries are arranged according to company asset size.

Annual Statement Studies. Robert Morris Associates: The Association of Lending and Credit Risk Professiona. • Annual. Free to members; non-members, $140.00. Median and quartile financial ratios are given for over 400 kinds of manufacturing, wholesale, retail, construction, and consumer finance establishments. Data is sorted by both asset size and sales volume. Includes a clearly written "Definition of Ratios" and an alphabetical industry index.

INTERNET DATABASES

Fedstats. Federal Interagency Council on Statistical Policy. Phone: (202)395-7254 • URL: http://www.fedstats.gov • Web site features an efficient search facility for full-text statistics produced by more than 70 federal agencies, including the Census Bureau, the Bureau of Economic Analysis, and the Bureau of Labor Statistics. Boolean searches can be made within one agency or for all agencies combined. Links are offered to international statistical bureaus, including the UN, IMF, OECD, UNESCO, Eurostat, and 20 individual countries. Fees: Free.

USDA. United States Department of Agriculture. Phone: (202)720-2791 E-mail: agsec@usda.gov • URL: http://www.usda.gov • The USDA home page has six sections: News and Information; What's New; About USDA; Agencies; Opportunities; Search and Help. Keyword searching is offered from the USDA home page and from various individual agency home pages. Agencies are the Economic Research Service, Agricultural Marketing Service, National Agricultural Statistics Service, National Agricultural Library, and about 12 others. Updating varies. Fees: Free.

ONLINE DATABASES

DRI U.S. Central Database. Data Products Division. • Provides more than 23,000 business, financial, demographic, economic, foreign trade, and industry-related time series for the U.S. Includes national income, population, retail-wholesale trade, price indexes, labor data, housing, industrial production, banking, interest rates, money supply, etc. Time period is generally 1947 to date (some data back to 1929). Updating varies. Inquire as to online cost and availability.

Food Science and Technology Abstracts [online]. IFIS North American Desk. • Produced by International Food Information Service. Provides about 500,000 online citations, with abstracts, to the international literature of food science, technology, commodities, engineering, and processing. Approximately 2,000 periodicals are covered. Time period is 1969 to date, with monthly updates. Inquire as to online cost and availability.

FOODS ADLIBRA. General Mills, Inc. • Contains online citations, with abstracts, to the technical and business literature of food processing and packaging. New products and new ingredients are featured. Covers about 250 trade journals and 500 research journals from 1974 to date, with monthly updates. Inquire as to online cost and availability.

PERIODICALS AND NEWSLETTERS

Journal of Dairy Science. American Dairy Science Association. • Monthly. $250.00 per year. Provides primary scientific research on all aspects of dairy foods and dairy cattle production and management.

Monthly Price Review. Urner Barry Publications Inc. • Monthly. $131.00 per year. Annual summary.

Weekly Insiders Dairy and Egg Letter. Urner Barry Publications, Inc. • Weekly. $173.00 per year.

PRICE SOURCES

Supermarket News: The Industry's Weekly Newspaper. Fairchild Publications. • Weekly. Individuals, $68.00 per year; instututions, $44.50 per year; corporations, $89.00 per year.

RESEARCH CENTERS AND INSTITUTES

Dairy Research and Education Center. Pennsylvania State University. University Park, PA 16802. Phone: (814)863-3665 Fax: (814)863-6042 • URL: http://www.das.psu.edu.

STATISTICS SOURCES

Agricultural Statistics. Available from U. S. Government Printing Office. • Annual. Produced by the National Agricultural Statistics Service, U. S. Department of Agriculture. Provides a wide variety of statistical data relating to agricultural production, supplies, consumption, prices/price-supports, foreign trade, costs, and returns, as well as farm labor, loans, income, and population. In many cases, historical data is shown annually for 10 years. In addition to farm data, includes detailed fishery statistics.

Annual Survey of Manufactures. Available from U. S. Government Printing Office. • Annual. Prices vary. Issued by the U. S. Census Bureau as an interim update to the *Census of Manufactures.* Includes data on number of manufacturing establishments in various industries, employment, labor costs, value of shipments, capital expenditures, inventories, energy costs, and assets. (See also Census Bureau home page, http://www.census.gov/.).

Business Statistics of the United States. Courtenay M. Slater, editor. Bernan Associates. • 1999. $74.00. Fifth edition. Based on *Business Statistics*, formerly issue by the Bureau of Economic Analysis, U. S. Department of Commerce. Provides basic data for a wide variety of U. S. industries, services, and economic indicators. Most statistics are shown annually for 29 years and monthly for the most recent four years.

Survey of Current Business. Available from U. S. Government Printing Office. • Monthly. $49.00 per year. Issued by Bureau of Economic Analysis, U. S. Department of Commerce. Presents a wide variety of business and economic data.

TRADE/PROFESSIONAL ASSOCIATIONS

American Butter Institute. 2102 Wilson Blvd., No. 900, Arlington, VA 22201-3009. Phone: (703)243-6113 Fax: (703)841-9328 E-mail: aminer@nmpf.org • URL: http://www.butterinstitute.org.

Certified Milk Producers Association of America. 8300 Pine Ave., Chino, CA 91710. Phone: (909)393-0960 Fax: (909)393-0284.

Dairy Society International. 7185 Ruritan Dr., Chambersburg, PA 17201. Phone: (717)375-4392.

Milk Industry Foundation. 1250 H St., N.W., Suite 900, Washington, DC 20005. Phone: (202)737-4332 Fax: (202)331-7820 • URL: http://www.idfa.org.

National Cheese Institute. 1250 H St., N.W., Suite 900, Washington, DC 20005. Phone: (202)737-4332 Fax: (202)331-7820 • URL: http://www.idfa.org.

National Dairy Council. 10255 W. Higgins Rd., Suite 900, Rosemont, IL 60018-5616. Phone: (847)803-2000 Fax: (847)803-2077 • URL: http://www.dairyinfo.com.

OTHER SOURCES

Major Food and Drink Companies of the World. Available from The Gale Group. • 2001. $855.00. Fourth edition. Two volumes. Published by Graham & Whiteside. Contains profiles and trade names for more than 9,000 important food and beverage companies in various countries. In addition to foods, includes both alcoholic and nonalcoholic drink products.

Thomas Food and Beverage Market Place. Grey House Publishing. • Annual. $295.00. Three volumes. Contains more than 40,000 entries covering food companies, beverages, food equipment, warehouse companies, food brokers, wholesalers, importers, and exporters. Formerly *Thomas Food Industry Register.*

DANGEROUS MATERIALS

See: HAZARDOUS MATERIALS

DATA BASES, ONLINE

See: ONLINE INFORMATION SYSTEMS

DATA COMMUNICATIONS

See: COMPUTER COMMUNICATIONS

DATA IDENTIFICATION SYSTEMS, AUTOMATIC

See: AUTOMATIC IDENTIFICATION SYSTEMS

DATA SYSTEMS

See: SYSTEMS IN MANAGEMENT

DATES (CHRONOLOGY)

See: CHRONOLOGY

DAY CARE CENTERS

See also: BABY SITTING

GENERAL WORKS

Expanding Services to Meet Community Needs in an Era of Change. American Association of Homes and Services for the Aging. • 1996. $30.00. Covers new, innovative models of home health care delivery, intergenerational day care, and senior housing services.

FINANCIAL RATIOS

Annual Statement Studies. Robert Morris Associates: The Association of Lending and Credit Risk Professiona. • Annual. Free to members; non-members, $140.00. Median and quartile financial ratios are given for over 400 kinds of manufacturing, wholesale, retail, construction, and consumer finance establishments. Data is sorted by both asset size and sales volume. Includes a clearly written "Definition of Ratios" and an alphabetical industry index.

HANDBOOKS AND MANUALS

Child Care Service. Entrepreneur Media, Inc. • Looseleaf. $59.50. A practical guide to starting a day care center for children. Covers profit potential, start-up costs, market size evaluation, owner's time required, site selection, pricing, accounting, advertising, promotion, etc. (Start-Up Business Guide No. E1058.).

Senior Day Care Center. Entrepreneur Media, Inc. • Looseleaf. $59.50. A practical guide to starting a day care center for older adults (supervised environment for frail individuals). Covers profit potential, start-up costs, market size evaluation, owner's time required, site selection, lease negotiation, pricing, accounting, advertising, promotion, etc. (Start-Up Business Guide No. E1335.).

PERIODICALS AND NEWSLETTERS

Day Care USA Newsletter: The Independent Biweekly Newsletter of Day Care Information Service. United Communications Group (UCG). • Biweekly. $294.00 per year. Newsletter. Provides current information on child day care center funding, legislation, and regulation.

TRADE/PROFESSIONAL ASSOCIATIONS

Comprehensive Day Care Programs. Stevens Administrative Center. Spring Garden at 13th St., Philadelphia, PA 19123. Phone: (215)351-7200 Fax: (215)351-7165.

DDT

See: PESTICIDE INDUSTRY

DEATH TAX

See: INHERITANCE TAX

DEATHS AND BIRTHS

See: VITAL STATISTICS

DEBATES AND DEBATING

See also: PUBLIC SPEAKING

GENERAL WORKS

How to Win Arguments; More Often Than Not. William A. Rusher. University Press of America. • 1985. $17.75.

Mastering Competitive Debate. Dana Hensley and Diana Carlin. Clark Publishing, Inc. • 1999. $38.00. Fith edition.

DIRECTORIES

American Forensic Association Newsletter - Directory. American Forensic Association. • Annual. Free with subscription; non-subscription, $7.50. List of 1,500 member teachers of argumentation and debate.

ONLINE DATABASES

CIS. Congressional Information Service, Inc. • Indexes publications of the United States Congress,

1970 to present. Inquire as to online cost and availability.

PERIODICALS AND NEWSLETTERS

Argumentation and Advocacy. American Forensic Association. • Quarterly. $55.00 per year. Formerly *American Forensic Association Journal.*

Spectra. National Communication Association. • Monthly. $45.00 per year.

TRADE/PROFESSIONAL ASSOCIATIONS

American Forensic Association. P.O. Box 256, River Falls, WI 54022. Phone: 800-228-5424 or (715)425-3198 Fax: (715)425-9533 E-mail: james.w.pratt@uwrf.edu.

National Forensic League. P.O. Box 38, Ripon, WI 54971-0038. Phone: (920)748-6206 or (920)748-6896 Fax: (920)748-9478 E-mail: nfl@mail.wiscnet.net • URL: http://www.debate.uvm.edu/nfl.html.

DEBENTURES

See: BONDS

DEBT COLLECTION

See: COLLECTING OF ACCOUNTS

DEBT, NATIONAL

See: NATIONAL DEBT

DECEPTIVE ADVERTISING

See: ADVERTISING LAW AND REGULATION

DECISION-MAKING

See also: OPERATIONS RESEARCH

GENERAL WORKS

Business Statistics: Contemporary Decision Making. Ken Black. South-Western Publishing Co. • 2000. $65.00. Third edition.

Case Studies in Financial Decision Making. Diana R. Harrington and Kenneth M. Eades. Dryden Press. • 1993. $63.50. Third edition.

Decision Making: Alternatives to Rational Choice Models. Mary Zey. Sage Publications, Inc. • 1992. $58.00. Eighteen contributors provide material on decision-making theory.

Decision Making and Forecasting: With Emphasis on Model Building and Policy Analysis. Kneale T. Marshall and Robert M. Oliver. McGraw-Hill. • 1995. $86.88.

The Dynamic Decision Maker: Five Decision Styles for Executive and Business Success. Michael J. Driver and others. HarperInformation. • 1993. $24.95. The five styles are decisive, flexible, hierarchial, integrative, and systemic.

Judgment in Managerial Decision Making. May H. Bazerman. John Wiley and Sons, Inc. • 1997. $40.95. Fourth edition.

The Psychology of Decision Making: People in Organizations. Lee R. Beach. Sage Publications, Inc. • 1997. $30.00. Includes references and index. (Foundations for Organizational Science).

Quantitative Methods for Business Decisions:with cases. Lawrence L. Lapin. Wadsworth Publishing Co. • 1995. $75.95. Sixth edition.

Smart Choices: A Practical Guide to Making Better Decisions. John S. Hammond and others. Harvard Business School Press. • 1998. $22.50. Provides a systematic approach to effective decision-making. Eight fundamentals of decision-analysis are described, involving problems, objectives, alternatives, consequences, tradeoffs, uncertainty, risks, and choices.

Systems and Decision Making: A Management Science Approach. Hans G. Daellenbach. John Wiley and Sons, Inc. • 1994. $118.95.

ABSTRACTS AND INDEXES

Psychological Abstracts. American Psychological Association. • Monthly. Members, $799.00 per year; individuals and institutions, $1,075.00 per year. Covers the international literature of psychology and the behavioral sciences. Includes journals, technical reports, dissertations, and other sources.

ENCYCLOPEDIAS AND DICTIONARIES

Blackwell Encyclopedic Dictionary of Strategic Management. Derek F. Channon, editor. Blackwell Publishers. • 1997. $110.00. The editor is associated with Imperial College, London. Contains definitions of key terms combined with longer articles written by various U. S. and foreign business educators. Includes bibliographies and index. (Blackwell Encyclopedia of Management Series.).

HANDBOOKS AND MANUALS

AMA Management Handbook. John J. Hampton, editor. AMACOM. • 1994. $110.00. Third edition. Provides 200 chapters in 16 major subject areas. Covers a wide variety of business and industrial management topics.

ONLINE DATABASES

PsycINFO. American Psychological Association. • Provides indexing and abstracting of the worldwide literature of psychology and the behavioral sciences. Time period is 1967 to date, with monthly updates. Inquire as to online cost and availability.

PERIODICALS AND NEWSLETTERS

Communication Briefings: A Monthly Idea Source for Decision Makers. Briefings Publishing Group. • Monthly. $100.00 per year. Newsletter. Presents useful ideas for communication, public relations, customer service, human resources, and employee training.

Decision Line. Decision Sciences Institute. • Five times a year. Free to members; non-members, $6.00 per year.

Decision Sciences. Decision Sciences Institute. • Bimonthly. $59.00 per year.

RESEARCH CENTERS AND INSTITUTES

Center for Decision Research. University of Chicago Graduate School of Business. 1101 E. 58th St., Chicago, IL 60637. Phone: (773)702-4877 Fax: (773)702-0458 E-mail: richardthaler@gsb.uchicago.edu • URL: http://www.gsbdrl.uchicago.edu.

Center for Research in Regulated Industries. Rutgers University. Graduate School of Management, 180 University Ave., Newark, NJ 07102. Phone: (973)353-5049 Fax: (973)353-1348 E-mail: crri@andromeda.rutgers.edu • URL: http://www.rci.rutgers.edu/~crri.

Western Management Science Institute. University of California, Los Angeles. John C. Anderson Graduate School of Management, 405 Hilgard, Room 6223, Los Angeles, CA 90024. Phone: (310)825-2562.

TRADE/PROFESSIONAL ASSOCIATIONS

Decision Sciences Institute. University Plaza, Atlanta, GA 30303. Phone: (404)651-4073 Fax: (404)651-2804 E-mail: dsi@gsu.edu • URL: http://www.dsi.gsu.edu.

North American Simulation and Gaming Association. P.O. Box 78636, Indianapolis, IN 46278. Phone: 888-432-4263 or (317)387-1424 Fax: (317)387-1921 E-mail: info@nasaga.org • URL: http://www.nasaga.org • Members are professionals interested in the use of games and simulations for problem solving and decision-making in all types of organizations.

DECORATION, INTERIOR

See: INTERIOR DECORATION

DEDUCTIONS (INCOME TAX)

See: INCOME TAX

DEFENSE CONTRACTS

See: GOVERNMENT CONTRACTS

DEFENSE INDUSTRIES

See also: AEROSPACE INDUSTRY; AVIATION INDUSTRY; GOVERNMENT CONTRACTS; MILITARY MARKET

ABSTRACTS AND INDEXES

Air University Library Index to Military Periodicals. U.S. Air Force. • Quarterly. Free to qualified personnel. Annual cumulation.

ALMANACS AND YEARBOOKS

Brassey's Defence Yearbook. Brassey's. • 1997. $55.00. Formerly *RUSI.*

United Nations Disarmament Yearbook. United Nations Publications. • Annual. $55.00.

BIBLIOGRAPHIES

Defense and Security. Available from U. S. Government Printing Office. • Annual. Free. Issued by the Superintendent of Documents. A list of government publications on defense and related topics. Formerly *Defense Supply and Logistics.* (Subject Bibliography No. 153.).

DIRECTORIES

Department of Defense Telephone Directory. Available from U. S. Government Printing Office. • Three times a year. $44.00 per year. An alphabetical directory of U. S. Department of Defense personnel, including Departments of the Army, Navy, and Air Force.

INTERNET DATABASES

Fedstats. Federal Interagency Council on Statistical Policy. Phone: (202)395-7254 • URL: http://www.fedstats.gov • Web site features an efficient search facility for full-text statistics produced by more than 70 federal agencies, including the Census Bureau, the Bureau of Economic Analysis, and the Bureau of Labor Statistics. Boolean searches can be made within one agency or for all agencies combined. Links are offered to international statistical bureaus, including the UN, IMF, OECD, UNESCO, Eurostat, and 20 individual countries. Fees: Free.

ONLINE DATABASES

Aerospace/Defense Markets and Technology. The Gale Group. • Abstracts of commerical aerospace/defense related literature, 1982 to date. Also includes information about major defense contracts awarded by the U. S. Department of Defense. International coverage. Inquire as to online cost and availability.

DRI U.S. Central Database. Data Products Division. • Provides more than 23,000 business, financial, demographic, economic, foreign trade, and industry-related time series for the U.S. Includes national income, population, retail-wholesale trade, price indexes, labor data, housing, industrial production, banking, interest rates, money supply, etc. Time period is generally 1947 to date (some data back to 1929). Updating varies. Inquire as to online cost and availability.

PERIODICALS AND NEWSLETTERS

Air Force Journal of Logistics. Available from U. S. Government Printing Office. • Quarterly. $15.00 per year. Issued by the Air Force Logistics Management Center, Air Force Department, Defense Department. Presents research and information of interest to professional Air Force logisticians.

Armed Forces Journal International. Armed Forces Journal International, Inc. • Monthly. $45.00 per year. A defense magazine for career military officers and industry executives. Covers defense events, plans, policies, budgets, and innovations.

Defense Daily: The Daily of Aerospace and Defense. Phillips Business Information, Inc. • Daily (five times a week). $1,697.00 per year. Newsletter.

Defense Industry Report. Phillips Publishing, Inc. • Biweekly. $795.00 per year. Newsletter.

Defense Monitor. Center for Defense Information. • Ten times a year. $35.00 per year.

Inside R and D: A Weekly Report on Technical Innovation. Technical Insights. • Weekly. $840.00 per year. Concentrates on new and significant developments. Formerly *Technolog Transfer Week.*

National Defense. National Defense Industrial Association. • 10 times a year. $35.00 per year.

Soldiers. Available from U. S. Government Printing Office. • Monthly. $28.00 per year. Provides information on the policies, plans, operations, and technical developments of the U.S. Department of the Army (http://www.army.mil).

RESEARCH CENTERS AND INSTITUTES

Applied Research Laboratory. Pennsylvania State University. P.O. Box 30, State College, PA 16804. Phone: (814)865-6343 Fax: (814)865-3105 E-mail: lrh3@psu.edu • URL: http://www.arl.psu.edu.

Center for Defense Information. 1779 Massachusetts Ave., N.W., Washington, DC 20036. Phone: (202)332-0600 Fax: (202)462-4559 E-mail: info@cdi.org • URL: http://www.cdi.org.

Institute for Defense Analyses. 1801 N. Beauregard St., Alexandria, VA 22311-1772. Phone: (703)845-2300 Fax: (703)845-2569 • URL: http://www.ida.org.

Structures and Composites Laboratory. Stanford University. Dept. of Aeronautics and Astronomy, Stanford, CA 94305. Phone: (415)723-3524 Fax: (415)723-0062 E-mail: gspringer@stanford.edu.

STATISTICS SOURCES

Business Statistics of the United States. Courtenay M. Slater, editor. Bernan Associates. • 1999. $74.00. Fifth edition. Based on *Business Statistics*, formerly issue by the Bureau of Economic Analysis, U. S. Department of Commerce. Provides basic data for a wide variety of U. S. industries, services, and economic indicators. Most statistics are shown annually for 29 years and monthly for the most recent four years.

Standard & Poor's Industry Surveys. Standard & Poor's. • Semiannual. $1,800.00. Two looseleaf volumes. Includes monthly supplements. Provides detailed, individual surveys of 52 major industry groups. Each survey is revised on a semiannual basis. Also includes "Monthly Investment Review" (industry group investment analysis) and monthly "Trends & Projections" (economic analysis).

Survey of Current Business. Available from U. S. Government Printing Office. • Monthly. $49.00 per year. Issued by Bureau of Economic Analysis, U. S. Department of Commerce. Presents a wide variety of business and economic data.

World Factbook. U.S. National Technical Information Service. • Annual. $83.00. Prepared by the Central Intelligence Agency. For all countries of the world, provides current economic, demographic, geographic, communications, government, defense force, and illicit drug trade information (where applicable).

TRADE/PROFESSIONAL ASSOCIATIONS

National Defense Industrial Association. 2111 Wilson Blvd., No. 400, Arlington, VA 22201-3061. Phone: (703)522-1820 or (703)247-2589 Fax: (703)522-1885 E-mail: info@india.org • URL: http://www.adpa.org • Concerned with industrial preparedness for national defense.

National Defense Transportation Association. 50 S. Pickett St., Suite 220, Alexandria, VA 22304-7296. Phone: (703)751-5011 Fax: (703)823-8761 E-mail: ndta@ndtahq.com • URL: http://www.web2volpe.dot.gov/ndta.

OTHER SOURCES

Aerospace America [online]. American Institute of Aeronautics and Astronautics. • Provides complete text of the periodical, *Aerospace America*, 1984 to date, with monthly updates. Also includes news from the *AIAA Bulletin.* Inquire as to online cost and availability.

Aerospace Database. American Institute of Aeronautics and Astronautics. • Contains abstracts of literature covering all aspects of the aerospace and aircraft in series 1983 to date. Semimonthly updates. Inquire as to online cost and availability.

Army AL&T: Acquisitions, Logistics, and Technology Bulletin. Available from U. S. Government Printing Office. • Bimonthly. $20.00 per year. Produced by the U. S. Army Materiel Command (http://www.amc.army.mil). Reports on Army research, development, and acquisition. Formerly *Army RD&A.*

Carroll's Defense Industry Charts. Carroll Publishing. • Quarterly. $1,150.00 per year. Provides 180 large, fold-out paper charts showing personnel relationships at more than 100 major U. S. defense contractors. Charts are also available online and on CD-ROM.

Government Contract Litigation Reporter: Covers Defense Procurement Fraud Litigation As Well as False Claims Acts (Qui Tam) Litigation. Andrews Publications. • Semimonthly. $875.00 per year. Provides reports on defense procurement fraud lawsuits.

DEFENSE MARKET

See: MILITARY MARKET

DEFICIT, FEDERAL

See: NATIONAL DEBT

DEHYDRATED FOODS

See: FOOD INDUSTRY

DEMOGRAPHY

See: MARKET STATISTICS; POPULATION; VITAL STATISTICS

DENTAL SUPPLY INDUSTRY

DIRECTORIES

American Dental Directory. American Dental Association. • Annual. $187.50. Contains brief information for over 170,000 dentists.

Dentistry Today: Equipment Buyers' Guide. Dentistry Today, Inc. • Annual. Price on application. Provides purchasing information for more than 500 dental products.

Proofs: Buyers' Guide and United States Manufacturers' Directory. Dental Economics Div. PennWell Corp., Industrial Div. • Annual. $40.00. List of over 600 manufacturers of dental products and equipment; coverage includes foreign listings.

Who's Who in the Dental Laboratory Industry. National Association of Dental Laboratories. • Annual. $55.00. About 3,300 dental laboratories; 12,000 certified dental technicians, manufacturers, and schools of dental technology.

PERIODICALS AND NEWSLETTERS

Dental Lab Products. MEDEC Dental Communications. • Bimonthly. $35.00 per year. Edited for dental laboratory managers. Covers new products and technical developments.

Dental Products Report Europe. MEDEC Dental Communications. • Bimonthly. $40.00 per year. Covers new dental products for the European market.

Dental Products Report: Trends in Industry. MEDEC Dental Communications. • 11 times a year. $90.00 per year. Provides information on new dental products, technology, and trends in dentistry.

Dental Trade Newsletter. American Dental Trade Association. • Bimonthly. Price on application.

Proofs: The Magazine of Dental Sales. PennWell Corp., Industrial Div. • 10 times a year. $35.00 per year.

STATISTICS SOURCES

U. S. Industry and Trade Outlook: The McGraw-Hill Companies and the U.S. Department of Commerce/ International Trade Administration. Datapso Research Corp. • Annual. $69.95. Produced by the International Trade Administration, U. S. Department of Commerce, in a "public-private" partnership with DRI/McGraw-Hill and Standard & Poor's. Provides basic data, outlook for the current year, and "Long-Term Prospects" (five-year projections) for a wide variety of products and services. Includes high technology industries. Formerly *U. S. Industrial Outlook.*

TRADE/PROFESSIONAL ASSOCIATIONS

American Dental Association. 211 E. Chicago Ave., Chicago, IL 60611-2678. Phone: (312)440-2500 Fax: (312)440-2800 E-mail: online@ada.org • URL: http://www.ada.org.

American Dental Trade Association. 4222 King St., W., Alexandria, VA 22302-1597. Phone: (703)379-7755 Fax: (703)931-9429 E-mail: npetrovic@adta.com.

Dental Dealers of America. 123 S. Broad St., Suite 2030, Philadelphia, PA 19109-1020. Phone: (215)731-9975 or (215)731-9982 Fax: (215)731-9984.

Dental Manufacturers of America. Fidelity Bldg., 123 S. Broad St., Suite 2030, Philadelphia, PA 19109-1020. Phone: (215)731-9975 or (215)731-9982 Fax: (215)731-9984 E-mail: staff@dmanews.org • URL: http://www.dmanews.org.

Health Industry Manufacturers Association. 1200 G St., N.W., Suite 400, Washington, DC 20005. Phone: (202)783-8700 Fax: (202)783-8750 • URL: http://www.himanet.com.

DEPARTMENT STORES

See also: CHAIN STORES; MARKETING; RETAIL TRADE

GENERAL WORKS

The Retail Revolution: Market Transformation, Investment, and Labor in the Modern Department Store. Barry Bluestone and others. Greenwood Publishing Group, Inc. • 1980. $52.95.

DIRECTORIES

Directory of Department Stores. Chain Store Guide. • Annual. $290.00. Lists over 350 department stores and 1,100 mail order firms.

Directory of Discount and General Merchandise Stores. Chain Store Guide. • Annual. $300.00. Includes retailers and wholesalers of housewares, giftwares, novelties, toys, hobby materials, crafts, and stationery. Formerly *Directory of Discount Stores Catalog Showrooms.*

European Directory of Retailers and Wholesalers. Available from The Gale Group. • 1997. $790.00. Second edition. Published by Euromonitor. Provides detailed information on more than 4,000 major retail and wholesale businesses in 17 countries of Western Europe. Contains 26 categories, such as supermarkets, superstores, department stores, discount stores, franchise operators, mail order, etc. Includes company, product, and geographic indexes.

Plunkett's Retail Industry Almanac: Complete Profiles on the Retail 500-The Leading Firms in Retail Stores, Services, Catalogs, and On-Line Sales. Available from Plunkett Research, Ltd. • Annual. $179.99. Provides detailed profiles of 500 major U. S. retailers. Industry trends are discussed.

Sheldon's Major Stores and Chains. Phelon Sheldon and Marsar, Inc. • Annual. $175.00. Lists department stores and chains in, women's specialty and chains, home furnishing chains and resident buying offices in the U.S. and Canada. Formerly *Sheldon's Retail Stores.*

FINANCIAL RATIOS

Annual Statement Studies. Robert Morris Associates: The Association of Lending and Credit Risk Professiona. • Annual. Free to members; non-members, $140.00. Median and quartile financial ratios are given for over 400 kinds of manufacturing, wholesale, retail, construction, and consumer finance establishments. Data is sorted by both asset size and sales volume. Includes a clearly written "Definition of Ratios" and an alphabetical industry index.

Financial and Operating Results of Department and Specialty Stores. National Retail Federation. John Wiley and Sons, Inc. • Annual. Members, $80.00; non-members, $100.00.

INTERNET DATABASES

Fedstats. Federal Interagency Council on Statistical Policy. Phone: (202)395-7254 • URL: http://www.fedstats.gov • Web site features an efficient search facility for full-text statistics produced by more than 70 federal agencies, including the Census Bureau, the Bureau of Economic Analysis, and the Bureau of Labor Statistics. Boolean searches can be made within one agency or for all agencies combined. Links are offered to international statistical bureaus, including the UN, IMF, OECD, UNESCO, Eurostat, and 20 individual countries. Fees: Free.

ONLINE DATABASES

DRI U.S. Central Database. Data Products Division. • Provides more than 23,000 business, financial, demographic, economic, foreign trade, and industry-related time series for the U.S. Includes national income, population, retail-wholesale trade, price indexes, labor data, housing, industrial production, banking, interest rates, money supply, etc. Time period is generally 1947 to date (some data back to 1929). Updating varies. Inquire as to online cost and availability.

PERIODICALS AND NEWSLETTERS

Chain Store Age: The Newsmagazine for Retail Executives. Lebhar-Friedman, Inc. • Monthly. $105.00 per year. Formerly *Chain Store Age Executive with Shopping Center Age.*

The Retail Management Letter. Management Facts Co. • Monthly. $167.00 per year.

Retailing Today. Robert Kahn and Associates. • Monthly. $70.00 per year. Newsletter. Written for retail chief executive officers and other top retail management.

Stores. National Retail Federation. N R F Enterprises, Inc. • Monthly. $49.00 per year.

RESEARCH CENTERS AND INSTITUTES

Center for Retail Management. J. L. Kellogg Graduate School of Management, Northwestern University, Evanston, IL 60208. Phone: (847)467-3600 Fax: (847)467-3620 • URL: http://www.retailing-network.com • Conducts research related to retail marketing and management.

Center for Retailing Studies. Texas A & M University, Department of Marketing, 4112 Tamus, College Station, TX 77843-4112. Phone: (979)845-0325 Fax: (979)845-5230 E-mail: berryle@tamu.edu • URL: http://www.crstamu.org • Research areas include retailing issues and consumer economics.

STATISTICS SOURCES

Business Statistics of the United States. Courtenay M. Slater, editor. Bernan Associates. • 1999. $74.00. Fifth edition. Based on *Business Statistics*, formerly issue by the Bureau of Economic Analysis, U. S. Department of Commerce. Provides basic data for a wide variety of U. S. industries, services, and economic indicators. Most statistics are shown annually for 29 years and monthly for the most recent four years.

Merchandise and Operating Results of Department and Specialty Stores. National Retail Federation. John Wiley and Sons, Inc. • Annual. Members, $80.00; non-members, $100.00.

Survey of Current Business. Available from U. S. Government Printing Office. • Monthly. $49.00 per year. Issued by Bureau of Economic Analysis, U. S. Department of Commerce. Presents a wide variety of business and economic data.

WEFA Industrial Monitor. John Wiley and Sons, Inc. • Annual. $65.00. Prepared by industry analysts at WEFA, an economic forecasting and consulting firm (originally Wharton Econometric Forecasting Associates). Contains discussions of the outlook for major U. S. industries, with many 10-year forecasts (WEFA Web site is http://www.wefa.com).

TRADE/PROFESSIONAL ASSOCIATIONS

International Mass Retail Association. 1700 N. Moore St., Suite 2250, Arlington, VA 22209. Phone: (703)841-2300 Fax: (703)841-1184 • URL: http://www.imra.org.

National Retail Federation. 325 Seventh St., N.W., Suite 1000, Washington, DC 20004-2802. Phone: 800-673-4692 or (202)783-7971 Fax: (202)737-2849 E-mail: nrf@nrf.com • URL: http://www.nrf.com.

North American Retail Dealers Association. 10 E. 22nd St., Suite 310, Lombard, IL 60148. Phone: 800-621-0298 or (630)953-8950 Fax: (630)953-8957 E-mail: nardahdq@aol.com • URL: http://www.narda.com.

Retail, Wholesale and Department Store Union. 30 E. 29th St., New York, NY 10016. Phone: (212)684-5300 Fax: (212)779-2809 E-mail: rwdsu@aol.com.

DEPRECIATION

See also: ACCOUNTING

HANDBOOKS AND MANUALS

CCH Guide to Car, Travel, Entertainment, and Home Office Deductions. CCH, Inc. • Annual. $42.00. Explains how to claim maximum tax deductions for common business expenses. Includes automobile depreciation tables, lease value tables, worksheets, and examples of filled-in tax forms.

Depreciation and Investment Credit Manual. Prentice Hall. • Annual. Price on application.

Depreciation Handbook. Matthew Bender & Co., Inc. • $180.00. Looseleaf service. Periodic supplementation. Treatment of depreciation in one volume.

Federal Tax Course: General Edition. CCH, Inc. • Annual. $123.00. Provides basic reference and training for various forms of federal taxation: individual, business, corporate, partnership, estate, gift, etc. Includes *Federal Taxation Study Manual.*

Federal Tax Manual. CCH, Inc. • Looseleaf. $175.00 per year. Covers "basic federal tax rules and forms affecting individuals and businesses." Includes a copy of *Annuity, Depreciation, and Withholding Tables.*

U. S. Master Depreciation Guide. CCH, Inc. • Annual. $49.00. Contains explanations of ADR (asset depreciation range), ACRS (accelerated cost recovery system), and MACRS (modified accelerated cost recovery system). Includes the historical background of depreciation.

RESEARCH CENTERS AND INSTITUTES

Center for International Education and Research in Accounting. University of Illinois at Urbana-Champaign. 1206 S. Sixth St., 320 Commerce West Bldg., Champaign, IL 61820. Phone: (217)333-4545 Fax: (217)244-6565 E-mail: b-smith@uiuc.edu • URL: http://www.cba.uiuc.edu/ciera.

National Bureau of Economic Research, Inc. 1050 Massachusetts Ave., Cambridge, MA 02138-5398. Phone: (617)868-3900 Fax: (617)868-2742 E-mail: msfeldst@nber.org • URL: http://www.nber.org.

STATISTICS SOURCES

Statistics of Income: Corporation Income Tax Returns. U.S. Internal Revenue Service. Available from U.S. Government Printing Office. • Annual. $26.00.

DEPRESSION

See: MENTAL HEALTH

DEPRESSIONS, BUSINESS

See: BUSINESS CYCLES

DERIVATIVE SECURITIES

GENERAL WORKS

FIASCO: Blood in the Water on Wall Street. Frank Partnoy. W. W. Norton & Co., Inc. • 1997. $25.00. Tells how Wall Street sold risky derivatives to clients who had no understanding of the product.

Financial Institutions and Markets. Robert W. Kolb and Ricardo J. Rodriguez. Blackwell Publishers. • 1996. $77.95. Contains 40 articles (chapters) by various authors on U. S. financial markets and other topics. Includes separate chapters on the International Monetary Fund, inflation, monetary policy, the national debt, bank failures, derivatives, stock prices, initial public offerings, government bonds, pensions, foreign exchange, international markets, and other subjects.

The Witch Doctor of Wall Street: A Noted Financial Expert Guides You Through Today's Voodoo Economics. Robert H. Parks. Prometheus Books. • 1996. $25.95. The author, a professor of finance at Pace University, discusses "Practice and Malpractice" in relation to the following: business forecasting, economic theory, interest rates, monetary policy, the stock market, and corporate finance. Includes "A Short Primer on Derivatives," as an appendix.

DIRECTORIES

Bond Buyer's Municipal Marketplace. Thomson Financial Publishing. • Annual. $180.00 per year. Provides information on municipal bond professionals, such as dealers, underwriters, attorneys, arbitrage specialists, derivatives specialists, rating agencies, regulators, etc.

Derivatives Desk Reference: Buyside and Sellside Profiles. Capital Access International. • Annual. $295.00. A directory of about 900 firms active in the use of such derivatives as options, futures, currency swaps, interest rate swaps, and structured notes. Includes names of derivatives specialists in each firm.

Futures Guide to Computerized Trading. Futures Magazine, Inc. • Annual. $10.00. "A directory of products and services for the computerized trader." Provides information on computer software applications for commodity traders and money managers, including trading methods and technical analysis.

Futures Magazine SourceBook: The Most Complete List of Exchanges, Companies, Regulators, Organizations, etc., Offering Products and Services to the Futures and Options Industry. Futures Magazine, Inc. • Annual. $19.50. Provides information on commodity futures brokers, trading method services, publications, and other items of interest to futures traders and money managers.

Thomson Derivatives and Risk Management Directory. Thomson Learning. • 1998. $297.00. Lists "over 9,000 contacts at more than 4,000 institutions.".

ENCYCLOPEDIAS AND DICTIONARIES

Dictionary of Finance and Investment Terms. John Downes and Jordan E. Goodman. Barron's Educational Series, Inc. • 1998. $12.95. Fifth revised edition. Provides clear explanations of more than 5,000 business, banking, financial, investment, and tax terms. Includes a separate list of financial abbreviations and acronyms.

HANDBOOKS AND MANUALS

Analysis and Use of Financial Statements. Gerald I. White and others. John Wiley and Sons, Inc. • 1997. $112.95. Second edition. Includes analysis of financial ratios, cash flow, inventories, assets, debt, etc. Also covered are employee benefits, corporate investments, multinational operations, financial derivatives, and hedging activities.

Corporate Fraud. Michael J. Comer. Available from Ashgate Publishing Co. • 1997. $113.95. Third edition. Examines new risks of corporate fraud related to "electronic commerce, derivatives, computerization, empowerment, downsizing, and other recent developments." Covers fraud detection, prevention, and internal control systems. Published by Gower in England.

Derivatives: A Comprehensive Resource for Options, Futures, Interest Rate Swaps, and Mortgage Securities. Fred D. Arditti. Harvard Business School Press. • 1996. $60.00. Published by Harvard Business School Press. Provides detailed explanations of various kinds of financial derivatives (options, futures, swaps, etc.) and their trading tactics, uses, and risks. (Financial Management Association Survey and Synthesis Series).

Derivatives Handbook: Risk Management and Control. Robert J. Schwartz and Clifford W. Smith. John Wiley and Sons, Inc. • 1997. $79.95. Some chapter topics are legal risk, risk measurement, and risk oversight. Includes "Derivatives Debacles: Case Studies of Losses in DerivativesMarkets." A glossary of derivatives terminology is provided. (Wiley Financial Engineering Series).

Econometrics of Financial Markets. John Y. Campbell and others. California Princeton Fulfillment Services. • 1997. $49.50. Written for advanced students and industry professionals. Includes chapters on "The Predictability of Asset Returns," "Derivative Pricing Models," and "Fixed-Income Securities." Provides a discussion of the random walk theory of investing and tests of the theory.

Guide to Federal Regulation of Derivatives. CCH, Inc. • 1998. $99.00. Explains the complex derivatives regulations of the Securities and Exchange Commission. Covers swap agreements, third-party derivatives, credit derivatives, mutual fund liquidity, and other topics.

Handbook of Alternative Investment Strategies. Thomas Schneeweis and Joseph F. Pescatore, editors. Institutional Investor. • 1999. $95.00. Covers various forms of alternative investment, including hedge funds, managed futures, derivatives, venture capital, and natural resource financing.

Handbook of Derivative Instruments: Investment Research, Analysis, and Portfolio Applications. Atsuo Konishi and Ravi E. Dattatreya, editors. McGraw-Hill Professional. • 1996. $80.00. Second revised edition. Contains 41 chapters by various authors on all aspects of derivative securities, including such esoterica as "Inverse Floaters," "Positive Convexity," "Exotic Options," and "How to Use the Holes in Black-Scholes.".

Handbook of Equity Derivatives. Jack C. Francis and others, editors. John Wiley and Sons, Inc. • 1999. $95.00. Contains 27 chapters by various authors. Covers options (puts and calls), stock index futures, warrants, convertibles, over-the-counter options, swaps, legal issues, taxation, etc. (Financial Engineering Series).

Interest Rate Risk Measurement and Management. Sanjay K. Nawalkha and Donald R. Chambers, editors. Institutional Investor, Inc. • 1999. $95.00. Provides interest rate risk models for fixed-income derivatives and for investments by various kinds of financial institutions.

An Introduction to the Mathematics of Financial Derivatives. Salih N. Neftci. Academic Press, Inc. • 2000. $59.95. Second edition. Covers the mathematical models underlying the pricing of derivatives. Includes explanations of basic financial calculus for students, derivatives traders, risk managers, and others concerned with derivatives.

Over-the-Counter Derivatives Products: A Guide to Legal Risk Management and Documentation. Robert M. McLaughlin. McGraw-Hill Professional. • 1998. $75.00.

Swap Literacy. Elizabeth Ungar. Bloomberg Press. • 1996. $40.00. Written for corporate finance officers. Provides basic information on arbitrage, hedging, and speculation, involving interest rate, currency, and other types of financial swaps. (Bloomberg Professional Library.).

Understanding Financial Derivatives: How to Protect Your Investments. Donald Strassheim. McGraw-Hill Professional. • 1996. $40.00. Covers three basic risk management instruments: options, futures, and swaps. Includes advice on equity index options, financial futures contracts, and over-the-counter derivatives markets.

INTERNET DATABASES

DBC Online: America's Leading Provider of Real-Time Market Data to the Individual Investor. Data Broadcasting Corp. Phone: (415)571-1800 E-mail: dbcinfo@dbc.com • URL: http://www.dbc.com • Web site provides a wide variety of real-time securities market prices, data, and charts. Covers bonds ("BondVu"), stocks, commodities, options, mutual funds, major indexes, industry indexes, international markets, etc. Also includes news, SEC documents ("Smart-Edgar"), and various other features. Fees: Both free and fee-based, depending on level of information.

Derivatives. Derivatives Strategy and Tactics. Phone: (212)366-9578 Fax: (212)366-0551 E-mail: office@derivatives.com • URL: http://www.derivatives.com • Web site provides articles from *Derivatives Strategy* magazine (three-month delay). Also includes "Derivatives Comix," explaining complex topics in comic book form. An example is "Boovis and Beethead Play the Yield Curve Game." Links to useful derivatives Web sites and descriptions of recommended books are provided. Fees: Free.

Futures Online. Oster Communications, Inc. Phone: 800-601-8907 or (319)277-1278 Fax: (319)277-7982 • URL: http://www.futuresmag.com • Web site presents updates of *Futures* magazine and links to other futures-related sites. Includes "Futures Industry News," "Technical Talk," "Today's Hot Markets," "Futures Talk" (forums), "Futures Library" (archives, 1993 to date), and other features. Keyword searching is available. Updating: daily. Fees: Free.

U. S. Securities and Exchange Commission. Phone: 800-732-0330 or (202)942-7040 Fax: (202)942-9634 E-mail: webmaster@sec.gov • URL: http://www.sec.gov • SEC Web site offers free access through EDGAR to text of official corporate filings, such as annual reports (10-K), quarterly reports (10-Q), and proxies. (EDGAR is "Electronic Data Gathering, Analysis, and Retrieval System.") An example is given of how to obtain executive compensation data from proxies. Text of the daily *SEC News Digest* is offered, as are links to other government sites, non-government market regulators, and U. S. stock exchanges. Search facilities are extensive. Fees: Free.

Wall Street Journal Interactive Edition. Dow Jones & Co., Inc. Phone: 800-369-2834 or (212)416-2000 Fax: (212)416-2658 E-mail: inquiries@interactive.wsj.com • URL: http://www.wsj.com • Fee-based Web site providing online searching of worldwide information from the *The Wall Street Journal.* Includes "Company Snapshots," "The Journal's Greatest Hits," "Index to Market Data," "14-Day Searchable Archive," "Journal Links," etc. Financial price quotes are available. Fees: $49.00 per year; $29.00 per year to print subscribers.

Web Finance: Covering the Electronic Evolution of Finance. Securities Data Publishing. Phone: (212)765-5311 or 800-455-5844 Fax: (212)321-2336 E-mail: webfinance@tfn.com • URL: http://www.webfinance.net • Bi-weekly print and daily web-site publication of financial services on the Web, including financial links, archives, brokerage stocks, deal financing, and other financial and investment news and information.

PERIODICALS AND NEWSLETTERS

Derivatives Quarterly. Institutional Investor. • Quarterly. $280.00 per year. Emphasis is on the practical use of derivatives. Includes case studies to demonstrate "real-life" risks and benefits.

Derivatives Strategy. Derivatives Strategy and Tactics. • Monthly. $245.00 per year. Provides practical explanations of financial derivatives for institutional investors, corporate treasury officers, dealers, and others.

Derivatives Tactics. Derivative Strategy and Tactics. • Semimonthly. $695.00 per year. Newsletter. Edited for institutional investors. Covers options, swaps, and other financial derivatives.

Derivatives Week: The Newsweekly on Derivatives Worldwide. Institutional Investor. • Weekly. $2,330.00 per year. Newsletter on financial derivatives linked to equities, interest rates, commodities, and currencies. Covers new products, investment opportunities, legalities, etc.

Financial Markets, Institutions, and Instruments. New York University, Salomon Center. Blackwell Publishers. • Five times a year. $219.00 per year. Edited to "bridge the gap between the academic and professional finance communities." Special fifth issue each year provides surveys of developments in four areas: money and banking, derivative securities, corporate finance, and fixed-income securities.

Financial Trader. Miller Freeman, Inc. • 11 times a year. $160.00 per year. Edited for professional traders. Covers fixed income securities, emerging markets, derivatives, options, futures, and equities.

Futures: News, Analysis, and Strategies for Futures, Options, and Derivatives Traders. Futures Magazine, Inc. • Monthly. $39.00 per year. Edited for institutional money managers and traders, brokers, risk managers, and individual investors or speculators. Includes special feature issues on interest rates, technical indicators, currencies, charts, precious metals, hedge funds, and derivatives. Supplements available.

Journal of Derivatives. Institutional Investor. • Quarterly. $280.00 per year. Covers the structure and management of financial derivatives. Includes graphs, equations, and detailed analyses.

Journal of Investing. Institutional Investor. • Quarterly. $310.00 per year. Edited for professional investors. Topics include equities, fixed-income securities, derivatives, asset allocation, and other institutional investment subjects.

Journal of Risk Finance: The Convergence of Financial Products and Insurance. Institutional Investor. • Quarterly. $395.00 per year. Covers the field of customized risk management, including securitization, insurance, hedging, derivatives, and credit arbitrage.

Journal of Taxation of Financial Products. CCH, Inc. • Bimonthly. $249.00 per year.

The Wall Street Journal. Dow Jones & Co., Inc. • Daily. $175.00 per year. Covers news and trends relating to business, industry, finance, the economy, and international commerce. Provides extensive price and other data for the securities, commodity, options, futures, foreign exchange, and money markets.

STATISTICS SOURCES

Statistical Information on the Financial Services Industry. American Bankers Association. • Annual. Members, $150.00; non-members, $275.00. Presents a wide variety of data relating to banking and financial services, including consumer economics, personal finance, credit, government loans, capital markets, and international banking.

TRADE/PROFESSIONAL ASSOCIATIONS

Emerging Markets Traders Association. 63 Wall St., 20th Fl., New York, NY 10005. Phone: (212)293-5000 • URL: http://www.emta.org • Promotes orderly trading markets for emerging market instruments. Includes Options/Derivatives Working Group.

OTHER SOURCES

Factiva. Dow Jones Reuters Business Interactive, LLC. • Fee-based Web site provides "global news and business information through Web sites and content integration solutions." Includes Dow Jones and Reuters newswires, The Wall Street Journal, and more than 7,000 other sources of current news, historical articles, market research reports, and investment analysis. Content includes 96 major U. S. newspapers, 900 non-English sources, trade publications, media transcripts, country profiles, news photos, etc.

Nexis.com. Lexis-Nexis Group. • Fee-based Web site offers searching of about 2.8 billion documents in some 30,000 news, business, and legal information sources. Features include a subject directory covering 1,200 topics in 34 categories and a Company Dossier containing information on more than 500,000 public and private companies. Boolean searching is offered.

Quantitative Finance. Available from IOP Publishing, Inc. • Bimonthly. $199.00 per year. Published in the UK by the Institute of Physics. A technical journal on the use of quantitative tools and applications in financial analysis and financial engineering. Covers such topics as portfolio theory, derivatives, asset allocation, return on assets, risk management, price volatility, financial econometrics, market anomalies, and trading systems.

DESALINATION INDUSTRY

ABSTRACTS AND INDEXES

Applied Science and Technology Index. H. W. Wilson Co. • 11 times a year. Quarterly and annual cumulations. Service basis for print edition; CD-ROM edition, $1,495.00 per year. Indexes a wide variety of English language technical, industrial, and engineering periodicals.

Current Contents: Engineering, Computing and Technology. Institute for Scientific Information. • Weekly. $730.00 per year. Reproductions of contents pages of technical journals. Includes *Author Index, Address Directory, Current Book Contents* and *Title Word Index.* Formerly *Current Contents: Engineering, Technology and Applied Sciences.*

Environment Abstracts. Congressional Information Service. • Monthly. Price varies. Provides multidisciplinary coverage of the world's environmental literature. Incorporates *Acid Rain Abstracts.*

Environment Abstracts Annual: A Guide to the Key Environmental Literature of the Year. Congressional Information Service. • Annual. $495.00. A yearly cumulation of *Environment Abstracts.*

Oceanic Abstracts. Cambridge Information Group. • Bimonthly. $1,045.00 per year. Covers oceanography, marine biology, ocean shipping, and a wide range of other marine-related subject areas.

BIBLIOGRAPHIES

Encyclopedia of Physical Science and Engineering Information. The Gale Group. • 1996. $160.00. Second edition. Includes print, electronic, and other information sources for a wide range of scientific, technical, and engineering topics.

CD-ROM DATABASES

COMPENDEX PLUS [CD-ROM]. Engineering Information, Inc. • Quarterly. $3,450.00 per year. Provides CD-ROM indexing and abstracting of the world's engineering and technical information appearing in journals, reports, books, and proceedings, 1985 to date.

Environment Abstracts on CD-ROM. Congressional Information Service, Inc. • Quarterly. $1,295.00 per year. Contains the following CD-ROM databases: *Environment Abstracts, Energy Abstracts,* and *Acid Rain Abstracts.* Length of coverage varies.

NTIS on SilverPlatter. Available from SilverPlatter Information, Inc. • Quarterly. $2,850.00 per year. Produced by the National Technical Information Service. Provides a CD-ROM guide to over 500,000 government reports on a wide variety of technical, industrial, and business topics.

Science Citation Index: Compact Disc Edition. Institute for Scientific Information. • Quarterly. Provides CD-ROM indexing of the world's scientific and technical literature. Corresponds to online *Scisearch* and printed *Science Citation Index.*

WILSONDISC: Applied Science and Technology Abstracts. H. W. Wilson Co. • Monthly. $1,495.00 per year, including unlimited access to the online version of *Applied Science and Technology Abstracts* through WILSONLINE. Provides CD-ROM indexing and abstracting of 400 prominent scientific, technical, engineering, and industrial periodicals. Indexing coverage is provided from 1983 to date and abstracting from 1993 to date.

DIRECTORIES

Desalination Directory: Desalination and Water Reuse. Elsevier Scientific. • Annual. Members, $160.00; non-members, $250.00. Lists business firms, institutes, associations, government agencies, and individuals involved in some way with desalination. International coverage. Published in Italy by the School of Scientific Communication. Text in English.

HANDBOOKS AND MANUALS

Desalination Technology: Developments and Practice. Andrew Porteous, editor. Elsevier Science. • 1983. $74.00.

ONLINE DATABASES

Applied Science and Technology Index Online. H. W. Wilson Co. • Provides online indexing of 400 major scientific, technical, industrial, and engineering periodicals. Time period is 1983 to date. Monthly updates. Inquire as to online cost and availability.

Enviroline. Congressional Information Service, Inc. • Provides online indexing and abstracting of worldwide environmental and natural resource literature from 1975 to date. Updated monthly. Inquire as to online cost and availability.

F & S Index. The Gale Group. • Contains about four million citations to worldwide business, financial, and industrial or consumer product literature appearing from 1972 to date. Weekly updates. Inquire as to online cost and availability.

Globalbase. The Gale Group. • Provides more than one million online summaries of business, industrial, and economic news reports from more than 1,000 publications worldwide. Covers a wide range of material appearing in international trade journals, professional magazines, and newspapers. Time period is 1984 to date, with weekly updates. Inquire as to online cost and availability.

NTIS Bibliographic Data Base. National Technical Information Service. • Contains citations and abstracts to unrestricted reports of government-sponsored research, 1964 to date. Covers a wide range of technical, engineering, business, and social science topics. Monthly updates. Inquire as to online cost and availability.

Oceanic Abstracts (Online). Cambridge Scientific Abstracts. • Oceanographic and other marine-related technical literature, 1981 to present.Monthly updates. Inquire as to online cost and availability.

PROMT: Predicasts Overview of Markets and Technology. The Gale Group. • Companies, products, applied technologies and markets. U.S. and international literature coverage, 1972 to date. Inquire as to online cost and availability. Provides abstracts from more than 1,600 publications. Weekly updates.

Scisearch. Institute for Scientific Information. • Broad, multidisciplinary index to the literature of science and technology, 1974 to present. Inquire as to online cost and availability. Coverage of literature is worldwide, with weekly updates.

PERIODICALS AND NEWSLETTERS

Water Desalination Report. Maria C. Smith. • Weekly. $325.00 per year. Newsletter.

RESEARCH CENTERS AND INSTITUTES

Pacific International Center for High Technology Research. 2800 Woodlawn Dr., Suite 180, Honolulu, HI 96822-1843. Phone: (808)539-3900 Fax: (808)539-3892 E-mail: keithm@htdc.org • URL: http://www.pichtr.htdc.org • Desalination is included as a field of research.

TRADE/PROFESSIONAL ASSOCIATIONS

International Desalination Association. P.O. Box 387, Topsfield, MA 01983. Phone: (978)887-0410 Fax: (978)887-0411 E-mail: idalpab@ix.netcom.com • URL: http://www.ida.bm • Members are users and suppliers of desalination equipment.

DESIGN AND MANUFACTURING, COMPUTER-AIDED

See: COMPUTER-AIDED DESIGN AND MANUFACTURING (CAD/CAM)

DESIGN IN INDUSTRY

See also: ART IN INDUSTRY; ARTS MANAGEMENT; COMMERCIAL ART; GRAPHIC ARTS INDUSTRY; OFFICE DESIGN

ABSTRACTS AND INDEXES

Art Index. H. W. Wilson Co. • Quarterly. Annual cumulations. Service basis for print edition; CD-ROM edition, $1,495.00 per year. Subject and author index to periodicals in art, architecture, industrial design, city planning, photography, and various related topics.

BIOGRAPHICAL SOURCES

Contemporary Designers. The Gale Group. • 1997. $175.00. Third edition. Profiles the careers and accomplishments of 685 designers from throughout the world.

DIRECTORIES

Design Firm Directory: A Listing of Firms and Consultants in Grap hic Design in the United States. Wefler & Associates, Inc. • Annual. $145.00. Three volumes. Provides information on more than 2,600 commercial, private, and consulting design firms. Includes graphic, interior, landscape, and environmental designers.

Design News OEM Directory. Cahners Business Information. • Annual. $60.00. About 6,000 manufacturers and suppliers of power transmission products, fluid power products and electrical/electronic componets to the OEM (Original Equipment Manufacturers). Included with subscription to *Design News.* Formerly *Design News.*

Directory of Minority-Owned Professional and Personnel Services Consultants. San Francisco Redevelopment Agency. • Annual. Free. About 650 minority firms in Northern California.

ENR-Top International Design Firms (Engineering News Record). McGraw-Hill. • Annual. $10.00. Lists 200 firms. Includes U. S. firms. Formerly *Engineering News Record-Top International Design Firms.*

The Top 500 Design Firms Sourcebook. McGraw-Hill. • Annual. $25.00. Lists 500 leading architectural, engineering and speciality design firms selected on basis of annual billings. Formerly *ENR Directory of Design Firms.*

HANDBOOKS AND MANUALS

Logo Power: How to Create Effective Company Logos. William Haig and Laurel Harper. John Wiley & Sons, Inc. • 1997. $39.95. Explains how to plan, develop, evaluate, and implement a company logo system.

The New Guide to Identity: How to Create and Sustain Change Through Managing Identity. Wally Olins. Ashgate Publishing Co. • 1996. $22.95. A guide to corporate identity through the effective use of industrial design and graphics. Includes color illustrations.

Office Interior Design Guide: An Introduction for Facility and Design. Julie K. Rayfield. John Wiley and Sons, Inc. • 1997. $59.95.

ONLINE DATABASES

Art Index Online. H. W. Wilson Co. • Indexes a wide variety of art-related periodicals, 1984 to date. Monthly updates. Inquire as to online cost and availability.

PERIODICALS AND NEWSLETTERS

Design Drafting News. American Design Drafting Association. • Bimonthly. Membership. Newsletter.

Design Management Journal. Design Management Institute. • Quarterly. $96.00 per year. Covers the management of product-related design.

Design Perspectives. Industrial Designers Society of America. • 10 times a year. $32.00 per year.

Engineering Design Graphics Journal. American Society for Engineering Education. • Three times a year. Members, $6.00 per year; non-members, $20.00 per year;institutions, $10.00 per year. Concerned with engineering graphics, computer graphics, geometric modeling, computer-aided drafting, etc.

Machine Design: Magazine of Applied Technology for Design Engineering. Penton Media, Inc. • 23 times a year. Free to qualified personnel; others, $105.00 per year. Includes *Machine Design Reference Issues* and *Penton Executive Network.*

Product Design and Development. Cahners Business Information. • Monthly. $60.00 per year. Edited for design engineers. Emphasis is on materials, components, and processes.

TRADE/PROFESSIONAL ASSOCIATIONS

American Design Drafting Association. P.O. Box 11937, Columbia, SC 29211. Phone: (803)771-0008 Fax: (803)771-4272 E-mail: national@adda.org • URL: http://www.adda.org.

American Institute of Building Design. 991 Post Rd., E., Westport, CT 06880. Phone: 800-366-2423 or (203)227-3640 Fax: (203)227-8624 E-mail: aibdnat@aol.com • URL: http://www.aibd.org.

Design Management Institute. 29 Temple Place, 2nd Fl., Boston, MA 02111. Phone: (617)338-6380 Fax: (617)338-6570 E-mail: dmistaff@dmi.org • URL: http://www.dmi.org • Membership includes firms concerned with various kinds of commercial design, including product, graphic, interior, exhibit, package, and architectural.

Industrial Designers Society of America. 1142 E.Walker Rd., Suite E, Great Falls, VA 22066. Phone: (703)759-0100 Fax: (703)759-7679 E-mail: idsa@erols.com • URL: http://www.idsa.org • A professional society of industrial designers.

International Council of Societies of Industrial Design. Erottajankatu 11A 18, FIN-00120 Helsinki, Finland. Phone: 358 9 6962290 or 358 9 69622910 E-mail: icsidsec@icsid.org • URL: http://www.icsid.org.

DESKTOP PUBLISHING

See also: MICROCOMPUTERS AND MINICOMPUTERS; WORD PROCESSING

ABSTRACTS AND INDEXES

Applied Science and Technology Index. H. W. Wilson Co. • 11 times a year. Quarterly and annual cumulations. Service basis for print edition; CD-ROM edition, $1,495.00 per year. Indexes a wide variety of English language technical, industrial, and engineering periodicals.

Business Periodicals Index. H. W. Wilson Co. • Monthly, except August, with quarterly and annual cumulations. Service basis for print edition; CD-ROM edition, $1,495.00 per year.

Computer and Control Abstracts. Available from INSPEC, Inc. • Monthly. $2,160.00 per year. Section C of *Science Abstracts.*

Computer and Information Systems Abstracts Journal: An Abstract Journal Pertaining to the Theory, Design, Fabrication and Application of Computer and Information Systems. Cambridge Information Group. • Monthly. $1,045 per year.

Computer Literature Index: A Subject/Author Index to Computer and Data Processing Literature. Applied Computer Research, Inc. • Quarterly, with annual cumulation. $245.00 per year. Contains brief abstracts of book and periodical literature covering all phases of computing, including approximately 70 specific application areas.

Current Contents: Engineering, Computing and Technology. Institute for Scientific Information. • Weekly. $730.00 per year. Reproductions of contents pages of technical journals. Includes *Author Index, Address Directory, Current Book Contents* and *Title Word Index.* Formerly *Current Contents: Engineering, Technology and Applied Sciences.*

Microcomputer Abstracts. Information Today, Inc. • Quarterly. $225.00 per year. Provides abstracts covering a wide variety of personal and business microcomputer literature. Formerly *Microcomputer Index.*

CD-ROM DATABASES

Computer Select. The Gale Group. • Monthly. $1,250.00 per year. Provides one year of full-text on CD-ROM for 120 leading computer-related publications. Also includes 70,000 product specifications and brief profiles of 13,000 computer product vendors and manufacturers.

DIRECTORIES

Business Organizations, Agencies, and Publications Directory. The Gale Group. • 1999. $425.00. 12th edition. Over 40,000 entries describing 39 types of business information sources. Classified by type of organization, publication, or serviceIncludes state, national, and international agencies and organizations. Master index to names and keywords. Also includes e-mail addresses and web site URL's.

Data Sources: The Comprehensive Guide to the Data Processing Industry Hardware, Data Communications Products, Software, Company Profiles. The Gale Group. • Semiannual. $495.00 per year. Two volumes. Describes hardware and software for all computer operating sysems, including prices and technical details. Lists about 75,000 products from 14,000 suppliers. Industry-specific software applications are described.

Faulkner Information Service. Faulkner Information Services, Inc. • Looseleaf. Monthly updates. Many titles and volumes, covering virtually all aspects of computer software and hardware. Gives descriptions and technical data for specific products, including producers' names and addresses. Prices and details on request. Formerly (The Auerbach Series).

MicroLeads Vendor Directory on Disk (Personal Computer Industry). Chromatic Communications Enterprises, Inc. • Annual. $495.00. Includes computer hardware manufacturers, software producers, book-periodical publishers, and franchised or company-owned chains of personal computer equipment retailers, support services and accessory manufacturers. Formerly *MicroLeads U.S. Vender Directory.*

The Software Encyclopedia: A Guide for Personal, Professional, and Business Users. R. R. Bowker. • Annual. $255.00. Two volumes. Volume one lists software programs by title and producer. Volume two provides information on programs according to application and operating system. Includes prices and requirements for hardware and memory.

ENCYCLOPEDIAS AND DICTIONARIES

Dictionary of Computing. Valerie Illingworth, editor. Oxford University Press, Inc. • 1996. $49.95. Fourth edition.

Dictionary of Information Technology and Computer Science. Tony Gunton. Blackwell Publishers. • 1994. $50.95. Second edition. Covers key words, phrases, abbreviations, and acronyms used in computing and data communications.

Graphically Speaking: An Illustrated Guide to the Working Language of Design and Publishing. Mark Beach. Coast to Coast Books. • 1992. $29.50. Provides practical definitions of 2,800 terms used in printing, graphic design, publishing, and desktop publishing. Over 300 illustrations are included, about 40 in color.

HANDBOOKS AND MANUALS

The Desktop Designer's Illustration Handbook. Marcelle L. Toor. John Wiley and Sons, Inc. • 1996. $29.95. Serves as a guide to locating, selecting, and using illustrations for desktop publications. (ITCP-U.S. Computer Science Series).

Desktop Publishing. Entrepreneur Media, Inc. • Looseleaf. $59.50. A practical guide to starting a desktop publishing service. Covers profit potential, start-up costs, market size evaluation, pricing, accounting, advertising, promotion, etc. (Start-Up Business Guide No. E1288.).

Desktop Publishing by Design: Everyone's Guide to Pagemaker 6. Ronnie Shushan and others. Microsoft Press. • 1996. $39.95. Fourth edition. (By Design Series).

How to Produce Creative Advertising: Traditional Techniques and Computer Applications. Thomas Bivins and Ann Keding. NTC/Contemporary Publishing. • 1993. $37.95. Covers copywriting, advertising design, and the use of desktop publishing techniques in advertising. (NTC Business Book Series).

How to Produce Creative Publications: Traditional Techniques and Computer Applications. Thomas Bivins and William E. Ryan. NTC/Contemporary Publishing. • 1994. $32.95. A practical guide to the writing, designing, and production of magazines, annual reports, brochures, and newsletters by traditional methods and by desktop publishing.

Looking Good in Print: A Guide to Basic Design for Desktop Publishing. Roger C. Parker. Ventana Communications Group, Inc. • 1999. $29.99. Tenth edition. Covers newsletters, advertisements, brochures, manuals, and correspondence.

Using Desktop Publishing to Create Newsletters, Library Guides, and Web Pages: A How-To-Do-It Manual for Librarians. John Maxymuk. Neal-Schuman Publishers, Inc. • 1997. $55.00. Includes more than 90 illustrations.

INTERNET DATABASES

InfoTech Trends. Data Analysis Group. Phone: (707)894-9100 Fax: (707)486-5618 E-mail: support@infotechtrends.com • URL: http://www.infotechtrends.com • Web site provides both free and fee-based market research data on the information technology industry, including computers, peripherals, telecommunications, the Internet, software, CD-ROM/DVD, e-commerce, and workstations. Fees: Free for current (most recent year) data; more extensive information has various fee structures. Formerly *Computer Industry Forecasts.*

Wired News. Wired Digital, Inc. Phone: (415)276-8400 Fax: (415)276-8499 E-mail: newsfeedback@wired.com • URL: http://www.wired.com • Provides summaries and full-text of "Top Stories" relating to the Internet, computers, multimedia, telecommunications, and the electronic information industry in general. These news stories are placed in the broad categories of Politics, Business, Culture, and Technology. Affiliated with *Wired* magazine. Fees: Free.

ONLINE DATABASES

Applied Science and Technology Index Online. H. W. Wilson Co. • Provides online indexing of 400 major scientific, technical, industrial, and engineering periodicals. Time period is 1983 to date. Monthly updates. Inquire as to online cost and availability.

Computer Database. The Gale Group. • Provides online citations with abstracts to material appearing in about 150 trade journals and newsletters in the subject areas of computers, telecommunications, and electronics. Time period is 1983 to date, with weekly updates. Inquire as to online cost and availability.

Internet and Personal Computing Abstracts. Information Today, Inc. • Contains abstracts covering a wide variety of personal and business microcomputer literature appearing in more than 100 journals and popular magazines. Time period is 1981 to date, with monthly updates. Formerly *Microcomputer Index.* Inquire as to online cost and availability.

PROMT: Predicasts Overview of Markets and Technology. The Gale Group. • Companies, products, applied technologies and markets. U.S. and international literature coverage, 1972 to date. Inquire as to online cost and availability. Provides abstracts from more than 1,600 publications. Weekly updates.

Wilson Business Abstracts Online. H. W. Wilson Co. • Indexes and abstracts 600 major business periodicals, plus the *Wall Street Journal* and the business section of the *New York Times.* Indexing is from 1982, abstracting from 1990, with the two newspapers included from 1993. Updated weekly. Inquire as to online cost and availability. (*Business Periodicals Index* without abstracts is also available online.).

PERIODICALS AND NEWSLETTERS

Computer Industry Report. International Data Corp. • Semimonthly. $495.00 per year. Newsletter. Annual supplement. Also known as "The Gray Sheet." Formerly *EDP Industry Report and Market Review.*

Desktop Communications. International Desktop Communications, Ltd. • Bimonthly. $24.00 per year. Emphasis on typeface selection and page layout. Formerly *ITC Desktop.*

Desktop Publishers Journal. Business Media Group LLC. • Ten times a year. $49.00 per year. Edited for professional publishers, graphic designers, and industry service providers. Covers new products and emerging technologies for the electronic publishing industry.

EDP Weekly: The Leading Weekly Computer News Summary. Computer Age and E D P News Services. • Weekly. $495.00 per year. Newsletter. Summarizes news from all areas of the computer and microcomputer industries.

Innovative Publisher: Publishing Strategies for New Markets. Emmelle Publishing Co., Inc. • Biweekly. $69.00 per year. Provides articles and news on electronic publishing (CD-ROM or online) and desktop publishing.

Micropublishing News: The Newsmonthly for Electronic Designers and Publishers. Cygnus Business Media. • Monthly. Free to qualified personnel. Price on application. Edited for business and professional users of electronic publishing products and services. Topics covered include document imaging, CD-ROM publishing, digital video, and multimedia services. Available in four regional editions.

National Association of Desktop Publishers. Journal. National Association of Desktop Publishers. Desktop Publishing Institute. • Monthly. Free to members; non-members, $48.00 per year. Covers desktop, electronic, and multimedia publishing.

The Page. Z-D Journals. • 10 times a year. $59.00 per year. Newsletter on the use of MacIntosh computers for desktop publishing.

PC Publishing and Presentations: Desktop Publishing. International Desktop Communications, Ltd. • Monthly. $36.00 per year. Formerly *PC Publishing.*

Seybold Report on Publishing Systems. Seybold Publications. • Semimonthly. $365.00 per year. Newsletter.

Step-By-Step Electronic Design: The How-To Newsletter for Electronic Designers. Dynamic Graphics, Inc. • Monthly. $48.00 per year;with*Step-by-Step Graphics*,$90.00 per year.

RESEARCH CENTERS AND INSTITUTES

Technical and Educational Center of the Graphic Arts and Imaging. Rochester Institute of Technology, 67 Lomb Memorial Dr., Rochester, NY 14623-5603. Phone: 800-724-2536 or (716)475-2680 Fax: (716)475-7000 E-mail: webmail@rit.edu • URL: http://www.rit.edu/cime/te.

OTHER SOURCES

DataWorld. Faulkner Information Services, Inc. • Four looseleaf volumes, with monthly supplements. $1,395.00 per year. Describes and evaluates both hardware and software relating to midrange, micro, and mainframe computers. Available on CD-ROM.

Teach Yourself Desktop Publishing. Christopher Lumgair. NTC/Contemporary Publishing Group. •

2001. $10.95. Describes current desktop publishing software and techniques.

DETERGENTS

See: CLEANING PRODUCTS INDUSTRY

DEVELOPING AREAS

See also: FOREIGN INVESTMENTS

GENERAL WORKS

Economic Development. Jan S. Hogendorn. Addison-Wesley Educational Publishers, Inc. • 1997. $81.00.

Global Economic Prospects 2000. The World Bank, Office of the Publisher. • 1999. $25.00. "..offers an in-depth analysis of the economic prospects of developing countries.." Emphasis is on the impact of recessions and financial crises. Regional statistical data is included.

Marketing in the Third World. Denise M. Johnson and Erdener Kaynak, editors. Haworth Press, Inc. • 1996. $29.95. Various authors discuss marketing, advertising, government regulations, and other topics relating to business promotion in developing countries. (Also published in the *Journal of Global Marketing*, vol. 9.).

Trade and Employment in Developing Countries. Anne O. Krueger, editor. University of Chicago Press. • Three volumes. Vol. 1, 1980, $66.00; Vol. 2, 1982, $35.00; Vol. 3, 1983, $16.00. (National Bureau of Economic Research Project Report Series).

The World Bank and the Poorest Countries: Support for Development in the 1990s. World Bank, The Office of the Publisher. • 1994. $22.00. Describes progress in poverty reduction, economic management, and environmental protection in the 70 poorest countries of the world.

ABSTRACTS AND INDEXES

World Agricultural Economics and Rural Sociology Abstracts: Abstracts of World Literature. Available from CABI Publishing. • Monthly. $1095.00 per year. Published in England by CABI Publishing. Provides worldwide coverage of the literature.

ALMANACS AND YEARBOOKS

Emerging Markets Analyst. • Monthly. $895.00 per year. Provides an annual overview of the emerging financial markets in 24 countries of Latin America, Asia, and Europe. Includes data on international mutual funds and closed-end funds.

World Development Report. The World Bank, Office of the Publisher. • Annual. $50.00. Covers history, conditions, and trends relating to economic globalization and localization. Includes selected data from *World Development Indicators* for 132 countries or economies. Key indicators are provided for 78 additional countries or economies.

Worldmark Yearbook. The Gale Group. • Annual. $305.00. Three volumes. Covers economic, social, and political events in about 230 countries. Includes statistical data, directories, and a bibliography.

BIBLIOGRAPHIES

Catalogue of Statistical Materials of Developing Countries. Institute of Developing Economies/Ajia Keizai Kenkyusho. • Semiannual. Price varies. Text in English and Japanese.

Regional Economic Development: Theories amd Strategies for Developing Countries. Marguerite N. Abd El-Shahid. Sage Publications, Inc. • 1994. $10.00.

CD-ROM DATABASES

World Development Report [CD-ROM]. The World Bank, Office of the Publisher. • Annual. Single-user, $375.00. Network version, $750.00. CD-ROM includes the current edition of *World Development Report* and 21 previous editions.

ENCYCLOPEDIAS AND DICTIONARIES

Worldmark Encyclopedia of National Economies. The Gale Group. • 2002. $295.00. Four volumes. Covers both the current and historical development of the economies of 200 foreign nations. Includes analysis and statistics.

HANDBOOKS AND MANUALS

Nations of the World: A Political, Economic, and Business Handbook. Grey House Publishing. • 2000. $135.00. Includes descriptive data on economic characteristics, population, gross domestic product (GDP), banking, inflation, agriculture, tourism, and other factors. Covers "all the nations of the world.".

Third World Handbook. Available from Fitzroy Dearborn Publications, Inc. • 1994. $45.00. Second revised edition. Published by Cassell Publications. Discusses background, organizations, and movements within each country and region. Includes maps and photographs.

ONLINE DATABASES

EconLit. American Economic Association. • Covers the worldwide literature of economics as contained in selected monographs and about 550 journals. Subjects include microeconomics, macroeconomics, economic history, inflation, money, credit, finance, accounting theory, trade, natural resource economics, and regional economics. Time period is 1969 to present, with monthly updates. Inquire as to online cost and availability.

PERIODICALS AND NEWSLETTERS

Development Business. United Nations Publications. • Semimonthly. $495.00 per year. Provides leads on contract opportunities worldwide for engineering firms and multinational corporations. Text in English, French, Portuguese, and Spanish.

Emerging Markets Debt Report. Securities Data Publishing. • Weekly. $895.00 per year. Newsletter. Provides information on new and prospective sovereign and corporate bond issues from developing countries. Includes an emerging market bond index and pricing data. (Securities Data Publishing is a unit of Thomson Financial.).

Emerging Markets Quarterly. Institutional Investor. • Quarterly. $325.00 per year. Newsletter on financial markets in developing areas, such as Africa, Latin America, Southeast Asia, and Eastern Europe. Topics include institutional investment opportunities and regulatory matters. Formerly *Emerging Markets Weekly.*

Global Commodity Markets. The World Bank, Office of the Publisher. • Quarterly. $645.00 per year. Covers international trends in the production, consumption, and trade patterns of primary commodities, including food, metals, minerals, energy, and fertilizers. Includes electronic monthly updates and electronic access to the quarterly.

Journal of Developing Areas. Western Illinois University. • Quarterly. Individuals, $29.00 per year; institutions, $39.00 per year.

The Journal of Development Studies. ISBS. • Bimonthy. Individuals, $75.00 per year; institutions, $320.00 per year.

Journal of East-West Business. Haworth Press, Inc. • Quarterly. Individuals, $60.00 per year; institutions, $120.00 per year; libraries, $174.00 per year. An academic and practical journal focusing on business in the developing regions of Asia and Eastern Europe.

The Journal of International Trade and Economic Development. Routledge Journals. • Quarterly. Individuals, $68.00 per year; institutions, $445.00 per year. Emphasizes the effect of trade on the economies of developing nations.

Market Research International. Euromonitor International. • Monthly. $1,130.00 per year. Emphasis is on international consumer market research. Includes International Market Review, Global Market Trends and Developments, USA Market Report, Japan Market Report, Emerging Markets, and Market Focus (concise country reports).

World Development. Elsevier Science. • Monthly. $1,548.00 per year.

RESEARCH CENTERS AND INSTITUTES

Center for International Policy. 1755 Massachusetts Ave., N. W., Suite 312, Washington, DC 20036. Phone: (202)232-3317 Fax: (202)232-3440 E-mail: cip@ciponline.org • URL: http://www.ciponline.org • Research subjects include the International Monetary Fund, the World Bank, and other international financial institutions. Analyzes the impact of policies on social and economic conditions in developing countries.

Program on International Studies in Planning. Cornell University, 200 W. Sibley Hall, Ithaca, NY 14853. Phone: (607)255-2186 Fax: (607)255-6681 E-mail: bdl5@cornell.edu • URL: http://www.inet.crp.cornell.edu/organizations/isp/default.htm • Research activities are related to international urban and regional planning, with emphasis on developing areas.

STATISTICS SOURCES

Emerging Stock Markets Factbook. International Finance Corporation, Capital Market Dept. • Annual. $100.00. Published by the International Finance Corporation (IFC). Provides statistical profiles of more than 26 emerging stock markets in various countries of the world. Includes regional, composite, and industry indexes.

Global Development Finance: Analysis and Summary Tables. World Bank, The Office of the Publisher. • Annual. $40.00. Provides an analysis of debt and equity financial flows to 136 countries that report to the World Bank's Debtor Reporting System. Contains summary statistical tables for 150 countries.

Global Development Finance: Country Tables. World Bank, The Office of the Publisher. • 1998. $300.00 (includes *Analysis and Summary Tables*). Contains detailed statistical tables for 136 countries, covering total external debt, long-term debt ratios, arrears, commitments, disbursements, repayments, etc. Includes "major economic aggregates.".

Global Development Finance: External Public Debt of Developing Countries. World Bank, The Office of the Publisher. • Irregular. Prices vary. Includes supplements. Contains detailed data from the International Bank for Reconstruction and Development (World Bank) on the external debt load of over 100 developing countries.

Handbook of International Economic Statistics. Available from National Technical Information Service. • Annual. $40.00. Prepared by U. S. Central Intelligence Agency. Provides basic statistics for comparing worldwide economic performance, with an emphasis on Europe, including Eastern Europe.

Handbook of International Trade and Development Statistics. United Nations Publications. • Annual. $80.00. Text in English and French.

Least Developed Countries. United Nations Publications. • Annual. $45.00 Report on least developed countries compiled by the United Nations

Conference on Trade and Development (UNCTAD). Contains basic data.

Monthly Bulletin of Statistics. United Nations Publications. • Monthly. $295.00 per year. Provides current data for about 200 countries on a wide variety of economic, industrial, and demographic subjects. Compiled by United Nations Statistical Office.

Short-Term Economic Indicators: Transition Economies. OECD Publications and Information Center. • Quarterly. Presents annual, quarterly, and monthly economic indicators for the developing countries of Eastern Europe and the New Independent States.

Statistical Abstract of the World. The Gale Group. • 1997. $80.00. Third edition. Provides data on a wide variety of economic, social, and political topics for about 200 countries. Arranged by country.

Statistical Handbook on Poverty in the Developing World. Chandrika Kaul. Oryx Press. • 1999. $65.00. Provides international coverage, including special sections on women and children, and on selected cities. (Statistical Handbook Series).

Statistical Yearbook. United Nations Publications. • Annual. $125.00. Contains statistics for about 200 countries on a wide variety of economic, industrial, and demographic topics. Compiled by United Nations Statistical Office.

UNESCO Statistical Yearbook. Bernan Press. • Annual. $95.00. Co-published by Bernan Press and the United Nations Educational, Scientific, and Cultural Organization (http://www.unesco.org). Presents statistical data from more than 200 countries on education, technology, research, broadcasting, cinema, book publishing, newspapers, libraries, museums, and population. Includes charts, maps, and graphs.

World Bank Atlas. The World Bank, Office of the Publisher. • Annual. Price on application. Contains "color maps, charts, and graphs representing the main social, economic, and environmental indicators for 209 countries and territories" (publisher).

World Development Indicators. World Bank, The Office of the Publisher. • Annual. $60.00. Provides data and information on the people, economy, environment, and markets of 148 countries. Emphasis is on statistics relating to major development issues.

World Statistics Pocketbook. United Nations Publications. • Annual. $10.00. Presents basic economic, social, and environmental indicators for about 200 countries and areas. Covers more than 50 items relating to population, economic activity, labor force, agriculture, industry, energy, trade, transportation, communication, education, tourism, and the environment. Statistical sources are noted.

TRADE/PROFESSIONAL ASSOCIATIONS

Commission on International Affairs. c/o National Association of State Universities and Land-Gran, 1307 New York Ave., Suite 400, Washington, DC 20005-4701. Phone: (202)478-6040 Fax: (202)478-6046 E-mail: sgluxman@nasulgc.org.

International Development Association. The World Bank, 1818 H St., N.W., Room E1227, Washington, DC 20433: Phone: (202)477-1234 Fax: (202)477-6391 • URL: http://www.worldbank.org • Promotes the economic development of poor countries.

Overseas Development Council. 1875 Connecticut Ave., N.W., Suite 1012, Washington, DC 20009. Phone: (202)234-8701 Fax: (202)745-0067 E-mail: giunta@odc.org • URL: http://www.odc.org.

Oxfam America. 26 West St., Boston, MA 02111-1206. Phone: 800-770-9326 or (617)482-1211 Fax: (617)728-2594 E-mail: info@oxfamamerica.org • URL:. http://www.oxfamamerica.org.

Peaceworkers. 721 Shrader St., San Francisco, CA 94117. Phone: (415)751-0302 Fax: (415)751-0302 E-mail: peaceworkers@igc.apc.org.

Society for International Development. 1875 Connecticut Ave., N.W., Washington, DC 20009. 1875 Connecticut Ave., N.W.,.

OTHER SOURCES

World Migration Report. United Nations Publications. • Annual. $39.00. Analyzes major trends in world migration, including individual country profiles.

DEVELOPMENT, COMMUNITY

See: COMMUNITY DEVELOPMENT

DEVELOPMENT CREDIT CORPORATIONS

See: CREDIT

DEVELOPMENT, INDUSTRIAL

See: INDUSTRIAL DEVELOPMENT

DEVELOPMENT, URBAN

See: URBAN DEVELOPMENT

DIAMOND INDUSTRY

See also: GEMS AND GEMSTONES; INDUSTRIAL DIAMONDS

GENERAL WORKS

Diamonds. Fred Ware. Gem Book Publishers. • 1998. $14.95. Revised edition. (Fred Ware Gem Book Series).

Diamonds and Precious Stones. Harry Emmanuel. Gordon Press Publishers. • 1977. $79.95.

ALMANACS AND YEARBOOKS

Diamond Manufacturers and Importers Association of America Yearbook. • Annual.

DIRECTORIES

Jewelers' Circular/Keystone-Jewelers' Directory. Cahners Business Information. • Annual. $33.95. About 8,500 manufacturers, importers and wholesale jewelers providing merchandise and supplies to the jewelry retailing industry; and related trade organizations. Included with subscription to *Jewelers' Circular Keystone.*

PERIODICALS AND NEWSLETTERS

Diamond World Review. World Federation of Diamond Bourses. International Diamond Publications, Ltd. • Bimonthly. $78.00 per year. Text in English.

Israel Diamond and Precious Stones. International Diamond Publications, Ltd. • Bimonthly. $78.00 per year. Text in English. Formerly *Israel Diamonds.*

STATISTICS SOURCES

Mineral Commodity Summaries. Available from U. S. Government Printing Office. • Annual. Published by the U. S. Geological Survey, Department of the Interior (http://www.usgs.gov). Contains detailed, five-year data for about 90 nonfuel minerals. Covers a wide range of statistics, including production, imports, exports, consumption, reserves, prices, tariff information, and industry employment. (Two pages are devoted to each mineral.).

TRADE/PROFESSIONAL ASSOCIATIONS

Diamond Council of America. c/o Jerry Fogel, 9140 Ward Parkway, Kansas City, MO 64114. Phone: (816)444-3500 Fax: (816)444-0330.

Diamond Dealers Club. 580 Fifth Ave., New York, NY 10036. Phone: (212)869-9777 Fax: (212)869-5164.

Industrial Diamond Association. P.O. Box 1070, Skyland, NC 28776. Phone: (704)684-1986 or (704)684-1988 Fax: (704)684-7372 E-mail: gray@juno.com • URL: http://www.superabrasives.org.

DIAMONDS, INDUSTRIAL

See: INDUSTRIAL DIAMONDS

DICTATING MACHINES

See: OFFICE EQUIPMENT AND SUPPLIES

DIE CASTING

See: TOOL INDUSTRY

DIESEL ENGINES

See: ENGINES

DIET

See also: HEALTH FOOD INDUSTRY; HERBS; VITAMINS

ABSTRACTS AND INDEXES

Nutrition Abstracts and Reviews, Series A: Human and Experimental. Available from CABI Publishing North America. • Monthly. $1,385.00 per year. Published in England by CABI Publishing. Provides worldwide coverage of the literature.

CD-ROM DATABASES

Consumers Reference Disc. National Information Services Corp. • Quarterly. Provides the CD-ROM version of *Consumer Health and Nutrition Index* from Oryx Press and *Consumers Index to Product Evaluations and Information Sources* from Pierian Press. Contains citations to consumer health articles and consumer product evaluations, tests, warnings, and recalls.

Health Reference Center. The Gale Group. • Monthly. Provides CD-ROM citations, abstracts, and selected full-text articles on many health-related subjects. Includes references to medical journals, general periodicals, newsletters, newspapers, pamphlets, and medical reference books.

Magazine Index Plus. The Gale Group. • Monthly. $4,000.00 per year (includes InfoTrac workstation). Provides full text on CD-ROM for about 100 popular, general interest magazines and indexing for 300 others. Includes special indexing of reviews and product evaluations. Time period is 1980 to date.

DIRECTORIES

American Society of Bariatric Physicians - Directory. American Society of Bariatric Physicians. • Annual. $50.00. Lists 1300 physicians concerned with obesity.

ENCYCLOPEDIAS AND DICTIONARIES

CRC Desk Reference for Nutrition. Carolyn D. Berdanier. CRC Press, Inc. • 1998. $69.95. Encyclopedic, alphabetical arrangement of topics.

Encyclopedia of Food Science, Food Technology, and Nutrition. Robert Macrae and others, editors.

Academic Press, Inc. • 1993. Eight volumes. $2,414.00.

Foods and Nutrition Encyclopedia. Audrey H. Ensminger and others. CRC Press, Inc. • 1993. $382.00. Second edition. Two volumes.

HANDBOOKS AND MANUALS

Advanced Nutrition: Micronutrients. Carolyn D. Berdanier and Mark L. Failla. CRC Press, Inc. • 2000. $99.95. Provides detailed coverage of essential vitamins and minerals. Written for professional dietitions and nutritionists. (Modern Nutrition Series).

Calories and Carbohydrates. Barbara Kraus. NAL. • 1999. $6.99. Revised edition.

Diet and Meal Planning. Entrepreneur Media, Inc. • Looseleaf. $59.50. A practical guide to starting a diet and meal planning service. Covers profit potential, start-up costs, market size evaluation, pricing, accounting, advertising, promotion, etc. (Start-Up Business Guide No. E2333.).

Mayo Clinic Diet Manual: A Handbook of Nutrition Practices. Jennifer K. Nelson and others. Harcourt Health Sciences. • 1994. $75.00. Seventh edition.

PDR Family Guide to Nutrition and Health: The Facts to Remember...The Claims to Forget. Medical Economics Co., Inc. • 1995. $25.95. Provides advice on diet, vitamins, minerals, fat, salt, cholesterol, and other topics related to nutrition.

Personal Health Reporter. The Gale Group. • 1992. $105.00. Two volumes. Volume one, $105.00; volume two, $105.00. Presents a collection of professional and popular articles on 150 topics relating to physical and mental health conditions and treatments.

INTERNET DATABASES

National Library of Medicine (NLM). National Institutes of Health (NIH). Phone: 888-346-3656 or (301)496-1131 Fax: (301)480-3537 E-mail: access@nlm.nih.gov • URL: http://www.nlm.nih.gov • NLM Web site offers free access through MEDLINE ("PubMed") to about nine million references to articles appearing in some 3,800 biomedical journals, with abstracts. Search interfaces range from "simple keywords to advanced Boolean expressions." The NLM site offers many links to other sources of biomedical and technical information (the National Center for Biotechnology Information, for example). Fees: Free.

ONLINE DATABASES

CAB Abstracts. CAB International North America. • Contains 46 specialized abstract collections covering over 10,000 journals and monographs in the areas of agriculture, horticulture, forest products, farm products, nutrition, dairy science, poultry, grains, animal health, entomology, etc. Time period is 1972 to date, with monthly updates. Inquire as to online cost and availability. *CAB Abstracts on CD-ROM* also available, with annual updating.

PERIODICALS AND NEWSLETTERS

American Dietetic Association Journal. American Dietetic Association. • Monthly. $125.00 per year.

American Journal of Clinical Nutrition: A Journal Reporting the Practical Application of Our World-Wide Knowledge of Nutrition. American Society for Clinical Nutrition, Inc. • Monthly. Individuals, $133.00 per year; institutions, $209.00 per year.

Family Economics and Nutrition Review. Available from U. S. Government Printing Office. • Quarterly. $19.00 per year. Issued by the Consumer and Food Economics Institute, U. S. Department of Agriculture. Provides articles on consumer expenditures and budgeting for food, clothing, housing, energy, education, etc.

International Journal for Vitamin and Nutrition Research. Hogrefe & Huber Publishers. • Quarterly. $198.00 per year.

Journal of Nutrition. American Institute of Nutrition. • Monthly. Individuals, $105.00 per year; institutions, $295.00 per year; students, $30.00 per year.

Journal of Nutrition Education. Society for Nutrition Education. Decker, Inc. • Bimonthly. Individuals, $129.00 per year; institutions, $170.00 per year.

Nutrition Reviews. International Life Science Institute. • Monthly. Individuals, $97.50 per year; institutions, $160.00 per year.

Nutrition Today. Williams and Wilkins. • Bimonthly. Individuals, $67.00 per year; institutions, $146.00 per year.

RESEARCH CENTERS AND INSTITUTES

Institute of Human Nutrition. Columbia University. College of Physicians and Surgeons, 630 W. 168th St., PH 15E, New York, NY 10032. Phone: (212)305-4808 Fax: (212)305-3079 E-mail: rjd20@columbia.edu • URL: http://www.cpmcnet.columbia.edu/dept/ihn/.

STATISTICS SOURCES

Agriculture Fact Book. Available from U. S. Government Printing Office. • Annual. Issued by the Office of Communications, U. S. Department of Agriculture. Includes data on U. S. agriculture, farmers, food, nutrition, and rural America. Programs of the Department of Agriculture in six areas are described: rural economic development, foreign trade, nutrition, the environment, inspection, and education.

TRADE/PROFESSIONAL ASSOCIATIONS

American Dietetic Association. 216 W. Jackson Blvd., Chicago, IL 60606-6695. Phone: (312)899-0040 Fax: (312)899-1079 E-mail: membrship@eatright.org • URL: http://www.eatright.org.

American Society for Nutritional Sciences. 9650 Rockville Pike, Bethesda, MD 20814-3990. Phone: (301)530-7050 Fax: (301)571-1892 E-mail: sec@asns.faseb.org • URL: http://www.faseb.org/asns/.

National Nutritional Foods Association. 3931 MacArthur Blvd., No. 101, Newport Beach, CA 92660-3021. Phone: (949)622-6272 Fax: (949)622-6266 E-mail: nnfa@aol.com • URL: http://www.nnfa.org.

OTHER SOURCES

Weight Loss and Diet Control Market. Available from MarketResearch.com. • 1999. $1,695.00. Market research report published by Marketdata Enterprises. Covers commercial diet programs, medical plans, nonprescription appetite suppressants low-calorie foods, artifical sweeteners, health clubs, and diet books. Includes forecasts to the year 2003.

DIGITAL COMPUTERS

See: COMPUTERS

DIGITAL MEDIA

See: ELECTRONIC PUBLISHING; MULTIMEDIA; ONLINE INFORMATION SYSTEMS; OPTICAL DISK STORAGE DEVICES

DINERS

See: RESTAURANTS, LUNCHROOMS, ETC.

DINNERWARE

See: TABLEWARE

DIPLOMATIC AND CONSULAR SERVICE

GENERAL WORKS

Safe Trip Abroad. Available from U. S. Government Printing Office. • 1996. $1.25. Issued by the Bureau of Consular Affairs, U. S. State Department (http://www.state.gov). Provides practical advice for international travel.

ABSTRACTS AND INDEXES

PAIS International in Print. Public Affairs Information Service, Inc. • Monthly. $650.00 per year; cumulations three times a year. Provides topical citations to the worldwide literature of public affairs, economics, demographics, sociology, and trade. Text in English; indexed materials in English, French, German, Italian, Portuguese and Spanish.

ALMANACS AND YEARBOOKS

The Statesman's Yearbook: Statistical and Historical Annual of the States of the World. Stockton Press Direct Marketing. • Annual. $65.00.

BIBLIOGRAPHIES

Diplomatic Bookshelf and Review. Arthur H. Thrower, Ltd. • Monthly.

CD-ROM DATABASES

Leadership Library on CD-ROM: Who's Who in the Leadership of the United States. Leadership Directories, Inc. • Quarterly. $2,641.00 per year, including access to Internet version (weekly updates). Contains all 14 *Yellow Book* personnel directories on CD-ROM, providing contact and brief biographical information for about 400,000 individuals. Covers business, government, financial institutions, news media, law firms, associations, foreign representatives, and nonprofit organizations. Includes photographs.

PAIS on CD-ROM. Public Affairs Information Service, Inc. • Quarterly. $1,995.00 per year. Provides a CD-ROM version of the online service, *PAIS International.* Contains over 400,000 citations to the literature of contemporary social, political, and economic issues.

DIRECTORIES

Diplomatic List. U.S. Department of State. Available from U.S. Government Printing Office. • Quarterly. $16.00 per year. List of foreign diplomats in and around Washington, D.C.

Foreign Consular Offices in the United States. U.S. Department of State. Available from U.S. Government Printing Office. • Semiannual. $13.00 per copy.

Foreign Representatives in the U. S. Yellow Book: Who's Who in the U. S. Offices of Foreign Corporations, Foreign Nations, the Foreign Press, and Intergovernmental Organizations. Leadership Directories, Inc. • Semiannual. $235.00 per year. Lists executives located in the U. S. for 1,300 foreign companies, 340 foreign banks and other financial institutions, 175 embassies and consulates, and 375 foreign press outlets. Includes five indexes.

United States Government Manual. National Archives and Records Administration. Available from U.S. Government Printing Office. • Annual. $46.00.

ONLINE DATABASES

PAIS International. Public Affairs Information Service, Inc. • Corresponds to the former printed publications, *PAIS Bulletin* (1976-90) and *PAIS Foreign Language Index* (1972-90), and to the current *PAIS International in Print* (1991 to date).

Covers economic, political, and sociological material appearing in periodicals, books, government documents, and other publications. Updating is monthly. Inquire as to online cost and availability.

PERIODICALS AND NEWSLETTERS

Diplomatic History. Society for Historians of American Foreign Relations. Blackwell Publishers. • Quarterly. $109.00 per year.

Diplomatic Observer. Institute for International Sociological Research. • Monthly. $16.50 per year.

Diplomatic World Bulletin and Delegates World Bulletin: Dedicated to Serving the United Nations and the International Community. Diplomatic World Bulletin Publications, Inc. • Biweekly. $45.00 per year.

Foreign Service Journal. American Foreign Service Association. • Monthly. $40.00 per year.

Society for Historians of American Foreign Relations Newsletter. Society for Historians of American Foreign Relations. • Quarterly.

RESEARCH CENTERS AND INSTITUTES

Center of International Studies. Princeton University. Bendheim Hall, Princeton, NJ 08544. Phone: (609)258-4851 Fax: (609)258-3988 • URL: http://www.princeton.edu/programs/cis.html.

TRADE/PROFESSIONAL ASSOCIATIONS

American Foreign Service Association. 2101 E St., N.W., Washington, DC 20037. Phone: 800-704-2372 or (202)338-3687 Fax: (202)338-6820 E-mail: afsa@afsa.org • URL: http://www.afsa.org.

Diplomatic and Consular Officers, Retired. 1801 F St., N.W., Washington, DC 20006. Phone: 800-344-9127 or (202)682-0500 Fax: (202)842-3295 E-mail: dacor@ix.netcom.com.

DIRECT COSTING

See: COST ACCOUNTING

DIRECT DEBIT SYSTEMS

See: POINT-OF-SALE SYSTEMS (POS)

DIRECT MAIL ADVERTISING

See also: ADVERTISING; MAIL ORDER BUSINESS; MAILING LISTS

DIRECTORIES

Directory of Mail Order Catalogs. Grey House Publishing. • Annual. $275.00. Contains 11,000 entries for mail order companies selling consumer products throughout the U.S.

Directory of Mailing List Companies. Todd Publications. • Biennial. $50.00. Lists and describes approximately 1,100 of the most active list brokers, owners, managers and compilers.

Mail Order Business Directory. B. Klein Publications. • Annual. $85.00. Provides 12,000 listings of mail order and catalog houses in the U.S.; international coverage.

Who's Who-Masa's Buyers' Guide to Blue Ribbon Mailing Service. Mail Advertising Service Association International. • Annual. Free. Member firms that provide printing, addressing, inserting, sorting, and other mailing services, and mailing list brokers.

FINANCIAL RATIOS

Annual Statement Studies. Robert Morris Associates: The Association of Lending and Credit Risk Professiona. • Annual. Free to members; non-members, $140.00. Median and quartile financial ratios are given for over 400 kinds of manufacturing, wholesale, retail, construction, and consumer finance establishments. Data is sorted by both asset size and sales volume. Includes a clearly written "Definition of Ratios" and an alphabetical industry index.

HANDBOOKS AND MANUALS

Do-It-Yourself Advertising: How to Produce Great Ads, Brochures, Catalogs, Direct Mail, and Much More!. Fred E. Hahn and Kenneth G. Mangun. John Wiley and Sons, Inc. • 1997. $45.00. Second edition. Covers magazines, newspapers, flyers, brochures, catalogs, direct mail, telemarketing, trade shows, and radio/TV promotions. Includes checklists. (Small Business Series).

The Greatest Direct Mail Sales Letters of All Time: Why They Succeed, How They Are Created, How You Can Create Great Sales Letters, Too. Richard S. Hodgson. Dartnell Corp. • 1995. $69.95. Second revised edition. About 100 direct mail sales lettes on a variety of products are reprinted and analyzed.

How to Start and Operate a Mail Order Business. Julian L. Simon. McGraw-Hill. • 1991. $42.95. Fifth edition.

The Perfect Sales Piece: A Complete Do-It-Yourself Guide to Creating Brochures, Catalogs, Fliers, and Pamphlets. Robert W. Bly. John Wiley and Sons, Inc. • 1994. $49.95. A guide to the use of various forms of printed literature for direct selling, sales promotion, and marketing. (Small Business Editions Series).

PERIODICALS AND NEWSLETTERS

Advertising Age: The International Newspaper of Marketing. Crain Communications, Inc. • Weekly. $109.00 per year. Includes supplement *Creativity.*

The Bullet. SRDS. • Bimonthly. Included with subscription to *Direct Marketing List Source.* Newsletter on direct mail advertising and mailing lists. Includes list updates and management changes.

Database Marketer. Intertec Publishing Co. • Monthly. $329.00 per year.

Direct Marketing: Using Direct Response Advertising to Enhance Marketing Database. Hoke Communications, Inc. • Monthly. $65.00 per year. Direct marketing to consumers and business.

DMA Washington Report: Federal and State Regulatory Issues of Concern. Direct Marketing Association. • Monthly. Membership.

Public Affairs Report. Institute of Govermental Studies. • Bimonthly. Free.

Target Marketing: The Leading Magazine for Integrated Database Marketing. North American Publishing Co. • Monthly. $65.00 per year. Dedicated to direct marketing excellence. Formerly *Zip Target Marketing.*

Who's Mailing What!: The Monthly Newsletter Analysis and Record of the Direct Mareting Archive. North American Publishing Co. • Monthly. $295.00 per year. Newsletter and listing of promotional mailings. Photocopies of mailings are available to subscribers.

STATISTICS SOURCES

DMA Statistical Fact Book. Direct Marketing Association, Inc. • Annual. $165.95 to non-members; $105.95 to members. Provides data in five sections covering direct response advertising, media, mailing lists, market applications, and "Practical Management Information." Includes material on interactive/online marketing. (Cover title: *Direct Marketing Association's Statistical Fact Book.*).

TRADE/PROFESSIONAL ASSOCIATIONS

Alliance of Nonprofit Mailers. 1211 Connecticut Ave., No. 620, Washington, DC 20036. Phone: (202)462-5132 Fax: (202)462-0423 E-mail: npmailers@aol.com • URL: http://www.nonprofitmailers.org.

Direct Marketing Association. 1120 Ave. of the Americas, New York, NY 10036-6700. Phone: (212)768-7277 Fax: (212)302-6714 E-mail: webmaster@the-dma.org • URL: http://www.the-dma.org.

Direct Marketing Educational Foundation. 1120 Ave. of the Americas, New York, NY 10036-6700. Phone: (212)768-7277 Fax: (212)302-6714 • URL: http://www.the-dma.org/dmef.

Mail Advertising Service Association International. 1421 Prince St., Alexandria, VA 22314. Phone: 800-333-6272 or (703)836-9200 Fax: (703)548-8204 E-mail: masa-mail@masa.org • URL: http://www.masa.org.

National Federation of Nonprofits. 815 15th St., N.W., Suite 822, Washington, DC 20005-2201. Phone: (202)628-4380 Fax: (202)628-4383.

DIRECT MARKETING

GENERAL WORKS

Creative Strategy in Direct Marketing. Susan K. Jones. NTC/Contemporary Publishing. • 1997. $39.95. Second edition.

Direct Marketing, Direct Selling, and the Mature Consumer: A Research Study. James R. Lumpkin and others. Greenwood Publishing Group, Inc. • 1989. $62.95. A study of older consumers and their use of mail order, telephone shopping, party-plans, etc.

Do-It-Yourself Direct Marketing: Secrets for Small Business. Mark S. Bacon. John Wiley and Sons, Inc. • 1997. $16.95. Second edition.

ABSTRACTS AND INDEXES

Business Periodicals Index. H. W. Wilson Co. • Monthly, except August, with quarterly and annual cumulations. Service basis for print edition; CD-ROM edition, $1,495.00 per year.

DIRECTORIES

AMA International Member and Marketing Services Guide. American Marketing Association. • Annual. $150.00. Lists professional members of the American Marketing Association. Also contains information on providers of marketing support services and products, including software, communications, direct marketing, promotion, research, and consulting companies. Includes geographical and alphabetical indexes. Formerly *Marketing Yellow Pages and AMA International Membership Directory.*

Catalog Age/Direct Sourcebook. Intertec Publishing Co. • Annual. $35.00. Lists of approximately 300 suppliers of products and services for direct marketing, especially catalog marketing.

Direct Marketing List Source. SRDS. • Bimonthly. $542.00 per year. Provides detailed information and rates for business, farm, and consumer mailing lists (U. S., Canadian, and international). Includes current postal information and directories of list brokers, compilers, and managers. Formerly *Direct Mail List Rates and Data.*

Direct Marketing Market Place: The Networking Source of the Direct Marketing Industry. National Register Publishing. • Annual. $269.00. Lists direct marketers, service companies, creative sources, professional groups, photographers, paper suppliers, etc.

WFDSA Directory of Members (World Federation of Direct Selling Association). World Federation of Direct Selling Associations. • Annual. Price on application.

HANDBOOKS AND MANUALS

Complete Direct Marketing Sourcebook: A Step-by-Step Guide to Organizing and Managing a Successful Direct Marketing Program. John Kremer. John Wiley and Sons, Inc. • 1992. $27.95. Includes checklists, sample direct mail letters, and the calculation of break-even points. (Small Business Editions Series).

Direct Marketing Success: What Works and Why. Freeman F. Gosden. John Wiley and Sons, Inc. • 1989. $24.95.

The New Direct Marketing: How to Implement a Profit-Driven Database Marketing Strategy. Spepard, Davis, Associates Staff. McGraw-Hill Professional. • 1998. $114.95. Third edition. Discusses the construction, analysis, practical use, and evaluation of direct marketing databases containing primary and/or secondary data.

Sales Manager's Handbook. John P. Steinbrink. Dartnell Corp. • 1989. $93.50. 14th edition.

ONLINE DATABASES

ABI/INFORM. Bell & Howell Information and Learning. • Provides online indexing to business-related material occurring in over 1,000 periodicals from 1971 to the present. Inquire as to online cost and availability.

Wilson Business Abstracts Online. H. W. Wilson Co. • Indexes and abstracts 600 major business periodicals, plus the *Wall Street Journal* and the business section of the *New York Times*. Indexing is from 1982, abstracting from 1990, with the two newspapers included from 1993. Updated weekly. Inquire as to online cost and availability. (*Business Periodicals Index* without abstracts is also available online.).

PERIODICALS AND NEWSLETTERS

Catalog Age. Cowles Business Media, Inc. • Monthly. $72.00 per year. Edited for catalog marketing and management personnel.

Direct: Magazine for Direct Marketing Management. Intertec Publinshing Co. • Monthly. Free to qualified personnel; others, $74.00 per year.

Direct Marketing: Using Direct Response Advertising to Enhance Marketing Database. Hoke Communications, Inc. • Monthly. $65.00 per year. Direct marketing to consumers and business.

Direct Selling Association World Federation News. Direct Selling Association. World Federation of Direct Selling Associations. • Six times a year. Membership.

DM News: The Newspaper of Direct Marketing. DM News Corp. • Weekly. $75.00 per year. Includes special feature issues on catalog marketing, telephone marketing, database marketing, and fundraising. Includes monthly supplements. *DM News International*, *DRTV News*, and *TeleServices*.

Journal of Interactive Marketing. Direct Marketing Educational Foundation. John Wiley and Sons, Inc., Journals Div. • Quarterly. Institutions, $550.00 per year. Exchange of ideas in the field of direct marketing. Formerly *Journal of Direct Marketing*.

Who's Mailing What!: The Monthly Newsletter Analysis and Record of the Direct Mareting Archive. North American Publishing Co. • Monthly. $295.00 per year. Newsletter and listing of promotional mailings. Photocopies of mailings are available to subscribers.

STATISTICS SOURCES

DMA Statistical Fact Book. Direct Marketing Association, Inc. • Annual. $165.95 to non-members; $105.95 to members. Provides data in five sections covering direct response advertising, media, mailing lists, market applications, and "Practical Management Information." Includes material on interactive/online marketing. (Cover title: *Direct Marketing Association's Statistical Fact Book.*).

TRADE/PROFESSIONAL ASSOCIATIONS

Direct Marketing Educational Foundation. 1120 Ave. of the Americas, New York, NY 10036-6700. Phone: (212)768-7277 Fax: (212)302-6714 • URL: http://www.the-dma.org/dmef.

Direct Selling Association. 1666 K St., N.W., Suite 1010, Washington, DC 20006-2808. Phone: (202)293-5760 Fax: (202)463-4569 E-mail: info@dsa.org • URL: http://www.dsa.org.

OTHER SOURCES

Fred Goss' What's Working in Direct Marketing. United Communications Group (UCG). • Biweekly. $242.00 per year. Newsletter. Provides ideas for direct marketing promotions.

DIRECT SELLING

See: DIRECT MARKETING

DIRECTORIES

See: CATALOGS AND DIRECTORIES

DIRECTORS

See: CORPORATE DIRECTORS AND OFFICERS

DISABILITY INSURANCE

See also: EMPLOYEE BENEFIT PLANS

GENERAL WORKS

Smarter Insurance Solutions. Janet Bamford. Bloomberg Press. • 1996. $19.95. Provides practical advice to consumers, with separate chapters on the following kinds of insurance: automobile, homeowners, health, disability, and life. (Bloomberg Personal Bookshelf Series).

Social Security, Medicare, and Pensions: Get the Most Out of Your Retirement and Medical Benefits. Joseph Matthews and Dorothy M. Berman. Nolo.com. • 1999. $21.95. Seventh edition. In addition to the basic topics, includes practical information on Supplemental Security Income (SSI), disability benefits, veterans benefits, 401(k) plans, Medicare HMOs, medigap insurance, Medicaid, and how to appeal decisions.

ABSTRACTS AND INDEXES

Business Periodicals Index. H. W. Wilson Co. • Monthly, except August, with quarterly and annual cumulations. Service basis for print edition; CD-ROM edition, $1,495.00 per year.

Current Law Index: Multiple Access to Legal Periodicals. The Gale Group. • Monthly. $650.00 per year. Produced in cooperation with the American Association of Law Libraries. Indexes more than 900 law journals, legal newspapers, and specialty publications from the U.S., Canada, U.K., Ireland, Australia, and New Zealand.

Index to Legal Periodicals and Books. H. W. Wilson Co. • Monthly. Quarterly and annual cumulations. $270.00 per year. CD-ROM version available at $1,495.00 per year.

Insurance Periodicals Index. Specials Libraries Association, Insurance and Employees Benefits Div. CCH/NILS Publishing Co. • Annual. $250.00. Compiled by the Insurance and Employee Benefits Div., Special Libraries Association. A yearly index of over 15,000 articles from about 35 insurance periodicals. Arrangement is by subject, with an index to authors.

ALMANACS AND YEARBOOKS

American Law Yearbook. The Gale Group. • Annual. $155.00. Serves as a yearly supplement to *West's Encyclopedia of American Law*. Describes new legal developments in many subject areas.

CD-ROM DATABASES

U. S. Insurance: Life, Accident, and Health. Sheshunoff Information Services, Inc. • Monthly. Price on application. CD-ROM provides detailed, current information on the financial characteristics of more than 2,300 life, accident, and health insurance companies.

WILSONDISC: Index to Legal Periodicals and Books. H. W. Wilson Co. • Monthly. Including unlimited online access to *Index to Legal Periodicals* through WILSONLINE. Contains CD-ROM indexing of more than 800 English language legal periodicals from 1981 to date and 2,500 books.

WILSONDISC: Wilson Business Abstracts. H. W. Wilson Co. • Monthly. $2,495.00 per year, including unlimited online access to *Wilson Business Abstracts* through WILSONLINE. Provides CD-ROM "cover-to-cover" abstracting and indexing of over 600 prominent business periodicals. Indexing is from 1982, abstracting from 1990. (*Business Periodicals Index* without abstracts is available on CD-ROM at $1,495 per year.).

ENCYCLOPEDIAS AND DICTIONARIES

West's Encyclopedia of American Law. Available from The Gale Group. • 1997. $995.00. Second edition. 12 volumes. Published by West Group. Covers a wide variety of legal topics for the general reader. Formerly *Guide to American Law: Everyone's Legal Encyclopedia* (1985).

HANDBOOKS AND MANUALS

The Complete Book of Insurance: The Consumer's Guide to Insuring Your Life, Health, Property, and Income. Ben G. Baldwin. McGraw-Hill Professional. • 1996. $24.95. Revised edition. Provides basic information and advice on various kinds of insurance: life, health, property (fire), disability, long-term care, automobile, liability, and annuities.

U. S. Master Employee Benefits Guide. CCH, Inc. • Annual. $49.00. Explains federal tax and labor laws relating to health care benefits, disability benefits, workers' compensation, employee assistance plans, etc.

INTERNET DATABASES

Social Security Online: The Official Web Site of the Social Security Administration. U. S. Social Security Administration. Phone: 800-772-1213 or (410)965-7700 • URL: http://www.ssa.gov • Web site provides a wide variety of online information relating to social security and Medicare. Topics include benefits, disability, employer wage reporting, personal earnings statements, statistics, government financing, social security law, and public welfare reform legislation.

ONLINE DATABASES

I.I.I. Data Base Search. Insurance Information Institute. • Provides online citations and abstracts of insurance-related literature in magazines, newspapers, trade journals, and books. Emphasis is on property and casualty insurance issues, including highway safety, product safety, and environmental liability. Inquire as to online cost and availability.

Index to Legal Periodicals and Books (Online). H. W. Wilson Co. • Broad coverage of law journals and books 1981 to date. Monthly updates. Inquire as to online cost and availability.

Management Contents. The Gale Group. • Covers a wide range of management, financial, marketing, personnel, and administrative topics. About 150 leading business journals are indexed and abstracted from 1974 to date, with monthly updating. Inquire as to online cost and availability.

Wilson Business Abstracts Online. H. W. Wilson Co. • Indexes and abstracts 600 major business periodicals, plus the *Wall Street Journal* and the business section of the *New York Times.* Indexing is from 1982, abstracting from 1990, with the two newspapers included from 1993. Updated weekly. Inquire as to online cost and availability. (*Business Periodicals Index* without abstracts is also available online.).

PERIODICALS AND NEWSLETTERS

Advisory Today. National Association of insurance and Finacial Advisors. • Monthly. Free to members; non-members, $7.00 per year. Edited for individual life and health insurance agents. Among the topics included are disability insurance and long-term care insurance. Formerly Life Association News.

Broker World. Insurance Publications, Inc. • Monthly. $6.00 per year. Edited for independent insurance agents and brokers. Special feature issue topics include annuities, disability insurance, estate planning, and life insurance.

Health Insurance Underwriter. National Association of Health Underwriters. • 11 times a year. Free to members; non-members, $25.00 per year. Includes special feature issues on long-term care insurance, disability insurance, managed health care, and insurance office management.

Jounal of Finacial Services Professionals. American Society of CLU and Ch F C. • Bimonthly. $38.00 per year. Provides information on life insurance and financial planning, including estate planning, retirement, tax planning, trusts, business insurance, long-term care insurance, disability insurance, and employee benefits. Formerly (American Society of CLU and Ch F C Journal).

RESEARCH CENTERS AND INSTITUTES

Lexis.com Research System. Lexis-Nexis Group. Phone: 800-227-9597 or (937)865-6800 Fax: (937)865-6909 E-mail: webmaster@prod.lexis-nexis.com • URL: http://www.lexis.com • Fee-based Web site offers extensive searching of a wide variety of legal sources. Additional features include Daily Opinion Service, lexis.com Bookstore, Career Center, CLE Center, Law Schools, and Practice Pages ("Pages specific to areas of specialty").

TRADE/PROFESSIONAL ASSOCIATIONS

Health Insurance Association of America. 555 13th St., N.W., Washington, DC 20004. Phone: (202)824-1600 Fax: (202)824-1722 • URL: http://www.hiaa.org • Members are commercial health insurers. Includes a Managed Care and Group Insurance Committee, a Disability Insurance Committee, a Medicare Administration Committee, and a Long-Term Care Task Force.

National Association Insurance and Financial Advisors. 1922 F St., N.W., Washington, DC 20006-4387. Phone: (202)331-6000 Fax: (202)835-9601 • URL: http://www.naifa.org.

National Association of Health Underwriters. 200 N. 14th St., Ste. 450, Arlington, VA 22201. Phone: (703)276-0220 Fax: (703)841-7797 • URL: http://www.nahu.org • Members are engaged in the sale of health and disability insurance.

DISABLED

See: HANDICAPPED WORKERS

DISCHARGED SERVICEMEN

See: VETERANS

DISCIPLINE OF EMPLOYEES

See: EMPLOYEE DISCIPLINE

DISCOUNT HOUSES

See also: CHAIN STORES; DEPARTMENT STORES; MARKETING; RETAIL TRADE

DIRECTORIES

Discount Store News - Top Chains. Chain Store Guide. • Annual. $79.00.

European Directory of Retailers and Wholesalers. Available from The Gale Group. • 1997. $790.00. Second edition. Published by Euromonitor. Provides detailed information on more than 4,000 major retail and wholesale businesses in 17 countries of Western Europe. Contains 26 categories, such as supermarkets, superstores, department stores, discount stores, franchise operators, mail order, etc. Includes company, product, and geographic indexes.

Phelon's Discount/Jobbing Trade. Phelon, Sheldon and Marsar, Inc. • Annual. $175.00. Up-to-date information on the discount and mass merchandising chains, clubs, outlets, stores and warehouses throughout the United States. Also wholesalers, jobbers and distributors of all kinds of goods.

Plunkett's Retail Industry Almanac: Complete Profiles on the Retail 500-The Leading Firms in Retail Stores, Services, Catalogs, and On-Line Sales. Available from Plunkett Research, Ltd. • Annual. $179.99. Provides detailed profiles of 500 major U. S. retailers. Industry trends are discussed.

PERIODICALS AND NEWSLETTERS

Chain Store Age: The Newsmagazine for Retail Executives. Lebhar-Friedman, Inc. • Monthly. $105.00 per year. Formerly *Chain Store Age Executive with Shopping Center Age.*

DSN Retailing Today (Discount Store News). Lebhar-Friedman, Inc. • Biweekly. $119.00 per year. Includes supplement *Apparel Merchandising.* Formerly Discount Store News.

Retail Merchandiser. Bill Communications, Communications Group. • Monthly. $55.00 per year. Mass merchandising retail industry. Formerly *Discount Merchandiser.*

Value Retail News: The Journal of Outlet and Off-Price Retail and Development. Off-Price Specialists, Inc. Value Retail News. • Monthly. Members $99.00 per year; non-members, $144.00 per year. Provides news of the off-price and outlet store industry. Emphasis is on real estate for outlet store centers.

RESEARCH CENTERS AND INSTITUTES

Center for Retail Management. J. L. Kellogg Graduate School of Management, Northwestern University, Evanston, IL 60208. Phone: (847)467-3600 Fax: (847)467-3620 • URL: http://www.retailing-network.com • Conducts research related to retail marketing and management.

Center for Retailing Studies. Texas A & M University, Department of Marketing, 4112 Tamus, College Station, TX 77843-4112. Phone: (979)845-0325 Fax: (979)845-5230 E-mail: berryle@tamu.edu • URL: http://www.crstamu.org • Research areas include retailing issues and consumer economics.

TRADE/PROFESSIONAL ASSOCIATIONS

International Mass Retail Association. 1700 N. Moore St., Suite 2250, Arlington, VA 22209. Phone: (703)841-2300 Fax: (703)841-1184 • URL: http://www.imra.org.

National Association of Wholesaler-Distributors. 1725 K St., N.W., Washington, DC 20006. Phone: (202)872-0885 Fax: (202)785-0586 E-mail: meetings@nawd.org • URL: http://www.nawmeetings.org.

DISCOVERIES, SCIENTIFIC AND TECHNOLOGICAL

See: INVENTIONS; PATENTS

DISCRIMINATION IN EMPLOYMENT

See: AFFIRMATIVE ACTION PROGRAMS

DISHWARE

See: TABLEWARE

DISINFECTION AND DISINFECTANT

See: SANITATION INDUSTRY

DISK STORAGE DEVICES, OPTICAL

See: OPTICAL DISK STORAGE DEVICES

DISMISSAL OF EMPLOYEES

See also: JOB HUNTING; UNEMPLOYMENT

GENERAL WORKS

Corporate Executions: The Ugly Truth About Layoffs. How Corporate Greed Is Shattering lives, Companies and Communities. Alan Downs. AMACOM. • 1995. $22.95. States that management layoffs are usually unnecessary and a detriment to the corporation.

Healing the Wounds: Overcoming the Trauma of Layoffs, and Revitalizing Downsized Organizations. David M. Noer. Jossey-Bass, Inc., Publishers. • 1993. $29.50. (Management Series).

PR News Casebook. The Gale Group. • 1993. $99.00. A collection of about 1,000 case studies covering major public relations campaigns and events, taken from the pages of *PR News.* Covers such issues as boycotts, new products, anniversaries, plant closings, downsizing, and stockholder relations.

When You Lose Your Job: Laid Off, Fired, Early Retired, Relocated, Demoted. Cliff Hakim. Berrett-Koehler Publishers, Inc. • 1993. $14.95. A guide to overcoming job loss. Covers emotional responses, as well as practical matters such as networking, resumes, and preparing for interviews.

ABSTRACTS AND INDEXES

Business Periodicals Index. H. W. Wilson Co. • Monthly, except August, with quarterly and annual cumulations. Service basis for print edition; CD-ROM edition, $1,495.00 per year.

Current Law Index: Multiple Access to Legal Periodicals. The Gale Group. • Monthly. $650.00 per year. Produced in cooperation with the American Association of Law Libraries. Indexes more than 900 law journals, legal newspapers, and specialty publications from the U.S., Canada, U.K., Ireland, Australia, and New Zealand.

Human Resources Abstracts: An International Information Service. Sage Publications, Inc. • Quarterly. Individuals, $150.00 per year; institutions, $610.00 per year.

Index to Legal Periodicals and Books. H. W. Wilson Co. • Monthly. Quarterly and annual cumulations. $270.00 per year. CD-ROM version available at $1,495.00 per year.

Personnel Management Abstracts. • Quarterly. $190.00 per year. Includes annual cumulation.

ALMANACS AND YEARBOOKS

American Law Yearbook. The Gale Group. • Annual. $155.00. Serves as a yearly supplement to *West's Encyclopedia of American Law.* Describes new legal developments in many subject areas.

CD-ROM DATABASES

WILSONDISC: Index to Legal Periodicals and Books. H. W. Wilson Co. • Monthly. Including unlimited online access to *Index to Legal Periodicals* through WILSONLINE. Contains CD-ROM indexing of more than 800 English language legal periodicals from 1981 to date and 2,500 books.

DIRECTORIES

Business Organizations, Agencies, and Publications Directory. The Gale Group. • 1999. $425.00. 12th edition. Over 40,000 entries describing 39 types of business information sources. Classified by type of organization, publication, or serviceIncludes state, national, and international agencies and organizations. Master index to names and keywords. Also includes e-mail addresses and web site URL's.

Directory of Outplacement and Career Management Firms. Kennedy Information, LLC. • Annual. $129.95. Contains profiles of more than 320 firms specialize in helping "downsized" executives find new employment.

ENCYCLOPEDIAS AND DICTIONARIES

Blackwell Encyclopedic Dictionary of Human Resource Management. Lawrence H. Peters and Charles R. Greer, editors. Blackwell Publishers. • 1996. $105.95. The editors are associated with Texas Christian University. Contains definitions of key terms combined with longer articles written by various U. S. and foreign business educators. Includes bibliographies and index. (Blackwell Encyclopedia of Management Series).

West's Encyclopedia of American Law. Available from The Gale Group. • 1997. $995.00. Second edition. 12 volumes. Published by West Group. Covers a wide variety of legal topics for the general reader. Formerly *Guide to American Law: Everyone's Legal Encyclopedia* (1985).

HANDBOOKS AND MANUALS

Employment Termination: Rights and Remedies. William J. Holloway and Michael J. Leech. BNA Books. • 1993. $145.00. Second edition. Discusses employment contracts and wrongful-discharge claims.

Fair, Square, and Legal: Safe Hiring, Managing, and Firing Practices to Keep You and Your Company Out of Court. Donald Weiss. AMACOM. • 1999. $29.95. Third edition. Covers recruiting, interviewing, sexual discrimination, evaluation of employees, disipline, defamation charges, and wrongful discharge.

The Federal Manager's Handbook: A Guide to Rehabilitating or Removing the Problem Employee. G. Jerry Shaw and William L. Bransford. FPMI Communications, Inc. • 1997. $24.95. Third revised edition.

The Hiring and Firing Book: A Complete Legal Guide for Employers. Steven M. Sack. Legal Strategies, Inc. • 1996. $149.95. Revised edition. Covers a wide range of legal considerations relative to employment and dismissal. Includes checklists, a glossary, and samples of applications, agreements, contracts, and other documents.

WARN Act: A Manager's Compliance Guide to Workforce Reductions. Joseph A. Brislin. BNA Plus Books. • 1990. $195.00.

INTERNET DATABASES

EBSCO Information Services. Ebsco Publishing. Phone: 800-871-8508 or (508)356-6500 Fax: (508)356-5640 E-mail: ep@epnet.com • URL: http://www.epnet.com • Fee-based Web site providing Internet access to a wide variety of databases, including business-related material. Full text is available for many periodical titles, with daily updates. Fees: Apply.

ProQuest Direct. Bell & Howell Information and Learning. Phone: 800-521-0600 or (313)761-4700 Fax: (313)973-9145 • URL: http://www.umi.com/proquest • Fee-based Web site providing Internet access to more than 3,000 periodicals, newspapers, and other publications. Many items are available full-text, with daily updates. Includes extensive corporate and financial information from Disclosure, Inc. Fees: Apply.

ONLINE DATABASES

Index to Legal Periodicals and Books (Online). H. W. Wilson Co. • Broad coverage of law journals and books 1981 to date. Monthly updates. Inquire as to online cost and availability.

Wilson Business Abstracts Online. H. W. Wilson Co. • Indexes and abstracts 600 major business periodicals, plus the *Wall Street Journal* and the business section of the *New York Times.* Indexing is from 1982, abstracting from 1990, with the two newspapers included from 1993. Updated weekly. Inquire as to online cost and availability. (*Business Periodicals Index* without abstracts is also available online.).

PERIODICALS AND NEWSLETTERS

Employee Terminations Law Bulletin. Quinlan Publishing Co., Inc. • Monthly. $89.00 per year. Newsletter.

HR Briefing (Human Resources). Bureau of Business Practice, Inc. • Semimonthly. $195.00 per year. Newsletter. Formerly *Personnel Manager's Letter.*

ReCareering Newsletter: An Idea and Resource Guide to Second Career and Relocation Planning. Publications Plus, Inc. • Monthly. $59.00 per year. Edited for "downsized managers, early retirees, and others in career transition after leaving traditional employment." Offers advice on second careers, franchises, starting a business, finances, education, training, skills assessment, and other matters of interest to the newly unemployed.

RESEARCH CENTERS AND INSTITUTES

Lexis.com Research System. Lexis-Nexis Group. Phone: 800-227-9597 or (937)865-6800 Fax: (937)865-6909 E-mail: webmaster@prod.lexis-nexis.com • URL: http://www.lexis.com • Fee-based Web site offers extensive searching of a wide variety of legal sources. Additional features include Daily Opinion Service, lexis.com Bookstore, Career Center, CLE Center, Law Schools, and Practice Pages ("Pages specific to areas of specialty").

TRADE/PROFESSIONAL ASSOCIATIONS

Association of Career Management Consulting Firms International. 204 E. St., N.E., Washington, DC 20002. Phone: (202)857-1185 Fax: (202)547-6348 • URL: http://www.aocfi.org • Promotes professional standards of competence, objectivity, and integrity in the service of clients.

OTHER SOURCES

Corporate Compliance Series. West Group. • Eleven looseleaf volumes, with periodic supplementation. $990.00. Covers criminal and civil liability problems for corporations. Includes employee safety, product liability, pension requirements, securities violations, equal employment opportunity issues, intellectual property, employee hiring and firing, and other corporate compliance topics.

Employment Litigation Reporter: The National Journal of Record for Termination Lawsuits Alleging Tort and Contract Claims Against Employers. Andrews Publications. • Semimonthly. $825.00 per year. Provides reports on wrongful dismissal lawsuits.

Employment Practice Guide. CCH, Inc. • Weekly. $999.00 per year. Four looseleaf volumes.

How to Interview Effectively. American Management Association Extension Institute. • Looseleaf. $110.00. Self-study course on employment, performance, evaluation, disciplinary, and exit interviewing. Emphasis is on practical explanations, examples, and problem solving. Quizzes and a case study are included.

InSite 2. Intelligence Data/Thomson Financial. • Fee-based Web site consolidates information in a "Base Pack" consisting of Business InSite, Market InSite, and Company InSite. Optional databases are Consumer InSite, Health and Wellness InSite, Newsletter InSite, and Computer InSite. Includes fulltext content from more than 2,500 trade publications, journals, newsletters, newspapers, analyst reports, and other sources. Continuous updating. Formerly produced by The Gale Group.

DISPLAY OF MERCHANDISE

See also: POINT-OF-PURCHASE ADVERTISING; TRADE SHOWS

DIRECTORIES

Creative's Illustrated Guide to P-O-P Exhibits and Promotion. Magazines Creative, Inc. • Annual. $25.00. Lists sources of point-of-purchase displays, signs, and exhibits and sources of other promotional materials and equipment. Available online.

HANDBOOKS AND MANUALS

Library Displays Handbook. Mark Schaeffer. H. W. Wilson Co. • 1991. $42.00. Provides detailed instructions for signs, posters, wall displays, bulletin boards, and exhibits.

The Successful Exhibitor's Handbook: Trade Show Techniques for Beginners and Pros. Barry Siskind. Self-Counsel Press, Inc. • 1996. $14.95. Third edition.

PERIODICALS AND NEWSLETTERS

Creative: The Magazine of Promotion and Marketing. Magazines Creative, Inc. • Bimonthly. $30.00 per year. Covers promotional materials, including exhibits, incentives, point-of-purchase advertising, premiums, and specialty advertising.

Journal of Convention and Exhibition Management. Haworth Press, Inc. • Quarterly. Individuals $50.00 per year; institutions, $85.00 per year; libraries, $95.00 per year.

Signs of the Times: The National Journal of Signs and Advertising Displays. ST Publications, Inc. • 13 times a year. $36.00 per year. For designers and manufacturers of all types of signs. Features how-to-tips. Includes *Sign Erection, Maintenance Directory* and annual *Buyer's Guide.*

VM & SD (Visual Merchandising and Store Design). International Authority on Visual Merchandising and Store Design. S T Publications, Inc. • Monthly. $39.00 per year. Ideas for retailers on store design and display. Includes *Buyers' Guide.* Formerly *Visual Merchandising.*

TRADE/PROFESSIONAL ASSOCIATIONS

National Association of Display Industries. 234 Fifth Ave., No. 407, New York, NY 10001-7607. Phone: 888-477-6234 or (212)725-4490.

Point-of-Purchase Advertising International. 1660 L St., N.W., 10th Fl., Washington, DC 20036. Phone: (202)530-3000 Fax: (202)530-3030 • URL: http://www.popai.com.

DISPOSABLE FABRICS

See: NONWOVEN FABRICS INDUSTRY

DISPUTES, LABOR

See: ARBITRATION; STRIKES AND LOCKOUTS

DISSERTATIONS

GENERAL WORKS

Doing Exemplary Research. Peter J. Frost and Ralph E. Stablein, editors. Sage Publications, Inc. • 1992. $48.00. Contains discussions of research methodologies.

Surviving Your Dissertation: A Comprehensive Guide to Content and Process. Kjell E. Rudestam and Rae R. Newton. Sage Publications, Inc. • 2000. Price on application. Provides general advice on how to successfully complete a dissertation or thesis.

ABSTRACTS AND INDEXES

Dissertation Abstracts International. UMI. • Monthly. Price on application. Section A: Humanities and Social Sciences. Author-written summaries of current doctoral dissertations from over 500 educational institutions.

HANDBOOKS AND MANUALS

The Chicago Manual of Style: The Essential Guide for Authors, Editors, and Publishers. University of Chicago Press. • 1993. $40.00. 14th edition.

Manual for Writers of Term Papers, Theses, and Dissertations. Kate L. Turabian. University of Chicago Press. • 1996. $27.50. Sixth edition. (Chicago Guides to Writing, Editing and Publishing Series).

MLA Handbook for Writers of Research Papers. Joseph Gibaldi. Modern Language Association of America. • 1999. $14.75. Fifth edition.

ONLINE DATABASES

Dissertation Abstracts Online. Bell & Howell Information and Learning. • Citations to all dissertations accepted for doctoral degrees by accredited U.S. educational institutions, 1861 to date. Includes British theses, 1988 to date. Inquire as to online cost and availability.

PERIODICALS AND NEWSLETTERS

American Doctoral Dissertations. Association of Research Libraries. UMI. • Annual. Price on application.

Resources in Education. Educational Resources Information Center. Available from U.S. Government Printing Office. • Monthly. $102.00 per year. Reports on educational research.

DISTILLING INDUSTRY

See also: BEVERAGE INDUSTRY; BREWING INDUSTRY; WINE INDUSTRY

ALMANACS AND YEARBOOKS

The U.S. Distilled Spirits Market: Impact Databank Market Review and Forecast. M. Shanken Communications, Inc. • Annual. $845.00. Includes industry commentary and statistics.

DIRECTORIES

Beverage Industry - Annual Manual. Stagnito Communications, Inc. • Annual. $55.00. Provides statistical information on multiple beverage markets. Includes an industry directory. Supplement to *Beverage Industry.*

The Beverage Marketing Directory. Beverage Marketing Corp. • Annual. $845.00. Provides information for approximately 11,000 beverage companies and suppliers to beverage companies. Includes sales volume and brand names. Formerly *National Beverage Marketing Directory.*

Brewers Digest Annual Buyers Guide and Brewery Directory. Siebel Publishing Co., Inc. • Annual. $50.00. Lists breweries throughout the western hemisphere.

National Licensed Beverage Association-Members Directory. National Licensed Beverage Association. • Annual. $40.00.

FINANCIAL RATIOS

Almanac of Business and Industrial Financial Ratios. Leo Troy. Prentice Hall. • Annual. $99.95. Contains financial ratios derived from federal tax returns. Ratios for each of about 200 industries are arranged according to company asset size.

Annual Statement Studies. Robert Morris Associates: The Association of Lending and Credit Risk Professiona. • Annual. Free to members; non-members, $140.00. Median and quartile financial ratios are given for over 400 kinds of manufacturing, wholesale, retail, construction, and consumer finance establishments. Data is sorted by both asset size and sales volume. Includes a clearly written "Definition of Ratios" and an alphabetical industry index.

HANDBOOKS AND MANUALS

Liquor Store. Entrepreneur Media, Inc. • Looseleaf. $59.50. A practical guide to starting a liquor store. Covers profit potential, start-up costs, market size evaluation, owner's time required, site selection, lease negotiation, pricing, accounting, advertising, promotion, etc. (Start-Up Business Guide No. E1024.).

INTERNET DATABASES

Fedstats. Federal Interagency Council on Statistical Policy. Phone: (202)395-7254 • URL: http://www.fedstats.gov • Web site features an efficient search facility for full-text statistics produced by more than 70 federal agencies, including the Census Bureau, the Bureau of Economic Analysis, and the Bureau of Labor Statistics. Boolean searches can be made within one agency or for all agencies combined. Links are offered to international statistical bureaus, including the UN, IMF, OECD, UNESCO, Eurostat, and 20 individual countries. Fees: Free.

ONLINE DATABASES

DRI U.S. Central Database. Data Products Division. • Provides more than 23,000 business, financial, demographic, economic, foreign trade, and industry-related time series for the U.S. Includes national income, population, retail-wholesale trade, price indexes, labor data, housing, industrial production, banking, interest rates, money supply, etc. Time period is generally 1947 to date (some data back to 1929). Updating varies. Inquire as to online cost and availability.

PERIODICALS AND NEWSLETTERS

American Society of Brewing Chemists Journal. American Society of Brewing Chemists. • Quarterly. Members, $95.00 per year; non-members, $137.00 per year; corporate members, $195.00 per year; student members, $25.00 per year.

ASBC Newsletter. American Society of Brewing Chemists. • Quarterly. Members, $95.00 per year; non-members, $130.00 per year; corporate members, $195.00 per year; student members, $26.00 per year.

Brewing and Distilling International. Brewery Traders Publications, Ltd. • Monthly. $160.00 per year.

Bureau of Alcohol, Tobacco, and Firearms Quarterly Bulletin. Bureau of Alcohol, Tobacco, and Firearms, U.S. Department of the Treasury. Available from U.S. Government Printing Office. • Quarterly. $18.00 per year. Laws and regulations.

Impact: U.S. News and Research for the Wine, Spirits, and Beer Industries. M. Shanken Communications, Inc. • Biweekly. $375.00 per year. Newsletter covering the marketing, economic, and financial aspects of alcoholic beverages.

Kane's Beverage Week: The Newsletter of Beverage Marketing. Whitaker Newsletters, Inc. • Weekly. $449.00 per year. Newsletter. Covers news relating to the alcoholic beverage industries, including social, health, and legal issues.

Malt Advocate. Malt Advocate, Inc. • Quarterly. $16.00 per year. Provides information for consumers of upscale whiskey and beer.

Master Brewer's Association of America. Communications. Master Brewer's Association of America. • Bimonthly. $60.00 per year. Included with membership.

STATISTICS SOURCES

Annual Survey of Manufactures. Available from U. S. Government Printing Office. • Annual. Prices vary. Issued by the U. S. Census Bureau as an interim update to the *Census of Manufactures.* Includes data on number of manufacturing establishments in various industries, employment, labor costs, value of shipments, capital expenditures, inventories, energy costs, and assets. (See also Census Bureau home page, http://www.census.gov/.).

Business Statistics of the United States. Courtenay M. Slater, editor. Bernan Associates. • 1999. $74.00. Fifth edition. Based on *Business Statistics*, formerly issue by the Bureau of Economic Analysis, U. S. Department of Commerce. Provides basic data for a wide variety of U. S. industries, services, and economic indicators. Most statistics are shown annually for 29 years and monthly for the most recent four years.

Impact Beverage Trends in America. M. Shanken Communications, Inc. • Annual. $695.00. Detailed compilations of data for various segments of the liquor, beer, and soft drink industries.

Monthly Statistical Release: Distilled Spirits. U. S. Bureau of Alcohol, Tobacco, and Firearms. • Monthly.

Standard & Poor's Industry Surveys. Standard & Poor's. • Semiannual. $1,800.00. Two looseleaf volumes. Includes monthly supplements. Provides detailed, individual surveys of 52 major industry groups. Each survey is revised on a semiannual basis. Also includes "Monthly Investment Review" (industry group investment analysis) and monthly "Trends & Projections" (economic analysis).

Survey of Current Business. Available from U. S. Government Printing Office. • Monthly. $49.00 per year. Issued by Bureau of Economic Analysis, U. S. Department of Commerce. Presents a wide variety of business and economic data.

TRADE/PROFESSIONAL ASSOCIATIONS

Distilled Spirits Council of the United States. 1250 Eye St., N.W., Suite 400, Washington, DC 20005. Phone: (202)628-3544 Fax: (202)682-8888 • URL: http://www.discus.health.org.

United Food and Commercial Workers International Union. 1775 K. St., N.W., Washington, DC 20006. Phone: (202)223-3111 Fax: (202)466-1562 • URL: http://www.ufcw.org.

OTHER SOURCES

Liquor Control Law Reports: Federal and All States. CCH, Inc. • $3,338.00 per year. Nine looseleaf volumes. Biweekly updates. Federal and state regulation and taxation of alcoholic beverages.

Major Food and Drink Companies of the World. Available from The Gale Group. • 2001. $855.00. Fourth edition. Two volumes. Published by Graham & Whiteside. Contains profiles and trade names for more than 9,000 important food and beverage companies in various countries. In addition to foods, includes both alcoholic and nonalcoholic drink products.

Thomas Food and Beverage Market Place. Grey House Publishing. • Annual. $295.00. Three volumes. Contains more than 40,000 entries covering food companies, beverages, food equipment, warehouse companies, food brokers, wholesalers, importers, and exporters. Formerly *Thomas Food Industry Register.*

DISTRIBUTION

See also: MARKETING; RACK JOBBERS; TRANSPORTATION INDUSTRY; TRUCKING INDUSTRY; WHOLESALE TRADE

ABSTRACTS AND INDEXES

Business Periodicals Index. H. W. Wilson Co. • Monthly, except August, with quarterly and annual cumulations. Service basis for print edition; CD-ROM edition, $1,495.00 per year.

BIBLIOGRAPHIES

Marketing Information Revolution. Robert C. Blattberg, editor. McGraw-Hill. • 1993. $39.95. Third edition. Includes a wide variety of sources for specific kinds of marketing.

DIRECTORIES

American Wholesalers and Distributors Directory. The Gale Group. • 2000. $215.00. Eighth edition. Lists more than 27,000 national, regional, state, and local wholesalesrs.

Grocery Distribution Magazine Directory of Warehouse Equipment, Fixtures, and Services. Trend Publishing, Inc. • Annual. $7.50. Covers products related to food warehousing, distribution, and storage.

Warehouse Management's Guide to Public Warehousing. Cahners Business Information. • Annual. $55.00. List of general merchandise,contract and refrigerated warehouses. Formerly *Distribution Guide to Public Warehousing.*

Warehousing Distribution Directory. Commonwealth Business Media. • Semiannual. $63.00. Lists about 800 warehousing and consolidation companies and firms offering trucking, trailer on flatcar, container on flatcar, and piggyback carriers services.

ENCYCLOPEDIAS AND DICTIONARIES

Blackwell Encyclopedic Dictionary of Marketing. Barbara R. Lewis and Dale Littler, editors. Blackwell Publishers. • 1996. $105.95. The editors are associated with the Manchester School of Management. Contains definitions of key terms combined with longer articles written by various U. S. and foreign business educators. Includes bibliographies and index. (Blackwell Encyclopedia of Management series.).

ONLINE DATABASES

ABI/INFORM. Bell & Howell Information and Learning. • Provides online indexing to business-related material occurring in over 1,000 periodicals from 1971 to the present. Inquire as to online cost and availability.

Wilson Business Abstracts Online. H. W. Wilson Co. • Indexes and abstracts 600 major business periodicals, plus the *Wall Street Journal* and the business section of the *New York Times.* Indexing is from 1982, abstracting from 1990, with the two newspapers included from 1993. Updated weekly. Inquire as to online cost and availability. (*Business Periodicals Index* without abstracts is also available online.).

PERIODICALS AND NEWSLETTERS

Advertising Age's B to B: News Monthly Concerning the How-To Strategic and Tact ical Marketing, Sales and Advertising of Business-to-Business Products and Services. Crain Communications, Inc. • Monthly. $49.00 per year. Formerly Business Marketing.

Chilton's Distribution: The Transportation and Business Logistics Magazine. Cahners Business Information. • Monthly. $65.00 per year.

Distribution Center Management. Alexander Communications Group, Inc. • Monthly. $139.00 per year.

Industrial Distribution: For Industrial Distributors and Their Sales Personnel. Cahners Business Information. • Monthly. $97.90 per year.

Journal of Marketing Channels: Distribution Systems, Strategy, and Management. Haworth Press, Inc. • Quarterly. Individuals, $60.00 per year; institutions, $75.00 per year; libraries, 175.00 per year. Subject matter has to do with the management of product distribution systems.

Marketing Management: Shaping the Profession of Marketing. American Marketing Association. • Quarterly. Members, $45.00 per year; non-members, $70.00 per year; institutions, $90.00 per year. Covers trends in the management of marketing, sales, and distribution.

Transportation and Distribution. Penton Media Inc. • Monthly. Free to qualified personnel; others, $50.00 per year. Essential information on transportation and distribution practices in domestic and international trade.

RESEARCH CENTERS AND INSTITUTES

Center for Research and Management Services. Indiana State University. School of Business, Terre Haute, IN 47809. Phone: (812)237-3232 Fax: (812)237-8720 E-mail: cfrminn@befac.indstate.edu.

Marketing Science Institute. 1000 Massachusetts Ave., Cambridge, MA 02138. Phone: (617)491-2060 Fax: (617)491-2065 • URL: http://www.msi.org.

TRADE/PROFESSIONAL ASSOCIATIONS

Council of Logistics Management. 2803 Butterfield Rd., No. 200, Oakbrook, IL 60523. Phone: (630)574-0985 Fax: (630)574-0989 E-mail: clmadmin@clm1.org • URL: http://www.clm1.org.

National Association of Wholesaler-Distributors. 1725 K St., N.W., Washington, DC 20006. Phone: (202)872-0885 Fax: (202)785-0586 E-mail: meetings@nawd.org • URL: http://www.nawmeetings.org.

OTHER SOURCES

Manufacturing and Distribution USA. The Gale Group. • 2000. $375.00. Three volumes. Replaces *Manufacturing USA* and *Wholesale and Retail Trade USA.* Presents statistics and projections relating to economic activity in more than 500 business classifications.

Product Distribution Law Guide. CCH, Inc. • Looseleaf. $199.00. Annual updates available. Covers the legal aspects of various methods of product distribution, including franchising.

DIVIDENDS

See also: INVESTMENTS; STOCKS

GENERAL WORKS

Dividend Investor: A Safe and Sure Way to Build Wealth with High-Yield Dividend Stocks. Harvey C. Knowles and Damon H. Petty. McGraw-Hill Professional. • 1992. $24.95.

How to Invest Wisely. Lawrence S. Pratt. American Institute for Economic Research. • 1998. $9.00. Presents a conservative policy of investing, with emphasis on dividend-paying common stocks. Gold and other inflation hedges are compared. Includes a reprint of *Toward an Optimal Stock Selection Strategy* (1997). (Economic Education Bulletin.).

Relative Dividend Yield: Common Stock Investing for Income and Appreciation. Anthony E. Spare and Paul Ciotti. John Wiley and Sons, Inc. • 1999. $59.95. Second edition. (Frontiers in Finance Series).

Toward an Optimal Stock Selection Strategy. Lawrence S. Pratt. American Institute for Economic Research. • 1997. $6.00. Second edition. Discusses the strategy of buying only the stocks in the Dow Jones Industrial Average that have the highest-yielding dividends. Includes detailed charts and tables. (Economic Education Bulletin.).

What Works on Wall Street: A Guide to the Best-Performing Investment Strategies of All Time. James P. O'Shaughnessy. McGraw-Hill. • 1998. $22.95. Second revised edition. Examines investment strategies over a 43-year period and concludes that large capitalization, high-dividend-yield stocks produce the best results.

DIRECTORIES

American Stock Exchange Directory. CCH, Inc. • 2000. $30.00.

Guide to Dividend Reinvestment Plans. Evergreen Enterprises. • Quarterly. $142.00 per year. Looseleaf. Provides detailed, current information on the dividend reinvestment programs of over 1,000 publicly traded corporations in the U. S. and Canada.

Moneypaper's Guide to Dividend Reinvestment Plans. Moneypaper. • Annual. $9.00. Provides details on about 900 corporate dividend reinvestment plans that permit optional cash investments.

Moody's Handbook of Dividend Achievers. Mergent. • Annual. $29.95. Compiled by Moody's Investors Service. Provides information on about 330 companies that have increased cash dividends for the past 10 consecutive years or more.

Standard and Poor's Security Dealers of North America. Standard & Poor's. • Semiannual. $480.00 per year; with *Supplements* every six weeks, $590.00 per year. Geographical listing of over 12,000 stock, bond, and commodity dealers.

FINANCIAL RATIOS

Quarterly Financial Report for Manufacturing, Mining, and Trade Corporations. U.S. Federal Trade

Commission and U.S. Securities and Exchange Commission. Available from U.S. Government Printing Office. • Quarterly. $39.00 per year.

HANDBOOKS AND MANUALS

Moody's Dividend Record and Annual Dividend Record. Information Services. • Semiweekly. $775.00 per year. Includes annual and cumulative supplement. Formerly *Moody's Dividend Record.*

Standard and Poor's Dividend Record. Standard and Poor's. • Daily. $825.00 per year.

INTERNET DATABASES

Fedstats. Federal Interagency Council on Statistical Policy. Phone: (202)395-7254 • URL: http://www.fedstats.gov • Web site features an efficient search facility for full-text statistics produced by more than 70 federal agencies, including the Census Bureau, the Bureau of Economic Analysis, and the Bureau of Labor Statistics. Boolean searches can be made within one agency or for all agencies combined. Links are offered to international statistical bureaus, including the UN, IMF, OECD, UNESCO, Eurostat, and 20 individual countries. Fees: Free.

ONLINE DATABASES

Disclosure SEC Database. Disclosure, Inc. • Provides information from records filed with the Securities and Exchange Commission by publicly owned corporations, 1977 to present. Weekly updates. Inquire as to online cost and availability.

Dow Jones Text Library. Dow Jones and Co., Inc. • Full text and edited news stories and articles on business affairs; 1984 to date. Inquire as to online cost and availability.

DRI U.S. Central Database. Data Products Division. • Provides more than 23,000 business, financial, demographic, economic, foreign trade, and industry-related time series for the U.S. Includes national income, population, retail-wholesale trade, price indexes, labor data, housing, industrial production, banking, interest rates, money supply, etc. Time period is generally 1947 to date (some data back to 1929). Updating varies. Inquire as to online cost and availability.

PERIODICALS AND NEWSLETTERS

Barron's: The Dow Jones Business and Financial Weekly. Dow Jones and Co., Inc. • Weekly. $145.00 per year.

Commercial and Financial Chronicle. William B. Dana Co. • Weekly. $140.00. per year.

DRIP Investor: Your Guide to Buying Stocks Without a Broker. Horizon Publishing, Co., LLC. • Monthly. $89.00 per year. Newsletter covering the dividend reinvestment plans (DRIPs) of various publicly-owned corporations. Includes model portfolios and *Directory of Dividend Reinvestment Plans.*

Investment Guide. American Investment Services. • Monthly. $49.00 per year. Newsletter. Emphasis is on blue-chip stocks with high dividend yields.

Moneypaper. • Monthly. $81.00 per year. Newsletter. Provides general investment advice, including summaries from other investment advisory services. Emphasis is on company-sponsored dividend reinvestment plans. Subscription includes annual directory: *The Moneypaper's Guide to Dividend Reinvestment Plans.*

Wall Street Transcript: A Professional Publication for the Business and Financial Community. Wall Street Transcript Corp. • Weekly. $1,890.00. per year. Provides reprints of investment research reports.

PRICE SOURCES

Stock Market Values and Yields for 1997. Research Institute of America. • 1997. $20.00. Revised edition. Gives year-end prices and dividends for tax purposes.

Stock Values and Dividends for Tax Purposes. CCH, Inc. • Annual. Gives year-end prices and dividends for tax purposes.

RESEARCH CENTERS AND INSTITUTES

Center for Research in Security Prices. University of Chicago, 725 S. Wells St., Suite 800, Chicago, IL 60607. Phone: (773)702-7467 Fax: (773)753-4797 E-mail: mail@crsp.uchicago.edu • URL: http://www.crsp.com.

Rodney L. White Center for Financial Research. University of Pennsylvania, 3254 Steinberg Hall-Dietrich Hall, Philadelphia, PA 19104. Phone: (215)898-7616 Fax: (215)573-8084 E-mail: rlwtcr@finance.wharton.upenn.edu • URL: http://www.finance.wharton.upenn.edu/~rlwctr • Research areas include financial management, money markets, real estate finance, and international finance.

STATISTICS SOURCES

Business Statistics of the United States. Courtenay M. Slater, editor. Bernan Associates. • 1999. $74.00. Fifth edition. Based on *Business Statistics*, formerly issue by the Bureau of Economic Analysis, U. S. Department of Commerce. Provides basic data for a wide variety of U. S. industries, services, and economic indicators. Most statistics are shown annually for 29 years and monthly for the most recent four years.

Survey of Current Business. Available from U. S. Government Printing Office. • Monthly. $49.00 per year. Issued by Bureau of Economic Analysis, U. S. Department of Commerce. Presents a wide variety of business and economic data.

OTHER SOURCES

Corporate Dividends and Stock Repurchases. Barbara Black. West Group. • $130.00. Looseleaf service. Periodic supplementation. Covers the law relating to dividends in general, illegal dividends, stock splits, stock dividends, corporate repurchases, and other dividend topics.

Mergent Company Data. Mergent FIS, Inc. • Monthly. Price on application. CD-ROM provides detailed financial statement information for more than 10,000 New York Stock Exchange, American Stock Exchange, and NASDAQ corporations. Includes balance sheets, income statements, dividend history, annual price ranges, stock splits, Moody's debt ratings, etc. Formerly *Moody's Company Data.*

DIVORCE

See also: FAMILY LAW

GENERAL WORKS

Economics of Divorce: The Effect on Parents and Children. Craig A. Everett. Haworth Press, Inc. • 1994. $39.95. (Journal of Divorce and Remarriage Series).

Smart Questions to Ask Your Financial Advisers. Lynn Brenner. Bloomberg Press. • 1997. $19.95. Provides practical advice on how to deal with financial planners, stockbrokers, insurance agents, and lawyers. Some of the areas covered are investments, estate planning, tax planning, house buying, prenuptial agreements, divorce arrangements, loss of a job, and retirement. (Bloomberg Personal Bookshelf Series Library.).

ABSTRACTS AND INDEXES

Current Law Index: Multiple Access to Legal Periodicals. The Gale Group. • Monthly. $650.00 per year. Produced in cooperation with the American Association of Law Libraries. Indexes more than 900 law journals, legal newspapers, and specialty publications from the U.S., Canada, U.K., Ireland, Australia, and New Zealand.

Index to Legal Periodicals and Books. H. W. Wilson Co. • Monthly. Quarterly and annual cumulations. $270.00 per year. CD-ROM version available at $1,495.00 per year.

Psychological Abstracts. American Psychological Association. • Monthly. Members, $799.00 per year; individuals and institutions, $1,075.00 per year. Covers the international literature of psychology and the behavioral sciences. Includes journals, technical reports, dissertations, and other sources.

Sage Family Studies Abstracts. Sage Publications, Inc. • Quarterly. Individuals, $125.00 per year; institutions, $575.00 per year.

Women Studies Abstracts. Transaction Publishers. • Quarterly. Individuals, $102.00 per year; institutions, $216.00 per year.

CD-ROM DATABASES

Magazine Index Plus. The Gale Group. • Monthly. $4,000.00 per year (includes InfoTrac workstation). Provides full text on CD-ROM for about 100 popular, general interest magazines and indexing for 300 others. Includes special indexing of reviews and product evaluations. Time period is 1980 to date.

DIRECTORIES

American Academy of Matrimonial Lawyers: List of Certified Fellows. American Academy of Matrimonial Lawyers. • Annual. Membership.

Where to Write for Vital Records: Births, Deaths, Marriages, and Divorces. Available from U. S. Government Printing Office. • 1999. $3.00. Issued by the National Center for Health Statistics, U. S. Department of Health and Human Services. Arranged by state. Provides addresses, telephone numbers, and cost of copies for various kinds of vital records or certificates. (DHHS Publication No. PHS 93-1142.).

HANDBOOKS AND MANUALS

Divorce Decisions Workbook: A Planning and Action Guide. Marjorie L. Engel and Diana D. Gould. McGraw-Hill. • 1992. $27.95. Covers the business, financial, legal, and tax aspects of divorce.

Divorce Taxation. Warren, Gorham and Lamont/RIA Group. • Looseleaf service. $515.00 per year. Monthly *Report Bulletins* and updates.

Divorce Yourself: The National No-Fault Divorce Kit. Daniel Sitarz. Nova Publishing Co. • 1996. $34.95. Third edition. Provides instructions, checklists, questionnaires, worksheets, and forms for use in uncomplicated divorce proceedings. Forms are also available on IBM or MAC diskettes. (Legal Self-Help Series).

Negotiating to Settlement in Divorce. Sanford N. Katz, editor. Aspen Law and Business. • 1987. $75.00. Looseleaf service.

Valuation Strategies in Divorce. Robert D. Feder. John Wiley and Sons, Inc. • 1997. Fourth edition. Two volumes. Price on application. Explains the basic principles of asset valuation in divorce cases. Discusses financial statements, tax returns, retirement benefits, real estate, and personal property.

ONLINE DATABASES

Contemporary Women's Issues. Responsive Database Services, Inc. • Provides fulltext articles online from 150 periodicals and a wide variety of additional sources relating to economic, legal, social, political, education, health, and other women's issues. Time span is 1992 to date. Weekly updates. Inquire as to online cost and availability. (Also available in a CD-ROM version.).

Index to Legal Periodicals and Books (Online). H. W. Wilson Co. • Broad coverage of law journals and books 1981 to date. Monthly updates. Inquire as to online cost and availability.

Legal Resource Index. The Gale Group. • Broad coverage of law literature appearing in legal, business, and other periodicals, 1980 to date. Monthly updates. Inquire as to online cost and availability.

LEXIS. LEXIS-NEXIS. • The various LEXIS databases provide full text and indexing for a wide variety of legal cases, statutes, orders, and opinions.

PsycINFO. American Psychological Association. • Provides indexing and abstracting of the worldwide literature of psychology and the behavioral sciences. Time period is 1967 to date, with monthly updates. Inquire as to online cost and availability.

PERIODICALS AND NEWSLETTERS

Family Advocate. American Bar Association, Family Law Section. • Quarterly. Members $39.50; non-members, $44.50 per year. Practical advice for attorneys practicing family law.

Journal of Divorce and Remarriage: Research and Clinical Studies in Family Theory, Family Law, Family Meditation and Family Therapy. Haworth Press, Inc. • Quarterly. Individuals, $60.00 per year; institutions, $140.00 per year; libraries, $400.00 per year. Two volumes.

RESEARCH CENTERS AND INSTITUTES

Lexis.com Research System. Lexis-Nexis Group. Phone: 800-227-9597 or (937)865-6800 Fax: (937)865-6909 E-mail: webmaster@prod.lexis-nexis.com • URL: http://www.lexis.com • Fee-based Web site offers extensive searching of a wide variety of legal sources. Additional features include Daily Opinion Service, lexis.com Bookstore, Career Center, CLE Center, Law Schools, and Practice Pages ("Pages specific to areas of specialty").

STATISTICS SOURCES

Current Population Reports: Population Characteristics, Special Studies, and Consumer Income, Series P-20, P-23, and P-60. Available from U. S. Government Printing Office. • Irregular. $39.00 per year. Issued by the U.S. Bureau of the Census (http://www.census.gov). Each issue covers a special topic relating to population or income. Series P-20, *Population Characteristics*, provides statistical studies on such items as mobility, fertility, education, and marital status. Series P-23, *Special Studies*, consists of occasional reports on methodology. Series P-60, *Consumer Income*, publishes reports on income in relation to age, sex, education, occupation, family size, etc.

Monthly Vital Statistics Report. U. S. Department of Health and Human Services, Data Dissemination Branch. • Monthly. Provides data on births, deaths, cause of death, marriage, and divorce.

Statistical Handbook on the American Family. Bruce A. Chadwick and Tim B. Heaton, editors. Oryx Press. • 1998. $65.00. Includes data on education, health, politics, employment, expenditures, social characteristics, the elderly, and women in the labor force. Historical statistics on marriage, birth, and divorce are shown from 1900 on. A list of sources and a subject index are provided. (Statistical Handbook Series).

TRADE/PROFESSIONAL ASSOCIATIONS

American Academy of Matrimonial Lawyers. 150 N. Michigan Ave., Suite 2040, Chicago, IL 60601. Phone: (312)263-6477 Fax: (312)263-7682 • URL: http://www.aaml.org • Members are attorneys specializing in family law.

National Organization for Men. 11 Park Place, Ste. 1100, New York, NY 10007. Phone: (212)686-6253 or (212)766-4030 Fax: (212)791-3056 • URL: http://www.tnom.com • Encourages rational and objective state and national divorce laws.

OTHER SOURCES

Divorce and Taxes. CCH, Inc. • 2000. $39.00. Second edition. In addition to tax problems, topics include alimony, division of property, and divorce decrees.

DO-IT-YOURSELF

See: HOME IMPROVEMENT INDUSTRY

DOCKS

See: PORTS

DOCTORS' DEGREES

See: ACADEMIC DEGREES

DOCUMENT IMAGING

See also: MICROFORMS

ABSTRACTS AND INDEXES

Applied Science and Technology Index. H. W. Wilson Co. • 11 times a year. Quarterly and annual cumulations. Service basis for print edition; CD-ROM edition, $1,495.00 per year. Indexes a wide variety of English language technical, industrial, and engineering periodicals.

Computer Literature Index: A Subject/Author Index to Computer and Data Processing Literature. Applied Computer Research, Inc. • Quarterly, with annual cumulation. $245.00 per year. Contains brief abstracts of book and periodical literature covering all phases of computing, including approximately 70 specific application areas.

F & S Index: United States. The Gale Group. • Monthly. $1,295.00 per year, including quarterly and annual cumulations. Provides annotated citations to marketing, business, financial, and industrial literature. Coverage of U. S. business activity includes trade journals, financial magazines, business newspapers, and special reports. Formerly *Predicasts F & S Index: United States.*

Imaging Abstracts. Royal Photographic Society of Great Britain, Imaging Science and Technology Grou. Elsevier Science. • Bimonthly. $792.00 per year. Formerly *Photographic Abstracts.*

Key Abstracts: Business Automation. Available from INSPEC, Inc. • Monthly. $240.00 per year. Provides international coverage of journal and proceedings literature. Published in England by the Institution of Electrical Engineers (IEE).

Microcomputer Abstracts. Information Today, Inc. • Quarterly. $225.00 per year. Provides abstracts covering a wide variety of personal and business microcomputer literature. Formerly *Microcomputer Index.*

NTIS Alerts: Computers, Control & Information Theory. National Technical Information Service. • Semimonthly. $235.00 per year. Provides descriptions of government-sponsored research reports and software, with ordering information. Covers computer hardware, software, control systems, pattern recognition, image processing, and related subjects. Formerly *Abstract Newsletter.*

CD-ROM DATABASES

Datapro on CD-ROM: Computer Systems Analyst. Gartner Group, Inc. • Monthly. Price on application. Includes detailed information on specific computer hardware and software products, such as peripherals, security systems, document imaging systems, and UNIX-related products.

F & S Index Plus Text. The Gale Group. • Monthly. $7,575.00 per year. Provides CD-ROM citations to worldwide business, marketing, and industrial material appearing in a large assortment of trade journals, newspapers, and other publications. Time period is four years.

WILSONDISC: Applied Science and Technology Abstracts. H. W. Wilson Co. • Monthly. $1,495.00 per year, including unlimited access to the online version of *Applied Science and Technology Abstracts* through WILSONLINE. Provides CD-ROM indexing and abstracting of 400 prominent scientific, technical, engineering, and industrial periodicals. Indexing coverage is provided from 1983 to date and abstracting from 1993 to date.

DIRECTORIES

Advanced Imaging Buyers Guide: The Most Comprehensive Worldwide Directory of Imaging Product and Equipment Vendors. Cygnus Business Media. • Annual. $19.95. List of about 800 electronic imaging companies and their products.

Better Buys for Business: The Independent Consumer Guide to Office Equipment. What to Buy for Business, Inc. • 10 times a year. $134.00 per year. Each issue is on a particular office product, with detailed evaluation of specific models: 1. Low-Volume Copier Guide, 2. Mid-Volume Copier Guide, 3. High-Volume Copier Guide, 4. Plain Paper Fax and Low-Volume Multifunctional Guide, 5. Mid/High-Volume Multifunctional Guide, 6. Laser Printer Guide, 7. Color Printer and Color Copier Guide, 8. Scan-to-File Guide, 9. Business Phone Systems Guide, 10. Postage Meter Guide, with a Short Guide to Shredders.

KMWorld Buyer's Guide. Knowledge Asset Media. • Semiannual. Controlled circulation as part of *KMWorld.* Contains corporate and product profiles related to various aspects of knowledge management and information systems. (Knowledge Asset Media is a an affiliate of Information Today, Inc.).

The Software Encyclopedia: A Guide for Personal, Professional, and Business Users. R. R. Bowker. • Annual. $255.00. Two volumes. Volume one lists software programs by title and producer. Volume two provides information on programs according to application and operating system. Includes prices and requirements for hardware and memory.

ENCYCLOPEDIAS AND DICTIONARIES

Every Manager's Guide to Information Technology: A Glossary of Key Terms and Concepts for Today's Business Leader. Peter G. W. Keen. Harvard Business School Press. • 1995. $18.95. Second edition. Provides definitions of terms related to computers, data communications, and information network systems. (Harvard Business Economist Reference Series).

HANDBOOKS AND MANUALS

Electronic Document Management Systems: A Practical Guide for Evaluators and Users. Thomas M. Koulopoulos. McGraw-Hill. • 1995. $45.00.

ONLINE DATABASES

Applied Science and Technology Index Online. H. W. Wilson Co. • Provides online indexing of 400 major scientific, technical, industrial, and engineering periodicals. Time period is 1983 to date. Monthly updates. Inquire as to online cost and availability.

F & S Index. The Gale Group. • Contains about four million citations to worldwide business, financial, and industrial or consumer product literature appearing from 1972 to date. Weekly updates. Inquire as to online cost and availability.

Internet and Personal Computing Abstracts. Information Today, Inc. • Contains abstracts covering a wide variety of personal and business microcomputer literature appearing in more than 100 journals and popular magazines. Time period is 1981 to date, with monthly updates. Formerly *Microcomputer Index*. Inquire as to online cost and availability.

Microcomputer Software Guide Online. R. R. Bowker. • Provides information on more than 30,000 microcomputer software applications from more than 4,000 producers. Corresponds to printed *Software Encyclopedia*, but with monthly updates. Inquire as to online cost and availability.

PROMT: Predicasts Overview of Markets and Technology. The Gale Group. • Companies, products, applied technologies and markets. U.S. and international literature coverage, 1972 to date. Inquire as to online cost and availability. Provides abstracts from more than 1,600 publications. Weekly updates.

PERIODICALS AND NEWSLETTERS

Advanced Imaging: Solutions for the Electronic Imaging Professional. Cygnus Business Media. • Monthly. Free to qualified personnel; others, $60.00 per year Covers document-based imaging technologies, products, systems, and services. Coverage is also devoted to multimedia and electronic printing and publishing.

Document Imaging Report. Corry Publishing, Inc. • Biweekly. $597.00 per year. Newsletter.

Document Processing Technology. RB Publishing Co. • Five times a year. Controlled circulation. Edited for "high volume document printing" professionals. Covers imaging, printing, and mailing.

IEEE Transactions on Visualization and Computer Graphics. Institute of Electrical and Electronics Engineers. • Quarterly. $490.00 per year. Topics include computer vision, computer graphics, image processing, signal processing, computer-aided design, animation, and virtual reality.

Imaging and Document Solutions. Miller Freeman, Inc. • Monthly. $17.95 per year. Emphasis is on descriptions of new imaging products, including CD-ROM items. Formerly *Imaging Magazines*.

Imaging Business: The Voice of the Document Imaging Channel. Phillips Business Information, Inc. • Monthly. Free to qualified personnel. Edited for resellers of document imaging equipment.

Imaging KM: Creating and Managing the Knowledge-Based Enterprise (Knowledge Management). Knowledge Asset Media. • 10 times a year. Free to qualified personnel; others, $48.00 per year. Covers automated and networked document image handling.

Item Processing Report. Phillips Business Information, Inc. • Biweekly. $695.00 per year. Newsletter for banks on check processing, document imaging, and optical character recognition.

KMWorld: Creating and Managing the Knowledge-Based Enterprise. Knowledge Asset Media. • Monthly. Controlled circulation. Provides articles on knowledge management, including business intelligence, multimedia content management, document management, e-business, and intellectual property. Emphasis is on business-to-business information technology. (Knowledge Asset Media is a an affiliate of Information Today, Inc.).

Knowledge Management. CurtCo Freedom Group. • Monthly. Controlled circulation. Covers applications of information technology and knowledge management strategy.

Micropublishing News: The Newsmonthly for Electronic Designers and Publishers. Cygnus Business Media. • Monthly. Free to qualified personnel. Price on application. Edited for business and professional users of electronic publishing products and services. Topics covered include document imaging, CD-ROM publishing, digital video, and multimedia services. Available in four regional editions.

Office Systems. Quality Publishing, Inc. • Monthly. Price on application. Special feature issue topics include document imaging, document management, office supplies, and office equipment. Incorporates *Managing Office Technology*.

RESEARCH CENTERS AND INSTITUTES

Bibliographical Center for Research, Inc., Rocky Mountain Region. 14394 E. Evans Ave., Aurora, CO 80014-1478. Phone: 800-397-1552 or (303)751-6277 Fax: (303)751-9787 E-mail: admin@bec.org • URL: http://www.ber.org • Fields of research include information retrieval systems, Internet technology, CD-ROM technology, document delivery, and library automation.

Center for Imaging Science. Rochester Institute of Technology, 54 Lomb Memorial Dr., Rochester, NY 14623. Phone: (716)475-5994 Fax: (716)475-5988 E-mail: gatley@cis.rit.edu • URL: http://www.cis.rit.edu • Activities include research in color science and digital image processing.

Center for Integrated Manufacturing Studies. Rochester Institute of Technology, 111 Lomb Memorial Dr., Rochester, NY 14623-5608. Phone: (716)475-5101 Fax: (716)475-5250 E-mail: wjsasp@rit.edu • URL: http://www.cims.rit.edu • Research areas include electronics, imaging, printing, and publishing.

Digital Image Analysis Laboratory. University of Arizona, Dept. of Electrical and Computer Engineering, Tucson, AZ 85721. Phone: (520)621-4554 Fax: (520)621-8076 E-mail: schowengerdt@ece.arizona.edu • URL: http://www.ece.arizona.edu/~dial • Research fields include image processing, computer vision, and artificial intelligence.

Graphics, Visualization, and Usability Center. Georgia Institute of Technology, Mail Code 0280, Atlanta, GA 30332-0280. Phone: (404)894-4488 Fax: (404)894-0673 E-mail: jarek@cc.gatech.edu • URL: http://www.cc.gatech.edu/gvu/ • Research areas include computer graphics, multimedia, image recognition, interactive graphics systems, animation, and virtual realities.

Image Science Research Group. Worcester Polytechnic Institute, Computer Science Department, 100 Institute Rd., Worcester, MA 01609. Phone: (508)831-5671 Fax: (508)831-5776 E-mail: isrg@cs.wpi.edu • URL: http://www.cs.wpi.edu/research/ • Areas of research include image processing, computer graphics, and computational vision.

Imaging Systems Laboratory. Carnegie Mellon University, Robotics Institute, 5000 Forbes Ave., Pittsburgh, PA 15213. Phone: (412)268-3824 Fax: (412)683-3763 E-mail: rht@cs.cmu.edu • Fields of research include computer vision and document interpretation.

Institute for Information Science and Technology. George Washington University, 801 22nd St., N. W., 6th Fl., Washington, DC 20052. Phone: (202)994-6208 Fax: (202)994-0227 E-mail: helgert@seas.gwu.edu • Research areas include computer graphics and image processing.

TRADE/PROFESSIONAL ASSOCIATIONS

Association for Information and Image Management. 1100 Wayne Ave., Suite 1100, Silver Spring, MD 20910-5603. Phone: (301)587-8202 Fax: (301)587-2711 E-mail: aiim@aiim.org • URL: http://www.aiim.org • Members are producers and users of image management equipment.

DOCUMENTATION (INFORMATION RETRIEVAL)

See: ONLINE INFORMATION SYSTEMS

DOCUMENTS

See: GOVERNMENT PUBLICATIONS

DOG FOOD

See: PET INDUSTRY

DOMESTIC APPLIANCES

See: ELECTRIC APPLIANCE INDUSTRY

DONATIONS, CHARITABLE

See: PHILANTHROPY

DOOR INDUSTRY

See also: BUILDING INDUSTRY

ABSTRACTS AND INDEXES

NTIS Alerts: Building Industry Technology. National Technical Information Service. • Semimonthly. $210.00 per year. Provides descriptions of government-sponsored research reports and software, with ordering information. Covers architecture, construction management, building materials, maintenance, furnishings, and related subjects. Formerly *Abstract Newsletter*.

ONLINE DATABASES

Trade & Industry Index. The Gale Group. • Provides indexing of business periodicals, January 1981 to date. Daily updates. (Full text articles from some periodicals are available online, 1983 to date, in the companion database, *Trade & Industry ASAP*.) Inquire as to online cost and availability.

PERIODICALS AND NEWSLETTERS

Door and Operator Industry. International Door Association. • Bimonthly. Free. Edited for garage door and opener dealers.

Door and Window Retailing. Jervis & Associates. • Bimonthly. $15.00 per year. Edited for door and window retailers. Formerly *Door and Window Business*.

Doors and Hardware. Door and Hardware Institute. • Monthly. $49.00 per year.

RESEARCH CENTERS AND INSTITUTES

Building Technology Center. Stevens Institute of Technology, Castle Point on the Hudson, Hoboken, NJ 07030. Phone: (201)420-5100 Fax: (201)420-5593.

TRADE/PROFESSIONAL ASSOCIATIONS

American Architectural Manufacturers Association. 1827 Walden Office Square, Suite 104, Schamburg, IL 60173. Phone: (847)303-5664 Fax: (847)303-5774 E-mail: webmaster@aamanet.org • URL: http://www.aamanet.org • Members are manufacturers of a wide variety of architectural products. Includes a Residential/Commercial Window and Door Committee.

Door and Access Systems Manufacturers Association International. 1300 Sumner Ave., Cleveland, OH 44115-2851. Phone: (216)241-7333 Fax: (216)241-0105 E-mail: dasma@taol.com • URL: http://www.dasma.com • Members are manufacturers of "upward-acting" garage doors and related products, both residential and commercial.

Door and Hardware Institute. 14170 Newbrook Dr., Ste. 200, Chantilly, VA 22021-2223. Phone: (703)222-2010 Fax: (703)222-2410 • URL: http://www.dhi.org.

International Door Association. P.O. Box 117, West Milton, OH 45383-0117. Phone: (937)698-4186 • Members are manufacturers, dealers, and installers of overhead garage door systems.

National Fenestration Rating Council. 1300 Spring St., Suite 500, Silver Spring, MD 20910. Phone: (301)589-6372 Fax: (301)588-0854 E-mail: nfrcusa@aol.com • URL: http://www.nfrc.org • Conducts insulation efficiency testing of doors and windows. Encourages informed purchase by consumers of windows, doors, and skylights.

National Sash and Door Jobbers Association. 10047 Robert Trent Jones Parkway, New Port Richey, FL 34655-4649. Phone: 800-786-7274 or (727)372-3665 Fax: (727)372-2879 E-mail: info@nsdja.com • URL: http://www.nsdja.com • Members are wholesale distributors of door and window products.

Steel Door Institute. 30200 Detroit Rd., Cleveland, OH 44145. Phone: (440)899-0010 Fax: (440)892-1404 • URL: http://www.steeldoor.org • Members are manufacturers of all-metal doors and frames.

Window and Door Manufactures Association. 1400 E Touhy Ave., No. 470, Des Plaines, IL 60018. Phone: 800-223-2301 or (847)299-5200 Fax: (847)299-1286 • URL: http://www.nwwda.org • Members are manufacturers of wooden door and window products.

OTHER SOURCES

Door Hardware. Available from MarketResearch.com. • 1997. $495.00. Market research report published by Specialists in Business Information. Covers locks, closers, doorknobs, security devices, and other door hardware. Presents market data relative to demographics, sales growth, shipments, exports, imports, price trends, and end-use. Includes company profiles.

Doors. Available from MarketResearch.com. • 1999. $2,250.00. Market research report published by Specialists in Business Information. Covers residential doors, including garage doors. Presents market data relative to demographics, sales growth, shipments, exports, imports, price trends, and end-use. Includes company profiles.

DOOR-TO-DOOR SELLING

See: DIRECT MARKETING

DOUGLAS FIR

See: LUMBER INDUSTRY

DOW THEORY

See also: INVESTMENTS; STOCKS; TECHNICAL ANALYSIS (FINANCE)

GENERAL WORKS

Dow Theory Today. Richard Russell. Fraser Publishing Co. • 1981. $12.00. Reprint of 1958 edition.

The Stock Market Barometer: A Study of Its Forecast Value Based on Charles H. Dow's Theory of the Price Movement, with an Analysis of the Market and Its History Since 1897. William P. Hamilton. Omnigraphics, Inc. • 1990. $45.00. Reprint of 1922 edition.

ONLINE DATABASES

Dow Jones Text Library. Dow Jones and Co., Inc. • Full text and edited news stories and articles on business affairs; 1984 to date. Inquire as to online cost and availability.

PERIODICALS AND NEWSLETTERS

Dow Theory Forecasts: Business and Stock Market. Dow Theory Forecasts, Inc. • Weekly. $233.00 per year. Provides information and advice on blue chip and income stocks.

Dow Theory Letters. Dow Theory Letters, Inc. • Biweekly. $250.00 per year. Newsletter on stock market trends, investing, and economic conditions.

STATISTICS SOURCES

Advance-Decline Album. Dow Theory Letters, Inc. • Annual. Contains one page for each year since 1931. Includes charts of the New York Stock Exchange advance-decline ratio and the Dow Jones industrial average.

Dow Jones Averages Chart Album. Dow Theory Letters, Inc. • Annual. Contains one page for each year since 1885. Includes line charts of the Dow Jones industrial, transportation, utilities, and bond averages. Important historical and economic dates are shown.

Dow Jones Averages 1885-1995. Phyllis S. Pierce, editor. McGraw-Hill. • 1996. $95.00. Fourth edition. Presents the daily Dow Jones stock price averages for more than 100 years.

DOWNSIZING

See: DISMISSAL OF EMPLOYEES

DRAFTING, MECHANICAL

See: MECHANICAL DRAWING

DRAPERY INDUSTRY

See: WINDOW COVERING INDUSTRY

DRIED FOODS

See: FOOD INDUSTRY

DRILLING AND BORING MACHINERY

See: MACHINERY

DRINKING AND TRAFFIC ACCIDENTS

See: TRAFFIC ACCIDENTS AND TRAFFIC SAFETY

DRIVE-IN AND CURB SERVICES

See also: RESTAURANTS, LUNCHROOMS, ETC.

DIRECTORIES

Directory of Chain Restaurant Operators. Chain Store Guide. • Annual. $300.00. Includes fast food establishments, and leading chain hotel copanies operating foodservice unit.

HANDBOOKS AND MANUALS

Donut Shop. Entrepreneur Media, Inc. • Looseleaf. $59.50. A practical guide to starting a doughnut shop. Covers profit potential, start-up costs, market size evaluation, owner's time required, site selection, lease negotiation, pricing, accounting, advertising, promotion, etc. (Start-Up Business Guide No. E1126.).

PERIODICALS AND NEWSLETTERS

QSR: The Magazine of Quick Service Restaurant Success. Journalistic, Inc. • Nine times a year. $32.00 per year. Provides news and management advice for quick-service restaurants, including franchisors and franchisees.

TRADE/PROFESSIONAL ASSOCIATIONS

National Frozen Food Dessert and Fast Food Association. P.O. Box 1116, Millbrook, NY 12545. Phone: 800-535-7748 or (914)677-9301 Fax: (914)677-3387.

DRUG ABUSE AND TRAFFIC

See also: ALCOHOLISM; NARCOTICS; PHARMACEUTICAL INDUSTRY

GENERAL WORKS

A Brief History of Cocaine. Steven B. Karch. CRC Press, Inc. • 1997. $24.95. Emphasizes the societal effects of cocaine abuse in various regions of the world.

The Chemistry of Mind-Altering Drugs: History, Pharmacology, and Cultural Context. Daniel M. Perrine. American Chemical Society. • 1996. $42.00. Contains detailed descriptions of the pharmacological and psychological effects of a wide variety of drugs, "from alcohol to zopiclone.".

Drugs of Abuse. Available from U. S. Government Printing Office. • 1997. $15.00. Issued by the Drug Enforcement Administration, U. S. Department of Justice (http://www.usdoj.gov). Provides detailed information on various kinds of narcotics, depressants, stimulants, hallucinogens, cannabis, steroids, and inhalants. Contains many color illustrations and a detailed summary of the Controlled Substances Act.

The Facts About Drug Use: Coping with Drugs and Alcohol in Your Family, at Work, in Your Community. Barry Stimmel, editor. The Haworth Press, Inc. • 1992. $14.95. A comprehensive overview of drug dependence, including alcoholism.

Family Therapy of Drug Abuse and Addiction. M. Duncan Stanton and Thomas C. Todd. Guilford Publications, Inc., Dept IT. • 1982. $55.00. (Family Therapy Series).

The United Nations and Drug Abuse Control. United Nations Publications. • 1992. An overview of international drug control efforts.

ABSTRACTS AND INDEXES

Excerpta Medica: Drug Dependence, Alcohol Abuse, and Alcoholism. Elsevier Science. • Bimonthly. $1,079.00 per year. Section 40 of *Excerpta Medica.*

CD-ROM DATABASES

Magazine Index Plus. The Gale Group. • Monthly. $4,000.00 per year (includes InfoTrac workstation). Provides full text on CD-ROM for about 100 popular, general interest magazines and indexing for 300 others. Includes special indexing of reviews and product evaluations. Time period is 1980 to date.

DIRECTORIES

Evaluation Guide to Health and Wellness Programs. The Corporate University. • $189.00. Looseleaf service. Semiannual updates, $49.00 each. Provides detailed descriptions and evaluations of more than 200 employee wellness programs that are available nationally. Covers 15 major topics, such as stress management, substance abuse, occupational safety, smoking cessation, blood pressure management, exercise/fitness, diet, and mental health. Programs are available from both profit and non-profit organizations.

ENCYCLOPEDIAS AND DICTIONARIES

American Drug Index. Facts and Comparison. • Annual. $49.95. Lists over 20,000 drug entries in dictionary style.

Encyclopedia of Crime and Justice. Available from The Gale Group. • 2001. $425.00. Second edition. Four volumes. Published by Macmillan Reference USA. Contains extensive information on a wide variety of topics pertaining to crime, criminology, social issues, and the courts. (A revision of 1982 edition.).

Encyclopedia of Drugs, Alcohol, and Addictive Behavior. Available from The Gale Group. • 2001. $425.00. Second edition. Four volumes. Published by Macmillan Reference USA. Covers the social, economic, political, and medical aspects of addiction.

HANDBOOKS AND MANUALS

Drug Abuse and the Law Sourcebook. Gerald F. Uelmen and Victor G. Haddox. West Group. • $240.00 per year. Two looseleaf volumes. Periodic supplementation. Covers drugs of abuse, criminal responsibility, possessory offenses, trafficking offenses, and related topics. (Criminal Law Series).

Drug Abuse Handbook. Steven B. Karch, editor. CRC Press, Inc. • 1997. $99.95. Provides comprehensive coverage of drug abuse issues and trends. Edited for healthcare professionals.

Drug Abuse in Society: A Reference Handbook. Geraldine Woods. ABC-CLIO, Inc. • 1993. $39.50. (Contemporary World Issues Series).

Drug Testing Legal Manual. Kevin B. Zeese. West Group. • Two looseleaf volumes. $210.00. Periodic supplementation. Covers methods of testing for illegal drugs, pre-employment drug testing, technological problems, testing of school students, and related topics. (Criminal Law Series).

Narcotics and Drug Abuse A to Z. Croner Publications, Inc. • Three volumes. Price on application. Lists treatment centers.

Substance Abuse: A Comprehensive Textbook. Joyce H. Lowinson and others. Lippincott Williams & Wilkins. • 1997. $155.00. Third edition. Covers the medical, psychological, socioeconomic, and public health aspects of drug and alcohol abuse.

ONLINE DATABASES

Mental Health Abstracts. IFI/Plenum Data Corp. • Provides indexing and abstracting of mental health and mental illness literature appearing in more than 1,200 journals and other sources from 1969 to date. Monthly updates. Inquire as to online cost and availability.

Pharmaceutical News Index. Bell & Howell Information and Learning. • Indexes major pharmaceutical industry newsletters, 1974 to present. Weekly updates. Inquire as to online cost and availability.

Toxline. National Library of Medicine. • Abstracting service covering human and animal toxicity studies, 1965 to present (older studies available in *Toxback* file). Monthly updates. Inquire as to online cost and availability.

PERIODICALS AND NEWSLETTERS

American Journal of Drug and Alcohol Abuse. Marcel Dekker Journals. • Quarterly. $750.00 per year.

Contemporary Drug Problems. Federal Legal Publications, Inc. • Quarterly. $45.00 per year.

Drug and Alcohol Abuse Education. Editorial Resources, Inc. • Monthly. $84.00 per year. Newsletter covering education, prevention, and treatment relating to abuse of drugs and alcohol.

Drugs and Society: A Journal of Contemporary Issues. Haworth Press, Inc. • Quarterly. Individuals, $42.00 per year; institutions, $90.00 per year;libraries, $200.00 per year. Edited for researchers and practitioners. Covers various areas of susbstance abuse, including alcoholism.

International Drug Report. International Narcotic Enforcement Officers Association. • Quarterly. $35.00 per year. Text in English, French and Spanish.

International Police Review. Jane's Information Group, Inc. • Bimonthy. Institutions, $215.00 per year. Covers "every aspect" of policing and security throughout the world, including organized crime, money laundering, drugs, illegal immigration, forensic science, and police technology.

Journal of Alcohol and Drug Education. American Alcohol and Drug Information Foundation. • Three times a year. Free to members; non-members, $45.00 per year.

Journal of Drug Education. Baywood Publishing Co., Inc. • Quarterly. $175.50 per year.

Journal of Drug Issues. Florida State University, School of Criminology and Criminal Justice. • Quarterly. Individuals, $80.00 per year; institutions, $105.00 per year.

Professional Counselor Magazine: Serving the Mental Health and Addictions Fields. Health Communications, Inc. • Bimonthly. $26.00 per year. Covers both clinical and societal aspects of substance abuse.

Workplace Substance Abuse Advisor. LRP Publications. • Biweekly. $377.00 per year. Newsletter. Covers federal and local laws relating to alcohol and drug use and testing. Provides information on employee assistance plans. Formerly *National Report on Substance Abuse.*

STATISTICS SOURCES

Crime in America's Top-Rated Cities: A Statistical Profile. Grey House Publishing. • Biennial. $125.00. Contains 20-year data for major crime categories in 75 cities, suburbs, metropolitan areas, and the U. S. Also includes statistics on correctional facilities, inmates, hate crimes, illegal drugs, and other crime-related matters.

Statistics on Alcohol, Drug, and Tobacco Use: A Selection of Statistical Charts, Graphs and Tables about Alcohol, Drug and Tobacco Use from a Variety of Published Sources with Explanatory Comments. The Gale Group. • 1995. $65.00. Includes graphs, charts, and tables arranged within subject chapters. Citations to data sources are provided.

World Factbook. U.S. National Technical Information Service. • Annual. $83.00. Prepared by the Central Intelligence Agency. For all countries of the world, provides current economic, demographic, geographic, communications, government, defense force, and illicit drug trade information (where applicable).

TRADE/PROFESSIONAL ASSOCIATIONS

American Pharmaceutical Association/Academy of Pharmacy Practice and Management. c/o Anne Burns, 2215 Constitution Ave., N.W., Washington, DC 20037-2895. Phone: 800-237-2742 or (202)628-4410 Fax: (202)783-2351 E-mail: apha-appm@mail.aphanet.org • URL: http://www.aphanet.org.

Drug, Chemical and Allied Trades Association. 510 Route 130, Suite B1, East Windsor, NJ 08520. Phone: (609)448-1000 Fax: (609)448-1944.

International Narcotic Enforcement Officers Association. 112 State St., Suite 1200, Albany, NY 12207. Phone: (518)463-6232 Fax: (518)432-3378 • URL: http://www.ineoa.org.

Section for Psychiatric and Substance Abuse Services. c/o American Hospital Association, One N. Franklin St., Chicago, IL 60606. Phone: 800-242-4890 or (312)422-3000 Fax: (312)422-4796 • URL: http://www.aha.org.

OTHER SOURCES

World Drug Report. United Nations Publications. • Annual. $25.00. Issued by the United Nations Office for Drug Control and Crime Prevention. Includes maps, graphs, charts, and tables.

World of Criminal Justice. The Gale Group. • 2001. $150.00. Two volumes. Contains both topical and biographical entries relating to the criminal justice system and criminology.

DRUG INDUSTRY

See: PHARMACEUTICAL INDUSTRY

DRUG STORES

See also: CHAIN STORES; DISCOUNT HOUSES; PHARMACEUTICAL INDUSTRY

GENERAL WORKS

Pharmaceutical Marketing in the 21st Century. Mickey C. Smith, editor. Haworth Press, Inc. • 1996. $49.95. Various authors discuss the marketing, pricing, distribution, and retailing of prescription drugs. (Pharmaceutical Marketing and Management Series, Vol. 10, Nos. 2,3&4).

ALMANACS AND YEARBOOKS

Family Almanac. National Association of Retail Druggists. Creative Publishing. • Annual. Free at participating pharmacies. Formerly *NARD Almanac and Health Guide.*

FINANCIAL RATIOS

Almanac of Business and Industrial Financial Ratios. Leo Troy. Prentice Hall. • Annual. $99.95. Contains financial ratios derived from federal tax returns. Ratios for each of about 200 industries are arranged according to company asset size.

NWDA Operating Survey. National Wholesale Druggists' Association. • Annual. Members, $30.00; non-members, $295.00. A 48-page report of financial and operating ratios for the wholesale drug industry.

HANDBOOKS AND MANUALS

Financial Management for Pharmacists: A Decision-Making Approach. Norman V. Carroll. Lippincott Williams & Wilkins. • 1997. $39.00. Second edition.

INTERNET DATABASES

Fedstats. Federal Interagency Council on Statistical Policy. Phone: (202)395-7254 • URL: http://www.fedstats.gov • Web site features an efficient search facility for full-text statistics produced by more than 70 federal agencies, including the Census Bureau, the Bureau of Economic Analysis, and the Bureau of Labor Statistics. Boolean searches can be made within one agency or for all agencies combined. Links are offered to international statistical bureaus, including the UN, IMF, OECD, UNESCO, Eurostat, and 20 individual countries. Fees: Free.

ONLINE DATABASES

DRI U.S. Central Database. Data Products Division. • Provides more than 23,000 business, financial, demographic, economic, foreign trade, and industry-related time series for the U.S. Includes national income, population, retail-wholesale trade, price indexes, labor data, housing, industrial production, banking, interest rates, money supply, etc. Time period is generally 1947 to date (some data back to 1929). Updating varies. Inquire as to online cost and availability.

PERIODICALS AND NEWSLETTERS

American Druggist. Press Corps, Inc. • Monthly. $44.00 per year. Provides news and analysis of major trends affecting pharmacists. Includes an annual "Generic Survey" (September).

America's Pharmacist. National Community Pharmacists Association. • Monthly. $50.00 per year. Formerly *N A R D Journal.*

Chain Drug Review: The Reporter for the Chain Drug Store Industry. Racher Press, Inc. • Biweekly. $136.00 per year. Covers news and trends of concern to the chain drug store industry. Includes special articles on OTC (over-the-counter) drugs.

Community Pharmacist: Meeting the Professional and Educational Needs of Today's Practitioner. ELF Publicatons, Inc. • Bimonthly. $25.00 per year. Edited for retail pharmacists in various settings, whether independent or chain-operated. Covers both pharmaceutical and business topics.

Computertalk: For Contemporary Pharmacy Management. Computertalk Associates, Inc. • Bimonthly. $50.00 per year. Provides detailed advice and information on computer systems for pharmacies, including a buyers' guide issue.

Drug Store News. Lebhar-Friedman Inc. • Biweekly. $95.00 per year.

Drug Topics. Medical Economics Co., Inc. • 23 times a year. $61.00 per year. Edited for retail pharmacists, hospital pharmacists, pharmacy chain store executives, wholesalers, buyers, and others concerned with drug dispensing and drug store management. Provides information on new products, including personal care items and cosmetics.

Pharmacy Times: Practical Information for Today's Pharmacists. Romaine Pierson Publishing Co. • Monthly. $43.00 per year. Edited for pharmacists. Covers store management, new products, regulations, home health care products, managed care issues, etc.

Retail Pharmacy News. McMahon Publishing Group. • Monthly. $70.00 per year. Featues include product news for pharmacists and financial news for chain store executives.

U. S. Pharmacist. Jobson Publishing LLC. • Monthly. $30.00 per year. Covers a wide variety of topics for independent, chain store, hospital, and other pharmacists.

Weekly Pharmacy Reports: The Green Sheet. F-D-C Reports, Inc. • Weekly. $82.00 per year. Newsletter for retailers and wholesalers of pharmaceutical products. Includes pricing developments and new drug announcements.

PRICE SOURCES

First DataBank Blue Book. Hearst Corp. • Annual. $65.00. List of manufacturers of prescription and over-the-counter drugs, sold in retail drug stores. Formerly *American Druggist Blue Book.*

RESEARCH CENTERS AND INSTITUTES

Pharmaceutical Marketing and Management Research Program. University of Mississippi, Waller Lab Complex, Room 101, University, MS 38677. Phone: (662)915-5948 Fax: (662)915-5262 E-mail: dgarner@olemiss.edu • URL: http://www.olemiss.edu/depts/rips/pmmrp/.

STATISTICS SOURCES

Business Statistics of the United States. Courtenay M. Slater, editor. Bernan Associates. • 1999. $74.00. Fifth edition. Based on *Business Statistics*, formerly issue by the Bureau of Economic Analysis, U. S. Department of Commerce. Provides basic data for a wide variety of U. S. industries, services, and economic indicators. Most statistics are shown annually for 29 years and monthly for the most recent four years.

Lilly Digest. Eli Lilly and Co. • Annual. $30.00. Includes drug store financial data.

Lilly Hospital Pharmacy Survey. Eli Lilly and Co. • Annual. $30.00. Includes financial data for drug stores located in hospitals.

Standard & Poor's Industry Surveys. Standard & Poor's. • Semiannual. $1,800.00. Two looseleaf volumes. Includes monthly supplements. Provides detailed, individual surveys of 52 major industry groups. Each survey is revised on a semiannual basis. Also includes "Monthly Investment Review" (industry group investment analysis) and monthly "Trends & Projections" (economic analysis).

Survey of Current Business. Available from U. S. Government Printing Office. • Monthly. $49.00 per year. Issued by Bureau of Economic Analysis, U. S. Department of Commerce. Presents a wide variety of business and economic data.

WEFA Industrial Monitor. John Wiley and Sons, Inc. • Annual. $65.00. Prepared by industry analysts at WEFA, an economic forecasting and consulting firm (originally Wharton Econometric Forecasting Associates). Contains discussions of the outlook for major U. S. industries, with many 10-year forecasts (WEFA Web site is http://www.wefa.com).

TRADE/PROFESSIONAL ASSOCIATIONS

American Pharmaceutical Association/Academy of Pharmacy Practice and Management. c/o Anne Burns, 2215 Constitution Ave., N.W., Washington, DC 20037-2895. Phone: 800-237-2742 or (202)628-4410 Fax: (202)783-2351 E-mail: apha-appm@mail.aphanet.org • URL: http://www.aphanet.org.

National Association of Chain Drug Stores. c/o Ronald L. Ziegler, P.O. Box 1417-D49, Alexandria, VA 22313-1480. Phone: (703)549-3001 Fax: (703)836-4869 E-mail: homepage_info@nacds.org • URL: http://www.nacds.org.

National Wholesale Druggists' Association. 1821 Michael Faraday Dr., Suite 400, Reston, VA 20190. Phone: (703)787-0000 Fax: (703)787-6930 E-mail: info@nwda.org • URL: http://www.nwda.org.

OTHER SOURCES

Mail Service Pharmacy Market. MarketResearch.com. • 1999. $3,250.00. Provides detailed market data, with forecasts to the year 2003.

DRUGS

See: DRUG ABUSE AND TRAFFIC; NARCOTICS; PHARMACEUTICAL INDUSTRY

DRUGS, GENERIC

See: GENERIC DRUG INDUSTRY

DRUGS, NONPRESCRIPTION

See: NONPRESCRIPTION DRUG INDUSTRY

DRUNKENNESS

See: ALCOHOLISM

DRY CLEANING INDUSTRY

See: CLEANING INDUSTRY

DUPLICATING MACHINES

See: COPYING MACHINE INDUSTRY

DUTIES

See: TARIFF; TAXATION

DYES AND DYEING

See also: TEXTILE INDUSTRY

GENERAL WORKS

Natural Dyes and Home Dyeing. Rita J. Adrosko. Dover Publications, Inc. • 1971. $5.95.

ABSTRACTS AND INDEXES

CPI Digest: Key to World Literature Serving the Coatings, Plastics, Fibers, Adhesives, and Related Industries (Chemical Process Industries). CPI Information Services. • Monthly. $397.00 per year. Abstracts of business and technical articles for polymer-based, chemical process industries. Includes a monthly list of relevant U. S. patents. International coverage.

Textile Chemist and Colorist. American Association of Textile Chemists and Colorists. • Monthly. Free to members; non-members, $60.00 per year. Annual *Buyer's Guide* available.

DIRECTORIES

OPD Chemical Buyers Directory. Schnell Publishing Co., Inc. • Annual. $129.00. Included in subscription to *Chemical Marketing Reporter.* About 1,500 suppliers of chemical process materials and more than 300 companies which transport and store chemicals in the U.S.

ONLINE DATABASES

CA Search. Chemical Abstracts Service. • Guide to chemical literature, 1967 to present. Inquire as to online cost and availability.

PERIODICALS AND NEWSLETTERS

International Dyer. World Textile Publications Ltd. • Monthly. $120.00 per year.

International Textile Bulletin: Dyeing-Printing-Finishing Edition. ITS Publishing, International Textile Service. • Quarterly. $170.00 per year. Editions in Chinese, English, French, German, Italian and Spanish.

TRADE/PROFESSIONAL ASSOCIATIONS

Textile Processors, Service Trades, Health Care, Professional and Technical Employees International Union. 303 E. Wacker Dr., Suite 1109, Chicago, IL 60601. Phone: (312)946-0450 Fax: (312)964-0453.

E

E-COMMERCE

See: ELECTRONIC COMMERCE

EATING FACILITIES, EMPLOYEES

See: EMPLOYEE LUNCHROOMS AND CAFETERIAS

EATING PLACES

See: RESTAURANTS, LUNCHROOMS, ETC.

ECOLOGY

See: ENVIRONMENT

ECONOMETRICS

See also: ECONOMIC RESEARCH; ECONOMIC STATISTICS; ECONOMICS

GENERAL WORKS

Advances in Econometrics and Quantitative Economics. Morris H. DeGroot and others. Blackwell Publishers. • 1995. $99.95.

An Introduction to the Theory and Practice of Econometrics. George G. Judge and others. John Wiley and Sons, Inc. • 1988. $108.95. Second edition.

The Theory and Practice of Econometrics. George G. Judge and others. John Wiley and Sons, Inc. • 1985. $111.95. Second edition. (Probability and Mathematical Statistics Series).

CD-ROM DATABASES

EconLit. Available from SilverPlatter Information, Inc. • Monthly. Single-user, $1,600.00 per year. Multi-user, $2,400.00 per year. Provides CD-ROM citations, with abstracts, to articles from more than 500 economics journals. Time period is 1969 to date. Produced by the American Economic Association.

ENCYCLOPEDIAS AND DICTIONARIES

Dictionary of Econometrics. Adrian C. Darnell. Edward Elgar Publishing, Inc. • 1994. $150.00. Published by Edward Elgar Publishing Co. (UK).

Dictionary of Economics. Jae K. Shim and Joel G. Siegel. John Wiley and Sons, Inc. • 1995. $79.95. Contains 2,200 definitions of economic terms. Includes graphs, charts, tables, and economic formulas. (Business Dictionary Series).

HANDBOOKS AND MANUALS

Econometric Analysis. William H. Greene. Prentice Hall. • 2000. Fourth edition. Price on application. Includes bibliographical references.

Econometric Analysis of Financial Markets. J. Kaehler and P. Kugler, editors. Springer-Verlag New York, Inc. • 1994. $71.95. (Studies in Empirical Economics Series).

Econometric Methods. John Johnston. McGraw-Hill. • 1996. $85.63. Fourth edition. Covers various models, equations, variables, relationships, and "A Smorgasbord of Computationally Intense Methods.".

Econometrics of Financial Markets. John Y. Campbell and others. California Princeton Fulfillment Services. • 1997. $49.50. Written for advanced students and industry professionals. Includes chapters on "The Predictability of Asset Returns," "Derivative Pricing Models," and "Fixed-Income Securities." Provides a discussion of the random walk theory of investing and tests of the theory.

Mathematics for Economic Analysis. Knut Sydsaeter and Peter J. Hammond. Prentice Hall. • 1994. $57.80.

Using Econometrics: A Practical Guide. A. H. Studenmund. Addison-Wesley Longman, Inc. • 2001. Fourth edition. Price on application.

ONLINE DATABASES

EconBase: Time Series and Forecasts. WEFA, Inc. • Presents online econometric data for business conditions, economics, demographics, industry, finance, employment, household income, interest rates, prices, etc. Includes two-year forecasts for a wide range of economic indicators. Time span is 1948 to date, with monthly updates. Inquire as to online cost and availability.

EconLit. American Economic Association. • Covers the worldwide literature of economics as contained in selected monographs and about 550 journals. Subjects include microeconomics, macroeconomics, economic history, inflation, money, credit, finance, accounting theory, trade, natural resource economics, and regional economics. Time period is 1969 to present, with monthly updates. Inquire as to online cost and availability.

PERIODICALS AND NEWSLETTERS

Econometric Theory. Cambridge University Press, Journals Dept. • Bimonthly. $280.00 Per year. Devoted to the advancement of theoretical research in econometrics.

Econometrica. Blackwell Publishers. • Bimonthly. $350.00 per year. Published in England by Basil Blackwell Ltd.

Journal of Applied Econometrics. John Wiley and Sons, Inc., Journals Div. • Bimonthly. Institutions, $870.00 per year.

Journal of Econometrics. Elsevier Science. • Monthly. $2,020.00 per year.

RESEARCH CENTERS AND INSTITUTES

Center for Mathematical Studies in Economics and Management Sciences. Northwestern University, Leverone Hall, Room 317, 2001 Sheridan Rd., Evanston, IL 60208-2014. Phone: (847)491-3527 Fax: (847)491-2530 E-mail: sreiter@casbah.acns.nwu.edu • URL: http://www.kellogg.nwu.edu/research/math.

Cowles Foundation for Research in Economics. Yale University. 30 Hillhouse Ave., New Haven, CT 06520-8281. Phone: (203)432-3704 Fax: (203)432-6167 E-mail: john.geanakoplos@yale.edu • URL: http://www.econ.yale.edu.

Econometric Research Program. Princeton University. 203 Fisher Hall, Princeton, NJ 08544-1021. Phone: (609)258-4014 Fax: (609)258-5561 E-mail: honore@princeton.edu • URL: http://www.princeton.edu/~erp.

TRADE/PROFESSIONAL ASSOCIATIONS

Econometric Society. Northwestern University, Dept. of Economics, Evanston, IL 60208-2600. Phone: (708)491-3615 • URL: http://www.econometricsociety.org.es.

Institute for Econometric Research. 2200 S.W. 10th St., Deerfield, FL 33442. Phone: 800-499-0066 or (954)421-1000 Fax: (954)421-8200 • URL: http://www.mfmag.com.

OTHER SOURCES

Quantitative Finance. Available from IOP Publishing, Inc. • Bimonthly. $199.00 per year. Published in the UK by the Institute of Physics. A technical journal on the use of quantitative tools and applications in financial analysis and financial engineering. Covers such topics as portfolio theory, derivatives, asset allocation, return on assets, risk management, price volatility, financial econometrics, market anomalies, and trading systems.

ECONOMIC BOTANY

See also: AGRICULTURE

ABSTRACTS AND INDEXES

Biological and Agricultural Index. H.W. Wilson Co. • 11 times a year. Annual and quarterly cumulations. Service basis.

ENCYCLOPEDIAS AND DICTIONARIES

Dictionary of Economic Plants. J.C. Uphof. Lubrecht and Cramer, Ltd. • 1968. $49.00. Second enlarged revised edition.

PERIODICALS AND NEWSLETTERS

American Journal of Botany: Devoted to All Branches of Plant Sciences. Botanical Society of America, Inc., Business Office. • Monthly. $195.00 per year. Includes *Plant Science Bulletin.*

The Botanical Review: Interpreting Botanical Progress. Society for Economic Botany. New York Botanical Garden Press. • Quarterly. $82.00 per year. Reviews articles in all fields of botany.

Economic Botany: Devoted to Applied Botany and Plant Utilization. Society for Economic Botany. New York Botanical Garden Press. • Quarterly. $88.00 per year. Includes *Plants and People.* Newsletter. Original research and review articles on the uses of plants.

Plant Science Bulletin. Botanical Society of America, Inc. • Quarterly. Membership.

RESEARCH CENTERS AND INSTITUTES

Morton Collectanea. University of Miami Dept. of Biology. P.O. Box 249118, Coral Gables, FL 33124-0421. Phone: (305)284-3973 Fax: (305)284-3039 E-mail: mgaines@umiami.ir.miami.edu • URL: http://www.fig.cox.miami.edu.

TRADE/PROFESSIONAL ASSOCIATIONS

Botanical Society of America. c/o Kimberly E. Hiser, 1735 Neil Ave., Columbus, OH 43210-1293. Phone: (614)292-3519 Fax: (614)292-3519 • URL: http://www.botany.org/bsa.

Society for Economic Botany. New York Botanical Gardens, Bronx, NY 10458. E-mail: dlentz@nybg.org • URL: http://www.econbot.org.

OTHER SOURCES

Global Seed Markets. Theta Reports/PJB Medical Publications, Inc. • 2000. $1,040.00. Market research data. Covers the major seed sectors, including cereal crops, legumes, oilseed crops, fibre crops, and beet crops. Provides analysis of biotechnology developments. (Theta Report No. DS208E.).

ECONOMIC CONDITIONS

See: BUSINESS CONDITIONS

ECONOMIC CYCLES

See: BUSINESS CYCLES

ECONOMIC DEVELOPMENT

See also: DEVELOPING AREAS; INDUSTRIAL DEVELOPMENT; URBAN DEVELOPMENT

GENERAL WORKS

Economic Development. Jan S. Hogendorn. Addison-Wesley Educational Publishers, Inc. • 1997. $81.00.

Economics of Development. Malcolm Gillis and others. W. W. Norton and Co., Inc. • 2000. Fifth edition. Price on application.

Global Economic Prospects and the Developing Countries, 1999-2000. World Bank, The Office of the Publisher. • 1999. $25.00. Examines the economic connections between industrial and developing countries, with a different theme in each edition.

Global Economic Prospects 2000. The World Bank, Office of the Publisher. • 1999. $25.00. "..offers an in-depth analysis of the economic prospects of developing countries.." Emphasis is on the impact of recessions and financial crises. Regional statistical data is included.

ABSTRACTS AND INDEXES

PAIS International in Print. Public Affairs Information Service, Inc. • Monthly. $650.00 per year; cumulations three times a year. Provides topical citations to the worldwide literature of public affairs, economics, demographics, sociology, and trade. Text in English; indexed materials in English, French, German, Italian, Portuguese and Spanish.

Social Sciences Index. H. W. Wilson Co. • Quarterly, with annual cumulation. Service basis for print edition; CD-ROM edition, $1,495 per year. Indexes more than 400 periodicals covering economics, environmental policy, government, insurance, labor, health care policy, plannning, public administration, public welfare, urban studies, women's issues, criminology, and related topics.

ALMANACS AND YEARBOOKS

Trade and Development Report and Overview. Available from United Nations Publications. • Annual. $45.00. Yearly overview of trends in international trade, including an analysis of the economic and trade situation in developing countries. Published by the United Nations Conference on Trade and Development (UNCTAD).

BIBLIOGRAPHIES

Regional Economic Development: Theories amd Strategies for Developing Countries. Marguerite N. Abd El-Shahid. Sage Publications, Inc. • 1994. $10.00.

CD-ROM DATABASES

PAIS on CD-ROM. Public Affairs Information Service, Inc. • Quarterly. $1,995.00 per year. Provides a CD-ROM version of the online service, *PAIS International.* Contains over 400,000 citations to the literature of contemporary social, political, and economic issues.

Social Science Source. EBSCO Publishing. • Monthly. $1,495.00 per year. Provides CD-ROM citations and abstracts to social science articles in more than 600 periodicals, with full text from 125 periodicals. Covers economics, political science, public policy, international relations, psychology, and other topics. Time period is most recent five years.

Social Sciences Citation Index: Compact Disc Edition with Abstracts. Institute for Scientific Information. • Quarterly. Provides CD-ROM indexing and abstracting of "significant articles" from 1,400 social science journals worldwide, with additional selections from 3,200 other journals, 1986 to date. Includes economics, business, finance, management, communications, demographics, information and library science, political science, sociology, and many other subjects.

WILSONDISC: Wilson Social Sciences Abstracts. H. W. Wilson Co. • Monthly. Including unlimited online access to *Social Sciences Index* through WILSONLINE. Provides CD-ROM indexing from 1983 and abstracting from 1994 of more than 400 periodicals covering economics, area studies, community health, public administration, public welfare, urban studies, and many other topics related to the social sciences.

DIRECTORIES

Funding Sources for Community and Economic Development: A Guide to Current Sources for Local Programs and Projects. Oryx Press. • 2000. $64.95. Sixth edition. Provides information on 2,600 funding sources. Includes "A Guide to Proposal Planning.".

ENCYCLOPEDIAS AND DICTIONARIES

Worldmark Encyclopedia of National Economies. The Gale Group. • 2002. $295.00. Four volumes. Covers both the current and historical development of the economies of 200 foreign nations. Includes analysis and statistics.

ONLINE DATABASES

Business and Industry. Responsive Database Services, Inc. • Contains online citations, abstracts, and selected fulltext from more than 1,000 trade journals, newspapers, and other publications. Provides general coverage of both manufacturing and service industries, including marketing, production, industry trends, key events, and information on specific companies. Time span is 1994 to date. Daily updates. Inquire as to online cost and availability. (Also available in a CD-ROM version.).

PAIS International. Public Affairs Information Service, Inc. • Corresponds to the former printed publications, *PAIS Bulletin* (1976-90) and *PAIS Foreign Language Index* (1972-90), and to the current *PAIS International in Print* (1991 to date). Covers economic, political, and sociological material appearing in periodicals, books, government documents, and other publications. Updating is monthly. Inquire as to online cost and availability.

Tablebase. Responsive Database Services, Inc. • Provides online numerical tabular data from a wide variety of business, organization, and government sources, including 900 trade journals. Includes industry and individual company statistics relating to products, market share, sales forecasts, production, exports, market trends, etc. Time span is 1997 to date. Weekly updates. Inquire as to online cost and availability. (Also available in a CD-ROM version.).

Wilson Social Sciences Abstracts Online. H. W. Wilson Co. • Provides online abstracting and indexing of more than 415 periodicals covering area studies, community health, public administration, public welfare, urban studies, and many other social science topics. Time period is 1994 to date for abstracts and 1983 to date for indexing, with updates monthly. Inquire as to online cost and availability.

PERIODICALS AND NEWSLETTERS

Economic Development and Cultural Change. University of Chicago Press, Journals Div. • Quarterly. Individuals, $44.00 per year; institutions, $138.00 per year. Examines the economic and social forces that affect development and the impact of development on culture.

Economic Development Monitor. Whitaker Newsletters, Inc. • Biweekly. $247.00 per year. Newsletter. Covers the news of U. S. economic and industrial development, including legislation, regulation, planning, and financing.

Economic Development Quarterly: The Journal of American Revitalization. Sage Publications, Inc. • Quarterly. Individuals, $75.00 per year; institutions, $325,00 per year.

Economic Development Review. American Economic Development Council. • Quarterly. Individuals, $60.00 per year; institutions, $48.00 per year.

Financial Flows and the Developing Countries. World Bank, The Office of the Publisher. • Quarterly. $150.00 per year. Concerned mainly with debt, capital markets, and foreign direct investment. Includes statistical tables.

The Journal of Development Economics. Elsevier Science. • Bimonthly. $1,223.00 per year.

The Journal of International Trade and Economic Development. Routledge Journals. • Quarterly. Individuals, $68.00 per year; institutions, $445.00 per year. Emphasizes the effect of trade on the economies of developing nations.

Plants, Sites, and Parks. Cahners Business Information. • Bimonthly. $30.00 per year. Covers economic development, site location, industrial parks, and industrial development programs.

RESEARCH CENTERS AND INSTITUTES

Center for International Policy. 1755 Massachusetts Ave., N. W., Suite 312, Washington, DC 20036. Phone: (202)232-3317 Fax: (202)232-3440 E-mail: cip@ciponline.org • URL: http://www.ciponline.org • Research subjects include the International Monetary Fund, the World Bank, and other international financial institutions. Analyzes the impact of policies on social and economic conditions in developing countries.

Center for Research in Economic Development. San Diego State University. Department of Economics, Mail Code 4485, San Diego, CA 92182. Phone: (858)594-5492 Fax: (858)594-5062 E-mail: madh@mail.sdsu.edu • URL: http://www.sdsu.edu.

Economic Growth Center. Yale University. P.O. Box 208269, New Haven, CT 06520-8269. Phone: (203)432-3610 Fax: (203)432-3898 E-mail: lucinda.gall@yale.edu • URL: http://www.econ.yale.edu/egcenter.

Regional Economic Development Center. University of Memphis. Johnson Hall, Room 226, Memphis, TN 38152. Phone: (901)678-2056 Fax: (901)678-4162 E-mail: gpearson@cc.memphis.edu • URL: http://www.people.memphis.edu/~crplan.

W. E. Upjohn Institute for Employment Research. 300 S. Westnedge Ave., Kalamazoo, MI 49007-4686. Phone: (616)343-5541 Fax: (616)343-3308 E-mail: eberts@we.upjohninst.org • URL: http://www.upjohninst.org • Research fields include unemployment, unemployment insurance, worker's compensation, labor productivity, profit sharing, the labor market, economic development, earnings, training, and other areas related to employment.

STATISTICS SOURCES

Encyclopedia of American Industries. The Gale Group. • 1998. $560.00. Second edition. Two volumes. $280.00 per volume. Volume one is *Manufacturing Industries* and volume two is *Service and Non-Manufacturing Industries.* Provides the history, development, and recent status of approximately 1,000 industries. Includes statistical graphs, with industry and general indexes.

Global Development Finance: Analysis and Summary Tables. World Bank, The Office of the Publisher. • Annual. $40.00. Provides an analysis of debt and equity financial flows to 136 countries that report to the World Bank's Debtor Reporting System. Contains summary statistical tables for 150 countries.

Global Development Finance: Country Tables. World Bank, The Office of the Publisher. • 1998. $300.00 (includes *Analysis and Summary Tables*). Contains detailed statistical tables for 136 countries, covering total external debt, long-term debt ratios, arrears, commitments, disbursements, repayments, etc. Includes "major economic aggregates.".

Handbook of International Economic Statistics. Available from National Technical Information Service. • Annual. $40.00. Prepared by U. S. Central Intelligence Agency. Provides basic statistics for comparing worldwide economic performance, with an emphasis on Europe, including Eastern Europe.

National Accounts of OECD Countries. OECD Publications and Information Center. • Annual. Two volumes. Price varies.

Short-Term Economic Indicators: Transition Economies. OECD Publications and Information Center. • Quarterly. Presents annual, quarterly, and monthly economic indicators for the developing countries of Eastern Europe and the New Independent States.

Social Indicators of Development. John Hopkins University Press. • 1996. $26.95. Provides social and economic statistics for over 170 countries. Includes population, labor force, income, poverty level, natural resources, medical care, education, the environment, and expenditures on living essentials. Covers a 30-year period. (World Bank Series).

TRADE/PROFESSIONAL ASSOCIATIONS

American Economic Development Council. 1030 Higgins Rd., Suite 301, Park Ridge, IL 60668. Phone: (847)692-9944 Fax: (847)696-2990 E-mail: aedc@interaccess.com • URL: http://www.aedc.org.

Bretton Woods Committee. 1990 M St., N.W., Suite 450, Washington, DC 20036. Phone: (202)331-1616 Fax: (202)785-9423 E-mail: info@brettonwoods.org • URL: http://www.brettonwoods.org • Members are corporate executives, government officials, college administrators, bankers, and other "National Leaders." Seeks to inform and educate the public as to the activities of the International Monetary Fund, the World Bank, and other multinational development banking organizations. Promotes U. S. participation in multinational banking.

Committee for Economic Development. 2000 L St., N.W., Suite 700, Washington, DC 20036. Phone: (202)296-5860 Fax: (202)223-0776 E-mail: ckolb@ced.org • URL: http://www.ced.org.

Council for Urban Economic Development. 1730 K St., N.W., Suite 700, Washington, DC 20006. Phone: (202)223-4735 Fax: (202)223-4745 E-mail: mail@urbandevelopment.com • URL: http://www.cued.org.

National Association of State Development Agencies. 750 First St., N.E., Suite 710, Washington, DC 20002. Phone: (202)898-1302 Fax: (202)898-1312.

National Policy Association. 1424 16th St., N.W., Suite 700, Washington, DC 20036. Phone: (202)265-7685 Fax: (202)797-5516 E-mail: npa@npa1.org • URL: http://www.npa1.org.

Organisation for Economic Co-Operation and Development. Two, rue Andre Pascal, F-75775 Paris Cedex 16, France. Phone: 33 1 45248200 Fax: 33 1 45248500 E-mail: news.contact@oecd.org • URL: http://www.oecd.org.

Society for International Development. 1875 Connecticut Ave., N.W., Washington, DC 20009. 1875 Connecticut Ave., N.W.,.

OTHER SOURCES

Towards a Sustainable Energy Future. Organization for Economic Cooperation and Development. • 2001. $100.00. Prepared by the International Energy Agency (IEA). Describes various policies for promoting sustainable energy, especially. Prepared by the International Energy Agency (IEA). Describes various policies for promoting sustainable energy, especially as related to economic development. Discusses "growing concerns about climate change and energy-supply security.".

The World Economy: A Millennial Perspective. Angus Maddison. Organization for Economic Cooperation and Development. • 2001. $63.00. "...covers the development of the entire world economy over the past 2000 years," including data on world population and gross domestic product (GDP) since the year 1000, and exports since 1820. Focuses primarily on the disparity in economic performance among nations over the very long term. More than 200 statistical tables and figures are provided (detailed information available at http://www.theworldeconomy.org).

World Investment Report. United Nations Publications. • Annual. $49.00. Concerned with foreign direct investment, economic development, regional trends, transnational corporations, and globalization.

ECONOMIC ENTOMOLOGY

See also: PESTICIDE INDUSTRY

ABSTRACTS AND INDEXES

Biological and Agricultural Index. H.W. Wilson Co. • 11 times a year. Annual and quarterly cumulations. Service basis.

Review of Agricultural Entomology: Consisting of Abstracts of Reviews of Current Literature on Applied Entomology Throughout the World. Available from CABI Publishing North America. • Monthly. $1220.00 per year. Published in England by CABI Publishing. Provides worldwide coverage of the literature. (Formerly *Review of Applied Entomology, Series A: Agricultural.*).

Review of Medical and Veterinary Entomology. Available from CABI Publishing North America. • Monthly. $710.00 per year. Provides worldwide coverage of the literature. Formerly *Review of Applied Entomology, Series B: Medical and Veterinary.*

ALMANACS AND YEARBOOKS

Annual Review of Entomology. Annual Reviews, Inc. • Annual. Individuals, $60.00, institutions, $120.00.

CD-ROM DATABASES

AGRICOLA on SilverPlatter. Available from SilverPlatter Information, Inc. • Quarterly. $825.00 per year. Produced by the National Agricultural Library. Provides about three million citations on CD-ROM to the literature of agriculture, agricultural economics, animal sciences, entomology, fertilizer, food, forestry, nutrition, pesticides, plant science, water resources, and other topics. Each quarterly disc covers the past ten years, with archival discs available from 1970.

ENCYCLOPEDIAS AND DICTIONARIES

Encyclopedia of Agriculture Science. Charles J. Arntzen and Ellen M. Ritter, editors. Academic Press, Inc. • 1994. $625.00. Four volumes.

HANDBOOKS AND MANUALS

Introduction to Insect Pest Management. Robert L. Metcalf and William H. Luckmann. John Wiley and Sons, Inc. • 1994. $125.00. Third edition. (Environmental Science and Technology Series).

ONLINE DATABASES

Derwent Crop Protection File. Derwent, Inc. • Provides citations to the international journal literature of agricultural chemicals and pesticides from 1968 to date, with updating eight times per year. Formerly *PESTDOC.* Inquire as to online cost and availability.

PERIODICALS AND NEWSLETTERS

American Entomologist: Entomological Articles of General Interest. Entomological Society of America. • Quarterly. Members, $15.00 per year; non-members, $36.00 per year, institutions, $64.00 per year. Formerly *Entomological Society of America Bulletin.*

Entomological Society of America Annals: Devoted to the Interest of Classical Entomology. Entomological Society of America. • Bimonthly. Members, $25.00 per year; non-members, $81.00 per year; institutions, $156.00 per year.

RESEARCH CENTERS AND INSTITUTES

Cattle Fever Tick Research Laboratory. U.S. Department of Agricultural Livestock Insects Laboratory, P.O. Box 1010, Edinburg, TX 78539. Phone: (210)580-7268 Fax: (210)580-7261 E-mail: rbdavey@rgv.net.

Center for Integrated Plant Systems. Michigan State University. East Lansing, MI 48824-1311. Phone: (517)353-9430 Fax: (517)353-5598 E-mail: hartl@msu.edu • URL: http://www.cips.msu.edu.

Food and Environmental Toxicology Laboratory. University of Florida. P.O. Box 110720, Gainesville, FL 32611-0720. Phone: (352)392-1978 Fax: (352)392-1988 E-mail: hamo@gnv.ifas.ufl.edu • URL: http://www.fshn.isas.ufl.edu/index.htm.

Integrated Plant Protection Center. Oregon State University. 2040 Cordley Hall, Corvallis, OR 97331-2915. Phone: (541)737-3541 Fax: (541)737-3080 E-mail: koganm@bcc.orst.edu • URL: http://www.ippc.orst.edu.

Laboratory for Pest Control Application Technology. Ohio State University, Ohio Agricultural Research and Development Center,

Wooster, OH 44691. Phone: (330)263-3726 Fax: (330)263-3686 E-mail: hall.1@osu.edu • URL: http://www.oardc.ohio-state.edu/lpcat/ • Conducts pest control research in cooperation with the U. S. Department of Agriculture.

Toxic Chemicals Laboratory. Cornell University. New York State College of Agriculture, Tower Rd., Ithaca, NY 14853-7401. Phone: (607)255-4538 Fax: (607)255-0599 E-mail: djl@cornell.edu.

TRADE/PROFESSIONAL ASSOCIATIONS

American Entomological Society. Academy of Natural Sciences of Philadelphia, 1900 Benjamin Franklin Parkway, Philadelphia, PA 19103-1195. Phone: (215)561-3978 Fax: (215)299-1028 E-mail: aes@say.acnatsci.org.

OTHER SOURCES

World Non-Agricultural Pesticide Markets. Theta Reports/PJB Medical Publications, Inc. • 2000. $1,670.00. Market research data. Includes home/garden pesticides, herbicides, professional pest-control products, and turf pesticides. (Theta Report No. DS191E.).

ECONOMIC FORECASTING

See: BUSINESS FORECASTING

ECONOMIC GEOLOGY

See also: MINES AND MINERAL RESOURCES

ENCYCLOPEDIAS AND DICTIONARIES

Glossary of Geology. Robert L. Bates and Julia A. Jackson. American Geological Institute. • 1997. $110.00. Fourth edition.

ONLINE DATABASES

GEOARCHIVE. Geosystems. • Citations to literature on geoscience and water. 1974 to present. Monthly updates. Inquire as to online cost and availability.

GEOREF. American Geological Institute. • Bibliography and index of geology and geosciences literature, 1785 to present. Inquire as to online cost and availability.

PERIODICALS AND NEWSLETTERS

Economic Geology and the Bulletin of the Society of Economic Geologists. Society of Economic Geologist. Economic Geology Publishing Co. • Irregular. Individuals, $75.00 per year; institutions, $145.00 per year.

RESEARCH CENTERS AND INSTITUTES

Bureau of Economic Geology. University of Texas at Austin. University Station, P.O. Box X, Austin, TX 78713-8924. Phone: 888-839-4365 or (512)471-1534 Fax: (512)471-0140 E-mail: begmail@begv.beg.utexas.edu • URL: http://www.utexas.edu/research/beg/.

Mineral Industry Research Laboratory. University of Alaska Fairbanks. Fairbanks, AK 99775-5960. Phone: (907)474-7366 Fax: (907)474-5400 E-mail: fysme@uaf.edu • URL: http://www.sme.uaf.edu.

TRADE/PROFESSIONAL ASSOCIATIONS

Society of Economic Geologists. 7811 Shaffer Pkwy., Littleton, CO 80127. Phone: (720)981-7882 Fax: (720)981-7874 E-mail: soceongeol@can.net • URL: http://www.segweb.org.

ECONOMIC HISTORY

See: BUSINESS HISTORY

ECONOMIC INDICATORS

GENERAL WORKS

Business Cycles: Theory, History, Indicators, and Forecasting. Victor Zarnowitz. University of Chicago Press. • 1992. $77.00.

Forecasting Business Trends. American Institute for Economic Research. • 2000. $6.00. Summarizes methods of economic forecasting, statistical indicators, methods of analyzing business cycles, and use of leading, coincident, and lagging indicators. Includes charts, tables, and a glossary of terms. (Economic Education Bulletin.).

Global Economic Prospects 2000. The World Bank, Office of the Publisher. • 1999. $25.00. "..offers an in-depth analysis of the economic prospects of developing countries.." Emphasis is on the impact of recessions and financial crises. Regional statistical data is included.

ALMANACS AND YEARBOOKS

World Development Report. The World Bank, Office of the Publisher. • Annual. $50.00. Covers history, conditions, and trends relating to economic globalization and localization. Includes selected data from *World Development Indicators* for 132 countries or economies. Key indicators are provided for 78 additional countries or economies.

CD-ROM DATABASES

World Development Report [CD-ROM]. The World Bank, Office of the Publisher. • Annual. Single-user, $375.00. Network version, $750.00. CD-ROM includes the current edition of *World Development Report* and 21 previous editions.

HANDBOOKS AND MANUALS

Guide to Economic Indicators. Norman Frumkin. M. E. Sharpe, Inc. • 2000. $64.95. Third edition. Provides detailed descriptions and sources of 50 economic indicators.

Guide to Everyday Economic Statistics. Gary E. Clayton and Martin G. Giesbrecht. McGraw-Hill. • 1997. $14.38. Fourth edition. Contains clear explanations of the commonly used economic indicators.

Investor's Guide to Economic Indicators. Charles R. Nelson. John Wiley and Sons, Inc. • 1989. $17.95.

INTERNET DATABASES

BanxQuote Banking, Mortgage, and Finance Center. BanxQuote, Inc. Phone: 800-765-3000 or (212)643-8000 Fax: (212)643-0020 E-mail: info@banx.com • URL: http://www.banx.com • Web site quotes interest rates paid by banks around the country on various savings products, as well as rates paid by consumers for automobile loans, mortgages, credit cards, home equity loans, and personal loans. Also provided: stock quotes, indexes, stock options, futures trading data, economic indicators, and links to many other financial sites. Daily updates. Fees: Free.

Bureau of Economic Analysis (BEA). U. S. Department of Commerce, Bureau of Economic Analysis. Phone: (202)606-9900 Fax: (202)606-5310 E-mail: webmaster@bea.doc.gov • URL: http://www.bea.doc.gov • Web site includes "News Release Information" covering national, regional, and international economic estimates from the BEA. Highlights of releases appear online the same day, complete text and tables appear the next day. "Recent News Releases" section provides titles for past nine months, with links. "BEA Data and Methodology" includes "Frequently Requested NIPA Data" (national income and product accounts, such as gross domestic product and personal income). Other statistics are available. Fees: Free.

Bureau of Labor Statistics (BLS). U. S. Department of Labor, Bureau of Labor Statistics. Phone: (202)523-1092 E-mail: labstat.helpdesk@bls.gov • URL: http://www.bls.gov • Web site provides a great variety of employment, wage, price, and economic data. Some links are "Data," "Economy at a Glance," "Keyword Search of BLS Web Pages," "Regional Information," and "Other Statistical Sites." Fees: Free.

Business Week Online. McGraw-Hill. Phone: (212)512-2762 Fax: (212)512-6590 • URL: http://www.businessweek.com • Web site provides complete contents of current issue of *Business Week* plus "BW Daily" with additonal business news, financial market quotes, and corporate information from Standard & Poor's. Includes various features, such as "Banking Center" with mortgage and interest data, and "Interactive Computer Buying Guide." The "Business Week Archive" is fully searchable back to 1991. Fees: Mostly free, but full-text archive articles are $2.00 each.

Fedstats. Federal Interagency Council on Statistical Policy. Phone: (202)395-7254 • URL: http://www.fedstats.gov • Web site features an efficient search facility for full-text statistics produced by more than 70 federal agencies, including the Census Bureau, the Bureau of Economic Analysis, and the Bureau of Labor Statistics. Boolean searches can be made within one agency or for all agencies combined. Links are offered to international statistical bureaus, including the UN, IMF, OECD, UNESCO, Eurostat, and 20 individual countries. Fees: Free.

U. S. Census Bureau: The Official Statistics. U. S. Bureau of the Census. Phone: (301)763-4100 Fax: (301)763-4794 • URL: http://www.census.gov • Web site is "Your Source for Social, Demographic, and Economic Information." Contains "Current U. S. Population Count," "Current Economic Indicators," and a wide variety of data under "Other Official Statistics." Keyword searching is provided. Fees: Free.

ONLINE DATABASES

DRI U.S. Central Database. Data Products Division. • Provides more than 23,000 business, financial, demographic, economic, foreign trade, and industry-related time series for the U.S. Includes national income, population, retail-wholesale trade, price indexes, labor data, housing, industrial production, banking, interest rates, money supply, etc. Time period is generally 1947 to date (some data back to 1929). Updating varies. Inquire as to online cost and availability.

EconBase: Time Series and Forecasts. WEFA, Inc. • Presents online econometric data for business conditions, economics, demographics, industry, finance, employment, household income, interest rates, prices, etc. Includes two-year forecasts for a wide range of economic indicators. Time span is 1948 to date, with monthly updates. Inquire as to online cost and availability.

OECD Main Economic Indicators. Organization for Economic Cooperation and Development. • International statistics provided by OECD, 1960 to date. Monthly updates. Inquire as to online cost and availability.

PERIODICALS AND NEWSLETTERS

Financial Times Currency Forecaster: Consensus Forecasts of the Worldwide Currency and Economic Outlook. Capitol Publications, Inc. • Monthly. $695.00 per year. Newsletter. Provides forecasts of foreign currency exchange rates and economic conditions. Supplement available: *Mid-Month Global Financial Report.*

Research Reports. American Institute for Economic Research. • Semimonthly. $59.00 per year. Newsletter. Alternate issues include charts of "Primary Leading Indicators," "Primary Roughly

Coincident Indicators," and "Primary Lagging Indicators," as issued by The Conference Board (formerly provided by the U. S. Department of Commerce).

RESEARCH CENTERS AND INSTITUTES

Conference Board, Inc. 845 Third Ave., New York, NY 10022. Phone: (212)759-0900 Fax: (212)980-7014 E-mail: richard.cavanaugh@conference-board.org • URL: http://www.conference-board.org.

STATISTICS SOURCES

The AIER Chart Book. AIER Research Staff. American Institute for Economic Research. • Annual. $3.00. A compact compilation of long-range charts ("Purchasing Power of the Dollar," for example, goes back to 1780) covering various aspects of the U. S. economy. Includes inflation, interest rates, debt, gold, taxation, stock prices, etc. (Economic Education Bulletin.).

Business Cycle Indicators. Conference Board, Inc. • Monthly. $120.00 per year. Contains detailed business and economic statistics in tables that were formerly published by the U. S. Department of Commerce in *Survey of Current Business*, and before that, in the discontinued *Business Conditions Digest*. Includes composite indexes of leading economic indicators, coincident indicators, and lagging indicators.

Business Statistics of the United States. Courtenay M. Slater, editor. Bernan Associates. • 1999. $74.00. Fifth edition. Based on *Business Statistics*, formerly issue by the Bureau of Economic Analysis, U. S. Department of Commerce. Provides basic data for a wide variety of U. S. industries, services, and economic indicators. Most statistics are shown annually for 29 years and monthly for the most recent four years.

Country Outlooks. Bank of America, World Information Services, Dept. 3015. • Looseleaf. $495.00 per year. Covers 30 major countries, with each country updated twice a year (60 issues per year). Provides detailed economic data and financial forecasts, including tables of key economic indicators.

Country Profile: Annual Survey of Political and Economic Background. Economist Intelligence Unit. • Annual. $225.00 per country or country group. Contains statistical tables "showing the last 6 year run of macro-economic indicators, and an overview of a country's politics, economy and industry." Covers 180 countries in 115 annual editions.

Economic and Budget Outlook: Fiscal Years 2000-2009. Available from U. S. Government Printing Office. • 1999. $15.00. Issued by the Congressional Budget Office (http://www.cbo.gov). Contains CBO economic projections and federal budget projections annually to 2009 in billions of dollars. An appendix contains "Historical Budget Data" annually from 1962 to 1998, including revenues, outlays, deficits, surpluses, and debt held by the public.

Economic Indicators. Council of Economic Advisors, Executive Office of the President. Available from U.S. Government Printing Office. • Monthly. $55.00 per year.

Economic Indicators Handbook: Time Series, Conversions, Documentation. The Gale Group. • 2000. $195.00. Sixth edition. Provides data for about 175 U. S. economic indicators, such as the consumer price index (CPI), gross national product (GNP), and the rate of inflation. Values for series are given since inception, in both original form and adjusted for inflation. A bibliography of sources is included.

Leading Economic Indicators and Related Composite Indexes. Conference Board, Inc. • Monthly. $24.00 per year. Shows monthly changes in the composite indexes of leading, coincident, and lagging economic indicators, formerly computed by the U. S. Department of Commerce. Tables present monthly data for up to 10 years, with a one-page line chart covering 18 years. (The Conference Board News.).

Main Economic Indicators. OECD Publication and Information Center. • Monthly. $450.00 per year. "The essential source of timely statistics for OECD member countries." Includes a wide variety of business, economic, and industrial data for the 29 OECD nations.

Main Economic Indicators: Historical Statistics. OECD Publications and Information Center. • Annual. $50.00.

Short-Term Economic Indicators: Transition Economies. OECD Publications and Information Center. • Quarterly. Presents annual, quarterly, and monthly economic indicators for the developing countries of Eastern Europe and the New Independent States.

Survey of Current Business. Available from U. S. Government Printing Office. • Monthly. $49.00 per year. Issued by Bureau of Economic Analysis, U. S. Department of Commerce. Presents a wide variety of business and economic data.

World Bank Atlas. The World Bank, Office of the Publisher. • Annual. Price on application. Contains "color maps, charts, and graphs representing the main social, economic, and environmental indicators for 209 countries and territories" (publisher).

World Development Indicators. World Bank, The Office of the Publisher. • Annual. $60.00. Provides data and information on the people, economy, environment, and markets of 148 countries. Emphasis is on statistics relating to major development issues.

TRADE/PROFESSIONAL ASSOCIATIONS

Institute for Economic Analysis. c/o Richard Atlee, P.O. Box 1510, Southwest Harbor, ME 04679-1510. Phone: (207)244-9590 Fax: (301)588-4569.

ECONOMIC PLANNING

See: ECONOMIC POLICY

ECONOMIC POLICY

See also: ECONOMIC DEVELOPMENT; ECONOMICS

GENERAL WORKS

Age of Diminished Expectations: U. S. Economic Policy in the 1990s. Paul Krugman. MIT Press. • 1997. $30.00. Third edition. States that the big problem is slow growth in productivity.

Economic Policy, Financial Markets, and Economic Growth. Benjamin Zycher and Lewis C. Solmon, editors. HarperCollins Publishers. • 1993. $63.00.

Money, Banking, and the Economy. Thomas Mayer and others. W. W. Norton & Co., Inc. • 1996. $85.50. Sixth edition.

Setting National Priorities: Budget Choices for the Next Century. Robert D. Reischauer and Henry J. Aaron, editors. Brookings Institution Press. • 1996. $42.95. Contains discussions of the federal budget, economic policy, and government spending policy.

ABSTRACTS AND INDEXES

Social Sciences Index. H. W. Wilson Co. • Quarterly, with annual cumulation. Service basis for print edition; CD-ROM edition, $1,495 per year. Indexes more than 400 periodicals covering economics, environmental policy, government, insurance, labor, health care policy, plannning, public administration, public welfare, urban studies, women's issues, criminology, and related topics.

CD-ROM DATABASES

Social Science Source. EBSCO Publishing. • Monthly. $1,495.00 per year. Provides CD-ROM citations and abstracts to social science articles in more than 600 periodicals, with full text from 125 periodicals. Covers economics, political science, public policy, international relations, psychology, and other topics. Time period is most recent five years.

Social Sciences Citation Index: Compact Disc Edition with Abstracts. Institute for Scientific Information. • Quarterly. Provides CD-ROM indexing and abstracting of "significant articles" from 1,400 social science journals worldwide, with additional selections from 3,200 other journals, 1986 to date. Includes economics, business, finance, management, communications, demographics, information and library science, political science, sociology, and many other subjects.

WILSONDISC: Wilson Social Sciences Abstracts. H. W. Wilson Co. • Monthly. Including unlimited online access to *Social Sciences Index* through WILSONLINE. Provides CD-ROM indexing from 1983 and abstracting from 1994 of more than 400 periodicals covering economics, area studies, community health, public administration, public welfare, urban studies, and many other topics related to the social sciences.

ENCYCLOPEDIAS AND DICTIONARIES

Blackwell Encyclopedic Dictionary of Managerial Economics. Robert McAuliffe, editor. Blackwell Publishers. • 1997. $105.95. The editor is associated with Boston College. Contains definitions of key terms combined with longer articles written by various U. S. and foreign business educators. Includes bibliographies and index. *Blackwell Encyclopedia of Management Series.*

Dictionary of Economics. Jae K. Shim and Joel G. Siegel. John Wiley and Sons, Inc. • 1995. $79.95. Contains 2,200 definitions of economic terms. Includes graphs, charts, tables, and economic formulas. (Business Dictionary Series).

INTERNET DATABASES

Wall Street Journal Interactive Edition. Dow Jones & Co., Inc. Phone: 800-369-2834 or (212)416-2000 Fax: (212)416-2658 E-mail: inquiries@interactive.wsj.com • URL: http://www.wsj.com • Fee-based Web site providing online searching of worldwide information from the *The Wall Street Journal*. Includes "Company Snapshots," "The Journal's Greatest Hits," "Index to Market Data," "14-Day Searchable Archive," "Journal Links," etc. Financial price quotes are available. Fees: $49.00 per year; $29.00 per year to print subscribers.

ONLINE DATABASES

Wilson Social Sciences Abstracts Online. H. W. Wilson Co. • Provides online abstracting and indexing of more than 415 periodicals covering area studies, community health, public administration, public welfare, urban studies, and many other social science topics. Time period is 1994 to date for abstracts and 1983 to date for indexing, with updates monthly. Inquire as to online cost and availability.

PERIODICALS AND NEWSLETTERS

Blue Chip Financial Forecasts: What Top Analysts are Saying About U. S. and Foreign Interest Rates, Monetary Policy, Inflation, and Economic Growth. Aspen Publishers, Inc. • Monthly. $654.00 per year. Newsletter. Gives forecasts about a year in advance for interest rates, inflation, currency exchange rates, monetary policy, and economic growth rates.

Challenge: The Magazine of Economic Affairs. M. E. Sharpe, Inc. • Bimonthly. Individuals, $45.00 per year; institutions, $146.00 per year. A nontechnical journal on current economic policy and economic trends.

International Monetary Fund Staff Papers. International Monetary Fund, Publication Services. • Quarterly. Individuals, $56.00 per year; students, $28.00 per year. Contains studies by IMF staff members on balance of payments, foreign exchange, fiscal policy, and related topics.

The Wall Street Journal. Dow Jones & Co., Inc. • Daily. $175.00 per year. Covers news and trends relating to business, industry, finance, the economy, and international commerce. Provides extensive price and other data for the securities, commodity, options, futures, foreign exchange, and money markets.

RESEARCH CENTERS AND INSTITUTES

Bradley Policy Research Center. University of Rochester, William E. Simon Graduate School of Business Administration, Rochester, NY 14627. Phone: (716)275-0834 Fax: (716)461-3309 E-mail: mullen@ssb.rochester.edu • Corporate control and corporate takeovers are among the research areas covered.

Brookings Institution. 1775 Massachusetts Ave., N.W., Washington, DC 20036-2188. Phone: (202)797-6000 Fax: (202)797-6004 E-mail: estinger@brookings.edu • URL: http://www.brookings.edu/.

TRADE/PROFESSIONAL ASSOCIATIONS

Hudson Institute. Herman Kahn Center, 5395 Emerson Way, Indianapolis, IN 46226. Phone: 800-483-7660 or (317)545-1000 Fax: (317)545-9639 E-mail: info@hudson.org • URL: http://www.hudson.org.

OTHER SOURCES

Factiva. Dow Jones Reuters Business Interactive, LLC. • Fee-based Web site provides "global news and business information through Web sites and content integration solutions." Includes Dow Jones and Reuters newswires, The Wall Street Journal, and more than 7,000 other sources of current news, historical articles, market research reports, and investment analysis. Content includes 96 major U. S. newspapers, 900 non-English sources, trade publications, media transcripts, country profiles, news photos, etc.

Nexis.com. Lexis-Nexis Group. • Fee-based Web site offers searching of about 2.8 billion documents in some 30,000 news, business, and legal information sources. Features include a subject directory covering 1,200 topics in 34 categories and a Company Dossier containing information on more than 500,000 public and private companies. Boolean searching is offered.

ECONOMIC RESEARCH

See also: BUREAUS OF BUSINESS RESEARCH; BUSINESS RESEARCH

ABSTRACTS AND INDEXES

Social Sciences Index. H. W. Wilson Co. • Quarterly, with annual cumulation. Service basis for print edition; CD-ROM edition, $1,495 per year. Indexes more than 400 periodicals covering economics, environmental policy, government, insurance, labor, health care policy, plannning, public administration, public welfare, urban studies, women's issues, criminology, and related topics.

ALMANACS AND YEARBOOKS

Research in Experimental Economics. JAI Press, Inc. • Irregular.$78.50. Supplement available *An Experiment in Non-Cooperative Oligopoly.*

Research in Law and Economics: A Research Annual. Richard O. Zerbe. JAI Press, Inc. • Irregular.$78.50. Supplement available:*Economics of Nonproprietary Organizations.*

BIBLIOGRAPHIES

Bibliographic Guide to Business and Economics. Available from The Gale Group. • Annual. $795.00. Three volumes. Published by G. K. Hall & Co. Lists business and economics publications cataloged by the New York Public Library and the Library of Congress.

Bibliographic Guide to Conference Publications. Available from The Gale Group. • Annual. $545.00. Two volumes. Published by G. K. Hall & Co., Lists a wide range of conference publications cataloged by the New York Public Library and the Library of Congress.

Business Information Sources. Lorna M. Daniells. California Princeton Fulfillment Services. • 1993. $42.50. Third revised edition. Basic business sources, with discussion and full annotations.

CD-ROM DATABASES

Profiles in Business and Management: An International Directory of Scholars and Their Research [CD-ROM]. Harvard Business School Publishing. • Annual. $595.00 per year. Fully searchable CD-ROM version of two-volume printed directory. Contains bibliographic and biographical information for over 5600 business and management experts active in 21 subject areas. Formerly *International Directory of Business and Management Scholars.*

Social Science Source. EBSCO Publishing. • Monthly. $1,495.00 per year. Provides CD-ROM citations and abstracts to social science articles in more than 600 periodicals, with full text from 125 periodicals. Covers economics, political science, public policy, international relations, psychology, and other topics. Time period is most recent five years.

Social Sciences Citation Index: Compact Disc Edition with Abstracts. Institute for Scientific Information. • Quarterly. Provides CD-ROM indexing and abstracting of "significant articles" from 1,400 social science journals worldwide, with additional selections from 3,200 other journals, 1986 to date. Includes economics, business, finance, management, communications, demographics, information and library science, political science, sociology, and many other subjects.

WILSONDISC: Wilson Social Sciences Abstracts. H. W. Wilson Co. • Monthly. Including unlimited online access to *Social Sciences Index* through WILSONLINE. Provides CD-ROM indexing from 1983 and abstracting from 1994 of more than 400 periodicals covering economics, area studies, community health, public administration, public welfare, urban studies, and many other topics related to the social sciences.

DIRECTORIES

Association for University Business and Economic Research Membership Directory. Association for University Business and Economic Research. • Annual. $10.00. Member institutions in the United States and abroad with centers, bureaus, departments, etc., concerned with business and economic research.

Profiles in Business and Management: An International Directory of Scholars and Their Research Version 2.0. Claudia Bruce, editor. Harvard Business School Press. • 1996. $495.00. Two volumes. Provides backgrounds, publications, and current research projects of more than 5,600 business and management experts.

HANDBOOKS AND MANUALS

Using Government Information Sources, Print and Electronic. Jean L. Sears and Marilyn K. Moody. Oryx Press. • 1994. $115.00. Second edition. Contains detailed information in four sections on subject searches, agency searches, statistical searches, and special techniques for searching. Appendixes give selected agency and publisher addresses, telephone numbers, and computer communications numbers.

ONLINE DATABASES

Current Contents Connect. Institute for Scientific Information. • Provides online abstracts of articles listed in the tables of contents of about 7,500 journals. Coverage is very broad, including science, social science, life science, technology, engineering, industry, agriculture, the environment, economics, and arts and humanities. Time period is two years, with weekly updates. Inquire as to online cost and availability.

Wilson Social Sciences Abstracts Online. H. W. Wilson Co. • Provides online abstracting and indexing of more than 415 periodicals covering area studies, community health, public administration, public welfare, urban studies, and many other social science topics. Time period is 1994 to date for abstracts and 1983 to date for indexing, with updates monthly. Inquire as to online cost and availability.

PERIODICALS AND NEWSLETTERS

Applied Economics Letters. Routledge Journals. • Monthly. $554.00 per year. Provides short accounts of new, original research in practical economics. Supplement to *Applied Economics.*

Mathematical Finance: An International Journal of Mathematics, Statistics, and Financial Economics. Blackwell Publishers. • Quarterly. $342.00 per year. Covers the use of sophisticated mathematical tools in financial research and practice.

Research Reports. American Institute for Economic Research. • Semimonthly. $59.00 per year. Newsletter. Alternate issues include charts of "Primary Leading Indicators," "Primary Roughly Coincident Indicators," and "Primary Lagging Indicators," as issued by The Conference Board (formerly provided by the U. S. Department of Commerce).

Review of Financial Economics. University of New Orleans,Lake Front, College of Business Administration, Busine. JAI Press Inc. • Three times a year. $266.00 per year. Formerly *Review of Business and Economic Research.*

RESEARCH CENTERS AND INSTITUTES

American Institute for Economic Research. P.O. Box 1000, Great Barrington, MA 01230. Phone: (413)528-1216 Fax: (413)528-0103 E-mail: info@aier.org • URL: http://www.aier.org.

Brookings Institution. 1775 Massachusetts Ave., N.W., Washington, DC 20036-2188. Phone: (202)797-6000 Fax: (202)797-6004 E-mail: estinger@brookings.edu • URL: http://www.brookings.edu/.

Bureau of Economic and Business Research. University of Illinois at Urbana-Champaign, 1206 S. Sixth St., Champaign, IL 61820. Phone: (217)333-2330 Fax: (217)244-7410 E-mail: g-oldman@uiuc.edu • URL: http://www.cba.uiuc.edu/research.

Bureau of Economic Research. Rutgers University. New Jersy Hall, 75 Hamilton St., New Brunswick, NJ 08903-5055. Phone: (732)932-7891 Fax: (732)932-7416 E-mail: berkowi@rci.rutgers.edu • URL: http://www.economic.rutgers.edu.

Cowles Foundation for Research in Economics. Yale University. 30 Hillhouse Ave., New Haven, CT 06520-8281. Phone: (203)432-3704 Fax: (203)432-

6167 E-mail: john.geanakoplos@yale.edu • URL: http://www.econ.yale.edu.

Institute for Economic Research. University of Washington. P.O. Box 353330, Seattle, WA 98195. Phone: (206)543-5945 Fax: (206)685-7477 • URL: http://www.econ.washington.edu/.

Institute of Business and Economic Research. University of California at Berkeley, School of Business, F502 Haas, Berkeley, CA 94720-1922. Phone: (510)642-1922 Fax: (510)642-5018 E-mail: barde@uclink4.berkeley.edu • URL: http://www.haas.berkeley.edu/groups/iber • Research fields are business administration, economics, finance, real estate, and international development.

National Bureau of Economic Research, Inc. 1050 Massachusetts Ave., Cambridge, MA 02138-5398. Phone: (617)868-3900 Fax: (617)868-2742 E-mail: msfeldst@nber.org • URL: http://www.nber.org.

National Opinion Research Center. 1155 E. 60th St., Chicago, IL 60637. Phone: (773)753-7500 Fax: (773)753-7886 E-mail: cloud.patricia@norcmail.uchicago.edu • URL: http://www.norc.uchicago.edu.

TRADE/PROFESSIONAL ASSOCIATIONS

National Association for Business Economics. 1233 20th St., N.W., Suite 505, Washington, DC 20036. Phone: (202)463-6223 Fax: (202)463-6239 E-mail: nabe@nabe.com • URL: http://www.nabe.com.

ECONOMIC RESPONSIBILITY

See: SOCIAL RESPONSIBILITY

ECONOMIC STATISTICS

See also: BUSINESS STATISTICS; ECONOMETRICS; ECONOMICS; MARKET STATISTICS; STATISTICAL METHODS; STATISTICS SOURCES

GENERAL WORKS

Business Statistics for Management and Economics. Wayne W. Daniel and James C. Terrell. Houghton Mifflin Co. • 2000. $19.47. Seventh edition.

ABSTRACTS AND INDEXES

Current Index to Statistics: Applications, Methods, and Theory. American Statistical Association. • Annual. Price on application. An index to journal articles on statistical applications and methodology.

Social Sciences Index. H. W. Wilson Co. • Quarterly, with annual cumulation. Service basis for print edition; CD-ROM edition, $1,495 per year. Indexes more than 400 periodicals covering economics, environmental policy, government, insurance, labor, health care policy, plannning, public administration, public welfare, urban studies, women's issues, criminology, and related topics.

ALMANACS AND YEARBOOKS

Irwin Business and Investment Almanac, 1996. Summer N. Levine and Caroline Levine. McGraw-Hill Professional. • 1995. $75.00. A review of last year's business activity. Covers a wide variety of business and economic data: stock market statistics, industrial information, commodity futures information, art market trends, comparative living costs for U. S. metropolitan areas, foreign stock market data, etc. Formerly *Business One Irwin Business and Investment Almanac.*

BIBLIOGRAPHIES

Global Data Locator. George T. Kurian. Bernan Associates. • 1997. $89.00. Provides detailed descriptions of international statistical sourcebooks and electronic databases. Covers a wide variety of trade, economic, and demographic topics.

Statistics Sources: A Subject Guide to Data on Industrial, Business, Social, Educational, Financial and Other Topics for the U. S. and Selected Foreign Countries. The Gale Group. • 2000. $475.00. 25th edition. Two volumes. Lists sources of statistical information for more than 20,000 topics.

World Directory of Non-Official Statistical Sources. Gale Group, Inc. • 2001. $590.00. Provides detailed descriptions of more than 4,000 regularly published, non-governmental statistics sources. Includes surveys, studies, market research reports, trade journals, databank compilations, and other print sources. Coverage is international, with four indexes.

CD-ROM DATABASES

National Trade Data Bank: The Export Connection. U. S. Department of Commerce. • Monthly. $575.00 per year. Provides over 150,000 trade-related data series on CD-ROM. Includes full text of many government publications. Specific data is included on national income, labor, price indexes, foreign exchange, technical standards, and international markets. Website address is http://www.stat-usa.gov/.

Social Science Source. EBSCO Publishing. • Monthly. $1,495.00 per year. Provides CD-ROM citations and abstracts to social science articles in more than 600 periodicals, with full text from 125 periodicals. Covers economics, political science, public policy, international relations, psychology, and other topics. Time period is most recent five years.

Social Sciences Citation Index: Compact Disc Edition with Abstracts. Institute for Scientific Information. • Quarterly. Provides CD-ROM indexing and abstracting of "significant articles" from 1,400 social science journals worldwide, with additional selections from 3,200 other journals, 1986 to date. Includes economics, business, finance, management, communications, demographics, information and library science, political science, sociology, and many other subjects.

Statistical Abstract of the United States on CD-ROM. Hoover's, Inc. • Annual. $49.95. Provides all statistics from official print version, plus expanded historical data, greater detail, and keyword searching features.

Statistical Masterfile. Congressional Information Service. • Quarterly. Price varies. Provides CD-ROM versions of *American Statistics Index, Index to International Statistics,* and *Statistical Reference Index.* Contains indexing and abstracting of a wide variety of published statistics sources, both governmental and private.

WILSONDISC: Wilson Social Sciences Abstracts. H. W. Wilson Co. • Monthly. Including unlimited online access to *Social Sciences Index* through WILSONLINE. Provides CD-ROM indexing from 1983 and abstracting from 1994 of more than 400 periodicals covering economics, area studies, community health, public administration, public welfare, urban studies, and many other topics related to the social sciences.

World Marketing Forecasts on CD-ROM. The Gale Group. • Annual. $2,500.00. Produced by Euromonitor. Provides detailed forecast data for the years to 2012 on CD-ROM for 54 countries in all parts of the world. Covers a wide range of social, demographic, economic, and market factors. Includes specific forecasts for many kinds of consumer products.

DIRECTORIES

The Internet Blue Pages: The Guide to Federal Government Web Sites. Information Today, Inc. • Annual. $34.95. Provides information on more than 900 Web sites used by various agencies of the federal government. Includes indexes to agencies and topics. Links to all Web sites listed are available at http://www.fedweb.com. (CyberAge Books.).

ENCYCLOPEDIAS AND DICTIONARIES

Knowledge Exchange Business Encyclopedia: Your Complete Business Advisor. Lorraine Spurge, editor. Knowledge Exchange LLC. • 1997. $45.00. Provides definitions of business terms and financial expressions, profiles of leading industries, tables of economic statistics, biographies of business leaders, and other business information. Includes "A Chronology of Business from 3000 B.C. Through 1995." Contains illustrations and three indexes.

HANDBOOKS AND MANUALS

Finding Statistics Online: How to Locate the Elusive Numbers You Need. Paula Berinstein. Information Today, Inc. • 1998. $29.95. Provides advice on efficient searching when looking for statistical data on the World Wide Web or from commercial online services and database producers. (CyberAge Books.).

Guide to Everyday Economic Statistics. Gary E. Clayton and Martin G. Giesbrecht. McGraw-Hill. • 1997. $14.38. Fourth edition. Contains clear explanations of the commonly used economic indicators.

INTERNET DATABASES

The Dismal Scientist. Dismal Sciences, Inc. Phone: (610)241-1000 Fax: (610)696-3836 E-mail: webmaster@dismal.com • URL: http://www.dismal.com • Web site contains a wide variety of economic data and rankings. A search feature provides detailed economic profiles of local areas by ZIP code. Major divisions of the site are Economy, Data, Thoughts, Forecasts, and Toolkit, with many specially written articles and currrent analysis by "recognized economists." Fees: Free.

Fedstats. Federal Interagency Council on Statistical Policy. Phone: (202)395-7254 • URL: http://www.fedstats.gov • Web site features an efficient search facility for full-text statistics produced by more than 70 federal agencies, including the Census Bureau, the Bureau of Economic Analysis, and the Bureau of Labor Statistics. Boolean searches can be made within one agency or for all agencies combined. Links are offered to international statistical bureaus, including the UN, IMF, OECD, UNESCO, Eurostat, and 20 individual countries. Fees: Free.

ONLINE DATABASES

ASI (American Statistics Index). Congressional Information Service. • A comprehensive online index, with abstracts, to the statistical publications of over 500 federal government offices and agencies from 1973 to date. A wide variety of information is indexed, with emphasis on demographic, economic, social, and natural resources data. Updated monthly. Inquire as to online cost and availability.

DRI U.S. Central Database. Data Products Division. • Provides more than 23,000 business, financial, demographic, economic, foreign trade, and industry-related time series for the U.S. Includes national income, population, retail-wholesale trade, price indexes, labor data, housing, industrial production, banking, interest rates, money supply, etc. Time period is generally 1947 to date (some data back to 1929). Updating varies. Inquire as to online cost and availability.

Euromonitor Market Research. Euromonitor International. • Provides the complete text online of Euromonitor market analysis reports. Covers consumer goods market research data for all major countries, with emphasis on specific product categories. Time period is current. Continuous updating. Inquire as to online cost and availability.

OECD Main Economic Indicators. Organization for Economic Cooperation and Development. • International statistics provided by OECD, 1960 to date. Monthly updates. Inquire as to online cost and availability.

Wilson Social Sciences Abstracts Online. H. W. Wilson Co. • Provides online abstracting and indexing of more than 415 periodicals covering area studies, community health, public administration, public welfare, urban studies, and many other social science topics. Time period is 1994 to date for abstracts and 1983 to date for indexing, with updates monthly. Inquire as to online cost and availability.

PERIODICALS AND NEWSLETTERS

Journal of Business and Economic Statistics. American Statistical Association. • Quarterly. Libraries, $90.00 per year. Emphasis is on statistical measurement and applications for business and economics.

STATISTICS SOURCES

American Business Climate and Economic Profiles. The Gale Group. • 1993. $135.00. Provides business, industrial, demographic, and economic figures for all states and 300 metropolitan areas. Includes production, taxation, population, growth rates, labor force data, incomes, total sales, etc.

Consumer Canada 1996. Available from The Gale Group. • 1996. $750.00. Published by Euromonitor. Provides consumer market, socioeconomic, and demographic data for Canada. Includes consumer market size (volume and value) for many specific kinds of products.

Consumer International 2000/2001. Available from The Gale Group. • 1998. $1,190.00. Seventh edition. Published by Euromonitor. Contains extensive consumer market, economic, and demographic data for 27 major, non-European countries, including the U. S. and Canada. Includes consumer market size (volume and value) for 150 product types in 14 categories (food, clothing, automobiles, cosmetics, appliances, etc.).

Country Data Forecasts. Bank of America, World Information Services, Dept. 3015. • Looseleaf, with semiannual updates. $495.00 per year. Provides detailed statistical tables for 80 countries, showing historical data and five-year forecasts of 23 key economic series. Includes population, inflation figures, debt, per capita income, foreign trade, exchange rates, and other data.

County and City Extra: Annual Metro, City and County Data Book. Mark Littman and Deirdre A. Gaquin. Bernan Press. • 1999. $109.00. Updates and augments data published irregularly in print form by the U. S. Census Bureau in *County and City Data Book.* Covers "every state, county, metropolitan area, and congressional district in the United States, as well as all U. S. cities with a 1990 population of 25,000 or more." Contains a wide range tic maps.

Current Population Reports: Household Economic Studies, Series P-70. Available from U. S. Government Printing Office. • Irregular. $16.00 per year. Issued by the U.S. Bureau of the Census (http://www.census.gov). Each issue covers a special topic relating to household socioeconomic characteristics.

Economic Indicators. Council of Economic Advisors, Executive Office of the President. Available from U.S. Government Printing Office. • Monthly. $55.00 per year.

Economic Report of the President: Together with the Annual Report of the Council of Economic Advisors. Available from U. S. Government Printing Office. • Annual. $29.00. Includes about 130 pages of "Statistical Tables Relating to Income, Employment, and Production." Tables cover national income, employment, wages, productivity, manufacturing, prices, credit, finance (public and private), corporate profits, and foreign trade.

European Marketing Forecasts 2001. Available from The Gale Group. • 2000. $1,190.00. Third edition. Published by Euromonitor. Contains demographic, economic, and market forecasts for the countries of Europe to the year 2010. Forecasts include market-size data for 15 consumer product sectors (food, clothing, automobiles, consumer electronics, etc.).

Handbook of International Economic Statistics. Available from National Technical Information Service. • Annual. $40.00. Prepared by U. S. Central Intelligence Agency. Provides basic statistics for comparing worldwide economic performance, with an emphasis on Europe, including Eastern Europe.

International Marketing Forecasts 2001. Available from The Gale Group. • 2000. $1,090.00. Third edition. Published by Euromonitor. Contains demographic, economic, and market forecasts to the year 2010 for major, non-European countries, including the U. S. and Canada. Forecasts include market-size data for 15 consumer product sectors, such as food, clothing, and automobiles.

Main Economic Indicators. OECD Publication and Information Center. • Monthly. $450.00 per year. "The essential source of timely statistics for OECD member countries." Includes a wide variety of business, economic, and industrial data for the 29 OECD nations.

Main Economic Indicators: Historical Statistics. OECD Publications and Information Center. • Annual. $50.00.

Metropolitan Life Insurance Co. Statistical Bulletin SB. Metropolitan Life Insurance Co. • Quarterly. Individuals, $50.00 per year. Covers a wide range of social, economic and demographic health concerns.

Monthly Bulletin of Statistics. United Nations Publications. • Monthly. $295.00 per year. Provides current data for about 200 countries on a wide variety of economic, industrial, and demographic subjects. Compiled by United Nations Statistical Office.

OECD Economic Outlook. OECD Publications and Information Center. • Semiannual. $95.00 per year. Contains a wide range of economic and monetary data relating to the member countries of the Organization for Economic Cooperation and Development. Includes about 100 statistical tables and graphs, with 24-month forecasts for each of the OECD countries. Provides extensive review and analysis of recent economic trends.

OECD Economic Survey of the United States. OECD Publications and Information Center. • Annual. $30.00.

Places, Towns, and Townships, 1998. Deirdre A. Gaquin and Richard W. Dodge, editors. Bernan Press. • 1997. $89.00. Second edition. Presents demographic and economic statistics from the U. S. Census Bureau and other government sources for places, cities, towns, villages, census designated places, and minor civil divisions. Contains more than 60 data categories.

Social Statistics of the United States. Mark S. Littman, editor. Bernan Press. • 2000. $65.00. Includes statistical data on population growth, labor force, occupations, environmental trends, leisure time use, income, poverty, taxes, and other economic or demographic topics.

Standard & Poor's Industry Surveys. Standard & Poor's. • Semiannual. $1,800.00. Two looseleaf volumes. Includes monthly supplements. Provides detailed, individual surveys of 52 major industry groups. Each survey is revised on a semiannual basis. Also includes "Monthly Investment Review" (industry group investment analysis) and monthly "Trends & Projections" (economic analysis).

State and Metropolitan Area Data Book. Available from U. S. Government Printing Office. • 1998. $31.00. Issued by the U. S. Bureau of the Census. Presents a wide variety of statistical data for U. S. regions, states, counties, metropolitan areas, and central cities, with ranking tables. Time period is 1970 to 1990.

Statistical Abstract of the United States. Available from U. S. Government Printing Office. • Annual. $51.00. Issued by the U. S. Bureau of the Census.

Statistical Abstract of the World. The Gale Group. • 1997. $80.00. Third edition. Provides data on a wide variety of economic, social, and political topics for about 200 countries. Arranged by country.

Statistical Forecasts of the United States. The Gale Group. • 1995. $99.00. Second edition. Provides both long-term and short-term statistical forecasts relating to basic items in the U. S.: population, employment, labor, crime, education, and health care. Data in the form of charts, graphs, and tables has been taken from a wide variety of government and private sources. Includes a subject index and an "Index of Forecast by Year.".

A Statistical Portrait of the United States: Social Conditions and Trends. Mark S. Littman, editor. Bernan Press. • 1998. $89.00. Covers "social, economic, and environmental trends in the United States over the past 25 years." Includes statistical tables, graphs, and analysis relating to such topics as population, income, poverty, wealth, labor, housing, education, healthcare, air/water quality, and government.

Statistical Yearbook. United Nations Publications. • Annual. $125.00. Contains statistics for about 200 countries on a wide variety of economic, industrial, and demographic topics. Compiled by United Nations Statistical Office.

The World Economic Factbook. Available from The Gale Group. • 2000. $450.00. Seventh edition. Published by Euromonitor. Presents key economic facts and figures for each of 200 countries, including details of chief industries, export-import trade, currency, political risk, household expenditures, and the economic situation in general.

World Economic Outlook: A Survey by the Staff of the International Monetary Fund. International Monetary Fund, Publications Services. • Semiannual. $62.00 per year. Presents international statistics combined with forecasts and analyses of the world economy. Editions available in Arabic, English, French and Spanish.

World Economic Prospects: A Planner's Guide to International Market Conditions. Available from The Gale Group. • 2000. $450.00. Second edition. Published by Euromonitor. Ranks 78 countries by specific economic characteristics, such as gross domestic product (GDP) per capita and short term growth prospects. Discusses the economic situation, prospects, and market potential of each of the countries.

World Statistics Pocketbook. United Nations Publications. • Annual. $10.00. Presents basic economic, social, and environmental indicators for about 200 countries and areas. Covers more than 50 items relating to population, economic activity, labor force, agriculture, industry, energy, trade, transportation, communication, education, tourism, and the environment. Statistical sources are noted.

TRADE/PROFESSIONAL ASSOCIATIONS

American Statistical Association. 1429 Duke St., Alexandria, VA 22314-3402. Phone: (703)684-1221

Fax: (703)684-2037 E-mail: asainfo@amstat.org • URL: http://www.amstat.org • A professional society concerned with statistical theory, methodology, and applications. Sections include Survey Research Methods, Government Statistics, and Business and Economic Statistics.

Econometric Society. Northwestern University, Dept. of Economics, Evanston, IL 60208-2600. Phone: (708)491-3615 • URL: http://www.econometricsociety.org.es.

Institute for Econometric Research. 2200 S.W. 10th St., Deerfield, FL 33442. Phone: 800-499-0066 or (954)421-1000 Fax: (954)421-8200 • URL: http://www.mfmag.com.

ECONOMICS

See also: BUSINESS RESEARCH; ECONOMETRICS

GENERAL WORKS

Behind the Veil of Economics: Essays in the Worldly Philosophy. Robert L. Heilbroner. W. W. Norton Co., Inc. • 1989. $7.95.

Economic History of the United States. M.E. Sharpe, Inc. • 1977. Seven volumes.

Economics. Paul A. Samuelson and William D. Nordhaus. McGraw-Hill. • 2000. $68.00. 17th edition.

Economics Explained: Everything You Need to Know About How the Economy Works and Where It's Going. Robert L. Heilbroner. Simon & Schuster Trade. • 1994. $12.00. Fourth revised edition.

Economics on Trial: Lies, Myths, and Realities. Mark Skousen. McGraw-Hill. • 1993. $17.50.

Economics: Principles, Problems, and Policies. Campbell R. McConnell and Stanley Lee Brue. McGraw-Hill. • 1998. $92.50. 13th edition.

Economics Today. Roger L. Miller. Addison-Wesley Longman, Inc. • 2000. 11th edition. Price on application.

Fundamentals of Managerial Economics. James L. and Mark Hirschey Pappas. Dryden Press. • 1997. $97.50. Sixth edition.

Managerial Economics. James R. McGuigan. South-Western Publishing Co. • 1998. $90.95. Eighth edition. (HT-Mangerial Economics Series).

Managerial Economics: Analysis, Problems, Cases. Dale Truett and Lila Truett. South-Western College Publishing. • 1995. $75.25. Fifth edition. (Principles of Economics Series).

Managerial Economics and Business Strategy. Michael R. Baye. McGraw-Hill Professional. • 2000. Third edition. Price on application.

Managerial Economics: Applied Microeconomics for Decision Making. Charles S. Maurice and Christopher R. Thomas. McGraw-Hill Higher Education. • 1994. $69.75. Fifth edition.

Modern Economics. Jan S. Hogendorn. Prentice Hall. • 1994. $75.00.

Principles of Economics. Richard G. Lipsey and K. Alec Chrystal. Oxford University Press, Inc. • 1999. Ninth edition. Price on application.

Principles of Macroeconomics. Gerry F. Welch. Harcourt Brace College Publishers. • 1998. $25.00.

Understanding Economics Today. Gary M. Walton and Frank C. Wykoff. McGraw-Hill Professional. • 2001. Seventh edition. Price on application.

The Witch Doctor of Wall Street: A Noted Financial Expert Guides You Through Today's Voodoo Economics. Robert H. Parks. Prometheus Books. • 1996. $25.95. The author, a professor of finance at Pace University, discusses "Practice and Malpractice" in relation to the following: business forecasting, economic theory, interest rates, monetary policy, the stock market, and corporate finance. Includes "A Short Primer on Derivatives," as an appendix.

ABSTRACTS AND INDEXES

Index of Economic Articles in Journals and Collective Volumes. American Economic Association. • Irregular. $160.00.

NTIS Alerts: Business & Economics. National Technical Information Service.

Social Sciences Citation Index. Institute for Scientific Information. • Three times a year. $6,900 per year. Annual cumulation. Includes *Source Index, Citation Index, Permuterm Subject Index,* and *Corporate Index.*

Social Sciences Index. H. W. Wilson Co. • Quarterly, with annual cumulation. Service basis for print edition; CD-ROM edition, $1,495 per year. Indexes more than 400 periodicals covering economics, environmental policy, government, insurance, labor, health care policy, plannning, public administration, public welfare, urban studies, women's issues, criminology, and related topics.

BIBLIOGRAPHIES

Bibliographic Guide to Business and Economics. Available from The Gale Group. • Annual. $795.00. Three volumes. Published by G. K. Hall & Co. Lists business and economics publications cataloged by the New York Public Library and the Library of Congress.

Bibliographic Guide to Conference Publications. Available from The Gale Group. • Annual. $545.00. Two volumes. Published by G. K. Hall & Co., Lists a wide range of conference publications cataloged by the New York Public Library and the Library of Congress.

Business Library Review: An International Journal. International Publishers Distributor. • Quarterly. Academic institutions, $318.00 per year;corporations, $501.00 per year.Incorporates *The Wall Street Review of Books* and *Economics and Business: An Annotated Bibliography.* Publishes scholarly reviews of books on a wide variety of topics in business, economics, and finance. Text in French.

International Bibliography of the Social Sciences: Economics. British Library of Political and Economic Science. Routledge. • Annual. $230.00.

CD-ROM DATABASES

Business Source Plus. EBSCO Information Services. • Monthly. $1,495.00 per year. Provides CD-ROM citations and abstracts to articles in about 650 business periodicals and newspapers, including *The Wall Street Journal.* Full text is provided from 200 selected periodicals. Covers accounting, communications, economics, finance, management, marketing, and other business subjects.

EconLit. Available from SilverPlatter Information, Inc. • Monthly. Single-user, $1,600.00 per year. Multi-user, $2,400.00 per year. Provides CD-ROM citations, with abstracts, to articles from more than 500 economics journals. Time period is 1969 to date. Produced by the American Economic Association.

Social Science Source. EBSCO Publishing. • Monthly. $1,495.00 per year. Provides CD-ROM citations and abstracts to social science articles in more than 600 periodicals, with full text from 125 periodicals. Covers economics, political science, public policy, international relations, psychology, and other topics. Time period is most recent five years.

Social Sciences Citation Index: Compact Disc Edition. Institute for Scientific Information. • Quarterly. Provides CD-ROM indexing of the world's social sciences literature, including economics, business, finance, management, communications, demographics, information and library science, political science, sociology, etc. Corresponds to online *Social Scisearch* and printed *Social Sciences Citation Index.*

Social Sciences Citation Index: Compact Disc Edition with Abstracts. Institute for Scientific Information. • Quarterly. Provides CD-ROM indexing and abstracting of "significant articles" from 1,400 social science journals worldwide, with additional selections from 3,200 other journals, 1986 to date. Includes economics, business, finance, management, communications, demographics, information and library science, political science, sociology, and many other subjects.

WILSONDISC: Wilson Social Sciences Abstracts. H. W. Wilson Co. • Monthly. Including unlimited online access to *Social Sciences Index* through WILSONLINE. Provides CD-ROM indexing from 1983 and abstracting from 1994 of more than 400 periodicals covering economics, area studies, community health, public administration, public welfare, urban studies, and many other topics related to the social sciences.

ENCYCLOPEDIAS AND DICTIONARIES

Blackwell Encyclopedic Dictionary of Managerial Economics. Robert McAuliffe, editor. Blackwell Publishers. • 1997. $105.95. The editor is associated with Boston College. Contains definitions of key terms combined with longer articles written by various U. S. and foreign business educators. Includes bibliographies and index. *Blackwell Encyclopedia of Management Series.*

Dictionary of Economics. Jae K. Shim and Joel G. Siegel. John Wiley and Sons, Inc. • 1995. $79.95. Contains 2,200 definitions of economic terms. Includes graphs, charts, tables, and economic formulas. (Business Dictionary Series).

Encyclopedia of American Economic History. Glenn Porter. Available from Gale Group. • 1980. $350.00. Three volumes. Individual volumes, $120.00.

Gale Encyclopedia of U.S. Economic History. The Gale Group. • 2000. $205.00. Two volumes. Contains about 1,000 alphabetically arranged entries. Includes industry profiles, biographies, social issue profiles, geographic profiles, and chronological tables.

Quadrilingual Economics Dictionary: English/ American, French, German, Dutch. Frits J. de Jong and others, editors. Kluwer Academic Publishers. • 1981. $234.00.

HANDBOOKS AND MANUALS

Handbook of Mathematical Economics, 1981-91. Elsevier Science. • 1981. $440.00. Four volumes.

INTERNET DATABASES

The Dismal Scientist. Dismal Sciences, Inc. Phone: (610)241-1000 Fax: (610)696-3836 E-mail: webmaster@dismal.com • URL: http://www.dismal.com • Web site contains a wide variety of economic data and rankings. A search feature provides detailed economic profiles of local areas by ZIP code. Major divisions of the site are Economy, Data, Thoughts, Forecasts, and Toolkit, with many specially written articles and currrent analysis by "recognized economists." Fees: Free.

ONLINE DATABASES

Dow Jones Text Library. Dow Jones and Co., Inc. • Full text and edited news stories and articles on business affairs; 1984 to date. Inquire as to online cost and availability.

EconLit. American Economic Association. • Covers the worldwide literature of economics as contained in selected monographs and about 550 journals. Subjects include microeconomics, macroeconomics, economic history, inflation, money, credit, finance, accounting theory, trade, natural resource economics, and regional economics. Time period is 1969 to present, with monthly updates. Inquire as to online cost and availability.

Newspaper and Periodical Abstracts. Bell & Howell Information and Learning. • Provides online coverage (citations and abstracts) of 25 major newspapers, 1,600 perodicals, and 70 TV programs. Covers business, economics, current affairs, health, fitness, sports, education, technology, government, consumer affairs, psychology, the arts, and the social sciences. Time period is 1986 to date, with daily updates. Inquire as to online cost and availability.

Social Scisearch. Institute for Scientific Information. • Broad, multidisciplinary index to the literature of the social sciences, 1972 to present. Weekly updates. Worldwide coverage. Inquire as to online cost and availability.

Wilson Social Sciences Abstracts Online. H. W. Wilson Co. • Provides online abstracting and indexing of more than 415 periodicals covering area studies, community health, public administration, public welfare, urban studies, and many other social science topics. Time period is 1994 to date for abstracts and 1983 to date for indexing, with updates monthly. Inquire as to online cost and availability.

PERIODICALS AND NEWSLETTERS

American Economic Review. American Economic Association. • Quarterly. Free to members; non-members, $135.00 per year. (Includes *Journal of Economic Literature* and *Journal of Economic Persepective*).

Applied Economics. Routledge Journals. • Monthly. $2,120.00 per year. Emphasizes quantitative studies having results of practical use. Supplements available, *Applied Financial Economics* and *Applied Economics Letters.*

Applied Economics Letters. Routledge Journals. • Monthly. $554.00 per year. Provides short accounts of new, original research in practical economics. Supplement to *Applied Economics.*

Applied Financial Economics. Routledge Journals. • Bimonthly. Individuals, $648.00 per year; institutions, $1,053.00 per year. Covers practical aspects of financial economics, banking, and monetary economics. Supplement to *Applied Economics.*

Blue Chip Economic Indicators: What Top Economists Are Saying About the U.S. Outlook for the Year Ahead. Aspen Publishers, Inc. • Monthly. $654.00 per year. Newsletter containing U. S. economic consensus forecasts.

Econometrica. Blackwell Publishers. • Bimonthly. $350.00 per year. Published in England by Basil Blackwell Ltd.

The Economist. Economist Intelligence Unit. • 51 times a year. Individuals, $130.00 per year; institutions, $125.00 per year.

International Review of Applied Economics. Carfax Publishing Co. • Three times a year. Individuals, $148.00 per year; institutions, $512.00 per year.

Journal of Economic Literature. American Economic Association. • Quarterly. $135.00 per year. Includes *American Economic Review* and *Journal of Economic Perspectives.*

Journal of Economics and Business. Temple University, School of Business Administration. Elsevier Science. • Bimonthly. $418.00 per year. Professional and academic research primarily in economics, finance and related business disciplines.

NABE News. National Association for Business Economics. • Bimonthly. $95.00 per year. Membership newsletter. Contains feature articles, news of local chapters and roundtables, reviews of seminars and meetings, personal notes and advertisements of interest to the business economist.

Quarterly Journal of Economics. Harvard University, Dept. of Economics. MIT Press. • Quarterly. Individuals, $40.00 per year; Instutions, $148.00 per year.

The Quarterly Review of Economics and Finance. University of Illinois at Urbana-Champaign, Bureau of Economics and Business Res. Available from JAI Press, Inc. • Five times a year. $349.00 per year. Includes annual supplement. Formerly *Quarterly Review of Economics and Business.*

Review of Social Economy. Association for Social Economics. Routledge Journals. • Quarterly. Individuals, $65.00 per year; institutions, $177.00 per year. Subject matter is concerned with the relationships between social values and economics. Includes articles on income distribution, poverty, labor, and class.

RESEARCH CENTERS AND INSTITUTES

American Institute for Economic Research. P.O. Box 1000, Great Barrington, MA 01230. Phone: (413)528-1216 Fax: (413)528-0103 E-mail: info@aier.org • URL: http://www.aier.org.

Bureau of Economic and Business Research. University of Florida. P.O. Box 117145, Gainesville, FL 32611-7145. Phone: (352)392-0171 Fax: (352)392-4739 E-mail: bebr@bebr.cba.ufl.edu • URL: http://www.bebr.ufl.edu.

Bureau of Economic Research. Rutgers University. New Jersy Hall, 75 Hamilton St., New Brunswick, NJ 08903-5055. Phone: (732)932-7891 Fax: (732)932-7416 E-mail: berkowi@rci.rutgers.edu • URL: http://www.economic.rutgers.edu.

Cowles Foundation for Research in Economics. Yale University. 30 Hillhouse Ave., New Haven, CT 06520-8281. Phone: (203)432-3704 Fax: (203)432-6167 E-mail: john.geanakoplos@yale.edu • URL: http://www.econ.yale.edu.

National Bureau of Economic Research, Inc. 1050 Massachusetts Ave., Cambridge, MA 02138-5398. Phone: (617)868-3900 Fax: (617)868-2742 E-mail: msfeldst@nber.org • URL: http://www.nber.org.

National Opinion Research Center. 1155 E. 60th St., Chicago, IL 60637. Phone: (773)753-7500 Fax: (773)753-7886 E-mail: cloud.patricia@norcmail.uchicago.edu • URL: http://www.norc.uchicago.edu.

STATISTICS SOURCES

Economic Indicators. Council of Economic Advisors, Executive Office of the President. Available from U.S. Government Printing Office. • Monthly. $55.00 per year.

TRADE/PROFESSIONAL ASSOCIATIONS

American Economic Association. 2014 Broadway, Suite 305, Nashville, TN 37203-2418. Phone: (615)322-2595 Fax: (615)343-7590 • URL: http://www.vanderbilt.edu/aea.

Econometric Society. Northwestern University, Dept. of Economics, Evanston, IL 60208-2600. Phone: (708)491-3615 • URL: http://www.econometricsociety.org.es.

Foundation for Economic Education. 30 S. Broadway, Irvington, NY 10533. Phone: 800-452-3518 or (914)591-7230 Fax: (914)591-8910 E-mail: iol@fee.org • URL: http://www.fee.org.

Hudson Institute. Herman Kahn Center, 5395 Emerson Way, Indianapolis, IN 46226. Phone: 800-483-7660 or (317)545-1000 Fax: (317)545-9639 E-mail: info@hudson.org • URL: http://www.hudson.org.

National Association for Business Economics. 1233 20th St., N.W., Suite 505, Washington, DC 20036. Phone: (202)463-6223 Fax: (202)463-6239 E-mail: nabe@nabe.com • URL: http://www.nabe.com.

National Council on Economic Education. 1140 Ave. of the Americas, New York, NY 10036. Phone: 800-338-1192 or (212)730-1792 Fax: (212)730-1793 E-mail: ncee@eaglobal.org • URL: http://www.nationalcouncil.org.

ECONOMICS, BUSINESS

See: BUSINESS ECONOMICS

ECONOMICS, MATHEMATICAL

See: ECONOMETRICS

EDITORS AND EDITING

See also: BUSINESS JOURNALISM; HOUSE ORGANS; JOURNALISM; NEWSPAPERS; PERIODICALS; PUBLISHING INDUSTRY

GENERAL WORKS

The Elements of Editing: A Modern Guide for Editors and Journalists. Arthur Plotnik. Pearson Education and Technology. • 1986. $9.95.

ALMANACS AND YEARBOOKS

Editor and Publisher International Yearbook: Encyclopedia of the Newspaper Industry. Editor and Publisher Co., Inc. • Annual. $125.00. Daily and Sunday newspapers in the United States and Canada.

BIBLIOGRAPHIES

Editing: An Annotated Bibliography. Bruce W. Speck. Greenwood Publishing Group, Inc. • 1991. $67.95. (Bibliographies and Indexes in Mass Media and Communications Series, No. 47).

CD-ROM DATABASES

Leadership Library on CD-ROM: Who's Who in the Leadership of the United States. Leadership Directories, Inc. • Quarterly. $2,641.00 per year, including access to Internet version (weekly updates). Contains all 14 *Yellow Book* personnel directories on CD-ROM, providing contact and brief biographical information for about 400,000 individuals. Covers business, government, financial institutions, news media, law firms, associations, foreign representatives, and nonprofit organizations. Includes photographs.

DIRECTORIES

Editor and Publisher Market Guide. Editor and Publisher Co., Inc. • Annual. $125.00. More than 1,700 newspaper markets in the Unite States and Canada.

Editor and Publisher Syndicate Directory: Annual Directory of Syndicate Services. Editor and Publisher Co., Inc. • Annual. $8.00. Directory of several hundred syndicates serving newspapers in the United States and abroad with news, columns, features, comic strips, editorial cartoons, etc.

International Literary Market Place: The Directory of the International Book Publishing Industry. R. R. Bowker. • Annual. $189.95. More than 10,370 publishers in over 180 countries outside the U.S.and Canada and about 1,150 trade and professional organizations related to publishing abroad.

Literary Market Place: The Directory of the American Book Publishing Industry. R. R. Bowker. • Annual. $199.95. Two volumes. Over 16,000 firms or organizations offering services related to the publishing industry.

Magazines Careers Directory: A Practical One-Stop Guide to Getting a Job in Publc Relations. Visible Ink Press. • 1993. $17.95. Fifth edition. Includes information on magazine publishing careers in art, editing, sales, and business management. Provides advice from "insiders," resume suggestions, a directory of companies that may offer entry-level positions, and a directory of career information sources. *Career Advisor Series.*

News Media Yellow Book: Who's Who Among Reporters, Writers, Editors, and Producers in the Leading National News Media. Leadership Directories, Inc. • Quarterly. $305.00 per year. Lists the staffs of major newspapers and news magazines, TV and radio networks, news services and bureaus, and feature syndicates. Includes syndicated columnists and programs. Seven specialized indexes are provided.

Working Press of the Nation. R. R. Bowker. • Annual. $450.00. Three volumes: (1) *Newspaper Directory*; (2) *Magazine and Internal Publications Directory*; (3) *Radio and Television Directory.* Includes names of editors and other personnel. Individual volumes, $249.00.

Writer's Guide to Book Editors, Publishers, and Literary Agents, 2000-2001: Who They Are, What They Want, and How to Win Them Over. Jeff Herman. Prima Publishing. • Annual. $27.95; with CD-ROM, $49.95. Directory for authors includes information on publishers' response times and pay rates.

HANDBOOKS AND MANUALS

The Chicago Manual of Style: The Essential Guide for Authors, Editors, and Publishers. University of Chicago Press. • 1993. $40.00. 14th edition.

MLA Handbook for Writers of Research Papers. Joseph Gibaldi. Modern Language Association of America. • 1999. $14.75. Fifth edition.

Writer's Handbook for Editing and Revision. Rick Wilber. NTC/Contemporary Publishing. • 1996. $19.95. Discusses rewrites and before-and-after drafts.

PERIODICALS AND NEWSLETTERS

American Editor. American Society of Newspaper Editors. • Nine times a year. $29.00 per year. Formerly *American Society of Newspaper Editors Bulletin.*

Copy Editor: Language News for the Publishing Profession. Mary Beth/Protomastro. • Bimonthly. $69.00 per year. Newsletter for professional copy editors and proofreaders. Includes such items as "Top Ten Resources for Copy Editors.".

Editor and Publisher - The Fourth Estate: Spot News and Features About Newspapers, Advertisers and Agencies. Editor and Publisher Co., Inc. • Weekly. $75.00 per year. Trade journal of the newspaper industry.

Folio: The Magazine for Magazine Management. Intertec Publishing Co. • 17 times a year. $96.00 per year.

Freelance Writer's Report. Dana K. Cassell, editor. CNW Publishing. • Monthly. $39.00 per year. Newsletter. Provides marketing tips and information on new markets for freelance writers. Includes interviews with editors and advice on taxation and legalities.

Quill: The Magazine for Journalists. Society of Professional Journalists. • Monthly. $29.00 per year. A magazine for journalists.

A S B P E Editor's Notes. American Society of Business Press Editors. • Bimonthly. Membership. Newsletter. Formerly (American Society of Business Press Editors).

Writing That Works: The Business Communications Report. Writing That Works. • Monthly. $119.00 per year.

TRADE/PROFESSIONAL ASSOCIATIONS

American Society of Business Press Editors. 107 W. Ogden Ave., LaGrange, IL 60525-2022. Phone: (708)352-6950 Fax: (708)352-3780 E-mail: 7114.34@compuserve.com • URL: http://www.asbpe.com.

American Society of Magazine Editors. 919 Third Ave., New York, NY 10022. Phone: (212)872-3700 Fax: (212)906-0128 E-mail: asme@magazine.org • URL: http://www.magazine.org.

American Society of Newspaper Editors. 11690 Sunrise Valley Dr., No. B, Reston, VA 20191-1409. Phone: (703)453-1122 Fax: (703)453-1133 E-mail: asne@asne.org • URL: http://www.infi.net/asne.

Associated Press Managing Editors. 50 Rockefeller Plaza, New York, NY 10020. Phone: (212)621-1552 Fax: (212)621-1567 E-mail: info@ap.org • URL: http://www.apme.com.

International Association of Business Communicators. One Hallidie Plaza, Suite 600, San Francisco, CA 94102. Phone: (415)544-4700 Fax: (415)544-4747 E-mail: leader-centre@iabc.com • URL: http://www.iabc.com.

EDUCATION

See: SCHOOLS

EDUCATION, BUSINESS

See: BUSINESS EDUCATION

EDUCATION, COMPUTERS IN

See: COMPUTERS IN EDUCATION

EDUCATION, EMPLOYEE

See: TRAINING OF EMPLOYEES

EDUCATION, EXECUTIVE

See: EXECUTIVE TRAINING AND DEVELOPMENT

EDUCATION, FEDERAL AID

See: FEDERAL AID

EDUCATION, HIGHER

See: COLLEGES AND UNIVERSITIES

EDUCATION, TECHNICAL

See: TECHNICAL EDUCATION

EDUCATION, VOCATIONAL

See: VOCATIONAL EDUCATION

EDUCATIONAL FILMS

See: AUDIOVISUAL AIDS IN EDUCATION

EFFICIENCY, INDUSTRIAL

See: TIME AND MOTION STUDY

EFTPOS (ELECTRONIC FUNDS TRANSFER POINT-OF-SALE SYSTEMS)

See: POINT-OF-SALE SYSTEMS (POS)

EFTS

See: ELECTRONIC FUNDS TRANSFER SYSTEMS (EFTS)

EGG INDUSTRY

See: POULTRY INDUSTRY

ELECTRIC APPARATUS

See: ELECTRICAL EQUIPMENT INDUSTRY

ELECTRIC APPLIANCE INDUSTRY

See also: CONSUMER ELECTRONICS

CD-ROM DATABASES

World Marketing Forecasts on CD-ROM. The Gale Group. • Annual. $2,500.00. Produced by Euromonitor. Provides detailed forecast data for the years to 2012 on CD-ROM for 54 countries in all parts of the world. Covers a wide range of social, demographic, economic, and market factors. Includes specific forecasts for many kinds of consumer products.

DIRECTORIES

Appliance - Appliance Industry Purchasing Directory. Dana Chase Publications, Inc. • Annual. $40.00. Suppliers to manufacturers of consumer, commercial, and business appliances.

Appliance Manufacturer Buyers Guide. Business News Publishing Co. • Annual. $25.00.

FINANCIAL RATIOS

Almanac of Business and Industrial Financial Ratios. Leo Troy. Prentice Hall. • Annual. $99.95. Contains financial ratios derived from federal tax returns. Ratios for each of about 200 industries are arranged according to company asset size.

Annual Statement Studies. Robert Morris Associates: The Association of Lending and Credit Risk Professiona. • Annual. Free to members; non-members, $140.00. Median and quartile financial ratios are given for over 400 kinds of manufacturing, wholesale, retail, construction, and consumer finance establishments. Data is sorted by both asset size and sales volume. Includes a clearly written "Definition of Ratios" and an alphabetical industry index.

NARDA's Cost of Doing Business Survey. North American Retail Dealers Association. • Annual. $250.00.

INTERNET DATABASES

Fedstats. Federal Interagency Council on Statistical Policy. Phone: (202)395-7254 • URL: http://

www.fedstats.gov • Web site features an efficient search facility for full-text statistics produced by more than 70 federal agencies, including the Census Bureau, the Bureau of Economic Analysis, and the Bureau of Labor Statistics. Boolean searches can be made within one agency or for all agencies combined. Links are offered to international statistical bureaus, including the UN, IMF, OECD, UNESCO, Eurostat, and 20 individual countries. Fees: Free.

ONLINE DATABASES

DRI U.S. Central Database. Data Products Division. • Provides more than 23,000 business, financial, demographic, economic, foreign trade, and industry-related time series for the U.S. Includes national income, population, retail-wholesale trade, price indexes, labor data, housing, industrial production, banking, interest rates, money supply, etc. Time period is generally 1947 to date (some data back to 1929). Updating varies. Inquire as to online cost and availability.

Euromonitor Market Research. Euromonitor International. • Provides the complete text online of Euromonitor market analysis reports. Covers consumer goods market research data for all major countries, with emphasis on specific product categories. Time period is current. Continuous updating. Inquire as to online cost and availability.

PERIODICALS AND NEWSLETTERS

Appliance. Dana Chase Publications, Inc. • Monthly. $75.00 per year.

Appliance Manufacturer. Business News Publishing Co. • Monthly. $55.00 per year.

Appliance Service News. Gamit Enterprises, Inc. • Monthly. $34.95.

Chilton's Product Design and Development. Cahners Business Information. • Monthly. $80.00 per year.

Dealerscope Consumer Electronics Marketplace: For CE,PC and Major Appliance Retailers. North American Publishing Co. • Monthly. Free to qualified personnel; others, $79.00 per year. Formerly *Dealerscope Merchandising.*

Global Appliance Report: A Monthly Digest of International News Affecting the Home Appliance Industry. Association of Home Appliance Manufacturers. • 22 times a year. Members, $300.00 per year; non-members, $500.00 per year.

NARDA Independent Retailer. North American Retail Dealers Association. • Monthly. $78.00. Formerly *NARDA News.*

STATISTICS SOURCES

Annual Survey of Manufactures. Available from U. S. Government Printing Office. • Annual. Prices vary. Issued by the U. S. Census Bureau as an interim update to the *Census of Manufactures.* Includes data on number of manufacturing establishments in various industries, employment, labor costs, value of shipments, capital expenditures, inventories, energy costs, and assets. (See also Census Bureau home page, http://www.census.gov/.).

Business Statistics of the United States. Courtenay M. Slater, editor. Bernan Associates. • 1999. $74.00. Fifth edition. Based on *Business Statistics*, formerly issue by the Bureau of Economic Analysis, U. S. Department of Commerce. Provides basic data for a wide variety of U. S. industries, services, and economic indicators. Most statistics are shown annually for 29 years and monthly for the most recent four years.

Consumer Canada 1996. Available from The Gale Group. • 1996. $750.00. Published by Euromonitor. Provides consumer market, socioeconomic, and demographic data for Canada. Includes consumer market size (volume and value) for many specific kinds of products.

Consumer International 2000/2001. Available from The Gale Group. • 1998. $1,190.00. Seventh edition. Published by Euromonitor. Contains extensive consumer market, economic, and demographic data for 27 major, non-European countries, including the U. S. and Canada. Includes consumer market size (volume and value) for 150 product types in 14 categories (food, clothing, automobiles, cosmetics, appliances, etc.).

European Marketing Forecasts 2001. Available from The Gale Group. • 2000. $1,190.00. Third edition. Published by Euromonitor. Contains demographic, economic, and market forecasts for the countries of Europe to the year 2010. Forecasts include market-size data for 15 consumer product sectors (food, clothing, automobiles, consumer electronics, etc.).

International Marketing Forecasts 2001. Available from The Gale Group. • 2000. $1,090.00. Third edition. Published by Euromonitor. Contains demographic, economic, and market forecasts to the year 2010 for major, non-European countries, including the U. S. and Canada. Forecasts include market-size data for 15 consumer product sectors, such as food, clothing, and automobiles.

Major Home Appliance Industry Fact Book: A Comprehensive Reference on the United States Major Home Appliance Industry. Association of Home Appliance Manufacturers. • Biennial. $35.00. Includes statistical data on manufacturing, industry shipments, distribution, and ownership.

Major Household Appliances. U.S. Bureau of the Census. • Annual. (Current Industrial Reports MA-36F.).

Manufacturing Profiles. Available from U. S. Government Printing Office. • Annual. Issued by the U. S. Census Bureau. A printed consolidation of the entire *Current Industrial Report* series, presenting "all the data compiled." Contains statistics on production, shipments, inventories, consumption, exports, imports, and orders for a wide variety of manufactured products. (See also Census Bureau home page, http://www.census.gov/.).

Standard & Poor's Industry Surveys. Standard & Poor's. • Semiannual. $1,800.00. Two looseleaf volumes. Includes monthly supplements. Provides detailed, individual surveys of 52 major industry groups. Each survey is revised on a semiannual basis. Also includes "Monthly Investment Review" (industry group investment analysis) and monthly "Trends & Projections" (economic analysis).

Survey of Current Business. Available from U. S. Government Printing Office. • Monthly. $49.00 per year. Issued by Bureau of Economic Analysis, U. S. Department of Commerce. Presents a wide variety of business and economic data.

TRADE/PROFESSIONAL ASSOCIATIONS

Appliance Parts Distributors Association. 6761 E. Ten Mile Rd., Centerline, MI 48015. Phone: (810)754-1818 Fax: (810)754-2260.

Association of Home Appliance Manufacturers. 1111 19th St., N.W., Washington, DC 20036. Phone: (202)872-5955 Fax: (202)872-9354 E-mail: ahamdc@aol.com • URL: http://www.aham.org.

National Appliance Service Association. 9247 N. Meridan St., Suite 216, Indianapolis, IN 46260-1813. Phone: (317)844-1602 Fax: (317)844-4745 E-mail: info@nasal.org • URL: http://www.nasal.org.

National Housewares Manufacturers Association. 6400 Shafer Court, Suite 650, Rosemont, IL 60018. Phone: 800-843-6462 or (847)292-4200 Fax: (847)292-4211 • URL: http://www.housewares.org • Members are manufacturers of housewares and small appliances.

North American Retail Dealers Association. 10 E. 22nd St., Suite 310, Lombard, IL 60148. Phone: 800-621-0298 or (630)953-8950 Fax: (630)953-8957 E-mail: nardahdq@aol.com • URL: http://www.narda.com.

ELECTRIC CONTRACTORS

See: ELECTRICAL CONSTRUCTION INDUSTRY

ELECTRIC LAMPS

See: LIGHTING

ELECTRIC LIGHTING

See: LIGHTING

ELECTRIC MOTOR INDUSTRY

See: ELECTRICAL EQUIPMENT INDUSTRY

ELECTRIC POWER

See: ELECTRIC UTILITIES

ELECTRIC POWER COGENERATION

See: COGENERATION OF ENERGY

ELECTRIC POWER PLANTS

See also: ELECTRIC UTILITIES; ELECTRICAL EQUIPMENT INDUSTRY; PUBLIC UTILITIES

GENERAL WORKS

Power System Operation. Robert H. Miller. McGraw-Hill. • 1994. $60.00. Third edition.

ABSTRACTS AND INDEXES

Key Abstracts: Computing in Electronics and Power. Available from INSPEC, Inc. • Monthly. $240.00 per year. Provides international coverage of journal and proceedings literature. Published in England by the Institution of Electrical Engineers (IEE).

Key Abstracts: Power Systems and Applications. Available from INSPEC, Inc. • Monthly. $240.00 per year. Provides international coverage of journal and proceedings literature, including publications on electric power apparatus and machines. Published in England by the Institution of Electrical Engineers (IEE).

DIRECTORIES

Electrical World Directory of Electric Power Producers and Distributors. • Annual. $395.00. Over 3,500 investor-owned, municipal, rural cooperative and government electric utility systems in the U.S. and Canada. Formerly *Electrical World-Directory of Electric Power Producers.*

FINANCIAL RATIOS

Annual Statement Studies. Robert Morris Associates: The Association of Lending and Credit Risk Professiona. • Annual. Free to members; non-members, $140.00. Median and quartile financial ratios are given for over 400 kinds of manufacturing, wholesale, retail, construction, and consumer finance establishments. Data is sorted by both asset size and sales volume. Includes a clearly written "Definition of Ratios" and an alphabetical industry index.

HANDBOOKS AND MANUALS

Power Plant Engineers Guide. Frank Graham and Charles Buffinghon. Pearson Education and Technology. • 1984. $32.50. Third edition.

Standard Handbook of Power Plant Engineering. Thomas C. Elliott. McGraw-Hill. • 1997. $115.00. Second edition.

PERIODICALS AND NEWSLETTERS

Electrical Construction and Maintenance (EC&M). Intertec Publishing Corp. • Monthly. Free to qualified personnel; individuals, $30.00 per year; libraries, $25.00 per year.

Independent Power Report: An Exclusive Biweekly Covering the Cogeneration and Small Power Market. McGraw-Hill, Energy and Business Newsletter. • Biweekly. $815.00 per year. Newsletter. Covers industry trends, new projects, new contracts, rate changes, and regulations, with emphasis on the Federal Energy Regulatory Commission (FERC). Formerly *Cogeneration Report.*

Power Engineering International. PennWell Corp., Industrial Div. • 10 times a year. $168.00 per year.

Private Power Executive. Pequot Publishing, Inc. • Bimonthly. $90.00 per year. Covers private power (non-utility) enterprises, including cogeneration projects and industrial self-generation.

STATISTICS SOURCES

Financial Statistics of Major Publicly Owned Electric Utilities in the U.S. U.S. Energy Information Administration, U.S. Department of Energy. Available from U.S. Government Printing Office. • Annual. $45.00.

Inventory of Electrtic Utility Power Plants in the United States. Energy Information Administration, U.S. Department of Energy. Available from U.S. Government Printing Office. • Annual. $33.00.

Statistical YearBook of the Electric Utility Industry. Edison Electric Institute. • Annual. $225.00.

Steam Electric Market Analysis. National Mining Association. • Monthly. $300.00 per year. Covers 400 major electric power plants, with detailed data on coal consumption and stockpiles. Shows percent of power generated by fuel type. (Publisher formerly National Coal Association.).

TRADE/PROFESSIONAL ASSOCIATIONS

Association of Edison Illuminating Companies. P.O. Box 2641, Birmingham, AL 35291-0992. Phone: (205)257-2530 Fax: (205)257-2540 E-mail: diraeic@abinter.net • URL: http://www.aeic.org.

Association of Energy Engineers. 4025 Pleasantdale Rd., Suite 420, Atlanta, GA 30340. Phone: (770)447-5083 Fax: (770)446-3969 E-mail: info@aeecenter.org • URL: http://www.aeecenter.org • Members are engineers and other professionals concerned with energy management and cogeneration.

Edison Electric Institute. 701 Pennsylvania Ave., N.W., Washington, DC 20004-2696. Phone: (202)508-5000 or (202)508-5454 Fax: (202)508-5360 • URL: http://www.eei.org.

Electrical Generating Systems Association. 1650 S. Dixie Highway, 5th Fl., Boca Raton, FL 33432. Phone: (561)750-5575 Fax: (561)395-8557.

ELECTRIC POWER, RURAL

See: RURAL ELECTRIFICATION

ELECTRIC RATES

See also: PUBLIC UTILITIES

PERIODICALS AND NEWSLETTERS

Electric Utility Week: The Electric Utility Industry Newsletter. McGraw-Hill, Chemical Engineering Div. • Weekly. $1,475.00 per year. Newsletter. Formerly *Electric Week.*

STATISTICS SOURCES

EIA Residential Electric Bills in Major Cities. Energy Information Administration. U.S. Department of Energy. • Annual.

ELECTRIC SIGNS

See: SIGNS AND SIGN BOARDS

ELECTRIC UTILITIES

See also: COGENERATION OF ENERGY; ELECTRIC POWER PLANTS; HYDROELECTRIC INDUSTRY; PUBLIC UTILITIES

GENERAL WORKS

Electricity Supply Industry: Structure, Ownership, and Regulation. OECD Publications and Information Center. • 1994. $113.00. Discusses the "extensive reform" of the electric utility industry that is underway worldwide. Includes profiles of the electricity supply industry.

ABSTRACTS AND INDEXES

Business Periodicals Index. H. W. Wilson Co. • Monthly, except August, with quarterly and annual cumulations. Service basis for print edition; CD-ROM edition, $1,495.00 per year.

NTIS Alerts: Energy. National Technical Information Service. • Semimonthly. $245.00 per year. Provides descriptions of government-sponsored research reports and software, with ordering information. Covers electric power, batteries, fuels, geothermal energy, heating/cooling systems, nuclear technology, solar energy, energy policy, and related subjects. Formerly *Abstract Newsletter.*

DIRECTORIES

Electrical World Directory of Electric Power Producers and Distributors. • Annual. $395.00. Over 3,500 investor-owned, municipal, rural cooperative and government electric utility systems in the U.S. and Canada. Formerly *Electrical World-Directory of Electric Power Producers.*

The International Competitive Power Industry Directory. PennWell Corp. • Annual. $75.00. Lists suppliers of services, products, and equipment for the hydro, geothermal, solar, and wind power industries.

Plunkett's Energy Industry Almanac: Complete Profiles on the Energy Industry 500 Companies. Plunkett Research Ltd. • Annual. $149.99. Includes major oil companies, utilities, pipelines, alternative energy companies, etc. Provides information on industry trends.

Public Power Annual Directory and Statistical Reprot. American Public Power Association. • Annual. $90.00. List of more than 2,000 local publicly owned electric utilities in United States and possessions. Formerly (Public Power Directory of Local Publicly Owned Electric Utilities).

Utility Automation Buying Guide. Pennwell Publishing Co. • Annual. Price on application. A directory of information technology products and services for electric utility companies.

ENCYCLOPEDIAS AND DICTIONARIES

Macmillan Encyclopedia of Energy. Available from The Gale Group. • 2001. $350.00. Three volumes. Published by Macmillan Reference USA. Covers the business, technology, and history of a wide variety of energy sources.

FINANCIAL RATIOS

Almanac of Business and Industrial Financial Ratios. Leo Troy. Prentice Hall. • Annual. $99.95. Contains financial ratios derived from federal tax returns. Ratios for each of about 200 industries are arranged according to company asset size.

HANDBOOKS AND MANUALS

Moody's Public Utility Manual. Financial Information Services. • Annual. $1,595.00. Two volumes. Supplemented twice weekly by *Moody's Public Utility News Reports.* Contains financial and other information concerning publicly-held utility companies (electric, gas, telephone, water).

INTERNET DATABASES

Fedstats. Federal Interagency Council on Statistical Policy. Phone: (202)395-7254 • URL: http://www.fedstats.gov • Web site features an efficient search facility for full-text statistics produced by more than 70 federal agencies, including the Census Bureau, the Bureau of Economic Analysis, and the Bureau of Labor Statistics. Boolean searches can be made within one agency or for all agencies combined. Links are offered to international statistical bureaus, including the UN, IMF, OECD, UNESCO, Eurostat, and 20 individual countries. Fees: Free.

ONLINE DATABASES

DRI U.S. Central Database. Data Products Division. • Provides more than 23,000 business, financial, demographic, economic, foreign trade, and industry-related time series for the U.S. Includes national income, population, retail-wholesale trade, price indexes, labor data, housing, industrial production, banking, interest rates, money supply, etc. Time period is generally 1947 to date (some data back to 1929). Updating varies. Inquire as to online cost and availability.

PERIODICALS AND NEWSLETTERS

Electric Perspectives. Edison Electric Institute. • Bimonthly. $50.00 per year. Covers business, financial, and operational aspects of the investor-owned electric utility industry. Edited for utility executives and managers.

Electric Utility Week: The Electric Utility Industry Newsletter. McGraw-Hill, Chemical Engineering Div. • Weekly. $1,475.00 per year. Newsletter. Formerly *Electric Week.*

Electrical Wholesaling. Intertec Publishing Corp. • Monthly. $20.00 per year.

Electrical World. McGraw-Hill. • Monthly. $99.00 per year.

Energy Services Marketing Letter: Covering Electric and Gas Utility Marketing Programs. • Monthly. $295.00 per year. Newsletter. Formerly *DSM Letter.*

EPRI Journal. Electric Power Research Institute. • Bimonthly. Free to members; non-members, $29.00 per year.

Public Power. American Public Power Association. • Bimonthly. $50.00 per year.

Public Power Weekly. American Public Power Association. • Weekly. $400.00 per year. Newsletter.

Utility Automation. PennWell Corp., Industrial Div. • Seven times a year. $48.00 per year. Covers new information technologies for electric utilities, including automated meter reading, distribution management systems, and customer information systems.

PRICE SOURCES

International Energy Agency. Energy Prices and Taxes. OECD Publications and Information Center. • Quarterly. $350.00 per year. Compiled by the International Energy Agency. Provides data on prices and taxation of petroleum products, natural gas, coal, and electricity. Diskette edition, $800.00. (Published in Paris).

PPI Detailed Report. Bureau of Labor Statistics, U.S. Department of Labor. Available from U.S. Government Printing Office. • Monthly. $55.00 per year. Formerly *Producer Price Indexes.*

RESEARCH CENTERS AND INSTITUTES

Laboratory for Electromagnetic and Electronic Systems. Massachusetts Institute of Technology, 77 Massachusetts Ave., Bldg. 10, Room 172, Cambridge, MA 02139. Phone: (617)253-4631 Fax: (617)258-6774 E-mail: jgk@mit.edu • URL: http://power.mit.edu/index.html • Research areas include heat transfer and cryogenics.

Lamme Power Systems Laboratory. Ohio State University. 2015 Neil Ave., Columbus, OH 43210. Phone: (614)292-7410 Fax: (614)292-7596 E-mail: sebo.1@osu.edu • URL: http://www.eng.ohio-state.edu/research.html.

STATISTICS SOURCES

Annual Energy Outlook [year], with Projections to [year]. Available from U. S. Government Printing Office. • Annual. Issued by the Energy Information Administration, U. S. Department of Energy (http://www.eia.doe.gov). Contains detailed statistics and 20-year projections for electricity, oil, natural gas, coal, and renewable energy. Text provides extensive discussion of energy issues and "Market Trends.".

Annual Energy Review. Available from U. S. Government Printing Office. • Annual Issued by the Energy Information Administration, Office of Energy Markets and End Use, U. S. Department of Energy. Presents long-term historical as well as recent data on production, consumption, stocks, imports, exports, and prices of the principal energy commodities in the U. S.

Business Statistics of the United States. Courtenay M. Slater, editor. Bernan Associates. • 1999. $74.00. Fifth edition. Based on *Business Statistics*, formerly issue by the Bureau of Economic Analysis, U. S. Department of Commerce. Provides basic data for a wide variety of U. S. industries, services, and economic indicators. Most statistics are shown annually for 29 years and monthly for the most recent four years.

Electric Power Monthly. Available from U. S. Government Printing Office. • Monthly. $115.00 per year. Issued by the Office of Coal and Electric Power Statistics, Energy Information Administration, U. S. Department of Energy. Contains statistical data relating to electric utility operation, capability, fuel use, and prices.

Electricity Information. OECD Publications and Information Center. • Annual. $130.00. Compiled by the International Energy Agency (IEA). Provides detailed electric power statistics for each OECD country, including data on prices, production, and consumption.

Energy Balances of OECD Countries. Organization for Economic Cooperation and Development. Available from OECD Publications and Information Center. • Irregular. $110.00. Presents two-year data on the supply and consumption of solid fuels, oil, gas, and electricity, expressed in oil equivalency terms. Historical tables are also provided. Relates to OECD member countries.

Financial Statistics of Major Publicly Owned Electric Utilities in the U.S. U.S. Energy Information Administration, U.S. Department of Energy. Available from U.S. Government Printing Office. • Annual. $45.00.

Inventory of Electrtic Utility Power Plants in the United States. Energy Information Administration, U.S. Department of Energy. Available from U.S. Government Printing Office. • Annual. $33.00.

OECD Nuclear Energy Data. Organization for Economic Cooperation and Development. Available from OECD Publications and Information Center. • Annual. $32.00. Produced by the OECD Nuclear Energy Agency. Provides a yearly compilation of basic statistics on electricity generation and nuclear power in OECD member countries. Text in English and French.

Standard & Poor's Industry Surveys. Standard & Poor's. • Semiannual. $1,800.00. Two looseleaf volumes. Includes monthly supplements. Provides detailed, individual surveys of 52 major industry groups. Each survey is revised on a semiannual basis. Also includes "Monthly Investment Review" (industry group investment analysis) and monthly "Trends & Projections" (economic analysis).

Statistical YearBook of the Electric Utility Industry. Edison Electric Institute. • Annual. $225.00.

Steam Electric Market Analysis. National Mining Association. • Monthly. $300.00 per year. Covers 400 major electric power plants, with detailed data on coal consumption and stockpiles. Shows percent of power generated by fuel type. (Publisher formerly National Coal Association.).

Survey of Current Business. Available from U. S. Government Printing Office. • Monthly. $49.00 per year. Issued by Bureau of Economic Analysis, U. S. Department of Commerce. Presents a wide variety of business and economic data.

World Energy Outlook. OECD Publications and Information Center. • Annual. $150.00. Provides detailed, 15-year projections by the International Energy Agency (IEA) for world energy supply and demand.

TRADE/PROFESSIONAL ASSOCIATIONS

American Public Power Association. 2301 M St., N.W., Washington, DC 20037. Phone: (202)467-2900 Fax: (202)467-2910 • URL: http://www.appanet.org.

Association of Edison Illuminating Companies. P.O. Box 2641, Birmingham, AL 35291-0992. Phone: (205)257-2530 Fax: (205)257-2540 E-mail: diraeic@abinter.net • URL: http://www.aeic.org.

Edison Electric Institute. 701 Pennsylvania Ave., N.W., Washington, DC 20004-2696. Phone: (202)508-5000 or (202)508-5454 Fax: (202)508-5360 • URL: http://www.eei.org.

International League of Electrical Associations. 2901 Metro Dr., Suite 203, Bloomington, MN 55425-1556. Phone: (612)854-4405 Fax: (612)854-7076.

OTHER SOURCES

Infrastructure Industries USA. The Gale Group. • 2001. $240.00. Replaces *Agriculture, Forestry, Fishing, Mining, and Construction USA* and *Transportation and Public Utilities USA.* Presents statistics and projections relating to economic activity in a wide variety of natural resource and construction industries.

Major Energy Companies of the World. Available from The Gale Group. • 2001. $855.00. Fourth edition. Published by Graham & Whiteside. Contains detailed information on more than 3,300 important energy companies in various countries. Industries include electricity generation, coal, natural gas, nuclear energy, petroleum, fuel distribution, and equipment for energy production.

Utilities Industry Litigation Reporter: National Coverage of the Many Types of Litigation Stemming From the Transmission and Distribution of Energy By Publicly and Privately Owned Utilities. Andrews Publications. • Monthly. $775.00 per year. Reports on legal cases involving the generation or distribution of energy.

ELECTRIC WIRE

See: WIRE INDUSTRY

ELECTRICAL CONSTRUCTION INDUSTRY

ALMANACS AND YEARBOOKS

EC&M's Electrical Products Yearbook (Electrical Construction and Maintenance). Intertec Publishing Corp. • Annual. Free to qualified personnel; others, $10.00.

BIBLIOGRAPHIES

Census of Construction: Subject Bibliography No. 157. Available from U. S. Government Printing Office. • Annual. Free. Lists government publications.

DIRECTORIES

Electrical Construction Materials Directory. Underwriters Laboratories, Inc. • Annual. $22.00. Lists construction materials manufacturers authorized to use UL label.

Plastics Recognized Component Directory. Underwriters Laboratories, Inc. • Annual. $46.00. Lists electrical component manufacturers authorized to use UL label. Formerly *Recognized Component Directory.*

FINANCIAL RATIOS

Almanac of Business and Industrial Financial Ratios. Leo Troy. Prentice Hall. • Annual. $99.95. Contains financial ratios derived from federal tax returns. Ratios for each of about 200 industries are arranged according to company asset size.

Annual Statement Studies. Robert Morris Associates: The Association of Lending and Credit Risk Professiona. • Annual. Free to members; non-members, $140.00. Median and quartile financial ratios are given for over 400 kinds of manufacturing, wholesale, retail, construction, and consumer finance establishments. Data is sorted by both asset size and sales volume. Includes a clearly written "Definition of Ratios" and an alphabetical industry index.

Construction Industry Annual Financial Survey. Construction Financial Management Association. • Annual. $149.00. Contains key financial ratios for various kinds and sizes of construction contractors.

HANDBOOKS AND MANUALS

CEE News Buyers' Guide. Intertec Publishing Corp. • Annual. $25.00. List of approximately 1,900 manufacturers of products used in the electrical construction industry; coverage includes Canada.

PERIODICALS AND NEWSLETTERS

CEE News. Intertec Publishing Corp. • Monthly. $30.00 per year. Formerly *Electrical Construction Technology.*

Electrical Construction and Maintenance (EC&M). Intertec Publishing Corp. • Monthly. Free to qualified personnel; individuals, $30.00 per year; libraries, $25.00 per year.

Electrical Contractor. National Electrical Contractors Association. • Monthly. Membership.

STATISTICS SOURCES

United States Census of Construction Industries. U.S. Bureau of the Census. • Quinquennial. Results presented in reports, tape, and CD-ROM files.

TRADE/PROFESSIONAL ASSOCIATIONS

Independent Electrical Contractors. 2010 A Eisenhower Ave., Alexandria, VA 22314. Phone: 800-456-4324 or (703)549-7351 Fax: (703)549-7448 E-mail: ieccasey@aol.com • URL: http://www.ieci.org.

International Association of Electrical Inspectors. P.O. Box 830848, Richardson, TX 75080-0848. Phone: 800-786-4234 or (972)235-1455 Fax: (972)235-3855 E-mail: iaei@compuserve.com • URL: http://www.iaei.com.

Joint Industry Board of the Electrical Industry. 158-11 Harry Van Arsdale, Jr. Ave., Flushing, NY 11365. Phone: (718)591-2000 Fax: (718)380-7741 • Concerned with labor-management relations of electrical contractors.

National Electrical Contractors Association. c/o Tim Welsh, Associated Builders and Contractors, 1300 N. 17th St., Ste. 800, Rosslyn, VA 22209. Phone: (703)827-2000 or (703)812-2017 Fax: (703)812-8235 • URL: http://www.abc.org.

Power and Communication Contractors Association. 6301 Stevenson Ave., Suite 1, Alexandria, VA 22304. Phone: 800-542-7222 or (703)823-1555 Fax: (703)823-5064 • URL: http://www.pccaweb.org.

ELECTRICAL ENGINEERING

ABSTRACTS AND INDEXES

Applied Science and Technology Index. H. W. Wilson Co. • 11 times a year. Quarterly and annual cumulations. Service basis for print edition; CD-ROM edition, $1,495.00 per year. Indexes a wide variety of English language technical, industrial, and engineering periodicals.

Engineering Index Monthly: Abstracting and Indexing Services Covering Sources of the World's Engineering Literature. Engineering Information, Inc. • Monthly. $2,300.00 per year. Provides indexing and abstracting of the world's engineering and technical literature.

BIBLIOGRAPHIES

Aslib Book Guide: A Monthly List of Recommended Scientific and Technical Books. Available from Information Today, Inc. • Monthly. Members, $164.00 per year; non-members, $204.00 per year. Published in London by Aslib: The Association for Information Management. Formerly *Aslib Book List.*

Encyclopedia of Physical Science and Engineering Information. The Gale Group. • 1996. $160.00. Second edition. Includes print, electronic, and other information sources for a wide range of scientific, technical, and engineering topics.

IEEE Publications Bulletin. Institute of Electrical and Electronics Engineers. • Quarterly. Free. Provides information on all IEEE journals, proceedings, and other publications.

BIOGRAPHICAL SOURCES

Who's Who in Science and Engineering. Marquis Who's Who. • Biennial. $269.00. Provides concise biographical information on 26,000 prominent engineers and scientists. International coverage, with geographical and professional indexes.

CD-ROM DATABASES

COMPENDEX PLUS [CD-ROM]. Engineering Information, Inc. • Quarterly. $3,450.00 per year. Provides CD-ROM indexing and abstracting of the world's engineering and technical information appearing in journals, reports, books, and proceedings, 1985 to date.

DIRECTORIES

IEEE Membership Directory. Institute of Electrical and Electronics Engineers, Inc. • Annual. $190.00.

Peterson's Computer Science and Electrical Engineering Programs. Peterson's. • 1996. $24.95. A guide to 900 accredited graduate degree programs related to computers or electrical engineering at colleges and universities in the U. S. and Canada.

Peterson's Graduate and Professional Programs: Engineering and Applied Sciences. Peterson's. • Annual. $37.95. Provides details of more than 3,400 graduate and professional programs in engineering and related fields at colleges and universities. Formerly *Peterson's Guide to Graduate Programs in Engineering and Professional Sciences.*

Plunkett's Engineering and Research Industry Almanac. Plunkett Research, Ltd. • Annual. $179.99. Contains detailed profiles of major engineering and technology corporations. Includes CD-ROM.

ENCYCLOPEDIAS AND DICTIONARIES

Wiley Encyclopedia of Electrical and Electronics Engineering. John G. Webster, editor. John Wiley and Sons, Inc. • 1999. $6,495.00. 24 volumes. Contains about 1,400 articles, each with bibliography. Arrangement is according to 64 categories.

HANDBOOKS AND MANUALS

Standard Handbook for Electrical Engineers. Douglas G. Fink and Wayne Beaty, editors. McGraw-Hill. • 1999. $150.00. 14th edtion.

ONLINE DATABASES

COMPENDEX PLUS. Engineering Information, Inc. • Provides online indexing and abstracting of the world's engineering and technical information appearing in journals, reports, books, and proceedings. Time period is 1970 to date, with weekly updates. Inquire as to online cost and availability.

Current Contents Connect. Institute for Scientific Information. • Provides online abstracts of articles listed in the tables of contents of about 7,500 journals. Coverage is very broad, including science, social science, life science, technology, engineering, industry, agriculture, the environment, economics, and arts and humanities. Time period is two years, with weekly updates. Inquire as to online cost and availability.

INSPEC. Institute of Electrical and Electronics Engineers (IEEE). • Provides indexing and abstracting of the worldwide literature of electrical engineering, electronics, physics, computer technology, information technology, and industrial controls. Time period is 1970 to date, with weekly updates. Inquire as to online cost and availability. (INSPEC is Information Services for the Physics and Engineering Communities.).

NTIS Bibliographic Data Base. National Technical Information Service. • Contains citations and abstracts to unrestricted reports of government-sponsored research, 1964 to date. Covers a wide range of technical, engineering, business, and social science topics. Monthly updates. Inquire as to online cost and availability.

Who's Who in Technology [Online]. The Gale Group. • Provides online biographical profiles of over 25,000 American scientists, engineers, and others in technology-related occupations. Inquire as to online cost and availability.

PERIODICALS AND NEWSLETTERS

Electronic Engineering Times: The Industry Newspaper for Engineers and Technical Management. CMP Publications, Inc. • Weekly. $199.00 per year.

IEEE Industry Applications Magazine. Institute of Electrical and Electronics Engineers. • Bimonthly. $190.00 per year. Covers new industrial applications of power conversion, drives, lighting, and control. Emphasis is on the petroleum, chemical, rubber, plastics, textile, and mining industries.

IEEE Proceedings-Circuits, Devices and Systems. Institute of Electrical and Electronics Engineers, Inc. • Monthly. $720.00 per year.

IEEE Spectrum. Institute of Electrical and Electronics Engineers, Inc. • Monthly. $195.00 per year. Supplement available *The Institute.*

RESEARCH CENTERS AND INSTITUTES

Communications and Signal Processing Laboratory. University of Michigan. EECS Bldg. 4240, North Campus, Ann Arbor, MI 48109-2122. Phone: (734)763-0564 Fax: (734)763-8041 E-mail: hero@eecsumich.edu • URL: http://www.eecs.umich.edu/systems/homecspl.com.

Electrical and Computer Engineering Industrial Institute. Purdue University School of Electrical and Computer Engineering. 1285 Electrical Engineering Bldg., West Lafayette, IN 47907-1285. Phone: (765)494-3441 Fax: (765)494-3554 E-mail: moyars@ecn.purdue.edu • URL: http://ece.www.ecn.purdue.edu.

Electrical Engineering Research Laboratory. University of Texas at Austin. 634 Engineering Science Bldg., Austin, TX 78712. Phone: (512)471-1072 Fax: (512)471-5445 E-mail: niekirk@mail • URL: http://www.utexas.edu.

Laboratory for Electromagnetic and Electronic Systems. Massachusetts Institute of Technology, 77 Massachusetts Ave., Bldg. 10, Room 172, Cambridge, MA 02139. Phone: (617)253-4631 Fax: (617)258-6774 E-mail: jgk@mit.edu • URL: http://power.mit.edu/index.html • Research areas include heat transfer and cryogenics.

TRADE/PROFESSIONAL ASSOCIATIONS

Institute of Electrical and Electronics Engineers. Three Park Ave., 17th Fl., New York, NY 10016-5997. Phone: (212)419-7900 Fax: (212)752-4929 • URL: http://www.ieee.org.

Joint Electron Device Engineering Council. 2500 Wilson Blvd., Arlington, VA 22201-3834. Phone: (703)907-7534 Fax: (703)907-7583 • URL: http://www.jedec.org.

ELECTRICAL EQUIPMENT INDUSTRY

See also: ELECTRIC APPLIANCE INDUSTRY; ELECTRIC POWER PLANTS

ABSTRACTS AND INDEXES

Applied Science and Technology Index. H. W. Wilson Co. • 11 times a year. Quarterly and annual cumulations. Service basis for print edition; CD-ROM edition, $1,495.00 per year. Indexes a wide variety of English language technical, industrial, and engineering periodicals.

Business Periodicals Index. H. W. Wilson Co. • Monthly, except August, with quarterly and annual cumulations. Service basis for print edition; CD-ROM edition, $1,495.00 per year.

Key Abstracts: Power Systems and Applications. Available from INSPEC, Inc. • Monthly. $240.00 per year. Provides international coverage of journal and proceedings literature, including publications on electric power apparatus and machines. Published in England by the Institution of Electrical Engineers (IEE).

DIRECTORIES

Building Supply Home Centers Retail Giants Report. Cahners Business Information. • Annual. $30.00. Lists major retailers of a wide variety of building and home improvement materials, products, fixtures, accessories, equipment, and tools.

Design News OEM Directory. Cahners Business Information. • Annual. $60.00. About 6,000 manufacturers and suppliers of power transmission products, fluid power products and electrical/ electronic componets to the OEM (Original Equipment Manufacturers). Included with subscription to *Design News.* Formerly *Design News.*

Directory of Electrical Wholesale Distributors. Intertec Publishing Corp. • Biennial. $695.00. Over 2,800 companies with over 9,000 locations.

Electrical Apparatus: Magazine of Electromechanical Operation and Maintenance. Barks Publications, Inc. • Monthly. $45.00. Lists 3,000 manufacturers and distributors of electrical and electronic products.

Thomas Register of American Manufacturers and Thomas Register Catalog File. Thomas Publishing Co., Inc. • Annual. $149.00. 34 volumes. A three-part system offering information on a wide variety of industrial equipment and supplies.

FINANCIAL RATIOS

Annual Statement Studies. Robert Morris Associates: The Association of Lending and Credit Risk Professiona. • Annual. Free to members; non-members, $140.00. Median and quartile financial ratios are given for over 400 kinds of manufacturing, wholesale, retail, construction, and consumer finance establishments. Data is sorted by both asset size and sales volume. Includes a clearly written "Definition of Ratios" and an alphabetical industry index.

HANDBOOKS AND MANUALS

CEE News Buyers' Guide. Intertec Publishing Corp. • Annual. $25.00. List of approximately 1,900 manufacturers of products used in the electrical construction industry; coverage includes Canada.

Guide to Energy Efficient Commercial Equipment. Margaret Suozzo and others. American Council for an Energy Efficient Economy. • 1997. $25.00. Provides information on specifying and purchasing energy-saving systems for buildings (heating, air conditioning, lighting, and motors).

ONLINE DATABASES

Business and Industry. Responsive Database Services, Inc. • Contains online citations, abstracts, and selected fulltext from more than 1,000 trade journals, newspapers, and other publications. Provides general coverage of both manufacturing and service industries, including marketing, production, industry trends, key events, and information on specific companies. Time span is 1994 to date. Daily updates. Inquire as to online cost and availability. (Also available in a CD-ROM version.).

Tablebase. Responsive Database Services, Inc. • Provides online numerical tabular data from a wide variety of business, organization, and government sources, including 900 trade journals. Includes industry and individual company statistics relating to products, market share, sales forecasts, production, exports, market trends, etc. Time span is 1997 to date. Weekly updates. Inquire as to online cost and availability. (Also available in a CD-ROM version.).

Thomas Register Online. Thomas Publishing Co., Inc. • Provides concise information on approximately 194,000 U. S. companies, mainly manufacturers, with over 50,000 product classifications. Indexes over 115,000 trade names. Information is updated semiannually. Inquire as to online cost and availability.

PERIODICALS AND NEWSLETTERS

Appliance Manufacturer. Business News Publishing Co. • Monthly. $55.00 per year.

Canadian Industrial Equipment News: Reader Service On New, Improved and Redesigned Industrial Equipment and Supplies. Southam Magazine Group. • Monthly. $62.95 per year. Supplement available. Formerly *Electrical Equipment News.*

CEE News. Intertec Publishing Corp. • Monthly. $30.00 per year. Formerly *Electrical Construction Technology.*

Dealerscope Consumer Electronics Marketplace: For CE,PC and Major Appliance Retailers. North American Publishing Co. • Monthly. Free to qualified personnel; others, $79.00 per year. Formerly *Dealerscope Merchandising.*

EE Product News (Electronics-Electrical). Penton Media Inc. • Monthly. Free to qualified personnel; others, $55.00 per year.

National Home Center News: News and Analysis for the Home Improvement, Building, Material Industry. Lebhar-Friedman, Inc. • 22 times a year. $99.00 per year. Includes special feature issues on hardware and tools, building materials, millwork, electrical supplies, lighting, and kitchens.

STATISTICS SOURCES

Annual Survey of Manufactures. Available from U. S. Government Printing Office. • Annual. Prices vary. Issued by the U. S. Census Bureau as an interim update to the *Census of Manufactures.* Includes data on number of manufacturing establishments in various industries, employment, labor costs, value of shipments, capital expenditures, inventories, energy costs, and assets. (See also Census Bureau home page, http://www.census.gov/.).

Encyclopedia of American Industries. The Gale Group. • 1998. $560.00. Second edition. Two volumes. $280.00 per volume. Volume one is *Manufacturing Industries* and volume two is *Service and Non-Manufacturing Industries.* Provides the history, development, and recent status of approximately 1,000 industries. Includes statistical graphs, with industry and general indexes.

Manufacturing Profiles. Available from U. S. Government Printing Office. • Annual. Issued by the U. S. Census Bureau. A printed consolidation of the entire *Current Industrial Report* series, presenting "all the data compiled." Contains statistics on production, shipments, inventories, consumption, exports, imports, and orders for a wide variety of manufactured products. (See also Census Bureau home page, http://www.census.gov/.).

Standard & Poor's Industry Surveys. Standard & Poor's. • Semiannual. $1,800.00. Two looseleaf volumes. Includes monthly supplements. Provides detailed, individual surveys of 52 major industry groups. Each survey is revised on a semiannual basis. Also includes "Monthly Investment Review" (industry group investment analysis) and monthly "Trends & Projections" (economic analysis).

U. S. Industry and Trade Outlook: The McGraw-Hill Companies and the U.S. Department of Commerce/ International Trade Administration. Datapso Research Corp. • Annual. $69.95. Produced by the International Trade Administration, U. S. Department of Commerce, in a "public-private" partnership with DRI/McGraw-Hill and Standard & Poor's. Provides basic data, outlook for the current year, and "Long-Term Prospects" (five-year projections) for a wide variety of products and services. Includes high technology industries. Formerly *U. S. Industrial Outlook.*

United States Census of Manufactures. U.S. Bureau of the Census. • Quinquennial. Results presented in reports, tape, CD-ROM, and Diskette files.

TRADE/PROFESSIONAL ASSOCIATIONS

Association of Home Appliance Manufacturers. 1111 19th St., N.W., Washington, DC 20036. Phone: (202)872-5955 Fax: (202)872-9354 E-mail: ahamdc@aol.com • URL: http://www.aham.org.

Electrical Equipment Representatives Association. P.O. Box 419264, Kansas City, MO 64141-6264. Phone: (816)561-5323 Fax: (816)561-1249 • URL: http://www.eera.org.

Electrical Generating Systems Association. 1650 S. Dixie Highway, 5th Fl., Boca Raton, FL 33432. Phone: (561)750-5575 Fax: (561)395-8557.

National Appliance Parts Suppliers Association. 16420 Se McGillivray, Ste. 103-133, Vancouver, WA 98683. Phone: (360)834-3805 Fax: (206)834-3507 • URL: http://www.napsa.repairnet.com.

National Electrical Manufacturers Association. 1300 N. 17th St., Suite 1847, Alexandria, VA 22209. Phone: (703)841-3200 Fax: (703)841-5900.

ELECTRONIC COMMERCE

See also: INTERNET

GENERAL WORKS

The E-Commerce Book: Building the E-Empire. Steffano Korper and Juanita Ellis. Academic Press. • 1999. $39.95. Covers the practical aspects of Internet commerce, including sales, marketing, advertising, payment systems, and security. Written for a general audience.

eBrands: Building an Internet Business at Breakneck Speed. Phil Carpenter. Harvard Business School Press. • 2000. $25.95. Emphasis is on the marketing aspects of electronic commerce.

Executive's Guide to E-Commerce. Martin Deise and Douglas Reagan. John Wiley and Sons, Inc. • 1999. $39.95. Covers the basic principles of doing business successfully by way of the Internet.

The Internet Bubble: Inside the Overvalued World of High-Tech Stocks, and What You Should Know to Avoid the Coming Catastrophe. Tony Perkins and Michael C. Perkins. HarperCollins Publishers, Inc. • 1999. $27.00. The authors predict a shakeout in e-commerce stocks and other Internet-related investments. (HarperBusiness.).

The Leap: A Memoir of Love and Madness in the Internet Gold Rush. Tom Ashbrook. Houghton Mifflin Co. • 2000. $25.00. The author relates his personal and family tribulations while attempting to obtain financing for an eventually successful e-business startup, HomePortfolio.com.

DIRECTORIES

Handbook of Internet Stocks. Mergent. • Annual. $19.95. Contains detailed financial information on more than 200 Internet-related corporations, including e-commerce firms and telecommunications hardware manufacturers. Lists and rankings are provided.

KMWorld Buyer's Guide. Knowledge Asset Media. • Semiannual. Controlled circulation as part of *KMWorld.* Contains corporate and product profiles related to various aspects of knowledge management and information systems. (Knowledge Asset Media is a an affiliate of Information Today, Inc.).

Plunkett's E-Commerce and Internet Business Almanac. Plunkett Research, Ltd. • Annual. $199.99. Contains detailed profiles of 250 large companies engaged in various areas of Internet commerce, including e-business Web sites, communications equipment manufacturers, and Internet service providers. Includes CD-ROM.

HANDBOOKS AND MANUALS

Cybertaxation: The Taxation of E-Commerce. Karl A. Frieden. CCH, Inc. • 2000. $75.00. Includes state sales and use tax issues and corporate income tax rules, as related to doing business over the Internet.

Developing E-Business Architectures: A Manager's Guide. Paul Harmon and others. Academic Press. • 2000. $34.95.

Guide to EU Information Sources on the Internet. Euroconfidentiel S. A. • Annual. $220.00. Contains descriptions of more than 1,700 Web sites providing information relating to the European Union and European commerce and industry. Includes a quarterly e-mail newsletter with new sites and address changes.

Guidelines for Consumer Protection in the Context of Electronic Commerce. Organization for Economic Cooperation and Development. • 2000. $20.00. Provides a guide to effective consumer protection in online business-to-consumer transactions.

Intellectual Property in the International Marketplace. Melvi Simensky and others. John Wiley and Sons, Inc. • 1999. $250.00. Two volumes. Volume one: *Valuation, Protection, and Electronic Commerce.* Volume two: *Exploitation and Country-by-Country Profiles.* Includes contributions from lawyers and consultants in various countries.

Learning Web Design: A Beginner's Guide to HTML, Graphics, and Beyond. Jennifer Niederst. O'Reilly & Associates, Inc. • 2001. $34.95. Written for beginners who have no previous knowledge of how Web design works.

Marketer's Guide to E-Commerce: Everything You Need to Know to Successfully Sell, Promote, and Market Your Business, Product, or Service Online. Arthur Bell and Vincent Leger. NTC/Contemporary Publishing Group. • 2001. $39.95. Covers website marketing strategies, including guidelines and examples. (NTC Business Books.).

Start Right in E-Business: A Step-by-Step Guide to Successful E-Business Implementation. Bennet P. Lientz and Kathryn P. Rea. Academic Press. • 2000. $44.95.

Web Style Guide: Basic Design Principles for Creating Web Sites. Patrick J. Lynch and Sarah Horton. Yale University Press. • 1999. $35.00. Covers design of content, interface, page layout, graphics, and multimedia aspects.

INTERNET DATABASES

Ebusiness Forum: Global Business Intelligence for the Digital Age. Economist Intelligence Unit (EIU), Economist Group. Phone: 800-938-4685 or (212)554-0600 Fax: (212)586-0248 E-mail: newyork@eiu.com • URL: http://www.ebusinessforum.com • Web site provides information relating to multinational business, with an emphasis on activities in specific countries. Includes rankings of countries for "e-business readiness," additional data on the political, economic, and business environment in 180 nations ("Doing Business in.."), and "Today's News Analysis." Fees: Free, but registration is required for access to all content. Daily updates.

Gomez. Gomez Advisors, Inc. Phone: (978)287-0095 E-mail: contact@gomez.com • URL: http://www.gomez.com • The Gomez Web site rates e-commerce companies providing products or services to consumers. Numerical scores are specific as to ease of use, customer confidence, resources, costs, etc. More than 30 product categories are covered, including books, music, videos, toys, sporting goods, gifts, travel, prescriptions, health information, online brokers, insurance, banks, and general merchandise. Fees: Free. (GomezPro, a service for e-commerce professionals, is also available.).

InfoTech Trends. Data Analysis Group. Phone: (707)894-9100 Fax: (707)486-5618 E-mail: support@infotechtrends.com • URL: http://www.infotechtrends.com • Web site provides both free and fee-based market research data on the information technology industry, including computers, peripherals, telecommunications, the Internet, software, CD-ROM/DVD, e-commerce, and workstations. Fees: Free for current (most recent year) data; more extensive information has various fee structures. Formerly *Computer Industry Forecasts.*

Interactive Week: The Internet's Newspaper. Ziff Davis Media, Inc. 28 E. 28th St., New York, NY 10016. Phone: (212)503-3500 Fax: (212)503-5680 E-mail: iweekinfo@zd.com • URL: http://www.zd.com • Weekly. $99.00 per year. Covers news and trends relating to Internet commerce, computer communications, and telecommunications.

PERIODICALS AND NEWSLETTERS

e-Business Advisor: Technology Strategies for Business Innovators. Advisor Media, Inc. • Monthly. $39.00 per year. Covers electronic commerce management and technology, including payment technology, Web development, knowledge management, and e-business market research.

E-Commerce Tax Alert. CCH, Inc. • Monthly. $397.00 per year. Newsletter. Edited for owners and managers of firms doing business through the Internet. Covers compliance with federal, state, local, and international tax regulations.

E-retailing World. Bill Communications, Inc. • Bimonthly. Controlled circulation. Covers various kinds of online retailing, including store-based, catalog-based, pure play, and "click-and-mortar." Includes both technology and management issues.

EC Software News. Faulkner & Gray, Inc. • Monthly. $59.95 per year. Newsletter. Covers the latest developments in e-commerce software, both business-to-business and business-to-consumer.

EC.COM Magazine: The Magazine for Electronic Commerce Management. Electronic Commerce Media, Inc. • Monthly. $48.00 per year. Covers both technical and business issues relating to e-commerce. information.

Electronic Commerce World. Faulkner & Gray, Inc. • Monthly. $45.00 per year. Provides practical information on the application of electronic commerce technology. Also covers such items as taxation of e-business, cash management, copyright, and legal issues.

eShopper. Ziff-Davis. • Bimonthly. $9.97 per year. A consumer magazine providing advice and information for "shopping on the Web.".

eWEEK: Building the .Com Enterprise. Ziff-Davis. • Weekly. Controlled circulation (free). Non-qualified: $195.00 per year. Serves as an "information source for companies undertaking e-commerce and Internet-based business initiatives." Formerly *PC Week.*

Financial Service Online. Faulkner & Gray, Inc. • Monthly. $95.00 per year. Covers the operation and management of interactive financial services to consumers in their homes for banking, investments, and bill-paying.

International Journal of Electronic Commerce. M. E. Sharpe, Inc. • Quarterly. Individuals, $64.00 per year. Institutions, $286.00 per year. A scholarly journal published to advance the understanding and practice of electronic commerce.

Journal of Internet Law. Aspen Law and Business. • Monthly. $295.00 per year. Covers such Internet and e-commerce topics as domain name disputes, copyright protection, Uniform Commercial Code issues, international law, privacy regulation, electronic records, digital signatures, liability, and security.

KMWorld: Creating and Managing the Knowledge-Based Enterprise. Knowledge Asset Media. • Monthly. Controlled circulation. Provides articles on knowledge management, including business intelligence, multimedia content management, document management, e-business, and intellectual property. Emphasis is on business-to-business information technology. (Knowledge Asset Media is a an affiliate of Information Today, Inc.).

Knowledge Management. CurtCo Freedom Group. • Monthly. Controlled circulation. Covers applications of information technology and knowledge management strategy.

Online Investor: Personal Investing for the Digital Age. Stock Trends, Inc. • Monthly. $24.95 per year. Provides advice and Web site reviews for online traders.

Silicon Alley Reporter. Rising Tide Studios. • Monthly. $29.95 per year. Covers the latest trends in e-commerce, multimedia, and the Internet.

Smart Business for the New Economy. Ziff-Davis. • Monthly. $12.00 per year. Provides practical advice for doing business in an economy dominated by technology and electronic commerce.

WebFinance. Securities Data Publishing. • Semimonthly. $995.00 per year. Newsletter (also available online at www.webfinance.net). Covers the Internet-based provision of online financial services by banks, online brokers, mutual funds, and insurance companies. Provides news stories, analysis, and descriptions of useful resources. (Securities Data Publishing is a unit of Thomson Financial.).

STATISTICS SOURCES

DMA State of the Catalog Industry Report. Direct Marketing Association, Inc. • Annual. $495.00. Provides merchandising, operating, and financial statistics on consumer and business-to-business marketing through both print and electronic (interactive) catalogs. (Produced in association with W. A. Dean & Associates.).

DMA Statistical Fact Book. Direct Marketing Association, Inc. • Annual. $165.95 to non-members; $105.95 to members. Provides data in five sections covering direct response advertising, media, mailing lists, market applications, and "Practical Management Information." Includes material on interactive/online marketing. (Cover title: *Direct Marketing Association's Statistical Fact Book.*).

OECD Information Technology Outlook 2000: ICTs, E-Commerce and the Information Economy. Organization for Economic Cooperation and Development. • 2000. $72.00. Provides data on information and communications technology (ICT) and electronic commerce in 11 OECD nations (includes U. S.). Coverage includes network infrastructure, electronic payment systems, financial transaction technologies, intelligent agents, global navigation systems, and portable flat panel display technologies.

OTHER SOURCES

Cyberfinance: Raising Capital for the E-Business. Martin B. Robins. CCH, Inc. • 2001. $79.00. Covers the taxation, financial, and legal aspects of raising money for new Internet-based ("dot.com") companies, including the three stages of startup, growth, and initial public offering.

Darwin: Business Evolving in the Information Age. CXO Media Inc. • Monthly. $44.95 per year. Presents non-technical explanations of information technology (IT) to corporate business executives. Uses a case study format.

DMA Direct and Interactive Marketing Buying Practices Study. Direct Marketing Association, Inc. • 2000. $1,295.00. Provides marketing research data relating to consumer purchasing from catalogs. "Incidence and profile of Internet buying" is also included. (Research conducted by Elrick & Lavidge.).

Dynamic E-Business Implementation Management: How to Effectively Manage E-Business Implementation. Bennet P. Lientz and Kathryn P. Rea. Academic Press. • 2000. $44.95.

eMarketer's eAdvertising Report. Available from MarketResearch.com. • 1999. $795.00. Market research data published by eMarketer. Covers the growth of the Internet online advertising market. Includes future trends and Internet users' attitudes.

Entrepreneurship.com. Tim Burns. Dearborn Financial Publishing. • 2000. $19.95. Provides basic advice and information on the topic of dot.com startups, including business plan creation and financing.

Factiva. Dow Jones Reuters Business Interactive, LLC. • Fee-based Web site provides "global news and business information through Web sites and content integration solutions." Includes Dow Jones and Reuters newswires, The Wall Street Journal, and more than 7,000 other sources of current news, historical articles, market research reports, and investment analysis. Content includes 96 major U. S. newspapers, 900 non-English sources, trade publications, media transcripts, country profiles, news photos, etc.

net.people: The Personalities and Passions Behind the Web Sites. Eric C. Steinert and Thomas E. Bleier. Information Today, Inc. • 2000. $19.95. Presents the personal stories of 36 Web "entrepreneurs and visionaries." (CyberAge Books.).

Nexis.com. Lexis-Nexis Group. • Fee-based Web site offers searching of about 2.8 billion documents in some 30,000 news, business, and legal information sources. Features include a subject directory covering 1,200 topics in 34 categories and a Company Dossier containing information on more than 500,000 public and private companies. Boolean searching is offered.

North American Interactive Television Markets. Available from MarketResearch.com. • 1999. $3,450.00. Published by Frost & Sullivan. Contains market research data on growth, end-user trends, and market strategies. Company profiles are included.

Sales and Use Taxation of E-Commerce: State Tax Administrators' Current Thinking, with CCH Commentary. CCH, Inc. • 2000. $129.00. Provides advice and information on the impact of state sales taxes on e-commerce activity.

ELECTRONIC COMPONENTS

See: ELECTRONICS INDUSTRY; SEMICONDUCTOR INDUSTRY

ELECTRONIC FUNDS TRANSFER POINT-OF-SALE SYSTEMS (EFTPOS)

See: POINT-OF-SALE SYSTEMS (POS)

ELECTRONIC FUNDS TRANSFER SYSTEMS (EFTS)

See also: BANK AUTOMATION; BANKS AND BANKING

DIRECTORIES

Bank Systems and Technology-Directory and Buyer's Guide. Miller Freeman, Inc. • Annual. $25.00. List of more than 1,800 manufacturers, distributors, and other suppliers of equipment and materials to the banking industry.

HANDBOOKS AND MANUALS

Deposit Accounts Regulation Manual. Kenneth F. Hall. West Group. • 1993. $135.00. Provides yearly coverage of federal laws and regulations governing bank deposit accounts, including Truth-in-Savings, Federal Deposit Insurance, Electronic Funds Transfers, fee disclosure, privacy issues, and reserve requirements. (Commercial Law Series).

The Law of Electronic Funds Transfer. Matthew Bender and Co., Inc. • Looseleaf service. Price on application. Periodic supplementation.

PERIODICALS AND NEWSLETTERS

Bank Systems and Technology: For Senior-Level Executives in Operations and Technology. Miller Freeman, Inc. • 13 times a year. $65.00 per year. Focuses on strategic planning for banking executives. Formerly *Bank Systems and Equipment.*

EFT Report (Electronic Funds Transfer). Phillips Business Information, Inc. • Biweekly. $695.00 per year. Newsletter on subject of electronic funds transfer.

Future Banker: The Vision of Leadership in an Electronic Age. American Banker. • Monthly. $79.00 per year. Covers technology innovation for the banking industry, including online banking.

Item Processing Report. Phillips Business Information, Inc. • Biweekly. $695.00 per year. Newsletter for banks on check processing, document imaging, and optical character recognition.

OTHER SOURCES

Endpoint Express. United Communications Group (UCG). • Biweekly. $355.00 per year. Newsletter. Covers bank payment systems, including checks, electronic funds transfer (EFT), point-of-sale (POS), and automated teller machine (ATM) operations. Formerly *Bank Office Bulletin.*

The U. S. Market for Plastic Payment Cards. Available from MarketResearch.com. • 1998. $2,500.00. Market research report published by Packaged Facts. Covers credit cards, charge cards, debit cards, and smart cards. Provides profiles of Visa, Mastercard, American Express, Discover, Diners Club, and others.

ELECTRONIC MAIL

See: COMPUTER COMMUNICATIONS

ELECTRONIC MEDIA

See: INTERACTIVE MEDIA; MULTIMEDIA

ELECTRONIC OPTICS

See: OPTOELECTRONICS

ELECTRONIC PUBLISHING

See also: MULTIMEDIA

GENERAL WORKS

Future Libraries: Dreams, Madness, and Reality. Walt Crawford and Michael Gorman. American Library Association. • 1995. $28.00. Discusses the "over-hyped virtual library" and electronic-publishing "fantasies." Presents the argument for the importance of books, physical libraries, and library personnel.

Towards Electronic Publishing: Realities for Scientists, Librarians, and Publishers. Carol Tenopir and Donald W. King. Special Libraries Association. • 2000. $59.00. Discusses 40-year developments, trends, and price escalation in the academic journal publishing system.

ABSTRACTS AND INDEXES

Computer Literature Index: A Subject/Author Index to Computer and Data Processing Literature. Applied Computer Research, Inc. • Quarterly, with annual cumulation. $245.00 per year. Contains brief abstracts of book and periodical literature covering all phases of computing, including approximately 70 specific application areas.

F & S Index: United States. The Gale Group. • Monthly. $1,295.00 per year, including quarterly and annual cumulations. Provides annotated citations to marketing, business, financial, and industrial literature. Coverage of U. S. business activity includes trade journals, financial magazines, business newspapers, and special reports. Formerly *Predicasts F & S Index: United States.*

Key Abstracts: Business Automation. Available from INSPEC, Inc. • Monthly. $240.00 per year. Provides international coverage of journal and proceedings literature. Published in England by the Institution of Electrical Engineers (IEE).

Microcomputer Abstracts. Information Today, Inc. • Quarterly. $225.00 per year. Provides abstracts covering a wide variety of personal and business microcomputer literature. Formerly *Microcomputer Index.*

ALMANACS AND YEARBOOKS

Communication Technology Update. Focal Press. • Annual. $32.95. A yearly review of developments in electronic media, telecommunications, and the Internet.

New Media Market Place and New Media Titles. Waterlow New Media Information. • 1996. $155.00. Provides a wide variety of information on multimedia industries, including CD-ROM publishing, digital video, interactive TV, portable information products, and video CD. Includes industry review articles, interviews, market data, profiles of 2,000 multimedia companies, product directories, and a bibliography.

CD-ROM DATABASES

Computer Select. The Gale Group. • Monthly. $1,250.00 per year. Provides one year of full-text on CD-ROM for 120 leading computer-related publications. Also includes 70,000 product specifications and brief profiles of 13,000 computer product vendors and manufacturers.

F & S Index Plus Text. The Gale Group. • Monthly. $7,575.00 per year. Provides CD-ROM citations to worldwide business, marketing, and industrial material appearing in a large assortment of trade journals, newspapers, and other publications. Time period is four years.

Hoover's Company Capsules on CD-ROM. Hoover's, Inc. • Quarterly. $349.95 per year (single-user). Provides the CD-ROM version of *Hoover's Handbook of American Business, Hoover's*

Handbook of Emerging Companies, Hoover's Handbook of World Business, Hoover's Guide to Computer Companies, Hoover's Guide to Media Companies, Hoover's Handbook of Private Companies, and various regional guides. Includes more than 11,000 profiles of companies.

DIRECTORIES

Advanced Imaging Buyers Guide: The Most Comprehensive Worldwide Directory of Imaging Product and Equipment Vendors. Cygnus Business Media. • Annual. $19.95. List of about 800 electronic imaging companies and their products.

CD-ROMS in Print. The Gale Group. • Annual. $175.00. Describes more than 13,000 currrently available reference and multimedia CD-ROM titles and provides contact information for about 4,000 CD-ROM publishing and distribution companies. Includes several indexes.

Data Sources: The Comprehensive Guide to the Data Processing Industry Hardware, Data Communications Products, Software, Company Profiles. The Gale Group. • Semiannual. $495.00 per year. Two volumes. Describes hardware and software for all computer operating sysems, including prices and technical details. Lists about 75,000 products from 14,000 suppliers. Industry-specific software applications are described.

The Software Encyclopedia: A Guide for Personal, Professional, and Business Users. R. R. Bowker. • Annual. $255.00. Two volumes. Volume one lists software programs by title and producer. Volume two provides information on programs according to application and operating system. Includes prices and requirements for hardware and memory.

ENCYCLOPEDIAS AND DICTIONARIES

Cyberspace Lexicon: An Illustrated Dictionary of Terms from Multimedia to Virtual Reality. Bob Cotton and Richard Oliver. Phaidon Press, Inc. • 1994. $29.95. Defines more than 800 terms, with manyillustrations. Includes a bibliography.

Cyberspeak: An Online Dictionary. Andy Ihnatko. Random House, Inc. • 1996. $12.95. An informal guide to the language of computers, multimedia, and the Internet.

Every Manager's Guide to Information Technology: A Glossary of Key Terms and Concepts for Today's Business Leader. Peter G. W. Keen. Harvard Business School Press. • 1995. $18.95. Second edition. Provides definitions of terms related to computers, data communications, and information network systems. (Harvard Business Economist Reference Series).

New Hacker's Dictionary. Eric S. Raymond. MIT Press. • 1996. $39.00. Third edition. Includes three classifications of hacker communication: slang, jargon, and "techspeak.".

HANDBOOKS AND MANUALS

The Art of Electronic Publishing: The Internet and Beyond. Sanford Ressler. Prentice Hall. • 1996. $39.95. Places emphasis on the World Wide Web. Includes information on document processors, standards, integration and management, with case studies.

Beyond Book Indexing: How to Get Started in Web Indexing, Embedded Indexing, and Other Computer-Based Media. Diane Brenner and Marilyn Rowland, editors. Information Today, Inc. • 2000. $31.25. Published for the American Society of Indexers. Contains 12 chapters written by professional indexers. Part one discusses making an index by marking items in an electronic document (embedded indexing); part two is on indexing to make Web pages more accessible; part three covers CD-ROM and multimedia indexing; part four provides career and promotional advice for professionals in the field. Includes an index by Janet Perlman and a glossary.

Developing and Managing E-Journal Collections: A How-To-DoIt Manual for Librarians. Donnelyn Curtis and others. Neal-Schuman Publishers, Inc. • 2000. $55.00. Covers the acquisition, management, and integration of journals published in electronic form.

Electronic Design and Publishing: Business Practices. Liane Sebastian. Allworth Press. • 1995. $19.95. Second edition.

Electronic Media Management. Peter K. Pringle and others. Butterworth-Heinemann. • 1999. $44.95. Fourth edition. (Focal Press).

Electronic Publishing: Applications and Implications. Elisabeth Logan and Myke Gluck, editors. Information Today, Inc. • 1997. $34.95. Provides information on copyright, preservation, standards, and other issues relating to the substitution of electronic media for paper-based print.

INTERNET DATABASES

InfoTech Trends. Data Analysis Group. Phone: (707)894-9100 Fax: (707)486-5618 E-mail: support@infotechtrends.com • URL: http://www.infotechtrends.com • Web site provides both free and fee-based market research data on the information technology industry, including computers, peripherals, telecommunications, the Internet, software, CD-ROM/DVD, e-commerce, and workstations. Fees: Free for current (most recent year) data; more extensive information has various fee structures. Formerly *Computer Industry Forecasts.*

Internet Publishing Magazine. North American Publishing Co. 401 North Broad St., Philadelphia, PA 19108. Phone: (215)238-5300 Fax: (215)238-5457 • URL: http://www.ipubmag.com • Eight times a year. Controlled circulation. Edited for print publishers, online-only publishers, web designers, advertising agencies, and others concerned with the publishing of content through the Web.

Wired News. Wired Digital, Inc. Phone: (415)276-8400 Fax: (415)276-8499 E-mail: newsfeedback@wired.com • URL: http://www.wired.com • Provides summaries and full-text of "Top Stories" relating to the Internet, computers, multimedia, telecommunications, and the electronic information industry in general. These news stories are placed in the broad categories of Politics, Business, Culture, and Technology. Affiliated with *Wired* magazine. Fees: Free.

ONLINE DATABASES

F & S Index. The Gale Group. • Contains about four million citations to worldwide business, financial, and industrial or consumer product literature appearing from 1972 to date. Weekly updates. Inquire as to online cost and availability.

Internet and Personal Computing Abstracts. Information Today, Inc. • Contains abstracts covering a wide variety of personal and business microcomputer literature appearing in more than 100 journals and popular magazines. Time period is 1981 to date, with monthly updates. Formerly *Microcomputer Index.* Inquire as to online cost and availability.

Microcomputer Software Guide Online. R. R. Bowker. • Provides information on more than 30,000 microcomputer software applications from more than 4,000 producers. Corresponds to printed *Software Encyclopedia,* but with monthly updates. Inquire as to online cost and availability.

PROMT: Predicasts Overview of Markets and Technology. The Gale Group. • Companies, products, applied technologies and markets. U.S. and international literature coverage, 1972 to date. Inquire as to online cost and availability. Provides abstracts from more than 1,600 publications. Weekly updates.

PERIODICALS AND NEWSLETTERS

Advanced Imaging: Solutions for the Electronic Imaging Professional. Cygnus Business Media. • Monthly. Free to qualified personnel; others, $60.00 per year Covers document-based imaging technologies, products, systems, and services. Coverage is also devoted to multimedia and electronic printing and publishing.

Desktop Publishers Journal. Business Media Group LLC. • Ten times a year. $49.00 per year. Edited for professional publishers, graphic designers, and industry service providers. Covers new products and emerging technologies for the electronic publishing industry.

Digital Publishing Technologies: How to Implement New Media Publishing. Information Today, Inc. • Monthly. $196.00 per year. Covers online and CD-ROM publishing, including industry news, new applications, new products, electronic publishing technology, and descriptions of completed publishing projects.

Educational Marketer: The Educational Publishing Industry's Voice of Authority Since 1968. SIMBA Information. • Three times a month. $479.00 per year. Newsletter. Edited for suppliers of educational materials to schools and colleges at all levels. Covers print and electronic publishing, software, audiovisual items, and multimedia. Includes corporate news and educational statistics.

Electronic Information Report: Empowering Industry Decision Makers Since 1979. SIMBA Information. • 46 times a year. $549.00 per year. Newsletter. Provides business and financial news and trends for online services, electronic publishing, storage media, multimedia, and voice services. Includes information on relevant IPOs (initial public offerings) and mergers. Formerly *Electronic Information Week.*

Electronic Publishing: For the Business Leaders Who Buy Technology. PennWell Corp., Advanced Technology Div. • Monthly. $45.00 per year. Edited for digital publishing professionals. New products are featured.

Interactive Content: Consumer Media Strategies Monthly. Jupiter Media Metrix. • Monthly. $675.00 per year; with online edition, $775.00 per year. Newsletter. Covers the broad field of providing content (information, news, entertainment) for the Internet/World Wide Web.

Micropublishing News: The Newsmonthly for Electronic Designers and Publishers. Cygnus Business Media. • Monthly. Free to qualified personnel. Price on application. Edited for business and professional users of electronic publishing products and services. Topics covered include document imaging, CD-ROM publishing, digital video, and multimedia services. Available in four regional editions.

National Association of Desktop Publishers. Journal. National Association of Desktop Publishers. Desktop Publishing Institute. • Monthly. Free to members; non-members, $48.00 per year. Covers desktop, electronic, and multimedia publishing.

Publish: The Magazine for Electronic Publishing Professionals. International Data Group. • Monthly. $39.90 per year. Edited for electronic publishing professionals. Covers new technologies and new products.

Silicon Alley Reporter. Rising Tide Studios. • Monthly. $29.95 per year. Covers the latest trends in e-commerce, multimedia, and the Internet.

Wired. Wired Ventures Ltd. • Monthly. $24.00 per year. Edited for creators and managers in various areas of electronic information and entertainment, including multimedia, the Internet, and video. Often considered to be the primary publication of the "digital generation.".

Yellow Pages and Directory Report: The Newsletter for the Yellow Page and Directory Publishing Industry. SIMBA Information. • 22 times a year. $579.00 per year. Newsletter. Covers the yellow pages publishing industry, including electronic directory publishing, directory advertising, and special interest directories.

RESEARCH CENTERS AND INSTITUTES

Center for Integrated Manufacturing Studies. Rochester Institute of Technology, 111 Lomb Memorial Dr., Rochester, NY 14623-5608. Phone: (716)475-5101 Fax: (716)475-5250 E-mail: wjsasp@rit.edu • URL: http://www.cims.rit.edu • Research areas include electronics, imaging, printing, and publishing.

International Data Corp. (IDC). Five Speen St., Framingham, MA 01701. Phone: (508)935-4389 Fax: (508)935-4789 • URL: http://www.idcresearch.com • Private research firm specializing in market research related to computers, multimedia, and telecommunications.

Media Laboratory. Massachusetts Institute of Technology, 20 Ames St., Room E-15, Cambridge, MA 02139. Phone: (617)253-0338 Fax: (617)258-6264 E-mail: casr@media.mit.edu • URL: http://www.media.mit.edu • Research areas include electronic publishing, spatial imaging, human-machine interface, computer vision, and advanced television.

STATISTICS SOURCES

By the Numbers: Electronic and Online Publishing. The Gale Group. • 1997. $385.00. Four volumes. $99.00 per volume. Covers "high-interest" industries: 1. *By the Numbers: Electronic and Online Publishing*; 2. *By the Numbers: Emerging Industries*; 3. *By the Numbers: Nonprofits*; 4. *By the Numbers: Publishing.* Each volume provides about 600 tabulations of industry data on revenues, market share, employment, trends, financial ratios, profits, salaries, and so forth. Citations to data sources are included.

Multimedia Title Publishing: Review, Trends, and Forecast. SIMBA Information. • Annual. $895.00. Provides industry statistics and market research data. Covers both business and consumer multimedia items, with emphasis on CD-ROM publishing.

OTHER SOURCES

Consumer Online Services Report. Jupiter Media Metrix. • Annual. $1,895.00. Market research report. Provides analysis of trends in the online information industry, with projections of growth in future years (five-year forecasts). Contains profiles of electronic media companies.

DVD Assessment, No. 3. Julie B. Schwerin and Theodore A. Pine, editors. InfoTech, Inc. • 1998. $1,295.00. Third edition. Provides detailed market research data on Digital Video Discs (also known as Digital Versatile Discs). Includes history of DVD, technical specifications, DVD publishing outlook, "Industry Overview," "Market Context," "Infrastructure Analysis," "Long-Range Forecast to 2005," and emerging technologies.

Optical Publishing Industry Assessment. Julie B. Schwerin and Theodore A. Pine, editors. InfoTech, Inc. • 1998. $1,295.00. Ninth edition. Provides market research data and forecasts to 2005 for DVD-ROM, "Hybrid ROM/Online Media," and other segments of the interactive entertainment, digital information, and consumer electronics industries. Covers both software (content) and hardware. Includes Video-CD, DVD- Video, CD-Audio, DVD-Audio, DVD-ROM, PC-Desktop, TV Set-Top, CD-R, CD-RW, DVD-R and DVD-RAM.

Towards Electronic Journals: Realities for Scientists, Librarians, and Publishers. Carol Tenopir and Donald W. King. Special Libraries Association. • 2000. $59.00. Discusses journals in electronic form vs. traditional (paper) scholarly journals, including the impact of subscription prices.

ELECTRONIC SECURITY SYSTEMS

See also: INDUSTRIAL SECURITY PROGRAMS

DIRECTORIES

Automotive Burglary Protection and Mechanical Equipment Directory. Underwriters Laboratories, Inc. • Annual. $10.00. Lists manufacturers authorized to use UL label.

National Burglar and Fire Alarm Association Members Services Directory. National Burglar and Fire Alarm Association. • Annual. Membership. Names and addresses of about 4,000 alarm security companies. Formerly *National Burglar and Fire Alarm Association-Directory of Members.*

Security Distributing and Marketing-Security Products and Services Locater. Cahners Business Information. • Annual. $50.00. Formerly *SDM: Security Distributing and Marketing-Security Products and Services Directory.*

Security: Product Service Suppliers Guide. Cahners Business Information. • Annual. $50.00 Includes computer and information protection products. Formerly *Security - World Product Directory.*

HANDBOOKS AND MANUALS

Burglar Alarm Sales and Installation. Entrepreneur Media, Inc. • Looseleaf. $59.50. A practical guide to starting a burglar alarm service. Covers profit potential, start-up costs, market size evaluation, owner's time required, pricing, accounting, advertising, promotion, etc. (Start-Up Business Guide No. E1091.).

Effective Physical Security: Design, Equipment, and Operations. Lawrence J. Fennelly, editor. Butterworth-Heinemann. • 1996. $36.95. Second edition. Contains chapters written by various U. S. security equipment specialists. Covers architectural considerations, locks, safes, alarms, intrusion detection systems, closed circuit television, identification systems, etc.

PERIODICALS AND NEWSLETTERS

9-1-1 Magazine: Public Safety Communications and Response. Official Publications, Inc. • Bimonthly. $31.95 per year. Covers technical information and applications for public safety communications personnel.

Security Distributing and Marketing. Cahners Business Information. • 13 times a year. $82.00 per year. Covers applications, merchandising, new technology and management.

Security Management. American Society for Industrial Security. • Monthly. Free to members; non-members, $48.00 per year. Articles cover the protection of corporate assets, including personnel property and information security.

Security Systems Administration. Cygnus Business Media. • Monthly. $10.00 per year.

Security: The Magazine for Buyers of Security Products, Systems and Service. Cahners Business Information. • Monthly. $82.90 per year.

TRADE/PROFESSIONAL ASSOCIATIONS

ASIS International (American Society for Industrial Security). 1625 Prince St., Alexandria, VA 22314-2818. Phone: (703)519-6200 Fax: (703)519-6299 • URL: http://www.asisonline.org.

Automatic Fire Alarm Association. P.O. Box 951807, Lake Mary, FL 32795-1807. Phone: (407)322-6288 Fax: (407)322-7488 • URL: http://www.afaa.org.

Central Station Alarm Association. 440 Maple Ave., Suite 201, Vienna, VA 22180-4723. Phone: (703)242-4670 Fax: (703)242-4675 E-mail: admin@csaaul.org.

National Burglar and Fire Alarm Association. 8300 Colesville Rd., Ste. 750, Silver Spring, MD 20910-6225. Phone: (301)907-3202 Fax: (301)907-7897 E-mail: staff@alarm.org • URL: http://www.alarm.org.

ELECTRONICS, AVIATION

See: AVIONICS

ELECTRONICS, CONSUMER

See: CONSUMER ECONOMICS

ELECTRONICS INDUSTRY

See also: AVIONICS; ELECTRICAL ENGINEERING; MEDICAL ELECTRONICS; OPTOELECTRONICS; RADIO EQUIPMENT INDUSTRY; SEMICONDUCTOR INDUSTRY; TELEVISION APPARATUS INDUSTRY

GENERAL WORKS

Basic Electronics. Bernard Grob. Pearson Education and Technology. • 1996. $84.75. Eight edition.

Electronics Fundamentals: Circuits, Devices, and Applications. Thomas L. Floyd. Prentice Hall. • 2000. $90.67. Fifth edition.

ABSTRACTS AND INDEXES

Applied Science and Technology Index. H. W. Wilson Co. • 11 times a year. Quarterly and annual cumulations. Service basis for print edition; CD-ROM edition, $1,495.00 per year. Indexes a wide variety of English language technical, industrial, and engineering periodicals.

Electrical and Electronic Abstracts. INSPEC, Inc. • Monthly. $3,435.00 per year, with annual cumulation. *Science Abstracts. Section B.*

Electronics and Communications Abstracts Journal: Comprehensive Coverage of Essential Scientific Literature. Cambridge Information Group. • Monthly. $1,045.00 per year.

Key Abstracts: Computing in Electronics and Power. Available from INSPEC, Inc. • Monthly. $240.00 per year. Provides international coverage of journal and proceedings literature. Published in England by the Institution of Electrical Engineers (IEE).

Key Abstracts: Electronic Circuits. INSPEC, Inc. • Monthly. $240.00 per year. Provides international coverage of journal and proceedings literature. Published in England by the Institution of Electrical Engineers (IEE).

Key Abstracts: Electronic Instrumentation. Available from INSPEC, Inc. • Monthly. $240.00 per year. Provides international coverage of journal and proceedings literature. Published in England by the Institution of Electrical Engineers (IEE).

NTIS Alerts: Electrotechnology. National Technical Information Service. • Semimonthly. $210.00 per year. Provides descriptions of government-sponsored research reports and software, with ordering information. Covers electronic components, semiconductors, antennas, circuits, optoelectronic devices, and related subjects. Formerly *Abstract Newsletter.*

Solid State and Superconductivity Abstracts. Cambridge Information Group. • Bimonthly. $1,045.00 per year. Formerly *Solid State Abstracts Journal.*

CD-ROM DATABASES

Electronic Strategies. Thomson Financial Securities Data. • Monthly. $2,995.00 per year. CD-ROM contains full text of investment analysts' reports on companies operating in the following fields: electronics, computers, semiconductors, and office products.

DIRECTORIES

Directory of Computer and Consumer Electronics. Chain Store Age. • Annual. $290.00. Includes 2,900 "leading" retailers and over 200 "top" distributors. Formerly *Directory of Consumer Electronics Retails and Distributors.*

ECN's Electronic Industry Telephone Directory. Cahners Business Information. • Annual. $55.00. Information on 30,000 electronic manufacturers, distributors, and representatives. Formerly *Electronic Industry Telephone Directory.*

ENCYCLOPEDIAS AND DICTIONARIES

Dictionary of Electronics. S.W. Amos and Roger Amos. Butterworth-Heinemann. • 1996. $34.95. Third edition.

McGraw-Hill Encyclopedia of Science & Technology. McGraw-Hill. • 1997. $1,995.00. Eighth edition. 20 volumes.

Modern Dictionary of Electronics. Rudolf F. Graf. Butterworth-Heineman. • 1999. $59.95. Seventh edition.

Wiley Encyclopedia of Electrical and Electronics Engineering. John G. Webster, editor. John Wiley and Sons, Inc. • 1999. $6,495.00. 24 volumes. Contains about 1,400 articles, each with bibliography. Arrangement is according to 64 categories.

FINANCIAL RATIOS

Almanac of Business and Industrial Financial Ratios. Leo Troy. Prentice Hall. • Annual. $99.95. Contains financial ratios derived from federal tax returns. Ratios for each of about 200 industries are arranged according to company asset size.

Annual Statement Studies. Robert Morris Associates: The Association of Lending and Credit Risk Professiona. • Annual. Free to members; non-members, $140.00. Median and quartile financial ratios are given for over 400 kinds of manufacturing, wholesale, retail, construction, and consumer finance establishments. Data is sorted by both asset size and sales volume. Includes a clearly written "Definition of Ratios" and an alphabetical industry index.

HANDBOOKS AND MANUALS

Electronic Instrument Handbook. Clyde F. Coombs. McGraw-Hill. • 1999. $125.00. Second edition. (Engineering Handbook Series).

Solid State Electronic Devices. Prentice Hall. • 2000. Fifth edition. Price on application.

ONLINE DATABASES

Hard Sciences. Cambridge Scientific Abstracts. • Provides the online version of *Computer and Information Systems Abstracts, Electronics and Communications Abstracts, Health and Safety Science Abstracts, ISMEC: Mechanical Engineering Abstracts (Information Service in Mechanical Engineering)* and *Solid State and Superconductivity Abstracts.* Time period is 1981 to date, with monthly updates. Inquire as to online cost and availability.

INSPEC. Institute of Electrical and Electronics Engineers (IEEE). • Provides indexing and abstracting of the worldwide literature of electrical engineering, electronics, physics, computer technology, information technology, and industrial controls. Time period is 1970 to date, with weekly updates. Inquire as to online cost and availability. (INSPEC is Information Services for the Physics and Engineering Communities.).

Who's Who in Technology [Online]. The Gale Group. • Provides online biographical profiles of over 25,000 American scientists, engineers, and others in technology-related occupations. Inquire as to online cost and availability.

PERIODICALS AND NEWSLETTERS

Electronic Business. Cahners Business Information. • Monthly. $83.90 per year. For the non-technical manager and executive in the electronics industry. Offers news, trends, figures and forecasts. Formerly *Electronic Business Today.*

Electronic Design. Penton Media Inc. • Biweekly. $100.00 per year. Provides technical information for U.S. design engineers and managers.

Electronic Industries Association's - Executive Report. Eletronic Industries Association. • Bimonthly. Free to members; non-members, $50.00 per year.

Electronic News. Cahners Business Information. • 51 times a year. $119.00 per year.

Electronic Products. Hearst Business Communications, Inc. UTP Div. • Monthly. $50.00 per year.

Mainly Marketing: The Schoonmaker Report to Technical Managements. Warren K. Schoonmaker, editor. Schoonmaker Associates. • Monthly. $200.00 per year. Report to technical managements focusing on methods of marketing high technology.

Medical Electronics. Measurements & Data Corp. • Bimonthly. $22.00 per year. Includes information on new medical electronic products, technology, industry news, and medical safety.

Medical Electronics and Equipment News. Reilly Publishing Co. • Bimonthly. Free to qualified personnel; others, $50.00 per year. Provides medical electronics industry news and new product information.

RESEARCH CENTERS AND INSTITUTES

Communications and Signal Processing Laboratory. University of Michigan. EECS Bldg. 4240, North Campus, Ann Arbor, MI 48109-2122. Phone: (734)763-0564 Fax: (734)763-8041 E-mail: hero@eecsumich.edu • URL: http://www.eecs.umich.edu/systems/homecspl.com.

Electronics Laboratory. Oklahoma State University. Stillwater, OK 74078-0116. Phone: (405)744-6788 Fax: (405)744-6187 E-mail: tberten@master.ceat.okstate.edu.

Electronics Research Laboratory. University of California at Berkeley. 253 Cory Hall, Berkeley, CA 94720. Phone: (510)642-2301 Fax: (510)643-8426 E-mail: sastry@eecs.berkeley.edu.

Laboratory for Electromagnetic and Electronic Systems. Massachusetts Institute of Technology, 77 Massachusetts Ave., Bldg. 10, Room 172, Cambridge, MA 02139. Phone: (617)253-4631 Fax: (617)258-6774 E-mail: jgk@mit.edu • URL: http://power.mit.edu/index.html • Research areas include heat transfer and cryogenics.

Research Laboratory of Electronics. Massachusetts Institute of Technology. Bldg. 36, Room 413, Cambridge, MA 02139-4307. Phone: (617)253-2509 Fax: (617)258-7864 E-mail: bpassero@rle.mit.edu • URL: http://www.rleweb.mit.edu.

SRI International. 333 Ravenswood Ave., Menlo Park, CA 94025-3493. Phone: (650)859-2000 Fax: (650)326-5512 E-mail: inquiryline@sri.com • URL: http://www.sri.com • Private research firm specializing in market research in high technology areas.

Telecommunications and Signal Processing Research Center. University of Texas at Austin. 439 Engineering Science Bldg., Austin, TX 78712-1084. Phone: (512)471-3954 Fax: (512)471-1856 E-mail: ejpowers@mail.utexas.edu • URL: http://www.ece.utexas.edu/projects/telecom/.

STATISTICS SOURCES

Annual Survey of Manufactures. Available from U. S. Government Printing Office. • Annual. Prices vary. Issued by the U. S. Census Bureau as an interim update to the *Census of Manufactures.* Includes data on number of manufacturing establishments in various industries, employment, labor costs, value of shipments, capital expenditures, inventories, energy costs, and assets. (See also Census Bureau home page, http://www.census.gov/.).

Communication Equipment, and Other Electronic Systems and Equipment. U. S. Bureau of the Census. • Annual. Provides data on shipments: value, quantity, imports, and exports. (Current Industrial Reports, MA-36P.).

Electromedical Equipment and Irradiation Equipment, Including X-Ray. U. S. Bureau of the Census. • Annual. Contains shipment quantity, value of shipment, export, and import data. (Current Industrial Report No. MA-38R.).

Electronic Market Data Book. Electronic Industries Association, Marketing Services Dept. • Annual. Members, $75.00; non-members, $125.00.

Manufacturing Profiles. Available from U. S. Government Printing Office. • Annual. Issued by the U. S. Census Bureau. A printed consolidation of the entire *Current Industrial Report* series, presenting "all the data compiled." Contains statistics on production, shipments, inventories, consumption, exports, imports, and orders for a wide variety of manufactured products. (See also Census Bureau home page, http://www.census.gov/.).

Semiconductors, Printed Circuit Boards, and Other Electronic Components. U. S. Bureau of the Census. • Annual. Provides data on shipments: value, quantity, imports, and exports. (Current Industrial Reports, MA-36Q.).

Standard & Poor's Industry Surveys. Standard & Poor's. • Semiannual. $1,800.00. Two looseleaf volumes. Includes monthly supplements. Provides detailed, individual surveys of 52 major industry groups. Each survey is revised on a semiannual basis. Also includes "Monthly Investment Review" (industry group investment analysis) and monthly "Trends & Projections" (economic analysis).

U. S. Industry and Trade Outlook: The McGraw-Hill Companies and the U.S. Department of Commerce/International Trade Administration. Datapso Research Corp. • Annual. $69.95. Produced by the International Trade Administration, U. S. Department of Commerce, in a "public-private" partnership with DRI/McGraw-Hill and Standard & Poor's. Provides basic data, outlook for the current year, and "Long-Term Prospects" (five-year projections) for a wide variety of products and services. Includes high technology industries. Formerly *U. S. Industrial Outlook.*

WEFA Industrial Monitor. John Wiley and Sons, Inc. • Annual. $65.00. Prepared by industry analysts at WEFA, an economic forecasting and consulting firm (originally Wharton Econometric Forecasting Associates). Contains discussions of the outlook for major U. S. industries, with many 10-year forecasts (WEFA Web site is http://www.wefa.com).

TRADE/PROFESSIONAL ASSOCIATIONS

American Electronics Association. 5201 Great American Parkway, Suite 520, Santa Clara, CA 95054. Phone: 800-284-4232 or (408)987-4200 Fax: (408)986-1247 • URL: http://www.aeanet.org.

ASM International. 9639 Kinsman Rd., Materials Park, OH 44073. Phone: 800-336-5152 or (216)338-5151 Fax: (216)338-4634 E-mail: memserv@po.asm-intl.org • URL: http://www.asm-intl.org • Members are materials engineers, metallurgists, industry executives, educators, and others concerned with a wide range of materials and metals. Divisions include Aerospace, Composites, Electronic Materials and Processing, Energy, Highway/Off-Highway Vehicle, Joining, Materials Testing and Quality Control, Society of Carbide and Tool Engineers, and Surface Engineering.

Electronic Industries Association. 2500 Wilson Blvd., Arlington, VA 22201. Phone: (703)907-7500 Fax: (703)907-7501 • URL: http://www.eia.org • Includes a Solid State Products Committee.

National Electronic Distributors Association. 1111 Alderman Dr., Ste. 400, Alpharetta, GA 30005-4143. Phone: 800-347-6332 or (678)393-9990 Fax: (678)393-9998 E-mail: info@nedassoc.org • URL: http://www.nedassoc.org.

OTHER SOURCES

Business & Company Resource Center. The Gale Group. • Fee-based Web site provides a wide range of business, industry, and specific company information. Access is offered to trade journal articles, market research data, insider trading activity, major shareholder data, corporate histories, emerging technology reports, corporate earnings estimates, press releases, and other sources. Provides detailed company profiles, industry overviews, and rankings. Offers integration of Predicasts PROMT, Newsletters ASAP, Investext Plus, Business Index ASAP, Brands and Their Companies, and other databases (many have full text).

Electronic Market Trends. Electronic Industries Association, Marketing Services Dept. • Monthly. Members, $100.00 per year; non-members, $150.00 per year.

ELECTRONICS, MEDICAL

See: MEDICAL ELECTRONICS

ELECTROPLATING

See: METAL FINISHING

ELEVATORS

See also: BUILDING INDUSTRY

DIRECTORIES

Elevator World-Source Issue. Elevator World, Inc. • Annual. $35.00. Lists about 450 elevator manufacturers and suppliers to the industry; consultants and 109 trade associations; international coverage.

PERIODICALS AND NEWSLETTERS

Commercial Building: Tranforming Plans into Buildings. Stamats Communications. • Bimonthly. $48.00 per year. Edited for building contractors, engineers, and architects. Includes special features on new products, climate control, plumbing, and vertical transportation.

Elevator World. Elevator World, Inc. • Monthly. $67.00 per year.

National Elevator Industry, Inc. Newsletter. National Elevator Industry, Inc. • Quarterly. Price on application.

TRADE/PROFESSIONAL ASSOCIATIONS

American Society of Mechanical Engineers. Three Park Ave., New York, NY 10016-5990. Phone: 800-843-2763 or (212)705-7722 Fax: (212)705-7674 E-mail: infocentral@asme.org • URL: http://www.asme.org.

National Association of Elevator Contractors. 1298 Wellbrook Circle, N.E., Suite A, Conyers, GA 30207. Phone: (770)760-9660 Fax: (770)760-9714 E-mail: naec@mindspring.com • URL: http://www.naec.org.

National Elevator Industry. 400 Frank W. Burr Blvd., Teaneck, NJ 07666. Phone: (201)928-2828 Fax: (201)928-4200.

EMBASSIES

See: DIPLOMATIC AND CONSULAR SERVICE

EMBEZZLEMENT

See: FRAUD AND EMBEZZLEMENT

EMERGING MARKETS

See: DEVELOPING AREAS

EMIGRATION

See: IMMIGRATION AND EMIGRATION

EMPLOYEE BENEFIT PLANS

See also: FRINGE BENEFITS; PENSIONS; PROFIT SHARING

GENERAL WORKS

Fundamentals of Employee Benefit Programs. Employee Benefit Research Institute. • 1996. $49.95. Fifth edition. Provides basic explanation of employee benefit programs in both the private and public sectors, including health insurance, pension plans, retirement planning, social security, and long-term care insurance.

ABSTRACTS AND INDEXES

Business Periodicals Index. H. W. Wilson Co. • Monthly, except August, with quarterly and annual cumulations. Service basis for print edition; CD-ROM edition, $1,495.00 per year.

Insurance Periodicals Index. Specials Libraries Association, Insurance and Employees Benefits Div. CCH/NILS Publishing Co. • Annual. $250.00. Compiled by the Insurance and Employee Benefits Div., Special Libraries Association. A yearly index of over 15,000 articles from about 35 insurance periodicals. Arrangement is by subject, with an index to authors.

BIBLIOGRAPHIES

Employee Assistance Programs: An Annotated Bibliography. Donna Kemp. Garland Publishing, Inc. • 1989. $15.00. (Public Affairs and Administration Series).

Insurance and Employee Benefits Literature. Special Libraries Association, Insurance and Employee Benefits Div. • Bimonthly. $15.00 per year.

DIRECTORIES

Business Insurance Directory of Corporate Buyers of Insurance, Benefit Plans and Risk Management Services. Crain Communications, Inc. • Annual. $95.00. More than 2,600 corporations. Includes names of corporate employee benefits managers.

Business Insurance: Employee Benefit Consultants. Crain Communications, Inc. • Annual. $4.00. List of about 130 firms that offer empolyee benefit counseling services.

EBN Benefits Sourcebook. Securities Data Publishing. • Annual. $36.95. Lists vendors of products and services for the employee benefits industry. Includes industry trends and statistics. (Securities Data Publishing is a unit of Thomson Financial.).

The Human Resource Executive's Market Resource. LRP Publications. • Annual. $25.00. A directory of services and products of use to personnel departments. Includes 20 categories, such as training, outplacement, health benefits, recognition awards, testing, workers' compensation, temporary staffing, recruitment, and human resources software.

Internet Tools of the Profession: A Guide for Information Professionals. Hope N. Tillman, editor. Special Libraries Association. • 1997. $49.00. Second edition. Consists of 14 sections by various authors or compilers. After two introductory articles on searching the Internet, there are 12 annotated lists of useful Web sites, covering the SLA, business and finance, chemistry, education, food and agriculture, information technology, insurance and employee benefits, law, library management, metals and materials, pharmaceuticals, and telecommunications. An index is provided.

ENCYCLOPEDIAS AND DICTIONARIES

Blackwell Encyclopedic Dictionary of Human Resource Management. Lawrence H. Peters and Charles R. Greer, editors. Blackwell Publishers. • 1996. $105.95. The editors are associated with Texas Christian University. Contains definitions of key terms combined with longer articles written by various U. S. and foreign business educators. Includes bibliographies and index. (Blackwell Encyclopedia of Management Series).

Employee Benefit Plans: A Glossary of Terms. Judith A. Sankey, editor. International Foundation of Employee Benefit Plans. • 1997. $32.00. Ninth edition. Contains updated and new definitions derived from all aspects of the employee benefits field in the U.S. and Canada.

HANDBOOKS AND MANUALS

Accountant's Guide to Employee Benefits. Paul Rosenfield. Warren, Gorham and Lamont/RIA Group. • $205.00. Periodic supplementation. Formerly *Accounting and Auditing for Employee Benefits.*

Employee Benefits Handbook. Warren, Gorham and Lamont/RIA Group. • Looseleaf service. $195.00. Semiannual updates.

Handbook of Employee Benefits: Design, Funding, and Administration. Jerry S. Rosenbloom, editor. McGraw-Hill Higher Education. • 2001. $95.00. Fourth edition.

Handbook of Executive Benefits. Towers Perrin. McGraw-Hill Higher Education. • 1995. $75.00.

Medicare: Employer Health Plans. Available from Consumer Information Center. • Free. Published by the U. S. Department of Health and Human Services. Explains the special rules that apply to Medicare beneficiaries who have employer group health plan coverage. (Publication No. 520-Y.).

U. S. Master Employee Benefits Guide. CCH, Inc. • Annual. $49.00. Explains federal tax and labor laws relating to health care benefits, disability benefits, workers' compensation, employee assistance plans, etc.

INTERNET DATABASES

Internet Tools of the Profession. Special Libraries Association. Phone: (202)234-4700 Fax: (202)265-9317 E-mail: hope@tiac.net • URL: http://www.sla.org/pubs/itotp • Web site is designed to update the printed *Internet Tools of the Profession.* Provides links to a wide range of useful databases in business, finance, industry, information technology, insurance, law, library management, telecommunications, and other subject areas. Fees: Free.

ONLINE DATABASES

ABI/INFORM. Bell & Howell Information and Learning. • Provides online indexing to business-related material occurring in over 1,000 periodicals from 1971 to the present. Inquire as to online cost and availability.

Accounting and Tax Database. Bell & Howell Information and Learning. • Provides indexing and abstracting of the literature of accounting, taxation, and financial management, 1971 to date. Updating is weekly. Especially covers accounting, auditing, banking, bankruptcy, employee compensation and benefits, cash management, financial planning, and credit. Inquire as to online cost and availability.

Employee Benefits Infosource. International Foundation of Employee Benefit Plans. • Provides citations and abstracts to the literature of employee benefits, 1986 to present. Monthly updates. Inquire as to online cost and availability.

Labordoc. International Labour Office. • Indexing of labor literature and the publications of the International Labour Organization, 1965 to present. Monthly updates. Inquire as to online cost and availability.

PAIS International. Public Affairs Information Service, Inc. • Corresponds to the former printed publications, *PAIS Bulletin* (1976-90) and *PAIS Foreign Language Index* (1972-90), and to the current *PAIS International in Print* (1991 to date). Covers economic, political, and sociological material appearing in periodicals, books, government documents, and other publications. Updating is monthly. Inquire as to online cost and availability.

Wilson Business Abstracts Online. H. W. Wilson Co. • Indexes and abstracts 600 major business periodicals, plus the *Wall Street Journal* and the business section of the *New York Times.* Indexing is from 1982, abstracting from 1990, with the two newspapers included from 1993. Updated weekly. Inquire as to online cost and availability. (*Business Periodicals Index* without abstracts is also available online.).

PERIODICALS AND NEWSLETTERS

Benefits News Analysis. Benefits News Analysis, Inc. • Bimonthly. $89.00. Analysis of corporate employee benefit practices. Includes review of benefit program changes at a number of large corporations.

Business and Health. Medical Economics Co., Inc. • Monthly. $99.00 per year. Edited for business, government, and other buyers of employee healthcare insurance or HMO coverage.

Business Insurance: News Magazine for Corporate Risk, Employee Benefit and Financial Executives. Crain Communications, Inc. • Weekly. $89.00 per year. Covers a wide variety of business insurance topics, including risk management, employee benefits, workers compensation, marine insurance, and casualty insurance.

Compensation and Benefits Management. Panel Publishers. • Quarterly. $164.00 per year. Timely articles and regular columns directed to the executive, manager or professional responsible for design, implementation and management of compensation programs.

Compensation and Benefits Update. Warren, Gorham and Lamont/RIA Group. • Monthly. $149.00 per year. Provides information on the latest ideas and developments in the field of employee benefits. In-depth exploration of popular benefits programs. Formerly *Benefits and Compensation Update.*

Contingencies: The Magazine of the Actuarial Profession. American Academy of Actuaries. • Bimonthly. $30.00 per year. Provides non-technical articles on the actuarial aspects of insurance, employee benefits, and pensions.

Employee Benefit News: The News Magazine for Employee Benefit Management. Securities Data Publishing. • Monthly. $94.00 per year. Edited for human relations directors and other managers of employee benefits. (Securities Data Publishing is a unit of Thomson Financial.).

Employee Benefit Plan Review. Charles D. Spencer and Associates, Inc. • Monthly. $75.00 per year. (Also *Spencer's Research Reports on Employee Benefits.* Looseleaf service. $585.00 per year). Provides a review of recent events affecting the administration of employee benefit programs.

Employee Benefits Digest. International Foundation of Employee Benefit Plans. • Monthly. $190.00 per year. Articles on timely topics and information on current employee benefits literature.

Employee Benefits Journal. International Foundation of Employee Benefit Plans. • Quarterly. $70.00 per year. Selected articles on timely and important benefit subjects.

Human Resource Executive. LRP Publications, Inc. • Monthly. $89.95 per year. Edited for directors of corporate human resource departments. Special issues emphasize training, benefits, retirement planning, recruitment, outplacement, workers' compensation, legal pitfalls, and oes emphasize training, benefits, retirement planning, recruitment, outplacement, workers' compensation, legal pitfalls, and other personnel topics.

IOMA's Report on Defined Contribution Plan Investing. Institute for Management and Administration, Inc. • Semimonthly. $1,156.90 per year. Newsletter. Edited for 401(k) and other defined contribution retirement plan managers, sponsors, and service providers. Reports on such items as investment manager performance, guaranteed investment contract (GIC) yields, and asset allocation trends.

Journal of Finacial Services Professionals. American Society of CLU and Ch F C. • Bimonthly. $38.00 per year. Provides information on life insurance and financial planning, including estate planning, retirement, tax planning, trusts, business insurance, long-term care insurance, disability insurance, and employee benefits. Formerly (American Society of CLU and Ch F C Journal).

Legal-Legislative Reporter News Bulletin. International Foundation of Employee Benefit Plans, Inc. • Monthly. $190.00 per year. Review of legislative developments, court cases, arbitration awards and administrative decisions of importance.

Pension Plan Guide. CCH, Inc. • Weekly. $1,129.00 per year. Newsletter. Formerly *Pension Plan Guide Summary.*

Risk and Insurance. LRP Publications. • Monthly. Price on application. Topics include risk management, workers' compensation, reinsurance, employee benefits, and managed care.

The Successful Benefits Communicator. Lawence Ragan Communications, Inc. • Monthly. $117.00 per year. Newsletter on techniques for providing useful information to employees about benefits. Formerly *Techniques for the Benefits Communicator.*

Workforce: The Business Magazine for Leaders in Human Resources. ACC Communications, Inc. • Monthly. $59.00 per year. Edited for human resources managers. Covers employee benefits, compensation, relocation, recruitment, training, personnel legalities, and related subjects. Supplements include bimonthly "New Product News" and semiannual "Recruitment/Staffing Sourcebook." Formerly *Personnel Journal.*

RESEARCH CENTERS AND INSTITUTES

Employee Benefit Research Institute. 2121 K St., N. W., Suite 600, Washington, DC 20037-1896. Phone: (202)659-0670 Fax: (202)775-6312 E-mail: salisbury@ebri.org • URL: http://www.ebri.org • Conducts research on employee benefits, including various kinds of pensions, individual retirement accounts (IRAs), health insurance, social security, and long-term health care benefits.

STATISTICS SOURCES

Compensation and Working Conditions. Available from U. S. Government Printing Office. • Quarterly. $18.00 per year. Issued by the Bureau of Labor Statistics, U. S. Department of Labor. Presents wage and benefit changes that result from collective bargaining settlements and unilateral management decisions. Includes statistical summaries and special reports on wage trends. Formerly *Current Wage Developments.*

EBRI Databook on Employee Benefits. Employee Benefit Research Institute. • 1997 $99.00. Fourth edition. Contains more than 350 tables and charts presenting data on employee benefits in the U. S., including pensions, health insurance, social security, and medicare. Includes a glossary of employee benefit terms.

Employee Benefits in Medium and Large Private Establishments. Available from U. S. Government Printing Office. • Biennial. Issued by Bureau of Labor Statistics, U. S. Department of Labor. Provides data on benefits provided by companies with 100 or more employees. Covers benefits for both full-time and part-time workers, including health insurance, pensions, a wide variety of paid time-off policies (holidays, vacations, personal leave, maternity leave, etc.), and other fringe benefits.

Employee Benefits in Small Private Establishments. Available from U. S. Government Printing Office. • Biennial. Issued by Bureau of Labor Statistics, U. S. Department of Labor. Supplies data on a wide variety of benefits provided by companies with fewer than 100 employees. Includes statistics for both full-time and part-time workers.

Report on the American Workforce. Available from U. S. Government Printing Office. • Annual. $15.00. Issued by the U. S. Department of Labor (http://www.dol.gov). Appendix contains tabular statistics, including employment, unemployment, price indexes, consumer expenditures, employee benefits (retirement, insurance, vacation, etc.), wages, productivity, hours of work, and occupational injuries. Annual figures are shown for up to 50 years.

Social Security Bulletin. Social Security Administration. Available from U.S. Government Printing Office. • Quarterly. $23.00 per year. Annual statistical supplement.

TRADE/PROFESSIONAL ASSOCIATIONS

American Society of Pension Actuaries. 4245 N. Fairfax Dr., Suite 750, Arlington, VA 22203. Phone: (703)516-9300 Fax: (703)516-9308 E-mail: aspa@aspa.org • URL: http://www.aspa.org • Members are involved in the pension and insurance aspects of employee benefits. Includes an Insurance and Risk Management Committee, and sponsors an annual 401(k) Workshop.

Association of Private Pension and Welfare Plans. 1212 New York Ave., N. W., Suite 1250, Washington, DC 20005-3987. Phone: (202)289-6700 Fax: (202)289-4582 • URL: http://www.appwp.org • Members are large and small business firms offering pension and other benefit plans for their employees.

Council on Employee Benefits. 1212 New York Ave., N.W., Suite 1225, Washington, DC 20005. Phone: (202)408-3192 Fax: (202)408-3289 E-mail: vschieber@ceb.org • URL: http://www.ceb.org.

Employers Council on Flexible Compensation. 927 15th St., N.W., Suite 1000, Washington, DC 20005. Phone: (202)659-4300 E-mail: infoefc@ecfc.org • URL: http://www.ecfc.org • Promotes flexible or "cafeteria" plans for employee compensation and benefits.

International Foundation of Employee Benefit Plans. P.O. Box 69, Brookfield, WI 53008. Phone: 888-334-3327 or (262)786-6700 Fax: (262)786-8670 E-mail: pr@ifebp.org • URL: http://www.ifebp.org.

International Society of Certified Employee Beneift Plan Specialists. P.O. Box 209, Brookfield, WI 53008-0209. Phone: (414)786-8771 Fax: (414)786-8650 E-mail: iscebs@ifebp.org • URL: http://www.ifebp.org/ishmpage.html • Affiliated with International Foundation of Employee Benefit Plans.

National Employee Benefits Institute. 1350 Connecticut Ave., N.W. No. 600, Washington, DC 20036. Phone: 888-822-1344 or (202)822-6432 Fax: (202)466-5109.

Profit Sharing/401(K) Education Foundation. 10 S. Riverside Plaza, No. 1610, Chicago, IL 60606. Phone: (312)441-8550 Fax: (312)441-8559 E-mail: psca@psca.org • URL: http://www.psca.org.

OTHER SOURCES

Employee Benefit Cases. Bureau of National Affairs, Inc. • 50 times a year. $1,141.00 per year. Looseleaf.

Employee Benefits Management. CCH, Inc. • Five looseleaf volumes. Newsletter and semimonthly updates. Emphasis on pension plans.

EMPLOYEE COUNSELING

See: COUNSELING

EMPLOYEE DISCIPLINE

ABSTRACTS AND INDEXES

Business Periodicals Index. H. W. Wilson Co. • Monthly, except August, with quarterly and annual cumulations. Service basis for print edition; CD-ROM edition, $1,495.00 per year.

Personnel Management Abstracts. • Quarterly. $190.00 per year. Includes annual cumulation.

DIRECTORIES

Business Organizations, Agencies, and Publications Directory. The Gale Group. • 1999. $425.00. 12th edition. Over 40,000 entries describing 39 types of business information sources. Classified by type of organization, publication, or serviceIncludes state, national, and international agencies and organizations. Master index to names and keywords. Also includes e-mail addresses and web site URL's.

HANDBOOKS AND MANUALS

Fair, Square, and Legal: Safe Hiring, Managing, and Firing Practices to Keep You and Your Company Out of Court. Donald Weiss. AMACOM. • 1999. $29.95. Third edition. Covers recruiting, interviewing, sexual discrimination, evaluation of employees, disipline, defamation charges, and wrongful discharge.

The Federal Manager's Handbook: A Guide to Rehabilitating or Removing the Problem Employee. G. Jerry Shaw and William L. Bransford. FPMI Communications, Inc. • 1997. $24.95. Third revised edition.

ONLINE DATABASES

Wilson Business Abstracts Online. H. W. Wilson Co. • Indexes and abstracts 600 major business periodicals, plus the *Wall Street Journal* and the business section of the *New York Times.* Indexing is from 1982, abstracting from 1990, with the two newspapers included from 1993. Updated weekly. Inquire as to online cost and availability. (*Business Periodicals Index* without abstracts is also available online.).

PERIODICALS AND NEWSLETTERS

Employee Relations Bulletin. Bureau of Business Practice, Inc. • Semimonthly. $199.00 per year. Newsletter. Formerly *Employee Relations and Human Resources Bulletin.*

HR Briefing (Human Resources). Bureau of Business Practice, Inc. • Semimonthly. $195.00 per year. Newsletter. Formerly *Personnel Manager's Letter.*

Labor Relations Bulletin. Bureau of Business Practice, Inc. • Monthly. $99.84 per year. Labor arbitration case analysis. Formerly *Discipline and Grievances.*

OTHER SOURCES

Employment Practice Guide. CCH, Inc. • Weekly. $999.00 per year. Four looseleaf volumes.

How to Interview Effectively. American Management Association Extension Institute. • Looseleaf. $110.00. Self-study course on employment, performance, evaluation, disciplinary, and exit interviewing. Emphasis is on practical explanations, examples, and problem solving. Quizzes and a case study are included.

EMPLOYEE DISMISSAL

See: DISMISSAL OF EMPLOYEES

EMPLOYEE EDUCATION

See: TRAINING OF EMPLOYEES

EMPLOYEE EFFICIENCY

See: TIME AND MOTION STUDY

EMPLOYEE HEALTH PROGRAMS

See: EMPLOYEE WELLNESS PROGRAMS

EMPLOYEE LUNCHROOMS AND CAFETERIAS

See also: RESTAURANTS, LUNCHROOMS, ETC.

GENERAL WORKS

Fundamentals of Professional Food Preparation: A Laboratory Text-Workbook. Donald V. Laconi. John Wiley and Sons, Inc. • 1995. $54.95.

PERIODICALS AND NEWSLETTERS

Chef. Talcott Communications Corp. • Monthly. $24.00 per year. Edited for executive chefs, food and beverage directors, caterers, banquet and club managers, and others responsible for food buying and food service. Special coverage of regional foods is provided.

TRADE/PROFESSIONAL ASSOCIATIONS

Society for Foodservice Management. 304 W. Liberty St., Suite 201, Louisville, KY 40202. Phone: (502)583-3783 Fax: (502)589-3602 E-mail: sfmhq@aol.com • URL: http://www.sfm-online.org.

EMPLOYEE MAGAZINES

See: HOUSE ORGANS

EMPLOYEE MANUALS

See: PROCEDURE MANUALS

EMPLOYEE MOTIVATION

See: MOTIVATION (PSYCHOLOGY)

EMPLOYEE PAMPHLETS

See: PAMPHLETS

EMPLOYEE PARTICIPATION

See: PARTICIPATIVE MANAGEMENT

EMPLOYEE RATING

See: RATING OF EMPLOYEES

EMPLOYEE RELOCATION

See: RELOCATION OF EMPLOYEES

EMPLOYEE REPRESENTATION IN MANAGEMENT

GENERAL WORKS

Employee Representation: Alternatives and Future Directions. Bruce E. Kaufman and Morris Kleiner, editors. University of Wisconsin, Industrial Realtions Research Assoc. • 1993. $28.00.

Worker Self-Management in Industry: The West European Experience. G. David Garson, editor. Greenwood Publishing Group, Inc. • 1977. $48.95. (Praeger Special Studies).

DIRECTORIES

Employee Involvement Association Membership Directory. Employee Involvement Association. • Annual. Membership.

ONLINE DATABASES

Labordoc. International Labour Office. • Indexing of labor literature and the publications of the International Labour Organization, 1965 to present. Monthly updates. Inquire as to online cost and availability.

Management Contents. The Gale Group. • Covers a wide range of management, financial, marketing, personnel, and administrative topics. About 150 leading business journals are indexed and abstracted from 1974 to date, with monthly updating. Inquire as to online cost and availability.

PERIODICALS AND NEWSLETTERS

New Horizons. Employee Involvement Association. • Quarterly. Membership. Newsletter.

STATISTICS SOURCES

Employee Involvement Association Statistical Report. Employee Involvement Association. • Annual. 150.00.

TRADE/PROFESSIONAL ASSOCIATIONS

Employee Involvement Association. 525 Fifth St., S.W., Ste. A, Des Moines, IA 50309-4501. Phone: (515)282-8192 Fax: (515)282-9117 E-mail: jbw@amg-inc.com • URL: http://www.eia.com • Members are business and government professionals dedicated to employee involvement processes, including suggestion systems.

EMPLOYEE SELECTION

See: RECRUITMENT OF PERSONNEL

EMPLOYEE STOCK OWNERSHIP PLANS

ABSTRACTS AND INDEXES

Business Periodicals Index. H. W. Wilson Co. • Monthly, except August, with quarterly and annual cumulations. Service basis for print edition; CD-ROM edition, $1,495.00 per year.

DIRECTORIES

Business Organizations, Agencies, and Publications Directory. The Gale Group. • 1999. $425.00. 12th edition. Over 40,000 entries describing 39 types of business information sources. Classified by type of organization, publication, or serviceIncludes state, national, and international agencies and organizations. Master index to names and keywords. Also includes e-mail addresses and web site URL's.

HANDBOOKS AND MANUALS

Employee Stock Ownership Plans: A Practical Guide to ESOPs and Other Broad Ownership Programs. Scott Rodrick, editor. Harcourt Brace, Legal and Professional Publications, Inc. • 1996. $79.00. Contains 19 articles by various authors on ESOPs, 401(k) plans, profit sharing, executive stock option plans, and related subjects.

The 401(k) Plan Handbook. Julie Jason. Prentice Hall. • 1997. $79.95. Provides technical, legal, administrative, and investment details of 401(k) retirement plans.

Handbook of 401(k) Plan Management. Towers, Perrin, Foster and Crosby Staff. McGraw-Hill Higher Education. • 1992. $70.00. Written for employers and pension plan administrators. In addition to legal details of 401(k) plans, employee stock ownership plans (ESOPs) and basic principles of asset investment are covered. Appendix contains "Sample 401(k) Savings Plan Document.".

U. S. Master Pension Guide. CCH, Inc. • Annual. $49.00. Explains IRS rules and regulations applying to 401(k) plans, 403(k) plans, ESOPs (employee stock ownership plans), IRAs, SEPs (simplified employee pension plans), Keogh plans, and nonqualified plans.

ONLINE DATABASES

Wilson Business Abstracts Online. H. W. Wilson Co. • Indexes and abstracts 600 major business periodicals, plus the *Wall Street Journal* and the business section of the *New York Times*. Indexing is from 1982, abstracting from 1990, with the two newspapers included from 1993. Updated weekly. Inquire as to online cost and availability. (*Business Periodicals Index* without abstracts is also available online.).

PERIODICALS AND NEWSLETTERS

Employee Ownership Report. National Center for Employee Ownership, Inc. • Bimonthly. Membership. Formerly *Employee Ownership*.

ESOP Report (Employee Stock Ownership Plan). ESOP Association. • Monthly. Membership. Newsletter.

Journal of Compensation and Benefits. Warren, Gorham & Lamont/RIA Group. • Bimonthly. $170.00 per year. Working advisor for benefits administrators, company specialists and consultants.

TRADE/PROFESSIONAL ASSOCIATIONS

ESOP Association. 1726 M St., N.W. Suite 501, Washington, DC 20036. Phone: (202)293-2971 Fax: (202)293-7568 E-mail: esop@esopassociation.org • URL: http://www.esopassociation.org • Members are companies with employee stock ownership plans.

National Center for Employee Ownership. 1736 Franklin St., 8th Fl., Oakland, CA 94612. Phone: (510)272-9461 or (510)208-1800 Fax: (510)272-9510 E-mail: nceo@nceo.org • URL: http://www.nceo.org.

EMPLOYEE SUGGESTIONS

See: SUGGESTION SYSTEMS

EMPLOYEE THEFT

See: CRIME AND CRIMINALS; FRAUD AND EMBEZZLEMENT

EMPLOYEE TRAINING

See: TRAINING OF EMPLOYEES

EMPLOYEE WELLNESS PROGRAMS

See also: HEALTH CARE INDUSTRY

GENERAL WORKS

Principles of Health and Hygiene in the Workplace. Timothy J. Key and Michael A. Mueller. Lewis Publishers. • Date not set. $69.95.

Work and Health: Strategies for Maintaining a Vital Workforce. Panel Publishers. • 1989. $79.00.

ABSTRACTS AND INDEXES

Excerpta Medica: Occupational Health and Industrial Medicine. Elsevier Science. • Monthly. $1,833.00 per year. Section 35 of *Excerpta Medica*.

Safety and Health at Work. International Labour Office. • Bimonthly. $240.00 per year. Formerly *Occupational Safety and Health Abstracts*.

DIRECTORIES

Evaluation Guide to Health and Wellness Programs. The Corporate University. • $189.00. Looseleaf service. Semiannual updates, $49.00 each. Provides detailed descriptions and evaluations of more than 200 employee wellness programs that are available nationally. Covers 15 major topics, such as stress management, substance abuse, occupational safety, smoking cessation, blood pressure management, exercise/fitness, diet, and mental health. Programs are available from both profit and non-profit organizations.

Fitness Management Products and Services Source Guide. Leisure Publications, Inc. • Annual. $30.00. A directory of fitness equipment manufacturers and suppliers of services. Includes a glossary of terms related to the fitness industry and employee wellness programs.

Preventive Care Sourcebook. Aspen Publishers, Inc. • Annual. $89.00. Lists sources of programs and materials on preventive care, community health, and employee wellness.

ENCYCLOPEDIAS AND DICTIONARIES

Encyclopedia of Occupational Health and Safety. Available from The Gale Group. • 1999. $495.00. Fourth edition. Four volumes. Published by the International Labor Office (http://www.ilo.org). Covers safety engineering, industrial medicine, ergonomics, hygiene, epidemiology, toxicology, industrial psychology, and related topics. Includes material related to specific chemical, textile, transport, construction, manufacturing, and other industries. Indexed by subject, chemical name, and author, with a "Directory of Experts.".

HANDBOOKS AND MANUALS

How to Cut Your Company's Health Care Costs. George Halvorson. Prentice Hall. • 1987. $27.50.

Stress and Well-Being at Work: Assessments and Interventions for Occupational Mental Health. James C. Quick and others, editors. American Psychological Association. • 1992. $19.95.

Worksite Wellness: A New and Practical Approach to Reducing Health Care Cost. David W. Jensen. Prentice Hall. • 1987. $25.00.

PERIODICALS AND NEWSLETTERS

Employee Health and Fitness: The Executive Update on Health Improvement Programs. American Health Consultants, Inc. • Monthly. $499.00 per year. Newsletter. Executive update on health improvement programs.

Fitness Management. Leisure Publications, Inc. • Monthly. $24.00 per year. Published for owners and managers of physical fitness centers, both commercial and corporate.

Job Safety and Health Quarterly. Available from U. S. Government Printing Office. • Quarterly. $17.00 per year. Issued by the Occupational Safety and Health Administration (OSHA), U. S. Department of Labor. Contains articles on employee safety and health, with information on current OSHA activities.

RESEARCH CENTERS AND INSTITUTES

Center for Health Promotion Research and Development. University of Texas, Houston Health Science Center, P.O. Box 20186, Houston, TX 77225. Phone: (713)500-9601 Fax: (713)500-9602 E-mail: guy@utsph.sph.uth.tmc.edu • URL: http://www.utsph.sph.uth.tmc.edu • Fields of study include worksite health promotion.

Center for Worksite Health Enhancement. Pennsylvania State University, One White Bldg., University Park, PA 16802. Phone: (814)863-0435 Fax: (814)863-8586 E-mail: ryr@psuvm.psu.edu • Evaluates health and fitness programs.

Health Policy Institute. University of Texas-Houston Health Science Center, P.O. Box 20186, Houston, TX 77225. Phone: (713)500-9485 Fax: (713)500-9493 E-mail: dlow@admin4.hsc.uth.tmc.edu • URL: http://www.sph.utu.tmc.edu/ctr/hpi/hpi.htm.

Health Research Institute. 3538 Torino Way, Concord, CA 94518. Phone: (510)676-2320 Fax: (510)676-2342 • Conducts applied research in health care financing and delivery of health services, with emphasis on cost containment.

National Wellness Institute, Inc. P.O. Box 827, Stevens Point, WI 54481. Phone: (715)342-2969 Fax: (715)342-2979 E-mail: nwi@wellnessnwi.org • URL: http://www.wellnessnwi.org/.

TRADE/PROFESSIONAL ASSOCIATIONS

Wellness Center. 145 W. 28th St., Room 9R, New York, NY 10001. Phone: (212)465-8062 • Members include business firms and organizations with wellness centers for employees.

EMPLOYEES, TEMPORARY

See: TEMPORARY EMPLOYEES

EMPLOYMENT

See also: JOB HUNTING; LABOR SUPPLY; OCCUPATIONS; UNEMPLOYMENT

GENERAL WORKS

Getting Ahead at Work: A Proven System for Advancing at Work, Regardless of Your Occupation. Gordon W. Green. Carol Publishing Group. • 1989. $9.95. Includes making a good impression in a new job.

The Human Marketplace: An Examination of Private Employment Agencies. Tomas Martinez. Transaction Publishers. • 1995. $34.95.

ABSTRACTS AND INDEXES

Human Resources Abstracts: An International Information Service. Sage Publications, Inc. • Quarterly. Individuals, $150.00 per year; institutions, $610.00 per year.

ALMANACS AND YEARBOOKS

Employment Outlook. OECD Publications and Information Center. • Annual. $50.00. Outlines the employment prospects for the coming year in OECD countries. Also discusses labor force growth, job creation, labor standards, and collective bargaining.

World Labour Report. International Labour Office. • Irregular. Price varies. Volume eight. International coverage. Reviews significant recent events and labor policy developments in the following areas: employment, human rights, labor relations, and working conditions.

CD-ROM DATABASES

Sourcebooks America CD-ROM. CACI Marketing Systems. • Annual. $1,250.00. Provides the CD-ROM version of *The Sourcebook of ZIP Code Demographics: Census Edition* and *The Sourcebook of County Demographics: Census Edition.*

WILSONDISC: Wilson Business Abstracts. H. W. Wilson Co. • Monthly. $2,495.00 per year, including unlimited online access to *Wilson Business Abstracts* through WILSONLINE. Provides CD-ROM "cover-to-cover" abstracting and indexing of over 600 prominent business periodicals. Indexing is from 1982, abstracting from 1990. (*Business Periodicals Index* without abstracts is available on CD-ROM at $1,495 per year.).

DIRECTORIES

Directory of Counseling Services. International Association of Counseling Services. • Annual. $50.00. About 200 accredited services in the United States and Canada concerned with psychological educational, and vocational counseling, including those at colleges and universities and public and private agencies.

NACE National Directory: Who's Who in Career Planning, Placement, and Recruitment. National Association of Colleges and Employers. • Annual. Members, $32.95; non-members, $47.95. Lists over 2,200 college placement offices and about 2,000 companies interested in recruiting college graduates. Gives names of placement and recruitment personnel. Formerly *CPC National Dierctory.*

National Directory of Personnel Service Firms. National Association of Personnel Services. • Annual. $15.95. Lists over 1,100 member private (for-profit) employment firms. Formerly *ACCESS.*

ENCYCLOPEDIAS AND DICTIONARIES

Selected Characteristics of Occupations Defined in the Revised Dictionary of Occupational Titles. Available from U. S. Government Printing Office. • 1993. Provides data on training time, physical demands, and environmental conditions for various occupations. (Employment and Training Administration, U. S. Department of Labor.).

HANDBOOKS AND MANUALS

Career Guide to Industries. Available from U. S. Government Printing Office. • 1998. $17.00. Issued by the Bureau of Labor Statistics, U. S. Department of Labor (http://www.bls.gov). Presents background career information (text) and statistics for the 40 industries that account for 70 percent of wage and salary jobs in the U. S. Includes nature of the industry, employment data, working conditions, training, earnings, rate of job growth, outlook, and other career factors. (BLS Bulletin 2503.).

Civil Service Handbook: How to Get a Civil Service Job. Pearson Education and Technology. • 1999. $12.95. 14th edition. (Arco Civil Service Series).

Law of the Workplace: Rights of Employers and Employees. James Hunt and Patricia Strongin. Bureau of National Affairs, Inc. • 1994. $45.00. Third edition. Wages, hours, working conditions, benefits, and so forth.

Legal Guide to Independent Contractor Status. Robert W. Wood. Panel Publishers. • 1999. $165.00. Third edition. A guide to the legal and tax-related differences between employers and independent contractors. Includes examples of both "safe" and "troublesome" independent contractor designations. Penalties and fines are discussed.

Occupational Outlook Handbook. Bureau of Labor Statistics, U.S. Department of Labor. Available from U.S. Government Printing Office. • Biennial. $53.00. Issued as one of the Bureau's *Bulletin* series and kept up to date by *Occupational Outlook Quarterly.*

Practical Guide to Tax Issues in Employment. Julia K. Brazelton. CCH, Inc. • 1999. $95.00. Covers income taxation as related to labor law and tax law, including settlements and awards. Written for tax professionals.

Standard Occupational Classification Manual. Available from Bernan Associates. • 2000. $38.00. Replaces the *Dictionary of Occupational Titles.* Produced by the federal Office of Management and Budget, Executive Office of the President. "Occupations are classified based on the work performed, and on the required skills, education, training, and credentials for each one." Six-digit codes contain elements for 23 Major Groups, 96 Minor Groups, 451 Broad Occupations, and 820 Detailed Occupations. Designed to reflect the occupational structure currently existing in the U. S.

INTERNET DATABASES

Bureau of Economic Analysis (BEA). U. S. Department of Commerce, Bureau of Economic Analysis. Phone: (202)606-9900 Fax: (202)606-5310 E-mail: webmaster@bea.doc.gov • URL: http://www.bea.doc.gov • Web site includes "News Release Information" covering national, regional, and international economic estimates from the BEA. Highlights of releases appear online the same day, complete text and tables appear the next day. "Recent News Releases" section provides titles for past nine months, with links. "BEA Data and Methodology" includes "Frequently Requested NIPA Data" (national income and product accounts, such as gross domestic product and personal income). Other statistics are available. Fees: Free.

Fedstats. Federal Interagency Council on Statistical Policy. Phone: (202)395-7254 • URL: http://www.fedstats.gov • Web site features an efficient search facility for full-text statistics produced by more than 70 federal agencies, including the Census Bureau, the Bureau of Economic Analysis, and the Bureau of Labor Statistics. Boolean searches can be made within one agency or for all agencies combined. Links are offered to international statistical bureaus, including the UN, IMF, OECD, UNESCO, Eurostat, and 20 individual countries. Fees: Free.

ONLINE DATABASES

DRI U.S. Central Database. Data Products Division. • Provides more than 23,000 business, financial, demographic, economic, foreign trade, and industry-related time series for the U.S. Includes national income, population, retail-wholesale trade, price indexes, labor data, housing, industrial production, banking, interest rates, money supply, etc. Time period is generally 1947 to date (some data back to 1929). Updating varies. Inquire as to online cost and availability.

EconBase: Time Series and Forecasts. WEFA, Inc. • Presents online econometric data for business conditions, economics, demographics, industry, finance, employment, household income, interest rates, prices, etc. Includes two-year forecasts for a wide range of economic indicators. Time span is 1948 to date, with monthly updates. Inquire as to online cost and availability.

Labordoc. International Labour Office. • Indexing of labor literature and the publications of the International Labour Organization, 1965 to present. Monthly updates. Inquire as to online cost and availability.

Wilson Business Abstracts Online. H. W. Wilson Co. • Indexes and abstracts 600 major business periodicals, plus the *Wall Street Journal* and the business section of the *New York Times.* Indexing is from 1982, abstracting from 1990, with the two newspapers included from 1993. Updated weekly. Inquire as to online cost and availability. (*Business Periodicals Index* without abstracts is also available online.).

PERIODICALS AND NEWSLETTERS

Human Resources Report. Bureau of National Affairs, Inc. • Weekly. $875.00 per year. Newsletter. Formerly *BNA'S Employee Relations Weekly.*

Occupational Outlook Quarterly. U.S. Department of Labor. Available from U.S. Government Printing Office. • Quarterly. $9.50 per year.

Recruiting Trends: The Monthly Newsletter for the Recruiting Executive. Kennedy Information LLC. • Monthly. $155.00 per year.

Vocational Training News: The Independent Weekly Report on Employment, Training, and Vocational Education. Aspen Publishers, Inc. • Weekly. $319.00 per year. Newsletter. Emphasis is on federal job training and vocational education programs. Formerly *Manpower and Vocational Education Weekly.*

RESEARCH CENTERS AND INSTITUTES

W. E. Upjohn Institute for Employment Research. 300 S. Westnedge Ave., Kalamazoo, MI 49007-4686. Phone: (616)343-5541 Fax: (616)343-3308 E-

For publishers addresses, refer to SOURCES CITED section at the back of the book.

mail: eberts@we.upjohninst.org • URL: http://www.upjohninst.org • Research fields include unemployment, unemployment insurance, worker's compensation, labor productivity, profit sharing, the labor market, economic development, earnings, training, and other areas related to employment.

STATISTICS SOURCES

Area Trends in Employment and Unemployment. Available from U. S. Government Printing Office. • Monthly. $60.00 per year. Issued by the U. S. Department of Labor (http://www.dol.gov). Includes a listing of labor surplus areas in the U. S.

Bulletin of Labour Statistics: Supplementing the Annual Data Presented in the Year Book of Labour Statistics. International Labour Ofice. ILO Publications Center. • Quarterly. $84.00 per year. Includes five *Supplements.* A supplement to *Yearbook of Labour Statistics.* Provides current labor and price index statistics for over 130 countries. Generally includes data for the most recent four years. Text in English, French and Spanish.

Business Statistics of the United States. Courtenay M. Slater, editor. Bernan Associates. • 1999. $74.00. Fifth edition. Based on *Business Statistics*, formerly issue by the Bureau of Economic Analysis, U. S. Department of Commerce. Provides basic data for a wide variety of U. S. industries, services, and economic indicators. Most statistics are shown annually for 29 years and monthly for the most recent four years.

County and City Extra: Annual Metro, City and County Data Book. Mark Littman and Deirdre A. Gaquin. Bernan Press. • 1999. $109.00. Updates and augments data published irregularly in print form by the U. S. Census Bureau in *County and City Data Book.* Covers "every state, county, metropolitan area, and congressional district in the United States, as well as all U. S. cities with a 1990 population of 25,000 or more." Contains a wide range tic maps.

County Business Patterns. Available from U. S. Government Printing Office. • Irregular. 52 issues containing annual data for each state, the District of Columbia, and a U. S. Summary. Produced by U.S. Bureau of the Census (http://www.census.gov). Provides local establishment and employment statistics by industry.

Demographics USA: County Edition. Market Statistics. • Annual. $435.00. Contains 200 statistical series for each of 3,000 counties. Includes population, household income, employment, retail sales, and consumer expenditures. Also provides Effective Buying Income, Buying Power Index, and data summaries by Metro Market, Media Market, and State. (CD-ROM version is available.).

Demographics USA: ZIP Edition. Market Statistics. • Annual. $435.00. Contains 50 statistical series for each of 40,000 ZIP codes. Includes population, household income, employment, retail sales, and consumer expenditures. Also provides Effective Buying Income, Business Characteristics, and data summaries by state, region, and the first three digits of ZIP codes. (CD-ROM version is available.).

Economic Report of the President: Together with the Annual Report of the Council of Economic Advisors. Available from U. S. Government Printing Office. • Annual. $29.00. Includes about 130 pages of "Statistical Tables Relating to Income, Employment, and Production." Tables cover national income, employment, wages, productivity, manufacturing, prices, credit, finance (public and private), corporate profits, and foreign trade.

Employment and Earnings. Available from U. S. Government Printing Office. • Monthly. $50.00 per year, including annual supplement. Produced by the Bureau of Labor Statistics, U. S. Department of Labor. Provides current data on employment, hours, and earnings for the U. S. as a whole, for states, and for more than 200 local areas.

Employment and Wages: Annual Averages. Available from U. S. Government Printing Office. • Annual. $48.00. Issued by the Bureau of Labor Statistics, U. S. Department of Labor. Presents a wide variety of data arranged by state and industry.

Employment Outlook, 1996-2006: A Summary of BLS Projections. Available from U. S. Government Printing Office. • 1998. $10.00. Issued by the Bureau of Labor Statistics, U. S. Department of Labor (http://www.bls.gov). Provides 1996 employment data and 2006 projections for a wide variety of managerial, professional, technical, marketing, clerical, service, agricultural, and production occupations. Includes factors affecting the employment growth of various industries. (Bureau of Labor Statistics Bulletin 2502.).

Gale City and Metro Rankings Reporter. The Gale Group. • 1996. $134.00. Second edition. Provides about 3,000 statistical ranking tables covering more than 1,500 U. S. cities and Metropolitan Statistical Areas. Covers economic, demographic, social, governmental, and cultural factors. Sources are private studies and government data.

Gale Country and World Rankings Reporter. The Gale Group. • 1997. $135.00. Second edition. Provides about 3,000 statistical ranking tables and charts covering more than 235 nations. Sources include the United Nations and various government publications.

Gale State Rankings Reporter. The Gale Group. • 1996. $110.00. Second edition Provides 3,000 ranked lists of states under 35 subject headings. Sources are newspapers, periodicals, books, research institute publications, and government publications.

Geographic Profile of Employment and Unemployment. Available from U. S. Government Printing Office. • Annual. Issued by Bureau of Labor Statistics, U. S. Department of Labor. Presents detailed, annual average employment, unemployment, and labor force data for regions, states, and metropolitan areas. Characteristics include sex, age, race, Hispanic origin, marital status, occupation, and type of industry.

Geographic Reference Report: Annual Report of Costs, Wages, salaries, and Human Resource Statistics for the United States and Canada. ERI. • Annual. $389.00. Provides demographic and other data for each of 298 North American metropolian areas, including local salaries, wage differentials, cost-of-living, housing costs, income taxation, employment, unemployment, population, major employers, crime rates, weather, etc.

Labour Force Statistics, 1977/1997: 1998 Edition. Organization for Economic Cooperation and Development. Available from OECD Publications and Information Center. • 1999. $98.00. Provides 21 years of data for OECD member countries on population, employment, unemployment, civilian labor force, armed forces, and other labor factors.

Monthly Labor Review. Available from U. S. Government Printing Office. • Monthly. $43.00 per year. Issued by the Bureau of Labor Statistics, U. S. Department of Labor. Contains data on the labor force, wages, work stoppages, price indexes, productivity, economic growth, and occupational injuries and illnesses.

Occupational Projections and Training Data. Available from U. S. Government Printing Office. • Biennial. $7.00. Issued by Bureau of Labor Statistics, U. S. Department of Labor. Contains projections of employment change and job openings over the next 15 years for about 500 specific occupations. Also includes the number of associate, bachelor's, master's, doctoral, and professional degrees awarded in a recent year for about 900 specific fields of study.

Quarterly Labour Force Statistics. Organization for Economic Cooperation and Development. Available from OECD Publications and Information Center. • Quarterly. $60.00 per year. Provides current data for OECD member countries on population, employment, unemployment, civilian labor force, armed forces, and other labor factors.

Report on the American Workforce. Available from U. S. Government Printing Office. • Annual. $15.00. Issued by the U. S. Department of Labor (http://www.dol.gov). Appendix contains tabular statistics, including employment, unemployment, price indexes, consumer expenditures, employee benefits (retirement, insurance, vacation, etc.), wages, productivity, hours of work, and occupational injuries. Annual figures are shown for up to 50 years.

Services: Statistics on Value Added and Employment. Organization for Economic Cooperation and Development. • Annual. $67.00. Provides 10-year data on service industry employment and output (value added) for all OECD countries. Covers such industries as telecommunications, business services, and information technology services.

State Profiles: The Population and Economy of Each U. S. State. Courtenay Slater and Martha Davis, editors. Bernan Press. • 1999. $74.00. Presents charts, tables, and text in an eight-page profile for each state. Covers population, labor force, income, poverty, employment, wages, industry, trade, housing, education, health, taxes, and government finances.

Statistical Abstract of the World. The Gale Group. • 1997. $80.00. Third edition. Provides data on a wide variety of economic, social, and political topics for about 200 countries. Arranged by country.

Statistical Forecasts of the United States. The Gale Group. • 1995. $99.00. Second edition. Provides both long-term and short-term statistical forecasts relating to basic items in the U. S.: population, employment, labor, crime, education, and health care. Data in the form of charts, graphs, and tables has been taken from a wide variety of government and private sources. Includes a subject index and an "Index of Forecast by Year.".

Statistical Handbook of Working America. The Gale Group. • 1997. $125.00. Second edition. Provides statistics, rankings, and forecasts relating to a wide variety of careers, occupations, and working conditions.

Statistical Handbook on the American Family. Bruce A. Chadwick and Tim B. Heaton, editors. Oryx Press. • 1998. $65.00. Includes data on education, health, politics, employment, expenditures, social characteristics, the elderly, and women in the labor force. Historical statistics on marriage, birth, and divorce are shown from 1900 on. A list of sources and a subject index are provided. (Statistical Handbook Series).

Survey of Current Business. Available from U. S. Government Printing Office. • Monthly. $49.00 per year. Issued by Bureau of Economic Analysis, U. S. Department of Commerce. Presents a wide variety of business and economic data.

World Statistics Pocketbook. United Nations Publications. • Annual. $10.00. Presents basic economic, social, and environmental indicators for about 200 countries and areas. Covers more than 50 items relating to population, economic activity, labor force, agriculture, industry, energy, trade, transportation, communication, education, tourism, and the environment. Statistical sources are noted.

Year Book of Labour Statistics. International Labour Office. • Annual. $168.00. Presents a wide range of labor and price data for most countries of the world. Supplement available *Sources and Methods. Labour Statistics.*

TRADE/PROFESSIONAL ASSOCIATIONS

Association of Master of Business Administration Executives. c/o AMBA Center, Five Summit Place, Branford, CT 06405. Phone: (203)315-5221 Fax: (203)483-6186.

International Association of Personnel in Employment Security. 1801 Louisville Rd., Frankfort, KY 40601. Phone: (502)223-4459 Fax: (502)233-4127 E-mail: iapes@aol.com • URL: http://www.iapes.org.

National Association of Personnel Services. 3133 Mount Vernon Ave., Alexandria, VA 22305. Phone: (703)684-0180 or (703)684-0181 Fax: (703)684-0071 E-mail: info@napsweb.org • URL: http://www.napsweb.org • Members are private employment agencies.

OTHER SOURCES

Employment and Training Reporter. MII Publications, Inc. • $747.00 per year. Looseleaf service. Weekly reports. Two volumes.

Employment Discrimination: Law and Litigation. Merrick T. Rossein. West Group. • $220.00 per year. Looseleaf service. Periodic supplementation. Covers employment provisions of the Civil Rights Act, the Equal Pay Act, and related topics.

Employment Litigation Reporter: The National Journal of Record for Termination Lawsuits Alleging Tort and Contract Claims Against Employers. Andrews Publications. • Semimonthly. $825.00 per year. Provides reports on wrongful dismissal lawsuits.

Labor Law Reports. CCH, Inc. • 16 looseleaf volumes. $2,151.00 per year, including weekly updates. Covers laborrelations, wages and hours, state labor laws, and employment practices. Supplement available *Guide to Fair Employment Practices.*

Working Americans, 1880-1999, Volume One: The Working Class. Grey House Publishing. • 2000. $135.00. Provides detailed information on the lifestyles and economic life of working class families in the 12 decades from 1880 to 1999. Includes such items as selected consumer prices, income, family finances, budgets, life at home, jobs, and working conditions. (Universal Reference Publications.).

Working Americans, 1880-1999, Volume Two: The Middle Class. Grey House Publishing. • 2000. $135.00. Furnishes details of the social and economic lives of middle class Americans during the years 1880 to 1999. Describes such items as selected consumer prices, income, family finances, budgets, life at home, jobs, and working conditions. (Universal Reference Publications.).

EMPLOYMENT AGENCIES AND SERVICES

See also: CIVIL SERVICE; COLLEGE PLACEMENT BUREAUS

DIRECTORIES

Directory of Executive Recruiters. Kennedy Information, LLC. • Annual. $44.95. Contains profiles of more than 4,000 executive recruiting firms in the U. S., Canada, and Mexico.

Directory of Outplacement and Career Management Firms. Kennedy Information, LLC. • Annual. $129.95. Contains profiles of more than 320 firms specialize in helping "downsized" executives find new employment.

50 Leading Retained Executive Search Firms in North America. Kennedy Information, LLC. • Annual. $15.00. Provides profiles of major search firms, including revenue data.

40 Largest Retained Executive Search Firms, U. S. & World. Kennedy Information, LLC. • Annual. $15.00. Rankings of search firms are by U. S. and world estimated revenues, with tables of staff sizes. Growth trends and market size estimates for the executive search industry are also provided.

Kennedy's Directory of Executive Temporary Placement Firms. Kennedy Information, LLC. • 1995. $24.95. Eighth revised edition. Provides information on about 225 executive search firms that have temporary placement as a specialty.

Key Women in Retained Executive Search. Kennedy Information, LLC. • 1994. Price on application. Lists about 600 women executives in 300 search firms in North America. Arranged by name of firm, with an index to names of individuals.

NACE National Directory: Who's Who in Career Planning, Placement, and Recruitment. National Association of Colleges and Employers. • Annual. Members, $32.95; non-members, $47.95. Lists over 2,200 college placement offices and about 2,000 companies interested in recruiting college graduates. Gives names of placement and recruitment personnel. Formerly *CPC National Dierctory.*

National Directory of Personnel Service Firms. National Association of Personnel Services. • Annual. $15.95. Lists over 1,100 member private (for-profit) employment firms. Formerly *ACCESS.*

HANDBOOKS AND MANUALS

Employment Agency. Entrepreneur Media, Inc. • Looseleaf. $59.50. A practical guide to starting an employment agency. Covers profit potential, start-up costs, market size evaluation, owner's time required, site selection, lease negotiation, pricing, accounting, advertising, promotion, etc. (Start-Up Business Guide No. E1051.).

Executive Recruiting Service. Entrepreneur Media, Inc. • Looseleaf. $59.50. A practical guide to starting an executive recruitment service. Covers profit potential, start-up costs, market size evaluation, owner's time required, pricing, accounting, advertising, promotion, etc. (Start-Up Business Guide No. E1228.).

Recruiter's Research Blue Book: A How-To Guide for Researchers, Search Consultants, Corporate Recruiters, Small Business Owners, Venture Capitalists, and Line Executives. Andrea A. Jupina. Kennedy Information. • 2000. $179.00. Second edition. Provides detailed coverage of the role that research plays in executive recruiting. Includes such practical items as "Telephone Interview Guide," "Legal Issues in Executive Search," and "How to Create an Execuive Search Library." Covers both person-to-person research and research using printed and online business information sources. Includes an extensive directory of recommended sources. Formerly *Handbook of Executive Search Research.*

Temporary Help Service. Entrepreneur Media, Inc. • Looseleaf. $59.50. A practical guide to starting an employment agency for temporary workers. Covers profit potential, start-up costs, market size evaluation, owner's time required, site selection, lease negotiation, pricing, accounting, advertising, promotion, etc. (Start-Up Business Guide No. E1189.).

INTERNET DATABASES

Bureau of Labor Statistics (BLS). U. S. Department of Labor, Bureau of Labor Statistics. Phone: (202)523-1092 E-mail: labstat.helpdesk@bls.gov • URL: http://www.bls.gov • Web site provides a great variety of employment, wage, price, and economic data. Some links are "Data," "Economy at a Glance," "Keyword Search of BLS Web Pages," "Regional Information," and "Other Statistical Sites." Fees: Free.

PERIODICALS AND NEWSLETTERS

Journal of Career Planning and Employment: The International Magazine of Placement and Recruitment. National Association of Colleges and Employers. • Quarterly. Free to members; non-members, $72.00 per year. Includes *Spotlight* newsletter. Formerly *Journal of College Placement.*

Recruiting Trends: The Monthly Newsletter for the Recruiting Executive. Kennedy Information LLC. • Monthly. $155.00 per year.

RESEARCH CENTERS AND INSTITUTES

Women Employed Institute. 22 W. Monroe St., Suite 1400, Chicago, IL 60603-2505. Phone: (312)782-3902 Fax: (312)782-5249 E-mail: info@womenemployed.org • URL: http://www.womenemployed.org • Research areas include the economic status of working women, sexual harassment in the workplace, equal employment opportunity, and career development.

STATISTICS SOURCES

An Analysis of Executive Search in North America. Kennedy Information, LLC. • Annual. $59.00. Includes ranking of leading executive search firms and estimates of market share and total revenue.

An Analysis of Outplacement Consulting in North America. Kennedy Information, LLC. • 1995. $35.00. Fourth edition. Includes ranking of leading outplacement consulting firms and estimates of market share and total revenue.

Handbook of U. S. Labor Statistics: Employment, Earnings, Prices, Productivity, and Other Labor Data. Eva E. Jacobs, editor. Bernan Associates. • 1999. $74.00. Based on *Handbook of Labor Statistics*, formerly issued by the Bureau of Labor Statistics, U. S. Department of Labor. Includes the Bureau's projections of employment in the U. S. by industry and occupation. Provides a wide variety of data on the work force, prices, fringe benefits, and consumer expenditures.

TRADE/PROFESSIONAL ASSOCIATIONS

American Staffing Association. 277 S. Washington St., Ste. 200, Alexandria, VA 22314-3119. Phone: (703)549-6287 Fax: (703)549-4808 E-mail: asa@staffingtoday.net • URL: http://www.staffingtoday.net • An association of private employment agencies for temporary workers.

Association of Career Management Consulting Firms International. 204 E. St., N.E., Washington, DC 20002. Phone: (202)857-1185 Fax: (202)547-6348 • URL: http://www.aocfi.org • Promotes professional standards of competence, objectivity, and integrity in the service of clients.

Association of Executive Search Consultants. 500 Fifth Ave., Suite 930, New York, NY 10110-0999. Phone: (212)398-9556 Fax: (212)398-9560 E-mail: aesc@aesc.org • URL: http://www.aesc.org.

National Association of Personnel Services. 3133 Mount Vernon Ave., Alexandria, VA 22305. Phone: (703)684-0180 or (703)684-0181 Fax: (703)684-0071 E-mail: info@napsweb.org • URL: http://www.napsweb.org • Members are private employment agencies.

Opportunities Industrialization Centers of America. 1415 N. Broad St., Philadelphia, PA 19122. Phone:

(215)236-4500 Fax: (215)236-7480 E-mail: oica@aol.com • URL: http://www.oicafamerica.org • Provides services for the hard core unemployed and under-employed.

EMPLOYMENT IN FOREIGN COUNTRIES

DIRECTORIES

American Jobs Abroad. The Gale Group. • 1996. $65.00. Provides information on more than 800 U. S. companies and 110 government agencies, associations, and other organizations that employ Americans overseas. (American Jobs Abroad Series).

Directory of American Firms Operating in Foreign Countries. Uniworld Business Publications Inc. • Biennial. $275.00. Three volumes. Lists approximately 2,450 American companies with more than 29,500 subsidiaries and affiliates in 138 foreign countries.

ONLINE DATABASES

Labordoc. International Labour Office. • Indexing of labor literature and the publications of the International Labour Organization, 1965 to present. Monthly updates. Inquire as to online cost and availability.

PERIODICALS AND NEWSLETTERS

International Employment Hotline. Cantrell Corp. • Monthly. $39.00 per year. Newsletter. Lists current overseas job openings by country and employer. Gives job titles and job descriptions as well as candidate qualificaitons.

Transitions Abroad: The Guide to Learning, Living, and Working Overseas. Transitions Abroad Publishing, Inc. • Bimonthly. $28.00 per year, including annual directory of information sources. Provides practical information and advice on foreign education and employment. Supplement available *Overseas Travel Planner.*

OTHER SOURCES

Foreign Labor Trends. Available from U. S. Government Printing Office. • Irregular (50 to 60 issues per year, each on an individual country). $38.00 per year. Prepared by various American Embassies. Issued by the Bureau of International Labor Affairs, U. S. Department of Labor. Covers labor developments in important foreign countries, including trends in wages, working conditions, labor supply, employment, and unemployment.

EMPLOYMENT INTERVIEWING

See: INTERVIEWING; JOB HUNTING

EMPLOYMENT MANAGEMENT

See: PERSONNEL MANAGEMENT

EMPLOYMENT OF OLDER WORKERS

See also: EQUAL EMPLOYMENT OPPORTUNITY; RETIREMENT

ALMANACS AND YEARBOOKS

Older Americans Information Directory. Group Grey House Publshing, Inc. • 2000. $190.00. Second edition. Presents articles (text) and sources of information on a wide variety of aging and retirement topics. Includes an index to personal names, organizations, and subjects.

DIRECTORIES

Older Americans Information Directory. Laura Mars, editor. Grey House Publishing, Inc. • 1998. $160.00. First edition. Provides information on about 5,000 organizations and agencies concerned with the needs of older people in the U. S.

ONLINE DATABASES

Labordoc. International Labour Office. • Indexing of labor literature and the publications of the International Labour Organization, 1965 to present. Monthly updates. Inquire as to online cost and availability.

STATISTICS SOURCES

Income of the Population 55 and Older. Available from U. S. Government Printing Office. • Biennial. $19.00. Issued by the Social Security Administration (http://www.ssa.gov). Covers major sources and amounts of income for the 55 and older population in the U. S., "with special emphasis on some aspects of the income of the population 65 and older.".

Social Security Bulletin. Social Security Administration. Available from U.S. Government Printing Office. • Quarterly. $23.00 per year. Annual statistical supplement.

Statistical Handbook on Aging Americans. Renee Schick, editor. Oryx Press. • 1994. $65.00. Second edition. Provides data on demographics, social characteristics, health, employment, economic conditions, income, pensions, and social security. Includes bibliographic information and a glossary. (Statistical Handbook Series).

Statistical Record of Older Americans. The Gale Group. • 1996. $109.00. Second edition. Includes income and pension data.

TRADE/PROFESSIONAL ASSOCIATIONS

Gerontological Society of America. 1030 15th St., N.W., Suite 250, Washington, DC 20005-1503. Phone: (202)842-1275 Fax: (202)842-1150 E-mail: webmaster@geron.org • URL: http://www.geron.org.

National Interfaith Coalition on Aging. 409 Third St., S.W., Suite 200, Washington, DC 20024. Phone: (202)479-1200 Fax: (202)479-0735 E-mail: info@ncoa.org • URL: http://www.ncoa.org.

OTHER SOURCES

Age Discrimination. Shepard's. • Three looseleaf volumes. $300.00. Annual supplementation. Emphasis on the Age Discrimination Act, the Age Discrimination in Employment Act, and the Equal Credit Opportunity Act.

EMPLOYMENT OF THE HANDICAPPED

See: HANDICAPPED WORKERS

EMPLOYMENT OF WOMEN

See also: EQUAL EMPLOYMENT OPPORTUNITY; WOMEN ACCOUNTANTS; WOMEN ENGINEERS; WOMEN IN THE WORK FORCE; WOMEN LAWYERS; WOMEN PHYSICIANS

GENERAL WORKS

Advancing Women in Business: The Catalyst Guide to Best Practices from the Corporate Leaders. Catalyst Staff. Available from Jossey-Bass, Inc., Publishers. • 1998. $26.00. Explains the human resources practices of corporations providing a favorable climate for the advancement of female employees.

Women and Careers: Issues, Pressures, and Challenges. Carol W. Konek and Sally L. Kitch, editors. Sage Publications, Inc. • 1993. $49.95. Based on a major survey assessing women's experiences in the workplace.

Women Breaking Through: Overcoming the Final 10 Obstacles at Work. Deborah J. Swiss. Peterson's. • 1996. $24.95. Discusses specific strategies for women to use to advance beyond the middle management level. Based on a survey of 300 women "on the leading edge of change.".

ABSTRACTS AND INDEXES

Women Studies Abstracts. Transaction Publishers. • Quarterly. Individuals, $102.00 per year; institutions, $216.00 per year.

BIOGRAPHICAL SOURCES

Who's Who of American Women. Marquis Who's Who. • Biennial. $259.00. Provides over 27,000 biographical profiles of important women, including individuals prominent in business, finance, and industry.

DIRECTORIES

Encyclopedia of Women's Associations Worldwide. The Gale Group. • 1998. $85.00. Second edition. Provides detailed information for more than 3,400 organizations throughout the world that relate to women and women's issues.

Women's Information Directory. The Gale Group. • 1992. $75.00. A guide to approximately 6,000 organizations, agencies, institutions, programs, and publications concerned with women in the United States. Includes subject and title indexes.

HANDBOOKS AND MANUALS

Women and the Law. Carol H. Lefcourt, editor. West Group. • $140.00. Looseleaf service. Periodic supplementation. Covers such topics as employment discrimination, pay equity (comparable worth), sexual harassment in the workplace, property rights, and child custody issues. (Civil Rights Series).

ONLINE DATABASES

Contemporary Women's Issues. Responsive Database Services, Inc. • Provides fulltext articles online from 150 periodicals and a wide variety of additional sources relating to economic, legal, social, political, education, health, and other women's issues. Time span is 1992 to date. Weekly updates. Inquire as to online cost and availability. (Also available in a CD-ROM version.).

Labordoc. International Labour Office. • Indexing of labor literature and the publications of the International Labour Organization, 1965 to present. Monthly updates. Inquire as to online cost and availability.

PERIODICALS AND NEWSLETTERS

AAUW Outlook. American Association of University Women. • Quarterly. Free to members; non-members, $15.00 per year. Formerly *Graduate Woman.*

The Equal Employer. Y. S. Publications, Inc. • Biweekly. $245.00 per year. Newsletter on fair employment practices.

Family Relations: State Capitals. Wakeman-Walworth, Inc. • Weekly. $245.00 per year. Newsletter. Formerly *From the State Capitals: Family Relations.*

Feminist Economics. International Association for Feminist Economics. Routledge Journals. • Three times a year. Individuals, $50.00 per year; institutions, $150.00 per year. Includes articles on issues relating to the employment and economic opportunities of women.

MS. Liberty Media for Women, L.L.C. • Bimonthly. $35.00 per year.

National Business Woman. National Federation of Business and Professional Women's Clubs, Inc. •

Quarterly. $10.00 per year. Focuses on the activities and interests of working women.

New Woman. Rodale Press, Inc. • Monthly. $27.60 per year.

Perspective. Catalyst, Inc. • Monthly. $60.00 per year. Newsletter. Covers leadership, mentoring, work/family programs, success stories, and other topics for women in the corporate world.

SFNOW Times. National Organization for Women, San Francisco Chapter. • Monthly. $4.50.

Women Today. M and O Communications. • Biweekly. $40.00 per year.

Women's Studies International Forum: A Multidisciplinary Journal for the Rapid Publication of Research Communications and Review Articles in Women's Studies. Elsevier Science. • Bimonthly. $479.00 per year.

Women's Studies Quarterly: The First U.S. Journal Devoted to Teaching about Women. Feminist Press. • Four times a year. Individuals, $30.00 per year; institutions, $40.00 per year. Provides coverage of issues and events in women's studies and feminist education, including in-depth articles on research about women and current projects to transform traditional curricula. Includes two double thematic issues.

Working Woman. MacDonald Communications Corp. • 10 times a year. $15.00 per year. Focuses on solutions of business problems.

RESEARCH CENTERS AND INSTITUTES

Business and Professional Women's Foundation. 2012 Massachusetts Ave., N.W., Washington, DC 20036. Phone: (202)293-1200 Fax: (202)861-0298 E-mail: gshaffer@bpwusa.org • URL: http://www.bpwusa.org.

Women Employed Institute. 22 W. Monroe St., Suite 1400, Chicago, IL 60603-2505. Phone: (312)782-3902 Fax: (312)782-5249 E-mail: info@womenemployed.org • URL: http://www.womenemployed.org • Research areas include the economic status of working women, sexual harassment in the workplace, equal employment opportunity, and career development.

STATISTICS SOURCES

Statistical Handbook on Women in America. Cynthia M. Taeuber, editor. Oryx Press. • 1996. $65.00. Includes data on demographics, employment, earnings, economic status, educational status, marriage, divorce, household units, health, and other topics. (Statistical Handbook Series).

Statistical Record of Women Worldwide. The Gale Group. • 1996. $125.00. Second edition. Includes employment data and other economic statistics relating to women in the U. S. and internationally.

United States Equal Employment Opportunity Commission Annual Report: Job Patterns for Minorities and Women in Private Industry. U.S. Equal Employment Opportunity Commission. • Annual.

Women in the World of Work: Statistical Analysis and Projections to the Year 2000. Shirley Nuss and others. International Labour Office. • 1989. $18.00. (Women, Work, and Development Series, No. 18).

TRADE/PROFESSIONAL ASSOCIATIONS

American Association of University Women. 1111 16th St., N.W., Washington, DC 20036. Phone: 800-326-2289 or (202)785-7700 Fax: (202)872-1425 E-mail: info@aauw.org • URL: http://www.aauw.org/index.html.

American Business Women's Association. P.O. Box 8728, Kansas City, MO 64114-0728. Phone: 800-228-0007 or (816)361-6621 Fax: (816)361-4991 E-mail: info@abwa.org • URL: http://www.abwahq.org.

Business and Professional Women USA. 2012 Massachusetts Ave., N.W., Washington, DC 20036. Phone: (202)293-1100 Fax: (202)861-0298 • URL: http://www.bpwwusa.org.

Catalyst. 120 Wall St., 5th Fl., New York, NY 10005-3904. Phone: (212)514-7600 Fax: (212)514-8470 E-mail: info@catalystwomen.org • URL: http://www.catalystwomen.org • Provides information, research, and publications relating to women's workplace issues. Promotes corporate leadership for women.

Coalition of Labor Union Women. 1126 16th St., N.W., Washington, DC 20036. Phone: (202)466-4610 Fax: (202)776-0537.

Federally Employed Women. P.O. Box 27687, Washington, DC 20005. Phone: (703)941-3390 Fax: (202)898-0998 E-mail: exec.dir@few.org • URL: http://www.few.org.

Federation of Organizations for Professional Women. P.O. Box 6234, Falls Church, VA 22040. Phone: (202)328-1415 Fax: (703)532-7295 E-mail: fopw@dgs-dgsys.com.

International Association for Feminist Economics. c/o Jean Schackleford, Dept. of Economics, Bucknell University, Lewisburg, PA 17837. Phone: (570)524-3441 Fax: (570)524-3451 E-mail: jshackle@bucknell.edu • Members are economists having a feminist viewpoint. Promotes greater economic opportunities for women.

International Federation of Business and Professional Women. Cloisters Business Center, Studio 16, Eight Battersea Park Rd., London SW8 4BG, England. Phone: 44 20 77388323 Fax: 44 20 76228528 E-mail: bpwhiq@cs.com • URL: http://www.bpwintl.com.

National Association for Female Executives. 135 W. 50th St., 16th Fl., New York, NY 10020. Phone: 800-634-6233 or (212)445-6233 or (212)445-6235 Fax: (212)445-6228 E-mail: nafe@nafe.com • URL: http://www.nafe.com.

National Association of Women Business Owners. 1411 K St., N.W., Washington, DC 20005. Phone: 800-556-2926 or (202)347-8686 Fax: (202)347-9210 E-mail: national@nawbo.org • URL: http://www.nawbo.org.

National Organization for Women. 733 15th St., N.W., 2nd Fl., Washington, DC 20005. Phone: (202)628-8669 Fax: (202)785-8576 E-mail: now@now.org • URL: http://www.now.org.

National Partnership for Women and Families. 1875 Connecticut Ave., N. W., Suite 710, Washington, DC 20009. Phone: (202)986-2600 Fax: (202)986-2539 E-mail: info@nationalpartnership.org • URL: http://www.nationalpartnership.org • Includes a Counseling on Employment Discrimination Committee. Offers telephone referral services.

National Women's Law Center. 11 Dupont Circle, N.W., Suite 800, Washington, DC 20036. Phone: (202)588-5180 Fax: (202)588-5185 E-mail: nwlcinfo@aol.com • Seeks protection and advancement of women's legal rights. Includes employment issues among areas of interest.

EMPLOYMENT RESUMES

See: JOB RESUMES

EMPLOYMENT SECURITY

See: UNEMPLOYMENT INSURANCE

EMPLOYMENT TESTS

See: PSYCHOLOGICAL TESTING

ENDOWMENTS

See: FOUNDATIONS

ENERGY COGENERATION

See: COGENERATION OF ENERGY

ENERGY, GEOTHERMAL

See: GEOTHERMAL ENERGY

ENERGY, NUCLEAR

See: NUCLEAR ENERGY

ENERGY, SOLAR

See: SOLAR ENERGY

ENERGY SOURCES

See also: COAL INDUSTRY; ELECTRIC UTILITIES; GEOTHERMAL ENERGY; NATURAL GAS; NUCLEAR ENERGY; PETROLEUM INDUSTRY; SOLAR ENERGY

GENERAL WORKS

Energy and Problems of a Technical Society. Jack J. Kraushaar and Robert A. Ristinen. John Wiley and Sons, Inc. • 1993. $58.95. Second edition.

Energy, Combustion and Environment. Norman Chigier. McGraw-Hill. • 1981. $86.25.

Energy Management. Paul Ocallaghan. McGraw-Hill. • 1993. $55.00.

Renewable Energy: Power for a Sustainable Future. Godfrey Boyle, editor. Available from Taylor & Francis. • 1996. $39.95. Published by Open University Press. Contains ten chapters, each on a particular renewable energy source, including solar, biomass, hydropower, wind, and geothermal.

ABSTRACTS AND INDEXES

Applied Science and Technology Index. H. W. Wilson Co. • 11 times a year. Quarterly and annual cumulations. Service basis for print edition; CD-ROM edition, $1,495.00 per year. Indexes a wide variety of English language technical, industrial, and engineering periodicals.

NTIS Alerts: Energy. National Technical Information Service. • Semimonthly. $245.00 per year. Provides descriptions of government-sponsored research reports and software, with ordering information. Covers electric power, batteries, fuels, geothermal energy, heating/cooling systems, nuclear technology, solar energy, energy policy, and related subjects. Formerly *Abstract Newsletter.*

ALMANACS AND YEARBOOKS

Annual Review of Energy and the Environment. Annual Reviews, Inc. • Annual. Individuals, $76.00; institutions, $152.00. Formerly *Annual Review of Energy.*

CD-ROM DATABASES

Environment Abstracts on CD-ROM. Congressional Information Service, Inc. • Quarterly. $1,295.00 per year. Contains the following CD-ROM databases: *Environment Abstracts, Energy Abstracts,* and *Acid Rain Abstracts.* Length of coverage varies.

DIRECTORIES

Financial Times Energy Yearbook: Mining 2000. Available from The Gale Group. • Annual. $320.00. Published by Financial Times Energy. Provides production and financial details for more than 800 major mining companies worldwide. Includes coverage of reserves, operations, properties, and growth rates. Formerly *Financial Times International Yearbook: Mining.*

Financial Times Energy Yearbook: Oil & Gas: 2000. Available from The Gale Group. • Annual. $320.00. Published by Financial Times Energy. Provides production and financial details for more than 800 major oil and gas companies worldwide. Includes coverage of reserves, operations, properties, and growth rates. Formerly *Financial Times Oil & Gas Yearbook.*

Institutional Buyers of Energy Stocks: A Targeted Directory. Investment Data Corp. • Annual. $645.00. Provides detailed profiles 555 institutional buyers of petroleum-related and other energy stocks. Includes names of financial analysts and portfolio managers.

Plunkett's Energy Industry Almanac: Complete Profiles on the Energy Industry 500 Companies. Plunkett Research Ltd. • Annual. $149.99. Includes major oil companies, utilities, pipelines, alternative energy companies, etc. Provides information on industry trends.

World Energy and Nuclear Directory. Allyn and Bacon/Longman. • 1996. Fifth edition. Price on application. Lists 5,000 public and private, international research and development organizations functioning in a wide variety of areas related to energy.

ENCYCLOPEDIAS AND DICTIONARIES

Macmillan Encyclopedia of Energy. Available from The Gale Group. • 2001. $350.00. Three volumes. Published by Macmillan Reference USA. Covers the business, technology, and history of a wide variety of energy sources.

Wiley Encyclopedia of Energy and the Environment. Frederick John Francis. John Wiley and Sons, Inc. • 1999. $1,500.00. Four volumes. Second edition. Covers a wide variety of energy and environmental topics, including legal and policy issues.

HANDBOOKS AND MANUALS

Energy Management Handbook. Wayne C. Turner. Prentice Hall. • 1996. $130.00. Third edition.

Energy Systems Handbook. Orjan Isacson and Edward Rideout. McGraw Hill. • 1999. $39.95.

INTERNET DATABASES

U. S. Census Bureau: The Official Statistics. U. S. Bureau of the Census. Phone: (301)763-4100 Fax: (301)763-4794 • URL: http://www.census.gov • Web site is "Your Source for Social, Demographic, and Economic Information." Contains "Current U. S. Population Count," "Current Economic Indicators," and a wide variety of data under "Other Official Statistics." Keyword searching is provided. Fees: Free.

ONLINE DATABASES

Applied Science and Technology Index Online. H. W. Wilson Co. • Provides online indexing of 400 major scientific, technical, industrial, and engineering periodicals. Time period is 1983 to date. Monthly updates. Inquire as to online cost and availability.

Energyline. Congressional Information Service, Inc. • Provides online citations and abstracts to the literature of all forms of energy: petroleum, natural gas, coal, nuclear power, solar energy, etc. Time period is 1971 to 1993 (closed file). Inquire as to online cost and availability.

PERIODICALS AND NEWSLETTERS

Energy and Fuels. American Chemical Society. • Bimonthly. Institutions, $728.00 per year; others, price on application. an interdisciplinary technical journal covering non-nuclear energy sources: petroleum, gas, synthetic fuels, etc.

Energy Conservation Digest. Editorial Resources, Inc. • Semimonthly. $176.00 per year. Newsletter on the conservation of energy resources. Includes legislation, research, new products, job opportunities, calendar of events, and energy economics.

Energy Conservation News. Business Communications Co., Inc. • Monthly. $375.00 per year. Newsletter.

Energy Conversion and Management. Elsevier Science. • 18 times a year. $2,835.00 per year. Presents a scholarly approach to alternative or renewable energy sources. Text in English, French and German.

Energy Daily. King Publishing Group, Inc. • Daily. $1,575.00 per year. Newsletter. News on the energy industry and its regulators.

Energy Magazine. Business Communications Co., Inc. • Five times a year. Institutions, $375.00 per year; others, price on application.

Energy Sources: Journal of Extraction, Conversion and the Environment. Taylor & Francis, Inc. • 10 times a year. Individuals, $423.00 per year; institutions, $938.00 per year.

Energy: The International Journal. Elsevier Science. • Monthly. $1,608.00 per year.

Independent Energy: The Power Industry's Business Magazine. PennWell Corp., Industrial Div. • 10 times a year. $127.00 per year. Covers non-utility electric power plants (cogeneration) and other alternative sources of electric energy.

International Journal of Energy Research. Available from John Wiley and Sons, Inc., Journals Div. • 15 times a year. Institutions, $2,735.00 per year. Published in England by John Wiley & Sons Ltd.

Renewable Energy News Digest. Sun Words. • Monthly. $60.00 per year. Newsletter. Covers geothermal, solar, wind, cogenerated, and other energy sources.

Resource and Energy Economics: A Journal Devoted to the Interdisciplinary Studies in the Allocation of Natural Resources. Elsevier Science. • Quarterly. $478.00 per year. Text in English.

World Environment Report: News and Information on International Resource Management. Business Publishers, Inc. • Biweekly. $494.00 per year. Newsletter on international developments having to do with the environment, energy, pollution control, waste management, and toxic substances.

PRICE SOURCES

International Energy Agency. Energy Prices and Taxes. OECD Publications and Information Center. • Quarterly. $350.00 per year. Compiled by the International Energy Agency. Provides data on prices and taxation of petroleum products, natural gas, coal, and electricity. Diskette edition, $800.00. (Published in Paris).

RESEARCH CENTERS AND INSTITUTES

Canadian Energy Research Institute. 3512 33rd St., N. W., Suite 150, Calgary, AB, Canada T2L 2A6. Phone: (403)282-1231 Fax: (403)284-4181 E-mail: ceri@ceri.ca • URL: http://www.ceri.ca • Conducts research on the economic aspects of various forms of energy, including petroleum, natural gas, coal, nuclear, and water power (hydroelectric).

Energy Laboratory. Massachusetts Institute of Technology. Bldg. E40-455, Cambridge, MA 02139-4307. Phone: (617)253-3401 Fax: (617)253-8013 E-mail: testerel@mit.edu • URL: http://www.web.mit.edu/energylab/www/.

Hawaii Natural Energy Institute. University of Hawaii at Manoa, 2540 Dole St., Holmes Hall 246, Honolulu, HI 96822. Phone: (808)956-8890 Fax: (808)956-2336 E-mail: hnei@hawaii.edu • URL: http://www.soest.hawaii.edu • Research areas include geothermal, wind, solar, hydroelectric, and other energy sources.

Oak Ridge National Laboratory. P.O. Box 2008, Oak Ridge, TN 37831-6255. Phone: (423)576-2900 Fax: (423)241-2967 E-mail: stairb@ornl.gov • URL: http://www.ornl.gov.

STATISTICS SOURCES

Annual Energy Outlook [year], with Projections to [year]. Available from U. S. Government Printing Office. • Annual. Issued by the Energy Information Administration, U. S. Department of Energy (http://www.eia.doe.gov). Contains detailed statistics and 20-year projections for electricity, oil, natural gas, coal, and renewable energy. Text provides extensive discussion of energy issues and "Market Trends.".

Annual Energy Review. Available from U. S. Government Printing Office. • Annual Issued by the Energy Information Administration, Office of Energy Markets and End Use, U. S. Department of Energy. Presents long-term historical as well as recent data on production, consumption, stocks, imports, exports, and prices of the principal energy commodities in the U. S.

Electric Power Monthly. Available from U. S. Government Printing Office. • Monthly. $115.00 per year. Issued by the Office of Coal and Electric Power Statistics, Energy Information Administration, U. S. Department of Energy. Contains statistical data relating to electric utility operation, capability, fuel use, and prices.

Energy Balances of OECD Countries. Organization for Economic Cooperation and Development. Available from OECD Publications and Information Center. • Irregular. $110.00. Presents two-year data on the supply and consumption of solid fuels, oil, gas, and electricity, expressed in oil equivalency terms. Historical tables are also provided. Relates to OECD member countries.

Energy Statistics of OECD Countries. Available from OECD Publications Center. • Annual. $110.00. Detailed energy supply and consumption data for OECD member countries.

Energy Statistics Yearbook. United Nations Dept. of Economic and Social Affairs. United Nations Publications. • Annual. $100.00. Text in English and French.

International Energy Annual. Available from U. S. Government Printing Office. • Annual. $34.00. Issued by the Energy Information Administration, U. S. Department of Energy. Provides production, consumption, import, and export data for primary energy commodities in more than 200 countries and areas. In addition to petroleum products and alcohol, renewable energy sources are covered (hydroelectric, geothermal, solar, and wind).

Monthly Bulletin of Statistics. United Nations Publications. • Monthly. $295.00 per year. Provides current data for about 200 countries on a wide variety of economic, industrial, and demographic subjects. Compiled by United Nations Statistical Office.

Monthly Energy Review. Available from U. S. Government Printing Office. • Monthly. $98.00 per year. Issued by the Energy Information Administration, Office of Energy Markets and End Use, U. S. Department of Energy. Contains current and historical statistics on U. S. production, storage, imports, and consumption of petroleum, natural gas, and coal.

Petroleum Supply Annual. Available from U. S. Government Printing Office. • Annual. $78.00. Two volumes. Produced by the Energy Information Administration, U. S. Department of Energy. Contains worldwide data on the petroleum industry and petroleum products.

Petroleum Supply Monthly. Available from U. S. Government Printing Office. • Monthly. $100.00 per year. Produced by the Energy Information Administration, U. S. Department of Energy. Provides worldwide statistics on a wide variety of petroleum products. Covers production, supplies, exports and imports, transportation, refinery operations, and other aspects of the petroleum industry.

Short-Term Energy Outlook: Quarterly Projections. Available from U. S. Government Printing Office. • Semiannual. $10.00 per year. Issued by Energy Information Administration, U. S. Department of Energy. Contains forecasts of U. S. energy supply, demand, and prices.

Social Statistics of the United States. Mark S. Littman, editor. Bernan Press. • 2000. $65.00. Includes statistical data on population growth, labor force, occupations, environmental trends, leisure time use, income, poverty, taxes, and other economic or demographic topics.

Statistical Abstract of the United States. Available from U. S. Government Printing Office. • Annual. $51.00. Issued by the U. S. Bureau of the Census.

A Statistical Portrait of the United States: Social Conditions and Trends. Mark S. Littman, editor. Bernan Press. • 1998. $89.00. Covers "social, economic, and environmental trends in the United States over the past 25 years." Includes statistical tables, graphs, and analysis relating to such topics as population, income, poverty, wealth, labor, housing, education, healthcare, air/water quality, and government.

Statistical Yearbook. United Nations Publications. • Annual. $125.00. Contains statistics for about 200 countries on a wide variety of economic, industrial, and demographic topics. Compiled by United Nations Statistical Office.

World Energy Outlook. OECD Publications and Information Center. • Annual. $150.00. Provides detailed, 15-year projections by the International Energy Agency (IEA) for world energy supply and demand.

World Statistics Pocketbook. United Nations Publications. • Annual. $10.00. Presents basic economic, social, and environmental indicators for about 200 countries and areas. Covers more than 50 items relating to population, economic activity, labor force, agriculture, industry, energy, trade, transportation, communication, education, tourism, and the environment. Statistical sources are noted.

TRADE/PROFESSIONAL ASSOCIATIONS

American Council for an Energy-Efficient Economy. 1001 Connecticut Ave., N. W., Suite 801, Washington, DC 20036. Phone: (202)429-0063 Fax: (202)429-0193 E-mail: info@aceee.org • URL: http://www.aceee.org • Promotes energy efficiency as a means of enhancing both economic prosperity and environmental protection. Publishes books, proceedings, and reports.

International Energy Agency. Nine rue de la Federation, F-75739 Paris Cedex 15, France. Phone: 33 1 40576551 Fax: 33 1 40576559 E-mail: info@iea.org • URL: http://www.iea.org.

U.S. Energy Association. 1620 Eye St., N.W., Suite 1000, Washington, DC 20006. Phone: (202)331-0415 Fax: (202)331-0418.

OTHER SOURCES

Energy Management and Federal Energy Guidelines. CCH, Inc. • Biweekly. $1,658.00 per year. Seven looseleaf volumes. Periodic supplementation. Reports on petroleum allocation rules, conservation efforts, new technology, and other energy concerns.

Major Energy Companies of the World. Available from The Gale Group. • 2001. $855.00. Fourth edition. Published by Graham & Whiteside. Contains detailed information on more than 3,300 important energy companies in various countries. Industries include electricity generation, coal, natural gas, nuclear energy, petroleum, fuel distribution, and equipment for energy production.

Towards a Sustainable Energy Future. Organization for Economic Cooperation and Development. • 2001. $100.00. Prepared by the International Energy Agency (IEA). Describes various policies for promoting sustainable energy, especially. Prepared by the International Energy Agency (IEA). Describes various policies for promoting sustainable energy, especially as related to economic development. Discusses "growing concerns about climate change and energy-supply security.".

ENGINEERING CONSULTANTS

See also: CONSULTANTS; MANAGEMENT CONSULTANTS

DIRECTORIES

American Consulting Engineers Council-Membership Directory. American Consulting Engineers Council. • Annual. $140.00. A state-by-state listing of ACEC's 5,200 consulting engineering firms with a total of over 180,000 employees.

Consulting Services. Association of Consulting Chemists and Chemical Engineers, Inc. • Biennial. $30.00. Directory containing one-page "scope sheet" for each member and an extensive classified directory.

Emerson's Directory of Leading U.S. Technology Consulting Firms. Available from Hoover's, Inc. • Biennial. $195.00. Published by the Emerson Company (http://www.emersoncompany.com). Provides information on 500 major consulting firms specializing in technology.

HANDBOOKS AND MANUALS

Architects and Engineers: Their Professional Responsibilities. James Acret. McGraw-Hill. • 1977. $95.00. Second edition. Covers legal responsibilities, liabilities, and malpractice.

The Consultant's Proposal, Fee, and Contract Problem-Solver. Ronald Tepper. John Wiley and Sons, Inc. • 1993. $24.95. Provides advice for consultants on fees, contracts, proposals, and client communications. Includes case histories in 10 specific fields, such as finance, marketing, engineering, and management.

How to Succeed as an Independent Consultant. Herman Holtz. John Wiley and Sons, Inc. • 1993. $34.95. Third edition. Covers a wide variety of marketing, financial, professional, and ethical issues for consultants. Includes bibliographic and organizational information.

PERIODICALS AND NEWSLETTERS

Consulting-Specifiying Engineer. Cahners Business Information. • 13 times a year. $86.90 per year. Formerly *Consulting Engineer.*

The Last Word. American Consulting Engineers Council. • Weekly. $149.00 per year.

STATISTICS SOURCES

Salaries of Scientists, Engineers, and Technicians: A Summary of Salary Surveys. Commission on Professionals in Science and Technology. CPST Publications. • Irregular. $100.00. A summary of salary surveys.

TRADE/PROFESSIONAL ASSOCIATIONS

American Consulting Engineers Council. 1015 15th St., N.W., Suite 802, Washington, DC 20005. Phone: (202)347-7474 Fax: (202)898-0068 E-mail: acec@acec.org • URL: http://www.acec.org.

APEC. Talbott Tower, Suite 318, 131 N. Ludlow St., Dayton, OH 45402-1164. Phone: (937)228-2602 Fax: (937)228-5652 E-mail: apecinc@worldnet.att.net.

Association of Consulting Chemists and Chemical Engineers. P.O. Box 297, Sparta, NJ 07871. Phone: (973)729-6671 Fax: (973)729-7088 E-mail: info@chemconsult.org • URL: http://www.chemconsult.org.

ENGINES

See also: LUBRICATION AND LUBRICANTS

DIRECTORIES

Diesel Progress North American Edition: For Engine, Drive and Hydraulic System Enginneering and Equipment Management. Diesel and Gas Turbine Publications. • Monthly. $75.00 per year. List of over 1,500 factory-authorized engine distributors and independent service keepers. Formerly *Diesel Progress Engines and Drives?.*

Fairplay World Shipping Directory. Available from Fairplay Publications, Inc. • Annual. $360.00. Published in the UK by Lloyd's Register-Fairplay Ltd. Provides information on more than 64,000 companies providing maritime services and products, including 1,600 shipbuilders and data on 55,000 individual ships. Includes shipowners, shipbrokers, engine builders, salvage companies, marine insurance companies, maritime lawyers, consultants, maritime schools, etc. Five indexes cover a total of 170,000 entries.

Lloyd's Maritime Directory. Available from Informa Publishing Group Ltd. • Annual. $468.00. Two volumes. Published in the UK by Lloyd's List (http://www.lloydslist.com). Lists more than 5,500 shipowners, container companies, salvage firms, towing services, shipbuilders, ship repairers, marine engine builders, ship management services, maritime lawyers, consultants, etc.

PERIODICALS AND NEWSLETTERS

Diesel and Gas Turbine Worldwide: The International Engine Power Systems Magazine. Joseph M. Kane, editor. Diesel & Gas Turbine Publications. • 10 times a year. $65.00 per year.

Gas Turbine World. Pequot Publishing, Inc. • Bimonthly. $90.00 per year.

RESEARCH CENTERS AND INSTITUTES

Davidson Laboratory. Stevens Institute of Technology. 711 Hudson St., Hoboken, NJ 07030. Phone: (201)216-5300 Fax: (201)216-8214 E-mail: m1bruno@stevens-tech.edu • URL: http://www.dl.stevens-tech.edu.

Engine Research Center. University of Wisconsin - Madison. 121 Engineering Research Bldg., 1500 Engineering Dr., Madison, WI 53706-1687. Phone: (608)263-2735 Fax: (608)263-9870 E-mail: farrell@engr.wisc.edu • URL: http://www.erc.wisc.edu/.

Mechanical Engineering Department. Stevens Institute of Technology. Castle Point on the Hudson, Hoboken, NJ 07030. Phone: (201)216-5591 Fax: (201)216-8315 E-mail: sthangem@stevens-tech.edu • URL: http://www.me.stevens-tech.edu.

Southwest Research Institute. P.O. Box 28510, San Antonio, TX 78228-0510. Phone: (210)684-5111 Fax: (210)522-3496 E-mail: jkittle@swri.org • URL: http://www.swri.org.

STATISTICS SOURCES

Annual Survey of Manufactures. Available from U. S. Government Printing Office. • Annual. Prices vary. Issued by the U. S. Census Bureau as an interim update to the *Census of Manufactures.* Includes data on number of manufacturing establishments in various industries, employment, labor costs, value of shipments, capital expenditures, inventories, energy costs, and assets. (See also Census Bureau home page, http://www.census.gov/.).

Manufacturing Profiles. Available from U. S. Government Printing Office. • Annual. Issued by the U. S. Census Bureau. A printed consolidation of the entire *Current Industrial Report* series, presenting "all the data compiled." Contains statistics on production, shipments, inventories, consumption, exports, imports, and orders for a wide variety of manufactured products. (See also Census Bureau home page, http://www.census.gov/.).

World Trade Annual. United Nations Statistical Office. Walker and Co. • Annual. Prices vary.

TRADE/PROFESSIONAL ASSOCIATIONS

Association of Diesel Specialists. 9140 Ward Parkway, Kansas City, MO 64114. Phone: (816)444-3500 Fax: (816)444-0330 E-mail: info@diesel.org • URL: http://www.diesel.org.

Engine Manufacturers Association. 401 N. Michigan Ave., Chicago, IL 60611. Phone: (312)644-6610 Fax: (312)321-5111 E-mail: ema@sba.com • URL: http://www.engine-manufacturers.com.

OTHER SOURCES

Lloyd's List. Available from Informa Publishing Group Ltd. • Daily. $1,665.00 per year. Published in the UK by Lloyd's List (http://www.lloydslist.com). Marine industry newspaper. Covers a wide variety of maritime topics, including global news, business/insurance, regulation, shipping markets, financial markets, shipping movements, freight logistics, and marine technology. (Also available weekly at $385.00 per year.).

ENTERTAINMENT INDUSTRY

See: AMUSEMENT INDUSTRY; SHOW BUSINESS

ENTOMOLOGY, ECONOMIC

See: ECONOMIC ENTOMOLOGY

ENTRANCE REQUIREMENTS

See: COLLEGE ENTRANCE REQUIREMENTS

ENTREPRENEURIAL CAPITAL

See: VENTURE CAPITAL

ENTREPRENEURIAL HISTORY

See: BUSINESS HISTORY

ENTREPRENEURS AND INTRAPRENEURS

See also: WOMEN EXECUTIVES

GENERAL WORKS

Innovation and Entrepreneurship: Practice and Principles. Peter F. Drucker. HarperInformation. • 1986. $14.50.

Is It Too Late to Run Away and Join the Circus? Finding the Life You Really Want. Marti Smye. Simon and Schuster Trade. • 1998. $14.95. Provides philosophical and inspirational advice on leaving corporate life and becoming self-employed as a consultant or whatever. Central theme is dealing with major changes in life style and career objectives. (Macmillan Business Book.).

The Leap: A Memoir of Love and Madness in the Internet Gold Rush. Tom Ashbrook. Houghton Mifflin Co. • 2000. $25.00. The author relates his personal and family tribulations while attempting to obtain financing for an eventually successful e-business startup, HomePortfolio.com.

Trends 2000: How to Prepare For and Profit From the Changes of the 21st Century. Gerald Celente. Little, Brown and Co. • 1998. $14.99. Emphasis is on economic, social, and political trends.

Women Entrepreneurs: Moving Beyond the Glass Ceiling. Dorothy P. Moore and E. Holly Buttner. Sage Publications, Inc. • 1997. $46.00. Contains profiles of "129 successful female entrepreneurs who previously worked in corporate environments.".

ABSTRACTS AND INDEXES

Business Periodicals Index. H. W. Wilson Co. • Monthly, except August, with quarterly and annual cumulations. Service basis for print edition; CD-ROM edition, $1,495.00 per year.

BIOGRAPHICAL SOURCES

Contemporary Entrepreneurs: Profiles of Entrepreneurs and the Businesses They Started, Representing 74 Companies in 30 Industries. Craig E. Aronoff and John L. Ward, editors. Omnigraphics, Inc. • 1992. $95.00.

CD-ROM DATABASES

Hoover's Company Capsules on CD-ROM. Hoover's, Inc. • Quarterly. $349.95 per year (single-user). Provides the CD-ROM version of *Hoover's Handbook of American Business, Hoover's Handbook of Emerging Companies, Hoover's Handbook of World Business, Hoover's Guide to Computer Companies, Hoover's Guide to Media Companies, Hoover's Handbook of Private Companies,* and various regional guides. Includes more than 11,000 profiles of companies.

DIRECTORIES

Business Organizations, Agencies, and Publications Directory. The Gale Group. • 1999. $425.00. 12th edition. Over 40,000 entries describing 39 types of business information sources. Classified by type of organization, publication, or serviceIncludes state, national, and international agencies and organizations. Master index to names and keywords. Also includes e-mail addresses and web site URL's.

Fitzroy Dearborn International Directory of Venture Capital Funds. Jennifer Schellinger, editor. Fitzroy Dearborn Publishers, Inc. • 1998. $175.00. Third edition. Provides detailed information on more than 1,000 sources of venture capital, with articles on entrepreneurship.

Hoover's Handbook of Emerging Companies: Profiles of America's Most Exciting Growth Enterprises. Hoover's, Inc. • 2000. $89.95. Contains detailed profiles of 300 rapidly growing corporations. Includes indexes by industry, location, executive name, company name, and brand name.

Venture Capital Directory (Small Business Administation). Forum Publishing Co. • Annual. $12.95. Over 500 members of the Small Business Administration and the Small Business Investment. Companies that provide funding for small and minority businesses.

ENCYCLOPEDIAS AND DICTIONARIES

Encyclopedia of Small Business. The Gale Group. • 1998. $395.00. Two volumes. Contains about 500 informative entries on a wide variety of topics affecting small business. Arrangement is alphabetical.

HANDBOOKS AND MANUALS

The Entrepreneur's Guide to Growing Up: Taking Your Small Company to the Next Level. Edna Sheedy. Self-Counsel Press, Inc. • 1993. $8.95. Discusses company structure, delegation, management information requirements, and other topics related to company growth. *Business Series.*

From Executive to Entrepreneur: Making the Transition. Gilbert Z. Zoghlin. AMACOM. • 1991. $24.95. A self-help guide offering psychological and financial advice to corporate employees who wish to go into business for themselves.

The Geek's Guide to Internet Business Success: The Definitive Business Blueprint for Internet Developers, Programmers, Consultants, Marketers, and Serivce Providers. Bob Schmidt. John Wiley and Sons, Inc. • 1997. $22.95. Written for beginning Internet entrepreneurs, especially those with technical expertise but little or no business experience. Covers fee or rate setting, developing new business, product mix, budgeting, partnerships, personnel, and planning. Includes checklists and worksheets.

How to Incorporate: A Handbook for Entrepreneurs and Professionals. Michael Diamond. John Wiley and Sons, Inc. • 1996. $49.95. Third edition.

Infopreneurs: Turning Data into Dollars. H. Skip Weitzen. John Wiley and Sons, Inc. • 1988. $27.95. Infopreneurs are entrepreneurs who market information. A how-to-do-it manual.

New Venture Creation: Entrepreneurship for the 21st Century. Jeffrey A. Timmons and others. McGraw-Hill Professional. • 1998. Fifth edition. Price on application.

Standard Business Forms for the Entrepreneur. Entrepreneur Media, Inc. • Looseleaf. $59.50. A practical collection of forms useful to entrepreneurial small businesses. (Start-Up Business Guide No. E1319.).

Start-Up Business Guides. Entrepreneur Media, Inc. • Looseleaf. $59.50 each. Practical guides to starting a wide variety of small businesses.

Startup: An Entrepreneur's Guide to Launching and Managing a New Business. William J. Stolze. Rock Beach Press. • 1989. $24.95.

Venture Capital: An Authoritative Guide for Investors, Entrepreneurs, and Managers. Douglas A. Lindgren. McGraw-Hill Professional. • 1998. $65.00.

INTERNET DATABASES

MBEMAG. Minority Business Entrepreneur Magazine. Phone: (310)540-9398 Fax: (310)792-8263 E-mail: webmaster@mbemag.com • URL: http://www.mbemag.com • Web site's main feature is the "MBE Business Resources Directory." This provides complete mailing addresses, phone, fax, and Web site addresses (URL) for more than 40 organizations and government agencies having information or assistance for ethnic minority and women business owners. Some other links are "Current Events," "Calendar of Events," and

"Business Opportunities." Updating is bimonthly. Fees: Free.

ONLINE DATABASES

Wilson Business Abstracts Online. H. W. Wilson Co. • Indexes and abstracts 600 major business periodicals, plus the *Wall Street Journal* and the business section of the *New York Times*. Indexing is from 1982, abstracting from 1990, with the two newspapers included from 1993. Updated weekly. Inquire as to online cost and availability. (*Business Periodicals Index* without abstracts is also available online.).

PERIODICALS AND NEWSLETTERS

Black Enterprise. Earl G. Graves Publishing Co. • Monthly. $21.95 per year. Covers careers, personal finances and leisure.

Business Start-Ups: Smart Ideas for Your Small Business. Entrepreneur Media, Inc. • Monthly. $14.97 per year. Provides advice for starting a small business. Includes business trends, new technology, E-commerce, and case histories ("real-life stories").

Business 2.0. Imagine Media, Inc. • Monthly. $12.00 per year. General business magazine emphasizing ideas and innovation.

Chief Executive Officers Newsletter: For the Entrepreneurial Manager and the Pr ofessionals Who Advise Him. Center for Entrepreneurial Management, Inc. • Monthly. $96.00 per year. Formerly *Entrepreneurial Manager's Newsletter*.

Entrepreneur: The Small Business Authority. Entrepreneur Media, Inc. • Monthly. $19.97 per year. Contains advice for small business owners and prospective owners. Includes numerous franchise advertisements.

Fast Company: How Smart Business Works. Fast Company Inc. • Monthly. $23.95 per year. Covers business management, with emphasis on creativity, leadership, innovation, career advancement, teamwork, the global economy, and the "new workplace.".

Income Opportunities: The Original Small Business - Home Office Magazine. Natcom, Inc. • Monthly. $31.95 per year.

Inc.: The Magazine for Growing Companies. Goldhirsh Group, Inc. • 18 times a year. $19.00 per year. Edited for small office and office-in-the-home businesses with from one to 25 employees. Covers management, office technology, and lifestyle. Incorporates *Self-Employed Professional*.

Journal of Business Venturing. Elsevier Science. • Bimonthly. $545.00 per year.

Minority Business Entrepreneur. • Bimonthly. $16.00 per year. Reports on issues "critical to the growth and development of minority and women-owned firms." Provides information on relevant legislation and profiles successful women and minority entrepreneurs.

Success: For the Innovative Entrepreneur. Success Holdings LLC. • Monthly. $19.97 per year. Provides information to help individuals advance in business.

Upside: People, Technology, Capital. Upside Publishing Co. • Monthly. $29.95 per year. Covers the business, investment, and entrepreneurial aspects of high technology.

Women's Business Exclusive: For Women Entrepreneurs. • Bimonthly. $39.00 per year. Newsletter. Reports news and information relating to financing, business procurement initiatives, technical assistance, and policy research. Provides advice on marketing, negotiating, and other management topics.

RESEARCH CENTERS AND INSTITUTES

Arthur M. Bank Center for Entrepreneurship. Babson College, Babson Park, MA 02157-0310. Phone: (617)239-4420 Fax: (617)239-4178 E-mail: spinelli@babson.edu • URL: http://www.babson.edu/entrep • Sponsors annual Babson College Entrepreneurship Research Conference.

Berkley Center for Entrepreneurial Studies. New York University, Management Education Center, Stern School of Business, 44 W. Fourth St., Suite 8-165 B, New York, NY 10012. Phone: (212)998-0070 Fax: (212)995-4211 E-mail: lpoole@stern.nyu.edu • URL: http://www.stern.nyu.edu/bces.

Bureau of Economic and Business Research. University of Illinois at Urbana-Champaign, 1206 S. Sixth St., Champaign, IL 61820. Phone: (217)333-2330 Fax: (217)244-7410 E-mail: g-oldman@uiuc.edu • URL: http://www.cba.uiuc.edu/research.

Center for Entrepreneurial Studies and Development, Inc. West Virginia University, College of Engineering and Mineral Resources, P.O. Box 6107, Morgantown, WV 26506-6107. Phone: (304)293-3612 Fax: (304)293-6707 E-mail: byrd@cemr.wvu.edu • URL: http://www.cesd.wvu.edu • Inventory control systems included as a research field.

Center for Private Enterprise. Baylor University, Hankamer School of Business, P.O. Box 98003, Waco, TX 76798-8003. Phone: (254)710-2263 Fax: (254)710-1092 E-mail: jimtruitt@baylor.edu • URL: http://129.62.162.136/enterprise/ • Includes studies of entrepreneurship and women entrepreneurs.

Center for the Study of Entrepreneurship. Marquette University, College of Business Administration, Milwaukee, WI 53201-1881. Phone: (414)288-5100 Fax: (414)288-1660.

National Association of Women Business Owners. 1100 Wayne Ave., Suite 830, Silver Spring, MD 20910-5603. Phone: (301)608-2590 Fax: (301)608-2596 E-mail: nawbohq@aol.com • URL: http://www.nfwbo.org • Provides research reports and statistical studies relating to various aspects of women-owned business enterprises. Affiliated with the National Association of Women Business Owners.

TRADE/PROFESSIONAL ASSOCIATIONS

Association of African-American Women Business Owners. c/o Brenda Alford, P.O. Box 13858, Silver Spring, MD 20911-0858. Phone: (301)585-8051.

Chief Executive Officers Club. 180 Varick St., Penthouse Suite, New York, NY 10014. Phone: (212)633-0060 or (212)633-0061 Fax: (212)633-0063 E-mail: ceoclubs@bway.net • URL: http://www.ceo-clubs.org • Serves as an information resource for small business owners and managers.

National Association of Minority Women in Business. 906 Grand Ave., Suite 200, Kansas City, MO 64106. Phone: (816)421-3335 Fax: (816)421-3336.

National Association of Women Business Owners. 1411 K St., N.W., Washington, DC 20005. Phone: 800-556-2926 or (202)347-8686 Fax: (202)347-9210 E-mail: national@nawbo.org • URL: http://www.nawbo.org.

National Business Incubation Association. 20 E. Circle Dr., Suite 190, Athens, OH 45701. Phone: (740)593-4331 Fax: (740)593-1996 E-mail: info@nbia.org • URL: http://www.nbia.org • Members are business assistance professionals concerned with business startups, entrepreneurship, and effective small business management.

OTHER SOURCES

Cyberfinance: Raising Capital for the E-Business. Martin B. Robins. CCH, Inc. • 2001. $79.00. Covers the taxation, financial, and legal aspects of raising money for new Internet-based ("dot.com") companies, including the three stages of startup, growth, and initial public offering.

Entrepreneurship.com. Tim Burns. Dearborn Financial Publishing. • 2000. $19.95. Provides basic advice and information on the topic of dot.com startups, including business plan creation and financing.

Home Business Magazine: The Home-Based Entrepreneur's Magazine. United Marketing and Research Co., Inc. • Bimonthly. $15.00 per year. Provides practical advice and ideas relating to the operation of a business in the home. Sections include "Marketing & Sales," "Money Corner" (financing), "Businesses & Opportunities," and "Home Office" (equipment, etc.). Includes an annual directory of more than 250 non-franchised home business opportunities, including start-up costs and information about providers.

net.people: The Personalities and Passions Behind the Web Sites. Eric C. Steinert and Thomas E. Bleier. Information Today, Inc. • 2000. $19.95. Presents the personal stories of 36 Web "entrepreneurs and visionaries." (CyberAge Books.).

ENVIRONMENT

See also: AIR POLLUTION; ENVIRONMENTAL LAW; WATER POLLUTION

GENERAL WORKS

Crisis Response: Inside Stories on Managing Image Under Siege. The Gale Group. • 1993. $60.00. Presents first-hand accounts by media relations professionals of major business crises and how they were handled. Topics include the following kinds of crises: environmental, governmental, corporate image, communications, and product.

Environmental Business Management: An Introduction. Klaus North. International Labour Office. • 1992. $24.75. (Management Development Series, No. 30).

Environmental Geology. Edward A. Keller. Prentice Hall. • 1999. $76.00. Eighth edition.

Introduction to Ecological Economics. Robert Costanza and others. Saint Lucie Press. • 1997. $54.95. Advocates environmental policy changes on local, regional, national, and international levels.

Pollution: Causes, Effects, and Control. R. M. Harrison, editor. American Chemical Society. • 1996. $71.00. Third edition. Published by The Royal Society of Chemistry. A basic introduction to pollution of air, water, and land. Includes discussions of pollution control technologies.

Recent Advances and Issues in Environmental Science. John R. Callahan. Oryx Press. • 2000. $44.95. Includes environmental economic problems, such as saving jobs vs. protecting the environment. (Oryx Frontiers of Science Series.).

Sustainability Perspectives for Resources and Business. Orie L. Loucks and others. Saint Lucie Press. • 1999. $44.95. Discusses the business and economic aspects of environmental protection.

World Environmental Business Handbook. Available from The Gale Group. • 1993. $190.00. Second edition. Published by Euromonitor. An overview of environmental business activities, trends, issues, and problems throughout the world.

ABSTRACTS AND INDEXES

Environment Abstracts. Congressional Information Service. • Monthly. Price varies. Provides multidisciplinary coverage of the world's environmental literature. Incorporates *Acid Rain Abstracts.*

Environment Abstracts Annual: A Guide to the Key Environmental Literature of the Year. Congressional Information Service. • Annual. $495.00. A yearly cumulation of *Environment Abstracts.*

Environmental Periodicals Bibliography: A Current Awareness Bibliography Featuring Citations of Scientific and Popular Articles in Serial Publications in the Area of the Environment. Environmental Studies Institute. International Academy at Santa Barbara. • Monthly. Price varies. An index to current environmental literature.

Excerpta Medica: Environmental Health and Pollution Control. Elsevier Science. • 16 times a year. 2,506.00 per year. Section 46 of *Excerpta Medica.* Covers air, water, and land pollution and noise control.

NTIS Alerts: Environmental Pollution & Control. National Technical Information Service. • Semimonthly. $245.00 per year. Provides descriptions of government-sponsored research reports and software, with ordering information. Covers the following categories of environmental pollution: air, water, solid wastes, radiation, pesticides, and noise. Formerly *Abstract Newsletter.*

Social Sciences Index. H. W. Wilson Co. • Quarterly, with annual cumulation. Service basis for print edition; CD-ROM edition, $1,495 per year. Indexes more than 400 periodicals covering economics, environmental policy, government, insurance, labor, health care policy, plannning, public administration, public welfare, urban studies, women's issues, criminology, and related topics.

ALMANACS AND YEARBOOKS

Earth Almanac: An Annual Geophysical Review of the State of the Planet. Natalie Goldstein. Oryx Press. • Annual. $65.00. Provides background information, statistics, and a summary of major events relating to the atmosphere, oceans, land, and fresh water.

Environmental Viewpoints. The Gale Group. • 1993. $195.00. Three volumes. $65.00 per volume. A compendium of excerpts of about 200 articles on a wide variety of environmental topics, selected from both popular and professional periodicals. Arranged alphabetically by topic, with a subject/keyword index.

Gale Environmental Almanac. The Gale Group. • 1994. $110.00. Contains 15 chapters, each on a broad topic related to the environment, such as "Waste and Recycling." Each chapter has a topical overview, charts, statistics, and illustrations. Includes a glossary of environmental terms and a bibliography.

Land Use and Environment Law Review, 1984. West Group. • Dates vary. $215.00. Five volumes.

BIBLIOGRAPHIES

The Ecology of Land Use: A Bibliographic Guide. Graham Trelstad. Sage Publications, Inc. • 1994. $10.00.

BIOGRAPHICAL SOURCES

World Who is Who and Does What in Environment and Conservation. Nicholas Polunin, editor. St. Martin's Press. • 1997. $75.00. Provides biographies of 1,300 individuals considered to be leaders in environmental and conservation areas.

CD-ROM DATABASES

Environment Abstracts on CD-ROM. Congressional Information Service, Inc. • Quarterly. $1,295.00 per year. Contains the following CD-ROM databases: *Environment Abstracts, Energy Abstracts,* and *Acid Rain Abstracts.* Length of coverage varies.

Magazine Index Plus. The Gale Group. • Monthly. $4,000.00 per year (includes InfoTrac workstation). Provides full text on CD-ROM for about 100 popular, general interest magazines and indexing for 300 others. Includes special indexing of reviews and product evaluations. Time period is 1980 to date.

Social Science Source. EBSCO Publishing. • Monthly. $1,495.00 per year. Provides CD-ROM citations and abstracts to social science articles in more than 600 periodicals, with full text from 125 periodicals. Covers economics, political science, public policy, international relations, psychology, and other topics. Time period is most recent five years.

Social Sciences Citation Index: Compact Disc Edition with Abstracts. Institute for Scientific Information. • Quarterly. Provides CD-ROM indexing and abstracting of "significant articles" from 1,400 social science journals worldwide, with additional selections from 3,200 other journals, 1986 to date. Includes economics, business, finance, management, communications, demographics, information and library science, political science, sociology, and many other subjects.

WILSONDISC: Wilson Social Sciences Abstracts. H. W. Wilson Co. • Monthly. Including unlimited online access to *Social Sciences Index* through WILSONLINE. Provides CD-ROM indexing from 1983 and abstracting from 1994 of more than 400 periodicals covering economics, area studies, community health, public administration, public welfare, urban studies, and many other topics related to the social sciences.

DIRECTORIES

Design Firm Directory: A Listing of Firms and Consultants in Grap hic Design in the United States. Wefler & Associates, Inc. • Annual. $145.00. Three volumes. Provides information on more than 2,600 commercial, private, and consulting design firms. Includes graphic, interior, landscape, and environmental designers.

Environmental Career Directory. Visible Ink Press. • 1993. $17.95. Includes career information relating to workers in conservation, recycling, wildlife management, pollution control, and other areas. Provides advice from "insiders," resume suggestions, a directory of companies that may offer entry-level positions, and a directory of career information sources. (Career Advisor Series.).

Gale Environmental Sourcebook: A Guide to Organizations, Agencies, and Publications. The Gale Group. • 1993. $95.00. Second edition. A directory of print and non-print information sources on a wide variety of environmental topics.

ENCYCLOPEDIAS AND DICTIONARIES

Encyclopedia of Environmental Science. John Mongillo and Linda Zierdt-Warshaw. Oryx Press. • 2000. $95.00. Provides information on more than 1,000 topics relating to the environment. Includes graphs, tables, maps, illustrations, and 400 Web site addresses.

Encyclopedia of Environmental Science and Engineering. James R. Pfafflin and Edward N. Ziegler, editors. Gordon and Breach Publishing Group. • $1,758.00. Three volumes.

Environmental Encyclopedia. The Gale Group. • 1998. $235.00. Second edition. Provides over 1,300 articles on all aspects of the environment. Written in non-technical style.

Macmillan Encyclopedia of the Environment. Stephen R. Kellert, editor. Pearson Education and Technology. • 1997. $300.00. Six volumes.

Unabridged Dictionary of Occupational and Environmental Safety and Health with CD-ROM. Jeffrey W. Vincoli and Kathryn L. Bazan. Lewis Publishers. • 1999. $89.95.

Wiley Encyclopedia of Energy and the Environment. Frederick John Francis. John Wiley and Sons, Inc. • 1999. $1,500.00. Four volumes. Second edition. Covers a wide variety of energy and environmental topics, including legal and policy issues.

HANDBOOKS AND MANUALS

Environmental Accounting: Current Issues, Abstracts, and Bibliography. United Nations Publications. • 1992. Provides guidelines for environmental disclosure in corporate annual reports.

Environmental Engineering. P. Aarne Vesilind and others. Butterworth-Heinemann. • 1994. $66.95. Third edition.

Handbook of Environmental Health and Safety: Principles and Practices. Herman Koren and Michael S. Bisesi. Lewis Publishers. • 1995. $199.90 Third edition. Two volumes. Volume one, $99.95; volume two, $99.95.

Industrial Pollution Prevention Handbook. Harry M. Freeman. McGraw-Hill. • 1992. $115.00.

Statistics for the Environment: Statistical Aspects of Health and the Environment. Vic Barnett and K. Feridun Turkman, editors. John Wiley and Sons, Inc. • 1999. $180.00. Contains articles on the statistical analysis and interpretation of environmental monitoring and sampling data. Areas covered include meteorology, pollution of the environment, and forest resources.

INTERNET DATABASES

E: The Environmental Magazine [online]. Earth Action Network, Inc. Phone: (203)854-5559 Fax: (203)866-0602 • URL: http://www.emagazine.com • Web site provides full-text articles from *E: The Environmental Magazine* for a period of about two years. Searching is provided. Alphabetical and subject links are shown for a wide variety of environmental Web sites. Fees: Free.

National Library of Medicine (NLM). National Institutes of Health (NIH). Phone: 888-346-3656 or (301)496-1131 Fax: (301)480-3537 E-mail: access@nlm.nih.gov • URL: http://www.nlm.nih.gov • NLM Web site offers free access through MEDLINE ("PubMed") to about nine million references to articles appearing in some 3,800 biomedical journals, with abstracts. Search interfaces range from "simple keywords to advanced Boolean expressions." The NLM site offers many links to other sources of biomedical and technical information (the National Center for Biotechnology Information, for example). Fees: Free.

ONLINE DATABASES

Aqualine. Water Research Centre. • Citations and abstracts of literature on aquatic environment, 1960 to present. Inquire as to online cost and availability.

Enviroline. Congressional Information Service, Inc. • Provides online indexing and abstracting of worldwide environmental and natural resource literature from 1975 to date. Updated monthly. Inquire as to online cost and availability.

Newspaper and Periodical Abstracts. Bell & Howell Information and Learning. • Provides online coverage (citations and abstracts) of 25 major newspapers, 1,600 perodicals, and 70 TV programs. Covers business, economics, current affairs, health, fitness, sports, education, technology, government, consumer affairs, psychology, the arts, and the social sciences. Time period is 1986 to date, with daily updates. Inquire as to online cost and availability.

Wilson Social Sciences Abstracts Online. H. W. Wilson Co. • Provides online abstracting and indexing of more than 415 periodicals covering area studies, community health, public administration, public welfare, urban studies, and many other social science topics. Time period is 1994 to date for abstracts and 1983 to date for indexing, with updates monthly. Inquire as to online cost and availability.

PERIODICALS AND NEWSLETTERS

E: The Environment Magazine. Earth Action Network, Inc. • Bimonthly. $20.00 per year. A popular, consumer magazine providing news, information, and commentary on a wide range of environmental issues.

Ecology. Ecological Society of America. • Eight times a year. $350.00 per year. All forms of life in relation to environment.

Ecology Law Quarterly. University of California at Berkeley, Boalt Hall School of Law. University of California Press, Journals Div. • Quarterly. Individuals, $30.00 per year; institutions, $54.00 per year; students, $22.00 per year.

Ecology USA. Business Publishers, Inc. • Biweekly. $135.00 per year.

EM: Environmental Solutions That Make Good Business Sense. Air and Waste Management Association. • Monthly. Individuals $99.00 per year; institutions, $130.00 per year. Newsletter. Provides news of regulations, legislation, and technology relating to the environment, recycling, and waste control. Formerly *Environmental Manager*.

Environment. Heldref Publications. • 10 times a year. Individuals, $39.00 per year; institutions, $79.00 per year.

Environment Reporter. The Bureau of National Affairs, Inc. Trends Publishing, Inc. • Weekly. $2,844.00 per year. Looseleaf. Provides information on the U.S. and international policies, plans, programs, projects, publications and events in environmental and pollution control topics.

Environmental Business Journal: Strategic Information for a Changing Industry. Environmental Business Publishing Co. • Monthly. $495.00 per year. Newsletter. Includes both industrial and financial information relating to individual companies and to the environmental industry in general. Covers air pollution, wat es, U. S. Department of Health and Human Services. Provides conference, workshop, and symposium proceedings, as well as extensive reviews of environmental prospects.

Environmental Health Perspectives. Available from U. S. Government Printing Office. • Monthly. $150.00 per year. Issued by the U.S. Department of Health and Human Services (http://www.dhhs.gov). Contains original research on various aspects of the environment and human health. Includes news of environment-related legislation, regulatory actions, and technological advances.

Environmental Health Perspectives Supplement. Available from U. S. Government Printing Office. • Bimonthly. $91.00 per year. Issued by the U.S. Department of Health and Human Services (http://www.dhhs.gov). Provides original, peer-reviewed monographs on environmental health topics. Includes an annual review of the field.

Environmental Science and Technology. Kluwer Academic Publishers. • Irregular. Price varies.

Friends of the Earth. • Bimonthly. $25.00 per year. Newsletter on environmental and natural resource issues and public policy.

Journal of Environmental Sciences. Chinese Academy of Sciences, Environmental Science Council. IOS Press, Inc. • Quarterly. $100.00 per year.

Journal of Industrial Ecology. Yale University, School of Forestry and Environmental Studies. MIT Press. • Quarterly. Individuals, $40.00 per year; institutions, $115.00 per year; students and retired persons, $30.00 per year. Contains multidisciplinary articles on the relationships between industrial activity and the environment.

Journal of Sustainable Agriculture: Innovations for the Long-Term and Lasting Maintenance and Enhancement of Agricultural Resources, Production and Environmental Quality. Haworth Press, Inc. • Quarterly. Individuals, $50.00 per year; institutions, $75.00 per year; libraries, $185.00 per year. Two volumes. An academic and practical journal concerned with resource depletion and environmental misuse.

Resources. Resources for the Future, Inc. • Quarterly. Free. Includes feature articles about environmental and natural resources issues as well as organizational news about books, research programs and related activities.

World Environment Report: News and Information on International Resource Management. Business Publishers, Inc. • Biweekly. $494.00 per year. Newsletter on international developments having to do with the environment, energy, pollution control, waste management, and toxic substances.

RESEARCH CENTERS AND INSTITUTES

Center for Energy and Environmental Studies. Carnegie Mellon University Department of Engineering and Public Policy. Baker Hall 128-A, Pittsburgh, PA 15213. Phone: (412)268-5897 Fax: (412)268-3757.

Environmental Hazards Management Institute. P.O. Box 932, Durham, NH 03824. Phone: (603)868-1496 Fax: (603)868-1547 E-mail: ehmi@aol.com • URL: http://www.ehmi.com.

Environmental Toxicology Center. University of Wisconsin-Madison, Enzyme Institute, Room 290, 1710 University Ave., Madison, WI 53705-4098. Phone: (608)263-4825 Fax: (608)262-5245 E-mail: jefcoate@facstaff.wisc.edu • URL: http://www.wisc.edu/etc/.

Urban Land Institute. 1025 Thomas Jefferson Ave. N.W., Suite 500W, Washington, DC 20004. Phone: (202)624-7000 Fax: (202)624-7140 E-mail: rlevitt@uli.org • URL: http://www.uli.org • Studies urban land planning and the growth and development of urbanized areas, including central city problems, industrial development, community development, residential development, taxation, shopping centers, and the effects of development on the environment.

STATISTICS SOURCES

Health and Environment in America's Top-Rated Cities: A Statistical Profile. Grey House Publishing. • Biennial. $195.00. Covers 75 U. S. cities. Includes statistical and other data on a wide variety of topics, such as air quality, water quality, recycling, hospitals, physicians, health care costs, death rates, infant mortality, accidents, and suicides.

Social Statistics of the United States. Mark S. Littman, editor. Bernan Press. • 2000. $65.00. Includes statistical data on population growth, labor force, occupations, environmental trends, leisure time use, income, poverty, taxes, and other economic or demographic topics.

A Statistical Portrait of the United States: Social Conditions and Trends. Mark S. Littman, editor. Bernan Press. • 1998. $89.00. Covers "social, economic, and environmental trends in the United States over the past 25 years." Includes statistical tables, graphs, and analysis relating to such topics as population, income, poverty, wealth, labor, housing, education, healthcare, air/water quality, and government.

Statistical Record of the Environment. The Gale Group. • 1996. $120.00. Third edition. Provides over 875 charts, tables, and graphs of major environmental statistics, arranged by subject. Covers population growth, hazardous waste, nuclear energy, acid rain, pesticides, and other subjects related to the environment. A keyword index is included.

U. S. Industry and Trade Outlook: The McGraw-Hill Companies and the U.S. Department of Commerce/International Trade Administration. Datapso Research Corp. • Annual. $69.95. Produced by the International Trade Administration, U. S. Department of Commerce, in a "public-private" partnership with DRI/McGraw-Hill and Standard & Poor's. Provides basic data, outlook for the current year, and "Long-Term Prospects" (five-year projections) for a wide variety of products and services. Includes high technology industries. Formerly *U. S. Industrial Outlook.*

World Bank Atlas. The World Bank, Office of the Publisher. • Annual. Price on application. Contains "color maps, charts, and graphs representing the main social, economic, and environmental indicators for 209 countries and territories" (publisher).

World Development Indicators. World Bank, The Office of the Publisher. • Annual. $60.00. Provides data and information on the people, economy, environment, and markets of 148 countries. Emphasis is on statistics relating to major development issues.

World Statistics Pocketbook. United Nations Publications. • Annual. $10.00. Presents basic economic, social, and environmental indicators for about 200 countries and areas. Covers more than 50 items relating to population, economic activity, labor force, agriculture, industry, energy, trade, transportation, communication, education, tourism, and the environment. Statistical sources are noted.

TRADE/PROFESSIONAL ASSOCIATIONS

Environmental Management Association. 530 W. Ionia St., Suite C, Lansing, MI 48933-1062. Phone: (517)485-5715 Fax: (517)371-1170.

Friends of the Earth. 1025 Vermont Ave., N.W., Suite. 300, Washington, DC 20005. Phone: (202)783-7400 Fax: (202)783-0444 E-mail: foe@foe.org • URL: http://www.foe.org • Promotes protection of the environment and conservation of natural resources.

National Association of Environmental Professionals. Three Adams St., South Portland, OR 04106. Phone: (207)767-1505 E-mail: naep@link.com • URL: http://www.enfo.com/naep.

OTHER SOURCES

Environment Reporter. Bureau of National Affairs, Inc. • Weekly. $2,844.00 per year. 18 volumes. Looseleaf. Covers legal aspects of wide variety of environmental concerns.

Environmental Law Reporter. Environmental Law Institute. • Monthly. $1,045.00 per year. Seven volumes. Looseleaf service.

Our National Parks and the Search for Sustainability. Bob R. O'Brien. University of Texas Press. • 1999. $40.00. Sustainability is defined as "a balance that allows as many people as possible to visit a park that is kept in as natural a state as possible.".

Towards a Sustainable Energy Future. Organization for Economic Cooperation and Development. • 2001. $100.00. Prepared by the International Energy Agency (IEA). Describes various policies for promoting sustainable energy, especially. Prepared by the International Energy Agency (IEA). Describes various policies for promoting sustainable energy, especially as related to economic development. Discusses "growing concerns about climate change and energy-supply security.".

ENVIRONMENTAL CONTROL

See: AIR POLLUTION; LAND UTILIZATION; WATER POLLUTION

ENVIRONMENTAL LAW

GENERAL WORKS

Environmental Law in a Nutshell. Roger W. Findley and Daniel A. Farber. West Publishing Co., College and School Div. • 1992. $15.50. Fourth edition. (Paralegal Series).

Environmental Policy in the 1990s: Reform or Reaction. Norman Vig and Michael Kraft. Congressional Quarterly, Inc. • 1996. $43.95 Third edition.

Environmental Politics and Policy. Walter A. Rosenbaum. Congressional Quarterly, Inc. • 1998. $31.95. Fourth edition.

Public Policies for Environmental Protection. Paul R. Portney, editor. Johns Hopkins University Press. • 2000. Second edition. Price on application. A discussion of issues, progress, and problems in the regulation of air pollution, water pollution, hazardous wastes, and toxic substances. Economic factors are emphasized.

ABSTRACTS AND INDEXES

Current Law Index: Multiple Access to Legal Periodicals. The Gale Group. • Monthly. $650.00 per year. Produced in cooperation with the American Association of Law Libraries. Indexes more than 900 law journals, legal newspapers, and specialty publications from the U.S., Canada, U.K., Ireland, Australia, and New Zealand.

Environment Abstracts. Congressional Information Service. • Monthly. Price varies. Provides multidisciplinary coverage of the world's environmental literature. Incorporates *Acid Rain Abstracts.*

Environment Abstracts Annual: A Guide to the Key Environmental Literature of the Year. Congressional Information Service. • Annual. $495.00. A yearly cumulation of *Environment Abstracts.*

Index to Legal Periodicals and Books. H. W. Wilson Co. • Monthly. Quarterly and annual cumulations. $270.00 per year. CD-ROM version available at $1,495.00 per year.

ALMANACS AND YEARBOOKS

Insurance Law Review. Pat Magarick. West Group. • 1990. $125.00. Provides review of legal topics within the casualty insurance area, including professional liability, product liability, and environmental issues.

BIBLIOGRAPHIES

Encyclopedia of Legal Information Sources. The Gale Group. • 1992. $180.00. Second edition. Lists more than 23,000 law-related information sources, including print, nonprint, and organizational.

CD-ROM DATABASES

Environment Abstracts on CD-ROM. Congressional Information Service, Inc. • Quarterly. $1,295.00 per year. Contains the following CD-ROM databases: *Environment Abstracts, Energy Abstracts*, and *Acid Rain Abstracts.* Length of coverage varies.

LegalTrac. The Gale Group. • Monthly. $5,000.00 per year. Price includes workstation. Provides CD-ROM indexing of periodical literature relating to legal matters from 1980 to date. Corresponds to online *Legal Resource Index.*

PAIS on CD-ROM. Public Affairs Information Service, Inc. • Quarterly. $1,995.00 per year. Provides a CD-ROM version of the online service, *PAIS International.* Contains over 400,000 citations to the literature of contemporary social, political, and economic issues.

WILSONDISC: Index to Legal Periodicals and Books. H. W. Wilson Co. • Monthly. Including unlimited online access to *Index to Legal Periodicals* through WILSONLINE. Contains CD-ROM indexing of more than 800 English language legal periodicals from 1981 to date and 2,500 books.

DIRECTORIES

Directory of Environmental Attorneys. Aspen Law and Business. • 1994. $195.00.

Law and Legal Information Directory. The Gale Group. • 2000. $405.00. 11th edition. Two volumes. Contains a wide range of sources of legal information, such as associations, law schools, courts, federal agencies, referral services, libraries, publishers, and research centers. There is a separate chapter for each of 23 types of information source or service.

Lawyer's Register International by Specialties and Fields of Law Including a Directory of Corporate Counsel. Lawyer's Register Publishing Co. • Annual. $329.00. Three volumes. Referral source for law firms.

HANDBOOKS AND MANUALS

Baxter's Environmental Compliance Manual: Procedures, Checklists, and Forms for Effective Compliance. West Group. • Three looseleaf volumes. $475.00. Periodic supplementation. Covers the creation, implementation, and management of corporate environmental compliance programs, so that liability exposure will be reduced. (Environmental Law Series).

Corporate Counsellor's Deskbook. Dennis J. Block and Michael A. Epstein, editors. Panel Publishing. • 1999. $220.00. Fifth edition. Looseleaf. Annual supplementation. Covers a wide variety of corporate legal issues, including internal investigations, indemnification, insider trading, intellectual property, executive compensation, antitrust, export-import, real estate, environmental law, government contracts, and bankruptcy.

ONLINE DATABASES

Enviroline. Congressional Information Service, Inc. • Provides online indexing and abstracting of worldwide environmental and natural resource literature from 1975 to date. Updated monthly. Inquire as to online cost and availability.

Environmental Law Reporter [online]. Environmental Law Institute. • Provides full text online of *Environmental Law Reporter*, covering administrative materials, news, pending legislation, statutes, bibliography, etc. Time periods vary. Inquire as to online cost and availability.

Index to Legal Periodicals and Books (Online). H. W. Wilson Co. • Broad coverage of law journals and books 1981 to date. Monthly updates. Inquire as to online cost and availability.

Legal Resource Index. The Gale Group. • Broad coverage of law literature appearing in legal, business, and other periodicals, 1980 to date. Monthly updates. Inquire as to online cost and availability.

LEXIS Environmental Law Library. LEXIS-NEXIS. • Provides legal decisions and regulatory material relating to the environment, as well as full text of *Environmental Law Reporter* and other legal publications dealing with the environment. Time period varies. Inquire as to online cost and availability.

PAIS International. Public Affairs Information Service, Inc. • Corresponds to the former printed publications, *PAIS Bulletin* (1976-90) and *PAIS Foreign Language Index* (1972-90), and to the current *PAIS International in Print* (1991 to date). Covers economic, political, and sociological material appearing in periodicals, books, government documents, and other publications. Updating is monthly. Inquire as to online cost and availability.

PERIODICALS AND NEWSLETTERS

Air-Water Pollution Report: The Weekly Report on Environmental Executives. Business Publishers, Inc. • Weekly. $667.00 per year. Newsletter covering legislation, regulation, business news, research news, etc. Formed by merger of *Environment Week* and *Air-Water Pollution Report.*

Environmental Health Perspectives. Available from U. S. Government Printing Office. • Monthly. $150.00 per year. Issued by the U.S. Department of Health and Human Services (http://www.dhhs.gov). Contains original research on various aspects of the environment and human health. Includes news of environment-related legislation, regulatory actions, and technological advances.

Environmental Law and Management. Available from John Wiley and Sons, Inc., Journals Div. • Bimonthly. Institutions, $650.00 per year. Provides international coverage of subject matter. Published in England by John Wiley and Sons Ltd. Formerly *Land Management and Environmental Law Report.*

Environmental Policy Alert. Inside Washington Publishers. • Biweekly. $645.00 per year. Newsletter on environmental legislation, regulation, and litigation.

RESEARCH CENTERS AND INSTITUTES

Environmental Law Institute. 1616 P St., N. W.,, Suite 200, Washington, DC 20036. Phone: (202)939-3800 Fax: (202)939-3868 E-mail: law@eli.org • URL: http://www.eli.org • Conducts research projects relating to environmental regulatory enforcement and reform.

Institute for Environmental Negotiation. University of Virginia, Campbell Hall, Charlottesville, VA 22903. Phone: (804)924-1970 Fax: (804)924-0231 E-mail: rcc3f@virginia.edu • URL: http://www.virginia/edu/~evening/ien.html • Research activities are related to the resolution of environmental disputes through negotiation, mediation, and consensus building.

Lexis.com Research System. Lexis-Nexis Group. Phone: 800-227-9597 or (937)865-6800 Fax: (937)865-6909 E-mail: webmaster@prod.lexis-nexis.com • URL: http://www.lexis.com • Fee-based Web site offers extensive searching of a wide variety of legal sources. Additional features include Daily Opinion Service, lexis.com Bookstore, Career Center, CLE Center, Law Schools, and Practice Pages ("Pages specific to areas of specialty").

Natural Resources Defense Council. 40 W. 20th St., New York, NY 10011. Phone: (212)727-2700 Fax: (212)727-1773 E-mail: nrdcinfo@nrdc.org • URL: http://www.nrdc.org • Studies the use of the judicial system to enforce environmental protection laws.

TRADE/PROFESSIONAL ASSOCIATIONS

Association of Local Air Pollution Control Officials. 444 N. Capitol St., N. W., Suite 307, Washington, DC 20001. Phone: (202)624-7864 Fax: (202)624-7863.

Association of State and Interstate Water Pollution Control Administrators. 750 First St., N.E., Suite 910, Washington, DC 20002. Phone: (202)898-0905

Fax: (202)898-0929 E-mail: admin1@asiwpca.org • URL: http://www.asiwpca.org.

National Conference of Local Environmental Health Administrators. 1359 Blue Tent Court, Cool, CA 95614-2120. Phone: (530)823-1736.

OTHER SOURCES

Environment Reporter. Bureau of National Affairs, Inc. • Weekly. $2,844.00 per year. 18 volumes. Looseleaf. Covers legal aspects of wide variety of environmental concerns.

Environmental Law Reporter. Environmental Law Institute. • Monthly. $1,045.00 per year. Seven volumes. Looseleaf service.

ENVIRONMENTAL POLLUTION

See: AIR POLLUTION; WATER POLLUTION

EQUAL EMPLOYMENT OPPORTUNITY

See also: AFFIRMATIVE ACTION PROGRAMS; EMPLOYMENT OF OLDER WORKERS; EMPLOYMENT OF WOMEN

GENERAL WORKS

EEO Law and Personnel Practices. Arthur Gutman. Sage Publications, Inc. • 1993. $58.00. Discusses the practical effect of federal regulations dealing with race, color, religion, sex, national origin, age, and disability. Explains administrative procedures, litigation actions, and penalties.

Equal Opportunity Law. David P. Twomey. South-Western Publishing Co. • 1996. $31.50. Third edition.

Labor and Employment Law: Text and Cases. David P. Twomey. South-Western Publishing Co. • 1993. $73.75. Ninth edition.

ABSTRACTS AND INDEXES

Human Resources Abstracts: An International Information Service. Sage Publications, Inc. • Quarterly. Individuals, $150.00 per year; institutions, $610.00 per year.

DIRECTORIES

National Directory of Minority-Owned Business Firms. Available from The Gale Group. • 2001. $285.00. 11th edition. Published by Business Research Services. Includes more than 47,000 minority-owned businesses.

National Directory of Women-Owned Business Firms. The Gale Group. • 2000. $285.00. 11th edition. Published by Business Research Services. Includes more than 28,000 businesses owned by women.

Regional Directory of Minority-and Women-Owned Business Firms. Business Research Services, Inc. • Annual. Three volumes. $175.00 per volume. Regional editions are Eastern, Central,and Western.

HANDBOOKS AND MANUALS

Defense of Equal Employment Claims. William L. Diedrich and William Gaus. Shepard's. • 1982. $105.00 per year. (Individual Rights Series).

Equal Employment Opportunity Compliance Manual: Procedures, Forms, Affirmative Action Programs, Laws, Regulations. Prentice Hall. • Two looseleaf volumes. Periodic supplementation. Price on application.

Equality in the Workplace: An Equal Opportunities Handbook for Trainers. Helen Collins. Blackwell Publishers. • 1995. $43.95. (Human Resource Management in Action Series).

Federal Civil Rights Acts. Rodney A. Smolla. West Group. • Two looseleaf volumes. $245.00. Covers current legislation relating to a wide range of civil rights issues, including discrimination in employment, housing, property rights, and voting. (Civil Right Series).

Manual on Employment Discrimination Law and Civil Rights Action in the Federal Courts. Charles R. Richey. West Group. • $100.00. Looseleaf service. Periodic supplementation.

ONLINE DATABASES

Labordoc. International Labour Office. • Indexing of labor literature and the publications of the International Labour Organization, 1965 to present. Monthly updates. Inquire as to online cost and availability.

PERIODICALS AND NEWSLETTERS

Employment Practices Update. West Group. • Monthly. $275.00 per year. Newsletter. Formerly *Equal Employment Compliance Update.*

The Equal Employer. Y. S. Publications, Inc. • Biweekly. $245.00 per year. Newsletter on fair employment practices.

Fair Employment Compliance: A Confidential Letter to Management. Management Resources, Inc. • Semimonthly. $245.00 per year. Newsletter.

Fair Employment Report. Business Publishers, Inc. • Biweekly. $327.00 per year. Formerly *Civil Rights Employment Reporter.*

PE Update. Project Equality. • Quarterly. Membership. Formerly *Project Equality Update.*

RESEARCH CENTERS AND INSTITUTES

Human Resources Institute. University of Alabama. P.O. 870225, Tuscaloosa, AL 35487. Phone: (205)348-8939 Fax: (205)348-6995 E-mail: tbain@cba.ua.edu • URL: http://www.ua.edu.

Industrial Relations Section. Princeton University, Firestone Library, Pinceton, NJ 08544. Phone: (609)258-4040 Fax: (609)258-2907 • URL: http://www.irs.princeton.edu/ • Fields of research include labor supply, manpower training, unemployment, and equal employment opportunity.

Institute of Labor and Industrial Relations. University of Illinois at Urbana-Champaign. 504 E. Armory Ave., Champaign, IL 61820. Phone: (217)333-1480 Fax: (217)244-9290 E-mail: feuille@uiuc.edu • URL: http://www.ilir.uiuc.edu.

Women Employed Institute. 22 W. Monroe St., Suite 1400, Chicago, IL 60603-2505. Phone: (312)782-3902 Fax: (312)782-5249 E-mail: info@womenemployed.org • URL: http://www.womenemployed.org • Research areas include the economic status of working women, sexual harassment in the workplace, equal employment opportunity, and career development.

TRADE/PROFESSIONAL ASSOCIATIONS

American Association for Affirmative Action. 5530 Wisconsin Ave., Ste. 1110, Chevy Chase, MD 20815-4330. Phone: 800-252-8952 Fax: (301)656-9008 E-mail: lsshaw@aol.com • URL: http://www.affirmativeaction.org.

OTHER SOURCES

BNA Fair Employment Practice Service. Bureau of National Affairs, Inc. • Weekly. $501.00 per year. Three volumes. Looseleaf.

Corporate Compliance Series. West Group. • Eleven looseleaf volumes, with periodic supplementation. $990.00. Covers criminal and civil liability problems for corporations. Includes employee safety, product liability, pension requirements, securities violations, equal employment opportunity issues, intellectual property, employee hiring and firing, and other corporate compliance topics.

EEOC Compliance Manual (Equal Employment Opportunity Commission). Bureau of National Affairs, Inc. • Irregular. $263.00 per year, including periodic updates. Two volumes. Looseleaf.Guide to federal Equal Employment Opportunity Commission activities.

Employment Discrimination. Matthew Bender & Co., Inc. • $1,260.00. Nine looseleaf volumes. Periodic supplementation, $849.00. Treatise on both substantive and procedural law governing employment discrimination based on sex, age, race, religion, national origin, etc.

Employment Discrimination: Law and Litigation. Merrick T. Rossein. West Group. • $220.00 per year. Looseleaf service. Periodic supplementation. Covers employment provisions of the Civil Rights Act, the Equal Pay Act, and related topics.

Human Resources Management Whole. CCH, Inc. • Nine looseleaf volumes. $1,572 per year. Includes monthly updates. Components are *Ideas and Trends Newsletter, Employment Relations, Compensation, Equal Employment Opportunity, Personnel Practices/Communications* and *OSHA Compliance.* Components are available separately.

EQUIPMENT LEASING

See also: RENTAL SERVICES

GENERAL WORKS

Lease or Buy? Principles for Sound Corporate Decision Making. James S. Schallheim. Harvard Business School Press. • 1994. $35.00. Discusses leasing arrangements, tax implications, accounting problems, net present value, and internal rate of return analysis. (Financial Management Association Survey and Synthesis Series).

ABSTRACTS AND INDEXES

Business Periodicals Index. H. W. Wilson Co. • Monthly, except August, with quarterly and annual cumulations. Service basis for print edition; CD-ROM edition, $1,495.00 per year.

CD-ROM DATABASES

WILSONDISC: Wilson Business Abstracts. H. W. Wilson Co. • Monthly. $2,495.00 per year, including unlimited online access to *Wilson Business Abstracts* through WILSONLINE. Provides CD-ROM "cover-to-cover" abstracting and indexing of over 600 prominent business periodicals. Indexing is from 1982, abstracting from 1990. (*Business Periodicals Index* without abstracts is available on CD-ROM at $1,495 per year.).

DIRECTORIES

Leasing Sourcebook: The Directory of the U. S. Capital Equipment Leasing Industry. Bibliotechnology Systems and Publishing Co. • Irregular. $135.00. Lists more than 5,200 capital equipment leasing companies.

Who's Who in Equipment Leasing. Equipment Leasing Association. • Annual. $350.00. Provides information on about 750 commercial equipment leasing companies.

HANDBOOKS AND MANUALS

Equipment Leasing. Matthew Bender and Co., Inc. • $405.00. Three looseleaf volumes. Periodic supplementation.

Equipment Leasing, Leveraged Leasing. Practising Law Institute. • Two looseleaf volumes. $295.00. Annual revisions. Contains "Practical analyses of the legal, tax, accounting, and financial aspects of equipment leasing." Includes forms, agreements, and checklists.

ONLINE DATABASES

ABI/INFORM. Bell & Howell Information and Learning. • Provides online indexing to business-related material occurring in over 1,000 periodicals from 1971 to the present. Inquire as to online cost and availability.

Management Contents. The Gale Group. • Covers a wide range of management, financial, marketing, personnel, and administrative topics. About 150 leading business journals are indexed and abstracted from 1974 to date, with monthly updating. Inquire as to online cost and availability.

Trade & Industry Index. The Gale Group. • Provides indexing of business periodicals, January 1981 to date. Daily updates. (Full text articles from some periodicals are available online, 1983 to date, in the companion database, *Trade & Industry ASAP.*) Inquire as to online cost and availability.

Wilson Business Abstracts Online. H. W. Wilson Co. • Indexes and abstracts 600 major business periodicals, plus the *Wall Street Journal* and the business section of the *New York Times*. Indexing is from 1982, abstracting from 1990, with the two newspapers included from 1993. Updated weekly. Inquire as to online cost and availability. (*Business Periodicals Index* without abstracts is also available online.).

STATISTICS SOURCES

WEFA Industrial Monitor. John Wiley and Sons, Inc. • Annual. $65.00. Prepared by industry analysts at WEFA, an economic forecasting and consulting firm (originally Wharton Econometric Forecasting Associates). Contains discussions of the outlook for major U. S. industries, with many 10-year forecasts (WEFA Web site is http://www.wefa.com).

OTHER SOURCES

How to Make the Right Leasing Decisions. American Management Association Extension Institute. • Looseleaf. $110.00. Self-study course. Emphasis is on practical explanations, examples, and problem solving. Quizzes and a case study are included.

ERGONOMICS

See: HUMAN ENGINEERING

ESSENTIAL OILS

See: ADDITIVES AND FLAVORINGS; PERFUME INDUSTRY

ESTATE PLANNING

See also: INHERITANCE TAX; TAX PLANNING

GENERAL WORKS

Investing During Retirement: The Vanguard Guide to Managing Your Retirement Assets. Vanguard Group. McGraw-Hill Professional. • 1996. $17.95. A basic, general guide to investing after retirement. Covers pension plans, basic principles of investing, types of mutual funds, asset allocation, retirement income planning, social security, estate planning, and contingencies. Includes glossary and worksheets for net worth, budget, and income.

Life Insurance in Estate Planning. James C. Munch, Jr. Aspen Books. • 1981. $80.00. Includes current supplement.

The Lifetime Book of Money Management. Grace W. Weinstein. Visible Ink Press. • 1993. $15.95. Third edition. Gives popularly-written advice on investments, life and health insurance, owning a home, credit, retirement, estate planning, and other personal finance topics.

Smart Questions to Ask Your Financial Advisers. Lynn Brenner. Bloomberg Press. • 1997. $19.95. Provides practical advice on how to deal with financial planners, stockbrokers, insurance agents, and lawyers. Some of the areas covered are investments, estate planning, tax planning, house buying, prenuptial agreements, divorce arrangements, loss of a job, and retirement. (Bloomberg Personal Bookshelf Series Library.).

Staying Wealthy: Strategies for Protecting Your Assets. Brian H. Breuel. Bloomberg Press. • 1998. $21.95. Presents ideas for estate planning and personal wealth preservation. Includes case studies. (Bloomberg Personal Bookshelf Series).

ABSTRACTS AND INDEXES

Insurance Periodicals Index. Specials Libraries Association, Insurance and Employees Benefits Div. CCH/NILS Publishing Co. • Annual. $250.00. Compiled by the Insurance and Employee Benefits Div., Special Libraries Association. A yearly index of over 15,000 articles from about 35 insurance periodicals. Arrangement is by subject, with an index to authors.

ALMANACS AND YEARBOOKS

University of Miami Law Center's Philip E. Heckerling Institute on Estate Planning. John T. Graubatz. Matthew Bender & Co., Inc. • Annual. Looseleaf service. Price on application. Review of estate, gift, generation-skipping transfer and income tax developments.

ENCYCLOPEDIAS AND DICTIONARIES

Dictionary of Finance and Investment Terms. John Downes and Jordan E. Goodman. Barron's Educational Series, Inc. • 1998. $12.95. Fifth revised edition. Provides clear explanations of more than 5,000 business, banking, financial, investment, and tax terms. Includes a separate list of financial abbreviations and acronyms.

Encyclopedia of Estate Planning. Robert S. Holzman. Boardroom Books. • 1995. $59.00. Second revised edition.

FINANCIAL RATIOS

Financial Planning for Older Clients. James E. Pearman. CCH, Inc. • 2000. $49.00. Covers income sources, social security, Medicare, Medicaid, investment planning, estate planning, and other retirement-related topics. Edited for accountants, attorneys, and other financial advisors.

HANDBOOKS AND MANUALS

Asset Protection Planning Guide: A State-of-the-Art Approach to Integrated Estate Planning. Barry S. Engel and others. CCH, Inc. • 2001. $99.00. Provides advice for attorneys, trust officers, accountants, and others engaged in financial planning for protection of assets.

CCH Financial and Estate Planning. CCH, Inc. • Semimonthly. $845.00 per year. Four looseleaf volumes.

CCH Financial and Estate Planning Guide [summary volume]. CCH, Inc. • Annual. $57.95. Contains four main parts: General Principles and Techniques, Special Situations, Building the Estate, and Planning Aids.

The Complete Probate Kit. Jen C. Appel and F. Bruce Gentry. John Wiley and Sons, Inc. • 1991. $29.95. A practical guide to settling estates. Provides summaries of the applicable state laws and definitions of relevant terms.

Estate and Retirement Planning Answer Book. William D. Mitchell. Aspen Publshers. • 1996. $118.00. Second edition. Basic questions and answers by a lawyer.

Estate Plan Book 2000. William S. Moore. American Institute for Economic Research. • 2000. $10.00. Revision of 1997 edition. Part one: "Basic Estate Planning." Part two: "Reducing Taxes on the Disposition of Your Estate." Part three: "Putting it All Together: Examples of Estate Plans." Provides succinct information on wills, trusts, tax planning, and gifts. (Economic Education Bulletin.).

Estate Planning Primer. Ralph G. Miller. CCH, Inc. • 1999. $99.00. Eighth edition. Written for attorneys and other estate planning professionals. Includes tables, sample tax forms, legal documents, and client letters. letters.

Estate Tax Techniques. Matthew Bender & Co., Inc. • $640.00. Three looseleaf volumes. Periodic supplementation.

How to Save Time and Taxes in Handling Estates. Matthew Bender & Co., Inc. • $235.00. Looseleaf servie. Periodic supplementation. (How to Save Time and Taxes Series).

How to Save Time and Taxes Preparing Fiduciary Income Tax Returns: Federal and State. Matthew Bender & Co., Inc. • $230.00. Looseleaf service. Periodic supplementation. (How to Save Time and Taxes Series).

Individual Retirement Account Answer Book. Donald R. Levy and Steven G. Lockwood. Panel Publishers. • 1999. $136.00. Sixth edition. Periodic supplementation available. Questions and answers include information about contributions, distributions, rollovers, Roth IRAs, SIMPLE IRAs (Savings Incentive Match Plans for Employees), Education IRAs, and SEPs (Simplified Employee Pension plans). Chapters are provided on retirement planning, estate planning, and tax planning.

Inheritor's Handbook: A Definitive Guide for Beneficiaries. Dan Rottenberg. Bloomberg Press. • 1998. $23.95. Covers both financial and emotional issues faced by beneficiaries. (Bloomberg Personal Bookshelf Series.).

Life Insurance Answer Book: For Qualified Plans and Estate Planning. Gary S. Lesser and Lawrence C. Starr, editors. Panel Publishers. • 1998. $118.00. Second edition. Four parts by various authors cover life insurance in general, qualified plans, fiduciary responsibility, and estate planning. Includes sample documents, worksheets, and information in Q&A form.

Modern Estate Planning. Ernest D. Fiore and M. Friedlich. Matthew Bender & Co., Inc. • $1,210.00. Seven looseleaf volumes. Updates, $875.00.

Tools and Techniques of Financial Planning. Stephan Leimberg and others. The National Underwriter Co. • 1993. $37.50. Fourth revised edition.

U. S. Master Estate and Gift Tax Guide. CCH, Inc. • Annual. $49.00. Covers federal estate and gift taxes, including generation-skipping transfer tax plans. Includes tax tables and sample filled-in tax return forms.

INTERNET DATABASES

CCH Essentials: An Internet Tax Research and Primary Source Library. CCH, Inc. Phone: 800-248-3248 or (773)866-6000 Fax: 800-224-8299 or (773)866-3608 E-mail: cust_serv@cch.com • URL: http://tax.cch.com/essentials • Fee-based Web site provides full-text coverage of federal tax law and regulations, including rulings, procedures, tax court decisions, and IRS publications, announcements, notices, and penalties. Includes explanation, analysis, tax planning guides, and a daily tax news service. Searching is offered, including citation search. Fee: $495.00 per year.

PERIODICALS AND NEWSLETTERS

Broker World. Insurance Publications, Inc. • Monthly. $6.00 per year. Edited for independent insurance agents and brokers. Special feature issue topics include annuities, disability insurance, estate planning, and life insurance.

Estate Planner's Alert. Research Institute of America, Inc. • Monthly. $140.00 per year. Newsletter. Covers the tax aspects of personal finance, including home ownership, investments, insurance, retirement planning, and charitable giving. Formerly *Estate and Financial Planners Alert.*

Estate Planning. Warren, Gorham and Lamont/RIA Group. • Bimonthly. $141.50 per year. Semiannual updates.

Estate Planning Review. CCH, Inc. • Monthly. $196.00 per year.

Financial Planning: The Magazine for Financial Service Professionals. Securities Data Publishing. • Monthly. $79.00 per year. Edited for independent financial planners and insurance agents. Covers retirement planning, estate planning, tax planning, and insurance, including long-term healthcare considerations. Special features include a Retirement Planning Issue, Mutual Fund Performance Survey, and Variable Life and Annuity Survey. (Securities Data Publishing is a unit of Thomson Financial.).

Jounal of Finacial Services Professionals. American Society of CLU and Ch F C. • Bimonthly. $38.00 per year. Provides information on life insurance and financial planning, including estate planning, retirement, tax planning, trusts, business insurance, long-term care insurance, disability insurance, and employee benefits. Formerly (American Society of CLU and Ch F C Journal).

Journal of Practical Estate Planning. CCH, Inc. • Bimonthly. $195.00 per year. Edited for attorneys and other estate planning professionals.

Journal of Retirement Planning. CCH, Inc. • Bimonthly. $169.00 per year. Emphasis is on retirement and estate planning advice provided by lawyers and accountants as part of their practices.

Worth: Financial Intelligence. Worth Media. • 10 times a year. $18.00 per year. Contains articles for affluent consumers on personal financial management, including investments, estate planning, and taxes.

OTHER SOURCES

Estate and Personal Financial Planning. Edward F. Koren. West Group. • Monthly. Newsletter. Price on application.

Estate Planning and Taxation Coordinator. Research Institute of America, Inc. • Nine looseleaf volumes. $760.00 per year. Biweekly updates. Includes *Estate Planner's Alert* and *Lifetime Planning Alert.*

Estate Planning for Farmers and Ranchers: A Guide to Family Businesses with Agricultural Holdings. Donald H. Kelley and David A. Ludtke. Shepard's. • 1995. Third edition. Price on application.

Estate Planning: Inheritance Taxes. Prentice Hall. • Five looseleaf volumes. Periodic supplementation. Price on application.

Estate Planning Program. Prentice Hall. • Two looseleaf volumes. Periodic supplementation. Price on application. Includes checklists and forms.

Estate Planning Strategies After Estate Tax Reform: Insights and Analysis. CCH, Inc. • 2001. $45.00. Produced by the Estate Planning Department of Schiff, Hardin & Waite. Covers estate planning techniques and opportunities resulting from tax legislation of 2001.

Estate Planning Under the New Law: What You Need to Know. CCH, Inc. • 2001. $7.00. Booklet summarizes significant changes in estate planning brought about by tax legislation of 2001.

Estate Planning: Wills, Trusts and Forms. Research Institute of America. • Looseleaf service. Includes bimonthly *Report Bulletins* and updates.

Federal Estate and Gift Tax Reports. CCH, Inc. • Weekly. $520.00. Three looseleaf volumes.

Fiduciary Tax Guide. CCH, Inc. • Monthly. $439.00 per year, Includes looseleaf monthly updates. Covers federal income taxation of estates, trusts, and beneficiaries. Provides information on gift and generation- skipping taxation.

Financial and Estate Planning: Analysis, Strategies and Checklists. CCH, Inc. • Looseleaf services. $200.00 per year.

How to Plan for a Secure Retirement. Elias Zuckerman and others. Consumer Reports Books. • 2000. $29.95. Covers pension plans, health insurance, estate planning, retirement communities, and related topics. (Consumer Reports Money Guide.).

ESTATE TAX

See: INHERITANCE TAX

ESTIMATING

GENERAL WORKS

Cost Estimating. Rodney D. Stewart. John Wiley and Sons, Inc. • 1991. $130.00. Second edition. Discusses high technology engineering cost forecasting, including the estimation of software costs.

Fundamentals of Construction Estimating. David Pratt. Delmar Publishing. • 1995. $78.95.

ABSTRACTS AND INDEXES

Business Periodicals Index. H. W. Wilson Co. • Monthly, except August, with quarterly and annual cumulations. Service basis for print edition; CD-ROM edition, $1,495.00 per year.

NTIS Alerts: Building Industry Technology. National Technical Information Service. • Semimonthly. $210.00 per year. Provides descriptions of government-sponsored research reports and software, with ordering information. Covers architecture, construction management, building materials, maintenance, furnishings, and related subjects. Formerly *Abstract Newsletter.*

CD-ROM DATABASES

ABI/INFORM Global. Bell & Howell Information and Learning. • Monthly. $6,500.00 per year. Provides CD-ROM indexing and abstracting of worldwide business literature appearing in over 1,200 periodicals for the most recent five years. Archival discs are available from 1971. Formerly *ABI/INFORM OnDisc.*

COMPENDEX PLUS [CD-ROM]. Engineering Information, Inc. • Quarterly. $3,450.00 per year. Provides CD-ROM indexing and abstracting of the world's engineering and technical information appearing in journals, reports, books, and proceedings, 1985 to date.

WILSONDISC: Business Periodicals Index. H. W. Wilson Co. • Monthly. $1,495.00 per year. Provides CD-ROM indexing of business periodicals from 1982 to date. Price includes online service.

DIRECTORIES

AACE International-Directory of Members. AACE International. • Annual. $10.00 per year. 6,000 cost engineers, estimators, and cost management professionals worldwide.

HANDBOOKS AND MANUALS

Basic Estimating for Construction. James A. S. Fatzinger. Prentice Hall. • 2000. $69.95. Covers electrical, plumbing, concrete, masonry, framing, etc. Includes a glossary and typical bid forms.

Construction Contractors' Survival Guide. Thomas C. Schleifer. John Wiley and Sons, Inc. • 1990. $80.00. (Practical Construction Guides Series).

Estimating for Home Builders. Jerry Householder. Home Builder Press. • 1998. $30.80. Third edition. Describes the process of developing complete cost estimates-and the shortcut methods-to ensure success in the building business.

Estimating in Building Construction. Frank R. Dagostino. Prentice Hall. • 1998. $81.00. Fifth edition.

Walker's Building Estimator's Reference Book. Scott Siddens, editor. Frank R. Walker Co. • 1999 $69.95. 26th revised edition.

ONLINE DATABASES

ABI/INFORM. Bell & Howell Information and Learning. • Provides online indexing to business-related material occurring in over 1,000 periodicals from 1971 to the present. Inquire as to online cost and availability.

Trade & Industry Index. The Gale Group. • Provides indexing of business periodicals, January 1981 to date. Daily updates. (Full text articles from some periodicals are available online, 1983 to date, in the companion database, *Trade & Industry ASAP.*) Inquire as to online cost and availability.

Wilson Business Abstracts Online. H. W. Wilson Co. • Indexes and abstracts 600 major business periodicals, plus the *Wall Street Journal* and the business section of the *New York Times.* Indexing is from 1982, abstracting from 1990, with the two newspapers included from 1993. Updated weekly. Inquire as to online cost and availability. (*Business Periodicals Index* without abstracts is also available online.).

PERIODICALS AND NEWSLETTERS

Cost Engineering: The Journal of Cost Estimating, Cost Control, and Project Management. American Association of Cost Engineers. • Monthly. $57.00 per year. Subjects include cost estimation and cost control.

Design Cost Data: The Cost Estimating Magazine for Architects, Builders and Specifiers. L. M. Rector Corp. • Bimonthly. $64.80 per year. Provides a preliminary cost estimating system for architects, contractors, builders, and developers, utilizing historical data. Includes case studies of actual costs. Formerly *Design Cost and Data.*

The National Estimator. Society of Cost Estimating and Analysis. • Semiannual. $30.00 per year. Covers government contract estimating.

PRICE SOURCES

Means Facilities Construction Cost Data. R.S. Means Co., Inc. • Annual. Price on application. Provides costs for use in building estimating.

Means Interior Cost Data. R.S. Means Co., Inc. • Annual. $79.95.

Means Repair and Remodeling Cost Data. R.S. Means Co., Inc. • Annual. $79.95.

Means Residential Cost Data. R.S. Means Co., Inc. • Annual. $72.95.

National Building Cost Manual. Craftsman Book Co. • Annual. $20.00.

National Construction Estimator. Martin Kiley and William Moselle. Craftsman Book Co. • Annual. $47.50.

RESEARCH CENTERS AND INSTITUTES

Construction Industry Institute. University of Texas at Austin, 3208 Red River, Suite 300, Austin, TX 78705-2697. Phone: (512)232-3000 Fax: (512)499-

8101 E-mail: k.eickman@mail.utexas.edu • URL: http://www.construction-institution.org • Research activities are related to the management, planning, and design aspects of construction project execution.

Construction Research Center. Georgia Institute of Technology, Atlanta, GA 30332-0245. Phone: (404)894-3013 Fax: (404)894-9140 E-mail: steve.johnson@mse.gatech.edu • URL: http://www.arch.gatech.edu/crc/ • Conducts interdisciplinary research in all aspects of construction, including planning, design, cost estimating, and management.

TRADE/PROFESSIONAL ASSOCIATIONS

American Society of Professional Estimators. 11141 Georgia Ave., Suite 412, Wheaton, MD 20902. Phone: (301)929-8848 Fax: (301)929-0231 E-mail: info@aspenational.com • URL: http://www.aspenational.com • Members are construction cost estimators and construction educators.

Professional Construction Estimators Association of America. P.O. Box 11626, Charlotte, NC 28220-1626. Phone: (704)522-6376 Fax: (704)522-7013 E-mail: pcea@pcea.com • URL: http://www.pcea.org • Members are building and construction cost estimators.

Society of Cost Estimating and Analysis. 101 S. Whiting St., Suite 201, Alexandria, VA 22304. Phone: (703)751-8069 Fax: (703)461-7328 E-mail: scea@erols.com • URL: http://www.scea.com • Members are engaged in government contract estimating and pricing.

OTHER SOURCES

AACE International. Transactions of the Annual Meetings. American Association of Cost Engineers. AACE International. • Annual. Price varies. Contains texts of papers presented at AACE meetings.

ETHICAL DRUG INDUSTRY

See: PHARMACEUTICAL INDUSTRY

ETHICS

See: BUSINESS ETHICS; SOCIAL RESPONSIBILITY

ETIQUETTE

HANDBOOKS AND MANUALS

Amy Vanderbilt's Complete Book of Etiquette. Nancy Tuckerman and Nancy Dunnan. Doubleday. • 1995. $32.00. Revised edition.

Business Etiquette. Marjorie Brody and Barbara Pachter. McGraw-Hill Professional. • 1994. $10.95.

Executive Etiquette in the New Workplace. Marjabelle Steward and Marian Faux. St. Martin's Press. • 1995. $14.95.

Little Black Book of Business Etiquette. Michael C. Thomsett. AMACOM. • 1991. $14.95. Covers company politics, chain of command, business lunches, dress codes, etc. (Little Black Book Series).

Snowdon's Official International Protocols: The Definitive Guide to Business and Social Customs of the World. Sondra Snowdon. McGraw-Hill Professional. • 1996. $75.00. Discusses the protocols of 60 nations: social customs, business climate, personal characteristics, relevant history, and politics.

EUROCURRENCY

See also: FOREIGN EXCHANGE

ABSTRACTS AND INDEXES

Banking Information Index. U M I Banking Information Index. • Monthly. Price on application. Covers a wide variety of banking, business, and financial subjects in periodicals. Formerly *Banking Literature Index.*

INTERNET DATABASES

Europa: The European Union's Server. European Union 352 4301 35 349. E-mail: pressoffice@eurostat.cec.be • URL: http://www.europa.eu.int • Web site provides access to a wide variety of EU information, including statistics (Eurostat), news, policies, publications, key issues, and official exchange rates for the euro. Includes links to the European Central Bank, the European Investment Bank, and other institutions. Fees: Free.

ONLINE DATABASES

Banking Information Source. Bell & Howell Information and Learning. • Provides indexing and abstracting of periodical and other literature from 1982 to date, with weekly updates. Covers the financial services industry: banks, savings institutions, investment houses, credit unions, insurance companies, and real estate organizations. Emphasis is on marketing and management. Inquire as to online cost and availability. (Formerly *FINIS: Financial Industry Information Service.*).

PERIODICALS AND NEWSLETTERS

Euromoney: The Monthly Journal of International Money and Capital Markets. American Educational Systems. • Monthly. $395.00 per year. Supplement available*Guide to World Equity Markets.*

Financial Times [London]. Available from FT Publications, Inc. • Daily, except Sunday. $184.00 per year. An international business and financial newspaper, featuring news from London, Paris, Frankfurt, New York, and Tokyo. Includes worldwide stock and bond market data, commodity market data, and monetary/currency exchange information.

International Currency Review. World Reports Ltd. • Quarterly. $475.00 per year.

Rundt's World Business Intelligence. S. J. Rundt and Associates, Inc. • Weekly. $695.00 per year. Formerly *Rundt's Weekly Intelligence.*

STATISTICS SOURCES

International Financial Statistics. International Monetary Fund, Publications Services. • Monthly. Individuals, $246.00 per year; libraries, $123.00 per year. Includes a wide variety of current data for individual countries in Europe and elsewhere. Annual issue available. Editions available in French and Spanish.

EURODOLLARS

See: EUROCURRENCY

EUROPEAN CONSUMER MARKET

See also: EUROPEAN MARKETS

ABSTRACTS AND INDEXES

Business Periodicals Index. H. W. Wilson Co. • Monthly, except August, with quarterly and annual cumulations. Service basis for print edition; CD-ROM edition, $1,495.00 per year.

CD-ROM DATABASES

ABI/INFORM Global. Bell & Howell Information and Learning. • Monthly. $6,500.00 per year. Provides CD-ROM indexing and abstracting of worldwide business literature appearing in over 1,200 periodicals for the most recent five years. Archival discs are available from 1971. Formerly *ABI/INFORM OnDisc.*

WILSONDISC: Business Periodicals Index. H. W. Wilson Co. • Monthly. $1,495.00 per year. Provides CD-ROM indexing of business periodicals from 1982 to date. Price includes online service.

World Consumer Markets. The Gale Group. • Annual. $2,500.00. Pblished by Euromonitor. Provides five- year historical data, current data, and forecasts, on CD-ROM for 330 consumer products in 55 countries. Market data is presented in a standardized format for each country.

World Database of Consumer Brands and Their Owners on CD-ROM. The Gale Group. • Annual. $3,190.00. Produced by Euromonitor. Provides detailed information on CD-ROM for about 10,000 companies and 80,000 brands around the world. Covers 1,000 product sectors.

World Marketing Forecasts on CD-ROM. The Gale Group. • Annual. $2,500.00. Produced by Euromonitor. Provides detailed forecast data for the years to 2012 on CD-ROM for 54 countries in all parts of the world. Covers a wide range of social, demographic, economic, and market factors. Includes specific forecasts for many kinds of consumer products.

DIRECTORIES

Continental Europe Market Guide. Dun and Bradstreet Information Services. • Semiannual. $1,600.00 per two volume set. Lists about 220,000 firms in 21 European countries. Includes financial strength and credit ratings. Geographic arrangement.

Directory of Consumer Brands and Their Owners: Eastern Europe. Available from The Gale Group. • 1998. $990.00. Published by Euromonitor. Provides information about brands available from major Eastern European companies. Descriptions of companies are also included.

Directory of Consumer Brands and Their Owners: Europe. Available from The Gale Group. • 1998. $990.00. Two volumes. Third edition. Published by Euromonitor. Provides information about brands available from major European companies. Descriptions of companies are also included.

European Directory of Retailers and Wholesalers. Available from The Gale Group. • 1997. $790.00. Second edition. Published by Euromonitor. Provides detailed information on more than 4,000 major retail and wholesale businesses in 17 countries of Western Europe. Contains 26 categories, such as supermarkets, superstores, department stores, discount stores, franchise operators, mail order, etc. Includes company, product, and geographic indexes.

European Food Marketing Directory. The Gale Group. • 1996. $430.00. Fourth edition. Volume four. Published by Euromonitor. Lists approximately 650 European food distributors and 1,600 food manufacturers. Covers more than 20 countries in all parts of Europe.

European Markets: A Guide to Company and Industry Information Sources. Washington Researchers. • 1996. $335.00. A directory of government offices, "experts," publications, and databases related to European markets and companies. Includes individual chapters on 18 nations of Europe.

International Brands and Their Companies. The Gale Group. • 1998. $295.00. Fifth edition. Contains about 84,000 worldwide (non-U. S.) entries for trade names, trademarks, and brand names of consumer-oriented products and their manufacturers, importers, distributors, or marketers. Formerly *International Trade Names Dictionary.*

International Media Guide: Consumer Magazines Worldwide. International Media Guides, Inc. • Annual. $285.00. Contains descriptions of 4,500 consumer magazines in 24 subject categories in 200 countries, including U. S. Provides details of advertising rates and circulation.

Major Market Share Companies: Europe. Available from The Gale Group. • 2000. $900.00. Published by Euromonitor (http://www.euromonitor.com). Provides consumer market share data and rankings for multinational and regional companies. Covers leading firms in 14 European countries.

Market Share Tracker. Available from The Gale Group. • 2000. $1,000.00. Published by Euromonitor (http://www.euromonitor.com). Provides consumer market share data for leading companies in 30 major countries.

World Retail Directory and Sourcebook 1999. Available from The Gale Group. • 1999. $590.00. Fourth edition. Published by Euromonitor. Provides information on more than 2,600 retailers around the world, with detailed profiles of the top 70. Information sources, conferences, trade fairs, and special libraries are also listed.

The World's Major Multinationals. Available from The Gale Group. • 2000. $1,100.00. Published by Euromonitor (http://www.euromonitor.com). Provides profiles of leading companies around the world selling branded products to consumers. Includes detailed financial data for each firm.

HANDBOOKS AND MANUALS

Consumer Price Indices: An ILO Manual. Ralph Turvey and others. International Labour Office. • 1990. $24.75.

The World's Largest Market: A Business Guide to Europe 1992. Robert Williams and others. AMACOM. • 1991. $19.95. Reprint edition. Provides information on agencies, organizations programs, and regulations relevant to the forthcoming 1992 unified European Community.

ONLINE DATABASES

ABI/INFORM. Bell & Howell Information and Learning. • Provides online indexing to business-related material occurring in over 1,000 periodicals from 1971 to the present. Inquire as to online cost and availability.

Euromonitor Journals. Euromonitor International. • Contains full-text reports online from *Market Research Europe, Market Research Great Britain, Market Research International*, and *Retail Monitor International*. Time period is 1995 to date, with monthly updates. Inquire as to online cost and availability.

Euromonitor Market Research. Euromonitor International. • Provides the complete text online of Euromonitor market analysis reports. Covers consumer goods market research data for all major countries, with emphasis on specific product categories. Time period is current. Continuous updating. Inquire as to online cost and availability.

F & S Index. The Gale Group. • Contains about four million citations to worldwide business, financial, and industrial or consumer product literature appearing from 1972 to date. Weekly updates. Inquire as to online cost and availability.

Globalbase. The Gale Group. • Provides more than one million online summaries of business, industrial, and economic news reports from more than 1,000 publications worldwide. Covers a wide range of material appearing in international trade journals, professional magazines, and newspapers. Time period is 1984 to date, with weekly updates. Inquire as to online cost and availability.

PROMT: Predicasts Overview of Markets and Technology. The Gale Group. • Companies, products, applied technologies and markets. U.S. and international literature coverage, 1972 to date. Inquire as to online cost and availability. Provides abstracts from more than 1,600 publications. Weekly updates.

Trade & Industry Index. The Gale Group. • Provides indexing of business periodicals, January 1981 to date. Daily updates. (Full text articles from some periodicals are available online, 1983 to date, in the companion database, *Trade & Industry ASAP.*) Inquire as to online cost and availability.

Wilson Business Abstracts Online. H. W. Wilson Co. • Indexes and abstracts 600 major business periodicals, plus the *Wall Street Journal* and the business section of the *New York Times*. Indexing is from 1982, abstracting from 1990, with the two newspapers included from 1993. Updated weekly. Inquire as to online cost and availability. (*Business Periodicals Index* without abstracts is also available online.).

PERIODICALS AND NEWSLETTERS

Advertising Age's Euromarketing. Crain Communications, Inc. • Weekly. $295.00 per year. Newsletter on European advertising and marketing.

Europa 2000: The American Business Report on Europe. Wolfe Publishing, Inc. • Monthly. $119.00 per year. Newsletter on consumer and industrial marketing in a unified European Economic Community. Includes classified business opportunity advertisements and a listing by country of forthcoming major trade shows in Europe.

Journal of Euromarketing. Haworth Press, Inc. • Quarterly. Individuals, $50.00 per year; institutions, $85.00 per year; libraries, $275.00 per year.

Journal of International Consumer Marketing. Haworth Press, Inc. • Quarterly. Individuals, $60.00 per year; institutions, $90.00 per year; libraries, $300.00 per year.

Pharma Business: The International Magazine of Pharmaceutical Business and Marketing. Engel Publishing Partners. • Eight times a year. $185.00 per year. Circulated mainly in European countries. Coverage includes worldwide industry news, new drug products, regulations, and research developments.

STATISTICS SOURCES

Consumer Eastern Europe. Available from The Gale Group. • 2001. $1,090.00. Eighth edition. Published by Euromonitor. Provides demographic and consumer market data for the countries of Eastern Europe.

Consumer Europe 2000/2001. Available from The Gale Group. • 2000. $1,190.00. 16th edition. Published by Euromonitor. Detailed statistical tables furnish five-year data on the production, sales, distribution, consumption, and other aspects of more than 240 consumer product categories. Thirteen countries of Western Europe are included.

European Compendium of Marketing Information. Available from The Gale Group. • 1996. $350.00. Second edition. Volume two. Published by Euromonitor. Provides marketing and production statistics relating to European consumer products and services.

European Economy, Series A: Recent Economic Trends. Commission of the European Communities. Bernan Associates. • Monthly. $65.00 per year. Published by the Commission of the European Communities, Luxembourg.

European Economy, Series B: Business and Consumer Survey Results. Commission of the European Communities. Available from Bernan Associates. • Monthly. Published by the Commission of the European Communities, Luxembourg. Editions in English, French, German, and Italian.

European Marketing Data and Statistics 2001. Available from The Gale Group. • 2001. $450.00. 36th edition. Published by Euromonitor. Presents essential marketing data, including demographics and consumer expenditure patterns, for 31 European countries.

European Marketing Forecasts 2001. Available from The Gale Group. • 2000. $1,190.00. Third edition. Published by Euromonitor. Contains demographic, economic, and market forecasts for the countries of Europe to the year 2010. Forecasts include market-size data for 15 consumer product sectors (food, clothing, automobiles, consumer electronics, etc.).

European Retail Statistics: 17 Countries. Available from European Business Publications, Inc. • Annual. $375.00. Published in London by Corporate Intelligence Research Publications Ltd. Presents national retail statistics for each of 17 major countries of Europe, including total sales, number of businesses, employment, the food sector, the non-food sector, and demographic data.

Regions Statistical Yearbook. Bernan Associates. • Annual. $45.00. Published by the Commission of European Communities. Provides data on the social and economic situation in specific European areas. Includes population, employment, migration, industry, living standards, etc.

Retail Trade International. The Gale Group. • 2000. $1,990.00. Second edition. Six volumes. Presents comprehensive data on retail trends in 51 countries. Includes textual analysis and profiles of major retailers. Covers Europe, Asia, the Middle East, Africa and the Americas.

World Consumer Income and Expenditure Patterns. Available from The Gale Group. • 2001. $650.00. Published by Euromonitor (http://www.euromonitor.com). Provides data on consumer income, earning power, and expenditures for 52 countries around the world.

TRADE/PROFESSIONAL ASSOCIATIONS

Association of International Marketing. P.O. Box 70, London E13 8BQ, England. Phone: 44 181 9867539 Fax: 44 181 9867539 • A multinational organization. Promotes the advancement and exchange of information and ideas in international marketing.

European Direct Marketing Association. 439 Ave. de Tervueren, B-1150 Brussels, Belgium. E-mail: edma@skynet.be • A multinational organization. Facilitates contacts and exchange of ideas and techniques among countries and members. Sponsors "Best of Europe" contest, with awards for best direct mail campaigns.

European Marketing Academy. c/o European Institute for Advanced Studies in Management, 13, rue d'Egmont, B-1000 32 Brussels, Belgium. E-mail: emac@eiasm.be • URL: http://www.eiasm.be/emac/emachp.html • A multinational organization. Promotes international exchange in the field of marketing.

European Marketing Association. 18 Saint Peters Hill, Brixham, Devon, England. 18 Saint Peters Hill, • A multinational organization. Promotes the marketing profession in Europe.

OTHER SOURCES

Disposable Paper Products. Available from MarketResearch.com. • 1998. $5,900.00. Published by Euromonitor Publications Ltd. Provides consumer market data and forecasts to 2001 for the United States, the United Kingdom, Germany, France, and Italy.

Fast Food. Available from MarketResearch.com. • 1998. $5,000.00. Published by Euromonitor Publications Ltd. Provides consumer market data for the United States, the United Kingdom, Germany, France, and Italy.

Frozen Foods. Available from MarketResearch.com. • 1997. $5,000.00. Published by Euromonitor Publications Ltd. Provides consumer market data and forecasts for the United States, the United Kingdom, Germany, France, and Italy. Contains market analyses for many kinds of frozen foods.

Fruit Juices. Available from MarketResearch.com. • 1998. $5,900.00. Published by Euromonitor Publications Ltd. Provides consumer market data and forecasts to 2002 for the United States, the United Kingdom, Germany, France, and Italy. Includes fresh, frozen, bottled, and canned fruit and vegetable juices.

Household Cleaning Agents. Available from MarketResearch.com. • 1998. $5,900.00. Published by Euromonitor Publications Ltd. Provides consumer market data and forecasts to 2002 for the United States, the United Kingdom, Germany, France, and Italy. Covers dishwashing detergents, floor cleaning products, scourers, polishes, bleaching products, etc.

Major Performance Rankings. Available from The Gale Group. • 2001. $1,100.00. Published by Euromonitor. Ranks 2,500 leading consumer product companies worldwide by various kinds of business and financial data, such as sales, profit, and market share. Includes international, regional, and country rankings.

World Consumer Income and Expenditure Patterns. Available from The Gale Group. • 2001. $990.00. Second edition. Two volumes. Published by Euromonitor. Provides data for 52 countries on consumer income, earning power, spending patterns, and savings. Expenditures are detailed for 75 product or service categories.

EUROPEAN ECONOMIC COMMUNITY

See: EUROPEAN MARKETS

EUROPEAN MARKETS

See also: EUROPEAN CONSUMER MARKET; INTERNATIONAL BUSINESS

ABSTRACTS AND INDEXES

Business Periodicals Index. H. W. Wilson Co. • Monthly, except August, with quarterly and annual cumulations. Service basis for print edition; CD-ROM edition, $1,495.00 per year.

F & S Index: Europe. The Gale Group. • Monthly. $1,295.00 per year, including quarterly and annual cumulations. Provides annotated citations to marketing, business, financial, and industrial literature. Coverage of European business activity includes trade journals, financial magazines, business newspapers, and special reports. Formerly *Predicasts F & S Index: Europe.*

ALMANACS AND YEARBOOKS

Economic Survey of Europe. United Nations Publications. • Three times a year. Price varies. Provides yearly analysis and review of the European economy, including Eastern Europe and the USSR. Text in English.

Euroguide Yearbook of the Institutions of the European Union and of the Other European Organiz. Bernan Associates. • Annual. Free. Published by Editions Delta. Information on public and private institutions in the European Union contributing to European integration.

European Union Annual Review of Activities. Blackwell Publishers. • 1998. $15.99.

BIOGRAPHICAL SOURCES

Who's Who of European Business: and Industry. Triumph Books. • Irregular. $295.00. Lists over 9,500 business executives from 36 countries in Eastern and Western Europe. Two volumes.

CD-ROM DATABASES

Baltia Kompass Business Disc. Available from Kompass USA, Inc. • Annual. $360.00. CD-ROM provides information on more than 22,000 companies in Estonia, Latvia, and Lithuania. Classification system covers approximately 50,000 products and services.

Benelux Kompass Business Disc. Available from Kompass USA, Inc. • Annual. $560.00. CD-ROM provides information on more than 54,000 companies in Belgium, Netherlands, and Luxembourg. Classification system covers approximately 50,000 products and services.

East European Kompass on Disc. Available from Kompass USA, Inc. • Annual. $1,280.00. CD-ROM provides information on more than 294,000 companies in Austria, Azerbaijan, Belarus, Croatia, Czech Republic, Estonia, Hungary, Latvia, Lithuania, Moldova, Poland, Romania, Russia, Slovakia, Slovenia, Ukraine, and Yugoslavia. Classification system covers approximately 50,000 products and services.

European Kompass on Disc. Available from Kompass USA, Inc. • Annual. $2,070.00. CD-ROM provides information on more than 350,000 companies in Belgium, Denmark, France, Germany, Ireland, Italy, Luxembourg, Netherlands, Norway, Spain, Sweden, and UK. Classification system covers approximately 50,000 products and services.

Hoover's Company Capsules on CD-ROM. Hoover's, Inc. • Quarterly. $349.95 per year (single-user). Provides the CD-ROM version of *Hoover's Handbook of American Business, Hoover's Handbook of Emerging Companies, Hoover's Handbook of World Business, Hoover's Guide to Computer Companies, Hoover's Guide to Media Companies, Hoover's Handbook of Private Companies,* and various regional guides. Includes more than 11,000 profiles of companies.

Kompass CD-ROM Editions. Available from Kompass USA, Inc. • Annual. Prices vary. CD-ROM versions of Kompass international trade directories are available for each of 30 major countries and eight world regions. Searching is provided for 50,000 product/service items and many company details.

Scandinavian Kompass on Disc. Available from Kompass USA, Inc. • Annual. $1,950.00. CD-ROM provides information on more than 66,000 companies in Denmark, Finland, Norway, and Sweden. Classification system covers approximately 50,000 products and services.

DIRECTORIES

Directory of EU Information Sources. Euroconfidentiel S. A. • Annual. $250.00. Lists more than 12,500 publications, associations, consultants, law firms, diplomats, jounalists, and other sources of information about Europe and the European Union.

Directory of Trade and Professional Associations in the European Union. Euroconfidentiel S. A. • Annual. $160.00. Includes more than 9,000 EU-related associations.

Eastern Europe: A Directory and Sourcebook. Available from The Gale Group. • 1999. $590.00. Second edition. Published by Euromonitor. Describes major companies in Eastern Europe. Sourcebook section provides marketing and business information sources.

European Markets: A Guide to Company and Industry Information Sources. Washington Researchers. • 1996. $335.00. A directory of government offices, "experts," publications, and databases related to European markets and companies. Includes individual chapters on 18 nations of Europe.

European Union Encyclopedia and Directory. Taylor and Francis, Inc. • 1999. $450.00. Second edition. Published by Europa. Provides directory information for major European Union organizations, with detailed descriptions of various groups or concepts in an "Encyclopedia" section. A statistics section contains a wide variety of data related to business, industry, and economics. Formerly *The European Communities Encyclopedia and Directory.*

Europe's Major Companies Directory. Available from The Gale Group. • 1997. $590.00. Second edition. Published by Euromonitor. Contains detailed financial and product information for about 6,000 major companies in 16 countries of Western Europe.

Europe's Medium-Sized Companies Directory. Available from The Gale Group. • 1997. $590.00. Published by Euromonitor. Contains detailed financial and product information on about 5,000 medium-sized companies in 16 countries of Western Europe.

Europe's Top Quoted Companies: A Comparative Directory from Seventeen European Stock Exchanges. Available from Hoover's, Inc. • Annual. $150.00. Published in the UK by COFISEM. Provides detailed, 5-year financial data on 700 major European companies that are publicly traded. Includes company addresses.

Hoover's Handbook of World Business: Profiles of Major European, Asian, Latin American, and Canadian Companies. Hoover's, Inc. • Annual. $99.95. Contains detailed profiles of more than 300 large foreign companies. Includes indexes by industry, location, executive name, company name, and brand name.

International Media Guide: Business Professional Publications: Europe. International Media Guides, Inc. • Annual. $285.00. Describes 6,000 trade journals from Eastern and Western Europe, with advertising rates and circulation data.

Kompass International Trade Directories. Available from MarketResearch.com. • Annual. Prices and volumes vary. Kompass directories are published internationally for each of more than 70 countries, from Algeria to Yugoslavia. The Kompass classification system covers 50,000 individual product and service categories. Most directories include a tradename index and company profiles.

Major Chemical and Petrochemical Companies of Europe. Kluwer Law International. • Annual. $315.00. Published by Graham & Whiteside Ltd., London. Includes financial, personnel, and product information for chemical companies in Western Europe.

Major Employers of Europe 2000/2001. Available from The Gale Group. • Annual. $270.00. Published by Graham & Whiteside. Provides concise information on the top 10,000 companies in Europe, according to number of employees. Firms are indexed by country and by business activity.

Major Financial Institutions of Europe. European Business Publications, Inc. • Annual. $495.00. Contains profiles of over 7,000 financial institutions in Europe such as banks, investment companies, and insurance companies. Formerly *Major Financial Institutions of Continental Europe*.

The Top 5,000 European Companies 2000/2001. Available from The Gale Group. • 2001. $630.00. Second edition. Published by Graham & Whiteside. In addition to about 5,000 manufacturing and service companies, includes the 500 largest banks in Europe and the 100 largest insurance companies.

Venture Capital Report Guide to Venture Capital in Europe. Pitman Publishing. • 1991. $125.00. Provides information on more than 500 European venture capital firms. Lists current investments.

ENCYCLOPEDIAS AND DICTIONARIES

Encyclopedia of Business. The Gale Group. • 2000. $425.00. Second edition. Two volumes. Contains more than 700 signed articles covering major business disciplines and concepts. International in scope.

Encyclopedia of the European Union. Desmond Dinan, editor. Lynne Rienner Publishers. • 2000. $110.00. Covers "virtually every aspect" of the EU. Includes "maps, glossaries, appendixes, and a comprehensive index.".

HANDBOOKS AND MANUALS

Guide to EU Information Sources on the Internet. Euroconfidentiel S. A. • Annual. $220.00. Contains descriptions of more than 1,700 Web sites providing information relating to the European Union and European commerce and industry. Includes a quarterly e-mail newsletter with new sites and address changes.

Practical Guide to Foreign Direct Investment in the European Union. Euroconfidentiel S. A. • Annual. $260.00. Provides coverage of national and EU business incentives. In addition to 70 charts and tables, includes EU country profiles of taxation, labor costs, and employment regulations.

Transnational Accounting. Dieter Ordelheide and others, editors. Groves Dictionaries. • 2000. $650.00. Three volumes. Published by Macmillan (UK). Provides detailed descriptions of financial accounting principles and practices in 14 major countries (10 European, plus the U. S., Canada, Australia, and Japan). Includes tables, exhibits, index, and a glossary of 244 accounting terms in eight languages.

INTERNET DATABASES

Europa: The European Union's Server. European Union 352 4301 35 349. E-mail: pressoffice@eurostat.cec.be • URL: http://www.europa.eu.int • Web site provides access to a wide variety of EU information, including statistics (Eurostat), news, policies, publications, key issues, and official exchange rates for the euro. Includes links to the European Central Bank, the European Investment Bank, and other institutions. Fees: Free.

Financial Times: Where Information Becomes Intelligence. FT Group. Phone: (212)752-4500 Fax: (212)688-8229 • URL: http://www.ft.com • Web site provides extensive data and information relating to international business and finance, with daily updates. Includes Markets Today, Company News, Economic Indicators, Equities, Currencies, Capital Markets, Euro Prices, etc. Fees: Free (registration required).

ONLINE DATABASES

ABI/INFORM. Bell & Howell Information and Learning. • Provides online indexing to business-related material occurring in over 1,000 periodicals from 1971 to the present. Inquire as to online cost and availability.

Globalbase. The Gale Group. • Provides more than one million online summaries of business, industrial, and economic news reports from more than 1,000 publications worldwide. Covers a wide range of material appearing in international trade journals, professional magazines, and newspapers. Time period is 1984 to date, with weekly updates. Inquire as to online cost and availability.

Management Contents. The Gale Group. • Covers a wide range of management, financial, marketing, personnel, and administrative topics. About 150 leading business journals are indexed and abstracted from 1974 to date, with monthly updating. Inquire as to online cost and availability.

PAIS International. Public Affairs Information Service, Inc. • Corresponds to the former printed publications, *PAIS Bulletin* (1976-90) and *PAIS Foreign Language Index* (1972-90), and to the current *PAIS International in Print* (1991 to date). Covers economic, political, and sociological material appearing in periodicals, books, government documents, and other publications. Updating is monthly. Inquire as to online cost and availability.

Trade & Industry Index. The Gale Group. • Provides indexing of business periodicals, January 1981 to date. Daily updates. (Full text articles from some periodicals are available online, 1983 to date, in the companion database, *Trade & Industry ASAP.*) Inquire as to online cost and availability.

PERIODICALS AND NEWSLETTERS

Bulletin of the European Union. Commision of the European Communities. Bernan Associates. • 11 times a year. $210.00 per year. Published by the Office of Official Publications of the European Communities. Covers all main events within the Union. Supplement available. Text in Danish, Dutch, English, French, German, Greek, Italian, Spanish, Portuguese. Formerly *Bulletin of the European Communities.*

Business Week International: The World's Only International Newsweekly of Business. McGraw-Hill. • Weekly. $105.00 per year.

Europa 2000: The American Business Report on Europe. Wolfe Publishing, Inc. • Monthly. $119.00 per year. Newsletter on consumer and industrial marketing in a unified European Economic Community. Includes classified business opportunity advertisements and a listing by country of forthcoming major trade shows in Europe.

European Access. European Commission-United Kingdom Offices, EL. Available from Chadwyck-Healey, Inc. • Bimonthly. $260.00 per year. Published in England. A journal providing general coverage of developments and trends within the European Community.

European Management Journal. Elsevier Science. • Bimonthly. $566.00 per year. Covers a wide variety of topics, including management problems of the European Single Market.

EuroWatch. Worldwide Trade Executives. • Biweekly. $799.00 per year. Newsletter.

Frankfurt Finance. Available from European Business Publications, Inc. • Monthly. $470.00 per year. Newsletter. Published in Germany by Frankfurter Allgemeine Zeitung GmbH Information Services. Presents news of German Bundesbank decisions and the European monetary system, including the European Monetary Union (EMU). Contains charts and tables. Formerly *Old Continent.*

Institutional Investor International Edition: The Magazine for International Finance and Investment. Institutional Investor. • Monthly. $415.00 per year. Covers the international aspects of professional investing and finance. Emphasis is on Europe, the Far East, and Latin America.

Journal of Business Strategy. Faulkner and Gray, Inc. • Bimonthly. $84.00 per year. Devoted to the theory and practice of strategy, planning, implementation and competitive analysis. Covers every aspect of business from advertising to systems design. Incorporates*Journal of European Business.*

Market Research Europe. Available from MarketResearch.com. • Monthly. $1,050.00 per year. Published by Euromonitor Publications. Newsletter on consumer spending in Europe.

Wall Street Journal/Europe. Dow Jones & Co., Inc. • Daily. $700.00 per year (air mail). Published in Europe. Text in English.

STATISTICS SOURCES

Basic Statistics of the European Union. Statistical Office of the European Communities. Available from Bernan Associates. • Annual. Provides European demographic, economic, and other basic data. The U. S., Canada, Japan, and the Soviet Union are included for comparative purposes. Text in Dutch, English, French, and German. Formerly *Basic Statistics of the European Community.*

The Book of European Forecasts. Available from The Gale Group. • 1996. $320.00. Second edition. Published by Euromonitor. Presents economic, commercial, demographic, and social forecasts for Europe, with statistical data and commentary.

The Book of European Regions. Available from The Gale Group. • 1992. $290.00. Second edition. Published by Euromonitor. Contains economic and demographic data for over 220 European regions. Maps and regional rankings are included.

Consumer Europe 2000/2001. Available from The Gale Group. • 2000. $1,190.00. 16th edition. Published by Euromonitor. Detailed statistical tables furnish five-year data on the production, sales, distribution, consumption, and other aspects of more than 240 consumer product categories. Thirteen countries of Western Europe are included.

European Economy, Series A: Recent Economic Trends. Commission of the European Communities. Bernan Associates. • Monthly. $65.00 per year. Published by the Commission of the European Communities, Luxembourg.

European Economy, Series B: Business and Consumer Survey Results. Commission of the European Communities. Available from Bernan Associates. • Monthly. Published by the Commission of the European Communities, Luxembourg. Editions in English, French, German, and Italian.

European Marketing Data and Statistics 2001. Available from The Gale Group. • 2001. $450.00. 36th edition. Published by Euromonitor. Presents essential marketing data, including demographics and consumer expenditure patterns, for 31 European countries.

European Marketing Forecasts 2001. Available from The Gale Group. • 2000. $1,190.00. Third edition. Published by Euromonitor. Contains demographic, economic, and market forecasts for the countries of Europe to the year 2010. Forecasts include market-size data for 15 consumer product sectors (food, clothing, automobiles, consumer electronics, etc.).

Handbook of International Economic Statistics. Available from National Technical Information Service. • Annual. $40.00. Prepared by U. S. Central Intelligence Agency. Provides basic statistics for comparing worldwide economic performance, with an emphasis on Europe, including Eastern Europe.

International Financial Statistics. International Monetary Fund, Publications Services. • Monthly.

Individuals, $246.00 per year; libraries, $123.00 per year. Includes a wide variety of current data for individual countries in Europe and elsewhere. Annual issue available. Editions available in French and Spanish.

Regions Statistical Yearbook. Bernan Associates. • Annual. $45.00. Published by the Commission of European Communities. Provides data on the social and economic situation in specific European areas. Includes population, employment, migration, industry, living standards, etc.

TRADE/PROFESSIONAL ASSOCIATIONS

European Union Office of Press and Public Affairs. 2300 M St., N.W., Washington, DC 20037. Phone: (202)862-9500 Fax: (202)429-1766 • URL: http://www.eurunion.org.

Trade Associations amd Professional Bodies of the Continental European Union. Available from The Gale Group. 27500 Drake Rd., Farmington Hills, MI 48331-3535. Phone: 800-877-GALE or (248)699-GALE Fax: 800-414-5043 or (248)699-8069 E-mail: galeord@galegroup.com • URL: http://www.galegroup.com • 2000. $280.00. Published by Graham & Whiteside. Provides detailed information on more than 3,600 business and professional organizations in Europe.

OTHER SOURCES

Access to European Union: Law, Economics, Policies. Euroconfidentiel S. A. • Annual. $62.00. Covers EU legislation and policy in major industrial and commercial sectors. Includes customs policy, the common market, monetary union, taxation, competition, "The EU in the World," and related topics. Contains more than 300 bibliographical references.

Common Market Reporter. CCH, Inc. • $1,070.00 per year, including weekly *Euromarket News.* Looseleaf service. Four volumes. Periodic supplementation.

The EU Institutions' Register. Euroconfidentiel S. A. • Annual. $130.00. Lists more than 5,000 key personnel in European Union institutions and decentralized agencies. Includes areas of responsibility.

Major Companies of Europe. Available from The Gale Group. • Annual. $1,780.00. Six volumes ($360.00 per volume). Published by Graham & Whiteside. Regional volumes provide detailed information on a total of more than 24,000 of Europe's largest companies: 1. Austria, Belgium, Cyprus, Denmark, Ireland, Finland. 2. France. 3. Germany. 4. Greece, Italy, Liechtenstein, Luxembourg, The Netherlands, Norway. 5. Portugal, Spain, Sweden, Switzerland. 6. United Kingdom.

The Rome, Maastricht, and Amsterdam Treaties: Comparative Texts. Euroconfidentiel S. A. • 1999. $42.00. Includes a comprehensive keyword index.

EUROPEAN UNION

See: EUROPEAN MARKETS

EVALUATION OF PERFORMANCE

See: RATING OF EMPLOYEES

EVENT PLANNING

See: SPECIAL EVENT PLANNING

EXCHANGE, FOREIGN

See: FOREIGN EXCHANGE

EXCHANGE RATES

See: CURRENCY EXCHANGE RATES

EXCHANGES, COMMODITY

See: COMMODITY FUTURES TRADING

EXCHANGES, STOCK

See: STOCK EXCHANGES

EXCISE TAX

HANDBOOKS AND MANUALS

Excise Taxes. Prentice Hall. • Looseleaf. $216.00. Monthly updates. (Information Services Series).

Internal Revenue Code: Income, Estate, Gift, Employment, and Excise Taxes. CCH, Inc. • Annual. $69.00. Two volumes. Provides full text of the Internal Revenue Code (5,000 pages), including procedural and administrative provisions.

U. S. Master Excise Tax Guide. CCH, Inc. • Annual. $49.00. Provides detailed explanations of significant excise tax regulations, rulings, and court decisions.

INTERNET DATABASES

CCH Essentials: An Internet Tax Research and Primary Source Library. CCH, Inc. Phone: 800-248-3248 or (773)866-6000 Fax: 800-224-8299 or (773)866-3608 E-mail: cust_serv@cch.com • URL: http://tax.cch.com/essentials • Fee-based Web site provides full-text coverage of federal tax law and regulations, including rulings, procedures, tax court decisions, and IRS publications, announcements, notices, and penalties. Includes explanation, analysis, tax planning guides, and a daily tax news service. Searching is offered, including citation search. Fee: $495.00 per year.

PERIODICALS AND NEWSLETTERS

The Journal of Taxation: A National Journal of Current Developments, Analysis and Commentary for Tax Professionals. Warren, Gorham & Lamont/RIA Group. • Monthly. $215.00 per year. Analysis of current tax developments for tax specialists.

RESEARCH CENTERS AND INSTITUTES

Center for Tax Policy Studies. Purdue University, 490 Krannert, West Lafayette, IN 47907-1310. Phone: (765)494-4442 Fax: (765)496-1778 E-mail: papke@mgmt.purdue.edu.

Tax Foundation. 1250 H St., N.W., Suite 750, Washington, DC 20005. Phone: (202)783-2760 Fax: (202)783-6868 E-mail: taxfnd@intr.net • URL: http://www.taxfoundation.org.

EXECUTIVE COMPENSATION

See also: ADMINISTRATION; EXECUTIVES

GENERAL WORKS

Compensation. George T. Milkovich. McGraw-Hill Professional. • 1998. $87.81. Sixth edition.

Compensation Management in a Knowledge-Based World. Richard I. Henderson. Prentice Hall. • 1999. $93.00. Eighth edition.

Executive Compensation: A Strategic Guide for the 1990s. Fred Foulkes, editor. Harvard Business School Press. • 1991. $75.00.

ABSTRACTS AND INDEXES

Business Periodicals Index. H. W. Wilson Co. • Monthly, except August, with quarterly and annual cumulations. Service basis for print edition; CD-ROM edition, $1,495.00 per year.

BIBLIOGRAPHIES

Available Pay Survey Reports: An Annotated Bibliography. Abbott, Langer and Associates. • 1995. U.S. volume, $450.00; international volume, $160.00. Fourth edition.

DIRECTORIES

Directory of Executive Compensation Consultants. Kennedy Information, LLC. • 1993. $47.50. Includes over 250 office locations maintained by about 65 executive compensation consulting firms.

HANDBOOKS AND MANUALS

Compensating Executives. Arthur H. Kroll. CCH, Inc. • 1998. $115.00. Covers the creation and implementation of executive compensation programs. Includes sample forms, plans, and checklists.

Corporate Counsellor's Deskbook. Dennis J. Block and Michael A. Epstein, editors. Panel Publishing. • 1999. $220.00. Fifth edition. Looseleaf. Annual supplementation. Covers a wide variety of corporate legal issues, including internal investigations, indemnification, insider trading, intellectual property, executive compensation, antitrust, export-import, real estate, environmental law, government contracts, and bankruptcy.

Employee Stock Ownership Plans: A Practical Guide to ESOPs and Other Broad Ownership Programs. Scott Rodrick, editor. Harcourt Brace, Legal and Professional Publications, Inc. • 1996. $79.00. Contains 19 articles by various authors on ESOPs, 401(k) plans, profit sharing, executive stock option plans, and related subjects.

Handbook of Executive Benefits. Towers Perrin. McGraw-Hill Higher Education. • 1995. $75.00.

How to Design and Install Management Incentive Compensation Plans: A Practical Guide to Installing Performance Bonus Plans. Dale Arahood. Dale Arahood and Associates. • 1996. $129.00. Revised edition. "This book focuses on how pay should be determined rather than how much should be paid.".

Personnel Management: Compensation. Prentice Hall. • Looseleaf. Periodic supplementation. Price on application.

U. S. Master Compensation Tax Guide. CCH, Inc. • Annual. $54.95. Provides concise coverage of taxes on salaries, bonuses, fringe benefits, other current compensation, and deferred compensation (qualified and nonqualified).

INTERNET DATABASES

U. S. Securities and Exchange Commission. Phone: 800-732-0330 or (202)942-7040 Fax: (202)942-9634 E-mail: webmaster@sec.gov • URL: http://www.sec.gov • SEC Web site offers free access through EDGAR to text of official corporate filings, such as annual reports (10-K), quarterly reports (10-Q), and proxies. (EDGAR is "Electronic Data Gathering, Analysis, and Retrieval System.") An example is given of how to obtain executive compensation data from proxies. Text of the daily *SEC News Digest* is offered, as are links to other government sites, non-government market regulators, and U. S. stock exchanges. Search facilities are extensive. Fees: Free.

Wageweb: Salary Survey Data On-Line. HRPDI: Human Resources Programs Development and Improvement. Phone: (609)254-5893 Fax: (856)232-6989 E-mail: salaries@wageweb.com • URL: http://www.wageweb.com • Web site provides salary information for more than 170 benchmark positions, including (for example) 29 information management jobs. Data shows average minimum, median, and average maximum compensation for each position, based on salary surveys. Fees: Free for national salary data; $169.00 per year for more detailed information (geographic, organization size, specific industries).

ONLINE DATABASES

ABI/INFORM. Bell & Howell Information and Learning. • Provides online indexing to business-related material occurring in over 1,000 periodicals from 1971 to the present. Inquire as to online cost and availability.

Disclosure SEC Database. Disclosure, Inc. • Provides information from records filed with the Securities and Exchange Commission by publicly owned corporations, 1977 to present. Weekly updates. Inquire as to online cost and availability.

Wilson Business Abstracts Online. H. W. Wilson Co. • Indexes and abstracts 600 major business periodicals, plus the *Wall Street Journal* and the business section of the *New York Times.* Indexing is from 1982, abstracting from 1990, with the two newspapers included from 1993. Updated weekly. Inquire as to online cost and availability. (*Business Periodicals Index* without abstracts is also available online.).

PERIODICALS AND NEWSLETTERS

Compensation and Benefits Review. Sage Publications, Inc. • Individuals, $240.00 per year; institutions, $240.00 per year.

Compensation and Benefits Update. Warren, Gorham and Lamont/RIA Group. • Monthly. $149.00 per year. Provides information on the latest ideas and developments in the field of employee benefits. In-depth exploration of popular benefits programs. Formerly *Benefits and Compensation Update.*

Tax Management Compensation Planning Journal. Bureau of National Affairs, Inc. • Monthly. $426.00 per year. Formerly *Compensation Planning Journal.*

STATISTICS SOURCES

Compensation Benchmarks for Private Practice Attorneys. Altman Weil Publications, Inc. • Annual. $295.00. Provides legal-office compensation standards arranged by region, firm size, legal specialty, and various other factors. Covers attorneys, paralegals, and other personnel.

Executive Remuneration. American Banker Newsletter, Thomson Financial Media. • Annual.

Forbes Chief Executive Compensation Survey. Forbes Magazine. • Annual. $4.95. List of 800 firms. May issue of *Forbes Magazine.*

Project Management Salary Survey. Project Management Institute. • Annual. $129.00. Gives compensation data for key project management positions in North America, according to job title, level of responsibility, number of employees supervised, and various other factors. Includes data on retirement plans and benefits.

Top Executive Compensation. Conference Board, Inc. • Annual. Members $30.00; non-members $120.00. Provides data on compensation of highest paid executives in major corporations.

TRADE/PROFESSIONAL ASSOCIATIONS

American Compensation Association. 14040 N. Northsight Blvd., Scottsdale, AZ 85260. Phone: 877-951-9191 or (480)951-9191 Fax: (480)483-8352 E-mail: aca@acaonline.org • URL: http://www.acaonline.org.

OTHER SOURCES

Business Rankings Annual. The Gale Group. • Annual. $305.00.Two volumes. Compiled by the Business Library Staff of the Brooklyn Public Library. This is a guide to lists and rankings appearing in major business publications. The top ten names are listed in each case.

Compensation. Bureau of National Affairs, Inc. • Weekly. $533.00 per year. Three volumes. Looseleaf. (BNA Policy and Practice Series.).

Executive Compensation. Arthur H. Kroll. Prentice Hall. • Three looseleaf volumes. Periodic supplementation. Price on application. Includes monthly newsletter.

Executive Compensation and Taxation Coordinator. Research Institute of America, Inc. • Three looseleaf volumes. $450.00 per year. Monthly updates.

EXECUTIVE EDUCATION

See: EXECUTIVE TRAINING AND DEVELOPMENT

EXECUTIVE RATING

See: RATING OF EMPLOYEES

EXECUTIVE RECRUITING

See: RECRUITMENT OF PERSONNEL

EXECUTIVE SALARIES

See: EXECUTIVE COMPENSATION

EXECUTIVE SEARCH SERVICES

See: EMPLOYMENT AGENCIES AND SERVICES; RECRUITMENT OF PERSONNEL

EXECUTIVE SECRETARIES

See: OFFICE PRACTICE

EXECUTIVE STRESS

See: STRESS (ANXIETY)

EXECUTIVE TRAINING AND DEVELOPMENT

See also: ADULT EDUCATION; BUSINESS EDUCATION; TRAINING OF EMPLOYEES

ABSTRACTS AND INDEXES

Business Periodicals Index. H. W. Wilson Co. • Monthly, except August, with quarterly and annual cumulations. Service basis for print edition; CD-ROM edition, $1,495.00 per year.

BIBLIOGRAPHIES

Management Education and Development: An Annotated Resource Book. Theodore T. Herbert and Edward Yost. Greenwood Publishing Group, Inc. • 1978. $59.95.

DIRECTORIES

Bricker's International Directory: Long-Term University- Based Executive Programs. Peterson's. • Annual. $295.00. Presents detailed information about executive education programs offered by 85 universities and nonprofit organizations in the U. S. and around the world. Includes general management and function-specific programs.

Training and Development Organizations Directory. The Gale Group. • 1994. $385.00. Sixth edition.

ENCYCLOPEDIAS AND DICTIONARIES

Dictionary of HRD. Angus Reynolds and others. • 1997. $67.95. Provides definitions of more than 3,000 terms related to human resource development. Includes acronyms, abbreviations, and a list of "100 Essential HRD Terms." Published by Gower in England.

HANDBOOKS AND MANUALS

Gower Handbook of Management Development. Alan Mumford, editor. Ashgate Publishing Co. • 1995. $113.95. Fourth edition. Consists of 28 chapters written by various authors. Published by Gower in England.

How to Conduct Training Seminars: A Complete Reference Guide for Training Managers. Lawrence S. Munson. McGraw-Hill. • 1992. $34.95. Second edition.

Sexual Harassment Awareness Training: 60 Practical Activities for Trainers. Andrea P. Baridon and David R. Eyler. McGraw-Hill. • 1996. $21.95. Discusses the kinds of sexual harassment, judging workplace behavior, application of the "reasonable person standard," employer liability, and related issues.

Studying Your Workforce: Applied Research Methods and Tools for the Training and Development Practitioner. Alan Clardy. Sage Publications, Inc. • 1997. $45.00. Describes how to apply specific research methods to common training problems. Emphasis is on data collection methods: testing, observation, surveys, and interviews. Topics include performance problems and assessment.

ONLINE DATABASES

ABI/INFORM. Bell & Howell Information and Learning. • Provides online indexing to business-related material occurring in over 1,000 periodicals from 1971 to the present. Inquire as to online cost and availability.

Wilson Business Abstracts Online. H. W. Wilson Co. • Indexes and abstracts 600 major business periodicals, plus the *Wall Street Journal* and the business section of the *New York Times.* Indexing is from 1982, abstracting from 1990, with the two newspapers included from 1993. Updated weekly. Inquire as to online cost and availability. (*Business Periodicals Index* without abstracts is also available online.).

PERIODICALS AND NEWSLETTERS

Business Education Forum. National Business Education Association. • Four times a year. Libraries, $70.00 per year. Includes *Yearbook* and *Keying In,* a newsletter.

Executive Excellence: The Newsletter of Personal Development Managerial Effectiveness, and Organizational Productivity. Kenneth M. Shelton, editor. Executive Excellence Publishing. • Monthly. $129.00 per year. Newsletter.

Journal of Management Education. Organizational Behavior Teaching Society. Sage Publications, Inc. • Quarterly. Individuals, $65.00 per year; institutions, $270.00 per year. A scholarly journal dealing with the teaching and training of business students and managers.

Training and Development. American Society for Training and Development. • Monthly. Free to members; non-members, $85.00 per year.

Training: The Magazine of Covering the Human Side of Business. Lakewood Publications, Inc. • Monthly. $78.00 per year.

TRADE/PROFESSIONAL ASSOCIATIONS
American Institute, Inc. 4301 Fairfax Dr., Suite 630, Arlington, VA 22203-1627. 4301 Fairfax Dr., Suite 630,.

American Society for Training and Development. P.O. Box 1443, Alexandria, VA 22313-2043. Phone: (703)683-8100 Fax: (703)683-8103 E-mail: csc4@astd.org • URL: http://www.astd.org.

EXECUTIVES

See also: ADMINISTRATION; BUSINESS; CORPORATE DIRECTORS AND OFFICERS

BIBLIOGRAPHIES
Thunderbird International Business Review. Thunderbird American Graduate School of International Management. John Wiley and Sons, Inc., Journals Div. • Bimonthly. Institutions, $320.00 per year. Formerly *International Executive.*

BIOGRAPHICAL SOURCES
The Highwaymen: Warriors on the Information Superhighway. Ken Auletta. Harcourt Trade Publications. • 1998. $13.00. Revised expanded edition. Contains critical articles about Ted Turner, Rupert Murdoch, Barry Diller, Michael Eisner, and other key figures in electronic communications, entertainment, and information.

Newsmakers. The Gale Group. • Annual. $145.00. Three softbound issues and one hardbound annual. Biographical information on individuals currently in the news. Includes photographs. Formerly *Contemporary Newsmakers.*

Who Knows Who: Networking Through Corporate Boards. Who Know Who Publishing. • 1994. $150.00. Fifth edition. Shows the connections between the board members of major U. S. corporations and major foundations and nonprofit organizations.

Who's Who in Finance and Industry. Marquis Who's Who. • Biennial. $295.00. Provides over 22,400 concise biographies of business leaders in all fields.

CD-ROM DATABASES
Profiles in Business and Management: An International Directory of Scholars and Their Research [CD-ROM]. Harvard Business School Publishing. • Annual. $595.00 per year. Fully searchable CD-ROM version of two-volume printed directory. Contains bibliographic and biographical information for over 5600 business and management experts active in 21 subject areas. Formerly *International Directory of Business and Management Scholars.*

The Tax Directory [CD-ROM]. Tax Analysts. • Quarterly. Provides *The Tax Directory* listings on CD-ROM, covering federal, state, and international tax officials, tax practitioners, and corporate tax executives.

WILSONDISC: Wilson Business Abstracts. H. W. Wilson Co. • Monthly. $2,495.00 per year, including unlimited online access to *Wilson Business Abstracts* through WILSONLINE. Provides CD-ROM "cover-to-cover" abstracting and indexing of over 600 prominent business periodicals. Indexing is from 1982, abstracting from 1990. (*Business Periodicals Index* without abstracts is available on CD-ROM at $1,495 per year.).

DIRECTORIES
Corporate Yellow Book: Who's Who at the Leading U.S. Companies. Leadership Directions, Inc. • Quarterly. $305.00 per year. Lists names and titles of over 51,000 key executives in major U. S. corporations. Includes four indexes: industry, personnel, geographic by state, and company/subsidiary. Companion volume to *Financial Yellow Book.*

Cyberhound's Guide to People on the Internet. The Gale Group. • 1997. $79.00. Second edition. Provides descriptions of about 5,500 Internet databases maintained by or for prominent individuals in business, the professions, entertainment, and sports. Indexed by name, subject, and keyword (master index).

D and B Million Dollar Directory. Dun and Bradstreet Information Services. • Annual. Commercial institutions, $1,395.00; libraries, $1,275.00. Lease basis.

Directory of Executive Recruiters. Kennedy Information, LLC. • Annual. $44.95. Contains profiles of more than 4,000 executive recruiting firms in the U. S., Canada, and Mexico.

Directory of Outplacement and Career Management Firms. Kennedy Information, LLC. • Annual. $129.95. Contains profiles of more than 320 firms specialize in helping "downsized" executives find new employment.

Executive Manpower Directory. 40 Plus Club of New York. • Monthly.

Financial Yellow Book: Who's Who at the Leading U. S. Financial Institutions. Leadership Directories, Inc. • Semiannual. $235.00. Gives the names and titles of over 31,000 key executives in financial institutions. Includes the areas of banking, investment, money management, and insurance. Five indexes are provided: institution, executive name, geographic by state, financial service segment, and parent company.

Profiles in Business and Management: An International Directory of Scholars and Their Research Version 2.0. Claudia Bruce, editor. Harvard Business School Press. • 1996. $495.00. Two volumes. Provides backgrounds, publications, and current research projects of more than 5,600 business and management experts.

Standard and Poor's Register of Corporations, Directors and Executives. Standard and Poor's. • Annual. $675.00. Periodic supplementation. Over 55,000 public and privately held corporations in the U.S. Three volumes. Three supplements.

The Tax Directory. Tax Analysts. • Annual. $299.00. ($399.00 with quarterly CD-ROM updates.) Four volumes: *Government Officials Worldwide* (lists 15,000 state, federal, and international tax officials, with basic corporate and individual income tax rates for 100 countries); *Private Sector Professionals Worldwide* (lists 25,000 U.S. and foreign tax practitioners: accountants, lawyers, enrolled agents, and actuarial firms); *Corporate Tax Managers Worldwide* (lists 10,000 tax managers employed by U.S. and foreign companies).

HANDBOOKS AND MANUALS
Kennedy's Pocket Guide to Working with Executive Recruiters. James H. Kennedy, editor. Kennedy Information, LLC. • 1996. $9.95. Second revised editon. Consists of 30 chapters written by various experts. Includes a glossary: "Lexicon of Executive Recruiting.".

INTERNET DATABASES
EBSCO Information Services. Ebsco Publishing. Phone: 800-871-8508 or (508)356-6500 Fax: (508)356-5640 E-mail: ep@epnet.com • URL: http://www.epnet.com • Fee-based Web site providing Internet access to a wide variety of databases, including business-related material. Full text is available for many periodical titles, with daily updates. Fees: Apply.

ProQuest Direct. Bell & Howell Information and Learning. Phone: 800-521-0600 or (313)761-4700 Fax: (313)973-9145 • URL: http://www.umi.com/proquest • Fee-based Web site providing Internet access to more than 3,000 periodicals, newspapers, and other publications. Many items are available full-text, with daily updates. Includes extensive corporate and financial information from Disclosure, Inc. Fees: Apply.

ONLINE DATABASES
Management Contents. The Gale Group. • Covers a wide range of management, financial, marketing, personnel, and administrative topics. About 150 leading business journals are indexed and abstracted from 1974 to date, with monthly updating. Inquire as to online cost and availability.

Standard & Poor's Register: Biographical. Standard & Poor's Corp. • Contains brief biographies of approximately 70,000 business executives and directors. Corresponds to the biographical volume of *Standard & Poor's Register of Corporations, Directors, and Executives.* Updated twice a year. Inquire as to online cost and availability.

Wilson Business Abstracts Online. H. W. Wilson Co. • Indexes and abstracts 600 major business periodicals, plus the *Wall Street Journal* and the business section of the *New York Times.* Indexing is from 1982, abstracting from 1990, with the two newspapers included from 1993. Updated weekly. Inquire as to online cost and availability. (*Business Periodicals Index* without abstracts is also available online.).

PERIODICALS AND NEWSLETTERS
The Academy of Management Executive. Oxford University Press, Journals. • Quarterly. $135.00 per year. Contains articles relating to the practical application of management principles and theory.

Administrative Science Quarterly. Cornell University Press, Johnson Graduate School of Management. • Individuals: $55.00 per year; institutions, $100.00 per year.

Business Finance. Duke Communications International. • Monthly. $59.00 per year. Covers trends in finance, technology, and economics for corporate financial executives.

CONTEXT: Business in a World Being Transformed by Technology. Diamond Technology Partners, Inc. • Quarterly. Price on application. Covers developments and trends in business and information technology for non-technical senior executives.

Daily Report for Executives. Bureau of National Affairs, Inc. • Daily. $6,927.00 per year. Newsletter. Covers legal, regulatory, economic, and tax developments affecting corporations.

Directors & Boards. • Quarterly. $295.00 per year. Edited for corporate board members and senior executive officers.

Director's Monthly. National Association of Corporate Directors. • Monthly. $350.00 per year. Newsletter.

Executive Wealth Advisory. National Institute of Business Management. • Monthly. $96.00 per year. Newsletter.

Management Review. American Management Association. • Membership.

TRADE/PROFESSIONAL ASSOCIATIONS
Academy of Management. P.O. Box 3020, Briarcliff Manor, NY 10510-3020. Phone: (914)923-2607 Fax: (914)923-2615 E-mail: aom@academy.pace.edu • URL: http://www.aom.pace.edu • Members are university professors of management and selected business executives.

American Association of Industrial Management. Stearns Bldg., Ste. 506, 293 Bridge St., Springfield, MA 01103. Phone: 888-698-1968 or (413)737-9725 or (413)737-8766 Fax: (413)737-9724 E-mail: aaimnmta@aol.com • URL: http://www.americanassocofindmgmt.com.

Association of Master of Business Administration Executives. c/o AMBA Center, Five Summit Place, Branford, CT 06405. Phone: (203)315-5221 Fax: (203)483-6186.

Chief Executives Organization. 7920 Norfolk Ave., Suite 400, Bethesda, MD 20814. Phone: (301)656-9220 Fax: (301)656-9221 E-mail: info@chiefexec.org.

International Executive Service Corps. 333 Ludlow St., Stamford, CT 06902. Phone: 800-243-2531 or (203)967-6000 Fax: (203)324-2531 E-mail: iesc@iesc.org • URL: http://www.iesc.org.

National Association for Female Executives. 135 W. 50th St., 16th Fl., New York, NY 10020. Phone: 800-634-6233 or (212)445-6233 or (212)445-6235 Fax: (212)445-6228 E-mail: nafe@nafe.com • URL: http://www.nafe.com.

National Association of Corporate Directors. 1701 L St., N.W., Suite 560, Washington, DC 20036. Phone: (202)775-0509 Fax: (202)775-4857 E-mail: info@nacdoline.org • URL: http://www.nacdonline.org.

Tax Analysts. 6830 N. Fairfax Dr., Arlington, VA 22213. Phone: 800-955-3444 or (703)533-4400 Fax: (703)533-4444 E-mail: webmaster@tax.org • URL: http://www.tax.org • An advocacy group reviewing U. S. and foreign income tax developments. Includes a Tax Policy Advisory Board.

Young Presidents' Organization. 451 S. Decker, Suite 200, Irving, TX 75062. Phone: (972)650-4600 Fax: (972)650-4777 E-mail: askypo@ypo.org • URL: http://www.ypo.org.

OTHER SOURCES

American Business Leaders: From Colonial Times to the Present. Neil A. Hamilton. ABC-CLIO, Inc. • 1999. $150.00. Two volumes. Contains biographies of 413 notable business figures. Historical coverage is from the 17th century to the 1990s.

Dun's Middle Market Disc. Dun & Bradstreet, Inc. • Quarterly. Price on application. CD-ROM provides information on more than 150,000 middle market U. S. private companies and their executives.

Dun's Million Dollar Disc. Dun & Bradstreet, Inc. • Quarterly. $3,800.00 per year to libraries; $5,500.00 per year to businesses. CD-ROM provides information on more than 240,000 public and private U. S. companies having sales volume of $5 million or more or 100 employees or more. Includes biographical data on more than 640,000 company executives.

InSite 2. Intelligence Data/Thomson Financial. • Fee-based Web site consolidates information in a "Base Pack" consisting of Business InSite, Market InSite, and Company InSite. Optional databases are Consumer InSite, Health and Wellness InSite, Newsletter InSite, and Computer InSite. Includes fulltext content from more than 2,500 trade publications, journals, newsletters, newspapers, analyst reports, and other sources. Continuous updating. Formerly produced by The Gale Group.

Standard & Poor's Corporations. Available from Dialog OnDisc. • Monthly. Price on application. Produced by Standard & Poor's. Contains three CD-ROM files: Executives, Private Companies, and Public Companies, providing detailed information on more than 70,000 business executives, 55,000 private companies, and 12,000 publicly-traded corporations.

EXECUTIVES, WOMEN

See: WOMEN EXECUTIVES

EXERCISE EQUIPMENT INDUSTRY

See: FITNESS INDUSTRY

EXHIBITS

See: DISPLAY OF MERCHANDISE; TRADE SHOWS

EXPENSE CONTROL

See: COST CONTROL

EXPERT SYSTEMS

See: ARTIFICIAL INTELLIGENCE

EXPLOSIVES INDUSTRY

ABSTRACTS AND INDEXES

Applied Science and Technology Index. H. W. Wilson Co. • 11 times a year. Quarterly and annual cumulations. Service basis for print edition; CD-ROM edition, $1,495.00 per year. Indexes a wide variety of English language technical, industrial, and engineering periodicals.

Engineering Index Monthly: Abstracting and Indexing Services Covering Sources of the World's Engineering Literature. Engineering Information, Inc. • Monthly. $2,300.00 per year. Provides indexing and abstracting of the world's engineering and technical literature.

F & S Index: United States. The Gale Group. • Monthly. $1,295.00 per year, including quarterly and annual cumulations. Provides annotated citations to marketing, business, financial, and industrial literature. Coverage of U. S. business activity includes trade journals, financial magazines, business newspapers, and special reports. Formerly *Predicasts F & S Index: United States.*

IMM Abstracts and Index: A Survey of World Literature on the Economic Geology and Mining of All Minerals (Except Coal), Mineral Processing, and Nonferrous Extraction Metallurgy. Institution of Mining and Metallurgy. • Bimonthly. Members, $142.00 per year; non-members, $215.00 per year. Provides international coverage of the literature of mining and nonferrous metallurgy. Includes mineral economics, tunnelling, and rock mechanics.

CD-ROM DATABASES

COMPENDEX PLUS [CD-ROM]. Engineering Information, Inc. • Quarterly. $3,450.00 per year. Provides CD-ROM indexing and abstracting of the world's engineering and technical information appearing in journals, reports, books, and proceedings, 1985 to date.

F & S Index Plus Text. The Gale Group. • Monthly. $7,575.00 per year. Provides CD-ROM citations to worldwide business, marketing, and industrial material appearing in a large assortment of trade journals, newspapers, and other publications. Time period is four years.

WILSONDISC: Applied Science and Technology Abstracts. H. W. Wilson Co. • Monthly. $1,495.00 per year, including unlimited access to the online version of *Applied Science and Technology Abstracts* through WILSONLINE. Provides CD-ROM indexing and abstracting of 400 prominent scientific, technical, engineering, and industrial periodicals. Indexing coverage is provided from 1983 to date and abstracting from 1993 to date.

ONLINE DATABASES

Aerospace/Defense Markets and Technology. The Gale Group. • Abstracts of commerical aerospace/defense related literature, 1982 to date. Also includes information about major defense contracts awarded by the U. S. Department of Defense. International coverage. Inquire as to online cost and availability.

Applied Science and Technology Index Online. H. W. Wilson Co. • Provides online indexing of 400 major scientific, technical, industrial, and engineering periodicals. Time period is 1983 to date. Monthly updates. Inquire as to online cost and availability.

COMPENDEX PLUS. Engineering Information, Inc. • Provides online indexing and abstracting of the world's engineering and technical information appearing in journals, reports, books, and proceedings. Time period is 1970 to date, with weekly updates. Inquire as to online cost and availability.

F & S Index. The Gale Group. • Contains about four million citations to worldwide business, financial, and industrial or consumer product literature appearing from 1972 to date. Weekly updates. Inquire as to online cost and availability.

Trade & Industry Index. The Gale Group. • Provides indexing of business periodicals, January 1981 to date. Daily updates. (Full text articles from some periodicals are available online, 1983 to date, in the companion database, *Trade & Industry ASAP.*) Inquire as to online cost and availability.

PERIODICALS AND NEWSLETTERS

Journal of Explosives Engineering. International Society of Explosives Engineers. • Bimonthly. $35.00 per year.

RESEARCH CENTERS AND INSTITUTES

Energetic Materials Research and Testing Center. New Mexico Institute of Mining and Technology, 801 Leroy Place, Socorro, NM 87801. Phone: (505)835-5312 Fax: (505)835-5630 E-mail: jcortez@emrtc.nmt.edu • URL: http://www.emrtc.nmt • Research areas include the development of industrial applications for explosives as energy sources.

New Mexico Engineering Research Institute. University of New Mexico. 901 University Blvd., S.E., Albuquerque, NM 87106-4339. Phone: (505)272-7200 Fax: (505)272-7203 E-mail: oneil@nmeri.umm.edu • URL: http://www.nmeri.umn.edu.

Rock Mechanics and Explosives Research Center. University of Missouri at Rolla, Rolla, MO 65401-0660. Phone: (573)341-4365 Fax: (573)341-4368 E-mail: vsnelson@umr.edu • URL: http://www.umr.edu/~rockmech.

TRADE/PROFESSIONAL ASSOCIATIONS

Institute of Makers of Explosives. 1120 19th St., N. W., Suite 310, Washington, DC 20036. Phone: (202)429-9280 Fax: (202)293-2420 E-mail: info@ime.org • URL: http://www.ime.org • Members are manufacturers of commercial explosives.

International Society of Explosives Engineers. 29100 Aurora Rd., Cleveland, OH 44139-1800. Phone: (216)349-4004 Fax: (216)349-3788 E-mail: isee@isee.org • URL: http://www.isee.org.

OTHER SOURCES

Aerospace Database. American Institute of Aeronautics and Astronautics. • Contains abstracts of literature covering all aspects of the aerospace and aircraft in series 1983 to date. Semimonthly updates. Inquire as to online cost and availability.

EXPORT-IMPORT TRADE

See also: CUSTOMS HOUSE, U.S. CUSTOMS SERVICE; FOREIGN TRADE

GENERAL WORKS

Exporting from the United States. U.S. Dept. of Commerce. Prima Publishing. • 1993. $14.95. Second revised edition.

ALMANACS AND YEARBOOKS

International Monetary Fund. Annual Report on Exhange Arrangements and Exchange Restrictions. International Monetary Fund Publications Services. • Annual. Individuals, $95.00; libraries, $47.50.

CD-ROM DATABASES

National Trade Data Bank: The Export Connection. U. S. Department of Commerce. • Monthly. $575.00 per year. Provides over 150,000 trade-related data series on CD-ROM. Includes full text of many government publications. Specific data is included on national income, labor, price indexes, foreign exchange, technical standards, and international markets. Website address is http://www.stat-usa.gov/.

U. S. Exports of Merchandise on CD-ROM. U. S. Bureau of the Census, Foreign Trade Div.,. • Monthly. $1,200 per year. Provides export data in the most extensive detail available, including product, quantity, value, shipping weight, country of destination, customs district of exportation, etc.

U. S. Imports of Merchandise (CD-ROM). U. S. Bureau of the Census, Foreign Trade Division. • Monthly. $1,200 per year. Provides import data in the most extensive detail available, including product, quantity, value, shipping weight, country of origin, customs district of entry, rate provision, etc.

World Trade Atlas CD-ROM. Global Trade Information Services, Inc. • Monthly. $4,920.00 per year. ($3,650.00 per year with quarterly updates.) Provides government statistics on trade between the U. S. and each of more than 200 countries. Includes import-export data, trade balances, product information, market share, price data, etc. Time period is the most recent three years.

World Trade Database. Statistics Canada, International Trade Division. • Annual. $3,500.00. CD-ROM provides 13 years of export-import data for 600 commodities traded by the 160 member countries of the United Nations.

DIRECTORIES

American Export Register. Available from Thomas Publishing Co., International Div. • Annual. $120.00. Two volumes. Supplement available *American Export Products.* Lists over 44,000 American firms with exporting programs. Includes *American Export Products.* Formerly *American Register of Exporters and Importers.*

Directory of United States Importers/Directory of United States Exporters. Journal of Commerce, Inc. • Annual. Two volumes. $450.00 per volume. Approximately 55,000 firms with import and export interests; export and import managers, agents, and merchants in the United States; World ports; consulates and embassies. Formerly *United States Importers and Exporters Directories.*

International Intertrade Index: New Foreign Products Marketing Techniques. John E. Felber. • Monthly. $45.00 per year. Lists new foreign products being offered to U.S. firms. Supplement available *Foreign Trade Fairs New Products.*

Kelly's Directory. Reed Business Information. • Annual. $400.00. Lists approximately 77,000 manufacturers and merchants. Formerly *Kelly's Business Directory.*

U.S. Custom House Guide. Commonwealth Business Media. • Annual. $475.00. Quarterly supplements. List of ports having custom facilities, customs officials, port authorities, chambers of commerce, embassies and consulates, foreign trade zones, and other organizations; related trade services.

ENCYCLOPEDIAS AND DICTIONARIES

Exporters' Encyclopedia. Dun and Bradstreet Information Services. • 1995. $495.00. Lease basis.

HANDBOOKS AND MANUALS

Arthur Andersen North American Business Sourcebook: The Most Comprehensive, Authoritative Reference Guide to Expanding Trade in the North American Market. Triumph Books. • 1993. $195.00. Includes statistical, regulatory, economic, and directory information relating to North American trade, including information on the North American Free Trade Agreement (NAFTA). Emphasis is on exporting to Mexico and Canada.

Basic Guide to Exporting. Available from U. S. Government Printing Office. • 1999. $16.00. Issued by the International Trade Administration, U. S. Department of Commerce. Discusses the costs, risks, and strategy of exporting. Includes sources of assistance and a glossary of terms used in the export business.

Corporate Counsellor's Deskbook. Dennis J. Block and Michael A. Epstein, editors. Panel Publishing. • 1999. $220.00. Fifth edition. Looseleaf. Annual supplementation. Covers a wide variety of corporate legal issues, including internal investigations, indemnification, insider trading, intellectual property, executive compensation, antitrust, export-import, real estate, environmental law, government contracts, and bankruptcy.

Export-Import Financing. Harry M. Vendikian and Gerald Warfield. John Wiley and Sons, Inc. • 1996. $79.95. Fourth edition.

Export Sales and Marketing Manual. Export Institute. • Looseleaf service. $295.00 Periodic supplementation. Provides detailed information on exporting from the U. S. Includes sections on licenses, markets, pricing, agreements, shipping, payment, and other export topics.

Exporting with the Internet. Peter J. Robinson and Jonathan Powell. John Wiley and Sons, Inc. • 1997. $39.95. Explains how the Internet can help with finding overseas buyers and expediting export shipments and payments. (Business Technology Series).

Import and Export. Entrepreneur Media, Inc. • Looseleaf. $59.50. A practical guide to starting an import/ export business. Covers profit potential, start-up costs, market size evaluation, owner's time required, pricing, accounting, advertising promotion, etc. (Start-Up Business Guide No. E1092.).

Importers Manual U. S. A.: The Single Source Reference for Importing to the United States. Edward G. Hinkelman. World Trade Press. • 1997. $87.00. Second edition. Published by World Trade Press. Covers U. S. customs regulations, letters of credit, contracts, shipping, insurance, and other items relating to importing. Includes 60 essays on practical aspects of importing.

Importing into the United States. Available from U. S. Government Printing Office. • 1998. $10.50. Issued by the U. S. Customs Service, Department of the Treasury. Formerly *Exporting to the United States.* Explains customs organization, entry of goods, invoices, assessment of duty, marking requirements, and other subjects.

International Standards Desk Reference: Your Passport to World Markets. Amy Zuckerman. AMACOM. • 1996. $35.00. Provides information on standards important in export-import trade, such as ISO 9000.

Reference Book for World Traders. Croner Publications, Inc. • $170.00. Three volumes. A looseleaf handbook covering information required for planning and executing exports and imports to and from all foreign countries; kept up to date by an amendment service.

United States Export Administration Regulations. Available from U. S. Government Printing Office. • $116.00. Looseleaf. Includes basic manual and supplementary bulletins for one year. Issued by the Bureau of Export Administration, U. S. Department of Commerce (http://www.doc.gov). Consists of export licensing rules and regulations.

INTERNET DATABASES

Fedstats. Federal Interagency Council on Statistical Policy. Phone: (202)395-7254 • URL: http://www.fedstats.gov • Web site features an efficient search facility for full-text statistics produced by more than 70 federal agencies, including the Census Bureau, the Bureau of Economic Analysis, and the Bureau of Labor Statistics. Boolean searches can be made within one agency or for all agencies combined. Links are offered to international statistical bureaus, including the UN, IMF, OECD, UNESCO, Eurostat, and 20 individual countries. Fees: Free.

ONLINE DATABASES

Business and Industry. Responsive Database Services, Inc. • Contains online citations, abstracts, and selected fulltext from more than 1,000 trade journals, newspapers, and other publications. Provides general coverage of both manufacturing and service industries, including marketing, production, industry trends, key events, and information on specific companies. Time span is 1994 to date. Daily updates. Inquire as to online cost and availability. (Also available in a CD-ROM version.).

DRI U.S. Central Database. Data Products Division. • Provides more than 23,000 business, financial, demographic, economic, foreign trade, and industry-related time series for the U.S. Includes national income, population, retail-wholesale trade, price indexes, labor data, housing, industrial production, banking, interest rates, money supply, etc. Time period is generally 1947 to date (some data back to 1929). Updating varies. Inquire as to online cost and availability.

Tablebase. Responsive Database Services, Inc. • Provides online numerical tabular data from a wide variety of business, organization, and government sources, including 900 trade journals. Includes industry and individual company statistics relating to products, market share, sales forecasts, production, exports, market trends, etc. Time span is 1997 to date. Weekly updates. Inquire as to online cost and availability. (Also available in a CD-ROM version.).

PERIODICALS AND NEWSLETTERS

AgExporter. Available from U. S. Government Printing Office. • Monthly. $44.00 per year. Issued by the Foreign Agricultural Service, U. S. Department of Agriculture. Edited for U. S. exporters of farm products. Provides practical information on exporting, including overseas trade opportunities.

Customs Bulletin and Decisions. Available from U. S. Government Printing Office. • Weekly. $220.00 per year. Issued by U. S. Customs Service, Department of the Treasury. Contains regulations, rulings, decisions, and notices relating to customs laws.

Export America. Available from U. S. Government Printing Office. • Monthly. $61.00 per year. Issued by the International Trade Administration, U. S. Department of Conmmerce (http://www.ita.doc.gov/). Contains articles written to help American exporters penetrate overseas markets. Provides information on opportunities for trade and methods of doing international business. Formerly *Business America*.

Export Today: The Global Business and Technology Magazine. Trade Communications, Inc. • Monthly. $49.00 per year. Edited for corporate executives to provide practical information on international business and exporting.

International Trade Alert. American Association of Exporters and Importers. • Weekly. Membership.

International Trade Reporter Export Reference Manual. Bureau of National Affairs, Inc. • Weekly. $874.00 per year. Looseleaf. Formerly *Export Shipping Manual.*

Outlook for United States Agricultural Trade. Available from U. S. Government Printing Office. • Quarterly. $10.00 per year. Issued by the Economic Research Service, U. S. Department of Agriculture. (Situation and Outlook Reports.).

Trade & Culture: How to Make it in the World Market. Key Communications Corp. • Quarterly. $29.95 per year. Edited for businesses actively involved in exporting or importing.

RESEARCH CENTERS AND INSTITUTES

Division of Business and Economic Research. University of New Orleans. New Orleans, LA 70148. Phone: (504)280-6240 Fax: (504)280-6094 E-mail: vlmbd@uno.edu.

International Tax Program. Harvard University, Pound Hall, Room 400, Cambridge, MA 02138. Phone: (617)495-4406 Fax: (617)495-0423 • URL: http://www.law.harvard.edu/programs/itp • Studies the worldwide problems of taxation, including tax law and tax administration.

STATISTICS SOURCES

Business Statistics of the United States. Courtenay M. Slater, editor. Bernan Associates. • 1999. $74.00. Fifth edition. Based on *Business Statistics*, formerly issue by the Bureau of Economic Analysis, U. S. Department of Commerce. Provides basic data for a wide variety of U. S. industries, services, and economic indicators. Most statistics are shown annually for 29 years and monthly for the most recent four years.

Foreign Agricultural Trade of the United States. Available from U. S. Government Printing Office. • Monthly. $50.00 per year. Issued by the Economic Research Service of the U. S. Department of Agriculture. Provides data on U. S. exports and imports of agricultural commodities.

Foreign Trade of the United States: Including State and Metro Area Export Data. Courtenay M. Slater, and James B. Rice, editors. Bernan Press. • 1999. $74.00. Provides detailed national, state, and local data relating to U. S. exports and imports.

International Trade Statistics Yearbook. United Nations Statistical Office. United Nations Publications. • Annual. $135.00. Two volumes.

Manufacturing Profiles. Available from U. S. Government Printing Office. • Annual. Issued by the U. S. Census Bureau. A printed consolidation of the entire *Current Industrial Report* series, presenting "all the data compiled." Contains statistics on production, shipments, inventories, consumption, exports, imports, and orders for a wide variety of manufactured products. (See also Census Bureau home page, http://www.census.gov/.).

North American Free Trade Agreement: Opportunities for U. S. Industries, NAFTA Industry Sector Reports. Available from U. S. Government Printing Office. • 1993. Issued by the International Trade Administration, U. S. Department of Commerce. Contains NAFTA Industry Sector Reports showing statistical data on exports from 36 U. S. manufacturing sectors to Mexico, Canada, and other parts of the world.

Survey of Current Business. Available from U. S. Government Printing Office. • Monthly. $49.00 per year. Issued by Bureau of Economic Analysis, U. S. Department of Commerce. Presents a wide variety of business and economic data.

United States Waterborne Exports and General Imports. U.S. Bureau of the Census. • Quarterly and annual.

TRADE/PROFESSIONAL ASSOCIATIONS

American Association of Exporters and Importers. 51 E. 42nd St., 7th Fl., New York, NY 10017-5404. Phone: (212)944-2230 Fax: (212)382-2606.

American League for Exports and Security Assistance. 122 C St., N.W., Suite 745, Washington, DC 20001. Phone: (202)783-0051 Fax: (202)737-4727 E-mail: alesa@erols.com.

National Association of Export Companies. P.O. Box 1330, Murray Hill Station, New York, NY 10156-1330. Phone: (504)490-9594 • URL: http://www.nexco.org.

National Customs Brokers and Forwarders Association of America. 1200 18th St., N.W., Suite 901, Washington, DC 20036. Phone: (202)466-0222 Fax: (202)466-0226 E-mail: staff@ncbfaa.org • URL: http://www.ncbfaa.org.

OTHER SOURCES

Customs Regulations of the United States. Available from U. S. Government Printing Office. • Looseleaf. $123.00. Issued by U. S. Customs Service, Department of the Treasury. Reprint of regulations published to carry out customs laws of the U. S. Includes supplementary material for an indeterminate period.

Going Global: Getting Started in International Trade. American Management Association Extension Institute. • Looseleaf. $130.00. Self-study course. Emphasis is on practical explanations, examples, and problem solving. Quizzes and a case study are included.

Investing, Licensing, and Trading. Economist Intelligence Unit. • Semiannual. $345.00 per year for each country. Key laws, rules, and licensing provisions are explained for each of 60 countries. Information is provided on political conditions, markets, price policies, foreign exchange practices, labor, and export-import.

Successful International Marketing: How to Gain the Global Advantage. American Management Association Extension Institute. • Looseleaf. $130.00. Self-study course. Emphasis is on practical explanations, examples, and problem solving. Quizzes and a case study are included.

U. S. Business Advisor. Small Business Administration. • Web site provides "a one-stop electronic link to all the information and services government provides for the business community." Covers about 60 federal agencies that exist to assist or regulate business. Detailed information is provided on financial assistance, workplace issues, taxes, regulations, international trade, and other business topics. Searching is offered. Fees: Free.

EXPOSITIONS

See: CONVENTIONS; FAIRS

EYECARE INDUSTRY

See: CONTACT LENS AND INTRAOCULAR LENS INDUSTRIES; OPHTHALMIC INDUSTRY

F

FABRICS, INDUSTRIAL

See: INDUSTRIAL FABRICS INDUSTRY

FABRICS, NONWOVEN

See: NONWOVEN FABRICS INDUSTRY

FACILITIES MANAGEMENT

See: FACTORY MANAGEMENT

FACSIMILE SYSTEMS

ABSTRACTS AND INDEXES

Applied Science and Technology Index. H. W. Wilson Co. • 11 times a year. Quarterly and annual cumulations. Service basis for print edition; CD-ROM edition, $1,495.00 per year. Indexes a wide variety of English language technical, industrial, and engineering periodicals.

Business Periodicals Index. H. W. Wilson Co. • Monthly, except August, with quarterly and annual cumulations. Service basis for print edition; CD-ROM edition, $1,495.00 per year.

DIRECTORIES

Better Buys for Business: The Independent Consumer Guide to Office Equipment. What to Buy for Business, Inc. • 10 times a year. $134.00 per year. Each issue is on a particular office product, with detailed evaluation of specific models: 1. Low-Volume Copier Guide, 2. Mid-Volume Copier Guide, 3. High-Volume Copier Guide, 4. Plain Paper Fax and Low-Volume Multifunctional Guide, 5. Mid/High-Volume Multifunctional Guide, 6. Laser Printer Guide, 7. Color Printer and Color Copier Guide, 8. Scan-to-File Guide, 9. Business Phone Systems Guide, 10. Postage Meter Guide, with a Short Guide to Shredders.

Essential Business Buyer's Guide, from Cellular Services and Overnight Mail to Internet Access Providers, 401(k) Plans, and Desktop Computers: The Ultimate Guide to Buying Office Equipment, Products, and Services. Sourcebooks, Inc. • 1996. $18.95. Compiled by the staff of *Business Consumer Guide*. Lists recommended brands of office equipment.

FaxUSA: A Directory of Facsimile Numbers for Business and Organizations Nationwide. Darren L. Smith, editor. Omnigraphics, Inc. • Annual. $130.00. Provides more than 111,500 listings, with fax numbers, telephone numbers, and addresses.

National E-Mail and Fax Directory. The Gale Group. • Annual. $150.00. Provides fax numbers, telephone numbers, and addresses for U. S. companies, organizations, government agencies, and libraries. Includes alphabetic listings and subject listings.

North American Fax Directory. Dial-A-Fax Directories Corp. • Annual. $289.00. Approximately 209,000 companies that possess facsimile machines. Formerly *Dial-A-Fax Directory*.

Telecommunications Directory. The Gale Group. • 2000. $595.00. 12th edition. National and international voice, data, facsimile, and video communications services. Formerly *Telecommunications Systems and Services Directory*.

HANDBOOKS AND MANUALS

Fax Handbook. Gerald V. Quinn. McGraw-Hill Professional. • 1989. $16.95.

Fax Modem Sourcebook. Andrew Margolis. John Wiley and Sons, Inc. • 1995. $85.00. Explains fax modem technology for both the novice and the experienced user. Includes technical programming information and international standards.

The Modem Reference: The Complete Guide to PC Communications. Michael A. Banks. Information Today, Inc. • 2000. $29.95. Fourth edition. Covers personal computer data communications technology, including fax transmissions, computer networks, modems, and the Internet. Popularly written.

ONLINE DATABASES

Applied Science and Technology Index Online. H. W. Wilson Co. • Provides online indexing of 400 major scientific, technical, industrial, and engineering periodicals. Time period is 1983 to date. Monthly updates. Inquire as to online cost and availability.

Wilson Business Abstracts Online. H. W. Wilson Co. • Indexes and abstracts 600 major business periodicals, plus the *Wall Street Journal* and the business section of the *New York Times*. Indexing is from 1982, abstracting from 1990, with the two newspapers included from 1993. Updated weekly. Inquire as to online cost and availability. (*Business Periodicals Index* without abstracts is also available online.).

PERIODICALS AND NEWSLETTERS

FAX Magazine. Technical Data Publishing Corp. • Quarterly. Price on application.

Internet Telephony Magazine: The Authority on Voice, Video, Fax, and Data Convergence. Technology Marketing Corp. • Monthly. $29.00 per year. Covers the business and technology of telephone and other communications service via the Internet.

TWICE: This Week in Consumer Electronics. Cahners Business Information, Broadcasting and Cable's International Group. • 29 times a year. Free to qualified personnel; others, $99.90 per year. Contains marketing and manufacturing news relating to a wide variety of consumer electronic products, including video, audio, telephone, and home office equipment.

FACTORY LOCATION

See: LOCATION OF INDUSTRY

FACTORY MAINTENANCE

See: MAINTENANCE OF BUILDINGS

FACTORY MANAGEMENT

See also: TIME AND MOTION STUDY

GENERAL WORKS

Contemporary Supervision: Managing People and Technology. Betty R. Ricks. McGraw-Hill. • 1994. $68.75.

ABSTRACTS AND INDEXES

Key Abstracts: Factory Automation. Available from INSPEC, Inc. • Monthly. $240.00 per year. Provides international coverage of journal and proceedings literature, including publications on CAD/CAM, materials handling, robotics, and factory management. Published in England by the Institution of Electrical Engineers (IEE).

ENCYCLOPEDIAS AND DICTIONARIES

Blackwell Encyclopedic Dictionary of Operations Management. Nigel Slack, editor. Blackwell Publishers. • 1997. $105.95. The editor is associated with the University of Warwick, England. Contains definitions of key terms combined with longer articles written by various U. S. and foreign business educators. Includes bibliographies and index. (Blackwell Encyclopedia of Management Series.).

HANDBOOKS AND MANUALS

Effective Supervisor's Handbook. Louis V. Imundo. AMACOM. • 1992. $16.95. Second edition.

Maintenance Engineering Handbook. Lindley R. Higgins. McGraw-Hill. • 1994. $125.00. Fifth edition. Contains about 60 chapters by various authors in 12 major sections covering all elements of industrial and plant maintenance.

Manager's Tool Kit: Practical Tips for Tackling 100 On-the-Job Problems. Cy Charney. AMACOM. • 1995. $17.95.

Managing Factory Maintenance. Joel Levitt. Industrial Press, Inc. • 1996. $39.95.

Standard Handbook of Plant Engineering. Robert C. Rosaler. McGraw-Hill. • 1991. $125.00. Second edition.

PERIODICALS AND NEWSLETTERS

AFE Newsline. Association for Facilities Engineering. • Bimonthly. Members, $7.00; non-members, $14.00. Covers national, regional and local chapter activities of the Association for Facilities Engineering. Formerly *AIPE Newsline*.

Industry Week: The Industry Management Magazine. Penton Media, Inc. • 18 times a year. Free to qualified personnel; others, $65.00 per year. Edited for industrial and business managers. Covers organizational and technological developments affecting industrial management.

Production. Gardner Publications, Inc. • Monthly. $48.00 per year. Covers the latest manufacturing management issues. Discusses the strategic and financial implications of various tecnologies as they impact factory management, quality and competitiveness.

RESEARCH CENTERS AND INSTITUTES

Carnegie Mellon Research Institute. Carnegie Mellon University, 700 Technology Dr., Pittsburgh, PA 15219. Phone: (412)268-3190 Fax: (412)268-3101 E-mail: twillke@emu.edu • Multidisciplinary research activities include expert systems applications, minicomputer and microcomputer systems design, genetic engineering, and transportation systems analysis.

Research Program in Takeovers and Corporate Restructuring. University of California, Los Angeles. John E. Anderson Graduate School of Management, 258 Tavistock Ave., Los Angeles, CA 90049-3229. Phone: (310)825-2200 Fax: (310)472-9471 E-mail: weston@anderson.ucla.edu • URL: http://www.agsm.ucla.edui/acadunit/finance/westonbio.ht.

TRADE/PROFESSIONAL ASSOCIATIONS

American Association of Industrial Management. Stearns Bldg., Ste. 506, 293 Bridge St., Springfield, MA 01103. Phone: 888-698-1968 or (413)737-9725 or (413)737-8766 Fax: (413)737-9724 E-mail: aaimnmta@aol.com • URL: http://www.americanassocofindmgmt.com.

American Society of Mechanical Engineers. Three Park Ave., New York, NY 10016-5990. Phone: 800-843-2763 or (212)705-7722 Fax: (212)705-7674 E-mail: infocentral@asme.org • URL: http://www.asme.org.

Association for Facilities Engineering. 8180 Corporate Park Dr., Suite 305, Cincinnati, OH 45242. Phone: 888-222-0155 or (513)489-2473 Fax: (513)247-7422 E-mail: mail@afe.org • URL: http://www.afe.org.

Institute of Industrial Engineers. 25 Technology Park, Norcross, GA 30092. Phone: 800-494-0460 or (770)449-0460 Fax: (770)441-3295 • URL: http://www.iienet.org.

Society for Advancement of Management. Texas A&M University-Corpus Christi, College of Business, 6300 Ocean Dr., Corpus Christi, TX 78412. Phone: 888-827-6077 or (361)825-6045 or (361)825-5574 Fax: (361)825-2725 E-mail: moustafa@falcon.tamucc.edu • URL: http://www.enterprise.tamucc.edu/sam/.

OTHER SOURCES

First-Line Supervision. American Management Association Extension Institute. • Looseleaf. $110.00. Self-study course. Emphasis is on practical explanations, examples, and problem solving. Quizzes and a case study are included.

FACTORY SECURITY

See: INDUSTRIAL SECURITY PROGRAMS

FAILURES, BANK

See: BANK FAILURES

FAILURES, BUSINESS

See: BUSINESS FAILURES

FAIR EMPLOYMENT PRACTICES

See: EQUAL EMPLOYMENT OPPORTUNITY; LABOR

FAIR TRADE

See: PRICES AND PRICING

FAIRS

See also: CONCESSIONS; CONVENTIONS

ABSTRACTS AND INDEXES

Holidays and Festivals Index. Helene Henderson and Barry Puckett, editors. Omnigraphics, Inc. • 1995. $84.00. Serves as an index to more than 3,000 holidays, festivals, celebrations, and other observances found in 27 standard reference works.

DIRECTORIES

Cavalcade of Acts and Attractions. BPI Communications, Amusement Business Div. • Annual. $92.00. Directory of personal appearance artists, touring shows and other specialized entertainment. Lists promoters, producers, managers and booking agents.

Directory of North American Fairs, Festivals and Expositions. BPI Communications, Amusement Business Div. • Annual. $65.00. Lists over 5,000 fairs, festivals and expositions in the U.S. and Canada which run three days or more. Formerly *Calvacade and Directory of Fairs.*

IAFE Directory. International Association of Fairs and Expositions. • Annual. Free to members; non-members, $85.00. Lists more than 1,300 member agricultural fairs in the United States and Canada. Formerly *International Association of Fairs and Expositions Directory.*

IEG Sponsorship Sourcebook. International Events Group, Inc. • Annual. $199.00. Provides information on about 3,000 festivals, celebrations, and sports events that are available for commercial sponsorship. Information is also given on public relations firms, sports marketing companies, fireworks suppliers, and other companies providing services for special events. Formerly *IEG Directory of Sponsorship Marketing.*

International Association of Amusement Parks and Attractions International Directory and Buyers Guide. International Association of Amusement Parks and Attractions. • Annual. $83.00. Over 1,800 member amusement parks, attractions and industry suppliers.

PERIODICALS AND NEWSLETTERS

Horseman and Fair World: Devoted to the Trotting and Pacing Horse. Horseman Publishing Co., Inc., Insite Communications. • Weekly. $80.00 per year.

IEG's Sponsorship Report: The International Newsletter of Event Sponsorship and Lifestyle Marketing. International Events Group, Inc. • Biweekly. $415.00 per year. Newsletter reporting on corporate sponsorship of special events: sports, music, festivals, and the arts. Edited for event producers, directors, and marketing personnel.

TRADE/PROFESSIONAL ASSOCIATIONS

International Association of Fairs and Expositions. P.O. Box 985, Springfield, MO 65801. Phone: 800-516-0313 or (417)862-5771 Fax: (417)862-0156 E-mail: iafg@iafenet.org.

FAMILY CORPORATIONS

See: CLOSELY HELD CORPORATIONS

FAMILY LAW

See also: DIVORCE

ABSTRACTS AND INDEXES

Current Law Index: Multiple Access to Legal Periodicals. The Gale Group. • Monthly. $650.00 per year. Produced in cooperation with the American Association of Law Libraries. Indexes more than 900 law journals, legal newspapers, and specialty publications from the U.S., Canada, U.K., Ireland, Australia, and New Zealand.

Readers' Guide to Periodical Literature. H. W. Wilson Co. • Monthly. $220.00 per year. CD-ROM edition, $1,495 per year, including annual cumulation. Indexes about 250 peridicals of general interest.

ALMANACS AND YEARBOOKS

American Law Yearbook. The Gale Group. • Annual. $155.00. Serves as a yearly supplement to *West's Encyclopedia of American Law.* Describes new legal developments in many subject areas.

BIBLIOGRAPHIES

Encyclopedia of Legal Information Sources. The Gale Group. • 1992. $180.00. Second edition. Lists more than 23,000 law-related information sources, including print, nonprint, and organizational.

DIRECTORIES

Directory of Judges with Juvenile/Family Law Jurisdiction. National Council of Juvenile and Family Court Judges. • Irregular. $25.00. 1,400 judges who have juvenile, family, or domestic relations jurisdiction.

ENCYCLOPEDIAS AND DICTIONARIES

West's Encyclopedia of American Law. Available from The Gale Group. • 1997. $995.00. Second edition. 12 volumes. Published by West Group. Covers a wide variety of legal topics for the general reader. Formerly *Guide to American Law: Everyone's Legal Encyclopedia* (1985).

HANDBOOKS AND MANUALS

Family Law in a Nutshell. Harry D. Krause. West Publishing Co., College and School Div. • 1995. $18.00. Third edition. (Paralegal Series).

Handbook of Family Law. Stuart J. Faber. Lega Books. • 1987. $56.50. Fifth revised edition. Two volumes.

Women and the Law. Carol H. Lefcourt, editor. West Group. • $140.00. Looseleaf service. Periodic supplementation. Covers such topics as employment discrimination, pay equity (comparable worth), sexual harassment in the workplace, property rights, and child custody issues. (Civil Rights Series).

ONLINE DATABASES

Contemporary Women's Issues. Responsive Database Services, Inc. • Provides fulltext articles online from 150 periodicals and a wide variety of additional sources relating to economic, legal, social, political, education, health, and other women's issues. Time span is 1992 to date. Weekly updates. Inquire as to online cost and availability. (Also available in a CD-ROM version.).

Readers' Guide Abstracts Online. H. W. Wilson Co. • Indexes and abstracts general interest periodicals, 1983 to date. Weekly updates. Inquire as to online cost and availability.

PERIODICALS AND NEWSLETTERS

Brandeis Law Journal. Louis D. Brandeis School of Law. University of Louisville. • Quarterly. $30.00 per year. Formerly *Journal of Family Law.*

Family Advocate. American Bar Association, Family Law Section. • Quarterly. Members $39.50; non-members, $44.50 per year. Practical advice for attorneys practicing family law.

Family Court Review. Association of Family and Conciliation Courts. Sage Publications, Inc. • Quarterly. $230.00 per year.

Family Law Quarterly. American Bar Association, Family Law Section. • Quarterly. Free to members; non-members, $49.95 per year.

Family Law Reporter. Bureau of National Affairs, Inc. • Weekly. $709.00 per year. Legal newsletter.

Family Relations: State Capitals. Wakeman-Walworth, Inc. • Weekly. $245.00 per year. Newsletter. Formerly *From the State Capitals: Family Relations.*

Journal of Social Welfare and Family Law. Routledge Journals. • Quarterly. Individuals, $83.00 per year; institutions, $324.00 per year.

The Liberator: Male Call. Men's Defense Association. • Monthly. $24.00 per year. Newsletter supporting men's rights in family law. Formerly *Legal Beagle.*

Matrimonial Strategist. American Lawyer Media, L.P. • Monthly. $175.00 per year. Newsletter on legal strategy and matrimonial law.

The Women's Advocate. National Center on Women and Family Law. • Irregular. Price on application. Manuals supporting women's rights in family law.

RESEARCH CENTERS AND INSTITUTES

Center for Governmental Responsibility. University of Florida, College of Law, P.O. Box 117629, Gainesville, FL 32611-7629. Phone: (352)392-2237 Fax: (352)392-1457 E-mail: jlmills@law.ufl.edu • URL: http://www.law.ufl.edu/college/cgr • Research fields include family law.

Lexis.com Research System. Lexis-Nexis Group. Phone: 800-227-9597 or (937)865-6800 Fax: (937)865-6909 E-mail: webmaster@prod.lexis-nexis.com • URL: http://www.lexis.com • Fee-based Web site offers extensive searching of a wide variety of legal sources. Additional features include Daily Opinion Service, lexis.com Bookstore, Career Center, CLE Center, Law Schools, and Practice Pages ("Pages specific to areas of specialty").

TRADE/PROFESSIONAL ASSOCIATIONS

Academy of Family Mediators. Five Militia Dr., Lexington, MA 02173. Phone: 800-292-4236 or (781)674-2663 Fax: (781)674-2690 E-mail: afmoffice@mediators.org • URL: http://www.mediators.org.

American Academy of Matrimonial Lawyers. 150 N. Michigan Ave., Suite 2040, Chicago, IL 60601. Phone: (312)263-6477 Fax: (312)263-7682 • URL: http://www.aaml.org • Members are attorneys specializing in family law.

American College of Counselors. 824 S. Park Ave., Springfield, IL 62704. Phone: (217)698-7668 Fax: (217)648-7668.

Association of Family and Conciliation Courts. c/o Ann Milne, 329 W. Wilson, Madison, WI 53703. Phone: (608)251-4001 Fax: (608)251-2231 E-mail: afcc@afccnet.org • Members are judges, attorneys, and family counselors. Promotes conciliation counseling as a complement to legal procedures.

National Council of Juvenile and Family Court Judges. 1041 N. Virginia St., Reno, NV 89557. Phone: (775)784-6012 Fax: (775)784-6628 • URL: http://www.ncjfcj.unr.edu.

NOW Legal Defense and Education Fund. 395 Hudson St., 5th Fl., New York, NY 10014-3669. Phone: (212)925-6635 Fax: (212)226-1066 • URL: http://www.nowldef.org.

Organization for the Enforcement of Child Support. 1712 Deer Park Rd., Finksburg, MD 21048. Phone: (410)876-1826 Fax: (410)876-1826 • Promotes more effective child support laws.

OTHER SOURCES

Family Law Tax Guide. CCH, Inc. • Monthly. $567.00 per year. Looseleaf service.

FARM BUSINESS

See: AGRIBUSINESS

FARM CREDIT

See: AGRICULTURAL CREDIT

FARM EQUIPMENT INDUSTRY

See: AGRICULTURAL MACHINERY

FARM IMPLEMENTS

See: AGRICULTURAL MACHINERY

FARM INCOME

See: AGRICULTURAL STATISTICS

FARM JOURNALS

See also: BUSINESS JOURNALISM

ABSTRACTS AND INDEXES

Biological and Agricultural Index. H.W. Wilson Co. • 11 times a year. Annual and quarterly cumulations. Service basis.

DIRECTORIES

Consumer Magazine and Advertising Source. SRDS. • Monthly. $661.00 per year. Contains advertising rates and other data for U. S. consumer magazines and agricultural publications. Also provides consumer market data for population, households, income, and retail sales. Formerly *Consumer Magazine and Agri-Media Source.*

PERIODICALS AND NEWSLETTERS

Agronomy Journal. American Society of Agronomy, Inc. • Bimonthly. Free to members; non-members, $171.00 per year.

Byline. • 11 times a year. $22.00 per year.

Farm Journal. Farm Journal, Inc. • 12 times a year. $18.00 per year. Includes Supplements.

TRADE/PROFESSIONAL ASSOCIATIONS

Agricultural Communicators in Education. P.O. Box 110811, Gainesville, FL 32611-0811. Phone: (352)392-9588 Fax: (352)392-7902 E-mail: ace@gnv.ifas.ufl.edu • URL: http://www.acceweb.org.

American Agricultural Editor's Association. P.O. Box 162585, Austin, TX 78716-2585. Phone: (512)451-5000 Fax: (512)323-3503 • URL: http://www.ageditors.com.

National Association of Agricultural Journalists. c/o Suzanne Steel, 216 Kottman Hall, 2021 Coffey Rd., Columbus, OH 43210. Phone: (614)292-9637 Fax: (614)292-2270 E-mail: steel@osu.edu.

OTHER SOURCES

Bacon's Newspaper/Magazine Directories. Bacon's Publishing Co. • Annual. $295.00 per year. Quarterly update. Two volumes: Magazines and Newspapers. Covers print media in the United States and Canada. Formerly *Bacon's Publicity Checker.*

FARM LABOR

See: FARMERS; LABOR

FARM MACHINERY

See: AGRICULTURAL MACHINERY

FARM MANAGEMENT

See also: AGRICULTURE

GENERAL WORKS

Farm Management. Ronald D. Kay and William M. Edwards. McGraw-Hill Higher Education. • 1999. Fourth edition. Price on application.

Farm Management: Principles, Budgets, Plans. John Herbst and Duane Erickson. Stipes Publishing L.L.C. • 1996. $25.80. 10th edition.

HANDBOOKS AND MANUALS

Farm Management. Michael D. Boehlje and Vernon R. Eidman. John Wiley and Sons, Inc. • 1984. $108.95.

PERIODICALS AND NEWSLETTERS

Ag Executive. Ag Executive, Inc. • Monthly. $84.00 per year. Newsletter. Topics include farm taxes, accounting, real estate, and financial planning.

FMRA News. American Society of Farm Managers and Rural Appraisers. • Bimonthly. $24.00.

Journal of Range Management: Covering the Study, Management, and Use of Rangeland Ecosystems and Range Resources. Society for Range Management. • Bimonthly. $95.00 per year., with *Rangelands,* $140.00 per year. Technical articles oriented towards research in range science and management.

TRADE/PROFESSIONAL ASSOCIATIONS

American Society of Farm Managers and Rural Appraisers. 950 S. Cherry St., Suite 508, Denver, CO 80246-2664. Phone: (303)758-3513 or (303)758-3514 Fax: (303)758-0190 E-mail: asfmra@agri-associations.org • URL: http://www.asfmra.org.

Northwest Farm Managers Association. P.O. Box 5437, Fargo, ND 58105. Phone: (701)231-7459 Fax: (701)231-1059.

Society for Range Management. 445 Union Blvd., Ste. 230, Lakewood, CO 80228. Phone: (303)355-7070 Fax: (303)355-5059 E-mail: srmden@ix.netcom.com • URL: http://www.srm.org.

OTHER SOURCES

Agricultural Law. Matthew Bender & Co., Inc. • $2,120.00 per year. 15 looseleaf volumes. Periodic supplementation. Covers all aspects of state and federal law relating to farms, ranches and other agricultural interests. Includes five volumes dealing with agricultural estate, tax and business planning.

FARM MARKETS

See also: MARKETING

GENERAL WORKS

Introduction to Agricultural Marketing. Robert E. Branson and Douglas G. Norvell. McGraw-Hill. • 1983. $43.74.

ALMANACS AND YEARBOOKS

Agricultural Policies, Markets, and Trade: Monitoring and Evaluation. Organization for Economic Cooperation and Development. Available from OECD Publications and Information Center. • Annual. $62.00. A yearly report on agricultural and trade policy developments in OECD member countries.

DIRECTORIES

Packer Produce Availability and Merchandising Guide. Vance Publishing Corp. • Annual. $35.00. A buyer's directory giving sources of fresh fruits and vegetables. Shippers are listed by location for each commodity.

ENCYCLOPEDIAS AND DICTIONARIES

Dictionary of Agriculture: From Abaca to Zoonosis. Kathryn L. Lipton. Lynne Rienner Publishers, Inc. • 1995. $75.00. Emphasis is on agricultural economics.

HANDBOOKS AND MANUALS

Handbook of Transportation and Marketing in Agriculture. Essex E. Finney, editor. Franklin Book Co., Inc. • 1981. Vol. 1, $252.00; vol. 2, $282.00. (CRC Agriculture Series).

PERIODICALS AND NEWSLETTERS

Agri Marketing: The Magazine for Professionals Selling to the Farm Market. Doane Agricultural Services. • 11 times a year. $30.00 per year.

Produce Merchandising: The Packer's Retailing and Merchandising Magazine. Vance Publishing Corp., Produce Div. • Monthly. $35.00 per year. Provides information and advice on the retail marketing and promotion of fresh fruits and vegetalbe.

RESEARCH CENTERS AND INSTITUTES

Giannini Foundation of Agricultural Economics. University of California. 248 Giannini Hall, No. 3310, Berkeley, CA 94720-3310. Phone: (510)642-7121 Fax: (510)643-8911 E-mail: dote@are.berkeley.edu • URL: http://www.are.berkeley.edu/library.

Texas Agricultural Market Research Center. Texas A & M University. Dept. of Agricultural Economics, College Station, TX 77843-2124. Phone: (979)845-5911 Fax: (979)845-6378 E-mail: tamrc@tamu.edu.

STATISTICS SOURCES

OECD Agricultural Outlook. Organization for Economic Cooperation and Development. • Annual. $31.00. Provides a five-year outlook for agricultural markets in various countries of the world, including the U. S., other OECD countries, and selected non-OECD nations.

TRADE/PROFESSIONAL ASSOCIATIONS

American Agricultural Marketing Association. 225 W. Touhy Ave., Park Ridge, IL 60068-5809. Phone: (312)399-5700 Fax: (312)399-5896.

North American Agricultural Marketing Officials. P.O. Box 146500, Salt Lake City, UT 84114-6500. E-mail: info@naamo.org • URL: http://www.naamo.org.

OTHER SOURCES

Global Seed Markets. Theta Reports/PJB Medical Publications, Inc. • 2000. $1,040.00. Market research data. Covers the major seed sectors, including cereal crops, legumes, oilseed crops, fibre crops, and beet crops. Provides analysis of biotechnology developments. (Theta Report No. DS208E.).

FARM PRODUCE

See also: AGRICULTURE

GENERAL WORKS

Agricultural Product Prices. William G. Tomek and Kenneth L. Robinson. Cornell University Press. • 1990. $35.00. Third edition.

ABSTRACTS AND INDEXES

Field Crop Abstracts: Monthly Abstract Journal on World Annual Cereal, Legume, Root, Oilseed and Fibre Crops. Available from CABI Publishing North America. • Monthly. $1,465.00 per year. Published in England by CABI Publishing, formerly Commonwealth Agricultural Bureaux. Provides worldwide coverage of the literature.

CD-ROM DATABASES

AGRICOLA on SilverPlatter. Available from SilverPlatter Information, Inc. • Quarterly. $825.00 per year. Produced by the National Agricultural Library. Provides about three million citations on CD-ROM to the literature of agriculture, agricultural economics, animal sciences, entomology, fertilizer, food, forestry, nutrition, pesticides, plant science, water resources, and other topics. Each quarterly disc covers the past ten years, with archival discs available from 1970.

WILSONDISC: Biological and Agricultural Index. H. W. Wilson Co. • Monthly. $1,495.00 per year, including unlimited online access to *Biological and Agricultural Index* through WILSONLINE. Provides CD-ROM indexing of over 250 periodicals covering agriculture, agricultural chemicals, biochemistry, biotechnology, entomology, horticulture, and related topics.

DIRECTORIES

American Fruit Grower Source Book. Meister Publishing Co. • Annual. $5.00.

American Vegetable Grower Source Book. Meister Publishing Co. • Annual. $2.75. Formerly *American Vegetable Grower Buyers' Guide.*

ENCYCLOPEDIAS AND DICTIONARIES

Encyclopedia of Agriculture Science. Charles J. Arntzen and Ellen M. Ritter, editors. Academic Press, Inc. • 1994. $625.00. Four volumes.

FINANCIAL RATIOS

Annual Statement Studies. Robert Morris Associates: The Association of Lending and Credit Risk Professiona. • Annual. Free to members; non-members, $140.00. Median and quartile financial ratios are given for over 400 kinds of manufacturing, wholesale, retail, construction, and consumer finance establishments. Data is sorted by both asset size and sales volume. Includes a clearly written "Definition of Ratios" and an alphabetical industry index.

INTERNET DATABASES

USDA. United States Department of Agriculture. Phone: (202)720-2791 E-mail: agsec@usda.gov • URL: http://www.usda.gov • The USDA home page has six sections: News and Information; What's New; About USDA; Agencies; Opportunities; Search and Help. Keyword searching is offered from the USDA home page and from various individual agency home pages. Agencies are the Economic Research Service, Agricultural Marketing Service, National Agricultural Statistics Service, National Agricultural Library, and about 12 others. Updating varies. Fees: Free.

ONLINE DATABASES

Agricola. U.S. National Agricultural Library. • Covers worldwide agricultural literature. Over 2.8 million citations, 1970 to present, with monthly updates. Inquire as to online cost and availability.

Biological and Agricultural Index Online. H. W. Wilson Co. • Indexes a wide variety of agricultural and biological periodicals, 1983 to date. Monthly updates. Inquire as to online cost and availability.

CAB Abstracts. CAB International North America. • Contains 46 specialized abstract collections covering over 10,000 journals and monographs in the areas of agriculture, horticulture, forest products, farm products, nutrition, dairy science, poultry, grains, animal health, entomology, etc. Time period is 1972 to date, with monthly updates. Inquire as to online cost and availability. *CAB Abstracts on CD-ROM* also available, with annual updating.

PERIODICALS AND NEWSLETTERS

Agricultural Research. Available from U. S. Government Printing Office. • Monthly. $45.00 per year. Issued by the Agricultural Research Service of the U. S. Department of Agriculture. Presents results of research projects related to a wide variety of farm crops and products.

Barron's: The Dow Jones Business and Financial Weekly. Dow Jones and Co., Inc. • Weekly. $145.00 per year.

Crop Science. Crop Science Society of America. • Bimonthly. Free to members, non-members, $241.00 per year.

RESEARCH CENTERS AND INSTITUTES

California Agricultural Experiment Station. University of California at Berkeley. 1111 Franklin St., 6th Fl., Oakland, CA 94607-5200. Phone: (510)987-0060 Fax: (510)451-2317 E-mail: wr.gomes@ucop.edu • URL: http://www.ucop.edu/anrhome/danr.html.

Florida Agricultural Experiment Station. University of Florida. Institute of Food and Agricultural Science, P.O. Box 110200, Gainesville, FL 32611-0200. Phone: (352)392-1784 Fax: (352)392-4965 E-mail: rlj@gnv.ifas.ufl.edu • URL: http://www.research.ifas.ufl.edu.

Kansas Agricultural Experiment Station - Performance Test Program. Kansas State University. Department of Agronomy, Throckmorton Hall, Manhattan, KS 66506. Phone: (785)532-6101 Fax: (785)532-6094 E-mail: dmengel@bear.agron.ksu.edu • URL: http://www.ksu.edu/kscpt.

Michigan Agricultural Experiment Station. Michigan State University. 109 Agricultural Hall, East Lansing, MI 48224-1039. Phone: (517)355-0123 Fax: (517)355-5406 E-mail: gray@pilot.msu.edu • URL: http://www.msu.edu.

Texas Agricultural Experiment Station at Sonora. Texas A & M University. P.O. Box 918, Sonora, TX 76950. Phone: (915)387-3168 Fax: (915)387-5045 E-mail: angora@sonoratx.net.

STATISTICS SOURCES

Agricultural Statistics. Available from U. S. Government Printing Office. • Annual. Produced by the National Agricultural Statistics Service, U. S. Department of Agriculture. Provides a wide variety of statistical data relating to agricultural production, supplies, consumption, prices/price-supports, foreign trade, costs, and returns, as well as farm labor, loans, income, and population. In many cases, historical data is shown annually for 10 years. In addition to farm data, includes detailed fishery statistics.

FAO Quarterly Bulletin of Statistics. Food and Agriculture Organization of the United Nations. Available from UNIPUB. • Quarterly. $20.00 per year. Provides international data on agricultural production, trade, and prices, covering the major commodities of many countries. Text in English, French, and Spanish. Formerly *FAO Monthly Bulletin of Statistics.*

Foreign Agricultural Trade of the United States. Available from U. S. Government Printing Office. • Monthly. $50.00 per year. Issued by the Economic Research Service of the U. S. Department of Agriculture. Provides data on U. S. exports and imports of agricultural commodities.

United States Census of Agriculture. U.S. Bureau of the Census. • Quinquennial. Results presented in reports, tape, CD-ROM, and Diskette files.

Vegetables and Specialties Situation and Outlook. Available from U. S. Government Printing Office. • Three times a year. $15.00 per year. Issued by the Economic Research Service of the U. S. Department of Agriculture. Provides current statistical information on supply, demand, and prices.

World Agricultural Supply and Demand Estimates. Available from U. S. Government Printing Office. • Monthly. $38.00 per year. Issued by the Economics and Statistics Service and the Foreign Agricultural Service of the U. S. Department of Agriculture. Consists mainly of statistical data and tables.

TRADE/PROFESSIONAL ASSOCIATIONS

National Association of Produce Market Managers. Administration Bldg., Rm. 110, 16 Forest Parkway, Forest Park, GA 30297. Phone: (404)366-6910 Fax: (404)362-4564.

Natural Food Associates. 8345 Walnut Hill Lane, Suite 225, Dallas, TX 75231-4205. 8345 Walnut Hill Lane, Suite 225, • Members are professionals and consumers interested in natural foods and organic farming.

Produce Marketing Association. P.O. Box 6036, Newark, DE 19714-6036. Phone: (302)738-7100 Fax: (302)731-2409 E-mail: pma@mail.pma.com • URL: http://www.pma.com.

FARMERS

See also: AGRICULTURE; LABOR

ABSTRACTS AND INDEXES

World Agricultural Economics and Rural Sociology Abstracts: Abstracts of World Literature. Available from CABI Publishing. • Monthly. $1095.00 per year. Published in England by CABI Publishing. Provides worldwide coverage of the literature.

INTERNET DATABASES

USDA. United States Department of Agriculture. Phone: (202)720-2791 E-mail: agsec@usda.gov • URL: http://www.usda.gov • The USDA home page has six sections: News and Information; What's New; About USDA; Agencies; Opportunities; Search and Help. Keyword searching is offered from the USDA home page and from various individual agency home pages. Agencies are the Economic Research Service, Agricultural Marketing Service, National Agricultural Statistics Service, National Agricultural Library, and about 12 others. Updating varies. Fees: Free.

PERIODICALS AND NEWSLETTERS

Agricultural Outlook. Available from U. S. Government Printing Office. • Monthly. $60.00 per year. Issued by the Economic Research Service of the U. S. Department of Agriculture. Provides analysis of agriculture and the economy.

Farm Industry News. Intertec Publishing Co., Agribusiness Div. • 12 times a year. $25.00 per year. Includes new products for farm use.

Farmer's Digest. Heartland Communictions Group, Inc. • 10 times a year. $17.95 per year. Current information on all phases of agriculture.

News for Family Farmers and Rural Americans. Farmers Educational and Cooperative Union of America. • Monthly. $10.00 per year. Formerly *National Farmers Union Washington Newsletter.*

Progressive Farmer. Progressive Farmer, Inc. • 18 times a year. $18.00 per year. 17 regional editions. Includes supplement *Rural Sportsman.*

STATISTICS SOURCES

Agricultural Statistics. Available from U. S. Government Printing Office. • Annual. Produced by the National Agricultural Statistics Service, U. S. Department of Agriculture. Provides a wide variety of statistical data relating to agricultural production, supplies, consumption, prices/price-supports, foreign trade, costs, and returns, as well as farm labor, loans, income, and population. In many cases, historical data is shown annually for 10 years. In addition to farm data, includes detailed fishery statistics.

Agriculture Fact Book. Available from U. S. Government Printing Office. • Annual. Issued by the Office of Communications, U. S. Department of Agriculture. Includes data on U. S. agriculture, farmers, food, nutrition, and rural America. Programs of the Department of Agriculture in six areas are described: rural economic development, foreign trade, nutrition, the environment, inspection, and education.

Farm Labor. U.S. Department of Agriculture. • Monthly.

TRADE/PROFESSIONAL ASSOCIATIONS

National Farmers Organization. 2505 Elmwood Dr., Ames, IA 50010-2000. Phone: (515)292-2000 Fax: (515)292-7106 E-mail: info@netins.net • URL: http://www.nfo.org.

National Farmers Union. 11900 E. Cornell Ave., Aurora, CO 80014-3194. Phone: 800-347-1961 or (303)337-5500 Fax: (303)368-1390 E-mail: nfu.denver@nfu.org • URL: http://www.nfu.org.

OTHER SOURCES

Estate Planning for Farmers and Ranchers: A Guide to Family Businesses with Agricultural Holdings. Donald H. Kelley and David A. Ludtke. Shepard's. • 1995. Third edition. Price on application.

FARMS

See: AGRICULTURE

FASHION INDUSTRY

See also: CLOTHING INDUSTRY; WOMEN'S APPAREL

GENERAL WORKS

Fashion Accessories: The Complete Twentieth Century Sourcebook. John Peacock. Macmillan Publishing Co., Inc. • 2000. $34.95.

Fashion and Merchandising Fads. Frank W. Hoffmann and William G. Bailey. Haworth Press, Inc. • 1994. $49.95. Contains descriptions of fashion industry fads or promotions from A to Z (A-2 Flight Jacket to Zipper).

Fashion Merchandising: An Introduction. Elaine Stone. McGraw-Hill. • 1989. $45.72. Fifth edition. (Marketing Series).

Marketing Today's Fashion. Carol Mueller. Prentice Hall. • 1994. $85.00. Third edition.

CD-ROM DATABASES

Magazine Index Plus. The Gale Group. • Monthly. $4,000.00 per year (includes InfoTrac workstation). Provides full text on CD-ROM for about 100 popular, general interest magazines and indexing for 300 others. Includes special indexing of reviews and product evaluations. Time period is 1980 to date.

DIRECTORIES

Accessories Resources Directory. Business Journals, Inc. • Annual. $30.00. 1,600 manufacturers, importers, and sales representatives producing or handling belts, gloves, handbags, scarves, hosiery, jewelry, sunglasses and umbrellas. Formerly *Accessories Directory.*

Contemporary Fashion. Richard Martin, editor. St. James Press. • $140.00. Second edition. Date not set. Provides detailed information on more than 400 fashion designers, milliners, footwear designers, apparel companies, and textile houses. Includes black-and-white photographs, biographical information, and bibliographies.

ENCYCLOPEDIAS AND DICTIONARIES

Fairchild's Dictionary of Fashion. Phyllis B. Tortora. Fairchild Books. • 1996. $75.00. Seventh edition.

HANDBOOKS AND MANUALS

Fashion Advertising and Promotion. Jay Diamond and Ellen Diamond. John Wiley and Sons, Inc. • 1995. $10.00 (Fashion Merchandising Series.).

Modern Fashion Drawing. Dora Shackell and W. Stuart Masters. Gordon Press Publishers. • 1978. $250.00. Reprint of the 1934 edition.

PERIODICALS AND NEWSLETTERS

DNR: The Men's Fashion Retail Textile Authority. Fairchild Publications. • Daily. $85.00 per year. Formerly *Daily News Record.*

GQ (Gentleman's Quarterly). Conde Nast Publications, Inc. • Monthly. Individuals, $19.97 per year; libraries, $12.50 per year.

Harper's Bazaar. Hearst Corp. • Monthly. $10.00 per year.

Mademoiselle. Conde Nast Publications, Inc.,. • Monthly. $16.00 per year.

Vogue. Conde Nast Publications, Inc. • Monthly. $28.00 per year.

WWD (Women's Wear Daily): The Retailer's Daily Newspaper. Fairchild Publications. • Daily. Institutions, $75.00 per year; corporations $195.00 per year.

TRADE/PROFESSIONAL ASSOCIATIONS

Council of Fashion Designers of America. 1412 Broadway, Suite 2006, New York, NY 10018. Phone: (212)302-1821 Fax: (212)768-0515.

Fashion Association. 475 Park Ave., S., 9th Fl., New York, NY 10016. Phone: (212)683-5665 Fax: (212)545-1709.

International Association of Clothing Designers and Executives. 475 Park Ave., S., 17th Fl., New York, NY 10016. Phone: (212)685-6602 Fax: (212)545-1709.

National Association of Fashion and Accessory Designers. 2180 E. 93rd St., Cleveland, OH 44106. Phone: (216)231-0375.

Union of Needletrades, Industrial and Textile Employees. 1710 Broadway, New York, NY 10019. Phone: (212)265-7000 Fax: (212)315-3803 • URL: http://www.uniteunion.org.

OTHER SOURCES

Fashion Calendar. Fashion Calendar International. • Bimonthly. $365.00 per year.

FAST FOOD INDUSTRY

See also: FROZEN FOOD INDUSTRY; RESTAURANTS, LUNCHROOMS, ETC.

DIRECTORIES

Directory of Chain Restaurant Operators. Chain Store Guide. • Annual. $300.00. Includes fast food establishments, and leading chain hotel copanies operating foodservice unit.

FINANCIAL RATIOS

Annual Statement Studies. Robert Morris Associates: The Association of Lending and Credit Risk Professiona. • Annual. Free to members; non-members, $140.00. Median and quartile financial ratios are given for over 400 kinds of manufacturing, wholesale, retail, construction, and consumer finance establishments. Data is sorted by both asset size and sales volume. Includes a clearly written "Definition of Ratios" and an alphabetical industry index.

HANDBOOKS AND MANUALS

Donut Shop. Entrepreneur Media, Inc. • Looseleaf. $59.50. A practical guide to starting a doughnut shop. Covers profit potential, start-up costs, market size evaluation, owner's time required, site selection, lease negotiation, pricing, accounting, advertising, promotion, etc. (Start-Up Business Guide No. E1126.).

Pizzeria. Entrepreneur Media, Inc. • Looseleaf. $59.50. A practical guide to starting a pizza shop. Covers profit potential, start-up costs, market size evaluation, owner's time required, site selection, lease negotiation, pricing, accounting, advertising, promotion, etc. (Start-Up Business Guide No. E1006.).

Sandwich Shop/Deli. Entrepreneur Media, Inc. • Looseleaf. $59.50. A practical guide to starting a sandwich shop and delicatessen. Covers profit potential, start-up costs, market size evaluation, owner's time required, site selection, lease negotiation, pricing, accounting, advertising, promotion, etc. (Start-Up Business Guide No. E1156.).

PERIODICALS AND NEWSLETTERS

Pizza Today. National Association of Pizza Operators. • Monthly. $30.00 per year. Covers both practical business topics and food topics for pizza establishments.

QSR: The Magazine of Quick Service Restaurant Success. Journalistic, Inc. • Nine times a year. $32.00 per year. Provides news and management advice for quick-service restaurants, including franchisors and franchisees.

Restaurant Business. Bill Communications, Inc. • 24 times a year. $110.00 per year.

TRADE/PROFESSIONAL ASSOCIATIONS

National Association of Pizza Operators. P.O. Box 1347, New Albany, IN 47151-1347. Phone: (812)949-0909 Fax: (812)941-9711 • URL: http://www.pizzatoday.com • Members are pizza establishment operators, food suppliers, and equipment manufacturers.

OTHER SOURCES

Fast Food. Available from MarketResearch.com. • 1998. $5,000.00. Published by Euromonitor Publications Ltd. Provides consumer market data for the United States, the United Kingdom, Germany, France, and Italy.

FASTENER INDUSTRY

See also: HARDWARE INDUSTRY

DIRECTORIES

Fastener Technology International Buyers' Guide. Initial Publications, Inc. • Annual. $35.00. List of over 2,000 international manufacturers and distributors of fasteners and precision-formed parts.

Macrae's Blue Book: Serving the Original Equipment Market. MacRae's Blue Book, Inc. • Annual. $170.00. Two volumes. Lists about 50,000 manufacturers of a wide variety of industrial equipment and supplies.

Thomas Register of American Manufacturers and Thomas Register Catalog File. Thomas Publishing Co., Inc. • Annual. $149.00. 34 volumes. A three-part system offering information on a wide variety of industrial equipment and supplies.

HANDBOOKS AND MANUALS

Assembly Buyer's Guide. Cahners Business Information. • Annual. $25.00. Lists manufacturers and suppliers of equipment relating to assembly automation, fasteners, adhesives, robotics, and power tools.

McGraw-Hill Machining and Metalworking Handbook. Ronald A. Walsh. McGraw-Hill. • 1998. $99.95. Second edition. Coverage includes machinery, machining techniques, machine tools, machine design, parts, fastening, and plating.

ONLINE DATABASES

Thomas Register Online. Thomas Publishing Co., Inc. • Provides concise information on approximately 194,000 U. S. companies, mainly manufacturers, with over 50,000 product classifications. Indexes over 115,000 trade names. Information is updated semiannually. Inquire as to online cost and availability.

PERIODICALS AND NEWSLETTERS

Fastener Technology International. Initial Publications. • Bimonthly. $35.00 per year.

Hardware Age. Cahners Business Information. • Monthly. $75.00 per year.

STATISTICS SOURCES

U. S. Industry and Trade Outlook: The McGraw-Hill Companies and the U.S. Department of Commerce/ International Trade Administration. Datapso Research Corp. • Annual. $69.95. Produced by the International Trade Administration, U. S. Department of Commerce, in a "public-private" partnership with DRI/McGraw-Hill and Standard & Poor's. Provides basic data, outlook for the current year, and "Long-Term Prospects" (five-year projections) for a wide variety of products and services. Includes high technology industries. Formerly *U. S. Industrial Outlook.*

TRADE/PROFESSIONAL ASSOCIATIONS

ASM International. 9639 Kinsman Rd., Materials Park, OH 44073. Phone: 800-336-5152 or (216)338-5151 Fax: (216)338-4634 E-mail: memserv@po.asm-intl.org • URL: http://www.asm-intl.org • Members are materials engineers, metallurgists, industry executives, educators, and others concerned with a wide range of materials and metals. Divisions include Aerospace, Composites, Electronic Materials and Processing, Energy, Highway/Off-Highway Vehicle, Joining, Materials Testing and Quality Control, Society of Carbide and Tool Engineers, and Surface Engineering.

Industrial Fasteners Institute. 1717 E. Ninth St., Suite 1105, Cleveland, OH 44114-2879. Phone: (216)241-1482 Fax: (216)241-5901 E-mail: indfast@aol.com • URL: http://www.industrial-fasteners.org.

National Fastener Distributors Association. 1717 E. 9th St., Suite 1185, Cleveland, OH 44114-2803. Phone: (216)579-1571 Fax: (216)579-1531 • URL: http://www.nfda-fastener.org.

Specialty Tools and Fasteners Distributors Association. P.O. Box 44, Elm Grove, WI 53122. Phone: 800-352-2981 or (414)784-4774 Fax: (414)784-5059 E-mail: stafda@execpc.com • URL: http://www.stafda.org.

Tubular Rivet and Machine Institute. 25 N. Broadway, Tarrytown, NY 10591. Phone: (914)332-0040 Fax: (914)332-1541.

OTHER SOURCES

Assembly. Cahners Business Information. • Monthly. $68.00 per year. Covers assembly, fastening, and joining systems. Includes information on automation and robotics.

FATS

See: OIL AND FATS INDUSTRY

FAX

See: FACSIMILE SYSTEMS

FEDERAL AID

See also: GRANTS-IN-AID

GENERAL WORKS

From Idea to Funded Project: Grant Proposals that Work. Jane C. Belcher and Julia M. Jacobsen. Oryx Press. • 1992. $26.50. Fourth edition. Formerly *A Process for the Development of Ideas.*

DIRECTORIES

Carroll's Federal Assistance Directory. Carroll Publishing. • Free Web site provides detailed information on more than 1,500 federal programs "disbursing financial and technical support to individuals and organizations." Simple or advanced searching is offered by popular name, federal agency, or keyword.

Catalog of Federal Domestic Assistance. U.S. Office of Management and Budget. Available from U.S. Government Printing Office. • Annual. $87.00. Looseleaf service. Includes up-dating service for indeterminate period. Summary of financial and nonfinanacial Federal programs, projects, services and activities that provide assistance or benefits to the American public.

Getting Yours; The Complete Guide to Government Money. Matthew Lesko. Viking Penguin. • 1987. $14.95 Third edition. (Handbook Series).

Government Assistance Almanac: The Guide to Federal, Domestic, Financial and Other Programs Covering Grants, Loans, Insurance, Personal Payments and Benefits. J. Robert Dumouchel, editor. Omnigraphics, Inc. • Annual. $190.00. Describes more than 1,300 federal assistance programs available from about 50 agencies. Includes statistics, a directory of 4,000 field offices, and comprehensive indexing.

Guide to Federal Funding for Education. Education Funding Research Council. • Quarterly. $297.00 per year. Describes approximately 407 federal education programs that award grants and contracts. Includes semimonthly supplement: *Grant Updates.*

Guide to Federal Funding for Governments and Non-Profits. Government Information Services. • Quarterly. $339.00 per year. Contains detailed descriptions of federal grant programs in economic development, housing, transportation, social services, science, etc. Semimonthly supplement available: *Federal Grant Deadline Calendar.*

HANDBOOKS AND MANUALS

Financing Graduate School: How to Get Money for Your Master's or Ph.D. Patricia McWade. Peterson's. • 1996. $16.95. Second revised edition. Discusses the practical aspects of various types of financial aid for graduate students. Includes bibliographic and directory information.

Grants Policy Directives. U.S. Dept. of Health, and Human Services. Available from U.S. Government Printing Office. • $219.00. Periodic supplementation. Provides guidelines on the fiscal and administrative aspects of grant management to all granting agencies of the Dept. of Health and Human Services.

How to Write Proposals that Produce. Joel P. Bowman and Bernadine P. Branchaw. Oryx Press. • 1992. $23.50. An extensive guide to effective proposal writing for both nonprofit organizations and businesses. Covers writing style, intended audience, format, use of graphs, charts, and tables, documentation, evaluation, oral presentation, and related topics.

Proposal Planning and Writing. Lynn E. Miner and others. Oryx Press. • 1998. $34.50. Second edition. Discusses the steps necessary to locate and obtain funding from the federal government, foundations, and corporations.

ONLINE DATABASES

Grants. Oryx Press. • References grants by federal, state, and local governments and other organizations; current file includes grants with deadlines within the next six months. Inquire as to online cost and availability.

PERIODICALS AND NEWSLETTERS

Federal Assistance Monitor. Community Development Services. CD Publications. • Semimonthly. $279.00 per year. Newsletter. Provides news of federal grant and loan programs for social, economic, and community purposes. Monitors grant announcements, funding, and availability.

Federal Grants and Contracts Weekly: Funding Opportunities in Research, Training and Services. Aspen Publishers, Inc. • Weekly. $394.00 per year.

Grantsmanship Center Magazine: A Compendium of Resources for Nonprofit Organizations. Grantsmanship Center. • Irregular. Free to qualified personnel. Contains a variety of concise articles on grant-related topics, such as program planning, proposal writing, fundraising, non-cash gifts, federal project grants, benchmarking, taxation, etc.

OTHER SOURCES

FedWorld: A Program of the United States Department of Commerce. National Technical Information Service. • Web site offers "a comprehensive central access point for searching, locating, ordering, and acquiring government and business information." Emphasis is on searching the Web pages, databases, and government reports of a wide variety of federal agencies. Fees: Free.

FirstGov: Your First Click to the U. S. Government. General Services Administration. • Free Web site provides extensive links to federal agencies covering a wide variety of topics, such as agriculture, business, consumer safety, education, the environment, government jobs, grants, health, social security, statistics sources, taxes, technology, travel, and world affairs. Also provides links to federal forms, including IRS tax forms. Searching is offered, both keyword and advanced.

U. S. Business Advisor. Small Business Administration. • Web site provides "a one-stop electronic link to all the information and services government provides for the business community." Covers about 60 federal agencies that exist to assist or regulate business. Detailed information is provided on financial assistance, workplace issues, taxes, regulations, international trade, and other business topics. Searching is offered. Fees: Free.

FEDERAL AID FOR EDUCATION

See: FEDERAL AID

FEDERAL AID TO RESEARCH

See: FEDERAL AID

FEDERAL BUDGET

See also: NATIONAL DEBT

GENERAL WORKS

Balanced Budgets and American Politics. James D. Savage. Cornell University Press. • 1988. $45.00. States the case for economic growth being more important than a balanced federal budget.

Setting National Priorities: Budget Choices for the Next Century. Robert D. Reischauer and Henry J. Aaron, editors. Brookings Institution Press. • 1996. $42.95. Contains discussions of the federal budget, economic policy, and government spending policy.

ABSTRACTS AND INDEXES

American Statistics Index: A Comprehensive Guide and Index to the Statistical Publications of the United States Government. Congressional Information Service, Inc. • Monthly. Quarterly and annual cumulations. Price varies.

ENCYCLOPEDIAS AND DICTIONARIES

International Encyclopedia of Public Policy and Administration. Jay M. Shafritz, editor. HarperCollins Publishers. • 1997. $550.00. Four volumes. Covers 20 major areas, such as public administration, government budgeting, industrial policy, nonprofit management, organizational theory, public finance, labor relations, and taxation. Includes a brief bibliography for each major entry and a comprehensive index.

FINANCIAL RATIOS

Financial Report of the United States Government. Available from U. S. Government Printing Office. • Annual. $14.00. Issued by the U. S. Treasury Department (http://www.treas.gov). Presents information about the financial condition and operations of the federal government. Program accounting systems of various government agencies provide data for the report.

HANDBOOKS AND MANUALS

Guide to the Federal Budget 1998. Stanley E. Collender. Rowman and Littlefield Publishers, Inc. • 1997. $56.00. A practical explanation of the federal budget for the most recent fiscal year.

INTERNET DATABASES

Fedstats. Federal Interagency Council on Statistical Policy. Phone: (202)395-7254 • URL: http://www.fedstats.gov • Web site features an efficient search facility for full-text statistics produced by more than 70 federal agencies, including the Census Bureau, the Bureau of Economic Analysis, and the Bureau of Labor Statistics. Boolean searches can be made within one agency or for all agencies combined. Links are offered to international statistical bureaus, including the UN, IMF, OECD, UNESCO, Eurostat, and 20 individual countries. Fees: Free.

ONLINE DATABASES

DRI U.S. Central Database. Data Products Division. • Provides more than 23,000 business, financial, demographic, economic, foreign trade, and industry-related time series for the U.S. Includes national income, population, retail-wholesale trade, price indexes, labor data, housing, industrial production, banking, interest rates, money supply, etc. Time period is generally 1947 to date (some data back to 1929). Updating varies. Inquire as to online cost and availability.

STATISTICS SOURCES

The AIER Chart Book. AIER Research Staff. American Institute for Economic Research. • Annual. $3.00. A compact compilation of long-range charts ("Purchasing Power of the Dollar," for example, goes back to 1780) covering various aspects of the U. S. economy. Includes inflation, interest rates, debt, gold, taxation, stock prices, etc. (Economic Education Bulletin.).

Budget of the United States Government. U.S. Office of Management and Budget. Available from U.S. Government Printing Office. • Annual.

Business Statistics of the United States. Courtenay M. Slater, editor. Bernan Associates. • 1999. $74.00. Fifth edition. Based on *Business Statistics*, formerly issue by the Bureau of Economic Analysis, U. S. Department of Commerce. Provides basic data for a wide variety of U. S. industries, services, and economic indicators. Most statistics are shown annually for 29 years and monthly for the most recent four years.

Citizen's Guide to the Federal Budget. Available from U. S. Government Printing Office. • Annual. $3.25. Issued by the Office of Management and Budget, Executive Office of the President (http://www.whitehouse.gov). Provides basic data for the general public about the budget of the U. S. government.

Economic and Budget Outlook: Fiscal Years 2000-2009. Available from U. S. Government Printing Office. • 1999. $15.00. Issued by the Congressional Budget Office (http://www.cbo.gov). Contains CBO economic projections and federal budget projections annually to 2009 in billions of dollars. An appendix contains "Historical Budget Data" annually from 1962 to 1998, including revenues, outlays, deficits, surpluses, and debt held by the public.

Historical Tables, Budget of the United States Government. Available from U. S. Government Printing Office. • Annual. Issued by the Office of Management and Budget, Executive Office of the President (http://www.whitehouse.gov). Provides statistical data on the federal budget for an extended period of about 60 years in the past to projections of four years in the future. Includes federal debt and federal employment.

Monthly Treasury Statement of Receipts and Outlays of the United States Government. Available from U. S. Government Printing Office. • Monthly. $40.00 per year. Issued by the Financial Management Service, U. S. Treasury Department.

Survey of Current Business. Available from U. S. Government Printing Office. • Monthly. $49.00 per year. Issued by Bureau of Economic Analysis, U. S. Department of Commerce. Presents a wide variety of business and economic data.

Treasury Bulletin. Available from U. S. Government Printing Office. • Quarterly. $39.00 per year. Issued by the Financial Management Service, U. S. Treasury Department. Provides data on the federal budget, government securities and yields, the national debt, and the financing of the federal government in general.

United States Budget in Brief. U.S. Office of Management and Budget, Executive Office of the President. Available from U.S. Government Printing Office. • Annual.

OTHER SOURCES

United States Government Annual Report, Fiscal Year... Available from U. S. Government Printing Office. • Annual. $5.00. Issued by the Financial Management Service, U. S. Treasury Department (http://www.fms.treas.gov). Contains the official report on the receipts and outlays of the federal government. Presents budgetary results at the summary level.

FEDERAL EMPLOYEES

See: BUREAUCRACY; GOVERNMENT EMPLOYEES

FEDERAL GOVERNMENT

GENERAL WORKS

American Government: Readings and Cases. Peter Woll. Addison-Wesley Longman, Inc. • 1998. $36.00. 13th edition.

Moving Power and Money: The Politics of Census Taking. Barbara E. Bryant and William Dunn. New

Strategist Publications, Inc. • 1995. $24.95. Barbara Everitt Bryant was Director of the U. S. Census Bureau from 1989 to 1993. She provides a plan for reducing the costs of census taking, improving accuracy, and overcoming public resistance to the census.

Unbridled Power: Inside the Secret Culture of the IRS. Shelley L. Davis. HarperCollins Publishers. • 1997. $25.00. A highly critical view of the Internal Revenue Service by its former historian.

ABSTRACTS AND INDEXES

Current Law Index: Multiple Access to Legal Periodicals. The Gale Group. • Monthly. $650.00 per year. Produced in cooperation with the American Association of Law Libraries. Indexes more than 900 law journals, legal newspapers, and specialty publications from the U.S., Canada, U.K., Ireland, Australia, and New Zealand.

Social Sciences Index. H. W. Wilson Co. • Quarterly, with annual cumulation. Service basis for print edition; CD-ROM edition, $1,495 per year. Indexes more than 400 periodicals covering economics, environmental policy, government, insurance, labor, health care policy, plannning, public administration, public welfare, urban studies, women's issues, criminology, and related topics.

BIBLIOGRAPHIES

Subject Bibliography Index: A Guide to U. S. Government Information. Available from U. S. Government Printing Office. • Annual. Free. Issued by the Superintendent of Documents. Lists currently available subject bibliographies by title and by topic. Each *Subject Bibliography* describes government books, periodicals, posters, pamphlets, and subscription services available for sale from the Government Printing Office.

CD-ROM DATABASES

Leadership Library on CD-ROM: Who's Who in the Leadership of the United States. Leadership Directories, Inc. • Quarterly. $2,641.00 per year, including access to Internet version (weekly updates). Contains all 14 *Yellow Book* personnel directories on CD-ROM, providing contact and brief biographical information for about 400,000 individuals. Covers business, government, financial institutions, news media, law firms, associations, foreign representatives, and nonprofit organizations. Includes photographs.

Social Science Source. EBSCO Publishing. • Monthly. $1,495.00 per year. Provides CD-ROM citations and abstracts to social science articles in more than 600 periodicals, with full text from 125 periodicals. Covers economics, political science, public policy, international relations, psychology, and other topics. Time period is most recent five years.

Social Sciences Citation Index: Compact Disc Edition with Abstracts. Institute for Scientific Information. • Quarterly. Provides CD-ROM indexing and abstracting of "significant articles" from 1,400 social science journals worldwide, with additional selections from 3,200 other journals, 1986 to date. Includes economics, business, finance, management, communications, demographics, information and library science, political science, sociology, and many other subjects.

Staff Directories on CD-ROM. CQ Staff Directories, Inc. • Three times a year. $495.00 per year. Provides the contents on CD-ROM of *Congressional Staff Directory, Federal Staff Directory*, and *Judicial Staff Directory.* Includes photographs and maps.

Statistical Masterfile. Congressional Information Service. • Quarterly. Price varies. Provides CD-ROM versions of *American Statistics Index, Index to International Statistics,* and *Statistical Reference Index.* Contains indexing and abstracting of a wide variety of published statistics sources, both governmental and private.

WILSONDISC: Wilson Social Sciences Abstracts. H. W. Wilson Co. • Monthly. Including unlimited online access to *Social Sciences Index* through WILSONLINE. Provides CD-ROM indexing from 1983 and abstracting from 1994 of more than 400 periodicals covering economics, area studies, community health, public administration, public welfare, urban studies, and many other topics related to the social sciences.

DIRECTORIES

Almanac of the Federal Judiciary. Publishers, Inc. • Annual. $295.00 per set. Two volumes. Volume one provides information on federal district judges; volume two relates to federal circuit judges.

Carroll's Federal & Federal Regional Directory: CD-ROM Edition. Carroll Publishing. • Bimonthly. $800.00 per year. Provides CD-ROM listings of more than 120,000 (55,000 high-level and 65,000 mid-level) U. S. government officials in Washington and throughout the country, including in military installations. Also available online.

Carroll's Federal Directory. Carroll Publishing. • Bimonthly. $325.00 per year. Lists 40,000 key U. S. officials, including members of Congress, Cabinet members, federal judges, Executive Office of the President personnel, and a wide variety of administrators.

Carroll's Federal Regional Directory. Carroll Publishing. • Semiannual. $255.00 per year. Lists more than 28,000 non-Washington based federal executives in administrative agencies, the courts, and military bases. Arranged in four sections: Alphabetical (last names), Organizational, Geographical, and Keyword. Includes maps.

Congressional Directory. U.S. Government Printing Office. • Biennial. $45.00.

Federal Agency Profiles for Students. The Gale Group. • 1999. $99.00. Provides detailed descriptions of about 200 prominent U.S. government agencies, including major activities, organizational structure, political issues, budget, and history. Includes a glossary, chronology, and index.

Federal Regional Yellow Book: Who's Who in the Federal Government's Departments, Agencies, Military Installations, and Service Academies Outside of Washington, DC. Leadership Directories, Inc. • Semiannual. $235.00 per year. Lists over 36,000 federal officials and support staff at 8,000 regional offices.

Federal Regulatory Directory. Congressional Quarterly, Inc. • Biennial. $149.95. Published by Congressional Quarterly, Inc. Provides detailed profiles of government agency functions and duties, and describes the laws each agency enforces. Includes extensive directory information.

Federal Staff Directory: With Biographical Information on Executive Staff Personnel. CQ Staff Directories, Inc. • Three times a year. $227.00 per year. Single copies, $89.00. Lists 40,000 staff members of federal departments and agencies, with biographies of 2,600 key executives. Includes keyword and name indexes.

Government Phone Book USA: Your Comprehensive Guide to Federal, State, County, and Local Government Offices in the United States. Omnigraphics, Inc. • Annual. $230.00. Contains more than 168,500 listings of federal, state, county, and local government offices and personnel, including legislatures. Formerly *Government Directory of Addresses and Phone Numbers.*

The Internet Blue Pages: The Guide to Federal Government Web Sites. Information Today, Inc. • Annual. $34.95. Provides information on more than 900 Web sites used by various agencies of the federal government. Includes indexes to agencies and topics. Links to all Web sites listed are available at http://www.fedweb.com. (CyberAge Books.).

Judicial Staff Directory: With Biographical Information on Judges and Key Court Staff. CQ Staff Directories, Inc. • Annual. $89.00 per no. Lists 16,000 federal court personnel, including 1,300 federal judges and their staffs, with biographies of judges and key executives. Includes maps of court jurisdictions.

Judicial Yellow Book: Who's Who in Federal and State Courts. Leadership Directories, Inc. • Semiannual. $235.00 per year. Lists more than 3,200 judges and staffs in various federal courts and 1,200 judges and staffs in state courts. Includes biographical profiles of judges.

United States Government Manual. National Archives and Records Administration. Available from U.S. Government Printing Office. • Annual. $46.00.

Washington Information Directory. Congressional Quarterly, Inc. • Annual. $119.00. Published by Congressional Quarterly, Inc. Lists names, addresses, phone numbers, fax numbers, and some Internet addresses for Congress, federal agencies, and nonprofit organizations in Washington, DC. Includes brief descriptions of each group and a subject index.

HANDBOOKS AND MANUALS

Government Auditing Standards. Available from U. S. Government Printing Office. • 1994. $6.50. Revised edition. Issued by the U. S. General Accounting Office (http://www.gao.gov). Contains standards for CPA firms to follow in financial and performance audits of federal government agencies and programs. Also known as the "Yellow Book.".

Office of Personnel Management Operating Manuals. Available from U. S. Government Printing Office. • Four looseleaf manuals at various prices ($25.00 to $190.00). Price of each manual includes updates for an indeterminate period. Manuals provides details of the federal wage system, the federal wage system "Nonappropriated Fund", personnel recordkeeping, personnel actions, qualification standards, and data reporting.

INTERNET DATABASES

Fedstats. Federal Interagency Council on Statistical Policy. Phone: (202)395-7254 • URL: http://www.fedstats.gov • Web site features an efficient search facility for full-text statistics produced by more than 70 federal agencies, including the Census Bureau, the Bureau of Economic Analysis, and the Bureau of Labor Statistics. Boolean searches can be made within one agency or for all agencies combined. Links are offered to international statistical bureaus, including the UN, IMF, OECD, UNESCO, Eurostat, and 20 individual countries. Fees: Free.

U. S. Census Bureau: The Official Statistics. U. S. Bureau of the Census. Phone: (301)763-4100 Fax: (301)763-4794 • URL: http://www.census.gov • Web site is "Your Source for Social, Demographic, and Economic Information." Contains "Current U. S. Population Count," "Current Economic Indicators," and a wide variety of data under "Other Official Statistics." Keyword searching is provided. Fees: Free.

ONLINE DATABASES

American Statistics Index: A Comprehensive Guide and Index to the Statistical Publications of the United States Government [Online]. Congressional

Information Service, Inc. • Indexes and abstracts, 1973 to date. Inquire as to online cost and availability.

GPO Monthly Catalog. U. S. Government Printing Office. • Contains over 375,000 online citations to U. S. government publications, 1976 to date, with monthly updates. Corresponds to the printed *Monthly Catalog of United States Government Publications.* Inquire as to online cost and availability.

GPO Publications Reference File. U. S. Government Printing Office. • An online guide to federal government publications in print (currently for sale), forthcoming, and recently out-of-print. Biweekly updates. Inquire as to online cost and availability.

Wilson Social Sciences Abstracts Online. H. W. Wilson Co. • Provides online abstracting and indexing of more than 415 periodicals covering area studies, community health, public administration, public welfare, urban studies, and many other social science topics. Time period is 1994 to date for abstracts and 1983 to date for indexing, with updates monthly. Inquire as to online cost and availability.

PERIODICALS AND NEWSLETTERS

Federal Computer Week: The Newspaper for the Government Systems Community. FCW Government Technology Group. • 41 times a year. $95.00 per year.

Government Executive: Federal Government's Business Magazine. National Journal Group, Inc. • Monthly. $48.00 per year. Includes management of computerized information systems in the federal government.

The Information Freeway Report: Free Business and Government Information Via Modem. Washington Researchers Ltd. • Monthly. $160.00 per year. Newsletter. Provides news of business and government databases that are available free of charge through the Internet or directly. Emphasis is on federal government databases and electronic bulletin boards (Fedworld).

National Journal: The Weekly on Politics and Government. National Journal Group, Inc. • Semiweekly. $1,197.00 per year. Includes semiannual supplement *Capital Source.* A non-partisan weekly magazine on politics and government.

RESEARCH CENTERS AND INSTITUTES

American Enterprise Institute. 1150 17th St., N.W., Washington, DC 20036. Phone: 800-862-5801 or (202)862-5800 Fax: (202)862-7177 • URL: http://www.aei.org.

Brookings Institution. 1775 Massachusetts Ave., N.W., Washington, DC 20036-2188. Phone: (202)797-6000 Fax: (202)797-6004 E-mail: estinger@brookings.edu • URL: http://www.brookings.edu/.

Lexis.com Research System. Lexis-Nexis Group. Phone: 800-227-9597 or (937)865-6800 Fax: (937)865-6909 E-mail: webmaster@prod.lexis-nexis.com • URL: http://www.lexis.com • Fee-based Web site offers extensive searching of a wide variety of legal sources. Additional features include Daily Opinion Service, lexis.com Bookstore, Career Center, CLE Center, Law Schools, and Practice Pages ("Pages specific to areas of specialty").

RAND. P.O. Box 2138, Santa Monica, CA 90407-2138. Phone: (310)393-0411 Fax: (310)393-4818 E-mail: correspondence@rand.org • URL: http://www.rand.org.

STATISTICS SOURCES

Social Statistics of the United States. Mark S. Littman, editor. Bernan Press. • 2000. $65.00. Includes statistical data on population growth, labor force, occupations, environmental trends, leisure time use, income, poverty, taxes, and other economic or demographic topics.

Statistical Abstract of the United States. Available from U. S. Government Printing Office. • Annual. $51.00. Issued by the U. S. Bureau of the Census.

A Statistical Portrait of the United States: Social Conditions and Trends. Mark S. Littman, editor. Bernan Press. • 1998. $89.00. Covers "social, economic, and environmental trends in the United States over the past 25 years." Includes statistical tables, graphs, and analysis relating to such topics as population, income, poverty, wealth, labor, housing, education, healthcare, air/water quality, and government.

OTHER SOURCES

Carroll's Defense Organization Charts. Carroll Publishing. • Quarterly. $1,470.00 per year. Provides more than 200 large, fold-out paper charts showing personnel relationships in 2,400 U. S. military offices. Charts are also available online and on CD-ROM.

Carroll's Federal Organization Charts. Carroll Publishing. • Quarterly. $950.00 per year. Provides 200 large, fold-out paper charts showing personnel relationships in 2,100 federal departments and agencies. Charts are also available online and on CD-ROM.

Federal Information Disclosure: Procedures, Forms and the Law. James T. O'Reilly. Shepard's. • 1977. $200.00. Second edition. Two volumes. Discusses legal aspects of getting information from the government.

Federal Trade Commission. Stephanie W. Kanwit. Shepard's. • 1979. $190.00. Two volumes. Discussion of regulations and procedures. (Regulatory Manual Series).

FedWorld: A Program of the United States Department of Commerce. National Technical Information Service. • Web site offers "a comprehensive central access point for searching, locating, ordering, and acquiring government and business information." Emphasis is on searching the Web pages, databases, and government reports of a wide variety of federal agencies. Fees: Free.

FirstGov: Your First Click to the U. S. Government. General Services Administration. • Free Web site provides extensive links to federal agencies covering a wide variety of topics, such as agriculture, business, consumer safety, education, the environment, government jobs, grants, health, social security, statistics sources, taxes, technology, travel, and world affairs. Also provides links to federal forms, including IRS tax forms. Searching is offered, both keyword and advanced.

Washington [year]. Columbia Books, Inc. • Annual. $129.00. Provides information on about 5,000 Washington, DC key businesses, government offices, non-profit organizations, and cultural institutions, with the names of about 25,000 principal executives. Includes Washington media, law offices, foundations, labor unions, international organizations, clubs, etc.

FEDERAL INSURANCE CONTRIBUTIONS ACT (FICA)

See: SOCIAL SECURITY

FEDERAL REGULATION

See: REGULATION OF INDUSTRY

FEDERAL RESERVE SYSTEM

See also: BANKS AND BANKING

GENERAL WORKS

Tight Money Timing: The Impact of Interest Rates and the Federal Reserve on the Stock Market. Wilfred R. George. Greenwood Publishing Group, Inc. • 1982. $55.00.

ABSTRACTS AND INDEXES

Banking Information Index. U M I Banking Information Index. • Monthly. Price on application. Covers a wide variety of banking, business, and financial subjects in periodicals. Formerly *Banking Literature Index.*

BIBLIOGRAPHIES

The FED in Print: Economics and Banking Topics. Federal Reserve Bank of Philadelphia. • Semiannual. Free. Business and banking topics.

Federal Reserve Board Publications. U.S. Board of Governors of the Federal Reserve System. • Semiannual. Free.

HANDBOOKS AND MANUALS

Federal Reserve Regulatory Service. U.S. Federal Reserve System, Board of Governors Publications Services Section, R. • Monthly. $200.00 per year. Looseleaf. Includes four handbooks updated monthly: *Consumer and Community Affairs, Monetary Policy and Reserve Requirements Securities, Credit Transactions and Payment Systems.* Irregular supplements.

Federal Reserve System: Purposes and Functions. U.S. Board of Governors of the Federal Reserve System. • Irregular.

INTERNET DATABASES

Fedstats. Federal Interagency Council on Statistical Policy. Phone: (202)395-7254 • URL: http://www.fedstats.gov • Web site features an efficient search facility for full-text statistics produced by more than 70 federal agencies, including the Census Bureau, the Bureau of Economic Analysis, and the Bureau of Labor Statistics. Boolean searches can be made within one agency or for all agencies combined. Links are offered to international statistical bureaus, including the UN, IMF, OECD, UNESCO, Eurostat, and 20 individual countries. Fees: Free.

ONLINE DATABASES

Banking Information Source. Bell & Howell Information and Learning. • Provides indexing and abstracting of periodical and other literature from 1982 to date, with weekly updates. Covers the financial services industry: banks, savings institutions, investment houses, credit unions, insurance companies, and real estate organizations. Emphasis is on marketing and management. Inquire as to online cost and availability. (Formerly *FINIS: Financial Industry Information Service.*).

DRI U.S. Central Database. Data Products Division. • Provides more than 23,000 business, financial, demographic, economic, foreign trade, and industry-related time series for the U.S. Includes national income, population, retail-wholesale trade, price indexes, labor data, housing, industrial production, banking, interest rates, money supply, etc. Time period is generally 1947 to date (some data back to 1929). Updating varies. Inquire as to online cost and availability.

PERIODICALS AND NEWSLETTERS

Central Banking: Policy, Markets, Supervision. Available from European Business Publications, Inc. • Quarterly. $350.00 per year, including annual *Central Banking Directory.* Published in England by Central Banking Publications. Reports and comments on the activities of central banks around the world. Also provides discussions of the International Monetary Fund (IMF), the Organization for Economic Cooperation and Development (OECD), the Bank for International Settlements (BIS), and the World Bank.

InvesTech Market Analyst: Technical and Monetary Investment Analysis. InvesTech Research. • Every three weeks. $190.00 per year. Newsletter. Provides interpretation of monetary statistics and Federal Reserve actions, especially as related to technical analysis of stock market price trends.

STATISTICS SOURCES

Business Indexes. Board of Governors of the Federal Reserve System. • Monthly.

Business Statistics of the United States. Courtenay M. Slater, editor. Bernan Associates. • 1999. $74.00. Fifth edition. Based on *Business Statistics*, formerly issue by the Bureau of Economic Analysis, U. S. Department of Commerce. Provides basic data for a wide variety of U. S. industries, services, and economic indicators. Most statistics are shown annually for 29 years and monthly for the most recent four years.

Consumer Installment Credit. Board of Governors. • Monthly. $5.00 per year.

Federal Reserve Bulletin. U.S. Federal Reserve System. • Monthly. $25.00 per year. Provides statistics on banking and the economy, including interest rates, money supply, and the Federal Reserve Board indexes of industrial production.

Survey of Current Business. Available from U. S. Government Printing Office. • Monthly. $49.00 per year. Issued by Bureau of Economic Analysis, U. S. Department of Commerce. Presents a wide variety of business and economic data.

FEDERAL STATISTICS

See: GOVERNMENT STATISTICS

FEED AND FEEDSTUFFS INDUSTRY

See also: CORN INDUSTRY; FARM PRODUCE

GENERAL WORKS

Feeds and Feeding. Arthur E. Cullison and Robert S. Lowrey. Prentice Hall. • 1998. $100.00. Fifth edition.

ABSTRACTS AND INDEXES

Field Crop Abstracts: Monthly Abstract Journal on World Annual Cereal, Legume, Root, Oilseed and Fibre Crops. Available from CABI Publishing North America. • Monthly. $1,465.00 per year. Published in England by CABI Publishing, formerly Commonwealth Agricultural Bureaux. Provides worldwide coverage of the literature.

Nutrition Abstracts and Reviews, Series B: Livestock Feeds and Feeding. Available from CABI Publishing North America. • Monthly. $930.00 per year. Published in England by CABI Publishing. Provides worldwide coverage of the literature.

CD-ROM DATABASES

AGRICOLA on SilverPlatter. Available from SilverPlatter Information, Inc. • Quarterly. $825.00 per year. Produced by the National Agricultural Library. Provides about three million citations on CD-ROM to the literature of agriculture, agricultural economics, animal sciences, entomology, fertilizer, food, forestry, nutrition, pesticides, plant science, water resources, and other topics. Each quarterly disc covers the past ten years, with archival discs available from 1970.

DIRECTORIES

Feed Industry Red Book: Reference Book and Buyer's Guide for the Manufacturing Industry. Moffat Publishing, Inc. • Annual. $40.00. List of over 200 firms involved in the large animal and pet food manufacturing and distribution business, including sources of feed ingredients and suppliers of feed materials handling equipment.

National Grain and Feed Association Directory. • Annual. Price on application.

ENCYCLOPEDIAS AND DICTIONARIES

Encyclopedia of Agriculture Science. Charles J. Arntzen and Ellen M. Ritter, editors. Academic Press, Inc. • 1994. $625.00. Four volumes.

FINANCIAL RATIOS

Annual Statement Studies. Robert Morris Associates: The Association of Lending and Credit Risk Professiona. • Annual. Free to members; non-members, $140.00. Median and quartile financial ratios are given for over 400 kinds of manufacturing, wholesale, retail, construction, and consumer finance establishments. Data is sorted by both asset size and sales volume. Includes a clearly written "Definition of Ratios" and an alphabetical industry index.

INTERNET DATABASES

USDA. United States Department of Agriculture. Phone: (202)720-2791 E-mail: agsec@usda.gov • URL: http://www.usda.gov • The USDA home page has six sections: News and Information; What's New; About USDA; Agencies; Opportunities; Search and Help. Keyword searching is offered from the USDA home page and from various individual agency home pages. Agencies are the Economic Research Service, Agricultural Marketing Service, National Agricultural Statistics Service, National Agricultural Library, and about 12 others. Updating varies. Fees: Free.

ONLINE DATABASES

Biological and Agricultural Index Online. H. W. Wilson Co. • Indexes a wide variety of agricultural and biological periodicals, 1983 to date. Monthly updates. Inquire as to online cost and availability.

CAB Abstracts. CAB International North America. • Contains 46 specialized abstract collections covering over 10,000 journals and monographs in the areas of agriculture, horticulture, forest products, farm products, nutrition, dairy science, poultry, grains, animal health, entomology, etc. Time period is 1972 to date, with monthly updates. Inquire as to online cost and availability. *CAB Abstracts on CD-ROM* also available, with annual updating.

PERIODICALS AND NEWSLETTERS

Feed and Feeding Digest. National Grain and Feed Association. • Monthly. Membership.

Feed Bulletin. Jacobsen Publishing Co. • Daily. $340.00 per year.

Grain and Feed Weekly Summary and Statistics. U.S. Dept. of Agriculture. Agricultural Marketing Service, Livestock and Seed Div. • Weekly. $85.00 per year. Formerly *Grain and Feed Market News.*

PRICE SOURCES

Feedstuffs: The Weekly Newspaper for Agribusiness. ABC, Inc. • Weekly. $109.00 per year.

RESEARCH CENTERS AND INSTITUTES

Food and Feed Grain Institute. Kansas State University. Waters Hall, Room 105, Manhattan, KS 66506-4030. Phone: (785)532-4057 Fax: (785)532-5861 E-mail: reb@ksu.edu • URL: http://www.ksu.edu.

Soil Testing Laboratory. University of Massachusetts at Amherst. West Experiment Station, Amherst, MA 01003-8020. Phone: (413)545-2311 Fax: (413)545-1931 • URL: http://www.umass.edu/t/soils/soiltest.

STATISTICS SOURCES

Agricultural Statistics. Available from U. S. Government Printing Office. • Annual. Produced by the National Agricultural Statistics Service, U. S. Department of Agriculture. Provides a wide variety of statistical data relating to agricultural production, supplies, consumption, prices/price-supports, foreign trade, costs, and returns, as well as farm labor, loans, income, and population. In many cases, historical data is shown annually for 10 years. In addition to farm data, includes detailed fishery statistics.

Annual Survey of Manufactures. Available from U. S. Government Printing Office. • Annual. Prices vary. Issued by the U. S. Census Bureau as an interim update to the *Census of Manufactures.* Includes data on number of manufacturing establishments in various industries, employment, labor costs, value of shipments, capital expenditures, inventories, energy costs, and assets. (See also Census Bureau home page, http://www.census.gov/.).

Foreign Agricultural Trade of the United States. Available from U. S. Government Printing Office. • Monthly. $50.00 per year. Issued by the Economic Research Service of the U. S. Department of Agriculture. Provides data on U. S. exports and imports of agricultural commodities.

World Agricultural Supply and Demand Estimates. Available from U. S. Government Printing Office. • Monthly. $38.00 per year. Issued by the Economics and Statistics Service and the Foreign Agricultural Service of the U. S. Department of Agriculture. Consists mainly of statistical data and tables.

TRADE/PROFESSIONAL ASSOCIATIONS

American Feed Industry Association. 1501 Wilson Blvd., Suite 1100, Arlington, VA 22209. Phone: (703)524-0810 Fax: (703)524-1921 E-mail: afia@afia.org • URL: http://www.feedsearch.com.

National Grain and Feed Association. 1201 New York Ave., N.W., Suite 830, Washington, DC 20005-3917. Phone: (202)289-0873 Fax: (202)289-5388 E-mail: ngfa@ngfa.org • URL: http://www.ngfa.org.

National Hay Association. 102 Treasury Island Causeway, Suite 201, Saint Petersburg, FL 33706. Phone: 800-707-0014 or (727)367-9702 Fax: (727)367-9608 E-mail: haynha@aol.com • URL: http://www.haynha.org.

U.S. Grains Council. 1400 K St., N.W., Suite 1200, Washington, DC 20005. Phone: (202)789-0789 Fax: (202)898-0522 E-mail: grains@grains.org • URL: http://www.grains.org.

FERTILIZER INDUSTRY

See also: AGRICULTURAL CHEMICALS; POTASH INDUSTRY

ALMANACS AND YEARBOOKS

Association of American Plant Food Control Officials Official Publication. Association of American Plant Food Control Officials, Inc. University of Kentucky. • Annual. $25.00.

CD-ROM DATABASES

AGRICOLA on SilverPlatter. Available from SilverPlatter Information, Inc. • Quarterly. $825.00 per year. Produced by the National Agricultural Library. Provides about three million citations on CD-ROM to the literature of agriculture, agricultural economics, animal sciences, entomology, fertilizer, food, forestry, nutrition, pesticides, plant science, water resources, and other topics. Each quarterly disc covers the past ten years, with archival discs available from 1970.

ENCYCLOPEDIAS AND DICTIONARIES

Encyclopedia of Agriculture Science. Charles J. Arntzen and Ellen M. Ritter, editors. Academic Press, Inc. • 1994. $625.00. Four volumes.

FINANCIAL RATIOS

Annual Statement Studies. Robert Morris Associates: The Association of Lending and Credit Risk Professiona. • Annual. Free to members; non-members, $140.00. Median and quartile financial ratios are given for over 400 kinds of manufacturing, wholesale, retail, construction, and consumer finance establishments. Data is sorted by both asset size and sales volume. Includes a clearly written "Definition of Ratios" and an alphabetical industry index.

INTERNET DATABASES

Fedstats. Federal Interagency Council on Statistical Policy. Phone: (202)395-7254 • URL: http://www.fedstats.gov • Web site features an efficient search facility for full-text statistics produced by more than 70 federal agencies, including the Census Bureau, the Bureau of Economic Analysis, and the Bureau of Labor Statistics. Boolean searches can be made within one agency or for all agencies combined. Links are offered to international statistical bureaus, including the UN, IMF, OECD, UNESCO, Eurostat, and 20 individual countries. Fees: Free.

USDA. United States Department of Agriculture. Phone: (202)720-2791 E-mail: agsec@usda.gov • URL: http://www.usda.gov • The USDA home page has six sections: News and Information; What's New; About USDA; Agencies; Opportunities; Search and Help. Keyword searching is offered from the USDA home page and from various individual agency home pages. Agencies are the Economic Research Service, Agricultural Marketing Service, National Agricultural Statistics Service, National Agricultural Library, and about 12 others. Updating varies. Fees: Free.

ONLINE DATABASES

CAB Abstracts. CAB International North America. • Contains 46 specialized abstract collections covering over 10,000 journals and monographs in the areas of agriculture, horticulture, forest products, farm products, nutrition, dairy science, poultry, grains, animal health, entomology, etc. Time period is 1972 to date, with monthly updates. Inquire as to online cost and availability. *CAB Abstracts on CD-ROM* also available, with annual updating.

DRI U.S. Central Database. Data Products Division. • Provides more than 23,000 business, financial, demographic, economic, foreign trade, and industry-related time series for the U.S. Includes national income, population, retail-wholesale trade, price indexes, labor data, housing, industrial production, banking, interest rates, money supply, etc. Time period is generally 1947 to date (some data back to 1929). Updating varies. Inquire as to online cost and availability.

PERIODICALS AND NEWSLETTERS

Ag Retailer Magazine. Doane Agricultural Service Co. • Nine times a year. Free. Published to meet the business needs of the retail fertilizer and agrichemical dealer industry.

Better Crops With Plant Food. Potash and Phosphate Institute. • Quarterly. $8.00.

Dealer and Applicator. Vance Publishing Corp. • Nine times a year. $35.00 per year. Formerly *Custom Applicator.*

Dealer Progress: How Smart Agribusiness is Growing. Clear Window, Inc. • Bimonthly. $40.00 per year. Published in association with the Fertilizer Institute. Includes information on fertilizers and agricultural chemicals, including farm pesticides. Formerly *Progress.*

Farm Chemicals. Meister Publishing Co. • Monthly. $47.00 per year.

PRICE SOURCES

The National Provisioner: Serving Meat, Poultry, and Seafood Processors. Stagnito Communications, Inc. • Monthly. Free to qualified personnel; others, $65.00 per year. Annual *Buyer's Guide* available. Meat, poultry and seafood newsletter.

Prices of Agricultural Products and Selected Inputs in Europe and North America. Economic Commission for Europe. United Nations Publications. • Annual.

RESEARCH CENTERS AND INSTITUTES

Agricultural Research Division. University of Nebraska - Lincoln. 207 Agricultural Hall, Lincoln, NE 68583-0704. Phone: (402)472-2045 Fax: (402)472-9071 E-mail: dnelson@.unl.edu • URL: http://ianrwww.unl.edu/ianr/ard/index.htm.

California Agricultural Experiment Station. University of California at Berkeley. 1111 Franklin St., 6th Fl., Oakland, CA 94607-5200. Phone: (510)987-0060 Fax: (510)451-2317 E-mail: wr.gomes@ucop.edu • URL: http://www.ucop.edu/anrhome/danr.html.

International Fertilizer Development Center. P.O. Box 2040, Muscle Shoals, AL 35662. Phone: (205)381-6600 Fax: (205)381-7408 E-mail: general@ifdc.org • URL: http://www.ifdc.org • Conducts research relating to all aspects of fertilizer production, marketing, and use. Supported by the United Nations, the World Bank, and other international agencies.

Sulphur Institute. 1140 Connecticut Ave., N.W., Suite. 612, Washington, DC 20036. Phone: (202)331-9660 Fax: (202)293-2940 E-mail: sulphur@sulphurinstitute.org • URL: http://www.sulphurinstitute.org.

Tennessee Agricultural Experiment Station. University of Tennessee, Knoxville. P.O. Box 1071, Knoxville, TN 37901-1071. Phone: (865)974-7121 Fax: (865)974-6479 E-mail: drichard@utk.edu • URL: http://www.funnelweb.utcc.utk.edu/~taescomm/default.html.

STATISTICS SOURCES

Agricultural Statistics. Available from U. S. Government Printing Office. • Annual. Produced by the National Agricultural Statistics Service, U. S. Department of Agriculture. Provides a wide variety of statistical data relating to agricultural production, supplies, consumption, prices/price-supports, foreign trade, costs, and returns, as well as farm labor, loans, income, and population. In many cases, historical data is shown annually for 10 years. In addition to farm data, includes detailed fishery statistics.

Annual Survey of Manufactures. Available from U. S. Government Printing Office. • Annual. Prices vary. Issued by the U. S. Census Bureau as an interim update to the *Census of Manufactures.* Includes data on number of manufacturing establishments in various industries, employment, labor costs, value of shipments, capital expenditures, inventories, energy costs, and assets. (See also Census Bureau home page, http://www.census.gov/.).

Business Statistics of the United States. Courtenay M. Slater, editor. Bernan Associates. • 1999. $74.00. Fifth edition. Based on *Business Statistics*, formerly issue by the Bureau of Economic Analysis, U. S. Department of Commerce. Provides basic data for a wide variety of U. S. industries, services, and economic indicators. Most statistics are shown annually for 29 years and monthly for the most recent four years.

FAO Fertilizer Yearbook. United Nations Food and Agriculture Organization. Bernan Associates. • Annual. $36.00. Text in English, French, and Spanish. Formerly *Annual Fertilizer Review.*

Fertilizer Facts and Figures. Fertilizer Institute. • Annual. Price on application.

Manufacturing Profiles. Available from U. S. Government Printing Office. • Annual. Issued by the U. S. Census Bureau. A printed consolidation of the entire *Current Industrial Report* series, presenting "all the data compiled." Contains statistics on production, shipments, inventories, consumption, exports, imports, and orders for a wide variety of manufactured products. (See also Census Bureau home page, http://www.census.gov/.).

Survey of Current Business. Available from U. S. Government Printing Office. • Monthly. $49.00 per year. Issued by Bureau of Economic Analysis, U. S. Department of Commerce. Presents a wide variety of business and economic data.

TRADE/PROFESSIONAL ASSOCIATIONS

Agricultural Retailers Association. 11701 Borman Dr., Suite 110, Saint Louis, MO 63146. Phone: 800-844-4900 or (314)567-6655 Fax: (314)567-6808 E-mail: ara@agretailerassn.org • URL: http://www.agretailerassn.org.

Association of American Plant Food Control Officials. University of Kentucky, Division of Regulatory Services, 103 Regional Services Bldg., Lexington, KY 40546-0275. Phone: (606)257-2668 or (606)257-2970 Fax: (606)257-7351 E-mail: dterry@ca.uky.edu • URL: http://www.uky.edu/agriculture/regulatoryservices/aapfco/htm.

Fertilizer Industry Round Table. 1914 Baldwin Mill Rd., Forest Hill, MD 21050. Phone: (410)557-8026 Fax: (410)592-5796.

The Fertilizer Institute. 501 Second St., N.E., Washington, DC 20002. Phone: (202)675-8250 Fax: (202)544-8123 • URL: http://www.tfi.org.

OTHER SOURCES

Major Chemical and Petrochemical Companies of the World. Available from The Gale Group. • 2001. $855.00. Third edition. Two volumes. Published by Graham & Whiteside. Contains profiles of more than 7,000 important chemical and petrochemical companies in various countries. Subject areas include general chemicals, specialty chemicals, agricultural chemicals, petrochemicals, industrial gases, and fertilizers.

FESTIVALS

See: ANNIVERSARIES AND HOLIDAYS; FAIRS

FIBER INDUSTRY

See also: COTTON INDUSTRY; JUTE INDUSTRY; SYNTHETIC TEXTILE FIBER INDUSTRY; WOOL AND WORSTED INDUSTRY

ABSTRACTS AND INDEXES

NTIS Alerts: Materials Sciences. National Technical Information Service. • Semimonthly. $220.00 per year. Provides descriptions of government-sponsored research reports and software, with ordering information. Covers ceramics, glass, coatings, composite materials, alloys, plastics, wood, paper, adhesives, fibers, lubricants, and related subjects. Formerly *Abstract Newsletter.*

Textile Technology Digest. Institute of Textile Technology. • Monthly. $535.00 per year. Provides indexing and abstracting of a wide variety of textile technology literature.

CD-ROM DATABASES

Textile Technology Digest [CD-ROM]. Textile Information Center, Institute of Textile Technology. • Quarterly. $1,700.00 per year. Provides CD-ROM indexing and abstracting of worldwide journals and monographs in various areas of textile technology, production, and management. Covers 1978 to date.

DIRECTORIES

America's Textiles International-Buyer's Guide. Billian Publishing, Inc. • Annual. $25.00. List of 2,800 suppliers for the textile industry.

Materials Research Centres: A World Directory of Organizations and Programmes in Materials Science. Allyn and Bacon/Longman. • 1991. $475.00. Fourth edition. Profiles of research centers in 75 countries. Materials include plastics, metals, fibers, etc.

ENCYCLOPEDIAS AND DICTIONARIES

Encyclopedia of Textiles. French and European Publications, Inc. • 1980. $39.95. Third edition.

Textile Terms and Definitions. J.E. McIntyre and Paul N. Daniels, editors. Available from State Mutual Book and Periodical Service Ltd., Trade Order Dept. • 1995. $110.00. 10th edition. Published by the Textile Insitute (UK). Includes more than 1,000 definitions of textile processes, fiber types, and end products. Illustrated.

ONLINE DATABASES

Textile Technology Digest [online]. Textile Information Center, Institute of Textile Technology. • Contains indexing and abstracting of more than 300 worldwide journals and monographs in various areas of textile technology, production, and management. Time period is 1978 to date, with monthly updating. Inquire as to online cost and availability.

World Textiles. Elsevier Science, Inc. • Provides abstracting and indexing from 1970 of worldwide textile literature (periodicals, books, pamphlets, and reports). Includes U. S., European, and British patent information. Updating is monthly. Inquire as to online cost and availability.

PERIODICALS AND NEWSLETTERS

Fiber Organon: Featuring Manufactured Fibers. Fiber Economics Bureau, Inc. • Monthly. $300.00 per year. Formerly *Textile Organon.*

Fibre Market News. Group Interest Enterprises. G.I.E., Inc., Publishers. • Bimonthly. $145.00 per year. Newsletter. Serves dealers, brokers and consumers of paper stock and all secondary fibers.

RESEARCH CENTERS AND INSTITUTES

Herty Research and Development Center. P.O. Box 7798, Savannah, GA 31418-7798. Phone: (912)963-2600 Fax: (912)963-2614 E-mail: hertyfound@aol.com • URL: http://www.members.aol.com/hertyfound/herty.html.

Institute of Textile Technology. 2551 Ivy Rd., Charlottesville, VA 22903-4614. Phone: (804)296-5511 Fax: (804)296-2957 E-mail: library@itt.edu • URL: http://www.itt.edu.

Texas Agricultural Market Research Center. Texas A & M University. Dept. of Agricultural Economics, College Station, TX 77843-2124. Phone: (979)845-5911 Fax: (979)845-6378 E-mail: tamrc@tamu.edu.

Textiles and Materials. Philadelphia University, Schoolhouse Lane and Henry Ave., Philadelphia, PA 19144. Phone: (215)951-2751 Fax: (215)951-2651 E-mail: brooksteind@philaau.edu • URL: http://www.philaau.edu • Many research areas, including industrial and nonwoven textiles.

STATISTICS SOURCES

Consumption on the Woolen System and Worsted Combing. U. S. Bureau of the Census. • Quarterly and annual. Provides data on consumption of fibers in woolen and worsted spinning mills, by class of fibers and end use. (Current Industrial Reports, MQ-22D.).

TRADE/PROFESSIONAL ASSOCIATIONS

American Fiber Manufacturers Association. 1150 17th St., N.W., Suite 310, Washington, DC 20036. Phone: (202)296-6508 Fax: (202)296-3052 • URL: http://www.fibersource.com.

Fiber Society. Clemson University, School of Textiles Fiber and Polymer Science, 161 Sirrine Hall, Clemson, SC 29634-1307. Phone: (864)656-5957 or (864)656-3176 Fax: (864)656-5973 E-mail: gbhuven@clemson.edu • URL: http://www.fibersoc.tfe.gatech.edu/.

Hard Fibres Association. c/o Metcalf Agency, P.O. Box 250, Skaneateles, NY 13152. Phone: (315)685-5088 Fax: (315)685-5077 E-mail: pfmetcalf@aol.com.

Textile Fibers and By-Products Association. P.O. 550326, Atlanta, GA 30355. Phone: (404)262-2477 Fax: (404)261-0628.

Textile Institute. Saint James Bldgs., 4th Fl., Oxford St., Manchester M1 6FQ, England. Phone: 44 161 2371188 Fax: 44 161 2361991 E-mail: tiihq@textileinst.org.uk • URL: http://www.texi.org • Members in 100 countries involved with textile industry management, marketing, science, and technology.

OTHER SOURCES

Textile Business Outlook. Statistikon Corp. • Quarterly. $985.00 per year. Analyzes current business, marketing, and financial conditions for the worldwide textile industry (fibers and fabrics). Includes statistical forecasts.

FIBER OPTICS INDUSTRY

GENERAL WORKS

Fiber Optic Systems: An Introduction and Business Overview. Terry Edwards. John Wiley and Sons, Inc. • 1989. $160.00.

Fundamentals of Optical Fibers. John A. Buck. John Wiley and Sons, Inc. • 1995. $84.95. (Pure and Applied Optics Series).

Future Trends in Telecommunications. R. J. Horrocks and R.W. Scarr. John Wiley and Sons, Inc. • 1993. $235.00. Includes fiber optics technology, local area networks, and satellite communications. Discusses the future of telecommunications for the consumer and for industry. *Communication and Distributed Systems Series.*

Introduction to Glass Science and Technology. J. E. Shelby. American Chemical Society. • 1997. $40.00. Covers the basics of glass manufacture, including the physical, optical, electrical, chemical, and mechanical properties of glass. (RCS Paperback Series).

ABSTRACTS AND INDEXES

Applied Science and Technology Index. H. W. Wilson Co. • 11 times a year. Quarterly and annual cumulations. Service basis for print edition; CD-ROM edition, $1,495.00 per year. Indexes a wide variety of English language technical, industrial, and engineering periodicals.

CA Selects: Fiber Optics and Optical Communication. Chemical Abstracts Service. • Semiweekly. $275.00 per year.

Key Abstracts: Optoelectronics. Available from INSPEC, Inc. • Monthly. $240.00 per year. Provides international coverage of journal and proceedings literature relating to fiber optics, lasers, and optoelectronics in general. Published in England by the Institution of Electrical Engineers (IEE).

BIBLIOGRAPHIES

Encyclopedia of Physical Science and Engineering Information. The Gale Group. • 1996. $160.00. Second edition. Includes print, electronic, and other information sources for a wide range of scientific, technical, and engineering topics.

CD-ROM DATABASES

COMPENDEX PLUS [CD-ROM]. Engineering Information, Inc. • Quarterly. $3,450.00 per year. Provides CD-ROM indexing and abstracting of the world's engineering and technical information appearing in journals, reports, books, and proceedings, 1985 to date.

Science Citation Index: Compact Disc Edition. Institute for Scientific Information. • Quarterly. Provides CD-ROM indexing of the world's scientific and technical literature. Corresponds to online *Scisearch* and printed *Science Citation Index.*

WILSONDISC: Applied Science and Technology Abstracts. H. W. Wilson Co. • Monthly. $1,495.00 per year, including unlimited access to the online version of *Applied Science and Technology Abstracts* through WILSONLINE. Provides CD-ROM indexing and abstracting of 400 prominent scientific, technical, engineering, and industrial periodicals. Indexing coverage is provided from 1983 to date and abstracting from 1993 to date.

DIRECTORIES

Fiberoptic Product News Buying Guide. Cahners Business Information, New Product Information. • Annual. $55.00. Lists over 500 manufacturers and suppliers of fiber optics products, equipment and services.

International Fiber Optics Yellow Pages. Information Gatekeepers, Inc. • Annual. $89.95. Includes manufacturers of fiber optics products. Provides a glossary and a discussion of current uses of fiber optics. Formerly *Fiber Optics Yellow Pages.*

Laser Focus World Buyers' Guide. PennWell Corp., Advanced Technology Div. • Annual. $125.00. Lists more than 2,000 suppliers of optoelectronic and laser products and services.

Lightwave Buyers Guide. PennWell Corp., Advanced Technology Div. • Annual. $68.00. Lists manufacturers and distributors of fiberoptic systems and components.

ENCYCLOPEDIAS AND DICTIONARIES

Encyclopedia of Materials: Science and Technology. K.H.J. Buschow and others, editors. Pergamon Press/Elsevier Science. • 2001. $6,875.00. Eleven volumes. Provides extensive technical information on a wide variety of materials, including metals, ceramics, plastics, optical materials, and building materials. Includes more than 2,000 articles and 5,000 illustrations.

HANDBOOKS AND MANUALS

Fiber Optic Communications Handbook. McGraw-Hill Professional. • 1990. $89.50. Second edition.

Handbook of Fiber Optics: Theory and Applications. Chai Yeh. Academic Press, Inc. • 1990. $116.00.

Optical Fibre Sensor Technology. Ken Grattan and Beverley Meggitt. Chapman and Hall. • 1999. Price on application.

ONLINE DATABASES

Applied Science and Technology Index Online. H. W. Wilson Co. • Provides online indexing of 400 major scientific, technical, industrial, and engineering periodicals. Time period is 1983 to date. Monthly updates. Inquire as to online cost and availability.

F & S Index. The Gale Group. • Contains about four million citations to worldwide business, financial, and industrial or consumer product literature appearing from 1972 to date. Weekly updates. Inquire as to online cost and availability.

Globalbase. The Gale Group. • Provides more than one million online summaries of business, industrial, and economic news reports from more than 1,000 publications worldwide. Covers a wide range of material appearing in international trade journals, professional magazines, and newspapers. Time period is 1984 to date, with weekly updates. Inquire as to online cost and availability.

PROMT: Predicasts Overview of Markets and Technology. The Gale Group. • Companies, products, applied technologies and markets. U.S. and international literature coverage, 1972 to date. Inquire as to online cost and availability. Provides abstracts from more than 1,600 publications. Weekly updates.

Scisearch. Institute for Scientific Information. • Broad, multidisciplinary index to the literature of science and technology, 1974 to present. Inquire as to online cost and availability. Coverage of literature is worldwide, with weekly updates.

PERIODICALS AND NEWSLETTERS

Fiber Optics and Communications. Information Gatekeepers, Inc. • Monthly. $675.00. Emphasis on the use of fiber optics in telecommunications.

Fiber Optics News. Phillips Business Information, Inc. • Weekly. $697.00 per year. Newsletter.

Fiberoptic Product News. Cahners Business Information New Product Information. • 13 times a year. $119.00 per year. Provides general coverage of the fiber optics industry, for both producers and users.

Laser Focus World: The World of Optoelectronics. PennWell Corp., Advanced Technology Div. • Monthly. $156.00 per year. Covers business and technical aspects of electro-optics, including lasers and fiberoptics. Includes *Buyer's Guide.*

Lightwave: Fiber Optics Technology and Applications Worldwide. PennWell Corp., Advaned Technology Div. • Monthly. $79.00 per year.

Optical Fiber Technology: Materials, Devices, and Systems. Academic Press, Inc., Journal Div. • Quarterly. $230.00 per year.

Optics and Photonics News. Optical Society of America, Inc. • Monthly. $99.00 per year.

RESEARCH CENTERS AND INSTITUTES

Edward L. Ginzton Laboratory. Stanford University, 450 Via Palou, Stanford, CA 94305-4085. Phone: (650)023-0111 Fax: (650)725-9355 E-mail: dabm@ee.stanford.edu • URL: http://www.stanford.edu/group/ginzton • Research fields include low-temperature physics and superconducting electronics.

Fiber and Electro Optics Research Center. Virginia Polytechnic Institute and State University, Dept. of Electrical Engineering, 106 Plantation Rd., Blacksburg, VA 24061. Phone: (540)231-7203 Fax: (540)231-4561 E-mail: roclaus@vt.edu.

Fiberoptic Materials Research Program. 607 Taylor Rd., College of Engineering, P.O. Box 909, Piscataway, NJ 08854-8065. Phone: (732)445-4729 Fax: (908)445-4545 E-mail: sigel@alumnia.rutgers.edu • Research fields include the communications and biomedical applications of fiber optics.

Laboratory for Information and Decision Systems. Massachusetts Institute of Technology, Bldg. 35, Room 308, Cambridge, MA 02139-4307. Phone: (617)253-2141 Fax: (617)253-3578 E-mail: chan@mit.edu • URL: http://www.justice.mit.edu • Research areas include data communication networks and fiber optic networks.

STATISTICS SOURCES

U. S. Industry and Trade Outlook: The McGraw-Hill Companies and the U.S. Department of Commerce/International Trade Administration. Datapso Research Corp. • Annual. $69.95. Produced by the International Trade Administration, U. S. Department of Commerce, in a "public-private" partnership with DRI/McGraw-Hill and Standard & Poor's. Provides basic data, outlook for the current year, and "Long-Term Prospects" (five-year projections) for a wide variety of products and services. Includes high technology industries. Formerly *U. S. Industrial Outlook.*

TRADE/PROFESSIONAL ASSOCIATIONS

IEEE Lasers and Electro-Optics Society. Institute of Electrical and Electronics Engineers, P.O. Box 1331, Piscataway, NJ 08855-1331. Phone: (732)981-0060 Fax: (732)981-1721 E-mail: g.walters@ieee.org • URL: http://www.ieee.org/leos • A society of the Institute of Electrical and Electronics Engineers. Fields of interest include lasers, fiber optics, optoelectronics, and photonics.

Optical Society of America. 2010 Massachusetts Ave., N.W., Washington, DC 20036-1023. Phone: (202)223-8130 Fax: (202)223-1096 • URL: http://www.osa.org.

SPIE-The International Society for Optical Engineering. P.O. Box 10, Bellingham, WA 98227-0010. Phone: (360)676-3290 Fax: (360)647-1445 E-mail: spie@spie.org • URL: http://www.spie.org.

OTHER SOURCES

Fiber Systems International. Available from IOP Publishing, Inc. • Monthly. Controlled circulation. Published in the UK by the Institute of Physics. "Covering the optical communications marketplace within the Americas and Asia." *Fibre Systems Europe* is also available, covering the business and marketing aspects of fiber optics communications in Europe.

FICTION, BUSINESS

See: BUSINESS IN FICTION

FILES AND FILING (DOCUMENTS)

See also: LIBRARY MANAGEMENT; OFFICE MANAGEMENT; OFFICE PRACTICE

GENERAL WORKS

Filing and Records Management. Nathan Krevolin. Prentice Hall. • 1986. $25.95.

CD-ROM DATABASES

LISA Plus: Library and Information Science Abstracts. Bowker-Saur, Reed Reference Publishing. • Quarterly. $1,450.00 per year. Provides CD-ROM abstracting and indexing of the world's library and information science literature. Covers a wide variety of topics.

ONLINE DATABASES

LISA Online: Library and Information Science Abstracts. Bowker-Saur, Reed Reference Publishing. • Provides abstracting and indexing of the world's library and information science literature from 1969 to the present. Covers a wide variety of topics in over 550 journals from 60 countries, with biweekly updates. Inquire as to online cost and availability.

TRADE/PROFESSIONAL ASSOCIATIONS

National Association of Professional Organizers. 1033 La Posada Drive, Suite 220, Austin, TX 78752. Phone: (512)454-8626 Fax: (512)454-3036 E-mail: napo@assnmgmt.com • URL: http://www.napo.net • Members are concerned with time management, productivity, and the efficient organization of documents and activities.

FILMS, MOTION PICTURE

See: MOTION PICTURE INDUSTRY

FILMSTRIPS

See: AUDIOVISUAL AIDS IN EDUCATION; AUDIOVISUAL AIDS IN INDUSTRY

FILTER INDUSTRY

ABSTRACTS AND INDEXES

Applied Science and Technology Index. H. W. Wilson Co. • 11 times a year. Quarterly and annual cumulations. Service basis for print edition; CD-ROM edition, $1,495.00 per year. Indexes a wide variety of English language technical, industrial, and engineering periodicals.

Current Contents: Engineering, Computing and Technology. Institute for Scientific Information. • Weekly. $730.00 per year. Reproductions of contents pages of technical journals. Includes *Author Index, Address Directory, Current Book Contents* and *Title Word Index.* Formerly *Current Contents: Engineering, Technology and Applied Sciences.*

DIRECTORIES

Macrae's Blue Book: Serving the Original Equipment Market. MacRae's Blue Book, Inc. • Annual. $170.00. Two volumes. Lists about 50,000 manufacturers of a wide variety of industrial equipment and supplies.

Thomas Register of American Manufacturers and Thomas Register Catalog File. Thomas Publishing Co., Inc. • Annual. $149.00. 34 volumes. A three-part system offering information on a wide variety of industrial equipment and supplies.

HANDBOOKS AND MANUALS

Filters and Filtration Handbook. T. Christopher Dickenson. Elsevier Science. • 1997. $243.00. Fourth edition.

ONLINE DATABASES

Applied Science and Technology Index Online. H. W. Wilson Co. • Provides online indexing of 400 major scientific, technical, industrial, and engineering periodicals. Time period is 1983 to date. Monthly updates. Inquire as to online cost and availability.

PROMT: Predicasts Overview of Markets and Technology. The Gale Group. • Companies, products, applied technologies and markets. U.S. and international literature coverage, 1972 to date. Inquire as to online cost and availability. Provides abstracts from more than 1,600 publications. Weekly updates.

Thomas Register Online. Thomas Publishing Co., Inc. • Provides concise information on approximately 194,000 U. S. companies, mainly manufacturers, with over 50,000 product classifications. Indexes over 115,000 trade names. Information is updated semiannually. Inquire as to online cost and availability.

PERIODICALS AND NEWSLETTERS

Fabric Filter. McIlvaine Co. • Monthly. $635.00 per year. Newsletter. Subscription includes "Knowledge Network": manual, catalog, video tapes, reprints, and other information sources relating to dry filter products and applications in various industries.

Filtration News. Eagle Publications, Inc. • Bimonthly. Controlled circulation. Emphasis is on new filtration products for industrial use.

Industrial Equipment News. Thomas Publishing Co. • Monthly. $95.00 per year. Free. What's new in equipment, parts and materials.

Liquid Filtration. McIlvaine Co. • Monthly. $635.00 per year. Newsletter. Subscription includes "Knowledge Network": manual, catalog, video tapes, reprints, and other information sources relating to the filtration of liquids.

New Equipment Digest Market. Penton Media Inc. • Monthly. Free to qualified personnel; others, $55.00 per year. Formerly *Material Handling Engineering.*

New Equipment Reporter: New Products Industrial News. De Roche Publications. • Monthly. Controlled circulation.

Processing. Putman Media. • 14 times a year. $54.00 per year. Emphasis is on descriptions of new products for all areas of industrial processing, including valves, controls, filters, pumps, compressors, fluidics, and instrumentation.

TRADE/PROFESSIONAL ASSOCIATIONS

Filter Manufacturers Council. P.O. Box 13966, Research Triangle Park, NC 27709-3966. Phone: 800-993-4583 or (919)549-4800 Fax: (919)549-4824 E-mail: bhazelett@mema.org • URL: http://www.filtercouncil.org.

OTHER SOURCES

Biotechnology Instrumentation Markets. Theta Reports/PJB Medical Publications, Inc. • 1999. $1,495.00. Contains market research data, with projections through the year 2002. Covers such products as specialized analytical instruments, filters/membranes, and mass spectrometers. (Theta Report No. 960.).

FINANCE

See also: ACCOUNTING; BUSINESS; COMPUTERS IN FINANCE; CORPORATE FINANCE; COUNTY FINANCE; FINANCIAL MANAGEMENT; INTERNATIONAL FINANCE; INVESTMENTS; MUNICIPAL FINANCE

GENERAL WORKS

Accounting and Finance for Non-Specialists. Peter Atrill and Eddie McLaney. Prentice Hall. • 2000. Third edition. Price on application. Includes the measurement and reporting of financial performance and cash flow.

Case Studies in Finance: Managing for Corporate Value Creation. Robert Bruner. McGraw-Hill Professional. • 1998. Third edition. Price on application.

Essentials of Managerial Finance. J. Fred Weston. Harcourt College Publishers. • 1999. $44.50. 12th edition.

Finance for the Nonfinancial Manager. Herbert T. Spiro. John Wiley and Sons, Inc. • 1996. $39.95. Fourth edition.

Financial Institutions, Markets and Money. David S. Kidwell and others. Dryden Press. • 1993. $56.00. Fifth edition.

Money, Banking, and Financial Markets. Lloyd Thomas. McGraw-Hill. • 1996. $82.50.

Winning Numbers: How to Use Business Facts and Figures to Make Your Point and Get Ahead. Michael C. Thomsett. AMACOM. • 1990. $22.95. A short course in financial communication, or finance for the nonfinancial manager.

ABSTRACTS AND INDEXES

Banking Information Index. U M I Banking Information Index. • Monthly. Price on application. Covers a wide variety of banking, business, and financial subjects in periodicals. Formerly *Banking Literature Index.*

Business Periodicals Index. H. W. Wilson Co. • Monthly, except August, with quarterly and annual cumulations. Service basis for print edition; CD-ROM edition, $1,495.00 per year.

Investment Statistics Locator. Linda H. Bentley and Jennifer J. Kiesl, editors. Oryx Press. • 1994. $69.95. Expanded revised edition. Provides detailed subject indexing of more than 50 of the most-used sources of financial and investment data. Includes an annotated bibliography.

NTIS Alerts: Business & Economics. National Technical Information Service.

BIBLIOGRAPHIES

Business Information Sources. Lorna M. Daniells. California Princeton Fulfillment Services. • 1993. $42.50. Third revised edition. Basic business sources, with discussion and full annotations.

Business Library Review: An International Journal. International Publishers Distributor. • Quarterly. Academic institutions, $318.00 per year;corporations, $501.00 per year.Incorporates *The Wall Street Review of Books* and *Economics and Business: An Annotated Bibliography.* Publishes scholarly reviews of books on a wide variety of topics in business, economics, and finance. Text in French.

Information Sources in Finance and Banking. R. G. Lester, editor. Bowker-Saur. • 1995. $125.00. Published by K. G. Saur. International coverage.

BIOGRAPHICAL SOURCES

Who's Who in Finance and Industry. Marquis Who's Who. • Biennial. $295.00. Provides over 22,400 concise biographies of business leaders in all fields.

CD-ROM DATABASES

Business Source Plus. EBSCO Information Services. • Monthly. $1,495.00 per year. Provides CD-ROM citations and abstracts to articles in about 650 business periodicals and newspapers, including *The Wall Street Journal.* Full text is provided from 200 selected periodicals. Covers accounting, communications, economics, finance, management, marketing, and other business subjects.

Social Sciences Citation Index: Compact Disc Edition with Abstracts. Institute for Scientific Information. • Quarterly. Provides CD-ROM indexing and abstracting of "significant articles" from 1,400 social science journals worldwide, with additional selections from 3,200 other journals, 1986 to date. Includes economics, business, finance, management, communications, demographics, information and library science, political science, sociology, and many other subjects.

WILSONDISC: Wilson Business Abstracts. H. W. Wilson Co. • Monthly. $2,495.00 per year, including unlimited online access to *Wilson Business Abstracts* through WILSONLINE. Provides CD-ROM "cover-to-cover" abstracting and indexing of over 600 prominent business periodicals. Indexing is from 1982, abstracting from 1990. (*Business Periodicals Index* without abstracts is available on CD-ROM at $1,495 per year.).

DIRECTORIES

Internet Tools of the Profession: A Guide for Information Professionals. Hope N. Tillman, editor. Special Libraries Association. • 1997. $49.00. Second edition. Consists of 14 sections by various authors or compilers. After two introductory articles on searching the Internet, there are 12 annotated lists of useful Web sites, covering the SLA, business and finance, chemistry, education, food and agriculture, information technology, insurance and employee benefits, law, library management, metals and materials, pharmaceuticals, and telecommunications. An index is provided.

Plunkett's On-Line Trading, Finance, and Investment Web Sites Almanac. Plunkett Research, Ltd. • Annual. $149.99. Provides profiles and usefulness rankings of financial Web sites. Sites are rated from 1 to 5 for specific uses. Includes diskette.

ENCYCLOPEDIAS AND DICTIONARIES

The A-Z Vocabulary for Investors. American Institute for Economic Research. • 1997. $7.00. Second half of book is a "General Glossary" of about 400 financial terms "most-commonly used" in investing. First half contains lengthier descriptions of types of banking institutions (commercial banks, thrift institutions, credit unions), followed by succinct explanations of various forms of investment: stocks, bonds, options, futures, commodities, and "Other Investments" (collectibles, currencies, mortgages, precious metals, real estate, charitable trusts). (Economic Education Bulletin.).

Blackwell Encyclopedic Dictionary of Finance. Dean Paxson and Douglas Wood, editors. Blackwell Publishers. • 1997. $110.00. The editors are associated with the University of Manchester. Contains definitions of key terms combined with longer articles written by various U. S. and foreign business educators. Includes bibliographies and index. (Blackwell Encyclopedia of Management Series).

Dictionary of Finance and Investment Terms. John Downes and Jordan E. Goodman. Barron's Educational Series, Inc. • 1998. $12.95. Fifth revised edition. Provides clear explanations of more than 5,000 business, banking, financial, investment, and tax terms. Includes a separate list of financial abbreviations and acronyms.

Encyclopedia of Banking and Finance. Charles J. Woelfel. McGraw-Hill Professional. • 1996. $50.00. 10th revised edition.

Encyclopedia of Business. The Gale Group. • 2000. $425.00. Second edition. Two volumes. Contains more than 700 signed articles covering major business disciplines and concepts. International in scope.

Encyclopedia of Business and Finance. Burton Kaliski, editor. Available from The Gale Group. • 2001. $240.00. Two volumes. Published by Macmillan Reference USA. Contains articles by various contributors on accounting, business administration, banking, finance, management information systems, and marketing.

International Dictionary of Accounting Acronyms. Thomas W. Morris, editor. Fitzroy Dearborn Publishers. • 1999. $45.00. Defines 2,000 acronyms used in worldwide accounting and finance.

Knowledge Exchange Business Encyclopedia: Your Complete Business Advisor. Lorraine Spurge, editor. Knowledge Exchange LLC. • 1997. $45.00. Provides definitions of business terms and financial expressions, profiles of leading industries, tables of economic statistics, biographies of business leaders, and other business information. Includes "A Chronology of Business from 3000 B.C. Through 1995." Contains illustrations and three indexes.

The New Palgrave Dictionary of Money and Finance. Peter Newman and others, editors. Groves Dictionaries. • 1998. $550.00. Three volumes. Consists of signed essays on over 1,000 financial topics, each with a bibliography. Covers a wide variety of financial, monetary, and investment areas. A detailed subject index is provided.

FINANCIAL RATIOS

Major Financial Institutions of the World. Available from The Gale Group. • 2001. $855.00. Fourth edition. Two volumes. Published by Graham & Whiteside. Contains detailed information on more than 7,500 important financial institutions in various countries. Includes banks, investment companies, and insurance companies.

Resumes for Banking and Financial Careers, With Sample Cover Letters. NTC/Contemporary Publishing Group. • 2001. $10.95. Second edition. Contains 100 sample resumes and 20 cover letters. (VGM Professional Resumes Series.).

HANDBOOKS AND MANUALS

Where to Go When the Bank Says No: Alternatives to Financing Your Business. David R. Evanson. Bloomberg Press. • 1998. $24.95. Emphasis is on obtaining business financing in the $250,000 to $15,000,000 range. Business plans are discussed. (Bloomberg Small Business Series).

INTERNET DATABASES

BanxQuote Banking, Mortgage, and Finance Center. BanxQuote, Inc. Phone: 800-765-3000 or (212)643-8000 Fax: (212)643-0020 E-mail: info@banx.com • URL: http://www.banx.com • Web site quotes interest rates paid by banks around the country on various savings products, as well as rates paid by consumers for automobile loans, mortgages, credit cards, home equity loans, and personal loans. Also provided: stock quotes, indexes, stock options, futures trading data, economic indicators, and links to many other financial sites. Daily updates. Fees: Free.

Business Week Online. McGraw-Hill. Phone: (212)512-2762 Fax: (212)512-6590 • URL: http://www.businessweek.com • Web site provides complete contents of current issue of *Business Week* plus "BW Daily" with additonal business news, financial market quotes, and corporate information from Standard & Poor's. Includes various features, such as "Banking Center" with mortgage and interest data, and "Interactive Computer Buying Guide." The "Business Week Archive" is fully searchable back to 1991. Fees: Mostly free, but full-text archive articles are $2.00 each.

EBSCO Information Services. Ebsco Publishing. Phone: 800-871-8508 or (508)356-6500 Fax: (508)356-5640 E-mail: ep@epnet.com • URL: http://www.epnet.com • Fee-based Web site providing Internet access to a wide variety of databases, including business-related material. Full text is available for many periodical titles, with daily updates. Fees: Apply.

Fedstats. Federal Interagency Council on Statistical Policy. Phone: (202)395-7254 • URL: http://www.fedstats.gov • Web site features an efficient search facility for full-text statistics produced by more than 70 federal agencies, including the Census Bureau, the Bureau of Economic Analysis, and the Bureau of Labor Statistics. Boolean searches can be made within one agency or for all agencies combined. Links are offered to international statistical bureaus, including the UN, IMF, OECD, UNESCO, Eurostat, and 20 individual countries. Fees: Free.

The Financial Post (Web site). National Post Online (Hollinger/CanWest). Phone: (244)383-2300 Fax: (416)383-2443 • URL: http://www.nationalpost.com/financialpost/ • Provides a broad range of Canadian business news online, with daily updates. Includes news, opinion, and special reports, as well as "Investing," "Money Rates," "Market Watch," and "Daily Mutual Funds." Allows advanced searching (Boolean operators), with links to various other sites. Fees: Free.

Internet Tools of the Profession. Special Libraries Association. Phone: (202)234-4700 Fax: (202)265-9317 E-mail: hope@tiac.net • URL: http://www.sla.org/pubs/itotp • Web site is designed to update the printed *Internet Tools of the Profession.* Provides links to a wide range of useful databases in business, finance, industry, information technology, insurance, law, library management, telecommunications, and other subject areas. Fees: Free.

ProQuest Direct. Bell & Howell Information and Learning. Phone: 800-521-0600 or (313)761-4700 Fax: (313)973-9145 • URL: http://www.umi.com/proquest • Fee-based Web site providing Internet access to more than 3,000 periodicals, newspapers, and other publications. Many items are available full-text, with daily updates. Includes extensive corporate and financial information from Disclosure, Inc. Fees: Apply.

Wall Street Journal Interactive Edition. Dow Jones & Co., Inc. Phone: 800-369-2834 or (212)416-2000 Fax: (212)416-2658 E-mail: inquiries@interactive.wsj.com • URL: http://www.wsj.com • Fee-based Web site providing online searching of worldwide information from the *The Wall Street Journal.* Includes "Company Snapshots," "The Journal's Greatest Hits," "Index to Market Data," "14-Day Searchable Archive," "Journal Links," etc. Financial price quotes are available. Fees: $49.00 per year; $29.00 per year to print subscribers.

Web Finance: Covering the Electronic Evolution of Finance. Securities Data Publishing. Phone: (212)765-5311 or 800-455-5844 Fax: (212)321-2336 E-mail: webfinance@tfn.com • URL: http://www.webfinance.net • Bi-weekly print and daily web-site publication of financial services on the Web, including financial links, archives, brokerage stocks, deal financing, and other financial and investment news and information.

ONLINE DATABASES

ABI/INFORM. Bell & Howell Information and Learning. • Provides online indexing to business-related material occurring in over 1,000 periodicals from 1971 to the present. Inquire as to online cost and availability.

Banking Information Source. Bell & Howell Information and Learning. • Provides indexing and abstracting of periodical and other literature from 1982 to date, with weekly updates. Covers the financial services industry: banks, savings institutions, investment houses, credit unions, insurance companies, and real estate organizations. Emphasis is on marketing and management. Inquire as to online cost and availability. (Formerly *FINIS: Financial Industry Information Service.*).

Compustat. Standard and Poor's. • Financial data on publicly held U.S. and some foreign corporations; data held for 20 years. Inquire as to online cost and availability.

Disclosure SEC Database. Disclosure, Inc. • Provides information from records filed with the Securities and Exchange Commission by publicly owned corporations, 1977 to present. Weekly updates. Inquire as to online cost and availability.

DRI Financial and Credit Statistics. Data Products Division. • Contains U. S. and international statistical data relating to money markets, interest rates, foreign exchange, banking, and stock and bond indexes. Time period is 1973 to date, with continuous updating. Inquire as to online cost and availability.

DRI U.S. Central Database. Data Products Division. • Provides more than 23,000 business, financial, demographic, economic, foreign trade, and industry-related time series for the U.S. Includes national income, population, retail-wholesale trade, price indexes, labor data, housing, industrial production, banking, interest rates, money supply, etc. Time period is generally 1947 to date (some data back to 1929). Updating varies. Inquire as to online cost and availability.

EconBase: Time Series and Forecasts. WEFA, Inc. • Presents online econometric data for business conditions, economics, demographics, industry, finance, employment, household income, interest rates, prices, etc. Includes two-year forecasts for a wide range of economic indicators. Time span is 1948 to date, with monthly updates. Inquire as to online cost and availability.

EconLit. American Economic Association. • Covers the worldwide literature of economics as contained in selected monographs and about 550 journals. Subjects include microeconomics, macroeconomics, economic history, inflation, money, credit, finance, accounting theory, trade, natural resource economics, and regional economics. Time period is 1969 to present, with monthly updates. Inquire as to online cost and availability.

Wilson Business Abstracts Online. H. W. Wilson Co. • Indexes and abstracts 600 major business periodicals, plus the *Wall Street Journal* and the business section of the *New York Times.* Indexing is from 1982, abstracting from 1990, with the two newspapers included from 1993. Updated weekly. Inquire as to online cost and availability. (*Business Periodicals Index* without abstracts is also available online.).

PERIODICALS AND NEWSLETTERS

Applied Financial Economics. Routledge Journals. • Bimonthly. Individuals, $648.00 per year; institutions, $1,053.00 per year. Covers practical aspects of financial economics, banking, and monetary economics. Supplement to *Applied Economics.*

Barron's: The Dow Jones Business and Financial Weekly. Dow Jones and Co., Inc. • Weekly. $145.00 per year.

Business Credit. National Association of Credit Management. • Monthly. $34.00 per year. Formerly *Credit and Financial Management.*

Commercial and Financial Chronicle. William B. Dana Co. • Weekly. $140.00. per year.

Financial History: Chronicling the History of America's Capital Markets. Museum of American Financial History. • Quarterly. Membership. Contains articles on early stock and bond markets and trading in the U. S., with photographs and other illustrations. Current trading in rare and unusual, obsolete stock and bond certificates is featured. Formerly *Friends or Financial History.*

Financial Markets, Institutions, and Instruments. New York University, Salomon Center. Blackwell Publishers. • Five times a year. $219.00 per year. Edited to "bridge the gap between the academic and professional finance communities." Special fifth issue each year provides surveys of developments in four areas: money and banking, derivative securities, corporate finance, and fixed-income securities.

Fortune Magazine. Time Inc., Business Information Group. • Biweekly. $59.95 per year. Edited for top executives and upper-level managers.

Journal of Finance. American Finance Association. Blackwell Publishers. • Bimonthly. $190.00 per year.

Journal of Financial and Quantitative Analysis. University of Washington, School of Business Administration. • Quarterly. Individuals, $45.00 per year; libraries, $95.00 per year; students, $25.00 per year.

Journal of Financial Economics. Elsevier Science. • Monthly. $1,429.00 per year.

Mathematical Finance: An International Journal of Mathematics, Statistics, and Financial Economics. Blackwell Publishers. • Quarterly. $342.00 per year. Covers the use of sophisticated mathematical tools in financial research and practice.

Paytech. American Payroll Association. • Bimonthly. Membership. Covers the details and technology of payroll administration.

The Quarterly Review of Economics and Finance. University of Illinois at Urbana-Champaign, Bureau of Economics and Business Res. Available from JAI Press, Inc. • Five times a year. $349.00 per year. Includes annual supplement. Formerly *Quarterly Review of Economics and Business.*

The Wall Street Journal. Dow Jones & Co., Inc. • Daily. $175.00 per year. Covers news and trends relating to business, industry, finance, the economy, and international commerce. Provides extensive price and other data for the securities, commodity, options, futures, foreign exchange, and money markets.

WebFinance. Securities Data Publishing. • Semimonthly. $995.00 per year. Newsletter (also available online at www.webfinance.net). Covers the Internet-based provision of online financial services by banks, online brokers, mutual funds, and insurance companies. Provides news stories, analysis, and descriptions of useful resources. (Securities Data Publishing is a unit of Thomson Financial.).

RESEARCH CENTERS AND INSTITUTES

American Institute for Economic Research. P.O. Box 1000, Great Barrington, MA 01230. Phone: (413)528-1216 Fax: (413)528-0103 E-mail: info@aier.org • URL: http://www.aier.org.

Conference Board, Inc. 845 Third Ave., New York, NY 10022. Phone: (212)759-0900 Fax: (212)980-7014 E-mail: richard.cavanaugh@conference-board.org • URL: http://www.conference-board.org.

Financial Executives Research Foundation. P.O. Box 1938, Morristown, NJ 07962-1938. Phone: (973)898-4608 Fax: (973)898-6636 E-mail: rcolson@fei.org • URL: http://www.ferf.org.

Salomon Center. New York University. Stern School of Business, 44 W. Fourth St., New York, NY 10012-1126. Phone: (212)998-0707 Fax: (212)995-4220 E-mail: iwalter@stern.nyu.edu • URL: http://www.stern.nyu.edu/salmon/.

STATISTICS SOURCES

Business Statistics of the United States. Courtenay M. Slater, editor. Bernan Associates. • 1999. $74.00. Fifth edition. Based on *Business Statistics*, formerly issue by the Bureau of Economic Analysis, U. S. Department of Commerce. Provides basic data for a wide variety of U. S. industries, services, and economic indicators. Most statistics are shown annually for 29 years and monthly for the most recent four years.

Economic Report of the President: Together with the Annual Report of the Council of Economic Advisors. Available from U. S. Government Printing Office. • Annual. $29.00. Includes about 130 pages of "Statistical Tables Relating to Income, Employment, and Production." Tables cover national income, employment, wages, productivity, manufacturing, prices, credit, finance (public and private), corporate profits, and foreign trade.

Statistical Information on the Financial Services Industry. American Bankers Association. • Annual. Members, $150.00; non-members, $275.00. Presents a wide variety of data relating to banking and financial services, including consumer economics, personal finance, credit, government loans, capital markets, and international banking.

Survey of Current Business. Available from U. S. Government Printing Office. • Monthly. $49.00 per year. Issued by Bureau of Economic Analysis, U. S. Department of Commerce. Presents a wide variety of business and economic data.

TRADE/PROFESSIONAL ASSOCIATIONS

Allied Finance Adjusters Conference. P.O. Box 16196, Pensacola, FL 32507. Phone: 800-843-1232 • URL: http://www.alliedfinanceadjusters.com.

American Finance Association. c/o Professor David Pyle, University of California Berkeley, Haas School of Business, 545 Student Services Bldg., Berkeley, CA 94720-1900. Phone: (510)642-4417 E-mail: pyle@haas.berkeley.edu • URL: http://www.afajof.org • Members are business educators and financial executives.

American Financial Services Association. 919 18th St., N.W., Washington, DC 20006. Phone: (202)296-5544 Fax: (202)223-0321 E-mail: afsa@afsamail.com • URL: http://www.americanfinsvcs.org.

American Payroll Association. 30 E. 33rd St., 5th Fl., New York, NY 10016. Phone: (212)686-2030 Fax: (212)686-4080 E-mail: apa@apa-ed.com • URL: http://www.americanpayroll.org • Members are payroll administrators and personnel managers.

Commercial Finance Association. 225 W. 34th St., Suite 1815, New York, NY 10122. Phone: (212)594-3490 Fax: (212)564-6053 • URL: http://www.csfa.com.

Financial Executives Institute. P.O. Box 1938, Morristown, NJ 07962-1938. Phone: (973)898-4600 Fax: (973)898-4649.

Government Finance Officers Association of the United States and Canada. 180 N. Michigan Ave., Chicago, IL 60601. Phone: (312)977-9700 • URL: http://www.gfoa.com.

OTHER SOURCES

BNA's Banking Report: Legal and Regulatory Developments in the Financial Services Industry. Bureau of National Affairs, Inc. • Weekly. $1,221.00 per year. Two volumes. Looseleaf. Emphasis on federal regulations.

Business & Company Resource Center. The Gale Group. • Fee-based Web site provides a wide range of business, industry, and specific company information. Access is offered to trade journal articles, market research data, insider trading activity, major shareholder data, corporate histories, emerging technology reports, corporate earnings estimates, press releases, and other sources. Provides detailed company profiles, industry overviews, and rankings. Offers integration of Predicasts PROMT, Newsletters ASAP, Investext Plus, Business Index ASAP, Brands and Their Companies, and other databases (many have full text).

Business Rankings Annual. The Gale Group. • Annual. $305.00.Two volumes. Compiled by the Business Library Staff of the Brooklyn Public Library. This is a guide to lists and rankings appearing in major business publications. The top ten names are listed in each case.

Factiva. Dow Jones Reuters Business Interactive, LLC. • Fee-based Web site provides "global news and business information through Web sites and content integration solutions." Includes Dow Jones and Reuters newswires, The Wall Street Journal, and more than 7,000 other sources of current news, historical articles, market research reports, and investment analysis. Content includes 96 major U. S. newspapers, 900 non-English sources, trade publications, media transcripts, country profiles, news photos, etc.

Fundamentals of Finance and Accounting for Nonfinancial Managers. American Management Association Extension Institute. • Looseleaf. $110.00. Self-study course. Emphasis is on practical explanations, examples, and problem solving. Quizzes and a case study are included.

Information, Finance, and Services USA. The Gale Group. • 2001. $240.00. Replaces *Service Industries USA* and *Finance, Insurance, and Real Estate USA.* Presents statistics and projections relating to economic activity in a wide variety of non-manufacturing areas.

InSite 2. Intelligence Data/Thomson Financial. • Fee-based Web site consolidates information in a "Base Pack" consisting of Business InSite, Market InSite, and Company InSite. Optional databases are Consumer InSite, Health and Wellness InSite, Newsletter InSite, and Computer InSite. Includes fulltext content from more than 2,500 trade publications, journals, newsletters, newspapers, analyst reports, and other sources. Continuous updating. Formerly produced by The Gale Group.

Nexis.com. Lexis-Nexis Group. • Fee-based Web site offers searching of about 2.8 billion documents in some 30,000 news, business, and legal information sources. Features include a subject directory covering 1,200 topics in 34 categories and a Company Dossier containing information on more than 500,000 public and private companies. Boolean searching is offered.

FINANCE, BANK

See: BANK LOANS

FINANCE COMPANIES

See also: CREDIT

FINANCIAL RATIOS

Almanac of Business and Industrial Financial Ratios. Leo Troy. Prentice Hall. • Annual. $99.95. Contains financial ratios derived from federal tax returns. Ratios for each of about 200 industries are arranged according to company asset size.

HANDBOOKS AND MANUALS

Moody's Bank and Finance Manual. Moody's Investor Service. • Annual. $995.00 per year. Four volumes. Includes biweekly supplements in *Moody's Bank and Finance News Report.*

PERIODICALS AND NEWSLETTERS

Consumer Credit and Truth-in-Lending Compliance Report. Warren, Gorham and Lamont/RIA Group. • Monthly. $183.75 per year. Newsletter. Focuses on the latest regulatory rulings and findings involving consumer lending and credit activity. Formerly *Bank Installment Lending Newsletter.*

Consumer Finance Newsletter. Financial Publishing Co. • Monthly. $24.50 per year. Covers changes in state and federal consumer lending regulations.

Credit. American Financial Services Association. • Bimonthly. Members, $12.00 per year; non-members, $22.00 per year.

Secured Lender. Commercial Finance Association. • Bimonthly. Members, $24.00 per year; non-members, $48.00 per year.

STATISTICS SOURCES

Consumer Installment Credit. Board of Governors. • Monthly. $5.00 per year.

Finance Companies. U. S. Federal Reserve System. • Monthly. $5.00 per year. (Federal Reserve Statistical Release, G.20.).

TRADE/PROFESSIONAL ASSOCIATIONS

American Financial Services Association. 919 18th St., N.W., Washington, DC 20006. Phone: (202)296-5544 Fax: (202)223-0321 E-mail: afsa@afsamail.com • URL: http://www.americanfinsvcs.org.

Commercial Finance Association. 225 W. 34th St., Suite 1815, New York, NY 10122. Phone: (212)594-3490 Fax: (212)564-6053 • URL: http://www.csfa.com.

National Foundation for Consumer Credit. 8611 Second Ave., Suite 100, Silver Spring, MD 20910-3372. Phone: 800-388-2227 or (301)589-5600 Fax: (301)495-5623 • URL: http://www.nfcc.org.

FINANCE, COMPUTERS IN

See: COMPUTERS IN FINANCE

FINANCE, CORPORATE

See: CORPORATE FINANCE

FINANCE, INTERNATIONAL

See: INTERNATIONAL FINANCE

FINANCE, PERSONAL

See: PERSONAL FINANCE

FINANCE, PUBLIC

See: PUBLIC FINANCE

FINANCIAL ANALYSIS

See also: COMPUTERS IN FINANCE; FINANCE; FINANCIAL RATIOS; TECHNICAL ANALYSIS (FINANCE)

GENERAL WORKS

Asset Allocation and Financial Market Timing: Techniques for Investment Professionals. Carroll D. Aby and Donald E. Vaughn. Greenwood Publishing Group, Inc. • 1995. $77.50.

Cases in Financial Statement Reporting and Analysis. Leopold A. Bernstein and Mostafa M. Maksy. McGraw-Hill Higher Education. • 1985. $36.95. Second edition.

Dow 36,000: The New Strategy for Profiting from the Coming Rise in the Stock Market. James K. Glassman and Kevin A. Hassett. Times Books. • 1999. $25.00. States that conventional measures of stock market value are obsolete.

Investments: An Introduction to Analysis and Management. Frederick Amling. Pearson Custom Publishing. • 1999. Seventh edition.

Market Efficiency: Stock Market Behavior in Theory and Practice. Andrew W. Lo, editor. Edward Elgar Publishing, Inc. • 1997. $430.00. Two volumes. Consists of reprints of 49 articles dating from 1937 to 1993, in five sections: "Theoretical Foundations," "The Random Walk Hypothesis," "Variance Bounds Tests," "Overreaction and Underreaction," and "Anomalies." (International Library of Critical Writings in Financial Economics Series: No. 3).

Modern Portfolio Theory and Investment Analysis. Edwin J. Elton and Martin J. Gruber. John Wiley and Sons, Inc. • 1995. $52.95. Fifth edition. The authors' central concern is that of mixing assets to achieve maximum overall return consonant with an acceptable level of risk. (Portfolio Management Series).

Security Analysis and Portfolio Management. Donald E. Fischer and Ronald L. Jordan. Prentice Hall. • 1995. $87.00. Sixth edition.

Understanding Financial Statements. Adlyn M. Fraser and Aileen Orminston. Prentice Hall. • 2000. Sixth edition. Price on application. Emphasis is on the evaluation and interpretation of financial statements.

ALMANACS AND YEARBOOKS

Advances in Investment Analysis and Portfolio Management. Chung-Few Lee, editor. JAI Press, Inc. • 1999. $78.50.

CD-ROM DATABASES

InvesText [CD-ROM]. Thomson Financial Securities Data. • Monthly. $5,000.00 per year. Contains full text on CD-ROM of investment research reports from about 250 sources, including leading brokers and investment bankers. Reports are available on both U. S. and international publicly traded corporations. Separate industry reports cover more than 50 industries. Time span is 1982 to date.

DIRECTORIES

Association for Investment Management and Research-Membership Directory. Association for Investment Management and Research. • Annual. $150.00. Members are professional investment managers and securities analysts.

Directory of Registered Investment Advisors. Money Market Directories, Inc. • Annual. $450.00. Lists over 14,000 investment advisors and advisory firms. Indicates services offered, personnel, and amount of assets being managed. Formerly *Directory of Registered Investment Advisors with the Securities and Exchange Commission.*

Institutional Buyers of Bank and Thrift Stocks: A Targeted Directory. Investment Data Corp. • Annual. $645.00. Provides detailed profiles of about 600 institutional buyers of bank and savings and loan stocks. Includes names of financial analysts and portfolio managers.

Institutional Buyers of Energy Stocks: A Targeted Directory. Investment Data Corp. • Annual. $645.00. Provides detailed profiles 555 institutional buyers of petroleum-related and other energy stocks. Includes names of financial analysts and portfolio managers.

Institutional Buyers of Foreign Stocks: A Targeted Directory. Investment Data Corp. • Annual. $595.00. Provides detailed profiles of institutional buyers of international stocks. Includes names of financial analysts and portfolio managers.

Institutional Buyers of REIT Securities: A Targeted Directory. Investment Data Corp. • Semiannual. $995.00 per year. Provides detailed profiles of about 500 institutional buyers of REIT securities. Includes names of financial analysts and portfolio managers.

Institutional Buyers of Small-Cap Stocks: A Targeted Directory. Investment Data Corp. • Annual. $295.00. Provides detailed profiles of more than 837 institutional buyers of small capitalization stocks. Includes names of financial analysts and portfolio managers.

Nelson's Directory of Investment Research. Wiesenberger/Thomson Financial. • Annual. $590.00. Three volumes. Provides information on 10,000 investment research analysts at more than 800 firms. Indexes include company name, industry, and name of person.

Zacks Analyst Directory: Listed by Broker. Zacks Investment Research. • Quarterly. $395.00 per year. Lists stockbroker investment analysts and gives the names of major U. S. corporations covered by those analysts.

Zacks Analyst Directory: Listed by Company. Zacks Investment Research. • Quarterly. $395.00 per year. Lists major U. S. corporations and gives the names of stockbroker investment analysts covering those companies.

Zacks EPS Calendar. Zacks Investment Research. • Biweekly. $1,250.00 per year. (Also available monthly at $895.00 per year.) Lists anticipated reporting dates of earnings per share for major U. S. corporations.

FINANCIAL RATIOS

Reliable Financial Reporting and Internal Control: A Global Implementation Guide. Dmitris N. Chorafas. John Wiley and Sons, Inc. • 2000. $65.00. Discusses financial reporting and control as related to doing business internationally.

HANDBOOKS AND MANUALS

Analysis and Use of Financial Statements. Gerald I. White and others. John Wiley and Sons, Inc. • 1997. $112.95. Second edition. Includes analysis of financial ratios, cash flow, inventories, assets, debt, etc. Also covered are employee benefits, corporate investments, multinational operations, financial derivatives, and hedging activities.

Analysis of Financial Statements. Leopold A. Bernstein and John J. Wild. McGraw-Hill. • 1999. $60.00. Fifth edition. Includes practical examples of analysis.

Analyst's Handbook: Composite Corporate Per Share Data by Industry. Standard and Poor's. • Annual. $795.00. Monthly updates.

Convertible Securities: The Latest Instruments, Portfolio Strategies, and Valuation Analysis. John P. Calamos. McGraw-Hill Professional. • 1998. $65.00. Second edition.

Corporate Financial Analysis: Decisions in a Global Environment. Diana R. Harrington and Brent D. Wilson. McGraw-Hill Professional. • 1993. $50.00. Fourth edition.

Econometrics of Financial Markets. John Y. Campbell and others. California Princeton Fulfillment Services. • 1997. $49.50. Written for advanced students and industry professionals. Includes chapters on "The Predictability of Asset Returns," "Derivative Pricing Models," and "Fixed-Income Securities." Provides a discussion of the random walk theory of investing and tests of the theory.

Financial Statement Analysis: A Practitioner's Guide. McGraw-Hill. • 1998. $60.00. Sixth edition.

Financial Statement Analysis: The Investor's Self Study Guide to Interpreting and Analyzing. Charles J. Woelfel. McGraw-Hill Professional. • 1993. $22.95. Revised edition.

Fixed Income Analytics: State-of-the-Art Analysis and Valuation Modeling. Ravi E. Dattatreya, editor. McGraw-Hill Professional. • 1991. $69.95. Discusses the yield curve, structure and value in corporate bonds, mortgage-backed securities, and other topics.

Guide to Financial Reporting and Analysis. Eugene E. Comiskey and Charles W. Mulford. John Wiley and Sons, Inc. • 2000. $75.00. Provides financial statement examples to illustrate the application of generally accepted accounting principles.

An Introduction to the Mathematics of Financial Derivatives. Salih N. Neftci. Academic Press, Inc. • 2000. $59.95. Second edition. Covers the mathematical models underlying the pricing of derivatives. Includes explanations of basic financial calculus for students, derivatives traders, risk managers, and others concerned with derivatives.

Manager's Guide to Financial Statement Analysis. Stephen F. Jablonsky and Noah P. Barsky. John Wiley and Sons, Inc. • 1998. $67.95. The two main sections are "Financial Statements and Business Strategy" and "Market Valuation and Business Strategy.".

The Numbers You Need. The Gale Group. • 1993. $55.00. Contains mathematical equations, formulas, charts, and graphs, including many that are related to business or finance. Explanations, step-by-step directions, and examples of use are provided.

Techniques of Financial Analysis: A Modern Approach. Erich A. Helfert. McGraw-Hill Higher Education. • 1996. $32.00. Ninth edition.

INTERNET DATABASES

FIS Online: The Preferred Source for Global Business and Financial Information. Mergent. Phone: 800-342-5647 or (212)413-7601 Fax: (212)413-7777 E-mail: fis@fisonline.com • URL: http://www.fisonline.com • Fee-based Web site provides detailed information on more than 10,000 publicly-owned corporations listed on the New York Stock Exchange, American Stock Exchange, NASDAQ, and U. S. regional exchanges. Searching is offered on eight financial variables and six text fields. Weekly updating. Fees: Rates on application. (Mergent is publisher of Moody's Manuals.).

ONLINE DATABASES

Compustat. Standard and Poor's. • Financial data on publicly held U.S. and some foreign corporations; data held for 20 years. Inquire as to online cost and availability.

Disclosure SEC Database. Disclosure, Inc. • Provides information from records filed with the Securities and Exchange Commission by publicly owned corporations, 1977 to present. Weekly updates. Inquire as to online cost and availability.

InvesText. Thomson Financial Securities Data. • Provides full text online of investment research reports from more than 300 sources, including leading brokers and investment bankers. Reports are available on approximately 50,000 U. S. and international corporations. Separate industry reports cover 54 industries. Time span is 1982 to date, with daily updates. Inquire as to online cost and availability.

Super Searchers on Wall Street: Top Investment Professionals Share Their Online Research Secrets. Amelia Kassel and Reva Basch. Information Today, Inc. • 2000. $24.95. Gives the results of interviews with "10 leading financial industry research experts." Explains how online information is used by stock brokers, investment bankers, and individual investors. Includes relevant Web sites and other sources. (CyberAge Books.).

PERIODICALS AND NEWSLETTERS

Consensus: National Futures and Financial Weekly. Consensus, Inc. • Weekly. $365.00 per year. Newspaper. Contains news, statistics, and special reports relating to agricultural, industrial, and financial futures markets. Features daily basis price charts, reprints of market advice, and "The Consensus Index of Bullish Market Opinion" (charts show percent bullish of advisors for various futures).

Financial Analysts Journal. Association for Investment Management and Research. • Bimonthly. $175.00 per year.

Institutional Investor: The Magazine for Finance and Investment. Institutional Investor. • Monthly. $475.00 per year. Edited for portfolio managers and other investment professionals. Special feature issues include "Country Credit Ratings," "Fixed Income Trading Ranking," "All-America Research Team," and "Global Banking Ranking.".

Journal of Financial Statement Analysis. Institutional Investor. • Quarterly. $280.00 per year. Covers the practical analysis and interpretation of corporate financial reports.

MPT Review; Specializing in Modern Portfolio Theory. Navellier and Associates, Inc. • Monthly. $275.00 per year. Newsletter. Provides specific stock selection and model portfolio advice (conservative, moderately aggressive, and aggressive) based on quantitative analysis and modern portfolio theory.

Zacks Analyst Watch. Zacks Investment Research. • Biweekly. $250.00 per year. Provides the results of research by stockbroker investment analysts on major U. S. corporations.

Zacks Earnings Forecaster. Zacks Investment Research. • Biweekly. $495.00 per year. (Also available monthly at $375.00 per year.) Provides estimates by stockbroker investment analysts of earnings per share of individual U. S. companies.

Zacks Profit Guide. Zacks Investment Research. • Quarterly. $375.00 per year. Provides analysis of total return and stock price performance of major U. S. companies.

RESEARCH CENTERS AND INSTITUTES

Institute for Quantitative Research in Finance. Church Street Station, P.O. Box 6194, New York, NY 10249-6194. Phone: (212)744-6825 Fax: (212)517-2259 E-mail: daleberman@compuserve • Financial research areas include quantitative methods, securities analysis, and the financial structure of industries. Also known as the "Q Group.".

TRADE/PROFESSIONAL ASSOCIATIONS

Association for Investment Management and Research. 560 Ray C. Hunt Dr., Charlottesville, VA 22903-0668. Phone: 800-247-8132 or (804)951-5499 Fax: (804)951-5262 E-mail: info@aimr.org • URL: http://www.aimr.org.

New York Society of Security Analysts. One World Trade Center, Suite 4447, New York, NY 10048. Phone: 800-248-0108 or (212)912-9249 Fax: (212)912-9310 E-mail: staff@nyssa.org • URL: http://www.nyssa.org.

OTHER SOURCES

Quantitative Finance. Available from IOP Publishing, Inc. • Bimonthly. $199.00 per year. Published in the UK by the Institute of Physics. A technical journal on the use of quantitative tools and applications in financial analysis and financial engineering. Covers such topics as portfolio theory, derivatives, asset allocation, return on assets, risk management, price volatility, financial econometrics, market anomalies, and trading systems.

FINANCIAL FUTURES TRADING

See also: STOCK INDEX TRADING

GENERAL WORKS

Financial Options: From Theory to Practice. Stephen Figlewski. McGraw-Hill Professional. • 1992. $29.95. Includes options on financial futures.

Futures Markets. A. G. Malliaris, editor. Edward Elgar Publishing, Inc. • 1997. $450.00. Three volumes. Consists of reprints of 70 articles dating from 1959 to 1993, on futures market volatility, speculation, hedging, stock indexes, portfolio insurance, interest rates, and foreign currencies. (International Library of Critical Writings in Financial Economics.).

Getting Started in Futures. Todd Lofton. John Wiley and Sons, Inc. • 1997. $18.95. Third edition. A general introduction to commodity and financial futures trading. Includes case studies and a glossary. (All About Series).

Introduction to Futures and Options Markets. John C. Hull. Prentice Hall. • 1997. $94.00. Third edition.

ABSTRACTS AND INDEXES

Business Periodicals Index. H. W. Wilson Co. • Monthly, except August, with quarterly and annual cumulations. Service basis for print edition; CD-ROM edition, $1,495.00 per year.

DIRECTORIES

Business Organizations, Agencies, and Publications Directory. The Gale Group. • 1999. $425.00. 12th edition. Over 40,000 entries describing 39 types of business information sources. Classified by type of organization, publication, or serviceIncludes state, national, and international agencies and organizations. Master index to names and keywords. Also includes e-mail addresses and web site URL's.

Futures Guide to Computerized Trading. Futures Magazine, Inc. • Annual. $10.00. "A directory of products and services for the computerized trader." Provides information on computer software applications for commodity traders and money managers, including trading methods and technical analysis.

Futures Magazine SourceBook: The Most Complete List of Exchanges, Companies, Regulators, Organizations, etc., Offering Products and Services to the Futures and Options Industry. Futures Magazine, Inc. • Annual. $19.50. Provides information on commodity futures brokers, trading method services, publications, and other items of interest to futures traders and money managers.

ENCYCLOPEDIAS AND DICTIONARIES

International Encyclopedia of Futures and Options. Michael R. Ryder, editor. Fitzroy Dearborn Publishers. • 2000. $275.00. Two volumes. Covers terminology, concepts, events, individuals, and markets.

HANDBOOKS AND MANUALS

Currency and Interest Rate Hedging: A User's Guide to Options, Futures, Swaps, and Forward Contracts. Torben J. Andersen. New York Institute of Finance. • 1993. $49.95. Second edition.

Currency Options: Hedging and Trading Strategies. Henry Clasing. McGraw-Hill Professional. • 1992. $70.00.

Derivatives: A Comprehensive Resource for Options, Futures, Interest Rate Swaps, and Mortgage Securities. Fred D. Arditti. Harvard Business School Press. • 1996. $60.00. Published by Harvard Business School Press. Provides detailed explanations of various kinds of financial derivatives (options, futures, swaps, etc.) and their trading tactics, uses, and risks. (Financial Management Association Survey and Synthesis Series).

Foreign Exchange Handbook: Managing Risk and Opportunity in Global Currency Markets. Paul Bishop and Don Dixon. McGraw-Hill. • 1992. $69.95. Discusses factors affecting currency value, currency price forecasting, options trading, futures, credit risk, and related subjects.

Handbook of Derivative Instruments: Investment Research, Analysis, and Portfolio Applications. Atsuo Konishi and Ravi E. Dattatreya, editors. McGraw-Hill Professional. • 1996. $80.00. Second revised edition. Contains 41 chapters by various authors on all aspects of derivative securities, including such esoterica as "Inverse Floaters," "Positive Convexity," "Exotic Options," and "How to Use the Holes in Black-Scholes.".

Handbook of Equity Derivatives. Jack C. Francis and others, editors. John Wiley and Sons, Inc. • 1999. $95.00. Contains 27 chapters by various authors. Covers options (puts and calls), stock index futures, warrants, convertibles, over-the-counter options, swaps, legal issues, taxation, etc. (Financial Engineering Series).

International Guide to Foreign Currency Management. Gary Shoup, editor. Fitzroy Dearborn Publishers. • 1998. $65.00. Written for corporate financial managers. Covers the market for currencies, price forecasting, exposure of various kinds, and risk management.

Money Management Strategies for Futures Traders. Nauzer J. Balsara. John Wiley and Sons, Inc. • 1992. $69.95. How to limit risk and avoid catastrophic losses. (Financial Editions Series).

Options, Futures, and Other Derivatives. John C. Hull. Prentice Hall. • 1999. $94.00. Fourth edition.

Options: The International Guide to Valuation and Trading Strategies. Gordon Gemmill. McGraw-Hill. • 1993. $37.95. Covers valuation techniques for American, European, and Asian options. Trading strategies are discussed for options on currencies, stock indexes, interest rates, and commodities.

Over-the-Counter Derivatives Products: A Guide to Legal Risk Management and Documentation. Robert M. McLaughlin. McGraw-Hill Professional. • 1998. $75.00.

Strategic Trading in the Foreign Exchange Markets. Gary Klopfenstein. Fitzroy Dearborn Publishers. • 1999. $65.00. Describes the tactics of successful foreign exchange traders.

Trading and Investing in Bond Options: Risk Management, Arbitrage, and Value Investing. Anthony M. Wong. John Wiley and Sons, Inc. • 1991. $55.00. Covers dealing, trading, and investing in U. S. government bond futures options (puts and calls).

Trading Financial Futures: Markets, Methods, Strategies, and Tactics. John W. Labuszewski and John E. Nyhoff. John Wiley and Sons, Inc. • 1997. $49.95. Second edition. (Wiley Finance Editions Series).

Trading Options on Futures: Markets, Methods, Strategies, and Tactics. John W. Labuszewski and John E. Nyhoff. John Wiley and Sons, Inc. • 1996. $39.95. Second edition.

Understanding Financial Derivatives: How to Protect Your Investments. Donald Strassheim. McGraw-Hill Professional. • 1996. $40.00. Covers three basic risk management instruments: options, futures, and swaps. Includes advice on equity index options, financial futures contracts, and over-the-counter derivatives markets.

INTERNET DATABASES

BanxQuote Banking, Mortgage, and Finance Center. BanxQuote, Inc. Phone: 800-765-3000 or (212)643-8000 Fax: (212)643-0020 E-mail: info@banx.com • URL: http://www.banx.com • Web site quotes interest rates paid by banks around the country on various savings products, as well as rates paid by consumers for automobile loans, mortgages, credit cards, home equity loans, and personal loans. Also provided: stock quotes, indexes, stock options, futures trading data, economic indicators, and links to many other financial sites. Daily updates. Fees: Free.

Chicago Board of Trade: The World's Leading Futures Exchange. Chicago Board of Trade. Phone: (312)345-3500 Fax: (312)341-3027 E-mail: comments@cbot.com • URL: http://www.cbot.com • Web site provides a wide variety of statistics, commentary, charts, and news relating to both agricultural and financial futures trading. For example, Web page "MarketPlex: Information MarketPlace to the World" offers prices & volume, contract specifications & margins, government reports, etc. The CBOT *Statistical Annual*, in book form for 109 years, is now offered online. Searching is available, with daily updates for current data. Fees: Mostly free (some specialized services are fee-based).

Futures Online. Oster Communications, Inc. Phone: 800-601-8907 or (319)277-1278 Fax: (319)277-7982 • URL: http://www.futuresmag.com • Web site presents updates of *Futures* magazine and links to other futures-related sites. Includes "Futures Industry News," "Technical Talk," "Today's Hot Markets," "Futures Talk" (forums), "Futures Library" (archives, 1993 to date), and other features. Keyword searching is available. Updating: daily. Fees: Free.

ONLINE DATABASES

Wilson Business Abstracts Online. H. W. Wilson Co. • Indexes and abstracts 600 major business periodicals, plus the *Wall Street Journal* and the business section of the *New York Times*. Indexing is from 1982, abstracting from 1990, with the two newspapers included from 1993. Updated weekly. Inquire as to online cost and availability. (*Business Periodicals Index* without abstracts is also available online.).

PERIODICALS AND NEWSLETTERS

Barron's: The Dow Jones Business and Financial Weekly. Dow Jones and Co., Inc. • Weekly. $145.00 per year.

Derivatives Tactics. Derivative Strategy and Tactics. • Semimonthly. $695.00 per year. Newsletter. Edited for institutional investors. Covers options, swaps, and other financial derivatives.

Financial Trader. Miller Freeman, Inc. • 11 times a year. $160.00 per year. Edited for professional traders. Covers fixed income securities, emerging markets, derivatives, options, futures, and equities.

Futures and OTC World: The Futures Portfolio Advisor (Over the Counter). R.R. Wasendorf, editor. Russell R. Wasendorf. • Weekly. $435.00 per year. Newsletter. Futures market information. Includes Daily Hotline Information to update advice. Formerly *Futures and Options Factors.*

Futures: News, Analysis, and Strategies for Futures, Options, and Derivatives Traders. Futures Magazine, Inc. • Monthly. $39.00 per year. Edited for institutional money managers and traders, brokers, risk managers, and individual investors or speculators. Includes special feature issues on interest rates, technical indicators, currencies, charts, precious metals, hedge funds, and derivatives. Supplements available.

Journal of Fixed Income. Institutional Investor. • Quarterly. $325.00 per year. Covers a wide range of fixed-income investments for institutions, including bonds, interest-rate options, high-yield securities, and mortgages.

Technical Analysis of Stocks & Commodities: The Trader's Magazine. Technical Analysis, Inc. • 13 times a year. $49.95 per year. Covers use of personal computers for stock trading, price movement analysis by means of charts, and other technical trading methods.

Timing Financial Advisory Service. William Jaeger. • Biweekly. $144.00 per year. Newsletter. Follows the financial markets with emphasis on futures. Also includes weather and its effect on agricultural commodities. Formerly*Timing Commodity and Financial Advisory Service.*

The Wall Street Journal. Dow Jones & Co., Inc. • Daily. $175.00 per year. Covers news and trends relating to business, industry, finance, the economy, and international commerce. Provides extensive price and other data for the securities, commodity, options, futures, foreign exchange, and money markets.

STATISTICS SOURCES

Statistical Annual: Interest Rates, Metals, Stock Indices, Options on Financial Futures, Options on Metals Futures. Chicago Board of Trade. • Annual. Includes historical data on GNMA CDR Futures, Cash-Settled GNMA Futures, U. S. Treasury Bond Futures, U. S. Treasury Note Futures, Options on Treasury Note Futures, NASDAQ-100 Futures, Major Market Index Futures, Major Market Index MAXI Futures, Municipal Bond Index Futures, 1,000-Ounce Silver Futures, Options on Silver Futures, and Kilo Gold Futures.

TRADE/PROFESSIONAL ASSOCIATIONS

Futures Industry Association. 2001 Pennsylvania, N.W., Suite 600, Washington, DC 20006-1807. Phone: (202)466-5460 Fax: (202)296-3184 E-mail: info@fiafii.org • URL: http://www.fiafii.org.

National Association of Securities Dealers. 1735 K St., N.W., Washington, DC 20006-1506. Phone: (202)728-8000 Fax: (202)293-6260 • URL: http://www.nasdr.com/1000.asp.

National Futures Association. 200 W. Madison St., Chicago, IL 60606-3447. Phone: 800-621-3570 or (312)781-1410 Fax: (312)781-1467 E-mail: public__affairs@nfa.futures.org • URL: http://www.nfa.futures.org.

Security Traders Association. One World Trade Center, Suite 4511, New York, NY 10048. Phone: (212)524-0484 Fax: (212)321-3449.

OTHER SOURCES

Managing Financial Risk with Forwards, Futures, Options, and Swaps. American Management Association Extension Institute. • Looseleaf. $130.00. Self-study course. Emphasis is on practical explanations, examples, and problem solving. Quizzes and a case study are included.

FINANCIAL MANAGEMENT

See also: COMPUTERS IN FINANCE; CORPORATE FINANCE; FINANCE

GENERAL WORKS

Analysis for Financial Management. Robert C. Higgins. McGraw-Hill. • 2000. $55.94. Sixth edition.

Case Studies in Financial Decision Making. Diana R. Harrington and Kenneth M. Eades. Dryden Press. • 1993. $63.50. Third edition.

Cases in Financial Mangement: Directed Versions. Eugene Brigham and Louis Gapenski. Dryden Press. • 1993. $32.00.

Financial Management: Theory and Practice. Eugene F. Brigham. Harcourt Trade Publishers. • 1998. $106.00. Nineth edition.

Foundations of Financial Management. Stanley R. Block and Geoffrey A. Hirt. McGraw-Hill Professional. • 1999. $67.00. Ninth edition (Finance Series).

Fundamentals of Financial Management. James C. Van Horne and John M. Wachowicz. Prentice Hall. • 1997. $80.00. 10th edition.

Introduction to Financial Management. Lawrence D. Schall. McGraw-Hill. • 1990. $83.75. Sixth edition.

ABSTRACTS AND INDEXES

Banking Information Index. U M I Banking Information Index. • Monthly. Price on application.

Covers a wide variety of banking, business, and financial subjects in periodicals. Formerly *Banking Literature Index*.

Business Periodicals Index. H. W. Wilson Co. • Monthly, except August, with quarterly and annual cumulations. Service basis for print edition; CD-ROM edition, $1,495.00 per year.

BIOGRAPHICAL SOURCES

Who's Who in Finance and Industry. Marquis Who's Who. • Biennial. $295.00. Provides over 22,400 concise biographies of business leaders in all fields.

CD-ROM DATABASES

ABI/INFORM Global. Bell & Howell Information and Learning. • Monthly. $6,500.00 per year. Provides CD-ROM indexing and abstracting of worldwide business literature appearing in over 1,200 periodicals for the most recent five years. Archival discs are available from 1971. Formerly *ABI/INFORM OnDisc*.

Corporate Affiliations Plus. National Register Publishing, Reed Reference Publishing. • Quarterly. $1,995.00 per year. Provides CD-ROM discs corresponding to *Directory of Corporate Affiliations* and *Corporate Finance Bluebook*. Contains corporate financial services information and worldwide data on subsidiaries and affiliates.

WILSONDISC: Business Periodicals Index. H. W. Wilson Co. • Monthly. $1,495.00 per year. Provides CD-ROM indexing of business periodicals from 1982 to date. Price includes online service.

DIRECTORIES

America's Corporate Finance Directory. National Register Publishing. • Annual. $699.00. A directory of financial executives employed at over 5,000 U. S. corporations. Includes a listing of the outside financial services (banks, pension managers, insurance firms, auditors) used by each corporation.

Business and Finance Career Directory. Visible Ink Press. • 1992. $17.95.

Financial Management Association: Membership/ Professional Directory. Financial Management Association. • Annual. Membership. Lists 4,800 corporate financial officers and professors of financial management.

Nelson's Directory of Investment Managers. Wiesenberger/Thomson Financial. • Annual. $545.00. Three volumes. Provides information on 2,600 investment management firms, both U.S. and foreign.

ENCYCLOPEDIAS AND DICTIONARIES

Blackwell Encyclopedic Dictionary of Finance. Dean Paxson and Douglas Wood, editors. Blackwell Publishers. • 1997. $110.00. The editors are associated with the University of Manchester. Contains definitions of key terms combined with longer articles written by various U. S. and foreign business educators. Includes bibliographies and index. (Blackwell Encyclopedia of Management Series).

HANDBOOKS AND MANUALS

Advanced Strategies in Financial Risk Management. Robert J. Schwartz and Clifford W. Smith, editors. Prentice Hall. • 1993. $65.00. Includes technical discussions of financial swaps and derivatives.

AMA Management Handbook. John J. Hampton, editor. AMACOM. • 1994. $110.00. Third edition. Provides 200 chapters in 16 major subject areas. Covers a wide variety of business and industrial management topics.

Banking and Finance on the Internet. Mary J. Cronin, editor. John Wiley and Sons, Inc. • 1997. $45.00. Contains articles on Internet services, written by bankers, money mangers, investment analysts, and stockbrokers. Emphasis is on operations management. (Communications Series).

Financial Management Handbook. Philip Vale. Ashgate Publishing Co. • 1988. $93.95. Third edition.

Financial Management: How to Make a Go of Your Business. Available from U. S. Government Printing Office. • 1986. $3.50. Published by U. S. Small Business Administration. (Small Business Management Series, No. 44.).

Financial Management Techniques for Small Business. Art R. DeThomas. PSI Research. • 1991. $19.95. (Successful Business Library Series).

Guide to Preparing Financial Statements. John R. Clay and others. Practitioners Publishing Co. • 1998. Three looseleaf volumes. Price on application.

Guide to Preparing Nonprofit Financial Statements. Harold L. Monk and others. Practitioners Publishing Co. • 1997. $177.00. Two looseleaf volumes.

McGraw-Hill Pocket Guide to Business Finance: 201 Decision- Making Tools for Managers. Joel G. Siegel and others. McGraw-Hill. • 1992. $14.95. Includes ratios, formulas, models, guidelines, instructions, strategies, and rules of thumb.

Swap Literacy. Elizabeth Ungar. Bloomberg Press. • 1996. $40.00. Written for corporate finance officers. Provides basic information on arbitrage, hedging, and speculation, involving interest rate, currency, and other types of financial swaps. (Bloomberg Professional Library.).

Swaps and Financial Engineering: A Self-Study Guide to Mastering and Applying Swaps and Financial Engineering. Coopers and Lybrand Staff. McGraw-Hill Professional. • 1994. $55.00.

Understanding and Managing Financial Information: The Non-Financial Manager's Guide. Michael M. Coltman. Self-Counsel Press, Inc. • 1993. $9.95. (Business Series).

ONLINE DATABASES

ABI/INFORM. Bell & Howell Information and Learning. • Provides online indexing to business-related material occurring in over 1,000 periodicals from 1971 to the present. Inquire as to online cost and availability.

Accounting and Tax Database. Bell & Howell Information and Learning. • Provides indexing and abstracting of the literature of accounting, taxation, and financial management, 1971 to date. Updating is weekly. Especially covers accounting, auditing, banking, bankruptcy, employee compensation and benefits, cash management, financial planning, and credit. Inquire as to online cost and availability.

American Banker Full Text. American Banker-Bond Buyer, Database Services. • Provides complete text online of the daily *American Banker*. Inquire as to online cost and availability.

Banking Information Source. Bell & Howell Information and Learning. • Provides indexing and abstracting of periodical and other literature from 1982 to date, with weekly updates. Covers the financial services industry: banks, savings institutions, investment houses, credit unions, insurance companies, and real estate organizations. Emphasis is on marketing and management. Inquire as to online cost and availability. (Formerly *FINIS: Financial Industry Information Service*.).

Management Contents. The Gale Group. • Covers a wide range of management, financial, marketing, personnel, and administrative topics. About 150 leading business journals are indexed and abstracted from 1974 to date, with monthly updating. Inquire as to online cost and availability.

Trade & Industry Index. The Gale Group. • Provides indexing of business periodicals, January 1981 to date. Daily updates. (Full text articles from some periodicals are available online, 1983 to date, in the companion database, *Trade & Industry ASAP*.) Inquire as to online cost and availability.

Wilson Business Abstracts Online. H. W. Wilson Co. • Indexes and abstracts 600 major business periodicals, plus the *Wall Street Journal* and the business section of the *New York Times*. Indexing is from 1982, abstracting from 1990, with the two newspapers included from 1993. Updated weekly. Inquire as to online cost and availability. (*Business Periodicals Index* without abstracts is also available online.).

PERIODICALS AND NEWSLETTERS

Bank Accounting and Finance. Institutional Investor. • Quarterly. $250.00 per year. Emphasis is on the practical aspects of bank accounting and bank financial management.

Business Finance. Duke Communications International. • Monthly. $59.00 per year. Covers trends in finance, technology, and economics for corporate financial executives.

CFO: The Magazine for Senior Financial Executives. CFO Publishing Corp., The Economist Group. • Monthly. Free to qualified subscribers; others, $50.00 per year.

Financial Executive. Financial Executives Institute. • Bimonthly. $45.00 per year. Published for corporate financial officers and managers.

FMC (Financial Management): Journal of the Financial Management Association. Financial Management Association International. • Quarterly. Individuals, $80.00 per year; libraries, $100.00 per year. Covers theory and practice of financial planning, international finance, investment banking, and portfolio management. Includes *Financial Practice* and *Education and Contempory Finance Digest*.

Fund Action. Institutional Investor. • Weekly. $2,220.00 per year. Newsletter. Edited for mutual fund executives. Covers competition among funds, aggregate statistics, new products, regulations, service providers, and other subjects of interest to fund managers.

Global Finance. Global Finance Media, Inc. • Monthly. $300.00 per year. Edited for corporate financial executives and money managers responsible for "cross-border" financial transactions.

Investment Management Weekly. Securities Data Publishing. • Weekly. $1,370.00 per year. Newsletter. Edited for money managers and other investment professionals. Covers personnel news, investment strategies, and industry trends. (Securities Data Publishing is a unit of Thomson Financial.).

IT Cost Management Strategies: The Planning Assistant for IT Directors. Computer Economics, Inc. • Monthly. $495.00 per year. Newsletter for information technology professionals. Covers data processing costs, budgeting, financial management, and related topics.

Operations Management. Institutional Investor. • Weekly. $2,105.00 per year. Newsletter. Edited for managers of securities clearance and settlement at financial institutions. Covers new products, technology, legalities, management practices, and other topics related to securities processing.

Strategic Finance. Institute of Management Accountants. • Monthly. $140.00 per year; non-profit institutions, $70.00 per year. Provides articles on corporate finance, cost control, cash flow, budgeting, corporate taxes, and other financial management topics.

RESEARCH CENTERS AND INSTITUTES

Financial Executives Research Foundation. P.O. Box 1938, Morristown, NJ 07962-1938. Phone: (973)898-4608 Fax: (973)898-6636 E-mail: rcolson@fei.org • URL: http://www.ferf.org.

Rodney L. White Center for Financial Research. University of Pennsylvania, 3254 Steinberg Hall-Dietrich Hall, Philadelphia, PA 19104. Phone: (215)898-7616 Fax: (215)573-8084 E-mail: rlwtcr@finance.wharton.upenn.edu • URL: http://www.finance.wharton.upenn.edu/~rlwctr • Research areas include financial management, money markets, real estate finance, and international finance.

TRADE/PROFESSIONAL ASSOCIATIONS

American Finance Association. c/o Professor David Pyle, University of California Berkeley, Haas School of Business, 545 Student Services Bldg., Berkeley, CA 94720-1900. Phone: (510)642-4417 E-mail: pyle@haas.berkeley.edu • URL: http://www.afajof.org • Members are business educators and financial executives.

Association for Financial Professionals. 7315 Wisconsin Ave., Suite 600-W, Bethesda, MD 20814-3211. Phone: (301)907-2862 Fax: (301)907-2864 E-mail: afp@afponline.org • URL: http://www.afponline.org • Members are corporate treasurers and other managers of business finance. Formerly Treasury Management Association.

Financial Executives Institute. P.O. Box 1938, Morristown, NJ 07962-1938. Phone: (973)898-4600 Fax: (973)898-4649.

Financial Management Association International. College of Business Administration, University of South Florida, Tampa, FL 33620-5500. Phone: (813)974-2084 Fax: (813)974-3318 E-mail: fma@coba.usf.edu • URL: http://www.fma.org • Members are corporate financial officers and professors of financial management.

Financial Managers Society. 230 W. Monroe, Ste. 2205, Chicago, IL 60606. Phone: 800-275-4367 or (312)578-1300 Fax: (312)578-1308 E-mail: lauriek@fmsinc.org • URL: http://www.fmsinc.org • Members are financial managers of financial institutions.

Financial Women's Association of New York. 215 Park Ave. S., Suite 1713, New York, NY 10003. Phone: (212)533-2141 Fax: (212)982-3008 E-mail: info@fwa.org • URL: http://www.fwa.org • Members are professional women in finance.

OTHER SOURCES

Fundamentals of Finance and Accounting for Nonfinancial Managers. American Management Association Extension Institute. • Looseleaf. $110.00. Self-study course. Emphasis is on practical explanations, examples, and problem solving. Quizzes and a case study are included.

How to Manage Corporate Cash. American Management Association Extension Institute. • Looseleaf. $110.00. Self-study course. Emphasis is on practical explanations, examples, and problem solving. Quizzes and a case study are included.

FINANCIAL PLANNING

See also: ESTATE PLANNING; PERSONAL FINANCE; TAX PLANNING

GENERAL WORKS

Financial Planning for the Utterly Confused. Joel Lerner. McGraw-Hill. • 1998. $12.00. Fifth edition. Covers annuities, certificates of deposit, bonds, mutual funds, insurance, home ownership, retirement, social security, wills, etc.

How to Avoid Financial Fraud. C. Edgar Murray. American Institute for Economic Research. • 1999. $3.00. Provides concise discussions of fraud victims, perpetrators, and sales tactics. Also includes practical advice on "Selecting a Financial Planner" and "Selecting a Broker." Contains a directory of state securities regulators and a glossary defining various fraudulant financial schemes. (Economic Education Bulletin.).

How to Plan Your Retirement Years. Kerry A. Lynch, editor. American Institute for Economic Research. • 1996. $6.00. Provides concise, conservative advice on retirement planning, savings, pensions, IRAs, Keogh plans, annuities, and making effective use of social security. (Economic Education Bulletin.).

Smart Questions to Ask Your Financial Advisers. Lynn Brenner. Bloomberg Press. • 1997. $19.95. Provides practical advice on how to deal with financial planners, stockbrokers, insurance agents, and lawyers. Some of the areas covered are investments, estate planning, tax planning, house buying, prenuptial agreements, divorce arrangements, loss of a job, and retirement. (Bloomberg Personal Bookshelf Series Library.).

ABSTRACTS AND INDEXES

Business Periodicals Index. H. W. Wilson Co. • Monthly, except August, with quarterly and annual cumulations. Service basis for print edition; CD-ROM edition, $1,495.00 per year.

DIRECTORIES

Business Organizations, Agencies, and Publications Directory. The Gale Group. • 1999. $425.00. 12th edition. Over 40,000 entries describing 39 types of business information sources. Classified by type of organization, publication, or serviceIncludes state, national, and international agencies and organizations. Master index to names and keywords. Also includes e-mail addresses and web site URL's.

Directory of Registered Investment Advisors. Money Market Directories, Inc. • Annual. $450.00. Lists over 14,000 investment advisors and advisory firms. Indicates services offered, personnel, and amount of assets being managed. Formerly *Directory of Registered Investment Advisors with the Securities and Exchange Commission.*

Plunkett's Financial Services Industry Almanac: The Leading Firms in Investments, Banking, and Financial Information. Available from Plunkett Research, Ltd. • Annual. $245.00. Discusses important trends in various sectors of the financial industry. Five hundred major banking, credit card, investment, and financial services companies are profiled.

ENCYCLOPEDIAS AND DICTIONARIES

Dictionary of Personal Finance. Joel G. Siegel and others. Pearson Education and Technology. • 1993. $20.00.

FINANCIAL RATIOS

The Financial Elite: Database of Financial Services Companies. Donnelley Marketing. • Quarterly. Price on application. Formerly compiled by Database America. Provides current information on CD-ROM for 500,000 major U. S. companies offering financial services. Data for each firm includes year started, type of financial service, annual revenues, name of top executive, and number of employees.

Financial Planning for Older Clients. James E. Pearman. CCH, Inc. • 2000. $49.00. Covers income sources, social security, Medicare, Medicaid, investment planning, estate planning, and other retirement-related topics. Edited for accountants, attorneys, and other financial advisors.

HANDBOOKS AND MANUALS

Asset Protection Planning Guide: A State-of-the-Art Approach to Integrated Estate Planning. Barry S. Engel and others. CCH, Inc. • 2001. $99.00. Provides advice for attorneys, trust officers, accountants, and others engaged in financial planning for protection of assets.

Best Practices for Financial Advisors. Mary Rowland. • 1997. $40.00. Provides advice for professional financial advisors on practice management, ethics, marketing, and legal concerns. (Bloomberg Professional Library.).

CCH Financial and Estate Planning Guide [summary volume]. CCH, Inc. • Annual. $57.95. Contains four main parts: General Principles and Techniques, Special Situations, Building the Estate, and Planning Aids.

Ernst & Young's Personal Financial Planning Guide. John Wiley and Sons, Inc. • 1999. $19.95. Third edition.

Estate and Retirement Planning Answer Book. William D. Mitchell. Aspen Publshers. • 1996. $118.00. Second edition. Basic questions and answers by a lawyer.

Financial Planning Applications. William J. Ruckstuhl. Maple-Vail Book, The Manufacturing Group. • 2000. $68.00. 16th edition. Emphasis on annuities and life insurance. (Huebner School Series.).

Financial Planning for Libraries. Ann E. Prentice. Scarecrow Press. • 1996. $39.95. Second edition. Includes examples of budgets for libraries. (Library Administration Series, No. 12).

Getting Started in Investment Planning Services. James E. Grant. CCH, Inc. • 1999. $85.00. Second edition. Provides advice and information for lawyers and accountants who are planning to initiate fee-based investment services.

Kiss Your Stockbroker Goodbye: A Guide to Independent Investing. John G. Wells. St. Martin's Press. • 1997. $25.95. The author believes that the small investor is throwing money away by using full-commission brokers when discount brokers and many sources of information are easily available. Contains separate chapters on stocks, bonds, mutual funds, asset allocation, financial planners, and related topics. Wells is a securities analyst (CFA) and portfolio manager.

Personal Financial Planning: The Advisor's Guide. Rolf Auster. CCH, Inc. • 1998. $55.95. Third edition. Covers personal taxes, investments, credit, mortgages, insurance, pensions, social security, estate planning, etc.

Personal Financial Planning: With Forms and Checklists. Jonathan Pond. Warren, Gorham & Lamont/RIA Group. • $165.00. Biennial supplementation. Designed for professional financial planners, accountants, attorneys, insurance marketers, brokers, and bankers.

Practicing Financial Planning: A Complete Guide for Professionals. Sid Mittra. Mittra and Associates. • 1993. $29.95. Approved for continuing education of financial planners by the International Board of Standards and Practices for Certified Financial Planners. Covers planning strategies, funds allocation, insurance considerations, risk management, ethics, and other topics.

Protecting Your Practice. Katherine Vessenes. Bloomberg Press. • 1997. $50.00. Discusses legal compliance issues for financial planners. (Bloomberg Professional Library.).

Retirement Planning Guide. Sidney Kess and Barbara Weltman. CCH, Inc. • 1999. $49.00. Presents an overview for attorneys, accountants, and other professionals of the various concepts involved in retirement planning. Includes checklists, tables, forms, and study questions.

The Touche Ross Personal Financial Planning and Investment Workbook. John R. Connell and others. Prentice Hall. • 1989. $39.95. Third edition.

Wall Street Journal Guide to Planning Your Financial Future: The Easy-to-Read Guide to Lifetime Planning for Retirement. Kenneth M. Morris. Simon & Schuster Trade. • 1998. $14.95. Revised edition. (Wall Street Journal Guides Series).

INTERNET DATABASES

Deloitte & Touche Online. Deloitte & Touche LLP, Financial Consulting Services Center. Phone: (513)784-7100 E-mail: webmaster@dtonline.com • URL: http://www.dtonline.com • Web site provides concise, full-text articles on taxes, personal finance, and business from a leading accounting firm. Includes "Tax News and Views," "Personal Finance Advisor," "Business Advisor: A Resource for Small Business Owners," "Financial Tip of the Week," and "This Week Online: Top of the News." Weekly updates. Fees: Free.

ONLINE DATABASES

Wilson Business Abstracts Online. H. W. Wilson Co. • Indexes and abstracts 600 major business periodicals, plus the *Wall Street Journal* and the business section of the *New York Times*. Indexing is from 1982, abstracting from 1990, with the two newspapers included from 1993. Updated weekly. Inquire as to online cost and availability. (*Business Periodicals Index* without abstracts is also available online.).

PERIODICALS AND NEWSLETTERS

Asset Management. Dow Jones Financial Publishing Corp. • Bimonthly. $345.00 per year. Covers the management of the assets of affluent, high net worth investors. Provides information on various financial products and services.

Estate Planner's Alert. Research Institute of America, Inc. • Monthly. $140.00 per year. Newsletter. Covers the tax aspects of personal finance, including home ownership, investments, insurance, retirement planning, and charitable giving. Formerly *Estate and Financial Planners Alert.*

Financial Counseling and Planning. Association for Financial Counseling and Planning Education. • Semiannual. Members, $60. per year; institutions, $100.00 per year; libraries, $60.00 per year. Disseminates scholarly research relating to finacial planning and counseling .

Financial Planning: The Magazine for Financial Service Professionals. Securities Data Publishing. • Monthly. $79.00 per year. Edited for independent financial planners and insurance agents. Covers retirement planning, estate planning, tax planning, and insurance, including long-term healthcare considerations. Special features include a Retirement Planning Issue, Mutual Fund Performance Survey, and Variable Life and Annuity Survey. (Securities Data Publishing is a unit of Thomson Financial.).

FMC (Financial Management): Journal of the Financial Management Association. Financial Management Association International. • Quarterly. Individuals, $80.00 per year; libraries, $100.00 per year. Covers theory and practice of financial planning, international finance, investment banking, and portfolio management. Includes *Financial Practice* and *Education and Contempory Finance Digest.*

Investment Advisor. Dow Jones Financial Publishing Corp. • Monthly. $79.00 per year. Edited for professional investment advisors, financial planners, stock brokers, bankers, and others concerned with the management of assets.

Investment News: The Weekly Newspaper for Financial Advisers. Crain Communications, Inc. • Weekly. $38.00 per year. Edited for both personal and institutional investment advisers, planners, and managers.

Jounal of Finacial Services Professionals. American Society of CLU and Ch F C. • Bimonthly. $38.00 per year. Provides information on life insurance and financial planning, including estate planning, retirement, tax planning, trusts, business insurance, long-term care insurance, disability insurance, and employee benefits. Formerly (American Society of CLU and Ch F C Journal).

Journal of Financial Planning. Financial Planning Association. • 12 times a year. Free to members; non-members, $90.00 per year. Edited for professional financial and investment planners.

Journal of Financial Planning Today. New Directions Publications, Inc. • Quarterly. $100.00 per year. Formerly *Financial Planning Today.*

Journal of Private Portfolio Management. Institutional Investor. • Quarterly. $280.00 per year. Edited for managers of wealthy individuals' investment portfolios.

Journal of Retirement Planning. CCH, Inc. • Bimonthly. $169.00 per year. Emphasis is on retirement and estate planning advice provided by lawyers and accountants as part of their practices.

Journal of Taxation of Financial Products. CCH, Inc. • Bimonthly. $249.00 per year.

Money. Time Inc. • Monthly. $39.95 per year. Covers all aspects of family finance; investments, careers, shopping, taxes, insurance, consumerism, etc.

On Wall Street. Securities Data Publishing. • Monthly. $96.00 per year. Edited for securities dealers. Includes articles on financial planning, retirement planning, variable annuities, and money management, with special coverage of 401(k) plans and IRAs. (Securities Data Publishing is a unit of Thomson Financial.).

Personal Financial Planning: Strategies for Professional Advisors. Warren, Gorham & Lamont/ RIA Group. • Bimonthly. $145.00 per year.

The Practical Accountant: Accounting and Taxes in Everyday Practice. Faulkner and Gray, Inc. • Monthly. $60.00 per year. Covers tax planning, financial planning, practice management, client relationships, and related topics.

Private Asset Management. Institutional Investor. • Biweekly. $2,105.00 per year. Newsletter. Edited for managers investing the private assets of wealthy ("high-net-worth") individuals. Includes marketing, taxation, regulation, and fee topics.

Treasury Manager's Report: Strategic Information for the Financial Executive. Phillips Business Information, Inc. • Biweekly. $595.00. Newsletter reporting on legal developments affecting the operations of banks, savings institutions, and other financial service organizations. Formerly *Financial Services Law Report.*

Worth: Financial Intelligence. Worth Media. • 10 times a year. $18.00 per year. Contains articles for affluent consumers on personal financial management, including investments, estate planning, and taxes.

RESEARCH CENTERS AND INSTITUTES

American Institute for Economic Research. P.O. Box 1000, Great Barrington, MA 01230. Phone: (413)528-1216 Fax: (413)528-0103 E-mail: info@aier.org • URL: http://www.aier.org.

TRADE/PROFESSIONAL ASSOCIATIONS

Association for Financial Counseling and Planning Education. 2121 Arlington Ave., Suite 5, Upper Arlington, OH 43221. Phone: (614)485-9650 Fax: (614)485-9621 E-mail: sburns@finsolve.com • URL: http://www.afcpe.org • Members are professional financial planners and academics.

Institute of Certified Financial Planners. 3801 E. Florida Ave., Ste. 708, Denver, CO 80210-2571. Phone: 800-322-4237 or (303)759-4900 Fax: (303)759-0749 • Members are Certified Financial Planners or are enrolled in programs accredited by the International Board of Standards and Practices for Certified Financial Planners.

International Association for Financial Planning. 5775 Glenridge Dr. N.E., Suite B-300, Atlanta, GA 30328-5364. Phone: 800-322-4237 or (404)845-0011 Fax: (404)845-3660 E-mail: membership@fpanet.org • URL: http://www.iafp.org • Members are individuals involved in some aspect of financial planning.

Investment Counsel Association of America. 1050 17th St., N.W., Suite 725, Washington, DC 20036-5503. Phone: (202)293-4222 Fax: (202)293-4223 E-mail: icaa@icaa.org • URL: http://www.icaa.org.

National Association of Personal Financial Advisors. 355 W. Dundee Rd., Suite 107, Buffalo Grove, IL 60089-3500. Phone: 800-366-2732 or (847)537-7722 Fax: (847)537-7740 E-mail: turfe@napfa.org • URL: http://www.napfa.org • Members are full-time financial planners who are compensated on a fee-only basis.

OTHER SOURCES

Estate and Personal Financial Planning. Edward F. Koren. West Group. • Monthly. Newsletter. Price on application.

Financial and Estate Planning: Analysis, Strategies and Checklists. CCH, Inc. • Looseleaf services. $200.00 per year.

FINANCIAL RATIOS

See also: FINANCIAL ANALYSIS

BIBLIOGRAPHIES

R3: Ratios, Ratings, and Reference. Anne L. Buchanan, editor. Available from American Library Association. • 1996. $20.00. Published by the Reference and User Services Association. Contains basic information on the construction and uses of financial ratios, with extensive listings of ratio data sources. (RUSA Occasional Papers, No. 20.).

FINANCIAL RATIOS

Almanac of Business and Industrial Financial Ratios. Leo Troy. Prentice Hall. • Annual. $99.95. Contains financial ratios derived from federal tax returns. Ratios for each of about 200 industries are arranged according to company asset size.

Annual Statement Studies. Robert Morris Associates: The Association of Lending and Credit Risk Professiona. • Annual. Free to members; non-members, $140.00. Median and quartile financial ratios are given for over 400 kinds of manufacturing, wholesale, retail, construction, and consumer finance establishments. Data is sorted by both asset size and sales volume. Includes a clearly written "Definition of Ratios" and an alphabetical industry index.

Industry Norms and Key Business Ratios. Desk Top Edition. Dun and Bradstreet Corp., Business Information Services. • Annual. Five volumes. $475.00 per volume. $1,890.00 per set. Covers over 800 kinds of businesses, arranged by Standard Industrial Classification number. More detailed editions covering longer periods of time are also available.

Quarterly Financial Report for Manufacturing, Mining, and Trade Corporations. U.S. Federal Trade Commission and U.S. Securities and Exchange Commission. Available from U.S. Government Printing Office. • Quarterly. $39.00 per year.

HANDBOOKS AND MANUALS

Analysis and Use of Financial Statements. Gerald I. White and others. John Wiley and Sons, Inc. • 1997. $112.95. Second edition. Includes analysis of financial ratios, cash flow, inventories, assets, debt, etc. Also covered are employee benefits, corporate investments, multinational operations, financial derivatives, and hedging activities.

Dun & Bradstreet/Gale Group Industry Handbooks. The Gale Group. • 2000. $630.00. Five volumes. $145.00 per volume. Each volume covers two or more major industries: 1. *Entertainment and Hospitality*; 2. *Construction and Agriculture*; 3. *Chemicals and Pharmaceuticals*; 4. *Computers & Software and Broadcasting & Telecommunications*; 5. *Insurance and Health & Medical Services.* The following are included for each industry: overview, statistics, financial ratios, rankings, merger information, company directory, directory of associations, and consultants directory.

How to Read a Financial Report: Wringing Cash Flow and Other Vital Signs Out of the Numbers. John A. Tracy. John Wiley and Sons, Inc. • 1999. $29.95. Fifth edition.

ONLINE DATABASES

Compustat. Standard and Poor's. • Financial data on publicly held U.S. and some foreign corporations; data held for 20 years. Inquire as to online cost and availability.

Disclosure SEC Database. Disclosure, Inc. • Provides information from records filed with the Securities and Exchange Commission by publicly owned corporations, 1977 to present. Weekly updates. Inquire as to online cost and availability.

STATISTICS SOURCES

By the Numbers: Electronic and Online Publishing. The Gale Group. • 1997. $385.00. Four volumes. $99.00 per volume. Covers "high-interest" industries: 1. *By the Numbers: Electronic and Online Publishing*; 2. *By the Numbers: Emerging Industries*; 3. *By the Numbers: Nonprofits*; 4. *By the Numbers: Publishing.* Each volume provides about 600 tabulations of industry data on revenues, market share, employment, trends, financial ratios, profits, salaries, and so forth. Citations to data sources are included.

OTHER SOURCES

Country Risk Monitor. Bank of America, World Information Services, Dept. 3015. • Looseleaf, with semiannual updates. $495.00 per year. Provides rankings of 80 countries according to current and future business risk. Utilizes key economic ratios and benchmarks for countries in a manner similar to financial ratio analysis for industries.

FINANCIAL SERVICES

See: INVESTMENT ADVISORY SERVICES

FINANCIAL STATEMENTS

See: CORPORATION REPORTS; FINANCIAL ANALYSIS

FIRE ALARMS

See: ELECTRONIC SECURITY SYSTEMS

FIRE INSURANCE

See also: INSURANCE

GENERAL WORKS

Smarter Insurance Solutions. Janet Bamford. Bloomberg Press. • 1996. $19.95. Provides practical advice to consumers, with separate chapters on the following kinds of insurance: automobile, homeowners, health, disability, and life. (Bloomberg Personal Bookshelf Series).

ABSTRACTS AND INDEXES

Insurance Periodicals Index. Specials Libraries Association, Insurance and Employees Benefits Div. CCH/NILS Publishing Co. • Annual. $250.00. Compiled by the Insurance and Employee Benefits Div., Special Libraries Association. A yearly index of over 15,000 articles from about 35 insurance periodicals. Arrangement is by subject, with an index to authors.

ALMANACS AND YEARBOOKS

Insurance Almanac: Who, What, When and Where in Insurance. Underwriter Printing and Publishing Co. • Annual. $145.00. Lists insurance agencies and brokerage firms; U.S. and Canadian insurance companies, adjusters, appraisers, auditors, investigators, insurance officials and insurance organizations.

CD-ROM DATABASES

U. S. Insurance: Property and Casualty. Sheshunoff Information Services, Inc. • Monthly. Price on application. CD-ROM provides detailed, current financial information on more than 3,200 property and casualty insurance companies.

DIRECTORIES

S & P's Insurance Book. Standard & Poor's Ratings Group, Insurance Rating Services. • Quarterly. Price on application. Contains detailed financial analyses and ratings of various kinds of insurance companies.

S & P's Insurance Digest: Property-Casualty and Reinsurance Edition. Standard & Poor's Ratings Group, Insurance Rating Services. • Quarterly. Contains concise financial analyses and ratings of property-casualty insurance companies.

ENCYCLOPEDIAS AND DICTIONARIES

Dictionary of Insurance. Lewis E. Davids. Rowman and Littlefield Publishers, Inc. • 1990. $17.95. Seventh revised edition.

Dictionary of Insurance Terms. Harvey W. Rubin. Barron's Educational Series, Inc. • 2000. $12.95. Fourth edition. Defines terms in a wide variety of insurance fields. Price on application.

Insurance Words and Their Meanings: A Dictionary of Insurance Terms. Diana Kowatch. The Rough Notes Co., Inc. • 1998. $38.50. 16th revised edition.

Rupp's Insurance and Risk Management Glossary. Richard V. Rupp. Available from CCH, Inc. • 1996. $35.00. Second edition. Published by NILS Publishing Co. Provides definitions of 6,400 insurance words and phrases. Includes a guide to acronyms and abbreviations.

HANDBOOKS AND MANUALS

The Complete Book of Insurance: The Consumer's Guide to Insuring Your Life, Health, Property, and Income. Ben G. Baldwin. McGraw-Hill Professional. • 1996. $24.95. Revised edition. Provides basic information and advice on various kinds of insurance: life, health, property (fire), disability, long-term care, automobile, liability, and annuities.

Insurance Smart: How to Buy the Right Insurance at the Right Price. Jeffrey P. O'Donnell. John Wiley and Sons, Inc. • 1991. $12.95. Advice for insurance buyers on automobile, homeowner, business, farm, health, and life coverage.

ONLINE DATABASES

Best's Company Reports. A. M. Best Co. • Provides full financial data online for U. S. insurance companies (life, health, property, casualty), including balance sheet data, income statements, expenses, premium income, losses, and investments. Includes *Best's Company Reports, Best's Insurance News,* and Best's ratings of insurance companies. Inquire as to online cost and availability.

I.I.I. Data Base Search. Insurance Information Institute. • Provides online citations and abstracts of insurance-related literature in magazines, newspapers, trade journals, and books. Emphasis is on property and casualty insurance issues, including highway safety, product safety, and environmental liability. Inquire as to online cost and availability.

PERIODICALS AND NEWSLETTERS

Fire, Casualty and Surety Bulletin. The National Underwriter Co. • Monthly. $420.00 per year. Five base volumes. Monthly updates.

NAMIC Magazine. National Association of Mutual Insurance Cos. • Bimonthly. $18.00 per year. Formerly *Mutual Insurance Bulletin.*

STATISTICS SOURCES

Best's Aggregates and Averages: Property-Casualty. A.M. Best Co. • Annual. $335.00. Statistical summary of composite property casualty business. 400 pages of historical data, underwriting expenses and underwriting experience by line.

Property-Casualty Insurance Facts. Insurance Information Institute. • Annual. $22.50. Formerly *Insurance Facts.*

TRADE/PROFESSIONAL ASSOCIATIONS

American Insurance Association. 1130 Connecticut Ave., N.W., Suite 1000, Washington, DC 20036. Phone: 800-242-2302 or (202)828-7100 or (202)828-7183 Fax: (202)293-1219.

CPCU Society. 720 Providence Rd., Malvern, PA 19355-0709. Phone: 800-932-2728 E-mail: cpcu@ansiweb.com • URL: http://www.cpcusociety.org.

OTHER SOURCES

Best's Insurance Reports: Property-Casualty. A.M. Best Co. • Annual. $745.00. Guide to over 1,750 major property/casualty companies.

BestWeek: Property-Casualty. A.M. Best Co. • Weekly. $495.00 per year. Newsletter. Focuses on key areas of the insurance industry. Formerly *Best's Insurance Management Reports: Property-Casualty.*

Fire and Casualty Insurance Law Reports. CCH, Inc. • $870.00 per year. Looseleaf service. Semimonthly updates.

FIRE PREVENTION

See also: FIRE PROTECTION

ABSTRACTS AND INDEXES

Applied Science and Technology Index. H. W. Wilson Co. • 11 times a year. Quarterly and annual cumulations. Service basis for print edition; CD-ROM edition, $1,495.00 per year. Indexes a wide variety of English language technical, industrial, and engineering periodicals.

ONLINE DATABASES

Applied Science and Technology Index Online. H. W. Wilson Co. • Provides online indexing of 400 major scientific, technical, industrial, and engineering periodicals. Time period is 1983 to date. Monthly updates. Inquire as to online cost and availability.

PERIODICALS AND NEWSLETTERS

Fire and Materials. Available from John Wiley and Sons, Inc., Journals Div. • Bimonthly. $495.00 per year. Published in England by John Wiley & Sons Ltd. Provides international coverage of subject matter.

Security Letter. • 22 times a year. $187.00 per year. News and insight on protection of assets from loss. Includes stock market and other data on the security industry.

STATISTICS SOURCES

NFPA Journal. National Fire Protection Association. • Bimonthly. Membership. Incorporates *Fire Journal* and *Fire Command.*

FIRE PROTECTION

See also: FIRE PREVENTION

DIRECTORIES

NFPA Buyer's Guide. National Fire Protection Association. • Annual. $12.00. Listing of fire protection equipment manufacturers. Formerly *Fire Protection Reference Directory.*

HANDBOOKS AND MANUALS

Fire Protection Handbook. National Fire Protection Association. • Irregular. Members, $112.50; non-members, $125.00.

National Fire Protection Association. National Fire Codes. National Fire Protection Association. • Annual. Members, $610.00; non-members, $675.00. Includes supplement. Lists over 270 codes.

PERIODICALS AND NEWSLETTERS

Fire Chief: Administration, Training, Operations. Intertec Publishing Corp. • Monthly. $54.00 per year.

Fire Engineering: The Journal of Fire Suppression and Protection. PennWell Corp., Industrial Div. • Monthly. $28.50 per year.

Fire International: The Journal of the World's Fire Protection Services. DMG World Media. • 10 times a year. $158.00 per year. Text in English. Summaries in French and German.

Fire Technology: An International Journal of Fire Protection Research and Engineering. National Fire Protection Association. • Quarterly. $39.50 per year.

STATISTICS SOURCES

NFPA Journal. National Fire Protection Association. • Bimonthly. Membership. Incorporates *Fire Journal* and *Fire Command.*

TRADE/PROFESSIONAL ASSOCIATIONS

International Association of Fire Chiefs. 4025 Fair Ridge Dr., Fairfax, VA 22033-2868. Phone: (703)273-0911 Fax: (703)273-9363 E-mail: dircomm.@iafc.org • URL: http://www.iafc.org.

International Association of Fire Fighters. 1750 New York Ave., N.W., 3rd Fl., Washington, DC 20006-5395. Phone: (202)737-8484 Fax: (202)737-8418.

International Fire Marshals Association. One Batterymarch Park, Quincy, MA 02269-9101. Phone: (617)984-7424 Fax: (617)984-7056.

International Fire Service Training Association. Oklahoma State University, 930 N. Willis, Stillwater, OK 74078-0118. Phone: 800-654-4055 or (405)744-5723 Fax: (405)744-8204 • URL: http://www.ifsta.org.

National Fire Protection Association. P.O. Box 9101, Quincy, MA 02269-9101. Phone: (617)770-3000 Fax: (617)770-0700 E-mail: library@nfpa.org • URL: http://www.nfpa.org.

Society of Fire Protection Engineers. 7315 Wisconsin Ave., No. 1225W, Bethesda, MD 20814-3202. Phone: (301)718-2910 Fax: (301)718-2242 E-mail: sfpehqtrs@sfpe.org • URL: http://www.sfpe.org.

FIREARMS INDUSTRY

See also: DEFENSE INDUSTRIES; MILITARY MARKET

DIRECTORIES

Guns Illustrated. DBI Books, Inc. • Annual. $20.95. Lists of national and international associations, manufacturers, importers, and distributors of firearms, shooting equipment and services.

Law and Order Magazine Police Equipment Buyer's Guide. Hendon, Inc. • Annual. $15.00. Lists manufacturers, dealers, and distributors of equipment and services for police departments.

Law Enforcement Technology Directory. Cygnus Business Media. • Annual. $60.00 per year. $6.00 per issue; a directory of products, equipment, services, and technology for police professionals. Includes weapons, uniforms, communications equipment, and software.

Shooting Industry-Buyers Guide. Publishers' Development Corp. • Annual. $15.00. Manufacturers, wholesalers, and importers of guns and related equipment and supplies.

HANDBOOKS AND MANUALS

Modern Guns: Identification and Values. Russell C. Quertermous and Steven C. Quertermous. Collector Books. • 2000. $14.95. 13th edition.

The Winchester Handbook. George Madis. Art and Reference House. • 1981. $24.95.

PERIODICALS AND NEWSLETTERS

American Firearms Industry. National Association of Federally Licensed Firearms Dealers. AFI Communications Group, Inc. • Monthly. $35.00 per year.

American Rifleman. National Rifle Association of America. NRA Publications. • Monthly. $35.00 per year.

Bureau of Alcohol, Tobacco, and Firearms Quarterly Bulletin. Bureau of Alcohol, Tobacco, and Firearms, U.S. Department of the Treasury. Available from U.S. Government Printing Office. • Quarterly. $18.00 per year. Laws and regulations.

Guns and Ammo. EMAP USA. • Monthly. $17.94 per year.

Guns Magazine: Finest in the Firearms Field. Publishers Development Corp. • Monthly. $19.95 per year. Annual *Supplement* available. Formerly *Guns.*

Law and Order Magazine: The Magazine for Police Management. Hendon Publishing Co. • Monthly. $22.00 per year. Edited for law enforcement officials. Includes special issues on communications, technology, weapons, and uniforms and equipment.

Law Enforcement Technology. Cygnus Business Media. • Monthly. $60.00 per year. Covers new products and technologies for police professionals. Includes special issues on weapons, uniforms, communications equipment, computers (hardware-software), vehicles, and enforcement of drug laws.

Shooting Industry. Publishers Development Corp. • Monthly. $25.00 per year.

STATISTICS SOURCES

Annual Survey of Manufactures. Available from U. S. Government Printing Office. • Annual. Prices vary. Issued by the U. S. Census Bureau as an interim update to the *Census of Manufactures.* Includes data on number of manufacturing establishments in various industries, employment, labor costs, value of shipments, capital expenditures, inventories, energy costs, and assets. (See also Census Bureau home page, http://www.census.gov/.).

Statistics on Weapons and Violence: A Selection of Statistical Charts, Graphs and Tables about Weapons and Violence from a Variety of Published Sources with Explanatory Comments. The Gale Group. • 1995. $65.00. Includes graphs, charts, and tables arranged within subject chapters. Citations to data sources are provided. (Statistics for Students Series).

TRADE/PROFESSIONAL ASSOCIATIONS

National Rifle Association of America. 11250 Waples Mill Rd., Fairfax, VA 22030. Phone: 800-672-3888 or (703)267-1000 Fax: (703)267-3989 E-mail: comm@nrahq.org • URL: http://www.nra.org.

National Shooting Sports Foundation. Flintlock Ridge Office Center, 11 Mile Hill Rd., Newton, CT 06470-2359. Phone: (203)426-1320 Fax: (203)426-1087 E-mail: info@nssf.org • URL: http://www.nssf.org.

Sporting Arms and Ammunition Manufacturers Institute. 11 Mile Hill Rd., Newtown, CT 06470-2359. Phone: (203)426-4358 Fax: (203)426-1087.

FIRING OF EMPLOYEES

See: DISMISSAL OF EMPLOYEES

FISH CULTURE

See: AQUACULTURE

FISH INDUSTRY

See also: SEAFOOD INDUSTRY

GENERAL WORKS

Water Quality Management for Pond Fish Culture. Claude E. Boyd. Elsevier Science. • 1982. $162.00. (Developments in Aquaculture and Fisheries Science Series: volume nine).

ABSTRACTS AND INDEXES

NTIS Alerts: Agriculture & Food. National Technical Information Service. • Semimonthly. $195.00 per year. Provides descriptions of government-sponsored research reports and software, with ordering information. Covers agricultural economics, horticulture, fisheries, veterinary medicine, food technology, and related subjects. Formerly *Abstract Newsletter.*

CD-ROM DATABASES

Food Science and Technology Abstracts [CD-ROM]. Available from SilverPlatter Information, Inc. • Quarterly. $3,700 per year. Produced by International Food Information Service (home page is http://www.ifis.org). Provides worldwide coverage on CD-ROM of the literature of food technology and production. Various types of publications are indexed, with abstracts, including about 1,800 periodicals. Time period is 1969 to date.

DIRECTORIES

The Seafood Business Annual Buyer's Guide. Diversified Business Communications. • Annual. Price on application. Lists about 1,300 North American fish and shellfish suppliers, distributors, importers and exporters and suppliers of related services and equipment. Formerly *Seafood Buyer's Sourcebook.*

INTERNET DATABASES

USDA. United States Department of Agriculture. Phone: (202)720-2791 E-mail: agsec@usda.gov • URL: http://www.usda.gov • The USDA home page has six sections: News and Information; What's New; About USDA; Agencies; Opportunities; Search and Help. Keyword searching is offered from the USDA home page and from various individual agency home pages. Agencies are the Economic Research Service, Agricultural Marketing Service, National Agricultural Statistics Service, National Agricultural Library, and about 12 others. Updating varies. Fees: Free.

ONLINE DATABASES

Food Science and Technology Abstracts [online]. IFIS North American Desk. • Produced by International Food Information Service. Provides about 500,000 online citations, with abstracts, to the international literature of food science, technology, commodities, engineering, and processing. Approximately 2,000 periodicals are covered. Time period is 1969 to date, with monthly updates. Inquire as to online cost and availability.

PRICE SOURCES

Seafood Price-Current. Urner Barry Publications, Inc. • Semiweekly. $295.00 per year.

RESEARCH CENTERS AND INSTITUTES

Darling Marine Center. University of Maine, 193 Clarks Cove Rd., Walpole, ME 04573. Phone: (207)563-3146 Fax: (207)563-3119 E-mail: kevin@maine.maine.edu • URL: http://server.dmc.maine.edu • *Formerly Ira C. Darling Center for Research, Teaching, and Service.*

Institute for Fisheries Research. 212 Museums Annex Bldg., 1109 N. University Ave., Ann Arbor, MI 48109-1084. Phone: (734)663-3554 Fax: (734)663-9399 E-mail: seelbacp@dnr.state.mi.us • URL: http://www.dnr.state.mi.us/www/ifr/ifrhome/index.htm.

Marine Life Research Group. University of California, San Diego. Scripps Institution of Oceanography, 9500 Gilman Dr., La Jolla, CA 92093-0227. Phone: (858)534-0731 Fax: (858)534-6500 E-mail: mmullin@ucsd.edu • URL: http://www.mlrg.ucsd.edu/.

Mote Marine Laboratory. 1600 Thompson Parkway, Sarasota, FL 33426. Phone: 800-691-6683 or (941)388-4441 Fax: (941)388-4312 E-mail: info@mote.org • URL: http://www.mote.org.

Scripps Institution of Oceanography, Center for Coastal Studies. University of California, San Diego. 9500 Gilman Dr., La Jolla, CA 92093-0209. Phone: (858)534-4333 Fax: (858)534-0300 E-mail: rguza@ucsd.edu.

STATISTICS SOURCES

Agricultural Statistics. Available from U. S. Government Printing Office. • Annual. Produced by the National Agricultural Statistics Service, U. S. Department of Agriculture. Provides a wide variety of statistical data relating to agricultural production, supplies, consumption, prices/price-supports, foreign trade, costs, and returns, as well as farm labor, loans, income, and population. In many cases, historical data is shown annually for 10 years. In addition to farm data, includes detailed fishery statistics.

Annual Survey of Manufactures. Available from U. S. Government Printing Office. • Annual. Prices vary. Issued by the U. S. Census Bureau as an interim update to the *Census of Manufactures.* Includes data on number of manufacturing establishments in various industries, employment, labor costs, value of shipments, capital expenditures, inventories, energy costs, and assets. (See also Census Bureau home page, http://www.census.gov/.).

FAO Fishery Series. Food and Agriculture Organization of the United States. Available from Bernan Associates. • Irregular. Price varies. Text in English, French, and Spanish. Incorporates *Yearbook of Fishery Statistics.*

Fisheries of the United States. Available from U. S. Government Printing Office. • Annual. $18.00. Issued by the National Marine Fisheries Service, National Oceanic and Atmospheric Administration, U. S. Department of Commerce.

Imports and Exports of Fishery Products. National Marine Fisheries Service. U.S. Department of Commerce. • Annual.

TRADE/PROFESSIONAL ASSOCIATIONS

American Fisheries Society. 5410 Grosvenor Lane, Suite 110, Bethesda, MD 20814. Phone: (301)897-8616 Fax: (301)897-8096 E-mail: main@fisheries.org • URL: http://www.fisheries.org.

OTHER SOURCES

Infrastructure Industries USA. The Gale Group. • 2001. $240.00. Replaces *Agriculture, Forestry, Fishing, Mining, and Construction USA* and *Transportation and Public Utilities USA.* Presents statistics and projections relating to economic activity in a wide variety of natural resource and construction industries.

Major Food and Drink Companies of the World. Available from The Gale Group. • 2001. $855.00. Fourth edition. Two volumes. Published by Graham & Whiteside. Contains profiles and trade names for more than 9,000 important food and beverage companies in various countries. In addition to foods, includes both alcoholic and nonalcoholic drink products.

The Seafood Market. MarketResearch.com. • 1997. $595.00. Market research report. Covers fresh, frozen, and canned seafood. Market projections are provided to the year 2001.

Thomas Food and Beverage Market Place. Grey House Publishing. • Annual. $295.00. Three volumes. Contains more than 40,000 entries covering food companies, beverages, food equipment, warehouse companies, food brokers, wholesalers, importers, and exporters. Formerly *Thomas Food Industry Register.*

FITNESS INDUSTRY

ABSTRACTS AND INDEXES

Readers' Guide to Periodical Literature. H. W. Wilson Co. • Monthly. $220.00 per year. CD-ROM edition, $1,495 per year, including annual cumulation. Indexes about 250 peridicals of general interest.

CD-ROM DATABASES

WILSONDISC: Readers' Guide to Periodical Literature. H. W. Wilson Co. • Monthly. $1,095.00 per year, including unlimited online access to *Readers' Guide to Periodical Literature* through WILSONLINE. Provides CD-ROM indexing of about 250 general interest periodicals. Covers 1983 to date. (*Readers' Guide Abstracts* also available on CD-ROM at $1,995 per year.).

DIRECTORIES

Club Industry: Buyers Guide. Intertec Publishing Corp. • Annual. $25.00. A directory of over 1,000 companies furnishing equipment, supplies, and services to health and fitness clubs.

Evaluation Guide to Health and Wellness Programs. The Corporate University. • $189.00. Looseleaf service. Semiannual updates, $49.00 each. Provides detailed descriptions and evaluations of more than 200 employee wellness programs that are available nationally. Covers 15 major topics, such as stress management, substance abuse, occupational safety, smoking cessation, blood pressure management, exercise/fitness, diet, and mental health. Programs are available from both profit and non-profit organizations.

Fitness Management Products and Services Source Guide. Leisure Publications, Inc. • Annual. $30.00. A directory of fitness equipment manufacturers and suppliers of services. Includes a glossary of terms related to the fitness industry and employee wellness programs.

Looking Fit Buyers Guide. Virgo Publishing, Inc. • Annual. $4.00. Lists suppliers of products and equipment for health clubs, aerobic studios, and tanning salons.

HANDBOOKS AND MANUALS

Children's Fitness Center. Entrepreneur Media, Inc. • Looseleaf. $59.50. A practical guide to starting a physical fitness center for children. Covers profit potential, start-up costs, market size evaluation, owner's time required, site selection, lease negotiation, pricing, accounting, advertising, promotion, etc. (Start-Up Business Guide No. E1351.).

Physical Fitness Center. Entrepreneur Media, Inc. • Looseleaf. $59.50. A practical guide to starting a physical fitness center. Covers profit potential, start-up costs, market size evaluation, owner's time required, site selection, lease negotiation, pricing, accounting, advertising, promotion, etc. (Start-Up Business Guide No. E1172.).

ONLINE DATABASES

Newspaper and Periodical Abstracts. Bell & Howell Information and Learning. • Provides online coverage (citations and abstracts) of 25 major newspapers, 1,600 perodicals, and 70 TV programs. Covers business, economics, current affairs, health, fitness, sports, education, technology, government, consumer affairs, psychology, the arts, and the social sciences. Time period is 1986 to date, with daily updates. Inquire as to online cost and availability.

PROMT: Predicasts Overview of Markets and Technology. The Gale Group. • Companies, products, applied technologies and markets. U.S. and international literature coverage, 1972 to date. Inquire as to online cost and availability. Provides abstracts from more than 1,600 publications. Weekly updates.

Readers' Guide Abstracts Online. H. W. Wilson Co. • Indexes and abstracts general interest periodicals, 1983 to date. Weekly updates. Inquire as to online cost and availability.

PERIODICALS AND NEWSLETTERS

Athletic Business. Athletic Business Publications, Inc. • Monthly. $50.00 per year. Published for those whose responsibility is the business of planning, financing and operating athletic/recreation/fitness programs and facilities.

Fitness Management. Leisure Publications, Inc. • Monthly. $24.00 per year. Published for owners and managers of physical fitness centers, both commercial and corporate.

Looking Fit. Virgo Publishing, Inc. • 14 times a year. $40.00 per year. Covers the business and marketing side of health clubs, aerobic studios, and tanning salons.

RESEARCH CENTERS AND INSTITUTES

Center for Exercise Science. University of Florida, 27 Florida Gym, Gainesville, FL 32611. Phone: (352)392-9575 Fax: (352)392-0316 E-mail: spowers@hhp.ufl.edu • Studies fitness as it relates to the general population and as it relates to athletic performance.

Health Management Research Center. University of Michigan, 1027 E. Huron St., Ann Arbor, MI 48109-1688. Phone: (734)763-2462 Fax: (734)763-2206 E-mail: dwe@umich.edu • URL: http://www.umich.edu/~hmrc.

High Technology Fitness Research Institute. 1510 W. Montana St., Chicago, IL 60614. Phone: (773)528-1000 Fax: (773)528-1043 E-mail: bgoldman@worldhalth.net • URL: http://www.worldhealth.net • Research activities include the analysis of health and fitness products and programs on the market.

Human Power, Biochemechanics, and Robotics Laboratory. Cornell University, Dept. of Theoretical and Applied Mechanics, 306 Kimball Hall, Ithaca, NY 14853. Phone: (607)255-7108 Fax: (607)255-2011 E-mail: ruina@cornell.edu • URL: http://www.tam.cornell.edu/~ruina • Conducts research relating to human muscle-powered machines, such as bicycles and rowers.

National Institute for Fitness and Sport. 250 University Blvd., Indianapolis, IN 46202-5192. Phone: (317)274-3432 Fax: (317)274-7408 • URL: http://www.nifs.org.

STATISTICS SOURCES

Profiles of Success. International Health, Racquet, and Sportsclub Association. • Annual. Members, $125.00; non-members, $500.00. Provides detailed financial statistics for commercial health clubs, sports clubs, and gyms.

United States Census of Service Industries. U.S. Bureau of the Census. • Quinquennial. Various reports available.

TRADE/PROFESSIONAL ASSOCIATIONS

Aerobics and Fitness Association of America. 15250 Ventura Blvd., Suite 200, Sherman Oaks, CA 91403. Phone: 800-446-2322 or (818)905-0040 Fax: (818)990-5468 E-mail: afaa@pop3.com • URL: http://www.afaa.com • Members are fitness professionals and aerobic exercise instructors.

American Fitness Association. 1945 Palo Verde Ave., Suite 202, Long Beach, CA 90815. Phone: (562)799-8333 Fax: (562)799-3355 E-mail: staff@nsfa-online.com • URL: http://www.nsfa-online.com • Members are health and fitness professionals.

American Spa and Health Resort Association. P.O. Box 585, Lake Forest, IL 60045. Phone: (847)234-8851 Fax: (847)295-7790 • Members are owners and operators of health spas.

Association for Worksite Health Promotion. 60 Revere Dr., Suite 500, Northbrook, IL 60062-1577. Phone: (847)480-9574 Fax: (847)480-9282 E-mail: awhp@awhp.com • URL: http://www.awhp.com • Members are physical fitness professionals hired by major corporations to conduct health and fitness programs.

Fitness Motivation Institute of America Association. 5221 Scotts Valley Dr., Scott Valley, CA 95066. Phone: 800-538-7790 or (408)439-9898 Fax: (408)439-9504 • URL: http://www.fmia.com • Seeks to motivate, educate, and evaluate individuals in the area of physical fitness. Members are health and fitness professionals.

IDEA, The Health and Fitness Source. 6190 Cornerstone Court E., Suite 204, San Diego, CA 92121. Phone: 800-999-4332 or (619)535-8979 Fax: (619)535-8234 E-mail: member@ideafit.com • URL: http://www.ideafit.com • An educational network and forum for fitness instructors, personal trainers, exercise club owners, and others.

International Health, Racquet and Sportsclub Association. 263 Summer St., Boston, MA 02210. Phone: 800-228-4772 or (617)951-0055 Fax: (617)951-0056 E-mail: info@ihrsa.org • URL: http://www.ihrsa.org • Members are for-profit health clubs, sports clubs, and gyms.

International Physical Fitness Association. 415 W. Court St., Flint, MI 48503. Phone: (810)239-2166 Fax: (810)239-9390 • Members are physical fitness centers of all types.

National Health Club Association. 12596 W. Bayaud Ave., Suite 160, Denver, CO 80228. Phone: 800-765-6422 or (303)753-6422 Fax: (303)986-6813 • Members are fitness centers, health clubs, spas, etc.

National Spa and Pool Institute. 2111 Eisenhower Ave., Alexandria, VA 22314. Phone: (703)838-0083 Fax: (703)549-0493 E-mail: memberserviceinfo@nspi.org • URL: http://www.nspi.org • Members include a wide variety of business firms and individuals involved in some way with health spas, swimming pools, or hot tubs.

United States Association of Independent Gymnastic Clubs. 235 Pinehurst Rd., Wilmington, DE 19803. Phone: (302)656-3706 Fax: (302)656-8929 • Members include gym clubs and manufacturers of gymnastic equipment.

OTHER SOURCES

Consumer Attitudes Toward Physical Fitness and Health Clubs. Available from MarketResearch.com. • 1999. $795.00. Published by American Sports Data, Inc. Contains market research information.

The Market for Physical Fitness and Exercise Equipment. MarketResearch.com. • 1999. $3,250.00. Provides consumer and institutional market data, with forecasts to the year 2003.

Superstudy of Sports Participation. Available from MarketResearch.com. • 1999. $650.00. Three volumes. Published by American Sports Data, Inc. Provides market research data on 102 sports and activities. Vol. 1: *Physical Fitness Activities.* Vol. 2: *Recreational Sports.* Vol. 3: *Outdoor Activities.* (Volumes are available separately at $275.00.).

Weight Loss and Diet Control Market. Available from MarketResearch.com. • 1999. $1,695.00. Market research report published by Marketdata Enterprises. Covers commercial diet programs, medical plans, nonprescription appetite suppressants low-calorie foods, artifical sweeteners, health clubs, and diet books. Includes forecasts to the year 2003.

FIXED INCOME SECURITIES

See: BONDS

FLAVORINGS

See: ADDITIVES AND FLAVORINGS

FLOOR COVERINGS

ALMANACS AND YEARBOOKS

Flooring Buying and Resource Guide. Douglas Publications, Inc. • Annual. $42.50. Lists of manufacturers, workroom manufacturers' representatives, and distributors of floor and other interior surfacing products and equipment; carpet inspection servicecompanies' and related trade associations in the United States and Canada. Formerly *Flooring Directory and Buying Guide.*

DIRECTORIES

Floor Covering Weekly Product Source Guide. Hearst Business Communications, Inc., FCW Div. • Annual. $29.00. Lists manufacturers and importers of carpeting, rugs, ceramic tile, and other floor coverings. Formerly *Floor Covering Weekly.*

ICS Cleaning Specialists Annual Trade Directory and Buying Guide. Business News Publishing Co., II, L.L.C. • Annual. $25.00. Lists about 6,000 manufacturers and distributors of floor covering installation and cleaning equipment. Formerly *Installation and Cleaning Specialists Trade Directory and Buying Guides.*

FINANCIAL RATIOS

Annual Statement Studies. Robert Morris Associates: The Association of Lending and Credit Risk Professiona. • Annual. Free to members; non-members, $140.00. Median and quartile financial ratios are given for over 400 kinds of manufacturing, wholesale, retail, construction, and consumer finance establishments. Data is sorted by both asset size and sales volume. Includes a clearly written "Definition of Ratios" and an alphabetical industry index.

ONLINE DATABASES

F & S Index. The Gale Group. • Contains about four million citations to worldwide business, financial, and industrial or consumer product literature appearing from 1972 to date. Weekly updates. Inquire as to online cost and availability.

PERIODICALS AND NEWSLETTERS

Carpet and Floorcoverings Review. Miller Freeman PLC. • Biweekly. $140.00 per year.

Carpet and Rug Industry. Rodman Publications. • Monthly. $42.00 per year. Edited for manufacturers and distributors of carpets and rugs.

Dalton Carpet Journal. Daily Citizen-News. • Monthly. $12.00. Covers the international tufted carpet market.

Floor Covering News. Roel Product Inc. • Biweekly. $25.00 per year. For retailers, distributors, contractors, and manufacturers.

Floor Covering Weekly. Hearst Business Communications, Inc., FCW Div. • 32 times a year. $54.00 per year.

Installation and Cleaning Specialist. Specialist Publications, Inc. • Monthly. $38.00 per year. Written for floor covering installers and cleaners.

Oriental Rug Review. Oriental Rug Auction Review, Inc. • Bimonthly. $48.00 per year.

Paint and Decorating Retailer. Paint and Decorating Retailers Association. • Monthly. $45.00 per year. Formerly *Decorating Retailer.*

STATISTICS SOURCES

Annual Survey of Manufactures. Available from U. S. Government Printing Office. • Annual. Prices vary. Issued by the U. S. Census Bureau as an interim update to the *Census of Manufactures.* Includes data on number of manufacturing establishments in various industries, employment, labor costs, value of shipments, capital expenditures, inventories, energy costs, and assets. (See also Census Bureau home page, http://www.census.gov/.).

Manufacturing Profiles. Available from U. S. Government Printing Office. • Annual. Issued by the U. S. Census Bureau. A printed consolidation of the entire *Current Industrial Report* series, presenting "all the data compiled." Contains statistics on production, shipments, inventories, consumption, exports, imports, and orders for a wide variety of manufactured products. (See also Census Bureau home page, http://www.census.gov/.).

U. S. Industry and Trade Outlook: The McGraw-Hill Companies and the U.S. Department of Commerce/International Trade Administration. Datapso Research Corp. • Annual. $69.95. Produced by the International Trade Administration, U. S. Department of Commerce, in a "public-private" partnership with DRI/McGraw-Hill and Standard & Poor's. Provides basic data, outlook for the current year, and "Long-Term Prospects" (five-year projections) for a wide variety of products and services. Includes high technology industries. Formerly *U. S. Industrial Outlook.*

United States Census of Manufactures. U.S. Bureau of the Census. • Quinquennial. Results presented in reports, tape, CD-ROM, and Diskette files.

WEFA Industrial Monitor. John Wiley and Sons, Inc. • Annual. $65.00. Prepared by industry analysts at WEFA, an economic forecasting and consulting firm (originally Wharton Econometric Forecasting Associates). Contains discussions of the outlook for major U. S. industries, with many 10-year forecasts (WEFA Web site is http://www.wefa.com).

TRADE/PROFESSIONAL ASSOCIATIONS

Carpet and Rug Institute. P.O. Box 2048, Dalton, GA 30722. Phone: 800-882-8846 or (706)278-3176 Fax: (706)278-8835 • URL: http://www.carpetrug.com.

Carpet Cushion Council. P.O. Box 546, Riverside, CT 06878. Phone: (203)637-1312 Fax: (203)698-1022 E-mail: carpetcushion@gcigrove.com • URL: http://www.carpetcushion.org.

Jute Carpet Backing Council and Burlap and Jute Association. c/o Textile Bag and Packaging Association, Drawer 8, Dayton, OH 45401-0008. Phone: (937)476-8272 Fax: (937)258-0029 E-mail: tbpa@aol.com.

OTHER SOURCES

Carpets and Rugs. Available from MarketResearch.com. • 1999. $3,300.00. Market research data. Published by the Freedonia Group. Provides both historical data and forecasts to 2007 for various kinds of carpeting.

Laminate Flooring. Available from MarketResearch.com. • 1997. $495.00. Market research report published by Specialists in Business Information. Presents laminate flooring market data relative to demographics, sales growth, shipments, exports, imports, price trends, and end-use. Includes company profiles.

U. S. Floor Coverings Industry. Available from MarketResearch.com. • 1999. $1,795.00. Market research report published by Specialists in Business Information. Covers carpets, hardwood flooring, and tile. Presents market data relative to demographics, sales growth, shipments, exports, imports, price trends, and end-use. Includes company profiles.

Vinyl Sheet and Floor Tile. Available from MarketResearch.com. • 1997. $495.00. Market research report published by Specialists in Business Information. Presents vinyl flooring market data relative to demographics, sales growth, shipments, exports, imports, price trends, and end-use. Includes company profiles.

Wood Flooring. Available from MarketResearch.com. • 1999. $2,250.00. Market research report published by Specialists in Business Information. Presents hardwood flooring market data relative to demographics, sales growth, shipments, exports, imports, price trends, and end-use. Includes company profiles.

FLORIST SHOPS

See also: NURSERIES (HORTICULTURAL)

GENERAL WORKS

Retail Florist Business. Peter B. Pfahl and P. Blair Pfahl. Interstate Publishers. • 1994. $48.75. Fifth edition.

DIRECTORIES

Florist-Buyers Directory. Florist's Transworld Delivery. • Annual. $6.00. Lists 1,200 suppliers in floral industry.

FMA Directory and Buyer's Guide. Floral Marketing Association. Produce Marketing Association. • Annual. $45.00. Mass-market growers, wholesalers, equipment manufacturers, accessory suppliers, and supermarket retailers handling flowers and foliage plants and related products. Formerly *Floral Marketing Directory and Buyer's Guide.*

Wholesale Florists and Florist Suppliers of America-Membership Directory. Wholesale Florists and Florist Suppliers of America. • Annual. $100.00. 1,275 listings.

FINANCIAL RATIOS

Annual Statement Studies. Robert Morris Associates: The Association of Lending and Credit Risk Professiona. • Annual. Free to members; non-members, $140.00. Median and quartile financial ratios are given for over 400 kinds of manufacturing, wholesale, retail, construction, and consumer finance establishments. Data is sorted by both asset size and sales volume. Includes a clearly written "Definition of Ratios" and an alphabetical industry index.

HANDBOOKS AND MANUALS

Flower Shop. Entrepreneur Media, Inc. • Looseleaf. $59.50. A practical guide to starting a retail flower shop. Covers profit potential, start-up costs, market size evaluation, owner's time required, site selection, lease negotiation, pricing, accounting, advertising, promotion, etc. (Start-Up Business Guide No. E1143.).

PERIODICALS AND NEWSLETTERS

Florafacts. Florafax International, Inc. • Monthly. $15.00 per year.

Florist. FTD Association. • Monthly. $39.00 per year.

Florists' Review. Florists' Review Enterprises. • Monthly. $39.00 per year.

Flowers: The Beautiful Magazine About the Business of Flowers. Teleflora, Inc. • Monthly. $38.95 per year.

STATISTICS SOURCES

United States Census of Retail Trade. U.S. Bureau of the Census. • Quinquennial.

TRADE/PROFESSIONAL ASSOCIATIONS

Society of American Florists. 1601 Duke St., Alexandria, VA 22314-3406. Phone: 800-336-4743 or (703)836-8700 Fax: (703)836-8705.

Wholesale Florists and Florist Suppliers of America. 410 Pine St., Vienna, VA 22180. Phone: (703)242-7000 Fax: (703)319-1647 E-mail: j.wanko@wffsa.org.

FLOUR INDUSTRY

See also: GRAIN INDUSTRY

ABSTRACTS AND INDEXES

Flour Milling and Baking Research Association Abstracts. Flour Milling and Baking Research Association. • Bimonthly. Membership.

CD-ROM DATABASES

Food Science and Technology Abstracts [CD-ROM]. Available from SilverPlatter Information, Inc. • Quarterly. $3,700 per year. Produced by International Food Information Service (home page is http://www.ifis.org). Provides worldwide coverage on CD-ROM of the literature of food technology and production. Various types of publications are indexed, with abstracts, including about 1,800 periodicals. Time period is 1969 to date.

INTERNET DATABASES

Fedstats. Federal Interagency Council on Statistical Policy. Phone: (202)395-7254 • URL: http://www.fedstats.gov • Web site features an efficient search facility for full-text statistics produced by more than 70 federal agencies, including the Census Bureau, the Bureau of Economic Analysis, and the Bureau of Labor Statistics. Boolean searches can be made within one agency or for all agencies combined. Links are offered to international statistical bureaus, including the UN, IMF, OECD, UNESCO, Eurostat, and 20 individual countries. Fees: Free.

USDA. United States Department of Agriculture. Phone: (202)720-2791 E-mail: agsec@usda.gov • URL: http://www.usda.gov • The USDA home page has six sections: News and Information; What's New; About USDA; Agencies; Opportunities; Search and Help. Keyword searching is offered from the USDA home page and from various individual agency home pages. Agencies are the Economic Research Service, Agricultural Marketing Service, National Agricultural Statistics Service, National Agricultural Library, and about 12 others. Updating varies. Fees: Free.

ONLINE DATABASES

DRI U.S. Central Database. Data Products Division. • Provides more than 23,000 business, financial, demographic, economic, foreign trade, and industry-related time series for the U.S. Includes national income, population, retail-wholesale trade, price indexes, labor data, housing, industrial production, banking, interest rates, money supply, etc. Time period is generally 1947 to date (some data back to 1929). Updating varies. Inquire as to online cost and availability.

Food Science and Technology Abstracts [online]. IFIS North American Desk. • Produced by International Food Information Service. Provides about 500,000 online citations, with abstracts, to the international literature of food science, technology, commodities, engineering, and processing. Approximately 2,000 periodicals are covered. Time period is 1969 to date, with monthly updates. Inquire as to online cost and availability.

PRICE SOURCES

Commercial Review. Oregon Feed and Grain Association. Commercial Review, Inc. • Weekly. $30.00 per year.

RESEARCH CENTERS AND INSTITUTES

Food and Feed Grain Institute. Kansas State University. Waters Hall, Room 105, Manhattan, KS 66506-4030. Phone: (785)532-4057 Fax: (785)532-5861 E-mail: reb@ksu.edu • URL: http://www.ksu.edu.

Plant Biotechnology Institute. National Research Council of Canada. 110 Gymnasium Place, Saskatoon, SK, Canada S7N OW9. Phone: (306)975-5575 Fax: (306)975-4839 E-mail: kkartha@pbi.nrc.ca • URL: http://www.pbi.nrc.ca.

STATISTICS SOURCES

Agricultural Statistics. Available from U. S. Government Printing Office. • Annual. Produced by the National Agricultural Statistics Service, U. S. Department of Agriculture. Provides a wide variety of statistical data relating to agricultural production, supplies, consumption, prices/price-supports, foreign trade, costs, and returns, as well as farm labor, loans, income, and population. In many cases, historical data is shown annually for 10 years. In addition to farm data, includes detailed fishery statistics.

Annual Survey of Manufactures. Available from U. S. Government Printing Office. • Annual. Prices vary. Issued by the U. S. Census Bureau as an interim update to the *Census of Manufactures.* Includes data on number of manufacturing establishments in various industries, employment, labor costs, value of shipments, capital expenditures, inventories, energy costs, and assets. (See also

Census Bureau home page, http://www.census.gov/.).

Business Statistics of the United States. Courtenay M. Slater, editor. Bernan Associates. • 1999. $74.00. Fifth edition. Based on *Business Statistics*, formerly issue by the Bureau of Economic Analysis, U. S. Department of Commerce. Provides basic data for a wide variety of U. S. industries, services, and economic indicators. Most statistics are shown annually for 29 years and monthly for the most recent four years.

Flour Milling Products. U. S. Bureau of the Census. • Monthly and annual. Covers production, mill stocks, exports, and imports of wheat and rye flour. (Current Industrial Reports, M20A.).

Manufacturing Profiles. Available from U. S. Government Printing Office. • Annual. Issued by the U. S. Census Bureau. A printed consolidation of the entire *Current Industrial Report* series, presenting "all the data compiled." Contains statistics on production, shipments, inventories, consumption, exports, imports, and orders for a wide variety of manufactured products. (See also Census Bureau home page, http://www.census.gov/.).

Survey of Current Business. Available from U. S. Government Printing Office. • Monthly. $49.00 per year. Issued by Bureau of Economic Analysis, U. S. Department of Commerce. Presents a wide variety of business and economic data.

TRADE/PROFESSIONAL ASSOCIATIONS

American Corn Millers' Federation. 600 Maryland Ave., S.W., Suite 305 W, Washington, DC 20024. Phone: (202)554-1614 Fax: (202)554-1616 E-mail: cornmiller@aol.com.

American Institute of Baking. P.O. Box 3999, Manhattan, KS 66502-3999. Phone: (785)537-4750 Fax: (785)537-1493 E-mail: mailbox@aibonline.org • URL: http://www.aibonline.org.

Association of Operative Millers. 5001 College Blvd., Suite 104, Leawood, KS 66211. Phone: (913)338-3377 Fax: (913)338-3553 E-mail: aom@sky.net.

National Association of Flour Distributors. c/o David Scruggs, P.O. Box 165067, Little Rock, AR 72216. Phone: (501)372-0636 Fax: (973)316-6668.

North American Millers' Association. 600 Maryland Ave., S.W., Suite 305-W, Washington, DC 20024-2573. Phone: (202)484-2200 Fax: (202)488-7416.

OTHER SOURCES

Major Food and Drink Companies of the World. Available from The Gale Group. • 2001. $855.00. Fourth edition. Two volumes. Published by Graham & Whiteside. Contains profiles and trade names for more than 9,000 important food and beverage companies in various countries. In addition to foods, includes both alcoholic and nonalcoholic drink products.

Thomas Food and Beverage Market Place. Grey House Publishing. • Annual. $295.00. Three volumes. Contains more than 40,000 entries covering food companies, beverages, food equipment, warehouse companies, food brokers, wholesalers, importers, and exporters. Formerly *Thomas Food Industry Register.*

FLUIDICS INDUSTRY

See also: HYDRAULIC ENGINEERING AND MACHINERY

ABSTRACTS AND INDEXES

Applied Science and Technology Index. H. W. Wilson Co. • 11 times a year. Quarterly and annual cumulations. Service basis for print edition; CD-ROM edition, $1,495.00 per year. Indexes a wide variety of English language technical, industrial, and engineering periodicals.

Current Contents: Engineering, Computing and Technology. Institute for Scientific Information. • Weekly. $730.00 per year. Reproductions of contents pages of technical journals. Includes *Author Index, Address Directory, Current Book Contents* and *Title Word Index.* Formerly *Current Contents: Engineering, Technology and Applied Sciences.*

Mechanical Engineering Abstracts. Cambridge Information Group. • Bimonthly. $975.00 per year. Formerly *ISMEC - Mechanical Engineering Abstracts.*

CD-ROM DATABASES

Science Citation Index: Compact Disc Edition. Institute for Scientific Information. • Quarterly. Provides CD-ROM indexing of the world's scientific and technical literature. Corresponds to online *Scisearch* and printed *Science Citation Index.*

DIRECTORIES

CEC Chemical Equipment Catalog: Equipment for the Process Industries. Cahners Business Information. • Annual. $60.00. Provides catalog descriptions of chemical processing equipment in 12 major product or service categories.

Fluid Power Association: Directory and Member Guide. National Fluid Power Association. • Annual. $150.00.

Fluid Power Handbook and Directory. Penton Media Inc. • Biennial. $80.00 per year. Over 1,500 manufacturers and 3,000 distributors of fluid power products in the United States and Canada.

Macrae's Blue Book: Serving the Original Equipment Market. MacRae's Blue Book, Inc. • Annual. $170.00. Two volumes. Lists about 50,000 manufacturers of a wide variety of industrial equipment and supplies.

Thomas Register of American Manufacturers and Thomas Register Catalog File. Thomas Publishing Co., Inc. • Annual. $149.00. 34 volumes. A three-part system offering information on a wide variety of industrial equipment and supplies.

ONLINE DATABASES

Applied Science and Technology Index Online. H. W. Wilson Co. • Provides online indexing of 400 major scientific, technical, industrial, and engineering periodicals. Time period is 1983 to date. Monthly updates. Inquire as to online cost and availability.

FLUIDEX. Available from Elsevier Science, Inc., Secondary Publishing Division. • Produced in the Netherlands by Elsevier Science B.V. Provides indexing and abstracting of the international literature of fluid engineering and technology, 1973 to date, with monthly updates. Also known as *Fluid Engineering Abstracts.* Inquire as to online cost and availability.

Hard Sciences. Cambridge Scientific Abstracts. • Provides the online version of *Computer and Information Systems Abstracts, Electronics and Communications Abstracts, Health and Safety Science Abstracts, ISMEC: Mechanical Engineering Abstracts (Information Service in Mechanical Engineering)* and *Solid State and Superconductivity Abstracts.* Time period is 1981 to date, with monthly updates. Inquire as to online cost and availability.

PROMT: Predicasts Overview of Markets and Technology. The Gale Group. • Companies, products, applied technologies and markets. U.S. and international literature coverage, 1972 to date. Inquire as to online cost and availability. Provides abstracts from more than 1,600 publications. Weekly updates.

Scisearch. Institute for Scientific Information. • Broad, multidisciplinary index to the literature of science and technology, 1974 to present. Inquire as to online cost and availability. Coverage of literature is worldwide, with weekly updates.

Thomas Register Online. Thomas Publishing Co., Inc. • Provides concise information on approximately 194,000 U. S. companies, mainly manufacturers, with over 50,000 product classifications. Indexes over 115,000 trade names. Information is updated semiannually. Inquire as to online cost and availability.

PERIODICALS AND NEWSLETTERS

FPDA News. Fluid Power Distributors Association. • Bimonthly. Membership newsletter. Formerly *FPDA Power Planner.*

Hydraulics and Pneumatics: The Magazine of Fluid Power and Motion Control Systems. Penton Media Inc. • Monthly. Free to qualified personnel; others, $55.00 per year.

Industrial Equipment News. Thomas Publishing Co. • Monthly. $95.00 per year. Free. What's new in equipment, parts and materials.

Journal of Fluid Control: Applications and Research on Fluid Control, Hydraulics and Pneumatics, Instrumentation, and Fluidics. David H. Tarumoto, editor. Delbridge Publishing Co. • Quarterly. $145.00 per volume.

National Fluid Power Association Reporter. National Fluid Power Association. • Bimonthly. $50.00 per year. Newsletter.

New Equipment Digest Market. Penton Media Inc. • Monthly. Free to qualified personnel; others, $55.00 per year. Formerly *Material Handling Engineering.*

New Equipment Reporter: New Products Industrial News. De Roche Publications. • Monthly. Controlled circulation.

Processing. Putman Media. • 14 times a year. $54.00 per year. Emphasis is on descriptions of new products for all areas of industrial processing, including valves, controls, filters, pumps, compressors, fluidics, and instrumentation.

RESEARCH CENTERS AND INSTITUTES

Fluid Power Institute. Milwaukee School of Engineering, Milwaukee, WI 53202. Phone: (414)277-7191 Fax: (414)277-7470 E-mail: wanke@msoe.edu • URL: http://www.msoe.edu.

Fluid Power Laboratory. Ohio State University, Mechanical Engineering Department, 206 W. 18th Ave., Columbus, OH 43210. Phone: (614)292-9044 Fax: (614)292-3163 E-mail: singh.3@osu.edu • URL: http://www.ohio-state.edu.

STATISTICS SOURCES

Annual Survey of Manufactures. Available from U. S. Government Printing Office. • Annual. Prices vary. Issued by the U. S. Census Bureau as an interim update to the *Census of Manufactures.* Includes data on number of manufacturing establishments in various industries, employment, labor costs, value of shipments, capital expenditures, inventories, energy costs, and assets. (See also Census Bureau home page, http://www.census.gov/.).

Manufacturing Profiles. Available from U. S. Government Printing Office. • Annual. Issued by the U. S. Census Bureau. A printed consolidation of the entire *Current Industrial Report* series, presenting "all the data compiled." Contains statistics on production, shipments, inventories, consumption, exports, imports, and orders for a wide variety of manufactured products. (See also Census Bureau home page, http://www.census.gov/.).

TRADE/PROFESSIONAL ASSOCIATIONS

Fluid Power Distributors Association. P.O. Box 1420, Cherry Hill, NJ 08034-0054. Phone: (609)424-8998 Fax: (609)424-9248 E-mail: fpda@howellmgt.com • URL: http://www.fpda.org.

Fluid Power Society. 2433 N. Mayfair Rd., Suite 111, Milwaukee, WI 53226. Phone: (414)257-0910 Fax: (414)257-4092 E-mail: fpsociety@aol.com • URL: http://www.ifps.org.

Institute for Fluitronics Education. P.O. Box 106, Elm Grove, WI 53122-0160. Phone: (414)782-0410 Fax: (414)786-0410 • Concerned with microcomputer control of fluid power.

National Conference on Fluid Power. 3333 N. Mayfair Rd., Milwaukee, WI 53222-3219. Phone: (414)778-3368 Fax: (414)778-3361 E-mail: bprueser@nfpa.com.

National Fluid Power Association. 3333 N. Mayfair Rd., Milwaukee, WI 53222-3219. Phone: (414)778-3344 Fax: (414)778-3361 E-mail: nfpa@nfpa.com • URL: http://www.nfpa.com • Manufacturers.

FLUORESCENT LIGHTING

See: LIGHTING

FLYING

See: AIR PILOTS; AIR TRAVEL; AIRLINE INDUSTRY; BUSINESS AVIATION

FM BROADCASTING

See: RADIO BROADCASTING INDUSTRY

FOCUS GROUPS

See: MARKET RESEARCH; SURVEY METHODS

FOOD ADDITIVES

See: ADDITIVES AND FLAVORINGS

FOOD EQUIPMENT AND MACHINERY

ABSTRACTS AND INDEXES

Applied Science and Technology Index. H. W. Wilson Co. • 11 times a year. Quarterly and annual cumulations. Service basis for print edition; CD-ROM edition, $1,495.00 per year. Indexes a wide variety of English language technical, industrial, and engineering periodicals.

Food Science and Technology Abstracts. International Food Information Service Publishing. • Monthly. $1,780.00 per year. Provides worldwide coverage of the literature of food technology and food production.

Foods Adlibra: Key to the World's Food Literature. Foods Adlibra Publications. • Semimonthly.Provides journal citations and abstracts to the literature of food technology and packaging.

ALMANACS AND YEARBOOKS

Almanac of the Canning, Freezing, Preserving Industries, Vol. Two. Edward E. Judge and Sons, Inc. • Annual. $71.00. Contains U. S. food laws and regulations and detailed production statistics.

CD-ROM DATABASES

Food Science and Technology Abstracts [CD-ROM]. Available from SilverPlatter Information, Inc. • Quarterly. $3,700 per year. Produced by International Food Information Service (home page is http://www.ifis.org). Provides worldwide coverage on CD-ROM of the literature of food technology and production. Various types of publications are indexed, with abstracts, including about 1,800 periodicals. Time period is 1969 to date.

DIRECTORIES

Food Master. Cahners Business Information. • Annual. $99.95. Over 5,000 manufacturers and distributors of food machinery and supplies. Formerly *Food Engineering Master.*

Food Processing Guide and Directory. Putman Publishing Co. • Annual. $75.00. Lists over 5,390 food ingredient and equipment manufacturers.

Foodservice Equipment and Supplies Product Source Guide. Cahners Business Information. • Annual. $35.00. Nearly 1,700 manufacturers of food service equipment and supplies. Formerly *Foodservice Equipment Buyer's Guide and Product Directory.*

Prepared Foods Food Industry Sourcebook. Cahners Business Information. • Annual. $35.00. Provides information on more than 3,000 manufacturers and suppliers of products, ingredients, supplies, and equipment for the food processing industry.

ENCYCLOPEDIAS AND DICTIONARIES

Wiley Encyclopedia of Packaging Technology. Aaron Brody and Kenneth Marsh, editors. John Wiley and Sons, Inc. • 1997. $190.00. Second edition.

HANDBOOKS AND MANUALS

Food and Beverage Market Place: Suppliers Guide. Grey House Publishing. • 2000. $225.00. Second editon. Contains details on companies providing the food industry with a wide variety of supplies, ingredients, packaging, equipment, machinery, instrumentation, chemicals, etc.

ONLINE DATABASES

Food Science and Technology Abstracts [online]. IFIS North American Desk. • Produced by International Food Information Service. Provides about 500,000 online citations, with abstracts, to the international literature of food science, technology, commodities, engineering, and processing. Approximately 2,000 periodicals are covered. Time period is 1969 to date, with monthly updates. Inquire as to online cost and availability.

FOODS ADLIBRA. General Mills, Inc. • Contains online citations, with abstracts, to the technical and business literature of food processing and packaging. New products and new ingredients are featured. Covers about 250 trade journals and 500 research journals from 1974 to date, with monthly updates. Inquire as to online cost and availability.

PERIODICALS AND NEWSLETTERS

Food Engineering International. Cahners Business Information. • Bimonthly. Price on application. Formerly *Chilton's Food Engineering International.*

Food Manufacturing. Cahners Business Information, New Product Information. • Monthly. $59.75 per year. Edited for food processing operations managers and food engineering managers. Includes end-of-year *Food Products and Equipment Literature Review.* Formerly *Food Products and Equipment.*

Food Processing. Putman Publishing Co. • Monthly. Free to qualified personnel; others, $98.00 per year. Edited for executive and operating personnel in the food processing industry.

Food Production/Management: Monthly Publication of the Canning, Glass-Packing Aseptic, and Frozen Food Industry. Arthur Judge, editor. CTI Publications, Inc. • Monthly. $35.00 per year.

Foodservice Equipment and Supplies. Cahners Business Information. • 13 times a year. $92.90 per year.

RESEARCH CENTERS AND INSTITUTES

Food Industries Center. Ohio State University, Howlett Hall, Suite 140, 2001 Fyffe Court, Columbus, OH 43210. Phone: (614)292-7004 Fax: (614)292-4233 E-mail: james.14@osu.edu • URL: http://www.osu.edu.

Institute of Food Science. Cornell University, 114 Stocking Hall, Ithaca, NY 14853. Phone: (607)255-7915 Fax: (607)254-4868 E-mail: mrm1@cornell.edu • URL: http://www.nysaes.cornell.edu/cifs/ • Research areas include the chemistry and processing of food commodities, food processing engineering, food packaging, and nutrition.

National Food Processors Association Research Foundation. 1350 Eye St., N.W., Suite 300, Washington, DC 20005. Phone: (202)639-5958 Fax: (202)639-5991 E-mail: rappleb@nfpa-food.org • URL: http://www.nfpa-food.org • Conducts research on food processing engineering, chemistry, microbiology, sanitation, preservation aspects, and public health factors.

STATISTICS SOURCES

Annual Survey of Manufactures. Available from U. S. Government Printing Office. • Annual. Prices vary. Issued by the U. S. Census Bureau as an interim update to the *Census of Manufactures.* Includes data on number of manufacturing establishments in various industries, employment, labor costs, value of shipments, capital expenditures, inventories, energy costs, and assets. (See also Census Bureau home page, http://www.census.gov/.).

U. S. Industry and Trade Outlook: The McGraw-Hill Companies and the U.S. Department of Commerce/International Trade Administration. Datapso Research Corp. • Annual. $69.95. Produced by the International Trade Administration, U. S. Department of Commerce, in a "public-private" partnership with DRI/McGraw-Hill and Standard & Poor's. Provides basic data, outlook for the current year, and "Long-Term Prospects" (five-year projections) for a wide variety of products and services. Includes high technology industries. Formerly *U. S. Industrial Outlook.*

TRADE/PROFESSIONAL ASSOCIATIONS

Commercial Food Equipment Service Association. 9247 N. Meridan St., Suite 216, Indianapolis, IN 46260. Phone: (317)844-4700 Fax: (317)844-4745.

FISA-Food Industry Suppliers Association. 1207 Sunset Dr., Greensboro, NC 27408. Phone: (336)274-6311 Fax: (336)691-1839.

Food Equipment Manufacturers Association. 401 N. Michigan Ave., Chicago, IL 60611. Phone: 800-336-0019 or (312)644-6610 Fax: (312)245-1566 E-mail: info@nafem.org • URL: http://www.nafem.org.

Food Processing Machinery and Supplies Association. 200 Daingerfield Rd., Alexandria, VA 22314-2800. Phone: 800-331-8816 or (703)684-1080 Fax: (703)548-6563 E-mail: info@fpmsa.org • URL: http://www.fpmsa.org.

Foodservice and Packaging Institute. 1550 Wilson Blvd., No. 701, Arlington, VA 22209. Phone: (703)527-7505 Fax: (703)527-7512 E-mail: fpi@fpi.org • URL: http://www.fpi.org • Members are manufacturers of one-time-use food containers.

Foodservice Equipment Distributors Association. 223 W. Jackson Blvd., Suite 620, Chicago, IL 60606. Phone: (312)427-9605 Fax: (312)427-9607.

International Association of Food Industry Suppliers. 1451 Dolley Madison Blvd., Mc Lean, VA 22101-3850. Phone: (703)761-2600 Fax:

(703)761-4334 E-mail: info@iafis.org • URL: http://www.iafis.org.

International Foodservice Manufacturers Association. Two Prudential Plaza, 180 N. Stetson Ave., Ste. 4400, Chicago, IL 60601. Phone: (312)540-4400 Fax: (312)540-4401 E-mail: ifma@ifmaworld.com • URL: http://www.ifmaworld.com.

Manufacturers' Agents for Food Service Industry. 2402 Mount Vernon Rd., Suite 110, Dunwood, GA 30338. Phone: (770)698-8994 Fax: (770)698-8043 E-mail: info@mafsi.org • URL: http://www.mafsi.org • Members are independent manufacturers' representatives who sell food service equipment and supplies.

North American Association of Food Equipment Manufacturers. 401 N. Michigan Ave., Chicago, IL 60601-4267. Phone: 800-336-0019 or (312)245-1566 Fax: (312)527-6658 E-mail: info@nafem.org • URL: http://www.nafem.org.

Research and Development Associates for Military Food and Packaging Systems. 16607 Blanco Rd., No. 1506, San Antonio, TX 78232. Phone: (210)493-8024 Fax: (210)493-8036 E-mail: rda50@flash.net • URL: http://www.militaryfood.org.

OTHER SOURCES

Major Food and Drink Companies of the World. Available from The Gale Group. • 2001. $855.00. Fourth edition. Two volumes. Published by Graham & Whiteside. Contains profiles and trade names for more than 9,000 important food and beverage companies in various countries. In addition to foods, includes both alcoholic and nonalcoholic drink products.

Thomas Food and Beverage Market Place. Grey House Publishing. • Annual. $295.00. Three volumes. Contains more than 40,000 entries covering food companies, beverages, food equipment, warehouse companies, food brokers, wholesalers, importers, and exporters. Formerly *Thomas Food Industry Register.*

FOOD INDUSTRY

See also: GROCERY BUSINESS

ABSTRACTS AND INDEXES

Applied Science and Technology Index. H. W. Wilson Co. • 11 times a year. Quarterly and annual cumulations. Service basis for print edition; CD-ROM edition, $1,495.00 per year. Indexes a wide variety of English language technical, industrial, and engineering periodicals.

Food Science and Technology Abstracts. International Food Information Service Publishing. • Monthly. $1,780.00 per year. Provides worldwide coverage of the literature of food technology and food production.

Foods Adlibra: Key to the World's Food Literature. Foods Adlibra Publications. • Semimonthly.Provides journal citations and abstracts to the literature of food technology and packaging.

NTIS Alerts: Agriculture & Food. National Technical Information Service. • Semimonthly. $195.00 per year. Provides descriptions of government-sponsored research reports and software, with ordering information. Covers agricultural economics, horticulture, fisheries, veterinary medicine, food technology, and related subjects. Formerly *Abstract Newsletter.*

Nutrition Abstracts and Reviews, Series A: Human and Experimental. Available from CABI Publishing North America. • Monthly. $1,385.00 per year. Published in England by CABI Publishing. Provides worldwide coverage of the literature.

ALMANACS AND YEARBOOKS

FAO Yearbook: Trade. Available from Bernan Associates. • Annual. Published by the Food and Agriculture Organization of the United Nations (FAO). A compliation of international trade statistics for agricultural, fishery, and forest products. Text in English, French, and Spanish.

The State of Food and Agriculture. Available from Bernan Associates. • Annual. Published by the Food and Agriculture Organization of the United Nations (FAO). A yearly review of world and regional agricultural and food activities. Includes tables and graphs. Text in English.

CD-ROM DATABASES

AGRICOLA on SilverPlatter. Available from SilverPlatter Information, Inc. • Quarterly. $825.00 per year. Produced by the National Agricultural Library. Provides about three million citations on CD-ROM to the literature of agriculture, agricultural economics, animal sciences, entomology, fertilizer, food, forestry, nutrition, pesticides, plant science, water resources, and other topics. Each quarterly disc covers the past ten years, with archival discs available from 1970.

Food Science and Technology Abstracts [CD-ROM]. Available from SilverPlatter Information, Inc. • Quarterly. $3,700 per year. Produced by International Food Information Service (home page is http://www.ifis.org). Provides worldwide coverage on CD-ROM of the literature of food technology and production. Various types of publications are indexed, with abstracts, including about 1,800 periodicals. Time period is 1969 to date.

World Marketing Forecasts on CD-ROM. The Gale Group. • Annual. $2,500.00. Produced by Euromonitor. Provides detailed forecast data for the years to 2012 on CD-ROM for 54 countries in all parts of the world. Covers a wide range of social, demographic, economic, and market factors. Includes specific forecasts for many kinds of consumer products.

DIRECTORIES

Food Business Mergers and Acquisitions. Food Institute. • Annual. $510.00. Gives names, locations, and industry categories of all companies involved in food business mergers during the previous year.

Food Chemicals News Directory. Food Chemical News. CRC Press, Inc. • Semiannual. $497.00. Over 2,000 subsidiaries belonging to nearly 250 corporate parents plus an additional 3,000 independent processors. Formerly *Hereld's 1,500.*

Food Engineering Database. Cahners Business Information. • Annual. $325.00. More than 17,000 food and beverage plants with 20 or more employees, food and beverage research and development facilities, and company headquarters. Formerly *Food Engineering Directory of U.S. Food and Beverage Plants.*

Food Master. Cahners Business Information. • Annual. $99.95. Over 5,000 manufacturers and distributors of food machinery and supplies. Formerly *Food Engineering Master.*

Food Processing Guide and Directory. Putman Publishing Co. • Annual. $75.00. Lists over 5,390 food ingredient and equipment manufacturers.

Internet Tools of the Profession: A Guide for Information Professionals. Hope N. Tillman, editor. Special Libraries Association. • 1997. $49.00. Second edition. Consists of 14 sections by various authors or compilers. After two introductory articles on searching the Internet, there are 12 annotated lists of useful Web sites, covering the SLA, business and finance, chemistry, education, food and agriculture, information technology, insurance and employee benefits, law, library management, metals and materials, pharmaceuticals, and telecommunications. An index is provided.

Prepared Foods Food Industry Sourcebook. Cahners Business Information. • Annual. $35.00. Provides information on more than 3,000 manufacturers and suppliers of products, ingredients, supplies, and equipment for the food processing industry.

World Food Marketing Directory. Available from The Gale Group. • 2001. $1,090.00. Second edition. Three volumes. Published by Euromonitor. Provides detailed information on the major food companies of the world, including specific brand data.

ENCYCLOPEDIAS AND DICTIONARIES

Consumers' Guide to Product Grades and Terms: From Grade A to VSOP-Definitions of 8,000 Terms Describing Food Housewares and Other Everyday Terms. The Gale Group. • 1992. $75.00. Includes product grades and classifications defined by government agencies, such as the Food and Drug Administration (FDA), and by voluntary standards organizations, such as the American National Standards Institute (ANSI).

Dictionary of Agriculture: From Abaca to Zoonosis. Kathryn L. Lipton. Lynne Rienner Publishers, Inc. • 1995. $75.00. Emphasis is on agricultural economics.

Dictionary of Food and Ingredients. Robert S. Igoe and Y.H. Hui. Aspen Publishers, Inc. • 1995. $30.00. Third edition.

Encyclopedia of Agriculture Science. Charles J. Arntzen and Ellen M. Ritter, editors. Academic Press, Inc. • 1994. $625.00. Four volumes.

Encyclopedia of Food Science, Food Technology, and Nutrition. Robert Macrae and others, editors. Academic Press, Inc. • 1993. Eight volumes. $2,414.00.

Foods and Nutrition Encyclopedia. Audrey H. Ensminger and others. CRC Press, Inc. • 1993. $382.00. Second edition. Two volumes.

FINANCIAL RATIOS

Almanac of Business and Industrial Financial Ratios. Leo Troy. Prentice Hall. • Annual. $99.95. Contains financial ratios derived from federal tax returns. Ratios for each of about 200 industries are arranged according to company asset size.

Food Marketing Industry Speaks. Food Marketing Institute. • Annual. Members, $30.00; non-members, $75.00. Provides data on overall food industry marketing performance, including retail distribution and store operations.

HANDBOOKS AND MANUALS

Trade Dimensions' Marketing Guidebook. Trade Dimensions. • Annual. $340.00. Over 850 major chain and independent food retailers and wholesalers in the United States and Canada; also includes food brokers, rack jobbers, candy and tobacco distributors, and magazine distributors. Formerly *Progressive Grocer's Marketing Guidebook.*

INTERNET DATABASES

Fedstats. Federal Interagency Council on Statistical Policy. Phone: (202)395-7254 • URL: http://www.fedstats.gov • Web site features an efficient search facility for full-text statistics produced by more than 70 federal agencies, including the Census Bureau, the Bureau of Economic Analysis, and the Bureau of Labor Statistics. Boolean searches can be made within one agency or for all agencies combined. Links are offered to international statistical bureaus, including the UN, IMF, OECD, UNESCO, Eurostat, and 20 individual countries. Fees: Free.

Internet Tools of the Profession. Special Libraries Association. Phone: (202)234-4700 Fax: (202)265-9317 E-mail: hope@tiac.net • URL: http://

www.sla.org/pubs/itotp • Web site is designed to update the printed *Internet Tools of the Profession.* Provides links to a wide range of useful databases in business, finance, industry, information technology, insurance, law, library management, telecommunications, and other subject areas. Fees: Free.

ONLINE DATABASES

Applied Science and Technology Index Online. H. W. Wilson Co. • Provides online indexing of 400 major scientific, technical, industrial, and engineering periodicals. Time period is 1983 to date. Monthly updates. Inquire as to online cost and availability.

DRI U.S. Central Database. Data Products Division. • Provides more than 23,000 business, financial, demographic, economic, foreign trade, and industry-related time series for the U.S. Includes national income, population, retail-wholesale trade, price indexes, labor data, housing, industrial production, banking, interest rates, money supply, etc. Time period is generally 1947 to date (some data back to 1929). Updating varies. Inquire as to online cost and availability.

Euromonitor Market Research. Euromonitor International. • Provides the complete text online of Euromonitor market analysis reports. Covers consumer goods market research data for all major countries, with emphasis on specific product categories. Time period is current. Continuous updating. Inquire as to online cost and availability.

Food Science and Technology Abstracts [online]. IFIS North American Desk. • Produced by International Food Information Service. Provides about 500,000 online citations, with abstracts, to the international literature of food science, technology, commodities, engineering, and processing. Approximately 2,000 periodicals are covered. Time period is 1969 to date, with monthly updates. Inquire as to online cost and availability.

FOODS ADLIBRA. General Mills, Inc. • Contains online citations, with abstracts, to the technical and business literature of food processing and packaging. New products and new ingredients are featured. Covers about 250 trade journals and 500 research journals from 1974 to date, with monthly updates. Inquire as to online cost and availability.

PERIODICALS AND NEWSLETTERS

FDA Consumer. Available from U. S. Government Printing Office. • Bimonthly. $23.00 per year. Issued by the U. S. Food and Drug Administration. Provides consumer information about FDA regulations and product safety.

Food Industry Newsletter: All the Food News That Matters. Newsletters, Inc. • 26 times a year. $245.00 per year. Irregular updates. A summary of key industry news for food executives.

Food Technology. Institute of Food Technologists. • Monthly. Free to members; non-members, $82.00 per year. Articles cover food product development, food ingredients, production, packaging, research, and regulation.

Journal of Agricultural and Food Information. Haworth Press, Inc. • Quarterly. Individuals, $45.00 per year; libraries and other institutions, $85.00 per year. A journal for librarians and others concerned with the acquisition of information on food and agriculture.

Journal of Food Products Marketing: Innovations in Food Advertising, Food Promotion, Food Publicity, Food Sales Promotion. Haworth Press, Inc. • Quarterly. Individuals, $60.00 per year; institutions, $95.00 per year; libraries, $175.00 per year.

Journal of Food Science. Institute of Food Technologists. • Bimonthly. Members, $20.00 per year; non-members, $100.00 per year. A peer-reviewed research journal.

Journal of International Food and Agribusiness Marketing. Haworth Press, Inc. • Quarterly. Individuals, $60.00 per year; institutions, $75.00 per year; libraries, $175.00 per year.

Prepared Foods. Cahners Business Information. • Monthly. $99.90 per year. Edited for food manufacturing management, marketing, and operations personnel.

Progressive Grocer: The Magazine of Supermarketing. Bill Communications, Inc. • Monthly. $99.00 per year.

Washington Agricultural Record. • Weekly. $65.00 per year. Newsletter.

Weekly Digest. American Institute of Food Distribution. • Weekly. $495.00. (Includes *Report on Food Markets, Food Distribution Digest* and *Washington Food Report*).

RESEARCH CENTERS AND INSTITUTES

Academy of Food Marketing. Saint Joseph's University. 5600 City Ave., Philadelphia, PA 19131. Phone: (610)660-1600 Fax: (610)660-1604 E-mail: cmallowe@sju.edu • URL: http://www.sju.edu.

Institute for Food Law and Regulations. Michigan State University, 165C National Food Safety and Toxicology Bldg., East Lansing, MI 48224. Phone: 888-579-3663 or (517)355-8295 Fax: (517)432-1492 E-mail: vhegarty@pilot.msu.edu • URL: http://www.msu.edu • Conducts research on the food industry, including processing, packaging, marketing, and new products.

Monell Chemical Senses Center. 3500 Market St., Philadelphia, PA 19104-3308. Phone: (215)898-8878 Fax: (215)898-2084 E-mail: beauchamp@monell.org • URL: http://www.monell.org • Does multidisciplinary research relating to taste and smell (the chemical senses), including investigation of the sensory qualities of food.

Texas Agricultural Market Research Center. Texas A & M University. Dept. of Agricultural Economics, College Station, TX 77843-2124. Phone: (979)845-5911 Fax: (979)845-6378 E-mail: tamrc@tamu.edu.

STATISTICS SOURCES

Agriculture Fact Book. Available from U. S. Government Printing Office. • Annual. Issued by the Office of Communications, U. S. Department of Agriculture. Includes data on U. S. agriculture, farmers, food, nutrition, and rural America. Programs of the Department of Agriculture in six areas are described: rural economic development, foreign trade, nutrition, the environment, inspection, and education.

Annual Survey of Manufactures. Available from U. S. Government Printing Office. • Annual. Prices vary. Issued by the U. S. Census Bureau as an interim update to the *Census of Manufactures.* Includes data on number of manufacturing establishments in various industries, employment, labor costs, value of shipments, capital expenditures, inventories, energy costs, and assets. (See also Census Bureau home page, http://www.census.gov/.).

Business Statistics of the United States. Courtenay M. Slater, editor. Bernan Associates. • 1999. $74.00. Fifth edition. Based on *Business Statistics*, formerly issue by the Bureau of Economic Analysis, U. S. Department of Commerce. Provides basic data for a wide variety of U. S. industries, services, and economic indicators. Most statistics are shown annually for 29 years and monthly for the most recent four years.

Consumer Canada 1996. Available from The Gale Group. • 1996. $750.00. Published by Euromonitor. Provides consumer market, socioeconomic, and demographic data for Canada. Includes consumer market size (volume and value) for many specific kinds of products.

Consumer International 2000/2001. Available from The Gale Group. • 1998. $1,190.00. Seventh edition. Published by Euromonitor. Contains extensive consumer market, economic, and demographic data for 27 major, non-European countries, including the U. S. and Canada. Includes consumer market size (volume and value) for 150 product types in 14 categories (food, clothing, automobiles, cosmetics, appliances, etc.).

European Marketing Forecasts 2001. Available from The Gale Group. • 2000. $1,190.00. Third edition. Published by Euromonitor. Contains demographic, economic, and market forecasts for the countries of Europe to the year 2010. Forecasts include market-size data for 15 consumer product sectors (food, clothing, automobiles, consumer electronics, etc.).

Food Review. Available from U. S. Government Printing Office. • Three times a year. $13.00 per year. Issued by the U. S. Department of Agriculture. Contains data on domestic and foreign food costs and production. Formerly *National Food Review.*

International Marketing Forecasts 2001. Available from The Gale Group. • 2000. $1,090.00. Third edition. Published by Euromonitor. Contains demographic, economic, and market forecasts to the year 2010 for major, non-European countries, including the U. S. and Canada. Forecasts include market-size data for 15 consumer product sectors, such as food, clothing, and automobiles.

Standard & Poor's Industry Surveys. Standard & Poor's. • Semiannual. $1,800.00. Two looseleaf volumes. Includes monthly supplements. Provides detailed, individual surveys of 52 major industry groups. Each survey is revised on a semiannual basis. Also includes "Monthly Investment Review" (industry group investment analysis) and monthly "Trends & Projections" (economic analysis).

Survey of Current Business. Available from U. S. Government Printing Office. • Monthly. $49.00 per year. Issued by Bureau of Economic Analysis, U. S. Department of Commerce. Presents a wide variety of business and economic data.

WEFA Industrial Monitor. John Wiley and Sons, Inc. • Annual. $65.00. Prepared by industry analysts at WEFA, an economic forecasting and consulting firm (originally Wharton Econometric Forecasting Associates). Contains discussions of the outlook for major U. S. industries, with many 10-year forecasts (WEFA Web site is http://www.wefa.com).

TRADE/PROFESSIONAL ASSOCIATIONS

American Institute of Food Distribution. 28-12 Broadway, Fair Lawn, NJ 07410-3913. Phone: (201)791-5570 Fax: (201)791-5222 E-mail: 70473.741@compuserve.com • URL: http://www.foodinstitute.com.

Association Sales and Marketing Companies. 2100 Reston Parkway, Suite 400, Reston, VA 20191-1218. Phone: (703)758-7790 Fax: (703)758-7787 E-mail: info@asmc.org • URL: http://www.asmc.org.

FISA-Food Industry Suppliers Association. 1207 Sunset Dr., Greensboro, NC 27408. Phone: (336)274-6311 Fax: (336)691-1839.

Institute of Food Technologists. 221 N. LaSalle St., Suite 300, Chicago, IL 60601. Phone: (312)782-8424 Fax: (312)782-8348 E-mail: info@ift.org • URL: http://www.ift.org • A professional society of food scientists active in government, academia, and industry.

United Food and Commercial Workers International Union. 1775 K. St., N.W., Washington, DC 20006. Phone: (202)223-3111 Fax: (202)466-1562 • URL: http://www.ufcw.org.

OTHER SOURCES

Business & Company Resource Center. The Gale Group. • Fee-based Web site provides a wide range of business, industry, and specific company information. Access is offered to trade journal articles, market research data, insider trading activity, major shareholder data, corporate histories, emerging technology reports, corporate earnings estimates, press releases, and other sources. Provides detailed company profiles, industry overviews, and rankings. Offers integration of Predicasts PROMT, Newsletters ASAP, Investext Plus, Business Index ASAP, Brands and Their Companies, and other databases (many have full text).

Food Law Reports. CCH, Inc. • Weekly. $1,349.00 per year. Six looseleaf volumes. Covers regulation of adulteration, packaging, labeling, and additives. Formerly *Food Drug Cosmetic Law Reports.*

Healthy Prepared Foods. MarketResearch.com. • 1999. $2,750.00. Consumer market data on foods that are low in calories, fat, cholesterol, sodium, and sugar or high in fiber and calcium, with forecasts to 2003.

Major Food and Drink Companies of the World. Available from The Gale Group. • 2001. $855.00. Fourth edition. Two volumes. Published by Graham & Whiteside. Contains profiles and trade names for more than 9,000 important food and beverage companies in various countries. In addition to foods, includes both alcoholic and nonalcoholic drink products.

The Market for Value-Added Fresh Produce. MarketResearch.com. • 1999. $2,750.00. Market research report. Covers packaged salad mixes, bulk salad mixes, pre-cut fruits, and pre-cut vegetables. Market projections are provided to the year 2003.

Thomas Food and Beverage Market Place. Grey House Publishing. • Annual. $295.00. Three volumes. Contains more than 40,000 entries covering food companies, beverages, food equipment, warehouse companies, food brokers, wholesalers, importers, and exporters. Formerly *Thomas Food Industry Register.*

FOOD MACHINERY

See: FOOD EQUIPMENT AND MACHINERY

FOOD PACKAGING

See: PACKAGING

FOOD, PROCESSED

See: PROCESSED FOOD INDUSTRY

FOOD PROCESSING

See: FOOD INDUSTRY; PROCESSED FOOD INDUSTRY

FOOD SERVICE INDUSTRY

See also: RESTAURANTS, LUNCHROOMS, ETC.

GENERAL WORKS

Fundamentals of Professional Food Preparation: A Laboratory Text-Workbook. Donald V. Laconi. John Wiley and Sons, Inc. • 1995. $54.95.

DIRECTORIES

Directory of Foodservice Distributors. Chain Store Guide. • Annual. $290.00. Covers distributors of food and equipment to restaurants and institutions.

Foodservice Consultants Society International: Membership Roster. Foodservice Consultants Society International. • Annual. $450.00. About 950 food service consultants.

Foodservice Equipment and Supplies Product Source Guide. Cahners Business Information. • Annual. $35.00. Nearly 1,700 manufacturers of food service equipment and supplies. Formerly *Foodservice Equipment Buyer's Guide and Product Directory.*

International Foodservice Manufacturers Association: Membership Directory. International Foodservice Manufacturers Association. • Annual. Membership. Manufacturers of processed foods equipment and supplies for schools, hospitals, hotels, restaurants, and institutions and related services in the foodservice industry.

School Foodservice Who's Who Directory. Information Central Inc. • Triennial. $675.00. Two volumes. Gives food service details for approximately 5,800 large school districts. Serves as a marketing information source for food and equipment suppliers.

HANDBOOKS AND MANUALS

Catering Service. Entrepreneur Media, Inc. • Looseleaf. $59.50. A practical guide to starting a food and beverage catering business. Covers profit potential, start-up costs, market size evaluation, owner's time required, site selection, pricing, accounting, advertising, promotion, etc. (Start-Up Business Guide No. E1215.).

Cooking for Fifty: The Complete Reference and Cookbook. Chet Holden. John Wiley and Sons, Inc. • 1993. $90.00. Discusses commercial cooking techniques and includes 300 "contemporary" recipes for institutional and commercial cooks.

Diet and Meal Planning. Entrepreneur Media, Inc. • Looseleaf. $59.50. A practical guide to starting a diet and meal planning service. Covers profit potential, start-up costs, market size evaluation, pricing, accounting, advertising, promotion, etc. (Start-Up Business Guide No. E2333.).

ONLINE DATABASES

PROMT: Predicasts Overview of Markets and Technology. The Gale Group. • Companies, products, applied technologies and markets. U.S. and international literature coverage, 1972 to date. Inquire as to online cost and availability. Provides abstracts from more than 1,600 publications. Weekly updates.

PERIODICALS AND NEWSLETTERS

Chef. Talcott Communications Corp. • Monthly. $24.00 per year. Edited for executive chefs, food and beverage directors, caterers, banquet and club managers, and others responsible for food buying and food service. Special coverage of regional foods is provided.

Food Management: Schools, Colleges, Hospitals, Nursing Home Contract Services. Penton Media Inc. • Monthly. Free to qualified personnel; others, $60.00 per year.

Foodservice Equipment and Supplies. Cahners Business Information. • 13 times a year. $92.90 per year.

Hospitality Technology: Infosystems for Foodservice and Lodging. Edgell Communications, Inc. • Monthly. $36.00 per year. Covers information technology, computer communications, and software for foodservice and lodging enterprises.

ID-The Voice of Foodservice Distribution. Bill Communications, Inc. • 14 times a year. $105.00 per year. For foodservice distribution executives and sales representatives. Formerly *Institutional Distribution.*

Journal of Restaurant and Foodservice Marketing. Haworth Press, Inc. • Quarterly. Individuals, $50.00 per year; institutions, $60.00 per year; libraries, $75.00 per year.

Restaurants and Institutions. Cahners Business Information. • Semimonthly. $136.90 per year. Features news, new products, recipes, menu concepts and merchandising ideas from the most successful foodservice operations around the U.S.

TRADE/PROFESSIONAL ASSOCIATIONS

American Correctional Food Service Association. 4248 Park Glen Rd., Minneapolis, MN 55416. Phone: (612)928-4658 Fax: (612)929-1318 E-mail: acfsa@corrections.com • URL: http://www.corrections.com/acfsa • Members are employees of food service operations at correctional institutions.

American School Food Service Association. 700 S. Washington St., Ste. 300, Alexandria, VA 22314. Phone: 800-877-8822 or (703)739-3900 Fax: (703)739-3915 E-mail: servicecenter@asfa.org • URL: http://www.asfsa.org.

American Society for Healthcare Food Service Administrators. c/o American Hospital Association, One N. Franklin St., Chicago, IL 60606. Phone: (312)422-3840 Fax: (312)422-4581 E-mail: sarmist1@aha.org • URL: http://www.ashfsa.org.

Dietary Managers Association. 406 Surrey Woods Dr., Saint Charles, IL 60174. Phone: 800-323-1908 or (630)587-6336 Fax: (630)587-6308 • URL: http://www.dmaonline.org.

Food Distributors International. 201 Park Washington Court, Falls Church, VA 22046. Phone: (703)532-9400 Fax: (703)538-4673 E-mail: staff@fdi.org • URL: http://www.fdi.org • Members are wholesale grocery companies catering to institutions.

Foodservice and Packaging Institute. 1550 Wilson Blvd., No. 701, Arlington, VA 22209. Phone: (703)527-7505 Fax: (703)527-7512 E-mail: fpi@fpi.org • URL: http://www.fpi.org • Members are manufacturers of one-time-use food containers.

Foodservice Consultants Society International. 304 W. Liberty St., Suite 201, Louisville, KY 40202-3068. Phone: (502)583-3783 Fax: (502)589-3602 E-mail: info@fcsi.org • URL: http://www.fcsi.org.

Foodservice Equipment Distributors Association. 223 W. Jackson Blvd., Suite 620, Chicago, IL 60606. Phone: (312)427-9605 Fax: (312)427-9607.

International Food Service Executive's Association. 3739 Mykonos Court, Boca Raton, FL 33498-1282. Phone: (561)998-7758 Fax: (561)998-3878 E-mail: hq@ifsea.org • URL: http://www.ifsea.org.

International Foodservice Editorial Council. P.O. Box 491, Hyde Park, NY 12538. Phone: (914)452-4345 Fax: (914)452-0532 E-mail: ifec@aol.com.

International Foodservice Manufacturers Association. Two Prudential Plaza, 180 N. Stetson Ave., Ste. 4400, Chicago, IL 60601. Phone:

(312)540-4400 Fax: (312)540-4401 E-mail: ifma@ifmaworld.com • URL: http://www.ifmaworld.com.

Manufacturers' Agents for Food Service Industry. 2402 Mount Vernon Rd., Suite 110, Dunwood, GA 30338. Phone: (770)698-8994 Fax: (770)698-8043 E-mail: info@mafsi.org • URL: http://www.mafsi.org • Members are independent manufacturers' representatives who sell food service equipment and supplies.

Mobile Industrial Caterers' Association. 1240 N. Jefferson St., Suite G, Anaheim, CA 92807. Phone: (714)632-6800 Fax: (714)632-5405.

National Council of Chain Restaurants. 325 Seventh St. N.W., Suite 1000, Washington, DC 20004. Phone: (202)626-8183 Fax: (202)626-8185.

National Food Service Association. 152 N. Drexel Ave., Columbus, OH 43209-1427. Phone: (614)263-3346 Fax: (614)263-3359.

National Restaurant Association Educational Foundation. 250 S. Wacker Dr., Chicago, IL 60606. Phone: 800-765-2122 or (812)215-1010 • URL: http://www.edfound.org.

Society for Foodservice Management. 304 W. Liberty St., Suite 201, Louisville, KY 40202. Phone: (502)583-3783 Fax: (502)589-3602 E-mail: sfmhq@aol.com • URL: http://www.sfm-online.org.

Unipro Foodservice. 280 Interstate N. Parkway, Suite 400, Atlanta, GA 30339. Phone: (770)952-0871 Fax: (770)952-0872.

FOOD SERVICE, INSTITUTIONAL

See: FOOD SERVICE INDUSTRY

FOOD, SNACK

See: SNACK FOOD INDUSTRY

FOOD, SPECIALTY

See: SPECIALTY FOOD INDUSTRY

FOOTWEAR

See: SHOE INDUSTRY

FORECASTING

See: BUSINESS FORECASTING; FUTURISTICS

FOREIGN AGRICULTURE

See also: AGRICULTURE

ONLINE DATABASES

CAB Abstracts. CAB International North America. • Contains 46 specialized abstract collections covering over 10,000 journals and monographs in the areas of agriculture, horticulture, forest products, farm products, nutrition, dairy science, poultry, grains, animal health, entomology, etc. Time period is 1972 to date, with monthly updates. Inquire as to online cost and availability. *CAB Abstracts on CD-ROM* also available, with annual updating.

PERIODICALS AND NEWSLETTERS

AgExporter. Available from U. S. Government Printing Office. • Monthly. $44.00 per year. Issued by the Foreign Agricultural Service, U. S. Department of Agriculture. Edited for U. S. exporters of farm products. Provides practical information on exporting, including overseas trade opportunities.

IFAP Newsletter. International Federation of Agricultural Producers. • Bimonthly. Price on application.

Outlook for United States Agricultural Trade. Available from U. S. Government Printing Office. • Quarterly. $10.00 per year. Issued by the Economic Research Service, U. S. Department of Agriculture. (Situation and Outlook Reports.).

STATISTICS SOURCES

Foreign Agricultural Trade of the United States. Available from U. S. Government Printing Office. • Monthly. $50.00 per year. Issued by the Economic Research Service of the U. S. Department of Agriculture. Provides data on U. S. exports and imports of agricultural commodities.

World Agricultural Supply and Demand Estimates. Available from U. S. Government Printing Office. • Monthly. $38.00 per year. Issued by the Economics and Statistics Service and the Foreign Agricultural Service of the U. S. Department of Agriculture. Consists mainly of statistical data and tables.

TRADE/PROFESSIONAL ASSOCIATIONS

International Agricultural Club. U.S. Dept. of Agriculture, 14th and Independence Ave., S.W., Room 5702, Washington, DC 20250. Phone: (202)720-7457.

FOREIGN AUTOMOBILES

See also: AUTOMOBILES

GENERAL WORKS

Auto Industries of Europe, U.S. and Japan. Richard Phillps and others. HarperInformation. • 1982. $32.00. (Economist Intelligence Series).

DIRECTORIES

Overseas Automotive Council Membership Roster. Overseas Automotive Council. • Annual. $50.00 per year. Lists over 700 U.S. and overseas members. Newsletter.

ONLINE DATABASES

Ward's AutoInfoBank. Ward's Communications, Inc. • Provides weekly, monthly, quarterly, and annual statistical data drom 1965 to date for U. S. and imported cars and trucks. Covers production, shipments, sales, inventories, optional equipment, etc. Updating varies by series. Inquire as to online cost and availability.

PERIODICALS AND NEWSLETTERS

Importcar: The Complete Import Service Magazine. Babcox Publications, Inc. • Monthly. $64.00 per year. Includes *Automotive Aftermarket Training Guide.* Formerly *Importcar and Truck.*

TRADE/PROFESSIONAL ASSOCIATIONS

American International Automobile Dealers Association. 99 Canal Center Plaza, Suite 500, Alexandria, VA 22314. Phone: 800-462-4232 or (703)519-7800 Fax: (703)519-7810 E-mail: goaiada@aiada.org • URL: http://www.aiada.org.

Association of International Automobile Manufacturers. 1001 19th St. N., Suite 1200, Arlington, VA 22209. Phone: (703)525-7788 Fax: (703)525-8817 • URL: http://www.aiam.org.

FOREIGN BUSINESS

See: INTERNATIONAL BUSINESS

FOREIGN COMMERCE

See: FOREIGN TRADE

FOREIGN CREDIT

See also: CREDIT; EXPORT-IMPORT TRADE; FOREIGN EXCHANGE

ABSTRACTS AND INDEXES

PAIS International in Print. Public Affairs Information Service, Inc. • Monthly. $650.00 per year; cumulations three times a year. Provides topical citations to the worldwide literature of public affairs, economics, demographics, sociology, and trade. Text in English; indexed materials in English, French, German, Italian, Portuguese and Spanish.

CD-ROM DATABASES

EconLit. Available from SilverPlatter Information, Inc. • Monthly. Single-user, $1,600.00 per year. Multi-user, $2,400.00 per year. Provides CD-ROM citations, with abstracts, to articles from more than 500 economics journals. Time period is 1969 to date. Produced by the American Economic Association.

PAIS on CD-ROM. Public Affairs Information Service, Inc. • Quarterly. $1,995.00 per year. Provides a CD-ROM version of the online service, *PAIS International.* Contains over 400,000 citations to the literature of contemporary social, political, and economic issues.

ONLINE DATABASES

DRI Financial and Credit Statistics. Data Products Division. • Contains U. S. and international statistical data relating to money markets, interest rates, foreign exchange, banking, and stock and bond indexes. Time period is 1973 to date, with continuous updating. Inquire as to online cost and availability.

PAIS International. Public Affairs Information Service, Inc. • Corresponds to the former printed publications, *PAIS Bulletin* (1976-90) and *PAIS Foreign Language Index* (1972-90), and to the current *PAIS International in Print* (1991 to date). Covers economic, political, and sociological material appearing in periodicals, books, government documents, and other publications. Updating is monthly. Inquire as to online cost and availability.

PERIODICALS AND NEWSLETTERS

Bank Letter: Newsletter of Commercial and Institutional Banking. Institutional Investor, Newsletters Div. • Weekly. $2,220.00 per year. Newsletter. Covers retail banking, commercial lending, foreign loans, bank technology, government regulations, and other topics related to banking.

Bondweek: The Newsweekly of Fixed Income and Credit Markets. Institutional Investor. • Weekly. $2,220.00 per year. Newsletter. Covers taxable, fixed-income securities for professional investors, including corporate, government, foreign, mortgage, and high-yield.

FCIB International Bulletin (Finance, Credit and International Business). Finance, Credit and International Business - National Association of Credit Mana. FCIB - NACM. • Monthly. Free.

Grant's Interest Rate Observer. James Grant, editor. Interest Rate Publishing Corp. • Biweekly. $495.00 per year. Newsletter containing detailed analysis of money-related topics, including interest rate trends, global credit markets, fixed-income investments, bank loan policies, and international money markets.

International Bank Credit Analyst. BCA Publications Ltd. • Monthly. $795.00 per year. "A monthly forecast and analysis of currency movements, interest rates, and stock market developments in the principal countries, based on a continuous appraisal of money and credit trends worldwide." Includes many charts and graphs providing international coverage of money, credit, and securities.

Project Finance: The Monthly Analysis of Export, Import and Project Finance. Institutional Investor. • Monthly. $635.00 per year. An analysis of the techniques and practice used in international trade and project finance. Supplements available *World Export Credit Guides* and *Project Finance Book of Lists*. Formed by the merger of *Infrastructure Finance* and *Project and Trade Finance*.

STATISTICS SOURCES

Statistical Information on the Financial Services Industry. American Bankers Association. • Annual. Members, $150.00; non-members, $275.00. Presents a wide variety of data relating to banking and financial services, including consumer economics, personal finance, credit, government loans, capital markets, and international banking.

TRADE/PROFESSIONAL ASSOCIATIONS

FCIB/NACM Corp. 8840 Columbia 100 Pkwy., Columbia, MD 21054-2158. Phone: 888-256-3242 or (732)283-8606 Fax: (732)283-8613 • URL: http://www.fcibglobal.com.

Foreign Credit Insurance Association. 40 Rector St., 11th Fl., New York, NY 10006. Phone: (212)306-5000 Fax: (212)513-4704.

OTHER SOURCES

Country Finance. Economist Intelligence Unit. • Semiannual (quarterly for "fast-changing countries"). $395.00 per year for each country. Discusses banking and financial conditions in each of 47 countries. Includes foreign exchange regulations, the currency outlook, sources of capital, financing techniques, and tax considerations. Formerly Financing Foreign Operations.

FOREIGN EMPLOYMENT

See: EMPLOYMENT IN FOREIGN COUNTRIES

FOREIGN EXCHANGE

See also: CURRENCY EXCHANGE RATES; MONEY; PAPER MONEY

GENERAL WORKS

Currency Risk Management. Gary Shoup, editor. Fitzroy Dearborn Publishers Inc. • 1998. $55.00.

Exchange Rate Determination and Adjustment. Jagdeep S. Bhandari. Greenwood Publishing Group, Inc. • 1982. $65.00.

Financial Institutions and Markets. Robert W. Kolb and Ricardo J. Rodriguez. Blackwell Publishers. • 1996. $77.95. Contains 40 articles (chapters) by various authors on U. S. financial markets and other topics. Includes separate chapters on the International Monetary Fund, inflation, monetary policy, the national debt, bank failures, derivatives, stock prices, initial public offerings, government bonds, pensions, foreign exchange, international markets, and other subjects.

Foreign Exchange Exposure Management: A Portfolio Approach. Niso Abuaf and Stephan Schoess. John Wiley and Sons, Inc. • 1994. $99.95.

The International Money Market: An Assessment of Forecasting Techniques and Market Efficiency. Richard M. Levich. JAI Press, Inc. • 1979. $78.50. (Contemporary Studies in Economic and Financial Analysis Series, Vol. 22).

ABSTRACTS AND INDEXES

Banking Information Index. U M I Banking Information Index. • Monthly. Price on application. Covers a wide variety of banking, business, and financial subjects in periodicals. Formerly *Banking Literature Index*.

ALMANACS AND YEARBOOKS

International Monetary Fund. Annual Report on Exhange Arrangements and Exchange Restrictions. International Monetary Fund Publications Services. • Annual. Individuals, $95.00; libraries, $47.50.

World Currrency Yearbook. International Currency Analysis, Inc. • Annual. $250.00. Directory of more than 110 central banks worldwide.

HANDBOOKS AND MANUALS

Foreign Exchange Handbook: Managing Risk and Opportunity in Global Currency Markets. Paul Bishop and Don Dixon. McGraw-Hill. • 1992. $69.95. Discusses factors affecting currency value, currency price forecasting, options trading, futures, credit risk, and related subjects.

International Guide to Foreign Currency Management. Gary Shoup, editor. Fitzroy Dearborn Publishers. • 1998. $65.00. Written for corporate financial managers. Covers the market for currencies, price forecasting, exposure of various kinds, and risk management.

Strategic Trading in the Foreign Exchange Markets. Gary Klopfenstein. Fitzroy Dearborn Publishers. • 1999. $65.00. Describes the tactics of successful foreign exchange traders.

INTERNET DATABASES

Europa: The European Union's Server. European Union 352 4301 35 349. E-mail: pressoffice@eurostat.cec.be • URL: http://www.europa.eu.int • Web site provides access to a wide variety of EU information, including statistics (Eurostat), news, policies, publications, key issues, and official exchange rates for the euro. Includes links to the European Central Bank, the European Investment Bank, and other institutions. Fees: Free.

Financial Times: Where Information Becomes Intelligence. FT Group. Phone: (212)752-4500 Fax: (212)688-8229 • URL: http://www.ft.com • Web site provides extensive data and information relating to international business and finance, with daily updates. Includes Markets Today, Company News, Economic Indicators, Equities, Currencies, Capital Markets, Euro Prices, etc. Fees: Free (registration required).

Wall Street Journal Interactive Edition. Dow Jones & Co., Inc. Phone: 800-369-2834 or (212)416-2000 Fax: (212)416-2658 E-mail: inquiries@interactive.wsj.com • URL: http://www.wsj.com • Fee-based Web site providing online searching of worldwide information from the *The Wall Street Journal*. Includes "Company Snapshots," "The Journal's Greatest Hits," "Index to Market Data," "14-Day Searchable Archive," "Journal Links," etc. Financial price quotes are available. Fees: $49.00 per year; $29.00 per year to print subscribers.

ONLINE DATABASES

DRI Financial and Credit Statistics. Data Products Division. • Contains U. S. and international statistical data relating to money markets, interest rates, foreign exchange, banking, and stock and bond indexes. Time period is 1973 to date, with continuous updating. Inquire as to online cost and availability.

PERIODICALS AND NEWSLETTERS

Financial Times [London]. Available from FT Publications, Inc. • Daily, except Sunday. $184.00 per year. An international business and financial newspaper, featuring news from London, Paris, Frankfurt, New York, and Tokyo. Includes worldwide stock and bond market data, commodity market data, and monetary/currency exchange information.

Foreign Exchange Letter. Institutional Investor, Newsletters Div. • Biweekly. $1,595.00 per year. Newsletter. Provides information on foreign exchange rates, trends, and opportunities. Edited for banks, multinational corporations, currency traders, and others concerned with money rates.

Foreign Exchange Rates. U.S. Federal Reserve System. • Weekly, $20.00 per year; monthly, $5.00 per year.

Frankfurt Finance. Available from European Business Publications, Inc. • Monthly. $470.00 per year. Newsletter. Published in Germany by Frankfurter Allgemeine Zeitung GmbH Information Services. Presents news of German Bundesbank decisions and the European monetary system, including the European Monetary Union (EMU). Contains charts and tables. Formerly *Old Continent*.

FX Manager (Foreign Exchange). American Educational Systems. • Monthly. $790.00 per year. Foreign exchange forecasts. Formerly *Euromoney Treasury Manager*.

International Market Alert. International Reports, Inc. • Daily. Prices varies. Newsletter. Covers activities of central banks, foreign exchange markets, and New York bond and money markets. Gives specific hedging advice for major currencies. Available online.

International Monetary Fund Staff Papers. International Monetary Fund, Publication Services. • Quarterly. Individuals, $56.00 per year; students, $28.00 per year. Contains studies by IMF staff members on balance of payments, foreign exchange, fiscal policy, and related topics.

Rundt's World Business Intelligence. S. J. Rundt and Associates, Inc. • Weekly. $695.00 per year. Formerly *Rundt's Weekly Intelligence*.

The Wall Street Journal. Dow Jones & Co., Inc. • Daily. $175.00 per year. Covers news and trends relating to business, industry, finance, the economy, and international commerce. Provides extensive price and other data for the securities, commodity, options, futures, foreign exchange, and money markets.

RESEARCH CENTERS AND INSTITUTES

Institute for International Economics. 11 Dupont Circle, N. W., Suite 620, Washington, DC 20036. Phone: (202)328-9000 Fax: (202)328-5432 • URL: http://www.iie.com • Research fields include a wide range of international economic issues, including foreign exchange rates.

STATISTICS SOURCES

Financial Market Trends. Organization for Economic Cooperation and Development. • Three times a year. $100.00 per year. Provides analysis of developments and trends in international and national capital markets. Includes charts and graphs on interest rates, exchange rates, stock market indexes, bank stock indexes, trading volumes, and loans outstanding. Data from OECD countries includes international direct investment, bank profitability, institutional investment, and privatization.

International Financial Statistics. International Monetary Fund, Publications Services. • Monthly. Individuals, $246.00 per year; libraries, $123.00 per year. Includes a wide variety of current data for individual countries in Europe and elsewhere. Annual issue available. Editions available in French and Spanish.

TRADE/PROFESSIONAL ASSOCIATIONS

International Monetary Fund. 700 19th St., N.W., Washington, DC 20431. Phone: (202)623-7000 Fax: (202)623-4661.

OTHER SOURCES

Factiva. Dow Jones Reuters Business Interactive, LLC. • Fee-based Web site provides "global news and business information through Web sites and content integration solutions." Includes Dow Jones and Reuters newswires, The Wall Street Journal, and more than 7,000 other sources of current news, historical articles, market research reports, and investment analysis. Content includes 96 major U. S. newspapers, 900 non-English sources, trade publications, media transcripts, country profiles, news photos, etc.

Nexis.com. Lexis-Nexis Group. • Fee-based Web site offers searching of about 2.8 billion documents in some 30,000 news, business, and legal information sources. Features include a subject directory covering 1,200 topics in 34 categories and a Company Dossier containing information on more than 500,000 public and private companies. Boolean searching is offered.

FOREIGN INVESTMENTS

See also: FOREIGN TRADE; INTERNATIONAL FINANCE; INVESTMENTS

ALMANACS AND YEARBOOKS

Emerging Markets Analyst. • Monthly. $895.00 per year. Provides an annual overview of the emerging financial markets in 24 countries of Latin America, Asia, and Europe. Includes data on international mutual funds and closed-end funds.

BIBLIOGRAPHIES

Thunderbird International Business Review. Thunderbird American Graduate School of International Management. John Wiley and Sons, Inc., Journals Div. • Bimonthly. Institutions, $320.00 per year. Formerly *International Executive.*

DIRECTORIES

Asia Pacific Securities Handbook. Available from Hoover's, Inc. • Annual. $99.95. Published in Hong Kong. Provides detailed descriptions of stock exchanges in 17 Asia Pacific countries, including Australia, China, Hong Kong, India, Japan, and Singapore. Lists largest public companies and most active stock issues.

Dow Jones Guide to the Global Stock Market. Dow Jones & Co., Inc. • Annual. $34.95. Three volumes. Presents concise profiles and three-year financial performance data for each of 3,000 publicly held companies in 35 countries. (Includes all Dow Jones Global Index companies.).

Europe's Top Quoted Companies: A Comparative Directory from Seventeen European Stock Exchanges. Available from Hoover's, Inc. • Annual. $150.00. Published in the UK by COFISEM. Provides detailed, 5-year financial data on 700 major European companies that are publicly traded. Includes company addresses.

Institutional Buyers of Foreign Stocks: A Targeted Directory. Investment Data Corp. • Annual. $595.00. Provides detailed profiles of institutional buyers of international stocks. Includes names of financial analysts and portfolio managers.

International Centre for Settlement of Investment Disputes - Annual Report. International Centre for Settlement of Investment Disputes. • Annual. Free. Editions available in French and Spanish.

HANDBOOKS AND MANUALS

Global Equity Selection Strategies. Ross P. Bruner, editor. Fitzroy Dearborn Publishers, Inc. • 1999. $65.00. Written by various professionals in the field of international investments. Contains six major sections covering growth, value, size, price momentum, sector rotation, and country allocation. (Glenlake Business Monographs).

Practical Guide to Foreign Direct Investment in the European Union. Euroconfidentiel S. A. • Annual. $260.00. Provides coverage of national and EU business incentives. In addition to 70 charts and tables, includes EU country profiles of taxation, labor costs, and employment regulations.

INTERNET DATABASES

CANOE: Canadian Online Explorer. Canoe Limited Partnership. Phone: (416)947-2027 Fax: (416)947-2209 • URL: http://www.canoe.ca • Web site provides a wide variety of Canadian news and information, including business and financial data. Includes "Money," "Your Investment," "Technology," and "Stock Quotes." Allows keyword searching, with links to many other sites. Daily updating. Fees: Free.

DBC Online: America's Leading Provider of Real-Time Market Data to the Individual Investor. Data Broadcasting Corp. Phone: (415)571-1800 E-mail: dbcinfo@dbc.com • URL: http://www.dbc.com • Web site provides a wide variety of real-time securities market prices, data, and charts. Covers bonds ("BondVu"), stocks, commodities, options, mutual funds, major indexes, industry indexes, international markets, etc. Also includes news, SEC documents ("Smart-Edgar"), and various other features. Fees: Both free and fee-based, depending on level of information.

PERIODICALS AND NEWSLETTERS

Emerging Markets Debt Report. Securities Data Publishing. • Weekly. $895.00 per year. Newsletter. Provides information on new and prospective sovereign and corporate bond issues from developing countries. Includes an emerging market bond index and pricing data. (Securities Data Publishing is a unit of Thomson Financial.).

Emerging Markets Quarterly. Institutional Investor. • Quarterly. $325.00 per year. Newsletter on financial markets in developing areas, such as Africa, Latin America, Southeast Asia, and Eastern Europe. Topics include institutional investment opportunities and regulatory matters. Formerly *Emerging Markets Weekly.*

Financial Times Global Investors' Digest. Capitol Publications, Inc. • Monthly. $695.00 per year. Newsletter. Contains information, forecasts, data, and analysis relating to international financial markets, including emerging markets. Supplement available *Mid-Month Global Financial Report.* Formerly *Global Investors' Digest.*

Financial Trader. Miller Freeman, Inc. • 11 times a year. $160.00 per year. Edited for professional traders. Covers fixed income securities, emerging markets, derivatives, options, futures, and equities.

Global Money Management. Institutional Investor. • Biweekly. $2,330.00 per year. Newsletter. Edited for international pension fund and investment company managers. Includes information on foreign investment opportunities and strategies.

Institutional Investor International Edition: The Magazine for International Finance and Investment. Institutional Investor. • Monthly. $415.00 per year. Covers the international aspects of professional investing and finance. Emphasis is on Europe, the Far East, and Latin America.

Institutional Investor: The Magazine for Finance and Investment. Institutional Investor. • Monthly. $475.00 per year. Edited for portfolio managers and other investment professionals. Special feature issues include "Country Credit Ratings," "Fixed Income Trading Ranking," "All-America Research Team," and "Global Banking Ranking.".

Journal of Alternative Investments. Institutional Investor. • Quarterly. $380.00 per year. Covers such items as hedge funds, private equity financing, funds of funds, real estate investment trusts, natural resource investments, foreign exchange, and emerging markets.

STATISTICS SOURCES

Financial Market Trends. Organization for Economic Cooperation and Development. • Three times a year. $100.00 per year. Provides analysis of developments and trends in international and national capital markets. Includes charts and graphs on interest rates, exchange rates, stock market indexes, bank stock indexes, trading volumes, and loans outstanding. Data from OECD countries includes international direct investment, bank profitability, institutional investment, and privatization.

International Direct Investment Statistics Yearbook. OECD Publications and Information Center. • Annual. $79.00. Provides direct investment inflow and outflow data for OECD countries.

International Guide to Securities Market Indices. Henry Shilling, editor. Fitzroy Dearborn Publishers. • 1996. $140.00. Describes 400 stock market, bond market, and other financial price indexes maintained in various countries of the world (300 of the indexes are described in detail, including graphs and 10-year data).

OTHER SOURCES

Investing in Latin America: Best Stocks, Best Funds. Michael Molinski. Bloomberg Press. • 1999. $24.95. Provides Latin American stock and mutual fund recommendations for individual investors. (Bloomberg Personal Bookshelf.).

Investing, Licensing, and Trading. Economist Intelligence Unit. • Semiannual. $345.00 per year for each country. Key laws, rules, and licensing provisions are explained for each of 60 countries. Information is provided on political conditions, markets, price policies, foreign exchange practices, labor, and export-import.

World Investment Report. United Nations Publications. • Annual. $49.00. Concerned with foreign direct investment, economic development, regional trends, transnational corporations, and globalization.

FOREIGN LANGUAGE PRESS AND NEWSPAPERS

See also: BUSINESS JOURNALISM; NEWSPAPERS

ALMANACS AND YEARBOOKS

Editor and Publisher International Yearbook: Encyclopedia of the Newspaper Industry. Editor and Publisher Co., Inc. • Annual. $125.00. Daily and Sunday newspapers in the United States and Canada.

DIRECTORIES

Bacon's International Media Directory. Bacon's Publishing Co., Inc. • Annual. $295.00. Covers print media in Western Europe. Formerly *Bacon's International Publicity Checker.*

Benn's Media Directories. Nichols Publishing Co. • Annual. $620.00. Three volumes. Over 47,000 daily and weekly newspapers, free newspapers, periodicals directories, major publishers, in-house periodicals, television and broadcasting stations, media associations and suppliers of services to the publishing and broadcasting industry. Formerly *Benn's Press Directory.*

Burrelle's Media Directory: Newspapers and Related Media. Burrelle's Information Services. • Annual. $275.00. Two volumes. *Daily Newspapers* volume lists more than 2,000 daily publications in the U. S., Canada, and Mexico. *Non-Daily Newspapers* volume lists more than 10,000 items published no more than three times a week. Provides detailed descriptions, including key personnel.

Hispanic Media and Market Source. SRDS. • Quarterly. $271.00 per year. Provides detailed information on the following Hispanic advertising media in the U. S.: TV, radio, newspapers, magazines, direct mail, outdoor, and special events. Formerly *Hispanic Media and Markets.*

International Media Guide: Newspapers Worldwide. International Media Guides, Inc. • Annual. $285.00. Provides advertising rates, circulation, and other details relating to newspapers in major cities of the world (covers 200 countries, including U. S.).

Willings Press Guide. Hollis Directories Ltd. • Annual. $325.00. Two volumes. Over 30,000 periodicals and newspapers, plus some annuals and directories published in the United Kingdom and Ireland, with listings for major publications in Europe, the Americas, Australasia, Africa, the Far East and the Middle East; also includes 3,000 services to publishers in the United Kingdom.

PERIODICALS AND NEWSLETTERS

International Press Journal: International Press News and Views. • Quarterly. $20.00 per year.

World Press Review: News and Views from Around the World. Stanley Foundation. • Monthly. $26.97 per year. International news and information on a wide variety of subjects that do not appear in other American publications.

TRADE/PROFESSIONAL ASSOCIATIONS

Foreign Press Association. 110 E. 59th St., Suite 2102A, New York, NY 10022. Phone: (212)751-3068 Fax: (212)751-3081 E-mail: fpanewyork@aol.com.

Overseas Writers. 2071 National Press Bldg., Washington, DC 20045. Phone: (301)229-2387 or (301)229-3748 Fax: (301)229-6704.

United Press International. 1510 H St., N.W., Suite 600, Washington, DC 20005. Phone: 800-796-4874 or (202)898-8000 Fax: (202)898-8057.

FOREIGN LAW

See: INTERNATIONAL LAW AND REGULATION

FOREIGN MARKETS

See: FOREIGN TRADE

FOREIGN OPERATIONS

See: INTERNATIONAL BUSINESS

FOREIGN RADIO AND TELEVISION

See also: FOREIGN LANGUAGE PRESS AND NEWSPAPERS; RADIO BROADCASTING INDUSTRY; TELEVISION BROADCASTING INDUSTRY

DIRECTORIES

International Radio and Television Society: Foundation-Roster Yearbook. International Radio and Television Society, Inc. • Annual. Membership. A directory of approximately 1,600 members (persons involved professionally with radio or television).

International Television and Video Almanac: Reference Tool of the Television and Home Video Industries. Quigley Publishing Co., Inc. • Annual. $119.00.

International Television Association-Membership Directory. International Television Association. • Annual. Membership.

PERIODICALS AND NEWSLETTERS

International Broadcast Engineer. DMG World Media. • Eight times a year. $180.00 per year.

ITVA News. International Television Association. • Bimonthly. Membership newsletter. Formerly *International Television News.*

Television International Magazine. Television International Publications, Ltd. • Bimonthly. $42.00 per year.

TRADE/PROFESSIONAL ASSOCIATIONS

International Radio and Television Society Foundation. 420 Lexington Ave., Suite 1714, New York, NY 10170. Phone: (212)867-6650 Fax: (212)867-6653 • URL: http://www.irts.org.

International Television Association. 9202 N. Meridian St., Suite 200, Indianapois, IN 46260-1810. Phone: 888-879-4882 or (317)816-6269 Fax: 800-801-8926 E-mail: chris@itva.org • URL: http://www.itva.org • Concerned with non-broadcast industrial television recording for business training and corporate communications.

FOREIGN SERVICE

See: DIPLOMATIC AND CONSULAR SERVICE

FOREIGN STUDY

See: STUDY ABROAD

FOREIGN TRADE

See also: EXPORT-IMPORT TRADE

GENERAL WORKS

Reciprocity, U. S. Trade Policy, and the GATT Regime. Carolyn Rhodes. Cornell University Press. • 1993. $37.50.

ABSTRACTS AND INDEXES

PAIS International in Print. Public Affairs Information Service, Inc. • Monthly. $650.00 per year; cumulations three times a year. Provides topical citations to the worldwide literature of public affairs, economics, demographics, sociology, and trade. Text in English; indexed materials in English, French, German, Italian, Portuguese and Spanish.

ALMANACS AND YEARBOOKS

Agricultural Policies, Markets, and Trade: Monitoring and Evaluation. Organization for Economic Cooperation and Development. Available from OECD Publications and Information Center. • Annual. $62.00. A yearly report on agricultural and trade policy developments in OECD member countries.

FAO Yearbook: Trade. Available from Bernan Associates. • Annual. Published by the Food and Agriculture Organization of the United Nations (FAO). A compliation of international trade statistics for agricultural, fishery, and forest products. Text in English, French, and Spanish.

Trade and Development Report and Overview. Available from United Nations Publications. • Annual. $45.00. Yearly overview of trends in international trade, including an analysis of the economic and trade situation in developing countries. Published by the United Nations Conference on Trade and Development (UNCTAD).

BIBLIOGRAPHIES

Global Data Locator. George T. Kurian. Bernan Associates. • 1997. $89.00. Provides detailed descriptions of international statistical sourcebooks and electronic databases. Covers a wide variety of trade, economic, and demographic topics.

CD-ROM DATABASES

National Trade Data Bank: The Export Connection. U. S. Department of Commerce. • Monthly. $575.00 per year. Provides over 150,000 trade-related data series on CD-ROM. Includes full text of many government publications. Specific data is included on national income, labor, price indexes, foreign exchange, technical standards, and international markets. Website address is http://www.stat-usa.gov/.

PAIS on CD-ROM. Public Affairs Information Service, Inc. • Quarterly. $1,995.00 per year. Provides a CD-ROM version of the online service, *PAIS International.* Contains over 400,000 citations to the literature of contemporary social, political, and economic issues.

WILSONDISC: Wilson Business Abstracts. H. W. Wilson Co. • Monthly. $2,495.00 per year, including unlimited online access to *Wilson Business Abstracts* through WILSONLINE. Provides CD-ROM "cover-to-cover" abstracting and indexing of over 600 prominent business periodicals. Indexing is from 1982, abstracting from 1990. (*Business Periodicals Index* without abstracts is available on CD-ROM at $1,495 per year.).

World Trade Atlas CD-ROM. Global Trade Information Services, Inc. • Monthly. $4,920.00 per year. ($3,650.00 per year with quarterly updates.) Provides government statistics on trade between the U. S. and each of more than 200 countries. Includes import-export data, trade balances, product information, market share, price data, etc. Time period is the most recent three years.

World Trade Organization Trade Policy Review. Bernan Press. • Annual. $95.00. CD-ROM provides detailed trade information for each of 40 countries. Includes search capabilities, hypertext links, charts, tables, and graphs.

DIRECTORIES

Directory of American Firms Operating in Foreign Countries. Uniworld Business Publications Inc. • Biennial. $275.00. Three volumes. Lists approximately 2,450 American companies with more than 29,500 subsidiaries and affiliates in 138 foreign countries.

Directory of Foreign Firms Operating in the United States. Uniworld Business Publications, Inc. • Biennial. $225.00. Lists about 2,400 foreign companies and 5,700 American affiliates. 75 countries are represented.

Internet Resources and Services for International Business: A Global Guide. Lewis-Guodo Liu. Oryx Press. • 1998. $49.95. Describes more than 2,500 business-related Web sites from 176 countries. Includes five major categories: general information, economics, business and trade, business travel, and contacts. Indexed by Web site name, country, and subject.

Principal International Businesses: The World Marketing Directory. Dun and Bradstreet Information Services. • Annual. $5000. Provides information about 50,000 major businesses located in over 140 countries. Geographic arrangement with company name and product indexes.

Trade Directories of the World. Croner Publications, Inc. • Annual. 100.00.Looseleaf. Monthly supplements. Lists over 3,300 publications.

U. S. Almanac of International Trade. Bernan Press. • 2000. $225.00. Fifth edition. Provides directory information on individuals and organizations concerned with foreign trade. Contains four sections dealing with: U. S. government, foreign governments, international organizations, and trade-related groups. Formerly *Washington Almanac of International Trade and Business.*

World Business Directory 2001. World Trade Centers Association. Available from The Gale Group. • 2000. $615.00. Ninth edition. Four volumes. Addresses and contact information for 300 world trade centers and affiliate organizations worldwide.

ENCYCLOPEDIAS AND DICTIONARIES

Blackwell Encyclopedic Dictionary of International Management. John J. O'Connell, editor. Blackwell Publishers. • 1997. $105.95. The editor is associated with the American Graduate School of International Management. Contains definitions of key terms combined with longer articles written by various U. S. and foreign business educators. Includes bibliographies and index. (Blackwell Encyclopedia of Management Series).

Encyclopedia of Business. The Gale Group. • 2000. $425.00. Second edition. Two volumes. Contains more than 700 signed articles covering major business disciplines and concepts. International in scope.

HANDBOOKS AND MANUALS

Arthur Andersen North American Business Sourcebook: The Most Comprehensive, Authoritative Reference Guide to Expanding Trade in the North American Market. Triumph Books. • 1993. $195.00. Includes statistical, regulatory, economic, and directory information relating to North American trade, including information on the North American Free Trade Agreement (NAFTA). Emphasis is on exporting to Mexico and Canada.

Reference Book for World Traders. Croner Publications, Inc. • $170.00. Three volumes. A looseleaf handbook covering information required for planning and executing exports and imports to and from all foreign countries; kept up to date by an amendment service.

INTERNET DATABASES

Bureau of Economic Analysis (BEA). U. S. Department of Commerce, Bureau of Economic Analysis. Phone: (202)606-9900 Fax: (202)606-5310 E-mail: webmaster@bea.doc.gov • URL: http://www.bea.doc.gov • Web site includes "News Release Information" covering national, regional, and international economic estimates from the BEA. Highlights of releases appear online the same day, complete text and tables appear the next day. "Recent News Releases" section provides titles for past nine months, with links. "BEA Data and Methodology" includes "Frequently Requested NIPA Data" (national income and product accounts, such as gross domestic product and personal income). Other statistics are available. Fees: Free.

Canadian American Trade Site: Promoting Trade Between Canada and the Southeastern United States. Small Business Development Center of South Carolina. Phone: 800-243-7232 or (803)777-4909 Fax: (803)777-4403 E-mail: canamtr@darla.badm.sc.edu • URL: http://canamtrade.badm.sc.edu • Web site provides information about trade between the U. S. and Canada. Includes links to other trade-related Web sites. Fees: Free.

EBSCO Information Services. Ebsco Publishing. Phone: 800-871-8508 or (508)356-6500 Fax: (508)356-5640 E-mail: ep@epnet.com • URL: http://www.epnet.com • Fee-based Web site providing Internet access to a wide variety of databases, including business-related material. Full text is available for many periodical titles, with daily updates. Fees: Apply.

Fedstats. Federal Interagency Council on Statistical Policy. Phone: (202)395-7254 • URL: http://www.fedstats.gov • Web site features an efficient search facility for full-text statistics produced by more than 70 federal agencies, including the Census Bureau, the Bureau of Economic Analysis, and the Bureau of Labor Statistics. Boolean searches can be made within one agency or for all agencies combined. Links are offered to international statistical bureaus, including the UN, IMF, OECD, UNESCO, Eurostat, and 20 individual countries. Fees: Free.

ProQuest Direct. Bell & Howell Information and Learning. Phone: 800-521-0600 or (313)761-4700 Fax: (313)973-9145 • URL: http://www.umi.com/proquest • Fee-based Web site providing Internet access to more than 3,000 periodicals, newspapers, and other publications. Many items are available full-text, with daily updates. Includes extensive corporate and financial information from Disclosure, Inc. Fees: Apply.

ONLINE DATABASES

DRI U.S. Central Database. Data Products Division. • Provides more than 23,000 business, financial, demographic, economic, foreign trade, and industry-related time series for the U.S. Includes national income, population, retail-wholesale trade, price indexes, labor data, housing, industrial production, banking, interest rates, money supply, etc. Time period is generally 1947 to date (some data back to 1929). Updating varies. Inquire as to online cost and availability.

EconLit. American Economic Association. • Covers the worldwide literature of economics as contained in selected monographs and about 550 journals. Subjects include microeconomics, macroeconomics, economic history, inflation, money, credit, finance, accounting theory, trade, natural resource economics, and regional economics. Time period is 1969 to present, with monthly updates. Inquire as to online cost and availability.

PAIS International. Public Affairs Information Service, Inc. • Corresponds to the former printed publications, *PAIS Bulletin* (1976-90) and *PAIS Foreign Language Index* (1972-90), and to the current *PAIS International in Print* (1991 to date). Covers economic, political, and sociological material appearing in periodicals, books, government documents, and other publications. Updating is monthly. Inquire as to online cost and availability.

Wilson Business Abstracts Online. H. W. Wilson Co. • Indexes and abstracts 600 major business periodicals, plus the *Wall Street Journal* and the business section of the *New York Times.* Indexing is from 1982, abstracting from 1990, with the two newspapers included from 1993. Updated weekly. Inquire as to online cost and availability. (*Business Periodicals Index* without abstracts is also available online.).

PERIODICALS AND NEWSLETTERS

Canada-U. S. Trade. Carswell. • Monthly. $185.00 per year. Newsletter on all current aspects of trade between the U. S. and Canada.

Direction of Trade Statistics. International Monetary Fund. International Monetary Fund Publications Services. • Quarterly. $110.00 per year. Includes *Yearbook.*

Economic Justice Report: Global Issues of Economic Justice. Ecumenical Coalition for Economic Justice. • Quarterly. Individuals, $30.00 per year; institutions, $40.00 per year. Reports on economic fairness in foreign trade. Formerly *Gatt-Fly Report.*

EuroWatch. Worldwide Trade Executives. • Biweekly. $799.00 per year. Newsletter.

International Trade Reporter Export Reference Manual. Bureau of National Affairs, Inc. • Weekly. $874.00 per year. Looseleaf. Formerly *Export Shipping Manual.*

The Journal of International Trade and Economic Development. Routledge Journals. • Quarterly. Individuals, $68.00 per year; institutions, $445.00 per year. Emphasizes the effect of trade on the economies of developing nations.

Journal of World Trade. Kluwer Law International. • Bimonthly. $609.60 per year. Includes online edition. Formerly *Journal of World Trade Law.*

Project Finance: The Monthly Analysis of Export, Import and Project Finance. Institutional Investor. • Monthly. $635.00 per year. An analysis of the techniques and practice used in international trade and project finance. Supplements available *World Export Credit Guides* and *Project Finance Book of Lists.* Formed by the merger of *Infrastructure Finance* and *Project and Trade Finance.*

World Trade: For the Executive with Global Vision. World Trade Magazine. • Monthly. $36.00 per year. Edited for senior management of U. S. companies engaged in international business and trade.

RESEARCH CENTERS AND INSTITUTES

Conference Board, Inc. 845 Third Ave., New York, NY 10022. Phone: (212)759-0900 Fax: (212)980-7014 E-mail: richard.cavanaugh@conference-board.org • URL: http://www.conference-board.org.

International Law Institute. 1615 New Hampshire Ave., N.W., Suite 100, Washington, DC 20009. Phone: (202)483-3036 Fax: (202)483-3029 E-mail: training@ili.org • URL: http://www.ili.org • Research in foreign trade law and in other areas of international law is done in cooperation with Georgetown University.

STATISTICS SOURCES

Agriculture Fact Book. Available from U. S. Government Printing Office. • Annual. Issued by the Office of Communications, U. S. Department of Agriculture. Includes data on U. S. agriculture, farmers, food, nutrition, and rural America. Programs of the Department of Agriculture in six areas are described: rural economic development, foreign trade, nutrition, the environment, inspection, and education.

Business Statistics of the United States. Courtenay M. Slater, editor. Bernan Associates. • 1999. $74.00. Fifth edition. Based on *Business Statistics*, formerly issue by the Bureau of Economic Analysis, U. S. Department of Commerce. Provides basic data for a wide variety of U. S. industries, services, and economic indicators. Most statistics are shown annually for 29 years and monthly for the most recent four years.

Economic Report of the President: Together with the Annual Report of the Council of Economic Advisors. Available from U. S. Government Printing Office. • Annual. $29.00. Includes about 130 pages of "Statistical Tables Relating to Income, Employment, and Production." Tables cover national income, employment, wages, productivity, manufacturing, prices, credit, finance (public and private), corporate profits, and foreign trade.

Foreign Agricultural Trade of the United States. Available from U. S. Government Printing Office. •

Monthly. $50.00 per year. Issued by the Economic Research Service of the U. S. Department of Agriculture. Provides data on U. S. exports and imports of agricultural commodities.

Foreign Trade by Commodities (Series C). OECD Publications and Information Center. • Annual. $625.00. Five volumes. Presents detailed five-year export-import data for specific commodities in OECD member countries.

Foreign Trade of the United States: Including State and Metro Area Export Data. Courtenay M. Slater, and James B. Rice, editors. Bernan Press. • 1999. $74.00. Provides detailed national, state, and local data relating to U. S. exports and imports.

Handbook of International Economic Statistics. Available from National Technical Information Service. • Annual. $40.00. Prepared by U. S. Central Intelligence Agency. Provides basic statistics for comparing worldwide economic performance, with an emphasis on Europe, including Eastern Europe.

Handbook of International Trade and Development Statistics. United Nations Publications. • Annual. $80.00. Text in English and French.

International Trade Statistics Yearbook. United Nations Statistical Office. United Nations Publications. • Annual. $135.00. Two volumes.

Monthly Bulletin of Statistics. United Nations Publications. • Monthly. $295.00 per year. Provides current data for about 200 countries on a wide variety of economic, industrial, and demographic subjects. Compiled by United Nations Statistical Office.

Monthly Statistics of Foreign Trade (Series A). OECD Publications and Information Center. • Monthly. $190.00 per year. Shows value of exports and imports in OECD member countries, including volume-of-trade indicators. Formerly *OECD Statistics of Foreign Trade (Series A).*

Services: Statistics on International Transactions. Organization for Economic Cooperation and Development. Available from OECD Publications and Information Center. • Annual. $71.00. Presents a compilation and assessment of data on OECD member countries' international trade in services. Covers four major categories for 20 years: travel, transportation, government services, and other services.

State Profiles: The Population and Economy of Each U. S. State. Courtenay Slater and Martha Davis, editors. Bernan Press. • 1999. $74.00. Presents charts, tables, and text in an eight-page profile for each state. Covers population, labor force, income, poverty, employment, wages, industry, trade, housing, education, health, taxes, and government finances.

Statistical Yearbook. United Nations Publications. • Annual. $125.00. Contains statistics for about 200 countries on a wide variety of economic, industrial, and demographic topics. Compiled by United Nations Statistical Office.

Survey of Current Business. Available from U. S. Government Printing Office. • Monthly. $49.00 per year. Issued by Bureau of Economic Analysis, U. S. Department of Commerce. Presents a wide variety of business and economic data.

World Statistics Pocketbook. United Nations Publications. • Annual. $10.00. Presents basic economic, social, and environmental indicators for about 200 countries and areas. Covers more than 50 items relating to population, economic activity, labor force, agriculture, industry, energy, trade, transportation, communication, education, tourism, and the environment. Statistical sources are noted.

World Trade Annual. United Nations Statistical Office. Walker and Co. • Annual. Prices vary.

TRADE/PROFESSIONAL ASSOCIATIONS

National Foreign Trade Council. 1270 Ave. of the Americas, New York, NY 10020. Phone: (212)399-7128 Fax: (212)399-7144.

World Trade Centers Association. One World Trade Center, Suite 7701, New York, NY 10048. Phone: (212)435-7168 Fax: (212)435-2810 • URL: http://www.wtca.org • Members are associated with centers devoted to the increase of international trade.

OTHER SOURCES

FedWorld: A Program of the United States Department of Commerce. National Technical Information Service. • Web site offers "a comprehensive central access point for searching, locating, ordering, and acquiring government and business information." Emphasis is on searching the Web pages, databases, and government reports of a wide variety of federal agencies. Fees: Free.

Foreign Tax and Trade Briefs. Matthew Bender & Co., Inc. • $470.00. Two looseleaf volumes. Periodic supplementation. The latest tax and trade information for over 100 foreign countries.

From GATT to the WTO: The Multilateral Trading System in the New Millennium. WTO Secretariat, editor. Available from Kluwer Academic Publishers. • 2000. $79.50. Published by the World Trade Organization (http://www.wto.org). A collection of essays on the future of world trade, written on the occasion of the 50th anniversary of the multilateral trading system (GATT/WTO). The authors are described as "important academics in international trade.".

Going Global: Getting Started in International Trade. American Management Association Extension Institute. • Looseleaf. $130.00. Self-study course. Emphasis is on practical explanations, examples, and problem solving. Quizzes and a case study are included.

InSite 2. Intelligence Data/Thomson Financial. • Fee-based Web site consolidates information in a "Base Pack" consisting of Business InSite, Market InSite, and Company InSite. Optional databases are Consumer InSite, Health and Wellness InSite, Newsletter InSite, and Computer InSite. Includes fulltext content from more than 2,500 trade publications, journals, newsletters, newspapers, analyst reports, and other sources. Continuous updating. Formerly produced by The Gale Group.

Successful International Marketing: How to Gain the Global Advantage. American Management Association Extension Institute. • Looseleaf. $130.00. Self-study course. Emphasis is on practical explanations, examples, and problem solving. Quizzes and a case study are included.

Trade Policy Reviews. Bernan Press. • Annual. Price varies for each country's review (31 are available). Each review describes "trade policies, practices, and macroeconomic situations." Prepared by the Trade Policy Review Board of the World Trade Organization.

World Trade Organization Annual Report. Available from Bernan Associates. • Annual. $80.00. Two volumes ($40.00 per volume). Published by the World Trade Organization. Volume one: *Annual Report.* Volume two: *International Trade Statistics.*

World Trade Organization Dispute Settlement Decisions: Bernan's Annotated Reporter. Bernan Press. • Dates vary. $75.00 per volume. Contains all World Trade Organization Panel Reports and Appellate Decisions since the establishment of the WTO in 1995. Includes such cases as "The Importation, Sale, and Distribution of Bananas.".

WTO Focus. World Trade Organization, Publications Service. • Newsletter. Free. 10 times a year. Text in English. Provides current news about activities relating to the World Trade Organization (WTO) and the General Agreement on Tariffs and Trade (GATT). Formerly *GATT Focus.*

FOREMEN

See: FACTORY MANAGEMENT

FOREST PRODUCTS

See also: HARDWOOD INDUSTRY; LUMBER INDUSTRY; PAPER INDUSTRY

GENERAL WORKS

Decision-Making in Forest Management. M. R. Williams. State Mutual Book and Periodical Service, Ltd. • 1988. $270.00.

Forest Products and Wood Science: An Introduction. John G. Haygreen and Jim L. Bowyer. Iowa State University Press. • 1996. $62.95. Third edition.

Introduction to Forest Science. Raymond A. Young. John Wiley and Sons, Inc. • 1990. $106.95. Second edition.

Managing the World's Forests: Looking for Balance Between Conservation and Development. Narendra P. Sharma. Kendall-Hunt Publishing Co. • 1992. $35.95. A study by The World Bank.

ABSTRACTS AND INDEXES

Forestry Abstracts: Compiled from World Literature. Available from CABI Publishing North America. • Monthly. $1,155 per year. Published in England by CABI Publishing. Provides worldwide coverage of the literature.

ALMANACS AND YEARBOOKS

Wood Technology-Equipment Catalog and Buyers' Guide. Miller Freeman, Inc. • Annual. $55.00. Formerly *Forest Industries-Lumber Review and Buyers' Guide.*

CD-ROM DATABASES

AGRICOLA on SilverPlatter. Available from SilverPlatter Information, Inc. • Quarterly. $825.00 per year. Produced by the National Agricultural Library. Provides about three million citations on CD-ROM to the literature of agriculture, agricultural economics, animal sciences, entomology, fertilizer, food, forestry, nutrition, pesticides, plant science, water resources, and other topics. Each quarterly disc covers the past ten years, with archival discs available from 1970.

DIRECTORIES

Directory of the Wood Products Industry. Miller Freeman, Inc. • Biennial. $295.00. Lists sawmills, panelmills, logging operations, plywood products, wood products, distributors, etc. Geographic arrangement, with an index to lumber specialities. Formerly *Directory of the Forest Products Industry.*

ENCYCLOPEDIAS AND DICTIONARIES

Encyclopedia of Agriculture Science. Charles J. Arntzen and Ellen M. Ritter, editors. Academic Press, Inc. • 1994. $625.00. Four volumes.

Encyclopedia of Wood: A Tree by Tree Guide to the World's Most Valuable Resource. Bill Lincoln and others. Facts on File, Inc. • 1989. $29.95.

INTERNET DATABASES

USDA. United States Department of Agriculture. Phone: (202)720-2791 E-mail: agsec@usda.gov • URL: http://www.usda.gov • The USDA home page has six sections: News and Information; What's New; About USDA; Agencies; Opportunities;

Search and Help. Keyword searching is offered from the USDA home page and from various individual agency home pages. Agencies are the Economic Research Service, Agricultural Marketing Service, National Agricultural Statistics Service, National Agricultural Library, and about 12 others. Updating varies. Fees: Free.

ONLINE DATABASES

Business and Industry. Responsive Database Services, Inc. • Contains online citations, abstracts, and selected fulltext from more than 1,000 trade journals, newspapers, and other publications. Provides general coverage of both manufacturing and service industries, including marketing, production, industry trends, key events, and information on specific companies. Time span is 1994 to date. Daily updates. Inquire as to online cost and availability. (Also available in a CD-ROM version.).

CAB Abstracts. CAB International North America. • Contains 46 specialized abstract collections covering over 10,000 journals and monographs in the areas of agriculture, horticulture, forest products, farm products, nutrition, dairy science, poultry, grains, animal health, entomology, etc. Time period is 1972 to date, with monthly updates. Inquire as to online cost and availability. *CAB Abstracts on CD-ROM* also available, with annual updating.

PaperChem Database. Information Services Div. • Worldwide coverage of the scientific and technical paper industry chemical literature, including patents, 1967 to present. Weekly updates. Inquire as to online cost and availability.

PIRA. Technical Centre for the Paper and Board, Printing and Packaging Industries. • Citations and abstracts pertaining to bookbinding and other pulp, paper, and packaging industries, 1975 to present. Weekly updates. Inquire as to online cost and availability.

Tablebase. Responsive Database Services, Inc. • Provides online numerical tabular data from a wide variety of business, organization, and government sources, including 900 trade journals. Includes industry and individual company statistics relating to products, market share, sales forecasts, production, exports, market trends, etc. Time span is 1997 to date. Weekly updates. Inquire as to online cost and availability. (Also available in a CD-ROM version.).

PERIODICALS AND NEWSLETTERS

Forest Products Journal. Forest Products Society. • 10 times a year. $135.00 per year.

Journal of Sustainable Forestry. Haworth Press, Inc. • Quarterly. Individuals, $65.00 per year; institutions, $95.00 per year; libraries, $135.00 per year. Two volumes. An academic and practical journal. Topics include forest management, forest economics, and wood science.

Wood Technology: Logging, Pulpwood, Forestry, Lumber, Panels. Miller Freeman, Inc. • Eight times a year. $120.00 per year. Formerly *Forest Industries.*

PRICE SOURCES

Official Board Markets: "The Yellow Sheet". Mark Arzoumanian. Advanstar Communications, Inc. • Weekly. $150.00 per year. Covers the corrugated container, folding carton, rigid box and waste paper industries.

RESEARCH CENTERS AND INSTITUTES

Forintek Canada Corporation. 2665 E. Mall, Vancouver, BC, Canada V6T 1W5. Phone: (604)224-3221 Fax: (604)222-5690 • URL: http://www.forintek.ca.

STATISTICS SOURCES

Agricultural Statistics. Available from U. S. Government Printing Office. • Annual. Produced by the National Agricultural Statistics Service, U. S. Department of Agriculture. Provides a wide variety of statistical data relating to agricultural production, supplies, consumption, prices/price-supports, foreign trade, costs, and returns, as well as farm labor, loans, income, and population. In many cases, historical data is shown annually for 10 years. In addition to farm data, includes detailed fishery statistics.

Encyclopedia of American Industries. The Gale Group. • 1998. $560.00. Second edition. Two volumes. $280.00 per volume. Volume one is *Manufacturing Industries* and volume two is *Service and Non-Manufacturing Industries.* Provides the history, development, and recent status of approximately 1,000 industries. Includes statistical graphs, with industry and general indexes.

Lumber Production and Mill Stocks. U.S. Bureau of the Census. • Annual. (Current Industrial Reports MA-24T).

Standard & Poor's Industry Surveys. Standard & Poor's. • Semiannual. $1,800.00. Two looseleaf volumes. Includes monthly supplements. Provides detailed, individual surveys of 52 major industry groups. Each survey is revised on a semiannual basis. Also includes "Monthly Investment Review" (industry group investment analysis) and monthly "Trends & Projections" (economic analysis).

Timber Bulletin. Economic Commission for Europe. United Nations Publications. • Irregular. Price on application. Contains international statistics on forest products, including price, production, and foreign trade data.

U. S. Industry and Trade Outlook: The McGraw-Hill Companies and the U.S. Department of Commerce/International Trade Administration. Datapso Research Corp. • Annual. $69.95. Produced by the International Trade Administration, U. S. Department of Commerce, in a "public-private" partnership with DRI/McGraw-Hill and Standard & Poor's. Provides basic data, outlook for the current year, and "Long-Term Prospects" (five-year projections) for a wide variety of products and services. Includes high technology industries. Formerly *U. S. Industrial Outlook.*

United States Timber Production, Trade, Consumption, And Price Statistics. Forest Service. U.S. Department of Agriculture. • Annual.

Yearbook of Forest Products. Food and Agriculture Organization of the United Nations. Available from Bernan Associates. • Annual. Test in English, French, and Spanish.

TRADE/PROFESSIONAL ASSOCIATIONS

American Forest and Paper Association. 1111 19th St., N.W., Ste. 800, Washington, DC 20036. Phone: (202)463-2700 Fax: (202)463-2785 E-mail: info@afandpa.org • URL: http://www.afandpa.org.

American Wood Preservers Institute. 2750 Prosperity Ave., Suite 550, Fairfax, VA 22031-4312. Phone: 800-356-2974 or (703)204-0500 Fax: (703)204-4610 E-mail: info@awpi.org • URL: http://www.awpi.org.

Forest Products Society. 2801 Marshall Court, Madison, WI 53705-2295. Phone: (608)231-1361 Fax: (608)231-2152 E-mail: info@forestprod.org • URL: http://www.forestprod.org.

National Hardwood Lumber Association. P.O. Box 34518, Memphis, TN 38184-0518. Phone: (901)377-1818 Fax: (901)382-6419 • URL: http://www.natlhardwood.org • Members are hardwood lumber and veneer manufacturers and distributors. Users of hardwood products are also members.

Wood Products Manufacturers Association. 175 State Rd., E., Westminster, MA 01473-1208. Phone: (978)874-5445 Fax: (978)874-9946 E-mail: woodprod@wpma.org • URL: http://www.wpma.org.

OTHER SOURCES

Infrastructure Industries USA. The Gale Group. • 2001. $240.00. Replaces *Agriculture, Forestry, Fishing, Mining, and Construction USA* and *Transportation and Public Utilities USA.* Presents statistics and projections relating to economic activity in a wide variety of natural resource and construction industries.

FORGERIES

See also: COUNTERFEITING; CRIME AND CRIMINALS; FRAUD AND EMBEZZLEMENT

ONLINE DATABASES

NCJRS: National Criminal Justice Reference Service. U.S. Department of Justice. • References print and non-print information on law enforcement and criminal justice, 1972 to present. Monthly updates. Inquire as to online cost and availability.

PERIODICALS AND NEWSLETTERS

FBI Law Enforcement Bulletin. Available from U. S. Government Printing Office. • Monthly. $36.00 per year. Issued by Federal Bureau of Investigation, U. S. Department of Justice. Contains articles on a wide variety of law enforcement and crime topics, including computer-related crime.

TRADE/PROFESSIONAL ASSOCIATIONS

American Association of Handwriting Analysts. P.O. Box 45, Southfield, MI 48037-0095,. Phone: (248)746-0740 Fax: (248)746-0756 E-mail: aahaoffice@aol.com • URL: http://www.handwriting.org/aaha/.

Handwriting Analysts, International. 1504 W. 29th St., Davenport, IA 52804. Phone: (319)391-7350 Fax: (319)391-1762.

FORGES

See: FOUNDRIES

FORMS AND BLANKS

DIRECTORIES

Business Forms, Labels, and Systems: Who's Who of Manufacturers and Suppliers. North American Publishing Co. • Annual. $20.00. Lists more than 800 suppliers and manufacturers of business forms, labels, and related equipment.

ENCYCLOPEDIAS AND DICTIONARIES

Nichols Cyclopedia of Legal Forms: Annotated; 1925-1990. West Group. • 31 volumes. $1,320.00. Periodic supplementation. Provides personal and business forms and alternative provisions for more than 250 subjects.

FINANCIAL RATIOS

Annual Statement Studies. Robert Morris Associates: The Association of Lending and Credit Risk Professiona. • Annual. Free to members; non-members, $140.00. Median and quartile financial ratios are given for over 400 kinds of manufacturing, wholesale, retail, construction, and consumer finance establishments. Data is sorted by both asset size and sales volume. Includes a clearly written "Definition of Ratios" and an alphabetical industry index.

HANDBOOKS AND MANUALS

Business Forms on File Collection. Facts on File Staff. Facts on File, Inc. • Annual. $125.00.

Checklists and Operating Forms for Small Businesses. John C. Wisdom. John Wiley and Sons, Inc. • 1997. $125.00. 19th edition. Includes disk.

Complete Book of Personal Legal Forms. Daniel Sitarz. Nova Publishing Co. • 1996. $29.95. Second revised edition. Provides more than 100 forms, including contracts, bills of sale, promissory notes, leases, deeds, receipts, and wills. Forms are also available on IBM or MAC diskettes. (Legal Self-Help Series).

Complete Book of Small Business Legal Forms. Daniel Sitarz. Nova Publishing Co. • 1996. $29.95. Second revised edition. Includes basic forms and instructions for use by small businesses in routine legal situations. Forms are also available on IBM or MAC diskettes. (Small Business Library Series).

Computer Law Forms Handbook: A Legal Guide to Drafting and Negotiating. Laurens R. Schwartz. West Group. • Annual. $162.00.

PMI Book of Project Management Forms. Project Management Institute. • 1997. $49.95. Contains more than 100 sample forms for use in project management. Includes checklists, reports, charts, agreements, schedules, requisitions, order forms, and other documents.

Standard Business Forms for the Entrepreneur. Entrepreneur Media, Inc. • Looseleaf. $59.50. A practical collection of forms useful to entrepreneurial small businesses. (Start-Up Business Guide No. E1319.).

Warren's Forms of Agreements. Matthew Bender & Co., Inc. • $940.00. Seven looseleaf volumes. Periodic supplementation. A compact source of forms that business transaction lawyers are most frequently asked to document.

West's Legal Forms. West Publishing Co., College and School Div. • Second edition. Multivolume set. Price on application. Periodic supplementation.

PERIODICALS AND NEWSLETTERS

Business Forms, Labels and Systems. North American Publishing Co. • Semimonthly. $95.00 per year. Formerly *Business Forms and Systems.*

Form: The Voice of the Independent Business Forms Industry. Document Management Industries Association. • Monthly. Members, $29.00 per year; non-members, $49.00 per year.

TRADE/PROFESSIONAL ASSOCIATIONS

Business Forms Management Association. 319 Washington St. S.W., No. 710, Portland, OR 97204. Phone: (503)227-3393 Fax: (503)274-7667 E-mail: bfma@bfma.org • URL: http://www.bfma.org.

Document Management Industries Association. 433 E. Monroe Ave., Alexandria, VA 22301. Phone: 800-336-4641 or (703)836-6232 Fax: (703)836-2241 E-mail: dmia@formmag.com • URL: http://www.dmia.org.

OTHER SOURCES

Basic Legal Forms with Commentary. Marvin Hyman. Warren, Gorham and Lamont/RIA Group. • Looseleaf. $105.00. Periodic supplementation. Forms for any type of legal transaction. Includes commentary.

Complete Federal Tax Forms. Research Institute of America, Inc. • Three looseleaf volumes. Periodic supplementations. Price on application. Contains more than 650 reprints of blank Internal Revenue Service forms, with instructions.

Current Legal Forms with Tax Analysis. Matthew Bender and Co., Inc. • Quarterly. $730.00 per year. 23 looseleaf volumes. Periodic supplementation, $1,685.00.

Fletcher Corporation Forms Annotated, 1980-1990. West Group. • $995.00. 12th edition. 21 volumes.

Forms and Agreements for Architects, Engineers and Contractors. Albert Dib. West Group. • Four looseleaf volumes. $495.00. Periodic supplementation. Covers evaluation of construction documents and alternative clauses. Includes pleadings for litigation and resolving of claims. (Real Property-Zoning Series).

Forms of Business Agreements and Resolutions-Annotated, Tax Tested. Prentice Hall. • Three looseleaf volumes. Periodic supplementation. Price on application.

Manual of Corporate Forms for Securities Practice. Arnold S. Jacobs. West Group. • $395.00. Three looseleaf volumes. Periodic supplementation. (Securitie Laws Series).

FORMS OF ADDRESS

See: ETIQUETTE

FORWARDING COMPANIES

See: FREIGHT TRANSPORT

FORWARDING FREIGHT

See: FREIGHT TRANSPORT

FOUNDATIONS

See also: ARTS MANAGEMENT; FUND-RAISING; GRANTS-IN-AID; NONPROFIT CORPORATIONS

GENERAL WORKS

Foundation Trusteeship: Service in the Public Interest. John Nason. The Foundation Center. • 1989. $19.95. Covers the roles and responsibilities of foundation boards.

ABSTRACTS AND INDEXES

Foundation Grants Index. The Foundation Center. • Irregular. $165.00 per year. Over 5,000 grants of $10,000 or more. Formerly *Foundation Grants Quarterly.*

BIBLIOGRAPHIES

Literature of the Nonprofit Sector: A Bibliography with Abstracts. The Foundation Center. • Dates vary. Six volumes. $45.00 per volume. Covers the literature of philanthropy, foundations, nonprofit organizations, fund-raising, and federal aid.

BIOGRAPHICAL SOURCES

Who Knows Who: Networking Through Corporate Boards. Who Know Who Publishing. • 1994. $150.00. Fifth edition. Shows the connections between the board members of major U. S. corporations and major foundations and nonprofit organizations.

CD-ROM DATABASES

Leadership Library on CD-ROM: Who's Who in the Leadership of the United States. Leadership Directories, Inc. • Quarterly. $2,641.00 per year, including access to Internet version (weekly updates). Contains all 14 *Yellow Book* personnel directories on CD-ROM, providing contact and brief biographical information for about 400,000 individuals. Covers business, government, financial institutions, news media, law firms, associations, foreign representatives, and nonprofit organizations. Includes photographs.

Prospector's Choice: The Electronic Product Profiling 10,000 Corporate and Foundation Grantmakers. The Gale Group. • Annual. $849.00. Provides detailed CD-ROM information on foundations and corporate philanthropies. Also known as *Corporate and Foundation Givers on Disk.*

DIRECTORIES

Corporate Foundation Profiles. The Foundation Center. • Biennial. $155.00 per year.

Corporate Giving Directory: Comprehensive Profiles of America's Major Corporate Foundations and Corporate Charitable Giving Programs. The Gale Group. • Annual. $485.00. Contains detailed descriptions of the philanthropic foundations of over 1,000 major U. S. corporations. Includes grant types, priorities for giving, recent grants, and advice on approaching corporate givers.

Cumulative List of Organizations Described in Section 170(c) of the Internal Revenue Code of 1986. Available from U. S. Government Printing Office. • Annual. $114.00 per year, including quarterly supplements. Lists about 300,000 organizations eligible for contributions deductible for federal income tax purposes. Provides name of each organization and city, but not complete address information. Arranged alphabetically by name of institution. (Office of Employee Plans and Exempt Organizations, Internal Revenue Service.).

Directory of Operating Grants. Research Grant Guides. • Annual. $59.50. Contains profiles for approximately 800 foundations that award grants to nonprofit organizations for such operating expenses as salaries, rent, and utilities. Geographical arrangement, with indexes.

Foundation Directory. The Foundation Center. • Annual. $215.00. Over 37,700 of the largest foundations in the United States, all having 2,000,000.00 or more assets or awarding $200,000 or more in grants in a recent year.

The Foundation 1000. The Foundation Center. • Annual. $295.00. Provides detailed descriptions of the 1,000 largest foundations in the U. S., responsible for 64% of all foundation giving. Indexing is by subject, type of support, location, and personnel.

The Foundation Reporter: Comprehensive Profiles and Giving Analyses of America's Major Private Foundations. The Taft Group. • Annual. $425.00. Provides detailed information on major U. S. foundations. Eight indexes (location, grant type, recipient type, personnel, etc.).

Grants for Libraries and Information Services. The Foundation Center. • Annual. $75.00. Foundations and organizations which have awarded grants made the preceding year for public, academic, research, special, and school libraries; for archives and information centers; for consumer information; and for philanthropy information centers.

The International Foundations Directory. Taylor and Francis, Inc. • 1998. $210.00. Eighth edition. Published by Europa. A directory of international foundations, trusts, and other nonprofit organizations.

National Directory of Corporate Giving: A Guide to Corporate Giving Programs and Corporate Foundations. The Foundation Center. • Biennial. $225.00. Provides information on 2,895 corporations that maintain philanthropic programs (direct giving programs or company-sponsored foundations).

National Guide to Funding for Libraries and Information Services. The Foundation Center. • 1997. $95.00. Contains detailed information on about 600 foundations and corporate direct giving programs providing funding to libraries. Includes indexing by type of support, subject field, location, and key personnel.

Nelson's Directory of Plan Sponsors. Wiesenberger/Thomson Financial. • Annual. $545.00. Three volumes. Available in two versions, alphabetic or geographic. Covers pension plan sponsors and pension funds, including more than 11,000 corporate funds, 4,000 endowment or foundation funds, 1,300 multi-employer funds, 1,000 hospital funds, and 900 public employee funds. Includes information on asset allocation and investment style. Eight indexes.

Nonprofit Sector Yellow Book: Who's Who in the Management of the Leading Foundations, Universities, Museums, and Other Nonprofit Organizations. Leadership Directories, Inc. • Semiannual. $235.00 per year. Covers management personnel and board members of about 1,000 prominent, nonprofit organizations: foundations, colleges, museums, performing arts groups, medical institutions, libraries, private preparatory schools, and charitable service organizations.

HANDBOOKS AND MANUALS

Corporate Contributions Handbook: Devoting Private Means to Public Needs. James P. Shannon, editor. Jossey-Bass, Inc., Publishers. • 1991. $48.95. Published jointly with the Council on Foundations. Provides practical management and legal advice for corporate philanthropic units. (Nonprofit Sector-Public Administration Series).

Foundation Fundamentals: A Guide for Grantseekers. The Foundation Center. • 1999. $34.75. Sixth edition.

Guide to Proposal Writing. Jane C. Geever and Patricia McNeil. The Foundation Center. • 1997. $34.95. Revised edition. An explanation of proposal-writing techniques. Includes interviews with foundation officials and examples of successful grant proposals.

INTERNET DATABASES

GaleNet: Your Information Community. The Gale Group. Phone: 800-877-GALE or (248)699-GALE Fax: 800-414-5043 or (248)699-8069 E-mail: galenet@gale.com • URL: http://www.galenet.com • Web site provides a wide variety of full-text information from Gale databases, Taft, and other sources. Covers associations, biography, business directories, education, the information industry, literature, publishing, and science. Fee-based subscriptions are available for individual databases (free demonstration). Includes Boolean search features and the BRS/Search user interface.

Welcome to the Foundation Center. The Foundation Center. Phone: (212)620-4230 Fax: (212)691-1828 E-mail: mfn@fdncenter.org • URL: http://www.fdncenter.org • Web site provides a wide variety of information about foundations, grants, and philanthropy, with links to philanthropic organizations. "Grantmaker Information" link furnishes descriptions of available funding. Fees: Free.

PERIODICALS AND NEWSLETTERS

Don Kramer's Nonprofit Issues. Don Kramer Publisher. • Monthly. $129.00 per year. Newsletter with legal emphasis. Covers the laws, rules, regulations, and taxes affecting nonprofit organizations.

Foundation News and Commentary: Philanthropy and the Nonprofit Sector. Council on Foundations. • Bimonthly. $48.00 per year. Formerly *Foundation News.*

RESEARCH CENTERS AND INSTITUTES

Foundation Center. 79 Fifth Ave., New York, NY 10003-3076. Phone: 800-424-9836 or (212)807-3690 Fax: (212)807-3691 • URL: http://www.fdncenter.org.

STATISTICS SOURCES

Giving U.S.A: The Annual Compilation of Total Philanthropic Giving Estimates. American Association of Fund-Raising Counsel. AAFRC Trust for Philanthropy. • Annual. $49.95.

TRADE/PROFESSIONAL ASSOCIATIONS

Council on Foundations. 1828 L St., N. W., Suite 300, Washington, DC 20036. Phone: (202)466-6512 Fax: (202)785-3926 E-mail: webmaster@cof.org • URL: http://www.cof.org.

Independent Sector. 1200 18th St., N.W., Suite 200, Washington, DC 20036. Phone: (202)467-6000 Fax: (202)416-6101.

OTHER SOURCES

Washington [year]. Columbia Books, Inc. • Annual. $129.00. Provides information on about 5,000 Washington, DC key businesses, government offices, non-profit organizations, and cultural institutions, with the names of about 25,000 principal executives. Includes Washington media, law offices, foundations, labor unions, international organizations, clubs, etc.

FOUNDRIES

See also: IRON AND STEEL INDUSTRY

ABSTRACTS AND INDEXES

Casting Digest. ASM International. • Bimonthly. $165.00 per year. Provides abstracts of the international literature of metal casting, forming, and molding.

DIRECTORIES

Directory of Steel Foundries and Buyers Guide. Steel Founders' Society of America. • Biennial. $95.00. Formerly *Directory of Steel Foundries in the United States, Canada, and Mexico.*

Foundry Directory and Register of Forges. Metal Bulletin, Inc. • Quarterly. $165.00. Foundries and forges in the United Kingdom and Europe.

Modern Casting-Buyer's Reference Issue. American Foundrymen's Society, Inc. • Annual. $25.00. About 1,700 manufacturers, suppliers, and distributors of foundry and metal casting equipment and products. Formerly *Modern Castings - Buyer's Guide.*

FINANCIAL RATIOS

Annual Statement Studies. Robert Morris Associates: The Association of Lending and Credit Risk Professiona. • Annual. Free to members; non-members, $140.00. Median and quartile financial ratios are given for over 400 kinds of manufacturing, wholesale, retail, construction, and consumer finance establishments. Data is sorted by both asset size and sales volume. Includes a clearly written "Definition of Ratios" and an alphabetical industry index.

HANDBOOKS AND MANUALS

Foundryman's Handbook: Facts, Figures, Formulae. Elsevier Science. • 1986. $119.00. Ninth edition.

PERIODICALS AND NEWSLETTERS

Foundry Management and Technology. Penton Media. • Monthly. Free to qualified personnel; others, $50.00 per year. Coverage includes nonferrous casting technology and production.

Modern Casting. American Foundrymen's Society, Inc. • Monthly. $50.00 per year.

RESEARCH CENTERS AND INSTITUTES

Cast Metals Laboratory. University of Wisconsin-Madison, 1509 University Ave., Madison, WI 53706. Phone: (608)262-2562 Fax: (608)262-8353 E-mail: loper@engr.wisc.edu • URL: http://www.msae.wisc.edu.

Metal Casting Laboratory. Pennsylvania State University, 207 Hammond Bldg., University Park, PA 16802. Phone: (814)863-7290 Fax: (814)863-4745 E-mail: rcv2@psu.edu • URL: http://www.ie.psu.edu/orgs/mcg/.

STATISTICS SOURCES

Nonferrous Castings. U. S. Bureau of the Census. • Annual. (Current Industrial Reports MA-33E.).

TRADE/PROFESSIONAL ASSOCIATIONS

American Foundrymen's Society. 505 State St., Des Plaines, IL 60016-8399. Phone: 800-537-4237 or (708)824-0181 Fax: (708)824-7848 • URL: http://www.afsinc.org.

Casting Industry Suppliers Association. 223 W. Jackson Blvd., Ste. 800, Chicago, IL 60606. Phone: (312)957-1701 Fax: (312)957-1702 E-mail: 74117.445@compuserve.com.

Non-Ferrous Founders Society. 1480 Renaissnace Dr., Ste. 310, Park Ridge, IL 60068. Phone: (847)299-0950 Fax: (847)299-3598 E-mail: staff@nffs.org • URL: http://www.nffs.org • Members are manufacturers of brass, bronze, aluminum and other nonferrous castings.

Steel Founders' Society of America. Cast Metals Federation Bldg., 455 State St., Des Plaines, IL 60016. Phone: (847)382-8240 Fax: (847)382-8287 E-mail: monroe@scra.org • URL: http://www.sfsa.org.

FOUNTAIN PENS

See: WRITING INSTRUMENTS

401(K) RETIREMENT PLANS

GENERAL WORKS

A Commonsense Guide to Your 401(k). Mary Rowland. Available from W.W. Norton and Co., Inc. • 1997. $19.95. Explains how to use a 401(k) plan as a foundation for financial planning. (Bloomberg Personal Bookshelf Series.).

Fundamentals of Employee Benefit Programs. Employee Benefit Research Institute. • 1996. $49.95. Fifth edition. Provides basic explanation of employee benefit programs in both the private and public sectors, including health insurance, pension plans, retirement planning, social security, and long-term care insurance.

Investing During Retirement: The Vanguard Guide to Managing Your Retirement Assets. Vanguard Group. McGraw-Hill Professional. • 1996. $17.95. A basic, general guide to investing after retirement. Covers pension plans, basic principles of investing, types of mutual funds, asset allocation, retirement income planning, social security, estate planning, and contingencies. Includes glossary and worksheets for net worth, budget, and income.

Retirement Security: Understanding and Planning Your Financial Future. David M. Walker. John Wiley and Sons, Inc. • 1996. $29.95. Topics include investments, social security, Medicare, health insurance, and employer retirement plans.

Social Security, Medicare, and Pensions: Get the Most Out of Your Retirement and Medical Benefits. Joseph Matthews and Dorothy M. Berman. Nolo.com. • 1999. $21.95. Seventh edition. In addition to the basic topics, includes practical information on Supplemental Security Income (SSI), disability benefits, veterans benefits, 401(k) plans, Medicare HMOs, medigap insurance, Medicaid, and how to appeal decisions.

Vanguard Retirement Investing Guide: Charting Your Course to a Secure Retirement. Vanguard Group. McGraw-Hill Professional. • 1995. $24.95. Second edition. Covers saving and investing for future retirement. Topics include goal setting, investment fundamentals, mutual funds, asset allocation, defined contribution retirement savings plans, social security, and retirement savings strategies. Includes glossary and worksheet for retirement saving.

You and Your 401(k): How to Manage Your 401(k) for Maximum Returns. Julie Jason. Simon & Schuster Trade. • 1996. $10.00. Presents popularly written advice and information concerning the key features of 401(k) plans and how to choose appropriate investments. Includes a glossary and sample forms. The author is an investment consultant.

DIRECTORIES

Business Insurance: Directory of 401(k) Plan Administrators. Crain Communications, Inc. • Annual. $4.00. Provides information on approximately 75 companies that administer 401(k) retirement plans.

HANDBOOKS AND MANUALS

Employee Stock Ownership Plans: A Practical Guide to ESOPs and Other Broad Ownership Programs. Scott Rodrick, editor. Harcourt Brace, Legal and Professional Publications, Inc. • 1996. $79.00. Contains 19 articles by various authors on ESOPs, 401(k) plans, profit sharing, executive stock option plans, and related subjects.

Estate Plan Book 2000. William S. Moore. American Institute for Economic Research. • 2000. $10.00. Revision of 1997 edition. Part one: "Basic Estate Planning." Part two: "Reducing Taxes on the Disposition of Your Estate." Part three: "Putting it All Together: Examples of Estate Plans." Provides succinct information on wills, trusts, tax planning, and gifts. (Economic Education Bulletin.).

401(k) Handbook. Thompson Publishing Group. • Looseleaf. $319.00 per year (includes monthly bulletin and updates). Provides detailed explanations of complex 401(k) rules and regulations.

The 401(k) Plan Handbook. Julie Jason. Prentice Hall. • 1997. $79.95. Provides technical, legal, administrative, and investment details of 401(k) retirement plans.

Handbook of 401(k) Plan Management. Towers, Perrin, Foster and Crosby Staff. McGraw-Hill Higher Education. • 1992. $70.00. Written for employers and pension plan administrators. In addition to legal details of 401(k) plans, employee stock ownership plans (ESOPs) and basic principles of asset investment are covered. Appendix contains "Sample 401(k) Savings Plan Document.".

How to Build Wealth with Tax-Sheltered Investments. Kerry Anne Lynch. American Institute for Economic Research. • 2000. $6.00. Provides practical information on conservative tax shelters, including defined-contribution pension plans, individual retirement accounts, Keogh plans, U. S. savings bonds, municipal bonds, and various kinds of annuities: deferred, variable-rate, immediate, and foreign-currency. (Economic Education Bulletin.).

The New Working Woman's Guide to Retirement Planning. Martha P. Patterson. University of Pennsylvania Press. • 1999. $17.50. Second edition. Provides retirement advice for employed women, including information on various kinds of IRAs, cash balance and other pension plans, 401(k) plans, and social security. Four case studies are provided to illustrate retirement planning at specific life and career stages.

Retirement Planning Guide. Sidney Kess and Barbara Weltman. CCH, Inc. • 1999. $49.00. Presents an overview for attorneys, accountants, and other professionals of the various concepts involved in retirement planning. Includes checklists, tables, forms, and study questions.

U. S. Master Pension Guide. CCH, Inc. • Annual. $49.00. Explains IRS rules and regulations applying to 401(k) plans, 403(k) plans, ESOPs (employee stock ownership plans), IRAs, SEPs (simplified employee pension plans), Keogh plans, and nonqualified plans.

INTERNET DATABASES

Bureau of Labor Statistics (BLS). U. S. Department of Labor, Bureau of Labor Statistics. Phone: (202)523-1092 E-mail: labstat.helpdesk@bls.gov • URL: http://www.bls.gov • Web site provides a great variety of employment, wage, price, and economic data. Some links are "Data," "Economy at a Glance," "Keyword Search of BLS Web Pages," "Regional Information," and "Other Statistical Sites." Fees: Free.

Mutual Funds Interactive. Brill Editorial Services, Inc. Phone: 877-442-7455 • URL: http://www.brill.com • Web site provides specific information on individual funds in addition to general advice on mutual fund investing and 401(k) plans. Searching is provided, including links to moderated newsgroups and a chat page. Fees: Free.

Small Business Retirement Savings Advisor. U. S. Department of Labor, Pension and Welfare Benefits Administration. Phone: (202)219-8921 • URL: http://www.dol.gov/elaws/pwbaplan.htm • Web site provides "answers to a variety of commonly asked questions about retirement saving options for small business employers." Includes a comparison chart and detailed descriptions of various plans: 401(k), SEP-IRA, SIMPLE-IRA, Payroll Deduction IRA, Keogh Profit-Sharing, Keogh Money Purchase, and Defined Benefit. Searching is offered. Fees: Free.

Web Finance: Covering the Electronic Evolution of Finance. Securities Data Publishing. Phone: (212)765-5311 or 800-455-5844 Fax: (212)321-2336 E-mail: webfinance@tfn.com • URL: http://www.webfinance.net • Bi-weekly print and daily web-site publication of financial services on the Web, including financial links, archives, brokerage stocks, deal financing, and other financial and investment news and information.

PERIODICALS AND NEWSLETTERS

Defined Contribution News. Institutional Investor. • Biweekly. $2,330.00 per year. Newsletter. Edited for financial institutions and others offering defined contribution pension plans.

Financial Planning: The Magazine for Financial Service Professionals. Securities Data Publishing. • Monthly. $79.00 per year. Edited for independent financial planners and insurance agents. Covers retirement planning, estate planning, tax planning, and insurance, including long-term healthcare considerations. Special features include a Retirement Planning Issue, Mutual Fund Performance Survey, and Variable Life and Annuity Survey. (Securities Data Publishing is a unit of Thomson Financial.).

401(k) Dimensions. Hearst Business Communications. • Quarterly. $15.00 per year. Newsletter. Edited for employees of companies offering 401(k) defined contribution retirement plans. Promotes sound investment principles.

IOMA's Report on Defined Contribution Plan Investing. Institute for Management and Administration, Inc. • Semimonthly. $1,156.90 per year. Newsletter. Edited for 401(k) and other defined contribution retirement plan managers, sponsors, and service providers. Reports on such items as investment manager performance, guaranteed investment contract (GIC) yields, and asset allocation trends.

IOMA's Report on Managing 401(k) Plans. Institute for Management and Administration. • Monthly. $275.95 per year. Newsletter for retirement plan managers.

On Wall Street. Securities Data Publishing. • Monthly. $96.00 per year. Edited for securities dealers. Includes articles on financial planning, retirement planning, variable annuities, and money management, with special coverage of 401(k) plans and IRAs. (Securities Data Publishing is a unit of Thomson Financial.).

Plan Sponsor. Asset International, Inc. • Monthly. $150.00 per year. Edited for professional pension plan managers and executives. Defined contribution plans are emphasized.

Retirement Plans Bulletin: Practical Explanations for the IRA and Retirement Plan Professional. Universal Pensions, Inc. • Monthly. $99.00 per year. Newsletter. Provides information on the rules and regulations governing qualified (tax-deferred) retirement plans.

RESEARCH CENTERS AND INSTITUTES

Center for Pension and Retirement Research. Miami University, Department of Economics, 109E Laws Hall, Oxford, OH 45056. Phone: (513)529-2850 Fax: (513)529-6992 E-mail: swilliamson@eh.net • URL: http://www.eh.net/~cprr • Research areas include pension economics, pension plans, and retirement decisions.

Employee Benefit Research Institute. 2121 K St., N. W., Suite 600, Washington, DC 20037-1896. Phone: (202)659-0670 Fax: (202)775-6312 E-mail: salisbury@ebri.org • URL: http://www.ebri.org • Conducts research on employee benefits, including various kinds of pensions, individual retirement accounts (IRAs), health insurance, social security, and long-term health care benefits.

Pension Research Council. University of Pennsylvania, 304 CPC, 3641 Locust Walk, Philadelphia, PA 19104-6218. Phone: (215)898-7620 Fax: (215)898-0310 E-mail: mitchelo@wharton.upenn.edu • URL: http://www.prc.wharton.upenn.edu/prc/prc.html • Research areas include various types of private sector and public employee pension plans.

STATISTICS SOURCES

EBRI Databook on Employee Benefits. Employee Benefit Research Institute. • 1997 $99.00. Fourth edition. Contains more than 350 tables and charts presenting data on employee benefits in the U. S., including pensions, health insurance, social security, and medicare. Includes a glossary of employee benefit terms.

Handbook of U. S. Labor Statistics: Employment, Earnings, Prices, Productivity, and Other Labor Data. Eva E. Jacobs, editor. Bernan Associates. • 1999. $74.00. Based on *Handbook of Labor Statistics*, formerly issued by the Bureau of Labor Statistics, U. S. Department of Labor. Includes the Bureau's projections of employment in the U. S. by industry and occupation. Provides a wide variety of data on the work force, prices, fringe benefits, and consumer expenditures.

Quarterly Pension Investment Report. Employee Benefit Research Institute. • Quarterly. $1,500.00 per year. $400.00 per year to nonprofit organizations. Provides aggregate financial asset data for U. S. private and public pension systems. Statistics are given for both defined contribution and defined benefit plans, including investment mixes (stocks, bonds, cash, other). Contains historical data for private trust, life insurance, and state and local government funds.

TRADE/PROFESSIONAL ASSOCIATIONS

American Society of Pension Actuaries. 4245 N. Fairfax Dr., Suite 750, Arlington, VA 22203. Phone: (703)516-9300 Fax: (703)516-9308 E-mail: aspa@aspa.org • URL: http://www.aspa.org • Members are involved in the pension and insurance aspects of employee benefits. Includes an Insurance and Risk Management Committee, and sponsors an annual 401(k) Workshop.

Association of Private Pension and Welfare Plans. 1212 New York Ave., N. W., Suite 1250, Washington, DC 20005-3987. Phone: (202)289-6700 Fax: (202)289-4582 • URL: http://www.appwp.org • Members are large and small business firms offering pension and other benefit plans for their employees.

Profit Sharing/401(K) Council of America. 10 S. Riverside Plaza, No. 1610, Chicago, IL 60606. Phone: (312)441-8550 Fax: (312)441-8559 E-mail: psca@psca.org • URL: http://www.psca.org • Members are business firms with profit sharing and/or 401(K) plans. Affiliated with the Profit Sharing/401(K) Education Foundation at the same address.

FRAGRANCE INDUSTRY

See: PERFUME INDUSTRY

FRANCHISES

See also: CHAIN STORES; CONCESSIONS

GENERAL WORKS

The Franchise Option: How to Expand Your Business Through Franchising. Kathryn Boe and others. International Franchise Association. • 1987. $24.00. Second edition.

Franchising: Realities and Remedies. Harold Brown. New York Law Publishing Co. • Looseleaf service. $90.00.

Tips and Traps When Buying a Franchise. Mary E. Tomzack. Source Book Publications. • 1999. $19.95. Second edition. Provides specific cautionary advice and information for prospective franchisees.

DIRECTORIES

Bond's Franchise Guide. Robert Bond. Sourcebook Publications. • Annual. $29.95. Contains listings of more than 2,300 franchises in 54 categories, with detailed profiles of over 1,000 major franchise companies. Profiles include information on services provided by franchisers and financing needed by franchisees. Formerly *Source Book of Franchise Opportunities*.

Directory of Franchising Organizations. Pilot Books. • Annual. $12.95. Lists the nation's top franchises with description and cost of investment.

Entrepreneur's Annual Franchise 500 Issue. Entrepreneur Media, Inc. • Annual. $4.95. Provides a ranking of 500 "top franchise opportunities," based on a combination of financial strength, growth rate, size, stability, number of years in business, litigation history, and other factors. Includes 17 major business categories, further divided into about 140 very specific groups (22 kinds of fast food, for example).

European Directory of Retailers and Wholesalers. Available from The Gale Group. • 1997. $790.00. Second edition. Published by Euromonitor. Provides detailed information on more than 4,000 major retail and wholesale businesses in 17 countries of Western Europe. Contains 26 categories, such as supermarkets, superstores, department stores, discount stores, franchise operators, mail order, etc. Includes company, product, and geographic indexes.

Franchise Annual: Complete Handbook and Directory. Info Press Inc. • Annual. $39.95. Over 4,200 franchises; international coverage.

Franchise Opportunities Guide: A Comprehensive Listing of the World's Leading Franchises. International Franchise Association. • Semiannual. $42.00 per year. More than 600 companies which offer franchises.

Franchise Opportunities Handbook. Available from U. S. Government Printing Office. • Annual. Prepared by the U. S. Department of Commerce. Contains descriptions of franchises available in the U. S. and advice for those who are considering investment in a franchise. Government assistance programs from various agencies are outlined.

ENCYCLOPEDIAS AND DICTIONARIES

Encyclopedia of Small Business. The Gale Group. • 1998. $395.00. Two volumes. Contains about 500 informative entries on a wide variety of topics affecting small business. Arrangement is alphabetical.

HANDBOOKS AND MANUALS

Blueprint for Franchising a Business. Steven S. Raab and Gregory Matusky. John Wiley and Sons, Inc. • 1987. $45.00.

Franchising and Licensing: Two Ways to Build Your Business. Andrew Sherman. AMACOM. • 1999. $45.00. Second edition. Written for the business person who wishes to become a franchiser. Tells how to raise capital, create a prototype, structure franchise agreements, develop operations manuals, market the franchise, and maintain good relations with franchisees.

Guide to Franchising. Martin Mendelsohn. Continuum International Publishing Group, Inc. • 1999. $32.95. Sixth edition.

Master Franchising: Selecting, Negotiating, and Operating a Master Franchise. Carl E. Zwisler. CCH, Inc. • 1999. $80.00. Written for franchisees, franchisers, and professional advisors. Emphasis is on international franchise transactions.

PERIODICALS AND NEWSLETTERS

Entrepreneur: The Small Business Authority. Entrepreneur Media, Inc. • Monthly. $19.97 per year. Contains advice for small business owners and prospective owners. Includes numerous franchise advertisements.

Franchise Times. Restaurant Finance Corp. • Biweekly. $35.00 per year. Formerly *Continental Franchise Review*.

Franchising World. International Franchise Association. • Bimonthly. $18.00 per year. Formerly *Franchising Opportunities*.

Info Franchise Newsletter. Info Franchise News Inc. • Monthly. $120.00 per year. Newsletter. New franchisors, litigation, legislation, trends, forecasts, etc.

QSR: The Magazine of Quick Service Restaurant Success. Journalistic, Inc. • Nine times a year. $32.00 per year. Provides news and management advice for quick-service restaurants, including franchisors and franchisees.

ReCareering Newsletter: An Idea and Resource Guide to Second Career and Relocation Planning. Publications Plus, Inc. • Monthly. $59.00 per year. Edited for "downsized managers, early retirees, and others in career transition after leaving traditional employment." Offers advice on second careers, franchises, starting a business, finances, education, training, skills assessment, and other matters of interest to the newly unemployed.

STATISTICS SOURCES

The Profile of Franchising: A Statistical Profile of the 1996 Uniform Franchise Offering Circular Data. International Franchise Association. • 1998. $175.00. Based on data from 1,156 franchise systems. Includes information on 30 characteristics of franchises.

TRADE/PROFESSIONAL ASSOCIATIONS

International Franchise Association. 1350 New York Ave., N.W., Suite 900, Washington, DC 20005. Phone: (202)628-8000 Fax: (202)628-0812 E-mail: ifa@franchise.org • URL: http://www.franchise.org.

OTHER SOURCES

Product Distribution Law Guide. CCH, Inc. • Looseleaf. $199.00. Annual updates available. Covers the legal aspects of various methods of product distribution, including franchising.

FRAUD AND EMBEZZLEMENT

See also: CRIME AND CRIMINALS; FORGERIES

GENERAL WORKS

Dirty Business: Exploring Corporate Misconduct: Analysis and Cases. Maurice Punch. Sage Publications, Inc. • 1996. $79.95. Covers organizational misbehavior and white-collar crime. Includes "Ten Cases of Corporate Deviance.".

How to Avoid Financial Fraud. C. Edgar Murray. American Institute for Economic Research. • 1999. $3.00. Provides concise discussions of fraud victims, perpetrators, and sales tactics. Also includes practical advice on "Selecting a Financial Planner" and "Selecting a Broker." Contains a directory of state securities regulators and a glossary defining various fraudulant financial schemes. (Economic Education Bulletin.).

Women Who Embezzle or Defraud: A Study of Convicted Felons. Dorothy Zietz. Greenwood Publishing Group, Inc. • 1981. $45.00.

ABSTRACTS AND INDEXES

Current Law Index: Multiple Access to Legal Periodicals. The Gale Group. • Monthly. $650.00 per year. Produced in cooperation with the American Association of Law Libraries. Indexes more than 900 law journals, legal newspapers, and specialty publications from the U.S., Canada, U.K., Ireland, Australia, and New Zealand.

ENCYCLOPEDIAS AND DICTIONARIES

Encyclopedia of Crime and Justice. Available from The Gale Group. • 2001. $425.00. Second edition. Four volumes. Published by Macmillan Reference USA. Contains extensive information on a wide variety of topics pertaining to crime, criminology, social issues, and the courts. (A revision of 1982 edition.).

HANDBOOKS AND MANUALS

Accountant's Handbook of Fraud and Commercial Crime. G. Jack Bologna and others. John Wiley and Sons, Inc. • 1992. $155.00. *1996 Supplement*, $65.00.

Banking Crimes: Fraud, Money Laundering, Embezzlement. John K. Villa. West Group. • Annual. $125.00. Covers fraud and embezzlement. Looseleaf.

Corporate Fraud. Michael J. Comer. Available from Ashgate Publishing Co. • 1997. $113.95. Third edition. Examines new risks of corporate fraud related to "electronic commerce, derivatives, computerization, empowerment, downsizing, and other recent developments." Covers fraud detection, prevention, and internal control systems. Published by Gower in England.

Financial Shenanigans: How to Detect Accounting Gimmicks and Fraud in Financial Reports. Howard M. Schilit. McGraw-Hill. • 1993. $22.95. Tells how to interpret the footnotes and fine print in corporate annual and other reports.

Private Investigator. Entrepreneur Media, Inc. • Looseleaf. $59.50. A practical guide to starting a private investigation agency. Covers profit potential, start-up costs, market size evaluation, pricing, accounting, advertising, promotion, etc. (Start-Up Business Guide No. E1320.).

Securities Crimes. Marvin Pickholz. West Group. • $145.00. Looseleaf service. Periodic supplementation. Analyzes the enfo of federal securities laws from the viewpoint of the defendant. Discusses Securities and Exchange Commission (SEC) investigations and federal sentencing guidelines.

U. S. Master Auditing Guide. CCH, Inc. • Annual. $65.00. Covers such topics as auditing standards, audit management, compliance, consulting, governmental audits, forensic auditing, and fraud. Includes checklists, charts, graphs, and sample reports.

ONLINE DATABASES

NCJRS: National Criminal Justice Reference Service. U.S. Department of Justice. • References print and non-print information on law enforcement and criminal justice, 1972 to present. Monthly updates. Inquire as to online cost and availability.

PERIODICALS AND NEWSLETTERS

Claims. IW Publications, Inc. • Monthly. $42.00 per year. Edited for insurance adjusters, risk managers, and claims professionals. Covers investigation, fraud, insurance law, and other claims-related topics.

FBI Law Enforcement Bulletin. Available from U. S. Government Printing Office. • Monthly. $36.00 per year. Issued by Federal Bureau of Investigation, U. S. Department of Justice. Contains articles on a wide variety of law enforcement and crime topics, including computer-related crime.

White-Collar Crime Reporter: Information and Analyses Concerning White-Collar Practice. Andrews Publications. • 10 times a year. $550.00 per year. Newsletter. Provides information on trends in white collar crime.

RESEARCH CENTERS AND INSTITUTES

Lexis.com Research System. Lexis-Nexis Group. Phone: 800-227-9597 or (937)865-6800 Fax: (937)865-6909 E-mail: webmaster@prod.lexis-nexis.com • URL: http://www.lexis.com • Fee-based Web site offers extensive searching of a wide variety of legal sources. Additional features include Daily Opinion Service, lexis.com Bookstore, Career Center, CLE Center, Law Schools, and Practice Pages ("Pages specific to areas of specialty").

STATISTICS SOURCES

Uniform Crime Reports for the United States. Federal Bureau of Investigation, U.S. Department of Justice. Available from U.S. Government Printing Office. • Annual. Price varies.

TRADE/PROFESSIONAL ASSOCIATIONS

American Society of Criminology. 1314 Kinnear Rd., Suite 212, Columbus, OH 43212. Phone: (614)292-9207 Fax: (614)292-6767.

OTHER SOURCES

Business Crime: Criminal Liability of the Business Community. Matthew Bender & Co., Inc. • $1,380.00. Seven looseleaf volumes. Periodic supplementation. Guide to the many criminal problems that can arise in modern business practice. Provides how-to guidance.

Consumer Protection and the Law. Dee Pridgen. West Group. • Looseleaf. $135.00. Periodic supplementation. Covers advertising, sales practices, unfair trade practices, consumer fraud, and product warranties.

Forensic Accounting and Financial Fraud. American Management Association Extension Institute. • Looseleaf. $130.00. Self-study course. Emphasis is on practical explanations, examples, and problem solving. Quizzes and a case study are included.

World of Criminal Justice. The Gale Group. • 2001. $150.00. Two volumes. Contains both topical and biographical entries relating to the criminal justice system and criminology.

FRAUD, COMPUTER

See: COMPUTER CRIME AND SECURITY

FREEDOM OF INFORMATION

ABSTRACTS AND INDEXES

Index to Legal Periodicals and Books. H. W. Wilson Co. • Monthly. Quarterly and annual cumulations. $270.00 per year. CD-ROM version available at $1,495.00 per year.

DIRECTORIES

American Society of Access Professionals-Membership Directory. American Society of Access Professionals. • Annual. Membership.

HANDBOOKS AND MANUALS

Citizen's Guide on Using the Freedom of Information Act and the Privacy Act of 1974 to Request Government Records. U. S. Government Printing Office. • 1997. $5.00.

Guidebook to the Freedom of Information and Privacy Acts. Justin D. Franklin and Robert F. Bouchard, editors. West Group. • $120.00 per year. Two looseleaf volumes. Periodic supplementation. Includes procedures for requesting and acquiring business and government data. (Civil Rights Series).

ONLINE DATABASES

Index to Legal Periodicals and Books (Online). H. W. Wilson Co. • Broad coverage of law journals and books 1981 to date. Monthly updates. Inquire as to online cost and availability.

Legal Resource Index. The Gale Group. • Broad coverage of law literature appearing in legal, business, and other periodicals, 1980 to date. Monthly updates. Inquire as to online cost and availability.

LEXIS. LEXIS-NEXIS. • The various LEXIS databases provide full text and indexing for a wide variety of legal cases, statutes, orders, and opinions.

PERIODICALS AND NEWSLETTERS

Access Reports: Freedom of Information. Access Reports, Inc. • Biweekly. $325.00 per year. Newsletter.

FTC Freedom of Information Log (Federal Trade Commission). Washington Regulatory Reporting Associates. • Weekly. $451.00 per year. Newsletter listing Freedom of Information Act requests that have been submitted to the Federal Trade Commission.

The IRE Journal. Investigative Reporters and Editors, Inc. • Bimonthly. $25.00 per year. Contains practical information relating to investigative journalism.

RESEARCH CENTERS AND INSTITUTES

Public Law Education Institute. 454 New Jersey Ave., S.E., Washington, DC 20003. Phone: (202)544-8646.

TRADE/PROFESSIONAL ASSOCIATIONS

American Society of Access Professionals. 1441 Eye St. N.W., 7th Fl., Washington, DC 20005-2210. Phone: (202)712-9054 Fax: (202)216-9646 E-mail: asap@7bostromdc.com • URL: http://www.podi.com/asap • Members are individuals concerned with safeguarding freedom of information, privacy, open meetings, and fair credit reporting laws.

Electronic Frontier Foundation. 1550 Bryant St., Suite 725, San Francisco, CA 94103. Phone: (415)436-9333 Fax: (415)436-9993 E-mail: info@eff.org • URL: http://www.eff.org • Members are individuals with an interest in computer-based communications. Promotes electronic communication civil liberties and First Amendment rights.

Freedom of Information Center. University of Missouri, 127 Neff Annex, Columbia, MO 65211. Phone: (573)882-4856 Fax: (573)882-9002 E-mail: foiww@showme.missouri.edu • URL: http://www.missouri.edu/~foiwww • Supported by the communications media.

Freedom of Information Clearinghouse. 1600 20th St., N.W., Washington, DC 20009. Phone: (202)588-1000 Fax: (202)588-7790 • Promotes citizen access to government-held information.

Investigative Reporters and Editors. School of Journalism, 138 Neff Annex, Columbia, MO 65211. Phone: (573)882-2042 Fax: (573)882-5431 E-mail: info@ire.org • URL: http://www.ire.org • Provides educational services to those engaged in investigative journalism.

National Center for Freedom of Information Studies. Loyola University of Chicago, 820 N. Michigan Ave., Chicago, IL 60611. Phone: (312)915-6549 Fax: (312)915-6520 • Legal emphasis.

Reporters Committee for Freedom of the Press. 1815 N. Fort Meyer Dr., Ste. 900, Arlington, VA 22209. Phone: (703)807-2100 Fax: (703)807-2109 E-mail: rcfp@rcfp.org • URL: http://www.rcfp.org/rcfp • Concerned with protecting freedom of information rights for the working press.

FREIGHT, AIR

See: AIR FREIGHT

FREIGHT FORWARDERS

See: FREIGHT TRANSPORT

FREIGHT RATES

See also: FREIGHT TRANSPORT

ALMANACS AND YEARBOOKS

FAO Yearbook: Trade. Available from Bernan Associates. • Annual. Published by the Food and Agriculture Organization of the United Nations (FAO). A compliation of international trade statistics for agricultural, fishery, and forest products. Text in English, French, and Spanish.

PERIODICALS AND NEWSLETTERS

International Freighting Weekly: Sea, Air, Rail, Road. Emap-Business International Ltd. • Weekly. Members, $165.00 per year; non-members, $325.00 per year.

FREIGHT SHIPS

See: SHIPS, SHIPPING AND SHIPBUILDING

FREIGHT TRANSPORT

See also: AIR FREIGHT; FREIGHT RATES; TRANSPORTATION INDUSTRY

DIRECTORIES

Air Freight Directory. Air Cargo, Inc. • Bimonthly. $84.00 per year. Air freight motor carriers.

American Motor Carrier Directory. Commonwealth Business Media. • Annual. $517.00 per year. Lists all licensed Less Than Truckload (LTL) general commodity carriers in the U. S., including specialized motor carriers and related services. Formerly *American Motor Carrier Directory.*

National Customs Brokers and Forwarders Association of America: Membership Directory. National Customs Brokers and Forwarders Association of America, Inc. • Annual. $25.00. Lists about 600 customs brokers, international air cargo agents, and freight forwarders in the U.S.

Official Directory of Industrial and Commercial Traffic Executives. Commonwealth Business Media. • Annual. $395.00. About 16,000 U.S. and Canadian commercial firms with full-time or part-time traffic/transportation departments, and 28,000 traffic executives.

ENCYCLOPEDIAS AND DICTIONARIES

Dictionary of Shipping Terms. Peter Brodie. Available from Informa Publishing Group Ltd. • 1997. $57.00. Third edition. Published in the UK by Lloyd's List (http://www.lloydslist.com). Defines more than 2,000 words, phrases, and abbreviations related to the shipping and maritime industries.

Illustrated Dictionary of Cargo Handling. Peter Brodie. Available from Informa Publishing Group Ltd. • 1996. $100.00. Second edition. Published in the UK by Lloyd's List (http://www.lloydslist.com). Provides definitions of about 600 terms relating to "the vessels and equipment used in modern cargo handling and shipping," including containerization.

Macmillan Encyclopedia of Transportation. Available from The Gale Group. • 2000. $375.00. Six volumes. Published by Macmillan Reference USA. Covers the business, technology, and history of transportation on land, on water, in the air, and in space. Includes definitions, cross-references, and 200 color illustrations.

FINANCIAL RATIOS

Annual Statement Studies. Robert Morris Associates: The Association of Lending and Credit Risk Professiona. • Annual. Free to members; non-members, $140.00. Median and quartile financial ratios are given for over 400 kinds of manufacturing, wholesale, retail, construction, and consumer finance establishments. Data is sorted by both asset size and sales volume. Includes a clearly written "Definition of Ratios" and an alphabetical industry index.

HANDBOOKS AND MANUALS

The Business of Shipping. Lane C. Kendall and James J. Buckley. Cornell Maritime Press, Inc. • 2000. $50.00. Seventh edition.

Freight Brokerage. Entrepreneur Media, Inc. • Looseleaf. $59.50. A practical guide to freight transportation brokering. Covers profit potential, start-up costs, market size evaluation, pricing, accounting, advertising, promotion, etc. (Start-Up Business Guide No. E1328.).

INTERNET DATABASES

Fedstats. Federal Interagency Council on Statistical Policy. Phone: (202)395-7254 • URL: http://www.fedstats.gov • Web site features an efficient search facility for full-text statistics produced by more than 70 federal agencies, including the Census Bureau, the Bureau of Economic Analysis, and the Bureau of Labor Statistics. Boolean searches can be made within one agency or for all agencies combined. Links are offered to international statistical bureaus, including the UN, IMF, OECD, UNESCO, Eurostat, and 20 individual countries. Fees: Free.

ONLINE DATABASES

DRI U.S. Central Database. Data Products Division. • Provides more than 23,000 business, financial, demographic, economic, foreign trade, and industry-related time series for the U.S. Includes national income, population, retail-wholesale trade, price indexes, labor data, housing, industrial production, banking, interest rates, money supply, etc. Time period is generally 1947 to date (some data back to 1929). Updating varies. Inquire as to online cost and availability.

STATISTICS SOURCES

Business Statistics of the United States. Courtenay M. Slater, editor. Bernan Associates. • 1999. $74.00. Fifth edition. Based on *Business Statistics*, formerly issue by the Bureau of Economic Analysis, U. S. Department of Commerce. Provides basic data for a wide variety of U. S. industries, services, and economic indicators. Most statistics are shown annually for 29 years and monthly for the most recent four years.

Survey of Current Business. Available from U. S. Government Printing Office. • Monthly. $49.00 per year. Issued by Bureau of Economic Analysis, U. S. Department of Commerce. Presents a wide variety of business and economic data.

TRADE/PROFESSIONAL ASSOCIATIONS

Transportation Institute. 5201 Auth Way, Camp Springs, MD 20746. Phone: (301)423-3335 Fax: (301)423-0634 E-mail: info@trans-inst.org • URL: http://www.trans-inst.org.

OTHER SOURCES

Federal Carriers Reports. CCH, Inc. • Biweekly. $1,372.00 per year. Four looseleaf volumes. Periodic supplementation. Federal rules and regulations for motor carriers, water carriers, and freight forwarders.

FRINGE AREAS

See: CITY PLANNING; URBAN DEVELOPMENT

FRINGE BENEFITS

See also: EMPLOYEE BENEFIT PLANS

ABSTRACTS AND INDEXES

Business Periodicals Index. H. W. Wilson Co. • Monthly, except August, with quarterly and annual cumulations. Service basis for print edition; CD-ROM edition, $1,495.00 per year.

ENCYCLOPEDIAS AND DICTIONARIES

Blackwell Encyclopedic Dictionary of Human Resource Management. Lawrence H. Peters and Charles R. Greer, editors. Blackwell Publishers. • 1996. $105.95. The editors are associated with Texas Christian University. Contains definitions of key terms combined with longer articles written by various U. S. and foreign business educators. Includes bibliographies and index. (Blackwell Encyclopedia of Management Series).

HANDBOOKS AND MANUALS

U. S. Master Compensation Tax Guide. CCH, Inc. • Annual. $54.95. Provides concise coverage of taxes on salaries, bonuses, fringe benefits, other current compensation, and deferred compensation (qualified and nonqualified).

INTERNET DATABASES

Bureau of Labor Statistics (BLS). U. S. Department of Labor, Bureau of Labor Statistics. Phone: (202)523-1092 E-mail: labstat.helpdesk@bls.gov • URL: http://www.bls.gov • Web site provides a great variety of employment, wage, price, and economic data. Some links are "Data," "Economy at a Glance," "Keyword Search of BLS Web Pages," "Regional Information," and "Other Statistical Sites." Fees: Free.

ONLINE DATABASES

ABI/INFORM. Bell & Howell Information and Learning. • Provides online indexing to business-related material occurring in over 1,000 periodicals from 1971 to the present. Inquire as to online cost and availability.

Wilson Business Abstracts Online. H. W. Wilson Co. • Indexes and abstracts 600 major business periodicals, plus the *Wall Street Journal* and the business section of the *New York Times.* Indexing is from 1982, abstracting from 1990, with the two newspapers included from 1993. Updated weekly. Inquire as to online cost and availability. (*Business Periodicals Index* without abstracts is also available online.).

STATISTICS SOURCES

Compensation and Working Conditions. Available from U. S. Government Printing Office. • Quarterly. $18.00 per year. Issued by the Bureau of Labor Statistics, U. S. Department of Labor. Presents wage and benefit changes that result from collective bargaining settlements and unilateral management decisions. Includes statistical summaries and special reports on wage trends. Formerly *Current Wage Developments.*

Employee Benefits in Medium and Large Private Establishments. Available from U. S. Government Printing Office. • Biennial. Issued by Bureau of Labor Statistics, U. S. Department of Labor. Provides data on benefits provided by companies with 100 or more employees. Covers benefits for both full-time and part-time workers, including health insurance, pensions, a wide variety of paid time-off policies (holidays, vacations, personal leave, maternity leave, etc.), and other fringe benefits.

Employee Benefits in Small Private Establishments. Available from U. S. Government Printing Office. • Biennial. Issued by Bureau of Labor Statistics, U. S. Department of Labor. Supplies data on a wide variety of benefits provided by companies with fewer than 100 employees. Includes statistics for both full-time and part-time workers.

Handbook of U. S. Labor Statistics: Employment, Earnings, Prices, Productivity, and Other Labor Data. Eva E. Jacobs, editor. Bernan Associates. • 1999. $74.00. Based on *Handbook of Labor Statistics*, formerly issued by the Bureau of Labor Statistics, U. S. Department of Labor. Includes the Bureau's projections of employment in the U. S. by industry and occupation. Provides a wide variety of data on the work force, prices, fringe benefits, and consumer expenditures.

OTHER SOURCES

Executive Compensation. Arthur H. Kroll. Prentice Hall. • Three looseleaf volumes. Periodic supplementation. Price on application. Includes monthly newsletter.

Executive Compensation and Taxation Coordinator. Research Institute of America, Inc. • Three looseleaf volumes. $450.00 per year. Monthly updates.

Fringe Benefits Tax Guide. CCH, Inc. • Monthly. Looseleaf.

FROZEN FOOD INDUSTRY

See also: CANNED FOOD INDUSTRY; FAST FOOD INDUSTRY; REFRIGERATION INDUSTRY

ABSTRACTS AND INDEXES

Food Science and Technology Abstracts. International Food Information Service Publishing. • Monthly. $1,780.00 per year. Provides worldwide coverage of the literature of food technology and food production.

Foods Adlibra: Key to the World's Food Literature. Foods Adlibra Publications. • Semimonthly.Provides journal citations and abstracts to the literature of food technology and packaging.

ALMANACS AND YEARBOOKS

Almanac of the Canning, Freezing, Preserving Industries, Vol. Two. Edward E. Judge and Sons, Inc. • Annual. $71.00. Contains U. S. food laws and regulations and detailed production statistics.

CD-ROM DATABASES

Food Science and Technology Abstracts [CD-ROM]. Available from SilverPlatter Information, Inc. • Quarterly. $3,700 per year. Produced by International Food Information Service (home page is http://www.ifis.org). Provides worldwide coverage on CD-ROM of the literature of food technology and production. Various types of publications are indexed, with abstracts, including about 1,800 periodicals. Time period is 1969 to date.

DIRECTORIES

American Frozen Food Institute-Membership Directory and Buyers Guide. American Frozen Food Institute. • Annual. $100.00. 550 member frozen food processors, suppliers, brokers, and distributors.

Directory of the Canning, Freezing, Preserving Industries. Edward E. Judge and Sons, Inc. • Biennial. $175.00. Provides information on about 2,950 packers of a wide variety of food products.

National Frozen Food Association Directory. National Frozen Food Association, Inc. • Annual. $195.00. Lists products, services and personnel.

Quick Frozen Foods Annual Directory of Frozen Food Processors and Buyers' Guide. Saul Beck Publications. • Annual. $130.00. Lists 10,500 frozen food processors; suppliers of freezing and food processing machinery, equipment, and supplies; broker locaters, refrigerated warehouses, truck and rail freight lines, and packaging systems handling frozen food.

ONLINE DATABASES

Food Science and Technology Abstracts [online]. IFIS North American Desk. • Produced by International Food Information Service. Provides about 500,000 online citations, with abstracts, to the international literature of food science, technology, commodities, engineering, and processing. Approximately 2,000 periodicals are covered. Time period is 1969 to date, with monthly updates. Inquire as to online cost and availability.

FOODS ADLIBRA. General Mills, Inc. • Contains online citations, with abstracts, to the technical and business literature of food processing and packaging. New products and new ingredients are featured. Covers about 250 trade journals and 500 research journals from 1974 to date, with monthly updates. Inquire as to online cost and availability.

PERIODICALS AND NEWSLETTERS

Quick Frozen Foods International. E.W. Williams Publications Co. • Quarterly. $38.00 per year. Text in English, summaries in French and German.

STATISTICS SOURCES

Annual Survey of Manufactures. Available from U. S. Government Printing Office. • Annual. Prices vary. Issued by the U. S. Census Bureau as an interim update to the *Census of Manufactures.* Includes data on number of manufacturing establishments in various industries, employment, labor costs, value of shipments, capital expenditures, inventories, energy costs, and assets. (See also Census Bureau home page, http://www.census.gov/.).

Frozen Food Pack Statistics. American Frozen Food Institute. • Annual. Members, $10.00; non-members, $100.00.

Statistics Summaries. American Frozen Food Institute. • Membership.

TRADE/PROFESSIONAL ASSOCIATIONS

American Association of Meat Processors. P.O. Box 269, Elizabethtown, PA 17022. Phone: (717)367-1168 Fax: (717)367-9096 E-mail: aamp@aamp.com • URL: http://www.aamp.com.

American Frozen Food Institute. 2000 Corporate Ridge, Suite 1000, McLean, VA 22102-7805. Phone: (703)821-0770 Fax: (703)821-1350 E-mail: affi@dn.net • URL: http://www.affi.net.

National Frozen Food Association. P.O. Box 6069, Harrisburg, PA 17112. Phone: (717)657-8601 Fax: (717)657-9862 E-mail: info@nffa.org • URL: http://www.nffa.org.

National Prepared Food Association. 485 Kinderkamack Rd., 2nd Fl., Oradell, NJ 07649. Phone: (201)634-1870 Fax: (201)634-1871 E-mail: star1870@aol.com.

OTHER SOURCES

Frozen Foods. Available from MarketResearch.com. • 1997. $5,000.00. Published by Euromonitor Publications Ltd. Provides consumer market data and forecasts for the United States, the United Kingdom, Germany, France, and Italy. Contains market analyses for many kinds of frozen foods.

Major Food and Drink Companies of the World. Available from The Gale Group. • 2001. $855.00. Fourth edition. Two volumes. Published by Graham & Whiteside. Contains profiles and trade names for more than 9,000 important food and beverage companies in various countries. In addition to foods, includes both alcoholic and nonalcoholic drink products.

Thomas Food and Beverage Market Place. Grey House Publishing. • Annual. $295.00. Three volumes. Contains more than 40,000 entries covering food companies, beverages, food equipment, warehouse companies, food brokers, wholesalers, importers, and exporters. Formerly *Thomas Food Industry Register.*

FRUIT INDUSTRY

See also: APPLE INDUSTRY; BANANA INDUSTRY; CITRUS FRUIT INDUSTRY

ABSTRACTS AND INDEXES

Food Science and Technology Abstracts. International Food Information Service Publishing. • Monthly. $1,780.00 per year. Provides worldwide coverage of the literature of food technology and food production.

Foods Adlibra: Key to the World's Food Literature. Foods Adlibra Publications. • Semimonthly.Provides journal citations and abstracts to the literature of food technology and packaging.

Horticultural Abstracts: Compiled from World Literature on Temperate and Tropical Fruits, Vegetables, Ornaments, Plantation Crops. Available from CABI Publishing North America. • Monthly. $1,605.00 per year. Published in England by CABI Publishing. Provides worldwide coverage of the literature of fruits, vegetables, flowers, plants, and all aspects of gardens and gardening.

VITIS: Viticulture and Enology Abstracts. Bundesanstalt fuer Zuechtungsforschungan an Kulturpflanzen Institut fuer Rebenzu. • Quarterly. $65.00 per year. Provides abstracts of journal and other literature relating to wine technology and the cultivation of grapes.

CD-ROM DATABASES

AGRICOLA on SilverPlatter. Available from SilverPlatter Information, Inc. • Quarterly. $825.00 per year. Produced by the National Agricultural Library. Provides about three million citations on CD-ROM to the literature of agriculture, agricultural economics, animal sciences, entomology, fertilizer, food, forestry, nutrition, pesticides, plant science, water resources, and other topics. Each quarterly disc covers the past ten years, with archival discs available from 1970.

Food Science and Technology Abstracts [CD-ROM]. Available from SilverPlatter Information, Inc. • Quarterly. $3,700 per year. Produced by International Food Information Service (home page is http://www.ifis.org). Provides worldwide coverage on CD-ROM of the literature of food technology and production. Various types of publications are indexed, with abstracts, including about 1,800 periodicals. Time period is 1969 to date.

DIRECTORIES

American Fruit Grower Source Book. Meister Publishing Co. • Annual. $5.00.

Packer Produce Availability and Merchandising Guide. Vance Publishing Corp. • Annual. $35.00. A buyer's directory giving sources of fresh fruits and vegetables. Shippers are listed by location for each commodity.

ENCYCLOPEDIAS AND DICTIONARIES

Encyclopedia of Agriculture Science. Charles J. Arntzen and Ellen M. Ritter, editors. Academic Press, Inc. • 1994. $625.00. Four volumes.

Foods and Nutrition Encyclopedia. Audrey H. Ensminger and others. CRC Press, Inc. • 1993. $382.00. Second edition. Two volumes.

INTERNET DATABASES

USDA. United States Department of Agriculture. Phone: (202)720-2791 E-mail: agsec@usda.gov • URL: http://www.usda.gov • The USDA home page has six sections: News and Information; What's New; About USDA; Agencies; Opportunities; Search and Help. Keyword searching is offered from the USDA home page and from various individual agency home pages. Agencies are the Economic Research Service, Agricultural Marketing Service, National Agricultural Statistics Service, National Agricultural Library, and about 12 others. Updating varies. Fees: Free.

ONLINE DATABASES

Food Science and Technology Abstracts [online]. IFIS North American Desk. • Produced by International Food Information Service. Provides about 500,000 online citations, with abstracts, to the international literature of food science, technology, commodities, engineering, and processing. Approximately 2,000 periodicals are covered. Time period is 1969 to date, with monthly updates. Inquire as to online cost and availability.

FOODS ADLIBRA. General Mills, Inc. • Contains online citations, with abstracts, to the technical and business literature of food processing and packaging. New products and new ingredients are featured. Covers about 250 trade journals and 500 research journals from 1974 to date, with monthly updates. Inquire as to online cost and availability.

PERIODICALS AND NEWSLETTERS

American Fruit Grower. Meister Publishing Co. • Monthly. $27.47 per year.

Fresh Produce Journal. Lockwood Press, Ltd. • Weekly. $148.00 per year. Formerly *Fruit Trades Journal.*

Fruit Varieties Journal. American Pomological Society. • Quarterly. $30.00 per year. Presents reports and general information on fruit varieties.

Journal of Tree Fruit Production. Haworth Press, Inc. • Semiannual. Individuals, $45.00 per year; institutions, $75.00 per year; libraries, $85.00 per year. A research journal for tree fruit growers.

The Packer: Devoted to the Interest of Commericial Growers, Packers, Shippers, Receivers and Retailers of Fruits, Vegetables and Other Products. Vance Publishing Corp., Produce Div. • Weekly. $65.00 per year. Supplments available, *Brand Directory* and *Fresh Trends, Packer's Produce Availiability and Merchandising Guide* and *Produce Services Sourcebooks.*

Produce Merchandising: The Packer's Retailing and Merchandising Magazine. Vance Publishing Corp., Produce Div. • Monthly. $35.00 per year. Provides information and advice on the retail marketing and promotion of fresh fruits and vegetalbe.

Small Fruits Review. Haworth Press, Inc. • Quarterly. Individuals, $36.00 per year; institutions, $48.00 per year; libraries, $125.00 per year. An academic and practical journal focusing on the marketing of grapes, berries, and other small fruit. Formerly *Journal of Small Fruits and Viticulture.*

Western Fruit Grower: The Business Magazines of the Western Produce Industry. Meister Publishing Co. • Monthly. $15.95 per year. Covers the commercial fruit industry in 13 western states.

PRICE SOURCES

PPI Detailed Report. Bureau of Labor Statistics, U.S. Department of Labor. Available from U.S. Government Printing Office. • Monthly. $55.00 per year. Formerly *Producer Price Indexes.*

RESEARCH CENTERS AND INSTITUTES

Washington State University. Agricultural Research Center, P.O. Box 646240, Pullman, WA 99164-6240. Phone: (509)335-4563 Fax: (509)335-6751 E-mail: cavalieri@wsu.edu • URL: http://www.arc.cahe.wsu.edu.

California Agricultural Experiment Station. University of California at Berkeley. 1111 Franklin St., 6th Fl., Oakland, CA 94607-5200. Phone: (510)987-0060 Fax: (510)451-2317 E-mail: wr.gomes@ucop.edu • URL: http://www.ucop.edu/anrhome/danr.html.

Hawaii Institute of Tropical Agriculture and Human Resources. University of Hawaii at Manoa, Honolulu, HI 96822. Phone: (808)956-8131 Fax: (808)956-9105 E-mail: tadean2@avax.ctahr.hawaii.edu • URL: http://www.ctahr.hawaii.edu • Concerned with the production and marketing of tropical food and ornamental plant products, including pineapples, bananas, coffee, and macadamia nuts.

New York State Agricultural Experiment Station. Cornell University. 630 W. North St., Geneva, NY 14456. Phone: (315)787-2211 Fax: (315)787-2276 E-mail: jeh3@cornell.edu • URL: http://www.nyseas.cornell.edu/.

STATISTICS SOURCES

Agricultural Statistics. Available from U. S. Government Printing Office. • Annual. Produced by the National Agricultural Statistics Service, U. S. Department of Agriculture. Provides a wide variety of statistical data relating to agricultural production, supplies, consumption, prices/price-supports, foreign trade, costs, and returns, as well as farm labor, loans, income, and population. In many cases, historical data is shown annually for 10 years. In addition to farm data, includes detailed fishery statistics.

FAO Quarterly Bulletin of Statistics. Food and Agriculture Organization of the United Nations. Available from UNIPUB. • Quarterly. $20.00 per year. Provides international data on agricultural production, trade, and prices, covering the major commodities of many countries. Text in English, French, and Spanish. Formerly *FAO Monthly Bulletin of Statistics.*

Foreign Agricultural Trade of the United States. Available from U. S. Government Printing Office. • Monthly. $50.00 per year. Issued by the Economic Research Service of the U. S. Department of Agriculture. Provides data on U. S. exports and imports of agricultural commodities.

Fruit and Tree Nuts Situation and Outlook Report. Available from U. S. Government Printing Office. • Three times a year. $13.00 per year. (Economic Research Service, U. S. Department of Agriculture.).

World Agricultural Supply and Demand Estimates. Available from U. S. Government Printing Office. • Monthly. $38.00 per year. Issued by the Economics and Statistics Service and the Foreign Agricultural Service of the U. S. Department of Agriculture. Consists mainly of statistical data and tables.

TRADE/PROFESSIONAL ASSOCIATIONS

National Association of Fruits, Flavors and Syrups. P.O. Box 545, Matawan, NJ 07747. Phone: (732)583-8272 Fax: (732)583-0798 E-mail: naffs@naffs.org • URL: http://www.naffs.org • Manufacturers of fruit and syrup toppings, flavors and stabilizers for the food industry.

Rare Fruit Council International. P.O. Box 561914, Miami, FL 33256-1914. Phone: (305)378-4457 Fax: (813)474-6133 E-mail: tfncws@gate.net • URL: http://www.gate.net/~tfnews.

United Fresh Fruit and Vegetable Association. 727 N. Washington St., Alexandria, VA 22314. Phone: (703)836-3410 Fax: (703)836-7745 E-mail: uffva@uffva.org.

OTHER SOURCES

Major Food and Drink Companies of the World. Available from The Gale Group. • 2001. $855.00. Fourth edition. Two volumes. Published by Graham & Whiteside. Contains profiles and trade names for more than 9,000 important food and beverage companies in various countries. In addition to foods, includes both alcoholic and nonalcoholic drink products.

The Market for Value-Added Fresh Produce. MarketResearch.com. • 1999. $2,750.00. Market research report. Covers packaged salad mixes, bulk salad mixes, pre-cut fruits, and pre-cut vegetables. Market projections are provided to the year 2003.

Thomas Food and Beverage Market Place. Grey House Publishing. • Annual. $295.00. Three volumes. Contains more than 40,000 entries covering food companies, beverages, food equipment, warehouse companies, food brokers, wholesalers, importers, and exporters. Formerly *Thomas Food Industry Register.*

FRUIT JUICE INDUSTRY

See: BEVERAGE INDUSTRY; CITRUS FRUIT INDUSTRY

FUEL

GENERAL WORKS

Biofuels. OECD Publications and Information Center. • 1994. $28.00. Produced by the International Energy Agency (IEA). Analyzes costs and greenhouse gas emissions resulting from the production and use of ethanol fuel. In addition to ethanol from corn, wheat, and sugar beets, consideration is given to diesel fuel from rapeseed oil and methanol from wood.

ABSTRACTS AND INDEXES

NTIS Alerts: Energy. National Technical Information Service. • Semimonthly. $245.00 per year. Provides descriptions of government-sponsored research reports and software, with ordering information. Covers electric power, batteries, fuels, geothermal energy, heating/cooling systems, nuclear technology, solar energy, energy policy, and related subjects. Formerly *Abstract Newsletter.*

CD-ROM DATABASES

Environment Abstracts on CD-ROM. Congressional Information Service, Inc. • Quarterly. $1,295.00 per year. Contains the following CD-ROM databases: *Environment Abstracts, Energy Abstracts,* and *Acid Rain Abstracts.* Length of coverage varies.

DIRECTORIES

Financial Times Energy Yearbook: Oil & Gas: 2000. Available from The Gale Group. • Annual. $320.00. Published by Financial Times Energy. Provides production and financial details for more than 800 major oil and gas companies worldwide. Includes coverage of reserves, operations, properties, and growth rates. Formerly *Financial Times Oil & Gas Yearbook.*

ENCYCLOPEDIAS AND DICTIONARIES

Macmillan Encyclopedia of Energy. Available from The Gale Group. • 2001. $350.00. Three volumes. Published by Macmillan Reference USA. Covers the business, technology, and history of a wide variety of energy sources.

ONLINE DATABASES

Energyline. Congressional Information Service, Inc. • Provides online citations and abstracts to the literature of all forms of energy: petroleum, natural gas, coal, nuclear power, solar energy, etc. Time period is 1971 to 1993 (closed file). Inquire as to online cost and availability.

PERIODICALS AND NEWSLETTERS

Barron's: The Dow Jones Business and Financial Weekly. Dow Jones and Co., Inc. • Weekly. $145.00 per year.

Energy and Fuels. American Chemical Society. • Bimonthly. Institutions, $728.00 per year; others, price on application. an interdisciplinary technical journal covering non-nuclear energy sources: petroleum, gas, synthetic fuels, etc.

Energy: The International Journal. Elsevier Science. • Monthly. $1,608.00 per year.

Fuel: Science and Technology of Fuel and Energy. Elsevier Science. • 15 times a year. $2,267.00 per year.

International Journal of Energy Research. Available from John Wiley and Sons, Inc., Journals Div. • 15 times a year. Institutions, $2,735.00 per year. Published in England by John Wiley & Sons Ltd.

RESEARCH CENTERS AND INSTITUTES

Argonne National Laboratory. 9700 S. Cass Ave., Argonne, IL 60439-4832. Phone: (630)252-2000 Fax: (630)252-7923 • URL: http://www.anl.gov.

Energy and Environmental Research Center. University of North Dakota. P.O. Box 9018, Grand Forks, ND 58202-9018. Phone: (701)777-5000 Fax: (701)777-5181 E-mail: ghg@eerc.und.nodak.edu.

Energy Laboratory. Massachusetts Institute of Technology. Bldg. E40-455, Cambridge, MA 02139-4307. Phone: (617)253-3401 Fax: (617)253-8013 E-mail: testerel@mit.edu • URL: http://www.web.mit.edu/energylab/www/.

Southwest Research Institute. P.O. Box 28510, San Antonio, TX 78228-0510. Phone: (210)684-5111 Fax: (210)522-3496 E-mail: jkittle@swri.org • URL: http://www.swri.org.

STATISTICS SOURCES

Annual Energy Outlook [year], with Projections to [year]. Available from U. S. Government Printing Office. • Annual. Issued by the Energy Information Administration, U. S. Department of Energy (http://www.eia.doe.gov). Contains detailed statistics and 20-year projections for electricity, oil, natural gas, coal, and renewable energy. Text provides extensive discussion of energy issues and "Market Trends.".

Energy Statistics Yearbook. United Nations Dept. of Economic and Social Affairs. United Nations Publications. • Annual. $100.00. Text in English and French.

International Energy Annual. Available from U. S. Government Printing Office. • Annual. $34.00. Issued by the Energy Information Administration, U. S. Department of Energy. Provides production, consumption, import, and export data for primary energy commodities in more than 200 countries and areas. In addition to petroleum products and alcohol, renewable energy sources are covered (hydroelectric, geothermal, solar, and wind).

Petroleum Statement, Annual Energy Report. Energy Information Administration. U.S. Department of Energy. • Annual.

Steam Electric Market Analysis. National Mining Association. • Monthly. $300.00 per year. Covers 400 major electric power plants, with detailed data on coal consumption and stockpiles. Shows percent of power generated by fuel type. (Publisher formerly National Coal Association.).

OTHER SOURCES

Major Energy Companies of the World. Available from The Gale Group. • 2001. $855.00. Fourth edition. Published by Graham & Whiteside. Contains detailed information on more than 3,300 important energy companies in various countries. Industries include electricity generation, coal, natural gas, nuclear energy, petroleum, fuel distribution, and equipment for energy production.

FUEL CELLS

See: BATTERY INDUSTRY

FUEL OIL INDUSTRY

FINANCIAL RATIOS

Annual Statement Studies. Robert Morris Associates: The Association of Lending and Credit Risk Professiona. • Annual. Free to members; non-members, $140.00. Median and quartile financial ratios are given for over 400 kinds of manufacturing, wholesale, retail, construction, and consumer finance establishments. Data is sorted by both asset size and sales volume. Includes a clearly written "Definition of Ratios" and an alphabetical industry index.

INTERNET DATABASES

Fedstats. Federal Interagency Council on Statistical Policy. Phone: (202)395-7254 • URL: http://www.fedstats.gov • Web site features an efficient search facility for full-text statistics produced by more than 70 federal agencies, including the Census Bureau, the Bureau of Economic Analysis, and the Bureau of Labor Statistics. Boolean searches can be made within one agency or for all agencies combined. Links are offered to international statistical bureaus, including the UN, IMF, OECD, UNESCO, Eurostat, and 20 individual countries. Fees: Free.

ONLINE DATABASES

DRI U.S. Central Database. Data Products Division. • Provides more than 23,000 business, financial, demographic, economic, foreign trade, and industry-related time series for the U.S. Includes national income, population, retail-wholesale trade, price indexes, labor data, housing, industrial production, banking, interest rates, money supply, etc. Time period is generally 1947 to date (some data back to 1929). Updating varies. Inquire as to online cost and availability.

Platt's Energy Prices. Data Products Division. • Contains daily high and low prices for crude oil and petroleum products, including gasoline, fuel oil, and liquefied petroleum gas (LPG). Coverage is international from 1983 to present, with daily updates. Inquire as to online cost and availability.

PERIODICALS AND NEWSLETTERS

Oil and Gas Journal. PennWell Corp., Industrial Div. • Weekly. $84.00 per year.

Oilheating. Industry Publications, Inc. • 12 times a year. $30.00 per year. Formerly *Fueloil and Oil Heat with Air Conditioning.*

STATISTICS SOURCES

Business Statistics of the United States. Courtenay M. Slater, editor. Bernan Associates. • 1999. $74.00. Fifth edition. Based on *Business Statistics*, formerly issue by the Bureau of Economic Analysis, U. S. Department of Commerce. Provides basic data for a wide variety of U. S. industries, services, and economic indicators. Most statistics are shown annually for 29 years and monthly for the most recent four years.

Fuel Oil News: Source Book. • Annual. $28.00. Provides fuel (heating) oil industry data.

Petroleum Supply Annual. Available from U. S. Government Printing Office. • Annual. $78.00. Two volumes. Produced by the Energy Information Administration, U. S. Department of Energy. Contains worldwide data on the petroleum industry and petroleum products.

Petroleum Supply Monthly. Available from U. S. Government Printing Office. • Monthly. $100.00 per year. Produced by the Energy Information Administration, U. S. Department of Energy. Provides worldwide statistics on a wide variety of petroleum products. Covers production, supplies, exports and imports, transportation, refinery operations, and other aspects of the petroleum industry.

Survey of Current Business. Available from U. S. Government Printing Office. • Monthly. $49.00 per year. Issued by Bureau of Economic Analysis, U. S. Department of Commerce. Presents a wide variety of business and economic data.

TRADE/PROFESSIONAL ASSOCIATIONS

Petroleum Marketers Association of America. 1901 N. Fort Meyer Dr., Suite 1200, Arlington, VA 22209. Phone: (703)351-8000 Fax: (703)351-9160 E-mail: http://www.pmaa.org.

FUEL, SYNTHETIC

See: SYNTHETIC FUELS

FUND-RAISING

See also: FEDERAL AID; FOUNDATIONS; GRANTS-IN-AID

GENERAL WORKS

Complete Guide to Corporate Fund Raising. Joseph Dermer and Stephen Wertheimer, editors. Fund Raising Institute. • 1991. $19.95. Discusses the art of obtaining grants from corporate sources. Written by nine fund raising counselors.

Fund Raising: The Guide to Raising Money from Private Sources. Thomas C. Broce. University of Oklahoma Press. • 1986. $27.95. Second enlarged revised edition.

BIBLIOGRAPHIES

Bibliography of Fund Raising and Philanthropy. National Catholic Development Conference. • 1982. $22.50. Second edition.

Management and Leadership Resources for Non-Profits. Available from Applied Research and Development Institute. • Annual. $3.50. Compiled by the Applied Research and Development Institute and published as a special issue of *The Journal of Philanthropy.* Lists and describes over 800 books, periodicals, and other publications in 14 categories (general management, finance, marketing, development, etc.). Includes a directory of publishers. No indexes.

The Non-Profit Handbook: Books, Periodicals, Software, Internet Sites, and Other Essential Resources for Non-Profit Leaders. Chronicle of Higher Education, Inc. • Annual. $5.00. A special issue of *Chronicle of Philanthropy.* Contains annotations of books, periodicals, and other material from various sources, relating to Advocacy, Boards, Communications and Marketing, Financial Management, Fund Raising, General Information, Managing, Philanthropic Tradition, Technology, and Volunteers. Includes index to titles.

DIRECTORIES

Charitable Organizations of the U. S.: A Descriptive and Financial Information Guide. The Gale Group. • 1991. $150.00. Second edition. Describes nearly 800 nonprofit groups active in soliciting funds from the American public. Includes nearly 800 data on sources of income, administrative expenses, and payout.

The Foundation Reporter: Comprehensive Profiles and Giving Analyses of America's Major Private Foundations. The Taft Group. • Annual. $425.00. Provides detailed information on major U. S. foundations. Eight indexes (location, grant type, recipient type, personnel, etc.).

Funding Sources for Community and Economic Development: A Guide to Current Sources for Local Programs and Projects. Oryx Press. • 2000. $64.95. Sixth edition. Provides information on 2,600 funding sources. Includes "A Guide to Proposal Planning.".

Guide to Federal Funding for Governments and Non-Profits. Government Information Services. • Quarterly. $339.00 per year. Contains detailed descriptions of federal grant programs in economic development, housing, transportation, social services, science, etc. Semimonthly supplement available: *Federal Grant Deadline Calendar.*

HANDBOOKS AND MANUALS

The Art of Asking: How to Solicit Philanthropic Gifts. Paul H. Schneiter. Fund Raising Institute. • 1985. $25.00.

The Art of Fund Raising. Irving R. Warner. Fund Raising Institute. • 1991. $19.95. Third edition. Includes case histories.

The Business of Special Events: Fundraising Strategies for Changing Times. Harry A. Freedman and Karen Feldman. Pineapple Press, Inc. • 1998. $21.95.

Conducting a Successful Capital Campaign: A Comprehensive Fundraising Guide for Nonprofit Organizations. Kent E. Dove. Jossey-Bass, Inc., Publishers. • 1988. $38.95. (Nonprofit Sector-Public Administration Series).

Fundraising: Hands-On Tactics for Nonprofit Groups. L. Peter Edles. McGraw-Hill. • 1992. $32.95. Covers fundamental premises, soliciting major gifts, small gift prospecting, canvassing, telephone appeals, creating publications, direct mail, and other fund-raising topics for nonprofit organizations.

Getting Funded: A Complete Guide to Proposal Writing. Mary S. Hall. Portland State University. • 1988. $23.95. Third edition. Proposal writing for public and private grants.

How to Write Proposals that Produce. Joel P. Bowman and Bernadine P. Branchaw. Oryx Press. • 1992. $23.50. An extensive guide to effective proposal writing for both nonprofit organizations and businesses. Covers writing style, intended audience, format, use of graphs, charts, and tables, documentation, evaluation, oral presentation, and related topics.

The Law of Fund-Raising. Bruce R. Hopkins. John Wiley and Sons, Inc. • 1995. $160.00. Second edition. Annual supplements available. Covers all aspects of state and federal nonprofit fund-raising law. Includes summaries of the relevant laws and regulations of each state. *Nonprofit Law, Finance and Management Series.*

The Law of Fund-Raising: 1999 Cumulative Supplement. Bruce R. Hopkins. John Wiley and Sons, Inc. • 1998. $65.00. *Nonprofit Law, Finance and Management Series.*

The Nonprofit Entrepreneur: Creating Ventures to Earn Income. Edward Skloot, editor. The Foundation Center. • 1988. $19.95. Advice on earning income through fees and service charges.

Raise More Money for Your Nonprofit Organization: A Guide to Evaluating and Improving Your Fundraising. Anne L. New. The Foundation Center. • 1991. $14.95.

INTERNET DATABASES

American Visions Non-Profit Center. American Visions Society/American Visions Magazine. Phone: (202)462-1779 Fax: (202)462-3997 • URL: http://www.americanvisions.com • Web site "Created by African Americans for African Americans..enables non-profit professionals to share ideas, provide assistance, seek funding, [and] browse for information.." Includes "Black Endowment," a monthly online newsletter covering people, grants, non-profit seminars, and non-profit news. Registration required, with two options: "Grantseeker" or "Grantmaker." Free 30-day trial available.

Welcome to the Foundation Center. The Foundation Center. Phone: (212)620-4230 Fax: (212)691-1828 E-mail: mfn@fdncenter.org • URL: http://www.fdncenter.org • Web site provides a wide variety of information about foundations, grants, and philanthropy, with links to philanthropic organizations. "Grantmaker Information" link furnishes descriptions of available funding. Fees: Free.

PERIODICALS AND NEWSLETTERS

DM News: The Newspaper of Direct Marketing. DM News Corp. • Weekly. $75.00 per year. Includes special feature issues on catalog marketing, telephone marketing, database marketing, and fundraising. Includes monthly supplements. *DM News International, DRTV News,* and *TeleServices.*

FRM Weekly (Fund Raising Management). Hoke Communications, Inc. • Weekly. $115.00 per year.

Giving USA Update. American Association of Fund-Raising Counsel. AAFRC Trust for Philanthropy. • Quarterly. $110.00 per year. Legal, economic and social essays on philanthropy.

Grantsmanship Center Magazine: A Compendium of Resources for Nonprofit Organizations. Grantsmanship Center. • Irregular. Free to qualified personnel. Contains a variety of concise articles on grant-related topics, such as program planning, proposal writing, fundraising, non-cash gifts, federal project grants, benchmarking, taxation, etc.

NSFRE News. National Society of Fund Raising Executives. • 6 times a year. Free to members; non-members, $25.00 per year. Information on events, people and issues in the fundraising profession.

Taft Monthly Portfolio. Taft Group. • Monthly. $75.00 per year. New ideas and proven techniques used by universitites, hospitals and a wide range of other nonprofit organizations to raise philanthropic gifts. Formerly *FRI Monthly Portfolio.*

RESEARCH CENTERS AND INSTITUTES

Foundation Center. 79 Fifth Ave., New York, NY 10003-3076. Phone: 800-424-9836 or (212)807-3690 Fax: (212)807-3691 • URL: http://www.fdncenter.org.

STATISTICS SOURCES

Giving U.S.A: The Annual Compilation of Total Philanthropic Giving Estimates. American Association of Fund-Raising Counsel. AAFRC Trust for Philanthropy. • Annual. $49.95.

United Way Annual Report. United Way of America. • Annual. Price on application.

TRADE/PROFESSIONAL ASSOCIATIONS

Alliance of Nonprofit Mailers. 1211 Connecticut Ave., No. 620, Washington, DC 20036. Phone: (202)462-5132 Fax: (202)462-0423 E-mail: npmailers@aol.com • URL: http://www.nonprofitmailers.org.

American Association of Fund-Raising Counsel. 37 E. 28th St., Rm. 902, New York, NY 10016-7919. Phone: 800-462-2372 or (212)481-6705 Fax: (212)481-7238 E-mail: aafrc@aol.com • URL: http://www.aafrc.org.

National Federation of Nonprofits. 815 15th St., N.W., Suite 822, Washington, DC 20005-2201. Phone: (202)628-4380 Fax: (202)628-4383.

National Society of Fund Raising Executives. 1101 King St., Suite 700, Alexandria, VA 22314. Phone: 800-666-5863 or (703)684-0410 Fax: (703)684-0540 E-mail: nsfre@nsfre.org • URL: http://www.nsfre.org.

OTHER SOURCES

Charitable Giving and Solicitation. Warren Gorham and Lamont/RIA Group. • $495.00 per year. Looseleaf service. Monthly bulletin discusses federal tax rules pertaining to charitable contributions.

Corporate Giving Watch: News and Ideas for Nonprofit Organizations Seeking Corporate Funds. Available from The Gale Group. • Monthly. $149.00 per year. Newsletter. Published by The Taft Group. Includes news, trends, and statistics related to corporate giving programs. "Corporate Profiles" insert contains profiles of individual programs.

FUNDS, COMMUNITY

See: COMMUNITY FUNDS

FUNDS, MUTUAL

See: INVESTMENT COMPANIES

FUNERAL HOMES AND DIRECTORS

DIRECTORIES

The American Blue Book of Funeral Directors. Kates-Bolyston Publications, Inc. • Biennial. $75.00. About 22,000 funeral homes primarily in the United States and Canada.

Funeral and Memorial Societies of America. • Annual. Free. Lists over 150 nonprofit memorial societies which assists members in obtaining simple funeral arrangements at reasonable cost. Includes members of the Memorial Society Association of Canada. Formerly *Continental Association of Funeral and Memorial Societies Directory of Member Societies.*

NFDA Directory of Members and Resource Guide. NFDA Publications, Inc. • Annual. $75.00. 20,000 members of state funeral director associations affiliated with the National Funeral Directors Association. Formerly *National Funeral Directors Association-Membership Listing and Resources.*

FINANCIAL RATIOS

Annual Statement Studies. Robert Morris Associates: The Association of Lending and Credit Risk Professiona. • Annual. Free to members; non-members, $140.00. Median and quartile financial ratios are given for over 400 kinds of manufacturing, wholesale, retail, construction, and consumer finance establishments. Data is sorted by both asset size and sales volume. Includes a clearly written "Definition of Ratios" and an alphabetical industry index.

HANDBOOKS AND MANUALS

Dealing Creatively with Death: A Manual of Death Education and Simple Burial. Ernest Morgan and Jennifer Morgan. Upper Access, Inc. • 2001. $12.95. 14th revised edition. A humanistic approach to dying and grieving; pursuing economy, simplicity and greater sensitivity in funeral practices.

PERIODICALS AND NEWSLETTERS

American Funeral Director. Kates-Bolyston Publications, Inc. • Monthly. $28.00 per year.

The Director. National Funeral Directors Association. NFDA Publications, Inc. • Monthly $30.00 per year.

Funeral Service Insider. Jean DeSapio, editor. Atcom, Inc. • Weekly. $255.00 per year. News and trends among death-care professionals.

TRADE/PROFESSIONAL ASSOCIATIONS

Funeral and Memorial Societies of America. P.O. Box 10, Hinesburg, VT 05461. Phone: 800-458-5563 or (802)482-3437 or (802)482-2879 Fax: (802)482-5246 E-mail: famsa@funerals.org • URL: http://www.funerals.org.famsa.

National Foundation of Funeral Service. 13625 Bishops Dr., Brookfield, WI 53005-6607. 13625 Bishops Dr.,.

National Funeral Directors and Morticians Association. 3951 Snapfinger Parkway, Suite 570, Omega World Center, Decatur, GA 30035. Phone: 800-434-0958 or (404)286-6680 Fax: (404)286-6573 E-mail: nfdma@mindspring.com • URL: http://www.nfdma.com.

National Funeral Directors Association. 13625 Bishops Dr., Brookfield, WI 53005-6600. Phone: 800-228-6332 or (262)789-1880 Fax: (262)789-6977 E-mail: nfda@nfda.org • URL: http://www.nfda.org.

National Selected Morticians. Five Revere Dr., Suite 340, Northbrook, IL 60062-8009. Phone: (847)559-9569 Fax: (847)559-9571 E-mail: info@nsm.org • URL: http://www.nsm.org.

OTHER SOURCES

The U. S. Market for Funeral and Cremation Services. Available from MarketResearch.com. • 1997. $2,350.00. Market research report published by Packaged Facts. Includes information on multinational funeral service chains.

FUR INDUSTRY

PERIODICALS AND NEWSLETTERS

Fur Age. Fur Vogue Publishing Co., Inc. • 10 times a year. $100.00 per year. Formerly *Fur Age Weekly.*

TRADE/PROFESSIONAL ASSOCIATIONS

American Fur Merchants' Association. 224 W. 30th St., 2nd Fl., New York, NY 10001. Phone: (212)564-5133 Fax: (212)643-9124.

Fur Information Council of America. 224 W. 30th St., 2nd Fl., New York, NY 10001. Phone: (212)564-5133 Fax: (212)643-9124.

OTHER SOURCES

Blue Book of Fur Farming. Becker Publishing. • Annual. $20.00. Lists manufacturers and suppliers of equipment and materials used in the raising of fur-bearing animals for the fur industry.

Fur Rancher. Becker Publishing. • Quarterly. $20.00 per year. Covers the farm raising of animals for fur.

Fur World: The Newsmagazine of Fur and Better Outerware. Creative Marketing Plus, Inc. • Semimonthly. $45.00 per year. Edited for fur retailers, ranchers, pelt dealers, and manufacturers. Provides news and statistics relating to the retail and wholesale fur business.

FURNISHINGS (MEN'S CLOTHING)

See: MEN'S CLOTHING INDUSTRY

FURNITURE INDUSTRY

See also: OFFICE FURNITURE INDUSTRY

ABSTRACTS AND INDEXES

NTIS Alerts: Building Industry Technology. National Technical Information Service. • Semimonthly. $210.00 per year. Provides descriptions of government-sponsored research reports and software, with ordering information. Covers architecture, construction management, building materials, maintenance, furnishings, and related subjects. Formerly *Abstract Newsletter.*

BIOGRAPHICAL SOURCES

Who's Who in the Southern Furniture Industry. American Furniture Manufacturers Association. • Annual. $50.00. Lists about 400 manufacturers of furniture and their suppliers.

CD-ROM DATABASES

World Marketing Forecasts on CD-ROM. The Gale Group. • Annual. $2,500.00. Produced by Euromonitor. Provides detailed forecast data for the years to 2012 on CD-ROM for 54 countries in all parts of the world. Covers a wide range of social, demographic, economic, and market factors. Includes specific forecasts for many kinds of consumer products.

DIRECTORIES

Directory of Home Furnishings Retailers. Chain Store Guide. • Annual. $290.00. Includes more than 4,800 furniture retailers and wholesalers.

FDM-The Source-Woodworking Industry Directory. Cahners Business Information. • Annual. $25.00. A product-classified listing of more than 1,800 suppliers to the furniture and cabinet industries. Includes Canada.

Juvenile Merchandising - Directory and Buyers Guide. E.W. Williams Publications Co. • Annual. $15.00. Manufacturers, suppliers, and distributors of products for juveniles, including furniture, bedding, pre-school toys, etc.; trade associations.

Wood Digest Showcase. Cygnus Publishing, Inc., Johnson Hill Press, Inc. • Annual. Controlled circulation. Formerly *Furniture Wood/Digest-Showcase.*

FINANCIAL RATIOS

Almanac of Business and Industrial Financial Ratios. Leo Troy. Prentice Hall. • Annual. $99.95. Contains financial ratios derived from federal tax returns. Ratios for each of about 200 industries are arranged according to company asset size.

Industry Norms and Key Business Ratios. Desk Top Edition. Dun and Bradstreet Corp., Business Information Services. • Annual. Five volumes. $475.00 per volume. $1,890.00 per set. Covers over 800 kinds of businesses, arranged by Standard Industrial Classification number. More detailed editions covering longer periods of time are also available.

HANDBOOKS AND MANUALS

PVC Furniture Manufacturing. Entrepreneur Media, Inc. • Looseleaf. $59.50. A practical guide to starting a business for the manufacture of plastic furniture. Covers profit potential, start-up costs, market size evaluation, owner's time required, site selection, lease negotiation, pricing, accounting, advertising, promotion, etc. (Start-Up Business Guide No. E1262.).

INTERNET DATABASES

Fedstats. Federal Interagency Council on Statistical Policy. Phone: (202)395-7254 • URL: http://www.fedstats.gov • Web site features an efficient search facility for full-text statistics produced by more than 70 federal agencies, including the Census Bureau, the Bureau of Economic Analysis, and the Bureau of Labor Statistics. Boolean searches can be made within one agency or for all agencies combined. Links are offered to international statistical bureaus, including the UN, IMF, OECD, UNESCO, Eurostat, and 20 individual countries. Fees: Free.

ONLINE DATABASES

DRI U.S. Central Database. Data Products Division. • Provides more than 23,000 business, financial, demographic, economic, foreign trade, and industry-related time series for the U.S. Includes national income, population, retail-wholesale trade, price indexes, labor data, housing, industrial production, banking, interest rates, money supply, etc. Time period is generally 1947 to date (some data back to 1929). Updating varies. Inquire as to online cost and availability.

Euromonitor Market Research. Euromonitor International. • Provides the complete text online of Euromonitor market analysis reports. Covers consumer goods market research data for all major countries, with emphasis on specific product categories. Time period is current. Continuous updating. Inquire as to online cost and availability.

PERIODICALS AND NEWSLETTERS

FDM: Furniture Design and Manufacturing: Serving the Upholstered Furniture Industry. Chartwell Communications, Inc. • Monthly. Free to qualified personnel. Edited for furniture executives, production managers, and designers. Covers the manufacturing of household, office, and institutional furniture, store fixtures, and kitchen and bathroom cabinets.

Furniture/Today: The Weekly Business Newspaper of the Furniture Industry. Cahners Business Newspapers. • Weekly. $139.97 per year.

Furniture World. Towse Publishing Co. • Monthly. $19.00 per year. Formerly *Furniture World and Furniture Buyer and Decorator.*

HFN (Home Furnishing Network). Fairchild Publications. • Weekly. Manufacturers, retailers, and agents $65.00 per year; other corporations, $80.00 per year.Formerly *H F D-Home Furnishing Daily.*

RESEARCH CENTERS AND INSTITUTES

Wood Research Laboratory. Purdue University, Department of Forestry and Natural Resources, West Lafayette, IN 47907-1200. Phone: (765)494-3615 Fax: (765)496-1344 E-mail: mhunt@fnr.purdue.edu • URL: http://www.fnr.purdue.edu.

STATISTICS SOURCES

Annual Survey of Manufactures. Available from U. S. Government Printing Office. • Annual. Prices vary. Issued by the U. S. Census Bureau as an interim update to the *Census of Manufactures.* Includes data on number of manufacturing establishments in various industries, employment, labor costs, value of shipments, capital expenditures, inventories, energy costs, and assets. (See also Census Bureau home page, http://www.census.gov/.).

Business Statistics of the United States. Courtenay M. Slater, editor. Bernan Associates. • 1999. $74.00. Fifth edition. Based on *Business Statistics,* formerly issue by the Bureau of Economic Analysis, U. S. Department of Commerce. Provides basic data for a wide variety of U. S. industries, services, and economic indicators. Most statistics are shown annually for 29 years and monthly for the most recent four years.

Consumer Canada 1996. Available from The Gale Group. • 1996. $750.00. Published by Euromonitor. Provides consumer market, socioeconomic, and demographic data for Canada. Includes consumer market size (volume and value) for many specific kinds of products.

Consumer International 2000/2001. Available from The Gale Group. • 1998. $1,190.00. Seventh edition. Published by Euromonitor. Contains extensive consumer market, economic, and demographic data for 27 major, non-European countries, including the U. S. and Canada. Includes consumer market size (volume and value) for 150 product types in 14 categories (food, clothing, automobiles, cosmetics, appliances, etc.).

European Marketing Forecasts 2001. Available from The Gale Group. • 2000. $1,190.00. Third edition. Published by Euromonitor. Contains demographic, economic, and market forecasts for the countries of Europe to the year 2010. Forecasts include market-size data for 15 consumer product sectors (food, clothing, automobiles, consumer electronics, etc.).

International Marketing Forecasts 2001. Available from The Gale Group. • 2000. $1,090.00. Third edition. Published by Euromonitor. Contains demographic, economic, and market forecasts to the year 2010 for major, non-European countries, including the U. S. and Canada. Forecasts include market-size data for 15 consumer product sectors, such as food, clothing, and automobiles.

Survey of Current Business. Available from U. S. Government Printing Office. • Monthly. $49.00 per year. Issued by Bureau of Economic Analysis, U. S. Department of Commerce. Presents a wide variety of business and economic data.

WEFA Industrial Monitor. John Wiley and Sons, Inc. • Annual. $65.00. Prepared by industry analysts at WEFA, an economic forecasting and consulting firm (originally Wharton Econometric Forecasting Associates). Contains discussions of the outlook for major U. S. industries, with many 10-year forecasts (WEFA Web site is http://www.wefa.com).

TRADE/PROFESSIONAL ASSOCIATIONS

American Furniture Manufacturers Association. P.O. Box HP-7, High Point, NC 27261. Phone: (336)884-5000 Fax: (336)884-5303 • URL: http://www.afma4u.org.

International Home Furnishings Representatives Association. P.O. Box 670, High Point, NC 27261-0670. Phone: (336)889-3920 Fax: (336)889-8245 E-mail: ihfra@aol.com • URL: http://www.ihfra.com.

National Home Furnishings Association. P.O. Box 2396, High Point, NC 27261. Phone: 800-888-9590 or (336)801-6100 Fax: (336)883-1195 E-mail: mail@nhfa.org • URL: http://www.nhfa.org.

United Furniture Workers Insurance Fund. P.O. Box 100037, Nashville, TN 37224. Phone: (615)889-8860 Fax: (615)391-0865.

FUTURES, FINANCIAL

See: FINANCIAL FUTURES TRADING

FUTURES TRADING

See: COMMODITY FUTURES TRADING

FUTURISTICS

GENERAL WORKS

The Age of Spiritual Machines: When Computers Exceed Human Intelligence. Ray Kurzweil. Viking Penguin. • 1999. $25.95. Provides speculation on the future of artificial intelligence and "computer consciousness.".

The Art of the Long View: Planning for the Future in an Uncertain World. Peter Schwartz. Doubleday. • 1991. $15.95. Covers strategic planning for corporations and smaller firms. Includes "The World in 2005: Three Scenarios.".

Being Digital. Nicholas Negroponte. Vintage Books. • 1995. $28.00. A kind of history of multimedia, with visions of future technology and public participation. Predicts how computers will affect society in years to come.

Cyberquake: How the Internet will Erase Profits, Topple Market Leaders, and Shatter Business Models. Michael Sullivan-Trainor. John Wiley & Sons, Inc. • 1997. $26.95. Predicts that the Internet will cause "an overwhelming shift in control of the worldwide marketplace" in the early 21st century. (Business Technology Series).

Data Smog: Surviving the Information Glut. David Shenk. HarperCollins Publishers. • 1997. $24.00. A critical view of both the electronic and print information industries. Emphasis is on information overload.

Dow 100,000: Fact or Fiction. Charles W. Kadlec. Prentice Hall. • 1999. $25.00. Predicts a level of 100,000 for the Dow Jones Industrial Average in the year 2020, based mainly on a technological revolution.

The 500 Year Delta: What Happens After What Comes Next. Jim Taylor and others. HarperCollins Publishers. • 1998. $14.00. Provides analysis of major corporate and political trends.

The Fortune Sellers: The Big Business of Buying and Selling Predictions. William A. Sherden. John Wiley and Sons, Inc. • 1997. $29.95. The author states that predictions are notoriously unreliable in any field, including the stock market, the economy, and the weather. (Forecasters in all areas don't have to be right; they just have to be interesting.).

Libraries and the Future: Essays on the Library in the Twenty-First Century. F. W. Lancaster, editor. Haworth Press, Inc. • 1993. $49.95. Emphasis is on information services in libraries of the future. (Original Book Series).

Megatrends Two Thousand: Ten New Directions for the 1990's. John Naisbitt and Patricia Aburdene. Avon Books. • 1991. $6.99. Social forecasting to the year 2000 and into the 21st century.

Predicting the Future: An Introduction to the Theory of Forecasting. Nicholas Rescher. State University of New York Press. • 1997. $65.50. Provides a general theory of prediction, including the principles and methodology of forecasting. Includes "The Evaluation of Predictions and Predictors.".

Preparing for the Twenty-First Century. Paul Kennedy. Villard Books. • 1993. $15.00. A somber view of the future.

Probable Tomorrows: How Science and Technology Will Transform Our Lives in the Next Twenty Years. Marvin J. Cetron and Owen L. Davies. St. Martin's Press. • 1997. $24.95. Predicts the developments in technological products, services, and "everyday conveniences" by the year 2017. Covers such items as personal computers, artificial intelligence, telecommunications, highspeed railroads, and healthcare.

The Shape of Things to Come: Seven Imperatives for Winning in the New World of Business. Richard W. Oliver. McGraw-Hill. • 1998. $24.95. Contains predictions relating to the influence of information technology on 21st century business. (Business Week Books.).

A Short History of the Future. W. Warren Wagar. University of Chicago Press. • 1989. $29.95.

Trends 2000: How to Prepare For and Profit From the Changes of the 21st Century. Gerald Celente. Little, Brown and Co. • 1998. $14.99. Emphasis is on economic, social, and political trends.

What Will Be: How the New World of Information Will Change Our Lives. Michael L. Dertouzos. HarperSan Francisco. • 1997. $25.00. A discussion of the "information market place" of the future, including telecommuting, virtual reality, and computer recognition of speech. The author is director of the MIT Laboratory for Computer Science.

The World in 2020: Power, Culture, and Prosperity. Hamish McRae. Harvard Business School Press. • 1995. $24.95. States that the best predictor of economic success will be a nation's creativity and social responsibility.

ABSTRACTS AND INDEXES

Future Survey: A Monthly Abstract of Books, Articles, and Reports Concerning Trends, Forecasts, and Ideas About the Future. World Future Society. • Monthly. Individuals, $89.00 per year; libraries, $129.00 per year. Includes author and subject indexes.

BIBLIOGRAPHIES

Future Survey Annual: A Guide to the Recent Literature of Trends, Forecasts, and Policy Proposals. World Future Society. • Annual. $35.00.

DIRECTORIES

World Futures Studies Federation Membership Directory. World Future Studies Federation. • Annual. $50.00. Lists over 700 member individuals and 60 institutions with an interest in the study of the world's future. Formerly *World Future Studies-Newsletter Membership Directory.*

PERIODICALS AND NEWSLETTERS

Futures Research Quarterly. World Future Society. • Quarterly. Members, $70.00 per year; others, $90.00 per year.

Futuretech. Technical Insights. • 18 times a year. $1,600.00 per year. Newsletter on newly emerging technologies and their markets.

The Futurist: A Journal of Forecasts, Trends, and Ideas About the Future. World Future Society. • Bimonthly. Members, $39.00 per year; non-members, $47.00 per year.

The Trends Journal: The Authority on Trends Management. Gerald Celente, editor. Trends Research Institute. • Quarterly. $185.00 per year. Newsletter. Provides forecasts on a wide variety of economic, social, and political topics. Includes "Hot Trends to Watch.".

21.C: Scanning the Future: A Magazine of Culture, Technology, and Science. International Publishers Distributors. • Quarterly. $24.00 per year. Contains multidisciplinary articles relating to the 21st century.

RESEARCH CENTERS AND INSTITUTES

Institute for Alternative Futures. 100 N. Pitt St., Suite 235, Alexandria, VA 22314. Phone: (703)684-5880 Fax: (703)684-0640 E-mail: futurist@altfutures.com • URL: http://www.altfutures.com • Conducts studies in the future of communications, health care, bioengineering, the legal system, etc.

TRADE/PROFESSIONAL ASSOCIATIONS

Academy of Arts and Sciences of the Americas. 9450 Old Cutler Rd., Miami, FL 33156. Phone: (305)663-9897 Fax: (305)667-8426 • Seeks an interdisciplinary approach to the 21st century.

Institute for the Future. 2744 Sand Hill Rd., Menlo Park, CA 94025-7020. Phone: (650)854-6322 Fax: (650)854-7850 • URL: http://www.iftf.org.

World Future Society. 7910 Woodmont Ave., Suite 450, Bethesda, MD 20814. Phone: 800-989-8274 or (301)656-8274 Fax: (301)951-0394 E-mail: info@wfs.org • URL: http://www.wfs.org • Members are individuals concerned with forecasts and ideas about the future.

World Futures Studies Federation. c/o WFSF Secretariat Office, Main Administration Bldg., 2nd Fl., University of Saint La Salle, Bacolod City 6100, Philippines. Phone: 63 34 4353857 Fax: 63 34 4353857 E-mail: secretariat@worldfutures.org • Members are institutions and individuals involved with study of the future.

OTHER SOURCES

MarketingClick Network: American Demographics. Intertec Publishing, a Primedia Co. • Web site provides full-text articles from *American Demographics*, *Marketing Tools*, and *Forecast*, with keyword searching. The *Marketing Tools Directory* can also be searched online, listing suppliers of products, information, and services for advertising, market research, and marketing. Fees: Free.

G

GAMBLING INDUSTRY

DIRECTORIES

International Gaming Resource Guide. Gem Communications. • Annual. $50.00. Includes gambling establishments, race tracks, racing commissions, etc. Formery International Gaming and Wagering Business Directory.

ENCYCLOPEDIAS AND DICTIONARIES

Dictionary of Gambling and Gaming. Thomas L. Clark. Lexik House Publishers. • 1988. $48.00.

Encyclopedia of Emerging Industries. The Gale Group. • 2000. $295.00. Fourth edition. Provides detailed information on 90 "newly flourishing" industries. Includes historical background, organizational structure, significant individuals, current conditions, major companies, work force, technology trends, research developments, and other industry facts.

HANDBOOKS AND MANUALS

Managing Casinos: A Guide for Entrepreneurs, Management Personnel, and Aspiring Managers. Ruben Martinez. Barricade Books, Inc. • 1995. $75.00. Covers such topics as the installation of profitable games, providing credit to players, casino business math, and understanding odds.

ONLINE DATABASES

PAIS International. Public Affairs Information Service, Inc. • Corresponds to the former printed publications, *PAIS Bulletin* (1976-90) and *PAIS Foreign Language Index* (1972-90), and to the current *PAIS International in Print* (1991 to date). Covers economic, political, and sociological material appearing in periodicals, books, government documents, and other publications. Updating is monthly. Inquire as to online cost and availability.

PERIODICALS AND NEWSLETTERS

The Bottomline. International Association of Hospitality Accountants. • Bimonthly. Free to members, educational institutions and libraries; others, $50.00 per year. Contains articles on accounting, finance, information technology, and management for hotels, resorts, casinos, clubs, and other hospitality businesses.

Casino Chronicle. Casino Chronicle, Inc. Ben Borowsky. • 48 times a year. $175.00 per year. Newsletter focusing on the Atlantic City gambling industry.

Gaming International Magazine. Boardwalker Magazine, Inc. • Quarterly. $28.00 per year.

Hospitality Technology: Infosystems for Foodservice and Lodging. Edgell Communications, Inc. • Monthly. $36.00 per year. Covers information technology, computer communications, and software for foodservice and lodging enterprises.

International Gaming and Wagering Business. Gem Communications. • Monthly. $60.00 per year.

WIN. Gambling Times, Inc. • Monthly. $44.00 per year. Formerly *Gambling Times.*

RESEARCH CENTERS AND INSTITUTES

Casino and Gaming Market Research Handbook. Available from MarketResearch.com. 641 Ave. of the Americas, Third Floor, New York, NY 10011. Phone: 800-298-5699 or (212)807-2629 Fax: (212)807-2642 E-mail: order@marketresearch.com • URL: http://www.marketresearch.com • 2001. $375.00. Fifth edition. Published by Richard K. Miller & Associates. Includes analysis and statistical data on casinos, lotteries, table games, electronic gaming machines, bingo, and online gambling.

STATISTICS SOURCES

Standard & Poor's Industry Surveys. Standard & Poor's. • Semiannual. $1,800.00. Two looseleaf volumes. Includes monthly supplements. Provides detailed, individual surveys of 52 major industry groups. Each survey is revised on a semiannual basis. Also includes "Monthly Investment Review" (industry group investment analysis) and monthly "Trends & Projections" (economic analysis).

TRADE/PROFESSIONAL ASSOCIATIONS

American Amusement Machine Association. 450 E. Higgins, Suite 201, Elk Grove Village, IL 60007-1417. Phone: (847)290-9088 Fax: (847)290-9121 E-mail: information@coin-op.org • URL: http://www.coin-op.org.

Gam-Anon International Service Office. P.O. Box 570157, Whitestone, NY 11357. Phone: (718)352-1671 Fax: (718)746-2571 • Affiliated with Gamblers Anonymous.

Gamblers Anonymous. P.O. Box 17173, Los Angeles, CA 90017. Phone: (213)386-8789 Fax: (213)386-0030 E-mail: isomain@gamblersanonymous.org • URL: http://www.gamblersanonymous.org.

Hospitality Financial and Technology Professionals. 11709 Boulder Lane, Suite 110, Austin, TX 78726. Phone: 800-646-4387 or (512)249-5333 Fax: (512)249-1533 E-mail: hftp@hftp.org • URL: http://www.hitecshow • Members are accounting and finance officers in the hotel, motel, casino, club, and other areas of the hospitality industry.

National Association of Off-Track Betting. Park Place, Pomona, NY 10970. Phone: (914)362-0400 Fax: (914)632-0419.

National Council on Problem Gambling. 10025 Governor Warfield Parkway, Ste. 311, Columbia, MD 21044. Phone: (410)730-8008 Fax: (410)730-0669 E-mail: ncpg@erols.com • URL: http://www.ncpgambling.org.

GAMES

See: TOY INDUSTRY

GAMES, MANAGEMENT

See: MANAGEMENT GAMES

GARAGES

See: GASOLINE SERVICE STATIONS

GARBAGE DISPOSAL

See: SANITATION INDUSTRY

GARDEN SUPPLY INDUSTRY

See also: LAWN CARE INDUSTRY

DIRECTORIES

Building Supply Home Centers Retail Giants Report. Cahners Business Information. • Annual. $30.00. Lists major retailers of a wide variety of building and home improvement materials, products, fixtures, accessories, equipment, and tools.

Yard and Garden. Cygnus Publishing, Inc., Johnson Hill Press, Inc. • Seven times a year. $48.00. Includes retailers and distributors of lawn and garden power equipment, lawn and plant care products, patio furniture, etc. Arranged by type of product. Includes a *Product* issue.

STATISTICS SOURCES

U. S. Industry and Trade Outlook: The McGraw-Hill Companies and the U.S. Department of Commerce/International Trade Administration. Datapso Research Corp. • Annual. $69.95. Produced by the International Trade Administration, U. S. Department of Commerce, in a "public-private" partnership with DRI/McGraw-Hill and Standard & Poor's. Provides basic data, outlook for the current year, and "Long-Term Prospects" (five-year projections) for a wide variety of products and services. Includes high technology industries. Formerly *U. S. Industrial Outlook.*

OTHER SOURCES

Lawn and Garden Market. Available from MarketResearch.com. • 1999. $2,850.00. Published by Packaged Facts. Provides market data on garden equipment, fertilizers and other substances, and professional lawn care services.

GARMENT INDUSTRY

See: CLOTHING INDUSTRY

GAS AND OIL ENGINES

See: ENGINES

GAS APPLIANCES

DIRECTORIES

Appliance - Appliance Industry Purchasing Directory. Dana Chase Publications, Inc. • Annual. $40.00. Suppliers to manufacturers of consumer, commercial, and business appliances.

Appliance Manufacturer Buyers Guide. Business News Publishing Co. • Annual. $25.00.

Kitchen and Bath Business Buyers' Guide. Miller Freeman, Inc. • Annual. $7.00. Guide to kitchen and bath products, supplies and services. Formerly *Kitchen and Bath Business and Buyers' Guide/ Almanac.*

PERIODICALS AND NEWSLETTERS

Appliance. Dana Chase Publications, Inc. • Monthly. $75.00 per year.

Appliance Manufacturer. Business News Publishing Co. • Monthly. $55.00 per year.

TRADE/PROFESSIONAL ASSOCIATIONS

American Society of Gas Engineers. 6867 Brecksville Rd., Independence, OH 44131. Phone: (714)666-0411 Fax: (714)666-0411 • URL: http://www.asge-national.org.

Gas Appliance Manufacturers Association. 1901 N. Moore St., Suite 1100, Arlington, VA 22209. Phone: (703)525-9565 Fax: (703)525-0718 E-mail: information@gamanet.org • URL: http://www.gamanet.org.

GAS COMPANIES

See: PUBLIC UTILITIES

GAS ENGINES

See: ENGINES

GAS INDUSTRY

See also: NATURAL GAS; PROPANE AND BUTANE GAS INDUSTRY; PUBLIC UTILITIES

ABSTRACTS AND INDEXES

Gas Abstracts. Institute of Gas Technology. • Monthly. $425.00 per year. Abstracts of gas and energy related articles from around the world.

ALMANACS AND YEARBOOKS

Annual Institute on Oil and Gas Law and Taxation. Matthew Bender & Co., Inc. • Annual. Price on application. Answers to current legal and tax problems, including cases and regulations implementing tax reduction and tax form.

DIRECTORIES

American Public Gas Association-Directory. American Public Gas Association. • Annual. $17.00. About 1,000 municipally owned gas systems throughout the United States.

Brown's Directory. Advanstar Communications, Inc. • Annual. $335.00.

Gas Industry Training Directory. American Gas Association. • Annual. Free. Lists over 600 programs available from gas transmission and distributions companies, manufacturers of gas-fired equipment, consultants, etc., and from gas associations.

Gas Utility Industry Worldwide. Midwest Publishing Co. • Annual. $115.00. Approximately 8,000 utility companies, contractors, engineering firms, equipment manufacturers, supply companies, underground natural gas storage facilities and regulatory agencies; international coverage.

Plunkett's Energy Industry Almanac: Complete Profiles on the Energy Industry 500 Companies. Plunkett Research Ltd. • Annual. $149.99. Includes major oil companies, utilities, pipelines, alternative energy companies, etc. Provides information on industry trends.

ENCYCLOPEDIAS AND DICTIONARIES

Manual of Oil and Gas Terms: Annotated. Matthew Bender & Co., Inc. • 1983. 10th edition. Periodic supplementation. Price on application. Defines technical, legal, and tax terms relating to the oil and gas industry.

FINANCIAL RATIOS

Almanac of Business and Industrial Financial Ratios. Leo Troy. Prentice Hall. • Annual. $99.95. Contains financial ratios derived from federal tax returns. Ratios for each of about 200 industries are arranged according to company asset size.

HANDBOOKS AND MANUALS

Ernst and Young's Oil and Gas Federal Income Taxation. John R. Braden and others. CCH, Inc. • Annual. $92.95. Formerly *Miller's Oil and Gas Federal Income Taxation.*

Moody's Public Utility Manual. Financial Information Services. • Annual. $1,595.00. Two volumes. Supplemented twice weekly by *Moody's Public Utility News Reports.* Contains financial and other information concerning publicly-held utility companies (electric, gas, telephone, water).

INTERNET DATABASES

Fedstats. Federal Interagency Council on Statistical Policy. Phone: (202)395-7254 • URL: http://www.fedstats.gov • Web site features an efficient search facility for full-text statistics produced by more than 70 federal agencies, including the Census Bureau, the Bureau of Economic Analysis, and the Bureau of Labor Statistics. Boolean searches can be made within one agency or for all agencies combined. Links are offered to international statistical bureaus, including the UN, IMF, OECD, UNESCO, Eurostat, and 20 individual countries. Fees: Free.

ONLINE DATABASES

DRI U.S. Central Database. Data Products Division. • Provides more than 23,000 business, financial, demographic, economic, foreign trade, and industry-related time series for the U.S. Includes national income, population, retail-wholesale trade, price indexes, labor data, housing, industrial production, banking, interest rates, money supply, etc. Time period is generally 1947 to date (some data back to 1929). Updating varies. Inquire as to online cost and availability.

F & S Index. The Gale Group. • Contains about four million citations to worldwide business, financial, and industrial or consumer product literature appearing from 1972 to date. Weekly updates. Inquire as to online cost and availability.

PERIODICALS AND NEWSLETTERS

American Gas. American Gas Association. • 11 times a year. $59.00 per year. Formerly *AGA Monthly.*

American Public Gas Association Public Gas News. American Public Gas Association. • Biweekly. $45.00 per year. Formerly, *American Public Gas Association Newsletter.*

Gas Utility and Pipeline Industries: The Executive, Administration, Operations Md Engineering Magazine of Gas Energy Supply, Risk Management, Pipeline Transmission, Utility Distribution. Gas Industries Inc. • Monthly. $20.00 per year. Includes semiannual *AGA News.* Formerly *Gas Industires Magazine.*

Oil and Gas Journal. PennWell Corp., Industrial Div. • Weekly. $84.00 per year.

Oil, Gas and Energy Quarterly. Matthew Bender & Shepard. • Quarterly. $165.00 per year. Formerly *Oil and Gas Tax Quarterly.*

PRICE SOURCES

The AGA Rate Service. American Gas Association. • Semiannual. Members, $175.00 per year; non-members, $300.00 per year.

STATISTICS SOURCES

Business Statistics of the United States. Courtenay M. Slater, editor. Bernan Associates. • 1999. $74.00. Fifth edition. Based on *Business Statistics,* formerly issue by the Bureau of Economic Analysis, U. S. Department of Commerce. Provides basic data for a wide variety of U. S. industries, services, and economic indicators. Most statistics are shown annually for 29 years and monthly for the most recent four years.

Energy Balances of OECD Countries. Organization for Economic Cooperation and Development. Available from OECD Publications and Information Center. • Irregular. $110.00. Presents two-year data on the supply and consumption of solid fuels, oil, gas, and electricity, expressed in oil equivalency terms. Historical tables are also provided. Relates to OECD member countries.

Gas Data Book. American Gas Association. • Annual.

Gas Facts: A Statistical Record of the Gas Utility Industry. American Gas Association, Dept. of Statistics. • Annual. Members, $40.00; non-members, $80.00.

Standard & Poor's Industry Surveys. Standard & Poor's. • Semiannual. $1,800.00. Two looseleaf volumes. Includes monthly supplements. Provides detailed, individual surveys of 52 major industry groups. Each survey is revised on a semiannual basis. Also includes "Monthly Investment Review" (industry group investment analysis) and monthly "Trends & Projections" (economic analysis).

Survey of Current Business. Available from U. S. Government Printing Office. • Monthly. $49.00 per year. Issued by Bureau of Economic Analysis, U. S. Department of Commerce. Presents a wide variety of business and economic data.

TRADE/PROFESSIONAL ASSOCIATIONS

American Gas Association. 444 N. Capitol St., N.W., Washington, DC 20001. Phone: (202)824-7000 Fax: (202)824-7115 • URL: http://www.aga.com.

American Public Gas Association. 11094-D Lee Highway, Suite 102, Fairfax, VA 22030. Phone: (703)352-3890 Fax: (703)352-1271 • URL: http://www.apga.org.

Institute of Gas Technology. 1700 S. Mount Prospect Rd., Des Plaines, IL 60018-1804. Phone: (847)768-0500 Fax: (847)768-0516 • URL: http://www.igt.org.

Interstate Natural Gas Association of America. 10 G St., N.E., Suite 700, Washington, DC 20002. Phone: (202)216-5900 Fax: (202)216-0877 • URL: http://www.ingaa.org.

National Propane Gas Association. 1600 Eisenhower Lane, Suite 100, Lisle, IL 60532. Phone: 800-457-4772 or (630)515-0600 Fax: (630)515-8774 E-mail: info@npga.org • URL: http://www.propanegas.com/npga.

OTHER SOURCES

Federal Taxation of Oil and Gas Transactions. Matthew Bender & Co., Inc. • $350.00. Two looseleaf volumes. Periodic supplementation.

Infrastructure Industries USA. The Gale Group. • 2001. $240.00. Replaces *Agriculture, Forestry, Fishing, Mining, and Construction USA* and *Transportation and Public Utilities USA.* Presents statistics and projections relating to economic activity in a wide variety of natural resource and construction industries.

Major Chemical and Petrochemical Companies of the World. Available from The Gale Group. • 2001. $855.00. Third edition. Two volumes. Published by Graham & Whiteside. Contains profiles of more than

7,000 important chemical and petrochemical companies in various countries. Subject areas include general chemicals, specialty chemicals, agricultural chemicals, petrochemicals, industrial gases, and fertilizers.

GAS, LIQUEFIED PETROLEUM

See: PROPANE AND BUTANE GAS INDUSTRY

GAS, NATURAL

See: NATURAL GAS

GAS PIPELINES

See: PIPELINE INDUSTRY

GAS RATES

See: GAS INDUSTRY

GASOHOL

See: FUEL

GASOLINE ENGINES

See: ENGINES

GASOLINE INDUSTRY

See also: GAS INDUSTRY; PETROLEUM INDUSTRY

DIRECTORIES

Financial Times Energy Yearbook: Oil & Gas: 2000. Available from The Gale Group. • Annual. $320.00. Published by Financial Times Energy. Provides production and financial details for more than 800 major oil and gas companies worldwide. Includes coverage of reserves, operations, properties, and growth rates. Formerly *Financial Times Oil & Gas Yearbook.*

Geophysical Directory. Claudia LaCalli, editor. Geophysical Directory, Inc. • Annual. $75.00. Worldwide coverage of about 4,500 companies and personnel using and providing supplies and services in petroleum and mineral exploration.

Worldwide Refining and Gas Processing Directory. PennWell Corp., Petroleum Div. • Annual. $165.00. Lists over 1,000 crude oil refineries, 1,300 gas processing plants and over 600 engineering and construction firms which build and service these plants; worldwide coverage.

INTERNET DATABASES

Fedstats. Federal Interagency Council on Statistical Policy. Phone: (202)395-7254 • URL: http://www.fedstats.gov • Web site features an efficient search facility for full-text statistics produced by more than 70 federal agencies, including the Census Bureau, the Bureau of Economic Analysis, and the Bureau of Labor Statistics. Boolean searches can be made within one agency or for all agencies combined. Links are offered to international statistical bureaus, including the UN, IMF, OECD, UNESCO, Eurostat, and 20 individual countries. Fees: Free.

ONLINE DATABASES

DRI U.S. Central Database. Data Products Division. • Provides more than 23,000 business, financial, demographic, economic, foreign trade, and industry-related time series for the U.S. Includes national income, population, retail-wholesale trade, price indexes, labor data, housing, industrial production, banking, interest rates, money supply, etc. Time period is generally 1947 to date (some data back to 1929). Updating varies. Inquire as to online cost and availability.

Platt's Energy Prices. Data Products Division. • Contains daily high and low prices for crude oil and petroleum products, including gasoline, fuel oil, and liquefied petroleum gas (LPG). Coverage is international from 1983 to present, with daily updates. Inquire as to online cost and availability.

PERIODICALS AND NEWSLETTERS

American Petroleum Institute. Division of Statistics. Weekly Statistical Bulletin. American Petroleum Institute. • Weekly. $115.00 per year. Includes *Monthly Statistical Report.*

Barron's: The Dow Jones Business and Financial Weekly. Dow Jones and Co., Inc. • Weekly. $145.00 per year.

International Oil News. William F. Bland Co. • Weekly. $579.00 per year. Reports news of prime interest to top executives in the international oil industry.

Lundberg Letter. Tele-Drop, Inc. • Semimonthly. $950.00 per year. Petroleum newsletter.

Oil and Gas Journal. PennWell Corp., Industrial Div. • Weekly. $84.00 per year.

Petroleum Newsletter. National Safety Council. • Bimonthly. Members, $15.00 per year; non-members, $19.00 per year.

PRICE SOURCES

CPI Detailed Report: Consumer Price Index. Available from U.S. Government Printing Office. • Monthly. $45.00 per year. Cost of living data.

STATISTICS SOURCES

Annual Energy Outlook [year], with Projections to [year]. Available from U. S. Government Printing Office. • Annual. Issued by the Energy Information Administration, U. S. Department of Energy (http://www.eia.doe.gov). Contains detailed statistics and 20-year projections for electricity, oil, natural gas, coal, and renewable energy. Text provides extensive discussion of energy issues and "Market Trends.".

Business Statistics of the United States. Courtenay M. Slater, editor. Bernan Associates. • 1999. $74.00. Fifth edition. Based on *Business Statistics*, formerly issue by the Bureau of Economic Analysis, U. S. Department of Commerce. Provides basic data for a wide variety of U. S. industries, services, and economic indicators. Most statistics are shown annually for 29 years and monthly for the most recent four years.

International Energy Annual. Available from U. S. Government Printing Office. • Annual. $34.00. Issued by the Energy Information Administration, U. S. Department of Energy. Provides production, consumption, import, and export data for primary energy commodities in more than 200 countries and areas. In addition to petroleum products and alcohol, renewable energy sources are covered (hydroelectric, geothermal, solar, and wind).

Petroleum Supply Annual. Available from U. S. Government Printing Office. • Annual. $78.00. Two volumes. Produced by the Energy Information Administration, U. S. Department of Energy. Contains worldwide data on the petroleum industry and petroleum products.

Petroleum Supply Monthly. Available from U. S. Government Printing Office. • Monthly. $100.00 per year. Produced by the Energy Information Administration, U. S. Department of Energy. Provides worldwide statistics on a wide variety of petroleum products. Covers production, supplies, exports and imports, transportation, refinery operations, and other aspects of the petroleum industry.

Standard & Poor's Industry Surveys. Standard & Poor's. • Semiannual. $1,800.00. Two looseleaf volumes. Includes monthly supplements. Provides detailed, individual surveys of 52 major industry groups. Each survey is revised on a semiannual basis. Also includes "Monthly Investment Review" (industry group investment analysis) and monthly "Trends & Projections" (economic analysis).

Survey of Current Business. Available from U. S. Government Printing Office. • Monthly. $49.00 per year. Issued by Bureau of Economic Analysis, U. S. Department of Commerce. Presents a wide variety of business and economic data.

Weekly Petroleum Status Report. Energy Information Administration. Available from U.S. Government Printing Office. • Weekly. $85.00 per year. Current statistics in the context of both historical information and selected prices and forecasts.

TRADE/PROFESSIONAL ASSOCIATIONS

Federation of Tax Administrators. 444 N. Capitol St., Suite 348, Washington, DC 20001. Phone: (202)624-5890 Fax: (202)624-7888 • URL: http://www.taxadmin.org.

Society of Independent Gasoline Marketers of America. 11911 Freedom Dr., Suite 590, Reston, VA 20190. Phone: (703)709-7000 Fax: (703)709-7007.

GASOLINE SERVICE STATIONS

See also: GASOLINE INDUSTRY

FINANCIAL RATIOS

Almanac of Business and Industrial Financial Ratios. Leo Troy. Prentice Hall. • Annual. $99.95. Contains financial ratios derived from federal tax returns. Ratios for each of about 200 industries are arranged according to company asset size.

Annual Statement Studies. Robert Morris Associates: The Association of Lending and Credit Risk Professiona. • Annual. Free to members; non-members, $140.00. Median and quartile financial ratios are given for over 400 kinds of manufacturing, wholesale, retail, construction, and consumer finance establishments. Data is sorted by both asset size and sales volume. Includes a clearly written "Definition of Ratios" and an alphabetical industry index.

INTERNET DATABASES

Fedstats. Federal Interagency Council on Statistical Policy. Phone: (202)395-7254 • URL: http://www.fedstats.gov • Web site features an efficient search facility for full-text statistics produced by more than 70 federal agencies, including the Census Bureau, the Bureau of Economic Analysis, and the Bureau of Labor Statistics. Boolean searches can be made within one agency or for all agencies combined. Links are offered to international statistical bureaus, including the UN, IMF, OECD, UNESCO, Eurostat, and 20 individual countries. Fees: Free.

ONLINE DATABASES

DRI U.S. Central Database. Data Products Division. • Provides more than 23,000 business, financial, demographic, economic, foreign trade, and industry-related time series for the U.S. Includes national income, population, retail-wholesale trade, price indexes, labor data, housing, industrial production, banking, interest rates, money supply, etc. Time period is generally 1947 to date (some data back to 1929). Updating varies. Inquire as to online cost and availability.

PERIODICALS AND NEWSLETTERS

Motor Age: For the Professional Automotive Import and Domestic Service Industry. Cahners Business Information. • Monthly. $49.00 per year. Published for independent automotive repair shops and gasoline service stations.

Oil Express: Inside Report on Trends in Petroleum Marketing Without the Influ nce of Advertising. Aspen Publishers, Inc. • Weekly. $337.00 per year. Newsletter. Provides news of trends in petroleum marketing and convenience store operations. Includes *U. S. Oil Week's Price Monitor* (petroleum product prices) and *C-Store Digest* (news concerning convenience stores operated by the major oil companies) and *Fuel Oil Update*. Formerly (U.S. Oil Week).

STATISTICS SOURCES

Business Statistics of the United States. Courtenay M. Slater, editor. Bernan Associates. • 1999. $74.00. Fifth edition. Based on *Business Statistics*, formerly issue by the Bureau of Economic Analysis, U. S. Department of Commerce. Provides basic data for a wide variety of U. S. industries, services, and economic indicators. Most statistics are shown annually for 29 years and monthly for the most recent four years.

Survey of Current Business. Available from U. S. Government Printing Office. • Monthly. $49.00 per year. Issued by Bureau of Economic Analysis, U. S. Department of Commerce. Presents a wide variety of business and economic data.

United States Census of Service Industries. U.S. Bureau of the Census. • Quinquennial. Various reports available.

TRADE/PROFESSIONAL ASSOCIATIONS

Automotive Service Association. P.O. Box 929, Bedford, TX 76095-0929. Phone: 800-272-7467 or (817)283-6205 Fax: (817)685-0225 E-mail: asainfo@asashop.org • URL: http://www.asashop.org • Members are body, paint, radiator, transmission, brake, and other shops or garages doing automotive repair work.

Gasoline and Automotive Service Dealers Association. 9520 Seaview Ave., Brooklyn, NY 11236. Phone: (718)241-1111 Fax: (718)763-6589 • Members are owners and operators of automobile service stations and repair shops.

GATT

See: GENERAL AGREEMENT ON TARIFFS AND TRADE (GATT)

GAUGES

See: TOOL INDUSTRY

GEAR INDUSTRY

See also: MACHINERY

ABSTRACTS AND INDEXES

Applied Science and Technology Index. H. W. Wilson Co. • 11 times a year. Quarterly and annual cumulations. Service basis for print edition; CD-ROM edition, $1,495.00 per year. Indexes a wide variety of English language technical, industrial, and engineering periodicals.

Engineering Index Monthly: Abstracting and Indexing Services Covering Sources of the World's Engineering Literature. Engineering Information, Inc. • Monthly. $2,300.00 per year. Provides indexing and abstracting of the world's engineering and technical literature.

F & S Index: United States. The Gale Group. • Monthly. $1,295.00 per year, including quarterly and annual cumulations. Provides annotated citations to marketing, business, financial, and industrial literature. Coverage of U. S. business activity includes trade journals, financial magazines, business newspapers, and special reports. Formerly *Predicasts F & S Index: United States.*

NTIS Alerts: Manufacturing Technology. National Technical Information Service. • Semimonthly. $265.00 per year. Provides descriptions of government-sponsored research reports and software, with ordering information. Covers computer-aided design and manufacturing (CAD/CAM), engineering materials, quality control, machine tools, robots, lasers, productivity, and related subjects. Formerly *Abstract Newsletter*.

CD-ROM DATABASES

COMPENDEX PLUS [CD-ROM]. Engineering Information, Inc. • Quarterly. $3,450.00 per year. Provides CD-ROM indexing and abstracting of the world's engineering and technical information appearing in journals, reports, books, and proceedings, 1985 to date.

F & S Index Plus Text. The Gale Group. • Monthly. $7,575.00 per year. Provides CD-ROM citations to worldwide business, marketing, and industrial material appearing in a large assortment of trade journals, newspapers, and other publications. Time period is four years.

WILSONDISC: Applied Science and Technology Abstracts. H. W. Wilson Co. • Monthly. $1,495.00 per year, including unlimited access to the online version of *Applied Science and Technology Abstracts* through WILSONLINE. Provides CD-ROM indexing and abstracting of 400 prominent scientific, technical, engineering, and industrial periodicals. Indexing coverage is provided from 1983 to date and abstracting from 1993 to date.

ENCYCLOPEDIAS AND DICTIONARIES

Encyclopedic Dictionary of Gears and Gearing. David W. South. McGraw-Hill. • 1992. $54.50.

HANDBOOKS AND MANUALS

Mechanical Engineer's Reference Book. E. H. Smith, editor. Society of Automotive Engineers, Inc. • 1994. $135.00. 12th edition. Covers mechanical engineering principles, computer integrated engineering systems, design standards, materials, power transmission, and many other engineering topics. (Authored Royalty Series).

ONLINE DATABASES

Applied Science and Technology Index Online. H. W. Wilson Co. • Provides online indexing of 400 major scientific, technical, industrial, and engineering periodicals. Time period is 1983 to date. Monthly updates. Inquire as to online cost and availability.

COMPENDEX PLUS. Engineering Information, Inc. • Provides online indexing and abstracting of the world's engineering and technical information appearing in journals, reports, books, and proceedings. Time period is 1970 to date, with weekly updates. Inquire as to online cost and availability.

F & S Index. The Gale Group. • Contains about four million citations to worldwide business, financial, and industrial or consumer product literature appearing from 1972 to date. Weekly updates. Inquire as to online cost and availability.

Trade & Industry Index. The Gale Group. • Provides indexing of business periodicals, January 1981 to date. Daily updates. (Full text articles from some periodicals are available online, 1983 to date, in the companion database, *Trade & Industry ASAP.*) Inquire as to online cost and availability.

PERIODICALS AND NEWSLETTERS

American Gear Manufacturers Association News Digest. American Gear Manufacturers Association. • Bimonthly. $50.00 per year. Newsletter. Covers business and research news relating to the gear industry.

Gear Technology: The Journal of Gear Manufacturing. Randall Publishing, Inc. • Bimonthly. $45.00 per year. Edited for manufacturers, engineers, and designers of gears.

RESEARCH CENTERS AND INSTITUTES

Gear Dynamics and Gear Noise Research Laboratory. Ohio State University, 1009 Robinson Laboratory, 206 W. 18th Ave., Columbus, OH 43210. Phone: (614)292-9044 Fax: (614)292-3163 E-mail: houser.4@osu.edu • URL: http://www.gearlab.eng.ohio-state.edu.

TRADE/PROFESSIONAL ASSOCIATIONS

American Gear Manufacturers Association. 1500 King St., Suite 201, Alexandria, VA 22314-2730. Phone: (703)684-0211 Fax: (703)684-0242 E-mail: webmaster@agma.org • URL: http://www.agma.org • Members are manufacturers of gears and gear-cutting equipment.

GEMS AND GEMSTONES

See also: JEWELRY BUSINESS

GENERAL WORKS

Gem Testing. Basil William Anderson and Alan Jobbins. Butterworth-Heinemann. • 1990. $34.95. Tenth revised edition.

Gemstones of the World. Walter Schumann. Sterling Publishing Co., Inc. • 2000. $24.95. Expanded revised edition.

Precious Stones and Gems. Edwin M. Streeter. Gordon Press Publishers. • 1977. $79.95.

HANDBOOKS AND MANUALS

Gem Identification Made Easy: A Hands-on Guide to More Confident Buying and Selling. Antoinette L. Matlins and Antonio C. Bonanno. Gem Stone Press. • 1997. $34.95. Second revised edition.

Handbook of Gem Identification. Richard T. Liddicoat, Jr. Gemological Institute of America. • 1987. $47.50. 12th edition.

Jewelry and Gems: The Buying Guide-How to Buy Diamonds, Pearls, Precious and Other Popular Gems with Confidence and Knowledge. Antoinette L. Matlins and Antonio C. Bonanno. GemStone Press. • 1998. $24.95. Fourth revised edition.

ONLINE DATABASES

GEOREF. American Geological Institute. • Bibliography and index of geology and geosciences literature, 1785 to present. Inquire as to online cost and availability.

PERIODICALS AND NEWSLETTERS

Gems and Gemology. Gemological Institute of America. • Quarterly. $69.95 per year.

Lapidary Journal. PRIMEDIA Special Interest Publications. • Monthly. $30.00.

Modern Jeweler. Cygnus Business Media. • Monthly. $60.00 per year. Edited for retail jewelers. Covers the merchandising of jewelry, gems, and watches. Supersedes in part *Modern Jeweler.*

Spectra. American Gem Society. • Monthly. Membership. Newsletter.

STATISTICS SOURCES

Mineral Commodity Summaries. Available from U. S. Government Printing Office. • Annual. Published by the U. S. Geological Survey, Department of the Interior (http://www.usgs.gov). Contains detailed, five-year data for about 90 nonfuel minerals. Covers a wide range of statistics, including production, imports, exports, consumption, reserves, prices, tariff information, and industry employment. (Two pages are devoted to each mineral.).

TRADE/PROFESSIONAL ASSOCIATIONS

American Gem and Mineral Suppliers Association. P.O. Box 4065, Santa Monica, CA 90411-4065. Phone: (909)794-1343 Fax: (909)794-1343.

American Gem Society. 8881 W. Sahara Ave., Las Vegas, NV 89117-5865. Phone: (702)255-6500 Fax: (702)255-7420 • URL: http://www.ags.org.

American Gem Trade Association. P.O. Box 420643, Dallas, TX 75342-0643. Phone: 800-972-1162 or (214)742-4367 Fax: (214)742-7334.

Gemological Institute of America. 5345 Armada Dr., Carlsbad, CA 92008. Phone: 800-421-7250 or (760)603-4000 Fax: (760)603-4080 • URL: http://www.gia.edu.

GENERAL AGREEMENT ON TARIFFS AND TRADE (GATT)

GENERAL WORKS

Reciprocity, U. S. Trade Policy, and the GATT Regime. Carolyn Rhodes. Cornell University Press. • 1993. $37.50.

ALMANACS AND YEARBOOKS

WTO Annual Report World Trade Organization. Available from Bernan Associates. • Annual. Review of activities. Published in Switzerland by GATT. Editions in English, French and Spanish. Formerly *GATT Activities.*

PERIODICALS AND NEWSLETTERS

Economic Justice Report: Global Issues of Economic Justice. Ecumenical Coalition for Economic Justice. • Quarterly. Individuals, $30.00 per year; institutions, $40.00 per year. Reports on economic fairness in foreign trade. Formerly *Gatt-Fly Report.*

RESEARCH CENTERS AND INSTITUTES

Institute for International Economics. 11 Dupont Circle, N. W., Suite 620, Washington, DC 20036. Phone: (202)328-9000 Fax: (202)328-5432 • URL: http://www.iie.com • Research fields include a wide range of international economic issues, including foreign exchange rates.

TRADE/PROFESSIONAL ASSOCIATIONS

World Trade Organization. Centre William Rappard. 154 rue de Lausanne, CH-1211 Geneva 21, Switzerland. Phone: 41 22 739511 Fax: 41 22 7395007 E-mail: enquires@wto.org • URL: http://www.wto.org.

OTHER SOURCES

Copyright Law in Business and Practice. John W. Hazard. West Group. • 1998. $160.00.

From GATT to the WTO: The Multilateral Trading System in the New Millennium. WTO Secretariat, editor. Available from Kluwer Academic Publishers. • 2000. $79.50. Published by the World Trade Organization (http://www.wto.org). A collection of essays on the future of world trade, written on the occasion of the 50th anniversary of the multilateral trading system (GATT/WTO). The authors are described as "important academics in international trade.".

World Trade Organization Annual Report. Available from Bernan Associates. • Annual. $80.00. Two volumes ($40.00 per volume). Published by the World Trade Organization. Volume one: *Annual Report.* Volume two: *International Trade Statistics.*

WTO Focus. World Trade Organization, Publications Service. • Newsletter. Free. 10 times a year. Text in English. Provides current news about activities relating to the World Trade Organization (WTO) and the General Agreement on Tariffs and Trade (GATT). Formerly *GATT Focus.*

GENERAL AVIATION

See: BUSINESS AVIATION

GENERATORS, ELECTRIC

See: ELECTRICAL EQUIPMENT INDUSTRY

GENERIC DRUG INDUSTRY

See also: PHARMACEUTICAL INDUSTRY

ABSTRACTS AND INDEXES

Business Periodicals Index. H. W. Wilson Co. • Monthly, except August, with quarterly and annual cumulations. Service basis for print edition; CD-ROM edition, $1,495.00 per year.

International Pharmaceutical Abstracts: Key to the World's Literature of Pharmacy. American Society of Health-System Pharmacists. • Semimonthly. Members, $142.95 per year; non-members, $552.50 per year.

CD-ROM DATABASES

ABI/INFORM Global. Bell & Howell Information and Learning. • Monthly. $6,500.00 per year. Provides CD-ROM indexing and abstracting of worldwide business literature appearing in over 1,200 periodicals for the most recent five years. Archival discs are available from 1971. Formerly *ABI/INFORM OnDisc.*

F & S Index Plus Text. The Gale Group. • Monthly. $7,575.00 per year. Provides CD-ROM citations to worldwide business, marketing, and industrial material appearing in a large assortment of trade journals, newspapers, and other publications. Time period is four years.

International Pharmaceutical Abstracts [CD-ROM]. American Society of Health-System Pharmacists. • Quarterly. $1,795.00 per year. Contains CD-ROM indexing and abstracting of international pharmaceutical literature from 1970 to date.

Physicians' Desk Reference Library on CD-ROM. Medical Economics. • Three times a year. $595.00 per year. Contains the CD-ROM equivalent of *Physicians' Desk Reference (PDR), Physicians' Desk Reference for Nonprescription Drugs, Physicians' Desk Reference for Opthalmology,* and other PDR publications.

WILSONDISC: Wilson Business Abstracts. H. W. Wilson Co. • Monthly. $2,495.00 per year, including unlimited online access to *Wilson Business Abstracts* through WILSONLINE. Provides CD-ROM "cover-to-cover" abstracting and indexing of over 600 prominent business periodicals. Indexing is from 1982, abstracting from 1990. (*Business Periodicals Index* without abstracts is available on CD-ROM at $1,495 per year.).

DIRECTORIES

Mosby's GenRx: The Complete Reference for Generic and Brand Drugs. Harcourt Health Sciences. • 1998. $72.95. Provides detailed information on a wide variety of generic and brand name prescription drugs. Includes color identification pictures, prescribing data, and price comparisons. Formerly *Physicians GenRx.*

The Red Book. Medical Economics Co., Inc. • Annual. $57.95 for basic volume or $99.00 per year with monthly updates. Provides product information and prices for more than 100,000 prescription and nonprescription drugs and other items sold by pharmacies. Also known as *Drug Topics Red Book.*

HANDBOOKS AND MANUALS

Approved Drug Products, with Therapeutic Equivalence Evaluations. Available from U. S. Government Printing Office. • $101.00 for basic manual and supplemental material for an indeterminate period. Issued by the Food and Drug Administration, U. S. Department of Health and Human Services. Lists prescription drugs that have been approved by the FDA. Includes therapeutic equivalents to aid in containment of health costs and to serve State drug selection laws.

Physicians' Desk Reference. Medical Economics Co., Inc. • Annual. $82.95. Generally known as "PDR". Provides detailed descriptions, effects, and adverse reactions for about 4,000 prescription drugs. Includes data on more than 250 drug manufacturers, with brand name and generic name indexes and drug identification photographs. Discontinued drugs are also listed.

INTERNET DATABASES

National Library of Medicine (NLM). National Institutes of Health (NIH). Phone: 888-346-3656 or (301)496-1131 Fax: (301)480-3537 E-mail: access@nlm.nih.gov • URL: http://www.nlm.nih.gov • NLM Web site offers free access through MEDLINE ("PubMed") to about nine million references to articles appearing in some 3,800 biomedical journals, with abstracts. Search interfaces range from "simple keywords to advanced Boolean expressions." The NLM site offers many links to other sources of biomedical and technical information (the National Center for Biotechnology Information, for example). Fees: Free.

RxList: The Internet Drug Index. Neil Sandow. Phone: (707)746-8754 E-mail: info@rxlist.com • URL: http://www.rxlist.com • Web site features detailed information (cost, usage, dosage, side effects, etc.) from Mosby, Inc. for about 300 major pharmaceutical products, representing two thirds of prescriptions filled in the U. S. (3,700 other products are listed). The "Top 200" drugs are ranked by number of prescriptions filled. Keyword searching is provided. Fees: Free.

ONLINE DATABASES

ABI/INFORM. Bell & Howell Information and Learning. • Provides online indexing to business-related material occurring in over 1,000 periodicals from 1971 to the present. Inquire as to online cost and availability.

Derwent Drug File. Derwent, Inc. • Provides indexing and abstracting of the world's pharmaceutical journal literature since 1964, with weekly updates. Formerly *RINGDOC.* Inquire as to online cost and availability.

F & S Index. The Gale Group. • Contains about four million citations to worldwide business, financial, and industrial or consumer product literature appearing from 1972 to date. Weekly updates. Inquire as to online cost and availability.

F-D-C Reports. FDC Reports, Inc. • An online version of "The Gray Sheet" (medical devices), "The Pink Sheet" (pharmaceuticals), "The Rose Sheet" (cosmetics), "The Blue Sheet" (biomedical), and "The Tan Sheet" (nonprescription). Contains full-text information on legal, technical, corporate, financial, and marketing developments from 1987 to date, with weekly updates. Inquire as to online cost and availability.

International Pharmaceutical Abstracts [online]. American Society of Health-System Pharmacists. •

Provides online indexing and abstracting of the world's pharmaceutical literature from 1970 to date. Monthly updates. Inquire as to online cost and availability.

Pharmaceutical News Index. Bell & Howell Information and Learning. • Indexes major pharmaceutical industry newsletters, 1974 to present. Weekly updates. Inquire as to online cost and availability.

PROMT: Predicasts Overview of Markets and Technology. The Gale Group. • Companies, products, applied technologies and markets. U.S. and international literature coverage, 1972 to date. Inquire as to online cost and availability. Provides abstracts from more than 1,600 publications. Weekly updates.

Trade & Industry Index. The Gale Group. • Provides indexing of business periodicals, January 1981 to date. Daily updates. (Full text articles from some periodicals are available online, 1983 to date, in the companion database, *Trade & Industry ASAP.*) Inquire as to online cost and availability.

Wilson Business Abstracts Online. H. W. Wilson Co. • Indexes and abstracts 600 major business periodicals, plus the *Wall Street Journal* and the business section of the *New York Times.* Indexing is from 1982, abstracting from 1990, with the two newspapers included from 1993. Updated weekly. Inquire as to online cost and availability. (*Business Periodicals Index* without abstracts is also available online.).

PERIODICALS AND NEWSLETTERS

American Druggist. Press Corps, Inc. • Monthly. $44.00 per year. Provides news and analysis of major trends affecting pharmacists. Includes an annual "Generic Survey" (September).

Drug Store News. Chain Pharmacy. Lebhar-Friedman, Inc. • Monthly. $36.00 per year. Formerly *Drug Store News for the Pharmacists.*

Generic Line. Washington Business Information, Inc. • Biweekly. $435.00 per year. Newsletter. Covers regulation, legislation, technology, marketing, and other issues affecting companies providing generic pharmaceuticals.

Prescription Pharmaceuticals and Biotechnology: The Pink Sheet. F-D-C Reports, Inc. • Weekly. $1,170 per year. Newsletter covering business and regulatory developments affecting the pharmaceutical and biotechnology industries. Provides information on generic drug approvals and includes a drug sector stock index.

Worst Pills Best Pills News. Public Citizen. • Monthly. $16.00 per year. Newsletter. Provides pharmaceutical news and information for consumers, with an emphasis on harmful drug interactions.

PRICE SOURCES

First DataBank Blue Book. Hearst Corp. • Annual. $65.00. List of manufacturers of prescription and over-the-counter drugs, sold in retail drug stores. Formerly *American Druggist Blue Book.*

RESEARCH CENTERS AND INSTITUTES

Pharmaceutical Marketing and Management Research Program. University of Mississippi, Waller Lab Complex, Room 101, University, MS 38677. Phone: (662)915-5948 Fax: (662)915-5262 E-mail: dgarner@olemiss.edu • URL: http://www.olemiss.edu/depts/rips/pmmrp/.

TRADE/PROFESSIONAL ASSOCIATIONS

Generic Pharmaceutical Industry Association. 1620 Eye St., N.W., Suite 800, Washington, DC 20006-4005. Phone: (202)833-9070 Fax: (202)833-9612 E-mail: info@gpia.org • URL: http://www.gpia.org • Members are manufacturers, wholesalers, and retailers of generic prescription drugs.

OTHER SOURCES

Business & Company Resource Center. The Gale Group. • Fee-based Web site provides a wide range of business, industry, and specific company information. Access is offered to trade journal articles, market research data, insider trading activity, major shareholder data, corporate histories, emerging technology reports, corporate earnings estimates, press releases, and other sources. Provides detailed company profiles, industry overviews, and rankings. Offers integration of Predicasts PROMT, Newsletters ASAP, Investext Plus, Business Index ASAP, Brands and Their Companies, and other databases (many have full text).

Major Pharmaceutical Companies of the World. Available from The Gale Group. • 2001. $885.00. Third edition. Published by Graham & Whiteside. Contains detailed information and trade names for more than 2,500 important pharmaceutical companies in various countries.

The Market for Generic Drugs. MarketResearch.com. • 2000. $3,000.00. Market research data. Includes a discussion of current trends in the use of generic prescription drugs to reduce healthcare costs, with forcasts to 2004.

Mosby's GenRx [year]. CME, Inc. • Annual. $99.00. CD-ROM contains detailed monographs for more than 2,200 generic and brand name prescription drugs. Includes color pill images and customizable patient education handouts.

GENERIC PRODUCTS

See: PRIVATE LABEL PRODUCTS

GENETIC ENGINEERING

See also: BIOTECHNOLOGY

GENERAL WORKS

Altered Fates: The Genetic Re-Engineering of Human Life. Jeff Lyon and Peter Gorner. W. W. Norton & Co., Inc. • 1995. $27.50. A discussion of recent progress in genetic engineering.

ABSTRACTS AND INDEXES

Applied Science and Technology Index. H. W. Wilson Co. • 11 times a year. Quarterly and annual cumulations. Service basis for print edition; CD-ROM edition, $1,495.00 per year. Indexes a wide variety of English language technical, industrial, and engineering periodicals.

Excerpta Medica: Human Genetics. Elsevier Science. • Semimonthly. $3,196.00 per year. Section 22 of *Excerpta Medica.*

Genetics Abstracts. Cambridge Information Group. • Monthly. $1,035.00 per year.

NTIS Alerts: Biomedical Technology & Human Factors Engineering. National Technical Information Service. • Semimonthly. $210.00 per year. Provides descriptions of government-sponsored research reports and software, with ordering information. Covers biotechnology, ergonomics, bionics, artificial intelligence, prosthetics, and related subjects. Formerly *Abstract Newsletter.*

ALMANACS AND YEARBOOKS

Plunkett's Biotech and Genetics Industry Almanac. Plunkett Research, Ltd. • Annual. $199.99. Provides detailed profiles of 400 leading biotech corporations. Includes information on current trends and research in the field of biotechnology/genetics.

BIBLIOGRAPHIES

Information Sources in the Life Sciences. H. V. Wyatt, editor. Bowker-Saur. • 1997. $95.00. Fourth edition. Includes an evaluation of biotechnology information sources. (Guides to Information Sources Series).

CD-ROM DATABASES

Biotechnology Abstracts on CD-ROM. Derwent, Inc. • Quarterly. Price on application. Provides CD-ROM indexing and abstracting of the world's biotechnology journal literature since 1982, including genetic engineering topics.

CSA Life Sciences Collection [CD-ROM]. Cambridge Scientific Abstracts. • Quarterly. Includes CD-ROM versions of *Biotechnology Research Abstracts, Entomology Abstracts, Genetics Abstracts,* and about 20 other abstract collections.

DIRECTORIES

BioScan: The Worldwide Biotech Industry Reporting Service. American Health Consultants, Inc. • Bimonthly. $1,395.00 per year. Looseleaf. Provides detailed information on over 900 U. S. and foreign companies broadly classified as biotechnological. In addition to medical technology and advanced pharmaceutical firms, includes firms doing research in food processing, waste management, agriculture, and veterinary science.

Corptech Directory of Technology Companies. Corporate Technology Information Services, Inc. c/o Eileen Kennedy. • Annual. $795.00. Four volumes. Profiles of more than 45,000 manufacturers and developers of high technology products. Includes private companies, publicly-held corporations, and subsidiaries. Formerly *Corporate Technology Directory.*

Genetic Engineering and Biotechnology Firms Worldwide Directory. Mega-Type Publishing. • Annual. $299.00. About 6,000 firms, including major firms with biotechnology divisions as well as small independent firms.

ENCYCLOPEDIAS AND DICTIONARIES

Encyclopedia of Emerging Industries. The Gale Group. • 2000. $295.00. Fourth edition. Provides detailed information on 90 "newly flourishing" industries. Includes historical background, organizational structure, significant individuals, current conditions, major companies, work force, technology trends, research developments, and other industry facts.

ONLINE DATABASES

Applied Science and Technology Index Online. H. W. Wilson Co. • Provides online indexing of 400 major scientific, technical, industrial, and engineering periodicals. Time period is 1983 to date. Monthly updates. Inquire as to online cost and availability.

CSA Life Sciences Collection. Cambridge Scientific Abstracts. • Includes online versions of *Biotechnology Research Abstracts, Entomology Abstracts, Genetics Abstracts,* and about 20 other abstract collections. Time period is 1978 to date, with monthly updates. Inquire as to online cost and availability.

Derwent Biotechnology Abstracts. Derwent, Inc. • Provides indexing and abstracting of the world's biotechnology journal literature since 1982, including genetic engineering topics. Monthly updates. Inquire as to online cost and availability.

PROMT: Predicasts Overview of Markets and Technology. The Gale Group. • Companies, products, applied technologies and markets. U.S. and international literature coverage, 1972 to date. Inquire as to online cost and availability. Provides abstracts from more than 1,600 publications. Weekly updates.

PERIODICALS AND NEWSLETTERS

Applied Genetics News. Business Communications Co., Inc. • Monthly. $415.00 per year. Newsletter on research developments.

BioWorld Today: The Daily Biotechnology Newspaper. American Health Consultants, Inc., BioWorld Publishing Group. • Daily. $1,897.00 per year. Covers news of the biotechnology and genetic engineering industries, with emphasis on finance, investments, and marketing.

BioWorld Week: The Weekly Biotechnology Report. American Health Consultants, Inc., BioWorld Publishing Group. • Weekly. $747.00 per year. Provides a weekly summary of business and financial news relating to the biotechnology and genetic engineering industries.

Genetic Engineering News: The Information Source of the Biotechnology Industry. Mary Ann Liebert, Inc. • Biweekly. Institutions, $397.00 per year. Newsletter. Business and financial coverage.

Genetic Technology News. Technical Insights. • 51 times a year. $885.00 per year. Reports on genetic engineering and its uses in the chemical, pharmaceutical, food processing and energy industries as well as in agriculture, animal breeding and medicine. Includes three supplements: *Patent Update*, *Strategic Partners Reports*, and *Market Forecasts*.

Health Policy and Biomedical Research: The Blue Sheet. F-D-C Reports, Inc. • 51 Times a year. $619.00 per year. Newsletter. Emphasis is on news of medical research agencies and institutions, especially the National Institutes of Health (NIH).

Washington Drug Letter. Washington Business Information, Inc. • Daily. $867.00 per year. Newsletter on legislative and regulatory concerns.

RESEARCH CENTERS AND INSTITUTES

Carnegie Mellon Research Institute. Carnegie Mellon University, 700 Technology Dr., Pittsburgh, PA 15219. Phone: (412)268-3190 Fax: (412)268-3101 E-mail: twillke@emu.edu • Multidisciplinary research activities include expert systems applications, minicomputer and microcomputer systems design, genetic engineering, and transportation systems analysis.

Department of Molecular and Human Genetics. Baylor College of Medicine, One Baylor Plaza, Room 904E, Houston, TX 77030. Phone: (713)798-6522 Fax: (713)798-6521 E-mail: abeaudet@bcm.tmc.edu • URL: http://www.ginger.bcm.tmc.edu:8088/.

Environmental Biotechnology Institute. University of Idaho, Food Research Center 103, Moscow, ID 83844-1052. Phone: (208)885-6580 Fax: (208)885-5741 E-mail: crawford@uidaho.edu • URL: http://www.image.fs.uidaho.edu/biotech/.

TRADE/PROFESSIONAL ASSOCIATIONS

American Genetic Association. P.O. Box 257, Buckeystown, MD 21717-0257. Phone: (301)695-9292 Fax: (301)695-9292 • Members are scientists engaged in genetics research.

Council for Responsible Genetics. Five Upland Rd., Suite 3, Cambridge, MA 02140. Phone: (617)868-0870 Fax: (617)491-5344 E-mail: crg@gene-watch.org • URL: http://www.gene-watch.org • Concerned with the social implications of genetic engineering.

Genetics Society of America. 9650 Rockville Pike, Bethesda, MD 20814-3998. Phone: (301)571-1825 Fax: (301)530-7079 E-mail: estraass@genetics.faseb.org • URL: http://www.faseb.org/genetics/ • Members are individuals and organizations with an interest in genetics.

OTHER SOURCES

New and Breaking Technologies in the Pharmaceutical and Medical Device Industries. Theta Reports/PJB Medical Publications, Inc. • 1999. $1,695.00. Contains market research predictions of medical technology trends over the next 5 to 10 years (2004-2009), including developments in biotechnology, genetic engineering, medical device technology, therapeutic vaccines, non-invasive diagnostics, and minimally-invasive surgery. (Theta Report No. 931.).

GEOTHERMAL ENERGY

GENERAL WORKS

Renewable Energy: Power for a Sustainable Future. Godfrey Boyle, editor. Available from Taylor & Francis. • 1996. $39.95. Published by Open University Press. Contains ten chapters, each on a particular renewable energy source, including solar, biomass, hydropower, wind, and geothermal.

ABSTRACTS AND INDEXES

Applied Science and Technology Index. H. W. Wilson Co. • 11 times a year. Quarterly and annual cumulations. Service basis for print edition; CD-ROM edition, $1,495.00 per year. Indexes a wide variety of English language technical, industrial, and engineering periodicals.

Engineering Index Monthly: Abstracting and Indexing Services Covering Sources of the World's Engineering Literature. Engineering Information, Inc. • Monthly. $2,300.00 per year. Provides indexing and abstracting of the world's engineering and technical literature.

Environment Abstracts. Congressional Information Service. • Monthly. Price varies. Provides multidisciplinary coverage of the world's environmental literature. Incorporates *Acid Rain Abstracts*.

Environment Abstracts Annual: A Guide to the Key Environmental Literature of the Year. Congressional Information Service. • Annual. $495.00. A yearly cumulation of *Environment Abstracts*.

NTIS Alerts: Energy. National Technical Information Service. • Semimonthly. $245.00 per year. Provides descriptions of government-sponsored research reports and software, with ordering information. Covers electric power, batteries, fuels, geothermal energy, heating/cooling systems, nuclear technology, solar energy, energy policy, and related subjects. Formerly *Abstract Newsletter*.

ALMANACS AND YEARBOOKS

Earth Almanac: An Annual Geophysical Review of the State of the Planet. Natalie Goldstein. Oryx Press. • Annual. $65.00. Provides background information, statistics, and a summary of major events relating to the atmosphere, oceans, land, and fresh water.

CD-ROM DATABASES

COMPENDEX PLUS [CD-ROM]. Engineering Information, Inc. • Quarterly. $3,450.00 per year. Provides CD-ROM indexing and abstracting of the world's engineering and technical information appearing in journals, reports, books, and proceedings, 1985 to date.

Environment Abstracts on CD-ROM. Congressional Information Service, Inc. • Quarterly. $1,295.00 per year. Contains the following CD-ROM databases: *Environment Abstracts, Energy Abstracts*, and *Acid Rain Abstracts*. Length of coverage varies.

WILSONDISC: Applied Science and Technology Abstracts. H. W. Wilson Co. • Monthly. $1,495.00 per year, including unlimited access to the online version of *Applied Science and Technology Abstracts* through WILSONLINE. Provides CD-ROM indexing and abstracting of 400 prominent scientific, technical, engineering, and industrial periodicals. Indexing coverage is provided from 1983 to date and abstracting from 1993 to date.

DIRECTORIES

The International Competitive Power Industry Directory. PennWell Corp. • Annual. $75.00. Lists suppliers of services, products, and equipment for the hydro, geothermal, solar, and wind power industries.

ENCYCLOPEDIAS AND DICTIONARIES

Macmillan Encyclopedia of Energy. Available from The Gale Group. • 2001. $350.00. Three volumes. Published by Macmillan Reference USA. Covers the business, technology, and history of a wide variety of energy sources.

Wiley Encyclopedia of Energy and the Environment. Frederick John Francis. John Wiley and Sons, Inc. • 1999. $1,500.00. Four volumes. Second edition. Covers a wide variety of energy and environmental topics, including legal and policy issues.

ONLINE DATABASES

Applied Science and Technology Index Online. H. W. Wilson Co. • Provides online indexing of 400 major scientific, technical, industrial, and engineering periodicals. Time period is 1983 to date. Monthly updates. Inquire as to online cost and availability.

COMPENDEX PLUS. Engineering Information, Inc. • Provides online indexing and abstracting of the world's engineering and technical information appearing in journals, reports, books, and proceedings. Time period is 1970 to date, with weekly updates. Inquire as to online cost and availability.

Current Contents Connect. Institute for Scientific Information. • Provides online abstracts of articles listed in the tables of contents of about 7,500 journals. Coverage is very broad, including science, social science, life science, technology, engineering, industry, agriculture, the environment, economics, and arts and humanities. Time period is two years, with weekly updates. Inquire as to online cost and availability.

Enviroline. Congressional Information Service, Inc. • Provides online indexing and abstracting of worldwide environmental and natural resource literature from 1975 to date. Updated monthly. Inquire as to online cost and availability.

PROMT: Predicasts Overview of Markets and Technology. The Gale Group. • Companies, products, applied technologies and markets. U.S. and international literature coverage, 1972 to date. Inquire as to online cost and availability. Provides abstracts from more than 1,600 publications. Weekly updates.

PERIODICALS AND NEWSLETTERS

Energy Conversion and Management. Elsevier Science. • 18 times a year. $2,835.00 per year. Presents a scholarly approach to alternative or renewable energy sources. Text in English, French and German.

Geothermics: International Journal of Geothermal Research and Its Applications. Elsevier Science. • Bimonthly. $921.00 per year. Covers theory, exploration, development, and utilization of geothermal energy. Text and summaries in English and French.

Independent Energy: The Power Industry's Business Magazine. PennWell Corp., Industrial Div. • 10 times a year. $127.00 per year. Covers non-utility electric power plants (cogeneration) and other alternative sources of electric energy.

Renewable Energy News Digest. Sun Words. • Monthly. $60.00 per year. Newsletter. Covers geothermal, solar, wind, cogenerated, and other energy sources.

RESEARCH CENTERS AND INSTITUTES

Geothermal Laboratory. Southern Methodist University, 217 Heroy Bldg., 3225 Daniels Ave., Dallas, TX 75206-0395. Phone: (214)768-2749 Fax: (214)768-2701 E-mail: blackwel@passion.isem.smu.edu • URL: http://www.smu.edu/~geothermal.

Hawaii Natural Energy Institute. University of Hawaii at Manoa, 2540 Dole St., Holmes Hall 246, Honolulu, HI 96822. Phone: (808)956-8890 Fax: (808)956-2336 E-mail: hnei@hawaii.edu • URL: http://www.soest.hawaii.edu • Research areas include geothermal, wind, solar, hydroelectric, and other energy sources.

STATISTICS SOURCES

Annual Energy Outlook [year], with Projections to [year]. Available from U. S. Government Printing Office. • Annual. Issued by the Energy Information Administration, U. S. Department of Energy (http://www.eia.doe.gov). Contains detailed statistics and 20-year projections for electricity, oil, natural gas, coal, and renewable energy. Text provides extensive discussion of energy issues and "Market Trends.".

International Energy Annual. Available from U. S. Government Printing Office. • Annual. $34.00. Issued by the Energy Information Administration, U. S. Department of Energy. Provides production, consumption, import, and export data for primary energy commodities in more than 200 countries and areas. In addition to petroleum products and alcohol, renewable energy sources are covered (hydroelectric, geothermal, solar, and wind).

TRADE/PROFESSIONAL ASSOCIATIONS

Geothermal Resources Council. P.O. Box 1350, Davis, CA 95617-1350. Phone: (916)758-2360 Fax: (916)758-2839 E-mail: carth307@concentric.net • URL: http://www.geothermal.org • Encourages research, development, and exploration for worldwide geothermal energy. Includes eight International Groups.

OTHER SOURCES

Business & Company Resource Center. The Gale Group. • Fee-based Web site provides a wide range of business, industry, and specific company information. Access is offered to trade journal articles, market research data, insider trading activity, major shareholder data, corporate histories, emerging technology reports, corporate earnings estimates, press releases, and other sources. Provides detailed company profiles, industry overviews, and rankings. Offers integration of Predicasts PROMT, Newsletters ASAP, Investext Plus, Business Index ASAP, Brands and Their Companies, and other databases (many have full text).

Major Energy Companies of the World. Available from The Gale Group. • 2001. $855.00. Fourth edition. Published by Graham & Whiteside. Contains detailed information on more than 3,300 important energy companies in various countries. Industries include electricity generation, coal, natural gas, nuclear energy, petroleum, fuel distribution, and equipment for energy production.

GIFT BUSINESS

DIRECTORIES

Directory of Discount and General Merchandise Stores. Chain Store Guide. • Annual. $300.00. Includes retailers and wholesalers of housewares, giftwares, novelties, toys, hobby materials, crafts, and stationery. Formerly *Directory of Discount Stores Catalog Showrooms.*

Gift and Decorative Accessory Buyers Directory. Geyer-McAllister Publications, Inc. • Annual. Included in subscription to *Gifts and Decorative Accessories.* Manufacturers, importers, jobbers, and manufacturers' representatives of gifts, china and glass, lamps and home accessories, stationery, greeting cards, and related products.

Nationwide Directory of Gift, Housewares and Home Textiles Buyers. Salesman's Guide. • Annual. $195.00.

FINANCIAL RATIOS

Annual Statement Studies. Robert Morris Associates: The Association of Lending and Credit Risk Professiona. • Annual. Free to members; non-members, $140.00. Median and quartile financial ratios are given for over 400 kinds of manufacturing, wholesale, retail, construction, and consumer finance establishments. Data is sorted by both asset size and sales volume. Includes a clearly written "Definition of Ratios" and an alphabetical industry index.

HANDBOOKS AND MANUALS

Gift/Specialty Store. Entrepreneur Media, Inc. • Looseleaf. $59.50. A practical guide to starting a gift shop. Covers profit potential, start-up costs, market size evaluation, owner's time required, site selection, lease negotiation, pricing, accounting, advertising, promotion, etc. (Start-Up Business Guide No. E1218.).

PERIODICALS AND NEWSLETTERS

Fancy Food. Talcott Communications Corp. • Monthly. $34.00 per year. Emphasizes new specialty food products and the business management aspects of the specialty food and confection industries. Includes special issues on wine, cheese, candy, "upscale" cookware, and gifts.

Gifts and Decorative Accessories: The International Business Magazine of Gifts, Tabletop, Gourmet, Home Accessories, Greeting Card and Social Stationery. Cahners Business Newspapers. • Monthly. $49.95 per year.

Gifts and Tablewares. Southam Magazine Group. • Seven times a year. $45.95 per year. Includes annual *Trade Directory.*

Giftware News: The International Magazine for Gifts, China and Glass, Stationery and Home Accessories. Talcott Communications Corp. • Monthly. $36.00 per year. Includes annual *Directory.*

Gourmet News: The Business Newspaper for the Gourmet Industry. United Publications, Inc. • Monthly. $55.00 per year. Provides news of the gourmet food industry, including specialty food stores, upscale cookware shops, and gift shops.

TRADE/PROFESSIONAL ASSOCIATIONS

Gift Association of America. P.O. Box 26696, Collegevile, PA 19426-0696. Phone: (610)831-1841.

Souvenir and Novelty Trade Association. 7000 Terminal Square, Suite 210, Upper Darby, PA 19082. Phone: (610)734-2420 Fax: (610)734-2423 E-mail: souvnormag.@aol.com.

OTHER SOURCES

Gifts and Decorative Accessories Market. Available from MarketResearch.com. • 1998. $1,795.00. Published by Unity Marketing. Market research report covering growth trends and projections.

GIFT TAX

GENERAL WORKS

How to Make Tax-Saving Gifts. William S. Moore. American Institute for Economic Research. • 1999. $3.00. Provides practical advice on the tax consequences of gifts, including gifts for college tuition expenses, gifts of real estate, charitable gifts, and the use of life insurance trusts. (Economic Education Bulletin.).

HANDBOOKS AND MANUALS

Corporate, Partnership, Estate, and Gift Taxation 1997. James W. Pratt and William Kulsrud, editors. McGraw-Hill Higher Education. • 1996. $71.25. 10th edition.

Federal Estate and Gift Taxation. Richard B. Stevens and Guy B. Maxfield. Warren, Gorham and Lamont/RIA Group. • $390.00. Looseleaf service. Semiannual supplementation. Clarification and guidance on estate tax laws.

Federal Estate and Gift Taxes: Code and Regulations, Including Related Income Tax Provisions. CCH, Inc. • Annual. $44.95. Provides full text of estate, gift, and generation-skipping tax provisions of the Internal Revenue Code.

Federal Tax Course: General Edition. CCH, Inc. • Annual. $123.00. Provides basic reference and training for various forms of federal taxation: individual, business, corporate, partnership, estate, gift, etc. Includes *Federal Taxation Study Manual.*

Internal Revenue Code: Income, Estate, Gift, Employment, and Excise Taxes. CCH, Inc. • Annual. $69.00. Two volumes. Provides full text of the Internal Revenue Code (5,000 pages), including procedural and administrative provisions.

Tax Examples. John C. Wisdom. West Group. • 1993. $125.00. Presents yearly examples, with forms, of a wide variety of tax problems and issues. Subjects include taxable income, deductions, alternative minimum tax, dependents, gift taxes, partnerships, and other problem areas. Includesaccounting method considerations. (Tax Series).

U. S. Master Estate and Gift Tax Guide. CCH, Inc. • Annual. $49.00. Covers federal estate and gift taxes, including generation-skipping transfer tax plans. Includes tax tables and sample filled-in tax return forms.

INTERNET DATABASES

The Digital Daily. Internal Revenue Service. Phone: (202)622-5000 Fax: (202)622-5844 • URL: http://www.irs.ustreas.gov • Web site provides a wide variety of tax information, including IRS forms and publications. Includes "Highlights of New Tax Law." Searching is available. Fees: Free.

Tax Analysts [Web site]. Tax Analysts. Phone: 800-955-3444 or (703)533-4400 Fax: (703)533-4444 • URL: http://www.tax.org • The three main sections of Tax Analysts home page are "Tax News" (Today's Tax News, Feature of the Week, Tax Snapshots, Tax Calendar); "Products & Services" (Product Catalog, Press Releases); and "Public Interest" (Discussion Groups, Tax Clinic, Tax History Project). Fees: Free for coverage of current tax events; fee-based for comprehensive information. Daily updating.

PERIODICALS AND NEWSLETTERS

Highlights and Documents. Tax Analysts. • Daily. $2,249.00 per year, including monthly indexes. Newsletter. Provides daily coverage of IRS, congressional, judicial, state, and international tax developments. Includes abstracts and citations for "all tax documents released within the previous 24 to 48 hours." Annual compilation available *Highlights and Documents on Microfiche.*

The Journal of Taxation: A National Journal of Current Developments, Analysis and Commentary for Tax Professionals. Warren, Gorham & Lamont/RIA Group. • Monthly. $215.00 per year. Analysis of current tax developments for tax specialists.

Tax Notes: The Weekly Tax Service. Tax Analysts. • Weekly. $1,699.00 per year. Includes an *Annual* and 1985-1996 compliations on CD-ROM. Newsletter. Covers "tax news from all federal sources," including congressional committees, tax courts, and the Internal Revenue Service. Each issue contains "summaries of every document that pertains to federal tax law," with citations. Commentary is provided.

Tax Practice. Tax Analysts. • Weekly. $199.00 per year. Newsletter. Covers news affecting tax practitioners and litigators, with emphasis on federal court decisions, rules and regulations, and tax petitions. Provides a guide to Internal Revenue Service audit issues.

RESEARCH CENTERS AND INSTITUTES

Center for Tax Policy Studies. Purdue University, 490 Krannert, West Lafayette, IN 47907-1310. Phone: (765)494-4442 Fax: (765)496-1778 E-mail: papke@mgmt.purdue.edu.

Tax Foundation. 1250 H St., N.W., Suite 750, Washington, DC 20005. Phone: (202)783-2760 Fax: (202)783-6868 E-mail: taxfnd@intr.net • URL: http://www.taxfoundation.org.

TRADE/PROFESSIONAL ASSOCIATIONS

National Tax Association. 725 15th St., N.W., No. 600, Washington, DC 20005-2109. Phone: (202)737-3325 Fax: (202)737-7308 E-mail: natltax@aol.com.

OTHER SOURCES

Fiduciary Tax Guide. CCH, Inc. • Monthly. $439.00 per year, Includes looseleaf monthly updates. Covers federal income taxation of estates, trusts, and beneficiaries. Provides information on gift and generation- skipping taxation.

GIRLS' CLOTHING

See: CHILDREN'S APPAREL INDUSTRY

GLASS CONTAINER INDUSTRY

See also: CONTAINER INDUSTRY; GLASS INDUSTRY; GLASSWARE INDUSTRY

ENCYCLOPEDIAS AND DICTIONARIES

Wiley Encyclopedia of Packaging Technology. Aaron Brody and Kenneth Marsh, editors. John Wiley and Sons, Inc. • 1997. $190.00. Second edition.

INTERNET DATABASES

Fedstats. Federal Interagency Council on Statistical Policy. Phone: (202)395-7254 • URL: http://www.fedstats.gov • Web site features an efficient search facility for full-text statistics produced by more than 70 federal agencies, including the Census Bureau, the Bureau of Economic Analysis, and the Bureau of Labor Statistics. Boolean searches can be made within one agency or for all agencies combined. Links are offered to international statistical bureaus, including the UN, IMF, OECD, UNESCO, Eurostat, and 20 individual countries. Fees: Free.

ONLINE DATABASES

DRI U.S. Central Database. Data Products Division. • Provides more than 23,000 business, financial, demographic, economic, foreign trade, and industry-related time series for the U.S. Includes national income, population, retail-wholesale trade, price indexes, labor data, housing, industrial production, banking, interest rates, money supply, etc. Time period is generally 1947 to date (some data back to 1929). Updating varies. Inquire as to online cost and availability.

STATISTICS SOURCES

Business Statistics of the United States. Courtenay M. Slater, editor. Bernan Associates. • 1999. $74.00. Fifth edition. Based on *Business Statistics*, formerly issue by the Bureau of Economic Analysis, U. S. Department of Commerce. Provides basic data for a wide variety of U. S. industries, services, and economic indicators. Most statistics are shown annually for 29 years and monthly for the most recent four years.

Survey of Current Business. Available from U. S. Government Printing Office. • Monthly. $49.00 per year. Issued by Bureau of Economic Analysis, U. S. Department of Commerce. Presents a wide variety of business and economic data.

TRADE/PROFESSIONAL ASSOCIATIONS

American Scientific Glassblowers Society. 302 Red Bud Lane, Thomasville, NC 27360. Phone: (336)882-0174 Fax: (336)882-0172.

Glass Molders, Pottery, Plastics and Allied Workers International Union. P.O. Box 607, Media, PA 19063. Phone: (610)565-5051 Fax: (610)565-0983.

Glass Packaging Institute. 1627 K St., N.W., Suite 800, Washington, DC 20006. Phone: (202)887-4850 Fax: (202)785-5377 E-mail: gpidc@erols.com • URL: http://www.gpi.org.

National Association of Container Distributors. 1900 Arch St., Philadelphia, PA 19103. Phone: (215)564-3484 Fax: (215)564-2175 E-mail: nacd@fernley.com • URL: http://www.nacd.net.

GLASS INDUSTRY

See also: GLASS CONTAINER INDUSTRY; GLASSWARE INDUSTRY; TABLEWARE

GENERAL WORKS

Glass Science. Robert H. Doremus. John Wiley and Sons, Inc. • 1994. $105.00. Second edition.

Introduction to Glass Science and Technology. J. E. Shelby. American Chemical Society. • 1997. $40.00. Covers the basics of glass manufacture, including the physical, optical, electrical, chemical, and mechanical properties of glass. (RCS Paperback Series).

ABSTRACTS AND INDEXES

NTIS Alerts: Materials Sciences. National Technical Information Service. • Semimonthly. $220.00 per year. Provides descriptions of government-sponsored research reports and software, with ordering information. Covers ceramics, glass, coatings, composite materials, alloys, plastics, wood, paper, adhesives, fibers, lubricants, and related subjects. Formerly *Abstract Newsletter.*

DIRECTORIES

Glass Digest Buyers' Guide. Ashlee Publishing Co., Inc. • Annual. $35.00. Included with *Glass Digest.* Formerly *International Glass/Metal Catalog.*

Glass Factory Directory of North America and U.S. Industry Factbook. LJV, Inc. • Annual. $25.00. Lists over 600 glass factory locations in the U.S., Canada and Mexico.

Glass Industry-Directory. Ashlee Publishing Co., Inc. • Annual. $35.00. Lists of primary and secondary glass manufacturers, suppliers to the glass industry, glass associations and unions, independent research labs, and glass educational institutions. International coverage.

U. S. Glass, Metal, and Glazing: Buyers Guide. Key Communications, Inc. • Annual. $20.00. A directory of supplies and equipment for the glass fabrication and installation industry.

FINANCIAL RATIOS

Almanac of Business and Industrial Financial Ratios. Leo Troy. Prentice Hall. • Annual. $99.95. Contains financial ratios derived from federal tax returns. Ratios for each of about 200 industries are arranged according to company asset size.

Annual Statement Studies. Robert Morris Associates: The Association of Lending and Credit Risk Professiona. • Annual. Free to members; non-members, $140.00. Median and quartile financial ratios are given for over 400 kinds of manufacturing, wholesale, retail, construction, and consumer finance establishments. Data is sorted by both asset size and sales volume. Includes a clearly written "Definition of Ratios" and an alphabetical industry index.

HANDBOOKS AND MANUALS

ASM Engineered Materials Reference Book. Michael L. Bauccio. ASM International. • 1994. $139.00. Second edition. Provides information on a wide range of materials, with special sections on ceramics, industrial glass products, and plastics.

The Handbook of Glass Manufacture. Fay V. Tooley, editor. Ashlee Publishing Co., Inc. • 1985. 195.00. Revised edition. Two volumes.

INTERNET DATABASES

Fedstats. Federal Interagency Council on Statistical Policy. Phone: (202)395-7254 • URL: http://www.fedstats.gov • Web site features an efficient search facility for full-text statistics produced by more than 70 federal agencies, including the Census Bureau, the Bureau of Economic Analysis, and the Bureau of Labor Statistics. Boolean searches can be made within one agency or for all agencies combined. Links are offered to international statistical bureaus, including the UN, IMF, OECD, UNESCO, Eurostat, and 20 individual countries. Fees: Free.

ONLINE DATABASES

DRI U.S. Central Database. Data Products Division. • Provides more than 23,000 business, financial, demographic, economic, foreign trade, and industry-related time series for the U.S. Includes national income, population, retail-wholesale trade, price indexes, labor data, housing, industrial production, banking, interest rates, money supply, etc. Time period is generally 1947 to date (some data back to 1929). Updating varies. Inquire as to online cost and availability.

PERIODICALS AND NEWSLETTERS

American Glass Review. Doctorow Communications, Inc. • Seven times a year. $25.00 per year. Covers the manufacture, distribution and processing of flat glass, industrial glass, scientific and optical glass, etc. Includes *American Glass Review Glass Factory Directory.*

Glass Digest: Trade Magazine Serving the Flat Glass, Architectural Metal an d Allied Products Industry. Ashlee Publishing Co., Inc. • Monthly. $40.00 per year.

Glass Magazine. National Glass Association. • Monthly. $34.95 per year.

U. S. Glass, Metal, and Glazing. Key Communications, Inc. • Monthly. $39.00 per year. Edited for glass fabricators, glaziers, distributors, and retailers. Special feature issues are devoted to architectural glass, mirror glass, windows, storefronts, hardware, machinery, sealants, and adhesives. Regular topics include automobile glass and fenestration (window design and placement).

RESEARCH CENTERS AND INSTITUTES

Physics Research Center and Vitreous State Laboratory. Catholic University of America. 620 Michigan Ave., N.E., 200 Hannan Hall, Washington, DC 20064. Phone: (202)319-5315 Fax: (202)319-

4448 E-mail: montrose@cua.edu • URL: http://www.arts-sciences.cua.edu/phys.

STATISTICS SOURCES

Annual Survey of Manufactures. Available from U. S. Government Printing Office. • Annual. Prices vary. Issued by the U. S. Census Bureau as an interim update to the *Census of Manufactures.* Includes data on number of manufacturing establishments in various industries, employment, labor costs, value of shipments, capital expenditures, inventories, energy costs, and assets. (See also Census Bureau home page, http://www.census.gov/.).

Business Statistics of the United States. Courtenay M. Slater, editor. Bernan Associates. • 1999. $74.00. Fifth edition. Based on *Business Statistics*, formerly issue by the Bureau of Economic Analysis, U. S. Department of Commerce. Provides basic data for a wide variety of U. S. industries, services, and economic indicators. Most statistics are shown annually for 29 years and monthly for the most recent four years.

Manufacturing Profiles. Available from U. S. Government Printing Office. • Annual. Issued by the U. S. Census Bureau. A printed consolidation of the entire *Current Industrial Report* series, presenting "all the data compiled." Contains statistics on production, shipments, inventories, consumption, exports, imports, and orders for a wide variety of manufactured products. (See also Census Bureau home page, http://www.census.gov/.).

Survey of Current Business. Available from U. S. Government Printing Office. • Monthly. $49.00 per year. Issued by Bureau of Economic Analysis, U. S. Department of Commerce. Presents a wide variety of business and economic data.

TRADE/PROFESSIONAL ASSOCIATIONS

ABG Division United Steel Worker. 3362 Hollenberg Dr., Bridgeton, MO 63044. Phone: (314)739-6142 Fax: (314)739-1216.

American Flint Glass Workers Union. 1440 S. Byrne Rd., Toledo, OH 43614. Phone: 800-742-8213 or (419)385-6687 Fax: (419)385-8839 E-mail: dlusetti@netzero.net.

Glass Association of North America. 2945 S.W. Wanamaker Dr., Suite A, Topeka, KS 66614. Phone: (785)271-0208 Fax: (785)271-0166 E-mail: gana@glasswebsite.com • URL: http://www.glasswebsite.com.

National Glass Association. 8200 Greensboro Dr., 3rd Fl., McLean, VA 22102. Phone: (703)442-4890 Fax: (703)442-0603 E-mail: nga@glass.org • URL: http://www.glass.org.

Sealed Insulating Glass Manufacturers Association. 401 N. Michigan Ave., Chicago, IL 60611-4267. Phone: (312)644-6610 Fax: (312)527-6783 E-mail: sigma@sba.com • URL: http://www.sigmaonline.org/sigma.

GLASSWARE INDUSTRY

See also: GLASS CONTAINER INDUSTRY; GLASS INDUSTRY; TABLEWARE

STATISTICS SOURCES

Annual Survey of Manufactures. Available from U. S. Government Printing Office. • Annual. Prices vary. Issued by the U. S. Census Bureau as an interim update to the *Census of Manufactures.* Includes data on number of manufacturing establishments in various industries, employment, labor costs, value of shipments, capital expenditures, inventories, energy costs, and assets. (See also Census Bureau home page, http://www.census.gov/.).

Manufacturing Profiles. Available from U. S. Government Printing Office. • Annual. Issued by the U. S. Census Bureau. A printed consolidation of the entire *Current Industrial Report* series, presenting "all the data compiled." Contains statistics on production, shipments, inventories, consumption, exports, imports, and orders for a wide variety of manufactured products. (See also Census Bureau home page, http://www.census.gov/.).

TRADE/PROFESSIONAL ASSOCIATIONS

Associated Glass and Pottery Manufacturers. c/o Custom Deco, 1343 Miami St., Toledo, OH 43605. Phone: (419)698-2900 Fax: (419)698-9928.

Glass Association of North America. 2945 S.W. Wanamaker Dr., Suite A, Topeka, KS 66614. Phone: (785)271-0208 Fax: (785)271-0166 E-mail: gana@glasswebsite.com • URL: http://www.glasswebsite.com.

National Glass Association. 8200 Greensboro Dr., 3rd Fl., McLean, VA 22102. Phone: (703)442-4890 Fax: (703)442-0603 E-mail: nga@glass.org • URL: http://www.glass.org.

Stained Glass Association of America. 4450 Fenton Rd., Hartland, MI 48353-1404. Phone: 800-888-7422 or (816)333-6690 Fax: (816)361-9173 E-mail: sgaofa@aol.com • URL: http://www.stainedglass.org.

OTHER SOURCES

The Tabletop Market. Available from MarketResearch.com. • 2000. $2,750.00. Published by Packaged Facts. Provides market data on dinnerware, glassware, and flatware, with projections to 2002.

GLOVE INDUSTRY

See also: CHILDREN'S APPAREL INDUSTRY; MEN'S CLOTHING INDUSTRY; WOMEN'S APPAREL

GENERAL WORKS

Fashion Accessories: The Complete Twentieth Century Sourcebook. John Peacock. Macmillan Publishing Co., Inc. • 2000. $34.95.

DIRECTORIES

Accessories Resources Directory. Business Journals, Inc. • Annual. $30.00. 1,600 manufacturers, importers, and sales representatives producing or handling belts, gloves, handbags, scarves, hosiery, jewelry, sunglasses and umbrellas. Formerly *Accessories Directory.*

STATISTICS SOURCES

Annual Survey of Manufactures. Available from U. S. Government Printing Office. • Annual. Prices vary. Issued by the U. S. Census Bureau as an interim update to the *Census of Manufactures.* Includes data on number of manufacturing establishments in various industries, employment, labor costs, value of shipments, capital expenditures, inventories, energy costs, and assets. (See also Census Bureau home page, http://www.census.gov/.).

Manufacturing Profiles. Available from U. S. Government Printing Office. • Annual. Issued by the U. S. Census Bureau. A printed consolidation of the entire *Current Industrial Report* series, presenting "all the data compiled." Contains statistics on production, shipments, inventories, consumption, exports, imports, and orders for a wide variety of manufactured products. (See also Census Bureau home page, http://www.census.gov/.).

TRADE/PROFESSIONAL ASSOCIATIONS

International Hand Protection Association. 7315 Wisconsin Ave., Suite 424, Bethesda, MD 20814. Phone: (301)961-8680 Fax: (301)961-8681.

National Industrial Glove Distributors Association. Fernley and Fernley, 1900 Arch St., Philadelphia, PA 19103. Phone: (215)564-3484 Fax: (215)564-2175 E-mail: assnhqt@netaxs.com • URL: http://www.nigda.org.

GLUE INDUSTRY

See: ADHESIVES

GOING PUBLIC

See: NEW ISSUES (FINANCE)

GOLD

See also: COINS AS AN INVESTMENT; MONEY

GENERAL WORKS

Gold and Liberty. Richard M. Salsman. American Institute for Economic Research. • 1995. $8.00. Mainly a conservative argument in favor of the gold standard and against central banking, but also contains historical background and 10 unique charts, such as "Purchasing Power of Gold and of the U. S. Dollar, 1792-1994." Includes a 16-page, classified bibliography on the origins of gold as money, the classical gold standard, political issues, gold as an investment, the future of gold, and other topics.

How to Invest Wisely. Lawrence S. Pratt. American Institute for Economic Research. • 1998. $9.00. Presents a conservative policy of investing, with emphasis on dividend-paying common stocks. Gold and other inflation hedges are compared. Includes a reprint of *Toward an Optimal Stock Selection Strategy* (1997). (Economic Education Bulletin.).

Money: Its Origins, Development, Debasement, and Prospects. John H. Wood. American Institute for Economic Research. • 1999. $10.00. A politically conservative view of monetary history, the gold standard, banking systems, and inflation. Includes a list of references. (Economic Education Bulletin.).

ALMANACS AND YEARBOOKS

World Currrency Yearbook. International Currency Analysis, Inc. • Annual. $250.00. Directory of more than 110 central banks worldwide.

DIRECTORIES

Financial Times Energy Yearbook: Mining 2000. Available from The Gale Group. • Annual. $320.00. Published by Financial Times Energy. Provides production and financial details for more than 800 major mining companies worldwide. Includes coverage of reserves, operations, properties, and growth rates. Formerly *Financial Times International Yearbook: Mining.*

Futures Guide to Computerized Trading. Futures Magazine, Inc. • Annual. $10.00. "A directory of products and services for the computerized trader." Provides information on computer software applications for commodity traders and money managers, including trading methods and technical analysis.

Futures Magazine SourceBook: The Most Complete List of Exchanges, Companies, Regulators, Organizations, etc., Offering Products and Services to the Futures and Options Industry. Futures Magazine, Inc. • Annual. $19.50. Provides information on commodity futures brokers, trading method services, publications, and other items of interest to futures traders and money managers.

HANDBOOKS AND MANUALS

Jake Bernstein's New Guide to Investing in Metals. Jacob Bernstein. John Wiley and Sons, Inc. • 1991.

$34.95. Covers bullion, coins, futures, options, mining stocks, and precious metal mutual funds. Includes the history of metals as an investment.

Looking for Gold: The Modern Prospector's Handbook. Bradford Angier. Stackpole Books, Inc. • 1995. $16.95.

INTERNET DATABASES

Fedstats. Federal Interagency Council on Statistical Policy. Phone: (202)395-7254 • URL: http://www.fedstats.gov • Web site features an efficient search facility for full-text statistics produced by more than 70 federal agencies, including the Census Bureau, the Bureau of Economic Analysis, and the Bureau of Labor Statistics. Boolean searches can be made within one agency or for all agencies combined. Links are offered to international statistical bureaus, including the UN, IMF, OECD, UNESCO, Eurostat, and 20 individual countries. Fees: Free.

Futures Online. Oster Communications, Inc. Phone: 800-601-8907 or (319)277-1278 Fax: (319)277-7982 • URL: http://www.futuresmag.com • Web site presents updates of *Futures* magazine and links to other futures-related sites. Includes "Futures Industry News," "Technical Talk," "Today's Hot Markets," "Futures Talk" (forums), "Futures Library" (archives, 1993 to date), and other features. Keyword searching is available. Updating: daily. Fees: Free.

ONLINE DATABASES

DRI U.S. Central Database. Data Products Division. • Provides more than 23,000 business, financial, demographic, economic, foreign trade, and industry-related time series for the U.S. Includes national income, population, retail-wholesale trade, price indexes, labor data, housing, industrial production, banking, interest rates, money supply, etc. Time period is generally 1947 to date (some data back to 1929). Updating varies. Inquire as to online cost and availability.

GEOREF. American Geological Institute. • Bibliography and index of geology and geosciences literature, 1785 to present. Inquire as to online cost and availability.

PERIODICALS AND NEWSLETTERS

American Gold News and Western Prospector. DeServices, Inc. • Monthly. $18.00 per year. Provides news about gold mining. Incorporates *Western Prospector*. Formerly *American Gold News*.

Bullion Report. Investor Metals Services, Inc. • Semimonthly. $90.00 per year.

Canadian Resources and PennyMines Analyst: The Canadian Newsletter for Penny-Mines Investors Who Insist on Geological Value. MPL Communication, Inc. • Weekly. $157.00 per year. Newsletter. Mainly on Canadian gold mine stocks. Formerly *Canadian PennyMines Analyst*.

Futures: News, Analysis, and Strategies for Futures, Options, and Derivatives Traders. Futures Magazine, Inc. • Monthly. $39.00 per year. Edited for institutional money managers and traders, brokers, risk managers, and individual investors or speculators. Includes special feature issues on interest rates, technical indicators, currencies, charts, precious metals, hedge funds, and derivatives. Supplements available.

Gold Newsletter. James U. Blanchard, editor. Jefferson Financial, Inc. • Monthly. $99.00 per year. Newsletter. Covers news of the international gold market and provides commentary on the price of gold.

Powell Monetary Analyst. Larson M. Powell, editor. Reserve Research Ltd. • Biweekly. $285.00 per year. Newsletters. Information on precious metals, coins and curriencies.

PRICE SOURCES

Metals Week. McGraw-Hill Commodity Services Group. • Weekly. $770.00 per year.

STATISTICS SOURCES

The AIER Chart Book. AIER Research Staff. American Institute for Economic Research. • Annual. $3.00. A compact compilation of long-range charts ("Purchasing Power of the Dollar," for example, goes back to 1780) covering various aspects of the U. S. economy. Includes inflation, interest rates, debt, gold, taxation, stock prices, etc. (Economic Education Bulletin.).

Business Statistics of the United States. Courtenay M. Slater, editor. Bernan Associates. • 1999. $74.00. Fifth edition. Based on *Business Statistics*, formerly issue by the Bureau of Economic Analysis, U. S. Department of Commerce. Provides basic data for a wide variety of U. S. industries, services, and economic indicators. Most statistics are shown annually for 29 years and monthly for the most recent four years.

London Currency Report. World Reports Ltd. • 10 times a year. $950.00 per year. Formerly *Gold and Silver Survey*.

Mineral Commodity Summaries. Available from U. S. Government Printing Office. • Annual. Published by the U. S. Geological Survey, Department of the Interior (http://www.usgs.gov). Contains detailed, five-year data for about 90 nonfuel minerals. Covers a wide range of statistics, including production, imports, exports, consumption, reserves, prices, tariff information, and industry employment. (Two pages are devoted to each mineral.).

Non-Ferrous Metal Data Yearbook. American Bureau of Metal Statistics. • Annual. $395.00. Provides about 200 statistical tables covering many nonferrous metals. Includes production, consumption, inventories, exports, imports, and other data.

Standard & Poor's Industry Surveys. Standard & Poor's. • Semiannual. $1,800.00. Two looseleaf volumes. Includes monthly supplements. Provides detailed, individual surveys of 52 major industry groups. Each survey is revised on a semiannual basis. Also includes "Monthly Investment Review" (industry group investment analysis) and monthly "Trends & Projections" (economic analysis).

Statistical Annual: Interest Rates, Metals, Stock Indices, Options on Financial Futures, Options on Metals Futures. Chicago Board of Trade. • Annual. Includes historical data on GNMA CDR Futures, Cash-Settled GNMA Futures, U. S. Treasury Bond Futures, U. S. Treasury Note Futures, Options on Treasury Note Futures, NASDAQ-100 Futures, Major Market Index Futures, Major Market Index MAXI Futures, Municipal Bond Index Futures, 1,000-Ounce Silver Futures, Options on Silver Futures, and Kilo Gold Futures.

Survey of Current Business. Available from U. S. Government Printing Office. • Monthly. $49.00 per year. Issued by Bureau of Economic Analysis, U. S. Department of Commerce. Presents a wide variety of business and economic data.

United States Census of Mineral Industries. Bureau of the Census, U.S. Department of Commerce. Available from U.S. Government Printing Office. • Quinquennial.

TRADE/PROFESSIONAL ASSOCIATIONS

American Bureau of Metal Statistics. P.O. Box 805, Chatham, NJ 07928. Phone: (973)701-2299 Fax: (973)701-2152 E-mail: info@abms.com • URL: http://www.abms.com • Members are metal companies. Compiles and publishes detailed statistical data on a wide variety of nonferrous metals: aluminum, copper, gold, lead, nickel, platinum, silver, tin, titanium, uranium, zinc, and others.

Gold Institute. 1112 16th St., N.W., Suite 240, Washington, DC 20036. Phone: (202)835-0185 Fax: (202)835-0155 E-mail: info@goldinstitute.org • URL: http://www.goldinstitute.org.

OTHER SOURCES

The Power of Gold: The History of an Obsession. Peter L. Bernstein. John Wiley and Sons, Inc. • 2000. $27.95. Covers the economic and financial history of gold from ancient times to the present.

GOLF INDUSTRY

DIRECTORIES

Directory of Golf. National Golf Foundation. • Annual $60.00. Lists golf course architects, contractors, builders, appraisers, and consulting firms. Golf equipment manufacturers are also included.

Driving Range Directory. National Golf Foundation. • 1998. $99.00. Lists about 1,700 golf driving ranges in the U. S.

Executive/Par-3 Golf Course Directory. National Golf Foundation. • 1998. $99.00. Lists about 1,700 U. S. golf courses of less than regulation size.

Golf Course Directory. National Golf Foundation. • 1998. $199.00. Two volumes (Alabama-Montana and Nebraska-Wyoming). Lists about 16,000 public and private golf facilities, with information as to size, number of holes, year opened, and practice ranges.

Golf Index. Ingledue Travel Publications. • Semiannual. $40.00 per year. Provides directory listings of golf courses and resorts around the world. Contains information on golf travel packages, tour operators, and tournaments.

Golf Magazine Golf Club Buyers' Guide. Times Mirror Magazines, Inc. • Annual. Price on application. Lists golf club manufacturers, with description of products and prices.

Golf Shop Operations: Buyer's Guide. New York Times Co., Magazine Group. • Annual. $10.00 Included in subscription. Lists golf equipment and apparel suppliers. Includes suggested retail prices of specific items.

Off-Course Golf Retail Stores Directory. National Golf Foundation. • 1998. $99.00. Lists about 2,000 retail stores selling golf equipment, but not located on a golf course.

Resorts and Parks Purchasing Guide. Klevens Publications, Inc. • Annual. $60.00. Lists suppliers of products and services for resorts and parks, including national parks, amusement parks, dude ranches, golf resorts, ski areas, and national monument areas.

HANDBOOKS AND MANUALS

Golf U.S.A.: A Guide to the Best Golf Courses and Resorts. Corey Sandler. NTC/Contemporary Publishing Group. • 2001. $17.95. Second edition. Describes 2,500 public and private golf courses. (Contemporary Books.).

Human Resource Management for Golf Course Superintendents. Robert A. Milligan and Thomas R. Maloney. Ann Arbor Press, Inc. • 1996. $34.95. Covers various personnel topics as related to golf course management, including organizational structure, recruitment, employee selection, training, motivation, and discipline.

PERIODICALS AND NEWSLETTERS

AGS Quarterly. American Golf Sponsors. • Quarterly. Membership newsletter for sponsors of major golf tournaments.

Golf Course Management. Golf Course Superintendents Association of America. • Monthly. $48.00 per year. Contains articles on golf course maintenance, equipment, landscaping, renovation, and management.

Golf Course News: The Newspaper for the Golf Course Industry. United Publications, Inc. • Nine times a year. Price on application. Edited for golf course superintendents, managers, architects, and developers.

Golf Digest: How to Play What to Play, Where to Play. New York Times Co., Magazine Group. • Monthly. $27.94 per year. A high circulation consumer magazine for golfers. Editions available in various languages. Supplement available *Golf Digest Woman.*

Golf Magazine. Times Mirror Magazines, Inc. • Monthly. $19.95 per year. Popular consumer magazine for golfers.

Golf Shop Operations. New York Times Co., Magazine Group. • 10 times a year. $72.00 per year. Edited for retailers of golf equipment.

Golfdom. Advanstar Communications, Inc. • Eight times a year. $25.00 per year. Covers marketing, financing, insurance, human resources, maintenance, environmental factors, and other aspects of golf course management. *Formerly Golf Business.*

Golfweek: America's Golf Newspaper. Turnstile Publishing Co. • Weekly. $69.95 per year. Includes biweekly supplement, "Golfweek's Strictly Business," covering business and marketing for the golfing industry.

RESEARCH CENTERS AND INSTITUTES

National Golf Foundation. 1150 S. U. S. Highway One, Suite 401, Jupiter, FL 33477. Phone: (561)744-6006 Fax: (561)744-6107 • URL: http://www.ngf.org • Research areas include golf consumers, golf course operations, and other aspects of the golf industry.

STATISTICS SOURCES

U. S. Industry and Trade Outlook: The McGraw-Hill Companies and the U.S. Department of Commerce/ International Trade Administration. Datapso Research Corp. • Annual. $69.95. Produced by the International Trade Administration, U. S. Department of Commerce, in a "public-private" partnership with DRI/McGraw-Hill and Standard & Poor's. Provides basic data, outlook for the current year, and "Long-Term Prospects" (five-year projections) for a wide variety of products and services. Includes high technology industries. Formerly *U. S. Industrial Outlook.*

TRADE/PROFESSIONAL ASSOCIATIONS

American Recreational Golf Association. P.O. Box 35189, Chicago, IL 60707-0189. Phone: (708)453-0080 Fax: (708)453-0083 • Evaluates golf equipment and offers equipment certification.

American Society of Golf Course Architects. 221 N. LaSalle St., Chicago, IL 60601. Phone: (312)372-7090 Fax: (312)372-6160 E-mail: asgca@selz.com • URL: http://www.golfdesign.org • Members are professional designers and architects of golf courses.

Association of Golf Merchandisers. P.O. Box 19899, Fountain Hills, AZ 85269. Phone: (480)373-8564 Fax: (480)373-8518 • Members are vendors of gold equipment and merchandise.

Golf Course Builders Association of America. 920 Airport Rd., Suite 210, Chapel Hill, NC 27514. Phone: (919)942-8922 Fax: (919)942-6955 E-mail: gcbaa@aol.com • URL: http://www.gcbaa.org • Members are golf course builders, designers, and suppliers.

Golf Course Superintendents Association of America. 1421 Research Park Dr., Lawrence, KS 66049-3859. Phone: 800-472-7878 or (785)841-2240 or (785)832-4430 Fax: (785)832-4488 E-mail: infobox@gcsaa.org • URL: http://www.gcsaa.org • Members are golf course superintendents and others concerned with golf course maintenance and improvement.

Golf Manufacturers and Distributors Association. P.O. Box 37324, Cincinnati, OH 45222. Phone: (513)631-4400 • Members are exhibitors at the Professional Golfers' Association annual trade show. Seeks to improve the "business habits" of professional golfers.

Ladies Professional Golf Association. 100 International Golf Dr., Daytona Beach, FL 32124-1092. Phone: (904)274-6200 Fax: (904)274-1099 • URL: http://www.lpga.com • Divisions are Teaching and Tournamemt.

National Golf Course Owners Association. 1470 Ben Sawyer Blvd., Suite 18, Mount Pleasant, SC 29464-4535. Phone: 800-933-4262 or (843)881-9956 Fax: (843)881-9958 E-mail: info@ngcoa.com • URL: http://www.ngcoa.com • Members are owners and operators of private golf courses.

PGA Tour Tournament Association. 13000 Sawgrass Village Circle, No. 36, Ponte Vedra Beach, FL 32082. Phone: (904)285-4222 Fax: (904)273-5726 E-mail: pgatourta@aol.com • URL: http://www.pgatta.org • Members are sponsors of major professional golf tournaments. Committees include Finance, Marketing, and Media Relations.

Professional Golfers' Association of America. 100 Ave. of Champions, Palm Beach Gardens, FL 33410-9601. Phone: (561)624-8400 Fax: (561)624-8430 E-mail: info@pga.com • URL: http://www.pga.com/.

United States Golf Association (USGA). P.O. Box 708, Far Hills, NJ 07931. Phone: (908)234-2300 Fax: (908)234-9687 E-mail: usga@usga.org • URL: http://www.usga.org • Members are established golf courses and clubs. Serves as governing body for golf in the U. S. and provides rules and regulations.

OTHER SOURCES

Golf Participation in the U. S. Available from MarketResearch.com. • 1998. $250.00. Published by the National Golf Foundation. Market research report on consumer attitudes and industry statistics.

Superstudy of Sports Participation. Available from MarketResearch.com. • 1999. $650.00. Three volumes. Published by American Sports Data, Inc. Provides market research data on 102 sports and activities. Vol. 1: *Physical Fitness Activities.* Vol. 2: *Recreational Sports.* Vol. 3: *Outdoor Activities.* (Volumes are available separately at $275.00.).

GOURMET FOODS

See: SPECIALTY FOOD INDUSTRY

GOVERNMENT ACCOUNTING

GENERAL WORKS

Accounting for Governmental and Non-Profit Entities. Earl R. Wilson and others. McGraw-Hill. • 2000. 12th edition. Price on application.

Essentials of Accounting for Governmental and Not-for-Profit Organizations. John H. Engstrom and Leon E. Hay. McGraw-Hill. • 1998. $53.44. Fifth edition.

ABSTRACTS AND INDEXES

Accounting and Tax Index. UMI. • Quarterly. Price on application. Includes annual cumulative bound volume. Indexes accounting, auditing, and taxation literature appearing in journals, books, pamphlets, conference proceedings, and newsletters. (UMI is University Microfilms International, a Bell & Howell Co.).

Accounting Articles. CCH, Inc. • Monthly. $594.00 per year. Looseleaf service.

PAIS International in Print. Public Affairs Information Service, Inc. • Monthly. $650.00 per year; cumulations three times a year. Provides topical citations to the worldwide literature of public affairs, economics, demographics, sociology, and trade. Text in English; indexed materials in English, French, German, Italian, Portuguese and Spanish.

Sage Public Administration Abstracts. Sage Publications, Inc. • Quarterly. Individuals, $150.00 per year; institutions, $575.00 per year.

ALMANACS AND YEARBOOKS

Research in Governmental and Nonprofit Accounting. JAI Press, Inc. • Irregular.$78.50.

CD-ROM DATABASES

PAIS on CD-ROM. Public Affairs Information Service, Inc. • Quarterly. $1,995.00 per year. Provides a CD-ROM version of the online service, *PAIS International.* Contains over 400,000 citations to the literature of contemporary social, political, and economic issues.

HANDBOOKS AND MANUALS

GAAP for Governments: Interpretation and Application of Generally Accepted Accounting Principles for State and Local Governments. John Wiley and Sons, Inc. • Annual. $134.00. (Includes CD-ROM.).

Government Auditing Standards. Available from U. S. Government Printing Office. • 1994. $6.50. Revised edition. Issued by the U. S. General Accounting Office (http://www.gao.gov). Contains standards for CPA firms to follow in financial and performance audits of federal government agencies and programs. Also known as the "Yellow Book.".

INTERNET DATABASES

Rutgers Accounting Web (RAW). Rutgers University Accounting Research Center. Phone: (201)648-5172 Fax: (201)648-1233 • URL: http://www.rutgers.edu/accounting • RAW Web site provides extensive links to sources of national and international accounting information, such as the Big Six accounting firms, the Financial Accounting Standards Board (FASB), SEC filings (EDGAR), journals, publishers, software, the International Accounting Network, and "Internet's largest list of accounting firms in USA." Searching is offered. Fees: Free.

ONLINE DATABASES

Accounting and Tax Database. Bell & Howell Information and Learning. • Provides indexing and abstracting of the literature of accounting, taxation, and financial management, 1971 to date. Updating is weekly. Especially covers accounting, auditing, banking, bankruptcy, employee compensation and benefits, cash management, financial planning, and credit. Inquire as to online cost and availability.

PAIS International. Public Affairs Information Service, Inc. • Corresponds to the former printed publications, *PAIS Bulletin* (1976-90) and *PAIS Foreign Language Index* (1972-90), and to the current *PAIS International in Print* (1991 to date). Covers economic, political, and sociological material appearing in periodicals, books, government documents, and other publications. Updating is monthly. Inquire as to online cost and availability.

PERIODICALS AND NEWSLETTERS

Governing: The States and Localities. • Monthly. $39.95 per year. Edited for state and local government officials. Covers finance, office management, computers, telecommunications, environmental concerns, etc.

Government Accountants Journal. Association of Government Accountants. • Quarterly. $60.00 per year.

TRADE/PROFESSIONAL ASSOCIATIONS

Association of Government Accountants. 2208 Mount Vernon Ave., Alexandria, VA 22301-1314. Phone: 800-242-7211 or (703)684-6931 Fax: (703)548-9367 • URL: http://www.agacgfm.org • Members are employed by federal, state, county, and city government agencies. Includes accountants, auditors, budget officers, and other government finance administrators and officials.

GOVERNMENT ADMINISTRATION

See: PUBLIC ADMINISTRATION

GOVERNMENT AGENCIES

See: FEDERAL GOVERNMENT; MUNICIPAL GOVERNMENT; STATE GOVERNMENT

GOVERNMENT AID

See: FEDERAL AID

GOVERNMENT AND BUSINESS

See: REGULATION OF INDUSTRY

GOVERNMENT BONDS

See also: BONDS; MUNICIPAL BONDS

GENERAL WORKS

Buying Treasury Securities: Bills, Notes, Bonds, Offerings Schedule, Conversions. Federal Reserve Bank of Philadelphia. • Revised as required. Free pamphlet. Provides clear definitions, information, and instructions relating to U. S. Treasury securities: short-term (bills), medium-term (notes), and long-term (bonds).

Financial Institutions and Markets. Robert W. Kolb and Ricardo J. Rodriguez. Blackwell Publishers. • 1996. $77.95. Contains 40 articles (chapters) by various authors on U. S. financial markets and other topics. Includes separate chapters on the International Monetary Fund, inflation, monetary policy, the national debt, bank failures, derivatives, stock prices, initial public offerings, government bonds, pensions, foreign exchange, international markets, and other subjects.

Fixed-Income Investment: Recent Research. Thomas S. Ho, editor. McGraw-Hill Professional. • 1994. $65.00. Discusses bond portfolio management, the yield curve, bond pricing methods, and related subjects.

ABSTRACTS AND INDEXES

Banking Information Index. U M I Banking Information Index. • Monthly. Price on application. Covers a wide variety of banking, business, and financial subjects in periodicals. Formerly *Banking Literature Index.*

ALMANACS AND YEARBOOKS

Fixed Income Almanac: The Bond Investor's Compendium of Key Market, Product, and Performance Data. Livingston G. Douglas. McGraw-Hill Professional. • 1993. $75.00. Presents 20 years of data in 350 graphs and charts. Covers bond market volatility, yield spreads, high-yield (junk) corporate bonds, default rates, and other items, such as Federal Reserve policy.

DIRECTORIES

Moody's Municipal and Government Manual. Financial Information Services. • Annual. $2,495.00 per year. Updated biweekly in *News Reports.*

ENCYCLOPEDIAS AND DICTIONARIES

Dictionary of Finance and Investment Terms. John Downes and Jordan E. Goodman. Barron's Educational Series, Inc. • 1998. $12.95. Fifth revised edition. Provides clear explanations of more than 5,000 business, banking, financial, investment, and tax terms. Includes a separate list of financial abbreviations and acronyms.

HANDBOOKS AND MANUALS

Fixed Income Analytics: State-of-the-Art Analysis and Valuation Modeling. Ravi E. Dattatreya, editor. McGraw-Hill Professional. • 1991. $69.95. Discusses the yield curve, structure and value in corporate bonds, mortgage-backed securities, and other topics.

Fixed Income Mathematics: Analytical and Statistical Techniques. Frank J. Fabozzi. McGraw-Hill Professional. • 1996. $60.00. Third edition. Covers the basics of fixed income analysis, as well as more advanced techniques used for complex securities.

How to Build Wealth with Tax-Sheltered Investments. Kerry Anne Lynch. American Institute for Economic Research. • 2000. $6.00. Provides practical information on conservative tax shelters, including defined-contribution pension plans, individual retirement accounts, Keogh plans, U. S. savings bonds, municipal bonds, and various kinds of annuities: deferred, variable-rate, immediate, and foreign-currency. (Economic Education Bulletin.).

Trading and Investing in Bond Options: Risk Management, Arbitrage, and Value Investing. Anthony M. Wong. John Wiley and Sons, Inc. • 1991. $55.00. Covers dealing, trading, and investing in U. S. government bond futures options (puts and calls).

INTERNET DATABASES

DBC Online: America's Leading Provider of Real-Time Market Data to the Individual Investor. Data Broadcasting Corp. Phone: (415)571-1800 E-mail: dbcinfo@dbc.com • URL: http://www.dbc.com • Web site provides a wide variety of real-time securities market prices, data, and charts. Covers bonds ("BondVu"), stocks, commodities, options, mutual funds, major indexes, industry indexes, international markets, etc. Also includes news, SEC documents ("Smart-Edgar"), and various other features. Fees: Both free and fee-based, depending on level of information.

Fedstats. Federal Interagency Council on Statistical Policy. Phone: (202)395-7254 • URL: http://www.fedstats.gov • Web site features an efficient search facility for full-text statistics produced by more than 70 federal agencies, including the Census Bureau, the Bureau of Economic Analysis, and the Bureau of Labor Statistics. Boolean searches can be made within one agency or for all agencies combined. Links are offered to international statistical bureaus, including the UN, IMF, OECD, UNESCO, Eurostat, and 20 individual countries. Fees: Free.

Wall Street Journal Interactive Edition. Dow Jones & Co., Inc. Phone: 800-369-2834 or (212)416-2000 Fax: (212)416-2658 E-mail: inquiries@interactive.wsj.com • URL: http://www.wsj.com • Fee-based Web site providing online searching of worldwide information from the *The Wall Street Journal.* Includes "Company Snapshots," "The Journal's Greatest Hits," "Index to Market Data," "14-Day Searchable Archive," "Journal Links," etc. Financial price quotes are available. Fees: $49.00 per year; $29.00 per year to print subscribers.

ONLINE DATABASES

DRI U.S. Central Database. Data Products Division. • Provides more than 23,000 business, financial, demographic, economic, foreign trade, and industry-related time series for the U.S. Includes national income, population, retail-wholesale trade, price indexes, labor data, housing, industrial production, banking, interest rates, money supply, etc. Time period is generally 1947 to date (some data back to 1929). Updating varies. Inquire as to online cost and availability.

PERIODICALS AND NEWSLETTERS

The Bond Buyer. American Banker Newsletter, Thomson Financial Media. • Daily edition, $1,897 per year. Weekly edition, $525.00 per year. Reports on new municipal bond issues.

Bondweek: The Newsweekly of Fixed Income and Credit Markets. Institutional Investor. • Weekly. $2,220.00 per year. Newsletter. Covers taxable, fixed-income securities for professional investors, including corporate, government, foreign, mortgage, and high-yield.

Journal of Fixed Income. Institutional Investor. • Quarterly. $325.00 per year. Covers a wide range of fixed-income investments for institutions, including bonds, interest-rate options, high-yield securities, and mortgages.

Moody's Bond Survey. Financial Information Services. • Weekly. $1,350.00 per year. Newsletter.

The Wall Street Journal. Dow Jones & Co., Inc. • Daily. $175.00 per year. Covers news and trends relating to business, industry, finance, the economy, and international commerce. Provides extensive price and other data for the securities, commodity, options, futures, foreign exchange, and money markets.

STATISTICS SOURCES

Business Statistics of the United States. Courtenay M. Slater, editor. Bernan Associates. • 1999. $74.00. Fifth edition. Based on *Business Statistics*, formerly issue by the Bureau of Economic Analysis, U. S. Department of Commerce. Provides basic data for a wide variety of U. S. industries, services, and economic indicators. Most statistics are shown annually for 29 years and monthly for the most recent four years.

Daily Treasury Statement: Cash and Debt Operations of the United States Treasury. Available from U. S. Government Printing Office. • Daily, except Saturdays, Sundays, and holidays. $855.00 per year. (Financial Management Service, U. S. Treasury Department.).

SBBI Monthly Market Reports. Ibbotson Associates. • Monthly. $995.00 per year. These reports provide current updating of stocks, bonds, bills, and inflation (SBBI) data. Each issue contains the most recent month's investment returns and index values for various kinds of securities, as well as monthly statistics for the past year. Analysis is included.

SBBI Quarterly Market Reports. Ibbotson Associates. • Quarterly. $495.00 per year. Each quarterly volume contains detailed updates to stocks, bonds, bills, and inflation (SBBI) data. Includes total and sector returns for the broad stock market, small company stocks, intermediate and long-term government bonds, long-term corporate bonds, and U. S. Treasury Bills. Analyses, tables, graphs, and market consensus forecasts are provided.

Statistical Annual: Interest Rates, Metals, Stock Indices, Options on Financial Futures, Options on Metals Futures. Chicago Board of Trade. • Annual. Includes historical data on GNMA CDR Futures, Cash-Settled GNMA Futures, U. S. Treasury Bond Futures, U. S. Treasury Note Futures, Options on Treasury Note Futures, NASDAQ-100 Futures,

Major Market Index Futures, Major Market Index MAXI Futures, Municipal Bond Index Futures, 1,000-Ounce Silver Futures, Options on Silver Futures, and Kilo Gold Futures.

Stocks, Bonds, Bills, and Inflation Yearbook. Ibbotson Associates. • Annual. $92.00. Provides detailed data from 1926 to the present on inflation and the returns from various kinds of financial investments, such as small-cap stocks and long-term government bonds.

Survey of Current Business. Available from U. S. Government Printing Office. • Monthly. $49.00 per year. Issued by Bureau of Economic Analysis, U. S. Department of Commerce. Presents a wide variety of business and economic data.

Treasury Bulletin. Available from U. S. Government Printing Office. • Quarterly. $39.00 per year. Issued by the Financial Management Service, U. S. Treasury Department. Provides data on the federal budget, government securities and yields, the national debt, and the financing of the federal government in general.

OTHER SOURCES

Factiva. Dow Jones Reuters Business Interactive, LLC. • Fee-based Web site provides "global news and business information through Web sites and content integration solutions." Includes Dow Jones and Reuters newswires, The Wall Street Journal, and more than 7,000 other sources of current news, historical articles, market research reports, and investment analysis. Content includes 96 major U. S. newspapers, 900 non-English sources, trade publications, media transcripts, country profiles, news photos, etc.

Fitch Insights. Fitch Investors Service, Inc. • Biweekly. $1,040.00 per year. Includes bond rating actions and explanation of actions. Provides commentary and Fitch's view of the financial markets.

Nexis.com. Lexis-Nexis Group. • Fee-based Web site offers searching of about 2.8 billion documents in some 30,000 news, business, and legal information sources. Features include a subject directory covering 1,200 topics in 34 categories and a Company Dossier containing information on more than 500,000 public and private companies. Boolean searching is offered.

Tables of Redemption Values for United States Savings Bonds, Series EE. Available from U. S. Government Printing Office. • Semiannual. $5.00 per year. Issued by the Public Debt Bureau, U. S. Treasury Department.

Tables of Redemption Values for United States Series E Savings Bonds and Saving Notes. Available from U. S. Government Printing Office. • Semiannual. $5.00 per year. Issued by the Public Debt Bureau, U. S. Treasury Department.

GOVERNMENT BUDGET

See: FEDERAL BUDGET

GOVERNMENT, COMPUTERS IN

See: COMPUTERS IN GOVERNMENT

GOVERNMENT CONTRACTS

See also: CONTRACTS; GOVERNMENT PURCHASING

GENERAL WORKS

Government Contracts and Subcontract Leads Directory. Government Data Publications, Inc. • Annual. $89.50. Firms which received prime contracts for production of goods or services from federal government agencies during the preceeding twelve months. Formerly *Government Contracts Directory.*

ABSTRACTS AND INDEXES

Current Law Index: Multiple Access to Legal Periodicals. The Gale Group. • Monthly. $650.00 per year. Produced in cooperation with the American Association of Law Libraries. Indexes more than 900 law journals, legal newspapers, and specialty publications from the U.S., Canada, U.K., Ireland, Australia, and New Zealand.

ALMANACS AND YEARBOOKS

Yearbook of Procurement Articles. Federal Publications, Inc. • Annual.

DIRECTORIES

Government Prime Contractors Directory. Government Data Publications, Inc. • Annual. $15.00. Organizations that received government prime contractors during the previous two years. Formerly *Government Production Prime Contractors.*

HANDBOOKS AND MANUALS

Contracting with the Federal Government. Margaret M. Worhtingotn and Louis P. Goldman. John Wiley and Sons, Inc. • 1998. $115.00. Fourth edition. Tells how to acquire federal contracts and execute them profitably.

Corporate Counsellor's Deskbook. Dennis J. Block and Michael A. Epstein, editors. Panel Publishing. • 1999. $220.00. Fifth edition. Looseleaf. Annual supplementation. Covers a wide variety of corporate legal issues, including internal investigations, indemnification, insider trading, intellectual property, executive compensation, antitrust, export-import, real estate, environmental law, government contracts, and bankruptcy.

Cost Accounting Standards Board Regulations. CCH, Inc. • 1999. $24.00. Covers Federal Acquisition Regulation (FAR) cost accounting standards for both defense and civilian government contracts. Provides the rules for estimating and reporting costs for contracts of more than $500,000.

How to Obtain Government Contracts. Entrepreneur Media, Inc. • Looseleaf. $59.50. A practical guide to acquiring and negotiating government contracts. (Start-Up Business Guide No. E1227.).

PERIODICALS AND NEWSLETTERS

Commerce Business Daily. Industry and Trade Administration, U.S. Department of Commerce. Available from U.S. Government Printing Office. • Daily. Priority, $324.00 per year; non-priority, $275.00 per year. Synopsis of *U.S. Government Proposed Procurement, Sales and Contract Awards.*

Federal Grants and Contracts Weekly: Funding Opportunities in Research, Training and Services. Aspen Publishers, Inc. • Weekly. $394.00 per year.

Government Contractor. Federal Publications, Inc. • Weekly. $1,032.00 per year.

Government Primecontracts Monthly. Government Data Publications, Inc. • Irregular. $96.00 per year.

MBI: The National Report on Minority, Women-Owned, and Disadvantaged Businesses. Community Development Services, Inc. CD Publications. • Semimonthly. $372.00 per year. Newsletter. Provides news of affirmative action, government contracts, minority business employment, and education/training for minorities in business. Formerly *Minorities in Business.*

The National Estimator. Society of Cost Estimating and Analysis. • Semiannual. $30.00 per year. Covers government contract estimating.

RESEARCH CENTERS AND INSTITUTES

Lexis.com Research System. Lexis-Nexis Group. Phone: 800-227-9597 or (937)865-6800 Fax: (937)865-6909 E-mail: webmaster@prod.lexis-nexis.com • URL: http://www.lexis.com • Fee-based Web site offers extensive searching of a wide variety of legal sources. Additional features include Daily Opinion Service, lexis.com Bookstore, Career Center, CLE Center, Law Schools, and Practice Pages ("Pages specific to areas of specialty").

TRADE/PROFESSIONAL ASSOCIATIONS

Contract Services Association of America. 1200 G St., N.W., Ste. 510, Washington, DC 20005-3802. Phone: (202)347-0600 Fax: (202)347-0608 E-mail: gary@csa-dc.org • URL: http://www.csa-dc.org.

National Contract Management Association. 1912 Woodford Rd., Vienna, VA 22182. Phone: 800-344-8096 or (703)448-9231 Fax: (703)448-0939 • URL: http://www.ncmahq.org.

Society of Cost Estimating and Analysis. 101 S. Whiting St., Suite 201, Alexandria, VA 22304. Phone: (703)751-8069 Fax: (703)461-7328 E-mail: scea@erols.com • URL: http://www.scea.com • Members are engaged in government contract estimating and pricing.

OTHER SOURCES

Federal Contracts Report. Bureau of National Affairs, Inc. • Weekly. $1,245.00 per year, Two volumes. Looseleaf. Developments affecting federal contracts and grants.

Federal Government Subcontract Forms. Robert J. English. West Group. • Three looseleaf volumes. $305.00. Periodic supplementation.

Government Contracts: Law, Administration and Procedure. Matthew Bender & Co., Inc. • $1,050.00. 17 looseleaf volumes. Periodic supplementation. Coverage of important aspects of government contracts.

Government Contracts Reports. CCH, Inc. • $2,249.00 per year. 10 looseleaf volumes. Weekly updates. Laws and regulations affecting government contracts.

Government Contracts Update: How to Target, Win, and Perform Government Contracts. United Communications Group (UCG). • Biweekly. $277.00 per year. Newsletter. Formerly *Federal Procurement Update.*

GOVERNMENT DOCUMENTS

See: GOVERNMENT PUBLICATIONS

GOVERNMENT EMPLOYEES

See also: BUREAUCRACY; CIVIL SERVICE; PUBLIC ADMINISTRATION

GENERAL WORKS

Improving Public Productivity: Concepts and Practice. Ellen D. Rosen. Sage Publications, Inc. • 1993. $52.00. A discussion of strategies for improving service quality and client satisfaction in public agencies at the local, state, and national level. Methods for measuring public sector productivity are included.

Performance Management in Government: Contemporary Illustrations. OECD Publications and Information Center. • 1996.

CD-ROM DATABASES

Leadership Library on CD-ROM: Who's Who in the Leadership of the United States. Leadership Directories, Inc. • Quarterly. $2,641.00 per year, including access to Internet version (weekly updates). Contains all 14 *Yellow Book* personnel directories on CD-ROM, providing contact and brief biographical information for about 400,000 individuals. Covers business, government, financial institutions, news media, law firms, associations, foreign representatives, and nonprofit organizations. Includes photographs.

Staff Directories on CD-ROM. CQ Staff Directories, Inc. • Three times a year. $495.00 per year. Provides the contents on CD-ROM of *Congressional Staff Directory, Federal Staff Directory*, and *Judicial Staff Directory*. Includes photographs and maps.

The Tax Directory [CD-ROM]. Tax Analysts. • Quarterly. Provides *The Tax Directory* listings on CD-ROM, covering federal, state, and international tax officials, tax practitioners, and corporate tax executives.

DIRECTORIES

The Almanac of the Executive Branch. Maximov Publications. • Annual. $149.00. Provides detailed information on more than 830 key staff memebers of the executive branch of the federal government. Includes educational background, previous employment, job responsibilities, etc.

Almanac of the Unelected: Staff of the U. S. Congress. Bernan Press. • Annual. $275.00. Provides detailed information on key staff members of the legislative branch of the federal government. Includes educational background, previous employment, job responsibilities, etc.

Carroll's County Directory. Carroll Publishing. • Semiannual. $255.00 per year. Lists about 42,000 officials in 3,100 U. S. counties, with expanded listings for counties having a population of over 50,000. Includes state maps.

Carroll's Federal & Federal Regional Directory: CD-ROM Edition. Carroll Publishing. • Bimonthly. $800.00 per year. Provides CD-ROM listings of more than 120,000 (55,000 high-level and 65,000 mid-level) U. S. government officials in Washington and throughout the country, including in military installations. Also available online.

Carroll's Federal Directory. Carroll Publishing. • Bimonthly. $325.00 per year. Lists 40,000 key U. S. officials, including members of Congress, Cabinet members, federal judges, Executive Office of the President personnel, and a wide variety of administrators.

Carroll's Federal Regional Directory. Carroll Publishing. • Semiannual. $255.00 per year. Lists more than 28,000 non-Washington based federal executives in administrative agencies, the courts, and military bases. Arranged in four sections: Alphabetical (last names), Organizational, Geographical, and Keyword. Includes maps.

Carroll's Municipal/County Directory: CD-ROM Edition. Carroll Publishing. • Semiannual. $750.00 per year. Provides CD-ROM listings of about 99,000 city, town, and county officials in the U. S. Also available online.

Carroll's Municipal Directory. Carroll Publishing. • Semiannual. $255.00 per year. Lists about 50,000 officials in 7,900 U. S. towns and cities, with expanded listings for cities having a population of over 25,000. Top 100 cities are ranked by population and size.

Carroll's State Directory. Carroll Publishing. • Three times a year. $300.00 per year. Lists about 42,000 individuals in executive, administrative, and legislative positions in 50 states, the District of Columbia, Puerto Rico, and the American Territories. Includes keyword and other indexing.

Carroll's State Directory: CD-ROM Edition. Carroll Publishing. • Three times a year. $600.00 per year. Provides CD-ROM listings of about 42,000 state officials, plus the text of all state constitutions and biographies of all governors. Also available online.

Congressional Directory. U.S. Government Printing Office. • Biennial. $45.00.

Congressional Staff Directory: With Biographical Information on Members and Key Congressional Staff. CQ Staff Directories, Inc. • Three times a year. $227.00 per year. Single copies, $89.00. Contains more than 3,200 detailed biographies of members of Congress and their staffs. Includes committees and subcommittees. Keyword and name indexes are provided.

Department of Defense Telephone Directory. Available from U. S. Government Printing Office. • Three times a year. $44.00 per year. An alphabetical directory of U. S. Department of Defense personnel, including Departments of the Army, Navy, and Air Force.

Federal Regional Yellow Book: Who's Who in the Federal Government's Departments, Agencies, Military Installations, and Service Academies Outside of Washington, DC. Leadership Directories, Inc. • Semiannual. $235.00 per year. Lists over 36,000 federal officials and support staff at 8,000 regional offices.

Federal Staff Directory: With Biographical Information on Executive Staff Personnel. CQ Staff Directories, Inc. • Three times a year. $227.00 per year. Single copies, $89.00. Lists 40,000 staff members of federal departments and agencies, with biographies of 2,600 key executives. Includes keyword and name indexes.

Federal Yellow Book: Who's Who in the Federal Departments and Agencies. Leadership Directories, Inc. • Quarterly. $305.00 per year. White House, Executive Office of the President and departments and agencies of the executive branch nationwide, plus 38,000 other personnel.

The Tax Directory. Tax Analysts. • Annual. $299.00. ($399.00 with quarterly CD-ROM updates.) Four volumes: *Government Officials Worldwide* (lists 15,000 state, federal, and international tax officials, with basic corporate and individual income tax rates for 100 countries); *Private Sector Professionals Worldwide* (lists 25,000 U.S. and foreign tax practitioners: accountants, lawyers, enrolled agents, and actuarial firms); *Corporate Tax Managers Worldwide* (lists 10,000 tax managers employed by U.S. and foreign companies).

United States Government Manual. National Archives and Records Administration. Available from U.S. Government Printing Office. • Annual. $46.00.

Worldwide Government Directory 2001. Available from The Gale Group. • 2001. $394.00. 19th edition. Published by Keesings Worldwide. Lists more than 32,000 key officials in the governments of over 199 countries.

ENCYCLOPEDIAS AND DICTIONARIES

International Encyclopedia of Public Policy and Administration. Jay M. Shafritz, editor. HarperCollins Publishers. • 1997. $550.00. Four volumes. Covers 20 major areas, such as public administration, government budgeting, industrial policy, nonprofit management, organizational theory, public finance, labor relations, and taxation. Includes a brief bibliography for each major entry and a comprehensive index.

HANDBOOKS AND MANUALS

The Federal Manager's Handbook: A Guide to Rehabilitating or Removing the Problem Employee. G. Jerry Shaw and William L. Bransford. FPMI Communications, Inc. • 1997. $24.95. Third revised edition.

Office of Personnel Management Operating Manuals. Available from U. S. Government Printing Office. • Four looseleaf manuals at various prices ($25.00 to $190.00). Price of each manual includes updates for an indeterminate period. Manuals provides details of the federal wage system, the federal wage system "Nonappropriated Fund", personnel recordkeeping, personnel actions, qualification standards, and data reporting.

INTERNET DATABASES

Bureau of Labor Statistics (BLS). U. S. Department of Labor, Bureau of Labor Statistics. Phone: (202)523-1092 E-mail: labstat.helpdesk@bls.gov • URL: http://www.bls.gov • Web site provides a great variety of employment, wage, price, and economic data. Some links are "Data," "Economy at a Glance," "Keyword Search of BLS Web Pages," "Regional Information," and "Other Statistical Sites." Fees: Free.

Fedstats. Federal Interagency Council on Statistical Policy. Phone: (202)395-7254 • URL: http://www.fedstats.gov • Web site features an efficient search facility for full-text statistics produced by more than 70 federal agencies, including the Census Bureau, the Bureau of Economic Analysis, and the Bureau of Labor Statistics. Boolean searches can be made within one agency or for all agencies combined. Links are offered to international statistical bureaus, including the UN, IMF, OECD, UNESCO, Eurostat, and 20 individual countries. Fees: Free.

U. S. Census Bureau: The Official Statistics. U. S. Bureau of the Census. Phone: (301)763-4100 Fax: (301)763-4794 • URL: http://www.census.gov • Web site is "Your Source for Social, Demographic, and Economic Information." Contains "Current U. S. Population Count," "Current Economic Indicators," and a wide variety of data under "Other Official Statistics." Keyword searching is provided. Fees: Free.

ONLINE DATABASES

DRI U.S. Central Database. Data Products Division. • Provides more than 23,000 business, financial, demographic, economic, foreign trade, and industry-related time series for the U.S. Includes national income, population, retail-wholesale trade, price indexes, labor data, housing, industrial production, banking, interest rates, money supply, etc. Time period is generally 1947 to date (some data back to 1929). Updating varies. Inquire as to online cost and availability.

PERIODICALS AND NEWSLETTERS

AFSCME Public Employee. American Federation of State, County, and Municipal Employees. • Bimonthly. Membership; free to libraries. Formerly *Public Employee Magazine*.

Employee Policy for the Private and Public Sector: State Capitals. Wakeman-Walworth, Inc. • Weekly. $245.00 per year. Newsletter. Formerly *From the State Capitals: Employee Policy for the Private and Public Sector.*

Federal Employee. National Federation of Federal Employees. • Monthly. $15.00 per year.

Federal Employee News Digest. Federal Employee News Digest, Inc. • Weekly. $59.00 per year.

Provides essential information for federal employees.

Federal Human Resources Week. LRP Publications. • 48 times a year. $325.00 per year. Newsletter. Covers federal personnel issues, including legislation, benefits, budgets, and downsizing.

Federal Jobs Digest. Breakthrough Publications, Inc. • Biweekly. Individuals, $125.00 per year; libraries, $112.50 per year. Lists 15,000 immediate job openings within the federal government in each issue.

Government Standard. American Federation of Government Employees. • Bimonthly. Membership.

Government Union Review. Public Service Research Foundation. • Quarterly. $20.00 per year. Academic quarterly covering the labor relations field.

RESEARCH CENTERS AND INSTITUTES

Office of Government Programs. Louisiana State University. Pleasant Hall, Room 379, Baton Rouge, LA 70803. Phone: (225)388-6746 Fax: (225)388-6200 E-mail: ogp@doce.lsu.edu • URL: http://www.doce.lsu.edu/government.

STATISTICS SOURCES

Business Statistics of the United States. Courtenay M. Slater, editor. Bernan Associates. • 1999. $74.00. Fifth edition. Based on *Business Statistics*, formerly issue by the Bureau of Economic Analysis, U. S. Department of Commerce. Provides basic data for a wide variety of U. S. industries, services, and economic indicators. Most statistics are shown annually for 29 years and monthly for the most recent four years.

Handbook of U. S. Labor Statistics: Employment, Earnings, Prices, Productivity, and Other Labor Data. Eva E. Jacobs, editor. Bernan Associates. • 1999. $74.00. Based on *Handbook of Labor Statistics*, formerly issued by the Bureau of Labor Statistics, U. S. Department of Labor. Includes the Bureau's projections of employment in the U. S. by industry and occupation. Provides a wide variety of data on the work force, prices, fringe benefits, and consumer expenditures.

Historical Tables, Budget of the United States Government. Available from U. S. Government Printing Office. • Annual. Issued by the Office of Management and Budget, Executive Office of the President (http://www.whitehouse.gov). Provides statistical data on the federal budget for an extended period of about 60 years in the past to projections of four years in the future. Includes federal debt and federal employment.

Public Employment. Bureau of the Census, U.S. Department of Commerce. Available from U.S. Government Printing Office. • Annual.

Social Statistics of the United States. Mark S. Littman, editor. Bernan Press. • 2000. $65.00. Includes statistical data on population growth, labor force, occupations, environmental trends, leisure time use, income, poverty, taxes, and other economic or demographic topics.

Statistical Abstract of the United States. Available from U. S. Government Printing Office. • Annual. $51.00. Issued by the U. S. Bureau of the Census.

A Statistical Portrait of the United States: Social Conditions and Trends. Mark S. Littman, editor. Bernan Press. • 1998. $89.00. Covers "social, economic, and environmental trends in the United States over the past 25 years." Includes statistical tables, graphs, and analysis relating to such topics as population, income, poverty, wealth, labor, housing, education, healthcare, air/water quality, and government.

Survey of Current Business. Available from U. S. Government Printing Office. • Monthly. $49.00 per year. Issued by Bureau of Economic Analysis, U. S. Department of Commerce. Presents a wide variety of business and economic data.

TRADE/PROFESSIONAL ASSOCIATIONS

American Federation of Government Employees. 80 F St., N.W., Washington, DC 20001. Phone: (202)737-8700 or (202)639-6419 Fax: (202)639-6441 E-mail: communications@afge.org • URL: http://www.afge.org.

American Federation of State, County and Municipal Employees. 1625 L St., N.W., Washington, DC 20036. Phone: (202)429-1000 Fax: (202)429-1293 • URL: http://www.afscme.org.

Civil Service Employees Association. P.O. Box 125, Albany, NY 12210. Phone: 800-342-4146 or (518)434-0191 Fax: (518)462-3639.

National Association of Government Employees. 159 Burgin Parkway, Quincy, MA 02169. Phone: (617)376-2220 Fax: (617)376-0285 E-mail: nage@erols.com • URL: http://www.nage.org.

National Federation of Federal Employees. 1016 16th St., N.W., Suite 300, Washington, DC 20036. Phone: (202)862-4400 Fax: (202)862-4432 • URL: http://www.nffe.org.

Tax Analysts. 6830 N. Fairfax Dr., Arlington, VA 22213. Phone: 800-955-3444 or (703)533-4400 Fax: (703)533-4444 E-mail: webmaster@tax.org • URL: http://www.tax.org • An advocacy group reviewing U. S. and foreign income tax developments. Includes a Tax Policy Advisory Board.

OTHER SOURCES

Carroll's Federal Organization Charts. Carroll Publishing. • Quarterly. $950.00 per year. Provides 200 large, fold-out paper charts showing personnel relationships in 2,100 federal departments and agencies. Charts are also available online and on CD-ROM.

Government Discrimination: Equal Protection Law and Litigation. James A. Kushner. West Group. • $140.00 per year. Looseleaf service. Periodic supplementation. Covers discrimination in employment, housing, and other areas by local, state, and federal offices or agencies. (Civil Rights Series).

Government Employee Relations Report. Bureau of National Affairs, Inc. • Weekly. $999.00 per year. Three volumes. Looseleaf. Concerned with labor relations in the public sector.

Opportunities in Government Careers. Neale J. Baxter. NTC/Contemporary Publishing Group. • 2001. $15.95. Edited for students and job seekers. Includes education requirements and salary data. (VGM Career Books.).

State Legislators' Occupations: 1994, A Survey. National Conference of State Legislatures. • 1994. $20.00. Presents survey results concerning the occupations of more than 7,000 state legislators. (Members of state legislatures usually combine government service with other occupations.).

GOVERNMENT EXPENDITURES

See: FEDERAL BUDGET

GOVERNMENT FINANCE

See: PUBLIC FINANCE

GOVERNMENT HOUSING PROJECTS

See: HOUSING

GOVERNMENT INVESTIGATIONS

GENERAL WORKS

Congressional Investigations: Law and Practice. John C. Grabow. Aspen Law and Business. • 1988. $95.00. Looseleaf service.

ABSTRACTS AND INDEXES

PAIS International in Print. Public Affairs Information Service, Inc. • Monthly. $650.00 per year; cumulations three times a year. Provides topical citations to the worldwide literature of public affairs, economics, demographics, sociology, and trade. Text in English; indexed materials in English, French, German, Italian, Portuguese and Spanish.

CD-ROM DATABASES

PAIS on CD-ROM. Public Affairs Information Service, Inc. • Quarterly. $1,995.00 per year. Provides a CD-ROM version of the online service, *PAIS International.* Contains over 400,000 citations to the literature of contemporary social, political, and economic issues.

ENCYCLOPEDIAS AND DICTIONARIES

Encyclopedia of Crime and Justice. Available from The Gale Group. • 2001. $425.00. Second edition. Four volumes. Published by Macmillan Reference USA. Contains extensive information on a wide variety of topics pertaining to crime, criminology, social issues, and the courts. (A revision of 1982 edition.).

Encyclopedia of Governmental Advisory Organizations. The Gale Group. • 2000. $615.00. 15th edition.

ONLINE DATABASES

CIS. Congressional Information Service, Inc. • Indexes publications of the United States Congress, 1970 to present. Inquire as to online cost and availability.

Newspaper and Periodical Abstracts. Bell & Howell Information and Learning. • Provides online coverage (citations and abstracts) of 25 major newspapers, 1,600 perodicals, and 70 TV programs. Covers business, economics, current affairs, health, fitness, sports, education, technology, government, consumer affairs, psychology, the arts, and the social sciences. Time period is 1986 to date, with daily updates. Inquire as to online cost and availability.

PAIS International. Public Affairs Information Service, Inc. • Corresponds to the former printed publications, *PAIS Bulletin* (1976-90) and *PAIS Foreign Language Index* (1972-90), and to the current *PAIS International in Print* (1991 to date). Covers economic, political, and sociological material appearing in periodicals, books, government documents, and other publications. Updating is monthly. Inquire as to online cost and availability.

TRADE/PROFESSIONAL ASSOCIATIONS

Federal Criminal Investigators Association. P.O. Box 23400, Washington, DC 20026. Phone: 800-961-7753 or (281)320-1242 Fax: (281)320-1242 E-mail: info@fedcia.org • URL: http://www.fedcia.org.

Society of Professional Investigators. 80 Eighth Ave., Suite 303, New York, NY 10011. Phone: (212)625-3533 or (718)331-7400 Fax: (718)259-2550 E-mail: admin@spionline.org • URL: http://www.spionline.org.

OTHER SOURCES

World of Criminal Justice. The Gale Group. • 2001. $150.00. Two volumes. Contains both topical and biographical entries relating to the criminal justice system and criminology.

GOVERNMENT OFFICIALS

See: BUREAUCRACY; GOVERNMENT EMPLOYEES

GOVERNMENT PROCUREMENT

See: GOVERNMENT PURCHASING

GOVERNMENT PUBLICATIONS

See also: CENSUS REPORTS

ABSTRACTS AND INDEXES

U. S. Government Periodicals Index. Congressional Information Service, Inc. • Quarterly. $995.00 per year. Annual cumulation. An index to approximately 180 periodicals issued by various agencies of the federal government.

BIBLIOGRAPHIES

Bibliographic Guide to Government Publications: Foreign. Available from The Gale Group. • Annual. $720.00. Two volumes. Published by G. K. Hall & Co. Lists government publications from countries other than the U. S.

Bibliographic Guide to Government Publications: U. S. Available from The Gale Group. • Annual. $620.00. Two volumes. Published by G. K. Hall & Co. Lists U. S. government publications.

Lesko's Info-PowerIII: Over 45,000 Free and Low Cost Sources of Information. Visible Ink Press. • 1996. $29.95. Third edition.

Monthly Catalog of United States Government Publications. U. S. Government Printing Office. • Monthly. $52.00 per year. Modified in 1996. Print edition now consists of very brief entries, indexed only by key words in titles.

State Government Research Checklist. Council of State Governments. • Bimonthly. $24.99 per year. Lists reports by state legislative research agencies, study committees, commissions, and independent organizations.

State Reference Publications: A Bibliographic Guide to State Blue Books, Legislative Manuals and Other General Reference Sources. Government Research Service. • Biennial. $70.00. State government directories, blue books, legislative manuals, statistical abstracts, judicial direcrories, local government directories, and other general publications; state capitols.

Subject Bibliography Index: A Guide to U. S. Government Information. Available from U. S. Government Printing Office. • Annual. Free. Issued by the Superintendent of Documents. Lists currently available subject bibliographies by title and by topic. Each *Subject Bibliography* describes government books, periodicals, posters, pamphlets, and subscription services available for sale from the Government Printing Office.

U. S. Government Books: Publications for Sale by the Government Printing Office. U. S. Government Printing Office. • Quarterly. Free. Describes best selling government documents and "new titles that reflect today's news and consumer issues.".

U. S. Government Information Catalog of New and Popular Titles. U. S. Government Printing Office. • Irregular. Free. Includes recently issued and popular publications, periodicals, and electronic products.

U. S. Government Information for Business. U. S. Government Printing Office. • Annual. Free. A selected list of currently available publications, periodicals, and electronic products on business, trade, labor, federal regulations, economics, and other topics. Also known as *Business Catalog.*

U.S. Government Subscriptions. U. S. Government Printing Office. • Quarterly. Free. Includes agency and subject indexes.

CD-ROM DATABASES

Monthly Catalog of United States Government Publications [CD-ROM]. U. S. Government Printing Office. • Monthly. $199.00 per year. Entries contain complete bibliographic information formerly appearing in the print edition of the *Monthly Catalog*. Each issue is cumulative, with author, title, and subject indexes. The January issue includes the *Periodicals Supplement*.

U. S. Government Periodicals Index (CD-ROM). Congressional Information Service, Inc. • Quarterly. $795.00 per year. Provides indexing on CD-ROM to about 180 federal government periodicals.

DIRECTORIES

Congressional Directory. U.S. Government Printing Office. • Biennial. $45.00.

Directory of Federal Libraries. William R. Evinger, editor. Oryx Press. • 1997. $97.50. Third edition.

Directory of Government Document Collections and Librarians. Government Documents Round Table. American Library Association, Washington Office. • Seventh edition. Price on application. A guide to federal, state, local, foreign, and international document collections in the U.S. Includes name of libratians and other government document professionals.

The Internet Blue Pages: The Guide to Federal Government Web Sites. Information Today, Inc. • Annual. $34.95. Provides information on more than 900 Web sites used by various agencies of the federal government. Includes indexes to agencies and topics. Links to all Web sites listed are available at http://www.fedweb.com. (CyberAge Books.).

National Five Digit Zip Code and Post Office Directory. U.S. Postal Service. • Annual. Two volumes. Formerly *National Zip Code and Post Office Directory-.*

United States Government Manual. National Archives and Records Administration. Available from U.S. Government Printing Office. • Annual. $46.00.

HANDBOOKS AND MANUALS

Guide to U. S. Government Publications. The Gale Group. • Annual. $360.00. Catalogs "important series, periodicals, and reference tools" published annually by the federal government. Includes references to annual reports of various agencies.

Standard Industrial Classification Manual. U.S. Department of Commerce, Bureau of the Census. Available from U.S. Government Printing Office. • 1987. $36.00.

Tapping the Government Grapevine: The User-Friendly Guide to U. S. Government Information Sources. Judith S. Robinson. Oryx Press. • 1998. $45.50. Third edition. Includes source information on statistics, regulations, patents, technology, nonprint items, bibliographies, and indexes. A special chapter by Karen Smith covers "Foreign and International Documents.".

United States Government Printing Office Style Manual. U. S. Government Printing Office. • 2000. $41.00. 29th edition. Supersedes the 1984 edition (28th). Designed to achieve uniformity in the style and form of government printing.

Using Government Documents: A How-To-Do-It Manual for School Librarians. Melody S. Kelly. Neal-Schuman Publishers, Inc. • 1992. $27.50. (How-to-Do-It Series).

Using Government Information Sources, Print and Electronic. Jean L. Sears and Marilyn K. Moody. Oryx Press. • 1994. $115.00. Second edition. Contains detailed information in four sections on subject searches, agency searches, statistical searches, and special techniques for searching. Appendixes give selected agency and publisher addresses, telephone numbers, and computer communications numbers.

INTERNET DATABASES

GPO Access: Keeping America Informed Electronically. U. S. Government Printing Office Sales Program, Bibliographic Systems Branch. Phone: 888-293-6498 or (202)512-1530 Fax: (202)512-1262 E-mail: gpoaccess@gpo.gov • URL: http://www.access.gpo.gov • Web site provides searching of the GPO's Sales Product Catalog (SPC), also known as Publications Reference File (PRF). Covers all "Government information products currently offered for sale by the Superintendent of Documents." There are also specialized search pages for individual databases, such as the *Code of Federal Regulations*, the *Federal Register*, and *Commerce Business Daily*. Updated daily. Fees: Free.

ONLINE DATABASES

American Statistics Index: A Comprehensive Guide and Index to the Statistical Publications of the United States Government [Online]. Congressional Information Service, Inc. • Indexes and abstracts, 1973 to date. Inquire as to online cost and availability.

CIS. Congressional Information Service, Inc. • Indexes publications of the United States Congress, 1970 to present. Inquire as to online cost and availability.

GPO Monthly Catalog. U. S. Government Printing Office. • Contains over 375,000 online citations to U. S. government publications, 1976 to date, with monthly updates. Corresponds to the printed *Monthly Catalog of United States Government Publications*. Inquire as to online cost and availability.

GPO Publications Reference File. U. S. Government Printing Office. • An online guide to federal government publications in print (currently for sale), forthcoming, and recently out-of-print. Biweekly updates. Inquire as to online cost and availability.

PERIODICALS AND NEWSLETTERS

Documents to the People. Government Documents Round Table. American Library Association. • Quarterly. $20.00 per year.

Federal Register. Office of the Federal Register. Available from U.S. Government Printing Office. • Daily except Saturday and Sunday. $697.00 per year. Publishes regulations and legal notices issued by federal agencies, including executive orders and presidential proclamations. Issued by the National Archives and Records Administration (http://www.nara.gov).

Government Publications News. Bernan Associates. • Monthly. Free. Controlled circulation newsletter providing information on recent publications from the U. S. Government Printing Office and selected international agencies.

Internet Connection: Your Guide to Government Resources. Glasser Legalworks. • 10 times a year. $89.00 per year. Newsletter (print) devoted to finding free or low-cost U. S. Government information on the Internet. Provides detailed descriptions of government Web sites.

Journal of Government Information: An International Review of Policy, Issues an d

Resources. Elsevier Science. • Bimonthly. $570.00 per year.

OTHER SOURCES

FedWorld: A Program of the United States Department of Commerce. National Technical Information Service. • Web site offers "a comprehensive central access point for searching, locating, ordering, and acquiring government and business information." Emphasis is on searching the Web pages, databases, and government reports of a wide variety of federal agencies. Fees: Free.

FirstGov: Your First Click to the U. S. Government. General Services Administration. • Free Web site provides extensive links to federal agencies covering a wide variety of topics, such as agriculture, business, consumer safety, education, the environment, government jobs, grants, health, social security, statistics sources, taxes, technology, travel, and world affairs. Also provides links to federal forms, including IRS tax forms. Searching is offered, both keyword and advanced.

GOVERNMENT PURCHASING

See also: GOVERNMENT CONTRACTS; GOVERNMENT PUBLICATIONS

DIRECTORIES

United States Government Manual. National Archives and Records Administration. Available from U.S. Government Printing Office. • Annual. $46.00.

United States Government Purchasing and Sales Directory. U.S. Small Business Administration. Available from U.S. Government Printing Office. • 1994.

ONLINE DATABASES

CIS. Congressional Information Service, Inc. • Indexes publications of the United States Congress, 1970 to present. Inquire as to online cost and availability.

PERIODICALS AND NEWSLETTERS

Commerce Business Daily. Industry and Trade Administration, U.S. Department of Commerce. Available from U.S. Government Printing Office. • Daily. Priority, $324.00 per year; non-priority, $275.00 per year. Synopsis of *U.S. Government Proposed Procurement, Sales and Contract Awards.*

Federal Register. Office of the Federal Register. Available from U.S. Government Printing Office. • Daily except Saturday and Sunday. $697.00 per year. Publishes regulations and legal notices issued by federal agencies, including executive orders and presidential proclamations. Issued by the National Archives and Records Administration (http://www.nara.gov).

Government Product News. Penton Media Inc. • Monthly. Free to qualified personnel; others, $50.00 per year.

Navy Supply Corps Newsletter. Available from U. S. Government Printing Office. • Bimonthly. $20.00 per year. Newsletter issued by U. S. Navy Supply Systems Command. Provides news of Navy supplies and stores activities.

TRADE/PROFESSIONAL ASSOCIATIONS

National Association of State Procurement Officials. c/o Association Management Resources, 167 W. Main St., Suite 600, Lexington, KY 40507. Phone: (606)231-1877 or (606)231-1963 Fax: (606)231-1928 E-mail: croberts@amrinc.net • URL: http://www.naspo.org • Purchasing officials of the states and territories.

National Institute of Government Purchasing. 151 Spring St., Herndon, VA 20170. Phone: 800-367-6447 or (703)736-8900 Fax: (703)736-9644 • URL: http://www.nigp.org.

OTHER SOURCES

Federal Contracts Report. Bureau of National Affairs, Inc. • Weekly. $1,245.00 per year, Two volumes. Looseleaf. Developments affecting federal contracts and grants.

Government Contracts Reports. CCH, Inc. • $2,249.00 per year. 10 looseleaf volumes. Weekly updates. Laws and regulations affecting government contracts.

Government Contracts Update: How to Target, Win, and Perform Government Contracts. United Communications Group (UCG). • Biweekly. $277.00 per year. Newsletter. Formerly *Federal Procurement Update.*

GOVERNMENT REGULATION OF INDUSTRY

See: REGULATION OF INDUSTRY

GOVERNMENT REGULATION OF RAILROADS

See: INTERSTATE COMMERCE

GOVERNMENT RESEARCH

See also: GOVERNMENT PUBLICATIONS; GOVERNMENT STATISTICS

ABSTRACTS AND INDEXES

NTIS Alerts: Business & Economics. National Technical Information Service.

NTIS Alerts: Government Inventions for Licensing. National Technical Information Service. • Semimonthly. $270.00 per year. Identifies new inventions available from various government agencies. Covers a wide variety of industrial and technical areas. Formerly *Abstract Newsletter.*

PAIS International in Print. Public Affairs Information Service, Inc. • Monthly. $650.00 per year; cumulations three times a year. Provides topical citations to the worldwide literature of public affairs, economics, demographics, sociology, and trade. Text in English; indexed materials in English, French, German, Italian, Portuguese and Spanish.

CD-ROM DATABASES

PAIS on CD-ROM. Public Affairs Information Service, Inc. • Quarterly. $1,995.00 per year. Provides a CD-ROM version of the online service, *PAIS International.* Contains over 400,000 citations to the literature of contemporary social, political, and economic issues.

DIRECTORIES

Government Research Directory. The Gale Group. • 2000. $530.00 14th edition. Lists more than 4,800 research facilities and programs of the United States and Canadian federal governments.

GRA Professional Directory of Who's Who in Governmental Research. Governmental Research Association, Inc. • Annual. $50.00. Lists information on governmental research organization throughout the country.

Unique 3-in-1 Research and Development Directory. Government Data Publications, Inc. • Annual. $15.00. Government contractors in the research and development fields. Included with subscription to *R and D Contracts Monthly.* Formerly *Research and Development Directory.*

ENCYCLOPEDIAS AND DICTIONARIES

Encyclopedia of Governmental Advisory Organizations. The Gale Group. • 2000. $615.00. 15th edition.

HANDBOOKS AND MANUALS

Using Government Information Sources, Print and Electronic. Jean L. Sears and Marilyn K. Moody. Oryx Press. • 1994. $115.00. Second edition. Contains detailed information in four sections on subject searches, agency searches, statistical searches, and special techniques for searching. Appendixes give selected agency and publisher addresses, telephone numbers, and computer communications numbers.

ONLINE DATABASES

NTIS Bibliographic Data Base. National Technical Information Service. • Contains citations and abstracts to unrestricted reports of government-sponsored research, 1964 to date. Covers a wide range of technical, engineering, business, and social science topics. Monthly updates. Inquire as to online cost and availability.

PAIS International. Public Affairs Information Service, Inc. • Corresponds to the former printed publications, *PAIS Bulletin* (1976-90) and *PAIS Foreign Language Index* (1972-90), and to the current *PAIS International in Print* (1991 to date). Covers economic, political, and sociological material appearing in periodicals, books, government documents, and other publications. Updating is monthly. Inquire as to online cost and availability.

Research Centers and Services Directories. The Gale Group. • Contains profiles of about 30,000 research centers, organizations, laboratories, and agencies in 147 countries. Corresponds to the printed *Research Centers Directory, International Research Centers Directory, Government Research Directory,* and *Research Services Directory.* Updating is semiannual. Inquire as to online cost and availability.

PERIODICALS AND NEWSLETTERS

Federal Research Report: Weekly Report on Federal Grants and Contracts to Research Institutions. Business Publishers, Inc. • Weekly. $270.00 per year.

GRA Reporter. Governmental Research Association, Inc. • Quarterly. $75.00 per year. Update on GRA-member agencies.

The Information Freeway Report: Free Business and Government Information Via Modem. Washington Researchers Ltd. • Monthly. $160.00 per year. Newsletter. Provides news of business and government databases that are available free of charge through the Internet or directly. Emphasis is on federal government databases and electronic bulletin boards (Fedworld).

R and D Contracts Monthly (Research and Development): A Continuously Up-dated Sales nd R and D Tool For All Research Organizations and Manufacturers. Government Data Publications, Inc. • Monthly. $96.00 per year. Lists recently awarded government contracts. Annual *Directory* available.

RESEARCH CENTERS AND INSTITUTES

Bureau of Governmental Research. University of Maryland. School of Public Affairs, 2101 Van Munching Hall, College Park, MD 20742. Phone: (301)405-6330 Fax: (301)403-4675.

Division of Government Research. University of New Mexico. 1920 Lomas Blvd., N.E., Room 166, Albuquerque, NM 87131-6025. Phone: (505)277-3305 Fax: (505)277-6540 E-mail: dgrint@unm.edu • URL: http://www.unm.edu/~dgrint/dgr.html.

Inter-University Consortium for Political and Social Research. University of Michigan. P.O. Box 1248,

Ann Arbor, MI 48106-1248. Phone: (734)998-9900 Fax: (734)998-9889 E-mail: netmail@icpsr.umich.edu • URL: http://www.icpsr.umich.edu.

TRADE/PROFESSIONAL ASSOCIATIONS
Governmental Research Association. 402 Samford Hall, Birmingham, AL 35229-7017. Phone: (205)726-2482 Fax: (205)726-2900.

OTHER SOURCES
FedWorld: A Program of the United States Department of Commerce. National Technical Information Service. • Web site offers "a comprehensive central access point for searching, locating, ordering, and acquiring government and business information." Emphasis is on searching the Web pages, databases, and government reports of a wide variety of federal agencies. Fees: Free.

FirstGov: Your First Click to the U. S. Government. General Services Administration. • Free Web site provides extensive links to federal agencies covering a wide variety of topics, such as agriculture, business, consumer safety, education, the environment, government jobs, grants, health, social security, statistics sources, taxes, technology, travel, and world affairs. Also provides links to federal forms, including IRS tax forms. Searching is offered, both keyword and advanced.

GOVERNMENT RESEARCH SUPPORT

See: FEDERAL AID

GOVERNMENT SERVICE

See: CIVIL SERVICE

GOVERNMENT, STATE

See: STATE GOVERNMENT

GOVERNMENT STATISTICS

See also: BUSINESS STATISTICS; GOVERNMENT PUBLICATIONS; STATISTICS SOURCES

ABSTRACTS AND INDEXES
American Statistics Index: A Comprehensive Guide and Index to the Statistical Publications of the United States Government. Congressional Information Service, Inc. • Monthly. Quarterly and annual cumulations. Price varies.

Current Index to Statistics: Applications, Methods, and Theory. American Statistical Association. • Annual. Price on application. An index to journal articles on statistical applications and methodology.

CD-ROM DATABASES
Statistical Masterfile. Congressional Information Service. • Quarterly. Price varies. Provides CD-ROM versions of *American Statistics Index, Index to International Statistics,* and *Statistical Reference Index.* Contains indexing and abstracting of a wide variety of published statistics sources, both governmental and private.

DIRECTORIES
Government Information on the Internet. Greg R. Notess. Bernan Associates. • Annual. $38.50. directory of publicly-accessible Internet sites maintained by the U. S. Government. Also includes selected foreign government sites, state sites, and non-government sites containing government-provided data.

HANDBOOKS AND MANUALS
Guide to Everyday Economic Statistics. Gary E. Clayton and Martin G. Giesbrecht. McGraw-Hill. • 1997. $14.38. Fourth edition. Contains clear explanations of the commonly used economic indicators.

Using Government Information Sources, Print and Electronic. Jean L. Sears and Marilyn K. Moody. Oryx Press. • 1994. $115.00. Second edition. Contains detailed information in four sections on subject searches, agency searches, statistical searches, and special techniques for searching. Appendixes give selected agency and publisher addresses, telephone numbers, and computer communications numbers.

INTERNET DATABASES
Fedstats. Federal Interagency Council on Statistical Policy. Phone: (202)395-7254 • URL: http://www.fedstats.gov • Web site features an efficient search facility for full-text statistics produced by more than 70 federal agencies, including the Census Bureau, the Bureau of Economic Analysis, and the Bureau of Labor Statistics. Boolean searches can be made within one agency or for all agencies combined. Links are offered to international statistical bureaus, including the UN, IMF, OECD, UNESCO, Eurostat, and 20 individual countries. Fees: Free.

ONLINE DATABASES
ASI (American Statistics Index). Congressional Information Service. • A comprehensive online index, with abstracts, to the statistical publications of over 500 federal government offices and agencies from 1973 to date. A wide variety of information is indexed, with emphasis on demographic, economic, social, and natural resources data. Updated monthly. Inquire as to online cost and availability.

STATISTICS SOURCES
Internal Revenue Service Data Book. Available from U. S. Government Printing Office. • Annual. $3.50. "Contains statistical tables and organizational information previously included in the Internal Revenue Service annual report." (Internal Revenue Service Publication, 55B.).

Revenue Statistics. OECD Publications and Information Center. • Annual. $65.00. Presents data on government revenues in OECD countries, classified by type of tax and level of government. Text in English and French.

Social Statistics of the United States. Mark S. Littman, editor. Bernan Press. • 2000. $65.00. Includes statistical data on population growth, labor force, occupations, environmental trends, leisure time use, income, poverty, taxes, and other economic or demographic topics.

Standard & Poor's Statistical Service. Current Statistics. Standard & Poor's. • Monthly. $688.00 per year. Includes 10 *Basic Statistics* sections, *Current Statistics Supplements* and *Annual Security Price Index Record.*

Statistical Abstract of the United States. Available from U. S. Government Printing Office. • Annual. $51.00. Issued by the U. S. Bureau of the Census.

A Statistical Portrait of the United States: Social Conditions and Trends. Mark S. Littman, editor. Bernan Press. • 1998. $89.00. Covers "social, economic, and environmental trends in the United States over the past 25 years." Includes statistical tables, graphs, and analysis relating to such topics as population, income, poverty, wealth, labor, housing, education, healthcare, air/water quality, and government.

TRADE/PROFESSIONAL ASSOCIATIONS
American Statistical Association. 1429 Duke St., Alexandria, VA 22314-3402. Phone: (703)684-1221 Fax: (703)684-2037 E-mail: asainfo@amstat.org • URL: http://www.amstat.org • A professional society concerned with statistical theory, methodology, and applications. Sections include Survey Research Methods, Government Statistics, and Business and Economic Statistics.

National Association for Public Health Statistics and Information Systems. 1220 19th St., N. W., Ste. 802, Washington, DC 20036. Phone: (202)463-8851 Fax: (202)463-4870 E-mail: tme.nq@naphsis.org • URL: http://www.naphsis.org • Members are officials of state and local health agencies.

OTHER SOURCES
FedWorld: A Program of the United States Department of Commerce. National Technical Information Service. • Web site offers "a comprehensive central access point for searching, locating, ordering, and acquiring government and business information." Emphasis is on searching the Web pages, databases, and government reports of a wide variety of federal agencies. Fees: Free.

FirstGov: Your First Click to the U. S. Government. General Services Administration. • Free Web site provides extensive links to federal agencies covering a wide variety of topics, such as agriculture, business, consumer safety, education, the environment, government jobs, grants, health, social security, statistics sources, taxes, technology, travel, and world affairs. Also provides links to federal forms, including IRS tax forms. Searching is offered, both keyword and advanced.

GOVERNMENT SURPLUS

See: SURPLUS PRODUCTS

GRADUATE WORK IN UNIVERSITIES

See also: ADULT EDUCATION; BUSINESS EDUCATION; COLLEGES AND UNIVERSITIES

GENERAL WORKS
Gravy Training: Inside the Business of Business Schools. Stuart Crainer and Des Dearlove. Jossey-Bass, Inc., Publishers. • 1999. $25.00. Provides a critical look at major American business schools.

Overeducation in the U.S. Labor Market. Russell W. Rumberger. Greenwood Publishing Group, Inc. • 1981. $57.95.

ABSTRACTS AND INDEXES
Current Index to Journals in Education (CIJE). Oryx Press. • Monthly. $245.00 per year. Semiannual cumulations, $475.00.

Education Index. H.W. Wilson Co. • 10 times a year. Service basis.

Educational Administration Abstracts. Corwin Press, Inc. • Quarterly. Indivduals, $110.00 per year; institutions, $475.00 per year.

CD-ROM DATABASES
College Blue Book CD-ROM. Available from The Gale Group. • Annual. $250.00. Produced by Macmillan Reference USA. Serves as electronic version of printed *College Blue Book.* Provides detailed information on programs, degrees, and financial aid sources in the U.S. and Canada.

DIRECTORIES
AACSB: The International Association for Management Education. American Assembly of Collegiate Schools of Business. • Annual. $15.00. Lists over 800 member institutions offering instructional programs in business administration at

the college level. Formerly (American Assembley of Collegiate Schools of Business Membership Directory).

Faculty White Pages. The Gale Group. • 1991. $135.00. "Telephone book" classified arrangement of over 537,000 U. S. college faculty members in 41 subject sections. A roster of institutions is included.

Peterson's Computer Science and Electrical Engineering Programs. Peterson's. • 1996. $24.95. A guide to 900 accredited graduate degree programs related to computers or electrical engineering at colleges and universities in the U. S. and Canada.

Peterson's Graduate and Professional Programs: Business, Education, Health, Information Studies, Law, and Social Work. Peterson's Magazine Group. • Annual. $27.95. Provides details of graduate and professional programs in business, law, information, and other fields at colleges and universities. Formerly *Peterson's Guide to Graduate Programs in Business, Education, Health, Information Studies, Law and Social Work.*

Peterson's Graduate and Professional Programs: Engineering and Applied Sciences. Peterson's. • Annual. $37.95. Provides details of more than 3,400 graduate and professional programs in engineering and related fields at colleges and universities. Formerly *Peterson's Guide to Graduate Programs in Engineering and Professional Sciences.*

Peterson's Guide to Graduate and Professional Programs: An Overview. Peterson's. • Annual. $27.95. Six volumes provide details of more than 31,000 graduate programs at 1,600 colleges and universities: 1. An Overview; 2. Humanities, Arts, and Social Sciences; 3. MBA; 4. Visual and Performing Arts; 5. Engineering and Applied Sciences; 6. Business, Education, Health, Information Studies, Law, and Social Work. (Volumes are available individually.).

Peterson's Guide to MBA Programs: The Most Comprehensive Guide to U. S., Canadian, and International Business Schools. Peterson's. • 1996. $21.95. Provides detailed information on about 850 graduate programs in business at 700 colleges and universities in the U. S., Canada, and other countries.

Peterson's Professional Degree Programs in the Visual and Performing Arts. Peterson's. • Annual. $24.95. A directory of more than 900 degree programs in art, music, theater, and dance at 600 colleges and professional schools.

The World of Learning. Available from The Gale Group. • $712.50. 50th edition. Covers about 26,000 colleges, libraries, museums, learned societies, academies, and research institutions throughout the world. Published by Europa Publications.

HANDBOOKS AND MANUALS

Directory of Graduate Programs. Educational Testing Service. • Irregular. $80.00. Four volumes. $20.00 per volume. 15th edition. Accredited institutions that offer advanced deree in 84 graduate program areas. Degrees not included are J.D., D.D.S., M.D. and some other professional degrees.

Financing Graduate School: How to Get Money for Your Master's or Ph.D. Patricia McWade. Peterson's. • 1996. $16.95. Second revised edition. Discusses the practical aspects of various types of financial aid for graduate students. Includes bibliographic and directory information.

Official Guide for GMAT Review (Graduate Management Admission Test). Graduate Management Admissions Council. Educational Testing Service. • Biennial. $11.95. Provides sample tests, answers, and explanations for the Graduate Management Admission Test (GMAT).

ONLINE DATABASES

Dissertation Abstracts Online. Bell & Howell Information and Learning. • Citations to all dissertations accepted for doctoral degrees by accredited U.S. educational institutions, 1861 to date. Includes British theses, 1988 to date. Inquire as to online cost and availability.

Education Index Online. H. W. Wilson Co. • Indexes a wide variety of periodicals related to schools, colleges, and education, 1984 to date. Monthly updates. Inquire as to online cost and availability.

PERIODICALS AND NEWSLETTERS

AACSB Newsline. American Assembly of Collegiate Schools of Business, The International Association for Management Education. • Quarterly. $15.00 per yer. Contains news of AACSB activities and developments i higher education for business and management.

Journal of Higher Education. Ohio State University Press. • Bimonthly. Individuals, $42.00 per year; institutions, $90.00 per year. Issues important to faculty administrators and program managers in higher education.

Resources in Education. Educational Resources Information Center. Available from U.S. Government Printing Office. • Monthly. $102.00 per year. Reports on educational research.

RESEARCH CENTERS AND INSTITUTES

Center for the Study of Higher Education. Pennsylvania State University. 403 S. Allen St., Suite 104, University Park, PA 16801-5252. Phone: (814)865-6346 Fax: (814)865-3638 E-mail: fxc2@psu.edu • URL: http://www.ed.psu.edu/cshe.

ERIC Clearinghouse on Higher Education. George Washington University. Graduate School of Education and Human Development, One Dupont Circle, Suite 630, Washington, DC 20036. Phone: 800-773-3742 or (202)296-2597 Fax: (202)452-1844 E-mail: akezar@eric-he.edu • URL: http://www.eriche.org.

STATISTICS SOURCES

Degrees and Other Awards Conferred by Institutions of Higher Education. Available from U. S. Government Printing Office. • Annual. Issued by the National Center for Education Statistics, U. S. Department of Education. Provides data on the number of degrees awarded at the associate's, bachelor's, master's, and doctor's levels. Includes fields of study and racial-ethnic-sex data by major field or discipline.

Digest of Education Statistics. Available from U. S. Government Printing Office. • Annual. $44.00. Covers all areas of education from kindergarten through graduate school. Includes data from both government and private sources. Compiled by National Center for Education Statistics, U. S. Department of Education.

Occupational Projections and Training Data. Available from U. S. Government Printing Office. • Biennial. $7.00. Issued by Bureau of Labor Statistics, U. S. Department of Labor. Contains projections of employment change and job openings over the next 15 years for about 500 specific occupations. Also includes the number of associate, bachelor's, master's, doctoral, and professional degrees awarded in a recent year for about 900 specific fields of study.

School Enrollment, Social and Economic Characteristics of Students. Available from U. S. Government Printing Office. • Annual. Issued by the U. S. Bureau of the Census. Presents detailed tabulations of data on school enrollment of the civilian noninstitutional population three years old and over. Covers nursery school, kindergarten, elementary school, high school, college, and graduate school. Information is provided on age, race, sex, family income, marital status, employment, and other characteristics.

Survey of Salaries. American Assembly of Collegiate Schools of Business. • Annual. $20.00, Reports aggregate salary data of business school administrators and faculty.

TRADE/PROFESSIONAL ASSOCIATIONS

AACSB - The International Association for Management Education. 600 Emerson Rd., Suite 300, St. Louis, MO 63141-6762. Phone: (314)872-8481 Fax: (314)872-8495 • URL: http://www.aacsb.edu.

Association of Graduate Schools in the Association of American Universities. 1200 New York Ave., Suite 550, Washington, DC 20005. Phone: (202)408-7500 Fax: (202)408-8184.

Association of Master of Business Administration Executives. c/o AMBA Center, Five Summit Place, Branford, CT 06405. Phone: (203)315-5221 Fax: (203)483-6186.

Consortium for Graduate Study in Management. 200 S. Hanley Rd., Suite 1102, Saint Louis, MO 63105-3415. Phone: 888-658-6814 or (314)935-5011 Fax: (314)935-5014 E-mail: cgsmfrontdesk@mail.olin.wustl.edu • URL: http://www.cgsm.wustl.edu:8010/.

Council of Graduate Schools. One Dupont Circle, N.W., Suite 430, Washington, DC 20036-1173. Phone: (202)223-3791 Fax: (202)331-7157 E-mail: ngaffney@cgs.nche.edu • URL: http://www.cgsnet.org.

Graduate Management Admission Council. 1750 Tysons Blvd., No. 1100, McLean, VA 22102-4220. Phone: (703)749-0131 Fax: (703)749-0169 E-mail: gmat@ets.org • URL: http://www.gmat.org • Members are graduate schools of business administration and management.

Graduate Record Examinations Board. 51-L Rosedale Rd., Princeton, NJ 08541. Phone: (609)683-2002 or (609)771-7670 Fax: (609)683-2040 E-mail: gre-info@rosedale.org • URL: http://www.gre.org.

OTHER SOURCES

American Universities and Colleges. Walter de Gruyter, Inc. • 2001. $249.50. 16th edition. Two volumes. Produced in collaboration with the American Council on Education. Provides full descriptions of more than 1,900 institutions of higher learning, including details of graduate and professional programs.

Educational Rankings Annual: A Compilation of Approximately 3,500 Published Rankings and Lists on Every Aspect of Education. The Gale Group. • 2000. $220.00. Provides national, regional, local, and international rankings of a wide variety of educational institutions, including business and professional schools.

GRAFT (POLITICS)

See: CRIME AND CRIMINALS

GRAIN DEALERS

See: GRAIN INDUSTRY

GRAIN ELEVATORS

See: GRAIN INDUSTRY

GRAIN INDUSTRY

ABSTRACTS AND INDEXES

Field Crop Abstracts: Monthly Abstract Journal on World Annual Cereal, Legume, Root, Oilseed and Fibre Crops. Available from CABI Publishing North America. • Monthly. $1,465.00 per year. Published in England by CABI Publishing, formerly Commonwealth Agricultural Bureaux. Provides worldwide coverage of the literature.

Food Science and Technology Abstracts. International Food Information Service Publishing. • Monthly. $1,780.00 per year. Provides worldwide coverage of the literature of food technology and food production.

Foods Adlibra: Key to the World's Food Literature. Foods Adlibra Publications. • Semimonthly.Provides journal citations and abstracts to the literature of food technology and packaging.

CD-ROM DATABASES

AGRICOLA on SilverPlatter. Available from SilverPlatter Information, Inc. • Quarterly. $825.00 per year. Produced by the National Agricultural Library. Provides about three million citations on CD-ROM to the literature of agriculture, agricultural economics, animal sciences, entomology, fertilizer, food, forestry, nutrition, pesticides, plant science, water resources, and other topics. Each quarterly disc covers the past ten years, with archival discs available from 1970.

Food Science and Technology Abstracts [CD-ROM]. Available from SilverPlatter Information, Inc. • Quarterly. $3,700 per year. Produced by International Food Information Service (home page is http://www.ifis.org). Provides worldwide coverage on CD-ROM of the literature of food technology and production. Various types of publications are indexed, with abstracts, including about 1,800 periodicals. Time period is 1969 to date.

DIRECTORIES

National Grain and Feed Association Directory. • Annual. Price on application.

North American Grain and Milling Annual. Sosland Publishing Co. • Annual. $95.00. Features listings of the major grain facilities in the U.S. and Canada. Provides an annual overview of the U.S. grain industry and a complete reference to equipment and service suppliers. Formerly *Milling Directory Buyer's Guide.*

ENCYCLOPEDIAS AND DICTIONARIES

Encyclopedia of Agriculture Science. Charles J. Arntzen and Ellen M. Ritter, editors. Academic Press, Inc. • 1994. $625.00. Four volumes.

FINANCIAL RATIOS

Almanac of Business and Industrial Financial Ratios. Leo Troy. Prentice Hall. • Annual. $99.95. Contains financial ratios derived from federal tax returns. Ratios for each of about 200 industries are arranged according to company asset size.

Annual Statement Studies. Robert Morris Associates: The Association of Lending and Credit Risk Professiona. • Annual. Free to members; non-members, $140.00. Median and quartile financial ratios are given for over 400 kinds of manufacturing, wholesale, retail, construction, and consumer finance establishments. Data is sorted by both asset size and sales volume. Includes a clearly written "Definition of Ratios" and an alphabetical industry index.

INTERNET DATABASES

Fedstats. Federal Interagency Council on Statistical Policy. Phone: (202)395-7254 • URL: http://www.fedstats.gov • Web site features an efficient search facility for full-text statistics produced by more than 70 federal agencies, including the Census Bureau, the Bureau of Economic Analysis, and the Bureau of Labor Statistics. Boolean searches can be made within one agency or for all agencies combined. Links are offered to international statistical bureaus, including the UN, IMF, OECD, UNESCO, Eurostat, and 20 individual countries. Fees: Free.

USDA. United States Department of Agriculture. Phone: (202)720-2791 E-mail: agsec@usda.gov • URL: http://www.usda.gov • The USDA home page has six sections: News and Information; What's New; About USDA; Agencies; Opportunities; Search and Help. Keyword searching is offered from the USDA home page and from various individual agency home pages. Agencies are the Economic Research Service, Agricultural Marketing Service, National Agricultural Statistics Service, National Agricultural Library, and about 12 others. Updating varies. Fees: Free.

ONLINE DATABASES

Agricola. U.S. National Agricultural Library. • Covers worldwide agricultural literature. Over 2.8 million citations, 1970 to present, with monthly updates. Inquire as to online cost and availability.

CAB Abstracts. CAB International North America. • Contains 46 specialized abstract collections covering over 10,000 journals and monographs in the areas of agriculture, horticulture, forest products, farm products, nutrition, dairy science, poultry, grains, animal health, entomology, etc. Time period is 1972 to date, with monthly updates. Inquire as to online cost and availability. *CAB Abstracts on CD-ROM* also available, with annual updating.

DRI U.S. Central Database. Data Products Division. • Provides more than 23,000 business, financial, demographic, economic, foreign trade, and industry-related time series for the U.S. Includes national income, population, retail-wholesale trade, price indexes, labor data, housing, industrial production, banking, interest rates, money supply, etc. Time period is generally 1947 to date (some data back to 1929). Updating varies. Inquire as to online cost and availability.

Food Science and Technology Abstracts [online]. IFIS North American Desk. • Produced by International Food Information Service. Provides about 500,000 online citations, with abstracts, to the international literature of food science, technology, commodities, engineering, and processing. Approximately 2,000 periodicals are covered. Time period is 1969 to date, with monthly updates. Inquire as to online cost and availability.

FOODS ADLIBRA. General Mills, Inc. • Contains online citations, with abstracts, to the technical and business literature of food processing and packaging. New products and new ingredients are featured. Covers about 250 trade journals and 500 research journals from 1974 to date, with monthly updates. Inquire as to online cost and availability.

PERIODICALS AND NEWSLETTERS

Grain and Feed Weekly Summary and Statistics. U.S. Dept. of Agriculture. Agricultural Marketing Service, Livestock and Seed Div. • Weekly. $85.00 per year. Formerly *Grain and Feed Market News.*

Milling and Baking News. Sosland Publishing Co. • Weekly. $122.00 per year. News magazine for the breadstuffs industry.

PRICE SOURCES

Commercial Review. Oregon Feed and Grain Association. Commercial Review, Inc. • Weekly. $30.00 per year.

Nebraska Farmer. Nebraska Farmer Co. Farm Progress Cos. • 15 times a year. $19.95 per year.

RESEARCH CENTERS AND INSTITUTES

Cereal Disease Laboratory U.S. Department of Agricultural Research Service. 1551 Lindig St., St. Paul, MN 55108. Phone: (612)625-6299 Fax: (612)649-5054 • URL: http://www.cdl.umn.edu/.

Food and Feed Grain Institute. Kansas State University. Waters Hall, Room 105, Manhattan, KS 66506-4030. Phone: (785)532-4057 Fax: (785)532-5861 E-mail: reb@ksu.edu • URL: http://www.ksu.edu.

STATISTICS SOURCES

Agricultural Statistics. Available from U. S. Government Printing Office. • Annual. Produced by the National Agricultural Statistics Service, U. S. Department of Agriculture. Provides a wide variety of statistical data relating to agricultural production, supplies, consumption, prices/price-supports, foreign trade, costs, and returns, as well as farm labor, loans, income, and population. In many cases, historical data is shown annually for 10 years. In addition to farm data, includes detailed fishery statistics.

Business Statistics of the United States. Courtenay M. Slater, editor. Bernan Associates. • 1999. $74.00. Fifth edition. Based on *Business Statistics*, formerly issue by the Bureau of Economic Analysis, U. S. Department of Commerce. Provides basic data for a wide variety of U. S. industries, services, and economic indicators. Most statistics are shown annually for 29 years and monthly for the most recent four years.

FAO Quarterly Bulletin of Statistics. Food and Agriculture Organization of the United Nations. Available from UNIPUB. • Quarterly. $20.00 per year. Provides international data on agricultural production, trade, and prices, covering the major commodities of many countries. Text in English, French, and Spanish. Formerly *FAO Monthly Bulletin of Statistics.*

Foreign Agricultural Trade of the United States. Available from U. S. Government Printing Office. • Monthly. $50.00 per year. Issued by the Economic Research Service of the U. S. Department of Agriculture. Provides data on U. S. exports and imports of agricultural commodities.

Statistical Annual: Grains, Options on Agricultural Futures. Chicago Board of Trade. • Annual. Includes historical data on Wheat Futures, Options on Wheat Futures, Corn Futures, Options on Corn Futures, Oats Futures, Soybean Futures, Options on Soybean Futures, Soybean Oil Futures, Soybean Meal Futures.

Survey of Current Business. Available from U. S. Government Printing Office. • Monthly. $49.00 per year. Issued by Bureau of Economic Analysis, U. S. Department of Commerce. Presents a wide variety of business and economic data.

United States Census of Agriculture. U.S. Bureau of the Census. • Quinquennial. Results presented in reports, tape, CD-ROM, and Diskette files.

World Agricultural Supply and Demand Estimates. Available from U. S. Government Printing Office. • Monthly. $38.00 per year. Issued by the Economics and Statistics Service and the Foreign Agricultural Service of the U. S. Department of Agriculture. Consists mainly of statistical data and tables.

TRADE/PROFESSIONAL ASSOCIATIONS

Grain Elevator and Processing Society. P.O. Box 15026, Minneapolis, MN 55415-0026. Phone: (612)339-4625 Fax: (612)339-4644 • URL: http://www.geaps.com.

National Grain and Feed Association. 1201 New York Ave., N.W., Suite 830, Washington, DC 20005-3917. Phone: (202)289-0873 Fax: (202)289-

5388 E-mail: ngfa@ngfa.org • URL: http://www.ngfa.org.

National Grain Trade Council. 1300 L St., N.W., Suite 925, Washington, DC 20005. Phone: (202)842-0400 Fax: (202)789-7223.

North American Export Grain Association. 1300 L St., N.W., Suite 900, Washington, DC 20005. Phone: (202)682-4030 Fax: (202)682-4033 E-mail: naega@cwixmail.com.

Transportation, Elevator and Grain Merchants Association. 1300 L St., N.W., Suite 925, Washington, DC 20005. Phone: (202)842-0400 Fax: (202)789-7223.

U.S. Grains Council. 1400 K St., N.W., Suite 1200, Washington, DC 20005. Phone: (202)789-0789 Fax: (202)898-0522 E-mail: grains@grains.org • URL: http://www.grains.org.

OTHER SOURCES

Major Food and Drink Companies of the World. Available from The Gale Group. • 2001. $855.00. Fourth edition. Two volumes. Published by Graham & Whiteside. Contains profiles and trade names for more than 9,000 important food and beverage companies in various countries. In addition to foods, includes both alcoholic and nonalcoholic drink products.

Thomas Food and Beverage Market Place. Grey House Publishing. • Annual. $295.00. Three volumes. Contains more than 40,000 entries covering food companies, beverages, food equipment, warehouse companies, food brokers, wholesalers, importers, and exporters. Formerly *Thomas Food Industry Register.*

GRANITE

See: QUARRYING

GRANTS-IN-AID

See also: ARTS MANAGEMENT; FEDERAL AID; FOUNDATIONS

GENERAL WORKS

A Casebook of Grant Proposals in the Humanities. William Coleman and others, editors. Neal-Schuman Publishers, Inc. • 1982. $45.00.

From Idea to Funded Project: Grant Proposals that Work. Jane C. Belcher and Julia M. Jacobsen. Oryx Press. • 1992. $26.50. Fourth edition. Formerly *A Process for the Development of Ideas.*

Grant Budgeting and Finance: Getting the Most Out of Your Grant Dollar. Frea E. Sladek and Eugene L. Stein. Perseus Publishing. • 1981. $65.00.

Grants for Arts, Culture, and the Humanities. The Foundation Center. • 1997. $75.00. (Grants Guides Series).

ABSTRACTS AND INDEXES

Foundation Grants Index. The Foundation Center. • Irregular. $165.00 per year. Over 5,000 grants of $10,000 or more. Formerly *Foundation Grants Quarterly.*

CD-ROM DATABASES

Grants on Disc. The Gale Group. • Quarterly. $695.00 per year. On CD-ROM, provides detailed information on about 410,000 grants. Describes up to 100 of the highest grants awarded by each of 6,000 large foundations and corporations.

DIRECTORIES

Directory of Operating Grants. Research Grant Guides. • Annual. $59.50. Contains profiles for approximately 800 foundations that award grants to nonprofit organizations for such operating expenses as salaries, rent, and utilities. Geographical arrangement, with indexes.

Directory of Research Grants. Oryx Press. • Annual. $135.00. More than 6,000 research grants available from government, business, foundation and private sources.

Foundation Grants to Individuals. The Foundation Center. • Biennial. $65.00. Over 3,300 foundations that make grants to individuals.

The Foundation Reporter: Comprehensive Profiles and Giving Analyses of America's Major Private Foundations. The Taft Group. • Annual. $425.00. Provides detailed information on major U. S. foundations. Eight indexes (location, grant type, recipient type, personnel, etc.).

Government Assistance Almanac: The Guide to Federal, Domestic, Financial and Other Programs Covering Grants, Loans, Insurance, Personal Payments and Benefits. J. Robert Dumouchel, editor. Omnigraphics, Inc. • Annual. $190.00. Describes more than 1,300 federal assistance programs available from about 50 agencies. Includes statistics, a directory of 4,000 field offices, and comprehensive indexing.

Grants for Libraries and Information Services. The Foundation Center. • Annual. $75.00. Foundations and organizations which have awarded grants made the preceding year for public, academic, research, special, and school libraries; for archives and information centers; for consumer information; and for philanthropy information centers.

Grants Register (Graduate Student Financial Aid). St. Martin's Press. • Annual. $120.00. About 2,000 sources in the United Kingdom, Ireland, Australia, Canada and the U.S. and other English-speaking areas which award financial aid for graduate study, research or travel.

Guide to Federal Funding for Governments and Non-Profits. Government Information Services. • Quarterly. $339.00 per year. Contains detailed descriptions of federal grant programs in economic development, housing, transportation, social services, science, etc. Semimonthly supplement available: *Federal Grant Deadline Calendar.*

Peterson's Scholarships, Grants, and Prizes: Your Complete Guide to College Aid from Private Sources. Peterson's. • 1998. $26.95. Second edition.

HANDBOOKS AND MANUALS

Foundation Fundamentals: A Guide for Grantseekers. The Foundation Center. • 1999. $34.75. Sixth edition.

Getting Funded: A Complete Guide to Proposal Writing. Mary S. Hall. Portland State University. • 1988. $23.95. Third edition. Proposal writing for public and private grants.

Guide to Proposal Writing. Jane C. Geever and Patricia McNeil. The Foundation Center. • 1997. $34.95. Revised edition. An explanation of proposal-writing techniques. Includes interviews with foundation officials and examples of successful grant proposals.

How to Write Proposals that Produce. Joel P. Bowman and Bernadine P. Branchaw. Oryx Press. • 1992. $23.50. An extensive guide to effective proposal writing for both nonprofit organizations and businesses. Covers writing style, intended audience, format, use of graphs, charts, and tables, documentation, evaluation, oral presentation, and related topics.

Proposal Planning and Writing. Lynn E. Miner and others. Oryx Press. • 1998. $34.50. Second edition. Discusses the steps necessary to locate and obtain funding from the federal government, foundations, and corporations.

INTERNET DATABASES

American Visions Non-Profit Center. American Visions Society/American Visions Magazine. Phone: (202)462-1779 Fax: (202)462-3997 • URL: http://www.americanvisions.com • Web site "Created by African Americans for African Americans..enables non-profit professionals to share ideas, provide assistance, seek funding, [and] browse for information.." Includes "Black Endowment," a monthly online newsletter covering people, grants, non-profit seminars, and non-profit news. Registration required, with two options: "Grantseeker" or "Grantmaker." Free 30-day trial available.

GaleNet: Your Information Community. The Gale Group. Phone: 800-877-GALE or (248)699-GALE Fax: 800-414-5043 or (248)699-8069 E-mail: galenet@gale.com • URL: http://www.galenet.com • Web site provides a wide variety of full-text information from Gale databases, Taft, and other sources. Covers associations, biography, business directories, education, the information industry, literature, publishing, and science. Fee-based subscriptions are available for individual databases (free demonstration). Includes Boolean search features and the BRS/Search user interface.

Welcome to the Foundation Center. The Foundation Center. Phone: (212)620-4230 Fax: (212)691-1828 E-mail: mfn@fdncenter.org • URL: http://www.fdncenter.org • Web site provides a wide variety of information about foundations, grants, and philanthropy, with links to philanthropic organizations. "Grantmaker Information" link furnishes descriptions of available funding. Fees: Free.

ONLINE DATABASES

Grants. Oryx Press. • References grants by federal, state, and local governments and other organizations; current file includes grants with deadlines within the next six months. Inquire as to online cost and availability.

PERIODICALS AND NEWSLETTERS

Federal Assistance Monitor. Community Development Services. CD Publications. • Semimonthly. $279.00 per year. Newsletter. Provides news of federal grant and loan programs for social, economic, and community purposes. Monitors grant announcements, funding, and availability.

Federal Grants and Contracts Weekly: Funding Opportunities in Research, Training and Services. Aspen Publishers, Inc. • Weekly. $394.00 per year.

Grantsmanship Center Magazine: A Compendium of Resources for Nonprofit Organizations. Grantsmanship Center. • Irregular. Free to qualified personnel. Contains a variety of concise articles on grant-related topics, such as program planning, proposal writing, fundraising, non-cash gifts, federal project grants, benchmarking, taxation, etc.

RESEARCH CENTERS AND INSTITUTES

Foundation Center. 79 Fifth Ave., New York, NY 10003-3076. Phone: 800-424-9836 or (212)807-3690 Fax: (212)807-3691 • URL: http://www.fdncenter.org.

TRADE/PROFESSIONAL ASSOCIATIONS

Council for Aid to Education. 342 Madison Ave., Suite 1532, New York, NY 10173. Phone: (212)661-5800 Fax: (212)661-9766 E-mail: ellen@cae.org • URL: http://www.cae.org.

National Association of Student Financial Aid Administrators. 1129 20th St., N.W. Ste 400, Washington, DC 20036-5020. Phone: (202)785-0453 Fax: (202)785-1487 E-mail: ask@nasfaa.org •

URL: http://www.nsfaa.org • Serves as a national forum for matters related to student aid.

National Grants Management Association. P.O. Box 5333, Rockville, MD 20854-5333. Phone: (301)871-0730 Fax: (301)460-9240 E-mail: ngma@erols.com • URL: http://www.ngma-grants.org.

OTHER SOURCES

FedWorld: A Program of the United States Department of Commerce. National Technical Information Service. • Web site offers "a comprehensive central access point for searching, locating, ordering, and acquiring government and business information." Emphasis is on searching the Web pages, databases, and government reports of a wide variety of federal agencies. Fees: Free.

FirstGov: Your First Click to the U. S. Government. General Services Administration. • Free Web site provides extensive links to federal agencies covering a wide variety of topics, such as agriculture, business, consumer safety, education, the environment, government jobs, grants, health, social security, statistics sources, taxes, technology, travel, and world affairs. Also provides links to federal forms, including IRS tax forms. Searching is offered, both keyword and advanced.

GRAPE INDUSTRY

See: FRUIT INDUSTRY

GRAPHIC ARTS INDUSTRY

See also: COMMERCIAL ART; DESIGN IN INDUSTRY; LITHOGRAPHY; PRINTING AND PRINTING EQUIPMENT INDUSTRIES

GENERAL WORKS

Institute of Paper Science and Technology Graphic Arts Bulletin. Institute of Paper Science and Technology. • Monthly. $400.00 per volume. Formerly *Graphic Arts Literature Abstracts.*

The Visual Display of Quantitative Information. Edward R. Tufte. Graphics Press. • 1992. $40.00. A classic work on the graphic display of numerical data, including many illustrations. The two parts are "Graphical Practice," and "Theory of Data Graphics.".

ABSTRACTS AND INDEXES

Art Index. H. W. Wilson Co. • Quarterly. Annual cumulations. Service basis for print edition; CD-ROM edition, $1,495.00 per year. Subject and author index to periodicals in art, architecture, industrial design, city planning, photography, and various related topics.

GATF World. Graphic Arts Technical Foundation. • Bimonthly. $75.00 per year. Technical articles of interest to the graphic communications industry. Incorporates *Graphic Arts Abstracts.*

DIRECTORIES

Design Firm Directory: A Listing of Firms and Consultants in Grap hic Design in the United States. Wefler & Associates, Inc. • Annual. $145.00. Three volumes. Provides information on more than 2,600 commercial, private, and consulting design firms. Includes graphic, interior, landscape, and environmental designers.

Graphic Arts Blue Book. A. F. Lewis and Co. Inc. • Auuual. $85.00. Eight regional editions. Printing plants, bookbinders, imagesetters, platemakers, paper merchants, paper manufacturers, printing machine manufacturers and dealers, and others serving the printing industry.

ENCYCLOPEDIAS AND DICTIONARIES

Dictionary of the Graphic Arts Industry. Wolfgang Muller. Elsevier Science. • 1981. $240.75. Text in English, French, German, Hungarian, and Polish.

Graphically Speaking: An Illustrated Guide to the Working Language of Design and Publishing. Mark Beach. Coast to Coast Books. • 1992. $29.50. Provides practical definitions of 2,800 terms used in printing, graphic design, publishing, and desktop publishing. Over 300 illustrations are included, about 40 in color.

NTC's Mass Media Dictionary. R. Terry Ellmore. NTC/Contemporary Publishing. • 1993. $24.95. Covers television, radio, newspapers, magazines, film, graphic arts, books, billboards, public relations, and advertising. Terms are related to production, research, audience measurement, audio-video engineering, printing, publishing, and other areas.

FINANCIAL RATIOS

Annual Statement Studies. Robert Morris Associates: The Association of Lending and Credit Risk Professiona. • Annual. Free to members; non-members, $140.00. Median and quartile financial ratios are given for over 400 kinds of manufacturing, wholesale, retail, construction, and consumer finance establishments. Data is sorted by both asset size and sales volume. Includes a clearly written "Definition of Ratios" and an alphabetical industry index.

PIA Financial Ratio Studies. Printing Industries of America, Inc. • Annual. Members, $650.00 set or $100.00 per volume; non-members, $995.00 set or $1,155.00 per volume. 14 volumes.

HANDBOOKS AND MANUALS

Getting It Printed: How to Work with Printers and Graphic Arts Services to Assure Quality, Stay on Schedule, and Control Costs. Mark Beach and Eric Kenly. F and W. Publications, Inc. • 1998. $32.99. Third edition.

Graphic Artists Guild Handbook of Pricing and Ethical Guidelines: Pricing and Ethical Guidelines. Graphic Artists Guild. • 2000. 32.95. 10th edition.

Graphic Designer's Production Handbook. Norman Sanders and William Bevington. Hastings House Publishers. • 1982. $12.95. (Visual Communication Books Series).

Newspaper Designer's Handbook. Timothy Harrower. McGraw-Hill Higher Education. • 1997. $28.25. Fourth edition.

ONLINE DATABASES

Art Index Online. H. W. Wilson Co. • Indexes a wide variety of art-related periodicals, 1984 to date. Monthly updates. Inquire as to online cost and availability.

PERIODICALS AND NEWSLETTERS

Color Publishing. PennWell Corp., Advanced Technology Div. • Bimonthly. $29.70 per year.

Desktop Publishers Journal. Business Media Group LLC. • Ten times a year. $49.00 per year. Edited for professional publishers, graphic designers, and industry service providers. Covers new products and emerging technologies for the electronic publishing industry.

Graphic Arts Monthly. Cahners Business Information. • Monthly. $110.00 per year.

In-Plant Graphics. North American Publishing Co. • Monthly. $79.00 per year. Formerly *In-Plant Reproductions.*

Step-By-Step Graphics: The How-To Reference Magazine for Visual Communicators. Dynamic Graphics, Inc. • Bimonthly. $42.00 per year; with *Step-by-Step Electronic Design*, $90.00 per year.

Taga Newsletter. Technical Association of the Graphic Arts. • Quarterly. Membership.

RESEARCH CENTERS AND INSTITUTES

Design Research Unit. Massachusetts College of Art, 621 Huntington Ave., Boston, MA 02115. Phone: (617)232-1492 Fax: (617)566-4034 • Conducts research related to the design of printed matter, including annual reports, letterheads, posters, and brochures.

Technical and Educational Center of the Graphic Arts and Imaging. Rochester Institute of Technology, 67 Lomb Memorial Dr., Rochester, NY 14623-5603. Phone: 800-724-2536 or (716)475-2680 Fax: (716)475-7000 E-mail: webmail@rit.edu • URL: http://www.rit.edu/cime/te.

TRADE/PROFESSIONAL ASSOCIATIONS

American Institute of Graphic Arts. 164 Fifth Ave., New York, NY 10010. Phone: 800-548-1634 or (212)807-1990 Fax: (212)807-1799 • URL: http://www.aiga.org.

Design Management Institute. 29 Temple Place, 2nd Fl., Boston, MA 02111. Phone: (617)338-6380 Fax: (617)338-6570 E-mail: dmistaff@dmi.org • URL: http://www.dmi.org • Membership includes firms concerned with various kinds of commercial design, including product, graphic, interior, exhibit, package, and architectural.

Graphic Artists Guild. 90 John St., Suite 403, New York, NY 10038-3202. Phone: 800-500-2627 or (212)791-3400 Fax: (212)791-0333 E-mail: pr@gag.com • URL: http://www.gag.org/.

Graphic Arts Technical Foundation. 200 Deer Run Rd., Sewickley, PA 15143-2600. Phone: 800-910-4283 or (412)741-6860 Fax: (412)741-2311 E-mail: info@gatf.org • URL: http://www.gatf.org.

Graphic Communications International Union. 1900 L St., N.W., Washington, DC 20036. Phone: (202)462-1400 Fax: (202)721-0600 • URL: http://www.gciu.org.

Research and Engineering Council of the Graphic Arts Industry. P.O. Box 1086, White Stone, VA 22578-1086. Phone: (804)436-9922 Fax: (804)436-9511 E-mail: recouncil@aol.com • URL: http://www.recouncil.org.

Society of American Graphic Artists. 32 Union Square, Room 1214, New York, NY 10003. Phone: (212)260-5706.

Technical Association of the Graphic Arts. 68 Lomb Memorial Dr., Rochester, NY 14623-5604. Phone: (716)475-7470 Fax: (716)475-2250 E-mail: info@taga.org • URL: http://www.taga.org.

GRAPHICS, COMPUTER

See: COMPUTER GRAPHICS

GRAPHS AND CHARTS

GENERAL WORKS

The Visual Display of Quantitative Information. Edward R. Tufte. Graphics Press. • 1992. $40.00. A classic work on the graphic display of numerical data, including many illustrations. The two parts are "Graphical Practice," and "Theory of Data Graphics.".

ENCYCLOPEDIAS AND DICTIONARIES

Information Graphics-A Comprehensive Illustrated Reference: Visual Tools for Analyzing, Managing, and Communicating. Robert L. Harris. Management Graphics. • 1996. $60.00. Provides more than 850 alphabetical entries and about 4,000 illustrations. Covers the practical application of charts, graphs, maps, diagrams, and tables.

HANDBOOKS AND MANUALS

Designing Infographics. Eric K. Meyer. Hayden. • 1997. $39.99. A basic handbook on the design and presentation of computer-generated charts, graphs, tables, maps, diagrams, etc.

Power Pitches: How to Produce Winning Presentations Using Charts, Slides, Video, and Multimedia. Alan L. Brown. McGraw-Hill Professional. • 1997. $39.95. Includes "Ten Rules of Power Pitching.".

PERIODICALS AND NEWSLETTERS

Harvard Management Communication Letter. Harvard Business School Press. • Monthly. $79.00 per year. Newsletter. Provides practical advice on both electronic and conventional business communication: e-mail, telephone, cell phones, memos, letters, written reports, speeches, meetings, and visual presentations (slides, flipcharts, easels, etc.). Also covers face-to-face communication, discussion, listening, and negotiation.

Presentations: Technology and Techniques for Effective Communication. Lakewood Publications, Inc. • Monthly. $50.00 per year. Covers the use of presentation hardware and software, including audiovisual equipment and computerized display systems. Includes an annual *"Buyers Guide to Presentation Products.".*

GRAPHITE

See: MINES AND MINERAL RESOURCES

GRAVEL INDUSTRY

See: QUARRYING

GREASE

See: LUBRICATION AND LUBRICANTS

GREETING CARD INDUSTRY

TRADE/PROFESSIONAL ASSOCIATIONS

Greeting Card Association. 1030 15th St., N.W., Suite 870, Washington, DC 20005. Phone: (202)393-1778 Fax: (202)393-0336 • URL: http://www.greetingcard.org.

OTHER SOURCES

The Greeting Card Market. Available from MarketResearch.com. • 1998. $2,750.00. Published by Packaged Facts. Provides market data for various kinds of greeting cards, with sales projections to 2002.

GRINDING AND POLISHING

See: ABRASIVES INDUSTRY

GROCERY BUSINESS

See also: CHAIN STORES; FOOD INDUSTRY; SUPERMARKETS

ALMANACS AND YEARBOOKS

Progressive Grocer Annual Report of the Grocery Industry. Bill Communications, Inc. • Annual. $15.00.

DIRECTORIES

Directory of Supermarket, Grocery, and Convenience Store Chains. Chain Store Guide. • Annual. $300.00. Provides information on about 2,200 food store chains operating 30,000 individual stores. Store locations are given.

Directory of Wholesale Grocers: Service Merchandisers. Chain Store Age. • Annual. $300.00. Profiles over 2,000 cooperatives, voluntaries, non-sponsoring wholesalers, cash and carry warehouses, and nearly 220 service merchandisers. Formerly *Directory of Cooperatives, Voluntaries, and Wholesale Grocers.*

Grocery Distribution Magazine Directory of Warehouse Equipment, Fixtures, and Services. Trend Publishing, Inc. • Annual. $7.50. Covers products related to food warehousing, distribution, and storage.

International Private Label Directory. E. W. Williams Publications Co. • Annual. $75.00. Provides information on over 2,000 suppliers of a wide variety of private label and generic products: food, over-the-counter health products, personal care items, and general merchandise. Formerly *Private Label Directory.*

Trade Dimensions' Market Scope. Trade Dimensions. • Annual. $325.00. Statistics of grocery distribution for 249 metropolitan areas. Formerly *Progressive Grocer's market Scope.*

FINANCIAL RATIOS

Almanac of Business and Industrial Financial Ratios. Leo Troy. Prentice Hall. • Annual. $99.95. Contains financial ratios derived from federal tax returns. Ratios for each of about 200 industries are arranged according to company asset size.

Food Marketing Industry Speaks. Food Marketing Institute. • Annual. Members, $30.00; non-members, $75.00. Provides data on overall food industry marketing performance, including retail distribution and store operations.

Operations Review. Food Marketing Institute. • Quarterly. $50.00 per year. Includes operating ratios for food retailing companies.

HANDBOOKS AND MANUALS

Convenience Food Store. Entrepreneur Media, Inc. • Looseleaf. $59.50. A practical guide to starting a convenience food store. Covers profit potential, start-up costs, market size evaluation, owner's time required, site selection, lease negotiation, pricing, accounting, advertising, promotion, etc. (Start-Up Business Guide No. E1173.).

Trade Dimensions' Marketing Guidebook. Trade Dimensions. • Annual. $340.00. Over 850 major chain and independent food retailers and wholesalers in the United States and Canada; also includes food brokers, rack jobbers, candy and tobacco distributors, and magazine distributors. Formerly *Progressive Grocer's Marketing Guidebook.*

INTERNET DATABASES

Fedstats. Federal Interagency Council on Statistical Policy. Phone: (202)395-7254 • URL: http://www.fedstats.gov • Web site features an efficient search facility for full-text statistics produced by more than 70 federal agencies, including the Census Bureau, the Bureau of Economic Analysis, and the Bureau of Labor Statistics. Boolean searches can be made within one agency or for all agencies combined. Links are offered to international statistical bureaus, including the UN, IMF, OECD, UNESCO, Eurostat, and 20 individual countries. Fees: Free.

ONLINE DATABASES

DRI U.S. Central Database. Data Products Division. • Provides more than 23,000 business, financial, demographic, economic, foreign trade, and industry-related time series for the U.S. Includes national income, population, retail-wholesale trade, price indexes, labor data, housing, industrial production, banking, interest rates, money supply, etc. Time period is generally 1947 to date (some data back to 1929). Updating varies. Inquire as to online cost and availability.

PERIODICALS AND NEWSLETTERS

Food and Beverage Newsletter. National Safety Council. • Bimonthly. Members, $15.00 per year; non-members, $19.00 per year.

Food Industry Newsletter: All the Food News That Matters. Newsletters, Inc. • 26 times a year. $245.00 per year. Irregular updates. A summary of key industry news for food executives.

Food Trade News. Best-Met Publishing Co., Inc. • Monthly. $36.00 per year. Reports on the retail food industry in Pennsylvania, Delaware, southern New Jersey and northern Maryland.

Griffin's Modern Grocer. Griffin Publishing Co., Inc. • Monthly. $45.00 per year. Formerly *Modern Grocer.*

Grocery Headquarters: The Newspaper for the Food Industry. Trend Publishing, Inc. • Monthly. $100.00 per year. Covers the sale and distribution of food products and other items sold in supermarkets and grocery stores. Edited mainly for retailers and wholesalers. Formerly *Grocery Marketing.*

Produce Merchandising: The Packer's Retailing and Merchandising Magazine. Vance Publishing Corp., Produce Div. • Monthly. $35.00 per year. Provides information and advice on the retail marketing and promotion of fresh fruits and vegetalbe.

Progressive Grocer: The Magazine of Supermarketing. Bill Communications, Inc. • Monthly. $99.00 per year.

STATISTICS SOURCES

Business Statistics of the United States. Courtenay M. Slater, editor. Bernan Associates. • 1999. $74.00. Fifth edition. Based on *Business Statistics*, formerly issue by the Bureau of Economic Analysis, U. S. Department of Commerce. Provides basic data for a wide variety of U. S. industries, services, and economic indicators. Most statistics are shown annually for 29 years and monthly for the most recent four years.

Survey of Current Business. Available from U. S. Government Printing Office. • Monthly. $49.00 per year. Issued by Bureau of Economic Analysis, U. S. Department of Commerce. Presents a wide variety of business and economic data.

WEFA Industrial Monitor. John Wiley and Sons, Inc. • Annual. $65.00. Prepared by industry analysts at WEFA, an economic forecasting and consulting firm (originally Wharton Econometric Forecasting Associates). Contains discussions of the outlook for major U. S. industries, with many 10-year forecasts (WEFA Web site is http://www.wefa.com).

TRADE/PROFESSIONAL ASSOCIATIONS

Association Sales and Marketing Companies. 2100 Reston Parkway, Suite 400, Reston, VA 20191-1218. Phone: (703)758-7790 Fax: (703)758-7787 E-mail: info@asmc.org • URL: http://www.asmc.org.

Food Distributors International. 201 Park Washington Court, Falls Church, VA 22046. Phone: (703)532-9400 Fax: (703)538-4673 E-mail: staff@fdi.org • URL: http://www.fdi.org • Members are wholesale grocery companies catering to institutions.

Food Marketing Institute. 800 Connecticut Ave., N.W., Washington, DC 20006. Phone: (202)452-8444 Fax: (202)429-4519 E-mail: fmi@fmi.org • URL: http://www.fm.org.

Grocery Manufacturers of America. 1010 Wisconsin Ave., N.W., Suite 900, Washington, DC 20007. Phone: (202)337-9400 Fax: (202)337-4508.

National Food Distributors Association. 401 N. Michigan Ave., Ste. 2200, Chicago, IL 60611-4267.

Phone: (312)644-6610 Fax: (312)321-6869 • URL: http://www.specialtyfoods.org/.

National Food Processors Association. 1301 Eye St., N.W., Ste. 300, Washington, DC 20005. Phone: (202)639-5900 Fax: (202)639-5932 E-mail: nfpa@nfpa-food.org • URL: http://www.nfpa-food.org.

National Grocers Association. 1825 Samuel Morse Dr., Reston, VA 22190-5317. Phone: (703)437-5300 Fax: (703)437-7768 E-mail: info@nationalgrocers.org • URL: http://www.nationalgrocers.org.

OTHER SOURCES

Thomas Food and Beverage Market Place. Grey House Publishing. • Annual. $295.00. Three volumes. Contains more than 40,000 entries covering food companies, beverages, food equipment, warehouse companies, food brokers, wholesalers, importers, and exporters. Formerly *Thomas Food Industry Register.*

GROSS NATIONAL PRODUCT

See also: NATIONAL ACCOUNTING

ENCYCLOPEDIAS AND DICTIONARIES

Worldmark Encyclopedia of National Economies. The Gale Group. • 2002. $295.00. Four volumes. Covers both the current and historical development of the economies of 200 foreign nations. Includes analysis and statistics.

HANDBOOKS AND MANUALS

Nations of the World: A Political, Economic, and Business Handbook. Grey House Publishing. • 2000. $135.00. Includes descriptive data on economic characteristics, population, gross domestic product (GDP), banking, inflation, agriculture, tourism, and other factors. Covers "all the nations of the world.".

INTERNET DATABASES

Bureau of Economic Analysis (BEA). U. S. Department of Commerce, Bureau of Economic Analysis. Phone: (202)606-9900 Fax: (202)606-5310 E-mail: webmaster@bea.doc.gov • URL: http://www.bea.doc.gov • Web site includes "News Release Information" covering national, regional, and international economic estimates from the BEA. Highlights of releases appear online the same day, complete text and tables appear the next day. "Recent News Releases" section provides titles for past nine months, with links. "BEA Data and Methodology" includes "Frequently Requested NIPA Data" (national income and product accounts, such as gross domestic product and personal income). Other statistics are available. Fees: Free.

Fedstats. Federal Interagency Council on Statistical Policy. Phone: (202)395-7254 • URL: http://www.fedstats.gov • Web site features an efficient search facility for full-text statistics produced by more than 70 federal agencies, including the Census Bureau, the Bureau of Economic Analysis, and the Bureau of Labor Statistics. Boolean searches can be made within one agency or for all agencies combined. Links are offered to international statistical bureaus, including the UN, IMF, OECD, UNESCO, Eurostat, and 20 individual countries. Fees: Free.

ONLINE DATABASES

DRI U.S. Central Database. Data Products Division. • Provides more than 23,000 business, financial, demographic, economic, foreign trade, and industry-related time series for the U.S. Includes national income, population, retail-wholesale trade, price indexes, labor data, housing, industrial production, banking, interest rates, money supply, etc. Time period is generally 1947 to date (some data back to 1929). Updating varies. Inquire as to online cost and availability.

STATISTICS SOURCES

Business Statistics of the United States. Courtenay M. Slater, editor. Bernan Associates. • 1999. $74.00. Fifth edition. Based on *Business Statistics*, formerly issue by the Bureau of Economic Analysis, U. S. Department of Commerce. Provides basic data for a wide variety of U. S. industries, services, and economic indicators. Most statistics are shown annually for 29 years and monthly for the most recent four years.

Economic Indicators Handbook: Time Series, Conversions, Documentation. The Gale Group. • 2000. $195.00. Sixth edition. Provides data for about 175 U. S. economic indicators, such as the consumer price index (CPI), gross national product (GNP), and the rate of inflation. Values for series are given since inception, in both original form and adjusted for inflation. A bibliography of sources is included.

Survey of Current Business. Available from U. S. Government Printing Office. • Monthly. $49.00 per year. Issued by Bureau of Economic Analysis, U. S. Department of Commerce. Presents a wide variety of business and economic data.

TRADE/PROFESSIONAL ASSOCIATIONS

Institute for Economic Analysis. c/o Richard Atlee, P.O. Box 1510, Southwest Harbor, ME 04679-1510. Phone: (207)244-9590 Fax: (301)588-4569.

OTHER SOURCES

The World Economy: A Millennial Perspective. Angus Maddison. Organization for Economic Cooperation and Development. • 2001. $63.00. "...covers the development of the entire world economy over the past 2000 years," including data on world population and gross domestic product (GDP) since the year 1000, and exports since 1820. Focuses primarily on the disparity in economic performance among nations over the very long term. More than 200 statistical tables and figures are provided (detailed information available at http://www.theworldeconomy.org).

GROUP INSURANCE

See: HEALTH INSURANCE

GROUP MEDICAL PRACTICE

See also: HEALTH CARE INDUSTRY; MEDICAL ECONOMICS (PRACTICE MANAGEMENT)

GENERAL WORKS

Management of Healthcare Organizations. Kerry D. Carson and others. Brooks/Cole Publishing Co. • Price on application. (SWC-Management Series).

ABSTRACTS AND INDEXES

NTIS Alerts: Health Care. National Technical Information Service. • Semimonthly. $210.00 per year. Provides descriptions of government-sponsored research reports and software, with ordering information. Covers a wide variety of health care topics, including quality assurance, delivery organization, economics (costs), technology, and legislation. Formerly *Abstract Newsletter.*

DIRECTORIES

AAHP/Dorland Directory of Health Plans. Dorland Healthcare Information. • Annual. $215.00. Published in association with the American Association of Health Plans (http://www.aahp.org). Lists more than 2,400 health plans, including Health Maintenance Organizations (HMOs), Preferred Provider Organizations (PPOs), and Point of Service plans (POS). Includes the names of about 9,000 health plan executives. Formerly *Managed Health Care Directory.*

American Medical Group Association Directory. American Group Practice Association. • Annual. $399.00. Lists about 250 private group medical practices and their professional staffs, totaling about 25,000 physicians and administrators. Formerly *American Group Practice Association Directory.*

Directory of Physician Groups and Networks. Dorland Healthcare Information. • Annual. $345.00. Lists more than 4,200 independent practice associations (IPAs), physician hospital organizations (PHOs), management service organizations (MSOs), physician practice management companies (PPMCs), and group practices having 20 or more physicians.

Medical Group Management Association Directory. Medical Group Management Association. • Annual. More than 16,000 individual members and 6,000 member groups representing over 130,000 physicians.

ENCYCLOPEDIAS AND DICTIONARIES

Guidebook to Managed Care and Practice Management Terminology. Norman Winegar and Michelle Hayter. Haworth Press, Inc. • 1998. $39.95. Provides definitions of managed care "terminology, jargon, and concepts.".

HANDBOOKS AND MANUALS

Healthcare Finance for the Non-Financial Manager: Basic Guide to Financial Analysis & Control. Louis Gapenski. McGraw-Hill Professional. • 1994. $47.50.

Managed Care Handbook: How to Prepare Your Medical Practice for the Managed Care Revolution. James Lyle and Hoyt Torras. Practice Management Information Corp. • 1994. $49.95. Second edition. A management guide for physicians in private practice.

PERIODICALS AND NEWSLETTERS

AHA News. Health Forum, Inc. • Weekly. $147.00 per year. Edited for hospital and health care industry administrators. Covers health care news events and legislative activity. An American Hospital Association publication (http://www.aha.org).

American Medical Group Association-Executive News Service. American Medical Group Association. • Monthly. Membership. Newsletter. Formerly *American Group Practice Association-Executive News Service.*

Group Practice Journal. American Medical Group Practice Association. • 10 times a year. $75.00 per year.

Health Forum. American Hospital Association. American Hospital Publishing, Inc. • Biweekly. $80.00 per year. Covers the general management of hospitals, nursing homes, and managed care organizations. Formerly *HospitalsHealthNetworks.*

HMO Magazine (Health Maintenance Organization). Group Health Association of America. • Bimonthly. $75.00 per year.

Medical Group Management Journal. Medical Group Management Association. • Bimonthly. $68.00 per year.

Modern Physician: Essential Business News for the Executive Physician. Crain Communications, Inc. • Monthly. $39.50. Edited for physicians responsible for business decisions at hospitals, clinics, HMOs, and other health groups. Includes special issues on managed care, practice management, legal issues, and finance.

TRADE/PROFESSIONAL ASSOCIATIONS

American College of Medical Practice Executives. 104 Inverness Terrace E., Englewood, CO 80112-5306. Phone: 877-275-6442 Fax: (303)643-4427 • URL: http://www.mgma.com.

American Medical Group Association. 1422 Duke St., Alexandria, VA 22314-3430. Phone: (703)838-

0033 Fax: (703)548-1890 E-mail: rconnor@amga.org • URL: http://www.amga.org.

Medical Group Management Association. 104 Inverness Terrace E., Englewood, CO 80112-5306. Phone: 888-608-5601 or (303)799-1111 Fax: (303)643-4439 • URL: http://www.mgma.com • Members are medical group managers.

GROWTH STOCKS

See: STOCKS

GUARANTEED WAGES

See: WAGES AND SALARIES

GUIDANCE

See: COUNSELING; VOCATIONAL GUIDANCE

GUIDED MISSILES

See: ROCKET INDUSTRY

GUMS AND RESINS

See: NAVAL STORES

GUNS

See: FIREARMS INDUSTRY

H

HABERDASHERY

See: MEN'S CLOTHING INDUSTRY

HAIR CARE PRODUCTS

See: COSMETICS INDUSTRY

HAIRDRESSERS

See: BARBER AND BEAUTY SHOPS

HALF-TONE PROCESS

See: PHOTOENGRAVING

HANDICAPPED WORKERS

See also: EQUAL EMPLOYMENT OPPORTUNITY

GENERAL WORKS

New Technologies and the Employment of Disabled Persons. H. Allan Hunt and Monroe Berkowitz, editors. International Labour Office. • 1992. $18.00. Discusses the development and use of new technologies to create job opportunities for the disabled in various countries.

DIRECTORIES

Complete Directory for People with Disabilities. Grey House Publishing. • Annual. $165.00. Provides information on a wide variety of products, goods, services, and facilities, including job training programs, rehabilitation services, and funding sources. Indexed by organization name, disability/ need, and location.

Directory of Grants for Organizations Serving People with Disabilities: A Guide to Sources of Funding in the United States for Programs and Services for Personswith Disabilities. Richard M. Eckstein. Research Grant Guides. • Biennial. $59.50. Lists over 800 foundations, associations, and government agencies that grant funds to non-profit organizations for projects related to handicapped persons. Formerly *Handicapped Funding Directory.*

HANDBOOKS AND MANUALS

ADA Compliance Guide (Americans with Disabilities Act). Thompson Publishing Group. • Looseleaf, with monthly updates and monthly news bulletin. $287.00 per year. Provides detailed information for employers and local governments on the requirements of the Americans with Disabilities Act.

Americans with Disabilities Act: A Practical and Legal Guide to Impact, Enforcement, and Compliance. BNA Plus. • 1990. $95.00. (Special Report Series).

Americans with Disabilities Act Handbook. Henry H. Perritt. John Wiley and Sons, Inc. • 1997. $360.00. Third edition. Two volumes. 1996 Cumulative Supplement, $78.00. Two Volumes. Provides analysis of the 1990 Americans with Disabilities Act (ADA). Discusses employment provisions and the requirements for physical access to public accommodations. An appendix contains the complete ADA text.

Employment Law Guide to the Americans with Disabilities Act. Mark Daniels. Prentice Hall. • 1992. $95.00.

Handbook of Services for the Handicapped. Alfred H. Katz and Knute Martin. Greenwood Publishing Group Inc. • 1982. $65.00.

Handicapped Requirements Handbook. Thompson Publishing Group. • $196.00. Looseleaf service. Monthly updates. $35.00 per chapter.

PERIODICALS AND NEWSLETTERS

GDL Alert. Warren, Gorham & Lamont/RIA Group. • Monthly. $110.98 per year. Newsletter. Covers current legal developments of interest to employers. Formerly *Disabilities in the Workplace Alert.*

RESEARCH CENTERS AND INSTITUTES

International Center for the Disabled. 340 E. 24th St., New York, NY 10010. Phone: (212)679-0100 Fax: (212)585-6161 E-mail: ccgodfrey@aol.com.

Rehabilitation Program. University of Arizona. College of Education, P.O. Box 210069, Tucson, AZ 85721. Phone: (520)621-7822 Fax: (520)621-3821.

Vocational and Rehabilitation Research Institute. 3304 33rd St., N.W., Calgary, AB, Canada T2L 2A6. Phone: (403)284-1121 Fax: (403)289-6427 E-mail: vrri@cadvision.com • URL: http://www.vrri.org • Associated with University of Calgary.

TRADE/PROFESSIONAL ASSOCIATIONS

Disability Rights Center. 2500 Q St., N.W., Washington, DC. Phone: (703)934-2020 or (703)934-2021 Fax: (703)352-5762 E-mail: drc@patriot.net.

Goodwill Industries of International. 9200 Rockville Pike, Bethesda, MD 20814. Phone: 800-664-6577 or (301)530-6500 Fax: (301)530-1516 E-mail: goodwill@goodwill.org • URL: http://www.goodwill.org.

National Association of the Physically Handicapped. Scarlet Oaks, No. GA4, 440 Lafayette Ave., Cincinnati, OH 45220-1000. Phone: 800-340-6274 or (513)961-8040 E-mail: hroudebush@worldnet.att.net • URL: http://www.naph.net.

Special Interest Group on Computers and the Physically Handicapped. c/o Association for Computing Machinery, 1515 Broadway, 17th Fl., New York, NY 10036. Phone: (212)869-7440 Fax: (212)302-5826 E-mail: acmhelp@acm.org • URL: http://www.acm.org/sigcaph • Members are physically disabled computer professionals.

OTHER SOURCES

Disability and Rehabilitation Products Markets. Theta Reports/PJB Medical Publications, Inc. • 1999. $1,295.00. Market research data. Covers the market for products designed to help differently-abled people lead more active lives. Includes such items as adaptive computers, augmentative communication devices, lifts/vans, and bath/home products. Profiles of leading suppliers are included. (Theta Report No. 800.).

HANDICRAFTS

See: GIFT BUSINESS; HOBBY INDUSTRY

HANDLING OF MATERIALS

See: MATERIALS HANDLING

HARASSMENT, SEXUAL

See: SEXUAL HARASSMENT IN THE WORKPLACE

HARBORS

See: PORTS

HARD FIBERS INDUSTRY

See: FIBER INDUSTRY

HARDWARE INDUSTRY

See also: FASTENER INDUSTRY; SAW INDUSTRY; TOOL INDUSTRY

DIRECTORIES

Directory of Building Products and Hardlines Distributors. Chain Store Guide. • Annual. $280.00. Includes hardware, houseware, and building supply distributors. Formerly *Directory of Hardline Distributors.*

Directory of Home Center Operators and Hardware Chains. Chain Store Age. • Annual. $300.00. Nearly 5,400 home center operators, paint and home decorating chains, and lumber and building materials companies.

ProSales Buyer's Guide. Hanley-Wood, LLC. • Annual. $5.00. A directory of equipment for professional builders.

Thomas Register of American Manufacturers and Thomas Register Catalog File. Thomas Publishing Co., Inc. • Annual. $149.00. 34 volumes. A three-part system offering information on a wide variety of industrial equipment and supplies.

FINANCIAL RATIOS

Almanac of Business and Industrial Financial Ratios. Leo Troy. Prentice Hall. • Annual. $99.95. Contains financial ratios derived from federal tax returns. Ratios for each of about 200 industries are arranged according to company asset size.

Annual Statement Studies. Robert Morris Associates: The Association of Lending and Credit Risk Professiona. • Annual. Free to members; non-members, $140.00. Median and quartile financial ratios are given for over 400 kinds of manufacturing, wholesale, retail, construction, and consumer finance establishments. Data is sorted by both asset size and sales volume. Includes a clearly written "Definition of Ratios" and an alphabetical industry index.

National Retail Hardware Association Management Report: Cost of Doing Business Survey. National Retail Hardware Association. • Annual. Members, $49.00; non-members, $98.00.

ONLINE DATABASES

Thomas Register Online. Thomas Publishing Co., Inc. • Provides concise information on approximately 194,000 U. S. companies, mainly manufacturers, with over 50,000 product classifications. Indexes over 115,000 trade names. Information is updated semiannually. Inquire as to online cost and availability.

PERIODICALS AND NEWSLETTERS

Do-it-Yourself Retailing: Serving Hardware, Home Center and Building Material Retailers. National Retail Hardware Association. • Monthly. $50.00 per year. Formerly *Hardware Retailing.*

Doors and Hardware. Door and Hardware Institute. • Monthly. $49.00 per year.

Hardware Age. Cahners Business Information. • Monthly. $75.00 per year.

TRADE/PROFESSIONAL ASSOCIATIONS

American Hardware Manufacturers Association. 810 N. Plaza Dr., Schaumburg, IL 60173. Phone: (847)605-1025 Fax: (847)605-1093 • URL: http://www.ahma.org.

Builders' Hardware Manufacturers Association. 355 Lexington Ave., 17th Fl., New York, NY 10017. Phone: (212)297-2100 Fax: (212)370-9047 E-mail: info@buildershardware.com • URL: http://www.buildershardware.com.

Door and Hardware Institute. 14170 Newbrook Dr., Ste. 200, Chantilly, VA 22021-2223. Phone: (703)222-2010 Fax: (703)222-2410 • URL: http://www.dhi.org.

International Hardware Distributors Association. 401 N. Michigan Ave., Suite 2200, Chicago, IL 60611-4267. Phone: (312)644-6610 Fax: (312)527-6640 E-mail: ihda@sba.com.

National Retail Hardware Association. 5822 W. 74th St., Indianapolis, IN 46278. Phone: 800-772-4424 or (317)290-0338 Fax: (317)328-4354 E-mail: nrha@iquest.net • URL: http://www.nrha.org.

OTHER SOURCES

Door Hardware. Available from MarketResearch.com. • 1997. $495.00. Market research report published by Specialists in Business Information. Covers locks, closers, doorknobs, security devices, and other door hardware. Presents market data relative to demographics, sales growth, shipments, exports, imports, price trends, and end-use. Includes company profiles.

The Home Improvement Market. Available from MarketResearch.com. • 1999. $2,750.00. Market research report published by Packaged Facts. Covers the market for lumber, finishing materials, tools, hardware, etc.

HARDWOOD INDUSTRY

See also: LUMBER INDUSTRY

GENERAL WORKS

Forest Products and Wood Science: An Introduction. John G. Haygreen and Jim L. Bowyer. Iowa State University Press. • 1996. $62.95. Third edition.

ABSTRACTS AND INDEXES

Forest Products Abstracts. CABI Publishing North America. • Bimonthly. $1,155.00 per year. Published in England by CABI Publishing. Provides worldwide coverage of forest products literature.

CD-ROM DATABASES

AGRICOLA on SilverPlatter. Available from SilverPlatter Information, Inc. • Quarterly. $825.00 per year. Produced by the National Agricultural Library. Provides about three million citations on CD-ROM to the literature of agriculture, agricultural economics, animal sciences, entomology, fertilizer, food, forestry, nutrition, pesticides, plant science, water resources, and other topics. Each quarterly disc covers the past ten years, with archival discs available from 1970.

WILSONDISC: Biological and Agricultural Index. H. W. Wilson Co. • Monthly. $1,495.00 per year, including unlimited online access to *Biological and Agricultural Index* through WILSONLINE. Provides CD-ROM indexing of over 250 periodicals covering agriculture, agricultural chemicals, biochemistry, biotechnology, entomology, horticulture, and related topics.

DIRECTORIES

Directory of the Wood Products Industry. Miller Freeman, Inc. • Biennial. $295.00. Lists sawmills, panelmills, logging operations, plywood products, wood products, distributors, etc. Geographic arrangement, with an index to lumber specialities. Formerly *Directory of the Forest Products Industry.*

Hardwood Manufacturers Association: Membership Directory. Hardwood Manufacturers Association. • Annual. Lists over 100 companies.

National Hardwood Lumber Association Membership Directory. National Hardwood Lumber Association. • Annual. $85.00. Members are hardwood lumber and veneer manufacturers, distributors, and users.

Where to Buy Hardwood Plywood and Veneer. Hardwood Plywood Manufacturers Association. • Annual. $20.00. Lists about 190 member manufacturers, prefinishers, and suppliers of hardwood veneer and plywood.

ENCYCLOPEDIAS AND DICTIONARIES

Encyclopedia of Agriculture Science. Charles J. Arntzen and Ellen M. Ritter, editors. Academic Press, Inc. • 1994. $625.00. Four volumes.

Encyclopedia of Wood. U.S. Dept. of Forestry Staff. Sterling Publishing Co., Inc. • 1989. $24.95. Revised edition.

Encyclopedia of Wood: A Tree by Tree Guide to the World's Most Valuable Resource. Bill Lincoln and others. Facts on File, Inc. • 1989. $29.95.

FINANCIAL RATIOS

Annual Statement Studies. Robert Morris Associates: The Association of Lending and Credit Risk Professiona. • Annual. Free to members; non-members, $140.00. Median and quartile financial ratios are given for over 400 kinds of manufacturing, wholesale, retail, construction, and consumer finance establishments. Data is sorted by both asset size and sales volume. Includes a clearly written "Definition of Ratios" and an alphabetical industry index.

Industry Norms and Key Business Ratios. Desk Top Edition. Dun and Bradstreet Corp., Business Information Services. • Annual. Five volumes. $475.00 per volume. $1,890.00 per set. Covers over 800 kinds of businesses, arranged by Standard Industrial Classification number. More detailed editions covering longer periods of time are also available.

INTERNET DATABASES

Fedstats. Federal Interagency Council on Statistical Policy. Phone: (202)395-7254 • URL: http://www.fedstats.gov • Web site features an efficient search facility for full-text statistics produced by more than 70 federal agencies, including the Census Bureau, the Bureau of Economic Analysis, and the Bureau of Labor Statistics. Boolean searches can be made within one agency or for all agencies combined. Links are offered to international statistical bureaus, including the UN, IMF, OECD, UNESCO, Eurostat, and 20 individual countries. Fees: Free.

USDA. United States Department of Agriculture. Phone: (202)720-2791 E-mail: agsec@usda.gov • URL: http://www.usda.gov • The USDA home page has six sections: News and Information; What's New; About USDA; Agencies; Opportunities; Search and Help. Keyword searching is offered from the USDA home page and from various individual agency home pages. Agencies are the Economic Research Service, Agricultural Marketing Service, National Agricultural Statistics Service, National Agricultural Library, and about 12 others. Updating varies. Fees: Free.

ONLINE DATABASES

Agricola. U.S. National Agricultural Library. • Covers worldwide agricultural literature. Over 2.8 million citations, 1970 to present, with monthly updates. Inquire as to online cost and availability.

Biological and Agricultural Index Online. H. W. Wilson Co. • Indexes a wide variety of agricultural and biological periodicals, 1983 to date. Monthly updates. Inquire as to online cost and availability.

CAB Abstracts. CAB International North America. • Contains 46 specialized abstract collections covering over 10,000 journals and monographs in the areas of agriculture, horticulture, forest products, farm products, nutrition, dairy science, poultry, grains, animal health, entomology, etc. Time period is 1972 to date, with monthly updates. Inquire as to online cost and availability. *CAB Abstracts on CD-ROM* also available, with annual updating.

DRI U.S. Central Database. Data Products Division. • Provides more than 23,000 business, financial, demographic, economic, foreign trade, and industry-related time series for the U.S. Includes national income, population, retail-wholesale trade, price indexes, labor data, housing, industrial production, banking, interest rates, money supply, etc. Time period is generally 1947 to date (some data back to 1929). Updating varies. Inquire as to online cost and availability.

Globalbase. The Gale Group. • Provides more than one million online summaries of business, industrial, and economic news reports from more than 1,000 publications worldwide. Covers a wide range of material appearing in international trade journals, professional magazines, and newspapers. Time period is 1984 to date, with weekly updates. Inquire as to online cost and availability.

PROMT: Predicasts Overview of Markets and Technology. The Gale Group. • Companies, products, applied technologies and markets. U.S. and international literature coverage, 1972 to date. Inquire as to online cost and availability. Provides abstracts from more than 1,600 publications. Weekly updates.

PERIODICALS AND NEWSLETTERS

Hardwood Floors. National Wood Flooring Association. Athletic Business Publications, Inc. • Bimonthly. $36.00 per year. Covers the marketing and installation of hardwood flooring. Published for contractors and retailers.

National Hardwood Magazine. Miller Publishing Co. • Monthly. $45.00 per year.

NHLA Newsletter. National Hardwood Lumber Association. • Monthly. Membership. Newsletter on hardwood products, industry trends, and legislation.

Wood Technology: Logging, Pulpwood, Forestry, Lumber, Panels. Miller Freeman, Inc. • Eight times a year. $120.00 per year. Formerly *Forest Industries*.

RESEARCH CENTERS AND INSTITUTES

Wood and Paper Science. North Carolina State University, P.O. Box 8005, Raleigh, NC 27695. Phone: (919)515-5807 Fax: (919)515-6302 E-mail: mikekocurek@ncsu.edu • URL: http://www.cfr.ncsu.edu/wps/ • Studies the mechanical and engineering properties of wood, wood finishing, wood anatomy, wood chemistry, etc.

Wood Research Laboratory. Purdue University, Department of Forestry and Natural Resources, West Lafayette, IN 47907-1200. Phone: (765)494-3615 Fax: (765)496-1344 E-mail: mhunt@fnr.purdue.edu • URL: http://www.fnr.purdue.edu.

STATISTICS SOURCES

AF and PA Statistical Roundup. American Forest and Paper Association. • Monthly. Members, $57.00 per year; non-members, $157.00 per year. Contains monthly statistical data for hardwood and softwood products. Formerly *NFPA Statistical Roundup*.

Agricultural Statistics. Available from U. S. Government Printing Office. • Annual. Produced by the National Agricultural Statistics Service, U. S. Department of Agriculture. Provides a wide variety of statistical data relating to agricultural production, supplies, consumption, prices/price-supports, foreign trade, costs, and returns, as well as farm labor, loans, income, and population. In many cases, historical data is shown annually for 10 years. In addition to farm data, includes detailed fishery statistics.

Annual Survey of Manufactures. Available from U. S. Government Printing Office. • Annual. Prices vary. Issued by the U. S. Census Bureau as an interim update to the *Census of Manufactures*. Includes data on number of manufacturing establishments in various industries, employment, labor costs, value of shipments, capital expenditures, inventories, energy costs, and assets. (See also Census Bureau home page, http://www.census.gov/.).

Business Statistics of the United States. Courtenay M. Slater, editor. Bernan Associates. • 1999. $74.00. Fifth edition. Based on *Business Statistics*, formerly issue by the Bureau of Economic Analysis, U. S. Department of Commerce. Provides basic data for a wide variety of U. S. industries, services, and economic indicators. Most statistics are shown annually for 29 years and monthly for the most recent four years.

Manufacturing Profiles. Available from U. S. Government Printing Office. • Annual. Issued by the U. S. Census Bureau. A printed consolidation of the entire *Current Industrial Report* series, presenting "all the data compiled." Contains statistics on production, shipments, inventories, consumption, exports, imports, and orders for a wide variety of manufactured products. (See also Census Bureau home page, http://www.census.gov/.).

Survey of Current Business. Available from U. S. Government Printing Office. • Monthly. $49.00 per year. Issued by Bureau of Economic Analysis, U. S. Department of Commerce. Presents a wide variety of business and economic data.

TRADE/PROFESSIONAL ASSOCIATIONS

American Forest and Paper Association. 1111 19th St., N.W., Ste. 800, Washington, DC 20036. Phone: (202)463-2700 Fax: (202)463-2785 E-mail: info@afandpa.org • URL: http://www.afandpa.org.

American Walnut Manufacturers Association. P.O. Box 5046, Zionsville, IN 46077. Phone: (317)873-8780 Fax: (317)873-8788 E-mail: larryfrye@compuserve.com.

Appalachian Hardwood Manufacturers, Inc. P.O. Box 427, High Point, NC 27261. Phone: (336)885-8315 Fax: (336)886-8865 E-mail: applumber@aol.com • Members are manufacturers interested in promoting the use of Appalachian hardwood.

Hardwood Distributors Association. P.O. Box 988, North Tonawanda, NY 14120. Phone: (716)694-0562 Fax: (716)694-0966.

Hardwood Manufacturers Association. 400 Penn Center Blvd., Suite 530, Pittsburgh, PA 15235. Phone: (412)829-0770 Fax: (412)829-0844 • Members are manufacturers of hardwood lumber and hardwood products.

Hardwood Plywood and Veneer Association. P.O. Box 2789, Reston, VA 20195-0789. Phone: (703)435-2900 Fax: (703)435-2537 E-mail: hpva@hpva.org • URL: http://www.hpva.org.

National Hardwood Lumber Association. P.O. Box 34518, Memphis, TN 38184-0518. Phone: (901)377-1818 Fax: (901)382-6419 • URL: http://www.natlhardwood.org • Members are hardwood lumber and veneer manufacturers and distributors. Users of hardwood products are also members.

Wood Component Manufacturers Association. 1000 Johnson Ferry Rd., Suite A-130, Marietta, GA 30068. Phone: (770)565-6660 • URL: http://www.woodcomponents.org • Members are manufacturers of prefabricated hardwood parts for the furniture industry.

OTHER SOURCES

U. S. Floor Coverings Industry. Available from MarketResearch.com. • 1999. $1,795.00. Market research report published by Specialists in Business Information. Covers carpets, hardwood flooring, and tile. Presents market data relative to demographics, sales growth, shipments, exports, imports, price trends, and end-use. Includes company profiles.

Wood Flooring. Available from MarketResearch.com. • 1999. $2,250.00. Market research report published by Specialists in Business Information. Presents hardwood flooring market data relative to demographics, sales growth, shipments, exports, imports, price trends, and end-use. Includes company profiles.

HARVESTING MACHINERY

See: AGRICULTURAL MACHINERY

HAT INDUSTRY

See: MEN'S CLOTHING INDUSTRY; MILLINERY INDUSTRY

HAY INDUSTRY

See: FEED AND FEEDSTUFFS INDUSTRY

HAZARDOUS MATERIALS

See also: INDUSTRIAL HYGIENE; WASTE MANAGEMENT

GENERAL WORKS

Hazardous Waste Management. McGraw-Hill. • 2000. $85.63. Second edition.

Management of Hazardous Materials and Wastes: Treatment, Minimization, and Environmental Impacts. Shyamal K. Majumdar and others, editors. Pennsylvania Academy of Science. • 1989. $45.00.

Understanding Toxicology: Chemicals, Their Benefits and Uses. H. Bruno Schiefer and others. CRC Press, Inc. • 1997. $34.95. Provides a basic introduction to chemical interactions and toxicology for the general reader.

ABSTRACTS AND INDEXES

Applied Science and Technology Index. H. W. Wilson Co. • 11 times a year. Quarterly and annual cumulations. Service basis for print edition; CD-ROM edition, $1,495.00 per year. Indexes a wide variety of English language technical, industrial, and engineering periodicals.

Current Contents: Engineering, Computing and Technology. Institute for Scientific Information. • Weekly. $730.00 per year. Reproductions of contents pages of technical journals. Includes *Author Index, Address Directory, Current Book Contents* and *Title Word Index*. Formerly *Current Contents: Engineering, Technology and Applied Sciences*.

Health and Safety Science Abstracts. Institute of Safety and Systems Management. Cambridge Information Group. • Quarterly. $775.00 per year. Formerly *Safety Science Abstracts Journal*.

NTIS Alerts: Environmental Pollution & Control. National Technical Information Service. • Semimonthly. $245.00 per year. Provides descriptions of government-sponsored research reports and software, with ordering information. Covers the following categories of environmental pollution: air, water, solid wastes, radiation, pesticides, and noise. Formerly *Abstract Newsletter*.

CD-ROM DATABASES

Chem-Bank. SilverPlatter Information, Inc. • Quarterly. $1,595.00 per year. Provides CD-ROM information on hazardous substances, including 140,000 chemicals in the *Registry of Toxic Effects of Chemical Substances* and 60,000 materials covered by the *Toxic Substances Control Act Initial Inventory*.

OSH-ROM: Occupational Safety and Health Information on CD-ROM. Available from SilverPlatter Information, Inc. • Price and frequency on application. Produced in Geneva by the International Occupational Safety and Health Information Centre, International Labour Organization (http://www.ilo.org). Provides about two million citations and abstracts to the worldwide literature of industrial safety, industrial hygiene, hazardous materials, and accident prevention. Material is included from journals, technical reports, books, government publications, and other sources. Time span varies.

DIRECTORIES

Best's Safety and Security Directory: Safety-Industrial Hygiene-Security. A.M. Best Co. • Annual. $95.00. A manual of current industrial safety practices with a directory of manufacturers and distributors of plant safety, security and industrial hygiene products and services listed by hazard. Formerly *Best's Safety Directory*.

EI Environmental Services Directory. Environmental Information Ltd. • Biennial. $1,250.00. Over 620 waste-handling facilities, 600 transportation firms, 500 spill response firms, 2,100 consultants, 470 laboratories, 450 soil boring/well drilling firms, incineration services, asbestos services, etc. Formerly *Industrial and Hazardous Waste Management Firms.*

Emergency Response Directory for Hazardous Materials Accidents. Odin Press. • Biennial. $36.00. Provides resources for the containment and cleanup of toxic spills. Lists government agencies, spill response contractors, chemical manufacturers, hot lines, etc.

Hazardous Substances Resource Guide. The Gale Group. • 1997. $225.00. Second edition. Provides detailed information on each of about 1,500 hazardous materials, including trade name, health hazard, use, and storage. Information on organizations and a glossary are also included. Written for the lay user.

Hazardous Waste Consultant Directory of Commercial Hazardous Waste Management Facilities. Elsevier Science. • Annual. $115.00. List of 170 facilities that process, store, and dispose of hazardous waste materials.

Pollution Equipment News Buyer's Guide. Rimbach Publishing, Inc. • Annual. $100.00. Over 3,000 manufacturers of pollution control equipment and products.

Waste Age Buyers' Guide. Intertec Publishing Corp. • Annual. $39.95. Manufacturers of equipment and supplies for the waste management industry.

ENCYCLOPEDIAS AND DICTIONARIES

Encyclopedia of Occupational Health and Safety. Available from The Gale Group. • 1999. $495.00. Fourth edition. Four volumes. Published by the International Labor Office (http://www.ilo.org). Covers safety engineering, industrial medicine, ergonomics, hygiene, epidemiology, toxicology, industrial psychology, and related topics. Includes material related to specific chemical, textile, transport, construction, manufacturing, and other industries. Indexed by subject, chemical name, and author, with a "Directory of Experts.".

Hazardous Materials Dictionary. Ronny J. Coleman. Technomic Publishing Co., Inc. • 1994. $79.95. Second revised edition.

HANDBOOKS AND MANUALS

Comprehensive Guide to the Hazardous Properties of Chemical Substances. Pradyot Patnaik. John Wiley and Sons, Inc. • 1998. $130.00. Second edition.

A Guide to Hazardous Materials Management: Physical Characteristics, Federal Regulations, and Response Alternatives. Aileen Schumacher. Greenwood Publishing Group Inc. • 1988. $72.95.

Handbook of Industrial Toxicology. E. R. Plunkett, editor. Chemical Publishing Co., Inc. • 1987. $100.00.

Hazardous and Toxic Materials: Safe Handling and Disposal. Howard H. Fawcett, editor. John Wiley and Sons, Inc. • 1988. $139.00. Second edition.

Hazardous Waste Management in Small Businesses: Regulating and Assisting the Small Generator. Robert E. Deyle. Greenwood Publishing Group, Inc. • 1989. $59.95. Emphasis on legal aspects.

Patty's Industrial Hygiene and Toxicology. George D. Clayton and Florence E. Clayton, editors. John Wiley and Sons, Inc. • 2000. $2,195.00. Three volumes in 10 parts. Provides broad coverage of environmental factors and stresses affecting the health of workers. Contains detailed information on the effects of specific substances.

Recommendations on the Transport of Dangerous Goods. United Nations Publications. • 1999. $120.00. 11th edition. Covers regulations imposed by various governments and international organizations.

Sax's Dangerous Properties of Industrial Materials. Richard J. Lewis. John Wiley and Sons, Inc. • 1999. $545.00. 10th edition. Three volumes. Provides detailed information on the chemical, physical, and toxicity characteristics of more than 22,000 industrial materials. Hazard ratings and safety profiles are specified.

Standard Handbook of Hazardous Waste Treatment and Disposal. Harry M. Freeman, editor. McGraw-Hill. • 1997. $140.00. Second expanded revised edition.

Toxic Substances Controls Guide. Mary D. Worobec and Cheryl Hogue. Bureau of National Affairs, Inc. • 1992. 45.00. Second edition. Emphasis on legal aspects.

ONLINE DATABASES

Applied Science and Technology Index Online. H. W. Wilson Co. • Provides online indexing of 400 major scientific, technical, industrial, and engineering periodicals. Time period is 1983 to date. Monthly updates. Inquire as to online cost and availability.

NIOSHTIC: National Institute for Occupational Safety and Health Technical Information Center Database. National Institute for Occupational Safety and Health, Technical Information Bra. • Provides citations and abstracts of technical literature in the areas of industrial safety, industrial hygiene, and toxicology. Covers 1890 to date, but mostly 1973 to date. Monthly updates. (Database is also known as *Occupational Safety and Health.*) Inquire as to online cost and availability.

PROMT: Predicasts Overview of Markets and Technology. The Gale Group. • Companies, products, applied technologies and markets. U.S. and international literature coverage, 1972 to date. Inquire as to online cost and availability. Provides abstracts from more than 1,600 publications. Weekly updates.

PERIODICALS AND NEWSLETTERS

American Industrial Hygiene Association Journal: A Publication for the Science of Occupational and Environmental Health. American Industrial Hygiene Association. • Monthly. Institutions, $160.00 per year.

Asbestos and Lead Abatement Report: Inspection, Analysis, Removal, Maintenance, Alternatives. Business Publishers, Inc. • Biweekly. $357.00 per year. Newsletter on legal issues relating to the removal or containment of asbestos and lead. Includes news of research activities.

Environment Advisor. J.J. Keller & Associates, Inc. • Monthly. $90.00 per year. Newsletter. Formerly *Hazardous Substances Advisor.*

Environmental Science and Technology. Kluwer Academic Publishers. • Irregular. Price varies.

Golob's Environmental Business. World Information Systems. • Weekly. $375.00 per year. Newsletter. Formerly *Hazardous Materials Intelligence Report.*

Hazardous Materials Newsletter. Hazardous Materials Publishing Co. • Bimonthly. $47.00 per year.

Hazardous Materials Transportation. Washington Business Information, Inc. • Biweekly. $797.00 per year. Looseleaf service. Newsletter on the responsibilities of shippers and carriers for the safe transportation of hazardous materials.

Hazardous Waste Business. McGraw-Hill, Energy and Business Newsletter. • Biweekly. $695.00 per year. Newsletter on the control and cleanup of hazardous waste from a business viewpoint. Covers regulation, new technology, corporate activities, and industry trends.

Hazardous Waste Consultant. Elsevier Science. • Seven times a year. $798.00 per year. Discusses the technical, regulatory and legal aspects of the hazardous waste industry.

Hazardous Waste News. Business Publishers, Inc. • Weekly. $687.00 per year. Newsletter. Incorporates *Lab Waste* and *Hazards Management.* Includes *Nuclear Waste Bulletin.*

Nuclear Waste News: Generation, Packaging, Transportation, Processing, Disposal. Business Publishers, Inc. • Weekly. $867.00. per year. Newsletter.

OSHA Required Safety Training for Supervisors. Occupational Safety and Health Administration. Business and Legal Reports, Inc. • Monthly. $99.00 per year. Newsletter. Formerly *Safetyworks for Supervisors.*

Pollution Engineering: Magazine of Environmental Control. Cahners Business Information. • 13 times a year. $85.90 per year. Includes *Product-Service Locater.*

Sludge Newsletter: The Newsletter on Municipal Wastewater and Biosolids. Business Publishers, Inc. • Biweekly. $409.00 per year. per year. Monitors sludge management developments in Washington and around the country.

Waste Management: Industrial-Radioactive-Hazardous. Elsevier Science. • Eight times a year. $1,350.00 per year. Formerly *Nuclear and Chemical Waste Management.*

World Environment Report: News and Information on International Resource Management. Business Publishers, Inc. • Biweekly. $494.00 per year. Newsletter on international developments having to do with the environment, energy, pollution control, waste management, and toxic substances.

World Wastes: The Independent Voice of the Industry. Intertec Publishing Corp. • Monthly. $52.00 per year. Includes annual catalog. Formerly *Management of World Wastes: The Independent Voice of the Industry.*

RESEARCH CENTERS AND INSTITUTES

Battelle Memorial Institute. 505 King Ave., Columbus, OH 43201-2693. Phone: 800-201-2011 or (614)424-6424 Fax: (614)424-3260 • URL: http://www.battelle.org • Multidisciplinary research facilities at various locations include: Microcomputer Applications and Technology Center; Battelle Industrial Technology Center; Technology and Society Research Center; Office of Transportation Systems and Planning; Office of Waste Technology Development; Materials Information Center; Office of Nuclear Waste Isolation.

Center for Geoenvironmental Science and Technology. University of Cincinnati, P.O. Box 210384, Cincinnati, OH 45221-0384. Phone: (513)556-2472 Fax: (513)556-2522.

Concurrent Technology Corporation. Regional Enterprise Tower, 28th Fl., 425 Sixth Ave., Pittsburgh, PA 15219. Phone: (412)577-2640 Fax: (412)577-2660 E-mail: ctc@ctc.com • URL: http://www.ctc.com.

Environmental Hazards Management Institute. P.O. Box 932, Durham, NH 03824. Phone: (603)868-1496 Fax: (603)868-1547 E-mail: ehmi@aol.com • URL: http://www.ehmi.com.

Environmental Toxicology Center. University of Wisconsin-Madison, Enzyme Institute, Room 290,

1710 University Ave., Madison, WI 53705-4098. Phone: (608)263-4825 Fax: (608)262-5245 E-mail: jefcoate@facstaff.wisc.edu • URL: http://www.wisc.edu/etc/.

Hazardous Substance Management Research Center. New Jersey Institute of Technology, Newark, NJ 07102. Phone: (973)596-3233 Fax: (973)802-1946 E-mail: lederman@admin.njit.edu • URL: http://www.hsmrc.org.

STATISTICS SOURCES

Health, United States, 1999: Health and Aging Chartbook. Available from U. S. Government Printing Office. • 1999. $37.00. Issued by the National Center for Health Statistics, U. S. Department of Health and Human Services. Contains 34 bar charts in color, with related statistical tables. Provides detailed data on persons over 65 years of age, including population, living arrangements, life expectancy, nursing home residence, poverty, health status, assistive devices, health insurance, and health care expenditures.

Statistical Record of the Environment. The Gale Group. • 1996. $120.00. Third edition. Provides over 875 charts, tables, and graphs of major environmental statistics, arranged by subject. Covers population growth, hazardous waste, nuclear energy, acid rain, pesticides, and other subjects related to the environment. A keyword index is included.

TRADE/PROFESSIONAL ASSOCIATIONS

American Conference of Governmental Industrial Hygienists. 1330 Kemper Meadow Dr., Cincinnati, OH 45240. Phone: (513)742-2020 Fax: (513)742-3355 E-mail: mail@acgih.org • URL: http://www.acgih.org • Members are government employees.

American Industrial Hygiene Association. 2700 Prosperity Ave., Suite 250, Fairfax, VA 22031. Phone: (703)849-8888 Fax: (703)207-3561 E-mail: infonet@aiha.org • URL: http://www.aiha.org.

Conference on Safe Transportation of Hazardous Articles. 7811 Carrleigh Parkway, Springfield, VA 22152. Phone: (703)451-4031 Fax: (703)451-4207 E-mail: mail@costha.com • URL: http://www.costha.org • Members are shipper associations concerned with the legal aspects of transporting hazardous materials.

Hazardous Materials Advisory Council. 1110 Vermont Ave., N.W., Suite 301, Washington, DC 20005. Phone: (202)289-4550 Fax: (202)289-4074 E-mail: hmacinfo@hmac.org • URL: http://www.hmac.org • Promotes safe transportation of materials.

National Solid Waste Management Association. c/o Environmental Industry Associates, 4301 Connecticut Ave., N.W., Suite 300, Washington, DC 20008. Phone: 800-424-2869 or (202)244-4700 Fax: (202)966-4818.

OTHER SOURCES

Hazardous Waste Litigation Reporter: The National Journal of Record of Hazardous Waste-Related Litigation. Andrews Publications. • Semimonthly. $875.00 per year. Reports on hazardous waste legal cases.

HEALTH CARE INDUSTRY

See also: HEALTH INSURANCE; HEALTH MAINTENANCE ORGANIZATIONS; HOME HEALTH CARE INDUSTRY; HOSPITAL ADMINISTRATION; MEDICARE; NURSING HOMES

GENERAL WORKS

Fundamentals of Strategic Planning for Healthcare Organizations. Stan Williamson and others. Haworth Press, Inc. • 1996. $49.95.

Health Care Cost Containment. Karen Davis and others. Johns Hopkins University Press. • 1990. $48.00. (Studies in Health Care Finance and Administrations).

Health Care Economics. Paul J. Feldstein. Delmar Publications. • 1998. $80.95. Fifth edition.

Management of Healthcare Organizations. Kerry D. Carson and others. Brooks/Cole Publishing Co. • Price on application. (SWC-Management Series).

Marketing Health Care into the Twenty-First Century: The Changing Dynamic. Alan K. Vitberg. Haworth Press, Inc. • 1996. $39.95.

Medical Care, Medical Costs: The Search for a Health Insurance Policy. Rashi Fein. Replica Books. • 1999. $26.95.

Reform of Health Care Systems: A Review of Seventeen OECD Countries. OECD Publications and Information Center. • 1994. An extensive review of attempts by major countries to control health care costs.

ABSTRACTS AND INDEXES

Business Periodicals Index. H. W. Wilson Co. • Monthly, except August, with quarterly and annual cumulations. Service basis for print edition; CD-ROM edition, $1,495.00 per year.

Cumulative Index to Nursing and Allied Health Literature. CINAHL Information Systems. • Quarterly. $365.00 per year. Annual cumulation.

Index Medicus. National Library of Medicine. Available from U. S. Government Printing Office. • Monthly. $522.00 per year. Bibliographic listing of references to current articles from approximately 3,000 of the world's biomedical journals.

Index to Health Information. Congressional Information Service, Inc. • Quarterly. $945.00 per year, including two-volume annual cumulation. Provides index and abstracts covering the medical and health field in general, with emphasis on statistical sources and government documents. Service with microfiche source documents, $4,995.00 per year.

NTIS Alerts: Health Care. National Technical Information Service. • Semimonthly. $210.00 per year. Provides descriptions of government-sponsored research reports and software, with ordering information. Covers a wide variety of health care topics, including quality assurance, delivery organization, economics (costs), technology, and legislation. Formerly *Abstract Newsletter*.

Science Citation Index. Institute for Scientific Information. • Bimonthly. $15,020.00 per year. Annual cumulation. Includes *Source Index, Citation Index, Permuterm Subject Index*, and *Corporate Index*.

Social Sciences Index. H. W. Wilson Co. • Quarterly, with annual cumulation. Service basis for print edition; CD-ROM edition, $1,495 per year. Indexes more than 400 periodicals covering economics, environmental policy, government, insurance, labor, health care policy, planning, public administration, public welfare, urban studies, women's issues, criminology, and related topics.

ALMANACS AND YEARBOOKS

Advances in Health Economics and Health Services Research. JAI Press, Inc. • Irregular. $73.25.

Annual Review of Medicine: Selected Topics in the Clinical Sciences. Annual Reviews, Inc. • Annual. Individuals, $60.00; institutions, $120.00.

Annual Review of Public Health. Annual Reviews, Inc. • Annual. Individuals, $64.00; institutions, $128.00.

BIBLIOGRAPHIES

Encyclopedia of Health Information Sources. The Gale Group. • 1993. $180.00. Second edition. Both print and nonprint sources of information are listed for 450 health-related topics.

Long-Term Care: An Annotated Bibliography. Theodore H. Koff. Greenwood Publishing Group, Inc. • 1995. $59.95.

Medical and Health Care Books and Serials in Print: An Index to Literature in Health Sciences. R. R. Bowker. • Annual. $265.95. Two volumes.

Vital and Health Statistics. Available from U. S. Government Printing Office. • Annual. Free. Lists government publications. (GPO Subject Bibliography Number 121).

BIOGRAPHICAL SOURCES

Dictionary of American Medical Biography. Martin Kaufman and others. Greenwood Publishing Group Inc. • 1984. $195.00. Two volumes. Vol. one, $100.00; vol. two, $100.00.

CD-ROM DATABASES

BioMed Strategies. Thomson Financial Securities Data. • Monthly. $2,995.00 per year. CD-ROM contains full text of investment analysts' reports on companies operating in the following fields: biotechnology, pharmaceuticals, medical products, and health care.

Health Reference Center. The Gale Group. • Monthly. Provides CD-ROM citations, abstracts, and selected full-text articles on many health-related subjects. Includes references to medical journals, general periodicals, newsletters, newspapers, pamphlets, and medical reference books.

Social Science Source. EBSCO Publishing. • Monthly. $1,495.00 per year. Provides CD-ROM citations and abstracts to social science articles in more than 600 periodicals, with full text from 125 periodicals. Covers economics, political science, public policy, international relations, psychology, and other topics. Time period is most recent five years.

Social Sciences Citation Index: Compact Disc Edition with Abstracts. Institute for Scientific Information. • Quarterly. Provides CD-ROM indexing and abstracting of "significant articles" from 1,400 social science journals worldwide, with additional selections from 3,200 other journals, 1986 to date. Includes economics, business, finance, management, communications, demographics, information and library science, political science, sociology, and many other subjects.

WILSONDISC: Wilson Social Sciences Abstracts. H. W. Wilson Co. • Monthly. Including unlimited online access to *Social Sciences Index* through WILSONLINE. Provides CD-ROM indexing from 1983 and abstracting from 1994 of more than 400 periodicals covering economics, area studies, community health, public administration, public welfare, urban studies, and many other topics related to the social sciences.

DIRECTORIES

American Dental Directory. American Dental Association. • Annual. $187.50. Contains brief information for over 170,000 dentists.

BioScan: The Worldwide Biotech Industry Reporting Service. American Health Consultants, Inc. • Bimonthly. $1,395.00 per year. Looseleaf. Provides detailed information on over 900 U. S. and foreign companies broadly classified as biotechnological. In addition to medical technology and advanced pharmaceutical firms, includes firms doing research in food processing, waste management, agriculture, and veterinary science.

Business Organizations, Agencies, and Publications Directory. The Gale Group. • 1999. $425.00. 12th edition. Over 40,000 entries describing 39 types of business information sources. Classified by type of organization, publication, or serviceIncludes state, national, and international agencies and organizations. Master index to names and keywords. Also includes e-mail addresses and web site URL's.

Buyers' Guide for the Health Care Market: A Directory of Products and Services for Health Care Institutions. American Hospital Association. Health Forum, Inc. • Annual. $17.95. Lists 1,200 suppliers and manufacturers of health care products and services for hospitals, nursing homes, and related organizations.

Detwiler's Directory of Health and Medical Resources. S. M. Detwiler and Associates. Hatherleigh Co., Ltd. • Annual. $220.00. Lists sources of information relating to the healthcare industry, including government agencies, medical experts, directories, newsletters, research groups, associations, and mailing list producers. Four indexes are provided: subject, publication, service, and acronym.

Directory of Health Care Professionals. Dorland Healthcare Information. • Annual. $299.00. Lists about 175,000 professional staff members at 7,000 U. S. hospitals and health systems.

Directory of Physician Groups and Networks. Dorland Healthcare Information. • Annual. $345.00. Lists more than 4,200 independent practice associations (IPAs), physician hospital organizations (PHOs), management service organizations (MSOs), physician practice management companies (PPMCs), and group practices having 20 or more physicians.

Directory of Physicians in the United States. American Medical Association. • Biennial. $595.00. Four volumes. Brief information for more than 686,000 physicians. Formerly*American Medical Directory.*

Encyclopedia of Medical Organizations and Agencies. The Gale Group. • 2000. $285.00. 11th edition. Information on over 14,000 public and private organizations in medicine and related fields.

The HCEA: A Directory of Health Care Meetings and Conventions. Healthcare Convention and Healthcare Exhibitors Association. • Semiannual. Free to members; non-members, $245.00 per year. Lists more than 2,400 health care meetings, most of which have an exhibit program. Formerly *Handbook-A Directory of Health Care Meetings and Conventions.*

Health Devices Sourcebook. ECRI (Emergency Care Research Institute). • Annual. Lists over 6,000 manufacturers of a wide variety of medical equipment and supplies, including clinical laboratory equipment, testing instruments, surgical instruments, patient care equipment, etc.

Health Industry Buyers Guide. Spring House. • Annual. $195.00. About 4,000 manufacturers of hospital and physician's supplies and equipment. Formerly *Surgical Trade Buyers Guide.*

Healthcare Career Directory: Nurses and Physicians: A Practical One-Stop Guide to Getting a Job in Public Relations. The Gale Group. • 1993. $17.95. Second edition. Includes information on careers in nursing, family medicine, surgery, and other medical areas. Provides advice from "insiders," resume suggestions, a directory of companies that may offer entry-level positions, and a directory of career information sources. *Career Advisor Series.*

Medical and Health Information Directory. The Gale Group. • 1999. $630.00. Three volumes. 12th edition. Vol. one covers medical organizations, agencies, and institutions; vol. two includes bibliographic, library, and database information; vol. three is a guide to services available for various medical and health problems.

Medical and Healthcare Marketplace Guide. Dorland Healthcare Information. • Annual. $690.00. Two volumes. Provides market survey summaries for about 500 specific product and service categories (volume one: "Research Reports"). Contains profiles of nearly 6,000 pharmaceutical, medical product, and healthcare service companies (volume two: "Company Profiles").

Medical Research Centres: A World Directory of Organizations and Programmes. Allyn and Bacon/ Longman. • Irregular. $535.00. Two volumes. Contains profiles of about 7,000 medical research facilities around the world. Includes medical, dental, nursing, pharmaceutical, psychiatric, and surgical research centers.

National Health Directory. Aspen Publishers, Inc. • 1997. $95.00. Lists about 10,000 federal and state public health care officials.

Nursing Home Report and Directory. SMG Marketing Group, Inc. • Annual. $525.00. Lists almost 4,000 nursing homes with 50 beds or more.

OB/GYN Reference Guide. Access Publishing Co. • Annual. Price on application. Includes directory information for obstetrical/gynecological equipment, supplies, pharmaceuticals, services, organizations, and publications.

Official ABMS Directory of Board Certified Medical Specialists. Marquis Who's Who. • Annual. $525.00. Four volumes. Published in conjunction with the American Board of Medical Specialties. Includes information on more than 565,000 specialists. Volumes are arranged by medical specialty and then geographically, with an overall index to physicians' names. Formerly *Directory of Medical Specialists.*

Plunkett's Health Care Industry Almanac: The Only Complete Guide to the Fastest-Changing Industry in America. Available from Plunkett Research, Ltd. • Biennial. $179.99. Includes detailed profiles of 500 large companies providing health care products or services, with indexes by products, services, and location. Provides statistical and trend information for the health insurance industry, HMOs, hospital utilization, Medicare, medical technology, and national health expenditures.

Radiology Reference Guide. Access Publishing Co. • Annual. Price on application. Includes directory information for radiological equipment, supplies, services, organizations, and publications.

Telehealth Buyer's Guide. Miller Freeman. • Annual. $10.00. Lists sources of telecommunications and information technology products and services for the health care industry.

FINANCIAL RATIOS

Industry Norms and Key Business Ratios. Desk Top Edition. Dun and Bradstreet Corp., Business Information Services. • Annual. Five volumes. $475.00 per volume. $1,890.00 per set. Covers over 800 kinds of businesses, arranged by Standard Industrial Classification number. More detailed editions covering longer periods of time are also available.

HANDBOOKS AND MANUALS

Advertising Handbook for Health Care Services. William J. Winston, editor. The Haworth Press, Inc. • 1986. $8.95. (Health Marketing Quarterly Series: Supplement No. 1).

The Consumer Health Information Source Book. Alan Rees, editor. Oryx Press. • 2000. $59.50. Sixth edition. Bibliography of current literature and guide to organizations.

Consumers' Guide to Health Plans. Center for the Study of Services. • 1996. $12.00. Revised edition. Presents the results of a consumer survey on satisfaction with specific managed care health insurance plans, and related information. Includes "Top-Rated Plans," "Health Plans That Chose Not to Have Their Members Surveyed," and other lists. General advice is provided on choosing a plan, finding a good doctor, getting good care, etc.

Dun & Bradstreet/Gale Group Industry Handbooks. The Gale Group. • 2000. $630.00. Five volumes. $145.00 per volume. Each volume covers two or more major industries: 1. *Entertainment and Hospitality*; 2. *Construction and Agriculture*; 3. *Chemicals and Pharmaceuticals*; 4. *Computers & Software and Broadcasting & Telecommunications*; 5. *Insurance and Health & Medical Services.* The following are included for each industry: overview, statistics, financial ratios, rankings, merger information, company directory, directory of associations, and consultants directory.

Health Law Handbook, 1992. Alice G. Gosfield, editor. West Group. • 1992. $75.00.

Healthcare Finance for the Non-Financial Manager: Basic Guide to Financial Analysis & Control. Louis Gapenski. McGraw-Hill Professional. • 1994. $47.50.

Long Term Care Administration; The Management of Institutional and Non-Institutional Components of the Continuum of Care. Ben Abramovice. The Haworth Press, Inc. • 1987. $39.95. Explores the multidisciplinary nature of long-term care. (Marketing and Health Services Administration, No. 1).

Management Accounting for Healthcare Organizations. Bruce R. Neumann and Keith E. Boles. Teach'em. • 1998. $65.00. Fifth revised edition.

INTERNET DATABASES

National Center for Health Statistics: Monitoring the Nation's Health. National Center for Health Statistics, Centers for Disease Control and Preventio. Phone: (301)458-4636 E-mail: nchsquery@cdc.gov • URL: http://www.cdc.gov/nchswww • Web site provides detailed data on diseases, vital statistics, and health care in the U. S. Includes a search facility and links to many other health-related Web sites. "Fastats A to Z" offers quick data on hundreds of topics from Accidents to Work-Loss Days, with links to Comprehensive Data and related sources. Frequent updates. Fees: Free.

National Library of Medicine (NLM). National Institutes of Health (NIH). Phone: 888-346-3656 or (301)496-1131 Fax: (301)480-3537 E-mail: access@nlm.nih.gov • URL: http://www.nlm.nih.gov • NLM Web site offers free access through MEDLINE ("PubMed") to about nine million references to articles appearing in some 3,800 biomedical journals, with abstracts. Search interfaces range from "simple keywords to advanced Boolean expressions." The NLM site offers many

For publishers addresses, refer to SOURCES CITED section at the back of the book.

links to other sources of biomedical and technical information (the National Center for Biotechnology Information, for example). Fees: Free.

ONLINE DATABASES

Embase. Elsevier Science, Inc. • Worldwide medical literature, 1974 to present. Weekly updates. Inquire as to online cost and availability.

F-D-C Reports. FDC Reports, Inc. • An online version of "The Gray Sheet" (medical devices), "The Pink Sheet" (pharmaceuticals), "The Rose Sheet" (cosmetics), "The Blue Sheet" (biomedical), and "The Tan Sheet" (nonprescription). Contains full-text information on legal, technical, corporate, financial, and marketing developments from 1987 to date, with weekly updates. Inquire as to online cost and availability.

Globalbase. The Gale Group. • Provides more than one million online summaries of business, industrial, and economic news reports from more than 1,000 publications worldwide. Covers a wide range of material appearing in international trade journals, professional magazines, and newspapers. Time period is 1984 to date, with weekly updates. Inquire as to online cost and availability.

Healthstar. Medlars Management Section. • Provides indexing and abstracting of non-clinical literature relating to health care delivery, 1975 to date. Monthly updates. Inquire as to online cost and availability.

Marketing and Advertising Reference Service (MARS). The Gale Group. • Provides abstracts of literature relating to consumer marketing and advertising, including all forms of advertising media. Time period is 1984 to date. Daily updates. Inquire as to online cost and availability.

Medline. Medlars Management Section. • Provides indexing and abstracting of worldwide medical literature, 1966 to date. Weekly updates. Inquire as to online cost and availability.

Newspaper and Periodical Abstracts. Bell & Howell Information and Learning. • Provides online coverage (citations and abstracts) of 25 major newspapers, 1,600 perodicals, and 70 TV programs. Covers business, economics, current affairs, health, fitness, sports, education, technology, government, consumer affairs, psychology, the arts, and the social sciences. Time period is 1986 to date, with daily updates. Inquire as to online cost and availability.

PAIS International. Public Affairs Information Service, Inc. • Corresponds to the former printed publications, *PAIS Bulletin* (1976-90) and *PAIS Foreign Language Index* (1972-90), and to the current *PAIS International in Print* (1991 to date). Covers economic, political, and sociological material appearing in periodicals, books, government documents, and other publications. Updating is monthly. Inquire as to online cost and availability.

PROMT: Predicasts Overview of Markets and Technology. The Gale Group. • Companies, products, applied technologies and markets. U.S. and international literature coverage, 1972 to date. Inquire as to online cost and availability. Provides abstracts from more than 1,600 publications. Weekly updates.

Scisearch. Institute for Scientific Information. • Broad, multidisciplinary index to the literature of science and technology, 1974 to present. Inquire as to online cost and availability. Coverage of literature is worldwide, with weekly updates.

Super Searchers on Health and Medicine: The Online Secrets of Top Health and Medical Researchers. Susan M. Detwiler and Reva Basch. Information Today, Inc. • 2000. $24.95. Provides the results of interviews with 10 experts in online searching for medical research data and healthcare information. Discusses both traditional sources and Web sites. (CyberAge Books.).

Wilson Business Abstracts Online. H. W. Wilson Co. • Indexes and abstracts 600 major business periodicals, plus the *Wall Street Journal* and the business section of the *New York Times*. Indexing is from 1982, abstracting from 1990, with the two newspapers included from 1993. Updated weekly. Inquire as to online cost and availability. (*Business Periodicals Index* without abstracts is also available online.).

Wilson Social Sciences Abstracts Online. H. W. Wilson Co. • Provides online abstracting and indexing of more than 415 periodicals covering area studies, community health, public administration, public welfare, urban studies, and many other social science topics. Time period is 1994 to date for abstracts and 1983 to date for indexing, with updates monthly. Inquire as to online cost and availability.

PERIODICALS AND NEWSLETTERS

AHA News. Health Forum, Inc. • Weekly. $147.00 per year. Edited for hospital and health care industry administrators. Covers health care news events and legislative activity. An American Hospital Association publication (http://www.aha.org).

American Dental Association Journal. American Dental Association. • Monthly. Free to members; non-members, $100.00 per year; institutions, $121.00 per year.

American Health Care Association: Provider. American Health Care Association. • Monthly. $48.00 per year. Formerly *American Health Care Association Journal.*

American Journal of Nursing. American Nurses Association. Lippincott Williams and Wilkins. • Monthly. Individuals, $29.95 per year; institutions, $79.95 per year. For registered nurses. Emphasis on the latest technological advances affecting nursing care.

American Medical News. American Medical Association. • 48 times a year. Individuals, $145.00 per year, institutions, $245.00 per year. Economic and legal news for the medical profession.

The BBI Newsletter: A Perceptive Analysis of the Healthcare Industry and Marketplace Focusing on New Technology, Strategic Planning, and Marketshare Projections. American Health Consultants. • Monthly. $827.00 per year.

Changing Medical Markets: The Monthly Newsletter for Executives in the Healthcare and Biotechnology Industries. Theta Reports/PJB Medical Publications, Inc. • Monthly. $295.00 per year. Newsletter. Covers developments in medical technology, new products, corporate trends, medical market research, mergers, personnel, and other healthcare topics.

Faulkner and Gray's Medicine and Health. Faulkner & Gray. • Weekly. $525.00 per year. Newsletter on socioeconomic developments relating to the health care industry. Formerly *McGraw-Hill's Washington Report on Medicine and Health.*

Health Care Financing Review. Available from U. S. Government Printing Office. • Quarterly. $30.00 per year. Issued by the Health Care Financing Administration, U. S. Department of Health and Human Services. Presents articles by professionals in the areas of health care costs and financing.

Health Care Strategic Management: The Newsletter for Hospital Strategies. Business Word, Inc. • Monthly. $249.00 per year. Planning, marketing and resource allocation.

Health Facilities Management. American Hospital Association. American Hospital Publishing, Inc. • Monthly. $40.00 per year. Covers building maintenance and engineering for hospitals and nursing homes.

Health Forum. American Hospital Association. American Hospital Publishing, Inc. • Biweekly. $80.00 per year. Covers the general management of hospitals, nursing homes, and managed care organizations. Formerly *HospitalsHealthNetworks.*

Health Grants and Contracts Weekly: Selected Federal Project Opportunities. Aspen Publishers, Inc. • Weekly. $379.00 per year. Lists new health-related federal contracts and grants.

Health Industry Today: The Market Letter for Health Care Industry Vendors. Business Word, Inc. • Monthly. $325.00 per year.

Health Letter. Sidney M. Wolfe, editor. Public Citizen, Inc. • Monthly. $18.00 per year. Newsletter for healthcare consumers.

Health Management Technology. Nelson Publishing, Inc. • Monthly. $38.00 per year. Formerly *Computers in Healthcare.*

Health Marketing Quarterly. The Haworth Press, Inc. • Quarterly. Individuals, $60.00 per year; institutions, $80.00 per year; libraries, $425.00 per year.

Health News Daily. F-D-C Reports, Inc. • Daily. $1,350.00 per year. Newsletter providing broad coverage of the healthcare business, including government policy, regulation, research, finance, and insurance. Contains news of pharmaceuticals, medical devices, biotechnology, and healthcare delivery in general.

Health Policy and Biomedical Research: The Blue Sheet. F-D-C Reports, Inc. • 51 Times a year. $619.00 per year. Newsletter. Emphasis is on news of medical research agencies and institutions, especially the National Institutes of Health (NIH).

Healthcare Business. Healthcare Business Media, Inc. • Bimonthly. $28.00 per year. Provides broad coverage of finance, marketing, management, and technology for executives in the health care industry. Includes "Roundtable" discussions of particular health care issues.

Healthcare Executive. American College of Healthcare Executives. • Bimonthly. $60.00 per year. Focuses on critical management issues.

Healthcare Financial Management. Healthcare Financial Management Association. • Monthly. $82.00 per year.

Healthcare Forum Journal: Leadership Strategies for Healthcare Executives. Healthcare Forum. • Bimonthly. $65.00 per year.

Healthcare Informatics: The Business of Healthcare Information Technology. McGraw-Hill. • Monthly. $40.00 per year. Covers various aspects of information and computer technology for the health care industry.

Healthcare Marketing Report. HMR Publication Group. • Monthly. Price on application.

Healthcare PR and Marketing News. Phillips Business Information, Inc. • Biweekly. $497.00 per year. Newsletter on public relations and client communications for the healthcare industry.

International Journal of Health Planning and Management. Available from John Wiley and Sons, Inc., Journals Div. • Quarterly. Institutions, $980.00 per year. Published in England by John Wiley and Sons Ltd.

JAMA: The Journal of the American Medical Association. American Medical Association. • 48 times a year. Two volumes. Individuals, $145.00 per year; institutions, $245.00 per year.

Journal of Healthcare Information Management. Healthcare Information and Management Systems Society. Jossey-Bass Inc., Publishers. • Quarterly. Institutions, $114.00 per year.

Marketing Health Services. American Marketing Association. • Quarterly. Members, $45.00 per year; non-members, $70.00 per year; institutions, $90.00 per year. Formerly*Journal of Health Care Marketing*.

Medical Devices, Diagnostics, and Instrumentation: The Gray Sheet Reports. F-D-C Reports, Inc. • Weekly. $955.00 per year. Newsletter. Provides industry and financial news, including a medical sector stock index. Monitors regulatory developments at the Center for Devices and Radiological Health of the U. S. Food and Drug Administration.

Medical Group Management Journal. Medical Group Management Association. • Bimonthly. $68.00 per year.

Medical Marketing and Media. CPS Communications, Inc. • Monthly. Individuals, $75.00 per year; institutions, $100.00 per person. Contains articles on marketing, direct marketing, advertising media, and sales personnel for the healthcare and pharmaceutical industries.

Medical Reference Services Quarterly. Haworth Press, Inc. • Quarterly. Individuals, $50.00 per year; libraries and other institutions, $175.00 per year. An academic and practical journal for medical reference librarians.

Medical Tribune: World News of Medicine and Its Practice. Press Corps, Inc. • Biweekly. Free to qualified personnel; others, $95.00 per year. Includes *Family Physicians, Internist and Cardiologist* and *Obstetetrician and Gynecologist.*

Medical Utilization Management. Faulkner & Gray. • Biweekly. $395.00 per year. Newsletter. Formerly *Medical Utilization Review.*

The Milbank Quarterly. Milbank Memorial Fund. Blackwell Publishers. • Quarterly. $101.00 per year. Formerly*Health and Society.*

Modern Healthcare: The Newsmagazine for Adminstrators and Managers in Hospitals and Other Healthcare Institutions. Crain Communications, Inc. • Weekly. $135.00 per year; students, $63.00 per year.

Modern Physician: Essential Business News for the Executive Physician. Crain Communications, Inc. • Monthly. $39.50. Edited for physicians responsible for business decisions at hospitals, clinics, HMOs, and other health groups. Includes special issues on managed care, practice management, legal issues, and finance.

New England Journal of Medicine. Massachusetts Medical Society, Publishing Div. • Weekly. Individuals, $135.00 per year; institutions, $349.00 per year. The offical journal of the Massachusetts Medical Society.

Patient Management. Cahners Business Information, New Product Information. • Nine times a year. $24.00 per year. Formerly *Medical Care Products.*

Physicians & Computers. Moorhead Publications Inc. • Monthly. $40.00 per year. Includes material on computer diagnostics, online research, medical and non-medical software, computer equipment, and practice management.

Services Marketing Quarterly. Haworth Press, Inc. • Semiannual. Two volumes. Individuals, $60.00 per year; institutions, $90.00 per year; libraries, $275.00 per year. Supplies "how to" marketing tools for specific sectors of the expanding service sector of the economy. Formerly *Journal of Professional Services Marketing.*

Strategic Health Care Marketing. Health Care Communications. • Monthly. $269.00 per year. Newsletter.

Telehealth Magazine. Miller Freeman. • Bimonthly. $50.00 per year. Covers Internet, wireless, and other telecommunications technologies for health care professionals.

RESEARCH CENTERS AND INSTITUTES

Bureau of Economic and Business Research. University of Illinois at Urbana-Champaign, 1206 S. Sixth St., Champaign, IL 61820. Phone: (217)333-2330 Fax: (217)244-7410 E-mail: g-oldman@uiuc.edu • URL: http://www.cba.uiuc.edu/research.

Center for Health Administration Studies. University of Chicago, 969 E. 60th St., Chicago, IL 60637. Phone: (773)702-7104 Fax: (773)702-7222 E-mail: chas@uchichago.edu • URL: http://www.chas.uchicago.edu.

Center for Health Policy Law and Management. Duke University, P.O. Box 90253, Durham, NC 27708. Phone: (919)684-3023 Fax: (919)684-6246 E-mail: fsloan@hpolicy.duke.edu • URL: http://www.hpolicy.duke.edu.

Center for Health Research. Wayne State University, College of Nursing, 5557 Cass Ave., Detroit, MI 48202. Phone: (313)577-4134 Fax: (313)577-5777 E-mail: ajacox@wayne.edu • URL: http://www.comm.wayne.edu/nursing/nursing.html • Studies innovation in health care organization and financing.

ECRI: Emergency Care Research Institute. 5200 Butler Pike, Plymouth Meeting, PA 19462. Phone: (610)825-6000 Fax: (610)834-1275 E-mail: ecri@hslc.org • URL: http://www.ecri.org • Major research area is health care technology.

Health Policy Institute. University of Texas-Houston Health Science Center, P.O. Box 20186, Houston, TX 77225. Phone: (713)500-9485 Fax: (713)500-9493 E-mail: dlow@admin4.hsc.uth.tmc.edu • URL: http://www.sph.utu.tmc.edu/ctr/hpi/hpi.htm.

Health Research Institute. 3538 Torino Way, Concord, CA 94518. Phone: (510)676-2320 Fax: (510)676-2342 • Conducts applied research in health care financing and delivery of health services, with emphasis on cost containment.

Institute for Health, Health Care Policy, and Aging Research. Rutgers University, 30 College Ave., New Brunswick, NJ 08903. Phone: (732)932-8413 Fax: (732)982-6872 E-mail: caboyer@rci.rutgers.edu • URL: http://www.ihhcpar.rutgers.edu/ • Areas of study include HMO use by older adults.

Institute for Health Services Research and Policy Studies. Northwestern University, 629 Noyes St., Evanston, IL 60208-4170. Phone: (847)491-5643 Fax: (847)491-2202 E-mail: k-kramer@nwu.edu • URL: http://www.edu/ihsrps.

Leonard Davis Institute of Health Economics. University of Pennsylvania, 3641 Locust Walk, Philadelphia, PA 19104-6218. Phone: (215)898-1655 Fax: (215)898-0229 E-mail: levyj@wharton.upenn.edu • URL: http://www.upenn.edu/ldi/ • Research fields include health care management and cost-quality trade-offs.

Malcolm Wiener Center for Social Policy. Harvard University, John F. Kennedy School of Government, 79 John F. Kennedy, Cambridge, MA 02138. Phone: (617)495-1461 Fax: (617)496-9053 E-mail: juliewilson@harvard.edu • URL: http://www.ksg.harvard.edu/socpol • Does multidisciplinary research on health care access and financing.

STATISTICS SOURCES

Health and Environment in America's Top-Rated Cities: A Statistical Profile. Grey House Publishing. • Biennial. $195.00. Covers 75 U. S. cities. Includes statistical and other data on a wide variety of topics, such as air quality, water quality, recycling, hospitals, physicians, health care costs, death rates, infant mortality, accidents, and suicides.

Health Care Costs. DRI/McGraw-Hill. • Quarterly. Price on application. Cost indexes for hospitals, nursing homes, and home healthcare agencies.

Social Statistics of the United States. Mark S. Littman, editor. Bernan Press. • 2000. $65.00. Includes statistical data on population growth, labor force, occupations, environmental trends, leisure time use, income, poverty, taxes, and other economic or demographic topics.

Standard & Poor's Industry Surveys. Standard & Poor's. • Semiannual. $1,800.00. Two looseleaf volumes. Includes monthly supplements. Provides detailed, individual surveys of 52 major industry groups. Each survey is revised on a semiannual basis. Also includes "Monthly Investment Review" (industry group investment analysis) and monthly "Trends & Projections" (economic analysis).

Statistical Forecasts of the United States. The Gale Group. • 1995. $99.00. Second edition. Provides both long-term and short-term statistical forecasts relating to basic items in the U. S.: population, employment, labor, crime, education, and health care. Data in the form of charts, graphs, and tables has been taken from a wide variety of government and private sources. Includes a subject index and an "Index of Forecast by Year.".

A Statistical Portrait of the United States: Social Conditions and Trends. Mark S. Littman, editor. Bernan Press. • 1998. $89.00. Covers "social, economic, and environmental trends in the United States over the past 25 years." Includes statistical tables, graphs, and analysis relating to such topics as population, income, poverty, wealth, labor, housing, education, healthcare, air/water quality, and government.

U. S. Industry and Trade Outlook: The McGraw-Hill Companies and the U.S. Department of Commerce/ International Trade Administration. Datapso Research Corp. • Annual. $69.95. Produced by the International Trade Administration, U. S. Department of Commerce, in a "public-private" partnership with DRI/McGraw-Hill and Standard & Poor's. Provides basic data, outlook for the current year, and "Long-Term Prospects" (five-year projections) for a wide variety of products and services. Includes high technology industries. Formerly *U. S. Industrial Outlook.*

Universal Healthcare Almanac: A Complete Guide for the Healthcare Professional - Facts, Figures, Analysis. Silver & Cherner, Ltd. • Looseleaf service. $195.00 per year. Quarterly updates. Includes a wide variety of health care statistics: national expenditures, hospital data, health insurance, health professionals, vital statistics, demographics, etc. Years of coverage vary, with long range forecasts provided in some cases.

WEFA Industrial Monitor. John Wiley and Sons, Inc. • Annual. $65.00. Prepared by industry analysts at WEFA, an economic forecasting and consulting firm (originally Wharton Econometric Forecasting Associates). Contains discussions of the outlook for major U. S. industries, with many 10-year forecasts (WEFA Web site is http://www.wefa.com).

TRADE/PROFESSIONAL ASSOCIATIONS

American Academy of Medical Administrators. 701 Lee St., Ste. 600, Des Plaines, IL 60016. Phone: (847)759-8601 Fax: (847)759-8602 E-mail: info@

aameda.org • URL: http://www.aameda.org • Members are executives and middle managers in health care administration.

American Association for Continuity of Care. P.O. Box 7073, North Brunswick, NJ 08902. Phone: 800-816-1575 Fax: (301)352-7086 • URL: http://www.continuitycare.com • Members are professionals concerned with continuity of care, health care after hospital discharge, and home health care.

American Association of Health Plans. 1129 20th St., N.W., Suite 600, Washington, DC 20036-3421. Phone: (202)728-3200 Fax: (202)331-7487 • URL: http://www.aahp.org • Members are alternate health care organizations, including HMOs.

American Association of Healthcare Consultants. 11208 Waples Mill Rd., Suite 109, Fairfax, VA 22030. Phone: 800-362-4674 or (703)691-2242 Fax: (703)691-2247 E-mail: consultahc@aol.com • URL: http://www.aahc.net • Members are professional consultants who specialize in the health care industry.

American Board of Medical Specialties. 1007 Church St., Suite 404, Evanston, IL 60201-5913. Phone: (847)491-9091 Fax: (847)328-3596 • URL: http://www.abms.org/abms • Functions as the parent organization for U. S. medical specialty boards.

American College of Health Care Administrators. 325 S. Patrick St., Alexandria, VA 22314. Phone: 888-882-2422 or (703)739-7900 Fax: (703)739-7901 E-mail: info@achca.org • URL: http://www.achca.org.

American College of Healthcare Executives. One N. Franklin, St., Suite 1700, Chicago, IL 60606-3491. Phone: (312)424-2800 Fax: (312)424-0023 • URL: http://www.ache.org.

American Dental Association. 211 E. Chicago Ave., Chicago, IL 60611-2678. Phone: (312)440-2500 Fax: (312)440-2800 E-mail: online@ada.org • URL: http://www.ada.org.

American Health Care Association. 1201 L St., N. W., Washington, DC 20005. Phone: (202)842-4444 Fax: (202)842-3860 • URL: http://www.ahca.org.

American Hospital Association. One N. Franklin St., Chicago, IL 60606. Phone: (312)422-3000 Fax: (312)422-4796 • URL: http://www.aha.org.

American Medical Association. 515 N. State St., Chicago, IL 60610. Phone: (312)464-5000 Fax: (312)464-4184 • URL: http://www.ama-assn.org/ • Concerned with retirement planning and other financial planning for physicians 55 years of age or older.

American Nurses Association. 600 Maryland Ave., S.W., Suite 100 W., Washington, DC 20024-2571. Phone: 800-274-4262 or (202)651-7000 Fax: (202)651-7001 • URL: http://www.nursingworld.org.

American Pharmaceutical Association/Academy of Pharmacy Practice and Management. c/o Anne Burns, 2215 Constitution Ave., N.W., Washington, DC 20037-2895. Phone: 800-237-2742 or (202)628-4410 Fax: (202)783-2351 E-mail: apha-appm@mail.aphanet.org • URL: http://www.aphanet.org.

Health Industry Distributors Association. 66 Canal Center Plaza, Suite 520, Alexandria, VA 22314-1591. Phone: (703)549-4432 Fax: (703)549-6495 • URL: http://www.hida.org.

Health Industry Manufacturers Association. 1200 G St., N.W., Suite 400, Washington, DC 20005. Phone: (202)783-8700 Fax: (202)783-8750 • URL: http://www.himanet.com.

Health Industry Representatives Association. 6740 E. Hampden Ave., Suite 306, Denver, CO 80224. Phone: 800-777-4472 or (303)756-8115 Fax: (303)756-5699 • URL: http://www.hira.org • Members are manufacturers' representatives working within the health care industry.

Healthcare Convention and Exhibitors Association. 5775 Peachtree-Dunwoody Rd., Suite 500-G, Atlanta, GA 30342. Phone: (404)252-3663 Fax: (404)252-0774 E-mail: hcea@assnhq.com • URL: http://www.hcea.org • Promotes more effective display of health care products at professional conventions.

Healthcare Financing Management Association. Two Westbrook Corporate Financial Center, Suite 700, Westchester, IL 60154-5700. Phone: 800-252-4362 E-mail: tarya@hfma.org • URL: http://www.hfma.org.

Healthcare Financing Study Group. 1919 Pennsylvania Ave., N.W., Suite 800, Washington, DC 20006. Phone: (202)887-1400 Fax: (202)466-3215 • Concerned with the provision of capital financing for health care institutions.

Independent Medical Distributors Association. 5800 Foxridge Dr., No. 115, Mission, KS 66202-2333. Phone: (913)262-4510 Fax: (913)262-0174 • URL: http://www.imda.org • Members are distributors of high technology health care products.

Medical Group Management Association. 104 Inverness Terrace E., Englewood, CO 80112-5306. Phone: 888-608-5601 or (303)799-1111 Fax: (303)643-4439 • URL: http://www.mgma.com • Members are medical group managers.

National Association for Medical Equipment Services. 625 Slaters Lane, Suite 200, Alexandria, VA 22314-1171. Phone: (703)836-6263 Fax: (703)836-6730 E-mail: info@names.org • URL: http://www.names.org • Members are durable medical equipment and oxygen suppliers, mainly for home health care. Has Legislative Affairs Committee that is concerned with Medicare/Medicaid benefits.

People's Medical Society. 462 Walnut St., Allentown, PA 18102. Phone: 800-624-8773 or (610)770-1670 Fax: (610)770-0607 E-mail: mad1@peoplesmed.org • URL: http://www.peoplesmed.org • A consumer affairs society concerned with the cost, quality, and management of the American health care system.

Pharmaceutical Research and Manufacturers Association. 1100 15th St., N.W., Suite 900, Washington, DC 20005. Phone: (202)835-3400 Fax: (202)835-3429 • URL: http://www.phrma.org.

Special Interest Group on Biomedical Computing. Association for Computing Machinery, 1515 Broadway, New York, NY 10036. Phone: (212)869-7440 Fax: (212)302-5826 E-mail: sigs@acm.org • URL: http://www.acm.org/sigbio • Concerned with medical informatics, molecular databases, medical multimedia, and computerization in general as related to the health and biological sciences.

OTHER SOURCES

The Competitive Edge. InterStudy Publications. • Semiannual. Price on application. Provides highly detailed statistical, directory, and market information on U. S. health maintenance organizations. Consists of three parts: *The HMO Directory, The HMO Industry Report*, and *The Regional Market Analysis.* (Emphasis is on market research. http://www.dresources.com/).

Health Care Products and Remedies. Available from MarketResearch.com. • 1997. $600.00 each. Consists of market reports published by Simmons Market Research Bureau on each of about 25 health care product categories. Examples are cold remedies, contraceptives, hearing aids, bandages, headache remedies, eyeglasses, contact lenses, and vitamins. Each report covers buying patterns and demographics.

HEALTH CLUB INDUSTRY

See: FITNESS INDUSTRY

HEALTH FOOD INDUSTRY

See also: DIET; FOOD INDUSTRY; HERBS; VITAMINS

ABSTRACTS AND INDEXES

Nutrition Abstracts and Reviews, Series A: Human and Experimental. Available from CABI Publishing North America. • Monthly. $1,385.00 per year. Published in England by CABI Publishing. Provides worldwide coverage of the literature.

DIRECTORIES

Health Products Business Purchasing Guide. Cygnus Business Media. • Annual. $35.00. Listing of manufacturers, importers, exclusive distributors, brokers, and wholesalers of health food products, publishers of health food related books and magazines, and associations interested in the health foods industry. Formerly Health Foods Business Purchasing Guide.

FINANCIAL RATIOS

Annual Statement Studies. Robert Morris Associates: The Association of Lending and Credit Risk Professiona. • Annual. Free to members; non-members, $140.00. Median and quartile financial ratios are given for over 400 kinds of manufacturing, wholesale, retail, construction, and consumer finance establishments. Data is sorted by both asset size and sales volume. Includes a clearly written "Definition of Ratios" and an alphabetical industry index.

HANDBOOKS AND MANUALS

Health Food/Vitamin Store. Entrepreneur Media, Inc. • Looseleaf. $59.50. A practical guide to starting a health food store. Covers profit potential, start-up costs, market size evaluation, owner's time required, site selection, lease negotiation, pricing, accounting, advertising, promotion, etc. (Start-Up Business Guide No. E1296.).

Health Foods: A Source Guide. Gordon Press Publishers. • 1991. $77.95.

Herbal Drugs and Phytopharmaceuticals. Max Wichtl and Norman G. Bisset, editors. CRC Press, Inc. • 1994. $190.00. Provides a scientific approach to the medicinal use of herbs. (English translation of original German edition.).

PERIODICALS AND NEWSLETTERS

Health Products Business: The Business Publication of the Natural Foods In dustry. Cygnus Business Media. • Monthly. $54.00 per year.

TRADE/PROFESSIONAL ASSOCIATIONS

Natural Food Associates. 8345 Walnut Hill Lane, Suite 225, Dallas, TX 75231-4205. 8345 Walnut Hill Lane, Suite 225, • Members are professionals and consumers interested in natural foods and organic farming.

OTHER SOURCES

The Health and Natural Product Store Market. Available from MarketResearch.com. • 1999. $2,750.00. Published by Packaged Facts. Contains market research data.

Healthy Prepared Foods. MarketResearch.com. • 1999. $2,750.00. Consumer market data on foods that are low in calories, fat, cholesterol, sodium, and sugar or high in fiber and calcium, with forecasts to 2003.

Market for Healthy Snacks. MarketResearch.com. • 1996. $1,250.00. Provides market data on granola bars, dried fruit, trail mix, rice cakes, etc.

HEALTH, INDUSTRIAL

See: INDUSTRIAL HYGIENE

HEALTH INSURANCE

See also: ACCIDENT INSURANCE; HEALTH MAINTENANCE ORGANIZATIONS; INSURANCE; LIFE INSURANCE; LONG-TERM CARE INSURANCE; MEDICARE

GENERAL WORKS

Compulsory Health Insurance: The Continuing American Debate. Ronald L. Numbers, editor. Greenwood Publishing Group Inc. • 1982. $49.95. (Contributions in Medical History Series, No.11).

Fundamentals of Employee Benefit Programs. Employee Benefit Research Institute. • 1996. $49.95. Fifth edition. Provides basic explanation of employee benefit programs in both the private and public sectors, including health insurance, pension plans, retirement planning, social security, and long-term care insurance.

Health Care Cost Containment. Karen Davis and others. Johns Hopkins University Press. • 1990. $48.00. (Studies in Health Care Finance and Administrations).

The Lifetime Book of Money Management. Grace W. Weinstein. Visible Ink Press. • 1993. $15.95. Third edition. Gives popularly-written advice on investments, life and health insurance, owning a home, credit, retirement, estate planning, and other personal finance topics.

Medical Care, Medical Costs: The Search for a Health Insurance Policy. Rashi Fein. Replica Books. • 1999. $26.95.

Medicare Made Easy: Everything You Need to Know to Make Medicare Work for You. Charles B. Inlander and Michael A. Danio. Fine Communications. • 1999. $19.98. Revised edition. Provides basic information on Medicare claims processing and the manner in which Medicare relates to other health insurance. The author is a consumer advocate and president of the People's Medical Society.

Retirement Security: Understanding and Planning Your Financial Future. David M. Walker. John Wiley and Sons, Inc. • 1996. $29.95. Topics include investments, social security, Medicare, health insurance, and employer retirement plans.

Smarter Insurance Solutions. Janet Bamford. Bloomberg Press. • 1996. $19.95. Provides practical advice to consumers, with separate chapters on the following kinds of insurance: automobile, homeowners, health, disability, and life. (Bloomberg Personal Bookshelf Series).

ABSTRACTS AND INDEXES

Index to Health Information. Congressional Information Service, Inc. • Quarterly. $945.00 per year, including two-volume annual cumulation. Provides index and abstracts covering the medical and health field in general, with emphasis on statistical sources and government documents. Service with microfiche source documents, $4,995.00 per year.

Insurance Periodicals Index. Specials Libraries Association, Insurance and Employees Benefits Div. CCH/NILS Publishing Co. • Annual. $250.00. Compiled by the Insurance and Employee Benefits Div., Special Libraries Association. A yearly index of over 15,000 articles from about 35 insurance periodicals. Arrangement is by subject, with an index to authors.

ALMANACS AND YEARBOOKS

Insurance Almanac: Who, What, When and Where in Insurance. Underwriter Printing and Publishing Co. • Annual. $145.00. Lists insurance agencies and brokerage firms; U.S. and Canadian insurance companies, adjusters, appraisers, auditors, investigators, insurance officials and insurance organizations.

BIBLIOGRAPHIES

List of Worthwhile Life and Health Insurance Books. American Council of Life Insurance. • Annual. Free. Books in print on life and health insurance and closely related subjects.

CD-ROM DATABASES

Magazine Index Plus. The Gale Group. • Monthly. $4,000.00 per year (includes InfoTrac workstation). Provides full text on CD-ROM for about 100 popular, general interest magazines and indexing for 300 others. Includes special indexing of reviews and product evaluations. Time period is 1980 to date.

U. S. Insurance: Life, Accident, and Health. Sheshunoff Information Services, Inc. • Monthly. Price on application. CD-ROM provides detailed, current information on the financial characteristics of more than 2,300 life, accident, and health insurance companies.

DIRECTORIES

HMO/PPO Directory. Medical Economics Co., Inc. • Annual. $215.00. Provides detailed information on managed care providers in the U. S., chiefly health maintenance organizations (HMOs) and preferred provider organizations (PPOs).

Who Writes What in Life and Health Insurance. The National Underwriter Co. • Annual. $9.95.

ENCYCLOPEDIAS AND DICTIONARIES

Dictionary of Insurance. Lewis E. Davids. Rowman and Littlefield Publishers, Inc. • 1990. $17.95. Seventh revised edition.

Dictionary of Insurance Terms. Harvey W. Rubin. Barron's Educational Series, Inc. • 2000. $12.95. Fourth edition. Defines terms in a wide variety of insurance fields. Price on application.

Health Insurance Terminology: A Glossary of Health Insurance Terms. Margaret Lynch, editor. Health Insurance Association of America. • 1992. $10.00.

Insurance Words and Their Meanings: A Dictionary of Insurance Terms. Diana Kowatch. The Rough Notes Co., Inc. • 1998. $38.50. 16th revised edition.

Rupp's Insurance and Risk Management Glossary. Richard V. Rupp. Available from CCH, Inc. • 1996. $35.00. Second edition. Published by NILS Publishing Co. Provides definitions of 6,400 insurance words and phrases. Includes a guide to acronyms and abbreviations.

HANDBOOKS AND MANUALS

The Complete Book of Insurance: The Consumer's Guide to Insuring Your Life, Health, Property, and Income. Ben G. Baldwin. McGraw-Hill Professional. • 1996. $24.95. Revised edition. Provides basic information and advice on various kinds of insurance: life, health, property (fire), disability, long-term care, automobile, liability, and annuities.

Guide to Health Insurance for People with Medicare. U. S. Health Care Financing Administration, Department of Health and Human Servi. • Annual. Free. Contains detailed information on private health insurance as a supplement to Medicare.

How to Cover the Gaps in Medicare: Health Insurance and Long-Term Care Options for the Retired. Robert A. Gilmour. American Institute for Economic Research. • 2000. $5.00. 12th revised edition. Four parts: "The Medicare Quandry," "How to Protect Yourself Against the Medigap," "Long-Term Care Options", and "End-of-Life Decisions" (living wills). Includes discussions of long-term care insurance, retirement communities, and HMO Medicare insurance, (Economic Education Bulletin Series, No. 10).

An Insurance Guide for Seniors. Insurance Forum, Inc. • 1997. $15.00. Provides concise advice and information on Medicare, Medicare supplement insurance, HMOs, long-term care insurance, automobile insurance, life insurance, annuities, and pensions. An appendix lists "Financially Strong Insurance Companies." (*The Insurance Forum*, vol. 24, no. 4.).

Insurance Handbook for the Medical Offices. Marilyn T. Fordney. Harcourt Health Sciences Group. • 1999. $43.95. Sixth edition.

Life and Health Insurance Law. William F. Meyer. West Group. • 1972. $125.00. Covers the legal aspects of life, health, and accident insurance.

McGill's Life Insurance. Edward E. Graves, editor. The American College. • 1998. $71.00. Second edition. Contains chapters by various authors on diverse kinds of life insurance, as well as annuities, disability insurance, long-term care insurance, risk management, reinsurance, and other insurance topics. Originally by Dan M. McGill.

Medical Claims Processing. Entrepreneur Media, Inc. • Looseleaf. $59.50. A practical guide to starting a medical claims processing service. Covers profit potential, start-up costs, market size evaluation, owner's time required, site selection, pricing, accounting, advertising, promotion, etc. (Start-Up Business Guide No. E1345.).

Medicare and Medicaid Claims and Procedures. Harvey L. McCormick. West Publishing Co., College and School Div. • 1986. Two volumes. Price on application. Periodic supplementation.

Medicare: Employer Health Plans. Available from Consumer Information Center. • Free. Published by the U. S. Department of Health and Human Services. Explains the special rules that apply to Medicare beneficiaries who have employer group health plan coverage. (Publication No. 520-Y.).

Medicare Explained. CCH, Inc. • Annual. $30.00.

Source Book of Health Insurance Data, 1997-1998. Health Insurance Association of America. • 1998. $35.00. Data on health insurance, medical care costs, morbidity and health manpower in the U. S.

INTERNET DATABASES

Bureau of Labor Statistics (BLS). U. S. Department of Labor, Bureau of Labor Statistics. Phone: (202)523-1092 E-mail: labstat.helpdesk@bls.gov • URL: http://www.bls.gov • Web site provides a great variety of employment, wage, price, and economic data. Some links are "Data," "Economy at a Glance," "Keyword Search of BLS Web Pages," "Regional Information," and "Other Statistical Sites." Fees: Free.

InsWeb. InsWeb Corp. Phone: (650)372-2129 E-mail: info@insweb.com • URL: http://www.insweb.com • Web site offers a wide variety of advice and information on automobile, life, health, and "other" insurance. Includes glossaries of insurance terms, Standard & Poor's ratings of individual insurance companies, and "Financial Needs Estimators." Searching is available. Fees: Free.

National Center for Health Statistics: Monitoring the Nation's Health. National Center for Health Statistics, Centers for Disease Control and Preventio.

Phone: (301)458-4636 E-mail: nchsquery@cdc.gov • URL: http://www.cdc.gov/nchswww • Web site provides detailed data on diseases, vital statistics, and health care in the U. S. Includes a search facility and links to many other health-related Web sites. "Fastats A to Z" offers quick data on hundreds of topics from Accidents to Work-Loss Days, with links to Comprehensive Data and related sources. Frequent updates. Fees: Free.

ONLINE DATABASES

Best's Company Reports. A. M. Best Co. • Provides full financial data online for U. S. insurance companies (life, health, property, casualty), including balance sheet data, income statements, expenses, premium income, losses, and investments. Includes *Best's Company Reports*, *Best's Insurance News*, and Best's ratings of insuarance companies. Inquire as to online cost and availability.

Healthstar. Medlars Management Section. • Provides indexing and abstracting of non-clinical literature relating to health care delivery, 1975 to date. Monthly updates. Inquire as to online cost and availability.

I.I.I. Data Base Search. Insurance Information Institute. • Provides online citations and abstracts of insurance-related literature in magazines, newspapers, trade journals, and books. Emphasis is on property and casualty insurance issues, including highway safety, product safety, and environmental liability. Inquire as to online cost and availability.

PERIODICALS AND NEWSLETTERS

Advisory Today. National Association of insurance and Finacial Advisors. • Monthly. Free to members; non-members, $7.00 per year. Edited for individual life and health insurance agents. Among the topics included are disability insurance and long-term care insurance. Formerly Life Association News.

Best's Review: Inurance Issues and Analysis. A.M. Best Co. • Monthly. $25.00 per year. Editorial coverage of significant industry trends, developments, and important events. Formerly Best's Review: Property-Casualty Insurance.

Business and Health. Medical Economics Co., Inc. • Monthly. $99.00 per year. Edited for business, government, and other buyers of employee healthcare insurance or HMO coverage.

Contingencies: The Magazine of the Actuarial Profession. American Academy of Actuaries. • Bimonthly. $30.00 per year. Provides non-technical articles on the actuarial aspects of insurance, employee benefits, and pensions.

Drug Benefit Trends: For Pharmacy Managers and Managed Healthcare Professionals. SCP Communications, Inc. • Monthly. Individuals, $72.00 per year; institutions, $120.00 per year. Covers the business of managed care drug benefits.

Guide to HMOs and Health Insurers: A Quarterly Compilation of Health Insurance Company Ratings and Analysis. Weiss Ratings, Inc. • Quarterly. $438.00 per year. Emphasis is on rating of financial safety and relative risk. Includes annual summary.

Guide to Life, Health, and Annuity Insurers: A Quarterly Compilation of Insurance Company Ratings and Analysis. Weiss Ratings, Inc. • Quarterly. $438.00 per year. Emphasis is on rating of financial safety and relative risk. Includes annual summary.

Health Care Financing Review. Available from U. S. Government Printing Office. • Quarterly. $30.00 per year. Issued by the Health Care Financing Administration, U. S. Department of Health and Human Services. Presents articles by professionals in the areas of health care costs and financing.

Health Data Management. Faulkner & Gray, Inc. • Monthly. $98.00 per year. Covers the management and automation of clinical data and health care insurance claims. Includes information on claims processors and third-party administrators.

Health Insurance Underwriter. National Association of Health Underwriters. • 11 times a year. Free to members; non-members, $25.00 per year. Includes special feature issues on long-term care insurance, disability insurance, managed health care, and insurance office management.

Health News Daily. F-D-C Reports, Inc. • Daily. $1,350.00 per year. Newsletter providing broad coverage of the healthcare business, including government policy, regulation, research, finance, and insurance. Contains news of pharmaceuticals, medical devices, biotechnology, and healthcare delivery in general.

Healthplan: The Magazine of Trends, Insights, and Best Practices. American Association of Health Plans. • Bimonthly. $75.00 per year. Edited for managed care executives.

Inquiry: The Journal of Health Care Organization, Provision, and Financing. Finger Lakes Blue Cross and Blue Shield Association. • Quarterly. Individuals, $50.00 per year; institutions, $70.00 per year.

Insurance and Technology. Miller Freeman. • Monthly. $65.00 per year. Covers information technology and systems management as applied to the operation of life, health, casualty, and property insurance companies.

The Insurance Forum: For the Unfettered Exchange of Ideas About Insurance. Joseph M. Belth, editor. Insurance Forum, Inc. • Monthly. $90.00 per year. Newsletter. Provides analysis of the insurance business, including occasional special issues showing the ratings of about 1,600 life-health insurance companies, as determined by four major rating services: Duff & Phelps Credit Rating Co., Moody's Investors Service, Standard & Poor's Corp., and Weiss Research, Inc.

Professional Agent. National Association of Professional Insurance Agents. • Monthly. Members, $12,00 per year; non-members, $24.00 per year. Provides sales and marketing advice for independent agents in various fields of insurance, including life, health, property, and casualty.

Risk and Insurance. LRP Publications. • Monthly. Price on application. Topics include risk management, workers' compensation, reinsurance, employee benefits, and managed care.

PRICE SOURCES

Medicare Supplement Price Survey. Weiss Ratings, Inc. • Continuous revision. Price on application. Available for individual geographic areas to provide detailed price information for various types of Medicare supplement health insurance policies issued by specific insurance companies.

RESEARCH CENTERS AND INSTITUTES

Center for Medical Economics Studies. Northeastern University. 185 Commodore Dr., Jupiter, FL 33477. Phone: (561)745-9145 E-mail: dolly321@aol.com.

Division of Health Services Research and Policy. University of Minnesota, P.O. Box 729, Minneapolis, MN 55455. Phone: (612)624-6151 Fax: (612)624-2196 E-mail: foote003@tc.umn.edu • URL: http://www.hsr.umn.edu • Fields of research include health insurance, consumer choice of health plans, quality of care, and long-term care.

Employee Benefit Research Institute. 2121 K St., N. W., Suite 600, Washington, DC 20037-1896. Phone: (202)659-0670 Fax: (202)775-6312 E-mail: salisbury@ebri.org • URL: http://www.ebri.org • Conducts research on employee benefits, including various kinds of pensions, individual retirement accounts (IRAs), health insurance, social security, and long-term health care benefits.

Health Management and Policy. University of Michigan, 109 S. Observatory St., Ann Arbor, MI 48109-2029. Phone: (734)763-9903 Fax: (734)764-4338 E-mail: weissert@umich.edu • URL: http://www.sph.umich.edu/ • Research fields include health care economics, health insurance, and long-term care.

Social Welfare Research Institute. Boston College. 140 Commonwealth Ave., 515 McGuinn Hall, Room 508, Chestnut Hill, MA 02167. Phone: (617)552-4070 Fax: (617)552-3903 E-mail: schervish@bc.edu • URL: http://www.bc.edu/swri.

STATISTICS SOURCES

DRG Handbook: Comparative Clinical and Financial Standards (Diagnosis Related Group). HCIA, Inc. (Health Care Investment Analysts). • Annual. $399.00. Presents summary data for all 477 DRGs (diagnosis-related groups) and the 23 MDCs (major diagnostic categories), based on information from more than 11 million Medicare patients. Ranks DRG information for 100 hospital groups according to number of beds, payor mix, case-mix, system affiliation, and profitability. Emphasis is financial. Formerly *Medicare DRG Handbook*.

EBRI Databook on Employee Benefits. Employee Benefit Research Institute. • 1997 $99.00. Fourth edition. Contains more than 350 tables and charts presenting data on employee benefits in the U. S., including pensions, health insurance, social security, and medicare. Includes a glossary of employee benefit terms.

Employee Benefits in Medium and Large Private Establishments. Available from U. S. Government Printing Office. • Biennial. Issued by Bureau of Labor Statistics, U. S. Department of Labor. Provides data on benefits provided by companies with 100 or more employees. Covers benefits for both full-time and part-time workers, including health insurance, pensions, a wide variety of paid time-off policies (holidays, vacations, personal leave, maternity leave, etc.), and other fringe benefits.

Employee Benefits in Small Private Establishments. Available from U. S. Government Printing Office. • Biennial. Issued by Bureau of Labor Statistics, U. S. Department of Labor. Supplies data on a wide variety of benefits provided by companies with fewer than 100 employees. Includes statistics for both full-time and part-time workers.

Handbook of U. S. Labor Statistics: Employment, Earnings, Prices, Productivity, and Other Labor Data. Eva E. Jacobs, editor. Bernan Associates. • 1999. $74.00. Based on *Handbook of Labor Statistics*, formerly issued by the Bureau of Labor Statistics, U. S. Department of Labor. Includes the Bureau's projections of employment in the U. S. by industry and occupation. Provides a wide variety of data on the work force, prices, fringe benefits, and consumer expenditures.

Health Insurance Company Financial Data. The National Underwriter Co. • Annual.

Health, United States, 1999: Health and Aging Chartbook. Available from U. S. Government Printing Office. • 1999. $37.00. Issued by the National Center for Health Statistics, U. S. Department of Health and Human Services. Contains 34 bar charts in color, with related statistical tables. Provides detailed data on persons over 65 years of age, including population, living arrangements, life expectancy, nursing home residence, poverty, health status, assistive devices, health insurance, and health care expenditures.

Insurance Statistics Yearbook. OECD Publications and Information Center. • Annual. $75.00. Presents detailed statistics on insurance premiums collected in OECD countries, by type of insurance.

Standard & Poor's Industry Surveys. Standard & Poor's. • Semiannual. $1,800.00. Two looseleaf volumes. Includes monthly supplements. Provides detailed, individual surveys of 52 major industry groups. Each survey is revised on a semiannual basis. Also includes "Monthly Investment Review" (industry group investment analysis) and monthly "Trends & Projections" (economic analysis).

TRADE/PROFESSIONAL ASSOCIATIONS

Blue Cross and Blue Shield Association. 225 N. Michigan Ave., Chicago, IL 60611. Phone: (312)297-6000 Fax: (312)297-6609 • URL: http://www.bluecares.com.

Health Insurance Association of America. 555 13th St., N.W., Washington, DC 20004. Phone: (202)824-1600 Fax: (202)824-1722 • URL: http://www.hiaa.org • Members are commercial health insurers. Includes a Managed Care and Group Insurance Committee, a Disability Insurance Committee, a Medicare Administration Committee, and a Long-Term Care Task Force.

National Association of Professional Insurance Agents. 400 N. Washington St., Alexandria, VA 22314. Phone: (703)836-9340 Fax: (703)836-1279 E-mail: piaweb@pianet.org • URL: http://www.pianet.com • Members are independent agents in various fields of insurance.

OTHER SOURCES

Best's Insurance Reports. A.M. Best Co. • Annual. $745.00 per edition. Two editions, Life-health insurance covering about 1,750 companies, and property-casualty insurance covering over 2,500 companies. Includes one year subscription to both *Best's Review* and *Best's Insurance Management Reports.*

Life, Health, and Accident Insurance Law Reports. CCH, Inc. • $835.00 per year. Looseleaf service. Monthly updates.

The Long-Term Care Market. MarketResearch.com. • 1999. $3,250.00. Market data with forecasts to the year 2005. Emphasis is on the over-85 age group. Covers health insurance, the nursing home industry, pharmaceuticals, healthcare supplies, etc.

HEALTH MAINTENANCE ORGANIZATIONS

See also: HEALTH CARE INDUSTRY; HEALTH INSURANCE

GENERAL WORKS

Choosing and Using an HMO. Ellyn Spragins. • 1997. $19.95. Includes advice on finding a doctor, going outside the plan, and avoiding excess costs. (Bloomberg Personal Bookshelf Series.).

Health Against Wealth: HMOs and the Breakdown of Medical Trust. George Anders. Houghton Mifflin Co. • 1996. $15.00. The author, a *Wall Street Journal* reporter, presents the negative side of HMO cost cutting.

Managed Care: The Vision and the Strategy. American Association of Homes and Services for the Aging. • 1996. $30.00. A report on an AAHSA national managed care summit. Topics include delivery models, regulatory conflicts, costs, finances, consumer choice, and related subjects.

Management of Healthcare Organizations. Kerry D. Carson and others. Brooks/Cole Publishing Co. • Price on application. (SWC-Management Series).

Social Security, Medicare, and Pensions: Get the Most Out of Your Retirement and Medical Benefits. Joseph Matthews and Dorothy M. Berman. Nolo.com. • 1999. $21.95. Seventh edition. In addition to the basic topics, includes practical information on Supplemental Security Income (SSI), disability benefits, veterans benefits, 401(k) plans, Medicare HMOs, medigap insurance, Medicaid, and how to appeal decisions.

BIBLIOGRAPHIES

AAHSA Resource Catalog. American Association of Homes and Services for the Aging. • Annual. Free. Provides descriptions of material relating to managed care, senior housing, assisted living, continuing care retirement communities (CCRCs), nursing facilities, and home health care. Publishers are AAHSA and others.

Encyclopedia of Health Information Sources. The Gale Group. • 1993. $180.00. Second edition. Both print and nonprint sources of information are listed for 450 health-related topics.

DIRECTORIES

AAHP/Dorland Directory of Health Plans. Dorland Healthcare Information. • Annual. $215.00. Published in association with the American Association of Health Plans (http://www.aahp.org). Lists more than 2,400 health plans, including Health Maintenance Organizations (HMOs), Preferred Provider Organizations (PPOs), and Point of Service plans (POS). Includes the names of about 9,000 health plan executives. Formerly *Managed Health Care Directory.*

Encyclopedia of Medical Organizations and Agencies. The Gale Group. • 2000. $285.00. 11th edition. Information on over 14,000 public and private organizations in medicine and related fields.

HMO/PPO Directory. Medical Economics Co., Inc. • Annual. $215.00. Provides detailed information on managed care providers in the U. S., chiefly health maintenance organizations (HMOs) and preferred provider organizations (PPOs).

HMO Report and Directory. SMG Marketing Group, Inc. • Annual. $525.00. Contains information relating to over 700 HMOs. Relevant market data is also provided.

Medical and Health Information Directory. The Gale Group. • 1999. $630.00. Three volumes. 12th edition. Vol. one covers medical organizations, agencies, and institutions; vol. two includes bibliographic, library, and database information; vol. three is a guide to services available for various medical and health problems.

National Directory of HMOs. Group Health Association of America. • Annual. $125.00. Includes names of key personnel and benefit options.

ENCYCLOPEDIAS AND DICTIONARIES

Guidebook to Managed Care and Practice Management Terminology. Norman Winegar and L. Michelle Hayter. Haworth Press, Inc. • 1998. $39.95. Provides definitions of managed care "terminology, jargon, and concepts.".

HANDBOOKS AND MANUALS

Consumers' Guide to Health Plans. Center for the Study of Services. • 1996. $12.00. Revised edition. Presents the results of a consumer survey on satisfaction with specific managed care health insurance plans, and related information. Includes "Top-Rated Plans," "Health Plans That Chose Not to Have Their Members Surveyed," and other lists. General advice is provided on choosing a plan, finding a good doctor, getting good care, etc.

Healthcare Finance for the Non-Financial Manager: Basic Guide to Financial Analysis & Control. Louis Gapenski. McGraw-Hill Professional. • 1994. $47.50.

How to Cover the Gaps in Medicare: Health Insurance and Long-Term Care Options for the Retired. Robert A. Gilmour. American Institute for Economic Research. • 2000. $5.00. 12th revised edition. Four parts: "The Medicare Quandry," "How to Protect Yourself Against the Medigap," "Long-Term Care Options", and "End-of-Life Decisions" (living wills). Includes discussions of long-term care insurance, retirement communities, and HMO Medicare insurance, (Economic Education Bulletin Series, No. 10).

An Insurance Guide for Seniors. Insurance Forum, Inc. • 1997. $15.00. Provides concise advice and information on Medicare, Medicare supplement insurance, HMOs, long-term care insurance, automobile insurance, life insurance, annuities, and pensions. An appendix lists "Financially Strong Insurance Companies." (*The Insurance Forum*, vol. 24, no. 4.).

The Managed Care Contracting Handbook: Planning and Negotiating the Managed Care Relationship. Maria K. Todd. Available from McGraw Hill Higher Education. • 1996. $65.00. Copublished by McGraw-Hill Healthcare Education Group and the Healthcare Financial Management Association. Covers managed care planning, proposals, strategy, negotiation, and contract law. Written for healthcare providers.

Managed Care Handbook: How to Prepare Your Medical Practice for the Managed Care Revolution. James Lyle and Hoyt Torras. Practice Management Information Corp. • 1994. $49.95. Second edition. A management guide for physicians in private practice.

Medicare and Coordinated Care Plans. Available from Consumer Information Center. • Free. Published by the U. S. Department of Health and Human Services. Contains detailed information on services to Medicare beneficiaries from health maintenance organizations (HMOs). (Publication No. 509-X.).

INTERNET DATABASES

InsWeb. InsWeb Corp. Phone: (650)372-2129 E-mail: info@insweb.com • URL: http://www.insweb.com • Web site offers a wide variety of advice and information on automobile, life, health, and "other" insurance. Includes glossaries of insurance terms, Standard & Poor's ratings of individual insurance companies, and "Financial Needs Estimators." Searching is available. Fees: Free.

PERIODICALS AND NEWSLETTERS

AHA News. Health Forum, Inc. • Weekly. $147.00 per year. Edited for hospital and health care industry administrators. Covers health care news events and legislative activity. An American Hospital Association publication (http://www.aha.org).

Business and Health. Medical Economics Co., Inc. • Monthly. $99.00 per year. Edited for business, government, and other buyers of employee healthcare insurance or HMO coverage.

Drug Benefit Trends: For Pharmacy Managers and Managed Healthcare Professionals. SCP Communications, Inc. • Monthly. Individuals, $72.00 per year; institutions, $120.00 per year. Covers the business of managed care drug benefits.

Effective Clinical Practice. American College of Physicians. • Bimonthly. Individuals, $54.00 per year; institutions, $70.00 per year. Formerly *HMO Practice.*

Group Practice Journal. American Medical Group Practice Association. • 10 times a year. $75.00 per year.

Guide to HMOs and Health Insurers: A Quarterly Compilation of Health Insurance Company Ratings and Analysis. Weiss Ratings, Inc. • Quarterly. $438.00 per year. Emphasis is on rating of financial safety and relative risk. Includes annual summary.

Health Forum. American Hospital Association. American Hospital Publishing, Inc. • Biweekly. $80.00 per year. Covers the general management of hospitals, nursing homes, and managed care organizations. Formerly *HospitalsHealthNetworks.*

Health Insurance Underwriter. National Association of Health Underwriters. • 11 times a year. Free to members; non-members, $25.00 per year. Includes special feature issues on long-term care insurance, disability insurance, managed health care, and insurance office management.

Healthcare Executive. American College of Healthcare Executives. • Bimonthly. $60.00 per year. Focuses on critical management issues.

Healthplan: The Magazine of Trends, Insights, and Best Practices. American Association of Health Plans. • Bimonthly. $75.00 per year. Edited for managed care executives.

HMO Magazine (Health Maintenance Organization). Group Health Association of America. • Bimonthly. $75.00 per year.

Managed Care: A Guide for Physicians. Stezzi Communicatons, Inc. • Monthly. $78.00 per year. Edited for physicians and managed care administrators. Includes advice on careers and the business aspects of managed care.

Managed Care Interface: Today's Experts Tomorrow's Health Care. Medicom International, Inc. • Monthly. $80.00 per year. Provides news and information on all aspects of the managed health care industry.

Managed Care Marketing. Engel Publishing Partners. • Quarterly. $24.00 per year. Edited for executives of managed health care companies and organizations.

Managed Care Outlook: The Insider's Business Briefing on Managed Health Care. Aspen Publishers, Inc. • 50 times a year. $499.00 per year. Newsletter relating to health maintenance organizations (HMOs), preferred provider organizations (PPOs), and other managed care systems.

Managed Healthcare News: The Managed Care Industry's News Authority. Quadrant HealthCom, Inc. • Monthly. $75.00 per year. Presents new developments and trends for medical directors, pharmacists, administrators, and others concerned with managed care.

Managed Healthcare: The News Magazine for Managers of Healthcare Costs and Quality, Advanstar Healthcare Croup. Advanstar Communications, Inc. • Monthly. $64.00 per year. Edited for managers of HMOs and other managed care organizations. Covers outcomes, quality assurance, technology, long term care, and trends in the health care industry.

Medical Benefits. Panel Publishers. • Semimonthly. $216.00 per year. Newsletter. Provides summaries of periodical articles.

Modern Physician: Essential Business News for the Executive Physician. Crain Communications, Inc. • Monthly. $39.50. Edited for physicians responsible for business decisions at hospitals, clinics, HMOs, and other health groups. Includes special issues on managed care, practice management, legal issues, and finance.

RESEARCH CENTERS AND INSTITUTES

Center for Health Administration Studies. University of Chicago, 969 E. 60th St., Chicago, IL 60637. Phone: (773)702-7104 Fax: (773)702-7222 E-mail: chas@uchichago.edu • URL: http://www.chas.uchicago.edu.

Center for Health Economics Research. Waverly Oaks Rd., Suite 330, Waltham, MA 02452. Phone: (781)788-8100 Fax: (781)788-8101 E-mail: jmitchell@cher.org • URL: http://www.her-cher.org • Studies the financing of Medicare.

Center for Health Policy Law and Management. Duke University, P.O. Box 90253, Durham, NC 27708. Phone: (919)684-3023 Fax: (919)684-6246 E-mail: fsloan@hpolicy.duke.edu • URL: http://www.hpolicy.duke.edu.

Center for Health Research. Wayne State University, College of Nursing, 5557 Cass Ave., Detroit, MI 48202. Phone: (313)577-4134 Fax: (313)577-5777 E-mail: ajacox@wayne.edu • URL: http://www.comm.wayne.edu/nursing/nursing.html • Studies innovation in health care organization and financing.

Center for Research in Ambulatory Health Care Administration. 104 Inverness Terrace E., Englewood, CO 80112-5306. Phone: (303)397-7879 Fax: (303)397-1827 E-mail: npiland@mgma.com • URL: http://www.mgma.com/research • Fields of research include medical group practice management.

Health Research Institute. 3538 Torino Way, Concord, CA 94518. Phone: (510)676-2320 Fax: (510)676-2342 • Conducts applied research in health care financing and delivery of health services, with emphasis on cost containment.

Health Services Research and Development Center. Johns Hopkins University, 624 N. Broadway, Room 482, Baltimore, MD 21205-1996. Phone: (410)955-3625 Fax: (410)955-0470 E-mail: dsteinwa@jhsph.edu.

Institute for Health, Health Care Policy, and Aging Research. Rutgers University, 30 College Ave., New Brunswick, NJ 08903. Phone: (732)932-8413 Fax: (732)982-6872 E-mail: caboyer@rci.rutgers.edu • URL: http://www.ihhcpar.rutgers.edu/ • Areas of study include HMO use by older adults.

Stratis Health. 2901 Metro Dr., Suite 400, Bloomington, MN 55425-1529. Phone: (612)854-3306 Fax: (612)853-8503 E-mail: info@stratishealth.org • URL: http://www.stratishealth.org.

STATISTICS SOURCES

Standard & Poor's Industry Surveys. Standard & Poor's. • Semiannual. $1,800.00. Two looseleaf volumes. Includes monthly supplements. Provides detailed, individual surveys of 52 major industry groups. Each survey is revised on a semiannual basis. Also includes "Monthly Investment Review" (industry group investment analysis) and monthly "Trends & Projections" (economic analysis).

TRADE/PROFESSIONAL ASSOCIATIONS

American Association of Health Plans. 1129 20th St., N.W., Suite 600, Washington, DC 20036-3421. Phone: (202)728-3200 Fax: (202)331-7487 • URL: http://www.aahp.org • Members are alternate health care organizations, including HMOs.

American Association of Preferred Provider Organizations. One Bridge Plaza, Suite 350, Fort Lee, NJ 07024. Phone: 800-642-2515 or (201)947-5545 Fax: (201)947-8406 • URL: http://www.aappo.org.

American Medical Group Association. 1422 Duke St., Alexandria, VA 22314-3430. Phone: (703)838-0033 Fax: (703)548-1890 E-mail: rconnor@amga.org • URL: http://www.amga.org.

OTHER SOURCES

The Competitive Edge. InterStudy Publications. • Semiannual. Price on application. Provides highly detailed statistical, directory, and market information on U. S. health maintenance organizations. Consists of three parts: *The HMO Directory, The HMO Industry Report*, and *The Regional Market Analysis.* (Emphasis is on market research. http://www.dresources.com/).

The Managed Medicare and Medicaid Market. MarketResearch.com. • 1997. $1,250.00. Market research report on medicare HMOs. Includes analysis of legal issues and the impact of managed care on older consumers. Providers such as Kaiser Permanente, Humana, and U. S. Healthcare are profiled.

HEALTH OF EMPLOYEES

See: EMPLOYEE WELLNESS PROGRAMS

HEATING AND VENTILATION

See also: AIR CONDITIONING INDUSTRY

ABSTRACTS AND INDEXES

NTIS Alerts: Energy. National Technical Information Service. • Semimonthly. $245.00 per year. Provides descriptions of government-sponsored research reports and software, with ordering information. Covers electric power, batteries, fuels, geothermal energy, heating/cooling systems, nuclear technology, solar energy, energy policy, and related subjects. Formerly *Abstract Newsletter.*

DIRECTORIES

Air Conditioning, Heating, and Refrigeration News-Directory. Business News Publishing Co. • Annual. $235.00.

The Wholesaler "Wholesaling 100". TMB Publishing, Inc. • Annual. $25.00. Provides information on the 100 leading wholesalers of plumbing, piping, heating, and air conditioning equipment.

ENCYCLOPEDIAS AND DICTIONARIES

Macmillan Encyclopedia of Energy. Available from The Gale Group. • 2001. $350.00. Three volumes. Published by Macmillan Reference USA. Covers the business, technology, and history of a wide variety of energy sources.

FINANCIAL RATIOS

American Supply Association Operating Performance Report. American Supply Association. • Annual. Members, $45.00; non-members, $150.00.

Annual Statement Studies. Robert Morris Associates: The Association of Lending and Credit Risk Professiona. • Annual. Free to members; non-members, $140.00. Median and quartile financial ratios are given for over 400 kinds of manufacturing, wholesale, retail, construction, and consumer finance establishments. Data is sorted by both asset size and sales volume. Includes a clearly written "Definition of Ratios" and an alphabetical industry index.

HANDBOOKS AND MANUALS

Guide to Energy Efficient Commercial Equipment. Margaret Suozzo and others. American Council for an Energy Efficient Economy. • 1997. $25.00. Provides information on specifying and purchasing energy-saving systems for buildings (heating, air conditioning, lighting, and motors).

No-Regrets Remodeling: Creating a Comfortable, Healthy Home That Saves Energy. Available from American Council for an Energy-Efficient Economy. • 1997. $19.95. Edited by *Home Energy* magazine. Serves as a home remodeling guide to efficient heating, cooling, ventilation, water heating, insulation, lighting, and windows.

PERIODICALS AND NEWSLETTERS

Air Conditioning, Heating, and Refrigeration News. Business News Publishing Co. • Weekly. $87.00 per year. Includes *Annual Directory* and *Statistical Summary.*

ASHRAE Journal: Heating, Refrigeration, Air Conditioning, Ventilation. American Society of Heating, Refrigerating and Air Conditioning Engineers, Inc. • Monthly. Free to members; non-members, $59.00 per year.

Heating/Piping/Air Conditioning Engineering: The Magazine of Mechanical Systems Engineering. Penton Media Inc. • Monthly. Free to qualified personnel; others, $65.00 per year. Covers design, specification, installation, operation, and maintenance for systems in industrial, commercial, and institutional buildings. Formerly Heating, Piping and Air Conditioning.

The Wholesaler. TMB Publishing, Inc. • Monthly. $75.00 per year. Edited for wholesalers and distributors of plumbing, piping, heating, and air conditioning equipment.

RESEARCH CENTERS AND INSTITUTES

Ray W. Herrick Laboratories. Purdue University, School of Mechanical Engineering, West Lafayette, IN 47907-1077. Phone: (765)494-2132 Fax: (765)494-0787 E-mail: rhlab@ecn.purdue.edu.

STATISTICS SOURCES

Annual Survey of Manufactures. Available from U. S. Government Printing Office. • Annual. Prices vary. Issued by the U. S. Census Bureau as an interim update to the *Census of Manufactures.* Includes data on number of manufacturing establishments in various industries, employment, labor costs, value of shipments, capital expenditures, inventories, energy costs, and assets. (See also Census Bureau home page, http://www.census.gov/.).

Manufacturing Profiles. Available from U. S. Government Printing Office. • Annual. Issued by the U. S. Census Bureau. A printed consolidation of the entire *Current Industrial Report* series, presenting "all the data compiled." Contains statistics on production, shipments, inventories, consumption, exports, imports, and orders for a wide variety of manufactured products. (See also Census Bureau home page, http://www.census.gov/.).

Refrigeration, Air Conditioning, and Warm Air Heating Equipment. U. S. Bureau of the Census. • Annual. Provides data on quantity and value of shipments by manufacturers. Formerly *Air Conditioning and Refrigeration Equipment.* (Current Industrial Reports, MA-35M.).

TRADE/PROFESSIONAL ASSOCIATIONS

American Society of Heating, Refrigerating and Air Conditioning Engineers. 1791 Tullie Circle, N.E., Atlanta, GA 30329. Phone: 800-527-4723 or (404)636-8400 Fax: (404)321-5478 E-mail: ashrae@ashrae.org • URL: http://www.ashrae.org.

Industrial Heating Equipment Association. 1111 N. 19th St., Ste. 425, Arlington, VA 22209. Phone: (703)525-2513 Fax: (703)525-2515 E-mail: ihea@ihea.org • URL: http://www.ihea.org.

International District Energy Association. 1200 19th St., N.W., Suite 300, Washington, DC 20036-2401. Phone: (202)429-5111 Fax: (202)429-5113 E-mail: idea@dc.sba.com.

OTHER SOURCES

HPAC Techlit Selector (Heating, Piping, Air Conditioning). Penton Media, Inc. • Semiannual. Free to qualified personnel. Manufacturers' catalogs and technical literature.

Major Energy Companies of the World. Available from The Gale Group. • 2001. $855.00. Fourth edition. Published by Graham & Whiteside. Contains detailed information on more than 3,300 important energy companies in various countries. Industries include electricity generation, coal, natural gas, nuclear energy, petroleum, fuel distribution, and equipment for energy production.

HELICOPTERS

See also: AEROSPACE INDUSTRY; AVIATION INDUSTRY

DIRECTORIES

The Helicopter Annual. Helicopter Association International. • Annual. Members, $20.00; non-members, $40.00.

Vertiflite-American Helicopter Society Membership Directory. American Helicopter Society, Inc. • Annual. $45.00. Lists over 6,000 individuals and 150 companies concerned with vertical take off and landing craft.

ENCYCLOPEDIAS AND DICTIONARIES

Macmillan Encyclopedia of Transportation. Available from The Gale Group. • 2000. $375.00. Six volumes. Published by Macmillan Reference USA. Covers the business, technology, and history of transportation on land, on water, in the air, and in space. Includes definitions, cross-references, and 200 color illustrations.

HANDBOOKS AND MANUALS

Operations and Management, Guide/Safety Manual. Helicopter Association International. • Annual.

PERIODICALS AND NEWSLETTERS

American Helicopter Society Journal. American Helicopter Society, Inc. • Quarterly. $60.00 per year.

Helicopter News. Phillips Business Information, Inc. • Biweekly. $697.00 per year. Newsletter.

Journal of Aircraft: Devoted to Aeronautical Science and Technology. American Institute of Aeronautics and Astronautics, Inc. • Bimonthly. Members, $50.00 per year; non-members, $175.00 per year; institutions, $350.00 per year.

Rotor and Wing International: Serving the Worldwide Helicopter Industry. Phillips Business Information, Inc. • Monthly. Free to qualified personnel; others, $49.00 per year. Includes supplement *World Helicopter Resources.*

Vertiflite. American Helicopter Society, Inc. • Bimonthly. $60.00 per year.

RESEARCH CENTERS AND INSTITUTES

Flight Mechanics Laboratory. Texas A & M University, College Station, TX 77843-3141. Phone: (409)845-1732 Fax: (409)845-6051 E-mail: ward@aero.tamu.edu.

Ohio Aerospace Institute. 22800 Cedar Point Rd., Cleveland, OH 44142. Phone: (440)962-3000 Fax: (440)962-3120 E-mail: michaelsalkind@oai.org • URL: http://www.oai.org • Aerospace-related research, education, and technology transfers.

STATISTICS SOURCES

Aerospace Facts and Figures. Aerospace Industries Association of America. • Annual. $35.00. Includes financial data for the aerospace industries.

FAA Statistical Handbook of Aviation. Federal Aviation Administration. Available from U. S. Government Printing Office. • Annual.

TRADE/PROFESSIONAL ASSOCIATIONS

American Helicopter Society. 217 N. Washington St., Alexandria, VA 22314-2538. Phone: (703)684-6777 Fax: (703)739-9279 E-mail: ahs703@aol.com • URL: http://www.vtol.org.

Helicopter Association International. 1635 Prince St., Alexandria, VA 22314-1818. Phone: (703)683-4646 Fax: (703)683-4745 E-mail: rotor@rotor.com • URL: http://www.rotor.com.

HENS

See: POULTRY INDUSTRY

HERBS

See also: DIET; HEALTH FOOD INDUSTRY

ALMANACS AND YEARBOOKS

Herbarist. Herb Society of America, Inc. • Annual. $5.00.

DIRECTORIES

PDR for Herbal Medicines. Medical Economics Co., Inc. • 1999. $59.95. Published in cooperation with PhytoPharm, U. S. Institute for Phytopharmaceuticals, Inc. Provdies detailed information on more than 600 herbal remedies, including scientific names, common names, indications, usage, adverse reactions, drug interaactions, and literature citations.

HANDBOOKS AND MANUALS

Herb Farming. Entrepreneur Media, Inc. • Looseleaf. $59.50. A practical guide to the business side of herb farming. Covers profit potential, start-up costs, market size evaluation, owner's time required, pricing, accounting, advertising, promotion, etc. (Start-Up Business Guide No. E1282.).

Herbal Drugs and Phytopharmaceuticals. Max Wichtl and Norman G. Bisset, editors. CRC Press, Inc. • 1994. $190.00. Provides a scientific approach to the medicinal use of herbs. (English translation of original German edition.).

The Herbalist. Joseph E. Mayer. Gordon Press Publishers. • 1992. $79.99. (Alternative Medicine Series).

The Honest Herbal: A Sensible Guide to the Use of Herbs and Related Remedies. Varro E. Tyler. The Haworth Press, Inc. • 1993. $49.95. Third edition.

PERIODICALS AND NEWSLETTERS

Health Supplement Retailer. Virgo Publishing, Inc. • Monthly. $38.00 per year. Covers all aspects of the vitamin and health supplement market, including new products. Includes an annual buyer's guide, an annual compilation of industry statistics, and annual guides to vitamins and herbs.

Herb Quarterly. Long Mountain Press. • Quarterly. $24.00 per year. A magazine for herb enthusiasts covering all aspects of herb uses.

Journal of Herbs, Spices and Medicinal Plants. Haworth Press, Inc. • Quarterly. Individuals, $45.00 per year; institutions, $65.00 per year; libraries, $175.00 per year. An academic and practical journal on production, marketing, and other aspects of herbs and spices.

Supplement Industry Executive. Vitamin Retailer Magazine, Inc. • Bimonthly. $25.00 per year. Edited for manufacturers of vitamins and other dietary supplements. Covers marketing, new products, industry trends, regulations, manufacturing procedures, and related topics. Includes a directory of suppliers to the industry.

Vitamin Retailer. Vitamin Retailer Magazine, Inc. • Monthly. $45.00 per year. Edited for retailers of vitamins, herbal remedies, minerals, antioxidants, essential fatty acids, and other food supplements.

TRADE/PROFESSIONAL ASSOCIATIONS

Herb Society of America. 9019 Kirtland-Chardon Rd., Kirtland, OH 44094. Phone: (440)256-0514 Fax: (440)256-0541 E-mail: herbs@herbsociety.org • URL: http://www.herbsociety.com.

OTHER SOURCES

Pharmacopeia of Herbs. CME, Inc. • $149.00. Frequently updated CD-ROM provides searchable data on a wide variety of herbal medicines, vitamins, and amino acids. Includes information on clinical studies, contraindications, side-effects, phytoactivity, and 534 therapeutic use categories. Contains a 1,000 word glossary.

U. S. Herbal Supplement Market. Available from MarketResearch.com. • 1999. $2,750.00. Market research data published by Packaged Facts. Includes forecasts to 2003.

HIDE INDUSTRY

See: CATTLE INDUSTRY

HIGH BLOOD PRESSURE

See: HYPERTENSION

HIGH FIDELITY/STEREO

See also: RADIO EQUIPMENT INDUSTRY; SOUND RECORDERS AND RECORDING

GENERAL WORKS

Sound and Recording: An Introduction. Francis Rumsey. Butterworth-Heinemann. • 1997. $39.95. Third edition. Covers the theory and principles of sound recording and reproduction, with chapters on amplifiers, microphones, mixers, and other components.

DIRECTORIES

Audio Annual Product Review Directory. Hachette Filipacchi Magazines, Inc. • Annual. $3.95.

Directory of Computer and Consumer Electronics. Chain Store Age. • Annual. $290.00. Includes 2,900 "leading" retailers and over 200 "top" distributors. Formerly *Directory of Consumer Electronics Retails and Distributors.*

Schwann Opus: The Classical Music Resource. Schwann Publications. • Annual. $27.45 per year. Lists classical music recordings by composer. Covers compact discs, minidiscs, and cassette tapes. Includes an extensive, alphabetical list of recording labels and distributors, with addresses and telephone numbers (many listings also include fax numbers and Internet addresses).

Schwann Spectrum: The Guide to Rock, Jazz, World...and Beyond. Schwann Publications. • Annual. $27.45 per year. Lists rock, jazz, country, folk, soundtrack, international, new age, religious, and other disc and tape popular recordings by performer. Includes an extensive, alphabetical list of recording labels and distributors, with addresses and telephone numbers (some listings also include fax numbers and Internet addresses).

HANDBOOKS AND MANUALS

Audio Electronics. John L. Hood. Butterworth-Heinemann. • 1999. $47.95. Second edition.

Audio Engineer's Reference Book. Michael Talbot-Smith, editor. Butterworth-Heinemann. • 1994. $165.00. Second edition.

Audio Recording and Reproduction: Practical Measures for Audio Enthusiasts. Michael Talbot-Smith. Butterworth-Heinemann. • 1994. $29.95.

Handbook for Sound Engineers: The New Audio Cyclopedia. Glen M. Ballou, editor. Butterworth-Heineman. • 1991. $120.00. Second edition. Covers fundamentals of sound, sound-system design, loudspeaker building, sound recording, audio circuits, and computer-generated music.

Home Entertainment Installation. Entrepreneur Media, Inc. • Looseleaf. $59.50. A practical guide to starting a home entertainment installation service. Covers profit potential, start-up costs, market size evaluation, owner's time required, pricing, accounting, advertising, promotion, etc. (Start-Up Business Guide No. E1349.).

PERIODICALS AND NEWSLETTERS

The Absolute Sound: The High End Journal of Audio and Music. Harry Pearson, editor. Absolute Multimedia Inc. • Six times a year. $42.00 per year.

Audio. Hachette Filipacchi Magazines, Inc. • Monthly. $26.00 per year. Includes annual directory *Product Review.*

Audio Week: The Authoritative News Service of the Audio Consumer Electronics Industry. • Weekly. $617.00. Newsletter. Provdies audio industry news, company news, and new product information.

High Performance Review: Definitive Magazine for Audiophiles and Music Lovers. High Performance Review Publishing. • Quarterly. $15.00 per year.

Poptronics. Gernsback Publications, Inc. • Monthly. $19.99 per year. Incorporates *Electronics Now.*

Sensible Sound. • Bimonthly. $29.00 per year. High fidelity equipment review.

Stereo Review's Sound & Vision: Home Theater-Audio- Video- MultimediaMovies- Music. Hachette Filipacchi Magazines, Inc. • 10 times a year. $24.00 per year. Popular magazine providing explanatory articles and critical reviews of equipment and media (CD-ROM, DVD, videocassettes, etc.). Supplement available *Stero Review's Sound and Vision Buyers Guide.* Replaces *Stereo Review* and *Video Magazine.*

Stereophile: For the High Fidelity Stereo Perfectionist. EMAP USA. • Monthly. $24.94 per year. Review of high-end audio products.

TWICE: This Week in Consumer Electronics. Cahners Business Information, Broadcasting and Cable's International Group. • 29 times a year. Free to qualified personnel; others, $99.90 per year. Contains marketing and manufacturing news relating to a wide variety of consumer electronic products, including video, audio, telephone, and home office equipment.

PRICE SOURCES

Orion Audio Blue Book. Orion Research Corp. • Annual. $179.00. Quotes retail and wholesale prices of used audio equipment. Original list prices and years of manufacture are also shown.

Orion Car Stereo Blue Book. Orion Research Corp. • Annual. $144.00. Quotes retail and wholesale prices of used stereo sound equipment for automobiles. Original list prices and years of manufacture are also shown.

Orion Guitars and Musical Instruments Blue Book. Orion Research Corp. • Annual. $179.00. List of manufacturers of guitars and musical instruments. Original list prices and years of manufacture are also shown. Formerly *Orion Professional Sound and Musical Instruments.*

TRADE/PROFESSIONAL ASSOCIATIONS

Electronic Industries Association. 2500 Wilson Blvd., Arlington, VA 22201. Phone: (703)907-7500 Fax: (703)907-7501 • URL: http://www.eia.org • Includes a Solid State Products Committee.

OTHER SOURCES

U. S. Home Theater Market. Available from MarketResearch.com. • 1997. $2,,500.00. Market research report published by Packaged Facts. Covers big-screen TV, high definition TV, audio equipment, and video sources. Market projections are provided to the year 2001.

HIGH TECHNOLOGY

See: TECHNOLOGY

HIGH YIELD BONDS

See: JUNK BOND FINANCING

HIGHER EDUCATION

See: COLLEGES AND UNIVERSITIES

HIGHWAY ACCIDENTS

See: TRAFFIC ACCIDENTS AND TRAFFIC SAFETY

HIGHWAYS

See: ROADS AND HIGHWAYS

HIRE PURCHASE PLAN

See: INSTALLMENT PLAN PURCHASING

HISPANIC MARKETS

See: MINORITY MARKETS

HISTORY, BUSINESS

See: BUSINESS HISTORY

HMOS

See: HEALTH MAINTENANCE ORGANIZATIONS

HOBBY INDUSTRY

DIRECTORIES

Craft and Needlework Age Trade Directory. Krause Publications, Inc. • Annual. $35.00. Lists of about 300 manufacturers and 50 publishers of books and periodicals in the craft and needlework industry.

Directory of Discount and General Merchandise Stores. Chain Store Guide. • Annual. $300.00. Includes retailers and wholesalers of housewares, giftwares, novelties, toys, hobby materials, crafts, and stationery. Formerly *Directory of Discount Stores Catalog Showrooms.*

FINANCIAL RATIOS

Annual Statement Studies. Robert Morris Associates: The Association of Lending and Credit Risk Professiona. • Annual. Free to members; non-members, $140.00. Median and quartile financial ratios are given for over 400 kinds of manufacturing, wholesale, retail, construction, and consumer finance establishments. Data is sorted by both asset size and sales volume. Includes a clearly written "Definition of Ratios" and an alphabetical industry index.

HANDBOOKS AND MANUALS

Collectibles Broker. Entrepreneur Media, Inc. • Looseleaf. $59.50. A practical guide to starting a brokerage service for collectibles. Covers profit potential, start-up costs, market size evaluation, owner's time required, pricing, accounting, advertising, promotion, etc. (Start-Up Business Guide No. E1360.).

Craft Businesses. Entrepreneur Media, Inc. • Looseleaf. $59.50. A practical guide to starting a handicrafts-related business. Covers profit potential, start-up costs, market size evaluation, owner's time required, site selection, lease negotiation, pricing, accounting, advertising, promotion, etc. (Start-Up Business Guide No. E1304.).

Hobby Shop. Entrepreneur Media, Inc. • Looseleaf. $59.50. A practical guide to starting a hobby shop. Covers profit potential, start-up costs, market size evaluation, owner's time required, site selection, lease negotiation, pricing, accounting, advertising, promotion, etc. (Start-Up Business Guide No. E1132.).

Start and Run a Profitable Craft Business: A Step-by-Step Business Plan. William G. Hynes. Self-Counsel Press, Inc. • 1996. $14.95. Sixth edition.

PERIODICALS AND NEWSLETTERS

Antiques and Collecting Magazine. Frances L. Graham, editor. Lightner Publishing Corp. • Monthly. $32.00 per year.

International Journal: The News and Views Paper for the Hobbyist. Levine Publications. • Quarterly. $52.50.

PRICE SOURCES

Kovels' Antiques and Collectibles. Ralph and Terry Kovel. Crown Publishers Group, Inc. • Annual. $19.95.

Pictorial Price Guide to American Antiques: 2000-2001. Dorothy Hammond. Viking Penguin. • 1999. $19.95. 21st edition.

STATISTICS SOURCES

Lifestyle Market Analyst. SRDS. • Annual. $391.00. Published in conjunction with NDL (National Demographics & Lifestyles). Provides extensive lifestyle data on interests, activities, and hobbies within specific geographic and demographic markets.

TRADE/PROFESSIONAL ASSOCIATIONS

Hobby Industry Association of America. 319 E. 54th St., Elmwood Park, NJ 07407. Phone: (201)794-1133 Fax: (201)797-0657 E-mail: hia@ix.netcom.com.

Society of Craft Designers. P.O. Box 2188, Zanesville, OH 43702-2188. Phone: (740)452-4541 Fax: (740)452-2552 E-mail: scd@offinger.com.

HOG INDUSTRY

See: LIVESTOCK INDUSTRY; SWINE INDUSTRY

HOISTING MACHINERY

See: CONVEYING MACHINERY; ELEVATORS

HOLIDAYS

See: ANNIVERSARIES AND HOLIDAYS

HOME APPLIANCES

See: ELECTRIC APPLIANCE INDUSTRY

HOME-BASED BUSINESSES

See: SELF-EMPLOYMENT

HOME BUILDING INDUSTRY

See: BUILDING INDUSTRY

HOME COMPUTERS

See: MICROCOMPUTERS AND MINICOMPUTERS

HOME DECORATION

See: INTERIOR DECORATION

HOME EDUCATION

See: CORRESPONDENCE SCHOOLS AND COURSES

HOME FREEZERS

See: FROZEN FOOD INDUSTRY

HOME FURNISHINGS

See: FLOOR COVERINGS; FURNITURE INDUSTRY; INTERIOR DECORATION

HOME FURNITURE INDUSTRY

See: FURNITURE INDUSTRY

HOME HEALTH CARE INDUSTRY

See also: HEALTH CARE INDUSTRY

GENERAL WORKS

Caring for Frail Elderly People: New Directions in Care. OECD Publications and Information Center. • 1994. $27.00. Discusses the problem in OECD countries of providing good quality care to the elderly at manageable cost. Includes trends in family care, housing policies, and private financing.

Expanding Services to Meet Community Needs in an Era of Change. American Association of Homes and Services for the Aging. • 1996. $30.00. Covers new, innovative models of home health care delivery, intergenerational day care, and senior housing services.

Long-Term Care and Its Alternatives. Charles B. Inlander. People's Medical Society. • 1996. $16.95. Provides practical advice on the financing of long-term health care. The author is a consumer advocate and president of the People's Medical Society.

Who Cares for Them? Workers in the Home Care Industry. Penny H. Feldman and others. Greenwood Publishing Group, Inc. • 1990. $55.00. (Contributions to the Study of Aging Series, No.16).

BIBLIOGRAPHIES

AAHSA Resource Catalog. American Association of Homes and Services for the Aging. • Annual. Free. Provides descriptions of material relating to managed care, senior housing, assisted living, continuing care retirement communities (CCRCs), nursing facilities, and home health care. Publishers are AAHSA and others.

Encyclopedia of Health Information Sources. The Gale Group. • 1993. $180.00. Second edition. Both print and nonprint sources of information are listed for 450 health-related topics.

DIRECTORIES

Encyclopedia of Medical Organizations and Agencies. The Gale Group. • 2000. $285.00. 11th edition. Information on over 14,000 public and private organizations in medicine and related fields.

Health Devices Sourcebook. ECRI (Emergency Care Research Institute). • Annual. Lists over 6,000 manufacturers of a wide variety of medical equipment and supplies, including clinical laboratory equipment, testing instruments, surgical instruments, patient care equipment, etc.

Health Industry Buyers Guide. Spring House. • Annual. $195.00. About 4,000 manufacturers of hospital and physician's supplies and equipment. Formerly *Surgical Trade Buyers Guide.*

Home Health Agencies Report and Directory. SMG Marketing Group, Inc. • Annual. $575.00. Lists over 13,000 home healthcare agencies and corporations. Includes a market analysis and growth projections.

Home Health Agency Chain Directory. SMG Marketing Group, Inc. • Annual. $595.00. Lists over 800 corporate home healthcare agencies which own two or more facilities. Includes an analysis of market trends.

HomeCare Magazine Buyers' Guide. Intertec Publishing Corp. • Annual. $25.00. Lists about 800 manufacturers and distributors of home health care and rehabilitation products. Includes key personnel and trade names. Formerly *Homecare Product Directory and Buyers' Guide.*

FINANCIAL RATIOS

Annual Statement Studies. Robert Morris Associates: The Association of Lending and Credit Risk Professiona. • Annual. Free to members; non-members, $140.00. Median and quartile financial ratios are given for over 400 kinds of manufacturing, wholesale, retail, construction, and consumer finance establishments. Data is sorted by both asset size and sales volume. Includes a clearly written "Definition of Ratios" and an alphabetical industry index.

HANDBOOKS AND MANUALS

Administrator's Handbook for Community Health and Home Care Services. Anne S. Smith. National League for Nursing Press. • 1988. $175.00.

Home Care Client Assessment Handbook. Janet E. Jackson and Marianne Neighbors. Aspen Publishers, Inc. • 1990. $69.00.

Home Care Management: Quality-Based Costing, Pricing, and Productivity. Roey Kirk and Deborah Kranz. Aspen Publishers, Inc. • 1988. $66.00.

Home Health Care Management. Lazelle E. Benefield. Prentice Hall. • 1988. $50.00.

An Insider's Guide to Home Health Care. Tova Navarra and Margaret Ferrer. SLACK, Inc. • 1996. $28.00. Covers "unexpected situations, cultural differences, and potential comflicts" for professionals in the home health care field. Emphasizes teamwork for optimal care management.

PERIODICALS AND NEWSLETTERS

Caring. National Association for Home Care. • Monthly. $45.00 per year. Provides articles on the business of home health care.

Continuing Care: Supporting the Transition into Post Hospital Care. Stevenson Publishing Corp. • Monthly. $99.00 per year. Topics include insurance, legal issues, health business news, ethics, and case management. Includes annual *Buyer's Guide*.

HME News. United Publications, Inc. • Monthly. Controlled circulation. Covers the home medical equipment business for dealers and manufacturers. Provides information on a wide variety of home health care supplies and equipment.

Home Health Care Dealer-Provider. Curant Communications, Inc. • Bimonthly. Controlled circulation. For home care dealer and home care pharmacies. Formerly *Home Health Care Dealer - Supplier*.

Home Health Care Services Quarterly: The Journal of Community Care. Haworth Press, Inc. • Quarterly. Individuals, $60.00 per year; institutions $120.00 per year;libraries, $375.00 per year. An academic and practical journal focusing on the marketing and administration of home care.

Home Health Line: The Home Care Industry's National Independent Newsletter. • 48 times a year. $399.00 per year. Newsletter on legislation and regulations affecting the home health care industry, with an emphasis on federal funding and Medicare programs.

Home Health Products. Stevens Publishing Corp. • 10 times a year. $99.00 per year. Covers new medical equipment products for the home care industry.

Home Healthcare Nurse. Lippincott Williams and Wilkins, Publishers. • 10 times a year. Individuals, $43.00 per year; institutions, $180.00 per year. For professional nurses in the home health care field.

Homecare News. National Association for Home Care. • Quarterly. $20.00 per year.

Homecare: The Business Magazine of the Home Health Industry. Intertec Publishing. • Monthly. $65.00 per year. Edited for dealers and suppliers of home medical equipment, including pharmacies and chain stores. Includes information on new products.

Hospital Home Health: The Monthly Updates for Executives and Health Care Professionals. American Health Consultants, Inc. • Monthly. $399.00 per year. Newsletter for hospital-based home health agencies.

RESEARCH CENTERS AND INSTITUTES

Stratis Health. 2901 Metro Dr., Suite 400, Bloomington, MN 55425-1529. Phone: (612)854-3306 Fax: (612)853-8503 E-mail: info@stratishealth.org • URL: http://www.stratishealth.org.

STATISTICS SOURCES

Health Care Costs. DRI/McGraw-Hill. • Quarterly. Price on application. Cost indexes for hospitals, nursing homes, and home healthcare agencies.

Health, United States, 1999: Health and Aging Chartbook. Available from U. S. Government Printing Office. • 1999. $37.00. Issued by the National Center for Health Statistics, U. S. Department of Health and Human Services. Contains 34 bar charts in color, with related statistical tables. Provides detailed data on persons over 65 years of age, including population, living arrangements, life expectancy, nursing home residence, poverty, health status, assistive devices, health insurance, and health care expenditures.

TRADE/PROFESSIONAL ASSOCIATIONS

American Association for Continuity of Care. P.O. Box 7073, North Brunswick, NJ 08902. Phone: 800-816-1575 Fax: (301)352-7086 • URL: http://www.continuitycare.com • Members are professionals concerned with continuity of care, health care after hospital discharge, and home health care.

American Federation of Home Health Agencies. 1320 Fenwick Lane,, Suite 100, Silver Spring, MD 20910. Phone: 800-234-4211 Fax: (301)588-4732 E-mail: afhha@his.com • URL: http://www.his.com/~afhha/usa.html • Promotes home health care.

National Association for Home Care. 228 Seventh St., S.E., Washington, DC 20003. Phone: (202)547-7424 Fax: (202)547-3540 E-mail: clc@nahc.org • URL: http://www.nahc.org • Promotes high standards of patient care in home care services. Members are home health care providers.

National Association for Medical Equipment Services. 625 Slaters Lane, Suite 200, Alexandria, VA 22314-1171. Phone: (703)836-6263 Fax: (703)836-6730 E-mail: info@names.org • URL: http://www.names.org • Members are durable medical equipment and oxygen suppliers, mainly for home health care. Has Legislative Affairs Committee that is concerned with Medicare/Medicaid benefits.

OTHER SOURCES

Disability and Rehabilitation Products Markets. Theta Reports/PJB Medical Publications, Inc. • 1999. $1,295.00. Market research data. Covers the market for products designed to help differently-abled people lead more active lives. Includes such items as adaptive computers, augmentative communication devices, lifts/vans, and bath/home products. Profiles of leading suppliers are included. (Theta Report No. 800.).

Home Care Products Market. MarketResearch.com. • 2001. $3,250.00. Market data with projections to 2005. Covers a wide variety of products: wheelchairs, crutches, beds, monitoring equipment, etc.

Home Care Services Market. MarketResearch.com. • 1999. $3,250.00. Market data with projections. Covers a wide variety of services: primary nursing, respiratory, dialysis, infusion, etc.

The U. S. Market for Home Medical Tests. Available from MarketResearch.com. • 1997. $2,350.00. Market research report published by Packaged Facts. Covers the market for diagnostic products used in the home and the effect of regulation.

HOME IMPROVEMENT INDUSTRY

See also: BUILDING INDUSTRY

DIRECTORIES

Builder: Buyer's Guide. Hanley-Wood, LLC. • Annual. $10.00. A directory of products and services for the home building and remodeling industry.

Building Supply Home Centers Retail Giants Report. Cahners Business Information. • Annual. $30.00. Lists major retailers of a wide variety of building and home improvement materials, products, fixtures, accessories, equipment, and tools.

Directory of Home Center Operators and Hardware Chains. Chain Store Age. • Annual. $300.00. Nearly 5,400 home center operators, paint and home decorating chains, and lumber and building materials companies.

Remodeling Product Guide. Hanley-Wood, LLC. • Annual. $10.00. A directory of products and services for the home remodeling industry. Formerly *Remodeling-Guide to Manufacturers*.

ENCYCLOPEDIAS AND DICTIONARIES

Illustrated Dictionary of Building Materials and Techniques: An Invaluable Sourcebook to the Tools, Terms, Materials, and Techniques Used by Building Professionals. Paul Bianchina. John Wiley and Sons, Inc. • 1993. $49.95. Contains 4,000 definitions of building and building materials terms, with 500 illustrations. Includes materials grades, measurements, and specifications.

HANDBOOKS AND MANUALS

No-Regrets Remodeling: Creating a Comfortable, Healthy Home That Saves Energy. Available from American Council for an Energy-Efficient Economy. • 1997. $19.95. Edited by *Home Energy* magazine. Serves as a home remodeling guide to efficient heating, cooling, ventilation, water heating, insulation, lighting, and windows.

Profiting from Real Estate Rehab. Sandra M. Brassfield. John Wiley and Sons, Inc. • 1992. $39.95. How to fix up old houses and sell them at a profit.

PERIODICALS AND NEWSLETTERS

Builder: Official Publication of the National Association of Home Builders. National Association of Home Builders of the United States. Hanley-Wood, LLC. • Monthly. $29.95 per year. Covers the home building and remodeling industry in general, including design, construction, and marketing.

Building Material Retailer. National Lumber and Building Material Dealers Association. • Monthly. $25.00 per year. Includes special feature issues on hand and power tools, lumber, roofing, kitchens, flooring, windows and doors, and insulation.

National Home Center News: News and Analysis for the Home Improvement, Building, Material Industry. Lebhar-Friedman, Inc. • 22 times a year. $99.00 per year. Includes special feature issues on hardware and tools, building materials, millwork, electrical supplies, lighting, and kitchens.

Remodeling: Excellence in Professional Remodeling. Hanley-Wood, LLC. • Monthly. $44.95 per year. Covers new products, construction, management, and marketing for remodelers.

STATISTICS SOURCES

Expenditures for Residential Improvements and Repairs. Available from U. S. Government Printing Office. • Quarterly. $14.00 per year. Bureau of the Census Construction Report, C50. Provides estimates of spending for housing maintenance, repairs, additions, alterations, and major replacements.

TRADE/PROFESSIONAL ASSOCIATIONS

National Association of the Remodeling Industry. 4900 Seminary Rd., Suite 320, Alexandria, VA 22311. Phone: (703)575-1100 Fax: (703)575-1121 E-mail: info@nari.org • URL: http://www.nari.org.

OTHER SOURCES

The Home Improvement Market. Available from MarketResearch.com. • 1999. $2,750.00. Market research report published by Packaged Facts. Covers the market for lumber, finishing materials, tools, hardware, etc.

HOME OWNERSHIP

See also: PERSONAL FINANCE

GENERAL WORKS

How to Sell Your Home for Top Dollar. Michael C. Thomsett. McGraw-Hill Professional. • 1989. $13.00. (One Hour Guides Series).

A New Housing Policy for America: Recapturing the American Dream. David C. Schwartz and others. Temple University Press. • 1988. $24.95.

CD-ROM DATABASES

Magazine Index Plus. The Gale Group. • Monthly. $4,000.00 per year (includes InfoTrac workstation). Provides full text on CD-ROM for about 100 popular, general interest magazines and indexing for 300 others. Includes special indexing of reviews and product evaluations. Time period is 1980 to date.

WILSONDISC: Readers' Guide to Periodical Literature. H. W. Wilson Co. • Monthly. $1,095.00 per year, including unlimited online access to *Readers' Guide to Periodical Literature* through WILSONLINE. Provides CD-ROM indexing of about 250 general interest periodicals. Covers 1983 to date. (*Readers' Guide Abstracts* also available on CD-ROM at $1,995 per year.).

HANDBOOKS AND MANUALS

Home Inspection Service. Entrepreneur Media, Inc. • Looseleaf. $59.50. A practical guide to starting a home inspection service. Covers profit potential, start-up costs, market size evaluation, owner's time required, pricing, accounting, advertising, promotion, etc. (Start-Up Business Guide No. E1334.).

Homeowner or Tenant? How to Make a Wise Choice. Lawrence S. Pratt. American Institute for Economic Research. • 1997. $6.00. Provides detailed information for making rent or buy decisions. Includes "Mortgage Arithmetic," "Hints for Buyers, Sellers, and Renters," worksheets, mortgage loan interest tables, and other data. (Economic Education Bulletin.).

How to Buy a House, Condo, or Co-op. Jean C. Thomsett. Consumers Union of the United States, Inc. • 1996. $84.75. Fifth edition.

Your Dream Home: A Comprehensive Guide to Buying a House, Condo, or Co-op. Marguerite Smith. Available from Little, Brown & Co. • 1997. $10.99. Published by Warner Books.

ONLINE DATABASES

PAIS International. Public Affairs Information Service, Inc. • Corresponds to the former printed publications, *PAIS Bulletin* (1976-90) and *PAIS Foreign Language Index* (1972-90), and to the current *PAIS International in Print* (1991 to date). Covers economic, political, and sociological material appearing in periodicals, books, government documents, and other publications. Updating is monthly. Inquire as to online cost and availability.

Readers' Guide Abstracts Online. H. W. Wilson Co. • Indexes and abstracts general interest periodicals, 1983 to date. Weekly updates. Inquire as to online cost and availability.

PERIODICALS AND NEWSLETTERS

Fine Homebuilding. Taunton Press, Inc. • Bimonthly $36.00. Special interest magazine written by builders for builders - professional and homeowners.

Ledger Quarterly: A Financial Review for Community Association Practitioners. Community Associations Institute. • Quarterly. Members, $40.00 per year; non-members, $67.00 per year. Newsletter. Provides current information on issues affecting the finances of condominium, cooperative, homeowner, apartment, and other community housing associations.

Metropolitan Home: Style for Our Generation. Hachette Filipacchi Magazines, Inc. • Bimonthly. $17.94 per year.

Unique Homes: The National Magazine of Luxury Real Estate. Unique Homes, Inc. • Eight times a year. $30.97 per year. Homes for sale.

STATISTICS SOURCES

American Housing Survey for the United States in [year]. Available from U. S. Government Printing Office. • Biennial. Issued by the U. S. Census Bureau (http://www.census.gov). Covers both owner-occupied and renter-occupied housing. Includes data on such factors as condition of building, type of mortgage, utility costs, and housing occupied by minorities. (Current Housing Reports, H150.).

Current Population Reports: Household Economic Studies, Series P-70. Available from U. S. Government Printing Office. • Irregular. $16.00 per year. Issued by the U.S. Bureau of the Census (http://www.census.gov). Each issue covers a special topic relating to household socioeconomic characteristics.

Housing Statistics of the United States. Patrick A. Simmons, editor. Bernan Press. • 2000. $74.00. Third edition. (Bernan Press U.S. Data Book Series).

New One-Family Houses Sold. Available from U. S. Government Printing Office. • Monthly. $45.00 per year. Bureau of the Census Construction Report, C25. Provides data on new, privately-owned, one-family homes sold during the month and for sale at the end of the month.

ULI Market Profiles: North America. Urban Land Institute. • Annual. Members, $249.95; non-members, $299.95. Provides real estate marketing data for residential, retail, office, and industrial sectors. Covers 76 U. S. metropolitan areas and 13 major foreign metropolitan areas.

TRADE/PROFESSIONAL ASSOCIATIONS

Community Associations Institute. 1630 Duke St., Alexandria, VA 22314. Phone: (703)548-8600 Fax: (703)684-1581 • URL: http://www.caionline.org • Members are condominium associations, homeowners associations, builders, property managers, developers, and others concerned with the common facilities and services in condominiums, townhouses, planned unit developments, and other planned communities.

National Foundation Manufactured Home Owners. c/o Debra Chapman, 62 Hawthorne Circle, Willow Street, PA 17584. Phone: (717)284-4520 Fax: (717)284-4250 E-mail: pamhoa@aol.com.

National Homeowners Association. P.O.Box 221225, Chantilly, VA 20153. Phone: (703)581-1515 Fax: (703)581-1234.

National Housing Conference. 815 15th St., N.W., Suite 538, Washington, DC 20005. Phone: (202)393-5772 Fax: (202)393-5656 E-mail: nhc@nhc.org • URL: http://www.nch.org.

National Rural Housing Coalition. 1250 Eye St., N.W., Ste. 902, Washington, DC 20005. Phone: (202)393-5229 Fax: (202)393-3034 E-mail: nrhc@rapoza.org.

HOME TEXTILES

See: LINEN INDUSTRY

HOMES FOR THE AGED

See: NURSING HOMES

HONEY INDUSTRY

ABSTRACTS AND INDEXES

Apicultural Abstracts. International Bee Research Association. • Quarterly. $295.00 per year. Up-to-date summary of world literature on bees and beekeeping.

Bee Culture. A. I. Root Co. • Monthly. $20.00 per year. Articles, reports and stories about beekeeping market. Latest industry news. Formerly *Gleanings in Bee Culture.*

INTERNET DATABASES

USDA. United States Department of Agriculture. Phone: (202)720-2791 E-mail: agsec@usda.gov • URL: http://www.usda.gov • The USDA home page has six sections: News and Information; What's New; About USDA; Agencies; Opportunities; Search and Help. Keyword searching is offered from the USDA home page and from various individual agency home pages. Agencies are the Economic Research Service, Agricultural Marketing Service, National Agricultural Statistics Service, National Agricultural Library, and about 12 others. Updating varies. Fees: Free.

ONLINE DATABASES

CAB Abstracts. CAB International North America. • Contains 46 specialized abstract collections covering over 10,000 journals and monographs in the areas of agriculture, horticulture, forest products, farm products, nutrition, dairy science, poultry, grains, animal health, entomology, etc. Time period is 1972 to date, with monthly updates. Inquire as to online cost and availability. *CAB Abstracts on CD-ROM* also available, with annual updating.

F & S Index. The Gale Group. • Contains about four million citations to worldwide business, financial, and industrial or consumer product literature appearing from 1972 to date. Weekly updates. Inquire as to online cost and availability.

PERIODICALS AND NEWSLETTERS

American Bee Journal. Dadant and Sons, Inc. • Monthly. $19.25 per year. Magazine for hobbyist and professional beekeepers.

American Beekeeping Federation Newsletter. American Beekeeping Federation. • Bimonthly. $25.00 per year. Newsletter.

Bee Craft: The Official Journal of the British BeeKeepers' Association. Bee Craft Ltd., The Secretary. • Monthly. $35.00 per year.

Bee World. International Bee Research Association. • Quarterly. $70.00 per year. Authoritative articles and reviews about recent scientific and technological developments.

Beekeeping. Devon Beekeepers Association. • Ten times a year. Free to members; non-members, $15.00 per year.

Journal of Apicultural Research. International Bee Research Association. • Quarterly. $170.00 per year. Primary research.

RESEARCH CENTERS AND INSTITUTES

Bee Biology and Systematics Laboratory. Utah State University. 5310 Old Main Hill, Logan, UT 84322-5310. Phone: (435)797-2524 Fax: (435)797-0461 E-mail: wkemp@cc.usu.edu • URL: http://www.loganbeelab.usu.edu.

Honey Bee Research Unit. U.S. Department of Agricultural Research Service, Carl Hayden Bee Research Center, 2000 E. Allen Rd., Tucson, AZ 85719. Phone: (520)670-6380 Fax: (520)670-6493 E-mail: eric@tucson.ars.ag.gov • URL: http://gears.tucson,ars.ag.gov/.

Kika de la Garza Subtropical Agricultural Research Center. U.S. Department of Agricultural Research Center, BIRU Bldg. 213, 2413 E. Highway 83, Weslaco, TX 78596. Phone: (956)969-5005 Fax: (956)969-5033 E-mail: dbrandenberger@weslaco.ars.usda.gov • URL: http://www.weslaco.ars.usda.gov.

Northeast Research and Extension Center. University of Arkansas. P.O. Box 48, Keiser, AR 72351. Phone: (501)526-2199 Fax: (501)526-2582 E-mail: bourland@comp.uark.edu.

STATISTICS SOURCES

Agricultural Statistics. Available from U. S. Government Printing Office. • Annual. Produced by the National Agricultural Statistics Service, U. S. Department of Agriculture. Provides a wide variety of statistical data relating to agricultural production, supplies, consumption, prices/price-supports, foreign trade, costs, and returns, as well as farm labor, loans, income, and population. In many cases, historical data is shown annually for 10 years. In addition to farm data, includes detailed fishery statistics.

Honey Production, Annual Summary. U.S. Department of Agriculture. • Annual.

Sugar and Sweetener Situation and Outlook. Available from U. S. Government Printing Office. • Three times per year. $11.00 per year. Issued by Economic Research Service, U. S. Department of Agriculture. Provides current statistical information on supply, demand, and prices.

TRADE/PROFESSIONAL ASSOCIATIONS

American Beekeeping Federation. P.O. Box 1038, Jesup, GA 31598-1038. Phone: (912)427-4233 Fax: (912)427-8447 E-mail: info@abfnet.org • URL: http://www.abfnet.org.

International Bee Research Association. 18 North Rd., Cardiff, S. Glam CF1 3DY 44, Wales. E-mail: ibra@cardiff.ac.uk • URL: http://www.cardiff.ac.uk/ibra/index.html.

International Federation of Beekeepers' Associations. Corso Vittorio Emanuele 101, I-00186 Rome, Italy. Phone: 39 6 685286 Fax: 39 6 6852286 E-mail: apimondia@mclink.it.

National Honey Packers and Dealers Association. P.O. Box 545, Matawan, NJ 07747. Phone: (732)583-8188 Fax: (732)583-0798.

HONG KONG

See: ASIAN MARKETS

HONORARY DEGREES

See: ACADEMIC DEGREES

HOPS

See: BREWING INDUSTRY

HOROLOGY

See: CLOCK AND WATCH INDUSTRY

HORTICULTURE

See: NURSERIES (HORTICULTURAL)

HOSIERY INDUSTRY

See also: CHILDREN'S APPAREL INDUSTRY; CLOTHING INDUSTRY; WOMEN'S APPAREL; TEXTILE INDUSTRY

DIRECTORIES

Accessories Resources Directory. Business Journals, Inc. • Annual. $30.00. 1,600 manufacturers, importers, and sales representatives producing or handling belts, gloves, handbags, scarves, hosiery, jewelry, sunglasses and umbrellas. Formerly *Accessories Directory.*

HANDBOOKS AND MANUALS

Sock Shop. Entrepreneur Media, Inc. • Looseleaf. $59.50. A practical guide to starting a store that sells stockings of various kinds. Covers profit potential, start-up costs, market size evaluation, owner's time required, site selection, lease negotiation, pricing, accounting, advertising, etc. (Start-Up Business Guide No. E1340.).

INTERNET DATABASES

Fedstats. Federal Interagency Council on Statistical Policy. Phone: (202)395-7254 • URL: http://www.fedstats.gov • Web site features an efficient search facility for full-text statistics produced by more than 70 federal agencies, including the Census Bureau, the Bureau of Economic Analysis, and the Bureau of Labor Statistics. Boolean searches can be made within one agency or for all agencies combined. Links are offered to international statistical bureaus, including the UN, IMF, OECD, UNESCO, Eurostat, and 20 individual countries. Fees: Free.

ONLINE DATABASES

DRI U.S. Central Database. Data Products Division. • Provides more than 23,000 business, financial, demographic, economic, foreign trade, and industry-related time series for the U.S. Includes national income, population, retail-wholesale trade, price indexes, labor data, housing, industrial production, banking, interest rates, money supply, etc. Time period is generally 1947 to date (some data back to 1929). Updating varies. Inquire as to online cost and availability.

PERIODICALS AND NEWSLETTERS

Hosiery News. Hosiery Association. • Monthly. Membership. Hosiery-related news including new offerings for retail, industry changes, legislative updates of hosiery-impacting laws, foreign trade and statistical information.

STATISTICS SOURCES

Business Statistics of the United States. Courtenay M. Slater, editor. Bernan Associates. • 1999. $74.00. Fifth edition. Based on *Business Statistics*, formerly issue by the Bureau of Economic Analysis, U. S. Department of Commerce. Provides basic data for a wide variety of U. S. industries, services, and economic indicators. Most statistics are shown annually for 29 years and monthly for the most recent four years.

Hosiery Statistics. Hosiery Association. • Annual. $50.00.

Survey of Current Business. Available from U. S. Government Printing Office. • Monthly. $49.00 per year. Issued by Bureau of Economic Analysis, U. S. Department of Commerce. Presents a wide variety of business and economic data.

TRADE/PROFESSIONAL ASSOCIATIONS

Amalgamated Clothing and Textile Workers Union. 1710 Broadway, New York, NY 10019. Phone: (212)265-7000 Fax: (212)265-3415.

The Hosiery Association. 3623 Latrobe Dr., Ste. 130, Charlotte, NC 28211. Phone: (704)365-0913 Fax: (704)362-2056 E-mail: hosierytha@aol.com • URL: http://www.hosieryassociation.com.

HOSPITAL ADMINISTRATION

See also: ADMINISTRATION; HEALTH CARE INDUSTRY; HOSPITAL EQUIPMENT

GENERAL WORKS

Basic Hospital Financial Management. Donald F. Beck. Aspen Publishers, Inc. • 1989. $62.00. Second edition.

The Financial Management of Hospitals. Howard J. Berman and others. Health Administration Press. • 1998. $52.00.

Fundamentals of Strategic Planning for Healthcare Organizations. Stan Williamson and others. Haworth Press, Inc. • 1996. $49.95.

Introduction to Hospital Accounting. L. Vann Seawell. Healthcare Financial Management Educational Foundation. • 1992. $45.00. Third edition.

Management of Healthcare Organizations. Kerry D. Carson and others. Brooks/Cole Publishing Co. • Price on application. (SWC-Management Series).

Predicting Successful Hospital Mergers and Acquisitions: A Financial and Analytical Marketing Tool. David P. Angrisani and Robert L. Goldman. Haworth Press, Inc. • 1997. $49.95.

ABSTRACTS AND INDEXES

Excerpta Medica: Health Policy, Economics and Management. Elsevier Science. • Bimonthly. $1,327.00 per year. Section 36 of *Excerpta Medica.*

DIRECTORIES

AHA Guide to the Health Care Field. American Hospital Association. American Hospital Publishing, Inc. • Annual. $280.00. A directory of hospitals and health care systems.

Directory of Health Care Professionals. Dorland Healthcare Information. • Annual. $299.00. Lists about 175,000 professional staff members at 7,000 U. S. hospitals and health systems.

Directory of Hospital Personnel. Medical Economics Co., Inc. • Annual. $325.00. Lists over 200,000 healthcare professionals in 7,000 U. S. hospitals. Geographic arrangement, with indexes by personnel, hospital name, and bed size.

Directory of Physician Groups and Networks. Dorland Healthcare Information. • Annual. $345.00. Lists more than 4,200 independent practice associations (IPAs), physician hospital organizations (PHOs), management service organizations (MSOs), physician practice management companies (PPMCs), and group practices having 20 or more physicians.

Directory of Privately-Owned Hospitals,Residential Treatment Facilities and Centers, Hospital Management Companies, and Health Systems. Federation of American Health Systems. • Annual. $125.00.

OB/GYN Reference Guide. Access Publishing Co. • Annual. Price on application. Includes directory information for obstetrical/gynecological equipment, supplies, pharmaceuticals, services, organizations, and publications.

Plunkett's Health Care Industry Almanac: The Only Complete Guide to the Fastest-Changing Industry in America. Available from Plunkett Research, Ltd. • Biennial. $179.99. Includes detailed profiles of 500 large companies providing health care products or services, with indexes by products, services, and location. Provides statistical and trend information for the health insurance industry, HMOs, hospital utilization, Medicare, medical technology, and national health expenditures.

Profiles of U. S. Hospitals. Dorland Healthcare Information. • Annual. $299.00. Contains profiles of more than 6,000 community, teaching, children's, specialty, psychiatric, and rehabilitation hospitals. Emphasis is on 50 key financial and performance measures. Annual CD-ROM version with key word searching is available at $395.00.

Radiology Reference Guide. Access Publishing Co. • Annual. Price on application. Includes directory information for radiological equipment, supplies, services, organizations, and publications.

Society for Health Strategy and Market Development-Directory of Membership and Services. Society for Healthcare Strategy and Market Development. American Hospital Association. • Annual. Membership. Formerly *American Society for Health Care Marketing and Public Relations-Membership Directory.*

FINANCIAL RATIOS

Almanac of Business and Industrial Financial Ratios. Leo Troy. Prentice Hall. • Annual. $99.95.

Contains financial ratios derived from federal tax returns. Ratios for each of about 200 industries are arranged according to company asset size.

Hospital Finance Almanac. Healthcare Financial Management Association. • Annual. $350.00. Provides five-year data relating to the financial and operating performance of the U. S. hospital industry. A consolidation of the former *Financial Report of the Hospital Industry* and *Performance Report of the Hospital Industry.*

HANDBOOKS AND MANUALS

Healthcare Finance for the Non-Financial Manager: Basic Guide to Financial Analysis & Control. Louis Gapenski. McGraw-Hill Professional. • 1994. $47.50.

Hospital Cost Management. Prentice Hall. • Looseleaf. Periodic supplementation. Price on application.

The Managed Care Contracting Handbook: Planning and Negotiating the Managed Care Relationship. Maria K. Todd. Available from McGraw Hill Higher Education. • 1996. $65.00. Copublished by McGraw-Hill Healthcare Education Group and the Healthcare Financial Management Association. Covers managed care planning, proposals, strategy, negotiation, and contract law. Written for healthcare providers.

Management Accounting for Healthcare Organizations. Bruce R. Neumann and Keith E. Boles. Teach'em. • 1998. $65.00. Fifth revised edition.

ONLINE DATABASES

Healthstar. Medlars Management Section. • Provides indexing and abstracting of non-clinical literature relating to health care delivery, 1975 to date. Monthly updates. Inquire as to online cost and availability.

PERIODICALS AND NEWSLETTERS

AHA News. Health Forum, Inc. • Weekly. $147.00 per year. Edited for hospital and health care industry administrators. Covers health care news events and legislative activity. An American Hospital Association publication (http://www.aha.org).

Health Facilities Management. American Hospital Association. American Hospital Publishing, Inc. • Monthly. $40.00 per year. Covers building maintenance and engineering for hospitals and nursing homes.

Health Forum. American Hospital Association. American Hospital Publishing, Inc. • Biweekly. $80.00 per year. Covers the general management of hospitals, nursing homes, and managed care organizations. Formerly *HospitalsHealthNetworks.*

Healthcare PR and Marketing News. Phillips Business Information, Inc. • Biweekly. $497.00 per year. Newsletter on public relations and client communications for the healthcare industry.

Hospital Pharmacist Report. Medical Economics Co., Inc. • Monthly. $39.00 per year. Covers both business and clinical topics for hospital pharmacists.

Hospital Revenue Report. United Communications Group. • 25 times a year. $379.00 per year. Newsletter. Advises hospitals on how to cut costs, increase patient revenue, and maximize Medicare income. Incorporates *Health Care Marketer.*

Journal of Healthcare Management. Foundation of the American College of Healthcare Executives. Health Administration Press. • Quarterly. $65.00 per year. Information on the latest trends, developments and innovations in the industry. Formerly (Hospital and Health Services Administration).

Journal of Hospital Marketing. Haworth Press, Inc. • Semiannual. Individuals, $45.00 per year; institutions, $85.00 per year; libraries, $275.00 per year.

Modern Physician: Essential Business News for the Executive Physician. Crain Communications, Inc. • Monthly. $39.50. Edited for physicians responsible for business decisions at hospitals, clinics, HMOs, and other health groups. Includes special issues on managed care, practice management, legal issues, and finance.

Report on Healthcare Information Management: A Strategic Guide to Technology and Data Integration. Aspen Publishers, Inc. • Monthly. $358.00 per year. Newsletter. Covers management information sytems for hospitals and physicians' groups.

Solid Waste Report: Resource Recovery-Recycling-Collection-Disposal. Business Publishers, Inc. • Weekly. $627.00 per year. Newsletter. Covers regulation, business news, technology, and international events relating to solid waste management.

Trustee: The Magazine for Hospital Governing Boards. American Hospital Association. American Hospital Publishing, Inc. • 10 times a year. $35.00 per year. Emphasis is on community health care.

RESEARCH CENTERS AND INSTITUTES

Center for Health Administration Studies. University of Chicago, 969 E. 60th St., Chicago, IL 60637. Phone: (773)702-7104 Fax: (773)702-7222 E-mail: chas@uchichago.edu • URL: http://www.chas.uchicago.edu.

Health Services Research and Development Center. Johns Hopkins University, 624 N. Broadway, Room 482, Baltimore, MD 21205-1996. Phone: (410)955-3625 Fax: (410)955-0470 E-mail: dsteinwa@jhsph.edu.

STATISTICS SOURCES

AHA Hospital Statistics. American Hospital Association. American Hospital Publishing, Inc. • Annual. Members, $59.00 per year; non-members $139.00 per year. Provides detailed statistical data on the nation's hospitals, including revenues, expenses, utilization, and personnel. Formerly *Hospital Statistics.*

Economic Trends. American Hospital Association. American Hospital Publishing, Inc. • Quarterly. Members, $85.00 per year; non-members $135.00 per year. Provides statistical data on the nation's hospitals, including revenues, expenses.

Health and Environment in America's Top-Rated Cities: A Statistical Profile. Grey House Publishing. • Biennial. $195.00. Covers 75 U. S. cities. Includes statistical and other data on a wide variety of topics, such as air quality, water quality, recycling, hospitals, physicians, health care costs, death rates, infant mortality, accidents, and suicides.

Health Care Costs. DRI/McGraw-Hill. • Quarterly. Price on application. Cost indexes for hospitals, nursing homes, and home healthcare agencies.

Lilly Hospital Pharmacy Survey. Eli Lilly and Co. • Annual. $30.00. Includes financial data for drug stores located in hospitals.

Standard & Poor's Industry Surveys. Standard & Poor's. • Semiannual. $1,800.00. Two looseleaf volumes. Includes monthly supplements. Provides detailed, individual surveys of 52 major industry groups. Each survey is revised on a semiannual basis. Also includes "Monthly Investment Review" (industry group investment analysis) and monthly "Trends & Projections" (economic analysis).

TRADE/PROFESSIONAL ASSOCIATIONS

American College of Healthcare Executives. One N. Franklin, St., Suite 1700, Chicago, IL 60606-3491. Phone: (312)424-2800 Fax: (312)424-0023 • URL: http://www.ache.org.

American Hospital Association. One N. Franklin St., Chicago, IL 60606. Phone: (312)422-3000 Fax: (312)422-4796 • URL: http://www.aha.org.

American Society of Health System Pharmacists. 7272 Wisconsin Ave., Bethesda, MD 20814. Phone: (301)657-3000 Fax: (301)657-1251 E-mail: pdiso@ashp.org • URL: http://www.ashp.org.

Healthcare Financing Management Association. Two Westbrook Corporate Financial Center, Suite 700, Westchester, IL 60154-5700. Phone: 800-252-4362 E-mail: tarya@hfma.org • URL: http://www.hfma.org.

Healthcare Information and Management Systems Society. 230 E. Ohio St., Suite 500, Chicago, IL 60611-3265. Phone: 800-252-4362 or (312)664-4467 Fax: (312)664-6143 E-mail: himss@himss.org • URL: http://www.himi.org.

OTHER SOURCES

Distressed Hospital Quarterly. Health Care Investment Analysts. • Quarterly. $500.00 per year. Names and provides information on specific distressed hospitals, which are defined as those "exhibiting substantial adverse changes" in such factors as capital structure, profitability, liquidity, payor mix, and utilization.

HOSPITAL EQUIPMENT

See also: SURGICAL INSTRUMENTS INDUSTRY; X-RAY EQUIPMENT INDUSTRY

CD-ROM DATABASES

Health Devices Alerts [CD-ROM]. ECRI. • Weekly. $2,450.00 per year. Provides CD-ROM reports of medical equipment defects, problems, failures, misuses, and recalls.

DIRECTORIES

Association for the Advancement of Medical Instrumentation Membership Directory. Association for the Advancement of Medical Instrumentation. • Annual. Membership. List 6,500 physicians, clinical engineers, biomedical engineersand technicians and nurses, researchers, and medical equipment manufacturers.

Buyers' Guide for the Health Care Market: A Directory of Products and Services for Health Care Institutions. American Hospital Association. Health Forum, Inc. • Annual. $17.95. Lists 1,200 suppliers and manufacturers of health care products and services for hospitals, nursing homes, and related organizations.

Health Devices Sourcebook. ECRI (Emergency Care Research Institute). • Annual. Lists over 6,000 manufacturers of a wide variety of medical equipment and supplies, including clinical laboratory equipment, testing instruments, surgical instruments, patient care equipment, etc.

Medical and Healthcare Marketplace Guide. Dorland Healthcare Information. • Annual. $690.00. Two volumes. Provides market survey summaries for about 500 specific product and service categories (volume one: "Research Reports"). Contains profiles of nearly 6,000 pharmaceutical, medical product, and healthcare service companies (volume two: "Company Profiles").

Society for Healthcare Strategy and Market Development-Directory of Membership and Service. Society for Healthcare Strategy and Market Development. American Hospital Association. • Annual. Membership.

INTERNET DATABASES

National Library of Medicine (NLM). National Institutes of Health (NIH). Phone: 888-346-3656 or (301)496-1131 Fax: (301)480-3537 E-mail:

access@nlm.nih.gov • URL: http://www.nlm.nih.gov • NLM Web site offers free access through MEDLINE ("PubMed") to about nine million references to articles appearing in some 3,800 biomedical journals, with abstracts. Search interfaces range from "simple keywords to advanced Boolean expressions." The NLM site offers many links to other sources of biomedical and technical information (the National Center for Biotechnology Information, for example). Fees: Free.

ONLINE DATABASES

F-D-C Reports. FDC Reports, Inc. • An online version of "The Gray Sheet" (medical devices), "The Pink Sheet" (pharmaceuticals), "The Rose Sheet" (cosmetics), "The Blue Sheet" (biomedical), and "The Tan Sheet" (nonprescription). Contains full-text information on legal, technical, corporate, financial, and marketing developments from 1987 to date, with weekly updates. Inquire as to online cost and availability.

Health Devices Alerts [online]. ECRI. • Provides online reports of medical equipment defects, problems, failures, misuses, and recalls. Time period is 1977 to date, with weekly updates. Inquire as to online cost and availability.

PERIODICALS AND NEWSLETTERS

Health Devices Alerts: A Summary of Reported Problems, Hazards, Recalls, and Updates. ECRI (Emergency Care Research Institute). • Weekly. Newsletter containing reviews of health equipment problems. Includes *Health Devices Alerts Action Items, Health Devices Alerts Abstracts, Health Devices Alerts FDA Data, Health Devices Alerts Implants, Health Devices Alerts Hazards Bulletin.*

Healthcare Purchasing News: A Magazine for Hospital Materials Management Central Service, Infection Control Practitioners. McKnight Medical Communications. • Monthly. $44.00 per year. Edited for personnel responsible for the purchase of medical, surgical, and hospital equipment and supplies. Features new purchasing techniques and new products. Includes news of the activities of two major purchasing associations, Health Care Material Management Society and International Association of Healthcare Central Service Materiel Management.

Medical Devices, Diagnostics, and Instrumentation: The Gray Sheet Reports. F-D-C Reports, Inc. • Weekly. $955.00 per year. Newsletter. Provides industry and financial news, including a medical sector stock index. Monitors regulatory developments at the Center for Devices and Radiological Health of the U. S. Food and Drug Administration.

Medical Product Manufacturing News. Canon Communications LLC. • 10 times a year. Free to qualified personnel; others, $125.00 per year. Directed at manufacturers of medical devices and medical electronic equipment. Covers industry news, service news, and new products.

Patient Management. Cahners Business Information, New Product Information. • Nine times a year. $24.00 per year. Formerly *Medical Care Products.*

Surgical Products. Cahners Business Information. • 10 times a year. $24.00 per year. Covers new Technology and products for surgeons and operation rooms.

STATISTICS SOURCES

Electromedical Equipment and Irradiation Equipment, Including X-Ray. U. S. Bureau of the Census. • Annual. Contains shipment quantity, value of shipment, export, and import data. (Current Industrial Report No. MA-38R.).

Standard & Poor's Industry Surveys. Standard & Poor's. • Semiannual. $1,800.00. Two looseleaf volumes. Includes monthly supplements. Provides detailed, individual surveys of 52 major industry groups. Each survey is revised on a semiannual basis. Also includes "Monthly Investment Review" (industry group investment analysis) and monthly "Trends & Projections" (economic analysis).

TRADE/PROFESSIONAL ASSOCIATIONS

Association for Healthcare Resource and Materials Management. c/o American Hospital Association, One N. Franklin St ., Chicago, IL 60606. Phone: (312)422-3840 Fax: (312)422-3573 E-mail: ahrmm@aha.org • URL: http://www.ahrmm.org • Members are involved with the purchasing and distribution of supplies and equipment for hospitals and other healthcare establishments. Affiliated with the American Hospital Association.

Health Care Resource Management Society. P.O. Box 29253, Cincinnati, OH 45229-0253. Phone: (513)520-1058 or (513)872-6315 Fax: (513)872-6158 E-mail: hcrms@choice.net • URL: http://www.hcrms.com • Members are materials management (purchasing) personnel in hospitals and the healthcare industry. The Society is concerned with hospital costs, distribution, logistics, recycling, and inventory management.

Health Industry Manufacturers Association. 1200 G St., N.W., Suite 400, Washington, DC 20005. Phone: (202)783-8700 Fax: (202)783-8750 • URL: http://www.himanet.com.

International Association of Healthcare Central Service Materiel Management. 213 W. Institute Place, Suite 307, Chicago, IL 60610. Phone: 800-962-8274 or (312)440-0078 Fax: (312)440-9474 E-mail: mailbox@iahcsmm.com • URL: http://www.iahcsmm.com • Members are professional personnel responsible for management and distribution of supplies from a central service material management (purchasing) department of a hospital.

National Association for Medical Equipment Services. 625 Slaters Lane, Suite 200, Alexandria, VA 22314-1171. Phone: (703)836-6263 Fax: (703)836-6730 E-mail: info@names.org • URL: http://www.names.org • Members are durable medical equipment and oxygen suppliers, mainly for home health care. Has Legislative Affairs Committee that is concerned with Medicare/Medicaid benefits.

OTHER SOURCES

Disposable Medical Supplies. Available from MarketResearch.com. • 1998. $3,500.00. Published by the Freedonia Group. Market data with forecasts to 2002 and 2007. Includes disposable syringes, catheters, kits, trays, etc.

New and Breaking Technologies in the Pharmaceutical and Medical Device Industries. Theta Reports/PJB Medical Publications, Inc. • 1999. $1,695.00. Contains market research predictions of medical technology trends over the next 5 to 10 years (2004-2009), including developments in biotechnology, genetic engineering, medical device technology, therapeutic vaccines, non-invasive diagnostics, and minimally-invasive surgery. (Theta Report No. 931.).

Nonwoven Disposables. Theta Reports/PJB Medical Publications, Inc. • 1999. $1,495.00. Provides market research data, including sales projections. Covers hospital disposable items, such as surgical drapes, masks, head covers, patient gowns, and incontinence products. (Theta Report No. 922.).

HOSPITALITY INDUSTRY

See: HOTEL AND MOTEL INDUSTRY; RESTAURANTS, LUNCHROOMS, ETC.; TRAVEL INDUSTRY

HOSPITALS

See: HOSPITAL ADMINISTRATION

HOTEL AND MOTEL INDUSTRY

See also: TRAVEL INDUSTRY

GENERAL WORKS

How Consumers Pick a Hotel: Strategic Segmentation and Target Marketing. Dennis J. Cahill. The Haworth Press, Inc. • 1997. $39.95.

The Lodging and Food Service Industry. Gerald W. Lattin and others. Educational Institute of the American Hotel & Motel Association. • 1998. $60.95. Fourth revised edition. General survey of the hospitality industry.

Management of Hotel and Motel Security. Harvey Burstein. Marcel Dekker, Inc. • 1980. $110.00. (Occupational Safety and Health Series).

Marketing Management for the Hospitality Industry: A Strategic Approach. Allen Z. Reich. John Wiley and Sons, Inc. • 1997. $59.95.

ABSTRACTS AND INDEXES

Leisure, Recreation, and Tourism Abstracts. Available from CABI Publishing North America. • Quarterly. $470.00 per year. Published in England by CABI Publishing. Provides coverage of the worldwide literature of travel, recreation, sports, and the hospitality industry. Emphasis is on research.

Lodging, Restaurant and Tourism Index. Distance Learning Service, Consumer and Faamily Sciences Library. Purdue University. • Quarterly. $225.00 per year. Provides subject indexing to 52 periodicals related to the hospitality industry. Annual bound cumulations are available. Formerly *Lodging and Restaurant Index.*

DIRECTORIES

AH & MA Buyers Guide. American Hotel and Motel Association. • Annual. $50.00. Contains more than 3,500 listings of suppliers of products and services for the lodging industry.

Almanac. Penton Media Inc. • Annual. $50.00. Lists equipment, products, and services for the hotel and motel industry.

Directory of Hotel and Motel Companies. American Hotel and Motel Association. • Annual. $79.00 per year. International coverage.

A Guide to College Programs in Hospitality and Tourism. Council on Hotel, Restaurant and Institutional Education. John Wiley and Sons, Inc. • 1995. $29.95. Fifth edition. About 400 secondary and technical institutes, colleges, and universities; international coverage.

Hotel and Travel Index: The World Wide Hotel Directory. Cahners Travel Group. • Quarterly. $130.00 per year. Contains concise information on more than 45,000 hotels in the U. S. and around the world. Includes 400 maps showing location of hotels and airports.

OAG Business Travel Planner: North America. Cahners Travel Group. • Quarterly. $149.00 per year. Arranged according to more than 14,700 destinations in the U. S., Canada, Mexico, and the Caribbean. Lists more than 32,000 hotels, with AAA ratings where available. Provides information on airports, ground transportation, coming events, and climate.

OAG Travel Planner: Asia Pacific. Cahners Travel Group. • Quarterly. $130.00 per year. Arranged according to more than 5,000 destinations throughout Asia and the Pacific. Lists about 5,000 hotels, with information on airports, ground transportation, coming events, and climate.

OAG Travel Planner: Europe. Cahners Travel Group. • Quarterly. $130.00 per year. Arranged according to more than 13,850 destinations in Europe. Lists more than 14,700 hotels, with information on airports, ground transportation, coming events, and climate.

Official Hotel Guide. Cahners Travel Group. • Annual. $229.00. Three volumes. Contains detailed descriptions of about 30,000 hotels and resorts worldwide, graded by a 10-level classification system. Includes more than 350 maps.

Resorts and Parks Purchasing Guide. Klevens Publications, Inc. • Annual. $60.00. Lists suppliers of products and services for resorts and parks, including national parks, amusement parks, dude ranches, golf resorts, ski areas, and national monument areas.

Star Service: The Critical Guide to Hotels and Cruise Ships. Cahners Travel Group. • $249.00. Looseleaf. Quarterly supplements. Provides "honest and unbiased descriptions of accommodations, facilities, amenities, ambience, appearance, and service" for more than 10,000 hotels worldwide and 150 cruise ships. Ship information includes history, passenger profiles, crew profiles, and other data.

ENCYCLOPEDIAS AND DICTIONARIES

Uniform System of Accounts for the Lodging Industry. Timothy J. Eaton, editor. Educational Institute of the American Hotel & Motel Association. • 1998. Tenth edition. Price on application.

FINANCIAL RATIOS

Almanac of Business and Industrial Financial Ratios. Leo Troy. Prentice Hall. • Annual. $99.95. Contains financial ratios derived from federal tax returns. Ratios for each of about 200 industries are arranged according to company asset size.

Annual Statement Studies. Robert Morris Associates: The Association of Lending and Credit Risk Professiona. • Annual. Free to members; non-members, $140.00. Median and quartile financial ratios are given for over 400 kinds of manufacturing, wholesale, retail, construction, and consumer finance establishments. Data is sorted by both asset size and sales volume. Includes a clearly written "Definition of Ratios" and an alphabetical industry index.

HANDBOOKS AND MANUALS

Check-In-Check-Out. Principles of Effective Front Office Management. Gary K. Vallen and Jerome J. Vallen. Brown and Benchmark. • $44.75. Looseleaf service.

Dun & Bradstreet/Gale Group Industry Handbooks. The Gale Group. • 2000. $630.00. Five volumes. $145.00 per volume. Each volume covers two or more major industries: 1. *Entertainment and Hospitality*; 2. *Construction and Agriculture*; 3. *Chemicals and Pharmaceuticals*; 4. *Computers & Software and Broadcasting & Telecommunications*; 5. *Insurance and Health & Medical Services*. The following are included for each industry: overview, statistics, financial ratios, rankings, merger information, company directory, directory of associations, and consultants directory.

Hospitality Industry Managerial Accounting. Raymond S. Schmidgall. Educational Institute of the American Hotel & Motel Association. • 1997. Fourth edition. Price on application. A reference to improve decision-making.

Hotel Development. Urban Land Institute. • 1996. $59.95. Provides practical information on developing, acquiring, and renovating hotels in urban areas. Covers market analysis, financing, construction, and management. Includes case studies.

Management of People in Hotels and Restaurants. Donald E. Lundberg and James P. Armatas. Brown and Benchmark. • 1992. $36.50. Fifth edition.

Managing Front Office Operations. Michael L. Kasavana and Richard M. Brooks. Educational Institute of the American Hotel & Motel Association. • 1998. $66.95. Fifth revised edition. Covers all aspects of the front office. Includes computer appliations throughout all phases of the guest cycle.

Professional Management of Housekeeping Operations. Robert J. Martin and Tom Jones. John Wiley and Sons, Inc. • 1998. $59.95. Third edition. For hotels and motels.

Resort Development Handbook. Dean Schwanke and others. Urban Land Institute. • 1997. $89.95. Covers a wide range of resort settings and amenities, with details of development, market analysis, financing, design, and operations. Includes color photographs and case studies. (ULI Development Handbook Series).

Strategic Hotel Motel Marketing. Christopher W. L. Hart and David Troy. Educational Institute of the American Hotel & Motel Association. • 1998. $59.95. Third edition. Price on application.

Supervision in the Hospitality Industry. Raphael R. Kavanaugh and Jack D. Ninemeier. Educational Institute of the American Hotel & Motel Association. • 1998. $59.95. Third edition. Principles of communication, motivation, recruiting, training, etc.

INTERNET DATABASES

Fedstats. Federal Interagency Council on Statistical Policy. Phone: (202)395-7254 • URL: http://www.fedstats.gov • Web site features an efficient search facility for full-text statistics produced by more than 70 federal agencies, including the Census Bureau, the Bureau of Economic Analysis, and the Bureau of Labor Statistics. Boolean searches can be made within one agency or for all agencies combined. Links are offered to international statistical bureaus, including the UN, IMF, OECD, UNESCO, Eurostat, and 20 individual countries. Fees: Free.

ONLINE DATABASES

DRI U.S. Central Database. Data Products Division. • Provides more than 23,000 business, financial, demographic, economic, foreign trade, and industry-related time series for the U.S. Includes national income, population, retail-wholesale trade, price indexes, labor data, housing, industrial production, banking, interest rates, money supply, etc. Time period is generally 1947 to date (some data back to 1929). Updating varies. Inquire as to online cost and availability.

PERIODICALS AND NEWSLETTERS

The Bottomline. International Association of Hospitality Accountants. • Bimonthly. Free to members, educational institutions and libraries; others, $50.00 per year. Contains articles on accounting, finance, information technology, and management for hotels, resorts, casinos, clubs, and other hospitality businesses.

The Cornell Hotel and Restaurant Administration Quarterly. Cornell University School of Hotel Administration. Elsevier Science. • Bimonthly. $258.00 per year.

Hospitality Technology: Infosystems for Foodservice and Lodging. Edgell Communications, Inc. • Monthly. $36.00 per year. Covers information technology, computer communications, and software for foodservice and lodging enterprises.

Hotel and Motel Management. Advanstar Communications, Inc. • 21 times a year. $45.00 per year.

Hotel Business. ICD Publications. • Semimonthly. $100.00 per year. Covers management, technology, design, business trends, new products, finance, and other topics for the hotel-motel industry.

International Journal of Hospitality and Tourism Administration: A Multinationaland Cross-Cultural Journal of Applied Research. Haworth Press, Inc. • Quarterly. Individuals, $36.00 per year; institutions, $48.00 per year; libraries, $85.00 per year. An academic journal with articles relating to lodging, food service, travel, tourism, and the hospitality/leisure industries in general. Formerly *Journal of International Hospitality, Leisure, and Tourism Management.*

Journal of Hospitality and Leisure Marketing: The International Forum for Research, Theory and Practice. Haworth Press, Inc. • Quarterly. Individuals, $60.00 per year; institutions, $95.00 per year; libraries, $175.00 per year. An academic and practical journal covering various aspects of hotel, restaurant, and recreational marketing.

Lodging. American Hotel and Motel Association. • Monthly. $49.00 per year. Editorial sections include news, finance, technology, foodservice, new products, human resources, marketing, design, and renovation.

Lodging Hospitality: Management Magazine for Hotels, Motels and Resorts. Penton Media Inc. • Monthly. $65.00 per year. Covers a wide variety of topics relating to hotels, motels, and resorts, including management, marketing, finance, operations, and technology.

Resort Management and Operations: The Resort Resource. Finan Publishing Co., Inc. • Quarterly. $21.95 per year. Edited for hospitality professionals at both large and small resort facilities.

Restaurant Hospitality. Penton Media Inc. • Monthly. Free to qualified personnel; others, $65.00 per year.

STATISTICS SOURCES

Business Statistics of the United States. Courtenay M. Slater, editor. Bernan Associates. • 1999. $74.00. Fifth edition. Based on *Business Statistics*, formerly issue by the Bureau of Economic Analysis, U. S. Department of Commerce. Provides basic data for a wide variety of U. S. industries, services, and economic indicators. Most statistics are shown annually for 29 years and monthly for the most recent four years.

International Hotel Trends: A Statistical Summary. PKF Consulting. • Annual. $125.00. Provides detailed financial analysis of hotel operations around the world. (PKF is Pannell Kerr Forster.).

Outlook for Travel and Tourism. Travel Industry Association of America. • Annual. Members, $100.00; non-members, $175.00. Contains forecasts of the performance of the U. S. travel industry, including air travel, business travel, recreation (attractions), and accomodations.

Standard & Poor's Industry Surveys. Standard & Poor's. • Semiannual. $1,800.00. Two looseleaf volumes. Includes monthly supplements. Provides detailed, individual surveys of 52 major industry groups. Each survey is revised on a semiannual basis. Also includes "Monthly Investment Review" (industry group investment analysis) and monthly "Trends & Projections" (economic analysis).

Survey of Current Business. Available from U. S. Government Printing Office. • Monthly. $49.00 per year. Issued by Bureau of Economic Analysis, U. S. Department of Commerce. Presents a wide variety of business and economic data.

Trends in the Hotel Industry: U. S. Edition. PKF Consulting. • Annual. $225.00. Provides detailed financial analysis of hotel operations in the U. S. (PKF is Pannell Kerr Forster.).

TRADE/PROFESSIONAL ASSOCIATIONS

American Hotel and Motel Association. 1201 New York Ave., N.W., Suite 600, Washington, DC 20005-3931. Phone: (202)289-3100 Fax: (202)289-3199 E-mail: infoctr@ahma.com • URL: http://www.ahma.com.

Hospitality Financial and Technology Professionals. 11709 Boulder Lane, Suite 110, Austin, TX 78726. Phone: 800-646-4387 or (512)249-5333 Fax: (512)249-1533 E-mail: hftp@hftp.org • URL: http://www.hitecshow • Members are accounting and finance officers in the hotel, motel, casino, club, and other areas of the hospitality industry.

Hospitality Sales and Marketing Association International. 1300 L St., N.W., Suite 1020, Washington, DC 20005. Phone: (202)789-0089 Fax: (202)789-1725 E-mail: bgilbert@hsmail.org • URL: http://www.hsmai.org.

OTHER SOURCES

The Laws of Innkeepers: For Hotels, Motels, Restaurants, and Clubs. J. E. H. Sherry. Cornell University Press. • 1993. $45.00. Third edition.

HOUSE BUYING AND SELLING

See: HOME OWNERSHIP

HOUSE DECORATION

See: INTERIOR DECORATION

HOUSE OF REPRESENTATIVES

See: UNITED STATES CONGRESS

HOUSE ORGANS

See also: BUSINESS JOURNALISM; EDITORS AND EDITING; JOURNALISM; NEWSLETTERS

ALMANACS AND YEARBOOKS

Editor and Publisher International Yearbook: Encyclopedia of the Newspaper Industry. Editor and Publisher Co., Inc. • Annual. $125.00. Daily and Sunday newspapers in the United States and Canada.

DIRECTORIES

Working Press of the Nation. R. R. Bowker. • Annual. $450.00. Three volumes: (1) *Newspaper Directory*; (2) *Magazine and Internal Publications Directory*; (3) *Radio and Television Directory*. Includes names of editors and other personnel. Individual volumes, $249.00.

HANDBOOKS AND MANUALS

Editing Your Newsletter: How to Produce an Effective Publication Using Traditional Tools and Computers. Mark Beach. F and W Publications, Inc. • 1995. $22.99. Fourth edition. Covers design, writing, editing, production and distribution. Emphasis on in-house publications.

Personnel Management: Communications. Prentice Hall. • Looseleaf. Periodic supplementation. Price on application. Includes how to write effectively and how to prepare employee publications.

HOUSE-TO-HOUSE SELLING

See: DIRECT MARKETING

HOUSEHOLD APPLIANCES

See: ELECTRIC APPLIANCE INDUSTRY

HOUSEHOLD FURNISHINGS

See: FURNITURE INDUSTRY

HOUSEHOLD PRODUCTS INDUSTRY

See: CLEANING PRODUCTS INDUSTRY

HOUSES, PREFABRICATED

See: PREFABRICATED HOUSE INDUSTRY

HOUSEWARES INDUSTRY

DIRECTORIES

Directory of Building Products and Hardlines Distributors. Chain Store Guide. • Annual. $280.00. Includes hardware, houseware, and building supply distributors. Formerly *Directory of Hardline Distributors.*

Directory of Discount and General Merchandise Stores. Chain Store Guide. • Annual. $300.00. Includes retailers and wholesalers of housewares, giftwares, novelties, toys, hobby materials, crafts, and stationery. Formerly *Directory of Discount Stores Catalog Showrooms.*

Housewares Retail Directory. American Business Directories. • Annual. Price on application. A listing of about 3,103 retailers. Compiled from telephone company yellow pages.

Nationwide Directory of Gift, Housewares and Home Textiles Buyers. Salesman's Guide. • Annual. $195.00.

PERIODICALS AND NEWSLETTERS

Fancy Food. Talcott Communications Corp. • Monthly. $34.00 per year. Emphasizes new specialty food products and the business management aspects of the specialty food and confection industries. Includes special issues on wine, cheese, candy, "upscale" cookware, and gifts.

Gourmet News: The Business Newspaper for the Gourmet Industry. United Publications, Inc. • Monthly. $55.00 per year. Provides news of the gourmet food industry, including specialty food stores, upscale cookware shops, and gift shops.

Gourmet Retailer. Bill Communications, Business Communications Group. • Monthly. $24.00 per year. Covers upscale food and housewares, including confectionery items, bakery operations, and coffee.

TRADE/PROFESSIONAL ASSOCIATIONS

Cookware Manufacturers Association. c/o Hugh J. Rushing, P.O. Box 531335, Mountain Brook, AL 35253. Phone: (205)802-7600 Fax: (205)802-7610 E-mail: hrushing@cookware.org • URL: http://www.cookware.org • Members are manufacturers of cooking utensils and accessories.

National Housewares Manufacturers Association. 6400 Shafer Court, Suite 650, Rosemont, IL 60018. Phone: 800-843-6462 or (847)292-4200 Fax: (847)292-4211 • URL: http://www.housewares.org • Members are manufacturers of housewares and small appliances.

OTHER SOURCES

Housing Discrimination: Law and Litigation. Robert G. Schwemm. West Group. • Looseleaf. $130.00. Periodic supplementation. Covers provisions of the Fair Housing Act and related topics. (Civil Rights Series).

HOUSING

See also: APARTMENT HOUSES; BUILDING INDUSTRY; CONDOMINIUMS; PREFABRICATED HOUSE INDUSTRY; REAL ESTATE BUSINESS

GENERAL WORKS

A New Housing Policy for America: Recapturing the American Dream. David C. Schwartz and others. Temple University Press. • 1988. $24.95.

Rethinking Rental Housing. John I. Gilderbloom and Richard P. Applebaum. Temple University Press. • 1987. $44.95. Emphasis on social and political factors.

BIBLIOGRAPHIES

AAHSA Resource Catalog. American Association of Homes and Services for the Aging. • Annual. Free. Provides descriptions of material relating to managed care, senior housing, assisted living, continuing care retirement communities (CCRCs), nursing facilities, and home health care. Publishers are AAHSA and others.

CD-ROM DATABASES

National Newspaper Index CD-ROM. The Gale Group. • Monthly. Provides comprehensive CD-ROM indexing of all material appearing in the late edition of the *New York Times*, the final edition of the *Washington Post*, the national edition of the *Christian Science Monitor*, the home edition of the *Los Angeles Times*, and the *Wall Street Journal*. Time period is four years. Also available online.

The New York Times Ondisc. New York Times Online Services. • Monthly. $2,650.00 per year. CD-ROM discs contain the full text of *The New York Times*, final edition. Inquire as to time period covered and availability of backfiles.

Newspaper Abstracts Ondisc. Bell & Howell Information and Learning. • Monthly. $2,950.00 per year (covers 1989 to date; archival discs are available for 1985-88). Provides cover-to-cover CD-ROM indexing and abstracting of 19 major newspapers, including the *New York Times, Wall Street Journal, Washington Post, Chicago Tribune,* and *Los Angeles Times*.

Sourcebooks America CD-ROM. CACI Marketing Systems. • Annual. $1,250.00. Provides the CD-ROM version of *The Sourcebook of ZIP Code Demographics: Census Edition* and *The Sourcebook of County Demographics: Census Edition.*

DIRECTORIES

Directory of Retirement Facilities. Dorland Healthcare Information. • Annual. $249.00. Lists more than 18,500 assisted living, congregate care, independent living, and continuing care facilities.

NAHRO Directory of Local Agencies and Resource Guide. • Triennial. Members, $85.00; non-members, $100.00. Formerly *Directory of Local Agencies: Housing, Community Development, Redevelopment.*

ENCYCLOPEDIAS AND DICTIONARIES

Encyclopedia of Housing. Willem van Vliet, editor. Sage Publications, Inc. • 1998. $169.95. Contains

500 entries covering all aspects of housing. Includes index of names and subjects.

HANDBOOKS AND MANUALS

Federal Civil Rights Acts. Rodney A. Smolla. West Group. • Two looseleaf volumes. $245.00. Covers current legislation relating to a wide range of civil rights issues, including discrimination in employment, housing, property rights, and voting. (Civil Right Series).

INTERNET DATABASES

Fedstats. Federal Interagency Council on Statistical Policy. Phone: (202)395-7254 • URL: http://www.fedstats.gov • Web site features an efficient search facility for full-text statistics produced by more than 70 federal agencies, including the Census Bureau, the Bureau of Economic Analysis, and the Bureau of Labor Statistics. Boolean searches can be made within one agency or for all agencies combined. Links are offered to international statistical bureaus, including the UN, IMF, OECD, UNESCO, Eurostat, and 20 individual countries. Fees: Free.

U. S. Census Bureau: The Official Statistics. U. S. Bureau of the Census. Phone: (301)763-4100 Fax: (301)763-4794 • URL: http://www.census.gov • Web site is "Your Source for Social, Demographic, and Economic Information." Contains "Current U. S. Population Count," "Current Economic Indicators," and a wide variety of data under "Other Official Statistics." Keyword searching is provided. Fees: Free.

ONLINE DATABASES

DRI U.S. Central Database. Data Products Division. • Provides more than 23,000 business, financial, demographic, economic, foreign trade, and industry-related time series for the U.S. Includes national income, population, retail-wholesale trade, price indexes, labor data, housing, industrial production, banking, interest rates, money supply, etc. Time period is generally 1947 to date (some data back to 1929). Updating varies. Inquire as to online cost and availability.

Information Bank Abstracts. New York Times Index Dept. • Provides indexing and abstracting of current affairs, primarily from the final late edition of *The New York Times* and the Eastern edition of *The Wall Street Journal*. Time period is 1969 to present, with daily updates. Inquire as to online cost and availability.

PERIODICALS AND NEWSLETTERS

Affordable Housing Finance. Alexander & Edwards Publishing. • Ten times a year. $119.00 per year. Provides advice and information on obtaining financing for lower-cost housing. Covers both government and private sources.

Builder: Official Publication of the National Association of Home Builders. National Association of Home Builders of the United States. Hanley-Wood, LLC. • Monthly. $29.95 per year. Covers the home building and remodeling industry in general, including design, construction, and marketing.

Housing Affairs Letter: The Weekly Washington Report on Housing. Community Services Development, Inc. C D Publications. • Weekly. $409.00 per year.

Journal of Housing and Community Development. National Association of Housing and Redevelopment Officials (NAHRO). • Bimonthly. $24.00 per year. Formerly *Journal of Housing*.

Journal of Housing Economics. Academic Press, Inc., Journal Div. • Quarterly. $245.00 per year.

RESEARCH CENTERS AND INSTITUTES

American Affordable Housing Institute. Rutgers University, 33 Livingston Ave., New Brunswick, NJ 08901-2009. Phone: (732)932-6812 Fax: (732)932-7974 • Conducts studies related to housing affordability and availability, especially for first-time homebuyers. Also does research on meeting the housing needs of America's senior citizens.

Center for Finance and Real Estate. University of California, Los Angeles, John E. Anderson Graduate School of Management, P.O. Box 951481, Los Angeles, CA 90095-1481. Phone: (310)825-1953 Fax: (310)206-5455 E-mail: wtorous@anderson.ucla.edu • URL: http://www.agsm.ucla.edu/acadunit/finance/realestate.

NAHB Research Center. 400 Prince George's Blvd., Upper Marlboro, MD 20772. Phone: 800-638-8556 or (301)249-4000 Fax: (301)430-6180 E-mail: lbowles@nahbrc.org • URL: http://www.nahbrc.com.

National Economic Development and Law Center. 2201 Broadway, Suite 815, Oakland, CA 94612. Phone: (510)251-2600 Fax: (510)251-0600 E-mail: pubinfo@nedlc.org • URL: http://www.nedlc.org.

School of Architecture-Building Research Council. University of Illinois at Urbana-Champaign. One E. Saint Mary's Rd., Champaign, IL 61820. Phone: 800-336-0616 or (217)333-1801 Fax: (217)244-2204 E-mail: kgallghr@cso.uiuc.edu • URL: http://www.arch.uiuc.edu/brc.

Urban Institute. 2100 M St., N. W., Washington, DC 20037. Phone: (202)833-7200 Fax: (202)728-0232 E-mail: paffairs@ui.urban.org • URL: http://www.urban.org • Research activities include the study of urban economic affairs, development, housing, productivity, and municipal finance.

STATISTICS SOURCES

American Housing Survey for the United States in [year]. Available from U. S. Government Printing Office. • Biennial. Issued by the U. S. Census Bureau (http://www.census.gov). Covers both owner-occupied and renter-occupied housing. Includes data on such factors as condition of building, type of mortgage, utility costs, and housing occupied by minorities. (Current Housing Reports, H150.).

Business Statistics of the United States. Courtenay M. Slater, editor. Bernan Associates. • 1999. $74.00. Fifth edition. Based on *Business Statistics*, formerly issue by the Bureau of Economic Analysis, U. S. Department of Commerce. Provides basic data for a wide variety of U. S. industries, services, and economic indicators. Most statistics are shown annually for 29 years and monthly for the most recent four years.

County and City Extra: Annual Metro, City and County Data Book. Mark Littman and Deirdre A. Gaquin. Bernan Press. • 1999. $109.00. Updates and augments data published irregularly in print form by the U. S. Census Bureau in *County and City Data Book.* Covers "every state, county, metropolitan area, and congressional district in the United States, as well as all U. S. cities with a 1990 population of 25,000 or more." Contains a wide range tic maps.

Expenditures for Residential Improvements and Repairs. Available from U. S. Government Printing Office. • Quarterly. $14.00 per year. Bureau of the Census Construction Report, C50. Provides estimates of spending for housing maintenance, repairs, additions, alterations, and major replacements.

Gale City and Metro Rankings Reporter. The Gale Group. • 1996. $134.00. Second edition. Provides about 3,000 statistical ranking tables covering more than 1,500 U. S. cities and Metropolitan Statistical Areas. Covers economic, demographic, social, governmental, and cultural factors. Sources are private studies and government data.

Gale Country and World Rankings Reporter. The Gale Group. • 1997. $135.00. Second edition. Provides about 3,000 statistical ranking tables and charts covering more than 235 nations. Sources include the United Nations and various government publications.

Gale State Rankings Reporter. The Gale Group. • 1996. $110.00. Second edition Provides 3,000 ranked lists of states under 35 subject headings. Sources are newspapers, periodicals, books, research institute publications, and government publications.

Housing Market Report: Forecasting Home Sales and Construction Trends Since 1976. Community Development Services, Inc. • Semimonthly. $347.00 per year. Real estate outlook for U.S. housing markets.

Housing Starts. U.S. Bureau of the Census. Available from U.S. Government Printing Office. • Monthly. $39.00 per year. Construction Reports: C-20.

Housing Statistics of the United States. Patrick A. Simmons, editor. Bernan Press. • 2000. $74.00. Third edition. (Bernan Press U.S. Data Book Series).

Monthly Bulletin of Statistics. United Nations Publications. • Monthly. $295.00 per year. Provides current data for about 200 countries on a wide variety of economic, industrial, and demographic subjects. Compiled by United Nations Statistical Office.

New One-Family Houses Sold. Available from U. S. Government Printing Office. • Monthly. $45.00 per year. Bureau of the Census Construction Report, C25. Provides data on new, privately-owned, one-family homes sold during the month and for sale at the end of the month.

Social Statistics of the United States. Mark S. Littman, editor. Bernan Press. • 2000. $65.00. Includes statistical data on population growth, labor force, occupations, environmental trends, leisure time use, income, poverty, taxes, and other economic or demographic topics.

State Profiles: The Population and Economy of Each U. S. State. Courtenay Slater and Martha Davis, editors. Bernan Press. • 1999. $74.00. Presents charts, tables, and text in an eight-page profile for each state. Covers population, labor force, income, poverty, employment, wages, industry, trade, housing, education, health, taxes, and government finances.

Statistical Abstract of the United States. Available from U. S. Government Printing Office. • Annual. $51.00. Issued by the U. S. Bureau of the Census.

A Statistical Portrait of the United States: Social Conditions and Trends. Mark S. Littman, editor. Bernan Press. • 1998. $89.00. Covers "social, economic, and environmental trends in the United States over the past 25 years." Includes statistical tables, graphs, and analysis relating to such topics as population, income, poverty, wealth, labor, housing, education, healthcare, air/water quality, and government.

Statistical Yearbook. United Nations Publications. • Annual. $125.00. Contains statistics for about 200 countries on a wide variety of economic, industrial, and demographic topics. Compiled by United Nations Statistical Office.

Survey of Current Business. Available from U. S. Government Printing Office. • Monthly. $49.00 per year. Issued by Bureau of Economic Analysis, U. S. Department of Commerce. Presents a wide variety of business and economic data.

U. S. Housing Markets. Hanley-Wood, Inc. • Monthly. $345.00 per year. Includes eight interim reports. Provides data on residential building

 For publishers addresses, refer to SOURCES CITED section at the back of the book.

permits, apartment building completions, rental vacancy rates, sales of existing homes, average home prices, housing affordability, etc. All major U. S. cities and areas are covered.

TRADE/PROFESSIONAL ASSOCIATIONS

Building Systems Councils of NAHB. 1201 15th St., N.W., Washington, DC 20005. Phone: 800-368-5242 or (202)822-0576 Fax: (202)861-2141.

National Association of Home Builders of the United States. 17120 N. Dallas Pkwy., Ste. 175, Dallas, TX 75248. Phone: 800-252-9001 or (972)732-0090 Fax: (972)732-6067 • URL: http://www.nahb.com.

National Association of Housing and Redevelopment Officials. 630 Eye St., N.W., Washington, DC 20001. Phone: (202)289-3500 Fax: (202)289-8181 E-mail: nahro@nahro.org • URL: http://www.nahro.org.

National Center for Housing Management. 1010 N. Glebe Rd., Ste. 160, Arlington, VA 22201. Phone: 800-368-5625 or (703)872-1717 Fax: (703)516-4069 • URL: http://www.nchm.com.

National Housing Conference. 815 15th St., N.W., Suite 538, Washington, DC 20005. Phone: (202)393-5772 Fax: (202)393-5656 E-mail: nhc@nhc.org • URL: http://www.nch.org.

OTHER SOURCES

Fair Housing: Discrimination in Real Estate, Community Development and Revitalization. James A. Kushner. Shepard's. • 1983. $140.00. Second edition. (Individual Rights Series).

HOUSING MANAGEMENT

See: PROPERTY MANAGEMENT

HUMAN ENGINEERING

GENERAL WORKS

Designing the User Interface: Strategies for Effective Human-Computer Interaction. Ben Shneiderman. Addison Wesley Longman, Inc. • 1997. $44.95. Third edition. Provides an introduction to computer user-interface design. Covers usability testing, dialog boxes, menus, command languages, interaction devices, tutorials, printed user manuals, and related subjects.

Ergonomics at Work. David A. Osbourne. Books on Demand. • 1995. $102.70. Third edition.

The Ergonomics Edge: Improving Safety, Quality, and Productivity. Dan MacLeod. John Wiley and Sons, Inc. • 1994. $80.00. (Industrial Health and Safety Series).

ABSTRACTS AND INDEXES

NTIS Alerts: Biomedical Technology & Human Factors Engineering. National Technical Information Service. • Semimonthly. $210.00 per year. Provides descriptions of government-sponsored research reports and software, with ordering information. Covers biotechnology, ergonomics, bionics, artificial intelligence, prosthetics, and related subjects. Formerly *Abstract Newsletter.*

ENCYCLOPEDIAS AND DICTIONARIES

Encyclopedia of Occupational Health and Safety. Available from The Gale Group. • 1999. $495.00. Fourth edition. Four volumes. Published by the International Labor Office (http://www.ilo.org). Covers safety engineering, industrial medicine, ergonomics, hygiene, epidemiology, toxicology, industrial psychology, and related topics. Includes material related to specific chemical, textile, transport, construction, manufacturing, and other industries. Indexed by subject, chemical name, and author, with a "Directory of Experts.".

HANDBOOKS AND MANUALS

Handbook of Human Factors and Ergonomics. Gavriel Salvendy. John Wiley and Sons, Inc. • 1997. $225.00. Second edition.

Human Factors Design Handbook. Wesley E. Woodson and others. McGraw-Hill. • 1991. $150.00. Second edition.

PERIODICALS AND NEWSLETTERS

Applied Ergonomics: Human Factors in Technology and Society. Elsevier Science. • Bimonthly $772.00 per year.

Ergonomics: An International Journal of Research and Practice in Human Factors and Ergonomics. Taylor and Francis, Inc. • Monthly. Individuals, $1,018.00 per year; institutions, $2,056 per year.

Human Factors and Ergonomics in Manufacturing. Available from John Wiley and Sons, Inc., Journals Div. • Quarterly. Institutions, $545.00 per year. Published in England by John Wiley and Sons Ltd. Formerly *International Journal of Human Factors in Manufacturing.*

RESEARCH CENTERS AND INSTITUTES

Human Factors/Ergonomics Laboratory. Kansas State University. Industrial Manufacturing Systems Engineering Department, Durland Hall, Room 237, Manhattan, KS 66506-5101. Phone: (785)532-5606 Fax: (785)532-7810 E-mail: malyrs@ksu.edu.

TRADE/PROFESSIONAL ASSOCIATIONS

Human Factors and Ergonomics Society. P.O. Box 1369, Santa Monica, CA 90406-1369. Phone: (310)394-1811 Fax: (310)394-2410 E-mail: hfes@compuserve.com • URL: http://www.hfes.org.

MTM Association for Standards and Research. 1111 E. Touhy Ave., Des Plaines, IL 60018. Phone: (847)299-1111 Fax: (847)299-3509 E-mail: mtm@mtm.org • URL: http://www.mtm.org.

HUMAN MOTIVATION

See: MOTIVATION (PSYCHOLOGY)

HUMAN RELATIONS

See also: INDUSTRIAL PSYCHOLOGY; INDUSTRIAL RELATIONS; PERSONNEL MANAGEMENT

GENERAL WORKS

Coping with Difficult People. Robert N. Bramson. Dell Publishing. • 1981. $17.50.

Dinosaur Brains: Dealing with All Those Impossible People at Work. Albert J. Bernstein and Sydney C. Rozen. John Wiley and Sons, Inc. • 1989. $29.95. How to cope with "lizard logic" and overcome the "reptile response." That is, how to deal with irrational, impulsive, and self-destructive work behavior. Covers problem bosses, manipulators, self-promoters, the old boy network, etc.

Human Behavior at Work. O. Jeff Harris and Sandra Hartman. West Publishing Co., College and School Div. • 1991. $55.50.

Human Relations. Andrew J. Dubrin. Prentice Hall. • 1996. $55.00. Sixth edition.

ABSTRACTS AND INDEXES

Current Contents: Social and Behavioral Sciences. Institute for Scientific Information. • Weekly. $730.00 per year. Includes *Author Index.*

Personnel Management Abstracts. • Quarterly. $190.00 per year. Includes annual cumulation.

Psychological Abstracts. American Psychological Association. • Monthly. Members, $799.00 per year; individuals and institutions, $1,075.00 per year. Covers the international literature of psychology and the behavioral sciences. Includes journals, technical reports, dissertations, and other sources.

Social Sciences Index. H. W. Wilson Co. • Quarterly, with annual cumulation. Service basis for print edition; CD-ROM edition, $1,495 per year. Indexes more than 400 periodicals covering economics, environmental policy, government, insurance, labor, health care policy, plannning, public administration, public welfare, urban studies, women's issues, criminology, and related topics.

Sociological Abstracts. Cambridge Information Group. • Bimonthly. $635.00 per year. A compendium of non-evaluative abstracts covering the field of sociology and related disciplines. Includes an annual *Index.*

CD-ROM DATABASES

Magazine Index Plus. The Gale Group. • Monthly. $4,000.00 per year (includes InfoTrac workstation). Provides full text on CD-ROM for about 100 popular, general interest magazines and indexing for 300 others. Includes special indexing of reviews and product evaluations. Time period is 1980 to date.

Social Science Source. EBSCO Publishing. • Monthly. $1,495.00 per year. Provides CD-ROM citations and abstracts to social science articles in more than 600 periodicals, with full text from 125 periodicals. Covers economics, political science, public policy, international relations, psychology, and other topics. Time period is most recent five years.

Social Sciences Citation Index: Compact Disc Edition with Abstracts. Institute for Scientific Information. • Quarterly. Provides CD-ROM indexing and abstracting of "significant articles" from 1,400 social science journals worldwide, with additional selections from 3,200 other journals, 1986 to date. Includes economics, business, finance, management, communications, demographics, information and library science, political science, sociology, and many other subjects.

WILSONDISC: Wilson Social Sciences Abstracts. H. W. Wilson Co. • Monthly. Including unlimited online access to *Social Sciences Index* through WILSONLINE. Provides CD-ROM indexing from 1983 and abstracting from 1994 of more than 400 periodicals covering economics, area studies, community health, public administration, public welfare, urban studies, and many other topics related to the social sciences.

ENCYCLOPEDIAS AND DICTIONARIES

Blackwell Encyclopedic Dictionary of Human Resource Management. Lawrence H. Peters and Charles R. Greer, editors. Blackwell Publishers. • 1996. $105.95. The editors are associated with Texas Christian University. Contains definitions of key terms combined with longer articles written by various U. S. and foreign business educators. Includes bibliographies and index. (Blackwell Encyclopedia of Management Series).

Encyclopedia of Human Behavior. Vangipuram S. Ramachandran, editor. Academic Press, Inc. • 1994. $685.00. Four volumes. Contains signed articles on aptitude testing, arbitration, career development, consumer psychology, crisis management, decision making, economic behavior, group dynamics, leadership, motivation, negotiation, organizational behavior, planning, problem solving, stress, work efficiency, and other human behavior topics applicable to business situations.

The Gale Encyclopedia of Psychology. The Gale Group. • 1998. $130.00. Includes bibliographies arranged by topic and a glossary.

HANDBOOKS AND MANUALS

Human Resource Skills for the Project Manager: The Human Aspects of Project Management, Volume Two. Vijay K. Verma. Project Management Institute. • 1996. $32.95. (Human Aspects of Project Management Series).

Managing the Project Team: The Human Aspects of Project Management, Volume Three. Vijay K. Verma. Project Management Institute. • 1997. $32.95. (Human Aspects of Project Management Series).

Negotiating and Influencing Skills: The Art of Creating and Claiming Value. Brad McRae. Sage Publications, Inc. • 1997. $42.00. Presents a practical approach to various circumstances, based on the Harvard Project on Negotiation. Chapters include "Dealing with Difficult People and Difficult Situations." Contains a bibliography and glossary of terms.

Organizing Projects for Success: The Human Aspects of Project Management, Volume One. Vijay K. Verma. Project Management Institute. • 1995. $32.95. (Human Aspects of Project Management Series).

Sexual Orientation in the Workplace: Gays, Lesbians, Bisexuals and Heterosexuals Working Together. Amy J. Zuckerman and George F. Simons. Sage Publications, Inc. • 1996. $18.95. A workbook containing "a variety of simple tools and exercises" to provide skills for "working realistically and effectively with diverse colleagues.".

ONLINE DATABASES

Newspaper and Periodical Abstracts. Bell & Howell Information and Learning. • Provides online coverage (citations and abstracts) of 25 major newspapers, 1,600 perodicals, and 70 TV programs. Covers business, economics, current affairs, health, fitness, sports, education, technology, government, consumer affairs, psychology, the arts, and the social sciences. Time period is 1986 to date, with daily updates. Inquire as to online cost and availability.

PsycINFO. American Psychological Association. • Provides indexing and abstracting of the worldwide literature of psychology and the behavioral sciences. Time period is 1967 to date, with monthly updates. Inquire as to online cost and availability.

Wilson Social Sciences Abstracts Online. H. W. Wilson Co. • Provides online abstracting and indexing of more than 415 periodicals covering area studies, community health, public administration, public welfare, urban studies, and many other social science topics. Time period is 1994 to date for abstracts and 1983 to date for indexing, with updates monthly. Inquire as to online cost and availability.

PERIODICALS AND NEWSLETTERS

American Behavioral Scientist. Sage Publications, Inc. • Monthly. Individuals, $125.00 per year; institutions, $775.00 per year.

Commitment-Plus Newsletter. Quality and Productivity Management Association. Pride Publications. • Monthly. $97.00 per year. The latest trends and developments in the behavorial sciences as they apply to business and industry. Formerly *Behavioral Sciences Newsletter.*

Communication Briefings: A Monthly Idea Source for Decision Makers. Briefings Publishing Group. • Monthly. $100.00 per year. Newsletter. Presents useful ideas for communication, public relations, customer service, human resources, and employee training.

Human Communication Research. International Communication Association. Oxford University Press, Journals. • Quarterly. Individuals, $74.00 per year; institutions, $243.00 per year. A scholarly journal of interpersonal communication.

Human Relations: Towards the Integration of Social Sciences. Tavistock Institute of Human Relations. Sage Publications, Inc. • Monthly. Individuals, $92.00 per year; institutions, $677.00 per year.

Human Resource Management. John Wiley and Sons, Inc. • Quarterly. Institutions, $390.00 per year.

Human Resources Report. Bureau of National Affairs, Inc. • Weekly. $875.00 per year. Newsletter. Formerly *BNA'S Employee Relations Weekly.*

Journal of Applied Behavioral Science. Sage Publications, Inc. • Individuals, $75.00 per year; institutions, $350.00 per year.

Journal of Organizational Behavior Management. Haworth Press, Inc. • Semiannual. Individuals, $50.00 per year; institutions, $160.00 per year; libraries, $325.00 per year.

Organizational Dynamics: A Quarterly Review of Organizational Behavior for Management Executives. American Management Association. • Quarterly. $74.00 per year. Covers the application of behavioral sciences to business management.

Teamwork: Your Personal Guide to Working Successfully with People. Dartnell Corp. • Biweekly. $76.70 per year. Provides advice for employees on human relations, motivation, and team spirit.

RESEARCH CENTERS AND INSTITUTES

Committee on Human Development. University of Chicago. 5730 Woodlawn Ave., Chicago, IL 60637. Phone: (773)702-3971 Fax: (773)702-0320 E-mail: sgsg@ccp.uchicago.edu.

OTHER SOURCES

How to Manage Conflict in the Organization. American Management Association Extension Institute. • Looseleaf. $110.00. Self-study course. Emphasis is on practical explanations, examples, and problem solving. Quizzes and a case study are included.

HUMAN RESOURCES MANAGEMENT

See: PERSONNEL MANAGEMENT

HUMAN RIGHTS

See: CIVIL RIGHTS

HUMOR AND JOKES

See also: PUBLIC SPEAKING; TOASTS

GENERAL WORKS

The New Yorker Book of Business Cartoons from the New Yorker. Robert Mankoff, editor. Bloomberg Press. • 1998. $21.95. Contains reprints of 110 cartoons relating to business and finance. Artists are Charles Addams, George Booth, Roz Chast, William Hamilton, Edward Sorel, and other *New Yorker* cartoonists.

ENCYCLOPEDIAS AND DICTIONARIES

Encyclopedia of 20th Century American Humor. Alleen P. Nilsen and Don L. F. Nilsen. Oryx Press. • 2000. $67.50. Provides an A-to-Z consideration of American humor in its various forms, from early vaudeville to the Internet. Includes a bibliography, subject index, illustrations, and numerous humorous examples.

HANDBOOKS AND MANUALS

How to Be the Life of the Podium: Openers, Closers and Everything in Between to Keep Them Listening. Sylvia Simmons. AMACOM. • 1992. $15.95. A collection of 1,000 quips, quotes, analogies, stories, proverbs, and one-liners.

Laffirmations: 1001 Ways to Add Humor to Your Life and Work. Joel Goodman. Health Communications, Inc. • 1995. $8.95. The author is director of the Humor Project, a private company promoting humor in the corporate workplace.

PERIODICALS AND NEWSLETTERS

Studies in American Humor. American Human Studies Association. • Annual. Membership.

TRADE/PROFESSIONAL ASSOCIATIONS

American Humor Studies Association. c/o David E.E. Sloane, University of New Haven, West Haven, CT 06516. Fax: (203)932-7371 • URL: http://www.newhaven.edu/unh/special/ahsa/ahsahomepage.htm.

International Association of Professional Bureaucrats. c/o Dr. James H. Boren, One Plaza S., Suite 129, Tahlequah, OK 74464. Phone: (918)456-1357 Fax: (918)458-0124 E-mail: mumbles@www.jimboren.com • URL: http://www.jimboren.com • Motto of Association: "When in doubt, mumble.".

International Save the Pun Foundation. Station A, P.O. Box 5040, Toronto, ON, Canada M5W 1N4. Phone: (416)223-3351 Fax: (416)223-2236 E-mail: ngilbert@netcom.ca • URL: http://www.punpunpun.com.

International Training in Communication. 2519 Woodland Dr., Anaheim, CA 92801. Phone: (714)995-3660 Fax: (714)995-6974 E-mail: itcintl@itcintl.org • URL: http://www.itcintl.org.

Puns Corps. c/o Robert L. Birch. P.O. Box 2364, Falls Church, VA 22042. Phone: (703)533-3668.

Toastmasters International. P.O. Box 9052, Mission Viejo, CA 92690. Phone: (949)858-8255 Fax: (949)858-1207 E-mail: tminfo@toastmasters.org • URL: http://www.toastmasters.org.

OTHER SOURCES

Bits and Pieces: A Monthly Mixture of Horse Sense and Common Sense About Working with People. Economics Press, Inc. • Monthly. $22.00 per year. Quantity rates available. Pamphlets contain inspirational humor for employees.

HYDRAULIC ENGINEERING AND MACHINERY

See also: CIVIL ENGINEERING; FLUIDICS INDUSTRY

GENERAL WORKS

Fundamentals of Hydraulic Engineering Systems. Ned H. Hwang and R.J. Houghtalen. Prentice Hall. • 1995. $105.00. Third edition.

Industrial Hydraulics. John H. Pippenger and Tyler G. Hicks. McGraw-Hill. • 1979. $102.50. Third edition.

ABSTRACTS AND INDEXES

Fluid Abstracts: Civil Engineering. Elsevier Science. • Monthly. $1,319.00 per year. Annual cumulation. Includes the literature of coastal structures.Published in England by Elsevier Science Publishing Ltd. Formerly *Civil Engineering Hydraulics Abstracts.*

ENCYCLOPEDIAS AND DICTIONARIES

Dictionary of Hydraulic Machinery. A. T. Troskolanski. Elsevier Science. • 1986. $289.00. Text in English, French, German, Italian, and Russian.

HANDBOOKS AND MANUALS

Handbook of Hydraulics. Ernest F. Brater and Horace Williams King. McGraw-Hill. • 1996. $79.95. Seventh edition.

Hydraulic Engineering. Michael A. Ports, editor. American Society of Civil Engineers. • 1988. $117.00.

ONLINE DATABASES

FLUIDEX. Available from Elsevier Science, Inc., Secondary Publishing Division. • Produced in the Netherlands by Elsevier Science B.V. Provides indexing and abstracting of the international literature of fluid engineering and technology, 1973 to date, with monthly updates. Also known as *Fluid Engineering Abstracts.* Inquire as to online cost and availability.

PERIODICALS AND NEWSLETTERS

Hydraulics and Pneumatics: The Magazine of Fluid Power and Motion Control Systems. Penton Media Inc. • Monthly. Free to qualified personnel; others, $55.00 per year.

Journal of Hydraulic Research. International Association for Hydraulic Research. • Bimonthly. $340.00 per year. Text in English; summaries in English and French.

RESEARCH CENTERS AND INSTITUTES

Environmental Fluid Mechanics Laboratory. Stanford University. Dept. of Civil Engineering, Campus Box 4020, Stanford, CA 94305-4020. Phone: (650)723-1825 Fax: (650)725-3133.

Foundation for Cross-Connection Control and Hydraulic Research. University of Southern California. Kaprielian 200, Los Angeles, CA 90089-2531. Phone: (213)740-2032 Fax: (213)740-8399 E-mail: fccchr@usc.edu • URL: http://www.usc.edu/dept/fccchr/.

Institute of Hydraulic Research. University of Iowa. Iowa City, IA 52242. Phone: (319)335-5237 Fax: (319)335-5238 E-mail: iihr@uiowa.edu • URL: http://www.iihr.uiowa.edu.

TRADE/PROFESSIONAL ASSOCIATIONS

Fluid Power Society. 2433 N. Mayfair Rd., Suite 111, Milwaukee, WI 53226. Phone: (414)257-0910 Fax: (414)257-4092 E-mail: fpsociety@aol.com • URL: http://www.ifps.org.

Hydraulic Institute. Nine Sylvan Way, Parsippany, NJ 07054-3802. Phone: 888-786-7744 or (973)267-9700 Fax: (973)267-9055 E-mail: publications@pumps.org • URL: http://www.pumps.org.

Hydraulic Tool Manufacturers Association. c/o Petersen Consultants, Inc., 1509 Rapids Dr., Racine, WI 53404-2383. Phone: (414)633-3454 Fax: (414)637-8582.

International Association of Hydraulic Engineering and Research. Rotterdamseweg 185, NL-2629 Delft HD, Netherlands. Phone: 31 15 2858557 or 31 15 2858879 Fax: 31 15 2858417 E-mail: iahr@iahr.org • URL: http://www.iahr.nl.

National Conference on Fluid Power. 3333 N. Mayfair Rd., Milwaukee, WI 53222-3219. Phone: (414)778-3368 Fax: (414)778-3361 E-mail: bprueser@nfpa.com.

HYDROCARBONS

See: PETROLEUM INDUSTRY

HYDROELECTRIC INDUSTRY

GENERAL WORKS

Renewable Energy: Power for a Sustainable Future. Godfrey Boyle, editor. Available from Taylor & Francis. • 1996. $39.95. Published by Open University Press. Contains ten chapters, each on a particular renewable energy source, including solar, biomass, hydropower, wind, and geothermal.

DIRECTORIES

Hydro Review Worldwide Industry Directory. HCI Publications. • Annual. $20.00. Lists more than 250 manufacturers and suppliers of products and services to the hydroelectric industry worldwide. Formerly *Hydro Review-Industry Directory.*

The International Competitive Power Industry Directory. PennWell Corp. • Annual. $75.00. Lists suppliers of services, products, and equipment for the hydro, geothermal, solar, and wind power industries.

ENCYCLOPEDIAS AND DICTIONARIES

Wiley Encyclopedia of Energy and the Environment. Frederick John Francis. John Wiley and Sons, Inc. • 1999. $1,500.00. Four volumes. Second edition. Covers a wide variety of energy and environmental topics, including legal and policy issues.

PERIODICALS AND NEWSLETTERS

Hydro Review: A Magazine Covering the North American Hydroelectric Industry. HCI Publications. • Eight times a year. $65.00 per year. Covers hydroelectric power generation in North America. Supplement available *Industry Directory.*

RESEARCH CENTERS AND INSTITUTES

Canadian Energy Research Institute. 3512 33rd St., N. W., Suite 150, Calgary, AB, Canada T2L 2A6. Phone: (403)282-1231 Fax: (403)284-4181 E-mail: ceri@ceri.ca • URL: http://www.ceri.ca • Conducts research on the economic aspects of various forms of energy, including petroleum, natural gas, coal, nuclear, and water power (hydroelectric).

Hawaii Natural Energy Institute. University of Hawaii at Manoa, 2540 Dole St., Holmes Hall 246, Honolulu, HI 96822. Phone: (808)956-8890 Fax: (808)956-2336 E-mail: hnei@hawaii.edu • URL: http://www.soest.hawaii.edu • Research areas include geothermal, wind, solar, hydroelectric, and other energy sources.

STATISTICS SOURCES

Annual Energy Outlook [year], with Projections to [year]. Available from U. S. Government Printing Office. • Annual. Issued by the Energy Information Administration, U. S. Department of Energy (http://www.eia.doe.gov). Contains detailed statistics and 20-year projections for electricity, oil, natural gas, coal, and renewable energy. Text provides extensive discussion of energy issues and "Market Trends.".

TRADE/PROFESSIONAL ASSOCIATIONS

National Hydropower Association. One Massachusetts Ave., N.W., Ste. 850, Washington, DC 20001. Phone: (202)682-1700 Fax: (202)682-9478 E-mail: info@hydro.org • URL: http://www.hydro.org • Members are utilities, developers, manufacturers, organizations, bankers, architects, and others with an active interest in hydropower. Promotes the development of hydroelectric energy.

HYGIENE

See: INDUSTRIAL HYGIENE

HYPERTENSION

See also: STRESS (ANXIETY)

CD-ROM DATABASES

Consumers Reference Disc. National Information Services Corp. • Quarterly. Provides the CD-ROM version of *Consumer Health and Nutrition Index* from Oryx Press and *Consumers Index to Product Evaluations and Information Sources* from Pierian Press. Contains citations to consumer health articles and consumer product evaluations, tests, warnings, and recalls.

DIRECTORIES

Evaluation Guide to Health and Wellness Programs. The Corporate University. • $189.00. Looseleaf service. Semiannual updates, $49.00 each. Provides detailed descriptions and evaluations of more than 200 employee wellness programs that are available nationally. Covers 15 major topics, such as stress management, substance abuse, occupational safety, smoking cessation, blood pressure management, exercise/fitness, diet, and mental health. Programs are available from both profit and non-profit organizations.

HANDBOOKS AND MANUALS

Personal Health Reporter. The Gale Group. • 1992. $105.00. Two volumes. Volume one, $105.00; volume two, $105.00. Presents a collection of professional and popular articles on 150 topics relating to physical and mental health conditions and treatments.

INTERNET DATABASES

National Library of Medicine (NLM). National Institutes of Health (NIH). Phone: 888-346-3656 or (301)496-1131 Fax: (301)480-3537 E-mail: access@nlm.nih.gov • URL: http://www.nlm.nih.gov • NLM Web site offers free access through MEDLINE ("PubMed") to about nine million references to articles appearing in some 3,800 biomedical journals, with abstracts. Search interfaces range from "simple keywords to advanced Boolean expressions." The NLM site offers many links to other sources of biomedical and technical information (the National Center for Biotechnology Information, for example). Fees: Free.

PERIODICALS AND NEWSLETTERS

Hypertension. American Heart Association. Available from Williams and Wilkins. • Individuals, $226.00 per year; institutions, $608.00 per year.

RESEARCH CENTERS AND INSTITUTES

Division of Hypertension. University of Michigan. 3918 Taubman Center, Ann Arbor, MI 48109-0356. Phone: (734)936-4790 Fax: (734)936-8898 E-mail: aweder@umich.edu • URL: http://www.med.umich.edu/intmed/hypertension.

Hypertension Research Center. Indiana University-Purdue University at Indianapolis. 541 Clinical Dr., Room 423, Indianapolis, IN 46202-5111. Phone: (317)274-8153 Fax: (317)278-0673 E-mail: mweinbe@indyvax.iupui.edu.

TRADE/PROFESSIONAL ASSOCIATIONS

Citizens for Public Action on Blood Pressure and Cholesterol. P.O. Box 30374, Bethesda, MD 20824-0374. Phone: (301)770-1711 or (301)770-1712 Fax: (301)770-1113.

National Institute of Hypertension Studies-Institute of Hypertension School of Research. P.O. Box 02006, Detroit, MI 48202. Phone: (313)872-0505 or (313)873-8360 Fax: (313)872-0505.

I

ICE CREAM INDUSTRY

See also: DAIRY INDUSTRY

ABSTRACTS AND INDEXES

Food Science and Technology Abstracts. International Food Information Service Publishing. • Monthly. $1,780.00 per year. Provides worldwide coverage of the literature of food technology and food production.

Foods Adlibra: Key to the World's Food Literature. Foods Adlibra Publications. • Semimonthly.Provides journal citations and abstracts to the literature of food technology and packaging.

CD-ROM DATABASES

Food Science and Technology Abstracts [CD-ROM]. Available from SilverPlatter Information, Inc. • Quarterly. $3,700 per year. Produced by International Food Information Service (home page is http://www.ifis.org). Provides worldwide coverage on CD-ROM of the literature of food technology and production. Various types of publications are indexed, with abstracts, including about 1,800 periodicals. Time period is 1969 to date.

DIRECTORIES

Dairy Foods Market Directory. Cahners Business Information. • Annual. $99.90. Lists a wide variety of suppliers to the dairy industry.

National Dipper Yellow Pages. U. S. Exposition Corp. • Annual. $10.00. Special directory issue of *The National Dipper.* Lists products and services for the ice cream retail industry.

HANDBOOKS AND MANUALS

Ice Cream Store. Entrepreneur Media, Inc. • Looseleaf. $59.50. A practical guide to starting an ice cream shop. Covers profit potential, start-up costs, market size evaluation, owner's time required, site selection, lease negotiation, pricing, accounting, advertising, promotion, etc. (Start-Up Business Guide No. E1187.).

ONLINE DATABASES

Food Science and Technology Abstracts [online]. IFIS North American Desk. • Produced by International Food Information Service. Provides about 500,000 online citations, with abstracts, to the international literature of food science, technology, commodities, engineering, and processing. Approximately 2,000 periodicals are covered. Time period is 1969 to date, with monthly updates. Inquire as to online cost and availability.

FOODS ADLIBRA. General Mills, Inc. • Contains online citations, with abstracts, to the technical and business literature of food processing and packaging. New products and new ingredients are featured. Covers about 250 trade journals and 500 research journals from 1974 to date, with monthly updates. Inquire as to online cost and availability.

PERIODICALS AND NEWSLETTERS

Dairy Field: Helping Processors Manage the Changing Industry. Stagnito Publishing Co. • Monthly. $65.00 per year. Annual *Buyers Guide* availble.

Dairy Foods: Innovative Ideas and Technologies for Dairy Processors. Cahners Business Information. • Monthly. $99.90 per year. Provides broad coverage of new developments in the dairy industry, including cheese and ice cream products. Includes an annual *Supplement.*

Ice Cream Reporter: The Newsletter for Ice Cream Executives. MarketResearch.com. • Monthly. $395.00 per year. Covers new products, mergers, research, packaging, etc.

The National Dipper: The Magazine for Ice Cream Retailers. U. S. Exposition Corp. • Bimonthly. $55.00 per year. Edited for ice cream store owners and managers. Includes industry news, new product information, statistics, and feature articles.

PRICE SOURCES

Supermarket News: The Industry's Weekly Newspaper. Fairchild Publications. • Weekly. Individuals, $68.00 per year; instutions, $44.50 per year; corporations, $89.00 per year.

TRADE/PROFESSIONAL ASSOCIATIONS

International Ice Cream Association. 1250 H St., N.W., Suite 900, Washington, DC 20005. Phone: (202)737-4332 Fax: (202)331-7820 • URL: http://www.idfa.org.

National Ice Cream and Yogurt Retailers Association. 1429 King Ave., Suite 210, Columbus, OH 43212. Phone: (614)486-1444 Fax: (614)486-4711 E-mail: nicyra@aol.com • URL: http://www.nicyra.org.

OTHER SOURCES

The Ice Cream Market. MarketResearch.com. • 2000. $2,500.00. Market data and forecasts to 2004 on ice cream and related products (ice milk, frozen yogurt, etc.).

Major Food and Drink Companies of the World. Available from The Gale Group. • 2001. $855.00. Fourth edition. Two volumes. Published by Graham & Whiteside. Contains profiles and trade names for more than 9,000 important food and beverage companies in various countries. In addition to foods, includes both alcoholic and nonalcoholic drink products.

The Market for Ice Cream and Other Frozen Desserts. MarketResearch.com. • 2000. $2,500.00. Provides market data and discusses the impact on the ice cream industry of new technology and the Nutrition Labeling and Education Act. Includes sales projections to 2004.

Thomas Food and Beverage Market Place. Grey House Publishing. • Annual. $295.00. Three volumes. Contains more than 40,000 entries covering food companies, beverages, food equipment, warehouse companies, food brokers, wholesalers, importers, and exporters. Formerly *Thomas Food Industry Register.*

IDENTIFICATION SYSTEMS, AUTOMATIC

See: AUTOMATIC IDENTIFICATION SYSTEMS

ILLEGAL ALIENS

See: IMMIGRATION AND EMIGRATION

IMAGE, CORPORATE

See: CORPORATE IMAGE

IMMIGRATION AND EMIGRATION

See also: CITIZENSHIP

ABSTRACTS AND INDEXES

Current Law Index: Multiple Access to Legal Periodicals. The Gale Group. • Monthly. $650.00 per year. Produced in cooperation with the American Association of Law Libraries. Indexes more than 900 law journals, legal newspapers, and specialty publications from the U.S., Canada, U.K., Ireland, Australia, and New Zealand.

BIBLIOGRAPHIES

International Migration of the Highly Qualified: A Bibliographic and Conceptual Itinerary. Anne Marie Gaillard and Jacques Gaillard. Center for Migration Studies. • 1998. Price on application. Includes more than 1,800 references from 1954 to 1995 on the migration patterns of skilled or highly qualified workers. (CMS Bibliographies and Documentation Series).

HANDBOOKS AND MANUALS

Immigration Fundamentals: A Guide to Law and Practice. Practising Law Institute. • Looseleaf. $110.00. Semiannual revisions. Includes the legal aspects of employment-based immigration, family-sponsored immigration, nonimmigrants, refugees, deportation, naturalization, and citizenship. (Basic Practice Skills Series).

Immigration Procedures Handbook; A How-To Guide for Legal and Business Professionals. Austin T. Fragomen and others. West Group. • 1993. $155.00. How to bring foreign nationals to the U. S. on a temporary or permanent basis.

United States Immigration Laws, General Information. U.S. Immigration and Naturalization Service. Available from U.S. Government Printing Office. • Irregular.

PERIODICALS AND NEWSLETTERS

Immigration Law Report. West Group. • 24 times a year. $310.00 per year. Newsletter.

International Migration Review: A Quarterly Studying Sociological, Demographic, Economic,

Historical, and Legislative Aspects of Human Migration Movements and Ethnic Group Relations. Center for Migration Studies. • Quarterly. Individuals, $39.50 per year; institutions, $80.00 per year.

Migration World: A Bimonthly Magazine Focusing on the Newest Immigrant and Refuee Groups; Policy and Legislation; Resources. Center for Migration Studies. • Five times a year. Individuals, $31.00 per year; institutions, $50.00 per year.

RESEARCH CENTERS AND INSTITUTES

Center for Migration Studies. 209 Flagg Place, Staten Island, NY 10304-1199. Phone: (718)351-8800 Fax: (718)667-4598 E-mail: cmslft@aol.com • URL: http://www.cmsny.org • A nonprofit institute "committed to encourage and facilitate the study of sociodemographic, economic, political..aspects of human migration and refugee movement.".

Immigration History Research Center. University of Minnesota. 222 21st Ave., S., 311 Andersen Library, St. Paul, MN 55455. Phone: (612)625-4800 E-mail: ihrc@tc.umn.edu • URL: http://www.umn.edu/ihrc.

Lexis.com Research System. Lexis-Nexis Group. Phone: 800-227-9597 or (937)865-6800 Fax: (937)865-6909 E-mail: webmaster@prod.lexis-nexis.com • URL: http://www.lexis.com • Fee-based Web site offers extensive searching of a wide variety of legal sources. Additional features include Daily Opinion Service, lexis.com Bookstore, Career Center, CLE Center, Law Schools, and Practice Pages ("Pages specific to areas of specialty").

STATISTICS SOURCES

Population Projections of the United States by Age, Sex, Race, and Hispanic Origin: 1995 to 2050. Available from U. S. Government Printing Office. • 1996. $8.50. Issued by the U. S. Bureau of the Census (http://www.census.gov). Contains charts and tables. Appendixes include detailed data on fertility rates by age, life expectancy, immigration, and armed forces population. (Current Population Reports, P25-1130.).

TRADE/PROFESSIONAL ASSOCIATIONS

American Immigration Lawyers Association. 1400 Eye St., N.W., Suite 1200, Washington, DC 20005. Phone: (202)371-9377 Fax: (202)371-9449 • URL: http://www.aila.org.

Hebrew Immigrant Aid Society. 333 Seventh Ave., New York, NY 10001-5004. Phone: (212)967-4100 Fax: (212)967-4483 E-mail: info@hias.org • URL: http://www.hias.org.

National Immigration Forum. 220 Eye St., N.E., Suite 220, Washington, DC 20002. Phone: (202)544-0004 Fax: (202)544-1905 • URL: http://www.immigrationforum.org.

OTHER SOURCES

Board of Immigration Appeals Interim Decisions. U.S. Immigration and Naturalization Service. Available from U.S. Government Printing Office. • Irregular.

Immigration Law and Business. Austin T. Fragomen and others. West Group. • Three looseleaf volumes. $345.00. Periodic supplementation. Covers labor certification, temporary workers, applications, petitions, etc.

Immigration Law and Crimes. National Lawyers Guild. West Group. • Looseleaf. $140.00. Periodic supplementation. Covers legal representation of the foreign-born criminal defendant.

Immigration Law and Defense. National Lawyers Guild. West Group. • Two looseleaf volumes. $235.00. Periodic supplementation. Covers legal defense of immigrants and aliens.

Immigration Law and Procedure. Matthew Bender & Co., Inc. • $1,600.00. 20 looseleaf volumes. Periodic supplementation.

Trends in International Migration. Organization for Economic Cooperation and Development. • Annual. $59.00. Contains detailed data on population migration flows, channels of immigration, and migrant nationalities. Includes demographic analysis.

World Migration Report. United Nations Publications. • Annual. $39.00. Analyzes major trends in world migration, including individual country profiles.

IMPORT TRADE

See: EXPORT-IMPORT TRADE

INCANDESCENT LAMPS

See: LIGHTING

INCENTIVE

See: MOTIVATION (PSYCHOLOGY)

INCENTIVE MERCHANDISING

See: PREMIUMS

INCOME

GENERAL WORKS

Money: Who Has How Much and Why. Andrew Hacker. Available from Simon & Schuster Trade. • 1998. $13.00. Published by Scribner's Reference. A discourse on the distribution of wealth in America, with emphasis on the gap between rich and poor.

ALMANACS AND YEARBOOKS

National Accounts Statistics: Main Aggregates and Detailed Tables. United Nations Publications. • Annual. $160.00.

CD-ROM DATABASES

Sourcebook America. The Gale Group. • Annual. $995.00. Produced by CACI Marketing Systems. A combination on CD-ROM of *The Sourcebook of ZIP Code Demographics* and *The Sourcebook of County Demographics.* Provides detailed population and socio-economic data (about 75 items) for each of 3,141 U. S. counties and approximately 30,000 ZIP codes, plus states, metropolitan areas, and media market areas. Includes forecasts to the year 2004.

Sourcebooks America CD-ROM. CACI Marketing Systems. • Annual. $1,250.00. Provides the CD-ROM version of *The Sourcebook of ZIP Code Demographics: Census Edition* and *The Sourcebook of County Demographics: Census Edition.*

HANDBOOKS AND MANUALS

Comparative Guide to American Suburbs. Grey House Publishing. • 2001. $130.00. Second edition. Contains detailed profiles of 1,800 suburban communities having a population of 10,000 or more and located within the 50 largest metropolitan areas. Includes ranking tables for income, unemployment, new housing permits, home prices, and crime, as well as information on school districts. (Universal Reference Publications.).

INTERNET DATABASES

Bureau of Economic Analysis (BEA). U. S. Department of Commerce, Bureau of Economic Analysis. Phone: (202)606-9900 Fax: (202)606-5310 E-mail: webmaster@bea.doc.gov • URL: http://www.bea.doc.gov • Web site includes "News Release Information" covering national, regional, and international economic estimates from the BEA. Highlights of releases appear online the same day, complete text and tables appear the next day. "Recent News Releases" section provides titles for past nine months, with links. "BEA Data and Methodology" includes "Frequently Requested NIPA Data" (national income and product accounts, such as gross domestic product and personal income). Other statistics are available. Fees: Free.

Bureau of Labor Statistics (BLS). U. S. Department of Labor, Bureau of Labor Statistics. Phone: (202)523-1092 E-mail: labstat.helpdesk@bls.gov • URL: http://www.bls.gov • Web site provides a great variety of employment, wage, price, and economic data. Some links are "Data," "Economy at a Glance," "Keyword Search of BLS Web Pages," "Regional Information," and "Other Statistical Sites." Fees: Free.

Fedstats. Federal Interagency Council on Statistical Policy. Phone: (202)395-7254 • URL: http://www.fedstats.gov • Web site features an efficient search facility for full-text statistics produced by more than 70 federal agencies, including the Census Bureau, the Bureau of Economic Analysis, and the Bureau of Labor Statistics. Boolean searches can be made within one agency or for all agencies combined. Links are offered to international statistical bureaus, including the UN, IMF, OECD, UNESCO, Eurostat, and 20 individual countries. Fees: Free.

ONLINE DATABASES

DRI U.S. Central Database. Data Products Division. • Provides more than 23,000 business, financial, demographic, economic, foreign trade, and industry-related time series for the U.S. Includes national income, population, retail-wholesale trade, price indexes, labor data, housing, industrial production, banking, interest rates, money supply, etc. Time period is generally 1947 to date (some data back to 1929). Updating varies. Inquire as to online cost and availability.

EconLit. American Economic Association. • Covers the worldwide literature of economics as contained in selected monographs and about 550 journals. Subjects include microeconomics, macroeconomics, economic history, inflation, money, credit, finance, accounting theory, trade, natural resource economics, and regional economics. Time period is 1969 to present, with monthly updates. Inquire as to online cost and availability.

PERIODICALS AND NEWSLETTERS

Review of Income and Wealth. International Association for Research in Income and Wealth. • Quarterly. $110.00 per year.

Review of Social Economy. Association for Social Economics. Routledge Journals. • Quarterly. Individuals, $65.00 per year; institutions, $177.00 per year. Subject matter is concerned with the relationships between social values and economics. Includes articles on income distribution, poverty, labor, and class.

STATISTICS SOURCES

American Business Climate and Economic Profiles. The Gale Group. • 1993. $135.00. Provides business, industrial, demographic, and economic figures for all states and 300 metropolitan areas. Includes production, taxation, population, growth rates, labor force data, incomes, total sales, etc.

Business Statistics of the United States. Courtenay M. Slater, editor. Bernan Associates. • 1999. $74.00. Fifth edition. Based on *Business Statistics,* formerly issue by the Bureau of Economic Analysis, U. S. Department of Commerce. Provides basic data for a wide variety of U. S. industries, services, and economic indicators. Most statistics are shown annually for 29 years and monthly for the most recent four years.

County and City Extra: Annual Metro, City and County Data Book. Mark Littman and Deirdre A. Gaquin. Bernan Press. • 1999. $109.00. Updates and augments data published irregularly in print form by the U. S. Census Bureau in *County and City Data Book.* Covers "every state, county, metropolitan area, and congressional district in the United States, as well as all U. S. cities with a 1990 population of 25,000 or more." Contains a wide range tic maps.

Current Population Reports: Household Economic Studies, Series P-70. Available from U. S. Government Printing Office. • Irregular. $16.00 per year. Issued by the U.S. Bureau of the Census (http://www.census.gov). Each issue covers a special topic relating to household socioeconomic characteristics.

Current Population Reports: Population Characteristics, Special Studies, and Consumer Income, Series P-20, P-23, and P-60. Available from U. S. Government Printing Office. • Irregular. $39.00 per year. Issued by the U.S. Bureau of the Census (http://www.census.gov). Each issue covers a special topic relating to population or income. Series P-20, *Population Characteristics*, provides statistical studies on such items as mobility, fertility, education, and marital status. Series P-23, *Special Studies*, consists of occasional reports on methodology. Series P-60, *Consumer Income*, publishes reports on income in relation to age, sex, education, occupation, family size, etc.

Demographics USA: County Edition. Market Statistics. • Annual. $435.00. Contains 200 statistical series for each of 3,000 counties. Includes population, household income, employment, retail sales, and consumer expenditures. Also provides Effective Buying Income, Buying Power Index, and data summaries by Metro Market, Media Market, and State. (CD-ROM version is available.).

Demographics USA: ZIP Edition. Market Statistics. • Annual. $435.00. Contains 50 statistical series for each of 40,000 ZIP codes. Includes population, household income, employment, retail sales, and consumer expenditures. Also provides Effective Buying Income, Business Characteristics, and data summaries by state, region, and the first three digits of ZIP codes. (CD-ROM version is available.).

Economic Report of the President: Together with the Annual Report of the Council of Economic Advisors. Available from U. S. Government Printing Office. • Annual. $29.00. Includes about 130 pages of "Statistical Tables Relating to Income, Employment, and Production." Tables cover national income, employment, wages, productivity, manufacturing, prices, credit, finance (public and private), corporate profits, and foreign trade.

Gale City and Metro Rankings Reporter. The Gale Group. • 1996. $134.00. Second edition. Provides about 3,000 statistical ranking tables covering more than 1,500 U. S. cities and Metropolitan Statistical Areas. Covers economic, demographic, social, governmental, and cultural factors. Sources are private studies and government data.

Gale Country and World Rankings Reporter. The Gale Group. • 1997. $135.00. Second edition. Provides about 3,000 statistical ranking tables and charts covering more than 235 nations. Sources include the United Nations and various government publications.

Gale State Rankings Reporter. The Gale Group. • 1996. $110.00. Second edition Provides 3,000 ranked lists of states under 35 subject headings. Sources are newspapers, periodicals, books, research institute publications, and government publications.

Handbook of U. S. Labor Statistics: Employment, Earnings, Prices, Productivity, and Other Labor Data. Eva E. Jacobs, editor. Bernan Associates. • 1999. $74.00. Based on *Handbook of Labor Statistics*, formerly issued by the Bureau of Labor Statistics, U. S. Department of Labor. Includes the Bureau's projections of employment in the U. S. by industry and occupation. Provides a wide variety of data on the work force, prices, fringe benefits, and consumer expenditures.

Household Spending: Who Spends How Much On What. Hoai Tran. New Strategist Publications, Inc. • 1999. $94.95. Fifth edition. Gives facts about the buying habits of U. S. consumers according to income, age, household type, and household size. Includes spending data for about 1,000 products and services.

Income of the Population 55 and Older. Available from U. S. Government Printing Office. • Biennial. $19.00. Issued by the Social Security Administration (http://www.ssa.gov). Covers major sources and amounts of income for the 55 and older population in the U. S., "with special emphasis on some aspects of the income of the population 65 and older.".

Individual Income Tax Returns. U.S. Department of the Treasury, Internal Revenue Service. Available from U.S. Government Printing Office. • Annual. $17.00.

Markets of the United States for Business Planners: Historical and Current Profiles of 183 U. S. Urban Economies by Major Section and Industry, with Maps, Graphics, and Commentary. Thomas F. Conroy, editor. Omnigraphics, Inc. • 1995. $240.00. Second edition. Two volumes. Based on statistics from the Personal Income and Earnings Database of the Bureau of Economic Analysis, U. S. Dept. of Commerce. Provides extensive personal income data for all urban market areas of the U. S.

Money Income in the United States. Available from U. S. Government Printing Office. • Annual. $19.00. Issued by the U. S. Bureau of the Census. Presents data on consumer income in current and constant dollars, both totals and averages (means, medians, distributions). Includes figures for a wide variety of demographic and occupational characteristics. (Current Population Reports, P60-209.).

Social Statistics of the United States. Mark S. Littman, editor. Bernan Press. • 2000. $65.00. Includes statistical data on population growth, labor force, occupations, environmental trends, leisure time use, income, poverty, taxes, and other economic or demographic topics.

Sourcebook of Zip Code Demographics. CACI Marketing Systems. • 2000. $495.00. 15th revised edition. Published by CACI, Inc. Provides data on 75 demographic and socio-economic characteristics for each ZIP code in the U. S.

State Profiles: The Population and Economy of Each U. S. State. Courtenay Slater and Martha Davis, editors. Bernan Press. • 1999. $74.00. Presents charts, tables, and text in an eight-page profile for each state. Covers population, labor force, income, poverty, employment, wages, industry, trade, housing, education, health, taxes, and government finances.

Statistical Abstract of the World. The Gale Group. • 1997. $80.00. Third edition. Provides data on a wide variety of economic, social, and political topics for about 200 countries. Arranged by country.

Statistical Handbook on Consumption and Wealth in the United States. Chandrika Kaul and Valerie Tomaselli-Moschovitis. Oryx Press. • 1999. $65.00. Provides more than 400 graphs, tables, and charts dealing with basic income levels, income inequalities, spending patterns, taxation, subsidies, etc. (Statistical Handbook Series).

Statistics of Income Bulletin. Available from U.S. Government Printing Office. • Quarterly. $35.00 per year. Current data compiled from tax returns relating to income, assets, and expenses of individuals and businesses. (U. S. Internal Revenue Service.).

Statistics of Income: Corporation Income Tax Returns. U.S. Internal Revenue Service. Available from U.S. Government Printing Office. • Annual. $26.00.

Survey of Current Business. Available from U. S. Government Printing Office. • Monthly. $49.00 per year. Issued by Bureau of Economic Analysis, U. S. Department of Commerce. Presents a wide variety of business and economic data.

World Consumer Income and Expenditure Patterns. Available from The Gale Group. • 2001. $650.00. Published by Euromonitor (http://www.euromonitor.com). Provides data on consumer income, earning power, and expenditures for 52 countries around the world.

World Statistics Pocketbook. United Nations Publications. • Annual. $10.00. Presents basic economic, social, and environmental indicators for about 200 countries and areas. Covers more than 50 items relating to population, economic activity, labor force, agriculture, industry, energy, trade, transportation, communication, education, tourism, and the environment. Statistical sources are noted.

TRADE/PROFESSIONAL ASSOCIATIONS

International Association for Research in Income and Wealth. c/o New York University, Dept. of Economics, Room 700, 269 Mercer St., New York, NY 10003. Phone: (212)924-4386 Fax: (212)366-5067 E-mail: iariw@econ.nyu.edu • URL: http://www.econ.nyu.edu/dept/iariw.

OTHER SOURCES

MarketingClick Network: American Demographics. Intertec Publishing, a Primedia Co. • Web site provides full-text articles from *American Demographics*, *Marketing Tools*, and *Forecast*, with keyword searching. The *Marketing Tools Directory* can also be searched online, listing suppliers of products, information, and services for advertising, market research, and marketing. Fees: Free.

Working Americans, 1880-1999, Volume One: The Working Class. Grey House Publishing. • 2000. $135.00. Provides detailed information on the lifestyles and economic life of working class families in the 12 decades from 1880 to 1999. Includes such items as selected consumer prices, income, family finances, budgets, life at home, jobs, and working conditions. (Universal Reference Publications.).

Working Americans, 1880-1999, Volume Two: The Middle Class. Grey House Publishing. • 2000. $135.00. Furnishes details of the social and economic lives of middle class Americans during the years 1880 to 1999. Describes such items as selected consumer prices, income, family finances, budgets, life at home, jobs, and working conditions. (Universal Reference Publications.).

World Consumer Income and Expenditure Patterns. Available from The Gale Group. • 2001. $990.00. Second edition. Two volumes. Published by Euromonitor. Provides data for 52 countries on consumer income, earning power, spending patterns, and savings. Expenditures are detailed for 75 product or service categories.

INCOME TAX

See also: CORPORATE INCOME TAX; STATE TAXES; TAX PLANNING; TAX SHELTERS; TAXATION

GENERAL WORKS

The Decline (and Fall?) of the Income Tax: How to Make Sense of the American Tax Mess and the Flat-Tax Cures That Are Supposed to Fix It. Michael J. Graetz. W. W. Norton & Co., Inc. • 1997. $27.50. The author, a former U. S. Treasury official, proposes a value-added tax (VAT) to augment federal income tax. He reviews recent tax history and provides entertaining tax anecdotes.

The Flat Tax. Robert E. Hall and Alvin Rabushka. Hoover Institution Press. • 1995. $14.95. Second edition. A favorable view of a flat tax as a replacement for the graduated federal income tax.

Unbridled Power: Inside the Secret Culture of the IRS. Shelley L. Davis. HarperCollins Publishers. • 1997. $25.00. A highly critical view of the Internal Revenue Service by its former historian.

What the IRS Doesn't Want You to Know: A CPA Reveals the Tricks of the Trade. Martin Kaplan and Naomi Weiss. Villard Books. • 1999. $15.95. Sixth edition. Explains how to legally pay as little income tax as possible.

ABSTRACTS AND INDEXES

Accounting and Tax Index. UMI. • Quarterly. Price on application. Includes annual cumulative bound volume. Indexes accounting, auditing, and taxation literature appearing in journals, books, pamphlets, conference proceedings, and newsletters. (UMI is University Microfilms International, a Bell & Howell Co.).

ALMANACS AND YEARBOOKS

Tax Year in Review. CCH, Inc. • Annual. Covers the year's "major new legislative and regulatory changes.".

CD-ROM DATABASES

Federal Tax Products. Available from U. S. Government Printing Office. • Annual. $20.00. CD-ROM issued by the Internal Revenue Service (http://www.irs.treas.gov/forms_pubs/). Provides current tax forms, instructions, and publications. Also includes older tax forms beginning with 1991.

The Tax Directory [CD-ROM]. Tax Analysts. • Quarterly. Provides *The Tax Directory* listings on CD-ROM, covering federal, state, and international tax officials, tax practitioners, and corporate tax executives.

U. S. Master Tax Guide on CD-ROM. CCH, Inc. • Annual. $97.95. CD-ROM version of the printed *U. S. Master Tax Guide.* Includes search commands, link commands, and on-screen prompts.

U. S. Master Tax Guide Plus: Federal CD. CCH, Inc. • Monthly. $199.00 per year. Includes *U. S. Master Tax Guide* on CD-ROM, plus the IRS Code, IRS Regulations, tax court opinions, tax cases, and other source material.

WILSONDISC: Wilson Business Abstracts. H. W. Wilson Co. • Monthly. $2,495.00 per year, including unlimited online access to *Wilson Business Abstracts* through WILSONLINE. Provides CD-ROM "cover-to-cover" abstracting and indexing of over 600 prominent business periodicals. Indexing is from 1982, abstracting from 1990. (*Business Periodicals Index* without abstracts is available on CD-ROM at $1,495 per year.).

DIRECTORIES

Cumulative List of Organizations Described in Section 170(c) of the Internal Revenue Code of 1986. Available from U. S. Government Printing Office. • Annual. $114.00 per year, including quarterly supplements. Lists about 300,000 organizations eligible for contributions deductible for federal income tax purposes. Provides name of each organization and city, but not complete address information. Arranged alphabetically by name of institution. (Office of Employee Plans and Exempt Organizations, Internal Revenue Service.).

The Tax Directory. Tax Analysts. • Annual. $299.00. ($399.00 with quarterly CD-ROM updates.) Four volumes: *Government Officials Worldwide* (lists 15,000 state, federal, and international tax officials, with basic corporate and individual income tax rates for 100 countries); *Private Sector Professionals Worldwide* (lists 25,000 U.S. and foreign tax practitioners: accountants, lawyers, enrolled agents, and actuarial firms); *Corporate Tax Managers Worldwide* (lists 10,000 tax managers employed by U.S. and foreign companies).

ENCYCLOPEDIAS AND DICTIONARIES

Dictionary of 1040 Deductions. Matthew Bender & Co., Inc. • Annual. Price on application. Organized by schedule and supported by thousands of citations. Designed to quickly answer all questions about deductions.

HANDBOOKS AND MANUALS

Bender's Payroll Tax Guide. Matthew Bender & Co., Inc. • Annual. $117.00. Guide to payroll tax planning. Includes procedures, forms, and examples.

Bender's Tax Return Manual. Ernest D. Fiore and others. Matthew Bender & Co., Inc. • Annual. Price on application. Includes all major federal tax forms and schedules.

CCH Analysis of Top Tax Issues: Return Preparation and Planning Guide. CCH, Inc. • Annual. $45.00. Covers yearly tax changes affecting business and personal transactions, planning, and returns.

CCH Guide to Car, Travel, Entertainment, and Home Office Deductions. CCH, Inc. • Annual. $42.00. Explains how to claim maximum tax deductions for common business expenses. Includes automobile depreciation tables, lease value tables, worksheets, and examples of filled-in tax forms.

Ernst & Young Tax Guide 2000: The Official IRS Tax Guide and Usable Forms, Plus Easy-to-Use Explanation and Tax Saving Tips from America's Leading Big Six Accounting Firms. Ernst & Young Staff. John Wiley and Sons, Inc. • Annual. $15.95. (Ernst and Young Tax Guide Series).

Essentials of Federal Income Taxation for Individuals and Business. CCH, Inc. • Annual. $59.00. Covers basic tax planning and tax reduction strategies as affected by tax law changes and IRS interpretations. Includes sample filled-in forms.

Estate Plan Book 2000. William S. Moore. American Institute for Economic Research. • 2000. $10.00. Revision of 1997 edition. Part one: "Basic Estate Planning." Part two: "Reducing Taxes on the Disposition of Your Estate." Part three: "Putting it All Together: Examples of Estate Plans." Provides succinct information on wills, trusts, tax planning, and gifts. (Economic Education Bulletin.).

Federal Income Tax Regulations. Prentice Hall. • 1984. Four volumes. Price on application.

Federal Income Taxation of Corporations and Shareholders. Boris I. Bittker and James S. Eustice. Warren, Gorham and Lamont/RIA Group. • Looseleaf service. $235.00. Two volumes. Periodic supplementation. Provides details concerning best methods for structuring various corporation transactions. Actual forms used by top tax specialists covering a diverse range of tax situations are shown.

Federal Tax Citations. Shepard's. • 1990. $990.00. 11 volumes. Supplements available.

Federal Tax Course: General Edition. CCH, Inc. • Annual. $123.00. Provides basic reference and training for various forms of federal taxation: individual, business, corporate, partnership, estate, gift, etc. Includes *Federal Taxation Study Manual.*

Federal Tax Manual. CCH, Inc. • Looseleaf. $175.00 per year. Covers "basic federal tax rules and forms affecting individuals and businesses." Includes a copy of *Annuity, Depreciation, and Withholding Tables.*

Federal Taxation Practice and Procedure. Robert E. Meldman and Richard J. Sideman. CCH, Inc. • 1998. $89.00. Fifth edition. Provides information on the administrative structure of the Internal Revenue Service. Includes discussions of penalties, ethical duties, statute of limitations, litigation, and IRS collection procedures. Contains IRS standardized letters and notices.

H & R Block Income Tax Guide. Simon & Schuster Trade. • 1997. $15.00.

How to Practice Before the New IRS. Robert S. Schriebman. CCH, Inc. • 1999. $115.00. Reflects changes made by the IRS Restructuring and Reform Act of 1998. Covers audits, appeals, tax court basics, refunds, penalties, etc., for tax professionals.

Income Tax Regulations. CCH, Inc. • Annual. $95.00. Six volumes. Contains full text of official Internal Revenue Code regulations (approximately 11,000 pages).

Individual Tax Return Guide, 1992. Research Institute of America, Inc. • 1993. $10.00. Revised edition.

Individual Taxation. James W. Pratt and William N. Kulsrud. McGraw-Hill Higher Education. • 1996. $69.95. Tenth edition. Focuses on the federal income tax.

Individual Taxes: Worldwide Summaries. PricewaterhouseCoopers. John Wiley and Sons, Inc. • 1999. $95.00. Summarizes the personal tax regulations of more than 125 countries. Provides information useful for international tax planning and foreign investments.

Individuals' Filled-In Tax Return Forms. CCH, Inc. • 1999. $29.50. Revised edition.

Internal Revenue Code: All the Income, Estate, Gift, Employment, and Excise Procedure and Administrative Provisions. Research Institute of America, Inc. • Semiannual $35.50 per edition.

Internal Revenue Code: Income, Estate, Gift, Employment, and Excise Taxes. CCH, Inc. • Annual. $69.00. Two volumes. Provides full text of the Internal Revenue Code (5,000 pages), including procedural and administrative provisions.

IRS Tax Collection Procedures. CCH, Inc. • Looseleaf. $189.00. Supplementation available. Covers IRS collection personnel, payment arrangements, penalties, abatements, summons, liens, etc.

J. K. Lasser's Your Income Tax, 2001. J. K. Lasser Tax Institute Staff. John Wiley and Sons, Inc. • 2000. $15.95.

Money Income Tax Handbook. Mary L. Sprouse, editor. Little, Brown & Co. • 1995. $13.99. (Title refers to *Money* magazine.).

New Federal Graduated Withholding Tax Tables. CCH, Inc. • Annual.

1040 Preparation. Sidney Kess and Ben Eisenberg. CCH, Inc. • 2001. $62.00. How to prepare individual federal income tax returns.

Practical Guide to Tax Issues in Employment. Julia K. Brazelton. CCH, Inc. • 1999. $95.00. Covers income taxation as related to labor law and tax law, including settlements and awards. Written for tax professionals.

RIA Federal Income Tax Regulations. Research Institute of America, Inc. • Annual. Contains the official U. S. Treasury Department interpretation of federal income tax law. Three volumes cover final and temporary regulations and one volume covers proposed regulations.

Tax Examples. John C. Wisdom. West Group. • 1993. $125.00. Presents yearly examples, with forms, of a wide variety of tax problems and issues. Subjects include taxable income, deductions, alternative minimum tax, dependents, gift taxes, partnerships, and other problem areas. Includesaccounting method considerations. (Tax Series).

Tax Guide for Small Business. U.S. Department of the Treasury, Internal Revenue Service. Available from U.S. Government Printing Office. • Annual. $5.00.

Tax Penalties and Interest Handbook. Howard Davidoff and David A. Minars. LEXIS Publishing. • $80.00. Looseleaf. Annual supplements.

Tax Preparation Service. Entrepreneur Media, Inc. • Looseleaf. $59.50. A practical guide to starting a business for the preparation of income tax returns. Covers profit potential, start-up costs, market size evaluation, owner's time required, site selection, lease negotiation, pricing, accounting, advertising, promotion, etc. (Start-Up Business Guide No. E2332.).

U. S. Master Compensation Tax Guide. CCH, Inc. • Annual. $54.95. Provides concise coverage of taxes on salaries, bonuses, fringe benefits, other current compensation, and deferred compensation (qualified and nonqualified).

U. S. Master Tax Guide. CCH, Inc. • Annual. $46.00. Provides concise information on personal and business income tax, with cross-references to the Internal Revenue Code and Income Tax Regulations.

Your Federal Income Tax. U.S. Department of the Treasury, Internal Revenue Service. Available from U.S. Government Printing Office. • Annual. $22.00. Layman's guide to income tax preparation.

INTERNET DATABASES

CCH Essentials: An Internet Tax Research and Primary Source Library. CCH, Inc. Phone: 800-248-3248 or (773)866-6000 Fax: 800-224-8299 or (773)866-3608 E-mail: cust_serv@cch.com • URL: http://tax.cch.com/essentials • Fee-based Web site provides full-text coverage of federal tax law and regulations, including rulings, procedures, tax court decisions, and IRS publications, announcements, notices, and penalties. Includes explanation, analysis, tax planning guides, and a daily tax news service. Searching is offered, including citation search. Fee: $495.00 per year.

Deloitte & Touche Online. Deloitte & Touche LLP, Financial Consulting Services Center. Phone: (513)784-7100 E-mail: webmaster@dtonline.com • URL: http://www.dtonline.com • Web site provides concise, full-text articles on taxes, personal finance, and business from a leading accounting firm. Includes "Tax News and Views," "Personal Finance Advisor," "Business Advisor: A Resource for Small Business Owners," "Financial Tip of the Week," and "This Week Online: Top of the News." Weekly updates. Fees: Free.

The Digital Daily. Internal Revenue Service. Phone: (202)622-5000 Fax: (202)622-5844 • URL: http://www.irs.ustreas.gov • Web site provides a wide variety of tax information, including IRS forms and publications. Includes "Highlights of New Tax Law." Searching is available. Fees: Free.

Fedstats. Federal Interagency Council on Statistical Policy. Phone: (202)395-7254 • URL: http://www.fedstats.gov • Web site features an efficient search facility for full-text statistics produced by more than 70 federal agencies, including the Census Bureau, the Bureau of Economic Analysis, and the Bureau of Labor Statistics. Boolean searches can be made within one agency or for all agencies combined. Links are offered to international statistical bureaus, including the UN, IMF, OECD, UNESCO, Eurostat, and 20 individual countries. Fees: Free.

Rutgers Accounting Web (RAW). Rutgers University Accounting Research Center. Phone: (201)648-5172 Fax: (201)648-1233 • URL: http://www.rutgers.edu/accounting • RAW Web site provides extensive links to sources of national and international accounting information, such as the Big Six accounting firms, the Financial Accounting Standards Board (FASB), SEC filings (EDGAR), journals, publishers, software, the International Accounting Network, and "Internet's largest list of accounting firms in USA." Searching is offered. Fees: Free.

Tax Analysts [Web site]. Tax Analysts. Phone: 800-955-3444 or (703)533-4400 Fax: (703)533-4444 • URL: http://www.tax.org • The three main sections of Tax Analysts home page are "Tax News" (Today's Tax News, Feature of the Week, Tax Snapshots, Tax Calendar); "Products & Services" (Product Catalog, Press Releases); and "Public Interest" (Discussion Groups, Tax Clinic, Tax History Project). Fees: Free for coverage of current tax events; fee-based for comprehensive information. Daily updating.

ONLINE DATABASES

Accounting and Tax Database. Bell & Howell Information and Learning. • Provides indexing and abstracting of the literature of accounting, taxation, and financial management, 1971 to date. Updating is weekly. Especially covers accounting, auditing, banking, bankruptcy, employee compensation and benefits, cash management, financial planning, and credit. Inquire as to online cost and availability.

DRI U.S. Central Database. Data Products Division. • Provides more than 23,000 business, financial, demographic, economic, foreign trade, and industry-related time series for the U.S. Includes national income, population, retail-wholesale trade, price indexes, labor data, housing, industrial production, banking, interest rates, money supply, etc. Time period is generally 1947 to date (some data back to 1929). Updating varies. Inquire as to online cost and availability.

Wilson Business Abstracts Online. H. W. Wilson Co. • Indexes and abstracts 600 major business periodicals, plus the *Wall Street Journal* and the business section of the *New York Times*. Indexing is from 1982, abstracting from 1990, with the two newspapers included from 1993. Updated weekly. Inquire as to online cost and availability. (*Business Periodicals Index* without abstracts is also available online.).

PERIODICALS AND NEWSLETTERS

Highlights and Documents. Tax Analysts. • Daily. $2,249.00 per year, including monthly indexes. Newsletter. Provides daily coverage of IRS, congressional, judicial, state, and international tax developments. Includes abstracts and citations for "all tax documents released within the previous 24 to 48 hours." Annual compilation available *Highlights and Documents on Microfiche*.

Internal Revenue Bulletin. Available from U. S. Government Printing Office. • Weekly. $230.00 per year. Issued by the Internal Revenue Service. Contains IRS rulings, Treasury Decisions, Executive Orders, tax legislation, and court decisions. (Semiannual *Cumulative Bulletins* are sold separately.).

Internal Revenue Cumulative Bulletin. Available from U. S. Government Printing Office. • Semiannual. Issued by the Internal Revenue Service. Cumulates all items of a "permanent nature" appearing in the weekly *Internal Revenue Bulletin*.

Journal of Tax Practice and Procedure. CCH, Inc. • Bimonthly. $195.00 per year. Covers the representation of taxpayers before the IRS, "from initial contact through litigation.".

Practical Tax Strategies. Warren, Gorham & Lamont/RIA Group. • Monthly. $125.00 per year. Provides advice and information on tax planning for tax accountants, attorneys, and advisers.

State Income Tax Alert. CCH, Inc. • Semimonthly. $247.00 per year. Newsletter. Provides nationwide coverage of latest state income tax laws, regulations, and court decisions.

Tax Notes: The Weekly Tax Service. Tax Analysts. • Weekly. $1,699.00 per year. Includes an *Annual* and 1985-1996 compliations on CD-ROM. Newsletter. Covers "tax news from all federal sources," including congressional committees, tax courts, and the Internal Revenue Service. Each issue contains "summaries of every document that pertains to federal tax law," with citations. Commentary is provided.

Tax Practice. Tax Analysts. • Weekly. $199.00 per year. Newsletter. Covers news affecting tax practitioners and litigators, with emphasis on federal court decisions, rules and regulations, and tax petitions. Provides a guide to Internal Revenue Service audit issues.

Weekly Alert. Research Institute of America, Inc. • Weekly. Newsletter. $175.00 per year. Federal tax trends and new legislation.

RESEARCH CENTERS AND INSTITUTES

Center for Tax Policy Studies. Purdue University, 490 Krannert, West Lafayette, IN 47907-1310. Phone: (765)494-4442 Fax: (765)496-1778 E-mail: papke@mgmt.purdue.edu.

Tax Foundation. 1250 H St., N.W., Suite 750, Washington, DC 20005. Phone: (202)783-2760 Fax: (202)783-6868 E-mail: taxfnd@intr.net • URL: http://www.taxfoundation.org.

STATISTICS SOURCES

Business Statistics of the United States. Courtenay M. Slater, editor. Bernan Associates. • 1999. $74.00. Fifth edition. Based on *Business Statistics*, formerly issue by the Bureau of Economic Analysis, U. S. Department of Commerce. Provides basic data for a wide variety of U. S. industries, services, and economic indicators. Most statistics are shown annually for 29 years and monthly for the most recent four years.

Individual Income Tax Returns. U.S. Department of the Treasury, Internal Revenue Service. Available from U.S. Government Printing Office. • Annual. $17.00.

Internal Revenue Service Data Book. Available from U. S. Government Printing Office. • Annual. $3.50. "Contains statistical tables and organizational information previously included in the Internal Revenue Service annual report." (Internal Revenue Service Publication, 55B.).

Statistics of Income: Corporation Income Tax Returns. U.S. Internal Revenue Service. Available from U.S. Government Printing Office. • Annual. $26.00.

Survey of Current Business. Available from U. S. Government Printing Office. • Monthly. $49.00 per year. Issued by Bureau of Economic Analysis, U. S. Department of Commerce. Presents a wide variety of business and economic data.

TRADE/PROFESSIONAL ASSOCIATIONS

Institute of Tax Consultants. 7500 212th St., S.W., No. 205, Edmonds, WA 98026. Phone: (425)774-3521 Fax: (425)672-0461.

National Association of Enrolled Federal Tax Accountants. P.O. Box 59-009, Chicago, IL 60659-0009. Phone: (773)463-5577 or (773)463-3355.

National Taxpayers Union. 108 N. Alfred St., Alexandria, VA 22314. Phone: 800-829-4258 or (703)683-5700 Fax: (703)683-5722 E-mail: ntu@ntu.org • URL: http://www.ntu.org.

Tax Analysts. 6830 N. Fairfax Dr., Arlington, VA 22213. Phone: 800-955-3444 or (703)533-4400 Fax: (703)533-4444 E-mail: webmaster@tax.org • URL: http://www.tax.org • An advocacy group reviewing U. S. and foreign income tax developments. Includes a Tax Policy Advisory Board.

OTHER SOURCES

Complete Federal Tax Forms. Research Institute of America, Inc. • Three looseleaf volumes. Periodic supplementations. Price on application. Contains more than 650 reprints of blank Internal Revenue Service forms, with instructions.

Executive Compensation and Taxation Coordinator. Research Institute of America, Inc. • Three looseleaf volumes. $450.00 per year. Monthly updates.

Factiva. Dow Jones Reuters Business Interactive, LLC. • Fee-based Web site provides "global news and business information through Web sites and content integration solutions." Includes Dow Jones and Reuters newswires, The Wall Street Journal, and more than 7,000 other sources of current news, historical articles, market research reports, and investment analysis. Content includes 96 major U. S. newspapers, 900 non-English sources, trade publications, media transcripts, country profiles, news photos, etc.

Federal Income, Gift and Estate Taxation. Matthew Bender & Co., Inc. • $1,070.00. Nine looseleaf volumes. Periodic supplementation.

Federal Tax Coordinator 2D. Research Institute of America, Inc. • 35 looseleaf volumes. $1,375.00 per year. Weekly updates. Includes *Weekly Alert* newsletter and *Internal Revenue Bulletin.* Covers federal income, estate, gift, and excise taxes. Formerly *Federal Tax Coordinator.*

Federal Tax Course. CCH, Inc. • Annual. $136.00. Looseleaf. Summarizes requirements of current federal income tax regulations, revenue codes, laws, and filing requirements.

Federal Tax Forms. CCH, Inc. • Irregular. Looseleaf service. Three volumes. Actual size reproductions of federal income tax forms.

Federal Tax Guide. CCH, Inc. • $850.00 per year. Looseleaf service. Monthly updates. Eight volumes. For everyday business and personal federal income tax questions. Explanation of federal tax system, income tax regulations, check lists, withholding tables, and charts.

Federal Tax Guide: Internal Revenue Code. Prentice Hall. • Looseleaf. Periodic supplementation. Price on application.

Federal Taxes: Internal Memoranda of the IRS. Prentice Hall. • Looseleaf. Periodic supplementation. Price on application.

FedWorld: A Program of the United States Department of Commerce. National Technical Information Service. • Web site offers "a comprehensive central access point for searching, locating, ordering, and acquiring government and business information." Emphasis is on searching the Web pages, databases, and government reports of a wide variety of federal agencies. Fees: Free.

FirstGov: Your First Click to the U. S. Government. General Services Administration. • Free Web site provides extensive links to federal agencies covering a wide variety of topics, such as agriculture, business, consumer safety, education, the environment, government jobs, grants, health, social security, statistics sources, taxes, technology, travel, and world affairs. Also provides links to federal forms, including IRS tax forms. Searching is offered, both keyword and advanced.

Income Taxation: Accounting Methods and Periods. George Bauernfeind. Shepard's. • 1983. $235.00. Two volumes. (Tax and Estate Planning Series).

Institute on Federal Taxation, New York University. Proceedings, 1942-1953. William S. Hein and Co., Inc. • $4,750.00. 51 volume set.

Internal Revenue Manual: Administration. CCH, Inc. • Six looseleaf volumes. Reproduces IRS tax administration provisions and procedures.

Internal Revenue Manual: Audit and Administration. CCH, Inc. • Irregular $1,156.00. Reproduces IRS audit provisions and procedures.

IRS Publications. CCH, Inc. • Irregular. Three looseleaf volumes. Periodic supplementation. Photographic reproductions of current Internal Revenue Service tax publications intended for public use.

Nexis.com. Lexis-Nexis Group. • Fee-based Web site offers searching of about 2.8 billion documents in some 30,000 news, business, and legal information sources. Features include a subject directory covering 1,200 topics in 34 categories and a Company Dossier containing information on more than 500,000 public and private companies. Boolean searching is offered.

Tax Legislation 2001: Highlights. CCH, Inc. • 2001. $7.00. Booklet summarizes significant changes in U. S. tax law resulting from the legislation of 2001.

Tax Legislation 2001: Law, Explanation, and Analysis. CCH, Inc. • 2001. $42.50. Provides explanation and interpretation of federal tax legislation enacted in 2001.

Tax Planning for Individuals and Small Businesses. Sidney Kess. CCH, Inc. • 2000. $49.00. Includes illustrations, charts, and sample client letters. Edited primarily for accountants and lawyers.

INCOME TAX, STATE

See: STATE TAXES

INCORPORATION

See also: CORPORATION LAW AND REGULATION

ABSTRACTS AND INDEXES

Business Periodicals Index. H. W. Wilson Co. • Monthly, except August, with quarterly and annual cumulations. Service basis for print edition; CD-ROM edition, $1,495.00 per year.

Current Law Index: Multiple Access to Legal Periodicals. The Gale Group. • Monthly. $650.00 per year. Produced in cooperation with the American Association of Law Libraries. Indexes more than 900 law journals, legal newspapers, and specialty publications from the U.S., Canada, U.K., Ireland, Australia, and New Zealand.

Index to Legal Periodicals and Books. H. W. Wilson Co. • Monthly. Quarterly and annual cumulations. $270.00 per year. CD-ROM version available at $1,495.00 per year.

ALMANACS AND YEARBOOKS

American Law Yearbook. The Gale Group. • Annual. $155.00. Serves as a yearly supplement to *West's Encyclopedia of American Law.* Describes new legal developments in many subject areas.

CD-ROM DATABASES

Business Source Plus. EBSCO Information Services. • Monthly. $1,495.00 per year. Provides CD-ROM citations and abstracts to articles in about 650 business periodicals and newspapers, including *The Wall Street Journal.* Full text is provided from 200 selected periodicals. Covers accounting, communications, economics, finance, management, marketing, and other business subjects.

WILSONDISC: Index to Legal Periodicals and Books. H. W. Wilson Co. • Monthly. Including unlimited online access to *Index to Legal Periodicals* through WILSONLINE. Contains CD-ROM indexing of more than 800 English language legal periodicals from 1981 to date and 2,500 books.

WILSONDISC: Wilson Business Abstracts. H. W. Wilson Co. • Monthly. $2,495.00 per year, including unlimited online access to *Wilson Business Abstracts* through WILSONLINE. Provides CD-ROM "cover-to-cover" abstracting and indexing of over 600 prominent business periodicals. Indexing is from 1982, abstracting from 1990. (*Business Periodicals Index* without abstracts is available on CD-ROM at $1,495 per year.).

ENCYCLOPEDIAS AND DICTIONARIES

Encyclopedia of Business. The Gale Group. • 2000. $425.00. Second edition. Two volumes. Contains more than 700 signed articles covering major business disciplines and concepts. International in scope.

West's Encyclopedia of American Law. Available from The Gale Group. • 1997. $995.00. Second edition. 12 volumes. Published by West Group. Covers a wide variety of legal topics for the general reader. Formerly *Guide to American Law: Everyone's Legal Encyclopedia* (1985).

HANDBOOKS AND MANUALS

Financing the Corporation. Richard A. Booth. West Group. • $110.00. Looseleaf service. Periodic supplementation. Covers a wide variety of corporate finance legal topics, from initial capital structure to public sale of securities.

How to Form a Nonprofit Corporation. Anthony Mancuso. Nolo.com. • 1997. $39.95. Fourth edition.

How to Incorporate: A Handbook for Entrepreneurs and Professionals. Michael Diamond. John Wiley and Sons, Inc. • 1996. $49.95. Third edition.

Incorporate Your Business: The National Corporation Kit. Daniel Sitarz. Nova Publishing Co. • 1996. $29.95. Second revised edition. Includes basic forms and instructions for incorporating a small business in any state. Forms are also available on IBM or MAC diskettes. (Small Business Library Series).

Incorporating in [state] Without a Lawyer. W. Dean Brown. Consumer Publishing, Inc. • Annual. $24.95. Available in separate editions for each of 32 states and the District of Columbia. Includes specific instructions for creating a simple corporation in a particular state, with legal forms and sample stock certificates.

Securities Counseling for New and Developing Companies. Stuart R. Cohn. West Group. • 1993. $130.00. Covers securities planning for new businesses, with an emphasis on the avoidance of legal violations and civil liabilities. (Corporate Law Series).

Small Business Incorporation Kit. Robert L. Davidson. John Wiley and Sons, Inc. • 1992. $16.95.

ONLINE DATABASES

ABI/INFORM. Bell & Howell Information and Learning. • Provides online indexing to business-related material occurring in over 1,000 periodicals from 1971 to the present. Inquire as to online cost and availability.

Index to Legal Periodicals and Books (Online). H. W. Wilson Co. • Broad coverage of law journals and books 1981 to date. Monthly updates. Inquire as to online cost and availability.

Management Contents. The Gale Group. • Covers a wide range of management, financial, marketing, personnel, and administrative topics. About 150 leading business journals are indexed and abstracted from 1974 to date, with monthly updating. Inquire as to online cost and availability.

Wilson Business Abstracts Online. H. W. Wilson Co. • Indexes and abstracts 600 major business periodicals, plus the *Wall Street Journal* and the business section of the *New York Times*. Indexing is from 1982, abstracting from 1990, with the two newspapers included from 1993. Updated weekly. Inquire as to online cost and availability. (*Business Periodicals Index* without abstracts is also available online.).

RESEARCH CENTERS AND INSTITUTES

Lexis.com Research System. Lexis-Nexis Group. Phone: 800-227-9597 or (937)865-6800 Fax: (937)865-6909 E-mail: webmaster@prod.lexis-nexis.com • URL: http://www.lexis.com • Fee-based Web site offers extensive searching of a wide variety of legal sources. Additional features include Daily Opinion Service, lexis.com Bookstore, Career Center, CLE Center, Law Schools, and Practice Pages ("Pages specific to areas of specialty").

OTHER SOURCES

How to Form Your Own Corporation Without a Lawyer for Under $75.00. Ted Nicholas and Sean P. Melvin. Dearborn Financial Publishing. • 1999. $19.95. 26th edition.

INDEPENDENT SCHOOLS

See: PRIVATE SCHOOLS

INDEX TRADING

See: STOCK INDEX TRADING

INDEXING

See also: FILES AND FILING (DOCUMENTS)

GENERAL WORKS

The Amazing Internet Challenge: How Leading Projects Use Library Skills to Organize the Web. Amy T. Wells and others. American Library Association. • 1999. $45.00. Presents profiles of 12 digital libraries, such as the Agriculture Network Information Center and the Social Science Information Gateway. Emphasis is on how online indexes were created.

Explorations in Indexing and Abstracting: Pointing, Virtue, and Power. Brian C. O'Connor. Libraries Unlimited. • 1996. $40.00. Presents a philosophy of indexing. (Library and Information Science Text Series).

Indexing: The State of Our Knowledge and the State of Our Ignorance. Bella H. Weinberg, editor. Information Today, Inc. • 1989. $30.00. Ten papers presented at the 1988 annual meeting of the American Society of Indexers.

Information Today, Inc. Anne Leach, editor. American Society of Indexers. • 1998. $20.00. Second edition.

ALMANACS AND YEARBOOKS

NFAIS Yearbook of the Information Industry. Arthur W. Elias, editor. Information Today, Inc. • 1993. $40.00. Compiled by the National Federation of Abstracting and Information Services (NFAIS). Summarizes and analyzes the impacts of each year's events on information, abstracting, and indexing activities.

BIBLIOGRAPHIES

Can You Recommend a Good Book on Indexing?. Bella H. Weinberg. Information Today, Inc. • 1998. $39.50. Contains reviews of books on indexing, classified of general works, theory, book indexing, databases, thesauri, and computer-assisted (automatic) indexing. (CyberAge Books.).

CD-ROM DATABASES

LISA Plus: Library and Information Science Abstracts. Bowker-Saur, Reed Reference Publishing. • Quarterly. $1,450.00 per year. Provides CD-ROM abstracting and indexing of the world's library and information science literature. Covers a wide variety of topics.

DIRECTORIES

The Indexer Locater. American Society of Indexers, Inc. • Annual. Members, $10.00; non-members, $15.00. Lists over 200 free-lance indexers in the U. S. and their subject specialties. Formerly *Register of Indexers*.

ENCYCLOPEDIAS AND DICTIONARIES

Words That Mean Business: Three Thousand Terms for Access to Business Information. Warner-Eddison Associates. Neal-Schuman Publishers, Inc. • 1981. $60.00.

HANDBOOKS AND MANUALS

Beyond Book Indexing: How to Get Started in Web Indexing, Embedded Indexing, and Other Computer-Based Media. Diane Brenner and Marilyn Rowland, editors. Information Today, Inc. • 2000. $31.25. Published for the American Society of Indexers. Contains 12 chapters written by professional indexers. Part one discusses making an index by marking items in an electronic document (embedded indexing); part two is on indexing to make Web pages more accessible; part three covers CD-ROM and multimedia indexing; part four provides career and promotional advice for professionals in the field. Includes an index by Janet Perlman and a glossary.

Indexing and Abstracting in Theory and Practice. F. Wilfrid Lancaster. University of Illinois. • 1998. $47.50. Second revised edition. Includes indexing and abstracting exercises.

Indexing from A to Z. Hans H. Wellisch. H. W. Wilson Co. • 1996. $40.00. Second enlarged revised edition. A practical guide to the indexing of books, periodicals, and non-print materials. Covers such technical topics as exhaustivity, specificity, thesauri, and keywords, and such mundane topics as contracts and fees.

Subject Indexing: An Introductory Guide. Trudi Bellardo. Special Libraries Association. • 1991. $85.00. A self-study guide to creating subject indices for a variety of materials and formats.

ONLINE DATABASES

LISA Online: Library and Information Science Abstracts. Bowker-Saur, Reed Reference Publishing. • Provides abstracting and indexing of the world's library and information science literature from 1969 to the present. Covers a wide variety of topics in over 550 journals from 60 countries, with biweekly updates. Inquire as to online cost and availability.

PERIODICALS AND NEWSLETTERS

The Indexer. American Society of Indexers. • Semiannual. $40.00 per year. Devoted specifically to all aspects of indexing.

The Keywords. American Society of Indexers. • Six times a year. Free to members; non-members, $40.00 per year. Formerly *American Society of Indexes Newsletter*.

TRADE/PROFESSIONAL ASSOCIATIONS

American Society of Indexers. 11250 Roger Bacon Dr., Ste. 8, Reston, VA 20190. Phone: (703)234-4147 Fax: (703)435-4390 E-mail: info@asindexing.org • URL: http://www.asindexing.org • Affiliated with the American Library Association, the American Society for Information Science, and other organizations.

National Federation of Abstracting and Information Services. 1518 Walnut St., Suite 307, Philadelphia, PA 19102-3403. Phone: (215)893-1561 Fax: (215)893-1564 E-mail: nfais@nfais.org • URL: http://www.nfais.org.

Society of Indexers. Globe Centre, Penistone Rd., Sheffield S6 3AE, England. Globe Centre, Penistone Rd.,.

INDICATORS, ECONOMIC

See: ECONOMIC INDICATORS

INDIVIDUAL RETIREMENT ACCOUNTS

GENERAL WORKS

Fundamentals of Employee Benefit Programs. Employee Benefit Research Institute. • 1996. $49.95. Fifth edition. Provides basic explanation of employee benefit programs in both the private and public sectors, including health insurance, pension plans, retirement planning, social security, and long-term care insurance.

Investing During Retirement: The Vanguard Guide to Managing Your Retirement Assets. Vanguard Group. McGraw-Hill Professional. • 1996. $17.95. A basic, general guide to investing after retirement. Covers pension plans, basic principles of investing, types of mutual funds, asset allocation, retirement income planning, social security, estate planning, and contingencies. Includes glossary and worksheets for net worth, budget, and income.

Retirement Security: Understanding and Planning Your Financial Future. David M. Walker. John Wiley and Sons, Inc. • 1996. $29.95. Topics include investments, social security, Medicare, health insurance, and employer retirement plans.

Vanguard Retirement Investing Guide: Charting Your Course to a Secure Retirement. Vanguard Group. McGraw-Hill Professional. • 1995. $24.95. Second edition. Covers saving and investing for future retirement. Topics include goal setting, investment fundamentals, mutual funds, asset allocation, defined contribution retirement savings plans, social security, and retirement savings strategies. Includes glossary and worksheet for retirement saving.

HANDBOOKS AND MANUALS

Estate Plan Book 2000. William S. Moore. American Institute for Economic Research. • 2000. $10.00. Revision of 1997 edition. Part one: "Basic Estate Planning." Part two: "Reducing Taxes on the Disposition of Your Estate." Part three: "Putting it

All Together: Examples of Estate Plans." Provides succinct information on wills, trusts, tax planning, and gifts. (Economic Education Bulletin.).

How to Build Wealth with Tax-Sheltered Investments. Kerry Anne Lynch. American Institute for Economic Research. • 2000. $6.00. Provides practical information on conservative tax shelters, including defined-contribution pension plans, individual retirement accounts, Keogh plans, U. S. savings bonds, municipal bonds, and various kinds of annuities: deferred, variable-rate, immediate, and foreign-currency. (Economic Education Bulletin.).

Individual Retirement Account Answer Book. Donald R. Levy and Steven G. Lockwood. Panel Publishers. • 1999. $136.00. Sixth edition. Periodic supplementation available. Questions and answers include information about contributions, distributions, rollovers, Roth IRAs, SIMPLE IRAs (Savings Incentive Match Plans for Employees), Education IRAs, and SEPs (Simplified Employee Pension plans). Chapters are provided on retirement planning, estate planning, and tax planning.

IRA Basics. Institute of Financial Education. • 1997. $34.95. Seventh edition. A guide for bank personnel.

The New Working Woman's Guide to Retirement Planning. Martha P. Patterson. University of Pennsylvania Press. • 1999. $17.50. Second edition. Provides retirement advice for employed women, including information on various kinds of IRAs, cash balance and other pension plans, 401(k) plans, and social security. Four case studies are provided to illustrate retirement planning at specific life and career stages.

Retirement Planning Guide. Sidney Kess and Barbara Weltman. CCH, Inc. • 1999. $49.00. Presents an overview for attorneys, accountants, and other professionals of the various concepts involved in retirement planning. Includes checklists, tables, forms, and study questions.

U. S. Master Pension Guide. CCH, Inc. • Annual. $49.00. Explains IRS rules and regulations applying to 401(k) plans, 403(k) plans, ESOPs (employee stock ownership plans), IRAs, SEPs (simplified employee pension plans), Keogh plans, and nonqualified plans.

INTERNET DATABASES

The Digital Daily. Internal Revenue Service. Phone: (202)622-5000 Fax: (202)622-5844 • URL: http://www.irs.ustreas.gov • Web site provides a wide variety of tax information, including IRS forms and publications. Includes "Highlights of New Tax Law." Searching is available. Fees: Free.

Small Business Retirement Savings Advisor. U. S. Department of Labor, Pension and Welfare Benefits Administration. Phone: (202)219-8921 • URL: http://www.dol.gov/elaws/pwbaplan.htm • Web site provides "answers to a variety of commonly asked questions about retirement saving options for small business employers." Includes a comparison chart and detailed descriptions of various plans: 401(k), SEP-IRA, SIMPLE-IRA, Payroll Deduction IRA, Keogh Profit-Sharing, Keogh Money Purchase, and Defined Benefit. Searching is offered. Fees: Free.

PERIODICALS AND NEWSLETTERS

Financial Planning: The Magazine for Financial Service Professionals. Securities Data Publishing. • Monthly. $79.00 per year. Edited for independent financial planners and insurance agents. Covers retirement planning, estate planning, tax planning, and insurance, including long-term healthcare considerations. Special features include a Retirement Planning Issue, Mutual Fund Performance Survey, and Variable Life and Annuity Survey. (Securities Data Publishing is a unit of Thomson Financial.).

IRA Reporter (Individual Retirement Account). Universal Pensions, Inc. • Monthly. $115.00 per year. Newsletter. Edited for financial planners. Provides information on the rules and regulations of individual retirement accounts (IRAs).

On Wall Street. Securities Data Publishing. • Monthly. $96.00 per year. Edited for securities dealers. Includes articles on financial planning, retirement planning, variable annuities, and money management, with special coverage of 401(k) plans and IRAs. (Securities Data Publishing is a unit of Thomson Financial.).

Retirement Plans Bulletin: Practical Explanations for the IRA and Retirement Plan Professional. Universal Pensions, Inc. • Monthly. $99.00 per year. Newsletter. Provides information on the rules and regulations governing qualified (tax-deferred) retirement plans.

RESEARCH CENTERS AND INSTITUTES

Employee Benefit Research Institute. 2121 K St., N. W., Suite 600, Washington, DC 20037-1896. Phone: (202)659-0670 Fax: (202)775-6312 E-mail: salisbury@ebri.org • URL: http://www.ebri.org • Conducts research on employee benefits, including various kinds of pensions, individual retirement accounts (IRAs), health insurance, social security, and long-term health care benefits.

STATISTICS SOURCES

EBRI Databook on Employee Benefits. Employee Benefit Research Institute. • 1997 $99.00. Fourth edition. Contains more than 350 tables and charts presenting data on employee benefits in the U. S., including pensions, health insurance, social security, and medicare. Includes a glossary of employee benefit terms.

TRADE/PROFESSIONAL ASSOCIATIONS

Institute of Financial Education. 55 W. Monroe St., Suite 2800, Chicago, IL 60603. Phone: 800-946-0488 or (312)364-0100 Fax: (312)364-0190 E-mail: ifego@theinstitute.com • URL: http://www.theinstitute.com • Provides courses in banking, lending, personal finance, and mortgages for personnel of banks and savings institutions.

INDUSTRIAL ADVERTISING

See also: ADVERTISING; INDUSTRIAL MARKETING

CD-ROM DATABASES

Advertiser and Agency Red Books Plus. National Register Publishing, Reed Reference Publishing. • Quarterly. $1,295.00 per year. The CD-ROM version of *Standard Directory of Advertisers, Standard Directory of Advertising Agencies*, and *Standard Directory of International Advertisers and Agencies.*

DIRECTORIES

BMA Membership Directory and Resource Guide. Business Marketing Association. • Annual. Academic, $75.00; business, $150.00. Lists professionals in business and industrial advertising and marketing. Formerly *BMA Membership Directory and Yellow Pages.*

Business Publication Advertising Source. SRDS. • Monthly. $682.00 per year. Issued in three parts: (1) U. S. Business Publications, (2) U. S. Healthcare Publications, and (3) International Publications. Provides detailed advertising rates, profiles of editorial content, management names, "Multiple Publications Publishers," circulation data, and other trade journal information. Formerly *Business Publication Rates and Data.*

Standard Directory of Advertisers: Business Classifications Edition. National Register Publishing. • Annual $659.00; with supplements, $759.00. Arranged by product or service. Provides information on the advertising programs of over 20,000 companies, including advertising/marketing personnel and the names of advertising agencies used.

Standard Directory of Advertisers: Geographic Edition. National Register Publishing. • Annual $659.00; with supplements, $759.00. Arranged geographically by state. Provides information on the advertising programs of over 10,000 companies, including advertising/marketing personnel and the names of advertising agencies used. Includes *Advertiser/Agency* supplement.

HANDBOOKS AND MANUALS

Business to Business Advertising: A Marketing Management Approach. Charles Patti and others. NTC/Contemporary Publishing. • 1994. $39.95. (NTC Business Book Series).

PERIODICALS AND NEWSLETTERS

Advertising Age's B to B: News Monthly Concerning the How-To Strategic and Tact ical Marketing, Sales and Advertising of Business-to-Business Products and Services. Crain Communications, Inc. • Monthly. $49.00 per year. Formerly Business Marketing.

MC: Technology Marketing Intelligence. BPI Communications, Inc. • Monthly. $47.00 per year. Edited for marketing executives in high technology industries. Covers both advertising and marketing.

TRADE/PROFESSIONAL ASSOCIATIONS

Association of National Advertisers. 708 Third Ave., New York, NY 10017-4270. Phone: (212)697-5950 Fax: (212)661-8057 • URL: http://www.ana.net.

Business Marketing Association. 400 N. Michigan Ave., 15th Fl., Chicago, IL 60611. Phone: 800-664-4262 or (312)409-4262 Fax: (312)409-4266 E-mail: bma@marketing.org • URL: http://www.marketing.org • Members are professionals in business and industrial advertising and marketing. Formerly known as Business/Professional Advertising Association.

INDUSTRIAL ARBITRATION

See: ARBITRATION; INDUSTRIAL RELATIONS

INDUSTRIAL COATINGS

See also: CORROSION CONTROL INDUSTRY; PAINT AND PAINTING

GENERAL WORKS

The Chemistry and Physics of Coatings. Alastair R. Marrion, editor. CRC Press, Inc. • 1994. $42.00. Published by The Royal Society of Chemistry. Provides an overview of paint science and technology, including environmental considerations.

ABSTRACTS AND INDEXES

Applied Science and Technology Index. H. W. Wilson Co. • 11 times a year. Quarterly and annual cumulations. Service basis for print edition; CD-ROM edition, $1,495.00 per year. Indexes a wide variety of English language technical, industrial, and engineering periodicals.

Corrosion Abstracts: Abstracts of the World's Literature on Corrosion and Corrosion Mitigation. National Association of Corrosion Engineers. Cambridge Information Group. • Bimonthly. Members, $215.00 per year; non-members, $250.00 per year. Provides abstracts of the worldwide literature of corrosion and corrosion control. Also available on CD-ROM.

CPI Digest: Key to World Literature Serving the Coatings, Plastics, Fibers, Adhesives, and Related Industries (Chemical Process Industries). CPI Information Services. • Monthly. $397.00 per year. Abstracts of business and technical articles for polymer-based, chemical process industries. Includes a monthly list of relevant U. S. patents. International coverage.

Current Contents: Engineering, Computing and Technology. Institute for Scientific Information. • Weekly. $730.00 per year. Reproductions of contents pages of technical journals. Includes *Author Index, Address Directory, Current Book Contents* and *Title Word Index.* Formerly *Current Contents: Engineering, Technology and Applied Sciences.*

NTIS Alerts: Materials Sciences. National Technical Information Service. • Semimonthly. $220.00 per year. Provides descriptions of government-sponsored research reports and software, with ordering information. Covers ceramics, glass, coatings, composite materials, alloys, plastics, wood, paper, adhesives, fibers, lubricants, and related subjects. Formerly *Abstract Newsletter.*

Surface Finishing Technology. ASM International. • Monthly. Members, $130.00 per year; non-members, $160.00 per year. Provides abstracts of the international literature of metallic and nonmetallic industrial coating and finishing. Formerly *Cleaning-Finishing-Coating Digest.*

DIRECTORIES

Federation of Societies for Coatings Technology: Year Book and Membership Directory. Federation of Societies for Coatings Technology. • Annual. $150.00. About 7,500 chemists, technicians, and supervisory production personnel in the decorative and protective coatings industry who are members of the 26 constituent societies of the federation. Formerly Federation of Societies for Paint Technology.

Industrial Paint and Powder Buyer's Guide. Cahners Business Information. • Annual. Free to qualified personnel; others, $15.00. List of about 2,000 manufacturers of finishing and formulating products. Formerly *Industrial Finishing Buyer's Guide.*

Macrae's Blue Book: Serving the Original Equipment Market. MacRae's Blue Book, Inc. • Annual. $170.00. Two volumes. Lists about 50,000 manufacturers of a wide variety of industrial equipment and supplies.

McCutcheon's Functional Materials: North American Edition. Publishing Co., McCutcheon Div. • Annual. $170.00. Two volumes. North American edition contains detailed information on surfactant-related products produced in North America. Examples are enzymes, lubricants, waxes, and corrosion inhibitors. Company names, addresses and telephone numbers are included. International edition contains detailed information on surfactant-related products produced in Europe and Asia. Examples are enzymes, lubricants, waxes, and corrosion inhibitors. Company names, addresses, and telephone numbers are included.

Paint Red Book. PTN Publishing Co. • Annual. $53.00. Lists manufacturers of paint, varnish, lacquer, and specialized coatings. Suppliers of raw materials, chemicals, and equipment are included.

Thomas Register of American Manufacturers and Thomas Register Catalog File. Thomas Publishing Co., Inc. • Annual. $149.00. 34 volumes. A three-part system offering information on a wide variety of industrial equipment and supplies.

HANDBOOKS AND MANUALS

Corrosion Control. Samuel A. Bradford. Chapman and Hall. • 1992. $80.50. Discusses basic corrosion theory, corrosion causes, coatings, plastics, metals, and many other highly detailed, technical topics. (Chapman & Hall.).

Industrial Coatings: Properties, Applications, Quality, and Environmental Compliance. ASM International. • 1992. $90.00.

Maintenance Engineering Handbook. Lindley R. Higgins. McGraw-Hill. • 1994. $125.00. Fifth edition. Contains about 60 chapters by various authors in 12 major sections covering all elements of industrial and plant maintenance.

ONLINE DATABASES

Applied Science and Technology Index Online. H. W. Wilson Co. • Provides online indexing of 400 major scientific, technical, industrial, and engineering periodicals. Time period is 1983 to date. Monthly updates. Inquire as to online cost and availability.

PROMT: Predicasts Overview of Markets and Technology. The Gale Group. • Companies, products, applied technologies and markets. U.S. and international literature coverage, 1972 to date. Inquire as to online cost and availability. Provides abstracts from more than 1,600 publications. Weekly updates.

Thomas Register Online. Thomas Publishing Co., Inc. • Provides concise information on approximately 194,000 U. S. companies, mainly manufacturers, with over 50,000 product classifications. Indexes over 115,000 trade names. Information is updated semiannually. Inquire as to online cost and availability.

World Surface Coatings Abstracts [Online]. Paint Research Association of Great Britain. • Indexing and abstracting of the literature of paint and surface coatings, 1976 to present. Monthly updates. Inquire as to online cost and availability.

PERIODICALS AND NEWSLETTERS

Advanced Coatings and Surface Technology. Technical Insights. • Monthly. $650.00 per year. Newsletter on technical developments relating to industrial coatings.

Coatings. Roger Media Publishing Ltd., Magazine Div. • Bimonthly. $75.00 per year.

Corrosion: Journal of Science and Engineering. National Association of Corrosion Engineers. NACE International. • Monthly. Members, $95.00 per year; non-members, $160.00 per year. Covers corrosion control science, theory, engineering, and practice.

Industrial Equipment News. Thomas Publishing Co. • Monthly. $95.00 per year. Free. What's new in equipment, parts and materials.

Industrial Paint and Powder: Coatings Manufacturing and Application. Cahners Business Information. • Monthly. $72.90 per year. Supplement available, *Annual Buyer's Guide.* Formerly *Industrial Finishing.*

JCT:Journal of Coatings Technology. Federation of Societies for Coatings Technology. • Monthly. $120.00 per year.

Journal of Industrial Textiles. Technomic Publishing Co., Inc. • Quarterly. $370.00 per year for print or electronic edition; $425.00 per year for print and electronic editions. Formerly *Journal of Coated Fabrics.*

Materials Performance: Articles on Corrosion Science and Engineering Solutions for Corrosion Problems. National Association of Corrosion Engineers. NACE International. • Monthly. $100.00 per year. Covers the protection and performance of materials in corrosive environments. Includes information on new materials and industrial coatings.

Modern Paint and Coatings. Chemical Week Associates. • Monthly. $52.00 per year.

New Equipment Digest Market. Penton Media Inc. • Monthly. Free to qualified personnel; others, $55.00 per year. Formerly *Material Handling Engineering.*

New Equipment Reporter: New Products Industrial News. De Roche Publications. • Monthly. Controlled circulation.

Paint and Coatings Industry. Business News Publishing Co. • Monthly. $55.00 per year. Includes annual *Raw Material* and *Equipment Directory and Buyers Guide.*

RESEARCH CENTERS AND INSTITUTES

Emulsion Polymers Institute. Lehigh University, Iacocca Hall, 111 Research Dr., Bethlehem, PA 18015. Phone: (610)758-3590 Fax: (610)758-5880 E-mail: mse0@lehigh.edu • URL: http://www.lehigh.edu/~esd0/epihome.html • Includes latex paint research.

Fontana Corrosion Center. Ohio State University, 477 Watts, 2041 College Rd., Columbus, OH 43210. Phone: (614)688-4128 Fax: (614)292-9857 E-mail: frankel.10@osu.edu • URL: http://www.erbs1.eng.ohio-state.edu/~frankel • Research areas include metal coatings and corrosion of alloys.

International Coatings and Formulation Institute. University of Southern Mississippi, Dept. of Polymer Science, P.O. Box 10037, Hattiesburg, MS 39406-0037. Phone: (601)266-4080 Fax: (601)266-5880 E-mail: shelby.f.thames@usm.edu • URL: http://www.psrc.usm.edu/icfi.

STATISTICS SOURCES

Paint, Varnish, and Lacquer. U. S. Bureau of the Census. • Quarterly and annual. Provides data on shipments: value, quantity, imports, and exports. Includes paint, varnish, lacquer, product finishes, and special purpose coatings. (Current Industrial Reports, MQ-28F.).

U. S. Industry and Trade Outlook: The McGraw-Hill Companies and the U.S. Department of Commerce/ International Trade Administration. Datapso Research Corp. • Annual. $69.95. Produced by the International Trade Administration, U. S. Department of Commerce, in a "public-private" partnership with DRI/McGraw-Hill and Standard & Poor's. Provides basic data, outlook for the current year, and "Long-Term Prospects" (five-year projections) for a wide variety of products and services. Includes high technology industries. Formerly *U. S. Industrial Outlook.*

TRADE/PROFESSIONAL ASSOCIATIONS

American Electroplaters' and Surface Finishers Society. 12644 Research Parkway, Orlando, FL 32826-3298. Phone: (407)281-6441 Fax: (407)281-6446 E-mail: aesf@aesf.org • URL: http://www.aesf.org.

Association for Finishing Processes of the Society of Manufacturing Engineers. P.O. Box 930, Dearborn, MI 48121-0930. Phone: 800-733-4863 or (313)271-1500 Fax: (313)271-2861 • URL: http://www.sme.org • Sponsored by the Society of Manufacturing Engineers.

Association of Industrial Metallizers, Coaters and Laminators. 2166 Hill Rd, Fort Mill, SC 29715. Phone: (803)802-7820 Fax: (803)802-7821 E-mail: aimcal@aimcal.org • URL: http://www.aimcal.org.

Chemical Coaters Association International. P.O. Box 54316, Cincinnati, OH 45254. Phone: (513)624-6767 Fax: (513)624-0601 E-mail: aygoyer@one.net • URL: http://www.finishing.com/ccai • Members are industrial users of organic finishing systems.

Federation of Societies for Coatings Technology. 492 Norristown Rd., Blue Bell, PA 19422-2307.

Phone: (215)940-0777 Fax: (215)940-0292 E-mail: fsct@coatingstech.org • URL: http://ww.coatingstech.org.

NACE International: The Corrosion Society. P.O. Box 218340, Houston, TX 77218-8340. Phone: (281)228-6223 Fax: (281)228-6300 E-mail: msd@mail.nace.org • URL: http://www.nace.org • Members are engineers, scientists, and technicians concerned with corrosion control and prevention.

National Association of Metal Finishers. 112 J Elden St., Herndon, VA 20170. Phone: (703)709-8299 Fax: (703)709-1036 E-mail: namf@erols.com • URL: http://www.namf.org • Members are management personnel of metal and plastic finishing companies. Finishing includes plating, coating, polishing, rustproofing, and other processes.

National Paint and Coatings Association. 1500 Rhode Island Ave., N.W., Washington, DC 20005-5597. Phone: (202)462-6272 Fax: (202)462-8549 E-mail: npca@paint.org • URL: http://www.paint.org.

Powder Coating Institute. 2121 Eisenhower Ave., Suite 401, Alexandria, VA 22314. Phone: (703)684-1770 Fax: (703)684-1771 E-mail: pci-info@powdercoating.org • URL: http://www.powdercoating.org.

Society of Vacuum Coaters. 71 Pinon Hill Place N.E., Albuquerque, NM 87122-1914. Phone: (505)856-7188 Fax: (505)856-6716 E-mail: svcinfo@svc.org • URL: http://www.svc.org.

INDUSTRIAL CONTROLS

See: CONTROL EQUIPMENT INDUSTRY

INDUSTRIAL COUNSELING

See: PERSONNEL MANAGEMENT; VOCATIONAL GUIDANCE

INDUSTRIAL DESIGN

See: DESIGN IN INDUSTRY

INDUSTRIAL DEVELOPMENT

See also: DEVELOPING AREAS; ECONOMIC DEVELOPMENT; LOCATION OF INDUSTRY

DIRECTORIES

Site Selection. Conway Data, Inc. • Bimonthly. Six volumes, $20.00 per volume. $85.00 per set. Each of the six issues per year is a separate directory: *Geo-Corporate* (facility planners), *Geo-Economic* (area development officials), *Geo-Labor* (labor force data), *Geo-Life* (quality of life information), *GeoPolitical* (government agencies), and *Geo-Sites* (industrial/office parks). Formerly *Site Selection and Industrial Development.*

PERIODICALS AND NEWSLETTERS

American Economic Development Council News. American Economic Development Council. • Six times per year. Membership.

Area Development Sites and Facility Planning: The Executive Magazine of Sites and Facility Planning. S H Publications, Inc. • Monthly. $65.00 per year. Site selection, facility planning, and plant relocation. Formerly *Area Development Magazines.*

Economic Development Monitor. Whitaker Newsletters, Inc. • Biweekly. $247.00 per year. Newsletter. Covers the news of U. S. economic and industrial development, including legislation, regulation, planning, and financing.

Plants, Sites, and Parks. Cahners Business Information. • Bimonthly. $30.00 per year. Covers economic development, site location, industrial parks, and industrial development programs.

Sales Prospector. Prospector Research Services, Inc. • Monthly. $495.00 per year. In 14 United States regional editions. Reports on expansions and relocations of manufacturing firms, distribution centers, and transportation terminals in new existing buildings.

RESEARCH CENTERS AND INSTITUTES

Center for International Policy. 1755 Massachusetts Ave., N. W., Suite 312, Washington, DC 20036. Phone: (202)232-3317 Fax: (202)232-3440 E-mail: cip@ciponline.org • URL: http://www.ciponline.org • Research subjects include the International Monetary Fund, the World Bank, and other international financial institutions. Analyzes the impact of policies on social and economic conditions in developing countries.

Urban Land Institute. 1025 Thomas Jefferson Ave. N.W., Suite 500W, Washington, DC 20004. Phone: (202)624-7000 Fax: (202)624-7140 E-mail: rlevitt@uli.org • URL: http://www.uli.org • Studies urban land planning and the growth and development of urbanized areas, including central city problems, industrial development, community development, residential development, taxation, shopping centers, and the effects of development on the environment.

STATISTICS SOURCES

Handbook of International Economic Statistics. Available from National Technical Information Service. • Annual. $40.00. Prepared by U. S. Central Intelligence Agency. Provides basic statistics for comparing worldwide economic performance, with an emphasis on Europe, including Eastern Europe.

Industrial Commodity Statistics Yearbook. United Nations Dept. of Economic and Social Affairs. United Nations Publications. • Annual.

TRADE/PROFESSIONAL ASSOCIATIONS

American Economic Development Council. 1030 Higgins Rd., Suite 301, Park Ridge, IL 60668. Phone: (847)692-9944 Fax: (847)696-2990 E-mail: aedc@interaccess.com • URL: http://www.aedc.org.

International Development Research Council. 35 Technology Park/Atlanta, Suite 150, Norcross, GA 30092. Phone: (770)446-8955 Fax: (770)263-8825.

National Association of Industrial and Office Properties. 2201 Cooperative Way, Herndon, VA 20171. Phone: 800-666-6780 or (703)904-7100 Fax: (703)904-7942 E-mail: naiop@naiop.org • URL: http://www.naiop.org • Members are owners and developers of business, industrial, office, and retail properties.

INDUSTRIAL DIAMONDS

ABSTRACTS AND INDEXES

Industrial Diamond Review. De Beers Industrial Diamond Div. • Bimonthly. Free to qualified personnel. Incorporating *Industrial Diamond Abstracts.*

STATISTICS SOURCES

Mineral Commodity Summaries. Available from U. S. Government Printing Office. • Annual. Published by the U. S. Geological Survey, Department of the Interior (http://www.usgs.gov). Contains detailed, five-year data for about 90 nonfuel minerals. Covers a wide range of statistics, including production, imports, exports, consumption, reserves, prices, tariff information, and industry employment. (Two pages are devoted to each mineral.).

TRADE/PROFESSIONAL ASSOCIATIONS

Industrial Diamond Association. P.O. Box 1070, Skyland, NC 28776. Phone: (704)684-1986 or (704)684-1988 Fax: (704)684-7372 E-mail: gray@juno.com • URL: http://www.superabrasives.org.

INDUSTRIAL DIRECTORIES

See: CATALOGS AND DIRECTORIES

INDUSTRIAL DISPUTES

See: ARBITRATION; STRIKES AND LOCKOUTS

INDUSTRIAL DISTRIBUTION

See: DISTRIBUTION

INDUSTRIAL EFFICIENCY

See: TIME AND MOTION STUDY

INDUSTRIAL ENGINEERING

See also: INDUSTRIAL MANAGEMENT

GENERAL WORKS

Lessons to be Learned Just in Time. James J. Cammarano. Engineering and Management Press. • 1997. $34.95. Discusses the background, theory, and practical application of just-in-time (JIT) inventory control in manufacturing.

ABSTRACTS AND INDEXES

Applied Science and Technology Index. H. W. Wilson Co. • 11 times a year. Quarterly and annual cumulations. Service basis for print edition; CD-ROM edition, $1,495.00 per year. Indexes a wide variety of English language technical, industrial, and engineering periodicals.

Business Periodicals Index. H. W. Wilson Co. • Monthly, except August, with quarterly and annual cumulations. Service basis for print edition; CD-ROM edition, $1,495.00 per year.

Engineering Index Monthly: Abstracting and Indexing Services Covering Sources of the World's Engineering Literature. Engineering Information, Inc. • Monthly. $2,300.00 per year. Provides indexing and abstracting of the world's engineering and technical literature.

BIBLIOGRAPHIES

Encyclopedia of Physical Science and Engineering Information. The Gale Group. • 1996. $160.00. Second edition. Includes print, electronic, and other information sources for a wide range of scientific, technical, and engineering topics.

CD-ROM DATABASES

COMPENDEX PLUS [CD-ROM]. Engineering Information, Inc. • Quarterly. $3,450.00 per year. Provides CD-ROM indexing and abstracting of the world's engineering and technical information appearing in journals, reports, books, and proceedings, 1985 to date.

WILSONDISC: Applied Science and Technology Abstracts. H. W. Wilson Co. • Monthly. $1,495.00 per year, including unlimited access to the online version of *Applied Science and Technology Abstracts* through WILSONLINE. Provides CD-ROM indexing and abstracting of 400 prominent scientific, technical, engineering, and industrial periodicals. Indexing coverage is provided from 1983 to date and abstracting from 1993 to date.

WILSONDISC: Business Periodicals Index. H. W. Wilson Co. • Monthly. $1,495.00 per year. Provides CD-ROM indexing of business periodicals from 1982 to date. Price includes online service.

DIRECTORIES

NAEDA Equipment Dealer Buyer's Guide. North American Equipment Dealers Association. • Annual. $28.00. List of manufacturers and suppliers of agricultural, lawn and garden, and light industrial machinery.

ENCYCLOPEDIAS AND DICTIONARIES

Blackwell Encyclopedic Dictionary of Operations Management. Nigel Slack, editor. Blackwell Publishers. • 1997. $105.95. The editor is associated with the University of Warwick, England. Contains definitions of key terms combined with longer articles written by various U. S. and foreign business educators. Includes bibliographies and index. (Blackwell Encyclopedia of Management Series.).

Industrial Engineering Terminology. Institute of Industrial Engineering Staff. McGraw-Hill. • 1992. $80.95. Revised edition.

HANDBOOKS AND MANUALS

Handbook of Industrial Engineering. Gavriel Salvendy, editor. John Wiley and Sons, Inc. • 2000. $175.00. Third edition.

Maynard's Industrial Engineering Handbook. Kjell B. Zandin. McGraw-Hill. • 2000. $150.00. Fifth edition.

Standard Handbook of Plant Engineering. Robert C. Rosaler. McGraw-Hill. • 1991. $125.00. Second edition.

Systems Engineering: Concepts and Applications. Andrew P. Sage. John Wiley and Sons, Inc. • 1992. $84.95. Discusses practical engineering techniques for use in given situations. (Systems Engineering Series).

ONLINE DATABASES

Applied Science and Technology Index Online. H. W. Wilson Co. • Provides online indexing of 400 major scientific, technical, industrial, and engineering periodicals. Time period is 1983 to date. Monthly updates. Inquire as to online cost and availability.

COMPENDEX PLUS. Engineering Information, Inc. • Provides online indexing and abstracting of the world's engineering and technical information appearing in journals, reports, books, and proceedings. Time period is 1970 to date, with weekly updates. Inquire as to online cost and availability.

Wilson Business Abstracts Online. H. W. Wilson Co. • Indexes and abstracts 600 major business periodicals, plus the *Wall Street Journal* and the business section of the *New York Times*. Indexing is from 1982, abstracting from 1990, with the two newspapers included from 1993. Updated weekly. Inquire as to online cost and availability. (*Business Periodicals Index* without abstracts is also available online.).

PERIODICALS AND NEWSLETTERS

Computers and Industrial Engineering: An International Journal. Elsevier Science. • Eight times a year. $2,113.00 per year.

IEE Solutions. Institute of Industrial Engineers. • Monthly. Free to members; non-members, $49.00 per year. Features articles on material handling, computers, quality control, production and inventory control, engineering economics, worker motivation, management strategies, and factory automation. Formerly *Industrial Engineers*.

Manufacturing Computer Solutions: The Management Magazine of Integrated Manufacturing. Findlay Publications Ltd. • Monthly. Formed by the merger of *Engineering Computers* and *Manufacturing Systems*.

NAEDA Equipment Dealer. North American Equipment Dealers Association. • Monthly. $40.00 per year. Covers power equipment for farm, outdoor, and industrial use. Formerly *Farm and Power Equipment Dealer*.

Production. Gardner Publications, Inc. • Monthly. $48.00 per year. Covers the latest manufacturing management issues. Discusses the strategic and financial implications of various tecnologies as they impact factory management, quality and competitiveness.

RESEARCH CENTERS AND INSTITUTES

Center for Quality and Productivity Improvement. University of Wisconsin-Madison, 610 N. Walnut St., 575 WARF Bldg., Madison, WI 53705. Phone: (608)263-2520 Fax: (608)263-1425 E-mail: quality@engr.wisc.edu • URL: http://www.engr.wisc.edu/centers/cqpi • Research areas include quality management and industrial engineering.

Engineering and Industrial Experiment Station, Department of Materials Science and Engineering. University of Florida, Gainesville, FL 32611-6400. Phone: (352)846-3301 Fax: (352)392-7219 E-mail: rabba@mse.ufl.edu • URL: http://www.mse.ufl.edu • Research fields include chemical, civil, electrical, industrial, mechanical, and other types of engineering.

Engineering Dean's Office. University of California at Berkeley, 308 Mclaughin Hall, No. 1702, Berkeley, CA 94720-1706. Phone: (510)642-7594 Fax: (510)643-8653 E-mail: dma@coe.berkeley.edu • Research fields include civil, electrical, industrial, mechanical, and other types of engineering.

Engineering Experiment Station. Purdue University, West Lafayette, IN 47907. Phone: (317)494-5340 Fax: (317)494-9321 E-mail: stevens@ecn.purdue.edu • URL: http://www.ecn.purdue.edu • Research fields include chemical, civil, electrical, industrial, mechanical, and other types of engineering.

STATISTICS SOURCES

United States Census of Service Industries. U.S. Bureau of the Census. • Quinquennial. Various reports available.

TRADE/PROFESSIONAL ASSOCIATIONS

Institute of Industrial Engineers. 25 Technology Park, Norcross, GA 30092. Phone: 800-494-0460 or (770)449-0460 Fax: (770)441-3295 • URL: http://www.iienet.org.

SAVE International. 60 Revere Dr., Suite 500, Northbrook, IL 60062. Phone: (847)480-1730 Fax: (847)480-9282 E-mail: value@value-eng.com • Members are value engineers and value analysts. Purpose is to achieve the necessary function of a product or service at the lowest cost, consistent with quality requirements.

SOLE-The International Society of Logistics. 8100 Professional Place, Suite 211, Hyattsville, MD 20785. Phone: (301)459-8446 Fax: (301)459-1522 • Concerned with designing, supplying, and maintaining resources to support objectives, plans, and operations.

INDUSTRIAL EQUIPMENT INDUSTRY

DIRECTORIES

My Little Salesman Heavy Equipment Catalog; New and Used Equipment Guide. MSL, Inc. • Monthly. $18.00 per year.

Thomas Register of American Manufacturers and Thomas Register Catalog File. Thomas Publishing Co., Inc. • Annual. $149.00. 34 volumes. A three-part system offering information on a wide variety of industrial equipment and supplies.

FINANCIAL RATIOS

Cost of Doing Business: Farm and Power Equipment Dealers, Industrial Dealers, and Outdoor Power Equipment Dealers. North American Equipment Dealers Association. • Annual. $50.00. Provides data on sales, profit margins, expenses, assets, and employee productivity.

ONLINE DATABASES

PROMT: Predicasts Overview of Markets and Technology. The Gale Group. • Companies, products, applied technologies and markets. U.S. and international literature coverage, 1972 to date. Inquire as to online cost and availability. Provides abstracts from more than 1,600 publications. Weekly updates.

Thomas Register Online. Thomas Publishing Co., Inc. • Provides concise information on approximately 194,000 U. S. companies, mainly manufacturers, with over 50,000 product classifications. Indexes over 115,000 trade names. Information is updated semiannually. Inquire as to online cost and availability.

PERIODICALS AND NEWSLETTERS

IEEE Industry Applications Magazine. Institute of Electrical and Electronics Engineers. • Bimonthly. $190.00 per year. Covers new industrial applications of power conversion, drives, lighting, and control. Emphasis is on the petroleum, chemical, rubber, plastics, textile, and mining industries.

Industrial Distribution: For Industrial Distributors and Their Sales Personnel. Cahners Business Information. • Monthly. $97.90 per year.

Industrial Equipment News. Thomas Publishing Co. • Monthly. $95.00 per year. Free. What's new in equipment, parts and materials.

New Equipment Digest Market. Penton Media Inc. • Monthly. Free to qualified personnel; others, $55.00 per year. Formerly *Material Handling Engineering*.

STATISTICS SOURCES

U. S. Industry and Trade Outlook: The McGraw-Hill Companies and the U.S. Department of Commerce/ International Trade Administration. Datapso Research Corp. • Annual. $69.95. Produced by the International Trade Administration, U. S. Department of Commerce, in a "public-private" partnership with DRI/McGraw-Hill and Standard & Poor's. Provides basic data, outlook for the current year, and "Long-Term Prospects" (five-year projections) for a wide variety of products and services. Includes high technology industries. Formerly *U. S. Industrial Outlook*.

TRADE/PROFESSIONAL ASSOCIATIONS

American Supply and Machinery Manufacturers Association. 1300 Sumner Ave., Cleveland, OH 44115-2851. Phone: (216)241-7333 Fax: (216)241-0105 E-mail: asmma@taol.com • URL: http://www.asmma.com.

Industrial Distribution Association. 1277 Lenox Park Blvd., Ste. 275, Atlanta, GA 30319. Phone: (404)261-3991 Fax: (404)266-8311 E-mail: idainc@pop.mindspring.com • URL: http://www.ida-assoc.org.

OTHER SOURCES

Industrial Pumps and Pumping Equipment. Available from MarketResearch.com. • 1997. $1,195.00. Market research report published by Specialists in Business Information. Covers centrifugal, rotary, turbine, reciprocating, and other types of pumps. Presents market data relative to sales growth, shipments, exports, imports, and end-use. Includes company profiles.

INDUSTRIAL EQUIPMENT LEASING

See: RENTAL SERVICES

INDUSTRIAL FABRICS INDUSTRY

See also: NONWOVEN FABRICS INDUSTRY

ABSTRACTS AND INDEXES

Applied Science and Technology Index. H. W. Wilson Co. • 11 times a year. Quarterly and annual cumulations. Service basis for print edition; CD-ROM edition, $1,495.00 per year. Indexes a wide variety of English language technical, industrial, and engineering periodicals.

Textile Technology Digest. Institute of Textile Technology. • Monthly. $535.00 per year. Provides indexing and abstracting of a wide variety of textile technology literature.

CD-ROM DATABASES

Textile Technology Digest [CD-ROM]. Textile Information Center, Institute of Textile Technology. • Quarterly. $1,700.00 per year. Provides CD-ROM indexing and abstracting of worldwide journals and monographs in various areas of textile technology, production, and management. Covers 1978 to date.

DIRECTORIES

Davison's Textile Blue Book. Davison Publishing Co. • Annual. $165.00. Over 8,400 companies in the textle industry in the United States, Canada, and Mexico, including about 4,400 textile plants.

Industrial Fabric Products Review Buyer's Guide: The Encyclopedia of Industrial Fabrics. Industrial Fabrics Association International. • Annual. $20.00. Includes manufacturers of fabrics, fibers, and end products. Included with subscriptions to *Industrial Fabric Products Review.*

Industrial Fabrics Association International Membership Directory. Industrial Fabrics Association International. • Annual. Free to members; non-members, $40.00.

ENCYCLOPEDIAS AND DICTIONARIES

Encyclopedia of Textiles. French and European Publications, Inc. • 1980. $39.95. Third edition.

Textile Terms and Definitions. J.E. McIntyre and Paul N. Daniels, editors. Available from State Mutual Book and Periodical Service Ltd., Trade Order Dept. • 1995. $110.00. 10th edition. Published by the Textile Insitute (UK). Includes more than 1,000 definitions of textile processes, fiber types, and end products. Illustrated.

FINANCIAL RATIOS

Industry Norms and Key Business Ratios. Desk Top Edition. Dun and Bradstreet Corp., Business Information Services. • Annual. Five volumes. $475.00 per volume. $1,890.00 per set. Covers over 800 kinds of businesses, arranged by Standard Industrial Classification number. More detailed editions covering longer periods of time are also available.

ONLINE DATABASES

Applied Science and Technology Index Online. H. W. Wilson Co. • Provides online indexing of 400 major scientific, technical, industrial, and engineering periodicals. Time period is 1983 to date. Monthly updates. Inquire as to online cost and availability.

Textile Technology Digest [online]. Textile Information Center, Institute of Textile Technology. • Contains indexing and abstracting of more than 300 worldwide journals and monographs in various areas of textile technology, production, and management. Time period is 1978 to date, with monthly updating. Inquire as to online cost and availability.

World Textiles. Elsevier Science, Inc. • Provides abstracting and indexing from 1970 of worldwide textile literature (periodicals, books, pamphlets, and reports). Includes U. S., European, and British patent information. Updating is monthly. Inquire as to online cost and availability.

PERIODICALS AND NEWSLETTERS

Industrial Fabric Products Review. Industrial Fabrics Association International. • Monthly. $47.00 per year. Includes *Buyers Guide.*

International Textile Bulletin: Nonwovens and Industrial Textiles Edition. ITS Publishing, International Textile Service. • Quarterly. $170.00 per year. Editions in Chinese, English, French, German, Italian and Spanish.

Journal of Industrial Textiles. Technomic Publishing Co., Inc. • Quarterly. $370.00 per year for print or electronic edition; $425.00 per year for print and electronic editions. Formerly *Journal of Coated Fabrics.*

RESEARCH CENTERS AND INSTITUTES

Fibrous Materials Research Center. Drexel University, Dept. of Materials Engineering, 3141 Chestnut St., Philadelphia, PA 19104. Phone: (215)895-1640 Fax: (215)895-6684 E-mail: fko@drexel.edul.edu • URL: http://www.fmac/coe.drexel.edu • Research fields include computer-aided design of nonwoven fabrics and design curves for industrial fibers.

Institute of Textile Technology. 2551 Ivy Rd., Charlottesville, VA 22903-4614. Phone: (804)296-5511 Fax: (804)296-2957 E-mail: library@itt.edu • URL: http://www.itt.edu.

International Textile Center. Texas Tech University. P.O. Box 45019, Lubbock, TX 79409-5019. Phone: (806)747-3790 Fax: (806)747-3796 E-mail: itc@ttu.edu • URL: http://www.itc.ttu.edu.

Textiles and Materials. Philadelphia University, Schoolhouse Lane and Henry Ave., Philadelphia, PA 19144. Phone: (215)951-2751 Fax: (215)951-2651 E-mail: brooksteind@philaau.edu • URL: http://www.philaau.edu • Many research areas, including industrial and nonwoven textiles.

TRI/Princeton. P.O. Box 625, Princeton, NJ 08542. Phone: (609)924-3150 Fax: (609)683-7149 E-mail: info@triprinceton.org • URL: http://www.triprinceton.org.

STATISTICS SOURCES

Broadwoven Fabrics (Gray). U.S. Bureau of the Census. • Quarterly. Provides statistical data on production, value, shipments, and consumption. Includes woolen and worsted fabrics, tire fabrics, cotton broadwoven fabrics, etc. (Current Industrial Reports, MQ-22T.).

TRADE/PROFESSIONAL ASSOCIATIONS

Industrial Fabrics Association International. 1801 Country Rd B W., Roseville, MN 55113-4061. Phone: 800-225-4324 or (651)222-2508 Fax: (651)631-9334 E-mail: generalinfo@ifai.com • URL: http://www.ifai.com • Members include nonwoven industrial fabric producers.

Textile Institute. Saint James Bldgs., 4th Fl., Oxford St., Manchester M1 6FQ, England. Phone: 44 161 2371188 Fax: 44 161 2361991 E-mail: tiihq@textileinst.org.uk • URL: http://www.texi.org • Members in 100 countries involved with textile industry management, marketing, science, and technology.

OTHER SOURCES

Textile Business Outlook. Statistikon Corp. • Quarterly. $985.00 per year. Analyzes current business, marketing, and financial conditions for the worldwide textile industry (fibers and fabrics). Includes statistical forecasts.

INDUSTRIAL FASTENERS

See: FASTENER INDUSTRY

INDUSTRIAL HYGIENE

See also: INDUSTRIAL MEDICINE; INDUSTRIAL SAFETY

GENERAL WORKS

Industrial Safety and Health Management. C. Ray Asfahl. Prentice Hall. • 1998. $92.00. Fourth edition.

Principles of Health and Hygiene in the Workplace. Timothy J. Key and Michael A. Mueller. Lewis Publishers. • Date not set. $69.95.

Understanding Toxicology: Chemicals, Their Benefits and Uses. H. Bruno Schiefer and others. CRC Press, Inc. • 1997. $34.95. Provides a basic introduction to chemical interactions and toxicology for the general reader.

ABSTRACTS AND INDEXES

Safety and Health at Work. International Labour Office. • Bimonthly. $240.00 per year. Formerly *Occupational Safety and Health Abstracts.*

CD-ROM DATABASES

Health Reference Center. The Gale Group. • Monthly. Provides CD-ROM citations, abstracts, and selected full-text articles on many health-related subjects. Includes references to medical journals, general periodicals, newsletters, newspapers, pamphlets, and medical reference books.

Occupational Safety and Health Administration (OSHA): Regulations, Documents, and Technical Information. Available from U. S. Government Printing Office. • Quarterly. $46.00 per year. CD-ROM contains all OSHA regulations and standards currently in force, with selected documents and technical information.

DIRECTORIES

Industrial Hygiene News Buyer's Guide. Rimbach Publishing, Inc. • Annual. $50.00. Lists about 1,000 manufacturers and suppliers of products, equipment, and services to the occupational health, industrial hygiene, and high-tech safety industry.

ENCYCLOPEDIAS AND DICTIONARIES

Encyclopedia of Occupational Health and Safety. Available from The Gale Group. • 1999. $495.00. Fourth edition. Four volumes. Published by the International Labor Office (http://www.ilo.org). Covers safety engineering, industrial medicine, ergonomics, hygiene, epidemiology, toxicology, industrial psychology, and related topics. Includes material related to specific chemical, textile, transport, construction, manufacturing, and other industries. Indexed by subject, chemical name, and author, with a "Directory of Experts.".

Encyclopedia of Occupational Health and Safety 1983. International Labour Office. • 1991. $270.00. Third revised edition. Two volumes.

Unabridged Dictionary of Occupational and Environmental Safety and Health with CD-ROM. Jeffrey W. Vincoli and Kathryn L. Bazan. Lewis Publishers. • 1999. $89.95.

HANDBOOKS AND MANUALS

Handbook of Industrial Toxicology. E. R. Plunkett, editor. Chemical Publishing Co., Inc. • 1987. $100.00.

Handbook of Toxic and Hazardous Chemicals and Carcinogens. Marshall Sittig. Noyes Data Corp,. • 1992. $249.00. Third edition. Two volumes.

Hazardous and Toxic Materials: Safe Handling and Disposal. Howard H. Fawcett, editor. John Wiley and Sons, Inc. • 1988. $139.00. Second edition.

Patty's Industrial Hygiene and Toxicology. George D. Clayton and Florence E. Clayton, editors. John Wiley and Sons, Inc. • 2000. $2,195.00. Three volumes in 10 parts. Provides broad coverage of environmental factors and stresses affecting the health of workers. Contains detailed information on the effects of specific substances.

INTERNET DATABASES

National Center for Health Statistics: Monitoring the Nation's Health. National Center for Health Statistics, Centers for Disease Control and Preventio. Phone: (301)458-4636 E-mail: nchsquery@cdc.gov • URL: http://www.cdc.gov/nchswww • Web site provides detailed data on diseases, vital statistics, and health care in the U. S. Includes a search facility and links to many other health-related Web sites. "Fastats A to Z" offers quick data on hundreds of topics from Accidents to Work-Loss Days, with links to Comprehensive Data and related sources. Frequent updates. Fees: Free.

ONLINE DATABASES

Embase. Elsevier Science, Inc. • Worldwide medical literature, 1974 to present. Weekly updates. Inquire as to online cost and availability.

Toxline. National Library of Medicine. • Abstracting service covering human and animal toxicity studies, 1965 to present (older studies available in *Toxback* file). Monthly updates. Inquire as to online cost and availability.

PERIODICALS AND NEWSLETTERS

American Industrial Hygiene Association Journal: A Publication for the Science of Occupational and Environmental Health. American Industrial Hygiene Association. • Monthly. Institutions, $160.00 per year.

Archives of Environmental Health. Helen Dwight Reid Educational Foundation. Heldref Publications. • Bimonthly. $137.00 per year. Objective documentation of the effects of environmental agents on human health.

BNA's Safetynet. Bureau of National Affairs, Inc. • Biweekly. $680.00 per year. Looseleaf. Formerly *Job Safety and Health.*

Environmental Toxicology: An International Journal. John Wiley and Sons, Inc. Journals Div. • Five times a year. Institutions, $545.00 per year. Formerly *Environmental Toxicology and Water Quality.*

Industrial Hygiene News. Rimbach Publishing, Inc. • Seven times a year. Free to qualified personnel.

Management OHS and E. Stevens Publishing Corp. • Monthly. Free to qualified personnel; others, $150.00 per year. Includes news, interviews, feature articles, legal developments, and reviews of literature. Includes *Buyer's Guide.*

Occupational Health and Safety Letter...Towards Productivity and Peace of Mind. Business Publishers, Inc. • Biweekly. $317.00 per year.

RESEARCH CENTERS AND INSTITUTES

Michigan Institute for Environmental and Health Sciences. School of Public Health, University of Michigan, 1420 Washington Heights, Ann Arbor, MI 48109-2029. Phone: (734)764-3188 Fax: (734)936-7283 E-mail: jhv@umich.edu.

TRADE/PROFESSIONAL ASSOCIATIONS

American Industrial Health Council. 2001 Pennsylvania Ave., N.W., Suite 760, Washington, DC 20006. Phone: (202)833-2131 Fax: (202)833-2201 E-mail: membershipservices@ainc.org • URL: http://www.aihc.org.

American Industrial Hygiene Association. 2700 Prosperity Ave., Suite 250, Fairfax, VA 22031. Phone: (703)849-8888 Fax: (703)207-3561 E-mail: infonet@aiha.org • URL: http://www.aiha.org.

INDUSTRIAL JOURNALISM

See: BUSINESS JOURNALISM

INDUSTRIAL LOCATION

See: LOCATION OF INDUSTRY

INDUSTRIAL MANAGEMENT

See also: ADMINISTRATION; FACTORY MANAGEMENT; INDUSTRIAL ENGINEERING; PROJECT MANAGEMENT; RECORDS MANAGEMENT; SALES MANAGEMENT; SYSTEMS IN MANAGEMENT; TRAFFIC MANAGEMENT (INDUSTRIAL)

GENERAL WORKS

Chaos on the Shop Floor: A Worker's View of Quality, Productivity, and Management. Tom Juravich. Temple University Press. • 1988. $19.95. (Labor and Social Change Series).

Contemporary Supervision: Managing People and Technology. Betty R. Ricks. McGraw-Hill. • 1994. $68.75.

Fundamentals of Management. James H. Donnelly. McGraw-Hill. • 1997. 10th edition. Price on application.

Management: Concepts, Practice, and Skills. Premeaux Mondy. South-Western College Publishing. • 1999. $39.95. Eighth edition. (SWC-General Business Series).

Management: Skills and Application. Leslie W. Rue and Lloyd L. Byars. McGraw-Hill. • 1999. $59.65. Ninth edition. An introductory text covering the principles of successful management. Arranged according to the following "Skills:" Planning, Organizing, Staffing, Directing, and Controlling. Includes a glossary of key terms and three indexes. (Irwin Professional Publishing.).

Managing the Small to Mid-Sized Company: Concepts and Cases. James C. Collins and William C. Lazier. McGraw-Hill Higher Education. • 1994. $68.95.

Psychology for Leaders: Using Motivation, Conflict, and Power to Manage More Effectively. Dean Tjosvold and Mary Tjosvold. John Wiley and Sons, Inc. • 1995. $32.95. (Portable MBS Series).

Reengineering Management: The Mandate for New Leadership. James Champy. DIANE Publishing Co. • 1998. $25.00.

Reengineering the Corporation: A Manifesto for Business Revolution. Michael Hammer and James Champy. HarperCollins Publishers, Inc. • 1999. $16.00. Revised edition.

ABSTRACTS AND INDEXES

Business Periodicals Index. H. W. Wilson Co. • Monthly, except August, with quarterly and annual cumulations. Service basis for print edition; CD-ROM edition, $1,495.00 per year.

BIBLIOGRAPHIES

Business Information Sources. Lorna M. Daniells. California Princeton Fulfillment Services. • 1993. $42.50. Third revised edition. Basic business sources, with discussion and full annotations.

CD-ROM DATABASES

Business Source Plus. EBSCO Information Services. • Monthly. $1,495.00 per year. Provides CD-ROM citations and abstracts to articles in about 650 business periodicals and newspapers, including *The Wall Street Journal.* Full text is provided from 200 selected periodicals. Covers accounting, communications, economics, finance, management, marketing, and other business subjects.

WILSONDISC: Wilson Business Abstracts. H. W. Wilson Co. • Monthly. $2,495.00 per year, including unlimited online access to *Wilson Business Abstracts* through WILSONLINE. Provides CD-ROM "cover-to-cover" abstracting and indexing of over 600 prominent business periodicals. Indexing is from 1982, abstracting from 1990. (*Business Periodicals Index* without abstracts is available on CD-ROM at $1,495 per year.).

DIRECTORIES

Reference Book of Corporate Managements. Dun and Bradstreet Information Services. • Annual. Libraries, $650.00 per year; others, $795.00 per year. Lease basis. Management executives at over 12,000 leading United States companies.

ENCYCLOPEDIAS AND DICTIONARIES

Blackwell Encyclopedic Dictionary of Operations Management. Nigel Slack, editor. Blackwell Publishers. • 1997. $105.95. The editor is associated with the University of Warwick, England. Contains definitions of key terms combined with longer articles written by various U. S. and foreign business educators. Includes bibliographies and index. (Blackwell Encyclopedia of Management Series.).

Dictionary of Business and Management. Jerry M. Rosenberg. John Wiley and Sons, Inc. • 1992. $14.95. Third edition. (Business Dictionary Series).

Every Manager's Guide to Business Processes: A Glossary of Key Terms and Concepts for Today's Business Leader. Peter G. W. Keen. Harvard Business School Press. • 1995. $14.95. Provides definitions of contemporary business terms, such as "outsourcing," "benchmarking," and "groupware.".

Field Guide to Business Terms: A Glossary of Essential Tools and Concepts for Today's Manager. Alistair D. Williamson, editor. Harvard Business School Press. • 1993. $16.95. Defines fundamental terms. (Harvard Business Economist Reference Series).

International Encyclopedia of Business and Management. Malcolm Warner, editor. Routledge, Inc. • 1996. $1,319.95. Six volumes. Contains more than 500 articles on global management issues. Includes extensive bibliographies, cross references, and an index of key words and phrases.

HANDBOOKS AND MANUALS

AMA Management Handbook. John J. Hampton, editor. AMACOM. • 1994. $110.00. Third edition. Provides 200 chapters in 16 major subject areas. Covers a wide variety of business and industrial management topics.

Creating a Flexible Workplace: How to Select and Manage Alternative Work Options. Barry Olmsted and Suzanne Smith. AMACOM. • 1994. $59.95. Covers ten work options, such as flextime, job sharing, and permanent part-time employment.

Effective Supervisor's Handbook. Louis V. Imundo. AMACOM. • 1992. $16.95. Second edition.

How To Be a Manager: A Practical Guide to Tips and Techniques. Robert W. Gallant. Lewis Publishers. • 1991. $49.95. A concise handbook of principles, techniques, and methods of problem solving. Covers negotiation, discipline, management ethics, training, and other subjects.

Management: Skills and Application. Leslie W. Rue. McGraw-Hill Higher Education. • 1996. $39.95. Eighth edition.

Manager's Tool Kit: Practical Tips for Tackling 100 On-the-Job Problems. Cy Charney. AMACOM. • 1995. $17.95.

Managing More Effectively: A Professional Approach to Get the Best Out of People. Madhurendra K. Varma. Sage Publications, Inc. • 1997. $28.00. Focuses on the daily and practical application of management principles.

Organization Charts: Structures of More Than 200 Businesses and Non-Profit Organizations. The Gale Group. • 1999. $165.00. Third edition. Includes an introductory discussion of the history and use of such charts.

Production and Operations Management: An Applied Modern Approach. Joseph S. Martinich. John Wiley and Sons, Inc. • 1996. $105.95. Covers capacity planning, facility location, process design, inventory planning, personnel scheduling, etc.

Reengineering Revolution: A Handbook. Michael Hammer and Steven Stanton. HarperInformation. • 1995. $16.00.

Teambuilding and Total Quality: A Guidebook to TQM Success. Gene Milas. Engineering and Management Press. • 1997. $29.95. A practical, how-to-do-it guide to total quality management in industry. The importance of employee involvement is stressed.

Work Simplification: An Analyst's Handbook. Pierre Theriault. Engineering and Management Press. • 1996. $25.00. A basic guide to work simplification as an industrial management technique.

ONLINE DATABASES

Business and Management Practices. Responsive Database Services, Inc. • Provides fulltext of management articles appearing in more than 350 relevant publications. Emphasis is on "the processes, methods, and strategies of managing a business." Time span is 1995 to date. Inquire as to online cost and availability. (Also available in a CD-ROM version.).

Management Contents. The Gale Group. • Covers a wide range of management, financial, marketing, personnel, and administrative topics. About 150 leading business journals are indexed and abstracted from 1974 to date, with monthly updating. Inquire as to online cost and availability.

Wilson Business Abstracts Online. H. W. Wilson Co. • Indexes and abstracts 600 major business periodicals, plus the *Wall Street Journal* and the business section of the *New York Times*. Indexing is from 1982, abstracting from 1990, with the two newspapers included from 1993. Updated weekly. Inquire as to online cost and availability. (*Business Periodicals Index* without abstracts is also available online.).

PERIODICALS AND NEWSLETTERS

Executive Excellence: The Newsletter of Personal Development Managerial Effectiveness, and Organizational Productivity. Kenneth M. Shelton, editor. Executive Excellence Publishing. • Monthly. $129.00 per year. Newsletter.

Human Factors and Ergonomics in Manufacturing. Available from John Wiley and Sons, Inc., Journals Div. • Quarterly. Institutions, $545.00 per year. Published in England by John Wiley and Sons Ltd. Formerly *International Journal of Human Factors in Manufacturing.*

IEE Solutions. Institute of Industrial Engineers. • Monthly. Free to members; non-members, $49.00 per year. Features articles on material handling, computers, quality control, production and inventory control, engineering economics, worker motivation, management strategies, and factory automation. Formerly *Industrial Engineers.*

Industry Week: The Industry Management Magazine. Penton Media, Inc. • 18 times a year. Free to qualified personnel; others, $65.00 per year. Edited for industrial and business managers. Covers organizational and technological developments affecting industrial management.

Journal of Economics and Management Strategy. MIT Press. • Quarterly. Individuals, $45.00 per year; institutions, $135.00 per year. Covers "theoretical and empirical industrial organization, applied game theory, and management strategy.".

Management Update. Harvard Business School Publishing. • Monthly. $99.00 per year. Newsletter. Covers "ideas, trends, and solutions" for middle management.

Manager's Intelligence Report: Insider's Fast Track to Better Management. Lawence Ragan Communications, Inc. • Monthly. $129.00 per year. Newsletter on various aspects of management, including strategy, employee morale, and time management.

People at Work. Professional Training Associates, Inc. • Monthly. $89.00 per year. Newsletter on common personnel problems of supervisors and office managers. Formerly *Practical Supervision.*

Production and Operations Management. Production and Operations Management Society. • Quarterly. Individuals, $60.00 per year; institutions, $90.00 per year.

The Professional Manager. Institute of Industrial Engineers. • Bimonthly. Free to members; non-members, $40.00 per year. Features articles on the latest problem-solving techniques and trends available to industrial managers. Formerly *Industrial Management.*

Sloan Management Review. Sloan Management Review Association. Massachusetts Institute of Technology, Sloan School of Management. • Quarterly. $89.00 per year.

RESEARCH CENTERS AND INSTITUTES

Board of Research. Babson College, Babson Park, MA 02457. Phone: (718)239-5339 Fax: (718)239-6416 • URL: http://www.babson.edu/bor • Research areas include management, entrepreneurial characteristics, and multi-product inventory analysis.

Research-Technology Management. Industrial Research Institute, Inc. 1550 M St., N. W., Suite 1100, Washington, DC 20005-1712. Phone: (202)296-8811 Fax: (202)776-0756 • URL: http://www.iriinc.org • Bimonthly. $150.00 per year. Covers both theoretical and practical aspects of the management of industrial research and development.

TRADE/PROFESSIONAL ASSOCIATIONS

American Association of Industrial Management. Stearns Bldg., Ste. 506, 293 Bridge St., Springfield, MA 01103. Phone: 888-698-1968 or (413)737-9725 or (413)737-8766 Fax: (413)737-9724 E-mail: aaimnmta@aol.com • URL: http://www.americanassocofindmgmt.com.

American Management Association. 1601 Broadway, New York, NY 10019-7420. Phone: 800-262-9699 or (212)586-8100 Fax: (212)903-8168 • URL: http://www.amanet.org.

Institute of Industrial Engineers. 25 Technology Park, Norcross, GA 30092. Phone: 800-494-0460 or (770)449-0460 Fax: (770)441-3295 • URL: http://www.iienet.org.

International Management Council of the YMCA. 430 S. 20th St., Suite 3, Omaha, NE 68102-2506. Phone: 800-688-9622 or (402)345-1904 Fax: (402)345-4480 E-mail: imcoffice@msn.com • URL: http://www.imc-ymca.org.

National Management Association. 2210 Arbor Blvd., Dayton, OH 45439. Phone: (937)294-0421 Fax: (937)294-2374.

Production and Operations Management Society. c/o Sushil Gupta. Florida International University, College of Engineering, EAS 2460, 10555 W. Flagler St., Miami, FL 33174. Phone: (305)348-1413 Fax: (305)348-6890 E-mail: poms@fiu.edu • URL: http://www.poms.org • Members are professionals and educators in fields related to operations management and production.

Society for Advancement of Management. Texas A&M University-Corpus Christi, College of Business, 6300 Ocean Dr., Corpus Christi, TX 78412. Phone: 888-827-6077 or (361)825-6045 or (361)825-5574 Fax: (361)825-2725 E-mail: moustafa@falcon.tamucc.edu • URL: http://www.enterprise.tamucc.edu/sam/.

OTHER SOURCES

Better Supervision; Some Old Ideas and a Few New Ones about How to be a Better Boss. Economics Press, Inc. • Biweekly. $35.00 per year. Motivational pamphlets for supervisors.

First-Line Supervision. American Management Association Extension Institute. • Looseleaf. $110.00. Self-study course. Emphasis is on practical explanations, examples, and problem solving. Quizzes and a case study are included.

INDUSTRIAL MARKETING

See also: INDUSTRIAL ADVERTISING; MARKETING

GENERAL WORKS

Business Marketing: A Global Approach. Robert W. Haas. McGraw-Hill Higher Education. • 1996. $68.95. Sixth revised edition.

Business Marketing Management. Frank G. Bingham. NTC/Contemporary Publishing. • 1997. $71.95.

Defining Your Market: Winning Strategies for High-Tech, Industrial, and Service Firms. Art Weinstein. Haworth Press, Inc. • 1998. $39.95. Includes "models, frameworks, and processes" for effective industrial marketing.

Industrial Marketing Strategy. Frederick E. Webster. John Wiley and Sons, Inc. • 1991. $114.95. Third edition. (Marketing Management Series).

BIBLIOGRAPHIES

Marketing Information Revolution. Robert C. Blattberg, editor. McGraw-Hill. • 1993. $39.95. Third edition. Includes a wide variety of sources for specific kinds of marketing.

DIRECTORIES

BMA Membership Directory and Resource Guide. Business Marketing Association. • Annual. Academic, $75.00; business, $150.00. Lists professionals in business and industrial advertising and marketing. Formerly *BMA Membership Directory and Yellow Pages.*

Directory of Business-to-Business Catalogs. Grey House Publishing. • Annual. $190.00. Provides over 6,000 listings of U. S. mail order companies selling business or industrial products and services.

ENCYCLOPEDIAS AND DICTIONARIES

Blackwell Encyclopedic Dictionary of Marketing. Barbara R. Lewis and Dale Littler, editors. Blackwell Publishers. • 1996. $105.95. The editors are associated with the Manchester School of

Management. Contains definitions of key terms combined with longer articles written by various U. S. and foreign business educators. Includes bibliographies and index. (Blackwell Encyclopedia of Management series.).

Field Guide to Marketing: A Glossary of Essential Tools and Concepts for Today's Manager. McGraw-Hill. • 1993. $29.95. Defines fundamental terms.

HANDBOOKS AND MANUALS

B to B Marketing: Creating and Implementing a Successful Business-to-Business Marketing Program. Philip G. Duffy. McGraw-Hill Professional. • 1992. $29.95.

Marketing Manager's Handbook. Sidney J. Levy and others. Prentice Hall. • 2000. Price on application. Contains 71 chapters by various authors on a wide variety of marketing topics, including market segmentation, market research, international marketing, industrial marketing, survey methods, customer service, advertising, pricing, planning, strategy, and ethics.

ONLINE DATABASES

PROMT: Predicasts Overview of Markets and Technology. The Gale Group. • Companies, products, applied technologies and markets. U.S. and international literature coverage, 1972 to date. Inquire as to online cost and availability. Provides abstracts from more than 1,600 publications. Weekly updates.

PERIODICALS AND NEWSLETTERS

Industrial Marketing Management: The International Journal of Marketing for Industrial and High Tech Firms. Elsevier Science. • Eight times a year. $669.00 per year.

Journal of Business-to-Business Marketing: Innovations in Basic and Applied Research for Industrial Marketing. Haworth Press, Inc. • Quarterly. Individuals, $60.00 per year; institutions, $95.00 per year; libraries, $175.00 per year.

MC: Technology Marketing Intelligence. BPI Communications, Inc. • Monthly. $47.00 per year. Edited for marketing executives in high technology industries. Covers both advertising and marketing.

RESEARCH CENTERS AND INSTITUTES

Institute for the Study of Business Markets. Pennsylvania State University, 402 Business Administration Bldg., University Park, PA 16802-3004. Phone: (814)863-2782 Fax: (814)863-0413 E-mail: isbm@psu.edu • URL: http://www.smeal.psu.edu/isbm/ • Research areas include international distribution channels.

TRADE/PROFESSIONAL ASSOCIATIONS

Business Marketing Association. 400 N. Michigan Ave., 15th Fl., Chicago, IL 60611. Phone: 800-664-4262 or (312)409-4262 Fax: (312)409-4266 E-mail: bma@marketing.org • URL: http://www.marketing.org • Members are professionals in business and industrial advertising and marketing. Formerly known as Business/Professional Advertising Association.

INDUSTRIAL MEDICINE

See also: INDUSTRIAL HYGIENE

GENERAL WORKS

Principles of Health and Hygiene in the Workplace. Timothy J. Key and Michael A. Mueller. Lewis Publishers. • Date not set. $69.95.

ABSTRACTS AND INDEXES

Excerpta Medica: Occupational Health and Industrial Medicine. Elsevier Science. • Monthly. $1,833.00 per year. Section 35 of *Excerpta Medica.*

DIRECTORIES

American College of Occupational and Environmental Medicine-Membership Directory. • Annual. $150.00. Lists 6,500 medical directories and plant physicians specializing in occupational medicine and surgery; coverage includes Canada and other foreign countries. Geographically arranged.

ENCYCLOPEDIAS AND DICTIONARIES

Attorneys' Dictionary of Medicine. J. E. Schmidt. Matthew Bender & Shepherd. • $570.00. Looseleaf service. Six volumes. Periodic supplementation. Includes common lay words that lead to correct medical terms.

Encyclopedia of Occupational Health and Safety. Available from The Gale Group. • 1999. $495.00. Fourth edition. Four volumes. Published by the International Labor Office (http://www.ilo.org). Covers safety engineering, industrial medicine, ergonomics, hygiene, epidemiology, toxicology, industrial psychology, and related topics. Includes material related to specific chemical, textile, transport, construction, manufacturing, and other industries. Indexed by subject, chemical name, and author, with a "Directory of Experts.".

HANDBOOKS AND MANUALS

Patty's Industrial Hygiene and Toxicology. George D. Clayton and Florence E. Clayton, editors. John Wiley and Sons, Inc. • 2000. $2,195.00. Three volumes in 10 parts. Provides broad coverage of environmental factors and stresses affecting the health of workers. Contains detailed information on the effects of specific substances.

INTERNET DATABASES

National Library of Medicine (NLM). National Institutes of Health (NIH). Phone: 888-346-3656 or (301)496-1131 Fax: (301)480-3537 E-mail: access@nlm.nih.gov • URL: http://www.nlm.nih.gov • NLM Web site offers free access through MEDLINE ("PubMed") to about nine million references to articles appearing in some 3,800 biomedical journals, with abstracts. Search interfaces range from "simple keywords to advanced Boolean expressions." The NLM site offers many links to other sources of biomedical and technical information (the National Center for Biotechnology Information, for example). Fees: Free.

ONLINE DATABASES

Embase. Elsevier Science, Inc. • Worldwide medical literature, 1974 to present. Weekly updates. Inquire as to online cost and availability.

Medline. Medlars Management Section. • Provides indexing and abstracting of worldwide medical literature, 1966 to date. Weekly updates. Inquire as to online cost and availability.

PERIODICALS AND NEWSLETTERS

American Journal of Industrial Medicine. John Wiley and Sons, Inc., Journals Div. • Monthly. Institutions, $2,620.00 per year.

Environmental Epidemiology and Toxicology. International Society of Occupational Medicine and Toxicology. Princeton Scientific Publishing Co., Inc. • Quarterly. Individuals, $97.00 per year; institutions, $210.00 per year. Formerly *International Journal of Occupational Medicine, Immunology and Toxicology.*

OTHER SOURCES

Attorneys' Textbook of Medicine. Matthew Bender & Co., Inc. • Annual. $2,760.00. 23 looseleaf volumes. Quarterly updates. Periodic supplementation. Medico-legal material.

INDUSTRIAL MORALE

See: HUMAN RELATIONS

INDUSTRIAL PARKS

See: INDUSTRIAL DEVELOPMENT

INDUSTRIAL PHOTOGRAPHY

See: COMMERCIAL PHOTOGRAPHY

INDUSTRIAL PRODUCTIVITY

See: PRODUCTIVITY

INDUSTRIAL PSYCHOLOGY

See also: MENTAL HEALTH; PSYCHOLOGICAL TESTING; STRESS (ANXIETY)

GENERAL WORKS

Industrial and Organizational Psychology: From Fundamentals to Practice. Paul E. Spector. John Wiley and Sons, Inc. • 1999. $83.95. Second edition.

Introduction to Industrial-Organization Psychology. Ronald E. Riggio, editor. Addison-Wesley Educational Publications, Inc. • 1999. $80.00. Third edition. Price on application.

Managing Workplace Stress. Susan Cartwright and Cary L. Cooper. Sage Publications, Inc. • 1996. $34.00. Includes references and indexes. *Advanced Topics in Organizational Behavior, vol. 1.*

Psychology for Leaders: Using Motivation, Conflict, and Power to Manage More Effectively. Dean Tjosvold and Mary Tjosvold. John Wiley and Sons, Inc. • 1995. $32.95. (Portable MBS Series).

Psychology in Industrial Organizations. Norman R. Maier and Gertrude Verser. Houghton Mifflin Co. • 1982. $79.96. Fifth edition. Five volumes.

ABSTRACTS AND INDEXES

Business Periodicals Index. H. W. Wilson Co. • Monthly, except August, with quarterly and annual cumulations. Service basis for print edition; CD-ROM edition, $1,495.00 per year.

Psychological Abstracts. American Psychological Association. • Monthly. Members, $799.00 per year; individuals and institutions, $1,075.00 per year. Covers the international literature of psychology and the behavioral sciences. Includes journals, technical reports, dissertations, and other sources.

ALMANACS AND YEARBOOKS

International Review of Industrial and Organizational Psychology. Available from John Wiley and Sons, Inc., Journals Div. • Annual. $155.00. Published in England by John Wiley and Sons Ltd.

BIBLIOGRAPHIES

Bibliographic Guide to Psychology. Available from The Gale Group. • Annual. $295.00. Published by G. K. Hall & Co. Lists psychology publications cataloged by the New York Public Library and the Library of Congress.

DIRECTORIES

Test Critques. Pro-Ed. • 1998. 11 volumes. Prices vary. Presents detailed evaluations of the validity of tests in psychology, education, and business. Published by ProEd, Inc.

Tests: A Comprehensive Reference for Assessments in Psychology, Education and Business. Available from The Gale Group. • 1997. $99.00. Fourth edition. List nearly 500 publishers for over 3,000 tests. Published by Pro-Ed Inc.

ENCYCLOPEDIAS AND DICTIONARIES

Blackwell Encyclopedic Dictionary of Organizational Behavior. Nigel Nicholson, editor.

Blackwell Publishers. • 1995. $105.95. The editor is associated with the London Business School. Contains definitions of key terms combined with longer articles written by various U. S. and foreign business educators. Includes bibliographies and index. *Blackwell Encyclopedia of Management Series.*

Encyclopedia of Human Behavior. Vangipuram S. Ramachandran, editor. Academic Press, Inc. • 1994. $685.00. Four volumes. Contains signed articles on aptitude testing, arbitration, career development, consumer psychology, crisis management, decision making, economic behavior, group dynamics, leadership, motivation, negotiation, organizational behavior, planning, problem solving, stress, work efficiency, and other human behavior topics applicable to business situations.

Encyclopedia of Occupational Health and Safety. Available from The Gale Group. • 1999. $495.00. Fourth edition. Four volumes. Published by the International Labor Office (http://www.ilo.org). Covers safety engineering, industrial medicine, ergonomics, hygiene, epidemiology, toxicology, industrial psychology, and related topics. Includes material related to specific chemical, textile, transport, construction, manufacturing, and other industries. Indexed by subject, chemical name, and author, with a "Directory of Experts.".

The Gale Encyclopedia of Psychology. The Gale Group. • 1998. $130.00. Includes bibliographies arranged by topic and a glossary.

HANDBOOKS AND MANUALS

Stress and Well-Being at Work: Assessments and Interventions for Occupational Mental Health. James C. Quick and others, editors. American Psychological Association. • 1992. $19.95.

ONLINE DATABASES

Mental Health Abstracts. IFI/Plenum Data Corp. • Provides indexing and abstracting of mental health and mental illness literature appearing in more than 1,200 journals and other sources from 1969 to date. Monthly updates. Inquire as to online cost and availability.

PsycINFO. American Psychological Association. • Provides indexing and abstracting of the worldwide literature of psychology and the behavioral sciences. Time period is 1967 to date, with monthly updates. Inquire as to online cost and availability.

PERIODICALS AND NEWSLETTERS

Journal of Business and Psychology. Business Psychology Research Institute. Kluwer Plenum Academic Publishers. • Quarterly. Institutions, $556.80 per year.

Journal of Occupational and Organizational Psychology. British Psychological Society. • Quarterly. $230.00 per year. Formerly *Journal of Occupational Psychology.*

TRADE/PROFESSIONAL ASSOCIATIONS

American Psychological Association: Industrial and Organizational Psychology Society. 750 First St., N.E., Washington, DC 20002-4242. Phone: 800-374-2721 or (202)336-5500 Fax: (202)336-5997 E-mail: executiveoffice@apa.org • URL: http://www.apa.org/.

INDUSTRIAL PURCHASING

See: PURCHASING

INDUSTRIAL REAL ESTATE

See also: PROPERTY TAX; TAX SHELTERS

ABSTRACTS AND INDEXES

Business Periodicals Index. H. W. Wilson Co. • Monthly, except August, with quarterly and annual cumulations. Service basis for print edition; CD-ROM edition, $1,495.00 per year.

DIRECTORIES

Executive Guide to Specialists in Industrial and Office Real Estate. Society of Industrial and Office Realtors. • Annual. $70.00. Approximately 1,800 specialist in industrial real estate.

U.S. Real Estate Register. Barry, Inc. • Annual. $87.50. Formerly *Industrial Real Estate Managers Directory.*

HANDBOOKS AND MANUALS

Corporate Counsellor's Deskbook. Dennis J. Block and Michael A. Epstein, editors. Panel Publishing. • 1999. $220.00. Fifth edition. Looseleaf. Annual supplementation. Covers a wide variety of corporate legal issues, including internal investigations, indemnification, insider trading, intellectual property, executive compensation, antitrust, export-import, real estate, environmental law, government contracts, and bankruptcy.

ONLINE DATABASES

Wilson Business Abstracts Online. H. W. Wilson Co. • Indexes and abstracts 600 major business periodicals, plus the *Wall Street Journal* and the business section of the *New York Times.* Indexing is from 1982, abstracting from 1990, with the two newspapers included from 1993. Updated weekly. Inquire as to online cost and availability. (*Business Periodicals Index* without abstracts is also available online.).

PERIODICALS AND NEWSLETTERS

Area Development Sites and Facility Planning: The Executive Magazine of Sites and Facility Planning. S H Publications, Inc. • Monthly. $65.00 per year. Site selection, facility planning, and plant relocation. Formerly *Area Development Magazines.*

Buildings: The Facilities Construction and Management Journal. Stamats Communications, Inc. • Monthly. $70.00 per year. Serves professional building ownership/management organizations.

Business Facilities. Group C Communications. • Monthly. $30.00 per year. Facility planning and site selection.

Development. National Association of Industrial and Office Properties. • Quarterly. Free to members; non-members, $65.00 per year. Focuses on issues, trends and new ideas affecting the commercial and industrial real estate development industry.

Marketscore. CB Richard Ellis. • Quarterly. Price on application. Newsletter. Provides proprietary forecasts of commercial real estate performance in metropolitan areas.

Quarterly Market Report. CB Richard Ellis. • Quarterly. Price on application. Newsletter. Reviews current prices, rents, capitalization rates, and occupancy trends for commercial real estate.

Real Estate Finance. Institutional Investor. • Quarterly. $225.00 per year. Covers real estate for professional investors. Provides information on complex financing, legalities, and industry trends.

Real Estate Finance and Investment. Institutional Investor. • Weekly. $2,105.00 per year. Newsletter for professional investors in commercial real estate. Includes information on financing, restructuring, strategy, and regulation.

Real Estate Forum. Real Estate Media, Inc. • Monthly. $55.00 per year. Emphasis on corporate and industrial real estate.

PRICE SOURCES

National Real Estate Index. CB Richard Ellis. • Price and frequency on application. Provides reports on commercial real estate prices, rents, capitalization rates, and trends in more than 65 metropolitan areas. Time span is 12 years. Includes urban office buildings, suburban offices, warehouses, retail properties, and apartments.

RESEARCH CENTERS AND INSTITUTES

Center for Real Estate Studies. Indiana University Bloomington, 1309 E. Tenth St., Suite 738, Bloomington, IN 47405. Phone: (812)855-7794 Fax: (812)855-9472 E-mail: cres@indiana.edu • URL: http://www.indiana.edu/~cres/.

Office of Real Estate Research. University of Illinois at Urbana-Chamapign, 1407 E. Gregory Dr., 304 David Kinley Hall, Champaign, IL 61820. Phone: (217)244-0591 Fax: (217)244-9867 E-mail: orer@uiuc.edu • URL: http://www.cba.uiuc.edu/orer/orer.htm.

Real Estate Research Center. University of Florida. College of Business Administration, P.O. Box 117168, Gainesville, FL 32611-7168. Phone: (352)392-9307 Fax: (352)392-0381 E-mail: ling@dale.cba.ufl.edu • URL: http://www.bear.cba.ufl.edu/centers/ufrealestate/cres.htm.

STATISTICS SOURCES

Comparative Statistics of Industrial Office Real Estate Markets. Society of Industrial and Office Realtors. • Annual. $100.00. Includes review and forecast section. Formerly *Guide to Industrial and Office Real Estate Markets.*

ULI Market Profiles: North America. Urban Land Institute. • Annual. Members, $249.95; non-members, $299.95. Provides real estate marketing data for residential, retail, office, and industrial sectors. Covers 76 U. S. metropolitan areas and 13 major foreign metropolitan areas.

TRADE/PROFESSIONAL ASSOCIATIONS

American Industrial Real Estate Association. 700 S. Flower St., Suite 600, Los Angeles, CA 90017. Phone: (213)687-8777 Fax: (213)687-8616 E-mail: rsurace@airea.com • URL: http://www.airea.com.

NACORE International. 440 Columbia Dr., Suite 100, West Palm Beach, FL 33409. Phone: 800-726-8111 or (561)683-8111 Fax: (561)697-4853 E-mail: nacore@nacore.com • URL: http://www.nacore.org.

National Association of Industrial and Office Properties. 2201 Cooperative Way, Herndon, VA 20171. Phone: 800-666-6780 or (703)904-7100 Fax: (703)904-7942 E-mail: naiop@naiop.org • URL: http://www.naiop.org • Members are owners and developers of business, industrial, office, and retail properties.

INDUSTRIAL RECREATION

ABSTRACTS AND INDEXES

Leisure, Recreation, and Tourism Abstracts. Available from CABI Publishing North America. • Quarterly. $470.00 per year. Published in England by CABI Publishing. Provides coverage of the worldwide literature of travel, recreation, sports, and the hospitality industry. Emphasis is on research.

DIRECTORIES

National Employee Services and Recreation Association Membership Directory. National Employee Services and Recreation Association. • Annual. Membership. Lists more than 4,500 personnel managers, recreation directors and certified administrators in employee recreation, fitness and services. Formerly *National Employee Services and Recreation Association Membership Directory*.

PERIODICALS AND NEWSLETTERS

Employee Services Management: The Journal of Employee Services, Recreation, Health and Education. National Employee Service and Recreation Association. • 10 times a year. $44.00 per year.

TRADE/PROFESSIONAL ASSOCIATIONS

National Employee Services and Recreation Association. 2211 York Rd., Suite 207, Oak Brook, IL 60521-2371. Phone: (630)368-1280 Fax: (630)368-1286 E-mail: nesrahq@aol.com • URL: http://www.nesra.org.

INDUSTRIAL RELATIONS

See also: NEGOTIATION

GENERAL WORKS

Collective Bargaining and Labor. Terry L. Leap. Prentice Hall. • 1994. $90.00. Second edition.

Labor-Management Relations. Daniel Q. Mills. McGraw-Hill. • 1993. $83.75. Fifth edition. (Management Series).

Labor Relations. Arthur A. Sloan and Fred Witney. Prentice Hall. • 1996. $91.00. Ninth edition. Emphasizes collective bargaining and arbitration.

Labor Relations: Development, Structure, Process. John A. Fossum. McGraw-Hill Professional. • 1999. Seventh edition. Price on application.

ABSTRACTS AND INDEXES

Business Periodicals Index. H. W. Wilson Co. • Monthly, except August, with quarterly and annual cumulations. Service basis for print edition; CD-ROM edition, $1,495.00 per year.

Human Resources Abstracts: An International Information Service. Sage Publications, Inc. • Quarterly. Individuals, $150.00 per year; institutions, $610.00 per year.

Index to Legal Periodicals and Books. H. W. Wilson Co. • Monthly. Quarterly and annual cumulations. $270.00 per year. CD-ROM version available at $1,495.00 per year.

Personnel Management Abstracts. • Quarterly. $190.00 per year. Includes annual cumulation.

BIBLIOGRAPHIES

Business Information Sources. Lorna M. Daniells. California Princeton Fulfillment Services. • 1993. $42.50. Third revised edition. Basic business sources, with discussion and full annotations.

Labor Arbitration: An Annotated Bibliography, 1991-1996. Charles J. Coleman and others, editors. Cornell Universtiy Press. • 1997. $25.00. (ILR Bibliography Series, No. 18).

BIOGRAPHICAL SOURCES

Biographical Dictionary of American Labor. Gary M. Fink, editor. Greenwood Publishing Group Inc. • 1984. $115.00.

DIRECTORIES

DIrectory of U. S. Labor Organizations. BNA Books. Bureau of National Affairs, Inc. • Biennial. $85.00. More than 200 national unions and professional and state employees associations engaged in labor representation.

ENCYCLOPEDIAS AND DICTIONARIES

Blackwell Encyclopedic Dictionary of Human Resource Management. Lawrence H. Peters and Charles R. Greer, editors. Blackwell Publishers. • 1996. $105.95. The editors are associated with Texas Christian University. Contains definitions of key terms combined with longer articles written by various U. S. and foreign business educators. Includes bibliographies and index. (Blackwell Encyclopedia of Management Series).

International Encyclopedia of Public Policy and Administration. Jay M. Shafritz, editor. HarperCollins Publishers. • 1997. $550.00. Four volumes. Covers 20 major areas, such as public administration, government budgeting, industrial policy, nonprofit management, organizational theory, public finance, labor relations, and taxation. Includes a brief bibliography for each major entry and a comprehensive index.

HANDBOOKS AND MANUALS

AMA Management Handbook. John J. Hampton, editor. AMACOM. • 1994. $110.00. Third edition. Provides 200 chapters in 16 major subject areas. Covers a wide variety of business and industrial management topics.

Labor-Management Relations: Strikes, Lockouts, and Boycotts. Douglas E. Ray and Emery W. Bartle. West Group. • Looseleaf. $110.00. Covers legal issues involved in labor-management confrontations. Includes recent decisions of the National Labor Relations Board (NLRB).

ONLINE DATABASES

Index to Legal Periodicals and Books (Online). H. W. Wilson Co. • Broad coverage of law journals and books 1981 to date. Monthly updates. Inquire as to online cost and availability.

Legal Resource Index. The Gale Group. • Broad coverage of law literature appearing in legal, business, and other periodicals, 1980 to date. Monthly updates. Inquire as to online cost and availability.

LEXIS. LEXIS-NEXIS. • The various LEXIS databases provide full text and indexing for a wide variety of legal cases, statutes, orders, and opinions.

Wilson Business Abstracts Online. H. W. Wilson Co. • Indexes and abstracts 600 major business periodicals, plus the *Wall Street Journal* and the business section of the *New York Times*. Indexing is from 1982, abstracting from 1990, with the two newspapers included from 1993. Updated weekly. Inquire as to online cost and availability. (*Business Periodicals Index* without abstracts is also available online.).

PERIODICALS AND NEWSLETTERS

Berkeley Journal of Employment and Labor Law. University of California at Berkeley. University of California Press, Journals Div. • Semiannual. Individuals, $34.00 per year; institutions, $43.00 per year. Formerly *Industrial Relations Law Journal*.

HR Magazine (Human Resources): Strategies and Solutions for Human Resource Professionals. Society for Human Resource Management. • Monthly. Free to members; non-members, $125.00 per year. Formerly *Personnel Administrator*.

Industrial and Labor Relations Review. Cornell University, New York State School of Industrial and Labor Relations. • Quarterly. Individuals, $26.00 per year; institutions, $43.00 per year; students, $13.00 per year.

Industrial Relations: A Journal of Economy and Society. University of California at Berkeley Institute of Industrial Relations. Blackwell Publishers. • Quarterly. $99.00 per year.

IRRA Newsletter. Industrial Relations Research Association. • Quarterly. $75.00 per year. Membership.

Weekly Summary of the National Labor Relations Board Cases. Available from U. S. Government Printing Office. • Weekly. $174.00 per year. Issued by the Division of Information, National Labor Relations Board.

RESEARCH CENTERS AND INSTITUTES

Center for Human Resources. University of Pennsylvania, The Wharton School, 3733 Spruce St., 309 Vance Hall, Philadelphia, PA 19104-6358. Phone: (215)898-2722 Fax: (215)898-5908 E-mail: cappelli@wharton.upenn.edu • URL: http://www.management.wharton.upenn.edu/chr/.

Industrial Relations Research Institute. University of Wisconsin-Madison, 4226 Social Science Bldg., Madison, WI 53706. Phone: (608)262-1882 Fax: (608)265-4591 • URL: http://www.polyglot.lss.wisc.edu/irr/irr.html.

Industrial Relations Section. Princeton University, Firestone Library, Pinceton, NJ 08544. Phone: (609)258-4040 Fax: (609)258-2907 • URL: http://www.irs.princeton.edu/ • Fields of research include labor supply, manpower training, unemployment, and equal employment opportunity.

Institute of Industrial Relations. University of California at Berkeley, 2521 Channing Way, Berkeley, CA 94720-5555. Phone: (510)642-5452 Fax: (510)642-6432 E-mail: lincoln@haas.berkeley.edu • URL: http://www.violet.berkeley.edu/~iir/.

Institute of Labor and Industrial Relations. University of Michigan, Victor Vaughn Bldg., 1111 E. Catherine St., Ann Arbor, MI 48109-2054. Phone: (734)763-3116 Fax: (734)763-0913 E-mail: lroot@umich.edu • URL: http://www.ilir.umich.edu.

TRADE/PROFESSIONAL ASSOCIATIONS

Council of Communication Management. 333 B Route 46 W., Suite B 201, Fairfield, NJ 07004. Phone: (973)575-1444 Fax: (973)575-1445.

Industrial Relations Research Association. 504 E. Armory Ave., Champaign, IL 61820. Phone: (217)333-0072 Fax: (217)265-5130 • URL: http://www.irra.uiuc.edu.

Society for Human Resource Management. 1800 Duke St., Alexandria, VA 22314-3499. Phone: 800-283-7476 or (703)548-3440 Fax: (703)535-6490 E-mail: shrm@shrm.org • URL: http://www.shrm.org.

OTHER SOURCES

How to Manage Conflict in the Organization. American Management Association Extension Institute. • Looseleaf. $110.00. Self-study course. Emphasis is on practical explanations, examples, and problem solving. Quizzes and a case study are included.

Labor Relations Reporter. Bureau of National Affairs, Inc. • Biweekly. $4,118.00 per year. Six volumes. Looseleaf. Legal service.

INDUSTRIAL RESEARCH

See also: RESEARCH AND DEVELOPMENT

GENERAL WORKS

Industry's Future: Changing Patterns of Industrial Research. Herbert I. Fusfeld. American Chemical Society. • 1994. $45.00.

The Innovator's Dilemma: When New Technologies Cause Great Firms to Fail. Clayton M. Christensen. Harvard Business School Press. • 1997. $27.50. Discusses management myths relating to innovation, change, and research and development. (Mangement of Innovation and Change Series).

ABSTRACTS AND INDEXES

Applied Science and Technology Index. H. W. Wilson Co. • 11 times a year. Quarterly and annual cumulations. Service basis for print edition; CD-ROM edition, $1,495.00 per year. Indexes a wide variety of English language technical, industrial, and engineering periodicals.

CD-ROM DATABASES

Profiles in Business and Management: An International Directory of Scholars and Their Research [CD-ROM]. Harvard Business School Publishing. • Annual. $595.00 per year. Fully searchable CD-ROM version of two-volume printed directory. Contains bibliographic and biographical information for over 5600 business and management experts active in 21 subject areas. Formerly *International Directory of Business and Management Scholars.*

Science Citation Index: Compact Disc Edition. Institute for Scientific Information. • Quarterly. Provides CD-ROM indexing of the world's scientific and technical literature. Corresponds to online *Scisearch* and printed *Science Citation Index.*

DIRECTORIES

Directory of American Research and Technology: Organizations Active in Product Development for Business. R. R. Bowker. • Annual. $359.95. Lists over 13,000 publicly and privately owned research facilities. Formerly *Industrial Research Laboratories of the U.S.*

Plunkett's Engineering and Research Industry Almanac. Plunkett Research, Ltd. • Annual. $179.99. Contains detailed profiles of major engineering and technology corporations. Includes CD-ROM.

Profiles in Business and Management: An International Directory of Scholars and Their Research Version 2.0. Claudia Bruce, editor. Harvard Business School Press. • 1996. $495.00. Two volumes. Provides backgrounds, publications, and current research projects of more than 5,600 business and management experts.

Unique 3-in-1 Research and Development Directory. Government Data Publications, Inc. • Annual. $15.00. Government contractors in the research and development fields. Included with subscription to *R and D Contracts Monthly.* Formerly *Research and Development Directory.*

ENCYCLOPEDIAS AND DICTIONARIES

Blackwell Encyclopedic Dictionary of Operations Management. Nigel Slack, editor. Blackwell Publishers. • 1997. $105.95. The editor is associated with the University of Warwick, England. Contains definitions of key terms combined with longer articles written by various U. S. and foreign business educators. Includes bibliographies and index. (Blackwell Encyclopedia of Management Series.).

ONLINE DATABASES

Applied Science and Technology Index Online. H. W. Wilson Co. • Provides online indexing of 400 major scientific, technical, industrial, and engineering periodicals. Time period is 1983 to date. Monthly updates. Inquire as to online cost and availability.

Current Contents Connect. Institute for Scientific Information. • Provides online abstracts of articles listed in the tables of contents of about 7,500 journals. Coverage is very broad, including science, social science, life science, technology, engineering, industry, agriculture, the environment, economics, and arts and humanities. Time period is two years, with weekly updates. Inquire as to online cost and availability.

NTIS Bibliographic Data Base. National Technical Information Service. • Contains citations and abstracts to unrestricted reports of government-sponsored research, 1964 to date. Covers a wide range of technical, engineering, business, and social science topics. Monthly updates. Inquire as to online cost and availability.

Scisearch. Institute for Scientific Information. • Broad, multidisciplinary index to the literature of science and technology, 1974 to present. Inquire as to online cost and availability. Coverage of literature is worldwide, with weekly updates.

Who's Who in Technology [Online]. The Gale Group. • Provides online biographical profiles of over 25,000 American scientists, engineers, and others in technology-related occupations. Inquire as to online cost and availability.

PERIODICALS AND NEWSLETTERS

Industrial and Engineering Chemistry Research. American Chemical Society. • Monthly. Institutions, $1,343 per year; others, price on application. Available on line . Fromerly *Industrial and Engineering Chemistry Product Research and Development.*

Research and Development: The Voice of the Research and Development Community. Cahners Business Information. • 13 times a year. $81.90 per year.

RESEARCH CENTERS AND INSTITUTES

Center for Industrial Research and Service. Iowa State University of Science and Technology. 2272 Howe Hall, No. 2620, Ames, IA 50011-0001. Phone: (515)294-3420 Fax: (515)294-4925 E-mail: ciras@exnet.iastate.edu • URL: http://www.ciras.iastate.edu.

TRADE/PROFESSIONAL ASSOCIATIONS

Industrial Research Institute. 1550 M St., N.W., Suite 1100, Washington, DC 20005-1712. Phone: (202)296-8811 Fax: (202)776-0756.

Society of Research Administrators. 1200 19th St., N.W., Ste. 300, Washington, DC 20036-2422. Phone: (202)857-1141 Fax: (202)828-6049 E-mail: sra@dc.sba.com • URL: http://www.sra.rams.com.

INDUSTRIAL ROBOTS

See: ROBOTS

INDUSTRIAL SAFETY

See also: INDUSTRIAL HYGIENE; SAFETY

GENERAL WORKS

Industrial Safety and Health Management. C. Ray Asfahl. Prentice Hall. • 1998. $92.00. Fourth edition.

Occupational Safety and Health Management. Thomas Anton. McGraw-Hill. • 1989. $88.44. Second edition.

ABSTRACTS AND INDEXES

Health and Safety Science Abstracts. Institute of Safety and Systems Management. Cambridge Information Group. • Quarterly. $775.00 per year. Formerly *Safety Science Abstracts Journal.*

Safety and Health at Work. International Labour Office. • Bimonthly. $240.00 per year. Formerly *Occupational Safety and Health Abstracts.*

CD-ROM DATABASES

Occupational Safety and Health Administration (OSHA): Regulations, Documents, and Technical Information. Available from U. S. Government Printing Office. • Quarterly. $46.00 per year. CD-ROM contains all OSHA regulations and standards currently in force, with selected documents and technical information.

OSH-ROM: Occupational Safety and Health Information on CD-ROM. Available from SilverPlatter Information, Inc. • Price and frequency on application. Produced in Geneva by the International Occupational Safety and Health Information Centre, International Labour Organization (http://www.ilo.org). Provides about two million citations and abstracts to the worldwide literature of industrial safety, industrial hygiene, hazardous materials, and accident prevention. Material is included from journals, technical reports, books, government publications, and other sources. Time span varies.

DIRECTORIES

Best's Safety and Security Directory: Safety-Industrial Hygiene-Security. A.M. Best Co. • Annual. $95.00. A manual of current industrial safety practices with a directory of manufacturers and distributors of plant safety, security and industrial hygiene products and services listed by hazard. Formerly *Best's Safety Directory.*

ENCYCLOPEDIAS AND DICTIONARIES

Encyclopedia of Occupational Health and Safety. Available from The Gale Group. • 1999. $495.00. Fourth edition. Four volumes. Published by the International Labor Office (http://www.ilo.org). Covers safety engineering, industrial medicine, ergonomics, hygiene, epidemiology, toxicology, industrial psychology, and related topics. Includes material related to specific chemical, textile, transport, construction, manufacturing, and other industries. Indexed by subject, chemical name, and author, with a "Directory of Experts.".

Encyclopedia of Occupational Health and Safety 1983. International Labour Office. • 1991. $270.00. Third revised edition. Two volumes.

Unabridged Dictionary of Occupational and Environmental Safety and Health with CD-ROM. Jeffrey W. Vincoli and Kathryn L. Bazan. Lewis Publishers. • 1999. $89.95.

HANDBOOKS AND MANUALS

Handbook of Occupational Safety and Health. Louis J. Diberardinis. John Wiley and Sons, Inc. • 1998. $149.00. Second edition.

Handbook of Safety and Health Engineering. Roger L. Bauer and Jeffrey W. Vincoli. Lewis Publishers. • 1999. $89.95.

Managing Worker's Compensation: A Guide to Injury Reduction and Effective Claim Management. Keith Wertz and C. Bradley Layton. Lewis Publishers. • Date not set. $59.95. (Occupation Safety and Health Guide Series).

Occupational Safety and Health Law. Mark A. Rothstein. West Publishing Co., College and School Div. • 1990. Third edition. Price on application. Periodic supplementation. Discusses requirements of the Occupational Safety and Health Act (OSHA). (Handbook Series).

Occupational Safety and Health Standards for General Industry. CCH, Inc. • Annual. $42.95.

Sax's Dangerous Properties of Industrial Materials. Richard J. Lewis. John Wiley and Sons, Inc. • 1999. $545.00. 10th edition. Three volumes. Provides detailed information on the chemical, physical, and toxicity characteristics of more than 22,000 industrial materials. Hazard ratings and safety profiles are specified.

ONLINE DATABASES

NIOSHTIC: National Institute for Occupational Safety and Health Technical Information Center Database. National Institute for Occupational Safety and Health, Technical Information Bra. • Provides citations and abstracts of technical literature in the areas of industrial safety, industrial hygiene, and toxicology. Covers 1890 to date, but mostly 1973 to date. Monthly updates. (Database is also known as *Occupational Safety and Health.*) Inquire as to online cost and availability.

PERIODICALS AND NEWSLETTERS

BNA's Safetynet. Bureau of National Affairs, Inc. • Biweekly. $680.00 per year. Looseleaf. Formerly *Job Safety and Health.*

Industrial Safety and Hygiene News: News of Safety, Health and Hygiene, Environmental, Fire, Security and Emergency Protection Equipment. Business News Publishing Co. • Monthly. Free to qualified personnel; others, $120.00 per year.

Job Safety and Health Quarterly. Available from U. S. Government Printing Office. • Quarterly. $17.00 per year. Issued by the Occupational Safety and Health Administration (OSHA), U. S. Department of Labor. Contains articles on employee safety and health, with information on current OSHA activities.

Labor Division Newsletter. National Safety Council. • Monthly. $19.00 per year.

Occupational Hazards: Magazine of Health and Environment. Penton Media Inc. • Monthly. $50.00 per year. Industrial safety and security management.

Professional Safety. American Society of Safety Engineers. • Monthly. $60.00 per year. Emphasis is on research and technology in the field of accident prevention.

Safety and Health: The International Safety Health and Environment Magazine. National Safety Council. • Monthly. Members, $80.00 per year; non-members, $91.00 per year. Formerly *National Safety and Health News.*

RESEARCH CENTERS AND INSTITUTES

Institute for Advanced Safety Studies. 5950 W. Touhy Ave., Niles, IL 60714. Phone: (847)647-1101 Fax: (847)647-2047.

National Safe Workplace Institute/safeplaces.com. 3008 Bishops Ridge, Monroe, NC 28110. Phone: 800-951-6794 or (704)282-1111 Fax: (704)289-6601 E-mail: jakinney@earthlink.net • URL: http://www.nsafewi.com.

STATISTICS SOURCES

Report on the American Workforce. Available from U. S. Government Printing Office. • Annual. $15.00. Issued by the U. S. Department of Labor (http://www.dol.gov). Appendix contains tabular statistics, including employment, unemployment, price indexes, consumer expenditures, employee benefits (retirement, insurance, vacation, etc.), wages, productivity, hours of work, and occupational injuries. Annual figures are shown for up to 50 years.

TRADE/PROFESSIONAL ASSOCIATIONS

American Society of Safety Engineers. 1800 E. Oakton St., Des Plaines, IL 60018-2187. Phone: (847)699-2929 Fax: (847)296-3769 E-mail: customerservice@asse.org • URL: http://www.asse.org.

International Association of Industrial Accident Boards and Commissions. 1201 Wakarusa Dr., Lawrence, KS 66049. Phone: (785)840-9103 Fax: (785)840-9107 E-mail: workcomp@iaiabc.org • URL: http://www.iaiabc.org • Members are government agencies, insurance companies, lawyers, unions, self-insurers, and others with an interest in industrial safety and the administration of workers' compensation laws.

ISEA: The Safety Equipment Association. 1901 N. Moore St., Suite 808, Arlington, VA 22209. Phone: (703)525-1695 Fax: (703)528-2148 E-mail: isea@safetycentral.org • URL: http://www.safetycentral.org/isea.

National Safety Council. 1121 Spring Lake Dr., Itasca, IL 60143-3201. Phone: 800-621-7615 or (630)285-1121 Fax: (630)285-1315 • URL: http://www.nsc.org.

OTHER SOURCES

Corporate Compliance Series. West Group. • Eleven looseleaf volumes, with periodic supplementation. $990.00. Covers criminal and civil liability problems for corporations. Includes employee safety, product liability, pension requirements, securities violations, equal employment opportunity issues, intellectual property, employee hiring and firing, and other corporate compliance topics.

Human Resources Management Whole. CCH, Inc. • Nine looseleaf volumes. $1,572 per year. Includes monthly updates. Components are *Ideas and Trends Newsletter, Employment Relations, Compensation, Equal Employment Opportunity, Personnel Practices/Communications* and *OSHA Compliance.* Components are available separately.

INDUSTRIAL SECURITY PROGRAMS

See also: ELECTRONIC SECURITY SYSTEMS; LOCKS AND KEYS

DIRECTORIES

Security: Product Service Suppliers Guide. Cahners Business Information. • Annual. $50.00 Includes computer and information protection products. Formerly *Security - World Product Directory.*

HANDBOOKS AND MANUALS

Effective Physical Security: Design, Equipment, and Operations. Lawrence J. Fennelly, editor. Butterworth-Heinemann. • 1996. $36.95. Second edition. Contains chapters written by various U. S. security equipment specialists. Covers architectural considerations, locks, safes, alarms, intrusion detection systems, closed circuit television, identification systems, etc.

National Industrial Security Program Operating Manual. U.S. Department of Defense. Available from U.S. Government Printing Office. • 1995. $14.00.

Private Investigator. Entrepreneur Media, Inc. • Looseleaf. $59.50. A practical guide to starting a private investigation agency. Covers profit potential, start-up costs, market size evaluation, pricing, accounting, advertising, promotion, etc. (Start-Up Business Guide No. E1320.).

Security Applications in Industry and Institutions. Lawrence J. Fennelly, editor. Butterworth-Heinemann. • 1992. $46.95. Contains 19 chapters written by various security professionals in the U. S. Covers bank security, hotel security, shoplifting, college campus crime prevention, security in office buildings, hospitals, museums, libraries, etc.

PERIODICALS AND NEWSLETTERS

Security Letter. • 22 times a year. $187.00 per year. News and insight on protection of assets from loss. Includes stock market and other data on the security industry.

Security Management. American Society for Industrial Security. • Monthly. Free to members; non-members, $48.00 per year. Articles cover the protection of corporate assets, including personnel property and information security.

TRADE/PROFESSIONAL ASSOCIATIONS

ASIS International (American Society for Industrial Security). 1625 Prince St., Alexandria, VA 22314-2818. Phone: (703)519-6200 Fax: (703)519-6299 • URL: http://www.asisonline.org.

International Security Management Association. 66 Charles St., Suite 280, Boston, MA 02114. Phone: (319)381-4008 Fax: (319)381-4283 E-mail: isma3@aol.com • URL: http://www.ismanet.com • Members are executives of security service companies and executives of security operations at large corporations.

INDUSTRIAL STATISTICS

See: BUSINESS STATISTICS; STATISTICAL METHODS

INDUSTRIAL TOXICOLOGY

See: INDUSTRIAL HYGIENE

INDUSTRIAL WELFARE

See: EMPLOYEE BENEFIT PLANS

INDUSTRY

See also: BUSINESS; CORPORATIONS

GENERAL WORKS

How Products Are Made. The Gale Group. • Dates vary. Three volumes. $99.00 per volume. Provides easy-to-read, step-by-step descriptions of how approximately 100 different products are manufactured. Items are of all kinds, both mechanical and non-mechanical.

The Organization of Industry. George J. Stigler. University of Chicago Press. • 1983. $14.95.

ABSTRACTS AND INDEXES

Applied Science and Technology Index. H. W. Wilson Co. • 11 times a year. Quarterly and annual cumulations. Service basis for print edition; CD-ROM edition, $1,495.00 per year. Indexes a wide variety of English language technical, industrial, and engineering periodicals.

ALMANACS AND YEARBOOKS

Irwin Business and Investment Almanac, 1996. Summer N. Levine and Caroline Levine. McGraw-Hill Professional. • 1995. $75.00. A review of last year's business activity. Covers a wide variety of business and economic data: stock market statistics, industrial information, commodity futures information, art market trends, comparative living costs for U. S. metropolitan areas, foreign stock market data, etc. Formerly *Business One Irwin Business and Investment Almanac.*

BIOGRAPHICAL SOURCES

Who's Who in Finance and Industry. Marquis Who's Who. • Biennial. $295.00. Provides over 22,400 concise biographies of business leaders in all fields.

CD-ROM DATABASES

F & S Index Plus Text. The Gale Group. • Monthly. $7,575.00 per year. Provides CD-ROM citations to worldwide business, marketing, and industrial material appearing in a large assortment of trade journals, newspapers, and other publications. Time period is four years.

Hoover's Company Capsules on CD-ROM. Hoover's, Inc. • Quarterly. $349.95 per year (single-user). Provides the CD-ROM version of *Hoover's Handbook of American Business, Hoover's Handbook of Emerging Companies, Hoover's Handbook of World Business, Hoover's Guide to Computer Companies, Hoover's Guide to Media Companies, Hoover's Handbook of Private Companies,* and various regional guides. Includes more than 11,000 profiles of companies.

National Trade Data Bank: The Export Connection. U. S. Department of Commerce. • Monthly. $575.00 per year. Provides over 150,000 trade-related data series on CD-ROM. Includes full text of many government publications. Specific data is included on national income, labor, price indexes, foreign exchange, technical standards, and international markets. Website address is http://www.stat-usa.gov/.

16 Million Businesses Phone Directory. Info USA. • Annual. $29.95. Provides more than 16 million yellow pages telephone directory listings on CD-ROM for all ZIP Code areas of the U. S.

Statistical Abstract of the United States on CD-ROM. Hoover's, Inc. • Annual. $49.95. Provides all statistics from official print version, plus expanded historical data, greater detail, and keyword searching features. .

DIRECTORIES

American Big Businesses Directory. American Business Directories. • Annual. $595.00. Lists 177,000 public and private U. S. companies in all fields having 100 or more employees. Includes sales volume, number of employees, and name of chief executive. Formerly *Big Businesses Directory.*

American Business Locations Directory. The Gale Group. • 1999. $575.00. Second edition. (Four U. S. regional volumes and index volume). Provides 150,000 specific site locations for the 1,000 largest industiral and service companies in the U. S. Entries include the following for each location: address, senior officer, number of employees, sales volume, Standard Industrial Classification (SIC) codes, and name of parent company.

American Manufacturers Directory. American Business Directories. • Annual. $595.00. Lists more than 150,000 public and private U. S. manufacturers having 20 or more employees. Includes sales volume, number of employees, and name of chief executive or owner.

America's Corporate Families and International Affliates. Dun and Bradstreet Information Services. • Annual. Libraries, $895.00; corporations, $1,020.00. Lease basis. Three Volumes U.S. parent companies with foreign affiliates and foreign parent companies with U.S. affiliates.

Canadian Trade Index. Alliance of Manufacturers Exporters and Importers Canada. • Annual. $190.00. Provides information on about 15,000 manufacturers in Canada, including key personnel. Indexed by trade name, product, and location.

The Corporate Directory of U.S. Public Companies. Walker's Western Research. • Annual. $360.00. Two volumes. Contains information on more than 10,000 publicly-traded companies, including names of executives and major subsidiaries. Includes financial and stock data.

D and B Million Dollar Directory. Dun and Bradstreet Information Services. • Annual. Commercial institutions, $1,395.00; libraries, $1,275.00. Lease basis.

Dun's Industrial Guide: The Metalworking Directory. Dun and Bradstreet Information Services Dun & Bradstreet Corp. • Annual. Libraries, $485; commercial institutions, $795.00. Lease basis. Three volumes. Lists about 65,000 U. S. manufacturing plants using metal and suppliers of metalworking equipment and materials. Includes names and titles of key personnel. Products, purchases, and processes are indicated.

Harris Manufacturers Directory: National Edition. Available from The Gale Group. • 1998. $520.00. Two volumes. Published by Harris InfoSource (http://www.harrisinfo.com). Provides statistical and descriptive information for about 46,000 U.S. industrial firms having 100 or more employees.

Hoover's Masterlist of Major U. S. Companies. Hoover's, Inc. • Biennial. $99.95. Provides brief information, including annual sales, number of employees, and chief executive, for about 5,100 U. S. companies, both public and private.

Kompass USA. Kompass USA, Inc. • Annual. $375.00. Four volumes. Includes information on about 125,000 U.S. companies. Classification system covers approximately 50,000 products and services. Product and tradename indexes are provided.

Macrae's Blue Book: Serving the Original Equipment Market. MacRae's Blue Book, Inc. • Annual. $170.00. Two volumes. Lists about 50,000 manufacturers of a wide variety of industrial equipment and supplies.

Standard and Poor's Register of Corporations, Directors and Executives. Standard and Poor's. • Annual. $675.00. Periodic supplementation. Over 55,000 public and privately held corporations in the U.S. Three volumes. Three supplements.

Thomas Register of American Manufacturers and Thomas Register Catalog File. Thomas Publishing Co., Inc. • Annual. $149.00. 34 volumes. A three-part system offering information on a wide variety of industrial equipment and supplies.

Ward's Business Directory of U. S. Private and Public Companies. The Gale Group. • 2000. $2,590.00. Eight volumes. *Ward's* contains basic information on about 120,000 business firms, of which 90 percent are private companies. Includes mid-year *Supplement.* Volumes available individually. Prices vary.

ENCYCLOPEDIAS AND DICTIONARIES

Encyclopedia of Emerging Industries. The Gale Group. • 2000. $295.00. Fourth edition. Provides detailed information on 90 "newly flourishing" industries. Includes historical background, organizational structure, significant individuals, current conditions, major companies, work force, technology trends, research developments, and other industry facts.

Knowledge Exchange Business Encyclopedia: Your Complete Business Advisor. Lorraine Spurge, editor. Knowledge Exchange LLC. • 1997. $45.00. Provides definitions of business terms and financial expressions, profiles of leading industries, tables of economic statistics, biographies of business leaders, and other business information. Includes "A Chronology of Business from 3000 B.C. Through 1995." Contains illustrations and three indexes.

HANDBOOKS AND MANUALS

Career Guide to Industries. Available from U. S. Government Printing Office. • 1998. $17.00. Issued by the Bureau of Labor Statistics, U. S. Department of Labor (http://www.bls.gov). Presents background career information (text) and statistics for the 40 industries that account for 70 percent of wage and salary jobs in the U. S. Includes nature of the industry, employment data, working conditions, training, earnings, rate of job growth, outlook, and other career factors. (BLS Bulletin 2503.).

Dun & Bradstreet/Gale Group Industry Handbooks. The Gale Group. • 2000. $630.00. Five volumes. $145.00 per volume. Each volume covers two or more major industries: 1. *Entertainment and Hospitality*; 2. *Construction and Agriculture*; 3. *Chemicals and Pharmaceuticals*; 4. *Computers & Software and Broadcasting & Telecommunications*; 5. *Insurance and Health & Medical Services.* The following are included for each industry: overview, statistics, financial ratios, rankings, merger information, company directory, directory of associations, and consultants directory.

Industry and Product Classification Manual (SIC Basis). Available from National Technical Information Service. • 1992. Issued by U. S. Bureau of the Census. Contains extended Standard Industrial Classification (SIC) numbers used by the Census Bureau to allow a more detailed classification of industry, services, and agriculture.

Manufacturing Processes Reference Guide. R. H. Todd and others, editors. Industrial Press, Inc. • 1994. $44.95. Describes 130 manufacturing processes used in industry.

North American Industry Classification System (NAICS). Available from Bernan Press. • 1998. $32.50. Issued by the Executive Office of the President, Office of Management and Budget (OMB). The 1997 NAICS six-digit classification scheme replaces the 1987 Standard Industrial Classification (SIC) four-digit system. Detailed information on NAICS is available at http://www.census.gov/epcd/www/naics.html.

Standard Industrial Classification Manual. U.S. Department of Commerce, Bureau of the Census. Available from U.S. Government Printing Office. • 1987. $36.00.

INTERNET DATABASES

Bureau of Economic Analysis (BEA). U. S. Department of Commerce, Bureau of Economic Analysis. Phone: (202)606-9900 Fax: (202)606-5310 E-mail: webmaster@bea.doc.gov • URL: http://www.bea.doc.gov • Web site includes "News Release Information" covering national, regional, and international economic estimates from the BEA. Highlights of releases appear online the same day, complete text and tables appear the next day. "Recent News Releases" section provides titles for past nine months, with links. "BEA Data and Methodology" includes "Frequently Requested NIPA Data" (national income and product accounts, such as gross domestic product and personal income). Other statistics are available. Fees: Free.

Bureau of Labor Statistics (BLS). U. S. Department of Labor, Bureau of Labor Statistics. Phone: (202)523-1092 E-mail: labstat.helpdesk@bls.gov • URL: http://www.bls.gov • Web site provides a great variety of employment, wage, price, and economic data. Some links are "Data," "Economy at a Glance," "Keyword Search of BLS Web Pages," "Regional Information," and "Other Statistical Sites." Fees: Free.

EBSCO Information Services. Ebsco Publishing. Phone: 800-871-8508 or (508)356-6500 Fax: (508)356-5640 E-mail: ep@epnet.com • URL: http://www.epnet.com • Fee-based Web site providing Internet access to a wide variety of databases, including business-related material. Full text is available for many periodical titles, with daily updates. Fees: Apply.

Fedstats. Federal Interagency Council on Statistical Policy. Phone: (202)395-7254 • URL: http://www.fedstats.gov • Web site features an efficient search facility for full-text statistics produced by more than 70 federal agencies, including the Census Bureau, the Bureau of Economic Analysis, and the Bureau of Labor Statistics. Boolean searches can be made within one agency or for all agencies combined. Links are offered to international statistical bureaus, including the UN, IMF, OECD, UNESCO, Eurostat, and 20 individual countries. Fees: Free.

1997 NAICS and 1987 SIC Correspondence Tables. U. S. Census Bureau. Phone: (301)457-4100 Fax: (301)457-1296 E-mail: naics@census.gov • URL: http://www.census.gov/epcd/www/naicstab.htm • Web site provides detailed tables for converting four-digit Standard Industrial Classification (SIC) numbers to the six-digit North American Industrial Classification System (NAICS) or vice versa: "1987 SIC Matched to 1997 NAICS" or "1997 NAICS Matched to 1987 SIC." Fees: Free.

ProQuest Direct. Bell & Howell Information and Learning. Phone: 800-521-0600 or (313)761-4700 Fax: (313)973-9145 • URL: http://www.umi.com/proquest • Fee-based Web site providing Internet access to more than 3,000 periodicals, newspapers, and other publications. Many items are available full-text, with daily updates. Includes extensive corporate and financial information from Disclosure, Inc. Fees: Apply.

Switchboard. Switchboard, Inc. Phone: (508)898-1000 Fax: (508)898-1755 E-mail: webmaster@switchboard.com • URL: http://www.switchboard.com • Web site provides telephone numbers and street addresses for more than 100 million business locations and residences in the U. S. Broad industry categories are available. Fees: Free.

U. S. Census Bureau: The Official Statistics. U. S. Bureau of the Census. Phone: (301)763-4100 Fax: (301)763-4794 • URL: http://www.census.gov • Web site is "Your Source for Social, Demographic, and Economic Information." Contains "Current U. S. Population Count," "Current Economic Indicators," and a wide variety of data under "Other Official Statistics." Keyword searching is provided. Fees: Free.

Wall Street Journal Interactive Edition. Dow Jones & Co., Inc. Phone: 800-369-2834 or (212)416-2000 Fax: (212)416-2658 E-mail: inquiries@interactive.wsj.com • URL: http://www.wsj.com • Fee-based Web site providing online searching of worldwide information from the *The Wall Street Journal.* Includes "Company Snapshots," "The Journal's Greatest Hits," "Index to Market Data," "14-Day Searchable Archive," "Journal Links," etc. Financial price quotes are available. Fees: $49.00 per year; $29.00 per year to print subscribers.

ONLINE DATABASES

Applied Science and Technology Index Online. H. W. Wilson Co. • Provides online indexing of 400 major scientific, technical, industrial, and engineering periodicals. Time period is 1983 to date. Monthly updates. Inquire as to online cost and availability.

Business and Industry. Responsive Database Services, Inc. • Contains online citations, abstracts, and selected fulltext from more than 1,000 trade journals, newspapers, and other publications. Provides general coverage of both manufacturing and service industries, including marketing, production, industry trends, key events, and information on specific companies. Time span is 1994 to date. Daily updates. Inquire as to online cost and availability. (Also available in a CD-ROM version.).

DRI U.S. Central Database. Data Products Division. • Provides more than 23,000 business, financial, demographic, economic, foreign trade, and industry-related time series for the U.S. Includes national income, population, retail-wholesale trade, price indexes, labor data, housing, industrial production, banking, interest rates, money supply, etc. Time period is generally 1947 to date (some data back to 1929). Updating varies. Inquire as to online cost and availability.

EconBase: Time Series and Forecasts. WEFA, Inc. • Presents online econometric data for business conditions, economics, demographics, industry, finance, employment, household income, interest rates, prices, etc. Includes two-year forecasts for a wide range of economic indicators. Time span is 1948 to date, with monthly updates. Inquire as to online cost and availability.

F & S Index. The Gale Group. • Contains about four million citations to worldwide business, financial, and industrial or consumer product literature appearing from 1972 to date. Weekly updates. Inquire as to online cost and availability.

Industry Insider. Thomson Financial Securities Data. • Contains full-text online industry research reports from more than 200 leading trade associations, covering 50 specific industries. Reports include extensive statistics and market research data. Inquire as to online cost and availability.

Market Share Reporter (MSR) [online]. The Gale Group. • Provides online market share data for individual companies, products, and services, covering all industries. Sources include various publications, trade journals, associations, government agencies, corporate reports, investment research reports, etc. Time period is 1991 to date, with annual updates. Inquire as to online cost and availability.

PROMT: Predicasts Overview of Markets and Technology. The Gale Group. • Companies, products, applied technologies and markets. U.S. and international literature coverage, 1972 to date. Inquire as to online cost and availability. Provides abstracts from more than 1,600 publications. Weekly updates.

Tablebase. Responsive Database Services, Inc. • Provides online numerical tabular data from a wide variety of business, organization, and government sources, including 900 trade journals. Includes industry and individual company statistics relating to products, market share, sales forecasts, production, exports, market trends, etc. Time span is 1997 to date. Weekly updates. Inquire as to online cost and availability. (Also available in a CD-ROM version.).

Thomas Register Online. Thomas Publishing Co., Inc. • Provides concise information on approximately 194,000 U. S. companies, mainly manufacturers, with over 50,000 product classifications. Indexes over 115,000 trade names. Information is updated semiannually. Inquire as to online cost and availability.

Trade & Industry Index. The Gale Group. • Provides indexing of business periodicals, January 1981 to date. Daily updates. (Full text articles from some periodicals are available online, 1983 to date, in the companion database, *Trade & Industry ASAP.*) Inquire as to online cost and availability.

PERIODICALS AND NEWSLETTERS

American Industry. Publications for Industry. • Monthly. $25.00 per year.

Fortune Magazine. Time Inc., Business Information Group. • Biweekly. $59.95 per year. Edited for top executives and upper-level managers.

IEEE Industry Applications Magazine. Institute of Electrical and Electronics Engineers. • Bimonthly. $190.00 per year. Covers new industrial applications of power conversion, drives, lighting, and control. Emphasis is on the petroleum, chemical, rubber, plastics, textile, and mining industries.

Industries in Transition; A Newsletter Written for Growth Directed Management and Business Planners. Business Communications Co., Inc. • Monthly. $375.00 per year. Newsletter. Formerly *Growth Industry News.*

Industry Week: The Industry Management Magazine. Penton Media, Inc. • 18 times a year. Free to qualified personnel; others, $65.00 per year. Edited for industrial and business managers. Covers organizational and technological developments affecting industrial management.

Journal of Industrial Ecology. Yale University, School of Forestry and Environmental Studies. MIT Press. • Quarterly. Individuals, $40.00 per year; institutions, $115.00 per year; students and retired persons, $30.00 per year. Contains multidisciplinary articles on the relationships between industrial activity and the environment.

The Levy Institute Forecast. Bard College, Jerome Levy Economics Institute. • 12 times a year. $295.00 per year. Looseleaf service. Includes quarterly supplement. Formerly *Industry Forecast.*

The Wall Street Journal. Dow Jones & Co., Inc. • Daily. $175.00 per year. Covers news and trends relating to business, industry, finance, the economy, and international commerce. Provides extensive price and other data for the securities, commodity, options, futures, foreign exchange, and money markets.

RESEARCH CENTERS AND INSTITUTES

Conference Board, Inc. 845 Third Ave., New York, NY 10022. Phone: (212)759-0900 Fax: (212)980-7014 E-mail: richard.cavanaugh@conference-board.org • URL: http://www.conference-board.org.

National Center for Manufacturing Sciences. 3025 Boardwalk, Ann Arbor, MI 48108. Phone: (734)995-0300 Fax: (734)995-4004 E-mail: johnd@ncms.org • URL: http://www.ncms.org • Research areas include process technology and control, machine mechanics, sensors, testing methods, and quality assurance.

STATISTICS SOURCES

American Business Climate and Economic Profiles. The Gale Group. • 1993. $135.00. Provides business, industrial, demographic, and economic figures for all states and 300 metropolitan areas. Includes production, taxation, population, growth rates, labor force data, incomes, total sales, etc.

Annual Survey of Manufactures. Available from U. S. Government Printing Office. • Annual. Prices vary. Issued by the U. S. Census Bureau as an interim update to the *Census of Manufactures.* Includes data on number of manufacturing establishments in various industries, employment, labor costs, value of shipments, capital expenditures, inventories, energy costs, and assets. (See also Census Bureau home page, http://www.census.gov/.).

Business Statistics of the United States. Courtenay M. Slater, editor. Bernan Associates. • 1999. $74.00. Fifth edition. Based on *Business Statistics*, formerly issue by the Bureau of Economic Analysis, U. S. Department of Commerce. Provides basic data for a wide variety of U. S. industries, services, and economic indicators. Most statistics are shown annually for 29 years and monthly for the most recent four years.

By the Numbers: Electronic and Online Publishing. The Gale Group. • 1997. $385.00. Four volumes. $99.00 per volume. Covers "high-interest" industries: 1. *By the Numbers: Electronic and Online Publishing*; 2. *By the Numbers: Emerging Industries*; 3. *By the Numbers: Nonprofits*; 4. *By the Numbers: Publishing.* Each volume provides about 600 tabulations of industry data on revenues, market share, employment, trends, financial ratios, profits, salaries, and so forth. Citations to data sources are included.

County Business Patterns. Available from U. S. Government Printing Office. • Irregular. 52 issues containing annual data for each state, the District of Columbia, and a U. S. Summary. Produced by U.S. Bureau of the Census (http://www.census.gov). Provides local establishment and employment statistics by industry.

Dun's Census of American Business. Dun and Bradstreet, Economic Analysis Dept. • Annual. $325.00.

Economic Report of the President: Together with the Annual Report of the Council of Economic Advisors.

Available from U. S. Government Printing Office. • Annual. $29.00. Includes about 130 pages of "Statistical Tables Relating to Income, Employment, and Production." Tables cover national income, employment, wages, productivity, manufacturing, prices, credit, finance (public and private), corporate profits, and foreign trade.

Encyclopedia of American Industries. The Gale Group. • 1998. $560.00. Second edition. Two volumes. $280.00 per volume. Volume one is *Manufacturing Industries* and volume two is *Service and Non-Manufacturing Industries.* Provides the history, development, and recent status of approximately 1,000 industries. Includes statistical graphs, with industry and general indexes.

Encyclopedia of Global Industries. The Gale Group. • 1999. $420.00. Second edition. Provides detailed statistical information on 115 industries. Coverage is international, with country and subject indexes.

Federal Reserve Bulletin. U.S. Federal Reserve System. • Monthly. $25.00 per year. Provides statistics on banking and the economy, including interest rates, money supply, and the Federal Reserve Board indexes of industrial production.

Handbook of North American Industry: NAFTA and the Economies of its Member Nations. John E. Cremeans, editor. Bernan Press. • 1999. $89.00. Second edition. Provides detailed industry statistics for the U.S., Canada, and Mexico.

Handbook of U. S. Labor Statistics: Employment, Earnings, Prices, Productivity, and Other Labor Data. Eva E. Jacobs, editor. Bernan Associates. • 1999. $74.00. Based on *Handbook of Labor Statistics,* formerly issued by the Bureau of Labor Statistics, U. S. Department of Labor. Includes the Bureau's projections of employment in the U. S. by industry and occupation. Provides a wide variety of data on the work force, prices, fringe benefits, and consumer expenditures.

Indicators of Industrial Activity. OECD Publications and Information Center. • Quarterly. $114.00 per year. Information on production, deliveries, orders, prices and employment for 17 industrial sectors in selected OECD member countries.

Industrial Commodity Statistics Yearbook. United Nations Dept. of Economic and Social Affairs. United Nations Publications. • Annual.

Manufacturers' Shipments, Inventories, and Orders. Available from U. S. Government Printing Office. • Monthly. $70.00 per year. Issued by Bureau of the Census, U. S. Department of Commerce. Includes monthly *Advance Report on Durable Goods.* Provides data on production, value, shipments, and consumption for a wide variety of manufactured products. (Current Industrial Reports, M3-1.).

Manufacturing Profiles. Available from U. S. Government Printing Office. • Annual. Issued by the U. S. Census Bureau. A printed consolidation of the entire *Current Industrial Report* series, presenting "all the data compiled." Contains statistics on production, shipments, inventories, consumption, exports, imports, and orders for a wide variety of manufactured products. (See also Census Bureau home page, http://www.census.gov/.).

Manufacturing Worldwide: Industry Analyses, Statistics, Products, Leading Companies and Countries. The Gale Group. • 1999. $220.00. Third edition. A guide to worldwide economic activity in 500 product lines within 140 countries. Includes 37 detailed industry profiles. Name, address, phone, fax, employment, and ranking are shown for major companies worldwide in each industry sector.

Monthly Bulletin of Statistics. United Nations Publications. • Monthly. $295.00 per year. Provides current data for about 200 countries on a wide variety of economic, industrial, and demographic subjects. Compiled by United Nations Statistical Office.

Social Statistics of the United States. Mark S. Littman, editor. Bernan Press. • 2000. $65.00. Includes statistical data on population growth, labor force, occupations, environmental trends, leisure time use, income, poverty, taxes, and other economic or demographic topics.

SRC Green Book of 35-Year Charts. • Annual. $119.00. Chart book presents statistical information on the stocks of 400 leading companies over a 35-year period. Each full page chart is in semi-log format to avoid visual distortion. Also includes charts of 12 leading market averages or indexes and 39 major industry groups.

Standard & Poor's Industry Surveys. Standard & Poor's. • Semiannual. $1,800.00. Two looseleaf volumes. Includes monthly supplements. Provides detailed, individual surveys of 52 major industry groups. Each survey is revised on a semiannual basis. Also includes "Monthly Investment Review" (industry group investment analysis) and monthly "Trends & Projections" (economic analysis).

State Profiles: The Population and Economy of Each U. S. State. Courtenay Slater and Martha Davis, editors. Bernan Press. • 1999. $74.00. Presents charts, tables, and text in an eight-page profile for each state. Covers population, labor force, income, poverty, employment, wages, industry, trade, housing, education, health, taxes, and government finances.

Statistical Abstract of the United States. Available from U. S. Government Printing Office. • Annual. $51.00. Issued by the U. S. Bureau of the Census.

A Statistical Portrait of the United States: Social Conditions and Trends. Mark S. Littman, editor. Bernan Press. • 1998. $89.00. Covers "social, economic, and environmental trends in the United States over the past 25 years." Includes statistical tables, graphs, and analysis relating to such topics as population, income, poverty, wealth, labor, housing, education, healthcare, air/water quality, and government.

Statistical Yearbook. United Nations Publications. • Annual. $125.00. Contains statistics for about 200 countries on a wide variety of economic, industrial, and demographic topics. Compiled by United Nations Statistical Office.

Survey of Current Business. Available from U. S. Government Printing Office. • Monthly. $49.00 per year. Issued by Bureau of Economic Analysis, U. S. Department of Commerce. Presents a wide variety of business and economic data.

U. S. Industry and Trade Outlook: The McGraw-Hill Companies and the U.S. Department of Commerce/ International Trade Administration. Datapso Research Corp. • Annual. $69.95. Produced by the International Trade Administration, U. S. Department of Commerce, in a "public-private" partnership with DRI/McGraw-Hill and Standard & Poor's. Provides basic data, outlook for the current year, and "Long-Term Prospects" (five-year projections) for a wide variety of products and services. Includes high technology industries. Formerly *U. S. Industrial Outlook.*

U. S. Industry Profiles: The Leading 100. The Gale Group. • 1998. $120.00. Second edition. Contains detailed profiles, with statistics, of 100 industries in the areas of manufacturing, construction, transportation, wholesale trade, retail trade, and entertainment.

U. S. Market Trends and Forecasts. The Gale Group. • 2000. $315.00. Second edition. Provides graphic representation of market statistics by means of pie charts and tables for each of 30 major industries and 400 market segments. Includes market forecasts and historical overviews.

United States Census of Manufactures. U.S. Bureau of the Census. • Quinquennial. Results presented in reports, tape, CD-ROM, and Diskette files.

World Statistics Pocketbook. United Nations Publications. • Annual. $10.00. Presents basic economic, social, and environmental indicators for about 200 countries and areas. Covers more than 50 items relating to population, economic activity, labor force, agriculture, industry, energy, trade, transportation, communication, education, tourism, and the environment. Statistical sources are noted.

TRADE/PROFESSIONAL ASSOCIATIONS

National Association of Manufacturers. 1331 Pennsylvania Ave., N.W., Suite 600, Washington, DC 20004. Phone: 800-814-8468 or (202)637-3000 Fax: (202)637-3182 E-mail: manufacting@nam.org • URL: http://www.nam.org.

OTHER SOURCES

Bizlink. Rogers Media. • Web site provides news and information from 30 Canadian business and industrial publications issued by Rogers Media (formerly Maclean Hunter). Keyword searching is available for "all of the Bizlink archive" or for each of seven areas: Industry, Financial, Construction, Retailing, Marketing, Media, and Agriculture. Updates are daily. Fees: Free.

Business & Company Resource Center. The Gale Group. • Fee-based Web site provides a wide range of business, industry, and specific company information. Access is offered to trade journal articles, market research data, insider trading activity, major shareholder data, corporate histories, emerging technology reports, corporate earnings estimates, press releases, and other sources. Provides detailed company profiles, industry overviews, and rankings. Offers integration of Predicasts PROMT, Newsletters ASAP, Investext Plus, Business Index ASAP, Brands and Their Companies, and other databases (many have full text).

The Business Elite: Database of Corporate America. Donnelley Marketing. • Quarterly. $795.00. Formerly compiled by Database America. Provides current information on CD-ROM for about 850,000 businesses, comprising all U. S. private and public companies having more than 20 employees or sales of more than $1 million. Data for each firm includes detailed industry classification, year started, annual sales, name of top executive, and number of employees.

Business Rankings Annual. The Gale Group. • Annual. $305.00.Two volumes. Compiled by the Business Library Staff of the Brooklyn Public Library. This is a guide to lists and rankings appearing in major business publications. The top ten names are listed in each case.

D & B Business Locator. Dun & Bradstreet, Inc. • Quarterly. $2,495.00 per year. CD-ROM provides concise information on more than 10 million U. S. companies or businesses. Includes data on number of employees.

Dun's Middle Market Disc. Dun & Bradstreet, Inc. • Quarterly. Price on application. CD-ROM provides information on more than 150,000 middle market U. S. private companies and their executives.

Dun's Million Dollar Disc. Dun & Bradstreet, Inc. • Quarterly. $3,800.00 per year to libraries; $5,500.00 per year to businesses. CD-ROM provides information on more than 240,000 public and private U. S. companies having sales volume of $5 million

 For publishers addresses, refer to SOURCES CITED section at the back of the book.

or more or 100 employees or more. Includes biographical data on more than 640,000 company executives.

Factiva. Dow Jones Reuters Business Interactive, LLC. • Fee-based Web site provides "global news and business information through Web sites and content integration solutions." Includes Dow Jones and Reuters newswires, The Wall Street Journal, and more than 7,000 other sources of current news, historical articles, market research reports, and investment analysis. Content includes 96 major U. S. newspapers, 900 non-English sources, trade publications, media transcripts, country profiles, news photos, etc.

Infogate. Infogate, Inc. • Web site provides current news and information on seven "channels": News, Fun, Sports, Info, Finance, Shop, and Travel. Among the content partners are Business Wire, CBS MarketWatch, CNN, Morningstar, Standard & Poor's, and Thomson Investors Network. Fees: Free, but downloading of Infogate software is required (includes personalized news feature). Updating is continuous. Formerly Pointcast Network.

InSite 2. Intelligence Data/Thomson Financial. • Fee-based Web site consolidates information in a "Base Pack" consisting of Business InSite, Market InSite, and Company InSite. Optional databases are Consumer InSite, Health and Wellness InSite, Newsletter InSite, and Computer InSite. Includes fulltext content from more than 2,500 trade publications, journals, newsletters, newspapers, analyst reports, and other sources. Continuous updating. Formerly produced by The Gale Group.

Manufacturing and Distribution USA. The Gale Group. • 2000. $375.00. Three volumes. Replaces *Manufacturing USA* and *Wholesale and Retail Trade USA.* Presents statistics and projections relating to economic activity in more than 500 business classifications.

Nexis.com. Lexis-Nexis Group. • Fee-based Web site offers searching of about 2.8 billion documents in some 30,000 news, business, and legal information sources. Features include a subject directory covering 1,200 topics in 34 categories and a Company Dossier containing information on more than 500,000 public and private companies. Boolean searching is offered.

World Business Rankings Annual. The Gale Group. • 1998. $189.00. Provides 2,500 ranked lists of international companies, compiled from a variety of published sources. Each list shows the "top ten" in a particular category. Keyword indexing, a country index, and citations are provided.

INDUSTRY, REGULATION OF

See: REGULATION OF INDUSTRY

INFANTS WEAR

See: CHILDREN'S APPAREL INDUSTRY

INFLATION

See also: MONEY; PRICES AND PRICING

GENERAL WORKS

Financial Institutions and Markets. Robert W. Kolb and Ricardo J. Rodriguez. Blackwell Publishers. • 1996. $77.95. Contains 40 articles (chapters) by various authors on U. S. financial markets and other topics. Includes separate chapters on the International Monetary Fund, inflation, monetary policy, the national debt, bank failures, derivatives, stock prices, initial public offerings, government bonds, pensions, foreign exchange, international markets, and other subjects.

Great Inflations of the 20th Century: Theories, Policies, and Evidence. Pierre L. Siklos, editor. Edward Elgar Publishing, Inc. • 1995. $95.00. Contains reprints of papers on the history and economic analysis of major inflations.

How to Invest Wisely. Lawrence S. Pratt. American Institute for Economic Research. • 1998. $9.00. Presents a conservative policy of investing, with emphasis on dividend-paying common stocks. Gold and other inflation hedges are compared. Includes a reprint of *Toward an Optimal Stock Selection Strategy* (1997). (Economic Education Bulletin.).

Inflation, Exchange Rates, and the World Economy: Lectures on International Monetary Economics. W. M. Corden. University of Chicago Press. • 1986. $22.50. Third edition. (Studies in Business and Society Series).

Money: Its Origins, Development, Debasement, and Prospects. John H. Wood. American Institute for Economic Research. • 1999. $10.00. A politically conservative view of monetary history, the gold standard, banking systems, and inflation. Includes a list of references. (Economic Education Bulletin.).

Reducing Inflation: Motivation and Strategy. Christina D. Romer and David H. Romer, editors. University of Chicago Press. • 1997. $58.00. Consists of 10 essays and comments by various economists on strategies for controlling inflation. *National Bureau of Economic Research Project Reports.*

Social Effects of Inflation. Marvin E. Wolfgang and Richard D. Lambert, editors. American Academy of Political and Social Science. • 1981. $28.00. (Annuals of the American Academy of Political and Social Science Series: No. 456).

ABSTRACTS AND INDEXES

Business Periodicals Index. H. W. Wilson Co. • Monthly, except August, with quarterly and annual cumulations. Service basis for print edition; CD-ROM edition, $1,495.00 per year.

Social Sciences Index. H. W. Wilson Co. • Quarterly, with annual cumulation. Service basis for print edition; CD-ROM edition, $1,495 per year. Indexes more than 400 periodicals covering economics, environmental policy, government, insurance, labor, health care policy, plannning, public administration, public welfare, urban studies, women's issues, criminology, and related topics.

CD-ROM DATABASES

Magazine Index Plus. The Gale Group. • Monthly. $4,000.00 per year (includes InfoTrac workstation). Provides full text on CD-ROM for about 100 popular, general interest magazines and indexing for 300 others. Includes special indexing of reviews and product evaluations. Time period is 1980 to date.

Social Science Source. EBSCO Publishing. • Monthly. $1,495.00 per year. Provides CD-ROM citations and abstracts to social science articles in more than 600 periodicals, with full text from 125 periodicals. Covers economics, political science, public policy, international relations, psychology, and other topics. Time period is most recent five years.

Social Sciences Citation Index: Compact Disc Edition with Abstracts. Institute for Scientific Information. • Quarterly. Provides CD-ROM indexing and abstracting of "significant articles" from 1,400 social science journals worldwide, with additional selections from 3,200 other journals, 1986 to date. Includes economics, business, finance, management, communications, demographics, information and library science, political science, sociology, and many other subjects.

WILSONDISC: Wilson Social Sciences Abstracts. H. W. Wilson Co. • Monthly. Including unlimited online access to *Social Sciences Index* through WILSONLINE. Provides CD-ROM indexing from 1983 and abstracting from 1994 of more than 400 periodicals covering economics, area studies, community health, public administration, public welfare, urban studies, and many other topics related to the social sciences.

HANDBOOKS AND MANUALS

Nations of the World: A Political, Economic, and Business Handbook. Grey House Publishing. • 2000. $135.00. Includes descriptive data on economic characteristics, population, gross domestic product (GDP), banking, inflation, agriculture, tourism, and other factors. Covers "all the nations of the world.".

INTERNET DATABASES

Fedstats. Federal Interagency Council on Statistical Policy. Phone: (202)395-7254 • URL: http://www.fedstats.gov • Web site features an efficient search facility for full-text statistics produced by more than 70 federal agencies, including the Census Bureau, the Bureau of Economic Analysis, and the Bureau of Labor Statistics. Boolean searches can be made within one agency or for all agencies combined. Links are offered to international statistical bureaus, including the UN, IMF, OECD, UNESCO, Eurostat, and 20 individual countries. Fees: Free.

ONLINE DATABASES

ABI/INFORM. Bell & Howell Information and Learning. • Provides online indexing to business-related material occurring in over 1,000 periodicals from 1971 to the present. Inquire as to online cost and availability.

DRI U.S. Central Database. Data Products Division. • Provides more than 23,000 business, financial, demographic, economic, foreign trade, and industry-related time series for the U.S. Includes national income, population, retail-wholesale trade, price indexes, labor data, housing, industrial production, banking, interest rates, money supply, etc. Time period is generally 1947 to date (some data back to 1929). Updating varies. Inquire as to online cost and availability.

EconBase: Time Series and Forecasts. WEFA, Inc. • Presents online econometric data for business conditions, economics, demographics, industry, finance, employment, household income, interest rates, prices, etc. Includes two-year forecasts for a wide range of economic indicators. Time span is 1948 to date, with monthly updates. Inquire as to online cost and availability.

EconLit. American Economic Association. • Covers the worldwide literature of economics as contained in selected monographs and about 550 journals. Subjects include microeconomics, macroeconomics, economic history, inflation, money, credit, finance, accounting theory, trade, natural resource economics, and regional economics. Time period is 1969 to present, with monthly updates. Inquire as to online cost and availability.

Wilson Business Abstracts Online. H. W. Wilson Co. • Indexes and abstracts 600 major business periodicals, plus the *Wall Street Journal* and the business section of the *New York Times.* Indexing is from 1982, abstracting from 1990, with the two newspapers included from 1993. Updated weekly. Inquire as to online cost and availability. (*Business Periodicals Index* without abstracts is also available online.).

Wilson Social Sciences Abstracts Online. H. W. Wilson Co. • Provides online abstracting and indexing of more than 415 periodicals covering area studies, community health, public administration, public welfare, urban studies, and many other social science topics. Time period is 1994 to date for abstracts and 1983 to date for indexing, with updates monthly. Inquire as to online cost and availability.

PERIODICALS AND NEWSLETTERS

Blue Chip Financial Forecasts: What Top Analysts are Saying About U. S. and Foreign Interest Rates, Monetary Policy, Inflation, and Economic Growth. Aspen Publishers, Inc. • Monthly. $654.00 per year. Newsletter. Gives forecasts about a year in advance for interest rates, inflation, currency exchange rates, monetary policy, and economic growth rates.

Forecasts and Strategies. Phillips Business Information, Inc. • Monthly. $99.00 per year. Covers inflation, taxes and government controls.

Personal Finance. Kephart Communications, Inc. • Biweekly. $118.00 per year. Investment advisory newsletter.

PRICE SOURCES

CPI Detailed Report: Consumer Price Index. Available from U.S. Government Printing Office. • Monthly. $45.00 per year. Cost of living data.

STATISTICS SOURCES

ACCRA Cost of Living Index (Association for Applied Community Reseach). ACCRA. • Quarterly. $130.00 per year. Compares price levels for 280-310 U.S. cities.

The AIER Chart Book. AIER Research Staff. American Institute for Economic Research. • Annual. $3.00. A compact compilation of long-range charts ("Purchasing Power of the Dollar," for example, goes back to 1780) covering various aspects of the U. S. economy. Includes inflation, interest rates, debt, gold, taxation, stock prices, etc. (Economic Education Bulletin.).

American Cost of Living Survey. The Gale Group. • 1995. $160.00. Second edition. Cost of living data is provided for 455 U.S. cities and metroploitan areas.

Business Statistics of the United States. Courtenay M. Slater, editor. Bernan Associates. • 1999. $74.00. Fifth edition. Based on *Business Statistics*, formerly issue by the Bureau of Economic Analysis, U. S. Department of Commerce. Provides basic data for a wide variety of U. S. industries, services, and economic indicators. Most statistics are shown annually for 29 years and monthly for the most recent four years.

Economic Indicators Handbook: Time Series, Conversions, Documentation. The Gale Group. • 2000. $195.00. Sixth edition. Provides data for about 175 U. S. economic indicators, such as the consumer price index (CPI), gross national product (GNP), and the rate of inflation. Values for series are given since inception, in both original form and adjusted for inflation. A bibliography of sources is included.

Prices and Earnings Around the Globe. Union Bank of Switzerland. • Irregular. Free. Published in Zurich. Compares prices and purchasing power in 48 major cities of the world. Wages and hours are also compared. Text in English, French, German, and Italian.

SBBI Monthly Market Reports. Ibbotson Associates. • Monthly. $995.00 per year. These reports provide current updating of stocks, bonds, bills, and inflation (SBBI) data. Each issue contains the most recent month's investment returns and index values for various kinds of securities, as well as monthly statistics for the past year. Analysis is included.

SBBI Quarterly Market Reports. Ibbotson Associates. • Quarterly. $495.00 per year. Each quarterly volume contains detailed updates to stocks, bonds, bills, and inflation (SBBI) data. Includes total and sector returns for the broad stock market, small company stocks, intermediate and long-term government bonds, long-term corporate bonds, and U. S. Treasury Bills. Analyses, tables, graphs, and market consensus forecasts are provided.

Stocks, Bonds, Bills, and Inflation Yearbook. Ibbotson Associates. • Annual. $92.00. Provides detailed data from 1926 to the present on inflation and the returns from various kinds of financial investments, such as small-cap stocks and long-term government bonds.

Survey of Current Business. Available from U. S. Government Printing Office. • Monthly. $49.00 per year. Issued by Bureau of Economic Analysis, U. S. Department of Commerce. Presents a wide variety of business and economic data.

The Value of a Dollar. Grey House Publishing, Inc. • 1999. $125.00.

World Cost of Living Survey. The Gale Group. • 1999. $255.00. Second edition. Arranged by country and then by city within each country. Provides cost of living data for many products and services. Includes indexes and an annotated bibliography.

OTHER SOURCES

The Value of a Dollar: Millennium Edition, 1860-1999. Grey House Publishing. • 1999. $135.00. Second edition. Shows the actual prices of thousands of items available to consumers from the Civil War era to recent years. Includes selected data on consumer expenditures, investments, income, and jobs. (Universal Reference Publications.).

INFORMATION BROKERS

See: INFORMATION INDUSTRY

INFORMATION, FREEDOM OF

See: FREEDOM OF INFORMATION

INFORMATION INDUSTRY

See also: ONLINE INFORMATION SYSTEMS

GENERAL WORKS

Artificial Intelligence: Its Role in the Information Industry. Peter Davies. Information Today, Inc. • 1991. $39.50.

Economics of Information: A Guide to Economic and Cost-Benefit Analysis for Information Professionals. Bruce R. Kingma. Libraries Unlimited, Inc. • 2000. $45.00. Second edition. A technical discussion of market forces affecting the information industry. (Library and Information Science Text Series).

Expanding Technologies, Expanding Careers: Librarianship in Transition. Ellis Mount, editor. Special Libraries Association. • 1997. $45.00. Contains articles on alternative, non-traditional career paths for librarians, whether as entrepreneurs or employees. All the careers are related to computer-based, information retrieval and technology.

Future Libraries: Dreams, Madness, and Reality. Walt Crawford and Michael Gorman. American Library Association. • 1995. $28.00. Discusses the "over-hyped virtual library" and electronic-publishing "fantasies." Presents the argument for the importance of books, physical libraries, and library personnel.

Highway of Dreams: A Critical View Along the Information Superhighway. A. Michael Noll. Lawrence Erlbaum Associates, Inc. • 1996. $49.95. States that such factors as consumer needs and finance are often of more importance to the information industry than technological utopia. Includes such chapter headings as "Historical Perspective," "History Repeats," "Business Considerations," and "The Internet Exposed." (LEA's Telecommunications Series).

Info Rich-Info Poor: Access and Exchange in the Global Information Society. Trevor Haywood. Bowker-Saur. • 1995. $60.00. Published by K. G. Saur.

Information Imagineering: Meeting at the Interface. Milton T. Wolf and others, editors. American Library Association. • 1997. $36.00. A collection of articles on the effect of information technology on libraries, museums, and other institutions.

Information Management for the Intelligent Organization: The Art of Scanning the Environment. Chun Wei Choo. Information Today, Inc. • 1998. $39.50. Second edition. Published on behalf of the American Society for Information Science (ASIS). Covers the general principles of acquiring, creating, organizing, and using information within organizations.

Information Science: An Integrated View. Anthony Debons and others. Pearson Education and Technology. • 1988. $35.00. History, theory, and methodology. (Professional Librarian Series).

Interface Culture: How New Technology Transforms the Way We Create and Communicate. Steven Johnson. HarperCollins Publishers. • 1997. $24.00. A discussion of how computer interfaces and online technology ("cyberspace") affect society in general.

Knowledge Management for the Information Professional. T. Kanti Srikantaiah and Michael Koenig, editors. Information Today, Inc. • 2000. $44.50. Contains articles by 26 contributors on the concept of "knowledge management.".

The Shape of Things to Come: Seven Imperatives for Winning in the New World of Business. Richard W. Oliver. McGraw-Hill. • 1998. $24.95. Contains predictions relating to the influence of information technology on 21st century business. (Business Week Books.).

Silicon Snake Oil: Second Thoughts on the Information Highway. Clifford Stoll. Doubleday. • 1996. $14.00. The author discusses the extravagant claims being made for online networks and multimedia.

ABSTRACTS AND INDEXES

Applied Science and Technology Index. H. W. Wilson Co. • 11 times a year. Quarterly and annual cumulations. Service basis for print edition; CD-ROM edition, $1,495.00 per year. Indexes a wide variety of English language technical, industrial, and engineering periodicals.

Business Periodicals Index. H. W. Wilson Co. • Monthly, except August, with quarterly and annual cumulations. Service basis for print edition; CD-ROM edition, $1,495.00 per year.

Computer and Information Systems Abstracts Journal: An Abstract Journal Pertaining to the Theory, Design, Fabrication and Application of Computer and Information Systems. Cambridge Information Group. • Monthly. $1,045 per year.

Computer Literature Index: A Subject/Author Index to Computer and Data Processing Literature. Applied Computer Research, Inc. • Quarterly, with annual cumulation. $245.00 per year. Contains brief abstracts of book and periodical literature covering all phases of computing, including approximately 70 specific application areas.

Information Science Abstracts. American Society for Information Science. Information Today, Inc. • 11 times a year. $685.00 per year.

Library Literature and Information Science: An Index to Library and Information Science Publications. H. W. Wilson Co. • Bimonthly. Annual cumulation. Service basis. Formerly *Library Literature.*

LISA: Library and Information Science Abstracts. Bowker-Saur. • Monthly. $800.00 per year. Annual cumulation.

Social Sciences Citation Index. Institute for Scientific Information. • Three times a year. $6,900 per year. Annual cumulation. Includes *Source Index, Citation Index, Permuterm Subject Index,* and *Corporate Index.*

ALMANACS AND YEARBOOKS

Annual Review of Information Science and Technology. Martha E. Williams, editor. Information Today, Inc. • Annual. Members, $79.95; non-members, $99.95. Published on behalf of the American Society for Information Science (ASIS). Covers trends in planning, basic techniques, applications, and the information profession in general.

Information Technology Outlook. OECD Publications and Information Center. • Biennial. $72.00. A review of recent developments in international markets for computer hardware, software, and services. Also examines current legal provisions for information systems security and privacy in OECD countries.

NFAIS Yearbook of the Information Industry. Arthur W. Elias, editor. Information Today, Inc. • 1993. $40.00. Compiled by the National Federation of Abstracting and Information Services (NFAIS). Summarizes and analyzes the impacts of each year's events on information, abstracting, and indexing activities.

CD-ROM DATABASES

Computer Select. The Gale Group. • Monthly. $1,250.00 per year. Provides one year of full-text on CD-ROM for 120 leading computer-related publications. Also includes 70,000 product specifications and brief profiles of 13,000 computer product vendors and manufacturers.

Information Science Abstracts. Information Today, Inc. • Quarterly. $1,095.00 per year. Presents CD-ROM abstracts of worldwide information science and library science literature from 1966 to date.

LISA Plus: Library and Information Science Abstracts. Bowker-Saur, Reed Reference Publishing. • Quarterly. $1,450.00 per year. Provides CD-ROM abstracting and indexing of the world's library and information science literature. Covers a wide variety of topics.

Social Sciences Citation Index: Compact Disc Edition. Institute for Scientific Information. • Quarterly. Provides CD-ROM indexing of the world's social sciences literature, including economics, business, finance, management, communications, demographics, information and library science, political science, sociology, etc. Corresponds to online *Social Scisearch* and printed *Social Sciences Citation Index.*

Social Sciences Citation Index: Compact Disc Edition with Abstracts. Institute for Scientific Information. • Quarterly. Provides CD-ROM indexing and abstracting of "significant articles" from 1,400 social science journals worldwide, with additional selections from 3,200 other journals, 1986 to date. Includes economics, business, finance, management, communications, demographics, information and library science, political science, sociology, and many other subjects.

WILSONDISC: Library Literature and Information Science Index. H. W. Wilson Co. • Quarterly. Including unlimited access to the online version of *Library Literature.* Provides CD-ROM indexing of about 300 periodicals, covering a wide range of topics having to do with libraries, library management, and the information industry.

DIRECTORIES

ASIS Handbook and Directory. American Society for Information Science. • Annual. Members, $25.00; non-members, $100.00.

Burwell World Directory of Information Brokers. Helen P. Burwell, editor. Burwell Enterprises, Inc. • Annual. $59.50. Lists nearly 1,800 information brokers, document delivery firms, free-lance librarians, and fee-based library services. Provides U. S. and international coverage (46 countries). Formerly *Directory of Fee-Based Information Services.*

Cyberstocks: An Investor's Guide to Internet Companies. Alan Chai. Hoover's, Inc. • 1996. $24.95. Provides detailed profiles of 101 publicly traded companies involved in one way or another with the Internet.

Data Sources: The Comprehensive Guide to the Data Processing Industry Hardware, Data Communications Products, Software, Company Profiles. The Gale Group. • Semiannual. $495.00 per year. Two volumes. Describes hardware and software for all computer operating sysems, including prices and technical details. Lists about 75,000 products from 14,000 suppliers. Industry-specific software applications are described.

Gale Directory of Databases. The Gale Group. • 2001. $400.00. Two volumes. Volume 1, $270.00; volume 2, $180.00. *Volume 1: Online Databases* and *Volume 2: CD-ROM, Diskette, Magnetic Tape, Handheld, and Batch Access Database Products.*

Information Industry Directory. The Gale Group. • 2000. $635.00. 22nd edition. Two volumes. Lists nearly 4,600 producers and vendors of electronic information and related services. Subject, geographic, and master indexes are provided.

Information Marketplace Directory. SIMBA Information. • 1996. $295.00. Second edition. Lists computer-based information processing and multimedia companies, including those engaged in animation, audio, video, and interactive video.

Information Sources: The Annual Directory of the Information Industry Association. Software and Information Industry Association. • Annual. Members, $75.00; non-members, $125.00.

Internet Tools of the Profession: A Guide for Information Professionals. Hope N. Tillman, editor. Special Libraries Association. • 1997. $49.00. Second edition. Consists of 14 sections by various authors or compilers. After two introductory articles on searching the Internet, there are 12 annotated lists of useful Web sites, covering the SLA, business and finance, chemistry, education, food and agriculture, information technology, insurance and employee benefits, law, library management, metals and materials, pharmaceuticals, and telecommunications. An index is provided.

KMWorld Buyer's Guide. Knowledge Asset Media. • Semiannual. Controlled circulation as part of *KMWorld.* Contains corporate and product profiles related to various aspects of knowledge management and information systems. (Knowledge Asset Media is a an affiliate of Information Today, Inc.).

Peterson's Graduate and Professional Programs: Business, Education, Health, Information Studies, Law, and Social Work. Peterson's Magazine Group. • Annual. $27.95. Provides details of graduate and professional programs in business, law, information, and other fields at colleges and universities. Formerly *Peterson's Guide to Graduate Programs in Business, Education, Health, Information Studies, Law and Social Work.*

Plunkett's InfoTech Industry Almanac: Complete Profiles on the InfoTech 500-the Leading Firms in the Movement and Management of Voice, Data, and Video. Available from Plunkett Research, Ltd. • Annual. $149.99. Five hundred major information companies are profiled, with corporate culture aspects. Discusses major trends in various sectors of the computer and information industry, including data on careers and job growth. Includes several indexes.

Research Services Directory: Commercial & Corporate Research Centers. Grey House Publishing. • 1999. $395.00. Seventh edition. Lists more than 6,200 independent commercial research centers and laboratories offering contract or fee-based services. Includes corporate research departments, market research companies, and information brokers.

ENCYCLOPEDIAS AND DICTIONARIES

Dictionary of Bibliometrics. Virgil Diodato. Haworth Press, Inc. • 1994. $39.95. Contains detailed explanations of 225 terms, with references. (Bibliometrics is "the application of mathematical and statistical techniques to the study of publishing and professional communication.").

Dictionary of Computing. Valerie Illingworth, editor. Oxford University Press, Inc. • 1996. $49.95. Fourth edition.

Dictionary of Information Technology and Computer Science. Tony Gunton. Blackwell Publishers. • 1994. $50.95. Second edition. Covers key words, phrases, abbreviations, and acronyms used in computing and data communications.

Encyclopedia of Communication and Information. Available from The Gale Group. • 2001. $325.00. Three volumes. Published by Macmillan Reference USA.

Encyclopedia of Emerging Industries. The Gale Group. • 2000. $295.00. Fourth edition. Provides detailed information on 90 "newly flourishing" industries. Includes historical background, organizational structure, significant individuals, current conditions, major companies, work force, technology trends, research developments, and other industry facts.

Encyclopedia of Library and Information Science. Allen Kent and others, editors. Marcel Dekker, Inc. • 66 volumes. $6,583.50. $99.75 per volume. Dates vary.

Every Manager's Guide to Information Technology: A Glossary of Key Terms and Concepts for Today's Business Leader. Peter G. W. Keen. Harvard Business School Press. • 1995. $18.95. Second edition. Provides definitions of terms related to computers, data communications, and information network systems. (Harvard Business Economist Reference Series).

The Librarians' Thesaurus: A Concise Guide to Library and Information Terms. Mary E. Soper and others. American Library Association. • 1990. $25.00.

World Encyclopedia of Library and Information Services. Robert Wedgeworth, editor. American Library Association. • 1993. $200.00. Third edition. Contains about 340 articles from various contributors.

HANDBOOKS AND MANUALS

Coyle's Information Highway Handbook: A Practical File on the New Information Order. Karen

Coyle. American Library Association. • 1997. $30.00. Provides useful "essays on copyright, access, privacy, censorship, and the information marketplace.".

How to Avoid Liability: The Information Professionals' Guide to Negligence and Warrant Risks. T. R. Halvorson. Burwell Enterprises, Inc. • 1998. $24.50. Second edition. Provides legal advice, cases, and decisions relating to information brokers and others in the information business.

Infopreneurs: Turning Data into Dollars. H. Skip Weitzen. John Wiley and Sons, Inc. • 1988. $27.95. Infopreneurs are entrepreneurs who market information. A how-to-do-it manual.

Information Broker. Entrepreneur Media, Inc. • Looseleaf. $59.50. A practical guide to starting an information retrieval business. Covers profit potential, start-up costs, market size evaluation, pricing, accounting, advertising, promotion, etc. (Start-Up Business Guide No. E1237.).

Information Brokering: A How-To-Do-It Manual for Librarians. Florence M. Mason and Chris Dobson. Neal-Schuman Publishers, Inc. • 1998. $45.00. A practical guide to business plans, location, costs, fees, billing, marketing, accounting, taxes, and legal issues. Covers information brokering as a small business enterprise.

Information Broker's Handbook. Sue Rugge and Alfred Glossbrenner. McGraw-Hill. • 1997. $49.95. Third edition. Covers a wide range of topics relating to the information business and specifically to information brokering as a career. Includes a diskette with sample forms, contracts, letters, and reports. (Windcrest Books.).

Information for Sale: How to Start and Operate Your Own Data Research Service. John H. Everett and Elizabeth P. Crowe. McGraw-Hill Professional. • 1988. $15.95. Second edition. A revision of *The Information Broker's Handbook.*

Legal Liability Problems in Cyberspace: Craters in the Information Highway. T. R. Halvorson. Burwell Enterprises, Inc. • 1998. $24.50. Covers the legal risks and liabilities involved in doing online research as a paid professional. Includes a table of cases.

Position Descriptions in Special Libraries. Del Sweeney and Karin Zilla, editors. Special Libraries Association. • 1996. $41.00. Third revised edition. Provides 87 descriptions of library and information management positions.

Recruiter's Research Blue Book: A How-To Guide for Researchers, Search Consultants, Corporate Recruiters, Small Business Owners, Venture Capitalists, and Line Executives. Andrea A. Jupina. Kennedy Information. • 2000. $179.00. Second edition. Provides detailed coverage of the role that research plays in executive recruiting. Includes such practical items as "Telephone Interview Guide," "Legal Issues in Executive Search," and "How to Create an Execuive Search Library." Covers both person-to-person research and research using printed and online business information sources. Includes an extensive directory of recommended sources. Formerly *Handbook of Executive Search Research.*

Sawyer's Success Tactics for Information Businesses. Deboorah C. Sawyer. Burwell Enterprises, Inc. • 1998. $24.50. Covers such items as pricing, costs, and service for information brokers and others in the fee-based information business.

Sawyer's Survival Guide for Information Brokers. Deborah C. Sawyer. Burwell Enterprises, Inc. • 1995. $39.50. Provides practical advice for information entrepreneurs.

Trade Secret Protection in an Information Age. Gale R. Peterson. Glasser Legalworks. • Looseleaf. $149.00, including sample forms on disk. Periodic supplementation available. Covers trade secret law relating to computer software, online databases, and multimedia products. Explanations are based on more than 1,000 legal cases. Sample forms on disk include work-for-hire examples and covenants not to compete.

INTERNET DATABASES

InfoTech Trends. Data Analysis Group. Phone: (707)894-9100 Fax: (707)486-5618 E-mail: support@infotechtrends.com • URL: http://www.infotechtrends.com • Web site provides both free and fee-based market research data on the information technology industry, including computers, peripherals, telecommunications, the Internet, software, CD-ROM/DVD, e-commerce, and workstations. Fees: Free for current (most recent year) data; more extensive information has various fee structures. Formerly *Computer Industry Forecasts.*

Internet Tools of the Profession. Special Libraries Association. Phone: (202)234-4700 Fax: (202)265-9317 E-mail: hope@tiac.net • URL: http://www.sla.org/pubs/itotp • Web site is designed to update the printed *Internet Tools of the Profession.* Provides links to a wide range of useful databases in business, finance, industry, information technology, insurance, law, library management, telecommunications, and other subject areas. Fees: Free.

Wired News. Wired Digital, Inc. Phone: (415)276-8400 Fax: (415)276-8499 E-mail: newsfeedback@wired.com • URL: http://www.wired.com • Provides summaries and full-text of "Top Stories" relating to the Internet, computers, multimedia, telecommunications, and the electronic information industry in general. These news stories are placed in the broad categories of Politics, Business, Culture, and Technology. Affiliated with *Wired* magazine. Fees: Free.

ONLINE DATABASES

Applied Science and Technology Index Online. H. W. Wilson Co. • Provides online indexing of 400 major scientific, technical, industrial, and engineering periodicals. Time period is 1983 to date. Monthly updates. Inquire as to online cost and availability.

Gale Directory of Databases [online]. The Gale Group. • Presents the online version of the printed *Gale Directory of Databases, Volume 1: Online Databases* and *Gale Directory of Databases, Volume 2: CD-ROM, Diskette, Magnetic Tape, Handheld, and Batch Access Database Products.* Semiannual updates. Inquire as to online cost and availability.

Information Science Abstracts [online]. Information Today, Inc. • Provides indexing and abstracting of the international literature of information science, including library science, from 1966 to date. Monthly updates. Inquire as to online cost and availability.

Library Literature Online. H. W. Wilson Co. • Contains online indexing of a wide variety of library and information science literature from 1984 to date, with updating quarterly. Inquire as to online cost and availability.

LISA Online: Library and Information Science Abstracts. Bowker-Saur, Reed Reference Publishing. • Provides abstracting and indexing of the world's library and information science literature from 1969 to the present. Covers a wide variety of topics in over 550 journals from 60 countries, with biweekly updates. Inquire as to online cost and availability.

PROMT: Predicasts Overview of Markets and Technology. The Gale Group. • Companies, products, applied technologies and markets. U.S. and international literature coverage, 1972 to date. Inquire as to online cost and availability. Provides abstracts from more than 1,600 publications. Weekly updates.

Scisearch. Institute for Scientific Information. • Broad, multidisciplinary index to the literature of science and technology, 1974 to present. Inquire as to online cost and availability. Coverage of literature is worldwide, with weekly updates.

Social Scisearch. Institute for Scientific Information. • Broad, multidisciplinary index to the literature of the social sciences, 1972 to present. Weekly updates. Worldwide coverage. Inquire as to online cost and availability.

Wilson Business Abstracts Online. H. W. Wilson Co. • Indexes and abstracts 600 major business periodicals, plus the *Wall Street Journal* and the business section of the *New York Times.* Indexing is from 1982, abstracting from 1990, with the two newspapers included from 1993. Updated weekly. Inquire as to online cost and availability. (*Business Periodicals Index* without abstracts is also available online.).

PERIODICALS AND NEWSLETTERS

Aslib Proceedings. Available from Information Today, Inc. • Ten times a year. Free to Members; non-members, $252.00 per year. Published in London by Aslib Covers a wide variety of information industry and library management topics.

CIO: The Magazine for Information Executives. CIO Communications. • Semimonthly. $89.00 per year. Edited for chief information officers. Includes a monthly "Web Business" section (incorporates the former *WebMaster* periodical) and a monthly "Enterprise" section for company executives other than CIOs.

Competitive Intelligence Review. Society of Competitive Intelligence Professionals. John Wiley and Sons, Inc. Journals Div. • Quarterly. Institutions, $345.00 per year.

Computer Industry Report. International Data Corp. • Semimonthly. $495.00 per year. Newsletter. Annual supplement. Also known as "The Gray Sheet." Formerly *EDP Industry Report and Market Review.*

CONTEXT: Business in a World Being Transformed by Technology. Diamond Technology Partners, Inc. • Quarterly. Price on application. Covers developments and trends in business and information technology for non-technical senior executives.

Corporate Library Update: News for Information Managers and Special Librarians. Cahners Business Information. • Biweekly. $95.00 per year. Newsletter. Covers information technology, management techniques, new products, trends, etc.

EContent. Online, Inc. • Bimonthly. $55.00 per year. Directed at professional online information searchers. Formerly *Database.*

Electronic Information Report: Empowering Industry Decision Makers Since 1979. SIMBA Information. • 46 times a year. $549.00 per year. Newsletter. Provides business and financial news and trends for online services, electronic publishing, storage media, multimedia, and voice services. Includes information on relevant IPOs (initial public offerings) and mergers. Formerly *Electronic Information Week.*

Healthcare Informatics: The Business of Healthcare Information Technology. McGraw-Hill. • Monthly. $40.00 per year. Covers various aspects of information and computer technology for the health care industry.

Inform: The Magazine of Information and Image Management. Association for Information and Image Management. • Monthly. $85.00 per year. Covers technologies, applications, and trends.

Information Broker. Helen P. Burwell, editor. Burwell Enterprises, Inc. • Bimonthly. $40.00 per year. Newsletter provides advice and news for those in the fee-based information business.

Information Hotline. Science Associates International, Inc. • 10 times a year. Individuals and corporations, $150.00 per year; non-profit organizations, $135.00 per year. Newsletter.

Information Outlook: The Monthly Magazine of the Special Libraries Association. Special Libraries Association. • Monthly. $65.00 per year. Topics include information technology, the Internet, copyright, research techniques, library management, and professional development. Replaces *Special Libraries* and *SpeciaList.*

Information Services and Use: An International Journal. I O S Press. • Quarterly. Individiuals, $100.00 per year; institutions, $257.00 per year.

The Information Society: An International Journal. Taylor & Francis, Inc. • Quarterly. Individuals, $89.00 per year; institutions, $194.00 per year.

Information Standards Quarterly: News About Library, Information Sciences, and Publishing Standards. National Information Standards Organization (NISO). • Quarterly. $80.00 per year. Newsletter. Reports on activities of the National Information Standards Organization.

Information Times. Software and Information Industry Association. • Monthly. Membership. Formerly *Friday Memo.*

Information Today: The Newspaper for Users and Producers of Electronic Information Services. Information Today, Inc. • 11 times a year. $57.95 per year.

Information Week: For Business and Technology Managers. CMP Publications, Inc. • Weekly. $149.00 per year. The magazine for information systems management.

Information World Review: The Information Community Newspaper. Information Today, Inc. • Monthly. $92.00 per year. International coverage. Includes columns in French, German, and Dutch.

InfoWorld: Defining Technology for Business. InfoWorld Publishing. • Weekly. $160.00 per year. For personal computing professionals.

Journal of Documentation: Devoted to the Recording, Organization and Dissemination of Specialized Knowledge. Information Today, Inc. • Five times a year. Members, $200.00 per year; non-members, $252.00 per year. Scholarly journal covering information science since 1945.

Journal of the American Society for Information Science. John Wiley and Sons, Inc., Journals Div. • Bimonthly. $456.00 per year.

KMWorld: Creating and Managing the Knowledge-Based Enterprise. Knowledge Asset Media. • Monthly. Controlled circulation. Provides articles on knowledge management, including business intelligence, multimedia content management, document management, e-business, and intellectual property. Emphasis is on business-to-business information technology. (Knowledge Asset Media is a an affiliate of Information Today, Inc.).

Knowledge Management. CurtCo Freedom Group. • Monthly. Controlled circulation. Covers applications of information technology and knowledge management strategy.

Library Computing. Sage Publications, Inc. • Quarterly. Individuals, $65.00 per year; institutions, $255.00 per year. Formerly *Library Software Review.*

Monitor: An Analytical Review of Current Events in the Online and Electronic Publishing Industry. Information Today, Inc. • Monthly. $290.00 per year. Newsletter. Covers the international industry.

Online Newsletter. Information Intelligence, Inc. • 10 times a year. Individuals, $43.75 per year; libraries, $62.50 per year; students, $25.00 per year. Covers the online and CD-ROM information industries, including news of mergers, acquisitions, personnel, meetings, new products, and new technology.

Online: The Leading Magazine for Information Professionals. Online, Inc. • Bimonthly. $110.00 per year. General coverage of the online information industry.

Report on Electronic Commerce: Online Business, Financial and Consumer Strategies and Trends. Telecommunications Reports International, Inc. • 23 times a year. $745.00 per year. Newsletter. Includes *Daily Multimedia News Service.* Incorporates *Interactive Services Report.*

Seybold Report on Publishing Systems. Seybold Publications. • Semimonthly. $365.00 per year. Newsletter.

Silicon Alley Reporter. Rising Tide Studios. • Monthly. $29.95 per year. Covers the latest trends in e-commerce, multimedia, and the Internet.

Telematics and Informatics: An International Journal. Elsevier Science. • Quarterly. $713.00 per year.

Upgrade. Software and Information Industry Association. • Monthly. $75.00 per year. Covers news and trends relating to the software, information, and Internet industries. Formerly *SPA News* from Software Publisers Association.

Wired. Wired Ventures Ltd. • Monthly. $24.00 per year. Edited for creators and managers in various areas of electronic information and entertainment, including multimedia, the Internet, and video. Often considered to be the primary publication of the "digital generation.".

RESEARCH CENTERS AND INSTITUTES

Library Research Center. University of Illinois at Urbana-Champaign. 501 E. Daniel, Room 321, Champaign, IL 61820-6212. Phone: (217)333-1980 Fax: (217)244-3302 E-mail: lrc@uiuc.edu • URL: http://www.alexia.lis.uiuc.edu/gslis/research/lrc.html.

STATISTICS SOURCES

By the Numbers: Electronic and Online Publishing. The Gale Group. • 1997. $385.00. Four volumes. $99.00 per volume. Covers "high-interest" industries: 1. *By the Numbers: Electronic and Online Publishing*; 2. *By the Numbers: Emerging Industries*; 3. *By the Numbers: Nonprofits*; 4. *By the Numbers: Publishing.* Each volume provides about 600 tabulations of industry data on revenues, market share, employment, trends, financial ratios, profits, salaries, and so forth. Citations to data sources are included.

Information Systems Spending: An Analysis of Trends and Strategies. Computer Economics, Inc. • Annual. $1,595.00. Three volumes. Based on "in-depth surveys of public and private companies amd government organizations." Provides detailed data on management information systems spending, budgeting, and benchmarks. Includes charts, graphs, and analysis.

Multimedia Title Publishing: Review, Trends, and Forecast. SIMBA Information. • Annual. $895.00. Provides industry statistics and market research data. Covers both business and consumer multimedia items, with emphasis on CD-ROM publishing.

OECD Information Technology Outlook 2000: ICTs, E-Commerce and the Information Economy. Organization for Economic Cooperation and Development. • 2000. $72.00. Provides data on information and communications technology (ICT) and electronic commerce in 11 OECD nations (includes U. S.). Coverage includes network infrastructure, electronic payment systems, financial transaction technologies, intelligent agents, global navigation systems, and portable flat panel display technologies.

U. S. Industry and Trade Outlook: The McGraw-Hill Companies and the U.S. Department of Commerce/ International Trade Administration. Datapso Research Corp. • Annual. $69.95. Produced by the International Trade Administration, U. S. Department of Commerce, in a "public-private" partnership with DRI/McGraw-Hill and Standard & Poor's. Provides basic data, outlook for the current year, and "Long-Term Prospects" (five-year projections) for a wide variety of products and services. Includes high technology industries. Formerly *U. S. Industrial Outlook.*

TRADE/PROFESSIONAL ASSOCIATIONS

American Society for Information Science. 8720 Georgia Ave., Suite 501, Silver Spring, MD 20910-3602. Phone: (301)495-0900 Fax: (301)495-0810 E-mail: asis@asis.org • URL: http://www.asis.org • Members are information managers, scientists, librarians, and others who are interested in the storage, retrieval, and use of information.

Association of Independent Information Professionals. 10290 Monroe Dr., Dallas, TX 75229. Phone: (609)730-8759 E-mail: aiipinfo@aiip.org • URL: http://www.aiip.org • Members are information brokers, document providers, librarians, consultants, database designers, webmasters, and other information professionals. Formerly International Association of Independent Information Brokers.

Association of Information and Dissemination Centers. P.O. Box 8105, Athens, GA 30603. Phone: (706)542-6820 E-mail: secretariat@asidic.org • URL: http://www.asidic.org.

Library and Information Technology Association. 50 E. Huron St., Chicago, IL 60611. Phone: 800-545-2433 or (312)280-4270 Fax: (312)280-3257 E-mail: lita@ala.org • URL: http://www.lita.org • The Library and Information Technology Association is a Division of the American Library Association.

National Federation of Abstracting and Information Services. 1518 Walnut St., Suite 307, Philadelphia, PA 19102-3403. Phone: (215)893-1561 Fax: (215)893-1564 E-mail: nfais@nfais.org • URL: http: //www.nfais.org.

National Information Standards Organization. 4733 Bethesda Ave., Suite 300, Bethesda, MD 20814-5248. Phone: (301)654-2512 Fax: (301)654-1721 E-mail: nisohq@niso.org • URL: http://www.niso.org • Develops and promotes technical standards for the information industry and libraries, including the Z39.50 protocol for Internet database searching.

Society of Competitive Intelligence Professionals. 1700 Diagonal Rd., Suite 600, Alexandria, VA 22314. Phone: (703)739-0696 Fax: (703)739-2524 E-mail: info@scip.org • URL: http://www.scip.org • Members are professionals involved in competitor intelligence and analysis.

Software and Information Industry Association. 1730 M St., N. W., Suite 700, Washington, DC

20036-4510. Phone: (202)452-1600 Fax: (202)223-8756 • URL: http://www.siia.net • A trade association for the software and digital content industry. Divisions are Content, Education, Enterprise, Financial Information Services, Global, and Internet. Includes an Online Content Committee. Formerly Software Publishers Association.

Special Interest Group on Information Retrieval. c/o Association for Computing Machinery, 1515 Broadway, New York, NY 10036. Phone: (212)869-7440 Fax: (212)302-5826 E-mail: sigs@acm.org • URL: http://www.acm.org/sigir/.

OTHER SOURCES

Darwin: Business Evolving in the Information Age. CXO Media Inc. • Monthly. $44.95 per year. Presents non-technical explanations of information technology (IT) to corporate business executives. Uses a case study format.

Information and Image Management: The State of the Industry. Association for Information and Image Management. • Annual. $130.00. Market data with five-year forecasts. Covers electronic imaging, micrographics supplies and equipment, software, and records management services.

Information, Finance, and Services USA. The Gale Group. • 2001. $240.00. Replaces *Service Industries USA* and *Finance, Insurance, and Real Estate USA.* Presents statistics and projections relating to economic activity in a wide variety of non-manufacturing areas.

Librarianship and Information Work Worldwide. Available from The Gale Group. • Annual. $189.00. Published by K. G. Saur. International coverage.

Major Information Technology Companies of the World. Available from The Gale Group. • 2001. $885.00. Third edition. Published by Graham & Whiteside. Contains profiles of more than 2,600 leading information technology companies in various countries.

The Quintessential Searcher: The Wit and Wisdom of Barbara Quint. Marylaine Block, editor. Information Today, Inc. • 2001. $19.95. Presents the sayings of Barbara Quint, editor of *Searcher* magazine, who is often critical of the online information industry. (CyberAge Books.).

Valuating Information Intangibles: Measuring the Bottom Line Contribution of Librarians and Information Professionals. Frank H. Portugal. Special Libraries Association. • 2000. $79.00. Focuses on the importance of the intangible aspects of appraising information resources and services.

INFORMATION MANAGEMENT SYSTEMS

See: MANAGEMENT INFORMATION SYSTEMS

INFORMATION RETRIEVAL (DOCUMENTATION)

See: ONLINE INFORMATION SYSTEMS

INFORMATION SOURCES

See also: STATISTICS SOURCES

BIBLIOGRAPHIES

Analyzing Your Competition: Simple, Low-Cost Techniques for Intelligence Gathering. Michael Strenges. MarketResearch.com. • 1997. $95.00. Third edition. Mainly an annotated listing of specific, business information sources, but also contains concise discussions of information-gathering techniques. Indexed by publisher and title.

The Basic Business Library: Core Resources. Bernard S. Schlessinger and June H. Schlessinger. Oryx Press. • 1994. $43.50. Third edition. Consists of three parts: (1) "Core List of Printed Business Reference Sources," (2) "The Literature of Business Reference and Business Libraries: 1976-1994," and (3) "Business Reference Sources and Services: Essays." Part one lists 200 basic titles, with annotations and evaluations.

Booklist. American Library Association. • 22 times a year. $74.50. Reviews library materials for school and public libraries. Incorporates *Reference Books Bulletin.*

Business Information: How to Find It, How to Use It. Michael R. Lavin. Oryx Press. • 2001. $61.00. Third edition. Combines discussions of business research techniques with detailed descriptions of major business publications and databases. Includes title and subject indexes.

Business Information Sources. Lorna M. Daniells. California Princeton Fulfillment Services. • 1993. $42.50. Third revised edition. Basic business sources, with discussion and full annotations.

Business Research Handbook: Methods and Sources for Lawyers and Business Professionals. Kathy E. Shimpock. Aspen Law and Business. • $145.00. Looseleaf. Periodic supplementation. Provides detailed advice on how to find business information. Describes a wide variety of data sources, both private and government.

Computing Information Directory: Comprehensive Guide to the Computing and Computer Engineering Literature. Peter A. Hildebrandt, Inc. • Annual. $229.95. Describes computer journals, newsletters, handbooks, dictionaries, indexing services, review resources, directories, and other computer information sources. Includes a directory of publishers and a master subject index.

Data Sources for Business and Market Analysis. John Ganly. Scarecrow Press, Inc. • 1994. $58.00. Fourth edition. Emphasis is on sources of statistics for market research, especially government sources. Relevant directories, periodicals, and research aids are included.

Encyclopedia of Health Information Sources. The Gale Group. • 1993. $180.00. Second edition. Both print and nonprint sources of information are listed for 450 health-related topics.

Encyclopedia of Legal Information Sources. The Gale Group. • 1992. $180.00. Second edition. Lists more than 23,000 law-related information sources, including print, nonprint, and organizational.

Guide to Reference Books. Robert Balay and others. American Library Association. • 1996. $275.00. 11th edition.

How to Find Chemical Information: A Guide for Practicing Chemists, Educators, and Students. Robert E. Maizell. John Wiley and Sons, Inc. • 1998. $69.95. Third edition.

International Business Information: How to Find It, How to Use It. Ruth Pagell and Michael Halperin. Oryx Press. • 1997. $84.50. Second revised edition.

Legal Information: How to Find It, How to Use It. Kent Olson. Oryx Press. • 1998. $59.95. Recommends sources for various kinds of legal information.

Lesko's Info-PowerIII: Over 45,000 Free and Low Cost Sources of Information. Visible Ink Press. • 1996. $29.95. Third edition.

Public Library Catalog: Guide to Reference Books and Adult Nonfiction. Juliette Yaakov, editor. H. W. Wilson Co. • Quinquennial. $230.00. Contains annotations for 8,000 of the "best" reference and other nonfiction books in English. Covers a wide range of topics, including many that are related to business, economics, finance, or industry. (Standard Catalog Series).

Reference Books Bulletin: A Compilation of Evaluations. Mary Ellen Quinn, editor. American Library Association. • Annual. $28.50. Contains reference book reviews that appeared during the year in *Booklist.*

Reference Sources for Small and Medium-sized Libraries. Scott E. Kennedy, editor. American Library Association. • 1999. $60.00. Sixth edition. Includes alternative (electronic) formats for reference works.

Statistics Sources: A Subject Guide to Data on Industrial, Business, Social, Educational, Financial and Other Topics for the U. S. and Selected Foreign Countries. The Gale Group. • 2000. $475.00. 25th edition. Two volumes. Lists sources of statistical information for more than 20,000 topics.

Subject Encyclopedias: User's Guide, Review Citations, and Keyword Index. Allan N. Mirwis. Oryx Press. • 1999. $135.00. Two volumes. Volume one describes 1,000 subject encyclopedias; volume two provides a keyword index to articles appearing in 100 selected encyclopedias.

Topical Reference Books: Authoritative Evaluations of Recommended Resources in Specialized Subject Areas. R. R. Bowker. • 1991. $109.00. Ranks 2,000 reference books ("Core Titles," "New and Noteworthy," "Supplementary"). (Buying Guide Series).

U. S. Government Information for Business. U. S. Government Printing Office. • Annual. Free. A selected list of currently available publications, periodicals, and electronic products on business, trade, labor, federal regulations, economics, and other topics. Also known as *Business Catalog.*

CD-ROM DATABASES

CDMARC: Bibliographic. U. S. Library of Congress. • Quarterly. $1,340.00 per year. Provides bibliographic records on CD-ROM for over five million books cataloged by the Library of Congress since 1968. (MARC is Machine Readable Cataloging.).

Fast Reference Facts. The Gale Group. • 1995. $400.00. Contains more than 5,000 CD-ROM entries, providing concise answers to a wide variety of "everyday" queries, within 13 broad subject areas (includes business and economics). Sources of questions and answers include public libraries.

Statistical Masterfile. Congressional Information Service. • Quarterly. Price varies. Provides CD-ROM versions of *American Statistics Index, Index to International Statistics,* and *Statistical Reference Index.* Contains indexing and abstracting of a wide variety of published statistics sources, both governmental and private.

World Database of Business Information Sources on CD-ROM. The Gale Group. • Annual. Produced by Euromonitor. Presents Euromonitor's entire information source database on CD-ROM. Contains a worldwide total of about 35,000 publications, organizations, libraries, trade fairs, and online databases.

DIRECTORIES

Business Organizations, Agencies, and Publications Directory. The Gale Group. • 1999. $425.00. 12th edition. Over 40,000 entries describing 39 types of business information sources. Classified by type of organization, publication, or serviceIncludes state, national, and international agencies and organizations. Master index to names and keywords. Also includes e-mail addresses and web site URL's.

CD-ROMS in Print. The Gale Group. • Annual. $175.00. Describes more than 13,000 currrently available reference and multimedia CD-ROM titles and provides contact information for about 4,000 CD-ROM publishing and distribution companies. Includes several indexes.

Detwiler's Directory of Health and Medical Resources. Dorland Healthcare Information. • Annual. $195.00. Lists a wide range of healthcare information resources, including more than 2,000 corporations, associations, government agencies, publishers, licensure organizations, market research firms, foundations, and institutes, as well as 6,000 publications. Indexed by type of information, publication, acronym, and 600 subject categories.

Directories in Print. The Gale Group. • Annual. $530.00. Three volumes. Includes interedition *Supplement.* An annotated guide to approximately 15,500 business, industrial, professional, and scientific directories. Formerly *Directory of Directories.*

The Directory of Business Information Resources: Associations, Newsletters, Magazine Trade Shows. Grey House Publishing, Inc. • Annual. $195.00. Provides concise information on associations, newsletters, magazines, and trade shows for each of 90 major industry groups. An "Entry & Company Index" serves as a guide to titles, publishers, and organizations.

Directory of EU Information Sources. Euroconfidentiel S. A. • Annual. $250.00. Lists more than 12,500 publications, associations, consultants, law firms, diplomats, jounalists, and other sources of information about Europe and the European Union.

Directory of Marketing Information Companies. American Demographics, Inc. • Annual. $10.00. Lists companies offering market research and information services, with a selection of the "Best 100 Sources of Marketing Information.".

Directory of Special Libraries and Information Centers. The Gale Group. • 1999. $845.00. 25th edition. Three volumes. Two available separately: volume one,*Directory of Special Libraries and Information Centers*, $610.00; volume two *Geographic and Personnel Indexes*, $510.00. Contains 24,000 entries from the U.S., Canada, and 80 other countries. A detailed subject index is included in volume one.

Findex: The Worldwide Directory of Market Research Reports, Studies, and Surveys. MarketResearch.com. • Annual. $400.00. Provides brief annotations of market research reports and related publications from about 1,000 publishers, arranged by topic. Back of book includes Report Titles by Publisher, Publishers/Distributors Directory, Subject Index, Geography Index, and Company Index. (Formerly published by Cambridge Information Group.).

Finding Business Research on the Web: A Guide to the Web's Most Valuable Sites. MarketResearch.com. • Looseleaf. $175.00. Includes detailed rating charts. Contains profiles of the "100 best web sites.".

Fulltext Sources Online. Information Today, Inc. • Semiannual. $199.00 per year; $119.50 per issue. Lists more than 8,000 journals, newspapers, magazines, newsletters, and newswires found online in fulltext through DIALOG, LEXIS-NEXIS, Dow Jones, Westlaw, etc. Includes journals that have free Internet archives. (Formerly published by BiblioData.).

Gale Guide to Internet Databases. The Gale Group. • 1999. $120.00. Sixth edition. Presents critical descriptions and ratings of more than 5,000 useful Internet databases (especially World Wide Web sites). Includes a glossary of Internet terms, a bibliography, and five indexes.

Great Scouts! CyberGuides to Subject Searching on the Web. Margot Williams and others. Independent Publishers Group. • 1999. $24.95. Contains descriptions of selected Web sites, arranged by subject. Covers business, investments, computers, travel, the environment, health, social issues, etc. (CyberAge Books.).

Information Sources: The Annual Directory of the Information Industry Association. Software and Information Industry Association. • Annual. Members, $75.00; non-members, $125.00.

Internet-Plus Directory of Express Library Services: Research and Document Delivery for Hire. American Library Association. • 1997. $49.50. Covers fee-based services of various U. S., Canadian, and international libraries. Paid services include online searches, faxed documents, and specialized professional research. Price ranges are quoted. (A joint production of FISCAL, the ALA/ ACRL Discussion Group of Fee-Based Information Service Centers in Academic Libraries, and FYI, the Professional Research and Rapid Information Delivery Service of the County of Los Angeles Public Library.) Formerly *FISCAL Directory of Fee-Based Information Services in Libraries.*

Library Journal: Reference [year]: Print, CD-ROM, Online. Cahners Business Information. • Annual. Issued in November as supplement to *Library Journal.* Lists new and updated reference material, including general and trade print titles, directories, annuals, CD-ROM titles, and online sources. Includes material from more than 150 publishers, arranged by company name, with an index by subject. Addresses include e-mail and World Wide Web information, where available.

Prentice Hall Directory of Online Business Information. Christopher Engholm and Scott Grimes. Prentice Hall. • Annual. $34.95. Contains reviews of about 1,000 World Wide Web sites related to business. Sites are rated according to content, speed, and other factors.

Subject Collections: A Guide to Special Book Collections and Subject Emphasis in Libraries. Lee Ash and William G. Miller, editors. R. R. Bowker. • Irregular. $275.00. Two volumes. A guide to special book collections and subject emphases as reported by university, college, public and special libraries in th United States and Canada.

Subject Directory of Special Libraries and Information Centers. The Gale Group. • Annual. $845.00. Three volumes, available separately: volume one, *Business, Government, and Law Libraries*, $595.00; volume two, *Computer, Engineering, and Law Libraries*, $595.00; volume three, *Health Sciences Libraries*, $340.00. Altogether, 14,000 entries from the *Directory of Special Libraries and Information Centers* are arranged in 14 subject chapters.

World Directory of Business Information Libraries. Available from The Gale Group. • 2000. $590.00. Fourth edition. Published by Euromonitor. Provides detailed information on 2,000 major business libraries in 145 countries. Emphasis is on collections relevant to consumer goods and services markets.

World Directory of Business Information Web Sites. Available from The Gale Group. • 2001. $650.00. Fourth edition. Published by Euromonitor. Provides detailed descriptions of a wide variety of business-related Web sites. More than 1,500 sites are included from around the world. Covers statistics sources, market research, company information, rankings, surveys, economic data, etc.

World Directory of Marketing Information Sources. Available from The Gale Group. • 2001. $590.00. Third edition. Published by Euromonitor. Provides details on more than 6,000 sources of marketing information, including publications, libraries, associations, market research companies, online databases, and governmental organizations. Coverage is worldwide.

HANDBOOKS AND MANUALS

Best Bet Internet: Reference and Research When You Don't Have Time to Mess Around. Shirley D. Kennedy. American Library Association. • 1997. $35.00. Provides advice for librarians and others on the effective use of World Wide Web information sources.

The Business Library and How to Use It: A Guide to Sources and Research Strategies for Information on Business and Management. Ernest L. Maier and others, editors. Omnigraphics, Inc. • 1996. $56.00. Explains library research methods and describes specific sources of business information. A revision of *How to Use the Business Library*, by H. Webster Johnson and others (fifth edition, 1984).

Guide to the Use of Libraries and Information Sources. Jean K. Gates. McGraw-Hill. • 1994. $32.19. Seventh edition.

How To Find Information About Companies: The Corporate Intelligence Source Book. Washington Researchers. • Annual. $885.00. In three parts. $395.00 per volume. In part one, over 9,000 sources of corporate intelligence, including federal, state and local repositories of company filings, individual industry experts, published sources, databases, CD-Rom products, and corporate research services. Parts two and three provide guidelines for company research.

Introduction to Reference Work. William A. Katz. McGraw-Hill. • 1996. $92.19. Seventh edition. Two volumes. Volume one, $48.13; volume two, $44.06.

Using Government Information Sources, Print and Electronic. Jean L. Sears and Marilyn K. Moody. Oryx Press. • 1994. $115.00. Second edition. Contains detailed information in four sections on subject searches, agency searches, statistical searches, and special techniques for searching. Appendixes give selected agency and publisher addresses, telephone numbers, and computer communications numbers.

INTERNET DATABASES

EBSCO Information Services. Ebsco Publishing. Phone: 800-871-8508 or (508)356-6500 Fax: (508)356-5640 E-mail: ep@epnet.com • URL: http://www.epnet.com • Fee-based Web site providing Internet access to a wide variety of databases, including business-related material. Full text is available for many periodical titles, with daily updates. Fees: Apply.

GPO Access: Keeping America Informed Electronically. U. S. Government Printing Office Sales Program, Bibliographic Systems Branch. Phone: 888-293-6498 or (202)512-1530 Fax: (202)512-1262 E-mail: gpoaccess@gpo.gov • URL: http://www.access.gpo.gov • Web site provides searching of the GPO's Sales Product Catalog (SPC), also known as Publications Reference File (PRF). Covers all "Government information products currently offered for sale by the Superintendent of Documents." There are also specialized search pages for individual databases, such as the *Code of Federal Regulations*, the *Federal Register*, and *Commerce Business Daily.* Updated daily. Fees: Free.

Intelligence Data. Thomson Financial. Phone: 800-654-0393 or (212)806-8023 Fax: (212)806-8004 • URL: http://www.intelligencedata.com • Fee-based Web site provides a wide variety of information relating to competitive intelligence, strategic planning, business development, mergers, acquisitions, sales, and marketing. "Intelliscope" feature offers searching of other Thomson units, such as Investext, MarkIntel, InSite 2, and Industry Insider. Weekly updating.

ProQuest Direct. Bell & Howell Information and Learning. Phone: 800-521-0600 or (313)761-4700 Fax: (313)973-9145 • URL: http://www.umi.com/proquest • Fee-based Web site providing Internet access to more than 3,000 periodicals, newspapers, and other publications. Many items are available full-text, with daily updates. Includes extensive corporate and financial information from Disclosure, Inc. Fees: Apply.

PubList.com: The Internet Directory of Publications. Bowes & Associates, Inc. Phone: (781)792-0999 Fax: (781)792-0988 E-mail: info@publist.com • URL: http://www.publist.com • "The premier online global resource for information about print and electronic publications." Provides online searching for information on more than 150,000 magazines, journals, newsletters, e-journals, and monographs. Database entries generally include title, publisher, format, address, editor, circulation, subject, and International Standard Serial Number (ISSN). Fees: Free.

Ulrichsweb.com. R. R. Bowker. Phone: 888-269-5372 or (908)464-6800 Fax: (908)464-3553 E-mail: info@bowker.com • URL: http://www.ulrichsweb.com • Web site provides fee-based access to about 250,000 serials records from the *Ulrich's International Periodicals Directory* database. Includes periodical evaluations from *Library Journal* and *Magazines for Libraries.* Monthly updates.

WilsonWeb Periodicals Databases. H. W. Wilson. Phone: 800-367-6770 or (718)588-8400 Fax: 800-590-1617 or (718)992-8003 E-mail: custserv@hwwilson.com • URL: http://www.hwwilson.com/ • Web sites provide fee-based access to *Wilson Business Full Text, Applied Science & Technology Full Text, Biological & Agricultural Index, Library Literature & Information Science Full Text,* and *Readers' Guide Full Text, Mega Edition.* Daily updates.

ONLINE DATABASES

American Statistics Index: A Comprehensive Guide and Index to the Statistical Publications of the United States Government [Online]. Congressional Information Service, Inc. • Indexes and abstracts, 1973 to date. Inquire as to online cost and availability.

FINDEX. Kalorama Information. • Provides online annotations of market research reports and related publications from about 1,000 publishers. Time period is 1972 to date, with quarterly updates. (Formerly produced by Cambridge Information Group.) Inquire as to online cost and availability.

GPO Monthly Catalog. U. S. Government Printing Office. • Contains over 375,000 online citations to U. S. government publications, 1976 to date, with monthly updates. Corresponds to the printed *Monthly Catalog of United States Government Publications.* Inquire as to online cost and availability.

GPO Publications Reference File. U. S. Government Printing Office. • An online guide to federal government publications in print (currently for sale), forthcoming, and recently out-of-print. Biweekly updates. Inquire as to online cost and availability.

LC MARC: Books. U. S. Library of Congress. • Contains online bibliographic records for over five million books cataloged by the Library of Congress since 1968. Updating is weekly or monthly. Inquire as to online cost and availability. (MARC is machine readable cataloging.).

Newsletter Database. The Gale Group. • Contains the full text of about 600 U. S. and international newsletters covering a wide range of business and industrial topics. Time period is 1988 to date, with daily updates. Inquire as to online cost and availability.

PERIODICALS AND NEWSLETTERS

Business Information Alert: Sources, Strategies and Signposts for Information Professionals. Donna T. Heroy, editor. Alert Publications, Inc. • 10 times per year. $152.00 per year. Newsletter for business librarians and information specialists.

INFO. Tulsa City-County Library, Business & Technology Dept. • Bimonthly. Free. Newsletter listing selected new books in business, economics, and technology.

The Information Advisor: Tips and Techniques for Smart Information Users. MarketResearch.com. • Monthly. $149.00 per year. Newsletter. Evaluates and discusses online, CD-ROM, and published sources of business, financial, and market research information.

The Information Report. Washington Researchers Ltd. • Monthly. $160.00 per year. Newsletter listing private and government sources of information, mainly on business or economics.

Internet Reference Services Quarterly: A Journal of Innovative Information Practice, Technologies, and Resources. Haworth Press, Inc. • Quarterly. Individuals, $36.00 per year; libraries and other institutions, $48.00 per year. Covers both theoretical research and practical applications.

Reference and User Services Quarterly. American Library Association. • Quarterly. $50.00 per year. Official publication of the Reference and User Services Association (RUSA), a division of the American Library Association. In addition to articles, includes reviews of databases, reference books, and library professional material. Formerly *RQ.*

RUSA Update. American Library Association. • Quarterly. Free to members; non-members, $20.00 per year. Serves as news letter for the Reference and User Services Association, a division of the American Library Association. Includes activities of the Business Reference and Services Section (BRASS). Formerly *RASD Update.*

TRADE/PROFESSIONAL ASSOCIATIONS

Association of Information and Dissemination Centers. P.O. Box 8105, Athens, GA 30603. Phone: (706)542-6820 E-mail: secretariat@asidic.org • URL: http://www.asidic.org.

OTHER SOURCES

Business & Company Resource Center. The Gale Group. • Fee-based Web site provides a wide range of business, industry, and specific company information. Access is offered to trade journal articles, market research data, insider trading activity, major shareholder data, corporate histories, emerging technology reports, corporate earnings estimates, press releases, and other sources. Provides detailed company profiles, industry overviews, and rankings. Offers integration of Predicasts PROMT, Newsletters ASAP, Investext Plus, Business Index ASAP, Brands and Their Companies, and other databases (many have full text).

Business Information Desk Reference: Where to Find Answers to Your Business Questions. Melvyn N. Freed and Virgil P. Diodato. Prentice Hall. • 1992. $20.00. Offers a unique, question and answer approach to business information sources. Covers print sources, online databases, trade associations, and government agencies.

Business Rankings Annual. The Gale Group. • Annual. $305.00.Two volumes. Compiled by the Business Library Staff of the Brooklyn Public Library. This is a guide to lists and rankings appearing in major business publications. The top ten names are listed in each case.

Federal Information Disclosure: Procedures, Forms and the Law. James T. O'Reilly. Shepard's. • 1977. $200.00. Second edition. Two volumes. Discusses legal aspects of getting information from the government.

The Information Catalog. MarketResearch.com. • Quarterly. Free. Mainly a catalog of market research reports from various publishers, but also includes business and marketing reference sources. Includes keyword title index. Formerly *The Information Catalog: Marketing Intelligence Studies, Competitor Reports, Business and Marketing Sources.*

InSite 2. Intelligence Data/Thomson Financial. • Fee-based Web site consolidates information in a "Base Pack" consisting of Business InSite, Market InSite, and Company InSite. Optional databases are Consumer InSite, Health and Wellness InSite, Newsletter InSite, and Computer InSite. Includes fulltext content from more than 2,500 trade publications, journals, newsletters, newspapers, analyst reports, and other sources. Continuous updating. Formerly produced by The Gale Group.

The Invisible Web: Uncovering Information Sources Search Engines Can't See. Chris Sherman and Gary Price. Information Today, Inc. • 2001. $29.95. A guide to Web sites from universities, libraries, associations, government agencies, and other sources that are inadequately covered by conventional search engines (see also http://www.invisible-web.net). (CyberAge Books.).

INFORMATION SYSTEMS, MANAGEMENT

See: MANAGEMENT INFORMATION SYSTEMS

INFORMATION SYSTEMS, ONLINE

See: ONLINE INFORMATION SYSTEMS

INHERITANCE TAX

See also: ESTATE PLANNING

HANDBOOKS AND MANUALS

Corporate, Partnership, Estate, and Gift Taxation 1997. James W. Pratt and William Kulsrud, editors. McGraw-Hill Higher Education. • 1996. $71.25. 10th edition.

Estate Plan Book 2000. William S. Moore. American Institute for Economic Research. • 2000. $10.00. Revision of 1997 edition. Part one: "Basic Estate Planning." Part two: "Reducing Taxes on the Disposition of Your Estate." Part three: "Putting it All Together: Examples of Estate Plans." Provides succinct information on wills, trusts, tax planning, and gifts. (Economic Education Bulletin.).

Estate Tax Techniques. Matthew Bender & Co., Inc. • $640.00. Three looseleaf volumes. Periodic supplementation.

Federal Estate and Gift Taxation. Richard B. Stevens and Guy B. Maxfield. Warren, Gorham and Lamont/RIA Group. • $390.00. Looseleaf service. Semiannual supplementation. Clarification and guidance on estate tax laws.

Federal Estate and Gift Taxes: Code and Regulations, Including Related Income Tax Provisions. CCH, Inc. • Annual. $44.95. Provides full text of estate, gift, and generation-skipping tax provisions of the Internal Revenue Code.

Federal Income Taxes of Decedents, Estates, and Trusts. CCH, Inc. • Annual. $45.00. Provides rules for preparing a decedent's final income tax return. Includes discussions of fiduciary duties, grantor trusts, and bankruptcy estates.

Federal Tax Course: General Edition. CCH, Inc. • Annual. $123.00. Provides basic reference and training for various forms of federal taxation: individual, business, corporate, partnership, estate, gift, etc. Includes *Federal Taxation Study Manual.*

How to Save Time and Taxes in Handling Estates. Matthew Bender & Co., Inc. • $235.00. Looseleaf servie. Periodic supplementation. (How to Save Time and Taxes Series).

How to Save Time and Taxes Preparing Fiduciary Income Tax Returns: Federal and State. Matthew Bender & Co., Inc. • $230.00. Looseleaf service. Periodic supplementation. (How to Save Time and Taxes Series).

Inheritor's Handbook: A Definitive Guide for Beneficiaries. Dan Rottenberg. Bloomberg Press. • 1998. $23.95. Covers both financial and emotional issues faced by beneficiaries. (Bloomberg Personal Bookshelf Series.).

Internal Revenue Code: Income, Estate, Gift, Employment, and Excise Taxes. CCH, Inc. • Annual. $69.00. Two volumes. Provides full text of the Internal Revenue Code (5,000 pages), including procedural and administrative provisions.

Law of Federal Estate and Gift Taxation, 1978-1990. David T. Link and Larry D. Soderquist. West Group. • $100.00. Revised edition.

Trust Administration and Taxation. Matthew Bender & Co., Inc. • $830.00. Four looseleaf volumes. Periodic supplementation. Text on establishment, administration, and taxation of trusts.

U. S. Master Estate and Gift Tax Guide. CCH, Inc. • Annual. $49.00. Covers federal estate and gift taxes, including generation-skipping transfer tax plans. Includes tax tables and sample filled-in tax return forms.

INTERNET DATABASES

CCH Essentials: An Internet Tax Research and Primary Source Library. CCH, Inc. Phone: 800-248-3248 or (773)866-6000 Fax: 800-224-8299 or (773)866-3608 E-mail: cust_serv@cch.com • URL: http://tax.cch.com/essentials • Fee-based Web site provides full-text coverage of federal tax law and regulations, including rulings, procedures, tax court decisions, and IRS publications, announcements, notices, and penalties. Includes explanation, analysis, tax planning guides, and a daily tax news service. Searching is offered, including citation search. Fee: $495.00 per year.

The Digital Daily. Internal Revenue Service. Phone: (202)622-5000 Fax: (202)622-5844 • URL: http://www.irs.ustreas.gov • Web site provides a wide variety of tax information, including IRS forms and publications. Includes "Highlights of New Tax Law." Searching is available. Fees: Free.

Tax Analysts [Web site]. Tax Analysts. Phone: 800-955-3444 or (703)533-4400 Fax: (703)533-4444 • URL: http://www.tax.org • The three main sections of Tax Analysts home page are "Tax News" (Today's Tax News, Feature of the Week, Tax Snapshots, Tax Calendar); "Products & Services" (Product Catalog, Press Releases); and "Public Interest" (Discussion Groups, Tax Clinic, Tax History Project). Fees: Free for coverage of current tax events; fee-based for comprehensive information. Daily updating.

PERIODICALS AND NEWSLETTERS

Estate Planner's Alert. Research Institute of America, Inc. • Monthly. $140.00 per year. Newsletter. Covers the tax aspects of personal finance, including home ownership, investments, insurance, retirement planning, and charitable giving. Formerly *Estate and Financial Planners Alert.*

Highlights and Documents. Tax Analysts. • Daily. $2,249.00 per year, including monthly indexes. Newsletter. Provides daily coverage of IRS, congressional, judicial, state, and international tax developments. Includes abstracts and citations for "all tax documents released within the previous 24 to 48 hours." Annual compilation available *Highlights and Documents on Microfiche.*

Tax Notes: The Weekly Tax Service. Tax Analysts. • Weekly. $1,699.00 per year. Includes an *Annual* and 1985-1996 compliations on CD-ROM. Newsletter. Covers "tax news from all federal sources," including congressional committees, tax courts, and the Internal Revenue Service. Each issue contains "summaries of every document that pertains to federal tax law," with citations. Commentary is provided.

Tax Practice. Tax Analysts. • Weekly. $199.00 per year. Newsletter. Covers news affecting tax practitioners and litigators, with emphasis on federal court decisions, rules and regulations, and tax petitions. Provides a guide to Internal Revenue Service audit issues.

OTHER SOURCES

Estate Planning and Taxation Coordinator. Research Institute of America, Inc. • Nine looseleaf volumes. $760.00 per year. Biweekly updates. Includes *Estate Planner's Alert* and *Lifetime Planning Alert.*

Estate Planning: Inheritance Taxes. Prentice Hall. • Five looseleaf volumes. Periodic supplementation. Price on application.

Estate Planning Strategies After Estate Tax Reform: Insights and Analysis. CCH, Inc. • 2001. $45.00. Produced by the Estate Planning Department of Schiff, Hardin & Waite. Covers estate planning techniques and opportunities resulting from tax legislation of 2001.

Estate Planning Under the New Law: What You Need to Know. CCH, Inc. • 2001. $7.00. Booklet summarizes significant changes in estate planning brought about by tax legislation of 2001.

Federal Estate and Gift Tax Reports. CCH, Inc. • Weekly. $520.00. Three looseleaf volumes.

Federal Income, Gift and Estate Taxation. Matthew Bender & Co., Inc. • $1,070.00. Nine looseleaf volumes. Periodic supplementation.

Fiduciary Tax Guide. CCH, Inc. • Monthly. $439.00 per year, Includes looseleaf monthly updates. Covers federal income taxation of estates, trusts, and beneficiaries. Provides information on gift and generation- skipping taxation.

INITIAL PUBLIC OFFERINGS

See: NEW ISSUES (FINANCE)

INJURIES

See: ACCIDENTS

INK

See: PRINTING INK INDUSTRY

INLAND MARINE INSURANCE

See: MARINE INSURANCE

INLAND WATERWAYS

See: WATERWAYS

INNOVATION, BUSINESS

See: BUSINESS INNOVATION

INNOVATION IN PRODUCTS

See: NEW PRODUCTS

INSECTICIDES

See: PESTICIDE INDUSTRY

INSECTS

See: ECONOMIC ENTOMOLOGY

INSERVICE TRAINING

See: TRAINING OF EMPLOYEES

INSIDER TRADING

See also: STOCKHOLDERS

ABSTRACTS AND INDEXES

Business Periodicals Index. H. W. Wilson Co. • Monthly, except August, with quarterly and annual cumulations. Service basis for print edition; CD-ROM edition, $1,495.00 per year.

Index to Legal Periodicals and Books. H. W. Wilson Co. • Monthly. Quarterly and annual cumulations. $270.00 per year. CD-ROM version available at $1,495.00 per year.

DIRECTORIES

National Directory of Investment Newsletters. GPS Co. • Biennial. $49.95. Describes about 800 investment newsletters, and their publishers.

HANDBOOKS AND MANUALS

Corporate Counsellor's Deskbook. Dennis J. Block and Michael A. Epstein, editors. Panel Publishing. • 1999. $220.00. Fifth edition. Looseleaf. Annual supplementation. Covers a wide variety of corporate legal issues, including internal investigations, indemnification, insider trading, intellectual property, executive compensation, antitrust, export-import, real estate, environmental law, government contracts, and bankruptcy.

Insider Trading: Regulation: Enforcement and Prevention. Donald C. Langevoort. West Group. • $145.00. Looseleaf service. (Securities Law Series).

Responsibilities of Corporate Officers and Directors Under Federal Securities Law. CCH, Inc. • Annual.

$55.00. Includes discussions of indemnification, "D & O" insurance, corporate governance, and insider liability.

INTERNET DATABASES

Thomson Investors Network. Thomson Financial. Phone: (212)807-3800 • URL: http://thomsoninvest.net • Web site provides detailed data on insider trading, institutional portfolios, and "First Call" earnings estimates. Includes a stock screening (filtering) application, a search facility, and price quotes on stocks, bonds, and mutual funds. Continuous updating. Fees: $34.95 per year for general service. First Call earnings service is $19.95 per month or $199.00 per year.

U. S. Securities and Exchange Commission. Phone: 800-732-0330 or (202)942-7040 Fax: (202)942-9634 E-mail: webmaster@sec.gov • URL: http://www.sec.gov • SEC Web site offers free access through EDGAR to text of official corporate filings, such as annual reports (10-K), quarterly reports (10-Q), and proxies. (EDGAR is "Electronic Data Gathering, Analysis, and Retrieval System.") An example is given of how to obtain executive compensation data from proxies. Text of the daily *SEC News Digest* is offered, as are links to other government sites, non-government market regulators, and U. S. stock exchanges. Search facilities are extensive. Fees: Free.

ONLINE DATABASES

Index to Legal Periodicals and Books (Online). H. W. Wilson Co. • Broad coverage of law journals and books 1981 to date. Monthly updates. Inquire as to online cost and availability.

Legal Resource Index. The Gale Group. • Broad coverage of law literature appearing in legal, business, and other periodicals, 1980 to date. Monthly updates. Inquire as to online cost and availability.

LEXIS. LEXIS-NEXIS. • The various LEXIS databases provide full text and indexing for a wide variety of legal cases, statutes, orders, and opinions.

Vickers On-Line. Vickers Stock Research Corp. • Provides detailed online information relating to insider trading and the securities holdings of institutional investors. Daily updates. Inquire as to online cost and availability.

Wilson Business Abstracts Online. H. W. Wilson Co. • Indexes and abstracts 600 major business periodicals, plus the *Wall Street Journal* and the business section of the *New York Times*. Indexing is from 1982, abstracting from 1990, with the two newspapers included from 1993. Updated weekly. Inquire as to online cost and availability. (*Business Periodicals Index* without abstracts is also available online.).

PERIODICALS AND NEWSLETTERS

Barron's: The Dow Jones Business and Financial Weekly. Dow Jones and Co., Inc. • Weekly. $145.00 per year.

The Insiders: America's Most Knowledgeable Investors. Institute for Econometric Research. • Semimonthly. $100.00 per year. Newsletter.

Official Summary of Security Transactions and Holdings. U. S. Securities and Exchange Commission. Available from U. S. Government Printing Office. • Monthly. $166.00 per year. Lists buying or selling of each publicly held corporation's stock by its officers, directors, or other insiders.

Vickers Weekly Insider Report. Vickers Stock Research Corp. • Weekly. $176.00 per year. Newsletter. Provides information on the trading activities of corporate officers and directors in their own companies' securities.

RESEARCH CENTERS AND INSTITUTES

Center for Research in Security Prices. University of Chicago, 725 S. Wells St., Suite 800, Chicago, IL 60607. Phone: (773)702-7467 Fax: (773)753-4797 E-mail: mail@crsp.uchicago.edu • URL: http://www.crsp.com.

Glucksman Institute. New York University. Salomon Center, Stern School of Business, 44 W. Fourth St., Room 9-65, New York, NY 10012-0267. Phone: (212)998-0714 Fax: (212)995-4220 E-mail: iwalter@stern.nyu.edu • URL: http://www.stern.nyu.edu/salomon.

Rodney L. White Center for Financial Research. University of Pennsylvania, 3254 Steinberg Hall-Dietrich Hall, Philadelphia, PA 19104. Phone: (215)898-7616 Fax: (215)573-8084 E-mail: rlwtcr@finance.wharton.upenn.edu • URL: http://www.finance.wharton.upenn.edu/~rlwctr • Research areas include financial management, money markets, real estate finance, and international finance.

TRADE/PROFESSIONAL ASSOCIATIONS

American Stock Exchange. 86 Trinity Place, New York, NY 10006. Phone: (212)306-1000 Fax: (212)306-1218.

National Association of Securities Dealers. 1735 K St., N.W., Washington, DC 20006-1506. Phone: (202)728-8000 Fax: (202)293-6260 • URL: http://www.nasdr.com/1000.asp.

New York Stock Exchange. 11 Wall St., New York, NY 10005. Phone: (212)656-3000 Fax: (212)656-3939.

North American Securities Administrators Association. 10 G St., N.E., Ste. 710, Washington, DC 20002. Phone: (202)737-0900 Fax: (202)783-3571 E-mail: info@nasaa.org • Members are state officials who administer "blue sky" securities laws.

Securities Industry Association. 120 Broadway, New York, NY 10271-0080. Phone: (212)608-1500 Fax: (212)608-1604 E-mail: info@sia.com • URL: http://www.sia.com.

Security Traders Association. One World Trade Center, Suite 4511, New York, NY 10048. Phone: (212)524-0484 Fax: (212)321-3449.

OTHER SOURCES

Business & Company Resource Center. The Gale Group. • Fee-based Web site provides a wide range of business, industry, and specific company information. Access is offered to trade journal articles, market research data, insider trading activity, major shareholder data, corporate histories, emerging technology reports, corporate earnings estimates, press releases, and other sources. Provides detailed company profiles, industry overviews, and rankings. Offers integration of Predicasts PROMT, Newsletters ASAP, Investext Plus, Business Index ASAP, Brands and Their Companies, and other databases (many have full text).

Securities Litigation and Regulation Reporter: The National Journal of Record ofCommodities Litigation. Andrews Publications. • Semimonthly. $1,294.00 per year. Provides reports on litigation involving the rules and decisions of the Commodity Futures Trading Commission. Formerly *Securities and Commodities Litigation Reporter*.

INSOLVENCY

See: BANKRUPTCY

INSTALLMENT PLAN PURCHASING

See also: CONSUMER CREDIT; FINANCE COMPANIES

PERIODICALS AND NEWSLETTERS

Consumer Finance Newsletter. Financial Publishing Co. • Monthly. $24.50 per year. Covers changes in state and federal consumer lending regulations.

OTHER SOURCES

Consumer and Commercial Credit: Installment Sales. Prentice Hall. • Three looseleaf volumes. Periodic supplementation. Price on application. Covers secured transactions under the Uniform Commercial Code and the Uniform Consumer Credit Code. Includes retail installment sales, home improvement loans, higher education loans, and other kinds of installment loans.

Installment Credit Survey Report. American Bankers Association. • Annual. Members, $225.00; non-members, $325.00. Information covers installment loans. Formerly*Installment Credit Report*.

INSTITUTIONAL FOOD SERVICE

See: FOOD SERVICE INDUSTRY

INSTITUTIONAL INVESTMENTS

See also: INVESTMENTS; TRUSTS AND TRUSTEES

GENERAL WORKS

Asset Allocation and Financial Market Timing: Techniques for Investment Professionals. Carroll D. Aby and Donald E. Vaughn. Greenwood Publishing Group, Inc. • 1995. $77.50.

Cases in Portfolio Management. John A. Quelch. McGraw-Hill Higher Education. • 1994. $52.99.

Financial Markets and Institutions. Jeff Madura. South-Western College Publishing Co. • 2000. $91.95. Fifth edition. (SWC-Economics Series).

Investments: An Introduction to Analysis and Management. Frederick Amling. Pearson Custom Publishing. • 1999. Seventh edition.

Market Efficiency: Stock Market Behavior in Theory and Practice. Andrew W. Lo, editor. Edward Elgar Publishing, Inc. • 1997. $430.00. Two volumes. Consists of reprints of 49 articles dating from 1937 to 1993, in five sections: "Theoretical Foundations," "The Random Walk Hypothesis," "Variance Bounds Tests," "Overreaction and Underreaction," and "Anomalies." (International Library of Critical Writings in Financial Economics Series: No. 3).

Modern Portfolio Theory and Investment Analysis. Edwin J. Elton and Martin J. Gruber. John Wiley and Sons, Inc. • 1995. $52.95. Fifth edition. The authors' central concern is that of mixing assets to achieve maximum overall return consonant with an acceptable level of risk. (Portfolio Management Series).

Portfolio Selection: Efficient Diversification of Investments. Harry M. Markowitz. Blackwell Publishers. • 1991. $52.95. Second edition. A standard work on diversification of investments for institutions. Provides a mathematical approach.

Security Analysis and Portfolio Management. Donald E. Fischer and Ronald L. Jordan. Prentice Hall. • 1995. $87.00. Sixth edition.

ABSTRACTS AND INDEXES

Banking Information Index. U M I Banking Information Index. • Monthly. Price on application. Covers a wide variety of banking, business, and financial subjects in periodicals. Formerly *Banking Literature Index.*

ALMANACS AND YEARBOOKS

Advances in Investment Analysis and Portfolio Management. Chung-Few Lee, editor. JAI Press, Inc. • 1999. $78.50.

CD-ROM DATABASES

BioMed Strategies. Thomson Financial Securities Data. • Monthly. $2,995.00 per year. CD-ROM contains full text of investment analysts' reports on companies operating in the following fields: biotechnology, pharmaceuticals, medical products, and health care.

Chemical Strategies. Thomson Financial Securities Data. • Monthly. $2,995.00 per year. CD-ROM contains full text of investment analysts' reports on companies active in the chemical industries.

Compact D/SEC. Disclosure, Inc. • Monthly. Contains three CD-ROM files. (1) Disclosure: Provides Securities and Exchange Commission filings for over 12,500 publicly held corporations. (2) Disclosure/Spectrum Ownership Profiles: Provides detailed corporate descriptions and complete ownership information for over 6,000 public companies. (3) Zacks Earnings Estimates: Provides earnings per share forecasts for about 4,000 U. S. corporations.

Electronic Strategies. Thomson Financial Securities Data. • Monthly. $2,995.00 per year. CD-ROM contains full text of investment analysts' reports on companies operating in the following fields: electronics, computers, semiconductors, and office products.

InvesText [CD-ROM]. Thomson Financial Securities Data. • Monthly. $5,000.00 per year. Contains full text on CD-ROM of investment research reports from about 250 sources, including leading brokers and investment bankers. Reports are available on both U. S. and international publicly traded corporations. Separate industry reports cover more than 50 industries. Time span is 1982 to date.

SEC Online on SilverPlatter. Available from SilverPlatter Information, Inc. • Quarterly. $3,950.00 per year to nonprofit organizations; $6,950.00 per year to businesses. Produced by Disclosure, Inc. Provides complete text on CD-ROM of documents filed with the Securities and Exchange Commission by over 5,000 publicly held corporations, including 10K forms (annual), 10Q forms (quarterly), and proxies. Also includes annual reports to stockholders.

Telecom Strategies. Thomson Financial Securities Data. • Monthly. $2,995.00 per year. CD-ROM contains full text of investment analysts' reports on companies operating in the following fields: telecommunications, broadcasting, and cable communications.

DIRECTORIES

Association for Investment Management and Research-Membership Directory. Association for Investment Management and Research. • Annual. $150.00. Members are professional investment managers and securities analysts.

Corporate Finance Sourcebook: The Guide to Major Capital Investment Source and Related Financial Services. R. R. Bowker. • Annual. $625.00. Lists more than 3,550 sources of corporate capital: investment bankers, securities firms, pension management companies, trust companies, insurance companies, and private lenders. Includes the names of over 13,000 key personnel.

Directory of Trust Banking. Thomson Financial Publishing. • Annual. $315.00. Contains profiles of bank affiliated trust companies, independent trust companies, trust investment advisors, and trust fund managers. Provides contact information for professional personnel at more than 3,000 banking and other financial institutions.

Financial Yellow Book: Who's Who at the Leading U. S. Financial Institutions. Leadership Directories, Inc. • Semiannual. $235.00. Gives the names and titles of over 31,000 key executives in financial institutions. Includes the areas of banking, investment, money management, and insurance. Five indexes are provided: institution, executive name, geographic by state, financial service segment, and parent company.

Futures Guide to Computerized Trading. Futures Magazine, Inc. • Annual. $10.00. "A directory of products and services for the computerized trader." Provides information on computer software applications for commodity traders and money managers, including trading methods and technical analysis.

Futures Magazine SourceBook: The Most Complete List of Exchanges, Companies, Regulators, Organizations, etc., Offering Products and Services to the Futures and Options Industry. Futures Magazine, Inc. • Annual. $19.50. Provides information on commodity futures brokers, trading method services, publications, and other items of interest to futures traders and money managers.

Institutional Buyers of Bank and Thrift Stocks: A Targeted Directory. Investment Data Corp. • Annual. $645.00. Provides detailed profiles of about 600 institutional buyers of bank and savings and loan stocks. Includes names of financial analysts and portfolio managers.

Institutional Buyers of Energy Stocks: A Targeted Directory. Investment Data Corp. • Annual. $645.00. Provides detailed profiles 555 institutional buyers of petroleum-related and other energy stocks. Includes names of financial analysts and portfolio managers.

Institutional Buyers of Foreign Stocks: A Targeted Directory. Investment Data Corp. • Annual. $595.00. Provides detailed profiles of institutional buyers of international stocks. Includes names of financial analysts and portfolio managers.

Institutional Buyers of REIT Securities: A Targeted Directory. Investment Data Corp. • Semiannual. $995.00 per year. Provides detailed profiles of about 500 institutional buyers of REIT securities. Includes names of financial analysts and portfolio managers.

Institutional Buyers of Small-Cap Stocks: A Targeted Directory. Investment Data Corp. • Annual. $295.00. Provides detailed profiles of more than 837 institutional buyers of small capitalization stocks. Includes names of financial analysts and portfolio managers.

Money Market Directory of Pension Funds and Their Investment Managers. Money Market Directories, Inc. • Annual. $995.00. Institutional funds and managers.

Nelson's Directory of Institutional Real Estate. Wiesenberger/Thomson Financial. • Annual. $335.00. Includes real estate investment managers, service firms, consultants, real estate investment trusts (REITs), and various institutional investors in real estate.

Nelson's Directory of Investment Managers. Wiesenberger/Thomson Financial. • Annual. $545.00. Three volumes. Provides information on 2,600 investment management firms, both U.S. and foreign.

Nelson's Directory of Investment Research. Wiesenberger/Thomson Financial. • Annual. $590.00. Three volumes. Provides information on 10,000 investment research analysts at more than 800 firms. Indexes include company name, industry, and name of person.

Nelson's Directory of Pension Fund Consultants. Wiesenberger/Thomson Financial. • Annual. $350.00. Covers the pension plan sponsor industry. More than 325 worldwide consulting firms are described.

Nelson's Directory of Plan Sponsors. Wiesenberger/Thomson Financial. • Annual. $545.00. Three volumes. Available in two versions, alphabetic or geographic. Covers pension plan sponsors and pension funds, including more than 11,000 corporate funds, 4,000 endowment or foundation funds, 1,300 multi-employer funds, 1,000 hospital funds, and 900 public employee funds. Includes information on asset allocation and investment style. Eight indexes.

Plunkett's Financial Services Industry Almanac: The Leading Firms in Investments, Banking, and Financial Information. Available from Plunkett Research, Ltd. • Annual. $245.00. Discusses important trends in various sectors of the financial industry. Five hundred major banking, credit card, investment, and financial services companies are profiled.

Vickers Directory of Institutional Investors. Vickers Stock Research Corp. • Semiannual. $195.00 per year. Detailed alphabetical listing of more than 4,000 U. S., Canadian, and foreign institutional investors. Includes insurance companies, banks, endowment funds, and investment companies. Formerly *Directory of Institutional Investors.*

Zacks Analyst Directory: Listed by Broker. Zacks Investment Research. • Quarterly. $395.00 per year. Lists stockbroker investment analysts and gives the names of major U. S. corporations covered by those analysts.

Zacks Analyst Directory: Listed by Company. Zacks Investment Research. • Quarterly. $395.00 per year. Lists major U. S. corporations and gives the names of stockbroker investment analysts covering those companies.

Zacks EPS Calendar. Zacks Investment Research. • Biweekly. $1,250.00 per year. (Also available monthly at $895.00 per year.) Lists anticipated reporting dates of earnings per share for major U. S. corporations.

ENCYCLOPEDIAS AND DICTIONARIES

Blackwell Encyclopedic Dictionary of Finance. Dean Paxson and Douglas Wood, editors. Blackwell Publishers. • 1997. $110.00. The editors are associated with the University of Manchester. Contains definitions of key terms combined with longer articles written by various U. S. and foreign business educators. Includes bibliographies and index. (Blackwell Encyclopedia of Management Series).

Dictionary of Finance and Investment Terms. John Downes and Jordan E. Goodman. Barron's Educational Series, Inc. • 1998. $12.95. Fifth revised edition. Provides clear explanations of more than 5,000 business, banking, financial, investment, and tax terms. Includes a separate list of financial abbreviations and acronyms.

International Encyclopedia of Futures and Options. Michael R. Ryder, editor. Fitzroy Dearborn Publishers. • 2000. $275.00. Two volumes. Covers terminology, concepts, events, individuals, and markets.

The New Palgrave Dictionary of Money and Finance. Peter Newman and others, editors. Groves

Dictionaries. • 1998. $550.00. Three volumes. Consists of signed essays on over 1,000 financial topics, each with a bibliography. Covers a wide variety of financial, monetary, and investment areas. A detailed subject index is provided.

FINANCIAL RATIOS

Major Financial Institutions of the World. Available from The Gale Group. • 2001. $855.00. Fourth edition. Two volumes. Published by Graham & Whiteside. Contains detailed information on more than 7,500 important financial institutions in various countries. Includes banks, investment companies, and insurance companies.

HANDBOOKS AND MANUALS

Active Portfolio Management: Quantitative Theory and Applications. Richard C. Grinold. McGraw-Hill. • 1999. $70.00. Second edition.

Bank Investments and Funds Management. Gerald O. Hatler. American Bankers Association. • 1991. $49.00. Second edition. Focuses on portfolio management, risk analysis, and investment strategy.

Convertible Securities: The Latest Instruments, Portfolio Strategies, and Valuation Analysis. John P. Calamos. McGraw-Hill Professional. • 1998. $65.00. Second edition.

Derivatives: A Comprehensive Resource for Options, Futures, Interest Rate Swaps, and Mortgage Securities. Fred D. Arditti. Harvard Business School Press. • 1996. $60.00. Published by Harvard Business School Press. Provides detailed explanations of various kinds of financial derivatives (options, futures, swaps, etc.) and their trading tactics, uses, and risks. (Financial Management Association Survey and Synthesis Series).

Dynamic Asset Allocation: Strategies for the Stock, Bond, and Money Markets. David A. Hammer. John Wiley and Sons, Inc. • 1991. $49.95. A practical guide to the distribution of investment portfolio funds among various kinds of assets. (Finance Editions Series).

Econometric Analysis of Financial Markets. J. Kaehler and P. Kugler, editors. Springer-Verlag New York, Inc. • 1994. $71.95. (Studies in Empirical Economics Series).

Econometrics of Financial Markets. John Y. Campbell and others. California Princeton Fulfillment Services. • 1997. $49.50. Written for advanced students and industry professionals. Includes chapters on "The Predictability of Asset Returns," "Derivative Pricing Models," and "Fixed-Income Securities." Provides a discussion of the random walk theory of investing and tests of the theory.

Global Equity Selection Strategies. Ross P. Bruner, editor. Fitzroy Dearborn Publishers, Inc. • 1999. $65.00. Written by various professionals in the field of international investments. Contains six major sections covering growth, value, size, price momentum, sector rotation, and country allocation. (Glenlake Business Monographs).

Handbook of Alternative Investment Strategies. Thomas Schneeweis and Joseph F. Pescatore, editors. Institutional Investor. • 1999. $95.00. Covers various forms of alternative investment, including hedge funds, managed futures, derivatives, venture capital, and natural resource financing.

Handbook of Derivative Instruments: Investment Research, Analysis, and Portfolio Applications. Atsuo Konishi and Ravi E. Dattatreya, editors. McGraw-Hill Professional. • 1996. $80.00. Second revised edition. Contains 41 chapters by various authors on all aspects of derivative securities, including such esoterica as "Inverse Floaters," "Positive Convexity," "Exotic Options," and "How to Use the Holes in Black-Scholes.".

Handbook of Fixed Income Securities. Frank J. Fabozzi. McGraw-Hill Higher Education. • 2000. $99.95. Sixth edition. Topics include risk measurement, valuation techniques, and portfolio strategy.

Indexing for Maximum Investment Results. Albert S. Neuberg. Fitzroy Dearborn Publishers. • 1998. $65.00. Covers the Standard & Poor's 500 and other indexing strategies for both individual and institutional investors.

Interest Rate Risk Measurement and Management. Sanjay K. Nawalkha and Donald R. Chambers, editors. Institutional Investor, Inc. • 1999. $95.00. Provides interest rate risk models for fixed-income derivatives and for investments by various kinds of financial institutions.

An Introduction to the Mathematics of Financial Derivatives. Salih N. Neftci. Academic Press, Inc. • 2000. $59.95. Second edition. Covers the mathematical models underlying the pricing of derivatives. Includes explanations of basic financial calculus for students, derivatives traders, risk managers, and others concerned with derivatives.

Pension Fund Investment Management: A Handbook for Sponsors and Their Advisors. Fran K. Fabozzi. McGraw-Hill Professional. • 1990. $65.00.

Portfolio Management Formulas: Mathematical Trading Methods for the Futures, Options, and Stock Markets. Ralph Vince. John Wiley and Sons, Inc. • 1990. $85.00. Discusses optimization of trading systems by exploiting the rules of probability and making use of the principles of modern portfolio management theory. Computer programs are included.

INTERNET DATABASES

Derivatives. Derivatives Strategy and Tactics. Phone: (212)366-9578 Fax: (212)366-0551 E-mail: office@derivatives.com • URL: http://www.derivatives.com • Web site provides articles from *Derivatives Strategy* magazine (three-month delay). Also includes "Derivatives Comix," explaining complex topics in comic book form. An example is "Boovis and Beethead Play the Yield Curve Game." Links to useful derivatives Web sites and descriptions of recommended books are provided. Fees: Free.

Futures Online. Oster Communications, Inc. Phone: 800-601-8907 or (319)277-1278 Fax: (319)277-7982 • URL: http://www.futuresmag.com • Web site presents updates of *Futures* magazine and links to other futures-related sites. Includes "Futures Industry News," "Technical Talk," "Today's Hot Markets," "Futures Talk" (forums), "Futures Library" (archives, 1993 to date), and other features. Keyword searching is available. Updating: daily. Fees: Free.

Thomson Investors Network. Thomson Financial. Phone: (212)807-3800 • URL: http://thomsoninvest.net • Web site provides detailed data on insider trading, institutional portfolios, and "First Call" earnings estimates. Includes a stock screening (filtering) application, a search facility, and price quotes on stocks, bonds, and mutual funds. Continuous updating. Fees: $34.95 per year for general service. First Call earnings service is $19.95 per month or $199.00 per year.

Web Finance: Covering the Electronic Evolution of Finance. Securities Data Publishing. Phone: (212)765-5311 or 800-455-5844 Fax: (212)321-2336 E-mail: webfinance@tfn.com • URL: http://www.webfinance.net • Bi-weekly print and daily web-site publication of financial services on the Web, including financial links, archives, brokerage stocks, deal financing, and other financial and investment news and information.

ONLINE DATABASES

Banking Information Source. Bell & Howell Information and Learning. • Provides indexing and abstracting of periodical and other literature from 1982 to date, with weekly updates. Covers the financial services industry: banks, savings institutions, investment houses, credit unions, insurance companies, and real estate organizations. Emphasis is on marketing and management. Inquire as to online cost and availability. (Formerly *FINIS: Financial Industry Information Service.*).

Fitch IBCA Ratings Delivery Service. Fitch IBCA, Inc. • Provides online delivery of Fitch financial ratings in three sectors: "Corporate Finance" (corporate bonds, insurance companies), "Structured Finance" (asset-backed securities), and "U.S. Public Finance" (municipal bonds). Daily updates. Inquire as to online cost and availability.

InvesText. Thomson Financial Securities Data. • Provides full text online of investment research reports from more than 300 sources, including leading brokers and investment bankers. Reports are available on approximately 50,000 U. S. and international corporations. Separate industry reports cover 54 industries. Time span is 1982 to date, with daily updates. Inquire as to online cost and availability.

LEXIS Financial Information Service. LEXIS-NEXIS. • Includes many business and financial files, including the full text of *SEC News Digest*, *Zacks Earnings Forecaster*, SEC filings, and brokerage house research reports. Various time spans and updating frequencies. Inquire as to online cost and availability.

Super Searchers on Wall Street: Top Investment Professionals Share Their Online Research Secrets. Amelia Kassel and Reva Basch. Information Today, Inc. • 2000. $24.95. Gives the results of interviews with "10 leading financial industry research experts." Explains how online information is used by stock brokers, investment bankers, and individual investors. Includes relevant Web sites and other sources. (CyberAge Books.).

Vickers On-Line. Vickers Stock Research Corp. • Provides detailed online information relating to insider trading and the securities holdings of institutional investors. Daily updates. Inquire as to online cost and availability.

Zacks Earnings Estimates. Zacks Investment Research. • Provides online earnings projections for about 6,000 U. S. corporations, based on investment analysts' reports. Data is mainly from 200 major brokerage firms. Time span varies according to online provider, with daily or weekly updates. Inquire as to online cost and availability.

PERIODICALS AND NEWSLETTERS

Asset Management. Dow Jones Financial Publishing Corp. • Bimonthly. $345.00 per year. Covers the management of the assets of affluent, high net worth investors. Provides information on various financial products and services.

Bloomberg: A Magazine for Market Professionals. Bloomberg L.P. • Monthly. Free to qualified personnel. Edited for securities dealers and investment managers.

Bondweek: The Newsweekly of Fixed Income and Credit Markets. Institutional Investor. • Weekly. $2,220.00 per year. Newsletter. Covers taxable, fixed-income securities for professional investors, including corporate, government, foreign, mortgage, and high-yield.

Commercial Lending Review. Institutional Investor. • Quarterly. $195.00 per year. Edited for senior-level lending officers. Includes specialized lending techniques, management issues, legal developments, and reviews of specific industries.

Derivatives Quarterly. Institutional Investor. • Quarterly. $280.00 per year. Emphasis is on the practical use of derivatives. Includes case studies to demonstrate "real-life" risks and benefits.

Derivatives Strategy. Derivatives Strategy and Tactics. • Monthly. $245.00 per year. Provides practical explanations of financial derivatives for institutional investors, corporate treasury officers, dealers, and others.

Derivatives Tactics. Derivative Strategy and Tactics. • Semimonthly. $695.00 per year. Newsletter. Edited for institutional investors. Covers options, swaps, and other financial derivatives.

Emerging Markets Debt Report. Securities Data Publishing. • Weekly. $895.00 per year. Newsletter. Provides information on new and prospective sovereign and corporate bond issues from developing countries. Includes an emerging market bond index and pricing data. (Securities Data Publishing is a unit of Thomson Financial.).

Emerging Markets Quarterly. Institutional Investor. • Quarterly. $325.00 per year. Newsletter on financial markets in developing areas, such as Africa, Latin America, Southeast Asia, and Eastern Europe. Topics include institutional investment opportunities and regulatory matters. Formerly *Emerging Markets Weekly.*

Financial Markets, Institutions, and Instruments. New York University, Salomon Center. Blackwell Publishers. • Five times a year. $219.00 per year. Edited to "bridge the gap between the academic and professional finance communities." Special fifth issue each year provides surveys of developments in four areas: money and banking, derivative securities, corporate finance, and fixed-income securities.

Financial Trader. Miller Freeman, Inc. • 11 times a year. $160.00 per year. Edited for professional traders. Covers fixed income securities, emerging markets, derivatives, options, futures, and equities.

FMC (Financial Management): Journal of the Financial Management Association. Financial Management Association International. • Quarterly. Individuals, $80.00 per year; libraries, $100.00 per year. Covers theory and practice of financial planning, international finance, investment banking, and portfolio management. Includes *Financial Practice* and *Education and Contempory Finance Digest.*

Futures: News, Analysis, and Strategies for Futures, Options, and Derivatives Traders. Futures Magazine, Inc. • Monthly. $39.00 per year. Edited for institutional money managers and traders, brokers, risk managers, and individual investors or speculators. Includes special feature issues on interest rates, technical indicators, currencies, charts, precious metals, hedge funds, and derivatives. Supplements available.

Global Money Management. Institutional Investor. • Biweekly. $2,330.00 per year. Newsletter. Edited for international pension fund and investment company managers. Includes information on foreign investment opportunities and strategies.

Guide to Equity Mutual Funds: A Quarterly Compilation of Mutual Fund Ratings and Analysis Covering Equity and Balanced Funds. Weiss Ratings, Inc. • Quarterly. $438.00 per year. Emphasis is on rating of financial safety and relative risk. Includes annual summary.

High Yield Report. Securities Data Publishing. • Weekly. $995.00 per year. Newsletter covering the junk bond market. (Securities Data Publishing is a unit of Thomson Financial.).

Institutional Investor International Edition: The Magazine for International Finance and Investment. Institutional Investor. • Monthly. $415.00 per year. Covers the international aspects of professional investing and finance. Emphasis is on Europe, the Far East, and Latin America.

Institutional Investor: The Magazine for Finance and Investment. Institutional Investor. • Monthly. $475.00 per year. Edited for portfolio managers and other investment professionals. Special feature issues include "Country Credit Ratings," "Fixed Income Trading Ranking," "All-America Research Team," and "Global Banking Ranking.".

Insurance Finance and Investment. Institutional Investor. • Biweekly. $1,885.00 per year. Newsletter. Edited for insurance company investment managers.

Investment Advisor. Dow Jones Financial Publishing Corp. • Monthly. $79.00 per year. Edited for professional investment advisors, financial planners, stock brokers, bankers, and others concerned with the management of assets.

Investment Dealers' Digest. Securities Data Publishing. • Weekly. $750.00 per year. Covers financial news, trends, new products, people, private placements, new issues of securities, and other aspects of the investment business. Includes feature stories. (Securities Data Publishing is a unit of Thomson Financial.).

Investment Management Weekly. Securities Data Publishing. • Weekly. $1,370.00 per year. Newsletter. Edited for money managers and other investment professionals. Covers personnel news, investment strategies, and industry trends. (Securities Data Publishing is a unit of Thomson Financial.).

Investment News: The Weekly Newspaper for Financial Advisers. Crain Communications, Inc. • Weekly. $38.00 per year. Edited for both personal and institutional investment advisers, planners, and managers.

Investor Relations Business. Securities Data Publishing. • Semimonthly. $435.00 per year. Covers the issues affecting stockholder relations, corporate public relations, and institutional investor relations. (Securities Data Publishing is a unit of Thomson Financial.).

IOMA's Report on Defined Contribution Plan Investing. Institute for Management and Administration, Inc. • Semimonthly. $1,156.90 per year. Newsletter. Edited for 401(k) and other defined contribution retirement plan managers, sponsors, and service providers. Reports on such items as investment manager performance, guaranteed investment contract (GIC) yields, and asset allocation trends.

Journal of Alternative Investments. Institutional Investor. • Quarterly. $380.00 per year. Covers such items as hedge funds, private equity financing, funds of funds, real estate investment trusts, natural resource investments, foreign exchange, and emerging markets.

Journal of Derivatives. Institutional Investor. • Quarterly. $280.00 per year. Covers the structure and management of financial derivatives. Includes graphs, equations, and detailed analyses.

Journal of Financial Statement Analysis. Institutional Investor. • Quarterly. $280.00 per year. Covers the practical analysis and interpretation of corporate financial reports.

Journal of Fixed Income. Institutional Investor. • Quarterly. $325.00 per year. Covers a wide range of fixed-income investments for institutions, including bonds, interest-rate options, high-yield securities, and mortgages.

Journal of Investing. Institutional Investor. • Quarterly. $310.00 per year. Edited for professional investors. Topics include equities, fixed-income securities, derivatives, asset allocation, and other institutional investment subjects.

Journal of Portfolio Management: The Journal for Investment Professionals. Institutional Investor. • Quarterly. $370.00 per year. Edited for professional portfolio managers. Contains articles on investment practice, theory, and models.

Journal of Private Equity: Strategies and Techniques for Venture Investing. Institutional Investor. • Quarterly. $355.00 per year. Includes venture capital case histories, financial applications, foreign opportunities, industry analysis, management methods, etc.

Journal of Private Portfolio Management. Institutional Investor. • Quarterly. $280.00 per year. Edited for managers of wealthy individuals' investment portfolios.

Journal of Project Finance. Institutional Investor. • Quarterly. $290.00 per year. Covers the financing of large-scale construction projects, such as power plants and convention centers.

Journal of Risk Finance: The Convergence of Financial Products and Insurance. Institutional Investor. • Quarterly. $395.00 per year. Covers the field of customized risk management, including securitization, insurance, hedging, derivatives, and credit arbitrage.

Latin Fund Management. Securities Data Publishing. • Monthly. $495.00 per year. Newsletter (also available online at www.latinfund.net). Provides news and analysis of Latin American mutual funds, pension funds, and annuities. (Securities Data Publishing is a unit of Thomson Financial.).

Money Management Letter: Bi-Weekly Newsletter Covering the Pensions and Money Maagement Industry. Institutional Investor. • Biweekly. $2,550.00 per year. Newsletter. Edited for pension fund investment managers.

Mortgage-Backed Securities Letter. Securities Data Publishing. • Weekly. $1,595.00 per year. Newsletter. Provides news and analysis of the mortgage-backed securities market, including performance reports. (Securities Data Publishing is a unit of Thomson Financial.).

MPT Review; Specializing in Modern Portfolio Theory. Navellier and Associates, Inc. • Monthly. $275.00 per year. Newsletter. Provides specific stock selection and model portfolio advice (conservative, moderately aggressive, and aggressive) based on quantitative analysis and modern portfolio theory.

Outstanding Investor Digest: Perspectives and Activities of the Nation's Most Successful Money Managers. Outstanding Investor Digest, Inc. • $395.00 for 10 issues. Newsletter. Each issue features interviews with leading money managers.

Project Finance: The Magazine for Global Development. Institutional Investor Journals. • Monthly. $635.00 per year. Provides articles on the financing of the infrastructure (transportation, utilities, communications, the environment, etc). Coverage is international. Supplements available *World Export Credit Guide* and *Project Finance Book of Lists.* Formed by the merger of *Infrastructure Finance* and *Project and Trade Finance.*

Real Estate Finance and Investment. Institutional Investor. • Weekly. $2,105.00 per year. Newsletter for professional investors in commercial real estate. Includes information on financing, restructuring, strategy, and regulation.

Traders Magazine. Securities Data Publishing. • Monthly. $60.00 per year. Edited for institutional buy side and sell side equity traders. Covers industry news, market trends, regulatory developments, and personnel news. Serves as the official publication of the Security Traders Association. (Securities Data Publishing is a unit of Thomson Financial.).

Zacks Analyst Watch. Zacks Investment Research. • Biweekly. $250.00 per year. Provides the results of research by stockbroker investment analysts on major U. S. corporations.

Zacks Earnings Forecaster. Zacks Investment Research. • Biweekly. $495.00 per year. (Also available monthly at $375.00 per year.) Provides estimates by stockbroker investment analysts of earnings per share of individual U. S. companies.

Zacks Profit Guide. Zacks Investment Research. • Quarterly. $375.00 per year. Provides analysis of total return and stock price performance of major U. S. companies.

RESEARCH CENTERS AND INSTITUTES
Institute for Quantitative Research in Finance. Church Street Station, P.O. Box 6194, New York, NY 10249-6194. Phone: (212)744-6825 Fax: (212)517-2259 E-mail: daleberman@compuserve • Financial research areas include quantitative methods, securities analysis, and the financial structure of industries. Also known as the "Q Group.".

STATISTICS SOURCES
Financial Market Trends. Organization for Economic Cooperation and Development. • Three times a year. $100.00 per year. Provides analysis of developments and trends in international and national capital markets. Includes charts and graphs on interest rates, exchange rates, stock market indexes, bank stock indexes, trading volumes, and loans outstanding. Data from OECD countries includes international direct investment, bank profitability, institutional investment, and privatization.

Life Insurance Fact Book. American Council of Life Insurance. • Biennial. $37.50 per year; with diskette, $55.00 per year.

The New Finance: The Case Against Efficient Markets. Robert A. Haugen. Prentice Hall. • 1999. $26.20. Second edition.

Quarterly Pension Investment Report. Employee Benefit Research Institute. • Quarterly. $1,500.00 per year. $400.00 per year to nonprofit organizations. Provides aggregate financial asset data for U. S. private and public pension systems. Statistics are given for both defined contribution and defined benefit plans, including investment mixes (stocks, bonds, cash, other). Contains historical data for private trust, life insurance, and state and local government funds.

TRADE/PROFESSIONAL ASSOCIATIONS
Association for Investment Management and Research. 560 Ray C. Hunt Dr., Charlottesville, VA 22903-0668. Phone: 800-247-8132 or (804)951-5499 Fax: (804)951-5262 E-mail: info@aimr.org • URL: http://www.aimr.org.

Council of Institutional Investors. 1730 Rhode Island Ave., N. W., Suite 512, Washington, DC 20036. Phone: (202)822-0800 Fax: (202)822-0801 E-mail: info@cii.org • URL: http://www.cii.org • Members are nonprofit organization pension plans and other nonprofit institutional investors.

Investment Counsel Association of America. 1050 17th St., N.W., Suite 725, Washington, DC 20036-5503. Phone: (202)293-4222 Fax: (202)293-4223 E-mail: icaa@icaa.org • URL: http://www.icaa.org.

OTHER SOURCES
Quantitative Finance. Available from IOP Publishing, Inc. • Bimonthly. $199.00 per year. Published in the UK by the Institute of Physics. A technical journal on the use of quantitative tools and applications in financial analysis and financial engineering. Covers such topics as portfolio theory, derivatives, asset allocation, return on assets, risk management, price volatility, financial econometrics, market anomalies, and trading systems.

INSTRUCTION OF EMPLOYEES

See: TRAINING OF EMPLOYEES

INSTRUCTION, PROGRAMMED

See: PROGRAMMED LEARNING

INSTRUMENTS, MUSICAL

See: MUSICAL INSTRUMENTS INDUSTRY

INSTRUMENTS, SCIENTIFIC

See: SCIENTIFIC APPARATUS AND INSTRUMENT INDUSTRIES

INSTRUMENTS, SURGICAL

See: SURGICAL INSTRUMENTS INDUSTRY

INSULATION

See also: BUILDING INDUSTRY

DIRECTORIES
Building Supply Home Centers Retail Giants Report. Cahners Business Information. • Annual. $30.00. Lists major retailers of a wide variety of building and home improvement materials, products, fixtures, accessories, equipment, and tools.

HANDBOOKS AND MANUALS
No-Regrets Remodeling: Creating a Comfortable, Healthy Home That Saves Energy. Available from American Council for an Energy-Efficient Economy. • 1997. $19.95. Edited by *Home Energy* magazine. Serves as a home remodeling guide to efficient heating, cooling, ventilation, water heating, insulation, lighting, and windows.

PERIODICALS AND NEWSLETTERS
Building Material Retailer. National Lumber and Building Material Dealers Association. • Monthly. $25.00 per year. Includes special feature issues on hand and power tools, lumber, roofing, kitchens, flooring, windows and doors, and insulation.

Contractor's Guide: The Guide to the Roofing, Insulation, Siding, Solar, and Window Industries. Century Communications Corp. • Monthly. $26.00 per year. For roofing and insulation contractors.

Journal of Thermal Enevelope and Building Science. Technomic Publishing Co., Inc. • Quarterly. $465.00 per year. Formerly *Journal of Thermal Insulation and Building Envelopes.*

RSI (Roofing, Siding, Insulation). Advanstar Communications, Inc. • Monthly. $39.00 per year.

TRADE/PROFESSIONAL ASSOCIATIONS
Insulation Contractors Association of America. 1321 Duke St., Ste. 303, Alexandria, VA 22314. Phone: (703)739-0356 Fax: (703)739-0412 E-mail: icca@insulate.org • URL: http://www.insulate.org.

National Fenestration Rating Council. 1300 Spring St., Suite 500, Silver Spring, MD 20910. Phone: (301)589-6372 Fax: (301)588-0854 E-mail: nfrcusa@aol.com • URL: http://www.nfrc.org • Conducts insulation efficiency testing of doors and windows. Encourages informed purchase by consumers of windows, doors, and skylights.

National Insulation Association. 99 Canal Center Plaza, Suite 222, Alexandria, VA 22314. Phone: (703)683-6422 Fax: (703)549-4838 E-mail: sbaker@insulation.org • URL: http://www.insulation.org.

North American Insulation Manufacturers Association. 44 Canal Center Plaza, Suite 310, Alexandria, VA 22314. Phone: (703)684-0084 Fax: (703)684-0427 E-mail: insulation@naima.org • URL: http://www.naima.org.

INSURANCE

See also: ACCIDENT INSURANCE; AUTOMOBILE INSURANCE; BUSINESS INTERRUPTION INSURANCE; CASUALTY INSURANCE; CREDIT INSURANCE; DISABILITY INSURANCE; FIRE INSURANCE; HEALTH INSURANCE; LIFE INSURANCE; LONG-TERM CARE INSURANCE; MARINE INSURANCE; PROPERTY AND LIABILITY INSURANCE; RISK MANAGEMENT; UNEMPLOYMENT INSURANCE

GENERAL WORKS
Smarter Insurance Solutions. Janet Bamford. Bloomberg Press. • 1996. $19.95. Provides practical advice to consumers, with separate chapters on the following kinds of insurance: automobile, homeowners, health, disability, and life. (Bloomberg Personal Bookshelf Series).

ABSTRACTS AND INDEXES
Banking Information Index. U M I Banking Information Index. • Monthly. Price on application. Covers a wide variety of banking, business, and financial subjects in periodicals. Formerly *Banking Literature Index.*

Business Periodicals Index. H. W. Wilson Co. • Monthly, except August, with quarterly and annual cumulations. Service basis for print edition; CD-ROM edition, $1,495.00 per year.

Insurance Periodicals Index. Specials Libraries Association, Insurance and Employees Benefits Div. CCH/NILS Publishing Co. • Annual. $250.00. Compiled by the Insurance and Employee Benefits Div., Special Libraries Association. A yearly index of over 15,000 articles from about 35 insurance periodicals. Arrangement is by subject, with an index to authors.

Social Sciences Citation Index. Institute for Scientific Information. • Three times a year. $6,900 per year. Annual cumulation. Includes *Source Index, Citation Index, Permuterm Subject Index,* and *Corporate Index.*

Social Sciences Index. H. W. Wilson Co. • Quarterly, with annual cumulation. Service basis for print edition; CD-ROM edition, $1,495 per year. Indexes more than 400 periodicals covering economics, environmental policy, government, insurance, labor, health care policy, plannning, public administration, public welfare, urban studies, women's issues, criminology, and related topics.

ALMANACS AND YEARBOOKS
Insurance Almanac: Who, What, When and Where in Insurance. Underwriter Printing and Publishing Co. • Annual. $145.00. Lists insurance agencies and

brokerage firms; U.S. and Canadian insurance companies, adjusters, appraisers, auditors, investigators, insurance officials and insurance organizations.

BIBLIOGRAPHIES

Business Information Sources. Lorna M. Daniells. California Princeton Fulfillment Services. • 1993. $42.50. Third revised edition. Basic business sources, with discussion and full annotations.

Insurance and Employee Benefits Literature. Special Libraries Association, Insurance and Employee Benefits Div. • Bimonthly. $15.00 per year.

CD-ROM DATABASES

Social Science Source. EBSCO Publishing. • Monthly. $1,495.00 per year. Provides CD-ROM citations and abstracts to social science articles in more than 600 periodicals, with full text from 125 periodicals. Covers economics, political science, public policy, international relations, psychology, and other topics. Time period is most recent five years.

Social Sciences Citation Index: Compact Disc Edition. Institute for Scientific Information. • Quarterly. Provides CD-ROM indexing of the world's social sciences literature, including economics, business, finance, management, communications, demographics, information and library science, political science, sociology, etc. Corresponds to online *Social Scisearch* and printed *Social Sciences Citation Index.*

Social Sciences Citation Index: Compact Disc Edition with Abstracts. Institute for Scientific Information. • Quarterly. Provides CD-ROM indexing and abstracting of "significant articles" from 1,400 social science journals worldwide, with additional selections from 3,200 other journals, 1986 to date. Includes economics, business, finance, management, communications, demographics, information and library science, political science, sociology, and many other subjects.

U. S. Insurance: Life, Accident, and Health. Sheshunoff Information Services, Inc. • Monthly. Price on application. CD-ROM provides detailed, current information on the financial characteristics of more than 2,300 life, accident, and health insurance companies.

U. S. Insurance: Property and Casualty. Sheshunoff Information Services, Inc. • Monthly. Price on application. CD-ROM provides detailed, current financial information on more than 3,200 property and casualty insurance companies.

WILSONDISC: Wilson Business Abstracts. H. W. Wilson Co. • Monthly. $2,495.00 per year, including unlimited online access to *Wilson Business Abstracts* through WILSONLINE. Provides CD-ROM "cover-to-cover" abstracting and indexing of over 600 prominent business periodicals. Indexing is from 1982, abstracting from 1990. (*Business Periodicals Index* without abstracts is available on CD-ROM at $1,495 per year.).

WILSONDISC: Wilson Social Sciences Abstracts. H. W. Wilson Co. • Monthly. Including unlimited online access to *Social Sciences Index* through WILSONLINE. Provides CD-ROM indexing from 1983 and abstracting from 1994 of more than 400 periodicals covering economics, area studies, community health, public administration, public welfare, urban studies, and many other topics related to the social sciences.

DIRECTORIES

America's Corporate Finance Directory. National Register Publishing. • Annual. $699.00. A directory of financial executives employed at over 5,000 U. S. corporations. Includes a listing of the outside financial services (banks, pension managers, insurance firms, auditors) used by each corporation.

Best's Directory of Recommended Insurance Attorneys and Adjusters. A. M. Best Co. • Annual. $1130.00. Two volumes. More than 5,000 American, Canadian, and foreign insurance defense law firms; lists 1,200 national and international insurance adjusting firms. Formerly *Best's Directory of Recommended Insurance Adjusters.*

Business and Finance Career Directory. Visible Ink Press. • 1992. $17.95.

Corporate Finance Sourcebook: The Guide to Major Capital Investment Source and Related Financial Services. R. R. Bowker. • Annual. $625.00. Lists more than 3,550 sources of corporate capital: investment bankers, securities firms, pension management companies, trust companies, insurance companies, and private lenders. Includes the names of over 13,000 key personnel.

Financial Times World Insurance Yearbook. Available from The Gale Group. • 1991. $196.00. Published by St. James Press. Provides information on over 1,150 insurance companies in many countries of the world. Includes a summary of recent developments in the insurance industry.

Financial Yellow Book: Who's Who at the Leading U. S. Financial Institutions. Leadership Directories, Inc. • Semiannual. $235.00. Gives the names and titles of over 31,000 key executives in financial institutions. Includes the areas of banking, investment, money management, and insurance. Five indexes are provided: institution, executive name, geographic by state, financial service segment, and parent company.

Hine's Directory of Insurance Adjusters, Investigators, and Appraisers. Hine's, Inc. • Annual. $25.00. Lists selected independent insurance adjusters in the United States and Canada.

Insurance Market Place: The Agents and Brokers Guide to Non-Standard and Specialty Lines, Aviation, Marine and International Insurance. Rough Notes Co., Inc. • Annual. $12.95. Lists specialty, excess, and surplus insurance lines.

Internet Tools of the Profession: A Guide for Information Professionals. Hope N. Tillman, editor. Special Libraries Association. • 1997. $49.00. Second edition. Consists of 14 sections by various authors or compilers. After two introductory articles on searching the Internet, there are 12 annotated lists of useful Web sites, covering the SLA, business and finance, chemistry, education, food and agriculture, information technology, insurance and employee benefits, law, library management, metals and materials, pharmaceuticals, and telecommunications. An index is provided.

Major Financial Institutions of Europe. European Business Publications, Inc. • Annual. $495.00. Contains profiles of over 7,000 financial institutions in Europe such as banks, investment companies, and insurance companies. Formerly *Major Financial Institutions of Continental Europe.*

S & P's Insurance Book. Standard & Poor's Ratings Group, Insurance Rating Services. • Quarterly. Price on application. Contains detailed financial analyses and ratings of various kinds of insurance companies.

S & P's Insurance Digest: Life Insurance Edition. Standard & Poor's Ratings Group, Insurance Rating Services. • Quarterly. Contains concise financial analyses and ratings of life insurance companies.

The Top 5,000 European Companies 2000/2001. Available from The Gale Group. • 2001. $630.00. Second edition. Published by Graham & Whiteside. In addition to about 5,000 manufacturing and service companies, includes the 500 largest banks in Europe and the 100 largest insurance companies.

The Top 5,000 Global Companies 2000/2001. Available from The Gale Group. • Published by Graham & Whiteside. Includes about 5,000 manufacturing and service companies worldwide, plus the world's 500 largest banks and 100 largest insurance companies.

Who Writes What in Life and Health Insurance. The National Underwriter Co. • Annual. $9.95.

ENCYCLOPEDIAS AND DICTIONARIES

Dictionary of Insurance. Lewis E. Davids. Rowman and Littlefield Publishers, Inc. • 1990. $17.95. Seventh revised edition.

Dictionary of Insurance Terms. Harvey W. Rubin. Barron's Educational Series, Inc. • 2000. $12.95. Fourth edition. Defines terms in a wide variety of insurance fields. Price on application.

Insurance Words and Their Meanings: A Dictionary of Insurance Terms. Diana Kowatch. The Rough Notes Co., Inc. • 1998. $38.50. 16th revised edition.

Rupp's Insurance and Risk Management Glossary. Richard V. Rupp. Available from CCH, Inc. • 1996. $35.00. Second edition. Published by NILS Publishing Co. Provides definitions of 6,400 insurance words and phrases. Includes a guide to acronyms and abbreviations.

FINANCIAL RATIOS

Almanac of Business and Industrial Financial Ratios. Leo Troy. Prentice Hall. • Annual. $99.95. Contains financial ratios derived from federal tax returns. Ratios for each of about 200 industries are arranged according to company asset size.

The Financial Elite: Database of Financial Services Companies. Donnelley Marketing. • Quarterly. Price on application. Formerly compiled by Database America. Provides current information on CD-ROM for 500,000 major U. S. companies offering financial services. Data for each firm includes year started, type of financial service, annual revenues, name of top executive, and number of employees.

Major Financial Institutions of the World. Available from The Gale Group. • 2001. $855.00. Fourth edition. Two volumes. Published by Graham & Whiteside. Contains detailed information on more than 7,500 important financial institutions in various countries. Includes banks, investment companies, and insurance companies.

HANDBOOKS AND MANUALS

Business Insurance Guide: How to Purchase the Best and Most Affordable Insurance. Jamie McLeroy. Summers Press, Inc. • Looseleaf service. $96.50.

The Complete Book of Insurance: The Consumer's Guide to Insuring Your Life, Health, Property, and Income. Ben G. Baldwin. McGraw-Hill Professional. • 1996. $24.95. Revised edition. Provides basic information and advice on various kinds of insurance: life, health, property (fire), disability, long-term care, automobile, liability, and annuities.

Dun & Bradstreet/Gale Group Industry Handbooks. The Gale Group. • 2000. $630.00. Five volumes. $145.00 per volume. Each volume covers two or more major industries: 1. *Entertainment and Hospitality*; 2. *Construction and Agriculture*; 3. *Chemicals and Pharmaceuticals*; 4. *Computers & Software and Broadcasting & Telecommunications*; 5. *Insurance and Health & Medical Services.* The following are included for each industry: overview, statistics, financial ratios, rankings, merger information, company directory, directory of associations, and consultants directory.

An Insurance Guide for Seniors. Insurance Forum, Inc. • 1997. $15.00. Provides concise advice and information on Medicare, Medicare supplement insurance, HMOs, long-term care insurance, automobile insurance, life insurance, annuities, and pensions. An appendix lists "Financially Strong Insurance Companies." (*The Insurance Forum*, vol. 24, no. 4.).

Insurance Smart: How to Buy the Right Insurance at the Right Price. Jeffrey P. O'Donnell. John Wiley and Sons, Inc. • 1991. $12.95. Advice for insurance buyers on automobile, homeowner, business, farm, health, and life coverage.

Insuring Your Business: What You Need to Know to Get the Best Insurance Coverage for Your Business. Sean Mooney. Insurance Information Institute. • 1992. $22.50.

INTERNET DATABASES

InsWeb. InsWeb Corp. Phone: (650)372-2129 E-mail: info@insweb.com • URL: http://www.insweb.com • Web site offers a wide variety of advice and information on automobile, life, health, and "other" insurance. Includes glossaries of insurance terms, Standard & Poor's ratings of individual insurance companies, and "Financial Needs Estimators." Searching is available. Fees: Free.

Internet Tools of the Profession. Special Libraries Association. Phone: (202)234-4700 Fax: (202)265-9317 E-mail: hope@tiac.net • URL: http://www.sla.org/pubs/itotp • Web site is designed to update the printed *Internet Tools of the Profession.* Provides links to a wide range of useful databases in business, finance, industry, information technology, insurance, law, library management, telecommunications, and other subject areas. Fees: Free.

ONLINE DATABASES

ABI/INFORM. Bell & Howell Information and Learning. • Provides online indexing to business-related material occurring in over 1,000 periodicals from 1971 to the present. Inquire as to online cost and availability.

Banking Information Source. Bell & Howell Information and Learning. • Provides indexing and abstracting of periodical and other literature from 1982 to date, with weekly updates. Covers the financial services industry: banks, savings institutions, investment houses, credit unions, insurance companies, and real estate organizations. Emphasis is on marketing and management. Inquire as to online cost and availability. (Formerly *FINIS: Financial Industry Information Service.*).

Best's Company Reports. A. M. Best Co. • Provides full financial data online for U. S. insurance companies (life, health, property, casualty), including balance sheet data, income statements, expenses, premium income, losses, and investments. Includes *Best's Company Reports, Best's Insurance News*, and Best's ratings of insuarance companies. Inquire as to online cost and availability.

Fitch IBCA Ratings Delivery Service. Fitch IBCA, Inc. • Provides online delivery of Fitch financial ratings in three sectors: "Corporate Finance" (corporate bonds, insurance companies), "Structured Finance" (asset-backed securities), and "U.S. Public Finance" (municipal bonds). Daily updates. Inquire as to online cost and availability.

I.I.I. Data Base Search. Insurance Information Institute. • Provides online citations and abstracts of insurance-related literature in magazines, newspapers, trade journals, and books. Emphasis is on property and casualty insurance issues, including highway safety, product safety, and environmental liability. Inquire as to online cost and availability.

Social Scisearch. Institute for Scientific Information. • Broad, multidisciplinary index to the literature of the social sciences, 1972 to present. Weekly updates. Worldwide coverage. Inquire as to online cost and availability.

Wilson Business Abstracts Online. H. W. Wilson Co. • Indexes and abstracts 600 major business periodicals, plus the *Wall Street Journal* and the business section of the *New York Times*. Indexing is from 1982, abstracting from 1990, with the two newspapers included from 1993. Updated weekly. Inquire as to online cost and availability. (*Business Periodicals Index* without abstracts is also available online.).

Wilson Social Sciences Abstracts Online. H. W. Wilson Co. • Provides online abstracting and indexing of more than 415 periodicals covering area studies, community health, public administration, public welfare, urban studies, and many other social science topics. Time period is 1994 to date for abstracts and 1983 to date for indexing, with updates monthly. Inquire as to online cost and availability.

PERIODICALS AND NEWSLETTERS

Bank Investment Product News. Institutional Investor, Newsletters Div. • Weekly. $1,195.00 per year. Newsletter. Edited for bank executives. Covers the marketing and regulation of financial products sold through banks, such as mutual funds, stock brokerage services, and insurance.

Claims. IW Publications, Inc. • Monthly. $42.00 per year. Edited for insurance adjusters, risk managers, and claims professionals. Covers investigation, fraud, insurance law, and other claims-related topics.

Contingencies: The Magazine of the Actuarial Profession. American Academy of Actuaries. • Bimonthly. $30.00 per year. Provides non-technical articles on the actuarial aspects of insurance, employee benefits, and pensions.

CPCU Journal. Chartered Property and Casualty Underwriters Society. • Quarterly. $25.00 per year. Published by the Chartered Property and Casualty Underwriters Society (CPCU). Edited for professional insurance underwriters and agents.

Guide to Life, Health, and Annuity Insurers: A Quarterly Compilation of Insurance Company Ratings and Analysis. Weiss Ratings, Inc. • Quarterly. $438.00 per year. Emphasis is on rating of financial safety and relative risk. Includes annual summary.

Guide to Property and Casualty Insurers: A Quarterly Compilation of Insurance Company Ratings and Analysis. Weiss Ratings, Inc. • Quarterly. $438.00 per year. Emphasis is on rating of financial safety and relative risk. Includes annual summary.

Insurance Advocate. Emanuel Levy, editor. Shea-Haarmann. • Weekly. $59.00 per year. News and features on all aspects of insurance business for industry professionals.

Insurance and Technology. Miller Freeman. • Monthly. $65.00 per year. Covers information technology and systems management as applied to the operation of life, health, casualty, and property insurance companies.

Insurance Finance and Investment. Institutional Investor. • Biweekly. $1,885.00 per year. Newsletter. Edited for insurance company investment managers.

The Insurance Forum: For the Unfettered Exchange of Ideas About Insurance. Joseph M. Belth, editor. Insurance Forum, Inc. • Monthly. $90.00 per year. Newsletter. Provides analysis of the insurance business, including occasional special issues showing the ratings of about 1,600 life-health insurance companies, as determined by four major rating services: Duff & Phelps Credit Rating Co., Moody's Investors Service, Standard & Poor's Corp., and Weiss Research, Inc.

Insurance Networking: Strategies and Solutions for Electronic Commerce. Faulkner & Gray, Inc. • 10 times a year. $63.95 per year. Covers information technology for the insurance industry, with emphasis on computer communications and the Internet.

InsuranceWeek. I.W. Publications, Inc. • Weekly. $30.00 per year.

Journal of Risk Finance: The Convergence of Financial Products and Insurance. Institutional Investor. • Quarterly. $395.00 per year. Covers the field of customized risk management, including securitization, insurance, hedging, derivatives, and credit arbitrage.

Risk and Insurance. LRP Publications. • Monthly. Price on application. Topics include risk management, workers' compensation, reinsurance, employee benefits, and managed care.

Risk Management. Risk and Insurance Management Society. Risk Management Society Publishing, Inc. • Monthly. $54.00 per year.

The Safe Money Report. Weiss Ratings, Inc. • Monthly. $148.00 per year. Newsletter. Provides financial advice and current safety ratings of various banks, savings and loan companies, insurance companies, and securities dealers.

RESEARCH CENTERS AND INSTITUTES

Center for Risk Management and Insurance Research. Georgia State University, P.O. Box 4036, Atlanta, GA 30302-4036. Phone: (404)651-4250 Fax: (404)651-1897 E-mail: rwklein@gsu.edu • URL: http://www.rmi.gsu.edu/.

S. S. Huebner Foundation. University of Pennsylvania, Vance Hall, Room 430, Philadelphia, PA 19104-6301. Phone: (215)898-9631 Fax: (215)573-2218 E-mail: cummins@wharton.upenn.edu • URL: http://www.rider.wharton.upenn.edu/~sshuebne/ • Awards grants for research in various areas of insurance.

STATISTICS SOURCES

Insurance Statistics Yearbook. OECD Publications and Information Center. • Annual. $75.00. Presents detailed statistics on insurance premiums collected in OECD countries, by type of insurance.

Property-Casualty Insurance Facts. Insurance Information Institute. • Annual. $22.50. Formerly *Insurance Facts.*

Standard & Poor's Industry Surveys. Standard & Poor's. • Semiannual. $1,800.00. Two looseleaf volumes. Includes monthly supplements. Provides detailed, individual surveys of 52 major industry groups. Each survey is revised on a semiannual basis. Also includes "Monthly Investment Review" (industry group investment analysis) and monthly "Trends & Projections" (economic analysis).

U. S. Industry and Trade Outlook: The McGraw-Hill Companies and the U.S. Department of Commerce/International Trade Administration. Datapso Research Corp. • Annual. $69.95. Produced by the International Trade Administration, U. S. Department of Commerce, in a "public-private" partnership with DRI/McGraw-Hill and Standard & Poor's. Provides basic data, outlook for the current year, and "Long-Term Prospects" (five-year projections) for a wide variety of products and services. Includes high technology industries. Formerly *U. S. Industrial Outlook.*

TRADE/PROFESSIONAL ASSOCIATIONS

Alliance of American Insurers. 3025 Highland Pkwy., Ste. 800, Downers Grove, IL 60515. Phone: (630)724-2100 Fax: (630)724-2190 E-mail:

library@allianceai.org • URL: http://www.allianceai.org.

American Risk and Insurance Association. P.O. Box 3028, Malvern, PA 19355-0728. Phone: (610)640-1997 Fax: (610)725-1007 E-mail: aria@cpcuiia.org • URL: http://www.aria.org • Promotes education and research in the science of risk and insurance.

Insurance Services Office. Seven World Trade Center, New York, NY 10048. Phone: (212)898-6000 Fax: (212)898-5525.

National Association of Independent Insurers. 2600 River Rd., Des Plaines, IL 60018. Phone: (847)297-7800 Fax: (847)297-5064 • URL: http://www.naii.org.

National Association of Insurance Women International. P.O. Box 4410, Tulsa, OK 74159. Phone: 800-766-6249 Fax: (918)743-1968 E-mail: national@naiw.org • URL: http://www.naiw.org.

National Association of Mutual Insurance Companies. P.O. Box 68700, Indianapolis, IN 46268-0700. Phone: 800-336-2642 or (317)875-5250 Fax: (317)879-8408 E-mail: pubaff@naminc.org • URL: http://www.namic.org.

National Insurance Association. 1133 Dessertshell Ave., Las Vegas, NV 89123-0230. Phone: (702)269-2445 Fax: (702)269-2446.

Risk and Insurance Management Society. 655 Third Ave., 2nd Fl., New York, NY 10017. Phone: (212)286-9292 Fax: (212)986-9716 • URL: http://www.rims.org.

OTHER SOURCES

Best's Insurance Reports. A.M. Best Co. • Annual. $745.00 per edition. Two editions, Life-health insurance covering about 1,750 companies, and property-casualty insurance covering over 2,500 companies. Includes one year subscription to both *Best's Review* and *Best's Insurance Management Reports.*

Best's Insurance Reports: Property-Casualty. A.M. Best Co. • Annual. $745.00. Guide to over 1,750 major property/casualty companies.

Federal Taxation of Insurance Companies. Dennis P. Van Mieghem and others. Prentice Hall. • $447.00 per year. Looseleaf service. Biweekly updates.

Fire and Casualty Insurance Law Reports. CCH, Inc. • $870.00 per year. Looseleaf service. Semimonthly updates.

Information, Finance, and Services USA. The Gale Group. • 2001. $240.00. Replaces *Service Industries USA* and *Finance, Insurance, and Real Estate USA.* Presents statistics and projections relating to economic activity in a wide variety of non-manufacturing areas.

Insurance Day. Available from Informa Publishing Group Ltd. • Three times a week. $440.00 per year. Published in the UK by Lloyd's List (http://www.lloydslist.com). A newspaper providing international coverage of property/casualty/liability insurance, reinsurance, and risk, with an emphasis on marine insurance.

Life, Health, and Accident Insurance Law Reports. CCH, Inc. • $835.00 per year. Looseleaf service. Monthly updates.

INSURANCE, ACCIDENT

See: ACCIDENT INSURANCE

INSURANCE ACTUARIES

See: ACTUARIAL SCIENCE

INSURANCE AGENTS

GENERAL WORKS

Smart Questions to Ask Your Financial Advisers. Lynn Brenner. Bloomberg Press. • 1997. $19.95. Provides practical advice on how to deal with financial planners, stockbrokers, insurance agents, and lawyers. Some of the areas covered are investments, estate planning, tax planning, house buying, prenuptial agreements, divorce arrangements, loss of a job, and retirement. (Bloomberg Personal Bookshelf Series Library.).

BIOGRAPHICAL SOURCES

Who's Who in Insurance. Underwriter Printing and Publishing Co. • Annual. $130.00. Contains over 5,000 biographies of insurance officials, leading agents and brokers, and high-ranking company officials.

FINANCIAL RATIOS

Almanac of Business and Industrial Financial Ratios. Leo Troy. Prentice Hall. • Annual. $99.95. Contains financial ratios derived from federal tax returns. Ratios for each of about 200 industries are arranged according to company asset size.

Annual Statement Studies. Robert Morris Associates: The Association of Lending and Credit Risk Professiona. • Annual. Free to members; non-members, $140.00. Median and quartile financial ratios are given for over 400 kinds of manufacturing, wholesale, retail, construction, and consumer finance establishments. Data is sorted by both asset size and sales volume. Includes a clearly written "Definition of Ratios" and an alphabetical industry index.

HANDBOOKS AND MANUALS

Responsibilities of Insurance Agents and Brokers. Matthew Bender & Co., Inc. • $750.00. Four looseleaf volumes. Semiannual updates, $520.00. Covers legal responsibilities of agents and federal tax consequences of insurance arrangements.

PERIODICALS AND NEWSLETTERS

Broker World. Insurance Publications, Inc. • Monthly. $6.00 per year. Edited for independent insurance agents and brokers. Special feature issue topics include annuities, disability insurance, estate planning, and life insurance.

Financial Planning: The Magazine for Financial Service Professionals. Securities Data Publishing. • Monthly. $79.00 per year. Edited for independent financial planners and insurance agents. Covers retirement planning, estate planning, tax planning, and insurance, including long-term healthcare considerations. Special features include a Retirement Planning Issue, Mutual Fund Performance Survey, and Variable Life and Annuity Survey. (Securities Data Publishing is a unit of Thomson Financial.).

GAMA International Journal. GAMA International. • Bimonthly. $30.00 per year. Contains practical articles on the management of life insurance agencies. (GAMA International was formerly General Agents and Managers Association.).

Health Insurance Underwriter. National Association of Health Underwriters. • 11 times a year. Free to members; non-members, $25.00 per year. Includes special feature issues on long-term care insurance, disability insurance, managed health care, and insurance office management.

Independent Agent. Independent Insurance Agents of North America, Inc. MSI. • Monthly. $24.00 per year.

Insurance Marketing: The Ins and Outs of Recruiting and Retaining More Agents. Agent Media Corp. • Bimonthly. Controlled circulation. Provides practical advice for insurance companies on how to hire and keep sales personnel.

Professional Agent. National Association of Professional Insurance Agents. • Monthly. Members, $12,00 per year; non-members, $24.00 per year. Provides sales and marketing advice for independent agents in various fields of insurance, including life, health, property, and casualty.

Resource: An Association Magazine for Life Insurance Management. LOMA. • Monthly. $36.00 per year. Covers management topics for life insurance home and field office personnel. (LOMA was formerly Life Office Management Association.).

Today's Insurance Woman. National Association of Insurance Women. • Quarterly. $15.00 per year. Provides advice on professional and personal development for women in the insurance business.

TRADE/PROFESSIONAL ASSOCIATIONS

American Association of Managing General Agents. 9140 Ward Parkway, Kansas City, MO 64114. Phone: (816)444-3500 Fax: (816)444-0330 • URL: http://www.iix.com/aamga.

GAMA International. 1922 F St., N. W., Washington, DC 20006. Phone: 800-345-2687 or (202)331-6088 Fax: (202)785-5712 E-mail: gamamail@gama.naifa.org • URL: http://www.gamaweb.com • Members are life insurance agents.

Independent Insurance Agents of America. 127 S. Peyton, Alexandria, VA 22314. Phone: 800-221-7917 or (703)683-4422 Fax: (703)683-7556 • URL: http://www.independentagent.com/index.

National Association of Professional Insurance Agents. 400 N. Washington St., Alexandria, VA 22314. Phone: (703)836-9340 Fax: (703)836-1279 E-mail: piaweb@pianet.org • URL: http://www.pianet.com • Members are independent agents in various fields of insurance.

INSURANCE, AUTOMOBILE

See: AUTOMOBILE INSURANCE

INSURANCE, BUSINESS INTERRUPTION

See: BUSINESS INTERRUPTION INSURANCE

INSURANCE, CASUALTY

See: CASUALTY INSURANCE

INSURANCE, DISABILITY

See: DISABILITY INSURANCE

INSURANCE, FIRE

See: FIRE INSURANCE

INSURANCE, HEALTH

See: HEALTH INSURANCE

INSURANCE LAW AND REGULATION

ABSTRACTS AND INDEXES

Current Law Index: Multiple Access to Legal Periodicals. The Gale Group. • Monthly. $650.00 per year. Produced in cooperation with the American

Association of Law Libraries. Indexes more than 900 law journals, legal newspapers, and specialty publications from the U.S., Canada, U.K., Ireland, Australia, and New Zealand.

Index to Legal Periodicals and Books. H. W. Wilson Co. • Monthly. Quarterly and annual cumulations. $270.00 per year. CD-ROM version available at $1,495.00 per year.

ALMANACS AND YEARBOOKS

American Law Yearbook. The Gale Group. • Annual. $155.00. Serves as a yearly supplement to *West's Encyclopedia of American Law.* Describes new legal developments in many subject areas.

Property and Casualty Insurance: Year in Review. CCH, Inc. • Annual. $75.00. Summarizes the year's significant legal and regulatory developments.

CD-ROM DATABASES

WILSONDISC: Index to Legal Periodicals and Books. H. W. Wilson Co. • Monthly. Including unlimited online access to *Index to Legal Periodicals* through WILSONLINE. Contains CD-ROM indexing of more than 800 English language legal periodicals from 1981 to date and 2,500 books.

DIRECTORIES

Best's Directory of Recommended Insurance Attorneys and Adjusters. A. M. Best Co. • Annual. $1130.00. Two volumes. More than 5,000 American, Canadian, and foreign insurance defense law firms; lists 1,200 national and international insurance adjusting firms. Formerly *Best's Directory of Recommended Insurance Adjusters.*

Hine's Insurance Counsel. Hine's, Inc. • Annual. $50.00. List of law firms and attorneys in the U. S. and Canada specializing in defense of insurance companies.

Insurance Bar Directory. The Bar List Publishing Co. • Annual. $80.00. Lists law firms that handle defense in insurance litigation.

ENCYCLOPEDIAS AND DICTIONARIES

Couch on Insurance. Ronald Anderson. West Group. • 1984. $2,900.00. Second edition. 33 volumes. An encyclopedic statement of all phases of insurance law.

West's Encyclopedia of American Law. Available from The Gale Group. • 1997. $995.00. Second edition. 12 volumes. Published by West Group. Covers a wide variety of legal topics for the general reader. Formerly *Guide to American Law: Everyone's Legal Encyclopedia* (1985).

ONLINE DATABASES

Index to Legal Periodicals and Books (Online). H. W. Wilson Co. • Broad coverage of law journals and books 1981 to date. Monthly updates. Inquire as to online cost and availability.

PERIODICALS AND NEWSLETTERS

Defense Counsel Journal. International Association of Defense Counsel. • Quarterly. $65.00 per year. Scholarly and practical articles dealing with defense of civil cases, particularly those involving insurance.

FICC Quarterly. Federation of Insurance and Corporate Counsel. • Quarterly. $26.00 per year. A journal dealing with the legal aspects of insurance.

Insurance Regulation: State Capitals. Wakeman-Walworth, Inc. • Weekly. $245.00 per year. Formerly *From the State Capitals: Insurance Regulation.*

Journal of Insurance Regulation. National Association of Insurance Commissioners. • Quarterly. $65.00 per year.

NAIC News. National Association of Insurance Commissioners. • Monthly. $200.00 per year. Newsletter covering insurance legislation and regulation.

National Insurance Law Review. CCH/NILS Publishing Co. • Quarterly. $95.00 per year. Contains insurance-related articles from major law reviews.

RESEARCH CENTERS AND INSTITUTES

Lexis.com Research System. Lexis-Nexis Group. Phone: 800-227-9597 or (937)865-6800 Fax: (937)865-6909 E-mail: webmaster@prod.lexis-nexis.com • URL: http://www.lexis.com • Fee-based Web site offers extensive searching of a wide variety of legal sources. Additional features include Daily Opinion Service, lexis.com Bookstore, Career Center, CLE Center, Law Schools, and Practice Pages ("Pages specific to areas of specialty").

TRADE/PROFESSIONAL ASSOCIATIONS

Association of Defense Trial Attorneys. 600 Bank One Bldg., Peoria, IL 61602. Phone: (309)676-0400 Fax: (309)676-3374 E-mail: jdg@hurwitzfine.com.

Association of Life Insurance Counsel. c/o J. Michael Keefer, 200 E. Berry St., Fort Wayne, IN 46802. Phone: (219)455-5582 Fax: (219)455-5403 • Members are attorneys for life insurance companies.

Federation of Insurance and Corporate Counsel. c/o Joseph R. Olshan, P.O. Box 111, Walpole, MA 02081. Phone: (508)668-6859 Fax: (508)668-6892 E-mail: jolshan@otw.com • URL: http://www.thefederation.org • Members are insurance lawyers and insurance company executives.

International Association for Insurance Law in the United States. P.O. Box 9001, Mount Vernon, NY 10552. Phone: (914)699-2020 Fax: (914)699-2025 • Members are attorneys and others concerned with the international aspects of insurance law.

International Association of Defense Counsel. One N. Franklin St., No. 2400, Chicago, IL 60606-3401. Phone: (312)368-1494 Fax: (312)368-1854 E-mail: office@iadclaw.org • URL: http://www.iadclaw.org.

National Association of Insurance Commissioners. 2301 McGee St., Ste. 800, Kansas City, MO 64108-2604. Phone: (816)842-3600 • URL: http://www.naic.org • Members are state officials involved in the regulation of insurance companies.

INSURANCE, LIABILITY

See: PROPERTY AND LIABILITY INSURANCE

INSURANCE, LIFE

See: LIFE INSURANCE

INSURANCE, LONG-TERM CARE

See: LONG-TERM CARE INSURANCE

INSURANCE, MARINE

See: MARINE INSURANCE

INSURANCE, PROPERTY

See: PROPERTY AND LIABILITY INSURANCE

INSURANCE, SOCIAL

See: SOCIAL SECURITY

INSURANCE, TITLE

See: TITLE INSURANCE

INSURANCE UNDERWRITERS

PERIODICALS AND NEWSLETTERS

Joural of Finacial Services Professionals. American Society of CLU and Ch F C. • Bimonthly. $38.00 per year. Provides information on life insurance and financial planning, including estate planning, retirement, tax planning, trusts, business insurance, long-term care insurance, disability insurance, and employee benefits. Formerly (American Society of CLU and Ch F C Journal).

National Underwriter. The National Underwriter Co. • Weekly. Two editions: *Life* or *Health.* $83.00 per year, each edition.

TRADE/PROFESSIONAL ASSOCIATIONS

American Institute for CPCU. P.O. Box 3016, Malvern, PA 19355-0716. Phone: 800-644-2101 or (610)644-2100 Fax: (610)640-9576 E-mail: cserv@cpuiia.org • URL: http://www.aicpcu.com.

American Insurance Association. 1130 Connecticut Ave., N.W., Suite 1000, Washington, DC 20036. Phone: 800-242-2302 or (202)828-7100 or (202)828-7183 Fax: (202)293-1219.

CPCU Society. 720 Providence Rd., Malvern, PA 19355-0709. Phone: 800-932-2728 E-mail: cpcu@ansiweb.com • URL: http://www.cpcusociety.org.

Inland Marine Underwriters Association. 111 Broadway, 15th Fl., New York, NY 10006. Phone: (212)233-7958 Fax: (212)732-3451 E-mail: imuargt@aol.com • URL: http://www.imua.org.

Insurance Services Office. Seven World Trade Center, New York, NY 10048. Phone: (212)898-6000 Fax: (212)898-5525.

National Association Insurance and Financial Advisors. 1922 F St., N.W., Washington, DC 20006-4387. Phone: (202)331-6000 Fax: (202)835-9601 • URL: http://www.naifa.org.

Society of Financial Service Professionals. 270 S. Bryn Mawr Ave., Bryn Mawr, PA 19010-2195. Phone: 888-243-2258 or (610)526-2500 Fax: (610)527-4010 E-mail: custserv@financialpro.org • URL: http://www.financialpro.org.

INSURANCE, UNEMPLOYMENT

See: UNEMPLOYMENT INSURANCE

INTEGRATED CIRCUITS

See: SEMICONDUCTOR INDUSTRY

INTEGRATED SYSTEMS

See: SYSTEMS INTEGRATION

INTELLECTUAL PROPERTY

See also: COPYRIGHT; LICENSING AGREEMENTS; TRADE SECRETS

GENERAL WORKS

Modern Intellectual Property. Michael A. Epstein. Aspen Law and Business. • 1995. Third edition. Price on application.

ABSTRACTS AND INDEXES

Current Law Index: Multiple Access to Legal Periodicals. The Gale Group. • Monthly. $650.00

per year. Produced in cooperation with the American Association of Law Libraries. Indexes more than 900 law journals, legal newspapers, and specialty publications from the U.S., Canada, U.K., Ireland, Australia, and New Zealand.

Index to Legal Periodicals and Books. H. W. Wilson Co. • Monthly. Quarterly and annual cumulations. $270.00 per year. CD-ROM version available at $1,495.00 per year.

ALMANACS AND YEARBOOKS

Intellectual Property Law Review. W. Bryan Forney, editor. West Group. • 1992. $115.00. Patent, trademark, and copyright practices.

DIRECTORIES

Attorneys and Agents Registered to Practice Before United States Patent and Trademark Office. U.S. Patent and Trademark Office. Available from U.S. Government Printing Office. • Annual. $56.00.

Directory of Intellectual Property Attorneys. Aspen Law and Business. • Annual. Price on application.

KMWorld Buyer's Guide. Knowledge Asset Media. • Semiannual. Controlled circulation as part of *KMWorld*. Contains corporate and product profiles related to various aspects of knowledge management and information systems. (Knowledge Asset Media is a an affiliate of Information Today, Inc.).

ENCYCLOPEDIAS AND DICTIONARIES

McCarthy's Desk Encyclopedia of Intellectual Property. J. Thomas McCarthy. BNA Books. • 1995. $75.00.Second edition. Defines legal terms relating to patents, trademarks, copyrights, trade secrets, entertainment, and the computer industry.

HANDBOOKS AND MANUALS

Clearance and Copyright: Everything the Independent Filmmaker Needs to Know. Michael C. Donaldson. Silman-James Press. • 1996. $26.95. Covers film rights problems in pre-production, production, post-production, and final release. Includes sample contracts and forms.

Corporate Counsellor's Deskbook. Dennis J. Block and Michael A. Epstein, editors. Panel Publishing. • 1999. $220.00. Fifth edition. Looseleaf. Annual supplementation. Covers a wide variety of corporate legal issues, including internal investigations, indemnification, insider trading, intellectual property, executive compensation, antitrust, export-import, real estate, environmental law, government contracts, and bankruptcy.

Intellectual Property in the International Marketplace. Melvi Simensky and others. John Wiley and Sons, Inc. • 1999. $250.00. Two volumes. Volume one: *Valuation, Protection, and Electronic Commerce.* Volume two: *Exploitation and Country-by-Country Profiles.* Includes contributions from lawyers and consultants in various countries.

Intellectual Property Infringement Damages: A Litigation Support Handbook. Russell L. Parr. John Wiley and Sons, Inc. • 1999. $145.00. Annual supplement, $60.00. Describes how to calculate damages for patent, trademark, and copyright infringement. (Intellectual Property Series).

Patent, Copyright, and Trademark: A Desk Reference to Intellectual Property Law. Stephen Elias. Nolo.com. • 1999. $24.95. Third revised edition. Contains practical explanations of the legalities of patents, copyrights, trademarks, and trade secrets. Includes examples of relevant legal forms. A 1985 version was called *Nolo's Intellectual Property Law Dictionary.* (Nolo Press Self-Help Law Series).

Patent, Trademark, and Copyright Laws, 2000. Jeffrey Samuels. BNA Books. • $95.00. Date not set. Contains text of "all pertinent intellectual property legislation to date.".

Protecting Trade Secrets, Patents, Copyrights, and Trademarks. Robert C. Dorr and Christopher H. Munch. Panel Publishers. • Looseleaf service. $165.00.

What Corporate and General Practitioners Should Know About Intellectual Property Litigation. Raphael V. Lupo and Donna M. Tanguay. American Law Institute-American Bar Association. • 1991. $34.00. A lawyer's guide to patents, trademarks, copyrights, and trade secrets.

ONLINE DATABASES

Index to Legal Periodicals and Books (Online). H. W. Wilson Co. • Broad coverage of law journals and books 1981 to date. Monthly updates. Inquire as to online cost and availability.

Legal Resource Index. The Gale Group. • Broad coverage of law literature appearing in legal, business, and other periodicals, 1980 to date. Monthly updates. Inquire as to online cost and availability.

LEXIS. LEXIS-NEXIS. • The various LEXIS databases provide full text and indexing for a wide variety of legal cases, statutes, orders, and opinions.

PERIODICALS AND NEWSLETTERS

BNA's Patent, Trademark and Copyright Journal. Bureau of National Affairs, Inc. • Weekly. $1,366.00 per year.

Intellectual Property Newsletter. LLP Professional Publishing. • Monthly. $460.00 per year.

Intellectual Property Today. Omega Communications. • Monthly. $48.00 per year. Covers legal developments in copyright, patents, trademarks, and licensing. Emphasizes the effect of new technology on intellectual property. Formerly *Law Works.*

KMWorld: Creating and Managing the Knowledge-Based Enterprise. Knowledge Asset Media. • Monthly. Controlled circulation. Provides articles on knowledge management, including business intelligence, multimedia content management, document management, e-business, and intellectual property. Emphasis is on business-to-business information technology. (Knowledge Asset Media is a an affiliate of Information Today, Inc.).

Knowledge Management. CurtCo Freedom Group. • Monthly. Controlled circulation. Covers applications of information technology and knowledge management strategy.

RESEARCH CENTERS AND INSTITUTES

Lexis.com Research System. Lexis-Nexis Group. Phone: 800-227-9597 or (937)865-6800 Fax: (937)865-6909 E-mail: webmaster@prod.lexis-nexis.com • URL: http://www.lexis.com • Fee-based Web site offers extensive searching of a wide variety of legal sources. Additional features include Daily Opinion Service, lexis.com Bookstore, Career Center, CLE Center, Law Schools, and Practice Pages ("Pages specific to areas of specialty").

PTC Research Foundation. Franklin Pierce Law Center. Two White St., Concord, NH 03301. Phone: (603)228-1541 Fax: (603)224-3342 E-mail: cblank@fplc.edu.

TRADE/PROFESSIONAL ASSOCIATIONS

American Intellectual Property Law Association. 2001 Jefferson Davis Highway, Suite 203, Arlington, VA 22202. Phone: (703)415-0780 or (703)415-0781 Fax: (703)415-0786 E-mail: aipla@aipla.org • URL: http://www.aipla.org.

Intellectual Property Owners. 1255 23rd St., N.W., Suite 200, Washington, DC 20037. Phone: (202)466-2396 Fax: (202)466-2893 E-mail: info@ipo.org • URL: http://www.ipo.org • Seeks to strengthen patent, trademark, and copyright laws.

International Intellectual Property Alliance. 1747 Pennsylvania Ave., N.W., Suite 825, Washington, DC 20006. Phone: (202)833-4198 Fax: (202)872-0546 E-mail: smimet@iipa.com • URL: http://www.iipa.com • Promotes global protection of intellectual property.

International Intellectual Property Association. 1255 23rd St. N.W., Suite 850, Washington, DC 20037. Phone: (202)785-1814 Fax: (202)466-2893.

International Licensing Industry Merchandisers' Association. 350 Fifth Ave., Suite 2309, New York, NY 10118. Phone: (212)244-1944 Fax: (212)563-6552 E-mail: info@licensing.org • URL: http://www.licensing.org • Promotes the legal protection of licensed properties.

Licensing Executives Society. 1800 Diagonal Rd., Suite 280, Alexandria, VA 22314-2840. Phone: (703)836-3106 Fax: (703)836-3107.

OTHER SOURCES

Corporate Compliance Series. West Group. • Eleven looseleaf volumes, with periodic supplementation. $990.00. Covers criminal and civil liability problems for corporations. Includes employee safety, product liability, pension requirements, securities violations, equal employment opportunity issues, intellectual property, employee hiring and firing, and other corporate compliance topics.

Forms and Agreements on Intellectual Property and International Licensing. Leslie W. Melville. West Group. • $375.00. Three looseleaf volumes. Periodic supplementation.

Intellectual Property and Antitrust Law. William C. Holmes. West Group. • Looseleaf. $145.00. Periodic supplementation. Includes patent, trademark, and copyright practices.

INTELLIGENCE, ARTIFICIAL

See: ARTIFICIAL INTELLIGENCE

INTERACTIVE MEDIA

See also: MULTIMEDIA

GENERAL WORKS

The Interactive Corporation: Using Interactive Media and Intranets to Enhance Business Performance. Roger Fetterman. Reference Information Publishing. • 1997. $30.00. Presents corporate case studies of successful "networked interactive media in business processes.".

Interactive Marketing: The Future Present. Edward Forrest and Richard Mizerski, editors. NTC/Contemporary Publishing. • 1995. $47.95. Contains articles on the collection and analysis of interactive marketing data, database management, interactive media, marketing research strategies, and related topics.(NTC Business Book Series).

Interface Culture: How New Technology Transforms the Way We Create and Communicate. Steven Johnson. HarperCollins Publishers. • 1997. $24.00. A discussion of how computer interfaces and online technology ("cyberspace") affect society in general.

ALMANACS AND YEARBOOKS

Communication Technology Update. Focal Press. • Annual. $32.95. A yearly review of developments in electronic media, telecommunications, and the Internet.

CD-ROM DATABASES

Computer Select. The Gale Group. • Monthly. $1,250.00 per year. Provides one year of full-text on CD-ROM for 120 leading computer-related publications. Also includes 70,000 product specifications and brief profiles of 13,000 computer product vendors and manufacturers.

Hoover's Company Capsules on CD-ROM. Hoover's, Inc. • Quarterly. $349.95 per year (single-user). Provides the CD-ROM version of *Hoover's Handbook of American Business, Hoover's Handbook of Emerging Companies, Hoover's Handbook of World Business, Hoover's Guide to Computer Companies, Hoover's Guide to Media Companies, Hoover's Handbook of Private Companies,* and various regional guides. Includes more than 11,000 profiles of companies.

DIRECTORIES

Data Sources: The Comprehensive Guide to the Data Processing Industry Hardware, Data Communications Products, Software, Company Profiles. The Gale Group. • Semiannual. $495.00 per year. Two volumes. Describes hardware and software for all computer operating sysems, including prices and technical details. Lists about 75,000 products from 14,000 suppliers. Industry-specific software applications are described.

Information Marketplace Directory. SIMBA Information. • 1996. $295.00. Second edition. Lists computer-based information processing and multimedia companies, including those engaged in animation, audio, video, and interactive video.

Interactive Multimedia Association Membership Directory. Interactive Multimedia Association. • Annual. $60.00. Includes membership listing and a *Buyer's Guide.*

Interactive Television Buyer's Guide and Directory. Chilton Co. • Annual. Price on application. (A special issue of the periodical *Convergence.*).

Plunkett's Entertainment and Media Industry Almanac. Available from Plunkett Research, Ltd. • Biennial. $149.99. Provides profiles of leading firms in online information, films, radio, television, cable, multimedia, magazines, and book publishing. Includes World Wide Web sites, where available, plus information on careers and industry trends.

Plunkett's InfoTech Industry Almanac: Complete Profiles on the InfoTech 500-the Leading Firms in the Movement and Management of Voice, Data, and Video. Available from Plunkett Research, Ltd. • Annual. $149.99. Five hundred major information companies are profiled, with corporate culture aspects. Discusses major trends in various sectors of the computer and information industry, including data on careers and job growth. Includes several indexes.

ENCYCLOPEDIAS AND DICTIONARIES

Cyberspeak: An Online Dictionary. Andy Ihnatko. Random House, Inc. • 1996. $12.95. An informal guide to the language of computers, multimedia, and the Internet.

Encyclopedia of Emerging Industries. The Gale Group. • 2000. $295.00. Fourth edition. Provides detailed information on 90 "newly flourishing" industries. Includes historical background, organizational structure, significant individuals, current conditions, major companies, work force, technology trends, research developments, and other industry facts.

New Hacker's Dictionary. Eric S. Raymond. MIT Press. • 1996. $39.00. Third edition. Includes three classifications of hacker communication: slang, jargon, and "techspeak.".

HANDBOOKS AND MANUALS

Digital Video Buyer's Guide. CMP Media, Inc. • Annual. $10.00. A directory of professional video products, ineluding digital cameras, monitors, editing systems, and software.

An Interactive Guide to Multimedia. Que Education and Training. • 1996. $85.00, including CD-ROM. Explains multimedia production and application, including graphics, text, video, sound, editing, etc.

Interactive Music Handbook. Jodi Summers, editor. Carronade Group. • 1996. $24.95. Covers interactive or enhanced music CD-ROMs and online music for producers, audio technicians, and musicians. Includes case studies and interviews.

INTERNET DATABASES

InfoTech Trends. Data Analysis Group. Phone: (707)894-9100 Fax: (707)486-5618 E-mail: support@infotechtrends.com • URL: http://www.infotechtrends.com • Web site provides both free and fee-based market research data on the information technology industry, including computers, peripherals, telecommunications, the Internet, software, CD-ROM/DVD, e-commerce, and workstations. Fees: Free for current (most recent year) data; more extensive information has various fee structures. Formerly *Computer Industry Forecasts.*

Interactive Week: The Internet's Newspaper. Ziff Davis Media, Inc. 28 E. 28th St., New York, NY 10016. Phone: (212)503-3500 Fax: (212)503-5680 E-mail: iweekinfo@zd.com • URL: http://www.zd.com • Weekly. $99.00 per year. Covers news and trends relating to Internet commerce, computer communications, and telecommunications.

Wired News. Wired Digital, Inc. Phone: (415)276-8400 Fax: (415)276-8499 E-mail: newsfeedback@wired.com • URL: http://www.wired.com • Provides summaries and full-text of "Top Stories" relating to the Internet, computers, multimedia, telecommunications, and the electronic information industry in general. These news stories are placed in the broad categories of Politics, Business, Culture, and Technology. Affiliated with *Wired* magazine. Fees: Free.

PERIODICALS AND NEWSLETTERS

Convergence: The Journal of Research Into New Media Technologies. Chilton Co. • Monthly. Individuals, $60,00 per year; institutions, $120.00 per year. Covers the merging of communications technologies. Includes telecommunications networks, interactive TV, multimedia, wireless phone service, and electronic information services.

Digital Publishing Technologies: How to Implement New Media Publishing. Information Today, Inc. • Monthly. $196.00 per year. Covers online and CD-ROM publishing, including industry news, new applications, new products, electronic publishing technology, and descriptions of completed publishing projects.

DV: Digital Video. Miller Freeman, Inc. • Monthly. $29.97 per year. Edited for producers and creators of digital media. Includes topics relating to video, audio, animation, multimedia, interactive design, and special effects. Covers both hardware and software, with product reviews. Formerly *Digital Video Magazine.*

InterActive Consumers. MarketResearch.com. • Monthly. $395.00 per year. Newsletter. Covers the emerging markets for digital content, products, and services. Includes market information on telecommuting, online services, the Internet, online investing, and other areas of electronic commerce.

Interactive Content: Consumer Media Strategies Monthly. Jupiter Media Metrix. • Monthly. $675.00 per year; with online edition, $775.00 per year. Newsletter. Covers the broad field of providing content (information, news, entertainment) for the Internet/World Wide Web.

Interactive Update. Alexander and Associates. • Semimonthly. $395.00 per year. Newsletter on the interactive entertainment industry.

Interactivity: Tools and Techniques for Interactive Media Developers. Miller Freeman, Inc. • Monthly. $59.95 per year. Edited for professional interactive media developers. Includes a special issue on computer animation.

Maxium PC (Personal Computer). Imagine Media, Inc. • Quarterly. $12.00 per year. Provides articles and reviews relating to multimedia hardware and software. Each issue includes a CD-ROM sampler (emphasis is on games). Formed by the merger of *Home PC* and *Boot.*

NewMedia: The Magazine for Creators of the Digital Future. HyperMedia Communications, Inc. • Monthly. $29.95 per year. Edited for multimedia professionals, with emphasis on digital video and Internet graphics, including animation. Contains reviews of new products. Formerly *NewMedia Age.*

Smart TV: For Selective and Interactive Viewers. Videomaker, Inc. • Bimonthly. $14.97 per year. Consumer magazine covering WebTV, PC/TV appliances, DVD players, "Smart TV," advanced VCRs, and other topics relating to interactive television, the Internet, and multimedia.

Stereo Review's Sound & Vision: Home Theater-Audio- Video- MultimediaMovies- Music. Hachette Filipacchi Magazines, Inc. • 10 times a year. $24.00 per year. Popular magazine providing explanatory articles and critical reviews of equipment and media (CD-ROM, DVD, videocassettes, etc.). Supplement available *Stero Review's Sound and Vision Buyers Guide.* Replaces *Stereo Review* and *Video Magazine.*

3D Design. Miller Freeman, Inc. • Monthly. $50.00 per year. Edited for computer graphics and multimedia professionals. Special features include "Animation Mania" and "Interactive 3D.".

PRICE SOURCES

Opportunities in Interactive TV Applications & Services: An Analysis of Market Interest & Price Sensitivity. Available from MarketResearch.com. • 2001. $1,395. Published by TechTrends, Inc. Market research data. Includes an analysis of how much consumers are willing to pay per month for each application.

RESEARCH CENTERS AND INSTITUTES

American Video Institute. Rochester Institute of Technology, P.O. Box 9887, Rochester, NY 14623-0887. Phone: (716)475-6969 Fax: (716)475-5804 • Conducts research relating to videodiscs and interactive media.

Electronic Visualization Laboratory. University of Illinois at Chicago, Engineering Research Facility, 842 W. Taylor St., Room 2032, Chicago, IL 60607-7053. Phone: (312)996-3002 Fax: (312)413-7585 E-mail: tom@eecs.uic.edu • URL: http://www.evl.uic.edu • Research areas include computer graphics, virtual reality, multimedia, and interactive techniques.

Graphics, Visualization, and Usability Center. Georgia Institute of Technology, Mail Code 0280, Atlanta, GA 30332-0280. Phone: (404)894-4488 Fax: (404)894-0673 E-mail: jarek@cc.gatech.edu • URL: http://www.cc.gatech.edu/gvu/ • Research areas include computer graphics, multimedia, image recognition, interactive graphics systems, animation, and virtual realities.

Institute for Studies in the Arts. Arizona State University, College of Fine Arts, P.O. Box 873302, Tempe, AZ 85287-3302. Phone: (602)965-9438 Fax: (602)965-0961 E-mail: loveless@asu.edu • URL: http://www.researchnet.vprc.asu.edu/isa • Research areas include the fine arts aspects of interactive media.

Integrated Media Systems Center. University of Southern California, 3740 McClintock Ave., Suite 131, Los Angeles, CA 90089-2561. Phone: (213)740-0877 Fax: (213)740-8931 E-mail: nikias@imsc.usc.edu • URL: http://www.imsc.usc.edu • Media areas for research include education, mass communication, and entertainment.

Inter-Arts Center. San Francisco State University, School of Creative Arts, 1600 Holloway Ave., San Francisco, CA 94132. Phone: (415)338-1478 Fax: (415)338-6159 E-mail: jimdavis@sfsu.edu • URL: http://www.sfsu.edu/~iac • Research areas include multimedia, computerized experimental arts processes, and digital sound.

International Data Corp. (IDC). Five Speen St., Framingham, MA 01701. Phone: (508)935-4389 Fax: (508)935-4789 • URL: http://www.idcresearch.com • Private research firm specializing in market research related to computers, multimedia, and telecommunications.

Media Laboratory. Massachusetts Institute of Technology, 20 Ames St., Room E-15, Cambridge, MA 02139. Phone: (617)253-0338 Fax: (617)258-6264 E-mail: casr@media.mit.edu • URL: http://www.media.mit.edu • Research areas include electronic publishing, spatial imaging, human-machine interface, computer vision, and advanced television.

Multimedia Communications Laboratory. Boston University, PHO 445, Eight Saint Mary's St., Boston, MA 02215. Phone: (617)353-8042 Fax: (617)353-6440 E-mail: mcl@spiderman.bu.edu • URL: http://www.hulk.bu.edu • Research areas include interactive multimedia applications.

Studio for Creative Inquiry. Carnegie Mellon University, College of Fine Arts, Pittsburgh, PA 15213-3890. Phone: (412)268-3454 Fax: (412)268-2829 E-mail: mmbm@andrew.cmu.edu/ • URL: http://www.cmu.edu/studio/ • Research areas include artificial intelligence, virtual reality, hypermedia, multimedia, and telecommunications, in relation to the arts.

STATISTICS SOURCES

DMA Statistical Fact Book. Direct Marketing Association, Inc. • Annual. $165.95 to non-members; $105.95 to members. Provides data in five sections covering direct response advertising, media, mailing lists, market applications, and "Practical Management Information." Includes material on interactive/online marketing. (Cover title: *Direct Marketing Association's Statistical Fact Book.*).

TRADE/PROFESSIONAL ASSOCIATIONS

Association for Interactive Media. 1301 Connecticut Ave. N.W., 5th Fl., Washington, DC 20036-5105. Phone: (202)408-0008 Fax: (202)408-0111 E-mail: info@interactivehg.org • URL: http://www.interactivehg.org • Members are companies engaged in various interactive enterprises, utilizing the Internet, interactive television, computer communications, and multimedia.

Interactive Digital Software Association. 1775 Eye St., N.W., Ste. 420, Washington, DC 20005. E-mail: info@idsa.com • URL: http://www.e3expo.com • Members are interactive entertainment software publishers concerned with rating systems, software piracy, government relations, and other industry issues.

International Interactive Communications Society. 4840 McKnight Rd., Suite A, Pittsburgh, PA 15237. Phone: (412)734-1928 Fax: (412)369-3507 E-mail: worldhq@iics.org • URL: http://www.iics.org • Members are interactive media professionals concerned with intetractive arts and technologies.

Internet Alliance. P.O. Box 65782, Washington, DC 20035-5782. Phone: (202)955-8091 Fax: (202)955-8081 E-mail: ia@internetalliance.org • URL: http://www.internetalliance.org • Members are companies associated with the online and Internet industry. Promotes the Internet as "the global mass market medium of the 21st century." Concerned with government regulation, public policy, industry advocacy, consumer education, and media relations. Formerly Interactive Services Association.

Special Interest Group on Computer Graphics and Interactive Techniques. Association for Computing Machinery, 1515 Broadway, New York, NY 10036. Phone: (212)869-7440 Fax: (212)302-5826 E-mail: sigs@acm.org • URL: http://www.acm.org/siggraph • Concerned with research, technology, and applications for the technical, academic, business, and art communities. Publishes the quarterly newsletter *Computer Graphics.*

OTHER SOURCES

Digital Video. CMP Media, Inc. • Monthly. $60.00 per year. Edited for professionals in the field of digital video production. Covers such topics as operating systems, videography, digital video cameras, audio, workstations, web video, software development, and interactive television.

DVD Assessment, No. 3. Julie B. Schwerin and Theodore A. Pine, editors. InfoTech, Inc. • 1998. $1,295.00. Third edition. Provides detailed market research data on Digital Video Discs (also known as Digital Versatile Discs). Includes history of DVD, technical specifications, DVD publishing outlook, "Industry Overview," "Market Context," "Infrastructure Analysis," "Long-Range Forecast to 2005," and emerging technologies.

The Market for Interactive Television. MarketResearch.com. • 2000. $995.00. Market research data.

North American Interactive Television Markets. Available from MarketResearch.com. • 1999. $3,450.00. Published by Frost & Sullivan. Contains market research data on growth, end-user trends, and market strategies. Company profiles are included.

Optical Publishing Industry Assessment. Julie B. Schwerin and Theodore A. Pine, editors. InfoTech, Inc. • 1998. $1,295.00. Ninth edition. Provides market research data and forecasts to 2005 for DVD-ROM, "Hybrid ROM/Online Media," and other segments of the interactive entertainment, digital information, and consumer electronics industries. Covers both software (content) and hardware. Includes Video-CD, DVD- Video, CD-Audio, DVD-Audio, DVD-ROM, PC-Desktop, TV Set-Top, CD-R, CD-RW, DVD-R and DVD-RAM.

INTERACTIVE TELEVISION

See: INTERACTIVE MEDIA; VIDEOTEX/TELETEXT

INTEREST

See also: MONEY

GENERAL WORKS

Futures Markets. A. G. Malliaris, editor. Edward Elgar Publishing, Inc. • 1997. $450.00. Three volumes. Consists of reprints of 70 articles dating from 1959 to 1993, on futures market volatility, speculation, hedging, stock indexes, portfolio insurance, interest rates, and foreign currencies. (International Library of Critical Writings in Financial Economics.).

History of Interest Rates. Sidney Homer and Richard Sylla. Rutgers University Press. • 1996. $79.00. Third revised edition.

The Witch Doctor of Wall Street: A Noted Financial Expert Guides You Through Today's Voodoo Economics. Robert H. Parks. Prometheus Books. • 1996. $25.95. The author, a professor of finance at Pace University, discusses "Practice and Malpractice" in relation to the following: business forecasting, economic theory, interest rates, monetary policy, the stock market, and corporate finance. Includes "A Short Primer on Derivatives," as an appendix.

ABSTRACTS AND INDEXES

Banking Information Index. U M I Banking Information Index. • Monthly. Price on application. Covers a wide variety of banking, business, and financial subjects in periodicals. Formerly *Banking Literature Index.*

ENCYCLOPEDIAS AND DICTIONARIES

Blackwell Encyclopedic Dictionary of Finance. Dean Paxson and Douglas Wood, editors. Blackwell Publishers. • 1997. $110.00. The editors are associated with the University of Manchester. Contains definitions of key terms combined with longer articles written by various U. S. and foreign business educators. Includes bibliographies and index. (Blackwell Encyclopedia of Management Series).

FINANCIAL RATIOS

Money of the Mind: Borrowing and Lending in America from the Civil War to Michael Milken. James Grant. Farrar, Straus, and Giroux, LLC. • 1992. $16.00. A critical anlysis by the editor of *Grant's Interest Rate Observer.*

HANDBOOKS AND MANUALS

Advanced Strategies in Financial Risk Management. Robert J. Schwartz and Clifford W. Smith, editors. Prentice Hall. • 1993. $65.00. Includes technical discussions of financial swaps and derivatives.

Currency and Interest Rate Hedging: A User's Guide to Options, Futures, Swaps, and Forward Contracts. Torben J. Andersen. New York Institute of Finance. • 1993. $49.95. Second edition.

Derivatives: A Comprehensive Resource for Options, Futures, Interest Rate Swaps, and Mortgage Securities. Fred D. Arditti. Harvard Business School Press. • 1996. $60.00. Published by Harvard Business School Press. Provides detailed explanations of various kinds of financial derivatives (options, futures, swaps, etc.) and their trading tactics, uses, and risks. (Financial Management Association Survey and Synthesis Series).

Fibonacci Applications and Strategies for Traders. Robert Fischer. John Wiley and Sons, Inc. • 1993. $49.95. Provides a new look at the Elliott Wave Theory and Fibonacci numbers as applied to commodity prices, business cycles, and interest rate movements. (Traders Library).

Fixed Income Analytics: State-of-the-Art Analysis and Valuation Modeling. Ravi E. Dattatreya, editor. McGraw-Hill Professional. • 1991. $69.95. Discusses the yield curve, structure and value in corporate bonds, mortgage-backed securities, and other topics.

Interest Rate Risk Measurement and Management. Sanjay K. Nawalkha and Donald R. Chambers, editors. Institutional Investor, Inc. • 1999. $95.00. Provides interest rate risk models for fixed-income derivatives and for investments by various kinds of financial institutions.

Options, Futures, and Other Derivatives. John C. Hull. Prentice Hall. • 1999. $94.00. Fourth edition.

Swap and Derivative Financing: The Global Reference to Products Pricing Applications and Markets. Satyajit Das. McGraw-Hill Professional. • 1993. $95.00. Second revised edition.

Swap Literacy. Elizabeth Ungar. Bloomberg Press. • 1996. $40.00. Written for corporate finance officers. Provides basic information on arbitrage, hedging, and speculation, involving interest rate, currency, and other types of financial swaps. (Bloomberg Professional Library.).

Swaps and Financial Engineering: A Self-Study Guide to Mastering and Applying Swaps and Financial Engineering. Coopers and Lybrand Staff. McGraw-Hill Professional. • 1994. $55.00.

INTERNET DATABASES

BanxQuote Banking, Mortgage, and Finance Center. BanxQuote, Inc. Phone: 800-765-3000 or (212)643-8000 Fax: (212)643-0020 E-mail: info@banx.com • URL: http://www.banx.com • Web site quotes interest rates paid by banks around the country on various savings products, as well as rates paid by consumers for automobile loans, mortgages, credit cards, home equity loans, and personal loans. Also provided: stock quotes, indexes, stock options, futures trading data, economic indicators, and links to many other financial sites. Daily updates. Fees: Free.

Bureau of Economic Analysis (BEA). U. S. Department of Commerce, Bureau of Economic Analysis. Phone: (202)606-9900 Fax: (202)606-5310 E-mail: webmaster@bea.doc.gov • URL: http://www.bea.doc.gov • Web site includes "News Release Information" covering national, regional, and international economic estimates from the BEA. Highlights of releases appear online the same day, complete text and tables appear the next day. "Recent News Releases" section provides titles for past nine months, with links. "BEA Data and Methodology" includes "Frequently Requested NIPA Data" (national income and product accounts, such as gross domestic product and personal income). Other statistics are available. Fees: Free.

Business Week Online. McGraw-Hill. Phone: (212)512-2762 Fax: (212)512-6590 • URL: http://www.businessweek.com • Web site provides complete contents of current issue of *Business Week* plus "BW Daily" with additonal business news, financial market quotes, and corporate information from Standard & Poor's. Includes various features, such as "Banking Center" with mortgage and interest data, and "Interactive Computer Buying Guide." The "Business Week Archive" is fully searchable back to 1991. Fees: Mostly free, but full-text archive articles are $2.00 each.

Fedstats. Federal Interagency Council on Statistical Policy. Phone: (202)395-7254 • URL: http://www.fedstats.gov • Web site features an efficient search facility for full-text statistics produced by more than 70 federal agencies, including the Census Bureau, the Bureau of Economic Analysis, and the Bureau of Labor Statistics. Boolean searches can be made within one agency or for all agencies combined. Links are offered to international statistical bureaus, including the UN, IMF, OECD, UNESCO, Eurostat, and 20 individual countries. Fees: Free.

ONLINE DATABASES

Banking Information Source. Bell & Howell Information and Learning. • Provides indexing and abstracting of periodical and other literature from 1982 to date, with weekly updates. Covers the financial services industry: banks, savings institutions, investment houses, credit unions, insurance companies, and real estate organizations. Emphasis is on marketing and management. Inquire as to online cost and availability. (Formerly *FINIS: Financial Industry Information Service*.).

DRI Financial and Credit Statistics. Data Products Division. • Contains U. S. and international statistical data relating to money markets, interest rates, foreign exchange, banking, and stock and bond indexes. Time period is 1973 to date, with continuous updating. Inquire as to online cost and availability.

DRI U.S. Central Database. Data Products Division. • Provides more than 23,000 business, financial, demographic, economic, foreign trade, and industry-related time series for the U.S. Includes national income, population, retail-wholesale trade, price indexes, labor data, housing, industrial production, banking, interest rates, money supply, etc. Time period is generally 1947 to date (some data back to 1929). Updating varies. Inquire as to online cost and availability.

EconBase: Time Series and Forecasts. WEFA, Inc. • Presents online econometric data for business conditions, economics, demographics, industry, finance, employment, household income, interest rates, prices, etc. Includes two-year forecasts for a wide range of economic indicators. Time span is 1948 to date, with monthly updates. Inquire as to online cost and availability.

PERIODICALS AND NEWSLETTERS

Bank Rate Monitor: The Weekly Financial Rate Reporter. Advertising News Service, Inc. • Weekly. $895.00 per year. Newsletter. Includes online addition and monthly supplement. Provides detailed information on interest rates currently paid by U. S. banks and savings institutions.

Barron's: The Dow Jones Business and Financial Weekly. Dow Jones and Co., Inc. • Weekly. $145.00 per year.

BCA Interest Rate Forecast: A Monthly Analysis and Forecast of U.S. Bond and Money Market Trades. BCA Publications. • Monthly. $695.00 per year. Formerly *Interest Rate Forecast.*

Blue Chip Financial Forecasts: What Top Analysts are Saying About U. S. and Foreign Interest Rates, Monetary Policy, Inflation, and Economic Growth. Aspen Publishers, Inc. • Monthly. $654.00 per year. Newsletter. Gives forecasts about a year in advance for interest rates, inflation, currency exchange rates, monetary policy, and economic growth rates.

Grant's Interest Rate Observer. James Grant, editor. Interest Rate Publishing Corp. • Biweekly. $495.00 per year. Newsletter containing detailed analysis of money-related topics, including interest rate trends, global credit markets, fixed-income investments, bank loan policies, and international money markets.

Income Fund Outlook. Institute for Econometric Research. • Monthly. $100.00 per year. Newsletter. Contains tabular data on money market funds, certificates of deposit, bond funds, and tax-free bond funds. Includes specific recommendations, fund news, and commentary on interest rates.

Interest Rate Service. World Reports Ltd. • 10 times a year. $950.00 per year.

Journal of Fixed Income. Institutional Investor. • Quarterly. $325.00 per year. Covers a wide range of fixed-income investments for institutions, including bonds, interest-rate options, high-yield securities, and mortgages.

Jumbo Rate News. Bauer Financial Newsletters, Inc. • Weekly. $445.00 per year. Newsletter. Lists more than 1,100 of the highest interest rates available for "jumbo" certificates of deposit ($100,000 or more).

Money Reporter: The Insider's Letter for Investors Whose Interest is More Interest. MPL Communication, Inc. • Biweekly. $197.00 per year. Newsletter. Supplement available, *Monthly Key Investment.*Canadian interest-bearing deposits and investments.

The Moneyletter. IBC-Donoghue, Inc. • Semimonthly. $109.00 per year. Newsletter giving specific advice on interest rates, trends, money market funds, bond funds, and equity mutual funds. Formerly *Donoghue's Moneyletter.*

One Hundred Highest Yields Among Federally-Insured Banks and Savings Institutions. Advertising News Service, Inc. • Weekly. $124.00 per year. Newsletter.

RateGram: A Compendium of the Nation's Highest Federally Insured Rates. Bradshaw Group Ltd. • Biweekly. Individuals, $395.00 per year; libraries, $195.00 per year. Newsletter. Quotes highest interest rates available, with safety ratings, according to a survey of about 10,000 federally insured banks and savings institutions. Covers a wide variety of rates, although most space is devoted to insured certificates of deposit. Also covers foreign exchange rates, foreign interest rates, and foreign government long term bond yields.

STATISTICS SOURCES

The AIER Chart Book. AIER Research Staff. American Institute for Economic Research. • Annual. $3.00. A compact compilation of long-range charts ("Purchasing Power of the Dollar," for example, goes back to 1780) covering various aspects of the U. S. economy. Includes inflation, interest rates, debt, gold, taxation, stock prices, etc. (Economic Education Bulletin.).

Business Statistics of the United States. Courtenay M. Slater, editor. Bernan Associates. • 1999. $74.00. Fifth edition. Based on *Business Statistics*, formerly issue by the Bureau of Economic Analysis, U. S. Department of Commerce. Provides basic data for a wide variety of U. S. industries, services, and economic indicators. Most statistics are shown annually for 29 years and monthly for the most recent four years.

Federal Reserve Bulletin. U.S. Federal Reserve System. • Monthly. $25.00 per year. Provides statistics on banking and the economy, including interest rates, money supply, and the Federal Reserve Board indexes of industrial production.

Financial Market Trends. Organization for Economic Cooperation and Development. • Three times a year. $100.00 per year. Provides analysis of developments and trends in international and national capital markets. Includes charts and graphs on interest rates, exchange rates, stock market indexes, bank stock indexes, trading volumes, and loans outstanding. Data from OECD countries includes international direct investment, bank profitability, institutional investment, and privatization.

Selected Interest Rates. U.S. Federal Reserve System. • Weekly release, $20.00 per year; monthly release, $5.00 per year.

Statistical Annual: Interest Rates, Metals, Stock Indices, Options on Financial Futures, Options on Metals Futures. Chicago Board of Trade. • Annual. Includes historical data on GNMA CDR Futures, Cash-Settled GNMA Futures, U. S. Treasury Bond Futures, U. S. Treasury Note Futures, Options on Treasury Note Futures, NASDAQ-100 Futures, Major Market Index Futures, Major Market Index MAXI Futures, Municipal Bond Index Futures, 1,000-Ounce Silver Futures, Options on Silver Futures, and Kilo Gold Futures.

Survey of Current Business. Available from U. S. Government Printing Office. • Monthly. $49.00 per year. Issued by Bureau of Economic Analysis, U. S. Department of Commerce. Presents a wide variety of business and economic data.

Treasury Bulletin. Available from U. S. Government Printing Office. • Quarterly. $39.00 per year. Issued by the Financial Management Service, U. S. Treasury Department. Provides data on the federal

 For publishers addresses, refer to SOURCES CITED section at the back of the book.

budget, government securities and yields, the national debt, and the financing of the federal government in general.

INTERIOR DECORATION

See also: WINDOW COVERING INDUSTRY

GENERAL WORKS

Professional Practice for Interior Design. Christine M. Piotrowski. John Wiley and Sons, Inc. • 1994. $64.95. Second edition. (interior Design Series).

ABSTRACTS AND INDEXES

Art Index. H. W. Wilson Co. • Quarterly. Annual cumulations. Service basis for print edition; CD-ROM edition, $1,495.00 per year. Subject and author index to periodicals in art, architecture, industrial design, city planning, photography, and various related topics.

BIOGRAPHICAL SOURCES

Who's Who in Interior Design. Baron's Who's Who. • Annual. $280.00. Contains biographical data for over 3,500 interior designers worldwide.

DIRECTORIES

American Society of Interior Designers - Membership List. American Society of Interior Designers. • Annual. Membership.

Design Firm Directory: A Listing of Firms and Consultants in Grap hic Design in the United States. Wefler & Associates, Inc. • Annual. $145.00. Three volumes. Provides information on more than 2,600 commercial, private, and consulting design firms. Includes graphic, interior, landscape, and environmental designers.

Directory of Home Furnishings Retailers. Chain Store Guide. • Annual. $290.00. Includes more than 4,800 furniture retailers and wholesalers.

Directory of the Decorating Products Industry. Painting and Decorating Retailers Association. • Annual. $595.00. Lists nearly 2,800 retailers of window treatments, wall coverings, floor coverings, etc. Formerly *Directory of Decorating Products Retailers.* Formerly National Decorating Products Association.

Home Fashions: Buyer's Guide. Fairchild Publications. • Annual. $10.00. Lists manufacturers, importers, and regional sales representatives supplying bed, bath, kitchen, and table linens; window treatments; wall coverings; and fibers and fabrics.

IDH: National Buying Guide and Directory of Interior Furnishings, Allied Products and Services. E.W. Williams Publications Co. • Semiannual. $20.00 per year. Over 5,000 manufacturers and distributors of furniture, accessories, floor coverings, fabrics, wallcoverings, etc., and services relatedto these products. Formerly *Interior Decorator's Handbook.*

Interior Design Buyers Guide. Cahners Business Information, Interior Design Group. • Annual. Included with subscription to *Interior Design.*

Interiors and Sources: Directory and Buyer's Guide. L. C. Clark Publishing Co., Inc. • Annual. $10.00. Lists sources of surface materials, furniture, lighting, etc., for interior designers.

ENCYCLOPEDIAS AND DICTIONARIES

Encyclopedia of Interior Design. Joanna Banham, editor. Fitzroy Dearborn Publishers. • 1997. $270.00. Two volumes. Contains more than 500 essays on interior design topics. Includes bibliographies.

HANDBOOKS AND MANUALS

Interior Designer. Entrepreneur Media, Inc. • Looseleaf. $59.50. A practical guide to starting an interior design and decoration business. Covers profit potential, start-up costs, market size evaluation, owner's time required, pricing, accounting, advertising, promotion, etc. (Start-Up Business Guide No. E1314.).

Office Interior Design Guide: An Introduction for Facility and Design. Julie K. Rayfield. John Wiley and Sons, Inc. • 1997. $59.95.

ONLINE DATABASES

Art Index Online. H. W. Wilson Co. • Indexes a wide variety of art-related periodicals, 1984 to date. Monthly updates. Inquire as to online cost and availability.

Avery Architecture Index. Avery Architectural and Fine Arts Library. • Indexes a wide range of periodicals related to architecture and design. Subjects include building design, building materials, interior design, housing, land use, and city planning. Time span: 1977 to date. *bul* URL: http://www-rlg.stanford.edu/cit-ave.html.

PERIODICALS AND NEWSLETTERS

Contract Design: The Business Magazine of Commercial and Institutional Interior Design, and Architecture, Planning and Construction. Miller Freeman, Inc. • Monthly. $65.00 per year. Firms engaged in specifying furniture and furnishings for commercial installations. Formerly *Contract.*

Home Fashions Magazine. Fairchild Fashion and Merchandising Group. • Monthly. $30.00 per year.

Interior Design. Cahners Business Information, Interior Design Group. • Monthly. $46.71 per year. For the professional designed, provides information on trends and new products. Includes annual*Buyers' Guide* and *Interior Design Market.*

Interiors and Sources. L. C. Clark Publishing Co., Inc. • Bimonthly. $18.00 per year. Promotes professionalism for interior designers and design firms. Includes special features on office systems, work stations, and office furniture.

Interiors: For the Contract Design Professional. BPI Communications, Inc. • Monthly. $42.00 per year.

Paint and Decorating Retailer. Paint and Decorating Retailers Association. • Monthly. $45.00 per year. Formerly *Decorating Retailer.*

Waland Window Trends. Cygnus Business Media. • Monthly $36.00 per year. Edited for retailers of interior decoration products, with an emphasis on wallcoverings. Formerly *Wallcoverings, Windows and Interior Fashion.*

RESEARCH CENTERS AND INSTITUTES

Interior Design Laboratory. Lambuth University, P.O. Box 431, Jackson, TN 38301. Phone: (901)425-3275 Fax: (901)425-3497.

TRADE/PROFESSIONAL ASSOCIATIONS

American Society of Interior Designers. 608 Massachusetts Ave., N.E., Washington, DC 20002. Phone: (202)546-3480 Fax: (202)546-3240 E-mail: asid@asid.org • URL: http://www.interiors.org.

Decorators Club. 306 E. 61st St., New York, NY 10021-6508. Phone: (212)399-4062 Fax: (212)399-4063.

International Interior Design Association. 341 Merchandise Mart, Chicago, IL 60654-1104. Phone: 888-799-4432 or (312)467-1950 Fax: (312)467-0779 E-mail: iidahq@aol.com • URL: http://www.iida.com.

INTERNAL AUDITING

See also: AUDITING

ABSTRACTS AND INDEXES

Business Periodicals Index. H. W. Wilson Co. • Monthly, except August, with quarterly and annual cumulations. Service basis for print edition; CD-ROM edition, $1,495.00 per year.

DIRECTORIES

Business Organizations, Agencies, and Publications Directory. The Gale Group. • 1999. $425.00. 12th edition. Over 40,000 entries describing 39 types of business information sources. Classified by type of organization, publication, or serviceIncludes state, national, and international agencies and organizations. Master index to names and keywords. Also includes e-mail addresses and web site URL's.

ENCYCLOPEDIAS AND DICTIONARIES

Blackwell Encyclopedic Dictionary of Accounting. Rashad Abdel-khalik. Blackwell Publishers. • 1997. $105.95. The editor is associated with the University of Florida. Contains definitions of key terms combined with longer articles written by various U. S. and foreign business educators. Includes bibliographies and index. (Blackwell Encyclopedia of Management Series).

Dictionary of Accounting Terms. Joel G. Siegel and Jae K. Shim. Barron's Educational Series, Inc. • 1995. $11.95. Second edition.

FINANCIAL RATIOS

Reliable Financial Reporting and Internal Control: A Global Implementation Guide. Dmitris N. Chorafas. John Wiley and Sons, Inc. • 2000. $65.00. Discusses financial reporting and control as related to doing business internationally.

HANDBOOKS AND MANUALS

Accountants' Handbook. Douglas R. Carmichael and others, editors. John Wiley and Sons, Inc. • 1999. $135.00. Ninth edition. Chapters are written by various accounting and auditing specialists.

Corporate Fraud. Michael J. Comer. Available from Ashgate Publishing Co. • 1997. $113.95. Third edition. Examines new risks of corporate fraud related to "electronic commerce, derivatives, computerization, empowerment, downsizing, and other recent developments." Covers fraud detection, prevention, and internal control systems. Published by Gower in England.

Internal Auditing Manual. Warren, Gorham & Lamont/RIA Group. • Quarterly. $195.00 per year.

Internal Auditor's Handbook. Paul E. Heeschen and others. Institute of Internal Auditors, Inc. • 1984. $43.75.

INTERNET DATABASES

Rutgers Accounting Web (RAW). Rutgers University Accounting Research Center. Phone: (201)648-5172 Fax: (201)648-1233 • URL: http://www.rutgers.edu/accounting • RAW Web site provides extensive links to sources of national and international accounting information, such as the Big Six accounting firms, the Financial Accounting Standards Board (FASB), SEC filings (EDGAR), journals, publishers, software, the International Accounting Network, and "Internet's largest list of accounting firms in USA." Searching is offered. Fees: Free.

ONLINE DATABASES

Wilson Business Abstracts Online. H. W. Wilson Co. • Indexes and abstracts 600 major business periodicals, plus the *Wall Street Journal* and the business section of the *New York Times.* Indexing is from 1982, abstracting from 1990, with the two newspapers included from 1993. Updated weekly. Inquire as to online cost and availability. (*Business*

Periodicals Index without abstracts is also available online.).

PERIODICALS AND NEWSLETTERS

Internal Auditing Alert. Warren, Gorham and Lamont/RIA Group. • Monthly. $180.00 per year. Newsletter. Focuses on the means of monitoring and controlling the accounting system used by any enterprise or organization. Gives hints, ideas and suggestions for administering operations and improving the usefulness of the internal audit function.

Internal Auditor. Institute of Internal Auditors, Inc. • Bimonthly. $60.00 per year.

TRADE/PROFESSIONAL ASSOCIATIONS

Institute of Internal Auditors. 249 Maitland Ave., Altamonte Springs, FL 32701-4201. Phone: (407)830-7600 Fax: (407)831-5171 E-mail: iia@theiia.org • URL: http://www.theiia.org.

INTERNAL PUBLICATIONS

See: HOUSE ORGANS

INTERNAL REVENUE SERVICE

See: INCOME TAX

INTERNATIONAL AGENCIES

See also: ASSOCIATIONS; ORGANIZATION FOR ECONOMIC COOPERATION AND DEVELOPMENT; UNITED NATIONS

ABSTRACTS AND INDEXES

PAIS International in Print. Public Affairs Information Service, Inc. • Monthly. $650.00 per year; cumulations three times a year. Provides topical citations to the worldwide literature of public affairs, economics, demographics, sociology, and trade. Text in English; indexed materials in English, French, German, Italian, Portuguese and Spanish.

UNDOC: Current Index (United Nations Documents). United Nations Publications. • Quarterly. $150.00. Annual cumulation on microfiche. Text in English.

BIBLIOGRAPHIES

Monthly Bibliography. United Nations Publications. • Monthly. $125.00 per year. Text in English and French.

CD-ROM DATABASES

PAIS on CD-ROM. Public Affairs Information Service, Inc. • Quarterly. $1,995.00 per year. Provides a CD-ROM version of the online service, *PAIS International.* Contains over 400,000 citations to the literature of contemporary social, political, and economic issues.

Statistical Masterfile. Congressional Information Service. • Quarterly. Price varies. Provides CD-ROM versions of *American Statistics Index, Index to International Statistics,* and *Statistical Reference Index.* Contains indexing and abstracting of a wide variety of published statistics sources, both governmental and private.

World Database of Business Information Sources on CD-ROM. The Gale Group. • Annual. Produced by Euromonitor. Presents Euromonitor's entire information source database on CD-ROM. Contains a worldwide total of about 35,000 publications, organizations, libraries, trade fairs, and online databases.

Yearbook of International Organizations PLUS. R. R. Bowker. • Annual. $1,500.00. Compiled by the Union of International Organizations, Brussels. Includes the *Yearbook of International Organizations* and *Who's Who in International Organizations.*

DIRECTORIES

Encyclopedia of Associations: International Organizations. The Gale Group. • Annual. $615.00. Two volumes. Includes detailed information on more than 20,600 international nonprofit membership organizations.

Europa World Yearbook. Taylor and Francis, Inc. • Annual. $815.00. Two volumes. Published by Europa Publications Ltd. Basic source of information on every country and some 1,650 international organizations. Includes detailed directories and surveys for each country.

World Directory of Marketing Information Sources. Available from The Gale Group. • 2001. $590.00. Third edition. Published by Euromonitor. Provides details on more than 6,000 sources of marketing information, including publications, libraries, associations, market research companies, online databases, and governmental organizations. Coverage is worldwide.

World Directory of Trade and Business Associations. Available from The Gale Group. • 2000. $595.00. Third edition. Published by Euromonitor. Provides detailed information on approximately 5,000 trade associations in various countries of the world. Includes subject and geographic indexes.

Yearbook of International Organizations. Available from The Gale Group. • Annual. $1,300.00. Four volumes: (1) *Organization Descriptions and Index* (32,000 organizations in 225 countries); (2) *International Organization Participation* (geographic arrangement); (3) *Global Action Networks* (a subject directory with 4,300 categories); (4) *Internationa Organization Bibliography and Resources.* Published by K. G. Saur.

INTERNET DATABASES

Fedstats. Federal Interagency Council on Statistical Policy. Phone: (202)395-7254 • URL: http://www.fedstats.gov • Web site features an efficient search facility for full-text statistics produced by more than 70 federal agencies, including the Census Bureau, the Bureau of Economic Analysis, and the Bureau of Labor Statistics. Boolean searches can be made within one agency or for all agencies combined. Links are offered to international statistical bureaus, including the UN, IMF, OECD, UNESCO, Eurostat, and 20 individual countries. Fees: Free.

Publishers' Catalogues Home Page. Northern Lights Internet Solutions Ltd. Phone: (306)931-0020 Fax: (306)931-7667 E-mail: info@lights.com • URL: http://www.lights.com/publisher • Provides links to the Web home pages of about 1,700 U. S. publishers (including about 80 University presses) and publishers in 48 foreign countries. "International/Multinational Publishers" are included, such as the International Monetary Fund, the World Bank, and the World Trade Organization. Publishers are arranged in convenient alphabetical lists. Searching is offered. Fees: Free.

ONLINE DATABASES

Encyclopedia of Associations [Online]. The Gale Group. • Provides detailed information on about 160,000 U. S. and International non-profit organizations. Semiannual updates. Inquire as to online cost and availability.

PAIS International. Public Affairs Information Service, Inc. • Corresponds to the former printed publications, *PAIS Bulletin* (1976-90) and *PAIS Foreign Language Index* (1972-90), and to the current *PAIS International in Print* (1991 to date). Covers economic, political, and sociological material appearing in periodicals, books, government documents, and other publications. Updating is monthly. Inquire as to online cost and availability.

Research Centers and Services Directories. The Gale Group. • Contains profiles of about 30,000 research centers, organizations, laboratories, and agencies in 147 countries. Corresponds to the printed *Research Centers Directory, International Research Centers Directory, Government Research Directory,* and *Research Services Directory.* Updating is semiannual. Inquire as to online cost and availability.

PERIODICALS AND NEWSLETTERS

Government Publications News. Bernan Associates. • Monthly. Free. Controlled circulation newsletter providing information on recent publications from the U. S. Government Printing Office and selected international agencies.

TRADE/PROFESSIONAL ASSOCIATIONS

Trade Associations amd Professional Bodies of the Continental European Union. Available from The Gale Group. 27500 Drake Rd., Farmington Hills, MI 48331-3535. Phone: 800-877-GALE or (248)699-GALE Fax: 800-414-5043 or (248)699-8069 E-mail: galeord@galegroup.com • URL: http://www.galegroup.com • 2000. $280.00. Published by Graham & Whiteside. Provides detailed information on more than 3,600 business and professional organizations in Europe.

United States Council for International Business. 1212 Ave. of the Americas, 21st Fl., New York, NY 10036-1689. Phone: (212)354-4480 Fax: (212)575-0327 E-mail: info@uscib.org • URL: http://www.uscib.org.

OTHER SOURCES

The EU Institutions' Register. Euroconfidentiel S. A. • Annual. $130.00. Lists more than 5,000 key personnel in European Union institutions and decentralized agencies. Includes areas of responsibility.

From GATT to the WTO: The Multilateral Trading System in the New Millennium. WTO Secretariat, editor. Available from Kluwer Academic Publishers. • 2000. $79.50. Published by the World Trade Organization (http://www.wto.org). A collection of essays on the future of world trade, written on the occasion of the 50th anniversary of the multilateral trading system (GATT/WTO). The authors are described as "important academics in international trade.".

Washington [year]. Columbia Books, Inc. • Annual. $129.00. Provides information on about 5,000 Washington, DC key businesses, government offices, non-profit organizations, and cultural institutions, with the names of about 25,000 principal executives. Includes Washington media, law offices, foundations, labor unions, international organizations, clubs, etc.

World Trade Organization Annual Report. Available from Bernan Associates. • Annual. $80.00. Two volumes ($40.00 per volume). Published by the World Trade Organization. Volume one: *Annual Report.* Volume two: *International Trade Statistics.*

World Trade Organization Dispute Settlement Decisions: Bernan's Annotated Reporter. Bernan Press. • Dates vary. $75.00 per volume. Contains all World Trade Organization Panel Reports and Appellate Decisions since the establishment of the WTO in 1995. Includes such cases as "The Importation, Sale, and Distribution of Bananas.".

INTERNATIONAL ASSOCIATIONS

See: INTERNATIONAL AGENCIES

INTERNATIONAL BUSINESS

See also: EUROPEAN MARKETS; FOREIGN INVESTMENTS; FOREIGN TRADE; INTERNATIONAL MARKETING; MULTINATIONAL CORPORATIONS

GENERAL WORKS

Bargaining Across Borders: How to Conduct Business Successfully Anywhere in th e World. Dean A. Foster. McGraw-Hill. • 1992. $14.95. Includes a consideration of non-negotiable cultural differences.

Doing Business Internationally: The Guide to Cross Cultural Success. Terence Brake. McGraw-Hill Professional. • 1994. $27.50.

International Business. M. Woods, editor. Chapman and Hall. • 1995. Price on application.

International Business and Multinational Enterprises. Stefan H. Robock and Kenneth Simmonds. McGraw-Hill Higher Education. • 1988. $68.50. Fourth edition.

International Marketing. Philip R. Cateora and John Graham. McGraw-Hill. • 1998. $84.38. 10th edition.

Managing Globally: A Complete Guide to Competing Worldwide. Carl A. Nelson. McGraw-Hill Professional. • 1993. $65.00. Emphasis is on global strategic management and tactics.

ABSTRACTS AND INDEXES

F & S Index: Europe. The Gale Group. • Monthly. $1,295.00 per year, including quarterly and annual cumulations. Provides annotated citations to marketing, business, financial, and industrial literature. Coverage of European business activity includes trade journals, financial magazines, business newspapers, and special reports. Formerly *Predicasts F & S Index: Europe.*

F & S Index: International. The Gale Group. • Monthly. $1,295.00 per year, including quarterly and annual cumulations. Provides annotated citations to marketing, business, financial, and industrial literature. Coverage of international business activity includes trade journals, financial magazines, business newspapers, and special reports. Areas included are Asia, Latin America, Africa, the Middle East, Oceania, and Canada. Formerly *Predicasts F & S Index: International.*

NTIS Alerts: Business & Economics. National Technical Information Service.

ALMANACS AND YEARBOOKS

Countries of the World and Their Leaders Yearbook. The Gale Group. • 2000. $235.00. Two volumes. Interedition supplement,$105.00. Based on U. S. State Department data covering nearly 170 countries. Features "Background Notes on countries of the World." Also includes the CIA's list of "Chiefs of State and Cabinet Members of Foreign Governments," as well as key officers at U.S. embassies and other information.

Irwin International Almanac: Business and Investments. McGraw-Hill Professional. • 1994. $95.00. Second edition. Covers trends in global business and summarizes trading in major foreign securities markets.

Political Risk Yearbook. The P R S Group. • Annual. $1,200.00. Eight regional volumes. Each volume covers a separate region of the world and assesses economic and political conditions as they relate to the risk of doing business.

Private Investments Abroad: Problems and Solutions in International Business. Southwestern Legal Foundation, International and Comparative Law Center. Matthew Bender & Co., Inc. • Annual. $153.00. Symposium on worthwhile investment opportunities abroad and explains the best methods of transacting international business by integrating professional knowledge from the fields of law, economics and business management.

Research in International Business and Finance. JAI Press, Inc. • Irregular.$78.50.

BIBLIOGRAPHIES

Business Information Sources. Lorna M. Daniells. California Princeton Fulfillment Services. • 1993. $42.50. Third revised edition. Basic business sources, with discussion and full annotations.

International Business Finance: A Bibliography of Selected Business and Academic Sources. Raj Aggarwal. Greenwood Publishing Group, Inc. • 1984. $65.00.

International Business Information: How to Find It, How to Use It. Ruth Pagell and Michael Halperin. Oryx Press. • 1997. $84.50. Second revised edition.

BIOGRAPHICAL SOURCES

Who's Who of European Business: and Industry. Triumph Books. • Irregular. $295.00. Lists over 9,500 business executives from 36 countries in Eastern and Western Europe. Two volumes.

CD-ROM DATABASES

Asia Pacific Kompass on Disc. Available from Kompass USA, Inc. • Annual. $2,190.00. CD-ROM provides information on more than 280,000 companies in Australia, China, Hong Kong, India, Korea, Malaysia, New Zealand, Philippines, Singapore, Thailand, and Taiwan. Classification system covers approximately 50,000 products and services.

Baltia Kompass Business Disc. Available from Kompass USA, Inc. • Annual. $360.00. CD-ROM provides information on more than 22,000 companies in Estonia, Latvia, and Lithuania. Classification system covers approximately 50,000 products and services.

Benelux Kompass Business Disc. Available from Kompass USA, Inc. • Annual. $560.00. CD-ROM provides information on more than 54,000 companies in Belgium, Netherlands, and Luxembourg. Classification system covers approximately 50,000 products and services.

Business Source Plus. EBSCO Information Services. • Monthly. $1,495.00 per year. Provides CD-ROM citations and abstracts to articles in about 650 business periodicals and newspapers, including *The Wall Street Journal.* Full text is provided from 200 selected periodicals. Covers accounting, communications, economics, finance, management, marketing, and other business subjects.

Corporate Affiliations Plus. National Register Publishing, Reed Reference Publishing. • Quarterly. $1,995.00 per year. Provides CD-ROM discs corresponding to *Directory of Corporate Affiliations* and *Corporate Finance Bluebook.* Contains corporate financial services information and worldwide data on subsidiaries and affiliates.

East European Kompass on Disc. Available from Kompass USA, Inc. • Annual. $1,280.00. CD-ROM provides information on more than 294,000 companies in Austria, Azerbaijan, Belarus, Croatia, Czech Republic, Estonia, Hungary, Latvia, Lithuania, Moldova, Poland, Romania, Russia, Slovakia, Slovenia, Ukraine, and Yugoslavia. Classification system covers approximately 50,000 products and services.

European Kompass on Disc. Available from Kompass USA, Inc. • Annual. $2,070.00. CD-ROM provides information on more than 350,000 companies in Belgium, Denmark, France, Germany, Ireland, Italy, Luxembourg, Netherlands, Norway, Spain, Sweden, and UK. Classification system covers approximately 50,000 products and services.

Hoover's Company Capsules on CD-ROM. Hoover's, Inc. • Quarterly. $349.95 per year (single-user). Provides the CD-ROM version of *Hoover's Handbook of American Business, Hoover's Handbook of Emerging Companies, Hoover's Handbook of World Business, Hoover's Guide to Computer Companies, Hoover's Guide to Media Companies, Hoover's Handbook of Private Companies,* and various regional guides. Includes more than 11,000 profiles of companies.

Kompass CD-ROM Editions. Available from Kompass USA, Inc. • Annual. Prices vary. CD-ROM versions of Kompass international trade directories are available for each of 30 major countries and eight world regions. Searching is provided for 50,000 product/service items and many company details.

Middle-East/Africa Kompass on Disc. Available from Kompass USA, Inc. • Annual. $1,540.00. CD-ROM provides information on more than 150,000 companies in Algeria, Bahrain, Cyprus, Egypt, Lebanon, Mauritania, Morocco, Oman, Saudi Arabia, South Africa, Tunisia, and United Arab Emirates. Classification system covers approximately 50,000 products and services.

Scandinavian Kompass on Disc. Available from Kompass USA, Inc. • Annual. $1,950.00. CD-ROM provides information on more than 66,000 companies in Denmark, Finland, Norway, and Sweden. Classification system covers approximately 50,000 products and services.

World Database of Business Information Sources on CD-ROM. The Gale Group. • Annual. Produced by Euromonitor. Presents Euromonitor's entire information source database on CD-ROM. Contains a worldwide total of about 35,000 publications, organizations, libraries, trade fairs, and online databases.

World Database of Consumer Brands and Their Owners on CD-ROM. The Gale Group. • Annual. $3,190.00. Produced by Euromonitor. Provides detailed information on CD-ROM for about 10,000 companies and 80,000 brands around the world. Covers 1,000 product sectors.

DIRECTORIES

Alphaphonetic Directory of International Trademarks. Available from Thomson & Thomson. • Annual, with three cumulative updates during the year. $1,914.00 per year. 15 volumes. Published in Belgium by Compu-Mark. Provides owner, registration, and classification information for more than one million trademarks registered with the World Intellectual Property Organization (WIPO).

China: A Directory and Sourcebook. Available from The Gale Group. • 1998. $590.00. Second edition. Published by Euromonitor. Describes about 800 companies in both China and Hong Kong. Sourcebook section provides 500 information sources.

Craighead's International Business, Travel, and Relocation Guide to 81 Countries. Available from The Gale Group. • 2000. $725.00. Tenth edition. Four volumes. Compiled by Craighead Publications, Inc. Provides a wide range of business travel and relocation information for 78 different countries, including details on currency, customs regulations, visas, passports, healthcare, transportation, shopping, insurance, travel safety, etc. Formerly *International Business Travel and RelocatDirectory.*

Directory of American Firms Operating in Foreign Countries. Uniworld Business Publications Inc. • Biennial. $275.00. Three volumes. Lists approximately 2,450 American companies with more than 29,500 subsidiaries and affiliates in 138 foreign countries.

Directory of Foreign Firms Operating in the United States. Uniworld Business Publications, Inc. • Biennial. $225.00. Lists about 2,400 foreign companies and 5,700 American affiliates. 75 countries are represented.

Dow Jones Guide to the Global Stock Market. Dow Jones & Co., Inc. • Annual. $34.95. Three volumes. Presents concise profiles and three-year financial performance data for each of 3,000 publicly held companies in 35 countries. (Includes all Dow Jones Global Index companies.).

Eastern Europe: A Directory and Sourcebook. Available from The Gale Group. • 1999. $590.00. Second edition. Published by Euromonitor. Describes major companies in Eastern Europe. Sourcebook section provides marketing and business information sources.

Europe's Major Companies Directory. Available from The Gale Group. • 1997. $590.00. Second edition. Published by Euromonitor. Contains detailed financial and product information for about 6,000 major companies in 16 countries of Western Europe.

Europe's Medium-Sized Companies Directory. Available from The Gale Group. • 1997. $590.00. Published by Euromonitor. Contains detailed financial and product information on about 5,000 medium-sized companies in 16 countries of Western Europe.

Global Company Handbook. C I F A R Publications, Inc. • Annual. $495.00. Two volumes. Provides detailed profiles of 7,500 publicly traded companies in 48 countries. Includes global rankings and five years of data.

Hoover's Handbook of World Business: Profiles of Major European, Asian, Latin American, and Canadian Companies. Hoover's, Inc. • Annual. $99.95. Contains detailed profiles of more than 300 large foreign companies. Includes indexes by industry, location, executive name, company name, and brand name.

International Brands and Their Companies. The Gale Group. • 1998. $295.00. Fifth edition. Contains about 84,000 worldwide (non-U. S.) entries for trade names, trademarks, and brand names of consumer-oriented products and their manufacturers, importers, distributors, or marketers. Formerly *International Trade Names Dictionary.*

International Directory of Consumer Brands and Their Owners. Available from The Gale Group. • 1997. $450.00. Published by Euromonitor. Contains detailed information on more than 38,000 consumer product brands and their companies in 62 countries of the world, excluding Europe.

Internet Resources and Services for International Business: A Global Guide. Lewis-Guodo Liu. Oryx Press. • 1998. $49.95. Describes more than 2,500 business-related Web sites from 176 countries. Includes five major categories: general information, economics, business and trade, business travel, and contacts. Indexed by Web site name, country, and subject.

Japan Trade Directory 2000-2001. Available from The Gale Group. • 2000. $350.00. 18th edition. Published by the Japan External Trade Organization (JETRO). Provides information on about 2,800 Japanese companies currently active in exporting or importing.

Japanese Affiliated Companies In the U.S. and Canada. Available from The Gale Group. • 1994. $190.00. Published by the Japan External Trade Organization (JETRO). Lists approximately 10,000 affiliates of Japanese companies operating in the U. S. and Canada. Provides North American and Japanese addresses. Six indexes.

Kelly's Directory. Reed Business Information. • Annual. $400.00. Lists approximately 77,000 manufacturers and merchants. Formerly *Kelly's Business Directory.*

Kompass International Trade Directories. Available from MarketResearch.com. • Annual. Prices and volumes vary. Kompass directories are published internationally for each of more than 70 countries, from Algeria to Yugoslavia. The Kompass classification system covers 50,000 individual product and service categories. Most directories include a tradename index and company profiles.

Latin America: A Directory and Sourcebook. Available from The Gale Group. • 1999. $590.00. Second edition. Published by Euromonitor. Describes major companies in Latin America. Sourcebook section provides marketing and business information sources.

Major Companies of South West Asia 2001. Available from The Gale Group. • 2001. $550.00. Fifth edition. Published by Graham and Whiteside. Provides information on 3,600 leading businesses in India and 2,500 in Turkey, Pakistan, Iran, and other countries of the region.

Major Companies of the Arab World 2001. Available from The Gale Group. • 1999. $890.00. 23rd edition. Contains basic information on 8,000 companies. Published by Graham & Whiteside, London.

Major Companies of the Far East and Australasia 2001. Available from The Gale Group. • 2001. $1,475.00. 17th edition. Three volumes. Published in London by Graham & Whiteside, Provides information on about 13,000 major companies. Volume one ($575.00): *South East Asia.* Volume two ($575.00): *East Asia.* Volume three *Australia, New Zealand, and Papua New Guinea.*($390.00).

Moody's International Manual. Financial Information Services. • Annual. $3,175.00 per year. Includes weekly *News Reports.* Financial and other information about 3,000 publicly-owned corporations in 95 countries.

Principal International Businesses: The World Marketing Directory. Dun and Bradstreet Information Services. • Annual. $5000. Provides information about 50,000 major businesses located in over 140 countries. Geographic arrangement with company name and product indexes.

Sell's Products and Services Directory. Miller Freeman Information Services. • Annual. $175.00. Approximately 60,000 firms in United Kingdom and Ireland. Formerly *Sell's Directory.*

Standard Directory of International Advertisers and Agencies: The International Red Book. R. R. Bowker. • Annual. $569.00. Includes about 8,000 foreign companies and their advertising agencies. Geographic, company name, personal name, and trade name indexes are provided.

The Top 5,000 European Companies 2000/2001. Available from The Gale Group. • 2001. $630.00. Second edition. Published by Graham & Whiteside. In addition to about 5,000 manufacturing and service companies, includes the 500 largest banks in Europe and the 100 largest insurance companies.

The Top 5,000 Global Companies 2000/2001. Available from The Gale Group. • Published by Graham & Whiteside. Includes about 5,000 manufacturing and service companies worldwide, plus the world's 500 largest banks and 100 largest insurance companies.

Trade Directories of the World. Croner Publications, Inc. • Annual. 100.00.Looseleaf. Monthly supplements. Lists over 3,300 publications.

Who Owns Whom. Dun and Bradstreet Information Services. • Annual. Four editions: Australasia and Far East; Continental, Europe, two volumes; North America; United Kingdom, two volumes. Prices vary.

World Business Directory. The Gale Group. • 2000. $615.00. Four volumes. Ninth edition. Covers about 140,000 companies in 180 countries.

World Retail Directory and Sourcebook 1999. Available from The Gale Group. • 1999. $590.00. Fourth edition. Published by Euromonitor. Provides information on more than 2,600 retailers around the world, with detailed profiles of the top 70. Information sources, conferences, trade fairs, and special libraries are also listed.

ENCYCLOPEDIAS AND DICTIONARIES

Blackwell Encyclopedic Dictionary of International Management. John J. O'Connell, editor. Blackwell Publishers. • 1997. $105.95. The editor is associated with the American Graduate School of International Management. Contains definitions of key terms combined with longer articles written by various U. S. and foreign business educators. Includes bibliographies and index. (Blackwell Encyclopedia of Management Series).

Dictionary of International Business Terms. Jae K. Shim and others, editors. Fitzroy Dearborn Publishers. • 1998. $45.00. Defines more than 2,000 terms currently used in international business.

International Encyclopedia of Business and Management. Malcolm Warner, editor. Routledge, Inc. • 1996. $1,319.95. Six volumes. Contains more than 500 articles on global management issues. Includes extensive bibliographies, cross references, and an index of key words and phrases.

HANDBOOKS AND MANUALS

Handbook of International Management. Ingo Walter. John Wiley and Sons, Inc. • 1988. $180.00.

Handbook of the Nations: A Brief Guide to the Economy, Government, Land, Demographics, Communications, and National Defense Establishments of Each of 206 Nations and Other Political Entities. The Gale Group. • 2000. $155.00. 20th edition. Includes maps and tables.

International Business Handbook. Vishnu H. Kirpalani, editor. Haworth Press, Inc. • 1990. $89.95. (International Business Series, No. 1).

International Business Information on the Web: Searcher Magazine's Guide to Sites and Strategies for Global Business Research. Sheri R. Lanza and Barbara Quint. Information Today, Inc. • 2001. $29.95. (CyberAge Books.).

International Public Relations: How to Establish Your Company's Product, Service, and Image in Foreign Markets. Joyce Wouters. Books on Demand. • 1991. $99.20.

Snowdon's Official International Protocols: The Definitive Guide to Business and Social Customs of the World. Sondra Snowdon. McGraw-Hill Professional. • 1996. $75.00. Discusses the protocols of 60 nations: social customs, business climate, personal characteristics, relevant history, and politics.

INTERNET DATABASES

Ebusiness Forum: Global Business Intelligence for the Digital Age. Economist Intelligence Unit (EIU), Economist Group. Phone: 800-938-4685 or

For publishers addresses, refer to SOURCES CITED section at the back of the book.

(212)554-0600 Fax: (212)586-0248 E-mail: newyork@eiu.com • URL: http://www.ebusinessforum.com • Web site provides information relating to multinational business, with an emphasis on activities in specific countries. Includes rankings of countries for "e-business readiness," additional data on the political, economic, and business environment in 180 nations ("Doing Business in.."), and "Today's News Analysis." Fees: Free, but registration is required for access to all content. Daily updates.

Financial Times: Where Information Becomes Intelligence. FT Group. Phone: (212)752-4500 Fax: (212)688-8229 • URL: http://www.ft.com • Web site provides extensive data and information relating to international business and finance, with daily updates. Includes Markets Today, Company News, Economic Indicators, Equities, Currencies, Capital Markets, Euro Prices, etc. Fees: Free (registration required).

GaleNet: Your Information Community. The Gale Group. Phone: 800-877-GALE or (248)699-GALE Fax: 800-414-5043 or (248)699-8069 E-mail: galenet@gale.com • URL: http://www.galenet.com • Web site provides a wide variety of full-text information from Gale databases, Taft, and other sources. Covers associations, biography, business directories, education, the information industry, literature, publishing, and science. Fee-based subscriptions are available for individual databases (free demonstration). Includes Boolean search features and the BRS/Search user interface.

Wall Street Journal Interactive Edition. Dow Jones & Co., Inc. Phone: 800-369-2834 or (212)416-2000 Fax: (212)416-2658 E-mail: inquiries@interactive.wsj.com • URL: http://www.wsj.com • Fee-based Web site providing online searching of worldwide information from the *The Wall Street Journal.* Includes "Company Snapshots," "The Journal's Greatest Hits," "Index to Market Data," "14-Day Searchable Archive," "Journal Links," etc. Financial price quotes are available. Fees: $49.00 per year; $29.00 per year to print subscribers.

ONLINE DATABASES

Country Report Services. The PRS Group. • Provides full text of reports describing the business risks and opportunities currently existing in more than 150 countries of the world. Contains a wide variety of statistics and forecasts relating to economics political and social conditions. Also includes demographics, tax, and currency information. Updated monthly. Inquire as to online cost and availability.

Globalbase. The Gale Group. • Provides more than one million online summaries of business, industrial, and economic news reports from more than 1,000 publications worldwide. Covers a wide range of material appearing in international trade journals, professional magazines, and newspapers. Time period is 1984 to date, with weekly updates. Inquire as to online cost and availability.

Moody's Corporate News: International. Moody's Investors Service, Inc. • Provides financial and other business news relating to over 5,000 corporations in 100 countries, excluding the U. S. Time period is 1983 to date, with weekly updates. Inquire as to online cost and availability.

Super Searchers Cover the World: The Online Secrets of International Business Researchers. Mary E. Bates and Reva Basch. Information Today, Inc. • 2001. $24.95. Presents interviews with 15 experts in the area of online searching for international business information. (CyberAge Books.).

PERIODICALS AND NEWSLETTERS

Business Week International: The World's Only International Newsweekly of Business. McGraw-Hill. • Weekly. $105.00 per year.

Canadian Business. Canadian Business Media. • 21 times a year. $34.70 per year. Edited for corporate managers and executives, this is a major periodical in Canada covering a variety of business, economic, and financial topics. Emphasis is on the top 500 Canadian corporations.

The Economist. Economist Intelligence Unit. • 51 times a year. Individuals, $130.00 per year; institutions, $125.00 per year.

EuroWatch. Worldwide Trade Executives. • Biweekly. $799.00 per year. Newsletter.

Export Today: The Global Business and Technology Magazine. Trade Communications, Inc. • Monthly. $49.00 per year. Edited for corporate executives to provide practical information on international business and exporting.

International Market Alert. International Reports, Inc. • Daily. Prices varies. Newsletter. Covers activities of central banks, foreign exchange markets, and New York bond and money markets. Gives specific hedging advice for major currencies. Available online.

International Tax Planners Alert. Research Institute of America, Inc. • Monthly. $150.00 per year. Newsletter.

Journal of Global Marketing. Haworth Press, Inc. • Quarterly. Individuals, $60.00 per year; institutions, $90.00 per year; libraries, $300.00 per year.

Journal of International Consumer Marketing. Haworth Press, Inc. • Quarterly. Individuals, $60.00 per year; institutions, $90.00 per year; libraries, $300.00 per year.

Journal of International Marketing. American Marketing Association. • Members $45.00; non-members, $80.00 per year institutions, $150.00 per year.

Journal of Teaching in International Business. Haworth Press, Inc. • Quarterly. Individuals, $50.00 per year; institutions, $75.00 per year; libraries, $185.00 per year.

Journal of World Business. Columbia University, Trustees of Columbia University. JAI Press, Inc. • Quarterly. $258.00 per year.

Political Risk Letter. Available from MarketResearch.com. • Monthly. $435.00 per year. Newsletter published by Political Risk Services. Contains forecasts of the political risks of doisg business in each of 100 countries.

United States Import-Export Publications Co. New Media Productions. • Monthly. $48.00 per year.

The Wall Street Journal. Dow Jones & Co., Inc. • Daily. $175.00 per year. Covers news and trends relating to business, industry, finance, the economy, and international commerce. Provides extensive price and other data for the securities, commodity, options, futures, foreign exchange, and money markets.

World Trade: For the Executive with Global Vision. World Trade Magazine. • Monthly. $36.00 per year. Edited for senior management of U. S. companies engaged in international business and trade.

RESEARCH CENTERS AND INSTITUTES

Bureau of Economic and Business Research. University of Illinois at Urbana-Champaign, 1206 S. Sixth St., Champaign, IL 61820. Phone: (217)333-2330 Fax: (217)244-7410 E-mail: g-oldman@uiuc.edu • URL: http://www.cba.uiuc.edu/research.

Huntsman Center for Global Competition and Innovation. University of Pennsylvania, 3620 Locust Walk, Suite 1400, Philadelphia, PA 19104. Phone: (215)898-2104 Fax: (215)573-2129 E-mail: dayg@wharton.upenn.edu • URL: http://www.fourps.wharton.upenn.edu/ • Conducts research related to international business.

International Business Institute. St. Louis University, 3674 Lindell Blvd., St. Louis, MO 63108. Phone: (314)977-3898 Fax: (314)977-7188 E-mail: iib@slu.edu • URL: http://www.slu.edu.

STATISTICS SOURCES

Consumer Asia 2001. Available from The Gale Group. • 2001. $970.00. Eighth edition. Published by Euromonitor. Provides statistical andanalytical surveys of factors affecting Asian consumer markets: energy, labor, population, finance, debt, tourism, consumer expenditures, household characteristics, etc. Emphasis is on Hong Kong, Singapore, Taiwan, South Korea, Indonesia, and Malaysia.

Country Data Forecasts. Bank of America, World Information Services, Dept. 3015. • Looseleaf, with semiannual updates. $495.00 per year. Provides detailed statistical tables for 80 countries, showing historical data and five-year forecasts of 23 key economic series. Includes population, inflation figures, debt, per capita income, foreign trade, exchange rates, and other data.

Encyclopedia of Global Industries. The Gale Group. • 1999. $420.00. Second edition. Provides detailed statistical information on 115 industries. Coverage is international, with country and subject indexes.

International Marketing Data and Statistics 2001. Available from The Gale Group. • 2001. $450.00. 25th edition. Published by Euromonitor. Contains statistics on population, economic factors, energy, consumer expenditures, prices, and other items affecting marketing in 158 countries of the world.

International Survey of Business Expectations. Dun & Bradstreet Corp., Economic Analysis Dept. • Quarterly. $40.00 per year. A survey of international business executives regarding their quarterly expectations for sales, profits, prices, inventories, employment, and new orders. Results are given for each of 14 major foreign countries and the U. S.

International Trade Statistics Yearbook. United Nations Statistical Office. United Nations Publications. • Annual. $135.00. Two volumes.

Manufacturing Worldwide: Industry Analyses, Statistics, Products, Leading Companies and Countries. The Gale Group. • 1999. $220.00. Third edition. A guide to worldwide economic activity in 500 product lines within 140 countries. Includes 37 detailed industry profiles. Name, address, phone, fax, employment, and ranking are shown for major companies worldwide in each industry sector.

OECD Information Technology Outlook 2000: ICTs, E-Commerce and the Information Economy. Organization for Economic Cooperation and Development. • 2000. $72.00. Provides data on information and communications technology (ICT) and electronic commerce in 11 OECD nations (includes U. S.). Coverage includes network infrastructure, electronic payment systems, financial transaction technologies, intelligent agents, global navigation systems, and portable flat panel display technologies.

Retail Trade International. The Gale Group. • 2000. $1,990.00. Second edition. Six volumes. Presents comprehensive data on retail trends in 51 countries. Includes textual analysis and profiles of major retailers. Covers Europe, Asia, the Middle East, Africa and the Americas.

Services: Statistics on Value Added and Employment. Organization for Economic Cooperation and Development. • Annual. $67.00. Provides 10-year data on service industry employment and output (value added) for all OECD countries. Covers such industries as telecommunications, business services, and information technology services.

TRADE/PROFESSIONAL ASSOCIATIONS

International Executive Service Corps. 333 Ludlow St., Stamford, CT 06902. Phone: 800-243-2531 or (203)967-6000 Fax: (203)324-2531 E-mail: iesc@iesc.org • URL: http://www.iesc.org.

OTHER SOURCES

Country Finance. Economist Intelligence Unit. • Semiannual (quarterly for "fast-changing countries"). $395.00 per year for each country. Discusses banking and financial conditions in each of 47 countries. Includes foreign exchange regulations, the currency outlook, sources of capital, financing techniques, and tax considerations. Formerly Financing Foreign Operations.

Country Forecasts. Economist Intelligence Unit. • Quarterly. $845.00 per year per country. Five-year forecasts are provided for each of 62 countries. Analyzes economic, political, and business prospects.

Country Reports. Economist Intelligence Unit. • Quarterly. $425.00 per year per country or country group. Comprehensive economic and political information is presented for 180 countries in 99 *Country Reports*, with 12 to 18 month forecasts. Each subscription includes an annual *Country Profile* containing statistical tables.

Country Risk Monitor. Bank of America, World Information Services, Dept. 3015. • Looseleaf, with semiannual updates. $495.00 per year. Provides rankings of 80 countries according to current and future business risk. Utilizes key economic ratios and benchmarks for countries in a manner similar to financial ratio analysis for industries.

Country Risk Service. Economist Intelligence Unit. • Quarterly. $625.00 per year per country. Two-year risk forecasts are provided for each of 82 countries. Business, political, economic, and credit risks are analyzed.

Factiva. Dow Jones Reuters Business Interactive, LLC. • Fee-based Web site provides "global news and business information through Web sites and content integration solutions." Includes Dow Jones and Reuters newswires, The Wall Street Journal, and more than 7,000 other sources of current news, historical articles, market research reports, and investment analysis. Content includes 96 major U. S. newspapers, 900 non-English sources, trade publications, media transcripts, country profiles, news photos, etc.

FedWorld: A Program of the United States Department of Commerce. National Technical Information Service. • Web site offers "a comprehensive central access point for searching, locating, ordering, and acquiring government and business information." Emphasis is on searching the Web pages, databases, and government reports of a wide variety of federal agencies. Fees: Free.

Foreign Labor Trends. Available from U. S. Government Printing Office. • Irregular (50 to 60 issues per year, each on an individual country). $38.00 per year. Prepared by various American Embassies. Issued by the Bureau of International Labor Affairs, U. S. Department of Labor. Covers labor developments in important foreign countries, including trends in wages, working conditions, labor supply, employment, and unemployment.

Foreign Tax and Trade Briefs. Matthew Bender & Co., Inc. • $470.00. Two looseleaf volumes. Periodic supplementation. The latest tax and trade information for over 100 foreign countries.

Global Company News Digest: A Monthly Publication of Corporate News Summaries and Financial Transactions of the Leading 10,000 Companies Worldwide. C I F A R Publications, Inc. • Monthly. $495.00 per year. Subscriptions are available according to region, company characteristics, news topic, or industry. Provides both financial and non-financial news and information.

Income Taxation of Foreign Related Transactions. Matthew Bender and Co., Inc. • Six looseleaf volumes. Annual supplements available. Price on application. All aspects of U.S. taxation of Americans doing business abroad and foreigners investing in the U.S.

International Business Planning: Law and Taxation (United States). William P. Streng and Jeswald W. Salacuse. Matthew Bender & Co., Inc. • $1,200.00. Six looseleaf volumes. Periodic supplementation. Formerly *Federal Taxes.*

International Company Data. Mergent FIS, Inc. • Monthly. Price on application. CD-ROM provides detailed financial statement information for more than 11,000 public corporations in 100 foreign countries. Formerly *Moody's International Company Data.*

International Country Risk Guide. The P R S Group. • Monthly. $3,595.00 per year. Each issue provides detailed analysis of a group of countries, covering financial risks, political trends, and economic developments. More than 130 countries are covered during the course of a year, with specific business risk point ratings assigned.

International Tax Planning Manual-Corporations. CCH, Inc. • Eight times a year. Price on application. Two looseleaf volumes. Periodic supplementation. Tax strategies for doing business in 38 major countries. Formerly *International Tax Planning Manual.*

Investing, Licensing, and Trading. Economist Intelligence Unit. • Semiannual. $345.00 per year for each country. Key laws, rules, and licensing provisions are explained for each of 60 countries. Information is provided on political conditions, markets, price policies, foreign exchange practices, labor, and export-import.

Law of Transnational Business Transactions. Ved P. Nanda. West Group. • $375 per year. Three looseleaf volumes. Periodic supplementation. (International Business and Law Series).

Major Companies of Europe. Available from The Gale Group. • Annual. $1,780.00. Six volumes ($360.00 per volume). Published by Graham & Whiteside. Regional volumes provide detailed information on a total of more than 24,000 of Europe's largest companies: 1. Austria, Belgium, Cyprus, Denmark, Ireland, Finland. 2. France. 3. Germany. 4. Greece, Italy, Liechtenstein, Luxembourg, The Netherlands, Norway. 5. Portugal, Spain, Sweden, Switzerland. 6. United Kingdom.

Major Performance Rankings. Available from The Gale Group. • 2001. $1,100.00. Published by Euromonitor. Ranks 2,500 leading consumer product companies worldwide by various kinds of business and financial data, such as sales, profit, and market share. Includes international, regional, and country rankings.

Nexis.com. Lexis-Nexis Group. • Fee-based Web site offers searching of about 2.8 billion documents in some 30,000 news, business, and legal information sources. Features include a subject directory covering 1,200 topics in 34 categories and a Company Dossier containing information on more than 500,000 public and private companies. Boolean searching is offered.

World Business Rankings Annual. The Gale Group. • 1998. $189.00. Provides 2,500 ranked lists of international companies, compiled from a variety of published sources. Each list shows the "top ten" in a particular category. Keyword indexing, a country index, and citations are provided.

INTERNATIONAL CORPORATIONS

See: MULTINATIONAL CORPORATIONS

INTERNATIONAL DEVELOPMENT

See: DEVELOPING AREAS

INTERNATIONAL ECONOMICS

See also: ECONOMICS; INTERNATIONAL BUSINESS

GENERAL WORKS

International Economics. McGraw-Hill. • 2000. $66.25. Fourth edition.

Managing World Economic Change: International Political Economy. Prentice Hall. • 2000. Third edition. Price on application.

Modern International Economics. Wilfred Ethier. W. W. Norton & Co., Inc. • 1995. $91.00. Third edition.

The World in 2020: Power, Culture, and Prosperity. Hamish McRae. Harvard Business School Press. • 1995. $24.95. States that the best predictor of economic success will be a nation's creativity and social responsibility.

ABSTRACTS AND INDEXES

PAIS International in Print. Public Affairs Information Service, Inc. • Monthly. $650.00 per year; cumulations three times a year. Provides topical citations to the worldwide literature of public affairs, economics, demographics, sociology, and trade. Text in English; indexed materials in English, French, German, Italian, Portuguese and Spanish.

ALMANACS AND YEARBOOKS

Economic Survey of Europe. United Nations Publications. • Three times a year. Price varies. Provides yearly analysis and review of the European economy, including Eastern Europe and the USSR. Text in English.

Worldmark Yearbook. The Gale Group. • Annual. $305.00. Three volumes. Covers economic, social, and political events in about 230 countries. Includes statistical data, directories, and a bibliography.

BIBLIOGRAPHIES

International Bibliography of the Social Sciences: Economics. British Library of Political and Economic Science. Routledge. • Annual. $230.00.

OECD Catalogue of Publications. Organization for Economic Cooperation and Development. Available from OECD Publications and Information Center. • Annual. Free. Supplements available.

CD-ROM DATABASES

EconLit. Available from SilverPlatter Information, Inc. • Monthly. Single-user, $1,600.00 per year. Multi-user, $2,400.00 per year. Provides CD-ROM citations, with abstracts, to articles from more than 500 economics journals. Time period is 1969 to date. Produced by the American Economic Association.

National Trade Data Bank: The Export Connection. U. S. Department of Commerce. • Monthly. $575.00 per year. Provides over 150,000 trade-related data series on CD-ROM. Includes full text of many government publications. Specific data is included on national income, labor, price indexes, foreign exchange, technical standards, and international markets. Website address is http://www.stat-usa.gov/.

PAIS on CD-ROM. Public Affairs Information Service, Inc. • Quarterly. $1,995.00 per year. Provides a CD-ROM version of the online service, *PAIS International.* Contains over 400,000 citations to the literature of contemporary social, political, and economic issues.

ENCYCLOPEDIAS AND DICTIONARIES

Blackwell Encyclopedic Dictionary of Managerial Economics. Robert McAuliffe, editor. Blackwell Publishers. • 1997. $105.95. The editor is associated with Boston College. Contains definitions of key terms combined with longer articles written by various U. S. and foreign business educators. Includes bibliographies and index. *Blackwell Encyclopedia of Management Series.*

Worldmark Encyclopedia of National Economies. The Gale Group. • 2002. $295.00. Four volumes. Covers both the current and historical development of the economies of 200 foreign nations. Includes analysis and statistics.

HANDBOOKS AND MANUALS

Nations of the World: A Political, Economic, and Business Handbook. Grey House Publishing. • 2000. $135.00. Includes descriptive data on economic characteristics, population, gross domestic product (GDP), banking, inflation, agriculture, tourism, and other factors. Covers "all the nations of the world.".

INTERNET DATABASES

Europa: The European Union's Server. European Union 352 4301 35 349. E-mail: pressoffice@eurostat.cec.be • URL: http://www.europa.eu.int • Web site provides access to a wide variety of EU information, including statistics (Eurostat), news, policies, publications, key issues, and official exchange rates for the euro. Includes links to the European Central Bank, the European Investment Bank, and other institutions. Fees: Free.

ONLINE DATABASES

EconLit. American Economic Association. • Covers the worldwide literature of economics as contained in selected monographs and about 550 journals. Subjects include microeconomics, macroeconomics, economic history, inflation, money, credit, finance, accounting theory, trade, natural resource economics, and regional economics. Time period is 1969 to present, with monthly updates. Inquire as to online cost and availability.

OECD Main Economic Indicators. Organization for Economic Cooperation and Development. • International statistics provided by OECD, 1960 to date. Monthly updates. Inquire as to online cost and availability.

PAIS International. Public Affairs Information Service, Inc. • Corresponds to the former printed publications, *PAIS Bulletin* (1976-90) and *PAIS Foreign Language Index* (1972-90), and to the current *PAIS International in Print* (1991 to date). Covers economic, political, and sociological material appearing in periodicals, books, government documents, and other publications. Updating is monthly. Inquire as to online cost and availability.

PERIODICALS AND NEWSLETTERS

Asia Pacific Economic Review: Bridging Pacific Rim Business and Society. Zencore, Inc. • Monthly. $35.00 per year. Includes special issues on individual countries: Taiwan, Malayasia, China/Hong Kong, Japan, and Korea.

The Economist. Economist Intelligence Unit. • 51 times a year. Individuals, $130.00 per year; institutions, $125.00 per year.

Financial Times Currency Forecaster: Consensus Forecasts of the Worldwide Currency and Economic Outlook. Capitol Publications, Inc. • Monthly. $695.00 per year. Newsletter. Provides forecasts of foreign currency exchange rates and economic conditions. Supplement available: *Mid-Month Global Financial Report.*

George Washington Journal of International Law and Economics. National Law Center. George Washington University. • Three times a year. $23.00 per year. Articles dealing with a variety of topics within the area of private international comparative law and economics.

International Economic Insights. Institute for International Economics. • Bimonthly. $60.00 per year.

International Economic Review. University of Pennsylvania, Dept. of Economics. Blackwell Publishers, Inc. • Quarterly. $192.00 per year.

International Review of Applied Economics. Carfax Publishing Co. • Three times a year. Individuals, $148.00 per year; institutions, $512.00 per year.

The Journal of International Trade and Economic Development. Routledge Journals. • Quarterly. Individuals, $68.00 per year; institutions, $445.00 per year. Emphasizes the effect of trade on the economies of developing nations.

Review of International Political Economy. Routledge Journals. • Quarterly. Individuals, $72.00 per year; institutions, $275.00 per year. Includes articles on international trade, finance, production, and consumption.

RESEARCH CENTERS AND INSTITUTES

Institute for International Economics. 11 Dupont Circle, N. W., Suite 620, Washington, DC 20036. Phone: (202)328-9000 Fax: (202)328-5432 • URL: http://www.iie.com • Research fields include a wide range of international economic issues, including foreign exchange rates.

STATISTICS SOURCES

Country Outlooks. Bank of America, World Information Services, Dept. 3015. • Looseleaf. $495.00 per year. Covers 30 major countries, with each country updated twice a year (60 issues per year). Provides detailed economic data and financial forecasts, including tables of key economic indicators.

Country Profile: Annual Survey of Political and Economic Background. Economist Intelligence Unit. • Annual. $225.00 per country or country group. Contains statistical tables "showing the last 6 year run of macro-economic indicators, and an overview of a country's politics, economy and industry." Covers 180 countries in 115 annual editions.

Economic Outlook. Available from Basil Blackwell, Inc. • Quarterly. $658.00 per year. Published by the London Business School. Includes country and global forecasts of over 170 economic and business variables. Actual data is shown for two years, with forecasts up to ten years.

Handbook of International Economic Statistics. Available from National Technical Information Service. • Annual. $40.00. Prepared by U. S. Central Intelligence Agency. Provides basic statistics for comparing worldwide economic performance, with an emphasis on Europe, including Eastern Europe.

Main Economic Indicators. OECD Publication and Information Center. • Monthly. $450.00 per year. "The essential source of timely statistics for OECD member countries." Includes a wide variety of business, economic, and industrial data for the 29 OECD nations.

Main Economic Indicators: Historical Statistics. OECD Publications and Information Center. • Annual. $50.00.

OECD Economic Outlook. OECD Publications and Information Center. • Semiannual. $95.00 per year. Contains a wide range of economic and monetary data relating to the member countries of the Organization for Economic Cooperation and Development. Includes about 100 statistical tables and graphs, with 24-month forecasts for each of the OECD countries. Provides extensive review and analysis of recent economic trends.

OECD Economic Surveys. OECD Publications and Information Center. • Annual. $30.00 each. These are separate, yearly reviews for each of the economies of the industrialized nations that comprise the OECD. Each edition includes forecasts, analyses, and detailed statistical tables for the country being surveyed. (The combined series, one annual volume for each nation, is available at $485.00.).

Services: Statistics on International Transactions. Organization for Economic Cooperation and Development. Available from OECD Publications and Information Center. • Annual. $71.00. Presents a compilation and assessment of data on OECD member countries' international trade in services. Covers four major categories for 20 years: travel, transportation, government services, and other services.

Statistical Handbook on Poverty in the Developing World. Chandrika Kaul. Oryx Press. • 1999. $65.00. Provides international coverage, including special sections on women and children, and on selected cities. (Statistical Handbook Series).

The World Economic Factbook. Available from The Gale Group. • 2000. $450.00. Seventh edition. Published by Euromonitor. Presents key economic facts and figures for each of 200 countries, including details of chief industries, export-import trade, currency, political risk, household expenditures, and the economic situation in general.

World Economic Outlook: A Survey by the Staff of the International Monetary Fund. International Monetary Fund, Publications Services. • Semiannual. $62.00 per year. Presents international statistics combined with forecasts and analyses of the world economy. Editions available in Arabic, English, French and Spanish.

World Economic Prospects: A Planner's Guide to International Market Conditions. Available from The Gale Group. • 2000. $450.00. Second edition. Published by Euromonitor. Ranks 78 countries by specific economic characteristics, such as gross domestic product (GDP) per capita and short term growth prospects. Discusses the economic situation, prospects, and market potential of each of the countries.

World Factbook. U.S. National Technical Information Service. • Annual. $83.00. Prepared by the Central Intelligence Agency. For all countries of the world, provides current economic, demographic, geographic, communications, government, defense force, and illicit drug trade information (where applicable).

World Statistics Pocketbook. United Nations Publications. • Annual. $10.00. Presents basic economic, social, and environmental indicators for about 200 countries and areas. Covers more than 50 items relating to population, economic activity, labor force, agriculture, industry, energy, trade, transportation, communication, education, tourism, and the environment. Statistical sources are noted.

TRADE/PROFESSIONAL ASSOCIATIONS

Organisation for Economic Co-Operation and Development. Two, rue Andre Pascal, F-75775 Paris Cedex 16, France. Phone: 33 1 45248200 Fax: 33 1 45248500 E-mail: news.contact@oecd.org • URL: http://www.oecd.org.

OTHER SOURCES

Capital for Shipping. Available from Informa Publishing Group Ltd. • Annual. $128.00. Published in the UK by Lloyd's List (http://www.lloydslist.com). Consists of a "Financial Directory" and a "Legal Directory," listing international ship finance providers and international law firms specializing in shipping. (Included with subscription to *Lloyd's Shipping Economist*.).

Consensus Forecasts: A Digest of International Economic Forecasts. Consensus Economics Inc. • Monthly. $565.00 per year. Provides a survey of more than 200 "prominent" financial and economic forecasters, covering 20 major countries. Two-year forecasts for each country include future growth, inflation, interest rates, and exchange rates. Each issue contains analysis of business conditions in various countries.

World Economic and Social Survey: Trends and Policies in the World Economy. United Nations Publications. • Annual. $55.00. Includes discussion and "an extensive statistical annex of economic, trade, and financial indicators, incorporating current data and forecasts.".

World Economic Situation and Prospects. United Nations Publications. • Annual. $15.00. Serves as a supplement and update to the UN *World Economic and Social Survey*.

The World Economy: A Millennial Perspective. Angus Maddison. Organization for Economic Cooperation and Development. • 2001. $63.00. "...covers the development of the entire world economy over the past 2000 years," including data on world population and gross domestic product (GDP) since the year 1000, and exports since 1820. Focuses primarily on the disparity in economic performance among nations over the very long term. More than 200 statistical tables and figures are provided (detailed information available at http://www.theworldeconomy.org).

INTERNATIONAL FINANCE

See also: FOREIGN EXCHANGE; FOREIGN INVESTMENTS; INTERNATIONAL MONETARY FUND (IMF); MONEY

GENERAL WORKS

Cases in International Finance. Gunter Duffey. Addison-Wesley Longman, Inc. • 2001. Price on application.

ABSTRACTS AND INDEXES

Banking Information Index. U M I Banking Information Index. • Monthly. Price on application. Covers a wide variety of banking, business, and financial subjects in periodicals. Formerly *Banking Literature Index*.

World Banking Abstracts: The International Journal of the Financial Services Industry. Basil Blackwell, Inc. • Bimonthly. $866.00 per year. Provides worldwide coverage of articles appearing in over 400 financial publications.

ALMANACS AND YEARBOOKS

The Bankers' Almanac. Reed Business Information. • Semiannual. $730.00. Six volumes. Lists more than 4,500 banks; international coverage. Lists more than 4,500 banks; international coverage. Formerly *Bankers' Almanac and Yearbook*.

Emerging Markets Analyst. • Monthly. $895.00 per year. Provides an annual overview of the emerging financial markets in 24 countries of Latin America, Asia, and Europe. Includes data on international mutual funds and closed-end funds.

International Monetary Fund. Annual Report on Exhange Arrangements and Exchange Restrictions. International Monetary Fund Publications Services. • Annual. Individuals, $95.00; libraries, $47.50.

National Accounts Statistics: Main Aggregates and Detailed Tables. United Nations Publications. • Annual. $160.00.

BIBLIOGRAPHIES

Information Sources in Finance and Banking. R. G. Lester, editor. Bowker-Saur. • 1995. $125.00. Published by K. G. Saur. International coverage.

BIOGRAPHICAL SOURCES

Who's Who in International Banking. Bowker-Saur. • Irregular. $400.00. Contains biographical sketches of about 4,000 bankers. Worldwide coverage.

CD-ROM DATABASES

InvesText [CD-ROM]. Thomson Financial Securities Data. • Monthly. $5,000.00 per year. Contains full text on CD-ROM of investment research reports from about 250 sources, including leading brokers and investment bankers. Reports are available on both U. S. and international publicly traded corporations. Separate industry reports cover more than 50 industries. Time span is 1982 to date.

Leadership Library on CD-ROM: Who's Who in the Leadership of the United States. Leadership Directories, Inc. • Quarterly. $2,641.00 per year, including access to Internet version (weekly updates). Contains all 14 *Yellow Book* personnel directories on CD-ROM, providing contact and brief biographical information for about 400,000 individuals. Covers business, government, financial institutions, news media, law firms, associations, foreign representatives, and nonprofit organizations. Includes photographs.

DIRECTORIES

Central Banking Directory. Available from European Business Publications, Inc. • Biennial. Published in England by Central Banking Publications. Provides detailed information on over 160 central banks around the world. A full page is devoted to each country included. Included in subscription to *Central Banking*.

Dow Jones Guide to the Global Stock Market. Dow Jones & Co., Inc. • Annual. $34.95. Three volumes. Presents concise profiles and three-year financial performance data for each of 3,000 publicly held companies in 35 countries. (Includes all Dow Jones Global Index companies.).

Europe's Top Quoted Companies: A Comparative Directory from Seventeen European Stock Exchanges. Available from Hoover's, Inc. • Annual. $150.00. Published in the UK by COFISEM. Provides detailed, 5-year financial data on 700 major European companies that are publicly traded. Includes company addresses.

Foreign Representatives in the U. S. Yellow Book: Who's Who in the U. S. Offices of Foreign Corporations, Foreign Nations, the Foreign Press, and Intergovernmental Organizations. Leadership Directories, Inc. • Semiannual. $235.00 per year. Lists executives located in the U. S. for 1,300 foreign companies, 340 foreign banks and other financial institutions, 175 embassies and consulates, and 375 foreign press outlets. Includes five indexes.

Major Financial Institutions of Europe. European Business Publications, Inc. • Annual. $495.00. Contains profiles of over 7,000 financial institutions in Europe such as banks, investment companies, and insurance companies. Formerly *Major Financial Institutions of Continental Europe*.

Morningstar American Depositary Receipts. Morningstar, Inc. • Biweekly. $195.00 per year. Looseleaf. Provides detailed profiles of 700 foreign companies having shares traded in the U. S. through American Depositary Receipts (ADRs).

Polk World Bank Directory. Thomson Financial Publishing. • Annual. $330.00. Contains detailed listings of banks around the world, including the top 1,000 U. S. banks. Includes performance ratios for the three most recent fiscal years (return on assets, return on equity, etc.).

Polk World Banking Profiles: 2,000 Major Banks of the World. Thomson Financial Publishing. • Annual. $319.00. Provides extensive, three-year financial data for 2,000 U. S. and foreign banks. Includes analysis of 12 financial ratios and credit ratings from five leading bank rating agencies.

Thomson Bank Directory. Thomson Financial Publishing. • Semiannual. $395.00 per year. Four volumes. Provides detailed information on head offices and branches of banks in the United States and foreign countries.

Venture Capital Report Guide to Venture Capital in Europe. Pitman Publishing. • 1991. $125.00. Provides information on more than 500 European venture capital firms. Lists current investments.

ENCYCLOPEDIAS AND DICTIONARIES

Blackwell Encyclopedic Dictionary of Finance. Dean Paxson and Douglas Wood, editors. Blackwell Publishers. • 1997. $110.00. The editors are associated with the University of Manchester. Contains definitions of key terms combined with longer articles written by various U. S. and foreign business educators. Includes bibliographies and index. (Blackwell Encyclopedia of Management Series).

International Dictionary of Accounting Acronyms. Thomas W. Morris, editor. Fitzroy Dearborn Publishers. • 1999. $45.00. Defines 2,000 acronyms used in worldwide accounting and finance.

FINANCIAL RATIOS

Reliable Financial Reporting and Internal Control: A Global Implementation Guide. Dmitris N. Chorafas. John Wiley and Sons, Inc. • 2000. $65.00. Discusses financial reporting and control as related to doing business internationally.

HANDBOOKS AND MANUALS

IAS: Interpretation and Application of International Accounting Standards. John Wiley and Sons, Inc. • Annual. $65.00. (Also available on CD-ROM.).

International Banking. Peter K. Oppenheim. American Bankers Association. • 1991. $51.00. Sixth edition. Covers letters of credit, money transfers, collections, and other aspects of global banking.

Library of Investment Banking. Robert L. Kuhn, editor. McGraw-Hill Professional. • 1990. $475.00. Seven volumes: 1. Investing and Risk Management; 2. Capital Raising and Financial Structure; 3. Corporate and Municipal Securities; 4. Mergers, Acquisitions, and Leveraged Buyouts; 5. Mortgage and Asset Securitization; 6. International Finance and Investing; 7. Index.

Options: The International Guide to Valuation and Trading Strategies. Gordon Gemmill. McGraw-Hill. • 1993. $37.95. Covers valuation techniques for

American, European, and Asian options. Trading strategies are discussed for options on currencies, stock indexes, interest rates, and commodities.

Swap and Derivative Financing: The Global Reference to Products Pricing Applications and Markets. Satyajit Das. McGraw-Hill Professional. • 1993. $95.00. Second revised edition.

Transnational Accounting. Dieter Ordelheide and others, editors. Groves Dictionaries. • 2000. $650.00. Three volumes. Published by Macmillan (UK). Provides detailed descriptions of financial accounting principles and practices in 14 major countries (10 European, plus the U. S., Canada, Australia, and Japan). Includes tables, exhibits, index, and a glossary of 244 accounting terms in eight languages.

INTERNET DATABASES

Europa: The European Union's Server. European Union 352 4301 35 349. E-mail: pressoffice@eurostat.cec.be • URL: http://www.europa.eu.int • Web site provides access to a wide variety of EU information, including statistics (Eurostat), news, policies, publications, key issues, and official exchange rates for the euro. Includes links to the European Central Bank, the European Investment Bank, and other institutions. Fees: Free.

Financial Times: Where Information Becomes Intelligence. FT Group. Phone: (212)752-4500 Fax: (212)688-8229 • URL: http://www.ft.com • Web site provides extensive data and information relating to international business and finance, with daily updates. Includes Markets Today, Company News, Economic Indicators, Equities, Currencies, Capital Markets, Euro Prices, etc. Fees: Free (registration required).

ONLINE DATABASES

Banking Information Source. Bell & Howell Information and Learning. • Provides indexing and abstracting of periodical and other literature from 1982 to date, with weekly updates. Covers the financial services industry: banks, savings institutions, investment houses, credit unions, insurance companies, and real estate organizations. Emphasis is on marketing and management. Inquire as to online cost and availability. (Formerly *FINIS: Financial Industry Information Service.*).

DRI Financial and Credit Statistics. Data Products Division. • Contains U. S. and international statistical data relating to money markets, interest rates, foreign exchange, banking, and stock and bond indexes. Time period is 1973 to date, with continuous updating. Inquire as to online cost and availability.

InvesText. Thomson Financial Securities Data. • Provides full text online of investment research reports from more than 300 sources, including leading brokers and investment bankers. Reports are available on approximately 50,000 U. S. and international corporations. Separate industry reports cover 54 industries. Time span is 1982 to date, with daily updates. Inquire as to online cost and availability.

PERIODICALS AND NEWSLETTERS

Applied Financial Economics. Routledge Journals. • Bimonthly. Individuals, $648.00 per year; institutions, $1,053.00 per year. Covers practical aspects of financial economics, banking, and monetary economics. Supplement to *Applied Economics.*

The Asian Wall Street Journal. Dow Jones & Co., Inc. • Daily. $610.00 per year (air mail). Published in Hong Kong. Also available in a weekly edition at $259.00 per year: *Asian Wall Street Journal Weekly.*

Central Banking: Policy, Markets, Supervision. Available from European Business Publications, Inc. • Quarterly. $350.00 per year, including annual *Central Banking Directory.* Published in England by Central Banking Publications. Reports and comments on the activities of central banks around the world. Also provides discussions of the International Monetary Fund (IMF), the Organization for Economic Cooperation and Development (OECD), the Bank for International Settlements (BIS), and the World Bank.

The Economist. Economist Intelligence Unit. • 51 times a year. Individuals, $130.00 per year; institutions, $125.00 per year.

Emerging Markets Debt Report. Securities Data Publishing. • Weekly. $895.00 per year. Newsletter. Provides information on new and prospective sovereign and corporate bond issues from developing countries. Includes an emerging market bond index and pricing data. (Securities Data Publishing is a unit of Thomson Financial.).

Emerging Markets Quarterly. Institutional Investor. • Quarterly. $325.00 per year. Newsletter on financial markets in developing areas, such as Africa, Latin America, Southeast Asia, and Eastern Europe. Topics include institutional investment opportunities and regulatory matters. Formerly *Emerging Markets Weekly.*

Euromoney: The Monthly Journal of International Money and Capital Markets. American Educational Systems. • Monthly. $395.00 per year. Supplement available*Guide to World Equity Markets.*

Finance and Development. International Monetary Fund, Publication Services. • Quarterly. Free. Edition available in English, French and Spanish.

Financial Flows and the Developing Countries. World Bank, The Office of the Publisher. • Quarterly. $150.00 per year. Concerned mainly with debt, capital markets, and foreign direct investment. Includes statistical tables.

Financial Times Global Investors' Digest. Capitol Publications, Inc. • Monthly. $695.00 per year. Newsletter. Contains information, forecasts, data, and analysis relating to international financial markets, including emerging markets. Supplement available *Mid-Month Global Financial Report.* Formerly *Global Investors' Digest.*

Financial Times [London]. Available from FT Publications, Inc. • Daily, except Sunday. $184.00 per year. An international business and financial newspaper, featuring news from London, Paris, Frankfurt, New York, and Tokyo. Includes worldwide stock and bond market data, commodity market data, and monetary/currency exchange information.

FMC (Financial Management): Journal of the Financial Management Association. Financial Management Association International. • Quarterly. Individuals, $80.00 per year; libraries, $100.00 per year. Covers theory and practice of financial planning, international finance, investment banking, and portfolio management. Includes *Financial Practice* and *Education and Contempory Finance Digest.*

Frankfurt Finance. Available from European Business Publications, Inc. • Monthly. $470.00 per year. Newsletter. Published in Germany by Frankfurter Allgemeine Zeitung GmbH Information Services. Presents news of German Bundesbank decisions and the European monetary system, including the European Monetary Union (EMU). Contains charts and tables. Formerly *Old Continent.*

FX Manager (Foreign Exchange). American Educational Systems. • Monthly. $790.00 per year. Foreign exchange forecasts. Formerly *Euromoney Treasury Manager.*

Global Finance. Global Finance Media, Inc. • Monthly. $300.00 per year. Edited for corporate financial executives and money managers responsible for "cross-border" financial transactions.

Institutional Investor International Edition: The Magazine for International Finance and Investment. Institutional Investor. • Monthly. $415.00 per year. Covers the international aspects of professional investing and finance. Emphasis is on Europe, the Far East, and Latin America.

Institutional Investor: The Magazine for Finance and Investment. Institutional Investor. • Monthly. $475.00 per year. Edited for portfolio managers and other investment professionals. Special feature issues include "Country Credit Ratings," "Fixed Income Trading Ranking," "All-America Research Team," and "Global Banking Ranking.".

International Bank Credit Analyst. BCA Publications Ltd. • Monthly. $795.00 per year. "A monthly forecast and analysis of currency movements, interest rates, and stock market developments in the principal countries, based on a continuous appraisal of money and credit trends worldwide." Includes many charts and graphs providing international coverage of money, credit, and securities.

International Currency Review. World Reports Ltd. • Quarterly. $475.00 per year.

International Financial Law Review. American Educational Systems. • Monthly. $695.00 per year.

International Monetary Fund Staff Papers. International Monetary Fund, Publication Services. • Quarterly. Individuals, $56.00 per year; students, $28.00 per year. Contains studies by IMF staff members on balance of payments, foreign exchange, fiscal policy, and related topics.

Latin Finance. Latin American Financial Publications, Inc. • Monthly. $215.00 per year. Covers finance, investment, venture capital, and banking in Latin America.

Project Finance: The Monthly Analysis of Export, Import and Project Finance. Institutional Investor. • Monthly. $635.00 per year. An analysis of the techniques and practice used in international trade and project finance. Supplements available *World Export Credit Guides* and *Project Finance Book of Lists.* Formed by the merger of *Infrastructure Finance* and *Project and Trade Finance.*

Standard and Poor's Ratings Handbook. Standard & Poor's. • Monthly. $275.00 per year. Newsletter. Provides news and analysis of international credit markets, including information on new bond issues. Formerly *Credit Week International Ratings.*

The Wall Street Journal. Dow Jones & Co., Inc. • Daily. $175.00 per year. Covers news and trends relating to business, industry, finance, the economy, and international commerce. Provides extensive price and other data for the securities, commodity, options, futures, foreign exchange, and money markets.

Wall Street Journal/Europe. Dow Jones & Co., Inc. • Daily. $700.00 per year (air mail). Published in Europe. Text in English.

RESEARCH CENTERS AND INSTITUTES

Catalyst Institute. 33 N. LaSalle St., Suite 1900, Chicago, IL 60602-2604. Phone: (312)541-5400 Fax: (312)541-5401 E-mail: postmaster@catalystinstitute.org • URL: http://www.dstcatalyst.com • Investigates the financial services industry, including bank failures and the domino effect, the liability crisis, and regulations designed to prevent bank failures.

International Finance Section. Princeton University. Fisher Hall, Princeton, NJ 08544-1021. Phone:

(609)258-4048 Fax: (609)258-6419 E-mail: pbkenen@princeton.edu • URL: http://www.princeton.edu.

Rodney L. White Center for Financial Research. University of Pennsylvania, 3254 Steinberg Hall-Dietrich Hall, Philadelphia, PA 19104. Phone: (215)898-7616 Fax: (215)573-8084 E-mail: rlwtcr@finance.wharton.upenn.edu • URL: http://www.finance.wharton.upenn.edu/~rlwctr • Research areas include financial management, money markets, real estate finance, and international finance.

STATISTICS SOURCES

Bank Profitability: Financial Statements of Banks. Organization for Economic Cooperation and Development. Available from OECD Publications and Information Center. • Annual. $60.00. Presents data for 10 years on bank profitability in OECD member countries.

Emerging Stock Markets Factbook. International Finance Corporation, Capital Market Dept. • Annual. $100.00. Published by the International Finance Corporation (IFC). Provides statistical profiles of more than 26 emerging stock markets in various countries of the world. Includes regional, composite, and industry indexes.

Financial Market Trends. Organization for Economic Cooperation and Development. • Three times a year. $100.00 per year. Provides analysis of developments and trends in international and national capital markets. Includes charts and graphs on interest rates, exchange rates, stock market indexes, bank stock indexes, trading volumes, and loans outstanding. Data from OECD countries includes international direct investment, bank profitability, institutional investment, and privatization.

Global Development Finance: Analysis and Summary Tables. World Bank, The Office of the Publisher. • Annual. $40.00. Provides an analysis of debt and equity financial flows to 136 countries that report to the World Bank's Debtor Reporting System. Contains summary statistical tables for 150 countries.

Global Development Finance: Country Tables. World Bank, The Office of the Publisher. • 1998. $300.00 (includes *Analysis and Summary Tables*). Contains detailed statistical tables for 136 countries, covering total external debt, long-term debt ratios, arrears, commitments, disbursements, repayments, etc. Includes "major economic aggregates.".

Global Development Finance: External Public Debt of Developing Countries. World Bank, The Office of the Publisher. • Irregular. Prices vary. Includes supplements. Contains detailed data from the International Bank for Reconstruction and Development (World Bank) on the external debt load of over 100 developing countries.

Global Stock Guide. C I F A R Publications, Inc. • Monthly. $445.00 per year. Provides financial variables for 10,000 publicly traded companies in 48 countries.

International Direct Investment Statistics Yearbook. OECD Publications and Information Center. • Annual. $79.00. Provides direct investment inflow and outflow data for OECD countries.

International Financial Statistics. International Monetary Fund, Publications Services. • Monthly. Individuals, $246.00 per year; libraries, $123.00 per year. Includes a wide variety of current data for individual countries in Europe and elsewhere. Annual issue available. Editions available in French and Spanish.

International Guide to Securities Market Indices. Henry Shilling, editor. Fitzroy Dearborn Publishers. • 1996. $140.00. Describes 400 stock market, bond market, and other financial price indexes maintained in various countries of the world (300 of the indexes are described in detail, including graphs and 10-year data).

Statistical Information on the Financial Services Industry. American Bankers Association. • Annual. Members, $150.00; non-members, $275.00. Presents a wide variety of data relating to banking and financial services, including consumer economics, personal finance, credit, government loans, capital markets, and international banking.

TRADE/PROFESSIONAL ASSOCIATIONS

International Monetary Fund. 700 19th St., N.W., Washington, DC 20431. Phone: (202)623-7000 Fax: (202)623-4661.

World Bank. 1818 H St., N. W., Washington, DC 20433. Phone: (202)477-1234 Fax: (202)477-6391 • URL: http://www.worldbank.org • Comprises the International Bank for Reconstruction and Development and the International Development Association, with over 130 member countries.

OTHER SOURCES

Country Finance. Economist Intelligence Unit. • Semiannual (quarterly for "fast-changing countries"). $395.00 per year for each country. Discusses banking and financial conditions in each of 47 countries. Includes foreign exchange regulations, the currency outlook, sources of capital, financing techniques, and tax considerations. Formerly Financing Foreign Operations.

International Capital Markets and Securities Regulation. Harold S. Bloomenthal. West Group. • Six looseleaf volumes. $795.00. Periodic supplementation. Securities regulation in industrialized nations. (Securities Law Series).

Law and Practice of International Finance. Philip Wood. West Group. • Two looseleaf volumes. $250.00. Periodic supplementation.

World Investment Report. United Nations Publications. • Annual. $49.00. Concerned with foreign direct investment, economic development, regional trends, transnational corporations, and globalization.

INTERNATIONAL INSTITUTIONS

See: INTERNATIONAL AGENCIES

INTERNATIONAL INVESTMENTS

See: FOREIGN INVESTMENTS

INTERNATIONAL LAW AND REGULATION

GENERAL WORKS

Business Law: The Legal, Ethical, and International Environment. Henry R. Cheesman. Prentice Hall. • 1997. $105.00. Third edition.

ABSTRACTS AND INDEXES

Current Law Index: Multiple Access to Legal Periodicals. The Gale Group. • Monthly. $650.00 per year. Produced in cooperation with the American Association of Law Libraries. Indexes more than 900 law journals, legal newspapers, and specialty publications from the U.S., Canada, U.K., Ireland, Australia, and New Zealand.

Index to Foreign Legal Periodicals. American Association of Law Libraries. University of California Press, Journals Div. • Quarterly. $630.00 per year. Annual cumulation.

Index to Legal Periodicals and Books. H. W. Wilson Co. • Monthly. Quarterly and annual cumulations. $270.00 per year. CD-ROM version available at $1,495.00 per year.

ALMANACS AND YEARBOOKS

British Year Book of International Law. Royal Institute of International Affairs. Oxford University Press, Inc. • Annual. Price varies.

Yearbook of the International Law Commission. Available from United Nations Publications. • Annual. $90.00. Two volumes. Volume one, $35.00; volume two, $55.00.

BIBLIOGRAPHIES

Basic Documents in International Law. Ian Brownlie. Oxford University Press, Inc. • 1995. $85.00. Fourth edition.

International Legal Books in Print. Bowker-Saur. • Irregular. $375.00. Two volumes. Covers English-language law books published or distributed within the United Kingdom, Europe, and current or former British Commonwealth countries.

CD-ROM DATABASES

WILSONDISC: Index to Legal Periodicals and Books. H. W. Wilson Co. • Monthly. Including unlimited online access to *Index to Legal Periodicals* through WILSONLINE. Contains CD-ROM indexing of more than 800 English language legal periodicals from 1981 to date and 2,500 books.

DIRECTORIES

Martindale-Hubbell Law Directory. Martindale-Hubbell. • Annual. $695.00. 25 volumes. Lists 800,000 lawyers in the U. S., Canada, and 150 other countries, with an index to areas of specialization. Three of the 25 volumes provide the *Martindale-Hubbell Law Digest*, summarizing the statutary laws of the U. S. (state and federal), Canada, and 61 other countries.

Worldwide Government Directory 2001. Available from The Gale Group. • 2001. $394.00. 19th edition. Published by Keesings Worldwide. Lists more than 32,000 key officials in the governments of over 199 countries.

ENCYCLOPEDIAS AND DICTIONARIES

Index to Legal Citations and Abbreviations. Donald Raistrick. Bowker-Saur. • 1993. $100.00. Second edition. Explains about 25,000 legal abbreviations and acronyms used in the U. S., U. K., and Europe.

ONLINE DATABASES

Index to Legal Periodicals and Books (Online). H. W. Wilson Co. • Broad coverage of law journals and books 1981 to date. Monthly updates. Inquire as to online cost and availability.

PERIODICALS AND NEWSLETTERS

American Journal of International Law. American Society of International Law. • Quarterly. $140.00 per year.

International and Comparative Law Quarterly. British Institute of International and Comparative Law. • Quarterly. $190.00 per year. Includes *Quarterly Newsletter.*

International Financial Law Review. American Educational Systems. • Monthly. $695.00 per year.

International Lawyer. American Bar Association. International Law and Practice Section. • Quarterly. Free to members; non-members, $35.00 per year.

International Legal Materials. American Society of International Law. • Bimonthly. $190.00 per year.

RESEARCH CENTERS AND INSTITUTES

International Law Institute. 1615 New Hampshire Ave., N.W., Suite 100, Washington, DC 20009.

Phone: (202)483-3036 Fax: (202)483-3029 E-mail: training@ili.org • URL: http://www.ili.org • Research in foreign trade law and in other areas of international law is done in cooperation with Georgetown University.

Lexis.com Research System. Lexis-Nexis Group. Phone: 800-227-9597 or (937)865-6800 Fax: (937)865-6909 E-mail: webmaster@prod.lexis-nexis.com • URL: http://www.lexis.com • Fee-based Web site offers extensive searching of a wide variety of legal sources. Additional features include Daily Opinion Service, lexis.com Bookstore, Career Center, CLE Center, Law Schools, and Practice Pages ("Pages specific to areas of specialty").

TRADE/PROFESSIONAL ASSOCIATIONS

American Society of International Law. 2223 Massachusetts Ave., N.W., Washington, DC 20008-2864. Phone: (202)939-6000 Fax: (202)797-7133 E-mail: services@asil.org • URL: http://www.asil.org.

International Bar Association. 271 Regent St., London WIR 7PA, England. E-mail: sbl@int-bar.org • URL: http://www.ibanet.org.

International Center for Law in Development. 777 United Nations Plaza, 7 E., New York, NY 10017. Phone: (212)687-0036 Fax: (212)370-9844.

International Law Association. Charles Clore House, 17 Russell Square, London WC1B 5DR 4, England. Phone: 44 20 73232978 Fax: 44 20 73233580.

OTHER SOURCES

Access to European Union: Law, Economics, Policies. Euroconfidentiel S. A. • Annual. $62.00. Covers EU legislation and policy in major industrial and commercial sectors. Includes customs policy, the common market, monetary union, taxation, competition, "The EU in the World," and related topics. Contains more than 300 bibliographical references.

International Capital Markets and Securities Regulation. Harold S. Bloomenthal. West Group. • Six looseleaf volumes. $795.00. Periodic supplementation. Securities regulation in industrialized nations. (Securities Law Series).

Law and Practice of International Finance. Philip Wood. West Group. • Two looseleaf volumes. $250.00. Periodic supplementation.

Law of Transnational Business Transactions. Ved P. Nanda. West Group. • $375 per year. Three looseleaf volumes. Periodic supplementation. (International Business and Law Series).

The Rome, Maastricht, and Amsterdam Treaties: Comparative Texts. Euroconfidentiel S. A. • 1999. $42.00. Includes a comprehensive keyword index.

World Trade Organization Dispute Settlement Decisions: Bernan's Annotated Reporter. Bernan Press. • Dates vary. $75.00 per volume. Contains all World Trade Organization Panel Reports and Appellate Decisions since the establishment of the WTO in 1995. Includes such cases as "The Importation, Sale, and Distribution of Bananas.".

INTERNATIONAL MARKETING

See also: ASIAN MARKETS; CANADIAN MARKETS; EUROPEAN CONSUMER MARKET; LATIN AMERICAN MARKETS

GENERAL WORKS

Applying Telecommunications and Technology from a Global Business Perspective. Jay J. Zajas and Olive D. Church. Haworth Press, Inc. • 1996. $49.95. Provides an international, multicultural perspective.

Global Economic Prospects 2000. The World Bank, Office of the Publisher. • 1999. $25.00. "..offers an in-depth analysis of the economic prospects of developing countries.." Emphasis is on the impact of recessions and financial crises. Regional statistical data is included.

International Advertising: Realities and Myths. John P. Jones, editor. Sage Publications, Inc. • 1999. $76.00. Includes articles by advertising professionals in 10 different countries.

Marketing in the Third World. Denise M. Johnson and Erdener Kaynak, editors. Haworth Press, Inc. • 1996. $29.95. Various authors discuss marketing, advertising, government regulations, and other topics relating to business promotion in developing countries. (Also published in the *Journal of Global Marketing*, vol. 9.).

ABSTRACTS AND INDEXES

Business Periodicals Index. H. W. Wilson Co. • Monthly, except August, with quarterly and annual cumulations. Service basis for print edition; CD-ROM edition, $1,495.00 per year.

F & S Index: Europe. The Gale Group. • Monthly. $1,295.00 per year, including quarterly and annual cumulations. Provides annotated citations to marketing, business, financial, and industrial literature. Coverage of European business activity includes trade journals, financial magazines, business newspapers, and special reports. Formerly *Predicasts F & S Index: Europe.*

F & S Index: International. The Gale Group. • Monthly. $1,295.00 per year, including quarterly and annual cumulations. Provides annotated citations to marketing, business, financial, and industrial literature. Coverage of international business activity includes trade journals, financial magazines, business newspapers, and special reports. Areas included are Asia, Latin America, Africa, the Middle East, Oceania, and Canada. Formerly *Predicasts F & S Index: International.*

NTIS Alerts: Business & Economics. National Technical Information Service.

PAIS International in Print. Public Affairs Information Service, Inc. • Monthly. $650.00 per year; cumulations three times a year. Provides topical citations to the worldwide literature of public affairs, economics, demographics, sociology, and trade. Text in English; indexed materials in English, French, German, Italian, Portuguese and Spanish.

ALMANACS AND YEARBOOKS

World Development Report. The World Bank, Office of the Publisher. • Annual. $50.00. Covers history, conditions, and trends relating to economic globalization and localization. Includes selected data from *World Development Indicators* for 132 countries or economies. Key indicators are provided for 78 additional countries or economies.

CD-ROM DATABASES

Business Source Plus. EBSCO Information Services. • Monthly. $1,495.00 per year. Provides CD-ROM citations and abstracts to articles in about 650 business periodicals and newspapers, including *The Wall Street Journal.* Full text is provided from 200 selected periodicals. Covers accounting, communications, economics, finance, management, marketing, and other business subjects.

F & S Index Plus Text. The Gale Group. • Monthly. $7,575.00 per year. Provides CD-ROM citations to worldwide business, marketing, and industrial material appearing in a large assortment of trade journals, newspapers, and other publications. Time period is four years.

PAIS on CD-ROM. Public Affairs Information Service, Inc. • Quarterly. $1,995.00 per year. Provides a CD-ROM version of the online service, *PAIS International.* Contains over 400,000 citations to the literature of contemporary social, political, and economic issues.

WILSONDISC: Wilson Business Abstracts. H. W. Wilson Co. • Monthly. $2,495.00 per year, including unlimited online access to *Wilson Business Abstracts* through WILSONLINE. Provides CD-ROM "cover-to-cover" abstracting and indexing of over 600 prominent business periodicals. Indexing is from 1982, abstracting from 1990. (*Business Periodicals Index* without abstracts is available on CD-ROM at $1,495 per year.).

World Consumer Markets. The Gale Group. • Annual. $2,500.00. Pblished by Euromonitor. Provides five- year historical data, current data, and forecasts, on CD-ROM for 330 consumer products in 55 countries. Market data is presented in a standardized format for each country.

World Development Report [CD-ROM]. The World Bank, Office of the Publisher. • Annual. Single-user, $375.00. Network version, $750.00. CD-ROM includes the current edition of *World Development Report* and 21 previous editions.

World Marketing Data and Statistics on CD-ROM. The Gale Group. • Annual. $1,750.00. Published by Euromonitor. Provides demographic, marketing, socioeconomic, and political data on CD-ROM for each of 209 countries.

World Marketing Forecasts on CD-ROM. The Gale Group. • Annual. $2,500.00. Produced by Euromonitor. Provides detailed forecast data for the years to 2012 on CD-ROM for 54 countries in all parts of the world. Covers a wide range of social, demographic, economic, and market factors. Includes specific forecasts for many kinds of consumer products.

DIRECTORIES

Directory of Consumer Brands and Their Owners: Asia Pacific. Available from The Gale Group. • 1998. $990.00. Published by Euromonitor. Provides information about brands available from major Asia Pacific companies. Descriptions of companies are also included.

Directory of Consumer Brands and Their Owners: Eastern Europe. Available from The Gale Group. • 1998. $990.00. Published by Euromonitor. Provides information about brands available from major Eastern European companies. Descriptions of companies are also included.

Directory of Consumer Brands and Their Owners: Europe. Available from The Gale Group. • 1998. $990.00. Two volumes. Third edition. Published by Euromonitor. Provides information about brands available from major European companies. Descriptions of companies are also included.

Directory of Consumer Brands and Their Owners: Latin America. Available from The Gale Group. • 1999. $990.00. Published by Euromonitor. Provides information about brands available from major Latin American companies. Descriptions of companies are also included.

International Media Guide: Business Professional Publications: Asia Pacific/Middle East/Africa. International Media Guides, Inc. • Annual. $285.00. Provides information on 3,000 trade journals "from Africa to the Pacific Rim," including advertising rates and circulation data.

International Media Guide: Business Professional Publications: Europe. International Media Guides, Inc. • Annual. $285.00. Describes 6,000 trade journals from Eastern and Western Europe, with advertising rates and circulation data.

International Media Guide: Business/Professional Publications: The Americas. International Media Guides, Inc. • Annual. $285.00. Describes trade journals from North, South, and Central America, with advertising rates and circulation data.

International Media Guide: Consumer Magazines Worldwide. International Media Guides, Inc. • Annual. $285.00. Contains descriptions of 4,500 consumer magazines in 24 subject categories in 200 countries, including U. S. Provides details of advertising rates and circulation.

International Media Guide: Newspapers Worldwide. International Media Guides, Inc. • Annual. $285.00. Provides advertising rates, circulation, and other details relating to newspapers in major cities of the world (covers 200 countries, including U. S.).

Major Market Share Companies: The Americas. Available from The Gale Group. • 2000. $900.00. Published by Euromonitor (http://www.euromonitor.com). Provides consumer market share data and rankings for multinational and regional companies. Covers leading firms in the U.S., Canada, Mexico, Brazil, Argentina, Venezuela, and Chile.

Market Share Tracker. Available from The Gale Group. • 2000. $1,000.00. Published by Euromonitor (http://www.euromonitor.com). Provides consumer market share data for leading companies in 30 major countries.

MRA Blue Book Research Services Directory. Marketing Research Association. • Annual. $169.95. Lists more than 1,200 international marketing research companies and survey services. Formerly *Directory of Research Services Provided by Members of the Marketing Research Association.*

World Directory of Marketing Information Sources. Available from The Gale Group. • 2001. $590.00. Third edition. Published by Euromonitor. Provides details on more than 6,000 sources of marketing information, including publications, libraries, associations, market research companies, online databases, and governmental organizations. Coverage is worldwide.

ENCYCLOPEDIAS AND DICTIONARIES

Blackwell Encyclopedic Dictionary of Marketing. Barbara R. Lewis and Dale Littler, editors. Blackwell Publishers. • 1996. $105.95. The editors are associated with the Manchester School of Management. Contains definitions of key terms combined with longer articles written by various U. S. and foreign business educators. Includes bibliographies and index. (Blackwell Encyclopedia of Management series.).

Encyclopedia of Business. The Gale Group. • 2000. $425.00. Second edition. Two volumes. Contains more than 700 signed articles covering major business disciplines and concepts. International in scope.

Field Guide to Marketing: A Glossary of Essential Tools and Concepts for Today's Manager. McGraw-Hill. • 1993. $29.95. Defines fundamental terms.

HANDBOOKS AND MANUALS

Marketing Manager's Handbook. Sidney J. Levy and others. Prentice Hall. • 2000. Price on application. Contains 71 chapters by various authors on a wide variety of marketing topics, including market segmentation, market research, international marketing, industrial marketing, survey methods, customer service, advertising, pricing, planning, strategy, and ethics.

ONLINE DATABASES

ABI/INFORM. Bell & Howell Information and Learning. • Provides online indexing to business-related material occurring in over 1,000 periodicals from 1971 to the present. Inquire as to online cost and availability.

Euromonitor Journals. Euromonitor International. • Contains full-text reports online from *Market Research Europe, Market Research Great Britain, Market Research International*, and *Retail Monitor International*. Time period is 1995 to date, with monthly updates. Inquire as to online cost and availability.

Euromonitor Market Research. Euromonitor International. • Provides the complete text online of Euromonitor market analysis reports. Covers consumer goods market research data for all major countries, with emphasis on specific product categories. Time period is current. Continuous updating. Inquire as to online cost and availability.

F & S Index. The Gale Group. • Contains about four million citations to worldwide business, financial, and industrial or consumer product literature appearing from 1972 to date. Weekly updates. Inquire as to online cost and availability.

Globalbase. The Gale Group. • Provides more than one million online summaries of business, industrial, and economic news reports from more than 1,000 publications worldwide. Covers a wide range of material appearing in international trade journals, professional magazines, and newspapers. Time period is 1984 to date, with weekly updates. Inquire as to online cost and availability.

Management Contents. The Gale Group. • Covers a wide range of management, financial, marketing, personnel, and administrative topics. About 150 leading business journals are indexed and abstracted from 1974 to date, with monthly updating. Inquire as to online cost and availability.

MarkIntel. Thomson Financial Securities Data. • Provides the current full text online of more than 45,000 market research reports covering 54 industries, from 43 leading research firms worldwide. Reports include extensive forecasts and market analysis. Inquire as to online cost and availability.

PAIS International. Public Affairs Information Service, Inc. • Corresponds to the former printed publications, *PAIS Bulletin* (1976-90) and *PAIS Foreign Language Index* (1972-90), and to the current *PAIS International in Print* (1991 to date). Covers economic, political, and sociological material appearing in periodicals, books, government documents, and other publications. Updating is monthly. Inquire as to online cost and availability.

PROMT: Predicasts Overview of Markets and Technology. The Gale Group. • Companies, products, applied technologies and markets. U.S. and international literature coverage, 1972 to date. Inquire as to online cost and availability. Provides abstracts from more than 1,600 publications. Weekly updates.

Wilson Business Abstracts Online. H. W. Wilson Co. • Indexes and abstracts 600 major business periodicals, plus the *Wall Street Journal* and the business section of the *New York Times*. Indexing is from 1982, abstracting from 1990, with the two newspapers included from 1993. Updated weekly. Inquire as to online cost and availability. (*Business Periodicals Index* without abstracts is also available online.).

PERIODICALS AND NEWSLETTERS

Advertising Age's Euromarketing. Crain Communications, Inc. • Weekly. $295.00 per year. Newsletter on European advertising and marketing.

Global Competitor. Faulkner & Gray, Inc. • Quarterly. $129.00 per year. Edited for executives of multinational corporations.

Journal of International Marketing. American Marketing Association. • Members $45.00; non-members, $80.00 per year institutions, $150.00 per year.

Market Research International. Euromonitor International. • Monthly. $1,130.00 per year. Emphasis is on international consumer market research. Includes International Market Review, Global Market Trends and Developments, USA Market Report, Japan Market Report, Emerging Markets, and Market Focus (concise country reports).

Pharma Business: The International Magazine of Pharmaceutical Business and Marketing. Engel Publishing Partners. • Eight times a year. $185.00 per year. Circulated mainly in European countries. Coverage includes worldwide industry news, new drug products, regulations, and research developments.

Retail Monitor International. Euromonitor International. • Monthly. $1,050.00 per year. Covers many aspects of international retailing, with emphasis on market research data. Includes profiles of leading retail groups, country profiles, retail news, trends, consumer credit information, and "Retail Factfile" (statistics).

Trade & Culture: How to Make it in the World Market. Key Communications Corp. • Quarterly. $29.95 per year. Edited for businesses actively involved in exporting or importing.

United States Import-Export Publications Co. New Media Productions. • Monthly. $48.00 per year.

RESEARCH CENTERS AND INSTITUTES

Institute for the Study of Business Markets. Pennsylvania State University, 402 Business Administration Bldg., University Park, PA 16802-3004. Phone: (814)863-2782 Fax: (814)863-0413 E-mail: isbm@psu.edu • URL: http://www.smeal.psu.edu/isbm/ • Research areas include international distribution channels.

STATISTICS SOURCES

Consumer Canada 1996. Available from The Gale Group. • 1996. $750.00. Published by Euromonitor. Provides consumer market, socioeconomic, and demographic data for Canada. Includes consumer market size (volume and value) for many specific kinds of products.

Consumer International 2000/2001. Available from The Gale Group. • 1998. $1,190.00. Seventh edition. Published by Euromonitor. Contains extensive consumer market, economic, and demographic data for 27 major, non-European countries, including the U. S. and Canada. Includes consumer market size (volume and value) for 150 product types in 14 categories (food, clothing, automobiles, cosmetics, appliances, etc.).

European Marketing Forecasts 2001. Available from The Gale Group. • 2000. $1,190.00. Third edition. Published by Euromonitor. Contains demographic, economic, and market forecasts for the countries of Europe to the year 2010. Forecasts include market-size data for 15 consumer product sectors (food, clothing, automobiles, consumer electronics, etc.).

Gale Country and World Rankings Reporter. The Gale Group. • 1997. $135.00. Second edition. Provides about 3,000 statistical ranking tables and charts covering more than 235 nations. Sources include the United Nations and various government publications.

International Marketing Forecasts 2001. Available from The Gale Group. • 2000. $1,090.00. Third edition. Published by Euromonitor. Contains demographic, economic, and market forecasts to the year 2010 for major, non-European countries, including the U. S. and Canada. Forecasts include market-size data for 15 consumer product sectors, such as food, clothing, and automobiles.

World Bank Atlas. The World Bank, Office of the Publisher. • Annual. Price on application. Contains "color maps, charts, and graphs representing the main social, economic, and environmental indicators for 209 countries and territories" (publisher).

World Consumer Income and Expenditure Patterns. Available from The Gale Group. • 2001. $650.00. Published by Euromonitor (http://www.euromonitor.com). Provides data on consumer income, earning power, and expenditures for 52 countries around the world.

World Development Indicators. World Bank, The Office of the Publisher. • Annual. $60.00. Provides data and information on the people, economy, environment, and markets of 148 countries. Emphasis is on statistics relating to major development issues.

World Market Share Reporter: A Compilation of Reported World Market Share Data and Rankngs on Companies, Products, and Services. The Gale Group. • 1999. $330.00. Fourth edition. Provides market share data for companies, products, and industries in countries or regions other than North America and Mexico.

World Retail Data and Statistics 1999/2000. Available from The Gale Group. • 2000. $1,190.00. Fourth edition. Published by Euromonitor. Provides detailed retail industry statistics for 51 countries.

OTHER SOURCES

Going Global: Getting Started in International Trade. American Management Association Extension Institute. • Looseleaf. $130.00. Self-study course. Emphasis is on practical explanations, examples, and problem solving. Quizzes and a case study are included.

Successful International Marketing: How to Gain the Global Advantage. American Management Association Extension Institute. • Looseleaf. $130.00. Self-study course. Emphasis is on practical explanations, examples, and problem solving. Quizzes and a case study are included.

World Consumer Income and Expenditure Patterns. Available from The Gale Group. • 2001. $990.00. Second edition. Two volumes. Published by Euromonitor. Provides data for 52 countries on consumer income, earning power, spending patterns, and savings. Expenditures are detailed for 75 product or service categories.

INTERNATIONAL MONETARY FUND (IMF)

GENERAL WORKS

Financial Institutions and Markets. Robert W. Kolb and Ricardo J. Rodriguez. Blackwell Publishers. • 1996. $77.95. Contains 40 articles (chapters) by various authors on U. S. financial markets and other topics. Includes separate chapters on the International Monetary Fund, inflation, monetary policy, the national debt, bank failures, derivatives, stock prices, initial public offerings, government bonds, pensions, foreign exchange, international markets, and other subjects.

ABSTRACTS AND INDEXES

PAIS International in Print. Public Affairs Information Service, Inc. • Monthly. $650.00 per year; cumulations three times a year. Provides topical citations to the worldwide literature of public affairs, economics, demographics, sociology, and trade. Text in English; indexed materials in English, French, German, Italian, Portuguese and Spanish.

BIBLIOGRAPHIES

International Monetary Fund: A Selected Bibliography. Anne C. Salda. Transaction Publishers. • 1992. $64.95.

CD-ROM DATABASES

PAIS on CD-ROM. Public Affairs Information Service, Inc. • Quarterly. $1,995.00 per year. Provides a CD-ROM version of the online service, *PAIS International.* Contains over 400,000 citations to the literature of contemporary social, political, and economic issues.

ONLINE DATABASES

PAIS International. Public Affairs Information Service, Inc. • Corresponds to the former printed publications, *PAIS Bulletin* (1976-90) and *PAIS Foreign Language Index* (1972-90), and to the current *PAIS International in Print* (1991 to date). Covers economic, political, and sociological material appearing in periodicals, books, government documents, and other publications. Updating is monthly. Inquire as to online cost and availability.

PERIODICALS AND NEWSLETTERS

Central Banking: Policy, Markets, Supervision. Available from European Business Publications, Inc. • Quarterly. $350.00 per year, including annual *Central Banking Directory.* Published in England by Central Banking Publications. Reports and comments on the activities of central banks around the world. Also provides discussions of the International Monetary Fund (IMF), the Organization for Economic Cooperation and Development (OECD), the Bank for International Settlements (BIS), and the World Bank.

IMF Survey. International Monetary Fund, Publication Services. • 23 times a year. $79.00 per year. Newsletter. Covers IMF activities in international finance, trade, commodities, and foreign exchange. Editions in English, French, and Spanish.

International Monetary Fund Staff Papers. International Monetary Fund, Publication Services. • Quarterly. Individuals, $56.00 per year; students, $28.00 per year. Contains studies by IMF staff members on balance of payments, foreign exchange, fiscal policy, and related topics.

RESEARCH CENTERS AND INSTITUTES

Center for International Policy. 1755 Massachusetts Ave., N. W., Suite 312, Washington, DC 20036. Phone: (202)232-3317 Fax: (202)232-3440 E-mail: cip@ciponline.org • URL: http://www.ciponline.org • Research subjects include the International Monetary Fund, the World Bank, and other international financial institutions. Analyzes the impact of policies on social and economic conditions in developing countries.

TRADE/PROFESSIONAL ASSOCIATIONS

Bretton Woods Committee. 1990 M St., N.W., Suite 450, Washington, DC 20036. Phone: (202)331-1616 Fax: (202)785-9423 E-mail: info@brettonwoods.org • URL: http://www.brettonwoods.org • Members are corporate executives, government officials, college administrators, bankers, and other "National Leaders." Seeks to inform and educate the public as to the activities of the International Monetary Fund, the World Bank, and other multinational development banking organizations. Promotes U. S. participation in multinational banking.

International Monetary Fund. 700 19th St., N.W., Washington, DC 20431. Phone: (202)623-7000 Fax: (202)623-4661.

INTERNATIONAL ORGANIZATIONS

See: INTERNATIONAL AGENCIES

INTERNATIONAL TAXATION

See also: MULTINATIONAL CORPORATIONS; TAX SHELTERS

GENERAL WORKS

Improving Access to Bank Information for Tax Purposes. Organization for Economic Cooperation and Development. • 2000. $66.00. Discusses ways to improve the international exchange of bank account information for tax determinations.

ABSTRACTS AND INDEXES

Accounting and Tax Index. UMI. • Quarterly. Price on application. Includes annual cumulative bound volume. Indexes accounting, auditing, and taxation literature appearing in journals, books, pamphlets, conference proceedings, and newsletters. (UMI is University Microfilms International, a Bell & Howell Co.).

Business Periodicals Index. H. W. Wilson Co. • Monthly, except August, with quarterly and annual cumulations. Service basis for print edition; CD-ROM edition, $1,495.00 per year.

Index to Legal Periodicals and Books. H. W. Wilson Co. • Monthly. Quarterly and annual cumulations. $270.00 per year. CD-ROM version available at $1,495.00 per year.

PAIS International in Print. Public Affairs Information Service, Inc. • Monthly. $650.00 per year; cumulations three times a year. Provides topical citations to the worldwide literature of public affairs, economics, demographics, sociology, and trade. Text in English; indexed materials in English, French, German, Italian, Portuguese and Spanish.

CD-ROM DATABASES

PAIS on CD-ROM. Public Affairs Information Service, Inc. • Quarterly. $1,995.00 per year. Provides a CD-ROM version of the online service, *PAIS International.* Contains over 400,000 citations to the literature of contemporary social, political, and economic issues.

The Tax Directory [CD-ROM]. Tax Analysts. • Quarterly. Provides *The Tax Directory* listings on CD-ROM, covering federal, state, and international tax officials, tax practitioners, and corporate tax executives.

DIRECTORIES

The Tax Directory. Tax Analysts. • Annual. $299.00. ($399.00 with quarterly CD-ROM updates.) Four volumes: *Government Officials Worldwide* (lists 15,000 state, federal, and international tax officials, with basic corporate and individual income tax rates for 100 countries); *Private Sector Professionals Worldwide* (lists 25,000 U.S. and foreign tax practitioners: accountants, lawyers, enrolled agents, and actuarial firms); *Corporate Tax Managers Worldwide* (lists 10,000 tax managers employed by U.S. and foreign companies).

ENCYCLOPEDIAS AND DICTIONARIES

Dictionary of Taxation. Simon James. Edward Elgar Publishing, Inc. • 1998. $65.00. Provides detailed definitions of terms relating to "various aspects of taxes and tax systems throughout the world.".

HANDBOOKS AND MANUALS

Corporate Taxes: Worldwide Summaries. Price Waterhouse Coopers. John Wiley and Sons, Inc. • 1999. $95.00. Summarizes the corporate tax regulations of more than 125 countries. Provides information useful for international tax planning and foreign investments.

Individual Taxes: Worldwide Summaries. PricewaterhouseCoopers. John Wiley and Sons, Inc. • 1999. $95.00. Summarizes the personal tax regulations of more than 125 countries. Provides information useful for international tax planning and foreign investments.

International Income Taxation: Code and Regulations, Selected Sections. CCH, Inc. • Annual. $66.95. Covers U. S. taxation of foreign entities and U. S. taxation of domestic entities having foreign income.

Practical Guide to U. S. Taxation of International Transactions. Robert E. Meldman and Michael S. Schadewald. CCH, Inc. • 2000. $99.00. Third edition. Contains three parts: Basic Principles, U. S. Taxation of Foreign Income, and U. S. Taxation of Foreign Persons.

INTERNET DATABASES

TAXNET. Carswell/Thomas Professional Publishing. Phone: 800-387-5164 or (416)609-3800 Fax: (416)298-5082 • URL: http://www.carswell.com/taxnet.htm • Fee-based Web site provides complete coverage of Canadian tax law and regulation, including income tax, provincial taxes, accounting, and payrolls. Daily updates. Base price varies according to product.

ONLINE DATABASES

Index to Legal Periodicals and Books (Online). H. W. Wilson Co. • Broad coverage of law journals and books 1981 to date. Monthly updates. Inquire as to online cost and availability.

Legal Resource Index. The Gale Group. • Broad coverage of law literature appearing in legal, business, and other periodicals, 1980 to date. Monthly updates. Inquire as to online cost and availability.

LEXIS. LEXIS-NEXIS. • The various LEXIS databases provide full text and indexing for a wide variety of legal cases, statutes, orders, and opinions.

PAIS International. Public Affairs Information Service, Inc. • Corresponds to the former printed publications, *PAIS Bulletin* (1976-90) and *PAIS Foreign Language Index* (1972-90), and to the current *PAIS International in Print* (1991 to date). Covers economic, political, and sociological material appearing in periodicals, books, government documents, and other publications. Updating is monthly. Inquire as to online cost and availability.

Wilson Business Abstracts Online. H. W. Wilson Co. • Indexes and abstracts 600 major business periodicals, plus the *Wall Street Journal* and the business section of the *New York Times.* Indexing is from 1982, abstracting from 1990, with the two newspapers included from 1993. Updated weekly. Inquire as to online cost and availability. (*Business Periodicals Index* without abstracts is also available online.).

PERIODICALS AND NEWSLETTERS

Highlights and Documents. Tax Analysts. • Daily. $2,249.00 per year, including monthly indexes. Newsletter. Provides daily coverage of IRS, congressional, judicial, state, and international tax developments. Includes abstracts and citations for "all tax documents released within the previous 24 to 48 hours." Annual compilation available *Highlights and Documents on Microfiche.*

International Tax Journal. Panel Publishers. • Quarterly. $195.00 per year. Articles, columns and tax notes pertaining to the international tax market.

International Tax Planners Alert. Research Institute of America, Inc. • Monthly. $150.00 per year. Newsletter.

International Tax Report: Maximizing Tax Opportunities Worldwide. I B C Donoghue Organization. • Monthly. $1,110.00 per year.

Journal of International Taxation. Warren, Gorham & Lamont/RIA Group. • Looseleaf service. $290.00 per year. Monthly updates. Edited for tax accountants and tax lawyers.

Tax Management International Forum. Bureau of National Affairs, Inc. • Quarterly. $370.00 per year.

Tax Management International Journal: A Monthly Professional Review of Current International Tax Developments. Bureau of National Affairs, Inc. • Monthly. $426.00 per year.

Tax Notes International. Tax Analysts. • Weekly. $949.00 per year. Newsletter. Provides "news and in-depth reports on a variety of international tax topics." Summarizes tax statutes, regulations, rulings, court decisions, and treaties from various countries of the world.

RESEARCH CENTERS AND INSTITUTES

International Tax Program. Harvard University, Pound Hall, Room 400, Cambridge, MA 02138. Phone: (617)495-4406 Fax: (617)495-0423 • URL: http://www.law.harvard.edu/programs/itp • Studies the worldwide problems of taxation, including tax law and tax administration.

STATISTICS SOURCES

Revenue Statistics. OECD Publications and Information Center. • Annual. $65.00. Presents data on government revenues in OECD countries, classified by type of tax and level of government. Text in English and French.

TRADE/PROFESSIONAL ASSOCIATIONS

International Tax Institute. 345 Park Ave., New York, NY 10154. Phone: (212)872-6729 Fax: (212)872-3311 • Mainly concerned with U. S. taxation of foreign income.

Tax Analysts. 6830 N. Fairfax Dr., Arlington, VA 22213. Phone: 800-955-3444 or (703)533-4400 Fax: (703)533-4444 E-mail: webmaster@tax.org • URL: http://www.tax.org • An advocacy group reviewing U. S. and foreign income tax developments. Includes a Tax Policy Advisory Board.

OTHER SOURCES

Foreign Tax and Trade Briefs. Matthew Bender & Co., Inc. • $470.00. Two looseleaf volumes. Periodic supplementation. The latest tax and trade information for over 100 foreign countries.

International Tax Agreements. United Nations Publications. • Irregular. Price varies. Looseleaf.

Manufacturers' Tax Alert. CCH, Inc. • Monthly. $297.00 per year. Newsletter. Covers the major tax issues affecting manufacturing companies. Includes current developments in various kind of federal, state, and international taxes: sales, use, franchise, property, and corporate income.

INTERNATIONAL TRADE

See: FOREIGN TRADE

INTERNET

See also: COMPUTER COMMUNICATIONS; ONLINE INFORMATION SYSTEMS; ELECTRONIC COMMERCE

GENERAL WORKS

The Amazing Internet Challenge: How Leading Projects Use Library Skills to Organize the Web. Amy T. Wells and others. American Library Association. • 1999. $45.00. Presents profiles of 12 digital libraries, such as the Agriculture Network Information Center and the Social Science Information Gateway. Emphasis is on how online indexes were created.

Corporate Internet Planning Guide: Aligning Internet Strategy with Business Goals. Richard J. Gascoyne and Koray Ozcubucku. John Wiley and Sons, Inc. • 1996. $34.95. Provides administrative advice on planning, developing, and managing corporate Internet or intranet functions. Emphasis is on strategic planning. (Business, Commerce, Management Series).

Cyberquake: How the Internet will Erase Profits, Topple Market Leaders, and Shatter Business Models. Michael Sullivan-Trainor. John Wiley & Sons, Inc. • 1997. $26.95. Predicts that the Internet will cause "an overwhelming shift in control of the worldwide marketplace" in the early 21st century. (Business Technology Series).

Digital Literacy: Personal Preparation for the Internet Age. Paul Gilster. John Wiley and Sons, Inc. • 1997. $22.95. Provides practical advice for the online consumer on how to evaluate various aspects of the Internet ("digital literacy" is required, as well as "print literacy").

The Emperor's Virtual Clothes: The Naked Truth About Internet Culture. Dinty Moore. Algonquin Books of Chapel Hill. • 1995. $17.95. A readable consideration of both positive and negative aspects of the Internet.

The Evolving Virtual Library: Practical and Philosophical Perspectives. Laverna M. Saunders, editor. Information Today, Inc. • 1999. $39.50. Second edition. Various authors cover trends in library and school use of the Internet, intranets, extranets, and electronic databases.

Highway of Dreams: A Critical View Along the Information Superhighway. A. Michael Noll. Lawrence Erlbaum Associates, Inc. • 1996. $49.95. States that such factors as consumer needs and finance are often of more importance to the information industry than technological utopia. Includes such chapter headings as "Historical Perspective," "History Repeats," "Business Considerations," and "The Internet Exposed." (LEA's Telecommunications Series).

The Individual Investor Revolution: Unlock the Secrets of Wall Street and Invest Like a Pro. Charles B. Carlson. McGraw-Hill. • 1998. $21.95. Emphasizes the growing importance of the individual investor, especially with regard to online trading (e-trading). Includes the author's favorite websites for investors and traders.

Interface Culture: How New Technology Transforms the Way We Create and Communicate. Steven Johnson. HarperCollins Publishers. • 1997. $24.00. A discussion of how computer interfaces and online technology ("cyberspace") affect society in general.

The Internet Bubble: Inside the Overvalued World of High-Tech Stocks, and What You Should Know to Avoid the Coming Catastrophe. Tony Perkins and Michael C. Perkins. HarperCollins Publishers, Inc. • 1999. $27.00. The authors predict a shakeout in e-commerce stocks and other Internet-related investments. (HarperBusiness.).

The Internet Initiative: Libraries Providing Internet Services and How They Plan, Pay, and Manage. Edward J. Valauskas and others. American Library Association. • 1995. $27.00. Provides 18 reports on Internet services in various kinds of libraries.

Librarians on the Internet: Impact on Reference Services. Robin Kinder, editor. Haworth Press, Inc. • 1994. $69.95. Contains discussions by various authors on library use of the Internet. (Reference Librarian Series, Nos. 41&42).

Management Information Systems: With Application Cases and Internet Primer. James A. O'Brien and others. McGraw-Hill Higher Education. • 1996. $85.00. Third edition. Includes CD-ROM.

Marketing on the Internet: Multimedia Strategies for the World Wide Web. Jill Ellsworth and Matthew Ellsworth. John Wiley and Sons, Inc. • 1996. $29.99. Second revised expanded edition.

Moving Toward More Effective Public Internet Access: The 1998 National Survey of Public Library Outlet Internet Connectivity. Available from U. S. Government Printing Office. • 1999. $16.00. Issued by the National Commission on Libraries and Information Science.

Net Curriculum: An Educator's Guide to Using the Internet. Linda Joseph. Information Today, Inc. • 1999. $29.95. Covers various educational aspects of the Internet. Written for K-12 teachers, librarians, and media specialists by a columnist for *Multimedia Schools.* (CyberAge Books.).

Net Income: Cut Costs, Boost Profits, and Enhance Operations Online. Wally Bock and Jeff Senne. John Wiley and Sons, Inc. • 1997. $29.95. "Net Income" in this case is hoped-for Internet income. Promotes the use of the Internet, intranet, and extranet to improve business operations or start new businesses. The authors take a nontechnical, business strategy approach.

Online Competitive Intelligence: Increase Your Profits Using Cyber-Intelligence. Helen P. Burwell. Facts on Demand Press. • 1999. $25.95. Covers the selection and use of online sources for competitive intelligence. Includes descriptions of many Internet Web sites, classified by subject.

Silicon Snake Oil: Second Thoughts on the Information Highway. Clifford Stoll. Doubleday. • 1996. $14.00. The author discusses the extravagant claims being made for online networks and multimedia.

Web Commerce: Building a Digital Business. Kate Maddox and Dana Blankenhorn. John Wiley and Sons, Inc. • 1998. $29.95. Provides advice on doing business or providing services through the Internet.

Web Visions: An Inside Look at Successful Business Strategies on the Net. Eugene Marlow. John Wiley and Sons, Inc. • 1996. $30.95. The author explains the techniques that have been used by various corporations for success on the World Wide Web.

Wired Neighborhood. Stephen Doheny-Farina. Yale University Press. • 1996. $32.00. The author examines both the hazards and the advantages of "making the computer the center of our public and private lives," as exemplified by the Internet and telecommuting.

ABSTRACTS AND INDEXES

Business Periodicals Index. H. W. Wilson Co. • Monthly, except August, with quarterly and annual cumulations. Service basis for print edition; CD-ROM edition, $1,495.00 per year.

Computer Literature Index: A Subject/Author Index to Computer and Data Processing Literature. Applied Computer Research, Inc. • Quarterly, with annual cumulation. $245.00 per year. Contains brief abstracts of book and periodical literature covering all phases of computing, including approximately 70 specific application areas.

F & S Index: United States. The Gale Group. • Monthly. $1,295.00 per year, including quarterly and annual cumulations. Provides annotated citations to marketing, business, financial, and industrial literature. Coverage of U. S. business activity includes trade journals, financial magazines, business newspapers, and special reports. Formerly *Predicasts F & S Index: United States.*

Key Abstracts: Computer Communications and Storage. Available from INSPEC, Inc. • Monthly. $240.00 per year. Provides international coverage of journal and proceedings literature, including material on optical disks and networks. Published in England by the Institution of Electrical Engineers (IEE).

Library Literature and Information Science: An Index to Library and Information Science Publications. H. W. Wilson Co. • Bimonthly. Annual cumulation. Service basis. Formerly *Library Literature.*

Microcomputer Abstracts. Information Today, Inc. • Quarterly. $225.00 per year. Provides abstracts covering a wide variety of personal and business microcomputer literature. Formerly *Microcomputer Index.*

ALMANACS AND YEARBOOKS

Annual Review of Information Science and Technology. Martha E. Williams, editor. Information Today, Inc. • Annual. Members, $79.95; non-members, $99.95. Published on behalf of the American Society for Information Science (ASIS). Covers trends in planning, basic techniques, applications, and the information profession in general.

Communication Technology Update. Butterworth-Heinemann. • Annual. $36.95. Reviews technological developments and statistical trends in five key areas: mass media, computers, consumer electronics, communications satellites, and telephony. Includes television, cellular phones, and the Internet. (Focal Press.).

CD-ROM DATABASES

Computer Select. The Gale Group. • Monthly. $1,250.00 per year. Provides one year of full-text on CD-ROM for 120 leading computer-related publications. Also includes 70,000 product specifications and brief profiles of 13,000 computer product vendors and manufacturers.

F & S Index Plus Text. The Gale Group. • Monthly. $7,575.00 per year. Provides CD-ROM citations to worldwide business, marketing, and industrial material appearing in a large assortment of trade journals, newspapers, and other publications. Time period is four years.

Hoover's Company Capsules on CD-ROM. Hoover's, Inc. • Quarterly. $349.95 per year (single-user). Provides the CD-ROM version of *Hoover's Handbook of American Business, Hoover's Handbook of Emerging Companies, Hoover's Handbook of World Business, Hoover's Guide to Computer Companies, Hoover's Guide to Media Companies, Hoover's Handbook of Private Companies,* and various regional guides. Includes more than 11,000 profiles of companies.

Multimedia Schools: A Practical Journal of Multimedia, CD-ROM, Online, and Internet in K-12. Information Today, Inc. • Bimonthly. $39.95 per year. Provides purchasing recommendations and technical advice relating to the use of high-tech multimedia products in schools.

WILSONDISC: Library Literature and Information Science Index. H. W. Wilson Co. • Quarterly. Including unlimited access to the online version of *Library Literature.* Provides CD-ROM indexing of about 300 periodicals, covering a wide range of topics having to do with libraries, library management, and the information industry.

WILSONDISC: Wilson Business Abstracts. H. W. Wilson Co. • Monthly. $2,495.00 per year, including unlimited online access to *Wilson Business Abstracts* through WILSONLINE. Provides CD-ROM "cover-to-cover" abstracting and indexing of over 600 prominent business periodicals. Indexing is from 1982, abstracting from 1990. (*Business Periodicals Index* without abstracts is available on CD-ROM at $1,495 per year.).

DIRECTORIES

Boardwatch Magazine Directory of Internet Service Providers. Penton Media Inc. • Monthly. $36.00 per year. Lists thousands of Internet service providers by state and telephone area code, with monthly fees, ISDN availability, and other information. Includes a "Glossary of Internet Terms" and detailed technical articles on accessing the Internet.

Cyberhound's Guide to Companies on the Internet. The Gale Group. • 1996. $79.00. Presents critical descriptions and ratings of more than 2,000 company or corporate Internet databases. Includes a glossary of Internet terms, a bibliography, and indexes.

Cyberhound's Guide to International Discussion Groups. Visible Ink Press. • 1996. $79.00 Second edition. Presents critical descriptions and ratings of more tha 4,400 Internet discussion groups (newsgroups) covering a wide variety of topics.

Cyberhound's Guide to Internet Libraries. The Gale Group. • 1996. 79.00. Presents critical descriptions and ratings of more than 2,000 library Internet databases. Includes a glossary of Internet terms, a bibliography, and indexes.

Cyberhound's Guide to People on the Internet. The Gale Group. • 1997. $79.00. Second edition. Provides descriptions of about 5,500 Internet databases maintained by or for prominent individuals in business, the professions, entertainment, and sports. Indexed by name, subject, and keyword (master index).

Cyberhound's Guide to Publications on the Internet. The Gale Group. • 1996. $79.00. First edition. Presents critical descriptions and ratings of more than 3,400 Internet databases of journals, newspapers, newsletters, and other publications. Includes a glossary of Internet terms, a bibliography, and three indexes.

Cyberstocks: An Investor's Guide to Internet Companies. Alan Chai. Hoover's, Inc. • 1996. $24.95. Provides detailed profiles of 101 publicly traded companies involved in one way or another with the Internet.

CyberTools for Business: Practical Web Sites that will Save You Time and Money. Wayne Harris. Hoover's, Inc. • 1997. $19.95. Describes 100 World Wide Web sites that are useful for business, investing, and job hunting. Also lists Web addresses for about 4,500 public and private companies.

Data Sources: The Comprehensive Guide to the Data Processing Industry Hardware, Data Communications Products, Software, Company Profiles. The Gale Group. • Semiannual. $495.00 per year. Two volumes. Describes hardware and software for all computer operating sysems, including prices and technical details. Lists about 75,000 products from 14,000 suppliers. Industry-specific software applications are described.

Dial Up! Gale's Bulletin Board Locator. The Gale Group. • 1996. $49.00. Contains access and other information for 10,000 computer bulletin boards in the U. S. Arranged geographically, with indexes to bulletin board names, organizations, and topics.

Finding Business Research on the Web: A Guide to the Web's Most Valuable Sites. MarketResearch.com. • Looseleaf. $175.00. Includes detailed rating charts. Contains profiles of the "100 best web sites.".

Fulltext Sources Online. Information Today, Inc. • Semiannual. $199.00 per year; $119.50 per issue. Lists more than 8,000 journals, newspapers, magazines, newsletters, and newswires found online in fulltext through DIALOG, LEXIS-NEXIS, Dow Jones, Westlaw, etc. Includes journals that have free Internet archives. (Formerly published by BiblioData.).

Gale Guide to Internet Databases. The Gale Group. • 1999. $120.00. Sixth edition. Presents critical descriptions and ratings of more than 5,000 useful Internet databases (especially World Wide Web sites). Includes a glossary of Internet terms, a bibliography, and five indexes.

Government Information on the Internet. Greg R. Notess. Bernan Associates. • Annual. $38.50. directory of publicly-accessible Internet sites maintained by the U. S. Government. Also includes selected foreign government sites, state sites, and non-government sites containing government-provided data.

Great Scouts! CyberGuides to Subject Searching on the Web. Margot Williams and others. Independent Publishers Group. • 1999. $24.95. Contains descriptions of selected Web sites, arranged by subject. Covers business, investments, computers, travel, the environment, health, social issues, etc. (CyberAge Books.).

Handbook of Internet Stocks. Mergent. • Annual. $19.95. Contains detailed financial information on more than 200 Internet-related corporations, including e-commerce firms and telecommunications hardware manufacturers. Lists and rankings are provided.

Harley Hahn's Internet and Web Yellow Pages. Harley Hahn. Osborne/McGraw-Hill. • Annual. $34.95. Lists World Wide Web sites in more than 100 categories.

Interactive Advertising Source. SRDS. • Quarterly. $561.00 per year. Provides descriptive profiles, rates, audience, personnel, etc., for producers of various forms of interactive or multimedia advertising: online/Internet, CD-ROM, interactive TV, interactive cable, interactive telephone, interactive kiosk, and others. Includes online supplement *SRDS' URlink.*

The Internet Blue Pages: The Guide to Federal Government Web Sites. Information Today, Inc. • Annual. $34.95. Provides information on more than 900 Web sites used by various agencies of the federal government. Includes indexes to agencies and topics. Links to all Web sites listed are available at http://www.fedweb.com. (CyberAge Books.).

The Internet Compendium: Guide to Resources by Subject: Subject Guides to Health and Science Resources. Joseph Jones and others, editors. Neal-Schuman Publishers, Inc. • 1995. $82.50. Editors are with the University of Michigan Internet Clearinghouse. Provides direct location access to "thousands" of Internet addresses, in a detailed subject arrangement, with critical analysis of content. Contains information databases, text archives, library catalogs, bulletin boards, newsletters, forums, etc. Includes topics in medicine, agriculture, biology, chemistry, mathematics, physics, engineering, computers, and science in general.

The Internet Compendium: Guide to Resources by Subject: Subject Guides to Social Sciences, Business, and Law Resources. Joseph James and others, editors. Neal-Schuman Publishers, Inc. • 1995. $82.50. Editors are with the University of Michigan Internet Clearinghouse. Provides direct location access to "thousands" of Internet addresses, in a detailed subject arrangement, with critical analysis of content. Contains information databases, text archives, library catalogs, bulletin boards, newsletters, forums, etc. Includes topics in economics, finance, taxation, history, population, civil rights law, law careers, women's studies, and so forth.

The Internet Compendium: Guide to Resources by Subject: Subject Guides to the Humanities. Louis Rosenfeld and others, editors. Neal-Schuman Publishers, Inc. • 1995. $82.50. Editors are with the University of Michigan Internet Clearinghouse. Provides direct location access to "thousands" of Internet addresses, in a detailed subject arrangement, with critical analysis of content. Contains information databases, text archives, library catalogs, bulletin boards, newsletters, forums, etc. Includes topics in literature, art, religion, philosophy, music, education, library science, games, magic, and the humanities in general.

Internet Industry Directory. Internet Industry Magazine. • Semiannual. Price on application. Lists products and services for Internet service providers. Includes Internet-related articles and interviews.

Internet Resources: A Subject Guide. Available from American Library Association. • 1995. $18.00. Published by Association of College and Research Libraries. Provides updated versions of Internet subject directories appearing originally in *College and Research Libraries News.*

Internet Resources and Services for International Business: A Global Guide. Lewis-Guodo Liu. Oryx Press. • 1998. $49.95. Describes more than 2,500 business-related Web sites from 176 countries. Includes five major categories: general information, economics, business and trade, business travel, and contacts. Indexed by Web site name, country, and subject.

Internet Tools of the Profession: A Guide for Information Professionals. Hope N. Tillman, editor. Special Libraries Association. • 1997. $49.00. Second edition. Consists of 14 sections by various authors or compilers. After two introductory articles on searching the Internet, there are 12 annotated lists of useful Web sites, covering the SLA, business and finance, chemistry, education, food and agriculture, information technology, insurance and employee benefits, law, library management, metals and materials, pharmaceuticals, and telecommunications. An index is provided.

Library Journal: Reference [year]: Print, CD-ROM, Online. Cahners Business Information. • Annual. Issued in November as supplement to *Library Journal.* Lists new and updated reference material, including general and trade print titles, directories, annuals, CD-ROM titles, and online sources. Includes material from more than 150 publishers, arranged by company name, with an index by subject. Addresses include e-mail and World Wide Web information, where available.

New Riders' Official World Wide Web Yellow Pages. Pearson Education and Technology. • 1997. $34.99. A broadly classified listing of Web sites, with brief descriptions of sites and a subject index to narrower topics. Includes a guide to using the Internet and a separate, alphabetical listing of more than 1,500 college and university Web sites, both U. S. and foreign. Includes CD-ROM.

OPAC Directory: A Guide to Internet-Accessible Online Public Access Catalogs. Information Today, Inc. • Annual. $70.00. Provides the Internet addresses of more than 1,400 online public access catalogs, U. S. and foreign. Includes information on library size, subject strengths, and search characteristics.

Plunkett's E-Commerce and Internet Business Almanac. Plunkett Research, Ltd. • Annual. $199.99. Contains detailed profiles of 250 large companies engaged in various areas of Internet commerce, including e-business Web sites, communications equipment manufacturers, and Internet service providers. Includes CD-ROM.

Plunkett's Employers' Internet Sites with Careers Information. Plunkett Research, Ltd. • Annual. $149.99. Includes diskette.

Plunkett's InfoTech Industry Almanac: Complete Profiles on the InfoTech 500-the Leading Firms in the Movement and Management of Voice, Data, and Video. Available from Plunkett Research, Ltd. • Annual. $149.99. Five hundred major information companies are profiled, with corporate culture aspects. Discusses major trends in various sectors of the computer and information industry, including data on careers and job growth. Includes several indexes.

Plunkett's On-Line Trading, Finance, and Investment Web Sites Almanac. Plunkett Research, Ltd. • Annual. $149.99. Provides profiles and usefulness rankings of financial Web sites. Sites are rated from 1 to 5 for specific uses. Includes diskette.

Prentice Hall Directory of Online Business Information. Christopher Engholm and Scott Grimes. Prentice Hall. • Annual. $34.95. Contains reviews of about 1,000 World Wide Web sites related to business. Sites are rated according to content, speed, and other factors.

The Software Encyclopedia: A Guide for Personal, Professional, and Business Users. R. R. Bowker. • Annual. $255.00. Two volumes. Volume one lists software programs by title and producer. Volume two provides information on programs according to application and operating system. Includes prices and requirements for hardware and memory.

Telehealth Buyer's Guide. Miller Freeman. • Annual. $10.00. Lists sources of telecommunications and information technology products and services for the health care industry.

Web Site Source Book: A Guide to Major U. S. Businesses, Organizations, Agencies, Institutions, and Other Information Resources on the World Wide Web. Omnigraphics, Inc. • Annual. $110.00. About 40,000 Web sites are arranged alphabetically by business or organization and by 1,350 subject categories. Surface mail addresses, phone numbers, fax numbers, and e-mail addresses are included.

World Directory of Business Information Web Sites. Available from The Gale Group. • 2001. $650.00. Fourth edition. Published by Euromonitor. Provides detailed descriptions of a wide variety of business-related Web sites. More than 1,500 sites are included from around the world. Covers statistics sources, market research, company information, rankings, surveys, economic data, etc.

ENCYCLOPEDIAS AND DICTIONARIES

Business Internet and Intranets: A Manager's Guide to Key Terms and Concepts. Peter G. W. Keen and others. Harvard Business School Press. • 1998. $39.95. Defines more than 100 words and phrases relating to the Internet or corporate intranets.

CyberDictionary: Your Guide to the Wired World. Knowledge Exchange LLC. • 1996. $17.95. Includes many illustrations.

Cyberspace Lexicon: An Illustrated Dictionary of Terms from Multimedia to Virtual Reality. Bob Cotton and Richard Oliver. Phaidon Press, Inc. • 1994. $29.95. Defines more than 800 terms, with manyillustrations. Includes a bibliography.

Cyberspeak: An Online Dictionary. Andy Ihnatko. Random House, Inc. • 1996. $12.95. An informal guide to the language of computers, multimedia, and the Internet.

Every Manager's Guide to Information Technology: A Glossary of Key Terms and Concepts for Today's Business Leader. Peter G. W. Keen. Harvard

Business School Press. • 1995. $18.95. Second edition. Provides definitions of terms related to computers, data communications, and information network systems. (Harvard Business Economist Reference Series).

Multimedia and the Web from A to Z. Patrick M. Dillon and David C. Leonard. Oryx Press. • 1998. $39.95. Second enlarged revised edition. Defines more than 1,500 terms relating to software and hardware in the areas of computing, online technology, telecommunications, audio, video, motion pictures, CD-ROM, and the Internet. Includes acronyms and an annotated bibliography. Formerly *Multimedia Technology from A to Z* (1994).

New Hacker's Dictionary. Eric S. Raymond. MIT Press. • 1996. $39.00. Third edition. Includes three classifications of hacker communication: slang, jargon, and "techspeak.".

HANDBOOKS AND MANUALS

The Art of Electronic Publishing: The Internet and Beyond. Sanford Ressler. Prentice Hall. • 1996. $39.95. Places emphasis on the World Wide Web. Includes information on document processors, standards, integration and management, with case studies.

Banking and Finance on the Internet. Mary J. Cronin, editor. John Wiley and Sons, Inc. • 1997. $45.00. Contains articles on Internet services, written by bankers, money mangers, investment analysts, and stockbrokers. Emphasis is on operations management. (Communications Series).

Basic Internet for Busy Librarians: A Quick Course for Catching Up. Laura K. Murray. American Library Association. • 1998. $26.00. A "practical crash-course primer" for learning how to effectively navigate the Internet and the World Wide Web.

Best Bet Internet: Reference and Research When You Don't Have Time to Mess Around. Shirley D. Kennedy. American Library Association. • 1997. $35.00. Provides advice for librarians and others on the effective use of World Wide Web information sources.

Beyond Book Indexing: How to Get Started in Web Indexing, Embedded Indexing, and Other Computer-Based Media. Diane Brenner and Marilyn Rowland, editors. Information Today, Inc. • 2000. $31.25. Published for the American Society of Indexers. Contains 12 chapters written by professional indexers. Part one discusses making an index by marking items in an electronic document (embedded indexing); part two is on indexing to make Web pages more accessible; part three covers CD-ROM and multimedia indexing; part four provides career and promotional advice for professionals in the field. Includes an index by Janet Perlman and a glossary.

Build a World Wide Web Commerce Center: Plan, Program, and Manage Internet Commerce for Your Company. Net-Genesis Staff. John Wiley and Sons, Inc. • 1996. $29.95. Covers business and marketing applications of the World Wide Web.

Building the Service-Based Library Web Site: A Step-by-Step Guide to Design and Options. Kristen L. Garlock and Sherry Piontek. American Library Association. • 1996. $30.00. Provides practical information for libraries planning a World Wide Web home page.

Click Here! Internet Advertising: How the Pros Attract, Design, Price, Place, and Measure Ads Online. Eugene Marlow. John Wiley and Sons, Inc. • 1997. $29.95. Covers pricing, effectiveness, Web site selection, content, and other aspects of Internet advertising. (Business Technology Series).

Compuserve Internet Tour Guide. Richard Wagner. Ventana Communications Group, Inc. • 1996. $34.95. A detailed guide to accessing various features of the Internet by way of the Compuserve online service.

The Cybrarian's Manual. Pat Ensor, editor. American Library Association. • 1996. $35.00. Provides information for librarians concerning the Internet, expert systems, computer networks, client/server architecture, Web pages, multimedia, information industry careers, and other "cyberspace" topics.

Electronic Selling: Twenty-Three Steps to E-Selling Profits. Brian Jamison and others. McGraw-Hill. • 1997. $24.95. Covers selling on the World Wide Web, including security and payment issues. Provides a glossary and directory information. The authors are consultants specializing in Web site production.

Electronic Styles: A Handbook for Citing Electronic Information. Xia Li and Nancy Crane. Information Today, Inc. • 1996. $19.99. Second edition. Covers the citing of text-based information, electronic journals, Web sites, CD-ROM items, multimedia products, and online documents.

The Essential Guide to Bulletin Board Systems. Patrick R. Dewey. Information Today, Inc. • 1998. $39.50. Provides details on the setup and operation of online bulletin board systems. Covers both hardware and software.

Exporting with the Internet. Peter J. Robinson and Jonathan Powell. John Wiley and Sons, Inc. • 1997. $39.95. Explains how the Internet can help with finding overseas buyers and expediting export shipments and payments. (Business Technology Series).

The Extreme Searcher's Guide to Web Search Engines: A Handbook for the Serious Searcher. Randolph Hock. Information Today, Inc. • 1999. $34.95. Provides detailed information and advice on effective use of the major Internet search engines. (CyberAge Books.).

Find It Online: The Complete Guide to Online Research. Alan M. Schlein and others. National Book Network. • 1998. $19.95. Presents the general principles of online searching for information about people, phone numbers, public records, news, business, investments, etc. Covers both free and fee-based sources. (BRB Publications.).

Finding It on the Internet: The Internet Navigator's Guide to Search Tools and Techniques. Paul Gilster. John Wiley and Sons, Inc. • 1996. $24.95. Second expanded revised edition. A basic guide to efficient use of the World Wide Web, search engines, e-mail, hypertext, and the Internet in general. Includes such programs or systems as Gopher, Archie, Veronica, and Jughead, with emphasis on information searching.

Finding Market Research on the Web: Best Practices of Professional Researchers. Robert I. Berkman. MarketResearch.com. • 1999. $235.00. Provides tips and techniques for locating useful market research data through the Internet.

Finding Statistics Online: How to Locate the Elusive Numbers You Need. Paula Berinstein. Information Today, Inc. • 1998. $29.95. Provides advice on efficient searching when looking for statistical data on the World Wide Web or from commercial online services and database producers. (CyberAge Books.).

The Geek's Guide to Internet Business Success: The Definitive Business Blueprint for Internet Developers, Programmers, Consultants, Marketers, and Serivce Providers. Bob Schmidt. John Wiley and Sons, Inc. • 1997. $22.95. Written for beginning Internet entrepreneurs, especially those with technical expertise but little or no business experience. Covers fee or rate setting, developing new business, product mix, budgeting, partnerships, personnel, and planning. Includes checklists and worksheets.

Guide to EU Information Sources on the Internet. Euroconfidentiel S. A. • Annual. $220.00. Contains descriptions of more than 1,700 Web sites providing information relating to the European Union and European commerce and industry. Includes a quarterly e-mail newsletter with new sites and address changes.

International Business Information on the Web: Searcher Magazine's Guide to Sites and Strategies for Global Business Research. Sheri R. Lanza and Barbara Quint. Information Today, Inc. • 2001. $29.95. (CyberAge Books.).

Internet Book: Everything You Need to Know About Computer Networking and How the Internet Works. Douglas Comer. Simon and Schuster Trade. • 1997. $32.50. Second edition.

Internet Business Handbook. Daniel Dern. Prentice Hall. • 1997. $29.95.

Internet Insider. Ruffin Prevost. Osborne/McGraw-Hill. • 1995. $14.95. A colorful presentation. (Internet Series).

Internet Power Tools. John Ross. Alfred A. Knopf, Inc. • 1995. $40.00.

Internet Research Guide: A Concise, Friendly, and Practical Handbook for Anyone Researching in the Wide World of Cyberspace. Timothy K. Maloy. Allworth Press. • 1999. $18.95. Revised edition. Provides "hype-free" advice on practical use of the World Wide Web.

The Internet Troubleshooter: Help for the Logged-On and Lost. Nancy R. John and Edward J. Valauskas. American Library Association. • 1994. $27.00. A basic question-and-answer guide to the Internet. Includes illustrations and a glossary.

Learning Web Design: A Beginner's Guide to HTML, Graphics, and Beyond. Jennifer Niederst. O'Reilly & Associates, Inc. • 2001. $34.95. Written for beginners who have no previous knowledge of how Web design works.

Legal Liability Problems in Cyberspace: Craters in the Information Highway. T. R. Halvorson. Burwell Enterprises, Inc. • 1998. $24.50. Covers the legal risks and liabilities involved in doing online research as a paid professional. Includes a table of cases.

Managing Public-Access Computers: A How-To-Do-It Manual for Librarians. Donald A. Barclay. Neal-Schuman Publishers, Inc. • 2000. $59.95. Part one covers hardware, software, and other components. Part two discusses computers users. Part three is about systems management, library policy, and legal issues.

More Internet Troubleshooter: New Help for the Logged-On and Lost. Nancy R. John and Edward J. Valauskas. American Library Association. • 1998. $36.00. A question-and-answer sequel to *Internet Troubleshooter: Help for the Logged-On and Lost.*

The Mosaic Navigator TM: The Essential Guide to the Internet Interface. Paul Gilster. John Wiley and Sons, Inc. • 1995. $16.95. Explains how to use the Mosaic graphical user interface.

NetResearch: Finding Information Online. Daniel J. Barrett. Thomson Learning. • 1997. $24.95. A guide to "power searching" on the Internet, with emphasis on the intricacies of search engines.

The New Internet Business Book. Jill H. Ellsworth and Matthew V. Ellsworth. John Wiley and Sons,

Inc. • 1996. $24.95. Second edition. A basic guide to internet business opportunities and market research.

The Official America Online Internet Guide. David Peal. Ventana Communications Group, Inc. • 1999. $24.95. Provides a detailed explanation of the various features of versio of America Online, including electronic mail procedures and "Using the Internet.".

Online Deskbook: Online Magazine's Essential Desk Reference for Online and Internet Searchers. Mary E. Bates. Information Today, Inc. • 1996. $29.95. Covers the World Wide Web, as well as America Online, CompuServe, Dialog, Lexis-Nexis, and all other major online services. (Pemberton Press Books.).

Online Marketing Handbook: How to Promote, Advertise and Sell, Your Products and Services on the Internet. Daniel S. Janal. John Wiley and Sons, Inc. • 1998. $29.95. Revised edition. Provides step-by-step instructions for utilizing online publicity, advertising, and sales promotion. Contains chapters on interactive marketing, online crisis communication, and Web home page promotion, with numerous examples and checklists.

Secrets of the Super Net Searchers: The Reflections, Revelations and Hard-Won Wisdom of 35 of the World's Top Internet Researchers. Reva Basch. Information Today, Inc. • 1996. $29.95. Tells how to find "cyber-gems" among the "cyber-junk." (Cyber Age Books.).

Web Style Guide: Basic Design Principles for Creating Web Sites. Patrick J. Lynch and Sarah Horton. Yale University Press. • 1999. $35.00. Covers design of content, interface, page layout, graphics, and multimedia aspects.

Windows Internet Tour Guide: Cruising the Internet the Easy Way. Michael Fraase and Phil James. Ventana Communications Group, Inc. • 1995. $29.95. Second edition., An introduction to the Internet via Windows software.

World Wide Web Troubleshooter: Help for the Ensnared and Entangled. Nancy R. John and Edward J. Valauskas. American Library Association. • 1998. $36.00. Covers all aspects of the WWW in question-and-answer format.

INTERNET DATABASES

InfoTech Trends. Data Analysis Group. Phone: (707)894-9100 Fax: (707)486-5618 E-mail: support@infotechtrends.com • URL: http://www.infotechtrends.com • Web site provides both free and fee-based market research data on the information technology industry, including computers, peripherals, telecommunications, the Internet, software, CD-ROM/DVD, e-commerce, and workstations. Fees: Free for current (most recent year) data; more extensive information has various fee structures. Formerly *Computer Industry Forecasts.*

Interactive Week: The Internet's Newspaper. Ziff Davis Media, Inc. 28 E. 28th St., New York, NY 10016. Phone: (212)503-3500 Fax: (212)503-5680 E-mail: iweekinfo@zd.com • URL: http://www.zd.com • Weekly. $99.00 per year. Covers news and trends relating to Internet commerce, computer communications, and telecommunications.

Internet Business Intelligence: How to Build a Big Company System on a Small Company Budget. David Vine. Information Today, Inc. 143 Old Marlton Pike, Medford, NJ 08055-8750. Phone: 800-300-9868 or (609)654-6266 Fax: (609)654-4309 E-mail: custserv@infotoday.com • URL: http://www.infotoday.com • 2000. $29.95. Covers the obtaining of valuable business intelligence data through use of the Internet.

Internet Publishing Magazine. North American Publishing Co. 401 North Broad St., Philadelphia, PA 19108. Phone: (215)238-5300 Fax: (215)238-5457 • URL: http://www.ipubmag.com • Eight times a year. Controlled circulation. Edited for print publishers, online-only publishers, web designers, advertising agencies, and others concerned with the publishing of content through the Web.

Internet Tools of the Profession. Special Libraries Association. Phone: (202)234-4700 Fax: (202)265-9317 E-mail: hope@tiac.net • URL: http://www.sla.org/pubs/itotp • Web site is designed to update the printed *Internet Tools of the Profession.* Provides links to a wide range of useful databases in business, finance, industry, information technology, insurance, law, library management, telecommunications, and other subject areas. Fees: Free.

Internet.com: The E-Business and Internet Technology Network. Internet.com Corp. Phone: (212)547-7900 Fax: (212)953-1733 E-mail: info@internet.com • URL: http://www.internet.com • Web site provides a wide variety of information relating to Internet commerce, search engines, news, Web design, servers, browsers, Java, service providers, advertising, marketing, etc. Online searching is offered. Fees: Free. (Formerly produced by Mecklermedia Corp.).

SAEGIS Internet Search. Thomson & Thomson. Phone: 800-692-8833 or (617)479-1600 Fax: (617)786-8273 E-mail: support@thomson-thomson.com • URL: http://www.thomson-thomson.com • Fee-based Web site provides extensive, common law screening of the World Wide Web for trademarks. Searches are performed offline, with final report delivered to user's "SAEGIS Inbox." Context of trademark within each relevant Web site is indicated, and links are provided.

Search Engine Watch: You Want Answers?. Internet.com Corp. Phone: (212)547-7900 Fax: (212)953-1733 • URL: http://www.searchenginewatch.com • Web site offers information on various aspects of search engines, including new developments, indexing systems, technology, ratings and reviews of major operators, specialty services, tutorials, news, history, "Search Engine EKGs," "Facts and Fun," etc. Online searching is provided. Fees: Free. Formerly *A Webmaster's Guide to Search Engines.*

Wired News. Wired Digital, Inc. Phone: (415)276-8400 Fax: (415)276-8499 E-mail: newsfeedback@wired.com • URL: http://www.wired.com • Provides summaries and full-text of "Top Stories" relating to the Internet, computers, multimedia, telecommunications, and the electronic information industry in general. These news stories are placed in the broad categories of Politics, Business, Culture, and Technology. Affiliated with *Wired* magazine. Fees: Free.

ONLINE DATABASES

F & S Index. The Gale Group. • Contains about four million citations to worldwide business, financial, and industrial or consumer product literature appearing from 1972 to date. Weekly updates. Inquire as to online cost and availability.

Globalbase. The Gale Group. • Provides more than one million online summaries of business, industrial, and economic news reports from more than 1,000 publications worldwide. Covers a wide range of material appearing in international trade journals, professional magazines, and newspapers. Time period is 1984 to date, with weekly updates. Inquire as to online cost and availability.

Internet and Personal Computing Abstracts. Information Today, Inc. • Contains abstracts covering a wide variety of personal and business microcomputer literature appearing in more than 100 journals and popular magazines. Time period is 1981 to date, with monthly updates. Formerly *Microcomputer Index.* Inquire as to online cost and availability.

Law of the Super Searchers: The Online Secrets of Top Legal Researchers. T. R. Halvorson and Reva Basch. Information Today, Inc. • 1999. $24.95. Eight law researchers explain how to find useful legal information online. (CyberAge Books.).

Library Literature Online. H. W. Wilson Co. • Contains online indexing of a wide variety of library and information science literature from 1984 to date, with updating quarterly. Inquire as to online cost and availability.

Mastering Online Investing: How to Use the Internet to Become a More Successful Investor. Michael C. Thomsett. Dearborn Financial Publishing. • 2001. $19.95. Emphasis is on the Internet as an information source for intelligent investing, avoiding "speculation and fads.".

Microcomputer Software Guide Online. R. R. Bowker. • Provides information on more than 30,000 microcomputer software applications from more than 4,000 producers. Corresponds to printed *Software Encyclopedia,* but with monthly updates. Inquire as to online cost and availability.

PROMT: Predicasts Overview of Markets and Technology. The Gale Group. • Companies, products, applied technologies and markets. U.S. and international literature coverage, 1972 to date. Inquire as to online cost and availability. Provides abstracts from more than 1,600 publications. Weekly updates.

Super Searchers Cover the World: The Online Secrets of International Business Researchers. Mary E. Bates and Reva Basch. Information Today, Inc. • 2001. $24.95. Presents interviews with 15 experts in the area of online searching for international business information. (CyberAge Books.).

Super Searchers in the News: The Online Secrets of Journalists and News Researchers. Paula J. Hane and Reva Basch. Information Today, Inc. • 2000. $24.95. Contains online searching advice from 10 professional news researchers and fact checkers. (CyberAge Books.).

Super Searchers on Health and Medicine: The Online Secrets of Top Health and Medical Researchers. Susan M. Detwiler and Reva Basch. Information Today, Inc. • 2000. $24.95. Provides the results of interviews with 10 experts in online searching for medical research data and healthcare information. Discusses both traditional sources and Web sites. (CyberAge Books.).

Super Searchers on Mergers & Acquisitions: The Online Secrets of Top Corporate Researchers and M & A Pros. Jan Tudor and Reva Basch. Information Today, Inc. • 2001. $24.95. Presents the results of interviews with 13 "top M & A information pros." Covers the finding, evaluating, and delivering of relevant data on companies and industries. (CyberAge Books.).

Super Searchers on Wall Street: Top Investment Professionals Share Their Online Research Secrets. Amelia Kassel and Reva Basch. Information Today, Inc. • 2000. $24.95. Gives the results of interviews with "10 leading financial industry research experts." Explains how online information is used by stock brokers, investment bankers, and individual investors. Includes relevant Web sites and other sources. (CyberAge Books.).

Wilson Business Abstracts Online. H. W. Wilson Co. • Indexes and abstracts 600 major business periodicals, plus the *Wall Street Journal* and the business section of the *New York Times*. Indexing is from 1982, abstracting from 1990, with the two newspapers included from 1993. Updated weekly. Inquire as to online cost and availability. (*Business Periodicals Index* without abstracts is also available online.).

PERIODICALS AND NEWSLETTERS

BiblioData's Price Watcher: The Researcher's Guide to Online Prices. BiblioData. • Semimonthly. Individuals $129.00 per year; institutions, $169.00 per year; nonprofit organizations, $129.00 per year. Newsletter. Provides detailed analysis and reviews of pricing schemes used by Internet and other online information providers.

Boardwatch Magazine: Guide to the Internet, World Wide Web, and BBS. Penton Media Inc. • Monthly. $72.00 per year. Covers World Wide Web publishing, Internet technology, educational aspects of online communication, Internet legalities, and other computer communication topics.

CIO: The Magazine for Information Executives. CIO Communications. • Semimonthly. $89.00 per year. Edited for chief information officers. Includes a monthly "Web Business" section (incorporates the former *WebMaster* periodical) and a monthly "Enterprise" section for company executives other than CIOs.

The CyberSkeptic's Guide to Internet Research. BiblioData. • 10 times a year. $104.00 per year; nonprofit organizations, $159.00 per year. Newsletter. Presents critical reviews of World Wide Web sites and databases, written by information professionals. Includes "Late Breaking News" of Web sites.

Digital Publishing Technologies: How to Implement New Media Publishing. Information Today, Inc. • Monthly. $196.00 per year. Covers online and CD-ROM publishing, including industry news, new applications, new products, electronic publishing technology, and descriptions of completed publishing projects.

EContent. Online, Inc. • Bimonthly. $55.00 per year. Directed at professional online information searchers. Formerly *Database*.

Financial Service Online. Faulkner & Gray, Inc. • Monthly. $95.00 per year. Covers the operation and management of interactive financial services to consumers in their homes for banking, investments, and bill-paying.

Future Banker: The Vision of Leadership in an Electronic Age. American Banker. • Monthly. $79.00 per year. Covers technology innovation for the banking industry, including online banking.

The Industry Standard: The Newsmagazine of the Internet Economy. International Data Group, Inc. • Weekly. $76.00 per year. Presents news and trends affecting the Internet and intranet industries.

InfoAlert: Your Expert Guide to Online Business Information. Economics Press, Inc. • Monthly. $129.00 per year. Newsletter. Provides information on recommended World Wide Web sites in various business, marketing, industrial, and financial areas.

The Information Freeway Report: Free Business and Government Information Via Modem. Washington Researchers Ltd. • Monthly. $160.00 per year. Newsletter. Provides news of business and government databases that are available free of charge through the Internet or directly. Emphasis is on federal government databases and electronic bulletin boards (Fedworld).

Information Outlook: The Monthly Magazine of the Special Libraries Association. Special Libraries Association. • Monthly. $65.00 per year. Topics include information technology, the Internet, copyright, research techniques, library management, and professional development. Replaces *Special Libraries* and *SpeciaList*.

Information Standards Quarterly: News About Library, Information Sciences, and Publishing Standards. National Information Standards Organization (NISO). • Quarterly. $80.00 per year. Newsletter. Reports on activities of the National Information Standards Organization.

InterActive Consumers. MarketResearch.com. • Monthly. $395.00 per year. Newsletter. Covers the emerging markets for digital content, products, and services. Includes market information on telecommuting, online services, the Internet, online investing, and other areas of electronic commerce.

Interactive Content: Consumer Media Strategies Monthly. Jupiter Media Metrix. • Monthly. $675.00 per year; with online edition, $775.00 per year. Newsletter. Covers the broad field of providing content (information, news, entertainment) for the Internet/World Wide Web.

Interactive Home: Consumer Technology Monthly. Jupiter Media Metrix. • Monthly. $625.00 per year. Newsletter on devices to bring the Internet into the average American home. Covers TV set-top boxes, game devices, telephones with display screens, handheld computer communication devices, the usual PCs, etc.

Interactive Marketing and P R News: News and Practical Advice on Using Interactive Advertising and Marketing to Sell Your Products. Phillips Business Information, Inc. • Biweekly. $495.00 per year. Newsletter. Provides information and guidance on merchandising via CD-ROM ("multimedia catalogs"), the Internet, and interactive TV. Topics include "cybermoney", addresses for e-mail marketing, "virtual malls," and other interactive subjects. Formerly *Interactive Marketing News*.

Internet and Electronic Commerce Strategies: Using Technology to Improve Your Bottom Line. Computer Economics, Inc. • Monthly. $387.00 per year. Newsletter on management strategies for making money from the Internet. Compares online marketing with traditional marketing.

Internet Business Report: Software, Tools and Platforms. Jupiter Media Metrix. • Semimonthly. $695.00 per year; with electronic software, $795.00 per year. Newsletter. Covers Internet advertising, fee collection, and attempts in general to make the Internet/World Wide Web profitable. Includes news of how businesses are using the Internet for sales promotion and public relations.

Internet Connection: Your Guide to Government Resources. Glasser Legalworks. • 10 times a year. $89.00 per year. Newsletter (print) devoted to finding free or low-cost U. S. Government information on the Internet. Provides detailed descriptions of government Web sites.

Internet Marketing and Technology Report: Advising Marketing, Sales, and Corporate Executives on Online Opportunities. Computer Economics, Inc. • Monthly. $387.00 per year. Newsletter. Covers strategic marketing, sales, advertising, public relations, and corporate communications, all in relation to the Internet. Includes information on "cutting-edge technology" for the Internet.

Internet Marketing Report: News and Advice to Help Companies Harness the Power of the Internet to Achieve Business Objectives. Progressive Business Publications. • Semimonthly. $299.00 per year. Newsletter. Covers Internet marketing strategy, site traffic, success stories, technology, cost control, and other Web site advertising and marketing topics.

Internet Reference Services Quarterly: A Journal of Innovative Information Practice, Technologies, and Resources. Haworth Press, Inc. • Quarterly. Individuals, $36.00 per year; libraries and other institutions, $48.00 per year. Covers both theoretical research and practical applications.

Internet Retailer: Merchandising in an Age of Virtual Stores. Faulkner & Gray, Inc. • Bimonthly. $82.95. Covers the selling of retail merchandise through the Internet.

Internet Search Advantage: Professional's Guide to Internet Searching. Z-D Journals. • Monthly. $199.00 per year. Newsletter. Covers Internet research, utilities, agents, configurations, subject searches, search theory, etc. Emphasis is on the efficient use of various kinds of search engines. Includes E-mail alert service.

Internet Telephony Magazine: The Authority on Voice, Video, Fax, and Data Convergence. Technology Marketing Corp. • Monthly. $29.00 per year. Covers the business and technology of telephone and other communications service via the Internet.

Internet World: The Voice of E-Business and Internet Technology. Internet World Media. • Semimonthly. Edited for "Internet professionals." Includes industry news, new products, e-business news, and technical developments. (Formerly *WebWeek*.).

Internetweek: The Newspaper for the Communications Industry. CMP Publications, Inc. • 48 times a year. $175.00 per year. Edited for professionals involved with the Internet, intranets, and extranets. Formerly *Communications Week*.

Journal of Internet Cataloging: The International Quarterly of Digital Organization, Classification, and Access. Haworth Press, Inc. • Quarterly. Individuals, $40.00 per year; libraries and other institutions, $85.00 per year.

Journal of Internet Law. Aspen Law and Business. • Monthly. $295.00 per year. Covers such Internet and e-commerce topics as domain name disputes, copyright protection, Uniform Commercial Code issues, international law, privacy regulation, electronic records, digital signatures, liability, and security.

Multimedia Schools: A Practical Journal of Multimedia, CD-Rom, Online and Internet in K-12. Information Today, Inc. • Five times a year. $39.95 per year. Edited for school librarians, media center directors, computer coordinators, and others concerned with educational multimedia. Coverage includes the use of CD-ROM sources, the Internet, online services, and library technology.

The Net: The Ultimate Guide to the Internet. Imagine Publishing, Inc. • Monthly. $24.95 per year. Consumer magazine for users of the Internet. Features reviews and ratings of Internet software, sites (destinations), and publications. Includes articles on basic procedures for beginners.

Network World: The Newsweekly of Enterprise Network Computing. Network World Inc. • Weekly. $129.00 per year. Includes special feature issues on enterprise Internets, network operating systems, network management, high-speed modems, LAN management systems, and Internet access providers.

Online Marketplace. Jupiter Media Metrix. • Monthly. $695.00 per year. Newsletter on the collection of electronic payments ("e-money") for goods and services offered through the Internet. Covers trends in retailing, banking, travel, and other areas.

Silicon Alley Reporter. Rising Tide Studios. • Monthly. $29.95 per year. Covers the latest trends in e-commerce, multimedia, and the Internet.

Tele.com: Business and Technology for Public Network Service Providers. CMP Publications, Inc. • 14 times a year. $125.00 per year. Edited for executives and managers at both traditional telephone companies and wireless communications companies. Also provides news and information for Internet services providers and cable TV operators.

Telecom Business: Opportunities for Network Service Providers, Resellers, and Suppliers in the Competitive Telecom Industry. MultiMedia Publishing Corp. • Monthly. $56.95 per year. Provides business and technical information for telecommunications executives in various fields.

Telehealth Magazine. Miller Freeman. • Bimonthly. $50.00 per year. Covers Internet, wireless, and other telecommunications technologies for health care professionals.

Upgrade. Software and Information Industry Association. • Monthly. $75.00 per year. Covers news and trends relating to the software, information, and Internet industries. Formerly *SPA News* from Software Publisers Association.

*Virtual City: *The City Magazine of Cyberspace.* Virtual Communications, Inc. • Quarterly. $11.80 per year. Covers new developments in World Wide Web sites, access, software, and hardware.

Web Feet: The Internet Traveler's Desk Reference. RockHill Communications. • Monthly. $165.00 per year. Looseleaf. Serves as a subject guide to the "best" Web sites.

Web Marketing Update: Quick, Actionable, Internet Intelligence for Marketing Executives. Computer Economics, Inc. • Monthly. $347.00 per year. Newsletter on various aspects of promoting or selling products and services through an Internet Web site: technology, advertising, strategy, customer base, cost projections, search engines, etc.

Web Techniques: Solutions for Internet and World Wide Web Developers. Miller Freeman, Inc. • Monthly. $34.95 per year. A technical magazine edited for Internet and World Wide Web professionals.

WebFinance. Securities Data Publishing. • Semimonthly. $995.00 per year. Newsletter (also available online at www.webfinance.net). Covers the Internet-based provision of online financial services by banks, online brokers, mutual funds, and insurance companies. Provides news stories, analysis, and descriptions of useful resources. (Securities Data Publishing is a unit of Thomson Financial.).

Wired. Wired Ventures Ltd. • Monthly. $24.00 per year. Edited for creators and managers in various areas of electronic information and entertainment, including multimedia, the Internet, and video. Often considered to be the primary publication of the "digital generation.".

Wireless Integration: Solutions for Enterprise Decision Makers. PennWell Corp., Advanced Technology Div. • Bimonthly. $48.00 per year. Edited for networking and communications managers. Special issues cover the wireless office, wireless intranet/Internet, mobile wireless, telemetry, and buyer's guide directory information.

Wireless Review: Intelligence for Competitive Providers. Intertec Publishing Corp. • Semimonthly. $48.00 per year. Covers business and technology developments for wireless service providers. Includes special issues on a wide variety of wireless topics. Formed by merger of *Cellular Business* and *Wireless World.*

RESEARCH CENTERS AND INSTITUTES

Advanced Networking Research Group. Washington University, Campus Box 1045, St. Louis, MO 63130-4899. Phone: (314)935-8552 Fax: (314)935-7302 E-mail: jst@cs.wustl.edu • Research fields include the design of high speed internetworks and the design of host interfaces.

Bibliographical Center for Research, Inc., Rocky Mountain Region. 14394 E. Evans Ave., Aurora, CO 80014-1478. Phone: 800-397-1552 or (303)751-6277 Fax: (303)751-9787 E-mail: admin@bec.org • URL: http://www.ber.org • Fields of research include information retrieval systems, Internet technology, CD-ROM technology, document delivery, and library automation.

Columbia Institute for Tele-Information. Columbia University, Columbia Business School, 3022 Broadway, Uris Hall, Suite 1A, New York, NY 10027. Phone: (212)854-4222 Fax: (212)932-1471 E-mail: noam@columbia.edu • URL: http://www.vii.org • Areas of research include private and public networking, the economics of networks, pricing of network access, and economics of technology adoption in the public network.

Information Sciences Institute. University of Southern California, 4676 Admiralty Way, Suite 1001, Marina del Rey, CA 90292. Phone: (310)822-1511 Fax: (310)823-6714 • URL: http://www.isi.edu • Research fields include online information and computer science, with emphasis on the World Wide Web.

Super Searchers Go to the Source: The Interviewing and Hands-On Information Strategies of Top Primary Researchers - Online, On the Phone, and In Person. Risa Sacks and Reva Basch. Information Today, Inc. 143 Old Marlton Pike, Medford, NJ 08055-8750. Phone: 800-300-9868 or (609)654-6266 Fax: (609)654-4309 E-mail: custserv@infotoday.com • URL: http://www.infotoday.com • 2001. $24.95. Explains how information-search experts use various print, electronic, and live sources for competitive intelligence and other purposes. (CyberAge Books.).

STATISTICS SOURCES

Inter-NOT: Online & Internet Statistics Reality Check. Bruce Kushnick. New Networks Institute. • Annual. $495.00. Compares, analyzes, and criticizes statistics issued by Nielsen Media, Forrester Research, FIND/SVP, Yankelovich Partners and many others relating to online and Internet activities. For example, estimates of the number of Internet users have ranged from about 40 million down to six million. Topics include "Adjusting for the Puffery" and "The Most Plausible Statistics.".

OECD Information Technology Outlook 2000: ICTs, E-Commerce and the Information Economy. Organization for Economic Cooperation and Development. • 2000. $72.00. Provides data on information and communications technology (ICT) and electronic commerce in 11 OECD nations (includes U. S.). Coverage includes network infrastructure, electronic payment systems, financial transaction technologies, intelligent agents, global navigation systems, and portable flat panel display technologies.

Standard & Poor's Industry Surveys. Standard & Poor's. • Semiannual. $1,800.00. Two looseleaf volumes. Includes monthly supplements. Provides detailed, individual surveys of 52 major industry groups. Each survey is revised on a semiannual basis. Also includes "Monthly Investment Review" (industry group investment analysis) and monthly "Trends & Projections" (economic analysis).

Statistical Handbook on Technology. Paula Berinstein, editor. Oryx Press. • 1999. $65.00. Provides statistical data on such items as the Internet, online services, computer technology, recycling, patents, prescription drug sales, telecommunications, and aerospace. Includes charts, tables, and graphs. Edited for the general reader. (Statistical Handbook Series).

TRADE/PROFESSIONAL ASSOCIATIONS

Association for Interactive Media. 1301 Connecticut Ave. N.W., 5th Fl., Washington, DC 20036-5105. Phone: (202)408-0008 Fax: (202)408-0111 E-mail: info@interactivehg.org • URL: http://www.interactivehg.org • Members are companies engaged in various interactive enterprises, utilizing the Internet, interactive television, computer communications, and multimedia.

Electronic Frontier Foundation. 1550 Bryant St., Suite 725, San Francisco, CA 94103. Phone: (415)436-9333 Fax: (415)436-9993 E-mail: info@eff.org • URL: http://www.eff.org • Members are individuals with an interest in computer-based communications. Promotes electronic communication civil liberties and First Amendment rights.

Internet Alliance. P.O. Box 65782, Washington, DC 20035-5782. Phone: (202)955-8091 Fax: (202)955-8081 E-mail: ia@internetalliance.org • URL: http://www.internetalliance.org • Members are companies associated with the online and Internet industry. Promotes the Internet as "the global mass market medium of the 21st century." Concerned with government regulation, public policy, industry advocacy, consumer education, and media relations. Formerly Interactive Services Association.

Internet Society. 11150 Sunset Hills Rd., Suite 100, Reston, VA 20190-5321. Phone: (703)326-9880 Fax: (703)326-9881 E-mail: membership@isoc.org • URL: http://www.isoc.org • Members are technical personnel, corporations, business people, students, and others with an interest in Internet applications and technology.

National Information Standards Organization. 4733 Bethesda Ave., Suite 300, Bethesda, MD 20814-5248. Phone: (301)654-2512 Fax: (301)654-1721 E-mail: nisohq@niso.org • URL: http://www.niso.org • Develops and promotes technical standards for the information industry and libraries, including the Z39.50 protocol for Internet database searching.

Software and Information Industry Association. 1730 M St., N. W., Suite 700, Washington, DC 20036-4510. Phone: (202)452-1600 Fax: (202)223-8756 • URL: http://www.siia.net • A trade association for the software and digital content industry. Divisions are Content, Education, Enterprise, Financial Information Services, Global, and Internet. Includes an Online Content Committee. Formerly Software Publishers Association.

Special Interest Group on Hypertext, Hypermedia, and Web. Association for Computing Machinery, 1515 Broadway, New York, NY 10036. Phone: (212)869-7440 Fax: (212)302-5826 E-mail: sigs@acm.org • URL: http://www.acm.org/sigweb • Concerned with the design, use, and evaluation of hypertext and hypermedia systems. Provides a multi-disciplinary forum for the promotion, dissemination, and exchange of ideas relating to research technologies and applications. Publishes the *SIGWEB Newsletter* three times a year.

OTHER SOURCES

Broadband Solutions. North American Publishing Co. • Monthly. Controlled circulation. Covers the high-bandwidth telecommunications industry, including new products and emerging technologies.

Broadband Week. Cahners Business Information. • Semimonthly. Controlled circulation. Provides news and trends for all parts of the evolving broadband industry, including operations, marketing, finance, and technology.

Consumer Internet Economy. Jupiter Media Metrix. • 1999. $3,495.00. Market research report. Provides data and forecasts relating to various hardware and software elements of the Internet, including browsers, provision of service, telephone line modems, cable modems, wireless access devices, online advertising, programming languages, and Internet chips. Includes company profiles.

Consumer Online Services Report. Jupiter Media Metrix. • Annual. $1,895.00. Market research report. Provides analysis of trends in the online information industry, with projections of growth in future years (five-year forecasts). Contains profiles of electronic media companies.

eMarketer's eAdvertising Report. Available from MarketResearch.com. • 1999. $795.00. Market research data published by eMarketer. Covers the growth of the Internet online advertising market. Includes future trends and Internet users'attitudes.

Fat Pipe: The Business of Marketing Broadband Services. Dagda Mor Media, Inc. • Monthly. Controlled circulation. Edited for those who plan, develop, and market broadband Internet and telecommunications services.

Infogate. Infogate, Inc. • Web site provides current news and information on seven "channels": News, Fun, Sports, Info, Finance, Shop, and Travel. Among the content partners are Business Wire, CBS MarketWatch, CNN, Morningstar, Standard & Poor's, and Thomson Investors Network. Fees: Free, but downloading of Infogate software is required (includes personalized news feature). Updating is continuous. Formerly Pointcast Network.

Inter-NOT: The Terrible Twos-Online Industry's Learning Curve. Bruce Kushnick. New Networks Institute. • 1996. $495.00. Second edition. A market research report discussing the growing pains of the online industry, especially with regard to the Internet. The importance of market segmentation and customer service is emphasized.

Internet Payments Report. Jupiter Media Metrix. • Annual. $1,095.00. Market research report. Provides data, comment, and forecasts on the collection of electronic payments ("e-money") for goods and services offered through the Internet.

The Invisible Web: Uncovering Information Sources Search Engines Can't See. Chris Sherman and Gary Price. Information Today, Inc. • 2001. $29.95. A guide to Web sites from universities, libraries, associations, government agencies, and other sources that are inadequately covered by conventional search engines (see also http://www.invisible-web.net). (CyberAge Books.).

Key Note Market Report: Home Shopping. Jupiter Media Metrix. • Irregular. $365.00. Market research report. Covers "interactive retailing," mainly through the Internet and television, with predictions of future trends. Formerly *Key Note Report: Home Shopping.*

Major Information Technology Companies of the World. Available from The Gale Group. • 2001. $885.00. Third edition. Published by Graham & Whiteside. Contains profiles of more than 2,600 leading information technology companies in various countries.

net.people: The Personalities and Passions Behind the Web Sites. Eric C. Steinert and Thomas E. Bleier. Information Today, Inc. • 2000. $19.95. Presents the personal stories of 36 Web "entrepreneurs and visionaries." (CyberAge Books.).

Online Advertising Report. Jupiter Media Metrix. • Annual. $750.00. Market research report. Provides five-year forecasts of Internet advertising and subscription revenue. Contains analysis of online advertising trends and practices, with company profiles.

Online Banking. MarketResearch.com. • 2000. $3,450.00. Market research report. Includes demographics relating to the users and nonusers of online banking services. Provides market forecasts.

The Quintessential Searcher: The Wit and Wisdom of Barbara Quint. Marylaine Block, editor. Information Today, Inc. • 2001. $19.95. Presents the sayings of Barbara Quint, editor of *Searcher* magazine, who is often critical of the online information industry. (CyberAge Books.).

Telecommunications Regulation: Cable, Broadcasting, Satellite, and the Internet. Matthew Bender & Co., Inc. • Looseleaf. $700.00. Four volumes. Semiannual updates. Covers local, state, and federal regulation, with emphasis on the Telecommunications Act of 1996. Includes regulation of television, telephone, cable, satellite, computer communication, and online services. Formerly *Cable Television Law.*

World Online Markets. Jupiter Media Metrix. • Annual. $1,895.00. Market research report. Provides broad coverage of worldwide Internet and online information business activities, including country-by-country data. Includes company profiles and five-year forecasts or trend projections.

INTERNET COMMERCE

See: ELECTRONIC COMMERCE

INTERNSHIP PROGRAMS

DIRECTORIES

The Internship Bible. Random House, Inc. • Annual. $25.00. Compiled by the staff of the Princeton Review. Lists internships in various fields.

National Directory of Internships. National Society for Experiential Education. • Biennial. $33.95. Lists many internships in 85 corporate, nonprofit, and government areas.

Peterson's Internships: More Than 40,000 Opportunities to Get an Edge in Today's Competitive Job Market. Peterson's. • Annual. $24.95. Lists about 40,000 career-oriented internships in a wide variety of fields, including business.

Yale Daily News Guide to Internships. Simon & Schuster Trade. • Annual. $25.00. Compiled by the staff of the Yale Daily News. Lists internships in various fields.

TRADE/PROFESSIONAL ASSOCIATIONS

National Society for Experiential Education. 1703 N. Beauregard St., Alexandria, VA 22311-1717. Phone: (919)787-3263 Fax: (919)787-3381 E-mail: info@nsee.org • URL: http://www.nsee.org • Members include representatives of internship programs.

INTERPERSONAL RELATIONS

See: HUMAN RELATIONS

INTERSTATE COMMERCE

See also: MOTOR VEHICLE LAW AND REGULATION

ENCYCLOPEDIAS AND DICTIONARIES

Macmillan Encyclopedia of Transportation. Available from The Gale Group. • 2000. $375.00. Six volumes. Published by Macmillan Reference USA. Covers the business, technology, and history of transportation on land, on water, in the air, and in space. Includes definitions, cross-references, and 200 color illustrations.

STATISTICS SOURCES

Transportation Statistics Annual Report. Available from U. S. Government Printing Office. • Annual. $21.00. Issued by Bureau of Transportation Statistics, U. S. Department of Transportation. Provides data on operating revenues, expenses, employees, passenger miles (where applicable), and other factors for airlines, automobiles, buses, local transit, pipelines, railroads, ships, and trucks.

TRADE/PROFESSIONAL ASSOCIATIONS

Association for Transportation Law, Logistics, and Policy. 19564 Club House Rd., Montgomery Village, MD 20886-3002. Phone: (301)670-6733 Fax: (301)670-6735 E-mail: atllp@aol.com • URL: http://www.transportlink.com/atllp.

OTHER SOURCES

Federal Carriers Reports. CCH, Inc. • Biweekly. $1,372.00 per year. Four looseleaf volumes. Periodic supplementation. Federal rules and regulations for motor carriers, water carriers, and freight forwarders.

INTERVIEWING

See also: COUNSELING

GENERAL WORKS

Encyclopedia of Careers and Vocational Guidance. Holli Cosgrove. Ferguson Publishing Co. • 2000. $159.95. 11th edition.

Interviewing Principles and Practices. Charles J. Stewart and William B. Cash. Brown and Benchmark. • 1997. $40.00. Eighth edition.

The Perfect Interview: How to Get the Job You Really Want. John D. Drake. AMACOM. • 1996. $17.95. Second edition. Contains advice for jobseekers on how to control an interview and deal with difficult questions. Includes examples of both successful and unsuccessful interviews.

Sweaty Palms: The Neglected Art of Being Interviewed. H. Anthony Medley. Ten Speed Press. • 1991. $8.95. Revised edition.

ABSTRACTS AND INDEXES

Psychological Abstracts. American Psychological Association. • Monthly. Members, $799.00 per year; individuals and institutions, $1,075.00 per year. Covers the international literature of psychology and the behavioral sciences. Includes journals, technical reports, dissertations, and other sources.

ENCYCLOPEDIAS AND DICTIONARIES

Blackwell Encyclopedic Dictionary of Human Resource Management. Lawrence H. Peters and Charles R. Greer, editors. Blackwell Publishers. • 1996. $105.95. The editors are associated with Texas Christian University. Contains definitions of key terms combined with longer articles written by various U. S. and foreign business educators. Includes bibliographies and index. (Blackwell Encyclopedia of Management Series).

HANDBOOKS AND MANUALS

Fair, Square, and Legal: Safe Hiring, Managing, and Firing Practices to Keep You and Your Company Out of Court. Donald Weiss. AMACOM. • 1999. $29.95. Third edition. Covers recruiting, interviewing, sexual discrimination, evaluation of employees, disipline, defamation charges, and wrongful discharge.

The Five Minute Interview: A New and Powerful Approach to Interviewing. Richard H. Beatty. John Wiley and Sons, Inc. • 1997. $14.95. Second edition. Advice for job applicants.

Hiring Right: A Practical Guide. Susan J. Herman. Sage Publications, Inc. • 1993. $46.00. A practical manual covering job definition, recruitment, interviewing, testing, and checking of references.

How to Get Results from Interviewing: A Practical Guide for Operating Management. James M. Black. Krieger Publishing Co. • 1982. $22.00. Reprint of 1970 edition.

Recruiter's Research Blue Book: A How-To Guide for Researchers, Search Consultants, Corporate Recruiters, Small Business Owners, Venture Capitalists, and Line Executives. Andrea A. Jupina. Kennedy Information. • 2000. $179.00. Second edition. Provides detailed coverage of the role that research plays in executive recruiting. Includes such practical items as "Telephone Interview Guide," "Legal Issues in Executive Search," and "How to Create an Execuive Search Library." Covers both person-to-person research and research using printed and online business information sources. Includes an extensive directory of recommended sources. Formerly *Handbook of Executive Search Research.*

Recruiting, Interviewing, Selecting, and Orienting New Employees. Diane Arthur. AMACOM. • 1998. $59.95. Third edition. A practical guide to the basics of hiring, including legal considerations and sample forms.

Studying Your Workforce: Applied Research Methods and Tools for the Training and Development Practitioner. Alan Clardy. Sage Publications, Inc. • 1997. $45.00. Describes how to apply specific research methods to common training problems. Emphasis is on data collection methods: testing, observation, surveys, and interviews. Topics include performance problems and assessment.

ONLINE DATABASES

PsycINFO. American Psychological Association. • Provides indexing and abstracting of the worldwide literature of psychology and the behavioral sciences. Time period is 1967 to date, with monthly updates. Inquire as to online cost and availability.

RESEARCH CENTERS AND INSTITUTES

Super Searchers Go to the Source: The Interviewing and Hands-On Information Strategies of Top Primary Researchers - Online, On the Phone, and In Person. Risa Sacks and Reva Basch. Information Today, Inc. 143 Old Marlton Pike, Medford, NJ 08055-8750. Phone: 800-300-9868 or (609)654-6266 Fax: (609)654-4309 E-mail: custserv@infotoday.com • URL: http://www.infotoday.com • 2001. $24.95. Explains how information-search experts use various print, electronic, and live sources for competitive intelligence and other purposes. (CyberAge Books.).

OTHER SOURCES

How to Interview Effectively. American Management Association Extension Institute. • Looseleaf. $110.00. Self-study course on employment, performance, evaluation, disciplinary, and exit interviewing. Emphasis is on practical explanations, examples, and problem solving. Quizzes and a case study are included.

INTRANETS (COMPUTER NETWORKS)

GENERAL WORKS

The Evolving Virtual Library: Practical and Philosophical Perspectives. Laverna M. Saunders, editor. Information Today, Inc. • 1999. $39.50. Second edition. Various authors cover trends in library and school use of the Internet, intranets, extranets, and electronic databases.

The Human Side of Intranets: Content, Style, and Politics. Thom Dupper. Saint Lucie Press. • 1997. $54.95. A nontechnical, general discussion of corporate intranets.

The Interactive Corporation: Using Interactive Media and Intranets to Enhance Business Performance. Roger Fetterman. Reference Information Publishing. • 1997. $30.00. Presents corporate case studies of successful "networked interactive media in business processes.".

Intranets: What's the Bottom Line?. Randy J. Hinrichs. Prentice Hall. • 1997. $29.95. Explains the practical value of intranets for business communication.

ENCYCLOPEDIAS AND DICTIONARIES

Business Internet and Intranets: A Manager's Guide to Key Terms and Concepts. Peter G. W. Keen and others. Harvard Business School Press. • 1998. $39.95. Defines more than 100 words and phrases relating to the Internet or corporate intranets.

HANDBOOKS AND MANUALS

Building and Managing the Corporate Intranet. Ronald L. Wagner and others. McGraw-Hill. • 1997. $34.95.

The Corporate Intranet: Create and Manage an Internal Web for your Organization. Ryan Bernard. John Wiley and Sons, Inc. • 1997. $29.99. Second edition.

Hands-On Intranets. Vasanthan S. Dasan and others. Prentice Hall. • 1997. $39.95. A realistic guide to setting up and administering an intranet.

Managing the Corporate Intranet. Mitra Miller and others. John Wiley and Sons, Inc. • 1998. $39.99. Written for intranet managers and administrators. Includes checklists.

The Modem Reference: The Complete Guide to PC Communications. Michael A. Banks. Information Today, Inc. • 2000. $29.95. Fourth edition. Covers personal computer data communications technology, including fax transmissions, computer networks, modems, and the Internet. Popularly written.

INTERNET DATABASES

InfoTech Trends. Data Analysis Group. Phone: (707)894-9100 Fax: (707)486-5618 E-mail: support@infotechtrends.com • URL: http://www.infotechtrends.com • Web site provides both free and fee-based market research data on the information technology industry, including computers, peripherals, telecommunications, the Internet, software, CD-ROM/DVD, e-commerce, and workstations. Fees: Free for current (most recent year) data; more extensive information has various fee structures. Formerly *Computer Industry Forecasts.*

PERIODICALS AND NEWSLETTERS

Business Communications Review. BCR Enterprises, Inc. • Bimonthly. $45.00 per year. Edited for communications managers in large end-user companies and institutions. Includes special feature issues on intranets and network management.

Communications News: Solutions for Today's Networking Decision Managers. Nelson Publishing, Inc. • Monthly. Free to qualified personnel; others, $79.00 per year. Includes coverage of "Internetworking" and "Intrenetworking." Emphasis is on emerging telecommunications technologies.

The Industry Standard: The Newsmagazine of the Internet Economy. International Data Group, Inc. • Weekly. $76.00 per year. Presents news and trends affecting the Internet and intranet industries.

Internetweek: The Newspaper for the Communications Industry. CMP Publications, Inc. • 48 times a year. $175.00 per year. Edited for professionals involved with the Internet, intranets, and extranets. Formerly *Communications Week.*

Intranet and Networking Strategies Report: Advising IT Decision Makers on Best Practices and Current Trends. Computer Economics, Inc. • Monthly. $395.00 per year. Newsletter. Edited for information technology managers. Covers news and trends relating to a variety of corporate computer network and management information systems topics. Emphasis is on costs.

Intranet News. Publications Resource Group. • Monthly. $545.00 per year. Newsletter. Covers intranet applications, products, services, and company implementation.

IntraNet Professional: IntraNet Applications and Knowledge Management for Libraries and Information Professionals. Information Today, Inc. • Bimonthly. $79.95 per year. Newsletter on the use of Internet technology for local library networks.

Wireless Integration: Solutions for Enterprise Decision Makers. PennWell Corp., Advanced Technology Div. • Bimonthly. $48.00 per year. Edited for networking and communications managers. Special issues cover the wireless office, wireless intranet/Internet, mobile wireless, telemetry, and buyer's guide directory information.

Wireless Review: Intelligence for Competitive Providers. Intertec Publishing Corp. • Semimonthly. $48.00 per year. Covers business and technology developments for wireless service providers. Includes special issues on a wide variety of wireless topics. Formed by merger of *Cellular Business* and *Wireless World.*

INTRAOCULAR LENS INDUSTRY

See: CONTACT LENS AND INTRAOCULAR LENS INDUSTRIES

INTRAPRENEURS

See: ENTREPRENEURS AND INTRAPRENEURS

INVENTIONS

See also: NEW PRODUCTS; PATENTS

GENERAL WORKS

World of Invention: History's Most Significant Inventions and the People Beh ind Them. The Gale Group. • 1999. $105.00. Second edition.

ABSTRACTS AND INDEXES

Index of Patents Issued from the United States Patent and Trademark Office, Part One: List of Patentees. Available from U. S. Government Printing Office. • Annual. Lists patentees and reissue patentees for each year.

Index of Patents Issued from the United States Patent and Trademark Office, Part Two: Index to Subjects of Invention. Available from U. S. Government Printing Office. • Annual. A subject index to patents issued each year, arranged by class and subclass numbers. Includes a list of patent and tradmark depository libraries.

NTIS Alerts: Government Inventions for Licensing. National Technical Information Service. • Semimonthly. $270.00 per year. Identifies new inventions available from various government agencies. Covers a wide variety of industrial and technical areas. Formerly *Abstract Newsletter.*

HANDBOOKS AND MANUALS

Inventing and Patenting Sourcebook. The Gale Group. • 1992. $95.00. Second edition. A general guide for inventors. Contains how-to-do-it text, information sources, and sample forms.

Inventors Desktop Companion: A Guide to Successfully Marketing and Protecting Your Ideas. Richard C. Levy. Visible Ink Press. • 1998. $24.95. Second edition. Explains how to patent, trademark, or copyright an idea. Includes a listing of 2,000 associations and services for inventors.

PERIODICALS AND NEWSLETTERS

Official Gazette of the United States Patent and Trademark Office: Patents. Available from U. S. Government Printing Office. • Weekly. $1,425.00 per year. ($1,700.00 per year by first class mail.) Contains the Patents, Patent Office Notices, and Designs issued each week (http://www.uspto.gov). Annual indexes are sold separately.

TRADE/PROFESSIONAL ASSOCIATIONS

American Society of Inventors. P.O. Box 58426, Philadelphia, PA 19102-8426. Phone: (215)546-6601 Fax: (610)623-2165.

Inventors Workshop International Education Foundation. 1029 Castillo St., Santa Barbara, CA 93101-3736. Phone: (805)967-5722 Fax: (805)899-4927 • URL: http://www.ideahelp.com.

INVENTORY CONTROL

See also: PRODUCTION CONTROL

GENERAL WORKS

Inventory Control and Management. C. D. Waters. John Wiley and Sons, Inc. • 1992. $129.95.

Lessons to be Learned Just in Time. James J. Cammarano. Engineering and Management Press. • 1997. $34.95. Discusses the background, theory, and practical application of just-in-time (JIT) inventory control in manufacturing.

Principles of Inventory and Materials Management. Richard J. Tersine. Prentice Hall. • 1993. $60.80. Fourth edition. Includes material on just-in-time inventory systems.

Strategic Supply Management: A Blueprint for Revitalizing the Manufacturer-Supplier Partnership. Keki R. Bhote. AMACOM. • 1989. $65.00. How to reduce the expense of supply management and improve quality, delivery time, and inventory control.

ABSTRACTS AND INDEXES

Business Periodicals Index. H. W. Wilson Co. • Monthly, except August, with quarterly and annual cumulations. Service basis for print edition; CD-ROM edition, $1,495.00 per year.

ENCYCLOPEDIAS AND DICTIONARIES

Blackwell Encyclopedic Dictionary of Operations Management. Nigel Slack, editor. Blackwell Publishers. • 1997. $105.95. The editor is associated with the University of Warwick, England. Contains definitions of key terms combined with longer articles written by various U. S. and foreign business educators. Includes bibliographies and index. (Blackwell Encyclopedia of Management Series.).

ONLINE DATABASES

Wilson Business Abstracts Online. H. W. Wilson Co. • Indexes and abstracts 600 major business periodicals, plus the *Wall Street Journal* and the business section of the *New York Times*. Indexing is from 1982, abstracting from 1990, with the two newspapers included from 1993. Updated weekly. Inquire as to online cost and availability. (*Business Periodicals Index* without abstracts is also available online.).

PERIODICALS AND NEWSLETTERS

Journal of Supply Chain Management: A Global Review of Purchasing and Supply. National Association of Purchasing Management. • Quarterly. $59.00 per year. Formerly *International Journal of Purchasing and Materials Management.*

Production and Inventory Management Journal. APICS: The Educational Society for Resource Management. • Quarterly. Members, $64.00 per year; non-members, $80.00 per year.

RESEARCH CENTERS AND INSTITUTES

Board of Research. Babson College, Babson Park, MA 02457. Phone: (718)239-5339 Fax: (718)239-6416 • URL: http://www.babson.edu/bor • Research areas include management, entrepreneurial characteristics, and multi-product inventory analysis.

Center for Business and Industrial Studies. University of Missouri-St. Louis, School of Business Administration, 8001 Natural Bridge Rd., St. Louis, MO 63121. Phone: (314)516-5857 Fax: (314)516-6420 E-mail: ldsmith@.umsl.edu • URL: http://www.umsl.edu/~cbis/cbis.html • Research fields include inventory and management control. Specific projects also include development of computer software for operations in public transit systems.

Center for Entrepreneurial Studies and Development, Inc. West Virginia University, College of Engineering and Mineral Resources, P.O. Box 6107, Morgantown, WV 26506-6107. Phone: (304)293-3612 Fax: (304)293-6707 E-mail: byrd@cemr.wvu.edu • URL: http://www.cesd.wvu.edu • Inventory control systems included as a research field.

Engineering Systems Research Center. University of California at Berkeley. 3115 Etcheverry Hall, No. 1750, Berkeley, CA 94720-1750. Phone: (510)642-4994 Fax: (510)643-8982 E-mail: esrc@esrc.berkeley.edu • URL: http://www.esrc.berkeley.edu/esrc/.

TRADE/PROFESSIONAL ASSOCIATIONS

APICS-The Educational Society for Resource Management. 5301 Shawnee Rd., Alexandria, VA 22312. Phone: 800-444-2742 or (703)354-8851 Fax: (703)354-8106 • URL: http://www.apics.org • Members are professional resource managers.

INVESTMENT ADVISORY SERVICES

See also: INVESTMENTS; STOCKS

GENERAL WORKS

The Fortune Sellers: The Big Business of Buying and Selling Predictions. William A. Sherden. John Wiley and Sons, Inc. • 1997. $29.95. The author states that predictions are notoriously unreliable in any field, including the stock market, the economy, and the weather. (Forecasters in all areas don't have to be right; they just have to be interesting.).

DIRECTORIES

Directory of Registered Investment Advisors. Money Market Directories, Inc. • Annual. $450.00. Lists over 14,000 investment advisors and advisory firms. Indicates services offered, personnel, and amount of assets being managed. Formerly *Directory of Registered Investment Advisors with the Securities and Exchange Commission.*

Investment Council of American Directory of Member Firms. Investment Counsel Association of America. • Annual. Free.

Money Market Directory of Pension Funds and Their Investment Managers. Money Market Directories, Inc. • Annual. $995.00. Institutional funds and managers.

SIE Guide to Investment Publications: The Only Directory of Investment Advisory Publications for Investors. George H. Wein, editor. Select Information Exchange. • Annual. Free. Provides descriptions and prices of about 100 financial newsletters covering stocks, bonds, mutual funds, commodity futures, options, gold, and foreign investments. Offers subscription services, including short trials of any 20 investment newsletters for a total of $11.95. Formerly *SIE Market Letter Directory.*

ONLINE DATABASES

F & S Index. The Gale Group. • Contains about four million citations to worldwide business, financial, and industrial or consumer product literature appearing from 1972 to date. Weekly updates. Inquire as to online cost and availability.

PERIODICALS AND NEWSLETTERS

Bull and Bear Financial Newspaper. • Monthly. $29.00 per year. Each issue includes a digest of advice from investment advisory newsletters.

Dick Davis Digest. Dick Davis Publishing, Inc. • Semimonthly. $180.00 per year. Newsletter. A digest of investment advisory services.

The Hulbert Financial Digest. Hulbert Financial Digest, Inc. • Monthly. $135.00 per year. Trial subscriptions available. Rates the performance of investment advisory newsletters and services. Includes a stock market sentiment index based on bullish, bearish, or neutral opinions of advisors. Subscription includes *HFD's Thirteen-Year Longer Term Performance Report* and *HFD's Financial Newsletter Directory.*

Investor's Digest. Institute for Econometric Research. • Monthly. $60.00 per year. Newsletter. Contains digests of investment advice from a wide variety of advisory services.

Investors Intelligence. Michael Burke, editor. Chartcraft, Inc. • Biweekly. $184.00 per year. Monitors about 130 investment advisory services and prints summaries of advice from about half of them in each issue. Provides numerical index of bearish sentiment among services.

Moneypaper. • Monthly. $81.00 per year. Newsletter. Provides general investment advice, including summaries from other investment advisory services. Emphasis is on company-sponsored dividend reinvestment plans. Subscription includes annual directory: *The Moneypaper's Guide to Dividend Reinvestment Plans.*

Wall Street Digest. Wall Street Digest, Inc. • Monthly. $150.00 per year. Digest of investment advice from leading financial advisors.

TRADE/PROFESSIONAL ASSOCIATIONS

Association for Investment Management and Research. 560 Ray C. Hunt Dr., Charlottesville, VA 22903-0668. Phone: 800-247-8132 or (804)951-5499 Fax: (804)951-5262 E-mail: info@aimr.org • URL: http://www.aimr.org.

Investment Counsel Association of America. 1050 17th St., N.W., Suite 725, Washington, DC 20036-5503. Phone: (202)293-4222 Fax: (202)293-4223 E-mail: icaa@icaa.org • URL: http://www.icaa.org.

INVESTMENT ANALYSIS

See: FINANCIAL ANALYSIS

INVESTMENT BANKING

BIOGRAPHICAL SOURCES

Who's Who in Finance and Industry. Marquis Who's Who. • Biennial. $295.00. Provides over 22,400 concise biographies of business leaders in all fields.

Who's Who in the Securities Industry. Securities Industry Association. Economist Publishing Co. •

Annual. Price on application about 1,000 investment bankers.

CD-ROM DATABASES

Buyout Financing Sources/M & A Intermediaries. Securities Data Publishing. • Annual. $895.00. Provides the CD-ROM combination of *Directory of Buyout Financing Sources* and *Directory of M & A Intermediaries.* Contains information on more than 1,000 financing sources (banks, insurance companies, venture capital firms, etc.) and 850 intermediaries (corporate acquirers, valuation firms, lawyers, accountants, etc.). Also includes back issues of *Buyouts Newsletter* and *Mergers & Acquisitions Report.* Fully searchable. (Securities Data Publishing is a unit of Thomson Financial.).

DIRECTORIES

Corporate Finance Sourcebook: The Guide to Major Capital Investment Source and Related Financial Services. R. R. Bowker. • Annual. $625.00. Lists more than 3,550 sources of corporate capital: investment bankers, securities firms, pension management companies, trust companies, insurance companies, and private lenders. Includes the names of over 13,000 key personnel.

Directory of Buyout Financing Sources. Securities Data Publishing. • Annual. $395.00. Describes more than 1,000 U. S. and foreign sources of financing for buyout deals. Indexed by personnel, company, industry, and location. (Securities Data Publishing is a unit of Thomson Financial.).

Directory of M & A Intermediaries. Securities Data Publishing. • Annual. $360.00. Lists more than 850 dealmakers for mergers and acquisitions, including investment banks, business brokers, and commercial banks. (Securities Data Publishing is a unit of Thomson Financial.).

Plunkett's Financial Services Industry Almanac: The Leading Firms in Investments, Banking, and Financial Information. Available from Plunkett Research, Ltd. • Annual. $245.00. Discusses important trends in various sectors of the financial industry. Five hundred major banking, credit card, investment, and financial services companies are profiled.

Securities Industry Yearbook. Securities Industry Association. • Annual. Members, $85.00; non-members, $125.00. Information about securities industry firms and capital markets.

ENCYCLOPEDIAS AND DICTIONARIES

Blackwell Encyclopedic Dictionary of Finance. Dean Paxson and Douglas Wood, editors. Blackwell Publishers. • 1997. $110.00. The editors are associated with the University of Manchester. Contains definitions of key terms combined with longer articles written by various U. S. and foreign business educators. Includes bibliographies and index. (Blackwell Encyclopedia of Management Series).

HANDBOOKS AND MANUALS

Investment Banking Handbook. J. Peter Williamson. John Wiley and Sons, Inc. • 1988. $175.00. (Professional Banking and Finance Series).

Library of Investment Banking. Robert L. Kuhn, editor. McGraw-Hill Professional. • 1990. $475.00. Seven volumes: 1. Investing and Risk Management; 2. Capital Raising and Financial Structure; 3. Corporate and Municipal Securities; 4. Mergers, Acquisitions, and Leveraged Buyouts; 5. Mortgage and Asset Securitization; 6. International Finance and Investing; 7. Index.

PERIODICALS AND NEWSLETTERS

Corporate Financing Week: The Newsweekly of Corporate Finance, Investment Banking and M and A. Institutional Investor. • Weekly. $2,550.00 per year. Newsletter for corporate finance officers. Emphasis is on debt and equity financing, mergers, leveraged buyouts, investment banking, and venture capital.

FMC (Financial Management): Journal of the Financial Management Association. Financial Management Association International. • Quarterly. Individuals, $80.00 per year; libraries, $100.00 per year. Covers theory and practice of financial planning, international finance, investment banking, and portfolio management. Includes *Financial Practice* and *Education and Contempory Finance Digest.*

Investment Management Weekly. Securities Data Publishing. • Weekly. $1,370.00 per year. Newsletter. Edited for money managers and other investment professionals. Covers personnel news, investment strategies, and industry trends. (Securities Data Publishing is a unit of Thomson Financial.).

TRADE/PROFESSIONAL ASSOCIATIONS

National Association of Securities Dealers. 1735 K St., N.W., Washington, DC 20006-1506. Phone: (202)728-8000 Fax: (202)293-6260 • URL: http://www.nasdr.com/1000.asp.

Securities Industry Association. 120 Broadway, New York, NY 10271-0080. Phone: (212)608-1500 Fax: (212)608-1604 E-mail: info@sia.com • URL: http://www.sia.com.

INVESTMENT CLUBS

HANDBOOKS AND MANUALS

Investors Manual. National Association of Investors Corporation. • Irregular. Price on application. Provides stock study tools and procedures for do-it-yourself equity investors.

PERIODICALS AND NEWSLETTERS

Better Investing. National Association of Investors Corp. • Monthly. $24.00 per year. Provides stock study ideas and information for do-it-yourself common stock investors.

TRADE/PROFESSIONAL ASSOCIATIONS

National Association of Investors Corporation. P.O. Box 220, Royal Oak, MI 48068. Phone: (810)583-6242 Fax: (810)583-4880 • URL: http://www.better_investing.org.

INVESTMENT COMPANIES

See also: CLOSED-END FUNDS

GENERAL WORKS

Beating the Street: The Best-Selling Author of "One Up on Wall Street" Shows You How to Pick Winning Stocks and Mutual Funds. Peter Lynch and John Rothchild. Simon & Schuster Trade. • 1993. $23.00.

Bogle on Mutual Funds: New Perspectives for the Intelligent Investor. John C. Bogle. McGraw-Hill Professional. • 1993. $25.00.

Common Sense on Mutual Funds: New Imperatives for the Intelligent Investor. John C. Bogle. John Wiley and Sons, Inc. • 1999. $24.95. Provides practical, conservative advice for the average investor. Topics include asset allocation, index funds, global investing, fund selection, and taxes.

The Death of the Banker: The Decline and Fall of the Great Financial Dynasties and the Triumph of the Small Investor. Ron Chernow. Vintage Books. • 1997. $12.00. Contains three essays: "J. Pierpont Morgan," "The Warburgs," and "The Death of the Banker" (discusses the decline of banks in personal finance and the rise of mutual funds and stock brokers).

Getting Started in Mutual Funds. Alvin D. Hall. John Wiley and Sons, Inc. • 1998. $18.95. (Getting Started In... Series).

Mutual Funds: Your Key to Sound Financial Planning. Lyle Allen. Morrow/Avon. • 1994. $10.00.

The New Commonsense Guide to Mutual Funds. Mary Rowland. Bloomberg Press. • 1998. $15.95. Revised edition. Includes "Do's and Don'ts" for mutual fund investors. (Bloomberg Personal Bookshelf Series).

One Up on Wall Street: How to Use What You Already Know to Make Money in the Market. Peter Lynch and John Rothchild. Viking Penguin. • 1990. $14.95.

The Only Investment Guide You'll Ever Need. Andrew Tobias. Harcourt Brace and Co. • 1999. $14.00. Expanded revised edition. An entertaining, optimistic look at investing, written for the "average" investor. Provides generally conservative advice, favoring no-load, low-expense index funds.

Straight Talk About Mutual Funds. Dian Vujovich. McGraw-Hill. • 1996. $12.95. Second revised edition. The author provides basic advice and information for both beginning and experienced investors in mutual funds. (Straight Talk Series).

What You Need to Know About Mutual Funds. Kenneth M. Lefkowitz. American Institute for Economic Research. • 1996. $6.00. Provides conservative advice on investing in mutual funds, unit investment trusts, closed-end investment companies, and other funds. Includes a glossary and lists of recommended information sources.

Yes, You Can Achieve Financial Independence. James E. Stowers and others. Stowers Innovations, Inc. • 2000. $34.00.

ALMANACS AND YEARBOOKS

Business Week's Guide to Mutual Funds. Jeffrey M. Laderman. McGraw-Hill. • 2000. $14.95. 10th edition. Includes basic information, ratings, and performance data.

Emerging Markets Analyst. • Monthly. $895.00 per year. Provides an annual overview of the emerging financial markets in 24 countries of Latin America, Asia, and Europe. Includes data on international mutual funds and closed-end funds.

Investment Companies Yearbook. Securities Data Publishing. • Annual. $310.00. Provides an "entire history of recent events in the mutual funds industry," with emphasis on changes during the past year. About 100 pages are devoted to general information and advice for fund investors. Includes 600 full-page profiles of popular mutual funds, with brief descriptions of 10,000 others, plus 7,000 variable annuities and 500 closed-end funds. Contains a glossary of technical terms, a Web site index, and an overall book index. Also known as *Wiesenberger Investment Companies Yearbook.* (Securities Data Publishing is a unit of Thomson Financial.).

Moneyletter's Mutual Funds Almanac. Agora, Inc. • Annual. $39.95. Lists more than 3,000 open and closed-end funds. Formerly *IBC/Donaghue's Mutual Funds Almanac.*

DIRECTORIES

Major Financial Institutions of Europe. European Business Publications, Inc. • Annual. $495.00. Contains profiles of over 7,000 financial institutions in Europe such as banks, investment companies, and insurance companies. Formerly *Major Financial Institutions of Continental Europe.*

Morningstar Closed-End Fund 250. Morningstar Staff. McGraw-Hill Professional. • 1996. $35.00. Provides detailed information on 50 actively traded closed-end investment companies. Past data is included for up to 12 years, depending on life of the fund.

Morningstar Mutual Funds. Morningstar, Inc. • Biweekly. $495.00 per year. Looseleaf. Contains detailed information and risk-adjusted ratings on over 1,240 load and no-load, equity and fixed-income mutual funds. Annual returns are provided for up to 12 years for each fund.

Morningstar No-Load Funds. Morningstar, Inc. • Monthly. $145.00 per year. Looseleaf. Provides detailed information and risk-adjusted ratings on about 600 no-load and low-load mutual funds. Includes up to eight years of quarterly returns and 12 years of annual returns for each fund.

Mutual Fund Profiles. Standard & Poor's. • Quarterly. $158.00 per year. Produced jointly with Lipper Analytical Services. Provides detailed information on approximately 800 of the largest stock funds and taxable bond funds. In addition, contains concise data on about 2,400 smaller funds and municipal bond funds.

Nelson's Directory of Investment Managers. Wiesenberger/Thomson Financial. • Annual. $545.00. Three volumes. Provides information on 2,600 investment management firms, both U.S. and foreign.

Value Line Mutual Fund Survey. Value Line Publishing, Inc. • Biweekly. $295.00 per year. Looseleaf. Provides ratings and detailed performance information for 2,300 equity and fixed income funds.

Vickers Directory of Institutional Investors. Vickers Stock Research Corp. • Semiannual. $195.00 per year. Detailed alphabetical listing of more than 4,000 U. S., Canadian, and foreign institutional investors. Includes insurance companies, banks, endowment funds, and investment companies. Formerly *Directory of Institutional Investors.*

FINANCIAL RATIOS

Almanac of Business and Industrial Financial Ratios. Leo Troy. Prentice Hall. • Annual. $99.95. Contains financial ratios derived from federal tax returns. Ratios for each of about 200 industries are arranged according to company asset size.

The Financial Elite: Database of Financial Services Companies. Donnelley Marketing. • Quarterly. Price on application. Formerly compiled by Database America. Provides current information on CD-ROM for 500,000 major U. S. companies offering financial services. Data for each firm includes year started, type of financial service, annual revenues, name of top executive, and number of employees.

Major Financial Institutions of the World. Available from The Gale Group. • 2001. $855.00. Fourth edition. Two volumes. Published by Graham & Whiteside. Contains detailed information on more than 7,500 important financial institutions in various countries. Includes banks, investment companies, and insurance companies.

HANDBOOKS AND MANUALS

Handbook for No-Load Fund Investors. Sheldon Jacobs. McGraw-Hill Professional. • 1996. $40.00. 16th edition. Includes data on individual funds.

Indexing for Maximum Investment Results. Albert S. Neuberg. Fitzroy Dearborn Publishers. • 1998. $65.00. Covers the Standard & Poor's 500 and other indexing strategies for both individual and institutional investors.

Kiss Your Stockbroker Goodbye: A Guide to Independent Investing. John G. Wells. St. Martin's Press. • 1997. $25.95. The author believes that the small investor is throwing money away by using full-commission brokers when discount brokers and many sources of information are easily available. Contains separate chapters on stocks, bonds, mutual funds, asset allocation, financial planners, and related topics. Wells is a securities analyst (CFA) and portfolio manager.

Moody's Bank and Finance Manual. Moody's Investor Service. • Annual. $995.00 per year. Four volumes. Includes biweekly supplements in *Moody's Bank and Finance News Report.*

Mutual Fund Buyer's Guide: Performance Ratings, Five Year Projections, Safety Ratings, Sales. Norman G. Fosback. McGraw-Hill Professional. • 1994. $17.95.

INTERNET DATABASES

DBC Online: America's Leading Provider of Real-Time Market Data to the Individual Investor. Data Broadcasting Corp. Phone: (415)571-1800 E-mail: dbcinfo@dbc.com • URL: http://www.dbc.com • Web site provides a wide variety of real-time securities market prices, data, and charts. Covers bonds ("BondVu"), stocks, commodities, options, mutual funds, major indexes, industry indexes, international markets, etc. Also includes news, SEC documents ("Smart-Edgar"), and various other features. Fees: Both free and fee-based, depending on level of information.

The Financial Post (Web site). National Post Online (Hollinger/CanWest). Phone: (244)383-2300 Fax: (416)383-2443 • URL: http://www.nationalpost.com/financialpost/ • Provides a broad range of Canadian business news online, with daily updates. Includes news, opinion, and special reports, as well as "Investing," "Money Rates," "Market Watch," and "Daily Mutual Funds." Allows advanced searching (Boolean operators), with links to various other sites. Fees: Free.

FundAlarm. Roy Weitz. URL: http://www.fundalarm.com • Web site subtitle: "Know when to hold'em, know when to fold'em, know when to walk away, know when to run." Provides lists of underperforming mutual funds ("3-ALARM Funds") and severely underperforming funds ("Most Alarming 3-ALARM Funds"). Performance is based on various benchmarks. Site also provides mutual fund news, recent manager changes, and basic data for each of about 2,100 funds. Monthly updates. Fees: Free.

Morningstar.com: Your First Second Opinion. Morningstar, Inc. Phone: 800-735-0700 or (312)696-6000 Fax: (312)696-6001 E-mail: productsupport@morningstar.com • URL: http://www.morningstar.com • Web site provides a broad selection of information and advice on both mutual funds and individual stocks, including financial news and articles on investment fundamentals. Basic service is free, with "Premium Membership" available at $49.00 per year. Annual fee provides personal portfolio analysis, screening tools, and more extensive profiles of funds and stocks.

Mutual Funds Interactive. Brill Editorial Services, Inc. Phone: 877-442-7455 • URL: http://www.brill.com • Web site provides specific information on individual funds in addition to general advice on mutual fund investing and 401(k) plans. Searching is provided, including links to moderated newsgroups and a chat page. Fees: Free.

TheStreet.com: Your Insider's Look at Wall Street. TheStreet.com, Inc. Phone: 800-562-9571 or (212)321-5000 Fax: (212)321-5016 • URL: http://www.thestreet.com • Web site offers "Free Sections" and "Premium Sections" ($9.95 per month). Both sections offer iconoclastic advice and comment on the stock market, but premium service displays a more comprehensive selection of news and analysis. There are many by-lined articles. "Search the Site" is included.

Thomson Investors Network. Thomson Financial. Phone: (212)807-3800 • URL: http://thomsoninvest.net • Web site provides detailed data on insider trading, institutional portfolios, and "First Call" earnings estimates. Includes a stock screening (filtering) application, a search facility, and price quotes on stocks, bonds, and mutual funds. Continuous updating. Fees: $34.95 per year for general service. First Call earnings service is $19.95 per month or $199.00 per year.

Thomson Real Time Quotes: Real Fast...Real Free...Real Quotes...Real Time. Thomson Financial. Phone: (212)807-3800 • URL: http://www.thomsonfn.com/ • Web site provides continuous updating of prices for stocks, bonds, mutual funds, and options. Includes headline business news and market analysis. Fees: Free.

U. S. Securities and Exchange Commission. Phone: 800-732-0330 or (202)942-7040 Fax: (202)942-9634 E-mail: webmaster@sec.gov • URL: http://www.sec.gov • SEC Web site offers free access through EDGAR to text of official corporate filings, such as annual reports (10-K), quarterly reports (10-Q), and proxies. (EDGAR is "Electronic Data Gathering, Analysis, and Retrieval System.") An example is given of how to obtain executive compensation data from proxies. Text of the daily *SEC News Digest* is offered, as are links to other government sites, non-government market regulators, and U. S. stock exchanges. Search facilities are extensive. Fees: Free.

Web Finance: Covering the Electronic Evolution of Finance. Securities Data Publishing. Phone: (212)765-5311 or 800-455-5844 Fax: (212)321-2336 E-mail: webfinance@tfn.com • URL: http://www.webfinance.net • Bi-weekly print and daily web-site publication of financial services on the Web, including financial links, archives, brokerage stocks, deal financing, and other financial and investment news and information.

ONLINE DATABASES

Vickers On-Line. Vickers Stock Research Corp. • Provides detailed online information relating to insider trading and the securities holdings of institutional investors. Daily updates. Inquire as to online cost and availability.

PERIODICALS AND NEWSLETTERS

Bank Investment Product News. Institutional Investor, Newsletters Div. • Weekly. $1,195.00 per year. Newsletter. Edited for bank executives. Covers the marketing and regulation of financial products sold through banks, such as mutual funds, stock brokerage services, and insurance.

Barron's: The Dow Jones Business and Financial Weekly. Dow Jones and Co., Inc. • Weekly. $145.00 per year.

Cabot's Mutual Fund Navigator: Your Guide to Investing for Profits and Safety in the Best Mutual Funds. Cabot Heritage Corp. • Monthly. $125.00 per year. Newsletter. Recommends various mutual fund portfolios.

Financial Planning: The Magazine for Financial Service Professionals. Securities Data Publishing. • Monthly. $79.00 per year. Edited for independent financial planners and insurance agents. Covers retirement planning, estate planning, tax planning, and insurance, including long-term healthcare considerations. Special features include a Retirement Planning Issue, Mutual Fund Performance Survey, and Variable Life and Annuity Survey. (Securities Data Publishing is a unit of Thomson Financial.).

The Financial Post: Canadian's Business Voice. Financial Post Datagroup. • Daily. $234.00 per year. Provides Canadian business, economic, financial, and investment news. Features extensive price quotes from all major Canadian markets: stocks, bonds, mutual funds, commodities, and currencies. Supplement available: *Financial Post 500*. Includes annual supplement.

Financial Services Marketing: Finding, Keeping, and Profiting From the Right Customers. American Banker. • Bimonthly. Price on application. Covers marketing for a variety of financial institutions, including banks, investment companies, securities dealers, and credit unions.

Fund Action. Institutional Investor. • Weekly. $2,220.00 per year. Newsletter. Edited for mutual fund executives. Covers competition among funds, aggregate statistics, new products, regulations, service providers, and other subjects of interest to fund managers.

Growth Fund Guide: The Investor's Guide to Dynamic Growth Funds. Growth Fund Research, Inc. • Monthly. $99.00 per year. Newsletter. Covers no-load growth mutual funds.

Guide to Equity Mutual Funds: A Quarterly Compilation of Mutual Fund Ratings and Analysis Covering Equity and Balanced Funds. Weiss Ratings, Inc. • Quarterly. $438.00 per year. Emphasis is on rating of financial safety and relative risk. Includes annual summary.

Income Fund Outlook. Institute for Econometric Research. • Monthly. $100.00 per year. Newsletter. Contains tabular data on money market funds, certificates of deposit, bond funds, and tax-free bond funds. Includes specific recommendations, fund news, and commentary on interest rates.

InvesTech Mutual Fund Advisor: Professional Portfolio Allocation. InvesTech Research. • Every three weeks. $190.00 per year. Newsletter. Contains model portfolio for mutual fund investing.

Latin Fund Management. Securities Data Publishing. • Monthly. $495.00 per year. Newsletter (also available online at www.latinfund.net). Provides news and analysis of Latin American mutual funds, pension funds, and annuities. (Securities Data Publishing is a unit of Thomson Financial.).

Louis Rukeyser's Mutual Funds. Louis Rukeyser's Wall Street Club. • Monthly. $79.00 per year. Newsletter. Provides conservative advice on mutual fund investing.

The Moneyletter. IBC-Donoghue, Inc. • Semimonthly. $109.00 per year. Newsletter giving specific advice on interest rates, trends, money market funds, bond funds, and equity mutual funds. Formerly *Donoghue's Moneyletter*.

Morningstar Fund Investor. Morningstar, Inc. • Monthly. $79.00 per year. Newsletter. Provides tables of statistical data and star ratings for leading mutual funds ("The Morningstar 500"). News of funds and financial planning advice for investors is also included.

Mutual Fund Advisor: The Top Performing Mutual Funds. Mutual Fund Advisor, Inc. • Monthly. $75.00 per year. Newsletter.

Mutual Fund Buyer's Guide. Institute for Econometric Research. • Monthly. $80.00 per year. Each issue provides tabular data for about 1,500 mutual funds. Includes performance figures for various time periods from one month to 10 years. Up-market and down-market ratings are also given.

Mutual Fund Forecaster: Profit and Projections and Risk Ratings for Traders and Investors. Institute for Econometric Research. • Monthly. $100.00 per year. Newsletter. Contains buy recommendations, profit projections, risk ratings, and past performance data for individual mutual funds and closed-end funds.

Mutual Fund Investing. Jay Schabacker, editor. Phillips Publishing, Inc. • Monthly. $127.00 per year. Newsletter.

Mutual Fund Letter. Investment Information Services, Inc. • Monthly. $125.00 per year. Newsletter. Provides mutual fund recommendations.

Mutual Fund Market News. Securities Data Publishing. • Weekly. $1,425 per year. Newsletter (also available online at www.mfmarketnews.com). Edited for executives concerned with mutual fund administration and management. Covers marketing, distribution, new funds, mergers, regulations, legal issues, pricing, Internet use, and related topics. (Securities Data Publishing is a unit of Thomson Financial.).

Mutual Fund Strategies. Progressive Investing, Inc. • Monthly. $127.00 per year. Newsletter.

Mutual Fund Trends. Growth Fund Research, Inc. • Monthly. $139.00 per year. Newsletter. Includes charts of mutual funds.

Mutual Funds Magazine: Your Monthly Guide to America's Best Investments. Institute for Econometric Research. • Monthly. $19.94 per year. Popular magazine for mutual fund investors. Regular features include "Platinum Funds: The Investor's Guide to America's Most Popular Funds" (full-page evaluations), "Hot Funds," "Funding Retirement," and book reviews.

Mutual Funds Update. Securities Data Publishing. • Monthly. $325.00 per year. Provides recent performance information and statistics for approximately 10,000 mutual funds, as compiled from the CDA/Wiesenberger database. Includes commentary and analysis relating to the mutual fund industry. Information is provided on new funds, name changes, mergers, and liquidations. (Securities Data Publishing is a unit of Thomson Financial.).

The No-Load Fund Investor. • Monthly. $139.00 per year without *Handbook*; *Handbook* included, $159.00 per year. Latest performance statistics for no-loads, specific fund recommendations, market forecasts, and timely fund news.

The Wall Street Journal. Dow Jones & Co., Inc. • Daily. $175.00 per year. Covers news and trends relating to business, industry, finance, the economy, and international commerce. Provides extensive price and other data for the securities, commodity, options, futures, foreign exchange, and money markets.

STATISTICS SOURCES

Morningstar Variable Annuity Performance Report. Morningstar, Inc. • Monthly. $125.00 per year. Provides detailed statistics and ratings for more than 2,000 variable annuities and variable-life products.

Mutual Fund Fact Book: Industry Trends and Statistics. Investment Company Institute. • 1997. $25.00. 37th edition. Industry trends and statistics.

Statistical Information on the Financial Services Industry. American Bankers Association. • Annual. Members, $150.00; non-members, $275.00. Presents a wide variety of data relating to banking and financial services, including consumer economics, personal finance, credit, government loans, capital markets, and international banking.

Trends in Mutual Fund Activity. Investment Company Institute. • Monthly. $225.00 per year. Contains statistical tables showing fund industry sales, redemptions, assets, cash, and other data.

U. S. Industry and Trade Outlook: The McGraw-Hill Companies and the U.S. Department of Commerce/ International Trade Administration. Datapso Research Corp. • Annual. $69.95. Produced by the International Trade Administration, U. S. Department of Commerce, in a "public-private" partnership with DRI/McGraw-Hill and Standard & Poor's. Provides basic data, outlook for the current year, and "Long-Term Prospects" (five-year projections) for a wide variety of products and services. Includes high technology industries. Formerly *U. S. Industrial Outlook*.

TRADE/PROFESSIONAL ASSOCIATIONS

Investment Company Institute. 1401 H St., N. W., 12th Fl., Washington, DC 20005-2148. Phone: (202)326-5800 Fax: (202)326-8309 E-mail: info@ici.com • URL: http://www.ici.com • Members are investment companies offering mutual funds (open-end) and closed-end funds. Includes a Closed-End Investment Company Division.

Mutual Fund Education Alliance (The Association of No-Load Funds). 100 N.W. Englewood Rd., No. 130, Kansas City, MO 64118. E-mail: mfeamail@mfea.com • URL: http://www.mea.com.

National Association of Real Estate Investment Trusts. 1875 Eye St., N.W. Ste. 600, Washington, DC 20006. Phone: 800-362-7348 or (202)739-9400 Fax: (202)739-9401 • URL: http://www.nareit.com.

OTHER SOURCES

Fund Watch: The Official Guide to High-Performance Mutual Funds. Institute for Econometric Research. • Monthly. $80.00 per year. A chart service. Each issue provides 10-year charts of "high-performance" and widely-held mutual funds.

I B C's Money Fund Report. IBC Financial Data, Inc. • Weekly. $975.00 per year. Looseleaf. Contains detailed information on about 1,000 U. S. money market funds, including portfolios and yields. Formerly *Money Fund Report*.

Lipper Mutual Fund Performance Analysis. Lipper Analytical Services, Inc. • Weekly. Available to institutional clients only. (For detailed summaries of Lipper data on about 6,000 funds, see "Lipper Mutual Funds Quarterly" in *Barron's*, usually in the second week of January, April, July, and October.).

Quarterly Report on Money Fund Performance. IBC-Donoghue, Inc. • Quarterly. $525.00 per year. Provides expense ratio and yield data for about 1,000 money market funds in the U. S.

The Winning Portfolio: Choosing Your 10 Best Mutual Funds. Paul B. Farrell. Bloomberg Press. • 1999. $15.95. Tells how to select 10 from among the 10,000 mutual funds that are available. (Bloomberg Personal Bookshelf.).

INVESTMENT COMPANIES, CLOSED-END

See: CLOSED-END FUNDS

INVESTMENT DEALERS

See: STOCK BROKERS

INVESTMENT SERVICES

See: INVESTMENT ADVISORY SERVICES

INVESTMENT TRUSTS

See: INVESTMENT COMPANIES

INVESTMENTS

GENERAL WORKS

The Bear Book: Survive and Profit in Ferocious Markets. John Rothchild. John Wiley and Sons, Inc.

• 1998. $24.95. Tells how to invest when the stock market is sinking.

The Craft of Investing. John Train. • 1994. $22.00. Presents conservative discussions of a wide variety of investment topics, including market timing, growth vs. value stocks, mutual funds, emerging markets, retirement planning, and estate planning.

Don't Die Broke: How to Turn Your Retirement Savings into Lasting Income. Margaret A. Malaspina. Available from W.W. Norton and Co., Inc. • 1999. $21.95. Provides advice on such matters as retirement portfolio asset allocation and retirement spending accounts. (Bloomberg Personal Bookshelf.).

Education of a Speculator. Victor Niederhoffer. John Wiley and Sons, Inc. • 1997. $29.95. An autobiography providing basic advice on speculation, investment, and the commodity futures market.

Everyone's Money Book: Everything You Need to Know About Investing Wisely, Buying a Home... Jordan E. Goodman. Dearborn, A Kaplan Professional Co. • 1998. $26.95. Covers investing, taxes, mortgages, retirement planning, and other personal finance topics. Jordan E. Goodman is a writer for *Money* magazine.

Fundamentals of Investing. Lawrence J. Gitman and Michael D. Joehnk. Addison-Wesley Longman, Inc. • 1998. $98.33. Seventh edition.

How to Invest Wisely. Lawrence S. Pratt. American Institute for Economic Research. • 1998. $9.00. Presents a conservative policy of investing, with emphasis on dividend-paying common stocks. Gold and other inflation hedges are compared. Includes a reprint of *Toward an Optimal Stock Selection Strategy* (1997). (Economic Education Bulletin.).

The Individual Investor Revolution: Unlock the Secrets of Wall Street and Invest Like a Pro. Charles B. Carlson. McGraw-Hill. • 1998. $21.95. Emphasizes the growing importance of the individual investor, especially with regard to online trading (e-trading). Includes the author's favorite websites for investors and traders.

Investing During Retirement: The Vanguard Guide to Managing Your Retirement Assets. Vanguard Group. McGraw-Hill Professional. • 1996. $17.95. A basic, general guide to investing after retirement. Covers pension plans, basic principles of investing, types of mutual funds, asset allocation, retirement income planning, social security, estate planning, and contingencies. Includes glossary and worksheets for net worth, budget, and income.

Investments: An Introduction to Analysis and Management. Frederick Amling. Pearson Custom Publishing. • 1999. Seventh edition.

Investments: Analysis and Management. Charles P. Jones. John Wiley and Sons, Inc. • 1997. $102.95. Sixth edition.

Learn to Earn: An Introduction to the Basics of Investing and Business. Peter Lynch and John Rothchild. Simon & Schuster Trade. • 1996. $13.00.

The Lifetime Book of Money Management. Grace W. Weinstein. Visible Ink Press. • 1993. $15.95. Third edition. Gives popularly-written advice on investments, life and health insurance, owning a home, credit, retirement, estate planning, and other personal finance topics.

Never Call Your Broker on Monday: And 300 Other Financial Lessons You Can't Afford Not to Know. Nancy Dunnan. HarperCollins Publishers. • 1996. $8.50. Presents a wide range of personal finance advice, covering investments, insurance, wills, credit, real estate, etc.

The Only Investment Guide You'll Ever Need. Andrew Tobias. Harcourt Brace and Co. • 1999. $14.00. Expanded revised edition. An entertaining, optimistic look at investing, written for the "average" investor. Provides generally conservative advice, favoring no-load, low-expense index funds.

A Random Walk Down Wall Street: Including a Life-Cycle Guide to Personal Investing. Burton G. Malkiel. W. W. Norton & Co., Inc. • 1999. $29.95. Seventh edition.

Secrets of the Street: The Dark Side of Making Money. Gene Marcial. McGraw-Hill. • 1996. $10.95. Explains how the small, individual investor can be taken advantage of by Wall Street professionals.

A Short History of Financial Euphoria. John Kenneth Galbraith. Viking Penguin. • 1994. $10.95. An analysis of speculative euphoria and subsequent crashes, from the Holland tulip mania in 1637 to the 1987 unpleasantness in the U. S. stock market.

Smart Questions to Ask Your Financial Advisers. Lynn Brenner. Bloomberg Press. • 1997. $19.95. Provides practical advice on how to deal with financial planners, stockbrokers, insurance agents, and lawyers. Some of the areas covered are investments, estate planning, tax planning, house buying, prenuptial agreements, divorce arrangements, loss of a job, and retirement. (Bloomberg Personal Bookshelf Series Library.).

Stocks for the Long Run: A Guide to Selecting Markets for Long-Term Growth. Jeremy J. Siegel. McGraw-Hill. • 1998. $29.95. Second expanded edition. A favorable view of a buy-and-hold strategy for stock market investors. *Business Week Books.*

Toward an Optimal Stock Selection Strategy. Lawrence S. Pratt. American Institute for Economic Research. • 1997. $6.00. Second edition. Discusses the strategy of buying only the stocks in the Dow Jones Industrial Average that have the highest-yielding dividends. Includes detailed charts and tables. (Economic Education Bulletin.).

Vanguard Retirement Investing Guide: Charting Your Course to a Secure Retirement. Vanguard Group. McGraw-Hill Professional. • 1995. $24.95. Second edition. Covers saving and investing for future retirement. Topics include goal setting, investment fundamentals, mutual funds, asset allocation, defined contribution retirement savings plans, social security, and retirement savings strategies. Includes glossary and worksheet for retirement saving.

Wealth in a Decade: Brett Matchtig's Proven System for Creating Wealth, Living Off Your Investments and Attaining a Financially Secure Life. Brett Machtig and Ryan D. Behrends. McGraw-Hill Professional. • 1996. $24.95. The authors advocate systematic saving, prudent investing, and no credit card debt. Advice is given on constructing a diversified investment portfolio.

What Works on Wall Street: A Guide to the Best-Performing Investment Strategies of All Time. James P. O'Shaughnessy. McGraw-Hill. • 1998. $22.95. Second revised edition. Examines investment strategies over a 43-year period and concludes that large capitalization, high-dividend-yield stocks produce the best results.

You and Your 401(k): How to Manage Your 401(k) for Maximum Returns. Julie Jason. Simon & Schuster Trade. • 1996. $10.00. Presents popularly written advice and information concerning the key features of 401(k) plans and how to choose appropriate investments. Includes a glossary and sample forms. The author is an investment consultant.

ABSTRACTS AND INDEXES

Investment Statistics Locator. Linda H. Bentley and Jennifer J. Kiesl, editors. Oryx Press. • 1994. $69.95. Expanded revised edition. Provides detailed subject indexing of more than 50 of the most-used sources of financial and investment data. Includes an annotated bibliography.

ALMANACS AND YEARBOOKS

Advances in Investment Analysis and Portfolio Management. Chung-Few Lee, editor. JAI Press, Inc. • 1999. $78.50.

Dun and Bradstreet Guide to Your Investments: The Year-Round Investment Sourc ebook for Managing Your Personal Finances. Nancy Dunnan, editor. HarperSan Francisco. • 1996. $35.00.

Irwin Business and Investment Almanac, 1996. Summer N. Levine and Caroline Levine. McGraw-Hill Professional. • 1995. $75.00. A review of last year's business activity. Covers a wide variety of business and economic data: stock market statistics, industrial information, commodity futures information, art market trends, comparative living costs for U. S. metropolitan areas, foreign stock market data, etc. Formerly *Business One Irwin Business and Investment Almanac.*

BIBLIOGRAPHIES

Business Information Sources. Lorna M. Daniells. California Princeton Fulfillment Services. • 1993. $42.50. Third revised edition. Basic business sources, with discussion and full annotations.

Business Library Review: An International Journal. International Publishers Distributor. • Quarterly. Academic institutions, $318.00 per year;corporations, $501.00 per year.Incorporates *The Wall Street Review of Books* and *Economics and Business: An Annotated Bibliography.* Publishes scholarly reviews of books on a wide variety of topics in business, economics, and finance. Text in French.

CD-ROM DATABASES

Business Source Plus. EBSCO Information Services. • Monthly. $1,495.00 per year. Provides CD-ROM citations and abstracts to articles in about 650 business periodicals and newspapers, including *The Wall Street Journal.* Full text is provided from 200 selected periodicals. Covers accounting, communications, economics, finance, management, marketing, and other business subjects.

Compact D/SEC. Disclosure, Inc. • Monthly. Contains three CD-ROM files. (1) Disclosure: Provides Securities and Exchange Commission filings for over 12,500 publicly held corporations. (2) Disclosure/Spectrum Ownership Profiles: Provides detailed corporate descriptions and complete ownership information for over 6,000 public companies. (3) Zacks Earnings Estimates: Provides earnings per share forecasts for about 4,000 U. S. corporations.

InvesText [CD-ROM]. Thomson Financial Securities Data. • Monthly. $5,000.00 per year. Contains full text on CD-ROM of investment research reports from about 250 sources, including leading brokers and investment bankers. Reports are available on both U. S. and international publicly traded corporations. Separate industry reports cover more than 50 industries. Time span is 1982 to date.

WILSONDISC: Wilson Business Abstracts. H. W. Wilson Co. • Monthly. $2,495.00 per year, including unlimited online access to *Wilson Business Abstracts* through WILSONLINE. Provides CD-ROM "cover-to-cover" abstracting and indexing of over 600 prominent business periodicals. Indexing is from 1982, abstracting from 1990. (*Business Periodicals Index* without abstracts is available on CD-ROM at $1,495 per year.).

DIRECTORIES

Association for Investment Management and Research-Membership Directory. Association for Investment Management and Research. • Annual. $150.00. Members are professional investment managers and securities analysts.

CyberTools for Business: Practical Web Sites that will Save You Time and Money. Wayne Harris. Hoover's, Inc. • 1997. $19.95. Describes 100 World Wide Web sites that are useful for business, investing, and job hunting. Also lists Web addresses for about 4,500 public and private companies.

Moody's International Manual. Financial Information Services. • Annual. $3,175.00 per year. Includes weekly *News Reports.* Financial and other information about 3,000 publicly-owned corporations in 95 countries.

National Directory of Investment Newsletters. GPS Co. • Biennial. $49.95. Describes about 800 investment newsletters, and their publishers.

Plunkett's On-Line Trading, Finance, and Investment Web Sites Almanac. Plunkett Research, Ltd. • Annual. $149.99. Provides profiles and usefulness rankings of financial Web sites. Sites are rated from 1 to 5 for specific uses. Includes diskette.

ENCYCLOPEDIAS AND DICTIONARIES

The A-Z Vocabulary for Investors. American Institute for Economic Research. • 1997. $7.00. Second half of book is a "General Glossary" of about 400 financial terms "most-commonly used" in investing. First half contains lengthier descriptions of types of banking institutions (commercial banks, thrift institutions, credit unions), followed by succinct explanations of various forms of investment: stocks, bonds, options, futures, commodities, and "Other Investments" (collectibles, currencies, mortgages, precious metals, real estate, charitable trusts). (Economic Education Bulletin.).

Blackwell Encyclopedic Dictionary of Finance. Dean Paxson and Douglas Wood, editors. Blackwell Publishers. • 1997. $110.00. The editors are associated with the University of Manchester. Contains definitions of key terms combined with longer articles written by various U. S. and foreign business educators. Includes bibliographies and index. (Blackwell Encyclopedia of Management Series).

Dictionary of Finance and Investment Terms. John Downes and Jordan E. Goodman. Barron's Educational Series, Inc. • 1998. $12.95. Fifth revised edition. Provides clear explanations of more than 5,000 business, banking, financial, investment, and tax terms. Includes a separate list of financial abbreviations and acronyms.

Dictionary of Investing. Jerry M. Rosenberg. John Wiley and Sons, Inc. • 1992. $79.95. (Business Dictionary Series).

Dictionary of Personal Finance. Joel G. Siegel and others. Pearson Education and Technology. • 1993. $20.00.

Knowledge Exchange Business Encyclopedia: Your Complete Business Advisor. Lorraine Spurge, editor. Knowledge Exchange LLC. • 1997. $45.00. Provides definitions of business terms and financial expressions, profiles of leading industries, tables of economic statistics, biographies of business leaders, and other business information. Includes "A Chronology of Business from 3000 B.C. Through 1995." Contains illustrations and three indexes.

The New Palgrave Dictionary of Money and Finance. Peter Newman and others, editors. Groves Dictionaries. • 1998. $550.00. Three volumes. Consists of signed essays on over 1,000 financial topics, each with a bibliography. Covers a wide variety of financial, monetary, and investment areas. A detailed subject index is provided.

Wall Street Words: The Basics and Beyond. Richard J. Maturi. McGraw-Hill Professional. • 1991. $14.95. (Investor's Quick Reference Series).

FINANCIAL RATIOS

Major Financial Institutions of the World. Available from The Gale Group. • 2001. $855.00. Fourth edition. Two volumes. Published by Graham & Whiteside. Contains detailed information on more than 7,500 important financial institutions in various countries. Includes banks, investment companies, and insurance companies.

HANDBOOKS AND MANUALS

The 401(k) Plan Handbook. Julie Jason. Prentice Hall. • 1997. $79.95. Provides technical, legal, administrative, and investment details of 401(k) retirement plans.

Getting Started in Investment Planning Services. James E. Grant. CCH, Inc. • 1999. $85.00. Second edition. Provides advice and information for lawyers and accountants who are planning to initiate fee-based investment services.

Handbook of Alternative Investment Strategies. Thomas Schneeweis and Joseph F. Pescatore, editors. Institutional Investor. • 1999. $95.00. Covers various forms of alternative investment, including hedge funds, managed futures, derivatives, venture capital, and natural resource financing.

Handbook of 401(k) Plan Management. Towers, Perrin, Foster and Crosby Staff. McGraw-Hill Higher Education. • 1992. $70.00. Written for employers and pension plan administrators. In addition to legal details of 401(k) plans, employee stock ownership plans (ESOPs) and basic principles of asset investment are covered. Appendix contains "Sample 401(k) Savings Plan Document.".

Indexing for Maximum Investment Results. Albert S. Neuberg. Fitzroy Dearborn Publishers. • 1998. $65.00. Covers the Standard & Poor's 500 and other indexing strategies for both individual and institutional investors.

Kiss Your Stockbroker Goodbye: A Guide to Independent Investing. John G. Wells. St. Martin's Press. • 1997. $25.95. The author believes that the small investor is throwing money away by using full-commission brokers when discount brokers and many sources of information are easily available. Contains separate chapters on stocks, bonds, mutual funds, asset allocation, financial planners, and related topics. Wells is a securities analyst (CFA) and portfolio manager.

The Prudent Speculator: Al Frank on Investing. Al Frank. McGraw-Hill Professional. • 1989. $30.00. How to be a sensible investor or speculator. Includes advice on the use of margin accounts and stock market timing.

Venture Capital: An Authoritative Guide for Investors, Entrepreneurs, and Managers. Douglas A. Lindgren. McGraw-Hill Professional. • 1998. $65.00.

Wall Street Journal Guide to Planning Your Financial Future: The Easy-to-Read Guide to Lifetime Planning for Retirement. Kenneth M. Morris. Simon & Schuster Trade. • 1998. $14.95. Revised edition. (Wall Street Journal Guides Series).

INTERNET DATABASES

Morningstar.com: Your First Second Opinion. Morningstar, Inc. Phone: 800-735-0700 or (312)696-6000 Fax: (312)696-6001 E-mail: productsupport@morningstar.com • URL: http://www.morningstar.com • Web site provides a broad selection of information and advice on both mutual funds and individual stocks, including financial news and articles on investment fundamentals. Basic service is free, with "Premium Membership" available at $49.00 per year. Annual fee provides personal portfolio analysis, screening tools, and more extensive profiles of funds and stocks.

TheStreet.com: Your Insider's Look at Wall Street. TheStreet.com, Inc. Phone: 800-562-9571 or (212)321-5000 Fax: (212)321-5016 • URL: http://www.thestreet.com • Web site offers "Free Sections" and "Premium Sections" ($9.95 per month). Both sections offer iconoclastic advice and comment on the stock market, but premium service displays a more comprehensive selection of news and analysis. There are many by-lined articles. "Search the Site" is included.

Thomson Investors Network. Thomson Financial. Phone: (212)807-3800 • URL: http://thomsoninvest.net • Web site provides detailed data on insider trading, institutional portfolios, and "First Call" earnings estimates. Includes a stock screening (filtering) application, a search facility, and price quotes on stocks, bonds, and mutual funds. Continuous updating. Fees: $34.95 per year for general service. First Call earnings service is $19.95 per month or $199.00 per year.

ONLINE DATABASES

InvesText. Thomson Financial Securities Data. • Provides full text online of investment research reports from more than 300 sources, including leading brokers and investment bankers. Reports are available on approximately 50,000 U. S. and international corporations. Separate industry reports cover 54 industries. Time span is 1982 to date, with daily updates. Inquire as to online cost and availability.

LEXIS Financial Information Service. LEXIS-NEXIS. • Includes many business and financial files, including the full text of *SEC News Digest*, *Zacks Earnings Forecaster*, SEC filings, and brokerage house research reports. Various time spans and updating frequencies. Inquire as to online cost and availability.

Mastering Online Investing: How to Use the Internet to Become a More Successful Investor. Michael C. Thomsett. Dearborn Financial Publishing. • 2001. $19.95. Emphasis is on the Internet as an information source for intelligent investing, avoiding "speculation and fads.".

Super Searchers on Wall Street: Top Investment Professionals Share Their Online Research Secrets. Amelia Kassel and Reva Basch. Information Today, Inc. • 2000. $24.95. Gives the results of interviews with "10 leading financial industry research experts." Explains how online information is used by stock brokers, investment bankers, and individual investors. Includes relevant Web sites and other sources. (CyberAge Books.).

Wilson Business Abstracts Online. H. W. Wilson Co. • Indexes and abstracts 600 major business periodicals, plus the *Wall Street Journal* and the business section of the *New York Times.* Indexing is from 1982, abstracting from 1990, with the two newspapers included from 1993. Updated weekly. Inquire as to online cost and availability. (*Business Periodicals Index* without abstracts is also available online.).

PERIODICALS AND NEWSLETTERS

AAII Journal. American Association of Individual Investors. • 10 times a year. $49.00 per year. Covers strategy and investment techniques.

Asset Management. Dow Jones Financial Publishing Corp. • Bimonthly. $345.00 per year. Covers the management of the assets of affluent, high net worth investors. Provides information on various financial products and services.

Bank Credit Analyst. BCA Publications Ltd. • Monthly. $695.00 per year. "The independent monthly forecast and analysis of trends in business conditions and major investment markets based on a continuous appraisal of money and credit flows." Includes many charts and graphs relating to money, credit, and securities in the U. S.

Bank Rate Monitor: The Weekly Financial Rate Reporter. Advertising News Service, Inc. • Weekly. $895.00 per year. Newsletter. Includes online addition and monthly supplement. Provides detailed information on interest rates currently paid by U. S. banks and savings institutions.

Barron's: The Dow Jones Business and Financial Weekly. Dow Jones and Co., Inc. • Weekly. $145.00 per year.

Bloomberg Personal Finance. Bloomberg L.P. • Monthly. $24.95 per year. Provides advice on personal finance, investments, travel, real estate, and maintaining an "upscale life style." Formerly *Bloomberg Personal.*

Commercial and Financial Chronicle. William B. Dana Co. • Weekly. $140.00. per year.

Financial Sentinel: Your Beacon to the World of Investing. Gulf Atlantic Publishing, Inc. • Monthly. $29.95 per year. Provides "The only complete listing of all OTC Bulletin Board stocks traded, with all issues listed on the Nasdaq SmallCap Market, the Toronto, and Vancouver Stock Exchanges." Also includes investment advice and recommendations of small capitalization stocks.

Forbes. Forbes, Inc. • Biweekly. $59.95 per year. Includes supplements: *Forbes ASAP* and *Forbes FYI.*

Investment Advisor. Dow Jones Financial Publishing Corp. • Monthly. $79.00 per year. Edited for professional investment advisors, financial planners, stock brokers, bankers, and others concerned with the management of assets.

Investment Dealers' Digest. Securities Data Publishing. • Weekly. $750.00 per year. Covers financial news, trends, new products, people, private placements, new issues of securities, and other aspects of the investment business. Includes feature stories. (Securities Data Publishing is a unit of Thomson Financial.).

Investment Guide. American Investment Services. • Monthly. $49.00 per year. Newsletter. Emphasis is on blue-chip stocks with high dividend yields.

Investment News: The Weekly Newspaper for Financial Advisers. Crain Communications, Inc. • Weekly. $38.00 per year. Edited for both personal and institutional investment advisers, planners, and managers.

Investment Reporter. MPL Communication, Inc. • Weekly. $279.00 per year. Newsletter. Monthly supplement, *Investment Planning Guide.* Recommendations for Canadian investments. Formerly *Personal Wealth Reporter.*

Investor's Business Daily. Investor's Business Daily, Inc. • Daily. $169.00 per year. Newspaper.

Journal of Alternative Investments. Institutional Investor. • Quarterly. $380.00 per year. Covers such items as hedge funds, private equity financing, funds of funds, real estate investment trusts, natural resource investments, foreign exchange, and emerging markets.

Journal of Private Portfolio Management. Institutional Investor. • Quarterly. $280.00 per year. Edited for managers of wealthy individuals' investment portfolios.

Louis Rukeyser's Wall Street. • Monthly. $79.00 per year. Newsletter. Gives recommendations for personal investing.

Mark Skousen's Forecasts & Strategies. Phillips Business Information, Inc. • Monthly. $99.00 per year. Newsletter.

Morningstar Stock Investor. Morningstar, Inc. • Monthly. $89.00 per year. Newsletter. Provides detailed information on the financial fundamentals of 450 selected, undervalued stocks. Estimated future worth of each stock is given, according to an "Intrinsic Value Measure.".

One Hundred Highest Yields Among Federally-Insured Banks and Savings Institutions. Advertising News Service, Inc. • Weekly. $124.00 per year. Newsletter.

Online Investor: Personal Investing for the Digital Age. Stock Trends, Inc. • Monthly. $24.95 per year. Provides advice and Web site reviews for online traders.

Outstanding Investor Digest: Perspectives and Activities of the Nation's Most Successful Money Managers. Outstanding Investor Digest, Inc. • $395.00 for 10 issues. Newsletter. Each issue features interviews with leading money managers.

Predictions: Specific Investment Forecasts and Recommendations from the World's Top Financial Experts. Lee Euler, editor. Agora, Inc. • Monthly. $78.00 per year. Newsletter.

Profit Investor Portfolio: The International Magazine of Money and Style. Profit Publications, Inc. • Bimonthly. $29.95 per year. A glossy consumer magazine featuring specific investment recommendations and articles on upscale travel and shopping.

Profitable Investing. Richard E. Band, editor. Phillips Business Information, Inc. • Monthly. $149.00 per year. Newsletter.

Richard C. Young's Intelligence Report. Phillips Publishing International, Inc. • Monthly. $99.00 per year. Newsletter. Provides conservative advice for investing in stocks, fixed-income securities, and mutual funds.

SmartMoney: The Wall Street Journal Magazine of Personal Business. Hearst Corp. • Monthly. $24.00 per year. Includes *Stock Trader's Almanac.*

Stanger Report: A Guide to Partnership Investing. Robert A. Stanger and Co. • Monthly. $447.00 per year. Newsletter providing analysis of limited partnership investments.

The Wall Street Journal. Dow Jones & Co., Inc. • Daily. $175.00 per year. Covers news and trends relating to business, industry, finance, the economy, and international commerce. Provides extensive price and other data for the securities, commodity, options, futures, foreign exchange, and money markets.

Wall Street Transcript: A Professional Publication for the Business and Financial Community. Wall Street Transcript Corp. • Weekly. $1,890.00. per year. Provides reprints of investment research reports.

Worth: Financial Intelligence. Worth Media. • 10 times a year. $18.00 per year. Contains articles for affluent consumers on personal financial management, including investments, estate planning, and taxes.

Your Money. Consumers Digest, Inc. • Bimonthly. $25.97 per year. Provides information and advice on personal finance and investments.

PRICE SOURCES

Bank and Quotation Record. William B. Dana Co. • Monthly. $130.00 per year.

STATISTICS SOURCES

Standard & Poor's Industry Surveys. Standard & Poor's. • Semiannual. $1,800.00. Two looseleaf volumes. Includes monthly supplements. Provides detailed, individual surveys of 52 major industry groups. Each survey is revised on a semiannual basis. Also includes "Monthly Investment Review" (industry group investment analysis) and monthly "Trends & Projections" (economic analysis).

TRADE/PROFESSIONAL ASSOCIATIONS

American Association of Individual Investors. 625 N. Michigan Ave., Suite 1900, Chicago, IL 60611. Phone: 800-428-2244 or (312)280-0170 Fax: (312)280-9883 E-mail: members@aaii.com • URL: http://www.aaii.com.

Association for Investment Management and Research. 560 Ray C. Hunt Dr., Charlottesville, VA 22903-0668. Phone: 800-247-8132 or (804)951-5499 Fax: (804)951-5262 E-mail: info@aimr.org • URL: http://www.aimr.org.

National Association of Securities Dealers. 1735 K St., N.W., Washington, DC 20006-1506. Phone: (202)728-8000 Fax: (202)293-6260 • URL: http://www.nasdr.com/1000.asp.

National Investor Relations Institute. 8045 Leesberg Pike, Suite 600, Vienna, VA 22182. Phone: (703)506-3570 Fax: (703)506-3571 E-mail: info@niri.org • URL: http://www.niri.org.

OTHER SOURCES

Business & Company Resource Center. The Gale Group. • Fee-based Web site provides a wide range of business, industry, and specific company information. Access is offered to trade journal articles, market research data, insider trading activity, major shareholder data, corporate histories, emerging technology reports, corporate earnings estimates, press releases, and other sources. Provides detailed company profiles, industry overviews, and rankings. Offers integration of Predicasts PROMT, Newsletters ASAP, Investext Plus, Business Index ASAP, Brands and Their Companies, and other databases (many have full text).

Factiva. Dow Jones Reuters Business Interactive, LLC. • Fee-based Web site provides "global news and business information through Web sites and content integration solutions." Includes Dow Jones and Reuters newswires, The Wall Street Journal, and more than 7,000 other sources of current news, historical articles, market research reports, and investment analysis. Content includes 96 major U. S. newspapers, 900 non-English sources, trade publications, media transcripts, country profiles, news photos, etc.

Nexis.com. Lexis-Nexis Group. • Fee-based Web site offers searching of about 2.8 billion documents in some 30,000 news, business, and legal information sources. Features include a subject directory covering 1,200 topics in 34 categories and a Company Dossier containing information on more than 500,000 public and private companies. Boolean searching is offered.

The Value Line Investment Survey. Value Line Publishing, Inc. • Weekly. $570.00 per year. Provides detailed information and ratings for 1,700 stocks actively-traded in the U. S.

INVESTMENTS, INSTITUTIONAL

See: INSTITUTIONAL INVESTMENTS

INVESTMENTS, REAL ESTATE

See: REAL ESTATE INVESTMENTS

IRAS

See: INDIVIDUAL RETIREMENT ACCOUNTS

IRON AND STEEL INDUSTRY

See also: FOUNDRIES; METAL INDUSTRY

ABSTRACTS AND INDEXES

Steels Alert. Cambridge Information Group. • Monthly. $340.00 per year. Provides citations to the business and industrial literature of iron and steel. (Materials Business Information Series).

CD-ROM DATABASES

METADEX Materials Collection: Metals-Polymers-Ceramics. Cambridge Scientific Abstracts. • Quarterly. $6,950.00 per year. Provides CD-ROM citations to the worldwide literature of materials science and metallurgy. Corresponds to *Metals Abstracts, Alloys Index, Steels Alert, Nonferrous Alert, Polymers/Ceramics/Composites Alert,* and *Engineered Materials Abstracts.* (Formerly produced by ASM International.).

DIRECTORIES

Directory of Iron and Steel Plants (The Black Book). Association of Iron and Steel Engineers. • Annual. $50.00. Lists executives and officials in the United States and selected overseas steel companies and plants.

Directory of Steel Foundries and Buyers Guide. Steel Founders' Society of America. • Biennial. $95.00. Formerly *Directory of Steel Foundries in the United States, Canada, and Mexico.*

FINANCIAL RATIOS

Annual Statement Studies. Robert Morris Associates: The Association of Lending and Credit Risk Professiona. • Annual. Free to members; non-members, $140.00. Median and quartile financial ratios are given for over 400 kinds of manufacturing, wholesale, retail, construction, and consumer finance establishments. Data is sorted by both asset size and sales volume. Includes a clearly written "Definition of Ratios" and an alphabetical industry index.

HANDBOOKS AND MANUALS

Corrosion of Stainless Steels. A. John Sedriks. John Wiley and Sons, Inc. • 1996. $86.50. Second edition. Covers the corrosion and corrosion control of stainless steels used in a variety of applications. (Corrosion Monograph Series).

Stainless Steels, 87: Proceedings of Conference, University of York, 14-16 September, 87. Available from Ashgate Publishing Co. • 1988. $94.50. Published by Inst Material.

INTERNET DATABASES

Fedstats. Federal Interagency Council on Statistical Policy. Phone: (202)395-7254 • URL: http://www.fedstats.gov • Web site features an efficient search facility for full-text statistics produced by more than 70 federal agencies, including the Census Bureau, the Bureau of Economic Analysis, and the Bureau of Labor Statistics. Boolean searches can be made within one agency or for all agencies combined. Links are offered to international statistical bureaus, including the UN, IMF, OECD, UNESCO, Eurostat, and 20 individual countries. Fees: Free.

ONLINE DATABASES

DRI U.S. Central Database. Data Products Division. • Provides more than 23,000 business, financial, demographic, economic, foreign trade, and industry-related time series for the U.S. Includes national income, population, retail-wholesale trade, price indexes, labor data, housing, industrial production, banking, interest rates, money supply, etc. Time period is generally 1947 to date (some data back to 1929). Updating varies. Inquire as to online cost and availability.

Materials Business File. Cambridge Scientific Abstracts. • Provides online abstracts and citations to worldwide materials literature, covering the business and industrial aspects of metals, plastics, ceramics, and composites. Corresponds to *Steels Alert, Nonferrous Metals Alert,* and *Polymers/Ceramics/Composites Alert.* Time period is 1985 to date, with monthly updates. (Formerly produced by ASM International.) Inquire as to online cost and availability.

METADEX. Cambridge Scientific Abstracts. • Covers the worldwide literature of metals, metallurgy, and materials science, 1966 to date. Includes detailed alloys indexing from 1974. Biweekly updating. Inquire as to online cost and availability. (Formerly produced by ASM International.).

PROMT: Predicasts Overview of Markets and Technology. The Gale Group. • Companies, products, applied technologies and markets. U.S. and international literature coverage, 1972 to date. Inquire as to online cost and availability. Provides abstracts from more than 1,600 publications. Weekly updates.

PERIODICALS AND NEWSLETTERS

Advanced Materials and Processes. ASM International. • Monthly. Free to members; non-members $250.00 per year; institutions, $250.00 per year. Incorporates *Metal Progress.*Technical information and reports on new developments in the technology of engineered materials and manufacturing processes.

A I S E Steel Technology. Association of Iron and Steel Engineers. • Monthly. $58.00 per year. Formerly (Iron and Steel Engineer).

Metal Bulletin. Metal Bulletin, Inc. • Semiweekly. $1,378 per year. Provides news of international trends, prices, and market conditions for both steel and non-ferrous metal industries. (Published in England.).

Metal Bulletin Monthly. Metal Bulletin, Inc. • Monthly. Price on application. Edited for international metal industry business executives and senior technical personnel. Covers business, economic, and technical developments. (Published in England.).

Modern Casting. American Foundrymen's Society, Inc. • Monthly. $50.00 per year.

New Steel: Mini and Integrated Mill Management and Technologies. Cahners Business Information. • Monthly. $89.00 per year. Covers the primary metals industry, both ferrous and nonferrous. Includes technical, marketing, and product development articles. Formerly *Iron Age.*

Steel Times International. DMG World Media. • Bimonthly. $252.00 per year. Includes *Iron and Steel Directory.*

33 Metalproducing: For Primary Producers of Steel, Aluminum, and Copper-Base Alloys. Penton Media, Inc. • Monthly. $65.00 per year. Covers metal production technology and methods and industry news. Includes a bimonthly *Nonferrous Supplement.*

STATISTICS SOURCES

American Iron and Steel Annual Statistical Report. American Iron and Steel Institute. • Annual. $100.00 per year.

Annual Survey of Manufactures. Available from U. S. Government Printing Office. • Annual. Prices vary. Issued by the U. S. Census Bureau as an interim update to the *Census of Manufactures.* Includes data on number of manufacturing establishments in various industries, employment, labor costs, value of shipments, capital expenditures, inventories, energy costs, and assets. (See also Census Bureau home page, http://www.census.gov/.).

Business Statistics of the United States. Courtenay M. Slater, editor. Bernan Associates. • 1999. $74.00. Fifth edition. Based on *Business Statistics,* formerly issue by the Bureau of Economic Analysis, U. S. Department of Commerce. Provides basic data for a wide variety of U. S. industries, services, and economic indicators. Most statistics are shown annually for 29 years and monthly for the most recent four years.

Manufacturing Profiles. Available from U. S. Government Printing Office. • Annual. Issued by the U. S. Census Bureau. A printed consolidation of the entire *Current Industrial Report* series, presenting "all the data compiled." Contains statistics on production, shipments, inventories, consumption, exports, imports, and orders for a wide variety of manufactured products. (See also Census Bureau home page, http://www.census.gov/.).

Mineral Commodity Summaries. Available from U. S. Government Printing Office. • Annual. Published by the U. S. Geological Survey, Department of the Interior (http://www.usgs.gov). Contains detailed, five-year data for about 90 nonfuel minerals. Covers a wide range of statistics, including production, imports, exports, consumption, reserves, prices, tariff information, and industry employment. (Two pages are devoted to each mineral.).

OECD Iron and Steel Industry. Organization for Economic Cooperation and Development. Available from OECD Publications and Information Center. • Annual. Price varies. Data for orders, production, manpower, imports, exports, consumption, prices and investment in the iron and steel industry in OECD member countries. Text in English and French.

OECD Steel Market and Outlook. Organization for Economic Cooperation and Development. OECD Publications and Information Center. • Annual. Price varies.

Standard & Poor's Industry Surveys. Standard & Poor's. • Semiannual. $1,800.00. Two looseleaf volumes. Includes monthly supplements. Provides detailed, individual surveys of 52 major industry groups. Each survey is revised on a semiannual basis. Also includes "Monthly Investment Review" (industry group investment analysis) and monthly "Trends & Projections" (economic analysis).

Statistics of World Trade in Steel. United Nations Economic Commission for Europe. Available from United Nations Publications. • Annual. $90.00.

Steel Mill Products. U.S. Bureau of the Census. • Annual. (Current Industrial Reports MA-33B).

Survey of Current Business. Available from U. S. Government Printing Office. • Monthly. $49.00 per year. Issued by Bureau of Economic Analysis, U. S. Department of Commerce. Presents a wide variety of business and economic data.

WEFA Industrial Monitor. John Wiley and Sons, Inc. • Annual. $65.00. Prepared by industry analysts at WEFA, an economic forecasting and consulting firm (originally Wharton Econometric Forecasting Associates). Contains discussions of the outlook for major U. S. industries, with many 10-year forecasts (WEFA Web site is http://www.wefa.com).

TRADE/PROFESSIONAL ASSOCIATIONS

American Foundrymen's Society. 505 State St., Des Plaines, IL 60016-8399. Phone: 800-537-4237 or (708)824-0181 Fax: (708)824-7848 • URL: http://www.afsinc.org.

American Iron and Steel Institute. 1101 17th St., N.W., Ste. 1300, Washington, DC 20036-4700. Phone: (202)452-7100 Fax: (202)463-6573 • URL: http://www.steel.org.

Association of Iron and Steel Engineers. Three Gateway Center, Suite 1900, Pittsburgh, PA 15222. Phone: (412)281-6323 Fax: (412)281-4657 • URL: http://www.aise.org.

Association of Steel Distributors. 401 N. Michigan Ave., Chicago, IL 60611. Phone: (312)644-6610 Fax: (312)527-6705 • URL: http://www.steeldistributors.org/asd/.

Institute of Scrap Recycling Industries. 1325 G St., N.W., Suite 1000, Washington, DC 20005-3104. Phone: (202)737-1770 Fax: (202)626-0900 E-mail: isri@isri.com • URL: http://www.isri.org.

Iron and Steel Society. 186 Thorn Hill Rd., Warrendale, PA 15086-7528. Phone: (724)776-1535 Fax: (724)776-0430 E-mail: mailbag@issource.org • URL: http://www.issource.org.

Steel Founders' Society of America. Cast Metals Federation Bldg., 455 State St., Des Plaines, IL 60016. Phone: (847)382-8240 Fax: (847)382-8287 E-mail: monroe@scra.org • URL: http://www.sfsa.org.

Steel Service Center Institute. 127 Public Square, Suite 2400, Cleveland, OH 44114-1216. Phone: (216)694-3630 • URL: http://www.ssci.org.

IRON AND STEEL SCRAP METAL INDUSTRY

DIRECTORIES

North American Scrap Metals Directory. G.I.E. Media, Inc. • Annual. $85.00. Lists more than 9,000 scrap metal processors, brokers, and dealers.

INTERNET DATABASES

Fedstats. Federal Interagency Council on Statistical Policy. Phone: (202)395-7254 • URL: http://www.fedstats.gov • Web site features an efficient search facility for full-text statistics produced by more than 70 federal agencies, including the Census Bureau, the Bureau of Economic Analysis, and the Bureau of Labor Statistics. Boolean searches can be made within one agency or for all agencies combined. Links are offered to international statistical bureaus, including the UN, IMF, OECD, UNESCO, Eurostat, and 20 individual countries. Fees: Free.

ONLINE DATABASES

DRI U.S. Central Database. Data Products Division. • Provides more than 23,000 business, financial, demographic, economic, foreign trade, and industry-related time series for the U.S. Includes national income, population, retail-wholesale trade, price indexes, labor data, housing, industrial production, banking, interest rates, money supply, etc. Time period is generally 1947 to date (some data back to 1929). Updating varies. Inquire as to online cost and availability.

PERIODICALS AND NEWSLETTERS

Scrap. Institute of Scrap Recycling Industries. • Bimonthly. Free to members; non-members, $32.95 per year. Formerly *Scrap Processing and Recycling.*

STATISTICS SOURCES

Business Statistics of the United States. Courtenay M. Slater, editor. Bernan Associates. • 1999. $74.00. Fifth edition. Based on *Business Statistics*, formerly issue by the Bureau of Economic Analysis, U. S. Department of Commerce. Provides basic data for a wide variety of U. S. industries, services, and economic indicators. Most statistics are shown annually for 29 years and monthly for the most recent four years.

Survey of Current Business. Available from U. S. Government Printing Office. • Monthly. $49.00 per year. Issued by Bureau of Economic Analysis, U. S. Department of Commerce. Presents a wide variety of business and economic data.

TRADE/PROFESSIONAL ASSOCIATIONS

Institute of Scrap Recycling Industries. 1325 G St., N.W., Suite 1000, Washington, DC 20005-3104. Phone: (202)737-1770 Fax: (202)626-0900 E-mail: isri@isri.com • URL: http://www.isri.org.

IRON FOUNDRIES

See: FOUNDRIES

IRRIGATION

ABSTRACTS AND INDEXES

Environment Abstracts. Congressional Information Service. • Monthly. Price varies. Provides multidisciplinary coverage of the world's environmental literature. Incorporates *Acid Rain Abstracts.*

Environment Abstracts Annual: A Guide to the Key Environmental Literature of the Year. Congressional Information Service. • Annual. $495.00. A yearly cumulation of *Environment Abstracts.*

Irrigation and Drainage Abstracts. Available from CABI Publishing North America. • Quarterly. $545.00 per year. Published in England by CABI Publishing. Provides worldwide coverage of the literature.

CD-ROM DATABASES

Environment Abstracts on CD-ROM. Congressional Information Service, Inc. • Quarterly. $1,295.00 per year. Contains the following CD-ROM databases: *Environment Abstracts, Energy Abstracts*, and *Acid Rain Abstracts.* Length of coverage varies.

DIRECTORIES

Irrigation Association Membership-Directory and Industry Buyers' Guide. Irrigation Association. • Annual. Free to members; non-members, $25.00. Includes manufacturing, distribution, contracting, consultation, research and educational information.

ONLINE DATABASES

CAB Abstracts. CAB International North America. • Contains 46 specialized abstract collections covering over 10,000 journals and monographs in the areas of agriculture, horticulture, forest products, farm products, nutrition, dairy science, poultry, grains, animal health, entomology, etc. Time period is 1972 to date, with monthly updates. Inquire as to online cost and availability. *CAB Abstracts on CD-ROM* also available, with annual updating.

Enviroline. Congressional Information Service, Inc. • Provides online indexing and abstracting of worldwide environmental and natural resource literature from 1975 to date. Updated monthly. Inquire as to online cost and availability.

TRADE/PROFESSIONAL ASSOCIATIONS

Irrigation Association. 8260 Willow Oak Corporation Dr., Fairfax, VA 22031. Phone: (703)573-3551 Fax: (703)573-1913 • URL: http://www.irrigation.org.

National Water Resources Association. 3800 N. Fairfax Dr., Suite 4, Arlington, VA 22203. Phone: (703)524-1544 Fax: (703)524-1548 E-mail: nwra@dgs.dgsys.com • URL: http://www.nwra.org.

U.S. Committee on Irrigation and Drainage. 1616 17th St., No. 483, Denver, CO 80202. Phone: (303)628-5430 Fax: (303)628-5431 E-mail: stephens@uscid.org • URL: http://www.2.privatei.com/~uscid.

ISO 9000 STANDARDS

See: TOTAL QUALITY MANAGEMENT (TQM)

ISOTOPES

GENERAL WORKS

Isotopes for Medicine and the Life Sciences. S. James Adelstein and Frederick J. Manning, editors. National Academy Press. • 1995. $30.00. Includes bibliographical references and a glossary.

PERIODICALS AND NEWSLETTERS

International Journal of Applied Radiation and Isotopes. Elsevier Science. • Monthly. $465.00 per year.

RESEARCH CENTERS AND INSTITUTES

Radioisotope Laboratory. Texas A&M University. Nuclear Engineering Dept., 129 Zachry Bldg., College Station, TX 77843-3133. Phone: (979)845-4107 Fax: (979)845-6443 E-mail: iah@trinity.tamu.edu.

J

JANITORIAL SERVICES

See: MAINTENANCE OF BUILDINGS

JAPAN

See: ASIAN MARKETS

JAVA (COMPUTER PROGRAM LANGUAGE)

HANDBOOKS AND MANUALS

Advanced Techniques for Java Developers. Daniel J. Berg and J. Steven Fritzinger. John Wiley and Sons, Inc. • 1998. $49.99. Second revised edition. Written for experienced Java programmers. CD-ROM included.

Developing Java Software. Russel Winder. John Wiley and Sons, Inc. • 2000. $49.99. Second edition.

Introduction to Object-Oriented Programming with Java. C. Thomas Wu. McGraw-Hill. • 2001. Second edition. Price on application.

Java FAQs. Clifford J. Berg. Prentice Hall. • 2001. $26.95.

Java for Students 1.2. Doug Bell and Mike Parr. Prentice Hall. • 1998. $62.00. A basic introduction to Java.

Java Primer. David Forster. Addison-Wesley Longman, Inc. • 1999. $10.01.

Java Tutorial: Object-Oriented Programming for the Internet. Mary Campione and Kathy Walrath. Addison-Wesley Longman, Inc. • 1996. $41.95. Third edition. Presents a self-guided tour of the Java programming language. CD-ROM included. (Java Tutorial Services).

Teach Yourself Advanced Java in 21 Days. Scott Williams. • Date not set. $35.00.

Understanding Object-Oriented Programming with Java. Timothy Budd. Addison-Wesley Longman, Inc. • 1999. $63.00. Second edition.

PERIODICALS AND NEWSLETTERS

Java Developer's Journal. Sys-Con Publications. • Monthly. $49.00 per year. Provides technical information for Java professionals.

Java Pro. Fawcette Technical Publications. • Monthly. $35.00 per year. Contains technical articles for Java developers.

Java Report: The Independent Source for Java Development. Sigs Publications, Inc. • Monthly. $329.00 per year. Covers Java programming and development for software professionals.

OTHER SOURCES

Java Cookbook: Solutions and Examples for Java Developers. Ian Darwin. O'Reilly & Associates, Inc. • 2001. $44.95. Presents a "comprehensive collection of problems, solutions, and practical examples" for Java developers.

Learning Java. Pat Niemeyer and Jonathan Knudsen. O'Reilly & Associates, Inc. • 2000. $34.95, including CD-ROM. Covers the essentials for programmers beginning to use Java.

Teach Yourself Java. Chris Wright. NTC/Contemporary Publishing Group. • 2001. $12.95. Second edition. Covers the basics of designing websites and interactive pages.

JET PROPULSION

See: ROCKET INDUSTRY

JEWELRY BUSINESS

See also: GEMS AND GEMSTONES

DIRECTORIES

Jewelers' Circular/Keystone-Jewelers' Directory. Cahners Business Information. • Annual. $33.95. About 8,500 manufacturers, importers and wholesale jewelers providing merchandise and supplies to the jewelry retailing industry; and related trade organizations. Included with subscription to *Jewelers' Circular Keystone.*

Manufacturing Jewelers Buyers' Guide. Manufacturing Jewelers and Suppliers of America. • Biennial. $25.00. Lists manufacturers and suppliers and has cross-reference by products listed.

ENCYCLOPEDIAS AND DICTIONARIES

Illustrated Dictionary of Jewelry. Harold Newman. W. W. Norton & Co., Inc. • 1994. $29.95.

Jewelers' Dictionary. Donald S. McNeil, editor. Jewelers' Circular/Keystone. • 1979. $39.95. Third edition.

FINANCIAL RATIOS

Annual Statement Studies. Robert Morris Associates: The Association of Lending and Credit Risk Professiona. • Annual. Free to members; non-members, $140.00. Median and quartile financial ratios are given for over 400 kinds of manufacturing, wholesale, retail, construction, and consumer finance establishments. Data is sorted by both asset size and sales volume. Includes a clearly written "Definition of Ratios" and an alphabetical industry index.

HANDBOOKS AND MANUALS

Jewelry and Gems: The Buying Guide-How to Buy Diamonds, Pearls, Precious and Other Popular Gems with Confidence and Knowledge. Antoinette L. Matlins and Antonio C. Bonanno. GemStone Press. • 1998. $24.95. Fourth revised edition.

ONLINE DATABASES

PROMT: Predicasts Overview of Markets and Technology. The Gale Group. • Companies, products, applied technologies and markets. U.S. and international literature coverage, 1972 to date. Inquire as to online cost and availability. Provides abstracts from more than 1,600 publications. Weekly updates.

PERIODICALS AND NEWSLETTERS

American Jewelry Manufacturer. Manufacturing Jewelers and Silversmiths of America, Inc. • Monthly. $36.00 per year.

Jewelers' Circular Keystone. Cahners Business Information. • Monthly. $90.00 per year.

Modern Jeweler. Cygnus Business Media. • Monthly. $60.00 per year. Edited for retail jewelers. Covers the merchandising of jewelry, gems, and watches. Supersedes in part *Modern Jeweler.*

National Jeweler. Miller Freeman, Inc. • 24 times a year. $100.00 per year. For jewelry retailers.

STATISTICS SOURCES

U. S. Industry and Trade Outlook: The McGraw-Hill Companies and the U.S. Department of Commerce/International Trade Administration. Datapso Research Corp. • Annual. $69.95. Produced by the International Trade Administration, U. S. Department of Commerce, in a "public-private" partnership with DRI/McGraw-Hill and Standard & Poor's. Provides basic data, outlook for the current year, and "Long-Term Prospects" (five-year projections) for a wide variety of products and services. Includes high technology industries. Formerly *U. S. Industrial Outlook.*

TRADE/PROFESSIONAL ASSOCIATIONS

Gemological Institute of America. 5345 Armada Dr., Carlsbad, CA 92008. Phone: 800-421-7250 or (760)603-4000 Fax: (760)603-4080 • URL: http://www.gia.edu.

Jewelers Board of Trade. 95 Jefferson Blvd., Warwick, RI 02888-1046. Phone: (401)467-0055 Fax: (401)467-1199 • URL: http://www.jewelersboard.com • A credit reporting and collection organization for the jewelry business.

Jewelers of America. 1185 Sixth Ave., 30th Fl., New York, NY 10036. Phone: 800-223-0673 or (212)768-8777 Fax: (212)768-8087 E-mail: jewelersam@aol.com • URL: http://www.jewelers.org.

Jewelers Security Alliance of the U.S. Six E. 45th St., New York, NY 10017. Phone: 800-537-0067 or (212)687-0328 Fax: (212)808-9168 E-mail: jsa@polygon.net • URL: http://www.jsa.polygon.net.

Jewelers Vigilance Committee. 25 W. 45th St., Suite 400, New York, NY 10036. Phone: (212)997-2002 Fax: (212)997-9148.

Jewelry Information Center. 1185 Ave. of the Americas, 30th Fl., New York, NY 10036. Phone: 800-459-0130 or (212)398-2319 Fax: (212)398-2324 E-mail: jic@jewelryinfo.org • URL: http://www.jewelryinfo.org.

Manufacturing Jewelers and Suppliers of America. 45 Royal Little Dr., Providence, RI 02908-5305. Phone: 800-444-6572 or (401)274-3840 Fax: (401)274-0265 E-mail: mjsa@mjsaimc.com.

OTHER SOURCES

Confidential Reference Book of the Jewelers Board of Trade. Jewelers Board of Trade. • Supplied on loan basis only to members of the Jewelers Board of Trade. Jewelry and allied product manufacturers, wholesalers and retailers; complete address, phone number and credit rating.

JOB DESCRIPTIONS

See also: OCCUPATIONS

ENCYCLOPEDIAS AND DICTIONARIES

BLR Encyclopedia of Prewritten Job Descriptions. Business and Legal Reports, Inc. • $159.95. Looseleaf. Two volumes. Covers all levels "from president to mail clerk.".

Selected Characteristics of Occupations Defined in the Revised Dictionary of Occupational Titles. Available from U. S. Government Printing Office. • 1993. Provides data on training time, physical demands, and environmental conditions for various occupations. (Employment and Training Administration, U. S. Department of Labor.).

HANDBOOKS AND MANUALS

Complete Guide to Performance Standards for Library Personnel. Carol F. Goodson. Neal-Schuman Publishers, Inc. • 1997. $55.00. Provides specific job descriptions and performance standards for both professional and paraprofessional library personnel. Includes a bibliography of performance evaluation literature, with annotations.

Hiring Right: A Practical Guide. Susan J. Herman. Sage Publications, Inc. • 1993. $46.00. A practical manual covering job definition, recruitment, interviewing, testing, and checking of references.

Position Descriptions in Special Libraries. Del Sweeney and Karin Zilla, editors. Special Libraries Association. • 1996. $41.00. Third revised edition. Provides 87 descriptions of library and information management positions.

Standard Occupational Classification Manual. Available from Bernan Associates. • 2000. $38.00. Replaces the *Dictionary of Occupational Titles.* Produced by the federal Office of Management and Budget, Executive Office of the President. "Occupations are classified based on the work performed, and on the required skills, education, training, and credentials for each one." Six-digit codes contain elements for 23 Major Groups, 96 Minor Groups, 451 Broad Occupations, and 820 Detailed Occupations. Designed to reflect the occupational structure currently existing in the U. S.

JOB HUNTING

See also: EMPLOYMENT AGENCIES AND SERVICES; JOB RESUMES

GENERAL WORKS

Encyclopedia of Careers and Vocational Guidance. Holli Cosgrove. Ferguson Publishing Co. • 2000. $159.95. 11th edition.

How to Win the Job You Really Want. Janice Weinberg. Henry Holt and Co.,LLC. • 1995. $11.95. Second edition.

Secrets of a Top Headhunter: How to Get the High-Paying Job You've Always Wanted. Lester Korn. Simon & Schuster Trade. • 1988. $17.45.

What Color is Your Parachute? 2001: A Practical Manual for Job Hunters and Career Changers. Richard N. Bolles. Ten Speed Press. • 2000. $24.95. Revised edition. Features non-traditional job searching methods.

When You Lose Your Job: Laid Off, Fired, Early Retired, Relocated, Demoted. Cliff Hakim. Berrett-Koehler Publishers, Inc. • 1993. $14.95. A guide to overcoming job loss. Covers emotional responses, as well as practical matters such as networking, resumes, and preparing for interviews.

ABSTRACTS AND INDEXES

Business Periodicals Index. H. W. Wilson Co. • Monthly, except August, with quarterly and annual cumulations. Service basis for print edition; CD-ROM edition, $1,495.00 per year.

Readers' Guide to Periodical Literature. H. W. Wilson Co. • Monthly. $220.00 per year. CD-ROM edition, $1,495 per year, including annual cumulation. Indexes about 250 peridicals of general interest.

BIBLIOGRAPHIES

Job & Career Books. Kennedy Information, LLC. • Annual. Free. Contains descriptions of selected books from various publishers on job searching and choice of career.

Job Hunter's Sourcebook: Where to Find Employment Leads and Other Job Search Resources. The Gale Group. • 1999. $99.00. Fourth edition. Covers 179 professions and occupations.

CD-ROM DATABASES

Magazine Index Plus. The Gale Group. • Monthly. $4,000.00 per year (includes InfoTrac workstation). Provides full text on CD-ROM for about 100 popular, general interest magazines and indexing for 300 others. Includes special indexing of reviews and product evaluations. Time period is 1980 to date.

DIRECTORIES

The Almanac of American Employers: The Only Complete Guide to the Hottest, Fastest-Growing Major Corporations. Plunkett Research, Ltd. • Annual. $149.99. Provides descriptions of 500 large corporations, including salaries/benefits ratings, corporate culture profiles, types of employment, and other company information for job-seekers. Includes four indexes.

Business and Finance Career Directory. Visible Ink Press. • 1992. $17.95.

Computing and Software Career Directory. The Gale Group. • 1993. $39.00. Includes career information relating to programmers, software engineers, technical writers, systems experts, and other computer specialists. Provides advice from "insiders," resume suggestions, a directory of companies that may offer entry-level positions, and a directory of career information sources. (Career Advisor Series.).

CyberTools for Business: Practical Web Sites that will Save You Time and Money. Wayne Harris. Hoover's, Inc. • 1997. $19.95. Describes 100 World Wide Web sites that are useful for business, investing, and job hunting. Also lists Web addresses for about 4,500 public and private companies.

D and B Employment Opportunities Directory Career Guide. Dun and Bradstreet Information Services. • Annual. Libraries, $495.00. Lists more than 5,000 companies that have career opportunities in various fields. A Dun & Bradstreet publication.

Environmental Career Directory. Visible Ink Press. • 1993. $17.95. Includes career information relating to workers in conservation, recycling, wildlife management, pollution control, and other areas. Provides advice from "insiders," resume suggestions, a directory of companies that may offer entry-level positions, and a directory of career information sources. (Career Advisor Series.).

Executive Employment Guide. AMACOM. • Monthly. $20.00. Concise listing of about 151 firms, such as executive search organizations and employment agencies, that assist executives in locating employment.

Healthcare Career Directory: Nurses and Physicians: A Practical One-Stop Guide to Getting a Job in Public Relations. The Gale Group. • 1993. $17.95. Second edition. Includes information on careers in nursing, family medicine, surgery, and other medical areas. Provides advice from "insiders," resume suggestions, a directory of companies that may offer entry-level positions, and a directory of career information sources. *Career Advisor Series.*

Job Seeker's Guide to Private and Public Companies. The Gale Group. • 1995. $365.00. Third edition. Four regional volumes: *The West, The Midwest, The Northeast,* and *The South.* Covers about 15,000 companies, providing information on personnel department contacts, corporate officials, company benefits, application procedures, etc. Regional volumes are available separately at $99.00.

Magazines Careers Directory: A Practical One-Stop Guide to Getting a Job in Publc Relations. Visible Ink Press. • 1993. $17.95. Fifth edition. Includes information on magazine publishing careers in art, editing, sales, and business management. Provides advice from "insiders," resume suggestions, a directory of companies that may offer entry-level positions, and a directory of career information sources. *Career Advisor Series.*

NACE National Directory: Who's Who in Career Planning, Placement, and Recruitment. National Association of Colleges and Employers. • Annual. Members, $32.95; non-members, $47.95. Lists over 2,200 college placement offices and about 2,000 companies interested in recruiting college graduates. Gives names of placement and recruitment personnel. Formerly *CPC National Dierctory.*

Peterson's Internships: More Than 40,000 Opportunities to Get an Edge in Today's Competitive Job Market. Peterson's. • Annual. $24.95. Lists about 40,000 career-oriented internships in a wide variety of fields, including business.

Peterson's Job Opportunities for Business Majors. Peterson's. • Annual. $21.95. Provides career information for the 2,000 largest U. S. employers in various industries.

Plunkett's Companion to the Almanac of American Employers: Mid-Size Firms. Plunkett Research, Ltd. • Annual. $149.99. Provides job-seekers with detailed information about fast-growing, medium-size corporations. Includes diskette.

Plunkett's Employers' Internet Sites with Careers Information. Plunkett Research, Ltd. • Annual. $149.99. Includes diskette.

HANDBOOKS AND MANUALS

Career Guide to Industries. Available from U. S. Government Printing Office. • 1998. $17.00. Issued by the Bureau of Labor Statistics, U. S. Department of Labor (http://www.bls.gov). Presents background career information (text) and statistics for the 40 industries that account for 70 percent of wage and salary jobs in the U. S. Includes nature of the industry, employment data, working conditions, training, earnings, rate of job growth, outlook, and other career factors. (BLS Bulletin 2503.).

Job Search: The Total System. Kenneth Dawson and Sheryl N. Dawson. John Wiley and Sons, Inc. • 1996. $15.95. Second edition.

The New Complete Job Search. Richard H. Beatty. John Wiley and Sons, Inc. • 1992. $12.95. Tells how to conduct an effective job hunting campaign. Resumes, making contacts, interviews, and decision-making are discussed.

The Only Job-Hunting Guide You'll Ever Need: The Most Comprehensive Guide for Job Hunters and Career Switchers. Kathryn Petras and Ross Petras.

Simon & Schuster Trade. • 1995. $15.00. Revised edition.

ONLINE DATABASES

Readers' Guide Abstracts Online. H. W. Wilson Co. • Indexes and abstracts general interest periodicals, 1983 to date. Weekly updates. Inquire as to online cost and availability.

Wilson Business Abstracts Online. H. W. Wilson Co. • Indexes and abstracts 600 major business periodicals, plus the *Wall Street Journal* and the business section of the *New York Times*. Indexing is from 1982, abstracting from 1990, with the two newspapers included from 1993. Updated weekly. Inquire as to online cost and availability. (*Business Periodicals Index* without abstracts is also available online.).

PERIODICALS AND NEWSLETTERS

Corporate Jobs Outlook!. Plunkett Research, Ltd. • Bimonthly. $179.99 per year. Newsletter. Presents data on job possibilities at fast-growing, mid-sized corporations. Supplement available *Almanac of American Employers.*

National Business Employment Weekly. Dow Jones and Co., Inc. • Weekly. $199.00 per year. In addition to employment advertisements reprinted from various editions of the *Wall Street Journal*, contains substantial articles on how to find a job.

ReCareering Newsletter: An Idea and Resource Guide to Second Career and Relocation Planning. Publications Plus, Inc. • Monthly. $59.00 per year. Edited for "downsized managers, early retirees, and others in career transition after leaving traditional employment." Offers advice on second careers, franchises, starting a business, finances, education, training, skills assessment, and other matters of interest to the newly unemployed.

RESEARCH CENTERS AND INSTITUTES

Center for Labor and Human Resource Studies. Temple University, School of Business and Management, Speakman Hall, Room 366, Philadelphia, PA 19122. Phone: (215)204-8029 Fax: (215)204-5698 • Investigates factors affecting labor market success.

National Institute for Work and Learning. Academy for Educational Development, 1875 Connecticut Ave., N.W., Washington, DC 20009. Phone: (202)884-8187 Fax: (202)884-8422 E-mail: ichaner@aed.org • URL: http://www.niwl.org • Research areas include adult education, training, unemployment insurance, and career development.

Women Employed Institute. 22 W. Monroe St., Suite 1400, Chicago, IL 60603-2505. Phone: (312)782-3902 Fax: (312)782-5249 E-mail: info@womenemployed.org • URL: http://www.womenemployed.org • Research areas include the economic status of working women, sexual harassment in the workplace, equal employment opportunity, and career development.

TRADE/PROFESSIONAL ASSOCIATIONS

Association of Executive Search Consultants. 500 Fifth Ave., Suite 930, New York, NY 10110-0999. Phone: (212)398-9556 Fax: (212)398-9560 E-mail: aesc@aesc.org • URL: http://www.aesc.org.

Council on Career Development for Minorities. 1341 W. Mockingbird Lane, Suite 722-E, Dallas, TX 75247. Phone: (214)631-3677 Fax: (214)905-2046 E-mail: ccdm35@aol.com • URL: http://www.ccdm.org • Seeks to improve career counseling and placement services for minority college students.

International Association of Personnel in Employment Security. 1801 Louisville Rd., Frankfort, KY 40601. Phone: (502)223-4459 Fax: (502)233-4127 E-mail: iapes@aol.com • URL: http://www.iapes.org.

National Association of Older Worker Employment Services. 409 Third St., S.W., Suite 200, Washington, DC 20024. Phone: (202)479-1200 Fax: (202)479-0735 • URL: http://www.ncoa.org • Seeks to improve employment opportunities for older workers.

National Association of Personnel Services. 3133 Mount Vernon Ave., Alexandria, VA 22305. Phone: (703)684-0180 or (703)684-0181 Fax: (703)684-0071 E-mail: info@napsweb.org • URL: http://www.napsweb.org • Members are private employment agencies.

National Center for Disablity Services. 201 I.U. Willets Rd., Albertson, NY 11507. Phone: (516)747-5400 Fax: (516)746-3298 • URL: http://www.ncds.org • Seeks to improve employment opportunities for persons with disabilities.

Options. 225 S. 15th St., Suite 1635, Philadelphia, PA 19102-3916. Phone: (215)735-2202 Fax: (215)735-8097 E-mail: lmwendell@opticscareers.org • URL: http://www.optionscareers.org • Helps men and women of all ages and backgrounds in career planning and job hunting techniques.

JOB INTERVIEWS

See: INTERVIEWING

JOB PERFORMANCE

See: RATING OF EMPLOYEES

JOB RESUMES

See also: EMPLOYMENT AGENCIES AND SERVICES; JOB HUNTING

FINANCIAL RATIOS

Resumes for Banking and Financial Careers, With Sample Cover Letters. NTC/Contemporary Publishing Group. • 2001. $10.95. Second edition. Contains 100 sample resumes and 20 cover letters. (VGM Professional Resumes Series.).

HANDBOOKS AND MANUALS

How to Write Better Resumes. Gary Grappo and Adele Lewis. Barron's Educational Series, Inc. • 1998. $11.95. Fifth edition.

175 High-Impact Cover Letters. Richard H. Beatty. John Wiley and Sons, Inc. • 1996. $10.95. Second edition. Provides samples of cover letters for resumes.

Power Resumes. Ronald Tepper. John Wiley and Sons, Inc. • 1998. $14.95. Third edition. Offers 71 techniques for more effective resumes.

Professional Resumes for Tax and Accounting Occupations. David H. Noble. CCH, Inc. • 1999. $49.95. Written for accounting, tax, law, and finance professionals. In addition to advice, provides 335 sample resumes and 22 cover letters.

The Resume Kit. Richard H. Beatty. John Wiley and Sons, Inc. • 2000. $12.95. Fourth edition. Includes information on the linear resume, a form said to be favored by outplacement firms.

Resume Writing: A Comprehensive How-To-Do-It Guide. Burdette Bostwick. John Wiley and Sons, Inc. • 1990. $14.95. Fourth edition.

Resume Writing and Career Counseling. Entrepreneur Media, Inc. • Looseleaf. $59.50. A practical guide to starting a resume writing and career counseling service. Covers profit potential, start-up costs, market size evaluation, owner's time required, site selection, pricing, accounting, advertising, promotion, etc. (Start-Up Business Guide No. E1260.).

Resumes That Get Jobs. Pearson Education and Technology. • 1998. $16.00. Includes CD-ROM.

Revising Your Resume. Nancy Schuman and William Lewis. John Wiley and Sons, Inc. • 1986. $12.95. How to emphasize positive factors.

Sure-Hire Resumes. Robbie M. Kaplan. Impact Publications. • 1998. $14.95. Includes sample cover letters and 25 sample resumes.

JOB SEARCHING

See: JOB HUNTING

JOB TRAINING

See: TRAINING OF EMPLOYEES

JOBBERS

See: RACK JOBBERS; WHOLESALE TRADE

JOBBERS, RACK

See: RACK JOBBERS

JOBLESS COMPENSATION

See: UNEMPLOYMENT INSURANCE

JOBS IN FOREIGN COUNTRIES

See: EMPLOYMENT IN FOREIGN COUNTRIES

JOKES

See: HUMOR AND JOKES

JOURNALISM

See also: EDITORS AND EDITING; NEWSPAPERS

ALMANACS AND YEARBOOKS

Editor and Publisher International Yearbook: Encyclopedia of the Newspaper Industry. Editor and Publisher Co., Inc. • Annual. $125.00. Daily and Sunday newspapers in the United States and Canada.

BIOGRAPHICAL SOURCES

Biographical Dictionary of American Journalism. Joseph P. McKerns, editor. Greenwood Publishing Group Inc. • 1989. $65.00. Covers major mass media: newspapers, radio, television, and magazines. Includes reporters, editors, columnists, cartoonists, commentators, etc.

Major 20th-Century Writers: A Selection of Sketches from Contemporary Authors. The Gale Group. • 1999. $314.00. Second edition. Five volumes. Includes important nonfiction writers and journalists.

DIRECTORIES

Accredited Journalism and Mass Communication Education. School of Journalism. Accrediting Council on Education for Journalism and Mass Communications. • Annual. Free. Lists about 109 accredited schools.

Editor and Publisher Journalism Awards and Fellowship Directory. Editor and Publisher Co., Inc.

• Annual. Price on application. Over 500 cash prizes scholarships, fellowships, and grants available to journalists and students for work on special subjects or in specific fields.

Journalism and Mass Communication Directory. Association for Education in Journalism and Mass Communication. • Annual $25.00. Schools and departments of journalism and mass communication.

Journalist's Road to Success: Career and Scholarship Guide. Dow Jones Newspaper Fund, Inc. • Annual. Price on application. Lists more than 400 colleges and universities offering journalism/mass communications; general journalism career information; section of minority scholarships and special training programs; section on fellowships for continuing education. Formerly *Journalism Career and Scholarship Guide.*

Working Press of the Nation. R. R. Bowker. • Annual. $450.00. Three volumes: (1) *Newspaper Directory*; (2) *Magazine and Internal Publications Directory*; (3) *Radio and Television Directory.* Includes names of editors and other personnel. Individual volumes, $249.00.

HANDBOOKS AND MANUALS

Rights and Liabilities of Publishers, Broadcasters, and Reporters. Slade R. Metcalf and Robin Bierstedt. Shepard's. • 1982. $200.00. Two volumes. A legal manual for the media.

ONLINE DATABASES

Super Searchers in the News: The Online Secrets of Journalists and News Researchers. Paula J. Hane and Reva Basch. Information Today, Inc. • 2000. $24.95. Contains online searching advice from 10 professional news researchers and fact checkers. (CyberAge Books.).

PERIODICALS AND NEWSLETTERS

Columbia Journalism Review. Columbia University, Graduate School of Journalism. • Bimonthly. $19.95 per year. Critical review of news media.

Editor and Publisher - The Fourth Estate: Spot News and Features About Newspapers, Advertisers and Agencies. Editor and Publisher Co., Inc. • Weekly. $75.00 per year. Trade journal of the newspaper industry.

The IRE Journal. Investigative Reporters and Editors, Inc. • Bimonthly. $25.00 per year. Contains practical information relating to investigative journalism.

Journalism and Mass Communication Quarterly: Devoted to Research and Commentary in Journalism and Mass Communication. Association for Education in Journalism and Mass Communication. • Quarterly. Individuals, $50.00 per year; institutions, $70.00 per year. Formerly *Journalism Quarterly.*

Quill: The Magazine for Journalists. Society of Professional Journalists. • Monthly. $29.00 per year. A magazine for journalists.

RESEARCH CENTERS AND INSTITUTES

Institute for Communications Research. Texas Tech University, P.O. Box 43082, Lubbock, TX 79409. Phone: (806)742-3385 Fax: (806)742-1085 E-mail: jerry.hudson@ttu.edu.

Knight Center for Specialized Journalism. University of Maryland, 290 University College, College Park, MD 20742-1645. Phone: (301)985-7279 Fax: (301)985-7840 E-mail: knight@umail.umd.edu • URL: http://www.inform.umd.edu/knight • Research area is media coverage of complex subjects, such as economics, law, science, and medicine.

Northwestern University-Media Management Center. 1007 Church St., No. 312, Evanston, IL 60201-5912. Phone: (847)491-4900 Fax: (847)491-5619 E-mail: nmc@nwu.edu • URL: http://www.nmc-nwu.org • Research areas are related to various business aspects of the newspaper industry: management, marketing, personnel, planning, accounting, and finance. A joint activity of the J. L. Kellogg Graduate School of Management and the Medill School of Journalism.

TRADE/PROFESSIONAL ASSOCIATIONS

Accrediting Council on Education in Journalism and Mass Communications. University of Kansas. School of Journalism, Stauffer-Flint Hall, Lawrence, KS 66045. Phone: (913)864-3973 Fax: (913)864-5225 • URL: http://www.ukans.edu/~acejmc.

Association for Education in Journalism and Mass Communication. 234 Outlet Pointe Blvd., Ste. A, Columbia, SC 29210. Phone: (803)798-0271 Fax: (803)772-3509 E-mail: aejmchq@vm.sc.edu • URL: http://www.aejmc.sc.edu/online/home.html.

Foreign Press Association. 110 E. 59th St., Suite 2102A, New York, NY 10022. Phone: (212)751-3068 Fax: (212)751-3081 E-mail: fpanewyork@aol.com.

Investigative Reporters and Editors. School of Journalism, 138 Neff Annex, Columbia, MO 65211. Phone: (573)882-2042 Fax: (573)882-5431 E-mail: info@ire.org • URL: http://www.ire.org • Provides educational services to those engaged in investigative journalism.

National Press Club. National Press Bldg., 529 14th St., N.W., Washington, DC 20045. Phone: (202)662-7500 Fax: (202)662-7512 E-mail: info@npcpress.org • URL: http://www.npc.press.org.

Overseas Writers. 2071 National Press Bldg., Washington, DC 20045. Phone: (301)229-2387 or (301)229-3748 Fax: (301)229-6704.

Society of Professional Journalists. 16 S. Jackson, Greencastle, IN 46135. Phone: (765)653-3333 Fax: (765)653-4631 E-mail: spj@spjhq.org • URL: http://www.spj.org.

OTHER SOURCES

Opportunities in Journalism Careers. Donald L. Ferguson and Jim Patten. NTC/Contemporary Publishing Group. • 2001. $15.95. Edited for students and job seekers. Includes education requirements and salary data. (VGM Career Books.).

JOURNALISM, BUSINESS

See: BUSINESS JOURNALISM

JOURNALS, TRADE

See: TRADE JOURNALS

JUDICIARY

See: COURTS

JUICE INDUSTRY

See: BEVERAGE INDUSTRY; CITRUS FRUIT INDUSTRY

JUKE BOXES

See: VENDING MACHINES

JUNIOR COLLEGES

DIRECTORIES

American Association of Community and Junior Colleges Directory. American Association of Community and Junior Colleges. • Annual. $35.00. Formerly *Community, Junior and Technical College Directory.*

Patterson's Schools Classified. Educational Directories, Inc. • Annual. $15.00. Lists more than 7,000 accredited colleges, universities, junior colleges, and vocational schools. Includes brief descriptions. Classified arrangement, with index to name of school. Included in *Patterson's American Education.*

Peterson's Guide to Two-Year Colleges. Peterson's. • Annual. $19.95. Provides information on more than 1,500 U. S. academic institutions granting associate degrees.

PERIODICALS AND NEWSLETTERS

Community and Junior College Libraries: The Journal for Learning Resources Centers. Haworth Press, Inc. • Semiannual. Individuals, $34.00 per year; institutions, $60.00 per year.

Community College Journal. American Association of Community and Junior Colleges. • Bimonthly. $28.00 per year. Formerly *Community, Technical and Junior College Journal.*

Community College Review. Dept. of Adult and Community College Education. North Carolina State University. • Quarterly. $55.00 per year.

Community College Week: The Independent Voice Serving Community, Technical and Junior Colleges. Cox, Matthews & Associates. • Biweekly. $40.00 per year. Covers a wide variety of current topics relating to the administration and operation of community colleges.

STATISTICS SOURCES

Digest of Education Statistics. Available from U. S. Government Printing Office. • Annual. $44.00. Covers all areas of education from kindergarten through graduate school. Includes data from both government and private sources. Compiled by National Center for Education Statistics, U. S. Department of Education.

TRADE/PROFESSIONAL ASSOCIATIONS

American Association of Community Colleges. National Center for Higher Education. One Dupont Circle, N.W., No. 410, Washington, DC 20036-1176. Phone: (202)728-0200 Fax: (202)833-2467 E-mail: mlatif@aacc.nche.edu • URL: http://www.aacc.nche.edu.

JUNK

See: WASTE PRODUCTS

JUNK BOND FINANCING

See also: BONDS; FINANCE; LEVERAGED BUYOUTS

GENERAL WORKS

Advances and Innovations in the Bond and Mortgage Markets. Frank J. Fabozzi, editor. McGraw-Hill Professional. • 1989. $65.00.

The First Junk Bond: A Story of Corporate Boom and Bust. Harlan D. Platt. M. E. Sharpe, Inc. • 1994. $76.95. Relates the development and history of Michael Milken's first low-quality bond issue at high interest rates. Includes a chapter, "What Have We Learned?".

The High Yield Debt Market: Investment Performance and Economic Impact. Edward I. Altman, editor. McGraw-Hill Professional. • 1990. $55.00.

Junk Bonds: How High Yield Securities Restructured Corporate America. Glenn Yago. Oxford University Press, Inc. • 1990. $25.00.

The Predator's Ball: The Inside Story of Drexel Burnham and the Rise of the Junk Bond Raiders. Connie Bruck. Viking Penguin. • 1989. $14.95.

Understanding Corporate Bonds. Harold Kerzner. McGraw-Hill Professional. • 1990. $24.95. A general introduction to investing in corporate bonds. Includes a discussion of high-risk (junk) bonds.

ABSTRACTS AND INDEXES

Business Periodicals Index. H. W. Wilson Co. • Monthly, except August, with quarterly and annual cumulations. Service basis for print edition; CD-ROM edition, $1,495.00 per year.

ALMANACS AND YEARBOOKS

Fixed Income Almanac: The Bond Investor's Compendium of Key Market, Product, and Performance Data. Livingston G. Douglas. McGraw-Hill Professional. • 1993. $75.00. Presents 20 years of data in 350 graphs and charts. Covers bond market volatility, yield spreads, high-yield (junk) corporate bonds, default rates, and other items, such as Federal Reserve policy.

DIRECTORIES

Standard and Poor's Security Dealers of North America. Standard & Poor's. • Semiannual. $480.00 per year; with *Supplements* every six weeks, $590.00 per year. Geographical listing of over 12,000 stock, bond, and commodity dealers.

FINANCIAL RATIOS

Money of the Mind: Borrowing and Lending in America from the Civil War to Michael Milken. James Grant. Farrar, Straus, and Giroux, LLC. • 1992. $16.00. A critical anlysis by the editor of *Grant's Interest Rate Observer.*

HANDBOOKS AND MANUALS

Bond Markets: Analysis and Stratgies. Frank J. Fabozzi. Prentice Hall. • 1999. $96.00. Fourth edition.

Corporate Financial Distress and Bankruptcy: A Complete Guide to Predicting and Avoiding Distress and Profiting from Bankruptcy. Edward I. Altman. John Wiley and Sons, Inc. • 1993. $99.95. Second edition. Provides practical advice on analyzing the financial position of a corporation, with case studies. Includes a discussion of the junk bond market.

Fixed Income Analytics: State-of-the-Art Analysis and Valuation Modeling. Ravi E. Dattatreya, editor. McGraw-Hill Professional. • 1991. $69.95. Discusses the yield curve, structure and value in corporate bonds, mortgage-backed securities, and other topics.

Fixed Income Mathematics: Analytical and Statistical Techniques. Frank J. Fabozzi. McGraw-Hill Professional. • 1996. $60.00. Third edition. Covers the basics of fixed income analysis, as well as more advanced techniques used for complex securities.

ONLINE DATABASES

Wilson Business Abstracts Online. H. W. Wilson Co. • Indexes and abstracts 600 major business periodicals, plus the *Wall Street Journal* and the business section of the *New York Times.* Indexing is from 1982, abstracting from 1990, with the two newspapers included from 1993. Updated weekly. Inquire as to online cost and availability. (*Business Periodicals Index* without abstracts is also available online.).

PERIODICALS AND NEWSLETTERS

The Bond Buyer. American Banker Newsletter, Thomson Financial Media. • Daily edition, $1,897 per year. Weekly edition, $525.00 per year. Reports on new municipal bond issues.

Bondweek: The Newsweekly of Fixed Income and Credit Markets. Institutional Investor. • Weekly. $2,220.00 per year. Newsletter. Covers taxable, fixed-income securities for professional investors, including corporate, government, foreign, mortgage, and high-yield.

CreditWeek. Standard and Poor's. • Weekly. $1,695.00 per year.

High Yield Report. Securities Data Publishing. • Weekly. $995.00 per year. Newsletter covering the junk bond market. (Securities Data Publishing is a unit of Thomson Financial.).

Journal of Fixed Income. Institutional Investor. • Quarterly. $325.00 per year. Covers a wide range of fixed-income investments for institutions, including bonds, interest-rate options, high-yield securities, and mortgages.

Moody's Bond Survey. Financial Information Services. • Weekly. $1,350.00 per year. Newsletter.

RESEARCH CENTERS AND INSTITUTES

Glucksman Institute. New York University. Salomon Center, Stern School of Business, 44 W. Fourth St., Room 9-65, New York, NY 10012-0267. Phone: (212)998-0714 Fax: (212)995-4220 E-mail: iwalter@stern.nyu.edu • URL: http://www.stern.nyu.edu/salomon.

Institute for Quantitative Research in Finance. Church Street Station, P.O. Box 6194, New York, NY 10249-6194. Phone: (212)744-6825 Fax: (212)517-2259 E-mail: daleberman@compuserve • Financial research areas include quantitative methods, securities analysis, and the financial structure of industries. Also known as the "Q Group.".

Investor Responsibility Research Center, Inc. 1350 Connecticut Ave., N. W., Suite 700, Washington, DC 20036. Phone: (202)833-0700 Fax: (202)833-3555 E-mail: sfenn@irrc.org • URL: http://www.irrc.org • Studies developments of interest to institutional investors.

Rodney L. White Center for Financial Research. University of Pennsylvania, 3254 Steinberg Hall-Dietrich Hall, Philadelphia, PA 19104. Phone: (215)898-7616 Fax: (215)573-8084 E-mail: rlwtcr@finance.wharton.upenn.edu • URL: http://www.finance.wharton.upenn.edu/~rlwctr • Research areas include financial management, money markets, real estate finance, and international finance.

TRADE/PROFESSIONAL ASSOCIATIONS

Securities Industry Association. 120 Broadway, New York, NY 10271-0080. Phone: (212)608-1500 Fax: (212)608-1604 E-mail: info@sia.com • URL: http://www.sia.com.

OTHER SOURCES

Fitch Insights. Fitch Investors Service, Inc. • Biweekly. $1,040.00 per year. Includes bond rating actions and explanation of actions. Provides commentary and Fitch's view of the financial markets.

JURIES

See: TRIALS AND JURIES

JURISTS

See: LAWYERS

JURORS

See: COURTS

JUTE INDUSTRY

PERIODICALS AND NEWSLETTERS

Jute and Jute Fabrics-Bangladesh. Bangladesh Jute Research Institute. • Monthly. $5.00 per year. Text in English.

TRADE/PROFESSIONAL ASSOCIATIONS

Burlap and Jute Association. c/o Susan Spiegel, Drawer 8, Dayton, OH 45401. Phone: (973)476-8272 Fax: (973)258-0029 E-mail: tbpa@aol.com.

OTHER SOURCES

International Agreement on Jute and Jute Products. United Nations Publications. • 1992. Second revised edition. An international trade agreement.

JUVENILES

See: YOUTH MARKET

K

KEOGH PLANS

See also: SELF-EMPLOYMENT; TAX SHELTERS

ABSTRACTS AND INDEXES

Business Periodicals Index. H. W. Wilson Co. • Monthly, except August, with quarterly and annual cumulations. Service basis for print edition; CD-ROM edition, $1,495.00 per year.

HANDBOOKS AND MANUALS

How to Build Wealth with Tax-Sheltered Investments. Kerry Anne Lynch. American Institute for Economic Research. • 2000. $6.00. Provides practical information on conservative tax shelters, including defined-contribution pension plans, individual retirement accounts, Keogh plans, U. S. savings bonds, municipal bonds, and various kinds of annuities: deferred, variable-rate, immediate, and foreign-currency. (Economic Education Bulletin.).

Tax Strategies for the Self-Employed. CCH, Inc. • Annual. $89.00 Covers tax-deferred retirement plans.

U. S. Master Pension Guide. CCH, Inc. • Annual. $49.00. Explains IRS rules and regulations applying to 401(k) plans, 403(k) plans, ESOPs (employee stock ownership plans), IRAs, SEPs (simplified employee pension plans), Keogh plans, and nonqualified plans.

INTERNET DATABASES

Small Business Retirement Savings Advisor. U. S. Department of Labor, Pension and Welfare Benefits Administration. Phone: (202)219-8921 • URL: http://www.dol.gov/elaws/pwbaplan.htm • Web site provides "answers to a variety of commonly asked questions about retirement saving options for small business employers." Includes a comparison chart and detailed descriptions of various plans: 401(k), SEP-IRA, SIMPLE-IRA, Payroll Deduction IRA, Keogh Profit-Sharing, Keogh Money Purchase, and Defined Benefit. Searching is offered. Fees: Free.

ONLINE DATABASES

Wilson Business Abstracts Online. H. W. Wilson Co. • Indexes and abstracts 600 major business periodicals, plus the *Wall Street Journal* and the business section of the *New York Times*. Indexing is from 1982, abstracting from 1990, with the two newspapers included from 1993. Updated weekly. Inquire as to online cost and availability. (*Business Periodicals Index* without abstracts is also available online.).

PERIODICALS AND NEWSLETTERS

Small Business Tax News. Inside Mortgage Finance Publications. • Monthly. $175.00 per year. Newsletter. Formerly *Small Business Tax Control*.

Small Business Tax Review. A/N Group, Inc. • Monthly. $84.00 per year. Newsletter. Contains articles on Federal taxes and other issues affecting businesses.

KEYLESS DATA ENTRY

See: AUTOMATIC IDENTIFICATION SYSTEMS

KEYS

See: LOCKS AND KEYS

KITCHENS

DIRECTORIES

Building Supply Home Centers Retail Giants Report. Cahners Business Information. • Annual. $30.00. Lists major retailers of a wide variety of building and home improvement materials, products, fixtures, accessories, equipment, and tools.

FDM-The Source-Woodworking Industry Directory. Cahners Business Information. • Annual. $25.00. A product-classified listing of more than 1,800 suppliers to the furniture and cabinet industries. Includes Canada.

FINANCIAL RATIOS

Kitchen Cabinet Manufacturers Association Income and Expense Study. Kitchen Cabinet Manufacturers Association. • Annual. Membership. Formerly National Kitchen Cabinet Association.

PERIODICALS AND NEWSLETTERS

Building Material Retailer. National Lumber and Building Material Dealers Association. • Monthly. $25.00 per year. Includes special feature issues on hand and power tools, lumber, roofing, kitchens, flooring, windows and doors, and insulation.

FDM: Furniture Design and Manufacturing: Serving the Upholstered Furniture Industry. Chartwell Communications, Inc. • Monthly. Free to qualified personnel. Edited for furniture executives, production managers, and designers. Covers the manufacturing of household, office, and institutional furniture, store fixtures, and kitchen and bathroom cabinets.

Kitchen and Bath Business. Miller Freeman, Inc. • Monthly. $70.00 per year.

National Home Center News: News and Analysis for the Home Improvement, Building, Material Industry. Lebhar-Friedman, Inc. • 22 times a year. $99.00 per year. Includes special feature issues on hardware and tools, building materials, millwork, electrical supplies, lighting, and kitchens.

TRADE/PROFESSIONAL ASSOCIATIONS

Kitchen Cabinet Manufacturers Association. 1899 Preston White Dr., Reston, VA 20191-5435. Phone: (703)264-1690 Fax: (703)620-6530 • URL: http://www.kcma.org.

National Kitchen and Bath Association. 687 Willow Grove St., Hackettstown, NJ 07840. Phone: (908)852-0033 Fax: (908)852-1695 • URL: http://www.nkba.org.

OTHER SOURCES

Kitchen Cabinets and Countertops. Available from MarketResearch.com. • 1999. $2,250.00. Market research report published by Specialists in Business Information. Covers both custom and stock cabinets. Presents market data relative to demographics, sales growth, shipments, exports, imports, price trends, and end-use. Includes company profiles.

KNIT GOODS INDUSTRY

See also: TEXTILE INDUSTRY

ABSTRACTS AND INDEXES

Textile Technology Digest. Institute of Textile Technology. • Monthly. $535.00 per year. Provides indexing and abstracting of a wide variety of textile technology literature.

CD-ROM DATABASES

Textile Technology Digest [CD-ROM]. Textile Information Center, Institute of Textile Technology. • Quarterly. $1,700.00 per year. Provides CD-ROM indexing and abstracting of worldwide journals and monographs in various areas of textile technology, production, and management. Covers 1978 to date.

DIRECTORIES

American Sportswear and Knitting Times Buyers' Guide. National Knitwear and Sportswear Association. • Annual. $25.00. Formerly *Knitting Times Buyers' Guide*.

ENCYCLOPEDIAS AND DICTIONARIES

Encyclopedia of Textiles. French and European Publications, Inc. • 1980. $39.95. Third edition.

Textile Terms and Definitions. J.E. McIntyre and Paul N. Daniels, editors. Available from State Mutual Book and Periodical Service Ltd., Trade Order Dept. • 1995. $110.00. 10th edition. Published by the Textile Insitute (UK). Includes more than 1,000 definitions of textile processes, fiber types, and end products. Illustrated.

FINANCIAL RATIOS

Annual Statement Studies. Robert Morris Associates: The Association of Lending and Credit Risk Professiona. • Annual. Free to members; non-members, $140.00. Median and quartile financial ratios are given for over 400 kinds of manufacturing, wholesale, retail, construction, and consumer finance establishments. Data is sorted by both asset size and sales volume. Includes a clearly written "Definition of Ratios" and an alphabetical industry index.

ONLINE DATABASES

Textile Technology Digest [online]. Textile Information Center, Institute of Textile Technology. • Contains indexing and abstracting of more than 300 worldwide journals and monographs in various areas of textile technology, production, and management. Time period is 1978 to date, with monthly updating. Inquire as to online cost and availability.

World Textiles. Elsevier Science, Inc. • Provides abstracting and indexing from 1970 of worldwide textile literature (periodicals, books, pamphlets, and reports). Includes U. S., European, and British patent information. Updating is monthly. Inquire as to online cost and availability.

PERIODICALS AND NEWSLETTERS

American Sportswear and Knitting Times. National Knitwear and Sportswear Association. • Monthly. $40.00 per year. Includes *American Sportswear and Knitting Times Buyer's Guide.* Formerly *Knitting Times.*

DNR: The Men's Fashion Retail Textile Authority. Fairchild Publications. • Daily. $85.00 per year. Formerly *Daily News Record.*

STATISTICS SOURCES

Annual Survey of Manufactures. Available from U. S. Government Printing Office. • Annual. Prices vary. Issued by the U. S. Census Bureau as an interim update to the *Census of Manufactures.* Includes data on number of manufacturing establishments in various industries, employment, labor costs, value of shipments, capital expenditures, inventories, energy costs, and assets. (See also Census Bureau home page, http://www.census.gov/.).

Knit Fabric Production. U.S. Bureau of the Census. • Annual. (Current Industrial Reports MA-22K.).

Manufacturing Profiles. Available from U. S. Government Printing Office. • Annual. Issued by the U. S. Census Bureau. A printed consolidation of the entire *Current Industrial Report* series, presenting "all the data compiled." Contains statistics on production, shipments, inventories, consumption, exports, imports, and orders for a wide variety of manufactured products. (See also Census Bureau home page, http://www.census.gov/.).

U. S. Industry and Trade Outlook: The McGraw-Hill Companies and the U.S. Department of Commerce/ International Trade Administration. Datapso Research Corp. • Annual. $69.95. Produced by the International Trade Administration, U. S. Department of Commerce, in a "public-private" partnership with DRI/McGraw-Hill and Standard & Poor's. Provides basic data, outlook for the current year, and "Long-Term Prospects" (five-year projections) for a wide variety of products and services. Includes high technology industries. Formerly *U. S. Industrial Outlook.*

WEFA Industrial Monitor. John Wiley and Sons, Inc. • Annual. $65.00. Prepared by industry analysts at WEFA, an economic forecasting and consulting firm (originally Wharton Econometric Forecasting Associates). Contains discussions of the outlook for major U. S. industries, with many 10-year forecasts (WEFA Web site is http://www.wefa.com).

TRADE/PROFESSIONAL ASSOCIATIONS

Association of Knitted Fabrics Manufacturers. One Penn Plaza, Ste. 4401, New York, NY 10119. Phone: (212)695-8100 Fax: (212)695-4013.

Knitwear Division - American Apparel Manufacturers Association. 2500 Wilson Blvd., Suite 301, Arlington, VA 22201. Phone: 800-520-2262 or (703)524-1864 Fax: (703)522-6741.

National Knitwear and Sportswear Association. 307 Seventh Ave., Rm. 1601, New York, NY 10001-6007. Phone: (212)366-9008 Fax: (212)366-4166 E-mail: yarn-cad@interport.net • URL: http://www.asktmag.org.

Textile Institute. Saint James Bldgs., 4th Fl., Oxford St., Manchester M1 6FQ, England. Phone: 44 161 2371188 Fax: 44 161 2361991 E-mail: tiihq@textileinst.org.uk • URL: http://www.texi.org • Members in 100 countries involved with textile industry management, marketing, science, and technology.

United Knitwear Manufacturers League. 500 Seventh Ave., New York, NY 10018. Phone: (212)819-1011 Fax: (212)819-1026.

OTHER SOURCES

Textile Business Outlook. Statistikon Corp. • Quarterly. $985.00 per year. Analyzes current business, marketing, and financial conditions for the worldwide textile industry (fibers and fabrics). Includes statistical forecasts.

KOSHER FOODS INDUSTRY

DIRECTORIES

Directory of Delicatessen Products. Pacific Rim Publishing Co. • Annual. Included with February issue of *Deli News.* Lists suppliers of cheeses, lunch meats, packaged fresh meats, kosher foods, gourmet-specialty items, and bakery products.

Kosher Directory :Directory of Kosher Products and Services. Union of Orthodox Jewish Congregations of America, Kashruth Div. • Annual. $10.00. Over 10,000 consumer, institutional and industrial products and services produced under the rabbinical supervision of the Union.

PERIODICALS AND NEWSLETTERS

Deli News. Delicatessen Council of Southern California, Inc. Pacific Rim Publishing Co. • Monthly. $25.00 per year. Includes product news and comment related to cheeses, lunch meats, packaged fresh meats, kosher foods, gourmet-specialty items, and bakery products.

Di Yiddishe Heim/Jewish Home. Kehot Publication Society. • Quarterly. $8.00 per year. Text in English and Yiddishe.

TRADE/PROFESSIONAL ASSOCIATIONS

Union of Orthodox Jewish Congregations of America. 333 Seventh Ave., 19th Fl., New York, NY 10001. Phone: (212)563-4000 Fax: (212)564-9058.

L

LABELS AND LABELING

See also: PACKAGING

DIRECTORIES

Business Forms, Labels, and Systems: Who's Who of Manufacturers and Suppliers. North American Publishing Co. • Annual. $20.00. Lists more than 800 suppliers and manufacturers of business forms, labels, and related equipment.

ENCYCLOPEDIAS AND DICTIONARIES

Consumers' Guide to Product Grades and Terms: From Grade A to VSOP-Definitions of 8,000 Terms Describing Food Housewares and Other Everyday Terms. The Gale Group. • 1992. $75.00. Includes product grades and classifications defined by government agencies, such as the Food and Drug Administration (FDA), and by voluntary standards organizations, such as the American National Standards Institute (ANSI).

ONLINE DATABASES

PIRA. Technical Centre for the Paper and Board, Printing and Packaging Industries. • Citations and abstracts pertaining to bookbinding and other pulp, paper, and packaging industries, 1975 to present. Weekly updates. Inquire as to online cost and availability.

PERIODICALS AND NEWSLETTERS

Package Printing: For Printers and Converters of Labels, Flexible Packaging and Folding Cartons. North American Publishing Co. • Monthly. Free to qualified personnel; others, $59.00 per year. Formerly Package Printing and Converting.

TRADE/PROFESSIONAL ASSOCIATIONS

Label Printing Industries of America. 100 Daingerfield Rd., Alexandria, VA 22314. Phone: (703)519-8122 Fax: (703)548-3227 E-mail: lpia@printing.org • URL: http://www.printing.org.

Tag and Label Manufacturers Institute. 40 Shuman Blvd., Suite 295, Naperville, IL 60563. Phone: 800-533-8564 or (630)357-9222 Fax: (630)357-0192 E-mail: office@timi.com • URL: http://www.tlmi.com.

OTHER SOURCES

Food Law Reports. CCH, Inc. • Weekly. $1,349.00 per year. Six looseleaf volumes. Covers regulation of adulteration, packaging, labeling, and additives. Formerly *Food Drug Cosmetic Law Reports*.

Labels. Available from MarketResearch.com. • 1998. $3,300.00. Market research report published by the Freedonia Group. Covers types of label materials, methods of application, printing technology, and end-use markets. Includes company profiles and forecasts to the year 2002.

LABOR

See also: INDUSTRIAL RELATIONS; LABOR LAW AND REGULATION; LABOR UNIONS

GENERAL WORKS

Labor-Management Relations. Daniel Q. Mills. McGraw-Hill. • 1993. $83.75. Fifth edition. (Management Series).

Labor Relations. Arthur A. Sloan and Fred Witney. Prentice Hall. • 1996. $91.00. Ninth edition. Emphasizes collective bargaining and arbitration.

Labor Relations: Development, Structure, Process. John A. Fossum. McGraw-Hill Professional. • 1999. Seventh edition. Price on application.

ABSTRACTS AND INDEXES

Social Sciences Citation Index. Institute for Scientific Information. • Three times a year. $6,900 per year. Annual cumulation. Includes *Source Index, Citation Index, Permuterm Subject Index*, and *Corporate Index.*

Social Sciences Index. H. W. Wilson Co. • Quarterly, with annual cumulation. Service basis for print edition; CD-ROM edition, $1,495 per year. Indexes more than 400 periodicals covering economics, environmental policy, government, insurance, labor, health care policy, plannning, public administration, public welfare, urban studies, women's issues, criminology, and related topics.

ALMANACS AND YEARBOOKS

Advances in Industrial and Labor Relations. David B. Lipsky and David Levin, editors. JAI Press, Inc. • Irregular. $78.50. *Supplement* available.

World Labour Report. International Labour Office. • Irregular. Price varies. Volume eight. International coverage. Reviews significant recent events and labor policy developments in the following areas: employment, human rights, labor relations, and working conditions.

CD-ROM DATABASES

Social Science Source. EBSCO Publishing. • Monthly. $1,495.00 per year. Provides CD-ROM citations and abstracts to social science articles in more than 600 periodicals, with full text from 125 periodicals. Covers economics, political science, public policy, international relations, psychology, and other topics. Time period is most recent five years.

Social Sciences Citation Index: Compact Disc Edition. Institute for Scientific Information. • Quarterly. Provides CD-ROM indexing of the world's social sciences literature, including economics, business, finance, management, communications, demographics, information and library science, political science, sociology, etc. Corresponds to online *Social Scisearch* and printed *Social Sciences Citation Index.*

Social Sciences Citation Index: Compact Disc Edition with Abstracts. Institute for Scientific Information. • Quarterly. Provides CD-ROM indexing and abstracting of "significant articles" from 1,400 social science journals worldwide, with additional selections from 3,200 other journals, 1986 to date. Includes economics, business, finance, management, communications, demographics, information and library science, political science, sociology, and many other subjects.

WILSONDISC: Wilson Business Abstracts. H. W. Wilson Co. • Monthly. $2,495.00 per year, including unlimited online access to *Wilson Business Abstracts* through WILSONLINE. Provides CD-ROM "cover-to-cover" abstracting and indexing of over 600 prominent business periodicals. Indexing is from 1982, abstracting from 1990. (*Business Periodicals Index* without abstracts is available on CD-ROM at $1,495 per year.).

WILSONDISC: Wilson Social Sciences Abstracts. H. W. Wilson Co. • Monthly. Including unlimited online access to *Social Sciences Index* through WILSONLINE. Provides CD-ROM indexing from 1983 and abstracting from 1994 of more than 400 periodicals covering economics, area studies, community health, public administration, public welfare, urban studies, and many other topics related to the social sciences.

DIRECTORIES

DIrectory of U. S. Labor Organizations. BNA Books. Bureau of National Affairs, Inc. • Biennial. $85.00. More than 200 national unions and professional and state employees associations engaged in labor representation.

ENCYCLOPEDIAS AND DICTIONARIES

Roberts' Dictionary of Industrial Relations. Books on Demand. • 1993. $85.00. Fourth edition.

Selected Characteristics of Occupations Defined in the Revised Dictionary of Occupational Titles. Available from U. S. Government Printing Office. • 1993. Provides data on training time, physical demands, and environmental conditions for various occupations. (Employment and Training Administration, U. S. Department of Labor.).

HANDBOOKS AND MANUALS

Guidebook to Labor Relations. CCH, Inc. • Annual. $12.00.

Personnel Management: Labor Relations Guide. Prentice Hall. • Three looseleaf volumes. Periodic supplementation. Price on application.

Primer of Labor Relations. Linda G. Kahn. BNA Books. • 1994. $45.00. 25th edition.

Standard Occupational Classification Manual. Available from Bernan Associates. • 2000. $38.00. Replaces the *Dictionary of Occupational Titles.* Produced by the federal Office of Management and Budget, Executive Office of the President. "Occupations are classified based on the work performed, and on the required skills, education, training, and credentials for each one." Six-digit codes contain elements for 23 Major Groups, 96 Minor Groups, 451 Broad Occupations, and 820

Detailed Occupations. Designed to reflect the occupational structure currently existing in the U. S.

INTERNET DATABASES

Bureau of Labor Statistics (BLS). U. S. Department of Labor, Bureau of Labor Statistics. Phone: (202)523-1092 E-mail: labstat.helpdesk@bls.gov • URL: http://www.bls.gov • Web site provides a great variety of employment, wage, price, and economic data. Some links are "Data," "Economy at a Glance," "Keyword Search of BLS Web Pages," "Regional Information," and "Other Statistical Sites." Fees: Free.

ONLINE DATABASES

Labordoc. International Labour Office. • Indexing of labor literature and the publications of the International Labour Organization, 1965 to present. Monthly updates. Inquire as to online cost and availability.

Social Scisearch. Institute for Scientific Information. • Broad, multidisciplinary index to the literature of the social sciences, 1972 to present. Weekly updates. Worldwide coverage. Inquire as to online cost and availability.

Wilson Business Abstracts Online. H. W. Wilson Co. • Indexes and abstracts 600 major business periodicals, plus the *Wall Street Journal* and the business section of the *New York Times*. Indexing is from 1982, abstracting from 1990, with the two newspapers included from 1993. Updated weekly. Inquire as to online cost and availability. (*Business Periodicals Index* without abstracts is also available online.).

Wilson Social Sciences Abstracts Online. H. W. Wilson Co. • Provides online abstracting and indexing of more than 415 periodicals covering area studies, community health, public administration, public welfare, urban studies, and many other social science topics. Time period is 1994 to date for abstracts and 1983 to date for indexing, with updates monthly. Inquire as to online cost and availability.

PERIODICALS AND NEWSLETTERS

Daily Labor Report. Bureau of National Affairs, Inc. • Daily. $6,530.00 per year. Comprehensive newsletter reporting on national labor developments. Includes full text of many official documents and decisions.

Human Resources Report. Bureau of National Affairs, Inc. • Weekly. $875.00 per year. Newsletter. Formerly *BNA'S Employee Relations Weekly*.

International Labour Review. International Labour Office. ILO Publications Center. • Bimonthly. $64.00. Editions in English, French and Spanish.

Labor Trends. Business Research Publishing, Inc. • Weekly. $259.00 per year. Provides labor relations/ personnel news.

Review of Social Economy. Association for Social Economics. Routledge Journals. • Quarterly. Individuals, $65.00 per year; institutions, $177.00 per year. Subject matter is concerned with the relationships between social values and economics. Includes articles on income distribution, poverty, labor, and class.

RESEARCH CENTERS AND INSTITUTES

Council on Employee Relations. University of Pennsylvania. 309 Vance Hall, 3733 Spruce St., Philadelphia, PA 19104-6358. Phone: (215)898-5605 Fax: (215)898-5908 E-mail: cappelli@wharton.upenn.edu • URL: http://www.management.wharton.upenn.edu/chrl.

Institute of Labor and Industrial Relations. University of Illinois at Urbana-Champaign. 504 E. Armory Ave., Champaign, IL 61820. Phone: (217)333-1480 Fax: (217)244-9290 E-mail: feuille@uiuc.edu • URL: http://www.ilir.uiuc.edu.

Labor Research Association. 145 W. 28th St., New York, NY 10001-6191. Phone: (212)714-1677 Fax: (212)714-1674 E-mail: info@lra-ny.com • URL: http://www.lra-ny.com.

STATISTICS SOURCES

Bulletin of Labour Statistics: Supplementing the Annual Data Presented in the Year Book of Labour Statistics. International Labour Ofice. ILO Publications Center. • Quarterly. $84.00 per year. Includes five *Supplements*. A supplement to *Yearbook of Labour Statistics*. Provides current labor and price index statistics for over 130 countries. Generally includes data for the most recent four years. Text in English, French and Spanish.

Gale Book of Averages. The Gale Group. • 1994. $70.00. Contains 1,100-1,200 statistical averages on a variety of topics, with references to published sources. Subjects include business, labor, consumption, crime, and other areas of contemporary society.

Handbook of U. S. Labor Statistics: Employment, Earnings, Prices, Productivity, and Other Labor Data. Eva E. Jacobs, editor. Bernan Associates. • 1999. $74.00. Based on *Handbook of Labor Statistics*, formerly issued by the Bureau of Labor Statistics, U. S. Department of Labor. Includes the Bureau's projections of employment in the U. S. by industry and occupation. Provides a wide variety of data on the work force, prices, fringe benefits, and consumer expenditures.

Monthly Labor Review. Available from U. S. Government Printing Office. • Monthly. $43.00 per year. Issued by the Bureau of Labor Statistics, U. S. Department of Labor. Contains data on the labor force, wages, work stoppages, price indexes, productivity, economic growth, and occupational injuries and illnesses.

Statistical Forecasts of the United States. The Gale Group. • 1995. $99.00. Second edition. Provides both long-term and short-term statistical forecasts relating to basic items in the U. S.: population, employment, labor, crime, education, and health care. Data in the form of charts, graphs, and tables has been taken from a wide variety of government and private sources. Includes a subject index and an "Index of Forecast by Year.".

Year Book of Labour Statistics. International Labour Office. • Annual. $168.00. Presents a wide range of labor and price data for most countries of the world. Supplement available *Sources and Methods. Labour Statistics.*

TRADE/PROFESSIONAL ASSOCIATIONS

AFL-CIO. 815 16th St., N.W., Rm. 703, Washington, DC 20006. Phone: (202)637-5000 Fax: (202)637-5058 E-mail: feedback@flcio.org • URL: http://www.aflcio.org/home.htm.

Labor Policy Association. 1015 15th St., N.W., Washington, DC 20005. Phone: (202)789-8670 Fax: (202)789-0064 E-mail: info@lpa.org • URL: http://www.lpa.org.

OTHER SOURCES

Labor Relations Reporter. Bureau of National Affairs, Inc. • Biweekly. $4,118.00 per year. Six volumes. Looseleaf. Legal service.

LABOR ARBITRATION

See: ARBITRATION

LABOR DISCIPLINE

See: EMPLOYEE DISCIPLINE

LABOR DISPUTES

See: ARBITRATION; STRIKES AND LOCKOUTS

LABOR FORCE

See: LABOR SUPPLY

LABOR LAW AND REGULATION

GENERAL WORKS

Labor and Employment Law: Text and Cases. David P. Twomey. South-Western Publishing Co. • 1993. $73.75. Ninth edition.

ABSTRACTS AND INDEXES

Current Law Index: Multiple Access to Legal Periodicals. The Gale Group. • Monthly. $650.00 per year. Produced in cooperation with the American Association of Law Libraries. Indexes more than 900 law journals, legal newspapers, and specialty publications from the U.S., Canada, U.K., Ireland, Australia, and New Zealand.

Index to Legal Periodicals and Books. H. W. Wilson Co. • Monthly. Quarterly and annual cumulations. $270.00 per year. CD-ROM version available at $1,495.00 per year.

ALMANACS AND YEARBOOKS

American Law Yearbook. The Gale Group. • Annual. $155.00. Serves as a yearly supplement to *West's Encyclopedia of American Law*. Describes new legal developments in many subject areas.

Labor Law Developments: Annual Institute. Matthew Bender & Co., Inc. • Annual. Price on application. Annual collection of papers presented at the SWLF Labor Law Institute, by practitioners, labor law professors and NRLB members.

CD-ROM DATABASES

WILSONDISC: Index to Legal Periodicals and Books. H. W. Wilson Co. • Monthly. Including unlimited online access to *Index to Legal Periodicals* through WILSONLINE. Contains CD-ROM indexing of more than 800 English language legal periodicals from 1981 to date and 2,500 books.

ENCYCLOPEDIAS AND DICTIONARIES

West's Encyclopedia of American Law. Available from The Gale Group. • 1997. $995.00. Second edition. 12 volumes. Published by West Group. Covers a wide variety of legal topics for the general reader. Formerly *Guide to American Law: Everyone's Legal Encyclopedia* (1985).

HANDBOOKS AND MANUALS

Employee and Union Member Guide to Labor Law. National Lawyers Guild. West Group. • Two looseleaf volumes. $235.00. Periodic supplementation. Labor law for union members.

Guidebook to Labor Relations. CCH, Inc. • Annual. $12.00.

Labor-Management Relations: Strikes, Lockouts, and Boycotts. Douglas E. Ray and Emery W. Bartle. West Group. • Looseleaf. $110.00. Covers legal issues involved in labor-management confrontations. Includes recent decisions of the National Labor Relations Board (NLRB).

Law of the Workplace: Rights of Employers and Employees. James Hunt and Patricia Strongin. Bureau of National Affairs, Inc. • 1994. $45.00. Third edition. Wages, hours, working conditions, benefits, and so forth.

Practical Guide to Tax Issues in Employment. Julia K. Brazelton. CCH, Inc. • 1999. $95.00. Covers income taxation as related to labor law and tax law, including settlements and awards. Written for tax professionals.

ONLINE DATABASES

Index to Legal Periodicals and Books (Online). H. W. Wilson Co. • Broad coverage of law journals and books 1981 to date. Monthly updates. Inquire as to online cost and availability.

Instant Computer Arbitration Search. LRP Publications. • Provides citations to U. S. labor arbitration cases and a detailed directory of about 2,500 public and private labor arbitrators. Weekly updates. Cases date from 1970. Inquire as to online cost and availability.

PERIODICALS AND NEWSLETTERS

The Canadian Employer. Carswell. • Monthly. $185.00 per year. Newsletter. Provides current information on Canadian employment and labor laws.

Daily Labor Report. Bureau of National Affairs, Inc. • Daily. $6,530.00 per year. Comprehensive newsletter reporting on national labor developments. Includes full text of many official documents and decisions.

Employee Policy for the Private and Public Sector: State Capitals. Wakeman-Walworth, Inc. • Weekly. $245.00 per year. Newsletter. Formerly *From the State Capitals: Employee Policy for the Private and Public Sector.*

Federal Register. Office of the Federal Register. Available from U.S. Government Printing Office. • Daily except Saturday and Sunday. $697.00 per year. Publishes regulations and legal notices issued by federal agencies, including executive orders and presidential proclamations. Issued by the National Archives and Records Administration (http://www.nara.gov).

Labor and Employment Law. Labor and Employment Law Section. American Bar Association. • Quarterly. Membership.

Labor and Employment Law Newsletter. Matthew Bender & Co., Inc. • Irregular. $275.00 per year. Newsletter.

Labor Law Journal: To Promote Sound Thinking on Labor Law Problems. CCH, Inc. • Monthly. $169.00 per year.

Weekly Summary of the National Labor Relations Board Cases. Available from U. S. Government Printing Office. • Weekly. $174.00 per year. Issued by the Division of Information, National Labor Relations Board.

RESEARCH CENTERS AND INSTITUTES

Lexis.com Research System. Lexis-Nexis Group. Phone: 800-227-9597 or (937)865-6800 Fax: (937)865-6909 E-mail: webmaster@prod.lexis-nexis.com • URL: http://www.lexis.com • Fee-based Web site offers extensive searching of a wide variety of legal sources. Additional features include Daily Opinion Service, lexis.com Bookstore, Career Center, CLE Center, Law Schools, and Practice Pages ("Pages specific to areas of specialty").

TRADE/PROFESSIONAL ASSOCIATIONS

International Society for Labor Law and Social Security. Case Postale 500, CH-1211 Geneva 22, Switzerland. Phone: 41 22 7996343 Fax: 41 22 7996260 E-mail: servais@ilo.ch • URL: http://www.ilo.org/isllss.

OTHER SOURCES

Labor Arbitration Reports. Bureau of National Affairs, Inc. • Weekly. $797 per year. Looseleaf.

Labor Law: Annual Institute. Theodore W. Kheel and others. Matthew Bender & Co., Inc. • $650.00. Eleven looseleaf volumes. Quarterly updates. Covers all aspects of labor relations.

Labor Law Reports. CCH, Inc. • 16 looseleaf volumes. $2,151.00 per year, including weekly updates. Covers laborrelations, wages and hours, state labor laws, and employment practices. Supplement available *Guide to Fair Employment Practices.*

Labor Relations Reporter. Bureau of National Affairs, Inc. • Biweekly. $4,118.00 per year. Six volumes. Looseleaf. Legal service.

LABOR MARKET

See: LABOR SUPPLY

LABOR ORGANIZATION

See: LABOR UNIONS

LABOR PRODUCTIVITY

See: PRODUCTIVITY

LABOR RELATIONS

See: INDUSTRIAL RELATIONS; LABOR

LABOR SUPPLY

ALMANACS AND YEARBOOKS

Employment Outlook. OECD Publications and Information Center. • Annual. $50.00. Outlines the employment prospects for the coming year in OECD countries. Also discusses labor force growth, job creation, labor standards, and collective bargaining.

BIBLIOGRAPHIES

International Migration of the Highly Qualified: A Bibliographic and Conceptual Itinerary. Anne Marie Gaillard and Jacques Gaillard. Center for Migration Studies. • 1998. Price on application. Includes more than 1,800 references from 1954 to 1995 on the migration patterns of skilled or highly qualified workers. (CMS Bibliographies and Documentation Series).

CD-ROM DATABASES

Sourcebooks America CD-ROM. CACI Marketing Systems. • Annual. $1,250.00. Provides the CD-ROM version of *The Sourcebook of ZIP Code Demographics: Census Edition* and *The Sourcebook of County Demographics: Census Edition.*

HANDBOOKS AND MANUALS

WARN Act: A Manager's Compliance Guide to Workforce Reductions. Joseph A. Brislin. BNA Plus Books. • 1990. $195.00.

INTERNET DATABASES

Bureau of Economic Analysis (BEA). U. S. Department of Commerce, Bureau of Economic Analysis. Phone: (202)606-9900 Fax: (202)606-5310 E-mail: webmaster@bea.doc.gov • URL: http://www.bea.doc.gov • Web site includes "News Release Information" covering national, regional, and international economic estimates from the BEA. Highlights of releases appear online the same day, complete text and tables appear the next day. "Recent News Releases" section provides titles for past nine months, with links. "BEA Data and Methodology" includes "Frequently Requested NIPA Data" (national income and product accounts, such as gross domestic product and personal income). Other statistics are available. Fees: Free.

Fedstats. Federal Interagency Council on Statistical Policy. Phone: (202)395-7254 • URL: http://www.fedstats.gov • Web site features an efficient search facility for full-text statistics produced by more than 70 federal agencies, including the Census Bureau, the Bureau of Economic Analysis, and the Bureau of Labor Statistics. Boolean searches can be made within one agency or for all agencies combined. Links are offered to international statistical bureaus, including the UN, IMF, OECD, UNESCO, Eurostat, and 20 individual countries. Fees: Free.

ONLINE DATABASES

DRI U.S. Central Database. Data Products Division. • Provides more than 23,000 business, financial, demographic, economic, foreign trade, and industry-related time series for the U.S. Includes national income, population, retail-wholesale trade, price indexes, labor data, housing, industrial production, banking, interest rates, money supply, etc. Time period is generally 1947 to date (some data back to 1929). Updating varies. Inquire as to online cost and availability.

PERIODICALS AND NEWSLETTERS

Journal of Human Resources: Education, Manpower and Welfare Economics. University of Wisconson at Madison, Industrial Relations Research Institute. University of Wisconsin Press. • Quarterly. Individuals, $54.00 per year; institutions, $124.00 per year. Articles on manpower, health and welfare policies as they relate to the labor market and to economic and social development.

Work and Occupations: An International Sociological Journal. Sage Publications, Inc. • Quarterly. Individuals, $70.00 per year; institutions, $310.00 per year.

RESEARCH CENTERS AND INSTITUTES

Industrial Relations Section. Princeton University, Firestone Library, Pinceton, NJ 08544. Phone: (609)258-4040 Fax: (609)258-2907 • URL: http://www.irs.princeton.edu/ • Fields of research include labor supply, manpower training, unemployment, and equal employment opportunity.

Office of Manpower Studies. Purdue University. School of Technology, Knoy Hall, West Lafayette, IN 47907-1410. Phone: (765)494-2559 Fax: (765)494-0486 E-mail: kdshell@tech.purdue.edu.

W. E. Upjohn Institute for Employment Research. 300 S. Westnedge Ave., Kalamazoo, MI 49007-4686. Phone: (616)343-5541 Fax: (616)343-3308 E-mail: eberts@we.upjohninst.org • URL: http://www.upjohninst.org • Research fields include unemployment, unemployment insurance, worker's compensation, labor productivity, profit sharing, the labor market, economic development, earnings, training, and other areas related to employment.

STATISTICS SOURCES

American Business Climate and Economic Profiles. The Gale Group. • 1993. $135.00. Provides business, industrial, demographic, and economic figures for all states and 300 metropolitan areas. Includes production, taxation, population, growth rates, labor force data, incomes, total sales, etc.

Area Trends in Employment and Unemployment. Available from U. S. Government Printing Office. • Monthly. $60.00 per year. Issued by the U. S. Department of Labor (http://www.dol.gov). Includes a listing of labor surplus areas in the U. S.

Business Statistics of the United States. Courtenay M. Slater, editor. Bernan Associates. • 1999. $74.00. Fifth edition. Based on *Business Statistics*, formerly issue by the Bureau of Economic Analysis, U. S. Department of Commerce. Provides basic data for a wide variety of U. S. industries, services, and economic indicators. Most statistics are shown annually for 29 years and monthly for the most recent four years.

Employment and Earnings. Available from U. S. Government Printing Office. • Monthly. $50.00 per year, including annual supplement. Produced by the Bureau of Labor Statistics, U. S. Department of Labor. Provides current data on employment, hours, and earnings for the U. S. as a whole, for states, and for more than 200 local areas.

Geographic Profile of Employment and Unemployment. Available from U. S. Government Printing Office. • Annual. Issued by Bureau of Labor Statistics, U. S. Department of Labor. Presents detailed, annual average employment, unemployment, and labor force data for regions, states, and metropolitan areas. Characteristics include sex, age, race, Hispanic origin, marital status, occupation, and type of industry.

Labour Force Statistics, 1977/1997: 1998 Edition. Organization for Economic Cooperation and Development. Available from OECD Publications and Information Center. • 1999. $98.00. Provides 21 years of data for OECD member countries on population, employment, unemployment, civilian labor force, armed forces, and other labor factors.

Monthly Bulletin of Statistics. United Nations Publications. • Monthly. $295.00 per year. Provides current data for about 200 countries on a wide variety of economic, industrial, and demographic subjects. Compiled by United Nations Statistical Office.

Monthly Labor Review. Available from U. S. Government Printing Office. • Monthly. $43.00 per year. Issued by the Bureau of Labor Statistics, U. S. Department of Labor. Contains data on the labor force, wages, work stoppages, price indexes, productivity, economic growth, and occupational injuries and illnesses.

Quarterly Labour Force Statistics. Organization for Economic Cooperation and Development. Available from OECD Publications and Information Center. • Quarterly. $60.00 per year. Provides current data for OECD member countries on population, employment, unemployment, civilian labor force, armed forces, and other labor factors.

Report on the American Workforce. Available from U. S. Government Printing Office. • Annual. $15.00. Issued by the U. S. Department of Labor (http://www.dol.gov). Appendix contains tabular statistics, including employment, unemployment, price indexes, consumer expenditures, employee benefits (retirement, insurance, vacation, etc.), wages, productivity, hours of work, and occupational injuries. Annual figures are shown for up to 50 years.

Social Statistics of the United States. Mark S. Littman, editor. Bernan Press. • 2000. $65.00. Includes statistical data on population growth, labor force, occupations, environmental trends, leisure time use, income, poverty, taxes, and other economic or demographic topics.

State Profiles: The Population and Economy of Each U. S. State. Courtenay Slater and Martha Davis, editors. Bernan Press. • 1999. $74.00. Presents charts, tables, and text in an eight-page profile for each state. Covers population, labor force, income, poverty, employment, wages, industry, trade, housing, education, health, taxes, and government finances.

Statistical Handbook of Working America. The Gale Group. • 1997. $125.00. Second edition. Provides statistics, rankings, and forecasts relating to a wide variety of careers, occupations, and working conditions.

Statistical Yearbook. United Nations Publications. • Annual. $125.00. Contains statistics for about 200 countries on a wide variety of economic, industrial, and demographic topics. Compiled by United Nations Statistical Office.

Survey of Current Business. Available from U. S. Government Printing Office. • Monthly. $49.00 per year. Issued by Bureau of Economic Analysis, U. S. Department of Commerce. Presents a wide variety of business and economic data.

World Statistics Pocketbook. United Nations Publications. • Annual. $10.00. Presents basic economic, social, and environmental indicators for about 200 countries and areas. Covers more than 50 items relating to population, economic activity, labor force, agriculture, industry, energy, trade, transportation, communication, education, tourism, and the environment. Statistical sources are noted.

OTHER SOURCES

Foreign Labor Trends. Available from U. S. Government Printing Office. • Irregular (50 to 60 issues per year, each on an individual country). $38.00 per year. Prepared by various American Embassies. Issued by the Bureau of International Labor Affairs, U. S. Department of Labor. Covers labor developments in important foreign countries, including trends in wages, working conditions, labor supply, employment, and unemployment.

LABOR UNIONS

See also: COLLECTIVE BARGAINING

GENERAL WORKS

Labor Relations: Development, Structure, Process. John A. Fossum. McGraw-Hill Professional. • 1999. Seventh edition. Price on application.

DIRECTORIES

Directory of U. S. Labor Organizations. BNA Books. Bureau of National Affairs, Inc. • Biennial. $85.00. More than 200 national unions and professional and state employees associations engaged in labor representation.

Profiles of American Labor Unions. The Gale Group. • 1998. $305.00. Second edition. Provides detailed information on more than 280 national labor unions. Includes descriptions of about 800 bargaining agreements and biographies of more than 170 union officials. Local unions are also listed. Four indexes. Formerly *American Directory of Organized Labor* (1992).

Trade Union. International Confederation of Free Trade Unions. • Monthly. Formerly *Free Labour World.*

Trade Unions of the World. John C. Turbine & Associates. • 2000. $99.00. Fifth edition. Trade union federations and affiliated unions.

ENCYCLOPEDIAS AND DICTIONARIES

Labor Unions. Gary M. Fink. Greenwood Publishing Group, Inc. • 1977. $50.95. Encyclopedia of trade union history. Essays on more than 200 unions. (Encyclopedia of American Institutions Series).

Roberts' Dictionary of Industrial Relations. Books on Demand. • 1993. $85.00. Fourth edition.

HANDBOOKS AND MANUALS

Employee and Union Member Guide to Labor Law. National Lawyers Guild. West Group. • Two looseleaf volumes. $235.00. Periodic supplementation. Labor law for union members.

PERIODICALS AND NEWSLETTERS

America at Work. AFL-CIO, Public Affairs Dept. • Monthly. $10.00 per year. Formerly *AFL-CIO News.*

Union Labor Report. Bureau of National Affairs, Inc. • Biweekly. $848.00 per year.

TRADE/PROFESSIONAL ASSOCIATIONS

AFL-CIO. 815 16th St., N.W., Rm. 703, Washington, DC 20006. Phone: (202)637-5000 Fax: (202)637-5058 E-mail: feedback@flcio.org • URL: http://www.aflcio.org/home.htm.

National Federation of Independent Unions. 1166 S. 11th St., Philadelphia, PA 19147. Phone: 800-595-6348 or (215)336-3300 Fax: (215)755-3542 • URL: http://www.nfiu.org.

OTHER SOURCES

Labor Relations Reporter. Bureau of National Affairs, Inc. • Biweekly. $4,118.00 per year. Six volumes. Looseleaf. Legal service.

Washington [year]. Columbia Books, Inc. • Annual. $129.00. Provides information on about 5,000 Washington, DC key businesses, government offices, non-profit organizations, and cultural institutions, with the names of about 25,000 principal executives. Includes Washington media, law offices, foundations, labor unions, international organizations, clubs, etc.

LABORATORIES

See also: CLINICAL LABORATORY INDUSTRY; RESEARCH AND DEVELOPMENT

CD-ROM DATABASES

Science Citation Index: Compact Disc Edition. Institute for Scientific Information. • Quarterly. Provides CD-ROM indexing of the world's scientific and technical literature. Corresponds to online *Scisearch* and printed *Science Citation Index.*

DIRECTORIES

American Laboratory Buyers' Guide. International Scientific Communications, Inc. • Annual. $25.00. Manufacturers of and dealers in scientific instruments, equipment, apparatus, and chemicals worldwide.

Directory of American Research and Technology: Organizations Active in Product Development for Business. R. R. Bowker. • Annual. $359.95. Lists over 13,000 publicly and privately owned research facilities. Formerly *Industrial Research Laboratories of the U.S.*

Directory of Standards Laboratories. National Conference of Standards Laboratories. • Biennial. Members, $30.00 per year; non-members, $120.00 per year. Lists about 1,500 measurement standards laboratories.

Research Services Directory: Commercial & Corporate Research Centers. Grey House Publishing. • 1999. $395.00. Seventh edition. Lists more than 6,200 independent commercial research centers and laboratories offering contract or fee-based services. Includes corporate research departments, market research companies, and information brokers.

ONLINE DATABASES

Research Centers and Services Directories. The Gale Group. • Contains profiles of about 30,000 research centers, organizations, laboratories, and agencies in 147 countries. Corresponds to the printed *Research Centers Directory, International Research Centers Directory, Government Research Directory,* and *Research Services Directory.* Updating is semiannual. Inquire as to online cost and availability.

Scisearch. Institute for Scientific Information. • Broad, multidisciplinary index to the literature of science and technology, 1974 to present. Inquire as to online cost and availability. Coverage of literature is worldwide, with weekly updates.

PERIODICALS AND NEWSLETTERS

American Laboratory. International Scientific Communications, Inc. • Monthly. $235.00 per year. Includes annual *Buyers' Guide.*

Laboratory Equipment. Cahners Business Information, New Product Information. • 13 times a year. $65.95 per year.

Today's Chemist at Work. American Chemical Society. • Monthly. Institutions, $160.00 per year; others, price on application. Provide pracrtical information for chemists on day-to-day operations. Product coverage includes chemicals, equipment, apparatus, instruments, and supplies.

TRADE/PROFESSIONAL ASSOCIATIONS

ACIL. 1629 K St., N.W., Washington, DC 20006. Phone: (202)887-5872 Fax: (202)887-0021 • URL: http://www.acil.org.

LABORATORIES, CLINICAL

See: CLINICAL LABORATORY INDUSTRY

LABORATORY EQUIPMENT

See: SCIENTIFIC APPARATUS AND INSTRUMENT INDUSTRIES

LACE INDUSTRY

ABSTRACTS AND INDEXES

Textile Technology Digest. Institute of Textile Technology. • Monthly. $535.00 per year. Provides indexing and abstracting of a wide variety of textile technology literature.

CD-ROM DATABASES

Textile Technology Digest [CD-ROM]. Textile Information Center, Institute of Textile Technology. • Quarterly. $1,700.00 per year. Provides CD-ROM indexing and abstracting of worldwide journals and monographs in various areas of textile technology, production, and management. Covers 1978 to date.

DIRECTORIES

Annual Embroidery and Laces Directory. I. Leonard Seiler, editor. Schiffli Lace and Embroidery Manufacturers Association. • Annual. $5.00. Embroidery and lace product merchandisers, producers, and industry service providers in the United States with limited international coverage. Formerly *Embroidery Directory.*

ENCYCLOPEDIAS AND DICTIONARIES

Encyclopedia of Textiles. French and European Publications, Inc. • 1980. $39.95. Third edition.

Textile Terms and Definitions. J.E. McIntyre and Paul N. Daniels, editors. Available from State Mutual Book and Periodical Service Ltd., Trade Order Dept. • 1995. $110.00. 10th edition. Published by the Textile Insitute (UK). Includes more than 1,000 definitions of textile processes, fiber types, and end products. Illustrated.

ONLINE DATABASES

Textile Technology Digest [online]. Textile Information Center, Institute of Textile Technology. • Contains indexing and abstracting of more than 300 worldwide journals and monographs in various areas of textile technology, production, and management. Time period is 1978 to date, with monthly updating. Inquire as to online cost and availability.

World Textiles. Elsevier Science, Inc. • Provides abstracting and indexing from 1970 of worldwide textile literature (periodicals, books, pamphlets, and reports). Includes U. S., European, and British patent information. Updating is monthly. Inquire as to online cost and availability.

PERIODICALS AND NEWSLETTERS

Embroidery News. I. Leonard Seiler, editor. Schiffli Lace and Embroidery Manufacturers Association. • Bimonthly. Free to qualified personnel; others, $10.00.

TRADE/PROFESSIONAL ASSOCIATIONS

Schiffli Embroidery Manufacturers Promotion Fund. 596 Anderson Ave., Ste. 203, Cliffside Park, NJ 07010-1831. Phone: (201)943-7730 Fax: (201)943-7793 • URL: http://www.schifliusa.com.

Textile Institute. Saint James Bldgs., 4th Fl., Oxford St., Manchester M1 6FQ, England. Phone: 44 161 2371188 Fax: 44 161 2361991 E-mail: tiihq@ textileinst.org.uk • URL: http://www.texi.org • Members in 100 countries involved with textile industry management, marketing, science, and technology.

OTHER SOURCES

Textile Business Outlook. Statistikon Corp. • Quarterly. $985.00 per year. Analyzes current business, marketing, and financial conditions for the worldwide textile industry (fibers and fabrics). Includes statistical forecasts.

LACQUER AND LACQUERING

See: PAINT AND PAINTING

LAMB INDUSTRY

See: SHEEP INDUSTRY

LAMPS

See: LIGHTING

LAND COMPANIES

See: REAL ESTATE BUSINESS

LAND UTILIZATION

GENERAL WORKS

Recent Advances and Issues in Environmental Science. John R. Callahan. Oryx Press. • 2000. $44.95. Includes environmental economic problems, such as saving jobs vs. protecting the environment. (Oryx Frontiers of Science Series.).

ABSTRACTS AND INDEXES

Environment Abstracts. Congressional Information Service. • Monthly. Price varies. Provides multidisciplinary coverage of the world's environmental literature. Incorporates *Acid Rain Abstracts.*

Environment Abstracts Annual: A Guide to the Key Environmental Literature of the Year. Congressional Information Service. • Annual. $495.00. A yearly cumulation of *Environment Abstracts.*

Environmental Periodicals Bibliography: A Current Awareness Bibliography Featuring Citations of Scientific and Popular Articles in Serial Publications in the Area of the Environment. Environmental Studies Institute. International Academy at Santa Barbara. • Monthly. Price varies. An index to current environmental literature.

ALMANACS AND YEARBOOKS

Earth Almanac: An Annual Geophysical Review of the State of the Planet. Natalie Goldstein. Oryx Press. • Annual. $65.00. Provides background information, statistics, and a summary of major events relating to the atmosphere, oceans, land, and fresh water.

Institute on Planning, Zoning and Eminent Domain, Southwestern Legal Foundation:Proceedings, 1971-1994. William S. Hein & Co., Inc. • 1971. $2,887.00. 24 volumes.

Land Use and Environment Law Review, 1984. West Group. • Dates vary. $215.00. Five volumes.

BIBLIOGRAPHIES

The Ecology of Land Use: A Bibliographic Guide. Graham Trelstad. Sage Publications, Inc. • 1994. $10.00.

NIMBYS and LULUs (Not-in-My-Back-Yard and Locally-Unwanted-Land-Uses). Jan Horah and Heather Scott. Sage Publications, Inc. • 1993. $10.00.

CD-ROM DATABASES

Environment Abstracts on CD-ROM. Congressional Information Service, Inc. • Quarterly. $1,295.00 per year. Contains the following CD-ROM databases: *Environment Abstracts, Energy Abstracts,* and *Acid Rain Abstracts.* Length of coverage varies.

ONLINE DATABASES

Enviroline. Congressional Information Service, Inc. • Provides online indexing and abstracting of worldwide environmental and natural resource literature from 1975 to date. Updated monthly. Inquire as to online cost and availability.

PERIODICALS AND NEWSLETTERS

Environmental Law and Management. Available from John Wiley and Sons, Inc., Journals Div. • Bimonthly. Institutions, $650.00 per year. Provides international coverage of subject matter. Published in England by John Wiley and Sons Ltd. Formerly *Land Management and Environmental Law Report.*

Land Use Digest. Urban Land Institute. • Monthly. Membership.

Land Use Law and Zoning Digest. American Planning Association. • Monthly. $275.00 per year. Covers judicial decisions and state laws affecting zoning and land use. Edited for city planners and lawyers. Monthly supplement available *Zoning News.*

Land Use Law Report. Business Publishers, Inc. • Biweekly. $367.00 per year. Provides current reports on planning issues affecting urban, suburban, agricultural and natural resources land jurisdictions. Formerly *Land Use Planning Report.*

OTHER SOURCES

American Land Planning Law. Norman Williams, and John Taylor. West Group. • $750.00. Eight volumes. Periodic supplementation. (Real Property and Zoning Series).

Federal Land Use Law: Limitations, Procedures, Remedies. Daniel R. Mandelker and others. West Group. • $145.00 per year. Looseleaf service. Annual supplementation.

LANDLORD AND TENANT

See: APARTMENT HOUSES; PROPERTY MANAGEMENT; REAL ESTATE BUSINESS

LANDSCAPE ARCHITECTURE

GENERAL WORKS

Landscape Architecture: An Illustrated History in Timelines, Site Plans, and Biography. William A. Mann. John Wiley and Sons, Inc. • 1993. $64.95. Includes illustrations of notable site plans and biographies of people important to landscape architecture history.

ABSTRACTS AND INDEXES

Art Index. H. W. Wilson Co. • Quarterly. Annual cumulations. Service basis for print edition; CD-ROM edition, $1,495.00 per year. Subject and author index to periodicals in art, architecture, industrial design, city planning, photography, and various related topics.

DIRECTORIES

ASLA Members Handbook. American Society of Landscape Architects. • Annual. Members $25.00; non-members, $195.00.

Design Firm Directory: A Listing of Firms and Consultants in Grap hic Design in the United States. Wefler & Associates, Inc. • Annual. $145.00. Three volumes. Provides information on more than 2,600 commercial, private, and consulting design firms. Includes graphic, interior, landscape, and environmental designers.

ENCYCLOPEDIAS AND DICTIONARIES

Penguin Dictionary of Architecture and Landscape Architecture. Nicolas Pevsner and others. Viking Penguin. • 2000. $16.95. Fifth edition.

FINANCIAL RATIOS

Annual Statement Studies. Robert Morris Associates: The Association of Lending and Credit Risk Professiona. • Annual. Free to members; non-members, $140.00. Median and quartile financial ratios are given for over 400 kinds of manufacturing, wholesale, retail, construction, and consumer finance establishments. Data is sorted by both asset size and sales volume. Includes a clearly written "Definition of Ratios" and an alphabetical industry index.

HANDBOOKS AND MANUALS

Landscape Planning: Environmental Applications. William M. Marsh. John Wiley and Sons, Inc. • 1997. $58.95. Third edition. A handbook on environmental problems associated with landscape design, land planning, and land use. Includes techniques for obtaining data.

ONLINE DATABASES

Art Index Online. H. W. Wilson Co. • Indexes a wide variety of art-related periodicals, 1984 to date. Monthly updates. Inquire as to online cost and availability.

PERIODICALS AND NEWSLETTERS

Landscape Architecture. American Society of Landscape Architects. • Monthly. $49.00 per year.

Landscape Architecture News Digest. American Society of Landscape Architects. • 10 times a year. Free to members; non-members, $32.00 per year.

Landscape Journal: Design, Planning, and Management of the Land. Council of Education in Landscape Architecture. University of Wisconsin Press, Journal Div. • Semiannual. Individuals, $34.00 per year; institutions, $92.00 per year.

Landscape Maintenance News. Landscape Information Services. • Monthly. $48.00 per year. Newsletter for landscape service companies.

Landscape Management: Commercial Magazine for Lawn, Landscape and Grounds Managers. Advanstar Communications, Inc. • Monthly. $41.00 per year.

RESEARCH CENTERS AND INSTITUTES

Landscape Architecture Foundation. 636 Eye St., N.W., Washington, DC 20001-3736. Phone: (202)216-2355 Fax: (202)898-1185 E-mail: severett@asla.org • URL: http://www.asla.org/asla.

TRADE/PROFESSIONAL ASSOCIATIONS

American Society of Landscape Architects. 636 Eye St., N.W., Washington, DC 20001-3736. Phone: (202)898-2444 Fax: (202)898-1185 • URL: http://www.asla.org/.

LAN

See: LOCAL AREA NETWORKS

LAPTOP COMPUTERS

See: PORTABLE COMPUTERS

LARD INDUSTRY

See: OIL AND FATS INDUSTRY

LASERDISKS

See: OPTICAL DISK STORAGE DEVICES

LASERS

GENERAL WORKS

Lasers. Joseph H. Eberly and Peter W. Milonni. John Wiley and Sons, Inc. • 1988. $125.00.

ABSTRACTS AND INDEXES

Journal of Current Laser Abstracts. PennWell Corp., Advanced Technology Div. • Monthly. $495.00 per year. Covers the world's literature of lasers: industrial, medical, and military. Subscription includes annual subject and author index.

Key Abstracts: Optoelectronics. Available from INSPEC, Inc. • Monthly. $240.00 per year. Provides international coverage of journal and proceedings literature relating to fiber optics, lasers, and optoelectronics in general. Published in England by the Institution of Electrical Engineers (IEE).

NTIS Alerts: Manufacturing Technology. National Technical Information Service. • Semimonthly. $265.00 per year. Provides descriptions of government-sponsored research reports and software, with ordering information. Covers computer-aided design and manufacturing (CAD/CAM), engineering materials, quality control, machine tools, robots, lasers, productivity, and related subjects. Formerly *Abstract Newsletter.*

Solid State and Superconductivity Abstracts. Cambridge Information Group. • Bimonthly. $1,045.00 per year. Formerly *Solid State Abstracts Journal.*

DIRECTORIES

Industrial Laser Buyers Guide. PennWell Corp., Advanced Technology Div. • Annual. $85.00. Lists industrial laser suppliers by category and geographic location. (Included with subscription to *Industrial Laser Solutions.*).

Laser Focus World Buyers' Guide. PennWell Corp., Advanced Technology Div. • Annual. $125.00. Lists more than 2,000 suppliers of optoelectronic and laser products and services.

HANDBOOKS AND MANUALS

Handbook of Lasers. Marvin J. Weber. CRC Press, Inc. • 1995. $89.95.

PERIODICALS AND NEWSLETTERS

Industrial Laser Solutions. PennWell Corp., Advanced Technology Div. • Monthly. $250.00 per year. Covers industrial laser technology, especially machine tool applications. (Subscription includes annual *Industrial Laser Buyers Guide.*).

Laser Focus World: The World of Optoelectronics. PennWell Corp., Advanced Technology Div. • Monthly. $156.00 per year. Covers business and technical aspects of electro-optics, including lasers and fiberoptics. Includes *Buyer's Guide.*

Lasers in Surgery and Medicine. John Wiley and Sons, Inc., Journals Div. • 11 times a year. $1,090.00 per year. Original articles in laser surgery and medicine.

Medical Laser Report. PennWell Corp., Advanced Technology Div. • Monthly. $345.00 per year. Newsletter. Covers the business and financial side of the medical laser industry, along with news of technological developments and clinical applications. Supplement available *Buyers' Guide.* Formerly *Medical Laser Industrial Report.*

Optics and Laser Technology. Elsevier Science. • Eight times a year. $981.00 per year.

RESEARCH CENTERS AND INSTITUTES

Center for Laser Applications. UT Space Institute Research Park, University of Tennessee, Tullahoma, TN 37388. Phone: (931)393-7485 Fax: (931)454-2271 E-mail: jlewis@utsi.edu • URL: http://view.utsi.edu/cla • In addition to research, provides technical assistance relating to the industrial use of lasers.

Center for Laser Studies. University of Southern California, Denney Research Bldg., University Park, Los Angeles, CA 90089-1112. Phone: (213)740-4235 Fax: (213)740-8158 • Concerned with commercial and military laser applications.

Center for Research and Education in Optics and Lasers. University of Central Florida, 4000 Central Florida Blvd., Orlando, FL 32816-2700. Phone: (407)823-6800 Fax: (407)823-6880 E-mail: ewvs@creol.ucf.edu • URL: http://www.creol.ucf.edu.

Laser Biomedical Research Center. Massachusetts Institute of Technology, 77 Massachusetts Ave., Cambridge, MA 02139. Phone: (617)253-7700 Fax: (617)253-4513 E-mail: msfeld@mit.edu • URL: http://www.web.mit.edu/spectroscopy/www/staff/msfeld.html • Concerned with the medical use of lasers.

TRADE/PROFESSIONAL ASSOCIATIONS

IEEE Lasers and Electro-Optics Society. Institute of Electrical and Electronics Engineers, P.O. Box 1331, Piscataway, NJ 08855-1331. Phone: (732)981-0060 Fax: (732)981-1721 E-mail: g.walters@ieee.org • URL: http://www.ieee.org/leos • A society of the Institute of Electrical and Electronics Engineers. Fields of interest include lasers, fiber optics, optoelectronics, and photonics.

Laser Institute of America. 12424 Research Parkway, Suite 125, Orlando, FL 32826. Phone: 800-345-2737 or (407)380-1553 Fax: (407)380-5588 E-mail: webmaster@laserinstitute.org • URL: http://www.laserinstitute.org.

Optical Society of America. 2010 Massachusetts Ave., N.W., Washington, DC 20036-1023. Phone: (202)223-8130 Fax: (202)223-1096 • URL: http://www.osa.org.

LATHING

See: PLASTER AND PLASTERING

LATIN AMERICAN MARKETS

See also: NORTH AMERICAN FREE TRADE AGREEMENT

GENERAL WORKS

Latin America's Economy: Diversity, Trends, and Conflicts. Eliana Cardoso and Ann Helwege. MIT Press. • 1995. $22.00.

ABSTRACTS AND INDEXES

Business Periodicals Index. H. W. Wilson Co. • Monthly, except August, with quarterly and annual cumulations. Service basis for print edition; CD-ROM edition, $1,495.00 per year.

F & S Index: International. The Gale Group. • Monthly. $1,295.00 per year, including quarterly and annual cumulations. Provides annotated citations to marketing, business, financial, and industrial literature. Coverage of international business activity includes trade journals, financial magazines, business newspapers, and special reports. Areas included are Asia, Latin America, Africa, the Middle East, Oceania, and Canada. Formerly *Predicasts F & S Index: International.*

Hispanic American Periodicals Index. University of California, Los Angeles, Latin American Studies Center. Latin American Studies Center Publication. • Annual. $400.00. Indexes about 250 periodicals that regularly include material on Latin America. Supplement available.

PAIS International in Print. Public Affairs Information Service, Inc. • Monthly. $650.00 per year; cumulations three times a year. Provides topical citations to the worldwide literature of public affairs, economics, demographics, sociology, and trade. Text in English; indexed materials in English, French, German, Italian, Portuguese and Spanish.

ALMANACS AND YEARBOOKS

Emerging Markets Analyst. • Monthly. $895.00 per year. Provides an annual overview of the emerging financial markets in 24 countries of Latin America, Asia, and Europe. Includes data on international mutual funds and closed-end funds.

CD-ROM DATABASES

F & S Index Plus Text. The Gale Group. • Monthly. $7,575.00 per year. Provides CD-ROM citations to worldwide business, marketing, and industrial material appearing in a large assortment of trade journals, newspapers, and other publications. Time period is four years.

Hoover's Company Capsules on CD-ROM. Hoover's, Inc. • Quarterly. $349.95 per year (single-user). Provides the CD-ROM version of *Hoover's Handbook of American Business, Hoover's Handbook of Emerging Companies, Hoover's Handbook of World Business, Hoover's Guide to Computer Companies, Hoover's Guide to Media Companies, Hoover's Handbook of Private Companies,* and various regional guides. Includes more than 11,000 profiles of companies.

Latin American Studies, Volume I: Multidisciplinary. National Information Services Corp. • Semiannual. Provides more than 700,000 CD-ROM citations to scholarly literature on a wide variety of Latin American topics, including agriculture, business, demography, economics, government, and politics. Producers are the University of Texas, the University of California, and the Library of Congress.

Latin American Studies, Volume II: Current Affairs and Law. National Information Services Corp. • Semiannual. Contains a wide variety of information on CD-ROM, from various producers, relating to Latin American business, current events, and legislation. Includes periodical citations and abstracts in *INFO-SOUTH*; the full-text newsletters, *Chronicle of Latin American Economic Affairs, Central America Update,* and *SourceMex*; and other databases. Time periods are typically 1986, 1988, or 1990 to date.

PAIS on CD-ROM. Public Affairs Information Service, Inc. • Quarterly. $1,995.00 per year. Provides a CD-ROM version of the online service, *PAIS International.* Contains over 400,000 citations to the literature of contemporary social, political, and economic issues.

WILSONDISC: Wilson Business Abstracts. H. W. Wilson Co. • Monthly. $2,495.00 per year, including unlimited online access to *Wilson Business Abstracts* through WILSONLINE. Provides CD-ROM "cover-to-cover" abstracting and indexing of over 600 prominent business periodicals. Indexing is from 1982, abstracting from 1990. (*Business Periodicals Index* without abstracts is available on CD-ROM at $1,495 per year.).

World Consumer Markets. The Gale Group. • Annual. $2,500.00. Pblished by Euromonitor. Provides five- year historical data, current data, and forecasts, on CD-ROM for 330 consumer products in 55 countries. Market data is presented in a standardized format for each country.

World Database of Consumer Brands and Their Owners on CD-ROM. The Gale Group. • Annual. $3,190.00. Produced by Euromonitor. Provides detailed information on CD-ROM for about 10,000 companies and 80,000 brands around the world. Covers 1,000 product sectors.

World Marketing Forecasts on CD-ROM. The Gale Group. • Annual. $2,500.00. Produced by Euromonitor. Provides detailed forecast data for the years to 2012 on CD-ROM for 54 countries in all parts of the world. Covers a wide range of social, demographic, economic, and market factors. Includes specific forecasts for many kinds of consumer products.

DIRECTORIES

Brazil Company Handbook: Data on Major Listed Companies. Hoovers, Inc. • Annual. $49.95. Published by IMF Editora. Contains profiles of publicly traded companies in Brazil. Includes information on local stock exchanges and the nation's economic situation.

Directory of Consumer Brands and Their Owners: Latin America. Available from The Gale Group. • 1999. $990.00. Published by Euromonitor. Provides information about brands available from major Latin American companies. Descriptions of companies are also included.

Hoover's Handbook of World Business: Profiles of Major European, Asian, Latin American, and Canadian Companies. Hoover's, Inc. • Annual. $99.95. Contains detailed profiles of more than 300 large foreign companies. Includes indexes by industry, location, executive name, company name, and brand name.

International Directory of Consumer Brands and Their Owners. Available from The Gale Group. • 1997. $450.00. Published by Euromonitor. Contains detailed information on more than 38,000 consumer product brands and their companies in 62 countries of the world, excluding Europe.

International Media Guide: Business/Professional Publications: The Americas. International Media Guides, Inc. • Annual. $285.00. Describes trade journals from North, South, and Central America, with advertising rates and circulation data.

Latin America: A Directory and Sourcebook. Available from The Gale Group. • 1999. $590.00. Second edition. Published by Euromonitor. Describes major companies in Latin America. Sourcebook section provides marketing and business information sources.

Major Companies of Latin America and the Caribbean 2001. Available from The Gale Group. • 2001. $795.00. Sixth edition. Published by Graham & Whiteside, London. Contains detailed information on 7,500 major companies in Central and South America. Includes manufacturers, exporters, importers, service companies, and financial institutions.

Major Market Share Companies: The Americas. Available from The Gale Group. • 2000. $900.00. Published by Euromonitor (http://www.euromonitor.com). Provides consumer market share data and rankings for multinational and regional companies. Covers leading firms in the U.S., Canada, Mexico, Brazil, Argentina, Venezuela, and Chile.

Mexico Company Handbook: Data on Major Listed Companies. Available from Hoovers, Inc. • Annual. $29.95. Published by IMF Editora. Contains profiles of publicly traded companies in Mexico. Includes information on local stock exchanges and the nation's economic situation.

Trade Directory of Mexico. Mexican Foreign Trade Bank. • Annual. $100.00. Provides information on more than 4,200 Mexican companies involved in foreign trade. Lists forwarding agencies, customs brokers, consulting groups, transportation companies, and other trade-related Mexican organizations.

Venezuela Company Handbook: Data on Major Listed Companies. Hoovers, Inc. • Annual. $29.95. Published by IMF Editora. Contains profiles of publicly traded companies in Venezuela. Includes information on local stock exchanges and the nation's economic situation. Text in English.

ENCYCLOPEDIAS AND DICTIONARIES

Encyclopedia of Business. The Gale Group. • 2000. $425.00. Second edition. Two volumes. Contains more than 700 signed articles covering major business disciplines and concepts. International in scope.

HANDBOOKS AND MANUALS

Investing and Selling in Latin America. Judith Evans and others. Morning Light Publishing Co. • 1995. $60.00. Consists of one chapter for each of 12 Latin American countries. Covers a wide variety of legal, economic, and practical information relating to doing business in the region.

Mexico Business: The Portable Encyclopedia for Doing Business with Mexico. World Trade Press. • 1994. $24.95. Covers economic data, import/export possibilities, basic tax and trade laws, travel information, and other useful facts for doing business with Mexico. Includes a special section on NAFTA. (Country Business Guides-Series).

ONLINE DATABASES

Chronicle of Latin American Economic Affairs [online]. Latin America Data Base. • Contains the complete text online of the weekly newsletter, *Chronicle of Latin American Economic Affairs.* Provides news and analysis of trade and economic developments in Latin America, including Caribbean countries. Time period is 1986 to date, with weekly updates. Inquire as to online cost and availability.

EcoCentral. Latin America Data Base. • An online newsletter covering economic, trade, political, and social issues in Central America, especially in Nicaragua and El Salvador. Time period is 1986 to date, with weekly updates. Inquire as to online cost and availability.

Euromonitor Market Research. Euromonitor International. • Provides the complete text online of Euromonitor market analysis reports. Covers consumer goods market research data for all major countries, with emphasis on specific product categories. Time period is current. Continuous updating. Inquire as to online cost and availability.

F & S Index. The Gale Group. • Contains about four million citations to worldwide business, financial, and industrial or consumer product literature appearing from 1972 to date. Weekly updates. Inquire as to online cost and availability.

Globalbase. The Gale Group. • Provides more than one million online summaries of business, industrial, and economic news reports from more than 1,000 publications worldwide. Covers a wide range of material appearing in international trade journals, professional magazines, and newspapers. Time period is 1984 to date, with weekly updates. Inquire as to online cost and availability.

PAIS International. Public Affairs Information Service, Inc. • Corresponds to the former printed publications, *PAIS Bulletin* (1976-90) and *PAIS Foreign Language Index* (1972-90), and to the current *PAIS International in Print* (1991 to date). Covers economic, political, and sociological material appearing in periodicals, books, government documents, and other publications. Updating is monthly. Inquire as to online cost and availability.

PROMT: Predicasts Overview of Markets and Technology. The Gale Group. • Companies, products, applied technologies and markets. U.S. and international literature coverage, 1972 to date. Inquire as to online cost and availability. Provides abstracts from more than 1,600 publications. Weekly updates.

SourceMex. Latin America Data Base. • An online newsletter covering economic conditions in Mexico, including foreign trade, public finances, foreign debt, agriculture, and the oil industry. Time period is 1990 to date, with weekly updates. Inquire as to online cost and availability.

Wilson Business Abstracts Online. H. W. Wilson Co. • Indexes and abstracts 600 major business periodicals, plus the *Wall Street Journal* and the business section of the *New York Times*. Indexing is from 1982, abstracting from 1990, with the two newspapers included from 1993. Updated weekly. Inquire as to online cost and availability. (*Business Periodicals Index* without abstracts is also available online.).

PERIODICALS AND NEWSLETTERS

Business Latin America: Weekly Report to Managers of Latin American Operations. Economist Intelligence Unit. • Weekly. $1,195.00 per year. Newsletter covering Latin American business trends, politics, regulations, exchange rates, economics, and finance. Provides statistical data on foreign debt, taxes, labor costs, gross domestic product (GDP), and inflation rates.

Business Week International: The World's Only International Newsweekly of Business. McGraw-Hill. • Weekly. $105.00 per year.

Caribbean Business. Casiano Communications. • Weekly. $45.00 per year. Text in English.

Emerging Markets Quarterly. Institutional Investor. • Quarterly. $325.00 per year. Newsletter on financial markets in developing areas, such as Africa, Latin America, Southeast Asia, and Eastern Europe. Topics include institutional investment opportunities and regulatory matters. Formerly *Emerging Markets Weekly.*

Institutional Investor International Edition: The Magazine for International Finance and Investment. Institutional Investor. • Monthly. $415.00 per year. Covers the international aspects of professional investing and finance. Emphasis is on Europe, the Far East, and Latin America.

Lagniappe Letter: Biweekly Report of Issues Affecting Business in Latin America. Latin American Information Services, Inc. • Biweekly. $675.00 per year. Newsletter on key trade, economic, business, financial, and political developments in Central and Latin America. Includes *Lagniappe Quarterly Monitor.*

Latin American Business Review: Journal of the Business Association of Latin American Studies. Haworth Press, Inc. • Quarterly. Individuals, $50.00 per year; institutions, $75.00 per year; libraries, $95.00 per year.

Latin Finance. Latin American Financial Publications, Inc. • Monthly. $215.00 per year. Covers finance, investment, venture capital, and banking in Latin America.

Latin Fund Management. Securities Data Publishing. • Monthly. $495.00 per year. Newsletter (also available online at www.latinfund.net). Provides news and analysis of Latin American mutual funds, pension funds, and annuities. (Securities Data Publishing is a unit of Thomson Financial.).

Latin Trade: Your Business Source for Latin America. Freedom Publications, Inc. • Monthly. $36.00 per year. English and Spanish editions. Covers various aspects of Latin American business and trade, including economic indicators, export-import, finance, commodity news, company profiles, and political developments. Formerly *U.S.-Latin Trade.*

Progreso. Vision, Inc. • Monthly. $64.00 per year. Covers developments in Latin America affecting business and trade. Text in Spanish.

Twin Plant News: The Magazine of the Maquiladora Industries. Nibbe, Hernandez and Associates, Inc. • Monthly. $85.00 per year. Focuses on Mexican labor laws, taxes, economics, industrial trends, and culture. Industries featured include electronic components, plastics, automotive supplies, metals, communications, and packaging.

Vision: La Revista Latinoamericana. Vision, Inc. • Semimonthly. $72.00 per year. Text in Spanish. A popular newsmagazine covering Latin American politics, economics, business, and culture.

RESEARCH CENTERS AND INSTITUTES

Center for Latin American Studies. University of Florida, P.O. Box 115530, Gainesville, FL 32611-5530. Phone: (352)392-0375 Fax: (352)392-7682 E-mail: cwood@latam.ufl.edu • URL: http://www.latam.ufl.edu • Research areas include Latin American business, with emphasis on the Caribbean and South America.

Latin American and Caribbean Center. Florida International University, University Park, DM 353, Miami, FL 33199. Phone: (305)348-2894 Fax: (305)348-3593 E-mail: lacc@fiu.edu • URL: http://www.lacc.fiu.edu • Research fields include economic development and trade.

Latin American Center, University of California, Los Angeles. 405 Hilgard Ave., Los Angeles, CA 90095-1447. Phone: (310)825-4571 Fax: (310)206-6859 E-mail: nmoss@isop.ucla.edu • URL: http://www.isop.ucla.edu/lac.

STATISTICS SOURCES

Consumer International 2000/2001. Available from The Gale Group. • 1998. $1,190.00. Seventh edition. Published by Euromonitor. Contains extensive consumer market, economic, and demographic data for 27 major, non-European countries, including the U. S. and Canada. Includes consumer market size (volume and value) for 150 product types in 14 categories (food, clothing, automobiles, cosmetics, appliances, etc.).

Consumer Latin America. Available from The Gale Group. • 2001. $970.00. Eighth edition. Published by Euromonitor. Contains a wide variety of consumer market data relating to the countries of Latin America. Includes market forecasts.

Consumer Mexico, 1996. Available from The Gale Group. • 1996. $750.00. Published by Euromonitor. Provides demographic and consumer market data for Mexico.

Economic and Social Progress in Latin America Report. Inter-American Development Bank. • Annual. $24.95. Includes surveys of economic conditions in individual Latin American countries. Text in English.

Emerging Stock Markets Factbook. International Finance Corporation, Capital Market Dept. • Annual. $100.00. Published by the International Finance Corporation (IFC). Provides statistical profiles of more than 26 emerging stock markets in various countries of the world. Includes regional, composite, and industry indexes.

Gale Country and World Rankings Reporter. The Gale Group. • 1997. $135.00. Second edition. Provides about 3,000 statistical ranking tables and charts covering more than 235 nations. Sources include the United Nations and various government publications.

International Marketing Forecasts 2001. Available from The Gale Group. • 2000. $1,090.00. Third edition. Published by Euromonitor. Contains demographic, economic, and market forecasts to the year 2010 for major, non-European countries, including the U. S. and Canada. Forecasts include market-size data for 15 consumer product sectors, such as food, clothing, and automobiles.

Latin America in Graphs: Demographic and Economic Trends. Inter-American Development Bank. • 1994. $12.50.

Latin American Advertising, Marketing, and Media Data. Available from The Gale Group. • 1995. $470.00. Published by Euromonitor. Provides country profiles, demographics, economic indicators, advertising data, and media data. Also lists advertising agencies, newspaper publishers, magazine publishers, and market research companies.

Retail Trade International. The Gale Group. • 2000. $1,990.00. Second edition. Six volumes. Presents comprehensive data on retail trends in 51 countries. Includes textual analysis and profiles of major retailers. Covers Europe, Asia, the Middle East, Africa and the Americas.

Statistical Abstract of Latin America. University of California, Los Angeles. • Annual. $325.00. Two volumes.

Statistical Yearbook for Latin America and the Caribbean. Available from United Nations Publications. • Annual. $79.00. Issued by the Economic Commission for Latin America and the Caribbean. Includes a wide variety of economic, industrial, and trade data for Latin American nations. Text in English and Spanish.

TRADE/PROFESSIONAL ASSOCIATIONS

Association of American Chambers of Commerce in Latin America. 1615 H St., N.W., Washington, DC 20062. Phone: (202)463-5485 Fax: (202)463-3126 E-mail: scotth@aaccla.org • URL: http://www.aaccla.org.

Brazilian-American Chamber of Commerce. 509 W. Madison Ave., Suite 304, New York, NY 10022. Phone: (212)751-4691 Fax: (212)751-7692 E-mail: info@brazilcham.com • URL: http://www.brazilcham.com • Promotes trade between Brazil and the U. S.

Brazilian Government Trade Bureau. 1185 Ave. of the Americas, 21st Fl., New York, NY 10036-2601. Phone: (212)916-3200 Fax: (212)573-9406 E-mail: info@braziltradeny.com • URL: http://www.braziltradeny.com • Offers assistance to American firms wishing to purchase Brazilian products, and promotes Brazilian firms and their exports.

Colombian American Association. 30 Vesey St., Rm. 506, New York, NY 10007. Phone: (212)233-7776 Fax: (212)233-7779 E-mail: andean@nyct.net

For publishers addresses, refer to SOURCES CITED section at the back of the book.

• Seeks to facilitate trade and commerce between the Republic of Colombia and the U. S.

Colombian Government Trade Bureau. 277 Park Ave., 47th Fl., New York, NY 10172-4797. Phone: (212)223-1120 Fax: (212)223-1325 E-mail: proexpny@nyct.net • URL: http://www.proexport.com.co • Promotes Colombian exports to the U. S.

Council of the Americas. 680 Park Ave., New York, NY 10021. Phone: (212)628-3200 Fax: (212)249-1880 • URL: http://www.counciloftheamericas.org • Members are U. S. corporations with business interests in Latin America.

Inter-American Development Bank. 1300 New York Ave., N. W., Washington, DC 20577. Phone: (202)623-1000 Fax: (202)623-3096 E-mail: webmaster@iadb.org • URL: http://www.iadb.org • Members are 27 Western Hemisphere countries and 17 other countries. Promotes economic development and investment in Latin America. Makes long-term, low-interest loans to less-developed Latin American countries.

United States-Mexico Chamber of Commerce. 1300 Pennsylvania Ave., Ste. 270, Washington, DC 20004-3021. Phone: (202)371-8680 Fax: (202)371-8686 E-mail: news-hq@susmcoc.org • Works to promote trade and investment between the U. S. and Mexico.

Venezuelan American Association of the United States. 30 Vesey St., Rm. 2015, New York, NY 10007. Phone: (212)233-7776 Fax: (212)233-7779 E-mail: andean@nyct.ent • Faciltates trade and investment between the U. S. and Venezuela.

OTHER SOURCES

Investing in Latin America: Best Stocks, Best Funds. Michael Molinski. Bloomberg Press. • 1999. $24.95. Provides Latin American stock and mutual fund recommendations for individual investors. (Bloomberg Personal Bookshelf.).

Latin America and the Caribbean in the World Economy. United Nations Publications. • 1999. $25.00. Discusses trade policy, trade activity, regional integration, and environmental protection issues.

Latin American Market Planning Report. Available from MarketResearch.com. • 2000. $750.00.Market research report published by Strategy Research Corporation. Provides results of U. S. Hispanic Market Study covering demographics, product usage, media usage, public opinion issues, and other items.

LAUNDRY INDUSTRY

See also: CLEANING INDUSTRY

ABSTRACTS AND INDEXES

Textile Technology Digest. Institute of Textile Technology. • Monthly. $535.00 per year. Provides indexing and abstracting of a wide variety of textile technology literature.

CD-ROM DATABASES

Textile Technology Digest [CD-ROM]. Textile Information Center, Institute of Textile Technology. • Quarterly. $1,700.00 per year. Provides CD-ROM indexing and abstracting of worldwide journals and monographs in various areas of textile technology, production, and management. Covers 1978 to date.

DIRECTORIES

The Coin Laundry Association Supplier Directory. Coin Laundry Association. • Annual. $30.00. Lists sources of equipment, supplies, and services for coin-operated laundries.

ENCYCLOPEDIAS AND DICTIONARIES

Encyclopedia of Textiles. French and European Publications, Inc. • 1980. $39.95. Third edition.

Textile Terms and Definitions. J.E. McIntyre and Paul N. Daniels, editors. Available from State Mutual Book and Periodical Service Ltd., Trade Order Dept. • 1995. $110.00. 10th edition. Published by the Textile Insitute (UK). Includes more than 1,000 definitions of textile processes, fiber types, and end products. Illustrated.

FINANCIAL RATIOS

Annual Statement Studies. Robert Morris Associates: The Association of Lending and Credit Risk Professiona. • Annual. Free to members; non-members, $140.00. Median and quartile financial ratios are given for over 400 kinds of manufacturing, wholesale, retail, construction, and consumer finance establishments. Data is sorted by both asset size and sales volume. Includes a clearly written "Definition of Ratios" and an alphabetical industry index.

HANDBOOKS AND MANUALS

Diaper Delivery Service. Entrepreneur Media, Inc. • Looseleaf. $59.50. A practical guide to starting a service for the laundering and delivery of all-cotton diapers. Covers profit potential, start-up costs, market size evaluation, owner's time required, site selection, pricing, accounting, advertising, promotion, etc. (Start-Up Business Guide No. E1364.).

Laundromat. Entrepreneur Media, Inc. • Looseleaf. $59.50. A practical guide to starting a coin-operated, self-service laundry business. Covers profit potential, start-up costs, market size evaluation, owner's time required, site selection, lease negotiation, pricing, accounting, advertising, promotion, etc. (Start-Up Business Guide No. E1162.).

ONLINE DATABASES

Textile Technology Digest [online]. Textile Information Center, Institute of Textile Technology. • Contains indexing and abstracting of more than 300 worldwide journals and monographs in various areas of textile technology, production, and management. Time period is 1978 to date, with monthly updating. Inquire as to online cost and availability.

Textiles Information Treatment Users' Service (TITUS). Institut Textile de France. • Citations and abstracts of the worldwide literature on textiles, 1968 to present. Monthly updates. Inquire as to online cost and availability.

PERIODICALS AND NEWSLETTERS

American Coin-Op: The Magazine for Coin-Operated Laundry and Drycleaning Businessmen. Crain Communications, Inc. • Monthly. $35.00 per year.

American Laundry News. Crain Communications, Inc. • Monthly. $35.00 per year. Formerly *Laundry News.*

Coin Launderer and Cleaner. Sheidko Corp. • Monthly. $25.00 per year.

Journal of the Coin Laundry and Drycleaning Industry. Coin Laundry Association. • Monthly. $24.00 per year. Edited for owners and operators of coinoperated laundries.

TRADE/PROFESSIONAL ASSOCIATIONS

Coin Laundry Association. 1315 Butterfield Rd., Suite 212, Downers Grove, IL 60515. Phone: (630)963-5547 Fax: (630)963-5864 E-mail: info@coinlaundry.org • URL: http://www.coinlaundry.org.

International Fabricare Institute. 12251 Tech Rd., Silver Spring, MD 20904. Phone: 800-638-2627 or (301)622-1900 Fax: (301)236-9320 E-mail: wecare@ifi.org • URL: http://www.ifi.org.

Multi-Housing Laundry Association. 4101 Lake Boone Trail, Suite 201, Raleigh, NC 27607. Phone: (919)787-5181 Fax: (919)787-4916.

National Association of Institutional Linen Management. 2130 Lexington Rd., Suite H, Richmond, KY 40475. Phone: (606)624-0177 Fax: (606)624-3580 E-mail: nailm@iclub.org • URL: http://www.nailm.com.

Textile Care Allied Trades Association. 271 U.S. Highway 46, No. 203-D, Fairfield, NJ 07004-2458. Phone: (973)244-1790 Fax: (973)244-4455 E-mail: tcata@ix.netcom.com.

Textile Institute. Saint James Bldgs., 4th Fl., Oxford St., Manchester M1 6FQ, England. Phone: 44 161 2371188 Fax: 44 161 2361991 E-mail: tiihq@textileinst.org.uk • URL: http://www.texi.org • Members in 100 countries involved with textile industry management, marketing, science, and technology.

Uniform and Textile Service Association. 1300 N. 17th St., Suite 750, Arlington, VA 22209. Phone: (703)247-2600 Fax: (703)841-4750 E-mail: info@utsa.com • URL: http://www.utsa.com.

OTHER SOURCES

Textile Business Outlook. Statistikon Corp. • Quarterly. $985.00 per year. Analyzes current business, marketing, and financial conditions for the worldwide textile industry (fibers and fabrics). Includes statistical forecasts.

LAW

GENERAL WORKS

Introduction to Law and the Legal System. Harold J. Grilliot. Houghton Mifflin Co. • 1995. $69.56. Sixth edition. Six volumes.

ABSTRACTS AND INDEXES

Current Law Index: Multiple Access to Legal Periodicals. The Gale Group. • Monthly. $650.00 per year. Produced in cooperation with the American Association of Law Libraries. Indexes more than 900 law journals, legal newspapers, and specialty publications from the U.S., Canada, U.K., Ireland, Australia, and New Zealand.

Index to Foreign Legal Periodicals. American Association of Law Libraries. University of California Press, Journals Div. • Quarterly. $630.00 per year. Annual cumulation.

Index to Legal Periodicals and Books. H. W. Wilson Co. • Monthly. Quarterly and annual cumulations. $270.00 per year. CD-ROM version available at $1,495.00 per year.

Index to Periodical Articles Related to Law. Glanville Publishers, Inc. • Quarterly. $95.00 per year. Selected from journals not included in the *Index to Legal Periodicals, Current Law Index, Index to Foreign Legal Periodicals, Legal Resolve Index or Legaltrac.*

ALMANACS AND YEARBOOKS

American Law Yearbook. The Gale Group. • Annual. $155.00. Serves as a yearly supplement to *West's Encyclopedia of American Law.* Describes new legal developments in many subject areas.

Annual Survey of American Law, 1942-1995. New York University Law Publications. Oceana Publications, Inc. • 1943. $2,367.50. 62 volumes.

BIBLIOGRAPHIES

Bibliographic Guide to Law. Available from The Gale Group. • Annual. $545.00. Two volumes. Published by G. K. Hall & Co. Lists legal publications cataloged by the New York Public Library and the Library of Congress.

Bowker's Law Books and Serials in Print: A Multimedia Sourcebook. R. R. Bowker. • Annual $725.00. Three volumes. Includes supplement.

Criminal Justice Information: How to Find It, How to Use It. Dennis C. Benamati and others. Oryx Press. • 1997. $59.95. A guide to print, electronic, and online criminal justice information resources. Includes statistical reports, directories, periodicals, monographs, databases, and other sources.

Encyclopedia of Legal Information Sources. The Gale Group. • 1992. $180.00. Second edition. Lists more than 23,000 law-related information sources, including print, nonprint, and organizational.

International Legal Books in Print. Bowker-Saur. • Irregular. $375.00. Two volumes. Covers English-language law books published or distributed within the United Kingdom, Europe, and current or former British Commonwealth countries.

Law Books in Print: Law Books in English Published Throughout the World. Glanville Publishers, Inc. • Triennial. $750.00. Supplement available, *Law Books Publisher.*

Law Books 1876-1981; Books and Serials on Law and its Related Subjects. R. R. Bowker. • Looseleaf service. $695.00. Three volumes. Annual supplementation. Lists publishers and producers of over 55,000 legal reference publications, periodicals, software, audio cassette titles and video cassettes.

Legal Information: How to Find It, How to Use It. Kent Olson. Oryx Press. • 1998. $59.95. Recommends sources for various kinds of legal information.

Pimsleur's Checklists of Basic American Legal Publications. American Association of Law Libraries. Fred B. Rothman and Co. • Irregular. Price varies. Looseleaf service.

CD-ROM DATABASES

LegalTrac. The Gale Group. • Monthly. $5,000.00 per year. Price includes workstation. Provides CD-ROM indexing of periodical literature relating to legal matters from 1980 to date. Corresponds to online *Legal Resource Index.*

WILSONDISC: Index to Legal Periodicals and Books. H. W. Wilson Co. • Monthly. Including unlimited online access to *Index to Legal Periodicals* through WILSONLINE. Contains CD-ROM indexing of more than 800 English language legal periodicals from 1981 to date and 2,500 books.

DIRECTORIES

Internet Tools of the Profession: A Guide for Information Professionals. Hope N. Tillman, editor. Special Libraries Association. • 1997. $49.00. Second edition. Consists of 14 sections by various authors or compilers. After two introductory articles on searching the Internet, there are 12 annotated lists of useful Web sites, covering the SLA, business and finance, chemistry, education, food and agriculture, information technology, insurance and employee benefits, law, library management, metals and materials, pharmaceuticals, and telecommunications. An index is provided.

Law and Legal Information Directory. The Gale Group. • 2000. $405.00. 11th edition. Two volumes. Contains a wide range of sources of legal information, such as associations, law schools, courts, federal agencies, referral services, libraries, publishers, and research centers. There is a separate chapter for each of 23 types of information source or service.

Peterson's Graduate and Professional Programs: Business, Education, Health, Information Studies, Law, and Social Work. Peterson's Magazine Group. • Annual. $27.95. Provides details of graduate and professional programs in business, law, information, and other fields at colleges and universities. Formerly *Peterson's Guide to Graduate Programs in Business, Education, Health, Information Studies, Law and Social Work.*

ENCYCLOPEDIAS AND DICTIONARIES

Black's Law Dictionary. Henry Campbell and Henry Black. West Publishing Co., College and School Div. • 1999. $69.90. Seventh edition. Definitions of the terms and phrases of American and English jurisprudence, ancient and modern.

Communicating with Legal Databases: Terms and Abbreviations for the Legal Researcher. Anne L. McDonald. Neal-Schuman Publishers, Inc. • 1987. $82.50.

Corpus Juris Secundum: Criminal Law. West Publishing Co., College and School Div. • Seven volumes. Price on application. Periodic supplementation. A complete restatement of the entire body of American law based on all reported cases from 1658 to date. Encyclopedic arrangement.

Encyclopedia of Crime and Justice. Available from The Gale Group. • 2001. $425.00. Second edition. Four volumes. Published by Macmillan Reference USA. Contains extensive information on a wide variety of topics pertaining to crime, criminology, social issues, and the courts. (A revision of 1982 edition.).

Index to Legal Citations and Abbreviations. Donald Raistrick. Bowker-Saur. • 1993. $100.00. Second edition. Explains about 25,000 legal abbreviations and acronyms used in the U. S., U. K., and Europe.

Law Dictionary for Non-Lawyers. Daniel Oran. West Publishing Co., College and School Div. • 1999. $31.95. Fourth edition.

Legal Thesaurus. William C. Burton, editor. Pearson Education and Technology. • 1992. $27.00. Second edition.

Words and Phrases Legally Defined. John B. Saunders, Editor. LEXIS Publishing. • 1990. $520.00. Third edition. Four volumes. Definitions taken from court cases.

HANDBOOKS AND MANUALS

Legal Checklists, 1965-1991. Benjamin Becker and others. West Group. • 1989. $240.00. Two volumes.

Restatement of the Law. American Law Institute. • Multivolume set. Periodic supplementation. Price varies. Statements of the common law-an overview, clarification, and simplification of American law.

INTERNET DATABASES

Internet Tools of the Profession. Special Libraries Association. Phone: (202)234-4700 Fax: (202)265-9317 E-mail: hope@tiac.net • URL: http://www.sla.org/pubs/itotp • Web site is designed to update the printed *Internet Tools of the Profession.* Provides links to a wide range of useful databases in business, finance, industry, information technology, insurance, law, library management, telecommunications, and other subject areas. Fees: Free.

ONLINE DATABASES

Auto-Cite. West Group. • Provides information concerning federal and state case law, administrative decisions, and taxation. Daily updates. Inquire as to online cost and availability.

Index to Legal Periodicals and Books (Online). H. W. Wilson Co. • Broad coverage of law journals and books 1981 to date. Monthly updates. Inquire as to online cost and availability.

Law of the Super Searchers: The Online Secrets of Top Legal Researchers. T. R. Halvorson and Reva Basch. Information Today, Inc. • 1999. $24.95. Eight law researchers explain how to find useful legal information online. (CyberAge Books.).

Legal Resource Index. The Gale Group. • Broad coverage of law literature appearing in legal, business, and other periodicals, 1980 to date. Monthly updates. Inquire as to online cost and availability.

PERIODICALS AND NEWSLETTERS

American Journal of Comparative Law. University of California. • Quarterly. $30.00 per year.

Harvard Law Review. Harvard Law Review Association. • Eight times a year. $45.00 per year.

Journal of Internet Law. Aspen Law and Business. • Monthly. $295.00 per year. Covers such Internet and e-commerce topics as domain name disputes, copyright protection, Uniform Commercial Code issues, international law, privacy regulation, electronic records, digital signatures, liability, and security.

Law and Contemporary Problems. Duke University, School of Law. • Quarterly. $48.00 per year.

Legal Information Alert: What's New in Legal Publications, Databases, and Research Techniques. Donna T. Heroy, editor. Alert Publications, Inc. • 10 times per year. $169.00 per year. Newsletter for law librarians and legal information specialists.

Legal Reference Services Quarterly. Haworth Press, Inc. • Quarterly. Individuals, $60.00 per year; institutions and libraries, $135.00 per year.

Legal Times. American Lawyer Media, L.P. • Weekly. Individuals, $249.00 per year; institutions, $635.00 per year.

National Law Journal: The Weekly Newspaper for the Profession. American Lawyer Media, L.P. • Weekly. $158.00 per year. News and analysis of the latest developments in the law and the law profession.

United States Law Week: A National Survey of Current Law. Bureau of National Affairs, Inc. • Weekly. $989.00 per year. Covers U.S. Supreme Court proceedings and gives full text of decisions. Also provides detailed reports on important legislative and regulatory actions.

Yale Law Journal. Yale Journal Co., Inc. • Eight times a year. $40.00 per year.

RESEARCH CENTERS AND INSTITUTES

Center for the Study of Law, Science, and Technology. Arizona State University, College of Law, P.O. Box 877906, Tempe, AZ 85287-7906. Phone: (602)965-2554 Fax: (602)965-2427 E-mail: daniel.strouse@asu.edu • URL: http://www.law.asu.edu • Studies the legal problems created by technological advances.

Lexis.com Research System. Lexis-Nexis Group. Phone: 800-227-9597 or (937)865-6800 Fax: (937)865-6909 E-mail: webmaster@prod.lexis-nexis.com • URL: http://www.lexis.com • Fee-based Web site offers extensive searching of a wide variety of legal sources. Additional features include Daily Opinion Service, lexis.com Bookstore, Career Center, CLE Center, Law Schools, and Practice Pages ("Pages specific to areas of specialty").

Morin Center for Banking and Financial Law. Boston University, School of Law, 765 Commonwealth Ave., Boston, MA 02215. Phone: (617)353-3023 Fax: (617)353-2444 E-mail: banklaw@bu.edu • URL: http://www.web.bu.edu/law • Research fields include banking law, regulation of depository institutions, and deposit insurance.

STATISTICS SOURCES

Statistics on Crime, Justice, and Punishment. The Gale Group. • 1996. $65.00. Volume three. Includes graphs, charts, and tables arranged within subject chapters. Citations to data sources are provided.

For publishers addresses, refer to SOURCES CITED section at the back of the book.

TRADE/PROFESSIONAL ASSOCIATIONS
American Bar Association. 750 N. Lake Shore Dr., Chicago, IL 60611. Phone: 800-285-2221 or (312)988-5000 Fax: (312)988-5528 E-mail: info@abanet.org • URL: http://www.abanet.org.

American Law Institute. 4025 Chestnut St., Philadelphia, PA 19104-3099. Phone: 800-253-6397 or (215)243-1600 Fax: (215)243-1664 • URL: http://www.ali.org.

American Society of Comparative Law. c/o Dr. Arthur T. von Mehren, Harvard Law School, Cambridge, MA 02138. Phone: (617)495-3193 or (617)496-1763 Fax: (617)495-1110 E-mail: vonmehre@hulawl.harvard.edu.

Practising Law Institute. 810 Seventh Ave., New York, NY 10019. Phone: 800-260-4754 or (212)824-5700 Fax: (212)581-4670.

OTHER SOURCES
World of Criminal Justice. The Gale Group. • 2001. $150.00. Two volumes. Contains both topical and biographical entries relating to the criminal justice system and criminology.

LAW, BUSINESS

See: BUSINESS LAW

LAW, COMPUTER

See: COMPUTER LAW

LAW ENFORCEMENT INDUSTRIES

See also: CRIME AND CRIMINALS

DIRECTORIES
Directory of Juvenile and Adult Correctional Departments, Institutions, Agencies, and Paroling Authorities. American Correctional Association. • Annual. $80.00. Provides information on approximately 4,000 correctional agencies and institutions in the U. S. and Canada.

Jane's Police and Security Equipment: The Complete Source on Worldwide Law Enforcement Equipment. Jane's Information Group. • Annual. $350.00. Provides information on sources of more than 2,000 items of law enforcement equipment. Covers traffic control, riot control, communications, personal protection, surveillance, and other equipment categories. Includes detailed product descriptions.

Law and Order Magazine Police Equipment Buyer's Guide. Hendon, Inc. • Annual. $15.00. Lists manufacturers, dealers, and distributors of equipment and services for police departments.

Law Enforcement Technology Directory. Cygnus Business Media. • Annual. $60.00 per year. $6.00 per issue; a directory of products, equipment, services, and technology for police professionals. Includes weapons, uniforms, communications equipment, and software.

National Directory of Law Enforcement Administrators and Correctional Institutions. National Public Safety Information Bureau. • Annual. $99.00. Lists a wide variety of law enforcement administrators and institutions, including city police departments, sheriffs, prosecutors, state agencies, federal agencies, correctional institutions, college campus police departments, airport police, and harbor police.

Police: Buyer's Guide. Bobit Publications. • Annual. $3.00. Lists suppliers of products and services for police departments.

Police Chief: Buyer's Guide. International Association of Chiefs of Police. • Annual. $3.00. Contains a list of suppliers of equipment and services for police departments.

ENCYCLOPEDIAS AND DICTIONARIES
Encyclopedia of American Prisons. Marilyn D. McShane and Frank P. Williams, editors. Garland Publishing, Inc. • 1996. $100.00. (Reference Library of the Humanities Series, Volume 17487).

PERIODICALS AND NEWSLETTERS
Correctional Building News. Emlen Publications, Inc. • Bimonthly. Controlled circulation. Edited for designers and builders of prisons.

Corrections Today. American Correctional Association. • Bimonthly. $25.00 per year. Includes "Annual Architecture, Construction, and Design Issue" on prisons and other correctional facilities.

ID World: The Magazine of Personal Identification and Biometrics. Faulkner & Gray, Inc. • Bimonthly. Controlled circulation. Covers personal identification systems, including smart cards and finger prints. Includes articles on legal, regulatory, and privacy issues.

International Police Review. Jane's Information Group, Inc. • Bimonthy. Institutions, $215.00 per year. Covers "every aspect" of policing and security throughout the world, including organized crime, money laundering, drugs, illegal immigration, forensic science, and police technology.

Law and Order Magazine: The Magazine for Police Management. Hendon Publishing Co. • Monthly. $22.00 per year. Edited for law enforcement officials. Includes special issues on communications, technology, weapons, and uniforms and equipment.

Law Enforcement Product News. General Communications, Inc. • Bimonthly. Free. Covers new products and equipment for police departments and other law enforcement and correctional agencies.

Law Enforcement Technology. Cygnus Business Media. • Monthly. $60.00 per year. Covers new products and technologies for police professionals. Includes special issues on weapons, uniforms, communications equipment, computers (hardware-software), vehicles, and enforcement of drug laws.

9-1-1 Magazine: Public Safety Communications and Response. Official Publications, Inc. • Bimonthly. $31.95 per year. Covers technical information and applications for public safety communications personnel.

Police Chief: Professional Voice of Law Enforcement. International Association of Chiefs of Police. • Monthly. $25.00 per year. Subject matter includes information on law enforcement technology and new products.

Police Science and Technology Review. Jane's Information Group. • Quarterly. $90.00 per year. Includes detailed information on technology relating to surveillance, forensics, and fingerprints.

Police: The Law Officer's Magazine. Bobit Publications. • Monthly. $38.95 per year. Edited for law enforcement professionals. Includes information on new technology and equipment.

RESEARCH CENTERS AND INSTITUTES
Association for Correctional Research and Information Management. 1129 Rivara Court, Sacramento, CA 95864-3720. Phone: (916)487-9334 Fax: (916)487-9929 E-mail: ajipres@aol.com • Research areas include the statistics of prisons and jails.

Municipal Technical Advisory Service Library. University of Tennessee, Knoxville, Conference Center Bldg.., Suite 120, Knoxville, TN 37996-4105. Phone: (423)974-0411 Fax: (423)974-0423 E-mail: rschwartz@utk.edu • URL: http://www.mtas.utk.edu • Research areas include municipal finance, police administration, and public works.

Police Executive Research Forum. 1120 Connecticut Ave., N. W., Suite 930, Washington, DC 20036. Phone: 877-576-5423 or (202)466-7820 Fax: (202)466-7826 E-mail: perf@policeforum.org • URL: http://www.policeforum.org • Research areas include police operational and administrative procedures. Provides consulting services to local governments.

STATISTICS SOURCES
Crime in America's Top-Rated Cities: A Statistical Profile. Grey House Publishing. • Biennial. $125.00. Contains 20-year data for major crime categories in 75 cities, suburbs, metropolitan areas, and the U. S. Also includes statistics on correctional facilities, inmates, hate crimes, illegal drugs, and other crime-related matters.

Sourcebook of Criminal Justice Statistics. Available from U. S. Government Printing Office. • Annual. $56.00. Issued by the Bureau of Justice Statistics, U. S. Department of Justice (http://www.usdoj.gov/bjs). Contains both crime data and corrections statistics.

TRADE/PROFESSIONAL ASSOCIATIONS
American Correctional Association. 4380 Forbes Blvd., Lanham, MD 20706-4322. Phone: 800-222-5646 or (301)918-1800 Fax: (301)918-1900 • URL: http://www.corrections.com/aca • Members are correctional administrators, prison wardens, parole boards, educators, and others with an interest in correctional institutions. Various departments are concerned with conventions, corporate relations, finance, administration, communications, and standards.

Correctional Industries Association. 1420 N. Charles St., Ste. CH415, Baltimore, MD 21201. Phone: (410)837-5036 Fax: (410)837-5039 E-mail: ciahq@worldnet.att.net • URL: http://www.corrections.com/industries • Members are managers and supervisors in prison-operated industries.

International Association of Chiefs of Police (IACP). 515 N. Washington St., Alexandria, VA 22314. Phone: 800-843-4227 or (703)836-6767 Fax: (703)836-4543 • URL: http://www.theiacp.org • The IACP Law Enforcement Information Management Section is concerned with law enforcement management information systems, including data processing, telecommunications, and automated systems.

International Security Management Association. 66 Charles St., Suite 280, Boston, MA 02114. Phone: (319)381-4008 Fax: (319)381-4283 E-mail: isma3@aol.com • URL: http://www.ismanet.com • Members are executives of security service companies and executives of security operations at large corporations.

OTHER SOURCES
The Corrections Market. Available from FIND/SVP, Inc. • 1996. $2,150.00. Market research report published by Packaged Facts. Covers the markets for prison food service, health care, private management, and telecommunications. Includes market growth projections to the year 2000.

Police Markets of North America and the European Union: Jane's Special Report. Jane's Information Group. • 1997. $695.00. Provides detailed market research data relative to the police and security industry. Covers a wide range of equipment and vehicle markets geographically for U. S. states, Canadian provinces, and countries. (Law Enforcement-Related Special Report Series).

LAW, ENVIRONMENTAL

See: ENVIRONMENTAL LAW

LAW, FAMILY

See: FAMILY LAW

LAW FIRMS

See: LAWYERS

LAW, STATE

See: STATE LAW

LAWN CARE INDUSTRY

See also: GARDEN SUPPLY INDUSTRY

ABSTRACTS AND INDEXES

Horticultural Abstracts: Compiled from World Literature on Temperate and Tropical Fruits, Vegetables, Ornaments, Plantation Crops. Available from CABI Publishing North America. • Monthly. $1,605.00 per year. Published in England by CABI Publishing. Provides worldwide coverage of the literature of fruits, vegetables, flowers, plants, and all aspects of gardens and gardening.

Readers' Guide to Periodical Literature. H. W. Wilson Co. • Monthly. $220.00 per year. CD-ROM edition, $1,495 per year, including annual cumulation. Indexes about 250 peridicals of general interest.

CD-ROM DATABASES

AGRICOLA on SilverPlatter. Available from SilverPlatter Information, Inc. • Quarterly. $825.00 per year. Produced by the National Agricultural Library. Provides about three million citations on CD-ROM to the literature of agriculture, agricultural economics, animal sciences, entomology, fertilizer, food, forestry, nutrition, pesticides, plant science, water resources, and other topics. Each quarterly disc covers the past ten years, with archival discs available from 1970.

WILSONDISC: Biological and Agricultural Index. H. W. Wilson Co. • Monthly. $1,495.00 per year, including unlimited online access to *Biological and Agricultural Index* through WILSONLINE. Provides CD-ROM indexing of over 250 periodicals covering agriculture, agricultural chemicals, biochemistry, biotechnology, entomology, horticulture, and related topics.

WILSONDISC: Readers' Guide to Periodical Literature. H. W. Wilson Co. • Monthly. $1,095.00 per year, including unlimited online access to *Readers' Guide to Periodical Literature* through WILSONLINE. Provides CD-ROM indexing of about 250 general interest periodicals. Covers 1983 to date. (*Readers' Guide Abstracts* also available on CD-ROM at $1,995 per year.).

DIRECTORIES

Yard and Garden. Cygnus Publishing, Inc., Johnson Hill Press, Inc. • Seven times a year. $48.00. Includes retailers and distributors of lawn and garden power equipment, lawn and plant care products, patio furniture, etc. Arranged by type of product. Includes a *Product* issue.

ENCYCLOPEDIAS AND DICTIONARIES

Encyclopedia of Agriculture Science. Charles J. Arntzen and Ellen M. Ritter, editors. Academic Press, Inc. • 1994. $625.00. Four volumes.

HANDBOOKS AND MANUALS

Lawn Care Service. Entrepreneur Media, Inc. • Looseleaf. $59.50. A practical guide to starting a lawn care business. Covers profit potential, start-up costs, market size evaluation, owner's time required, pricing, accounting, advertising, promotion, etc. (Start-Up Business Guide No. E1198.).

ONLINE DATABASES

Agricola. U.S. National Agricultural Library. • Covers worldwide agricultural literature. Over 2.8 million citations, 1970 to present, with monthly updates. Inquire as to online cost and availability.

Biological and Agricultural Index Online. H. W. Wilson Co. • Indexes a wide variety of agricultural and biological periodicals, 1983 to date. Monthly updates. Inquire as to online cost and availability.

CAB Abstracts. CAB International North America. • Contains 46 specialized abstract collections covering over 10,000 journals and monographs in the areas of agriculture, horticulture, forest products, farm products, nutrition, dairy science, poultry, grains, animal health, entomology, etc. Time period is 1972 to date, with monthly updates. Inquire as to online cost and availability. *CAB Abstracts on CD-ROM* also available, with annual updating.

Globalbase. The Gale Group. • Provides more than one million online summaries of business, industrial, and economic news reports from more than 1,000 publications worldwide. Covers a wide range of material appearing in international trade journals, professional magazines, and newspapers. Time period is 1984 to date, with weekly updates. Inquire as to online cost and availability.

PROMT: Predicasts Overview of Markets and Technology. The Gale Group. • Companies, products, applied technologies and markets. U.S. and international literature coverage, 1972 to date. Inquire as to online cost and availability. Provides abstracts from more than 1,600 publications. Weekly updates.

Readers' Guide Abstracts Online. H. W. Wilson Co. • Indexes and abstracts general interest periodicals, 1983 to date. Weekly updates. Inquire as to online cost and availability.

PERIODICALS AND NEWSLETTERS

Journal of Turfgrass Management: Developments in Basic and Applied Turfgrass Research. Haworth Press, Inc. • Quarterly. Individuals, $45.00 per year; institutions, $65.00 per year; libraries, $75.00 per year. An applied research journal.

Landscape Management: Commercial Magazine for Lawn, Landscape and Grounds Managers. Advanstar Communications, Inc. • Monthly. $41.00 per year.

Lawn and Landscape. Group Interest Enterprises. G.I.E., Media Inc. • Monthly. $30.00 per year. Supplement available. Formerly *Lawn and Landscape Maintenance.*

PRO. Cygnus Publishing, Inc., Johnson Hill Press, Inc. • Seven times a year. $48.00 per year. For owners and operators of lawn maintenance service firms. Includes annual *Product* issue.

RESEARCH CENTERS AND INSTITUTES

Landscape Architecture Foundation. 636 Eye St., N.W., Washington, DC 20001-3736. Phone: (202)216-2355 Fax: (202)898-1185 E-mail: severett@asla.org • URL: http://www.asla.org/asla.

TRADE/PROFESSIONAL ASSOCIATIONS

Lawn Institute. 1509 N.E. Johnson Ferry Rd., Suite 190, Marietta, GA 30062-8122. Phone: (404)977-5492 Fax: (404)977-8205 • Members are producers of lawn seed and lawn care products.

Outdoor Power Equipment Institute. 341 S. Patrick St., Alexandria, VA 22314. Phone: (703)549-7600 Fax: (703)549-7604 • Members are manufacturers of lawn mowers, garden tractors, snow throwers, leaf vacuums, power trimmers, etc.

Professional Lawn Care Association of America. 1000 Johnson Ferry Rd., Suite C-135, Marietta, GA 30068. Phone: 800-458-3466 or (770)977-5222 Fax: (770)578-6071 E-mail: plcaa@plcaa.org • URL: http://www.plcaa.org • Members are active in the business of treating lawns with chemicals.

LAWS

See also: LAW

GENERAL WORKS

How Our Laws Are Made. Available from U. S. Government Printing Office. • 2000. $3.75. 22nd edition. Issued by U. S. House of Representatives.

Lawmaking and the Legislative Process: Committees, Connections, and Compromises. Tommy Neal. Oryx Press. • 1996. $26.50. Explains how bills are enacted into laws through the state legislative process. Provides step-by-step examples, using fictitious bills.

ABSTRACTS AND INDEXES

Congressional Index. CCH, Inc. • Weekly when Congress is in session. $1,283.00 per year. Index to action on Public Bills from introduction to final disposition. Subject, author, and bill number indexes.

Current Law Index: Multiple Access to Legal Periodicals. The Gale Group. • Monthly. $650.00 per year. Produced in cooperation with the American Association of Law Libraries. Indexes more than 900 law journals, legal newspapers, and specialty publications from the U.S., Canada, U.K., Ireland, Australia, and New Zealand.

ALMANACS AND YEARBOOKS

Advertising Law: Year in Review. CCH, Inc. • Annual. $85.00. Summarizes the year's significant legal and regulatory developments.

Property and Casualty Insurance: Year in Review. CCH, Inc. • Annual. $75.00. Summarizes the year's significant legal and regulatory developments.

Securities, Commodities, and Banking: Year in Review. CCH, Inc. • Annual. $55.00. Summarizes the year's significant legal and regulatory developments.

Suggested State Legislation. Council of State Governments. • Annual. $59.00. A source of legislative ideas and drafting assistance for state government officials.

DIRECTORIES

Federal Regulatory Directory. Congressional Quarterly, Inc. • Biennial. $149.95. Published by Congressional Quarterly, Inc. Provides detailed profiles of government agency functions and duties, and describes the laws each agency enforces. Includes extensive directory information.

Martindale-Hubbell Law Directory. Martindale-Hubbell. • Annual. $695.00. 25 volumes. Lists 800,000 lawyers in the U. S., Canada, and 150 other countries, with an index to areas of specialization. Three of the 25 volumes provide the *Martindale-Hubbell Law Digest*, summarizing the statutary laws of the U. S. (state and federal), Canada, and 61 other countries.

HANDBOOKS AND MANUALS

Code of Federal Regulations. Office of the Federal Register, U.S. General Services Administration.

For publishers addresses, refer to SOURCES CITED section at the back of the book.

Available from U.S. Government Printing Office. • $1,094.00 per year. Complete service.

National Survey of State Laws. The Gale Group. • 1999. $85.00. Third edition. Provides concise state-by-state comparisons of current state laws on a wide variety of topics. Includes references to specific codes or statutes.

United States Code. U.S. Congress. Available from U.S. Government Printing Office. • Continual supplements. Price varies. Permanent and general public law of the United States from 1789 to the codification date.

United States Code Annotated: Crimes and Criminal Procedures. West Publishing Co., College and School Div. • 15 volumes. Price on application. Arranged in parallel fashion to *United States Code.* Gives abstracts of relevant federal and state court decisions pertaining to each section of the code. Supplemented by annual pocket parts.

United States Code Service: Lawyers Edition. West Group. • 1991. $2,000.00. 184 volumes. All federal laws of a general and permanent nature arranged in accordance with the section numbering of the *United States Code* and the supplements thereto. Each code is annotated. Annual pocket supplements.

United States Statutes at Large. U.S. Office of the Federal Register. Available from U.S. Government Printing Office. • Annual. Price varies. Congressional acts and presidential proclamations issued during the Congressional session. For all laws in force at a specific date, refer to *United States Code.*

INTERNET DATABASES

FindLaw: Internet Legal Resources. FindLaw, Inc. Phone: (650)322-8430 E-mail: info@findlaw.com • URL: http://www.findlaw.com • Web site provides a wide variety of information and links relating to laws, law schools, professional development, lawyers, the U. S. Supreme Court, consultants (experts), law reviews, legal news, etc. Online searching is provided. Fees: Free.

ONLINE DATABASES

CIS. Congressional Information Service, Inc. • Indexes publications of the United States Congress, 1970 to present. Inquire as to online cost and availability.

PERIODICALS AND NEWSLETTERS

Congressional Record. U.S. Congress. Available from U.S. Government Printing Office. • Daily. $357.00 per year. Indexes give names, subjects, and history of bills. Texts of bills not included.

Congressional Record Scanner. Congressional Quarterly, Inc. • 180 times a year. $395.00 per year. Abstract of each day's Congressional Record.

Federal Register. Office of the Federal Register. Available from U.S. Government Printing Office. • Daily except Saturday and Sunday. $697.00 per year. Publishes regulations and legal notices issued by federal agencies, including executive orders and presidential proclamations. Issued by the National Archives and Records Administration (http://www.nara.gov).

United States Law Week: A National Survey of Current Law. Bureau of National Affairs, Inc. • Weekly. $989.00 per year. Covers U.S. Supreme Court proceedings and gives full text of decisions. Also provides detailed reports on important legislative and regulatory actions.

RESEARCH CENTERS AND INSTITUTES

Lexis.com Research System. Lexis-Nexis Group. Phone: 800-227-9597 or (937)865-6800 Fax: (937)865-6909 E-mail: webmaster@prod.lexis-nexis.com • URL: http://www.lexis.com • Fee-based Web site offers extensive searching of a wide variety of legal sources. Additional features include Daily Opinion Service, lexis.com Bookstore, Career Center, CLE Center, Law Schools, and Practice Pages ("Pages specific to areas of specialty").

LAWS, ADVERTISING

See: ADVERTISING LAW AND REGULATION

LAWS, BANKING

See: BANKING LAW AND REGULATION

LAWYERS

See also: WOMEN LAWYERS

GENERAL WORKS

The Betrayed Profession: Lawyering at the End of the Twentieth Century. Sol M. Linowitz and Martin Mayer. John Hopkins University Press. • 1996. $15.95. Reprint edition. A critical view of present-day lawyers and law firms.

Smart Questions to Ask Your Financial Advisers. Lynn Brenner. Bloomberg Press. • 1997. $19.95. Provides practical advice on how to deal with financial planners, stockbrokers, insurance agents, and lawyers. Some of the areas covered are investments, estate planning, tax planning, house buying, prenuptial agreements, divorce arrangements, loss of a job, and retirement. (Bloomberg Personal Bookshelf Series Library.).

ALMANACS AND YEARBOOKS

The Lawyer's Almanac; An Encyclopedia of Information about Law, Lawyers, and the Profession. Harcourt Trade. • 1985. $60.00.

BIOGRAPHICAL SOURCES

Who's Who in American Law. Marquis Who's Who. • Biennial. $285.00. Contains over 22,000 concise biographies of American lawyers, judges, and others in the legal field.

CD-ROM DATABASES

Martindale-Hubbell Law Directory on CD-ROM. Martindale-Hubbell, Reed Reference Publishing. • Quarterly. $995.00 per year. Provides CD-ROM information on over 900,000 lawyers. International coverage.

The Tax Directory [CD-ROM]. Tax Analysts. • Quarterly. Provides *The Tax Directory* listings on CD-ROM, covering federal, state, and international tax officials, tax practitioners, and corporate tax executives.

DIRECTORIES

American Bar Association Directory. American Bar Association. • Annual. $14.95. Lists about 7,500 lawyers.

Best's Directory of Recommended Insurance Attorneys and Adjusters. A. M. Best Co. • Annual. $1130.00. Two volumes. More than 5,000 American, Canadian, and foreign insurance defense law firms; lists 1,200 national and international insurance adjusting firms. Formerly *Best's Directory of Recommended Insurance Adjusters.*

Campbell's List: A Directory of Selected Lawyers and Includes Court Reporters and Process Servers. Campbell's List, Inc. • Annual. $10.00. September supplement. About 1,000 selected out-of-town lawyers in the United States, Canada, and foreign countries who are willing to handle correspondent work for other lawyers and businesses.

Directory of Environmental Attorneys. Aspen Law and Business. • 1994. $195.00.

Directory of Intellectual Property Attorneys. Aspen Law and Business. • Annual. Price on application.

Directory of Litigation Attorneys. Aspen Law and Business. • 1993. $450.00. Two volumes. Includes about 40,000 attorneys, 15,000 law firms, and 100 areas of litigation specialization.

Emerson's Directory of Leading U.S. Law Firms. Available from Hoover's, Inc. • Biennial. $195.00. Published by the Emerson Company (http://www.emersoncompany.com). Provides information on 500 major law firms.

Law Firms Yellow Book: Who's Who in the Management of the Leading U. S. Law Firms. Leadership Directories, Inc. • Semiannual. $235.00 per year. Provides detailed information on more than 800 major U. S. law firms. Includes domestic offices, foreign offices, subsidiaries, and affiliates. There are seven indexes: geographic, subject specialty, management, administrative, law school attended, personnel, and law firm.

Lawyers' List. CCH, Inc. • Annual. $75.00. About 2,500 lawyers engaged in general, corporate, trial, patent, trademark, copyright practices in the United States.

Lawyer's Register International by Specialties and Fields of Law Including a Directory of Corporate Counsel. Lawyer's Register Publishing Co. • Annual. $329.00. Three volumes. Referral source for law firms.

Martindale-Hubbell Bar Register of Preeminent Lawyers. Martindale-Hubbell. • Annual. $195.00. Lists over 10,000 "outstanding members of the bar" in general practice and in 28 specific fields. Covers the U. S. and Canada.

Martindale-Hubbell Law Directory. Martindale-Hubbell. • Annual. $695.00. 25 volumes. Lists 800,000 lawyers in the U. S., Canada, and 150 other countries, with an index to areas of specialization. Three of the 25 volumes provide the *Martindale-Hubbell Law Digest,* summarizing the statutary laws of the U. S. (state and federal), Canada, and 61 other countries.

National Directory of Corporate Distress Specialists: A Comprehensive Guide to Firms and Professionals Providing Services in Bankruptcies, Workouts, Turnarounds, and Distressed Investments. Joel W. Lustig, editor. Lustig Data Research, Inc. • Annual. $245.00. Provides information on 1,400 specialist firms in 17 subject areas-attorneys, accountants, financial advisors, investors, valuation consultants, turnaround managers, liquidators, etc. Nine indexes are included.

NLADA Directory of Legal Aid and Defender Offices in the United States and Territories. National Legal Aid and Defender Association. • Biennial. $70.00. Geographical list of approximately 3,600 legal aid and defender offices and their branches. Formerly *NLADA Directory Legal Aid and Defender Offices in the United States.*

The Tax Directory. Tax Analysts. • Annual. $299.00. ($399.00 with quarterly CD-ROM updates.) Four volumes: *Government Officials Worldwide* (lists 15,000 state, federal, and international tax officials, with basic corporate and individual income tax rates for 100 countries); *Private Sector Professionals Worldwide* (lists 25,000 U.S. and foreign tax practitioners: accountants, lawyers, enrolled agents, and actuarial firms); *Corporate Tax Managers Worldwide* (lists 10,000 tax managers employed by U.S. and foreign companies).

FINANCIAL RATIOS

Almanac of Business and Industrial Financial Ratios. Leo Troy. Prentice Hall. • Annual. $99.95.

Contains financial ratios derived from federal tax returns. Ratios for each of about 200 industries are arranged according to company asset size.

Annual Statement Studies. Robert Morris Associates: The Association of Lending and Credit Risk Professiona. • Annual. Free to members; non-members, $140.00. Median and quartile financial ratios are given for over 400 kinds of manufacturing, wholesale, retail, construction, and consumer finance establishments. Data is sorted by both asset size and sales volume. Includes a clearly written "Definition of Ratios" and an alphabetical industry index.

HANDBOOKS AND MANUALS

ABA/BNA Lawyer's Manual on Professional Conduct. American Bar Association. Bureau of National Affairs, Inc. • Biweekly. $845.00 per year. Looseleaf. Covers American Bar Association's model rules governing ethical practice of law.

Accounting Systems for Law Offices. William J. Burke and Carl W. Bradbury. Matthew Bender & Co., Inc. • Looseleaf Service. $220.00. Periodic supplementation.

The Business of Law: A Handbook on How to Manage Law Firms. Aspen Law and Business. • $95.00. 1990. Looseleaf service.

Career Legal Secretary. National Association of Legal Secretaries. West Publishing Co., College and School Div. • 1997. $35.50. Fourth edition.

Getting Started in Investment Planning Services. James E. Grant. CCH, Inc. • 1999. $85.00. Second edition. Provides advice and information for lawyers and accountants who are planning to initiate fee-based investment services.

How to Manage Your Law Office. Matthew Bender & Co., Inc. • $210.00 Two looseleaf volumes. Periodic supplementation.

Law Office Automation and Technology. Matthew Bender & Co., Inc. • $180.00. Looseleaf. Periodic supplementation.

Law Office Economics and Management Manual, 1970-1990. Paul S. Hoffman, editor. West Group. • $200.00. Two volumes. Collection of articles by experts exploring the management and financial issues facing law firms.

Legal Assistant's Handbook. Thomas W. Brunner and others. Bureau of National Affairs, Inc. • 1988. $44.00. Second edition.

Legal Malpractice: Liability, Prevention, Litigation, Insurance. Ronald E. Mallen and Jeffrey M. Smith. West Publishing Co., College and School Div. • 1995. Fourth edition. Three volumes. Price on application. Periodic supplementation.

Managing People in Today's Law Firm: The Human Resources Approach to Surviving Change. Ellen Weisbord and others. Greenwood Publishing Group, Inc. • 1995. $62.95.

Managing the Law Library 1999: Forging Effective Relationships in Today's Law Office. Practising Law Institute. • 1999. $99.00. Produced to provide background material for PLI seminars on the role of libraries and librarians in law firms.

Manual for Managing the Law Office. Prentice Hall. • Looseleaf service. Price on application. (Information Services Series).

A Primer for New Corporate Lawyers: What Business Lawyers Do. Clifford R. Ennico. West Group. • 1990. $39.95. Covers client relations, client counseling, negotiation, managing business transactions, and other topics.

Professional Resumes for Tax and Accounting Occupations. David H. Noble. CCH, Inc. • 1999. $49.95. Written for accounting, tax, law, and finance professionals. In addition to advice, provides 335 sample resumes and 22 cover letters.

Professional's Guide to Successful Management: The Eight Essentials for Running Your Firm, Practice, or Partnership. Carol A. O'Connor. McGraw-Hill. • 1994. Price on application.

Valuing Professional Practices: A Practitioner's Guide. Robert Reilly and Robert Schweihs. CCH, Inc. • 1997. $99.00. Provides a basic introduction to estimating the dollar value of practices in various professional fields.

INTERNET DATABASES

FindLaw: Internet Legal Resources. FindLaw, Inc. Phone: (650)322-8430 E-mail: info@findlaw.com • URL: http://www.findlaw.com • Web site provides a wide variety of information and links relating to laws, law schools, professional development, lawyers, the U. S. Supreme Court, consultants (experts), law reviews, legal news, etc. Online searching is provided. Fees: Free.

PERIODICALS AND NEWSLETTERS

ABA Journal: The Lawyers Magazine. American Bar Association. • Monthly. Free to members; non-members, $66.00 per year. Includes five regular sections: news affecting lawyers, practical applications of court decisions, pratice management advice, feature articles, and lifestyle stories.

The American Lawyer. American Lawyer Media L.P. • 10 times a year. $149.00 per year. General information for American attorneys.

Law Firm Governance: Journal of Practice Managment, Development, and Technology. Aspen Law and Business. • Quarterly. $196.00 per year. Covers project management, strategic planning, compensation systems, advertising, etc. Regular columns include "Best Practices," "Technology Trends," and "Professional Development." Formerly *Law Governance Review.*

Law Office Economics and Management. West Group. • Quarterly. $150.00 per year.

Marketing for Lawyers. Leader Publications. • Monthly. $138.00 per year. Newsletter. Provides advice for law firms on attracting new clients and providing good service to present clients.

National Law Journal: The Weekly Newspaper for the Profession. American Lawyer Media, L.P. • Weekly. $158.00 per year. News and analysis of the latest developments in the law and the law profession.

Of Counsel: The Monthly Legal Practice Report. Aspen Law and Business. • Monthly. $426.00 per year. Newsletter on the management, marketing, personnel, and compensation of law firms.

The Practical Lawyer. Committee on Continuing Professional Education. American Law Institute-American Bar Association. • Eight times a year. $40.00 per year.

The Practical Real Estate Lawyer. American Law Institute-American Bar Association, Committee on Continuing Profess. • Bimonthly. $37.00 per year. Frequently includes legal forms for use in real estate practice.

Tax Practice. Tax Analysts. • Weekly. $199.00 per year. Newsletter. Covers news affecting tax practitioners and litigators, with emphasis on federal court decisions, rules and regulations, and tax petitions. Provides a guide to Internal Revenue Service audit issues.

Taxation for Lawyers. Warren, Gorham & Lamont/ RIA Group. • Bimonthly. $114.98 per year. Edited for attorneys who are not tax specialists. Emphasis is on tax planning, estates, trusts, partnerships, and taxation of real estate.

STATISTICS SOURCES

Compensation Benchmarks for Private Practice Attorneys. Altman Weil Publications, Inc. • Annual. $295.00. Provides legal-office compensation standards arranged by region, firm size, legal specialty, and various other factors. Covers attorneys, paralegals, and other personnel.

Small Law Firm Economic Survey. Altman Weil Publications, Inc. • Annual. $295.00. Provides aggregate data (benchmarks) on the economics, finances, billing, and staffing of law offices in the U. S. having "less than 12 lawyers.".

Survey of Law Firm Economics: A Management and Planning Tool. Altman Weil Publications, Inc. • Annual. $595.00. Provides aggregate economic statistics and financial data (benchmarks) relating to the legal profession in the U. S. Includes income, expenses, hourly rates, billable hours, compensation, staffing, data by states, and trends. Most information is arranged by region, firm size, years of experience, and other factors.

U. S. Industry and Trade Outlook: The McGraw-Hill Companies and the U.S. Department of Commerce/ International Trade Administration. Datapso Research Corp. • Annual. $69.95. Produced by the International Trade Administration, U. S. Department of Commerce, in a "public-private" partnership with DRI/McGraw-Hill and Standard & Poor's. Provides basic data, outlook for the current year, and "Long-Term Prospects" (five-year projections) for a wide variety of products and services. Includes high technology industries. Formerly *U. S. Industrial Outlook.*

WEFA Industrial Monitor. John Wiley and Sons, Inc. • Annual. $65.00. Prepared by industry analysts at WEFA, an economic forecasting and consulting firm (originally Wharton Econometric Forecasting Associates). Contains discussions of the outlook for major U. S. industries, with many 10-year forecasts (WEFA Web site is http://www.wefa.com).

TRADE/PROFESSIONAL ASSOCIATIONS

American Bar Association. 750 N. Lake Shore Dr., Chicago, IL 60611. Phone: 800-285-2221 or (312)988-5000 Fax: (312)988-5528 E-mail: info@ abanet.org • URL: http://www.abanet.org.

American College of Trial Lawyers. 8001 Irvine Center Dr., Suite 960, Irvine, CA 92718. Phone: (949)727-3194 Fax: (949)727-3894.

Association of Trial Lawyers of America. 1050 31st St., N. W., Washington, DC 20007. Phone: 800-424-2725 or (202)965-3500 Fax: (202)625-7312.

Defense Research International. 130 N. Michigan Ave., Chicago, IL 60601. Phone: 800-667-8108 or (312)795-1101 Fax: (312)795-0747 E-mail: custservice@dri.org • URL: http://www.dri.org • Members are attorneys, insurance companies, insurance adjusters, and others. Includes Product Liability and Professional Liability Committees.

National Lawyers Guild. 126 University Place, New York, NY 10013-4538. Phone: (212)627-2656 Fax: (212)627-2404 E-mail: nlgno@nlg.org • URL: http:/ /www.nlg.org.

National Legal Aid and Defender Association. 1625 K St., N.W., Suite 800, Washington, DC 20006-1604. Phone: (202)452-0620 Fax: (202)872-1031 E-mail: info@nlada.org • URL: http://www.nlada.org.

Tax Analysts. 6830 N. Fairfax Dr., Arlington, VA 22213. Phone: 800-955-3444 or (703)533-4400 Fax: (703)533-4444 E-mail: webmaster@tax.org • URL: http://www.tax.org • An advocacy group reviewing U. S. and foreign income tax developments. Includes a Tax Policy Advisory Board.

OTHER SOURCES

Andrews' Professional Liability Litigation Reporter. Andrews Publications. • Monthly. $550.00 per year. Provides reports on lawsuits against attorneys, accountants, and investment professionals.

Avoiding Tax Malpractice. Robert Feinschreiber and Margaret Kent. CCH, Inc. • 2000. $75.00. Covers malpractice considerations for professional tax practitioners.

Capital for Shipping. Available from Informa Publishing Group Ltd. • Annual. $128.00. Published in the UK by Lloyd's List (http://www.lloydslist.com). Consists of a "Financial Directory" and a "Legal Directory," listing international ship finance providers and international law firms specializing in shipping. (Included with subscription to *Lloyd's Shipping Economist*.).

Washington [year]. Columbia Books, Inc. • Annual. $129.00. Provides information on about 5,000 Washington, DC key businesses, government offices, non-profit organizations, and cultural institutions, with the names of about 25,000 principal executives. Includes Washington media, law offices, foundations, labor unions, international organizations, clubs, etc.

LAYOFFS

See: DISMISSAL OF EMPLOYEES

LEAD INDUSTRY

ABSTRACTS AND INDEXES

IMM Abstracts and Index: A Survey of World Literature on the Economic Geology and Mining of All Minerals (Except Coal), Mineral Processing, and Nonferrous Extraction Metallurgy. Institution of Mining and Metallurgy. • Bimonthly. Members, $142.00 per year; non-members, $215.00 per year. Provides international coverage of the literature of mining and nonferrous metallurgy. Includes mineral economics, tunnelling, and rock mechanics.

Leadscan: A Review of Recent Technical Literature on the Uses of lead and its Products. Clive Larson,ed. C and C Associates. • Quarterly. $110.00 per year. Provides technical articles and abstracts of recent technical and market related literature on lead and its uses.

Nonferrous Metals Alert. Cambridge Information Group. • Monthly. $340.00 per year. Provides citations to the business and industrial literature of nonferrous metals. (Materials Business Information Series).

CD-ROM DATABASES

METADEX Materials Collection: Metals-Polymers-Ceramics. Cambridge Scientific Abstracts. • Quarterly. $6,950.00 per year. Provides CD-ROM citations to the worldwide literature of materials science and metallurgy. Corresponds to *Metals Abstracts, Alloys Index, Steels Alert, Nonferrous Alert, Polymers/Ceramics/Composites Alert,* and *Engineered Materials Abstracts.* (Formerly produced by ASM International.).

ONLINE DATABASES

Materials Business File. Cambridge Scientific Abstracts. • Provides online abstracts and citations to worldwide materials literature, covering the business and industrial aspects of metals, plastics, ceramics, and composites. Corresponds to *Steels Alert, Nonferrous Metals Alert,* and *Polymers/Ceramics/Composites Alert.* Time period is 1985 to date, with monthly updates. (Formerly produced by ASM International.) Inquire as to online cost and availability.

METADEX. Cambridge Scientific Abstracts. • Covers the worldwide literature of metals, metallurgy, and materials science, 1966 to date. Includes detailed alloys indexing from 1974. Biweekly updating. Inquire as to online cost and availability. (Formerly produced by ASM International.).

STATISTICS SOURCES

Lead and Zinc Statistics. International Lead and Zinc Study Group. • Monthly. $370.00 per year. Supplement available *Advance Data Service.* Text in English and French.

Mineral Commodity Summaries. Available from U. S. Government Printing Office. • Annual. Published by the U. S. Geological Survey, Department of the Interior (http://www.usgs.gov). Contains detailed, five-year data for about 90 nonfuel minerals. Covers a wide range of statistics, including production, imports, exports, consumption, reserves, prices, tariff information, and industry employment. (Two pages are devoted to each mineral.).

Non-Ferrous Metal Data Yearbook. American Bureau of Metal Statistics. • Annual. $395.00. Provides about 200 statistical tables covering many nonferrous metals. Includes production, consumption, inventories, exports, imports, and other data.

U. S. Industry and Trade Outlook: The McGraw-Hill Companies and the U.S. Department of Commerce/International Trade Administration. Datapso Research Corp. • Annual. $69.95. Produced by the International Trade Administration, U. S. Department of Commerce, in a "public-private" partnership with DRI/McGraw-Hill and Standard & Poor's. Provides basic data, outlook for the current year, and "Long-Term Prospects" (five-year projections) for a wide variety of products and services. Includes high technology industries. Formerly *U. S. Industrial Outlook.*

WEFA Industrial Monitor. John Wiley and Sons, Inc. • Annual. $65.00. Prepared by industry analysts at WEFA, an economic forecasting and consulting firm (originally Wharton Econometric Forecasting Associates). Contains discussions of the outlook for major U. S. industries, with many 10-year forecasts (WEFA Web site is http://www.wefa.com).

TRADE/PROFESSIONAL ASSOCIATIONS

American Bureau of Metal Statistics. P.O. Box 805, Chatham, NJ 07928. Phone: (973)701-2299 Fax: (973)701-2152 E-mail: info@abms.com • URL: http://www.abms.com • Members are metal companies. Compiles and publishes detailed statistical data on a wide variety of nonferrous metals: aluminum, copper, gold, lead, nickel, platinum, silver, tin, titanium, uranium, zinc, and others.

International Lead Zinc Research Organization. P.O. Box 12036, Research Triangle Park, NC 27709. Phone: (919)361-4647 Fax: (919)361-1957 E-mail: jcole@ilzro.org • URL: http://www.ilzro.com.

Lead Industries Association. 13 Main St., Sparta, NJ 07871. Phone: (973)726-5323 Fax: (973)726-4484 E-mail: miller@leadinfo.com • URL: http://www.leadinfo.com.

Non-Ferrous Metals Producers Committee. c/o Kenneth Button, Economic Consulting Service, 2030 M. St., N.W., Suite 800, Washington, DC 20036. Phone: (202)466-7720 Fax: (202)466-2710 • Members are copper, lead, and zinc producers. Promotes the copper, lead, and zinc mining and metal industries.

LEADERSHIP

GENERAL WORKS

The Art and Science of Leadership. Afsaneh Nahavandi. Prentice Hall. • 1999. $55.00. Second edition. Includes a discussion of participative management. Emphasis is on strategic leadership.

Innovation: Leadership Strategies for the Competitive Edge. Thomas D. Kuczmarski. NTC/Contemporary Publishing. • 1995. $37.95. (NTC Business Book Series).

The Leader of the Future: New Essays by World-Class Leaders and Thinkers. Jossey-Bass, Inc., Publishers. • 1996. $25.00. Contains 32 articles on leadership by "executives, consultants, and commentators." (Management Series).

Leaders, Fools, and Imposters: Essays on the Psychology of Leadership. Manfred F. R. Kets de Vries. Jossey-Bass, Inc., Publishers. • 1993. $30.95. (Management Series).

Leadership: Theory and Practice. Peter G. Northouse. Sage Publications, Inc. • 1997. $48.00. Considers the strengths and criticisms of specific leadership approaches, such as trait, style, situational, transformational, psychodynamic, path-goal, and others.

Psychology for Leaders: Using Motivation, Conflict, and Power to Manage More Effectively. Dean Tjosvold and Mary Tjosvold. John Wiley and Sons, Inc. • 1995. $32.95. (Portable MBS Series).

Why Leaders Can't Lead: The Unconscious Conspiracy Continues. Warren Bennis. Jossey-Bass, Inc., Publishers. • 1997. $30.00. (Management Series).

ENCYCLOPEDIAS AND DICTIONARIES

Blackwell Encyclopedic Dictionary of Organizational Behavior. Nigel Nicholson, editor. Blackwell Publishers. • 1995. $105.95. The editor is associated with the London Business School. Contains definitions of key terms combined with longer articles written by various U. S. and foreign business educators. Includes bibliographies and index. *Blackwell Encyclopedia of Management Series.*

Encyclopedia of Human Behavior. Vangipuram S. Ramachandran, editor. Academic Press, Inc. • 1994. $685.00. Four volumes. Contains signed articles on aptitude testing, arbitration, career development, consumer psychology, crisis management, decision making, economic behavior, group dynamics, leadership, motivation, negotiation, organizational behavior, planning, problem solving, stress, work efficiency, and other human behavior topics applicable to business situations.

HANDBOOKS AND MANUALS

Tough-Minded Leadership. Joe D. Batten. AMACOM. • 1989. $15.95.

PERIODICALS AND NEWSLETTERS

Executive Excellence: The Newsletter of Personal Development Managerial Effectiveness, and Organizational Productivity. Kenneth M. Shelton, editor. Executive Excellence Publishing. • Monthly. $129.00 per year. Newsletter.

Fast Company: How Smart Business Works. Fast Company Inc. • Monthly. $23.95 per year. Covers business management, with emphasis on creativity, leadership, innovation, career advancement, teamwork, the global economy, and the "new workplace.".

Leader to Leader. Peter F. Drucker Foundation for Nonprofit Management. Jossey-Bass Publishers. • Quarterly. Individuals, $149.00 per year; institutions, $149.00 per year. Contains articles on "management, leadership, and strategy" written by "leading executives, thinkers, and consultants." Covers both business and nonprofit issues.

Perspective. Catalyst, Inc. • Monthly. $60.00 per year. Newsletter. Covers leadership, mentoring, work/family programs, success stories, and other topics for women in the corporate world.

Positive Leadership: Improving Performance Through Value-Centered Management. Lawence Ragan Communications, Inc. • Monthly. $119.00 per year. Newsletter. Emphasis is on employee motivation, family issues, ethics, and community relations.

TRADE/PROFESSIONAL ASSOCIATIONS

Future Business Leaders of America-Phi Beta Lambda. 1912 Association Dr., Reston, VA 22091-1591. Phone: 800-325-2946 or (703)860-3334 Fax: (703)758-0749 E-mail: general@fbla.org • URL: http://www.fbla-pbl.org.

OTHER SOURCES

Leadership Skills for Managers. American Management Association Extension Institute. • Looseleaf. $110.00. Self-study course. Emphasis is on practical explanations, examples, and problem solving. Quizzes and a case study are included.

Leadership Strategies: The Tools to Help You Lead Effectively. Georgetown Publishing House. • Monthly. $99.00 per year. Newsletter. Includes concise articles on change management, delegation of authority, team building, conflict resolution, and other leadership topics.

LEADING INDICATORS

See: ECONOMIC INDICATORS

LEARNING, PROGRAMMED

See: PROGRAMMED LEARNING

LEASING SERVICES

See: AUTOMOBILE LEASE AND RENTAL SERVICES; EQUIPMENT LEASING; RENTAL SERVICES

LEATHER INDUSTRY

See also: LUGGAGE INDUSTRY; SHOE INDUSTRY; TANNING INDUSTRY

DIRECTORIES

American Leather Chemists Association-Directory. American Leather Chemists Association. • Annual. $20.00. About 1,000 chemists, leather technologists, and educators concerned with the tanning and leather industry.

Leather Manufacturer Directory. Shoe Trades Publishing Co. • Annual. $55.00. Lists hide processors, tanners and leather finishers in the U.S. and Canada.

Travelware Suppliers Directory. Business Journals, Inc. • Annual. $20.00. Lists 500 manufacturers and importers of components to the luggage and leather goods industry.

FINANCIAL RATIOS

Annual Statement Studies. Robert Morris Associates: The Association of Lending and Credit Risk Professiona. • Annual. Free to members; non-members, $140.00. Median and quartile financial ratios are given for over 400 kinds of manufacturing, wholesale, retail, construction, and consumer finance establishments. Data is sorted by both asset size and sales volume. Includes a clearly written "Definition of Ratios" and an alphabetical industry index.

INTERNET DATABASES

Fedstats. Federal Interagency Council on Statistical Policy. Phone: (202)395-7254 • URL: http://www.fedstats.gov • Web site features an efficient search facility for full-text statistics produced by more than 70 federal agencies, including the Census Bureau, the Bureau of Economic Analysis, and the Bureau of Labor Statistics. Boolean searches can be made within one agency or for all agencies combined. Links are offered to international statistical bureaus, including the UN, IMF, OECD, UNESCO, Eurostat, and 20 individual countries. Fees: Free.

ONLINE DATABASES

DRI U.S. Central Database. Data Products Division. • Provides more than 23,000 business, financial, demographic, economic, foreign trade, and industry-related time series for the U.S. Includes national income, population, retail-wholesale trade, price indexes, labor data, housing, industrial production, banking, interest rates, money supply, etc. Time period is generally 1947 to date (some data back to 1929). Updating varies. Inquire as to online cost and availability.

PERIODICALS AND NEWSLETTERS

American Leather Chemists Association Journal. American Leather Chemists Association. • Monthly. Free to members; non-members, $115.00 per year.

Leather Manufacturer. Shoe Trades Publishing Co. • Monthly. $52.00 per year. Edited for hide processors, tanners and leather finishers in the U.S. and Canada.

RESEARCH CENTERS AND INSTITUTES

Leather Industries Research Laboratory. P.O. Box 210014, Cincinnati, OH 45221-0014. Phone: (513)556-1200 Fax: (513)556-2377 E-mail: corynj@uc.edu • URL: http://www.leather.usa.com.

STATISTICS SOURCES

Annual Survey of Manufactures. Available from U. S. Government Printing Office. • Annual. Prices vary. Issued by the U. S. Census Bureau as an interim update to the *Census of Manufactures.* Includes data on number of manufacturing establishments in various industries, employment, labor costs, value of shipments, capital expenditures, inventories, energy costs, and assets. (See also Census Bureau home page, http://www.census.gov/.).

Business Statistics of the United States. Courtenay M. Slater, editor. Bernan Associates. • 1999. $74.00. Fifth edition. Based on *Business Statistics*, formerly issue by the Bureau of Economic Analysis, U. S. Department of Commerce. Provides basic data for a wide variety of U. S. industries, services, and economic indicators. Most statistics are shown annually for 29 years and monthly for the most recent four years.

Leather Industry Statistics. Leather Industries of America. • Annual. Free to members; non-members, $25.00. Provides detailed analysis of domestic and foreign trade.

Survey of Current Business. Available from U. S. Government Printing Office. • Monthly. $49.00 per year. Issued by Bureau of Economic Analysis, U. S. Department of Commerce. Presents a wide variety of business and economic data.

TRADE/PROFESSIONAL ASSOCIATIONS

American Leather Chemists Association. Texas Tech University, P.O. Box 41061, Lubbock, TX 79409-1061. Phone: (806)742-4138 Fax: (806)742-4139 E-mail: alca@leatherchemists.org • URL: http://www.leatherchemists.org.

Leather Industries of America. 1000 Thomas Jefferson St., N.W., Suite 515, Washington, DC 20007. Phone: (202)342-8086 Fax: (202)342-9063 E-mail: info@leatherusa.com • URL: http://www.leatherusa.com.

U.S. Hide, Skin and Leather Association. 1700 N. Moore St., Suite 1600, Arlington, VA 22209. Phone: (703)841-5485 Fax: (703)841-9656 E-mail: lcandon@ushsla.org • URL: http://www.mratami.org.

LEGAL FORMS

See: FORMS AND BLANKS

LEGAL HOLIDAYS

See: ANNIVERSARIES AND HOLIDAYS

LEGAL PROFESSION

See: LAWYERS

LEGAL RIGHTS

See: CIVIL RIGHTS

LEGATIONS

See: DIPLOMATIC AND CONSULAR SERVICE

LEGISLATION

See: LAWS

LEGISLATIVE INVESTIGATIONS

See: GOVERNMENT INVESTIGATIONS

LEGISLATIVE PROCEDURE

GENERAL WORKS

American Legislative Process: Congress and the States. William J. Keefe and Morris Ogul, editors. Prentice Hall. • 2000. $44.00. 10th edition.

How Our Laws Are Made. Available from U. S. Government Printing Office. • 2000. $3.75. 22nd edition. Issued by U. S. House of Representatives.

Legislative Process. Abner J. Mikva. Aspen Publishers, Inc. • 1995. $62.00.

ABSTRACTS AND INDEXES

Current Law Index: Multiple Access to Legal Periodicals. The Gale Group. • Monthly. $650.00 per year. Produced in cooperation with the American Association of Law Libraries. Indexes more than 900 law journals, legal newspapers, and specialty publications from the U.S., Canada, U.K., Ireland, Australia, and New Zealand.

BIBLIOGRAPHIES

Legislative Reference Services and Sources. Kathleen Low. Haworth Press, Inc. • 1994. $39.95. Describes more than 100 reference sources that are frequently consulted in providing information to legislators and their staffs. Includes a discussion of online services used for legislative reference.

RESEARCH CENTERS AND INSTITUTES

Harvard Legislative Research Bureau. Harvard Law School, 1541 Massachusetts Ave., Cambridge, MA

02138. Phone: (617)495-4400 Fax: (617)495-1110 • Concerned with federal and state legislation in all fields.

Lexis.com Research System. Lexis-Nexis Group. Phone: 800-227-9597 or (937)865-6800 Fax: (937)865-6909 E-mail: webmaster@prod.lexis-nexis.com • URL: http://www.lexis.com • Fee-based Web site offers extensive searching of a wide variety of legal sources. Additional features include Daily Opinion Service, lexis.com Bookstore, Career Center, CLE Center, Law Schools, and Practice Pages ("Pages specific to areas of specialty").

LEGISLATURES

GENERAL WORKS

Lawmaking and the Legislative Process: Committees, Connections, and Compromises. Tommy Neal. Oryx Press. • 1996. $26.50. Explains how bills are enacted into laws through the state legislative process. Provides step-by-step examples, using fictitious bills.

ALMANACS AND YEARBOOKS

Suggested State Legislation. Council of State Governments. • Annual. $59.00. A source of legislative ideas and drafting assistance for state government officials.

BIOGRAPHICAL SOURCES

Who's Who in American Politics. Marquis Who's Who. • Biennial. $275.00. Two volumes. Contains about 27,000 biographical sketches of local, state, and national elected or appointed individuals.

DIRECTORIES

CSG State Directories: I State Elective Officials. Council of State Governments. • Annual. $45.00. Lists about 8,000 state legislators, state executive branch elected officials, and state supreme court judges. Formerly *Book of the States, Supplement One: State Elective Officials and the Legislatures.*

Election Results Directory Supplement. National Conference of State Legislatures. • Annual. $35.00. Provides names, addresses, telephone numbers, and e-mail addresses of state legislators and executive officials.

PERIODICALS AND NEWSLETTERS

State Legislatures. National Conference of State Legislatures. • Monthly. $49.00 per year. Newsletter. Covers state legislative issues and politics.

TRADE/PROFESSIONAL ASSOCIATIONS

Council of State Governments. c/o Julia Nienaber, P.O. Box 11910, Lexington, KY 40578-1910. Phone: 800-800-1910 or (606)244-8000 or (606)244-8111 Fax: (606)244-8001 E-mail: info@csg.org • URL: http://www.csg.org.

National Conference of State Legislatures. 1560 Broadway, Suite 700, Denver, CO 80202. Phone: (303)830-2200 Fax: (303)863-8003 • URL: http://www.ncsl.org.

OTHER SOURCES

State Legislators' Occupations: 1994, A Survey. National Conference of State Legislatures. • 1994. $20.00. Presents survey results concerning the occupations of more than 7,000 state legislators. (Members of state legislatures usually combine government service with other occupations.).

LEISURE INDUSTRY

See: AMUSEMENT INDUSTRY; RECREATION INDUSTRY; SHOW BUSINESS; SPORTS BUSINESS

LEMONS

See: CITRUS FRUIT INDUSTRY

LENSES, CONTACT

See: CONTACT LENS AND INTRAOCULAR LENS INDUSTRIES

LENSES, INTRAOCULAR

See: CONTACT LENS AND INTRAOCULAR LENS INDUSTRIES

LETTER WRITING

See: BUSINESS CORRESPONDENCE

LEVERAGED BUYOUTS

See also: JUNK BOND FINANCING; MERGERS AND ACQUISITIONS

GENERAL WORKS

Cases in Corporate Acquisitions, Buyouts, Mergers, and Takeovers. The Gale Group. • 1999. $310.00. Reviews and analyzes about 300 cases of both success and failure in corporate acquisitiveness.

Mergers, Acquisitions, and Corporate Restructurings. Patrick A. Gaughan. John Wiley and Sons, Inc. • 1999. $75.00. Second edition. Covers mergers, acquisitions, divestitures, internal reorganizations, joint ventures, leveraged buyouts, bankruptcy workouts, and recapitalizations.

ABSTRACTS AND INDEXES

Business Periodicals Index. H. W. Wilson Co. • Monthly, except August, with quarterly and annual cumulations. Service basis for print edition; CD-ROM edition, $1,495.00 per year.

CD-ROM DATABASES

Buyout Financing Sources/M & A Intermediaries. Securities Data Publishing. • Annual. $895.00. Provides the CD-ROM combination of *Directory of Buyout Financing Sources* and *Directory of M & A Intermediaries.* Contains information on more than 1,000 financing sources (banks, insurance companies, venture capital firms, etc.) and 850 intermediaries (corporate acquirers, valuation firms, lawyers, accountants, etc.). Also includes back issues of *Buyouts Newsletter* and *Mergers & Acquisitions Report.* Fully searchable. (Securities Data Publishing is a unit of Thomson Financial.).

DIRECTORIES

Directory of Buyout Financing Sources. Securities Data Publishing. • Annual. $395.00. Describes more than 1,000 U. S. and foreign sources of financing for buyout deals. Indexed by personnel, company, industry, and location. (Securities Data Publishing is a unit of Thomson Financial.).

HANDBOOKS AND MANUALS

The Art of M & A: A Merger-Acquisition-Buyout Guide. Stanley F. Reed and Aleandra R. Lajoux. McGraw-Hill Professional. • 1998. $179.95. Second edition. A how-to-do-it guide for merger and acquisition ventures. Emphasis is on legal issues.

Corporate Acquisitions, Mergers, and Divestitures. Lewis D. Solomon. Prentice Hall. • Looseleaf. Periodic supplementation. Price on application. Includes how to buy a company with its own assets or earnings.

A Management Guide to Leveraged Buyouts. Edward K. Crawford. John Wiley and Sons, Inc. • 1987. $110.00. (Professional Banking and Finance Series).

Publicly Traded Corporations: Governance, Operation, and Regulation. John H. Matheson. West Group. • 1993. $130.00. Covers a wide range of corporate legal problems and issues, including shareholder communications and "tender offers and change of control transactions." (Corporate Law Series).

Tax Planning for Dispositions of Business Interests. Theodore Ness and William Indoe. Warren, Gorham & Lamont/RIA Group. • $145.00. Biennial supplementation.

ONLINE DATABASES

Wilson Business Abstracts Online. H. W. Wilson Co. • Indexes and abstracts 600 major business periodicals, plus the *Wall Street Journal* and the business section of the *New York Times.* Indexing is from 1982, abstracting from 1990, with the two newspapers included from 1993. Updated weekly. Inquire as to online cost and availability. (*Business Periodicals Index* without abstracts is also available online.).

PERIODICALS AND NEWSLETTERS

Buyouts: The Newsletter for Management Buyouts, Leveraged Aquisitions, and Special Situations. Securities Data Publishing. • Biweekly. $1,265.00 per year. Newsletter. Covers news and trends for the buyout industry. Provides information on deal makers and current buyout activity. (Securities Data Publishing is a unit of Thomson Financial.).

Corporate Acquisitions. A R C H Group. • Weekly. $425.00 per year. Newsletter.

Corporate Control Alert; A Report on Current Changes for Corporate Control. American Lawyer Media, L.P. • Monthly. $1,595 per year. A monthly mergers and acquisitions newsletter.

Corporate Financing Week: The Newsweekly of Corporate Finance, Investment Banking and M and A. Institutional Investor. • Weekly. $2,550.00 per year. Newsletter for corporate finance officers. Emphasis is on debt and equity financing, mergers, leveraged buyouts, investment banking, and venture capital.

Corporate Growth. Princeton Research Institute. • Monthly. $198.00 per year.

Corporate Growth Report. Quality Services Co. • Weekly. $895.00 per year. Newsletter. Gives details of current merger and buyout transactions or negotiations. Includes lists of companies wishing to buy and companies wishing to be bought. Formerly *Acquisition-Divestiture Weekly Report.*

F W's Corporate Finance: The Magazine fo the Financing Strategist. Financial World Partners. • Quarterly. $50.00 per year. Edited for financial executives of U. S. corporations. Covers leveraged buyouts, mergers, insurance, pensions, risk management, and other corporate topics. Includes case studies. Formerly *Corporate Finance.*

RESEARCH CENTERS AND INSTITUTES

Bradley Policy Research Center. University of Rochester, William E. Simon Graduate School of Business Administration, Rochester, NY 14627. Phone: (716)275-0834 Fax: (716)461-3309 E-mail: mullen@ssb.rochester.edu • Corporate control and corporate takeovers are among the research areas covered.

Center for the Study of American Business. Washington University in Saint Louis. Campus Box 1027, St. Louis, MO 63130-4899. Phone: (314)935-5630 Fax: (314)935-5688 • URL: http://csab.wustl.edu • Research activity includes the study of corporate takeovers.

Investor Responsibility Research Center, Inc. 1350 Connecticut Ave., N. W., Suite 700, Washington, DC 20036. Phone: (202)833-0700 Fax: (202)833-3555 E-mail: sfenn@irrc.org • URL: http://www.irrc.org • Studies developments of interest to institutional investors.

Rodney L. White Center for Financial Research. University of Pennsylvania, 3254 Steinberg Hall-Dietrich Hall, Philadelphia, PA 19104. Phone: (215)898-7616 Fax: (215)573-8084 E-mail: rlwtcr@finance.wharton.upenn.edu • URL: http://www.finance.wharton.upenn.edu/~rlwctr • Research areas include financial management, money markets, real estate finance, and international finance.

TRADE/PROFESSIONAL ASSOCIATIONS

International Merger and Acquisition Professionals. 3232 Cobb Parkway, Suite 437, Atlanta, GA 30339. Phone: (770)319-7797 Fax: (770)319-9838 E-mail: imap@mindspring.com • URL: http://www.imap.com • Mainly concerned with medium-sized businesses having annual sales of less than 50 million dollars.

LIABILITY INSURANCE

See: PROPERTY AND LIABILITY INSURANCE; PROFESSIONAL LIABILITY

LIABILITY, PRODUCT

See: PRODUCT SAFETY AND LIABILITY

LIABILITY, PROFESSIONAL

See: PROFESSIONAL LIABILITY

LIBRARIANS

GENERAL WORKS

Expanding Technologies, Expanding Careers: Librarianship in Transition. Ellis Mount, editor. Special Libraries Association. • 1997. $45.00. Contains articles on alternative, non-traditional career paths for librarians, whether as entrepreneurs or employees. All the careers are related to computer-based, information retrieval and technology.

Extending the Librarian's Domain: A Survey of Emerging Occupational Opportunities for Librarians and Information Professionals. Forest W. Horton. Special Libraries Association. • 1994. $38.00. An examination of non-traditional career possibilities for special librarians. (Occasional Papers: No. 4).

Opening New Doors: Alternative Careers for Librarians. Ellis Mount, editor. Special Libraries Association. • 1992. $39.00. Information professionals in careers outside the library field discuss the nature of their work, qualifications, rewards, finding a job, etc.

Stress and Burnout in Library Service. Janette S. Caputo. Oryx Press. • 1991. $24.95. Discusses symptoms of stress in library staff members and ways of dealing with stress. Includes self-help checklists and a list of references for further information.

ABSTRACTS AND INDEXES

Library Literature and Information Science: An Index to Library and Information Science Publications. H. W. Wilson Co. • Bimonthly. Annual cumulation. Service basis. Formerly *Library Literature.*

CD-ROM DATABASES

Leadership Library on CD-ROM: Who's Who in the Leadership of the United States. Leadership Directories, Inc. • Quarterly. $2,641.00 per year, including access to Internet version (weekly updates). Contains all 14 *Yellow Book* personnel directories on CD-ROM, providing contact and brief biographical information for about 400,000 individuals. Covers business, government, financial institutions, news media, law firms, associations, foreign representatives, and nonprofit organizations. Includes photographs.

LISA Plus: Library and Information Science Abstracts. Bowker-Saur, Reed Reference Publishing. • Quarterly. $1,450.00 per year. Provides CD-ROM abstracting and indexing of the world's library and information science literature. Covers a wide variety of topics.

WILSONDISC: Library Literature and Information Science Index. H. W. Wilson Co. • Quarterly. Including unlimited access to the online version of *Library Literature.* Provides CD-ROM indexing of about 300 periodicals, covering a wide range of topics having to do with libraries, library management, and the information industry.

DIRECTORIES

American Library Association Handbook of Organization. American Library Association. • Annual. $30.00. Lists about 52,000 librarians. Formerly *American Library Association Membership Directory.*

Burwell World Directory of Information Brokers. Helen P. Burwell, editor. Burwell Enterprises, Inc. • Annual. $59.50. Lists nearly 1,800 information brokers, document delivery firms, free-lance librarians, and fee-based library services. Provides U. S. and international coverage (46 countries). Formerly *Directory of Fee-Based Information Services.*

Guide to Employment Sources in the Library and Information Professions. American Library Association. • Annual. Free. Associations and agencies offering library placement services. Formerly *Guide to Library Placement Sources.*

Nonprofit Sector Yellow Book: Who's Who in the Management of the Leading Foundations, Universities, Museums, and Other Nonprofit Organizations. Leadership Directories, Inc. • Semiannual. $235.00 per year. Covers management personnel and board members of about 1,000 prominent, nonprofit organizations: foundations, colleges, museums, performing arts groups, medical institutions, libraries, private preparatory schools, and charitable service organizations.

Who's Who in Special Libraries. Special Libraries Association. • Annual. Free to members; non-members, $45.00. About 14,000 librarians of libraries and special collections having a specific subject focus.

HANDBOOKS AND MANUALS

Complete Guide to Performance Standards for Library Personnel. Carol F. Goodson. Neal-Schuman Publishers, Inc. • 1997. $55.00. Provides specific job descriptions and performance standards for both professional and paraprofessional library personnel. Includes a bibliography of performance evaluation literature, with annotations.

Evaluating Library Staff: A Performance Appraisal System. Patricia Belcastro. American Library Association. • 1998. $35.00. Provides information on an appraisal system applicable to a wide variety of jobs in all types of libraries. Includes guidelines, performance appraisal forms, sample employee profiles, and a "Code of Service.".

How to Avoid Liability: The Information Professionals' Guide to Negligence and Warrant Risks. T. R. Halvorson. Burwell Enterprises, Inc. • 1998. $24.50. Second edition. Provides legal advice, cases, and decisions relating to information brokers and others in the information business.

Information Brokering: A How-To-Do-It Manual for Librarians. Florence M. Mason and Chris Dobson. Neal-Schuman Publishers, Inc. • 1998. $45.00. A practical guide to business plans, location, costs, fees, billing, marketing, accounting, taxes, and legal issues. Covers information brokering as a small business enterprise.

Legal Liability Problems in Cyberspace: Craters in the Information Highway. T. R. Halvorson. Burwell Enterprises, Inc. • 1998. $24.50. Covers the legal risks and liabilities involved in doing online research as a paid professional. Includes a table of cases.

Position Descriptions in Special Libraries. Del Sweeney and Karin Zilla, editors. Special Libraries Association. • 1996. $41.00. Third revised edition. Provides 87 descriptions of library and information management positions.

Recruiting Library Staff: A How-To-Do-It Manual for Librarians. Kathleen Low. Neal-Schuman Publishers, Inc. • 2000. $45.00. Includes position description forms, sample announcements, and checklists. Discusses job fairs and other career events.

Sawyer's Success Tactics for Information Businesses. Deboorah C. Sawyer. Burwell Enterprises, Inc. • 1998. $24.50. Covers such items as pricing, costs, and service for information brokers and others in the fee-based information business.

Sawyer's Survival Guide for Information Brokers. Deborah C. Sawyer. Burwell Enterprises, Inc. • 1995. $39.50. Provides practical advice for information entrepreneurs.

The SOLO Librarian's Sourcebook. Judith A. Siess. Information Today, Inc. • 1997. $39.50. Covers management and other aspects of one-librarian libraries.

ONLINE DATABASES

Library Literature Online. H. W. Wilson Co. • Contains online indexing of a wide variety of library and information science literature from 1984 to date, with updating quarterly. Inquire as to online cost and availability.

LISA Online: Library and Information Science Abstracts. Bowker-Saur, Reed Reference Publishing. • Provides abstracting and indexing of the world's library and information science literature from 1969 to the present. Covers a wide variety of topics in over 550 journals from 60 countries, with biweekly updates. Inquire as to online cost and availability.

PERIODICALS AND NEWSLETTERS

American Libraries. American Library Association. • 11 times a year. Institutions and libraries only, $60.00 per year. Current news and information concerning the library industry.

Information Broker. Helen P. Burwell, editor. Burwell Enterprises, Inc. • Bimonthly. $40.00 per year. Newsletter provides advice and news for those in the fee-based information business.

Library Administrator's Digest. BCPL Friends. • 10 times a year. $39.00 per year. Newsletter.

Library Hotline. Cahners Business Information. • 50 times a year. $95.00 per year. News and developments affecting libraries and librarians.

Library Personnel News. Office for Library Personnel Resources. American Library

Association. • Six times a year. $20.00 per year. Newsletter covering personnel trends and issues.

The One-Person Library: A Newsletter for Librarians and Management. Information Bridges International, Inc. • Monthly. $85.00 per year. Newsletter for librarians working alone or with minimal assistance. Contains reports on library literature, management advice, case studies, book reviews, and general information.

School Library Journal: The Magazine of Children, Young Adults and School Librarians. Cahners Business Information, Printing and Publishing Div. • Monthly. $97.50 per year. Supplement available *Sourcebook.*

STATISTICS SOURCES

ALA Survey of Librarian Salaries. American Library Association. • Annual. $55.00. Provides data on salaries paid to librarians in academic and public libraries. Position categories range from beginning librarian to director.

SLA Salary Survey. Special Libraries Association. • Annual. Members, $36.00; non-members, $45.00. Provides data on salaries for special librarians in the U. S. and Canada, according to location, job title, industry, budget, and years of experience.

TRADE/PROFESSIONAL ASSOCIATIONS

American Association of School Librarians. 50 E. Huron St., Chicago, IL 60611. Phone: 800-545-2433 or (312)280-4386 Fax: (312)664-7459 E-mail: aasl@ala.org • URL: http://www.ala.org/aasl • A division of the American Library Association.

American Library Association. 50 E. Huron St., Chicago, IL 60611. Phone: 800-545-2433 or (312)944-7298 Fax: (312)440-9374 • URL: http://www.ala.org.

American Library Association Social Responsibilities Round-Table/Gay, Lesbian and Bisexual Task Force. 50 E. Huron St., Chicago, IL 60611. Phone: 800-545-2433 or (312)280-4294 Fax: (312)280-3256 • URL: http://www.ala.org • A division of the Social Responsibilities Round Table of the American Library Association.

Asian/Pacific American Librarians Association. Clark/Atlanta University, 223 James P. Brawley Dr., S.W., Atlanta, GA 30314-4391. Phone: (404)880-8701 or (404)557-8862 Fax: (404)880-8977 E-mail: akabir@cau.edu • URL: http://www.apala.edu.

Association of Independent Information Professionals. 10290 Monroe Dr., Dallas, TX 75229. Phone: (609)730-8759 E-mail: aiipinfo@aiip.org • URL: http://www.aiip.org • Members are information brokers, document providers, librarians, consultants, database designers, webmasters, and other information professionals. Formerly International Association of Independent Information Brokers.

Black Caucus of the American Library Association. c/o Gregory L. Reese, East Cleveland Public Library, East Cleveland, OH 44112. Phone: (216)541-1428 Fax: (216)541-1798 E-mail: glr@ccpl.lib.oh.us.

Catholic Library Association. 100 North St., Suite 224, Pittsfield, MA 01201-5109. Phone: (413)447-2252 Fax: (413)442-2252 E-mail: cla@vgernet.net • URL: http://www.caathla.org.

Chinese-American Librarians Association. c/o Sheila Lai, CSU, Sacramento, 2000 State Unversity Dr., E., Room 2503, Sacramento, CA 95819-6039. Phone: (916)278-6201 Fax: (916)363-0868 E-mail: cala@csd.uwm.edu • URL: http://www.cala.org.

Council of Planning Librarians. 101 N. Wacker Dr., No. CM-190, Chicago, IL 60606. Phone: (312)409-3349 Fax: (312)263-7417 E-mail: dahm@concentric.net • Members are libraries, librarians, and professional planners concerned with urban and regional planning. Affiliated with the American Planning Association.

Italian American Librarians Caucus. Six Peter Cooper Rd., Apt. 11-G, New York, NY 10010. Phone: (212)228-8438.

Middle East Librarians' Association. c/o Janet Heineck, P.O. Box 352900, University of Washington Library, Seattle, WA 98195-2900. Phone: (206)543-8407 Fax: (206)685-8049 E-mail: janeth@u.washington.edu.

Special Libraries Association. 1700 18th St., N.W., Washington, DC 20009-2514. Phone: (202)234-4700 Fax: (202)265-9317 E-mail: sla@sla.org • URL: http://www.sla.org/.

OTHER SOURCES

The Best of Times: A Personal and Occupational Odyssey. Paul Wasserman. Omnigraphics, Inc. • 2000. $35.00. Autobiography of a well known librarian, educator, and reference book editor. Foreward by Frederick G. Ruffner.

The Unabashed Librarian: The "How I Run My Library Good" Letter. Maurice J. Freedman. • Quarterly. $57.50 per year. Newsletter. Provides practical library management ideas and library humor.

Valuating Information Intangibles: Measuring the Bottom Line Contribution of Librarians and Information Professionals. Frank H. Portugal. Special Libraries Association. • 2000. $79.00. Focuses on the importance of the intangible aspects of appraising information resources and services.

LIBRARIES

See also: LIBRARY MANAGEMENT

GENERAL WORKS

Future Libraries: Dreams, Madness, and Reality. Walt Crawford and Michael Gorman. American Library Association. • 1995. $28.00. Discusses the "over-hyped virtual library" and electronic-publishing "fantasies." Presents the argument for the importance of books, physical libraries, and library personnel.

Introduction to Librarianship. Jean K. Gates. Neal-Schuman Publishers, Inc. • 1990. $38.50. Third edition.

Libraries and the Future: Essays on the Library in the Twenty-First Century. F. W. Lancaster, editor. Haworth Press, Inc. • 1993. $49.95. Emphasis is on information services in libraries of the future. (Original Book Series).

Moving Toward More Effective Public Internet Access: The 1998 National Survey of Public Library Outlet Internet Connectivity. Available from U. S. Government Printing Office. • 1999. $16.00. Issued by the National Commission on Libraries and Information Science.

ABSTRACTS AND INDEXES

Library Literature and Information Science: An Index to Library and Information Science Publications. H. W. Wilson Co. • Bimonthly. Annual cumulation. Service basis. Formerly *Library Literature.*

LISA: Library and Information Science Abstracts. Bowker-Saur. • Monthly. $800.00 per year. Annual cumulation.

ALMANACS AND YEARBOOKS

Bowker Annual: Library and Book Trade Almanac. R. R. Bowker. • Annual. $175.00. Lists of accredited library schools; scholarships for education in library science; library organizations; major libraries; publishing and book sellers organizations. Includes statistics and news of the book business.

CD-ROM DATABASES

CDMARC: Bibliographic. U. S. Library of Congress. • Quarterly. $1,340.00 per year. Provides bibliographic records on CD-ROM for over five million books cataloged by the Library of Congress since 1968. (MARC is Machine Readable Cataloging.).

ERIC on SilverPlatter. Available from SilverPlatter Information, Inc. • Quarterly. $700.00 per year. Produced by the Office of Educational Research and Improvement, U. S. Dept. of Education. Provides CD-ROM indexing and abstracting of a wide variety of literature relating to education. Archival discs are available from 1966.

Information Science Abstracts. Information Today, Inc. • Quarterly. $1,095.00 per year. Presents CD-ROM abstracts of worldwide information science and library science literature from 1966 to date.

LISA Plus: Library and Information Science Abstracts. Bowker-Saur, Reed Reference Publishing. • Quarterly. $1,450.00 per year. Provides CD-ROM abstracting and indexing of the world's library and information science literature. Covers a wide variety of topics.

WILSONDISC: Library Literature and Information Science Index. H. W. Wilson Co. • Quarterly. Including unlimited access to the online version of *Library Literature.* Provides CD-ROM indexing of about 300 periodicals, covering a wide range of topics having to do with libraries, library management, and the information industry.

DIRECTORIES

ALA Handbook of Organization. American Library Association. • Annual. $30.00. Includes information on ALA officers, committees, divisions, sections, round tables, and state chapters. (Issued as a supplement to *American Libraries.*).

American Library Directory. R. R. Bowker. • Annual. $269.95. Two volumes. Includes *Library Resource Guide.* Information on more than 36,000 public, academic, special and government libraries and library-related organizations in the U.S., Canada, and Mexico.

Cyberhound's Guide to Internet Libraries. The Gale Group. • 1996. 79.00. Presents critical descriptions and ratings of more than 2,000 library Internet databases. Includes a glossary of Internet terms, a bibliography, and indexes.

Directory of Government Document Collections and Librarians. Government Documents Round Table. American Library Association, Washington Office. • Seventh edition. Price on application. A guide to federal, state, local, foreign, and international document collections in the U.S. Includes name of librarians and other government document professionals.

Grants for Libraries and Information Services. The Foundation Center. • Annual. $75.00. Foundations and organizations which have awarded grants made the preceding year for public, academic, research, special, and school libraries; for archives and information centers; for consumer information; and for philanthropy information centers.

National Guide to Funding for Libraries and Information Services. The Foundation Center. • 1997. $95.00. Contains detailed information on about 600 foundations and corporate direct giving programs providing funding to libraries. Includes indexing by type of support, subject field, location, and key personnel.

Subject Collections: A Guide to Special Book Collections and Subject Emphasis in Libraries. Lee

Ash and William G. Miller, editors. R. R. Bowker. • Irregular. $275.00. Two volumes. A guide to special book collections and subject emphases as reported by university, college, public and special libraries in th United States and Canada.

Who's Who in Special Libraries. Special Libraries Association. • Annual. Free to members; non-members, $45.00. About 14,000 librarians of libraries and special collections having a specific subject focus.

World Guide to Libraries. Available from The Gale Group. • Biennial. $450.00. Two volumes. Provides information on more than 44,000 academic, government, and public libraries in 196 countries. Published by K. G. Saur.

ENCYCLOPEDIAS AND DICTIONARIES

Encyclopedia of Library and Information Science. Allen Kent and others, editors. Marcel Dekker, Inc. • 66 volumes. $6,583.50. $99.75 per volume. Dates vary.

The Librarians' Thesaurus: A Concise Guide to Library and Information Terms. Mary E. Soper and others. American Library Association. • 1990. $25.00.

World Encyclopedia of Library and Information Services. Robert Wedgeworth, editor. American Library Association. • 1993. $200.00. Third edition. Contains about 340 articles from various contributors.

HANDBOOKS AND MANUALS

Buying Books: A How-To-Do-It Manual for Librarians. Audrey Eaglen. Neal-Schuman Publishers, Inc. • 2000. $45.00. Second edition. Discusses vendor selection and book ordering in the age of electronic commerce. Covers both print and electronic bibliographic sources. (How-to-Do-It Manual for Librarians Series).

Buying Serials: A How-To-Do-It Manual for Librarians. N. Bernard Basch and Judy McQueen. Neal-Schuman Publishers, Inc. • 1990. $49.95. (How-to-Do-It Series).

Copyright Primer for Librarians and Educators. Janis H. Bruwelheide. American Library Association. • 1995. $25.00. Second edition.

Coyle's Information Highway Handbook: A Practical File on the New Information Order. Karen Coyle. American Library Association. • 1997. $30.00. Provides useful "essays on copyright, access, privacy, censorship, and the information marketplace.".

Creating Newsletters, Brochures, and Pamphlets: A How-To-Do-It Manual for Librarians. Barbara A. Radke and Barbara Stein. Neal-Schuman Publishers, Inc. • 1992. $39.95. Includes desktop publishing. (How-to-Do-It Series).

Friends of Libraries Sourcebook. Sandy Dolnick. American Library Association. • 1996. $32.00. Third edition. Provides information and guidance relating to Friends of Libraries support groups.

INTERNET DATABASES

GaleNet: Your Information Community. The Gale Group. Phone: 800-877-GALE or (248)699-GALE Fax: 800-414-5043 or (248)699-8069 E-mail: galenet@gale.com • URL: http://www.galenet.com • Web site provides a wide variety of full-text information from Gale databases, Taft, and other sources. Covers associations, biography, business directories, education, the information industry, literature, publishing, and science. Fee-based subscriptions are available for individual databases (free demonstration). Includes Boolean search features and the BRS/Search user interface.

WilsonWeb Periodicals Databases. H. W. Wilson. Phone: 800-367-6770 or (718)588-8400 Fax: 800-590-1617 or (718)992-8003 E-mail: custserv@hwwilson.com • URL: http://www.hwwilson.com/ • Web sites provide fee-based access to *Wilson Business Full Text, Applied Science & Technology Full Text, Biological & Agricultural Index, Library Literature & Information Science Full Text,* and *Readers' Guide Full Text, Mega Edition.* Daily updates.

ONLINE DATABASES

American Library Directory Online. R. R. Bowker. • Provides information on over 37,000 U. S. and Canadian libraries, including college, special, and public. Annual updates. Inquire as to online cost and availability.

ERIC. Educational Resources Information Center. • Broad range of educational literature, 1966 to present. Monthly updates. Inquire as to online cost and availability.

Information Science Abstracts [online]. Information Today, Inc. • Provides indexing and abstracting of the international literature of information science, including library science, from 1966 to date. Monthly updates. Inquire as to online cost and availability.

LC MARC: Books. U. S. Library of Congress. • Contains online bibliographic records for over five million books cataloged by the Library of Congress since 1968. Updating is weekly or monthly. Inquire as to online cost and availability. (MARC is machine readable cataloging.).

Library Literature Online. H. W. Wilson Co. • Contains online indexing of a wide variety of library and information science literature from 1984 to date, with updating quarterly. Inquire as to online cost and availability.

LISA Online: Library and Information Science Abstracts. Bowker-Saur, Reed Reference Publishing. • Provides abstracting and indexing of the world's library and information science literature from 1969 to the present. Covers a wide variety of topics in over 550 journals from 60 countries, with biweekly updates. Inquire as to online cost and availability.

OCLC Online Union Catalog. OCLC, Inc. • Online cooperative library cataloging service. Daily updates. Inquire as to online cost and availability.

PERIODICALS AND NEWSLETTERS

American Libraries. American Library Association. • 11 times a year. Institutions and libraries only, $60.00 per year. Current news and information concerning the library industry.

The Journal of Academic Librarianship: Articles, Features, and Book Reviews for the Academic Librarian Professional. Jai Press, Inc. • Bimonthly. $208.00 per year.

Library Hotline. Cahners Business Information. • 50 times a year. $95.00 per year. News and developments affecting libraries and librarians.

Library Journal. Cahners Business Information, Broadcasting and Cable's International Group. • 20 times a year. $109.00 per year.

The Library Quarterly: A Journal of Investigation and Discussion in the Field of Library Science. University of Chicago Graduate Library School. University of Chicago Press, Journals Div. • Quarterly. Individuals, $36.00 per year; institutions, $76.00 per year.

Library Trends. University of Illinois at Urbana-Champaign, Graduate School of Library and Information Science, Publications Office. University of Illinois Press. • Quarterly. Individuals, $60.00 per year; institutions; $85.00 per year.

Public Library Quarterly. The Haworth Press, Inc. • Quarterly. Individuals, $40.00 per year; institutions, $140.00 per year; libraries, $140.00 per year.

RESEARCH CENTERS AND INSTITUTES

Library Research Center. University of Illinois at Urbana-Champaign. 501 E. Daniel, Room 321, Champaign, IL 61820-6212. Phone: (217)333-1980 Fax: (217)244-3302 E-mail: lrc@uiuc.edu • URL: http://www.alexia.lis.uiuc.edu/gslis/research/lrc.html.

STATISTICS SOURCES

Digest of Education Statistics. Available from U. S. Government Printing Office. • Annual. $44.00. Covers all areas of education from kindergarten through graduate school. Includes data from both government and private sources. Compiled by National Center for Education Statistics, U. S. Department of Education.

Librarian's Companion: A Handbook of Thousands of Facts on Libraries, Librarians, Books, Newspapers, Publishers, Booksellers. Vladimir F. Wertsman. Greenwood Publishing Group, Inc. • 1996. $67.95. Second edition. Provides international statistics on libraries and publishing. Includes directory and biographical information.

UNESCO Statistical Yearbook. Bernan Press. • Annual. $95.00. Co-published by Bernan Press and the United Nations Educational, Scientific, and Cultural Organization (http://www.unesco.org). Presents statistical data from more than 200 countries on education, technology, research, broadcasting, cinema, book publishing, newspapers, libraries, museums, and population. Includes charts, maps, and graphs.

TRADE/PROFESSIONAL ASSOCIATIONS

American Library Association. 50 E. Huron St., Chicago, IL 60611. Phone: 800-545-2433 or (312)944-7298 Fax: (312)440-9374 • URL: http://www.ala.org.

Special Libraries Association. 1700 18th St., N.W., Washington, DC 20009-2514. Phone: (202)234-4700 Fax: (202)265-9317 E-mail: sla@sla.org • URL: http://www.sla.org/.

OTHER SOURCES

Advances in Librarianship. Academic Press, Inc., Journal Div. • Annual. Prices vary.

Librarianship and Information Work Worldwide. Available from The Gale Group. • Annual. $189.00. Published by K. G. Saur. International coverage.

LIBRARIES, COLLEGE AND UNIVERSITY

See: COLLEGE AND UNIVERSITY LIBRARIES

LIBRARIES, PUBLIC

See: LIBRARIES

LIBRARIES, SPECIAL

See: SPECIAL LIBRARIES

LIBRARY AUTOMATION

See also: ONLINE INFORMATION SYSTEMS

GENERAL WORKS

The Amazing Internet Challenge: How Leading Projects Use Library Skills to Organize the Web. Amy T. Wells and others. American Library

Association. • 1999. $45.00. Presents profiles of 12 digital libraries, such as the Agriculture Network Information Center and the Social Science Information Gateway. Emphasis is on how online indexes were created.

Electronic Library: The Promise and the Process. Kenneth E. Dowlin. Neal-Schuman Publishers, Inc. • 1984. $45.00. (Applications in Information Management and Technology Series).

The Evolving Virtual Library: Practical and Philosophical Perspectives. Laverna M. Saunders, editor. Information Today, Inc. • 1999. $39.50. Second edition. Various authors cover trends in library and school use of the Internet, intranets, extranets, and electronic databases.

Information Imagineering: Meeting at the Interface. Milton T. Wolf and others, editors. American Library Association. • 1997. $36.00. A collection of articles on the effect of information technology on libraries, museums, and other institutions.

Introduction to Automation for Librarians. William Saffady. American Library Association. • 1999. $60.00. Fourth edition. Provides basic information on electronic technology (computers, telecommunications) and library applications of technology.

Optical Discs in Libraries: Uses and Trends. Ching-chih Chen. Information Today, Inc. • 1991. $79.50. Includes summaries of over 250 use studies.

Wired for the Future: Developing Your Library Technology Plan. Diane Mayo and others. American Library Association. • 1998. $38.00. Describes various technologies and applications available to libraries.

ABSTRACTS AND INDEXES

Information Science Abstracts. American Society for Information Science. Information Today, Inc. • 11 times a year. $685.00 per year.

Library Literature and Information Science: An Index to Library and Information Science Publications. H. W. Wilson Co. • Bimonthly. Annual cumulation. Service basis. Formerly *Library Literature*.

LISA: Library and Information Science Abstracts. Bowker-Saur. • Monthly. $800.00 per year. Annual cumulation.

ALMANACS AND YEARBOOKS

Advances in Library Automation and Networking. JAI Press, Inc. • Annual. $73.25.

CD-ROM DATABASES

Information Science Abstracts. Information Today, Inc. • Quarterly. $1,095.00 per year. Presents CD-ROM abstracts of worldwide information science and library science literature from 1966 to date.

LISA Plus: Library and Information Science Abstracts. Bowker-Saur, Reed Reference Publishing. • Quarterly. $1,450.00 per year. Provides CD-ROM abstracting and indexing of the world's library and information science literature. Covers a wide variety of topics.

WILSONDISC: Library Literature and Information Science Index. H. W. Wilson Co. • Quarterly. Including unlimited access to the online version of *Library Literature*. Provides CD-ROM indexing of about 300 periodicals, covering a wide range of topics having to do with libraries, library management, and the information industry.

DIRECTORIES

ASIS Handbook and Directory. American Society for Information Science. • Annual. Members, $25.00; non-members, $100.00.

Computers in Libraries: Buyer's Guide and Consultant Directory. Information Today, Inc. • Annual. $30.00. Price on application.

Directory of Library Automation Software, Systems, and Services. Information Today, Inc. • Biennial. $89.00. Provides detailed descriptions of about 330 software programs and software services for libraries.

Librarian's Yellow Pages: Publications, Products, and Services for Libraries and Information Centers. Garance, Inc. • Irregular. Free to librains; others, $15.00. A classified compilation of advertisements. for library items from more than 1,000 U. S. and Canadian companies. Major sections cover audio, automation, books, CD-ROMs, periodicals, and video. Subject and company indexes are included.

Library Journal Sourcebook: The Reference for Library Products and Services. Cahners Business Information. • Annual. $5.75. Includes "Directory of Products and Services" (alphabetical by product) and "Directory of Suppliers" (alphabetical by company). Formerly *Library Journal Buyers' Guide*.

Library Resource Guide: A Catalog of Services and Suppliers for the Library Community. R. R. Bowker. • Irregular. Free to qualified personnel. An advertising directory listing several hundred manufacturers or distributors of library supplies, services, and equipment in such areas as audiovisual, automation, bar codes, binding, furniture, microfilm, shelving, and storage. Some book dealers, document delivery services, online services, and publishers are also included.

OPAC Directory: A Guide to Internet-Accessible Online Public Access Catalogs. Information Today, Inc. • Annual. $70.00. Provides the Internet addresses of more than 1,400 online public access catalogs, U. S. and foreign. Includes information on library size, subject strengths, and search characteristics.

303 Software Programs to Use in Your Library: Descriptions, Evaluations, and Practical Advice. Patrick R. Dewey. American Library Association. • 1997. $36.00. Contains profiles of a wide variety of software (21 categories) that may be useful in libraries. Includes prices, company addresses, glossary, bibliography, and an index.

HANDBOOKS AND MANUALS

Automating the Small Library. William Saffady. American Library Association. • 1991. $8.00. A concise overview of computer applications appropriate to small libraries. Covers circulation, cataloging, reference, acquisitions, and administration.

Basic Internet for Busy Librarians: A Quick Course for Catching Up. Laura K. Murray. American Library Association. • 1998. $26.00. A "practical crash-course primer" for learning how to effectively navigate the Internet and the World Wide Web.

Building the Service-Based Library Web Site: A Step-by-Step Guide to Design and Options. Kristen L. Garlock and Sherry Piontek. American Library Association. • 1996. $30.00. Provides practical information for libraries planning a World Wide Web home page.

Buying and Maintaining Personal Computers: A How-To-Do-It Manual for Librarians. Norman Howden. Neal-Schuman Publishers, Inc. • 2000. $45.00. Covers various aspects of buying PCs or MACs for library use, including choice of hardware, software selection, warranties, backup systems, staffing, and dealing with vendors.

CD-ROM Primer: The ABCs of CD-ROM. Cheryl LaGuardia. Neal-Schuman Publishers, Inc. • 1994. $49.95. Provides advice for librarians and others on CD-ROM equipment, selection, collecting, and maintenance. Includes a glossary, bibliography, and directory of suppliers.

The Cybrarian's Manual. Pat Ensor, editor. American Library Association. • 1996. $35.00. Provides information for librarians concerning the Internet, expert systems, computer networks, client/server architecture, Web pages, multimedia, information industry careers, and other "cyberspace" topics.

Developing and Managing E-Journal Collections: A How-To-DoIt Manual for Librarians. Donnelyn Curtis and others. Neal-Schuman Publishers, Inc. • 2000. $55.00. Covers the acquisition, management, and integration of journals published in electronic form.

Improving Online Public Access Catalogs. Martha M. Yee and Sara S. Layne. American Library Association. • 1998. $48.00. A practical guide to developing user-friendly online catalogs (OPACs).

The Internet Troubleshooter: Help for the Logged-On and Lost. Nancy R. John and Edward J. Valauskas. American Library Association. • 1994. $27.00. A basic question-and-answer guide to the Internet. Includes illustrations and a glossary.

Introduction to the Use of Computers in Libraries: A Textbook for the Non-Technical Student. Harold C. Ogg. Information Today, Inc. • 1997. $42.50. Provides basic information on computer programs for libraries, including spreadsheets, database applications, desktop publishing, automated circulation systems, and public access online catalogs.

The Library Administrator's Automation Handbook. Richard Boss. Information Today, Inc. • 1997. $39.50. Covers the library administrator's role in the planning, selection, and implementation of hardware and software for automated library systems.

Library Manager's Guide to Automation. Richard Boss. Pearson Education and Technology. • 1990. $45.00. Third edition. (Professional Librarian Series).

Managing Public-Access Computers: A How-To-Do-It Manual for Librarians. Donald A. Barclay. Neal-Schuman Publishers, Inc. • 2000. $59.95. Part one covers hardware, software, and other components. Part two discusses computers users. Part three is about systems management, library policy, and legal issues.

More Internet Troubleshooter: New Help for the Logged-On and Lost. Nancy R. John and Edward J. Valauskas. American Library Association. • 1998. $36.00. A question-and-answer sequel to *Internet Troubleshooter: Help for the Logged-On and Lost*.

Online Deskbook: Online Magazine's Essential Desk Reference for Online and Internet Searchers. Mary E. Bates. Information Today, Inc. • 1996. $29.95. Covers the World Wide Web, as well as America Online, CompuServe, Dialog, Lexis-Nexis, and all other major online services. (Pemberton Press Books.).

PC Management: A How-To-Do-It Manual for Librarians. Michael Schuyler and Jake Hoffman. Neal-Schuman Publishers, Inc. • 1990. $45.00. Covers the use of personal computers for library routines. Includes evaluations of software. (How-to-Do-It Series).

Using Desktop Publishing to Create Newsletters, Library Guides, and Web Pages: A How-To-Do-It Manual for Librarians. John Maxymuk. Neal-Schuman Publishers, Inc. • 1997. $55.00. Includes more than 90 illustrations.

Using Windows for Library Administration. Kenneth E. Marks and Steven P. Nielson. Information Today,

Inc. • 1997. $34.95. Contains details on the use of Microsoft Windows software applications for library management: spreadsheets, desktop publishing, project planning, forms, etc.

World Wide Web Troubleshooter: Help for the Ensnared and Entangled. Nancy R. John and Edward J. Valauskas. American Library Association. • 1998. $36.00. Covers all aspects of the WWW in question-and-answer format.

ONLINE DATABASES

Computer Database. The Gale Group. • Provides online citations with abstracts to material appearing in about 150 trade journals and newsletters in the subject areas of computers, telecommunications, and electronics. Time period is 1983 to date, with weekly updates. Inquire as to online cost and availability.

Information Science Abstracts [online]. Information Today, Inc. • Provides indexing and abstracting of the international literature of information science, including library science, from 1966 to date. Monthly updates. Inquire as to online cost and availability.

Library Literature Online. H. W. Wilson Co. • Contains online indexing of a wide variety of library and information science literature from 1984 to date, with updating quarterly. Inquire as to online cost and availability.

LISA Online: Library and Information Science Abstracts. Bowker-Saur, Reed Reference Publishing. • Provides abstracting and indexing of the world's library and information science literature from 1969 to the present. Covers a wide variety of topics in over 550 journals from 60 countries, with biweekly updates. Inquire as to online cost and availability.

PERIODICALS AND NEWSLETTERS

Aslib Proceedings. Available from Information Today, Inc. • Ten times a year. Free to Members; non-members, $252.00 per year. Published in London by Aslib Covers a wide variety of information industry and library management topics.

Computers in Libraries. Information Today, Inc. • 10 times a year. $89.95 per year.

The Electronic Library. Information Today, Inc. • Bimonthly. $269.00 per year.

Information Processing and Management: An International Journal. Elsevier Science. • Bimonthly. $981.00 per year. Text in English, French, German and Italian.

Information Standards Quarterly: News About Library, Information Sciences, and Publishing Standards. National Information Standards Organization (NISO). • Quarterly. $80.00 per year. Newsletter. Reports on activities of the National Information Standards Organization.

IntraNet Professional: IntraNet Applications and Knowledge Management for Libraries and Information Professionals. Information Today, Inc. • Bimonthly. $79.95 per year. Newsletter on the use of Internet technology for local library networks.

Journal of Internet Cataloging: The International Quarterly of Digital Organization, Classification, and Access. Haworth Press, Inc. • Quarterly. Individuals, $40.00 per year; libraries and other institutions, $85.00 per year.

Library Computing. Sage Publications, Inc. • Quarterly. Individuals, $65.00 per year; institutions, $255.00 per year. Formerly *Library Software Review.*

Library Systems Newsletter. Library Technology Reports. American Library Association. • Monthly. $55.00 per year. Articles and news briefs covering all aspects of library automation.

Multimedia Schools: A Practical Journal of Multimedia, CD-Rom, Online and Internet in K-12. Information Today, Inc. • Five times a year. $39.95 per year. Edited for school librarians, media center directors, computer coordinators, and others concerned with educational multimedia. Coverage includes the use of CD-ROM sources, the Internet, online services, and library technology.

Online Libraries and Microcomputers. Information Intelligence, Inc. • Monthly. Individuals $43.75 per year; libraries. $62.50 per year. Newsletter. Covers library automation and electronic information (online, CD-ROM). Reviews or describes new computer hardware and software for library use.

Program: Electronic Library and Information Systems. Available from Information Today, Inc. • Quarterly. Members, $175.00 per year; non-members, $214.00 per year. Published in London by Aslib: The Association for Information Management. Discusses computer applications for libraries.

Technical Services Quarterly: New Trends in Computers, Automation, and Advanced Technologies in the Technical Operation of Libraries and Information Centers. Haworth Press, Inc. • Quarterly. Individuals, $45.00 per year; institutions, $225.00 per year; libraries, $225.00 per year.

RESEARCH CENTERS AND INSTITUTES

Bibliographical Center for Research, Inc., Rocky Mountain Region. 14394 E. Evans Ave., Aurora, CO 80014-1478. Phone: 800-397-1552 or (303)751-6277 Fax: (303)751-9787 E-mail: admin@bec.org • URL: http://www.ber.org • Fields of research include information retrieval systems, Internet technology, CD-ROM technology, document delivery, and library automation.

Center for Study of Librarianship. Kent State University, P.O. Box 5190, Kent, OH 44242-0001. Phone: (330)672-2782 Fax: (330)672-7965 E-mail: rubin@slis.kent.edu • URL: http://www.web.slis.kent.edu.

TRADE/PROFESSIONAL ASSOCIATIONS

American Society for Information Science. 8720 Georgia Ave., Suite 501, Silver Spring, MD 20910-3602. Phone: (301)495-0900 Fax: (301)495-0810 E-mail: asis@asis.org • URL: http://www.asis.org • Members are information managers, scientists, librarians, and others who are interested in the storage, retrieval, and use of information.

Association for Library Collections and Technical Services. c/o American Library Association, 50 E. Huron St., Chicago, IL 60611. Phone: 800-545-2433 or (312)280-5308 Fax: (312)280-5033 E-mail: alcts@ala.org • URL: http://www.ala8.ala.org/alcts/.

Library and Information Technology Association. 50 E. Huron St., Chicago, IL 60611. Phone: 800-545-2433 or (312)280-4270 Fax: (312)280-3257 E-mail: lita@ala.org • URL: http://www.lita.org • The Library and Information Technology Association is a Division of the American Library Association.

National Information Standards Organization. 4733 Bethesda Ave., Suite 300, Bethesda, MD 20814-5248. Phone: (301)654-2512 Fax: (301)654-1721 E-mail: nisohq@niso.org • URL: http://www.niso.org • Develops and promotes technical standards for the information industry and libraries, including the Z39.50 protocol for Internet database searching.

Public Library Association; Technology Committee. c/o American Library Association, 50 E. Huron St., Chicago, IL 60611. Phone: 800-545-2433 or (312)280-5752 Fax: (312)280-5029 E-mail: pla@pla.org • URL: http://www.pla.org • The Public Library Association is a Division of the American Library Association.

Reference and User Services Association of the American Library Association: Machine Assisted Reference Section. c/o American Library Association, 50 E. Huron. St., Chicago, IL 60611. Phone: 800-545-2433 or (312)280-4398 Fax: (312)944-8085 E-mail: rusa@ala.org • URL: http://www.ala8.org/rusa/.

Special Libraries Association; Information Technology Division. 1700 18th St., N.W., Washington, DC 20009-2514. Phone: (202)234-4700 Fax: (202)265-9317 E-mail: sla@sla.org • URL: http://www.sla.org/.

OTHER SOURCES

Library Technology Reports: Evaluative Information on Library Systems, Equipment and Supplies. American Library Association. • Bimonthly. $225.00 per year.

Towards Electronic Journals: Realities for Scientists, Librarians, and Publishers. Carol Tenopir and Donald W. King. Special Libraries Association. • 2000. $59.00. Discusses journals in electronic form vs. traditional (paper) scholarly journals, including the impact of subscription prices.

LIBRARY MANAGEMENT

See also: LIBRARIES

GENERAL WORKS

Administration of the Public Library. Alice Gertzog and Edwin Beckerman. Scarecrow Press, Inc. • 1994. $62.50.

The Best of OPL, II: Selected Readings from the One-Person Library: 1990-1994. Guy St. Clair and Andrew Berner. Special Libraries Association. • 1996. $36.00. Contains reprints of useful material from *The One-Person Library: A Newsletter for Librarians and Management.*

Corporate Library Excellence. James M. Matarazzo. Special Libraries Association. • 1990. $28.00.

Future-Driven Library Marketing. Darlene E. Weingand. American Library Association. • 1998. $25.00. The author discusses progressive marketing strategies for libraries. An annotated bibliography is included.

Human Resource Management in Libraries: Theory and Practice. Richard Rubin. Neal-Schuman Publishers, Inc. • 1991. $55.00. Covers such topics as performance rating, pay equity, and collective bargaining.

Library Management Without Bias. Ching-Chih Chen. JAI Press, Inc. • 1981. $78.50. (Foundations in Library and Information Science).

Management of a Public Library. Harold R. Jenkins. JAI Press, Inc. • 1980 $78.50. (Foundations in Library and Information Science Series, Vol. 87).

Management Strategies for Libraries: A Basic Reader. Beverly Lynch, editor. Neal-Schuman Publishers, Inc. • 1985. $55.00.

Organizational Structure of Libraries. Lowell A. Martin. Scarecrow Press, Inc. • 1996. $39.50.

Personnel Administration in Libraries. Sheila Creth and Frederick Duda, editors. Neal-Schuman Publishers, Inc. • 1989. $55.00. Second edition.

Special Libraries: A Guide for Management. Cathy A. Porter and Elin B. Christianson. Special Libraries Association. • 1997. $42.00. Fourth edition. Provides basic information for the managers of business and other organizations on starting, staffing, and maintaining a special library.

Strategic Management for Today's Libraries. Marilyn G. Mason. American Library Association. • 1999. $35.00.

ABSTRACTS AND INDEXES

Library Literature and Information Science: An Index to Library and Information Science Publications. H. W. Wilson Co. • Bimonthly. Annual cumulation. Service basis. Formerly *Library Literature.*

ALMANACS AND YEARBOOKS

Advances in Library Administration and Organization. JAI Press, Inc. • Annual. $78.50.

CD-ROM DATABASES

Leadership Library on CD-ROM: Who's Who in the Leadership of the United States. Leadership Directories, Inc. • Quarterly. $2,641.00 per year, including access to Internet version (weekly updates). Contains all 14 *Yellow Book* personnel directories on CD-ROM, providing contact and brief biographical information for about 400,000 individuals. Covers business, government, financial institutions, news media, law firms, associations, foreign representatives, and nonprofit organizations. Includes photographs.

LISA Plus: Library and Information Science Abstracts. Bowker-Saur, Reed Reference Publishing. • Quarterly. $1,450.00 per year. Provides CD-ROM abstracting and indexing of the world's library and information science literature. Covers a wide variety of topics.

WILSONDISC: Library Literature and Information Science Index. H. W. Wilson Co. • Quarterly. Including unlimited access to the online version of *Library Literature.* Provides CD-ROM indexing of about 300 periodicals, covering a wide range of topics having to do with libraries, library management, and the information industry.

DIRECTORIES

Internet Tools of the Profession: A Guide for Information Professionals. Hope N. Tillman, editor. Special Libraries Association. • 1997. $49.00. Second edition. Consists of 14 sections by various authors or compilers. After two introductory articles on searching the Internet, there are 12 annotated lists of useful Web sites, covering the SLA, business and finance, chemistry, education, food and agriculture, information technology, insurance and employee benefits, law, library management, metals and materials, pharmaceuticals, and telecommunications. An index is provided.

Nonprofit Sector Yellow Book: Who's Who in the Management of the Leading Foundations, Universities, Museums, and Other Nonprofit Organizations. Leadership Directories, Inc. • Semiannual. $235.00 per year. Covers management personnel and board members of about 1,000 prominent, nonprofit organizations: foundations, colleges, museums, performing arts groups, medical institutions, libraries, private preparatory schools, and charitable service organizations.

HANDBOOKS AND MANUALS

Accounting for Libraries and Other Not-for-Profit Organizations. G. Stevenson Smith. American Library Association. • 1999. $82.00. Second edition. Covers accounting fundamentals for nonprofit organizations. Includes a glossary.

Assessing Service Quality: Satisfying the Expectations of Library Customers. Peter Hernon and Ellen Altman. American Library Association. • 1998. $40.00. Discusses surveys, focus groups, and other data collection methods for measuring the quality of library service. Includes sample forms and an annotated bibliography.

Budgeting: A How-to-Do-it Manual for Librarians. Alice S. Warner. Neal-Schuman Publishers, Inc. • 1998. $49.95. Explains six forms of budgeting suitable for various kinds of libraries. Includes a bibliography. (How-to-Do-It Series).

Buying Books: A How-To-Do-It Manual for Librarians. Audrey Eaglen. Neal-Schuman Publishers, Inc. • 2000. $45.00. Second edition. Discusses vendor selection and book ordering in the age of electronic commerce. Covers both print and electronic bibliographic sources. (How-to-Do-It Manual for Librarians Series).

Complete Guide to Performance Standards for Library Personnel. Carol F. Goodson. Neal-Schuman Publishers, Inc. • 1997. $55.00. Provides specific job descriptions and performance standards for both professional and paraprofessional library personnel. Includes a bibliography of performance evaluation literature, with annotations.

Control of Administrative and Financial Operations in Special Libraries. Madeline J. Daubert. Special Libraries Association. • 1996. $75.00. Self-study workbook.

Creating a Financial Plan: A How-To-Do-It Manual for Librarians. Betty J. Turock amd Andrea Pedolsky. Neal-Schuman Publishers, Inc. • 1992. $49.95. (How-to-Do-It Series).

Customer Service Excellence: A Concise Guide for Librarians. Darlene E. Weingand. American Library Association. • 1997. $30.00. Includes information on quality of service benchmarks, teamwork, patron-librarian conflict management, "customer service language," and other library service topics.

Descriptive Statistical Techniques for Librarians. Arthur W. Hafner. American Library Association. • 1997. $55.00 Second edition.

Evaluating Library Staff: A Performance Appraisal System. Patricia Belcastro. American Library Association. • 1998. $35.00. Provides information on an appraisal system applicable to a wide variety of jobs in all types of libraries. Includes guidelines, performance appraisal forms, sample employee profiles, and a "Code of Service.".

Financial Planning for Libraries. Ann E. Prentice. Scarecrow Press. • 1996. $39.95. Second edition. Includes examples of budgets for libraries. (Library Administration Series, No. 12).

The Library Administrator's Automation Handbook. Richard Boss. Information Today, Inc. • 1997. $39.50. Covers the library administrator's role in the planning, selection, and implementation of hardware and software for automated library systems.

Library Displays Handbook. Mark Schaeffer. H. W. Wilson Co. • 1991. $42.00. Provides detailed instructions for signs, posters, wall displays, bulletin boards, and exhibits.

Library Forms Illustrated Handbook. Elizabeth Futas. Neal-Schuman Publishers, Inc. • Looseleaf service $125.00 per year. Contains forms for acquisition, cataloging, circulation, reference, online searching, interlibrary loan, bibliographic instruction, personnel, administration, budgets, software control, hardware control, statistics, and special collections.

Library Manager's Deskbook: 102 Expert Solutions to 101 Common Dilemmas. Paula P. Carson and others. American Library Association. • 1995. $32.00. "..focuses on issues relevant to today's administrators and supervisors in all types and sizes of libraries.".

Library Personnel Administration. Lowell A. Martin. Scarecrow Press, Inc. • 1994. $31.00. (Library Administration Series, No. 11).

Library Space Planning: A How-To-Do-It Manual for Assessing, Allocating and Recognizing Collections, Resources, and Physical Facilities. Ruth A. Fraley and Carol Lee Anderson. Neal-Schuman Publishers, Inc. • 1990. $45.00. Second edition.

Managing Public-Access Computers: A How-To-Do-It Manual for Librarians. Donald A. Barclay. Neal-Schuman Publishers, Inc. • 2000. $59.95. Part one covers hardware, software, and other components. Part two discusses computers users. Part three is about systems management, library policy, and legal issues.

Managing the Law Library 1999: Forging Effective Relationships in Today's Law Office. Practising Law Institute. • 1999. $99.00. Produced to provide background material for PLI seminars on the role of libraries and librarians in law firms.

Marketing: A How-To-Do-It Manual for Librarians. Suzanne Walters. Neal-Schuman Publishers, Inc. • 1992. $45.00. Includes a sample library marketing plan with worksheets. Covers market research, strategies, tactics, and evaluation. (How-to-Do-It Series).

Moving and Reorganizing a Library. Marianna Wells and Rosemary Young. Ashgate Publishing Co. • 1997. $74.95. "This book provides detailed guidance on how to plan, design, prepare, and implement the move of a small or medium sized library from the time of the project's inception to its completion." Includes a case study and checklists. Published by Gower in England.

Performance Analysis and Appraisal: A How-To-Do-It Manual for Librarians. Robert D. Stueart and Maureen Sullivan. Neal-Schuman Publishers, Inc. • 1991. $49.95. (How-to-Do-It Series).

Recruiting Library Staff: A How-To-Do-It Manual for Librarians. Kathleen Low. Neal-Schuman Publishers, Inc. • 2000. $45.00. Includes position description forms, sample announcements, and checklists. Discusses job fairs and other career events.

Small Libraries: A Handbook for Successful Management. Sally G. Reed. McFarland and Co., Inc., Publishers. • 1991. $28.50. Covers personnel (including volunteers), buildings, collections, service policies, community politics, and other topics.

Strategic Management for Academic Libraries: A Handbook. Robert M. Hayes. Greenwood Publishing Group, Inc. • 1993. $65.00. (Library Management Collection).

Strategic Management for Public Libraries: A Handbook. Robert M. Hayes and Virginia A. Walter. Greenwood Publishing Group, Inc. • 1996. $65.00. (Library Management Collection).

Strategic Planning: A How-To-Do-It Manual for Librarians. M. E. Jacob. Neal-Schuman Publishers, Inc. • 1990. $45.00. (How-to-Do-It Series).

Using Windows for Library Administration. Kenneth E. Marks and Steven P. Nielson. Information Today, Inc. • 1997. $34.95. Contains details on the use of Microsoft Windows software applications for library management: spreadsheets, desktop publishing, project planning, forms, etc.

INTERNET DATABASES

Internet Tools of the Profession. Special Libraries Association. Phone: (202)234-4700 Fax: (202)265-9317 E-mail: hope@tiac.net • URL: http://www.sla.org/pubs/itotp • Web site is designed to update the printed *Internet Tools of the Profession.* Provides links to a wide range of useful databases in business, finance, industry, information technology, insurance, law, library management, telecommunications, and other subject areas. Fees: Free.

ONLINE DATABASES

Library Literature Online. H. W. Wilson Co. • Contains online indexing of a wide variety of library and information science literature from 1984 to date, with updating quarterly. Inquire as to online cost and availability.

LISA Online: Library and Information Science Abstracts. Bowker-Saur, Reed Reference Publishing. • Provides abstracting and indexing of the world's library and information science literature from 1969 to the present. Covers a wide variety of topics in over 550 journals from 60 countries, with biweekly updates. Inquire as to online cost and availability.

PERIODICALS AND NEWSLETTERS

The Bottom Line: A Financial Magazine for Librarians. Neal-Schuman Publishers, Inc. • Quarterly. $49.95 per year. Provides articles on the financial management of libraries: budgeting, funding, cost analysis, etc.

Collection Management: A Quarterly Journal Devoted to the Management of Library Collections. Haworth Press, Inc. • Quarterly. Individuals, $60.00 per year; institutions, $150.00 per year; libraries, $150.00 per year.

Information Management Report: An International Newsletter for Information Professionals and Librarians. R. R. Bowker. • Monthly. $470.00 per year. Incorporates *Outlook on Research Libraries.*

Information Outlook: The Monthly Magazine of the Special Libraries Association. Special Libraries Association. • Monthly. $65.00 per year. Topics include information technology, the Internet, copyright, research techniques, library management, and professional development. Replaces *Special Libraries* and *SpeciaList.*

Journal of Library Administration. Haworth Press, Inc. • Quarterly. Individuals, $45.00 per year; libraries and other institutions, $125.00 per year. Two volumes. Supplement available *Monographic.* Demonstrates the application of theory to everyday problems faced by library administrators.

Library Computing. Sage Publications, Inc. • Quarterly. Individuals, $65.00 per year; institutions, $255.00 per year. Formerly *Library Software Review.*

Library Systems Newsletter. Library Technology Reports. American Library Association. • Monthly. $55.00 per year. Articles and news briefs covering all aspects of library automation.

MLS (Marketing Library Services). Information Today, Inc. • Eight times a year. $69.95 per year. Newsletter. Provides advice on public relations, publicity, promotion of new services, and other library marketing topics.

The One-Person Library: A Newsletter for Librarians and Management. Information Bridges International, Inc. • Monthly. $85.00 per year. Newsletter for librarians working alone or with minimal assistance. Contains reports on library literature, management advice, case studies, book reviews, and general information.

TRADE/PROFESSIONAL ASSOCIATIONS

Library Administration and Management Association. 50 E. Huron St., Chicago, IL 60611. Phone: 800-545-2433 or (312)944-6780 Fax: (312)280-5033 E-mail: lama@ala.org • URL: http://www.ala8.ala.org/alsc/.

OTHER SOURCES

The Unabashed Librarian: The "How I Run My Library Good" Letter. Maurice J. Freedman. • Quarterly. $57.50 per year. Newsletter. Provides practical library management ideas and library humor.

LIBRARY RESEARCH

See also: ONLINE INFORMATION SYSTEMS

GENERAL WORKS

Doing Exemplary Research. Peter J. Frost and Ralph E. Stablein, editors. Sage Publications, Inc. • 1992. $48.00. Contains discussions of research methodologies.

Librarians on the Internet: Impact on Reference Services. Robin Kinder, editor. Haworth Press, Inc. • 1994. $69.95. Contains discussions by various authors on library use of the Internet. (Reference Librarian Series, Nos. 41&42).

Surviving Your Dissertation: A Comprehensive Guide to Content and Process. Kjell E. Rudestam and Rae R. Newton. Sage Publications, Inc. • 2000. Price on application. Provides general advice on how to successfully complete a dissertation or thesis.

ALMANACS AND YEARBOOKS

Bowker Annual: Library and Book Trade Almanac. R. R. Bowker. • Annual. $175.00. Lists of accredited library schools; scholarships for education in library science; library organizations; major libraries; publishing and book sellers organizations. Includes statistics and news of the book business.

BIBLIOGRAPHIES

American Reference Books Annual. Bohdan S. Wynar others, editors. Libraries Unlimited, Inc. • Annual. $110.00.

The Basic Business Library: Core Resources. Bernard S. Schlessinger and June H. Schlessinger. Oryx Press. • 1994. $43.50. Third edition. Consists of three parts: (1) "Core List of Printed Business Reference Sources," (2) "The Literature of Business Reference and Business Libraries: 1976-1994," and (3) "Business Reference Sources and Services: Essays." Part one lists 200 basic titles, with annotations and evaluations.

Reference Books Bulletin: A Compilation of Evaluations. Mary Ellen Quinn, editor. American Library Association. • Annual. $28.50. Contains reference book reviews that appeared during the year in *Booklist.*

Reference Sources for Small and Medium-sized Libraries. Scott E. Kennedy, editor. American Library Association. • 1999. $60.00. Sixth edition. Includes alternative (electronic) formats for reference works.

Subject Encyclopedias: User's Guide, Review Citations, and Keyword Index. Allan N. Mirwis. Oryx Press. • 1999. $135.00. Two volumes. Volume one describes 1,000 subject encyclopedias; volume two provides a keyword index to articles appearing in 100 selected encyclopedias.

Topical Reference Books: Authoritative Evaluations of Recommended Resources in Specialized Subject Areas. R. R. Bowker. • 1991. $109.00. Ranks 2,000 reference books ("Core Titles," "New and Noteworthy," "Supplementary"). (Buying Guide Series).

CD-ROM DATABASES

Fast Reference Facts. The Gale Group. • 1995. $400.00. Contains more than 5,000 CD-ROM entries, providing concise answers to a wide variety of "everyday" queries, within 13 broad subject areas (includes business and economics). Sources of questions and answers include public libraries.

DIRECTORIES

Directory of Special Libraries and Information Centers. The Gale Group. • 1999. $845.00. 25th edition. Three volumes. Two available separately: volume one,*Directory of Special Libraries and Information Centers,* $610.00; volume two *Geographic and Personnel Indexes,* $510.00. Contains 24,000 entries from the U.S., Canada, and 80 other countries. A detailed subject index is included in volume one.

Internet-Plus Directory of Express Library Services: Research and Document Delivery for Hire. American Library Association. • 1997. $49.50. Covers fee-based services of various U. S., Canadian, and international libraries. Paid services include online searches, faxed documents, and specialized professional research. Price ranges are quoted. (A joint production of FISCAL, the ALA/ACRL Discussion Group of Fee-Based Information Service Centers in Academic Libraries, and FYI, the Professional Research and Rapid Information Delivery Service of the County of Los Angeles Public Library.) Formerly *FISCAL Directory of Fee-Based Information Services in Libraries.*

Library Journal: Reference [year]: Print, CD-ROM, Online. Cahners Business Information. • Annual. Issued in November as supplement to *Library Journal.* Lists new and updated reference material, including general and trade print titles, directories, annuals, CD-ROM titles, and online sources. Includes material from more than 150 publishers, arranged by company name, with an index by subject. Addresses include e-mail and World Wide Web information, where available.

Subject Directory of Special Libraries and Information Centers. The Gale Group. • Annual. $845.00. Three volumes, available separately: volume one, *Business, Government, and Law Libraries,* $595.00; volume two, *Computer, Engineering, and Law Libraries,* $595.00; volume three, *Health Sciences Libraries,* $340.00. Altogether, 14,000 entries from the *Directory of Special Libraries and Information Centers* are arranged in 14 subject chapters.

HANDBOOKS AND MANUALS

Best Bet Internet: Reference and Research When You Don't Have Time to Mess Around. Shirley D. Kennedy. American Library Association. • 1997. $35.00. Provides advice for librarians and others on the effective use of World Wide Web information sources.

Building the Reference Collection: A How-To-Do-It Manual for School and Public Librarians. Neal-Schuman Publishers, Inc. • 1992. $38.50. Includes a list of 300 basic reference sources. (How-to-Do-It Series).

Developing Reference Collections and Services in an Electronic Age: A How-To-Do-It Manual for Librarians. Kay A. Cassell. Neal-Schuman Publishers, Inc. • 1999. $55.00. Discusses print vs. electronic media for library reference services.

Electronic Styles: A Handbook for Citing Electronic Information. Xia Li and Nancy Crane. Information Today, Inc. • 1996. $19.99. Second edition. Covers the citing of text-based information, electronic journals, Web sites, CD-ROM items, multimedia products, and online documents.

Guide to the Use of Libraries and Information Sources. Jean K. Gates. McGraw-Hill. • 1994. $32.19. Seventh edition.

Information Broker. Entrepreneur Media, Inc. • Looseleaf. $59.50. A practical guide to starting an information retrieval business. Covers profit potential, start-up costs, market size evaluation, pricing, accounting, advertising, promotion, etc. (Start-Up Business Guide No. E1237.).

Introduction to Reference Work. William A. Katz. McGraw-Hill. • 1996. $92.19. Seventh edition. Two volumes. Volume one, $48.13; volume two, $44.06.

Introductory CD-ROM Searching: The Key to Effective Ondisc Searching. Joseph Meloche. Haworth Press, Inc. • 1994. $49.95. Covers basic search strategies, with specific suggestions for Dialog OnDisc, Silverplatter, Wilsondisc, UMI, and others.

Oxford Guide to Library Research. Thomas Mann. Oxford University Press, Inc. • 1998. $35.00. Covers print sources, electronic sources, and "nine research methods.".

Recruiter's Research Blue Book: A How-To Guide for Researchers, Search Consultants, Corporate Recruiters, Small Business Owners, Venture Capitalists, and Line Executives. Andrea A. Jupina. Kennedy Information. • 2000. $179.00. Second edition. Provides detailed coverage of the role that research plays in executive recruiting. Includes such practical items as "Telephone Interview Guide," "Legal Issues in Executive Search," and "How to Create an Execuive Search Library." Covers both person-to-person research and research using printed and online business information sources. Includes an extensive directory of recommended sources. Formerly *Handbook of Executive Search Research.*

Working with Faculty to Design Undergraduate Information Literacy Programs: A How-To-Do-It Manual for Librarians. Rosemary M. Young and Stephana Harmony. Neal-Schuman Publishers, Inc. • 1999. $45.00. Includes sample forms, surveys, evaluations, and assignments for credit courses or single sessions.

PERIODICALS AND NEWSLETTERS

BiblioData's Price Watcher: The Researcher's Guide to Online Prices. BiblioData. • Semimonthly. Individuals $129.00 per year; institutions, $169.00 per year; nonprofit organizations, $129.00 per year. Newsletter. Provides detailed analysis and reviews of pricing schemes used by Internet and other online information providers.

College and Research Libraries (CRL). Association of College and Research Libraries. American Library Association. • Bimonthly. $60.00 per year. Supplement available *C and R L News.*

College and Research Libraries News. Association of College and Research Libraries. American Library Association. • 11 times per year. Free to members; non-members, $35.00 per year. Supplement to *College and Research Libraries.*

The CyberSkeptic's Guide to Internet Research. BiblioData. • 10 times a year. $104.00 per year; nonprofit organizations, $159.00 per year. Newsletter. Presents critical reviews of World Wide Web sites and databases, written by information professionals. Includes "Late Breaking News" of Web sites.

Focus: On the Center for Research Libraries. Center for Research Libraries. • Bimonthly. Free. Newsletter. Provides news of Center activites.

Internet Reference Services Quarterly: A Journal of Innovative Information Practice, Technologies, and Resources. Haworth Press, Inc. • Quarterly. Individuals, $36.00 per year; libraries and other institutions, $48.00 per year. Covers both theoretical research and practical applications.

Reference and User Services Quarterly. American Library Association. • Quarterly. $50.00 per year. Official publication of the Reference and User Services Association (RUSA), a division of the American Library Association. In addition to articles, includes reviews of databases, reference books, and library professional material. Formerly *RQ.*

Reference Librarian. Haworth Press, Inc. • Semiannual. Individuals, $60.00 per year; libraries and other institutions, $225.00 per year. Two volumes.

Research Strategies: A Journal of Library Concepts and Instruction. JAI Press, Inc. • Quarterly. $135.00 per year. Edited for librarians involved in bibliographic or library instruction.

RUSA Update. American Library Association. • Quarterly. Free to members; non-members, $20.00 per year. Serves as news letter for the Reference and User Services Association, a division of the American Library Association. Includes activities of the Business Reference and Services Section (BRASS). Formerly *RASD Update.*

OTHER SOURCES

The Invisible Web: Uncovering Information Sources Search Engines Can't See. Chris Sherman and Gary Price. Information Today, Inc. • 2001. $29.95. A guide to Web sites from universities, libraries, associations, government agencies, and other sources that are inadequately covered by conventional search engines (see also http://www.invisible-web.net). (CyberAge Books.).

LICENSE PLATES

See: MOTOR VEHICLE LAW AND REGULATION

LICENSES

DIRECTORIES

Professional and Occupational Licensing Directory. The Gale Group. • 1996. $120.00. Second edition. Provides detailed national and state information on the requirements for obtaining a license in each of about 500 occupations. Information needed to contact the appropriate licensing agency or organization is included in each case.

PERIODICALS AND NEWSLETTERS

CLEAR News. Council on Licensure, Enforcement, and Regulation. • Quarterly. Price on application. Newsletter on occupational and professional licenses and licensing.

The Licensing Letter. EPM Communications, Inc. • Monthly. $447.00 per year. Newsletter. Covers all aspects of licensed merchandising (compensation of a person or an organization for being associated with a product or service).

TRADE/PROFESSIONAL ASSOCIATIONS

Council on Licensure, Enforcement and Regulation. 403 Marquis Ave., Suite 100, Lexington, KY 40502. Phone: (606)269-1289 E-mail: clear@uky.compuscw.net • URL: http://www.clearhq.org • Members are state government occupational and professional licensing officials.

OTHER SOURCES

Broker-Dealer Regulation. David A. Lipton. West Group. • $145.00 per year. Looseleaf service. Annual supplementation. Focuses on the basics of stockbroker license application procedure, registration, regulation, and responsibilities.

LICENSING AGREEMENTS

See also: INTELLECTUAL PROPERTY

ABSTRACTS AND INDEXES

Current Law Index: Multiple Access to Legal Periodicals. The Gale Group. • Monthly. $650.00 per year. Produced in cooperation with the American Association of Law Libraries. Indexes more than 900 law journals, legal newspapers, and specialty publications from the U.S., Canada, U.K., Ireland, Australia, and New Zealand.

Index to Legal Periodicals and Books. H. W. Wilson Co. • Monthly. Quarterly and annual cumulations. $270.00 per year. CD-ROM version available at $1,495.00 per year.

NTIS Alerts: Government Inventions for Licensing. National Technical Information Service. • Semimonthly. $270.00 per year. Identifies new inventions available from various government agencies. Covers a wide variety of industrial and technical areas. Formerly *Abstract Newsletter.*

DIRECTORIES

Licensing Executives Society Membership Directory. Licensing Executives Society International. • Annual. Membership.

HANDBOOKS AND MANUALS

Licensing Law Handbook. West Group. • Annual. $175.00.

ONLINE DATABASES

Index to Legal Periodicals and Books (Online). H. W. Wilson Co. • Broad coverage of law journals and books 1981 to date. Monthly updates. Inquire as to online cost and availability.

Legal Resource Index. The Gale Group. • Broad coverage of law literature appearing in legal, business, and other periodicals, 1980 to date. Monthly updates. Inquire as to online cost and availability.

LEXIS. LEXIS-NEXIS. • The various LEXIS databases provide full text and indexing for a wide variety of legal cases, statutes, orders, and opinions.

PERIODICALS AND NEWSLETTERS

Intellectual Property Today. Omega Communications. • Monthly. $48.00 per year. Covers legal developments in copyright, patents, trademarks, and licensing. Emphasizes the effect of new technology on intellectual property. Formerly *Law Works.*

International New Product Newsletter. INPN, Inc. • Monthly. $175.00 per year. Includes licensing opportunities.

LES Nouvelles. Licensing Executives Society. • Quarterly. Free to members; libraries, $35.00 per year. Concerned with licensing agreements, patents, and trademarks.

The Licensing Book. Adventure Publishing. • Monthly. $36.00 per year. Contains articles about licensed product merchandising.

Licensing Law and Business Report. West Group. • Bimonthly. $323.00 per year. Newsletter.

World Technology: Patent Licensing Gazette. Techni Research Associates, Inc. • Bimonthly. $165.00 per year. Lists items available for license or acquisition.

RESEARCH CENTERS AND INSTITUTES

Lexis.com Research System. Lexis-Nexis Group. Phone: 800-227-9597 or (937)865-6800 Fax: (937)865-6909 E-mail: webmaster@prod.lexis-nexis.com • URL: http://www.lexis.com • Fee-based Web site offers extensive searching of a wide variety of legal sources. Additional features include Daily Opinion Service, lexis.com Bookstore, Career Center, CLE Center, Law Schools, and Practice Pages ("Pages specific to areas of specialty").

TRADE/PROFESSIONAL ASSOCIATIONS

International Licensing Industry Merchandisers' Association. 350 Fifth Ave., Suite 2309, New York, NY 10118. Phone: (212)244-1944 Fax: (212)563-6552 E-mail: info@licensing.org • URL: http://www.licensing.org • Promotes the legal protection of licensed properties.

Licensing Executives Society. 1800 Diagonal Rd., Suite 280, Alexandria, VA 22314-2840. Phone: (703)836-3106 Fax: (703)836-3107.

OTHER SOURCES

Eckstrom's Licensing Law Library. Lawrence J. Eckstrom. West Group. • 12 looseleaf volumes. $1,570.00. Periodic supplementation. Covers foreign and domestic operations and joint ventures, with forms and agreements.

Investing, Licensing, and Trading. Economist Intelligence Unit. • Semiannual. $345.00 per year for each country. Key laws, rules, and licensing provisions are explained for each of 60 countries. Information is provided on political conditions, markets, price policies, foreign exchange practices, labor, and export-import.

LIFE INSURANCE

See also: ACCIDENT INSURANCE; HEALTH INSURANCE; INSURANCE

GENERAL WORKS

Life Insurance in Estate Planning. James C. Munch, Jr. Aspen Books. • 1981. $80.00. Includes current supplement.

The Lifetime Book of Money Management. Grace W. Weinstein. Visible Ink Press. • 1993. $15.95. Third edition. Gives popularly-written advice on investments, life and health insurance, owning a home, credit, retirement, estate planning, and other personal finance topics.

Smarter Insurance Solutions. Janet Bamford. Bloomberg Press. • 1996. $19.95. Provides practical advice to consumers, with separate chapters on the following kinds of insurance: automobile, homeowners, health, disability, and life. (Bloomberg Personal Bookshelf Series).

Your Life Insurance Options. Alan Lavine. John Wiley and Sons, Inc. • 1993. $12.95. Tells how to buy life insurance, including the selection of a company and agent. Describes term life, whole life, variable life, universal life, and annuities. Includes a glossary of insurance terms and jargon. (ICFP Personal Wealth Building Guide Series).

ABSTRACTS AND INDEXES

Insurance Periodicals Index. Specials Libraries Association, Insurance and Employees Benefits Div. CCH/NILS Publishing Co. • Annual. $250.00. Compiled by the Insurance and Employee Benefits Div., Special Libraries Association. A yearly index of over 15,000 articles from about 35 insurance periodicals. Arrangement is by subject, with an index to authors.

BIBLIOGRAPHIES

Insurance and Employee Benefits Literature. Special Libraries Association, Insurance and Employee Benefits Div. • Bimonthly. $15.00 per year.

List of Worthwhile Life and Health Insurance Books. American Council of Life Insurance. • Annual. Free. Books in print on life and health insurance and closely related subjects.

CD-ROM DATABASES

U. S. Insurance: Life, Accident, and Health. Sheshunoff Information Services, Inc. • Monthly. Price on application. CD-ROM provides detailed, current information on the financial characteristics of more than 2,300 life, accident, and health insurance companies.

DIRECTORIES

Ratings Guide to Life, Health and Annuity Insurers. Weiss Ratings, Inc. • Quarterly. $438.00 per year. Rates life insurance companies for overall safety and financial stability. Formerly *Weiss Ratings' Guide to Life, Health and Annuity Insurers.*

S & P's Insurance Book. Standard & Poor's Ratings Group, Insurance Rating Services. • Quarterly. Price on application. Contains detailed financial analyses and ratings of various kinds of insurance companies.

S & P's Insurance Digest: Life Insurance Edition. Standard & Poor's Ratings Group, Insurance Rating Services. • Quarterly. Contains concise financial analyses and ratings of life insurance companies.

Who Writes What in Life and Health Insurance. The National Underwriter Co. • Annual. $9.95.

ENCYCLOPEDIAS AND DICTIONARIES

Dictionary of Insurance. Lewis E. Davids. Rowman and Littlefield Publishers, Inc. • 1990. $17.95. Seventh revised edition.

Dictionary of Insurance Terms. Harvey W. Rubin. Barron's Educational Series, Inc. • 2000. $12.95. Fourth edition. Defines terms in a wide variety of insurance fields. Price on application.

Insurance Words and Their Meanings: A Dictionary of Insurance Terms. Diana Kowatch. The Rough Notes Co., Inc. • 1998. $38.50. 16th revised edition.

Rupp's Insurance and Risk Management Glossary. Richard V. Rupp. Available from CCH, Inc. • 1996. $35.00. Second edition. Published by NILS Publishing Co. Provides definitions of 6,400 insurance words and phrases. Includes a guide to acronyms and abbreviations.

FINANCIAL RATIOS

Almanac of Business and Industrial Financial Ratios. Leo Troy. Prentice Hall. • Annual. $99.95. Contains financial ratios derived from federal tax returns. Ratios for each of about 200 industries are arranged according to company asset size.

HANDBOOKS AND MANUALS

The Complete Book of Insurance: The Consumer's Guide to Insuring Your Life, Health, Property, and Income. Ben G. Baldwin. McGraw-Hill Professional. • 1996. $24.95. Revised edition. Provides basic information and advice on various kinds of insurance: life, health, property (fire), disability, long-term care, automobile, liability, and annuities.

Financial Planning Applications. William J. Ruckstuhl. Maple-Vail Book, The Manufacturing Group. • 2000. $68.00. 16th edition. Emphasis on annuities and life insurance. (Huebner School Series.).

An Insurance Guide for Seniors. Insurance Forum, Inc. • 1997. $15.00. Provides concise advice and information on Medicare, Medicare supplement insurance, HMOs, long-term care insurance, automobile insurance, life insurance, annuities, and pensions. An appendix lists "Financially Strong Insurance Companies." (*The Insurance Forum*, vol. 24, no. 4.).

Life and Health Insurance Law. William F. Meyer. West Group. • 1972. $125.00. Covers the legal aspects of life, health, and accident insurance.

Life Insurance and Annuities from the Buyer's Point of View. American Institute for Economic Research. • Annual. $10.00.

Life Insurance Answer Book: For Qualified Plans and Estate Planning. Gary S. Lesser and Lawrence C. Starr, editors. Panel Publishers. • 1998. $118.00. Second edition. Four parts by various authors cover life insurance in general, qualified plans, fiduciary responsibility, and estate planning. Includes sample documents, worksheets, and information in Q&A form.

McGill's Life Insurance. Edward E. Graves, editor. The American College. • 1998. $71.00. Second edition. Contains chapters by various authors on diverse kinds of life insurance, as well as annuities, disability insurance, long-term care insurance, risk management, reinsurance, and other insurance topics. Originally by Dan M. McGill.

INTERNET DATABASES

InsWeb. InsWeb Corp. Phone: (650)372-2129 E-mail: info@insweb.com • URL: http://www.insweb.com • Web site offers a wide variety of advice and information on automobile, life, health, and "other" insurance. Includes glossaries of insurance terms, Standard & Poor's ratings of individual insurance companies, and "Financial Needs Estimators." Searching is available. Fees: Free.

ONLINE DATABASES

Best's Company Reports. A. M. Best Co. • Provides full financial data online for U. S. insurance companies (life, health, property, casualty), including balance sheet data, income statements, expenses, premium income, losses, and investments. Includes *Best's Company Reports*, *Best's Insurance News*, and Best's ratings of insuarance companies. Inquire as to online cost and availability.

PERIODICALS AND NEWSLETTERS

Advisory Today. National Association of insurance and Finacial Advisors. • Monthly. Free to members; non-members, $7.00 per year. Edited for individual life and health insurance agents. Among the topics included are disability insurance and long-term care insurance. Formerly Life Association News.

Annuity and Life Insurance Shopper. United States Annuities. • Quarterly. $65.00 per year. Provides information on rates and performance for fixed annuities, variable annuities, and term life policies issued by more than 250 insurance companies.

Best's Review: Inurance Issues and Analysis. A.M. Best Co. • Monthly. $25.00 per year. Editorial coverage of significant industry trends, developments, and important events. Formerly Best's Review: Property-Casualty Insurance.

Broker World. Insurance Publications, Inc. • Monthly. $6.00 per year. Edited for independent insurance agents and brokers. Special feature issue topics include annuities, disability insurance, estate planning, and life insurance.

Contingencies: The Magazine of the Actuarial Profession. American Academy of Actuaries. • Bimonthly. $30.00 per year. Provides non-technical articles on the actuarial aspects of insurance, employee benefits, and pensions.

GAMA International Journal. GAMA International. • Bimonthly. $30.00 per year. Contains practical articles on the management of life insurance agencies. (GAMA International was formerly General Agents and Managers Association.).

Guide to Life, Health, and Annuity Insurers: A Quarterly Compilation of Insurance Company Ratings and Analysis. Weiss Ratings, Inc. • Quarterly. $438.00 per year. Emphasis is on rating of financial safety and relative risk. Includes annual summary.

Insurance and Technology. Miller Freeman. • Monthly. $65.00 per year. Covers information technology and systems management as applied to the operation of life, health, casualty, and property insurance companies.

The Insurance Forum: For the Unfettered Exchange of Ideas About Insurance. Joseph M. Belth, editor. Insurance Forum, Inc. • Monthly. $90.00 per year. Newsletter. Provides analysis of the insurance business, including occasional special issues showing the ratings of about 1,600 life-health insurance companies, as determined by four major rating services: Duff & Phelps Credit Rating Co., Moody's Investors Service, Standard & Poor's Corp., and Weiss Research, Inc.

Insurance Marketing: The Ins and Outs of Recruiting and Retaining More Agents. Agent Media Corp. • Bimonthly. Controlled circulation. Provides practical advice for insurance companies on how to hire and keep sales personnel.

Jounal of Finacial Services Professionals. American Society of CLU and Ch F C. • Bimonthly. $38.00 per year. Provides information on life insurance and financial planning, including estate planning, retirement, tax planning, trusts, business insurance, long-term care insurance, disability insurance, and employee benefits. Formerly (American Society of CLU and Ch F C Journal).

National Underwriter. The National Underwriter Co. • Weekly. Two editions: *Life* or *Health.* $83.00 per year, each edition.

Professional Agent. National Association of Professional Insurance Agents. • Monthly. Members, $12,00 per year; non-members, $24.00 per year. Provides sales and marketing advice for independent agents in various fields of insurance, including life, health, property, and casualty.

Resource: An Association Magazine for Life Insurance Management. LOMA. • Monthly. $36.00 per year. Covers management topics for life insurance home and field office personnel. (LOMA was formerly Life Office Management Association.).

The Safe Money Report. Weiss Ratings, Inc. • Monthly. $148.00 per year. Newsletter. Provides financial advice and current safety ratings of various banks, savings and loan companies, insurance companies, and securities dealers.

RESEARCH CENTERS AND INSTITUTES

S. S. Huebner Foundation. University of Pennsylvania, Vance Hall, Room 430, Philadelphia, PA 19104-6301. Phone: (215)898-9631 Fax: (215)573-2218 E-mail: cummins@wharton.upenn.edu • URL: http://www.rider.wharton.upenn.edu/~sshuebne/ • Awards grants for research in various areas of insurance.

STATISTICS SOURCES

Insurance Statistics Yearbook. OECD Publications and Information Center. • Annual. $75.00. Presents detailed statistics on insurance premiums collected in OECD countries, by type of insurance.

Life Insurance Fact Book. American Council of Life Insurance. • Biennial. $37.50 per year; with diskette, $55.00 per year.

Morningstar Variable Annuity Performance Report. Morningstar, Inc. • Monthly. $125.00 per year. Provides detailed statistics and ratings for more than 2,000 variable annuities and variable-life products.

Standard & Poor's Industry Surveys. Standard & Poor's. • Semiannual. $1,800.00. Two looseleaf volumes. Includes monthly supplements. Provides detailed, individual surveys of 52 major industry groups. Each survey is revised on a semiannual basis. Also includes "Monthly Investment Review" (industry group investment analysis) and monthly "Trends & Projections" (economic analysis).

Statistical Information on the Financial Services Industry. American Bankers Association. • Annual. Members, $150.00; non-members, $275.00. Presents a wide variety of data relating to banking and financial services, including consumer economics, personal finance, credit, government loans, capital markets, and international banking.

U. S. Industry and Trade Outlook: The McGraw-Hill Companies and the U.S. Department of Commerce/ International Trade Administration. Datapso Research Corp. • Annual. $69.95. Produced by the International Trade Administration, U. S. Department of Commerce, in a "public-private" partnership with DRI/McGraw-Hill and Standard & Poor's. Provides basic data, outlook for the current year, and "Long-Term Prospects" (five-year projections) for a wide variety of products and services. Includes high technology industries. Formerly *U. S. Industrial Outlook.*

TRADE/PROFESSIONAL ASSOCIATIONS

American Council of Life Insurance. 1001 Pennsylvania Ave., N.W., Washington, DC 20004-2599. Phone: (202)624-2000 Fax: (202)624-2319 E-mail: acli@acli.com • URL: http://www.acli.com.

Association of Life Insurance Counsel. c/o J. Michael Keefer, 200 E. Berry St., Fort Wayne, IN 46802. Phone: (219)455-5582 Fax: (219)455-5403 • Members are attorneys for life insurance companies.

GAMA International. 1922 F St., N. W., Washington, DC 20006. Phone: 800-345-2687 or (202)331-6088 Fax: (202)785-5712 E-mail: gamamail@gama.naifa.org • URL: http://www.gamaweb.com • Members are life insurance agents.

Life Communicators Association. P.O.Box 196, Zionsville, IN 46077. Phone: (317)873-5916 Fax: (317)873-0049 E-mail: nclca@aol.com • URL: http://www.lcaonline.org.

Life Office Management Association. 2300 Windy Ridge Parkway, Suite 600, Atlanta, GA 30339-8443. Phone: (770)951-1770 Fax: (770)984-0441 E-mail: marketing@loma.org • URL: http://www.loma.org.

LIMRA International. 300 Day Hill Rd., Windsor, CT 06095. Phone: 800-235-4672 or (860)688-3358 Fax: (860)298-9555 • URL: http://www.limra.org.

National Association Insurance and Financial Advisors. 1922 F St., N.W., Washington, DC 20006-4387. Phone: (202)331-6000 Fax: (202)835-9601 • URL: http://www.naifa.org.

National Association of Professional Insurance Agents. 400 N. Washington St., Alexandria, VA 22314. Phone: (703)836-9340 Fax: (703)836-1279 E-mail: piaweb@pianet.org • URL: http://www.pianet.com • Members are independent agents in various fields of insurance.

Society of Financial Service Professionals. 270 S. Bryn Mawr Ave., Bryn Mawr, PA 19010-2195. Phone: 888-243-2258 or (610)526-2500 Fax: (610)527-4010 E-mail: custserv@financialpro.org • URL: http://www.financialpro.org.

OTHER SOURCES

Best's Insurance Reports. A.M. Best Co. • Annual. $745.00 per edition. Two editions, Life-health insurance covering about 1,750 companies, and property-casualty insurance covering over 2,500 companies. Includes one year subscription to both *Best's Review* and *Best's Insurance Management Reports.*

Federal Income Taxation of Life Insurance Companies. Matthew Bender & Co., Inc. • $630.00. Three looseleaf volumes. Periodic supplementation.

Information, Finance, and Services USA. The Gale Group. • 2001. $240.00. Replaces *Service Industries USA* and *Finance, Insurance, and Real Estate USA.* Presents statistics and projections relating to economic activity in a wide variety of non-manufacturing areas.

Life, Health, and Accident Insurance Law Reports. CCH, Inc. • $835.00 per year. Looseleaf service. Monthly updates.

LIFT TRUCKS

See: MATERIALS HANDLING

LIGHTING

DIRECTORIES

Home Lighting and Accessories Suppliers Directory. Doctorow Communications, Inc. • Semiannual. $6.00 per issue. Lists suppliers of residential lighting fixtures and accessories.

L D & A: Lighting Equipment and Accessories Directory. Illuminating Engineering Society. • Annual. $10.00. Lists over 800 manufacturers of lighting fixtures, controls, components, mounting devices, maintenance equipment, etc.

FINANCIAL RATIOS

Annual Statement Studies. Robert Morris Associates: The Association of Lending and Credit Risk Professiona. • Annual. Free to members; non-members, $140.00. Median and quartile financial ratios are given for over 400 kinds of manufacturing, wholesale, retail, construction, and consumer finance establishments. Data is sorted by both asset size and sales volume. Includes a clearly written "Definition of Ratios" and an alphabetical industry index.

HANDBOOKS AND MANUALS

I.E.S. Lighting Handbook. Illuminating Engineering Society. • Quadrennial. $389.00.

Lighting Design: An Introductory Guide for Professionals. Carl Gardner and Barry Hannaford. Ashgate Publishing Co. • 1993. $96.95. Includes project case studies and product/effect examples. Emphasis is on commercial interior and exterior lighting. Published by Design Council Books.

No-Regrets Remodeling: Creating a Comfortable, Healthy Home That Saves Energy. Available from American Council for an Energy-Efficient Economy. • 1997. $19.95. Edited by *Home Energy* magazine. Serves as a home remodeling guide to efficient heating, cooling, ventilation, water heating, insulation, lighting, and windows.

PERIODICALS AND NEWSLETTERS

Home Lighting and Accessories. Doctorow Communications, Inc. • Monthly. $30.00 per year. Trade magazine of the residential lighting industry for retailers, distributors, designers, architects, specifiers, manufacturers and all lighting professionals.

IEEE Industry Applications Magazine. Institute of Electrical and Electronics Engineers. • Bimonthly. $190.00 per year. Covers new industrial applications of power conversion, drives, lighting, and control. Emphasis is on the petroleum, chemical, rubber, plastics, textile, and mining industries.

LD & A: (Lighting Design and Application). Illuminating Engineering Society. • Monthly. $39.00 per year. Information on current events, products, projects and people in the lighting industry.

National Home Center News: News and Analysis for the Home Improvement, Building, Material Industry. Lebhar-Friedman, Inc. • 22 times a year. $99.00 per year. Includes special feature issues on hardware and tools, building materials, millwork, electrical supplies, lighting, and kitchens.

STATISTICS SOURCES

Annual Survey of Manufactures. Available from U. S. Government Printing Office. • Annual. Prices vary. Issued by the U. S. Census Bureau as an interim update to the *Census of Manufactures.* Includes data on number of manufacturing establishments in various industries, employment, labor costs, value of shipments, capital expenditures, inventories, energy costs, and assets. (See also Census Bureau home page, http://www.census.gov/.).

Electric Lamps. U. S. Bureau of the Census. • Quarterly and annual. Provides data on shipments:

value, quantity, imports, and exports. (Current Industrial Reports, MQ-36B.).

Manufacturing Profiles. Available from U. S. Government Printing Office. • Annual. Issued by the U. S. Census Bureau. A printed consolidation of the entire *Current Industrial Report* series, presenting "all the data compiled." Contains statistics on production, shipments, inventories, consumption, exports, imports, and orders for a wide variety of manufactured products. (See also Census Bureau home page, http://www.census.gov/.).

U. S. Industry and Trade Outlook: The McGraw-Hill Companies and the U.S. Department of Commerce/ International Trade Administration. Datapso Research Corp. • Annual. $69.95. Produced by the International Trade Administration, U. S. Department of Commerce, in a "public-private" partnership with DRI/McGraw-Hill and Standard & Poor's. Provides basic data, outlook for the current year, and "Long-Term Prospects" (five-year projections) for a wide variety of products and services. Includes high technology industries. Formerly *U. S. Industrial Outlook.*

TRADE/PROFESSIONAL ASSOCIATIONS

American Lighting Association. P.O. Box 420288, Dallas, TX 75342-0288. Phone: 800-274-4448 or (214)698-9898 or (214)698-9901 Fax: (214)698-9899 E-mail: webmaster@americanlightingassoc.com • URL: http://www.americnlightingassoc.com.

Illuminating Engineering Society of North America. 120 Wall St., 17th Fl., New York, NY 10005-4001. Phone: (212)248-5000 Fax: (212)248-5017 E-mail: bbay@iesna.org • URL: http://www.iesna.org • Members are lighting engineers, designers, architects, and manufacturers.

LIMESTONE INDUSTRY

See also: QUARRYING

FINANCIAL RATIOS

Annual Statement Studies. Robert Morris Associates: The Association of Lending and Credit Risk Professiona. • Annual. Free to members; non-members, $140.00. Median and quartile financial ratios are given for over 400 kinds of manufacturing, wholesale, retail, construction, and consumer finance establishments. Data is sorted by both asset size and sales volume. Includes a clearly written "Definition of Ratios" and an alphabetical industry index.

PERIODICALS AND NEWSLETTERS

Building Stone Magazine. Building Stone Institute. • Bimonthly. $65.00 per year.

TRADE/PROFESSIONAL ASSOCIATIONS

National Stone Association. 1415 Elliot Place, N.W., Washington, DC 20007. Phone: 800-342-1415 or (202)342-1100 Fax: (202)342-0702 • URL: http://www.aggregates.org.

LIMITED PARTNERSHIPS

See: PARTNERSHIP

LINEAR PROGRAMMING

GENERAL WORKS

An Introduction to Linear Programming and Game Theory. Paul R. Thie. John Wiley and Sons, Inc. • 1988. $102.95. Second edition.

Introduction to Practical Linear Programming. David J. Pannell. John Wiley and Sons, Inc. • 1996. $84.95. Explains how to apply linear programming to real-world situations in various areas, such as agriculture, manufacturing, finance, and advertising. Includes an IBM PC diskette containing "user-friendly" software.

ONLINE DATABASES

INSPEC. Institute of Electrical and Electronics Engineers (IEEE). • Provides indexing and abstracting of the worldwide literature of electrical engineering, electronics, physics, computer technology, information technology, and industrial controls. Time period is 1970 to date, with weekly updates. Inquire as to online cost and availability. (INSPEC is Information Services for the Physics and Engineering Communities.).

LINEN INDUSTRY

ABSTRACTS AND INDEXES

Textile Technology Digest. Institute of Textile Technology. • Monthly. $535.00 per year. Provides indexing and abstracting of a wide variety of textile technology literature.

CD-ROM DATABASES

Textile Technology Digest [CD-ROM]. Textile Information Center, Institute of Textile Technology. • Quarterly. $1,700.00 per year. Provides CD-ROM indexing and abstracting of worldwide journals and monographs in various areas of textile technology, production, and management. Covers 1978 to date.

DIRECTORIES

LDB Interior Textiles Buyer's Guide. E.W. Williams Publications Co. • Annual. $40.00. Includes over 2,000 manufacturers, distributors, and importers of curtains, draperies, hard window treatments, bedspreads, pillows, etc. Formerly *LDB Interior Textiles Directory.*

Nationwide Directory of Gift, Housewares and Home Textiles Buyers. Salesman's Guide. • Annual. $195.00.

ENCYCLOPEDIAS AND DICTIONARIES

Encyclopedia of Textiles. French and European Publications, Inc. • 1980. $39.95. Third edition.

Textile Terms and Definitions. J.E. McIntyre and Paul N. Daniels, editors. Available from State Mutual Book and Periodical Service Ltd., Trade Order Dept. • 1995. $110.00. 10th edition. Published by the Textile Insitute (UK). Includes more than 1,000 definitions of textile processes, fiber types, and end products. Illustrated.

ONLINE DATABASES

Textile Technology Digest [online]. Textile Information Center, Institute of Textile Technology. • Contains indexing and abstracting of more than 300 worldwide journals and monographs in various areas of textile technology, production, and management. Time period is 1978 to date, with monthly updating. Inquire as to online cost and availability.

World Textiles. Elsevier Science, Inc. • Provides abstracting and indexing from 1970 of worldwide textile literature (periodicals, books, pamphlets, and reports). Includes U. S., European, and British patent information. Updating is monthly. Inquire as to online cost and availability.

PERIODICALS AND NEWSLETTERS

LDB Interior Textiles. E.W. Williams Publications Co. • Monthly. $66.00 per year. Supplement available *Linens, Domestics and Baths-Interior Textile Annual Buyer's Guide.* Formerly *Interior Textiles.*

STATISTICS SOURCES

Annual Survey of Manufactures. Available from U. S. Government Printing Office. • Annual. Prices vary. Issued by the U. S. Census Bureau as an interim update to the *Census of Manufactures.* Includes data on number of manufacturing establishments in various industries, employment, labor costs, value of shipments, capital expenditures, inventories, energy costs, and assets. (See also Census Bureau home page, http://www.census.gov/.).

Manufacturing Profiles. Available from U. S. Government Printing Office. • Annual. Issued by the U. S. Census Bureau. A printed consolidation of the entire *Current Industrial Report* series, presenting "all the data compiled." Contains statistics on production, shipments, inventories, consumption, exports, imports, and orders for a wide variety of manufactured products. (See also Census Bureau home page, http://www.census.gov/.).

TRADE/PROFESSIONAL ASSOCIATIONS

Textile Institute. Saint James Bldgs., 4th Fl., Oxford St., Manchester M1 6FQ, England. Phone: 44 161 2371188 Fax: 44 161 2361991 E-mail: tiihq@textileinst.org.uk • URL: http://www.texi.org • Members in 100 countries involved with textile industry management, marketing, science, and technology.

OTHER SOURCES

Textile Business Outlook. Statistikon Corp. • Quarterly. $985.00 per year. Analyzes current business, marketing, and financial conditions for the worldwide textile industry (fibers and fabrics). Includes statistical forecasts.

LINGERIE INDUSTRY

See: UNDERWEAR INDUSTRY

LIQUEFIED PETROLEUM GAS

See: PROPANE AND BUTANE GAS INDUSTRY

LIQUOR INDUSTRY

See: DISTILLING INDUSTRY

LIQUOR LAW AND REGULATION

ABSTRACTS AND INDEXES

Current Law Index: Multiple Access to Legal Periodicals. The Gale Group. • Monthly. $650.00 per year. Produced in cooperation with the American Association of Law Libraries. Indexes more than 900 law journals, legal newspapers, and specialty publications from the U.S., Canada, U.K., Ireland, Australia, and New Zealand.

Index to Legal Periodicals and Books. H. W. Wilson Co. • Monthly. Quarterly and annual cumulations. $270.00 per year. CD-ROM version available at $1,495.00 per year.

ALMANACS AND YEARBOOKS

American Law Yearbook. The Gale Group. • Annual. $155.00. Serves as a yearly supplement to *West's Encyclopedia of American Law.* Describes new legal developments in many subject areas.

CD-ROM DATABASES

WILSONDISC: Index to Legal Periodicals and Books. H. W. Wilson Co. • Monthly. Including unlimited online access to *Index to Legal Periodicals* through WILSONLINE. Contains CD-ROM indexing of more than 800 English language legal periodicals from 1981 to date and 2,500 books.

ENCYCLOPEDIAS AND DICTIONARIES

West's Encyclopedia of American Law. Available from The Gale Group. • 1997. $995.00. Second edition. 12 volumes. Published by West Group. Covers a wide variety of legal topics for the general reader. Formerly *Guide to American Law: Everyone's Legal Encyclopedia* (1985).

ONLINE DATABASES

Index to Legal Periodicals and Books (Online). H. W. Wilson Co. • Broad coverage of law journals and books 1981 to date. Monthly updates. Inquire as to online cost and availability.

PERIODICALS AND NEWSLETTERS

Alcoholic Beverage Control: State Capitals. Wakeman-Walworth Inc. • Weekly. $245.00 per year. Formerly *From the State Capitals: Alcoholic Beverage Control.*

RESEARCH CENTERS AND INSTITUTES

Lexis.com Research System. Lexis-Nexis Group. Phone: 800-227-9597 or (937)865-6800 Fax: (937)865-6909 E-mail: webmaster@prod.lexis-nexis.com • URL: http://www.lexis.com • Fee-based Web site offers extensive searching of a wide variety of legal sources. Additional features include Daily Opinion Service, lexis.com Bookstore, Career Center, CLE Center, Law Schools, and Practice Pages ("Pages specific to areas of specialty").

STATISTICS SOURCES

Statistical Reports. National Alcoholic Beverage Control Association. • Monthly. Price on application. Includes quarterly and annual cumulations.

Uniform Crime Reports for the United States. Federal Bureau of Investigation, U.S. Department of Justice. Available from U.S. Government Printing Office. • Annual. Price varies.

TRADE/PROFESSIONAL ASSOCIATIONS

Joint Committee of the States to Study Alcoholic Beverage Laws. c/o National Alcoholic Beverage Control Association, 4216 King St., W., Alexandria, VA 22302. Phone: (703)578-4200 Fax: (703)820-3551.

National Alcohol Beverage Control Association. 4216 King St., Alexandria, VA 22302. Phone: (703)578-4200 Fax: (703)820-3551.

National Conference of State Liquor Administrators. c/o Charles D. Sapienza, New Jersey Dept. of Law and Public Safety, Division of Alcholic Beverage Control, P.O. Box 087, Trenton, NJ 08625-0087. Phone: (609)984-2598 Fax: (609)633-6078.

OTHER SOURCES

Liquor Control Law Reports: Federal and All States. CCH, Inc. • $3,338.00 per year. Nine looseleaf volumes. Biweekly updates. Federal and state regulation and taxation of alcoholic beverages.

LIQUOR STORES

FINANCIAL RATIOS

Almanac of Business and Industrial Financial Ratios. Leo Troy. Prentice Hall. • Annual. $99.95. Contains financial ratios derived from federal tax returns. Ratios for each of about 200 industries are arranged according to company asset size.

Annual Statement Studies. Robert Morris Associates: The Association of Lending and Credit Risk Professiona. • Annual. Free to members; non-members, $140.00. Median and quartile financial ratios are given for over 400 kinds of manufacturing, wholesale, retail, construction, and consumer finance establishments. Data is sorted by both asset size and sales volume. Includes a clearly written "Definition of Ratios" and an alphabetical industry index.

PRICE SOURCES

Beverage Media. Beverage Media, Ltd. • Monthly. $78.00 per year. Wholesale prices.

TRADE/PROFESSIONAL ASSOCIATIONS

National Association of Beverage Retailers. 5101 River Rd., Suite 108, Bethesda, MD 20816. Phone: 888-656-3241 or (301)656-1494 Fax: (301)656-7539 • URL: http://www.nabronline.org.

LITERARY AGENTS

See: WRITERS AND WRITING

LITERARY PROPERTY

See: COPYRIGHT

LITERATURE SEARCHING, ONLINE

See: ONLINE INFORMATION SYSTEMS

LITHOGRAPHY

See also: GRAPHIC ARTS INDUSTRY; PRINTING AND PRINTING EQUIPMENT INDUSTRIES

FINANCIAL RATIOS

PIA Financial Ratio Studies. Printing Industries of America, Inc. • Annual. Members, $650.00 set or $100.00 per volume; non-members, $995.00 set or $1,155.00 per volume. 14 volumes.

ONLINE DATABASES

PIRA. Technical Centre for the Paper and Board, Printing and Packaging Industries. • Citations and abstracts pertaining to bookbinding and other pulp, paper, and packaging industries, 1975 to present. Weekly updates. Inquire as to online cost and availability.

PERIODICALS AND NEWSLETTERS

American Printer. Intertec Publishing Corp. • Monthly. Free to qualified personnel; others, $65.00 per year. Serves the printing and lithographic industries and allied manufacturing and service segments.

TRADE/PROFESSIONAL ASSOCIATIONS

National Association of Printers and Lithographers. 75 W. Century Rd., Paramus, NJ 07652-1408. Phone: 800-642-6275 or (201)634-9600 E-mail: info@napl.org • URL: http://www.napl.org.

LIVESTOCK INDUSTRY

See also: CATTLE INDUSTRY; MEAT INDUSTRY; SWINE INDUSTRY

ABSTRACTS AND INDEXES

Animal Breeding Abstracts: A Monthly Abstract of World Literature. Available from CABI Publishing North America. • Monthly. $1095.00 per year. Published in England by CABI Publishing. Provides worldwide coverage of the literature.

Index Veterinarius: Comprehensive Monthly and Author Index to the World's Veterinary Literature. Availabe in Print and on the Internet. Available from CABI Publishing North America. • Monthly. $1,450.00 per year. Published in England by CABI Publishing. Provides worldwide coverage of the literature.

Nutrition Abstracts and Reviews, Series B: Livestock Feeds and Feeding. Available from CABI Publishing North America. • Monthly. $930.00 per year. Published in England by CABI Publishing. Provides worldwide coverage of the literature.

HANDBOOKS AND MANUALS

Stockman's Handbook. R. M. Ensminger. Interstate Publishers, Inc. • 1992. $91.25. Seventh edition.

INTERNET DATABASES

BEEF. National Cattlemen's Beef Association. Phone: (303)694-0305 Fax: (303)694-2851 E-mail: cows@beef.org • URL: http://www.beef.org • Web site provides detailed information from the "Cattle and Beef Handbook," including "Beef Economics" (production, sales, consumption, retail value, foreign competition, etc.). Text of monthly newsletter is also available: "The Beef Brief-Issues & Trends in the Cattle Industry." Keyword searching is offered. Fees: Free.

Fedstats. Federal Interagency Council on Statistical Policy. Phone: (202)395-7254 • URL: http://www.fedstats.gov • Web site features an efficient search facility for full-text statistics produced by more than 70 federal agencies, including the Census Bureau, the Bureau of Economic Analysis, and the Bureau of Labor Statistics. Boolean searches can be made within one agency or for all agencies combined. Links are offered to international statistical bureaus, including the UN, IMF, OECD, UNESCO, Eurostat, and 20 individual countries. Fees: Free.

USDA. United States Department of Agriculture. Phone: (202)720-2791 E-mail: agsec@usda.gov • URL: http://www.usda.gov • The USDA home page has six sections: News and Information; What's New; About USDA; Agencies; Opportunities; Search and Help. Keyword searching is offered from the USDA home page and from various individual agency home pages. Agencies are the Economic Research Service, Agricultural Marketing Service, National Agricultural Statistics Service, National Agricultural Library, and about 12 others. Updating varies. Fees: Free.

ONLINE DATABASES

Biological and Agricultural Index Online. H. W. Wilson Co. • Indexes a wide variety of agricultural and biological periodicals, 1983 to date. Monthly updates. Inquire as to online cost and availability.

CAB Abstracts. CAB International North America. • Contains 46 specialized abstract collections covering over 10,000 journals and monographs in the areas of agriculture, horticulture, forest products, farm products, nutrition, dairy science, poultry, grains, animal health, entomology, etc. Time period is 1972 to date, with monthly updates. Inquire as to online cost and availability. *CAB Abstracts on CD-ROM* also available, with annual updating.

DRI U.S. Central Database. Data Products Division. • Provides more than 23,000 business, financial, demographic, economic, foreign trade, and industry-related time series for the U.S. Includes national income, population, retail-wholesale trade, price indexes, labor data, housing, industrial production, banking, interest rates, money supply, etc. Time period is generally 1947 to date (some data back to 1929). Updating varies. Inquire as to online cost and availability.

PERIODICALS AND NEWSLETTERS

Doane's Agricultural Report. Doane Agricultural Services. • Weekly. $98.00 per year. Edited for "high volume document printing" professionals. Covers imaging, printing, and mailing.

Journal of Animal Science. American Society of Animal Science. • Monthly. $250.00 per year.

Large Animal Practice: Covering Health and Nutrition. Fancy Publications, Inc. • Bimonthly. $40.00 per year. Services the large animal veterinary (food animal) field.

Livestock Production Science. Elsevier Science. • Monthly. $1,288.00.

PRICE SOURCES

The National Provisioner: Serving Meat, Poultry, and Seafood Processors. Stagnito Communications, Inc. • Monthly. Free to qualified personnel; others, $65.00 per year. Annual *Buyer's Guide* available. Meat, poultry and seafood newsletter.

STATISTICS SOURCES

Agricultural Statistics. Available from U. S. Government Printing Office. • Annual. Produced by the National Agricultural Statistics Service, U. S. Department of Agriculture. Provides a wide variety of statistical data relating to agricultural production, supplies, consumption, prices/price-supports, foreign trade, costs, and returns, as well as farm labor, loans, income, and population. In many cases, historical data is shown annually for 10 years. In addition to farm data, includes detailed fishery statistics.

Business Statistics of the United States. Courtenay M. Slater, editor. Bernan Associates. • 1999. $74.00. Fifth edition. Based on *Business Statistics*, formerly issue by the Bureau of Economic Analysis, U. S. Department of Commerce. Provides basic data for a wide variety of U. S. industries, services, and economic indicators. Most statistics are shown annually for 29 years and monthly for the most recent four years.

Livestock, Meat, Wool, Market News. U.S. Department of Agriculture. • Weekly.

Survey of Current Business. Available from U. S. Government Printing Office. • Monthly. $49.00 per year. Issued by Bureau of Economic Analysis, U. S. Department of Commerce. Presents a wide variety of business and economic data.

WEFA Industrial Monitor. John Wiley and Sons, Inc. • Annual. $65.00. Prepared by industry analysts at WEFA, an economic forecasting and consulting firm (originally Wharton Econometric Forecasting Associates). Contains discussions of the outlook for major U. S. industries, with many 10-year forecasts (WEFA Web site is http://www.wefa.com).

TRADE/PROFESSIONAL ASSOCIATIONS

American Society of Animal Science. c/o Ellen Bergfeld, 111 N. Dunlap St., Savoy, IL 61874-9604. Phone: (217)356-3182 Fax: (217)398-4119 E-mail: asas@assochq.org • URL: http://www.asas.edu.

Livestock Marketing Association. 7509 Tiffany Springs Parkway, Kansas City, MO 64153-2315. Phone: 800-821-2048 or (816)891-0502 Fax: (816)891-0552.

National Cattlemen's Beef Association. P.O. Box 3469, Englewood, CO 80155. Phone: (312)467-5520 Fax: (312)467-9767 E-mail: cattle@beef.org • URL: http://www.beef.org/ncba.htm.

LOAN COMPANIES

See: FINANCE COMPANIES; SAVINGS AND LOAN ASSOCIATIONS

LOANS

See: BANK LOANS; CONSUMER CREDIT; CREDIT

LOANS, BANK

See: BANK LOANS

LOANS, COMMERCIAL

See: COMMERCIAL LENDING

LOANS, STUDENT

See: SCHOLARSHIPS AND STUDENT AID

LOBBYING

See: PRESSURE GROUPS

LOBSTER INDUSTRY

See also: SHELLFISH INDUSTRY

ABSTRACTS AND INDEXES

Oceanic Abstracts. Cambridge Information Group. • Bimonthly. $1,045.00 per year. Covers oceanography, marine biology, ocean shipping, and a wide range of other marine-related subject areas.

ONLINE DATABASES

Oceanic Abstracts (Online). Cambridge Scientific Abstracts. • Oceanographic and other marine-related technical literature, 1981 to present.Monthly updates. Inquire as to online cost and availability.

STATISTICS SOURCES

Fisheries of the United States. Available from U. S. Government Printing Office. • Annual. $18.00. Issued by the National Marine Fisheries Service, National Oceanic and Atmospheric Administration, U. S. Department of Commerce.

TRADE/PROFESSIONAL ASSOCIATIONS

Maine Lobstermen's Association. 41 RT 103, York, ME 03909. Phone: (207)337-1676 Fax: (207)363-6783 E-mail: pfarrey.loa.com.

LOCAL AREA NETWORKS

See also: COMPUTER COMMUNICATIONS; MICROCOMPUTERS AND MINICOMPUTERS

GENERAL WORKS

Computer Networks. Andrew S. Tanenbaum. Prentice Hall. • 1996. $85.00. Third edition.

Future Trends in Telecommunications. R. J. Horrocks and R.W. Scarr. John Wiley and Sons, Inc. • 1993. $235.00. Includes fiber optics technology, local area networks, and satellite communications. Discusses the future of telecommunications for the consumer and for industry. *Communication and Distributed Systems Series.*

Local Area Networks. David A. Stamper. Prentice Hall. • 2000. $69.33. Third edition.

ABSTRACTS AND INDEXES

Business Periodicals Index. H. W. Wilson Co. • Monthly, except August, with quarterly and annual cumulations. Service basis for print edition; CD-ROM edition, $1,495.00 per year.

Computer and Control Abstracts. Available from INSPEC, Inc. • Monthly. $2,160.00 per year. Section C of *Science Abstracts.*

Computer and Information Systems Abstracts Journal: An Abstract Journal Pertaining to the Theory, Design, Fabrication and Application of Computer and Information Systems. Cambridge Information Group. • Monthly. $1,045 per year.

Computer Literature Index: A Subject/Author Index to Computer and Data Processing Literature. Applied Computer Research, Inc. • Quarterly, with annual cumulation. $245.00 per year. Contains brief abstracts of book and periodical literature covering all phases of computing, including approximately 70 specific application areas.

Key Abstracts: Computer Communications and Storage. Available from INSPEC, Inc. • Monthly. $240.00 per year. Provides international coverage of journal and proceedings literature, including material on optical disks and networks. Published in England by the Institution of Electrical Engineers (IEE).

Microcomputer Abstracts. Information Today, Inc. • Quarterly. $225.00 per year. Provides abstracts covering a wide variety of personal and business microcomputer literature. Formerly *Microcomputer Index.*

CD-ROM DATABASES

Datapro on CD-ROM: Communications Analyst. Gartner Group, Inc. • Monthly. Price on application. Provides detailed information on products and services for communications systems, including local area networks and voice systems.

DIRECTORIES

Faulkner Information Service. Faulkner Information Services, Inc. • Looseleaf. Monthly updates. Many titles and volumes, covering virtually all aspects of computer software and hardware. Gives descriptions and technical data for specific products, including producers' names and addresses. Prices and details on request. Formerly (The Auerbach Series).

Network Buyers Guide. Miller Freeman. • Annual. $5.00. Lists suppliers of products for local and wide area computer networks. Formerly *LAN Buyers Guide Issue.*

ENCYCLOPEDIAS AND DICTIONARIES

Dictionary of Information Technology and Computer Science. Tony Gunton. Blackwell Publishers. • 1994. $50.95. Second edition. Covers key words, phrases, abbreviations, and acronyms used in computing and data communications.

Dictionary of PC Hardware and Data Communications Terms. Mitchell Shnier. Thomson Learning. • 1996. $19.95. (Online updates to print version available at http://www.ora.com/reference/dictionary.).

Every Manager's Guide to Information Technology: A Glossary of Key Terms and Concepts for Today's Business Leader. Peter G. W. Keen. Harvard Business School Press. • 1995. $18.95. Second edition. Provides definitions of terms related to computers, data communications, and information network systems. (Harvard Business Economist Reference Series).

HANDBOOKS AND MANUALS

Local Area Networks: A Client/Server Approach. James E. Goldman. John Wiley and Sons, Inc. • 1996. $86.95. A business-oriented guide to local area networks and client server architecture. Covers technology, installation, and management, including a glossary of LAN terms.

Local Area Networks in Information Management. Harry M. Kibrige. Greenwood Publishing Group, Inc. • 1989. $55.00. (New Directions in Information Management Series).

Networking Windows for Workgroups. Barry Nance. John Wiley and Sons, Inc. • 1993. $22.95. Designed for small businesses or small groups. Covers the installation and troubleshooting of local area networks using Microsoft's Windows for Workgroups.

ONLINE DATABASES

Internet and Personal Computing Abstracts. Information Today, Inc. • Contains abstracts covering a wide variety of personal and business microcomputer literature appearing in more than 100 journals and popular magazines. Time period is 1981 to date, with monthly updates. Formerly *Microcomputer Index.* Inquire as to online cost and availability.

PROMT: Predicasts Overview of Markets and Technology. The Gale Group. • Companies,

products, applied technologies and markets. U.S. and international literature coverage, 1972 to date. Inquire as to online cost and availability. Provides abstracts from more than 1,600 publications. Weekly updates.

Wilson Business Abstracts Online. H. W. Wilson Co. • Indexes and abstracts 600 major business periodicals, plus the *Wall Street Journal* and the business section of the *New York Times*. Indexing is from 1982, abstracting from 1990, with the two newspapers included from 1993. Updated weekly. Inquire as to online cost and availability. (*Business Periodicals Index* without abstracts is also available online.).

PERIODICALS AND NEWSLETTERS

Computer Reseller News: The Newspaper for Microcomputer Reselling. CMP Publications, Inc. • Weekly. $209.00 per year. Includes bimonthly supplement. Incorporates *Computer Reseller Sources and Macintosh News*. Formerly *Computer Retailer News*.

EDP Weekly: The Leading Weekly Computer News Summary. Computer Age and E D P News Services. • Weekly. $495.00 per year. Newsletter. Summarizes news from all areas of the computer and microcomputer industries.

Exploring Windows NT: Tips & Techniques for Microsoft Windows NT Professionals. Z-D Journals. • Monthly. $99.00 per year. Newsletter on the Windows operating system for networks.

Industrial Computing. ISA Services, Inc. • Monthly. $50.00 per year. Published by the Instrument Society of America. Edited for engineering managers and systems integrators. Subject matter includes industrial software, programmable controllers, artificial intelligence systems, and industrial computer networking systems.

Insurance Networking: Strategies and Solutions for Electronic Commerce. Faulkner & Gray, Inc. • 10 times a year. $63.95 per year. Covers information technology for the insurance industry, with emphasis on computer communications and the Internet.

Intranet and Networking Strategies Report: Advising IT Decision Makers on Best Practices and Current Trends. Computer Economics, Inc. • Monthly. $395.00 per year. Newsletter. Edited for information technology managers. Covers news and trends relating to a variety of corporate computer network and management information systems topics. Emphasis is on costs.

Local Area Networks: Newsletter Covering Worldwide Technology Trends, Applications and Markets. Information Gatekeepers, Inc. • Monthly. $695.00 per year. Cover new developments, new products, and marketing.

Managing Automation. Thomas Publishing Co. • Monthly. Free to qualified personnel. Coverage includes software for manufacturing, systems planning, integration in process industry automation, computer integrated manufacturing (CIM), computer networks for manufacturing, management problems, industry news, and new products.

Network Computing: Computing in a Network Environment. CMP Publications, Inc. • Semimonthly. $95.00 per year.

Network: Strategies and Solutions for the Network Professional. Miller Freeman. • Monthly. $29.95 per year. Covers network products and peripherals for computer professionals. Includes annual network managers salary survey and annual directory issue. Formerly *LAN: The Network Solutions Magazine*.

Network World: The Newsweekly of Enterprise Network Computing. Network World Inc. • Weekly. $129.00 per year. Includes special feature issues on enterprise Internets, network operating systems, network management, high-speed modems, LAN management systems, and Internet access providers.

Wireless Data News. Phillips Business Information, Inc. • 25 times a year. $797.00 per year. Newsletter. Covers the wireless data communications industry, including wireless LANs.

RESEARCH CENTERS AND INSTITUTES

Center for Advanced Technology in Computers and Information Systems. Columbia University, 161 Fort Washington Ave., AP1310, New York, NY 10032. Phone: (212)305-2944 Fax: (212)305-0196 E-mail: d1330@columbia.edu • URL: http://www.cpmc.columbia.edu/catc/.

Center for Research in Computing Technology. Harvard University, Pierce Hall, 29 Oxford St., Cambridge, MA 02138. Phone: (617)495-2832 Fax: (617)495-9837 E-mail: cheatham@das.harvard.edu • URL: http://www.das.harvard.edu/cs.grafs.html • Conducts research in computer vision, robotics, artificial intelligence, systems programming, programming languages, operating systems, networks, graphics, database management systems, and telecommunications.

Laboratory for Information and Decision Systems. Massachusetts Institute of Technology, Bldg. 35, Room 308, Cambridge, MA 02139-4307. Phone: (617)253-2141 Fax: (617)253-3578 E-mail: chan@mit.edu • URL: http://www.justice.mit.edu • Research areas include data communication networks and fiber optic networks.

STATISTICS SOURCES

Standard & Poor's Industry Surveys. Standard & Poor's. • Semiannual. $1,800.00. Two looseleaf volumes. Includes monthly supplements. Provides detailed, individual surveys of 52 major industry groups. Each survey is revised on a semiannual basis. Also includes "Monthly Investment Review" (industry group investment analysis) and monthly "Trends & Projections" (economic analysis).

U. S. Industry and Trade Outlook: The McGraw-Hill Companies and the U.S. Department of Commerce/International Trade Administration. Datapso Research Corp. • Annual. $69.95. Produced by the International Trade Administration, U. S. Department of Commerce, in a "public-private" partnership with DRI/McGraw-Hill and Standard & Poor's. Provides basic data, outlook for the current year, and "Long-Term Prospects" (five-year projections) for a wide variety of products and services. Includes high technology industries. Formerly *U. S. Industrial Outlook*.

TRADE/PROFESSIONAL ASSOCIATIONS

Computer and Communications Industry Association. 666 11th St., N.W., Suite 600, Washington, DC 20001. Phone: (202)783-0070 Fax: (202)783-0534 E-mail: ccianet@aol.com • URL: http://www.ccianet.org.

Instrument Society of America (ISA). P.O. Box 12277, Research Triangle Park, NC 27709. Phone: (919)549-8411 Fax: (919)549-8288 E-mail: info@isa.org • URL: http://www.isa.org • Members are engineers and others concerned with industrial instrumentation, systems, computers, and automation.

International Council for Computer Communication. P.O. Box 9745, Washington, DC 20016-9745. Phone: (703)836-7787 Fax: (703)836-7787 E-mail: iccc@icccgovernors.org • URL: http://www.icccgovernors.org.

OTHER SOURCES

DataWorld. Faulkner Information Services, Inc. • Four looseleaf volumes, with monthly supplements. $1,395.00 per year. Describes and evaluates both hardware and software relating to midrange, micro, and mainframe computers. Available on CD-ROM.

Faulkner's Local Area Networking. Faulkner Information Services, Inc. • Looseleaf, with monthly updates. $715.00 per year. Contains product reports and other information relating to PC networking, including security, gateways/bridges, and emerging standards. Formerly *Microcomputer Communications*.

LOCAL GOVERNMENT

See: COUNTY GOVERNMENT; MUNICIPAL GOVERNMENT; STATE GOVERNMENT

LOCATION OF INDUSTRY

See also: INDUSTRIAL DEVELOPMENT

GENERAL WORKS

Industrial Location: Principles and Policies. J.W. Harrington and Barney Warf. Routledge. • 1995. $85.00. Second revised edition.

DIRECTORIES

Site Selection. Conway Data, Inc. • Bimonthly. Six volumes, $20.00 per volume. $85.00 per set. Each of the six issues per year is a separate directory: *Geo-Corporate* (facility planners), *Geo-Economic* (area development officials), *Geo-Labor* (labor force data), *Geo-Life* (quality of life information), *GeoPolitical* (government agencies), and *Geo-Sites* (industrial/office parks). Formerly *Site Selection and Industrial Development*.

PERIODICALS AND NEWSLETTERS

Area Development Sites and Facility Planning: The Executive Magazine of Sites and Facility Planning. S H Publications, Inc. • Monthly. $65.00 per year. Site selection, facility planning, and plant relocation. Formerly *Area Development Magazines*.

Business Facilities. Group C Communications. • Monthly. $30.00 per year. Facility planning and site selection.

Expansion Management: Growth Strategies for Companies on the Move. Penton Media Inc., Industry Div. • Monthly. Free qualified personnel; others, $40.00 per year. Subject matter is concerned with expansion and relocation of industrial facilities.

Insulation Outlook: Business Solutions for Expanding or Relocating Companies. National Insulation Association. • $45.00 per year. Covers site selection and related topics.

New Plant Report. Conway Data Inc. • Monthly. $1,800.00 per year. Provides geographical listings of annoucements of corporate facility location plans and facility expansions. International coverage.

Plants, Sites, and Parks. Cahners Business Information. • Bimonthly. $30.00 per year. Covers economic development, site location, industrial parks, and industrial development programs.

STATISTICS SOURCES

Ernst & Young Almanac and Guide to U. S. Business Cities: 65 Leading Places to Do Business. John Wiley and Sons, Inc. • 1994. $16.95. Provides demographic, business, economic, and site selection data for 65 major U. S. cities.

LOCKOUTS

See: STRIKES AND LOCKOUTS

LOCKS AND KEYS

See also: INDUSTRIAL SECURITY PROGRAMS

DIRECTORIES

Locksmith Ledger-International Directory. Locksmith Publishing Corp. • Annual. $28.00 per year. Formerly *Locksmith Ledger-Security Guide and Directory.*

HANDBOOKS AND MANUALS

Complete Course in Professional Locksmithing. Robert L. Robinson. Burnham, Inc. • 1973. $68.95.

Effective Physical Security: Design, Equipment, and Operations. Lawrence J. Fennelly, editor. Butterworth-Heinemann. • 1996. $36.95. Second edition. Contains chapters written by various U. S. security equipment specialists. Covers architectural considerations, locks, safes, alarms, intrusion detection systems, closed circuit television, identification systems, etc.

PERIODICALS AND NEWSLETTERS

Keynotes. Associated Locksmiths of America, Inc. • Monthly. Membership.

Locksmith Ledger International. Locksmith Publishing Corp. • Monthly. $38.00 per year. Includes *Directory* issue. Formerly *Locksmith Ledger.*

National Locksmith. National Publishing Co. • Monthly. $41.00.

TRADE/PROFESSIONAL ASSOCIATIONS

Associated Locksmiths of America. 3003 Live Oak St., Dallas, TX 75204. Phone: 800-532-2562 or (214)827-1701 Fax: (214)827-1810 E-mail: aloa@aloa.org • URL: http://www.aloa.org.

Security Hardwear Distributors Association. 1900 Arch St., Philadelphia, PA 19103-1498. Phone: (215)564-3484 Fax: (215)564-2175 E-mail: assnhqt@netaxs.com.

LOCOMOTIVES

See: RAILROADS

LOGGING

See: LUMBER INDUSTRY

LOGISTIC RESEARCH

See: OPERATIONS RESEARCH

LOGOS

See: CORPORATE IMAGE; TRADEMARKS AND TRADE NAMES

LONG-TERM CARE INSURANCE

See also: HEALTH INSURANCE; NURSING HOMES

GENERAL WORKS

Caring for Frail Elderly People: New Directions in Care. OECD Publications and Information Center. • 1994. $27.00. Discusses the problem in OECD countries of providing good quality care to the elderly at manageable cost. Includes trends in family care, housing policies, and private financing.

Fundamentals of Employee Benefit Programs. Employee Benefit Research Institute. • 1996. $49.95. Fifth edition. Provides basic explanation of employee benefit programs in both the private and public sectors, including health insurance, pension plans, retirement planning, social security, and long-term care insurance.

Long-Term Care and Its Alternatives. Charles B. Inlander. People's Medical Society. • 1996. $16.95. Provides practical advice on the financing of long-term health care. The author is a consumer advocate and president of the People's Medical Society.

Managed Care: The Vision and the Strategy. American Association of Homes and Services for the Aging. • 1996. $30.00. A report on an AAHSA national managed care summit. Topics include delivery models, regulatory conflicts, costs, finances, consumer choice, and related subjects.

Sharing the Burden: Strategies for Public and Private Long-Term Care Insurance. Joshua M. Wiener and others. Brookings Institution Press. • 1994. $42.95.

A Shopper's Guide to Long-Term Care Insurance. DIANE Publishing Co. • 1995. $15.00. Revised edition. Provides impartial, consumer-oriented information and advice on long-term care insurance policies. Includes worksheets.

ABSTRACTS AND INDEXES

Insurance Periodicals Index. Specials Libraries Association, Insurance and Employees Benefits Div. CCH/NILS Publishing Co. • Annual. $250.00. Compiled by the Insurance and Employee Benefits Div., Special Libraries Association. A yearly index of over 15,000 articles from about 35 insurance periodicals. Arrangement is by subject, with an index to authors.

Readers' Guide to Periodical Literature. H. W. Wilson Co. • Monthly. $220.00 per year. CD-ROM edition, $1,495 per year, including annual cumulation. Indexes about 250 peridicals of general interest.

BIBLIOGRAPHIES

Long-Term Care: An Annotated Bibliography. Theodore H. Koff. Greenwood Publishing Group, Inc. • 1995. $59.95.

ENCYCLOPEDIAS AND DICTIONARIES

Rupp's Insurance and Risk Management Glossary. Richard V. Rupp. Available from CCH, Inc. • 1996. $35.00. Second edition. Published by NILS Publishing Co. Provides definitions of 6,400 insurance words and phrases. Includes a guide to acronyms and abbreviations.

HANDBOOKS AND MANUALS

The Complete Book of Insurance: The Consumer's Guide to Insuring Your Life, Health, Property, and Income. Ben G. Baldwin. McGraw-Hill Professional. • 1996. $24.95. Revised edition. Provides basic information and advice on various kinds of insurance: life, health, property (fire), disability, long-term care, automobile, liability, and annuities.

How to Cover the Gaps in Medicare: Health Insurance and Long-Term Care Options for the Retired. Robert A. Gilmour. American Institute for Economic Research. • 2000. $5.00. 12th revised edition. Four parts: "The Medicare Quandry," "How to Protect Yourself Against the Medigap," "Long-Term Care Options", and "End-of-Life Decisions" (living wills). Includes discussions of long-term care insurance, retirement communities, and HMO Medicare insurance, (Economic Education Bulletin Series, No. 10).

An Insurance Guide for Seniors. Insurance Forum, Inc. • 1997. $15.00. Provides concise advice and information on Medicare, Medicare supplement insurance, HMOs, long-term care insurance, automobile insurance, life insurance, annuities, and pensions. An appendix lists "Financially Strong Insurance Companies." (*The Insurance Forum*, vol. 24, no. 4.).

The Managed Care Contracting Handbook: Planning and Negotiating the Managed Care Relationship. Maria K. Todd. Available from McGraw Hill Higher Education. • 1996. $65.00. Copublished by McGraw-Hill Healthcare Education Group and the Healthcare Financial Management Association. Covers managed care planning, proposals, strategy, negotiation, and contract law. Written for healthcare providers.

INTERNET DATABASES

InsWeb. InsWeb Corp. Phone: (650)372-2129 E-mail: info@insweb.com • URL: http://www.insweb.com • Web site offers a wide variety of advice and information on automobile, life, health, and "other" insurance. Includes glossaries of insurance terms, Standard & Poor's ratings of individual insurance companies, and "Financial Needs Estimators." Searching is available. Fees: Free.

ONLINE DATABASES

Ageline. American Association of Retired Persons. • Provides indexing and abstracting of the literature of social gerontology, including consumer aspects, financial planning, employment, housing, health care services, mental health, social security, and retirement. Time period is 1978 to date. Inquire as to online cost and availability.

Readers' Guide Abstracts Online. H. W. Wilson Co. • Indexes and abstracts general interest periodicals, 1983 to date. Weekly updates. Inquire as to online cost and availability.

PERIODICALS AND NEWSLETTERS

Advisory Today. National Association of insurance and Finacial Advisors. • Monthly. Free to members; non-members, $7.00 per year. Edited for individual life and health insurance agents. Among the topics included are disability insurance and long-term care insurance. Formerly Life Association News.

Financial Planning: The Magazine for Financial Service Professionals. Securities Data Publishing. • Monthly. $79.00 per year. Edited for independent financial planners and insurance agents. Covers retirement planning, estate planning, tax planning, and insurance, including long-term healthcare considerations. Special features include a Retirement Planning Issue, Mutual Fund Performance Survey, and Variable Life and Annuity Survey. (Securities Data Publishing is a unit of Thomson Financial.).

Health Insurance Underwriter. National Association of Health Underwriters. • 11 times a year. Free to members; non-members, $25.00 per year. Includes special feature issues on long-term care insurance, disability insurance, managed health care, and insurance office management.

Jounal of Finacial Services Professionals. American Society of CLU and Ch F C. • Bimonthly. $38.00 per year. Provides information on life insurance and financial planning, including estate planning, retirement, tax planning, trusts, business insurance, long-term care insurance, disability insurance, and employee benefits. Formerly (American Society of CLU and Ch F C Journal).

RESEARCH CENTERS AND INSTITUTES

Division of Health Services Research and Policy. University of Minnesota, P.O. Box 729, Minneapolis, MN 55455. Phone: (612)624-6151 Fax: (612)624-2196 E-mail: foote003@tc.umn.edu • URL: http://www.hsr.umn.edu • Fields of research include health insurance, consumer choice of health plans, quality of care, and long-term care.

Employee Benefit Research Institute. 2121 K St., N. W., Suite 600, Washington, DC 20037-1896. Phone: (202)659-0670 Fax: (202)775-6312 E-mail: salisbury@ebri.org • URL: http://www.ebri.org • Conducts research on employee benefits, including various kinds of pensions, individual retirement accounts (IRAs), health insurance, social security, and long-term health care benefits.

Health Management and Policy. University of Michigan, 109 S. Observatory St., Ann Arbor, MI 48109-2029. Phone: (734)763-9903 Fax: (734)764-4338 E-mail: weissert@umich.edu • URL: http://www.sph.umich.edu/ • Research fields include health care economics, health insurance, and long-term care.

Institute for Health Policy Research. Health Science Center, J. Hillis Miller Health Center, University of Florida, P.O. Box 100177, Gainesville, FL 32610-0177. Phone: (352)395-8039 Fax: (352)395-8047 E-mail: admin@hpe.ufl.edu • URL: http://www.hpe.ufl.edu • Research areas include health economics, financing, and long-term care considerations.

STATISTICS SOURCES

EBRI Databook on Employee Benefits. Employee Benefit Research Institute. • 1997 $99.00. Fourth edition. Contains more than 350 tables and charts presenting data on employee benefits in the U. S., including pensions, health insurance, social security, and medicare. Includes a glossary of employee benefit terms.

TRADE/PROFESSIONAL ASSOCIATIONS

Families U. S. A. Foundation. 1334 G St., N. W., Washington, DC 20005. Phone: (202)628-3030 Fax: (202)347-2417 E-mail: info@familiesusa.org • URL: http://www.familiesusa.org • Fields of interest are health care and long-term health care, including insurance.

Health Insurance Association of America. 555 13th St., N.W., Washington, DC 20004. Phone: (202)824-1600 Fax: (202)824-1722 • URL: http://www.hiaa.org • Members are commercial health insurers. Includes a Managed Care and Group Insurance Committee, a Disability Insurance Committee, a Medicare Administration Committee, and a Long-Term Care Task Force.

Long-Term Care Campaign. P.O. Box 27394, Washington, DC 20038. Phone: (202)434-3744 or (202)434-3829 Fax: (202)434-6403 E-mail: info@ltccampaign.org • URL: http://www.ltccampaign.org • Promotes legislation that would provide social insurance for long-term health care.

National Association Insurance and Financial Advisors. 1922 F St., N.W., Washington, DC 20006-4387. Phone: (202)331-6000 Fax: (202)835-9601 • URL: http://www.naifa.org.

National Association of Health Underwriters. 200 N. 14th St., Ste. 450, Arlington, VA 22201. Phone: (703)276-0220 Fax: (703)841-7797 • URL: http://www.nahu.org • Members are engaged in the sale of health and disability insurance.

National Institute on Community-Based Long-Term Care. c/o National Council on the Aging, 409 Third St., S.W., Suite 200, Washington, DC 20024. Phone: (202)479-1200 Fax: (202)479-0735 E-mail: info@ncoa.org • URL: http://www.ncoa.org • Affiliated with the National Council on the Aging. Seeks to promote and develop a comprehensive long-term health care system.

OTHER SOURCES

The Long-Term Care Market. MarketResearch.com. • 1999. $3,250.00. Market data with forecasts to the year 2005. Emphasis is on the over-85 age group. Covers health insurance, the nursing home industry, pharmaceuticals, healthcare supplies, etc.

LONG-TERM HEALTH CARE INDUSTRY

See: HEALTH CARE INDUSTRY; NURSING HOMES

LOW TEMPERATURE TECHNOLOGY

See: CRYOGENICS

LUBRICATION AND LUBRICANTS

See also: PETROLEUM INDUSTRY

ABSTRACTS AND INDEXES

NLGI Spokesman. National Lubricating Grease Institute. • Monthly. $24.00 per year. Information about the lubricating grease industry.

NTIS Alerts: Materials Sciences. National Technical Information Service. • Semimonthly. $220.00 per year. Provides descriptions of government-sponsored research reports and software, with ordering information. Covers ceramics, glass, coatings, composite materials, alloys, plastics, wood, paper, adhesives, fibers, lubricants, and related subjects. Formerly *Abstract Newsletter.*

DIRECTORIES

McCutcheon's Functional Materials: North American Edition. Publishing Co., McCutcheon Div. • Annual. $170.00. Two volumes. North American edition contains detailed information on surfactant-related products produced in North America. Examples are enzymes, lubricants, waxes, and corrosion inhibitors. Company names, addresses and telephone numbers are included. International edition contains detailed information on surfactant-related products produced in Europe and Asia. Examples are enzymes, lubricants, waxes, and corrosion inhibitors. Company names, addresses, and telephone numbers are included.

FINANCIAL RATIOS

Annual Statement Studies. Robert Morris Associates: The Association of Lending and Credit Risk Professiona. • Annual. Free to members; non-members, $140.00. Median and quartile financial ratios are given for over 400 kinds of manufacturing, wholesale, retail, construction, and consumer finance establishments. Data is sorted by both asset size and sales volume. Includes a clearly written "Definition of Ratios" and an alphabetical industry index.

HANDBOOKS AND MANUALS

Maintenance Engineering Handbook. Lindley R. Higgins. McGraw-Hill. • 1994. $125.00. Fifth edition. Contains about 60 chapters by various authors in 12 major sections covering all elements of industrial and plant maintenance.

PERIODICALS AND NEWSLETTERS

Journal of Tribology. American Society of Mechanical Engineers. • Quarterly. Members, $40.00 per year; non-members, $255.00 per year. Details lubrication and lubricants.

Lubrication Engineering. Society of Tribiologists and Lubrication Engineers. • Monthly. $70.00 per year.

Tribology International; The Practice and Technology of Lubrication, Wear Prevention and Friction Control. Elsevier Science. • Bimonthly. $1,253. 00 per year.

TRADE/PROFESSIONAL ASSOCIATIONS

National Lubricating Grease Institute. 4635 Wyandotte St., Kansas City, MO 64112. Phone: (816)931-9480 Fax: (816)753-5026.

Society of Tribologists and Lubrication Engineers. 840 Busse Highway, Park Ridge, IL 60068-2376. Phone: (847)825-5536 Fax: (847)825-1456 E-mail: esalek@stle.org • URL: http://www.stle.org.

LUGGAGE INDUSTRY

DIRECTORIES

Travelware Resources Directory. Business Journals, Inc. • Annual. $20.00. Manufacturers of trunks, luggage, brief cases, and personal leather goods are listed. Formerly *Luggage and Travelware Directory.*

FINANCIAL RATIOS

Annual Statement Studies. Robert Morris Associates: The Association of Lending and Credit Risk Professiona. • Annual. Free to members; non-members, $140.00. Median and quartile financial ratios are given for over 400 kinds of manufacturing, wholesale, retail, construction, and consumer finance establishments. Data is sorted by both asset size and sales volume. Includes a clearly written "Definition of Ratios" and an alphabetical industry index.

PERIODICALS AND NEWSLETTERS

Newsbreak. Leather Industries of America. • Free to members and other qualified personnel. Reports on issues and events in the luggage industry.

Travelware. Business Journals, Inc. • Seven times a year. $32.00. Formerly *Luggage and Travelware.*

STATISTICS SOURCES

U. S. Industry and Trade Outlook: The McGraw-Hill Companies and the U.S. Department of Commerce/ International Trade Administration. Datapso Research Corp. • Annual. $69.95. Produced by the International Trade Administration, U. S. Department of Commerce, in a "public-private" partnership with DRI/McGraw-Hill and Standard & Poor's. Provides basic data, outlook for the current year, and "Long-Term Prospects" (five-year projections) for a wide variety of products and services. Includes high technology industries. Formerly *U. S. Industrial Outlook.*

TRADE/PROFESSIONAL ASSOCIATIONS

Luggage and Leather Goods Manufacturers of America. 350 Fifth Ave., Suite 2624, New York, NY 10118. Phone: 800-826-4224 or (212)695-2340 Fax: (212)643-8021 E-mail: llgma@llgma.org • URL: http://www.llgma.org.

National Luggage Dealers Association. 3338 W. Lake Ave., Glenview, IL 60025. Phone: (847)998-6869 Fax: (847)998-6884.

LUMBER INDUSTRY

See also: FOREST PRODUCTS; HARDWOOD INDUSTRY; PLYWOOD INDUSTRY; WOODWORKING INDUSTRIES

GENERAL WORKS

Managing the World's Forests: Looking for Balance Between Conservation and Development. Narendra P. Sharma. Kendall-Hunt Publishing Co. • 1992. $35.95. A study by The World Bank.

ABSTRACTS AND INDEXES

Forest Products Abstracts. CABI Publishing North America. • Bimonthly. $1,155.00 per year. Published in England by CABI Publishing. Provides worldwide coverage of forest products literature.

Forestry Abstracts: Compiled from World Literature. Available from CABI Publishing North

America. • Monthly. $1,155 per year. Published in England by CABI Publishing. Provides worldwide coverage of the literature.

DIRECTORIES

Building Supply Home Centers Retail Giants Report. Cahners Business Information. • Annual. $30.00. Lists major retailers of a wide variety of building and home improvement materials, products, fixtures, accessories, equipment, and tools.

Directory of the Wood Products Industry. Miller Freeman, Inc. • Biennial. $295.00. Lists sawmills, panelmills, logging operations, plywood products, wood products, distributors, etc. Geographic arrangement, with an index to lumber specialities. Formerly *Directory of the Forest Products Industry.*

Lumbermens Red Book: Reference Book of the Lumbermens Credit Association. Lumbermens Credit Association. • Semiannual $2,057.00 per year. Weekly supplements. Lists United States firms in the lumber and woodworking industries, with credit ratings.

Timber Harvesting Loggers' Resource Guide. Hatton Brown Publishers, Inc. • Annual. $10.00. List of industrial timber corporations; manufacturers and distributors of equipment used in harvesting and handling timber. Formerly *Timber Harvesting-Wood and Woodlands Directory.*

ENCYCLOPEDIAS AND DICTIONARIES

Encyclopedia of Wood: A Tree by Tree Guide to the World's Most Valuable Resource. Bill Lincoln and others. Facts on File, Inc. • 1989. $29.95.

Illustrated Dictionary of Building Materials and Techniques: An Invaluable Sourcebook to the Tools, Terms, Materials, and Techniques Used by Building Professionals. Paul Bianchina. John Wiley and Sons, Inc. • 1993. $49.95. Contains 4,000 definitions of building and building materials terms, with 500 illustrations. Includes materials grades, measurements, and specifications.

FINANCIAL RATIOS

Almanac of Business and Industrial Financial Ratios. Leo Troy. Prentice Hall. • Annual. $99.95. Contains financial ratios derived from federal tax returns. Ratios for each of about 200 industries are arranged according to company asset size.

Cost of Doing Business and Financial Position Survey of the Retail Lumber and Building Material Dealers of the Northeastern States. Northeastern Retail Lumber Association. • Annual. Free to members; non-members, $300.00. Includes sales figures, profit margins, pricing methods, rates of return, and other financial data for retailers of lumber and building supplies in the Northeast.

HANDBOOKS AND MANUALS

Timber Construction Manual. American Institute of Timber Construction Staff. John Wiley and Sons, Inc. • 1994. $130.00. Fourth edition.

INTERNET DATABASES

Fedstats. Federal Interagency Council on Statistical Policy. Phone: (202)395-7254 • URL: http://www.fedstats.gov • Web site features an efficient search facility for full-text statistics produced by more than 70 federal agencies, including the Census Bureau, the Bureau of Economic Analysis, and the Bureau of Labor Statistics. Boolean searches can be made within one agency or for all agencies combined. Links are offered to international statistical bureaus, including the UN, IMF, OECD, UNESCO, Eurostat, and 20 individual countries. Fees: Free.

USDA. United States Department of Agriculture. Phone: (202)720-2791 E-mail: agsec@usda.gov • URL: http://www.usda.gov • The USDA home page has six sections: News and Information; What's New; About USDA; Agencies; Opportunities; Search and Help. Keyword searching is offered from the USDA home page and from various individual agency home pages. Agencies are the Economic Research Service, Agricultural Marketing Service, National Agricultural Statistics Service, National Agricultural Library, and about 12 others. Updating varies. Fees: Free.

ONLINE DATABASES

DRI U.S. Central Database. Data Products Division. • Provides more than 23,000 business, financial, demographic, economic, foreign trade, and industry-related time series for the U.S. Includes national income, population, retail-wholesale trade, price indexes, labor data, housing, industrial production, banking, interest rates, money supply, etc. Time period is generally 1947 to date (some data back to 1929). Updating varies. Inquire as to online cost and availability.

PROMT: Predicasts Overview of Markets and Technology. The Gale Group. • Companies, products, applied technologies and markets. U.S. and international literature coverage, 1972 to date. Inquire as to online cost and availability. Provides abstracts from more than 1,600 publications. Weekly updates.

PERIODICALS AND NEWSLETTERS

Building Material Retailer. National Lumber and Building Material Dealers Association. • Monthly. $25.00 per year. Includes special feature issues on hand and power tools, lumber, roofing, kitchens, flooring, windows and doors, and insulation.

Lumber Co-Operator. Northeastern Retail Lumber Association. • Bimonthly. Members, $35.00 per year; non-members, $40.00 per year.

Random Lengths: The Weekly Report on North American Forest Products Markets. Random Lengths Publications, Inc. • Weekly. $249.50 per year. Newsletter. Information covering the wood products industry. Supplement available *Random Lengths Midweek Market Report.*

Southern Lumberman. Greysmith Publishing, Inc. • 13 times a year. $23.00 per year. A magazine for the sawmill industry.

Timber Harvesting. Hatton Brown Publishers, Inc. • 10 times a year. $40.00 per year.

Tree Planters' Notes. Available from U. S. Government Printing Office. • Quarterly. $10.00 per year. Issued by the Forest Service, U. S. Department of Agriculture. Covers reforestation and related forestry issues.

Wood and Wood Products: Furniture, Cabinets, Woodworking and Allied Products Management and Operations. Vance Publishing Corp. • 13 times a year. $50.00 per year.

Wood Technology: Logging, Pulpwood, Forestry, Lumber, Panels. Miller Freeman, Inc. • Eight times a year. $120.00 per year. Formerly *Forest Industries.*

STATISTICS SOURCES

Agricultural Statistics. Available from U. S. Government Printing Office. • Annual. Produced by the National Agricultural Statistics Service, U. S. Department of Agriculture. Provides a wide variety of statistical data relating to agricultural production, supplies, consumption, prices/price-supports, foreign trade, costs, and returns, as well as farm labor, loans, income, and population. In many cases, historical data is shown annually for 10 years. In addition to farm data, includes detailed fishery statistics.

Annual Survey of Manufactures. Available from U. S. Government Printing Office. • Annual. Prices vary. Issued by the U. S. Census Bureau as an interim update to the *Census of Manufactures.* Includes data on number of manufacturing establishments in various industries, employment, labor costs, value of shipments, capital expenditures, inventories, energy costs, and assets. (See also Census Bureau home page, http://www.census.gov/.).

Business Statistics of the United States. Courtenay M. Slater, editor. Bernan Associates. • 1999. $74.00. Fifth edition. Based on *Business Statistics*, formerly issue by the Bureau of Economic Analysis, U. S. Department of Commerce. Provides basic data for a wide variety of U. S. industries, services, and economic indicators. Most statistics are shown annually for 29 years and monthly for the most recent four years.

Lumber Production and Mill Stocks. U.S. Bureau of the Census. • Annual. (Current Industrial Reports MA-24T).

Manufacturing Profiles. Available from U. S. Government Printing Office. • Annual. Issued by the U. S. Census Bureau. A printed consolidation of the entire *Current Industrial Report* series, presenting "all the data compiled." Contains statistics on production, shipments, inventories, consumption, exports, imports, and orders for a wide variety of manufactured products. (See also Census Bureau home page, http://www.census.gov/.).

Survey of Current Business. Available from U. S. Government Printing Office. • Monthly. $49.00 per year. Issued by Bureau of Economic Analysis, U. S. Department of Commerce. Presents a wide variety of business and economic data.

Timber Bulletin. Economic Commission for Europe. United Nations Publications. • Irregular. Price on application. Contains international statistics on forest products, including price, production, and foreign trade data.

WEFA Industrial Monitor. John Wiley and Sons, Inc. • Annual. $65.00. Prepared by industry analysts at WEFA, an economic forecasting and consulting firm (originally Wharton Econometric Forecasting Associates). Contains discussions of the outlook for major U. S. industries, with many 10-year forecasts (WEFA Web site is http://www.wefa.com).

TRADE/PROFESSIONAL ASSOCIATIONS

American Hardware Export Council. 1111 19th St., N.W., Suite 800, Washington, DC 20036. Phone: (202)463-2720 Fax: (202)463-2787 E-mail: andrew-roberts@afandpa.org • URL: http://www.ahec.org.

American Lumber Standards Committee. P.O. Box 210, Germantown, MD 20875. Phone: (301)972-1700 Fax: (301)540-8004 E-mail: alsc@alsc.org.

National Hardwood Lumber Association. P.O. Box 34518, Memphis, TN 38184-0518. Phone: (901)377-1818 Fax: (901)382-6419 • URL: http://www.natlhardwood.org • Members are hardwood lumber and veneer manufacturers and distributors. Users of hardwood products are also members.

National Lumber and Building Materials Dealers Association. 40 Ivy St., S.E., Washington, DC 20003. Phone: 800-634-8695 or (202)547-2230 Fax: (202)547-8645.

LUNCHROOMS

See: RESTAURANTS, LUNCHROOMS, ETC.

LUNCHROOMS, EMPLOYEE

See: EMPLOYEE LUNCHROOMS AND CAFETERIAS

M

MACARONI

PRICE SOURCES

Supermarket News: The Industry's Weekly Newspaper. Fairchild Publications. • Weekly. Individuals, $68.00 per year; instututions, $44.50 per year; corporations, $89.00 per year.

TRADE/PROFESSIONAL ASSOCIATIONS

National Pasta Association. 2101 Wilson Blvd., No. 920, Arlington, VA 22201. Phone: (703)841-0818 Fax: (703)528-6507 E-mail: npa@ibm.net • URL: http://www.ilovepasta.org.

MACHINE DESIGN

See also: MECHANICAL ENGINEERING

HANDBOOKS AND MANUALS

Design of Machine Elements. Merhyle F. Spotts and Terry E. Shoup. Prentice Hall. • 1997. $105.00. Seventh edition.

McGraw-Hill Machining and Metalworking Handbook. Ronald A. Walsh. McGraw-Hill. • 1998. $99.95. Second edition. Coverage includes machinery, machining techniques, machine tools, machine design, parts, fastening, and plating.

Mechanical Engineering Design. Charles R. Mischke. McGraw-Hill. • 2000. $85.00. Sixth edition. (Mechanical Engineering Series).

Mechanical Engineer's Reference Book. E. H. Smith, editor. Society of Automotive Engineers, Inc. • 1994. $135.00. 12th edition. Covers mechanical engineering principles, computer integrated engineering systems, design standards, materials, power transmission, and many other engineering topics. (Authored Royalty Series).

PERIODICALS AND NEWSLETTERS

Advanced Manufacturing Technology: Monthly Report. Technical Insights. • Monthly. $695.00 per year. Newsletter. Covers technological developments relating to robotics, computer graphics, automation, computer-integrated manufacturing, and machining.

International Journal of Machine Tools and Manufacture: Design, Research and Application. Elsevier Science. • Monthly. $2,273 per year.

Journal of Mechanical Design. American Society of Mechanical Engineers. • Quarterly. Members, $40.00 per year; non-members, $215.00 per year. Formerly *Journal of Mechanisms, Transmissions and Automation in Design.*

Machine Design: Magazine of Applied Technology for Design Engineering. Penton Media, Inc. • 23 times a year. Free to qualified personnel; others, $105.00 per year. Includes *Machine Design Reference Issues* and *Penton Executive Network.*

Mechanism and Machine Theory. Elsevier Science. • Eight times a year $2,106.00 per year.

MACHINE SHOPS

DIRECTORIES

Dun's Industrial Guide: The Metalworking Directory. Dun and Bradstreet Information Services Dun & Bradstreet Corp. • Annual. Libraries, $485; commercial institutions, $795.00. Lease basis. Three volumes. Lists about 65,000 U. S. manufacturing plants using metal and suppliers of metalworking equipment and materials. Includes names and titles of key personnel. Products, purchases, and processes are indicated.

FINANCIAL RATIOS

Annual Statement Studies. Robert Morris Associates: The Association of Lending and Credit Risk Professiona. • Annual. Free to members; non-members, $140.00. Median and quartile financial ratios are given for over 400 kinds of manufacturing, wholesale, retail, construction, and consumer finance establishments. Data is sorted by both asset size and sales volume. Includes a clearly written "Definition of Ratios" and an alphabetical industry index.

HANDBOOKS AND MANUALS

Machine Shop Operations and Setups. Orville D. Lascoe and others. American Technical Publishers, Inc. • 1973. $25.96. Fourth edition.

Machine Shop Practice. K. H. Meltrecht. Industrial Press, Inc. • 1981. $41.90. Second edition. Two volumes. Vol. one, $20.95; vol. two, $20.95.

McGraw-Hill Machining and Metalworking Handbook. Ronald A. Walsh. McGraw-Hill. • 1998. $99.95. Second edition. Coverage includes machinery, machining techniques, machine tools, machine design, parts, fastening, and plating.

PERIODICALS AND NEWSLETTERS

Modern Machine Shop. Gardner Publications, Inc. • Monthly. $50.00 per year.

MACHINE TOOL INDUSTRY

See also: TOOL INDUSTRY

ABSTRACTS AND INDEXES

Cutting Technology. Penton Media, Inc. • Monthly. Controlled circulation. Provides abstracts of the international literature of metal cutting and machining. Formerly *Cutting Tool-Mchine Digest.*

NTIS Alerts: Manufacturing Technology. National Technical Information Service. • Semimonthly. $265.00 per year. Provides descriptions of government-sponsored research reports and software, with ordering information. Covers computer-aided design and manufacturing (CAD/CAM), engineering materials, quality control, machine tools, robots, lasers, productivity, and related subjects. Formerly *Abstract Newsletter.*

DIRECTORIES

Dun's Industrial Guide: The Metalworking Directory. Dun and Bradstreet Information Services Dun & Bradstreet Corp. • Annual. Libraries, $485; commercial institutions, $795.00. Lease basis. Three volumes. Lists about 65,000 U. S. manufacturing plants using metal and suppliers of metalworking equipment and materials. Includes names and titles of key personnel. Products, purchases, and processes are indicated.

Industrial Laser Buyers Guide. PennWell Corp., Advanced Technology Div. • Annual. $85.00. Lists industrial laser suppliers by category and geographic location. (Included with subscription to *Industrial Laser Solutions.*).

Modern Machine Shop Material Working Technology Guide. Gardner Publications, Inc. • Annual. $15.00. Lists products and services for the metalworking industry. Formerly *Modern Machine Shop CNC and Software Guide.*

FINANCIAL RATIOS

Annual Statement Studies. Robert Morris Associates: The Association of Lending and Credit Risk Professiona. • Annual. Free to members; non-members, $140.00. Median and quartile financial ratios are given for over 400 kinds of manufacturing, wholesale, retail, construction, and consumer finance establishments. Data is sorted by both asset size and sales volume. Includes a clearly written "Definition of Ratios" and an alphabetical industry index.

HANDBOOKS AND MANUALS

Machine Tool Practices. Richard R. Kibbe. Prentice Hall. • 1998. $90.67. Sixth edition.

INTERNET DATABASES

Fedstats. Federal Interagency Council on Statistical Policy. Phone: (202)395-7254 • URL: http://www.fedstats.gov • Web site features an efficient search facility for full-text statistics produced by more than 70 federal agencies, including the Census Bureau, the Bureau of Economic Analysis, and the Bureau of Labor Statistics. Boolean searches can be made within one agency or for all agencies combined. Links are offered to international statistical bureaus, including the UN, IMF, OECD, UNESCO, Eurostat, and 20 individual countries. Fees: Free.

ONLINE DATABASES

DRI U.S. Central Database. Data Products Division. • Provides more than 23,000 business, financial, demographic, economic, foreign trade, and industry-related time series for the U.S. Includes national income, population, retail-wholesale trade, price indexes, labor data, housing, industrial production, banking, interest rates, money supply, etc. Time period is generally 1947 to date (some data back to 1929). Updating varies. Inquire as to online cost and availability.

PROMT: Predicasts Overview of Markets and Technology. The Gale Group. • Companies, products, applied technologies and markets. U.S. and international literature coverage, 1972 to date. Inquire as to online cost and availability. Provides abstracts from more than 1,600 publications. Weekly updates.

PERIODICALS AND NEWSLETTERS

Industrial Laser Solutions. PennWell Corp., Advanced Technology Div. • Monthly. $250.00 per year. Covers industrial laser technology, especially machine tool applications. (Subscription includes annual *Industrial Laser Buyers Guide.*).

International Journal of Machine Tools and Manufacture: Design, Research and Application. Elsevier Science. • Monthly. $2,273 per year.

Manufacturing Engineering. Society of Manufacturing Engineers. • Monthly. $60.00 per year.

RESEARCH CENTERS AND INSTITUTES

Advanced Manufacturing Engineering Institute. University of Hartford, United Technologies Hall, Room 215, West Hartford, CT 06117. Phone: 800-678-4844 or (860)768-4615 Fax: (860)768-5073 E-mail: shetty@mail.hartford.edu • URL: http://www.uharay.hartford.edu/eau.

Machinability Laboratory. Pennsylvania State University. 310 Leohnard Bldg., University Park, PA 16802. Phone: (814)863-2357 Fax: (814)865-7601 E-mail: phc3@psu.edu.

STATISTICS SOURCES

Annual Survey of Manufactures. Available from U. S. Government Printing Office. • Annual. Prices vary. Issued by the U. S. Census Bureau as an interim update to the *Census of Manufactures.* Includes data on number of manufacturing establishments in various industries, employment, labor costs, value of shipments, capital expenditures, inventories, energy costs, and assets. (See also Census Bureau home page, http://www.census.gov/.).

Business Statistics of the United States. Courtenay M. Slater, editor. Bernan Associates. • 1999. $74.00. Fifth edition. Based on *Business Statistics*, formerly issue by the Bureau of Economic Analysis, U. S. Department of Commerce. Provides basic data for a wide variety of U. S. industries, services, and economic indicators. Most statistics are shown annually for 29 years and monthly for the most recent four years.

Survey of Current Business. Available from U. S. Government Printing Office. • Monthly. $49.00 per year. Issued by Bureau of Economic Analysis, U. S. Department of Commerce. Presents a wide variety of business and economic data.

TRADE/PROFESSIONAL ASSOCIATIONS

American Machine Tool Distributors' Association. 1445 Research Blvd., No. 450, Rockville, MD 20850-8125. Phone: 800-878-2683 or (301)738-1200 Fax: (301)738-9499 E-mail: jallen@amtda.org • URL: http://www.amtda.org.

ASM International. 9639 Kinsman Rd., Materials Park, OH 44073. Phone: 800-336-5152 or (216)338-5151 Fax: (216)338-4634 E-mail: memserv@po.asm-intl.org • URL: http://www.asm-intl.org • Members are materials engineers, metallurgists, industry executives, educators, and others concerned with a wide range of materials and metals. Divisions include Aerospace, Composites, Electronic Materials and Processing, Energy, Highway/Off-Highway Vehicle, Joining, Materials Testing and Quality Control, Society of Carbide and Tool Engineers, and Surface Engineering.

National Tooling and Machining Association. 9300 Livingston Rd., Fort Washington, MD 20744. Phone: 800-248-6862 or (301)248-6200 Fax: (301)248-7104 • URL: http://www.ntma.org.

Society of Manufacturing Engineers. P.O. Box 930, Dearborn, MI 48121-0930. Phone: 800-733-4763 or (313)271-1500 Fax: (313)271-2861 • URL: http://www.sme.org.

MACHINE TRANSLATING

ALMANACS AND YEARBOOKS

Translating and the Computer. Available from Information Today, Inc. • Annual. $49.00. Published in London by Aslib: The Association for Information Management. Includes papers from the annual International Conference on Translating and the Computer.

PERIODICALS AND NEWSLETTERS

Computational Linguistics. Association for Computational Linguistics. MIT Press. • Quarterly. Institutions, $128.00 per year. Covers developments in research and applications of natural language processing.

TRADE/PROFESSIONAL ASSOCIATIONS

Association for Computational Linguistics. c/o Pricilla Rasmussen, 75 Paterson St., Ste. 9, New Burnswick, NJ 08901-2116. Phone: (732)342-9100 Fax: (732)342-9339 E-mail: acl@aclweb.org.

MACHINE VISION

See also: AUTOMATION; ROBOTS

ABSTRACTS AND INDEXES

Applied Science and Technology Index. H. W. Wilson Co. • 11 times a year. Quarterly and annual cumulations. Service basis for print edition; CD-ROM edition, $1,495.00 per year. Indexes a wide variety of English language technical, industrial, and engineering periodicals.

CompuMath Citation Index. Institute for Scientific Information. • Three times a year. $1,090.00 per year. Provides citations to the worldwide literature of computer science and mathematics.

Computer and Information Systems Abstracts Journal: An Abstract Journal Pertaining to the Theory, Design, Fabrication and Application of Computer and Information Systems. Cambridge Information Group. • Monthly. $1,045 per year.

Computer Literature Index: A Subject/Author Index to Computer and Data Processing Literature. Applied Computer Research, Inc. • Quarterly, with annual cumulation. $245.00 per year. Contains brief abstracts of book and periodical literature covering all phases of computing, including approximately 70 specific application areas.

Engineering Index Monthly: Abstracting and Indexing Services Covering Sources of the World's Engineering Literature. Engineering Information, Inc. • Monthly. $2,300.00 per year. Provides indexing and abstracting of the world's engineering and technical literature.

Key Abstracts: Machine Vision. Available from INSPEC, Inc. • Monthly. $240.00 per year. Provides international coverage of journal and proceedings literature on optical noncontact sensing. Published in England by the Institution of Electrical Engineers (IEE).

NTIS Alerts: Computers, Control & Information Theory. National Technical Information Service. • Semimonthly. $235.00 per year. Provides descriptions of government-sponsored research reports and software, with ordering information. Covers computer hardware, software, control systems, pattern recognition, image processing, and related subjects. Formerly *Abstract Newsletter.*

NTIS Alerts: Manufacturing Technology. National Technical Information Service. • Semimonthly. $265.00 per year. Provides descriptions of government-sponsored research reports and software, with ordering information. Covers computer-aided design and manufacturing (CAD/CAM), engineering materials, quality control, machine tools, robots, lasers, productivity, and related subjects. Formerly *Abstract Newsletter.*

CD-ROM DATABASES

COMPENDEX PLUS [CD-ROM]. Engineering Information, Inc. • Quarterly. $3,450.00 per year. Provides CD-ROM indexing and abstracting of the world's engineering and technical information appearing in journals, reports, books, and proceedings, 1985 to date.

Computer Select. The Gale Group. • Monthly. $1,250.00 per year. Provides one year of full-text on CD-ROM for 120 leading computer-related publications. Also includes 70,000 product specifications and brief profiles of 13,000 computer product vendors and manufacturers.

WILSONDISC: Applied Science and Technology Abstracts. H. W. Wilson Co. • Monthly. $1,495.00 per year, including unlimited access to the online version of *Applied Science and Technology Abstracts* through WILSONLINE. Provides CD-ROM indexing and abstracting of 400 prominent scientific, technical, engineering, and industrial periodicals. Indexing coverage is provided from 1983 to date and abstracting from 1993 to date.

DIRECTORIES

Data Sources: The Comprehensive Guide to the Data Processing Industry Hardware, Data Communications Products, Software, Company Profiles. The Gale Group. • Semiannual. $495.00 per year. Two volumes. Describes hardware and software for all computer operating sysems, including prices and technical details. Lists about 75,000 products from 14,000 suppliers. Industry-specific software applications are described.

Frontline Solutions Buyer's Guide. Advanstar Communications, Inc. • Annual. $34.95. Provides information on manufacturers and suppliers of bar code, magnetic stripe, machine vision, optical character recognition, voice data, smart card, radio frequency, and other automatic identification systems. Formerly (Automatic I.D. News Buyer's Guide).

Machine Vision and Robotics Industry Directory. Society of Manufacturing Engineers. • Biennial. $25.00. Provides information on suppliers of machine vision systems, services, and equipment. Formerly *Machine Vision Industry Directory.*

Manufacturing Systems: Buyers Guide. Cahners Business Information. • Annual. Price on application. Contains information on companies manufacturing or supplying materials handling systems, CAD/CAM systems, specialized software for manufacturing, programmable controllers, machine vision systems, and automatic identification systems.

Sensors Buyers Guide. Advanstar Communications. • Annual. Price on application. Provides information on over 1,400 manufacturers of high technology sensors.

HANDBOOKS AND MANUALS

Handbook of Machine Vision Engineering. Michael Burke. John Wiley and Sons, Inc. • $159.90. Two volumes. Volume two, $79.95; volume three, $79.95.

ONLINE DATABASES

Applied Science and Technology Index Online. H. W. Wilson Co. • Provides online indexing of 400 major scientific, technical, industrial, and engineering periodicals. Time period is 1983 to date. Monthly updates. Inquire as to online cost and availability.

COMPENDEX PLUS. Engineering Information, Inc. • Provides online indexing and abstracting of the world's engineering and technical information appearing in journals, reports, books, and proceedings. Time period is 1970 to date, with weekly updates. Inquire as to online cost and availability.

Computer Database. The Gale Group. • Provides online citations with abstracts to material appearing in about 150 trade journals and newsletters in the subject areas of computers, telecommunications, and electronics. Time period is 1983 to date, with weekly updates. Inquire as to online cost and availability.

Current Contents Connect. Institute for Scientific Information. • Provides online abstracts of articles listed in the tables of contents of about 7,500 journals. Coverage is very broad, including science, social science, life science, technology, engineering, industry, agriculture, the environment, economics, and arts and humanities. Time period is two years, with weekly updates. Inquire as to online cost and availability.

Hard Sciences. Cambridge Scientific Abstracts. • Provides the online version of *Computer and Information Systems Abstracts, Electronics and Communications Abstracts, Health and Safety Science Abstracts, ISMEC: Mechanical Engineering Abstracts (Information Service in Mechanical Engineering)* and *Solid State and Superconductivity Abstracts.* Time period is 1981 to date, with monthly updates. Inquire as to online cost and availability.

PROMT: Predicasts Overview of Markets and Technology. The Gale Group. • Companies, products, applied technologies and markets. U.S. and international literature coverage, 1972 to date. Inquire as to online cost and availability. Provides abstracts from more than 1,600 publications. Weekly updates.

PERIODICALS AND NEWSLETTERS

IEEE Transactions on Visualization and Computer Graphics. Institute of Electrical and Electronics Engineers. • Quarterly. $490.00 per year. Topics include computer vision, computer graphics, image processing, signal processing, computer-aided design, animation, and virtual reality.

International Journal of Intelligent Systems. John Wiley and Sons, Inc. • Monthly. Institutions, $1,549.00 per year.

Manufacturing Computer Solutions. Hitchcock Publishing. • Monthly. Free to qualified personnel; others; $75.00 per year. Edited for managers of factory automation, emphasizing the integration of systems in manufacturing. Subjects include materials handling, CAD/CAM, specialized software for manufacturing, programmable controllers, machine vision, and automatic identification systems. Formerly *Manufacturing Systems.*

Sensors: The Journal of Applied Sensing Technology. Advanstar Communications. • Monthly. $62.00 per year. Edited for design, production, and manufacturing engineers involved with sensing systems. Emphasis is on emerging technology.

RESEARCH CENTERS AND INSTITUTES

Artificial Intelligence and Computer Vision Laboratory. University of Cincinnati, Dept. of Electrical, Computer Engineering and Computer Scien, 802 Rhodes Hall, Cincinnati, OH 45221-0030. Phone: (513)556-4778 Fax: (513)556-7326 E-mail: william.wee@uc.edu • Fields of research include computer vision, computer graphics, and artificial intelligence.

Center for Research in Computing Technology. Harvard University, Pierce Hall, 29 Oxford St., Cambridge, MA 02138. Phone: (617)495-2832 Fax: (617)495-9837 E-mail: cheatham@das.harvard.edu • URL: http://www.das.harvard.edu/cs.grafs.html • Conducts research in computer vision, robotics, artificial intelligence, systems programming, programming languages, operating systems, networks, graphics, database management systems, and telecommunications.

Computer Vision Laboratory. University of Arizona, Department of Electrical and Computer Engineering, ECE Bldg. 404, Room 230, Tucson, AZ 85721. Phone: (520)621-6191 Fax: (520)621-8076 E-mail: strickland@ece.arizona.edu • URL: http://www.ece.arizona.edu • Research areas include computer vision and speech synthesis.

Digital Image Analysis Laboratory. University of Arizona, Dept. of Electrical and Computer Engineering, Tucson, AZ 85721. Phone: (520)621-4554 Fax: (520)621-8076 E-mail: schowengerdt@ece.arizona.edu • URL: http://www.ece.arizona.edu/~dial • Research fields include image processing, computer vision, and artificial intelligence.

Image Science Research Group. Worcester Polytechnic Institute, Computer Science Department, 100 Institute Rd., Worcester, MA 01609. Phone: (508)831-5671 Fax: (508)831-5776 E-mail: isrg@cs.wpi.edu • URL: http://www.cs.wpi.edu/research/ • Areas of research include image processing, computer graphics, and computational vision.

Imaging and Computer Vision Center-Computer Vision Center for Vertebrate Brain Mapping. Drexel University, 32nd and Market Sts., Room 110-7, Philadelphia, PA 19104. Phone: (215)895-2279 Fax: (215)895-4987 • URL: http://www.drexel.icvc.com • Fields of research include computer vision, robot vision, and expert systems.

Imaging Systems Laboratory. Carnegie Mellon University, Robotics Institute, 5000 Forbes Ave., Pittsburgh, PA 15213. Phone: (412)268-3824 Fax: (412)683-3763 E-mail: rht@cs.cmu.edu • Fields of research include computer vision and document interpretation.

Media Laboratory. Massachusetts Institute of Technology, 20 Ames St., Room E-15, Cambridge, MA 02139. Phone: (617)253-0338 Fax: (617)258-6264 E-mail: casr@media.mit.edu • URL: http://www.media.mit.edu • Research areas include electronic publishing, spatial imaging, human-machine interface, computer vision, and advanced television.

Stanford Integrated Manufacturing Association. Stanford University, Bldg. 02-530, Stanford, CA 94305-3036. Phone: (650)723-9038 Fax: (650)723-5034 E-mail: susan.hansen@stanford.edu • URL: http://www.sima.stanford.edu/ • Consists of four research centers: Center for Automation and Manufacturing Science, Center for Design Research, Center for Materials Formability and Processing Science, and Center for Teaching and Research in Integrated Manufacturing Systems. Research fields include automation, robotics, intelligent systems, computer vision, design in manufacturing, materials science, composite materials, and ceramics.

TRADE/PROFESSIONAL ASSOCIATIONS

AIM U.S.A. 634 Alpha Dr., Pittsburgh, PA 15238-2802. Phone: 800-338-0206 or (412)963-8588 Fax: (412)963-8753 E-mail: info@aimglobal.org • URL: http://www.aimusa.org • Members are companies concerned with automatic identification and data capture, including bar code systems, magnetic stripes, machine vision, voice technology, optical character recognition, and systems integration technology.

Automated Imaging Association. P.O. Box 3724, Ann Arbor, MI 48106. Phone: (313)994-6088 Fax: (313)994-3338 E-mail: aia@automated-imaging.org • URL: http://www.automated-imaging.org • Promotes the use of machine vision technology.

Automatic Identification Manufacturers International. 623 Alpha Dr., Pittsburgh, PA 15238. Phone: (412)936-8009 Fax: (412)963-8753 • Members are automatic identification manufacturers and suppliers. Systems may utilize bar codes, magnetic stripes, radio frequencies, machine vision, voice technology, optical character recognition, or systems integration.

Machine Vision Association of the Society of Manufacturing Engineers. P.O. Box 930, Dearborn, MI 48121-0930. Phone: (313)271-1500 Fax: (313)271-2861 • URL: http://www.sme.org/mva • Members are professional engineers, managers, and students. Promotes the effective use of machine vision (optical sensing of actual scenes for use in machine control).

MACHINERY

ABSTRACTS AND INDEXES

Applied Science and Technology Index. H. W. Wilson Co. • 11 times a year. Quarterly and annual cumulations. Service basis for print edition; CD-ROM edition, $1,495.00 per year. Indexes a wide variety of English language technical, industrial, and engineering periodicals.

DIRECTORIES

Dun's Industrial Guide: The Metalworking Directory. Dun and Bradstreet Information Services Dun & Bradstreet Corp. • Annual. Libraries, $485; commercial institutions, $795.00. Lease basis. Three volumes. Lists about 65,000 U. S. manufacturing plants using metal and suppliers of metalworking equipment and materials. Includes names and titles of key personnel. Products, purchases, and processes are indicated.

Machinery Buyers Guide: The Annual Directory of Engineering and Products Services. Findlay Publications Ltd. • Annual. $200.00. About 6,000 firms offering machine tool, engineering products, machinery, industrial equipment and services worldwide.

Thomas Register of American Manufacturers and Thomas Register Catalog File. Thomas Publishing Co., Inc. • Annual. $149.00. 34 volumes. A three-part system offering information on a wide variety of industrial equipment and supplies.

Used Equipment Directory. Penton Media Inc. • Monthly. $30.00 per year. Lists of 800 dealers, in used metalworking, electrical power, process, and material handling equipment, machine tools, etc.

FINANCIAL RATIOS

Almanac of Business and Industrial Financial Ratios. Leo Troy. Prentice Hall. • Annual. $99.95. Contains financial ratios derived from federal tax returns. Ratios for each of about 200 industries are arranged according to company asset size.

Annual Statement Studies. Robert Morris Associates: The Association of Lending and Credit Risk Professiona. • Annual. Free to members; non-members, $140.00. Median and quartile financial ratios are given for over 400 kinds of manufacturing, wholesale, retail, construction, and consumer finance establishments. Data is sorted by both asset size and sales volume. Includes a clearly written "Definition of Ratios" and an alphabetical industry index.

HANDBOOKS AND MANUALS

Machinery's Handbook. E. Oberg and others. Industrial Press, Inc. • 2000. $99.95. 26th edition. Reference book for the mechanical engineer, draftsman, toolmaker, and machinist.

INTERNET DATABASES

Fedstats. Federal Interagency Council on Statistical Policy. Phone: (202)395-7254 • URL: http://www.fedstats.gov • Web site features an efficient search facility for full-text statistics produced by more than 70 federal agencies, including the Census Bureau, the Bureau of Economic Analysis, and the Bureau of Labor Statistics. Boolean searches can be made within one agency or for all agencies combined. Links are offered to international statistical bureaus, including the UN, IMF, OECD, UNESCO, Eurostat, and 20 individual countries. Fees: Free.

ONLINE DATABASES

Applied Science and Technology Index Online. H. W. Wilson Co. • Provides online indexing of 400 major scientific, technical, industrial, and engineering periodicals. Time period is 1983 to date. Monthly updates. Inquire as to online cost and availability.

Business and Industry. Responsive Database Services, Inc. • Contains online citations, abstracts, and selected fulltext from more than 1,000 trade journals, newspapers, and other publications. Provides general coverage of both manufacturing and service industries, including marketing, production, industry trends, key events, and information on specific companies. Time span is 1994 to date. Daily updates. Inquire as to online cost and availability. (Also available in a CD-ROM version.).

DRI U.S. Central Database. Data Products Division. • Provides more than 23,000 business, financial, demographic, economic, foreign trade, and industry-related time series for the U.S. Includes national income, population, retail-wholesale trade, price indexes, labor data, housing, industrial production, banking, interest rates, money supply, etc. Time period is generally 1947 to date (some data back to 1929). Updating varies. Inquire as to online cost and availability.

Tablebase. Responsive Database Services, Inc. • Provides online numerical tabular data from a wide variety of business, organization, and government sources, including 900 trade journals. Includes industry and individual company statistics relating to products, market share, sales forecasts, production, exports, market trends, etc. Time span is 1997 to date. Weekly updates. Inquire as to online cost and availability. (Also available in a CD-ROM version.).

Thomas Register Online. Thomas Publishing Co., Inc. • Provides concise information on approximately 194,000 U. S. companies, mainly manufacturers, with over 50,000 product classifications. Indexes over 115,000 trade names. Information is updated semiannually. Inquire as to online cost and availability.

PERIODICALS AND NEWSLETTERS

American Machinist. Penton Media Inc. • Monthly. Free to qualified personnel; others, $75.00 per year.

Processing. Putman Media. • 14 times a year. $54.00 per year. Emphasis is on descriptions of new products for all areas of industrial processing, including valves, controls, filters, pumps, compressors, fluidics, and instrumentation.

RESEARCH CENTERS AND INSTITUTES

National Center for Manufacturing Sciences. 3025 Boardwalk, Ann Arbor, MI 48108. Phone: (734)995-0300 Fax: (734)995-4004 E-mail: johnd@ncms.org • URL: http://www.ncms.org • Research areas include process technology and control, machine mechanics, sensors, testing methods, and quality assurance.

STATISTICS SOURCES

Annual Survey of Manufactures. Available from U. S. Government Printing Office. • Annual. Prices vary. Issued by the U. S. Census Bureau as an interim update to the *Census of Manufactures.* Includes data on number of manufacturing establishments in various industries, employment, labor costs, value of shipments, capital expenditures, inventories, energy costs, and assets. (See also Census Bureau home page, http://www.census.gov/.).

Business Statistics of the United States. Courtenay M. Slater, editor. Bernan Associates. • 1999. $74.00. Fifth edition. Based on *Business Statistics*, formerly issue by the Bureau of Economic Analysis, U. S. Department of Commerce. Provides basic data for a wide variety of U. S. industries, services, and economic indicators. Most statistics are shown annually for 29 years and monthly for the most recent four years.

Encyclopedia of American Industries. The Gale Group. • 1998. $560.00. Second edition. Two volumes. $280.00 per volume. Volume one is *Manufacturing Industries* and volume two is *Service and Non-Manufacturing Industries.* Provides the history, development, and recent status of approximately 1,000 industries. Includes statistical graphs, with industry and general indexes.

Survey of Current Business. Available from U. S. Government Printing Office. • Monthly. $49.00 per year. Issued by Bureau of Economic Analysis, U. S. Department of Commerce. Presents a wide variety of business and economic data.

United States Census of Manufactures. U.S. Bureau of the Census. • Quinquennial. Results presented in reports, tape, CD-ROM, and Diskette files.

WEFA Industrial Monitor. John Wiley and Sons, Inc. • Annual. $65.00. Prepared by industry analysts at WEFA, an economic forecasting and consulting firm (originally Wharton Econometric Forecasting Associates). Contains discussions of the outlook for major U. S. industries, with many 10-year forecasts (WEFA Web site is http://www.wefa.com).

TRADE/PROFESSIONAL ASSOCIATIONS

American Supply and Machinery Manufacturers Association. 1300 Sumner Ave., Cleveland, OH 44115-2851. Phone: (216)241-7333 Fax: (216)241-0105 E-mail: asmma@taol.com • URL: http://www.asmma.com.

Machinery Dealers National Association. 315 S. Patrick St., Alexandria, VA 22314-3501. Phone: 800-872-7807 or (703)836-9300 Fax: (703)836-9303 E-mail: office@mdna.com • URL: http://www.mdna.com.

Manufacturers Alliance/MAPI Inc. 1525 Wilson Blvd., Suite 900, Arlington, VA 22209. Phone: (703)841-9000 Fax: (703)841-9514.

MACHINERY, USED

See: SURPLUS PRODUCTS

MAGAZINE CIRCULATION

See: CIRCULATION MANAGEMENT (PUBLISHING)

MAGAZINES

See: PERIODICALS

MAGNESIUM INDUSTRY

DIRECTORIES

International Magnesium Association-Buyers Guide. International Magnesium Association. • Biennial. $40.00 per year.

STATISTICS SOURCES

Mineral Commodity Summaries. Available from U. S. Government Printing Office. • Annual. Published by the U. S. Geological Survey, Department of the Interior (http://www.usgs.gov). Contains detailed, five-year data for about 90 nonfuel minerals. Covers a wide range of statistics, including production, imports, exports, consumption, reserves, prices, tariff information, and industry employment. (Two pages are devoted to each mineral.).

Non-Ferrous Metal Data Yearbook. American Bureau of Metal Statistics. • Annual. $395.00. Provides about 200 statistical tables covering many nonferrous metals. Includes production, consumption, inventories, exports, imports, and other data.

Nonferrous Castings. U. S. Bureau of the Census. • Annual. (Current Industrial Reports MA-33E.).

TRADE/PROFESSIONAL ASSOCIATIONS

American Bureau of Metal Statistics. P.O. Box 805, Chatham, NJ 07928. Phone: (973)701-2299 Fax: (973)701-2152 E-mail: info@abms.com • URL: http://www.abms.com • Members are metal companies. Compiles and publishes detailed statistical data on a wide variety of nonferrous metals: aluminum, copper, gold, lead, nickel, platinum, silver, tin, titanium, uranium, zinc, and others.

International Magnesium Association. 1303 Vincent Place., Suite 1, McLean, VA 22101. Phone: (703)442-8888 Fax: (703)821-1824 E-mail: ima@bellatlantic.net • URL: http://www.intlmag.org/.

MAGNETIC RECORDS AND RECORDINGS

See: SOUND RECORDERS AND RECORDING

MAIL ORDER BUSINESS

See also: DIRECT MAIL ADVERTISING

CD-ROM DATABASES

MediaFinder CD-ROM: Oxbridge Directories of Print Media and Catalogs. Oxbridge Communications, Inc. • Quarterly. $1,695.00 per year. CD-ROM includes about 100,000 listings from *Standard Periodical Directory, National Directory of Catalogs, National Directory of British Mail Order Catalogs, National Directory of German Mail Order Catalogs, Oxbridge Directory of Newsletters, National Directory of Mailing Lists, College Media Directory*, and *National Directory of Magazines.*

DIRECTORIES

Catalog Age/Direct Sourcebook. Intertec Publishing Co. • Annual. $35.00. Lists of approximately 300 suppliers of products and services for direct marketing, especially catalog marketing.

Catalog of Catalogs: The Complete Mail-Order Directory. Edward L. Palder. Woodbine House. • Biennial. $25.95. Provides information on more than 14,000 U. S. and Canadian companies that issue catalogs and sell through the mail. Arrangement is by product, with an index to company names.

Directory of Business-to-Business Catalogs. Grey House Publishing. • Annual. $190.00. Provides over 6,000 listings of U. S. mail order companies selling business or industrial products and services.

Directory of Mail Order Catalogs. Grey House Publishing. • Annual. $275.00. Contains 11,000 entries for mail order companies selling consumer products throughout the U.S.

Drop Shipping Source Directory of Major Consumer Product Lines. Drop Shipping News. • Annual. $15.00. Lists over 700 firms of a wide variety of consumer products that can be drop shipped.

European Directory of Retailers and Wholesalers. Available from The Gale Group. • 1997. $790.00. Second edition. Published by Euromonitor. Provides detailed information on more than 4,000 major retail and wholesale businesses in 17 countries of Western Europe. Contains 26 categories, such as supermarkets, superstores, department stores, discount stores, franchise operators, mail order, etc. Includes company, product, and geographic indexes.

Mail Order Business Directory. B. Klein Publications. • Annual. $85.00. Provides 12,000 listings of mail order and catalog houses in the U.S.; international coverage.

The National Directory of Catalogs. Oxbridge Communications. • Annual. $595.00. Describes over 7,000 catalogs within 78 subject areas. Includes CD-ROM.

FINANCIAL RATIOS

Annual Statement Studies. Robert Morris Associates: The Association of Lending and Credit Risk Professiona. • Annual. Free to members; non-members, $140.00. Median and quartile financial ratios are given for over 400 kinds of manufacturing, wholesale, retail, construction, and consumer finance establishments. Data is sorted by both asset size and sales volume. Includes a clearly written "Definition of Ratios" and an alphabetical industry index.

HANDBOOKS AND MANUALS

Building a Mail Order Business: A Complete Manual for Success. William A. Cohen. John Wiley and Sons, Inc. • 1996. $42.95. Fourth edition.

Drop Shipping as a Marketing Function: A Handbook of Methods and Policies. Nicholas T. Scheel. Greenwood Publishing Group, Inc. • 1990. $59.95.

Mail Order Business. Entrepreneur Media, Inc. • Looseleaf. $59.50. A practical guide to starting a mail order business. Covers profit potential, start-up costs, pricing, market size evaluation, accounting, advertising, promotion, etc. (Start-Up Business Guide No. E1015.).

PERIODICALS AND NEWSLETTERS

Catalog Age. Cowles Business Media, Inc. • Monthly. $72.00 per year. Edited for catalog marketing and management personnel.

The Catalog Marketer. Maxwell Sroge Publishing, Inc. • Biweekly. $199.00 per year. Newsletter. "How-to" for catalog producers.

DM News: The Newspaper of Direct Marketing. DM News Corp. • Weekly. $75.00 per year. Includes special feature issues on catalog marketing, telephone marketing, database marketing, and fundraising. Includes monthly supplements. *DM News International, DRTV News,* and *TeleServices.*

Drop Shipping News. • Monthly. Price on application. Newsletter.

Non-Store Marketing Report. Maxwell Sroge Publishing, Inc. • Biweekly. $275.00 per year. Newsletter covering mail order, telephone selling, and direct selling.

STATISTICS SOURCES

WEFA Industrial Monitor. John Wiley and Sons, Inc. • Annual. $65.00. Prepared by industry analysts at WEFA, an economic forecasting and consulting firm (originally Wharton Econometric Forecasting Associates). Contains discussions of the outlook for major U. S. industries, with many 10-year forecasts (WEFA Web site is http://www.wefa.com).

TRADE/PROFESSIONAL ASSOCIATIONS

Mail Order Association of America. 1877 Bourne Court, Wantagh, NY 11793. Phone: (516)221-8257 Fax: (516)221-5697.

OTHER SOURCES

Mail Service Pharmacy Market. MarketResearch.com. • 1999. $3,250.00. Provides detailed market data, with forecasts to the year 2003.

The U. S. Market for Catalog Shopping. Available from MarketResearch.com. • 1997. $2,250.00. Market research report published by Packaged Facts. Includes analysis of catalog shopping market by age, ethnic groups, and income.

MAIL SERVICE

See: POSTAL SERVICES

MAILING LISTS

See also: DIRECT MAIL ADVERTISING

CD-ROM DATABASES

MediaFinder CD-ROM: Oxbridge Directories of Print Media and Catalogs. Oxbridge Communications, Inc. • Quarterly. $1,695.00 per year. CD-ROM includes about 100,000 listings from *Standard Periodical Directory, National Directory of Catalogs, National Directory of British Mail Order Catalogs, National Directory of German Mail Order Catalogs, Oxbridge Directory of Newsletters, National Directory of Mailing Lists, College Media Directory,* and *National Directory of Magazines.*

DIRECTORIES

Direct Marketing List Source. SRDS. • Bimonthly. $542.00 per year. Provides detailed information and rates for business, farm, and consumer mailing lists (U. S., Canadian, and international). Includes current postal information and directories of list brokers, compilers, and managers. Formerly *Direct Mail List Rates and Data.*

Directory of Mailing List Companies. Todd Publications. • Biennial. $50.00. Lists and describes approximately 1,100 of the most active list brokers, owners, managers and compilers.

National Directory of Mailing Lists 1997. Oxbridge Communications, Inc. • Annual. $695.00. Describes over 15,000 mailing lists in about 200 categories. Includes CD-ROM.

PERIODICALS AND NEWSLETTERS

The Bullet. SRDS. • Bimonthly. Included with subscription to *Direct Marketing List Source.* Newsletter on direct mail advertising and mailing lists. Includes list updates and management changes.

Database Marketer. Intertec Publishing Co. • Monthly. $329.00 per year.

Direct Marketing: Using Direct Response Advertising to Enhance Marketing Database. Hoke Communications, Inc. • Monthly. $65.00 per year. Direct marketing to consumers and business.

Target Marketing: The Leading Magazine for Integrated Database Marketing. North American Publishing Co. • Monthly. $65.00 per year. Dedicated to direct marketing excellence. Formerly *Zip Target Marketing.*

STATISTICS SOURCES

DMA Statistical Fact Book. Direct Marketing Association, Inc. • Annual. $165.95 to non-members; $105.95 to members. Provides data in five sections covering direct response advertising, media, mailing lists, market applications, and "Practical Management Information." Includes material on interactive/online marketing. (Cover title: *Direct Marketing Association's Statistical Fact Book.*).

MAINTENANCE OF BUILDINGS

See also: BUILDING INDUSTRY

DIRECTORIES

Concrete Repair Digest Buyers' Guide. The Aberdeen Group. • Annual. $3.00. Lists sources of products and services for concrete repair and maintenance specialists.

ICS Cleaning Specialists Annual Trade Directory and Buying Guide. Business News Publishing Co., II, L.L.C. • Annual. $25.00. Lists about 6,000 manufacturers and distributors of floor covering installation and cleaning equipment. Formerly *Installation and Cleaning Specialists Trade Directory and Buying Guides.*

Maintenance Supplies Buyers' Guide. Cygnus Business Media. • Annual. $15.00. Approximately 1,000 manufacturers and associations for commercial, industrial, and institutional janitorial supplies; international coverage. Formerly *Maintenance Supplies Annual.*

Sanitary Maintenance Buyers' Guide. Trade Press Publishing Corp. • Annual. $20.00.

FINANCIAL RATIOS

Annual Statement Studies. Robert Morris Associates: The Association of Lending and Credit Risk Professiona. • Annual. Free to members; non-members, $140.00. Median and quartile financial ratios are given for over 400 kinds of manufacturing, wholesale, retail, construction, and consumer finance establishments. Data is sorted by both asset size and sales volume. Includes a clearly written "Definition of Ratios" and an alphabetical industry index.

HANDBOOKS AND MANUALS

Carpet Cleaning Service. Entrepreneur Media, Inc. • Looseleaf. $59.50. A practical guide to starting a carpet cleaning business. Covers profit potential, start-up costs, market size evaluation, owner's time required, pricing, accounting, advertising, promotion, etc. (Start-Up Business Guide No. E1053.).

Everything You Need to Know to Start a House Cleaning Service. Mary P. Johnson. Cleaning Consultant Services, Inc. • 1999. $38.00 Revised edition.

Home Inspection Service. Entrepreneur Media, Inc. • Looseleaf. $59.50. A practical guide to starting a home inspection service. Covers profit potential, start-up costs, market size evaluation, owner's time required, pricing, accounting, advertising, promotion, etc. (Start-Up Business Guide No. E1334.).

House Painting. Entrepreneur Media, Inc. • Looseleaf. $59.50. A practical guide to starting a house painting business. Covers profit potential, start-up costs, market size evaluation, owner's time required, pricing, accounting, advertising, promotion, etc. (Start-Up Business Guide No. E1249.).

Janitorial Service. Entrepreneur Media, Inc. • Looseleaf. $59.50. A practical guide to starting a janitorial service business. Covers profit potential, start-up costs, market size evaluation, owner's time required, site selection, lease negotiation, pricing, accounting, advertising, promotion, etc. (Start-Up Business Guide No. E1034.).

Maintenance Engineering Handbook. Lindley R. Higgins. McGraw-Hill. • 1994. $125.00. Fifth edition. Contains about 60 chapters by various authors in 12 major sections covering all elements of industrial and plant maintenance.

Managing Factory Maintenance. Joel Levitt. Industrial Press, Inc. • 1996. $39.95.

Window Washing Service. Entrepreneur Media, Inc. • Looseleaf. $59.50. A practical guide to starting a window cleaning business. Covers profit potential, start-up costs, market size evaluation, owner's time required, pricing, accounting, advertising, promotion, etc. (Start-Up Business Guide No. E1012.).

PERIODICALS AND NEWSLETTERS

Building Operating Management: The National Magazine for Commercial and Institutional Buildings Construction, Renoration, Facility Management. Trade Press Publishing Corp. • Monthly. $55.00 per year.

Cleaning Business: Published Monthly for the Self-Employed Cleaning and Maintenance Professionals. William R. Griffin, Publisher. • Monthly. $20.00 per year. Formerly *Service Business.*

Industrial Maintenance and Plant Operation. Cahners Business Information. • Monthly. $39.00 per year.

Installation and Cleaning Specialist. Specialist Publications, Inc. • Monthly. $38.00 per year. Written for floor covering installers and cleaners.

Maintenance Supplies. Cygnus Publishing Co. • Monthly. $60.00 per year. Geared to distributors of sanitary supplies, maintenance equipment, etc.

Plant Services. Putman Media. • Monthly. $95.00 per year.

Sanitary Maintenance: The Journal of the Sanitary Supply Industry. Trade Press Publishing Corp. • Monthly. $55.00 per year.

TRADE/PROFESSIONAL ASSOCIATIONS

Building Service Contractors Association International. 10201 Lee Highway, Suite 225, Fairfax, VA 22030. Phone: 800-368-3414 or (703)359-7090 Fax: (703)352-0493 • URL: http://www.bscai.org.

International Maintenance Institute. P.O. Box 751896, Houston, TX 77275-1896. Phone: (281)481-0869 Fax: (281)481-8337 E-mail: iminst@swbell.net.

OTHER SOURCES

U. S. Commercial and Residential Cleaning Services Industry. Available from MarketResearch.com. • 1999. $1,395.00. Market research report published by Marketdata Enterprises. Covers commercial contract cleaning services and residential services. Provides actual industry and market statistics for 1987 to 1996, estimates for 1997-98, and forecasts to the year 2003.

MALLS, SHOPPING

See: SHOPPING CENTERS

MALPRACTICE

See: PROFESSIONAL LIABILITY

MANAGED CARE

See: HEALTH INSURANCE; HEALTH MAINTENANCE ORGANIZATIONS

MANAGEMENT

See: ADMINISTRATION; FACTORY MANAGEMENT; FINANCIAL MANAGEMENT; INDUSTRIAL MANAGEMENT; MANAGEMENT THEORY; OFFICE MANAGEMENT; PUBLIC ADMINISTRATION; SALES MANAGEMENT

MANAGEMENT, BANK

See: BANK MANAGEMENT

MANAGEMENT BY OBJECTIVES

See: INDUSTRIAL MANAGEMENT

MANAGEMENT CONSULTANTS

See also: CONSULTANTS

GENERAL WORKS

Dangerous Company: The Secret Story of the Consulting Powerhouses and the Corporations They Save and Ruin. James O'Shea and Charles Madigan. Random House, Inc. • 1997. $27.50. A critical view of the major consulting firms in the U. S. and how they influence large corporations.

The Witch Doctors: Making Sense of the Management Gurus. John Micklethwait and Adrian Wooldridge. Crown Publishing Group, Inc. • 1996. $25.00. A critical, iconoclastic, and practical view of consultants, business school professors, and modern management theory, written by two members of the editorial staff of *The Economist.*

ABSTRACTS AND INDEXES

Business Periodicals Index. H. W. Wilson Co. • Monthly, except August, with quarterly and annual cumulations. Service basis for print edition; CD-ROM edition, $1,495.00 per year.

BIBLIOGRAPHIES

Management Consultant Books. Kennedy Information, LLC. • Annual. Free. Contains descriptions of selected books from various publishers on management consulting.

DIRECTORIES

Business and Finance Career Directory. Visible Ink Press. • 1992. $17.95.

Consultants and Consulting Organizations Directory. The Gale Group. • 2001. $795.00. 23rd edition. Three volumes. Includes mid-year *Supplement.*

Directory of Management Consultants. Kennedy Information, LLC. • Annual. $149.00. Contains profiles of more than 1,800 general and specialty management consulting firms in the U. S., Canada, and Mexico.

Dun's Consultants Directory. Dun and Bradstreet Information Services. • 1996. $425.00. Lease basis. Lists about 25,000 top consulting firms in more than 200 fields.

40 Largest Management Consulting Firms, U. S. & World. Kennedy Information, LLC. • Annual. $15.00. Rankings of consulting firms are by U. S. and world estimated revenues, with tables of staff sizes. Growth trends and market size estimates for the management consulting industry are also provided.

100 Leading Management Consulting Firms in U. S. Kennedy Information, LLC. • Annual. $15.00. Includes company profiles and revenue data. These are "best firms in the business" as selected by Kennedy Publications.

FINANCIAL RATIOS

Annual Statement Studies. Robert Morris Associates: The Association of Lending and Credit Risk Professiona. • Annual. Free to members; non-members, $140.00. Median and quartile financial ratios are given for over 400 kinds of manufacturing, wholesale, retail, construction, and consumer finance establishments. Data is sorted by both asset size and sales volume. Includes a clearly written "Definition of Ratios" and an alphabetical industry index.

HANDBOOKS AND MANUALS

Business Plan Guide for Independent Consultants. Herman Holtz. John Wiley and Sons, Inc. • 1994. $115.00.

The Consultant's Proposal, Fee, and Contract Problem-Solver. Ronald Tepper. John Wiley and Sons, Inc. • 1993. $24.95. Provides advice for consultants on fees, contracts, proposals, and client communications. Includes case histories in 10 specific fields, such as finance, marketing, engineering, and management.

Consulting Business. Entrepreneur Media, Inc. • Looseleaf. $59.50. A practical guide to becoming a business consultant. Covers profit potential, start-up costs, market size evaluation, pricing, accounting, advertising, promotion, etc. (Start-Up Business Guide No. E1151.).

How to Become a Successful Consultant in Your Own Field. Hubert Bermont. Prima Publishing. • 1991. $21.95. Third enlarged revised edition.

How to Succeed as an Independent Consultant. Herman Holtz. John Wiley and Sons, Inc. • 1993. $34.95. Third edition. Covers a wide variety of marketing, financial, professional, and ethical issues for consultants. Includes bibliographic and organizational information.

ONLINE DATABASES

ABI/INFORM. Bell & Howell Information and Learning. • Provides online indexing to business-related material occurring in over 1,000 periodicals from 1971 to the present. Inquire as to online cost and availability.

Wilson Business Abstracts Online. H. W. Wilson Co. • Indexes and abstracts 600 major business periodicals, plus the *Wall Street Journal* and the business section of the *New York Times.* Indexing is from 1982, abstracting from 1990, with the two newspapers included from 1993. Updated weekly. Inquire as to online cost and availability. (*Business Periodicals Index* without abstracts is also available online.).

PERIODICALS AND NEWSLETTERS

Consultants News. Kennedy Information, LLC. • Monthly. $229.00 per year. Newsletter. News and ideas for management consultants.

STATISTICS SOURCES

An Analysis of the Management Consulting Business in the U. S. Today. Kennedy Information, LLC. • Annual. $35.00. Includes ranking of leading management consulting firms and estimates of market share and total revenue.

U. S. Industry and Trade Outlook: The McGraw-Hill Companies and the U.S. Department of Commerce/International Trade Administration. Datapso Research Corp. • Annual. $69.95. Produced by the International Trade Administration, U. S. Department of Commerce, in a "public-private" partnership with DRI/McGraw-Hill and Standard & Poor's. Provides basic data, outlook for the current year, and "Long-Term Prospects" (five-year projections) for a wide variety of products and services. Includes high technology industries. Formerly *U. S. Industrial Outlook.*

TRADE/PROFESSIONAL ASSOCIATIONS

Association of Management Consulting Firms. 380 Lexington Ave., No. 1699, New York, NY 10168-0002. Phone: (212)697-9693 Fax: (212)949-6571 E-mail: info@amcf.org • URL: http://www.amcf.org • Members are management consultants. One of the two divisions of the Council of Consulting Organizations.

Institute of Management Consultants. 1200 19th St., N.W., Suite 300, Washington, DC 20036-2422. Phone: 800-221-2557 or (202)857-5334 Fax: (202)857-5337 E-mail: office@imcusa.org • URL: http://www.imcusa.org • Provides professional services and certification to management consultants. One of the two divisions of the Council of Consulting Organizations.

OTHER SOURCES

Fee and Expense Policies: Statements of 46 Management Consulting Firms. James H. Kennedy, editor. Kennedy Information, LLC. • 1992. $67.00. Presents actual copies of billing and expense policies, including hourly and per diem rates. (Identification of firms has been removed.).

MANAGEMENT DEVELOPMENT

See: EXECUTIVE TRAINING AND DEVELOPMENT

MANAGEMENT, FINANCIAL

See: FINANCIAL MANAGEMENT

MANAGEMENT GAMES

GENERAL WORKS

Games, Strategies, and Managers: How Managers Can Use Game Theory to Make Better Business Decisions. John McMillan. Oxford University Press, Inc. • 1992. $17.95.

HANDBOOKS AND MANUALS

Business Policy Game: An International Simulation: Player's Manual. Richard V. Cotter and David J. Fritzsche. Prentice Hall. • 1995. $42.00. Fourth edition.

Handbook of Management Games and Simulations. Chris Elgood, editor. Ashgate Publishing Co. • 1997. $96.95. Sixth edition. Published by Gower in England.

Imaginative Events: A Sourcebook of Innovative Simulations, Exercises, Puzzles, and Games. Ken Jones. McGraw-Hill. • 1992. $110.00. Two volumes. (Training Series).

PERIODICALS AND NEWSLETTERS

Journal of Economics and Management Strategy. MIT Press. • Quarterly. Individuals, $45.00 per year; institutions, $135.00 per year. Covers "theoretical and empirical industrial organization, applied game theory, and management strategy.".

Simulation & Gaming: An International Journal of Theory, Design and Research. Sage Publications, Inc. • Quarterly. Individuals, $75.00 per year; institutions, $355.00 per year.

TRADE/PROFESSIONAL ASSOCIATIONS

Association for Business Simulation and Experiential Learning. c/o Hugh M. Cannon, Dept. of Marketing, Wayne State University, 5201 Cass Ave., Ste. 300, Detroit, MI 48202. Phone: (313)577-4551 Fax: (313)577-5486 E-mail: hughcannon@aol.com • URL: http://www.towson.edu/~absel/.

North American Simulation and Gaming Association. P.O. Box 78636, Indianapolis, IN 46278. Phone: 888-432-4263 or (317)387-1424 Fax: (317)387-1921 E-mail: info@nasaga.org • URL: http://www.nasaga.org • Members are professionals interested in the use of games and simulations for problem solving and decision-making in all types of organizations.

MANAGEMENT INFORMATION SYSTEMS

See also: COMPUTERS; SYSTEMS IN MANAGEMENT

GENERAL WORKS

Cases in the Management of Information Systems and Information Technology. Richard Lorette and Howard Walton. McGraw-Hill Higher Education. • 1994. $40.95.

Computers and Information Processing. South-Western Publishing Co. • 1998. $29.95. Seventh edition.

Information Management for the Intelligent Organization: The Art of Scanning the Environment. Chun Wei Choo. Information Today, Inc. • 1998. $39.50. Second edition. Published on behalf of the American Society for Information Science (ASIS). Covers the general principles of acquiring, creating, organizing, and using information within organizations.

Information Systems Concepts for Management. Henry C. Lucas. McGraw-Hill. • 1994. $25.00. Fifth edition.

Introduction to Information Systems. James A. O'Brien. McGraw-Hill. • 1999. $63.25. Ninth edition.

Knowledge Management for the Information Professional. T. Kanti Srikantaiah and Michael Koenig, editors. Information Today, Inc. • 2000. $44.50. Contains articles by 26 contributors on the concept of "knowledge management.".

Management Information Systems. Raymond McLeod and George Schell. Prentice Hall. • 2000. $89.33. Sixth edition.

Management Information Systems: Managing Information. Fritz J. Erickson and James A. O'Brien. McGraw-Hill Higher Education. • 1996. $72.25. Third edition.

Management Information Systems: The Manager's View. Robert A. Schultheis. McGraw-Hill Higher Education. • 1997. $62.00. Fourth edition.

Management Information Systems: With Application Cases and Internet Primer. James A. O'Brien and others. McGraw-Hill Higher Education. • 1996. $85.00. Third edition. Includes CD-ROM.

ABSTRACTS AND INDEXES

Business Periodicals Index. H. W. Wilson Co. • Monthly, except August, with quarterly and annual cumulations. Service basis for print edition; CD-ROM edition, $1,495.00 per year.

CD-ROM DATABASES

Computer Select. The Gale Group. • Monthly. $1,250.00 per year. Provides one year of full-text on CD-ROM for 120 leading computer-related publications. Also includes 70,000 product specifications and brief profiles of 13,000 computer product vendors and manufacturers.

Datapro on CD-ROM: Computer Systems Analyst. Gartner Group, Inc. • Monthly. Price on application. Includes detailed information on specific computer hardware and software products, such as peripherals, security systems, document imaging systems, and UNIX-related products.

DIRECTORIES

Data Communications Production Selection Guide. McGraw-Hill. • Semiannual. $25.00. List of networking vendors. Formerly *Data Communications Buyer's Guide.*

Data Sources: The Comprehensive Guide to the Data Processing Industry Hardware, Data Communications Products, Software, Company Profiles. The Gale Group. • Semiannual. $495.00 per year. Two volumes. Describes hardware and software for all computer operating sysems, including prices and technical details. Lists about 75,000 products from 14,000 suppliers. Industry-specific software applications are described.

Directory of Top Computer Executives. Applied Computer Research, Inc. • Semiannual. Price varies. Two volumes. Lists large companies and government agencies, with names of their data and systems executives.

KMWorld Buyer's Guide. Knowledge Asset Media. • Semiannual. Controlled circulation as part of *KMWorld.* Contains corporate and product profiles related to various aspects of knowledge management and information systems. (Knowledge Asset Media is a an affiliate of Information Today, Inc.).

ENCYCLOPEDIAS AND DICTIONARIES

Blackwell Encyclopedic Dictionary of Management Information Systems. Gordon B. Davis, editor. Blackwell Publishers. • 1996. $110.00. The editor is associated with the University of Minnesota. Contains definitions of key terms combined with longer articles written by various U. S. and foreign business educators. Includes bibliographies and index. *Blackwell Encyclopedia of Management Series.*

Encyclopedia of Business and Finance. Burton Kaliski, editor. Available from The Gale Group. • 2001. $240.00. Two volumes. Published by Macmillan Reference USA. Contains articles by various contributors on accounting, business administration, banking, finance, management information systems, and marketing.

HANDBOOKS AND MANUALS

Accountant's Handbook of Information Technology. G. Jack Bologna and Anthony M. Walsh. John Wiley and Sons, Inc. • 1997. $125.00.

Managing Information Systems and Technologies; A Basic Guide for Design, Selection, Evaluation and Use. Edwin M. Cortez and Edward J. Kazlauskas. Neal-Schuman Publishers, Inc. • 1985. $45.00.

INTERNET DATABASES

InfoTech Trends. Data Analysis Group. Phone: (707)894-9100 Fax: (707)486-5618 E-mail: support@infotechtrends.com • URL: http://www.infotechtrends.com • Web site provides both free and fee-based market research data on the information technology industry, including computers, peripherals, telecommunications, the Internet, software, CD-ROM/DVD, e-commerce, and workstations. Fees: Free for current (most recent year) data; more extensive information has various fee structures. Formerly *Computer Industry Forecasts.*

ONLINE DATABASES

ABI/INFORM. Bell & Howell Information and Learning. • Provides online indexing to business-related material occurring in over 1,000 periodicals from 1971 to the present. Inquire as to online cost and availability.

Hard Sciences. Cambridge Scientific Abstracts. • Provides the online version of *Computer and Information Systems Abstracts, Electronics and*

Communications Abstracts, Health and Safety Science Abstracts, ISMEC: Mechanical Engineering Abstracts (Information Service in Mechanical Engineering) and *Solid State and Superconductivity Abstracts.* Time period is 1981 to date, with monthly updates. Inquire as to online cost and availability.

SoftBase: Reviews, Companies, and Products. Information Sources, Inc. • Describes and reviews business software packages. Inquire as to online cost and availability.

Wilson Business Abstracts Online. H. W. Wilson Co. • Indexes and abstracts 600 major business periodicals, plus the *Wall Street Journal* and the business section of the *New York Times.* Indexing is from 1982, abstracting from 1990, with the two newspapers included from 1993. Updated weekly. Inquire as to online cost and availability. (*Business Periodicals Index* without abstracts is also available online.).

PERIODICALS AND NEWSLETTERS

CIO: The Magazine for Information Executives. CIO Communications. • Semimonthly. $89.00 per year. Edited for chief information officers. Includes a monthly "Web Business" section (incorporates the former *WebMaster* periodical) and a monthly "Enterprise" section for company executives other than CIOs.

Computer Economics Report: The Financial Advisor of Data Processing Users. Computer Economics, Inc. • Monthly. $595.00 per year. Newsletter on lease/purchase decisions, prices, discounts, residual value forecasts, personnel allocation, cost control, and other corporate computer topics. Edited for information technology (IT) executives.

Computerworld: Newsweekly for Information Technology Leaders. Computerworld, Inc. • Weekly. $39.95 per year.

Information and Management; International Journal of Information Systems Applications. Elsevier Science. • Bimonthly. $382.00 per year.

Information Executive: A Monthly Publication for DPMA and the Information Systems Profession. AITP-Association of Information Technology Professional. • Monthly. $45.00 per year. Articles reporting developmental and technical aspects of EDP services, supplies, equipment, accessories and related contemporary trends and issues. Formerly *Inside DPMA.*

Information Strategy: The Executive's Journal. Auerbach Publications. • Quarterly. $195.00 per year.

Information Systems; Data Bases: Their Creation, Management and Utilization. Elsevier Science. • Eight times a year. $1,194.00 per year.

Information Systems Management. Auerbach Publications. • Quarterly. $175.00 per year. Formerly *Journal of Information Systems Management.*

Information Week: For Business and Technology Managers. CMP Publications, Inc. • Weekly. $149.00 per year. The magazine for information systems management.

Intranet and Networking Strategies Report: Advising IT Decision Makers on Best Practices and Current Trends. Computer Economics, Inc. • Monthly. $395.00 per year. Newsletter. Edited for information technology managers. Covers news and trends relating to a variety of corporate computer network and management information systems topics. Emphasis is on costs.

IT Cost Management Strategies: The Planning Assistant for IT Directors. Computer Economics, Inc. • Monthly. $495.00 per year. Newsletter for information technology professionals. Covers data processing costs, budgeting, financial management, and related topics.

Journal of Management Information Systems. M. E. Sharpe, Inc. • Quarterly. Individuals, $75.00 per year; institutions, $380.00 per year. Includes analysis, case studies, and current research.

Journal of Systems Management. Association for Systems Management. • Monthly. $60.00 per year.

KMWorld: Creating and Managing the Knowledge-Based Enterprise. Knowledge Asset Media. • Monthly. Controlled circulation. Provides articles on knowledge management, including business intelligence, multimedia content management, document management, e-business, and intellectual property. Emphasis is on business-to-business information technology. (Knowledge Asset Media is a an affiliate of Information Today, Inc.).

Knowledge Management. CurtCo Freedom Group. • Monthly. Controlled circulation. Covers applications of information technology and knowledge management strategy.

Manufacturing Computer Solutions: The Management Magazine of Integrated Manufacturing. Findlay Publications Ltd. • Monthly. Formed by the merger of *Engineering Computers* and *Manufacturing Systems.*

MIS Quarterly (Management Information Systems). University of Minnesota School of Management. MIS Research Center, University of Minnesota, Carlson School of Management. • Quarterly. $80.00 per year.

Network Computing: Computing in a Network Environment. CMP Publications, Inc. • Semimonthly. $95.00 per year.

Report on Healthcare Information Management: A Strategic Guide to Technology and Data Integration. Aspen Publishers, Inc. • Monthly. $358.00 per year. Newsletter. Covers management information sytems for hospitals and physicians' groups.

Systems User. Caulfield Publishing Ltd. • Monthly. $62.00 per year.

RESEARCH CENTERS AND INSTITUTES

Center for Information Systems Research. Massachusetts Institute of Technology. Sloan School of Management, 77 Massachusetts Ave., MIT E40-193, Cambridge, MA 02139. Phone: (617)253-2348 Fax: (617)253-4424 E-mail: cisr@mit.edu • URL: http://web.mit.edu/cisr/www/.

Management Information Systems Research Center. University of Minnesota. Carlson School of Management, 321 19th Ave., S., Minneapolis, MN 55455-0430. Phone: (612)624-6565 Fax: (612)624-2056 • URL: http://www.misrc.umn.edu.

STATISTICS SOURCES

Information Systems Spending: An Analysis of Trends and Strategies. Computer Economics, Inc. • Annual. $1,595.00. Three volumes. Based on "in-depth surveys of public and private companies amd government organizations." Provides detailed data on management information systems spending, budgeting, and benchmarks. Includes charts, graphs, and analysis.

TRADE/PROFESSIONAL ASSOCIATIONS

Association for Data Center, Networking and Enterprise Systems. 742 E. Chapman Ave., Orange, CA 92666. Phone: (714)997-7966 Fax: (714)997-9743 E-mail: afcom@afcom.com • URL: http://www.afcom.com • Members are data processing operations management professionals.

Government Management Information Sciences. c/o Herschel E. Strickland, P.O. Box 421, Kennesaw, GA 30144-0421. Phone: 800-460-7454 or (770)975-0729 Fax: (770)975-0719 E-mail: gmishdqrs@mindspring.com • URL: http://www.gmis.org • Members are state and local government agencies.

Institute for the Management of Information Systems. Five Kingfisher House, New Mill Rd., Orpington, Kent BR5 3QG, England. Phone: 44 70 00023456 Fax: 44 70 00023023 E-mail: central@imis.org.uk.

Society for Information Management. 401 N. Michigan Ave., Chicago, IL 60621-4267. Phone: 800-387-9746 or (312)527-6734 or (312)644-6610 Fax: (312)245-1081 E-mail: info@simnet.org • URL: http://www.simnet.org.

Special Interest Group on Management Information Systems. Association for Computing Machinery, 1515 Broadway, New York, NY 10036. Phone: (212)869-7440 Fax: (212)302-5826 E-mail: sigs@acm.org • URL: http://www.acm.org/sigmis • Concerned with research, development, and innovation in business information technology. Publishes the *Database Quarterly.*

Special Interest Group on Management of Data. Association for Computing Machinery, 1515 Broadway, New York, NY 10036. Phone: (212)869-7440 Fax: (212)302-5826 E-mail: sigs@acm.org • URL: http://www.acm.org/sigmod • Concerned with database management systems. Publishes the quarterly newsletter *SIGMOD Record.*

OTHER SOURCES

Darwin: Business Evolving in the Information Age. CXO Media Inc. • Monthly. $44.95 per year. Presents non-technical explanations of information technology (IT) to corporate business executives. Uses a case study format.

Major Information Technology Companies of the World. Available from The Gale Group. • 2001. $885.00. Third edition. Published by Graham & Whiteside. Contains profiles of more than 2,600 leading information technology companies in various countries.

MANAGEMENT OF FACTORIES

See: FACTORY MANAGEMENT

MANAGEMENT, OPERATIONS

See: OPERATIONS MANAGEMENT

MANAGEMENT, PARTICIPATIVE

See: PARTICIPATIVE MANAGEMENT

MANAGEMENT, PRODUCTION

See: OPERATIONS MANAGEMENT

MANAGEMENT, SCIENTIFIC

See: TIME AND MOTION STUDY

MANAGEMENT SYSTEMS

See: SYSTEMS IN MANAGEMENT

MANAGEMENT THEORY

See also: ADMINISTRATION

GENERAL WORKS

Images of Organization. Gareth Morgan. Sage Publications, Inc. • 1996. $59.95. Second edition. Includes bibliography and index.

The Logic of Organizations. Bengt Abrahamsson. Sage Publications, Inc. • 1993. $42.00. Consists of two major sections: "The Emergence of Bureaucracy.." and "Administration Theory..".

Management: Theory, Process, and Practice. Richard M. Hodgetts. harcourt Trade Publishers. • 1989. Fifth edition. Price on application.

Modern Organizations: Administrative Theory in Contemporary Society. Ali Farazmand. Greenwood Publishing Group, Inc. • 1994. $59.95.

A Primer on Organizational Behavior. James L. Bowditch and Anthony F. Buono. John Wiley and Sons, Inc. • 1996. $48.95. Fourth edition. Price on application. Includes a discussion of participative management. Emphasis is on research and the theory of organizations. (Wiley Management Series).

Rethinking Organization: New Directions in Organization Theory and Analysis. Michael Reed and Michael Hughes. Sage Publications, Inc. • 1992. $62.00.

The Witch Doctors: Making Sense of the Management Gurus. John Micklethwait and Adrian Wooldridge. Crown Publishing Group, Inc. • 1996. $25.00. A critical, iconoclastic, and practical view of consultants, business school professors, and modern management theory, written by two members of the editorial staff of *The Economist.*

ABSTRACTS AND INDEXES

Business Periodicals Index. H. W. Wilson Co. • Monthly, except August, with quarterly and annual cumulations. Service basis for print edition; CD-ROM edition, $1,495.00 per year.

Social Sciences Citation Index. Institute for Scientific Information. • Three times a year. $6,900 per year. Annual cumulation. Includes *Source Index, Citation Index, Permuterm Subject Index,* and *Corporate Index.*

Social Sciences Index. H. W. Wilson Co. • Quarterly, with annual cumulation. Service basis for print edition; CD-ROM edition, $1,495 per year. Indexes more than 400 periodicals covering economics, environmental policy, government, insurance, labor, health care policy, plannning, public administration, public welfare, urban studies, women's issues, criminology, and related topics.

CD-ROM DATABASES

Profiles in Business and Management: An International Directory of Scholars and Their Research [CD-ROM]. Harvard Business School Publishing. • Annual. $595.00 per year. Fully searchable CD-ROM version of two-volume printed directory. Contains bibliographic and biographical information for over 5600 business and management experts active in 21 subject areas. Formerly *International Directory of Business and Management Scholars.*

Social Science Source. EBSCO Publishing. • Monthly. $1,495.00 per year. Provides CD-ROM citations and abstracts to social science articles in more than 600 periodicals, with full text from 125 periodicals. Covers economics, political science, public policy, international relations, psychology, and other topics. Time period is most recent five years.

Social Sciences Citation Index: Compact Disc Edition. Institute for Scientific Information. • Quarterly. Provides CD-ROM indexing of the world's social sciences literature, including economics, business, finance, management, communications, demographics, information and library science, political science, sociology, etc. Corresponds to online *Social Scisearch* and printed *Social Sciences Citation Index.*

Social Sciences Citation Index: Compact Disc Edition with Abstracts. Institute for Scientific Information. • Quarterly. Provides CD-ROM indexing and abstracting of "significant articles" from 1,400 social science journals worldwide, with additional selections from 3,200 other journals, 1986 to date. Includes economics, business, finance, management, communications, demographics, information and library science, political science, sociology, and many other subjects.

WILSONDISC: Wilson Social Sciences Abstracts. H. W. Wilson Co. • Monthly. Including unlimited online access to *Social Sciences Index* through WILSONLINE. Provides CD-ROM indexing from 1983 and abstracting from 1994 of more than 400 periodicals covering economics, area studies, community health, public administration, public welfare, urban studies, and many other topics related to the social sciences.

DIRECTORIES

Profiles in Business and Management: An International Directory of Scholars and Their Research Version 2.0. Claudia Bruce, editor. Harvard Business School Press. • 1996. $495.00. Two volumes. Provides backgrounds, publications, and current research projects of more than 5,600 business and management experts.

ENCYCLOPEDIAS AND DICTIONARIES

Blackwell Encyclopedic Dictionary of Organizational Behavior. Nigel Nicholson, editor. Blackwell Publishers. • 1995. $105.95. The editor is associated with the London Business School. Contains definitions of key terms combined with longer articles written by various U. S. and foreign business educators. Includes bibliographies and index. *Blackwell Encyclopedia of Management Series.*

International Encyclopedia of Business and Management. Malcolm Warner, editor. Routledge, Inc. • 1996. $1,319.95. Six volumes. Contains more than 500 articles on global management issues. Includes extensive bibliographies, cross references, and an index of key words and phrases.

International Encyclopedia of Public Policy and Administration. Jay M. Shafritz, editor. HarperCollins Publishers. • 1997. $550.00. Four volumes. Covers 20 major areas, such as public administration, government budgeting, industrial policy, nonprofit management, organizational theory, public finance, labor relations, and taxation. Includes a brief bibliography for each major entry and a comprehensive index.

HANDBOOKS AND MANUALS

Handbook of Organization Studies. Stewart R. Clegg and others, editors. Sage Publications, Inc. • 1996. $95.00. Consists of 29 chapters by various authors. Covers "theory, research, and practice in organization studies," including such topics as organizational economics, leadership, decision making, communication, and innovation.

ONLINE DATABASES

ABI/INFORM. Bell & Howell Information and Learning. • Provides online indexing to business-related material occurring in over 1,000 periodicals from 1971 to the present. Inquire as to online cost and availability.

Business and Management Practices. Responsive Database Services, Inc. • Provides fulltext of management articles appearing in more than 350 relevant publications. Emphasis is on "the processes, methods, and strategies of managing a business." Time span is 1995 to date. Inquire as to online cost and availability. (Also available in a CD-ROM version.).

Management Contents. The Gale Group. • Covers a wide range of management, financial, marketing, personnel, and administrative topics. About 150 leading business journals are indexed and abstracted from 1974 to date, with monthly updating. Inquire as to online cost and availability.

Social Scisearch. Institute for Scientific Information. • Broad, multidisciplinary index to the literature of the social sciences, 1972 to present. Weekly updates. Worldwide coverage. Inquire as to online cost and availability.

Wilson Business Abstracts Online. H. W. Wilson Co. • Indexes and abstracts 600 major business periodicals, plus the *Wall Street Journal* and the business section of the *New York Times.* Indexing is from 1982, abstracting from 1990, with the two newspapers included from 1993. Updated weekly. Inquire as to online cost and availability. (*Business Periodicals Index* without abstracts is also available online.).

Wilson Social Sciences Abstracts Online. H. W. Wilson Co. • Provides online abstracting and indexing of more than 415 periodicals covering area studies, community health, public administration, public welfare, urban studies, and many other social science topics. Time period is 1994 to date for abstracts and 1983 to date for indexing, with updates monthly. Inquire as to online cost and availability.

PERIODICALS AND NEWSLETTERS

The Academy of Management Executive. Oxford University Press, Journals. • Quarterly. $135.00 per year. Contains articles relating to the practical application of management principles and theory.

Academy of Management Journal. Academy of Management. • Bimonthly. $95.00 per year. Presents research papers on management-related topics.

Academy of Management Review. Academy of Management. • Quarterly. $80.00 per year. A scholarly journal concerned with the theory of management and organizations.

Administrative Science Quarterly. Cornell University Press, Johnson Graduate School of Management. • Individuals: $55.00 per year; institutions, $100.00 per year.

Chief Executive Magazine. Chief Executive Group, Inc. • 10 times a year. $95.00 per year.

Harvard Business Review. Harvard University, Graduate School of Business Administration. Harvard Businss School Publishing. • Bimonthly. $95.00 per year.

The Journal of Business. University of Chicago Press, Journals Div. • Quarterly. Individuals, $27.00 per year; institutions, $65.00 per year; students, $17.00 per year.

Journal of Economics and Management Strategy. MIT Press. • Quarterly. Individuals, $45.00 per year; institutions, $135.00 per year. Covers "theoretical and empirical industrial organization, applied game theory, and management strategy.".

Management Review. American Management Association. • Membership.

Management Science. Institute for Operations Research and the Management Sciences. • Monthly. Individuals, $143.00 per year; institutions, $327.00 per year. Provides an interchange of information between management and management scientists in industry, academia, the military and government.

Organizational Dynamics: A Quarterly Review of Organizational Behavior for Management Executives. American Management Association. • Quarterly. $74.00 per year. Covers the application of behavioral sciences to business management.

Sloan Management Review. Sloan Management Review Association. Massachusetts Institute of Technology, Sloan School of Management. • Quarterly. $89.00 per year.

RESEARCH CENTERS AND INSTITUTES

Board of Research. Babson College, Babson Park, MA 02457. Phone: (718)239-5339 Fax: (718)239-6416 • URL: http://www.babson.edu/bor • Research areas include management, entrepreneurial characteristics, and multi-product inventory analysis.

Bureau of Economic and Business Research. University of Illinois at Urbana-Champaign, 1206 S. Sixth St., Champaign, IL 61820. Phone: (217)333-2330 Fax: (217)244-7410 E-mail: g-oldman@uiuc.edu • URL: http://www.cba.uiuc.edu/research.

Executive Education. University of Wisconsin-Madison, School of Business, 975 University Ave., Madison, WI 53706-1323. Phone: 800-292-8964 or (608)441-7305 Fax: (608)441-7325 E-mail: dantonioni@bus.wisc.edu • URL: http://www.uwexeced.com/antonioni.

SEI Center for Advanced Studies in Management. University of Pennsylvania, 1400 Steinberg Hall-Dietrich, 3620 Locust Walk, Philadelphia, PA 19104-6371. Phone: (215)898-2349 Fax: (215)898-1703 E-mail: seicenter@wharton.upenn.edu • URL: http://www.marketing.wharton.upenn.edu/seicenter • Conducts interdisciplinary management studies.

TRADE/PROFESSIONAL ASSOCIATIONS

Academy of Management. P.O. Box 3020, Briarcliff Manor, NY 10510-3020. Phone: (914)923-2607 Fax: (914)923-2615 E-mail: aom@academy.pace.edu • URL: http://www.aom.pace.edu • Members are university professors of management and selected business executives.

American Management Association. 1601 Broadway, New York, NY 10019-7420. Phone: 800-262-9699 or (212)586-8100 Fax: (212)903-8168 • URL: http://www.amanet.org.

Society for Advancement of Management. Texas A&M University-Corpus Christi, College of Business, 6300 Ocean Dr., Corpus Christi, TX 78412. Phone: 888-827-6077 or (361)825-6045 or (361)825-5574 Fax: (361)825-2725 E-mail: moustafa@falcon.tamucc.edu • URL: http://www.enterprise.tamucc.edu/sam/.

MANPOWER

See: LABOR SUPPLY

MANUALS, PROCEDURE

See: PROCEDURE MANUALS

MANUFACTURED HOUSING

See: PREFABRICATED HOUSE INDUSTRY

MANUFACTURERS

See: CORPORATIONS; INDUSTRY; PRIVATE COMPANIES

MANUFACTURERS' AGENTS

DIRECTORIES

Manufacturers' Agents National Association - Directory of Manufacturers' Sales Agencies. Manufacturers' Agents National Association. • Annual. $129.00. Lists over 6,500 independent agents and firms. Price includes one year subscription to *Agency Sales Magazines.* Formerly *Manufacturers' Agents National Association-Directory of Members.*

HANDBOOKS AND MANUALS

Sales Representative Law Guide. CCH, Inc. • Looseleaf. $149.00 per year (updated annually). Covers state laws on independent sales representation. Includes checklists and forms.

PERIODICALS AND NEWSLETTERS

Agency Sales: The Marketing Magazine for Manufacturers' Agencies and Their Principals. Manufacturers' Agents National Association. • Monthly. $49.00 per year.

Rep-Letter. Manufacturers' Agents National Association. • Monthly. $37.50. A bound-in monthly feature of *Agency Sales Magazine.*

TRADE/PROFESSIONAL ASSOCIATIONS

Manufacturers' Agents National Association. P.O. Box 3467, Laguna Hills, CA 92654. Phone: (949)859-4040 Fax: (949)855-2973 E-mail: mana@manaonline.org • URL: http://www.manaonline.org.

MANUFACTURING

See: INDUSTRY

MANUFACTURING, COMPUTER-AIDED

See: COMPUTER-AIDED DESIGN AND MANUFACTURING (CAD/CAM)

MAPS

GENERAL WORKS

World Cartography. United Nations, Department of Economic and Social Affairs. United Nations Publications. • Various volumes. Price on application.

ABSTRACTS AND INDEXES

Geographical Abstracts: Human and Physical Geography. Elsevier Science. • Monthly. $3,253 per year. *Human Geography* $1,407.00 per year. Annual cumulation. *Physical Geography* $1,846.00 per year. Annual cumulation.

BIBLIOGRAPHIES

Bibliographic Guide to Maps and Atlases. Available from The Gale Group. • Annual. $295.00. Published by G. K. Hall & Co. Lists maps and atlases cataloged by the New York Public Library and the Library of Congress.

HANDBOOKS AND MANUALS

Map Librarianship: An Introduction. Libraries Unlimited, Inc. • 1998. $68.50. Third edition.

ONLINE DATABASES

GEOARCHIVE. Geosystems. • Citations to literature on geoscience and water. 1974 to present. Monthly updates. Inquire as to online cost and availability.

PERIODICALS AND NEWSLETTERS

Cartography and Geographic Information Science. American Congress on Surveying and Mapping. • Quarterly. Free to members; non-members, $90.00 per year.

Surveying and Land Information Systems: Devoted to the Advancement of the Sciences of Surveying and Mapping. American Congress on Surveying and Mapping. • Quarterly. Free to members; non-members, $90.00 per year. Formerly *Surveying and Mapping.*

STATISTICS SOURCES

World Bank Atlas. The World Bank, Office of the Publisher. • Annual. Price on application. Contains "color maps, charts, and graphs representing the main social, economic, and environmental indicators for 209 countries and territories" (publisher).

TRADE/PROFESSIONAL ASSOCIATIONS

American Congress on Surveying and Mapping. 5410 Grosvenor Lane, Suite 100, Bethesda, MD 20814-2144. Phone: (301)493-0200 Fax: (301)493-8245 E-mail: infoacsm@mindspring.com • URL: http://www.survmap.com.

OTHER SOURCES

Atlas & Gazetteer Series. DeLorme Mapping Co. • Dates vary. $649.95 complete ($74.95 per region). Consists of 50 volumes covering all areas of the U. S. Includes detailed maps, as well as descriptions of attractions, natural areas, and historic sites. (CD-ROM versions available.).

Columbia Gazetteer of North America. Saul B. Cohen, editor. Columbia University Press. • 2000. $250.00. Contains information on 50,000 places within the U. S., Canada, Mexico, and the Caribbean. Includes 24 pages of color maps. Provides brief descriptions of natural resources and industrial activities.

Columbia Gazetteer of the World. Saul B. Cohen, editor. Columbia University Press. • 1998. $750.00. Three volumes. Also available online (http://www.columbiagazetteer.org) and on CD-ROM.

Commercial Atlas and Marketing Guide. Rand McNally. • Annual. $395.00. Includes maps and marketing data: population, transportation, communication, and local area business statistics. Provides information on more than 128,000 U.S. locations.

Lloyd's Maritime Atlas of World Ports and Shipping Places. Available from Informa Publishing Group Ltd. • Annual. $119.00. Published in the UK by Lloyd's List (http://www.lloydslist.com). Contains more than 70 pages of world, ocean, regional, and port maps in color. Provides additional information for the planning of world shipping routes, including data on distances, port facilities, recurring weather hazards at sea, international load line zones, and sailing times.

Maps on File. Facts on File. • Annual. $195.00. Update, $45.00. 300 country and other maps in looseleaf binder.

Township Atlas of the United States. The Gale Group. • 2000. $85.00. Fourth edition. Covers the 48 contiguous states. Includes state maps, county maps, townships, subdivisions, and indexes.

Zip Code Mapbook of Metropolitan Areas. CACI Marketing Systems. • 1992. $195.00. Second edition. Contains Zip Code two-color maps of 326 metropolitan areas. Includes summary statistical profiles of each area: population characteristics, employment, housing, and income.

MARBLE

See also: QUARRYING

PERIODICALS AND NEWSLETTERS

Building Stone Magazine. Building Stone Institute. • Bimonthly. $65.00 per year.

TRADE/PROFESSIONAL ASSOCIATIONS

International Cast Polymer Association. 8201 Greensboro Dr., Suite 300, McLean, VA 22102-

3810. Phone: 800-414-4272 or (703)610-9034 Fax: (703)610-9005 E-mail: icpa@icpa-hq.com • URL: http://www.icpa-hq.com.

Marble Institute of America. 30 Eden Alley, Suite 301, Columbus, OH 43215. Phone: (614)228-6194 Fax: (614)461-1497 E-mail: miaadmin@marble-institute.com • URL: http://www.marble-institute.com.

MARGARINE INDUSTRY

CD-ROM DATABASES

Food Science and Technology Abstracts [CD-ROM]. Available from SilverPlatter Information, Inc. • Quarterly. $3,700 per year. Produced by International Food Information Service (home page is http://www.ifis.org). Provides worldwide coverage on CD-ROM of the literature of food technology and production. Various types of publications are indexed, with abstracts, including about 1,800 periodicals. Time period is 1969 to date.

INTERNET DATABASES

USDA. United States Department of Agriculture. Phone: (202)720-2791 E-mail: agsec@usda.gov • URL: http://www.usda.gov • The USDA home page has six sections: News and Information; What's New; About USDA; Agencies; Opportunities; Search and Help. Keyword searching is offered from the USDA home page and from various individual agency home pages. Agencies are the Economic Research Service, Agricultural Marketing Service, National Agricultural Statistics Service, National Agricultural Library, and about 12 others. Updating varies. Fees: Free.

ONLINE DATABASES

Food Science and Technology Abstracts [online]. IFIS North American Desk. • Produced by International Food Information Service. Provides about 500,000 online citations, with abstracts, to the international literature of food science, technology, commodities, engineering, and processing. Approximately 2,000 periodicals are covered. Time period is 1969 to date, with monthly updates. Inquire as to online cost and availability.

STATISTICS SOURCES

Agricultural Statistics. Available from U. S. Government Printing Office. • Annual. Produced by the National Agricultural Statistics Service, U. S. Department of Agriculture. Provides a wide variety of statistical data relating to agricultural production, supplies, consumption, prices/price-supports, foreign trade, costs, and returns, as well as farm labor, loans, income, and population. In many cases, historical data is shown annually for 10 years. In addition to farm data, includes detailed fishery statistics.

TRADE/PROFESSIONAL ASSOCIATIONS

National Association of Margarine Manufacturers. 1101 15th St., N.W., Suite 202, Washington, DC 20005. Phone: (202)785-3232 Fax: (202)223-9741 E-mail: namm@assnhq.com • URL: http://www.assnhq.com.

OTHER SOURCES

Major Food and Drink Companies of the World. Available from The Gale Group. • 2001. $855.00. Fourth edition. Two volumes. Published by Graham & Whiteside. Contains profiles and trade names for more than 9,000 important food and beverage companies in various countries. In addition to foods, includes both alcoholic and nonalcoholic drink products.

Thomas Food and Beverage Market Place. Grey House Publishing. • Annual. $295.00. Three volumes. Contains more than 40,000 entries covering food companies, beverages, food equipment, warehouse companies, food brokers, wholesalers, importers, and exporters. Formerly *Thomas Food Industry Register.*

MARINAS

ABSTRACTS AND INDEXES

Fluid Abstracts: Civil Engineering. Elsevier Science. • Monthly. $1,319.00 per year. Annual cumulation. Includes the literature of coastal structures.Published in England by Elsevier Science Publishing Ltd. Formerly *Civil Engineering Hydraulics Abstracts.*

Oceanic Abstracts. Cambridge Information Group. • Bimonthly. $1,045.00 per year. Covers oceanography, marine biology, ocean shipping, and a wide range of other marine-related subject areas.

Readers' Guide to Periodical Literature. H. W. Wilson Co. • Monthly. $220.00 per year. CD-ROM edition, $1,495 per year, including annual cumulation. Indexes about 250 peridicals of general interest.

CD-ROM DATABASES

WILSONDISC: Readers' Guide to Periodical Literature. H. W. Wilson Co. • Monthly. $1,095.00 per year, including unlimited online access to *Readers' Guide to Periodical Literature* through WILSONLINE. Provides CD-ROM indexing of about 250 general interest periodicals. Covers 1983 to date. (*Readers' Guide Abstracts* also available on CD-ROM at $1,995 per year.).

DIRECTORIES

Waterway Guide: The Yachtman's Bible. Intertec Publishing Corp. • Annual. $33.95 per edition. Three regional editions: Northern, and Middle Atlantic, Southern. Provides detailed information concerning marinas on inland and coastal waterways.

ONLINE DATABASES

Oceanic Abstracts (Online). Cambridge Scientific Abstracts. • Oceanographic and other marine-related technical literature, 1981 to present.Monthly updates. Inquire as to online cost and availability.

Readers' Guide Abstracts Online. H. W. Wilson Co. • Indexes and abstracts general interest periodicals, 1983 to date. Weekly updates. Inquire as to online cost and availability.

PERIODICALS AND NEWSLETTERS

Boating Industry: The Management Magazine of the Boating Industry. Intertec Publishing Corp. • Monthly. $38.00 per year. Supplement available: *Boating Industry Marine Buyer's Guide.*

Marina Dock Age. Preston Publications, Inc. • Bimonthly. $24.00 per year. Published for owners and managers of marinas and boatyards.

RESEARCH CENTERS AND INSTITUTES

National Ports and Waterways Institute. Louisiana State University, 2300 Claredon Blvd., Suite 300, Arlington, VA 22201. Phone: (703)276-7101 Fax: (703)276-7102 E-mail: npwi@seas.gwu.edu • URL: http://www.members.tripod.com/~npwi.

TRADE/PROFESSIONAL ASSOCIATIONS

American Boat Builders and Repairers Association. 425 E. 79th St., No. 11B, New York, NY 10021-1006. Phone: (212)396-4246 Fax: (212)396-4243 E-mail: abbra2@aol.com • URL: http://www.abbrayacht.com.

MARINE ENGINEERING

ABSTRACTS AND INDEXES

NTIS Alerts: Ocean Sciences and Technology. National Technical Information Service. • Semimonthly. $210.00 per year. Provides descriptions of government-sponsored research reports and software, with ordering information. Formerly *Abstract Newsletter.*

DIRECTORIES

Fairplay World Shipping Directory. Available from Fairplay Publications, Inc. • Annual. $360.00. Published in the UK by Lloyd's Register-Fairplay Ltd. Provides information on more than 64,000 companies providing maritime services and products, including 1,600 shipbuilders and data on 55,000 individual ships. Includes shipowners, shipbrokers, engine builders, salvage companies, marine insurance companies, maritime lawyers, consultants, maritime schools, etc. Five indexes cover a total of 170,000 entries.

Lloyd's Maritime Directory. Available from Informa Publishing Group Ltd. • Annual. $468.00. Two volumes. Published in the UK by Lloyd's List (http://www.lloydslist.com). Lists more than 5,500 shipowners, container companies, salvage firms, towing services, shipbuilders, ship repairers, marine engine builders, ship management services, maritime lawyers, consultants, etc.

Motor Ship Directory of Shipowners and Shipbuilders. Reed Business Information. • Annual. $120.00. Formerly *Directory of Shipowners, Shipbuilders and Marine Engineers.*

ENCYCLOPEDIAS AND DICTIONARIES

Dictionary of Marine Technology. Cyril Hughes. Available from Informa Publishing Group Ltd. • 1997. $108.00. Published in the UK by Lloyd's List (http://www.lloydslist.com). Includes more than 1,000 terms and acronyms in the fields of ship operation, technology, marine construction, maritime safety, environmental issues, and government regulation of shipping.

Illustrated Dictionary of Cargo Handling. Peter Brodie. Available from Informa Publishing Group Ltd. • 1996. $100.00. Second edition. Published in the UK by Lloyd's List (http://www.lloydslist.com). Provides definitions of about 600 terms relating to "the vessels and equipment used in modern cargo handling and shipping," including containerization.

HANDBOOKS AND MANUALS

Lloyd's List Marine Equipment Buyers' Guide. Available from Informa Publishing Group Ltd. • Annual. $270.00. Published in the UK by Lloyd's List (http://www.lloydslist.com). Lists more than 6,000 companies worldwide supplying over 2,000 types of marine products and services, including offshore equipment.

PERIODICALS AND NEWSLETTERS

Global Positioning and Navigation News. Phillips Business Information, Inc. • Biweekly. $597.00. Newsletter. Formerly *Marine Technology News.*

Journal of Ship Research. Society of Naval Architects and Marine Engineers. • Quarterly. Individuals, $25.00 per year; institutions, $98.00 per year.

Marine Engineers Review: Journal of the Institute of Marine Engineers. Available from Information Today, Inc. • Monthly. $140.00 per year. Published in London by the Institute of Marine Engineers. Covers marine engineering, offshore industries, and ocean shipping. Supplement available *Directory of Marine Diesel Engines.*

Marine Log. Simmons-Boardman Publishing Corp. • Monthly. $35.00 per year. Formerly *Marine Engineering-Log.*

Marine Management Holdings: Transactions. Available from Information Today, Inc. • Bimonthly. $220.00 per year. Published in London by Marine Management Holdings Ltd. Contains technical and regulatory material on a wide variety of marine and offshore topics. Formerly *Institute of Marine Engineers: Transactions.*

Marine Technology and SNAME News. Society of Naval Architects and Marine Engineers. •

Bimonthly. Individuals, $25.00 per year; institutions, $98.00 per year. Formerly *Marine Technology.*

Maritime Reporter and Engineering News. Maritime Activity Reports, Inc. • Monthly. $44.00 per year.

Naval Engineers Journal. American Society of Naval Engineers, Inc. • Bimonthly. $100 per year.

TRADE/PROFESSIONAL ASSOCIATIONS

American Society of Naval Engineers. 1452 Duke St., Alexandria, VA 22314. Phone: (703)836-6727 Fax: (703)836-7491 E-mail: asnehq@navalengineers.org • URL: http://www.navalengineers.org.

Institute of Marine Engineers. 76 Mark Lane, London EC3R 7JN, England. Phone: 44 207 3822600 Fax: 44 207 3822670 E-mail: mic@imare.org.uk • URL: http://www.imare.org.uk • An international organization of marine engineers, offshore engineers, and naval architects.

Marine Technology Society. 1828 L St., N.W., Suite 906, Washington, DC 20036. Phone: (202)775-5966 Fax: (202)429-9417 E-mail: mtsadmin@erols.com • URL: http://www.mtsociety.org.

Society of Naval Architects and Marine Engineers. 601 Pavonia Ave., Suite 400, Jersey City, NJ 07306. Phone: 800-798-2188 or (201)798-4800 Fax: (201)798-4975 • URL: http://www.sname.org.

OTHER SOURCES

Lloyd's List. Available from Informa Publishing Group Ltd. • Daily. $1,665.00 per year. Published in the UK by Lloyd's List (http://www.lloydslist.com). Marine industry newspaper. Covers a wide variety of maritime topics, including global news, business/insurance, regulation, shipping markets, financial markets, shipping movements, freight logistics, and marine technology. (Also available weekly at $385.00 per year.).

Lloyd's Ship Manager. Available from Informa Publishing Group Ltd. • Monthly. $251.00 per year, including annual supplementary guides and directories. Published in the UK by Lloyd's List (http://www.lloydslist.com). Covers all management, technical, and operational aspects of ocean-going shipping.

MARINE INSURANCE

CD-ROM DATABASES

U. S. Insurance: Property and Casualty. Sheshunoff Information Services, Inc. • Monthly. Price on application. CD-ROM provides detailed, current financial information on more than 3,200 property and casualty insurance companies.

DIRECTORIES

Fairplay World Shipping Directory. Available from Fairplay Publications, Inc. • Annual. $360.00. Published in the UK by Lloyd's Register-Fairplay Ltd. Provides information on more than 64,000 companies providing maritime services and products, including 1,600 shipbuilders and data on 55,000 individual ships. Includes shipowners, shipbrokers, engine builders, salvage companies, marine insurance companies, maritime lawyers, consultants, maritime schools, etc. Five indexes cover a total of 170,000 entries.

Lloyd's Maritime Directory. Available from Informa Publishing Group Ltd. • Annual. $468.00. Two volumes. Published in the UK by Lloyd's List (http://www.lloydslist.com). Lists more than 5,500 shipowners, container companies, salvage firms, towing services, shipbuilders, ship repairers, marine engine builders, ship management services, maritime lawyers, consultants, etc.

ENCYCLOPEDIAS AND DICTIONARIES

Marine Encyclopaedic Dictionary. Eric Sullivan. Available from Informa Publishing Group Ltd. • 1996. $110.00. Fifth edition. Published in the UK by Lloyd's List (http://www.lloydslist.com). Provides more than 20,000 marine-related definitions, including 2,000 technical terms. Covers all operational aspects of the shipping business: shipbroking, chartering, insurance, freight forwarding, maritime law, etc.

HANDBOOKS AND MANUALS

Marine Claims Handbook. N. Geoffry Hudson and Jeffrey Allen. Available from Informa Publishing Group Ltd. • 1996. $60.00. Fifth edition. Published in the UK by Lloyd's List (http://www.lloydslist.com). Covers the basic principles of marine insurance claims, including "correct procedural steps" and documentation.

ONLINE DATABASES

I.I.I. Data Base Search. Insurance Information Institute. • Provides online citations and abstracts of insurance-related literature in magazines, newspapers, trade journals, and books. Emphasis is on property and casualty insurance issues, including highway safety, product safety, and environmental liability. Inquire as to online cost and availability.

PERIODICALS AND NEWSLETTERS

Business Insurance: News Magazine for Corporate Risk, Employee Benefit and Financial Executives. Crain Communications, Inc. • Weekly. $89.00 per year. Covers a wide variety of business insurance topics, including risk management, employee benefits, workers compensation, marine insurance, and casualty insurance.

STATISTICS SOURCES

Property-Casualty Insurance Facts. Insurance Information Institute. • Annual. $22.50. Formerly *Insurance Facts.*

TRADE/PROFESSIONAL ASSOCIATIONS

American Institute of Marine Underwriters. 14 Wall St., New York, NY 10005. Phone: (212)233-0550 Fax: (212)227-5102 E-mail: aimu@aimu.org.

OTHER SOURCES

Insurance Day. Available from Informa Publishing Group Ltd. • Three times a week. $440.00 per year. Published in the UK by Lloyd's List (http://www.lloydslist.com). A newspaper providing international coverage of property/casualty/liability insurance, reinsurance, and risk, with an emphasis on marine insurance.

Lloyd's List. Available from Informa Publishing Group Ltd. • Daily. $1,665.00 per year. Published in the UK by Lloyd's List (http://www.lloydslist.com). Marine industry newspaper. Covers a wide variety of maritime topics, including global news, business/insurance, regulation, shipping markets, financial markets, shipping movements, freight logistics, and marine technology. (Also available weekly at $385.00 per year.).

Modern Law of Marine Insurance. D. Rhidian Thomas, editor. Available from Informa Publishing Group Ltd. • 1996. $160.00. Published in the UK by Lloyd's List (http://www.lloydslist.com). Contains contributions from both academics and practitioners on contracts, clauses, perils, proof, losses, seaworthiness, causation, insurance brokers, etc.

MARINE LAW

See: MARITIME LAW AND REGULATION

MARITIME INDUSTRY

See: SHIPS, SHIPPING AND SHIPBUILDING

MARITIME LAW AND REGULATION

ABSTRACTS AND INDEXES

Index to Legal Periodicals and Books. H. W. Wilson Co. • Monthly. Quarterly and annual cumulations. $270.00 per year. CD-ROM version available at $1,495.00 per year.

BIBLIOGRAPHIES

Law of the Sea: A Select Bibliography. United Nations Publications. • Annual. $17.00. Includes 23 subject categories.

Law of the Sea Bulletin. United Nations Publications. • Three times per year. $15.00 per issue. $40.00 per year.

DIRECTORIES

Fairplay World Shipping Directory. Available from Fairplay Publications, Inc. • Annual. $360.00. Published in the UK by Lloyd's Register-Fairplay Ltd. Provides information on more than 64,000 companies providing maritime services and products, including 1,600 shipbuilders and data on 55,000 individual ships. Includes shipowners, shipbrokers, engine builders, salvage companies, marine insurance companies, maritime lawyers, consultants, maritime schools, etc. Five indexes cover a total of 170,000 entries.

Lloyd's Maritime Directory. Available from Informa Publishing Group Ltd. • Annual. $468.00. Two volumes. Published in the UK by Lloyd's List (http://www.lloydslist.com). Lists more than 5,500 shipowners, container companies, salvage firms, towing services, shipbuilders, ship repairers, marine engine builders, ship management services, maritime lawyers, consultants, etc.

ENCYCLOPEDIAS AND DICTIONARIES

Dictionary of Shipping Terms. Peter Brodie. Available from Informa Publishing Group Ltd. • 1997. $57.00. Third edition. Published in the UK by Lloyd's List (http://www.lloydslist.com). Defines more than 2,000 words, phrases, and abbreviations related to the shipping and maritime industries.

Marine Encyclopaedic Dictionary. Eric Sullivan. Available from Informa Publishing Group Ltd. • 1996. $110.00. Fifth edition. Published in the UK by Lloyd's List (http://www.lloydslist.com). Provides more than 20,000 marine-related definitions, including 2,000 technical terms. Covers all operational aspects of the shipping business: shipbroking, chartering, insurance, freight forwarding, maritime law, etc.

PERIODICALS AND NEWSLETTERS

American Maritime Cases. American Maritime Cases, Inc. • 10 times a year. $637.50 per year.

Journal of Maritime Law and Commerce. Jefferson Law Book Co. • Quarterly. $150.00 per year.

Ocean Development and International Law; The Journal of Marine Affairs. Taylor & Francis, Inc. • Quarterly. Individuals, $191.00 per year; institutions, $385.00 per year.

Tulane Maritime Law Journal. Tulane University, School of Law, John Giffen Weinmann Hall. • Semiannual. $28.00 per year. Formerly *Maritime Lawyer.*

United States Coast Guard Marine Safety Council Proceedings. U.S. Coast Guard. • Bimonthly.

TRADE/PROFESSIONAL ASSOCIATIONS

Maritime Law Association of the U.S. 80 Pine St., New York, NY 10005-1759. Phone: (212)425-1900 Fax: (212)425-1901 E-mail: bonner@freehill.com.

OTHER SOURCES

Benedict on Admiralty. Matthew Bender & Co., Inc. • $2,660.00. 25 looseleaf volumes. Periodic supplementation. Covers American law of the sea and shipping.

Capital for Shipping. Available from Informa Publishing Group Ltd. • Annual. $128.00. Published in the UK by Lloyd's List (http://www.lloydslist.com). Consists of a "Financial Directory" and a "Legal Directory," listing international ship finance providers and international law firms specializing in shipping. (Included with subscription to *Lloyd's Shipping Economist.*).

Lloyd's List. Available from Informa Publishing Group Ltd. • Daily. $1,665.00 per year. Published in the UK by Lloyd's List (http://www.lloydslist.com). Marine industry newspaper. Covers a wide variety of maritime topics, including global news, business/insurance, regulation, shipping markets, financial markets, shipping movements, freight logistics, and marine technology. (Also available weekly at $385.00 per year.).

Lloyd's Maritime and Commercial Law Quarterly. Available from Informa Publishing Group Ltd. • Quarterly. $245.00 per year. Published in the UK by Lloyd's List (http://www.lloydslist.com). Provides international coverage of relevant cases, decisions, and developments.

Lloyd's Maritime Law, North American Edition: Incorporating Court Case Digest, Maritime Personal Injury Report, and Arbitration Awards Digest. Available from Informa Publishing Group Ltd. • Biweekly. $630.00 per year. Newsletter. Published in the UK by Lloyd's List (http://www.lloydslist.com). Provides "in-depth analysis of developments in U. S. maritimne law and maritime trends.".

Modern Law of Marine Insurance. D. Rhidian Thomas, editor. Available from Informa Publishing Group Ltd. • 1996. $160.00. Published in the UK by Lloyd's List (http://www.lloydslist.com). Contains contributions from both academics and practitioners on contracts, clauses, perils, proof, losses, seaworthiness, causation, insurance brokers, etc.

MARKET RESEARCH

See also: CONSUMER SURVEYS; INTERVIEWING; MARKET STATISTICS; MARKETING; MOTIVATION (PSYCHOLOGY); STATISTICS SOURCES; SURVEY METHODS

GENERAL WORKS

Breaking Up America: Advertisers and the New Media World. Joseph Turow. University of Chicago Press. • 1997. $22.50. A social criticism of target marketing, market segmentation, and customized media.

Exploring Marketing Research. William G. Zikmund. Harcourt Trade Publications. • 1999. $94.50. Seventh edition.

How Consumers Pick a Hotel: Strategic Segmentation and Target Marketing. Dennis J. Cahill. The Haworth Press, Inc. • 1997. $39.95.

Interactive Marketing: The Future Present. Edward Forrest and Richard Mizerski, editors. NTC/Contemporary Publishing. • 1995. $47.95. Contains articles on the collection and analysis of interactive marketing data, database management, interactive media, marketing research strategies, and related topics.(NTC Business Book Series).

Look Before You Leap: Market Research Made Easy-How to Find Out What You Really Need to Know to Make Your Business Grow. Don Doman and others. Self-Counsel Press, Inc. • 1993. $14.95.

Marketing Research. David A. Aaker and others. John Wiley and Sons, Inc. • 2000. Seventh edition. Price on application. Covers data collection methods, data analysis, advanced data analysis, and applications of market research.

Marketing Research: An Applied Approach. Thomas C. Kinnear and James R. Taylor. McGraw-Hill. • 1995. $80.50. Fifth edition. Includes CD-ROM.

Marketing Research in a Marketing Environment. William R. Dillion and others. McGraw-Hill Higher Education. • 1993. $67.50. Third edition.

Marketing Research Process. Len T. Wright and Margaret Crimp. Prentice Hall. • 2000. Fifth edition. Price on application.

Marketing Research That Pays Off: Case Histories of Marketing Research Leading to Success in the Marketplace. Larry Percy, editor. Haworth Press, Inc. • 1997. $49.95.

ALMANACS AND YEARBOOKS

Research Alert Yearbook: Vital Facts on Consumer Behavior and Attitudes. EPM Communications, Inc. • Annual. $295.00. Provides summaries of consumer market research from the newsletters *Research Alert, Youth Markets Alert, and Minority Markets Alert.* Includes tables, charts, graphs, and textual summaries for 41 subject categories. Sources include reports, studies, polls, and focus groups.

Research in Marketing: An Annual Compilation of Research. Jagdish N. Sheth, editor. JAI Press, Inc. • Annual. Institutions, $78.50. Supplement available *Choice Models for Buyer Behavior.*

BIBLIOGRAPHIES

Data Sources for Business and Market Analysis. John Ganly. Scarecrow Press, Inc. • 1994. $58.00. Fourth edition. Emphasis is on sources of statistics for market research, especially government sources. Relevant directories, periodicals, and research aids are included.

Marketing Power: Your Guide to Successful Research. American Demographics, Inc. • Quarterly. Issued as a supplement to *American Demographics* and *Marketing Tools.* Describes a wide variety of current market research material issued by various publishers and available from American Demographics, Inc.

CD-ROM DATABASES

FINDEX [cd-rom]. Available from SilverPlatter Information, Inc. • Quarterly. $995.00 per year. Produced by Kalorama Information. Formerly produced by Cambridge Scientific Abstracts. Serves as the CD-ROM version of *Findex: The Worldwide Directory of Market Research Reports, Studies, and Surveys.*

Profiles in Business and Management: An International Directory of Scholars and Their Research [CD-ROM]. Harvard Business School Publishing. • Annual. $595.00 per year. Fully searchable CD-ROM version of two-volume printed directory. Contains bibliographic and biographical information for over 5600 business and management experts active in 21 subject areas. Formerly *International Directory of Business and Management Scholars.*

DIRECTORIES

Bradford's International Directory of Marketing Research Agencies n the United States and the World. Business Research Services, Inc. • Annual. $90.00. Over 1,800 marketing research agencies and management consultants in market research. Formerly *Bradford's Directory of Marketing Research Agencies and Management Consultants.*

Directory of Marketing Information Companies. American Demographics, Inc. • Annual. $10.00. Lists companies offering market research and information services, with a selection of the "Best 100 Sources of Marketing Information.".

Findex: The Worldwide Directory of Market Research Reports, Studies, and Surveys. MarketResearch.com. • Annual. $400.00. Provides brief annotations of market research reports and related publications from about 1,000 publishers, arranged by topic. Back of book includes Report Titles by Publisher, Publishers/Distributors Directory, Subject Index, Geography Index, and Company Index. (Formerly published by Cambridge Information Group.).

Focus Group Directory: International Directory of Focus Group Companies and Services. New York AMA-Green Book. • Annual. $80.00. Contains information on companies offering focus group facilities, including recruiting, moderating, and transcription services.

GreenBook: Worldwide Directory of Marketing Research Companies and Services. New York Ama-Green Book. • Annual. $145.00. Contains information in 300 categories on more than 2,500 market research companies, consultants, field services, computer services, survey research companies, etc. Indexed by specialty, industry, company, computer program, and personnel. Formerly (Greenbook Worldwide International Directory of Marketing Research Companies and Services).

Medical and Healthcare Marketplace Guide. Dorland Healthcare Information. • Annual. $690.00. Two volumes. Provides market survey summaries for about 500 specific product and service categories (volume one: "Research Reports"). Contains profiles of nearly 6,000 pharmaceutical, medical product, and healthcare service companies (volume two: "Company Profiles").

MRA Blue Book Research Services Directory. Marketing Research Association. • Annual. $169.95. Lists more than 1,200 international marketing research companies and survey services. Formerly *Directory of Research Services Provided by Members of the Marketing Research Association.*

Profiles in Business and Management: An International Directory of Scholars and Their Research Version 2.0. Claudia Bruce, editor. Harvard Business School Press. • 1996. $495.00. Two volumes. Provides backgrounds, publications, and current research projects of more than 5,600 business and management experts.

Research Services Directory: Commercial & Corporate Research Centers. Grey House Publishing. • 1999. $395.00. Seventh edition. Lists more than 6,200 independent commercial research centers and laboratories offering contract or fee-based services. Includes corporate research departments, market research companies, and information brokers.

World Directory of Marketing Information Sources. Available from The Gale Group. • 2001. $590.00. Third edition. Published by Euromonitor. Provides details on more than 6,000 sources of marketing information, including publications, libraries, associations, market research companies, online databases, and governmental organizations. Coverage is worldwide.

ENCYCLOPEDIAS AND DICTIONARIES

Blackwell Encyclopedic Dictionary of Marketing. Barbara R. Lewis and Dale Littler, editors. Blackwell Publishers. • 1996. $105.95. The editors are associated with the Manchester School of Management. Contains definitions of key terms combined with longer articles written by various U. S. and foreign business educators. Includes bibliographies and index. (Blackwell Encyclopedia of Management series.).

HANDBOOKS AND MANUALS

Do-it-Yourself Marketing Research. George Breen and Albert B. Blankenship. Replica Books. • 1998. $44.95. Third edition.

Finding Market Research on the Web: Best Practices of Professional Researchers. Robert I. Berkman. MarketResearch.com. • 1999. $235.00. Provides tips and techniques for locating useful market research data through the Internet.

Focus Group Kit. David L. Morgan and Richard A. Krueger, editors. Sage Publications, Inc. • 1997. $99.95. Six volumes. Various authors cover the basics of focus group research, including planning, developing questions, moderating, and analyzing results.

Focus Groups: A Practical Guide for Applied Research. Richard A. Krueger and Mary Anne Casey. Sage Publications, Inc. • 2000. $69.95. Third edition. A step-by-step guide to obtaining useful research data from a focus group.

Handbook for Focus Group Research. Thomas L. Greenbaum. Sage Publications, Inc. • 1997. $49.95. Second edition. Includes glossary and index.

How to Find Market Research Online. Robert I. Berkman. MarketResearch.com. • Looseleaf. $182.50, including updates for one year. Analyzes and compares the online products of 80 market research publishers. Describes popular Internet search engines and provides information on useful World Wide Web sites.

Market Research Toolbox: A Concise Guide for Beginners. Edward F. McQuarrie. Sage Publications, Inc. • 1996. $46.00.

Marketing Manager's Handbook. Sidney J. Levy and others. Prentice Hall. • 2000. Price on application. Contains 71 chapters by various authors on a wide variety of marketing topics, including market segmentation, market research, international marketing, industrial marketing, survey methods, customer service, advertising, pricing, planning, strategy, and ethics.

Marketing Research Guide. Robert E. Stevens and others. Haworth Press, Inc. • 1997. $79.95. A practical guide to the preparation of a market research report, including worksheets, sample proposals, questionnaires, and an example of a final report.

Marketing Research Project Manual. Glen R. Jarboe. South-Western Publishing Co. • 1998. $27.95. Fourth edition. Covers the methodology of market research surveys.(SWC-Marketing Series).

The New Direct Marketing: How to Implement a Profit-Driven Database Marketing Strategy. Spepard, Davis, Associates Staff. McGraw-Hill Professional. • 1998. $114.95. Third edition. Discusses the construction, analysis, practical use, and evaluation of direct marketing databases containing primary and/or secondary data.

Survey Research Handbook: Guidelines and Strategies for Conducting a Survey. Pamela L. Alreck and Robert B. Settle. McGraw-Hill Higher Education. • 1994. $50.00. Second edition. Consists of four major parts: 1. Planning and Designing the Survey, 2. Developing Survey Instruments, 3. Collecting and Processing Data, 4. Interpreting and Reporting Results. Includes a glossary and index. (Marketing Series).

INTERNET DATABASES

Intelligence Data. Thomson Financial. Phone: 800-654-0393 or (212)806-8023 Fax: (212)806-8004 • URL: http://www.intelligencedata.com • Fee-based Web site provides a wide variety of information relating to competitive intelligence, strategic planning, business development, mergers, acquisitions, sales, and marketing. "Intelliscope" feature offers searching of other Thomson units, such as Investext, MarkIntel, InSite 2, and Industry Insider. Weekly updating.

ONLINE DATABASES

Euromonitor Journals. Euromonitor International. • Contains full-text reports online from *Market Research Europe, Market Research Great Britain, Market Research International*, and *Retail Monitor International.* Time period is 1995 to date, with monthly updates. Inquire as to online cost and availability.

Euromonitor Market Research. Euromonitor International. • Provides the complete text online of Euromonitor market analysis reports. Covers consumer goods market research data for all major countries, with emphasis on specific product categories. Time period is current. Continuous updating. Inquire as to online cost and availability.

FIND/SVP Market Research Reports. Kalorama Information. • Provides online full text of market research reports produced by FIND/SVP, Packaged Facts, Specialists in Business Information and others. Contains market data for a wide variety of industries, products, and services, including market size, forecasts, trends, structure, and opportunities. Inquire as to online cost and availability.

FINDEX. Kalorama Information. • Provides online annotations of market research reports and related publications from about 1,000 publishers. Time period is 1972 to date, with quarterly updates. (Formerly produced by Cambridge Information Group.) Inquire as to online cost and availability.

Frost & Sullivan Market Research Reports. Frost & Sullivan. • Contains full text of Frost & Sullivan market research reports on various industries and products. Each report includes a five-year forecast.

MarkIntel. Thomson Financial Securities Data. • Provides the current full text online of more than 45,000 market research reports covering 54 industries, from 43 leading research firms worldwide. Reports include extensive forecasts and market analysis. Inquire as to online cost and availability.

PROMT: Predicasts Overview of Markets and Technology. The Gale Group. • Companies, products, applied technologies and markets. U.S. and international literature coverage, 1972 to date. Inquire as to online cost and availability. Provides abstracts from more than 1,600 publications. Weekly updates.

Simmons Study of Media and Markets. Simmons Market Research Bureau. • Market and media survey data relating to the American consumer. Inquire as to online cost and availability.

PERIODICALS AND NEWSLETTERS

American Demographics: Consumer Trends for Business Leaders. Intertec Publishing Co. • Monthly. $69.00 per year.

The Boomer Report: The Insights You Need to Reach America's Most Influential Consumer Group. Age Wave Communications Corp. • Monthly. $195.00 per year. Newsletter. Presents market research relating to the "baby boomers," an age group generally defined as having been born between 1950 and 1970.

Brandweek. BPI Communications, Inc. • 47 times a year. $145.00 per year. Includes articles and case studies on mass marketing and mass media. Formerly *Adweek's Marketing Week.*

Database Marketer. Intertec Publishing Co. • Monthly. $329.00 per year.

The Information Advisor: Tips and Techniques for Smart Information Users. MarketResearch.com. • Monthly. $149.00 per year. Newsletter. Evaluates and discusses online, CD-ROM, and published sources of business, financial, and market research information.

Journal of Consumer Research; An Interdisciplinary Quarterly. University of Chicago Press, Journals Div. • Quarterly. Members, $45.00 per year; institutions, $99.00 per year; students, $25.00. Covers various aspects of consumer behavior.

Journal of Marketing Research. American Marketing Association. • Quarterly. Members, $45.00 per year; non-members, $80.00 per year; institutions, $200.00 per year. Provides analysis of marketing research theory and practice.

Market Research International. Euromonitor International. • Monthly. $1,130.00 per year. Emphasis is on international consumer market research. Includes International Market Review, Global Market Trends and Developments, USA Market Report, Japan Market Report, Emerging Markets, and Market Focus (concise country reports).

Marketing Research: A Magazine of Management and Applications. American Marketing Association. • Quarterly. Members, $45.00 per year; non-members, $70.00 per year; institutions,$120.00 per year.

Marketing to the Emerging Minorities. EPM Communications, Inc. • Monthly. $295.00 per year. Newsletter on market research relating to African American, Asian American, and U. S. Hispanic populations.

Research Alert: A Bi-Weekly Report of Consumer Marketing Studies. EPM Communications, Inc. • Semimonthly. $369.00 per year. Newsletter. Provides descriptions (abstracts) of new, consumer market research reports from private, government, and academic sources. Includes sample charts and tables.

Retail Monitor International. Euromonitor International. • Monthly. $1,050.00 per year. Covers many aspects of international retailing, with emphasis on market research data. Includes profiles of leading retail groups, country profiles, retail news, trends, consumer credit information, and "Retail Factfile" (statistics).

Youth Markets Alert. EPM Communications, Inc. • Monthly. $295.00 per year. Newsletter on youth market research. Covers age groups from elementary school to college years.

STATISTICS SOURCES

DMA Statistical Fact Book. Direct Marketing Association, Inc. • Annual. $165.95 to non-members; $105.95 to members. Provides data in five sections covering direct response advertising, media, mailing lists, market applications, and "Practical Management Information." Includes material on interactive/online marketing. (Cover title: *Direct Marketing Association's Statistical Fact Book.*).

TRADE/PROFESSIONAL ASSOCIATIONS

American Marketing Association. 311 S. Wacker Dr., Suite 5800, Chicago, IL 60606. Phone: 800-262-1150 or (312)542-9000 Fax: (312)542-9001 E-mail: info@ama.org • URL: http://www.ama.org.

Chemical Management and Resources Association. 60 Bay St., Suite 702, Staten Island, NY 10301. Phone: (718)876-8800 • Members are individuals engaged in chemical market research.

Marketing Research Association. 1344 Silas Deane Hwy., Ste. 306, Rocky Hill, CT 06067-0230. Phone: (860)257-4008 Fax: (860)257-3990 E-mail: email@mra-net.org • URL: http://www.mra-net.org.

Sales and Marketing Executives. 5500 Interstate N. Parkway, No. 545, Atlanta, GA 30328. Phone:

(770)661-8500 Fax: (770)661-8512 E-mail: smeihq@smei.org • URL: http://www.smei.org.

OTHER SOURCES

Business & Company Resource Center. The Gale Group. • Fee-based Web site provides a wide range of business, industry, and specific company information. Access is offered to trade journal articles, market research data, insider trading activity, major shareholder data, corporate histories, emerging technology reports, corporate earnings estimates, press releases, and other sources. Provides detailed company profiles, industry overviews, and rankings. Offers integration of Predicasts PROMT, Newsletters ASAP, Investext Plus, Business Index ASAP, Brands and Their Companies, and other databases (many have full text).

Factiva. Dow Jones Reuters Business Interactive, LLC. • Fee-based Web site provides "global news and business information through Web sites and content integration solutions." Includes Dow Jones and Reuters newswires, The Wall Street Journal, and more than 7,000 other sources of current news, historical articles, market research reports, and investment analysis. Content includes 96 major U. S. newspapers, 900 non-English sources, trade publications, media transcripts, country profiles, news photos, etc.

The Information Catalog. MarketResearch.com. • Quarterly. Free. Mainly a catalog of market research reports from various publishers, but also includes business and marketing reference sources. Includes keyword title index. Formerly *The Information Catalog: Marketing Intelligence Studies, Competitor Reports, Business and Marketing Sources.*

InSite 2. Intelligence Data/Thomson Financial. • Fee-based Web site consolidates information in a "Base Pack" consisting of Business InSite, Market InSite, and Company InSite. Optional databases are Consumer InSite, Health and Wellness InSite, Newsletter InSite, and Computer InSite. Includes fulltext content from more than 2,500 trade publications, journals, newsletters, newspapers, analyst reports, and other sources. Continuous updating. Formerly produced by The Gale Group.

MarketingClick Network: American Demographics. Intertec Publishing, a Primedia Co. • Web site provides full-text articles from *American Demographics, Marketing Tools,* and *Forecast,* with keyword searching. The *Marketing Tools Directory* can also be searched online, listing suppliers of products, information, and services for advertising, market research, and marketing. Fees: Free.

MARKET STATISTICS

See also: BUSINESS STATISTICS; MARKET RESEARCH; MARKETING; PURCHASING POWER; STATISTICS SOURCES

GENERAL WORKS

Global Economic Prospects 2000. The World Bank, Office of the Publisher. • 1999. $25.00. "..offers an in-depth analysis of the economic prospects of developing countries.." Emphasis is on the impact of recessions and financial crises. Regional statistical data is included.

ALMANACS AND YEARBOOKS

World Development Report. The World Bank, Office of the Publisher. • Annual. $50.00. Covers history, conditions, and trends relating to economic globalization and localization. Includes selected data from *World Development Indicators* for 132 countries or economies. Key indicators are provided for 78 additional countries or economies.

BIBLIOGRAPHIES

Data Sources for Business and Market Analysis. John Ganly. Scarecrow Press, Inc. • 1994. $58.00. Fourth edition. Emphasis is on sources of statistics for market research, especially government sources. Relevant directories, periodicals, and research aids are included.

Global Data Locator. George T. Kurian. Bernan Associates. • 1997. $89.00. Provides detailed descriptions of international statistical sourcebooks and electronic databases. Covers a wide variety of trade, economic, and demographic topics.

Statistics Sources: A Subject Guide to Data on Industrial, Business, Social, Educational, Financial and Other Topics for the U. S. and Selected Foreign Countries. The Gale Group. • 2000. $475.00. 25th edition. Two volumes. Lists sources of statistical information for more than 20,000 topics.

World Directory of Non-Official Statistical Sources. Gale Group, Inc. • 2001. $590.00. Provides detailed descriptions of more than 4,000 regularly published, non-governmental statistics sources. Includes surveys, studies, market research reports, trade journals, databank compilations, and other print sources. Coverage is international, with four indexes.

CD-ROM DATABASES

F & S Index Plus Text. The Gale Group. • Monthly. $7,575.00 per year. Provides CD-ROM citations to worldwide business, marketing, and industrial material appearing in a large assortment of trade journals, newspapers, and other publications. Time period is four years.

Sourcebook America. The Gale Group. • Annual. $995.00. Produced by CACI Marketing Systems. A combination on CD-ROM of *The Sourcebook of ZIP Code Demographics* and *The Sourcebook of County Demographics.* Provides detailed population and socio-economic data (about 75 items) for each of 3,141 U. S. counties and approximately 30,000 ZIP codes, plus states, metropolitan areas, and media market areas. Includes forecasts to the year 2004.

Sourcebooks America CD-ROM. CACI Marketing Systems. • Annual. $1,250.00. Provides the CD-ROM version of *The Sourcebook of ZIP Code Demographics: Census Edition* and *The Sourcebook of County Demographics: Census Edition.*

Statistical Masterfile. Congressional Information Service. • Quarterly. Price varies. Provides CD-ROM versions of *American Statistics Index, Index to International Statistics,* and *Statistical Reference Index.* Contains indexing and abstracting of a wide variety of published statistics sources, both governmental and private.

World Consumer Markets. The Gale Group. • Annual. $2,500.00. Pblished by Euromonitor. Provides five- year historical data, current data, and forecasts, on CD-ROM for 330 consumer products in 55 countries. Market data is presented in a standardized format for each country.

World Development Report [CD-ROM]. The World Bank, Office of the Publisher. • Annual. Single-user, $375.00. Network version, $750.00. CD-ROM includes the current edition of *World Development Report* and 21 previous editions.

World Marketing Data and Statistics on CD-ROM. The Gale Group. • Annual. $1,750.00. Published by Euromonitor. Provides demographic, marketing, socioeconomic, and political data on CD-ROM for each of 209 countries.

World Marketing Forecasts on CD-ROM. The Gale Group. • Annual. $2,500.00. Produced by Euromonitor. Provides detailed forecast data for the years to 2012 on CD-ROM for 54 countries in all parts of the world. Covers a wide range of social, demographic, economic, and market factors. Includes specific forecasts for many kinds of consumer products.

DIRECTORIES

Editor and Publisher Market Guide. Editor and Publisher Co., Inc. • Annual. $125.00. More than 1,700 newspaper markets in the Unite States and Canada.

Marketing Know-How: Your Guide to the Best Marketing Tools and Sources. Intertec Publishing. • 1996. $49.95. Describes more than 700 public and private sources of consumer marketing data. Also discusses market trends and provides information on such marketing techniques as cluster analysis, focus groups, and geodemographic analysis.

HANDBOOKS AND MANUALS

Finding Statistics Online: How to Locate the Elusive Numbers You Need. Paula Berinstein. Information Today, Inc. • 1998. $29.95. Provides advice on efficient searching when looking for statistical data on the World Wide Web or from commercial online services and database producers. (CyberAge Books.).

ONLINE DATABASES

EconBase: Time Series and Forecasts. WEFA, Inc. • Presents online econometric data for business conditions, economics, demographics, industry, finance, employment, household income, interest rates, prices, etc. Includes two-year forecasts for a wide range of economic indicators. Time span is 1948 to date, with monthly updates. Inquire as to online cost and availability.

F & S Index. The Gale Group. • Contains about four million citations to worldwide business, financial, and industrial or consumer product literature appearing from 1972 to date. Weekly updates. Inquire as to online cost and availability.

Industry Insider. Thomson Financial Securities Data. • Contains full-text online industry research reports from more than 200 leading trade associations, covering 50 specific industries. Reports include extensive statistics and market research data. Inquire as to online cost and availability.

Market Share Reporter (MSR) [online]. The Gale Group. • Provides online market share data for individual companies, products, and services, covering all industries. Sources include various publications, trade journals, associations, government agencies, corporate reports, investment research reports, etc. Time period is 1991 to date, with annual updates. Inquire as to online cost and availability.

PROMT: Predicasts Overview of Markets and Technology. The Gale Group. • Companies, products, applied technologies and markets. U.S. and international literature coverage, 1972 to date. Inquire as to online cost and availability. Provides abstracts from more than 1,600 publications. Weekly updates.

Tablebase. Responsive Database Services, Inc. • Provides online numerical tabular data from a wide variety of business, organization, and government sources, including 900 trade journals. Includes industry and individual company statistics relating to products, market share, sales forecasts, production, exports, market trends, etc. Time span is 1997 to date. Weekly updates. Inquire as to online cost and availability. (Also available in a CD-ROM version.).

STATISTICS SOURCES

American Business Climate and Economic Profiles. The Gale Group. • 1993. $135.00. Provides business, industrial, demographic, and economic figures for all states and 300 metropolitan areas. Includes production, taxation, population, growth rates, labor force data, incomes, total sales, etc.

Consumer Canada 1996. Available from The Gale Group. • 1996. $750.00. Published by Euromonitor. Provides consumer market, socioeconomic, and demographic data for Canada. Includes consumer market size (volume and value) for many specific kinds of products.

Consumer International 2000/2001. Available from The Gale Group. • 1998. $1,190.00. Seventh edition. Published by Euromonitor. Contains extensive consumer market, economic, and demographic data for 27 major, non-European countries, including the U. S. and Canada. Includes consumer market size (volume and value) for 150 product types in 14 categories (food, clothing, automobiles, cosmetics, appliances, etc.).

Consumer Power: How Americans Spend. Margaret Ambry. McGraw-Hill Professional. • 1992. $27.50. Contains detailed statistics on consumer income and spending. Nine major categories of products and services are covered, with spending data and dollar size of market for each item.

Consumer USA 2000. Available from The Gale Group. • 2000. $900.00. Fifth edition. Published by Euromonitor. Provides demographic and consumer market data for the United States. Forecasts to the year 2005.

County and City Data Book, a Statistical Abstract Supplement. U.S. Bureau of the Census. Available from U.S. Government Printing Office. • 1994. $60.00.

Current Population Reports: Household Economic Studies, Series P-70. Available from U. S. Government Printing Office. • Irregular. $16.00 per year. Issued by the U.S. Bureau of the Census (http://www.census.gov). Each issue covers a special topic relating to household socioeconomic characteristics.

Demographics USA: County Edition. Market Statistics. • Annual. $435.00. Contains 200 statistical series for each of 3,000 counties. Includes population, household income, employment, retail sales, and consumer expenditures. Also provides Effective Buying Income, Buying Power Index, and data summaries by Metro Market, Media Market, and State. (CD-ROM version is available.).

Demographics USA: ZIP Edition. Market Statistics. • Annual. $435.00. Contains 50 statistical series for each of 40,000 ZIP codes. Includes population, household income, employment, retail sales, and consumer expenditures. Also provides Effective Buying Income, Business Characteristics, and data summaries by state, region, and the first three digits of ZIP codes. (CD-ROM version is available.).

European Marketing Data and Statistics 2001. Available from The Gale Group. • 2001. $450.00. 36th edition. Published by Euromonitor. Presents essential marketing data, including demographics and consumer expenditure patterns, for 31 European countries.

European Marketing Forecasts 2001. Available from The Gale Group. • 2000. $1,190.00. Third edition. Published by Euromonitor. Contains demographic, economic, and market forecasts for the countries of Europe to the year 2010. Forecasts include market-size data for 15 consumer product sectors (food, clothing, automobiles, consumer electronics, etc.).

Gale City and Metro Rankings Reporter. The Gale Group. • 1996. $134.00. Second edition. Provides about 3,000 statistical ranking tables covering more than 1,500 U. S. cities and Metropolitan Statistical Areas. Covers economic, demographic, social, governmental, and cultural factors. Sources are private studies and government data.

Gale Country and World Rankings Reporter. The Gale Group. • 1997. $135.00. Second edition. Provides about 3,000 statistical ranking tables and charts covering more than 235 nations. Sources include the United Nations and various government publications.

Gale State Rankings Reporter. The Gale Group. • 1996. $110.00. Second edition Provides 3,000 ranked lists of states under 35 subject headings. Sources are newspapers, periodicals, books, research institute publications, and government publications.

Geographic Reference Report: Annual Report of Costs, Wages, salaries, and Human Resource Statistics for the United States and Canada. ERI. • Annual. $389.00. Provides demographic and other data for each of 298 North American metropolian areas, including local salaries, wage differentials, cost-of-living, housing costs, income taxation, employment, unemployment, population, major employers, crime rates, weather, etc.

Household Spending: Who Spends How Much On What. Hoai Tran. New Strategist Publications, Inc. • 1999. $94.95. Fifth edition. Gives facts about the buying habits of U. S. consumers according to income, age, household type, and household size. Includes spending data for about 1,000 products and services.

International Marketing Data and Statistics 2001. Available from The Gale Group. • 2001. $450.00. 25th edition. Published by Euromonitor. Contains statistics on population, economic factors, energy, consumer expenditures, prices, and other items affecting marketing in 158 countries of the world.

International Marketing Forecasts 2001. Available from The Gale Group. • 2000. $1,090.00. Third edition. Published by Euromonitor. Contains demographic, economic, and market forecasts to the year 2010 for major, non-European countries, including the U. S. and Canada. Forecasts include market-size data for 15 consumer product sectors, such as food, clothing, and automobiles.

Lifestyle Market Analyst. SRDS. • Annual. $391.00. Published in conjunction with NDL (National Demographics & Lifestyles). Provides extensive lifestyle data on interests, activities, and hobbies within specific geographic and demographic markets.

Market Share Reporter: An Annual Compilation of Reported Market Share Data on Companies, Products, and Services. The Gale Group. • Annual. $265.00. Contains summaries of market share reports. Actual data is given, with many charts and graphs. List more than 2,000 entries.

Markets of the United States for Business Planners: Historical and Current Profiles of 183 U. S. Urban Economies by Major Section and Industry, with Maps, Graphics, and Commentary. Thomas F. Conroy, editor. Omnigraphics, Inc. • 1995. $240.00. Second edition. Two volumes. Based on statistics from the Personal Income and Earnings Database of the Bureau of Economic Analysis, U. S. Dept. of Commerce. Provides extensive personal income data for all urban market areas of the U. S.

Moving and Relocation Sourcebook and Directory: Reference Guide to the 100 Largest Metropolitan Areas in the United States. Kay Gill, editor. Omnigraphics, Inc. • 1998. $185.00. Second edition. Provides extensive statistical and other descriptive data for the 100 largest metropolitan areas in the U. S. Includes maps and a discussion of factors to be considered when relocating.

Sales and Marketing Management Survey of Buying Power. Bill Communications, Inc. • Annual. $150.00.

The Sourcebook of ZIP Code Demographics. Available from The Gale Group. • 2000. $495.00. 15th edition. Published by CACI Marketing Systems. Presents detailed statistical profiles of every ZIP code in America, based on the 1990 census. Each profile contains data on more than 70 variables.

Statistical Handbook on Consumption and Wealth in the United States. Chandrika Kaul and Valerie Tomaselli-Moschovitis. Oryx Press. • 1999. $65.00. Provides more than 400 graphs, tables, and charts dealing with basic income levels, income inequalities, spending patterns, taxation, subsidies, etc. (Statistical Handbook Series).

U. S. Market Trends and Forecasts. The Gale Group. • 2000. $315.00. Second edition. Provides graphic representation of market statistics by means of pie charts and tables for each of 30 major industries and 400 market segments. Includes market forecasts and historical overviews.

World Bank Atlas. The World Bank, Office of the Publisher. • Annual. Price on application. Contains "color maps, charts, and graphs representing the main social, economic, and environmental indicators for 209 countries and territories" (publisher).

World Consumer Income and Expenditure Patterns. Available from The Gale Group. • 2001. $650.00. Published by Euromonitor (http://www.euromonitor.com). Provides data on consumer income, earning power, and expenditures for 52 countries around the world.

World Development Indicators. World Bank, The Office of the Publisher. • Annual. $60.00. Provides data and information on the people, economy, environment, and markets of 148 countries. Emphasis is on statistics relating to major development issues.

The World Economic Factbook. Available from The Gale Group. • 2000. $450.00. Seventh edition. Published by Euromonitor. Presents key economic facts and figures for each of 200 countries, including details of chief industries, export-import trade, currency, political risk, household expenditures, and the economic situation in general.

World Economic Prospects: A Planner's Guide to International Market Conditions. Available from The Gale Group. • 2000. $450.00. Second edition. Published by Euromonitor. Ranks 78 countries by specific economic characteristics, such as gross domestic product (GDP) per capita and short term growth prospects. Discusses the economic situation, prospects, and market potential of each of the countries.

World Market Share Reporter: A Compilation of Reported World Market Share Data and Rankngs on Companies, Products, and Services. The Gale Group. • 1999. $330.00. Fourth edition. Provides market share data for companies, products, and industries in countries or regions other than North America and Mexico.

World Retail Data and Statistics 1999/2000. Available from The Gale Group. • 2000. $1,190.00. Fourth edition. Published by Euromonitor. Provides detailed retail industry statistics for 51 countries.

OTHER SOURCES

Commercial Atlas and Marketing Guide. Rand McNally. • Annual. $395.00. Includes maps and marketing data: population, transportation, communication, and local area business statistics. Provides information on more than 128,000 U.S. locations.

Major Performance Rankings. Available from The Gale Group. • 2001. $1,100.00. Published by Euromonitor. Ranks 2,500 leading consumer product companies worldwide by various kinds of business and financial data, such as sales, profit, and market share. Includes international, regional, and country rankings.

World Consumer Income and Expenditure Patterns. Available from The Gale Group. • 2001. $990.00. Second edition. Two volumes. Published by Euromonitor. Provides data for 52 countries on consumer income, earning power, spending patterns, and savings. Expenditures are detailed for 75 product or service categories.

Zip Code Mapbook of Metropolitan Areas. CACI Marketing Systems. • 1992. $195.00. Second edition. Contains Zip Code two-color maps of 326 metropolitan areas. Includes summary statistical profiles of each area: population characteristics, employment, housing, and income.

MARKET SURVEYS

See: CONSUMER SURVEYS; MARKET RESEARCH; SURVEY METHODS

MARKET TESTING OF NEW PRODUCTS

See: CONSUMER SURVEYS; MARKET RESEARCH

MARKETING

See also: CHAIN STORES; DISTRIBUTION; MARKET RESEARCH; MARKET STATISTICS; SALESMEN AND SALESMANSHIP

GENERAL WORKS

Cases in Marketing Management. Kenneth L. Bernhardt and Thomas C. Kinnear. McGraw-Hill Higher Education. • 1997. Ninth edition. Price on application.

Cases in Strategic Marketing: An Integrated Approach. William J. McDonald. Pearson Education and Technology. • 1997. $53.00. Second edition.

Cyberquake: How the Internet will Erase Profits, Topple Market Leaders, and Shatter Business Models. Michael Sullivan-Trainor. John Wiley & Sons, Inc. • 1997. $26.95. Predicts that the Internet will cause "an overwhelming shift in control of the worldwide marketplace" in the early 21st century. (Business Technology Series).

Future-Driven Library Marketing. Darlene E. Weingand. American Library Association. • 1998. $25.00. The author discusses progressive marketing strategies for libraries. An annotated bibliography is included.

International Marketing. Philip R. Cateora and John Graham. McGraw-Hill. • 1998. $84.38. 10th edition.

Marketing. Damico Zikmund. Thomson Learning. • 2000. $65.00 Seventh edition. (SWC-General Business Series).

Marketing: Contemporary Concepts and Practices. William F. Schoell. Allyn and Bacon, Inc. • 1995. $87.00. Sixth edition.

Marketing for Nonmarketers: Principles and Tactics That Everyone in Bu siness Must Know. Houston G. Elamand and Norton Paley. Books on Demand. • 1992. $78.50. Second edition.

Marketing Management: Knowledge and Skills. J. Paul Peter. McGraw-Hill Professional. • 2000. $85.63. Sixth edition.

Marketing Management: Text and Cases. Douglas J. Dalrymple and Leonard J. Parsons. John Wiley and Sons, Inc. • 1994. $92.95. Sixth edition.

Marketing on the Internet: Multimedia Strategies for the World Wide Web. Jill Ellsworth and Matthew Ellsworth. John Wiley and Sons, Inc. • 1996. $29.99. Second revised expanded edition.

Marketing Planning. William Cohen. John Wiley and Sons, Inc. • 1997. Second edition. Price on application.

Marketing: Principles and Perspectives. William O. Bearden. McGraw-Hill. • 1994. $68.95. Second edition. (Marketing Series).

Marketing Strategy. Orville C. Walker and others. McGraw Hill. • 1998. $61.56. Third edition.

Marketing Strategy: Relationships, Offerings, Timing, and Resource Allocations. Devanathan Sudharshan. Prentice Hall. • 1995. $98.00.

Marketing Today. Gordon Oliver. Harcourt College Publishers. • 1994. $30.25. Third edition.

A Preface to Marketing Management. J. Paul Peter and James H. Donnelly. McGraw-Hill Higher Education. • 1997. $37.50. Seventh edition. (Marketing Series).

Strategic Market Management. David A. Aaker. John Wiley and Sons, Inc. • 1998. $79.00. Fifth edition.

Strategic Marketing. David W. Cravens. McGraw-Hill Professional. • 2000. Sixth edition. Price on application.

Strategic Marketing Problems: Cases and Comments. Roger A. Kerin and Robert A. Peterson. Prentice Hall. • 2000. $91.33. Ninth edition.

ABSTRACTS AND INDEXES

Business Periodicals Index. H. W. Wilson Co. • Monthly, except August, with quarterly and annual cumulations. Service basis for print edition; CD-ROM edition, $1,495.00 per year.

NTIS Alerts: Business & Economics. National Technical Information Service.

What's New in Advertising and Marketing. Special Libraries Association, Advertising and Marketing Div. • Quarterly. Non-profit organizations, $20.00 per year; corporations, $30.00 per year. Lists and briefly describes a wide variety of free or inexpensive material relating to advertising, marketing, and media.

ALMANACS AND YEARBOOKS

Major Marketing Campaigns Annual. The Gale Group. • Annual. $140.00. Describes in detail "100 major marketing initiatives of the previous calendar year." Includes illustrations.

BIBLIOGRAPHIES

Business Information Sources. Lorna M. Daniells. California Princeton Fulfillment Services. • 1993. $42.50. Third revised edition. Basic business sources, with discussion and full annotations.

Marketing Information Revolution. Robert C. Blattberg, editor. McGraw-Hill. • 1993. $39.95. Third edition. Includes a wide variety of sources for specific kinds of marketing.

CD-ROM DATABASES

Business Source Plus. EBSCO Information Services. • Monthly. $1,495.00 per year. Provides CD-ROM citations and abstracts to articles in about 650 business periodicals and newspapers, including *The Wall Street Journal.* Full text is provided from 200 selected periodicals. Covers accounting, communications, economics, finance, management, marketing, and other business subjects.

WILSONDISC: Wilson Business Abstracts. H. W. Wilson Co. • Monthly. $2,495.00 per year, including unlimited online access to *Wilson Business Abstracts* through WILSONLINE. Provides CD-ROM "cover-to-cover" abstracting and indexing of over 600 prominent business periodicals. Indexing is from 1982, abstracting from 1990. (*Business Periodicals Index* without abstracts is available on CD-ROM at $1,495 per year.).

DIRECTORIES

AMA International Member and Marketing Services Guide. American Marketing Association. • Annual. $150.00. Lists professional members of the American Marketing Association. Also contains information on providers of marketing support services and products, including software, communications, direct marketing, promotion, research, and consulting companies. Includes geographical and alphabetical indexes. Formerly *Marketing Yellow Pages and AMA International Membership Directory.*

Incentive-Merchandise and Travel Directory. Bill Communications, Inc. • Annual. $5.00. A special issue of *Incentive* magazine.

The PROMO 100 Promotion Agency Ranking. Intertec Publishing Co. • Annual. $9.95. Provides information on 100 leading product promotion agencies.

ENCYCLOPEDIAS AND DICTIONARIES

Blackwell Encyclopedic Dictionary of Marketing. Barbara R. Lewis and Dale Littler, editors. Blackwell Publishers. • 1996. $105.95. The editors are associated with the Manchester School of Management. Contains definitions of key terms combined with longer articles written by various U. S. and foreign business educators. Includes bibliographies and index. (Blackwell Encyclopedia of Management series.).

Complete Multilingual Dictionary of Advertising, Marketing, and Communications. Hans W. Paetzel, editor. NTC/Contemporary Publishing. • 1994. $49.95. Provides translations of about 8,000 technical and general terms. English, French and German terms.

Dictionary of Marketing and Advertising. Jerry M. Rosenberg. John Wiley and Sons, Inc. • 1995. $79.95. (Business Dictionary Series).

Dictionary of Marketing Terms. Betsy-Ann Toffler. Barron's Educational Series, Inc. • 2000. $12.95. Third edition. Business Dictionaries Series.

Encyclopedia of Business. The Gale Group. • 2000. $425.00. Second edition. Two volumes. Contains more than 700 signed articles covering major business disciplines and concepts. International in scope.

Encyclopedia of Business and Finance. Burton Kaliski, editor. Available from The Gale Group. • 2001. $240.00. Two volumes. Published by Macmillan Reference USA. Contains articles by various contributors on accounting, business administration, banking, finance, management information systems, and marketing.

Encyclopedia of Major Marketing Campaigns. The Gale Group. • 2000. $265.00. Covers 500 major marketing and advertising campaigns "of the 20th century." Examines historical context, target market, expectations, competition, strategy, development, and outcomes. Includes illustrations.

Field Guide to Marketing: A Glossary of Essential Tools and Concepts for Today's Manager. McGraw-Hill. • 1993. $29.95. Defines fundamental terms.

HANDBOOKS AND MANUALS

Creating Winning Marketing Plans: What Today's Managers Must Do to Succeed. Sidney J. Levy, editor. Dartnell Corp. • 1996. $39.95. Consists of articles by 25 "Top Experts." Covers marketing objectives, customer needs, market segmentation, database marketing, consumer scanning, and other topics.

Hispanic Market Handbook. The Gale Group. • 1995. $85.00. Provides advice on marketing consumer items to Hispanic Americans. Includes case studies and demographic profiles.

How to Write a Successful Marketing Plan: A Disciplined and Comprehensive Approach. Roman G. Hiebing. Prentice Hall. • 1999. $79.95. Second edition. The four main sections cover marketing background, the marketing plan, plan execution, and evaluation. Includes worksheets and formats.

Marketer's Guide to E-Commerce: Everything You Need to Know to Successfully Sell, Promote, and Market Your Business, Product, or Service Online. Arthur Bell and Vincent Leger. NTC/Contemporary Publishing Group. • 2001. $39.95. Covers website marketing strategies, including guidelines and examples. (NTC Business Books.).

Marketing Manager's Handbook. Sidney J. Levy and others. Prentice Hall. • 2000. Price on application. Contains 71 chapters by various authors on a wide variety of marketing topics, including market segmentation, market research, international marketing, industrial marketing, survey methods, customer service, advertising, pricing, planning, strategy, and ethics.

Marketing Planning Guide. Robert E. Stevens and others. Haworth Press, Inc. • 1997. $49.95. Second edition. Covers market segmentation, product positioning, and other marketing planning topics.

Marketing Plans: How to Prepare Them, How to Use Them. Malcolm H. McDonald. Butterworth-Heinemann. • 1999. $44.95. Fourth edition. (Professional Development Series).

Marketing Without Advertising. Michael Phillips and Salli Rasberry. Nolo.com. • 1996. $19.00. Second revised edition. How to market a small business economically.

Online Marketing Handbook: How to Promote, Advertise and Sell, Your Products and Services on the Internet. Daniel S. Janal. John Wiley and Sons, Inc. • 1998. $29.95. Revised edition. Provides step-by-step instructions for utilizing online publicity, advertising, and sales promotion. Contains chapters on interactive marketing, online crisis communication, and Web home page promotion, with numerous examples and checklists.

Promotional Marketing. Entrepreneur, Inc. • Looseleaf. $59.50. A practical guide to sales promotion and marketing for small businesses. (Start-Up Business Guide No. E1111.).

INTERNET DATABASES

EBSCO Information Services. Ebsco Publishing. Phone: 800-871-8508 or (508)356-6500 Fax: (508)356-5640 E-mail: ep@epnet.com • URL: http://www.epnet.com • Fee-based Web site providing Internet access to a wide variety of databases, including business-related material. Full text is available for many periodical titles, with daily updates. Fees: Apply.

ProQuest Direct. Bell & Howell Information and Learning. Phone: 800-521-0600 or (313)761-4700 Fax: (313)973-9145 • URL: http://www.umi.com/proquest • Fee-based Web site providing Internet access to more than 3,000 periodicals, newspapers, and other publications. Many items are available full-text, with daily updates. Includes extensive corporate and financial information from Disclosure, Inc. Fees: Apply.

ONLINE DATABASES

ABI/INFORM. Bell & Howell Information and Learning. • Provides online indexing to business-related material occurring in over 1,000 periodicals from 1971 to the present. Inquire as to online cost and availability.

Business and Industry. Responsive Database Services, Inc. • Contains online citations, abstracts, and selected fulltext from more than 1,000 trade journals, newspapers, and other publications. Provides general coverage of both manufacturing and service industries, including marketing, production, industry trends, key events, and information on specific companies. Time span is 1994 to date. Daily updates. Inquire as to online cost and availability. (Also available in a CD-ROM version.).

Management Contents. The Gale Group. • Covers a wide range of management, financial, marketing, personnel, and administrative topics. About 150 leading business journals are indexed and abstracted from 1974 to date, with monthly updating. Inquire as to online cost and availability.

Marketing and Advertising Reference Service (MARS). The Gale Group. • Provides abstracts of literature relating to consumer marketing and advertising, including all forms of advertising media. Time period is 1984 to date. Daily updates. Inquire as to online cost and availability.

Wilson Business Abstracts Online. H. W. Wilson Co. • Indexes and abstracts 600 major business periodicals, plus the *Wall Street Journal* and the business section of the *New York Times*. Indexing is from 1982, abstracting from 1990, with the two newspapers included from 1993. Updated weekly. Inquire as to online cost and availability. (*Business Periodicals Index* without abstracts is also available online.).

PERIODICALS AND NEWSLETTERS

Database Marketer. Intertec Publishing Co. • Monthly. $329.00 per year.

Entertainment Marketing Letter. EPM Communications, Inc. • 22 times a year. $319.00 per year. Newsletter. Covers the marketing of various entertainment products. Includes television broadcasting, videocassettes, celebrity tours and tie-ins, radio broadcasting, and the music business.

Financial Services Marketing: Finding, Keeping, and Profiting From the Right Customers. American Banker. • Bimonthly. Price on application. Covers marketing for a variety of financial institutions, including banks, investment companies, securities dealers, and credit unions.

Incentive: Managing and Marketing Through Motivation. Bill Communications, Inc. • Monthly. $55.00 per year.

Interactive Marketing and P R News: News and Practical Advice on Using Interactive Advertising and Marketing to Sell Your Products. Phillips Business Information, Inc. • Biweekly. $495.00 per year. Newsletter. Provides information and guidance on merchandising via CD-ROM ("multimedia catalogs"), the Internet, and interactive TV. Topics include "cybermoney", addresses for e-mail marketing, "virtual malls," and other interactive subjects. Formerly *Interactive Marketing News*.

Internet Marketing Report: News and Advice to Help Companies Harness the Power of the Internet to Achieve Business Objectives. Progressive Business Publications. • Semimonthly. $299.00 per year. Newsletter. Covers Internet marketing strategy, site traffic, success stories, technology, cost control, and other Web site advertising and marketing topics.

Journal of Global Marketing. Haworth Press, Inc. • Quarterly. Individuals, $60.00 per year; institutions, $90.00 per year; libraries, $300.00 per year.

Journal of International Consumer Marketing. Haworth Press, Inc. • Quarterly. Individuals, $60.00 per year; institutions, $90.00 per year; libraries, $300.00 per year.

Journal of International Marketing. American Marketing Association. • Members $45.00; non-members, $80.00 per year institutions, $150.00 per year.

Journal of Marketing. American Marketing Association. • Quarterly. Members, $45.00; per year; non-members, $80.00 per year; institutions, $200.00 per year. Covers both marketing theory and marketing practice.

Journal of Marketing Channels: Distribution Systems, Strategy, and Management. Haworth Press, Inc. • Quarterly. Individuals, $60.00 per year; institutions, $75.00 per year; libraries, 175.00 per year. Subject matter has to do with the management of product distribution systems.

Journal of Public Policy and Marketing. American Marketing Association. • Semiannual. Members, $50.00 per year; non-members, $70.00 per year; institutions, $100.00 per year. Devoted to the social and cultural impact of marketing activities.

The Licensing Letter. EPM Communications, Inc. • Monthly. $447.00 per year. Newsletter. Covers all aspects of licensed merchandising (compensation of a person or an organization for being associated with a product or service).

Marketing Magazine. Maclean Hunter Business Publications. • Weekly. $60.00 per year. "Canada's national weekly publication dedicated to the businesses of marketing, advertising, and media." Includes annual Marketing Awards, quarterly Digital Marketing (emerging technology), Promo Marketing, and PR Quarterly (special issues on public relations).

Marketing Management: Shaping the Profession of Marketing. American Marketing Association. • Quarterly. Members, $45.00 per year; non-members, $70.00 per year; institutions, $90.00 per year. Covers trends in the management of marketing, sales, and distribution.

Marketing News: Reporting on Marketing and Its Association. American Marketing Association. • Biweekly. Free to members; non-members, $100.00 per year; institutions, $130.00 per year.

The Marketing Report: The Best Time-Saving Information Source for Marketing Execcutives. Progressive Business Publications. • Semimonthly. $264.00 per year. Newsletter. Covers marketing ideas, problem solving, and new product development. Includes case histories.

Marketing Times. Sales and Marketing Executives International. • Quarterly. Membership.

MC: Technology Marketing Intelligence. BPI Communications, Inc. • Monthly. $47.00 per year. Edited for marketing executives in high technology industries. Covers both advertising and marketing.

Potentials: Ideas and Products that Motivate. Lakewood Publications, Inc. • 10 times a year. $24.00 per year. Covers incentives, premiums, awards, and gifts as related to promotional activities. Formerly *Potentials in Marketing*.

PROMO: Promotion Marketing Worldwide. Simba Information Inc. • Monthly. $65.00 per year. Edited for companies and agencies that utilize couponing, point-of-purchase advertising, special events, games, contests, premiums, product samples, and other unique promotional items.

Psychology and Marketing. John Wiley and Sons, Inc., Journals Div. • Eight times a year. $780.00 per year. Spots the latest social, economic, and cultural trends that affect marketing decisions.

Sales and Marketing Management. Bill Communications, Inc. • Monthly. $48.00 per year.

Sales & Marketing Report: Practical Ideas for Successful Selling. Lawence Ragan Communications, Inc. • Monthly. $119.00 per year. Newsletter. Emphasis is on sales training, staff morale, and marketing productivity.

Web Marketing Update: Quick, Actionable, Internet Intelligence for Marketing Executives. Computer Economics, Inc. • Monthly. $347.00 per year. Newsletter on various aspects of promoting or selling products and services through an Internet Web site: technology, advertising, strategy, customer base, cost projections, search engines, etc.

RESEARCH CENTERS AND INSTITUTES

Marketing Science Institute. 1000 Massachusetts Ave., Cambridge, MA 02138. Phone: (617)491-2060 Fax: (617)491-2065 • URL: http://www.msi.org.

TRADE/PROFESSIONAL ASSOCIATIONS

American Marketing Association. 311 S. Wacker Dr., Suite 5800, Chicago, IL 60606. Phone: 800-262-1150 or (312)542-9000 Fax: (312)542-9001 E-mail: info@ama.org • URL: http://www.ama.org.

OTHER SOURCES

How to Write a Marketing Plan. American Management Association Extension Institute. • Looseleaf. $130.00. Self-study course. Emphasis is on practical explanations, examples, and problem solving. Quizzes and a case study are included.

InSite 2. Intelligence Data/Thomson Financial. • Fee-based Web site consolidates information in a "Base Pack" consisting of Business InSite, Market InSite, and Company InSite. Optional databases are Consumer InSite, Health and Wellness InSite, Newsletter InSite, and Computer InSite. Includes fulltext content from more than 2,500 trade publications, journals, newsletters, newspapers, analyst reports, and other sources. Continuous updating. Formerly produced by The Gale Group.

MARKETING, BANK

See: BANK MARKETING

MARKETING, CHEMICAL

See: CHEMICAL MARKETING

MARKETING, DIRECT

See: DIRECT MARKETING

MARKETING, INDUSTRIAL

See: INDUSTRIAL MARKETING

MARKETING, INTERNATIONAL

See: INTERNATIONAL MARKETING

MARKETING, MULTILEVEL

See: MULTILEVEL MARKETING

MARKING MACHINES

DIRECTORIES

Marking Products and Equipment Buyer's Guide. Marking Devices Publishing Co., Inc. • Annual. $30.00. Included in subscription to *Marking Industry Magazine.*

PERIODICALS AND NEWSLETTERS

Marking Industry Magazine. Marking Devices Publishing, Inc. • Monthly. $44.00 per year. Includes annual buyer's guide *Marking Products and Equipment.*

MASONRY

DIRECTORIES

Magazine of Masonry Construction Buyers' Guide. The Aberdeen Group. • Annual. $3.00. Lists manufacturers or suppliers of products and services related to masonry construction.

FINANCIAL RATIOS

Annual Statement Studies. Robert Morris Associates: The Association of Lending and Credit Risk Professiona. • Annual. Free to members; non-members, $140.00. Median and quartile financial ratios are given for over 400 kinds of manufacturing, wholesale, retail, construction, and consumer finance establishments. Data is sorted by both asset size and sales volume. Includes a clearly written "Definition of Ratios" and an alphabetical industry index.

PERIODICALS AND NEWSLETTERS

The Aberdeen's Magazine of Masonry Construction. Aberdeen Group. • Monthly. $30.00 per year. Covers the business, production, and marketing aspects of various kind of masonry construction: brick, concrete block, glass block, etc.

Masonry. Mason Contractors Association of America. • Bimonthly. $20.00 per year.

Masonry Design West. Pleasanton Publishing Co. • Bimonthly. Price on application.

TRADE/PROFESSIONAL ASSOCIATIONS

International Masonry Institute. The James Price House, 42 E St., Annapolis, MD 21401. Phone: 800-464-0988 or (410)280-1305 Fax: (410)261-2855 E-mail: nbradford@imiweb.org • URL: http://www.imiweb.org.

Mason Contractors Association of America. 1910 S. Highland Ave., Suite 101, Lombard, IL 60148. Phone: 800-536-2225 or (630)705-4200 Fax: (630)705-4209 E-mail: info@masoncontractors.com • URL: http://www.masoncontractor.com.

National Concrete Masonry Association. 2302 Horse Pen Rd., Herndon, VA 20171-3499. Phone: (703)713-1900 Fax: (703)713-1910 E-mail: ncma@ncma.org • URL: http://www.ncma.org.

MASS MEDIA

See also: ADVERTISING MEDIA; MEDIA RESEARCH

GENERAL WORKS

Breaking Up America: Advertisers and the New Media World. Joseph Turow. University of Chicago Press. • 1997. $22.50. A social criticism of target marketing, market segmentation, and customized media.

Crisis Response: Inside Stories on Managing Image Under Siege. The Gale Group. • 1993. $60.00. Presents first-hand accounts by media relations professionals of major business crises and how they were handled. Topics include the following kinds of crises: environmental, governmental, corporate image, communications, and product.

Interface Culture: How New Technology Transforms the Way We Create and Communicate. Steven Johnson. HarperCollins Publishers. • 1997. $24.00. A discussion of how computer interfaces and online technology ("cyberspace") affect society in general.

The Media Monopoly. Ben H. Bagdikian. Beacon Press. • 1997. $17.50. Fifth edition.

Media Systems Society. Joseph Turow. Addison-Wesley Longman, Inc. • 1997. $67.50. Second edition. Provides commentary on the role of U.S. mass media in a global economy.

ABSTRACTS AND INDEXES

Business Periodicals Index. H. W. Wilson Co. • Monthly, except August, with quarterly and annual cumulations. Service basis for print edition; CD-ROM edition, $1,495.00 per year.

Communication Abstracts. Sage Publications, Inc. • Bimonthly. Individuals, $185.00 per year; institutions, $805.00 per year. Provides broad coverage of the literature of communications, including broadcasting and advertising.

Readers' Guide to Periodical Literature. H. W. Wilson Co. • Monthly. $220.00 per year. CD-ROM edition, $1,495 per year, including annual cumulation. Indexes about 250 peridicals of general interest.

What's New in Advertising and Marketing. Special Libraries Association, Advertising and Marketing Div. • Quarterly. Non-profit organizations, $20.00 per year; corporations, $30.00 per year. Lists and briefly describes a wide variety of free or inexpensive material relating to advertising, marketing, and media.

ALMANACS AND YEARBOOKS

Communication Technology Update. Butterworth-Heinemann. • Annual. $36.95. Reviews technological developments and statistical trends in five key areas: mass media, computers, consumer electronics, communications satellites, and telephony. Includes television, cellular phones, and the Internet. (Focal Press.).

BIBLIOGRAPHIES

Communication Booknotes Quarlterly : Recent Titles in Telecommunications, Informmation, and Media. Lawrence Erlbaum Associates, Inc. • Bimonthly. Individuals, $45.00 per year; institutions, $95.00 per year. Contains descriptive reviews of new publications. Formerly *Mass Media Booknotes.*

BIOGRAPHICAL SOURCES

The Highwaymen: Warriors on the Information Superhighway. Ken Auletta. Harcourt Trade Publications. • 1998. $13.00. Revised expanded edition. Contains critical articles about Ted Turner, Rupert Murdoch, Barry Diller, Michael Eisner, and other key figures in electronic communications, entertainment, and information.

CD-ROM DATABASES

ABI/INFORM Global. Bell & Howell Information and Learning. • Monthly. $6,500.00 per year. Provides CD-ROM indexing and abstracting of worldwide business literature appearing in over 1,200 periodicals for the most recent five years. Archival discs are available from 1971. Formerly *ABI/INFORM OnDisc.*

Hoover's Company Capsules on CD-ROM. Hoover's, Inc. • Quarterly. $349.95 per year (single-user). Provides the CD-ROM version of *Hoover's Handbook of American Business, Hoover's Handbook of Emerging Companies, Hoover's Handbook of World Business, Hoover's Guide to Computer Companies, Hoover's Guide to Media Companies, Hoover's Handbook of Private Companies,* and various regional guides. Includes more than 11,000 profiles of companies.

Leadership Library on CD-ROM: Who's Who in the Leadership of the United States. Leadership Directories, Inc. • Quarterly. $2,641.00 per year, including access to Internet version (weekly updates). Contains all 14 *Yellow Book* personnel directories on CD-ROM, providing contact and brief biographical information for about 400,000 individuals. Covers business, government, financial institutions, news media, law firms, associations, foreign representatives, and nonprofit organizations. Includes photographs.

PAIS on CD-ROM. Public Affairs Information Service, Inc. • Quarterly. $1,995.00 per year. Provides a CD-ROM version of the online service, *PAIS International.* Contains over 400,000 citations to the literature of contemporary social, political, and economic issues.

WILSONDISC: Business Periodicals Index. H. W. Wilson Co. • Monthly. $1,495.00 per year. Provides CD-ROM indexing of business periodicals from 1982 to date. Price includes online service.

WILSONDISC: Readers' Guide to Periodical Literature. H. W. Wilson Co. • Monthly. $1,095.00 per year, including unlimited online access to *Readers' Guide to Periodical Literature* through WILSONLINE. Provides CD-ROM indexing of about 250 general interest periodicals. Covers 1983 to date. (*Readers' Guide Abstracts* also available on CD-ROM at $1,995 per year.).

DIRECTORIES

Burrelle's Media Directory: Broadcast Media. Burrelle's Information Services. • Annual. $275.00. Two volumes. *Radio* volume lists more than 12,000 radio stations in the U. S. and Canada. *Television and Cable* volume lists more than 1,700 television stations and cable systems. Provides detailed descriptions, including programming and key personnel.

Burrelle's Media Directory: Magazines and Newsletters. Burrelle's Information Services. • Annual. $275.00. Provides detailed descriptions of more than 13,500 magazines and newsletters published in the U. S., Canada, and Mexico. Categories are professional, consumer, trade, and college.

Burrelle's Media Directory: Newspapers and Related Media. Burrelle's Information Services. • Annual. $275.00. Two volumes. *Daily Newspapers* volume lists more than 2,000 daily publications in the U. S., Canada, and Mexico. *Non-Daily Newspapers* volume lists more than 10,000 items published no more than three times a week. Provides detailed descriptions, including key personnel.

Gale Directory of Publications and Broadcast Media. The Gale Group. • Annual. $650.00. Five volumes. A guide to publications and broadcasting stations in the U. S. and Canada, including newspapers, magazines, journals, radio stations, television stations, and cable systems. Geographic arrangement. Volume three consists of statistical tables, maps, subject indexes, and title index. Formerly *Ayer Directory of Publications.*

Gale's Guide to the Media: A Gale Ready Reference Handbook. The Gale Group. • 2000. $125.00. Provides profiles of a wide variety of media-related organizations, publications, broadcasters, agencies, and databases, of interest to nonprofit groups. Contains three indexes and a glossary.

Marketer's Guide to Media. BPI Communications, Inc. • Quarterly. $105.00. Presents cost, circulation, and audience statistics for various mass media segments, including television, radio, magazines, newspapers, telephone yellow pages, and cinema. Formerly *Mediaweek's Guide to Media.*

News Media Yellow Book: Who's Who Among Reporters, Writers, Editors, and Producers in the Leading National News Media. Leadership Directories, Inc. • Quarterly. $305.00 per year. Lists the staffs of major newspapers and news magazines, TV and radio networks, news services and bureaus, and feature syndicates. Includes syndicated columnists and programs. Seven specialized indexes are provided.

Plunkett's Entertainment and Media Industry Almanac. Available from Plunkett Research, Ltd. • Biennial. $149.99. Provides profiles of leading firms in online information, films, radio, television, cable, multimedia, magazines, and book publishing. Includes World Wide Web sites, where available, plus information on careers and industry trends.

Power Media "Selects". Broadcast Interview Source. • Annual. $166.50. A directory of approximately 3,000 important newswire services, syndicates, national newspapers, magazines, radio and TV talk shows, etc.

ENCYCLOPEDIAS AND DICTIONARIES

Encyclopedia of Communication and Information. Available from The Gale Group. • 2001. $325.00. Three volumes. Published by Macmillan Reference USA.

NTC's Mass Media Dictionary. R. Terry Ellmore. NTC/Contemporary Publishing. • 1993. $24.95. Covers television, radio, newspapers, magazines, film, graphic arts, books, billboards, public relations, and advertising. Terms are related to production, research, audience measurement, audio-video engineering, printing, publishing, and other areas.

HANDBOOKS AND MANUALS

Mass Media Law and Regulation. William E. Francois. Waveland Press, Inc. • 1994. $45.95. Sixth revised edition.

Media for Business. Robert H. Amend and Michael A. Schrader. Butterworth-Heinemann. • 1991. $44.95.

INTERNET DATABASES

Wired News. Wired Digital, Inc. Phone: (415)276-8400 Fax: (415)276-8499 E-mail: newsfeedback@wired.com • URL: http://www.wired.com • Provides summaries and full-text of "Top Stories" relating to the Internet, computers, multimedia, telecommunications, and the electronic information industry in general. These news stories are placed in the broad categories of Politics, Business, Culture, and Technology. Affiliated with *Wired* magazine. Fees: Free.

ONLINE DATABASES

ABI/INFORM. Bell & Howell Information and Learning. • Provides online indexing to business-related material occurring in over 1,000 periodicals from 1971 to the present. Inquire as to online cost and availability.

Globalbase. The Gale Group. • Provides more than one million online summaries of business, industrial, and economic news reports from more than 1,000 publications worldwide. Covers a wide range of material appearing in international trade journals, professional magazines, and newspapers. Time period is 1984 to date, with weekly updates. Inquire as to online cost and availability.

Marketing and Advertising Reference Service (MARS). The Gale Group. • Provides abstracts of literature relating to consumer marketing and advertising, including all forms of advertising media. Time period is 1984 to date. Daily updates. Inquire as to online cost and availability.

PAIS International. Public Affairs Information Service, Inc. • Corresponds to the former printed publications, *PAIS Bulletin* (1976-90) and *PAIS Foreign Language Index* (1972-90), and to the current *PAIS International in Print* (1991 to date). Covers economic, political, and sociological material appearing in periodicals, books, government documents, and other publications. Updating is monthly. Inquire as to online cost and availability.

Readers' Guide Abstracts Online. H. W. Wilson Co. • Indexes and abstracts general interest periodicals, 1983 to date. Weekly updates. Inquire as to online cost and availability.

Trade & Industry Index. The Gale Group. • Provides indexing of business periodicals, January 1981 to date. Daily updates. (Full text articles from some periodicals are available online, 1983 to date, in the companion database, *Trade & Industry ASAP.*) Inquire as to online cost and availability.

Wilson Business Abstracts Online. H. W. Wilson Co. • Indexes and abstracts 600 major business periodicals, plus the *Wall Street Journal* and the business section of the *New York Times.* Indexing is from 1982, abstracting from 1990, with the two newspapers included from 1993. Updated weekly. Inquire as to online cost and availability. (*Business Periodicals Index* without abstracts is also available online.).

PERIODICALS AND NEWSLETTERS

Brandweek. BPI Communications, Inc. • 47 times a year. $145.00 per year. Includes articles and case studies on mass marketing and mass media. Formerly *Adweek's Marketing Week.*

Brill's Content: The Independent Voice of the Information Age. Brill Media Ventures, L.P. • Eight times a year. $19.95 per year. Presents a critical, iconoclastic view of various forms of news media, including TV, magazines, newspapers, and websites.

Media Industry Newsletter. Phillips Business Information, Inc. • Weekly. $595.00 per year. News of advertising, broadcasting, and publishing. Reports on the number of advertising pages in major magazines.

Media Mergers and Acquisitions. Paul Kagan Associates, Inc. • Monthly. $695.00 per year. Newsletter on media merger activity. Covers broadcasting, motion pictures, advertising, and publishing.

Mediaweek: Incorporating Marketing and Media Decisions. BPI Communications, Inc. • 47 times a year. $145.00 per year. Published for advertising media buyers and managers.

NewsInc.: The Business of the Newspapers Business. The Cole Group. • Biweekly. $425.00 per year. Newsletter. Reports on trends in mass media, especially with regard to newspaper publishing. Articles on cable TV and other competitive media are included.

Wired. Wired Ventures Ltd. • Monthly. $24.00 per year. Edited for creators and managers in various areas of electronic information and entertainment, including multimedia, the Internet, and video. Often considered to be the primary publication of the "digital generation.".

RESEARCH CENTERS AND INSTITUTES

Center for Mass Media Research. Marquette University, 1131 W. Wisconsin Ave., Milwaukee, WI 53233. Phone: (414)288-3453 E-mail: griffinr@marquette.edu.

Freedom Forum Media Studies Center. Columbia University, 580 Madison Ave., 42nd Fl., New York, NY 10022. Phone: (212)317-6501 Fax: (212)317-6573 E-mail: b.giles@mediastudies.org • URL: http://www.mediastudies.org • Research fields include mass communication and technological change, including mass media and the public trust.

For publishers addresses, refer to SOURCES CITED section at the back of the book.

Integrated Media Systems Center. University of Southern California, 3740 McClintock Ave., Suite 131, Los Angeles, CA 90089-2561. Phone: (213)740-0877 Fax: (213)740-8931 E-mail: nikias@imsc.usc.edu • URL: http://www.imsc.usc.edu • Media areas for research include education, mass communication, and entertainment.

Mass Communications Research Center. University of Wisconsin-Madison, 821 University Ave., 5050 Vilas Hall, Madison, WI 53706. Phone: (608)263-3381 Fax: (608)262-1361.

STATISTICS SOURCES

Kagan Media Index. Paul Kagan Associates, Inc. • Monthly. $675.00 per year. Provides electronic and entertainment media industry statistics. Includes television, radio, motion pictures, and home video.

Media Market Guide. Media Market Resources. • Quarterly. $675.00 per year. Presents circulation and cost data for television, radio, magazines, newspapers and outdoor markets.

UNESCO Statistical Yearbook. Bernan Press. • Annual. $95.00. Co-published by Bernan Press and the United Nations Educational, Scientific, and Cultural Organization (http://www.unesco.org). Presents statistical data from more than 200 countries on education, technology, research, broadcasting, cinema, book publishing, newspapers, libraries, museums, and population. Includes charts, maps, and graphs.

TRADE/PROFESSIONAL ASSOCIATIONS

Accuracy in Media. 4455 Connecticut Ave., N.W.,, Suite 330, Washington, DC 20008. Phone: 800-787-0044 or (202)364-4401 Fax: (202)371-4098 E-mail: ar@aim.org • URL: http://www.aim.org • A nonpartisan organization that receives and researches complaints from the public relating to factual errors made by the news media.

Association of Schools of Journalism and Mass Communication. c/o Jennifer H. McGill, 234 Outlet Pointe Blvd., Columbia, SC 29210-5667. Phone: (803)798-0271 Fax: (803)772-3509 E-mail: aejmc@vm.sc.edu.

Foundation for American Communications. 78-85 S. Grand Ave., Pasadena, CA 91105-1602. Phone: (213)851-7372 Fax: (213)851-9186 • Conducts Business/News Media Conferences involving business executives and journalists in an effort to improve the participants' understanding of the news media.

Minorities in Media. P.O. Box 9198, Petersburg, VA 23806. Phone: (804)524-5924 • Members are minority media professionals.

OTHER SOURCES

Washington [year]. Columbia Books, Inc. • Annual. $129.00. Provides information on about 5,000 Washington, DC key businesses, government offices, non-profit organizations, and cultural institutions, with the names of about 25,000 principal executives. Includes Washington media, law offices, foundations, labor unions, international organizations, clubs, etc.

MASS TRANSPORTATION

See: PUBLIC TRANSPORTATION; TRANSPORTATION INDUSTRY

MATERIALS

ABSTRACTS AND INDEXES

Engineered Materials Abstracts. Cambridge Information Group. • Monthly. $995.00 per year. Provides citations to the technical and engineering literature of plastic, ceramic, and composite materials.

Key Abstracts: Advanced Materials. Available from INSPEC, Inc. • Monthly. $240.00 per year. Provides international coverage of journal and proceedings literature, including publications on ceramics and composite materials. Published in England by the Institution of Electrical Engineers (IEE).

NTIS Alerts: Manufacturing Technology. National Technical Information Service. • Semimonthly. $265.00 per year. Provides descriptions of government-sponsored research reports and software, with ordering information. Covers computer-aided design and manufacturing (CAD/CAM), engineering materials, quality control, machine tools, robots, lasers, productivity, and related subjects. Formerly *Abstract Newsletter*.

NTIS Alerts: Materials Sciences. National Technical Information Service. • Semimonthly. $220.00 per year. Provides descriptions of government-sponsored research reports and software, with ordering information. Covers ceramics, glass, coatings, composite materials, alloys, plastics, wood, paper, adhesives, fibers, lubricants, and related subjects. Formerly *Abstract Newsletter*.

Polymers/Ceramics/Composites Alert. Cambridge Information Group. • Monthly. $340.00 per year. Provides citations to the business and industrial literature of plastic, ceramic, and composite materials. (Materials Business Information Series).

ALMANACS AND YEARBOOKS

Progress in Materials Science: An International Review Journal. Elsevier Science. • Bimonthly. $992.00 per year.

BIBLIOGRAPHIES

ASTM List of Publications. American Society for Testing and Materials (ASTM). • Annual.

CD-ROM DATABASES

International Plastics Selector. Data Business Publishing. • Semiannual. CD-ROM index version (technical data only), $695.00 per year or $495.00 per disc. CD-ROM image version (technical data and specification sheet images), $1,295.00 per year or $995.00 per disc. Provides detailed information on the properties of 20,000 types of plastic, both current and obsolete. Time period is 1977 to date. Includes trade names and supplier names and addresses.

METADEX Materials Collection: Metals-Polymers-Ceramics. Cambridge Scientific Abstracts. • Quarterly. $6,950.00 per year. Provides CD-ROM citations to the worldwide literature of materials science and metallurgy. Corresponds to *Metals Abstracts, Alloys Index, Steels Alert, Nonferrous Alert, Polymers/Ceramics/Composites Alert,* and *Engineered Materials Abstracts.* (Formerly produced by ASM International.).

DIRECTORIES

Internet Tools of the Profession: A Guide for Information Professionals. Hope N. Tillman, editor. Special Libraries Association. • 1997. $49.00. Second edition. Consists of 14 sections by various authors or compilers. After two introductory articles on searching the Internet, there are 12 annotated lists of useful Web sites, covering the SLA, business and finance, chemistry, education, food and agriculture, information technology, insurance and employee benefits, law, library management, metals and materials, pharmaceuticals, and telecommunications. An index is provided.

Materials Research Centres: A World Directory of Organizations and Programmes in Materials Science. Allyn and Bacon/Longman. • 1991. $475.00. Fourth edition. Profiles of research centers in 75 countries. Materials include plastics, metals, fibers, etc.

ENCYCLOPEDIAS AND DICTIONARIES

ASM Materials Engineering Dictionary. Joseph R. Davis, editor. ASM International. • 1992. $146.00. Contains 10,000 entries, 700 illustrations, and 150 tables relating to metals, plastics, ceramics, composites, and adhesives. Includes "Technical Briefs" on 64 key material groups.

Encyclopedia of Advanced Materials. David Bloor and others. Elsevier Science. • 1994. $1,811.25. Four volumes.

Encyclopedia of Materials: Science and Technology. K.H.J. Buschow and others, editors. Pergamon Press/Elsevier Science. • 2001. $6,875.00. Eleven volumes. Provides extensive technical information on a wide variety of materials, including metals, ceramics, plastics, optical materials, and building materials. Includes more than 2,000 articles and 5,000 illustrations.

Materials Science and Technology: A Comprehensive Treatment. R. W. Cahn and others, editors. John Wiley and Sons, Inc. • 1997. $7,349.00. 18 volumes. Each volume covers a particular area of high-performance materials technology.

HANDBOOKS AND MANUALS

ASM Engineered Materials Reference Book. Michael L. Bauccio. ASM International. • 1994. $139.00. Second edition. Provides information on a wide range of materials, with special sections on ceramics, industrial glass products, and plastics.

Corrosion Control. Samuel A. Bradford. Chapman and Hall. • 1992. $80.50. Discusses basic corrosion theory, corrosion causes, coatings, plastics, metals, and many other highly detailed, technical topics. (Chapman & Hall.).

Materials Handbook. George S. Brady and others. McGraw-Hill. • 1996. $99.00. 14th edition.

INTERNET DATABASES

Internet Tools of the Profession. Special Libraries Association. Phone: (202)234-4700 Fax: (202)265-9317 E-mail: hope@tiac.net • URL: http://www.sla.org/pubs/itotp • Web site is designed to update the printed *Internet Tools of the Profession.* Provides links to a wide range of useful databases in business, finance, industry, information technology, insurance, law, library management, telecommunications, and other subject areas. Fees: Free.

ONLINE DATABASES

Engineered Materials Abstracts [online]. Cambridge Scientific Abstracts. • Provides online citations to the technical and engineering literature of plastic, ceramic, and composite materials. Time period is 1986 to date, with monthly updates. (Formerly produced by ASM International.) Inquire as to online cost and availability.

Materials Business File. Cambridge Scientific Abstracts. • Provides online abstracts and citations to worldwide materials literature, covering the business and industrial aspects of metals, plastics, ceramics, and composites. Corresponds to *Steels Alert, Nonferrous Metals Alert,* and *Polymers/Ceramics/Composites Alert.* Time period is 1985 to date, with monthly updates. (Formerly produced by ASM International.) Inquire as to online cost and availability.

METADEX. Cambridge Scientific Abstracts. • Covers the worldwide literature of metals, metallurgy, and materials science, 1966 to date. Includes detailed alloys indexing from 1974. Biweekly updating. Inquire as to online cost and availability. (Formerly produced by ASM International.).

PERIODICALS AND NEWSLETTERS

ASTM Standardization News. American Society for Testing and Materials. • Monthly. $18.00 per year.

High-Tech Materials Alert: Advanced Materials-Their Uses and Manufacture. Technical Insights. • Monthly. $695.00 per year. Newsletter on technical developments relating to high-performance materials, including metals and ceramics. Includes market forecasts.

International Materials Review. ASM International, Materials Information. • Bimonthly. Members, $305.00 per year; non-members, $734.00 per year. Provides technical and research coverage of metals, alloys, and advanced materials. Formerly *International Metals Review.*

Journal of Advanced Materials. Society for the Advancement of Material and Process Engineering. • Quarterly. Members $20.00 per year; non-members, $60.00 per year. Contains technical and research articles. Formerly *SAMPE Quarterly.*

Journal of Materials Research. Materials Research Society. • Monthly. Members, $80.00 per year; non-members, $750.00 per year. Covers the preparation, properties, and processing of advanced materials.

Materials Evaluation. American Society for Nondestructive Testing. • Monthly. $105.00 per year. Provides up-to-date information about NDT applications and technical articles addressing nondestructive testing applications.

Materials Performance: Articles on Corrosion Science and Engineering Solutions for Corrosion Problems. National Association of Corrosion Engineers. NACE International. • Monthly. $100.00 per year. Covers the protection and performance of materials in corrosive environments. Includes information on new materials and industrial coatings.

Materials Science Center. University of Wisconsin - Madison.

Metallurgical and Materials Transactions A: Physical Metallurgy and Materials Sc. ASM International. • Monthly. Members, $75.00 per year; non-members, $1,361.00 per year; students, $35.00 per year. Formerly *Metallurgical Transactions APhysical Metallurgy and Materials Science.*

SAMPE Journal. Society for the Advancement of Material and Process Engineering. • Bimonthly. $65.00 per year. Provides technical information.

RESEARCH CENTERS AND INSTITUTES

Center for Advanced Materials Research. Brown University. P.O. Box M, Providence, RI 02912. Phone: (401)863-1386 Fax: (401)863-1387 E-mail: artonurmikko@brown.edu.

Materials Processing Center. Massachusetts Institute of Technology, 77 Massachusetts Ave., Room 12-007, Cambridge, MA 02139-4307. Phone: (617)253-5179 Fax: (617)258-6900 E-mail: fmpage@.mit.edu • URL: http://www.web.mit.edu/mpc/www/ • Conducts processing, engineering, and economic research in ferrous and nonferrous metals, ceramics, polymers, photonic materials, superconductors, welding, composite materials, and other materials.

Materials Research Center. Lehigh University. Five E. Packer Ave., Bethlehem, PA 18015. Phone: (610)758-4227 Fax: (610)758-3526 E-mail: mph2@lehigh.edu • URL: http://www.lehigh.edu/~inmatsci/inmatsci.html.

TRADE/PROFESSIONAL ASSOCIATIONS

ASM International. 9639 Kinsman Rd., Materials Park, OH 44073. Phone: 800-336-5152 or (216)338-5151 Fax: (216)338-4634 E-mail: memserv@po.asm-intl.org • URL: http://www.asm-intl.org • Members are materials engineers, metallurgists, industry executives, educators, and others concerned with a wide range of materials and metals. Divisions include Aerospace, Composites, Electronic Materials and Processing, Energy, Highway/Off-Highway Vehicle, Joining, Materials Testing and Quality Control, Society of Carbide and Tool Engineers, and Surface Engineering.

Materials Research Society. 506 Keystone Dr., Warrendale, PA 15086-7537. Phone: (724)779-3003 Fax: (724)779-8313 E-mail: info@mrs.org • URL: http://www.mrs.org • Members are individuals concerned with multidisciplinary research in the technology of advanced materials.

Minerals, Metals and Materials Society. 184 Thorn Hill Dr., Warrendale, PA 15086-7528. Phone: 800-759-4867 or (724)776-9000 Fax: (724)776-3770 E-mail: tmsgeneral@tms.org • URL: http://www.tms.org • Members are metallurgists, metallurgical engineers, and materials scientists. Divisions include Light Metals and Electronic, Magnetic, and Photonic Materials.

National Materials Advisory Board. c/o National Research Council, Harris Bldg, 2101 Constitution Avw., N.W., Rm. 262, Washington, DC 20418. Phone: (202)334-3505 Fax: (202)334-3718 E-mail: nmab@nas.edu • URL: http://www2.nas.edu/nmab.

Society for the Advancement of Material and Process Engineering. P.O. Box 2459, Covina, CA 91722-8459. Phone: 800-562-7360 or (626)331-0616 Fax: (626)332-8929 E-mail: sampeibo@aol.com • URL: http://www.sampe.org.

MATERIALS, BUILDING

See: BUILDING MATERIALS INDUSTRY

MATERIALS, COMPOSITE

See: COMPOSITE MATERIALS

MATERIALS HANDLING

ABSTRACTS AND INDEXES

Key Abstracts: Factory Automation. Available from INSPEC, Inc. • Monthly. $240.00 per year. Provides international coverage of journal and proceedings literature, including publications on CAD/CAM, materials handling, robotics, and factory management. Published in England by the Institution of Electrical Engineers (IEE).

DIRECTORIES

Manufacturing Systems: Buyers Guide. Cahners Business Information. • Annual. Price on application. Contains information on companies manufacturing or supplying materials handling systems, CAD/CAM systems, specialized software for manufacturing, programmable controllers, machine vision systems, and automatic identification systems.

Modern Materials Handling Casebook Directory. Cahners Business Information. • Annual. $25.00. Lists about 2,300 manufacturers of equipment and supplies in the materials handling industry. Supplement to *Modern Materials Handling.*

ENCYCLOPEDIAS AND DICTIONARIES

Illustrated Dictionary of Cargo Handling. Peter Brodie. Available from Informa Publishing Group Ltd. • 1996. $100.00. Second edition. Published in the UK by Lloyd's List (http://www.lloydslist.com). Provides definitions of about 600 terms relating to "the vessels and equipment used in modern cargo handling and shipping," including containerization.

HANDBOOKS AND MANUALS

Plant Layout and Materials Handling. James M. Apple. Krieger Publishing Co. • 1991. $59.50. Reprint edition.

INTERNET DATABASES

Fedstats. Federal Interagency Council on Statistical Policy. Phone: (202)395-7254 • URL: http://www.fedstats.gov • Web site features an efficient search facility for full-text statistics produced by more than 70 federal agencies, including the Census Bureau, the Bureau of Economic Analysis, and the Bureau of Labor Statistics. Boolean searches can be made within one agency or for all agencies combined. Links are offered to international statistical bureaus, including the UN, IMF, OECD, UNESCO, Eurostat, and 20 individual countries. Fees: Free.

ONLINE DATABASES

DRI U.S. Central Database. Data Products Division. • Provides more than 23,000 business, financial, demographic, economic, foreign trade, and industry-related time series for the U.S. Includes national income, population, retail-wholesale trade, price indexes, labor data, housing, industrial production, banking, interest rates, money supply, etc. Time period is generally 1947 to date (some data back to 1929). Updating varies. Inquire as to online cost and availability.

PERIODICALS AND NEWSLETTERS

Manufacturing Computer Solutions. Hitchcock Publishing. • Monthly. Free to qualified personnel; others; $75.00 per year. Edited for managers of factory automation, emphasizing the integration of systems in manufacturing. Subjects include materials handling, CAD/CAM, specialized software for manufacturing, programmable controllers, machine vision, and automatic identification systems. Formerly *Manufacturing Systems.*

Material Handling Management: Educating Industry on Product Handling, Flow Strategies, and Automation Technology. Penton Media Inc. • 13 times a year. Free to qualified personnel; other, $50.00 per year. Formerly *Material Handling Engineering.*

Modern Materials Handling. Cahners Publishing Co., Inc. • 14 times a year. $92.90 per year. For managers and engineers who buy or specify equipment used to move, store, control and protect products throughout the manufacturing and warehousing cycles. Includes *Casebook Directory* and *Planning Guide.* Also includes *ADC News and Solutions.*

STATISTICS SOURCES

Business Statistics of the United States. Courtenay M. Slater, editor. Bernan Associates. • 1999. $74.00. Fifth edition. Based on *Business Statistics,* formerly issue by the Bureau of Economic Analysis, U. S. Department of Commerce. Provides basic data for a wide variety of U. S. industries, services, and economic indicators. Most statistics are shown annually for 29 years and monthly for the most recent four years.

Survey of Current Business. Available from U. S. Government Printing Office. • Monthly. $49.00 per year. Issued by Bureau of Economic Analysis, U. S. Department of Commerce. Presents a wide variety of business and economic data.

TRADE/PROFESSIONAL ASSOCIATIONS

Industrial Truck Association. 1750 K St., N.W., Suite 460, Washington, DC 20006. Phone: (202)296-9880 Fax: (202)296-9884 E-mail: indtruck@earthlink.net • URL: http://www.indtrk.org.

Material Handling Equipment Distributors Association. 201 Route 45, Vernon Hills, IL 60061. Phone: (847)680-3500 Fax: (847)362-6989 E-mail: connect@mheda.org • URL: http://www.mheda.com.

Material Handling Industry. 8720 Red Oak Blvd., Suite 201, Charlotte, NC 28217. Phone: 800-345-1815 or (704)676-1190 Fax: (704)676-1199 E-mail: vwheller@mhia.org • URL: http://www.mhia.org.

Materials Handling and Management Society. 8720 Red Oak Blvd., Suite 201, Charlotte, NC 28217. Phone: (704)676-1183 Fax: (704)676-1199 E-mail: bcurtis@smhia.org • URL: http://www.mhia.org/mhms.

MATERIALS, HAZARDOUS

See: HAZARDOUS MATERIALS

MATHEMATICAL STATISTICS

See: STATISTICAL METHODS

MATHEMATICS, BUSINESS

See: BUSINESS MATHEMATICS

MATURE CONSUMER MARKET

GENERAL WORKS

Direct Marketing, Direct Selling, and the Mature Consumer: A Research Study. James R. Lumpkin and others. Greenwood Publishing Group, Inc. • 1989. $62.95. A study of older consumers and their use of mail order, telephone shopping, party-plans, etc.

Marketing Strategies for the Mature Market. George P. Moschis. Greenwood Publishing Group, Inc. • 1994. $59.95.

ABSTRACTS AND INDEXES

Business Periodicals Index. H. W. Wilson Co. • Monthly, except August, with quarterly and annual cumulations. Service basis for print edition; CD-ROM edition, $1,495.00 per year.

Readers' Guide to Periodical Literature. H. W. Wilson Co. • Monthly. $220.00 per year. CD-ROM edition, $1,495 per year, including annual cumulation. Indexes about 250 peridicals of general interest.

ALMANACS AND YEARBOOKS

Older Americans Information Directory. Group Grey House Publshing, Inc. • 2000. $190.00. Second edition. Presents articles (text) and sources of information on a wide variety of aging and retirement topics. Includes an index to personal names, organizations, and subjects.

CD-ROM DATABASES

ABI/INFORM Global. Bell & Howell Information and Learning. • Monthly. $6,500.00 per year. Provides CD-ROM indexing and abstracting of worldwide business literature appearing in over 1,200 periodicals for the most recent five years. Archival discs are available from 1971. Formerly *ABI/INFORM OnDisc.*

WILSONDISC: Business Periodicals Index. H. W. Wilson Co. • Monthly. $1,495.00 per year. Provides CD-ROM indexing of business periodicals from 1982 to date. Price includes online service.

WILSONDISC: Readers' Guide to Periodical Literature. H. W. Wilson Co. • Monthly. $1,095.00 per year, including unlimited online access to *Readers' Guide to Periodical Literature* through WILSONLINE. Provides CD-ROM indexing of about 250 general interest periodicals. Covers 1983 to date. (*Readers' Guide Abstracts* also available on CD-ROM at $1,995 per year.).

HANDBOOKS AND MANUALS

Marketing to Older Consumers: A Handbook of Information for Strategy Development. George P. Moschis. Greenwood Publishing Group, Inc. • 1992. $69.50.

ONLINE DATABASES

ABI/INFORM. Bell & Howell Information and Learning. • Provides online indexing to business-related material occurring in over 1,000 periodicals from 1971 to the present. Inquire as to online cost and availability.

Ageline. American Association of Retired Persons. • Provides indexing and abstracting of the literature of social gerontology, including consumer aspects, financial planning, employment, housing, health care services, mental health, social security, and retirement. Time period is 1978 to date. Inquire as to online cost and availability.

Globalbase. The Gale Group. • Provides more than one million online summaries of business, industrial, and economic news reports from more than 1,000 publications worldwide. Covers a wide range of material appearing in international trade journals, professional magazines, and newspapers. Time period is 1984 to date, with weekly updates. Inquire as to online cost and availability.

Marketing and Advertising Reference Service (MARS). The Gale Group. • Provides abstracts of literature relating to consumer marketing and advertising, including all forms of advertising media. Time period is 1984 to date. Daily updates. Inquire as to online cost and availability.

PROMT: Predicasts Overview of Markets and Technology. The Gale Group. • Companies, products, applied technologies and markets. U.S. and international literature coverage, 1972 to date. Inquire as to online cost and availability. Provides abstracts from more than 1,600 publications. Weekly updates.

Readers' Guide Abstracts Online. H. W. Wilson Co. • Indexes and abstracts general interest periodicals, 1983 to date. Weekly updates. Inquire as to online cost and availability.

Trade & Industry Index. The Gale Group. • Provides indexing of business periodicals, January 1981 to date. Daily updates. (Full text articles from some periodicals are available online, 1983 to date, in the companion database, *Trade & Industry ASAP.*) Inquire as to online cost and availability.

Wilson Business Abstracts Online. H. W. Wilson Co. • Indexes and abstracts 600 major business periodicals, plus the *Wall Street Journal* and the business section of the *New York Times.* Indexing is from 1982, abstracting from 1990, with the two newspapers included from 1993. Updated weekly. Inquire as to online cost and availability. (*Business Periodicals Index* without abstracts is also available online.).

PERIODICALS AND NEWSLETTERS

Selling to Seniors: The Monthly Report on Marketing. Community Development Services, Inc. CD Publications. • Monthly. $225.00 per year. Newsletter on effective ways to reach the "over 50" market.

RESEARCH CENTERS AND INSTITUTES

Center for Mature Consumer Studies. Georgia State University, Broad St., Atlanta, GA 30303. Phone: (404)651-4177 Fax: (404)651-4198 E-mail: gmoschis@gsu.edu • URL: http://www.gsu.edu/~mkteer/cmcs.html • Serves as an information resource, assisting in strategy development for reaching the mature consumer market.

Consumer Research Center. The Conference Board, Inc., 845 Third Ave., New York, NY 10022. Phone: (212)759-0900 Fax: (212)980-7014 E-mail: franco@conference-board.org • URL: http://www.crc-conquest.org • Conducts research on the consumer market, including elderly and working women segments.

STATISTICS SOURCES

Income of the Population 55 and Older. Available from U. S. Government Printing Office. • Biennial. $19.00. Issued by the Social Security Administration (http://www.ssa.gov). Covers major sources and amounts of income for the 55 and older population in the U. S., "with special emphasis on some aspects of the income of the population 65 and older.".

The Sourcebook of County Demographics. Available from The Gale Group. • 1999. $395.00. 13th edition. Published by CACI. Marketing Systems. Contains demographic and socio-economic data (70 characteristics) for each U. S. county. Formerly *Sourcebook of Demographics and Buying Power for Every County in the USA.*

The Sourcebook of ZIP Code Demographics. Available from The Gale Group. • 2000. $495.00. 15th edition. Published by CACI Marketing Systems. Presents detailed statistical profiles of every ZIP code in America, based on the 1990 census. Each profile contains data on more than 70 variables.

Statistical Handbook on Aging Americans. Renee Schick, editor. Oryx Press. • 1994. $65.00. Second edition. Provides data on demographics, social characteristics, health, employment, economic conditions, income, pensions, and social security. Includes bibliographic information and a glossary. (Statistical Handbook Series).

Statistical Record of Older Americans. The Gale Group. • 1996. $109.00. Second edition. Includes income and pension data.

TRADE/PROFESSIONAL ASSOCIATIONS

National Alliance of Senior Citizens. 1700 18th St.,N.W., Suite 401, Washington, DC 20009. Phone: (202)986-0117 Fax: (202)986-2974 • Members are individuals concerned with the needs of older Americans. Includes a Consumerism Advisory Council.

MEASURES

See: WEIGHTS AND MEASURES

MEAT INDUSTRY

See also: CATTLE INDUSTRY; LIVESTOCK INDUSTRY; SHEEP INDUSTRY; SWINE INDUSTRY

ABSTRACTS AND INDEXES

Food Science and Technology Abstracts. International Food Information Service Publishing. • Monthly. $1,780.00 per year. Provides worldwide coverage of the literature of food technology and food production.

Foods Adlibra: Key to the World's Food Literature. Foods Adlibra Publications. • Semimonthly.Provides journal citations and abstracts to the literature of food technology and packaging.

CD-ROM DATABASES

Food Science and Technology Abstracts [CD-ROM]. Available from SilverPlatter Information, Inc. • Quarterly. $3,700 per year. Produced by International Food Information Service (home page is http://www.ifis.org). Provides worldwide coverage on CD-ROM of the literature of food technology and production. Various types of publications are indexed, with abstracts, including about 1,800 periodicals. Time period is 1969 to date.

DIRECTORIES

Directory of Delicatessen Products. Pacific Rim Publishing Co. • Annual. Included with February issue of *Deli News.* Lists suppliers of cheeses, lunch meats, packaged fresh meats, kosher foods, gourmet-specialty items, and bakery products.

Meat and Poultry Inspection Directory. U.S. Department of Agriculture. Available from U.S. Government Printing Office. • Semiannual. $42.00 per year.

Meat Processing-Buyer's Guide. Watt Publishing Co. • Annual. $8.00. In-depth statistical review of the meat, poultry, and seafood industries with easy-to-read graphs and tables; governmental phonebook; listing of meat associations, list of suppliers to the industry; list of equipment, services, and supplies, list of meat processors and their respective products.

Specialty Food Industry Directory. Phoenix Media Network, Inc. • Annual. Included in subscription to Food Distribution Magazine. Lists manufacturers and suppliers of specialty foods, and services and equipment for the specialty food industry. Featured food products include legumes, sauces, spices, upscale cheese, specialty beverages, snack foods, baked goods, ethnic foods, and specialty meats.

ENCYCLOPEDIAS AND DICTIONARIES

Foods and Nutrition Encyclopedia. Audrey H. Ensminger and others. CRC Press, Inc. • 1993. $382.00. Second edition. Two volumes.

FINANCIAL RATIOS

Almanac of Business and Industrial Financial Ratios. Leo Troy. Prentice Hall. • Annual. $99.95. Contains financial ratios derived from federal tax returns. Ratios for each of about 200 industries are arranged according to company asset size.

Annual Statement Studies. Robert Morris Associates: The Association of Lending and Credit Risk Professiona. • Annual. Free to members; non-members, $140.00. Median and quartile financial ratios are given for over 400 kinds of manufacturing, wholesale, retail, construction, and consumer finance establishments. Data is sorted by both asset size and sales volume. Includes a clearly written "Definition of Ratios" and an alphabetical industry index.

HANDBOOKS AND MANUALS

Meat and Poultry Inspection Regulations. U.S. Department of Agriculture. Available from U.S. Government Printing Office. • Looseleaf. $297.00. Monthly updates included. Regulations for slaughter and processing of livestock and poultry as well as for certain voluntary services and humane slaughter.

INTERNET DATABASES

BEEF. National Cattlemen's Beef Association. Phone: (303)694-0305 Fax: (303)694-2851 E-mail: cows@beef.org • URL: http://www.beef.org • Web site provides detailed information from the "Cattle and Beef Handbook," including "Beef Economics" (production, sales, consumption, retail value, foreign competition, etc.). Text of monthly newsletter is also available: "The Beef Brief-Issues & Trends in the Cattle Industry." Keyword searching is offered. Fees: Free.

Fedstats. Federal Interagency Council on Statistical Policy. Phone: (202)395-7254 • URL: http://www.fedstats.gov • Web site features an efficient search facility for full-text statistics produced by more than 70 federal agencies, including the Census Bureau, the Bureau of Economic Analysis, and the Bureau of Labor Statistics. Boolean searches can be made within one agency or for all agencies combined. Links are offered to international statistical bureaus, including the UN, IMF, OECD, UNESCO, Eurostat, and 20 individual countries. Fees: Free.

USDA. United States Department of Agriculture. Phone: (202)720-2791 E-mail: agsec@usda.gov • URL: http://www.usda.gov • The USDA home page has six sections: News and Information; What's New; About USDA; Agencies; Opportunities; Search and Help. Keyword searching is offered from the USDA home page and from various individual agency home pages. Agencies are the Economic Research Service, Agricultural Marketing Service, National Agricultural Statistics Service, National Agricultural Library, and about 12 others. Updating varies. Fees: Free.

ONLINE DATABASES

DRI U.S. Central Database. Data Products Division. • Provides more than 23,000 business, financial, demographic, economic, foreign trade, and industry-related time series for the U.S. Includes national income, population, retail-wholesale trade, price indexes, labor data, housing, industrial production, banking, interest rates, money supply, etc. Time period is generally 1947 to date (some data back to 1929). Updating varies. Inquire as to online cost and availability.

Food Science and Technology Abstracts [online]. IFIS North American Desk. • Produced by International Food Information Service. Provides about 500,000 online citations, with abstracts, to the international literature of food science, technology, commodities, engineering, and processing. Approximately 2,000 periodicals are covered. Time period is 1969 to date, with monthly updates. Inquire as to online cost and availability.

FOODS ADLIBRA. General Mills, Inc. • Contains online citations, with abstracts, to the technical and business literature of food processing and packaging. New products and new ingredients are featured. Covers about 250 trade journals and 500 research journals from 1974 to date, with monthly updates. Inquire as to online cost and availability.

PERIODICALS AND NEWSLETTERS

Deli News. Delicatessen Council of Southern California, Inc. Pacific Rim Publishing Co. • Monthly. $25.00 per year. Includes product news and comment related to cheeses, lunch meats, packaged fresh meats, kosher foods, gourmet-specialty items, and bakery products.

Food Distribution Magazine. Phoenix Media Network, Inc. • Monthly. $49.00 per year. Edited for marketers and buyers of domestic and imported, specialty or gourmet food products, including ethnic foods, seasonings, and bakery items.

Meat and Poultry: The Business Journal of the Meat and Poultry Industry. Sosland Publishing Co. • Monthly. $42.00 per year.

Meat Processing. Watt Publishing Co. • Monthly. Free to qualified personnel; others, $72.00 per year.

PRICE SOURCES

The National Provisioner: Serving Meat, Poultry, and Seafood Processors. Stagnito Communications, Inc. • Monthly. Free to qualified personnel; others, $65.00 per year. Annual *Buyer's Guide* available. Meat, poultry and seafood newsletter.

STATISTICS SOURCES

Agricultural Statistics. Available from U. S. Government Printing Office. • Annual. Produced by the National Agricultural Statistics Service, U. S. Department of Agriculture. Provides a wide variety of statistical data relating to agricultural production, supplies, consumption, prices/price-supports, foreign trade, costs, and returns, as well as farm labor, loans, income, and population. In many cases, historical data is shown annually for 10 years. In addition to farm data, includes detailed fishery statistics.

Annual Survey of Manufactures. Available from U. S. Government Printing Office. • Annual. Prices vary. Issued by the U. S. Census Bureau as an interim update to the *Census of Manufactures.* Includes data on number of manufacturing establishments in various industries, employment, labor costs, value of shipments, capital expenditures, inventories, energy costs, and assets. (See also Census Bureau home page, http://www.census.gov/.).

Business Statistics of the United States. Courtenay M. Slater, editor. Bernan Associates. • 1999. $74.00. Fifth edition. Based on *Business Statistics*, formerly issue by the Bureau of Economic Analysis, U. S. Department of Commerce. Provides basic data for a wide variety of U. S. industries, services, and economic indicators. Most statistics are shown annually for 29 years and monthly for the most recent four years.

Livestock, Meat, Wool, Market News. U.S. Department of Agriculture. • Weekly.

Meat Balances in OECD Countries. Organization for Economic Cooperation and Development. Available from OECD Publications and Information Center. • Irregular. Price varies. Presents data for seven years on meat production, trade, and consumption. Covers various categories of meat in OECD member countries.

Survey of Current Business. Available from U. S. Government Printing Office. • Monthly. $49.00 per year. Issued by Bureau of Economic Analysis, U. S. Department of Commerce. Presents a wide variety of business and economic data.

TRADE/PROFESSIONAL ASSOCIATIONS

American Meat Institute. 1700 N. Moore St., Ste. 1600, Arlington, VA 22209. Phone: (703)841-2400 Fax: (703)527-0938 E-mail: memberservices@meatami.org • URL: http://www.meatami.org.

Meat Industry Suppliers Association. 111 Park Place, Falls Church, VA 22046-4513. Phone: (703)538-1793 Fax: (703)241-5603.

National Cattlemen's Beef Association. P.O. Box 3469, Englewood, CO 80155. Phone: (312)467-5520 Fax: (312)467-9767 E-mail: cattle@beef.org • URL: http://www.beef.org/ncba.htm.

North American Meat Processors Association. 1920 Association Dr., Suite 400, Reston, VA 20191-1547. Phone: (703)758-1900 Fax: (703)758-8001 E-mail: namp@ix.netcom.com • URL: http://www.namp.com.

OTHER SOURCES

Major Food and Drink Companies of the World. Available from The Gale Group. • 2001. $855.00. Fourth edition. Two volumes. Published by Graham & Whiteside. Contains profiles and trade names for more than 9,000 important food and beverage companies in various countries. In addition to foods, includes both alcoholic and nonalcoholic drink products.

Thomas Food and Beverage Market Place. Grey House Publishing. • Annual. $295.00. Three volumes. Contains more than 40,000 entries covering food companies, beverages, food equipment, warehouse companies, food brokers, wholesalers, importers, and exporters. Formerly *Thomas Food Industry Register.*

MEAT PACKING INDUSTRY

See: MEAT INDUSTRY

MECHANICAL DRAWING

GENERAL WORKS

Fundamentals of Engineering Drawing: With an Introduction to Interactive Computer Graphics for Design and Production. Warren J. Luzadder and Jon M. Duff. Prentice Hall. • 1992. $91.00. 11th edition.

PERIODICALS AND NEWSLETTERS

Engineering Design Graphics Journal. American Society for Engineering Education. • Three times a year. Members, $6.00 per year; non-members, $20.00 per year;institutions, $10.00 per year. Concerned with engineering graphics, computer graphics, geometric modeling, computer-aided drafting, etc.

TRADE/PROFESSIONAL ASSOCIATIONS

American Design Drafting Association. P.O. Box 11937, Columbia, SC 29211. Phone: (803)771-0008 Fax: (803)771-4272 E-mail: national@adda.org • URL: http://www.adda.org.

MECHANICAL ENGINEERING

See also: MACHINE DESIGN

ABSTRACTS AND INDEXES

Applied Mechanics Reviews: An Assessment of World Literature in Engineering Sciences. American Society of Mechanical Engineers. • Monthly. Members, $126.00 per year; non-members, $663.00 per year.

Engineering Index Monthly: Abstracting and Indexing Services Covering Sources of the World's Engineering Literature. Engineering Information, Inc. • Monthly. $2,300.00 per year. Provides indexing and abstracting of the world's engineering and technical literature.

Mechanical Engineering Abstracts. Cambridge Information Group. • Bimonthly. $975.00 per year. Formerly *ISMEC - Mechanical Engineering Abstracts.*

BIBLIOGRAPHIES

Encyclopedia of Physical Science and Engineering Information. The Gale Group. • 1996. $160.00. Second edition. Includes print, electronic, and other information sources for a wide range of scientific, technical, and engineering topics.

BIOGRAPHICAL SOURCES

Who's Who in Science and Engineering. Marquis Who's Who. • Biennial. $269.00. Provides concise biographical information on 26,000 prominent engineers and scientists. International coverage, with geographical and professional indexes.

CD-ROM DATABASES

COMPENDEX PLUS [CD-ROM]. Engineering Information, Inc. • Quarterly. $3,450.00 per year. Provides CD-ROM indexing and abstracting of the world's engineering and technical information appearing in journals, reports, books, and proceedings, 1985 to date.

DIRECTORIES

Peterson's Graduate and Professional Programs: Engineering and Applied Sciences. Peterson's. • Annual. $37.95. Provides details of more than 3,400 graduate and professional programs in engineering and related fields at colleges and universities. Formerly *Peterson's Guide to Graduate Programs in Engineering and Professional Sciences.*

HANDBOOKS AND MANUALS

Mechanical Engineering Design. Charles R. Mischke. McGraw-Hill. • 2000. $85.00. Sixth edition. (Mechanical Engineering Series).

Mechanical Engineers' Handbook. Myer P. Kutz, editor. John Wiley and Sons, Inc. • 1998. $250.00. Second edition.

Mechanical Engineer's Reference Book. E. H. Smith, editor. Society of Automotive Engineers, Inc. • 1994. $135.00. 12th edition. Covers mechanical engineering principles, computer integrated engineering systems, design standards, materials, power transmission, and many other engineering topics. (Authored Royalty Series).

ONLINE DATABASES

COMPENDEX PLUS. Engineering Information, Inc. • Provides online indexing and abstracting of the world's engineering and technical information appearing in journals, reports, books, and proceedings. Time period is 1970 to date, with weekly updates. Inquire as to online cost and availability.

Hard Sciences. Cambridge Scientific Abstracts. • Provides the online version of *Computer and Information Systems Abstracts, Electronics and Communications Abstracts, Health and Safety Science Abstracts, ISMEC: Mechanical Engineering Abstracts (Information Service in Mechanical Engineering)* and *Solid State and Superconductivity Abstracts.* Time period is 1981 to date, with monthly updates. Inquire as to online cost and availability.

NTIS Bibliographic Data Base. National Technical Information Service. • Contains citations and abstracts to unrestricted reports of government-sponsored research, 1964 to date. Covers a wide range of technical, engineering, business, and social science topics. Monthly updates. Inquire as to online cost and availability.

Who's Who in Technology [Online]. The Gale Group. • Provides online biographical profiles of over 25,000 American scientists, engineers, and others in technology-related occupations. Inquire as to online cost and availability.

PERIODICALS AND NEWSLETTERS

International Journal of Mechanical Sciences. Elsevier Science. • Monthly. $2,197.00 per year.

Journal of Applied Mechanics. American Society of Mechanical Engineers. • Quarterly. Members, $40.00 per year; non-members, $250.00 per year. Series E of the *Transactions of the ASME.*

Journal of Heat Transfer. American Society of Mechanical Engineers. • Quarterly. Members, $40.00 per year; non-members, $250.00 per year.

Journal of Turbomachinery. American Society of Mechanical Engineers. • Quarterly. Members, $40.00 per year; non-members, $215.00 per year. Series A of the *Transactions of the ASME.* Formerly *Journal of Gas Turbines.*

Mechanical Engineering. American Society of Mechanical Engineers. • Monthly. $100.00 per year.

RESEARCH CENTERS AND INSTITUTES

Engineering Dean's Office. University of California at Berkeley, 308 Mclaughin Hall, No. 1702, Berkeley, CA 94720-1706. Phone: (510)642-7594 Fax: (510)643-8653 E-mail: dma@coe.berkeley.edu • Research fields include civil, electrical, industrial, mechanical, and other types of engineering.

TRADE/PROFESSIONAL ASSOCIATIONS

American Society of Mechanical Engineers. Three Park Ave., New York, NY 10016-5990. Phone: 800-843-2763 or (212)705-7722 Fax: (212)705-7674 E-mail: infocentral@asme.org • URL: http://www.asme.org.

MECHANICAL POWER TRANSMISSION

See: POWER (MECHANICAL)

MEDIA, INTERACTIVE

See: INTERACTIVE MEDIA

MEDIA LAW

See: ADVERTISING LAW AND REGULATION; MASS MEDIA

MEDIA, MASS

See: MASS MEDIA

MEDIA RESEARCH

See also: ADVERTISING RESEARCH; MASS MEDIA

GENERAL WORKS

Electronic Media Ratings. Karen Buzzard. Butterworth-Heinemann. • 1992. $22.95. Provides basic information about TV and radio audience-rating techniques. Includes glossary and bibliography. (Electronic Media Guide Series).

ABSTRACTS AND INDEXES

Business Periodicals Index. H. W. Wilson Co. • Monthly, except August, with quarterly and annual cumulations. Service basis for print edition; CD-ROM edition, $1,495.00 per year.

Communication Abstracts. Sage Publications, Inc. • Bimonthly. Individuals, $185.00 per year; institutions, $805.00 per year. Provides broad coverage of the literature of communications, including broadcasting and advertising.

Electronics and Communications Abstracts Journal: Comprehensive Coverage of Essential Scientific Literature. Cambridge Information Group. • Monthly. $1,045.00 per year.

DIRECTORIES

Marketer's Guide to Media. BPI Communications, Inc. • Quarterly. $105.00. Presents cost, circulation, and audience statistics for various mass media segments, including television, radio, magazines, newspapers, telephone yellow pages, and cinema. Formerly *Mediaweek's Guide to Media.*

ONLINE DATABASES

Marketing and Advertising Reference Service (MARS). The Gale Group. • Provides abstracts of literature relating to consumer marketing and advertising, including all forms of advertising media. Time period is 1984 to date. Daily updates. Inquire as to online cost and availability.

Nielsen Station Index. Nielsen Media Research. • Measures local television station audiences in about 220 U. S. geographic areas. Includes current and some historical data. Inquire as to online cost and availability.

Nielsen Television Index. Nielsen Media Research. • Measures national television program audiences by sampling approximately 4,000 U. S. households. Time period is 1970 to date, with weekly updates.

Simmons Study of Media and Markets. Simmons Market Research Bureau. • Market and media survey data relating to the American consumer. Inquire as to online cost and availability.

Wilson Business Abstracts Online. H. W. Wilson Co. • Indexes and abstracts 600 major business periodicals, plus the *Wall Street Journal* and the business section of the *New York Times.* Indexing is from 1982, abstracting from 1990, with the two newspapers included from 1993. Updated weekly. Inquire as to online cost and availability. (*Business*

Periodicals Index without abstracts is also available online.).

PERIODICALS AND NEWSLETTERS

American Demographics: Consumer Trends for Business Leaders. Intertec Publishing Co. • Monthly. $69.00 per year.

Journal of Advertising Research. Advertising Research Foundation. • Bimonthly. $100.00 per year.

Journal of Applied Communication Research. National Communication Association. • Quarterly. $110.00 per year.

The Marketing Pulse: The Exclusive Insight Provider to the Entertainment, Marketing, Advertising and Media Industries. Unlimited Positive Communications, Inc. • Monthly. $300.00 per year. Newsletter concerned with advertising media forecasts and analyses. Emphasis is on TV and radio.

Mediaweek: Incorporating Marketing and Media Decisions. BPI Communications, Inc. • 47 times a year. $145.00 per year. Published for advertising media buyers and managers.

RESEARCH CENTERS AND INSTITUTES

Center for Communication Research. University of Wisconsin, 821 University Ave., Madison, WI 53706. Phone: (608)262-2543 Fax: (608)262-9953 E-mail: jdillard@facstaff.wisc.edu.

Center for Media and Public Affairs. 2100 L St., N. W., Suite 300, Washington, DC 20037. Phone: (202)223-2942 Fax: (202)872-4014 E-mail: cmpamm@aol.com • URL: http://www.cmpa.com.

Integrated Media Systems Center. University of Southern California, 3740 McClintock Ave., Suite 131, Los Angeles, CA 90089-2561. Phone: (213)740-0877 Fax: (213)740-8931 E-mail: nikias@imsc.usc.edu • URL: http://www.imsc.usc.edu • Media areas for research include education, mass communication, and entertainment.

Knight Center for Specialized Journalism. University of Maryland, 290 University College, College Park, MD 20742-1645. Phone: (301)985-7279 Fax: (301)985-7840 E-mail: knight@umail.umd.edu • URL: http://www.inform.umd.edu/knight • Research area is media coverage of complex subjects, such as economics, law, science, and medicine.

Mass Communications Research Center. University of Wisconsin-Madison, 821 University Ave., 5050 Vilas Hall, Madison, WI 53706. Phone: (608)263-3381 Fax: (608)262-1361.

TRADE/PROFESSIONAL ASSOCIATIONS

Advertising Research Foundation. 641 Lexington Ave., New York, NY 10022. Phone: (212)751-5656 Fax: (212)319-5265 E-mail: email@arfsite.org • URL: http://www.arfsite.org.

American Marketing Association. 311 S. Wacker Dr., Suite 5800, Chicago, IL 60606. Phone: 800-262-1150 or (312)542-9000 Fax: (312)542-9001 E-mail: info@ama.org • URL: http://www.ama.org.

Marketing Research Association. 1344 Silas Deane Hwy., Ste. 306, Rocky Hill, CT 06067-0230. Phone: (860)257-4008 Fax: (860)257-3990 E-mail: email@mra-net.org • URL: http://www.mra-net.org.

MEDIATION

See: ARBITRATION

MEDICAL CARE INDUSTRY

See: HEALTH CARE INDUSTRY

MEDICAL ECONOMICS (PRACTICE MANAGEMENT)

See also: GROUP MEDICAL PRACTICE; HEALTH CARE INDUSTRY

GENERAL WORKS

Management of Healthcare Organizations. Kerry D. Carson and others. Brooks/Cole Publishing Co. • Price on application. (SWC-Management Series).

BIBLIOGRAPHIES

Medical and Health Care Books and Serials in Print: An Index to Literature in Health Sciences. R. R. Bowker. • Annual. $265.95. Two volumes.

DIRECTORIES

Directory of Physician Groups and Networks. Dorland Healthcare Information. • Annual. $345.00. Lists more than 4,200 independent practice associations (IPAs), physician hospital organizations (PHOs), management service organizations (MSOs), physician practice management companies (PPMCs), and group practices having 20 or more physicians.

Encyclopedia of Medical Organizations and Agencies. The Gale Group. • 2000. $285.00. 11th edition. Information on over 14,000 public and private organizations in medicine and related fields.

Medical and Health Information Directory. The Gale Group. • 1999. $630.00. Three volumes. 12th edition. Vol. one covers medical organizations, agencies, and institutions; vol. two includes bibliographic, library, and database information; vol. three is a guide to services available for various medical and health problems.

Society of Medical-Dental Management Consultants: Membership Directory. Society of Medical-Dental Management Consultants. • Annual. Free. About 100 consultants in business and financial aspects of the management of medical and dental practices.

ENCYCLOPEDIAS AND DICTIONARIES

Guidebook to Managed Care and Practice Management Terminology. Norman Winegar and L. Michelle Hayter. Haworth Press, Inc. • 1998. $39.95. Provides definitions of managed care "terminology, jargon, and concepts.".

FINANCIAL RATIOS

Almanac of Business and Industrial Financial Ratios. Leo Troy. Prentice Hall. • Annual. $99.95. Contains financial ratios derived from federal tax returns. Ratios for each of about 200 industries are arranged according to company asset size.

Annual Statement Studies. Robert Morris Associates: The Association of Lending and Credit Risk Professiona. • Annual. Free to members; non-members, $140.00. Median and quartile financial ratios are given for over 400 kinds of manufacturing, wholesale, retail, construction, and consumer finance establishments. Data is sorted by both asset size and sales volume. Includes a clearly written "Definition of Ratios" and an alphabetical industry index.

Industry Norms and Key Business Ratios. Desk Top Edition. Dun and Bradstreet Corp., Business Information Services. • Annual. Five volumes. $475.00 per volume. $1,890.00 per set. Covers over 800 kinds of businesses, arranged by Standard Industrial Classification number. More detailed editions covering longer periods of time are also available.

HANDBOOKS AND MANUALS

Healthcare Finance for the Non-Financial Manager: Basic Guide to Financial Analysis & Control. Louis Gapenski. McGraw-Hill Professional. • 1994. $47.50.

Managed Care Handbook: How to Prepare Your Medical Practice for the Managed Care Revolution. James Lyle and Hoyt Torras. Practice Management Information Corp. • 1994. $49.95. Second edition. A management guide for physicians in private practice.

ONLINE DATABASES

Healthstar. Medlars Management Section. • Provides indexing and abstracting of non-clinical literature relating to health care delivery, 1975 to date. Monthly updates. Inquire as to online cost and availability.

PERIODICALS AND NEWSLETTERS

Dental Economics. Pennwell Publishing Co., Dental Economics Div. • Monthly. $78.00 per year.

Dental Practice and Finance. MEDEC Dental Communications. • Bimonthly. $55.00 per year. Covers practice management and financial topics for dentists. Includes investment advice.

Group Practice Journal. American Medical Group Practice Association. • 10 times a year. $75.00 per year.

Health Care Strategic Management: The Newsletter for Hospital Strategies. Business Word, Inc. • Monthly. $249.00 per year. Planning, marketing and resource allocation.

Health Marketing Quarterly. The Haworth Press, Inc. • Quarterly. Individuals, $60.00 per year; institutions, $80.00 per year; libraries, $425.00 per year.

Hospital Revenue Report. United Communications Group. • 25 times a year. $379.00 per year. Newsletter. Advises hospitals on how to cut costs, increase patient revenue, and maximize Medicare income. Incorporates *Health Care Marketer*.

Journal of Medical Practice Management. Williams and Wilkins. • Bimonthly. Individuals, $159.00 per year; institutions, $199.00 per year.

Life in Medicine: Business and Lifestyle Issues for New Physicians. Dynamic Graphics, Inc. • Bimonthly. $42.00 per year. Covers practice management and financial topics for new physicians.

Medical Economics. Medical Economics Co., Inc. • 25 times a year. $109.00 per year. Covers the financial, economic, insurance, administrative, and other non-clinical aspects of private medical practice. Provides investment and estate planning advice.

Medical Economics General Surgery-Orthopedic Surgery. Medical Economics Co., Inc. • Monthly. $65.00 per year. Provides information and advice on practice management (non-clinical) for surgeons. Formerly *Medical Economics for Surgeons*.

Medical Group Management Journal. Medical Group Management Association. • Bimonthly. $68.00 per year.

Medicare Compliance Alert. United Communications Group. • Biweekly. $370.00 per year. Newsletter. Supplement available, *Civil Money Penalties Reporter*. Newsletter. Provides news of changes in Medicare regulations and legislation. Advises physicians on Medicare rules relating to physician investments, joint ventures, limited partnerships, and patient referrals.

Modern Physician: Essential Business News for the Executive Physician. Crain Communications, Inc. • Monthly. $39.50. Edited for physicians responsible for business decisions at hospitals, clinics, HMOs, and other health groups. Includes special issues on managed care, practice management, legal issues, and finance.

Nursing Economics: Business Perspectives for Nurses. Jannetti Publications, Inc. • Bimonthly.

Individuals, $45.00 per year; institutions, $60.00 per year.

Nursing Management. Springhouse Corp. • Monthly. Individuals, $38.00 per year; institutions, $60.00 per year. Non-clinical subject matter.

Optometric Management: The Business and Marketing Magazine for Optometry. Boucher Communications, Inc. • Monthly. $48.00 per year. Provides information and advice for optometrists on practice management and marketing.

Physicians & Computers. Moorhead Publications Inc. • Monthly. $40.00 per year. Includes material on computer diagnostics, online research, medical and non-medical software, computer equipment, and practice management.

Physicians Financial News. McGraw-Hill. • Monthly. $105.00 per year.

Physician's Marketing and Management. American Health Consultants, Inc. • Monthly. Individuals, $299.00 per year; institutions, $323.00 per year. Formerly*Physician's Marketing.*

Podiatry Management. Kane Communications, Inc. • Nine times a year. $30.00 per year. Non-clinical subject matter.

Private Practice. Congress of County Medical Societies (CCMS) Publishing Co. • Monthly. $18.00 per year.

Resident and Staff Physician. Romaine Pierson Publishers, Inc. • Monthly. $62.00 per year.

Services Marketing Quarterly. Haworth Press, Inc. • Semiannual. Two volumes. Individuals, $60.00 per year; institutions, $90.00 per year; libraries, $275.00 per year. Supplies "how to" marketing tools for specific sectors of the expanding service sector of the economy. Formerly *Journal of Professional Services Marketing.*

TRADE/PROFESSIONAL ASSOCIATIONS

American Academy of Dental Group Practice. 2525 E. Arizona Biltmore Circle, Ste. 127, Phoenix, AZ 85016-2129. Phone: (602)381-1185 Fax: (602)381-1093 • URL: http://www.aadgp.org.

American Academy of Dental Practice Administration. c/o Kathleen Uebel, 1063 Whippoorwill Lane, Palatine, IL 60067. Phone: (847)934-4404 E-mail: aadpa@aol.com • URL: http://www.aadpa.org.

American Academy of Family Physicians. 11400 Tomahawk Creek Parkway, Leawood, MO 66211-2672. Phone: 800-274-2237 or (913)906-6000 Fax: (816)822-0580 E-mail: fp@aafp.org • URL: http://www.aafp.org.

American College of Medical Practice Executives. 104 Inverness Terrace E., Englewood, CO 80112-5306. Phone: 877-275-6442 Fax: (303)643-4427 • URL: http://www.mgma.com.

American Medical Association. 515 N. State St., Chicago, IL 60610. Phone: (312)464-5000 Fax: (312)464-4184 • URL: http://www.ama-assn.org/ • Concerned with retirement planning and other financial planning for physicians 55 years of age or older.

American Medical Group Association. 1422 Duke St., Alexandria, VA 22314-3430. Phone: (703)838-0033 Fax: (703)548-1890 E-mail: rconnor@amga.org • URL: http://www.amga.org.

American Professional Practice Association. Hillsboro Executive Center N., 350 Fairway Dr., Suite 200, Deerfield Park, FL 33441-1834. Phone: 800-221-2168 or (954)571-1877 Fax: (954)571-8582 E-mail: membership@assnservices.com • URL: http://www.appa-assn.com • Concerned with financial planning for physicians and dentists.

Medical Group Management Association. 104 Inverness Terrace E., Englewood, CO 80112-5306. Phone: 888-608-5601 or (303)799-1111 Fax: (303)643-4439 • URL: http://www.mgma.com • Members are medical group managers.

Society of Medical-Dental Management Consultants. 3646 E. Ray Rd. B16-45, Phoenix, AZ 85044. Phone: 800-826-2264 Fax: (602)759-3530 E-mail: chuck@smdmc.org • URL: http://www.smdmc.org.

MEDICAL ELECTRONICS

See also: MEDICAL TECHNOLOGY

ABSTRACTS AND INDEXES

Applied Science and Technology Index. H. W. Wilson Co. • 11 times a year. Quarterly and annual cumulations. Service basis for print edition; CD-ROM edition, $1,495.00 per year. Indexes a wide variety of English language technical, industrial, and engineering periodicals.

Excerpta Medica: Biophysics, Bioengineering, and Medical Instrumentation. Elsevier Science. • 16 times a year. $2,207.00 per year. Section 27 of *Excerpta Medica.*

NTIS Alerts: Biomedical Technology & Human Factors Engineering. National Technical Information Service. • Semimonthly. $210.00 per year. Provides descriptions of government-sponsored research reports and software, with ordering information. Covers biotechnology, ergonomics, bionics, artificial intelligence, prosthetics, and related subjects. Formerly *Abstract Newsletter.*

CD-ROM DATABASES

Health Devices Alerts [CD-ROM]. ECRI. • Weekly. $2,450.00 per year. Provides CD-ROM reports of medical equipment defects, problems, failures, misuses, and recalls.

WILSONDISC: Applied Science and Technology Abstracts. H. W. Wilson Co. • Monthly. $1,495.00 per year, including unlimited access to the online version of *Applied Science and Technology Abstracts* through WILSONLINE. Provides CD-ROM indexing and abstracting of 400 prominent scientific, technical, engineering, and industrial periodicals. Indexing coverage is provided from 1983 to date and abstracting from 1993 to date.

DIRECTORIES

Health Devices Sourcebook. ECRI (Emergency Care Research Institute). • Annual. Lists over 6,000 manufacturers of a wide variety of medical equipment and supplies, including clinical laboratory equipment, testing instruments, surgical instruments, patient care equipment, etc.

Medical Product Manufacturing News Buyers Guide. Canon Communications LLC. • Annual. Controlled circulation. A directory of over 3,000 medical device and medical electronic equipment. Formerly *Medical Product Manufacturing News-Buyer's Guide and Designer's Sourcebook.*

ENCYCLOPEDIAS AND DICTIONARIES

Wiley Encyclopedia of Electrical and Electronics Engineering. John G. Webster, editor. John Wiley and Sons, Inc. • 1999. $6,495.00. 24 volumes. Contains about 1,400 articles, each with bibliography. Arrangement is according to 64 categories.

ONLINE DATABASES

Applied Science and Technology Index Online. H. W. Wilson Co. • Provides online indexing of 400 major scientific, technical, industrial, and engineering periodicals. Time period is 1983 to date. Monthly updates. Inquire as to online cost and availability.

Current Contents Connect. Institute for Scientific Information. • Provides online abstracts of articles listed in the tables of contents of about 7,500 journals. Coverage is very broad, including science, social science, life science, technology, engineering, industry, agriculture, the environment, economics, and arts and humanities. Time period is two years, with weekly updates. Inquire as to online cost and availability.

F-D-C Reports. FDC Reports, Inc. • An online version of "The Gray Sheet" (medical devices), "The Pink Sheet" (pharmaceuticals), "The Rose Sheet" (cosmetics), "The Blue Sheet" (biomedical), and "The Tan Sheet" (nonprescription). Contains full-text information on legal, technical, corporate, financial, and marketing developments from 1987 to date, with weekly updates. Inquire as to online cost and availability.

Health Devices Alerts [online]. ECRI. • Provides online reports of medical equipment defects, problems, failures, misuses, and recalls. Time period is 1977 to date, with weekly updates. Inquire as to online cost and availability.

PROMT: Predicasts Overview of Markets and Technology. The Gale Group. • Companies, products, applied technologies and markets. U.S. and international literature coverage, 1972 to date. Inquire as to online cost and availability. Provides abstracts from more than 1,600 publications. Weekly updates.

PERIODICALS AND NEWSLETTERS

Health Devices Alerts: A Summary of Reported Problems, Hazards, Recalls, and Updates. ECRI (Emergency Care Research Institute). • Weekly. Newsletter containing reviews of health equipment problems. Includes *Health Devices Alerts Action Items, Health Devices Alerts Abstracts, Health Devices Alerts FDA Data, Health Devices Alerts Implants, Health Devices Alerts Hazards Bulletin.*

Medical Electronics. Measurements & Data Corp. • Bimonthly. $22.00 per year. Includes information on new medical electronic products, technology, industry news, and medical safety.

Medical Electronics and Equipment News. Reilly Publishing Co. • Bimonthly. Free to qualified personnel; others, $50.00 per year. Provides medical electronics industry news and new product information.

Medical Laser Report. PennWell Corp., Advanced Technology Div. • Monthly. $345.00 per year. Newsletter. Covers the business and financial side of the medical laser industry, along with news of technological developments and clinical applications. Supplement available *Buyers' Guide.* Formerly *Medical Laser Industrial Report.*

Medical Product Manufacturing News. Canon Communications LLC. • 10 times a year. Free to qualified personnel; others, $125.00 per year. Directed at manufacturers of medical devices and medical electronic equipment. Covers industry news, service news, and new products.

Physicians & Computers. Moorhead Publications Inc. • Monthly. $40.00 per year. Includes material on computer diagnostics, online research, medical and non-medical software, computer equipment, and practice management.

RESEARCH CENTERS AND INSTITUTES

Laboratory of Electronics. Rockefeller University, 1230 York Ave., New York, NY 10021. Phone: (212)327-8613 Fax: (212)327-7613 E-mail: ros@rockvax.rockefeller.edu • Studies the application of computer engineering and electronics to biomedicine.

Medical Electronics Laboratory. University of Wisconsin, 1300 University Ave., Madison, WI 53706. Phone: (608)262-1326 Fax: (608)262-2327 E-mail: yee@physiology.wisc.edu • Develops electronic instrumentation for medical and biological research.

STATISTICS SOURCES

Annual Survey of Manufactures. Available from U. S. Government Printing Office. • Annual. Prices vary. Issued by the U. S. Census Bureau as an interim update to the *Census of Manufactures.* Includes data on number of manufacturing establishments in various industries, employment, labor costs, value of shipments, capital expenditures, inventories, energy costs, and assets. (See also Census Bureau home page, http://www.census.gov/.).

Manufacturing Profiles. Available from U. S. Government Printing Office. • Annual. Issued by the U. S. Census Bureau. A printed consolidation of the entire *Current Industrial Report* series, presenting "all the data compiled." Contains statistics on production, shipments, inventories, consumption, exports, imports, and orders for a wide variety of manufactured products. (See also Census Bureau home page, http://www.census.gov/.).

U. S. Industry and Trade Outlook: The McGraw-Hill Companies and the U.S. Department of Commerce/International Trade Administration. Datapso Research Corp. • Annual. $69.95. Produced by the International Trade Administration, U. S. Department of Commerce, in a "public-private" partnership with DRI/McGraw-Hill and Standard & Poor's. Provides basic data, outlook for the current year, and "Long-Term Prospects" (five-year projections) for a wide variety of products and services. Includes high technology industries. Formerly *U. S. Industrial Outlook.*

TRADE/PROFESSIONAL ASSOCIATIONS

Association for the Advancement of Medical Instrumentation. 3330 Washington Blvd., Suite 400, Arlington, VA 22201. Phone: 800-332-2264 or (703)525-4890 Fax: (703)276-0793 • Members are engineers, technicians, physicians, manufacturers, and others with an interest in medical instrumentation.

Health Industry Manufacturers Association. 1200 G St., N.W., Suite 400, Washington, DC 20005. Phone: (202)783-8700 Fax: (202)783-8750 • URL: http://www.himanet.com.

Institute of Electrical and Electronics Engineers-Engineering in Medicine and Biology Society. Three Park Ave., 17th Fl., New York, NY 10017-2394. Phone: (212)419-7900 Fax: (212)752-4929 • URL: http://www.ieee.org • Members are engineers, technicians, physicians, manufacturers, and others with an interest in medical instrumentation.

OTHER SOURCES

Business & Company Resource Center. The Gale Group. • Fee-based Web site provides a wide range of business, industry, and specific company information. Access is offered to trade journal articles, market research data, insider trading activity, major shareholder data, corporate histories, emerging technology reports, corporate earnings estimates, press releases, and other sources. Provides detailed company profiles, industry overviews, and rankings. Offers integration of Predicasts PROMT, Newsletters ASAP, Investext Plus, Business Index ASAP, Brands and Their Companies, and other databases (many have full text).

Digital X-Ray Markets: Imaging in the 21st Century. Theta Reports/PJB Medical Publications, Inc. • 2000. $1,995.00. Market research data. Covers digital filmless radiography as a replacement for traditional x-ray technology. (Theta Report No. 1027.).

MEDICAL EQUIPMENT

See: HOSPITAL EQUIPMENT; SURGICAL INSTRUMENTS INDUSTRY

MEDICAL INSURANCE

See: HEALTH INSURANCE

MEDICAL LABORATORIES

See: CLINICAL LABORATORY INDUSTRY

MEDICAL LIABILITY

See: PROFESSIONAL LIABILITY

MEDICAL SERVICE, INDUSTRIAL

See: INDUSTRIAL MEDICINE

MEDICAL TECHNOLOGY

See also: MEDICAL TECHNOLOGY; SURGICAL INSTRUMENTS INDUSTRY; X-RAY EQUIPMENT INDUSTRY

GENERAL WORKS

Health Care, Technology, and the Competitive Environment. Henry P. Brehm and Ross M. Mullner, editors. Greenwood Publishing Group, Inc. • 1989. $69.50.

Medical Technology and Society: An Interdisciplinary Perspective. Joseph Bronzino and Vincent Smith. MIT Press. • 1990. $50.00.

ABSTRACTS AND INDEXES

Excerpta Medica: Biophysics, Bioengineering, and Medical Instrumentation. Elsevier Science. • 16 times a year. $2,207.00 per year. Section 27 of *Excerpta Medica.*

BIBLIOGRAPHIES

Encyclopedia of Physical Science and Engineering Information. The Gale Group. • 1996. $160.00. Second edition. Includes print, electronic, and other information sources for a wide range of scientific, technical, and engineering topics.

CD-ROM DATABASES

BioMed Strategies. Thomson Financial Securities Data. • Monthly. $2,995.00 per year. CD-ROM contains full text of investment analysts' reports on companies operating in the following fields: biotechnology, pharmaceuticals, medical products, and health care.

NTIS on SilverPlatter. Available from SilverPlatter Information, Inc. • Quarterly. $2,850.00 per year. Produced by the National Technical Information Service. Provides a CD-ROM guide to over 500,000 government reports on a wide variety of technical, industrial, and business topics.

DIRECTORIES

Association for the Advancement of Medical Instrumentation Membership Directory. Association for the Advancement of Medical Instrumentation. • Annual. Membership. List 6,500 physicians, clinical engineers, biomedical engineersand technicians and nurses, researchers, and medical equipment manufacturers.

BioScan: The Worldwide Biotech Industry Reporting Service. American Health Consultants, Inc. • Bimonthly. $1,395.00 per year. Looseleaf. Provides detailed information on over 900 U. S. and foreign companies broadly classified as biotechnological. In addition to medical technology and advanced pharmaceutical firms, includes firms doing research in food processing, waste management, agriculture, and veterinary science.

Health Devices Sourcebook. ECRI (Emergency Care Research Institute). • Annual. Lists over 6,000 manufacturers of a wide variety of medical equipment and supplies, including clinical laboratory equipment, testing instruments, surgical instruments, patient care equipment, etc.

Medical and Healthcare Marketplace Guide. Dorland Healthcare Information. • Annual. $690.00. Two volumes. Provides market survey summaries for about 500 specific product and service categories (volume one: "Research Reports"). Contains profiles of nearly 6,000 pharmaceutical, medical product, and healthcare service companies (volume two: "Company Profiles").

Medical Device Register. Medical Economics. • Annual. $325.00. Lists more than 12,000 suppliers of a wide variety of medical devices and clinical laboratory products.

Plunkett's Health Care Industry Almanac: The Only Complete Guide to the Fastest-Changing Industry in America. Available from Plunkett Research, Ltd. • Biennial. $179.99. Includes detailed profiles of 500 large companies providing health care products or services, with indexes by products, services, and location. Provides statistical and trend information for the health insurance industry, HMOs, hospital utilization, Medicare, medical technology, and national health expenditures.

FINANCIAL RATIOS

Industry Norms and Key Business Ratios. Desk Top Edition. Dun and Bradstreet Corp., Business Information Services. • Annual. Five volumes. $475.00 per volume. $1,890.00 per set. Covers over 800 kinds of businesses, arranged by Standard Industrial Classification number. More detailed editions covering longer periods of time are also available.

HANDBOOKS AND MANUALS

Physicians' Desk Reference for Ophthalmology. Medical Economics Publishing Co., Inc. • Irregular. $49.95. Provides detailed descriptions of ophthalmological instrumentation, equipment, supplies, lenses, and prescription drugs. Indexed by manufacturer, product name, product category, active drug ingredient, and instrumentation. Editorial discussion is included.

INTERNET DATABASES

National Library of Medicine (NLM). National Institutes of Health (NIH). Phone: 888-346-3656 or (301)496-1131 Fax: (301)480-3537 E-mail: access@nlm.nih.gov • URL: http://www.nlm.nih.gov • NLM Web site offers free access through MEDLINE ("PubMed") to about nine million references to articles appearing in some 3,800 biomedical journals, with abstracts. Search interfaces range from "simple keywords to advanced Boolean expressions." The NLM site offers many links to other sources of biomedical and technical information (the National Center for Biotechnology Information, for example). Fees: Free.

ONLINE DATABASES

F-D-C Reports. FDC Reports, Inc. • An online version of "The Gray Sheet" (medical devices), "The Pink Sheet" (pharmaceuticals), "The Rose Sheet" (cosmetics), "The Blue Sheet" (biomedical), and "The Tan Sheet" (nonprescription). Contains full-text information on legal, technical, corporate, financial, and marketing developments from 1987 to date, with weekly updates. Inquire as to online cost and availability.

Globalbase. The Gale Group. • Provides more than one million online summaries of business, industrial, and economic news reports from more than 1,000 publications worldwide. Covers a wide range of material appearing in international trade journals, professional magazines, and newspapers. Time period is 1984 to date, with weekly updates. Inquire as to online cost and availability.

NTIS Bibliographic Data Base. National Technical Information Service. • Contains citations and abstracts to unrestricted reports of government-sponsored research, 1964 to date. Covers a wide range of technical, engineering, business, and social science topics. Monthly updates. Inquire as to online cost and availability.

PROMT: Predicasts Overview of Markets and Technology. The Gale Group. • Companies, products, applied technologies and markets. U.S. and international literature coverage, 1972 to date. Inquire as to online cost and availability. Provides abstracts from more than 1,600 publications. Weekly updates.

Super Searchers on Health and Medicine: The Online Secrets of Top Health and Medical Researchers. Susan M. Detwiler and Reva Basch. Information Today, Inc. • 2000. $24.95. Provides the results of interviews with 10 experts in online searching for medical research data and healthcare information. Discusses both traditional sources and Web sites. (CyberAge Books.).

Who's Who in Technology [Online]. The Gale Group. • Provides online biographical profiles of over 25,000 American scientists, engineers, and others in technology-related occupations. Inquire as to online cost and availability.

PERIODICALS AND NEWSLETTERS

The BBI Newsletter: A Perceptive Analysis of the Healthcare Industry and Marketplace Focusing on New Technology, Strategic Planning, and Marketshare Projections. American Health Consultants. • Monthly. $827.00 per year.

Biomedical Instrumentation and Technology. Association for the Advancement of Medical Instrumentation. Hanley and Belfus, Inc. • Bimonthly. Individuals, $106.00 per year; institutions, $136.00 per year.

Biomedical Products. Cahners Business Information, New Product Information. • Monthly. $43.90 per year. Features new products and services.

Biomedical Technology Information Service. Aspen Publishers, Inc. • Semimonthly. Individuals, $335.00 per year; institutions, $385.00 per year. Newsletter on developments in medical devices and medical electronics.

Health Devices Alerts: A Summary of Reported Problems, Hazards, Recalls, and Updates. ECRI (Emergency Care Research Institute). • Weekly. Newsletter containing reviews of health equipment problems. Includes *Health Devices Alerts Action Items, Health Devices Alerts Abstracts, Health Devices Alerts FDA Data, Health Devices Alerts Implants, Health Devices Alerts Hazards Bulletin.*

Health News Daily. F-D-C Reports, Inc. • Daily. $1,350.00 per year. Newsletter providing broad coverage of the healthcare business, including government policy, regulation, research, finance, and insurance. Contains news of pharmaceuticals, medical devices, biotechnology, and healthcare delivery in general.

Healthcare Informatics: The Business of Healthcare Information Technology. McGraw-Hill. • Monthly. $40.00 per year. Covers various aspects of information and computer technology for the health care industry.

HME News. United Publications, Inc. • Monthly. Controlled circulation. Covers the home medical equipment business for dealers and manufacturers. Provides information on a wide variety of home health care supplies and equipment.

IEEE Engineering in Medicine and Biology Magazine. Institute of Electrical and Electronics Engineers, Inc. • Bimonthly. $176.00 per year. Published for biomedical engineers.

Medical Design Technology. Cahners Business Information. • Monthly. $70.00 per year. Edited for medical technology personnel. Includes new product introductions and applications.

Medical Device and Diagnostic Industry. Canon Communications LLC. • Monthly. Free to qualified personnel; others, $125.00 per year.

Medical Device Technology. Advanstar Communications, Inc. • Ten times a year. Free to qualified personnel; others, $180.00 per year.

Medical Devices, Diagnostics, and Instrumentation: The Gray Sheet Reports. F-D-C Reports, Inc. • Weekly. $955.00 per year. Newsletter. Provides industry and financial news, including a medical sector stock index. Monitors regulatory developments at the Center for Devices and Radiological Health of the U. S. Food and Drug Administration.

Medical Electronics and Equipment News. Reilly Publishing Co. • Bimonthly. Free to qualified personnel; others, $50.00 per year. Provides medical electronics industry news and new product information.

Medical Product Manufacturing News. Canon Communications LLC. • 10 times a year. Free to qualified personnel; others, $125.00 per year. Directed at manufacturers of medical devices and medical electronic equipment. Covers industry news, service news, and new products.

Medical Technology Stock Letter. Piedmont Venture Group. • Semimonthly. $320.00 per year. Newsletter. Provides health care industry investment recommendations, including information on initial public offerings.

Seminars in Ultrasound, CT, and MR (Computerized Tomography and Magnetic Resonance. Harcourt Health Sciences. • Bimonthly. $169.00 per year.

Surgical Products. Cahners Business Information. • 10 times a year. $24.00 per year. Covers new Technology and products for surgeons and operation rooms.

RESEARCH CENTERS AND INSTITUTES

ECRI: Emergency Care Research Institute. 5200 Butler Pike, Plymouth Meeting, PA 19462. Phone: (610)825-6000 Fax: (610)834-1275 E-mail: ecri@hslc.org • URL: http://www.ecri.org • Major research area is health care technology.

Medical Electronics Laboratory. University of Wisconsin, 1300 University Ave., Madison, WI 53706. Phone: (608)262-1326 Fax: (608)262-2327 E-mail: yee@physiology.wisc.edu • Develops electronic instrumentation for medical and biological research.

Medical Instrumentation Laboratory. University of Wisconsin-Madison, 1415 Engineering Dr., Madison, WI 53706. Phone: (608)263-1574 Fax: (608)265-9239 E-mail: webster@engr.wisc.edu • URL: http://www.engr.wisc.edu/bme/faculty/websterjohn.html • Research subjects include medical electrodes, medical amplifiers, bioimpedance techniques, and miniature tactile pressure sensors.

STATISTICS SOURCES

Electromedical Equipment and Irradiation Equipment, Including X-Ray. U. S. Bureau of the Census. • Annual. Contains shipment quantity, value of shipment, export, and import data. (Current Industrial Report No. MA-38R.).

TRADE/PROFESSIONAL ASSOCIATIONS

American Institute for Medical and Biological Engineering. 1901 Pennsylvania Ave., N.W., Suite 401, Washington, DC 20006. Phone: (202)496-9660 Fax: (202)466-8489.

Association for the Advancement of Medical Instrumentation. 3330 Washington Blvd., Suite 400, Arlington, VA 22201. Phone: 800-332-2264 or (703)525-4890 Fax: (703)276-0793 • Members are engineers, technicians, physicians, manufacturers, and others with an interest in medical instrumentation.

Health Industry Manufacturers Association. 1200 G St., N.W., Suite 400, Washington, DC 20005. Phone: (202)783-8700 Fax: (202)783-8750 • URL: http://www.himanet.com.

Special Interest Group on Biomedical Computing. Association for Computing Machinery, 1515 Broadway, New York, NY 10036. Phone: (212)869-7440 Fax: (212)302-5826 E-mail: sigs@acm.org • URL: http://www.acm.org/sigbio • Concerned with medical informatics, molecular databases, medical multimedia, and computerization in general as related to the health and biological sciences.

OTHER SOURCES

Biotechnology Instrumentation Markets. Theta Reports/PJB Medical Publications, Inc. • 1999. $1,495.00. Contains market research data, with projections through the year 2002. Covers such products as specialized analytical instruments, filters/membranes, and mass spectrometers. (Theta Report No. 960.).

Computer Assisted Surgery: Automation, Virtual Reality, Robotics, and Radiosurgery. Theta Reports/PJB Medical Publications, Inc. • 2000. $2,295.00. Contains market research data relating to surgical systems technology. (Theta Report No. 1105.).

New and Breaking Technologies in the Pharmaceutical and Medical Device Industries. Theta Reports/PJB Medical Publications, Inc. • 1999. $1,695.00. Market research data. Includes forecasts of medical technology and drug developments to 2005-2010.

New Ophthalmology: Treatments and Technologies. Theta Reports/PJB Medical Publications, Inc. • 2000. $1,695. Provides market research data relating to eye surgery, including LASIK, cataract surgery, and associated technology. (Theta Report No. 911.).

Pharmaceutical Litigation Reporter: The National Journal of Record of Pharmaceutical Litigation. Andrews Publications. • Monthly. $775.00 per year. Reports on a wide variety of legal cases involving the pharmaceutical and medical device industries. Includes product liability lawsuits.

MEDICARE

See also: HEALTH CARE INDUSTRY; HEALTH INSURANCE; SOCIAL SECURITY

GENERAL WORKS

Medical Care, Medical Costs: The Search for a Health Insurance Policy. Rashi Fein. Replica Books. • 1999. $26.95.

Medicare Made Easy: Everything You Need to Know to Make Medicare Work for You. Charles B. Inlander and Michael A. Danio. Fine Communications. • 1999. $19.98. Revised edition. Provides basic information on Medicare claims processing and the manner in which Medicare relates to other health insurance. The author is a consumer advocate and president of the People's Medical Society.

Retirement Security: Understanding and Planning Your Financial Future. David M. Walker. John Wiley and Sons, Inc. • 1996. $29.95. Topics include investments, social security, Medicare, health insurance, and employer retirement plans.

Social Security, Medicare, and Pensions: Get the Most Out of Your Retirement and Medical Benefits. Joseph Matthews and Dorothy M. Berman. Nolo.com. • 1999. $21.95. Seventh edition. In addition to the basic topics, includes practical information on Supplemental Security Income (SSI), disability benefits, veterans benefits, 401(k) plans, Medicare HMOs, medigap insurance, Medicaid, and how to appeal decisions.

ABSTRACTS AND INDEXES

Index to Health Information. Congressional Information Service, Inc. • Quarterly. $945.00 per year, including two-volume annual cumulation. Provides index and abstracts covering the medical and health field in general, with emphasis on statistical sources and government documents. Service with microfiche source documents, $4,995.00 per year.

NTIS Alerts: Health Care. National Technical Information Service. • Semimonthly. $210.00 per year. Provides descriptions of government-sponsored research reports and software, with ordering information. Covers a wide variety of health care topics, including quality assurance, delivery organization, economics (costs), technology, and legislation. Formerly *Abstract Newsletter*.

Readers' Guide to Periodical Literature. H. W. Wilson Co. • Monthly. $220.00 per year. CD-ROM edition, $1,495 per year, including annual cumulation. Indexes about 250 peridicals of general interest.

BIBLIOGRAPHIES

Encyclopedia of Health Information Sources. The Gale Group. • 1993. $180.00. Second edition. Both print and nonprint sources of information are listed for 450 health-related topics.

CD-ROM DATABASES

WILSONDISC: Readers' Guide to Periodical Literature. H. W. Wilson Co. • Monthly. $1,095.00 per year, including unlimited online access to *Readers' Guide to Periodical Literature* through WILSONLINE. Provides CD-ROM indexing of about 250 general interest periodicals. Covers 1983 to date. (*Readers' Guide Abstracts* also available on CD-ROM at $1,995 per year.).

DIRECTORIES

Encyclopedia of Medical Organizations and Agencies. The Gale Group. • 2000. $285.00. 11th edition. Information on over 14,000 public and private organizations in medicine and related fields.

Medical and Health Information Directory. The Gale Group. • 1999. $630.00. Three volumes. 12th edition. Vol. one covers medical organizations, agencies, and institutions; vol. two includes bibliographic, library, and database information; vol. three is a guide to services available for various medical and health problems.

Plunkett's Health Care Industry Almanac: The Only Complete Guide to the Fastest-Changing Industry in America. Available from Plunkett Research, Ltd. • Biennial. $179.99. Includes detailed profiles of 500 large companies providing health care products or services, with indexes by products, services, and location. Provides statistical and trend information for the health insurance industry, HMOs, hospital utilization, Medicare, medical technology, and national health expenditures.

ENCYCLOPEDIAS AND DICTIONARIES

Rupp's Insurance and Risk Management Glossary. Richard V. Rupp. Available from CCH, Inc. • 1996. $35.00. Second edition. Published by NILS Publishing Co. Provides definitions of 6,400 insurance words and phrases. Includes a guide to acronyms and abbreviations.

HANDBOOKS AND MANUALS

All About Medicare. The National Underwriter Co. • Annual. $12.25.

Complete and Easy Guide to Social Security and Medicare. Faustin Tehle. Fraser-Vance Publishing Co. • 1996. $12.95. 13th unabridged edition.

Guide to Health Insurance for People with Medicare. U. S. Health Care Financing Administration, Department of Health and Human Servi. • Annual. Free. Contains detailed information on private health insurance as a supplement to Medicare.

How to Cover the Gaps in Medicare: Health Insurance and Long-Term Care Options for the Retired. Robert A. Gilmour. American Institute for Economic Research. • 2000. $5.00. 12th revised edition. Four parts: "The Medicare Quandry," "How to Protect Yourself Against the Medigap," "Long-Term Care Options", and "End-of-Life Decisions" (living wills). Includes discussions of long-term care insurance, retirement communities, and HMO Medicare insurance, (Economic Education Bulletin Series, No. 10).

An Insurance Guide for Seniors. Insurance Forum, Inc. • 1997. $15.00. Provides concise advice and information on Medicare, Medicare supplement insurance, HMOs, long-term care insurance, automobile insurance, life insurance, annuities, and pensions. An appendix lists "Financially Strong Insurance Companies." (*The Insurance Forum*, vol. 24, no. 4.).

Medical Claims Processing. Entrepreneur Media, Inc. • Looseleaf. $59.50. A practical guide to starting a medical claims processing service. Covers profit potential, start-up costs, market size evaluation, owner's time required, site selection, pricing, accounting, advertising, promotion, etc. (Start-Up Business Guide No. E1345.).

Medicare and Coordinated Care Plans. Available from Consumer Information Center. • Free. Published by the U. S. Department of Health and Human Services. Contains detailed information on services to Medicare beneficiaries from health maintenance organizations (HMOs). (Publication No. 509-X.).

Medicare: Employer Health Plans. Available from Consumer Information Center. • Free. Published by the U. S. Department of Health and Human Services. Explains the special rules that apply to Medicare beneficiaries who have employer group health plan coverage. (Publication No. 520-Y.).

Medicare Explained. CCH, Inc. • Annual. $30.00.

Social Security Handbook. Available from U. S. Government Printing Office. • Annual. $45.00. Issued by the Social Security Administration (http://www.ssa.gov). Provides detailed information about social security programs, including Medicare, with brief descriptions of related programs administered by agencies other than the Social Security Administration.

Your Medicare Handbook. Available from U. S. Government Printing Office. • Annual. Issued by the Health Care Financing Administration, U. S. Department of Health and Human Services. Provides information on Medicare hospital insurance and medical insurance, including benefits, options, and rights. Discusses the functions of Medigap insurance, managed care plans, peer review organizations, and Medicare insurance carriers. Formerly *Medicare Handbook*.

INTERNET DATABASES

InsWeb. InsWeb Corp. Phone: (650)372-2129 E-mail: info@insweb.com • URL: http://www.insweb.com • Web site offers a wide variety of advice and information on automobile, life, health, and "other" insurance. Includes glossaries of insurance terms, Standard & Poor's ratings of individual insurance companies, and "Financial Needs Estimators." Searching is available. Fees: Free.

Medicare: The Official U. S. Government Site for Medicare Information. Health Care Financing Administration (HCFA). Phone: (410)786-3151 • URL: http://www.medicare.gov • Web site provides extensive information on Medicare health plans, publications, fraud, nursing homes, top 20 questions and answers, etc. Includes access to the National Nursing Home Database, providing summary compliance information on "every Medicare and Medicaid certified nursing home in the country." Online searching is offered. Fees: Free.

Social Security Online: The Official Web Site of the Social Security Administration. U. S. Social Security Administration. Phone: 800-772-1213 or (410)965-7700 • URL: http://www.ssa.gov • Web site provides a wide variety of online information relating to social security and Medicare. Topics include benefits, disability, employer wage reporting, personal earnings statements, statistics, government financing, social security law, and public welfare reform legislation.

ONLINE DATABASES

Readers' Guide Abstracts Online. H. W. Wilson Co. • Indexes and abstracts general interest periodicals, 1983 to date. Weekly updates. Inquire as to online cost and availability.

PERIODICALS AND NEWSLETTERS

American Health Care Association: Provider. American Health Care Association. • Monthly. $48.00 per year. Formerly *American Health Care Association Journal*.

Health Care Financing Review. Available from U. S. Government Printing Office. • Quarterly. $30.00 per year. Issued by the Health Care Financing Administration, U. S. Department of Health and Human Services. Presents articles by professionals in the areas of health care costs and financing.

Health Policy and Biomedical Research: The Blue Sheet. F-D-C Reports, Inc. • 51 Times a year. $619.00 per year. Newsletter. Emphasis is on news of medical research agencies and institutions, especially the National Institutes of Health (NIH).

Home Health Line: The Home Care Industry's National Independent Newsletter. • 48 times a year. $399.00 per year. Newsletter on legislation and regulations affecting the home health care industry, with an emphasis on federal funding and Medicare programs.

Hospital Revenue Report. United Communications Group. • 25 times a year. $379.00 per year. Newsletter. Advises hospitals on how to cut costs, increase patient revenue, and maximize Medicare income. Incorporates *Health Care Marketer*.

Medical Benefits. Panel Publishers. • Semimonthly. $216.00 per year. Newsletter. Provides summaries of periodical articles.

Medical Utilization Management. Faulkner & Gray. • Biweekly. $395.00 per year. Newsletter. Formerly *Medical Utilization Review*.

Medicare Compliance Alert. United Communications Group. • Biweekly. $370.00 per year. Newsletter. Supplement available, *Civil Money Penalties Reporter*. Newsletter. Provides news of changes in Medicare regulations and legislation. Advises physicians on Medicare rules relating to physician investments, joint ventures, limited partnerships, and patient referrals.

Older Americans Report. Business Publishers, Inc. • Weekly. $432.00 per year. Newsletter on health, economic, and social services for the aging, including social security, medicare, pensions, housing, nursing homes, and programs under the Older Americans Act. Edited for service providers.

PRICE SOURCES

Medicare Supplement Price Survey. Weiss Ratings, Inc. • Continuous revision. Price on application. Available for individual geographic areas to provide detailed price information for various types of Medicare supplement health insurance policies issued by specific insurance companies.

RESEARCH CENTERS AND INSTITUTES

Center for Health Administration Studies. University of Chicago, 969 E. 60th St., Chicago, IL 60637. Phone: (773)702-7104 Fax: (773)702-7222 E-mail: chas@uchichago.edu • URL: http://www.chas.uchicago.edu.

Center for Health Economics Research. Waverly Oaks Rd., Suite 330, Waltham, MA 02452. Phone: (781)788-8100 Fax: (781)788-8101 E-mail: jmitchell@cher.org • URL: http://www.her-cher.org • Studies the financing of Medicare.

Center for Health Research. Wayne State University, College of Nursing, 5557 Cass Ave., Detroit, MI 48202. Phone: (313)577-4134 Fax: (313)577-5777 E-mail: ajacox@wayne.edu • URL: http://www.comm.wayne.edu/nursing/nursing.html • Studies innovation in health care organization and financing.

Center for the Study of Aging. University of Bridgeport, Division of Counseling and Human Services, Carlson Hall, 303 University Ave., Bridgeport, CT 06601. Phone: (203)576-4175 Fax: (203)576-4200 • Research activities include the study of Medicare and Medicaid.

Health Services Research and Development Center. Johns Hopkins University, 624 N. Broadway, Room 482, Baltimore, MD 21205-1996. Phone: (410)955-3625 Fax: (410)955-0470 E-mail: dsteinwa@jhsph.edu.

Institute for Health, Health Care Policy, and Aging Research. Rutgers University, 30 College Ave., New Brunswick, NJ 08903. Phone: (732)932-8413 Fax: (732)982-6872 E-mail: caboyer@rci.rutgers.edu • URL: http://www.ihhcpar.rutgers.edu/ • Areas of study include HMO use by older adults.

Malcolm Wiener Center for Social Policy. Harvard University, John F. Kennedy School of Government, 79 John F. Kennedy, Cambridge, MA 02138. Phone: (617)495-1461 Fax: (617)496-9053 E-mail: juliewilson@harvard.edu • URL: http://www.ksg.harvard.edu/socpol • Does multidisciplinary research on health care access and financing.

Michigan Health and Social Security Research Institute. 8000 E. Jefferson Ave., Detroit, MI 48214-2699. Phone: (313)926-5563 Fax: (313)824-7220 • Studies the health and social security problems of trade union members.

National Center for Policy Analysis. 12655 N. Central Expressway, Suite 720, Dallas, TX 75243-1739. Phone: (972)386-6272 Fax: (972)386-0924 E-mail: jgoodman@ncpa.public-policy.org • URL: http://www.ncpa.org • Includes studies on medicare.

Stratis Health. 2901 Metro Dr., Suite 400, Bloomington, MN 55425-1529. Phone: (612)854-3306 Fax: (612)853-8503 E-mail: info@stratishealth.org • URL: http://www.stratishealth.org.

Thomas A. Roe Institute for Economic Policy Studies. Heritage Foundation, 214 Massachusetts Ave., N. E., Washington, DC 20002. Phone: (202)546-4400 Fax: (202)546-5421 E-mail: angela.antonelli@heritage.org • URL: http://www.heritage.org • Concerned with the financing of Medicare.

STATISTICS SOURCES

DRG Handbook: Comparative Clinical and Financial Standards (Diagnosis Related Group). HCIA, Inc. (Health Care Investment Analysts). • Annual. $399.00. Presents summary data for all 477 DRGs (diagnosis-related groups) and the 23 MDCs (major diagnostic categories), based on information from more than 11 million Medicare patients. Ranks DRG information for 100 hospital groups according to number of beds, payor mix, case-mix, system affiliation, and profitability. Emphasis is financial. Formerly *Medicare DRG Handbook*.

Health, United States, 1999: Health and Aging Chartbook. Available from U. S. Government Printing Office. • 1999. $37.00. Issued by the National Center for Health Statistics, U. S. Department of Health and Human Services. Contains 34 bar charts in color, with related statistical tables. Provides detailed data on persons over 65 years of age, including population, living arrangements, life expectancy, nursing home residence, poverty, health status, assistive devices, health insurance, and health care expenditures.

Statistical Handbook on Aging Americans. Renee Schick, editor. Oryx Press. • 1994. $65.00. Second edition. Provides data on demographics, social characteristics, health, employment, economic conditions, income, pensions, and social security. Includes bibliographic information and a glossary. (Statistical Handbook Series).

TRADE/PROFESSIONAL ASSOCIATIONS

Health Insurance Association of America. 555 13th St., N.W., Washington, DC 20004. Phone: (202)824-1600 Fax: (202)824-1722 • URL: http://www.hiaa.org • Members are commercial health insurers. Includes a Managed Care and Group Insurance Committee, a Disability Insurance Committee, a Medicare Administration Committee, and a Long-Term Care Task Force.

National Association for Medical Equipment Services. 625 Slaters Lane, Suite 200, Alexandria, VA 22314-1171. Phone: (703)836-6263 Fax: (703)836-6730 E-mail: info@names.org • URL: http://www.names.org • Members are durable medical equipment and oxygen suppliers, mainly for home health care. Has Legislative Affairs Committee that is concerned with Medicare/Medicaid benefits.

National Committee to Preserve Social Security and Medicare. 10 G St., N.E., Ste. 600, Washington, DC 20002. Phone: 800-966-1935 or (202)216-0420 Fax: (202)216-0451 • Members are individuals concerned with Medicare and social security programs.

OTHER SOURCES

The Managed Medicare and Medicaid Market. MarketResearch.com. • 1997. $1,250.00. Market research report on medicare HMOs. Includes analysis of legal issues and the impact of managed care on older consumers. Providers such as Kaiser Permanente, Humana, and U. S. Healthcare are profiled.

MEDICINE, INDUSTRIAL

See: INDUSTRIAL MEDICINE

MEETING MANAGEMENT

ABSTRACTS AND INDEXES

Business Periodicals Index. H. W. Wilson Co. • Monthly, except August, with quarterly and annual cumulations. Service basis for print edition; CD-ROM edition, $1,495.00 per year.

CD-ROM DATABASES

ABI/INFORM Global. Bell & Howell Information and Learning. • Monthly. $6,500.00 per year. Provides CD-ROM indexing and abstracting of worldwide business literature appearing in over 1,200 periodicals for the most recent five years. Archival discs are available from 1971. Formerly *ABI/INFORM OnDisc*.

WILSONDISC: Business Periodicals Index. H. W. Wilson Co. • Monthly. $1,495.00 per year. Provides CD-ROM indexing of business periodicals from 1982 to date. Price includes online service.

DIRECTORIES

Directory of Association Meeting Planners and Conference/Convention Directors. Salesman's Guide. • Annual. $259.95. Lists about 13,600 planners of meetings for over 8,100 national associations. Provides past and future convention locations, dates held, number of attendees, exhibit space required, and other convention information. Formerly *Association Meeting Planners*.

Directory of Corporate Meeting Planners. Salesman's Guide. • Annual. $385.00. Lists about 18,000 planners of off-site meetings for over 11,000 U. S. and Canadian corporations. Provides information on number of attendees and professional speaker usage.

Protocol (Corporate Meetings, Entertainment, and Special Events). Protocol Directory, Inc. • Annual. $48.00. Provides information on about 4,000 suppliers of products and services for special events, shows (entertainment), and business meetings. Geographic arrangement.

HANDBOOKS AND MANUALS

Big Meetings, Big Results. Tom McMahon. NTC/Contemporary Publishing. • 1994. $19.95. Includes checklists and diagrams. (NTC Business Book Series).

Formal Meeting: How to Prepare and Participate. Alice N. Pohl. NTC/Contemporary Publishing. • 1992. $10.95. (NTC Business Book Series).

How to Develop and Promote Successful Seminars and Workshops: A Definitive Guide to Creating and Marketing Seminars, Workshops, Classes, and Conferences. Howard L. Shenson. John Wiley and Sons, Inc. • 1990. $99.50.

How to Run Better Business Meetings: A Reference Guide for Managers. McGraw-Hill. • 1987. Price on application. Compiled by the 3M Meeting Management Team. Covers the planning, formatting, and executing of various kinds of business meetings. Charts, checklists, diagrams, and case studies are included.

Little Black Book of Business Meetings. Michael C. Thomsett. AMACOM. • 1989. $14.95. How to run a business meeting. (Little Black Book Series).

Seminar Promoting. Entrepreneur Media, Inc. • Looseleaf. $59.50. A practical guide to starting a seminar promotion business. Covers profit potential, start-up costs, market size evaluation, owner's time required, site selection, pricing, accounting, advertising, promotion, etc. (Start-Up Business Guide No. E1071.).

INTERNET DATABASES

Trade Show Central: The Internet's Leading Trade Show Information Resource!. Trade Show Central. Phone: (781)235-8095 Fax: (781)416-4500 • URL: http://www.tscentral.com • Web site provides information on "more than 30,000 Trade Shows, Conferences, and Seminars, 5,000 service providers, and 5,000 venues and facilities around the world." Searching is offered by trade show name, industry category, date, and location. Results may be sorted by event name, city, country, or date. Includes a "Career Center" for trade show personnel. Continuous updating. Fees: Free.

ONLINE DATABASES

ABI/INFORM. Bell & Howell Information and Learning. • Provides online indexing to business-related material occurring in over 1,000 periodicals from 1971 to the present. Inquire as to online cost and availability.

Management Contents. The Gale Group. • Covers a wide range of management, financial, marketing, personnel, and administrative topics. About 150 leading business journals are indexed and abstracted from 1974 to date, with monthly updating. Inquire as to online cost and availability.

Trade & Industry Index. The Gale Group. • Provides indexing of business periodicals, January 1981 to date. Daily updates. (Full text articles from some periodicals are available online, 1983 to date, in the companion database, *Trade & Industry ASAP.*) Inquire as to online cost and availability.

Wilson Business Abstracts Online. H. W. Wilson Co. • Indexes and abstracts 600 major business periodicals, plus the *Wall Street Journal* and the business section of the *New York Times*. Indexing is from 1982, abstracting from 1990, with the two newspapers included from 1993. Updated weekly. Inquire as to online cost and availability. (*Business Periodicals Index* without abstracts is also available online.).

PERIODICALS AND NEWSLETTERS

Harvard Management Communication Letter. Harvard Business School Press. • Monthly. $79.00 per year. Newsletter. Provides practical advice on both electronic and conventional business communication: e-mail, telephone, cell phones, memos, letters, written reports, speeches, meetings, and visual presentations (slides, flipcharts, easels, etc.). Also covers face-to-face communication, discussion, listening, and negotiation.

Journal of Convention and Exhibition Management. Haworth Press, Inc. • Quarterly. Individuals $50.00 per year; institutions, $85.00 per year; libraries, $95.00 per year.

Meeting and Conference Executives. MCEA. • Monthly. $99.00 per year. Newsletter. Formerly *Meeting Planners Alert.*

The Meeting Professional. Meeting Professionals International. • Monthly. $50.00 per year. Published for professionals in the meeting and convention industry. Contains news, features, and how-to's for domestic and international meetings management. Formerly *Meeting Manager.*

TRADE/PROFESSIONAL ASSOCIATIONS

Meeting Professionals International. 4455 LBJ Freeway, Suite 1200, Dallas, TX 75244-5903. Phone: (972)702-3000 Fax: (972)702-3070 • URL: http://www.mpiweb.org • Members are fee-based meeting planners, meeting consultants, and providers of meeting services.

Society of Corporate Meeting Professionals. 2965 Flowers Rd. S., Ste. 105, Atlanta, GA 30341. Phone: (770)457-9212 Fax: (770)458-3314 E-mail: assnhq@mindspring.com • URL: http://www.scmp.org • Members are company and corporate meeting planners.

Society of Government Meeting Professionals. Six Clouser Rd., Mechanicsburg, PA 17055-9735. Six Clouser Rd., • Members are individuals involved in the planning of government meetings.

MEETINGS

See: CONFERENCES, WORKSHOPS, AND SEMINARS

MEETINGS, SALES

See: SALES CONVENTIONS

MEN'S CLOTHING INDUSTRY

DIRECTORIES

Directory of Apparel Specialty Stores. Chain Store Guide. • Annual. $260.00. Lists over 5,000 women's, men's, family and sporting goods retailers.

Garment Manufacturer's Index. Klevens Publications, Inc. • Annual. $60.00. A directory of about 8,000 manufacturers and suppliers of products and services used in the making of men's, women's, and children's clothing. Includes fabrics, trimmings, factory equipment, and other supplies.

Hat Life Directory: Directory of Men's Hat, Ladie's Hat and Cap Industry. • Annual. $22.00. About 1,000 hat manufacturers, wholesalers, renovators, and importer's of men's headwear, plus trade suppliers. Formerly *Hat Life Yearbook and Directory.*

Nationwide Directory of Men's and Boys' Wear Buyers. Salesman's Guide. • Annual. $229.00. About 6,000 retail stores selling men's and boys' clothing, sportswear, furnishings, and accessories; coverage does not include New York metropolitan area.

FINANCIAL RATIOS

Annual Statement Studies. Robert Morris Associates: The Association of Lending and Credit Risk Professiona. • Annual. Free to members; non-members, $140.00. Median and quartile financial ratios are given for over 400 kinds of manufacturing, wholesale, retail, construction, and consumer finance establishments. Data is sorted by both asset size and sales volume. Includes a clearly written "Definition of Ratios" and an alphabetical industry index.

Special Statistical Report on Profit, Production and Sales Trends in the Men's and Boy's Tailored Clothing Industry. Clothing Manufacturers Association of the U.S.A. • 1983. $15.00.

INTERNET DATABASES

Fedstats. Federal Interagency Council on Statistical Policy. Phone: (202)395-7254 • URL: http://www.fedstats.gov • Web site features an efficient search facility for full-text statistics produced by more than 70 federal agencies, including the Census Bureau, the Bureau of Economic Analysis, and the Bureau of Labor Statistics. Boolean searches can be made within one agency or for all agencies combined. Links are offered to international statistical bureaus, including the UN, IMF, OECD, UNESCO, Eurostat, and 20 individual countries. Fees: Free.

ONLINE DATABASES

DRI U.S. Central Database. Data Products Division. • Provides more than 23,000 business, financial, demographic, economic, foreign trade, and industry-related time series for the U.S. Includes national income, population, retail-wholesale trade, price indexes, labor data, housing, industrial production, banking, interest rates, money supply, etc. Time period is generally 1947 to date (some data back to 1929). Updating varies. Inquire as to online cost and availability.

PROMT: Predicasts Overview of Markets and Technology. The Gale Group. • Companies, products, applied technologies and markets. U.S. and international literature coverage, 1972 to date. Inquire as to online cost and availability. Provides abstracts from more than 1,600 publications. Weekly updates.

PERIODICALS AND NEWSLETTERS

DNR: The Men's Fashion Retail Textile Authority. Fairchild Publications. • Daily. $85.00 per year. Formerly *Daily News Record.*

GQ (Gentleman's Quarterly). Conde Nast Publications, Inc. • Monthly. Individuals, $19.97 per year; libraries, $12.50 per year.

STATISTICS SOURCES

Annual Business Survey. Menswear Retailers of America. • Annual. $35.00.

Annual Survey of Manufactures. Available from U. S. Government Printing Office. • Annual. Prices vary. Issued by the U. S. Census Bureau as an interim update to the *Census of Manufactures.* Includes data on number of manufacturing establishments in various industries, employment, labor costs, value of shipments, capital expenditures, inventories, energy costs, and assets. (See also Census Bureau home page, http://www.census.gov/.).

Business Statistics of the United States. Courtenay M. Slater, editor. Bernan Associates. • 1999. $74.00. Fifth edition. Based on *Business Statistics*, formerly issue by the Bureau of Economic Analysis, U. S. Department of Commerce. Provides basic data for a wide variety of U. S. industries, services, and economic indicators. Most statistics are shown annually for 29 years and monthly for the most recent four years.

Manufacturing Profiles. Available from U. S. Government Printing Office. • Annual. Issued by the U. S. Census Bureau. A printed consolidation of the entire *Current Industrial Report* series, presenting "all the data compiled." Contains statistics on production, shipments, inventories, consumption, exports, imports, and orders for a wide variety of manufactured products. (See also Census Bureau home page, http://www.census.gov/.).

Survey of Current Business. Available from U. S. Government Printing Office. • Monthly. $49.00 per year. Issued by Bureau of Economic Analysis, U. S. Department of Commerce. Presents a wide variety of business and economic data.

TRADE/PROFESSIONAL ASSOCIATIONS

Bureau of Wholesale Sales Representatives. 1100 Spring St. N.W., Suite 700, Atlanta, GA 30309. Phone: 800-877-1808 or (404)870-7600 Fax: (404)870-7601 E-mail: repline@aol.com • URL: http://www.bwsr.com.

Clothing Manufacturers of the U.S.A. 730 Broadway, 9th Fl., New York, NY 10003. Phone: (212)529-0823 Fax: (212)529-1443.

Fashion Association. 475 Park Ave., S., 9th Fl., New York, NY 10016. Phone: (212)683-5665 Fax: (212)545-1709.

MENTAL HEALTH

See also: INDUSTRIAL PSYCHOLOGY; STRESS (ANXIETY)

GENERAL WORKS

Psychological Symptoms. Frank J. Bruno. John Wiley and Sons, Inc. • 1994. $24.95. Explains the meaning of common mental symptoms, what may cause them, and how to deal with them.

ABSTRACTS AND INDEXES

Psychological Abstracts. American Psychological Association. • Monthly. Members, $799.00 per year; individuals and institutions, $1,075.00 per year. Covers the international literature of psychology and the behavioral sciences. Includes journals, technical reports, dissertations, and other sources.

BIBLIOGRAPHIES

Bibliographic Guide to Psychology. Available from The Gale Group. • Annual. $295.00. Published by G. K. Hall & Co. Lists psychology publications cataloged by the New York Public Library and the Library of Congress.

CD-ROM DATABASES

Consumers Reference Disc. National Information Services Corp. • Quarterly. Provides the CD-ROM version of *Consumer Health and Nutrition Index* from Oryx Press and *Consumers Index to Product Evaluations and Information Sources* from Pierian Press. Contains citations to consumer health articles and consumer product evaluations, tests, warnings, and recalls.

Health Reference Center. The Gale Group. • Monthly. Provides CD-ROM citations, abstracts, and selected full-text articles on many health-related subjects. Includes references to medical journals, general periodicals, newsletters, newspapers, pamphlets, and medical reference books.

DIRECTORIES

Complete Mental Health Directory. Grey House Publishing. • 2001. $165.00. Second edition. Listings include mental health associations, support groups, facilities, media, HMOs, and government agencies. Includes basic descriptions of 25 mental health disorders. (Sedgwick Press.).

Evaluation Guide to Health and Wellness Programs. The Corporate University. • $189.00. Looseleaf service. Semiannual updates, $49.00 each. Provides detailed descriptions and evaluations of more than 200 employee wellness programs that are available nationally. Covers 15 major topics, such as stress management, substance abuse, occupational safety, smoking cessation, blood pressure management, exercise/fitness, diet, and mental health. Programs are available from both profit and non-profit organizations.

ENCYCLOPEDIAS AND DICTIONARIES

The Gale Encyclopedia of Psychology. The Gale Group. • 1998. $130.00. Includes bibliographies arranged by topic and a glossary.

HANDBOOKS AND MANUALS

International Handbook on Mental Health Policy. Donna R. Kemp, editor. Greenwood Publishing Group, Inc. • 1993. $125.00. Provides information on critical mental health issues in 20 countries.

Personal Health Reporter. The Gale Group. • 1992. $105.00. Two volumes. Volume one, $105.00; volume two, $105.00. Presents a collection of professional and popular articles on 150 topics relating to physical and mental health conditions and treatments.

Stress and Well-Being at Work: Assessments and Interventions for Occupational Mental Health. James C. Quick and others, editors. American Psychological Association. • 1992. $19.95.

INTERNET DATABASES

National Library of Medicine (NLM). National Institutes of Health (NIH). Phone: 888-346-3656 or (301)496-1131 Fax: (301)480-3537 E-mail: access@nlm.nih.gov • URL: http://www.nlm.nih.gov • NLM Web site offers free access through MEDLINE ("PubMed") to about nine million references to articles appearing in some 3,800 biomedical journals, with abstracts. Search interfaces range from "simple keywords to advanced Boolean expressions." The NLM site offers many links to other sources of biomedical and technical information (the National Center for Biotechnology Information, for example). Fees: Free.

ONLINE DATABASES

Mental Health Abstracts. IFI/Plenum Data Corp. • Provides indexing and abstracting of mental health and mental illness literature appearing in more than 1,200 journals and other sources from 1969 to date. Monthly updates. Inquire as to online cost and availability.

Newspaper and Periodical Abstracts. Bell & Howell Information and Learning. • Provides online coverage (citations and abstracts) of 25 major newspapers, 1,600 perodicals, and 70 TV programs. Covers business, economics, current affairs, health, fitness, sports, education, technology, government, consumer affairs, psychology, the arts, and the social sciences. Time period is 1986 to date, with daily updates. Inquire as to online cost and availability.

PsycINFO. American Psychological Association. • Provides indexing and abstracting of the worldwide literature of psychology and the behavioral sciences. Time period is 1967 to date, with monthly updates. Inquire as to online cost and availability.

PERIODICALS AND NEWSLETTERS

Employee Assistance Quarterly. Haworth Press, Inc. • Quarterly. Individuals, $40.00 per year; institutions. $80.00 per year; libraries, $375.00 per year. An academic and practical journal focusing on employee alcoholism and mental health problems. Formerly *Labor-Management Alcoholism Journal.*

Journal of Behavioral Health Services and Research. Association of Behaviorial Healthcare Management. Sage Publications, Inc. • Quarterly. Individuals, $63.00 per year; institutions, $233.00 per year. Pertains to the financing and organization of behavioral health services. Formerly *Journal of Mental Health Administration.*

Journal of Business and Psychology. Business Psychology Research Institute. Kluwer Plenum Academic Publishers. • Quarterly. Institutions, $556.80 per year.

Journal of Mental Health Counseling. American Counseling Association. • Quarterly.$131.00 per year. The official journal of the American Mental Health Counselors Association.

Mental Health Report. Business Publishers, Inc. • Biweekly. $396.00 per year.

Occupational Therapy in Mental Health: A Journal of Psychosocial Practice and Research. Haworth Press, Inc. • Quarterly. Individuals, $50.00 per year; institutions, $120.00 per year; libraries, $250.00 per year.

Psychology Today. Sussex Publishers Inc. • Bimonthly. $18.00 per year.

TRADE/PROFESSIONAL ASSOCIATIONS

American Mental Health Counselors Association. 801 N. Fairfax St. Suite 304, Alexandria, VA 22314. Phone: 800-326-2642 or (703)548-6002 Fax: (703)548-5233 • URL: http://www.amhca.org.

National Mental Health Association. 1021 Prince St., Arlington, VA 22314-2971. Phone: 800-969-6642 or (703)684-7722 Fax: (703)684-5968 • URL: http://www.nmha.org.

OTHER SOURCES

The Treatment of Mental Illness in an Evolving Health Care System. Available from MarketResearch.com. • 1997. $995.00. Market research report published by Theta Corporation. Provides market data on drugs and therapy used for treatment of mood, anxiety, and psychotic disorders. Includes pharmaceutical company profiles and forecasts to the year 2001.

MENTAL INSTITUTIONS

ABSTRACTS AND INDEXES

Psychological Abstracts. American Psychological Association. • Monthly. Members, $799.00 per year; individuals and institutions, $1,075.00 per year. Covers the international literature of psychology and the behavioral sciences. Includes journals, technical reports, dissertations, and other sources.

DIRECTORIES

Buyers' Guide for the Health Care Market: A Directory of Products and Services for Health Care Institutions. American Hospital Association. Health Forum, Inc. • Annual. $17.95. Lists 1,200 suppliers and manufacturers of health care products and services for hospitals, nursing homes, and related organizations.

ONLINE DATABASES

PsycINFO. American Psychological Association. • Provides indexing and abstracting of the worldwide literature of psychology and the behavioral sciences. Time period is 1967 to date, with monthly updates. Inquire as to online cost and availability.

PERIODICALS AND NEWSLETTERS

AHA News. Health Forum, Inc. • Weekly. $147.00 per year. Edited for hospital and health care industry administrators. Covers health care news events and legislative activity. An American Hospital Association publication (http://www.aha.org).

Health Facilities Management. American Hospital Association. American Hospital Publishing, Inc. • Monthly. $40.00 per year. Covers building maintenance and engineering for hospitals and nursing homes.

Health Forum. American Hospital Association. American Hospital Publishing, Inc. • Biweekly. $80.00 per year. Covers the general management of hospitals, nursing homes, and managed care organizations. Formerly *HospitalsHealthNetworks.*

Psychiatric Services. American Psychiatric Association. American Psychiatric Press, Inc., Journals Div. • Monthly. Individuals, $51.00 per year; Institutions, $85.00 per year. Formerly *Hospital and Community Psychiatry.*

TRADE/PROFESSIONAL ASSOCIATIONS

National Association of Psychiatric Health Systems. 325 Seventh St., N.W., Ste 625, Washington, DC 20004-2802. Phone: (202)393-6700 Fax: (202)783-6041 E-mail: naphs@naphs.org • URL: http://www.naphs.org.

National Association of State Mental Health Program Directors. 66 Canal Center Plaza, Suite 302, Alexandria, VA 22314. Phone: (703)739-9333 Fax: (703)548-9517 E-mail: bob.glover@nasmhpd.org • URL: http://www.nasmhpd.org.

Section for Psychiatric and Substance Abuse Services. c/o American Hospital Association, One N. Franklin St., Chicago, IL 60606. Phone: 800-242-4890 or (312)422-3000 Fax: (312)422-4796 • URL: http://www.aha.org.

MERCHANDISING

See: MARKETING; RETAIL TRADE

MERCHANT MARINE

See: SHIPS, SHIPPING AND SHIPBUILDING

MERCHANTS

See: RETAIL TRADE

MERGERS AND ACQUISITIONS

See also: LEVERAGED BUYOUTS

GENERAL WORKS

Cases in Corporate Acquisitions, Buyouts, Mergers, and Takeovers. The Gale Group. • 1999. $310.00. Reviews and analyzes about 300 cases of both success and failure in corporate acquisitiveness.

Mergers, Acquisitions, and Corporate Restructurings. Patrick A. Gaughan. John Wiley and Sons, Inc. • 1999. $75.00. Second edition. Covers mergers, acquisitions, divestitures, internal reorganizations, joint ventures, leveraged buyouts, bankruptcy workouts, and recapitalizations.

Predicting Successful Hospital Mergers and Acquisitions: A Financial and Analytical Marketing Tool. David P. Angrisani and Robert L. Goldman. Haworth Press, Inc. • 1997. $49.95.

ALMANACS AND YEARBOOKS

Merger Yearbook. Securities Data Publishing. • Annual. $595.00. Provides detailed information on mergers and acquisitions announced or completed during the year. Includes many charts. (Securities Data Publishing is a unit of Thomson Financial.).

CD-ROM DATABASES

Buyout Financing Sources/M & A Intermediaries. Securities Data Publishing. • Annual. $895.00. Provides the CD-ROM combination of *Directory of Buyout Financing Sources* and *Directory of M & A Intermediaries*. Contains information on more than 1,000 financing sources (banks, insurance companies, venture capital firms, etc.) and 850 intermediaries (corporate acquirers, valuation firms, lawyers, accountants, etc.). Also includes back issues of *Buyouts Newsletter* and *Mergers & Acquisitions Report*. Fully searchable. (Securities Data Publishing is a unit of Thomson Financial.).

Corporate Affiliations Plus. National Register Publishing, Reed Reference Publishing. • Quarterly. $1,995.00 per year. Provides CD-ROM discs corresponding to *Directory of Corporate Affiliations* and *Corporate Finance Bluebook*. Contains corporate financial services information and worldwide data on subsidiaries and affiliates.

DIRECTORIES

Directory of Corporate Affiliations. National Register Publishing. • Annual. $1,159.00. Five volumes. Volumes one and two: Master Index; volume three: U.S. Public Companies; volume four: U.S. Private Companies; volume five: International Public and Private Companies.

Directory of M & A Intermediaries. Securities Data Publishing. • Annual. $360.00. Lists more than 850 dealmakers for mergers and acquisitions, including investment banks, business brokers, and commercial banks. (Securities Data Publishing is a unit of Thomson Financial.).

Mergerstat Transaction Roster. Mergerstat. • Annual. $299.00. A directory of all U. S. companies that were involved in merger and acquisition activity during the year covered. Includes details of each transaction.

HANDBOOKS AND MANUALS

The Art of M & A: A Merger-Acquisition-Buyout Guide. Stanley F. Reed and Aleandra R. Lajoux. McGraw-Hill Professional. • 1998. $179.95. Second edition. A how-to-do-it guide for merger and acquisition ventures. Emphasis is on legal issues.

Corporate Acquisitions and Mergers. Byron E. Fox and Eleanor M. Fox. Kluwer Law International. • $405.00. Two looseleaf volumes. Quarterly supplements. A guide to the antiturst, tax, corporate, securities and financial aspects of business combinations. Includes extensive forms, charts and tables.

Corporate Acquisitions, Mergers, and Divestitures. Lewis D. Solomon. Prentice Hall. • Looseleaf. Periodic supplementation. Price on application. Includes how to buy a company with its own assets or earnings.

Library of Investment Banking. Robert L. Kuhn, editor. McGraw-Hill Professional. • 1990. $475.00. Seven volumes: 1. Investing and Risk Management; 2. Capital Raising and Financial Structure; 3. Corporate and Municipal Securities; 4. Mergers, Acquisitions, and Leveraged Buyouts; 5. Mortgage and Asset Securitization; 6. International Finance and Investing; 7. Index.

Mergers and Acquisitions Handbook. Milton L. Rock and Martin Sikora. McGraw-Hill. • 1994. $84.95. Second edition. The first and last word on successful mergers and acquisitions, from putting together an m&a team and targeting acquistion candidates to merging managements and benefits plans-and every step in between.

Publicly Traded Corporations: Governance, Operation, and Regulation. John H. Matheson. West Group. • 1993. $130.00. Covers a wide range of corporate legal problems and issues, including shareholder communications and "tender offers and change of control transactions." (Corporate Law Series).

INTERNET DATABASES

Intelligence Data. Thomson Financial. Phone: 800-654-0393 or (212)806-8023 Fax: (212)806-8004 • URL: http://www.intelligencedata.com • Fee-based Web site provides a wide variety of information relating to competitive intelligence, strategic planning, business development, mergers, acquisitions, sales, and marketing. "Intelliscope" feature offers searching of other Thomson units, such as Investext, MarkIntel, InSite 2, and Industry Insider. Weekly updating.

Web Finance: Covering the Electronic Evolution of Finance. Securities Data Publishing. Phone: (212)765-5311 or 800-455-5844 Fax: (212)321-2336 E-mail: webfinance@tfn.com • URL: http://www.webfinance.net • Bi-weekly print and daily web-site publication of financial services on the Web, including financial links, archives, brokerage stocks, deal financing, and other financial and investment news and information.

ONLINE DATABASES

Super Searchers on Mergers & Acquisitions: The Online Secrets of Top Corporate Researchers and M & A Pros. Jan Tudor and Reva Basch. Information Today, Inc. • 2001. $24.95. Presents the results of interviews with 13 "top M & A information pros." Covers the finding, evaluating, and delivering of relevant data on companies and industries. (CyberAge Books.).

PERIODICALS AND NEWSLETTERS

Bank Mergers & Acquisitions: The Authoritative Newsletter Providing In-Depth Analysis of the Restructuring of American Banking. SNL Securities. • Monthly. $795.00 per year. Newsletter. Includes information on transactions assisted by the Federal Deposit Insurance Corporation (FDIC) for commercial banks or by the Resolution Trust Corporation (RTC) for savings and loan institutions.

Business and Acquisition Newsletter. Newsletters International, Inc. • Monthly. $300.00 per year. Information about firms that want to buy or sell companies, divisions, subsidiaries, product lines, patents, etc.

Business Strategies Bulletin. CCH, Inc. • Monthly. $166.00 per year. Newsletter.

F W's Corporate Finance: The Magazine fo the Financing Strategist. Financial World Partners. • Quarterly. $50.00 per year. Edited for financial executives of U. S. corporations. Covers leveraged buyouts, mergers, insurance, pensions, risk management, and other corporate topics. Includes case studies. Formerly *Corporate Finance*.

Media Mergers and Acquisitions. Paul Kagan Associates, Inc. • Monthly. $695.00 per year. Newsletter on media merger activity. Covers broadcasting, motion pictures, advertising, and publishing.

Mergers & Acquisitions Report. Securities Data Publishing. • Weekly. $1,295.00 per year. Newsletter. Covers pending and ongoing mergers, acquisitions, restructurings, and bankruptcies. (Securities Data Publishing is a unit of Thomson Financial.).

Mergers & Acquisitions: The Dealmaker's Journal. Securities Data Publishing. • Bimonthly. $475.00 per year. Provides articles on various aspects of M & A, including valuation, pricing, taxes, and strategy. Current M & A deals are listed and described. (Securities Data Publishing is a unit of Thomson Financial.).

Mergerstat Quarterly Reports. Houlihan Lokey Howard & Zukin. • Quarterly. $100.00 per year. Newsletter. Provides details and analysis of recent corporate merger activity. Includes "Top deals year-to-date" and rankings of financial and legal advisors.

STATISTICS SOURCES

Mergerstat Review. Mergerstat. • Annual. $299.00. Provides analysis of merger and acquisition activity and trends during the year. Contains statistical, industry, and geographical data, including a 25-year historical review.

OTHER SOURCES

Acquisitions and Mergers: Negotiated and Contested Transactions. Simon M. Lorne. West Group. • Four looseleaf volumes. $445.00. Periodic supplementation. Includes legal forms and documents. (Securities Law Series).

Business Strategies. CCH, Inc. • Semimonthly. $819.00 per year. Four looseleaf volumes. Semimonthly updates. Legal, tax, and accounting aspects of business planning and decision-making. Provides information on start-ups, forms of ownership (partnerships, corporations), failing businesses, reorganizations, acquisitions, and so forth. Includes *Business Strategies Bulletin*, a monthly newsletter.

Capital Changes Reports. CCH, Inc. • Weekly. $1,310.00. Six looseleaf volumes. Arranged alphabetically by company. This service presents a chronological capital history that includes reorganizations, mergers and consolidations. Recent actions are found in Volume One - "New Matters.".

InSite 2. Intelligence Data/Thomson Financial. • Fee-based Web site consolidates information in a "Base Pack" consisting of Business InSite, Market InSite, and Company InSite. Optional databases are

Consumer InSite, Health and Wellness InSite, Newsletter InSite, and Computer InSite. Includes fulltext content from more than 2,500 trade publications, journals, newsletters, newspapers, analyst reports, and other sources. Continuous updating. Formerly produced by The Gale Group.

MERIT RATING

See: RATING OF EMPLOYEES

METAL FINISHING

ABSTRACTS AND INDEXES

Surface Finishing Technology. ASM International. • Monthly. Members, $130.00 per year; non-members, $160.00 per year. Provides abstracts of the international literature of metallic and nonmetallic industrial coating and finishing. Formerly *Cleaning-Finishing-Coating Digest.*

Surface Treatment Technology Abstracts. Finishing Publications Ltd. • Bimonthly. $880.00 per year. Includes *Printed Circuits* and *Electronics Coating Abstracts.*

DIRECTORIES

AESF Shop Guide-A Directory of Surface Finishing Shops. American Electroplaters' and Surface Finishers Society. • Annual. Price on application. List of over 1,700 electroplating, coating, and other surface finishing firms.

Dun's Industrial Guide: The Metalworking Directory. Dun and Bradstreet Information Services Dun & Bradstreet Corp. • Annual. Libraries, $485; commercial institutions, $795.00. Lease basis. Three volumes. Lists about 65,000 U. S. manufacturing plants using metal and suppliers of metalworking equipment and materials. Includes names and titles of key personnel. Products, purchases, and processes are indicated.

Metal Finishing Guidebook and Directory. Elsevier Science. • Annual. Price on application. Included with subscription to *Metal Finishing.* Lists manufacturers and suppliers to the industry.

Products Finishing Directory. Gardner Publications, Inc. • Annual. $15.00. Lists manufacturers and suppliers of equipment and processes which finish metal, plastics and composites.

HANDBOOKS AND MANUALS

McGraw-Hill Machining and Metalworking Handbook. Ronald A. Walsh. McGraw-Hill. • 1998. $99.95. Second edition. Coverage includes machinery, machining techniques, machine tools, machine design, parts, fastening, and plating.

PERIODICALS AND NEWSLETTERS

Finishers' Management. Publication Management, Inc. • 10 times a year. $35.00 per year.

Industrial Paint and Powder: Coatings Manufacturing and Application. Cahners Business Information. • Monthly. $72.90 per year. Supplement available, *Annual Buyer's Guide.* Formerly *Industrial Finishing.*

Metal Finishing: Devoted Exclusively to Metallic Surface Treatments. Elsevier Science. • Monthly. $64.00 per year. Includes annual *Metal Finishing Guidebook and Directory.*

Modern Metals. Trend Publishing, Inc. • Monthly. $95.00 per year. Covers management and production for plants that fabricate and finish metals of various kinds.

Plating and Surface Finishing: Electroplating, Finishing of Metals, Organic Finishing. American Electroplaters and Surface Finishers Society. • Monthly. Members, $16.00 per year; non-members, $60.00 per year.

Products Finishing. Gardner Publications, Inc. • Monthly. $40.00 per year.

TRADE/PROFESSIONAL ASSOCIATIONS

American Electroplaters' and Surface Finishers Society. 12644 Research Parkway, Orlando, FL 32826-3298. Phone: (407)281-6441 Fax: (407)281-6446 E-mail: aesf@aesf.org • URL: http://www.aesf.org.

Metal Finishing Suppliers' Association. 112 J Elden St., Herndon, VA 20170-4832. Phone: (703)709-5729 Fax: (703)709-1036 E-mail: dtrin@erols.com • URL: http://www.mfsa.org.

National Association of Metal Finishers. 112 J Elden St., Herndon, VA 20170. Phone: (703)709-8299 Fax: (703)709-1036 E-mail: namf@erols.com • URL: http://www.namf.org • Members are management personnel of metal and plastic finishing companies. Finishing includes plating, coating, polishing, rustproofing, and other processes.

METAL INDUSTRY

ABSTRACTS AND INDEXES

IMM Abstracts and Index: A Survey of World Literature on the Economic Geology and Mining of All Minerals (Except Coal), Mineral Processing, and Nonferrous Extraction Metallurgy. Institution of Mining and Metallurgy. • Bimonthly. Members, $142.00 per year; non-members, $215.00 per year. Provides international coverage of the literature of mining and nonferrous metallurgy. Includes mineral economics, tunnelling, and rock mechanics.

Metals Abstracts. Cambridge Information Group. • Monthly. $2,305.00 per year.

DIRECTORIES

Dun's Industrial Guide: The Metalworking Directory. Dun and Bradstreet Information Services Dun & Bradstreet Corp. • Annual. Libraries, $485; commercial institutions, $795.00. Lease basis. Three volumes. Lists about 65,000 U. S. manufacturing plants using metal and suppliers of metalworking equipment and materials. Includes names and titles of key personnel. Products, purchases, and processes are indicated.

Internet Tools of the Profession: A Guide for Information Professionals. Hope N. Tillman, editor. Special Libraries Association. • 1997. $49.00. Second edition. Consists of 14 sections by various authors or compilers. After two introductory articles on searching the Internet, there are 12 annotated lists of useful Web sites, covering the SLA, business and finance, chemistry, education, food and agriculture, information technology, insurance and employee benefits, law, library management, metals and materials, pharmaceuticals, and telecommunications. An index is provided.

Materials Research Centres: A World Directory of Organizations and Programmes in Materials Science. Allyn and Bacon/Longman. • 1991. $475.00. Fourth edition. Profiles of research centers in 75 countries. Materials include plastics, metals, fibers, etc.

North American Scrap Metals Directory. G.I.E. Media, Inc. • Annual. $85.00. Lists more than 9,000 scrap metal processors, brokers, and dealers.

ENCYCLOPEDIAS AND DICTIONARIES

ASM Materials Engineering Dictionary. Joseph R. Davis, editor. ASM International. • 1992. $146.00. Contains 10,000 entries, 700 illustrations, and 150 tables relating to metals, plastics, ceramics, composites, and adhesives. Includes "Technical Briefs" on 64 key material groups.

Encyclopedia of Materials: Science and Technology. K.H.J. Buschow and others, editors. Pergamon Press/Elsevier Science. • 2001. $6,875.00. Eleven volumes. Provides extensive technical information on a wide variety of materials, including metals, ceramics, plastics, optical materials, and building materials. Includes more than 2,000 articles and 5,000 illustrations.

FINANCIAL RATIOS

Almanac of Business and Industrial Financial Ratios. Leo Troy. Prentice Hall. • Annual. $99.95. Contains financial ratios derived from federal tax returns. Ratios for each of about 200 industries are arranged according to company asset size.

HANDBOOKS AND MANUALS

ASM Metals Reference Book. Michael L. Bauccio, editor. ASM International. • 1993. $144.00. Third edition. Includes glossary, tables, formulas, and diagrams. Covers a wide range of ferrous and nonferrous metals.

INTERNET DATABASES

Fedstats. Federal Interagency Council on Statistical Policy. Phone: (202)395-7254 • URL: http://www.fedstats.gov • Web site features an efficient search facility for full-text statistics produced by more than 70 federal agencies, including the Census Bureau, the Bureau of Economic Analysis, and the Bureau of Labor Statistics. Boolean searches can be made within one agency or for all agencies combined. Links are offered to international statistical bureaus, including the UN, IMF, OECD, UNESCO, Eurostat, and 20 individual countries. Fees: Free.

Internet Tools of the Profession. Special Libraries Association. Phone: (202)234-4700 Fax: (202)265-9317 E-mail: hope@tiac.net • URL: http://www.sla.org/pubs/itotp • Web site is designed to update the printed *Internet Tools of the Profession.* Provides links to a wide range of useful databases in business, finance, industry, information technology, insurance, law, library management, telecommunications, and other subject areas. Fees: Free.

ONLINE DATABASES

Business and Industry. Responsive Database Services, Inc. • Contains online citations, abstracts, and selected fulltext from more than 1,000 trade journals, newspapers, and other publications. Provides general coverage of both manufacturing and service industries, including marketing, production, industry trends, key events, and information on specific companies. Time span is 1994 to date. Daily updates. Inquire as to online cost and availability. (Also available in a CD-ROM version.).

DRI U.S. Central Database. Data Products Division. • Provides more than 23,000 business, financial, demographic, economic, foreign trade, and industry-related time series for the U.S. Includes national income, population, retail-wholesale trade, price indexes, labor data, housing, industrial production, banking, interest rates, money supply, etc. Time period is generally 1947 to date (some data back to 1929). Updating varies. Inquire as to online cost and availability.

Materials Business File. Cambridge Scientific Abstracts. • Provides online abstracts and citations to worldwide materials literature, covering the business and industrial aspects of metals, plastics, ceramics, and composites. Corresponds to *Steels Alert, Nonferrous Metals Alert,* and *Polymers/Ceramics/Composites Alert.* Time period is 1985 to date, with monthly updates. (Formerly produced by ASM International.) Inquire as to online cost and availability.

METADEX. Cambridge Scientific Abstracts. • Covers the worldwide literature of metals, metallurgy, and materials science, 1966 to date.

Includes detailed alloys indexing from 1974. Biweekly updating. Inquire as to online cost and availability. (Formerly produced by ASM International.).

PROMT: Predicasts Overview of Markets and Technology. The Gale Group. • Companies, products, applied technologies and markets. U.S. and international literature coverage, 1972 to date. Inquire as to online cost and availability. Provides abstracts from more than 1,600 publications. Weekly updates.

Tablebase. Responsive Database Services, Inc. • Provides online numerical tabular data from a wide variety of business, organization, and government sources, including 900 trade journals. Includes industry and individual company statistics relating to products, market share, sales forecasts, production, exports, market trends, etc. Time span is 1997 to date. Weekly updates. Inquire as to online cost and availability. (Also available in a CD-ROM version.).

PERIODICALS AND NEWSLETTERS

Advanced Materials and Processes. ASM International. • Monthly. Free to members; non-members $250.00 per year; institutions, $250.00 per year. Incorporates *Metal Progress.*Technical information and reports on new developments in the technology of engineered materials and manufacturing processes.

Cantech International. Trend Publishing. • Bimonthly. $70.00 per year. Covers metal can manufacturing, tooling, and decorating.

JOM: Journal of Metals. Minerals, Metals, and Materials Society. • Monthly. Individuals. $79.00 per year; institutions, $154.00 per year. A scholarly journal covering all phases of metals and metallurgy.

Metal Bulletin. Metal Bulletin, Inc. • Semiweekly. $1,378 per year. Provides news of international trends, prices, and market conditions for both steel and non-ferrous metal industries. (Published in England.).

Metal Bulletin Monthly. Metal Bulletin, Inc. • Monthly. Price on application. Edited for international metal industry business executives and senior technical personnel. Covers business, economic, and technical developments. (Published in England.).

Metal Center News. Hitchcock Publishing. • 13 times a year. $89.00 per year.

Modern Metals. Trend Publishing, Inc. • Monthly. $95.00 per year. Covers management and production for plants that fabricate and finish metals of various kinds.

New Steel: Mini and Integrated Mill Management and Technologies. Cahners Business Information. • Monthly. $89.00 per year. Covers the primary metals industry, both ferrous and nonferrous. Includes technical, marketing, and product development articles. Formerly *Iron Age.*

33 Metalproducing: For Primary Producers of Steel, Aluminum, and Copper-Base Alloys. Penton Media, Inc. • Monthly. $65.00 per year. Covers metal production technology and methods and industry news. Includes a bimonthly *Nonferrous Supplement.*

PRICE SOURCES

Metals Week. McGraw-Hill Commodity Services Group. • Weekly. $770.00 per year.

STATISTICS SOURCES

Annual Survey of Manufactures. Available from U. S. Government Printing Office. • Annual. Prices vary. Issued by the U. S. Census Bureau as an interim update to the *Census of Manufactures.* Includes data on number of manufacturing establishments in various industries, employment, labor costs, value of shipments, capital expenditures, inventories, energy costs, and assets. (See also Census Bureau home page, http:// www.census.gov/.).

Business Statistics of the United States. Courtenay M. Slater, editor. Bernan Associates. • 1999. $74.00. Fifth edition. Based on *Business Statistics*, formerly issue by the Bureau of Economic Analysis, U. S. Department of Commerce. Provides basic data for a wide variety of U. S. industries, services, and economic indicators. Most statistics are shown annually for 29 years and monthly for the most recent four years.

Encyclopedia of American Industries. The Gale Group. • 1998. $560.00. Second edition. Two volumes. $280.00 per volume. Volume one is *Manufacturing Industries* and volume two is *Service and Non-Manufacturing Industries.* Provides the history, development, and recent status of approximately 1,000 industries. Includes statistical graphs, with industry and general indexes.

Metal Statistics. Cahners Business Information. • Annual. $250.00. Provides statistical data on a wide variety of metals, metal products, ores, alloys, and scrap metal. Includes data on prices, production, consumption, shipments, imports, and exports.

Mineral Commodity Summaries. Available from U. S. Government Printing Office. • Annual. Published by the U. S. Geological Survey, Department of the Interior (http://www.usgs.gov). Contains detailed, five-year data for about 90 nonfuel minerals. Covers a wide range of statistics, including production, imports, exports, consumption, reserves, prices, tariff information, and industry employment. (Two pages are devoted to each mineral.).

Non-Ferrous Metal Data Yearbook. American Bureau of Metal Statistics. • Annual. $395.00. Provides about 200 statistical tables covering many nonferrous metals. Includes production, consumption, inventories, exports, imports, and other data.

Standard & Poor's Industry Surveys. Standard & Poor's. • Semiannual. $1,800.00. Two looseleaf volumes. Includes monthly supplements. Provides detailed, individual surveys of 52 major industry groups. Each survey is revised on a semiannual basis. Also includes "Monthly Investment Review" (industry group investment analysis) and monthly "Trends & Projections" (economic analysis).

Survey of Current Business. Available from U. S. Government Printing Office. • Monthly. $49.00 per year. Issued by Bureau of Economic Analysis, U. S. Department of Commerce. Presents a wide variety of business and economic data.

World Metal Statistics. World Bureau of Metal Statistics. • Monthly. $1,930.00 per year.

TRADE/PROFESSIONAL ASSOCIATIONS

American Bureau of Metal Statistics. P.O. Box 805, Chatham, NJ 07928. Phone: (973)701-2299 Fax: (973)701-2152 E-mail: info@abms.com • URL: http://www.abms.com • Members are metal companies. Compiles and publishes detailed statistical data on a wide variety of nonferrous metals: aluminum, copper, gold, lead, nickel, platinum, silver, tin, titanium, uranium, zinc, and others.

ASM International. 9639 Kinsman Rd., Materials Park, OH 44073. Phone: 800-336-5152 or (216)338-5151 Fax: (216)338-4634 E-mail: memserv@ po.asm-intl.org • URL: http://www.asm-intl.org • Members are materials engineers, metallurgists, industry executives, educators, and others concerned with a wide range of materials and metals. Divisions include Aerospace, Composites, Electronic Materials and Processing, Energy, Highway/Off-Highway Vehicle, Joining, Materials Testing and Quality Control, Society of Carbide and Tool Engineers, and Surface Engineering.

METAL INDUSTRY, NONFERROUS

See: NONFERROUS METAL INDUSTRY

METAL PLATING

See: METAL FINISHING

METAL POWDERS

See: POWDER METALLURGY INDUSTRY

METAL WORKING INDUSTRY

See also: MACHINE TOOL INDUSTRY

ABSTRACTS AND INDEXES

Casting Digest. ASM International. • Bimonthly. $165.00 per year. Provides abstracts of the international literature of metal casting, forming, and molding.

Cutting Technology. Penton Media, Inc. • Monthly. Controlled circulation. Provides abstracts of the international literature of metal cutting and machining. Formerly *Cutting Tool-Mchine Digest.*

Metalforming Digest. Cambridge Information Group. • Monthly. Provides abstracts of the international literature of metal forming, including powder metallurgy, stamping, extrusion, forging, etc.

DIRECTORIES

Dun's Industrial Guide: The Metalworking Directory. Dun and Bradstreet Information Services Dun & Bradstreet Corp. • Annual. Libraries, $485; commercial institutions, $795.00. Lease basis. Three volumes. Lists about 65,000 U. S. manufacturing plants using metal and suppliers of metalworking equipment and materials. Includes names and titles of key personnel. Products, purchases, and processes are indicated.

FMA's Who's Who in Metal Forming and Fabricating (Fabricator's and ManufacturersAssociation). Fabricators and Manufacturers Association International. • Annual. Free to members; non-members, $200.00. Lists about 2,000 members of the Fabricators and Manufacturers Association (FMA), International; and 1,000 members of the Tube and Pipe Association. Includes five indexes. Formerly *FMA Member Resource Directory.*

HANDBOOKS AND MANUALS

McGraw-Hill Machining and Metalworking Handbook. Ronald A. Walsh. McGraw-Hill. • 1998. $99.95. Second edition. Coverage includes machinery, machining techniques, machine tools, machine design, parts, fastening, and plating.

PERIODICALS AND NEWSLETTERS

The Fabricator. Fabricators and Manufacturers Association International. Croydon Group, Ltd. • Monthly. $75.00 per year. Covers the manufacture of sheet, coil, tube, pipe, and structural metal shapes.

Metalworking Digest. Cahners Business Information, New Product Information. • Monthly. $36.90. Includes *Metalworking Digest Literature Review.*

RESEARCH CENTERS AND INSTITUTES

Advanced Manufacturing Engineering Institute. University of Hartford, United Technologies Hall,

Room 215, West Hartford, CT 06117. Phone: 800-678-4844 or (860)768-4615 Fax: (860)768-5073 E-mail: shetty@mail.hartford.edu • URL: http://www.uharay.hartford.edu/eau.

Institute for Metal Forming. Lehigh University. Whitaker Laboratory 5, Bethlehem, PA 18015. Phone: (610)758-4252 Fax: (610)758-4244 E-mail: wzm2@lehigh.edu.

STATISTICS SOURCES

Annual Survey of Manufactures. Available from U. S. Government Printing Office. • Annual. Prices vary. Issued by the U. S. Census Bureau as an interim update to the *Census of Manufactures.* Includes data on number of manufacturing establishments in various industries, employment, labor costs, value of shipments, capital expenditures, inventories, energy costs, and assets. (See also Census Bureau home page, http://www.census.gov/.).

Manufacturing Profiles. Available from U. S. Government Printing Office. • Annual. Issued by the U. S. Census Bureau. A printed consolidation of the entire *Current Industrial Report* series, presenting "all the data compiled." Contains statistics on production, shipments, inventories, consumption, exports, imports, and orders for a wide variety of manufactured products. (See also Census Bureau home page, http://www.census.gov/.).

U. S. Industry and Trade Outlook: The McGraw-Hill Companies and the U.S. Department of Commerce/ International Trade Administration. Datapso Research Corp. • Annual. $69.95. Produced by the International Trade Administration, U. S. Department of Commerce, in a "public-private" partnership with DRI/McGraw-Hill and Standard & Poor's. Provides basic data, outlook for the current year, and "Long-Term Prospects" (five-year projections) for a wide variety of products and services. Includes high technology industries. Formerly *U. S. Industrial Outlook.*

TRADE/PROFESSIONAL ASSOCIATIONS

American Machine Tool Distributors' Association. 1445 Research Blvd., No. 450, Rockville, MD 20850-8125. Phone: 800-878-2683 or (301)738-1200 Fax: (301)738-9499 E-mail: jallen@amtda.org • URL: http://www.amtda.org.

Fabricators and Manufacturers Association International. 833 Featherstone Rd., Rockford, IL 61107-6302. Phone: (815)399-8700 Fax: (815)399-7279 E-mail: info@fmametal.fab.org • URL: http://www.fmametalfab.org • Members are individuals concerned with metal forming, cutting, and fabricating. Includes a Sheet Metal Division and the Tube and Pipe Fabricators Association.

Precision Metalforming Association. 6363 Oak Tree Blvd., Cleveland, OH 44131-2556. Phone: (216)901-8800 Fax: (213)901-9190 E-mail: pma@pma.org • URL: http://www.metalforming.com.

METALLURGY

See also: METAL INDUSTRY; POWDER METALLURGY INDUSTRY

ABSTRACTS AND INDEXES

Alloys Index. Cambridge Information Group. • Monthly. $445.00 per year. Annual cumulation, $760.00 per year. Auxiliary publication to *Metals Abstracts* and *Metals Abstracts Index.*

Applied Science and Technology Index. H. W. Wilson Co. • 11 times a year. Quarterly and annual cumulations. Service basis for print edition; CD-ROM edition, $1,495.00 per year. Indexes a wide variety of English language technical, industrial, and engineering periodicals.

IMM Abstracts and Index: A Survey of World Literature on the Economic Geology and Mining of All Minerals (Except Coal), Mineral Processing, and Nonferrous Extraction Metallurgy. Institution of Mining and Metallurgy. • Bimonthly. Members, $142.00 per year; non-members, $215.00 per year. Provides international coverage of the literature of mining and nonferrous metallurgy. Includes mineral economics, tunnelling, and rock mechanics.

Metals Abstracts. Cambridge Information Group. • Monthly. $2,305.00 per year.

NTIS Alerts: Materials Sciences. National Technical Information Service. • Semimonthly. $220.00 per year. Provides descriptions of government-sponsored research reports and software, with ordering information. Covers ceramics, glass, coatings, composite materials, alloys, plastics, wood, paper, adhesives, fibers, lubricants, and related subjects. Formerly *Abstract Newsletter.*

CD-ROM DATABASES

METADEX Materials Collection: Metals-Polymers-Ceramics. Cambridge Scientific Abstracts. • Quarterly. $6,950.00 per year. Provides CD-ROM citations to the worldwide literature of materials science and metallurgy. Corresponds to *Metals Abstracts, Alloys Index, Steels Alert, Nonferrous Alert, Polymers/Ceramics/Composites Alert,* and *Engineered Materials Abstracts.* (Formerly produced by ASM International.).

ENCYCLOPEDIAS AND DICTIONARIES

Encyclopedia of Materials: Science and Technology. K.H.J. Buschow and others, editors. Pergamon Press/Elsevier Science. • 2001. $6,875.00. Eleven volumes. Provides extensive technical information on a wide variety of materials, including metals, ceramics, plastics, optical materials, and building materials. Includes more than 2,000 articles and 5,000 illustrations.

HANDBOOKS AND MANUALS

Fundamentals of Metallurgical Processes. L. Coudurier and others. Franklin Book Co., Inc. • 1985. $187.00. Second edition. (International Monographs on Materials and Technology Series: Volume 27).

Smithells Metals Reference Book. Colin J. Smithells. Butterworth-Heinemann. • 1998. $125.00. Seventh edition. (Engineering Materials Selector Series).

ONLINE DATABASES

Applied Science and Technology Index Online. H. W. Wilson Co. • Provides online indexing of 400 major scientific, technical, industrial, and engineering periodicals. Time period is 1983 to date. Monthly updates. Inquire as to online cost and availability.

METADEX. Cambridge Scientific Abstracts. • Covers the worldwide literature of metals, metallurgy, and materials science, 1966 to date. Includes detailed alloys indexing from 1974. Biweekly updating. Inquire as to online cost and availability. (Formerly produced by ASM International.).

PERIODICALS AND NEWSLETTERS

ACTA Materalia: An International Journal for the Science of Materials. Elsevier Science. • Monthly. $1,135.00 per year. Formerly *ACTA Metallutgical et Materalia.*

High-Tech Materials Alert: Advanced Materials-Their Uses and Manufacture. Technical Insights. • Monthly. $695.00 per year. Newsletter on technical developments relating to high-performance materials, including metals and ceramics. Includes market forecasts.

International Materials Review. ASM International, Materials Information. • Bimonthly. Members, $305.00 per year; non-members, $734.00 per year. Provides technical and research coverage of metals, alloys, and advanced materials. Formerly *International Metals Review.*

JOM: Journal of Metals. Minerals, Metals, and Materials Society. • Monthly. Individuals. $79.00 per year; institutions, $154.00 per year. A scholarly journal covering all phases of metals and metallurgy.

Metallurgia, The Journal of Metals Technology, Metal Forming and Thermal Processing. British Forging Industry Association. DMG World Media. • Monthly. $275.00 per year.

Metallurgical and Materials Transactions A: Physical Metallurgy and Materials Sc. ASM International. • Monthly. Members, $75.00 per year; non-members, $1,361.00 per year; students, $35.00 per year. Formerly *Metallurgical Transactions APhysical Metallurgy and Materials Science.*

Metallurgical and Materials Transactions B: Process Metallurgy. ASM International, Materials Information. • Nine times a year. Members, $58.00 per year; non-members, $978.00 per year; students, $26.00 per year. Formerly *Metallurgical Transactions B: Process Metallurgy.*

Scripta Materialia. Acta Metallurgica, Inc. Elsevier Science. • Semimonthly. $1,188.00 per year.

RESEARCH CENTERS AND INSTITUTES

Basic Metals Processing Research Institute. University of Pittsburgh, School of Engineering, 848 Benedum Hall, Pittsburgh, PA 15261. Phone: (412)624-9737 Fax: (412)624-1543 E-mail: deardo@pitt.edu.

Cooperative Program in Metallurgy. Pennsylvania State University, Mineral Engineering Dept., University Park, PA 16802. Phone: (814)865-4882 Fax: (814)865-2917 E-mail: asare@ems.psu.edu/metals/.

Materials Processing Center. Massachusetts Institute of Technology, 77 Massachusetts Ave., Room 12-007, Cambridge, MA 02139-4307. Phone: (617)253-5179 Fax: (617)258-6900 E-mail: fmpage@.mit.edu • URL: http://www.web.mit.edu/mpc/www/ • Conducts processing, engineering, and economic research in ferrous and nonferrous metals, ceramics, polymers, photonic materials, superconductors, welding, composite materials, and other materials.

TRADE/PROFESSIONAL ASSOCIATIONS

ASM International. 9639 Kinsman Rd., Materials Park, OH 44073. Phone: 800-336-5152 or (216)338-5151 Fax: (216)338-4634 E-mail: memserv@po.asm-intl.org • URL: http://www.asm-intl.org • Members are materials engineers, metallurgists, industry executives, educators, and others concerned with a wide range of materials and metals. Divisions include Aerospace, Composites, Electronic Materials and Processing, Energy, Highway/Off-Highway Vehicle, Joining, Materials Testing and Quality Control, Society of Carbide and Tool Engineers, and Surface Engineering.

Minerals, Metals and Materials Society. 184 Thorn Hill Dr., Warrendale, PA 15086-7528. Phone: 800-759-4867 or (724)776-9000 Fax: (724)776-3770 E-mail: tmsgeneral@tms.org • URL: http://www.tms.org • Members are metallurgists, metallurgical engineers, and materials scientists. Divisions include Light Metals and Electronic, Magnetic, and Photonic Materials.

Mining and Metallurgical Society of America. 476 Wilson Ave., Novato, CA 94947-4236. Phone: (415)898-4508 Fax: (415)899-0262 E-mail: akburton@worldnet.att.net • URL: http://www.mmsa.net.

Society for Mining, Metallurgy, and Exploration. P.O. Box 625002, Littleton, CO 80162-5002. Phone:

800-763-3132 or (303)973-9550 or (303)948-4210 Fax: (303)973-3845 E-mail: sme@smenet.org • URL: http://www.smenet.org.

METALS, PRECIOUS

See: GOLD; METAL INDUSTRY; PLATINUM INDUSTRY; SILVER INDUSTRY

METALS, RARE EARTH

See: RARE EARTH METALS

METEOROLOGY

See: WEATHER AND WEATHER FORECASTING

METRIC SYSTEM

See: WEIGHTS AND MEASURES

METROPOLITAN AREAS

See: CITIES AND TOWNS; CITY PLANNING; MARKET STATISTICS; URBAN DEVELOPMENT

MEXICO

See: LATIN AMERICAN MARKETS

MICROCOMPUTERS AND MINICOMPUTERS

See also: ARTIFICIAL INTELLIGENCE; COMPUTER COMMUNICATIONS; COMPUTER CRIME AND SECURITY; COMPUTER PERIPHERALS AND ACCESSORIES; COMPUTER SOFTWARE INDUSTRY; COMPUTERS; COMPUTERS IN EDUCATION; DESKTOP PUBLISHING; OPTICAL DISK STORAGE DEVICES; PORTABLE COMPUTERS; WORD PROCESSING

GENERAL WORKS

Using Computers: Gateway to Information. Gary B. Shelley and T. Cashman. South-Western Publishing Co. • 1995. $44.65. Second edition.

ABSTRACTS AND INDEXES

Applied Science and Technology Index. H. W. Wilson Co. • 11 times a year. Quarterly and annual cumulations. Service basis for print edition; CD-ROM edition, $1,495.00 per year. Indexes a wide variety of English language technical, industrial, and engineering periodicals.

Business Periodicals Index. H. W. Wilson Co. • Monthly, except August, with quarterly and annual cumulations. Service basis for print edition; CD-ROM edition, $1,495.00 per year.

Computer and Control Abstracts. Available from INSPEC, Inc. • Monthly. $2,160.00 per year. Section C of *Science Abstracts.*

Computer and Information Systems Abstracts Journal: An Abstract Journal Pertaining to the Theory, Design, Fabrication and Application of Computer and Information Systems. Cambridge Information Group. • Monthly. $1,045 per year.

Computer Literature Index: A Subject/Author Index to Computer and Data Processing Literature. Applied Computer Research, Inc. • Quarterly, with annual cumulation. $245.00 per year. Contains brief abstracts of book and periodical literature covering all phases of computing, including approximately 70 specific application areas.

Current Contents: Engineering, Computing and Technology. Institute for Scientific Information. • Weekly. $730.00 per year. Reproductions of contents pages of technical journals. Includes *Author Index, Address Directory, Current Book Contents* and *Title Word Index.* Formerly *Current Contents: Engineering, Technology and Applied Sciences.*

LAMP (Literature Analysis of Microcomputer Publications). Soft Images. • Bimonthly. $89.95 per year. Annual cumulation.

Microcomputer Abstracts. Information Today, Inc. • Quarterly. $225.00 per year. Provides abstracts covering a wide variety of personal and business microcomputer literature. Formerly *Microcomputer Index.*

Science Citation Index. Institute for Scientific Information. • Bimonthly. $15,020.00 per year. Annual cumulation. Includes *Source Index, Citation Index, Permuterm Subject Index,* and *Corporate Index.*

ALMANACS AND YEARBOOKS

Computer Industry Almanac. Egil Juliussen and Karen Petska. Computer Industry Almanac, Inc. • Annual. $63.00. Analyzes recent trends in various segments of the computer industry, with forecasts, employment data and industry salary information. Includes directories of computer companies, industry organizations, and publications.

Information Technology Outlook. OECD Publications and Information Center. • Biennial. $72.00. A review of recent developments in international markets for computer hardware, software, and services. Also examines current legal provisions for information systems security and privacy in OECD countries.

BIBLIOGRAPHIES

Computer Book Review. • Quarterly. $30.00 per year. Includes annual index. Reviews new computer books. Back issues available.

Computing Information Directory: Comprehensive Guide to the Computing and Computer Engineering Literature. Peter A. Hildebrandt, Inc. • Annual. $229.95. Describes computer journals, newsletters, handbooks, dictionaries, indexing services, review resources, directories, and other computer information sources. Includes a directory of publishers and a master subject index.

CD-ROM DATABASES

Computer Select. The Gale Group. • Monthly. $1,250.00 per year. Provides one year of full-text on CD-ROM for 120 leading computer-related publications. Also includes 70,000 product specifications and brief profiles of 13,000 computer product vendors and manufacturers.

Datapro on CD-ROM: Computer Systems Hardware and Software. Gartner Group, Inc. • Monthly. Price on application. CD-ROM provides product specifications, product reports, user surveys, and market forecasts for a wide range of computer hardware and software.

Hoover's Company Capsules on CD-ROM. Hoover's, Inc. • Quarterly. $349.95 per year (single-user). Provides the CD-ROM version of *Hoover's Handbook of American Business, Hoover's Handbook of Emerging Companies, Hoover's Handbook of World Business, Hoover's Guide to Computer Companies, Hoover's Guide to Media Companies, Hoover's Handbook of Private Companies,* and various regional guides. Includes more than 11,000 profiles of companies.

WILSONDISC: Wilson Business Abstracts. H. W. Wilson Co. • Monthly. $2,495.00 per year, including unlimited online access to *Wilson Business Abstracts* through WILSONLINE. Provides CD-ROM "cover-to-cover" abstracting and indexing of over 600 prominent business periodicals. Indexing is from 1982, abstracting from 1990. (*Business Periodicals Index* without abstracts is available on CD-ROM at $1,495 per year.).

DIRECTORIES

Computing and Software Career Directory. The Gale Group. • 1993. $39.00. Includes career information relating to programmers, software engineers, technical writers, systems experts, and other computer specialists. Provides advice from "insiders," resume suggestions, a directory of companies that may offer entry-level positions, and a directory of career information sources. (Career Advisor Series.).

Control Engineering Buyers Guide. Cahners Business Information. • Annual. Free to qualified personnel. Contains specifications, prices, and manufacturers' listings for computer software, as related to control engineering.

Corptech Directory of Technology Companies. Corporate Technology Information Services, Inc. c/o Eileen Kennedy. • Annual. $795.00. Four volumes. Profiles of more than 45,000 manufacturers and developers of high technology products. Includes private companies, publicly-held corporations, and subsidiaries. Formerly *Corporate Technology Directory.*

Data Sources: The Comprehensive Guide to the Data Processing Industry Hardware, Data Communications Products, Software, Company Profiles. The Gale Group. • Semiannual. $495.00 per year. Two volumes. Describes hardware and software for all computer operating sysems, including prices and technical details. Lists about 75,000 products from 14,000 suppliers. Industry-specific software applications are described.

Essential Business Buyer's Guide, from Cellular Services and Overnight Mail to Internet Access Providers, 401(k) Plans, and Desktop Computers: The Ultimate Guide to Buying Office Equipment, Products, and Services. Sourcebooks, Inc. • 1996. $18.95. Compiled by the staff of *Business Consumer Guide.* Lists recommended brands of office equipment.

Faulkner Information Service. Faulkner Information Services, Inc. • Looseleaf. Monthly updates. Many titles and volumes, covering virtually all aspects of computer software and hardware. Gives descriptions and technical data for specific products, including producers' names and addresses. Prices and details on request. Formerly (The Auerbach Series).

MicroLeads Vendor Directory on Disk (Personal Computer Industry). Chromatic Communications Enterprises, Inc. • Annual. $495.00. Includes computer hardware manufacturers, software producers, book-periodical publishers, and franchised or company-owned chains of personal computer equipment retailers, support services and accessory manufacturers. Formerly *MicroLeads U.S. Vender Directory.*

The Software Encyclopedia: A Guide for Personal, Professional, and Business Users. R. R. Bowker. • Annual. $255.00. Two volumes. Volume one lists software programs by title and producer. Volume two provides information on programs according to application and operating system. Includes prices and requirements for hardware and memory.

ENCYCLOPEDIAS AND DICTIONARIES

Business Dictionary of Computers. Jerry M. Rosenberg. John Wiley and Sons, Inc. • 1993.

$14.95. Third edition. Provides concise definitions of over 7,500 computer terms, including slang terms, abbreviations, acronyms, and technical jargon. (Business Dictionary Series).

Computer Dictionary. Donald D. Spencer. Camelot Publishing Co. • 1993. $24.95. Fourth edition.

Cyberspeak: An Online Dictionary. Andy Ihnatko. Random House, Inc. • 1996. $12.95. An informal guide to the language of computers, multimedia, and the Internet.

Dictionary of Computer Terms. Brian Phaffenberger. Pearson Education and Technology. • 1997. $10.95. Sixth edition.

Dictionary of Computing. Valerie Illingworth, editor. Oxford University Press, Inc. • 1996. $49.95. Fourth edition.

Dictionary of Information Technology and Computer Science. Tony Gunton. Blackwell Publishers. • 1994. $50.95. Second edition. Covers key words, phrases, abbreviations, and acronyms used in computing and data communications.

Dictionary of PC Hardware and Data Communications Terms. Mitchell Shnier. Thomson Learning. • 1996. $19.95. (Online updates to print version available at http://www.ora.com/reference/dictionary.).

Encyclopedia of Microcomputers. Allen Kent and James G. Williams, editors. Marcel Dekker, Inc. • Dates vary. Prices vary. 24 volumes. Contains scholarly articles written by microcomputer experts. Includes bibliographies. Index available, $230.00.

Illustrated Dictionary of Microcomputers. Michael Hordeski. McGraw Hill Professional. • 1990. $19.95. Third edition.

New Hacker's Dictionary. Eric S. Raymond. MIT Press. • 1996. $39.00. Third edition. Includes three classifications of hacker communication: slang, jargon, and "techspeak.".

FINANCIAL RATIOS

Industry Norms and Key Business Ratios. Desk Top Edition. Dun and Bradstreet Corp., Business Information Services. • Annual. Five volumes. $475.00 per volume. $1,890.00 per set. Covers over 800 kinds of businesses, arranged by Standard Industrial Classification number. More detailed editions covering longer periods of time are also available.

HANDBOOKS AND MANUALS

Buying and Maintaining Personal Computers: A How-To-Do-It Manual for Librarians. Norman Howden. Neal-Schuman Publishers, Inc. • 2000. $45.00. Covers various aspects of buying PCs or MACs for library use, including choice of hardware, software selection, warranties, backup systems, staffing, and dealing with vendors.

Computer Buying Guide. Consumer Guide Editors. Publications International Ltd. • Annual. $9.99.

Computer Repair Service. Entrepreneur Media, Inc. • Looseleaf. $59.50. A practical guide to starting a computer repair service. Covers profit potential, start-up costs, market size evaluation, owner's time required, site selection, lease negotiation, pricing, accounting, advertising, promotion, etc. (Start-Up Business Guide No. E1256.).

Dun & Bradstreet/Gale Group Industry Handbooks. The Gale Group. • 2000. $630.00. Five volumes. $145.00 per volume. Each volume covers two or more major industries: 1. *Entertainment and Hospitality*; 2. *Construction and Agriculture*; 3. *Chemicals and Pharmaceuticals*; 4. *Computers & Software and Broadcasting & Telecommunications*; 5. *Insurance and Health & Medical Services.* The following are included for each industry: overview, statistics, financial ratios, rankings, merger information, company directory, directory of associations, and consultants directory.

Microcomputer Engineering. Gene H. Miller. Prentice Hall. • 1998. $100.00. Second edition.

The Modem Reference: The Complete Guide to PC Communications. Michael A. Banks. Information Today, Inc. • 2000. $29.95. Fourth edition. Covers personal computer data communications technology, including fax transmissions, computer networks, modems, and the Internet. Popularly written.

INTERNET DATABASES

InfoTech Trends. Data Analysis Group. Phone: (707)894-9100 Fax: (707)486-5618 E-mail: support@infotechtrends.com • URL: http://www.infotechtrends.com • Web site provides both free and fee-based market research data on the information technology industry, including computers, peripherals, telecommunications, the Internet, software, CD-ROM/DVD, e-commerce, and workstations. Fees: Free for current (most recent year) data; more extensive information has various fee structures. Formerly *Computer Industry Forecasts.*

Wired News. Wired Digital, Inc. Phone: (415)276-8400 Fax: (415)276-8499 E-mail: newsfeedback@wired.com • URL: http://www.wired.com • Provides summaries and full-text of "Top Stories" relating to the Internet, computers, multimedia, telecommunications, and the electronic information industry in general. These news stories are placed in the broad categories of Politics, Business, Culture, and Technology. Affiliated with *Wired* magazine. Fees: Free.

ONLINE DATABASES

Applied Science and Technology Index Online. H. W. Wilson Co. • Provides online indexing of 400 major scientific, technical, industrial, and engineering periodicals. Time period is 1983 to date. Monthly updates. Inquire as to online cost and availability.

Computer Database. The Gale Group. • Provides online citations with abstracts to material appearing in about 150 trade journals and newsletters in the subject areas of computers, telecommunications, and electronics. Time period is 1983 to date, with weekly updates. Inquire as to online cost and availability.

Globalbase. The Gale Group. • Provides more than one million online summaries of business, industrial, and economic news reports from more than 1,000 publications worldwide. Covers a wide range of material appearing in international trade journals, professional magazines, and newspapers. Time period is 1984 to date, with weekly updates. Inquire as to online cost and availability.

Internet and Personal Computing Abstracts. Information Today, Inc. • Contains abstracts covering a wide variety of personal and business microcomputer literature appearing in more than 100 journals and popular magazines. Time period is 1981 to date, with monthly updates. Formerly *Microcomputer Index.* Inquire as to online cost and availability.

Microcomputer Software Guide Online. R. R. Bowker. • Provides information on more than 30,000 microcomputer software applications from more than 4,000 producers. Corresponds to printed *Software Encyclopedia*, but with monthly updates. Inquire as to online cost and availability.

PROMT: Predicasts Overview of Markets and Technology. The Gale Group. • Companies, products, applied technologies and markets. U.S. and international literature coverage, 1972 to date. Inquire as to online cost and availability. Provides abstracts from more than 1,600 publications. Weekly updates.

Scisearch. Institute for Scientific Information. • Broad, multidisciplinary index to the literature of science and technology, 1974 to present. Inquire as to online cost and availability. Coverage of literature is worldwide, with weekly updates.

Wilson Business Abstracts Online. H. W. Wilson Co. • Indexes and abstracts 600 major business periodicals, plus the *Wall Street Journal* and the business section of the *New York Times.* Indexing is from 1982, abstracting from 1990, with the two newspapers included from 1993. Updated weekly. Inquire as to online cost and availability. (*Business Periodicals Index* without abstracts is also available online.).

PERIODICALS AND NEWSLETTERS

Andrew Seybold's Outlook: A Monthly Perspective of Issues Affecting the Mobile Computer and Communications Industries. Andrew Seybold's Outlook. • Monthly. $395.00 per year. Newsletter. Provides analysis of the computer industry to corporate buyers and to end users. Reports on hardware, software trends and future products. Formerly *Andrew Seybold's Outlook on Communications and Computing.*

Computer Industry Report. International Data Corp. • Semimonthly. $495.00 per year. Newsletter. Annual supplement. Also known as "The Gray Sheet." Formerly *EDP Industry Report and Market Review.*

Computer Shopper: The Computer Magazine for Direct Buyers. Ziff-Davis Publishing Co. • Monthly. $24.97 per year. Nationwide marketplace for computer equipment.

Computerworld: Newsweekly for Information Technology Leaders. Computerworld, Inc. • Weekly. $39.95 per year.

EDP Weekly: The Leading Weekly Computer News Summary. Computer Age and E D P News Services. • Weekly. $495.00 per year. Newsletter. Summarizes news from all areas of the computer and microcomputer industries.

Home Office Computing: Building Better Businesses with Technology. Freedom Technology Media Group. • Monthly. $16.97 per year. Office automation for the self-employed and small businesses. Formerly *Family and Home Office Computing.*

IEEE Micro. Institute of Electrical and Electronics Engineers, Inc. • Bimonthly. Free to members; non members, $455.00 per year.

InfoWorld: Defining Technology for Business. InfoWorld Publishing. • Weekly. $160.00 per year. For personal computing professionals.

Macworld. Mac Publishing, L.L.C. • Monthly. $30.00 per year. For Macintosh personal computer users.

Microprocessor Report: The Insiders' Guide to Microprocessor Hardware. Micro Design Resources. • 17 times a year. $695.00 per year. Newsletter. Covers the technical aspects of microprocessors from Intel, IBM, Cyrix, Motorola, and others.

Online Libraries and Microcomputers. Information Intelligence, Inc. • Monthly. Individuals $43.75 per year; libraries. $62.50 per year. Newsletter. Covers library automation and electronic information (online, CD-ROM). Reviews or describes new computer hardware and software for library use.

PC Letter: The Insider's Guide to the Personal Computer Industry. David Coursey, editor. Stewart Alsop. • 22 times a year. $495.00 per year.

Newsletter. Includes reviews of new PC hardware and software.

PC Magazine: The Independent Guide to Personal Computing and the Internet. Ziff-Davis Publishing Co. • Biweekly. $49.97 per year.

PC World: The No. 1 Source for Definitive How-to-Buy, How-to-Use Advice on Personal Computing Systems and Software. PC World Communications, Inc. • Monthly. $29.90 per year.

PlugIn Datamation: Profit and Value from Information Technology. Earth Web, Inc., Datamation. • Monthly. Price on application. Technical, semi-technical and general news covering EDP topics.

Release 1.0: Esther Dyson's Monthly Report. EDventure Holdings, Computer Publications Div. • 15 times a year. $695.00 per year. Newsletter.

Software Magazine. Wiesner Publishing, Inc. • Monthly. $42.00 per year.

PRICE SOURCES

Computer Price Guide: The Blue Book of Used IBM Computer Prices. Computer Economics, Inc. • Quarterly. $140.00 per year. Provides average prices of used IBM computer equipment, including "complete lists of obsolete IBM equipment." Includes a newsletter on trends in the used computer market. Edited for dealers, leasing firms, and business computer buyers.

Orion Computer Blue Book. Orion Research Corp. • Quarterly. $516.00 per year. $129.00 per issue. Quotes retail and wholesale prices of used computers and equipment. Original list prices and years of manufacture are also shown.

RESEARCH CENTERS AND INSTITUTES

Battelle Memorial Institute. 505 King Ave., Columbus, OH 43201-2693. Phone: 800-201-2011 or (614)424-6424 Fax: (614)424-3260 • URL: http://www.battelle.org • Multidisciplinary research facilities at various locations include: Microcomputer Applications and Technology Center; Battelle Industrial Technology Center; Technology and Society Research Center; Office of Transportation Systems and Planning; Office of Waste Technology Development; Materials Information Center; Office of Nuclear Waste Isolation.

Carnegie Mellon Research Institute. Carnegie Mellon University, 700 Technology Dr., Pittsburgh, PA 15219. Phone: (412)268-3190 Fax: (412)268-3101 E-mail: twillke@emu.edu • Multidisciplinary research activities include expert systems applications, minicomputer and microcomputer systems design, genetic engineering, and transportation systems analysis.

Center for Advanced Technology in Computers and Information Systems. Columbia University, 161 Fort Washington Ave., AP1310, New York, NY 10032. Phone: (212)305-2944 Fax: (212)305-0196 E-mail: d1330@columbia.edu • URL: http://www.cpmc.columbia.edu/catc/.

Center for Microelectronic and Computer Engineering. Rochester Institute of Technology, 82 Lomb Memorial Dr., Rochester, NY 14623-5604. Phone: (716)475-2035 Fax: (716)475-5041 E-mail: lffeee@rit.edu • URL: http://www.microe.rit.edu • Facilities include digital computer organization/microcomputer laboratory.

Center for Research in Computing Technology. Harvard University, Pierce Hall, 29 Oxford St., Cambridge, MA 02138. Phone: (617)495-2832 Fax: (617)495-9837 E-mail: cheatham@das.harvard.edu • URL: http://www.das.harvard.edu/cs.grafs.html • Conducts research in computer vision, robotics, artificial intelligence, systems programming, programming languages, operating systems, networks, graphics, database management systems, and telecommunications.

Technology Based Learning and Research. Arizona State University, College of Education, Community Service Center, Tempe, AZ 85287-0908. Phone: (480)965-4960 Fax: (480)946-1423 E-mail: bitter@asu.edu • URL: http://tblr.ed.asu.edu/projects.html • Research activities are related to computer literacy.

STATISTICS SOURCES

Computers and Office and Accounting Machines. U. S. Bureau of the Census. • Annual. Provides data on shipments: value, quantity, imports, and exports. (Current Industrial Reports, MA-35R.).

Standard & Poor's Industry Surveys. Standard & Poor's. • Semiannual. $1,800.00. Two looseleaf volumes. Includes monthly supplements. Provides detailed, individual surveys of 52 major industry groups. Each survey is revised on a semiannual basis. Also includes "Monthly Investment Review" (industry group investment analysis) and monthly "Trends & Projections" (economic analysis).

U. S. Industry and Trade Outlook: The McGraw-Hill Companies and the U.S. Department of Commerce/International Trade Administration. Datapso Research Corp. • Annual. $69.95. Produced by the International Trade Administration, U. S. Department of Commerce, in a "public-private" partnership with DRI/McGraw-Hill and Standard & Poor's. Provides basic data, outlook for the current year, and "Long-Term Prospects" (five-year projections) for a wide variety of products and services. Includes high technology industries. Formerly *U. S. Industrial Outlook.*

TRADE/PROFESSIONAL ASSOCIATIONS

Association of Minicomputer Users. 363 E. Central St., Franklin, MA 02038. Phone: (508)520-1555 Fax: (508)520-1558 E-mail: imstrain@ix.netcom.com.

Computing Technology Industry Association. 450 E. 22nd St., Suite 230, Lombard, IL 60148-6158. Phone: (630)268-1818 Fax: (630)268-1384 E-mail: info@comptia.org • URL: http://www.comptia.org • Members are resellers of various kinds of microcomputers and computer equipment.

IEEE Computer Society. 1730 Massachusetts Ave., N. W., Washington, DC 20036. Phone: (202)371-0101 Fax: (202)728-9614 E-mail: csinfo@computer.org • URL: http://www.computer.org • A society of the Institute of Electrical and Electronics Engineers. Said to be the world's largest organization of computer professionals. Some of the specific committees are: Computer Communications; Computer Graphics; Computers in Education; Design Automation; Office Automation; Personal Computing; Robotics; Security and Privacy; Software Engineering.

Information Technology Association of America. c/o ITAA, 1616 N. Fort Myer Dr., Suite 1300, Arlington, VA 22209-9998. Phone: (703)522-5055 Fax: (703)525-2279 • Members are computer software and services companies. Maintains an Information Systems Integration Services Section.

Microcomputer Investors Association. 902 Anderson Dr., Fredericksburg, VA 22405. Phone: (703)371-5474 • Members are professional investors who make use of microcomputers for portfolio management.

Society for Computer Simulation International. P.O. Box 17900, San Diego, CA 92177-1810. Phone: (858)277-3888 Fax: (858)277-3930 E-mail: info@scs.org • URL: http://www.scs.org.

OTHER SOURCES

DataWorld. Faulkner Information Services, Inc. • Four looseleaf volumes, with monthly supplements. $1,395.00 per year. Describes and evaluates both hardware and software relating to midrange, micro, and mainframe computers. Available on CD-ROM.

World of Computer Science. The Gale Group. • 2001. $150.00. Alphabetical arrangement. Contains 650 entries covering discoveries, theories, concepts, issues, ethics, and people in the broad area of computer science and technology.

MICROFICHE

See: MICROFORMS

MICROFILM

See: MICROFORMS

MICROFORMS

See also: DOCUMENT IMAGING

BIBLIOGRAPHIES

Guide to Microforms in Print: Author-Title. R. R. Bowker. • Annual. $475.00. Provides international coverage of authors and titles.

Guide to Microforms in Print: Subject Guide. Available from The Gale Group. • Annual. $450.00. Provides international coverage under 135 subject headings. Published by K. G. Saur.

Micropublishers' Trade List Annual. Chadwyck-Healey, Inc. • Annual. $375.00. About 250 publishers of microfilm and microfiche and their catalogs. Worldwide coverage.

Serials in Microform. UMI. • Annual. Free to libraries.

CD-ROM DATABASES

LISA Plus: Library and Information Science Abstracts. Bowker-Saur, Reed Reference Publishing. • Quarterly. $1,450.00 per year. Provides CD-ROM abstracting and indexing of the world's library and information science literature. Covers a wide variety of topics.

DIRECTORIES

AIIM Buying Guide. Association for Information and Image Management. • Annual. $64.00. 460 manufacturers, suppliers, service companies and consultants in the information management industry. Formerly *Buyer's Guide to Micrographic Equipment, Products and Services.*

Microform Market Place: An International Directory of Micropublishing. Available from Reed Reference Publishing. • Biennial. $75.00. Published by K. G. Saur. International coverage. Lists microform publishers by name, by subject area of specialization, and by country.

HANDBOOKS AND MANUALS

Preservation Microfilming: A Guide for Librarians and Archivists. Nancy E. Gwinn. Books on Demand. • 1995. $73.80. Second edition. Covers all aspects of planning and managing a microfilming operation.

ONLINE DATABASES

LISA Online: Library and Information Science Abstracts. Bowker-Saur, Reed Reference Publishing. • Provides abstracting and indexing of the world's library and information science literature from 1969 to the present. Covers a wide variety of topics in over 550 journals from 60 countries, with biweekly updates. Inquire as to online cost and availability.

Scisearch. Institute for Scientific Information. • Broad, multidisciplinary index to the literature of science and technology, 1974 to present. Inquire as to online cost and availability. Coverage of literature is worldwide, with weekly updates.

PERIODICALS AND NEWSLETTERS

Inform: The Magazine of Information and Image Management. Association for Information and Image Management. • Monthly. $85.00 per year. Covers technologies, applications, and trends.

Microform and Imaging Review. R. R. Bowker. • Quarterly. $165.00 per year. Evaluates scholarly micropublications for libraries. Includes articles on microform management.

Micrographics and Hybrid Imaging Systems Newsletter: Monthly Report for Busines Excutives Who Use of Market Microfilm Services and Hybrid Imaging Services and Equipment. Microfilm Publishing. Inc. • Monthly. $168.30 per year. A report for business executives who use or market microfilm services and equipment. Formerly *Micrographics Newsletter*.

TRADE/PROFESSIONAL ASSOCIATIONS

Association for Information and Image Management. 1100 Wayne Ave., Suite 1100, Silver Spring, MD 20910-5603. Phone: (301)587-8202 Fax: (301)587-2711 E-mail: aiim@aiim.org • URL: http://www.aiim.org • Members are producers and users of image management equipment.

International Information Management Congress. 1100 Wayne Ave., Ste. 1100, Silver Spring, MD 20910-5603. Phone: (301)587-8202 Fax: (301)587-2711 E-mail: aiim@aiim.org • URL: http://www.iimc.org.

OTHER SOURCES

Information and Image Management: The State of the Industry. Association for Information and Image Management. • Annual. $130.00. Market data with five-year forecasts. Covers electronic imaging, micrographics supplies and equipment, software, and records management services.

MICROGRAPHICS

See: MICROFORMS

MICROPHOTOGRAPHY

See: MICROFORMS

MICROPROCESSORS

See: MICROCOMPUTERS AND MINICOMPUTERS

MICROSOFT WINDOWS

See: WINDOWS (SOFTWARE)

MICROWAVES

ABSTRACTS AND INDEXES

Key Abstracts: Microwave Technology. Available from INSPEC, Inc. • Monthly. $240.00 per year. Provides international coverage of journal and proceedings literature. Published in England by the Institution of Electrical Engineers (IEE).

DIRECTORIES

Microwaves and RF Directory. Penton Media Inc. • Annual. $125.00. About 2,000 manufacturers of high frequency equipment components. International coverage. Formerly *Microwaves and RF Product Data Directory.*

PERIODICALS AND NEWSLETTERS

Journal of Microwave Power and Electromagnetic Energy. International Microwave Power Institute. • Quarterly. $195.00 per year. Formerly *Journal of Microwave Power.*

Microwave and Optical Technology Letters. John Wiley and Sons, Inc., Journals Div. • 24 times a year. $1,540.00 per year.

Microwave Journal. Horizon House Publications, Inc. • Monthly. $110.00 per year. International coverage.

Wireless Week. Cahners Business Information. • 51 times a year. $59.00 per year. Covers news of cellular telephones, mobile radios, communications satellites, microwave transmission, and the wireless industry in general.

RESEARCH CENTERS AND INSTITUTES

Microwave Device and Physical Electronics Laboratory. University of Utah. Electrical Engineering Dept., 50 S. Central Campus Dr., Room 3280, Salt Lake City, UT 84112. Phone: (801)581-6941 Fax: (801)581-5281 E-mail: grow@ee.utah.edu • URL: http://www.elen.utah.edu.

STATISTICS SOURCES

Electronic Market Data Book. Electronic Industries Association, Marketing Services Dept. • Annual. Members, $75.00; non-members, $125.00.

U. S. Industry and Trade Outlook: The McGraw-Hill Companies and the U.S. Department of Commerce/ International Trade Administration. Datapso Research Corp. • Annual. $69.95. Produced by the International Trade Administration, U. S. Department of Commerce, in a "public-private" partnership with DRI/McGraw-Hill and Standard & Poor's. Provides basic data, outlook for the current year, and "Long-Term Prospects" (five-year projections) for a wide variety of products and services. Includes high technology industries. Formerly *U. S. Industrial Outlook.*

TRADE/PROFESSIONAL ASSOCIATIONS

International Microwave Power Institute. 10210 Leatherleaf Court, Manassas, VA 20111. Phone: (703)257-1415 Fax: (703)257-0213 E-mail: info@impi.org • URL: http://www.impi.org.

MIGRATION

See: IMMIGRATION AND EMIGRATION

MIGRATION OF INDUSTRY

See: LOCATION OF INDUSTRY

MILITARY COMMISSARIES

See: POST EXCHANGES

MILITARY MARKET

See also: DEFENSE INDUSTRIES

BIBLIOGRAPHIES

Defense and Security. Available from U. S. Government Printing Office. • Annual. Free. Issued by the Superintendent of Documents. A list of government publications on defense and related topics. Formerly *Defense Supply and Logistics.* (Subject Bibliography No. 153.).

DIRECTORIES

ECN's Electronic Industry Telephone Directory. Cahners Business Information. • Annual. $55.00. Information on 30,000 electronic manufacturers, distributors, and representatives. Formerly *Electronic Industry Telephone Directory.*

Military Retailing Directory. Military Retailing Publisher. • Semiannual. $95.00 per year. Edited for use by military commissaries in making purchasing decisions. Lists sources of goods and sevices, with official military department and retail order numbers.

World Aviation Directory. McGraw-Hill Aviation Week Group. • Semiannual. $225.00 per year. Two volumes. Lists aviation, aerospace, and missile manufacturers. Includes *World Aviation Directory Buyer's Guide.*

FINANCIAL RATIOS

Industry Norms and Key Business Ratios. Desk Top Edition. Dun and Bradstreet Corp., Business Information Services. • Annual. Five volumes. $475.00 per volume. $1,890.00 per set. Covers over 800 kinds of businesses, arranged by Standard Industrial Classification number. More detailed editions covering longer periods of time are also available.

HANDBOOKS AND MANUALS

International Defense Electronic Systems Handbook. Intertec Publishing. • Annual. $195.00. Includes information concerning federal budget for electronic military equipment. Gives descriptions of equipment.

ONLINE DATABASES

Aerospace/Defense Markets and Technology. The Gale Group. • Abstracts of commerical aerospace/ defense related literature, 1982 to date. Also includes information about major defense contracts awarded by the U. S. Department of Defense. International coverage. Inquire as to online cost and availability.

PAIS International. Public Affairs Information Service, Inc. • Corresponds to the former printed publications, *PAIS Bulletin* (1976-90) and *PAIS Foreign Language Index* (1972-90), and to the current *PAIS International in Print* (1991 to date). Covers economic, political, and sociological material appearing in periodicals, books, government documents, and other publications. Updating is monthly. Inquire as to online cost and availability.

PERIODICALS AND NEWSLETTERS

Aerospace America. American Institute of Aeronautics and Astronautics, Inc. • Monthly. Free to members; non-members, $75.00 per year. Provides coverage of key issues affecting the aerospace field.

Aerospace and Defense Science. Aerospace and Defense Science, Inc. • Quarterly. $24.00 per year. Provides executive overviews and insights into defense and aerospace technologies and future applications.

Aviation Week and Space Technology. McGraw-Hill Aviation Week Group. • Monthly. $89.00 per year.

Defense Electronics. Intertec Publishing Corp. • Monthly. $52.00 per year.

Defense Systems Review and Military Communications. Cosgriff-Martin Publishing Group, Inc. • Monthly. $35.00 per year.

Flight International. Reed Business Information. • Weekly. $170.00 per year. Technical aerospace coverage.

Inside R and D: A Weekly Report on Technical Innovation. Technical Insights. • Weekly. $840.00 per year. Concentrates on new and significant developments. Formerly *Technolog Transfer Week.*

Interservice. American Logistics Association. • Quarterly. $20.00 per year. Official Journal of the American Logistics Association.

Journal of Electronic Defense. Association of Old Crows. Horizon-House Publications, Inc. • Monthly. Free to members; non-members, $120.00 per year.

Military Grocer. Downey Communications, Inc. • Bimonthly. $40.00 per year. Edited for managers and employees of supermarkets on military bases. (These are supermarkets administered by the Defense Commissary Agency.).

Military Market: Magazine for the Military Retail System. Army Times Publishing Co. • Monthly. $79.00 per year. Aimed at officials who buy for and operate military base stores. *Buyers Guide* and *Almanac and Directory* available, $10.00 each.

National Defense. National Defense Industrial Association. • 10 times a year. $35.00 per year.

Navy Supply Corps Newsletter. Available from U. S. Government Printing Office. • Bimonthly. $20.00 per year. Newsletter issued by U. S. Navy Supply Systems Command. Provides news of Navy supplies and stores activities.

TRADE/PROFESSIONAL ASSOCIATIONS

Aerospace Industries Association of America. 1250 Eye St., N.W., Washington, DC 20005. Phone: (202)371-8400 Fax: (202)371-8470 E-mail: aia@aia-aerospace.org • URL: http://www.aia-aerospace.org.

American Institute of Aeronautics and Astronautics. 1801 Alexander Bell Dr., Suite 500, c/o Michael Lewis, Reston, VA 20191-4344. Phone: 800-639-2422 or (703)264-7500 Fax: (703)264-7551 E-mail: customerserv@aiaa.org • URL: http://www.aiaa.org.

American Logistics Association. 1133 15th St., N.W., Suite 640, Washington, DC 20005. Phone: (202)466-2520 Fax: (202)296-4419 • URL: http://www.ala-national.org • Members are armed forces purchasing agencies and commercial firms.

National Defense Industrial Association. 2111 Wilson Blvd., No. 400, Arlington, VA 22201-3061. Phone: (703)522-1820 or (703)247-2589 Fax: (703)522-1885 E-mail: info@india.org • URL: http://www.adpa.org • Concerned with industrial preparedness for national defense.

Research and Development Associates for Military Food and Packaging Systems. 16607 Blanco Rd., No. 1506, San Antonio, TX 78232. Phone: (210)493-8024 Fax: (210)493-8036 E-mail: rda50@flash.net • URL: http://www.militaryfood.org.

OTHER SOURCES

Aerospace America [online]. American Institute of Aeronautics and Astronautics. • Provides complete text of the periodical, *Aerospace America*, 1984 to date, with monthly updates. Also includes news from the *AIAA Bulletin*. Inquire as to online cost and availability.

Aerospace Database. American Institute of Aeronautics and Astronautics. • Contains abstracts of literature covering all aspects of the aerospace and aircraft in series 1983 to date. Semimonthly updates. Inquire as to online cost and availability.

Carroll's Defense Organization Charts. Carroll Publishing. • Quarterly. $1,470.00 per year. Provides more than 200 large, fold-out paper charts showing personnel relationships in 2,400 U. S. military offices. Charts are also available online and on CD-ROM.

Jane's All the World's Aircraft. Jane's Information Group, Inc. • Annual. $300.00; CD-Rom edition, $425.00.

MILK INDUSTRY

See: DAIRY INDUSTRY

MILLERS AND MILLING

See: FLOUR INDUSTRY

MILLINERY INDUSTRY

DIRECTORIES

Contemporary Fashion. Richard Martin, editor. St. James Press. • $140.00. Second edition. Date not set. Provides detailed information on more than 400 fashion designers, milliners, footwear designers, apparel companies, and textile houses. Includes black-and-white photographs, biographical information, and bibliographies.

Garment Manufacturer's Index. Klevens Publications, Inc. • Annual. $60.00. A directory of about 8,000 manufacturers and suppliers of products and services used in the making of men's, women's, and children's clothing. Includes fabrics, trimmings, factory equipment, and other supplies.

HANDBOOKS AND MANUALS

Women's Accessories Store. Entrepreneur Media, Inc. • Looseleaf. $59.50. A practical guide to starting a women's clothing accessories shop. Covers profit potential, start-up costs, market size evaluation, owner's time required, site selection, lease negotiation, pricing, accounting, advertising, promotion, etc. (Start-Up Business Guide No. E1333.).

TRADE/PROFESSIONAL ASSOCIATIONS

Headwear Information Bureau. 302 W. 12th St., PH-C, New York, NY 10014. Phone: (212)627-8333 Fax: (212)627-0067 E-mail: milicase@aol.com • URL: http://www.hatsny.com.

MILLWORK

See: WOODWORKING INDUSTRIES

MINERALOGY

See also: METALLURGY; MINES AND MINERAL RESOURCES

ABSTRACTS AND INDEXES

Mineralogical Abstracts: A Quarterly Journal of Abstracts in English, Covering the World Literature of Mineralogy and Related Subjects. Mineralogical Society. • Quarterly. $350.00 per year.

HANDBOOKS AND MANUALS

Field Guide to Rocks and Minerals. Roger T. Peterson. Houghton Mifflin Co. • 1998. $28.00. Sixth edition. Data on where to find rocks and minerals, how to collect them, physical properties and various types. (Peterson Field Guide Series).

Manual of Mineralogy:With Minerals and Rock Exercises in Crystallography Mineralogy and Hand Speciman Petrology. Cornelius Klein and Cornelius Hurlburt. John Wiley and Sons, Inc. • 1998. $102.95. Revised edition.

ONLINE DATABASES

Scisearch. Institute for Scientific Information. • Broad, multidisciplinary index to the literature of science and technology, 1974 to present. Inquire as to online cost and availability. Coverage of literature is worldwide, with weekly updates.

PERIODICALS AND NEWSLETTERS

American Mineralogist. Mineralogical Society of America. • Bimonthly. $430.00 per year.

Rocks and Minerals: Mineralogy, Geology, Lapidary. Helen Dwight Reid Educational Foundation. Helderf Publications. • Bimonthly. Individuals, $38.00. per year; institutions, $74.00 per year.

TRADE/PROFESSIONAL ASSOCIATIONS

American Federation of Mineralogical Societies. P.O. Box 26523, Oklahoma City, OK 73126-0523. Phone: (405)682-2151.

Mineralogical Society of America. 1015 18th St., N.W., Suite 601, Washington, DC 20036-5274. Phone: (202)775-4344 Fax: (202)775-0018 E-mail: business@minsocam.org • URL: http://www.minsocam.org.

Minerals, Metals and Materials Society. 184 Thorn Hill Dr., Warrendale, PA 15086-7528. Phone: 800-759-4867 or (724)776-9000 Fax: (724)776-3770 E-mail: tmsgeneral@tms.org • URL: http://www.tms.org • Members are metallurgists, metallurgical engineers, and materials scientists. Divisions include Light Metals and Electronic, Magnetic, and Photonic Materials.

MINES AND MINERAL RESOURCES

See also: MINERALOGY; NATURAL RESOURCES

ABSTRACTS AND INDEXES

IMM Abstracts and Index: A Survey of World Literature on the Economic Geology and Mining of All Minerals (Except Coal), Mineral Processing, and Nonferrous Extraction Metallurgy. Institution of Mining and Metallurgy. • Bimonthly. Members, $142.00 per year; non-members, $215.00 per year. Provides international coverage of the literature of mining and nonferrous metallurgy. Includes mineral economics, tunnelling, and rock mechanics.

BIOGRAPHICAL SOURCES

Mining Engineering. Society for Mining, Metallurgy and Exploration. • Monthly. $125.00 per year. Includes *Who's Who in Mining Engineering*.

CD-ROM DATABASES

Environment Abstracts on CD-ROM. Congressional Information Service, Inc. • Quarterly. $1,295.00 per year. Contains the following CD-ROM databases: *Environment Abstracts, Energy Abstracts*, and *Acid Rain Abstracts*. Length of coverage varies.

DIRECTORIES

Canadian Mines Handbook. Southam Magazine Group. • Annual. $65.00. About 2,000 mining companies in Canada; also includes smelters, refineries, trade associations, related government agencies and similar organizations.

E & M J International Directory of Mining. Intertec Publishing Corp., Mining Information Services. • Annual. $140.00. Lists 2,100 companies and 3,000 mines and plants producing metals and nonmetallic minerals worldwide.

Engineering and Mining Journal Annual Buyers' Guide. Intertec Publishing Corp. • Annual. Free to qualified personnel; others, $69.00. List of manufacturers and suppliers of mining equipment; international coverage. Formerly *Engineering and Mining Journal Buying Directory*.

Financial Times Energy Yearbook: Mining 2000. Available from The Gale Group. • Annual. $320.00. Published by Financial Times Energy. Provides production and financial details for more than 800 major mining companies worldwide. Includes coverage of reserves, operations, properties, and growth rates. Formerly *Financial Times International Yearbook: Mining*.

FINANCIAL RATIOS

Almanac of Business and Industrial Financial Ratios. Leo Troy. Prentice Hall. • Annual. $99.95. Contains financial ratios derived from federal tax returns. Ratios for each of about 200 industries are arranged according to company asset size.

Quarterly Financial Report for Manufacturing, Mining, and Trade Corporations. U.S. Federal Trade Commission and U.S. Securities and Exchange

Commission. Available from U.S. Government Printing Office. • Quarterly. $39.00 per year.

INTERNET DATABASES
Fedstats. Federal Interagency Council on Statistical Policy. Phone: (202)395-7254 • URL: http://www.fedstats.gov • Web site features an efficient search facility for full-text statistics produced by more than 70 federal agencies, including the Census Bureau, the Bureau of Economic Analysis, and the Bureau of Labor Statistics. Boolean searches can be made within one agency or for all agencies combined. Links are offered to international statistical bureaus, including the UN, IMF, OECD, UNESCO, Eurostat, and 20 individual countries. Fees: Free.

NMA. National Mining Association. Phone: (202)463-2625 Fax: (202)463-6152 • URL: http://www.nma.org • Web site provides information on the U. S. coal and mineral industries. Includes "Salient Statistics of the Mining Industry," showing a wide variety of annual data (six years) for coal and non-fuel minerals. Publications of the National Mining Association are described and links are provided to other sites. (National Mining Association formerly known as National Coal Association.) Fees: Free.

ONLINE DATABASES
DRI U.S. Central Database. Data Products Division. • Provides more than 23,000 business, financial, demographic, economic, foreign trade, and industry-related time series for the U.S. Includes national income, population, retail-wholesale trade, price indexes, labor data, housing, industrial production, banking, interest rates, money supply, etc. Time period is generally 1947 to date (some data back to 1929). Updating varies. Inquire as to online cost and availability.

Energyline. Congressional Information Service, Inc. • Provides online citations and abstracts to the literature of all forms of energy: petroleum, natural gas, coal, nuclear power, solar energy, etc. Time period is 1971 to 1993 (closed file). Inquire as to online cost and availability.

GEOARCHIVE. Geosystems. • Citations to literature on geoscience and water. 1974 to present. Monthly updates. Inquire as to online cost and availability.

GEOREF. American Geological Institute. • Bibliography and index of geology and geosciences literature, 1785 to present. Inquire as to online cost and availability.

PERIODICALS AND NEWSLETTERS
Canadian Resources and PennyMines Analyst: The Canadian Newsletter for Penny-Mines Investors Who Insist on Geological Value. MPL Communication, Inc. • Weekly. $157.00 per year. Newsletter. Mainly on Canadian gold mine stocks. Formerly *Canadian PennyMines Analyst.*

Colorado School of Mines Quarterly Review. Colorado School of Mines Press. • Quarterly. $65.00 per year. Formerly *Colorado School of Mines Quarterly.*

Earth and Mineral Sciences. College of Earth and Mineral Sciences. Pennsylvania State University. • Semiannual. Free. Current research in material science, mineral engineering, geosciences, meteorology, geography and mineral economics.

Engineering and Mining Journal (E&MJ). Intertec Publishing Corp. • Monthly. $69.00 per year.

Mines Magazine. Colorado School of Mines Alumni Association, Inc. • Seven times a year. Free to members; other, $30.00 per year.

The Mining Record. Howell International Enterprises. • Weekly. $45.00 per year.

Mining Voice. National Mining Association. • Bimonthly. $36.00 per year. Covers U. S. mining issues and trends, with emphasis on coal. Formerly *Coal Voice.*

Mining Week. National Mining Association. • Weekly. Free to members; non-members, $100.00 per year. Newsletter. Covers legislative, business, research, and other developments of interest to the mining industry.

The Northern Miner: Devoted to the Mineral Resources Industry of Canada. Southam Magazine Group. • Weekly. $87.00 per year.

RESEARCH CENTERS AND INSTITUTES
Colorado School of Mines. Office of Research Development, Golden, CO 80401. Phone: (303)273-3767 Fax: (303)273-3244 E-mail: promig@mines.edu • URL: http://magma.mines.edu/research/.

STATISTICS SOURCES
Annual Survey of Manufactures. Available from U. S. Government Printing Office. • Annual. Prices vary. Issued by the U. S. Census Bureau as an interim update to the *Census of Manufactures.* Includes data on number of manufacturing establishments in various industries, employment, labor costs, value of shipments, capital expenditures, inventories, energy costs, and assets. (See also Census Bureau home page, http://www.census.gov/.).

Business Statistics of the United States. Courtenay M. Slater, editor. Bernan Associates. • 1999. $74.00. Fifth edition. Based on *Business Statistics*, formerly issue by the Bureau of Economic Analysis, U. S. Department of Commerce. Provides basic data for a wide variety of U. S. industries, services, and economic indicators. Most statistics are shown annually for 29 years and monthly for the most recent four years.

Manufacturing Profiles. Available from U. S. Government Printing Office. • Annual. Issued by the U. S. Census Bureau. A printed consolidation of the entire *Current Industrial Report* series, presenting "all the data compiled." Contains statistics on production, shipments, inventories, consumption, exports, imports, and orders for a wide variety of manufactured products. (See also Census Bureau home page, http://www.census.gov/.).

Mineral Commodity Summaries. Available from U. S. Government Printing Office. • Annual. Published by the U. S. Geological Survey, Department of the Interior (http://www.usgs.gov). Contains detailed, five-year data for about 90 nonfuel minerals. Covers a wide range of statistics, including production, imports, exports, consumption, reserves, prices, tariff information, and industry employment. (Two pages are devoted to each mineral.).

Minerals Yearbook. Available from U.S. Government Printing Office. • Annual. Three volumes.

Mining Machinery and Equipment. U.S. Bureau of the Census. • Annual. (Current Industrial Reports MA35F.).

Monthly Bulletin of Statistics. United Nations Publications. • Monthly. $295.00 per year. Provides current data for about 200 countries on a wide variety of economic, industrial, and demographic subjects. Compiled by United Nations Statistical Office.

Quarterly Mining Review. National Mining Association. • Quarterly. $300.00 per year. Contains detailed data on production, shipments, consumption, stockpiles, and trade for coal and various minerals. (Publisher formerly National Coal Association.).

Statistical Yearbook. United Nations Publications. • Annual. $125.00. Contains statistics for about 200 countries on a wide variety of economic, industrial, and demographic topics. Compiled by United Nations Statistical Office.

Survey of Current Business. Available from U. S. Government Printing Office. • Monthly. $49.00 per year. Issued by Bureau of Economic Analysis, U. S. Department of Commerce. Presents a wide variety of business and economic data.

United States Census of Mineral Industries. Bureau of the Census, U.S. Department of Commerce. Available from U.S. Government Printing Office. • Quinquennial.

WEFA Industrial Monitor. John Wiley and Sons, Inc. • Annual. $65.00. Prepared by industry analysts at WEFA, an economic forecasting and consulting firm (originally Wharton Econometric Forecasting Associates). Contains discussions of the outlook for major U. S. industries, with many 10-year forecasts (WEFA Web site is http://www.wefa.com).

TRADE/PROFESSIONAL ASSOCIATIONS
Mining and Metallurgical Society of America. 476 Wilson Ave., Novato, CA 94947-4236. Phone: (415)898-4508 Fax: (415)899-0262 E-mail: akburton@worldnet.att.net • URL: http://www.mmsa.net.

Society for Mining, Metallurgy, and Exploration. P.O. Box 625002, Littleton, CO 80162-5002. Phone: 800-763-3132 or (303)973-9550 or (303)948-4210 Fax: (303)973-3845 E-mail: sme@smenet.org • URL: http://www.smenet.org.

OTHER SOURCES
American Law of Mining: The Rocky Mountain Mineral Law Foundation. Matthew Bender & Co., Inc. • $650.00. Six looseleaf volumes. Annual update.

Infrastructure Industries USA. The Gale Group. • 2001. $240.00. Replaces *Agriculture, Forestry, Fishing, Mining, and Construction USA* and *Transportation and Public Utilities USA*. Presents statistics and projections relating to economic activity in a wide variety of natural resource and construction industries.

MINICOMPUTERS

See: MICROCOMPUTERS AND MINICOMPUTERS

MINING

See: MINES AND MINERAL RESOURCES

MINISTERS OF STATE

See: DIPLOMATIC AND CONSULAR SERVICE

MINORITY BUSINESS

GENERAL WORKS
The Black Manager: Making It in the Corporate World. Floyd Dickens and Jacqueline B. Dickens. AMACOM. • 1991. $22.95. Revised edition. Covers the four following career phases: entry, adjusting, planned growth, and success. Advice on personal and professional development is included.

History of Black Business in America: Capitalism, Race, Entrepreneurship. Juliet E. K. Walker. Available from The Gale Group. • 1998. $45.00. Published by Twayne Publishers. Includes profiles of African American business pioneers. (Evolution of Modern Business Series.).

Women Entrepreneurs: Moving Beyond the Glass Ceiling. Dorothy P. Moore and E. Holly Buttner. Sage Publications, Inc. • 1997. $46.00. Contains profiles of "129 successful female entrepreneurs who previously worked in corporate environments.".

ABSTRACTS AND INDEXES

NTIS Alerts: Business & Economics. National Technical Information Service.

BIOGRAPHICAL SOURCES

African-American Business Leaders: A Biographical Dictionary. John N. Ingham and Lynne B. Feldman. Greenwood Publishing Group, Inc. • 1993. $115.00. Contains extended biographical profiles of 123 African-American individuals prominent in business, from early days in America to recent times.

Who's Who Among African Americans. The Gale Group. • 2000. $175.00. 13th edition. Includes many business leaders.

DIRECTORIES

Black Enterprise: Top Black Businesses. Earl G. Graves Publishing Co. • Annual. $3.95. Lists of 100 black-owned businesses, banks, savings and loan associations, and insurance companies.

D & B Minority-Owned Business Directory. Dun & Bradstreet Information Services. • 2000. Price on application. Regional editions.

National Directory of Minority-Owned Business Firms. Available from The Gale Group. • 2001. $285.00. 11th edition. Published by Business Research Services. Includes more than 47,000 minority-owned businesses.

Regional Directory of Minority-and Women-Owned Business Firms. Business Research Services, Inc. • Annual. Three volumes. $175.00 per volume. Regional editions are Eastern, Central,and Western.

Try Us: National Minority Business Directory. Try Us Resources, Inc. • Annual. $69.00. Over 7,000 minority-owned companies, capable of supplying their goods and services on national or regional levels.

INTERNET DATABASES

MBEMAG. Minority Business Entrepreneur Magazine. Phone: (310)540-9398 Fax: (310)792-8263 E-mail: webmaster@mbemag.com • URL: http://www.mbemag.com • Web site's main feature is the "MBE Business Resources Directory." This provides complete mailing addresses, phone, fax, and Web site addresses (URL) for more than 40 organizations and government agencies having information or assistance for ethnic minority and women business owners. Some other links are "Current Events," "Calendar of Events," and "Business Opportunities." Updating is bimonthly. Fees: Free.

PERIODICALS AND NEWSLETTERS

Black Enterprise. Earl G. Graves Publishing Co. • Monthly. $21.95 per year. Covers careers, personal finances and leisure.

MBI: The National Report on Minority, Women-Owned, and Disadvantaged Businesses. Community Development Services, Inc. CD Publications. • Semimonthly. $372.00 per year. Newsletter. Provides news of affirmative action, government contracts, minority business employment, and education/training for minorities in business. Formerly *Minorities in Business.*

Minority Business Entrepreneur. • Bimonthly. $16.00 per year. Reports on issues "critical to the growth and development of minority and women-owned firms." Provides information on relevant legislation and profiles successful women and minority entrepreneurs.

Women's Business Exclusive: For Women Entrepreneurs. • Bimonthly. $39.00 per year. Newsletter. Reports news and information relating to financing, business procurement initiatives, technical assistance, and policy research. Provides advice on marketing, negotiating, and other management topics.

TRADE/PROFESSIONAL ASSOCIATIONS

Interracial Council for Business Opportunity. 550 Fifth Ave., Suite 2202, New York, NY 10118-2202. Phone: (212)779-4360 Fax: (212)779-4365 • Provides technical and financial assistance to minority business people.

National Association of Minority Women in Business. 906 Grand Ave., Suite 200, Kansas City, MO 64106. Phone: (816)421-3335 Fax: (816)421-3336.

National Minority Supplier Development Council. 1040 W. Sixth Ave., 2nd Fl., New York, NY 10018. Phone: (212)944-2430 Fax: (212)719-9611 • URL: http://www.nmsdcus.org.

Try Us Resources. 2105 Central Ave., N.E., Minneapolis, MN 55418. Phone: (612)781-6819 Fax: (612)781-0109 E-mail: tryusdir.mr.net • URL: http://www.tryusdir.com.

MINORITY MARKETS

ALMANACS AND YEARBOOKS

Research Alert Yearbook: Vital Facts on Consumer Behavior and Attitudes. EPM Communications, Inc. • Annual. $295.00. Provides summaries of consumer market research from the newsletters *Research Alert, Youth Markets Alert, and Minority Markets Alert.* Includes tables, charts, graphs, and textual summaries for 41 subject categories. Sources include reports, studies, polls, and focus groups.

HANDBOOKS AND MANUALS

Hispanic Market Handbook. The Gale Group. • 1995. $85.00. Provides advice on marketing consumer items to Hispanic Americans. Includes case studies and demographic profiles.

PERIODICALS AND NEWSLETTERS

Journal of Ethnic and Multicultural Marketing. Haworth Press, Inc. • Quarterly. Price on application.

Marketing to the Emerging Minorities. EPM Communications, Inc. • Monthly. $295.00 per year. Newsletter on market research relating to African American, Asian American, and U. S. Hispanic populations.

STATISTICS SOURCES

Statistical Handbook on U. S. Hispanics. Frank L. Schick and Renee Schick, editors. Oryx Press. • 1991. $65.00. Includes data on demographics, employment, income, assets, etc. (Statistical Handbook Series).

Statistical Record of Black America. The Gale Group. • 1996. $115.00. Fourth edition. Contains more than 1,000 statistical graphs, tables, and lists arranged in 16 broad subject chapters. Covers population, housing, business, income, education, etc. Includes an extensive bibliography and a detailed subject index.

TRADE/PROFESSIONAL ASSOCIATIONS

National Minority Supplier Development Council. 1040 W. Sixth Ave., 2nd Fl., New York, NY 10018. Phone: (212)944-2430 Fax: (212)719-9611 • URL: http://www.nmsdcus.org.

OTHER SOURCES

The African American Market. Available from MarketResearch.com. • 2000. $2,750.00. Published by Packaged Facts. Provides consumer market data and demographics, with projections to 2004.

The Hispanic Market. Available from MarketResearch.com. • 1999. $2,750.00. Published by Packaged Facts. Provides consumer market data and demographics, with projections to 2004.

MINORITY NEWSPAPERS

GENERAL WORKS

Survey of Black Newspapers in America. Mercer House Press. • 1980. $6.00. (Mass Communication and Journalism Series).

CD-ROM DATABASES

Newspaper Abstracts Ondisc. Bell & Howell Information and Learning. • Monthly. $2,950.00 per year (covers 1989 to date; archival discs are available for 1985-88). Provides cover-to-cover CD-ROM indexing and abstracting of 19 major newspapers, including the *New York Times, Wall Street Journal, Washington Post, Chicago Tribune,* and *Los Angeles Times.*

DIRECTORIES

Hispanic Media and Market Source. SRDS. • Quarterly. $271.00 per year. Provides detailed information on the following Hispanic advertising media in the U. S.: TV, radio, newspapers, magazines, direct mail, outdoor, and special events. Formerly *Hispanic Media and Markets.*

TRADE/PROFESSIONAL ASSOCIATIONS

National Newspaper Publishers Association. 3200 13th St., N.W., Washington, DC 20010. Phone: (202)588-8764 Fax: (202)588-5029 E-mail: nnpadc@nnpa.org • URL: http://www.nnpa.org.

MISSILE INDUSTRY

See: ROCKET INDUSTRY

MOBILE HOME INDUSTRY

See also: PREFABRICATED HOUSE INDUSTRY; RECREATIONAL VEHICLE INDUSTRY

CD-ROM DATABASES

Sourcebooks America CD-ROM. CACI Marketing Systems. • Annual. $1,250.00. Provides the CD-ROM version of *The Sourcebook of ZIP Code Demographics: Census Edition* and *The Sourcebook of County Demographics: Census Edition.*

DIRECTORIES

Manufactured Home Merchandiser Manufactured Home Producers Guide. RLD Group, Inc. • Annual. $10.00. Lists about 163 manufacturers of mobil homes, modular homes and other types of manufactured housing. Includes trade associations. Formerly *Mobile/Manufactured Home Merchandiser Manufactured Home Producers Guide.*

FINANCIAL RATIOS

Annual Statement Studies. Robert Morris Associates: The Association of Lending and Credit Risk Professiona. • Annual. Free to members; non-members, $140.00. Median and quartile financial ratios are given for over 400 kinds of manufacturing, wholesale, retail, construction, and consumer finance establishments. Data is sorted by both asset size and sales volume. Includes a clearly written "Definition of Ratios" and an alphabetical industry index.

INTERNET DATABASES

Fedstats. Federal Interagency Council on Statistical Policy. Phone: (202)395-7254 • URL: http://www.fedstats.gov • Web site features an efficient search facility for full-text statistics produced by more than 70 federal agencies, including the Census Bureau, the Bureau of Economic Analysis, and the

Bureau of Labor Statistics. Boolean searches can be made within one agency or for all agencies combined. Links are offered to international statistical bureaus, including the UN, IMF, OECD, UNESCO, Eurostat, and 20 individual countries. Fees: Free.

ONLINE DATABASES

DRI U.S. Central Database. Data Products Division. • Provides more than 23,000 business, financial, demographic, economic, foreign trade, and industry-related time series for the U.S. Includes national income, population, retail-wholesale trade, price indexes, labor data, housing, industrial production, banking, interest rates, money supply, etc. Time period is generally 1947 to date (some data back to 1929). Updating varies. Inquire as to online cost and availability.

PRICE SOURCES

NADA Appraisal Guides. National Automobile Dealers Association. • Prices and frequencies vary. Guides to prices of used cars, old used cars, motorcycles, mobile homes, recreational vehicles, and mopeds.

STATISTICS SOURCES

Business Statistics of the United States. Courtenay M. Slater, editor. Bernan Associates. • 1999. $74.00. Fifth edition. Based on *Business Statistics*, formerly issue by the Bureau of Economic Analysis, U. S. Department of Commerce. Provides basic data for a wide variety of U. S. industries, services, and economic indicators. Most statistics are shown annually for 29 years and monthly for the most recent four years.

Survey of Current Business. Available from U. S. Government Printing Office. • Monthly. $49.00 per year. Issued by Bureau of Economic Analysis, U. S. Department of Commerce. Presents a wide variety of business and economic data.

TRADE/PROFESSIONAL ASSOCIATIONS

Manufactured Housing Institute. 2101 Wilson Blvd., Suite 610, Arlington, VA 22201-3062. Phone: 800-505-5500 or (703)558-0400 Fax: (703)558-0401 E-mail: info@mfghome.org • URL: http://www.mfghome.org.

MOBILE TELEPHONE INDUSTRY

ABSTRACTS AND INDEXES

Applied Science and Technology Index. H. W. Wilson Co. • 11 times a year. Quarterly and annual cumulations. Service basis for print edition; CD-ROM edition, $1,495.00 per year. Indexes a wide variety of English language technical, industrial, and engineering periodicals.

ALMANACS AND YEARBOOKS

Communication Technology Update. Butterworth-Heinemann. • Annual. $36.95. Reviews technological developments and statistical trends in five key areas: mass media, computers, consumer electronics, communications satellites, and telephony. Includes television, cellular phones, and the Internet. (Focal Press.).

DIRECTORIES

Telecommunications Directory. The Gale Group. • 2000. $595.00. 12th edition. National and international voice, data, facsimile, and video communications services. Formerly *Telecommunications Systems and Services Directory.*

Wireless Industry Directory. Phillips Business Information, Inc. • Annual. $249.00. Lists over 4,000 radio common carriers offering mobile telephone services. Formerly *Cellular Mobile Communications Directory.*

ENCYCLOPEDIAS AND DICTIONARIES

Telecom Lingo Guide. Warren Communication News. • 1996. $60.00. Eighth edition. Defines more than 1,000 words, phrases, and acronyms frequently used in the telecommunications industry.

HANDBOOKS AND MANUALS

Cellular Phone Service. Entrepreneur Media, Inc. • Looseleaf. $59.50. A practical guide to starting a business for the servicing of cellular (mobile) telephones. Covers profit potential, start-up costs, market size evaluation, owner's time required, site selection, lease negotiation, pricing, accounting, advertising, promotion, etc. (Start-Up Business Guide No. E1268.).

Digital Cellular Telecommunications Systems. Douglas A. Kerr. McGraw-Hill. • 1997. $50.00.

Inside Cellular: An Operating Manual for Dealers, Carriers, and Investors. Kim A. Mayyasi. Brick House Publishing Co. • $95.00. Looseleaf.

Satellite-Based Cellular Communications. Bruno Pattan. McGraw-Hill. • 1997. $69.00. (Telecommunications Series).

ONLINE DATABASES

Applied Science and Technology Index Online. H. W. Wilson Co. • Provides online indexing of 400 major scientific, technical, industrial, and engineering periodicals. Time period is 1983 to date. Monthly updates. Inquire as to online cost and availability.

PERIODICALS AND NEWSLETTERS

Convergence: The Journal of Research Into New Media Technologies. Chilton Co. • Monthly. Individuals, $60,00 per year; institutions, $120.00 per year. Covers the merging of communications technologies. Includes telecommunications networks, interactive TV, multimedia, wireless phone service, and electronic information services.

Mobile Computing and Communication. EMAP USA. • Monthly. $11.97 per year. Covers cellular phones, notebook computers, and other portable electronic items. New products are featured. Formerly *Mobile Office.*

PICA Bulletin: News and Analysis for the Personal Communication Industry. Personal Communications Industry Association. • Weekly. $550.00 per year.

RCR (Radio Communications Report): The Newspaper for the Wireless Communications Industry. RCR Publications/Crain Communications. • Weekly. $39.00 per year. Covers news of the wireless communications industry, including business and financial developments.

Wireless Business and Technology: Products and Systems for the Mobile Communicattions Marketplace. Phillips Business Information, Inc. • Monthly. Free to qualified personnel. Trade journal for mobile radio and telephone dealers. Incorporates *Wireless Product News.*

Wireless Integration: Solutions for Enterprise Decision Makers. PennWell Corp., Advanced Technology Div. • Bimonthly. $48.00 per year. Edited for networking and communications managers. Special issues cover the wireless office, wireless intranet/Internet, mobile wireless, telemetry, and buyer's guide directory information.

Wireless Review: Intelligence for Competitive Providers. Intertec Publishing Corp. • Semimonthly. $48.00 per year. Covers business and technology developments for wireless service providers. Includes special issues on a wide variety of wireless topics. Formed by merger of *Cellular Business* and *Wireless World.*

Wireless Week. Cahners Business Information. • 51 times a year. $59.00 per year. Covers news of cellular telephones, mobile radios, communications satellites, microwave transmission, and the wireless industry in general.

STATISTICS SOURCES

U. S. Industry and Trade Outlook: The McGraw-Hill Companies and the U.S. Department of Commerce/ International Trade Administration. Datapso Research Corp. • Annual. $69.95. Produced by the International Trade Administration, U. S. Department of Commerce, in a "public-private" partnership with DRI/McGraw-Hill and Standard & Poor's. Provides basic data, outlook for the current year, and "Long-Term Prospects" (five-year projections) for a wide variety of products and services. Includes high technology industries. Formerly *U. S. Industrial Outlook.*

TRADE/PROFESSIONAL ASSOCIATIONS

Cellular Telecommunications Industry Association. 1250 Connecticut Ave., N.W., Suite 200, Washington, DC 20036. Phone: (202)785-0081 Fax: (202)785-0721 • Promotes the commercial development of cellular radiotelephone communications.

Personal Communications Industry Association. 500 Montgomery St., No. 700, Alexandria, VA 22314. Phone: 800-759-0300 or (703)739-0300 Fax: (703)836-1608 • URL: http://www.pcia.com • Promotes development of industry standards for mobile telephone systems. Also concerned with the advertising and marketing of mobile telephones.

Wireless Dealers Association. 9746 Tappanbeck Dr., Houston, TX 77055. Phone: 800-624-6918 Fax: 800-820-2284 E-mail: mail@wirelessindustry.com • URL: http://www.wirelessindustry.com • Members are individuals working within the cellular mobile telephone industry.

OTHER SOURCES

Major Telecommunications Companies of the World. Available from The Gale Group. • 2001. $855.00. Fourth edition. Published by Graham & Whiteside. Contains detailed information and trade names for more than 4,000 important telecommunications companies in various countries.

Wireless Data Networks. Warren Publishing Inc. • 1998. $1,995.00. Fourth edition. Presents market research information relating to cellular data networks, paging networks, packet radio networks, satellite systems, and other areas of wireless communication. Contains "summaries of recent developments and trends in wireless markets.".

MODEMS

See: COMPUTER COMMUNICATIONS

MODULAR CONSTRUCTION

See: PREFABRICATED HOUSE INDUSTRY

MOLASSES INDUSTRY

INTERNET DATABASES

USDA. United States Department of Agriculture. Phone: (202)720-2791 E-mail: agsec@usda.gov • URL: http://www.usda.gov • The USDA home page has six sections: News and Information; What's New; About USDA; Agencies; Opportunities; Search and Help. Keyword searching is offered from the USDA home page and from various individual agency home pages. Agencies are the Economic Research Service, Agricultural Marketing Service, National Agricultural Statistics Service, National Agricultural Library, and about 12 others. Updating varies. Fees: Free.

PERIODICALS AND NEWSLETTERS

Molasses Market News. U.S. Dept. of Agriculture, Agricultural Marketing Service. • Weekly. Provides the market news on molasses and its imports and exports.

PRICE SOURCES

Feedstuffs: The Weekly Newspaper for Agribusiness. ABC, Inc. • Weekly. $109.00 per year.

STATISTICS SOURCES

Agricultural Statistics. Available from U. S. Government Printing Office. • Annual. Produced by the National Agricultural Statistics Service, U. S. Department of Agriculture. Provides a wide variety of statistical data relating to agricultural production, supplies, consumption, prices/price-supports, foreign trade, costs, and returns, as well as farm labor, loans, income, and population. In many cases, historical data is shown annually for 10 years. In addition to farm data, includes detailed fishery statistics.

Sugar and Sweetener Situation and Outlook. Available from U. S. Government Printing Office. • Three times per year. $11.00 per year. Issued by Economic Research Service, U. S. Department of Agriculture. Provides current statistical information on supply, demand, and prices.

MONETARY POLICY

See: ECONOMIC POLICY; MONEY

MONEY

See also: COINS AS AN INVESTMENT; FOREIGN EXCHANGE; INFLATION; INTEREST; PAPER MONEY

GENERAL WORKS

Financial Institutions and Markets. Robert W. Kolb and Ricardo J. Rodriguez. Blackwell Publishers. • 1996. $77.95. Contains 40 articles (chapters) by various authors on U. S. financial markets and other topics. Includes separate chapters on the International Monetary Fund, inflation, monetary policy, the national debt, bank failures, derivatives, stock prices, initial public offerings, government bonds, pensions, foreign exchange, international markets, and other subjects.

Money, Banking, and Financial Markets. Lloyd Thomas. McGraw-Hill. • 1996. $82.50.

Money, Banking, and the Economy. Thomas Mayer and others. W. W. Norton & Co., Inc. • 1996. $85.50. Sixth edition.

Money: Its Origins, Development, Debasement, and Prospects. John H. Wood. American Institute for Economic Research. • 1999. $10.00. A politically conservative view of monetary history, the gold standard, banking systems, and inflation. Includes a list of references. (Economic Education Bulletin.).

Money Madness: Strange Manias and Extraordinary Schemes On and Off Wall Street. John M. Waggoner. McGraw-Hill Professional. • 1990. $26.00.

Money: Who Has How Much and Why. Andrew Hacker. Available from Simon & Schuster Trade. • 1998. $13.00. Published by Scribner's Reference. A discourse on the distribution of wealth in America, with emphasis on the gap between rich and poor.

ABSTRACTS AND INDEXES

Banking Information Index. U M I Banking Information Index. • Monthly. Price on application. Covers a wide variety of banking, business, and financial subjects in periodicals. Formerly *Banking Literature Index.*

Business Periodicals Index. H. W. Wilson Co. • Monthly, except August, with quarterly and annual cumulations. Service basis for print edition; CD-ROM edition, $1,495.00 per year.

ALMANACS AND YEARBOOKS

World Currrency Yearbook. International Currency Analysis, Inc. • Annual. $250.00. Directory of more than 110 central banks worldwide.

CD-ROM DATABASES

EconLit. Available from SilverPlatter Information, Inc. • Monthly. Single-user, $1,600.00 per year. Multi-user, $2,400.00 per year. Provides CD-ROM citations, with abstracts, to articles from more than 500 economics journals. Time period is 1969 to date. Produced by the American Economic Association.

DIRECTORIES

Futures Guide to Computerized Trading. Futures Magazine, Inc. • Annual. $10.00. "A directory of products and services for the computerized trader." Provides information on computer software applications for commodity traders and money managers, including trading methods and technical analysis.

Futures Magazine SourceBook: The Most Complete List of Exchanges, Companies, Regulators, Organizations, etc., Offering Products and Services to the Futures and Options Industry. Futures Magazine, Inc. • Annual. $19.50. Provides information on commodity futures brokers, trading method services, publications, and other items of interest to futures traders and money managers.

Money Market Directory of Pension Funds and Their Investment Managers. Money Market Directories, Inc. • Annual. $995.00. Institutional funds and managers.

Plunkett's Financial Services Industry Almanac: The Leading Firms in Investments, Banking, and Financial Information. Available from Plunkett Research, Ltd. • Annual. $245.00. Discusses important trends in various sectors of the financial industry. Five hundred major banking, credit card, investment, and financial services companies are profiled.

ENCYCLOPEDIAS AND DICTIONARIES

Blackwell Encyclopedic Dictionary of Finance. Dean Paxson and Douglas Wood, editors. Blackwell Publishers. • 1997. $110.00. The editors are associated with the University of Manchester. Contains definitions of key terms combined with longer articles written by various U. S. and foreign business educators. Includes bibliographies and index. (Blackwell Encyclopedia of Management Series).

Dictionary of Finance and Investment Terms. John Downes and Jordan E. Goodman. Barron's Educational Series, Inc. • 1998. $12.95. Fifth revised edition. Provides clear explanations of more than 5,000 business, banking, financial, investment, and tax terms. Includes a separate list of financial abbreviations and acronyms.

Encyclopedia of Banking and Finance. Charles J. Woelfel. McGraw-Hill Professional. • 1996. $50.00. 10th revised edition.

The New Palgrave Dictionary of Money and Finance. Peter Newman and others, editors. Groves Dictionaries. • 1998. $550.00. Three volumes. Consists of signed essays on over 1,000 financial topics, each with a bibliography. Covers a wide variety of financial, monetary, and investment areas. A detailed subject index is provided.

FINANCIAL RATIOS

Major Financial Institutions of the World. Available from The Gale Group. • 2001. $855.00. Fourth edition. Two volumes. Published by Graham & Whiteside. Contains detailed information on more than 7,500 important financial institutions in various countries. Includes banks, investment companies, and insurance companies.

Money of the Mind: Borrowing and Lending in America from the Civil War to Michael Milken. James Grant. Farrar, Straus, and Giroux, LLC. • 1992. $16.00. A critical anlysis by the editor of *Grant's Interest Rate Observer.*

HANDBOOKS AND MANUALS

Derivatives: A Comprehensive Resource for Options, Futures, Interest Rate Swaps, and Mortgage Securities. Fred D. Arditti. Harvard Business School Press. • 1996. $60.00. Published by Harvard Business School Press. Provides detailed explanations of various kinds of financial derivatives (options, futures, swaps, etc.) and their trading tactics, uses, and risks. (Financial Management Association Survey and Synthesis Series).

Dynamic Asset Allocation: Strategies for the Stock, Bond, and Money Markets. David A. Hammer. John Wiley and Sons, Inc. • 1991. $49.95. A practical guide to the distribution of investment portfolio funds among various kinds of assets. (Finance Editions Series).

Monetary Policy and Reserve Requirements Handbook. U.S. Federal Reserve System. Board of Governors Publications Services, Room MS-1. • Annual. $75.00.

INTERNET DATABASES

BanxQuote Banking, Mortgage, and Finance Center. BanxQuote, Inc. Phone: 800-765-3000 or (212)643-8000 Fax: (212)643-0020 E-mail: info@banx.com • URL: http://www.banx.com • Web site quotes interest rates paid by banks around the country on various savings products, as well as rates paid by consumers for automobile loans, mortgages, credit cards, home equity loans, and personal loans. Also provided: stock quotes, indexes, stock options, futures trading data, economic indicators, and links to many other financial sites. Daily updates. Fees: Free.

Bureau of Economic Analysis (BEA). U. S. Department of Commerce, Bureau of Economic Analysis. Phone: (202)606-9900 Fax: (202)606-5310 E-mail: webmaster@bea.doc.gov • URL: http://www.bea.doc.gov • Web site includes "News Release Information" covering national, regional, and international economic estimates from the BEA. Highlights of releases appear online the same day, complete text and tables appear the next day. "Recent News Releases" section provides titles for past nine months, with links. "BEA Data and Methodology" includes "Frequently Requested NIPA Data" (national income and product accounts, such as gross domestic product and personal income). Other statistics are available. Fees: Free.

Fedstats. Federal Interagency Council on Statistical Policy. Phone: (202)395-7254 • URL: http://www.fedstats.gov • Web site features an efficient search facility for full-text statistics produced by more than 70 federal agencies, including the Census Bureau, the Bureau of Economic Analysis, and the Bureau of Labor Statistics. Boolean searches can be made within one agency or for all agencies combined. Links are offered to international statistical bureaus, including the UN, IMF, OECD, UNESCO, Eurostat, and 20 individual countries. Fees: Free.

The Financial Post (Web site). National Post Online (Hollinger/CanWest). Phone: (244)383-2300 Fax: (416)383-2443 • URL: http://www.nationalpost.com/financialpost/ • Provides a broad range of Canadian business news online, with daily updates. Includes news, opinion, and special reports, as well as "Investing," "Money Rates,"

"Market Watch," and "Daily Mutual Funds." Allows advanced searching (Boolean operators), with links to various other sites. Fees: Free.

Futures Online. Oster Communications, Inc. Phone: 800-601-8907 or (319)277-1278 Fax: (319)277-7982 • URL: http://www.futuresmag.com • Web site presents updates of *Futures* magazine and links to other futures-related sites. Includes "Futures Industry News," "Technical Talk," "Today's Hot Markets," "Futures Talk" (forums), "Futures Library" (archives, 1993 to date), and other features. Keyword searching is available. Updating: daily. Fees: Free.

Wall Street Journal Interactive Edition. Dow Jones & Co., Inc. Phone: 800-369-2834 or (212)416-2000 Fax: (212)416-2658 E-mail: inquiries@interactive.wsj.com • URL: http://www.wsj.com • Fee-based Web site providing online searching of worldwide information from the *The Wall Street Journal.* Includes "Company Snapshots," "The Journal's Greatest Hits," "Index to Market Data," "14-Day Searchable Archive," "Journal Links," etc. Financial price quotes are available. Fees: $49.00 per year; $29.00 per year to print subscribers.

ONLINE DATABASES

ABI/INFORM. Bell & Howell Information and Learning. • Provides online indexing to business-related material occurring in over 1,000 periodicals from 1971 to the present. Inquire as to online cost and availability.

Banking Information Source. Bell & Howell Information and Learning. • Provides indexing and abstracting of periodical and other literature from 1982 to date, with weekly updates. Covers the financial services industry: banks, savings institutions, investment houses, credit unions, insurance companies, and real estate organizations. Emphasis is on marketing and management. Inquire as to online cost and availability. (Formerly *FINIS: Financial Industry Information Service.*).

DRI Financial and Credit Statistics. Data Products Division. • Contains U. S. and international statistical data relating to money markets, interest rates, foreign exchange, banking, and stock and bond indexes. Time period is 1973 to date, with continuous updating. Inquire as to online cost and availability.

DRI U.S. Central Database. Data Products Division. • Provides more than 23,000 business, financial, demographic, economic, foreign trade, and industry-related time series for the U.S. Includes national income, population, retail-wholesale trade, price indexes, labor data, housing, industrial production, banking, interest rates, money supply, etc. Time period is generally 1947 to date (some data back to 1929). Updating varies. Inquire as to online cost and availability.

EconLit. American Economic Association. • Covers the worldwide literature of economics as contained in selected monographs and about 550 journals. Subjects include microeconomics, macroeconomics, economic history, inflation, money, credit, finance, accounting theory, trade, natural resource economics, and regional economics. Time period is 1969 to present, with monthly updates. Inquire as to online cost and availability.

Wilson Business Abstracts Online. H. W. Wilson Co. • Indexes and abstracts 600 major business periodicals, plus the *Wall Street Journal* and the business section of the *New York Times*. Indexing is from 1982, abstracting from 1990, with the two newspapers included from 1993. Updated weekly. Inquire as to online cost and availability. (*Business Periodicals Index* without abstracts is also available online.).

PERIODICALS AND NEWSLETTERS

Applied Financial Economics. Routledge Journals. • Bimonthly. Individuals, $648.00 per year; institutions, $1,053.00 per year. Covers practical aspects of financial economics, banking, and monetary economics. Supplement to *Applied Economics*.

Bank Credit Analyst. BCA Publications Ltd. • Monthly. $695.00 per year. "The independent monthly forecast and analysis of trends in business conditions and major investment markets based on a continuous appraisal of money and credit flows." Includes many charts and graphs relating to money, credit, and securities in the U. S.

Bank Rate Monitor: The Weekly Financial Rate Reporter. Advertising News Service, Inc. • Weekly. $895.00 per year. Newsletter. Includes online addition and monthly supplement. Provides detailed information on interest rates currently paid by U. S. banks and savings institutions.

Blue Chip Financial Forecasts: What Top Analysts are Saying About U. S. and Foreign Interest Rates, Monetary Policy, Inflation, and Economic Growth. Aspen Publishers, Inc. • Monthly. $654.00 per year. Newsletter. Gives forecasts about a year in advance for interest rates, inflation, currency exchange rates, monetary policy, and economic growth rates.

Financial Markets, Institutions, and Instruments. New York University, Salomon Center. Blackwell Publishers. • Five times a year. $219.00 per year. Edited to "bridge the gap between the academic and professional finance communities." Special fifth issue each year provides surveys of developments in four areas: money and banking, derivative securities, corporate finance, and fixed-income securities.

Financial Times [London]. Available from FT Publications, Inc. • Daily, except Sunday. $184.00 per year. An international business and financial newspaper, featuring news from London, Paris, Frankfurt, New York, and Tokyo. Includes worldwide stock and bond market data, commodity market data, and monetary/currency exchange information.

Futures: News, Analysis, and Strategies for Futures, Options, and Derivatives Traders. Futures Magazine, Inc. • Monthly. $39.00 per year. Edited for institutional money managers and traders, brokers, risk managers, and individual investors or speculators. Includes special feature issues on interest rates, technical indicators, currencies, charts, precious metals, hedge funds, and derivatives. Supplements available.

Global Finance. Global Finance Media, Inc. • Monthly. $300.00 per year. Edited for corporate financial executives and money managers responsible for "cross-border" financial transactions.

Grant's Interest Rate Observer. James Grant, editor. Interest Rate Publishing Corp. • Biweekly. $495.00 per year. Newsletter containing detailed analysis of money-related topics, including interest rate trends, global credit markets, fixed-income investments, bank loan policies, and international money markets.

IMF Survey. International Monetary Fund, Publication Services. • 23 times a year. $79.00 per year. Newsletter. Covers IMF activities in international finance, trade, commodities, and foreign exchange. Editions in English, French, and Spanish.

International Bank Credit Analyst. BCA Publications Ltd. • Monthly. $795.00 per year. "A monthly forecast and analysis of currency movements, interest rates, and stock market developments in the principal countries, based on a continuous appraisal of money and credit trends worldwide." Includes many charts and graphs providing international coverage of money, credit, and securities.

International Currency Review. World Reports Ltd. • Quarterly. $475.00 per year.

International Market Alert. International Reports, Inc. • Daily. Prices varies. Newsletter. Covers activities of central banks, foreign exchange markets, and New York bond and money markets. Gives specific hedging advice for major currencies. Available online.

InvesTech Market Analyst: Technical and Monetary Investment Analysis. InvesTech Research. • Every three weeks. $190.00 per year. Newsletter. Provides interpretation of monetary statistics and Federal Reserve actions, especially as related to technical analysis of stock market price trends.

Journal of Money, Credit and Banking. Paul D. Evans, editor. Ohio State University Press. • Quarterly. Individuals $48.00 per year; institutions, $135.00 per year. Reports major findings in the study of financial markets, monetary and fiscal policy credit markets, money and banking, portfolio management and related subjects.

Money. Time Inc. • Monthly. $39.95 per year. Covers all aspects of family finance; investments, careers, shopping, taxes, insurance, consumerism, etc.

Money Reporter: The Insider's Letter for Investors Whose Interest is More Interest. MPL Communication, Inc. • Biweekly. $197.00 per year. Newsletter. Supplement available, *Monthly Key Investment.*Canadian interest-bearing deposits and investments.

The Moneyletter. IBC-Donoghue, Inc. • Semimonthly. $109.00 per year. Newsletter giving specific advice on interest rates, trends, money market funds, bond funds, and equity mutual funds. Formerly *Donoghue's Moneyletter.*

One Hundred Highest Yields Among Federally-Insured Banks and Savings Institutions. Advertising News Service, Inc. • Weekly. $124.00 per year. Newsletter.

Powell Monetary Analyst. Larson M. Powell, editor. Reserve Research Ltd. • Biweekly. $285.00 per year. Newsletters. Information on precious metals, coins and curriencies.

The Wall Street Journal. Dow Jones & Co., Inc. • Daily. $175.00 per year. Covers news and trends relating to business, industry, finance, the economy, and international commerce. Provides extensive price and other data for the securities, commodity, options, futures, foreign exchange, and money markets.

Your Money. Consumers Digest, Inc. • Bimonthly. $25.97 per year. Provides information and advice on personal finance and investments.

RESEARCH CENTERS AND INSTITUTES

Financial Institutions Center. University of Florida, College of Business Administration, 327 Business Bldg., Gainesville, FL 32611. Phone: (352)392-2610 • Studies monetary policy and the regulation of financial institutions.

Ludwig Von Mises Institute for Austrian Economics. 518 W. Magnolia Ave., Auburn, AL 36832. Phone: (334)321-2100 Fax: (334)321-2119 E-mail: mail@mises.org • URL: http://www.mises.org.

Rodney L. White Center for Financial Research. University of Pennsylvania, 3254 Steinberg Hall-Dietrich Hall, Philadelphia, PA 19104. Phone: (215)898-7616 Fax: (215)573-8084 E-mail: rlwtcr@finance.wharton.upenn.edu • URL: http://www.finance.wharton.upenn.edu/~rlwctr • Research areas include financial management, money markets, real estate finance, and international finance.

STATISTICS SOURCES

The AIER Chart Book. AIER Research Staff. American Institute for Economic Research. • Annual. $3.00. A compact compilation of long-range charts ("Purchasing Power of the Dollar," for example, goes back to 1780) covering various aspects of the U. S. economy. Includes inflation, interest rates, debt, gold, taxation, stock prices, etc. (Economic Education Bulletin.).

Business Statistics of the United States. Courtenay M. Slater, editor. Bernan Associates. • 1999. $74.00. Fifth edition. Based on *Business Statistics*, formerly issue by the Bureau of Economic Analysis, U. S. Department of Commerce. Provides basic data for a wide variety of U. S. industries, services, and economic indicators. Most statistics are shown annually for 29 years and monthly for the most recent four years.

Daily Treasury Statement: Cash and Debt Operations of the United States Treasury. Available from U. S. Government Printing Office. • Daily, except Saturdays, Sundays, and holidays. $855.00 per year. (Financial Management Service, U. S. Treasury Department.).

Federal Reserve Bulletin. U.S. Federal Reserve System. • Monthly. $25.00 per year. Provides statistics on banking and the economy, including interest rates, money supply, and the Federal Reserve Board indexes of industrial production.

International Financial Statistics. International Monetary Fund, Publications Services. • Monthly. Individuals, $246.00 per year; libraries, $123.00 per year. Includes a wide variety of current data for individual countries in Europe and elsewhere. Annual issue available. Editions available in French and Spanish.

Money Stock Liquid Assets, and Debt Measures, in Billions of Dollars. U.S. Federal Reserve System. U.S. Board of Governors. • Weekly. $35.00 per year.

Selected Interest Rates. U.S. Federal Reserve System. • Weekly release, $20.00 per year; monthly release, $5.00 per year.

Survey of Current Business. Available from U. S. Government Printing Office. • Monthly. $49.00 per year. Issued by Bureau of Economic Analysis, U. S. Department of Commerce. Presents a wide variety of business and economic data.

Treasury Bulletin. Available from U. S. Government Printing Office. • Quarterly. $39.00 per year. Issued by the Financial Management Service, U. S. Treasury Department. Provides data on the federal budget, government securities and yields, the national debt, and the financing of the federal government in general.

TRADE/PROFESSIONAL ASSOCIATIONS

International Monetary Fund. 700 19th St., N.W., Washington, DC 20431. Phone: (202)623-7000 Fax: (202)623-4661.

OTHER SOURCES

Factiva. Dow Jones Reuters Business Interactive, LLC. • Fee-based Web site provides "global news and business information through Web sites and content integration solutions." Includes Dow Jones and Reuters newswires, The Wall Street Journal, and more than 7,000 other sources of current news, historical articles, market research reports, and investment analysis. Content includes 96 major U. S. newspapers, 900 non-English sources, trade publications, media transcripts, country profiles, news photos, etc.

I B C's Money Fund Report. IBC Financial Data, Inc. • Weekly. $975.00 per year. Looseleaf. Contains detailed information on about 1,000 U. S. money market funds, including portfolios and yields. Formerly *Money Fund Report.*

Infogate. Infogate, Inc. • Web site provides current news and information on seven "channels": News, Fun, Sports, Info, Finance, Shop, and Travel. Among the content partners are Business Wire, CBS MarketWatch, CNN, Morningstar, Standard & Poor's, and Thomson Investors Network. Fees: Free, but downloading of Infogate software is required (includes personalized news feature). Updating is continuous. Formerly Pointcast Network.

Nexis.com. Lexis-Nexis Group. • Fee-based Web site offers searching of about 2.8 billion documents in some 30,000 news, business, and legal information sources. Features include a subject directory covering 1,200 topics in 34 categories and a Company Dossier containing information on more than 500,000 public and private companies. Boolean searching is offered.

Quarterly Report on Money Fund Performance. IBC-Donoghue, Inc. • Quarterly. $525.00 per year. Provides expense ratio and yield data for about 1,000 money market funds in the U. S.

The Value of a Dollar: Millennium Edition, 1860-1999. Grey House Publishing. • 1999. $135.00. Second edition. Shows the actual prices of thousands of items available to consumers from the Civil War era to recent years. Includes selected data on consumer expenditures, investments, income, and jobs. (Universal Reference Publications.).

MONEY MARKET

See: MONEY

MONEY MARKET FUNDS

See: INVESTMENT COMPANIES

MONEY RAISING

See: BUSINESS START-UP PLANS AND PROPOSALS; FUND-RAISING; VENTURE CAPITAL

MONEY RATES

See: INTEREST

MONOPOLIES

See: ANTITRUST ACTIONS

MORALE, INDUSTRIAL

See: HUMAN RELATIONS

MORTALITY

See: VITAL STATISTICS

MORTGAGE BANKS

See also: MORTGAGES

DIRECTORIES

Crittenden Directory of Real Estate Financing. Crittenden Research, Inc. • Semiannual. $399.00 per year. Included with subscription to weekly *Crittenden Report on Real Estate Financing.* Provides information on major U. S. real estate lenders.

Directory of State and Local Mortgage Bankers Association. Mortgage Bankers Association of America. • Irregular. $50.00.

FINANCIAL RATIOS

MBA Mortgage Banking Performance Report. Mortgage Bankers Association of America. • Quarterly. $400.00 per year, including annual summary. Annual summary only is $175.00. Contains the following kinds of data for mortgage banking companies: balance sheet, income statement, operating ratios, performance ratios.

HANDBOOKS AND MANUALS

Residential Mortgage Lending: From Application to Servicing. Institute of Financial Education. • 1998. $64.95. Fifth edition. A guide for bankers.

PERIODICALS AND NEWSLETTERS

Crittenden Report on Real Estate Financing: The Nation's Leading Weekly Newsletter on Real Estate Finance. Crittenden Research, Inc. • Weekly. $395.00 per year. Newsletter on real estate lending and mortgages. Includes semiannual *Crittenden Directory of Real Estate Financing.*

Mortgage Banking. Mortgage Bankers Association of America. • Monthly. $45.00 per year.

TRADE/PROFESSIONAL ASSOCIATIONS

Mortgage Bankers Association of America. c/o Janice Stango, 1125 15th St., N.W., Washington, DC 20005. Phone: (202)861-6500 Fax: (202)785-2967.

OTHER SOURCES

Information, Finance, and Services USA. The Gale Group. • 2001. $240.00. Replaces *Service Industries USA* and *Finance, Insurance, and Real Estate USA.* Presents statistics and projections relating to economic activity in a wide variety of non-manufacturing areas.

MORTGAGES

See also: MORTGAGE BANKS; REAL ESTATE INVESTMENTS

GENERAL WORKS

The Lifetime Book of Money Management. Grace W. Weinstein. Visible Ink Press. • 1993. $15.95. Third edition. Gives popularly-written advice on investments, life and health insurance, owning a home, credit, retirement, estate planning, and other personal finance topics.

Real Estate Finance and Investments. William B. Brueggeman and Jeffrey Fisher. McGraw-Hill. • 1996. $68.25. 10th edition. Covers mortgage loans, financing, risk analysis, income properties, land development, real estate investment trusts, and related topics.

Tips and Traps When Mortgage Hunting. Robert Irwin. McGraw-Hill. • 1995. $12.95. Second revised edition. Contains practical advice for home buyers and small real estate investors.

DIRECTORIES

Crittenden Directory of Real Estate Financing. Crittenden Research, Inc. • Semiannual. $399.00 per year. Included with subscription to weekly *Crittenden Report on Real Estate Financing.* Provides information on major U. S. real estate lenders.

Mortgage & Asset-Based Desk Reference: U. S. Buyside and Sellside Profiles. Capital Access International. • Annual. $395.00. Provides "detailed buyside and sellside profiles and contacts" for the mortgage and asset-based securities market.

Thomson National Directory of Mortgage Brokers. Thomson Financial Publishing. • Semiannual. $295.00 per year. Provides detailed information on 11,000 mortgage brokers in the U. S.

ENCYCLOPEDIAS AND DICTIONARIES

Dictionary of Real Estate. Jae K. Shim and others. John Wiley and Sons, Inc. • 1995. $80.00. Contains 3,000 definitions of commercial and residential real estate terms. Covers appraisal, escrow, investment, finance, mortgages, property management, construction, legal aspects, etc. Includes illustrations and formulas. (Business Dictionaries Series).

Real Estate Dictionary. Michael C. Thomsett. McFarland and Co., Inc., Publishers. • 1988. $38.50.

St. James Encyclopedia of Mortgage and Real Estate Finance. James Newell, editor. St. James Press. • 1991. $55.00. Defines over 1,000 terms related to the buying, selling, and financing of real estate. Includes charts and graphs.

HANDBOOKS AND MANUALS

Derivatives: A Comprehensive Resource for Options, Futures, Interest Rate Swaps, and Mortgage Securities. Fred D. Arditti. Harvard Business School Press. • 1996. $60.00. Published by Harvard Business School Press. Provides detailed explanations of various kinds of financial derivatives (options, futures, swaps, etc.) and their trading tactics, uses, and risks. (Financial Management Association Survey and Synthesis Series).

Handbook of Mortgage-Backed Securities. Frank J. Fabozzi, editor. McGraw-Hill Professional. • 1995. $85.00. Fourth edition.

Homeowner or Tenant? How to Make a Wise Choice. Lawrence S. Pratt. American Institute for Economic Research. • 1997. $6.00. Provides detailed information for making rent or buy decisions. Includes "Mortgage Arithmetic," "Hints for Buyers, Sellers, and Renters," worksheets, mortgage loan interest tables, and other data. (Economic Education Bulletin.).

Modern Real Estate and Mortgage Forms: Basic Forms and Agreements. Alvin L. Arnold. Warren, Gorham and Lamont/RIA Group. • Looseleaf. $130.00. Annual supplementation. Over 1,000 pages of forms.

Monthly Payment Direct Reduction Loan Schedules. Financial Publishing Co. • $75.00. 13th edition.

Mortgage-Backed Securities: Developments and Trends in the Secondary Mortgage Market. Kenneth G. Lore. West Group. • Annual. $196.00.

Mortgage Loan Disclosure Handbook: A Step-by-Step Guide with Forms. West Group. • Annual. $210.00. Covers disclosure requirements that lenders must meet under federal laws and regulations. Discusses the Truth-in-Lending Act, RESPA (Real Estate Settlement Procedures Act), the Equal Credit Opportunity Act, and the Fair Credit Reporting Act.

Real Estate Finance and Investment Manual. Jack Cummings. Prentice Hall. • 1997. $34.95. Second edition.

Real Estate Taxation: A Practitioner's Guide. David F. Windish. CCH, Inc. • 1998. $125.00. Second edition. Serves as a guide to the federal tax consequences of real estate ownership and operation. Covers mortgages, rental agreements, interest, landlord income, forms of ownership, and other tax-oriented topics.

Secondary Mortgage Market: Strategies for Surviving and Thriving in Today's Challenging Markets. McGraw-Hill Professional. • 1992. $70.00. Revised edition.

INTERNET DATABASES

BanxQuote Banking, Mortgage, and Finance Center. BanxQuote, Inc. Phone: 800-765-3000 or (212)643-8000 Fax: (212)643-0020 E-mail: info@banx.com • URL: http://www.banx.com • Web site quotes interest rates paid by banks around the country on various savings products, as well as rates paid by consumers for automobile loans, mortgages, credit cards, home equity loans, and personal loans. Also provided: stock quotes, indexes, stock options, futures trading data, economic indicators, and links to many other financial sites. Daily updates. Fees: Free.

Business Week Online. McGraw-Hill. Phone: (212)512-2762 Fax: (212)512-6590 • URL: http://www.businessweek.com • Web site provides complete contents of current issue of *Business Week* plus "BW Daily" with additonal business news, financial market quotes, and corporate information from Standard & Poor's. Includes various features, such as "Banking Center" with mortgage and interest data, and "Interactive Computer Buying Guide." The "Business Week Archive" is fully searchable back to 1991. Fees: Mostly free, but full-text archive articles are $2.00 each.

Fedstats. Federal Interagency Council on Statistical Policy. Phone: (202)395-7254 • URL: http://www.fedstats.gov • Web site features an efficient search facility for full-text statistics produced by more than 70 federal agencies, including the Census Bureau, the Bureau of Economic Analysis, and the Bureau of Labor Statistics. Boolean searches can be made within one agency or for all agencies combined. Links are offered to international statistical bureaus, including the UN, IMF, OECD, UNESCO, Eurostat, and 20 individual countries. Fees: Free.

ONLINE DATABASES

DRI U.S. Central Database. Data Products Division. • Provides more than 23,000 business, financial, demographic, economic, foreign trade, and industry-related time series for the U.S. Includes national income, population, retail-wholesale trade, price indexes, labor data, housing, industrial production, banking, interest rates, money supply, etc. Time period is generally 1947 to date (some data back to 1929). Updating varies. Inquire as to online cost and availability.

PERIODICALS AND NEWSLETTERS

Affordable Housing Finance. Alexander & Edwards Publishing. • Ten times a year. $119.00 per year. Provides advice and information on obtaining financing for lower-cost housing. Covers both government and private sources.

Apartment Finance Today. Alexander & Edwards Publishing. • Bimonthly. $29.00 per year. Covers mortgages and financial services for apartment developers, builders, and owners.

Crittenden Report on Real Estate Financing: The Nation's Leading Weekly Newsletter on Real Estate Finance. Crittenden Research, Inc. • Weekly. $395.00 per year. Newsletter on real estate lending and mortgages. Includes semiannual *Crittenden Directory of Real Estate Financing.*

Housing Affairs Letter: Weekly Washington Report on Housing. Community Development Services, Inc. CD Publications. • Weekly. $409.00 per year. Newsletter. Covers mortgage activity news, including forecasts of mortgage rates.

Journal of Fixed Income. Institutional Investor. • Quarterly. $325.00 per year. Covers a wide range of fixed-income investments for institutions, including bonds, interest-rate options, high-yield securities, and mortgages.

Mortgage and Real Estate Executives Report. Warren, Gorham and Lamont/RIA Group. • Semimonthly. $159.75 per year. Newsletter. Source of ideas and new updates. Covers the latest opportunities and developments.

Mortgage-Backed Securities Letter. Securities Data Publishing. • Weekly. $1,595.00 per year. Newsletter. Provides news and analysis of the mortgage-backed securities market, including performance reports. (Securities Data Publishing is a unit of Thomson Financial.).

National Mortgage News. Faulkner and Gray. • Weekly. $198.00 per year. Newsletter.

Real Estate Finance. Institutional Investor. • Quarterly. $225.00 per year. Covers real estate for professional investors. Provides information on complex financing, legalities, and industry trends.

Real Estate Finance and Investment. Institutional Investor. • Weekly. $2,105.00 per year. Newsletter for professional investors in commercial real estate. Includes information on financing, restructuring, strategy, and regulation.

RESEARCH CENTERS AND INSTITUTES

Center for Finance and Real Estate. University of California, Los Angeles, John E. Anderson Graduate School of Management, P.O. Box 951481, Los Angeles, CA 90095-1481. Phone: (310)825-1953 Fax: (310)206-5455 E-mail: wtorous@anderson.ucla.edu • URL: http://www.agsm.ucla.edu/acadunit/finance/realestate.

STATISTICS SOURCES

American Housing Survey for the United States in [year]. Available from U. S. Government Printing Office. • Biennial. Issued by the U. S. Census Bureau (http://www.census.gov). Covers both owner-occupied and renter-occupied housing. Includes data on such factors as condition of building, type of mortgage, utility costs, and housing occupied by minorities. (Current Housing Reports, H150.).

Business Statistics of the United States. Courtenay M. Slater, editor. Bernan Associates. • 1999. $74.00. Fifth edition. Based on *Business Statistics*, formerly issue by the Bureau of Economic Analysis, U. S. Department of Commerce. Provides basic data for a wide variety of U. S. industries, services, and economic indicators. Most statistics are shown annually for 29 years and monthly for the most recent four years.

Housing Statistics of the United States. Patrick A. Simmons, editor. Bernan Press. • 2000. $74.00. Third edition. (Bernan Press U.S. Data Book Series).

MBA National Delinquency Survey. Mortgage Bankers Association of America. • Quarterly. $30.00 per year. Provides delinquency and foreclosure data for single-family mortgage loans.

Statistical Information on the Financial Services Industry. American Bankers Association. • Annual. Members, $150.00; non-members, $275.00. Presents a wide variety of data relating to banking and financial services, including consumer economics, personal finance, credit, government loans, capital markets, and international banking.

Survey of Current Business. Available from U. S. Government Printing Office. • Monthly. $49.00 per year. Issued by Bureau of Economic Analysis, U. S. Department of Commerce. Presents a wide variety of business and economic data.

Survey of Mortgage Lending Activity. U.S. Department of Housing and Urban Development. • Monthly.

TRADE/PROFESSIONAL ASSOCIATIONS

Mortgage Insurance Companies of America. 727 15th St., N.W., 12th Fl., Washington, DC 20005. Phone: (202)393-5566 Fax: (202)393-5557.

MOTEL INDUSTRY

See: HOTEL AND MOTEL INDUSTRY

MOTION PICTURE CAMERAS

See: CAMERA INDUSTRY

MOTION PICTURE INDUSTRY

See also: MOTION PICTURE PHOTOGRAPHY; MOTION PICTURE THEATERS

ALMANACS AND YEARBOOKS

Annual Index to Motion Picture Credits. Academy of Motion Picture Arts and Sciences. • Annual. $50.00.

International Motion Picture Almanac: Reference Tool of the Film Industry. Quigley Publishing Co., Inc. • Annual. $100.00. Reference covering the motion picture industry.

Magill's Cinema Annual. The Gale Group. • Annual. $115.00. Provides reviews and facts for new films released each year in the United States. Typically covers about 300 movies, with nine indexes to title, director, screenwriter, actor, music, etc. Includes awards, obituaries, and "up-and- coming" performers of the year.

The Motion Picture Guide Annual. Available from R. R. Bowker. • Annual. $162.00. Published by CineBooks (http://www.cinebooks.com). Provides detailed information on every domestic and foreign film released theatrically in the U. S. during the year covered. Includes annual Academy Award listings and film industry obituaries. Yearly volumes are available for older movies, beginning with the 1987 edition for films of 1986.

BIBLIOGRAPHIES

Films and Audiovisual Information. Available from U. S. Government Printing Office. • Annual. Free. Issued by the Superintendent of Documents. A list of government publications on motion picture and audiovisual topics. Formerly *Motion Pictures, Films and Audiovisual Information.* (Subject Bibliography No. 73.).

BIOGRAPHICAL SOURCES

Celebrity Register. The Gale Group. • 1989. $99.00. Fifth edition. Compiled by Celebrity Services International (Earl Blackwell). Contains profiles of 1,300 famous individuals in the performing arts, sports, politics, business, and other fields.

The Highwaymen: Warriors on the Information Superhighway. Ken Auletta. Harcourt Trade Publications. • 1998. $13.00. Revised expanded edition. Contains critical articles about Ted Turner, Rupert Murdoch, Barry Diller, Michael Eisner, and other key figures in electronic communications, entertainment, and information.

CD-ROM DATABASES

Bowker's Complete Video Directory on Disc. Bowker Electronic Publishing. • Quarterly. $520.00 per year. An extensive CD-ROM directory of video tapes and laserdisks. Includes film reviews from *Variety.*

Hoover's Company Capsules on CD-ROM. Hoover's, Inc. • Quarterly. $349.95 per year (single-user). Provides the CD-ROM version of *Hoover's Handbook of American Business, Hoover's Handbook of Emerging Companies, Hoover's Handbook of World Business, Hoover's Guide to Computer Companies, Hoover's Guide to Media Companies, Hoover's Handbook of Private Companies,* and various regional guides. Includes more than 11,000 profiles of companies.

DIRECTORIES

Celebrity Directory: How to Reach Over 9,000 Movie, TV Stars and Other Famous Celebrities. Axiom Information Resources. • Annual. $39.95. Stars, agents, networks, studios, and other celebrities. Gives names and addresses.

Directors Guild of America Directory of Members. Directors Guild of America. • Annual. $25.00.

Hollywood Creative Directory. • Three times a year. $129.95 per year.$54.95 per issue. Lists more than 1,700 motion picture and television development and production companies in the U. S. (mainly California and New York). Includes names of studio and TV network executives.

Index to AV Producers and Distributors (Educational Audiovisual Materials). National Information Center for Educational Media. c/o Plexus Publishing, Inc. • Biennial. $89.00. A directory listing about 23,300 producers and distributors of all types of audiovisual educational materials.

International Dictionary of Film and Filmmakers. St. James Press. • 1996. $510.00. Second edition. Five volumes. Vol. 1:*Films.* Vol. 2: *Directors.* Vol. 3: *Actors and Actresses.* Vol. 4: *Writers and Production Artists.* Vol. 5: *Title Index.*

International Film Guide. Silman-James Press. • Annual. $24.95. Film production companies, distributors, organizations and government agencies. Also includes film festivals, non-theatrical distributors in the U.S., sources of films for collectors, film archives, services for the industry and film schools.

Plunkett's Entertainment and Media Industry Almanac. Available from Plunkett Research, Ltd. • Biennial. $149.99. Provides profiles of leading firms in online information, films, radio, television, cable, multimedia, magazines, and book publishing. Includes World Wide Web sites, where available, plus information on careers and industry trends.

ENCYCLOPEDIAS AND DICTIONARIES

Film Finance and Distribution: A Dictionary of Terms. John W. Cones. Silman-James Press. • 1992. $24.95. Includes commentary on practical approaches to financing and distribution for novice filmmakers.

Filmmaker's Dictionary. Ralph S. Singleton and James Conrad. National Book Network. • 2000. $22.95. Second edition. Defines technical terms, legal terms, industry jargon, and film slang.

International Film, Television, and Video Acronyms. Matthew Stevens, editor. Greenwood Publishing Group, Inc. • 1993. $85.00. A guide to 3,400 acronyms and 1,400 technical terms.

Multimedia and the Web from A to Z. Patrick M. Dillon and David C. Leonard. Oryx Press. • 1998. $39.95. Second enlarged revised edition. Defines more than 1,500 terms relating to software and hardware in the areas of computing, online technology, telecommunications, audio, video, motion pictures, CD-ROM, and the Internet. Includes acronyms and an annotated bibliography. Formerly *Multimedia Technology from A to Z* (1994).

NTC's Mass Media Dictionary. R. Terry Ellmore. NTC/Contemporary Publishing. • 1993. $24.95. Covers television, radio, newspapers, magazines, film, graphic arts, books, billboards, public relations, and advertising. Terms are related to production, research, audience measurement, audio-video engineering, printing, publishing, and other areas.

FINANCIAL RATIOS

Almanac of Business and Industrial Financial Ratios. Leo Troy. Prentice Hall. • Annual. $99.95. Contains financial ratios derived from federal tax returns. Ratios for each of about 200 industries are arranged according to company asset size.

Annual Statement Studies. Robert Morris Associates: The Association of Lending and Credit Risk Professiona. • Annual. Free to members; non-members, $140.00. Median and quartile financial ratios are given for over 400 kinds of manufacturing, wholesale, retail, construction, and consumer finance establishments. Data is sorted by both asset size and sales volume. Includes a clearly written "Definition of Ratios" and an alphabetical industry index.

The Biz: The Basic Business, Legal, and Financial Aspects of the Film Industry. Schuyler M. Moore. Silman-James Press. • 2000. $26.95. Provides information for independent filmmakers on raising money, business structure, budgeting, loans, legalities, taxation, industry jargon, and other topics. The author is an entertainment industry lawyer.

HANDBOOKS AND MANUALS

Clearance and Copyright: Everything the Independent Filmmaker Needs to Know. Michael C. Donaldson. Silman-James Press. • 1996. $26.95. Covers film rights problems in pre-production, production, post-production, and final release. Includes sample contracts and forms.

Contracts for the Film and Television Industry. Mark Litwak. Silman-James Press. • 1999. $35.95. Second expanded edition. Contains a wide variety of sample entertainment contracts. Includes material on rights, employment, joint ventures, music, financing, production, distribution, merchandising, and the retaining of attorneys.

Entertainment Law. Robert Fremlin. West Group. • $560.00. Looseleaf service. Includes updates. (Entertainment and Communicat Law Series).

Variety International Film Guide. Peter Cowie, editor. Silman-James Press. • Annual. $23.95. Covers the "who, what, where, and when of the international film scene." Includes information from 70 countries on film festivals, top-grossing films, awards, schools, etc.

ONLINE DATABASES

PROMT: Predicasts Overview of Markets and Technology. The Gale Group. • Companies, products, applied technologies and markets. U.S. and international literature coverage, 1972 to date. Inquire as to online cost and availability. Provides abstracts from more than 1,600 publications. Weekly updates.

PERIODICALS AND NEWSLETTERS

Daily Variety: News of the Entertainment Industry. Cahners Business Information. • Daily. $219.00 per year.

Film Journal: International. Sunshine Group. • Monthly. $65.00 per year. Formerly *Film Journal.*

Film Quarterly. University of California Press, Journals Div. • Quarterly. Individuals, $26.00 per year; institutions, $70.00 per year.

The Hollywood Reporter. • Daily. $219.00 per year. Covers the latest news in film, TV, cable, multimedia, music, and theatre. Includes box office grosses and entertainment industry financial data.

SMPTE Journal. Society of Motion Picture and Television Engineers. • Monthly. $125.00 per year.

Variety: The International Entertainment Weekly. Cahners Business Information, Broadcasting and Cable's International Group. • Weekly. $219.00 per year. Contains national and international news of show business, with emphasis on motion pictures and television.

RESEARCH CENTERS AND INSTITUTES

Wisconsin Center for Film and Theater Research. University of Wisconsin-Madison, 816 State St., Madison, WI 53706. Phone: (608)264-6466 Fax: (608)264-6472 E-mail: tbalio@facstaff.wisc.edu • URL: http://www.shsw.wisc.edu/archives/wcftr • Studies the performing arts in America, including theater, cinema, radio, and television.

STATISTICS SOURCES

Standard & Poor's Industry Surveys. Standard & Poor's. • Semiannual. $1,800.00. Two looseleaf volumes. Includes monthly supplements. Provides detailed, individual surveys of 52 major industry groups. Each survey is revised on a semiannual basis. Also includes "Monthly Investment Review" (industry group investment analysis) and monthly "Trends & Projections" (economic analysis).

U. S. Industry and Trade Outlook: The McGraw-Hill Companies and the U.S. Department of Commerce/ International Trade Administration. Datapso Research Corp. • Annual. $69.95. Produced by the International Trade Administration, U. S. Department of Commerce, in a "public-private" partnership with DRI/McGraw-Hill and Standard & Poor's. Provides basic data, outlook for the current year, and "Long-Term Prospects" (five-year projections) for a wide variety of products and services. Includes high technology industries. Formerly *U. S. Industrial Outlook.*

UNESCO Statistical Yearbook. Bernan Press. • Annual. $95.00. Co-published by Bernan Press and the United Nations Educational, Scientific, and Cultural Organization (http://www.unesco.org). Presents statistical data from more than 200 countries on education, technology, research, broadcasting, cinema, book publishing, newspapers, libraries, museums, and population. Includes charts, maps, and graphs.

TRADE/PROFESSIONAL ASSOCIATIONS

Academy of Motion Picture Arts and Sciences. 8949 Wilshire Blvd., Beverly Hills, CA 90211. Phone: (310)247-3000 Fax: (310)247-2600 E-mail: ampas@oscars.org • URL: http://www.oscars.org.

Alliance of Motion Picture and Television Producers. 15503 Ventura Blvd., Encino, CA 91436-3140. Phone: (818)995-3600 Fax: (818)382-1793.

Association of Cinema and Video Laboratories. c/o Frank Ricotta, Technicolor, Inc., 4050 Lankershin Blvd., North Hollywood, CA 91608. Phone: (818)769-8500 Fax: (818)761-4835.

Directors Guild of America. 7920 Sunset Blvd., Hollywood, CA 90046. Phone: (310)289-2000 Fax: (310)289-2024 • URL: http://www.dga.org.

Motion Picture Association of America. 1600 Eye St., N.W., Washington, DC 20006. Phone: (202)293-1966 Fax: (202)296-7410 • URL: http:// www.mpaa.org.

Producers Guild of America. 6363 Sunset Blvd., 9th Fl., Los Angeles, CA 90028. Phone: (310)557-0807 Fax: (310)557-0436 E-mail: thepga@pacbell.net • URL: http://www.producersguild.com.

Society of Motion Picture and Television Engineers. 595 W. Hartsdale Ave., White Plains, NY 10607. Phone: (914)761-1100 Fax: (914)761-3115 E-mail: smpte@smpte.org • URL: http://www.smpte.org.

OTHER SOURCES

Creativity Rules! A Writer's Workbook. John Vorhaus. Silman-James Press. • 2000. $15.95. Covers the practical process of conceiving, outlining, and developing a story, especially for TV or film scripts. Includes "tactics and exercises.".

Movie Money: Understanding Hollywood's Creative Accounting Practices. Bill Daniels and others. Silman-James Press. • 1998. $19.95. Explains the numerous amd mysterious accounting methods used by the film industry to arrive at gross and net profit figures. The authors also discuss profit participation, audits, claims, and negotiating.

Sports and Entertainment Litigation Reporter: National Journal of Record Covering Crititcal Issues in Entertainment Law Field. Andrews Publications. • Monthly. $775.00 per year. Provides reports on lawsuits involving films, TV, cable broadcasting, stage productions, radio, and other areas of the entertainment business.Formerly *Entertainment Litigation Reporter.*

MOTION PICTURE PHOTOGRAPHY

See also: CAMERA INDUSTRY; PHOTOGRAPHIC INDUSTRY

ABSTRACTS AND INDEXES

Art Index. H. W. Wilson Co. • Quarterly. Annual cumulations. Service basis for print edition; CD-ROM edition, $1,495.00 per year. Subject and author index to periodicals in art, architecture, industrial design, city planning, photography, and various related topics.

BIBLIOGRAPHIES

Films and Audiovisual Information. Available from U. S. Government Printing Office. • Annual. Free. Issued by the Superintendent of Documents. A list of government publications on motion picture and audiovisual topics. Formerly *Motion Pictures, Films and Audiovisual Information.* (Subject Bibliography No. 73.).

DIRECTORIES

The SHOOT Directory for Commercial Production and Postproduction. BPI Communications. • Annual. $79.00. Lists production companies, advertising agencies, and sources of professional television, motion picture, and audio equipment.

ENCYCLOPEDIAS AND DICTIONARIES

Film-Video Terms and Concepts: A Focal Handbook. Steven Browne. Butterworth-Heinemann. • 1992. $31.95. Defines production terms, techniques, and jargon relating to motion pictures, television, and the video industry. (Focal Handbook).

Focal Encyclopedia of Photography. Leslie Stroebel and Richard D. Zakia, editors. Butterworth-Heinemann. • 1993. $56.95. Third edition.

HANDBOOKS AND MANUALS

American Cinematographer Manual. Rod Ryan, editor. ASC Holding Corp. • 1993. $49.95. Seventh edition. A pocket size encyclopedia of practical information about cameras, lenses, films, exposure, depth of field, lighting, special effects, etc.

ONLINE DATABASES

Art Index Online. H. W. Wilson Co. • Indexes a wide variety of art-related periodicals, 1984 to date. Monthly updates. Inquire as to online cost and availability.

PERIODICALS AND NEWSLETTERS

American Cinematographer: International Journal of Motion Picture Production Techniques. American Society of Cinematographers. ASC Holding Corp. • Monthly. $40.00 per year.

SHOOT: The Leading Newsweekly for Commercial Production and Postproduction. BPI Communications. • Weekly. $115.00 per year. Covers animation, music, sound design, computer graphics, visual effects, cinematography, and other aspects of television and motion picture production, with emphasis on TV commercials.

SMPTE Journal. Society of Motion Picture and Television Engineers. • Monthly. $125.00 per year.

TRADE/PROFESSIONAL ASSOCIATIONS

American Society of Cinematographers. P.O. Box 2230, Hollywood, CA 90028. Phone: 800-448-0145 or (323)969-4333 Fax: (323)876-4973.

Society of Motion Picture and Television Engineers. 595 W. Hartsdale Ave., White Plains, NY 10607. Phone: (914)761-1100 Fax: (914)761-3115 E-mail: smpte@smpte.org • URL: http://www.smpte.org.

OTHER SOURCES

Videography. United Entertainment Media, Inc. • Monthly. $30.00 per year. Edited for the professional video production industry. Covers trends in technique and technology.

MOTION PICTURE THEATERS

DIRECTORIES

Motion Picture TV and Theatre Directory: For Services and Products. MPE Publications, Inc. • Semiannual. $15.20. Companies providing products and services to the motion picture and television industries.

FINANCIAL RATIOS

Almanac of Business and Industrial Financial Ratios. Leo Troy. Prentice Hall. • Annual. $99.95. Contains financial ratios derived from federal tax returns. Ratios for each of about 200 industries are arranged according to company asset size.

Annual Statement Studies. Robert Morris Associates: The Association of Lending and Credit Risk Professiona. • Annual. Free to members; non-members, $140.00. Median and quartile financial ratios are given for over 400 kinds of manufacturing, wholesale, retail, construction, and consumer finance establishments. Data is sorted by both asset size and sales volume. Includes a clearly written "Definition of Ratios" and an alphabetical industry index.

PERIODICALS AND NEWSLETTERS

Boxoffice: The Business Magazine of the Global Motion Picture Industry. RLD Communication. • Monthly. $40.00 per year.

Film Journal: International. Sunshine Group. • Monthly. $65.00 per year. Formerly *Film Journal.*

TRADE/PROFESSIONAL ASSOCIATIONS

International Theatre Equipment Association. 244 W. 49th St., Suite 200, New York, NY 10019. Phone: (212)246-6460 Fax: (212)265-6428.

National Association of Theatre Owners. 4605 Lankershim Blvd., Suite 340, North Hollywood, CA 91602. Phone: (818)506-1778 Fax: (818)506-0269 E-mail: nato@chq.com • URL: http:// www.hollywood.com/nato.

MOTION PICTURES IN EDUCATION

See: AUDIOVISUAL AIDS IN EDUCATION

MOTION PICTURES IN INDUSTRY

See: AUDIOVISUAL AIDS IN INDUSTRY

MOTION STUDY

See: TIME AND MOTION STUDY

MOTIVATION (PSYCHOLOGY)

See also: INDUSTRIAL PSYCHOLOGY

GENERAL WORKS

Contemporary Sales Force Management. Tony Carter. Haworth Press, Inc. • 1997. $49.95. Emphasis is on motivation of sales personnel. Includes case studies.

ABSTRACTS AND INDEXES

Psychological Abstracts. American Psychological Association. • Monthly. Members, $799.00 per year; individuals and institutions, $1,075.00 per year. Covers the international literature of psychology and the behavioral sciences. Includes journals, technical reports, dissertations, and other sources.

ENCYCLOPEDIAS AND DICTIONARIES

Blackwell Encyclopedic Dictionary of Organizational Behavior. Nigel Nicholson, editor. Blackwell Publishers. • 1995. $105.95. The editor is associated with the London Business School. Contains definitions of key terms combined with longer articles written by various U. S. and foreign business educators. Includes bibliographies and index. *Blackwell Encyclopedia of Management Series.*

Encyclopedia of Human Behavior. Vangipuram S. Ramachandran, editor. Academic Press, Inc. • 1994. $685.00. Four volumes. Contains signed articles on aptitude testing, arbitration, career development, consumer psychology, crisis management, decision making, economic behavior, group dynamics, leadership, motivation, negotiation, organizational behavior, planning, problem solving, stress, work efficiency, and other human behavior topics applicable to business situations.

HANDBOOKS AND MANUALS

Why This Horse Won't Drink: How to Win and Keep Employee Commitment. Ken Matejka. AMACOM. • 1990. $22.95. How to set up programs to build trust and change behavior.

ONLINE DATABASES

PsycINFO. American Psychological Association. • Provides indexing and abstracting of the worldwide literature of psychology and the behavioral sciences. Time period is 1967 to date, with monthly updates. Inquire as to online cost and availability.

PERIODICALS AND NEWSLETTERS

Incentive: Managing and Marketing Through Motivation. Bill Communications, Inc. • Monthly. $55.00 per year.

Learning and Motivation. Academic Press, Inc. Journal Div. • Quarterly. $425.00 per year.

Motivation and Emotion. Plenum Publishing Corp. • Quarterly. $385.00 per year.

The Motivational Manager: Strategies to Increase Morale and Productivity in the Workplace. Lawence Ragan Communications, Inc. • Monthly. $119.00 per year. Newsletter. Emphasis is on participative management.

Positive Leadership: Improving Performance Through Value-Centered Management. Lawence Ragan Communications, Inc. • Monthly. $119.00 per year. Newsletter. Emphasis is on employee motivation, family issues, ethics, and community relations.

Teamwork: Your Personal Guide to Working Successfully with People. Dartnell Corp. • Biweekly. $76.70 per year. Provides advice for employees on human relations, motivation, and team spirit.

MOTIVATION PAMPHLETS

See: PAMPHLETS

MOTIVATION POSTERS

See: POSTERS

MOTOR BUS LINES TIME TABLES

See: TIMETABLES

MOTOR BUSES

See also: TRANSPORTATION INDUSTRY

DIRECTORIES

Russell's Official National Motor Coach Guide: Official Publications of Bus Lines for the United States and Canada. Russell's Guides, Inc. • Monthly. $100.35 per year. Publications of bus lines for the U.S., Canada, and Mexico.

ENCYCLOPEDIAS AND DICTIONARIES

Macmillan Encyclopedia of Transportation. Available from The Gale Group. • 2000. $375.00. Six volumes. Published by Macmillan Reference USA. Covers the business, technology, and history of transportation on land, on water, in the air, and in space. Includes definitions, cross-references, and 200 color illustrations.

FINANCIAL RATIOS

Annual Statement Studies. Robert Morris Associates: The Association of Lending and Credit Risk Professiona. • Annual. Free to members; non-members, $140.00. Median and quartile financial ratios are given for over 400 kinds of manufacturing, wholesale, retail, construction, and consumer finance establishments. Data is sorted by both asset size and sales volume. Includes a clearly written "Definition of Ratios" and an alphabetical industry index.

ONLINE DATABASES

TRIS: Transportation Research Information Service. National Research Council. • Contains abstracts and citations to a wide range of transportation literature, 1968 to present, with monthly updates. Includes references to the literature of air transportation, highways, ships and shipping, railroads, trucking, and urban mass transportation. Formerly *TRIS-ON-LINE.* Inquire as to online cost and availability.

PERIODICALS AND NEWSLETTERS

Bus Ride. Friendship Publications, Inc. • 10 times a year. $35.00 per year.

Commercial Carrier Journal: For Fleet Management. Cahners Business Information. • Monthly. $45.00 per year. Formerly *Chilton's CCJ.*

Fleet Owner. Intertec Publishing Corp. • Monthly. $45.00 per year.

School Bus Fleet. Bobit Publishing Corp. • Bimonthly. $25.00 per year. Includes *Factbook.*

STATISTICS SOURCES

Transit Fact Book. American Public Transit Association. • Annual.

Transportation Statistics Annual Report. Available from U. S. Government Printing Office. • Annual. $21.00. Issued by Bureau of Transportation Statistics, U. S. Department of Transportation. Provides data on operating revenues, expenses, employees, passenger miles (where applicable), and other factors for airlines, automobiles, buses, local transit, pipelines, railroads, ships, and trucks.

TRADE/PROFESSIONAL ASSOCIATIONS

American Bus Association. 1100 New York Ave., N.W., Suite 1050, Washington, DC 20005-3934. Phone: 800-283-2877 or (202)842-1645 Fax: (202)842-0850 E-mail: abainfo@buses.org • URL: http://www.buses.org.

MOTOR CARS

See: AUTOMOBILES

MOTOR HOME INDUSTRY

See: MOBILE HOME INDUSTRY; RECREATIONAL VEHICLE INDUSTRY

MOTOR TRANSPORT

See: TRUCKING INDUSTRY

MOTOR TRUCK INDUSTRY

See: TRUCKING INDUSTRY

MOTOR TRUCK TRAILERS

See: TRUCK TRAILERS

MOTOR TRUCKS

See: TRUCKS (MANUFACTURING)

MOTOR VEHICLE EQUIPMENT INDUSTRY

See: AUTOMOBILE EQUIPMENT INDUSTRY

MOTOR VEHICLE LAW AND REGULATION

See also: INTERSTATE COMMERCE

GENERAL WORKS

What Your Car Really Costs: How to Keep a Financially Safe Driving Record. American Institute for Economic Research. • 1999. $6.00. Contains "Should You Buy or Lease?," "Should You Buy New or Used?," "Dealer Trade-in or Private Sale?," "Lemon Laws," and other car buying information. Includes rankings of specific models for resale value, 1992 to 1998. (Economic Education Bulletin.).

ABSTRACTS AND INDEXES

Current Law Index: Multiple Access to Legal Periodicals. The Gale Group. • Monthly. $650.00 per year. Produced in cooperation with the American Association of Law Libraries. Indexes more than 900 law journals, legal newspapers, and specialty publications from the U.S., Canada, U.K., Ireland, Australia, and New Zealand.

DIRECTORIES

American Association of Motor Vehicle Administrators: Membership Directory. American Association of Motor Vehicle Administrators. • Annual. $100.00.

PERIODICALS AND NEWSLETTERS

AAMVA Bulletin. American Association of Motor Vehicle Administrators. • Monthly. $25.00.

Motor Vehicle Regulation: State Capitals. Wakeman-Walworth, Inc. • Weekly. $245.00 per year. Formerly *From the State Capitals: Motor Vehicle Regulation.*

RESEARCH CENTERS AND INSTITUTES

Lexis.com Research System. Lexis-Nexis Group. Phone: 800-227-9597 or (937)865-6800 Fax: (937)865-6909 E-mail: webmaster@prod.lexis-nexis.com • URL: http://www.lexis.com • Fee-based

Web site offers extensive searching of a wide variety of legal sources. Additional features include Daily Opinion Service, lexis.com Bookstore, Career Center, CLE Center, Law Schools, and Practice Pages ("Pages specific to areas of specialty").

TRADE/PROFESSIONAL ASSOCIATIONS

American Association of Motor Vehicle Administrators. 4301 Wilson Blvd. Suite 400, Arlington, VA 22203-1800. Phone: (703)522-4200 Fax: (703)522-1553 • URL: http://www.aamva.org.

National Committee on Uniform Traffic Laws and Ordinances. 107 S. West St., No. 110, Alexandria, VA 22314. Phone: 800-807-5290 or (540)465-4701 Fax: (540)465-5383 E-mail: ncutloceo@rica.net • URL: http://www.ncutlo.org.

OTHER SOURCES

Federal Carriers Reports. CCH, Inc. • Biweekly. $1,372.00 per year. Four looseleaf volumes. Periodic supplementation. Federal rules and regulations for motor carriers, water carriers, and freight forwarders.

MOTOR VEHICLE LICENSES

See: MOTOR VEHICLE LAW AND REGULATION

MOTOR VEHICLE PARKING

See: PARKING

MOTOR VEHICLE PARTS INDUSTRY

See: AUTOMOBILE EQUIPMENT INDUSTRY

MOTOR VEHICLES

See: AUTOMOBILES; MOTOR BUSES; TRUCKS (MANUFACTURING)

MOTOR VEHICLES, FOREIGN

See: FOREIGN AUTOMOBILES

MOTOR VEHICLES, USED

See: USED CAR INDUSTRY

MOTORCYCLES

DIRECTORIES

Dealernews Buyers Guide. Advnastar Communications, Inc. • Annual. $25.00. List of manufacturers, distributors, OEMs, and service organizations serving the motorcycle, all-terrain vehicle, and watercraft industries.

Motorcycle Product News Trade Directory. Intertec Publishing Corp. • Annual. $25.00. Provides information on approximately 1,300 companies related to the motorcycle business.

PERIODICALS AND NEWSLETTERS

American Motorcyclist. American Motorcyclist Association. • Monthly. $12.50 per year.

Cycle World. Hachette Filipacchi Magazines, Inc. • Monthly. $19.94 per year. Incorporates *Cycle.*

Dealernews: The Voice of the Powersports Vehicle Industry. Advanstar Communications, Inc. • Monthly. Free to qualified personnel; others, $40.00 per year. News concerning the power sports motor vehicle industry.

Motorcycle Product News. Athletic Business Publications, Inc. • Monthly. $50.00 per year. Edited for wholesalers and retailers of motorcycles and supplies.

Motorcycle Shopper: The Source for Motorcycles, Parts, Accessories, Sidecars, Tools, Clubs, Events, and More. Payne Corp. • Monthly. $19.95 per year. Contains consumer advertisements for buying, selling, and trading motorcycles and parts.

Motorcyclist. EMAP USA. • Monthly. $11.97 per year.

PRICE SOURCES

NADA Appraisal Guides. National Automobile Dealers Association. • Prices and frequencies vary. Guides to prices of used cars, old used cars, motorcycles, mobile homes, recreational vehicles, and mopeds.

STATISTICS SOURCES

U. S. Industry and Trade Outlook: The McGraw-Hill Companies and the U.S. Department of Commerce/ International Trade Administration. Datapso Research Corp. • Annual. $69.95. Produced by the International Trade Administration, U. S. Department of Commerce, in a "public-private" partnership with DRI/McGraw-Hill and Standard & Poor's. Provides basic data, outlook for the current year, and "Long-Term Prospects" (five-year projections) for a wide variety of products and services. Includes high technology industries. Formerly *U. S. Industrial Outlook.*

TRADE/PROFESSIONAL ASSOCIATIONS

American Motorcyclist Association. 13515 Yarmouth Dr., Pickerington, OH 43147. Phone: (614)856-1900 Fax: (614)856-1920 E-mail: ama@aama-cycle.org • URL: http://www.ama-cycle.org.

Motorcycle Industry Council. Two Jenner St., Suite 150, Irvine, CA 92718. Phone: (949)727-4211 Fax: (949)727-3313 • URL: http://www.mic.org.

MOTORS

See: ENGINES

MOVING OF EMPLOYEES

See: RELOCATION OF EMPLOYEES

MOVING PICTURE INDUSTRY

See: MOTION PICTURE INDUSTRY

MULTIFAMILY HOUSING

See: APARTMENT HOUSES; CONDOMINIUMS

MULTILEVEL MARKETING

ABSTRACTS AND INDEXES

Business Periodicals Index. H. W. Wilson Co. • Monthly, except August, with quarterly and annual cumulations. Service basis for print edition; CD-ROM edition, $1,495.00 per year.

HANDBOOKS AND MANUALS

Get Rich Through Multi-Level Selling: Build Your Own Sales and Distribution Organization. Gini G. Scott. Self-Counsel Press, Inc. • 1998. $19.95. Third revised edition. (Business Series).

How to Develop Multilevel Marketing Sales. Entrepreneur Media, Inc. • Looseleaf. $59.50. A practical guide to starting a multilevel marketing business. Covers profit potential, start-up costs, owner's time required, pricing, accounting, advertising, market size evaluation, promotion, etc. (Start-Up Business Guide No. E1222.).

How to Make Big Money in Multilevel Marketing. Dave Roller. Prentice Hall. • 1989. $14.95.

ONLINE DATABASES

Marketing and Advertising Reference Service (MARS). The Gale Group. • Provides abstracts of literature relating to consumer marketing and advertising, including all forms of advertising media. Time period is 1984 to date. Daily updates. Inquire as to online cost and availability.

Wilson Business Abstracts Online. H. W. Wilson Co. • Indexes and abstracts 600 major business periodicals, plus the *Wall Street Journal* and the business section of the *New York Times.* Indexing is from 1982, abstracting from 1990, with the two newspapers included from 1993. Updated weekly. Inquire as to online cost and availability. (*Business Periodicals Index* without abstracts is also available online.).

MULTIMEDIA

See also: ELECTRONIC PUBLISHING; INTERACTIVE MEDIA; OPTICAL DISK STORAGE DEVICES

GENERAL WORKS

Being Digital. Nicholas Negroponte. Vintage Books. • 1995. $28.00. A kind of history of multimedia, with visions of future technology and public participation. Predicts how computers will affect society in years to come.

Future Libraries: Dreams, Madness, and Reality. Walt Crawford and Michael Gorman. American Library Association. • 1995. $28.00. Discusses the "over-hyped virtual library" and electronic-publishing "fantasies." Presents the argument for the importance of books, physical libraries, and library personnel.

Interface Culture: How New Technology Transforms the Way We Create and Communicate. Steven Johnson. HarperCollins Publishers. • 1997. $24.00. A discussion of how computer interfaces and online technology ("cyberspace") affect society in general.

Marketing on the Internet: Multimedia Strategies for the World Wide Web. Jill Ellsworth and Matthew Ellsworth. John Wiley and Sons, Inc. • 1996. $29.99. Second revised expanded edition.

Net Curriculum: An Educator's Guide to Using the Internet. Linda Joseph. Information Today, Inc. • 1999. $29.95. Covers various educational aspects of the Internet. Written for K-12 teachers, librarians, and media specialists by a columnist for *Multimedia Schools.* (CyberAge Books.).

Silicon Snake Oil: Second Thoughts on the Information Highway. Clifford Stoll. Doubleday. • 1996. $14.00. The author discusses the extravagant claims being made for online networks and multimedia.

ABSTRACTS AND INDEXES

Business Periodicals Index. H. W. Wilson Co. • Monthly, except August, with quarterly and annual cumulations. Service basis for print edition; CD-ROM edition, $1,495.00 per year.

Computer Literature Index: A Subject/Author Index to Computer and Data Processing Literature. Applied Computer Research, Inc. • Quarterly, with annual cumulation. $245.00 per year. Contains brief abstracts of book and periodical literature covering all phases of computing, including approximately 70 specific application areas.

F & S Index: United States. The Gale Group. • Monthly. $1,295.00 per year, including quarterly and annual cumulations. Provides annotated citations to marketing, business, financial, and industrial literature. Coverage of U. S. business activity includes trade journals, financial magazines, business newspapers, and special reports. Formerly *Predicasts F & S Index: United States.*

Library Literature and Information Science: An Index to Library and Information Science Publications. H. W. Wilson Co. • Bimonthly. Annual cumulation. Service basis. Formerly *Library Literature.*

Microcomputer Abstracts. Information Today, Inc. • Quarterly. $225.00 per year. Provides abstracts covering a wide variety of personal and business microcomputer literature. Formerly *Microcomputer Index.*

Readers' Guide to Periodical Literature. H. W. Wilson Co. • Monthly. $220.00 per year. CD-ROM edition, $1,495 per year, including annual cumulation. Indexes about 250 peridicals of general interest.

ALMANACS AND YEARBOOKS

Communication Technology Update. Focal Press. • Annual. $32.95. A yearly review of developments in electronic media, telecommunications, and the Internet.

New Media Market Place and New Media Titles. Waterlow New Media Information. • 1996. $155.00. Provides a wide variety of information on multimedia industries, including CD-ROM publishing, digital video, interactive TV, portable information products, and video CD. Includes industry review articles, interviews, market data, profiles of 2,000 multimedia companies, product directories, and a bibliography.

BIOGRAPHICAL SOURCES

The Highwaymen: Warriors on the Information Superhighway. Ken Auletta. Harcourt Trade Publications. • 1998. $13.00. Revised expanded edition. Contains critical articles about Ted Turner, Rupert Murdoch, Barry Diller, Michael Eisner, and other key figures in electronic communications, entertainment, and information.

CD-ROM DATABASES

Computer Select. The Gale Group. • Monthly. $1,250.00 per year. Provides one year of full-text on CD-ROM for 120 leading computer-related publications. Also includes 70,000 product specifications and brief profiles of 13,000 computer product vendors and manufacturers.

F & S Index Plus Text. The Gale Group. • Monthly. $7,575.00 per year. Provides CD-ROM citations to worldwide business, marketing, and industrial material appearing in a large assortment of trade journals, newspapers, and other publications. Time period is four years.

Hoover's Company Capsules on CD-ROM. Hoover's, Inc. • Quarterly. $349.95 per year (single-user). Provides the CD-ROM version of *Hoover's Handbook of American Business, Hoover's Handbook of Emerging Companies, Hoover's Handbook of World Business, Hoover's Guide to Computer Companies, Hoover's Guide to Media Companies, Hoover's Handbook of Private Companies,* and various regional guides. Includes more than 11,000 profiles of companies.

Multimedia Schools: A Practical Journal of Multimedia, CD-ROM, Online, and Internet in K-12. Information Today, Inc. • Bimonthly. $39.95 per year. Provides purchasing recommendations and technical advice relating to the use of high-tech multimedia products in schools.

WILSONDISC: Library Literature and Information Science Index. H. W. Wilson Co. • Quarterly. Including unlimited access to the online version of *Library Literature.* Provides CD-ROM indexing of about 300 periodicals, covering a wide range of topics having to do with libraries, library management, and the information industry.

WILSONDISC: Wilson Business Abstracts. H. W. Wilson Co. • Monthly. $2,495.00 per year, including unlimited online access to *Wilson Business Abstracts* through WILSONLINE. Provides CD-ROM "cover-to-cover" abstracting and indexing of over 600 prominent business periodicals. Indexing is from 1982, abstracting from 1990. (*Business Periodicals Index* without abstracts is available on CD-ROM at $1,495 per year.).

DIRECTORIES

Advanced Imaging Buyers Guide: The Most Comprehensive Worldwide Directory of Imaging Product and Equipment Vendors. Cygnus Business Media. • Annual. $19.95. List of about 800 electronic imaging companies and their products.

CD-ROMS in Print. The Gale Group. • Annual. $175.00. Describes more than 13,000 currrently available reference and multimedia CD-ROM titles and provides contact information for about 4,000 CD-ROM publishing and distribution companies. Includes several indexes.

Data Sources: The Comprehensive Guide to the Data Processing Industry Hardware, Data Communications Products, Software, Company Profiles. The Gale Group. • Semiannual. $495.00 per year. Two volumes. Describes hardware and software for all computer operating sysems, including prices and technical details. Lists about 75,000 products from 14,000 suppliers. Industry-specific software applications are described.

Information Marketplace Directory. SIMBA Information. • 1996. $295.00. Second edition. Lists computer-based information processing and multimedia companies, including those engaged in animation, audio, video, and interactive video.

Interactive Advertising Source. SRDS. • Quarterly. $561.00 per year. Provides descriptive profiles, rates, audience, personnel, etc., for producers of various forms of interactive or multimedia advertising: online/Internet, CD-ROM, interactive TV, interactive cable, interactive telephone, interactive kiosk, and others. Includes online supplement *SRDS' URlink.*

Interactive Multimedia Association Membership Directory. Interactive Multimedia Association. • Annual. $60.00. Includes membership listing and a *Buyer's Guide.*

KMWorld Buyer's Guide. Knowledge Asset Media. • Semiannual. Controlled circulation as part of *KMWorld.* Contains corporate and product profiles related to various aspects of knowledge management and information systems. (Knowledge Asset Media is a an affiliate of Information Today, Inc.).

Multimedia and CD-ROM Directory: The Global Source of Information for the Multimedia and CD-ROM Industries. Available from Omnigraphics, Inc. • Annual. $390.00. Two volumes: vol. 1, *New Media Companies* ($195.00); vol. 2, *New Media Titles* ($195.00). Published in London by Macmillan Reference Ltd. Volume one consists of statistics ("Facts and Figures"), articles on multimedia publishing, market profiles (countries), interviews, company directory, bibliography, and indexes. Volume two describes more than 19,000 CD-ROM titles, with publisher directory, indexes, and glossary. Formerly *CD-ROM Directory.*

Peterson's Guide to Distance Learning. Peterson's. • 1996. $24.95. Provides detailed information on accredited college and university programs available through television, radio, computer, videocassette, and audiocassette resources. Covers 700 U. S. and Canadian institutions. Formerly *The Electronic University.*

Plunkett's Entertainment and Media Industry Almanac. Available from Plunkett Research, Ltd. • Biennial. $149.99. Provides profiles of leading firms in online information, films, radio, television, cable, multimedia, magazines, and book publishing. Includes World Wide Web sites, where available, plus information on careers and industry trends.

Plunkett's InfoTech Industry Almanac: Complete Profiles on the InfoTech 500-the Leading Firms in the Movement and Management of Voice, Data, and Video. Available from Plunkett Research, Ltd. • Annual. $149.99. Five hundred major information companies are profiled, with corporate culture aspects. Discusses major trends in various sectors of the computer and information industry, including data on careers and job growth. Includes several indexes.

The Software Encyclopedia: A Guide for Personal, Professional, and Business Users. R. R. Bowker. • Annual. $255.00. Two volumes. Volume one lists software programs by title and producer. Volume two provides information on programs according to application and operating system. Includes prices and requirements for hardware and memory.

ENCYCLOPEDIAS AND DICTIONARIES

CyberDictionary: Your Guide to the Wired World. Knowledge Exchange LLC. • 1996. $17.95. Includes many illustrations.

Cyberspace Lexicon: An Illustrated Dictionary of Terms from Multimedia to Virtual Reality. Bob Cotton and Richard Oliver. Phaidon Press, Inc. • 1994. $29.95. Defines more than 800 terms, with manyillustrations. Includes a bibliography.

Cyberspeak: An Online Dictionary. Andy Ihnatko. Random House, Inc. • 1996. $12.95. An informal guide to the language of computers, multimedia, and the Internet.

Dictionary of Multimedia: Terms and Acronyms. Brad Hansen, editor. Fitzroy Dearborn Publishers. • 1998. $55.00. Second edition.

Every Manager's Guide to Information Technology: A Glossary of Key Terms and Concepts for Today's Business Leader. Peter G. W. Keen. Harvard Business School Press. • 1995. $18.95. Second edition. Provides definitions of terms related to computers, data communications, and information network systems. (Harvard Business Economist Reference Series).

Multimedia and the Web from A to Z. Patrick M. Dillon and David C. Leonard. Oryx Press. • 1998. $39.95. Second enlarged revised edition. Defines more than 1,500 terms relating to software and hardware in the areas of computing, online technology, telecommunications, audio, video, motion pictures, CD-ROM, and the Internet. Includes acronyms and an annotated bibliography. Formerly *Multimedia Technology from A to Z* (1994).

New Hacker's Dictionary. Eric S. Raymond. MIT Press. • 1996. $39.00. Third edition. Includes three classifications of hacker communication: slang, jargon, and "techspeak.".

HANDBOOKS AND MANUALS

Business Multimedia Explained: A Manager's Guide to Key Terms and Concepts. Peter G. W. Keen. Harvard Business School Press. • 1997. $39.95.

CD-ROM Handbook. Chris Sherman. McGraw-Hill. • 1993. $70.50. Second edition. Covers technology (audio, video, and multimedia), design, production, and economics of the CD-ROM industry.

The Cybrarian's Manual. Pat Ensor, editor. American Library Association. • 1996. $35.00. Provides information for librarians concerning the Internet, expert systems, computer networks, client/server architecture, Web pages, multimedia, information industry careers, and other "cyberspace" topics.

Digital Audio and Compact Disk Technology. Luc Baert and others. Butterworth-Heinemann. • 1995. $57.95. Third edition.

Electronic Media Management. Peter K. Pringle and others. Butterworth-Heinemann. • 1999. $44.95. Fourth edition. (Focal Press).

Interactive Computer Systems: Videotex and Multimedia. Antone F. Alber. Perseus Publishing. • 1993. $79.50.

An Interactive Guide to Multimedia. Que Education and Training. • 1996. $85.00, including CD-ROM. Explains multimedia production and application, including graphics, text, video, sound, editing, etc.

Learning Web Design: A Beginner's Guide to HTML, Graphics, and Beyond. Jennifer Niederst. O'Reilly & Associates, Inc. • 2001. $34.95. Written for beginners who have no previous knowledge of how Web design works.

Music Technology Buyer's Guide. United Entertainment Media, Inc. • $7.95. Annual. Lists more than 4,000 hardware and software music production products from 350 manufacturers. Includes synthesizers, MIDI hardware and software, mixers, microphones, music notation software, etc. Produced by the editorial staffs of *Keyboard* and *EQ* magazines.

Power Pitches: How to Produce Winning Presentations Using Charts, Slides, Video, and Multimedia. Alan L. Brown. McGraw-Hill Professional. • 1997. $39.95. Includes "Ten Rules of Power Pitching.".

Trade Secret Protection in an Information Age. Gale R. Peterson. Glasser Legalworks. • Looseleaf. $149.00, including sample forms on disk. Periodic supplementation available. Covers trade secret law relating to computer software, online databases, and multimedia products. Explanations are based on more than 1,000 legal cases. Sample forms on disk include work-for-hire examples and covenants not to compete.

INTERNET DATABASES

InfoTech Trends. Data Analysis Group. Phone: (707)894-9100 Fax: (707)486-5618 E-mail: support@infotechtrends.com • URL: http://www.infotechtrends.com • Web site provides both free and fee-based market research data on the information technology industry, including computers, peripherals, telecommunications, the Internet, software, CD-ROM/DVD, e-commerce, and workstations. Fees: Free for current (most recent year) data; more extensive information has various fee structures. Formerly *Computer Industry Forecasts.*

Interactive Week: The Internet's Newspaper. Ziff Davis Media, Inc. 28 E. 28th St., New York, NY 10016. Phone: (212)503-3500 Fax: (212)503-5680 E-mail: iweekinfo@zd.com • URL: http://www.zd.com • Weekly. $99.00 per year. Covers news and trends relating to Internet commerce, computer communications, and telecommunications.

Wired News. Wired Digital, Inc. Phone: (415)276-8400 Fax: (415)276-8499 E-mail: newsfeedback@wired.com • URL: http://www.wired.com • Provides summaries and full-text of "Top Stories" relating to the Internet, computers, multimedia, telecommunications, and the electronic information industry in general. These news stories are placed in the broad categories of Politics, Business, Culture, and Technology. Affiliated with *Wired* magazine. Fees: Free.

ONLINE DATABASES

F & S Index. The Gale Group. • Contains about four million citations to worldwide business, financial, and industrial or consumer product literature appearing from 1972 to date. Weekly updates. Inquire as to online cost and availability.

Gale Directory of Databases [online]. The Gale Group. • Presents the online version of the printed *Gale Directory of Databases, Volume 1: Online Databases* and *Gale Directory of Databases, Volume 2: CD-ROM, Diskette, Magnetic Tape, Handheld, and Batch Access Database Products.* Semiannual updates. Inquire as to online cost and availability.

Globalbase. The Gale Group. • Provides more than one million online summaries of business, industrial, and economic news reports from more than 1,000 publications worldwide. Covers a wide range of material appearing in international trade journals, professional magazines, and newspapers. Time period is 1984 to date, with weekly updates. Inquire as to online cost and availability.

Internet and Personal Computing Abstracts. Information Today, Inc. • Contains abstracts covering a wide variety of personal and business microcomputer literature appearing in more than 100 journals and popular magazines. Time period is 1981 to date, with monthly updates. Formerly *Microcomputer Index.* Inquire as to online cost and availability.

Library Literature Online. H. W. Wilson Co. • Contains online indexing of a wide variety of library and information science literature from 1984 to date, with updating quarterly. Inquire as to online cost and availability.

Microcomputer Software Guide Online. R. R. Bowker. • Provides information on more than 30,000 microcomputer software applications from more than 4,000 producers. Corresponds to printed *Software Encyclopedia,* but with monthly updates. Inquire as to online cost and availability.

PROMT: Predicasts Overview of Markets and Technology. The Gale Group. • Companies, products, applied technologies and markets. U.S. and international literature coverage, 1972 to date. Inquire as to online cost and availability. Provides abstracts from more than 1,600 publications. Weekly updates.

Readers' Guide Abstracts Online. H. W. Wilson Co. • Indexes and abstracts general interest periodicals, 1983 to date. Weekly updates. Inquire as to online cost and availability.

Wilson Business Abstracts Online. H. W. Wilson Co. • Indexes and abstracts 600 major business periodicals, plus the *Wall Street Journal* and the business section of the *New York Times.* Indexing is from 1982, abstracting from 1990, with the two newspapers included from 1993. Updated weekly. Inquire as to online cost and availability. (*Business Periodicals Index* without abstracts is also available online.).

PERIODICALS AND NEWSLETTERS

Advanced Imaging: Solutions for the Electronic Imaging Professional. Cygnus Business Media. • Monthly. Free to qualified personnel; others, $60.00 per year Covers document-based imaging technologies, products, systems, and services. Coverage is also devoted to multimedia and electronic printing and publishing.

Computer Music Journal. MIT Press. • Quarterly. Individuals, $48.00 per year; instutitions, $158.00 per year. Covers digital soound and the musical applications of computers.

Desktop Video Communications. BCR Enterprises, Inc,. • Bimonthly. $55.00 per year. Covers multimedia technologies, with emphasis on video conferencing and the "virtual office." Formerly *Virtual Workgroups.*

Digital Publishing Technologies: How to Implement New Media Publishing. Information Today, Inc. • Monthly. $196.00 per year. Covers online and CD-ROM publishing, including industry news, new applications, new products, electronic publishing technology, and descriptions of completed publishing projects.

DV: Digital Video. Miller Freeman, Inc. • Monthly. $29.97 per year. Edited for producers and creators of digital media. Includes topics relating to video, audio, animation, multimedia, interactive design, and special effects. Covers both hardware and software, with product reviews. Formerly *Digital Video Magazine.*

Educational Marketer: The Educational Publishing Industry's Voice of Authority Since 1968. SIMBA Information. • Three times a month. $479.00 per year. Newsletter. Edited for suppliers of educational materials to schools and colleges at all levels. Covers print and electronic publishing, software, audiovisual items, and multimedia. Includes corporate news and educational statistics.

Electronic Information Report: Empowering Industry Decision Makers Since 1979. SIMBA Information. • 46 times a year. $549.00 per year. Newsletter. Provides business and financial news and trends for online services, electronic publishing, storage media, multimedia, and voice services. Includes information on relevant IPOs (initial public offerings) and mergers. Formerly *Electronic Information Week.*

IEEE Multimedia Magazine. Institute of Electrical and Electronic Engineers. • Quarterly. Free to members; non-members, $390.00 per year. Provides a wide variety of technical information relating to multimedia systems and applications. Articles cover research, advanced applications, working systems, and theory.

Interactive Content: Consumer Media Strategies Monthly. Jupiter Media Metrix. • Monthly. $675.00 per year; with online edition, $775.00 per year. Newsletter. Covers the broad field of providing content (information, news, entertainment) for the Internet/World Wide Web.

KMWorld: Creating and Managing the Knowledge-Based Enterprise. Knowledge Asset Media. • Monthly. Controlled circulation. Provides articles on knowledge management, including business intelligence, multimedia content management, document management, e-business, and intellectual property. Emphasis is on business-to-business information technology. (Knowledge Asset Media is a an affiliate of Information Today, Inc.).

Knowledge Management. CurtCo Freedom Group. • Monthly. Controlled circulation. Covers applications of information technology and knowledge management strategy.

Maxium PC (Personal Computer). Imagine Media, Inc. • Quarterly. $12.00 per year. Provides articles and reviews relating to multimedia hardware and software. Each issue includes a CD-ROM sampler (emphasis is on games). Formed by the merger of *Home PC* and *Boot.*

Micropublishing News: The Newsmonthly for Electronic Designers and Publishers. Cygnus

Business Media. • Monthly. Free to qualified personnel. Price on application. Edited for business and professional users of electronic publishing products and services. Topics covered include document imaging, CD-ROM publishing, digital video, and multimedia services. Available in four regional editions.

Multimedia Schools: A Practical Journal of Multimedia, CD-Rom, Online and Internet in K-12. Information Today, Inc. • Five times a year. $39.95 per year. Edited for school librarians, media center directors, computer coordinators, and others concerned with educational multimedia. Coverage includes the use of CD-ROM sources, the Internet, online services, and library technology.

Multimedia Week. Phillips Business Information, Inc. • 50 times a year. $697.00 per year. Newsletter. Covers industry news and trends in multimedia hardware and software.

National Association of Desktop Publishers. Journal. National Association of Desktop Publishers. Desktop Publishing Institute. • Monthly. Free to members; non-members, $48.00 per year. Covers desktop, electronic, and multimedia publishing.

NewMedia: The Magazine for Creators of the Digital Future. HyperMedia Communications, Inc. • Monthly. $29.95 per year. Edited for multimedia professionals, with emphasis on digital video and Internet graphics, including animation. Contains reviews of new products. Formerly *NewMedia Age*.

Silicon Alley Reporter. Rising Tide Studios. • Monthly. $29.95 per year. Covers the latest trends in e-commerce, multimedia, and the Internet.

Stereo Review's Sound & Vision: Home Theater-Audio- Video- MultimediaMovies- Music. Hachette Filipacchi Magazines, Inc. • 10 times a year. $24.00 per year. Popular magazine providing explanatory articles and critical reviews of equipment and media (CD-ROM, DVD, videocassettes, etc.). Supplement available *Stero Review's Sound and Vision Buyers Guide*. Replaces *Stereo Review* and *Video Magazine*.

3D Design. Miller Freeman, Inc. • Monthly. $50.00 per year. Edited for computer graphics and multimedia professionals. Special features include "Animation Mania" and "Interactive 3D.".

Upgrade. Software and Information Industry Association. • Monthly. $75.00 per year. Covers news and trends relating to the software, information, and Internet industries. Formerly *SPA News* from Software Publisers Association.

*Virtual City: *The City Magazine of Cyberspace.* Virtual Communications, Inc. • Quarterly. $11.80 per year. Covers new developments in World Wide Web sites, access, software, and hardware.

Wired. Wired Ventures Ltd. • Monthly. $24.00 per year. Edited for creators and managers in various areas of electronic information and entertainment, including multimedia, the Internet, and video. Often considered to be the primary publication of the "digital generation.".

RESEARCH CENTERS AND INSTITUTES

Electronic Visualization Laboratory. University of Illinois at Chicago, Engineering Research Facility, 842 W. Taylor St., Room 2032, Chicago, IL 60607-7053. Phone: (312)996-3002 Fax: (312)413-7585 E-mail: tom@eecs.uic.edu • URL: http://www.evl.uic.edu • Research areas include computer graphics, virtual reality, multimedia, and interactive techniques.

Graphics, Visualization, and Usability Center. Georgia Institute of Technology, Mail Code 0280, Atlanta, GA 30332-0280. Phone: (404)894-4488 Fax: (404)894-0673 E-mail: jarek@cc.gatech.edu • URL: http://www.cc.gatech.edu/gvu/ • Research areas include computer graphics, multimedia, image recognition, interactive graphics systems, animation, and virtual realities.

Integrated Media Systems Center. University of Southern California, 3740 McClintock Ave., Suite 131, Los Angeles, CA 90089-2561. Phone: (213)740-0877 Fax: (213)740-8931 E-mail: nikias@imsc.usc.edu • URL: http://www.imsc.usc.edu • Media areas for research include education, mass communication, and entertainment.

Inter-Arts Center. San Francisco State University, School of Creative Arts, 1600 Holloway Ave., San Francisco, CA 94132. Phone: (415)338-1478 Fax: (415)338-6159 E-mail: jimdavis@sfsu.edu • URL: http://www.sfsu.edu/~iac • Research areas include multimedia, computerized experimental arts processes, and digital sound.

International Data Corp. (IDC). Five Speen St., Framingham, MA 01701. Phone: (508)935-4389 Fax: (508)935-4789 • URL: http://www.idcresearch.com • Private research firm specializing in market research related to computers, multimedia, and telecommunications.

Media Laboratory. Massachusetts Institute of Technology, 20 Ames St., Room E-15, Cambridge, MA 02139. Phone: (617)253-0338 Fax: (617)258-6264 E-mail: casr@media.mit.edu • URL: http://www.media.mit.edu • Research areas include electronic publishing, spatial imaging, human-machine interface, computer vision, and advanced television.

Multimedia Communications Laboratory. Boston University, PHO 445, Eight Saint Mary's St., Boston, MA 02215. Phone: (617)353-8042 Fax: (617)353-6440 E-mail: mcl@spiderman.bu.edu • URL: http://www.hulk.bu.edu • Research areas include interactive multimedia applications.

Studio for Creative Inquiry. Carnegie Mellon University, College of Fine Arts, Pittsburgh, PA 15213-3890. Phone: (412)268-3454 Fax: (412)268-2829 E-mail: mmbm@andrew.cmu.edu/ • URL: http://www.cmu.edu/studio/ • Research areas include artificial intelligence, virtual reality, hypermedia, multimedia, and telecommunications, in relation to the arts.

STATISTICS SOURCES

Multimedia Title Publishing: Review, Trends, and Forecast. SIMBA Information. • Annual. $895.00. Provides industry statistics and market research data. Covers both business and consumer multimedia items, with emphasis on CD-ROM publishing.

TRADE/PROFESSIONAL ASSOCIATIONS

Association for Interactive Media. 1301 Connecticut Ave. N.W., 5th Fl., Washington, DC 20036-5105. Phone: (202)408-0008 Fax: (202)408-0111 E-mail: info@interactivehg.org • URL: http://www.interactivehg.org • Members are companies engaged in various interactive enterprises, utilizing the Internet, interactive television, computer communications, and multimedia.

International Interactive Communications Society. 4840 McKnight Rd., Suite A, Pittsburgh, PA 15237. Phone: (412)734-1928 Fax: (412)369-3507 E-mail: worldhq@iics.org • URL: http://www.iics.org • Members are interactive media professionals concerned with intetractive arts and technologies.

Internet Alliance. P.O. Box 65782, Washington, DC 20035-5782. Phone: (202)955-8091 Fax: (202)955-8081 E-mail: ia@internetalliance.org • URL: http://www.internetalliance.org • Members are companies associated with the online and Internet industry. Promotes the Internet as "the global mass market medium of the 21st century." Concerned with government regulation, public policy, industry advocacy, consumer education, and media relations. Formerly Interactive Services Association.

Software and Information Industry Association. 1730 M St., N. W., Suite 700, Washington, DC 20036-4510. Phone: (202)452-1600 Fax: (202)223-8756 • URL: http://www.siia.net • A trade association for the software and digital content industry. Divisions are Content, Education, Enterprise, Financial Information Services, Global, and Internet. Includes an Online Content Committee. Formerly Software Publishers Association.

Special Interest Group on Electronic Sound Technology. Association for Computing Machinery, 1515 Broadway, New York, NY 10036. Phone: (212)869-7440 Fax: (212)302-5826 E-mail: sigs@acm.org • URL: http://www.acm.org/sigsound • Concerned with software, algorithms, hardware, and applications relating to digitally generated audio.

Special Interest Group on Multimedia. Association for Computing Machinery, 1515 Broadway, New York, NY 10036. Phone: (212)869-7440 Fax: (212)302-5826 E-mail: sigs@acm.org • URL: http://www.acm.org/sigmm • Concerned with multimedia computing, communication, storage, and applications.

OTHER SOURCES

Consumer Online Services Report. Jupiter Media Metrix. • Annual. $1,895.00. Market research report. Provides analysis of trends in the online information industry, with projections of growth in future years (five-year forecasts). Contains profiles of electronic media companies.

DVD Assessment, No. 3. Julie B. Schwerin and Theodore A. Pine, editors. InfoTech, Inc. • 1998. $1,295.00. Third edition. Provides detailed market research data on Digital Video Discs (also known as Digital Versatile Discs). Includes history of DVD, technical specifications, DVD publishing outlook, "Industry Overview," "Market Context," "Infrastructure Analysis," "Long-Range Forecast to 2005," and emerging technologies.

EQ: The Project Recording and Sound Magazine. United Entertainment Media, Inc. • Monthly. $36.00 per year. Provides advice on professional music recording equipment and technique.

Keyboard: Making Music with Technology. United Entertainment Media, Inc. • Monthly. $36.00 per year. Emphasis is on recording systems, keyboard technique, and computer-assisted music (MIDI) systems.

Optical Publishing Industry Assessment. Julie B. Schwerin and Theodore A. Pine, editors. InfoTech, Inc. • 1998. $1,295.00. Ninth edition. Provides market research data and forecasts to 2005 for DVD-ROM, "Hybrid ROM/Online Media," and other segments of the interactive entertainment, digital information, and consumer electronics industries. Covers both software (content) and hardware. Includes Video-CD, DVD- Video, CD-Audio, DVD-Audio, DVD-ROM, PC-Desktop, TV Set-Top, CD-R, CD-RW, DVD-R and DVD-RAM.

MULTINATIONAL CORPORATIONS

See also: CORPORATIONS; INTERNATIONAL BUSINESS; INTERNATIONAL TAXATION

GENERAL WORKS

International Business and Multinational Enterprises. Stefan H. Robock and Kenneth Simmonds. McGraw-Hill Higher Education. • 1988. $68.50. Fourth edition.

ABSTRACTS AND INDEXES

Business Periodicals Index. H. W. Wilson Co. • Monthly, except August, with quarterly and annual cumulations. Service basis for print edition; CD-ROM edition, $1,495.00 per year.

CD-ROM DATABASES

Business Source Plus. EBSCO Information Services. • Monthly. $1,495.00 per year. Provides CD-ROM citations and abstracts to articles in about 650 business periodicals and newspapers, including *The Wall Street Journal.* Full text is provided from 200 selected periodicals. Covers accounting, communications, economics, finance, management, marketing, and other business subjects.

Corporate Affiliations Plus. National Register Publishing, Reed Reference Publishing. • Quarterly. $1,995.00 per year. Provides CD-ROM discs corresponding to *Directory of Corporate Affiliations* and *Corporate Finance Bluebook.* Contains corporate financial services information and worldwide data on subsidiaries and affiliates.

Hoover's Company Capsules on CD-ROM. Hoover's, Inc. • Quarterly. $349.95 per year (single-user). Provides the CD-ROM version of *Hoover's Handbook of American Business, Hoover's Handbook of Emerging Companies, Hoover's Handbook of World Business, Hoover's Guide to Computer Companies, Hoover's Guide to Media Companies, Hoover's Handbook of Private Companies,* and various regional guides. Includes more than 11,000 profiles of companies.

InvesText [CD-ROM]. Thomson Financial Securities Data. • Monthly. $5,000.00 per year. Contains full text on CD-ROM of investment research reports from about 250 sources, including leading brokers and investment bankers. Reports are available on both U. S. and international publicly traded corporations. Separate industry reports cover more than 50 industries. Time span is 1982 to date.

Leadership Library on CD-ROM: Who's Who in the Leadership of the United States. Leadership Directories, Inc. • Quarterly. $2,641.00 per year, including access to Internet version (weekly updates). Contains all 14 *Yellow Book* personnel directories on CD-ROM, providing contact and brief biographical information for about 400,000 individuals. Covers business, government, financial institutions, news media, law firms, associations, foreign representatives, and nonprofit organizations. Includes photographs.

National Newspaper Index CD-ROM. The Gale Group. • Monthly. Provides comprehensive CD-ROM indexing of all material appearing in the late edition of the *New York Times*, the final edition of the *Washington Post*, the national edition of the *Christian Science Monitor*, the home edition of the *Los Angeles Times*, and the *Wall Street Journal.* Time period is four years. Also available online.

The New York Times Ondisc. New York Times Online Services. • Monthly. $2,650.00 per year. CD-ROM discs contain the full text of *The New York Times*, final edition. Inquire as to time period covered and availability of backfiles.

Newspaper Abstracts Ondisc. Bell & Howell Information and Learning. • Monthly. $2,950.00 per year (covers 1989 to date; archival discs are available for 1985-88). Provides cover-to-cover CD-ROM indexing and abstracting of 19 major newspapers, including the *New York Times, Wall Street Journal, Washington Post, Chicago Tribune,* and *Los Angeles Times.*

DIRECTORIES

American Big Businesses Directory. American Business Directories. • Annual. $595.00. Lists 177,000 public and private U. S. companies in all fields having 100 or more employees. Includes sales volume, number of employees, and name of chief executive. Formerly *Big Businesses Directory.*

America's Corporate Families and International Affiates. Dun and Bradstreet Information Services. • Annual. Libraries, $895.00; corporations, $1,020.00. Lease basis. Three Volumes U.S. parent companies with foreign affiliates and foreign parent companies with U.S. affiliates.

Business Organizations, Agencies, and Publications Directory. The Gale Group. • 1999. $425.00. 12th edition. Over 40,000 entries describing 39 types of business information sources. Classified by type of organization, publication, or serviceIncludes state, national, and international agencies and organizations. Master index to names and keywords. Also includes e-mail addresses and web site URL's.

Directory of American Firms Operating in Foreign Countries. Uniworld Business Publications Inc. • Biennial. $275.00. Three volumes. Lists approximately 2,450 American companies with more than 29,500 subsidiaries and affiliates in 138 foreign countries.

Directory of Corporate Affiliations. National Register Publishing. • Annual. $1,159.00. Five volumes. Volumes one and two: Master Index; volume three: U.S. Public Companies; volume four: U.S. Private Companies; volume five: International Public and Private Companies.

Directory of Foreign Firms Operating in the United States. Uniworld Business Publications, Inc. • Biennial. $225.00. Lists about 2,400 foreign companies and 5,700 American affiliates. 75 countries are represented.

Directory of Japanese-Affiliated Companies in the USA and Canada. Available from The Gale Group. • Annual. $375.00. Published by the Japanese External Trade Organization (JETRO). Provides data on more than 5,000 Japanese-affiliated companies located in the U. S. and Canada. (CD-ROM version included with printed directory.).

Directory of Multinationals. Available from The Gale Group. • 1998. $695.00. Two volumes. Fifth edition. Published by Waterlow Specialist Information Publishing. Provides detailed information on multinational firms with total annual sales in excess of one billion dollars and overseas sales in excess of $500 million. Includes narrative company descriptions and statistical data.

Dow Jones Guide to the Global Stock Market. Dow Jones & Co., Inc. • Annual. $34.95. Three volumes. Presents concise profiles and three-year financial performance data for each of 3,000 publicly held companies in 35 countries. (Includes all Dow Jones Global Index companies.).

Europe's Major Companies Directory. Available from The Gale Group. • 1997. $590.00. Second edition. Published by Euromonitor. Contains detailed financial and product information for about 6,000 major companies in 16 countries of Western Europe.

Foreign Representatives in the U. S. Yellow Book: Who's Who in the U. S. Offices of Foreign Corporations, Foreign Nations, the Foreign Press, and Intergovernmental Organizations. Leadership Directories, Inc. • Semiannual. $235.00 per year. Lists executives located in the U. S. for 1,300 foreign companies, 340 foreign banks and other financial institutions, 175 embassies and consulates, and 375 foreign press outlets. Includes five indexes.

Global Company Handbook. C I F A R Publications, Inc. • Annual. $495.00. Two volumes. Provides detailed profiles of 7,500 publicly traded companies in 48 countries. Includes global rankings and five years of data.

Hoover's Handbook of World Business: Profiles of Major European, Asian, Latin American, and Canadian Companies. Hoover's, Inc. • Annual. $99.95. Contains detailed profiles of more than 300 large foreign companies. Includes indexes by industry, location, executive name, company name, and brand name.

Japanese Affiliated Companies In the U.S. and Canada. Available from The Gale Group. • 1994. $190.00. Published by the Japan External Trade Organization (JETRO). Lists approximately 10,000 affiliates of Japanese companies operating in the U. S. and Canada. Provides North American and Japanese addresses. Six indexes.

Major Market Share Companies: Asia Pacific. Available from The Gale Group. • 2000. $900.00. Published by Euromonitor (http://www.euromonitor.com). Provides consumer market share data and rankings for multinational and regional companies. Covers leading firms in Japan, China, Australia, South Korea, Indonesia, Malaysia, Philippines, and Thailand.

Major Market Share Companies: Europe. Available from The Gale Group. • 2000. $900.00. Published by Euromonitor (http://www.euromonitor.com). Provides consumer market share data and rankings for multinational and regional companies. Covers leading firms in 14 European countries.

Major Market Share Companies: The Americas. Available from The Gale Group. • 2000. $900.00. Published by Euromonitor (http://www.euromonitor.com). Provides consumer market share data and rankings for multinational and regional companies. Covers leading firms in the U.S., Canada, Mexico, Brazil, Argentina, Venezuela, and Chile.

Market Share Tracker. Available from The Gale Group. • 2000. $1,000.00. Published by Euromonitor (http://www.euromonitor.com). Provides consumer market share data for leading companies in 30 major countries.

Morningstar American Depositary Receipts. Morningstar, Inc. • Biweekly. $195.00 per year. Looseleaf. Provides detailed profiles of 700 foreign companies having shares traded in the U. S. through American Depositary Receipts (ADRs).

Standard Directory of International Advertisers and Agencies: The International Red Book. R. R. Bowker. • Annual. $569.00. Includes about 8,000 foreign companies and their advertising agencies. Geographic, company name, personal name, and trade name indexes are provided.

The World's Major Multinationals. Available from The Gale Group. • 2000. $1,100.00. Published by Euromonitor (http://www.euromonitor.com). Provides profiles of leading companies around the world selling branded products to consumers. Includes detailed financial data for each firm.

Worldwide Branch Locations of Multinational Companies. The Gale Group. • 1993. $200.00. A guide to subsidiaries, sales offices, manufacturing facilities, and other corporate units operating outside the headquarters country. Includes over 500 leading multinational companies and their 20,000 branch locations.

ENCYCLOPEDIAS AND DICTIONARIES

Blackwell Encyclopedic Dictionary of International Management. John J. O'Connell, editor. Blackwell Publishers. • 1997. $105.95. The editor is associated with the American Graduate School of International Management. Contains definitions of key terms combined with longer articles written by various U.

S. and foreign business educators. Includes bibliographies and index. (Blackwell Encyclopedia of Management Series).

HANDBOOKS AND MANUALS

International Business Handbook. Vishnu H. Kirpalani, editor. Haworth Press, Inc. • 1990. $89.95. (International Business Series, No. 1).

Multinational Financial Management. Alan C. Shapiro. Prentice Hall. • 1999. $74.67. Sixth edition.

INTERNET DATABASES

EBSCO Information Services. Ebsco Publishing. Phone: 800-871-8508 or (508)356-6500 Fax: (508)356-5640 E-mail: ep@epnet.com • URL: http://www.epnet.com • Fee-based Web site providing Internet access to a wide variety of databases, including business-related material. Full text is available for many periodical titles, with daily updates. Fees: Apply.

Ebusiness Forum: Global Business Intelligence for the Digital Age. Economist Intelligence Unit (EIU), Economist Group. Phone: 800-938-4685 or (212)554-0600 Fax: (212)586-0248 E-mail: newyork@eiu.com • URL: http://www.ebusinessforum.com • Web site provides information relating to multinational business, with an emphasis on activities in specific countries. Includes rankings of countries for "e-business readiness," additional data on the political, economic, and business environment in 180 nations ("Doing Business in.."), and "Today's News Analysis." Fees: Free, but registration is required for access to all content. Daily updates.

ProQuest Direct. Bell & Howell Information and Learning. Phone: 800-521-0600 or (313)761-4700 Fax: (313)973-9145 • URL: http://www.umi.com/proquest • Fee-based Web site providing Internet access to more than 3,000 periodicals, newspapers, and other publications. Many items are available full-text, with daily updates. Includes extensive corporate and financial information from Disclosure, Inc. Fees: Apply.

ONLINE DATABASES

Information Bank Abstracts. New York Times Index Dept. • Provides indexing and abstracting of current affairs, primarily from the final late edition of *The New York Times* and the Eastern edition of *The Wall Street Journal*. Time period is 1969 to present, with daily updates. Inquire as to online cost and availability.

InvesText. Thomson Financial Securities Data. • Provides full text online of investment research reports from more than 300 sources, including leading brokers and investment bankers. Reports are available on approximately 50,000 U. S. and international corporations. Separate industry reports cover 54 industries. Time span is 1982 to date, with daily updates. Inquire as to online cost and availability.

Wilson Business Abstracts Online. H. W. Wilson Co. • Indexes and abstracts 600 major business periodicals, plus the *Wall Street Journal* and the business section of the *New York Times*. Indexing is from 1982, abstracting from 1990, with the two newspapers included from 1993. Updated weekly. Inquire as to online cost and availability. (*Business Periodicals Index* without abstracts is also available online.).

PERIODICALS AND NEWSLETTERS

Business Week International: The World's Only International Newsweekly of Business. McGraw-Hill. • Weekly. $105.00 per year.

Canadian Business. Canadian Business Media. • 21 times a year. $34.70 per year. Edited for corporate managers and executives, this is a major periodical in Canada covering a variety of business, economic, and financial topics. Emphasis is on the top 500 Canadian corporations.

Chief Executive Magazine. Chief Executive Group, Inc. • 10 times a year. $95.00 per year.

Financial Times [London]. Available from FT Publications, Inc. • Daily, except Sunday. $184.00 per year. An international business and financial newspaper, featuring news from London, Paris, Frankfurt, New York, and Tokyo. Includes worldwide stock and bond market data, commodity market data, and monetary/currency exchange information.

Fortune Magazine. Time Inc., Business Information Group. • Biweekly. $59.95 per year. Edited for top executives and upper-level managers.

Global Finance. Global Finance Media, Inc. • Monthly. $300.00 per year. Edited for corporate financial executives and money managers responsible for "cross-border" financial transactions.

Harvard Business Review. Harvard University, Graduate School of Business Administration. Harvard Businss School Publishing. • Bimonthly. $95.00 per year.

The International Information Report: The International Industry Dossier. Washington Researchers Ltd. • Monthly. $160.00 per year.

International Trade and Investment Letter: Trends in U.S Policies, Trade Finance and Trading Operations. International Business Affairs Corp. • Monthly. $240.00 per year. Newsletter.

Journal of Transnational Management Development: The Official Publication of the International Management Development Association. International Management Development Association. Haworth Press, Inc. • Quarterly. Individuals, $50.00 per year; institutions, $80.00 per year; libraries, $225.00 per year.

Multinational Monitor. Essential Information. • Monthly. Individuals, $25.00 per year; non-profit organizations, $30.00 per year; corporations, $40.00 per year. Track the activities of multinational corporations and their effects on the Third World, labor and the environment.

Multinational P R Report. Pigafetta Press. • Monthly. $85.00 per year. International public relations newsletter.

Transnational Corporations. United Nations Conference on Trade and Development. United Nations Publications. • Three times a year. $45.00 per year. Reports on both governmental and non-governmental aspects of multinational corporations. Issued by the United Nations Centre on Transnational Corporations (UNCTC). Formerly *CTC Reporter*.

Washington International Business Report: An Analytical Review and Outlook on Major Government Developments Impacting International Trade and Investment. International Business-Government Counsellors, Inc. • Monthly. $288.00 per year. Newsletter.

RESEARCH CENTERS AND INSTITUTES

Center for Human Resources. University of Pennsylvania, The Wharton School, 3733 Spruce St., 309 Vance Hall, Philadelphia, PA 19104-6358. Phone: (215)898-2722 Fax: (215)898-5908 E-mail: cappelli@wharton.upenn.edu • URL: http://www.management.wharton.upenn.edu/chr/.

Conference Board, Inc. 845 Third Ave., New York, NY 10022. Phone: (212)759-0900 Fax: (212)980-7014 E-mail: richard.cavanaugh@conference-board.org • URL: http://www.conference-board.org.

STATISTICS SOURCES

Global Stock Guide. C I F A R Publications, Inc. • Monthly. $445.00 per year. Provides financial variables for 10,000 publicly traded companies in 48 countries.

Manufacturing Worldwide: Industry Analyses, Statistics, Products, Leading Companies and Countries. The Gale Group. • 1999. $220.00. Third edition. A guide to worldwide economic activity in 500 product lines within 140 countries. Includes 37 detailed industry profiles. Name, address, phone, fax, employment, and ranking are shown for major companies worldwide in each industry sector.

TRADE/PROFESSIONAL ASSOCIATIONS

United States Council for International Business. 1212 Ave. of the Americas, 21st Fl., New York, NY 10036-1689. Phone: (212)354-4480 Fax: (212)575-0327 E-mail: info@uscib.org • URL: http://www.uscib.org.

OTHER SOURCES

Business & Company Resource Center. The Gale Group. • Fee-based Web site provides a wide range of business, industry, and specific company information. Access is offered to trade journal articles, market research data, insider trading activity, major shareholder data, corporate histories, emerging technology reports, corporate earnings estimates, press releases, and other sources. Provides detailed company profiles, industry overviews, and rankings. Offers integration of Predicasts PROMT, Newsletters ASAP, Investext Plus, Business Index ASAP, Brands and Their Companies, and other databases (many have full text).

Factiva. Dow Jones Reuters Business Interactive, LLC. • Fee-based Web site provides "global news and business information through Web sites and content integration solutions." Includes Dow Jones and Reuters newswires, The Wall Street Journal, and more than 7,000 other sources of current news, historical articles, market research reports, and investment analysis. Content includes 96 major U. S. newspapers, 900 non-English sources, trade publications, media transcripts, country profiles, news photos, etc.

Global Company News Digest: A Monthly Publication of Corporate News Summaries and Financial Transactions of the Leading 10,000 Companies Worldwide. C I F A R Publications, Inc. • Monthly. $495.00 per year. Subscriptions are available according to region, company characteristics, news topic, or industry. Provides both financial and non-financial news and information.

InSite 2. Intelligence Data/Thomson Financial. • Fee-based Web site consolidates information in a "Base Pack" consisting of Business InSite, Market InSite, and Company InSite. Optional databases are Consumer InSite, Health and Wellness InSite, Newsletter InSite, and Computer InSite. Includes fulltext content from more than 2,500 trade publications, journals, newsletters, newspapers, analyst reports, and other sources. Continuous updating. Formerly produced by The Gale Group.

International Company Data. Mergent FIS, Inc. • Monthly. Price on application. CD-ROM provides detailed financial statement information for more than 11,000 public corporations in 100 foreign countries. Formerly *Moody's International Company Data*.

Major Performance Rankings. Available from The Gale Group. • 2001. $1,100.00. Published by Euromonitor. Ranks 2,500 leading consumer product companies worldwide by various kinds of business and financial data, such as sales, profit, and market share. Includes international, regional, and country rankings.

Nexis.com. Lexis-Nexis Group. • Fee-based Web site offers searching of about 2.8 billion documents in some 30,000 news, business, and legal information sources. Features include a subject directory covering 1,200 topics in 34 categories and a Company Dossier containing information on more than 500,000 public and private companies. Boolean searching is offered.

World Business Rankings Annual. The Gale Group. • 1998. $189.00. Provides 2,500 ranked lists of international companies, compiled from a variety of published sources. Each list shows the "top ten" in a particular category. Keyword indexing, a country index, and citations are provided.

World Investment Report. United Nations Publications. • Annual. $49.00. Concerned with foreign direct investment, economic development, regional trends, transnational corporations, and globalization.

MULTIPLE DWELLINGS

See: APARTMENT HOUSES; CONDOMINIUMS

MUNICIPAL BONDS

See also: BONDS; MUNICIPAL FINANCE

ALMANACS AND YEARBOOKS

Fixed Income Almanac: The Bond Investor's Compendium of Key Market, Product, and Performance Data. Livingston G. Douglas. McGraw-Hill Professional. • 1993. $75.00. Presents 20 years of data in 350 graphs and charts. Covers bond market volatility, yield spreads, high-yield (junk) corporate bonds, default rates, and other items, such as Federal Reserve policy.

DIRECTORIES

Bond Buyer's Municipal Marketplace. Thomson Financial Publishing. • Annual. $180.00 per year. Provides information on municipal bond professionals, such as dealers, underwriters, attorneys, arbitrage specialists, derivatives specialists, rating agencies, regulators, etc.

Moody's Municipal and Government Manual. Financial Information Services. • Annual. $2,495.00 per year. Updated biweekly in *News Reports.*

Municipal Issuer's Registry. The Bond Buyer's Municipal Marketplace. • Annual. $235.00. Provides contact information relating to 6,000 issuers of municipal debt, including individuals responsible for municipal bond assignments.

ENCYCLOPEDIAS AND DICTIONARIES

Dictionary of Finance and Investment Terms. John Downes and Jordan E. Goodman. Barron's Educational Series, Inc. • 1998. $12.95. Fifth revised edition. Provides clear explanations of more than 5,000 business, banking, financial, investment, and tax terms. Includes a separate list of financial abbreviations and acronyms.

HANDBOOKS AND MANUALS

Fixed Income Analytics: State-of-the-Art Analysis and Valuation Modeling. Ravi E. Dattatreya, editor. McGraw-Hill Professional. • 1991. $69.95. Discusses the yield curve, structure and value in corporate bonds, mortgage-backed securities, and other topics.

Fixed Income Mathematics: Analytical and Statistical Techniques. Frank J. Fabozzi. McGraw-Hill Professional. • 1996. $60.00. Third edition. Covers the basics of fixed income analysis, as well as more advanced techniques used for complex securities.

Fundamentals of Municipal Bonds: A Basic, Definitive Text on the Municipal Securities Market. The Bond Market Association. • 1990. $29.95. Fourth revised edition.

Handbook for Muni Bond Issuers. Joe Mysak. Bloomberg Press. • 1998. $40.00. Written primarily for the officers and attorneys of municipalities. Provides a practical explanation of the municipal bond market. (Bloomberg Professional Library.).

How to Build Wealth with Tax-Sheltered Investments. Kerry Anne Lynch. American Institute for Economic Research. • 2000. $6.00. Provides practical information on conservative tax shelters, including defined-contribution pension plans, individual retirement accounts, Keogh plans, U. S. savings bonds, municipal bonds, and various kinds of annuities: deferred, variable-rate, immediate, and foreign-currency. (Economic Education Bulletin.).

Municipal Bonds: The Comprehensive Review of Municipal Securities and Public Finance. Robert Lamb and Stephen Rappaport. McGraw-Hill. • 1987. $34.95.

INTERNET DATABASES

DBC Online: America's Leading Provider of Real-Time Market Data to the Individual Investor. Data Broadcasting Corp. Phone: (415)571-1800 E-mail: dbcinfo@dbc.com • URL: http://www.dbc.com • Web site provides a wide variety of real-time securities market prices, data, and charts. Covers bonds ("BondVu"), stocks, commodities, options, mutual funds, major indexes, industry indexes, international markets, etc. Also includes news, SEC documents ("Smart-Edgar"), and various other features. Fees: Both free and fee-based, depending on level of information.

Fedstats. Federal Interagency Council on Statistical Policy. Phone: (202)395-7254 • URL: http://www.fedstats.gov • Web site features an efficient search facility for full-text statistics produced by more than 70 federal agencies, including the Census Bureau, the Bureau of Economic Analysis, and the Bureau of Labor Statistics. Boolean searches can be made within one agency or for all agencies combined. Links are offered to international statistical bureaus, including the UN, IMF, OECD, UNESCO, Eurostat, and 20 individual countries. Fees: Free.

Wall Street Journal Interactive Edition. Dow Jones & Co., Inc. Phone: 800-369-2834 or (212)416-2000 Fax: (212)416-2658 E-mail: inquiries@interactive.wsj.com • URL: http://www.wsj.com • Fee-based Web site providing online searching of worldwide information from the *The Wall Street Journal.* Includes "Company Snapshots," "The Journal's Greatest Hits," "Index to Market Data," "14-Day Searchable Archive," "Journal Links," etc. Financial price quotes are available. Fees: $49.00 per year; $29.00 per year to print subscribers.

ONLINE DATABASES

DRI U.S. Central Database. Data Products Division. • Provides more than 23,000 business, financial, demographic, economic, foreign trade, and industry-related time series for the U.S. Includes national income, population, retail-wholesale trade, price indexes, labor data, housing, industrial production, banking, interest rates, money supply, etc. Time period is generally 1947 to date (some data back to 1929). Updating varies. Inquire as to online cost and availability.

Fitch IBCA Ratings Delivery Service. Fitch IBCA, Inc. • Provides online delivery of Fitch financial ratings in three sectors: "Corporate Finance" (corporate bonds, insurance companies), "Structured Finance" (asset-backed securities), and "U.S. Public Finance" (municipal bonds). Daily updates. Inquire as to online cost and availability.

PERIODICALS AND NEWSLETTERS

The Bond Buyer. American Banker Newsletter, Thomson Financial Media. • Daily edition, $1,897 per year. Weekly edition, $525.00 per year. Reports on new municipal bond issues.

CreditWeek Municipal Edition. Standard & Poor's. • Weekly. $2,200.00 per year. Newsletter. Provides news and analysis of the municipal bond market, including information on new issues.

Grant's Municipal Bond Observer. James Grant, editor. Interest Rate Publishing Corp. • Biweekly. $650.00 per year. Newsletter. Provides detailed analysis of the municipal bond market.

Income Fund Outlook. Institute for Econometric Research. • Monthly. $100.00 per year. Newsletter. Contains tabular data on money market funds, certificates of deposit, bond funds, and tax-free bond funds. Includes specific recommendations, fund news, and commentary on interest rates.

Lynch Municipal Bond Advisory. James F. Lynch., ed. Lynch Municipal Bond Advisory,Inc. • Monthly. $250.00 per year. Newsletter covering events and trends in the municipal bond market.

MuniStatements. American Banker Newsletter, Thomson Financial Services Co. • Microfiche. Monthly shipments of Official Statements of municipal bond offerings. Back files available. Price on application.

The Wall Street Journal. Dow Jones & Co., Inc. • Daily. $175.00 per year. Covers news and trends relating to business, industry, finance, the economy, and international commerce. Provides extensive price and other data for the securities, commodity, options, futures, foreign exchange, and money markets.

PRICE SOURCES

Bank and Quotation Record. William B. Dana Co. • Monthly. $130.00 per year.

STATISTICS SOURCES

Business Statistics of the United States. Courtenay M. Slater, editor. Bernan Associates. • 1999. $74.00. Fifth edition. Based on *Business Statistics,* formerly issue by the Bureau of Economic Analysis, U. S. Department of Commerce. Provides basic data for a wide variety of U. S. industries, services, and economic indicators. Most statistics are shown annually for 29 years and monthly for the most recent four years.

S & P's Municipal Bond Book, with Notes, Commercial Paper, & IRBs. Standard & Poor's. • Bimonthly. $965.00 per year. Includes ratings and statistical information for about 20,000 municipal bonds, notes, commercial paper issues, and industrial revenue bonds (IRBs). The creditworthiness ("Rationales") of 200 selected municipalities and other issuers is discussed. Securities "under surveillance" by S & P are listed.

Statistical Annual: Interest Rates, Metals, Stock Indices, Options on Financial Futures, Options on Metals Futures. Chicago Board of Trade. • Annual. Includes historical data on GNMA CDR Futures, Cash-Settled GNMA Futures, U. S. Treasury Bond Futures, U. S. Treasury Note Futures, Options on Treasury Note Futures, NASDAQ-100 Futures, Major Market Index Futures, Major Market Index MAXI Futures, Municipal Bond Index Futures, 1,000-Ounce Silver Futures, Options on Silver Futures, and Kilo Gold Futures.

Survey of Current Business. Available from U. S. Government Printing Office. • Monthly. $49.00 per year. Issued by Bureau of Economic Analysis, U. S. Department of Commerce. Presents a wide variety of business and economic data.

TRADE/PROFESSIONAL ASSOCIATIONS
Bond Market Association. 40 Broad St., 12th Fl., New York, NY 10004-2373. Phone: (212)809-7000 Fax: (212)440-5260 • URL: http://www.psa.com.

OTHER SOURCES
Blue List of Current Municipal and Corporate Bond Offerings. Standard and Poor's. • Daily. $940.00 per year. Compendium of municipal and corporate bond offers.

Factiva. Dow Jones Reuters Business Interactive, LLC. • Fee-based Web site provides "global news and business information through Web sites and content integration solutions." Includes Dow Jones and Reuters newswires, The Wall Street Journal, and more than 7,000 other sources of current news, historical articles, market research reports, and investment analysis. Content includes 96 major U. S. newspapers, 900 non-English sources, trade publications, media transcripts, country profiles, news photos, etc.

Fitch Insights. Fitch Investors Service, Inc. • Biweekly. $1,040.00 per year. Includes bond rating actions and explanation of actions. Provides commentary and Fitch's view of the financial markets.

Nexis.com. Lexis-Nexis Group. • Fee-based Web site offers searching of about 2.8 billion documents in some 30,000 news, business, and legal information sources. Features include a subject directory covering 1,200 topics in 34 categories and a Company Dossier containing information on more than 500,000 public and private companies. Boolean searching is offered.

MUNICIPAL EMPLOYEES

See: CIVIL SERVICE; MUNICIPAL GOVERNMENT

MUNICIPAL FINANCE

See also: MUNICIPAL BONDS; MUNICIPAL GOVERNMENT; PUBLIC FINANCE

HANDBOOKS AND MANUALS
Miller Governmental GAAP Guide: A Comprehensive Interpretation of All Current Promulgated Governmental Generally Accepted Accounting Principles for State and Local and Local Governments. Larry P. Bailey. Harcourt Brace Professional Publishing. • Annual. $79.00. Includes reporting standards for hospitals, colleges, and other non-profit organizations. Provides a model comprehensive annual financial report.

ONLINE DATABASES
Social Scisearch. Institute for Scientific Information. • Broad, multidisciplinary index to the literature of the social sciences, 1972 to present. Weekly updates. Worldwide coverage. Inquire as to online cost and availability.

PERIODICALS AND NEWSLETTERS
Government Finance Review. Government Finance Officers Association. • Bimonthly. $30.00. per year.

Journal of Project Finance. Institutional Investor. • Quarterly. $290.00 per year. Covers the financing of large-scale construction projects, such as power plants and convention centers.

Municipal Finance Journal. Panel Publishers. • Quarterly. $260.00 per year. Recent tax and legal trends affecting both large and small state municipalities.

Nation's Cities Weekly. National League of Cities. • Weekly. $96.00 per year. Topics covered by special issues include city budgets, surface transportation, water supply, economic development, finances, telecommunications, and computers.

Project Finance: The Magazine for Global Development. Institutional Investor Journals. • Monthly. $635.00 per year. Provides articles on the financing of the infrastructure (transportation, utilities, communications, the environment, etc). Coverage is international. Supplements available *World Export Credit Guide* and *Project Finance Book of Lists.* Formed by the merger of *Infrastructure Finance* and *Project and Trade Finance.*

Public Finance Review. Sage Publications, Inc. • Quarterly. Individuals, $85.00 per year, institutions, $450.00 per year. Formerly *Public Finance Quarterly.*

RESEARCH CENTERS AND INSTITUTES
Municipal Technical Advisory Service Library. University of Tennessee, Knoxville, Conference Center Bldg.,, Suite 120, Knoxville, TN 37996-4105. Phone: (423)974-0411 Fax: (423)974-0423 E-mail: rschwartz@utk.edu • URL: http://www.mtas.utk.edu • Research areas include municipal finance, police administration, and public works.

Urban Institute. 2100 M St., N. W., Washington, DC 20037. Phone: (202)833-7200 Fax: (202)728-0232 E-mail: paffairs@ui.urban.org • URL: http://www.urban.org • Research activities include the study of urban economic affairs, development, housing, productivity, and municipal finance.

STATISTICS SOURCES
County and City Extra: Annual Metro, City and County Data Book. Mark Littman and Deirdre A. Gaquin. Bernan Press. • 1999. $109.00. Updates and augments data published irregularly in print form by the U. S. Census Bureau in *County and City Data Book.* Covers "every state, county, metropolitan area, and congressional district in the United States, as well as all U. S. cities with a 1990 population of 25,000 or more." Contains a wide range tic maps.

Facts and Figures on Government Finance. Tax Foundation, Inc. • Annual. $60.00.

Gale City and Metro Rankings Reporter. The Gale Group. • 1996. $134.00. Second edition. Provides about 3,000 statistical ranking tables covering more than 1,500 U. S. cities and Metropolitan Statistical Areas. Covers economic, demographic, social, governmental, and cultural factors. Sources are private studies and government data.

S & P's Municipal Bond Book, with Notes, Commercial Paper, & IRBs. Standard & Poor's. • Bimonthly. $965.00 per year. Includes ratings and statistical information for about 20,000 municipal bonds, notes, commercial paper issues, and industrial revenue bonds (IRBs). The creditworthiness ("Rationales") of 200 selected municipalities and other issuers is discussed. Securities "under surveillance" by S & P are listed.

TRADE/PROFESSIONAL ASSOCIATIONS
Association of Government Accountants. 2208 Mount Vernon Ave., Alexandria, VA 22301-1314. Phone: 800-242-7211 or (703)684-6931 Fax: (703)548-9367 • URL: http://www.agacgfm.org • Members are employed by federal, state, county, and city government agencies. Includes accountants, auditors, budget officers, and other government finance administrators and officials.

Government Finance Officers Association of the United States and Canada. 180 N. Michigan Ave., Chicago, IL 60601. Phone: (312)977-9700 • URL: http://www.gfoa.com.

MUNICIPAL GOVERNMENT

See also: CITIES AND TOWNS; CITY PLANNING; COUNTY GOVERNMENT; PUBLIC ADMINISTRATION

ABSTRACTS AND INDEXES
Social Sciences Citation Index. Institute for Scientific Information. • Three times a year. $6,900 per year. Annual cumulation. Includes *Source Index, Citation Index, Permuterm Subject Index,* and *Corporate Index.*

Social Sciences Index. H. W. Wilson Co. • Quarterly, with annual cumulation. Service basis for print edition; CD-ROM edition, $1,495 per year. Indexes more than 400 periodicals covering economics, environmental policy, government, insurance, labor, health care policy, plannning, public administration, public welfare, urban studies, women's issues, criminology, and related topics.

ALMANACS AND YEARBOOKS
Municipal Year Book. International City/County Management Association. • Annual. $84.95. An authoritative resume of activities and statistical data of American cities.

BIOGRAPHICAL SOURCES
Who's Who in American Politics. Marquis Who's Who. • Biennial. $275.00. Two volumes. Contains about 27,000 biographical sketches of local, state, and national elected or appointed individuals.

CD-ROM DATABASES
Social Science Source. EBSCO Publishing. • Monthly. $1,495.00 per year. Provides CD-ROM citations and abstracts to social science articles in more than 600 periodicals, with full text from 125 periodicals. Covers economics, political science, public policy, international relations, psychology, and other topics. Time period is most recent five years.

Social Sciences Citation Index: Compact Disc Edition. Institute for Scientific Information. • Quarterly. Provides CD-ROM indexing of the world's social sciences literature, including economics, business, finance, management, communications, demographics, information and library science, political science, sociology, etc. Corresponds to online *Social Scisearch* and printed *Social Sciences Citation Index.*

Social Sciences Citation Index: Compact Disc Edition with Abstracts. Institute for Scientific Information. • Quarterly. Provides CD-ROM indexing and abstracting of "significant articles" from 1,400 social science journals worldwide, with additional selections from 3,200 other journals, 1986 to date. Includes economics, business, finance, management, communications, demographics, information and library science, political science, sociology, and many other subjects.

WILSONDISC: Wilson Social Sciences Abstracts. H. W. Wilson Co. • Monthly. Including unlimited online access to *Social Sciences Index* through WILSONLINE. Provides CD-ROM indexing from 1983 and abstracting from 1994 of more than 400 periodicals covering economics, area studies, community health, public administration, public welfare, urban studies, and many other topics related to the social sciences.

DIRECTORIES
American City and County Municipal Index: Purchasing Guide for City, Township, County Officials and Consulting Engineers. Intertec Publishing Corp. • Annual. $61.95. Includes a directory of city and county governments with populations of 10,000 or more. Names and telephone numbers of municipal purchasing officials are listed. Also includes a directory of manufacturers and

suppliers of materials, equipment, and services for municipalities.

Carroll's Municipal/County Directory: CD-ROM Edition. Carroll Publishing. • Semiannual. $750.00 per year. Provides CD-ROM listings of about 99,000 city, town, and county officials in the U. S. Also available online.

Carroll's Municipal Directory. Carroll Publishing. • Semiannual. $255.00 per year. Lists about 50,000 officials in 7,900 U. S. towns and cities, with expanded listings for cities having a population of over 25,000. Top 100 cities are ranked by population and size.

Government Phone Book USA: Your Comprehensive Guide to Federal, State, County, and Local Government Offices in the United States. Omnigraphics, Inc. • Annual. $230.00. Contains more than 168,500 listings of federal, state, county, and local government offices and personnel, including legislatures. Formerly *Government Directory of Addresses and Phone Numbers.*

Mayors of America's Principal Cities. United States Conference of Mayors. • Semiannual. About 1,000 mayors of cities with populations of 30,000 or more.

Moody's Municipal and Government Manual. Financial Information Services. • Annual. $2,495.00 per year. Updated biweekly in *News Reports.*

Municipal Yellow Book: Who's Who in the Leading City and County Governments and Local Authorities. Leadership Directories, Inc. • Semiannual. $235.00 per year. Lists approximately 32,000 key personnel in city and county departments, agencies, subdivisions, and branches.

HANDBOOKS AND MANUALS

Municipal Management Series. International City/County Management Association. • 14 volumes. Various dates, 1968 to 1988. Finance, planning, training, public relations, and other subjects.

ONLINE DATABASES

Social Scisearch. Institute for Scientific Information. • Broad, multidisciplinary index to the literature of the social sciences, 1972 to present. Weekly updates. Worldwide coverage. Inquire as to online cost and availability.

Wilson Social Sciences Abstracts Online. H. W. Wilson Co. • Provides online abstracting and indexing of more than 415 periodicals covering area studies, community health, public administration, public welfare, urban studies, and many other social science topics. Time period is 1994 to date for abstracts and 1983 to date for indexing, with updates monthly. Inquire as to online cost and availability.

PERIODICALS AND NEWSLETTERS

American City and County: Administration, Engineering and Operations in Relation to Local Government. Intertec Publishing Corp. • Monthly. $58.00 per year. Edited for mayors, city managers, and other local officials. Emphasis is on equipment and basic services.

Current Municipal Problems. West Group. • Quarterly. $153.50 per year. Annual cumulation. Full text journal articles on municipal law and administration. Indexing included.

Governing: The States and Localities. • Monthly. $39.95 per year. Edited for state and local government officials. Covers finance, office management, computers, telecommunications, environmental concerns, etc.

Government Technology: Solutions for State and Local Government in the Information Age. • Monthly. Free to qualified personnel.

ICMA Newsletter. International City/County Management Association. • Biweekly. $175.00 per year. Covers news of developments in local government, professional municipal management, and federal regulation applied to municipalities.

McQuillan Municipal Law Report: A Monthly Review for Lawyers, Administrators and Officials. West Group. • Monthly. $277.00 per year. Newsletter. Summary of recent court decisions affecting municipalities.

National Civic Review. National Civic League, Inc. Jossey-Bass Inc., Publishers. • Quarterly. Institutions, $83.00 per year. Presents civic strategies for improving local government operations and community life.

Nation's Cities Weekly. National League of Cities. • Weekly. $96.00 per year. Topics covered by special issues include city budgets, surface transportation, water supply, economic development, finances, telecommunications, and computers.

Public Management: Devoted to the Conduct of Local Government. International City-County Management Association. • Monthly. $34.00 per year.

Public Risk. Public Risk Management Association. • 10 times a year. $125.00 per year. Covers risk management for state and local governments, including various kinds of liabilities.

U.S. Mayor. United States Conference of Mayors. • Biweekly. $35.00 per year. Formerly*Mayor.*

STATISTICS SOURCES

County and City Data Book, a Statistical Abstract Supplement. U.S. Bureau of the Census. Available from U.S. Government Printing Office. • 1994. $60.00.

Facts About the Cities. Allan Carpenter and Carl Provorse. H. W. Wilson Co. • 1996. $65.00. Second edition. Contains a wide variety of information on 300 American cities, including cities in Puerto Rico, Guam, and the U. S. Virgin Islands. Data is provided on the workplace, taxes, revenues, cost of living, population, climate, housing, transportation, etc.

Gale City and Metro Rankings Reporter. The Gale Group. • 1996. $134.00. Second edition. Provides about 3,000 statistical ranking tables covering more than 1,500 U. S. cities and Metropolitan Statistical Areas. Covers economic, demographic, social, governmental, and cultural factors. Sources are private studies and government data.

TRADE/PROFESSIONAL ASSOCIATIONS

International City/County Management Association. 777 N. Capitol St., N. E., Suite 500, Washington, DC 20002-4201. Phone: (202)289-4262 Fax: (202)962-3500 • URL: http://www.icma.org • Members are administrators and assistant administrators of cities, counties, and regions. Formerly known as the International City Managers' Association (ICMA).

International Institute of Municipal Clerks. 1221 N. San Dimas Canyon Rd., San Dimas, CA 91773-1223. Phone: (909)592-4462 Fax: (909)592-1555 E-mail: hq@iimc.com • URL: http://www.iimc.com.

International Municipal Lawyers Association. 1110 Vermont Ave., N.W., Suite 200, Washington, DC 20005. Phone: (202)466-5424 Fax: (202)785-0152 E-mail: info@imla.org • URL: http://www.imla.org.

National Civic League National Headquarters. 1445 Market, Suite 300, Denver, CO 80202-1728. Phone: 800-223-6004 or (303)571-4343 Fax: (303)571-4404 E-mail: ncl@ncl.org • URL: http://www.ncl.org/ncl.

National League of Cities. 1301 Pennsylvania Ave., N.W., Washington, DC 20004-1763. Phone: (202)626-3000 Fax: (202)626-3043 E-mail: pa@nlc.org • URL: http://www.nlc.org.

Public Risk Management Association. 1815 N. Fort Meyer Dr., Ste. 1020, Arlington, VA 22209-1805. Phone: (703)528-7701 Fax: (703)528-7966 E-mail: info@primacentral.org • URL: http://www.primacentral.org • Members are state and local government officials concerned with risk management and public liabilities.

United States Conference of Mayors. 1620 Eye St., N. W., Washington, DC 20006. Phone: (202)293-7330 Fax: (202)293-2352 E-mail: info@usmayors.org • URL: http://www.usmayors.org • Promotes improved municipal government, with emphasis on federal cooperation.

OTHER SOURCES

Local Government Law. Chester J. Antieau. Matthew Bender & Co., Inc. • $1,070.00. Seven looseleaf volumes. Periodic supplementation. States the principle of law for all types of local governments, and backs those principles with case citations from all jurisdictions. Examines the laws and their impact in three primary cases.

MUSHROOM INDUSTRY

INTERNET DATABASES

USDA. United States Department of Agriculture. Phone: (202)720-2791 E-mail: agsec@usda.gov • URL: http://www.usda.gov • The USDA home page has six sections: News and Information; What's New; About USDA; Agencies; Opportunities; Search and Help. Keyword searching is offered from the USDA home page and from various individual agency home pages. Agencies are the Economic Research Service, Agricultural Marketing Service, National Agricultural Statistics Service, National Agricultural Library, and about 12 others. Updating varies. Fees: Free.

PERIODICALS AND NEWSLETTERS

Mushroom Journal. Mushroom Growers' Association. • Monthly. Membership.

Mushroom News. American Mushroom Institute. • Monthly. $275.00. Includes *News Flash.*

STATISTICS SOURCES

Agricultural Statistics. Available from U. S. Government Printing Office. • Annual. Produced by the National Agricultural Statistics Service, U. S. Department of Agriculture. Provides a wide variety of statistical data relating to agricultural production, supplies, consumption, prices/price-supports, foreign trade, costs, and returns, as well as farm labor, loans, income, and population. In many cases, historical data is shown annually for 10 years. In addition to farm data, includes detailed fishery statistics.

TRADE/PROFESSIONAL ASSOCIATIONS

American Mushroom Institute. One Massachusetts Ave. N.W., Suite 800, Washington, DC 20001. Phone: (202)842-4344 Fax: (202)408-7763 • URL: http://www.americanmushroominst.com.

MUSIC INDUSTRY

See also: MUSICAL INSTRUMENTS INDUSTRY; PHONOGRAPH AND PHONOGRAPH RECORD INDUSTRIES

ABSTRACTS AND INDEXES

Music Index: A Subject-Author Guide to Over 300 Current International Periodicals. Harmonie Park Press. • Quarterly. $1,850.00 per year. Annual cummulation. Supplement available: *Music Index Subject Heading List.* Guide to current periodicals. Entries are in language of country issuing the index.

BIBLIOGRAPHIES

Information Sources in Music. Lewis Foreman, editor. Bowker-Saur. • 2001. $100.00. Evaluates information sources on a wide range of music topics, including copyright, music publishing, reprographics, and the use of computers in music publishing. (Guides to Information Sources Series).

Women in American Music; A Bibliography of Music and Literature. Adrienne Fried Block and Carol Neuls-Bates, editors. Greenwood Publishing Group, Inc. • 1979. $59.95.

BIOGRAPHICAL SOURCES

Celebrity Register. The Gale Group. • 1989. $99.00. Fifth edition. Compiled by Celebrity Services International (Earl Blackwell). Contains profiles of 1,300 famous individuals in the performing arts, sports, politics, business, and other fields.

Contemporary Musicians: Profiles of the People in Music. Available from The Gale Group. • 2001. $2,880.00. 32 volumes in print. $81.00 per volume.

DIRECTORIES

Billboard's International Buyer's Guide. Billboard Books. • Annual. $141.00. Record companies; music publishers; record and tape wholesalers; services and supplies for the music-record-tape-video industry; record and tape dealer accessories, fixtures, and merchandising products; includes United States and over 65 countries.

Grey House Performing Arts Directory. Grey House Publishing. • 2001. $220.00. Contains more than 7,700 entries covering dance, instrumental music, vocal music, theatre, performance series, festivals, performance facilities, and media sources.

MixPlus: Music and Audio Resources for the U. S. and Canada. Intertec Publishing Corp. • Annual. $14.95 for each regional edition (East, West, Central). A professional directory for the recording and music businesses, listing concert promoters, rehearsal halls, consultants, record labels, recording studios, tape and disc mastering services, legal services, facility designers, music education programs, and other music and audio services.

Music Address Book: How to Reach Anyone Who's Anyone in the Music Business. Michael Levine. HarperCollins Publishers. • 1994. $16.00. Second editon.

Musical America International Directory of the Performing Arts. Commonwealth Business Media. • Annual. $105.00. Covers United States and Canada.

Peterson's Professional Degree Programs in the Visual and Performing Arts. Peterson's. • Annual. $24.95. A directory of more than 900 degree programs in art, music, theater, and dance at 600 colleges and professional schools.

Phonolog Reporter: All-in-One Reporter. i2 Technologies. • Weekly. $486.00 per year. Looseleaf. Contains over one million listings of recorded music (compact discs, cassette tapes, and phonograph records). Includes both popular and classical releases. Popular music is classified by title, artist, and album; classical performances are accessible by title, artist, and composer.

Purchasers Guide to the Music Industries. Music Trades Corp. • Annual. Available only with subscription to *Music Trades.*

Recording Industry Sourcebook. Intertec Publishing. • Annual. $79.95. Provides more than 12,000 listings in 57 categories of record/tape/compact disc labels, producers, distributors, managers, equipment suppliers, and others.

Schwann Opus: The Classical Music Resource. Schwann Publications. • Annual. $27.45 per year. Lists classical music recordings by composer. Covers compact discs, minidiscs, and cassette tapes. Includes an extensive, alphabetical list of recording labels and distributors, with addresses and telephone numbers (many listings also include fax numbers and Internet addresses).

Schwann Spectrum: The Guide to Rock, Jazz, World...and Beyond. Schwann Publications. • Annual. $27.45 per year. Lists rock, jazz, country, folk, soundtrack, international, new age, religious, and other disc and tape popular recordings by performer. Includes an extensive, alphabetical list of recording labels and distributors, with addresses and telephone numbers (some listings also include fax numbers and Internet addresses).

ENCYCLOPEDIAS AND DICTIONARIES

Encyclopedia of Popular Music. Colin Larkin, editor. Groves Dictionaries, Inc. • 1998. $500.00. Third edition. Eight volumes. Covers a wide variety of music forms and pop culture. Includes bibliography and index.

HANDBOOKS AND MANUALS

All You Need to Know About the Music Business: Revised and Updated for the 21st Century. Donald S. Passman. Simon & Schuster Trade. • 2000. Price on application. Covers the practical and legal aspects of record contracts, music publishing, management agreements, touring, and other music business topics.

Entertainment Law. Howard Siegel, editor. New York State Bar Association. • 1990. $60.00. Contains chapters by various authors on the legal aspects of television, motion pictures, theatre, music, phonograph records, and related topics.

Interactive Music Handbook. Jodi Summers, editor. Carronade Group. • 1996. $24.95. Covers interactive or enhanced music CD-ROMs and online music for producers, audio technicians, and musicians. Includes case studies and interviews.

Music Technology Buyer's Guide. United Entertainment Media, Inc. • $7.95. Annual. Lists more than 4,000 hardware and software music production products from 350 manufacturers. Includes synthesizers, MIDI hardware and software, mixers, microphones, music notation software, etc. Produced by the editorial staffs of *Keyboard* and *EQ* magazines.

ONLINE DATABASES

PROMT: Predicasts Overview of Markets and Technology. The Gale Group. • Companies, products, applied technologies and markets. U.S. and international literature coverage, 1972 to date. Inquire as to online cost and availability. Provides abstracts from more than 1,600 publications. Weekly updates.

PERIODICALS AND NEWSLETTERS

Billboard: The International Newsweekly of Music, Video, and Home Entertainment. BPI Communications, Inc. • 51 times a year. $289.00 per year. Newsweekly for the music and home entertainment industries.

BMI: Music World. Broadcast Music, Inc. • Quarterly. Free to qualified personnel. Formerly *BMI: The Many Worlds of Music.*

Cash Box: The International Music-Record Weekly. Cash Box Publishing Co., Inc. • Weekly. $185.00 per year.

Computer Music Journal. MIT Press. • Quarterly. Individuals, $48.00 per year; instutitions, $158.00 per year. Covers digital soound and the musical applications of computers.

Down Beat: Jazz, Blues and Beyond. Maher Publications, Inc. • Monthly. $35.00 per year. Contemporary music.

Entertainment Marketing Letter. EPM Communications, Inc. • 22 times a year. $319.00 per year. Newsletter. Covers the marketing of various entertainment products. Includes television broadcasting, videocassettes, celebrity tours and tie-ins, radio broadcasting, and the music business.

Mix Magazine: Professional Recording, Sound, and Music Production. Intertec Publishing Corp. • Monthly. $34.95 per year.

Music Inc. Maher Publications, Inc. • 11 times a year. $16.00. per year. Music and sound retailing. Formerly *Up Beat Monthly.*

Music Journal. Incorporated Society of Musicians. • Monthly. $50.00 per year.

Music Reference Services Quarterly. Haworth Press, Inc. • Quarterly. Individuals, $40.00 per year; libraries and other institutions, $75.00 per year. An academic journal for music librarians.

Music Trades. Music Trades Corp. • Monthly. $14.00 per year. Includes *Purchaser's Guide to the Music Industries.*

Stereo Review's Sound & Vision: Home Theater-Audio- Video- MultimediaMovies- Music. Hachette Filipacchi Magazines, Inc. • 10 times a year. $24.00 per year. Popular magazine providing explanatory articles and critical reviews of equipment and media (CD-ROM, DVD, videocassettes, etc.). Supplement available *Stero Review's Sound and Vision Buyers Guide.* Replaces *Stereo Review* and *Video Magazine.*

STATISTICS SOURCES

U. S. Industry and Trade Outlook: The McGraw-Hill Companies and the U.S. Department of Commerce/ International Trade Administration. Datapso Research Corp. • Annual. $69.95. Produced by the International Trade Administration, U. S. Department of Commerce, in a "public-private" partnership with DRI/McGraw-Hill and Standard & Poor's. Provides basic data, outlook for the current year, and "Long-Term Prospects" (five-year projections) for a wide variety of products and services. Includes high technology industries. Formerly *U. S. Industrial Outlook.*

TRADE/PROFESSIONAL ASSOCIATIONS

American Society of Composers, Authors and Publishers. One Lincoln Plaza, New York, NY 10023. Phone: (212)621-6000 Fax: (212)724-9064 E-mail: info@ascap.com • URL: http://www.ascap.com.

Broadcast Music, Inc. 320 W. 57th St., New York, NY 10019. Phone: (212)586-2000 Fax: (212)956-2059.

Music Industry Conference. c/o MENC: The National Association for Music, 1806 Robert Fulton Dr., Reston, VA 20191. Phone: 800-336-3768 or (703)860-4000 Fax: (703)860-1531 E-mail: sandraf@menc.org • URL: http://www.menc.org.

National Association of Music Merchants. 5790 Arnada Dr., Carlsbad, CA 92008. Phone: 800-767-6266 or (619)438-8001 Fax: (619)438-7327.

OTHER SOURCES

EQ: The Project Recording and Sound Magazine. United Entertainment Media, Inc. • Monthly. $36.00 per year. Provides advice on professional music recording equipment and technique.

Keyboard: Making Music with Technology. United Entertainment Media, Inc. • Monthly. $36.00 per year. Emphasis is on recording systems, keyboard technique, and computer-assisted music (MIDI) systems.

Lindey on Entertainment, Publishing and the Arts: Agreements and the Law. Alexander Lindey, editor. West Group. • $673.00 per year. Looseleaf service. Periodic supplementation. Provides basic forms, applicable law, and guidance. (Entertainment and Communication Law Series).

Radio & Records. Radio & Records, Inc. • Weekly. $299.00 per year. Provides news and information relating to the record industry and to regional and national radio broadcasting. Special features cover specific types of programming, such as "classic rock," "adult alternative," "oldies," "country," and "news/talk." Radio station business and management topics are included.

Schwann Inside: Jazz and Classical. Schwann Publications. • Monthly. $55.95 per year. Provides reviews and listings of new classical and jazz recordings. Includes "Billboard Charts" of top selling jazz, contemporary jazz, classical, classical crossover, classical midline, and classical budget albums.

MUSICAL INSTRUMENTS INDUSTRY

See also: MUSIC INDUSTRY

DIRECTORIES

Musical Merchandise Review: Directory of Musical Instrument Dealers. Larkin Publications, Inc. • Annual. $125.00. Lists retailers of musical instruments and supplies.

Musical Merchandise Review: Music Industry Directory. Larkin Publications, Inc. • Annual. $25.00. Lists about 1,500 manufacturers and distributors of musical instruments and supplies. Includes indexes to products and trade names.

Purchasers Guide to the Music Industries. Music Trades Corp. • Annual. Available only with subscription to *Music Trades.*

FINANCIAL RATIOS

Annual Statement Studies. Robert Morris Associates: The Association of Lending and Credit Risk Professiona. • Annual. Free to members; non-members, $140.00. Median and quartile financial ratios are given for over 400 kinds of manufacturing, wholesale, retail, construction, and consumer finance establishments. Data is sorted by both asset size and sales volume. Includes a clearly written "Definition of Ratios" and an alphabetical industry index.

PERIODICALS AND NEWSLETTERS

Electronic Musician. Intertec Publishing Corp. • Monthly. $23.95 per year.

Instrumentalist: A Magazine for School and College Band and Orchestra Directors, Professional Instrumentalist, Teacher-Training Specialists in Instrumental Music Education and Instrumental Teachers. Instrumentalist Co. • Monthly. $22.00 per year. Professional journal for school band and orchestra directors and teachers of instruments in those ensembles.

Music Trades. Music Trades Corp. • Monthly. $14.00 per year. Includes *Purchaser's Guide to the Music Industries.*

PRICE SOURCES

Orion Guitars and Musical Instruments Blue Book. Orion Research Corp. • Annual. $179.00. List of manufacturers of guitars and musical instruments. Original list prices and years of manufacture are also shown. Formerly *Orion Professional Sound and Musical Instruments.*

STATISTICS SOURCES

U. S. Industry and Trade Outlook: The McGraw-Hill Companies and the U.S. Department of Commerce/International Trade Administration. Datapso Research Corp. • Annual. $69.95. Produced by the International Trade Administration, U. S. Department of Commerce, in a "public-private" partnership with DRI/McGraw-Hill and Standard & Poor's. Provides basic data, outlook for the current year, and "Long-Term Prospects" (five-year projections) for a wide variety of products and services. Includes high technology industries. Formerly *U. S. Industrial Outlook.*

TRADE/PROFESSIONAL ASSOCIATIONS

American Music Conference. 5790 Armada Dr., Carlsbad, CA 92008-4391. Phone: (760)431-9124 or (760)366-5260 Fax: (760)438-7327 E-mail: info@amc-music.com • URL: http://www.amc-music.com.

Music Distributors Association. c/o J&D Music Services, 38 W. 21st St., 11th Fl., New York, NY 10010-6906. Phone: (212)924-9175 Fax: (212)675-3577 E-mail: assnhdqs@aol.com • URL: http://www.musicdistributors.org.

National Association of Band Instrument Manufacturers. 38 W. 21st St., Rm. 1106, New York, NY 10010-6906. Phone: (212)924-9175 Fax: (212)675-3577 E-mail: assnhdqs@aol.com.

National Association of Music Merchants. 5790 Arnada Dr., Carlsbad, CA 92008. Phone: 800-767-6266 or (619)438-8001 Fax: (619)438-7327.

OTHER SOURCES

Music and Sound Retailer. Testa Communications. • Monthly. $18.00 per year. Provides news and advice on the retailing of a wide range of music and sound products, including musical instruments, electronic keyboards, sound amplification systems, music software, and recording equipment.

Musical Merchandise Review. Larkin Publications, Inc. • Monthly. $24.00 per year. Edited for musical instrument dealers selling pianos, organs, band/orchestra instruments, electronic keyboards, guitars, music amplifiers, microphones, sheet music, and other musical merchandise.

MUTUAL FUNDS

See: INVESTMENT COMPANIES

MUTUAL SAVINGS BANKS

See: SAVINGS BANKS

N

NAFTA

See: NORTH AMERICAN FREE TRADE AGREEMENT

NARCOTICS

See also: DRUG ABUSE AND TRAFFIC; PHARMACEUTICAL INDUSTRY

GENERAL WORKS

A Brief History of Cocaine. Steven B. Karch. CRC Press, Inc. • 1997. $24.95. Emphasizes the societal effects of cocaine abuse in various regions of the world.

The Chemistry of Mind-Altering Drugs: History, Pharmacology, and Cultural Context. Daniel M. Perrine. American Chemical Society. • 1996. $42.00. Contains detailed descriptions of the pharmacological and psychological effects of a wide variety of drugs, "from alcohol to zopiclone.".

Drugs of Abuse. Available from U. S. Government Printing Office. • 1997. $15.00. Issued by the Drug Enforcement Administration, U. S. Department of Justice (http://www.usdoj.gov). Provides detailed information on various kinds of narcotics, depressants, stimulants, hallucinogens, cannabis, steroids, and inhalants. Contains many color illustrations and a detailed summary of the Controlled Substances Act.

ALMANACS AND YEARBOOKS

Report of the International Narcotics Control Board on Its Work. United Nations Publications. • Annual. $20.00.

CD-ROM DATABASES

International Pharmaceutical Abstracts [CD-ROM]. American Society of Health-System Pharmacists. • Quarterly. $1,795.00 per year. Contains CD-ROM indexing and abstracting of international pharmaceutical literature from 1970 to date.

ENCYCLOPEDIAS AND DICTIONARIES

Encyclopedia of Drugs, Alcohol, and Addictive Behavior. Available from The Gale Group. • 2001. $425.00. Second edition. Four volumes. Published by Macmillan Reference USA. Covers the social, economic, political, and medical aspects of addiction.

HANDBOOKS AND MANUALS

Drug Abuse and the Law Sourcebook. Gerald F. Uelmen and Victor G. Haddox. West Group. • $240.00 per year. Two looseleaf volumes. Periodic supplementation. Covers drugs of abuse, criminal responsibility, possessory offenses, trafficking offenses, and related topics. (Criminal Law Series).

Drug Abuse Handbook. Steven B. Karch, editor. CRC Press, Inc. • 1997. $99.95. Provides comprehensive coverage of drug abuse issues and trends. Edited for healthcare professionals.

Narcotics and Drug Abuse A to Z. Croner Publications, Inc. • Three volumes. Price on application. Lists treatment centers.

Substance Abuse: A Comprehensive Textbook. Joyce H. Lowinson and others. Lippincott Williams & Wilkins. • 1997. $155.00. Third edition. Covers the medical, psychological, socioeconomic, and public health aspects of drug and alcohol abuse.

ONLINE DATABASES

International Pharmaceutical Abstracts [online]. American Society of Health-System Pharmacists. • Provides online indexing and abstracting of the world's pharmaceutical literature from 1970 to date. Monthly updates. Inquire as to online cost and availability.

Pharmaceutical News Index. Bell & Howell Information and Learning. • Indexes major pharmaceutical industry newsletters, 1974 to present. Weekly updates. Inquire as to online cost and availability.

Toxline. National Library of Medicine. • Abstracting service covering human and animal toxicity studies, 1965 to present (older studies available in *Toxback* file). Monthly updates. Inquire as to online cost and availability.

PERIODICALS AND NEWSLETTERS

Bulletin on Narcotics. United Nations Publications. • Quarterly. $10.00 per issue. Editions in Chinese, French, Russian and Spanish.

STATISTICS SOURCES

Narcotic Drugs: Estimated World Requirements. International Narcotics Control Board. United Nations Publications. • Annual. $38.00. Includes production and utilization data relating to legal narcotics. Text in French, English and Spanish.

Psychotropic Substances. United Nations Publications. • Annual. $42.00.

Statistics on Alcohol, Drug, and Tobacco Use: A Selection of Statistical Charts, Graphs and Tables about Alcohol, Drug and Tobacco Use from a Variety of Published Sources with Explanatory Comments. The Gale Group. • 1995. $65.00. Includes graphs, charts, and tables arranged within subject chapters. Citations to data sources are provided.

TRADE/PROFESSIONAL ASSOCIATIONS

The Health Connection. 55 W. Oak Ridge Dr., Hagerstown, MD 21740. Phone: 800-548-8700 or (301)790-9735 Fax: (301)790-9733 E-mail: sales@healthconnection.org • URL: http://www.healthconnection.org.

OTHER SOURCES

Defense of Narcotics Cases. David Bernheim. Matthew Bender & Co., Inc. • $590.00. Three looseleaf volumes. Periodic supplementation. Up-to-date coverage of all aspects of narcotics cases and related matters.

NATIONAL ACCOUNTING

See also: ECONOMIC POLICY; ECONOMIC STATISTICS; ECONOMICS

ABSTRACTS AND INDEXES

Social Sciences Index. H. W. Wilson Co. • Quarterly, with annual cumulation. Service basis for print edition; CD-ROM edition, $1,495 per year. Indexes more than 400 periodicals covering economics, environmental policy, government, insurance, labor, health care policy, plannning, public administration, public welfare, urban studies, women's issues, criminology, and related topics.

ALMANACS AND YEARBOOKS

National Accounts Statistics: Main Aggregates and Detailed Tables. United Nations Publications. • Annual. $160.00.

CD-ROM DATABASES

EconLit. Available from SilverPlatter Information, Inc. • Monthly. Single-user, $1,600.00 per year. Multi-user, $2,400.00 per year. Provides CD-ROM citations, with abstracts, to articles from more than 500 economics journals. Time period is 1969 to date. Produced by the American Economic Association.

Social Science Source. EBSCO Publishing. • Monthly. $1,495.00 per year. Provides CD-ROM citations and abstracts to social science articles in more than 600 periodicals, with full text from 125 periodicals. Covers economics, political science, public policy, international relations, psychology, and other topics. Time period is most recent five years.

Social Sciences Citation Index: Compact Disc Edition with Abstracts. Institute for Scientific Information. • Quarterly. Provides CD-ROM indexing and abstracting of "significant articles" from 1,400 social science journals worldwide, with additional selections from 3,200 other journals, 1986 to date. Includes economics, business, finance, management, communications, demographics, information and library science, political science, sociology, and many other subjects.

WILSONDISC: Wilson Social Sciences Abstracts. H. W. Wilson Co. • Monthly. Including unlimited online access to *Social Sciences Index* through WILSONLINE. Provides CD-ROM indexing from 1983 and abstracting from 1994 of more than 400 periodicals covering economics, area studies, community health, public administration, public welfare, urban studies, and many other topics related to the social sciences.

INTERNET DATABASES

Fedstats. Federal Interagency Council on Statistical Policy. Phone: (202)395-7254 • URL: http://www.fedstats.gov • Web site features an efficient search facility for full-text statistics produced by more than 70 federal agencies, including the Census Bureau, the Bureau of Economic Analysis, and the Bureau of Labor Statistics. Boolean searches can be made within one agency or for all agencies combined. Links are offered to international statistical bureaus, including the UN, IMF, OECD, UNESCO, Eurostat, and 20 individual countries. Fees: Free.

U. S. Census Bureau: The Official Statistics. U. S. Bureau of the Census. Phone: (301)763-4100 Fax: (301)763-4794 • URL: http://www.census.gov • Web site is "Your Source for Social, Demographic, and Economic Information." Contains "Current U. S. Population Count," "Current Economic Indicators," and a wide variety of data under "Other Official Statistics." Keyword searching is provided. Fees: Free.

ONLINE DATABASES

DRI U.S. Central Database. Data Products Division. • Provides more than 23,000 business, financial, demographic, economic, foreign trade, and industry-related time series for the U.S. Includes national income, population, retail-wholesale trade, price indexes, labor data, housing, industrial production, banking, interest rates, money supply, etc. Time period is generally 1947 to date (some data back to 1929). Updating varies. Inquire as to online cost and availability.

EconLit. American Economic Association. • Covers the worldwide literature of economics as contained in selected monographs and about 550 journals. Subjects include microeconomics, macroeconomics, economic history, inflation, money, credit, finance, accounting theory, trade, natural resource economics, and regional economics. Time period is 1969 to present, with monthly updates. Inquire as to online cost and availability.

Wilson Social Sciences Abstracts Online. H. W. Wilson Co. • Provides online abstracting and indexing of more than 415 periodicals covering area studies, community health, public administration, public welfare, urban studies, and many other social science topics. Time period is 1994 to date for abstracts and 1983 to date for indexing, with updates monthly. Inquire as to online cost and availability.

STATISTICS SOURCES

Business Statistics of the United States. Courtenay M. Slater, editor. Bernan Associates. • 1999. $74.00. Fifth edition. Based on *Business Statistics*, formerly issue by the Bureau of Economic Analysis, U. S. Department of Commerce. Provides basic data for a wide variety of U. S. industries, services, and economic indicators. Most statistics are shown annually for 29 years and monthly for the most recent four years.

Monthly Bulletin of Statistics. United Nations Publications. • Monthly. $295.00 per year. Provides current data for about 200 countries on a wide variety of economic, industrial, and demographic subjects. Compiled by United Nations Statistical Office.

National Accounts of OECD Countries. OECD Publications and Information Center. • Annual. Two volumes. Price varies.

OECD Quarterly National Accounts Bulletin. OECD Publications and Information Center. • Quarterly. $120.00 per year. National accounts data of OECD countries.

Social Statistics of the United States. Mark S. Littman, editor. Bernan Press. • 2000. $65.00. Includes statistical data on population growth, labor force, occupations, environmental trends, leisure time use, income, poverty, taxes, and other economic or demographic topics.

Statistical Abstract of the United States. Available from U. S. Government Printing Office. • Annual. $51.00. Issued by the U. S. Bureau of the Census.

A Statistical Portrait of the United States: Social Conditions and Trends. Mark S. Littman, editor. Bernan Press. • 1998. $89.00. Covers "social, economic, and environmental trends in the United States over the past 25 years." Includes statistical tables, graphs, and analysis relating to such topics as population, income, poverty, wealth, labor, housing, education, healthcare, air/water quality, and government.

Statistical Yearbook. United Nations Publications. • Annual. $125.00. Contains statistics for about 200 countries on a wide variety of economic, industrial, and demographic topics. Compiled by United Nations Statistical Office.

Survey of Current Business. Available from U. S. Government Printing Office. • Monthly. $49.00 per year. Issued by Bureau of Economic Analysis, U. S. Department of Commerce. Presents a wide variety of business and economic data.

NATIONAL BRANDS

See: TRADEMARKS AND TRADE NAMES

NATIONAL DEBT

See also: FEDERAL BUDGET

GENERAL WORKS

Financial Institutions and Markets. Robert W. Kolb and Ricardo J. Rodriguez. Blackwell Publishers. • 1996. $77.95. Contains 40 articles (chapters) by various authors on U. S. financial markets and other topics. Includes separate chapters on the International Monetary Fund, inflation, monetary policy, the national debt, bank failures, derivatives, stock prices, initial public offerings, government bonds, pensions, foreign exchange, international markets, and other subjects.

ABSTRACTS AND INDEXES

Business Periodicals Index. H. W. Wilson Co. • Monthly, except August, with quarterly and annual cumulations. Service basis for print edition; CD-ROM edition, $1,495.00 per year.

Readers' Guide to Periodical Literature. H. W. Wilson Co. • Monthly. $220.00 per year. CD-ROM edition, $1,495 per year, including annual cumulation. Indexes about 250 peridicals of general interest.

INTERNET DATABASES

Fedstats. Federal Interagency Council on Statistical Policy. Phone: (202)395-7254 • URL: http://www.fedstats.gov • Web site features an efficient search facility for full-text statistics produced by more than 70 federal agencies, including the Census Bureau, the Bureau of Economic Analysis, and the Bureau of Labor Statistics. Boolean searches can be made within one agency or for all agencies combined. Links are offered to international statistical bureaus, including the UN, IMF, OECD, UNESCO, Eurostat, and 20 individual countries. Fees: Free.

ONLINE DATABASES

DRI U.S. Central Database. Data Products Division. • Provides more than 23,000 business, financial, demographic, economic, foreign trade, and industry-related time series for the U.S. Includes national income, population, retail-wholesale trade, price indexes, labor data, housing, industrial production, banking, interest rates, money supply, etc. Time period is generally 1947 to date (some data back to 1929). Updating varies. Inquire as to online cost and availability.

Readers' Guide Abstracts Online. H. W. Wilson Co. • Indexes and abstracts general interest periodicals, 1983 to date. Weekly updates. Inquire as to online cost and availability.

Wilson Business Abstracts Online. H. W. Wilson Co. • Indexes and abstracts 600 major business periodicals, plus the *Wall Street Journal* and the business section of the *New York Times*. Indexing is from 1982, abstracting from 1990, with the two newspapers included from 1993. Updated weekly. Inquire as to online cost and availability. (*Business Periodicals Index* without abstracts is also available online.).

PERIODICALS AND NEWSLETTERS

OMB Watcher (Office of Management and Budget). O M B Watch. • Bimonthly. Individuals, $35.00 per year. Monitors operations of the federal Office of Management and Budget.

RESEARCH CENTERS AND INSTITUTES

League of Women Voters Education Fund. 1730 M St., N. W., Suite 1000, Washington, DC 20036. Phone: (202)429-1965 Fax: (202)429-0854 E-mail: lwv@lwv.orgc • URL: http://www.lwv.org • Research fields include federal deficit issues.

Tax Foundation. 1250 H St., N.W., Suite 750, Washington, DC 20005. Phone: (202)783-2760 Fax: (202)783-6868 E-mail: taxfnd@intr.net • URL: http://www.taxfoundation.org.

STATISTICS SOURCES

The AIER Chart Book. AIER Research Staff. American Institute for Economic Research. • Annual. $3.00. A compact compilation of long-range charts ("Purchasing Power of the Dollar," for example, goes back to 1780) covering various aspects of the U. S. economy. Includes inflation, interest rates, debt, gold, taxation, stock prices, etc. (Economic Education Bulletin.).

Business Statistics of the United States. Courtenay M. Slater, editor. Bernan Associates. • 1999. $74.00. Fifth edition. Based on *Business Statistics*, formerly issue by the Bureau of Economic Analysis, U. S. Department of Commerce. Provides basic data for a wide variety of U. S. industries, services, and economic indicators. Most statistics are shown annually for 29 years and monthly for the most recent four years.

Daily Treasury Statement: Cash and Debt Operations of the United States Treasury. Available from U. S. Government Printing Office. • Daily, except Saturdays, Sundays, and holidays. $855.00 per year. (Financial Management Service, U. S. Treasury Department.).

Economic and Budget Outlook: Fiscal Years 2000-2009. Available from U. S. Government Printing Office. • 1999. $15.00. Issued by the Congressional Budget Office (http://www.cbo.gov). Contains CBO economic projections and federal budget projections annually to 2009 in billions of dollars. An appendix contains "Historical Budget Data" annually from 1962 to 1998, including revenues, outlays, deficits, surpluses, and debt held by the public.

Historical Tables, Budget of the United States Government. Available from U. S. Government Printing Office. • Annual. Issued by the Office of Management and Budget, Executive Office of the President (http://www.whitehouse.gov). Provides statistical data on the federal budget for an extended period of about 60 years in the past to projections of four years in the future. Includes federal debt and federal employment.

Monthly Statement of the Public Debt of the United States. U. S. Dept. of the Treasury, Public Debt Bureau. Available from U. S. Government Printing Office. • Monthly. $29.00 per year.

Survey of Current Business. Available from U. S. Government Printing Office. • Monthly. $49.00 per year. Issued by Bureau of Economic Analysis, U. S. Department of Commerce. Presents a wide variety of business and economic data.

Treasury Bulletin. Available from U. S. Government Printing Office. • Quarterly. $39.00 per year. Issued by the Financial Management Service, U. S. Treasury Department. Provides data on the federal budget, government securities and yields, the national debt, and the financing of the federal government in general.

TRADE/PROFESSIONAL ASSOCIATIONS

Committee for a Responsible Federal Budget. 220 1/2 E St., N. E., Washington, DC 20002. Phone: (202)547-4484 Fax: (202)547-4476 E-mail: crfb@aol.com • Members are corporations and others seeking to improve the federal budget process.

Private Sector Council. 1101 16th St., N.W., Suite 300, Washington, DC 20036. Phone: (202)822-3910 Fax: (202)822-0638 • URL: http://www.privatesectorcouncil.org • Members are officers of large corporations who seek to facilitate reduction of the federal deficit.

NATIONAL HOLIDAYS

See: ANNIVERSARIES AND HOLIDAYS

NATIONAL INCOME

See: INCOME; NATIONAL ACCOUNTING

NATIONAL PLANNING

See: ECONOMIC POLICY

NATIONAL PRODUCT

See: GROSS NATIONAL PRODUCT

NATIONS, LAW OF

See: INTERNATIONAL LAW AND REGULATION

NATURAL GAS

See also: GAS INDUSTRY; PETROLEUM INDUSTRY; PROPANE AND BUTANE GAS INDUSTRY

ABSTRACTS AND INDEXES

Gas Abstracts. Institute of Gas Technology. • Monthly. $425.00 per year. Abstracts of gas and energy related articles from around the world.

DIRECTORIES

Brown's Directory. Advanstar Communications, Inc. • Annual. $335.00.

Financial Times Energy Yearbook: Oil & Gas: 2000. Available from The Gale Group. • Annual. $320.00. Published by Financial Times Energy. Provides production and financial details for more than 800 major oil and gas companies worldwide. Includes coverage of reserves, operations, properties, and growth rates. Formerly *Financial Times Oil & Gas Yearbook.*

Refining and Gas Processing Industry Worldwide. PennWell Publishing Co. • Annual. $165.00. International coverage. Formerly *Refining and Gas Processing.*

ONLINE DATABASES

Energyline. Congressional Information Service, Inc. • Provides online citations and abstracts to the literature of all forms of energy: petroleum, natural gas, coal, nuclear power, solar energy, etc. Time period is 1971 to 1993 (closed file). Inquire as to online cost and availability.

Tulsa (Petroleum Abstracts). Information Services. • Worldwide literature in the petroleum and natural gas areas, 1965 to present. Inquire as to online cost and availability. Includes petroleum exploration patents. Updated weekly. Over 600,000 entries.

PERIODICALS AND NEWSLETTERS

AGA American Gas. American Gas Association. • 11 times a year. $39.00 per year. Formerly *American Gas Association Monthly.*

Energy and Fuels. American Chemical Society. • Bimonthly. Institutions, $728.00 per year; others, price on application. an interdisciplinary technical journal covering non-nuclear energy sources: petroleum, gas, synthetic fuels, etc.

Gas Digest: The Magazine of Gas Operations. T-P Graphics. • Quarterly. Free. Articles and data relating to operations and management phases of natural gas operations.

Gas Utility and Pipeline Industries: The Executive, Administration, Operations Md Engineering Magazine of Gas Energy Supply, Risk Management, Pipeline Transmission, Utility Distribution. Gas Industries Inc. • Monthly. $20.00 per year. Includes semiannual *AGA News.* Formerly *Gas Industires Magazine.*

Natural Gas: The Monthly Journal for Producers, Marketers, Pipeline, Distributors and End Users. John Wiley and Sons, Inc. • Monthly. Institution, $649.00 per year. Newsletter. Covers business, economic, regulatory, and high-technology news relating to the natural gas industry.

The Oilman Weekly Newsletter. PennWell Corp., Petroleum Div. • Weekly. $1360.00 per year. Newsletter. Provides news of developments concerning the North Sea and European oil and gas businesses. Each issue contains four pages of statistical data.

PRICE SOURCES

The AGA Rate Service. American Gas Association. • Semiannual. Members, $175.00 per year; non-members, $300.00 per year.

International Energy Agency. Energy Prices and Taxes. OECD Publications and Information Center. • Quarterly. $350.00 per year. Compiled by the International Energy Agency. Provides data on prices and taxation of petroleum products, natural gas, coal, and electricity. Diskette edition, $800.00. (Published in Paris).

RESEARCH CENTERS AND INSTITUTES

Canadian Energy Research Institute. 3512 33rd St., N. W., Suite 150, Calgary, AB, Canada T2L 2A6. Phone: (403)282-1231 Fax: (403)284-4181 E-mail: ceri@ceri.ca • URL: http://www.ceri.ca • Conducts research on the economic aspects of various forms of energy, including petroleum, natural gas, coal, nuclear, and water power (hydroelectric).

STATISTICS SOURCES

Annual Energy Outlook [year], with Projections to [year]. Available from U. S. Government Printing Office. • Annual. Issued by the Energy Information Administration, U. S. Department of Energy (http://www.eia.doe.gov). Contains detailed statistics and 20-year projections for electricity, oil, natural gas, coal, and renewable energy. Text provides extensive discussion of energy issues and "Market Trends.".

Annual Energy Review. Available from U. S. Government Printing Office. • Annual Issued by the Energy Information Administration, Office of Energy Markets and End Use, U. S. Department of Energy. Presents long-term historical as well as recent data on production, consumption, stocks, imports, exports, and prices of the principal energy commodities in the U. S.

Energy Balances of OECD Countries. Organization for Economic Cooperation and Development. Available from OECD Publications and Information Center. • Irregular. $110.00. Presents two-year data on the supply and consumption of solid fuels, oil, gas, and electricity, expressed in oil equivalency terms. Historical tables are also provided. Relates to OECD member countries.

Gas Facts: A Statistical Record of the Gas Utility Industry. American Gas Association, Dept. of Statistics. • Annual. Members, $40.00; non-members, $80.00.

International Energy Annual. Available from U. S. Government Printing Office. • Annual. $34.00. Issued by the Energy Information Administration, U. S. Department of Energy. Provides production, consumption, import, and export data for primary energy commodities in more than 200 countries and areas. In addition to petroleum products and alcohol, renewable energy sources are covered (hydroelectric, geothermal, solar, and wind).

Monthly Energy Review. Available from U. S. Government Printing Office. • Monthly. $98.00 per year. Issued by the Energy Information Administration, Office of Energy Markets and End Use, U. S. Department of Energy. Contains current and historical statistics on U. S. production, storage, imports, and consumption of petroleum, natural gas, and coal.

Natural Gas Monthly. Energy Information Administration. Available from U.S. Government Printing Office. • Monthly. $89.00 per year. Annual cumulation. State and national data on production, storage, imports, exports and consumption of natural gas.

Petroleum Supply Annual. Available from U. S. Government Printing Office. • Annual. $78.00. Two volumes. Produced by the Energy Information Administration, U. S. Department of Energy. Contains worldwide data on the petroleum industry and petroleum products.

Petroleum Supply Monthly. Available from U. S. Government Printing Office. • Monthly. $100.00 per year. Produced by the Energy Information Administration, U. S. Department of Energy. Provides worldwide statistics on a wide variety of petroleum products. Covers production, supplies, exports and imports, transportation, refinery operations, and other aspects of the petroleum industry.

Standard & Poor's Industry Surveys. Standard & Poor's. • Semiannual. $1,800.00. Two looseleaf volumes. Includes monthly supplements. Provides detailed, individual surveys of 52 major industry groups. Each survey is revised on a semiannual basis. Also includes "Monthly Investment Review" (industry group investment analysis) and monthly "Trends & Projections" (economic analysis).

U. S. Industry and Trade Outlook: The McGraw-Hill Companies and the U.S. Department of Commerce/International Trade Administration. Datapso Research Corp. • Annual. $69.95. Produced by the International Trade Administration, U. S. Department of Commerce, in a "public-private" partnership with DRI/McGraw-Hill and Standard & Poor's. Provides basic data, outlook for the current year, and "Long-Term Prospects" (five-year projections) for a wide variety of products and services. Includes high technology industries. Formerly *U. S. Industrial Outlook.*

WEFA Industrial Monitor. John Wiley and Sons, Inc. • Annual. $65.00. Prepared by industry analysts at WEFA, an economic forecasting and consulting firm (originally Wharton Econometric Forecasting Associates). Contains discussions of the outlook for major U. S. industries, with many 10-year forecasts (WEFA Web site is http://www.wefa.com).

TRADE/PROFESSIONAL ASSOCIATIONS

American Gas Association. 444 N. Capitol St., N.W., Washington, DC 20001. Phone: (202)824-7000 Fax: (202)824-7115 • URL: http://www.aga.com.

Institute of Gas Technology. 1700 S. Mount Prospect Rd., Des Plaines, IL 60018-1804. Phone: (847)768-0500 Fax: (847)768-0516 • URL: http://www.igt.org.

Interstate Natural Gas Association of America. 10 G St., N.E., Suite 700, Washington, DC 20002. Phone: (202)216-5900 Fax: (202)216-0877 • URL: http://www.ingaa.org.

Natural Energy Services Association. 7600 W. Tidwell, Ste. 804, Houston, TX 77040. Phone: (713)939-9200 Fax: (713)690-7969 • URL: http://www.nesanet.org.

OTHER SOURCES

Infrastructure Industries USA. The Gale Group. • 2001. $240.00. Replaces *Agriculture, Forestry, Fishing, Mining, and Construction USA* and *Transportation and Public Utilities USA.* Presents statistics and projections relating to economic activity in a wide variety of natural resource and construction industries.

NATURAL RESOURCES

See also: FOREST PRODUCTS; GAS INDUSTRY; MINES AND MINERAL RESOURCES; PETROLEUM INDUSTRY; RECYCLING

ALMANACS AND YEARBOOKS

Environmental Viewpoints. The Gale Group. • 1993. $195.00. Three volumes. $65.00 per volume. A compendium of excerpts of about 200 articles on a wide variety of environmental topics, selected from both popular and professional periodicals. Arranged alphabetically by topic, with a subject/keyword index.

Gale Environmental Almanac. The Gale Group. • 1994. $110.00. Contains 15 chapters, each on a broad topic related to the environment, such as "Waste and Recycling." Each chapter has a topical overview, charts, statistics, and illustrations. Includes a glossary of environmental terms and a bibliography.

BIBLIOGRAPHIES

Resources for the Future: An International Annotated Bibliography. Alan J. Mayne. Greenwood Publishing Group, Inc. • 1993. $79.50. (Bibliographies and Indexes in Economics and Economic History Series, No 13).

BIOGRAPHICAL SOURCES

World Who is Who and Does What in Environment and Conservation. Nicholas Polunin, editor. St. Martin's Press. • 1997. $75.00. Provides biographies of 1,300 individuals considered to be leaders in environmental and conservation areas.

CD-ROM DATABASES

Environment Abstracts on CD-ROM. Congressional Information Service, Inc. • Quarterly. $1,295.00 per year. Contains the following CD-ROM databases: *Environment Abstracts, Energy Abstracts,* and *Acid Rain Abstracts.* Length of coverage varies.

DIRECTORIES

Conservation Directory: A Listing of Organizations, Agencies and Officials Concerned with Natural Resource Use and Management. Rue Gordon, editor. National Wildlife Federation. • Annual. Members, $54.90; non-members, $61.00. Lists agencies and private organizations in U.S. and Canada concerned with conservation and natural resource management.

Environmental Career Directory. Visible Ink Press. • 1993. $17.95. Includes career information relating to workers in conservation, recycling, wildlife management, pollution control, and other areas. Provides advice from "insiders," resume suggestions, a directory of companies that may offer entry-level positions, and a directory of career information sources. (Career Advisor Series.).

ENCYCLOPEDIAS AND DICTIONARIES

Environmental Encyclopedia. The Gale Group. • 1998. $235.00. Second edition. Provides over 1,300 articles on all aspects of the environment. Written in non-technical style.

HANDBOOKS AND MANUALS

Income Taxation of Natural Resources. Research Institute of America, Inc. • 2000. $99.00. Revised edition.

Statistics for the Environment: Statistical Aspects of Health and the Environment. Vic Barnett and K. Feridun Turkman, editors. John Wiley and Sons, Inc. • 1999. $180.00. Contains articles on the statistical analysis and interpretation of environmental monitoring and sampling data. Areas covered include meteorology, pollution of the environment, and forest resources.

INTERNET DATABASES

U. S. Census Bureau: The Official Statistics. U. S. Bureau of the Census. Phone: (301)763-4100 Fax: (301)763-4794 • URL: http://www.census.gov • Web site is "Your Source for Social, Demographic, and Economic Information." Contains "Current U. S. Population Count," "Current Economic Indicators," and a wide variety of data under "Other Official Statistics." Keyword searching is provided. Fees: Free.

ONLINE DATABASES

Energyline. Congressional Information Service, Inc. • Provides online citations and abstracts to the literature of all forms of energy: petroleum, natural gas, coal, nuclear power, solar energy, etc. Time period is 1971 to 1993 (closed file). Inquire as to online cost and availability.

Enviroline. Congressional Information Service, Inc. • Provides online indexing and abstracting of worldwide environmental and natural resource literature from 1975 to date. Updated monthly. Inquire as to online cost and availability.

PERIODICALS AND NEWSLETTERS

Energy Conservation Digest. Editorial Resources, Inc. • Semimonthly. $176.00 per year. Newsletter on the conservation of energy resources. Includes legislation, research, new products, job opportunities, calendar of events, and energy economics.

Environmental Business Journal: Strategic Information for a Changing Industry. Environmental Business Publishing Co. • Monthly. $495.00 per year. Newsletter. Includes both industrial and financial information relating to individual companies and to the environmental industry in general. Covers air pollution, wat es, U. S. Department of Health and Human Services. Provides conference, workshop, and symposium proceedings, as well as extensive reviews of environmental prospects.

Friends of the Earth. • Bimonthly. $25.00 per year. Newsletter on environmental and natural resource issues and public policy.

The Natural Resources Journal. University of New Mexico School of Law. • Quarterly. $40.00 per year.

Nature and Resources: International News about Research on Environment, Resources, and Conservation of Nature. Parthenon Publishing Group. • Quarterly. $92.00 per year.

Resources Policy; The International Journal on the Economics, Planning and Use of Non-Renewable Resources. Elsevier Science. • Quarterly. $647.00 per year.

World Environment Report: News and Information on International Resource Management. Business Publishers, Inc. • Biweekly. $494.00 per year. Newsletter on international developments having to do with the environment, energy, pollution control, waste management, and toxic substances.

RESEARCH CENTERS AND INSTITUTES

Natural Resources Defense Council. 40 W. 20th St., New York, NY 10011. Phone: (212)727-2700 Fax: (212)727-1773 E-mail: nrdcinfo@nrdc.org • URL: http://www.nrdc.org • Studies the use of the judicial system to enforce environmental protection laws.

STATISTICS SOURCES

Social Statistics of the United States. Mark S. Littman, editor. Bernan Press. • 2000. $65.00. Includes statistical data on population growth, labor force, occupations, environmental trends, leisure time use, income, poverty, taxes, and other economic or demographic topics.

Statistical Abstract of the United States. Available from U. S. Government Printing Office. • Annual. $51.00. Issued by the U. S. Bureau of the Census.

A Statistical Portrait of the United States: Social Conditions and Trends. Mark S. Littman, editor. Bernan Press. • 1998. $89.00. Covers "social, economic, and environmental trends in the United States over the past 25 years." Includes statistical tables, graphs, and analysis relating to such topics as population, income, poverty, wealth, labor, housing, education, healthcare, air/water quality, and government.

TRADE/PROFESSIONAL ASSOCIATIONS

Friends of the Earth. 1025 Vermont Ave., N.W., Suite. 300, Washington, DC 20005. Phone: (202)783-7400 Fax: (202)783-0444 E-mail: foe@foe.org • URL: http://www.foe.org • Promotes protection of the environment and conservation of natural resources.

National Wildlife Federation. 8925 Leesburg Pike, Vienna, VA 22184. Phone: (703)790-4000 • URL: http://www.nwf.org.

OTHER SOURCES

Energy Management and Federal Energy Guidelines. CCH, Inc. • Biweekly. $1,658.00 per year. Seven looseleaf volumes. Periodic supplementation. Reports on petroleum allocation rules, conservation efforts, new technology, and other energy concerns.

NAVAL LAW

See: MARITIME LAW AND REGULATION

NAVAL STORES

PERIODICALS AND NEWSLETTERS

Forest Chemicals Review. Kriedt Enterprises Ltd. • Bimonthly. $98.00 per year. Formerly *Naval Stores Review.*

NAVY

CD-ROM DATABASES

Leadership Library on CD-ROM: Who's Who in the Leadership of the United States. Leadership

Directories, Inc. • Quarterly. $2,641.00 per year, including access to Internet version (weekly updates). Contains all 14 *Yellow Book* personnel directories on CD-ROM, providing contact and brief biographical information for about 400,000 individuals. Covers business, government, financial institutions, news media, law firms, associations, foreign representatives, and nonprofit organizations. Includes photographs.

DIRECTORIES

Carroll's Federal & Federal Regional Directory: CD-ROM Edition. Carroll Publishing. • Bimonthly. $800.00 per year. Provides CD-ROM listings of more than 120,000 (55,000 high-level and 65,000 mid-level) U. S. government officials in Washington and throughout the country, including in military installations. Also available online.

Carroll's Federal Regional Directory. Carroll Publishing. • Semiannual. $255.00 per year. Lists more than 28,000 non-Washington based federal executives in administrative agencies, the courts, and military bases. Arranged in four sections: Alphabetical (last names), Organizational, Geographical, and Keyword. Includes maps.

Department of Defense Telephone Directory. Available from U. S. Government Printing Office. • Three times a year. $44.00 per year. An alphabetical directory of U. S. Department of Defense personnel, including Departments of the Army, Navy, and Air Force.

Directory of U.S. Military Bases Worldwide. William R. Evinger, editor. Oryx Press. • 1998. $125.00. Third edition.

Federal Regional Yellow Book: Who's Who in the Federal Government's Departments, Agencies, Military Installations, and Service Academies Outside of Washington, DC. Leadership Directories, Inc. • Semiannual. $235.00 per year. Lists over 36,000 federal officials and support staff at 8,000 regional offices.

Jane's Fighting Ships. Jane's Information Group, Inc. • Annual. $405.00; CD-Rom edition, $650.00 Navies of the world and ship details, weapons fits and specifications.

Ships and Aircraft of the United States Fleet. James C. Fahey, editor. Naval Institute Press. • Dates vary. $63.90. Two volumes.

HANDBOOKS AND MANUALS

Division Officer's Guide. James Stavridis. Naval Institute Press. • 1995. $19.95. 10th revised edition.

Watch Officer's Guide: A Handbook for All Deck Watch Offices. James Stavridis. Naval Institute Press. • 1999. $19.95. 14th edition.

PERIODICALS AND NEWSLETTERS

All Hands: Magazine of the United States Navy. Available from U. S. Government Printing Office. • Monthly. $42.00 per year. Contains articles of general interest concerning the U. S. Navy (http://www.navy.mil).

Armed Forces Journal International. Armed Forces Journal International, Inc. • Monthly. $45.00 per year. A defense magazine for career military officers and industry executives. Covers defense events, plans, policies, budgets, and innovations.

Naval Affairs: In the Interest of the Enlisted Active Duty Reserve, and Retired Personnel of the U.S. Navy, Marine Corps and Coast Guard. Fleet Reserve Association. • Free to members; non-members, $7.00 per year.

Naval Aviation News. Chief of Naval Operations Bureau of Aeronautics. Available from U.S. Government Printing Office. • Bimonthly. $16.00 per year. Articles on all phases on Navy and Marine activity.

Naval Engineers Journal. American Society of Naval Engineers, Inc. • Bimonthly. $100 per year.

Naval Research Logistics: An International Journal. John Wiley and Sons, Inc. • Eight times a year. $945.00 per year.

Naval Review: Annual Review of World Seapower. U.S. Naval Institute. Naval Institute Press. • Annual. Price on application. Covers the previous year's events. May issue of *U.S. Naval Institute Proceedings.*

Navy Supply Corps Newsletter. Available from U. S. Government Printing Office. • Bimonthly. $20.00 per year. Newsletter issued by U. S. Navy Supply Systems Command. Provides news of Navy supplies and stores activities.

Navy Times: Marine Corps, Navy, Coast Guard. Army Times Publishing Co. • Weekly. $52.00 per year. In two editions: Domestic and International.

Sea Power. Navy League of the United States. • Monthly. Free to members; non-members $25.00 per year. Includes annual *Almanac of Seapower.*

STATISTICS SOURCES

Annual Report of the Secretary of Defense. U.S. Department of Defense, Office of the Secretary. • Annual.

Budget of the United States Government. U.S. Office of Management and Budget. Available from U.S. Government Printing Office. • Annual.

TRADE/PROFESSIONAL ASSOCIATIONS

Fleet Reserve Association. 125 N. West St., Alexandria, VA 22314-2754. Phone: 800-372-1924 or (703)683-1400 Fax: (703)549-6610 E-mail: news-fra@fra.org • URL: http://www.fra.org.

Naval Historical Foundation. Washington Navy Yard, 1306 Dahlgren Ave., S.E., Washington, DC 20374-0571. Phone: (202)678-4333 or (202)678-4431 Fax: (202)889-3565 E-mail: nhfwny@msn.com • URL: http://www.mil.log/navyhist/.

Navy Club of the United States of America. 10701 S. Eastern Ave., Ste. 1611, Henderson, NV 89012. Phone: 800-628-7265 or (702)897-8729 Fax: (702)897-1939.

Navy League of the United States. 2300 Wilson Blvd., Arlington, VA 22201. Phone: 800-356-5760 or (703)528-1775 Fax: (703)528-2333 • URL: http://www.navyleague.org.

United States Naval Institute. 291 Wood Rd., Annapolis, MD 21402. Phone: 800-233-8764 or (410)268-6110 Fax: (410)269-7940 • URL: http://www.usni.org.

OTHER SOURCES

Carroll's Defense Organization Charts. Carroll Publishing. • Quarterly. $1,470.00 per year. Provides more than 200 large, fold-out paper charts showing personnel relationships in 2,400 U. S. military offices. Charts are also available online and on CD-ROM.

Department of the Navy Annual Report to the Congress. U.S. Department of the Navy. • Annual.

NEGOTIATION

See also: INDUSTRIAL RELATIONS

GENERAL WORKS

Bargaining Across Borders: How to Conduct Business Successfully Anywhere in th e World. Dean A. Foster. McGraw-Hill. • 1992. $14.95. Includes a consideration of non-negotiable cultural differences.

Business Negotiating Basics. Peter Economy. McGraw-Hill Higher Education. • 1993. $19.95.

Negotiation. Roy J. Lewicki and others. McGraw-Hill Higher Education. • 1994. $51.95. Second edition.

Negotiation Basics: Concepts, Skills, and Exercises. Ralph A. Johnson. Sage Publications, Inc. • 1993. $42.00. Topics include goal building, the role of information, cost-benefit decision making, strategy, and creating a positive negotiating climate.

Negotiation: Strategies for Mutual Gain - The Basic Seminar of the Harvard Program on Negotiation. Lavina Hall, editor. Sage Publications, Inc. • 1992. $48.00. Fourteen contributors provide practical advice on the art of negotiation.

Win-Win Negotiating: Turning Conflict into Agreement. Fred E. Jandt. John Wiley and Sons, Inc. • 1987. $19.95. (Sound Business Cassette Books).

ABSTRACTS AND INDEXES

Index to Legal Periodicals and Books. H. W. Wilson Co. • Monthly. Quarterly and annual cumulations. $270.00 per year. CD-ROM version available at $1,495.00 per year.

Personnel Management Abstracts. • Quarterly. $190.00 per year. Includes annual cumulation.

ENCYCLOPEDIAS AND DICTIONARIES

Blackwell Encyclopedic Dictionary of Strategic Management. Derek F. Channon, editor. Blackwell Publishers. • 1997. $110.00. The editor is associated with Imperial College, London. Contains definitions of key terms combined with longer articles written by various U. S. and foreign business educators. Includes bibliographies and index. (Blackwell Encyclopedia of Management Series.).

Field Guide to Negotiation: A Glossary of Essential Tools and Concepts for Today's Manager. Gavin Kennedy. McGraw-Hill. • 1993. $29.95. Defines fundamental terms.

HANDBOOKS AND MANUALS

Manager's Negotiating Answer Book. George Fuller. DIANE Publishing Co. • 1999. $40.00.

Negotiating and Influencing Skills: The Art of Creating and Claiming Value. Brad McRae. Sage Publications, Inc. • 1997. $42.00. Presents a practical approach to various circumstances, based on the Harvard Project on Negotiation. Chapters include "Dealing with Difficult People and Difficult Situations." Contains a bibliography and glossary of terms.

Negotiating for Business Results. Judith E. Fisher. McGraw-Hill Professional. • 1993. $10.95. (Business Skills Express Series).

Negotiating to Settlement in Divorce. Sanford N. Katz, editor. Aspen Law and Business. • 1987. $75.00. Looseleaf service.

Selling Through Negotiation: The Handbook of Sales Negotiation. Homer B. Smith. Marketing Education Associates. • 1988. $14.95.

ONLINE DATABASES

Index to Legal Periodicals and Books (Online). H. W. Wilson Co. • Broad coverage of law journals and books 1981 to date. Monthly updates. Inquire as to online cost and availability.

Legal Resource Index. The Gale Group. • Broad coverage of law literature appearing in legal, business, and other periodicals, 1980 to date. Monthly updates. Inquire as to online cost and availability.

LEXIS. LEXIS-NEXIS. • The various LEXIS databases provide full text and indexing for a wide variety of legal cases, statutes, orders, and opinions.

PERIODICALS AND NEWSLETTERS

Inside Negotiations. EFR Corp. • Monthly. $98.00 per year. Newsletter. Labor negotiations.

Negotiation Journal: On the Process of Dispute Settlement. Program on Negotiation. Plenum Publishing Corp. • Quarterly. $330.00 per year.

RESEARCH CENTERS AND INSTITUTES

Center for Negotiation and Conflict Resolution. Rutgers University, BSPPP 33 Livingston Ave., Suite 104, New Brunswick, NJ 08901-1985. Phone: (732)932-2487 Fax: (732)932-2493 E-mail: cncr@rci.rutgers.edu • URL: http://www.policy.rutgers.edu/cncr/.

Harvard Negotiation Project. Harvard University. Harvard Law School, Pound Hall Room 500, Cambridge, MA 02138. Phone: (617)495-1684 Fax: (617)495-7818 E-mail: info@pon.law.harvard.edu • Seeks to improve the theory and practice of negotiation.

OTHER SOURCES

Successful Negotiating. American Management Association Extension Institute. • Looseleaf. $110.00. Self-study course. Emphasis is on practical explanations, examples, and problem solving. Quizzes and a case study are included.

NETWORKS, COMPUTER

See: COMPUTER COMMUNICATIONS; LOCAL AREA NETWORKS

NEW ISSUES (FINANCE)

GENERAL WORKS

Financial Institutions and Markets. Robert W. Kolb and Ricardo J. Rodriguez. Blackwell Publishers. • 1996. $77.95. Contains 40 articles (chapters) by various authors on U. S. financial markets and other topics. Includes separate chapters on the International Monetary Fund, inflation, monetary policy, the national debt, bank failures, derivatives, stock prices, initial public offerings, government bonds, pensions, foreign exchange, international markets, and other subjects.

Investing in the Over-the-Counter Markets: Stocks, Bonds, IPOs. Alvin D. Hall. John Wiley and Sons, Inc. • 1995. $29.95. Provides advice and information on investing in "unlisted" or NASDAQ (National Association of Securities Dealers Automated Quotation System) stocks, bonds, and initial public offerings (IPOs).

CD-ROM DATABASES

Compact D/New Issues. Disclosure, Inc. • Monthly, $4,500.00 per year. Provides CD-ROM financial and other information relating to initial public offerings, spinoffs, recapitalizations, exchange offers, and other registrations filed with the Securities and Exchange Commission in compliance with the Securities Act of 1933. Time period is 1990 to date.

HANDBOOKS AND MANUALS

Financing the Corporation. Richard A. Booth. West Group. • $110.00. Looseleaf service. Periodic supplementation. Covers a wide variety of corporate finance legal topics, from initial capital structure to public sale of securities.

Going Public Handbook: Going Public, the Integrated Disclosure System, and Exempt Financing, 1992. Harold S. Bloomenthal. West Group. • 1993. $97.50. Covers public financing from initiation of underwriting to closing.

How to Prepare an Initial Public Offering. Practising Law Institute. • 1997. $129.00. (Corporate Law and Practice Course Handbook Series).

Initial Public Offerings: All You Need to Know About Taking a Company Public. David Sutton and M. William Benedetto. McGraw-Hill Professional. • 1990. $24.95. (Entrepreneur's Guide Series).

Securities Counseling for New and Developing Companies. Stuart R. Cohn. West Group. • 1993. $130.00. Covers securities planning for new businesses, with an emphasis on the avoidance of legal violations and civil liabilities. (Corporate Law Series).

Securities: Public and Private Offerings. William W. Prifti. West Group. • $250.00. Two looseleaf volumes. Periodic supplementation. How to issue securities. (Securities Law Series).

INTERNET DATABASES

Business Week Online. McGraw-Hill. Phone: (212)512-2762 Fax: (212)512-6590 • URL: http://www.businessweek.com • Web site provides complete contents of current issue of *Business Week* plus "BW Daily" with additonal business news, financial market quotes, and corporate information from Standard & Poor's. Includes various features, such as "Banking Center" with mortgage and interest data, and "Interactive Computer Buying Guide." The "Business Week Archive" is fully searchable back to 1991. Fees: Mostly free, but full-text archive articles are $2.00 each.

DBC Online: America's Leading Provider of Real-Time Market Data to the Individual Investor. Data Broadcasting Corp. Phone: (415)571-1800 E-mail: dbcinfo@dbc.com • URL: http://www.dbc.com • Web site provides a wide variety of real-time securities market prices, data, and charts. Covers bonds ("BondVu"), stocks, commodities, options, mutual funds, major indexes, industry indexes, international markets, etc. Also includes news, SEC documents ("Smart-Edgar"), and various other features. Fees: Both free and fee-based, depending on level of information.

IPOfn. IPO Financial Network. Phone: (973)379-5100 Fax: (973)379-1696 E-mail: info@ipofinancial.com • URL: http://www.ipofinancial.com • Web site provides free information on initial public offerings: "Pricing Recap" (price performance), "Calendar Update" (weekly listing of new offerings), "Company Roster" (Web sites), "Stock Brokers" (IPO dealers), and "Brokerage Firms" (underwriters). Fees: Basic data is free. Extensive analysis and recommendations are available through fee-based telephone, fax, and database services. Daily updates.

Web Finance: Covering the Electronic Evolution of Finance. Securities Data Publishing. Phone: (212)765-5311 or 800-455-5844 Fax: (212)321-2336 E-mail: webfinance@tfn.com • URL: http://www.webfinance.net • Bi-weekly print and daily web-site publication of financial services on the Web, including financial links, archives, brokerage stocks, deal financing, and other financial and investment news and information.

ONLINE DATABASES

Public Corporate New Issues. Thomson Financial Securities Data. • Provides detailed online information relating to initial public stock offerings (new issues) from 1970 to date. Updating is daily. Inquire as to online cost and availability. Inquire as to online cost and availability.

PERIODICALS AND NEWSLETTERS

The Bond Buyer. American Banker Newsletter, Thomson Financial Media. • Daily edition, $1,897 per year. Weekly edition, $525.00 per year. Reports on new municipal bond issues.

Emerging and Special Situations. Standard & Poor's. • Monthly. $210.00 per year. Newsletter.

Individual Investor. Individual Investor Group. • Monthly. $22.95 per year. Emphasis is on stocks selling for less than ten dollars a share. Includes a "Guide to Insider Transactions" and "New Issue Alert.".

Investment Dealers' Digest. Securities Data Publishing. • Weekly. $750.00 per year. Covers financial news, trends, new products, people, private placements, new issues of securities, and other aspects of the investment business. Includes feature stories. (Securities Data Publishing is a unit of Thomson Financial.).

IPO Reporter. Securities Data Publishing. • Weekly. $1,295.00 per year. Newsletter. Provides detailed information on new and upcoming initial public offerings. Includes aftermarket data and market trend analysis. (Securities Data Publishing is a unit of Thomson Financial.).

Medical Technology Stock Letter. Piedmont Venture Group. • Semimonthly. $320.00 per year. Newsletter. Provides health care industry investment recommendations, including information on initial public offerings.

New Issues: The Investor's Guide to Initial Public Offerings. Norman G. Fosback. Institute for Econometric Research. • Monthly. $200.00 per year. Newsletter. Includes "Penny Stock Calendar".

The Red Herring: The Business of Technology. Herring Communications, Inc.. • Monthly. $49.00 per year. Contains ars on investing in high technology, especially within the computer, communications, and information industries. Initial public offerings (IPOs) are emphasized. Includes technology stock listings and the Red Herring "Tech 250" stock index.

TRADE/PROFESSIONAL ASSOCIATIONS

National Association of Securities Dealers. 1735 K St., N.W., Washington, DC 20006-1506. Phone: (202)728-8000 Fax: (202)293-6260 • URL: http://www.nasdr.com/1000.asp.

Securities Industry Association. 120 Broadway, New York, NY 10271-0080. Phone: (212)608-1500 Fax: (212)608-1604 E-mail: info@sia.com • URL: http://www.sia.com.

Security Traders Association. One World Trade Center, Suite 4511, New York, NY 10048. Phone: (212)524-0484 Fax: (212)321-3449.

OTHER SOURCES

Cyberfinance: Raising Capital for the E-Business. Martin B. Robins. CCH, Inc. • 2001. $79.00. Covers the taxation, financial, and legal aspects of raising money for new Internet-based ("dot.com") companies, including the three stages of startup, growth, and initial public offering.

Going Public and the Public Corporation. Harold S. Bloomenthal. West Group. • $495.00 per year. Four looseleaf volumes. Periodic supplementation. Includes legal forms and documents. (Securities Law Series).

Investing in IPOs: New Paths to Profit with Initial Public Offerings. Tom Taulli. Bloomberg Press. • 1999. $24.95. Explains how individual investors can invest profitably in new stock offerings. (Bloomberg Personal Bookshelf.).

NEW PRODUCTS

See also: INVENTIONS; PATENTS

HANDBOOKS AND MANUALS

Design and Marketing of New Products. Glen L. Urban and John R. Hauser. Simon and Schuster Trade. • 1993. $97.00. Second edition.

Faster New Product Development: Getting the Right Product to Market Quickly. Milton D. Rosenau. AMACOM. • 1990. $55.00. A guide to new product development for companies of all sizes and kinds.

New Product Development and Marketing: A Practical Guide. Italo S. Servi. Greenwood

Publishing Group, Inc. • 1990. $55.00. Looseleaf. A practical guide to the creation, testing, and marketing of a new product.

New Product Development Checklists: From Mission to Market. George Gruenwald. NTC/Contemporary Publishing. • 1994. $22.95. (NTC Business Book Series).

New Products Management. Merle C. Crawford. McGraw-Hill Higher Education. • 1996. $86.25. Fifth edition.

ONLINE DATABASES

New Product Announcements Plus. The Gale Group. • Contains the full text of new product and corporate activity press releases, with special emphasis on high technology and emerging industries. Covers 1985 to date. Weekly updates. Inquire as to online cost and availability.

PROMT: Predicasts Overview of Markets and Technology. The Gale Group. • Companies, products, applied technologies and markets. U.S. and international literature coverage, 1972 to date. Inquire as to online cost and availability. Provides abstracts from more than 1,600 publications. Weekly updates.

PERIODICALS AND NEWSLETTERS

Chilton's Product Design and Development. Cahners Business Information. • Monthly. $80.00 per year.

Industrial Equipment News. Thomas Publishing Co. • Monthly. $95.00 per year. Free. What's new in equipment, parts and materials.

International New Product Newsletter. INPN, Inc. • Monthly. $175.00 per year. Includes licensing opportunities.

Journal of Product Innovation Management: An International Publication of the Product Development and Management Association. Product Development and Management Association. Elsevier Science. • Bimonthly. $425.00 per year. Covers new product planning and development.

New Equipment Digest Market. Penton Media Inc. • Monthly. Free to qualified personnel; others, $55.00 per year. Formerly *Material Handling Engineering*.

New Equipment Reporter: New Products Industrial News. De Roche Publications. • Monthly. Controlled circulation.

Potentials: Ideas and Products that Motivate. Lakewood Publications, Inc. • 10 times a year. $24.00 per year. Covers incentives, premiums, awards, and gifts as related to promotional activities. Formerly *Potentials in Marketing*.

OTHER SOURCES

How to Evaluate a New Product. American Management Association Extension Institute. • Looseleaf. $130.00. Self-study course. Emphasis is on practical explanations, examples, and problem solving. Quizzes are included.

Industrial Literature Review: Presents Catalogs and Brochures to Buyers and Specifiers in the United States Industrial Marketplace. Thomas Publishing Co. • Quarterly. Controlled circulation. Describes new catalogs and other new industrial literature.

InSite 2. Intelligence Data/Thomson Financial. • Fee-based Web site consolidates information in a "Base Pack" consisting of Business InSite, Market InSite, and Company InSite. Optional databases are Consumer InSite, Health and Wellness InSite, Newsletter InSite, and Computer InSite. Includes fulltext content from more than 2,500 trade publications, journals, newsletters, newspapers, analyst reports, and other sources. Continuous updating. Formerly produced by The Gale Group.

NEW YORK STOCK EXCHANGE

See: STOCK EXCHANGES

NEWSLETTERS

See also: INVESTMENT ADVISORY SERVICES; PERIODICALS

CD-ROM DATABASES

MediaFinder CD-ROM: Oxbridge Directories of Print Media and Catalogs. Oxbridge Communications, Inc. • Quarterly. $1,695.00 per year. CD-ROM includes about 100,000 listings from *Standard Periodical Directory, National Directory of Catalogs, National Directory of British Mail Order Catalogs, National Directory of German Mail Order Catalogs, Oxbridge Directory of Newsletters, National Directory of Mailing Lists, College Media Directory*, and *National Directory of Magazines.*

DIRECTORIES

Books and Periodicals Online: The Guide to Business and Legal Information on Databases and CD-ROM's. Nuchine Nobari, editor. Library Technology Alliance, Inc. • Annual. $365.00 per year. 97,000 periodicals available as part of online and CD-ROM databases; international coverage.

Burrelle's Media Directory: Magazines and Newsletters. Burrelle's Information Services. • Annual. $275.00. Provides detailed descriptions of more than 13,500 magazines and newsletters published in the U. S., Canada, and Mexico. Categories are professional, consumer, trade, and college.

The Directory of Business Information Resources: Associations, Newsletters, Magazine Trade Shows. Grey House Publishing, Inc. • Annual. $195.00. Provides concise information on associations, newsletters, magazines, and trade shows for each of 90 major industry groups. An "Entry & Company Index" serves as a guide to titles, publishers, and organizations.

Hudson's Subscription Newsletter Directory. Newsletter Clearinghouse. • Annual. $189.00. About 4,800 newsletters available by subscription.

Newsletters in Print. The Gale Group. • 2000. $285.00. 14th edition. Details 11,500 sources of information on a wide range of topics.

Oxbridge Directory of Newsletters. Oxbridge Communications, Inc. • Annual. $705.00. Lists approximately 20,000 newsletters in the United States and Canada.

SIE Guide to Investment Publications: The Only Directory of Investment Advisory Publications for Investors. George H. Wein, editor. Select Information Exchange. • Annual. Free. Provides descriptions and prices of about 100 financial newsletters covering stocks, bonds, mutual funds, commodity futures, options, gold, and foreign investments. Offers subscription services, including short trials of any 20 investment newsletters for a total of $11.95. Formerly *SIE Market Letter Directory*.

HANDBOOKS AND MANUALS

Creating Newsletters, Brochures, and Pamphlets: A How-To-Do-It Manual for Librarians. Barbara A. Radke and Barbara Stein. Neal-Schuman Publishers, Inc. • 1992. $39.95. Includes desktop publishing. (How-to-Do-It Series).

Editing Your Newsletter: How to Produce an Effective Publication Using Traditional Tools and Computers. Mark Beach. F and W Publications, Inc. • 1995. $22.99. Fourth edition. Covers design, writing, editing, production and distribution. Emphasis on in-house publications.

Home-Based Newsletter Publishing: A Success Guide for Entrepreneurs. William J. Bond. McGraw-Hill. • 1991. $14.95.

How to Produce Creative Advertising: Traditional Techniques and Computer Applications. Thomas Bivins and Ann Keding. NTC/Contemporary Publishing. • 1993. $37.95. Covers copywriting, advertising design, and the use of desktop publishing techniques in advertising. (NTC Business Book Series).

How to Produce Creative Publications: Traditional Techniques and Computer Applications. Thomas Bivins and William E. Ryan. NTC/Contemporary Publishing. • 1994. $32.95. A practical guide to the writing, designing, and production of magazines, annual reports, brochures, and newsletters by traditional methods and by desktop publishing.

Newsletter Publishing. Entrepreneur Media, Inc. • Looseleaf. $59.50. A practical guide to starting a newsletter. Covers profit potential, start-up costs, market size evaluation, pricing, accounting, advertising, promotion, etc. (Start-Up Business Guide No. E1067.).

Using Desktop Publishing to Create Newsletters, Library Guides, and Web Pages: A How-To-Do-It Manual for Librarians. John Maxymuk. Neal-Schuman Publishers, Inc. • 1997. $55.00. Includes more than 90 illustrations.

INTERNET DATABASES

PubList.com: The Internet Directory of Publications. Bowes & Associates, Inc. Phone: (781)792-0999 Fax: (781)792-0988 E-mail: info@publist.com • URL: http://www.publist.com • "The premier online global resource for information about print and electronic publications." Provides online searching for information on more than 150,000 magazines, journals, newsletters, e-journals, and monographs. Database entries generally include title, publisher, format, address, editor, circulation, subject, and International Standard Serial Number (ISSN). Fees: Free.

Ulrichsweb.com. R. R. Bowker. Phone: 888-269-5372 or (908)464-6800 Fax: (908)464-3553 E-mail: info@bowker.com • URL: http://www.ulrichsweb.com • Web site provides fee-based access to about 250,000 serials records from the *Ulrich's International Periodicals Directory* database. Includes periodical evaluations from *Library Journal* and *Magazines for Libraries*. Monthly updates.

ONLINE DATABASES

Gale Database of Publications and Broadcast Media. The Gale Group. • An online directory containing detailed information on over 67,000 periodicals, newspapers, broadcast stations, cable systems, directories, and newsletters. Corresponds to the following print sources: *Gale Directory of Publications and Broadcast Media; Directories in Print; City and State Directories in Print; Newsletters in Print.* Semiannual updates. Inquire as to online cost and availability.

Newsletter Database. The Gale Group. • Contains the full text of about 600 U. S. and international newsletters covering a wide range of business and industrial topics. Time period is 1988 to date, with daily updates. Inquire as to online cost and availability.

PERIODICALS AND NEWSLETTERS

Circulation Management. Intertec Publishing Co. • Monthly. $39.00 per year. Edited for circulation professionals in the magazine and newsletter publishing industry. Covers marketing, planning, promotion, management, budgeting, and related topics.

The Hulbert Financial Digest. Hulbert Financial Digest, Inc. • Monthly. $135.00 per year. Trial subscriptions available. Rates the performance of investment advisory newsletters and services. Includes a stock market sentiment index based on bullish, bearish, or neutral opinions of advisors. Subscription includes *HFD's Thirteen-Year Longer Term Performance Report* and *HFD's Financial Newsletter Directory.*

Ideas Unlimited: For Editors. Omniprints, Inc. • Monthly. $195.00 per year. Contains fillers for company newsletters: articles, cartoons, jokes, seasonal items, etc.

Newsletter on Newsletters: Reporting on the Newsletter World: Editing, Graphics, Management, Promotion, Newsletter Reviews, and Surveys. • Bimonthly. $196.00 per year.

STATISTICS SOURCES

Computer Publishing Market Forecast. SIMBA Information. • Annual. $1,995.00. Provides market data on computer-related books, magazines, newsletters, and other publications. Includes profiles of major publishers of computer-related material.

TRADE/PROFESSIONAL ASSOCIATIONS

Newsletter Publishers Association. 1501 Wilson Blvd., Suite 509, Arlington, VA 22209-2403. Phone: 800-356-9302 or (703)527-2333 Fax: (703)841-0629 E-mail: npa@newsletter.org.

OTHER SOURCES

Business & Company Resource Center. The Gale Group. • Fee-based Web site provides a wide range of business, industry, and specific company information. Access is offered to trade journal articles, market research data, insider trading activity, major shareholder data, corporate histories, emerging technology reports, corporate earnings estimates, press releases, and other sources. Provides detailed company profiles, industry overviews, and rankings. Offers integration of Predicasts PROMT, Newsletters ASAP, Investext Plus, Business Index ASAP, Brands and Their Companies, and other databases (many have full text).

NEWSPAPER CLIPPINGS

See: CLIPPING SERVICES

NEWSPAPER MARKET RESEARCH

See also: MARKET RESEARCH

DIRECTORIES

Editor and Publisher Market Guide. Editor and Publisher Co., Inc. • Annual. $125.00. More than 1,700 newspaper markets in the Unite States and Canada.

TRADE/PROFESSIONAL ASSOCIATIONS

International Newspaper Marketing Association. 10300 N. Central Expressway, Ste. 467, Dallas, TX 75231-8621. Phone: (214)373-9111 Fax: (214)343-9112 • URL: http://www.inma.org.

NEWSPAPER WORK

See: JOURNALISM

NEWSPAPERS

See also: COLLEGE AND SCHOOL NEWSPAPERS; FOREIGN LANGUAGE PRESS AND NEWSPAPERS; JOURNALISM; MINORITY NEWSPAPERS

ABSTRACTS AND INDEXES

Canadian Index. Micromedia Ltd. • Monthly, with annual cumulation. Price varies. Indexes approximately 500 Canadian periodicals of all kinds, including business magazines and trade journals. Ten daily Canadian newspapers are also indexed.

Newsbank. Newsbank, Inc. • Monthly. Price varies. Quarterly and annual cumulations. Index to articles of current interest from over 500 U.S. newspapers. Full text available on microfiche.

ALMANACS AND YEARBOOKS

Editor and Publisher International Yearbook: Encyclopedia of the Newspaper Industry. Editor and Publisher Co., Inc. • Annual. $125.00. Daily and Sunday newspapers in the United States and Canada.

BIOGRAPHICAL SOURCES

Biographical Dictionary of American Journalism. Joseph P. McKerns, editor. Greenwood Publishing Group Inc. • 1989. $65.00. Covers major mass media: newspapers, radio, television, and magazines. Includes reporters, editors, columnists, cartoonists, commentators, etc.

CD-ROM DATABASES

Leadership Library on CD-ROM: Who's Who in the Leadership of the United States. Leadership Directories, Inc. • Quarterly. $2,641.00 per year, including access to Internet version (weekly updates). Contains all 14 *Yellow Book* personnel directories on CD-ROM, providing contact and brief biographical information for about 400,000 individuals. Covers business, government, financial institutions, news media, law firms, associations, foreign representatives, and nonprofit organizations. Includes photographs.

MediaFinder CD-ROM: Oxbridge Directories of Print Media and Catalogs. Oxbridge Communications, Inc. • Quarterly. $1,695.00 per year. CD-ROM includes about 100,000 listings from *Standard Periodical Directory, National Directory of Catalogs, National Directory of British Mail Order Catalogs, National Directory of German Mail Order Catalogs, Oxbridge Directory of Newsletters, National Directory of Mailing Lists, College Media Directory*, and *National Directory of Magazines.*

National Newspaper Index CD-ROM. The Gale Group. • Monthly. Provides comprehensive CD-ROM indexing of all material appearing in the late edition of the *New York Times*, the final edition of the *Washington Post*, the national edition of the *Christian Science Monitor*, the home edition of the *Los Angeles Times*, and the *Wall Street Journal.* Time period is four years. Also available online.

The New York Times Ondisc. New York Times Online Services. • Monthly. $2,650.00 per year. CD-ROM discs contain the full text of *The New York Times*, final edition. Inquire as to time period covered and availability of backfiles.

Newspaper Abstracts Ondisc. Bell & Howell Information and Learning. • Monthly. $2,950.00 per year (covers 1989 to date; archival discs are available for 1985-88). Provides cover-to-cover CD-ROM indexing and abstracting of 19 major newspapers, including the *New York Times, Wall Street Journal, Washington Post, Chicago Tribune,* and *Los Angeles Times.*

DIRECTORIES

Burrelle's Media Directory: Newspapers and Related Media. Burrelle's Information Services. • Annual. $275.00. Two volumes. *Daily Newspapers* volume lists more than 2,000 daily publications in the U. S., Canada, and Mexico. *Non-Daily Newspapers* volume lists more than 10,000 items published no more than three times a week. Provides detailed descriptions, including key personnel.

CARD The Media Information Network (Canadian Advertising Rates and Data). Available from SRDS. • Biennial. $225.00 per issue. Published by Maclean Hunter Publishing Ltd. (Toronto). Provides advertising rates and other information relating to Canadian media: daily newspapers, weekly community newspapers, consumer magazines, business publications, school publications, religious publications, radio, and television.

Community Publication Advertising Source. SRDS. • Semiannual. $161.00 per issue. Provides advertising rates for weekly community newspapers, shopping guides, and religious newspapers, with circulation data and other information. Formerly *Community Publication Rates and Data.*

Cyberhound's Guide to Publications on the Internet. The Gale Group. • 1996. $79.00. First edition. Presents critical descriptions and ratings of more than 3,400 Internet databases of journals, newspapers, newsletters, and other publications. Includes a glossary of Internet terms, a bibliography, and three indexes.

Fulltext Sources Online. Information Today, Inc. • Semiannual. $199.00 per year; $119.50 per issue. Lists more than 8,000 journals, newspapers, magazines, newsletters, and newswires found online in fulltext through DIALOG, LEXIS-NEXIS, Dow Jones, Westlaw, etc. Includes journals that have free Internet archives. (Formerly published by BiblioData.).

Gale Directory of Publications and Broadcast Media. The Gale Group. • Annual. $650.00. Five volumes. A guide to publications and broadcasting stations in the U. S. and Canada, including newspapers, magazines, journals, radio stations, television stations, and cable systems. Geographic arrangement. Volume three consists of statistical tables, maps, subject indexes, and title index. Formerly *Ayer Directory of Publications.*

International Media Guide: Newspapers Worldwide. International Media Guides, Inc. • Annual. $285.00. Provides advertising rates, circulation, and other details relating to newspapers in major cities of the world (covers 200 countries, including U. S.).

National Directory of Community Newspapers. American Newspaper Representatives, Inc. • Annual. $105.00. Supersedes *National Directory of Weekly Newspapers.*

News Media Yellow Book: Who's Who Among Reporters, Writers, Editors, and Producers in the Leading National News Media. Leadership Directories, Inc. • Quarterly. $305.00 per year. Lists the staffs of major newspapers and news magazines, TV and radio networks, news services and bureaus, and feature syndicates. Includes syndicated columnists and programs. Seven specialized indexes are provided.

Newspaper Advertising Source. SRDS. • Monthly. $662.00 per year. Lists newspapers geographically, with detailed information on advertising rates, special features, personnel, circulation, etc. Includes a section on college newspapers. Also provides consumer market data for population, households, income, and retail sales. Formerly *Newspaper Rates and Data.*

Print Media Production Source. SRDS. • Quarterly. $401.00 per year. Contains details of printing and mechanical production requirements for advertising in specific trade journals, consumer magazines, and newspapers. Formerly *Print Media Production Data*.

Working Press of the Nation. R. R. Bowker. • Annual. $450.00. Three volumes: (1) *Newspaper Directory*; (2) *Magazine and Internal Publications Directory*; (3) *Radio and Television Directory*. Includes names of editors and other personnel. Individual volumes, $249.00.

ENCYCLOPEDIAS AND DICTIONARIES

NTC's Mass Media Dictionary. R. Terry Ellmore. NTC/Contemporary Publishing. • 1993. $24.95. Covers television, radio, newspapers, magazines, film, graphic arts, books, billboards, public relations, and advertising. Terms are related to production, research, audience measurement, audio-video engineering, printing, publishing, and other areas.

FINANCIAL RATIOS

Almanac of Business and Industrial Financial Ratios. Leo Troy. Prentice Hall. • Annual. $99.95. Contains financial ratios derived from federal tax returns. Ratios for each of about 200 industries are arranged according to company asset size.

Annual Statement Studies. Robert Morris Associates: The Association of Lending and Credit Risk Professiona. • Annual. Free to members; non-members, $140.00. Median and quartile financial ratios are given for over 400 kinds of manufacturing, wholesale, retail, construction, and consumer finance establishments. Data is sorted by both asset size and sales volume. Includes a clearly written "Definition of Ratios" and an alphabetical industry index.

HANDBOOKS AND MANUALS

Newspaper Designer's Handbook. Timothy Harrower. McGraw-Hill Higher Education. • 1997. $28.25. Fourth edition.

Rights and Liabilities of Publishers, Broadcasters, and Reporters. Slade R. Metcalf and Robin Bierstedt. Shepard's. • 1982. $200.00. Two volumes. A legal manual for the media.

INTERNET DATABASES

GaleNet: Your Information Community. The Gale Group. Phone: 800-877-GALE or (248)699-GALE Fax: 800-414-5043 or (248)699-8069 E-mail: galenet@gale.com • URL: http://www.galenet.com • Web site provides a wide variety of full-text information from Gale databases, Taft, and other sources. Covers associations, biography, business directories, education, the information industry, literature, publishing, and science. Fee-based subscriptions are available for individual databases (free demonstration). Includes Boolean search features and the BRS/Search user interface.

Wall Street Journal Interactive Edition. Dow Jones & Co., Inc. Phone: 800-369-2834 or (212)416-2000 Fax: (212)416-2658 E-mail: inquiries@interactive.wsj.com • URL: http://www.wsj.com • Fee-based Web site providing online searching of worldwide information from the *The Wall Street Journal*. Includes "Company Snapshots," "The Journal's Greatest Hits," "Index to Market Data," "14-Day Searchable Archive," "Journal Links," etc. Financial price quotes are available. Fees: $49.00 per year; $29.00 per year to print subscribers.

ONLINE DATABASES

Gale Database of Publications and Broadcast Media. The Gale Group. • An online directory containing detailed information on over 67,000 periodicals, newspapers, broadcast stations, cable systems, directories, and newsletters. Corresponds to the following print sources: *Gale Directory of Publications and Broadcast Media; Directories in Print; City and State Directories in Print; Newsletters in Print*. Semiannual updates. Inquire as to online cost and availability.

Information Bank Abstracts. New York Times Index Dept. • Provides indexing and abstracting of current affairs, primarily from the final late edition of *The New York Times* and the Eastern edition of *The Wall Street Journal*. Time period is 1969 to present, with daily updates. Inquire as to online cost and availability.

National Newspaper Index. The Gale Group. • Citations to news items in five major newspapers, 1970 to present. Weekly updates. Inquire as to online cost and availability.

Newspaper and Periodical Abstracts. Bell & Howell Information and Learning. • Provides online coverage (citations and abstracts) of 25 major newspapers, 1,600 perodicals, and 70 TV programs. Covers business, economics, current affairs, health, fitness, sports, education, technology, government, consumer affairs, psychology, the arts, and the social sciences. Time period is 1986 to date, with daily updates. Inquire as to online cost and availability.

Super Searchers in the News: The Online Secrets of Journalists and News Researchers. Paula J. Hane and Reva Basch. Information Today, Inc. • 2000. $24.95. Contains online searching advice from 10 professional news researchers and fact checkers. (CyberAge Books.).

PERIODICALS AND NEWSLETTERS

Brill's Content: The Independent Voice of the Information Age. Brill Media Ventures, L.P. • Eight times a year. $19.95 per year. Presents a critical, iconoclastic view of various forms of news media, including TV, magazines, newspapers, and websites.

Editor and Publisher - The Fourth Estate: Spot News and Features About Newspapers, Advertisers and Agencies. Editor and Publisher Co., Inc. • Weekly. $75.00 per year. Trade journal of the newspaper industry.

NewsInc.: The Business of the Newspapers Business. The Cole Group. • Biweekly. $425.00 per year. Newsletter. Reports on trends in mass media, especially with regard to newspaper publishing. Articles on cable TV and other competitive media are included.

Newspaper Financial Executives Journal. International Newspaper Financial Executives. • 10 times a year. $100.00. Provides financially related information to newspaper executives.

Publishers' Auxiliary. National Newspaper Association. • Biweekly. $85.00 per year.

The Wall Street Journal. Dow Jones & Co., Inc. • Daily. $175.00 per year. Covers news and trends relating to business, industry, finance, the economy, and international commerce. Provides extensive price and other data for the securities, commodity, options, futures, foreign exchange, and money markets.

RESEARCH CENTERS AND INSTITUTES

Northwestern University-Media Management Center. 1007 Church St., No. 312, Evanston, IL 60201-5912. Phone: (847)491-4900 Fax: (847)491-5619 E-mail: nmc@nwu.edu • URL: http://www.nmc-nwu.org • Research areas are related to various business aspects of the newspaper industry: management, marketing, personnel, planning, accounting, and finance. A joint activity of the J. L. Kellogg Graduate School of Management and the Medill School of Journalism.

STATISTICS SOURCES

Circulation [year]. SRDS. • Annual. $256.00. Contains detailed statistical analysis of newspaper circulation by metropolitan area or county and data on television viewing by area. Includes maps.

U. S. Industry and Trade Outlook: The McGraw-Hill Companies and the U.S. Department of Commerce/International Trade Administration. Datapso Research Corp. • Annual. $69.95. Produced by the International Trade Administration, U. S. Department of Commerce, in a "public-private" partnership with DRI/McGraw-Hill and Standard & Poor's. Provides basic data, outlook for the current year, and "Long-Term Prospects" (five-year projections) for a wide variety of products and services. Includes high technology industries. Formerly *U. S. Industrial Outlook*.

UNESCO Statistical Yearbook. Bernan Press. • Annual. $95.00. Co-published by Bernan Press and the United Nations Educational, Scientific, and Cultural Organization (http://www.unesco.org). Presents statistical data from more than 200 countries on education, technology, research, broadcasting, cinema, book publishing, newspapers, libraries, museums, and population. Includes charts, maps, and graphs.

TRADE/PROFESSIONAL ASSOCIATIONS

American Society of Newspaper Editors. 11690 Sunrise Valley Dr., No. B, Reston, VA 20191-1409. Phone: (703)453-1122 Fax: (703)453-1133 E-mail: asne@asne.org • URL: http://www.infi.net/asne.

International Newspaper Financial Executives. 21525 Ridgetop Circle, Suite 200, Sterling, VA 20166. Phone: (703)421-4060 Fax: (703)421-4068 E-mail: infe@infe.org • URL: http://www.infe.org.

National Federation of Press Women. P.O. Box 5556, Arlington, VA 22205-0056. Phone: (703)534-2500 Fax: 800-780-2715 E-mail: presswomen@aol.com.

National Newspaper Association. 1010 N. Glebe Rd., Ste. 450, Arlington, VA 22209. Phone: 800-829-4662 or (703)907-7900 Fax: (703)907-7901 E-mail: info@nna.org • URL: http://www.nna.org.

National Press Club. National Press Bldg., 529 14th St., N.W., Washington, DC 20045. Phone: (202)662-7500 Fax: (202)662-7512 E-mail: info@npcpress.org • URL: http://www.npc.press.org.

Newsletter Publishers Association. 1501 Wilson Blvd., Suite 509, Arlington, VA 22209-2403. Phone: 800-356-9302 or (703)527-2333 Fax: (703)841-0629 E-mail: npa@newsletter.org.

The Newspaper Guild. 501 Third St., N.W., 2nd Fl., Washington, DC 20001-2760. E-mail: lgildersleeve@cwa-union.org • URL: http://www.newsguild.org.

OTHER SOURCES

Factiva. Dow Jones Reuters Business Interactive, LLC. • Fee-based Web site provides "global news and business information through Web sites and content integration solutions." Includes Dow Jones and Reuters newswires, The Wall Street Journal, and more than 7,000 other sources of current news, historical articles, market research reports, and investment analysis. Content includes 96 major U. S. newspapers, 900 non-English sources, trade publications, media transcripts, country profiles, news photos, etc.

Nexis.com. Lexis-Nexis Group. • Fee-based Web site offers searching of about 2.8 billion documents in some 30,000 news, business, and legal information sources. Features include a subject directory covering 1,200 topics in 34 categories and a Company Dossier containing information on more than 500,000 public and private companies. Boolean searching is offered.

NEWSPAPERS, SCHOOL

See: COLLEGE AND SCHOOL NEWSPAPERS

NEWSPRINT PAPER INDUSTRY

See: PAPER INDUSTRY

NICKEL INDUSTRY

See: METAL INDUSTRY

NOISE CONTROL

ABSTRACTS AND INDEXES

Environment Abstracts. Congressional Information Service. • Monthly. Price varies. Provides multidisciplinary coverage of the world's environmental literature. Incorporates *Acid Rain Abstracts.*

Environment Abstracts Annual: A Guide to the Key Environmental Literature of the Year. Congressional Information Service. • Annual. $495.00. A yearly cumulation of *Environment Abstracts.*

Environmental Periodicals Bibliography: A Current Awareness Bibliography Featuring Citations of Scientific and Popular Articles in Serial Publications in the Area of the Environment. Environmental Studies Institute. International Academy at Santa Barbara. • Monthly. Price varies. An index to current environmental literature.

Excerpta Medica: Environmental Health and Pollution Control. Elsevier Science. • 16 times a year. 2,506.00 per year. Section 46 of *Excerpta Medica.* Covers air, water, and land pollution and noise control.

NTIS Alerts: Environmental Pollution & Control. National Technical Information Service. • Semimonthly. $245.00 per year. Provides descriptions of government-sponsored research reports and software, with ordering information. Covers the following categories of environmental pollution: air, water, solid wastes, radiation, pesticides, and noise. Formerly *Abstract Newsletter.*

Pollution Abstracts. Cambridge Information Group. • Monthly. $895.00 per year; with index, $985.00 per year.

CD-ROM DATABASES

Environment Abstracts on CD-ROM. Congressional Information Service, Inc. • Quarterly. $1,295.00 per year. Contains the following CD-ROM databases: *Environment Abstracts, Energy Abstracts,* and *Acid Rain Abstracts.* Length of coverage varies.

DIRECTORIES

Sound and Vibration Buyer's Guide. Acoustical Publications, Inc. • Annual. Free to qualified personnel. Lists of manufacturers of products for noise and vibration control, dynamic measurements instrumentation, and dynamic testing equipment.

ENCYCLOPEDIAS AND DICTIONARIES

Encyclopedia of Acoustics. Malcolm J. Crocker. John Wiley and Sons, Inc. • 1997. $650.00. Four volumes.

ONLINE DATABASES

Enviroline. Congressional Information Service, Inc. • Provides online indexing and abstracting of worldwide environmental and natural resource literature from 1975 to date. Updated monthly. Inquire as to online cost and availability.

PERIODICALS AND NEWSLETTERS

Acoustical Society of America Journal. American Institute of Physics. • Monthly. $1,020.00 per year.

Noise Control Engineering Journal. Institute of Noise Control Engineering. • Bimonthly. $70.00 per year.

Noise Regulation Report: The Nation's Only Noise Control Publication. Business Publishers, Inc. • Monthly. $487.00 per year. Newsletter. Covers federal and state rules and regulations for the control of excessive noise.

Sound and Vibration (S/V). Acoustical Publications, Inc. • Monthly. Free to qualified personnel; others, $60.00 per year.

RESEARCH CENTERS AND INSTITUTES

Center for Acoustics and Vibration. Pennsylvania State University. 157 Hammond Bldg., University Park, PA 16802. Phone: (814)865-2761 Fax: (814)863-7222 E-mail: ghk@kirkof.psu.edu • URL: http://kirkof.psu.edu.80/cav/.

Joint Institute for Advancement of Flight Sciences. George Washington University, NASA Langley Research Center, Mail Stop 269, Hampton, VA 23681-2199. Phone: (757)864-1982 Fax: (757)864-5894 E-mail: jiafs@seas.gwu.edu • URL: http://www.seas.gwu.edu/seas/jiafs • Conducts research in aeronautics, astronautics, and acoustics (flight-produced noise).

TRADE/PROFESSIONAL ASSOCIATIONS

Acoustical Society of America. Two Huntington Quadrangle, Ste. 1N01, Melville, NY 11797-4502. Phone: (516)576-2360 Fax: (516)576-2377 E-mail: asa@aip.org • URL: http://www.asa.aip.org.

Institute of Noise Control Engineering. P.O. Box 220, Saddle River, NJ 07458. Phone: (201)760-1101 Fax: (201)236-1210 E-mail: hq@ince.org.

Noise Control Association. 680 Rainier Lane, Port Ludlow, WA 98365-9775. Phone: (360)437-0814 Fax: (360)437-0814 E-mail: daharrisa@tolypen.com.

NONFERROUS METAL INDUSTRY

See also: METAL INDUSTRY

ABSTRACTS AND INDEXES

Applied Science and Technology Index. H. W. Wilson Co. • 11 times a year. Quarterly and annual cumulations. Service basis for print edition; CD-ROM edition, $1,495.00 per year. Indexes a wide variety of English language technical, industrial, and engineering periodicals.

F & S Index: United States. The Gale Group. • Monthly. $1,295.00 per year, including quarterly and annual cumulations. Provides annotated citations to marketing, business, financial, and industrial literature. Coverage of U. S. business activity includes trade journals, financial magazines, business newspapers, and special reports. Formerly *Predicasts F & S Index: United States.*

IMM Abstracts and Index: A Survey of World Literature on the Economic Geology and Mining of All Minerals (Except Coal), Mineral Processing, and Nonferrous Extraction Metallurgy. Institution of Mining and Metallurgy. • Bimonthly. Members, $142.00 per year; non-members, $215.00 per year. Provides international coverage of the literature of mining and nonferrous metallurgy. Includes mineral economics, tunnelling, and rock mechanics.

Nonferrous Metals Alert. Cambridge Information Group. • Monthly. $340.00 per year. Provides citations to the business and industrial literature of nonferrous metals. (Materials Business Information Series).

CD-ROM DATABASES

F & S Index Plus Text. The Gale Group. • Monthly. $7,575.00 per year. Provides CD-ROM citations to worldwide business, marketing, and industrial material appearing in a large assortment of trade journals, newspapers, and other publications. Time period is four years.

WILSONDISC: Applied Science and Technology Abstracts. H. W. Wilson Co. • Monthly. $1,495.00 per year, including unlimited access to the online version of *Applied Science and Technology Abstracts* through WILSONLINE. Provides CD-ROM indexing and abstracting of 400 prominent scientific, technical, engineering, and industrial periodicals. Indexing coverage is provided from 1983 to date and abstracting from 1993 to date.

DIRECTORIES

North American Scrap Metals Directory. G.I.E. Media, Inc. • Annual. $85.00. Lists more than 9,000 scrap metal processors, brokers, and dealers.

HANDBOOKS AND MANUALS

ASM Metals Reference Book. Michael L. Bauccio, editor. ASM International. • 1993. $144.00. Third edition. Includes glossary, tables, formulas, and diagrams. Covers a wide range of ferrous and nonferrous metals.

ONLINE DATABASES

Applied Science and Technology Index Online. H. W. Wilson Co. • Provides online indexing of 400 major scientific, technical, industrial, and engineering periodicals. Time period is 1983 to date. Monthly updates. Inquire as to online cost and availability.

F & S Index. The Gale Group. • Contains about four million citations to worldwide business, financial, and industrial or consumer product literature appearing from 1972 to date. Weekly updates. Inquire as to online cost and availability.

Trade & Industry Index. The Gale Group. • Provides indexing of business periodicals, January 1981 to date. Daily updates. (Full text articles from some periodicals are available online, 1983 to date, in the companion database, *Trade & Industry ASAP.*) Inquire as to online cost and availability.

PERIODICALS AND NEWSLETTERS

Foundry Management and Technology. Penton Media. • Monthly. Free to qualified personnel; others, $50.00 per year. Coverage includes nonferrous casting technology and production.

JOM: Journal of Metals. Minerals, Metals, and Materials Society. • Monthly. Individuals. $79.00 per year; institutions, $154.00 per year. A scholarly journal covering all phases of metals and metallurgy.

Light Metal Age. Fellom Publishing Co. • Bimonthly. $40.00 per year. Edited for production and engineering executives of the aluminum industry and other nonferrous light metal industries.

Metal Bulletin. Metal Bulletin, Inc. • Semiweekly. $1,378 per year. Provides news of international trends, prices, and market conditions for both steel and non-ferrous metal industries. (Published in England.).

Metal Bulletin Monthly. Metal Bulletin, Inc. • Monthly. Price on application. Edited for international metal industry business executives and senior technical personnel. Covers business, economic, and technical developments. (Published in England.).

Modern Metals. Trend Publishing, Inc. • Monthly. $95.00 per year. Covers management and production for plants that fabricate and finish metals of various kinds.

New Steel: Mini and Integrated Mill Management and Technologies. Cahners Business Information. • Monthly. $89.00 per year. Covers the primary metals industry, both ferrous and nonferrous. Includes technical, marketing, and product development articles. Formerly *Iron Age.*

33 Metalproducing: For Primary Producers of Steel, Aluminum, and Copper-Base Alloys. Penton Media, Inc. • Monthly. $65.00 per year. Covers metal production technology and methods and industry news. Includes a bimonthly *Nonferrous Supplement.*

RESEARCH CENTERS AND INSTITUTES

Cast Metals Laboratory. University of Wisconsin-Madison, 1509 University Ave., Madison, WI 53706. Phone: (608)262-2562 Fax: (608)262-8353 E-mail: loper@engr.wisc.edu • URL: http://www.msae.wisc.edu.

Materials Processing Center. Massachusetts Institute of Technology, 77 Massachusetts Ave., Room 12-007, Cambridge, MA 02139-4307. Phone: (617)253-5179 Fax: (617)258-6900 E-mail: fmpage@.mit.edu • URL: http://www.web.mit.edu/mpc/www/ • Conducts processing, engineering, and economic research in ferrous and nonferrous metals, ceramics, polymers, photonic materials, superconductors, welding, composite materials, and other materials.

Metal Casting Laboratory. Pennsylvania State University, 207 Hammond Bldg., University Park, PA 16802. Phone: (814)863-7290 Fax: (814)863-4745 E-mail: rcv2@psu.edu • URL: http://www.ie.psu.edu/orgs/mcg/.

STATISTICS SOURCES

Annual Survey of Manufactures. Available from U. S. Government Printing Office. • Annual. Prices vary. Issued by the U. S. Census Bureau as an interim update to the *Census of Manufactures.* Includes data on number of manufacturing establishments in various industries, employment, labor costs, value of shipments, capital expenditures, inventories, energy costs, and assets. (See also Census Bureau home page, http://www.census.gov/.).

Manufacturing Profiles. Available from U. S. Government Printing Office. • Annual. Issued by the U. S. Census Bureau. A printed consolidation of the entire *Current Industrial Report* series, presenting "all the data compiled." Contains statistics on production, shipments, inventories, consumption, exports, imports, and orders for a wide variety of manufactured products. (See also Census Bureau home page, http://www.census.gov/.).

Metal Statistics. Cahners Business Information. • Annual. $250.00. Provides statistical data on a wide variety of metals, metal products, ores, alloys, and scrap metal. Includes data on prices, production, consumption, shipments, imports, and exports.

Non-Ferrous Metal Data Yearbook. American Bureau of Metal Statistics. • Annual. $395.00. Provides about 200 statistical tables covering many nonferrous metals. Includes production, consumption, inventories, exports, imports, and other data.

Nonferrous Castings. U. S. Bureau of the Census. • Annual. (Current Industrial Reports MA-33E.).

TRADE/PROFESSIONAL ASSOCIATIONS

American Bureau of Metal Statistics. P.O. Box 805, Chatham, NJ 07928. Phone: (973)701-2299 Fax: (973)701-2152 E-mail: info@abms.com • URL: http://www.abms.com • Members are metal companies. Compiles and publishes detailed statistical data on a wide variety of nonferrous metals: aluminum, copper, gold, lead, nickel, platinum, silver, tin, titanium, uranium, zinc, and others.

Minerals, Metals and Materials Society. 184 Thorn Hill Dr., Warrendale, PA 15086-7528. Phone: 800-759-4867 or (724)776-9000 Fax: (724)776-3770 E-mail: tmsgeneral@tms.org • URL: http://www.tms.org • Members are metallurgists, metallurgical engineers, and materials scientists. Divisions include Light Metals and Electronic, Magnetic, and Photonic Materials.

Non-Ferrous Founders Society. 1480 Renaissnace Dr., Ste. 310, Park Ridge, IL 60068. Phone: (847)299-0950 Fax: (847)299-3598 E-mail: staff@nffs.org • URL: http://www.nffs.org • Members are manufacturers of brass, bronze, aluminum and other nonferrous castings.

Non-Ferrous Metals Producers Committee. c/o Kenneth Button, Economic Consulting Service, 2030 M. St., N.W., Suite 800, Washington, DC 20036. Phone: (202)466-7720 Fax: (202)466-2710 • Members are copper, lead, and zinc producers. Promotes the copper, lead, and zinc mining and metal industries.

NON-FOODS MERCHANDISERS

See: RACK JOBBERS

NONPRESCRIPTION DRUG INDUSTRY

See also: PHARMACEUTICAL INDUSTRY

CD-ROM DATABASES

World Marketing Forecasts on CD-ROM. The Gale Group. • Annual. $2,500.00. Produced by Euromonitor. Provides detailed forecast data for the years to 2012 on CD-ROM for 54 countries in all parts of the world. Covers a wide range of social, demographic, economic, and market factors. Includes specific forecasts for many kinds of consumer products.

DIRECTORIES

PDR for Herbal Medicines. Medical Economics Co., Inc. • 1999. $59.95. Published in cooperation with PhytoPharm, U. S. Institute for Phytopharmaceuticals, Inc. Provdies detailed information on more than 600 herbal remedies, including scientific names, common names, indications, usage, adverse reactions, drug interaactions, and literature citations.

Physicians' Desk Reference for Nonprescription Drugs and Dietary Supplements. Medical Economics Co., Inc. • Annual. $82.95. Contains detailed descriptions of "commonly used" over-the-counter drug products. Includes drug identification photographs. Indexing is by product category, product name, manufacturer, and active ingredient. Formerly *Physicians' Desk Reference for Nonprescription Drugs.*

The Red Book. Medical Economics Co., Inc. • Annual. $57.95 for basic volume or $99.00 per year with monthly updates. Provides product information and prices for more than 100,000 prescription and nonprescription drugs and other items sold by pharmacies. Also known as *Drug Topics Red Book.*

HANDBOOKS AND MANUALS

Herbal Drugs and Phytopharmaceuticals. Max Wichtl and Norman G. Bisset, editors. CRC Press, Inc. • 1994. $190.00. Provides a scientific approach to the medicinal use of herbs. (English translation of original German edition.).

ONLINE DATABASES

Euromonitor Market Research. Euromonitor International. • Provides the complete text online of Euromonitor market analysis reports. Covers consumer goods market research data for all major countries, with emphasis on specific product categories. Time period is current. Continuous updating. Inquire as to online cost and availability.

F-D-C Reports. FDC Reports, Inc. • An online version of "The Gray Sheet" (medical devices), "The Pink Sheet" (pharmaceuticals), "The Rose Sheet" (cosmetics), "The Blue Sheet" (biomedical), and "The Tan Sheet" (nonprescription). Contains full-text information on legal, technical, corporate, financial, and marketing developments from 1987 to date, with weekly updates. Inquire as to online cost and availability.

PERIODICALS AND NEWSLETTERS

Chain Drug Review: The Reporter for the Chain Drug Store Industry. Racher Press, Inc. • Biweekly. $136.00 per year. Covers news and trends of concern to the chain drug store industry. Includes special articles on OTC (over-the-counter) drugs.

Health Supplement Retailer. Virgo Publishing, Inc. • Monthly. $38.00 per year. Covers all aspects of the vitamin and health supplement market, including new products. Includes an annual buyer's guide, an annual compilation of industry statistics, and annual guides to vitamins and herbs.

Nonprescription Pharmaceuticals and Nutritionals: The Tan Sheet. F-D-C Reports, Inc. • Weekly. $860.00 per year. Newsletter covering over-the-counter drugs and vitamin supplements. Emphasis is on regulatory activities of the U. S. Food and Drug Administration (FDA).

Supplement Industry Executive. Vitamin Retailer Magazine, Inc. • Bimonthly. $25.00 per year. Edited for manufacturers of vitamins and other dietary supplements. Covers marketing, new products, industry trends, regulations, manufacturing procedures, and related topics. Includes a directory of suppliers to the industry.

Vitamin Retailer. Vitamin Retailer Magazine, Inc. • Monthly. $45.00 per year. Edited for retailers of vitamins, herbal remedies, minerals, antioxidants, essential fatty acids, and other food supplements.

STATISTICS SOURCES

Consumer Canada 1996. Available from The Gale Group. • 1996. $750.00. Published by Euromonitor. Provides consumer market, socioeconomic, and demographic data for Canada. Includes consumer market size (volume and value) for many specific kinds of products.

Consumer International 2000/2001. Available from The Gale Group. • 1998. $1,190.00. Seventh edition. Published by Euromonitor. Contains extensive consumer market, economic, and demographic data for 27 major, non-European countries, including the U. S. and Canada. Includes consumer market size (volume and value) for 150 product types in 14 categories (food, clothing, automobiles, cosmetics, appliances, etc.).

European Marketing Forecasts 2001. Available from The Gale Group. • 2000. $1,190.00. Third edition. Published by Euromonitor. Contains demographic, economic, and market forecasts for the countries of Europe to the year 2010. Forecasts include market-size data for 15 consumer product sectors (food, clothing, automobiles, consumer electronics, etc.).

International Marketing Forecasts 2001. Available from The Gale Group. • 2000. $1,090.00. Third edition. Published by Euromonitor. Contains demographic, economic, and market forecasts to the year 2010 for major, non-European countries, including the U. S. and Canada. Forecasts include market-size data for 15 consumer product sectors, such as food, clothing, and automobiles.

TRADE/PROFESSIONAL ASSOCIATIONS

Consumer Health Product Association. 1150 Connecticut Ave., N. W., Washington, DC 20036. Phone: (202)429-9260 Fax: (202)233-6835 • Members are over-the-counter drug manufacturers and suppliers.

OTHER SOURCES

Health Care Products and Remedies. Available from MarketResearch.com. • 1997. $600.00 each. Consists of market reports published by Simmons Market Research Bureau on each of about 25 health care product categories. Examples are cold remedies, contraceptives, hearing aids, bandages, headache remedies, eyeglasses, contact lenses, and vitamins. Each report covers buying patterns and demographics.

Major Pharmaceutical Companies of the World. Available from The Gale Group. • 2001. $885.00. Third edition. Published by Graham & Whiteside. Contains detailed information and trade names for more than 2,500 important pharmaceutical companies in various countries.

The Market for Rx-to-OTC Switched Drugs. MarketResearch.com. • 2000. $3,250.00. Market research report. Covers the market for over-the-counter drugs that were formerly available only by prescription. Includes profiles of relevant pharmaceutical companies.

Pharmacopeia of Herbs. CME, Inc. • $149.00. Frequently updated CD-ROM provides searchable data on a wide variety of herbal medicines, vitamins, and amino acids. Includes information on clinical studies, contraindications, side-effects, phytoactivity, and 534 therapeutic use categories. Contains a 1,000 word glossary.

NONPROFIT CORPORATIONS

See also: ASSOCIATIONS; FOUNDATIONS

GENERAL WORKS

The Leader of the Future: New Essays by World-Class Leaders and Thinkers. Jossey-Bass, Inc., Publishers. • 1996. $25.00. Contains 32 articles on leadership by "executives, consultants, and commentators." (Management Series).

Management Control in Nonprofit Organizations. Robert N. Anthony and David W. Young. McGraw-Hill. • 1998. $89.06. Sixth edition.

Managing the Non-Profit Organization: Practices and Principles. Peter F. Drucker. HarperInformation. • 1992. $23.00. General advice on strategy, leadership, marketing, and human relations for the non-profit manager.

ALMANACS AND YEARBOOKS

Nonprofit Almanac: A Publication Independent Sector. Virginia A. Hodgkinson and others. Jossey-Bass, Inc., Publishers. • 1996. $25.95. Provides trends and statistics for nonprofit wages, finances, employment, and giving patterns. Includes a glossary.

BIBLIOGRAPHIES

Literature of the Nonprofit Sector: A Bibliography with Abstracts. The Foundation Center. • Dates vary. Six volumes. $45.00 per volume. Covers the literature of philanthropy, foundations, nonprofit organizations, fund-raising, and federal aid.

Management and Leadership Resources for Non-Profits. Available from Applied Research and Development Institute. • Annual. $3.50. Compiled by the Applied Research and Development Institute and published as a special issue of *The Journal of Philanthropy.* Lists and describes over 800 books, periodicals, and other publications in 14 categories (general management, finance, marketing, development, etc.). Includes a directory of publishers. No indexes.

The Non-Profit Handbook: Books, Periodicals, Software, Internet Sites, and Other Essential Resources for Non-Profit Leaders. Chronicle of Higher Education, Inc. • Annual. $5.00. A special issue of *Chronicle of Philanthropy.* Contains annotations of books, periodicals, and other material from various sources, relating to Advocacy, Boards, Communications and Marketing, Financial Management, Fund Raising, General Information, Managing, Philanthropic Tradition, Technology, and Volunteers. Includes index to titles.

Resource Center Catalog. Society for Nonprofit Organizations. • Included in subscription to *Nonprofit World.*

BIOGRAPHICAL SOURCES

Who Knows Who: Networking Through Corporate Boards. Who Know Who Publishing. • 1994. $150.00. Fifth edition. Shows the connections between the board members of major U. S. corporations and major foundations and nonprofit organizations.

CD-ROM DATABASES

Leadership Library on CD-ROM: Who's Who in the Leadership of the United States. Leadership Directories, Inc. • Quarterly. $2,641.00 per year, including access to Internet version (weekly updates). Contains all 14 *Yellow Book* personnel directories on CD-ROM, providing contact and brief biographical information for about 400,000 individuals. Covers business, government, financial institutions, news media, law firms, associations, foreign representatives, and nonprofit organizations. Includes photographs.

DIRECTORIES

Charitable Organizations of the U. S.: A Descriptive and Financial Information Guide. The Gale Group. • 1991. $150.00. Second edition. Describes nearly 800 nonprofit groups active in soliciting funds from the American public. Includes nearly 800 data on sources of income, administrative expenses, and payout.

Cumulative List of Organizations Described in Section 170(c) of the Internal Revenue Code of 1986. Available from U. S. Government Printing Office. • Annual. $114.00 per year, including quarterly supplements. Lists about 300,000 organizations eligible for contributions deductible for federal income tax purposes. Provides name of each organization and city, but not complete address information. Arranged alphabetically by name of institution. (Office of Employee Plans and Exempt Organizations, Internal Revenue Service.).

Directory of Operating Grants. Research Grant Guides. • Annual. $59.50. Contains profiles for approximately 800 foundations that award grants to nonprofit organizations for such operating expenses as salaries, rent, and utilities. Geographical arrangement, with indexes.

Gale's Guide to Nonprofits: A Gale Ready Reference Handbook. The Gale Group. • 2000. $135.00. Serves to provide a wide variety of information sources of interest to nonprofit organizations, including publications, online databases, and associations. Contains three indexes and a glossary.

Gale's Guide to the Arts: A Gale Ready Reference Handbook. The Gale Group. • 2000. $125.00. Contains descriptions of information sources of interest to nonprofit art groups, including publications, online databases, museums, government agencies, and associations. Three indexes and a glossary are provided.

Gale's Guide to the Media: A Gale Ready Reference Handbook. The Gale Group. • 2000. $125.00. Provides profiles of a wide variety of media-related organizations, publications, broadcasters, agencies, and databases, of interest to nonprofit groups. Contains three indexes and a glossary.

Guide to Federal Funding for Governments and Non-Profits. Government Information Services. • Quarterly. $339.00 per year. Contains detailed descriptions of federal grant programs in economic development, housing, transportation, social services, science, etc. Semimonthly supplement available: *Federal Grant Deadline Calendar.*

National Directory of Nonprofit Organizations 2002. Available from The Gale Group. • 2001. $535.00. 13th edition. Two volumes. Volume one, $370.00; volume two, $240.00. Contains over 250,000 listings of nonprofit organizations, indexed by 260 areas of activity. Indicates income range and IRS tax filing status for each organization.

Nonprofit Sector Yellow Book: Who's Who in the Management of the Leading Foundations, Universities, Museums, and Other Nonprofit Organizations. Leadership Directories, Inc. • Semiannual. $235.00 per year. Covers management personnel and board members of about 1,000 prominent, nonprofit organizations: foundations, colleges, museums, performing arts groups, medical institutions, libraries, private preparatory schools, and charitable service organizations.

ENCYCLOPEDIAS AND DICTIONARIES

International Encyclopedia of Public Policy and Administration. Jay M. Shafritz, editor. HarperCollins Publishers. • 1997. $550.00. Four volumes. Covers 20 major areas, such as public administration, government budgeting, industrial policy, nonprofit management, organizational theory, public finance, labor relations, and taxation. Includes a brief bibliography for each major entry and a comprehensive index.

HANDBOOKS AND MANUALS

Accounting and Budgeting in Public and Non-profit Organizations: A Manager's Guide. C. William Garner. Jossey-Bass, Inc. Publishers. • Date not set. $39.95. An accounting primer for non-profit executives with no formal training in accounting. Includes an explanation of Generally Accepted Accounting Principles (GAAP) as applied to non-profit organizations. (Public Administration-Non Profit Sector Series).

Accounting for Libraries and Other Not-for-Profit Organizations. G. Stevenson Smith. American Library Association. • 1999. $82.00. Second edition. Covers accounting fundamentals for nonprofit organizations. Includes a glossary.

Conducting a Successful Capital Campaign: A Comprehensive Fundraising Guide for Nonprofit Organizations. Kent E. Dove. Jossey-Bass, Inc., Publishers. • 1988. $38.95. (Nonprofit Sector-Public Administration Series).

Financial and Accounting Guide for Not-for-Profit Organizations, Cumulative Supplement. Malvern J. Gross and others. John Wiley and Sons, Inc. • 2000. $145.00. Sixth edition. Covers key concepts, financial statement preparation, accounting guidelines, and financial control. Includes tax laws and forms.

Guide to Preparing Nonprofit Financial Statements. Harold L. Monk and others. Practitioners Publishing Co. • 1997. $177.00. Two looseleaf volumes.

How to Form a Nonprofit Corporation. Anthony Mancuso. Nolo.com. • 1997. $39.95. Fourth edition.

How to Write Proposals that Produce. Joel P. Bowman and Bernadine P. Branchaw. Oryx Press. • 1992. $23.50. An extensive guide to effective proposal writing for both nonprofit organizations and businesses. Covers writing style, intended audience, format, use of graphs, charts, and tables, documentation, evaluation, oral presentation, and related topics.

Law of Tax-Exempt Organizations. Bruce R. Hopkins. John Wiley and Sons, Inc. • 1998. $165.00.

Seventh edition.(Nonprofit Law, Finance and Management Series).

The Management of Nonprofit Organizations. Sharon M. Oster, editor. Ashgate Publishing Co. • 1994. $235.95. Published by Dartmouth Publisher.

The Nonprofit Entrepreneur: Creating Ventures to Earn Income. Edward Skloot, editor. The Foundation Center. • 1988. $19.95. Advice on earning income through fees and service charges.

Nonprofit Management Handbook: Operating Policies and Procedures. Tracy D. Connors. John Wiley and Sons, Inc. • 1999. $65.00. Second edition. Includes sample forms.

Not-for-Profit GAAP: Interpretation and Application of Generally Accepted Accounting Principles for Not-for-Profit Organizations. John Wiley and Sons, Inc. • Annual. $65.00. (Also available on CD-ROM.).

Parliamentary Law and Practice for Nonprofit Organizations. Howard L. Oleck and Cami Green. American Law Institute-American Bar Association. • 1991. $20.00. Second edition. Covers meeting procedures, motions, debate, voting, nominations, elections, committees, duties of officers, rights of members, and other topics.

Planning Tax-Exempt Organizations. Shepard's. • 1983. $210.00. Two volumes. How to form a nonprofit organization. (Tax and Estate Planning Series).

Raise More Money for Your Nonprofit Organization: A Guide to Evaluating and Improving Your Fundraising. Anne L. New. The Foundation Center. • 1991. $14.95.

Starting and Running a Nonprofit Organization. Joan Hummel. University of Minnesota Press. • 1996. $14.95. Second revised edition.

Strategic Management in Non-Profit Organizations: An Administrator's Handbook. Robert D. Hay. Greenwood Publishing Group, Inc. • 1990. $75.00.

Tax Planning and Compliance for Tax-Exempt Organizations: Forms, Checklists, Procedures. Jody Blazek. John Wiley and Sons, Inc. • 1999. $135.00. Third edition. Annual supplements available. (Wiley Nonprofit, Law, Finance, and Management Series).

INTERNET DATABASES

American Visions Non-Profit Center. American Visions Society/American Visions Magazine. Phone: (202)462-1779 Fax: (202)462-3997 • URL: http://www.americanvisions.com • Web site "Created by African Americans for African Americans..enables non-profit professionals to share ideas, provide assistance, seek funding, [and] browse for information.." Includes "Black Endowment," a monthly online newsletter covering people, grants, non-profit seminars, and non-profit news. Registration required, with two options: "Grantseeker" or "Grantmaker." Free 30-day trial available.

ONLINE DATABASES

Encyclopedia of Associations [Online]. The Gale Group. • Provides detailed information on about 160,000 U. S. and International non-profit organizations. Semiannual updates. Inquire as to online cost and availability.

PERIODICALS AND NEWSLETTERS

Board Member: The Periodical for Members of the National Center for Nonprofit Boards. National Center for Nonprofit Boards. • 10 times a year. Membership. Newsletter for trustees of nonprofit organizations.

Don Kramer's Nonprofit Issues. Don Kramer Publisher. • Monthly. $129.00 per year. Newsletter with legal emphasis. Covers the laws, rules, regulations, and taxes affecting nonprofit organizations.

Journal of Nonprofit and Public Sector Marketing. Haworth Press, Inc. • Quarterly. Individuals, $60.00 per year; institutions, $120.00 per year; libraries, $225.00 per year. Subject matter has to do with the promotion or marketing of the services of nonprofit organizations and governmental agencies.

Leader to Leader. Peter F. Drucker Foundation for Nonprofit Management. Jossey-Bass Publishers. • Quarterly. Individuals, $149.00 per year; institutions, $149.00 per year. Contains articles on "management, leadership, and strategy" written by "leading executives, thinkers, and consultants." Covers both business and nonprofit issues.

Non-Profit Legal and Tax Letter. Organization Management Inc. • 18 times a year. $235.00 per year. Newsletter. Covers fund raising, taxation, management, postal regulations, and other topics for nonprofit organizations.

Nonprofit Counsel. John Wiley and Sons, Inc., Journals Div. • Monthly. Institutions, $275.00 per year. Newsletter.

Nonprofit Management and Leadership. Jossey-Bass, Inc., Publishers. • Quarterly. Individuals, $56.00 per year; institutions, $125.00 per year. Sample issue free to librarians.

Nonprofit Times. NPT Publishing Group. • 18 times a year. $59.00 per year. Edited for executives of nonprofit organizations. Covers fund raising, personnel, management, and technology topics. Includes an annual nonprofit salary survey.

Nonprofit World: The National Bi-Monthly Nonprofit Leadership and Management Journal. Society for Nonprofit Organizations. • Bimonthly. $79.00 per year. Includes *National Directory of Service and Product Providers to Nonprofit Organizations* and *Resource Center Catalog*.

RESEARCH CENTERS AND INSTITUTES

Mandel Center for Nonprofit Organizations. Case Western Reserve University. 10900 Euclid Ave., Cleveland, OH 44106-7167. Phone: (216)368-2275 Fax: (216)368-8592 E-mail: jps@po.cwru.eduu • URL: http://www.cwru.edu/mandelcenter • Engages in research relating to the management of nonprofit organizations.

STATISTICS SOURCES

By the Numbers: Electronic and Online Publishing. The Gale Group. • 1997. $385.00. Four volumes. $99.00 per volume. Covers "high-interest" industries: 1. *By the Numbers: Electronic and Online Publishing*; 2. *By the Numbers: Emerging Industries*; 3. *By the Numbers: Nonprofits*; 4. *By the Numbers: Publishing*. Each volume provides about 600 tabulations of industry data on revenues, market share, employment, trends, financial ratios, profits, salaries, and so forth. Citations to data sources are included.

TRADE/PROFESSIONAL ASSOCIATIONS

Alliance for Nonprofit Management. 1899 L. St., N.W., 6th Fl., Washington, DC 20036. Phone: (202)955-8406 E-mail: alliance@allianceonline.org • URL: http://www.allianceonline.org.

Alliance of Nonprofit Mailers. 1211 Connecticut Ave., No. 620, Washington, DC 20036. Phone: (202)462-5132 Fax: (202)462-0423 E-mail: npmailers@aol.com • URL: http://www.nonprofitmailers.org.

Council of Institutional Investors. 1730 Rhode Island Ave., N. W., Suite 512, Washington, DC 20036. Phone: (202)822-0800 Fax: (202)822-0801 E-mail: info@cii.org • URL: http://www.cii.org • Members are nonprofit organization pension plans and other nonprofit institutional investors.

National Center for Nonprofit Boards. 1828 L St., N. W., Suite 900, Washington, DC 20036. Phone: 800-883-6262 or (202)452-6262 Fax: (202)452-6299 E-mail: ncnb@ncnb.org • URL: http://www.ncnb.org • Seeks to improve the effectiveness of nonprofit boards of trustees.

National Federation of Nonprofits. 815 15th St., N.W., Suite 822, Washington, DC 20005-2201. Phone: (202)628-4380 Fax: (202)628-4383.

Society for Nonprofit Organizations. 6314 Odana Rd., Suite 1, Madison, WI 53719. Phone: 800-424-7367 or (608)274-9777 Fax: (608)274-9978 E-mail: snpo@danenet.wicip.org • URL: http://www.danenet.wicip.org/snpo.

OTHER SOURCES

Charitable Giving and Solicitation. Warren Gorham and Lamont/RIA Group. • $495.00 per year. Looseleaf service. Monthly bulletin discusses federal tax rules pertaining to charitable contributions.

Corporate Giving Watch: News and Ideas for Nonprofit Organizations Seeking Corporate Funds. Available from The Gale Group. • Monthly. $149.00 per year. Newsletter. Published by The Taft Group. Includes news, trends, and statistics related to corporate giving programs. "Corporate Profiles" insert contains profiles of individual programs.

Managing Nonprofit Organizations in the 20th Century. James P. Gelatt. Oryx Press. • 1992. $29.95. The author "emphasizes successful ideas and working solutions." Includes charts and tables.

NON-WAGE PAYMENTS

See: EMPLOYEE BENEFIT PLANS; FRINGE BENEFITS

NONWOVEN FABRICS INDUSTRY

See also: INDUSTRIAL FABRICS INDUSTRY

ABSTRACTS AND INDEXES

Applied Science and Technology Index. H. W. Wilson Co. • 11 times a year. Quarterly and annual cumulations. Service basis for print edition; CD-ROM edition, $1,495.00 per year. Indexes a wide variety of English language technical, industrial, and engineering periodicals.

Textile Technology Digest. Institute of Textile Technology. • Monthly. $535.00 per year. Provides indexing and abstracting of a wide variety of textile technology literature.

CD-ROM DATABASES

Textile Technology Digest [CD-ROM]. Textile Information Center, Institute of Textile Technology. • Quarterly. $1,700.00 per year. Provides CD-ROM indexing and abstracting of worldwide journals and monographs in various areas of textile technology, production, and management. Covers 1978 to date.

DIRECTORIES

International Directory of the Nonwoven Fabrics Industry. INDA Association of the Nonwoven Fabrics Industry. • Biennial. Members, $135.00 per year; non-members, $195.00 per year. Lists about 3,000 manufacturers of nonwoven fabrics and suppliers of raw material and equipment.

ENCYCLOPEDIAS AND DICTIONARIES

Encyclopedia of Textiles. French and European Publications, Inc. • 1980. $39.95. Third edition.

Textile Terms and Definitions. J.E. McIntyre and Paul N. Daniels, editors. Available from State Mutual Book and Periodical Service Ltd., Trade

Order Dept. • 1995. $110.00. 10th edition. Published by the Textile Insitute (UK). Includes more than 1,000 definitions of textile processes, fiber types, and end products. Illustrated.

ONLINE DATABASES

Textile Technology Digest [online]. Textile Information Center, Institute of Textile Technology. • Contains indexing and abstracting of more than 300 worldwide journals and monographs in various areas of textile technology, production, and management. Time period is 1978 to date, with monthly updating. Inquire as to online cost and availability.

World Textiles. Elsevier Science, Inc. • Provides abstracting and indexing from 1970 of worldwide textile literature (periodicals, books, pamphlets, and reports). Includes U. S., European, and British patent information. Updating is monthly. Inquire as to online cost and availability.

PERIODICALS AND NEWSLETTERS

International Textile Bulletin: Nonwovens and Industrial Textiles Edition. ITS Publishing, International Textile Service. • Quarterly. $170.00 per year. Editions in Chinese, English, French, German, Italian and Spanish.

Nonwovens Industry: The International Magazine for the Nonwoven Fabrics and Disposable Soft Goods Industry. Rodman Publications. • Monthly. $48.00 per year.

RESEARCH CENTERS AND INSTITUTES

Fibrous Materials Research Center. Drexel University, Dept. of Materials Engineering, 3141 Chestnut St., Philadelphia, PA 19104. Phone: (215)895-1640 Fax: (215)895-6684 E-mail: fko@drexel.edul.edu • URL: http://www.fmac/coe.drexel.edu • Research fields include computer-aided design of nonwoven fabrics and design curves for industrial fibers.

Textiles and Materials. Philadelphia University, Schoolhouse Lane and Henry Ave., Philadelphia, PA 19144. Phone: (215)951-2751 Fax: (215)951-2651 E-mail: brooksteind@philaau.edu • URL: http://www.philaau.edu • Many research areas, including industrial and nonwoven textiles.

TRADE/PROFESSIONAL ASSOCIATIONS

INDA: Association of the Nonwoven Fabrics Industry. P.O. Box 1288, Cary, NC 27513. Phone: (919)233-1210 Fax: (919)233-1282 • URL: http://www.inda.com.

Industrial Fabrics Association International. 1801 Country Rd B W., Roseville, MN 55113-4061. Phone: 800-225-4324 or (651)222-2508 Fax: (651)631-9334 E-mail: generalinfo@ifai.com • URL: http://www.ifai.com • Members include nonwoven industrial fabric producers.

Institutional and Service Textile Distributors Association. 1609 Connecticut Ave., Washington, DC 20009. Phone: (202)986-0105 Fax: (202)986-0448 • Members are wholesalers of textile products to hospitals, hotels, airlines, etc.

Textile Institute. Saint James Bldgs., 4th Fl., Oxford St., Manchester M1 6FQ, England. Phone: 44 161 2371188 Fax: 44 161 2361991 E-mail: tiihq@textileinst.org.uk • URL: http://www.texi.org • Members in 100 countries involved with textile industry management, marketing, science, and technology.

OTHER SOURCES

Nonwoven Disposables. Theta Reports/PJB Medical Publications, Inc. • 1999. $1,495.00. Provides market research data, including sales projections. Covers hospital disposable items, such as surgical drapes, masks, head covers, patient gowns, and incontinence products. (Theta Report No. 922.).

Textile Business Outlook. Statistikon Corp. • Quarterly. $985.00 per year. Analyzes current business, marketing, and financial conditions for the worldwide textile industry (fibers and fabrics). Includes statistical forecasts.

NORTH AMERICAN FREE TRADE AGREEMENT

See also: LATIN AMERICAN MARKETS

GENERAL WORKS

Study on the Operation and Effects of the North American Free Trade Agreement. Available from U. S. Government Printing Office. • 1997. $17.00. Produced by the Executive Office of the President (http://www.whitehouse.gov). Presents a generally favorable view of the effects of NAFTA on the U. S. and Mexican economies.

ABSTRACTS AND INDEXES

Business Periodicals Index. H. W. Wilson Co. • Monthly, except August, with quarterly and annual cumulations. Service basis for print edition; CD-ROM edition, $1,495.00 per year.

PAIS International in Print. Public Affairs Information Service, Inc. • Monthly. $650.00 per year; cumulations three times a year. Provides topical citations to the worldwide literature of public affairs, economics, demographics, sociology, and trade. Text in English; indexed materials in English, French, German, Italian, Portuguese and Spanish.

Readers' Guide to Periodical Literature. H. W. Wilson Co. • Monthly. $220.00 per year. CD-ROM edition, $1,495 per year, including annual cumulation. Indexes about 250 peridicals of general interest.

CD-ROM DATABASES

F & S Index Plus Text. The Gale Group. • Monthly. $7,575.00 per year. Provides CD-ROM citations to worldwide business, marketing, and industrial material appearing in a large assortment of trade journals, newspapers, and other publications. Time period is four years.

PAIS on CD-ROM. Public Affairs Information Service, Inc. • Quarterly. $1,995.00 per year. Provides a CD-ROM version of the online service, *PAIS International.* Contains over 400,000 citations to the literature of contemporary social, political, and economic issues.

WILSONDISC: Wilson Business Abstracts. H. W. Wilson Co. • Monthly. $2,495.00 per year, including unlimited online access to *Wilson Business Abstracts* through WILSONLINE. Provides CD-ROM "cover-to-cover" abstracting and indexing of over 600 prominent business periodicals. Indexing is from 1982, abstracting from 1990. (*Business Periodicals Index* without abstracts is available on CD-ROM at $1,495 per year.).

ENCYCLOPEDIAS AND DICTIONARIES

Encyclopedia of Business. The Gale Group. • 2000. $425.00. Second edition. Two volumes. Contains more than 700 signed articles covering major business disciplines and concepts. International in scope.

HANDBOOKS AND MANUALS

Mexico Business: The Portable Encyclopedia for Doing Business with Mexico. World Trade Press. • 1994. $24.95. Covers economic data, import/export possibilities, basic tax and trade laws, travel information, and other useful facts for doing business with Mexico. Includes a special section on NAFTA. (Country Business Guides-Series).

NAFTA: The North American Free Trade Agreement, A Guide to Customs Procedures. Available from U. S. Government Printing Office. • 1994. $7.00. Revised edition. Issued by the Customs Service, U. S. Treasury Department. Provides a summary of NAFTA customs requirements and benefits. (Customs Publication No. 571.).

North American Free Trade Agreement Between the Government of the United States of America, the Government of Canada, and the Government of the United Mexican States. Available from U. S. Government Printing Office. • 1993. $40.00. Two volumes. Cover title: "The NAFTA." Issued by the Office of the United States Trade Representative, Executive Office of the President. Contains full legal text of the trade agreement, including objectives and definitions.

ONLINE DATABASES

F & S Index. The Gale Group. • Contains about four million citations to worldwide business, financial, and industrial or consumer product literature appearing from 1972 to date. Weekly updates. Inquire as to online cost and availability.

PAIS International. Public Affairs Information Service, Inc. • Corresponds to the former printed publications, *PAIS Bulletin* (1976-90) and *PAIS Foreign Language Index* (1972-90), and to the current *PAIS International in Print* (1991 to date). Covers economic, political, and sociological material appearing in periodicals, books, government documents, and other publications. Updating is monthly. Inquire as to online cost and availability.

PROMT: Predicasts Overview of Markets and Technology. The Gale Group. • Companies, products, applied technologies and markets. U.S. and international literature coverage, 1972 to date. Inquire as to online cost and availability. Provides abstracts from more than 1,600 publications. Weekly updates.

Readers' Guide Abstracts Online. H. W. Wilson Co. • Indexes and abstracts general interest periodicals, 1983 to date. Weekly updates. Inquire as to online cost and availability.

Wilson Business Abstracts Online. H. W. Wilson Co. • Indexes and abstracts 600 major business periodicals, plus the *Wall Street Journal* and the business section of the *New York Times*. Indexing is from 1982, abstracting from 1990, with the two newspapers included from 1993. Updated weekly. Inquire as to online cost and availability. (*Business Periodicals Index* without abstracts is also available online.).

RESEARCH CENTERS AND INSTITUTES

Lowe Institute of Political Economy. Claremont McKenna College, 850 Columbia Ave., Claremont, CA 91711. Phone: (909)621-8012 Fax: (909)607-8008 E-mail: lowe@mckenna.edu • URL: http://www.lowe.research.mckenna.edu • Research topics include NAFTA.

STATISTICS SOURCES

Handbook of North American Industry: NAFTA and the Economies of its Member Nations. John E. Cremeans, editor. Bernan Press. • 1999. $89.00. Second edition. Provides detailed industry statistics for the U.S., Canada, and Mexico.

North American Free Trade Agreement: Opportunities for U. S. Industries, NAFTA Industry Sector Reports. Available from U. S. Government Printing Office. • 1993. Issued by the International Trade Administration, U. S. Department of Commerce. Contains NAFTA Industry Sector Reports showing statistical data on exports from 36 U. S. manufacturing sectors to Mexico, Canada, and other parts of the world.

OTHER SOURCES

NAFTA Watch. CCH Canadian Ltd. • Semimonthly. $350.00 per year. Looseleaf. Legal and business

For publishers addresses, refer to SOURCES CITED section at the back of the book.

service covering the North American Free Trade Agreement.

NAFTA Works for America: Administration Update on the North American Free Trade Agreement, 1993-1998. Available from U. S. Government Printing Office. • 1999. $7.00. Cover title: *Bridging into the 21st Century.* Issued by the Office of the U. S. Trade Representative, Executive Office of the President (http://www.ustr.gov). Summarizes the accomplishment of NAFTA over its first five years.

NOTARIES

ENCYCLOPEDIAS AND DICTIONARIES

Notary Public Practices and Glossary. National Notary Association. • 1998. $22.00.

HANDBOOKS AND MANUALS

Anderson's Manual for Notaries Public: A Complete Guide for Notaries Public and Commissioners. Anderson Publishing Co. • 1999. $25.00. Eighth edition.

PERIODICALS AND NEWSLETTERS

American Notary. American Society of Notaries. • Quarterly. $26.00 per year. Provides information on new legislation, court decisions and other matters of interest to notaries public.

National Notary. National Notary Association. • Bimonthly. $34.00 per year.

Notary Bulletin. National Notary Association. • Bimonthly. $34.00 per year. Formerly *State Notary Bulletin.*

TRADE/PROFESSIONAL ASSOCIATIONS

American Society of Notaries. P.O. Box 5707, Tallahassee, FL 32314-5707. Phone: 800-522-3392 or (850)671-5164 Fax: (850)671-5165 E-mail: mail@notaries.org • URL: http://www.notaries.org.

National Notary Association. P.O. Box 2402, Chatsworth, CA 91313-2402. Phone: 800-876-6827 or (818)713-4000 Fax: 800-833-1211 E-mail: info@nationalnotary.org • URL: http://www.nationalnotary.org.

NOTEBOOK COMPUTERS

See: PORTABLE COMPUTERS

NOTIONS

See: GIFT BUSINESS

NUCLEAR ENERGY

See also: ENERGY SOURCES

GENERAL WORKS

Structural Materials in Nuclear Power Systems. J.T. Roberts, editor. Perseus Publishing. • 1981. $89.50. (Modern Perspectives in Energy Series).

ABSTRACTS AND INDEXES

Applied Science and Technology Index. H. W. Wilson Co. • 11 times a year. Quarterly and annual cumulations. Service basis for print edition; CD-ROM edition, $1,495.00 per year. Indexes a wide variety of English language technical, industrial, and engineering periodicals.

Environmental Periodicals Bibliography: A Current Awareness Bibliography Featuring Citations of Scientific and Popular Articles in Serial Publications in the Area of the Environment. Environmental Studies Institute. International Academy at Santa Barbara. • Monthly. Price varies. An index to current environmental literature.

NTIS Alerts: Energy. National Technical Information Service. • Semimonthly. $245.00 per year. Provides descriptions of government-sponsored research reports and software, with ordering information. Covers electric power, batteries, fuels, geothermal energy, heating/cooling systems, nuclear technology, solar energy, energy policy, and related subjects. Formerly *Abstract Newsletter.*

Science Citation Index. Institute for Scientific Information. • Bimonthly. $15,020.00 per year. Annual cumulation. Includes *Source Index, Citation Index, Permuterm Subject Index,* and *Corporate Index.*

ALMANACS AND YEARBOOKS

Annual Review of Nuclear and Particle Science. Annual Reviews, Inc. • Annual. Individuals, $70.00; institutions, $140.00.

BIBLIOGRAPHIES

Nuclear Power. Available from U. S. Government Printing Office. • Annual. Free. Lists government publications. GPO Subject Bibliography Number 200.

BIOGRAPHICAL SOURCES

Energy and Nuclear Sciences International Who's Who. Allyn and Bacon/Longman. • 1990. $310.00. Third edition.

CD-ROM DATABASES

Science Citation Index: Compact Disc Edition. Institute for Scientific Information. • Quarterly. Provides CD-ROM indexing of the world's scientific and technical literature. Corresponds to online *Scisearch* and printed *Science Citation Index.*

DIRECTORIES

Companies Holding Nuclear Certificates of Authorization. Boiler and Pressure Vessel Control Committee. • Bimonthly. $65.00 per year. Lists about 700 manufacturers certified for production of nuclear pressure vessels.

Electrical World Directory of Electric Power Producers and Distributors. • Annual. $395.00. Over 3,500 investor-owned, municipal, rural cooperative and government electric utility systems in the U.S. and Canada. Formerly *Electrical World-Directory of Electric Power Producers.*

Nuclear News Buyers Guide. American Nuclear Society. • Annual. $77.00. Lists approximately 1,600 manufacturers and suppliers of nuclear components. Included with subscription to *Nuclear News.*

Nuclear News-World List of Nuclear Power Plants. American Nuclear Society. • Annual. $19.00 per copy. List of over 100 U. S. and foreign nuclear power plants that are in operation, under construction, or on order.

World Energy and Nuclear Directory. Allyn and Bacon/Longman. • 1996. Fifth edition. Price on application. Lists 5,000 public and private, international research and development organizations functioning in a wide variety of areas related to energy.

ENCYCLOPEDIAS AND DICTIONARIES

Macmillan Encyclopedia of Energy. Available from The Gale Group. • 2001. $350.00. Three volumes. Published by Macmillan Reference USA. Covers the business, technology, and history of a wide variety of energy sources.

Wiley Encyclopedia of Energy and the Environment. Frederick John Francis. John Wiley and Sons, Inc. • 1999. $1,500.00. Four volumes. Second edition. Covers a wide variety of energy and environmental topics, including legal and policy issues.

HANDBOOKS AND MANUALS

Moody's Public Utility Manual. Financial Information Services. • Annual. $1,595.00. Two volumes. Supplemented twice weekly by *Moody's Public Utility News Reports.* Contains financial and other information concerning publicly-held utility companies (electric, gas, telephone, water).

ONLINE DATABASES

Energyline. Congressional Information Service, Inc. • Provides online citations and abstracts to the literature of all forms of energy: petroleum, natural gas, coal, nuclear power, solar energy, etc. Time period is 1971 to 1993 (closed file). Inquire as to online cost and availability.

Globalbase. The Gale Group. • Provides more than one million online summaries of business, industrial, and economic news reports from more than 1,000 publications worldwide. Covers a wide range of material appearing in international trade journals, professional magazines, and newspapers. Time period is 1984 to date, with weekly updates. Inquire as to online cost and availability.

PAIS International. Public Affairs Information Service, Inc. • Corresponds to the former printed publications, *PAIS Bulletin* (1976-90) and *PAIS Foreign Language Index* (1972-90), and to the current *PAIS International in Print* (1991 to date). Covers economic, political, and sociological material appearing in periodicals, books, government documents, and other publications. Updating is monthly. Inquire as to online cost and availability.

PROMT: Predicasts Overview of Markets and Technology. The Gale Group. • Companies, products, applied technologies and markets. U.S. and international literature coverage, 1972 to date. Inquire as to online cost and availability. Provides abstracts from more than 1,600 publications. Weekly updates.

Scisearch. Institute for Scientific Information. • Broad, multidisciplinary index to the literature of science and technology, 1974 to present. Inquire as to online cost and availability. Coverage of literature is worldwide, with weekly updates.

PERIODICALS AND NEWSLETTERS

American Nuclear Society Transactions. American Nuclear Society. • Two times a year. $450.00 per year. Supplement available.

Annals of Nuclear Energy. Elsevier Science. • 18 times a year. $2,709 per year. Text and summaries in English, French and German.

Atomic Energy. Russian Academy of Sciences, RU. Plenum Publishing Corp. • Monthly. $2,286.00 per year. Formerly *Soviet Atomic Energy.*

Bulletin of the Atomic Scientists: Magazine of Science and World Affairs. Educational Foundation for Nuclear Science. • Bimonthly. $36.00 per year.

Energy: The International Journal. Elsevier Science. • Monthly. $1,608.00 per year.

INIS Newsletter. International Atomic Energy Agency, Division of Publications. • Irregular. Free. Newsletter of the International Nuclear Information System (INIS).

Journal of Nuclear Materials Management. Institute of Nuclear Materials Management, Inc. • Quarterly. $100.00 per year. Summaries in England Japanese.

Nuclear Engineering International. Wilmington Publishers Ltd. • Monthly. $341.00 per year. Text in English; summaries in French and German.

Nuclear Fuel. McGraw-Hill. • Biweekly. $1,035.00 per year. Newsletter.

Nuclear News. American Nuclear Society. • Monthly. $224.00 per year. Includes *Nuclear News Buyers Guide and 3 Special Issues.*

Nuclear Plant Journal. Newal K. Agnihotri, editor. EQES, Inc. • Bimonthly. $120.00 per year.

Nuclear Science and Engineering: Research and Development Related to Peaceful Utilization of Nuclear Energy. American Nuclear Society. • Three volumes per year. $585.00 per year.

Nuclear Standards News. American Nuclear Society. • Monthly. $295.00 per year.

Nuclear Technology: Applications for Nuclear Science, Nuclear Engineering and Related Arts. American Nuclear Society. • Monthly. $595.00 per year.

Nucleonics Week. McGraw-Hill, Energy & Business Newsletters. • Weekly. $1,395.00 per year. Newsletter.

Power. McGraw-Hill. • Monthly. Free to qualified personnel; others, $55.00 per year.

RESEARCH CENTERS AND INSTITUTES

Canadian Energy Research Institute. 3512 33rd St., N. W., Suite 150, Calgary, AB, Canada T2L 2A6. Phone: (403)282-1231 Fax: (403)284-4181 E-mail: ceri@ceri.ca • URL: http://www.ceri.ca • Conducts research on the economic aspects of various forms of energy, including petroleum, natural gas, coal, nuclear, and water power (hydroelectric).

Center for Energy and Combustion Research. University of California, San Diego. 9500 Gillman Dr., MC 0411, La Jolla, CA 92093-0411. Phone: (858)534-4285 Fax: (858)534-5354 E-mail: nbastian@ames.ucsd.edu • URL: http://www-ames.ucsd.edu/research-units/cecr/welcome.html.

Energy Laboratory. Massachusetts Institute of Technology. Bldg. E40-455, Cambridge, MA 02139-4307. Phone: (617)253-3401 Fax: (617)253-8013 E-mail: testerel@mit.edu • URL: http://www.web.mit.edu/energylab/www/.

Laboratory for Nuclear Science. Massachusetts Institute of Technology, Bldg. 26, Room 505, Cambridge, MA 02139. Phone: (617)253-2361 Fax: (617)253-0111 • URL: http://www.lims.mit.edu.

Los Alamos National Laboratory. P.O. Box 1663, Los Alamos, NM 87545. Phone: (505)667-5061 Fax: (505)667-2997 E-mail: browne@lanl.gov • URL: http://www.lanl.com.

Michigan Memorial-Phoenix Project. University of Michigan, Phoenix Memorial Laboratory, Ford Nuclear Reactor, 2301 Bonisteel Blvd., Ann Arbor, MI 48109-2100. Phone: (734)764-6200 Fax: (734)936-1571 E-mail: jcl@umich.edu • URL: http://www.umich.edu/~mmpp • Conducts research in peaceful uses of nuclear energy.

Oak Ridge National Laboratory. P.O. Box 2008, Oak Ridge, TN 37831-6255. Phone: (423)576-2900 Fax: (423)241-2967 E-mail: stairb@ornl.gov • URL: http://www.ornl.gov.

STATISTICS SOURCES

Annual Energy Outlook [year], with Projections to [year]. Available from U. S. Government Printing Office. • Annual. Issued by the Energy Information Administration, U. S. Department of Energy (http://www.eia.doe.gov). Contains detailed statistics and 20-year projections for electricity, oil, natural gas, coal, and renewable energy. Text provides extensive discussion of energy issues and "Market Trends.".

Annual Energy Review. Available from U. S. Government Printing Office. • Annual Issued by the Energy Information Administration, Office of Energy Markets and End Use, U. S. Department of Energy. Presents long-term historical as well as recent data on production, consumption, stocks, imports, exports, and prices of the principal energy commodities in the U. S.

Budget of the United States Government. U.S. Office of Management and Budget. Available from U.S. Government Printing Office. • Annual.

Licensed Operating Reactors; Status Summary Report. Nuclear Regulatory Commission. Available from U. S. Government Printing Office. • Annual. Provides data on the operation of nuclear units.

OECD Nuclear Energy Data. Organization for Economic Cooperation and Development. Available from OECD Publications and Information Center. • Annual. $32.00. Produced by the OECD Nuclear Energy Agency. Provides a yearly compilation of basic statistics on electricity generation and nuclear power in OECD member countries. Text in English and French.

Statistical Record of the Environment. The Gale Group. • 1996. $120.00. Third edition. Provides over 875 charts, tables, and graphs of major environmental statistics, arranged by subject. Covers population growth, hazardous waste, nuclear energy, acid rain, pesticides, and other subjects related to the environment. A keyword index is included.

TRADE/PROFESSIONAL ASSOCIATIONS

American Nuclear Insurers. 29 S. Main St., Suite 300-S, West Hartford, CT 06107-2445. Phone: (860)561-3443 Fax: (860)561-4655 • URL: http://www.amnucins.com • Member companies provide property and liability insurance to the nuclear energy industry.

American Nuclear Society. 555 N. Kensington Ave., La Grange Park, IL 60526. Phone: (708)352-6611 Fax: (708)352-0499 • URL: http://www.ans.org • Purpose is to advance science and engineering in the nuclear power industry.

Citizen's Energy Council. P.O. Box U, Hewitt, NJ 07421. Phone: (201)728-2322 Fax: (201)728-7664 E-mail: nonukes@canoemail.com • Concerned with hazards of nuclear power.

Educational Foundation for Nuclear Science. 6042 S. Kimbark, Chicago, IL 60637. Phone: (773)702-2555 Fax: (773)702-0725 • URL: http://www.bullatomsci.org.

Environmental Coalition on Nuclear Power. 433 Orlando Ave., State College, PA 16803. Phone: (814)237-3900 Fax: (814)237-3900 • Seeks establishment of non-nuclear energy policy.

Institute of Electrical and Electronics Engineers; Nuclear and Plasma Sciences Society. Three Park Ave., 17th Fl., New York, NY 10017. Phone: (212)419-7900 Fax: (212)752-4929 • URL: http://www.ieee.org.

Institute of Nuclear Materials Management. 60 Revere Dr., Suite 500, Northbrook, IL 60062. Phone: (847)480-9573 Fax: (847)480-9282 E-mail: inmm@inmm.org • URL: http://www.inmm.org.

Institute of Nuclear Power Operations. 700 Galleria Parkway, Atlanta, GA 30339-5957. Phone: (770)644-8000 Fax: (770)644-8549 • An organization of electric utilities operating nuclear power plants.

Mutual Atomic Energy Liability Underwriters. 330 N. Wabash, Suite 2600, Chicago, IL 60611. Phone: (312)467-0003 Fax: (312)467-0774 • Members are mutual casualty insurance companies writing nuclear energy liability policies.

Nuclear Energy Institute. 1776 Eye St., N.W., Suite 400, Washington, DC 20006. Phone: (202)739-8000 Fax: (202)785-4019 E-mail: webmaster@nei.org • URL: http://www.nei.org • Consists mainly of industrial firms engaged in the development of nuclear energy for constructive purposes.

Nuclear Information and Records Management Association. 210 Fifth Ave., New York, NY 10010. Phone: (603)432-6476 Fax: (603)432-3024 • URL: http://www.nirma.org • Concerned with the maintenance of nuclear industry corporate records.

Nuclear Information and Resource Service. 1424 16th St., N.W., No. 404, Washington, DC 20036. Phone: (202)328-0002 Fax: (202)462-2183 E-mail: nirsnet@nirs.org • URL: http://www.nirs.org • Promotes alternatives to nuclear power.

Nuclear Suppliers Association. P.O. Box 2038, Springfield, VA 22152. Phone: (703)451-1912 Fax: (703)451-2334 E-mail: nsa_news@aol.com • URL: http://www.nuclearsuppliers.org.

Oak Ridge Associated Universities. P.O. Box 117, Oak Ridge, TN 37831-0117. Phone: (423)576-3000 Fax: (423)576-3643 E-mail: townsenr@orau.org • URL: http://www.orau.gov • Consortium of 87 universities operating under direct contract with the U. S. Department of Energy. Purpose is to further nuclear energy education and research.

Professional Reactor Operator Society. P.O. Box 484, Byron, IL 61010-0484. Phone: 800-422-2725 or (815)234-4175 Fax: (815)234-4175.

Public Citizen's Critical Mass Energy Project. 215 Pennsylvania Ave., S.E., Washington, DC 20003. Phone: (202)546-4996 Fax: (202)547-7392 E-mail: cmep@citizens.org • URL: http://www.citizens.org/cmep • Maintains national network of anti-nuclear groups.

OTHER SOURCES

Major Energy Companies of the World. Available from The Gale Group. • 2001. $855.00. Fourth edition. Published by Graham & Whiteside. Contains detailed information on more than 3,300 important energy companies in various countries. Industries include electricity generation, coal, natural gas, nuclear energy, petroleum, fuel distribution, and equipment for energy production.

NUMERICAL CONTROL OF MACHINERY (NC))

See: COMPUTER-AIDED DESIGN AND MANUFACTURING (CAD/CAM)

NUMISMATICS

See: COINS AS AN INVESTMENT

NURSERIES (HORTICULTURAL)

See also: FLORIST SHOPS

ABSTRACTS AND INDEXES

Horticultural Abstracts: Compiled from World Literature on Temperate and Tropical Fruits, Vegetables, Ornaments, Plantation Crops. Available from CABI Publishing North America. • Monthly. $1,605.00 per year. Published in England by CABI Publishing. Provides worldwide coverage of the literature of fruits, vegetables, flowers, plants, and all aspects of gardens and gardening.

NTIS Alerts: Agriculture & Food. National Technical Information Service. • Semimonthly. $195.00 per year. Provides descriptions of government-sponsored research reports and software, with ordering information. Covers agricultural economics, horticulture, fisheries, veterinary medicine, food technology, and related subjects. Formerly *Abstract Newsletter*.

DIRECTORIES

American Nursery and Landscape Association Membership Directory. American Nursery and Landscape Association. • Annual. Free to members; non-members, $250.00 per year. Lists 2,200 member firms. Formerly *American Association of Nurserymen Membership Directory*.

Nursery Stock and Supply Locator. American Association of Nurserymen. • Annual. $3.00.

ENCYCLOPEDIAS AND DICTIONARIES

New York Botanical Garden Illustrated Encyclopedia of Horticulture. Thomas H. Everett. Garland Publishing, Inc. • 1980. $1,070.00. Ten volumes.

ONLINE DATABASES

CAB Abstracts. CAB International North America. • Contains 46 specialized abstract collections covering over 10,000 journals and monographs in the areas of agriculture, horticulture, forest products, farm products, nutrition, dairy science, poultry, grains, animal health, entomology, etc. Time period is 1972 to date, with monthly updates. Inquire as to online cost and availability. *CAB Abstracts on CD-ROM* also available, with annual updating.

PERIODICALS AND NEWSLETTERS

American Nurseryman. American Nurseryman Publishing Co. • Semimonthly. $45.00 per year.

Greenhouse Grower. Meister Publishing Co. • 14 times a year. $37.45 per year. Concerned with all crops grown under glass or plastic.

Horticulture: The Art of American Gardening. PRIMEDIA Consumer Magazines and Internet Group. • 10 times a year. $28.00 per year.

Nursery Business Retailer. Brantwood Publications. • Bimonthly. Price on application.

TRADE/PROFESSIONAL ASSOCIATIONS

American Nursery and Landscape Association. 1250 Eye St., N.W., Suite 500, Washington, DC 20005-3922. Phone: (202)789-2900 Fax: (202)789-1893 • URL: http://www.anla.org.

Wholesale Nursery Growers of America. 1250 Eye St., N.W., Suite 500, Washington, DC 20005-3922. Phone: (202)789-2900 Fax: (202)789-1893 • URL: http://www.anla.org.

NURSERY SCHOOLS

See: DAY CARE CENTERS

NURSING HOMES

See also: LONG-TERM CARE INSURANCE; RETIREMENT COMMUNITIES

GENERAL WORKS

Caring for Frail Elderly People: New Directions in Care. OECD Publications and Information Center. • 1994. $27.00. Discusses the problem in OECD countries of providing good quality care to the elderly at manageable cost. Includes trends in family care, housing policies, and private financing.

Long-Term Care and Its Alternatives. Charles B. Inlander. People's Medical Society. • 1996. $16.95. Provides practical advice on the financing of long-term health care. The author is a consumer advocate and president of the People's Medical Society.

Managed Care: The Vision and the Strategy. American Association of Homes and Services for the Aging. • 1996. $30.00. A report on an AAHSA national managed care summit. Topics include delivery models, regulatory conflicts, costs, finances, consumer choice, and related subjects.

Management of Healthcare Organizations. Kerry D. Carson and others. Brooks/Cole Publishing Co. • Price on application. (SWC-Management Series).

BIBLIOGRAPHIES

AAHSA Resource Catalog. American Association of Homes and Services for the Aging. • Annual. Free. Provides descriptions of material relating to managed care, senior housing, assisted living, continuing care retirement communities (CCRCs), nursing facilities, and home health care. Publishers are AAHSA and others.

Long-Term Care: An Annotated Bibliography. Theodore H. Koff. Greenwood Publishing Group, Inc. • 1995. $59.95.

DIRECTORIES

Buyers' Guide for the Health Care Market: A Directory of Products and Services for Health Care Institutions. American Hospital Association. Health Forum, Inc. • Annual. $17.95. Lists 1,200 suppliers and manufacturers of health care products and services for hospitals, nursing homes, and related organizations.

Consumers' Directory of Continuing Care Retirement Communities. American Association of Homes and Services for the Aging. • 1997. $30.00. Contains information on fees, services, and accreditation of about 500 U. S. retirement facilities providing lifetime housing, meals, and health care. Introductory text discusses factors to be considered in selecting a continuing care community.

Contemporary Long Term Care Fax Directory. Bill Communications, Inc. • Annual. $10.50. Lists approximately 900 manufacturers and suppliers of equipment, products, and services for retirement communities and nursing homes. Formerly *Contemporary Administration for Long-Term Care Product Directory and Buyer's Guide.*

Directory of Nursing Homes. Dorland Healthcare Information. • Annual. $249.00. Provides information on admission requirements, resident facilities, and staff at more than 16,500 nursing homes.

McKnight's Long-Term Care News Industry Guide. McKnight Medical Communications Co. • Annual. $49.95. Lists suppliers of goods and services for retirement homes and nursing homes.

Nursing Home Report and Directory. SMG Marketing Group, Inc. • Annual. $525.00. Lists almost 4,000 nursing homes with 50 beds or more.

Provider: LTC Buyers' Guide. American Health Care Association. • Annual. $10.00. Lists several hundred manufacturers and suppliers of products and services for long term care (LTC) facilities.

FINANCIAL RATIOS

Annual Statement Studies. Robert Morris Associates: The Association of Lending and Credit Risk Professiona. • Annual. Free to members; non-members, $140.00. Median and quartile financial ratios are given for over 400 kinds of manufacturing, wholesale, retail, construction, and consumer finance establishments. Data is sorted by both asset size and sales volume. Includes a clearly written "Definition of Ratios" and an alphabetical industry index.

HANDBOOKS AND MANUALS

The Continuing Care Retirement Community, a Guidebook for Consumers. American Association of Homes and Services for the Aging. • 1984. $6.95. Provieds information for the evaluation of continuing care retirement communities and nursing facilities, including services and finances.

Healthcare Finance for the Non-Financial Manager: Basic Guide to Financial Analysis & Control. Louis Gapenski. McGraw-Hill Professional. • 1994. $47.50.

How to Cover the Gaps in Medicare: Health Insurance and Long-Term Care Options for the Retired. Robert A. Gilmour. American Institute for Economic Research. • 2000. $5.00. 12th revised edition. Four parts: "The Medicare Quandry," "How to Protect Yourself Against the Medigap," "Long-Term Care Options", and "End-of-Life Decisions" (living wills). Includes discussions of long-term care insurance, retirement communities, and HMO Medicare insurance, (Economic Education Bulletin Series, No. 10).

The Managed Care Contracting Handbook: Planning and Negotiating the Managed Care Relationship. Maria K. Todd. Available from McGraw Hill Higher Education. • 1996. $65.00. Copublished by McGraw-Hill Healthcare Education Group and the Healthcare Financial Management Association. Covers managed care planning, proposals, strategy, negotiation, and contract law. Written for healthcare providers.

INTERNET DATABASES

Medicare: The Official U. S. Government Site for Medicare Information. Health Care Financing Administration (HCFA). Phone: (410)786-3151 • URL: http://www.medicare.gov • Web site provides extensive information on Medicare health plans, publications, fraud, nursing homes, top 20 questions and answers, etc. Includes access to the National Nursing Home Database, providing summary compliance information on "every Medicare and Medicaid certified nursing home in the country." Online searching is offered. Fees: Free.

PERIODICALS AND NEWSLETTERS

AHA News. Health Forum, Inc. • Weekly. $147.00 per year. Edited for hospital and health care industry administrators. Covers health care news events and legislative activity. An American Hospital Association publication (http://www.aha.org).

American Health Care Association: Provider. American Health Care Association. • Monthly. $48.00 per year. Formerly *American Health Care Association Journal.*

Assisted Living Success. Virgo Publishing, Inc. • Monthly. $55.00 per year. Edited for owners, operators, and managers of assisted living facilities.

Assisted Living Today. Assisted Living Federation of America. • Nine times a year. $30.00 per year. Covers the management, marketing, and financing of assisted living residences.

Balance. American College of Health Care Administrators. • Eight times a year. Free to members; non-members, $80.00 per year. Includes research papers and articles on the administration of long term care facilities. Formerly*Continnum.*

Contemporary Long Term Care. Bill Communications, Inc. • Monthly. $72.00 per year. Edited for the long term health care industry, including retirement centers with life care, continuing care communities, and nursing homes.

Continuing Care: Supporting the Transition into Post Hospital Care. Stevenson Publishing Corp. • Monthly. $99.00 per year. Topics include insurance, legal issues, health business news, ethics, and case management. Includes annual *Buyer's Guide.*

Geriatric Care News. Frances Greer, editor. DRS Geriatric Publishing Co. • Monthly. $89.00 per year. Latest information for health care professionals in the geriatric field. Formerly *Geriatric and Residential Care Newsmonthly.*

Health Facilities Management. American Hospital Association. American Hospital Publishing, Inc. • Monthly. $40.00 per year. Covers building maintenance and engineering for hospitals and nursing homes.

Health Forum. American Hospital Association. American Hospital Publishing, Inc. • Biweekly. $80.00 per year. Covers the general management of hospitals, nursing homes, and managed care organizations. Formerly *HospitalsHealthNetworks.*

Housing the Elderly Report. Community Development Services, Inc. CD Publications. • Monthly. $197.00 per year. Newsletter. Edited for retirement communities, apartment projects, and nursing homes. Covers news relative to business and property management issues.

McKnight's Long Term Care News. McKnight Medical Communications, Inc. • Monthly. $44.95 per year. Edited for retirement housing directors and nursing home administrators.

Modern Healthcare: The Newsmagazine for Adminstrators and Managers in Hospitals and Other Healthcare Institutions. Crain Communications, Inc. • Weekly. $135.00 per year; students, $63.00 per year.

Nursing Homes: Long Term Care Management. Medquest Communications, LLC. • Monthly. $95.00 per year. Covers business, finance, and management topics for nursing home directors and administrators.

Older Americans Report. Business Publishers, Inc. • Weekly. $432.00 per year. Newsletter on health, economic, and social services for the aging, including social security, medicare, pensions, housing, nursing homes, and programs under the Older Americans Act. Edited for service providers.

Provider: For Long Term Care Professionals. American Health Care Association. • Monthly. $48.00 per year. Edited for medical directors, administrators, owners, and others concerned with extended care facilities and nursing homes. Covers business management, legal issues, financing, reimbursement, care planning, ethics, human resources, etc.

STATISTICS SOURCES

Guide to the Nursing Home Industry. Dorland Healthcare Information. • Annual. $249.00. Analyzes the financial and operational performance of the U. S. nursing home industry on both national and state levels. Includes detailed statistics and 19 financial performance indicators (aggregate data). Annual CD-ROM version with key word searching is available at $335.00.

Health Care Costs. DRI/McGraw-Hill. • Quarterly. Price on application. Cost indexes for hospitals, nursing homes, and home healthcare agencies.

Health, United States, 1999: Health and Aging Chartbook. Available from U. S. Government Printing Office. • 1999. $37.00. Issued by the National Center for Health Statistics, U. S. Department of Health and Human Services. Contains 34 bar charts in color, with related statistical tables. Provides detailed data on persons over 65 years of age, including population, living arrangements, life expectancy, nursing home residence, poverty, health status, assistive devices, health insurance, and health care expenditures.

Standard & Poor's Industry Surveys. Standard & Poor's. • Semiannual. $1,800.00. Two looseleaf volumes. Includes monthly supplements. Provides detailed, individual surveys of 52 major industry groups. Each survey is revised on a semiannual basis. Also includes "Monthly Investment Review" (industry group investment analysis) and monthly "Trends & Projections" (economic analysis).

TRADE/PROFESSIONAL ASSOCIATIONS

American Association for Continuity of Care. P.O. Box 7073, North Brunswick, NJ 08902. Phone: 800-816-1575 Fax: (301)352-7086 • URL: http://www.continuitycare.com • Members are professionals concerned with continuity of care, health care after hospital discharge, and home health care.

American Association of Homes and Services for the Aging. 901 E. St., N.W., Suite 500, Washington, DC 20004-2011. Phone: (202)783-2242 Fax: (202)783-2255 E-mail: info@aahsa.org • URL: http://www.aahsa.org.

American College of Health Care Administrators. 325 S. Patrick St., Alexandria, VA 22314. Phone: 888-882-2422 or (703)739-7900 Fax: (703)739-7901 E-mail: info@achca.org • URL: http://www.achca.org.

American Health Care Association. 1201 L St., N. W., Washington, DC 20005. Phone: (202)842-4444 Fax: (202)842-3860 • URL: http://www.ahca.org.

OTHER SOURCES

The Long-Term Care Market. MarketResearch.com. • 1999. $3,250.00. Market data with forecasts to the year 2005. Emphasis is on the over-85 age group. Covers health insurance, the nursing home industry, pharmaceuticals, healthcare supplies, etc.

The U. S. Market for Assisted-Living Facilities. MarketResearch.com. • 1997. $1,125.00. Market research report. Includes market demographics and estimates of future revenues. Facility operators such as Emeritus, Manor Care, and Marriott Senior Living are profiled.

NUT INDUSTRY

ABSTRACTS AND INDEXES

Food Science and Technology Abstracts. International Food Information Service Publishing. • Monthly. $1,780.00 per year. Provides worldwide coverage of the literature of food technology and food production.

Foods Adlibra: Key to the World's Food Literature. Foods Adlibra Publications. • Semimonthly.Provides journal citations and abstracts to the literature of food technology and packaging.

CD-ROM DATABASES

Food Science and Technology Abstracts [CD-ROM]. Available from SilverPlatter Information, Inc. • Quarterly. $3,700 per year. Produced by International Food Information Service (home page is http://www.ifis.org). Provides worldwide coverage on CD-ROM of the literature of food technology and production. Various types of publications are indexed, with abstracts, including about 1,800 periodicals. Time period is 1969 to date.

INTERNET DATABASES

USDA. United States Department of Agriculture. Phone: (202)720-2791 E-mail: agsec@usda.gov • URL: http://www.usda.gov • The USDA home page has six sections: News and Information; What's New; About USDA; Agencies; Opportunities; Search and Help. Keyword searching is offered from the USDA home page and from various individual agency home pages. Agencies are the Economic Research Service, Agricultural Marketing Service, National Agricultural Statistics Service, National Agricultural Library, and about 12 others. Updating varies. Fees: Free.

ONLINE DATABASES

Food Science and Technology Abstracts [online]. IFIS North American Desk. • Produced by International Food Information Service. Provides about 500,000 online citations, with abstracts, to the international literature of food science, technology, commodities, engineering, and processing. Approximately 2,000 periodicals are covered. Time period is 1969 to date, with monthly updates. Inquire as to online cost and availability.

FOODS ADLIBRA. General Mills, Inc. • Contains online citations, with abstracts, to the technical and business literature of food processing and packaging. New products and new ingredients are featured. Covers about 250 trade journals and 500 research journals from 1974 to date, with monthly updates. Inquire as to online cost and availability.

PERIODICALS AND NEWSLETTERS

Nutshell. Northern Nut Growers Association. • Four times a year. Membership.

Peanut Journal and Nut World. Virginia-Carolina Peanut Association. Peanut Journal Publishing Co. • Monthly. $8.00 per year.

RESEARCH CENTERS AND INSTITUTES

Hawaii Institute of Tropical Agriculture and Human Resources. University of Hawaii at Manoa, Honolulu, HI 96822. Phone: (808)956-8131 Fax: (808)956-9105 E-mail: tadean2@avax.ctahr.hawaii.edu • URL: http://www.ctahr.hawaii.edu • Concerned with the production and marketing of tropical food and ornamental plant products, including pineapples, bananas, coffee, and macadamia nuts.

STATISTICS SOURCES

Agricultural Statistics. Available from U. S. Government Printing Office. • Annual. Produced by the National Agricultural Statistics Service, U. S. Department of Agriculture. Provides a wide variety of statistical data relating to agricultural production, supplies, consumption, prices/price-supports, foreign trade, costs, and returns, as well as farm labor, loans, income, and population. In many cases, historical data is shown annually for 10 years. In addition to farm data, includes detailed fishery statistics.

Fruit and Tree Nuts Situation and Outlook Report. Available from U. S. Government Printing Office. • Three times a year. $13.00 per year. (Economic Research Service, U. S. Department of Agriculture.).

TRADE/PROFESSIONAL ASSOCIATIONS

Northern Nut Growers Association. R.R. 1, Niagara-on-the-Lake, ON, Canada L0S 1J0. Phone: (905)262-4927.

OTHER SOURCES

Major Food and Drink Companies of the World. Available from The Gale Group. • 2001. $855.00. Fourth edition. Two volumes. Published by Graham & Whiteside. Contains profiles and trade names for more than 9,000 important food and beverage companies in various countries. In addition to foods, includes both alcoholic and nonalcoholic drink products.

The Market for Salted Snacks. MarketResearch.com. • 2000. $2,750.00. Market research report. Covers potato chips, corn chips, popcorn, nuts, pretzels, and other salted snacks. Market projections are provided to the year 2004.

Thomas Food and Beverage Market Place. Grey House Publishing. • Annual. $295.00. Three volumes. Contains more than 40,000 entries covering food companies, beverages, food equipment, warehouse companies, food brokers, wholesalers, importers, and exporters. Formerly *Thomas Food Industry Register.*

NUTRITION

See: DIET

NYLON

See: SYNTHETIC TEXTILE FIBER INDUSTRY

O

OATS INDUSTRY

See: FEED AND FEEDSTUFFS INDUSTRY; GRAIN INDUSTRY

OBSOLETE SECURITIES

DIRECTORIES

Directory of Obsolete Securities. Financial Information, Inc. • Annual. Qualified personnel, $595.00.

PERIODICALS AND NEWSLETTERS

Financial History: Chronicling the History of America's Capital Markets. Museum of American Financial History. • Quarterly. Membership. Contains articles on early stock and bond markets and trading in the U. S., with photographs and other illustrations. Current trading in rare and unusual, obsolete stock and bond certificates is featured. Formerly *Friends or Financial History.*

PRICE SOURCES

National Bond Summary. National Quotation Bureau, Inc. • Monthly. $420.00 per year. Semiannual cumulations. Includes price quotes for both active and inactive issues.

National Stock Summary. National Quotation Bureau, Inc. • Monthly. $480.00 per year. Semiannual cumulations. Includes price quotes for both active and inactive issues, with transfer agents, market makers (brokers), and other information. (The National Quotation Bureau also provides daily and weekly stock price services.).

OTHER SOURCES

Capital Changes Reports. CCH, Inc. • Weekly. $1,310.00. Six looseleaf volumes. Arranged alphabetically by company. This service presents a chronological capital history that includes reorganizations, mergers and consolidations. Recent actions are found in Volume One - "New Matters.".

OCCUPATIONAL HEALTH

See: INDUSTRIAL HYGIENE

OCCUPATIONAL SAFETY

See: INDUSTRIAL SAFETY

OCCUPATIONAL THERAPY

ABSTRACTS AND INDEXES

Psychological Abstracts. American Psychological Association. • Monthly. Members, $799.00 per year; individuals and institutions, $1,075.00 per year. Covers the international literature of psychology and the behavioral sciences. Includes journals, technical reports, dissertations, and other sources.

HANDBOOKS AND MANUALS

Conditions in Occupational Therapy: Effect on Occupational Performance. Ruth Hansen and Ben Atchison. Lippincott Williams & Wilkins. • 1999. $42.00. Second edition. Each chapter "describes a major condition that occupational therapists frequently treat." Includes case studies.

ONLINE DATABASES

PsycINFO. American Psychological Association. • Provides indexing and abstracting of the worldwide literature of psychology and the behavioral sciences. Time period is 1967 to date, with monthly updates. Inquire as to online cost and availability.

PERIODICALS AND NEWSLETTERS

American Journal of Occupational Therapy. American Occupational Therapy Association. • Six times a year. $120.00 per year.

Occupational Therapy in Health Care: A Journal of Contemporary Practice. Haworth Press, Inc. • Quarterly. Individuals, $50.00 per year; institutions, $75.00 per year; libraries, $150.00 per year.

Occupational Therapy in Mental Health: A Journal of Psychosocial Practice and Research. Haworth Press, Inc. • Quarterly. Individuals, $50.00 per year; institutions, $120.00 per year; libraries, $250.00 per year.

TRADE/PROFESSIONAL ASSOCIATIONS

American Occupational Therapy Association. P.O. Box 31220, Bethesda, MD 20824-1220. Phone: 800-377-8555 or (301)652-2682 Fax: (301)652-7711 E-mail: praota@aota.org • URL: http://www.aota.org.

OCCUPATIONS

See also: EMPLOYMENT; JOB DESCRIPTIONS; JOB RESUMES; VOCATIONAL EDUCATION; VOCATIONAL GUIDANCE

GENERAL WORKS

Encyclopedia of Careers and Vocational Guidance. Holli Cosgrove. Ferguson Publishing Co. • 2000. $159.95. 11th edition.

Is It Too Late to Run Away and Join the Circus? Finding the Life You Really Want. Marti Smye. Simon and Schuster Trade. • 1998. $14.95. Provides philosophical and inspirational advice on leaving corporate life and becoming self-employed as a consultant or whatever. Central theme is dealing with major changes in life style and career objectives. (Macmillan Business Book.).

Women of the Street: Making It on Wall Street-the World's Toughest Business. Sue Herera. John Wiley and Sons, Inc. • 1997. $24.95. The author is a CNBC business television anchorperson.

BIBLIOGRAPHIES

Job Hunter's Sourcebook: Where to Find Employment Leads and Other Job Search Resources. The Gale Group. • 1999. $99.00. Fourth edition. Covers 179 professions and occupations.

Professional Careers Sourcebook. The Gale Group. • 1999. $105.00. Sixth edition. Includes information sources for 122 professions or occupations.

Vocational Careers Sourcebook. The Gale Group. • 1999. $110.00. Fourth edition. A companion volume to *Professional Careers Sourcebook.* Includes information sources for 1345 occupations that typically do not require a four-year college degree. Compiled in cooperation with InfoPLACE of the Cuyahoga County Public Library, Ohio.

CD-ROM DATABASES

Magazine Index Plus. The Gale Group. • Monthly. $4,000.00 per year (includes InfoTrac workstation). Provides full text on CD-ROM for about 100 popular, general interest magazines and indexing for 300 others. Includes special indexing of reviews and product evaluations. Time period is 1980 to date.

Sourcebooks America CD-ROM. CACI Marketing Systems. • Annual. $1,250.00. Provides the CD-ROM version of *The Sourcebook of ZIP Code Demographics: Census Edition* and *The Sourcebook of County Demographics: Census Edition.*

DIRECTORIES

NACE National Directory: Who's Who in Career Planning, Placement, and Recruitment. National Association of Colleges and Employers. • Annual. Members, $32.95; non-members, $47.95. Lists over 2,200 college placement offices and about 2,000 companies interested in recruiting college graduates. Gives names of placement and recruitment personnel. Formerly *CPC National Dierctory.*

Peterson's Job Opportunities for Business Majors. Peterson's. • Annual. $21.95. Provides career information for the 2,000 largest U. S. employers in various industries.

Professional and Occupational Licensing Directory. The Gale Group. • 1996. $120.00. Second edition. Provides detailed national and state information on the requirements for obtaining a license in each of about 500 occupations. Information needed to contact the appropriate licensing agency or organization is included in each case.

ENCYCLOPEDIAS AND DICTIONARIES

Selected Characteristics of Occupations Defined in the Revised Dictionary of Occupational Titles. Available from U. S. Government Printing Office. • 1993. Provides data on training time, physical demands, and environmental conditions for various occupations. (Employment and Training Administration, U. S. Department of Labor.).

HANDBOOKS AND MANUALS

Career Guide to Industries. Available from U. S. Government Printing Office. • 1998. $17.00. Issued by the Bureau of Labor Statistics, U. S. Department of Labor (http://www.bls.gov). Presents background career information (text) and statistics for the 40 industries that account for 70 percent of wage and salary jobs in the U. S. Includes nature of the industry, employment data, working conditions, training, earnings, rate of job growth, outlook, and other career factors. (BLS Bulletin 2503.).

Occupational Outlook Handbook. Bureau of Labor Statistics, U.S. Department of Labor. Available from U.S. Government Printing Office. • Biennial. $53.00. Issued as one of the Bureau's *Bulletin* series and kept up to date by *Occupational Outlook Quarterly.*

Peterson's Guide to Colleges for Careers in Computing: The Only Combined Career and College Guide for Future Computer Professionals. Peterson's. • 1996. $14.95. Describes career possibilities in various fields related to computers.

Specialty Occupational Outlook: Professions. The Gale Group. • 1995. $70.00. Provides information on 150 professional occupations.

Specialty Occupational Outlook: Trade and Technical. The Gale Group. • 1996. $70.00. Provides information on 150 "high-interest" careers that do not require a bachelor's degree.

Standard Occupational Classification Manual. Available from Bernan Associates. • 2000. $38.00. Replaces the *Dictionary of Occupational Titles.* Produced by the federal Office of Management and Budget, Executive Office of the President. "Occupations are classified based on the work performed, and on the required skills, education, training, and credentials for each one." Six-digit codes contain elements for 23 Major Groups, 96 Minor Groups, 451 Broad Occupations, and 820 Detailed Occupations. Designed to reflect the occupational structure currently existing in the U. S.

INTERNET DATABASES

Bureau of Labor Statistics (BLS). U. S. Department of Labor, Bureau of Labor Statistics. Phone: (202)523-1092 E-mail: labstat.helpdesk@bls.gov • URL: http://www.bls.gov • Web site provides a great variety of employment, wage, price, and economic data. Some links are "Data," "Economy at a Glance," "Keyword Search of BLS Web Pages," "Regional Information," and "Other Statistical Sites." Fees: Free.

PERIODICALS AND NEWSLETTERS

Career World. Weekly Reader Corp. • Six times a year. $9.25. per year. Up-to-the-minute, important career and vocational news for students in grades 7 thru 12.

Journal of Career Planning and Employment: The International Magazine of Placement and Recruitment. National Association of Colleges and Employers. • Quarterly. Free to members; non-members, $72.00 per year. Includes *Spotlight* newsletter. Formerly *Journal of College Placement.*

Occupational Outlook Quarterly. U.S. Department of Labor. Available from U.S. Government Printing Office. • Quarterly. $9.50 per year.

ReCareering Newsletter: An Idea and Resource Guide to Second Career and Relocation Planning. Publications Plus, Inc. • Monthly. $59.00 per year. Edited for "downsized managers, early retirees, and others in career transition after leaving traditional employment." Offers advice on second careers, franchises, starting a business, finances, education, training, skills assessment, and other matters of interest to the newly unemployed.

Techniques. Association for Career and Technical Education. • Eight times a year. Free to members; non-members, $39.00 per year. Formerly *Vocational Educational Journal.*

Work and Occupations: An International Sociological Journal. Sage Publications, Inc. • Quarterly. Individuals, $70.00 per year; institutions, $310.00 per year.

STATISTICS SOURCES

Employment Outlook, 1996-2006: A Summary of BLS Projections. Available from U. S. Government Printing Office. • 1998. $10.00. Issued by the Bureau of Labor Statistics, U. S. Department of Labor (http://www.bls.gov). Provides 1996 employment data and 2006 projections for a wide variety of managerial, professional, technical, marketing, clerical, service, agricultural, and production occupations. Includes factors affecting the employment growth of various industries. (Bureau of Labor Statistics Bulletin 2502.).

Handbook of U. S. Labor Statistics: Employment, Earnings, Prices, Productivity, and Other Labor Data. Eva E. Jacobs, editor. Bernan Associates. • 1999. $74.00. Based on *Handbook of Labor Statistics,* formerly issued by the Bureau of Labor Statistics, U. S. Department of Labor. Includes the Bureau's projections of employment in the U. S. by industry and occupation. Provides a wide variety of data on the work force, prices, fringe benefits, and consumer expenditures.

National Compensation Survey. Available from U. S. Government Printing Office. • Irregular. $300.00 per year. Consists of bulletins reporting on earnings for jobs in clerical, professional, technical, and other fields in 70 major metropolitan areas. Formerly *Occupational Compensation Survey.*

Occupational Projections and Training Data. Available from U. S. Government Printing Office. • Biennial. $7.00. Issued by Bureau of Labor Statistics, U. S. Department of Labor. Contains projections of employment change and job openings over the next 15 years for about 500 specific occupations. Also includes the number of associate, bachelor's, master's, doctoral, and professional degrees awarded in a recent year for about 900 specific fields of study.

Social Statistics of the United States. Mark S. Littman, editor. Bernan Press. • 2000. $65.00. Includes statistical data on population growth, labor force, occupations, environmental trends, leisure time use, income, poverty, taxes, and other economic or demographic topics.

Statistical Handbook of Working America. The Gale Group. • 1997. $125.00. Second edition. Provides statistics, rankings, and forecasts relating to a wide variety of careers, occupations, and working conditions.

TRADE/PROFESSIONAL ASSOCIATIONS

Association for Career and Technical Education. 1410 King St., Alexandria, VA 22314. Phone: 800-826-9772 or (703)683-3111 Fax: (703)683-7424 E-mail: acte@acteonline.org • URL: http://www.acteonline.org.

OTHER SOURCES

Chronicle Occupational Briefs. Chronicle Guidance Publications, Inc. • Pamphlets about various occupations.

Opportunities in Government Careers. Neale J. Baxter. NTC/Contemporary Publishing Group. • 2001. $15.95. Edited for students and job seekers. Includes education requirements and salary data. (VGM Career Books.).

Opportunities in Journalism Careers. Donald L. Ferguson and Jim Patten. NTC/Contemporary Publishing Group. • 2001. $15.95. Edited for students and job seekers. Includes education requirements and salary data. (VGM Career Books.).

Opportunities in Visual Arts Careers. Mark Salmon. NTC/Contemporary Publishing Group. • 2001. $15.95. Edited for students and job seekers. Includes education requirements and salary data. (VGM Career Books.).

State Legislators' Occupations: 1994, A Survey. National Conference of State Legislatures. • 1994. $20.00. Presents survey results concerning the occupations of more than 7,000 state legislators. (Members of state legislatures usually combine government service with other occupations.).

OCEAN LINERS

See: STEAMSHIP LINES

OCEANOGRAPHIC INDUSTRIES

See also: MARINE ENGINEERING

GENERAL WORKS

Recent Advances and Issues in Environmental Science. John R. Callahan. Oryx Press. • 2000. $44.95. Includes environmental economic problems, such as saving jobs vs. protecting the environment. (Oryx Frontiers of Science Series.).

Renewable Energy: Power for a Sustainable Future. Godfrey Boyle, editor. Available from Taylor & Francis. • 1996. $39.95. Published by Open University Press. Contains ten chapters, each on a particular renewable energy source, including solar, biomass, hydropower, wind, and geothermal.

ABSTRACTS AND INDEXES

Applied Science and Technology Index. H. W. Wilson Co. • 11 times a year. Quarterly and annual cumulations. Service basis for print edition; CD-ROM edition, $1,495.00 per year. Indexes a wide variety of English language technical, industrial, and engineering periodicals.

Meteorological and Geoastrophysical Abstracts. American Meteorological Society. • Monthly. $1.120.00 per year.

NTIS Alerts: Ocean Sciences and Technology. National Technical Information Service. • Semimonthly. $210.00 per year. Provides descriptions of government-sponsored research reports and software, with ordering information. Formerly *Abstract Newsletter.*

Oceanic Abstracts. Cambridge Information Group. • Bimonthly. $1,045.00 per year. Covers oceanography, marine biology, ocean shipping, and a wide range of other marine-related subject areas.

ALMANACS AND YEARBOOKS

Earth Almanac: An Annual Geophysical Review of the State of the Planet. Natalie Goldstein. Oryx Press. • Annual. $65.00. Provides background information, statistics, and a summary of major events relating to the atmosphere, oceans, land, and fresh water.

DIRECTORIES

Sea Technology Buyers Guide/Directory. Compass Publications, Inc. • Annual. $25.50. Manufacturing, service, research and development, engineering, construction, drilling, equipment lease and rental firms, and testing organizations providing goods and services to the oceanographic, offshore, marine sciences, and undersea defense industries. Formerly *Sea Technology Handbook/Directory.*

ENCYCLOPEDIAS AND DICTIONARIES

Water Encyclopedia. Frits Von Der Leeden and others, editors. Lewis Publishers. • 1990. $179.00. Second edition. Covers a wide variety of topics relating to water. (Geraghty and Miller Ground Water Series).

ONLINE DATABASES

Applied Science and Technology Index Online. H. W. Wilson Co. • Provides online indexing of 400 major scientific, technical, industrial, and engineering periodicals. Time period is 1983 to date. Monthly updates. Inquire as to online cost and availability.

GEOARCHIVE. Geosystems. • Citations to literature on geoscience and water. 1974 to present. Monthly updates. Inquire as to online cost and availability.

Oceanic Abstracts (Online). Cambridge Scientific Abstracts. • Oceanographic and other marine-related technical literature, 1981 to present.Monthly updates. Inquire as to online cost and availability.

PERIODICALS AND NEWSLETTERS

Marine Policy; The International Journal on the Organization, Management and Regulation of the Multiple Use of Ocean Space. Elsevier Science. • Bimonthly. $723.00 per year.

Ocean Development and International Law; The Journal of Marine Affairs. Taylor & Francis, Inc. • Quarterly. Individuals, $191.00 per year; institutions, $385.00 per year.

Ocean Engineering: An International Journal of Research and Development. Elsevier Science. • 12 times a year. $1,798.00 per year.

Progress in Oceanography. Elsevier Science. • 16 times a year. $1,962.00 per year.

Sea Technology: For Design Engineering and Application of Equipment and Services for the Marine Environment. Compass Publications, Inc. • Monthly. $35.00 per year.

TRADE/PROFESSIONAL ASSOCIATIONS

International Oceanographic Foundation. 4600 Rickenbacker Causeway, Miami, FL 33149-1098. Phone: (305)361-4888 or (305)361-4697 Fax: (305)361-4711.

Marine Technology Society. 1828 L St., N.W., Suite 906, Washington, DC 20036. Phone: (202)775-5966 Fax: (202)429-9417 E-mail: mtsadmin@erols.com • URL: http://www.mtsociety.org.

National Ocean Industries Association. 1120 G St., N.W., Suite 900, Washington, DC 20005. Phone: (202)347-6900 Fax: (202)347-8650 E-mail: noai@noai.org.

OECD

See: ORGANIZATION FOR ECONOMIC COOPERATION AND DEVELOPMENT

OFF-PRICE RETAILERS

See: DISCOUNT HOUSES

OFFICE APPLIANCES

See: OFFICE EQUIPMENT AND SUPPLIES

OFFICE AUTOMATION

See also: DESKTOP PUBLISHING; FACSIMILE SYSTEMS; MICROCOMPUTERS AND MINICOMPUTERS; WORD PROCESSING

ABSTRACTS AND INDEXES

Business Periodicals Index. H. W. Wilson Co. • Monthly, except August, with quarterly and annual cumulations. Service basis for print edition; CD-ROM edition, $1,495.00 per year.

Computer and Control Abstracts. Available from INSPEC, Inc. • Monthly. $2,160.00 per year. Section C of *Science Abstracts.*

Computer and Information Systems Abstracts Journal: An Abstract Journal Pertaining to the Theory, Design, Fabrication and Application of Computer and Information Systems. Cambridge Information Group. • Monthly. $1,045 per year.

Computer Literature Index: A Subject/Author Index to Computer and Data Processing Literature. Applied Computer Research, Inc. • Quarterly, with annual cumulation. $245.00 per year. Contains brief abstracts of book and periodical literature covering all phases of computing, including approximately 70 specific application areas.

Key Abstracts: Business Automation. Available from INSPEC, Inc. • Monthly. $240.00 per year. Provides international coverage of journal and proceedings literature. Published in England by the Institution of Electrical Engineers (IEE).

Microcomputer Abstracts. Information Today, Inc. • Quarterly. $225.00 per year. Provides abstracts covering a wide variety of personal and business microcomputer literature. Formerly *Microcomputer Index.*

DIRECTORIES

Faulkner Information Service. Faulkner Information Services, Inc. • Looseleaf. Monthly updates. Many titles and volumes, covering virtually all aspects of computer software and hardware. Gives descriptions and technical data for specific products, including producers' names and addresses. Prices and details on request. Formerly (The Auerbach Series).

The Software Encyclopedia: A Guide for Personal, Professional, and Business Users. R. R. Bowker. • Annual. $255.00. Two volumes. Volume one lists software programs by title and producer. Volume two provides information on programs according to application and operating system. Includes prices and requirements for hardware and memory.

ENCYCLOPEDIAS AND DICTIONARIES

Dictionary of Computer Terms. Brian Phaffenberger. Pearson Education and Technology. • 1997. $10.95. Sixth edition.

HANDBOOKS AND MANUALS

Electronic Office Machines. William R. Pasewark. South-Western Publishing Co. • 1995. $14.25. Seventh edition.

Procedures for the Automated Office. Sharon Burton and others. Prentice Hall. • 2000. $46.67. Fifth edition.

ONLINE DATABASES

Internet and Personal Computing Abstracts. Information Today, Inc. • Contains abstracts covering a wide variety of personal and business microcomputer literature appearing in more than 100 journals and popular magazines. Time period is 1981 to date, with monthly updates. Formerly *Microcomputer Index.* Inquire as to online cost and availability.

PROMT: Predicasts Overview of Markets and Technology. The Gale Group. • Companies, products, applied technologies and markets. U.S. and international literature coverage, 1972 to date. Inquire as to online cost and availability. Provides abstracts from more than 1,600 publications. Weekly updates.

Wilson Business Abstracts Online. H. W. Wilson Co. • Indexes and abstracts 600 major business periodicals, plus the *Wall Street Journal* and the business section of the *New York Times.* Indexing is from 1982, abstracting from 1990, with the two newspapers included from 1993. Updated weekly. Inquire as to online cost and availability. (*Business Periodicals Index* without abstracts is also available online.).

PERIODICALS AND NEWSLETTERS

EDP Weekly: The Leading Weekly Computer News Summary. Computer Age and E D P News Services. • Weekly. $495.00 per year. Newsletter. Summarizes news from all areas of the computer and microcomputer industries.

Home Office Computing: Building Better Businesses with Technology. Freedom Technology Media Group. • Monthly. $16.97 per year. Office automation for the self-employed and small businesses. Formerly *Family and Home Office Computing.*

Office Dealer: Updating the Office Industry's Products. Quality Publishing, Inc. • Six times a year. $36.00 per year. Supplies information on new products for dealers in office automation equipment and systems. Formerly *Office Systems Dealer.*

Office Products Analyst: A Monthly Report Devoted to the Analysis of Office Products. Industry Analysts, Inc. • Monthly. $195.00 per year. Newsletter. Includes user ratings of office automation equipment.

Office Systems. Quality Publishing, Inc. • Monthly. Price on application. Special feature issue topics include document imaging, document management, office supplies, and office equipment. Incorporates *Managing Office Technology.*

Wireless Integration: Solutions for Enterprise Decision Makers. PennWell Corp., Advanced Technology Div. • Bimonthly. $48.00 per year. Edited for networking and communications managers. Special issues cover the wireless office, wireless intranet/Internet, mobile wireless, telemetry, and buyer's guide directory information.

Wireless Review: Intelligence for Competitive Providers. Intertec Publishing Corp. • Semimonthly. $48.00 per year. Covers business and technology developments for wireless service providers. Includes special issues on a wide variety of wireless topics. Formed by merger of *Cellular Business* and *Wireless World.*

RESEARCH CENTERS AND INSTITUTES

Collaboratory for Research on Electronic Work. University of Michigan, 1075 Beal Ave., Ann Arbor, MI 48109-2112. Phone: (734)647-4948 Fax: (734)936-3168 E-mail: finholt@umich.edu • URL: http://crew.umich.edu/ • Concerned with the design and use of computer-based tools for thinking and planning in the professional office.

TRADE/PROFESSIONAL ASSOCIATIONS

IEEE Computer Society. 1730 Massachusetts Ave., N. W., Washington, DC 20036. Phone: (202)371-0101 Fax: (202)728-9614 E-mail: csinfo@computer.org • URL: http://www.computer.org • A society of the Institute of Electrical and Electronics Engineers. Said to be the world's largest organization of computer professionals. Some of the specific committees are: Computer Communications; Computer Graphics; Computers in Education; Design Automation; Office Automation; Personal Computing; Robotics; Security and Privacy; Software Engineering.

OTHER SOURCES

DataWorld. Faulkner Information Services, Inc. • Four looseleaf volumes, with monthly supplements. $1,395.00 per year. Describes and evaluates both hardware and software relating to midrange, micro, and mainframe computers. Available on CD-ROM.

OFFICE BUILDINGS

DIRECTORIES

National Real Estate Investor Sourcebook. Intertec Publishing Corp. • Annual. $79.95. List about 7,000 companies and individuals in eighteen real estate fields. Formerly *National Real Estate Investor Directory*.

HANDBOOKS AND MANUALS

Guide to Energy Efficient Commercial Equipment. Margaret Suozzo and others. American Council for an Energy Efficient Economy. • 1997. $25.00. Provides information on specifying and purchasing energy-saving systems for buildings (heating, air conditioning, lighting, and motors).

Managing the Office Building. Mark Ingerbretsen, editor. Institute of Real Estate Management. • 1985. $62.95. Revised edition.

Office Interior Design Guide: An Introduction for Facility and Design. Julie K. Rayfield. John Wiley and Sons, Inc. • 1997. $59.95.

Office Planning and Design Desk Reference: A Guide for Architects and Design Professionals. James Rappoport and others, editors. John Wiley and Sons, Inc. • 1991. $120.00. Covers the planning and designing of new or retrofitted office space.

PERIODICALS AND NEWSLETTERS

Building Operating Management: The National Magazine for Commercial and Institutional Buildings Construction, Renoration, Facility Management. Trade Press Publishing Corp. • Monthly. $55.00 per year.

Business Facilities. Group C Communications. • Monthly. $30.00 per year. Facility planning and site selection.

Commercial Building: Tranforming Plans into Buildings. Stamats Communications. • Bimonthly. $48.00 per year. Edited for building contractors, engineers, and architects. Includes special features on new products, climate control, plumbing, and vertical transportation.

Marketscore. CB Richard Ellis. • Quarterly. Price on application. Newsletter. Provides proprietary forecasts of commercial real estate performance in metropolitan areas.

National Real Estate Investor. Intertec Publishing Corp. • Monthly. $85.00 per year. Includes annual *Directory*. Market surveys by city.

Office Relocation Magazine. ORM Group. • Bimonthly. $39.00 per year. Provides articles on the relocation of office facilities.

Quarterly Market Report. CB Richard Ellis. • Quarterly. Price on application. Newsletter. Reviews current prices, rents, capitalization rates, and occupancy trends for commercial real estate.

Real Estate Economics: Journal of the American Real Estate and Urban Economics Association. MIT Press. • Quarterly. Institutions, $165.00 per year.

PRICE SOURCES

National Real Estate Index. CB Richard Ellis. • Price and frequency on application. Provides reports on commercial real estate prices, rents, capitalization rates, and trends in more than 65 metropolitan areas. Time span is 12 years. Includes urban office buildings, suburban offices, warehouses, retail properties, and apartments.

STATISTICS SOURCES

ULI Market Profiles: North America. Urban Land Institute. • Annual. Members, $249.95; non-members, $299.95. Provides real estate marketing data for residential, retail, office, and industrial sectors. Covers 76 U. S. metropolitan areas and 13 major foreign metropolitan areas.

TRADE/PROFESSIONAL ASSOCIATIONS

American Real Estate and Urban Economics Association. Indiana University School of Business, 1309 E. 10th St., Suite 738, Bloomington, IN 47405-1701. Phone: (812)855-7794 Fax: (812)855-8679 E-mail: areuea@indiana.edu • URL: http://www.areuea.org • Members are real estate teachers, researchers, economists, and others concerned with urban real estate and investment.

Building Owners and Managers Association International. 1201 New York Ave., N.W., Suite 300, Washington, DC 20005. Phone: (202)408-2662 Fax: (202)371-0181 E-mail: soppen@boma.org • URL: http://www.boma.org.

National Association of Industrial and Office Properties. 2201 Cooperative Way, Herndon, VA 20171. Phone: 800-666-6780 or (703)904-7100 Fax: (703)904-7942 E-mail: naiop@naiop.org • URL: http://www.naiop.org • Members are owners and developers of business, industrial, office, and retail properties.

OFFICE DESIGN

GENERAL WORKS

Color in the Office: Design Trends from 1950 to 1990 and Beyond. Sara O. Marberry. John Wiley & Sons, Inc. • 1993. $75.00. Presents past, present, and future color trends in corporate office design. Features color photographs of traditional, postmodern, and neoclassical office designs. (Architecture Series).

New Office: Designs for Corporations, People, and Technology. Karin Tetlow. PBC International. • 1997. $47.50. Includes 200 color pictures by leading international photographers.

DIRECTORIES

Interiors and Sources: Directory and Buyer's Guide. L. C. Clark Publishing Co., Inc. • Annual. $10.00. Lists sources of surface materials, furniture, lighting, etc., for interior designers.

ENCYCLOPEDIAS AND DICTIONARIES

Encyclopedia of Interior Design. Joanna Banham, editor. Fitzroy Dearborn Publishers. • 1997. $270.00. Two volumes. Contains more than 500 essays on interior design topics. Includes bibliographies.

HANDBOOKS AND MANUALS

Facilities and Workplace Design: An Illustrated Guide. Quarterman Lee and others. Engineering and Management Press. • 1996. $25.00. Written for both new and experienced designers. Features "25 illustrated tasks that can be applied to most projects."(Engineers in Business Series).

Home Office Design: Everything You Need to Know about Planning, Organizing, and Furnishing Your Work Space. Neal Zimmerman. John Wiley and Sons, Inc. • 1996. $19.95. Covers furniture, seating, workstations, filing, storage, task lighting, etc.

PERIODICALS AND NEWSLETTERS

Facilities Design and Management. Miller Freeman, Inc. • Monthly. $65.00 per year. Edited for planners, designers, and managers of major office facilities. Subject matter includes open plan systems, space allocation, office remodeling, office furniture, and related topics.

FM Data Monthly. Tradeline, Inc. • Monthly. $248.00 per year. Newsletter. Covers the planning, design, construction, and renovation of of a variety of corporate facilities. Formerly *Facilities Planning News*.

Interiors and Sources. L. C. Clark Publishing Co., Inc. • Bimonthly. $18.00 per year. Promotes professionalism for interior designers and design firms. Includes special features on office systems, work stations, and office furniture.

Today's Facility Manager: The Magazine of Facilities-Interior Planning Team. Group C Communications, Inc. • Monthly. $30.00 per year. Covers office design, furnishings, and furniture, including open plan systems. Formerly *Business Interiors*.

RESEARCH CENTERS AND INSTITUTES

Office Systems Research Association. Morehead State University, Dept. of Information Systems, Morehead, KY 40351-1689. Phone: (606)783-2724 Fax: (606)783-5025 E-mail: dikizzier@moreheadst.edu • URL: http://www.osra.org • Research areas include the analysis, design, and administration of office systems.

Operations Management Education and Research Foundation. P.O. Box 661, Rockford, MI 49341. Phone: (616)732-5543 • Research focuses on office operations, environment, and physical structures, including furniture fixtures.

TRADE/PROFESSIONAL ASSOCIATIONS

Office Planners and Users Group. P.O. Box 11182, Philadelphia, PA 19136. Phone: (215)335-9400 • Members include office designers, space planners, and architects.

OFFICE EQUIPMENT AND SUPPLIES

See also: COMPUTERS; OFFICE FURNITURE INDUSTRY; WORD PROCESSING

CD-ROM DATABASES

Electronic Strategies. Thomson Financial Securities Data. • Monthly. $2,995.00 per year. CD-ROM contains full text of investment analysts' reports on companies operating in the following fields: electronics, computers, semiconductors, and office products.

DIRECTORIES

Better Buys for Business: The Independent Consumer Guide to Office Equipment. What to Buy for Business, Inc. • 10 times a year. $134.00 per year. Each issue is on a particular office product, with detailed evaluation of specific models: 1. Low-Volume Copier Guide, 2. Mid-Volume Copier Guide, 3. High-Volume Copier Guide, 4. Plain Paper Fax and Low-Volume Multifunctional Guide, 5. Mid/High-Volume Multifunctional Guide, 6. Laser Printer Guide, 7. Color Printer and Color Copier Guide, 8. Scan-to-File Guide, 9. Business Phone Systems Guide, 10. Postage Meter Guide, with a Short Guide to Shredders.

Business Products Industry Association Membership Directory and Buyer's Guide. Business Products Industry Association. • Annual. Members, $20.00; Free to members; non-members, $80.00. 9,000 manufacturers, wholesalers, retailers and sales and marketing representatives in the office products industry.

Directory of Discount and General Merchandise Stores. Chain Store Guide. • Annual. $300.00. Includes retailers and wholesalers of housewares, giftwares, novelties, toys, hobby materials, crafts, and stationery. Formerly *Directory of Discount Stores Catalog Showrooms*.

Essential Business Buyer's Guide, from Cellular Services and Overnight Mail to Internet Access Providers, 401(k) Plans, and Desktop Computers: The Ultimate Guide to Buying Office Equipment, Products, and Services. Sourcebooks, Inc. • 1996. $18.95. Compiled by the staff of *Business Consumer Guide*. Lists recommended brands of office equipment.

HANDBOOKS AND MANUALS

Guide to Energy Efficient Office Equipment. Loretta A. Smith and others. American Council for an Energy Efficient Economy. • 1996. $12.00. Second edition. Provides information on selecting, purchasing, and using energy-saving computers, monitors, printers, copiers, and other office devices.

Office Equipment Adviser: The Essential What-to-Buy and How-to-Buy Resource for Offices with One to 100 People. What to Buy for Business, Inc. • 1995. $24.95. Third revised edition.

ONLINE DATABASES

PROMT: Predicasts Overview of Markets and Technology. The Gale Group. • Companies, products, applied technologies and markets. U.S. and international literature coverage, 1972 to date. Inquire as to online cost and availability. Provides abstracts from more than 1,600 publications. Weekly updates.

PERIODICALS AND NEWSLETTERS

The Business Consumer's Advisor. Buyers Laboratory, Inc. • Monthly. $175.00 per year. Newsletter.

Office Systems. Quality Publishing, Inc. • Monthly. Price on application. Special feature issue topics include document imaging, document management, office supplies, and office equipment. Incorporates *Managing Office Technology.*

PRICE SOURCES

Orion Copier Blue Book. Orion Research Corp. • Annual. $39.00. Quotes retail and wholesale prices of used office equipment. Original list prices and years of manufacture are also shown. Formerly *Orion Office Equipment Blue Book.*

STATISTICS SOURCES

Computers and Office and Accounting Machines. U. S. Bureau of the Census. • Annual. Provides data on shipments: value, quantity, imports, and exports. (Current Industrial Reports, MA-35R.).

TRADE/PROFESSIONAL ASSOCIATIONS

Business Products Industry Association. 301 N. Fairfax St., Alexandria, VA 22314. Phone: 800-542-6672 or (703)549-9040 Fax: (703)683-7552 • URL: http://www.bpia.org.

Business Technology Association. 12411 Wornall Rd., Kansas City, MO 64145. Phone: 800-247-2176 or (816)941-3100 Fax: (816)941-2829 E-mail: info@bta.org • URL: http://www.btanet.org.

Information Technology Industry Council. 1250 Eye St., N.W., Suite 200, Washington, DC 20005. Phone: (202)737-8888 Fax: (202)638-4922 E-mail: webmaster@itic.org • URL: http://www.itic.org.

OTHER SOURCES

Business Automation Reference Service: Office Equipment. Alltech Publishing Co. • Monthly. $100.00 per year. Looseleaf service.

Business Consumers's Network. Buyers Laboratory Inc. • Monthly. $795.00 per year. Looseleaf service. Tests office equipment and issues reports. Formerly *Buyers Laboratory Report on Office Products.*

OFFICE FORMS

See: FORMS AND BLANKS

OFFICE FURNITURE INDUSTRY

DIRECTORIES

FDM-The Source-Woodworking Industry Directory. Cahners Business Information. • Annual. $25.00. A product-classified listing of more than 1,800 suppliers to the furniture and cabinet industries. Includes Canada.

FINANCIAL RATIOS

Annual Statement Studies. Robert Morris Associates: The Association of Lending and Credit Risk Professiona. • Annual. Free to members; non-members, $140.00. Median and quartile financial ratios are given for over 400 kinds of manufacturing, wholesale, retail, construction, and consumer finance establishments. Data is sorted by both asset size and sales volume. Includes a clearly written "Definition of Ratios" and an alphabetical industry index.

HANDBOOKS AND MANUALS

Office Interior Design Guide: An Introduction for Facility and Design. Julie K. Rayfield. John Wiley and Sons, Inc. • 1997. $59.95.

PERIODICALS AND NEWSLETTERS

Contract Design: The Business Magazine of Commercial and Institutional Interior Design, and Architecture, Planning and Construction. Miller Freeman, Inc. • Monthly. $65.00 per year. Firms engaged in specifying furniture and furnishings for commercial installations. Formerly *Contract.*

FDM: Furniture Design and Manufacturing: Serving the Upholstered Furniture Industry. Chartwell Communications, Inc. • Monthly. Free to qualified personnel. Edited for furniture executives, production managers, and designers. Covers the manufacturing of household, office, and institutional furniture, store fixtures, and kitchen and bathroom cabinets.

Office World News. BUS Publications. • Monthly. $50.00 per year. Formerly *Office Products News.*

STATISTICS SOURCES

Annual Survey of Manufactures. Available from U. S. Government Printing Office. • Annual. Prices vary. Issued by the U. S. Census Bureau as an interim update to the *Census of Manufactures.* Includes data on number of manufacturing establishments in various industries, employment, labor costs, value of shipments, capital expenditures, inventories, energy costs, and assets. (See also Census Bureau home page, http://www.census.gov/.).

TRADE/PROFESSIONAL ASSOCIATIONS

Business and Institutional Furniture Manufacturers Association. 2680 Horizon, S.E., Suite A1, Grand Rapids, MI 49546-7500. Phone: (616)285-3963 Fax: (616)285-3765 E-mail: email@bifma.com • URL: http://www.bifma.com.

OFFICE IN THE HOME

See: SELF-EMPLOYMENT

OFFICE MACHINES

See: OFFICE EQUIPMENT AND SUPPLIES

OFFICE MANAGEMENT

See also: ADMINISTRATION; SYSTEMS IN MANAGEMENT; WORD PROCESSING

GENERAL WORKS

Administrative Office Management: An Introduction. Zane B. Quible. Prentice Hall. • 2000. $52.00. 7th edition. (KU-Office Procedures Series).

ABSTRACTS AND INDEXES

Business Periodicals Index. H. W. Wilson Co. • Monthly, except August, with quarterly and annual cumulations. Service basis for print edition; CD-ROM edition, $1,495.00 per year.

CD-ROM DATABASES

WILSONDISC: Wilson Business Abstracts. H. W. Wilson Co. • Monthly. $2,495.00 per year, including unlimited online access to *Wilson Business Abstracts* through WILSONLINE. Provides CD-ROM "cover-to-cover" abstracting and indexing of over 600 prominent business periodicals. Indexing is from 1982, abstracting from 1990. (*Business Periodicals Index* without abstracts is available on CD-ROM at $1,495 per year.).

HANDBOOKS AND MANUALS

AMA Management Handbook. John J. Hampton, editor. AMACOM. • 1994. $110.00. Third edition. Provides 200 chapters in 16 major subject areas. Covers a wide variety of business and industrial management topics.

ONLINE DATABASES

ABI/INFORM. Bell & Howell Information and Learning. • Provides online indexing to business-related material occurring in over 1,000 periodicals from 1971 to the present. Inquire as to online cost and availability.

Management Contents. The Gale Group. • Covers a wide range of management, financial, marketing, personnel, and administrative topics. About 150 leading business journals are indexed and abstracted from 1974 to date, with monthly updating. Inquire as to online cost and availability.

Wilson Business Abstracts Online. H. W. Wilson Co. • Indexes and abstracts 600 major business periodicals, plus the *Wall Street Journal* and the business section of the *New York Times.* Indexing is from 1982, abstracting from 1990, with the two newspapers included from 1993. Updated weekly. Inquire as to online cost and availability. (*Business Periodicals Index* without abstracts is also available online.).

PERIODICALS AND NEWSLETTERS

Nine to Five Newsletter. National Association of Working Women. • Five times a year. Free to members; individuals, $25.00 per year. A newsletter dealing with the rights and concerns of women office workers.

People at Work. Professional Training Associates, Inc. • Monthly. $89.00 per year. Newsletter on common personnel problems of supervisors and office managers. Formerly *Practical Supervision.*

TRADE/PROFESSIONAL ASSOCIATIONS

National Association of Professional Organizers. 1033 La Posada Drive, Suite 220, Austin, TX 78752. Phone: (512)454-8626 Fax: (512)454-3036 E-mail: napo@assnmgmt.com • URL: http://www.napo.net • Members are concerned with time management, productivity, and the efficient organization of documents and activities.

Nine to Five: National Association of Working Women. 231 W. Wisconsin Ave., Suite 900, Milwaukee, WI 53203. Phone: 800-522-0925 or (414)274-0925 Fax: (414)272-2870 E-mail: naww9to5@execpc.com • Members are women office workers. Strives for the improvement of office working conditions for women and the elimination of sex and race discrimination.

Special Interest Group on Supporting Group Work. Association for Computing, 1515 Broadway, 17th Fl., New York, NY 10036. Phone: (212)869-7440 Fax: (212)302-5826 E-mail: rivkin@acm.org • URL: http://www.acm.org/siggroup/ • Concerned with office automation and computer communications.

OTHER SOURCES

Electronic Office: Management and Technology. Faulkner Information Services, Inc. • Two looseleaf volumes, with monthly updates. $990.00 per year. Contains product reports and other information relating to automated office and integrated services.

OFFICE PRACTICE

See also: WORD PROCESSING

ENCYCLOPEDIAS AND DICTIONARIES

Professional Secretary's Encyclopedic Dictionary. Prentice Hall. • 1994. $29.95. Fifth edition.

HANDBOOKS AND MANUALS

Career Legal Secretary. National Association of Legal Secretaries. West Publishing Co., College and School Div. • 1997. $35.50. Fourth edition.

Complete Secretary's Handbook. Mary A. De Vries. Prentice Hall. • 1993. $24.95. Seventh edition.

Office Professional's Quick Reference Handbook. Sheryl Lindsell-Roberts. Pearson Education and Technology. • 1995. $9.00. Fifth revised edition.

Secretarial/Word Processing Service. Entrepreneur Media, Inc. • Looseleaf. $59.50. A practical guide to starting a secretarial and word processing business. Covers profit potential, start-up costs, market size evaluation, owner's time required, site selection, pricing, accounting, advertising, promotion, etc. (Start-Up Business Guide No. E1136.).

PERIODICALS AND NEWSLETTERS

Administrative Assistant's Update. Carswell Thomson Professional Publishing. • Monthly. $139.00 per year. Newsletter. Advice and information for secretaries and office workers. Formerly *Secretary's Update.*

OfficePro. Stratton Publishing and Marketing Inc. • Nine times a year. $25.00 per year. Provides statistics and other information about secretaries and office trends. Formerly *Secretary.*

The Take-Charge Assistant. American Management Association. • Monthly. $75.00 per year. Newsletter. Provides advice on personal and professional skills for office assistants.

TRADE/PROFESSIONAL ASSOCIATIONS

International Association of Administrative Professionals. P.O. Box 20404, Kansas City, MO 64195-0404. Phone: (816)891-6600 Fax: (816)891-9118 E-mail: exec.director@iaap-hq.org.

OFFICE SUPPLIES

See: OFFICE EQUIPMENT AND SUPPLIES

OFFICE SYSTEMS

See: SYSTEMS IN MANAGEMENT; WORD PROCESSING

OFFICIAL PUBLICATIONS

See: GOVERNMENT PUBLICATIONS

OFFICIALS AND EMPLOYEES

See: GOVERNMENT EMPLOYEES

OFFSET PRINTING

See: GRAPHIC ARTS INDUSTRY; PRINTING AND PRINTING EQUIPMENT INDUSTRIES

OFFSHORE PETROLEUM INDUSTRY

See also: PETROLEUM INDUSTRY

ABSTRACTS AND INDEXES

Applied Science and Technology Index. H. W. Wilson Co. • 11 times a year. Quarterly and annual cumulations. Service basis for print edition; CD-ROM edition, $1,495.00 per year. Indexes a wide variety of English language technical, industrial, and engineering periodicals.

DIRECTORIES

Financial Times Energy Yearbook: Oil & Gas: 2000. Available from The Gale Group. • Annual. $320.00. Published by Financial Times Energy. Provides production and financial details for more than 800 major oil and gas companies worldwide. Includes coverage of reserves, operations, properties, and growth rates. Formerly *Financial Times Oil & Gas Yearbook.*

Worldwide Offshore Petroleum Directory. PennWell Corp., Petroleum Div. • Annual. $165.00. Lists about 3,500 companies with 13,000 personnel.

HANDBOOKS AND MANUALS

Lloyd's List Marine Equipment Buyers' Guide. Available from Informa Publishing Group Ltd. • Annual. $270.00. Published in the UK by Lloyd's List (http://www.lloydslist.com). Lists more than 6,000 companies worldwide supplying over 2,000 types of marine products and services, including offshore equipment.

PERIODICALS AND NEWSLETTERS

Marine Engineers Review: Journal of the Institute of Marine Engineers. Available from Information Today, Inc. • Monthly. $140.00 per year. Published in London by the Institute of Marine Engineers. Covers marine engineering, offshore industries, and ocean shipping. Supplement available *Directory of Marine Diesel Engines.*

Marine Management Holdings: Transactions. Available from Information Today, Inc. • Bimonthly. $220.00 per year. Published in London by Marine Management Holdings Ltd. Contains technical and regulatory material on a wide variety of marine and offshore topics. Formerly *Institute of Marine Engineers: Transactions.*

Ocean Oil Weekly Report: News, Analysis, and Market Trends of the Worldwide Offshore Oil and Gas Industry. PennWell Corp., Petroleum Div. • Weekly. $495.00 per year. Newsletter with emphasis on the Gulf of Mexico offshore oil industry. Includes statistics.

Offshore: Incorporating The Oilman. PennWell Corp., Industrial Div. • Monthly. $75.00 per year.

The Oilman Weekly Newsletter. PennWell Corp., Petroleum Div. • Weekly. $1360.00 per year. Newsletter. Provides news of developments concerning the North Sea and European oil and gas businesses. Each issue contains four pages of statistical data.

RESEARCH CENTERS AND INSTITUTES

Geotechnical Engineering Center. University of Texas at Austin, Dept. of Civil Engineering, Austin, TX 78712. Phone: (512)471-4929 Fax: (512)471-6548 E-mail: swright@mail.utexas.edu • Areas of research include offshore complexes.

Southwest Research Institute. P.O. Box 28510, San Antonio, TX 78228-0510. Phone: (210)684-5111 Fax: (210)522-3496 E-mail: jkittle@swri.org • URL: http://www.swri.org.

TRADE/PROFESSIONAL ASSOCIATIONS

American Petroleum Institute. 1220 L St., N.W., Washington, DC 20005. Phone: (202)682-8000 Fax: (202)682-8029 • URL: http://www.api.org.

Institute of Marine Engineers. 76 Mark Lane, London EC3R 7JN, England. Phone: 44 207 3822600 Fax: 44 207 3822670 E-mail: mic@imare.org.uk • URL: http://www.imare.org.uk • An international organization of marine engineers, offshore engineers, and naval architects.

International Association of Drilling Contractors. P.O. Box 4287, Houston, TX 77210-4287. Phone: (281)578-7171 Fax: (281)578-0589 E-mail: info@iadc.org • URL: http://www.iadc.org • Includes an Offshore Committee.

Offshore Marine Service Association. 990 N. Corporate Dr., Suite 210, Harahan, LA 70123. Phone: (504)734-7622 Fax: (504)734-7134 • Members are owners and operators of vessels servicing offshore oil installations.

OIL

See: OIL AND FATS INDUSTRY; PETROLEUM INDUSTRY

OIL AND FATS INDUSTRY

ABSTRACTS AND INDEXES

Food Science and Technology Abstracts. International Food Information Service Publishing. • Monthly. $1,780.00 per year. Provides worldwide coverage of the literature of food technology and food production.

Foods Adlibra: Key to the World's Food Literature. Foods Adlibra Publications. • Semimonthly.Provides journal citations and abstracts to the literature of food technology and packaging.

CD-ROM DATABASES

Food Science and Technology Abstracts [CD-ROM]. Available from SilverPlatter Information, Inc. • Quarterly. $3,700 per year. Produced by International Food Information Service (home page is http://www.ifis.org). Provides worldwide coverage on CD-ROM of the literature of food technology and production. Various types of publications are indexed, with abstracts, including about 1,800 periodicals. Time period is 1969 to date.

DIRECTORIES

OPD Chemical Buyers Directory. Schnell Publishing Co., Inc. • Annual. $129.00. Included in subscription to *Chemical Marketing Reporter.* About 1,500 suppliers of chemical process materials and more than 300 companies which transport and store chemicals in the U.S.

HANDBOOKS AND MANUALS

Bailey's Industrial Oil and Fat Products. Alton E. Bailey. John Wiley and Sons, Inc. • 1996. $610.00. Five volumes. Fifth edition.

INTERNET DATABASES

Fedstats. Federal Interagency Council on Statistical Policy. Phone: (202)395-7254 • URL: http://www.fedstats.gov • Web site features an efficient search facility for full-text statistics produced by more than 70 federal agencies, including the Census Bureau, the Bureau of Economic Analysis, and the Bureau of Labor Statistics. Boolean searches can be made within one agency or for all agencies combined. Links are offered to international statistical bureaus, including the UN, IMF, OECD, UNESCO, Eurostat, and 20 individual countries. Fees: Free.

USDA. United States Department of Agriculture. Phone: (202)720-2791 E-mail: agsec@usda.gov • URL: http://www.usda.gov • The USDA home page has six sections: News and Information; What's New; About USDA; Agencies; Opportunities; Search and Help. Keyword searching is offered from the USDA home page and from various individual agency home pages. Agencies are the Economic Research Service, Agricultural Marketing Service, National Agricultural Statistics Service, National Agricultural Library, and about 12 others. Updating varies. Fees: Free.

ONLINE DATABASES

CAB Abstracts. CAB International North America. • Contains 46 specialized abstract collections covering over 10,000 journals and monographs in the areas of agriculture, horticulture, forest products, farm products, nutrition, dairy science, poultry, grains, animal health, entomology, etc. Time period is 1972 to date, with monthly updates. Inquire as to online cost and availability. *CAB Abstracts on CD-ROM* also available, with annual updating.

DRI U.S. Central Database. Data Products Division. • Provides more than 23,000 business, financial, demographic, economic, foreign trade, and industry-related time series for the U.S. Includes national income, population, retail-wholesale trade, price indexes, labor data, housing, industrial production, banking, interest rates, money supply, etc. Time period is generally 1947 to date (some data back to 1929). Updating varies. Inquire as to online cost and availability.

Food Science and Technology Abstracts [online]. IFIS North American Desk. • Produced by International Food Information Service. Provides about 500,000 online citations, with abstracts, to the international literature of food science, technology, commodities, engineering, and processing. Approximately 2,000 periodicals are covered. Time period is 1969 to date, with monthly updates. Inquire as to online cost and availability.

FOODS ADLIBRA. General Mills, Inc. • Contains online citations, with abstracts, to the technical and business literature of food processing and packaging. New products and new ingredients are featured. Covers about 250 trade journals and 500 research journals from 1974 to date, with monthly updates. Inquire as to online cost and availability.

PERIODICALS AND NEWSLETTERS

American Oil Chemists' Society Journal. American Oil Chemists' Society. AOCS Press. • Monthly. Individuals, $145.00 per year; institutions, $195.00 per year. Includes *INFORM: International News on Fats, Oils and Related Materials.*

Inform: International News on Fats, Oils, and Related Materials. American Oil Chemists Society. • Monthly. $115.00 per year. Covers a wide range of technical and business topics relating to the processing and utilization of edible oils, essential oils, and oilseeds.

RESEARCH CENTERS AND INSTITUTES

Food Research Center. Texas A & M University. College Station, TX 77843-2476. Phone: (409)845-2741 Fax: (409)845-2744 E-mail: kcrhee@tamu.edu • URL: http://www.tamu.edu/food-protein/.

STATISTICS SOURCES

Agricultural Statistics. Available from U. S. Government Printing Office. • Annual. Produced by the National Agricultural Statistics Service, U. S. Department of Agriculture. Provides a wide variety of statistical data relating to agricultural production, supplies, consumption, prices/price-supports, foreign trade, costs, and returns, as well as farm labor, loans, income, and population. In many cases, historical data is shown annually for 10 years. In addition to farm data, includes detailed fishery statistics.

Annual Survey of Manufactures. Available from U. S. Government Printing Office. • Annual. Prices vary. Issued by the U. S. Census Bureau as an interim update to the *Census of Manufactures.* Includes data on number of manufacturing establishments in various industries, employment, labor costs, value of shipments, capital expenditures, inventories, energy costs, and assets. (See also Census Bureau home page, http://www.census.gov/.).

Business Statistics of the United States. Courtenay M. Slater, editor. Bernan Associates. • 1999. $74.00. Fifth edition. Based on *Business Statistics*, formerly issue by the Bureau of Economic Analysis, U. S. Department of Commerce. Provides basic data for a wide variety of U. S. industries, services, and economic indicators. Most statistics are shown annually for 29 years and monthly for the most recent four years.

Fats and Oils: Oilseed Crushings. U. S. Bureau of the Census. • Monthly and annual. Provides data on shipments of cottonseed oil and soybean oil: value, quantity, imports, and exports. (Current Industrial Reports, M20J.).

Fats and Oils: Production, Consumption, and Stocks. U. S. Bureau of the Census. • Monthly and annual. Covers the supply and distribution of cottonseed, soybean, and palm oils, and selected inedible products. (Current Industrial Reports, M20K.).

Manufacturing Profiles. Available from U. S. Government Printing Office. • Annual. Issued by the U. S. Census Bureau. A printed consolidation of the entire *Current Industrial Report* series, presenting "all the data compiled." Contains statistics on production, shipments, inventories, consumption, exports, imports, and orders for a wide variety of manufactured products. (See also Census Bureau home page, http://www.census.gov/.).

Survey of Current Business. Available from U. S. Government Printing Office. • Monthly. $49.00 per year. Issued by Bureau of Economic Analysis, U. S. Department of Commerce. Presents a wide variety of business and economic data.

TRADE/PROFESSIONAL ASSOCIATIONS

American Oil Chemists' Society. 2211 W. Bradley Ave., Champaign, IL 61821-1827. Phone: (217)359-2344 Fax: (217)351-8091 E-mail: general@aocs.org • URL: http://www.aocs.org.

Institute of Shortening and Edible Oils. 1750 New York Ave., N.W., Suite 120, Washington, DC 20006. Phone: (202)783-7960 Fax: (202)393-1367 E-mail: info@iseo.org • URL: http://www.iseo.org.

National Cottonseed Products Association. P.O. Box 172267, Memphis, TN 38187-2267. Phone: (901)682-0800 Fax: (901)682-2856 E-mail: info@cottonseed.com • URL: http://www.cottonseed.com.

National Institute of Oilseed Products. 1101 15th St. N.W., Suite 202, Washington, DC 20005. Phone: (202)785-8450 or (202)785-8452 Fax: (202)223-9741 • URL: http://www.assnhq.com.

National Renderers Association. 801 N. Fairfax St., Suite 207, Alexandria, VA 22314. Phone: (703)683-0155 Fax: (703)683-2626 E-mail: renderers@aol.com • URL: http://www.renderers.org.

OTHER SOURCES

Major Food and Drink Companies of the World. Available from The Gale Group. • 2001. $855.00. Fourth edition. Two volumes. Published by Graham & Whiteside. Contains profiles and trade names for more than 9,000 important food and beverage companies in various countries. In addition to foods, includes both alcoholic and nonalcoholic drink products.

Thomas Food and Beverage Market Place. Grey House Publishing. • Annual. $295.00. Three volumes. Contains more than 40,000 entries covering food companies, beverages, food equipment, warehouse companies, food brokers, wholesalers, importers, and exporters. Formerly *Thomas Food Industry Register.*

OIL BURNER INDUSTRY

See: FUEL OIL INDUSTRY

OIL FIELD MACHINERY

See: PETROLEUM EQUIPMENT INDUSTRY

OIL FUEL INDUSTRY

See: FUEL OIL INDUSTRY

OIL INDUSTRY

See: PETROLEUM INDUSTRY

OIL MARKETING

See: PETROLEUM MARKETING

OIL TANKERS

See: TANK SHIPS

OILSEED INDUSTRY

See: OIL AND FATS INDUSTRY

OLD AGE

See: RETIREMENT

OLD AGE AND SURVIVORS INSURANCE

See: SOCIAL SECURITY

OLD AGE HOMES

See: NURSING HOMES

OLDER CONSUMERS

See: MATURE CONSUMER MARKET

OLDER WORKERS

See: EMPLOYMENT OF OLDER WORKERS

OLEOMARGARINE INDUSTRY

See: MARGARINE INDUSTRY

OLIVE OIL INDUSTRY

CD-ROM DATABASES

Food Science and Technology Abstracts [CD-ROM]. Available from SilverPlatter Information, Inc. • Quarterly. $3,700 per year. Produced by International Food Information Service (home page is http://www.ifis.org). Provides worldwide coverage on CD-ROM of the literature of food technology and production. Various types of publications are indexed, with abstracts, including about 1,800 periodicals. Time period is 1969 to date.

INTERNET DATABASES

USDA. United States Department of Agriculture. Phone: (202)720-2791 E-mail: agsec@usda.gov • URL: http://www.usda.gov • The USDA home page has six sections: News and Information; What's New; About USDA; Agencies; Opportunities; Search and Help. Keyword searching is offered from the USDA home page and from various individual agency home pages. Agencies are the Economic Research Service, Agricultural Marketing Service, National Agricultural Statistics Service, National Agricultural Library, and about 12 others. Updating varies. Fees: Free.

ONLINE DATABASES

Food Science and Technology Abstracts [online]. IFIS North American Desk. • Produced by International Food Information Service. Provides about 500,000 online citations, with abstracts, to the international literature of food science, technology, commodities, engineering, and processing. Approximately 2,000 periodicals are covered. Time period is 1969 to date, with monthly updates. Inquire as to online cost and availability.

STATISTICS SOURCES

Agricultural Statistics. Available from U. S. Government Printing Office. • Annual. Produced by the National Agricultural Statistics Service, U. S. Department of Agriculture. Provides a wide variety of statistical data relating to agricultural production, supplies, consumption, prices/price-supports, foreign trade, costs, and returns, as well as farm labor, loans, income, and population. In many cases, historical data is shown annually for 10 years. In addition to farm data, includes detailed fishery statistics.

TRADE/PROFESSIONAL ASSOCIATIONS

Association of Food Industries. P.O. Box 545, Matawan, NJ 07747. Phone: (732)583-8188 Fax: (732)583-0798 E-mail: afi@afius.org • URL: http://www.afius.org.

OTHER SOURCES

International Agreement on Olive Oil and Table Olives. United Nations Publications. • 1986. Trade agreements.

Major Food and Drink Companies of the World. Available from The Gale Group. • 2001. $855.00. Fourth edition. Two volumes. Published by Graham & Whiteside. Contains profiles and trade names for more than 9,000 important food and beverage companies in various countries. In addition to foods, includes both alcoholic and nonalcoholic drink products.

Thomas Food and Beverage Market Place. Grey House Publishing. • Annual. $295.00. Three volumes. Contains more than 40,000 entries covering food companies, beverages, food equipment, warehouse companies, food brokers, wholesalers, importers, and exporters. Formerly *Thomas Food Industry Register.*

ON-THE-JOB TRAINING

See: TRAINING OF EMPLOYEES

ONION INDUSTRY

INTERNET DATABASES

USDA. United States Department of Agriculture. Phone: (202)720-2791 E-mail: agsec@usda.gov • URL: http://www.usda.gov • The USDA home page has six sections: News and Information; What's New; About USDA; Agencies; Opportunities; Search and Help. Keyword searching is offered from the USDA home page and from various individual agency home pages. Agencies are the Economic Research Service, Agricultural Marketing Service, National Agricultural Statistics Service, National Agricultural Library, and about 12 others. Updating varies. Fees: Free.

PERIODICALS AND NEWSLETTERS

Onion Newsletter. National Onion Association. • Monthly. Free to members.

STATISTICS SOURCES

Agricultural Statistics. Available from U. S. Government Printing Office. • Annual. Produced by the National Agricultural Statistics Service, U. S. Department of Agriculture. Provides a wide variety of statistical data relating to agricultural production, supplies, consumption, prices/price-supports, foreign trade, costs, and returns, as well as farm labor, loans, income, and population. In many cases, historical data is shown annually for 10 years. In addition to farm data, includes detailed fishery statistics.

TRADE/PROFESSIONAL ASSOCIATIONS

National Onion Association. 822 Seventh St., No. 510, Greeley, CO 80631. Phone: (970)353-5895 Fax: (970)353-5897 E-mail: wmininger@onions-usa.org • URL: http://www.onions-usa.org.

ONLINE COMMERCE

See: ELECTRONIC COMMERCE

ONLINE INFORMATION SYSTEMS

See also: COMPUTER COMMUNICATIONS; INFORMATION INDUSTRY; INTERNET

GENERAL WORKS

Current Trends in Information: Research and Theory. Bill Katz and Robin Kinder, editors. The Haworth Press, Inc. • 1987. $49.95. (Reference Librarian Series, No. 18).

Data Smog: Surviving the Information Glut. David Shenk. HarperCollins Publishers. • 1997. $24.00. A critical view of both the electronic and print information industries. Emphasis is on information overload.

The Evolving Virtual Library: Practical and Philosophical Perspectives. Laverna M. Saunders, editor. Information Today, Inc. • 1999. $39.50. Second edition. Various authors cover trends in library and school use of the Internet, intranets, extranets, and electronic databases.

The Internet Initiative: Libraries Providing Internet Services and How They Plan, Pay, and Manage. Edward J. Valauskas and others. American Library Association. • 1995. $27.00. Provides 18 reports on Internet services in various kinds of libraries.

Managing Online Reference Services. Ethel Auster, editor. Neal-Schuman Publishers, Inc. • 1986. $45.00. Articles and bibliographies.

Moving Toward More Effective Public Internet Access: The 1998 National Survey of Public Library Outlet Internet Connectivity. Available from U. S. Government Printing Office. • 1999. $16.00. Issued by the National Commission on Libraries and Information Science.

Online Retrieval: A Dialogue of Theory and Practice. Geraldene Walker and Joseph Janes. Libraries Unlimited. • 1999. $55.00. Second edition. Edited by Carol Tenopir. Covers a wide variety of online information topics, with emphasis on bibliographic databases. (Database Searching Series.).

Secrets of the Super Searchers: The Accumulated Wisdom of 23 of the World's Top Online Searchers. Reva Basch. Information Today, Inc. • 1993. $39.95. Contains interviews with experienced online searchers, covering such topics as pre-search interviewing, search strategy, full-text considerations, search limiting, and client relations.

Silicon Snake Oil: Second Thoughts on the Information Highway. Clifford Stoll. Doubleday. • 1996. $14.00. The author discusses the extravagant claims being made for online networks and multimedia.

Super Searchers Do Business: The Online Secrets of Top Business Researchers. Mary E.Bates and Reva Basch. Information Today, Inc. • 1999. $24.95. Presents the results of interviews with "11 leading researchers who use the Internet and online services to find critical business information." (CyberAge Books.).

What Will Be: How the New World of Information Will Change Our Lives. Michael L. Dertouzos. HarperSan Francisco. • 1997. $25.00. A discussion of the "information market place" of the future, including telecommuting, virtual reality, and computer recognition of speech. The author is director of the MIT Laboratory for Computer Science.

ABSTRACTS AND INDEXES

Computer and Information Systems Abstracts Journal: An Abstract Journal Pertaining to the Theory, Design, Fabrication and Application of Computer and Information Systems. Cambridge Information Group. • Monthly. $1,045 per year.

Computer Literature Index: A Subject/Author Index to Computer and Data Processing Literature. Applied Computer Research, Inc. • Quarterly, with annual cumulation. $245.00 per year. Contains brief abstracts of book and periodical literature covering all phases of computing, including approximately 70 specific application areas.

Information Science Abstracts. American Society for Information Science. Information Today, Inc. • 11 times a year. $685.00 per year.

Library Literature and Information Science: An Index to Library and Information Science Publications. H. W. Wilson Co. • Bimonthly. Annual cumulation. Service basis. Formerly *Library Literature.*

LISA: Library and Information Science Abstracts. Bowker-Saur. • Monthly. $800.00 per year. Annual cumulation.

ALMANACS AND YEARBOOKS

Annual Review of Information Science and Technology. Martha E. Williams, editor. Information Today, Inc. • Annual. Members, $79.95; non-members, $99.95. Published on behalf of the American Society for Information Science (ASIS). Covers trends in planning, basic techniques, applications, and the information profession in general.

Business-Professional Online Services: Review, Trends, and Forecast. SIMBA Information, Inc. • Annual. $1,295.00 Provides a review of current conditions in the online information industry. Profiles of major database producers and online services are included. Formerly*Online Services: Review, Trends and Forecast.*

BIBLIOGRAPHIES

Computer Book Review. • Quarterly. $30.00 per year. Includes annual index. Reviews new computer books. Back issues available.

CD-ROM DATABASES

Computer Select. The Gale Group. • Monthly. $1,250.00 per year. Provides one year of full-text on CD-ROM for 120 leading computer-related publications. Also includes 70,000 product specifications and brief profiles of 13,000 computer product vendors and manufacturers.

Information Science Abstracts. Information Today, Inc. • Quarterly. $1,095.00 per year. Presents CD-ROM abstracts of worldwide information science and library science literature from 1966 to date.

LISA Plus: Library and Information Science Abstracts. Bowker-Saur, Reed Reference Publishing. • Quarterly. $1,450.00 per year. Provides CD-ROM abstracting and indexing of the world's library and information science literature. Covers a wide variety of topics.

WILSONDISC: Library Literature and Information Science Index. H. W. Wilson Co. • Quarterly. Including unlimited access to the online version of *Library Literature*. Provides CD-ROM indexing of about 300 periodicals, covering a wide range of topics having to do with libraries, library management, and the information industry.

World Database of Business Information Sources on CD-ROM. The Gale Group. • Annual. Produced by Euromonitor. Presents Euromonitor's entire information source database on CD-ROM. Contains a worldwide total of about 35,000 publications, organizations, libraries, trade fairs, and online databases.

DIRECTORIES

ASIS Handbook and Directory. American Society for Information Science. • Annual. Members, $25.00; non-members, $100.00.

Books and Periodicals Online: The Guide to Business and Legal Information on Databases and CD-ROM's. Nuchine Nobari, editor. Library Technology Alliance, Inc. • Annual. $365.00 per year. 97,000 periodicals available as part of online and CD-ROM databases; international coverage.

Data Sources: The Comprehensive Guide to the Data Processing Industry Hardware, Data Communications Products, Software, Company Profiles. The Gale Group. • Semiannual. $495.00 per year. Two volumes. Describes hardware and software for all computer operating sysems, including prices and technical details. Lists about 75,000 products from 14,000 suppliers. Industry-specific software applications are described.

Dial Up! Gale's Bulletin Board Locator. The Gale Group. • 1996. $49.00. Contains access and other information for 10,000 computer bulletin boards in the U. S. Arranged geographically, with indexes to bulletin board names, organizations, and topics.

Fulltext Sources Online. Information Today, Inc. • Semiannual. $199.00 per year; $119.50 per issue. Lists more than 8,000 journals, newspapers, magazines, newsletters, and newswires found online in fulltext through DIALOG, LEXIS-NEXIS, Dow Jones, Westlaw, etc. Includes journals that have free Internet archives. (Formerly published by BiblioData.).

Gale Directory of Databases. The Gale Group. • 2001. $400.00. Two volumes. Volume 1, $270.00; volume 2, $180.00. *Volume 1: Online Databases* and *Volume 2: CD-ROM, Diskette, Magnetic Tape, Handheld, and Batch Access Database Products.*

Information Industry Directory. The Gale Group. • 2000. $635.00. 22nd edition. Two volumes. Lists nearly 4,600 producers and vendors of electronic information and related services. Subject, geographic, and master indexes are provided.

Interactive Advertising Source. SRDS. • Quarterly. $561.00 per year. Provides descriptive profiles, rates, audience, personnel, etc., for producers of various forms of interactive or multimedia advertising: online/Internet, CD-ROM, interactive TV, interactive cable, interactive telephone, interactive kiosk, and others. Includes online supplement *SRDS' URlink.*

The Internet Compendium: Guide to Resources by Subject: Subject Guides to Health and Science Resources. Joseph Jones and others, editors. Neal-Schuman Publishers, Inc. • 1995. $82.50. Editors are with the University of Michigan Internet Clearinghouse. Provides direct location access to "thousands" of Internet addresses, in a detailed subject arrangement, with critical analysis of content. Contains information databases, text archives, library catalogs, bulletin boards, newsletters, forums, etc. Includes topics in medicine, agriculture, biology, chemistry, mathematics, physics, engineering, computers, and science in general.

The Internet Compendium: Guide to Resources by Subject: Subject Guides to Social Sciences, Business, and Law Resources. Joseph James and others, editors. Neal-Schuman Publishers, Inc. • 1995. $82.50. Editors are with the University of Michigan Internet Clearinghouse. Provides direct location access to "thousands" of Internet addresses, in a detailed subject arrangement, with critical analysis of content. Contains information databases, text archives, library catalogs, bulletin boards, newsletters, forums, etc. Includes topics in economics, finance, taxation, history, population, civil rights law, law careers, women's studies, and so forth.

The Internet Compendium: Guide to Resources by Subject: Subject Guides to the Humanities. Louis Rosenfeld and others, editors. Neal-Schuman Publishers, Inc. • 1995. $82.50. Editors are with the University of Michigan Internet Clearinghouse. Provides direct location access to "thousands" of Internet addresses, in a detailed subject arrangement, with critical analysis of content. Contains information databases, text archives, library catalogs, bulletin boards, newsletters, forums, etc. Includes topics in literature, art, religion, philosophy, music, education, library science, games, magic, and the humanities in general.

Internet-Plus Directory of Express Library Services: Research and Document Delivery for Hire. American Library Association. • 1997. $49.50. Covers fee-based services of various U. S., Canadian, and international libraries. Paid services include online searches, faxed documents, and specialized professional research. Price ranges are quoted. (A joint production of FISCAL, the ALA/ ACRL Discussion Group of Fee-Based Information Service Centers in Academic Libraries, and FYI, the Professional Research and Rapid Information Delivery Service of the County of Los Angeles Public Library.) Formerly *FISCAL Directory of Fee-Based Information Services in Libraries.*

Internet Tools of the Profession: A Guide for Information Professionals. Hope N. Tillman, editor. Special Libraries Association. • 1997. $49.00. Second edition. Consists of 14 sections by various authors or compilers. After two introductory articles on searching the Internet, there are 12 annotated lists of useful Web sites, covering the SLA, business and finance, chemistry, education, food and agriculture, information technology, insurance and employee benefits, law, library management, metals and materials, pharmaceuticals, and telecommunications. An index is provided.

Library Journal: Reference [year]: Print, CD-ROM, Online. Cahners Business Information. • Annual. Issued in November as supplement to *Library Journal.* Lists new and updated reference material, including general and trade print titles, directories, annuals, CD-ROM titles, and online sources. Includes material from more than 150 publishers, arranged by company name, with an index by subject. Addresses include e-mail and World Wide Web information, where available.

The Online 100: Online Magazine's Field Guide to the 100 Most Important Online Databases. Mick O'Leary. Information Today, Inc. • 1996. $22.95. Provides detailed descriptions of 100 "important and useful" online databases in various subject areas.

OPAC Directory: A Guide to Internet-Accessible Online Public Access Catalogs. Information Today, Inc. • Annual. $70.00. Provides the Internet addresses of more than 1,400 online public access catalogs, U. S. and foreign. Includes information on library size, subject strengths, and search characteristics.

Plunkett's Entertainment and Media Industry Almanac. Available from Plunkett Research, Ltd. • Biennial. $149.99. Provides profiles of leading firms in online information, films, radio, television, cable, multimedia, magazines, and book publishing. Includes World Wide Web sites, where available, plus information on careers and industry trends.

World Directory of Marketing Information Sources. Available from The Gale Group. • 2001. $590.00. Third edition. Published by Euromonitor. Provides details on more than 6,000 sources of marketing information, including publications, libraries, associations, market research companies, online databases, and governmental organizations. Coverage is worldwide.

ENCYCLOPEDIAS AND DICTIONARIES

Communicating with Legal Databases: Terms and Abbreviations for the Legal Researcher. Anne L. McDonald. Neal-Schuman Publishers, Inc. • 1987. $82.50.

CyberDictionary: Your Guide to the Wired World. Knowledge Exchange LLC. • 1996. $17.95. Includes many illustrations.

Cyberspace Lexicon: An Illustrated Dictionary of Terms from Multimedia to Virtual Reality. Bob Cotton and Richard Oliver. Phaidon Press, Inc. • 1994. $29.95. Defines more than 800 terms, with manyillustrations. Includes a bibliography.

Encyclopedia of Communication and Information. Available from The Gale Group. • 2001. $325.00. Three volumes. Published by Macmillan Reference USA.

Encyclopedia of Emerging Industries. The Gale Group. • 2000. $295.00. Fourth edition. Provides detailed information on 90 "newly flourishing" industries. Includes historical background, organizational structure, significant individuals, current conditions, major companies, work force, technology trends, research developments, and other industry facts.

World Encyclopedia of Library and Information Services. Robert Wedgeworth, editor. American Library Association. • 1993. $200.00. Third edition. Contains about 340 articles from various contributors.

HANDBOOKS AND MANUALS

Best Bet Internet: Reference and Research When You Don't Have Time to Mess Around. Shirley D. Kennedy. American Library Association. • 1997. $35.00. Provides advice for librarians and others on the effective use of World Wide Web information sources.

Beyond Book Indexing: How to Get Started in Web Indexing, Embedded Indexing, and Other Computer-Based Media. Diane Brenner and Marilyn Rowland, editors. Information Today, Inc. • 2000. $31.25. Published for the American Society of Indexers. Contains 12 chapters written by professional indexers. Part one discusses making an index by marking items in an electronic document (embedded indexing); part two is on indexing to make Web pages more accessible; part three covers CD-ROM and multimedia indexing; part four provides career and promotional advice for professionals in the field. Includes an index by Janet Perlman and a glossary.

Compuserve Internet Tour Guide. Richard Wagner. Ventana Communications Group, Inc. • 1996. $34.95. A detailed guide to accessing various features of the Internet by way of the Compuserve online service.

The Cybrarian's Manual. Pat Ensor, editor. American Library Association. • 1996. $35.00. Provides information for librarians concerning the Internet, expert systems, computer networks, client/server architecture, Web pages, multimedia, information industry careers, and other "cyberspace" topics.

Electronic Styles: A Handbook for Citing Electronic Information. Xia Li and Nancy Crane. Information Today, Inc. • 1996. $19.99. Second edition. Covers the citing of text-based information, electronic journals, Web sites, CD-ROM items, multimedia products, and online documents.

The Essential Guide to Bulletin Board Systems. Patrick R. Dewey. Information Today, Inc. • 1998. $39.50. Provides details on the setup and operation of online bulletin board systems. Covers both hardware and software.

Find It Online: The Complete Guide to Online Research. Alan M. Schlein and others. National Book Network. • 1998. $19.95. Presents the general principles of online searching for information about people, phone numbers, public records, news, business, investments, etc. Covers both free and fee-based sources. (BRB Publications.).

Finding Statistics Online: How to Locate the Elusive Numbers You Need. Paula Berinstein. Information Today, Inc. • 1998. $29.95. Provides advice on efficient searching when looking for statistical data on the World Wide Web or from commercial online services and database producers. (CyberAge Books.).

How to Find Market Research Online. Robert I. Berkman. MarketResearch.com. • Looseleaf. $182.50, including updates for one year. Analyzes and compares the online products of 80 market research publishers. Describes popular Internet search engines and provides information on useful World Wide Web sites.

Improving Online Public Access Catalogs. Martha M. Yee and Sara S. Layne. American Library Association. • 1998. $48.00. A practical guide to developing user-friendly online catalogs (OPACs).

International Business Information on the Web: Searcher Magazine's Guide to Sites and Strategies for Global Business Research. Sheri R. Lanza and Barbara Quint. Information Today, Inc. • 2001. $29.95. (CyberAge Books.).

Managing Information Systems and Technologies; A Basic Guide for Design, Selection, Evaluation and Use. Edwin M. Cortez and Edward J. Kazlauskas. Neal-Schuman Publishers, Inc. • 1985. $45.00.

Managing Public-Access Computers: A How-To-Do-It Manual for Librarians. Donald A. Barclay. Neal-Schuman Publishers, Inc. • 2000. $59.95. Part one covers hardware, software, and other components. Part two discusses computers users. Part three is about systems management, library policy, and legal issues.

NetResearch: Finding Information Online. Daniel J. Barrett. Thomson Learning. • 1997. $24.95. A guide to "power searching" on the Internet, with emphasis on the intricacies of search engines.

The Official America Online Internet Guide. David Peal. Ventana Communications Group, Inc. • 1999. $24.95. Provides a detailed explanation of the various features of versio of America Online, including electronic mail procedures and "Using the Internet.".

Online Deskbook: Online Magazine's Essential Desk Reference for Online and Internet Searchers. Mary E. Bates. Information Today, Inc. • 1996. $29.95. Covers the World Wide Web, as well as America Online, CompuServe, Dialog, Lexis-Nexis, and all other major online services. (Pemberton Press Books.).

INTERNET DATABASES

GaleNet: Your Information Community. The Gale Group. Phone: 800-877-GALE or (248)699-GALE Fax: 800-414-5043 or (248)699-8069 E-mail: galenet@gale.com • URL: http://www.galenet.com • Web site provides a wide variety of full-text information from Gale databases, Taft, and other sources. Covers associations, biography, business directories, education, the information industry, literature, publishing, and science. Fee-based subscriptions are available for individual databases (free demonstration). Includes Boolean search features and the BRS/Search user interface.

InfoTech Trends. Data Analysis Group. Phone: (707)894-9100 Fax: (707)486-5618 E-mail: support@infotechtrends.com • URL: http://www.infotechtrends.com • Web site provides both free and fee-based market research data on the information technology industry, including computers, peripherals, telecommunications, the Internet, software, CD-ROM/DVD, e-commerce, and workstations. Fees: Free for current (most recent year) data; more extensive information has various fee structures. Formerly *Computer Industry Forecasts.*

Interactive Week: The Internet's Newspaper. Ziff Davis Media, Inc. 28 E. 28th St., New York, NY 10016. Phone: (212)503-3500 Fax: (212)503-5680 E-mail: iweekinfo@zd.com • URL: http://www.zd.com • Weekly. $99.00 per year. Covers news and trends relating to Internet commerce, computer communications, and telecommunications.

Internet Business Intelligence: How to Build a Big Company System on a Small Company Budget. David Vine. Information Today, Inc. 143 Old Marlton Pike, Medford, NJ 08055-8750. Phone: 800-300-9868 or (609)654-6266 Fax: (609)654-4309 E-mail: custserv@infotoday.com • URL: http://www.infotoday.com • 2000. $29.95. Covers the obtaining of valuable business intelligence data through use of the Internet.

Internet Tools of the Profession. Special Libraries Association. Phone: (202)234-4700 Fax: (202)265-9317 E-mail: hope@tiac.net • URL: http://www.sla.org/pubs/itotp • Web site is designed to update the printed *Internet Tools of the Profession.* Provides links to a wide range of useful databases in business, finance, industry, information technology, insurance, law, library management, telecommunications, and other subject areas. Fees: Free.

Search Engine Watch: You Want Answers?. Internet.com Corp. Phone: (212)547-7900 Fax: (212)953-1733 • URL: http://www.searchenginewatch.com • Web site offers information on various aspects of search engines, including new developments, indexing systems, technology, ratings and reviews of major operators, specialty services, tutorials, news, history, "Search Engine EKGs," "Facts and Fun," etc. Online searching is provided. Fees: Free. Formerly *A Webmaster's Guide to Search Engines.*

Wired News. Wired Digital, Inc. Phone: (415)276-8400 Fax: (415)276-8499 E-mail: newsfeedback@wired.com • URL: http://www.wired.com • Provides summaries and full-text of "Top Stories" relating to the Internet, computers, multimedia, telecommunications, and the electronic information industry in general. These news stories are placed in the broad categories of Politics, Business, Culture, and Technology. Affiliated with *Wired* magazine. Fees: Free.

ONLINE DATABASES

Computer Database. The Gale Group. • Provides online citations with abstracts to material appearing in about 150 trade journals and newsletters in the subject areas of computers, telecommunications, and electronics. Time period is 1983 to date, with weekly updates. Inquire as to online cost and availability.

Gale Directory of Databases [online]. The Gale Group. • Presents the online version of the printed *Gale Directory of Databases, Volume 1: Online Databases* and *Gale Directory of Databases, Volume 2: CD-ROM, Diskette, Magnetic Tape, Handheld, and Batch Access Database Products.* Semiannual updates. Inquire as to online cost and availability.

Information Science Abstracts [online]. Information Today, Inc. • Provides indexing and abstracting of the international literature of information science, including library science, from 1966 to date. Monthly updates. Inquire as to online cost and availability.

Law of the Super Searchers: The Online Secrets of Top Legal Researchers. T. R. Halvorson and Reva Basch. Information Today, Inc. • 1999. $24.95. Eight law researchers explain how to find useful legal information online. (CyberAge Books.).

Library Literature Online. H. W. Wilson Co. • Contains online indexing of a wide variety of library and information science literature from 1984 to date, with updating quarterly. Inquire as to online cost and availability.

LISA Online: Library and Information Science Abstracts. Bowker-Saur, Reed Reference Publishing. • Provides abstracting and indexing of the world's library and information science literature from 1969 to the present. Covers a wide variety of topics in over 550 journals from 60 countries, with biweekly updates. Inquire as to online cost and availability.

Mastering Online Investing: How to Use the Internet to Become a More Successful Investor. Michael C. Thomsett. Dearborn Financial Publishing. • 2001. $19.95. Emphasis is on the Internet as an information source for intelligent investing, avoiding "speculation and fads.".

Super Searchers Cover the World: The Online Secrets of International Business Researchers. Mary E. Bates and Reva Basch. Information Today, Inc. • 2001. $24.95. Presents interviews with 15 experts in the area of online searching for international business information. (CyberAge Books.).

Super Searchers in the News: The Online Secrets of Journalists and News Researchers. Paula J. Hane and Reva Basch. Information Today, Inc. • 2000. $24.95. Contains online searching advice from 10 professional news researchers and fact checkers. (CyberAge Books.).

Super Searchers on Health and Medicine: The Online Secrets of Top Health and Medical Researchers. Susan M. Detwiler and Reva Basch. Information Today, Inc. • 2000. $24.95. Provides the results of interviews with 10 experts in online searching for medical research data and healthcare information. Discusses both traditional sources and Web sites. (CyberAge Books.).

Super Searchers on Mergers & Acquisitions: The Online Secrets of Top Corporate Researchers and M & A Pros. Jan Tudor and Reva Basch. Information Today, Inc. • 2001. $24.95. Presents the results of interviews with 13 "top M & A information pros." Covers the finding, evaluating, and delivering of relevant data on companies and industries. (CyberAge Books.).

Super Searchers on Wall Street: Top Investment Professionals Share Their Online Research Secrets. Amelia Kassel and Reva Basch. Information Today, Inc. • 2000. $24.95. Gives the results of interviews with "10 leading financial industry research experts." Explains how online information is used by stock brokers, investment bankers, and individual investors. Includes relevant Web sites and other sources. (CyberAge Books.).

PERIODICALS AND NEWSLETTERS

American Society for Information Science Journal. John Wiley and Sons, Inc. • 14 times a year. $1,259.00 per year.

Aslib Proceedings. Available from Information Today, Inc. • Ten times a year. Free to Members; non-members, $252.00 per year. Published in London by Aslib Covers a wide variety of information industry and library management topics.

Digital Publishing Technologies: How to Implement New Media Publishing. Information Today, Inc. • Monthly. $196.00 per year. Covers online and CD-ROM publishing, including industry news, new applications, new products, electronic publishing technology, and descriptions of completed publishing projects.

EContent. Online, Inc. • Bimonthly. $55.00 per year. Directed at professional online information searchers. Formerly *Database*.

Electronic Information Report: Empowering Industry Decision Makers Since 1979. SIMBA Information. • 46 times a year. $549.00 per year. Newsletter. Provides business and financial news and trends for online services, electronic publishing, storage media, multimedia, and voice services. Includes information on relevant IPOs (initial public offerings) and mergers. Formerly *Electronic Information Week*.

The Electronic Library. Information Today, Inc. • Bimonthly. $269.00 per year.

InfoAlert: Your Expert Guide to Online Business Information. Economics Press, Inc. • Monthly. $129.00 per year. Newsletter. Provides information on recommended World Wide Web sites in various business, marketing, industrial, and financial areas.

Information Hotline. Science Associates International, Inc. • 10 times a year. Individuals and corporations, $150.00 per year; non-profit organizations, $135.00 per year. Newsletter.

Information Outlook: The Monthly Magazine of the Special Libraries Association. Special Libraries Association. • Monthly. $65.00 per year. Topics include information technology, the Internet, copyright, research techniques, library management, and professional development. Replaces *Special Libraries* and *SpeciaList*.

Information Processing and Management: An International Journal. Elsevier Science. • Bimonthly. $981.00 per year. Text in English, French, German and Italian.

Information Retrieval and Library Automation. Lomond Publications, Inc. • Monthly. $75.00 per year. Summarizes research events and literature worldwide.

Information Sciences; An International Journal. Elsevier Science. • 36 times a year. $2,917.00 per year. Three sections, A: Informatics and Computer Science, B: Intelligent Systems, C: Applications.

Information Systems; Data Bases: Their Creation, Management and Utilization. Elsevier Science. • Eight times a year. $1,194.00 per year.

Information Today: The Newspaper for Users and Producers of Electronic Information Services. Information Today, Inc. • 11 times a year. $57.95 per year.

Innovative Publisher: Publishing Strategies for New Markets. Emmelle Publishing Co., Inc. • Biweekly. $69.00 per year. Provides articles and news on electronic publishing (CD-ROM or online) and desktop publishing.

Internet Reference Services Quarterly: A Journal of Innovative Information Practice, Technologies, and Resources. Haworth Press, Inc. • Quarterly. Individuals, $36.00 per year; libraries and other institutions, $48.00 per year. Covers both theoretical research and practical applications.

Journal of Information Science: Principles and Practice. Institute of Information Scientists. Elsivier Science. • Bimonthly. $310.00 per year.

Journal of Internet Cataloging: The International Quarterly of Digital Organization, Classification, and Access. Haworth Press, Inc. • Quarterly. Individuals, $40.00 per year; libraries and other institutions, $85.00 per year.

Link-Up: The Newsmagazine for Users of Online Services, CD-Rom, and the Internet. Information Today, Inc. • Bimonthly. $29.95 per year.

Multimedia Schools: A Practical Journal of Multimedia, CD-Rom, Online and Internet in K-12. Information Today, Inc. • Five times a year. $39.95 per year. Edited for school librarians, media center directors, computer coordinators, and others concerned with educational multimedia. Coverage includes the use of CD-ROM sources, the Internet, online services, and library technology.

Online and CD Notes. Available from Information Today, Inc. • 10 times a year. Members $80.00 per year; non-members, $140.00 per year. Published in London by Aslib: The Association for Information Management. Contains news and reviews of the online information industry. Formerly *Online and CD-ROM Notes*.

Online Information Review: The International Journal of Digital Information Research and Use. Information Today, Inc. • Bimonthly. $154.00 per year. Provides peer-reviewed research papers and online information industry news. Formerly *Online and CD-ROM Review*.

Online Investor: Personal Investing for the Digital Age. Stock Trends, Inc. • Monthly. $24.95 per year. Provides advice and Web site reviews for online traders.

Online Libraries and Microcomputers. Information Intelligence, Inc. • Monthly. Individuals $43.75 per year; libraries. $62.50 per year. Newsletter. Covers library automation and electronic information (online, CD-ROM). Reviews or describes new computer hardware and software for library use.

Online Newsletter. Information Intelligence, Inc. • 10 times a year. Individuals, $43.75 per year; libraries, $62.50 per year; students, $25.00 per year. Covers the online and CD-ROM information industries, including news of mergers, acquisitions, personnel, meetings, new products, and new technology.

Online: The Leading Magazine for Information Professionals. Online, Inc. • Bimonthly. $110.00 per year. General coverage of the online information industry.

Physicians & Computers. Moorhead Publications Inc. • Monthly. $40.00 per year. Includes material on computer diagnostics, online research, medical and non-medical software, computer equipment, and practice management.

Searcher: The Magazine for Database Professionals. Information Today, Inc. • 10 times per year. $64.95 per year. Covers a wide range of topics relating to online and CD-ROM database searching.

Silicon Alley Reporter. Rising Tide Studios. • Monthly. $29.95 per year. Covers the latest trends in e-commerce, multimedia, and the Internet.

Upgrade. Software and Information Industry Association. • Monthly. $75.00 per year. Covers news and trends relating to the software, information, and Internet industries. Formerly *SPA News* from Software Publisers Association.

WebFinance. Securities Data Publishing. • Semimonthly. $995.00 per year. Newsletter (also available online at www.webfinance.net). Covers the Internet-based provision of online financial services by banks, online brokers, mutual funds, and insurance companies. Provides news stories, analysis, and descriptions of useful resources. (Securities Data Publishing is a unit of Thomson Financial.).

Wired. Wired Ventures Ltd. • Monthly. $24.00 per year. Edited for creators and managers in various areas of electronic information and entertainment, including multimedia, the Internet, and video. Often considered to be the primary publication of the "digital generation.".

RESEARCH CENTERS AND INSTITUTES

Bibliographical Center for Research, Inc., Rocky Mountain Region. 14394 E. Evans Ave., Aurora, CO 80014-1478. Phone: 800-397-1552 or (303)751-6277 Fax: (303)751-9787 E-mail: admin@bec.org • URL: http://www.ber.org • Fields of research include information retrieval systems, Internet technology, CD-ROM technology, document delivery, and library automation.

Computer and Information Science Research Center. Ohio State University. 2015 Neil Ave., Columbus, OH 43210. Phone: (614)292-5813 Fax: (614)292-2911 E-mail: tfletch@cis.ohio-state.edu • URL: http://www.cis.ohio.state.edu.

Information Sciences Institute. University of Southern California, 4676 Admiralty Way, Suite 1001, Marina del Rey, CA 90292. Phone: (310)822-1511 Fax: (310)823-6714 • URL: http://www.isi.edu • Research fields include online information and computer science, with emphasis on the World Wide Web.

Laboratory for Computer Science. Massachusetts Institute of Technology, 545 Technology Square, Bldg. NE43, Cambridge, MA 02139. Phone: (617)253-5851 Fax: (617)258-8682 E-mail: mld@hq.lcs.mit.edu • URL: http://www.lcs.mit.edu/ • Research is in four areas: Intelligent Systems; Parallel Systems; Systems, Languages, and Networks; and Theory. Emphasis is on the application of online computing.

Management Information Systems Research Center. University of Minnesota. Carlson School of Management, 321 19th Ave., S., Minneapolis, MN

55455-0430. Phone: (612)624-6565 Fax: (612)624-2056 • URL: http://www.misrc.umn.edu.

NERAC, Inc. One Technology Dr., Tolland, CT 06084. Phone: (860)872-7000 Fax: (860)875-1749 E-mail: duwilde@nerac.com • URL: http://www.nerac.com.

Super Searchers Go to the Source: The Interviewing and Hands-On Information Strategies of Top Primary Researchers - Online, On the Phone, and In Person. Risa Sacks and Reva Basch. Information Today, Inc. 143 Old Marlton Pike, Medford, NJ 08055-8750. Phone: 800-300-9868 or (609)654-6266 Fax: (609)654-4309 E-mail: custserv@infotoday.com • URL: http://www.infotoday.com • 2001. $24.95. Explains how information-search experts use various print, electronic, and live sources for competitive intelligence and other purposes. (CyberAge Books.).

STATISTICS SOURCES

By the Numbers: Electronic and Online Publishing. The Gale Group. • 1997. $385.00. Four volumes. $99.00 per volume. Covers "high-interest" industries: 1. *By the Numbers: Electronic and Online Publishing*; 2. *By the Numbers: Emerging Industries*; 3. *By the Numbers: Nonprofits*; 4. *By the Numbers: Publishing*. Each volume provides about 600 tabulations of industry data on revenues, market share, employment, trends, financial ratios, profits, salaries, and so forth. Citations to data sources are included.

Inter-NOT: Online & Internet Statistics Reality Check. Bruce Kushnick. New Networks Institute. • Annual. $495.00. Compares, analyzes, and criticizes statistics issued by Nielsen Media, Forrester Research, FIND/SVP, Yankelovich Partners and many others relating to online and Internet activities. For example, estimates of the number of Internet users have ranged from about 40 million down to six million. Topics include "Adjusting for the Puffery" and "The Most Plausible Statistics.".

OECD Information Technology Outlook 2000: ICTs, E-Commerce and the Information Economy. Organization for Economic Cooperation and Development. • 2000. $72.00. Provides data on information and communications technology (ICT) and electronic commerce in 11 OECD nations (includes U. S.). Coverage includes network infrastructure, electronic payment systems, financial transaction technologies, intelligent agents, global navigation systems, and portable flat panel display technologies.

Statistical Handbook on Technology. Paula Berinstein, editor. Oryx Press. • 1999. $65.00. Provides statistical data on such items as the Internet, online services, computer technology, recycling, patents, prescription drug sales, telecommunications, and aerospace. Includes charts, tables, and graphs. Edited for the general reader. (Statistical Handbook Series).

TRADE/PROFESSIONAL ASSOCIATIONS

American Society for Information Science. 8720 Georgia Ave., Suite 501, Silver Spring, MD 20910-3602. Phone: (301)495-0900 Fax: (301)495-0810 E-mail: asis@asis.org • URL: http://www.asis.org • Members are information managers, scientists, librarians, and others who are interested in the storage, retrieval, and use of information.

Association of Information and Dissemination Centers. P.O. Box 8105, Athens, GA 30603. Phone: (706)542-6820 E-mail: secretariat@asidic.org • URL: http://www.asidic.org.

Electronic Frontier Foundation. 1550 Bryant St., Suite 725, San Francisco, CA 94103. Phone: (415)436-9333 Fax: (415)436-9993 E-mail: info@eff.org • URL: http://www.eff.org • Members are individuals with an interest in computer-based communications. Promotes electronic communication civil liberties and First Amendment rights.

International Federation for Information and Documentation. Postbos 90402, NL-2509 LK The Hague, Netherlands. Phone: 31 70 3140671 Fax: 31 70 3140677 E-mail: fid@python.konbib.nl.

International Federation for Information Processing. IFIP Secretariat, Hofstrasse 3, CH-1204 43 Laxenburg A-2361, Switzerland. Phone: 43 2336 73616 Fax: 43 2336 736169 E-mail: ifip@ifip.or.at • URL: http://www.ifip.or.at.

Internet Alliance. P.O. Box 65782, Washington, DC 20035-5782. Phone: (202)955-8091 Fax: (202)955-8081 E-mail: ia@internetalliance.org • URL: http://www.internetalliance.org • Members are companies associated with the online and Internet industry. Promotes the Internet as "the global mass market medium of the 21st century." Concerned with government regulation, public policy, industry advocacy, consumer education, and media relations. Formerly Interactive Services Association.

Library and Information Technology Association. 50 E. Huron St., Chicago, IL 60611. Phone: 800-545-2433 or (312)280-4270 Fax: (312)280-3257 E-mail: lita@ala.org • URL: http://www.lita.org • The Library and Information Technology Association is a Division of the American Library Association.

Reference and User Services Association of the American Library Association: Machine Assisted Reference Section. c/o American Library Association, 50 E. Huron. St., Chicago, IL 60611. Phone: 800-545-2433 or (312)280-4398 Fax: (312)944-8085 E-mail: rusa@ala.org • URL: http://www.ala8.org/rusa/.

Software and Information Industry Association. 1730 M St., N. W., Suite 700, Washington, DC 20036-4510. Phone: (202)452-1600 Fax: (202)223-8756 • URL: http://www.siia.net • A trade association for the software and digital content industry. Divisions are Content, Education, Enterprise, Financial Information Services, Global, and Internet. Includes an Online Content Committee. Formerly Software Publishers Association.

Special Interest Group on Hypertext, Hypermedia, and Web. Association for Computing Machinery, 1515 Broadway, New York, NY 10036. Phone: (212)869-7440 Fax: (212)302-5826 E-mail: sigs@acm.org • URL: http://www.acm.org/sigweb • Concerned with the design, use, and evaluation of hypertext and hypermedia systems. Provides a multi-disciplinary forum for the promotion, dissemination, and exchange of ideas relating to research technologies and applications. Publishes the *SIGWEB Newsletter* three times a year.

Special Interest Group on Information Retrieval. c/o Association for Computing Machinery, 1515 Broadway, New York, NY 10036. Phone: (212)869-7440 Fax: (212)302-5826 E-mail: sigs@acm.org • URL: http://www.acm.org/sigir/.

Special Libraries Association; Information Technology Division. 1700 18th St., N.W., Washington, DC 20009-2514. Phone: (202)234-4700 Fax: (202)265-9317 E-mail: sla@sla.org • URL: http://www.sla.org/.

OTHER SOURCES

Consumer Online Services Report. Jupiter Media Metrix. • Annual. $1,895.00. Market research report. Provides analysis of trends in the online information industry, with projections of growth in future years (five-year forecasts). Contains profiles of electronic media companies.

Home Banking Report. Jupiter Media Metrix. • Annual. $695.00. Market research report. Covers banking from home by phone or online, with projections of growth in future years.

Infogate. Infogate, Inc. • Web site provides current news and information on seven "channels": News, Fun, Sports, Info, Finance, Shop, and Travel. Among the content partners are Business Wire, CBS MarketWatch, CNN, Morningstar, Standard & Poor's, and Thomson Investors Network. Fees: Free, but downloading of Infogate software is required (includes personalized news feature). Updating is continuous. Formerly Pointcast Network.

Information, Finance, and Services USA. The Gale Group. • 2001. $240.00. Replaces *Service Industries USA* and *Finance, Insurance, and Real Estate USA*. Presents statistics and projections relating to economic activity in a wide variety of non-manufacturing areas.

Inter-NOT: The Terrible Twos-Online Industry's Learning Curve. Bruce Kushnick. New Networks Institute. • 1996. $495.00. Second edition. A market research report discussing the growing pains of the online industry, especially with regard to the Internet. The importance of market segmentation and customer service is emphasized.

The Invisible Web: Uncovering Information Sources Search Engines Can't See. Chris Sherman and Gary Price. Information Today, Inc. • 2001. $29.95. A guide to Web sites from universities, libraries, associations, government agencies, and other sources that are inadequately covered by conventional search engines (see also http://www.invisible-web.net). (CyberAge Books.).

Major Information Technology Companies of the World. Available from The Gale Group. • 2001. $885.00. Third edition. Published by Graham & Whiteside. Contains profiles of more than 2,600 leading information technology companies in various countries.

Major Telecommunications Companies of the World. Available from The Gale Group. • 2001. $855.00. Fourth edition. Published by Graham & Whiteside. Contains detailed information and trade names for more than 4,000 important telecommunications companies in various countries.

net.people: The Personalities and Passions Behind the Web Sites. Eric C. Steinert and Thomas E. Bleier. Information Today, Inc. • 2000. $19.95. Presents the personal stories of 36 Web "entrepreneurs and visionaries." (CyberAge Books.).

Online Advertising Report. Jupiter Media Metrix. • Annual. $750.00. Market research report. Provides five-year forecasts of Internet advertising and subscription revenue. Contains analysis of online advertising trends and practices, with company profiles.

The Quintessential Searcher: The Wit and Wisdom of Barbara Quint. Marylaine Block, editor. Information Today, Inc. • 2001. $19.95. Presents the sayings of Barbara Quint, editor of *Searcher* magazine, who is often critical of the online information industry. (CyberAge Books.).

Towards Electronic Journals: Realities for Scientists, Librarians, and Publishers. Carol Tenopir and Donald W. King. Special Libraries Association. • 2000. $59.00. Discusses journals in electronic form vs. traditional (paper) scholarly journals, including the impact of subscription prices.

World Online Markets. Jupiter Media Metrix. • Annual. $1,895.00. Market research report. Provides broad coverage of worldwide Internet and online information business activities, including country-by-country data. Includes company profiles and five-year forecasts or trend projections.

OPERATING RATIOS

See: FINANCIAL RATIOS

OPERATIONS MANAGEMENT

GENERAL WORKS

Principles of Operation Management. Barry Render. Thomson Learning. • 2000. $35.00. Sixth edition. (SWC-Management Series).

ENCYCLOPEDIAS AND DICTIONARIES

Blackwell Encyclopedic Dictionary of Operations Management. Nigel Slack, editor. Blackwell Publishers. • 1997. $105.95. The editor is associated with the University of Warwick, England. Contains definitions of key terms combined with longer articles written by various U. S. and foreign business educators. Includes bibliographies and index. (Blackwell Encyclopedia of Management Series.).

HANDBOOKS AND MANUALS

Banking and Finance on the Internet. Mary J. Cronin, editor. John Wiley and Sons, Inc. • 1997. $45.00. Contains articles on Internet services, written by bankers, money mangers, investment analysts, and stockbrokers. Emphasis is on operations management. (Communications Series).

Production and Operations Management: An Applied Modern Approach. Joseph S. Martinich. John Wiley and Sons, Inc. • 1996. $105.95. Covers capacity planning, facility location, process design, inventory planning, personnel scheduling, etc.

PERIODICALS AND NEWSLETTERS

Fee Income Growth Strategies. Siefer Consultants, Inc. • Monthly. $329.00 per year. Newsletter. Covers operations management for banks and other financial institutions. Formerly *Noninterest Income Growth Strategies.*

Operations Management. Institutional Investor. • Weekly. $2,105.00 per year. Newsletter. Edited for managers of securities clearance and settlement at financial institutions. Covers new products, technology, legalities, management practices, and other topics related to securities processing.

Production and Operations Management. Production and Operations Management Society. • Quarterly. Individuals, $60.00 per year; institutions, $90.00 per year.

RESEARCH CENTERS AND INSTITUTES

Operations Management Education and Research Foundation. P.O. Box 661, Rockford, MI 49341. Phone: (616)732-5543 • Research focuses on office operations, environment, and physical structures, including furniture fixtures.

TRADE/PROFESSIONAL ASSOCIATIONS

Association for Data Center, Networking and Enterprise Systems. 742 E. Chapman Ave., Orange, CA 92666. Phone: (714)997-7966 Fax: (714)997-9743 E-mail: afcom@afcom.com • URL: http://www.afcom.com • Members are data processing operations management professionals.

Production and Operations Management Society. c/o Sushil Gupta. Florida International University, College of Engineering, EAS 2460, 10555 W. Flagler St., Miami, FL 33174. Phone: (305)348-1413 Fax: (305)348-6890 E-mail: poms@fiu.edu • URL: http://www.poms.org • Members are professionals and educators in fields related to operations management and production.

OPERATIONS RESEARCH

See also: AUTOMATION; SYSTEMS IN MANAGEMENT

ABSTRACTS AND INDEXES

International Abstracts in Operations Research. International Federation of Operational Research Societies. Elsevier Science. • Bimonthly. $589.00 per year.

PERIODICALS AND NEWSLETTERS

Operational Research Society Journal. Groves Dictionaries, Inc. • Monthly. $846.00 per year. Covers various applications of operations research, including forecasting, inventory, logistics, project management, and scheduling. Includes technical approaches (simulation, mathematical programming, expert systems, etc.).

Operations Research. Institute for Operations Research and the Management Sciences. • Bimonthly. Individuals, $109.00 per year; institutions, $227.00 per year.

Operations Research Letters. Elsevier Science. • 10 times a year. $472.00 per year.

RESEARCH CENTERS AND INSTITUTES

Engineering Systems Research Center. University of California at Berkeley. 3115 Etcheverry Hall, No. 1750, Berkeley, CA 94720-1750. Phone: (510)642-4994 Fax: (510)643-8982 E-mail: esrc@esrc.berkeley.edu • URL: http://www.esrc.berkeley.edu/esrc/.

OPHTHALMIC INDUSTRY

See also: CONTACT LENS AND INTRAOCULAR LENS INDUSTRIES

ABSTRACTS AND INDEXES

Index Medicus. National Library of Medicine. Available from U. S. Government Printing Office. • Monthly. $522.00 per year. Bibliographic listing of references to current articles from approximately 3,000 of the world's biomedical journals.

Science Citation Index. Institute for Scientific Information. • Bimonthly. $15,020.00 per year. Annual cumulation. Includes *Source Index, Citation Index, Permuterm Subject Index,* and *Corporate Index.*

BIBLIOGRAPHIES

Medical and Health Care Books and Serials in Print: An Index to Literature in Health Sciences. R. R. Bowker. • Annual. $265.95. Two volumes.

BIOGRAPHICAL SOURCES

Dictionary of American Medical Biography. Martin Kaufman and others. Greenwood Publishing Group Inc. • 1984. $195.00. Two volumes. Vol. one, $100.00; vol. two, $100.00.

CD-ROM DATABASES

Physicians' Desk Reference Library on CD-ROM. Medical Economics. • Three times a year. $595.00 per year. Contains the CD-ROM equivalent of *Physicians' Desk Reference (PDR), Physicians' Desk Reference for Nonprescription Drugs, Physicians' Desk Reference for Opthalmology,* and other PDR publications.

DIRECTORIES

Encyclopedia of Medical Organizations and Agencies. The Gale Group. • 2000. $285.00. 11th edition. Information on over 14,000 public and private organizations in medicine and related fields.

Guild of Prescription Opticians of America-Guild Reference Directory. Guild of Prescription Opticians of America. Opticians Association of America. • Annual. $60.00. Lists 250 member firms with a total of 350 retail locations. Formerly *Guild of Prescription Opticians of America-Reference List of Guild Opticians.*

Medical and Health Information Directory. The Gale Group. • 1999. $630.00. Three volumes. 12th edition. Vol. one covers medical organizations, agencies, and institutions; vol. two includes bibliographic, library, and database information; vol. three is a guide to services available for various medical and health problems.

Optometry and Vision Science-Geographical Directory, American Academy of Optometry. American Academy of Optometry. • Biennial. $25.00. List of 3,400 members; international coverage.

OSA/SPIE/OSJ Membership Directory. Optical Society of America, Inc. • Annual. List of over 20,000 persons interested in any branch of optics. Formerly *Optical Society of America-Membership Directory.* Includes coverage of the Optical Society of America, the Optical Society of Japan, and the International Society for Optical Engineering.

Photonics Directory. Laurin Publishing Co., Inc. • Annual. $138.00. Four volumes. Volume one is a corporate guide; volume two is a buyer's guide; volume three is a designer's handbook; volume four is a dictionary. Formerly *Photonics Industry and System Purchasing Directory.*

FINANCIAL RATIOS

Almanac of Business and Industrial Financial Ratios. Leo Troy. Prentice Hall. • Annual. $99.95. Contains financial ratios derived from federal tax returns. Ratios for each of about 200 industries are arranged according to company asset size.

Annual Statement Studies. Robert Morris Associates: The Association of Lending and Credit Risk Professiona. • Annual. Free to members; non-members, $140.00. Median and quartile financial ratios are given for over 400 kinds of manufacturing, wholesale, retail, construction, and consumer finance establishments. Data is sorted by both asset size and sales volume. Includes a clearly written "Definition of Ratios" and an alphabetical industry index.

HANDBOOKS AND MANUALS

The Consumer Health Information Source Book. Alan Rees, editor. Oryx Press. • 2000. $59.50. Sixth edition. Bibliography of current literature and guide to organizations.

Physicians' Desk Reference for Ophthalmology. Medical Economics Publishing Co., Inc. • Irregular. $49.95. Provides detailed descriptions of ophthalmological instrumentation, equipment, supplies, lenses, and prescription drugs. Indexed by manufacturer, product name, product category, active drug ingredient, and instrumentation. Editorial discussion is included.

ONLINE DATABASES

Embase. Elsevier Science, Inc. • Worldwide medical literature, 1974 to present. Weekly updates. Inquire as to online cost and availability.

Globalbase. The Gale Group. • Provides more than one million online summaries of business, industrial, and economic news reports from more than 1,000 publications worldwide. Covers a wide range of material appearing in international trade journals, professional magazines, and newspapers. Time period is 1984 to date, with weekly updates. Inquire as to online cost and availability.

Medline. Medlars Management Section. • Provides indexing and abstracting of worldwide medical literature, 1966 to date. Weekly updates. Inquire as to online cost and availability.

Scisearch. Institute for Scientific Information. • Broad, multidisciplinary index to the literature of science and technology, 1974 to present. Inquire as to online cost and availability. Coverage of literature is worldwide, with weekly updates.

PERIODICALS AND NEWSLETTERS

American Journal of Ophthalmology. Elsevier Science Inc. • Monthly. $324.00 per year.

American Optometric Association News. American Optometric Association. • Semimonthly. Free to members; non-members, $76.00 per year.

Eyecare Business: The Magazine for Progressive Dispensing. Boucher Communications, Inc. • Monthly. Free to qualified personnel; others, $90.00 per year. Covers the business side of optometry and optical retailing. Each issue features "Frames and Fashion.".

Ophthalmology. American Academy of Opthalmology. Elsevier Science Inc. • Monthly. $342.00 per year.

Ophthalmology Times: All the Clinical News in Sight. Advanstar Communications, Inc. • Semimonthly. $190.00 per year.

Optometric Management: The Business and Marketing Magazine for Optometry. Boucher Communications, Inc. • Monthly. $48.00 per year. Provides information and advice for optometrists on practice management and marketing.

Optometry: Journal of the American Optometric Society. American Optometric Association. • Monthly. Free to members; non-members, $90.00 per year. Formerly (American Optometric Association Journal).

RESEARCH CENTERS AND INSTITUTES

Francis I. Proctor Foundation for Research in Ophthalmology. University of California, San Francisco, 95 Kirkham St., San Francisco, CA 94143-0944. Phone: (415)476-1442 Fax: (415)502-2521.

Howe Laboratory of Ophthalmology. Harvard University. Massachusetts Eye and Ear Infirmary, 243 Charles St., Boston, MA 02114. Phone: (617)573-3963 Fax: (617)573-4290 • URL: http://www.howelaboratory.harvard.edu • A research unit of Harvard Medical School.

Vision Research Center in Ophthalmology. Mount Sinai School of Medicine of City University of New Yor, k, One Gustave L. Levy Place, New York, NY 10029. Phone: (212)241-6249 Fax: (212)289-5945 E-mail: oscarc@worldnet.att.net • URL: http://www.mssm.edu/ophth/.

Visual Sciences Center. University of Chicago, 939 E. 57th St., Chicago, IL 60637. Phone: (773)702-8888 Fax: (773)702-8094 E-mail: jernest@midway.uchicago.edu • URL: http://www.bsd.uchicago.edu/oph/index.html.

STATISTICS SOURCES

Annual Survey of Manufactures. Available from U. S. Government Printing Office. • Annual. Prices vary. Issued by the U. S. Census Bureau as an interim update to the *Census of Manufactures.* Includes data on number of manufacturing establishments in various industries, employment, labor costs, value of shipments, capital expenditures, inventories, energy costs, and assets. (See also Census Bureau home page, http://www.census.gov/.).

U. S. Industry and Trade Outlook: The McGraw-Hill Companies and the U.S. Department of Commerce/International Trade Administration. Datapso Research Corp. • Annual. $69.95. Produced by the International Trade Administration, U. S. Department of Commerce, in a "public-private" partnership with DRI/McGraw-Hill and Standard & Poor's. Provides basic data, outlook for the current year, and "Long-Term Prospects" (five-year projections) for a wide variety of products and services. Includes high technology industries. Formerly *U. S. Industrial Outlook.*

TRADE/PROFESSIONAL ASSOCIATIONS

American Academy of Optometry. 6110 Executive Blvd., Suite 506, Rockville, MD 20852. Phone: (301)984-1441 Fax: (301)984-4737 E-mail: aaoptom@aol.com • URL: http://www.aaopt.org.

American Board of Ophthalmology. 111 Presidential Blvd., Suite 241, Bala Cynwyd, PA 19004. Phone: (610)664-1175 Fax: (610)664-6503.

American Optometric Association. 243 N. Lindbergh Blvd., St. Louis, MO 63141. Phone: (314)991-4100 Fax: (314)991-4101 • URL: http://www.aoanet.org/.

American Optometric Foundation. 6110 Executive Blvd., Suite 506, Bethesda, MD 20852. Phone: 800-368-6263 or (301)984-4734 Fax: (301)984-4737 E-mail: christine@aapotom.org • URL: http://www.ezell.org.

American Society of Contemporary Ophthalmology. 4711 W. Golf Rd., Suite 408, Skokie, IL 60076. Phone: 800-621-4002 or (847)568-1500 Fax: (847)568-1527 E-mail: iaos@aol.com.

Better Vision Institute. 1655 N. Fort Meyer Dr. Suite 200, Arlington, VA 22209. Phone: 800-424-8422 or (703)243-1508 Fax: (703)243-1537 E-mail: wca@visionsite.org • URL: http://www.visionsite.org.

National Academy of Opticianry. 8401 Corporate Dr. Ste. 605, Landover, MD 20785. Phone: (301)577-4828 Fax: (301)577-3880.

National Association of Optometrists and Opticians. P.O. Box 479, Marble Head, OH 43440. Phone: (419)798-4071 Fax: (419)798-5548.

National Optometric Association. P.O. Box F, East Chicago, IN 46312. Phone: (219)398-1832 Fax: (219)398-1077 • URL: http://www.natoptassoc.org.

Ophthalmic Research Institute. 6110 Executive Blvd., Suite 506, Rockville, MD 20852. Phone: (301)984-4785 Fax: (301)656-0989.

Optical Industry Association. 6055A Arlington Blvd., Falls Church, VA 22044. Phone: (703)237-8433 Fax: (703)237-0643 E-mail: omaassoc@aol.com.

Optical Laboratories Association. P.O. Box 2000, Merrifield, VA 22116-2000. Phone: (703)359-2830 Fax: (703)359-2834.

Opticians Association of America. 7023 Little River Turnpike, No. 207, Annandale, VA 22003. Phone: (703)916-8856 Fax: (703)691-3929.

OTHER SOURCES

Health Care Products and Remedies. Available from MarketResearch.com. • 1997. $600.00 each. Consists of market reports published by Simmons Market Research Bureau on each of about 25 health care product categories. Examples are cold remedies, contraceptives, hearing aids, bandages, headache remedies, eyeglasses, contact lenses, and vitamins. Each report covers buying patterns and demographics.

The Market for Ophthalmic Pharmaceuticals. MarketResearch.com. • 1997. $2,500.00. Market research report. Covers topical and internal drugs for eye disorders, with market estimates. Includes pharmaceutical company profiles.

New Ophthalmology: Treatments and Technologies. Theta Reports/PJB Medical Publications, Inc. • 2000. $1,695. Provides market research data relating to eye surgery, including LASIK, cataract surgery, and associated technology. (Theta Report No. 911.).

World Contact and Intraocular Lenses and Ophthalmic Devices Markets. Available from MarketResearch.com. • 1996. $995.00. Published by Theta Corporation. Provides market data on soft contact lenses, hard lenses, and lens care products, with forecasts to 2000.

OPIATES

See: NARCOTICS

OPINION POLLS

See: PUBLIC OPINION

OPTICAL DISK STORAGE DEVICES

See also: INFORMATION INDUSTRY; MICROCOMPUTERS AND MINICOMPUTERS; MULTIMEDIA

GENERAL WORKS

Optical Discs in Libraries: Uses and Trends. Ching-chih Chen. Information Today, Inc. • 1991. $79.50. Includes summaries of over 250 use studies.

ABSTRACTS AND INDEXES

Applied Science and Technology Index. H. W. Wilson Co. • 11 times a year. Quarterly and annual cumulations. Service basis for print edition; CD-ROM edition, $1,495.00 per year. Indexes a wide variety of English language technical, industrial, and engineering periodicals.

Business Periodicals Index. H. W. Wilson Co. • Monthly, except August, with quarterly and annual cumulations. Service basis for print edition; CD-ROM edition, $1,495.00 per year.

Computer and Control Abstracts. Available from INSPEC, Inc. • Monthly. $2,160.00 per year. Section C of *Science Abstracts.*

Computer and Information Systems Abstracts Journal: An Abstract Journal Pertaining to the Theory, Design, Fabrication and Application of Computer and Information Systems. Cambridge Information Group. • Monthly. $1,045 per year.

Current Contents: Engineering, Computing and Technology. Institute for Scientific Information. • Weekly. $730.00 per year. Reproductions of contents pages of technical journals. Includes *Author Index, Address Directory, Current Book Contents* and *Title Word Index.* Formerly *Current Contents: Engineering, Technology and Applied Sciences.*

Electronics and Communications Abstracts Journal: Comprehensive Coverage of Essential Scientific Literature. Cambridge Information Group. • Monthly. $1,045.00 per year.

Key Abstracts: Computer Communications and Storage. Available from INSPEC, Inc. • Monthly. $240.00 per year. Provides international coverage of journal and proceedings literature, including material on optical disks and networks. Published in England by the Institution of Electrical Engineers (IEE).

Library Literature and Information Science: An Index to Library and Information Science Publications. H. W. Wilson Co. • Bimonthly. Annual cumulation. Service basis. Formerly *Library Literature.*

Microcomputer Abstracts. Information Today, Inc. • Quarterly. $225.00 per year. Provides abstracts covering a wide variety of personal and business microcomputer literature. Formerly *Microcomputer Index.*

CD-ROM DATABASES

Information Science Abstracts. Information Today, Inc. • Quarterly. $1,095.00 per year. Presents CD-ROM abstracts of worldwide information science and library science literature from 1966 to date.

LISA Plus: Library and Information Science Abstracts. Bowker-Saur, Reed Reference Publishing. • Quarterly. $1,450.00 per year. Provides CD-ROM abstracting and indexing of the world's library and information science literature. Covers a wide variety of topics.

Multimedia Schools: A Practical Journal of Multimedia, CD-ROM, Online, and Internet in K-12. Information Today, Inc. • Bimonthly. $39.95 per year. Provides purchasing recommendations and technical advice relating to the use of high-tech multimedia products in schools.

WILSONDISC: Library Literature and Information Science Index. H. W. Wilson Co. • Quarterly. Including unlimited access to the online version of *Library Literature*. Provides CD-ROM indexing of about 300 periodicals, covering a wide range of topics having to do with libraries, library management, and the information industry.

DIRECTORIES

Broadcast Engineering: Equipment Reference Manual. Intertec Publishing Corp. • Annual. $20.00. Lists manufacturers and distributors of radio and TV broadcast and recording equipment. Included in subscription to *Broadcast Engineering*.

CD-ROM Finder. Information Today, Inc. • Irregular. $69.50. Describes over 2,300 CD-ROM titles. Formerly *Optical Electronic Publishing Directory*.

CD-ROMS in Print. The Gale Group. • Annual. $175.00. Describes more than 13,000 currrently available reference and multimedia CD-ROM titles and provides contact information for about 4,000 CD-ROM publishing and distribution companies. Includes several indexes.

Faulkner Information Service. Faulkner Information Services, Inc. • Looseleaf. Monthly updates. Many titles and volumes, covering virtually all aspects of computer software and hardware. Gives descriptions and technical data for specific products, including producers' names and addresses. Prices and details on request. Formerly (The Auerbach Series).

Faxon Guide to Electronic Media. Faxon Co., Inc. • Annual. Free to qualified personnel; others, $12.00. Provides brief descriptions of currently available CD-ROM databases. Formerly *Faxon Guide to CD-ROM*.

Gale Directory of Databases. The Gale Group. • 2001. $400.00. Two volumes. Volume 1, $270.00; volume 2, $180.00. *Volume 1: Online Databases* and *Volume 2: CD-ROM, Diskette, Magnetic Tape, Handheld, and Batch Access Database Products*.

Interactive Advertising Source. SRDS. • Quarterly. $561.00 per year. Provides descriptive profiles, rates, audience, personnel, etc., for producers of various forms of interactive or multimedia advertising: online/Internet, CD-ROM, interactive TV, interactive cable, interactive telephone, interactive kiosk, and others. Includes online supplement *SRDS' URlink*.

Laserlog Reporter: CD Reporter. Phonlog Publishing. • Biweekly. $228.00 per year. Looseleaf. Contains detailed listings of currently available compact disc music recordings, both popular and classical.

Library Journal: Reference [year]: Print, CD-ROM, Online. Cahners Business Information. • Annual. Issued in November as supplement to *Library Journal*. Lists new and updated reference material, including general and trade print titles, directories, annuals, CD-ROM titles, and online sources. Includes material from more than 150 publishers, arranged by company name, with an index by subject. Addresses include e-mail and World Wide Web information, where available.

MicroLeads Vendor Directory on Disk (Personal Computer Industry). Chromatic Communications Enterprises, Inc. • Annual. $495.00. Includes computer hardware manufacturers, software producers, book-periodical publishers, and franchised or company-owned chains of personal computer equipment retailers, support services and accessory manufacturers. Formerly *MicroLeads U.S. Vender Directory*.

Multimedia and CD-ROM Directory: The Global Source of Information for the Multimedia and CD-ROM Industries. Available from Omnigraphics, Inc. • Annual. $390.00. Two volumes: vol. 1, *New Media Companies* ($195.00); vol. 2, *New Media Titles* ($195.00). Published in London by Macmillan Reference Ltd. Volume one consists of statistics ("Facts and Figures"), articles on multimedia publishing, market profiles (countries), interviews, company directory, bibliography, and indexes. Volume two describes more than 19,000 CD-ROM titles, with publisher directory, indexes, and glossary. Formerly *CD-ROM Directory*.

Recording Industry Sourcebook. Intertec Publishing. • Annual. $79.95. Provides more than 12,000 listings in 57 categories of record/tape/compact disc labels, producers, distributors, managers, equipment suppliers, and others.

ENCYCLOPEDIAS AND DICTIONARIES

Dictionary of Information Technology and Computer Science. Tony Gunton. Blackwell Publishers. • 1994. $50.95. Second edition. Covers key words, phrases, abbreviations, and acronyms used in computing and data communications.

Multimedia and the Web from A to Z. Patrick M. Dillon and David C. Leonard. Oryx Press. • 1998. $39.95. Second enlarged revised edition. Defines more than 1,500 terms relating to software and hardware in the areas of computing, online technology, telecommunications, audio, video, motion pictures, CD-ROM, and the Internet. Includes acronyms and an annotated bibliography. Formerly *Multimedia Technology from A to Z* (1994).

HANDBOOKS AND MANUALS

CD-ROM Handbook. Chris Sherman. McGraw-Hill. • 1993. $70.50. Second edition. Covers technology (audio, video, and multimedia), design, production, and economics of the CD-ROM industry.

CD-ROM Primer: The ABCs of CD-ROM. Cheryl LaGuardia. Neal-Schuman Publishers, Inc. • 1994. $49.95. Provides advice for librarians and others on CD-ROM equipment, selection, collecting, and maintenance. Includes a glossary, bibliography, and directory of suppliers.

Compact Disc Handbook. Ken C. Pohlmann. A-R Editions, Inc. • 1992. $34.95. Second edition. A guide to compact disc technology, including player design and disc manufacturing. (Computer Music and Digital Audio Series).

Digital Audio and Compact Disk Technology. Luc Baert and others. Butterworth-Heinemann. • 1995. $57.95. Third edition.

Interactive Music Handbook. Jodi Summers, editor. Carronade Group. • 1996. $24.95. Covers interactive or enhanced music CD-ROMs and online music for producers, audio technicians, and musicians. Includes case studies and interviews.

Introductory CD-ROM Searching: The Key to Effective Ondisc Searching. Joseph Meloche. Haworth Press, Inc. • 1994. $49.95. Covers basic search strategies, with specific suggestions for Dialog OnDisc, Silverplatter, Wilsondisc, UMI, and others.

INTERNET DATABASES

InfoTech Trends. Data Analysis Group. Phone: (707)894-9100 Fax: (707)486-5618 E-mail: support@infotechtrends.com • URL: http://www.infotechtrends.com • Web site provides both free and fee-based market research data on the information technology industry, including computers, peripherals, telecommunications, the Internet, software, CD-ROM/DVD, e-commerce, and workstations. Fees: Free for current (most recent year) data; more extensive information has various fee structures. Formerly *Computer Industry Forecasts*.

Interactive Week: The Internet's Newspaper. Ziff Davis Media, Inc. 28 E. 28th St., New York, NY 10016. Phone: (212)503-3500 Fax: (212)503-5680 E-mail: iweekinfo@zd.com • URL: http://www.zd.com • Weekly. $99.00 per year. Covers news and trends relating to Internet commerce, computer communications, and telecommunications.

ONLINE DATABASES

Applied Science and Technology Index Online. H. W. Wilson Co. • Provides online indexing of 400 major scientific, technical, industrial, and engineering periodicals. Time period is 1983 to date. Monthly updates. Inquire as to online cost and availability.

Computer Database. The Gale Group. • Provides online citations with abstracts to material appearing in about 150 trade journals and newsletters in the subject areas of computers, telecommunications, and electronics. Time period is 1983 to date, with weekly updates. Inquire as to online cost and availability.

Gale Directory of Databases [online]. The Gale Group. • Presents the online version of the printed *Gale Directory of Databases, Volume 1: Online Databases* and *Gale Directory of Databases, Volume 2: CD-ROM, Diskette, Magnetic Tape, Handheld, and Batch Access Database Products.* Semiannual updates. Inquire as to online cost and availability.

Information Science Abstracts [online]. Information Today, Inc. • Provides indexing and abstracting of the international literature of information science, including library science, from 1966 to date. Monthly updates. Inquire as to online cost and availability.

Internet and Personal Computing Abstracts. Information Today, Inc. • Contains abstracts covering a wide variety of personal and business microcomputer literature appearing in more than 100 journals and popular magazines. Time period is 1981 to date, with monthly updates. Formerly *Microcomputer Index*. Inquire as to online cost and availability.

Library Literature Online. H. W. Wilson Co. • Contains online indexing of a wide variety of library and information science literature from 1984 to date, with updating quarterly. Inquire as to online cost and availability.

LISA Online: Library and Information Science Abstracts. Bowker-Saur, Reed Reference Publishing. • Provides abstracting and indexing of the world's library and information science literature from 1969 to the present. Covers a wide variety of topics in over 550 journals from 60 countries, with biweekly updates. Inquire as to online cost and availability.

PROMT: Predicasts Overview of Markets and Technology. The Gale Group. • Companies, products, applied technologies and markets. U.S. and international literature coverage, 1972 to date. Inquire as to online cost and availability. Provides abstracts from more than 1,600 publications. Weekly updates.

Wilson Business Abstracts Online. H. W. Wilson Co. • Indexes and abstracts 600 major business periodicals, plus the *Wall Street Journal* and the business section of the *New York Times*. Indexing is from 1982, abstracting from 1990, with the two newspapers included from 1993. Updated weekly. Inquire as to online cost and availability. (*Business Periodicals Index* without abstracts is also available online.).

PERIODICALS AND NEWSLETTERS

CD-ROM Information Products: The Evaluative Guide. Ashgate Publishing Co. • Quarterly. $110.00 per year. Provides detailed evaluations of new CD-ROM information products.

CD-ROM World: The Magazine and Review for CD-ROM Users. PC World Communications, Inc. • 10 times a year. $29.00 per year.

Computer Music Journal. MIT Press. • Quarterly. Individuals, $48.00 per year; instutitions, $158.00 per year. Covers digital sooound and the musical applications of computers.

Digital Publishing Technologies: How to Implement New Media Publishing. Information Today, Inc. • Monthly. $196.00 per year. Covers online and CD-ROM publishing, including industry news, new applications, new products, electronic publishing technology, and descriptions of completed publishing projects.

E Media. Online, Inc. • Bimonthly. Individuals, $55.00 per year; institutions, $98.00 per year. Contains "how-to" articles and reviews of CD-ROMs and equipment. Formerly *E Media Professional.*

EDP Weekly: The Leading Weekly Computer News Summary. Computer Age and E D P News Services. • Weekly. $495.00 per year. Newsletter. Summarizes news from all areas of the computer and microcomputer industries.

Innovative Publisher: Publishing Strategies for New Markets. Emmelle Publishing Co., Inc. • Biweekly. $69.00 per year. Provides articles and news on electronic publishing (CD-ROM or online) and desktop publishing.

Interactive Marketing and P R News: News and Practical Advice on Using Interactive Advertising and Marketing to Sell Your Products. Phillips Business Information, Inc. • Biweekly. $495.00 per year. Newsletter. Provides information and guidance on merchandising via CD-ROM ("multimedia catalogs"), the Internet, and interactive TV. Topics include "cybermoney", addresses for e-mail marketing, "virtual malls," and other interactive subjects. Formerly *Interactive Marketing News.*

Mass Storage News: Opportunities and Trends in Data Storage and Retrieval. Corry Publishing, Inc. • Biweekly. $597.00 per year. Newsletter. Provides descriptions of products and systems using optical storage. Formerly *Optical Memory News.*

Maxium PC (Personal Computer). Imagine Media, Inc. • Quarterly. $12.00 per year. Provides articles and reviews relating to multimedia hardware and software. Each issue includes a CD-ROM sampler (emphasis is on games). Formed by the merger of *Home PC* and *Boot.*

Micropublishing News: The Newsmonthly for Electronic Designers and Publishers. Cygnus Business Media. • Monthly. Free to qualified personnel. Price on application. Edited for business and professional users of electronic publishing products and services. Topics covered include document imaging, CD-ROM publishing, digital video, and multimedia services. Available in four regional editions.

Monitor: An Analytical Review of Current Events in the Online and Electronic Publishing Industry. Information Today, Inc. • Monthly. $290.00 per year. Newsletter. Covers the international industry.

NewMedia: The Magazine for Creators of the Digital Future. HyperMedia Communications, Inc. • Monthly. $29.95 per year. Edited for multimedia professionals, with emphasis on digital video and Internet graphics, including animation. Contains reviews of new products. Formerly *NewMedia Age.*

Online: The Leading Magazine for Information Professionals. Online, Inc. • Bimonthly. $110.00 per year. General coverage of the online information industry.

Searcher: The Magazine for Database Professionals. Information Today, Inc. • 10 times per year. $64.95 per year. Covers a wide range of topics relating to online and CD-ROM database searching.

Stereo Review's Sound & Vision: Home Theater-Audio- Video- MultimediaMovies- Music. Hachette Filipacchi Magazines, Inc. • 10 times a year. $24.00 per year. Popular magazine providing explanatory articles and critical reviews of equipment and media (CD-ROM, DVD, videocassettes, etc.). Supplement available *Stero Review's Sound and Vision Buyers Guide.* Replaces *Stereo Review* and *Video Magazine.*

RESEARCH CENTERS AND INSTITUTES

Bibliographical Center for Research, Inc., Rocky Mountain Region. 14394 E. Evans Ave., Aurora, CO 80014-1478. Phone: 800-397-1552 or (303)751-6277 Fax: (303)751-9787 E-mail: admin@bec.org • URL: http://www.ber.org • Fields of research include information retrieval systems, Internet technology, CD-ROM technology, document delivery, and library automation.

Communications and Information Processing Group. Rensselaer Polytechnic Institute, Electrical, Computer, and Systems Engineering Dept., Troy, NY 12180-3590. Phone: (518)276-6823 Fax: (518)276-6261 E-mail: modestino@ipl.rpi.edu • URL: http://www.rpi.edu • Includes Optical Signal Processing Laboratory and Speech Processing Laboratory.

Institute for Information Storage Technology, Santa Clara University, IIST Engineering Bldg., Santa Clara, CA 95053. Phone: (408)554-6853 Fax: (408)554-7841 E-mail: hoagland@siist.scu.edu • URL: http://www.iist.scu.edu.

STATISTICS SOURCES

Multimedia Title Publishing: Review, Trends, and Forecast. SIMBA Information. • Annual. $895.00. Provides industry statistics and market research data. Covers both business and consumer multimedia items, with emphasis on CD-ROM publishing.

TRADE/PROFESSIONAL ASSOCIATIONS

Association for Information and Image Management. 1100 Wayne Ave., Suite 1100, Silver Spring, MD 20910-5603. Phone: (301)587-8202 Fax: (301)587-2711 E-mail: aiim@aiim.org • URL: http://www.aiim.org • Members are producers and users of image management equipment.

Interactive Digital Software Association. 1775 Eye St., N.W., Ste. 420, Washington, DC 20005. E-mail: info@idsa.com • URL: http://www.e3expo.com • Members are interactive entertainment software publishers concerned with rating systems, software piracy, government relations, and other industry issues.

OTHER SOURCES

DataWorld. Faulkner Information Services, Inc. • Four looseleaf volumes, with monthly supplements. $1,395.00 per year. Describes and evaluates both hardware and software relating to midrange, micro, and mainframe computers. Available on CD-ROM.

DVD Assessment, No. 3. Julie B. Schwerin and Theodore A. Pine, editors. InfoTech, Inc. • 1998. $1,295.00. Third edition. Provides detailed market research data on Digital Video Discs (also known as Digital Versatile Discs). Includes history of DVD, technical specifications, DVD publishing outlook, "Industry Overview," "Market Context," "Infrastructure Analysis," "Long-Range Forecast to 2005," and emerging technologies.

Optical Publishing Industry Assessment. Julie B. Schwerin and Theodore A. Pine, editors. InfoTech, Inc. • 1998. $1,295.00. Ninth edition. Provides market research data and forecasts to 2005 for DVD-ROM, "Hybrid ROM/Online Media," and other segments of the interactive entertainment, digital information, and consumer electronics industries. Covers both software (content) and hardware. Includes Video-CD, DVD- Video, CD-Audio, DVD-Audio, DVD-ROM, PC-Desktop, TV Set-Top, CD-R, CD-RW, DVD-R and DVD-RAM.

OPTICAL ENGINEERING

See: OPTICS INDUSTRY

OPTICAL FIBERS

See: FIBER OPTICS INDUSTRY

OPTICAL PUBLISHING SYSTEMS

See: OPTICAL DISK STORAGE DEVICES

OPTICS INDUSTRY

See also: FIBER OPTICS INDUSTRY

GENERAL WORKS

Introduction to Glass Science and Technology. J. E. Shelby. American Chemical Society. • 1997. $40.00. Covers the basics of glass manufacture, including the physical, optical, electrical, chemical, and mechanical properties of glass. (RCS Paperback Series).

CD-ROM DATABASES

Science Citation Index: Compact Disc Edition. Institute for Scientific Information. • Quarterly. Provides CD-ROM indexing of the world's scientific and technical literature. Corresponds to online *Scisearch* and printed *Science Citation Index.*

DIRECTORIES

Photonics Directory. Laurin Publishing Co., Inc. • Annual. $138.00. Four volumes. Volume one is a corporate guide; volume two is a buyer's guide; volume three is a designer's handbook; volume four is a dictionary. Formerly *Photonics Industry and System Purchasing Directory.*

HANDBOOKS AND MANUALS

Optics. Miles V. Klein and Thomas Furtak. John Wiley and Sons, Inc. • 1988. $106.95. Second edition. (Manchester Physics Series).

ONLINE DATABASES

PROMT: Predicasts Overview of Markets and Technology. The Gale Group. • Companies, products, applied technologies and markets. U.S. and international literature coverage, 1972 to date. Inquire as to online cost and availability. Provides abstracts from more than 1,600 publications. Weekly updates.

Scisearch. Institute for Scientific Information. • Broad, multidisciplinary index to the literature of science and technology, 1974 to present. Inquire as to online cost and availability. Coverage of literature is worldwide, with weekly updates.

PERIODICALS AND NEWSLETTERS

Applied Optics. Optical Society of America, Inc. • 36 times a year. $1,910.00 per year.

Fiber Optics News. Phillips Business Information, Inc. • Weekly. $697.00 per year. Newsletter.

Optical Engineering. Interational Society of Optical Engineering. • Monthly. Free to members; non-members and institutions, $340.00 per year. Technical papers and letters.

Optical Society of America Journal. Optical Society of America, Inc. • Monthly. Part A, $1,075.00 per year; Part B, $1,075.00 per year.

Photonics Spectra. Laurin Publishing Co., Inc. • Monthly. $112.00 per year.

RESEARCH CENTERS AND INSTITUTES

Institute of Optics. University of Rochester, Rochester, NY 14627. Phone: (716)275-2134 Fax: (716)273-1072 E-mail: hall@optics.rochester.edu • URL: http://www.optics.rochester.edu.

Optical Sciences Center. University of Arizona, 1630 E. University Blvd., Tucson, AZ 85721. Phone: (520)621-6997 Fax: (520)621-9613 E-mail: jcwyant@u.arizona.edu • URL: http://www.optics.arizona.edu.

TRADE/PROFESSIONAL ASSOCIATIONS

Optical Industry Association. 6055A Arlington Blvd., Falls Church, VA 22044. Phone: (703)237-8433 Fax: (703)237-0643 E-mail: omaassoc@aol.com.

Optical Laboratories Association. P.O. Box 2000, Merrifield, VA 22116-2000. Phone: (703)359-2830 Fax: (703)359-2834.

Optical Society of America. 2010 Massachusetts Ave., N.W., Washington, DC 20036-1023. Phone: (202)223-8130 Fax: (202)223-1096 • URL: http://www.osa.org.

SPIE-The International Society for Optical Engineering. P.O. Box 10, Bellingham, WA 98227-0010. Phone: (360)676-3290 Fax: (360)647-1445 E-mail: spie@spie.org • URL: http://www.spie.org.

OPTIONS (PUTS AND CALLS)

See: STOCK OPTION CONTRACTS

OPTOELECTRONICS

See also: ELECTRONICS INDUSTRY; OPTICS INDUSTRY; PHOTONICS

GENERAL WORKS

Advances in Optotronics and Avionics Technologies. M. Garcia, editor. John Wiley and Sons, Inc. • 1996. $90.00.

Fundamentals of Optoelectronics. Clifford R. Pollock. McGraw-Hill Higher Education. • 1994. $77.50.

Optoelectronics: An Introduction. John Wilson. Prentice Hall. • 1998. $86.00.

ABSTRACTS AND INDEXES

Applied Science and Technology Index. H. W. Wilson Co. • 11 times a year. Quarterly and annual cumulations. Service basis for print edition; CD-ROM edition, $1,495.00 per year. Indexes a wide variety of English language technical, industrial, and engineering periodicals.

Key Abstracts: Optoelectronics. Available from INSPEC, Inc. • Monthly. $240.00 per year. Provides international coverage of journal and proceedings literature relating to fiber optics, lasers, and optoelectronics in general. Published in England by the Institution of Electrical Engineers (IEE).

NTIS Alerts: Electrotechnology. National Technical Information Service. • Semimonthly. $210.00 per year. Provides descriptions of government-sponsored research reports and software, with ordering information. Covers electronic components, semiconductors, antennas, circuits, optoelectronic devices, and related subjects. Formerly *Abstract Newsletter.*

Science Citation Index. Institute for Scientific Information. • Bimonthly. $15,020.00 per year. Annual cumulation. Includes *Source Index, Citation Index, Permuterm Subject Index,* and *Corporate Index.*

CD-ROM DATABASES

Science Citation Index: Compact Disc Edition. Institute for Scientific Information. • Quarterly. Provides CD-ROM indexing of the world's scientific and technical literature. Corresponds to online *Scisearch* and printed *Science Citation Index.*

DIRECTORIES

ID Systems Buyers Guide. Helmers Publishing, Inc. • Annual. Price on application. Provides information on over 750 companies manufacturing automatic identification equipment, including scanners, data collection terminals, and bar code systems.

Laser Focus World Buyers' Guide. PennWell Corp., Advanced Technology Div. • Annual. $125.00. Lists more than 2,000 suppliers of optoelectronic and laser products and services.

OSA/SPIE/OSJ Membership Directory. Optical Society of America, Inc. • Annual. List of over 20,000 persons interested in any branch of optics. Formerly *Optical Society of America-Membership Directory.* Includes coverage of the Optical Society of America, the Optical Society of Japan, and the International Society for Optical Engineering.

Photonics Directory. Laurin Publishing Co., Inc. • Annual. $138.00. Four volumes. Volume one is a corporate guide; volume two is a buyer's guide; volume three is a designer's handbook; volume four is a dictionary. Formerly *Photonics Industry and System Purchasing Directory.*

ENCYCLOPEDIAS AND DICTIONARIES

Wiley Encyclopedia of Electrical and Electronics Engineering. John G. Webster, editor. John Wiley and Sons, Inc. • 1999. $6,495.00. 24 volumes. Contains about 1,400 articles, each with bibliography. Arrangement is according to 64 categories.

HANDBOOKS AND MANUALS

Optoelectronic Devices. Safa Kasap. Addison Wesley Longman, Inc. • 2000. $87.00.

ONLINE DATABASES

Globalbase. The Gale Group. • Provides more than one million online summaries of business, industrial, and economic news reports from more than 1,000 publications worldwide. Covers a wide range of material appearing in international trade journals, professional magazines, and newspapers. Time period is 1984 to date, with weekly updates. Inquire as to online cost and availability.

Scisearch. Institute for Scientific Information. • Broad, multidisciplinary index to the literature of science and technology, 1974 to present. Inquire as to online cost and availability. Coverage of literature is worldwide, with weekly updates.

PERIODICALS AND NEWSLETTERS

Laser Focus World: The World of Optoelectronics. PennWell Corp., Advanced Technology Div. • Monthly. $156.00 per year. Covers business and technical aspects of electro-optics, including lasers and fiberoptics. Includes *Buyer's Guide.*

Microwave and Optical Technology Letters. John Wiley and Sons, Inc., Journals Div. • 24 times a year. $1,540.00 per year.

OE Reports (Optical Engineering). International Society for Optical Engineering. • Monthly. $25.00 per year. News and articles on optical and optoelectronic applied science and engineering. Formerly *Optical Engineering Reports.*

Optical Engineering. Interational Society of Optical Engineering. • Monthly. Free to members; non-members and institutions, $340.00 per year. Technical papers and letters.

Photonics Spectra. Laurin Publishing Co., Inc. • Monthly. $112.00 per year.

RESEARCH CENTERS AND INSTITUTES

Center for Photonics and Optoelectronic Materials. Princeton University, Engineering Quadrangle, School of Engineering and Applied Science, Princeton, NJ 08544. Phone: (609)258-4454 Fax: (609)258-1954 E-mail: poem@princeton.edu • URL: http://www.poem.princeton.edu/.

Center for Research and Education in Optics and Lasers. University of Central Florida, 4000 Central Florida Blvd., Orlando, FL 32816-2700. Phone: (407)823-6800 Fax: (407)823-6880 E-mail: ewvs@creol.ucf.edu • URL: http://www.creol.ucf.edu.

Fiber and Electro Optics Research Center. Virginia Polytechnic Institute and State University, Dept. of Electrical Engineering, 106 Plantation Rd., Blacksburg, VA 24061. Phone: (540)231-7203 Fax: (540)231-4561 E-mail: roclaus@vt.edu.

Institute of Optics. University of Rochester, Rochester, NY 14627. Phone: (716)275-2134 Fax: (716)273-1072 E-mail: hall@optics.rochester.edu • URL: http://www.optics.rochester.edu.

TRADE/PROFESSIONAL ASSOCIATIONS

IEEE Lasers and Electro-Optics Society. Institute of Electrical and Electronics Engineers, P.O. Box 1331, Piscataway, NJ 08855-1331. Phone: (732)981-0060 Fax: (732)981-1721 E-mail: g.walters@ieee.org • URL: http://www.ieee.org/leos • A society of the Institute of Electrical and Electronics Engineers. Fields of interest include lasers, fiber optics, optoelectronics, and photonics.

Instrument Society of America: Electro-Optics Division. P.O. Box 12277, Durham, NC 27709. Phone: (919)549-8411 Fax: (919)549-8288 E-mail: info@isa.org • URL: http://www.isa.org.

SPIE-The International Society for Optical Engineering. P.O. Box 10, Bellingham, WA 98227-0010. Phone: (360)676-3290 Fax: (360)647-1445 E-mail: spie@spie.org • URL: http://www.spie.org.

OTHER SOURCES

Fiber Systems International. Available from IOP Publishing, Inc. • Monthly. Controlled circulation. Published in the UK by the Institute of Physics. "Covering the optical communications marketplace within the Americas and Asia." *Fibre Systems Europe* is also available, covering the business and marketing aspects of fiber optics communications in Europe.

OPTOMETRIC INDUSTRY

See: OPHTHALMIC INDUSTRY

ORANGE INDUSTRY

See: CITRUS FRUIT INDUSTRY

ORDNANCE MARKET

See: MILITARY MARKET

ORGANIZATION

See: INDUSTRIAL MANAGEMENT

ORGANIZATION FOR ECONOMIC COOPERATION AND DEVELOPMENT

See also: FOREIGN TRADE

BIBLIOGRAPHIES

OECD Catalogue of Publications. Organization for Economic Cooperation and Development. Available from OECD Publications and Information Center. • Annual. Free. Supplements available.

DIRECTORIES

Europa World Yearbook. Taylor and Francis, Inc. • Annual. $815.00. Two volumes. Published by Europa Publications Ltd. Basic source of information on every country and some 1,650 international organizations. Includes detailed directories and surveys for each country.

PERIODICALS AND NEWSLETTERS

Central Banking: Policy, Markets, Supervision. Available from European Business Publications, Inc. • Quarterly. $350.00 per year, including annual *Central Banking Directory.* Published in England by Central Banking Publications. Reports and comments on the activities of central banks around the world. Also provides discussions of the International Monetary Fund (IMF), the Organization for Economic Cooperation and Development (OECD), the Bank for International Settlements (BIS), and the World Bank.

News from OECD. Available from OECD Publications and Information Center. • Monthly. Free. Lists OECD's calender of activities.

OECD Observer. Available from OECD Publications and Information Center. • Bimonthly. Price on application.

STATISTICS SOURCES

Main Economic Indicators. OECD Publication and Information Center. • Monthly. $450.00 per year. "The essential source of timely statistics for OECD member countries." Includes a wide variety of business, economic, and industrial data for the 29 OECD nations.

TRADE/PROFESSIONAL ASSOCIATIONS

Organisation for Economic Co-Operation and Development. Two, rue Andre Pascal, F-75775 Paris Cedex 16, France. Phone: 33 1 45248200 Fax: 33 1 45248500 E-mail: news.contact@oecd.org • URL: http://www.oecd.org.

ORGANIZATION FOR EUROPEAN ECONOMIC COOPERATION

See: ORGANIZATION FOR ECONOMIC COOPERATION AND DEVELOPMENT

ORGANIZATION THEORY

See: MANAGEMENT THEORY

ORGANIZATIONS

See: ASSOCIATIONS

ORGANIZED LABOR

See: LABOR UNIONS

ORIENTAL RUG INDUSTRY

DIRECTORIES

Floor Covering Weekly Product Source Guide. Hearst Business Communications, Inc., FCW Div. • Annual. $29.00. Lists manufacturers and importers of carpeting, rugs, ceramic tile, and other floor coverings. Formerly *Floor Covering Weekly.*

PERIODICALS AND NEWSLETTERS

Oriental Rug Review. Oriental Rug Auction Review, Inc. • Bimonthly. $48.00 per year.

TRADE/PROFESSIONAL ASSOCIATIONS

Oriental Rug Importers Association. 100 Park Plaza Dr., Secaucus, NJ 07094. Phone: (201)866-5054 Fax: (201)866-6169 • URL: http://www.oria.org.

OTHER SOURCES

Carpets and Rugs. Available from MarketResearch.com. • 1999. $3,300.00. Market research data. Published by the Freedonia Group. Provides both historical data and forecasts to 2007 for various kinds of carpeting.

ORTHOPEDIC APPLIANCE INDUSTRY

See: PROSTHETICS INDUSTRY

OUTDOOR ADVERTISING

See also: SIGNS AND SIGN BOARDS

DIRECTORIES

Buyers Guide to Outdoor Advertising. Competitive Media Reporting. • Semiannual. $425.00 per year. Lists more than 800 outdoor advertising companies and their market rates, etc.

Out-of-Home Advertising Source. SRDS. • Annual. $299.00. Provides detailed information on non-traditional or "out-of-home" advertising media: outdoor, aerial, airport, mass transit, bus benches, school, hotel, in-flight, in-store, theater, stadium, taxi, truckstop, kiosk, shopping malls, and others.

ENCYCLOPEDIAS AND DICTIONARIES

NTC's Mass Media Dictionary. R. Terry Ellmore. NTC/Contemporary Publishing. • 1993. $24.95. Covers television, radio, newspapers, magazines, film, graphic arts, books, billboards, public relations, and advertising. Terms are related to production, research, audience measurement, audio-video engineering, printing, publishing, and other areas.

FINANCIAL RATIOS

Annual Statement Studies. Robert Morris Associates: The Association of Lending and Credit Risk Professiona. • Annual. Free to members; non-members, $140.00. Median and quartile financial ratios are given for over 400 kinds of manufacturing, wholesale, retail, construction, and consumer finance establishments. Data is sorted by both asset size and sales volume. Includes a clearly written "Definition of Ratios" and an alphabetical industry index.

PERIODICALS AND NEWSLETTERS

Signs of the Times: The National Journal of Signs and Advertising Displays. ST Publications, Inc. • 13 times a year. $36.00 per year. For designers and manufacturers of all types of signs. Features how-to-tips. Includes *Sign Erection, Maintenance Directory* and annual *Buyer's Guide.*

TRADE/PROFESSIONAL ASSOCIATIONS

Outdoor Advertising Association of America. 1850 M St., N.W., Suite 1040, Washington, DC 20036-5803. Phone: (202)833-5566 Fax: (202)833-1522 E-mail: info@oaaa.org • URL: http://www.oaaa.org.

Outdoor Advertising of America/Marketing Div. 420 Lexington Ave., Rm. 2520, New York, NY 10170-2599. Phone: (212)688-3667 Fax: (212)752-1687.

OUTDOOR AMUSEMENTS

See: AMUSEMENT INDUSTRY

OUTPLACEMENT CONSULTANTS

See: EMPLOYMENT AGENCIES AND SERVICES

OVER-THE-COUNTER DRUGS

See: NONPRESCRIPTION DRUG INDUSTRY

OVER-THE-COUNTER SECURITIES INDUSTRY

See also: SECURITIES; STOCK BROKERS; STOCKS

GENERAL WORKS

Investing in Small-Cap Stocks. Christopher Graja and Elizabeth Ungar. Bloomberg Press. • 1999. $26.95. Second expanded revised edition. Provides a practical strategy for investing in small-capitalization stocks. (Bloomberg Personal Bookshelf Series.).

Investing in the Over-the-Counter Markets: Stocks, Bonds, IPOs. Alvin D. Hall. John Wiley and Sons, Inc. • 1995. $29.95. Provides advice and information on investing in "unlisted" or NASDAQ (National Association of Securities Dealers Automated Quotation System) stocks, bonds, and initial public offerings (IPOs).

Over-the-Counter Securities Markets. Julian G. Buckley and Leo M. Loll. Prentice Hall. • 1986. $33.95. Third edition.

DIRECTORIES

Institutional Buyers of Small-Cap Stocks: A Targeted Directory. Investment Data Corp. • Annual. $295.00. Provides detailed profiles of more than 837 institutional buyers of small capitalization stocks. Includes names of financial analysts and portfolio managers.

Standard and Poor's Security Dealers of North America. Standard & Poor's. • Semiannual. $480.00 per year; with *Supplements* every six weeks, $590.00 per year. Geographical listing of over 12,000 stock, bond, and commodity dealers.

Standard & Poor's SmallCap 600 Guide. McGraw-Hill. • Annual. $24.95. Contains detailed profiles of the companies included in Standard & Poor's SmallCap 600 Index of stock prices. Includes income and balance sheet data for up to 10 years, with growth and stability rankings for 600 small capitalization corporations.

Walker's Manual of Unlisted Stocks. Harry K. Eisenberg, editor. Walker's Manual, LLC. • Annual.

$85.00. Provides information on 500 over-the-counter stocks,including many "penny stocks" trading at less than $5.00 per share.

ENCYCLOPEDIAS AND DICTIONARIES

Dictionary of Finance and Investment Terms. John Downes and Jordan E. Goodman. Barron's Educational Series, Inc. • 1998. $12.95. Fifth revised edition. Provides clear explanations of more than 5,000 business, banking, financial, investment, and tax terms. Includes a separate list of financial abbreviations and acronyms.

HANDBOOKS AND MANUALS

Handbook of Derivative Instruments: Investment Research, Analysis, and Portfolio Applications. Atsuo Konishi and Ravi E. Dattatreya, editors. McGraw-Hill Professional. • 1996. $80.00. Second revised edition. Contains 41 chapters by various authors on all aspects of derivative securities, including such esoterica as "Inverse Floaters," "Positive Convexity," "Exotic Options," and "How to Use the Holes in Black-Scholes.".

Handbook of Equity Derivatives. Jack C. Francis and others, editors. John Wiley and Sons, Inc. • 1999. $95.00. Contains 27 chapters by various authors. Covers options (puts and calls), stock index futures, warrants, convertibles, over-the-counter options, swaps, legal issues, taxation, etc. (Financial Engineering Series).

Moody's Handbook of NASDAQ Stocks (National Association of Securities Dealers Automated Quotations). Financial Information Services. • Quarterly. $375.00 per year. Formerly *Moody's Handbook of O-T-C Stocks.*

Moody's OTC Industrial Manual. Financial Information Services. • Annual, $1,675.00 per year. Includes biweekly *Moody's OTC Industrial News Report.*

Moody's OTC Unlisted Manual (Over the Counter). Financial Information Services. • Annual, $1,550.00 per year. Includes supplement *Moody's OTC Unlisted News Report.*

NASD Manual. National Association of Securities Dealers, Inc. Available from CCH, Inc. • Quarterly. $430.00 per year.

Over-the-Counter Derivatives Products: A Guide to Legal Risk Management and Documentation. Robert M. McLaughlin. McGraw-Hill Professional. • 1998. $75.00.

Understanding Financial Derivatives: How to Protect Your Investments. Donald Strassheim. McGraw-Hill Professional. • 1996. $40.00. Covers three basic risk management instruments: options, futures, and swaps. Includes advice on equity index options, financial futures contracts, and over-the-counter derivatives markets.

INTERNET DATABASES

DBC Online: America's Leading Provider of Real-Time Market Data to the Individual Investor. Data Broadcasting Corp. Phone: (415)571-1800 E-mail: dbcinfo@dbc.com • URL: http://www.dbc.com • Web site provides a wide variety of real-time securities market prices, data, and charts. Covers bonds ("BondVu"), stocks, commodities, options, mutual funds, major indexes, industry indexes, international markets, etc. Also includes news, SEC documents ("Smart-Edgar"), and various other features. Fees: Both free and fee-based, depending on level of information.

TheStreet.com: Your Insider's Look at Wall Street. TheStreet.com, Inc. Phone: 800-562-9571 or (212)321-5000 Fax: (212)321-5016 • URL: http://www.thestreet.com • Web site offers "Free Sections" and "Premium Sections" ($9.95 per month). Both sections offer iconoclastic advice and comment on the stock market, but premium service displays a more comprehensive selection of news and analysis. There are many by-lined articles. "Search the Site" is included.

Wall Street Journal Interactive Edition. Dow Jones & Co., Inc. Phone: 800-369-2834 or (212)416-2000 Fax: (212)416-2658 E-mail: inquiries@interactive.wsj.com • URL: http://www.wsj.com • Fee-based Web site providing online searching of worldwide information from the *The Wall Street Journal.* Includes "Company Snapshots," "The Journal's Greatest Hits," "Index to Market Data," "14-Day Searchable Archive," "Journal Links," etc. Financial price quotes are available. Fees: $49.00 per year; $29.00 per year to print subscribers.

Web Finance: Covering the Electronic Evolution of Finance. Securities Data Publishing. Phone: (212)765-5311 or 800-455-5844 Fax: (212)321-2336 E-mail: webfinance@tfn.com • URL: http://www.webfinance.net • Bi-weekly print and daily web-site publication of financial services on the Web, including financial links, archives, brokerage stocks, deal financing, and other financial and investment news and information.

ONLINE DATABASES

Disclosure SEC Database. Disclosure, Inc. • Provides information from records filed with the Securities and Exchange Commission by publicly owned corporations, 1977 to present. Weekly updates. Inquire as to online cost and availability.

PERIODICALS AND NEWSLETTERS

America's Fastest Growing Companies. Individual Investor Group, Inc. • Monthly. $165.00 per year. Newsletter. Provides investment information on about 150 publicly-held corporations that are showing rapidly expanding sales and earnings. Formerly *America's Fastest Growing Corporations.*

Barron's: The Dow Jones Business and Financial Weekly. Dow Jones and Co., Inc. • Weekly. $145.00 per year.

Equities: Investment News of Promising Public Companies. Equities Magazine LLC. • Seven times a year. $21.00 per year. Formerly *OTC Review.*

Financial Sentinel: Your Beacon to the World of Investing. Gulf Atlantic Publishing, Inc. • Monthly. $29.95 per year. Provides "The only complete listing of all OTC Bulletin Board stocks traded, with all issues listed on the Nasdaq SmallCap Market, the Toronto, and Vancouver Stock Exchanges." Also includes investment advice and recommendations of small capitalization stocks.

Individual Investor. Individual Investor Group. • Monthly. $22.95 per year. Emphasis is on stocks selling for less than ten dollars a share. Includes a "Guide to Insider Transactions" and "New Issue Alert.".

New Issues: The Investor's Guide to Initial Public Offerings. Norman G. Fosback. Institute for Econometric Research. • Monthly. $200.00 per year. Newsletter. Includes "Penny Stock Calendar".

Penny Fortune Newsletter. James M. Fortune, editor. • Monthly. $79.00 per year. Reports on special situations and low- priced stocks. Includes charts and graphs.

Special Situations Newsletter: In-depth Survey of Under-Valued Stocks. Charles Howard Kaplan. • Monthly. $75.00 per year. Newsletter. Principal content is "This Month's Recommendation," a detailed analysis of one special situation stock.

The Wall Street Journal. Dow Jones & Co., Inc. • Daily. $175.00 per year. Covers news and trends relating to business, industry, finance, the economy, and international commerce. Provides extensive price and other data for the securities, commodity, options, futures, foreign exchange, and money markets.

PRICE SOURCES

Bank and Quotation Record. William B. Dana Co. • Monthly. $130.00 per year.

National Stock Summary. National Quotation Bureau, Inc. • Monthly. $480.00 per year. Semiannual cumulations. Includes price quotes for both active and inactive issues, with transfer agents, market makers (brokers), and other information. (The National Quotation Bureau also provides daily and weekly stock price services.).

STATISTICS SOURCES

Nasdaq Fact Book and Company Directory. National Association of Security Dealers, Inc. Corporate Communications. • Annual. $20.00. Contains statistical data relating to the Nasdaq Stock Market. Also provides corporate address, phone, symbol, stock price, and trading volume information for more than 5,000 securities traded through the National Association of Securities Dealers Automated Quotation System (Nasdaq), including Small-Cap Issues. Includes indexing by Standard Industrial Classification (SIC) number.

TRADE/PROFESSIONAL ASSOCIATIONS

Association of Publicly Traded Companies. 1200 G St., N.W., Suite 800, Washington, DC 20005. Phone: (202)434-8983 Fax: (202)434-8707 E-mail: aptc@aptc.org • URL: http://www.aptc.org.

National Association of Securities Dealers. 1735 K St., N.W., Washington, DC 20006-1506. Phone: (202)728-8000 Fax: (202)293-6260 • URL: http://www.nasdr.com/1000.asp.

Security Traders Association. One World Trade Center, Suite 4511, New York, NY 10048. Phone: (212)524-0484 Fax: (212)321-3449.

OTHER SOURCES

Factiva. Dow Jones Reuters Business Interactive, LLC. • Fee-based Web site provides "global news and business information through Web sites and content integration solutions." Includes Dow Jones and Reuters newswires, The Wall Street Journal, and more than 7,000 other sources of current news, historical articles, market research reports, and investment analysis. Content includes 96 major U. S. newspapers, 900 non-English sources, trade publications, media transcripts, country profiles, news photos, etc.

Nexis.com. Lexis-Nexis Group. • Fee-based Web site offers searching of about 2.8 billion documents in some 30,000 news, business, and legal information sources. Features include a subject directory covering 1,200 topics in 34 categories and a Company Dossier containing information on more than 500,000 public and private companies. Boolean searching is offered.

OVERSEAS EMPLOYMENT

See: EMPLOYMENT IN FOREIGN COUNTRIES

OXYACETYLENE WELDING

See: WELDING

OYSTER INDUSTRY

See also: SEAFOOD INDUSTRY; SHELLFISH INDUSTRY

STATISTICS SOURCES

Fisheries of the United States. Available from U. S. Government Printing Office. • Annual. $18.00.

Issued by the National Marine Fisheries Service, National Oceanic and Atmospheric Administration, U. S. Department of Commerce.

TRADE/PROFESSIONAL ASSOCIATIONS

Molluscan Shellfish Institute. 1901 N. Fort Meyer Dr., Suite 700, Arlington, VA 22209. Phone: (703)524-8883 Fax: (703)524-4619 E-mail: office@nfi.org.

National Shellfisheries Association. c/o Nancy C. Lewis, P.O. Box 350, Wachapreague, VA 23480. Phone: (757)787-5816 Fax: (757)787-5831 E-mail: nlewis@vims.edu • URL: http://www.shellfish.org.

Pacific Coast Oyster Growers Association. 120 State Ave., N.E., No. 142, Olympia, WA 98501. Phone: (360)754-2744 Fax: (360)754-2743 E-mail: pcsga@olywa.net • URL: http://www.olywa,net/pcoga/pcoga.html.

P

PACKAGING

See also: CONTAINER INDUSTRY; PAPER BOX AND PAPER CONTAINER INDUSTRIES; PAPERBOARD AND PAPERBOARD PACKAGING INDUSTRIES

GENERAL WORKS

The Total Package: The Secret History and Hidden Meanings of Boxes, Bottles, Cans, and Other Persuasive Containers. Thomas Hine. Little, Brown and Co. • 1997. $14.95. A popularly written history of packaging.

ABSTRACTS AND INDEXES

Foods Adlibra: Key to the World's Food Literature. Foods Adlibra Publications. • Semimonthly.Provides journal citations and abstracts to the literature of food technology and packaging.

BIOGRAPHICAL SOURCES

Who's Who and What's What in Packaging. Institute of Packaging Professionals. • Annual. Price on application.

DIRECTORIES

Household and Personal Products Industry - Buyers Guide. Rodman Publications. • Annual. $12.00. Lists of suppliers to manufacturers of cosmetics, toiletries, soaps, detergents, and related household and personal products.

Household and Personal Products Industry Contract Packaging and Private Label Directory. Rodman Publications. • Annual. $12.00. Provides information on about 450 companies offering private label or contract packaged household and personal care products, such as detergents, cosmetics, polishes, insecticides, and various aerosol items.

Official Container Directory. Advanstar Communications, Inc. • Semiannual. $75.00. About 3,000 manufacturers of corrugated and solid fiber containers, folding cartons, rigid boxes, fiber cans and tubes, and fiber drums. Includes a buying guide.

Packaging Digest Machinery/Materials Guide. Cahners Business Information. • Annual. $46.00. List of more than 3,100 manufacturers of machinery and materials for the packaging industry, and about 260 contract packagers.

ENCYCLOPEDIAS AND DICTIONARIES

Wiley Encyclopedia of Packaging Technology. Aaron Brody and Kenneth Marsh, editors. John Wiley and Sons, Inc. • 1997. $190.00. Second edition.

ONLINE DATABASES

FOODS ADLIBRA. General Mills, Inc. • Contains online citations, with abstracts, to the technical and business literature of food processing and packaging. New products and new ingredients are featured. Covers about 250 trade journals and 500 research journals from 1974 to date, with monthly updates. Inquire as to online cost and availability.

PIRA. Technical Centre for the Paper and Board, Printing and Packaging Industries. • Citations and abstracts pertaining to bookbinding and other pulp, paper, and packaging industries, 1975 to present. Weekly updates. Inquire as to online cost and availability.

PERIODICALS AND NEWSLETTERS

Household and Personal Products Industry: The Magazine for the Detergent, Soap, Cosmetic and Toiletry, Wax, Polish and Aerosol Industries. Rodman Publications. • Monthly. $48.00 per year. Covers marketing, packaging, production, technical innovations, private label developments, and aerosol packaging for soap, detergents, cosmetics, insecticides, and a variety of other household products.

Packaging Digest. Cahners Business Information. • 13 times a year. $92.90 per year.

Packaging Technology and Science. Available from John Wiley and Sons, Inc., Journals Div. • Bimonthly. $995.00 per year. Provides international coverage of subject matter. Published in England by John Wiley & Sons Ltd.

RESEARCH CENTERS AND INSTITUTES

Institute for Food Law and Regulations. Michigan State University, 165C National Food Safety and Toxicology Bldg., East Lansing, MI 48224. Phone: 888-579-3663 or (517)355-8295 Fax: (517)432-1492 E-mail: vhegarty@pilot.msu.edu • URL: http://www.msu.edu • Conducts research on the food industry, including processing, packaging, marketing, and new products.

Institute of Food Science. Cornell University, 114 Stocking Hall, Ithaca, NY 14853. Phone: (607)255-7915 Fax: (607)254-4868 E-mail: mrm1@cornell.edu • URL: http://www.nysaes.cornell.edu/cifs/ • Research areas include the chemistry and processing of food commodities, food processing engineering, food packaging, and nutrition.

TRADE/PROFESSIONAL ASSOCIATIONS

Flexible Packaging Association. 1090 Vermont Ave., N.W., Suite 500, Washington, DC 20005-4960. Phone: (202)842-3880 Fax: (202)842-3841 E-mail: fpa@flexpack.org.

Institute of Packaging Professionals. 481 Carlisle Dr., Herndon, VA 20170. Phone: 800-432-4085 or (703)318-8970 Fax: (703)814-4961 E-mail: iopp@pkgmatters.com • URL: http://www.iopp.org.

National Beverage Packaging Association. c/o Gary Lile, No. 1 Busch Place, OSC-2N, St. Louis, MO 63118. Phone: (314)577-2443 Fax: (314)577-2972 E-mail: gary.lileoanheuser-busch.com • Members are concerned with the packaging of soft drinks, beer, and juices.

OTHER SOURCES

Converted Flexible Packaging. Available from MarketResearch.com. • 1998. $3,400.00. Published by the Freedonia Group. Market data with forecasts to the year 2006. Covers plastic, paper, and foil packaging for food and non-food products.

Food Law Reports. CCH, Inc. • Weekly. $1,349.00 per year. Six looseleaf volumes. Covers regulation of adulteration, packaging, labeling, and additives. Formerly *Food Drug Cosmetic Law Reports.*

PACKAGING LABELS

See: LABELS AND LABELING

PACKAGING MACHINERY

DIRECTORIES

Packaging Digest Machinery/Materials Guide. Cahners Business Information. • Annual. $46.00. List of more than 3,100 manufacturers of machinery and materials for the packaging industry, and about 260 contract packagers.

PMMI: Official Packaging Machinery Directory. Packaging Machinery Manufacturers Institute. • Biennial. $25.00 per year.

ENCYCLOPEDIAS AND DICTIONARIES

Wiley Encyclopedia of Packaging Technology. Aaron Brody and Kenneth Marsh, editors. John Wiley and Sons, Inc. • 1997. $190.00. Second edition.

PERIODICALS AND NEWSLETTERS

Packaging Digest. Cahners Business Information. • 13 times a year. $92.90 per year.

STATISTICS SOURCES

U. S. Industry and Trade Outlook: The McGraw-Hill Companies and the U.S. Department of Commerce/International Trade Administration. Datapso Research Corp. • Annual. $69.95. Produced by the International Trade Administration, U. S. Department of Commerce, in a "public-private" partnership with DRI/McGraw-Hill and Standard & Poor's. Provides basic data, outlook for the current year, and "Long-Term Prospects" (five-year projections) for a wide variety of products and services. Includes high technology industries. Formerly *U. S. Industrial Outlook.*

TRADE/PROFESSIONAL ASSOCIATIONS

Packaging Machinery Manufacturers Institute. 4350 N. Fairfax Dr., Suite 600, Arlington, VA 22203. Phone: (703)243-8555 Fax: (703)243-8556 • URL: http://www.packexpo.com.

PACKAGING, PRESSURE

See: PRESSURE PACKAGING

PACKING INDUSTRY

See: MEAT INDUSTRY

PAINT AND PAINTING

See also: INDUSTRIAL COATINGS; VARNISH AND VARNISHING

GENERAL WORKS

The Chemistry and Physics of Coatings. Alastair R. Marrion, editor. CRC Press, Inc. • 1994. $42.00. Published by The Royal Society of Chemistry. Provides an overview of paint science and technology, including environmental considerations.

ABSTRACTS AND INDEXES

CPI Digest: Key to World Literature Serving the Coatings, Plastics, Fibers, Adhesives, and Related Industries (Chemical Process Industries). CPI Information Services. • Monthly. $397.00 per year. Abstracts of business and technical articles for polymer-based, chemical process industries. Includes a monthly list of relevant U. S. patents. International coverage.

World Surface Coatings Abstracts. Paint Research Association. • 13 times a year. Members, $1,260.00 per year; non-members, $1,980.00 per year.

DIRECTORIES

Building Supply Home Centers Retail Giants Report. Cahners Business Information. • Annual. $30.00. Lists major retailers of a wide variety of building and home improvement materials, products, fixtures, accessories, equipment, and tools.

Directory of Home Center Operators and Hardware Chains. Chain Store Age. • Annual. $300.00. Nearly 5,400 home center operators, paint and home decorating chains, and lumber and building materials companies.

Paint Red Book. PTN Publishing Co. • Annual. $53.00. Lists manufacturers of paint, varnish, lacquer, and specialized coatings. Suppliers of raw materials, chemicals, and equipment are included.

Rauch Guide to the U.S. Paint Industry. Carl Verbanic and Donald Dykes. Impact Marketing Consultants. • $389.00. Looseleaf. Includes market data in addition to directory information. Formerly *Kline Guide to the Paint Industry.*

FINANCIAL RATIOS

Almanac of Business and Industrial Financial Ratios. Leo Troy. Prentice Hall. • Annual. $99.95. Contains financial ratios derived from federal tax returns. Ratios for each of about 200 industries are arranged according to company asset size.

Annual Statement Studies. Robert Morris Associates: The Association of Lending and Credit Risk Professiona. • Annual. Free to members; non-members, $140.00. Median and quartile financial ratios are given for over 400 kinds of manufacturing, wholesale, retail, construction, and consumer finance establishments. Data is sorted by both asset size and sales volume. Includes a clearly written "Definition of Ratios" and an alphabetical industry index.

HANDBOOKS AND MANUALS

House Painting. Entrepreneur Media, Inc. • Looseleaf. $59.50. A practical guide to starting a house painting business. Covers profit potential, start-up costs, market size evaluation, owner's time required, pricing, accounting, advertising, promotion, etc. (Start-Up Business Guide No. E1249.).

Maintenance Engineering Handbook. Lindley R. Higgins. McGraw-Hill. • 1994. $125.00. Fifth edition. Contains about 60 chapters by various authors in 12 major sections covering all elements of industrial and plant maintenance.

Paint Handbook. Guy E. Weismantel, editor. McGraw-Hill. • 1981. $89.95.

Surface Coatings: Science and Technology. Swaraj Paul. John Wiley and Sons, Inc. • 1996. $225.00. Second edition.

INTERNET DATABASES

Fedstats. Federal Interagency Council on Statistical Policy. Phone: (202)395-7254 • URL: http://www.fedstats.gov • Web site features an efficient search facility for full-text statistics produced by more than 70 federal agencies, including the Census Bureau, the Bureau of Economic Analysis, and the Bureau of Labor Statistics. Boolean searches can be made within one agency or for all agencies combined. Links are offered to international statistical bureaus, including the UN, IMF, OECD, UNESCO, Eurostat, and 20 individual countries. Fees: Free.

ONLINE DATABASES

DRI U.S. Central Database. Data Products Division. • Provides more than 23,000 business, financial, demographic, economic, foreign trade, and industry-related time series for the U.S. Includes national income, population, retail-wholesale trade, price indexes, labor data, housing, industrial production, banking, interest rates, money supply, etc. Time period is generally 1947 to date (some data back to 1929). Updating varies. Inquire as to online cost and availability.

World Surface Coatings Abstracts [Online]. Paint Research Association of Great Britain. • Indexing and abstracting of the literature of paint and surface coatings, 1976 to present. Monthly updates. Inquire as to online cost and availability.

PERIODICALS AND NEWSLETTERS

American Painting Contractor. Douglas Publications, Inc. • Nine times a year. $30.00 per year.

Modern Paint and Coatings. Chemical Week Associates. • Monthly. $52.00 per year.

Paint and Coatings Industry. Business News Publishing Co. • Monthly. $55.00 per year. Includes annual *Raw Material* and *Equipment Directory and Buyers Guide.*

Paint and Decorating Retailer. Paint and Decorating Retailers Association. • Monthly. $45.00 per year. Formerly *Decorating Retailer.*

RESEARCH CENTERS AND INSTITUTES

Emulsion Polymers Institute. Lehigh University, Iacocca Hall, 111 Research Dr., Bethlehem, PA 18015. Phone: (610)758-3590 Fax: (610)758-5880 E-mail: mse0@lehigh.edu • URL: http://www.lehigh.edu/~esd0/epihome.html • Includes latex paint research.

STATISTICS SOURCES

Annual Survey of Manufactures. Available from U. S. Government Printing Office. • Annual. Prices vary. Issued by the U. S. Census Bureau as an interim update to the *Census of Manufactures.* Includes data on number of manufacturing establishments in various industries, employment, labor costs, value of shipments, capital expenditures, inventories, energy costs, and assets. (See also Census Bureau home page, http://www.census.gov/.).

Business Statistics of the United States. Courtenay M. Slater, editor. Bernan Associates. • 1999. $74.00. Fifth edition. Based on *Business Statistics,* formerly issue by the Bureau of Economic Analysis, U. S. Department of Commerce. Provides basic data for a wide variety of U. S. industries, services, and economic indicators. Most statistics are shown annually for 29 years and monthly for the most recent four years.

Manufacturing Profiles. Available from U. S. Government Printing Office. • Annual. Issued by the U. S. Census Bureau. A printed consolidation of the entire *Current Industrial Report* series, presenting "all the data compiled." Contains statistics on production, shipments, inventories, consumption, exports, imports, and orders for a wide variety of manufactured products. (See also Census Bureau home page, http://www.census.gov/.).

Paint, Varnish, and Lacquer. U. S. Bureau of the Census. • Quarterly and annual. Provides data on shipments: value, quantity, imports, and exports. Includes paint, varnish, lacquer, product finishes, and special purpose coatings. (Current Industrial Reports, MQ-28F.).

Survey of Current Business. Available from U. S. Government Printing Office. • Monthly. $49.00 per year. Issued by Bureau of Economic Analysis, U. S. Department of Commerce. Presents a wide variety of business and economic data.

TRADE/PROFESSIONAL ASSOCIATIONS

Federation of Societies for Coatings Technology. 492 Norristown Rd., Blue Bell, PA 19422-2307. Phone: (215)940-0777 Fax: (215)940-0292 E-mail: fsct@coatingstech.org • URL: http://ww.coatingstech.org.

National Paint and Coatings Association. 1500 Rhode Island Ave., N.W., Washington, DC 20005-5597. Phone: (202)462-6272 Fax: (202)462-8549 E-mail: npca@paint.org • URL: http://www.paint.org.

Painting and Decorating Contractors of America. 3913 Old Lee Highway, Suite 33B, Fairfax, VA 22030-2433. Phone: 800-332-7322 or (703)359-0826 Fax: (703)359-2576 • URL: http://www.pdca.org.

OTHER SOURCES

Coatings. National Paint and Coatings Association. • 10 times a year. $62.00 per year.

PAMPHLETS

ABSTRACTS AND INDEXES

Vertical File Index: Guide to Pamphlets and References to Current Topics. H.W. Wilson Co. • 11 times a year. $50.00 per year. A subject and title index to selected pamphlet material.

HANDBOOKS AND MANUALS

How to Produce Creative Advertising: Traditional Techniques and Computer Applications. Thomas Bivins and Ann Keding. NTC/Contemporary Publishing. • 1993. $37.95. Covers copywriting, advertising design, and the use of desktop publishing techniques in advertising. (NTC Business Book Series).

How to Produce Creative Publications: Traditional Techniques and Computer Applications. Thomas Bivins and William E. Ryan. NTC/Contemporary Publishing. • 1994. $32.95. A practical guide to the writing, designing, and production of magazines, annual reports, brochures, and newsletters by traditional methods and by desktop publishing.

The Perfect Sales Piece: A Complete Do-It-Yourself Guide to Creating Brochures, Catalogs, Fliers, and Pamphlets. Robert W. Bly. John Wiley and Sons, Inc. • 1994. $49.95. A guide to the use of various forms of printed literature for direct selling, sales promotion, and marketing. (Small Business Editions Series).

RESEARCH CENTERS AND INSTITUTES

Design Research Unit. Massachusetts College of Art, 621 Huntington Ave., Boston, MA 02115. Phone: (617)232-1492 Fax: (617)566-4034 • Conducts research related to the design of printed matter, including annual reports, letterheads, posters, and brochures.

OTHER SOURCES

Bits and Pieces: A Monthly Mixture of Horse Sense and Common Sense About Working with People. Economics Press, Inc. • Monthly. $22.00 per year. Quantity rates available. Pamphlets contain inspirational humor for employees.

PAPER BAG INDUSTRY

DIRECTORIES

Sources of Supply/Buyers Guide. William O. Dannhausen Corp. • Annual. $90.00. About 2,200 mills and converters, 2,700 merchants and 500 manufacturers' representatives in paper, films, foils, and allied lines.

PERIODICALS AND NEWSLETTERS

Paper, Film and Foil Converter. Intertec Publishing Corp. • Monthly. $62.50 per year.

STATISTICS SOURCES

Annual Survey of Manufactures. Available from U. S. Government Printing Office. • Annual. Prices vary. Issued by the U. S. Census Bureau as an interim update to the *Census of Manufactures.* Includes data on number of manufacturing establishments in various industries, employment, labor costs, value of shipments, capital expenditures, inventories, energy costs, and assets. (See also Census Bureau home page, http://www.census.gov/.).

TRADE/PROFESSIONAL ASSOCIATIONS

Paper Shipping Sack Manufacturers Association. 505 White Plains Rd., No. 206, Tarrytown, NY 10591. Phone: (914)631-0909 Fax: (914)631-0333.

PAPER BOARD INDUSTRY

See: PAPERBOARD AND PAPERBOARD PACKAGING INDUSTRIES

PAPER BOX AND PAPER CONTAINER INDUSTRIES

See also: BOX INDUSTRY; CONTAINER INDUSTRY; PAPERBOARD AND PAPERBOARD PACKAGING INDUSTRIES

DIRECTORIES

National Paperbox Association Membership Directory. National Paperbox Association. • Annual. $125.00.

Official Container Directory. Advanstar Communications, Inc. • Semiannual. $75.00. About 3,000 manufacturers of corrugated and solid fiber containers, folding cartons, rigid boxes, fiber cans and tubes, and fiber drums. Includes a buying guide.

Sources of Supply/Buyers Guide. William O. Dannhausen Corp. • Annual. $90.00. About 2,200 mills and converters, 2,700 merchants and 500 manufacturers' representatives in paper, films, foils, and allied lines.

ONLINE DATABASES

PIRA. Technical Centre for the Paper and Board, Printing and Packaging Industries. • Citations and abstracts pertaining to bookbinding and other pulp, paper, and packaging industries, 1975 to present. Weekly updates. Inquire as to online cost and availability.

PERIODICALS AND NEWSLETTERS

Boxboard Containers International. Intertec Publishing Corp. • Monthly. $28.00 per year. Formerly *Boxboard Containers.*

STATISTICS SOURCES

U. S. Industry and Trade Outlook: The McGraw-Hill Companies and the U.S. Department of Commerce/International Trade Administration. Datapso Research Corp. • Annual. $69.95. Produced by the International Trade Administration, U. S. Department of Commerce, in a "public-private" partnership with DRI/McGraw-Hill and Standard & Poor's. Provides basic data, outlook for the current year, and "Long-Term Prospects" (five-year projections) for a wide variety of products and services. Includes high technology industries. Formerly *U. S. Industrial Outlook.*

TRADE/PROFESSIONAL ASSOCIATIONS

Fibre Box Association. 2850 Golf Rd., Rolling Meadows, IL 60008. Phone: (847)364-9600 Fax: (847)364-9639 • URL: http://www.fibrebox.org.

National Paperbox Association. 801 N. Fairfax St., Suite 211, Alexandria, VA 22314-1757. Phone: (703)684-2212 Fax: (703)683-6920 E-mail: boxmaker@paperbox.org • URL: http://www.paperbox.org.

PAPER CONTAINERS

See: PAPER BOX AND PAPER CONTAINER INDUSTRIES

PAPER INDUSTRY

See also: PAPERBOARD AND PAPERBOARD PACKAGING INDUSTRIES; WOODPULP INDUSTRY

ABSTRACTS AND INDEXES

Institute of Paper Science and Technology. Abstract Bulletin. Institute of Paper Science and Technology. • Monthly. Worldwide coverage of the scientific and technical literature of interest to the pulp and paper industry.

NTIS Alerts: Materials Sciences. National Technical Information Service. • Semimonthly. $220.00 per year. Provides descriptions of government-sponsored research reports and software, with ordering information. Covers ceramics, glass, coatings, composite materials, alloys, plastics, wood, paper, adhesives, fibers, lubricants, and related subjects. Formerly *Abstract Newsletter.*

CD-ROM DATABASES

World Marketing Forecasts on CD-ROM. The Gale Group. • Annual. $2,500.00. Produced by Euromonitor. Provides detailed forecast data for the years to 2012 on CD-ROM for 54 countries in all parts of the world. Covers a wide range of social, demographic, economic, and market factors. Includes specific forecasts for many kinds of consumer products.

DIRECTORIES

Lockwood-Post's Directory of the Pulp, Paper and Allied Trades. Miller Freeman, Inc. • Annual. $277.00. Formerly *Lockwood's Directory of the Paper and Allied Trades.*

Pulp and Paper Buyer's Guide. Miller Freeman, Inc. • Annual. $155.00. Supplies and equipment.

Sources of Supply/Buyers Guide. William O. Dannhausen Corp. • Annual. $90.00. About 2,200 mills and converters, 2,700 merchants and 500 manufacturers' representatives in paper, films, foils, and allied lines.

Walden's ABC Guide and Paper Production Yearbook. Walden-Mott Corp. • Annual. $145.00. Detailed listings on about 7,662 paper manufacturers, converters and distributors in North America.

FINANCIAL RATIOS

Almanac of Business and Industrial Financial Ratios. Leo Troy. Prentice Hall. • Annual. $99.95. Contains financial ratios derived from federal tax returns. Ratios for each of about 200 industries are arranged according to company asset size.

HANDBOOKS AND MANUALS

Paper Basics: Forestry, Manufacture, Selection, Purchasing, Mathematics and Metrics, Recycling. David Saltman. Krieger Publishing Co. • 1991. $29.50. Reprint of 1978 edition.

INTERNET DATABASES

Fedstats. Federal Interagency Council on Statistical Policy. Phone: (202)395-7254 • URL: http://www.fedstats.gov • Web site features an efficient search facility for full-text statistics produced by more than 70 federal agencies, including the Census Bureau, the Bureau of Economic Analysis, and the Bureau of Labor Statistics. Boolean searches can be made within one agency or for all agencies combined. Links are offered to international statistical bureaus, including the UN, IMF, OECD, UNESCO, Eurostat, and 20 individual countries. Fees: Free.

ONLINE DATABASES

Business and Industry. Responsive Database Services, Inc. • Contains online citations, abstracts, and selected fulltext from more than 1,000 trade journals, newspapers, and other publications. Provides general coverage of both manufacturing and service industries, including marketing, production, industry trends, key events, and information on specific companies. Time span is 1994 to date. Daily updates. Inquire as to online cost and availability. (Also available in a CD-ROM version.).

DRI U.S. Central Database. Data Products Division. • Provides more than 23,000 business, financial, demographic, economic, foreign trade, and industry-related time series for the U.S. Includes national income, population, retail-wholesale trade, price indexes, labor data, housing, industrial production, banking, interest rates, money supply, etc. Time period is generally 1947 to date (some data back to 1929). Updating varies. Inquire as to online cost and availability.

Euromonitor Market Research. Euromonitor International. • Provides the complete text online of Euromonitor market analysis reports. Covers consumer goods market research data for all major countries, with emphasis on specific product categories. Time period is current. Continuous updating. Inquire as to online cost and availability.

PaperChem Database. Information Services Div. • Worldwide coverage of the scientific and technical paper industry chemical literature, including patents, 1967 to present. Weekly updates. Inquire as to online cost and availability.

PIRA. Technical Centre for the Paper and Board, Printing and Packaging Industries. • Citations and abstracts pertaining to bookbinding and other pulp, paper, and packaging industries, 1975 to present. Weekly updates. Inquire as to online cost and availability.

Tablebase. Responsive Database Services, Inc. • Provides online numerical tabular data from a wide variety of business, organization, and government sources, including 900 trade journals. Includes industry and individual company statistics relating to products, market share, sales forecasts, production, exports, market trends, etc. Time span is 1997 to date. Weekly updates. Inquire as to online cost and availability. (Also available in a CD-ROM version.).

PERIODICALS AND NEWSLETTERS

Paper Age. Global Publications. • Monthly. $20.00 per year.

Pulp and Paper. Miller Freeman, Inc. • Monthly. $135.00 per year.

Pulp and Paper Week. Miller Freeman, Inc. • 48 times a year. $737.00 per year. Newsletter.

TAPPI Journal. Technical Association of the Pulp and Paper Industry, Inc. • Monthly. Membership.

RESEARCH CENTERS AND INSTITUTES

Pulp and Paper Laboratory. North Carolina State University. Dept. of Wood and Paper Science, P.O. 8005, Raleigh, NC 27695. Phone: (919)515-5807 Fax: (919)515-6302 E-mail: mikekocurek@ncsu.edu • URL: http://www.cfr.ncsu.edu/wps/.

STATISTICS SOURCES

Annual Survey of Manufactures. Available from U. S. Government Printing Office. • Annual. Prices vary. Issued by the U. S. Census Bureau as an interim update to the *Census of Manufactures.* Includes data on number of manufacturing establishments in various industries, employment, labor costs, value of shipments, capital expenditures, inventories, energy costs, and assets. (See also Census Bureau home page, http://www.census.gov/.).

Business Statistics of the United States. Courtenay M. Slater, editor. Bernan Associates. • 1999. $74.00. Fifth edition. Based on *Business Statistics*, formerly issue by the Bureau of Economic Analysis, U. S. Department of Commerce. Provides basic data for a wide variety of U. S. industries, services, and economic indicators. Most statistics are shown annually for 29 years and monthly for the most recent four years.

Consumer Canada 1996. Available from The Gale Group. • 1996. $750.00. Published by Euromonitor. Provides consumer market, socioeconomic, and demographic data for Canada. Includes consumer market size (volume and value) for many specific kinds of products.

Consumer International 2000/2001. Available from The Gale Group. • 1998. $1,190.00. Seventh edition. Published by Euromonitor. Contains extensive consumer market, economic, and demographic data for 27 major, non-European countries, including the U. S. and Canada. Includes consumer market size (volume and value) for 150 product types in 14 categories (food, clothing, automobiles, cosmetics, appliances, etc.).

Encyclopedia of American Industries. The Gale Group. • 1998. $560.00. Second edition. Two volumes. $280.00 per volume. Volume one is *Manufacturing Industries* and volume two is *Service and Non-Manufacturing Industries.* Provides the history, development, and recent status of approximately 1,000 industries. Includes statistical graphs, with industry and general indexes.

European Marketing Forecasts 2001. Available from The Gale Group. • 2000. $1,190.00. Third edition. Published by Euromonitor. Contains demographic, economic, and market forecasts for the countries of Europe to the year 2010. Forecasts include market-size data for 15 consumer product sectors (food, clothing, automobiles, consumer electronics, etc.).

International Marketing Forecasts 2001. Available from The Gale Group. • 2000. $1,090.00. Third edition. Published by Euromonitor. Contains demographic, economic, and market forecasts to the year 2010 for major, non-European countries, including the U. S. and Canada. Forecasts include market-size data for 15 consumer product sectors, such as food, clothing, and automobiles.

The Pulp and Paper Industry in the OECD Member Countries. Organization for Economic Cooperation and Development. Available from OECD Publications and Information Center. • Annual. $31.00. Presents annual data on production, consumption, capacity, utilization, and foreign trade. Covers 33 pulp and paper products in OECD countries. Text in English and French.

Standard & Poor's Industry Surveys. Standard & Poor's. • Semiannual. $1,800.00. Two looseleaf volumes. Includes monthly supplements. Provides detailed, individual surveys of 52 major industry groups. Each survey is revised on a semiannual basis. Also includes "Monthly Investment Review" (industry group investment analysis) and monthly "Trends & Projections" (economic analysis).

Statistics of Paper, Paperboard and Wood Pulp. American Forest and Paper Association. • Annual. $395.00. Formerly *Statistics of Paper and Paperboard.*

Survey of Current Business. Available from U. S. Government Printing Office. • Monthly. $49.00 per year. Issued by Bureau of Economic Analysis, U. S. Department of Commerce. Presents a wide variety of business and economic data.

WEFA Industrial Monitor. John Wiley and Sons, Inc. • Annual. $65.00. Prepared by industry analysts at WEFA, an economic forecasting and consulting firm (originally Wharton Econometric Forecasting Associates). Contains discussions of the outlook for major U. S. industries, with many 10-year forecasts (WEFA Web site is http://www.wefa.com).

TRADE/PROFESSIONAL ASSOCIATIONS

American Forest and Paper Association. 1111 19th St., N.W., Ste. 800, Washington, DC 20036. Phone: (202)463-2700 Fax: (202)463-2785 E-mail: info@afandpa.org • URL: http://www.afandpa.org.

National Paper Trade Association. c/o John J. Buckley, 111 Great Neck Rd., Great Neck, NY 11021. Phone: (516)829-3070 Fax: (516)829-3074 • URL: http://www.gonpta.com.

Paper Industry Management Association. 1699 Wall St., Suite 212, Mount Prospect, IL 60056-5782. Phone: (847)956-0250 Fax: (847)956-0520 • URL: http://www.pima-online.org.

TAPPI. P.O. Box 105113, Atlanta, GA 30348-5113. Phone: 800-332-8686 or (770)446-1400 Fax: (770)446-6947 E-mail: serviceline@tappi.org • URL: http://www.tappi.org.

OTHER SOURCES

Business & Company Resource Center. The Gale Group. • Fee-based Web site provides a wide range of business, industry, and specific company information. Access is offered to trade journal articles, market research data, insider trading activity, major shareholder data, corporate histories, emerging technology reports, corporate earnings estimates, press releases, and other sources. Provides detailed company profiles, industry overviews, and rankings. Offers integration of Predicasts PROMT, Newsletters ASAP, Investext Plus, Business Index ASAP, Brands and Their Companies, and other databases (many have full text).

Disposable Paper Products. Available from MarketResearch.com. • 1998. $5,900.00. Published by Euromonitor Publications Ltd. Provides consumer market data and forecasts to 2001 for the United States, the United Kingdom, Germany, France, and Italy.

PAPER MONEY

See also: MONEY

ALMANACS AND YEARBOOKS

World Currrency Yearbook. International Currency Analysis, Inc. • Annual. $250.00. Directory of more than 110 central banks worldwide.

HANDBOOKS AND MANUALS

Comprehensive Catalog of United States Paper Money. Gene Hessler. BNR Press. • 1992. $42.50. Fifth edtion.

Paper Money of the United States: A Complete Guide with Valuations. Arthur L. Friedberg and others. Coin and Currency Institute, Inc. • 1998. $35.00. 15th revised edition.

PERIODICALS AND NEWSLETTERS

Paper Money. Society of Paper Money Collectors, Inc. • Bimonthly. $20.00 per year.

TRADE/PROFESSIONAL ASSOCIATIONS

Society of Paper Money Collectors. P.O. Box 79341, Dallas, TX 75379-3941. URL: http://www.spmc.org.

PAPERBACK BOOKS

See: PAPERBOUND BOOK INDUSTRY

PAPERBOARD AND PAPERBOARD PACKAGING INDUSTRIES

See also: CONTAINER INDUSTRY; PAPER BOX AND PAPER CONTAINER INDUSTRIES; PAPER INDUSTRY

DIRECTORIES

Official Container Directory. Advanstar Communications, Inc. • Semiannual. $75.00. About 3,000 manufacturers of corrugated and solid fiber containers, folding cartons, rigid boxes, fiber cans and tubes, and fiber drums. Includes a buying guide.

ENCYCLOPEDIAS AND DICTIONARIES

Wiley Encyclopedia of Packaging Technology. Aaron Brody and Kenneth Marsh, editors. John Wiley and Sons, Inc. • 1997. $190.00. Second edition.

FINANCIAL RATIOS

Annual Statement Studies. Robert Morris Associates: The Association of Lending and Credit Risk Professiona. • Annual. Free to members; non-members, $140.00. Median and quartile financial ratios are given for over 400 kinds of manufacturing, wholesale, retail, construction, and consumer finance establishments. Data is sorted by both asset size and sales volume. Includes a clearly written "Definition of Ratios" and an alphabetical industry index.

INTERNET DATABASES

Fedstats. Federal Interagency Council on Statistical Policy. Phone: (202)395-7254 • URL: http://www.fedstats.gov • Web site features an efficient search facility for full-text statistics produced by more than 70 federal agencies, including the Census Bureau, the Bureau of Economic Analysis, and the Bureau of Labor Statistics. Boolean searches can be made within one agency or for all agencies combined. Links are offered to international statistical bureaus, including the UN, IMF, OECD, UNESCO, Eurostat, and 20 individual countries. Fees: Free.

ONLINE DATABASES

DRI U.S. Central Database. Data Products Division. • Provides more than 23,000 business, financial, demographic, economic, foreign trade, and industry-related time series for the U.S. Includes national income, population, retail-wholesale trade, price indexes, labor data, housing, industrial production, banking, interest rates, money supply, etc. Time period is generally 1947 to date (some data back to 1929). Updating varies. Inquire as to online cost and availability.

PIRA. Technical Centre for the Paper and Board, Printing and Packaging Industries. • Citations and abstracts pertaining to bookbinding and other pulp, paper, and packaging industries, 1975 to present. Weekly updates. Inquire as to online cost and availability.

PERIODICALS AND NEWSLETTERS

Paperboard Packaging Worldwide. Advanstar Communications, Inc. • Monthly. $39.00 per year.

PRICE SOURCES

Official Board Markets: "The Yellow Sheet". Mark Arzoumanian. Advanstar Communications, Inc. • Weekly. $150.00 per year. Covers the corrugated container, folding carton, rigid box and waste paper industries.

STATISTICS SOURCES

Annual Survey of Manufactures. Available from U. S. Government Printing Office. • Annual. Prices vary. Issued by the U. S. Census Bureau as an interim update to the *Census of Manufactures.* Includes data on number of manufacturing establishments in various industries, employment, labor costs, value of shipments, capital expenditures, inventories, energy costs, and assets. (See also Census Bureau home page, http://www.census.gov/.).

Business Statistics of the United States. Courtenay M. Slater, editor. Bernan Associates. • 1999. $74.00. Fifth edition. Based on *Business Statistics*, formerly issue by the Bureau of Economic Analysis, U. S. Department of Commerce. Provides basic data for a wide variety of U. S. industries, services, and economic indicators. Most statistics are shown annually for 29 years and monthly for the most recent four years.

Statistics of Paper, Paperboard and Wood Pulp. American Forest and Paper Association. • Annual. $395.00. Formerly *Statistics of Paper and Paperboard.*

Survey of Current Business. Available from U. S. Government Printing Office. • Monthly. $49.00 per year. Issued by Bureau of Economic Analysis, U. S. Department of Commerce. Presents a wide variety of business and economic data.

TRADE/PROFESSIONAL ASSOCIATIONS

Paperboard Packaging Council. 201 N. Union St., Ste 200, Alexandria, VA 22314. Phone: (703)836-3300 Fax: (703)836-3290 E-mail: paperboardpackaging@ppcnet.org • URL: http://www.ppcnet.org.

PAPERBOUND BOOK INDUSTRY

See also: BOOK INDUSTRY; PUBLISHING INDUSTRY

ALMANACS AND YEARBOOKS

Bowker Annual: Library and Book Trade Almanac. R. R. Bowker. • Annual. $175.00. Lists of accredited library schools; scholarships for education in library science; library organizations; major libraries; publishing and book sellers organizations. Includes statistics and news of the book business.

CD-ROM DATABASES

Books in Print On Disc: The Complete Books in Print System on Compact Laser Disc. Bowker Electronic Publishing. • Monthly. $1195.00 per year. The CD-ROM version of *Books in Print, Forthcoming Books*, and other Bowker bibliographic publications: lists the books of over 50,000 U.S. publishers. Includes books recently declared out-of-print. Also available with full text book reviews.

INTERNET DATABASES

Amazon.com. Amazon.com, Inc. Phone: 800-201-7575 or (206)346-2992 Fax: (206)346-2950 E-mail: info@amazon.com • URL: http://www.amazon.com • "Welcome to Earth's Biggest Bookstore." Amazon.com claims to have more than 2.5 million titles that can be ordered online, but only through the Web site - no orders by mail, telephone, fax, or E-mail. Discounts are generally 30% for hardcovers and 20% for paperbacks. Efficient search facilities, including Boolean, make this Web site useful for reference (many titles have online reviews). Fees: Free.

ONLINE DATABASES

Books in Print Online. Bowker Electronic Publishing. • The online version of *Books in Print, Forthcoming Books, Paperbound Books in Print*, and other Bowker bibliographic publications: lists the books of over 50,000 U. S. publishers. Includes books recently declared out-of-print. Updated monthly. Inquire as to online cost and availability.

PERIODICALS AND NEWSLETTERS

Publishers Weekly: The International News Magazine of Book Publishing. Cahners Business Information, Broadcasting and Cables International Group. • Weekly. $189.00 per year. The international news magazine of book publishing.

PAPERWORK MANAGEMENT

See: OFFICE MANAGEMENT; RECORDS MANAGEMENT

PARKING

BIBLIOGRAPHIES

Parking Publications for Planners. Dennis Jenks. Sage Publications, Inc. • 1993. $10.00.

HANDBOOKS AND MANUALS

Urban Parks and Open Space. Gayle L. Berens and others. Urban Land Institute. • 1997. Price on application. Covers financing, design, management, and public-private partnerships relative to the development of open space for new urban parks. Includes color illustrations and the history of urban parks.

PERIODICALS AND NEWSLETTERS

Downtown Idea Exchange: Essential Information for Downtown Research and Development Center. Downtown Research and Development Center. Alexander Communications Group, Inc. • Semimonthly. $157.00 per year. Newsletter for those concerned with central business districts. Provides news and other information on planning, development, parking, mass transit, traffic, funding, and other topics.

Parking: The Magazine of the Parking Industry. National Parking Association. • 10 times a year. $95.00 per year. Includes *Product and Services Directory.*

TRADE/PROFESSIONAL ASSOCIATIONS

National Parking Association. 1112 16th St., N.W., Suite 300, Washington, DC 20036. Phone: 800-647-7275 or (202)296-4336 Fax: (202)331-8523 E-mail: info@npapark.org • URL: http://www.npaparks.org.

PARKS

See also: AMUSEMENT INDUSTRY

ABSTRACTS AND INDEXES

Environment Abstracts. Congressional Information Service. • Monthly. Price varies. Provides multidisciplinary coverage of the world's environmental literature. Incorporates *Acid Rain Abstracts.*

Environment Abstracts Annual: A Guide to the Key Environmental Literature of the Year. Congressional Information Service. • Annual. $495.00. A yearly cumulation of *Environment Abstracts.*

Environmental Periodicals Bibliography: A Current Awareness Bibliography Featuring Citations of Scientific and Popular Articles in Serial Publications in the Area of the Environment. Environmental Studies Institute. International Academy at Santa Barbara. • Monthly. Price varies. An index to current environmental literature.

CD-ROM DATABASES

Environment Abstracts on CD-ROM. Congressional Information Service, Inc. • Quarterly. $1,295.00 per year. Contains the following CD-ROM databases: *Environment Abstracts, Energy Abstracts*, and *Acid Rain Abstracts.* Length of coverage varies.

DIRECTORIES

Parks and Recreation Buyers' Guide. National Recreation and Park Association. • Annual. Price upon application. List of 800 companies supplying products and services to private and governmental park and recreation agencies.

Parks Directory of the United States: A Guide to 4,700 National and State Parks, Recreation Areas, Historic Sites, Battlefields, Monuments, Forests, Preserves, Memorials, Seashores...and Other Designated Recreation Areas in the United State. Darren L. Smith, editor. Omnigraphics, Inc. • Biennial. $145.00. Consists of three sections: National Parks, State Parks, and Park-Related Organizations and Agencies. Includes an alphabetical index and a park classification index.

Resorts and Parks Purchasing Guide. Klevens Publications, Inc. • Annual. $60.00. Lists suppliers of products and services for resorts and parks, including national parks, amusement parks, dude ranches, golf resorts, ski areas, and national monument areas.

HANDBOOKS AND MANUALS

Evaluating Urban Parks and Recreation. William S. Hendon. Greenwood Publishing Group, Inc. • 1981. $65.00.

The Nature of Recreation: A Handbook in Honor of Frederick Law Olmsted. Richard S. Wurman and others. MIT Press. • 1972. $12.95.

ONLINE DATABASES

Enviroline. Congressional Information Service, Inc. • Provides online indexing and abstracting of worldwide environmental and natural resource literature from 1975 to date. Updated monthly. Inquire as to online cost and availability.

TRADE/PROFESSIONAL ASSOCIATIONS

National Association of County Park and Recreation Officials. c/o Genessee County Parks and Recreation Commission, 5045 Stanley Rd., Flint, MI 48506. Phone: (810)736-7100 Fax: (810)736-7220.

National Recreation and Park Association. 22377 Belmont Ridge Rd., Ashburn, VA 20148-4501. Phone: (703)858-0784 Fax: (703)858-0794 E-mail: info@nrpa.org • URL: http://www.nrpa.org/nrpa.

OTHER SOURCES

Atlas & Gazetteer Series. DeLorme Mapping Co. • Dates vary. $649.95 complete ($74.95 per region). Consists of 50 volumes covering all areas of the U. S. Includes detailed maps, as well as descriptions of attractions, natural areas, and historic sites. (CD-ROM versions available.).

Our National Parks and the Search for Sustainability. Bob R. O'Brien. University of Texas Press. • 1999. $40.00. Sustainability is defined as "a balance that allows as many people as possible to visit a park that is kept in as natural a state as possible.".

PARLIAMENTARY PROCEDURE

ABSTRACTS AND INDEXES

Current Law Index: Multiple Access to Legal Periodicals. The Gale Group. • Monthly. $650.00 per year. Produced in cooperation with the American Association of Law Libraries. Indexes more than 900 law journals, legal newspapers, and specialty publications from the U.S., Canada, U.K., Ireland, Australia, and New Zealand.

ENCYCLOPEDIAS AND DICTIONARIES

Encyclopedia of Corporate Meetings, Minutes and Resolutions. William Sardell, editor. Prentice Hall. • 1985. $125.00. Third edition. Two volumes.

HANDBOOKS AND MANUALS

Formal Meeting: How to Prepare and Participate. Alice N. Pohl. NTC/Contemporary Publishing. • 1992. $10.95. (NTC Business Book Series).

Mason's Manual of Legislative Procedure. American Society of Legislative Clerks and Secretaries. National Conference of State Legislatures. • 1989. $40.00. Revised edition. Contains parliamentary law and rules, rules of debate, rules governing motions, how to conduct business, etc.

Modern Parliamentary Procedure. Ray E. Keesey. American Psychological Association. • 1994. $24.95. Revised edition. A modernization and simplification of traditional, complex rules of procedure. Written for associations, clubs, community groups, and other deliberative bodies.

Parliamentary Law and Practice for Nonprofit Organizations. Howard L. Oleck and Cami Green. American Law Institute-American Bar Association. • 1991. $20.00. Second edition. Covers meeting procedures, motions, debate, voting, nominations, elections, committees, duties of officers, rights of members, and other topics.

Robert's Rules of Order. Henry M. Roberts and William J. Evans, editors. HarperCollins Publishers. • 2000. $17.00. 10th edition.

PERIODICALS AND NEWSLETTERS

National Parliamentarian. National Association of Parliamentarians. • Quarterly. $20.00 per year. Articles and questions with answers on parliamentary procedure.

Parliamentary Journal. American Institute of Parliamentarians. • Quarterly. $20.00 per year.

RESEARCH CENTERS AND INSTITUTES

Lexis.com Research System. Lexis-Nexis Group. Phone: 800-227-9597 or (937)865-6800 Fax: (937)865-6909 E-mail: webmaster@prod.lexis-nexis.com • URL: http://www.lexis.com • Fee-based Web site offers extensive searching of a wide variety of legal sources. Additional features include Daily Opinion Service, lexis.com Bookstore, Career Center, CLE Center, Law Schools, and Practice Pages ("Pages specific to areas of specialty").

TRADE/PROFESSIONAL ASSOCIATIONS

American Institute of Parliamentarians. P.O. Box 2173, Wilmington, DE 19899-2173. Phone: 888-664-0428 or (302)762-1811 or (302)762-1811 Fax: (302)762-2170 E-mail: aip@aipparlipro.org • URL: http://www.aipparlipro.org.

National Association of Parliamentarians. 213 S. Main St., Independence, MO 64050-3808. Phone: 888-627-2929 or (816)833-3892 Fax: (816)833-3893 E-mail: nap2@prodigy.net • URL: http://www.parliamentarians.org.

PARTICIPATIVE MANAGEMENT

GENERAL WORKS

The Art and Science of Leadership. Afsaneh Nahavandi. Prentice Hall. • 1999. $55.00. Second edition. Includes a discussion of participative management. Emphasis is on strategic leadership.

Participative Management: An Analysis of Its Affect on Productivity. Michael H. Swearingen. Garland Publishing, Inc. • 1997. $35.00. (Garland Studies on Industrial Productivity).

A Primer on Organizational Behavior. James L. Bowditch and Anthony F. Buono. John Wiley and Sons, Inc. • 1996. $48.95. Fourth edition. Price on application. Includes a discussion of participative management. Emphasis is on research and the theory of organizations. (Wiley Management Series).

DIRECTORIES

Employee Involvement Association Membership Directory. Employee Involvement Association. • Annual. Membership.

PERIODICALS AND NEWSLETTERS

IPA Magazine. Involvement and Participation Association. • Quarterly. $60.00 per year. Formerly *Involvement of Participation and Industrial Participation.*

The Motivational Manager: Strategies to Increase Morale and Productivity in the Workplace. Lawence Ragan Communications, Inc. • Monthly. $119.00 per year. Newsletter. Emphasis is on participative management.

New Horizons. Employee Involvement Association. • Quarterly. Membership. Newsletter.

Team Leader. Dartnell Corp. • Biweekly. $76.70 per year. Newsletter. Includes coverage of self-directed work groups.

RESEARCH CENTERS AND INSTITUTES

Institute of Management, Innovation and Organization. University of California, Berkeley, F402 Haas School of Business, Berkeley, CA 94720-1930. Phone: (510)642-4041 Fax: (510)273-1072 E-mail: teece@haas.berkeley.edu • URL: http://www.haasberkeley.edu/~imio • Research areas include a wide range of business management functions.

STATISTICS SOURCES

Employee Involvement Association Statistical Report. Employee Involvement Association. • Annual. 150.00.

TRADE/PROFESSIONAL ASSOCIATIONS

Employee Involvement Association. 525 Fifth St., S.W., Ste. A, Des Moines, IA 50309-4501. Phone: (515)282-8192 Fax: (515)282-9117 E-mail: jbw@amg-inc.com • URL: http://www.eia.com • Members are business and government professionals dedicated to employee involvement processes, including suggestion systems.

Involvement and Participation Association. 42 Colebrooke Row, London N1 8AF, England. Phone: 44 171 3548040 Fax: 44 171 3548041 • Promotes employee participation in the workplace.

OTHER SOURCES

Creating a Culture of Competence. Michael Zwell. John Wiley and Sons, Inc. • 2000. $35.95. Emphasizes employee participation to arrive at a desired change in organizational culture.

PART-TIME EMPLOYEES

See: TEMPORARY EMPLOYEES

PARTNERSHIP

ABSTRACTS AND INDEXES

Current Law Index: Multiple Access to Legal Periodicals. The Gale Group. • Monthly. $650.00 per year. Produced in cooperation with the American Association of Law Libraries. Indexes more than 900 law journals, legal newspapers, and specialty publications from the U.S., Canada, U.K., Ireland, Australia, and New Zealand.

DIRECTORIES

CPB's Directory of Limited Partnerships. American Partnership Board, Inc. • Published periodically. Free booklet listing the names of more than 1,000 limited partnerships in which the Chicago Partnership Board "typically maintains trading information and auctioneering services.".

Directory of Partnership Sponsors. American Partnership Board, Inc. • Annual. $199.00. A directory of more than 400 major sponsors of publicly registered and private placement limited partnerships.

HANDBOOKS AND MANUALS

Corporate, Partnership, Estate, and Gift Taxation 1997. James W. Pratt and William Kulsrud, editors. McGraw-Hill Higher Education. • 1996. $71.25. 10th edition.

Corporation and Partnership Tax Return Guide. Research Institute of America Inc. • 2000. $16.50. Revised edition.

Corporation-Partnership-Fiduciary Filled-in Tax Return Forms, 1999. CCH, Inc. • 1999. $21.50.

Federal Tax Course: General Edition. CCH, Inc. • Annual. $123.00. Provides basic reference and training for various forms of federal taxation: individual, business, corporate, partnership, estate, gift, etc. Includes *Federal Taxation Study Manual.*

How to Save Time and Taxes Preparing the Federal Partnership Return. Matthew Bender & Co., Inc. • Looseleaf. Price on application. Periodic supplementation. (How to Save Time and Taxes Series).

Partnership Book: How You and a Friend Can Legally Start Your Own Business. Denis Clifford and Ralph Warner. Nolo.com. • 2000. Sixth edition. Price on application.

Professional's Guide to Successful Management: The Eight Essentials for Running Your Firm, Practice, or Partnership. Carol A. O'Connor. McGraw-Hill. • 1994. Price on application.

Tax Examples. John C. Wisdom. West Group. • 1993. $125.00. Presents yearly examples, with forms, of a wide variety of tax problems and issues. Subjects include taxable income, deductions, alternative minimum tax, dependents, gift taxes, partnerships, and other problem areas. Includesaccounting method considerations. (Tax Series).

PERIODICALS AND NEWSLETTERS

Business Strategies Bulletin. CCH, Inc. • Monthly. $166.00 per year. Newsletter.

Stanger Report: A Guide to Partnership Investing. Robert A. Stanger and Co. • Monthly. $447.00 per year. Newsletter providing analysis of limited partnership investments.

PRICE SOURCES

CPB's Partnership Trade Prices. American Partnership Board, Inc. • Quarterly. $299.00 per year. Provides actual high, low, and last auction trade prices for more than 800 limited partnerships. Valuations by general partners are also shown where available.

NAPEX Trade Price Reporter. National Partnership Exchange, Inc. • Quarterly. $160.00 per year.

Provides high, low, and last-trade prices (resale prices) for about 500 limited partnerships, including many that have invested primarily in real estate.

Units Available for Purchase. American Partnership Board, Inc. • Weekly. $99.00 per year. Lists limited partnership units being offered for purchase, with current offering price, original price, most recent distribution (annualized), most recent general partner valuation where available, and brief description.

RESEARCH CENTERS AND INSTITUTES

Lexis.com Research System. Lexis-Nexis Group. Phone: 800-227-9597 or (937)865-6800 Fax: (937)865-6909 E-mail: webmaster@prod.lexis-nexis.com • URL: http://www.lexis.com • Fee-based Web site offers extensive searching of a wide variety of legal sources. Additional features include Daily Opinion Service, lexis.com Bookstore, Career Center, CLE Center, Law Schools, and Practice Pages ("Pages specific to areas of specialty").

OTHER SOURCES

Business Strategies. CCH, Inc. • Semimonthly. $819.00 per year. Four looseleaf volumes. Semimonthly updates. Legal, tax, and accounting aspects of business planning and decision-making. Provides information on start-ups, forms of ownership (partnerships, corporations), failing businesses, reorganizations, acquisitions, and so forth. Includes *Business Strategies Bulletin,* a monthly newsletter.

Business Transactions: Tax Analysis. Research Institute of America. • Three looseleaf volumes. Biweekly updates. Price on application. Analyzes the tax consequences of various business decisions for sole proprietorships, partnerships, S corporations, and other corporations.

Business Transactions: Tax Planning. Research Institute of America, Inc. • Four looseleaf volumes. Monthly updates. Price on application. Covers the tax planning aspects of business decisions for sole proprietorships, partnerships, S corporations, and other corporations.

Federal Taxation of Partnerships and Partners. William S. McKee and others. Warren, Gorham and Lamont/RIA Group. • Looseleaf, $215.00. Two volumes. Quarterly supplementation. Provides guidance on every aspect of partnership taxation.

Investment Limited Partnerships. Robert J. Haft and Peter M. Fass. West Group. • Six looseleaf volumes. $795.00. Periodic supplementation. Provides extensive coverage of both the tax and securities law aspects of tax motivated investments. (Securities Law Series).

Partnerships and LLCs: Tax Practice and Analysis. Thomas G. Manolakas. CCH, Inc. • 2001. $99.00. Covers the taxation of partnerships and limited liability companies.

PARTY PLAN SELLING

See: DIRECT MARKETING

PASSPORTS

GENERAL WORKS

Safe Trip Abroad. Available from U. S. Government Printing Office. • 1996. $1.25. Issued by the Bureau of Consular Affairs, U. S. State Department (http://www.state.gov). Provides practical advice for international travel.

PASTA INDUSTRY

ABSTRACTS AND INDEXES

Food Science and Technology Abstracts. International Food Information Service Publishing. • Monthly. $1,780.00 per year. Provides worldwide coverage of the literature of food technology and food production.

Foods Adlibra: Key to the World's Food Literature. Foods Adlibra Publications. • Semimonthly.Provides journal citations and abstracts to the literature of food technology and packaging.

CD-ROM DATABASES

Food Science and Technology Abstracts [CD-ROM]. Available from SilverPlatter Information, Inc. • Quarterly. $3,700 per year. Produced by International Food Information Service (home page is http://www.ifis.org). Provides worldwide coverage on CD-ROM of the literature of food technology and production. Various types of publications are indexed, with abstracts, including about 1,800 periodicals. Time period is 1969 to date.

DIRECTORIES

Pasta Industry Directory. National Pasta Association. • Annual. $50.00. Lists pasta manufacturers and industry suppliers in various categories. (A special issue of *Pasta Journal.*).

ENCYCLOPEDIAS AND DICTIONARIES

Foods and Nutrition Encyclopedia. Audrey H. Ensminger and others. CRC Press, Inc. • 1993. $382.00. Second edition. Two volumes.

INTERNET DATABASES

I Love Pasta. National Pasta Association. Phone: (703)841-0818 Fax: (703)528-6507 E-mail: npa@ilovepasta.org • URL: http://www.ilovepasta.org • Web site provides a wide variety of information about pasta and the pasta industry. Includes 250 pasta recipes, pasta FAQs, and nutritional data. Industry statistics can be displayed, including data on imports, production, and per capita use in various countries. Extensive durum wheat data is provided.

ONLINE DATABASES

Food Science and Technology Abstracts [online]. IFIS North American Desk. • Produced by International Food Information Service. Provides about 500,000 online citations, with abstracts, to the international literature of food science, technology, commodities, engineering, and processing. Approximately 2,000 periodicals are covered. Time period is 1969 to date, with monthly updates. Inquire as to online cost and availability.

FOODS ADLIBRA. General Mills, Inc. • Contains online citations, with abstracts, to the technical and business literature of food processing and packaging. New products and new ingredients are featured. Covers about 250 trade journals and 500 research journals from 1974 to date, with monthly updates. Inquire as to online cost and availability.

PROMT: Predicasts Overview of Markets and Technology. The Gale Group. • Companies, products, applied technologies and markets. U.S. and international literature coverage, 1972 to date. Inquire as to online cost and availability. Provides abstracts from more than 1,600 publications. Weekly updates.

PERIODICALS AND NEWSLETTERS

Fancy Food. Talcott Communications Corp. • Monthly. $34.00 per year. Emphasizes new specialty food products and the business management aspects of the specialty food and confection industries. Includes special issues on wine, cheese, candy, "upscale" cookware, and gifts.

National Pasta Association FYI Newsletter. National Pasta Association. • Weekly. Membership.

Pasta Journal. National Pasta Association. • Bimonthly. $35.00 per year.

TRADE/PROFESSIONAL ASSOCIATIONS

National Pasta Association. 2101 Wilson Blvd., No. 920, Arlington, VA 22201. Phone: (703)841-0818 Fax: (703)528-6507 E-mail: npa@ibm.net • URL: http://www.ilovepasta.org.

OTHER SOURCES

Major Food and Drink Companies of the World. Available from The Gale Group. • 2001. $855.00. Fourth edition. Two volumes. Published by Graham & Whiteside. Contains profiles and trade names for more than 9,000 important food and beverage companies in various countries. In addition to foods, includes both alcoholic and nonalcoholic drink products.

The Market for Pasta. MarketResearch.com. • 2000. $2,250.00. Provides market data on various kinds of pasta, with sales forecasts to 2004.

Thomas Food and Beverage Market Place. Grey House Publishing. • Annual. $295.00. Three volumes. Contains more than 40,000 entries covering food companies, beverages, food equipment, warehouse companies, food brokers, wholesalers, importers, and exporters. Formerly *Thomas Food Industry Register.*

PATENTS

See also: INVENTIONS; NEW PRODUCTS; TECHNOLOGY TRANSFER

GENERAL WORKS

General Information Concerning Patents. Available from U. S. Government Printing Office. • 1997. $4.75. Issued by Patent and Trademark Office, U. S. Department of Commerce. Provides basic information on patent applications, fees, searches, specifications, and infringement. Includes "Answers to Questions Frequently Asked.".

Patents. Matthew Bender & Co., Inc. • 1,735.00. 13 looseleaf volumes. Periodic supplementation. An analysis of patent law in the U. S. Includes bibliography and glossary.

Patents, Trademarks and Related Rights: National and International Protection. Stephen Ladas. Harvard University Press. • 1975. $197.00. Three volumes.

ABSTRACTS AND INDEXES

CPI Digest: Key to World Literature Serving the Coatings, Plastics, Fibers, Adhesives, and Related Industries (Chemical Process Industries). CPI Information Services. • Monthly. $397.00 per year. Abstracts of business and technical articles for polymer-based, chemical process industries. Includes a monthly list of relevant U. S. patents. International coverage.

Index of Patents Issued from the United States Patent and Trademark Office, Part One: List of Patentees. Available from U. S. Government Printing Office. • Annual. Lists patentees and reissue patentees for each year.

Index of Patents Issued from the United States Patent and Trademark Office, Part Two: Index to Subjects of Invention. Available from U. S. Government Printing Office. • Annual. A subject index to patents issued each year, arranged by class and subclass numbers. Includes a list of patent and tradmark depository libraries.

World Patent Information: International Journal for Patent Documentation, Clasification and Statistics. Commission of the European Communities. Elsevier Science. • Quarterly. $538.00 per year.

ALMANACS AND YEARBOOKS

Intellectual Property Law Review. W. Bryan Forney, editor. West Group. • 1992. $115.00. Patent, trademark, and copyright practices.

Patent Law Annual, Southwestern Legal Foundation: Proceedings, lst-26th, 1963-1988. William S. Hein and Co., Inc. • 1963. $1,300.00 per set. Latest problem-solving information.

BIBLIOGRAPHIES

Information Sources in Patents. Peter Auger, editor. Bowker-Saur. • 1992. $75.00. Published by K. G. Saur. International coverage. (Guides to Information Sources Series).

CD-ROM DATABASES

CASSIS (Patents). U. S. Patent and Trademark Office, Office of Electronic Information Products. • A series of CD-ROM products, including *Patents ASSIGN* (assignment deeds, quarterly), *Patents ASSIST* (search tools, quarterly), *Patents BIB* (abstracts and search information, bimonthly), *Patents CLASS* (classifications, 1790 to date, bimonthly), *Patents SNAP* (serial number concordance, annual).

U. S. FullText. MicroPatent. • Monthly. Contains complete text on CD-ROM of all patents issued by the U. S. Patent and Trademark Office. Archival discs are available from 1975.

USAPat: Facsimile Images of United States Patents. U. S. Patent and Trademark Office, Office of Electronic Information Products. • Weekly (3 or 4 discs per week). $2,400.00 per year. Allows computer laser printing of original patent documents, including drawings. Calendar-year backfiles available from 1994. (Not a search system; documents are retrieved by patent number only.).

DIRECTORIES

Attorneys and Agents Registered to Practice Before United States Patent and Trademark Office. U.S. Patent and Trademark Office. Available from U.S. Government Printing Office. • Annual. $56.00.

Directory of Intellectual Property Attorneys. Aspen Law and Business. • Annual. Price on application.

ENCYCLOPEDIAS AND DICTIONARIES

Attorney's Dictionary of Patent Claims: Legal Materials and Practice Commentaries. Irwin M. Aisenberg. Matthew Bender & Co., Inc. • Looseleaf service. Two volumes. $470.00. Periodic supplementation. Operational guidance for bank officers, with analysis of statutory law and agency regulations.

McCarthy's Desk Encyclopedia of Intellectual Property. J. Thomas McCarthy. BNA Books. • 1995. $75.00.Second edition. Defines legal terms relating to patents, trademarks, copyrights, trade secrets, entertainment, and the computer industry.

Modern Patent Law Precedent: Dictionary of Key Terms and Concepts. Irwin M. Alsenberg. Glasser Legalworks. • 1997. $175.00. Third edition. Dictionary covers "3,000 relevant cases in which words and phrases are interpreted by decision-makers." Sources include the U. S. Code, patent examiners, terms of art, and general legal concepts relating to patent practice.

HANDBOOKS AND MANUALS

Copyrights, Patents, and Trademarks: Protect Your Rights Worldwide. Hoyt L. Barber. McGraw-Hill. • 1996. $32.95. Second edition.

Drafting Patent License Agreements, 1992-1993. Brian G. Brunsvold. Bureau of National Affairs, Inc. • 1998. $125.00. Fourth edition.

How to Write a Patent Application. Practising Law Institute. • Looseleaf. $195.00. Annual revisions. Edited for "both novice and experienced patent attorneys." Includes consideration of specific kinds of patent applications, such as design, electrical, software, chemical, and biotechnological. Checklists, sample forms, and case citations are provided.

Intellectual Property Infringement Damages: A Litigation Support Handbook. Russell L. Parr. John Wiley and Sons, Inc. • 1999. $145.00. Annual supplement, $60.00. Describes how to calculate damages for patent, trademark, and copyright infringement. (Intellectual Property Series).

Inventing and Patenting Sourcebook. The Gale Group. • 1992. $95.00. Second edition. A general guide for inventors. Contains how-to-do-it text, information sources, and sample forms.

Inventors Desktop Companion: A Guide to Successfully Marketing and Protecting Your Ideas. Richard C. Levy. Visible Ink Press. • 1998. $24.95. Second edition. Explains how to patent, trademark, or copyright an idea. Includes a listing of 2,000 associations and services for inventors.

Manual of Classification. U.S. Patent Office. Available from U.S. Government Printing Office. • $177.00. Two volumes. Index and revised looseleaf pages for an indefinite period. Lists patent classes and subclasses.

Manual of Patent Examining Procedure. U.S. Patent Office. Available from U.S. Government Printing Office. • Looseleaf. $248.00. Periodic supplementation included. Information on the practices and procedures relative to the prosecution of patent applications before the Patent and Trademark Office.

Patent, Copyright, and Trademark: A Desk Reference to Intellectual Property Law. Stephen Elias. Nolo.com. • 1999. $24.95. Third revised edition. Contains practical explanations of the legalities of patents, copyrights, trademarks, and trade secrets. Includes examples of relevant legal forms. A 1985 version was called *Nolo's Intellectual Property Law Dictionary.* (Nolo Press Self-Help Law Series).

Patent It Yourself. David R. Pressman. Nolo.com. • 2000. Eighth edition. Price on application.

Patent Law Basics. Peter D. Rosenberg. West Group. • $125.00. Looseleaf service. Periodic supplement. Overs Patent and Trademark Office applications, patent ownership, rights, protection, infringement, litigation, and other fundamentals of patent law.

Patent Law Handbook. West Group. • Annual. $167.00.

Patent, Trademark, and Copyright Laws, 2000. Jeffrey Samuels. BNA Books. • $95.00. Date not set. Contains text of "all pertinent intellectual property legislation to date.".

Protecting Trade Secrets, Patents, Copyrights, and Trademarks. Robert C. Dorr and Christopher H. Munch. Panel Publishers. • Looseleaf service. $165.00.

ONLINE DATABASES

CLAIMS. IFI/Plenum Data Corp. • Includes seven separate databases: *CLAIMS/Citation, CLAIMS/ Compound Registry, CLAIMS/Comprehensive Data Base, CLAIMS/Reassignment & Reexamination, CLAIMS/Reference, CLAIMS/U. S. Patent Abstracts,* and *CLAIMS/Uniterm.* Provides extensive current and historical information on U. S. Patents. Inquire as to online cost and availability.

Derwent U. S. Patents. Derwent, Inc. • Provides citations and abstracts for more then one million U. S. patents issued since 1971. Weekly updates. Inquire as to online cost and availability.

Derwent World Patents Index. Derwent, Inc. • Contains abstracts of more than 20 million patent documents from many countries. Time span varies. Weekly updates. Inquire as to online cost and availability.

U. S. Patents Fulltext. Available from DIALOG. • Contains complete text of patents issued by the U. S. Patent and Trademark Office since 1971. Weekly updates. Inquire as to online cost and availability.

PERIODICALS AND NEWSLETTERS

BNA's Patent, Trademark and Copyright Journal. Bureau of National Affairs, Inc. • Weekly. $1,366.00 per year.

Intellectual Property Today. Omega Communications. • Monthly. $48.00 per year. Covers legal developments in copyright, patents, trademarks, and licensing. Emphasizes the effect of new technology on intellectual property. Formerly *Law Works.*

LES Nouvelles. Licensing Executives Society. • Quarterly. Free to members; libraries, $35.00 per year. Concerned with licensing agreements, patents, and trademarks.

Official Gazette of the United States Patent and Trademark Office: Patents. Available from U. S. Government Printing Office. • Weekly. $1,425.00 per year. ($1,700.00 per year by first class mail.) Contains the Patents, Patent Office Notices, and Designs issued each week (http://www.uspto.gov). Annual indexes are sold separately.

Patent and Trademark Office Society Journal. Patent and Trademark Office Society. • Individuals, $40.00 per year; associates $47.00 per year; students, $26.00 per year.

STATISTICS SOURCES

Commissioner of Patents Annual Report. U.S. Patent Office. Available from U.S. Government Printing Office. • Annual.

Statistical Handbook on Technology. Paula Berinstein, editor. Oryx Press. • 1999. $65.00. Provides statistical data on such items as the Internet, online services, computer technology, recycling, patents, prescription drug sales, telecommunications, and aerospace. Includes charts, tables, and graphs. Edited for the general reader. (Statistical Handbook Series).

TRADE/PROFESSIONAL ASSOCIATIONS

American Intellectual Property Law Association. 2001 Jefferson Davis Highway, Suite 203, Arlington, VA 22202. Phone: (703)415-0780 or (703)415-0781 Fax: (703)415-0786 E-mail: aipla@aipla.org • URL: http://www.aipla.org.

International Intellectual Property Association. 1255 23rd St. N.W., Suite 850, Washington, DC 20037. Phone: (202)785-1814 Fax: (202)466-2893.

OTHER SOURCES

Intellectual Property and Antitrust Law. William C. Holmes. West Group. • Looseleaf. $145.00. Periodic supplementation. Includes patent, trademark, and copyright practices.

PAY PLANNING

See: EXECUTIVE COMPENSATION; WAGES AND SALARIES

PAYROLL ADMINISTRATION

See: WAGES AND SALARIES

PEACH INDUSTRY

See also: FRUIT INDUSTRY

CD-ROM DATABASES

Food Science and Technology Abstracts [CD-ROM]. Available from SilverPlatter Information, Inc. • Quarterly. $3,700 per year. Produced by International Food Information Service (home page is http://www.ifis.org). Provides worldwide coverage on CD-ROM of the literature of food technology and production. Various types of publications are indexed, with abstracts, including about 1,800 periodicals. Time period is 1969 to date.

INTERNET DATABASES

USDA. United States Department of Agriculture. Phone: (202)720-2791 E-mail: agsec@usda.gov • URL: http://www.usda.gov • The USDA home page has six sections: News and Information; What's New; About USDA; Agencies; Opportunities; Search and Help. Keyword searching is offered from the USDA home page and from various individual agency home pages. Agencies are the Economic Research Service, Agricultural Marketing Service, National Agricultural Statistics Service, National Agricultural Library, and about 12 others. Updating varies. Fees: Free.

ONLINE DATABASES

Food Science and Technology Abstracts [online]. IFIS North American Desk. • Produced by International Food Information Service. Provides about 500,000 online citations, with abstracts, to the international literature of food science, technology, commodities, engineering, and processing. Approximately 2,000 periodicals are covered. Time period is 1969 to date, with monthly updates. Inquire as to online cost and availability.

PERIODICALS AND NEWSLETTERS

Journal of Tree Fruit Production. Haworth Press, Inc. • Semiannual. Individuals, $45.00 per year; institutions, $75.00 per year; libraries, $85.00 per year. A research journal for tree fruit growers.

Peach-Times. National Peach Council. • Quarterly. Membership.

STATISTICS SOURCES

Agricultural Statistics. Available from U. S. Government Printing Office. • Annual. Produced by the National Agricultural Statistics Service, U. S. Department of Agriculture. Provides a wide variety of statistical data relating to agricultural production, supplies, consumption, prices/price-supports, foreign trade, costs, and returns, as well as farm labor, loans, income, and population. In many cases, historical data is shown annually for 10 years. In addition to farm data, includes detailed fishery statistics.

TRADE/PROFESSIONAL ASSOCIATIONS

National Peach Council. 12 Nicklaus Lane, Suite 101, Columbia, SC 29229. Phone: (803)788-7101 E-mail: charleswalker@worldnet.att.net.

OTHER SOURCES

Major Food and Drink Companies of the World. Available from The Gale Group. • 2001. $855.00. Fourth edition. Two volumes. Published by Graham & Whiteside. Contains profiles and trade names for more than 9,000 important food and beverage companies in various countries. In addition to foods, includes both alcoholic and nonalcoholic drink products.

Thomas Food and Beverage Market Place. Grey House Publishing. • Annual. $295.00. Three volumes. Contains more than 40,000 entries covering food companies, beverages, food equipment, warehouse companies, food brokers, wholesalers, importers, and exporters. Formerly *Thomas Food Industry Register.*

PEANUT AND PEANUT OIL INDUSTRIES

See also: NUT INDUSTRY; OIL AND FATS INDUSTRY

CD-ROM DATABASES

Food Science and Technology Abstracts [CD-ROM]. Available from SilverPlatter Information, Inc. • Quarterly. $3,700 per year. Produced by International Food Information Service (home page is http://www.ifis.org). Provides worldwide coverage on CD-ROM of the literature of food technology and production. Various types of publications are indexed, with abstracts, including about 1,800 periodicals. Time period is 1969 to date.

DIRECTORIES

American Peanut Council-Membership Directory. National Peanut Council, Inc. • Annual. $100.00. About 250 growers, shellers, processors, manufacturers, brokes and allied businesses providing goods and services to the peanut industry.

INTERNET DATABASES

USDA. United States Department of Agriculture. Phone: (202)720-2791 E-mail: agsec@usda.gov • URL: http://www.usda.gov • The USDA home page has six sections: News and Information; What's New; About USDA; Agencies; Opportunities; Search and Help. Keyword searching is offered from the USDA home page and from various individual agency home pages. Agencies are the Economic Research Service, Agricultural Marketing Service, National Agricultural Statistics Service, National Agricultural Library, and about 12 others. Updating varies. Fees: Free.

ONLINE DATABASES

Food Science and Technology Abstracts [online]. IFIS North American Desk. • Produced by International Food Information Service. Provides about 500,000 online citations, with abstracts, to the international literature of food science, technology, commodities, engineering, and processing. Approximately 2,000 periodicals are covered. Time period is 1969 to date, with monthly updates. Inquire as to online cost and availability.

PERIODICALS AND NEWSLETTERS

The Peanut Farmer: For Commercial Growers of Peanuts and Related Agribusiness. SpecComm International, Inc. • Seven times a year. $15.00 per year.

Peanut Journal and Nut World. Virginia-Carolina Peanut Association. Peanut Journal Publishing Co. • Monthly. $8.00 per year.

Peanut Science. American Peanut Research and Education Association. • Semiannual. $40.00 per issue.

STATISTICS SOURCES

Agricultural Statistics. Available from U. S. Government Printing Office. • Annual. Produced by the National Agricultural Statistics Service, U. S. Department of Agriculture. Provides a wide variety of statistical data relating to agricultural production, supplies, consumption, prices/price-supports, foreign trade, costs, and returns, as well as farm labor, loans, income, and population. In many cases, historical data is shown annually for 10 years. In addition to farm data, includes detailed fishery statistics.

TRADE/PROFESSIONAL ASSOCIATIONS

American Peanut Council. 1500 King St., Suite 301, Alexandria, VA 22314. Phone: (703)838-9500 Fax: (703)838-9089 E-mail: peanutsusa@aol.com • URL: http://www.peanutusa.com.

American Peanut Research and Education Society. Oklahoma State University, 376 AG Hall, Stillwater, OK 74078. Phone: (405)744-9634 Fax: (405)744-5269 E-mail: nickel@okway.okstate.edu.

Peanut and Tree Nut Processors Association. P.O. Box 59811, Potomac, MD 20859-9811. Phone: (301)365-2521 Fax: (301)365-7705 • URL: http://www.ptnpa.org.

OTHER SOURCES

Major Food and Drink Companies of the World. Available from The Gale Group. • 2001. $855.00. Fourth edition. Two volumes. Published by Graham & Whiteside. Contains profiles and trade names for more than 9,000 important food and beverage companies in various countries. In addition to foods, includes both alcoholic and nonalcoholic drink products.

Thomas Food and Beverage Market Place. Grey House Publishing. • Annual. $295.00. Three volumes. Contains more than 40,000 entries covering food companies, beverages, food equipment, warehouse companies, food brokers, wholesalers, importers, and exporters. Formerly *Thomas Food Industry Register.*

PEAR INDUSTRY

See also: FRUIT INDUSTRY

CD-ROM DATABASES

Food Science and Technology Abstracts [CD-ROM]. Available from SilverPlatter Information, Inc. • Quarterly. $3,700 per year. Produced by International Food Information Service (home page is http://www.ifis.org). Provides worldwide coverage on CD-ROM of the literature of food technology and production. Various types of publications are indexed, with abstracts, including about 1,800 periodicals. Time period is 1969 to date.

INTERNET DATABASES

USDA. United States Department of Agriculture. Phone: (202)720-2791 E-mail: agsec@usda.gov • URL: http://www.usda.gov • The USDA home page has six sections: News and Information; What's New; About USDA; Agencies; Opportunities; Search and Help. Keyword searching is offered from the USDA home page and from various individual agency home pages. Agencies are the Economic Research Service, Agricultural Marketing Service, National Agricultural Statistics Service, National Agricultural Library, and about 12 others. Updating varies. Fees: Free.

ONLINE DATABASES

Food Science and Technology Abstracts [online]. IFIS North American Desk. • Produced by International Food Information Service. Provides about 500,000 online citations, with abstracts, to the international literature of food science, technology, commodities, engineering, and processing. Approximately 2,000 periodicals are covered. Time period is 1969 to date, with monthly updates. Inquire as to online cost and availability.

PERIODICALS AND NEWSLETTERS

Journal of Tree Fruit Production. Haworth Press, Inc. • Semiannual. Individuals, $45.00 per year; institutions, $75.00 per year; libraries, $85.00 per year. A research journal for tree fruit growers.

STATISTICS SOURCES

Agricultural Statistics. Available from U. S. Government Printing Office. • Annual. Produced by the National Agricultural Statistics Service, U. S. Department of Agriculture. Provides a wide variety of statistical data relating to agricultural production, supplies, consumption, prices/price-supports, foreign trade, costs, and returns, as well as farm labor, loans, income, and population. In many cases, historical data is shown annually for 10 years. In addition to farm data, includes detailed fishery statistics.

OTHER SOURCES

Major Food and Drink Companies of the World. Available from The Gale Group. • 2001. $855.00. Fourth edition. Two volumes. Published by Graham & Whiteside. Contains profiles and trade names for more than 9,000 important food and beverage companies in various countries. In addition to foods, includes both alcoholic and nonalcoholic drink products.

Thomas Food and Beverage Market Place. Grey House Publishing. • Annual. $295.00. Three volumes. Contains more than 40,000 entries covering food companies, beverages, food equipment, warehouse companies, food brokers, wholesalers, importers, and exporters. Formerly *Thomas Food Industry Register.*

PECAN INDUSTRY

See also: NUT INDUSTRY

CD-ROM DATABASES

Food Science and Technology Abstracts [CD-ROM]. Available from SilverPlatter Information, Inc. • Quarterly. $3,700 per year. Produced by International Food Information Service (home page is http://www.ifis.org). Provides worldwide coverage on CD-ROM of the literature of food technology and production. Various types of publications are indexed, with abstracts, including about 1,800 periodicals. Time period is 1969 to date.

INTERNET DATABASES

USDA. United States Department of Agriculture. Phone: (202)720-2791 E-mail: agsec@usda.gov • URL: http://www.usda.gov • The USDA home page has six sections: News and Information; What's New; About USDA; Agencies; Opportunities; Search and Help. Keyword searching is offered from the USDA home page and from various individual agency home pages. Agencies are the Economic Research Service, Agricultural Marketing Service, National Agricultural Statistics Service, National Agricultural Library, and about 12 others. Updating varies. Fees: Free.

ONLINE DATABASES

Food Science and Technology Abstracts [online]. IFIS North American Desk. • Produced by International Food Information Service. Provides about 500,000 online citations, with abstracts, to the international literature of food science, technology, commodities, engineering, and processing. Approximately 2,000 periodicals are covered. Time period is 1969 to date, with monthly updates. Inquire as to online cost and availability.

PERIODICALS AND NEWSLETTERS

Pecan South. Texas Pecan Growers Association, Inc. • Monthly. $18.00 per year.

STATISTICS SOURCES

Agricultural Statistics. Available from U. S. Government Printing Office. • Annual. Produced by the National Agricultural Statistics Service, U. S. Department of Agriculture. Provides a wide variety of statistical data relating to agricultural production, supplies, consumption, prices/price-supports, foreign trade, costs, and returns, as well as farm labor, loans, income, and population. In many cases, historical data is shown annually for 10 years. In addition to farm data, includes detailed fishery statistics.

Fruit and Tree Nuts Situation and Outlook Report. Available from U. S. Government Printing Office. • Three times a year. $13.00 per year. (Economic Research Service, U. S. Department of Agriculture.).

TRADE/PROFESSIONAL ASSOCIATIONS

National Pecan Shellers Association. 5775 Peachtree-Dunwoody Rd., Suite 500-G, Atlanta, GA 30342. Phone: (404)252-3663 Fax: (404)252-0774 E-mail: npsa@assnhq.com • URL: http://www.ilovepecans.com.

OTHER SOURCES

Major Food and Drink Companies of the World. Available from The Gale Group. • 2001. $855.00. Fourth edition. Two volumes. Published by Graham & Whiteside. Contains profiles and trade names for more than 9,000 important food and beverage companies in various countries. In addition to foods, includes both alcoholic and nonalcoholic drink products.

Thomas Food and Beverage Market Place. Grey House Publishing. • Annual. $295.00. Three volumes. Contains more than 40,000 entries covering food companies, beverages, food equipment, warehouse companies, food brokers, wholesalers, importers, and exporters. Formerly *Thomas Food Industry Register.*

PENCILS

See: WRITING INSTRUMENTS

PENNY STOCKS

See: OVER-THE-COUNTER SECURITIES INDUSTRY

PENS

See: WRITING INSTRUMENTS

PENSIONS

See also: EMPLOYEE BENEFIT PLANS; ESTATE PLANNING; 401(K) RETIREMENT PLANS; INDIVIDUAL RETIREMENT ACCOUNTS; RETIREMENT; TRUSTS AND TRUSTEES

GENERAL WORKS

Financial Institutions and Markets. Robert W. Kolb and Ricardo J. Rodriguez. Blackwell Publishers. • 1996. $77.95. Contains 40 articles (chapters) by various authors on U. S. financial markets and other topics. Includes separate chapters on the International Monetary Fund, inflation, monetary policy, the national debt, bank failures, derivatives, stock prices, initial public offerings, government bonds, pensions, foreign exchange, international markets, and other subjects.

Fundamentals of Employee Benefit Programs. Employee Benefit Research Institute. • 1996. $49.95. Fifth edition. Provides basic explanation of employee benefit programs in both the private and public sectors, including health insurance, pension plans, retirement planning, social security, and long-term care insurance.

Fundamentals of Private Pensions. Dan McGill and others. University of Pennsylvania Press. • 1996. $79.95. Seventh revised edition.

How to Plan Your Retirement Years. Kerry A. Lynch, editor. American Institute for Economic Research. • 1996. $6.00. Provides concise, conservative advice on retirement planning, savings, pensions, IRAs, Keogh plans, annuities, and making effective use of social security. (Economic Education Bulletin.).

Investing During Retirement: The Vanguard Guide to Managing Your Retirement Assets. Vanguard Group. McGraw-Hill Professional. • 1996. $17.95. A basic, general guide to investing after retirement. Covers pension plans, basic principles of investing, types of mutual funds, asset allocation, retirement income planning, social security, estate planning, and contingencies. Includes glossary and worksheets for net worth, budget, and income.

Retirement Security: Understanding and Planning Your Financial Future. David M. Walker. John Wiley and Sons, Inc. • 1996. $29.95. Topics include investments, social security, Medicare, health insurance, and employer retirement plans.

Social Security, Medicare, and Pensions: Get the Most Out of Your Retirement and Medical Benefits. Joseph Matthews and Dorothy M. Berman. Nolo.com. • 1999. $21.95. Seventh edition. In addition to the basic topics, includes practical information on Supplemental Security Income (SSI), disability benefits, veterans benefits, 401(k) plans, Medicare HMOs, medigap insurance, Medicaid, and how to appeal decisions.

Vanguard Retirement Investing Guide: Charting Your Course to a Secure Retirement. Vanguard Group. McGraw-Hill Professional. • 1995. $24.95. Second edition. Covers saving and investing for future retirement. Topics include goal setting, investment fundamentals, mutual funds, asset allocation, defined contribution retirement savings plans, social security, and retirement savings strategies. Includes glossary and worksheet for retirement saving.

ABSTRACTS AND INDEXES

Insurance Periodicals Index. Specials Libraries Association, Insurance and Employees Benefits Div. CCH/NILS Publishing Co. • Annual. $250.00. Compiled by the Insurance and Employee Benefits Div., Special Libraries Association. A yearly index of over 15,000 articles from about 35 insurance periodicals. Arrangement is by subject, with an index to authors.

ALMANACS AND YEARBOOKS

Older Americans Information Directory. Group Grey House Publshing, Inc. • 2000. $190.00. Second edition. Presents articles (text) and sources of information on a wide variety of aging and retirement topics. Includes an index to personal names, organizations, and subjects.

DIRECTORIES

America's Corporate Finance Directory. National Register Publishing. • Annual. $699.00. A directory of financial executives employed at over 5,000 U. S. corporations. Includes a listing of the outside financial services (banks, pension managers, insurance firms, auditors) used by each corporation.

Corporate Finance Sourcebook: The Guide to Major Capital Investment Source and Related Financial Services. R. R. Bowker. • Annual. $625.00. Lists more than 3,550 sources of corporate capital: investment bankers, securities firms, pension management companies, trust companies, insurance companies, and private lenders. Includes the names of over 13,000 key personnel.

Money Market Directory of Pension Funds and Their Investment Managers. Money Market Directories, Inc. • Annual. $995.00. Institutional funds and managers.

Nelson's Directory of Pension Fund Consultants. Wiesenberger/Thomson Financial. • Annual. $350.00. Covers the pension plan sponsor industry. More than 325 worldwide consulting firms are described.

Nelson's Directory of Plan Sponsors. Wiesenberger/Thomson Financial. • Annual. $545.00. Three volumes. Available in two versions, alphabetic or geographic. Covers pension plan sponsors and pension funds, including more than 11,000 corporate funds, 4,000 endowment or foundation funds, 1,300 multi-employer funds, 1,000 hospital funds, and 900 public employee funds. Includes information on asset allocation and investment style. Eight indexes.

Pensions and Investments 1000 Largest Retirement Funds. Crain Communications, Inc. • Annual. $50.00. List of the largest retirement plans in terms of total assets. Formerly *Pensions and Investments Top 100 Retirement Funds.*

ENCYCLOPEDIAS AND DICTIONARIES

Dictionary of Finance and Investment Terms. John Downes and Jordan E. Goodman. Barron's Educational Series, Inc. • 1998. $12.95. Fifth revised edition. Provides clear explanations of more than 5,000 business, banking, financial, investment, and tax terms. Includes a separate list of financial abbreviations and acronyms.

FINANCIAL RATIOS

Financial Planning for Older Clients. James E. Pearman. CCH, Inc. • 2000. $49.00. Covers income sources, social security, Medicare, Medicaid, investment planning, estate planning, and other retirement-related topics. Edited for accountants, attorneys, and other financial advisors.

HANDBOOKS AND MANUALS

ERISA: The Law and the Code (Employee Retirement Income Security Act). Bureau of National Affairs, Inc. • Irregular. $75.00. The Employee Retirement Income Security Act, as amended, withrelevant provisions of the Internal Revenue Code.

Estate Plan Book 2000. William S. Moore. American Institute for Economic Research. • 2000. $10.00. Revision of 1997 edition. Part one: "Basic Estate Planning." Part two: "Reducing Taxes on the Disposition of Your Estate." Part three: "Putting it All Together: Examples of Estate Plans." Provides succinct information on wills, trusts, tax planning, and gifts. (Economic Education Bulletin.).

Guide to Pension and Profit Sharing Plans: Taxation, Selection, and Design. Donald S. Dunkle. Shepard's. • 1984. $115.00. (Commercial Law Publications).

Guidebook to Pension Planning. CCH, Inc. • Annual.

How to Build Wealth with Tax-Sheltered Investments. Kerry Anne Lynch. American Institute for Economic Research. • 2000. $6.00. Provides practical information on conservative tax shelters, including defined-contribution pension plans, individual retirement accounts, Keogh plans, U. S. savings bonds, municipal bonds, and various kinds of annuities: deferred, variable-rate, immediate, and foreign-currency. (Economic Education Bulletin.).

An Insurance Guide for Seniors. Insurance Forum, Inc. • 1997. $15.00. Provides concise advice and information on Medicare, Medicare supplement insurance, HMOs, long-term care insurance, automobile insurance, life insurance, annuities, and pensions. An appendix lists "Financially Strong Insurance Companies." (*The Insurance Forum*, vol. 24, no. 4.).

The New Working Woman's Guide to Retirement Planning. Martha P. Patterson. University of Pennsylvania Press. • 1999. $17.50. Second edition. Provides retirement advice for employed women, including information on various kinds of IRAs, cash balance and other pension plans, 401(k) plans, and social security. Four case studies are provided to illustrate retirement planning at specific life and career stages.

Pension and Employee Benefits: Code-ERISA-Regulations. CCH, Inc. • Three volumes. Looseleaf.

Pension and Profit Sharing Plans. Matthew Bender & Co., Inc. • Six looseleaf volumes. Periodic supplementation. Price on application. Full treatment of pension and profit sharing plans, including forms and legal analysis.

Pension and Profit Sharing Plans for Small or Medium Size Businesses. Panel Publishers, Inc. • Monthly. $191.50 per year. Newsletter. Topics of interest and concern to professionals who serve small and medium size pension and profit sharing plans.

Pension Fund Investment Management: A Handbook for Sponsors and Their Advisors. Fran K. Fabozzi. McGraw-Hill Professional. • 1990. $65.00.

Pension Planning: Pensions, Profit Sharing, and Other Deferred Compensation Plans. Everett T. Allen and others. McGraw-Hill Higher Education. • 1992. $69.75. Seventh edition.

Retirement Benefits Tax Guide. CCH, Inc. • Looseleaf. $199.00. Supplementation available.

U. S. Master Pension Guide. CCH, Inc. • Annual. $49.00. Explains IRS rules and regulations applying to 401(k) plans, 403(k) plans, ESOPs (employee stock ownership plans), IRAs, SEPs (simplified employee pension plans), Keogh plans, and nonqualified plans.

INTERNET DATABASES

Bureau of Labor Statistics (BLS). U. S. Department of Labor, Bureau of Labor Statistics. Phone: (202)523-1092 E-mail: labstat.helpdesk@bls.gov • URL: http://www.bls.gov • Web site provides a great variety of employment, wage, price, and economic data. Some links are "Data," "Economy at a Glance," "Keyword Search of BLS Web Pages," "Regional Information," and "Other Statistical Sites." Fees: Free.

EBSCO Information Services. Ebsco Publishing. Phone: 800-871-8508 or (508)356-6500 Fax: (508)356-5640 E-mail: ep@epnet.com • URL: http://www.epnet.com • Fee-based Web site providing Internet access to a wide variety of databases, including business-related material. Full text is available for many periodical titles, with daily updates. Fees: Apply.

InsWeb. InsWeb Corp. Phone: (650)372-2129 E-mail: info@insweb.com • URL: http://www.insweb.com • Web site offers a wide variety of advice and information on automobile, life, health, and "other" insurance. Includes glossaries of insurance terms, Standard & Poor's ratings of individual insurance companies, and "Financial Needs Estimators." Searching is available. Fees: Free.

ProQuest Direct. Bell & Howell Information and Learning. Phone: 800-521-0600 or (313)761-4700 Fax: (313)973-9145 • URL: http://www.umi.com/proquest • Fee-based Web site providing Internet access to more than 3,000 periodicals, newspapers, and other publications. Many items are available full-text, with daily updates. Includes extensive corporate and financial information from Disclosure, Inc. Fees: Apply.

Small Business Retirement Savings Advisor. U. S. Department of Labor, Pension and Welfare Benefits Administration. Phone: (202)219-8921 • URL: http://www.dol.gov/elaws/pwbaplan.htm • Web site provides "answers to a variety of commonly asked questions about retirement saving options for small business employers." Includes a comparison chart and detailed descriptions of various plans: 401(k), SEP-IRA, SIMPLE-IRA, Payroll Deduction IRA, Keogh Profit-Sharing, Keogh Money Purchase, and Defined Benefit. Searching is offered. Fees: Free.

PERIODICALS AND NEWSLETTERS

Contingencies: The Magazine of the Actuarial Profession. American Academy of Actuaries. • Bimonthly. $30.00 per year. Provides non-technical articles on the actuarial aspects of insurance, employee benefits, and pensions.

Defined Contribution News. Institutional Investor. • Biweekly. $2,330.00 per year. Newsletter. Edited for financial institutions and others offering defined contribution pension plans.

Employee Benefit Plan Review. Charles D. Spencer and Associates, Inc. • Monthly. $75.00 per year. (Also *Spencer's Research Reports on Employee Benefits.* Looseleaf service. $585.00 per year). Provides a review of recent events affecting the administration of employee benefit programs.

Journal of Pension Planning and Compliance. Panel Publishers. • Quarterly. $195.00 per year. Technical articles and regular columns on major issues confronting the pension community.

Journal of Retirement Planning. CCH, Inc. • Bimonthly. $169.00 per year. Emphasis is on retirement and estate planning advice provided by lawyers and accountants as part of their practices.

Money Management Letter: Bi-Weekly Newsletter Covering the Pensions and Money Maagement Industry. Institutional Investor. • Biweekly. $2,550.00 per year. Newsletter. Edited for pension fund investment managers.

Older Americans Report. Business Publishers, Inc. • Weekly. $432.00 per year. Newsletter on health, economic, and social services for the aging, including social security, medicare, pensions, housing, nursing homes, and programs under the Older Americans Act. Edited for service providers.

Pensions and Investments: The Newspaper of Corporate and Institutional Investing. Crain Communications, Inc. • Biweekly. $215.00 per year. Formerly *Pensions and Investment Age.*

Retirement Plans Bulletin: Practical Explanations for the IRA and Retirement Plan Professional. Universal Pensions, Inc. • Monthly. $99.00 per year. Newsletter. Provides information on the rules and regulations governing qualified (tax-deferred) retirement plans.

RESEARCH CENTERS AND INSTITUTES

Center for Pension and Retirement Research. Miami University, Department of Economics, 109E Laws Hall, Oxford, OH 45056. Phone: (513)529-2850 Fax: (513)529-6992 E-mail: swilliamson@eh.net • URL: http://www.eh.net/~cprr • Research areas include pension economics, pension plans, and retirement decisions.

Employee Benefit Research Institute. 2121 K St., N. W., Suite 600, Washington, DC 20037-1896. Phone: (202)659-0670 Fax: (202)775-6312 E-mail: salisbury@ebri.org • URL: http://www.ebri.org • Conducts research on employee benefits, including various kinds of pensions, individual retirement accounts (IRAs), health insurance, social security, and long-term health care benefits.

Pension Research Council. University of Pennsylvania, 304 CPC, 3641 Locust Walk, Philadelphia, PA 19104-6218. Phone: (215)898-7620 Fax: (215)898-0310 E-mail: mitchelo@wharton.upenn.edu • URL: http://www.prc.wharton.upenn.edu/prc/prc.html • Research areas include various types of private sector and public employee pension plans.

STATISTICS SOURCES

EBRI Databook on Employee Benefits. Employee Benefit Research Institute. • 1997 $99.00. Fourth edition. Contains more than 350 tables and charts presenting data on employee benefits in the U. S., including pensions, health insurance, social security, and medicare. Includes a glossary of employee benefit terms.

Employee Benefits in Medium and Large Private Establishments. Available from U. S. Government Printing Office. • Biennial. Issued by Bureau of Labor Statistics, U. S. Department of Labor. Provides data on benefits provided by companies with 100 or more employees. Covers benefits for both full-time and part-time workers, including health insurance, pensions, a wide variety of paid time-off policies (holidays, vacations, personal leave, maternity leave, etc.), and other fringe benefits.

Employee Benefits in Small Private Establishments. Available from U. S. Government Printing Office. • Biennial. Issued by Bureau of Labor Statistics, U. S. Department of Labor. Supplies data on a wide variety of benefits provided by companies with fewer than 100 employees. Includes statistics for both full-time and part-time workers.

Handbook of U. S. Labor Statistics: Employment, Earnings, Prices, Productivity, and Other Labor Data. Eva E. Jacobs, editor. Bernan Associates. • 1999. $74.00. Based on *Handbook of Labor Statistics*, formerly issued by the Bureau of Labor Statistics, U. S. Department of Labor. Includes the Bureau's projections of employment in the U. S. by industry and occupation. Provides a wide variety of data on the work force, prices, fringe benefits, and consumer expenditures.

Pension Facts. American Council of Life Insurance. • Biennial. Free.

Private Pensions in OECD Countries: The United States. OECD Publications and Information Center. • 1993. $22.00. Provides data relating to the characteristics of private pension arrangements in the U. S.

Quarterly Pension Investment Report. Employee Benefit Research Institute. • Quarterly. $1,500.00 per year. $400.00 per year to nonprofit organizations. Provides aggregate financial asset data for U. S. private and public pension systems. Statistics are given for both defined contribution and defined benefit plans, including investment mixes (stocks, bonds, cash, other). Contains historical data for private trust, life insurance, and state and local government funds.

Statistical Handbook on Aging Americans. Renee Schick, editor. Oryx Press. • 1994. $65.00. Second edition. Provides data on demographics, social characteristics, health, employment, economic conditions, income, pensions, and social security. Includes bibliographic information and a glossary. (Statistical Handbook Series).

Statistical Record of Older Americans. The Gale Group. • 1996. $109.00. Second edition. Includes income and pension data.

TRADE/PROFESSIONAL ASSOCIATIONS

American Society of Pension Actuaries. 4245 N. Fairfax Dr., Suite 750, Arlington, VA 22203. Phone: (703)516-9300 Fax: (703)516-9308 E-mail: aspa@aspa.org • URL: http://www.aspa.org • Members are involved in the pension and insurance aspects of employee benefits. Includes an Insurance and Risk Management Committee, and sponsors an annual 401(k) Workshop.

Association of Private Pension and Welfare Plans. 1212 New York Ave., N. W., Suite 1250, Washington, DC 20005-3987. Phone: (202)289-6700 Fax: (202)289-4582 • URL: http://www.appwp.org • Members are large and small business firms offering pension and other benefit plans for their employees.

Council of Institutional Investors. 1730 Rhode Island Ave., N. W., Suite 512, Washington, DC 20036. Phone: (202)822-0800 Fax: (202)822-0801 E-mail: info@cii.org • URL: http://www.cii.org • Members are nonprofit organization pension plans and other nonprofit institutional investors.

OTHER SOURCES

BNA Pension and Benefits Reporter. Bureau of National Affairs, Inc. • Weekly. $996.00 per year. Three looseleaf volumes. Legal developments affecting pensions. Formerly *BNA Pension Reporter.*

Corporate Compliance Series. West Group. • Eleven looseleaf volumes, with periodic supplementation. $990.00. Covers criminal and civil liability problems for corporations. Includes employee safety, product liability, pension requirements, securities violations, equal employment opportunity issues, intellectual property, employee hiring and firing, and other corporate compliance topics.

Employee Benefits Management. CCH, Inc. • Five looseleaf volumes. Newsletter and semimonthly updates. Emphasis on pension plans.

How to Plan for a Secure Retirement. Elias Zuckerman and others. Consumer Reports Books. • 2000. $29.95. Covers pension plans, health insurance, estate planning, retirement communities, and related topics. (Consumer Reports Money Guide.).

How to Set Up a Qualified Pension Plan Practice. American Management Association Extension Institute. • Looseleaf. $130.00. Self-study course. Emphasis is on practical explanations, examples, and problem solving. Quizzes and a case study are included. Covers pension plan consulting and administration for small and medium-sized companies.

Individual Retirement Plans Guide. CCH, Inc. • $230.00 per year. Looseleaf service. Monthly updates. Covers IRA plans (Individual Retirement Accounts), SEP plans (Simplified Employee Pensions), and Keogh plans (self-employed retirement accounts).

InSite 2. Intelligence Data/Thomson Financial. • Fee-based Web site consolidates information in a "Base Pack" consisting of Business InSite, Market InSite, and Company InSite. Optional databases are Consumer InSite, Health and Wellness InSite, Newsletter InSite, and Computer InSite. Includes fulltext content from more than 2,500 trade publications, journals, newsletters, newspapers, analyst reports, and other sources. Continuous updating. Formerly produced by The Gale Group.

Lieber on Pensions. William M. Lieber. Aspen Law and Business. • 1991. $595.00. Five volumes. Looseleaf periodic supplementation available. Organizes, describes, and analyzes ERISA and IRS pension rules. Topical arrangement.

Pension Fund Litigation Reporter. Andrews Publications. • Monthly. $750.00 per year. Contains reports on legal cases involving pension fund fiduciaries (trustees).

PEPPER INDUSTRY

See: SPICE INDUSTRY

PERFORMANCE EVALUATION

See: RATING OF EMPLOYEES

PERFORMING ARTS

See: SHOW BUSINESS

PERFUME INDUSTRY

See also: COSMETICS INDUSTRY

DIRECTORIES

Fragrance Foundation Reference Guide. Fragrance Foundation. • Annual. $85.00. Manufacturers of over 1,100 fragances available in the United States.

Who's Who: The CTFA Membership Directory (Cosmetics Industry). Cosmetic, Toiletry, and Fragrance Association. • Annual. $100.00. Lists about 1,000 member companies, with key personnel, products, and services.

World Cosmetics and Toiletries Directory. Available from The Gale Group. • 2001. $1,90.00. Second edition. Three volumes. Published by Euromonitor. Provides detailed descriptions of the world's cosmetics and toiletries companies. Includes consumers market research data.

HANDBOOKS AND MANUALS

The Chemistry of Fragrances. D. Pybus and C. Sell. Available from American Chemical Society. • 1998. $39.00. Published by The Royal Society of Chemistry.

Formulary of Cosmetic Preparations. Anthony L. Hunting, editor. Micelle Press, Inc. • 1991. $135.00. Two volumes. Volume one, *Decorative Cosmetics* $60.00; volume two *Creams, Lotions and Milks* $95.00.

ONLINE DATABASES

F-D-C Reports. FDC Reports, Inc. • An online version of "The Gray Sheet" (medical devices), "The Pink Sheet" (pharmaceuticals), "The Rose Sheet" (cosmetics), "The Blue Sheet" (biomedical), and "The Tan Sheet" (nonprescription). Contains full-text information on legal, technical, corporate, financial, and marketing developments from 1987 to date, with weekly updates. Inquire as to online cost and availability.

PROMT: Predicasts Overview of Markets and Technology. The Gale Group. • Companies, products, applied technologies and markets. U.S. and international literature coverage, 1972 to date. Inquire as to online cost and availability. Provides abstracts from more than 1,600 publications. Weekly updates.

PERIODICALS AND NEWSLETTERS

CTFA News. Cosmetic, Toiletry, and Fragrance Association. • Bimonthly. Newsletter.

Perfumer and Flavorist. Allured Publishing Corp. • Bimonthly. $135.00 per year. Provides information on the art and technology of flavors and fragrances, including essential oils, aroma chemicals, and spices.

Toiletries, Fragrances, and Skin Care: The Rose Sheet. F-D-C Reports, Inc. • Weekly. $710.00 per year. Newsletter. Provides industry news, regulatory news, market data, and a "Weekly Trademark Review" for the cosmetics industry.

STATISTICS SOURCES

Synthetic Organic Chemicals: United States Production and Sales. International Trade Commission. Available from U.S. Government Printing Office. • Annual.

TRADE/PROFESSIONAL ASSOCIATIONS

Cosmetic, Toiletry and Fragrance Association. 1101 17th St., N.W., Suite 300, Washington, DC 20036. Phone: (202)331-1770 Fax: (202)331-1969 • URL: http://www.ctfa.org/.

Fragrance Foundation. 145 E. 32nd St., 8th and 9th Fls., New York, NY 10016. Phone: (212)725-2755 Fax: (212)779-9058 E-mail: info@fragrance.org • URL: http://www.fragrance.org.

PERIODICAL CIRCULATION

See: CIRCULATION MANAGEMENT (PUBLISHING)

PERIODICALS

See also: CIRCULATION MANAGEMENT (PUBLISHING); HOUSE ORGANS; NEWSLETTERS; NEWSPAPERS; TRADE JOURNALS

GENERAL WORKS

Business Journals of the United States: Historical Guides to the World's Periodicals and Newspapers. William Fisher, editor. Greenwood Publishing Group, Inc. • 1991. $75.00. Contains historical and descriptive essays covering over 100 leading business publications.

Introduction to Serial Management. Marcia Tuttle. JAI Press, Inc. • 1978. $78.50. (Foundations in Library and Information Science Series, Vol. 11).

ABSTRACTS AND INDEXES

Applied Science and Technology Index. H. W. Wilson Co. • 11 times a year. Quarterly and annual cumulations. Service basis for print edition; CD-ROM edition, $1,495.00 per year. Indexes a wide variety of English language technical, industrial, and engineering periodicals.

Business Periodicals Index. H. W. Wilson Co. • Monthly, except August, with quarterly and annual cumulations. Service basis for print edition; CD-ROM edition, $1,495.00 per year.

Canadian Index. Micromedia Ltd. • Monthly, with annual cumulation. Price varies. Indexes approximately 500 Canadian periodicals of all kinds, including business magazines and trade journals. Ten daily Canadian newspapers are also indexed.

Canadian Periodical Index. The Gale Group. • Monthly. $515.00 per year. Annual cumulation. Indexes more than 400 English and French language periodicals.

Humanities Index. H.W. Wilson Co. • Quarterly. Annual cumulation. Service basis.

Readers' Guide to Periodical Literature. H. W. Wilson Co. • Monthly. $220.00 per year. CD-ROM edition, $1,495 per year, including annual cumulation. Indexes about 250 peridicals of general interest.

Social Sciences Index. H. W. Wilson Co. • Quarterly, with annual cumulation. Service basis for print edition; CD-ROM edition, $1,495 per year. Indexes more than 400 periodicals covering economics, environmental policy, government, insurance, labor, health care policy, plannning, public administration, public welfare, urban studies, women's issues, criminology, and related topics.

U. S. Government Periodicals Index. Congressional Information Service, Inc. • Quarterly. $995.00 per year. Annual cumulation. An index to approximately 180 periodicals issued by various agencies of the federal government.

BIBLIOGRAPHIES

Free Magazines for Libraries. Adeline M. Smith. McFarland & Co. Inc., Publishers. • 1994. $32.50. Fourth edition.

Guide to Special Issues and Indexes of Periodicals. Miriam Uhlan and Doris B. Katz, editors. Special Libraries Association. • 1994. $59.00. Fourth edition. A listing, with prices, of the special issues of over 1700 U. S. and Canadian periodicals in business, industry, technology, science, and the arts. Includes a comprehensive subject index.

Magazines for Libraries: For the General Reader and School, Junior College, University and Public Libraries. Bill Katz and Linda Steinberg Katz. R. R. Bowker. • 2000. $185.00. 10th edition. About 7,300 periodicals listed.

Serials for Libraries; An Annotated Guide to Continuations, Annuals, Yearbooks, Almanacs, Transactions, Proceedings, Directories, Services. Diane Sciattara. Neal-Schuman Publishers, Inc. • 1985. $85.00. Second edition.

Serials in Microform. UMI. • Annual. Free to libraries.

U.S. Government Subscriptions. U. S. Government Printing Office. • Quarterly. Free. Includes agency and subject indexes.

CD-ROM DATABASES

CPI.Q: The Canadian Periodical Index Full-Text on CD-ROM. The Gale Group. • Bimonthly. Provides CD-ROM citations from 1988 to date for more than 400 English and French language periodicals. Contains full-text coverage from 1995 to date for 150 periodicals.

Leadership Library on CD-ROM: Who's Who in the Leadership of the United States. Leadership Directories, Inc. • Quarterly. $2,641.00 per year, including access to Internet version (weekly updates). Contains all 14 *Yellow Book* personnel directories on CD-ROM, providing contact and brief biographical information for about 400,000 individuals. Covers business, government, financial institutions, news media, law firms, associations, foreign representatives, and nonprofit organizations. Includes photographs.

Magazine Index Plus. The Gale Group. • Monthly. $4,000.00 per year (includes InfoTrac workstation). Provides full text on CD-ROM for about 100 popular, general interest magazines and indexing for 300 others. Includes special indexing of reviews and product evaluations. Time period is 1980 to date.

MediaFinder CD-ROM: Oxbridge Directories of Print Media and Catalogs. Oxbridge Communications, Inc. • Quarterly. $1,695.00 per year. CD-ROM includes about 100,000 listings from *Standard Periodical Directory, National Directory of Catalogs, National Directory of British Mail Order Catalogs, National Directory of German Mail Order Catalogs, Oxbridge Directory of Newsletters, National Directory of Mailing Lists, College Media Directory*, and *National Directory of Magazines.*

Monthly Catalog of United States Government Publications [CD-ROM]. U. S. Government Printing Office. • Monthly. $199.00 per year. Entries contain complete bibliographic information formerly appearing in the print edition of the *Monthly Catalog*. Each issue is cumulative, with author, title, and subject indexes. The January issue includes the *Periodicals Supplement.*

Serials Directory: EBSCO CD-ROM. Ebsco Publishing. • Quarterly. $525.00 per year. The CD-ROM version of Ebsco's *The Serials Directory: An International Reference Book.*

Social Science Source. EBSCO Publishing. • Monthly. $1,495.00 per year. Provides CD-ROM citations and abstracts to social science articles in more than 600 periodicals, with full text from 125 periodicals. Covers economics, political science, public policy, international relations, psychology, and other topics. Time period is most recent five years.

Social Sciences Citation Index: Compact Disc Edition with Abstracts. Institute for Scientific Information. • Quarterly. Provides CD-ROM indexing and abstracting of "significant articles" from 1,400 social science journals worldwide, with additional selections from 3,200 other journals, 1986 to date. Includes economics, business, finance, management, communications, demographics, information and library science, political science, sociology, and many other subjects.

U. S. Government Periodicals Index (CD-ROM). Congressional Information Service, Inc. • Quarterly. $795.00 per year. Provides indexing on CD-ROM to about 180 federal government periodicals.

Ulrich's on Disc: The Complete International Serials Database on Compact Laser Disc. Bowker Electronic Publishing. • Quarterly. $850.00 per year. The CD-ROM version of *Ulrich's International Periodicals Directory* and *Magazines for Libraries.*

WILSONDISC: Wilson Social Sciences Abstracts. H. W. Wilson Co. • Monthly. Including unlimited online access to *Social Sciences Index* through WILSONLINE. Provides CD-ROM indexing from 1983 and abstracting from 1994 of more than 400 periodicals covering economics, area studies, community health, public administration, public welfare, urban studies, and many other topics related to the social sciences.

DIRECTORIES

Books and Periodicals Online: The Guide to Business and Legal Information on Databases and CD-ROM's. Nuchine Nobari, editor. Library Technology Alliance, Inc. • Annual. $365.00 per year. 97,000 periodicals available as part of online and CD-ROM databases; international coverage.

Burrelle's Media Directory: Magazines and Newsletters. Burrelle's Information Services. • Annual. $275.00. Provides detailed descriptions of more than 13,500 magazines and newsletters published in the U. S., Canada, and Mexico. Categories are professional, consumer, trade, and college.

Cabell's Directory of Publishing Opportunities in Economics, and Finance. Cabell Publishing Co. • 1997. $89.95. Provides editorial policies of commercial and scholarly periodicals in the areas of business and economics. Formerly *Cabell's Directory of Publishing Opportunities in Accounting, Economics, and Finance.*

Cabell's Directory of Publishing Opportunities in Education. Cabell Publishing Co. • 1998. $89.95. Over 430 journals in education which will consider manuscripts forpublication.

Cabell's Directory of Publishing Opportunities in Management. Cabell Publishing Co. • 1997. $89.95. Provides editorial policies of more than 300 management periodicals. Emphasis is on publishing opportunities for college faculty members. Formerly *Cabell's Directory of Publishing Opportunities Business and Economics.*

CARD The Media Information Network (Canadian Advertising Rates and Data). Available from SRDS. • Biennial. $225.00 per issue. Published by Maclean Hunter Publishing Ltd. (Toronto). Provides advertising rates and other information relating to Canadian media: daily newspapers, weekly community newspapers, consumer magazines, business publications, school publications, religious publications, radio, and television.

College Media Directory. Oxbridge Communications, Inc. • 1997. $245.00. Lists more than 6,000 publications from about 3,500 colleges and universities.

Consumer Magazine and Advertising Source. SRDS. • Monthly. $661.00 per year. Contains advertising rates and other data for U. S. consumer magazines and agricultural publications. Also provides consumer market data for population, households, income, and retail sales. Formerly *Consumer Magazine and Agri-Media Source*.

Cyberhound's Guide to Publications on the Internet. The Gale Group. • 1996. $79.00. First edition. Presents critical descriptions and ratings of more than 3,400 Internet databases of journals, newspapers, newsletters, and other publications. Includes a glossary of Internet terms, a bibliography, and three indexes.

The Directory of Business Information Resources: Associations, Newsletters, Magazine Trade Shows. Grey House Publishing, Inc. • Annual. $195.00. Provides concise information on associations, newsletters, magazines, and trade shows for each of 90 major industry groups. An "Entry & Company Index" serves as a guide to titles, publishers, and organizations.

Fulltext Sources Online. Information Today, Inc. • Semiannual. $199.00 per year; $119.50 per issue. Lists more than 8,000 journals, newspapers, magazines, newsletters, and newswires found online in fulltext through DIALOG, LEXIS-NEXIS, Dow Jones, Westlaw, etc. Includes journals that have free Internet archives. (Formerly published by BiblioData.).

Gale Directory of Publications and Broadcast Media. The Gale Group. • Annual. $650.00. Five volumes. A guide to publications and broadcasting stations in the U. S. and Canada, including newspapers, magazines, journals, radio stations, television stations, and cable systems. Geographic arrangement. Volume three consists of statistical tables, maps, subject indexes, and title index. Formerly *Ayer Directory of Publications*.

International Directory of Little Magazines and Small Presses. Dustbooks. • Annual. $40.00. Over 6,000 small, independent magazines, presses, and papers.

International Media Guide: Consumer Magazines Worldwide. International Media Guides, Inc. • Annual. $285.00. Contains descriptions of 4,500 consumer magazines in 24 subject categories in 200 countries, including U. S. Provides details of advertising rates and circulation.

Magazines Careers Directory: A Practical One-Stop Guide to Getting a Job in Publc Relations. Visible Ink Press. • 1993. $17.95. Fifth edition. Includes information on magazine publishing careers in art, editing, sales, and business management. Provides advice from "insiders," resume suggestions, a directory of companies that may offer entry-level positions, and a directory of career information sources. *Career Advisor Series.*

News Media Yellow Book: Who's Who Among Reporters, Writers, Editors, and Producers in the Leading National News Media. Leadership Directories, Inc. • Quarterly. $305.00 per year. Lists the staffs of major newspapers and news magazines, TV and radio networks, news services and bureaus, and feature syndicates. Includes syndicated columnists and programs. Seven specialized indexes are provided.

Print Media Production Source. SRDS. • Quarterly. $401.00 per year. Contains details of printing and mechanical production requirements for advertising in specific trade journals, consumer magazines, and newspapers. Formerly *Print Media Production Data.*

Samir Husni's Guide to New Consumer Magazines. Oxbridge Communications, Inc. • Annual. $95.00. A directory of more than 500 consumer magazines that began publication during the previous year. Includes names of key personnel.

Serials Directory: An International Reference Book. EBSCO Industries, Inc. • Annual. $339.00. Five volumes. Include cumulative updates. Over 155,000 current and ceased periodicals and serials worldwide.

The Standard Periodical Directory 2001. Available from The Gale Group. • 2000. $1,095.00. 24rd edition. Published by Oxbridge Communications. Covers 75,000 periodicals published in the United States and Canada arranged into more than 250 major subjects.

Ulrich's International Periodicals Directory. R. R. Bowker. • Annual. $595.00. Five volumes. Over 165,000 current periodicals published worldwide; 7,000 newspapers published in the United States. Approximately 10,000 periodicals that have ceased or suspended publication. Includes *Ulrich's Update.* Incorporates information from *Irregular Serials and Annuals.*

Working Press of the Nation. R. R. Bowker. • Annual. $450.00. Three volumes: (1) *Newspaper Directory*; (2) *Magazine and Internal Publications Directory*; (3) *Radio and Television Directory.* Includes names of editors and other personnel. Individual volumes, $249.00.

ENCYCLOPEDIAS AND DICTIONARIES

NTC's Mass Media Dictionary. R. Terry Ellmore. NTC/Contemporary Publishing. • 1993. $24.95. Covers television, radio, newspapers, magazines, film, graphic arts, books, billboards, public relations, and advertising. Terms are related to production, research, audience measurement, audio-video engineering, printing, publishing, and other areas.

Periodical Title Abbreviations. The Gale Group. • 2000. $735.00. 13th edition. Two volumes. $245.00 per volume Vol. 1 *By Abbreviation*; vol. 2 *By Title.* Lists more than 145,000 different abbreviations.

FINANCIAL RATIOS

Almanac of Business and Industrial Financial Ratios. Leo Troy. Prentice Hall. • Annual. $99.95. Contains financial ratios derived from federal tax returns. Ratios for each of about 200 industries are arranged according to company asset size.

Annual Statement Studies. Robert Morris Associates: The Association of Lending and Credit Risk Professiona. • Annual. Free to members; non-members, $140.00. Median and quartile financial ratios are given for over 400 kinds of manufacturing, wholesale, retail, construction, and consumer finance establishments. Data is sorted by both asset size and sales volume. Includes a clearly written "Definition of Ratios" and an alphabetical industry index.

HANDBOOKS AND MANUALS

Buying Serials: A How-To-Do-It Manual for Librarians. N. Bernard Basch and Judy McQueen. Neal-Schuman Publishers, Inc. • 1990. $49.95. (How-to-Do-It Series).

Developing and Managing E-Journal Collections: A How-To-DoIt Manual for Librarians. Donnelyn Curtis and others. Neal-Schuman Publishers, Inc. • 2000. $55.00. Covers the acquisition, management, and integration of journals published in electronic form.

INTERNET DATABASES

EBSCO Information Services. Ebsco Publishing. Phone: 800-871-8508 or (508)356-6500 Fax: (508)356-5640 E-mail: ep@epnet.com • URL: http://www.epnet.com • Fee-based Web site providing Internet access to a wide variety of databases, including business-related material. Full text is available for many periodical titles, with daily updates. Fees: Apply.

GaleNet: Your Information Community. The Gale Group. Phone: 800-877-GALE or (248)699-GALE Fax: 800-414-5043 or (248)699-8069 E-mail: galenet@gale.com • URL: http://www.galenet.com • Web site provides a wide variety of full-text information from Gale databases, Taft, and other sources. Covers associations, biography, business directories, education, the information industry, literature, publishing, and science. Fee-based subscriptions are available for individual databases (free demonstration). Includes Boolean search features and the BRS/Search user interface.

ProQuest Direct. Bell & Howell Information and Learning. Phone: 800-521-0600 or (313)761-4700 Fax: (313)973-9145 • URL: http://www.umi.com/proquest • Fee-based Web site providing Internet access to more than 3,000 periodicals, newspapers, and other publications. Many items are available full-text, with daily updates. Includes extensive corporate and financial information from Disclosure, Inc. Fees: Apply.

PubList.com: The Internet Directory of Publications. Bowes & Associates, Inc. Phone: (781)792-0999 Fax: (781)792-0988 E-mail: info@publist.com • URL: http://www.publist.com • "The premier online global resource for information about print and electronic publications." Provides online searching for information on more than 150,000 magazines, journals, newsletters, e-journals, and monographs. Database entries generally include title, publisher, format, address, editor, circulation, subject, and International Standard Serial Number (ISSN). Fees: Free.

Ulrichsweb.com. R. R. Bowker. Phone: 888-269-5372 or (908)464-6800 Fax: (908)464-3553 E-mail: info@bowker.com • URL: http://www.ulrichsweb.com • Web site provides fee-based access to about 250,000 serials records from the *Ulrich's International Periodicals Directory* database. Includes periodical evaluations from *Library Journal* and *Magazines for Libraries.* Monthly updates.

WilsonWeb Periodicals Databases. H. W. Wilson. Phone: 800-367-6770 or (718)588-8400 Fax: 800-590-1617 or (718)992-8003 E-mail: custserv@hwwilson.com • URL: http://www.hwwilson.com/ • Web sites provide fee-based access to *Wilson Business Full Text, Applied Science & Technology Full Text, Biological & Agricultural Index, Library Literature & Information Science Full Text,* and *Readers' Guide Full Text, Mega Edition.* Daily updates.

ONLINE DATABASES

ABI/INFORM. Bell & Howell Information and Learning. • Provides online indexing to business-related material occurring in over 1,000 periodicals from 1971 to the present. Inquire as to online cost and availability.

Gale Database of Publications and Broadcast Media. The Gale Group. • An online directory containing detailed information on over 67,000 periodicals, newspapers, broadcast stations, cable systems, directories, and newsletters. Corresponds to the following print sources: *Gale Directory of Publications and Broadcast Media; Directories in Print; City and State Directories in Print; Newsletters in Print.* Semiannual updates. Inquire as to online cost and availability.

Magazine Index. The Gale Group. • General magazine indexing (popular literature), 1973 to present. Daily updates. Inquire as to online cost and availability.

Newspaper and Periodical Abstracts. Bell & Howell Information and Learning. • Provides online coverage (citations and abstracts) of 25 major newspapers, 1,600 perodicals, and 70 TV programs. Covers business, economics, current affairs, health, fitness, sports, education, technology, government, consumer affairs, psychology, the arts, and the social sciences. Time period is 1986 to date, with daily updates. Inquire as to online cost and availability.

Trade & Industry Index. The Gale Group. • Provides indexing of business periodicals, January 1981 to date. Daily updates. (Full text articles from some periodicals are available online, 1983 to date, in the companion database, *Trade & Industry ASAP.*) Inquire as to online cost and availability.

Ulrich's International Periodicals Directory Online. Bowker Electronic Publishing. • Includes over 250,000 periodicals currently published worldwide and publications discontinued. Corresponds to *Ulrich's International Periodcals Directory, Irregular Serials and Annuals, Bowker International Serials Database Update,* and *Sources of Serials.* Inquire as to online cost and availability.

Wilson Social Sciences Abstracts Online. H. W. Wilson Co. • Provides online abstracting and indexing of more than 415 periodicals covering area studies, community health, public administration, public welfare, urban studies, and many other social science topics. Time period is 1994 to date for abstracts and 1983 to date for indexing, with updates monthly. Inquire as to online cost and availability.

PERIODICALS AND NEWSLETTERS

Circulation Management. Intertec Publishing Co. • Monthly. $39.00 per year. Edited for circulation professionals in the magazine and newsletter publishing industry. Covers marketing, planning, promotion, management, budgeting, and related topics.

Computer Publishing and Advertising Report: The Biweekly Newsletter for Publishing and Advertising Executives in the Computer Field. SIMBA Information, Inc. • Biweekly. $549.00 per year. Newsletter. Covers computer book publishing and computer-related advertising in periodicals and other media. Provides data on computer book sales and advertising in computer magazines.

Ebsco Bulletin of Serials Changes. EBSCO Industries, Inc.,Title Information Dept. • Bimonthly. $20.00 per year. New titles, discontinuations, title changes, mergers, etc.

Folio: The Magazine for Magazine Management. Intertec Publishing Co. • 17 times a year. $96.00 per year.

Magazine and Bookseller: The Retailer's Guide to Magazines and Paperbacks. North American Publishing Co. • Bimonthly. Free to qualified personnel; others, $59.00 per year.

Serials Librarian: The International Quarterly Journal of Serials Management. Haworth Press, Inc. • Quarterly. Individuals, $45.00 per year; institutions, $180.00 per year; libraries, $180.00 per year. Supplement available: *Serials Librarian.*

Serials Review. JAI Press. • Quarterly. $224.00 per year.

PRICE SOURCES

Faxon Guide to Serials, Including Annuals, Continuations, GPO Publications, Monographic Series, Newspapers, Periodicals, Proceedings, Transactions, and Yearbooks, and CD-ROM. Faxon Co., Inc. • Annual. Free to qualified personnel; others, $25.00. Gives prices and frequency, but no addresses.

STATISTICS SOURCES

Computer Publishing Market Forecast. SIMBA Information. • Annual. $1,995.00. Provides market data on computer-related books, magazines, newsletters, and other publications. Includes profiles of major publishers of computer-related material.

U. S. Industry and Trade Outlook: The McGraw-Hill Companies and the U.S. Department of Commerce/ International Trade Administration. Datapso Research Corp. • Annual. $69.95. Produced by the International Trade Administration, U. S. Department of Commerce, in a "public-private" partnership with DRI/McGraw-Hill and Standard & Poor's. Provides basic data, outlook for the current year, and "Long-Term Prospects" (five-year projections) for a wide variety of products and services. Includes high technology industries. Formerly *U. S. Industrial Outlook.*

TRADE/PROFESSIONAL ASSOCIATIONS

American Society of Magazine Editors. 919 Third Ave., New York, NY 10022. Phone: (212)872-3700 Fax: (212)906-0128 E-mail: asme@magazine.org • URL: http://www.magazine.org.

Audit Bureau of Circulations. 900 N. Meacham Rd., Schaumburg, IL 60173-4968. Phone: (847)605-0909 Fax: (847)605-0483 • URL: http://www.accessabvs.com • Verifies newspaper and periodical circulation statements. Includes a Business Publications Industry Committee and a Magazine Directors Advisory Committee.

BPA International. 270 Madison Ave., New York, NY 10016-0699. Phone: (212)779-3200 Fax: (212)779-3615 • URL: http://www.bpai.com • Verifies business and consumer periodical circulation statements. Includes a Circulation Managers Committee. *Formerly Business Publications Audit of Circulation.*

Magazine Publishers of America. 919 Third Ave., 22nd Fl., New York, NY 10022. Phone: (212)872-3700 Fax: (212)888-4217 E-mail: infocenter@magazine.org • URL: http://www.magazine.org • Members are publishers of consumer and other periodicals.

Publishers Information Bureau. 919 Third Ave., New York, NY 10022. Phone: (212)872-3700 Fax: (212)888-4217 E-mail: trobinson@magazine.org.

OTHER SOURCES

Bacon's Newspaper/Magazine Directories. Bacon's Publishing Co. • Annual. $295.00 per year. Quarterly update. Two volumes: Magazines and Newspapers. Covers print media in the United States and Canada. Formerly *Bacon's Publicity Checker.*

Towards Electronic Journals: Realities for Scientists, Librarians, and Publishers. Carol Tenopir and Donald W. King. Special Libraries Association. • 2000. $59.00. Discusses journals in electronic form vs. traditional (paper) scholarly journals, including the impact of subscription prices.

PERIODICALS, BUSINESS

See: TRADE JOURNALS

PERSONAL CARE PRODUCTS

See: COSMETICS INDUSTRY

PERSONAL COMPUTERS

See: MICROCOMPUTERS AND MINICOMPUTERS; PORTABLE COMPUTERS

PERSONAL FINANCE

See also: ESTATE PLANNING; FINANCIAL PLANNING; HOME OWNERSHIP; INVESTMENTS; LIFE INSURANCE; PENSIONS; TAX SHELTERS

GENERAL WORKS

Consumer Reports Money Book: How to Get It, Save It, and Spend It Wisely. Janet Bamford and others. Consumers Union of the United States, Inc. • 1997. $29.95. Revised edition. Covers budgeting, retirement planning, bank accounts, insurance, and other personal finance topics.

The Death of the Banker: The Decline and Fall of the Great Financial Dynasties and the Triumph of the Small Investor. Ron Chernow. Vintage Books. • 1997. $12.00. Contains three essays: "J. Pierpont Morgan," "The Warburgs," and "The Death of the Banker" (discusses the decline of banks in personal finance and the rise of mutual funds and stock brokers).

Don't Die Broke: How to Turn Your Retirement Savings into Lasting Income. Margaret A. Malaspina. Available from W.W. Norton and Co., Inc. • 1999. $21.95. Provides advice on such matters as retirement portfolio asset allocation and retirement spending accounts. (Bloomberg Personal Bookshelf.).

Everyone's Money Book: Everything You Need to Know About Investing Wisely, Buying a Home... Jordan E. Goodman. Dearborn, A Kaplan Professional Co. • 1998. $26.95. Covers investing, taxes, mortgages, retirement planning, and other personal finance topics. Jordan E. Goodman is a writer for *Money* magazine.

Financial Planning for the Utterly Confused. Joel Lerner. McGraw-Hill. • 1998. $12.00. Fifth edition. Covers annuities, certificates of deposit, bonds, mutual funds, insurance, home ownership, retirement, social security, wills, etc.

The Lifetime Book of Money Management. Grace W. Weinstein. Visible Ink Press. • 1993. $15.95. Third edition. Gives popularly-written advice on investments, life and health insurance, owning a home, credit, retirement, estate planning, and other personal finance topics.

Never Call Your Broker on Monday: And 300 Other Financial Lessons You Can't Afford Not to Know. Nancy Dunnan. HarperCollins Publishers. • 1996. $8.50. Presents a wide range of personal finance advice, covering investments, insurance, wills, credit, real estate, etc.

A Random Walk Down Wall Street: Including a Life-Cycle Guide to Personal Investing. Burton G. Malkiel. W. W. Norton & Co., Inc. • 1999. $29.95. Seventh edition.

Staying Wealthy: Strategies for Protecting Your Assets. Brian H. Breuel. Bloomberg Press. • 1998. $21.95. Presents ideas for estate planning and personal wealth preservation. Includes case studies. (Bloomberg Personal Bookshelf Series).

Wealth in a Decade: Brett Matchtig's Proven System for Creating Wealth, Living Off Your Investments and Attaining a Financially Secure Life. Brett Machtig and Ryan D. Behrends. McGraw-Hill Professional. • 1996. $24.95. The authors advocate systematic saving, prudent investing, and no credit card debt. Advice is given on constructing a diversified investment portfolio.

ABSTRACTS AND INDEXES

Banking Information Index. U M I Banking Information Index. • Monthly. Price on application. Covers a wide variety of banking, business, and financial subjects in periodicals. Formerly *Banking Literature Index.*

CD-ROM DATABASES

Magazine Index Plus. The Gale Group. • Monthly. $4,000.00 per year (includes InfoTrac workstation). Provides full text on CD-ROM for about 100 popular, general interest magazines and indexing for 300 others. Includes special indexing of reviews and product evaluations. Time period is 1980 to date.

National Newspaper Index CD-ROM. The Gale Group. • Monthly. Provides comprehensive CD-ROM indexing of all material appearing in the late edition of the *New York Times*, the final edition of the *Washington Post*, the national edition of the *Christian Science Monitor*, the home edition of the *Los Angeles Times*, and the *Wall Street Journal*. Time period is four years. Also available online.

The New York Times Ondisc. New York Times Online Services. • Monthly. $2,650.00 per year. CD-ROM discs contain the full text of *The New York Times*, final edition. Inquire as to time period covered and availability of backfiles.

Newspaper Abstracts Ondisc. Bell & Howell Information and Learning. • Monthly. $2,950.00 per year (covers 1989 to date; archival discs are available for 1985-88). Provides cover-to-cover CD-ROM indexing and abstracting of 19 major newspapers, including the *New York Times, Wall Street Journal, Washington Post, Chicago Tribune,* and *Los Angeles Times.*

WILSONDISC: Readers' Guide to Periodical Literature. H. W. Wilson Co. • Monthly. $1,095.00 per year, including unlimited online access to *Readers' Guide to Periodical Literature* through WILSONLINE. Provides CD-ROM indexing of about 250 general interest periodicals. Covers 1983 to date. (*Readers' Guide Abstracts* also available on CD-ROM at $1,995 per year.).

DIRECTORIES

Plunkett's On-Line Trading, Finance, and Investment Web Sites Almanac. Plunkett Research, Ltd. • Annual. $149.99. Provides profiles and usefulness rankings of financial Web sites. Sites are rated from 1 to 5 for specific uses. Includes diskette.

ENCYCLOPEDIAS AND DICTIONARIES

Dictionary of Personal Finance. Joel G. Siegel and others. Pearson Education and Technology. • 1993. $20.00.

FINANCIAL RATIOS

Financial Planning for Older Clients. James E. Pearman. CCH, Inc. • 2000. $49.00. Covers income sources, social security, Medicare, Medicaid, investment planning, estate planning, and other retirement-related topics. Edited for accountants, attorneys, and other financial advisors.

HANDBOOKS AND MANUALS

Best Practices for Financial Advisors. Mary Rowland. • 1997. $40.00. Provides advice for professional financial advisors on practice management, ethics, marketing, and legal concerns. (Bloomberg Professional Library.).

Complete Book of Personal- Legal Forms. Daniel Sitarz. Nova Publishing Co. • 1996. $29.95. Second revised edition. Provides more than 100 forms, including contracts, bills of sale, promissory notes, leases, deeds, receipts, and wills. Forms are also available on IBM or MAC diskettes. (Legal Self-Help Series).

Credit Consulting. Entrepreneur Media, Inc. • Looseleaf. $59.50. A practical guide to starting a consumer credit and debt counseling and consulting service. Covers profit potential, start-up costs, market size evaluation, owner's time required, pricing, accounting, advertising, promotion, etc. (Start-Up Business Guide No. E1321.).

Ernst & Young's Personal Financial Planning Guide. John Wiley and Sons, Inc. • 1999. $19.95. Third edition.

Estate and Retirement Planning Answer Book. William D. Mitchell. Aspen Publshers. • 1996. $118.00. Second edition. Basic questions and answers by a lawyer.

Getting Started in Investment Planning Services. James E. Grant. CCH, Inc. • 1999. $85.00. Second edition. Provides advice and information for lawyers and accountants who are planning to initiate fee-based investment services.

Homeowner or Tenant? How to Make a Wise Choice. Lawrence S. Pratt. American Institute for Economic Research. • 1997. $6.00. Provides detailed information for making rent or buy decisions. Includes "Mortgage Arithmetic," "Hints for Buyers, Sellers, and Renters," worksheets, mortgage loan interest tables, and other data. (Economic Education Bulletin.).

Personal Finance. Jack R. Kapoor and others. McGraw-Hill. • 2000. $82.50 Sixth edition.

Personal Financial Planning. G. Victor Hallman. McGraw-Hill. • 2000. $42.95. Sixth edition.

Personal Financial Planning: The Advisor's Guide. Rolf Auster. CCH, Inc. • 1998. $55.95. Third edition. Covers personal taxes, investments, credit, mortgages, insurance, pensions, social security, estate planning, etc.

Tools and Techniques of Financial Planning. Stephan Leimberg and others. The National Underwriter Co. • 1993. $37.50. Fourth revised edition.

Wall Street Journal Guide to Planning Your Financial Future: The Easy-to-Read Guide to Lifetime Planning for Retirement. Kenneth M. Morris. Simon & Schuster Trade. • 1998. $14.95. Revised edition. (Wall Street Journal Guides Series).

INTERNET DATABASES

BanxQuote Banking, Mortgage, and Finance Center. BanxQuote, Inc. Phone: 800-765-3000 or (212)643-8000 Fax: (212)643-0020 E-mail: info@banx.com • URL: http://www.banx.com • Web site quotes interest rates paid by banks around the country on various savings products, as well as rates paid by consumers for automobile loans, mortgages, credit cards, home equity loans, and personal loans. Also provided: stock quotes, indexes, stock options, futures trading data, economic indicators, and links to many other financial sites. Daily updates. Fees: Free.

DBC Online: America's Leading Provider of Real-Time Market Data to the Individual Investor. Data Broadcasting Corp. Phone: (415)571-1800 E-mail: dbcinfo@dbc.com • URL: http://www.dbc.com • Web site provides a wide variety of real-time securities market prices, data, and charts. Covers bonds ("BondVu"), stocks, commodities, options, mutual funds, major indexes, industry indexes, international markets, etc. Also includes news, SEC documents ("Smart-Edgar"), and various other features. Fees: Both free and fee-based, depending on level of information.

Deloitte & Touche Online. Deloitte & Touche LLP, Financial Consulting Services Center. Phone: (513)784-7100 E-mail: webmaster@dtonline.com • URL: http://www.dtonline.com • Web site provides concise, full-text articles on taxes, personal finance, and business from a leading accounting firm. Includes "Tax News and Views," "Personal Finance Advisor," "Business Advisor: A Resource for Small Business Owners," "Financial Tip of the Week," and "This Week Online: Top of the News." Weekly updates. Fees: Free.

ONLINE DATABASES

Banking Information Source. Bell & Howell Information and Learning. • Provides indexing and abstracting of periodical and other literature from 1982 to date, with weekly updates. Covers the financial services industry: banks, savings institutions, investment houses, credit unions, insurance companies, and real estate organizations. Emphasis is on marketing and management. Inquire as to online cost and availability. (Formerly *FINIS: Financial Industry Information Service.*).

Information Bank Abstracts. New York Times Index Dept. • Provides indexing and abstracting of current affairs, primarily from the final late edition of *The New York Times* and the Eastern edition of *The Wall Street Journal.* Time period is 1969 to present, with daily updates. Inquire as to online cost and availability.

PAIS International. Public Affairs Information Service, Inc. • Corresponds to the former printed publications, *PAIS Bulletin* (1976-90) and *PAIS Foreign Language Index* (1972-90), and to the current *PAIS International in Print* (1991 to date). Covers economic, political, and sociological material appearing in periodicals, books, government documents, and other publications. Updating is monthly. Inquire as to online cost and availability.

Readers' Guide Abstracts Online. H. W. Wilson Co. • Indexes and abstracts general interest periodicals, 1983 to date. Weekly updates. Inquire as to online cost and availability.

PERIODICALS AND NEWSLETTERS

Asset Management. Dow Jones Financial Publishing Corp. • Bimonthly. $345.00 per year. Covers the management of the assets of affluent, high net worth investors. Provides information on various financial products and services.

Barron's: The Dow Jones Business and Financial Weekly. Dow Jones and Co., Inc. • Weekly. $145.00 per year.

Bloomberg Personal Finance. Bloomberg L.P. • Monthly. $24.95 per year. Provides advice on personal finance, investments, travel, real estate, and maintaining an "upscale life style." Formerly *Bloomberg Personal.*

Bottom Line-Personal. Bottom Line Information, Inc. • Semimonthly. $29.95 per year. Provides information to help sophisticated people lead more productive lives.

Estate Planner's Alert. Research Institute of America, Inc. • Monthly. $140.00 per year. Newsletter. Covers the tax aspects of personal finance, including home ownership, investments, insurance, retirement planning, and charitable giving. Formerly *Estate and Financial Planners Alert.*

Family Economics and Nutrition Review. Available from U. S. Government Printing Office. • Quarterly. $19.00 per year. Issued by the Consumer and Food Economics Institute, U. S. Department of Agriculture. Provides articles on consumer expenditures and budgeting for food, clothing, housing, energy, education, etc.

Financial Counseling and Planning. Association for Financial Counseling and Planning Education. • Semiannual. Members, $60. per year; institutions, $100.00 per year; libraries, $60.00 per year. Disseminates scholarly research relating to finacial planning and counseling .

Forbes. Forbes, Inc. • Biweekly. $59.95 per year. Includes supplements: *Forbes ASAP* and *Forbes FYI.*

Income Fund Outlook. Institute for Econometric Research. • Monthly. $100.00 per year. Newsletter. Contains tabular data on money market funds, certificates of deposit, bond funds, and tax-free bond funds. Includes specific recommendations, fund news, and commentary on interest rates.

Investment Advisor. Dow Jones Financial Publishing Corp. • Monthly. $79.00 per year. Edited for professional investment advisors, financial planners, stock brokers, bankers, and others concerned with the management of assets.

Investment News: The Weekly Newspaper for Financial Advisers. Crain Communications, Inc. • Weekly. $38.00 per year. Edited for both personal and institutional investment advisers, planners, and managers.

Investment Reporter. MPL Communication, Inc. • Weekly. $279.00 per year. Newsletter. Monthly supplement, *Investment Planning Guide.* Recommendations for Canadian investments. Formerly *Personal Wealth Reporter.*

Journal of Private Portfolio Management. Institutional Investor. • Quarterly. $280.00 per year. Edited for managers of wealthy individuals' investment portfolios.

Kiplinger's Personal Finance Magazine. Kiplinger Washington Editors, Inc. • Monthly. $23.95 per year. Formerly *Changing Times.*

Money. Time Inc. • Monthly. $39.95 per year. Covers all aspects of family finance; investments, careers, shopping, taxes, insurance, consumerism, etc.

New Century Family Money Book: Your Comprehensive Guide to a Lifetime of Financial Security. Jonathan D. Pond. Dell Publishing Co., Inc. • 1995. $19.95.

Personal Finance. Kephart Communications, Inc. • Biweekly. $118.00 per year. Investment advisory newsletter.

Predictions: Specific Investment Forecasts and Recommendations from the World's Top Financial Experts. Lee Euler, editor. Agora, Inc. • Monthly. $78.00 per year. Newsletter.

Private Asset Management. Institutional Investor. • Biweekly. $2,105.00 per year. Newsletter. Edited for managers investing the private assets of wealthy ("high-net-worth") individuals. Includes marketing, taxation, regulation, and fee topics.

Working Woman. MacDonald Communications Corp. • 10 times a year. $15.00 per year. Focuses on solutions of business problems.

Worth: Financial Intelligence. Worth Media. • 10 times a year. $18.00 per year. Contains articles for affluent consumers on personal financial management, including investments, estate planning, and taxes.

Your Money. Consumers Digest, Inc. • Bimonthly. $25.97 per year. Provides information and advice on personal finance and investments.

RESEARCH CENTERS AND INSTITUTES

American Institute for Economic Research. P.O. Box 1000, Great Barrington, MA 01230. Phone: (413)528-1216 Fax: (413)528-0103 E-mail: info@aier.org • URL: http://www.aier.org.

C.V. Starr Center for Applied Economics. New York University, 269 Mercer St., 3rd Fl., New York, NY 10003. Phone: (212)998-8943 Fax: (212)995-3932 E-mail: william.baumol@nyu.edu • URL: http://www.econ.nyu.edu/cvstarr.

STATISTICS SOURCES

Consumer Expenditure Survey. Available from U. S. Government Printing Office. • Biennial. Issued by the Bureau of Labor Statistics, U. S. Department of Labor (http://www.bls.gov). Contains data on various kinds of consumer spending, according to household income, education, etc. (Bureau of Labor Statistics Bulletin.).

Current Population Reports: Household Economic Studies, Series P-70. Available from U. S. Government Printing Office. • Irregular. $16.00 per year. Issued by the U.S. Bureau of the Census (http://www.census.gov). Each issue covers a special topic relating to household socioeconomic characteristics.

Statistical Information on the Financial Services Industry. American Bankers Association. • Annual. Members, $150.00; non-members, $275.00. Presents a wide variety of data relating to banking and financial services, including consumer economics, personal finance, credit, government loans, capital markets, and international banking.

Statistics of Income Bulletin. Available from U.S. Government Printing Office. • Quarterly. $35.00 per year. Current data compiled from tax returns relating to income, assets, and expenses of individuals and businesses. (U. S. Internal Revenue Service.).

TRADE/PROFESSIONAL ASSOCIATIONS

Association for Financial Counseling and Planning Education. 2121 Arlington Ave., Suite 5, Upper Arlington, OH 43221. Phone: (614)485-9650 Fax: (614)485-9621 E-mail: sburns@finsolve.com • URL: http://www.afcpe.org • Members are professional financial planners and academics.

Conference on Consumer Finance Law. c/o Lawrence X. Pusateri, Peterson and Ross, 200 E. Randolph Dr., Suite 7300, Chicago, IL 60601. Phone: (312)861-1400 or (312)946-4653 Fax: (312)565-0832 E-mail: lpusateri@petersonross.com.

Institute of Certified Financial Planners. 3801 E. Florida Ave., Ste. 708, Denver, CO 80210-2571. Phone: 800-322-4237 or (303)759-4900 Fax: (303)759-0749 • Members are Certified Financial Planners or are enrolled in programs accredited by the International Board of Standards and Practices for Certified Financial Planners.

International Association for Financial Planning. 5775 Glenridge Dr. N.E., Suite B-300, Atlanta, GA 30328-5364. Phone: 800-322-4237 or (404)845-0011 Fax: (404)845-3660 E-mail: membership@fpanet.org • URL: http://www.iafp.org • Members are individuals involved in some aspect of financial planning.

OTHER SOURCES

Divorce and Taxes. CCH, Inc. • 2000. $39.00. Second edition. In addition to tax problems, topics include alimony, division of property, and divorce decrees.

Family Law Tax Guide. CCH, Inc. • Monthly. $567.00 per year. Looseleaf service.

Financial Planning and Financial Planning Ideas. Prentice Hall. • Two looseleaf volumes. Periodic supplementation. Price on application.

The Fragile Middle Class: Americans in Debt. Teresa A. Sullivan and others. Yale University Press. • 2000. $32.50. Provides an analysis of a 1991 survey of personal bankruptcies in five states of the U. S. Serves as a sequel to the authors' *As We Forgive Our Debtors* (1989), an analysis of 1981 bankruptcies.

Individual Retirement Plans Guide. CCH, Inc. • $230.00 per year. Looseleaf service. Monthly updates. Covers IRA plans (Individual Retirement Accounts), SEP plans (Simplified Employee Pensions), and Keogh plans (self-employed retirement accounts).

Infogate. Infogate, Inc. • Web site provides current news and information on seven "channels": News, Fun, Sports, Info, Finance, Shop, and Travel. Among the content partners are Business Wire, CBS MarketWatch, CNN, Morningstar, Standard & Poor's, and Thomson Investors Network. Fees: Free, but downloading of Infogate software is required (includes personalized news feature). Updating is continuous. Formerly Pointcast Network.

Working Americans, 1880-1999, Volume One: The Working Class. Grey House Publishing. • 2000. $135.00. Provides detailed information on the lifestyles and economic life of working class families in the 12 decades from 1880 to 1999. Includes such items as selected consumer prices, income, family finances, budgets, life at home, jobs, and working conditions. (Universal Reference Publications.).

Working Americans, 1880-1999, Volume Two: The Middle Class. Grey House Publishing. • 2000. $135.00. Furnishes details of the social and economic lives of middle class Americans during the years 1880 to 1999. Describes such items as selected consumer prices, income, family finances, budgets, life at home, jobs, and working conditions. (Universal Reference Publications.).

PERSONAL FINANCE COMPANIES

See: FINANCE COMPANIES

PERSONNEL INTERVIEWING

See: INTERVIEWING

PERSONNEL MANAGEMENT

See also: HUMAN RELATIONS; INDUSTRIAL RELATIONS

GENERAL WORKS

Advancing Women in Business: The Catalyst Guide to Best Practices from the Corporate Leaders. Catalyst Staff. Available from Jossey-Bass, Inc., Publishers. • 1998. $26.00. Explains the human resources practices of corporations providing a favorable climate for the advancement of female employees.

EEO Law and Personnel Practices. Arthur Gutman. Sage Publications, Inc. • 1993. $58.00. Discusses the practical effect of federal regulations dealing with race, color, religion, sex, national origin, age, and disability. Explains administrative procedures, litigation actions, and penalties.

Human Resource Management. George T. Milkovich and John W. Boudreau. McGraw-Hill. • 1999. $63.25. Ninth edition.

Human Resource Management: A Strategic and Global Perspective. John B. Miner and Donald P. Crane. Addison-Wesley Educational Publications, Inc. • 1997. Price on application.

Human Resource Management: An Economic Approach. David Lewin and Daniel J. Mitchell. South-Western Publishing Co. • 1989. $57.25. Second edition.

Human Resources and Personnel Management. William B. Werther and Keith Davis. McGraw-Hill. • 1995. $82.50. Fifth edition.

Managing Human Resources. Arthur W. Sherman and George Bohlander. Thomson Learning. • 2000. $50.50. 12th edition. (SWC-Management Series).

ABSTRACTS AND INDEXES

Business Periodicals Index. H. W. Wilson Co. • Monthly, except August, with quarterly and annual cumulations. Service basis for print edition; CD-ROM edition, $1,495.00 per year.

Human Resources Abstracts: An International Information Service. Sage Publications, Inc. • Quarterly. Individuals, $150.00 per year; institutions, $610.00 per year.

Personnel Management Abstracts. • Quarterly. $190.00 per year. Includes annual cumulation.

ALMANACS AND YEARBOOKS

Human Resources Yearbook. Prentice Hall. • Annual. $75.00.

Research in Personnel and Human Resources Management. Gerald D. Ferris, editor. JAI Press, Inc. • Irregular. $78.50.

BIBLIOGRAPHIES

Business Information Sources. Lorna M. Daniells. California Princeton Fulfillment Services. • 1993. $42.50. Third revised edition. Basic business sources, with discussion and full annotations.

CD-ROM DATABASES

WILSONDISC: Wilson Business Abstracts. H. W. Wilson Co. • Monthly. $2,495.00 per year, including unlimited online access to *Wilson Business Abstracts* through WILSONLINE. Provides CD-ROM "cover-to-cover" abstracting and indexing of over 600 prominent business periodicals. Indexing is from 1982, abstracting from 1990. (*Business Periodicals Index* without abstracts is available on CD-ROM at $1,495 per year.).

DIRECTORIES

The Human Resource Executive's Market Resource. LRP Publications. • Annual. $25.00. A directory of services and products of use to personnel departments. Includes 20 categories, such as training, outplacement, health benefits, recognition awards, testing, workers' compensation, temporary staffing, recruitment, and human resources software.

ENCYCLOPEDIAS AND DICTIONARIES

Blackwell Encyclopedic Dictionary of Human Resource Management. Lawrence H. Peters and Charles R. Greer, editors. Blackwell Publishers. • 1996. $105.95. The editors are associated with Texas Christian University. Contains definitions of key terms combined with longer articles written by various U. S. and foreign business educators. Includes bibliographies and index. (Blackwell Encyclopedia of Management Series).

BLR Encyclopedia of Prewritten Job Descriptions. Business and Legal Reports, Inc. • $159.95. Looseleaf. Two volumes. Covers all levels "from president to mail clerk.".

Dictionary of HRD. Angus Reynolds and others. • 1997. $67.95. Provides definitions of more than 3,000 terms related to human resource development. Includes acronyms, abbreviations, and a list of "100 Essential HRD Terms." Published by Gower in England.

Encyclopedia of Business. The Gale Group. • 2000. $425.00. Second edition. Two volumes. Contains more than 700 signed articles covering major business disciplines and concepts. International in scope.

Encyclopedia of Human Behavior. Vangipuram S. Ramachandran, editor. Academic Press, Inc. • 1994. $685.00. Four volumes. Contains signed articles on aptitude testing, arbitration, career development, consumer psychology, crisis management, decision making, economic behavior, group dynamics, leadership, motivation, negotiation, organizational behavior, planning, problem solving, stress, work efficiency, and other human behavior topics applicable to business situations.

HR Words You Gotta Know! Essential Human Resources, Terms, Laws, Acronyms and Abbreviations for Everyone in Business. William R. Tracey, editor. AMACOM. • 1994. $17.95. Explains important human relations management terms.

Human Resources Glossary: A Complete Desk Reference for HR Executives, Managers and Practitioners. William R. Tracey. Saint Lucie Press. • 1997. $69.95. Second edition. (First edition published in 1991 by Amacom.).

HANDBOOKS AND MANUALS

AMA Management Handbook. John J. Hampton, editor. AMACOM. • 1994. $110.00. Third edition. Provides 200 chapters in 16 major subject areas. Covers a wide variety of business and industrial management topics.

Company Policy and Personnel Workbook. Ardella Ramey. PSI Research. • 1999. $29.95. Fourth edition. Contains about 50 model company personnel policies for use as examples in developing a personnel manual. Explains the basic laws governing employee-employer relationships. (Successful Business Library Series).

Fair, Square, and Legal: Safe Hiring, Managing, and Firing Practices to Keep You and Your Company Out of Court. Donald Weiss. AMACOM. • 1999. $29.95. Third edition. Covers recruiting, interviewing, sexual discrimination, evaluation of employees, disipline, defamation charges, and wrongful discharge.

Hiring Right: A Practical Guide. Susan J. Herman. Sage Publications, Inc. • 1993. $46.00. A practical manual covering job definition, recruitment, interviewing, testing, and checking of references.

Hiring Winners. Richard J. Pinsker. AMACOM. • 1991. $19.95. Presents a practical system for finding and hiring people who will be ideal for a particular company or situation.

How to Design and Install Management Incentive Compensation Plans: A Practical Guide to Installing Performance Bonus Plans. Dale Arahood. Dale Arahood and Associates. • 1996. $129.00. Revised edition. "This book focuses on how pay should be determined rather than how much should be paid.".

How to Develop a Personnel Policy Manual. Joseph Lawson. AMACOM. • 1998. $75.00. Sixth edition.

How to Develop an Employee Handbook. Joseph W. Lawson. AMACOM. • 1997. $75.00. Second edition. Includes sample handbooks, personnel policy statements, and forms.

Human Resources Management and Development Handbook. William R. Tracey, editor. AMACOM. • 1993. $99.00. Second edition.

Kennedy's Pocket Guide to Working with Executive Recruiters. James H. Kennedy, editor. Kennedy Information, LLC. • 1996. $9.95. Second revised editon. Consists of 30 chapters written by various experts. Includes a glossary: "Lexicon of Executive Recruiting.".

Library Personnel Administration. Lowell A. Martin. Scarecrow Press, Inc. • 1994. $31.00. (Library Administration Series, No. 11).

Managing Human Resource Issues: Confronting Challenges. William J. Heisler and others. Jossey-Bass. • 1999. $32.95.

Office of Personnel Management Operating Manuals. Available from U. S. Government Printing Office. • Four looseleaf manuals at various prices ($25.00 to $190.00). Price of each manual includes updates for an indeterminate period. Manuals provides details of the federal wage system, the federal wage system "Nonappropriated Fund", personnel recordkeeping, personnel actions, qualification standards, and data reporting.

Personnel Management: Communications. Prentice Hall. • Looseleaf. Periodic supplementation. Price on application. Includes how to write effectively and how to prepare employee publications.

Personnel Management: Compensation. Prentice Hall. • Looseleaf. Periodic supplementation. Price on application.

Personnel Management: Labor Relations Guide. Prentice Hall. • Three looseleaf volumes. Periodic supplementation. Price on application.

Personnel Management: Policies and Practices. Prentice Hall. • Looseleaf. Periodic supplementation. Price on application.

Recruiting, Interviewing, Selecting, and Orienting New Employees. Diane Arthur. AMACOM. • 1998. $59.95. Third edition. A practical guide to the basics of hiring, including legal considerations and sample forms.

Sexual Orientation in the Workplace: Gays, Lesbians, Bisexuals and Heterosexuals Working Together. Amy J. Zuckerman and George F. Simons. Sage Publications, Inc. • 1996. $18.95. A workbook containing "a variety of simple tools and exercises" to provide skills for "working realistically and effectively with diverse colleagues.".

Studying Your Workforce: Applied Research Methods and Tools for the Training and Development Practitioner. Alan Clardy. Sage Publications, Inc. • 1997. $45.00. Describes how to apply specific research methods to common training problems. Emphasis is on data collection methods: testing, observation, surveys, and interviews. Topics include performance problems and assessment.

Turning Your Human Resources Department into a Profit Center. Michael W. Mercer. AMACOM. • 1989. $59.95. Concerned with costs, employee efficiency, and productivity.

INTERNET DATABASES

Wageweb: Salary Survey Data On-Line. HRPDI: Human Resources Programs Development and Improvement. Phone: (609)254-5893 Fax: (856)232-6989 E-mail: salaries@wageweb.com • URL: http://www.wageweb.com • Web site provides salary information for more than 170 benchmark positions, including (for example) 29 information management jobs. Data shows average minimum, median, and average maximum compensation for each position, based on salary surveys. Fees: Free for national salary data; $169.00 per year for more detailed information (geographic, organization size, specific industries).

ONLINE DATABASES

ABI/INFORM. Bell & Howell Information and Learning. • Provides online indexing to business-related material occurring in over 1,000 periodicals from 1971 to the present. Inquire as to online cost and availability.

Wilson Business Abstracts Online. H. W. Wilson Co. • Indexes and abstracts 600 major business periodicals, plus the *Wall Street Journal* and the business section of the *New York Times*. Indexing is from 1982, abstracting from 1990, with the two newspapers included from 1993. Updated weekly. Inquire as to online cost and availability. (*Business Periodicals Index* without abstracts is also available online.).

PERIODICALS AND NEWSLETTERS

HR Focus: The Hands-On Tool for Human Resources Professionals. American Management Association. • Monthly. $99.00 per year. Newsletter. Covers "all aspects of HR management," including corporate culture, the impact of technology, recruiting strategies, and training. Formerly *Personnel*.

HR Magazine (Human Resources): Strategies and Solutions for Human Resource Professionals. Society for Human Resource Management. • Monthly. Free to members; non-members, $125.00 per year. Formerly *Personnel Administrator*.

Human Resource Executive. LRP Publications, Inc. • Monthly. $89.95 per year. Edited for directors of corporate human resource departments. Special issues emphasize training, benefits, retirement planning, recruitment, outplacement, workers' compensation, legal pitfalls, and oes emphasize training, benefits, retirement planning, recruitment, outplacement, workers' compensation, legal pitfalls, and other personnel topics.

Human Resource Management. John Wiley and Sons, Inc. • Quarterly. Institutions, $390.00 per year.

Human Resource Manager's Legal Reporter. Business and Legal Reports, Inc. • Monthly. $95.00 per year. Reports and advises on the practical aspects of EEO and human resource compliance. Formerly *Manager's Legal Reporter.*

Human Resource Planning. Human Resource Planning Society. • Quarterly. $90.00 per year.

Human Resources Report. Bureau of National Affairs, Inc. • Weekly. $875.00 per year. Newsletter. Formerly *BNA'S Employee Relations Weekly.*

Personnel Psychology. Personnel Psychology, Inc. • Quarterly. $65.00 per year. Publishes research articles and book reviews.

Perspective. Catalyst, Inc. • Monthly. $60.00 per year. Newsletter. Covers leadership, mentoring, work/family programs, success stories, and other topics for women in the corporate world.

Public Personnel Management. International Personnel Management Association. • Quarterly. $50.00 per year.

Workforce: The Business Magazine for Leaders in Human Resources. ACC Communications, Inc. • Monthly. $59.00 per year. Edited for human resources managers. Covers employee benefits, compensation, relocation, recruitment, training, personnel legalities, and related subjects. Supplements include bimonthly "New Product News" and semiannual "Recruitment/Staffing Sourcebook." Formerly *Personnel Journal.*

RESEARCH CENTERS AND INSTITUTES

Center for Human Resources. Brandeis University, Heller Graduate School, 60 Turner St., Waltham, MA 02453. Phone: (781)736-3770 Fax: (781)736-3773 E-mail: curnan@brandeis.org • URL: http://www.heller.brandeis.edu/chr.

Human Resources Research Organization. 66 Canal Center Plaza, Suite 400, Alexandria, VA 22314. Phone: (703)549-3611 Fax: (703)549-9025 E-mail: lwise@mail.humrro.org • URL: http://www.humrro.org.

TRADE/PROFESSIONAL ASSOCIATIONS

Catalyst. 120 Wall St., 5th Fl., New York, NY 10005-3904. Phone: (212)514-7600 Fax: (212)514-8470 E-mail: info@catalystwomen.org • URL: http://www.catalystwomen.org • Provides information, research, and publications relating to women's workplace issues. Promotes corporate leadership for women.

Human Resource Planning Society. 317 Madison Ave., Suite 1509, New York, NY 10017. Phone: (212)490-6387 Fax: (212)682-6851 • Members are corporate human resource planning professionals and others concerned with employee recruitment, development, and utilization.

International Personnel Management Association. 1617 Duke St., Alexandria, VA 22314. Phone: (703)549-7100 Fax: (703)684-0948 E-mail: ipma@impa-hr.org • URL: http://www.ipma-hr.org.

National Human Resource Association. 6767 W. Greenfield Ave., Milwaukee, WI 53214-4967. Phone: (414)453-7499 Fax: (414)475-5959.

Society for Human Resource Management. 1800 Duke St., Alexandria, VA 22314-3499. Phone: 800-283-7476 or (703)548-3440 Fax: (703)535-6490 E-mail: shrm@shrm.org • URL: http://www.shrm.org.

Special Interest Group for Computer Personnel Research. c/o Association for Computing Machinery, 1515 Broadway, 17th Fl., New York, NY 10036. Phone: (212)869-7440 Fax: (212)302-5826 E-mail: acmhelp@acm.org • URL: http://www.acm.org/sigcpr • Concerned with the selection, training, and evaluation of computer personnel.

OTHER SOURCES

BNA Policy and Practice Series. Bureau of National Affairs, Inc. • Weekly. $1,749.00 per year. Five volumes. Looseleaf. Includes personnel management, labor relations, fair employment practice, compensation, and wage-hour laws.

Fundamentals of Human Resources. American Management Association Extension Institute. • Looseleaf. $110.00. Self-study course on a wide range of personnel topics. Emphasis is on practical explanations, examples, and problem solving. Quizzes and a case study are included.

How to Interview Effectively. American Management Association Extension Institute. • Looseleaf. $110.00. Self-study course on employment, performance, evaluation, disciplinary, and exit interviewing. Emphasis is on practical explanations, examples, and problem solving. Quizzes and a case study are included.

Human Resources Management Whole. CCH, Inc. • Nine looseleaf volumes. $1,572 per year. Includes monthly updates. Components are *Ideas and Trends Newsletter, Employment Relations, Compensation, Equal Employment Opportunity, Personnel Practices/Communications* and *OSHA Compliance.* Components are available separately.

PERSONNEL MANUALS

See: PROCEDURE MANUALS

PERSONNEL RECRUITMENT

See: RECRUITMENT OF PERSONNEL

PERSONNEL TESTING

See: PSYCHOLOGICAL TESTING; RATING OF EMPLOYEES

PERT (PROGRAM EVALUATION AND REVIEW TECHNIQUE)

See: CRITICAL PATH METHOD/PERT (PROGRAM EVALUATION AND REVIEW TECHNIQUE)

PEST CONTROL INDUSTRY

See also: PESTICIDE INDUSTRY

ABSTRACTS AND INDEXES

Biological and Agricultural Index. H.W. Wilson Co. • 11 times a year. Annual and quarterly cumulations. Service basis.

Entomology Abstracts. Cambridge Information Group. • Monthly. $985.00 per year.

CD-ROM DATABASES

CSA Life Sciences Collection [CD-ROM]. Cambridge Scientific Abstracts. • Quarterly. Includes CD-ROM versions of *Biotechnology Research Abstracts, Entomology Abstracts, Genetics Abstracts*, and about 20 other abstract collections.

WILSONDISC: Biological and Agricultural Index. H. W. Wilson Co. • Monthly. $1,495.00 per year, including unlimited online access to *Biological and Agricultural Index* through WILSONLINE. Provides CD-ROM indexing of over 250 periodicals covering agriculture, agricultural chemicals, biochemistry, biotechnology, entomology, horticulture, and related topics.

HANDBOOKS AND MANUALS

Handbook of Pest Management in Agriculture. David Pimentel, editor. CRC Press, Inc. • 1990. $975.00. Second edition. Three volumes.

INTERNET DATABASES

PestWeb: The Pest Control Industry Website. Van Waters & Rogers, Inc. Phone: 800-888-4897 or (425)889-3941 E-mail: webmaster@pestweb.com • URL: http://www.pestweb.com • Web site provides a wide variety of information on pest control products, manufacturers, associations, news, and education. Includes "Insects and Other Organisms," featuring details on 27 different kinds of pests, from ants to wasps. Online searching is offered. Fees: Free.

ONLINE DATABASES

Biological and Agricultural Index Online. H. W. Wilson Co. • Indexes a wide variety of agricultural and biological periodicals, 1983 to date. Monthly updates. Inquire as to online cost and availability.

CAB Abstracts. CAB International North America. • Contains 46 specialized abstract collections covering over 10,000 journals and monographs in the areas of agriculture, horticulture, forest products, farm products, nutrition, dairy science, poultry, grains, animal health, entomology, etc. Time period is 1972 to date, with monthly updates. Inquire as to online cost and availability. *CAB Abstracts on CD-ROM* also available, with annual updating.

CSA Life Sciences Collection. Cambridge Scientific Abstracts. • Includes online versions of *Biotechnology Research Abstracts, Entomology Abstracts, Genetics Abstracts*, and about 20 other abstract collections. Time period is 1978 to date, with monthly updates. Inquire as to online cost and availability.

PERIODICALS AND NEWSLETTERS

Pest Control. Advanstar Communications, Inc. • Monthly. $39.00 per year.

Pest Control Technology. G. I. E., Inc., Publishers. • Monthly. $32.00 per year. Provides technical and business management information for pest control personnel.

RESEARCH CENTERS AND INSTITUTES

Center for Urban and Industrial Pest Management. Purdue University, 1158 Entomology Hall, West Lafayette, IN 47907. Phone: (765)494-4564 Fax: (765)494-2152 E-mail: gbennett@entm.purdue.edu • URL: http://www.purdue.edu/entomology/urbancenter/home.html • Conducts research on the control of household and structural insect pests.

Laboratory for Pest Control Application Technology. Ohio State University, Ohio Agricultural Research and Development Center, Wooster, OH 44691. Phone: (330)263-3726 Fax: (330)263-3686 E-mail: hall.1@osu.edu • URL: http://www.oardc.ohio-state.edu/lpcat/ • Conducts pest control research in cooperation with the U. S. Department of Agriculture.

TRADE/PROFESSIONAL ASSOCIATIONS

National Pest Control Association. 8100 Oak St., Dunn Loring, VA 22027. Phone: 800-678-6722 or (703)573-8330 Fax: (703)573-4116.

OTHER SOURCES

Business & Company Resource Center. The Gale Group. • Fee-based Web site provides a wide range of business, industry, and specific company information. Access is offered to trade journal articles, market research data, insider trading activity, major shareholder data, corporate histories, emerging technology reports, corporate earnings estimates, press releases, and other sources. Provides detailed company profiles, industry overviews, and rankings. Offers integration of Predicasts PROMT, Newsletters ASAP, Investext Plus, Business Index ASAP, Brands and Their Companies, and other databases (many have full text).

PESTICIDE INDUSTRY

See also: AGRICULTURAL CHEMICALS; PEST CONTROL INDUSTRY

ABSTRACTS AND INDEXES

NTIS Alerts: Environmental Pollution & Control. National Technical Information Service. • Semimonthly. $245.00 per year. Provides descriptions of government-sponsored research reports and software, with ordering information. Covers the following categories of environmental pollution: air, water, solid wastes, radiation, pesticides, and noise. Formerly *Abstract Newsletter.*

Review of Agricultural Entomology: Consisting of Abstracts of Reviews of Current Literature on Applied Entomology Throughout the World. Available from CABI Publishing North America. • Monthly. $1220.00 per year. Published in England by CABI Publishing. Provides worldwide coverage of the literature. (Formerly *Review of Applied Entomology, Series A: Agricultural.*).

Review of Medical and Veterinary Entomology. Available from CABI Publishing North America. • Monthly. $710.00 per year. Provides worldwide coverage of the literature. Formerly *Review of Applied Entomology, Series B: Medical and Veterinary.*

CD-ROM DATABASES

AGRICOLA on SilverPlatter. Available from SilverPlatter Information, Inc. • Quarterly. $825.00 per year. Produced by the National Agricultural Library. Provides about three million citations on CD-ROM to the literature of agriculture, agricultural economics, animal sciences, entomology, fertilizer, food, forestry, nutrition, pesticides, plant science, water resources, and other topics. Each quarterly disc covers the past ten years, with archival discs available from 1970.

DIRECTORIES

Household and Personal Products Industry - Buyers Guide. Rodman Publications. • Annual. $12.00. Lists of suppliers to manufacturers of cosmetics, toiletries, soaps, detergents, and related household and personal products.

Household and Personal Products Industry Contract Packaging and Private Label Directory. Rodman Publications. • Annual. $12.00. Provides information on about 450 companies offering private label or contract packaged household and personal care products, such as detergents, cosmetics, polishes, insecticides, and various aerosol items.

Insect Control Guide. Meister Publishing Co. • Semiannual. $59.00. Includes trade names and usage information. Formerly *Insecticide Product Guide.*

World Directory of Pesticide Control Organizations. Springler-Verlag New York, Inc. • 1996. $85.00. Third edition. Published by The Royal Society of Chemistry. Provides detailed information on organizations and authorities concerned with the use and control of pesticides in 180 countries.

ENCYCLOPEDIAS AND DICTIONARIES

Encyclopedia of Agriculture Science. Charles J. Arntzen and Ellen M. Ritter, editors. Academic Press, Inc. • 1994. $625.00. Four volumes.

HANDBOOKS AND MANUALS

Crop Protection Chemicals Reference. Chemical and Pharmaceutical Press, Inc. • 1994. $130.00. 10th edition. Contains the complete text of product labels. Indexed by manufacturer, product category, pest use, crop use, chemical name, and brand name.

Pesticide Litigation Manual. John M. Johnson and George W. Ware. West Group. • Annual. $193.00. Discusses liability and other legal issues related to the manufacture and use of pesticides. Includes a guide to FIFRA (Federal Insecticide, Fungicide, and Rodenticide Act).

ONLINE DATABASES

Derwent Crop Protection File. Derwent, Inc. • Provides citations to the international journal literature of agricultural chemicals and pesticides from 1968 to date, with updating eight times per year. Formerly *PESTDOC.* Inquire as to online cost and availability.

PERIODICALS AND NEWSLETTERS

Dealer Progress: How Smart Agribusiness is Growing. Clear Window, Inc. • Bimonthly. $40.00 per year. Published in association with the Fertilizer Institute. Includes information on fertilizers and agricultural chemicals, including farm pesticides. Formerly *Progress.*

Household and Personal Products Industry: The Magazine for the Detergent, Soap, Cosmetic and Toiletry, Wax, Polish and Aerosol Industries. Rodman Publications. • Monthly. $48.00 per year. Covers marketing, packaging, production, technical innovations, private label developments, and aerosol packaging for soap, detergents, cosmetics, insecticides, and a variety of other household products.

Pest Control. Advanstar Communications, Inc. • Monthly. $39.00 per year.

Pest Control Technology. G. I. E., Inc., Publishers. • Monthly. $32.00 per year. Provides technical and business management information for pest control personnel.

Pesticide Biochemistry and Physiology: An International Journal. Academic Press, Inc. Journal Div. • Nine times a year. $820.00 per year.

STATISTICS SOURCES

Statistical Record of the Environment. The Gale Group. • 1996. $120.00. Third edition. Provides over 875 charts, tables, and graphs of major environmental statistics, arranged by subject. Covers population growth, hazardous waste, nuclear energy, acid rain, pesticides, and other subjects related to the environment. A keyword index is included.

Synthetic Organic Chemicals: United States Production and Sales. International Trade Commission. Available from U.S. Government Printing Office. • Annual.

TRADE/PROFESSIONAL ASSOCIATIONS

American Entomological Society. Academy of Natural Sciences of Philadelphia, 1900 Benjamin Franklin Parkway, Philadelphia, PA 19103-1195. Phone: (215)561-3978 Fax: (215)299-1028 E-mail: aes@say.acnatsci.org.

Association of American Pesticide Control Officials. Office of the Secretary, P.O. Box 1249, Hardwick, VT 05843. Phone: (802)472-6956 Fax: (802)472-6957 E-mail: aapco@plainfield.bypass.com.

National Pest Control Association. 8100 Oak St., Dunn Loring, VA 22027. Phone: 800-678-6722 or (703)573-8330 Fax: (703)573-4116.

United Products Formulators and Distributors Association. 2034 Beaver Ruin Rd., Norcross, GA 30071. 2034 Beaver Ruin Rd.,.

OTHER SOURCES

Agrochemical Companies Fact File. Theta Reports/PJB Medical Publications, Inc. • Annual. $1,460.00. Provides detailed profiles of more than 360 crop protection companies worldwide, including manufacturers of agrochemicals and biopesticides. Coverage includes finances, products, and joint ventures. Major agrochemical trading companies are also profiled. (Theta Report No. DS190E.).

Major Chemical and Petrochemical Companies of the World. Available from The Gale Group. • 2001. $855.00. Third edition. Two volumes. Published by Graham & Whiteside. Contains profiles of more than 7,000 important chemical and petrochemical companies in various countries. Subject areas include general chemicals, specialty chemicals, agricultural chemicals, petrochemicals, industrial gases, and fertilizers.

World Agrochemical Markets. Theta Reports/PJB Medical Publications, Inc. • 2000. $1,040.00. Market research data. Covers the demand for crop protection products in 11 countries having major markets and 20 countries having minor markets. (Theta Report No. DS196E.).

World Non-Agricultural Pesticide Markets. Theta Reports/PJB Medical Publications, Inc. • 2000. $1,670.00. Market research data. Includes home/garden pesticides, herbicides, professional pest-control products, and turf pesticides. (Theta Report No. DS191E.).

PET FOOD

See: PET INDUSTRY

PET INDUSTRY

See also: VETERINARY PRODUCTS

DIRECTORIES

Food Chemicals News Directory. Food Chemical News. CRC Press, Inc. • Semiannual. $497.00. Over 2,000 subsidiaries belonging to nearly 250 corporate parents plus an additional 3,000 independent processors. Formerly *Hereld's 1,500.*

Pet Dealer Purchasing Guide. Cygnus Business Media. • Annual. $35.00. Lists of manufacturers and importers of pet supplies; distributors and wholesalers of pet supples; wholesalers, breeders, and importers of pets (livestock); trade associations; publishers of pet books, records, and educational and training materials; pet care schools.

HANDBOOKS AND MANUALS

Pet Shop. Entrepreneur Media, Inc. • Looseleaf. $59.50. A practical guide to starting a pet store. Covers profit potential, start-up costs, market size evaluation, owner's time required, site selection, lease negotiation, pricing, accounting, advertising, promotion, etc. (Start-Up Business Guide No. E1007.).

PERIODICALS AND NEWSLETTERS

Pet Age: The Magazine for the Professional Retailer. Karen Long MacLeod, editor. H.H. Backer Associates, Inc. • Monthly. $25.00 per year.

Pet Product News. Fancy Publications, Inc. • Free to qualified personnel; others, $118.00 per year. Supplement available *Pet Product News Buyer's Guide.*

Petfood Industry. Watt Publishing Co. • Bimonthly. $36.00 per year.

Pets Supplies Marketing. Fancy Publications. • Quarterly. $250.00 per year.

TRADE/PROFESSIONAL ASSOCIATIONS

American Pet Products Manufacturers Association. 255 Glenville Rd., Greenwich, CT 06831. Phone: 800-452-1225 or (203)532-3602 Fax: (203)532-0551 E-mail: aferrante@appma.org • URL: http://www.appma.org.

Pet Food Institute. 1200 19th St., N.W., Suite 300, Washington, DC 20036. Phone: (202)857-1120 Fax: (202)857-1186 E-mail: pfi@dc.sba.com.

Pet Industry Distributors Association. 5024-R Campbell Blvd., Baltimore, MD 21236. Phone: (410)931-8100 Fax: (410)931-8111 E-mail: sking@unidial.com • URL: http://www.pida.org.

Pet Industry Joint Advisory Council. 1220 19th St., N.W., Suite 400, Washington, DC 20036. Phone: 800-553-7387 or (202)452-1525 Fax: (202)293-4377 • URL: http://www.pijac.org.

World Wide Pet Supply Association. 406 S. First Ave., Arcadia, CA 91006-3829. Phone: (626)447-2222 Fax: (626)447-8350 E-mail: info@wwpsa.com • URL: http://www.wwpsa.com.

OTHER SOURCES

Pet Supplies Market. Available from MarketResearch.com. • 1999. $2,750.00. Published by Packaged Facts. Provides market data with projections to 2001 on products for dogs, cats, fish, birds, and other pets.

PETROCHEMICAL INDUSTRY

See also: CHEMICAL INDUSTRIES; PETROLEUM INDUSTRY

GENERAL WORKS

Petrochemicals: The Rise of an Industry. Peter H. Spitz. John Wiley and Sons, Inc. • 1988. $125.00.

ABSTRACTS AND INDEXES

Applied Science and Technology Index. H. W. Wilson Co. • 11 times a year. Quarterly and annual cumulations. Service basis for print edition; CD-ROM edition, $1,495.00 per year. Indexes a wide variety of English language technical, industrial, and engineering periodicals.

ALMANACS AND YEARBOOKS

Worldwide Petrochemical Directory. PennWell Corp., Petroleum Div. • Annual. $165.00. Do more than 3,400 petrochemical plants; separate section on new construction; worldwide coverage. Formerly *Refining and Petrochemical Technology Yearbook.*

BIOGRAPHICAL SOURCES

Who's Who in World Petrochemicals and Plastics. Available from Reed Business Information. • Annual. $175.00. Names, addresses, telephone numbers, and company affiliations of individuals active in the petrochemical business. Formerly *Who's Who in World Petrochemicals.*

CD-ROM DATABASES

Chemical Strategies. Thomson Financial Securities Data. • Monthly. $2,995.00 per year. CD-ROM contains full text of investment analysts' reports on companies active in the chemical industries.

DIRECTORIES

Chemcyclopedia. American Chemical Society. • Annual. $60.00. Lists 10,000 chemicals in 12 product groups, produced by 900 manufacturers. Includes chemical characteristics, trade names, and indexes.

Major Chemical and Petrochemical Companies of Europe. Kluwer Law International. • Annual. $315.00. Published by Graham & Whiteside Ltd., London. Includes financial, personnel, and product information for chemical companies in Western Europe.

Petroprocess Directory. Atlantic Communications. • Annual. $69.00. Provides information on petrochemical companies and their products. Includes 24 industry categories.

ENCYCLOPEDIAS AND DICTIONARIES

Kirk-Othmer Encyclopedia of Chemical Technology. John Wiley and Sons, Inc. • 1991-97. $7,350.00, prepaid. 21 volumes. Fourth edition. Four volumes are scheduled to be published each year, with individual volumes available at $350.00.

FINANCIAL RATIOS

Industry Norms and Key Business Ratios. Desk Top Edition. Dun and Bradstreet Corp., Business Information Services. • Annual. Five volumes. $475.00 per volume. $1,890.00 per set. Covers over 800 kinds of businesses, arranged by Standard Industrial Classification number. More detailed editions covering longer periods of time are also available.

HANDBOOKS AND MANUALS

Handbook of Petrochemicals and Processes. G. Margaret Wells. Ashgate Publishing Co. • 1991. $122.95. Published by Gower in England.

ONLINE DATABASES

PROMT: Predicasts Overview of Markets and Technology. The Gale Group. • Companies, products, applied technologies and markets. U.S. and international literature coverage, 1972 to date. Inquire as to online cost and availability. Provides abstracts from more than 1,600 publications. Weekly updates.

PERIODICALS AND NEWSLETTERS

Hydrocarbon Processing. Gulf Publishing Co. • Monthly. Free to qualified personnel; others, $28.00 per year. International edition available.

Oil, Gas and Petrochem Equipment. PennWell Corp., Industrial Div. • Monthly. $35.00 per year.

PetroChemical News: A Weekly News Service in English Devoted to the Worldwide Petrochemical Industry. William F. Bland Co. • Weekly. $739.00 per year. Report of current and significant news about the petrochemical business worldwide.

TRADE/PROFESSIONAL ASSOCIATIONS

American Chemical Society. 1155 16th St., N.W., Washington, DC 20036. Phone: 800-227-5558 or (202)872-4600 Fax: (202)872-4615 E-mail: meminfo@acs.org • URL: http://www.acs.org.

Synthetic Organic Chemical Manufacturers Association. 1850 M St., N.W., Suite 700, Washington, DC 20036. Phone: (202)721-4100 Fax: (202)296-8120 • URL: http://www.socma.com • Members are manufacturers of synthetic organic chemicals, many of which are made from petroleum or natural gas.

OTHER SOURCES

Major Chemical and Petrochemical Companies of the World. Available from The Gale Group. • 2001. $855.00. Third edition. Two volumes. Published by Graham & Whiteside. Contains profiles of more than 7,000 important chemical and petrochemical companies in various countries. Subject areas include general chemicals, specialty chemicals, agricultural chemicals, petrochemicals, industrial gases, and fertilizers.

PETROLEUM EQUIPMENT INDUSTRY

ALMANACS AND YEARBOOKS

Petroleum Engineer International Drilling and Production Yearbook. Hart Publications, Inc. • Annual. $10.00.

DIRECTORIES

Composite Catalog of Oil Field Equipment and Services. Gulf Publishing Co. • Biennial. Price on application.

Financial Times Energy Yearbook: Oil & Gas: 2000. Available from The Gale Group. • Annual. $320.00. Published by Financial Times Energy. Provides production and financial details for more than 800 major oil and gas companies worldwide. Includes coverage of reserves, operations, properties, and growth rates. Formerly *Financial Times Oil & Gas Yearbook.*

Petroleum Equipment Directory. Petroleum Equipment Institute. • Annual. $100.00. Listing of over 1,600 member manufacturers, distributors and installers of petroleum marketing equipment worldwide.

Supply, Distribution Manufacturing and Service: Supply and Service Companies and Equipment Manufacturers. Midwest Publishing Co. • Annual. $115.00. 8,000 oil well supply stores, service companies, and equipment manufacturers. Formerly *Directory of Oil Well Supply Companies.*

FINANCIAL RATIOS

Annual Statement Studies. Robert Morris Associates: The Association of Lending and Credit Risk Professiona. • Annual. Free to members; non-members, $140.00. Median and quartile financial ratios are given for over 400 kinds of manufacturing, wholesale, retail, construction, and consumer finance establishments. Data is sorted by both asset size and sales volume. Includes a clearly written "Definition of Ratios" and an alphabetical industry index.

PERIODICALS AND NEWSLETTERS

Journal of Petroleum Technology. Society of Petroleum Engineers, Inc. • Monthly. Free to members; non-members, $45.00 per year. Covers oil and gas exploration, drilling and production, engineering management, resevoir engineering, geothermal energy sources and emerging technologies. Also includes society news, programs, events and activities. Supplement available *SPE Computer Applications.*

Oil, Gas and Petrochem Equipment. PennWell Corp., Industrial Div. • Monthly. $35.00 per year.

Petroleum Engineer International: The Worldwide Magazine of Drilling, Production,and Reservoir Technology. Hart Publications, Inc. • Monthly. $99.00 per year. Edited for "decision makers" in petroleum exploration and production. Emphasis is on technology.

STATISTICS SOURCES

Annual Survey of Manufactures. Available from U. S. Government Printing Office. • Annual. Prices vary. Issued by the U. S. Census Bureau as an interim update to the *Census of Manufactures.* Includes data on number of manufacturing establishments in various industries, employment, labor costs, value of shipments, capital expenditures, inventories, energy costs, and assets. (See also Census Bureau home page, http://www.census.gov/.).

Standard & Poor's Industry Surveys. Standard & Poor's. • Semiannual. $1,800.00. Two looseleaf volumes. Includes monthly supplements. Provides detailed, individual surveys of 52 major industry groups. Each survey is revised on a semiannual basis. Also includes "Monthly Investment Review" (industry group investment analysis) and monthly "Trends & Projections" (economic analysis).

U. S. Industry and Trade Outlook: The McGraw-Hill Companies and the U.S. Department of Commerce/ International Trade Administration. Datapso Research Corp. • Annual. $69.95. Produced by the

International Trade Administration, U. S. Department of Commerce, in a "public-private" partnership with DRI/McGraw-Hill and Standard & Poor's. Provides basic data, outlook for the current year, and "Long-Term Prospects" (five-year projections) for a wide variety of products and services. Includes high technology industries. Formerly *U. S. Industrial Outlook*.

TRADE/PROFESSIONAL ASSOCIATIONS

Petroleum Equipment Institute. P.O. Box 2380, Tulsa, OK 74101. Phone: (918)494-9696 Fax: (918)491-9895 E-mail: pei@peinet.com • URL: http://www.pei.org.

Petroleum Equipment Suppliers Association. 9225 Katy Freeway, Suite 310, Houston, TX 77024. Phone: (713)932-0168 Fax: (713)932-0497 • URL: http://www.pesa.org.

Society of Petroleum Engineers. 222 Palisades Creek Dr., Richardson, TX 75080-3836. Phone: (972)952-9393 Fax: (972)952-9435 E-mail: dadamson@spe.org • URL: http://www.spe.org.

PETROLEUM INDUSTRY

See also: FUEL OIL INDUSTRY; GASOLINE INDUSTRY; OFFSHORE PETROLEUM INDUSTRY; PETROCHEMICAL INDUSTRY; PETROLEUM EQUIPMENT INDUSTRY; PETROLEUM MARKETING; PIPELINE INDUSTRY; PROPANE AND BUTANE GAS INDUSTRY

ABSTRACTS AND INDEXES

Fuel and Energy Abstracts: A Summary of World Literature on All Scientific, Technical, Commercial and Environmental Aspects of Fuel and Energy. Elsevier Science. • Bimonthly. $1,583.00 per year.

NTIS Alerts: Energy. National Technical Information Service. • Semimonthly. $245.00 per year. Provides descriptions of government-sponsored research reports and software, with ordering information. Covers electric power, batteries, fuels, geothermal energy, heating/cooling systems, nuclear technology, solar energy, energy policy, and related subjects. Formerly *Abstract Newsletter*.

Petroleum Abstracts. University of Tulsa, Information Services Div. • 50 times a year. Service basis. Worldwide literature related to petroleum exploration and production.

Petroleum/Energy Business News Index. API Encompass. • Monthly. Members, $475.00 per year; non-members, $950.00 per year.

ALMANACS AND YEARBOOKS

Annual Institute on Oil and Gas Law and Taxation. Matthew Bender & Co., Inc. • Annual. Price on application. Answers to current legal and tax problems, including cases and regulations implementing tax reduction and tax form.

Petroleum Engineer International Drilling and Production Yearbook. Hart Publications, Inc. • Annual. $10.00.

DIRECTORIES

Financial Times Energy Yearbook: Oil & Gas: 2000. Available from The Gale Group. • Annual. $320.00. Published by Financial Times Energy. Provides production and financial details for more than 800 major oil and gas companies worldwide. Includes coverage of reserves, operations, properties, and growth rates. Formerly *Financial Times Oil & Gas Yearbook*.

Geophysical Directory. Claudia LaCalli, editor. Geophysical Directory, Inc. • Annual. $75.00. Worldwide coverage of about 4,500 companies and personnel using and providing supplies and services in petroleum and mineral exploration.

Institutional Buyers of Energy Stocks: A Targeted Directory. Investment Data Corp. • Annual. $645.00. Provides detailed profiles 555 institutional buyers of petroleum-related and other energy stocks. Includes names of financial analysts and portfolio managers.

Plunkett's Energy Industry Almanac: Complete Profiles on the Energy Industry 500 Companies. Plunkett Research Ltd. • Annual. $149.99. Includes major oil companies, utilities, pipelines, alternative energy companies, etc. Provides information on industry trends.

Refining and Gas Processing Industry Worldwide. PennWell Publishing Co. • Annual. $165.00. International coverage. Formerly *Refining and Gas Processing*.

ENCYCLOPEDIAS AND DICTIONARIES

International Petroleum Encyclopedia. PennWell Publishing. • Annual. $95.00. A worldwide petroleum directory. Features statistics and a complete atlas of the international petroleum market.

Macmillan Encyclopedia of Energy. Available from The Gale Group. • 2001. $350.00. Three volumes. Published by Macmillan Reference USA. Covers the business, technology, and history of a wide variety of energy sources.

Manual of Oil and Gas Terms: Annotated. Matthew Bender & Co., Inc. • 1983. 10th edition. Periodic supplementation. Price on application. Defines technical, legal, and tax terms relating to the oil and gas industry.

FINANCIAL RATIOS

Almanac of Business and Industrial Financial Ratios. Leo Troy. Prentice Hall. • Annual. $99.95. Contains financial ratios derived from federal tax returns. Ratios for each of about 200 industries are arranged according to company asset size.

HANDBOOKS AND MANUALS

Ernst and Young's Oil and Gas Federal Income Taxation. John R. Braden and others. CCH, Inc. • Annual. $92.95. Formerly *Miller's Oil and Gas Federal Income Taxation*.

Summers on Oil and Gas. West Publishing Co., College and School Div. • Price on application. Periodic supplementation. Legal aspects of the petroleum industry.

INTERNET DATABASES

Fedstats. Federal Interagency Council on Statistical Policy. Phone: (202)395-7254 • URL: http://www.fedstats.gov • Web site features an efficient search facility for full-text statistics produced by more than 70 federal agencies, including the Census Bureau, the Bureau of Economic Analysis, and the Bureau of Labor Statistics. Boolean searches can be made within one agency or for all agencies combined. Links are offered to international statistical bureaus, including the UN, IMF, OECD, UNESCO, Eurostat, and 20 individual countries. Fees: Free.

ONLINE DATABASES

Business and Industry. Responsive Database Services, Inc. • Contains online citations, abstracts, and selected fulltext from more than 1,000 trade journals, newspapers, and other publications. Provides general coverage of both manufacturing and service industries, including marketing, production, industry trends, key events, and information on specific companies. Time span is 1994 to date. Daily updates. Inquire as to online cost and availability. (Also available in a CD-ROM version.).

DRI U.S. Central Database. Data Products Division. • Provides more than 23,000 business, financial, demographic, economic, foreign trade, and industry-related time series for the U.S. Includes national income, population, retail-wholesale trade, price indexes, labor data, housing, industrial production, banking, interest rates, money supply, etc. Time period is generally 1947 to date (some data back to 1929). Updating varies. Inquire as to online cost and availability.

Energyline. Congressional Information Service, Inc. • Provides online citations and abstracts to the literature of all forms of energy: petroleum, natural gas, coal, nuclear power, solar energy, etc. Time period is 1971 to 1993 (closed file). Inquire as to online cost and availability.

Platt's Energy Prices. Data Products Division. • Contains daily high and low prices for crude oil and petroleum products, including gasoline, fuel oil, and liquefied petroleum gas (LPG). Coverage is international from 1983 to present, with daily updates. Inquire as to online cost and availability.

Tablebase. Responsive Database Services, Inc. • Provides online numerical tabular data from a wide variety of business, organization, and government sources, including 900 trade journals. Includes industry and individual company statistics relating to products, market share, sales forecasts, production, exports, market trends, etc. Time span is 1997 to date. Weekly updates. Inquire as to online cost and availability. (Also available in a CD-ROM version.).

Tulsa (Petroleum Abstracts). Information Services. • Worldwide literature in the petroleum and natural gas areas, 1965 to present. Inquire as to online cost and availability. Includes petroleum exploration patents. Updated weekly. Over 600,000 entries.

PERIODICALS AND NEWSLETTERS

Energy and Fuels. American Chemical Society. • Bimonthly. Institutions, $728.00 per year; others, price on application. an interdisciplinary technical journal covering non-nuclear energy sources: petroleum, gas, synthetic fuels, etc.

International Journal of Energy Research. Available from John Wiley and Sons, Inc., Journals Div. • 15 times a year. Institutions, $2,735.00 per year. Published in England by John Wiley & Sons Ltd.

International Oil News. William F. Bland Co. • Weekly. $579.00 per year. Reports news of prime interest to top executives in the international oil industry.

Lundberg Letter. Tele-Drop, Inc. • Semimonthly. $950.00 per year. Petroleum newsletter.

Oil and Gas Investor. Hart Publications, Inc. • Monthly. $195.00 per year.

Oil and Gas Journal. PennWell Corp., Industrial Div. • Weekly. $84.00 per year.

Oil Daily: Daily Newspaper of the Petroleum Industry. Energy Intelligence Group. • Daily. $1,145.00 per year. Newspaper for the petroleum industry.

Oil, Gas and Energy Quarterly. Matthew Bender & Shepard. • Quarterly. $165.00 per year. Formerly *Oil and Gas Tax Quarterly*.

The Oilman Weekly Newsletter. PennWell Corp., Petroleum Div. • Weekly. $1360.00 per year. Newsletter. Provides news of developments concerning the North Sea and European oil and gas businesses. Each issue contains four pages of statistical data.

PetroChemical News: A Weekly News Service in English Devoted to the Worldwide Petrochemical Industry. William F. Bland Co. • Weekly. $739.00 per year. Report of current and significant news about the petrochemical business worldwide.

For publishers addresses, refer to SOURCES CITED section at the back of the book.

Petroleum Engineer International: The Worldwide Magazine of Drilling, Production,and Reservoir Technology. Hart Publications, Inc. • Monthly. $99.00 per year. Edited for "decision makers" in petroleum exploration and production. Emphasis is on technology.

World Oil. Gulf Publishing Co. • Monthly. Free to qualified personnel; others, $34.00 per year. Covers worldwide oil and gas exploration, drilling and production.

PRICE SOURCES

International Energy Agency. Energy Prices and Taxes. OECD Publications and Information Center. • Quarterly. $350.00 per year. Compiled by the International Energy Agency. Provides data on prices and taxation of petroleum products, natural gas, coal, and electricity. Diskette edition, $800.00. (Published in Paris).

Oil Price Information Service. United Comunications Group. • Weekly. $545.00 per year. Regional editions available at $150.00 per year. Quotes wholesale terminal prices for various petroleum products.

Platt's Oilgram Price Report: an International Daily Oil-Gas Price and Marketing Letter. McGraw-Hill. • Daily. $1,517.00 per year. Prices and marketing intelligence for petroleum products. Includes weekly statistical summaries. Worldwide coverage.

RESEARCH CENTERS AND INSTITUTES

Canadian Energy Research Institute. 3512 33rd St., N. W., Suite 150, Calgary, AB, Canada T2L 2A6. Phone: (403)282-1231 Fax: (403)284-4181 E-mail: ceri@ceri.ca • URL: http://www.ceri.ca • Conducts research on the economic aspects of various forms of energy, including petroleum, natural gas, coal, nuclear, and water power (hydroelectric).

STATISTICS SOURCES

Annual Energy Outlook [year], with Projections to [year]. Available from U. S. Government Printing Office. • Annual. Issued by the Energy Information Administration, U. S. Department of Energy (http://www.eia.doe.gov). Contains detailed statistics and 20-year projections for electricity, oil, natural gas, coal, and renewable energy. Text provides extensive discussion of energy issues and "Market Trends.".

Annual Energy Review. Available from U. S. Government Printing Office. • Annual Issued by the Energy Information Administration, Office of Energy Markets and End Use, U. S. Department of Energy. Presents long-term historical as well as recent data on production, consumption, stocks, imports, exports, and prices of the principal energy commodities in the U. S.

Annual Survey of Manufactures. Available from U. S. Government Printing Office. • Annual. Prices vary. Issued by the U. S. Census Bureau as an interim update to the *Census of Manufactures.* Includes data on number of manufacturing establishments in various industries, employment, labor costs, value of shipments, capital expenditures, inventories, energy costs, and assets. (See also Census Bureau home page, http://www.census.gov/.).

Basic Petroleum Data Book. American Petroleum Institute. • Three times a year. $230.00 per year.

Business Statistics of the United States. Courtenay M. Slater, editor. Bernan Associates. • 1999. $74.00. Fifth edition. Based on *Business Statistics*, formerly issue by the Bureau of Economic Analysis, U. S. Department of Commerce. Provides basic data for a wide variety of U. S. industries, services, and economic indicators. Most statistics are shown annually for 29 years and monthly for the most recent four years.

Encyclopedia of American Industries. The Gale Group. • 1998. $560.00. Second edition. Two volumes. $280.00 per volume. Volume one is *Manufacturing Industries* and volume two is *Service and Non-Manufacturing Industries.* Provides the history, development, and recent status of approximately 1,000 industries. Includes statistical graphs, with industry and general indexes.

Energy Balances of OECD Countries. Organization for Economic Cooperation and Development. Available from OECD Publications and Information Center. • Irregular. $110.00. Presents two-year data on the supply and consumption of solid fuels, oil, gas, and electricity, expressed in oil equivalency terms. Historical tables are also provided. Relates to OECD member countries.

International Energy Annual. Available from U. S. Government Printing Office. • Annual. $34.00. Issued by the Energy Information Administration, U. S. Department of Energy. Provides production, consumption, import, and export data for primary energy commodities in more than 200 countries and areas. In addition to petroleum products and alcohol, renewable energy sources are covered (hydroelectric, geothermal, solar, and wind).

International Petroleum Monthly. Available from U. S. Government Printing Office. • Monthly. $70.00 per year. Issued by the Energy Information Administration, U. S. Department of Energy. Contains data on worldwide petroleum production, consumption, imports, exports, and available stocks.

Metropolitan Life Insurance Co. Statistical Bulletin SB. Metropolitan Life Insurance Co. • Quarterly. Individuals, $50.00 per year. Covers a wide range of social, economic and demographic health concerns.

Monthly Energy Review. Available from U. S. Government Printing Office. • Monthly. $98.00 per year. Issued by the Energy Information Administration, Office of Energy Markets and End Use, U. S. Department of Energy. Contains current and historical statistics on U. S. production, storage, imports, and consumption of petroleum, natural gas, and coal.

OECD Oil and Gas Information. Available from OECD Publications and Information Center. • Annual. Price varies. Data on oil and gas balances, supplies, consumption by end use sector and trade of OECD countries. Text in English and French.

The Oil and Natural Gas Producing Industry in Your State. Independent Petroleum Association of America. Petroleum Independent Publishers, Inc. • Annual. $75.00. Statistical issue of *Petroleum Independent.*

Oil/Energy Statistics Bulletin: And Canadian Oil Reports. Oil Statistics Co., Inc. • Biweekly. $185.00 per year.

Petroleum Supply Annual. Available from U. S. Government Printing Office. • Annual. $78.00. Two volumes. Produced by the Energy Information Administration, U. S. Department of Energy. Contains worldwide data on the petroleum industry and petroleum products.

Petroleum Supply Monthly. Available from U. S. Government Printing Office. • Monthly. $100.00 per year. Produced by the Energy Information Administration, U. S. Department of Energy. Provides worldwide statistics on a wide variety of petroleum products. Covers production, supplies, exports and imports, transportation, refinery operations, and other aspects of the petroleum industry.

Reserves of Crude Oil, Natural Gas Liquids and Natural Gas in the United States and Canada and United States Productive Capacity. American Gas Association. • Annual. Price on application.

Short-Term Energy Outlook: Quarterly Projections. Available from U. S. Government Printing Office. • Semiannual. $10.00 per year. Issued by Energy Information Administration, U. S. Department of Energy. Contains forecasts of U. S. energy supply, demand, and prices.

Standard & Poor's Industry Surveys. Standard & Poor's. • Semiannual. $1,800.00. Two looseleaf volumes. Includes monthly supplements. Provides detailed, individual surveys of 52 major industry groups. Each survey is revised on a semiannual basis. Also includes "Monthly Investment Review" (industry group investment analysis) and monthly "Trends & Projections" (economic analysis).

Survey of Current Business. Available from U. S. Government Printing Office. • Monthly. $49.00 per year. Issued by Bureau of Economic Analysis, U. S. Department of Commerce. Presents a wide variety of business and economic data.

Weekly Petroleum Status Report. Energy Information Administration. Available from U.S. Government Printing Office. • Weekly. $85.00 per year. Current statistics in the context of both historical information and selected prices and forecasts.

WEFA Industrial Monitor. John Wiley and Sons, Inc. • Annual. $65.00. Prepared by industry analysts at WEFA, an economic forecasting and consulting firm (originally Wharton Econometric Forecasting Associates). Contains discussions of the outlook for major U. S. industries, with many 10-year forecasts (WEFA Web site is http://www.wefa.com).

TRADE/PROFESSIONAL ASSOCIATIONS

American Independent Refiners Association. 3315 Cummings Lane, Chevy Chase, MD 20815. Phone: (301)913-9012 Fax: (301)913-9041.

American Petroleum Institute. 1220 L St., N.W., Washington, DC 20005. Phone: (202)682-8000 Fax: (202)682-8029 • URL: http://www.api.org.

Independent Petroleum Association of America. 1101 16th St., N.W., Washington, DC 20036. Phone: (202)857-4722 Fax: (202)857-4799 E-mail: rholmes@ipaa.org • URL: http://www.ipaa.org.

National Petrochemical and Refiners Association. 1899 L St., N.W., Suite 1000, Washington, DC 20036-3896. Phone: (202)457-0480 Fax: (202)457-0486 • URL: http://www.npradc.org.

National Petroleum Council. 1625 K St., N.W., Suite 600, Washington, DC 20006. Phone: (202)393-6100 Fax: (202)331-8539 • URL: http://www.npc.org.

OTHER SOURCES

Energy Management and Federal Energy Guidelines. CCH, Inc. • Biweekly. $1,658.00 per year. Seven looseleaf volumes. Periodic supplementation. Reports on petroleum allocation rules, conservation efforts, new technology, and other energy concerns.

Federal Taxation of Oil and Gas Transactions. Matthew Bender & Co., Inc. • $350.00. Two looseleaf volumes. Periodic supplementation.

Major Energy Companies of the World. Available from The Gale Group. • 2001. $855.00. Fourth edition. Published by Graham & Whiteside. Contains detailed information on more than 3,300 important energy companies in various countries. Industries include electricity generation, coal, natural gas, nuclear energy, petroleum, fuel distribution, and equipment for energy production.

PETROLEUM INDUSTRY, OFFSHORE

See: OFFSHORE PETROLEUM INDUSTRY

PETROLEUM MARKETING

See also: PETROLEUM INDUSTRY

DIRECTORIES

Geophysical Directory. Claudia LaCalli, editor. Geophysical Directory, Inc. • Annual. $75.00. Worldwide coverage of about 4,500 companies and personnel using and providing supplies and services in petroleum and mineral exploration.

U.S.A. Oil Industry Directory. PennWell Corp., Petroleum Div. • Annual. $125.00.

ENCYCLOPEDIAS AND DICTIONARIES

International Petroleum Encyclopedia. PennWell Publishing. • Annual. $95.00. A worldwide petroleum directory. Features statistics and a complete atlas of the international petroleum market.

FINANCIAL RATIOS

Industry Norms and Key Business Ratios. Desk Top Edition. Dun and Bradstreet Corp., Business Information Services. • Annual. Five volumes. $475.00 per volume. $1,890.00 per set. Covers over 800 kinds of businesses, arranged by Standard Industrial Classification number. More detailed editions covering longer periods of time are also available.

ONLINE DATABASES

PROMT: Predicasts Overview of Markets and Technology. The Gale Group. • Companies, products, applied technologies and markets. U.S. and international literature coverage, 1972 to date. Inquire as to online cost and availability. Provides abstracts from more than 1,600 publications. Weekly updates.

PERIODICALS AND NEWSLETTERS

The Marketer: Official Voice of Petroleum Marketers in Oklahoma. Oklahoma Petroleum Marketers Association. • Quarterly. $12.00 per year.

Oil and Gas Journal. PennWell Corp., Industrial Div. • Weekly. $84.00 per year.

Oil Daily: Daily Newspaper of the Petroleum Industry. Energy Intelligence Group. • Daily. $1,145.00 per year. Newspaper for the petroleum industry.

Oil Express: Inside Report on Trends in Petroleum Marketing Without the Influ nce of Advertising. Aspen Publishers, Inc. • Weekly. $337.00 per year. Newsletter. Provides news of trends in petroleum marketing and convenience store operations. Includes *U. S. Oil Week's Price Monitor* (petroleum product prices) and *C-Store Digest* (news concerning convenience stores operated by the major oil companies) and *Fuel Oil Update*. Formerly (U.S. Oil Week).

Oil Express: Inside Report on Trends in Petroleum Marketing without the Influence of Advertising. United Communications Group. • Weekly. $337.00 per year. Newsletter for petroleum marketers.

Platt's Oil Marketing Bulletin. McGraw-Hill. • Weekly. $427.00 per year. Newsletter. Marketing information service.

Platt's Oilgram News. McGraw-Hill, Commodity Services Group. • Daily. $1,347.00 per year. Covers oil industry in general.

STATISTICS SOURCES

Petroleum Marketing Monthly. Available from U. S. Government Printing Office. • Monthly. $116.00 per year. Current information and statistics relating to a wide variety of petroleum products. (Office of Oil and Gas, Energy Information Administration, U. S. Department of Energy.).

Standard & Poor's Industry Surveys. Standard & Poor's. • Semiannual. $1,800.00. Two looseleaf volumes. Includes monthly supplements. Provides detailed, individual surveys of 52 major industry groups. Each survey is revised on a semiannual basis. Also includes "Monthly Investment Review" (industry group investment analysis) and monthly "Trends & Projections" (economic analysis).

Standard & Poor's Statistical Service. Current Statistics. Standard & Poor's. • Monthly. $688.00 per year. Includes 10 *Basic Statistics* sections, *Current Statistics Supplements* and *Annual Security Price Index Record.*

TRADE/PROFESSIONAL ASSOCIATIONS

American Petroleum Institute. 1220 L St., N.W., Washington, DC 20005. Phone: (202)682-8000 Fax: (202)682-8029 • URL: http://www.api.org.

Petroleum Marketers Association of America. 1901 N. Fort Meyer Dr., Suite 1200, Arlington, VA 22209. Phone: (703)351-8000 Fax: (703)351-9160 E-mail: http://www.pmaa.org.

Society of Independent Gasoline Marketers of America. 11911 Freedom Dr., Suite 590, Reston, VA 20190. Phone: (703)709-7000 Fax: (703)709-7007.

PHARMACEUTICAL INDUSTRY

See also: DRUG STORES; GENERIC DRUG INDUSTRY; NONPRESCRIPTION DRUG INDUSTRY

GENERAL WORKS

The Chemistry of Mind-Altering Drugs: History, Pharmacology, and Cultural Context. Daniel M. Perrine. American Chemical Society. • 1996. $42.00. Contains detailed descriptions of the pharmacological and psychological effects of a wide variety of drugs, "from alcohol to zopiclone.".

Pharmaceutical Marketing in the 21st Century. Mickey C. Smith, editor. Haworth Press, Inc. • 1996. $49.95. Various authors discuss the marketing, pricing, distribution, and retailing of prescription drugs. (Pharmaceutical Marketing and Management Series, Vol. 10, Nos. 2,3&4).

ABSTRACTS AND INDEXES

Applied Science and Technology Index. H. W. Wilson Co. • 11 times a year. Quarterly and annual cumulations. Service basis for print edition; CD-ROM edition, $1,495.00 per year. Indexes a wide variety of English language technical, industrial, and engineering periodicals.

Index to Health Information. Congressional Information Service, Inc. • Quarterly. $945.00 per year, including two-volume annual cumulation. Provides index and abstracts covering the medical and health field in general, with emphasis on statistical sources and government documents. Service with microfiche source documents, $4,995.00 per year.

International Pharmaceutical Abstracts: Key to the World's Literature of Pharmacy. American Society of Health-System Pharmacists. • Semimonthly. Members, $142.95 per year; non-members, $552.50 per year.

Science Citation Index. Institute for Scientific Information. • Bimonthly. $15,020.00 per year. Annual cumulation. Includes *Source Index*, *Citation Index*, *Permuterm Subject Index*, and *Corporate Index*.

ALMANACS AND YEARBOOKS

Annual Review of Pharmacology and Toxicology. Annual Reviews, Inc. • Annual. Individuals, $60.00; institutions, $120.00.

BIBLIOGRAPHIES

Medical and Health Care Books and Serials in Print: An Index to Literature in Health Sciences. R. R. Bowker. • Annual. $265.95. Two volumes.

BIOGRAPHICAL SOURCES

Dictionary of American Medical Biography. Martin Kaufman and others. Greenwood Publishing Group Inc. • 1984. $195.00. Two volumes. Vol. one, $100.00; vol. two, $100.00.

CD-ROM DATABASES

BioMed Strategies. Thomson Financial Securities Data. • Monthly. $2,995.00 per year. CD-ROM contains full text of investment analysts' reports on companies operating in the following fields: biotechnology, pharmaceuticals, medical products, and health care.

International Pharmaceutical Abstracts [CD-ROM]. American Society of Health-System Pharmacists. • Quarterly. $1,795.00 per year. Contains CD-ROM indexing and abstracting of international pharmaceutical literature from 1970 to date.

Physicians' Desk Reference Library on CD-ROM. Medical Economics. • Three times a year. $595.00 per year. Contains the CD-ROM equivalent of *Physicians' Desk Referenc (PDR), Physicians' Desk Reference for Nonprescription Drugs, Physicians' Desk Reference for Opthalmology*, and other PDR publications.

DIRECTORIES

BioScan: The Worldwide Biotech Industry Reporting Service. American Health Consultants, Inc. • Bimonthly. $1,395.00 per year. Looseleaf. Provides detailed information on over 900 U. S. and foreign companies broadly classified as biotechnological. In addition to medical technology and advanced pharmaceutical firms, includes firms doing research in food processing, waste management, agriculture, and veterinary science.

Encyclopedia of Medical Organizations and Agencies. The Gale Group. • 2000. $285.00. 11th edition. Information on over 14,000 public and private organizations in medicine and related fields.

Internet Tools of the Profession: A Guide for Information Professionals. Hope N. Tillman, editor. Special Libraries Association. • 1997. $49.00. Second edition. Consists of 14 sections by various authors or compilers. After two introductory articles on searching the Internet, there are 12 annotated lists of useful Web sites, covering the SLA, business and finance, chemistry, education, food and agriculture, information technology, insurance and employee benefits, law, library management, metals and materials, pharmaceuticals, and telecommunications. An index is provided.

Medical and Health Information Directory. The Gale Group. • 1999. $630.00. Three volumes. 12th edition. Vol. one covers medical organizations, agencies, and institutions; vol. two includes bibliographic, library, and database information; vol. three is a guide to services available for various medical and health problems.

Medical and Healthcare Marketplace Guide. Dorland Healthcare Information. • Annual. $690.00. Two volumes. Provides market survey summaries for about 500 specific product and service categories (volume one: "Research Reports"). Contains profiles of nearly 6,000 pharmaceutical, medical product, and healthcare service companies (volume two: "Company Profiles").

Mosby's GenRx: The Complete Reference for Generic and Brand Drugs. Harcourt Health

Sciences. • 1998. $72.95. Provides detailed information on a wide variety of generic and brand name prescription drugs. Includes color identification pictures, prescribing data, and price comparisons. Formerly *Physicians GenRx*.

NDA Pipeline(New Drug Approval). F-D-C Reports, Inc. • Annual. $965.00. Provides information on U. S. drugs in the development stage and products receiving new drug approval (NDA) from the Food and Drug Administration. Listings are company-by-company and by generic name, with orphan drug designations. Includes an industry directory.

Pharmaceutical Marketers Directory. CPS Communications, Inc., Directories Div. • Annual. $175.00. About 15,000 personnel of pharmaceutical, medical products and equipment, and biotechnology companies; advertising agencies with clients in the medical field; health care publications; alternative media and medical industry suppliers.

Pharmaceutical Processing Annual Buyers Guide. Cahners Business Information. • Annual. Price on application. Lists makers and distributors of supplies and equipment for the pharmaceutical manufacturing industry.

The Red Book. Medical Economics Co., Inc. • Annual. $57.95 for basic volume or $99.00 per year with monthly updates. Provides product information and prices for more than 100,000 prescription and nonprescription drugs and other items sold by pharmacies. Also known as *Drug Topics Red Book*.

ENCYCLOPEDIAS AND DICTIONARIES

American Drug Index. Facts and Comparison. • Annual. $49.95. Lists over 20,000 drug entries in dictionary style.

Pharmacological and Chemical Synonyms: A Collection of Names of Drugs, Pesticides, and Other Compounds Drawn from the Medical Literature of the World. E. E. Marler. Elsevier Science. • 1994. $292.00. Tenth edition.

USAN and the USP Dictionary of Drug Names. United States Pharmacopeial Convention. • Annual. $105.00. Adopted names, brand names, compendial and other generic names, CAS Registry Numbers, molecular weights, and other information.

FINANCIAL RATIOS

Almanac of Business and Industrial Financial Ratios. Leo Troy. Prentice Hall. • Annual. $99.95. Contains financial ratios derived from federal tax returns. Ratios for each of about 200 industries are arranged according to company asset size.

Annual Statement Studies. Robert Morris Associates: The Association of Lending and Credit Risk Professiona. • Annual. Free to members; non-members, $140.00. Median and quartile financial ratios are given for over 400 kinds of manufacturing, wholesale, retail, construction, and consumer finance establishments. Data is sorted by both asset size and sales volume. Includes a clearly written "Definition of Ratios" and an alphabetical industry index.

NWDA Operating Survey. National Wholesale Druggists' Association. • Annual. Members, $30.00; non-members, $295.00. A 48-page report of financial and operating ratios for the wholesale drug industry.

Quarterly Financial Report for Manufacturing, Mining, and Trade Corporations. U.S. Federal Trade Commission and U.S. Securities and Exchange Commission. Available from U.S. Government Printing Office. • Quarterly. $39.00 per year.

HANDBOOKS AND MANUALS

AHFS Drug Information. American Hospital Formulary Service. American Society of Health-System Pharmacists. • $162.95 per year. Looseleaf service. Detailed information about drugs and groups of drugs.

Approved Drug Products, with Therapeutic Equivalence Evaluations. Available from U. S. Government Printing Office. • $101.00 for basic manual and supplemental material for an indeterminate period. Issued by the Food and Drug Administration, U. S. Department of Health and Human Services. Lists prescription drugs that have been approved by the FDA. Includes therapeutic equivalents to aid in containment of health costs and to serve State drug selection laws.

Complete Guide to Prescription and Non-Prescription Drugs: Side Effects, Warnings, and Vital Data for Safe Use. H. Winter Griffith. Berkley Publishing Group. • Annual. $16.95. A guide for consumers.

The Consumer Health Information Source Book. Alan Rees, editor. Oryx Press. • 2000. $59.50. Sixth edition. Bibliography of current literature and guide to organizations.

Dun & Bradstreet/Gale Group Industry Handbooks. The Gale Group. • 2000. $630.00. Five volumes. $145.00 per volume. Each volume covers two or more major industries: 1. *Entertainment and Hospitality*; 2. *Construction and Agriculture*; 3. *Chemicals and Pharmaceuticals*; 4. *Computers & Software and Broadcasting & Telecommunications*; 5. *Insurance and Health & Medical Services*. The following are included for each industry: overview, statistics, financial ratios, rankings, merger information, company directory, directory of associations, and consultants directory.

Financial Management for Pharmacists: A Decision-Making Approach. Norman V. Carroll. Lippincott Williams & Wilkins. • 1997. $39.00. Second edition.

Handbook of Nonprescription Drugs. Tom R. Covington and others, editors. American Pharmaceutical Association. • 2000. $120.00. 12th edition. Contains comprehensive, technical information on over-the-counter drugs.

Handbook of Over-the-Counter Drugs. Max Leber and others. Celestial Arts Publishing Co. • 1992. $22.95. Provides detailed, consumer information on the ingredients of nonprescription drugs and popular cosmetics.

PDR Guide to Drug Interactions, Side Effects, Indications. American Medical Association. Medical Economics Co., Inc. • Annual. $48.95. Includes a list of prescription drugs by "precise clinical situation.".

Physicians' Desk Reference. Medical Economics Co., Inc. • Annual. $82.95. Generally known as "PDR". Provides detailed descriptions, effects, and adverse reactions for about 4,000 prescription drugs. Includes data on more than 250 drug manufacturers, with brand name and generic name indexes and drug identification photographs. Discontinued drugs are also listed.

Physicians' Desk Reference for Ophthalmology. Medical Economics Publishing Co., Inc. • Irregular. $49.95. Provides detailed descriptions of ophthalmological instrumentation, equipment, supplies, lenses, and prescription drugs. Indexed by manufacturer, product name, product category, active drug ingredient, and instrumentation. Editorial discussion is included.

United States Pharmacopeia National Formulary. United States Pharmacopeial Convention. • Quinquennial. $450.00. Includes annual: *Supplement.*

INTERNET DATABASES

Internet Tools of the Profession. Special Libraries Association. Phone: (202)234-4700 Fax: (202)265-9317 E-mail: hope@tiac.net • URL: http://www.sla.org/pubs/itotp • Web site is designed to update the printed *Internet Tools of the Profession.* Provides links to a wide range of useful databases in business, finance, industry, information technology, insurance, law, library management, telecommunications, and other subject areas. Fees: Free.

National Library of Medicine (NLM). National Institutes of Health (NIH). Phone: 888-346-3656 or (301)496-1131 Fax: (301)480-3537 E-mail: access@nlm.nih.gov • URL: http://www.nlm.nih.gov • NLM Web site offers free access through MEDLINE ("PubMed") to about nine million references to articles appearing in some 3,800 biomedical journals, with abstracts. Search interfaces range from "simple keywords to advanced Boolean expressions." The NLM site offers many links to other sources of biomedical and technical information (the National Center for Biotechnology Information, for example). Fees: Free.

RxList: The Internet Drug Index. Neil Sandow. Phone: (707)746-8754 E-mail: info@rxlist.com • URL: http://www.rxlist.com • Web site features detailed information (cost, usage, dosage, side effects, etc.) from Mosby, Inc. for about 300 major pharmaceutical products, representing two thirds of prescriptions filled in the U. S. (3,700 other products are listed). The "Top 200" drugs are ranked by number of prescriptions filled. Keyword searching is provided. Fees: Free.

ONLINE DATABASES

Derwent Drug File. Derwent, Inc. • Provides indexing and abstracting of the world's pharmaceutical journal literature since 1964, with weekly updates. Formerly *RINGDOC*. Inquire as to online cost and availability.

Drug Information Fulltext. American Society of Health-System Pharmacists. • Provides full text monographs from the *American Hospital Formulary Service* and the *Handbook On Injectable Drugs*. Inquire as to online cost and availability.

F-D-C Reports. FDC Reports, Inc. • An online version of "The Gray Sheet" (medical devices), "The Pink Sheet" (pharmaceuticals), "The Rose Sheet" (cosmetics), "The Blue Sheet" (biomedical), and "The Tan Sheet" (nonprescription). Contains full-text information on legal, technical, corporate, financial, and marketing developments from 1987 to date, with weekly updates. Inquire as to online cost and availability.

Globalbase. The Gale Group. • Provides more than one million online summaries of business, industrial, and economic news reports from more than 1,000 publications worldwide. Covers a wide range of material appearing in international trade journals, professional magazines, and newspapers. Time period is 1984 to date, with weekly updates. Inquire as to online cost and availability.

International Pharmaceutical Abstracts [online]. American Society of Health-System Pharmacists. • Provides online indexing and abstracting of the world's pharmaceutical literature from 1970 to date. Monthly updates. Inquire as to online cost and availability.

Pharmaceutical News Index. Bell & Howell Information and Learning. • Indexes major pharmaceutical industry newsletters, 1974 to present. Weekly updates. Inquire as to online cost and availability.

PROMT: Predicasts Overview of Markets and Technology. The Gale Group. • Companies,

products, applied technologies and markets. U.S. and international literature coverage, 1972 to date. Inquire as to online cost and availability. Provides abstracts from more than 1,600 publications. Weekly updates.

Scisearch. Institute for Scientific Information. • Broad, multidisciplinary index to the literature of science and technology, 1974 to present. Inquire as to online cost and availability. Coverage of literature is worldwide, with weekly updates.

PERIODICALS AND NEWSLETTERS

American Journal of Health System Pharmacy. American Society of Health-System Pharmacists. • Semimonthly. $165.00 per year. Formerly American Society of Hospital Pharmacists. Formerly *American Journal of Hospital Pharmacy.*

Clin-Alert. Technomic Publishing Co. Inc. • 24 times a year. $155.00 per year for print or electronic edition; $175.00 per year for print and electronics edition. Newsletter. Contains current abstracts of drug adverse reactions and interactions reported in over 600 medical journals. Includes quarterly cumulative indexes.

Community Pharmacist: Meeting the Professional and Educational Needs of Today's Practitioner. ELF Publicatons, Inc. • Bimonthly. $25.00 per year. Edited for retail pharmacists in various settings, whether independent or chain-operated. Covers both pharmaceutical and business topics.

Drug Benefit Trends: For Pharmacy Managers and Managed Healthcare Professionals. SCP Communications, Inc. • Monthly. Individuals, $72.00 per year; institutions, $120.00 per year. Covers the business of managed care drug benefits.

Drug Development Research. John Wiley and Sons, Inc. • Monthly. $3,395.00 per year.

Drug Topics. Medical Economics Co., Inc. • 23 times a year. $61.00 per year. Edited for retail pharmacists, hospital pharmacists, pharmacy chain store executives, wholesalers, buyers, and others concerned with drug dispensing and drug store management. Provides information on new products, including personal care items and cosmetics.

FDA Consumer. Available from U. S. Government Printing Office. • Bimonthly. $23.00 per year. Issued by the U. S. Food and Drug Administration. Provides consumer information about FDA regulations and product safety.

Health News Daily. F-D-C Reports, Inc. • Daily. $1,350.00 per year. Newsletter providing broad coverage of the healthcare business, including government policy, regulation, research, finance, and insurance. Contains news of pharmaceuticals, medical devices, biotechnology, and healthcare delivery in general.

Healthcare Distributor: The Industry's Multi-Market Information Resource. ELF Publications. • Monthly. $30.00 per year. Formerly *Wholesale Drugs Magazine.*

Hospital Pharmacist Report. Medical Economics Co., Inc. • Monthly. $39.00 per year. Covers both business and clinical topics for hospital pharmacists.

Journal of Pharmaceutical Marketing and Management. Haworth Press, Inc. • Quarterly. Individuals, $60.00 per year; institutions, $90.00 per year; libraries, $275.00 per year.

Journal of Research in Pharmaceutical Economics. Haworth Press, Inc. • Quarterly. Individuals, $60.00 per year; institutions, $120.00 per year; libraries, $275.00 per year.

Med Ad News. Engel Publishing Partners. • Monthly. $150.00 per year. Covers the field of pharmaceutical advertising and marketing.

Medical Marketing and Media. CPS Communications, Inc. • Monthly. Individuals, $75.00 per year; institutions, $100.00 per person. Contains articles on marketing, direct marketing, advertising media, and sales personnel for the healthcare and pharmaceutical industries.

Nonprescription Pharmaceuticals and Nutritionals: The Tan Sheet. F-D-C Reports, Inc. • Weekly. $860.00 per year. Newsletter covering over-the-counter drugs and vitamin supplements. Emphasis is on regulatory activities of the U. S. Food and Drug Administration (FDA).

Pharma Business: The International Magazine of Pharmaceutical Business and Marketing. Engel Publishing Partners. • Eight times a year. $185.00 per year. Circulated mainly in European countries. Coverage includes worldwide industry news, new drug products, regulations, and research developments.

Pharma Marketletter. Marketletter Publications Ltd. • Weekly. $700.00 per year. Newsletter. Formerly *Marketletter.*

Pharmaceutical Engineering. International Society for Pharmaceutical Engineering, Inc. • Bimonthly. $60.00 per year. Feature articles provide practical application and specification information on the design, construction, supervision and maintenance of process equipment, plant systems, instrumentation and pharmaceutical facilities.

Pharmaceutical Executive: For Global Business and Marketing Leaders. Advanstar Communications, Inc. • Monthly. $64.00 per year.

Pharmaceutical Processing. Cahners Business Information, New Product Information. • Monthly. $69.95 per year. Formerly *Pharmaceutical and Cosmetic Equipment.*

Pharmaceutical Representative. McKnight Medical Communications. • Monthly. $35.95 per year. Edited for drug company salespeople and sales managers.

Pharmaceutical Technology. Advanstar Communications, Inc. • Monthly. $64.00 per year. Practical hands on information about the manufacture of pharmaceutical products, focusing on applied technology.

Pharmacopeial Forum. United States Pharmacopeial Convention, Inc. • Bimonthly. $310.00 per year.

Prescription Pharmaceuticals and Biotechnology: The Pink Sheet. F-D-C Reports, Inc. • Weekly. $1,170 per year. Newsletter covering business and regulatory developments affecting the pharmaceutical and biotechnology industries. Provides information on generic drug approvals and includes a drug sector stock index.

Weekly Pharmacy Reports: The Green Sheet. F-D-C Reports, Inc. • Weekly. $82.00 per year. Newsletter for retailers and wholesalers of pharmaceutical products. Includes pricing developments and new drug announcements.

Worst Pills Best Pills News. Public Citizen. • Monthly. $16.00 per year. Newsletter. Provides pharmaceutical news and information for consumers, with an emphasis on harmful drug interactions.

PRICE SOURCES

First DataBank Blue Book. Hearst Corp. • Annual. $65.00. List of manufacturers of prescription and over-the-counter drugs, sold in retail drug stores. Formerly *American Druggist Blue Book.*

RESEARCH CENTERS AND INSTITUTES

Pharmaceutical Marketing and Management Research Program. University of Mississippi, Waller Lab Complex, Room 101, University, MS 38677. Phone: (662)915-5948 Fax: (662)915-5262 E-mail: dgarner@olemiss.edu • URL: http://www.olemiss.edu/depts/rips/pmmrp/.

Pharmacology Research Laboratory. Indiana University-Purdue University at Indianapolis, School of Medicine, 635 Barnhill Dr., Indianapolis, IN 46202-5120. Phone: (317)274-7844 Fax: (317)274-7714 E-mail: besch@iupui.edu • URL: http://www.iupui.edu/~iuphtx/home1.html.

Upjohn Center for Clinical Pharmacology. University of Michigan. 3709 Upjohn Center, School of Medicine, Ann Arbor, MI 48109-0504. Phone: (734)764-9121 Fax: (734)763-3438.

STATISTICS SOURCES

Annual Survey of Manufactures. Available from U. S. Government Printing Office. • Annual. Prices vary. Issued by the U. S. Census Bureau as an interim update to the *Census of Manufactures.* Includes data on number of manufacturing establishments in various industries, employment, labor costs, value of shipments, capital expenditures, inventories, energy costs, and assets. (See also Census Bureau home page, http://www.census.gov/.).

Manufacturing Profiles. Available from U. S. Government Printing Office. • Annual. Issued by the U. S. Census Bureau. A printed consolidation of the entire *Current Industrial Report* series, presenting "all the data compiled." Contains statistics on production, shipments, inventories, consumption, exports, imports, and orders for a wide variety of manufactured products. (See also Census Bureau home page, http://www.census.gov/.).

Narcotic Drugs: Estimated World Requirements. International Narcotics Control Board. United Nations Publications. • Annual. $38.00. Includes production and utilization data relating to legal narcotics. Text in French, English and Spanish.

Pharmaceutical Research Manufacturers Association Annual Fact Book. Pharmaceutical Research and Manufacturers Association. • Annual.

Standard & Poor's Industry Surveys. Standard & Poor's. • Semiannual. $1,800.00. Two looseleaf volumes. Includes monthly supplements. Provides detailed, individual surveys of 52 major industry groups. Each survey is revised on a semiannual basis. Also includes "Monthly Investment Review" (industry group investment analysis) and monthly "Trends & Projections" (economic analysis).

Standard & Poor's Statistical Service. Current Statistics. Standard & Poor's. • Monthly. $688.00 per year. Includes 10 *Basic Statistics* sections, *Current Statistics Supplements* and *Annual Security Price Index Record.*

Statistical Handbook on Technology. Paula Berinstein, editor. Oryx Press. • 1999. $65.00. Provides statistical data on such items as the Internet, online services, computer technology, recycling, patents, prescription drug sales, telecommunications, and aerospace. Includes charts, tables, and graphs. Edited for the general reader. (Statistical Handbook Series).

U. S. Industry and Trade Outlook: The McGraw-Hill Companies and the U.S. Department of Commerce/ International Trade Administration. Datapso Research Corp. • Annual. $69.95. Produced by the International Trade Administration, U. S. Department of Commerce, in a "public-private" partnership with DRI/McGraw-Hill and Standard & Poor's. Provides basic data, outlook for the current year, and "Long-Term Prospects" (five-year projections) for a wide variety of products and services. Includes high technology industries. Formerly *U. S. Industrial Outlook.*

TRADE/PROFESSIONAL ASSOCIATIONS

American College of Apothecaries. P.O. Box 341266, Memphis, TN 38184-1266. Phone: (901)383-8119 Fax: (901)383-8882 • A professional society of pharmacists.

American Pharmaceutical Association/Academy of Pharmacy Practice and Management. c/o Anne Burns, 2215 Constitution Ave., N.W., Washington, DC 20037-2895. Phone: 800-237-2742 or (202)628-4410 Fax: (202)783-2351 E-mail: apha-appm@mail.aphanet.org • URL: http://www.aphanet.org.

American Society of Health System Pharmacists. 7272 Wisconsin Ave., Bethesda, MD 20814. Phone: (301)657-3000 Fax: (301)657-1251 E-mail: pdiso@ashp.org • URL: http://www.ashp.org.

Council on Family Health. 1155 Connecticut Ave., Suite 400, Washington, DC 20036. Phone: (202)429-6600 E-mail: sdibartolo@chpa-info.org • URL: http://www.cfhinfo.org • Members are drug manufacturers. Concerned with proper use of medications.

Drug, Chemical and Allied Trades Association. 510 Route 130, Suite B1, East Windsor, NJ 08520. Phone: (609)448-1000 Fax: (609)448-1944.

Drug Information Association. 501 Office Center Dr., Suite 450, Fort Washington, PA 19034-3211. Phone: (215)628-2288 Fax: (215)641-1229 E-mail: dia@diahome.org • URL: http://www.diahome.org • Concerned with the technology of drug information processing.

Generic Pharmaceutical Industry Association. 1620 Eye St., N.W., Suite 800, Washington, DC 20006-4005. Phone: (202)833-9070 Fax: (202)833-9612 E-mail: info@gpia.org • URL: http://www.gpia.org • Members are manufacturers, wholesalers, and retailers of generic prescription drugs.

Instrument Society of America: Food and Pharmaceutical Division. P.O. Box 12277, Durham, NC 27709. Phone: (919)549-8411 Fax: (919)549-8288 E-mail: info@isa.org • URL: http://www.isa.org.

International Society for Pharmaceutical Engineering. 3816 W. Linebaugh Ave., No. 412, Tampa, FL 33624. Phone: (813)960-2105 Fax: (813)264-2816 • URL: http://www.ispc.org.

National Association of Boards of Pharmacy. 700 Busse Highway, Park Ridge, IL 60068. Phone: (847)698-6227 Fax: (847)698-0124 • URL: http://www.nabp.net.

National Association of Chain Drug Stores. c/o Ronald L. Ziegler, P.O. Box 1417-D49, Alexandria, VA 22313-1480. Phone: (703)549-3001 Fax: (703)836-4869 E-mail: homepage_info@nacds.org • URL: http://www.nacds.org.

National Association of Pharmaceutical Manufacturers. 320 Old Country Rd., Suite 205, Garden City, NY 11530-1752. Phone: (516)741-3699 Fax: (516)741-3696 E-mail: napmgenrx@aol.com • URL: http://www.napmnet.org.

National Council for Prescription Drug Programs. 4201 N. 24th St., Suite 365, Phoenix, AZ 85016-6268. Phone: (602)957-9105 Fax: (602)955-0749 E-mail: ncpdp@ncpdp.org • URL: http://www.ncpdp.org • Concerned with standardization of third party prescription drug programs.

National Pharmaceutical Association. 107 Kilmayne Dr., Ste. C, Cary, NC 27511. Phone: 800-944-6742 or (919)831-5368 Fax: (919)469-5870 • A professional society of African-American pharmacists and pharmacy students.

National Pharmaceutical Council. 1894 Preston White Dr., Reston, VA 20191. Phone: (703)620-6390 Fax: (703)476-0904 • URL: http://www.npcnow.org • Members are drug manufacturers producing prescription medication.

National Wholesale Druggists' Association. 1821 Michael Faraday Dr., Suite 400, Reston, VA 20190. Phone: (703)787-0000 Fax: (703)787-6930 E-mail: info@nwda.org • URL: http://www.nwda.org.

Pharmaceutical Research and Manufacturers Association. 1100 15th St., N.W., Suite 900, Washington, DC 20005. Phone: (202)835-3400 Fax: (202)835-3429 • URL: http://www.phrma.org.

United States Pharmacopeia. 12601 Twinbrook Parkway, Rockville, MD 20852. Phone: 800-822-8772 or (301)881-0666 Fax: (301)816-8247 E-mail: webmaster@usp.org • URL: http://www.usp.org.

OTHER SOURCES

Drug Product Liability. Matthew Bender & Co., Inc. • $680.00. Three looseleaf volumes. Periodic supplementation. All aspects of drugs: manufacturing, marketing, distribution, quality control, multiple prescription problems, drug identification, FDA coverage, etc.

Food Law Reports. CCH, Inc. • Weekly. $1,349.00 per year. Six looseleaf volumes. Covers regulation of adulteration, packaging, labeling, and additives. Formerly *Food Drug Cosmetic Law Reports.*

Mail Service Pharmacy Market. MarketResearch.com. • 1999. $3,250.00. Provides detailed market data, with forecasts to the year 2003.

Major Pharmaceutical Companies of the World. Available from The Gale Group. • 2001. $885.00. Third edition. Published by Graham & Whiteside. Contains detailed information and trade names for more than 2,500 important pharmaceutical companies in various countries.

The Market for Generic Drugs. MarketResearch.com. • 2000. $3,000.00. Market research data. Includes a discussion of current trends in the use of generic prescription drugs to reduce healthcare costs, with forcasts to 2004.

The Market for Ophthalmic Pharmaceuticals. MarketResearch.com. • 1997. $2,500.00. Market research report. Covers topical and internal drugs for eye disorders, with market estimates. Includes pharmaceutical company profiles.

The Market for Rx-to-OTC Switched Drugs. MarketResearch.com. • 2000. $3,250.00. Market research report. Covers the market for over-the-counter drugs that were formerly available only by prescription. Includes profiles of relevant pharmaceutical companies.

The Market for Stress Management Products and Services. Available from MarketResearch.com. • 1996. $1,195.00. Market research report published by Marketdata Enterprises. Covers anti-anxiety drugs, stress management clinics, biofeedback centers, devices, seminars, workshops, spas, institutes, etc. Includes market size projections to the year 2000.

Mosby's GenRx [year]. CME, Inc. • Annual. $99.00. CD-ROM contains detailed monographs for more than 2,200 generic and brand name prescription drugs. Includes color pill images and customizable patient education handouts.

New and Breaking Technologies in the Pharmaceutical and Medical Device Industries. Theta Reports/PJB Medical Publications, Inc. • 1999. $1,695.00. Market research data. Includes forecasts of medical technology and drug developments to 2005-2010.

Pharmaceutical Litigation Reporter: The National Journal of Record of Pharmaceutical Litigation. Andrews Publications. • Monthly. $775.00 per year. Reports on a wide variety of legal cases involving the pharmaceutical and medical device industries. Includes product liability lawsuits.

The Treatment of Mental Illness in an Evolving Health Care System. Available from MarketResearch.com. • 1997. $995.00. Market research report published by Theta Corporation. Provides market data on drugs and therapy used for treatment of mood, anxiety, and psychotic disorders. Includes pharmaceutical company profiles and forecasts to the year 2001.

PHARMACIES

See: DRUG STORES

PHILANTHROPY

ABSTRACTS AND INDEXES

Index to Legal Periodicals and Books. H. W. Wilson Co. • Monthly. Quarterly and annual cumulations. $270.00 per year. CD-ROM version available at $1,495.00 per year.

BIBLIOGRAPHIES

Literature of the Nonprofit Sector: A Bibliography with Abstracts. The Foundation Center. • Dates vary. Six volumes. $45.00 per volume. Covers the literature of philanthropy, foundations, nonprofit organizations, fund-raising, and federal aid.

Management and Leadership Resources for Non-Profits. Available from Applied Research and Development Institute. • Annual. $3.50. Compiled by the Applied Research and Development Institute and published as a special issue of *The Journal of Philanthropy.* Lists and describes over 800 books, periodicals, and other publications in 14 categories (general management, finance, marketing, development, etc.). Includes a directory of publishers. No indexes.

The Non-Profit Handbook: Books, Periodicals, Software, Internet Sites, and Other Essential Resources for Non-Profit Leaders. Chronicle of Higher Education, Inc. • Annual. $5.00. A special issue of *Chronicle of Philanthropy.* Contains annotations of books, periodicals, and other material from various sources, relating to Advocacy, Boards, Communications and Marketing, Financial Management, Fund Raising, General Information, Managing, Philanthropic Tradition, Technology, and Volunteers. Includes index to titles.

Philanthropy and Voluntarism: An Annotated Bibliography. Daphne N. Layton. The Foundation Center. • 1987. $18.50.

CD-ROM DATABASES

Leadership Library on CD-ROM: Who's Who in the Leadership of the United States. Leadership Directories, Inc. • Quarterly. $2,641.00 per year, including access to Internet version (weekly updates). Contains all 14 *Yellow Book* personnel directories on CD-ROM, providing contact and brief biographical information for about 400,000 individuals. Covers business, government, financial institutions, news media, law firms, associations, foreign representatives, and nonprofit organizations. Includes photographs.

Prospector's Choice: The Electronic Product Profiling 10,000 Corporate and Foundation Grantmakers. The Gale Group. • Annual. $849.00. Provides detailed CD-ROM information on foundations and corporate philanthropies. Also known as *Corporate and Foundation Givers on Disk.*

DIRECTORIES

Charitable Organizations of the U. S.: A Descriptive and Financial Information Guide. The Gale Group.

• 1991. $150.00. Second edition. Describes nearly 800 nonprofit groups active in soliciting funds from the American public. Includes nearly 800 data on sources of income, administrative expenses, and payout.

Corporate Giving Directory: Comprehensive Profiles of America's Major Corporate Foundations and Corporate Charitable Giving Programs. The Gale Group. • Annual. $485.00. Contains detailed descriptions of the philanthropic foundations of over 1,000 major U. S. corporations. Includes grant types, priorities for giving, recent grants, and advice on approaching corporate givers.

Cumulative List of Organizations Described in Section 170(c) of the Internal Revenue Code of 1986. Available from U. S. Government Printing Office. • Annual. $114.00 per year, including quarterly supplements. Lists about 300,000 organizations eligible for contributions deductible for federal income tax purposes. Provides name of each organization and city, but not complete address information. Arranged alphabetically by name of institution. (Office of Employee Plans and Exempt Organizations, Internal Revenue Service.).

Directory of International Corporate Giving in America and Abroad. Available from The Gale Group. • 1997. $205.00. Contains details of the philanthropic activities of over 650 major foreign corporations with operations in the U. S. Includes 18 indexes.

Foundation Directory. The Foundation Center. • Annual. $215.00. Over 37,700 of the largest foundations in the United States, all having 2,000,000.00 or more assets or awarding $200,000 or more in grants in a recent year.

Guide to Private Fortunes. Available from The Gale Group. • 1994. $255.00. Third edition. Published by The Taft Group. Provides biographical information and philanthropic histories for 1,250 individuals with a net worth of over $25 million or who have demonstrated a pattern of substantial charitable giving. Formerly *Fund Raiser's Guide to Private Fortunes*, and before that, *America's Wealthiest People*.

National Directory of Corporate Giving: A Guide to Corporate Giving Programs and Corporate Foundations. The Foundation Center. • Biennial. $225.00. Provides information on 2,895 corporations that maintain philanthropic programs (direct giving programs or company-sponsored foundations).

Nonprofit Sector Yellow Book: Who's Who in the Management of the Leading Foundations, Universities, Museums, and Other Nonprofit Organizations. Leadership Directories, Inc. • Semiannual. $235.00 per year. Covers management personnel and board members of about 1,000 prominent, nonprofit organizations: foundations, colleges, museums, performing arts groups, medical institutions, libraries, private preparatory schools, and charitable service organizations.

Wise Giving Guide. National Charities Information Bureau, Inc. • Quarterly. Single copy free; individuals, $25.00 per year. Evaluates 400 national charities against a set of standards concerning management, government and budget.

HANDBOOKS AND MANUALS

Charitable Planning Primer. Ralph G. Miller and Adam Smalley. CCH, Inc. • 1999. $99.00. Covers the legal and tax aspects of charitable giving and planned gifts. Includes annuity documents, tax forms, tables, and examples.

Corporate Contributions Handbook: Devoting Private Means to Public Needs. James P. Shannon, editor. Jossey-Bass, Inc., Publishers. • 1991. $48.95. Published jointly with the Council on Foundations. Provides practical management and legal advice for corporate philanthropic units. (Nonprofit Sector-Public Administration Series).

Fundraising: Hands-On Tactics for Nonprofit Groups. L. Peter Edles. McGraw-Hill. • 1992. $32.95. Covers fundamental premises, soliciting major gifts, small gift prospecting, canvassing, telephone appeals, creating publications, direct mail, and other fund-raising topics for nonprofit organizations.

The Law of Fund-Raising. Bruce R. Hopkins. John Wiley and Sons, Inc. • 1995. $160.00. Second edition. Annual supplements available. Covers all aspects of state and federal nonprofit fund-raising law. Includes summaries of the relevant laws and regulations of each state. *Nonprofit Law, Finance and Management Series.*

The Law of Fund-Raising: 1999 Cumulative Supplement. Bruce R. Hopkins. John Wiley and Sons, Inc. • 1998. $65.00. *Nonprofit Law, Finance and Management Series.*

INTERNET DATABASES

Welcome to the Foundation Center. The Foundation Center. Phone: (212)620-4230 Fax: (212)691-1828 E-mail: mfn@fdncenter.org • URL: http://www.fdncenter.org • Web site provides a wide variety of information about foundations, grants, and philanthropy, with links to philanthropic organizations. "Grantmaker Information" link furnishes descriptions of available funding. Fees: Free.

ONLINE DATABASES

Index to Legal Periodicals and Books (Online). H. W. Wilson Co. • Broad coverage of law journals and books 1981 to date. Monthly updates. Inquire as to online cost and availability.

Legal Resource Index. The Gale Group. • Broad coverage of law literature appearing in legal, business, and other periodicals, 1980 to date. Monthly updates. Inquire as to online cost and availability.

LEXIS. LEXIS-NEXIS. • The various LEXIS databases provide full text and indexing for a wide variety of legal cases, statutes, orders, and opinions.

PERIODICALS AND NEWSLETTERS

Chronicle of Philanthropy:The Newspaper of the Non-Profit World. Chronicle of Higher Education, Inc. • Biweekly. $67.50 per year.

Corporate Philanthropy Report. Capitol Publications, Inc. • Monthly. $229.00 per year. Newsletter. Reports on trends in corporate giving and provides information on potential sources of corporate philanthropy.

Don Kramer's Nonprofit Issues. Don Kramer Publisher. • Monthly. $129.00 per year. Newsletter with legal emphasis. Covers the laws, rules, regulations, and taxes affecting nonprofit organizations.

Foundation News and Commentary: Philanthropy and the Nonprofit Sector. Council on Foundations. • Bimonthly. $48.00 per year. Formerly *Foundation News.*

Philanthropic Digest. Philanthropic Digest, Inc. • Monthly. $79.50 per year. Reports on current grants given to non-profit organizations by foundations, corporations and individuals.

Trusts and Estates. Intertec Publishing Corp. • Monthly. $129.00 per year. Includes annual *Directory.*

RESEARCH CENTERS AND INSTITUTES

Center for Corporate Community Relations. Boston College, 55 Lee Rd., Chestnut Hill, MA 02467. Phone: (617)552-4545 Fax: (617)552-8499 E-mail: cccr@bc.edu • URL: http://www.bc.edu/cccr • Areas of study include corporate images within local communities, corporate community relations, social vision, and philanthropy.

Foundation Center. 79 Fifth Ave., New York, NY 10003-3076. Phone: 800-424-9836 or (212)807-3690 Fax: (212)807-3691 • URL: http://www.fdncenter.org.

STATISTICS SOURCES

Giving U.S.A: The Annual Compilation of Total Philanthropic Giving Estimates. American Association of Fund-Raising Counsel. AAFRC Trust for Philanthropy. • Annual. $49.95.

Survey of Corporate Contributions. Conference Board, Inc. • Annual.

TRADE/PROFESSIONAL ASSOCIATIONS

American Association of Fund-Raising Counsel. 37 E. 28th St., Rm. 902, New York, NY 10016-7919. Phone: 800-462-2372 or (212)481-6705 Fax: (212)481-7238 E-mail: aafrc@aol.com • URL: http://www.aafrc.org.

Council of Better Business Bureaus. 4200 Wilson Blvd., Suite 800, Arlington, VA 22203-1838. Phone: (703)276-0100 Fax: (703)525-8277 E-mail: bbb@bbb.org • URL: http://www.bbb.org.

Council on Foundations. 1828 L St., N. W., Suite 300, Washington, DC 20036. Phone: (202)466-6512 Fax: (202)785-3926 E-mail: webmaster@cof.org • URL: http://www.cof.org.

Independent Sector. 1200 18th St., N.W., Suite 200, Washington, DC 20036. Phone: (202)467-6000 Fax: (202)416-6101.

National Association of State Charity Officials. c/o Richard C. Allen, Office of Attorney General, One Ashburton Place, Boston, MA 02108. Phone: (617)727-2200 Fax: (617)727-2920 • Members are state officials responsible for the administration of charitable solicitation laws.

National Charities Information Bureau. 19 Union Square, W., 6th Fl., New York, NY 10003-3395. Phone: (212)929-6300 Fax: (212)463-7083 E-mail: ncib@bway.net • URL: http://www.give.org • Sets accountability standards and provides information for nonprofit organizations that solicit contributions from the public.

National Committee for Responsive Philanthropy. 2001 S St., N.W., Suite 620, Washington, DC 20009. Phone: (202)387-9177 Fax: (202)332-5084 E-mail: info@ncrp.org • URL: http://www.ncrp.org • Promotes charitable giving to new organizations working for social change or controversial issues.

National Society of Fund Raising Executives. 1101 King St., Suite 700, Alexandria, VA 22314. Phone: 800-666-5863 or (703)684-0410 Fax: (703)684-0540 E-mail: nsfre@nsfre.org • URL: http://www.nsfre.org.

Women and Philanthropy. 1015 18th St., N.W., Suite 202, Washington, DC 20036. Phone: (202)887-9660 Fax: (202)861-5483 • URL: http://www.womenphil.org • Purpose is to increase the amount of money given to programs benefiting women.

OTHER SOURCES

Corporate Giving Watch: News and Ideas for Nonprofit Organizations Seeking Corporate Funds. Available from The Gale Group. • Monthly. $149.00 per year. Newsletter. Published by The Taft Group. Includes news, trends, and statistics related to corporate giving programs. "Corporate Profiles" insert contains profiles of individual programs.

For publishers addresses, refer to SOURCES CITED section at the back of the book.

PHILATELY

See: STAMPS AS AN INVESTMENT

PHONOGRAPH AND PHONOGRAPH RECORD INDUSTRIES

See also: HIGH FIDELITY/STEREO; SOUND RECORDERS AND RECORDING

GENERAL WORKS

America on Record: A History of Recorded Sound. Andre Millard. Cambridge University Press. • 1995. $18.95.

ABSTRACTS AND INDEXES

Music Library Association Notes. Music Library Association. • Quarterly. Individuals, $70.00 per year; institutions, $80.00 per year. Indexes record reviews (classical).

DIRECTORIES

Billboard's International Buyer's Guide. Billboard Books. • Annual. $141.00. Record companies; music publishers; record and tape wholesalers; services and supplies for the music-record-tape-video industry; record and tape dealer accessories, fixtures, and merchandising products; includes United States and over 65 countries.

Directory of Computer and Consumer Electronics. Chain Store Age. • Annual. $290.00. Includes 2,900 "leading" retailers and over 200 "top" distributors. Formerly *Directory of Consumer Electronics Retails and Distributors.*

International Tape/Disc Directory. Billboard. • Annual. $75.00. Tape/Audio/Video professional equipment manufacturers, audio/video duplicators; pre-recorded tape, tape service and supply companies; video music producers, production facilities, and video program suppliers. Primarily U.S. and Canadian coverage, with some international listings.

Phonolog Reporter: All-in-One Reporter. i2 Technologies. • Weekly. $486.00 per year. Looseleaf. Contains over one million listings of recorded music (compact discs, cassette tapes, and phonograph records). Includes both popular and classical releases. Popular music is classified by title, artist, and album; classical performances are accessible by title, artist, and composer.

Record Retailing Directory. BPI Communications. • Annual. $169.00. Lists record (music CD-ROMs) dealers, both independent and chain-owned.

Schwann Opus: The Classical Music Resource. Schwann Publications. • Annual. $27.45 per year. Lists classical music recordings by composer. Covers compact discs, minidiscs, and cassette tapes. Includes an extensive, alphabetical list of recording labels and distributors, with addresses and telephone numbers (many listings also include fax numbers and Internet addresses).

Schwann Spectrum: The Guide to Rock, Jazz, World...and Beyond. Schwann Publications. • Annual. $27.45 per year. Lists rock, jazz, country, folk, soundtrack, international, new age, religious, and other disc and tape popular recordings by performer. Includes an extensive, alphabetical list of recording labels and distributors, with addresses and telephone numbers (some listings also include fax numbers and Internet addresses).

HANDBOOKS AND MANUALS

Modern Recording Techniques. David M. Huber and Robert Runstein. Butterworth-Heinemann. • 1995. $29.95. Fourth edition.

Releasing an Independent Record: How to Successfully Start and Run Your Own Record Label in the 1990s. Gary Hustwit. Rockpress Publishing. • 1998. $26.95. Sixth edition.

PERIODICALS AND NEWSLETTERS

Audio. Hachette Filipacchi Magazines, Inc. • Monthly. $26.00 per year. Includes annual directory *Product Review.*

Billboard: The International Newsweekly of Music, Video, and Home Entertainment. BPI Communications, Inc. • 51 times a year. $289.00 per year. Newsweekly for the music and home entertainment industries.

Cash Box: The International Music-Record Weekly. Cash Box Publishing Co., Inc. • Weekly. $185.00 per year.

Dealerscope Consumer Electronics Marketplace: For CE,PC and Major Appliance Retailers. North American Publishing Co. • Monthly. Free to qualified personnel; others, $79.00 per year. Formerly *Dealerscope Merchandising.*

PRICE SOURCES

Orion Audio Blue Book. Orion Research Corp. • Annual. $179.00. Quotes retail and wholesale prices of used audio equipment. Original list prices and years of manufacture are also shown.

TRADE/PROFESSIONAL ASSOCIATIONS

National Academy of Recording Arts and Sciences. 3402 Pico Blvd., Santa Monica, CA 90405. Phone: (310)392-3777 Fax: (310)392-9262 • URL: http://www.grammy.com.

National Association of Recording Merchandisers. Nine Eves Dr., Suite 120, Marlton, NJ 08053. Phone: (609)596-2221 Fax: (609)596-3268 • URL: http://www.narm.com.

Recording Industry Association of America. 1330 Connecticut Ave., Suite 300, Washington, DC 20036. Phone: (202)775-0101 Fax: (202)775-7253 E-mail: websmaster@riaa.com • URL: http://www.riaa.com.

OTHER SOURCES

Radio & Records. Radio & Records, Inc. • Weekly. $299.00 per year. Provides news and information relating to the record industry and to regional and national radio broadcasting. Special features cover specific types of programming, such as "classic rock," "adult alternative," "oldies," "country," and "news/talk." Radio station business and management topics are included.

Schwann Inside: Jazz and Classical. Schwann Publications. • Monthly. $55.95 per year. Provides reviews and listings of new classical and jazz recordings. Includes "Billboard Charts" of top selling jazz, contemporary jazz, classical, classical crossover, classical midline, and classical budget albums.

PHOTOCOPYING INDUSTRY

See: COPYING MACHINE INDUSTRY

PHOTOENGRAVING

See also: PRINTING AND PRINTING EQUIPMENT INDUSTRIES

PERIODICALS AND NEWSLETTERS

Prepress Bulletin. Bessie Halfacre, editor. International Prepress Association. • Bimonthly. $15.00 per year. Provides management and technical information on the graphic arts prepress industry.

TRADE/PROFESSIONAL ASSOCIATIONS

International Prepress Association. 7200 France Ave., S., Suite 327, Edina, MN 55435. Phone: (612)896-1908 Fax: (612)896-0181 E-mail: ipampls@aol.com • URL: http://www.ipa.org.

PHOTOGRAPHIC INDUSTRY

See also: CAMERA INDUSTRY; COMMERCIAL PHOTOGRAPHY; GRAPHIC ARTS INDUSTRY; MOTION PICTURE PHOTOGRAPHY

ABSTRACTS AND INDEXES

Art Index. H. W. Wilson Co. • Quarterly. Annual cumulations. Service basis for print edition; CD-ROM edition, $1,495.00 per year. Subject and author index to periodicals in art, architecture, industrial design, city planning, photography, and various related topics.

Imaging Abstracts. Royal Photographic Society of Great Britain, Imaging Science and Technology Grou. Elsevier Science. • Bimonthly. $792.00 per year. Formerly *Photographic Abstracts.*

BIOGRAPHICAL SOURCES

Contemporary Photographers. Available from The Gale Group. • 1995. $175.00. Provides biographical and critical information on more than 850 international photographers.

DIRECTORIES

Who's Who in Professional Imaging. Professional Photographers of America, Inc. • Annual. $110.00. Lists over 18,000 members. Formerly *Buyers Guide to Qualified Photographers.*

ENCYCLOPEDIAS AND DICTIONARIES

Focal Encyclopedia of Photography. Leslie Stroebel and Richard D. Zakia, editors. Butterworth-Heinemann. • 1993. $56.95. Third edition.

FINANCIAL RATIOS

Cost of Doing Business Survey. Photo Marketing Association International. • Biennial. $225.00. Emphasis is on photographic retailing.

HANDBOOKS AND MANUALS

One-Hour Photo Processing Lab. Entrepreneur Media, Inc. • Looseleaf. $59.50. A practical guide to starting a film developing and printing business. Covers profit potential, start-up costs, market size evaluation, owner's time required, site selection, lease negotiation, pricing, accounting, advertising, promotion, etc. (Start-Up Business Guide No. E1209.).

ONLINE DATABASES

Art Index Online. H. W. Wilson Co. • Indexes a wide variety of art-related periodicals, 1984 to date. Monthly updates. Inquire as to online cost and availability.

F & S Index. The Gale Group. • Contains about four million citations to worldwide business, financial, and industrial or consumer product literature appearing from 1972 to date. Weekly updates. Inquire as to online cost and availability.

PERIODICALS AND NEWSLETTERS

The Journal of Imaging Science and Technology. Society for Imaging Science and Technolgy. • Bimonthly. $135.00 per year. Formerly *Journal of Imaging Technology.*

Photo Marketing. Photo Marketing Association International. • Monthly. Membership.

Shutterbug. Patch Communications. • Monthly. $17.95 per year. Articles about new equipment, test reports on film accessories, how-to articles, etc. Annual *Buying Guide* available.

PRICE SOURCES

Orion Camera Blue Book. Orion Research Corp. • Annual. $144.00. Published by Orion Research Corporation. Quotes retail and wholesale prices of used cameras and equipment. Original list prices and years of manufacture are also shown.

STATISTICS SOURCES

Annual Survey of Manufactures. Available from U. S. Government Printing Office. • Annual. Prices vary. Issued by the U. S. Census Bureau as an interim update to the *Census of Manufactures.* Includes data on number of manufacturing establishments in various industries, employment, labor costs, value of shipments, capital expenditures, inventories, energy costs, and assets. (See also Census Bureau home page, http://www.census.gov/.).

U. S. Industry and Trade Outlook: The McGraw-Hill Companies and the U.S. Department of Commerce/ International Trade Administration. Datapso Research Corp. • Annual. $69.95. Produced by the International Trade Administration, U. S. Department of Commerce, in a "public-private" partnership with DRI/McGraw-Hill and Standard & Poor's. Provides basic data, outlook for the current year, and "Long-Term Prospects" (five-year projections) for a wide variety of products and services. Includes high technology industries. Formerly *U. S. Industrial Outlook.*

TRADE/PROFESSIONAL ASSOCIATIONS

Photo Marketing Association International. 3000 Picture Place, Jackson, MI 49201. Phone: (517)788-8100 Fax: (517)788-8371 • URL: http://www.pmai.org.

Photographic and Imaging Manufacturers Association. 550 Mamaroneck Ave., Ste. 307, Harrison, NY 10528-1612. Phone: (914)698-7603 Fax: (914)698-7609 E-mail: pima@pima.net • URL: http://www.pima.net.

Photographic Society of America. 3000 United Founders Blvd., Suite 103, Oklahoma City, OK 73112. Phone: (405)843-1437 Fax: (405)843-1438 E-mail: psahq@theshop.net • URL: http://www.psa-photo.org.

Photoimaging Manufacturers and Distributors Association. 109 White Oak Lane, Ste. 72F, Old Bridge, NJ 08857. Phone: (732)679-3460 Fax: (732)679-2294 E-mail: bclarkpmda@aol.com.

Professional Photographers of America. 229 Peachtree St., N.E., Suite 2200, Atlanta, GA 30303. Phone: 800-786-6277 or (404)522-8600 Fax: (404)614-6404 E-mail: dmmahon@ppa.com • URL: http://www.ppa.com.

Society for Imaging Science and Technology. 7003 Kilworth Lane, Springfield, VA 22151. Phone: (703)642-9090 Fax: (703)642-9094 E-mail: info@imaging.org • URL: http://www.imaging.org.

PHOTOGRAPHY, COMMERCIAL

See: COMMERCIAL PHOTOGRAPHY

PHOTOGRAPHY, INDUSTRIAL

See: COMMERCIAL PHOTOGRAPHY

PHOTOMECHANICAL PROCESSES

See: GRAPHIC ARTS INDUSTRY

PHOTONICS

See also: OPTOELECTRONICS

GENERAL WORKS

Fundamentals of Photonics. Bahaa E. Seleh and Malvin C. Teich. John Wiley and Sons, Inc. • 1991. $105.00. (Pure and Applied Optics Series).

ABSTRACTS AND INDEXES

Applied Science and Technology Index. H. W. Wilson Co. • 11 times a year. Quarterly and annual cumulations. Service basis for print edition; CD-ROM edition, $1,495.00 per year. Indexes a wide variety of English language technical, industrial, and engineering periodicals.

DIRECTORIES

Corptech Directory of Technology Companies. Corporate Technology Information Services, Inc. c/o Eileen Kennedy. • Annual. $795.00. Four volumes. Profiles of more than 45,000 manufacturers and developers of high technology products. Includes private companies, publicly-held corporations, and subsidiaries. Formerly *Corporate Technology Directory.*

Photonics Directory. Laurin Publishing Co., Inc. • Annual. $138.00. Four volumes. Volume one is a corporate guide; volume two is a buyer's guide; volume three is a designer's handbook; volume four is a dictionary. Formerly *Photonics Industry and System Purchasing Directory.*

ENCYCLOPEDIAS AND DICTIONARIES

Wiley Encyclopedia of Electrical and Electronics Engineering. John G. Webster, editor. John Wiley and Sons, Inc. • 1999. $6,495.00. 24 volumes. Contains about 1,400 articles, each with bibliography. Arrangement is according to 64 categories.

HANDBOOKS AND MANUALS

Applied Photonics. Chai Yeh, editor. Academic Press, Inc. • 1994. $73.00.

Photonic Devices and Systems. R. G. Hunsperger. Marcel Dekker, Inc. • 1994. $165.00. (Optical Engineering Series: Vol. 45).

ONLINE DATABASES

Applied Science and Technology Index Online. H. W. Wilson Co. • Provides online indexing of 400 major scientific, technical, industrial, and engineering periodicals. Time period is 1983 to date. Monthly updates. Inquire as to online cost and availability.

PROMT: Predicasts Overview of Markets and Technology. The Gale Group. • Companies, products, applied technologies and markets. U.S. and international literature coverage, 1972 to date. Inquire as to online cost and availability. Provides abstracts from more than 1,600 publications. Weekly updates.

PERIODICALS AND NEWSLETTERS

Optics and Photonics News. Optical Society of America, Inc. • Monthly. $99.00 per year.

Photonics Spectra. Laurin Publishing Co., Inc. • Monthly. $112.00 per year.

RESEARCH CENTERS AND INSTITUTES

Center for Advanced Phototonic and Electronic Materials. State University of New York at Buffalo, 217 C Bonner Hall, Buffalo, NY 14260. Phone: (716)645-2422 Fax: (716)645-5964 E-mail: waanders@eng.buffalo.edu • URL: http://www.ee.buffalo.edu • Does integrated optics research, including photonic circuitry.

Center for Advanced Technology in Telecommunications. Polytechnic University, Five Metrotech Center, Brooklyn, NY 11201. Phone: (718)260-3050 Fax: (718)260-3074 E-mail: panwar@poly.edu • URL: http://www.catt.poly.edu • Research fields include active media for optical communication.

Center for Photonics and Optoelectronic Materials. Princeton University, Engineering Quadrangle, School of Engineering and Applied Science, Princeton, NJ 08544. Phone: (609)258-4454 Fax: (609)258-1954 E-mail: poem@princeton.edu • URL: http://www.poem.princeton.edu/.

Communications and Information Processing Group. Rensselaer Polytechnic Institute, Electrical, Computer, and Systems Engineering Dept., Troy, NY 12180-3590. Phone: (518)276-6823 Fax: (518)276-6261 E-mail: modestino@ipl.rpi.edu • URL: http://www.rpi.edu • Includes Optical Signal Processing Laboratory and Speech Processing Laboratory.

Materials Processing Center. Massachusetts Institute of Technology, 77 Massachusetts Ave., Room 12-007, Cambridge, MA 02139-4307. Phone: (617)253-5179 Fax: (617)258-6900 E-mail: fmpage@.mit.edu • URL: http://www.web.mit.edu/mpc/www/ • Conducts processing, engineering, and economic research in ferrous and nonferrous metals, ceramics, polymers, photonic materials, superconductors, welding, composite materials, and other materials.

Mediphotonics Laboratory. City College of City University of New York, 138th and Convent Ave., New York, NY 10031. Phone: (212)650-5531 Fax: (212)650-5530 E-mail: alfano@scsun.sci.ccny.cuny.edu.

Optoelectronic Computing Systems Center. University of Colorado at Boulder, Campus Box 525, Boulder, CO 80309. Phone: (303)492-7967 Fax: (303)492-3674 E-mail: jneff@colorado.edu • URL: http://www.ocs.colorado.edu • Explores the advantages of optics over electronics for information processing.

Photonics Research Laboratory. University of Florida, Hall 339 Larsen, Gainesville, FL 32611. Phone: (352)392-9265 Fax: (352)392-4963 E-mail: ramu@eng.ufl.edu • URL: http://www.nervm.nerdc.ufl.edu/~photon.

TRADE/PROFESSIONAL ASSOCIATIONS

IEEE Lasers and Electro-Optics Society. Institute of Electrical and Electronics Engineers, P.O. Box 1331, Piscataway, NJ 08855-1331. Phone: (732)981-0060 Fax: (732)981-1721 E-mail: g.walters@ieee.org • URL: http://www.ieee.org/leos • A society of the Institute of Electrical and Electronics Engineers. Fields of interest include lasers, fiber optics, optoelectronics, and photonics.

Minerals, Metals and Materials Society. 184 Thorn Hill Dr., Warrendale, PA 15086-7528. Phone: 800-759-4867 or (724)776-9000 Fax: (724)776-3770 E-mail: tmsgeneral@tms.org • URL: http://www.tms.org • Members are metallurgists, metallurgical engineers, and materials scientists. Divisions include Light Metals and Electronic, Magnetic, and Photonic Materials.

Optical Society of America. 2010 Massachusetts Ave., N.W., Washington, DC 20036-1023. Phone: (202)223-8130 Fax: (202)223-1096 • URL: http://www.osa.org.

SPIE-The International Society for Optical Engineering. P.O. Box 10, Bellingham, WA 98227-0010. Phone: (360)676-3290 Fax: (360)647-1445 E-mail: spie@spie.org • URL: http://www.spie.org.

OTHER SOURCES

Fiber Systems International. Available from IOP Publishing, Inc. • Monthly. Controlled circulation. Published in the UK by the Institute of Physics. "Covering the optical communications marketplace within the Americas and Asia." *Fibre Systems*

Europe is also available, covering the business and marketing aspects of fiber optics communications in Europe.

PHYSICAL DISTRIBUTION

See: DISTRIBUTION

PHYSICAL FITNESS INDUSTRY

See: FITNESS INDUSTRY

PICKETING

See: STRIKES AND LOCKOUTS

PIERS

See: PORTS

PIG INDUSTRY

See: SWINE INDUSTRY

PIGGYBACK TRANSPORT

See: TRUCK TRAILERS

PILOTS

See: AIR PILOTS

PINEAPPLE INDUSTRY

See also: FRUIT INDUSTRY

RESEARCH CENTERS AND INSTITUTES

Hawaii Institute of Tropical Agriculture and Human Resources. University of Hawaii at Manoa, Honolulu, HI 96822. Phone: (808)956-8131 Fax: (808)956-9105 E-mail: tadean2@avax.ctahr.hawaii.edu • URL: http://www.ctahr.hawaii.edu • Concerned with the production and marketing of tropical food and ornamental plant products, including pineapples, bananas, coffee, and macadamia nuts.

TRADE/PROFESSIONAL ASSOCIATIONS

Pineapple Growers Association of Hawaii. 1116 Whitmore Ave., Wahiawa, HI 96786. Phone: (808)877-3855 Fax: (808)871-0953 • Promotes the sale of pineapple products.

PIPE

See also: PLUMBING INDUSTRY

DIRECTORIES

FMA's Who's Who in Metal Forming and Fabricating (Fabricator's and ManufacturersAssociation). Fabricators and Manufacturers Association International. • Annual. Free to members; non-members, $200.00. Lists about 2,000 members of the Fabricators and Manufacturers Association (FMA), International; and 1,000 members of the Tube and Pipe Association. Includes five indexes. Formerly *FMA Member Resource Directory.*

Heating/Piping/Air Conditioning Info-Dex. Penton Media Inc. • Annual. $30.00. The HVAC/R industry's directory of products, manufacturers, and trade names and a composite of catalog data for mechanical systems engineering professionals.

The Wholesaler "Wholesaling 100". TMB Publishing, Inc. • Annual. $25.00. Provides information on the 100 leading wholesalers of plumbing, piping, heating, and air conditioning equipment.

FINANCIAL RATIOS

Annual Statement Studies. Robert Morris Associates: The Association of Lending and Credit Risk Professiona. • Annual. Free to members; non-members, $140.00. Median and quartile financial ratios are given for over 400 kinds of manufacturing, wholesale, retail, construction, and consumer finance establishments. Data is sorted by both asset size and sales volume. Includes a clearly written "Definition of Ratios" and an alphabetical industry index.

HANDBOOKS AND MANUALS

Piping Guide: A Compact Reference for the Design and Drafting of Piping Systems. David R. Sherwood and Dennis J. Whistance. SYNTEC, Inc. • 1991. $89.00. Second edition.

INTERNET DATABASES

Fedstats. Federal Interagency Council on Statistical Policy. Phone: (202)395-7254 • URL: http://www.fedstats.gov • Web site features an efficient search facility for full-text statistics produced by more than 70 federal agencies, including the Census Bureau, the Bureau of Economic Analysis, and the Bureau of Labor Statistics. Boolean searches can be made within one agency or for all agencies combined. Links are offered to international statistical bureaus, including the UN, IMF, OECD, UNESCO, Eurostat, and 20 individual countries. Fees: Free.

ONLINE DATABASES

DRI U.S. Central Database. Data Products Division. • Provides more than 23,000 business, financial, demographic, economic, foreign trade, and industry-related time series for the U.S. Includes national income, population, retail-wholesale trade, price indexes, labor data, housing, industrial production, banking, interest rates, money supply, etc. Time period is generally 1947 to date (some data back to 1929). Updating varies. Inquire as to online cost and availability.

PERIODICALS AND NEWSLETTERS

The Fabricator. Fabricators and Manufacturers Association International. Croydon Group, Ltd. • Monthly. $75.00 per year. Covers the manufacture of sheet, coil, tube, pipe, and structural metal shapes.

Heating/Piping/Air Conditioning Engineering: The Magazine of Mechanical Systems Engineering. Penton Media Inc. • Monthly. Free to qualified personnel; others, $65.00 per year. Covers design, specification, installation, operation, and maintenance for systems in industrial, commercial, and institutional buildings. Formerly Heating, Piping and Air Conditioning.

The Wholesaler. TMB Publishing, Inc. • Monthly. $75.00 per year. Edited for wholesalers and distributors of plumbing, piping, heating, and air conditioning equipment.

STATISTICS SOURCES

American Iron and Steel Annual Statistical Report. American Iron and Steel Institute. • Annual. $100.00 per year.

Business Statistics of the United States. Courtenay M. Slater, editor. Bernan Associates. • 1999. $74.00. Fifth edition. Based on *Business Statistics*, formerly issue by the Bureau of Economic Analysis, U. S. Department of Commerce. Provides basic data for a wide variety of U. S. industries, services, and economic indicators. Most statistics are shown annually for 29 years and monthly for the most recent four years.

Survey of Current Business. Available from U. S. Government Printing Office. • Monthly. $49.00 per year. Issued by Bureau of Economic Analysis, U. S. Department of Commerce. Presents a wide variety of business and economic data.

TRADE/PROFESSIONAL ASSOCIATIONS

Ductile Iron Pipe Research Association. 245 Riverchase Parkway, E., Suite 0, Birmingham, AL 35244. Phone: (205)402-8700 Fax: (205)402-8730 E-mail: info@dipra.org • URL: http://www.dipra.org.

Fabricators and Manufacturers Association International. 833 Featherstone Rd., Rockford, IL 61107-6302. Phone: (815)399-8700 Fax: (815)399-7279 E-mail: info@fmametal.fab.org • URL: http://www.fmametalfab.org • Members are individuals concerned with metal forming, cutting, and fabricating. Includes a Sheet Metal Division and the Tube and Pipe Fabricators Association.

Manufacturers Standardization Society of the Valve and Fittings Industry. 127 Park St., N. E., Vienna, VA 22180. Phone: (703)281-6613 Fax: (703)281-6671 E-mail: info@mss-hq.com • URL: http://www.mss-hq.com • Members are valve and fitting companies. Publishes standards and specifications.

National Certified Pipe Welding Bureau. 1385 Piccard Dr., Rockville, MD 20850-4329. Phone: 800-556-3653 or (301)869-5800 Fax: (301)990-9690 E-mail: nick@mcaa.org • URL: http://www.mcaa.org.

National Clay Pipe Institute. P.O. Box 759, Lake Geneva, WI 53147. Phone: (414)248-9094 Fax: (414)248-1564 E-mail: info@ncpi.org • URL: http://www.ncpi.org.

National Corrugated Steel Pipe Association. 1255 23rd St., N.W., Suite 200, Washington, DC 20037-1174. Phone: (202)452-1700 Fax: (202)833-3636 E-mail: csp@ncspa.org • URL: http://www.ncspa.org.

Plastics Pipe Institute. 1825 Connecticut Ave., N.W., Washington, DC 20009. Phone: 888-314-6774 or (202)462-9607 Fax: (202)462-9779 • URL: http://www.plasticpipe.org.

PIPELINE INDUSTRY

ABSTRACTS AND INDEXES

NTIS Alerts: Transportation. National Technical Information Service. • Semimonthly. $210.00 per year. Provides descriptions of government-sponsored research reports and software, with ordering information. Covers air, marine, highway, inland waterway, pipeline, and railroad transportation. Formerly *Abstract Newsletter.*

DIRECTORIES

Pipeline and Gas Journal Buyer's Guide. Oildom Publishing Co. of Texas, Inc. • Annual. $75.00. Supplies and services. Lists over 700 companies supplying products and services used in construction and operation of cross-country pipeline and gas distribution systems.

Plunkett's Energy Industry Almanac: Complete Profiles on the Energy Industry 500 Companies. Plunkett Research Ltd. • Annual. $149.99. Includes major oil companies, utilities, pipelines, alternative energy companies, etc. Provides information on industry trends.

Worldwide Pipelines and Contractors Directory. PennWell Corp., Petroleum Div. • Annual. $145.00. More than 4,000 companies, subsidiaries, branch offices, and engineering-construction services worldwide active in natural gas, crude oil, and products pipeline.

FINANCIAL RATIOS

Almanac of Business and Industrial Financial Ratios. Leo Troy. Prentice Hall. • Annual. $99.95. Contains financial ratios derived from federal tax returns. Ratios for each of about 200 industries are arranged according to company asset size.

PERIODICALS AND NEWSLETTERS

Pipe Line and Gas Industry: Crude Oil and Products Pipelines, Gas Transmission and Gas Distribution. Gulf Publishing Co. • Monthly. Free to qualified personnel; others, $29.00 per year. International edition available.

Pipeline and Gas Journal: Energy Construction, Transportation and Distribution. Oildom Publishing of Texas, Inc. • Monthly. $33.00 per year. Covers engineering and operating methods on cross-country pipelines that transport crude oil products and natural gas. Includes *Energy Management Report.* Incorporates *Pipeline.*

STATISTICS SOURCES

Transportation Statistics Annual Report. Available from U. S. Government Printing Office. • Annual. $21.00. Issued by Bureau of Transportation Statistics, U. S. Department of Transportation. Provides data on operating revenues, expenses, employees, passenger miles (where applicable), and other factors for airlines, automobiles, buses, local transit, pipelines, railroads, ships, and trucks.

TRADE/PROFESSIONAL ASSOCIATIONS

Association of Oil Pipe Lines. 1101 Vermont Ave., N.W., Suite 604, Washington, DC 20005. Phone: (202)408-7970 Fax: (202)408-7983 E-mail: aopl@aopl.org • URL: http://www.aopl.org.

Pipe Line Contractors Association. 1700 Pacific Ave., Suite 4100, Dallas, TX 75201. Phone: (214)969-2700 Fax: (214)969-2705.

OTHER SOURCES

Infrastructure Industries USA. The Gale Group. • 2001. $240.00. Replaces *Agriculture, Forestry, Fishing, Mining, and Construction USA* and *Transportation and Public Utilities USA.* Presents statistics and projections relating to economic activity in a wide variety of natural resource and construction industries.

PIPES (SMOKING)

See: TOBACCO AND TOBACCO INDUSTRY

PISTOLS

See: FIREARMS INDUSTRY

PLACEMENT BUREAUS

See: COLLEGE PLACEMENT BUREAUS

PLANNED ECONOMY

See: ECONOMIC POLICY

PLANNING

GENERAL WORKS

The Art of the Long View: Planning for the Future in an Uncertain World. Peter Schwartz. Doubleday. • 1991. $15.95. Covers strategic planning for corporations and smaller firms. Includes "The World in 2005: Three Scenarios.".

Corporate Internet Planning Guide: Aligning Internet Strategy with Business Goals. Richard J. Gascoyne and Koray Ozcubucku. John Wiley and Sons, Inc. • 1996. $34.95. Provides administrative advice on planning, developing, and managing corporate Internet or intranet functions. Emphasis is on strategic planning. (Business, Commerce, Management Series).

Strategic Planning Plus: An Organizational Guide. Roger Kaufman. Sage Publications, Inc. • 1992. $48.00.

ABSTRACTS AND INDEXES

Social Sciences Index. H. W. Wilson Co. • Quarterly, with annual cumulation. Service basis for print edition; CD-ROM edition, $1,495 per year. Indexes more than 400 periodicals covering economics, environmental policy, government, insurance, labor, health care policy, plannning, public administration, public welfare, urban studies, women's issues, criminology, and related topics.

CD-ROM DATABASES

Social Science Source. EBSCO Publishing. • Monthly. $1,495.00 per year. Provides CD-ROM citations and abstracts to social science articles in more than 600 periodicals, with full text from 125 periodicals. Covers economics, political science, public policy, international relations, psychology, and other topics. Time period is most recent five years.

Social Sciences Citation Index: Compact Disc Edition with Abstracts. Institute for Scientific Information. • Quarterly. Provides CD-ROM indexing and abstracting of "significant articles" from 1,400 social science journals worldwide, with additional selections from 3,200 other journals, 1986 to date. Includes economics, business, finance, management, communications, demographics, information and library science, political science, sociology, and many other subjects.

WILSONDISC: Wilson Business Abstracts. H. W. Wilson Co. • Monthly. $2,495.00 per year, including unlimited online access to *Wilson Business Abstracts* through WILSONLINE. Provides CD-ROM "cover-to-cover" abstracting and indexing of over 600 prominent business periodicals. Indexing is from 1982, abstracting from 1990. (*Business Periodicals Index* without abstracts is available on CD-ROM at $1,495 per year.).

WILSONDISC: Wilson Social Sciences Abstracts. H. W. Wilson Co. • Monthly. Including unlimited online access to *Social Sciences Index* through WILSONLINE. Provides CD-ROM indexing from 1983 and abstracting from 1994 of more than 400 periodicals covering economics, area studies, community health, public administration, public welfare, urban studies, and many other topics related to the social sciences.

ENCYCLOPEDIAS AND DICTIONARIES

Blackwell Encyclopedic Dictionary of Strategic Management. Derek F. Channon, editor. Blackwell Publishers. • 1997. $110.00. The editor is associated with Imperial College, London. Contains definitions of key terms combined with longer articles written by various U. S. and foreign business educators. Includes bibliographies and index. (Blackwell Encyclopedia of Management Series.).

HANDBOOKS AND MANUALS

AMA Management Handbook. John J. Hampton, editor. AMACOM. • 1994. $110.00. Third edition. Provides 200 chapters in 16 major subject areas. Covers a wide variety of business and industrial management topics.

Handbook of Strategic Planning. Bernard Taylor and Kevin Hawkins, editors. Books on Demand. • 1986. $148.20.

How to Write a Successful Marketing Plan: A Disciplined and Comprehensive Approach. Roman G. Hiebing. Prentice Hall. • 1999. $79.95. Second edition. The four main sections cover marketing background, the marketing plan, plan execution, and evaluation. Includes worksheets and formats.

Marketing Planning Guide. Robert E. Stevens and others. Haworth Press, Inc. • 1997. $49.95. Second edition. Covers market segmentation, product positioning, and other marketing planning topics.

Marketing Plans: How to Prepare Them, How to Use Them. Malcolm H. McDonald. Butterworth-Heinemann. • 1999. $44.95. Fourth edition. (Professional Development Series).

Strategic Planning: A Practical Guide. Peter Rea and Harold Kerzner. John Wiley and Sons, Inc. • 1997. $69.95. Covers strategic planning for manufacturing firms, small businesses, and large corporations. (Industrial Engineering Series).

Total Business Planning: A Step-by-Step Guide with Forms. James E. Burton and W. Blan McBride. John Wiley and Sons, Inc. • 1999. $29.95. Second edition. How to construct and activate an internal business plan, whether short-term or long-term. Includes CD-ROM.

INTERNET DATABASES

Intelligence Data. Thomson Financial. Phone: 800-654-0393 or (212)806-8023 Fax: (212)806-8004 • URL: http://www.intelligencedata.com • Fee-based Web site provides a wide variety of information relating to competitive intelligence, strategic planning, business development, mergers, acquisitions, sales, and marketing. "Intelliscope" feature offers searching of other Thomson units, such as Investext, MarkIntel, InSite 2, and Industry Insider. Weekly updating.

ONLINE DATABASES

Management Contents. The Gale Group. • Covers a wide range of management, financial, marketing, personnel, and administrative topics. About 150 leading business journals are indexed and abstracted from 1974 to date, with monthly updating. Inquire as to online cost and availability.

Wilson Business Abstracts Online. H. W. Wilson Co. • Indexes and abstracts 600 major business periodicals, plus the *Wall Street Journal* and the business section of the *New York Times.* Indexing is from 1982, abstracting from 1990, with the two newspapers included from 1993. Updated weekly. Inquire as to online cost and availability. (*Business Periodicals Index* without abstracts is also available online.).

Wilson Social Sciences Abstracts Online. H. W. Wilson Co. • Provides online abstracting and indexing of more than 415 periodicals covering area studies, community health, public administration, public welfare, urban studies, and many other social science topics. Time period is 1994 to date for abstracts and 1983 to date for indexing, with updates monthly. Inquire as to online cost and availability.

PERIODICALS AND NEWSLETTERS

Business Strategies Bulletin. CCH, Inc. • Monthly. $166.00 per year. Newsletter.

Futures; The Journal of Forecasting, Planning and Policy. Elsevier Science. • 10 times a year. $764.00 per year.

Journal of Business Strategy. Faulkner and Gray, Inc. • Bimonthly. $84.00 per year. Devoted to the theory and practice of strategy, planning, implementation and competitive analysis. Covers every aspect of business from advertising to systems design. Incorporates*Journal of European Business.*

Long Range Planning. Strategic Planning Society. Elsevier Science. • Bimonthly. $1,104.00 per year.

Planning. American Planning Association. • Monthly. Free to members; non-members, $60.00 per year.

Strategy and Business. Booz-Allen & Hamilton. • Quarterly. $38.00 per year.

RESEARCH CENTERS AND INSTITUTES

Institute of State and Regional Affairs. Pennsylvania State University at Harrisburg, 777 W. Harrisburg Pike, Middletown, PA 17057-4898. Phone: (717)948-6178 Fax: (717)948-6306 E-mail: xvc@psu.edu • URL: http://www.psdc.hbg.psu.edu/isra • Conducts research in environmental, general, and socioeconomic planning. Zoning is included.

Program on International Studies in Planning. Cornell University, 200 W. Sibley Hall, Ithaca, NY 14853. Phone: (607)255-2186 Fax: (607)255-6681 E-mail: bdl5@cornell.edu • URL: http://www.inet.crp.cornell.edu/organizations/isp/default.htm • Research activities are related to international urban and regional planning, with emphasis on developing areas.

TRADE/PROFESSIONAL ASSOCIATIONS

American Institute of Certified Planners. 1776 Massachusetts Ave., N.W., Suite 400, Washington, DC 20036. Phone: 800-954-1669 or (202)872-0611 Fax: (202)872-0643 E-mail: aicp@planning.org • URL: http://www.planning.org.

American Planning Association. 122 S. Michigan Ave., Suite. 1600, Chicago, IL 60603-6107. Phone: (312)431-9100 Fax: (312)431-9985 E-mail: research@planning.org • URL: http://www.planning.org.

National Policy Association. 1424 16th St., N.W., Suite 700, Washington, DC 20036. Phone: (202)265-7685 Fax: (202)797-5516 E-mail: npa@npa1.org • URL: http://www.npa1.org.

Strategic Leadership Forum. 435 N. Michigan Ave., Suite 1717, Chicago, IL 60611-4067. Phone: 800-873-5995 or (312)644-0829 Fax: (312)644-8557 • URL: http://www.slfnet.org.

OTHER SOURCES

Business Strategies. CCH, Inc. • Semimonthly. $819.00 per year. Four looseleaf volumes. Semimonthly updates. Legal, tax, and accounting aspects of business planning and decision-making. Provides information on start-ups, forms of ownership (partnerships, corporations), failing businesses, reorganizations, acquisitions, and so forth. Includes *Business Strategies Bulletin,* a monthly newsletter.

How to Write a Business Plan. American Management Association Extension Institute. • Looseleaf. $130.00. Self-study course. Emphasis is on practical explanations, examples, and problem solving. Quizzes and a case study are included.

How to Write a Marketing Plan. American Management Association Extension Institute. • Looseleaf. $130.00. Self-study course. Emphasis is on practical explanations, examples, and problem solving. Quizzes and a case study are included.

Macroeconomics and Company Planning. Continuing Professional Education Div. American Institute of Certified Public Accountants. • Looseleaf. Self-study course.

PLANS, BUSINESS

See: BUSINESS START-UP PLANS AND PROPOSALS; PLANNING

PLANT ENGINEERING

See: FACTORY MANAGEMENT

PLANT LOCATION

See: LOCATION OF INDUSTRY

PLANT MAINTENANCE

See: MAINTENANCE OF BUILDINGS

PLANT MANAGEMENT

See: FACTORY MANAGEMENT

PLANT PROTECTION

See: INDUSTRIAL SECURITY PROGRAMS

PLANT SITES

See: LOCATION OF INDUSTRY

PLASTER AND PLASTERING

DIRECTORIES

Who's Who in the Wall and Ceiling Industry. Association of the Wall and Ceiling Industries International. • Annual. Price on application. Contractors, manufacturers, suppliers, unions, organizations, and periodicals affiliated with the industry.

FINANCIAL RATIOS

Annual Statement Studies. Robert Morris Associates: The Association of Lending and Credit Risk Professiona. • Annual. Free to members; non-members, $140.00. Median and quartile financial ratios are given for over 400 kinds of manufacturing, wholesale, retail, construction, and consumer finance establishments. Data is sorted by both asset size and sales volume. Includes a clearly written "Definition of Ratios" and an alphabetical industry index.

PERIODICALS AND NEWSLETTERS

ENR Connecting the Industry Worldwide (Engineering News-Record). McGraw-Hill. • Weekly. $74.00 per year.

TRADE/PROFESSIONAL ASSOCIATIONS

Association of Wall and Ceiling Industries - International. 803 W. Broad St., Suite 600, Falls Church, VA 22046-3108. Phone: (703)534-8300 Fax: (703)534-8307 E-mail: info@awci.org • URL: http://www.awci.org.

International Institute for Lath and Plaster. 1043 Stuart St., No. 2, Lafayette, CA 94549. Phone: (925)283-5160 Fax: (925)283-5161.

PLASTIC CONTAINERS

See: CONTAINER INDUSTRY

PLASTICS INDUSTRY

See also: COMPOSITE MATERIALS

GENERAL WORKS

The Development of Plastics. S. Mossman and P. Morris, editors. CRC Press, Inc. • 1994. $68.00. Published by The Royal Society of Chemistry. Covers the history of plastics from the Victorian era to the present. Includes technical, scientific, and cultural perspectives.

ABSTRACTS AND INDEXES

Applied Science and Technology Index. H. W. Wilson Co. • 11 times a year. Quarterly and annual cumulations. Service basis for print edition; CD-ROM edition, $1,495.00 per year. Indexes a wide variety of English language technical, industrial, and engineering periodicals.

CPI Digest: Key to World Literature Serving the Coatings, Plastics, Fibers, Adhesives, and Related Industries (Chemical Process Industries). CPI Information Services. • Monthly. $397.00 per year. Abstracts of business and technical articles for polymer-based, chemical process industries. Includes a monthly list of relevant U. S. patents. International coverage.

Engineered Materials Abstracts. Cambridge Information Group. • Monthly. $995.00 per year. Provides citations to the technical and engineering literature of plastic, ceramic, and composite materials.

NTIS Alerts: Materials Sciences. National Technical Information Service. • Semimonthly. $220.00 per year. Provides descriptions of government-sponsored research reports and software, with ordering information. Covers ceramics, glass, coatings, composite materials, alloys, plastics, wood, paper, adhesives, fibers, lubricants, and related subjects. Formerly *Abstract Newsletter.*

Polymers/Ceramics/Composites Alert. Cambridge Information Group. • Monthly. $340.00 per year. Provides citations to the business and industrial literature of plastic, ceramic, and composite materials. (Materials Business Information Series).

RAPRA Abstracts. RAPRA Technology Ltd. • Monthly. $2,465.00 per year. Up-to-date survey of current international information relevant to the rubber, plastics and associated industries.

CD-ROM DATABASES

International Plastics Selector. Data Business Publishing. • Semiannual. CD-ROM index version (technical data only), $695.00 per year or $495.00 per disc. CD-ROM image version (technical data and specification sheet images), $1,295.00 per year or $995.00 per disc. Provides detailed information on the properties of 20,000 types of plastic, both current and obsolete. Time period is 1977 to date. Includes trade names and supplier names and addresses.

METADEX Materials Collection: Metals-Polymers-Ceramics. Cambridge Scientific Abstracts. • Quarterly. $6,950.00 per year. Provides CD-ROM citations to the worldwide literature of materials science and metallurgy. Corresponds to *Metals Abstracts, Alloys Index, Steels Alert, Nonferrous Alert, Polymers/Ceramics/Composites Alert,* and *Engineered Materials Abstracts.* (Formerly produced by ASM International.).

DIRECTORIES

Engineering Plastics and Composites. William A. Woishnis and others, editors. ASM International. • 1993. $149.00. Second edition. In four sections: (1) Trade names of plastics, reinforced plastics, and resin composites; (2) Index to materials, with suppliers and other information; (3) Suppliers alphabetically, with trade names; (4) Supplier contact information. (Materials Data Series).

Materials Research Centres: A World Directory of Organizations and Programmes in Materials Science. Allyn and Bacon/Longman. • 1991. $475.00. Fourth edition. Profiles of research centers in 75 countries. Materials include plastics, metals, fibers, etc.

Plastics Technology Manufacturing Handbook and Buyers' Guide. Bill Communications, Inc. • Annual. Over 4,000 manufacturers of plastics processing equipment and materials. Included in subscription to *Plastics Technology.*

ENCYCLOPEDIAS AND DICTIONARIES

ASM Materials Engineering Dictionary. Joseph R. Davis, editor. ASM International. • 1992. $146.00. Contains 10,000 entries, 700 illustrations, and 150 tables relating to metals, plastics, ceramics, composites, and adhesives. Includes "Technical Briefs" on 64 key material groups.

Dictionary of Plastics Technology. H. D. Junge. John Wiley and Sons, Inc. • 1987. $150.00.

Encyclopedia of Advanced Materials. David Bloor and others. Elsevier Science. • 1994. $1,811.25. Four volumes.

Encyclopedia of Emerging Industries. The Gale Group. • 2000. $295.00. Fourth edition. Provides detailed information on 90 "newly flourishing" industries. Includes historical background, organizational structure, significant individuals, current conditions, major companies, work force, technology trends, research developments, and other industry facts.

Encyclopedia of Materials: Science and Technology. K.H.J. Buschow and others, editors. Pergamon Press/Elsevier Science. • 2001. $6,875.00. Eleven volumes. Provides extensive technical information on a wide variety of materials, including metals, ceramics, plastics, optical materials, and building materials. Includes more than 2,000 articles and 5,000 illustrations.

Encyclopedia of Polymer Science and Engineering. H.F. Mark and others. John Wiley and Sons, Inc. • 1985. $5,035.00. 19 volumes, volume 22. $295.00 per volume. Second edition.

Kirk-Othmer Encyclopedia of Chemical Technology. John Wiley and Sons, Inc. • 1991-97. $7,350.00, prepaid. 21 volumes. Fourth edition. Four volumes are scheduled to be published each year, with individual volumes available at $350.00.

Modern Plastics Encyclopedia. McGraw-Hill. • Annual. $125.00. List of about 5,000 suppliers of over 350 types of products and services to the plastic industry in the U.S. and Canada. Included with subscription to *Modern Plastics.*

Whittington's Dictionary of Plastics. Society of Plastics Engineers. Available from Technomic Publishing Co. • 1993. $99.95. Third expanded revised edition.

FINANCIAL RATIOS

Annual Statement Studies. Robert Morris Associates: The Association of Lending and Credit Risk Professiona. • Annual. Free to members; non-members, $140.00. Median and quartile financial ratios are given for over 400 kinds of manufacturing, wholesale, retail, construction, and consumer finance establishments. Data is sorted by both asset size and sales volume. Includes a clearly written "Definition of Ratios" and an alphabetical industry index.

HANDBOOKS AND MANUALS

Advanced Polymer Composites: Principles and Applications. Bor Z. Jang. ASM International. • 1994. $93.00.

ASM Engineered Materials Reference Book. Michael L. Bauccio. ASM International. • 1994. $139.00. Second edition. Provides information on a wide range of materials, with special sections on ceramics, industrial glass products, and plastics.

Plastics Extrusion Technology Handbook. Sidney Levy and others. Industrial Press, Inc. • 1989. $44.95. Second edition.

Plastics Processing Technology. Edward A. Muccio. ASM International. • 1994. $87.00. Contains basic terminology and information on plastics for engineers, managers, technicians, purchasing agents, and students. Written to serve as a primer on plastics technology and processing.

Polymer Processing: Principles and Design. Donald G. Baird and Dimitria I. Collias. John Wiley and Sons, Inc. • 1998. $94.95. A practical guide to thermoplastics.

INTERNET DATABASES

Fedstats. Federal Interagency Council on Statistical Policy. Phone: (202)395-7254 • URL: http://www.fedstats.gov • Web site features an efficient search facility for full-text statistics produced by more than 70 federal agencies, including the Census Bureau, the Bureau of Economic Analysis, and the Bureau of Labor Statistics. Boolean searches can be made within one agency or for all agencies combined. Links are offered to international statistical bureaus, including the UN, IMF, OECD, UNESCO, Eurostat, and 20 individual countries. Fees: Free.

ONLINE DATABASES

Applied Science and Technology Index Online. H. W. Wilson Co. • Provides online indexing of 400 major scientific, technical, industrial, and engineering periodicals. Time period is 1983 to date. Monthly updates. Inquire as to online cost and availability.

Business and Industry. Responsive Database Services, Inc. • Contains online citations, abstracts, and selected fulltext from more than 1,000 trade journals, newspapers, and other publications. Provides general coverage of both manufacturing and service industries, including marketing, production, industry trends, key events, and information on specific companies. Time span is 1994 to date. Daily updates. Inquire as to online cost and availability. (Also available in a CD-ROM version.).

DRI U.S. Central Database. Data Products Division. • Provides more than 23,000 business, financial, demographic, economic, foreign trade, and industry-related time series for the U.S. Includes national income, population, retail-wholesale trade, price indexes, labor data, housing, industrial production, banking, interest rates, money supply, etc. Time period is generally 1947 to date (some data back to 1929). Updating varies. Inquire as to online cost and availability.

Engineered Materials Abstracts [online]. Cambridge Scientific Abstracts. • Provides online citations to the technical and engineering literature of plastic, ceramic, and composite materials. Time period is 1986 to date, with monthly updates. (Formerly produced by ASM International.) Inquire as to online cost and availability.

Materials Business File. Cambridge Scientific Abstracts. • Provides online abstracts and citations to worldwide materials literature, covering the business and industrial aspects of metals, plastics, ceramics, and composites. Corresponds to *Steels Alert, Nonferrous Metals Alert,* and *Polymers/Ceramics/Composites Alert.* Time period is 1985 to date, with monthly updates. (Formerly produced by ASM International.) Inquire as to online cost and availability.

METADEX. Cambridge Scientific Abstracts. • Covers the worldwide literature of metals, metallurgy, and materials science, 1966 to date. Includes detailed alloys indexing from 1974. Biweekly updating. Inquire as to online cost and availability. (Formerly produced by ASM International.).

Tablebase. Responsive Database Services, Inc. • Provides online numerical tabular data from a wide variety of business, organization, and government sources, including 900 trade journals. Includes industry and individual company statistics relating to products, market share, sales forecasts, production, exports, market trends, etc. Time span is 1997 to date. Weekly updates. Inquire as to online cost and availability. (Also available in a CD-ROM version.).

PERIODICALS AND NEWSLETTERS

Advances in Polymer Technology. Polymer Processing Institute. John Wiley and Sons, Inc., Journals Div. • Quarterly. Institutions, $765.00 per year.

Journal of Applied Polymer Science. John Wiley and Sons, Inc., Journals Div. • 56 times a year. Institutions, $11,570.00 per year.

Journal of Elastomers and Plastics. Technomic Publishing Co., Inc. • Quarterly. $340.00 per year.

Molding Systems. Society of Manufacturing Engineers. • Monthly. $100.00. Formerly *Plastics World.*

Plastics Engineering. Society of Plastics Engineers, Inc. • Monthly. $110.00 per year.

Plastics News: Crain's International Newspaper for the Plastics Industry. Crain Communications, Inc. • Weekly. $62.00 per year.

Plastics Technology: The Only Magazine for Plastics Processors. Bill Communications, Inc. • 13 times a year. $89.00 per year.

Plastics Week: The Global Newsletter. McGraw-Hill Chemicals and Plastics Information Services. • Weekly. $530.00 per year. Newsletter. Covers international trends in plastics production, technology, research, and legislation.

Polymer Engineering and Science. Society of Plastics Engineers, Inc. • Monthly. $220.00 per year. Includes six special issues.

Urethanes Technology. Crain Communications, Inc. • Bimonthly. $175.00 per year. Covers the international polyurethane industry.

RESEARCH CENTERS AND INSTITUTES

Materials Processing Center. Massachusetts Institute of Technology, 77 Massachusetts Ave., Room 12-007, Cambridge, MA 02139-4307. Phone: (617)253-5179 Fax: (617)258-6900 E-mail: fmpage@.mit.edu • URL: http://www.web.mit.edu/mpc/www/ • Conducts processing, engineering, and economic research in ferrous and nonferrous metals, ceramics, polymers, photonic materials, superconductors, welding, composite materials, and other materials.

Plastics Institute of America. 333 Aiken St., Lowell, MA 01854. Phone: (978)934-3130 Fax: (978)459-9420 E-mail: pia@cae.uml.edu • URL: http://www.plasticsinstitute.org.

Polymer Research Center. University of Cincinnati. College of Engineering, 644 Baldwin Hall, Cincinnati, OH 45221-0018. Phone: (513)556-5430 Fax: (513)556-5007 E-mail: sclarson@uceng.uc.edu.

Polymer Research Laboratory. University of Michigan. 2014 H.H. Dow Bldg., Ann Arbor, MI 48109. Phone: (734)763-9867 Fax: (734)763-4788 E-mail: rer@umich.edu.

STATISTICS SOURCES

Annual Survey of Manufactures. Available from U. S. Government Printing Office. • Annual. Prices vary. Issued by the U. S. Census Bureau as an interim update to the *Census of Manufactures.* Includes data on number of manufacturing establishments in various industries, employment, labor costs, value of shipments, capital expenditures, inventories, energy costs, and assets. (See also Census Bureau home page, http://www.census.gov/.).

Business Statistics of the United States. Courtenay M. Slater, editor. Bernan Associates. • 1999. $74.00.

For publishers addresses, refer to SOURCES CITED section at the back of the book.

Fifth edition. Based on *Business Statistics*, formerly issue by the Bureau of Economic Analysis, U. S. Department of Commerce. Provides basic data for a wide variety of U. S. industries, services, and economic indicators. Most statistics are shown annually for 29 years and monthly for the most recent four years.

Encyclopedia of American Industries. The Gale Group. • 1998. $560.00. Second edition. Two volumes. $280.00 per volume. Volume one is *Manufacturing Industries* and volume two is *Service and Non-Manufacturing Industries.* Provides the history, development, and recent status of approximately 1,000 industries. Includes statistical graphs, with industry and general indexes.

Standard & Poor's Industry Surveys. Standard & Poor's. • Semiannual. $1,800.00. Two looseleaf volumes. Includes monthly supplements. Provides detailed, individual surveys of 52 major industry groups. Each survey is revised on a semiannual basis. Also includes "Monthly Investment Review" (industry group investment analysis) and monthly "Trends & Projections" (economic analysis).

Survey of Current Business. Available from U. S. Government Printing Office. • Monthly. $49.00 per year. Issued by Bureau of Economic Analysis, U. S. Department of Commerce. Presents a wide variety of business and economic data.

TRADE/PROFESSIONAL ASSOCIATIONS

International Association of Plastic Distributors. 4707 College Blvd., Suite 105, Leawood, KS 66211. Phone: (913)345-1005 Fax: (913)345-1006 E-mail: iapd@iapd.org • URL: http://www.iapd.org.

Society of Plastics Engineers. 14 Fairfield Dr., Brookfield, CT 06804-0403. Phone: (203)775-0471 Fax: (203)775-8490 E-mail: info@4spe.org • URL: http://www.4spe.org.

Society of the Plastics Industry. 1801 K St., N.W., Suite 600K, Washington, DC 20006. Phone: (202)974-5200 Fax: (202)296-7005 E-mail: feedback@socplas.org • URL: http://www.socplas.org.

PLATING

See: METAL FINISHING

PLATINUM INDUSTRY

ABSTRACTS AND INDEXES

Nonferrous Metals Alert. Cambridge Information Group. • Monthly. $340.00 per year. Provides citations to the business and industrial literature of nonferrous metals. (Materials Business Information Series).

HANDBOOKS AND MANUALS

Jake Bernstein's New Guide to Investing in Metals. Jacob Bernstein. John Wiley and Sons, Inc. • 1991. $34.95. Covers bullion, coins, futures, options, mining stocks, and precious metal mutual funds. Includes the history of metals as an investment.

PERIODICALS AND NEWSLETTERS

Platinum Metals Review. Johnson, Matthey PLC. • Quarterly. Free. Text in English and Japanese.

STATISTICS SOURCES

Mineral Commodity Summaries. Available from U. S. Government Printing Office. • Annual. Published by the U. S. Geological Survey, Department of the Interior (http://www.usgs.gov). Contains detailed, five-year data for about 90 nonfuel minerals. Covers a wide range of statistics, including production, imports, exports, consumption, reserves, prices, tariff information, and industry employment. (Two pages are devoted to each mineral.).

Non-Ferrous Metal Data Yearbook. American Bureau of Metal Statistics. • Annual. $395.00. Provides about 200 statistical tables covering many nonferrous metals. Includes production, consumption, inventories, exports, imports, and other data.

Standard & Poor's Industry Surveys. Standard & Poor's. • Semiannual. $1,800.00. Two looseleaf volumes. Includes monthly supplements. Provides detailed, individual surveys of 52 major industry groups. Each survey is revised on a semiannual basis. Also includes "Monthly Investment Review" (industry group investment analysis) and monthly "Trends & Projections" (economic analysis).

TRADE/PROFESSIONAL ASSOCIATIONS

American Bureau of Metal Statistics. P.O. Box 805, Chatham, NJ 07928. Phone: (973)701-2299 Fax: (973)701-2152 E-mail: info@abms.com • URL: http://www.abms.com • Members are metal companies. Compiles and publishes detailed statistical data on a wide variety of nonferrous metals: aluminum, copper, gold, lead, nickel, platinum, silver, tin, titanium, uranium, zinc, and others.

PLUMBING INDUSTRY

See also: HEATING AND VENTILATION

DIRECTORIES

Directory of Building Products and Hardlines Distributors. Chain Store Guide. • Annual. $280.00. Includes hardware, houseware, and building supply distributors. Formerly *Directory of Hardline Distributors.*

The Wholesaler "Wholesaling 100". TMB Publishing, Inc. • Annual. $25.00. Provides information on the 100 leading wholesalers of plumbing, piping, heating, and air conditioning equipment.

FINANCIAL RATIOS

Almanac of Business and Industrial Financial Ratios. Leo Troy. Prentice Hall. • Annual. $99.95. Contains financial ratios derived from federal tax returns. Ratios for each of about 200 industries are arranged according to company asset size.

American Supply Association Operating Performance Report. American Supply Association. • Annual. Members, $45.00; non-members, $150.00.

Annual Statement Studies. Robert Morris Associates: The Association of Lending and Credit Risk Professiona. • Annual. Free to members; non-members, $140.00. Median and quartile financial ratios are given for over 400 kinds of manufacturing, wholesale, retail, construction, and consumer finance establishments. Data is sorted by both asset size and sales volume. Includes a clearly written "Definition of Ratios" and an alphabetical industry index.

HANDBOOKS AND MANUALS

National Plumbing Code Handbook. R. Dodge Woodson. McGraw-Hill. • 1997. $49.95. Second revised edition.

Plumbers Handbook. Howard C. Massey. Craftsman Book Co. • 1998. $32.00. Third Revised edition.

PERIODICALS AND NEWSLETTERS

Plumbing Engineer. American Society of Plumbing Engineers. TMB Publishing. • Monthly. $50.00 per year.

The Wholesaler. TMB Publishing, Inc. • Monthly. $75.00 per year. Edited for wholesalers and distributors of plumbing, piping, heating, and air conditioning equipment.

RESEARCH CENTERS AND INSTITUTES

Building Technology Center. Stevens Institute of Technology, Castle Point on the Hudson, Hoboken, NJ 07030. Phone: (201)420-5100 Fax: (201)420-5593.

STATISTICS SOURCES

Annual Survey of Manufactures. Available from U. S. Government Printing Office. • Annual. Prices vary. Issued by the U. S. Census Bureau as an interim update to the *Census of Manufactures.* Includes data on number of manufacturing establishments in various industries, employment, labor costs, value of shipments, capital expenditures, inventories, energy costs, and assets. (See also Census Bureau home page, http://www.census.gov/.).

Manufacturing Profiles. Available from U. S. Government Printing Office. • Annual. Issued by the U. S. Census Bureau. A printed consolidation of the entire *Current Industrial Report* series, presenting "all the data compiled." Contains statistics on production, shipments, inventories, consumption, exports, imports, and orders for a wide variety of manufactured products. (See also Census Bureau home page, http://www.census.gov/.).

Plumbing Fixtures. U. S. Bureau of the Census. • Quarterly and annual. Provides data on shipments: value, quantity, imports, and exports. Includes both metal and plastic fixtures. (Current Industrial Reports, MQ-34E.).

U. S. Industry and Trade Outlook: The McGraw-Hill Companies and the U.S. Department of Commerce/ International Trade Administration. Datapso Research Corp. • Annual. $69.95. Produced by the International Trade Administration, U. S. Department of Commerce, in a "public-private" partnership with DRI/McGraw-Hill and Standard & Poor's. Provides basic data, outlook for the current year, and "Long-Term Prospects" (five-year projections) for a wide variety of products and services. Includes high technology industries. Formerly *U. S. Industrial Outlook.*

TRADE/PROFESSIONAL ASSOCIATIONS

American Society of Plumbing Engineers. 3617 Thousand Oaks Blvd., No. 210, Westlake Village, CA 91362-3649. Phone: (805)495-7120 Fax: (805)495-4861 E-mail: aspehq@aol.com • URL: http://www.aspe.org.

American Supply Association. 222 Merchandise Mart, Suite 1360, Chicago, IL 60654. Phone: 800-464-0314 or (312)464-0090 Fax: (312)464-0091 E-mail: asa@asa.net • URL: http://www.asa.net.

National Association of Plumbing-Heating-Cooling Contractors. P.O. Box 6808, Falls Church, VA 22040. Phone: 800-533-7694 or (703)237-8100 Fax: (703)237-7442 E-mail: naphcc@naphcc.org • URL: http://www.naphcc.org.

Plumbing and Drainage Institute. c/o W.C. Whitehead, 45 Bristol Dr., Suite 101, South Easton, MA 02375-1916. Phone: 800-589-8956 or (508)230-3516 Fax: (508)230-3529 E-mail: info@pdionline.org • URL: http://www.pdionline.org.

PLYWOOD INDUSTRY

See also: LUMBER INDUSTRY

ABSTRACTS AND INDEXES

Forest Products Abstracts. CABI Publishing North America. • Bimonthly. $1,155.00 per year. Published in England by CABI Publishing. Provides worldwide coverage of forest products literature.

DIRECTORIES

Directory of the Wood Products Industry. Miller Freeman, Inc. • Biennial. $295.00. Lists sawmills, panelmills, logging operations, plywood products, wood products, distributors, etc. Geographic arrangement, with an index to lumber specialities. Formerly *Directory of the Forest Products Industry*.

Panel World Directory and Buyers' Guide. Hatton-Brown Publisher, Inc. • Annual. $10.00. Included with subscription to *Paper, Film and Foil Converter*. Supersedes *Plywood and Panel World Directory and Buyer's Guide*.

Where to Buy Hardwood Plywood and Veneer. Hardwood Plywood Manufacturers Association. • Annual. $20.00. Lists about 190 member manufacturers, prefinishers, and suppliers of hardwood veneer and plywood.

ENCYCLOPEDIAS AND DICTIONARIES

Illustrated Dictionary of Building Materials and Techniques: An Invaluable Sourcebook to the Tools, Terms, Materials, and Techniques Used by Building Professionals. Paul Bianchina. John Wiley and Sons, Inc. • 1993. $49.95. Contains 4,000 definitions of building and building materials terms, with 500 illustrations. Includes materials grades, measurements, and specifications.

PERIODICALS AND NEWSLETTERS

ENR Connecting the Industry Worldwide (Engineering News-Record). McGraw-Hill. • Weekly. $74.00 per year.

Panel World. Hatton-Brown Publishers, Inc. • Bimonthly. $28.00. Formerly *Plywood and Panel World*.

STATISTICS SOURCES

Annual Survey of Manufactures. Available from U. S. Government Printing Office. • Annual. Prices vary. Issued by the U. S. Census Bureau as an interim update to the *Census of Manufactures*. Includes data on number of manufacturing establishments in various industries, employment, labor costs, value of shipments, capital expenditures, inventories, energy costs, and assets. (See also Census Bureau home page, http://www.census.gov/.).

U. S. Industry and Trade Outlook: The McGraw-Hill Companies and the U.S. Department of Commerce/International Trade Administration. Datapso Research Corp. • Annual. $69.95. Produced by the International Trade Administration, U. S. Department of Commerce, in a "public-private" partnership with DRI/McGraw-Hill and Standard & Poor's. Provides basic data, outlook for the current year, and "Long-Term Prospects" (five-year projections) for a wide variety of products and services. Includes high technology industries. Formerly *U. S. Industrial Outlook*.

TRADE/PROFESSIONAL ASSOCIATIONS

APA: The Engineered Wood Association. P.O. Box 11700, Tacoma, WA 98411. Phone: (253)565-6600 Fax: (253)565-7265 • URL: http://www.apawood.org.

Engineered Wood Research Foundation. P.O. Box 11700, Tacoma, WA 98411. Phone: (253)565-6600 Fax: (253)565-7265.

Hardwood Plywood and Veneer Association. P.O. Box 2789, Reston, VA 20195-0789. Phone: (703)435-2900 Fax: (703)435-2537 E-mail: hpva@hpva.org • URL: http://www.hpva.org.

POINT-OF-PURCHASE ADVERTISING

See also: DISPLAY OF MERCHANDISE

DIRECTORIES

Creative's Illustrated Guide to P-O-P Exhibits and Promotion. Magazines Creative, Inc. • Annual. $25.00. Lists sources of point-of-purchase displays, signs, and exhibits and sources of other promotional materials and equipment. Available online.

Out-of-Home Advertising Source. SRDS. • Annual. $299.00. Provides detailed information on non-traditional or "out-of-home" advertising media: outdoor, aerial, airport, mass transit, bus benches, school, hotel, in-flight, in-store, theater, stadium, taxi, truckstop, kiosk, shopping malls, and others.

The PROMO 100 Promotion Agency Ranking. Intertec Publishing Co. • Annual. $9.95. Provides information on 100 leading product promotion agencies.

PERIODICALS AND NEWSLETTERS

Creative: The Magazine of Promotion and Marketing. Magazines Creative, Inc. • Bimonthly. $30.00 per year. Covers promotional materials, including exhibits, incentives, point-of-purchase advertising, premiums, and specialty advertising.

P-O-P Design (Point-of-Purchase): Products and News for High-Volume Pro ducers and Designers of Displays, Signs and Fixtures. Hoyt Publishing Co. • Bimonthly. $59.00 per year.

PROMO: Promotion Marketing Worldwide. Simba Information Inc. • Monthly. $65.00 per year. Edited for companies and agencies that utilize couponing, point-of-purchase advertising, special events, games, contests, premiums, product samples, and other unique promotional items.

TRADE/PROFESSIONAL ASSOCIATIONS

Point-of-Purchase Advertising International. 1660 L St., N.W., 10th Fl., Washington, DC 20036. Phone: (202)530-3000 Fax: (202)530-3030 • URL: http://www.popai.com.

POINT-OF-SALE SYSTEMS (POS)

See also: AUTOMATIC IDENTIFICATION SYSTEMS

GENERAL WORKS

Using Bar Code: Why It's Taking Over. David J. Collins and Nancy N. Whipple. Data Capture Press. • 1994. $34.95. Second edition.

DIRECTORIES

ID Systems Buyers Guide. Helmers Publishing, Inc. • Annual. Price on application. Provides information on over 750 companies manufacturing automatic identification equipment, including scanners, data collection terminals, and bar code systems.

PERIODICALS AND NEWSLETTERS

Bank Network News; News and Analysis of Shared EFT Networks. Faulkner & Gray, Inc. • Semimonthly. $395.00 per year. Newsletter.

Corporate EFT Report (Electronic Funds Tranfer). Phillips Business Information, Inc. • Biweekly. $595.00 per year. Newsletter on subject of electronic funds transfer.

Debit Card News: Newsletter for Retail Electronic Payments. Faulkner & Gray, Inc. • Monthly. $245.00 per year. Includes three special issues. Formerly *POS News*.

EFT Report (Electronic Funds Transfer). Phillips Business Information, Inc. • Biweekly. $695.00 per year. Newsletter on subject of electronic funds transfer.

STATISTICS SOURCES

Statistical Information on the Financial Services Industry. American Bankers Association. • Annual. Members, $150.00; non-members, $275.00. Presents a wide variety of data relating to banking and financial services, including consumer economics, personal finance, credit, government loans, capital markets, and international banking.

TRADE/PROFESSIONAL ASSOCIATIONS

Electronic Funds Transfer Association. 950 Herndon Parkway, Suite 390, Herndon, VA 22170. Phone: (703)435-9800 Fax: (703)435-7157 E-mail: efta@aol.com • URL: http://www.efta.org.

Uniform Code Council. 7887 Washington Village Dr., Ste. 300, Dayton, OH 45459-8605. Phone: (937)435-3870 Fax: (937)435-7317 E-mail: info@uc-council.org • URL: http://www.uc-council.org • Concerned with developing a universal product coding system to assign a unique identification number to every product sold in the United States.

OTHER SOURCES

Endpoint Express. United Communications Group (UCG). • Biweekly. $355.00 per year. Newsletter. Covers bank payment systems, including checks, electronic funds transfer (EFT), point-of-sale (POS), and automated teller machine (ATM) operations. Formerly *Bank Office Bulletin*.

POLICE EQUIPMENT

See: LAW ENFORCEMENT INDUSTRIES

POLICY MANUALS

See: PROCEDURE MANUALS

POLITICAL ECONOMY

See: ECONOMICS

POLLS, OPINION

See: PUBLIC OPINION

POLLUTION OF AIR

See: AIR POLLUTION

POLLUTION OF WATER

See: WATER POLLUTION

POLYMERS

See: CHEMICAL INDUSTRIES; PLASTICS INDUSTRY

POPCORN INDUSTRY

See: SNACK FOOD INDUSTRY

POPULATION

See also: CENSUS REPORTS; VITAL STATISTICS

GENERAL WORKS

Global Economic Prospects 2000. The World Bank, Office of the Publisher. • 1999. $25.00. "..offers an in-depth analysis of the economic prospects of developing countries.." Emphasis is on the impact of recessions and financial crises. Regional statistical data is included.

Moving Power and Money: The Politics of Census Taking. Barbara E. Bryant and William Dunn. New

Strategist Publications, Inc. • 1995. $24.95. Barbara Everitt Bryant was Director of the U. S. Census Bureau from 1989 to 1993. She provides a plan for reducing the costs of census taking, improving accuracy, and overcoming public resistance to the census.

ABSTRACTS AND INDEXES

PAIS International in Print. Public Affairs Information Service, Inc. • Monthly. $650.00 per year; cumulations three times a year. Provides topical citations to the worldwide literature of public affairs, economics, demographics, sociology, and trade. Text in English; indexed materials in English, French, German, Italian, Portuguese and Spanish.

Population Abstract of the U. S. The Gale Group. • 2000. $185.00. Historical emphasis. Includes a "breakdown of urban and rural population from the earliest census to the present.".

Social Sciences Citation Index. Institute for Scientific Information. • Three times a year. $6,900 per year. Annual cumulation. Includes *Source Index, Citation Index, Permuterm Subject Index,* and *Corporate Index.*

Social Sciences Index. H. W. Wilson Co. • Quarterly, with annual cumulation. Service basis for print edition; CD-ROM edition, $1,495 per year. Indexes more than 400 periodicals covering economics, environmental policy, government, insurance, labor, health care policy, plannning, public administration, public welfare, urban studies, women's issues, criminology, and related topics.

ALMANACS AND YEARBOOKS

Research in Population Economics. JAI Press, Inc. • Irregular. $90.25.

World Development Report. The World Bank, Office of the Publisher. • Annual. $50.00. Covers history, conditions, and trends relating to economic globalization and localization. Includes selected data from *World Development Indicators* for 132 countries or economies. Key indicators are provided for 78 additional countries or economies.

BIBLIOGRAPHIES

Census Catalog and Guide. U. S. Government Printing Office. • Annual. Lists publications and electronic media products currently available from the U. S. Bureau of the Census, along with some out of print items. Includes comprehensive title and subject indexes. Formerly *Bureau of the Census Catalog.*

Global Data Locator. George T. Kurian. Bernan Associates. • 1997. $89.00. Provides detailed descriptions of international statistical sourcebooks and electronic databases. Covers a wide variety of trade, economic, and demographic topics.

Monthly Product Announcement. U. S. Bureau of the Census, Customer Services. • Monthly. Lists Census Bureau publications and products that became available during the previous month.

CD-ROM DATABASES

PAIS on CD-ROM. Public Affairs Information Service, Inc. • Quarterly. $1,995.00 per year. Provides a CD-ROM version of the online service, *PAIS International.* Contains over 400,000 citations to the literature of contemporary social, political, and economic issues.

Social Science Source. EBSCO Publishing. • Monthly. $1,495.00 per year. Provides CD-ROM citations and abstracts to social science articles in more than 600 periodicals, with full text from 125 periodicals. Covers economics, political science, public policy, international relations, psychology, and other topics. Time period is most recent five years.

Social Sciences Citation Index: Compact Disc Edition. Institute for Scientific Information. • Quarterly. Provides CD-ROM indexing of the world's social sciences literature, including economics, business, finance, management, communications, demographics, information and library science, political science, sociology, etc. Corresponds to online *Social Scisearch* and printed *Social Sciences Citation Index.*

Social Sciences Citation Index: Compact Disc Edition with Abstracts. Institute for Scientific Information. • Quarterly. Provides CD-ROM indexing and abstracting of "significant articles" from 1,400 social science journals worldwide, with additional selections from 3,200 other journals, 1986 to date. Includes economics, business, finance, management, communications, demographics, information and library science, political science, sociology, and many other subjects.

Sourcebook America. The Gale Group. • Annual. $995.00. Produced by CACI Marketing Systems. A combination on CD-ROM of *The Sourcebook of ZIP Code Demographics* and *The Sourcebook of County Demographics.* Provides detailed population and socio-economic data (about 75 items) for each of 3,141 U. S. counties and approximately 30,000 ZIP codes, plus states, metropolitan areas, and media market areas. Includes forecasts to the year 2004.

Sourcebooks America CD-ROM. CACI Marketing Systems. • Annual. $1,250.00. Provides the CD-ROM version of *The Sourcebook of ZIP Code Demographics: Census Edition* and *The Sourcebook of County Demographics: Census Edition.*

Statistical Abstract of the United States on CD-ROM. Hoover's, Inc. • Annual. $49.95. Provides all statistics from official print version, plus expanded historical data, greater detail, and keyword searching features.

WILSONDISC: Wilson Social Sciences Abstracts. H. W. Wilson Co. • Monthly. Including unlimited online access to *Social Sciences Index* through WILSONLINE. Provides CD-ROM indexing from 1983 and abstracting from 1994 of more than 400 periodicals covering economics, area studies, community health, public administration, public welfare, urban studies, and many other topics related to the social sciences.

World Development Report [CD-ROM]. The World Bank, Office of the Publisher. • Annual. Single-user, $375.00. Network version, $750.00. CD-ROM includes the current edition of *World Development Report* and 21 previous editions.

World Marketing Data and Statistics on CD-ROM. The Gale Group. • Annual. $1,750.00. Published by Euromonitor. Provides demographic, marketing, socioeconomic, and political data on CD-ROM for each of 209 countries.

World Marketing Forecasts on CD-ROM. The Gale Group. • Annual. $2,500.00. Produced by Euromonitor. Provides detailed forecast data for the years to 2012 on CD-ROM for 54 countries in all parts of the world. Covers a wide range of social, demographic, economic, and market factors. Includes specific forecasts for many kinds of consumer products.

DIRECTORIES

Where to Write for Vital Records: Births, Deaths, Marriages, and Divorces. Available from U. S. Government Printing Office. • 1999. $3.00. Issued by the National Center for Health Statistics, U. S. Department of Health and Human Services. Arranged by state. Provides addresses, telephone numbers, and cost of copies for various kinds of vital records or certificates. (DHHS Publication No. PHS 93-1142.).

HANDBOOKS AND MANUALS

Comparative Guide to American Suburbs. Grey House Publishing. • 2001. $130.00. Second edition. Contains detailed profiles of 1,800 suburban communities having a population of 10,000 or more and located within the 50 largest metropolitan areas. Includes ranking tables for income, unemployment, new housing permits, home prices, and crime, as well as information on school districts. (Universal Reference Publications.).

Nations of the World: A Political, Economic, and Business Handbook. Grey House Publishing. • 2000. $135.00. Includes descriptive data on economic characteristics, population, gross domestic product (GDP), banking, inflation, agriculture, tourism, and other factors. Covers "all the nations of the world.".

INTERNET DATABASES

Bureau of Labor Statistics (BLS). U. S. Department of Labor, Bureau of Labor Statistics. Phone: (202)523-1092 E-mail: labstat.helpdesk@bls.gov • URL: http://www.bls.gov • Web site provides a great variety of employment, wage, price, and economic data. Some links are "Data," "Economy at a Glance," "Keyword Search of BLS Web Pages," "Regional Information," and "Other Statistical Sites." Fees: Free.

Fedstats. Federal Interagency Council on Statistical Policy. Phone: (202)395-7254 • URL: http://www.fedstats.gov • Web site features an efficient search facility for full-text statistics produced by more than 70 federal agencies, including the Census Bureau, the Bureau of Economic Analysis, and the Bureau of Labor Statistics. Boolean searches can be made within one agency or for all agencies combined. Links are offered to international statistical bureaus, including the UN, IMF, OECD, UNESCO, Eurostat, and 20 individual countries. Fees: Free.

ONLINE DATABASES

EconBase: Time Series and Forecasts. WEFA, Inc. • Presents online econometric data for business conditions, economics, demographics, industry, finance, employment, household income, interest rates, prices, etc. Includes two-year forecasts for a wide range of economic indicators. Time span is 1948 to date, with monthly updates. Inquire as to online cost and availability.

Euromonitor Market Research. Euromonitor International. • Provides the complete text online of Euromonitor market analysis reports. Covers consumer goods market research data for all major countries, with emphasis on specific product categories. Time period is current. Continuous updating. Inquire as to online cost and availability.

PAIS International. Public Affairs Information Service, Inc. • Corresponds to the former printed publications, *PAIS Bulletin* (1976-90) and *PAIS Foreign Language Index* (1972-90), and to the current *PAIS International in Print* (1991 to date). Covers economic, political, and sociological material appearing in periodicals, books, government documents, and other publications. Updating is monthly. Inquire as to online cost and availability.

Social Scisearch. Institute for Scientific Information. • Broad, multidisciplinary index to the literature of the social sciences, 1972 to present. Weekly updates. Worldwide coverage. Inquire as to online cost and availability.

Wilson Social Sciences Abstracts Online. H. W. Wilson Co. • Provides online abstracting and indexing of more than 415 periodicals covering area studies, community health, public administration, public welfare, urban studies, and many other social science topics. Time period is 1994 to date for abstracts and 1983 to date for indexing, with updates monthly. Inquire as to online cost and availability.

PERIODICALS AND NEWSLETTERS

American Demographics: Consumer Trends for Business Leaders. Intertec Publishing Co. • Monthly. $69.00 per year.

Demography. Population Association of America. • Quarterly. $85.00 per year.

Population Bulletin. Population Reference Bureau, Inc. • Quarterly. $7.00 per issue.

The ZPG Reporter. Zero Population Growth, Inc. • Bimonthly. $25.00 per year. Special reports on global issues and domestic issues as they relate to over population and its social, environmental and economic consequences. 20180.

RESEARCH CENTERS AND INSTITUTES

Center for Population and Development Studies. Harvard University. Nine Bow St., Cambridge, MA 02138. Phone: (617)495-2021 Fax: (617)495-5418 E-mail: cpds@hsph.harvard.edu • URL: http://www.hsph.harvard.edu/hcpds.

Population Research Center. University of Chicago. 1155 E. 60th St., Chicago, IL 60637. Phone: (773)256-6315 Fax: (773)256-6313 E-mail: marpari@apc.uchicago.edu • URL: http://www.spc.uchicago.edu/orgs/prc.

Populations Studies Center. University of Michigan. P.O. Box 1248, Ann Arbor, MI 48106-1248. Phone: (734)998-7275 Fax: (734)998-7415 E-mail: david1@umich.edu • URL: http://www.psc.lsa.umich.edu.

STATISTICS SOURCES

American Business Climate and Economic Profiles. The Gale Group. • 1993. $135.00. Provides business, industrial, demographic, and economic figures for all states and 300 metropolitan areas. Includes production, taxation, population, growth rates, labor force data, incomes, total sales, etc.

American Places Dictionary: A Guide to 45,000 Populated Places, Natural Features, and Other United States Places. Frank R. Abate, editor. Omnigraphics, Inc. • 1994. $400.00. Four regional volumes: Northeast, South, Midwest, and West. Provides statistical data and other information on 45,000 U. S. cities, towns, townships, boroughs, and villages. Includes detailed state profiles, county profiles, and more than 10,000 name origins. Arranged by state, then by county. (Individual regional volumes are available at $100.00.).

Consumer Canada 1996. Available from The Gale Group. • 1996. $750.00. Published by Euromonitor. Provides consumer market, socioeconomic, and demographic data for Canada. Includes consumer market size (volume and value) for many specific kinds of products.

Consumer International 2000/2001. Available from The Gale Group. • 1998. $1,190.00. Seventh edition. Published by Euromonitor. Contains extensive consumer market, economic, and demographic data for 27 major, non-European countries, including the U. S. and Canada. Includes consumer market size (volume and value) for 150 product types in 14 categories (food, clothing, automobiles, cosmetics, appliances, etc.).

County and City Extra: Annual Metro, City and County Data Book. Mark Littman and Deirdre A. Gaquin. Bernan Press. • 1999. $109.00. Updates and augments data published irregularly in print form by the U. S. Census Bureau in *County and City Data Book.* Covers "every state, county, metropolitan area, and congressional district in the United States, as well as all U. S. cities with a 1990 population of 25,000 or more." Contains a wide range tic maps.

Current Population Reports: Household Economic Studies, Series P-70. Available from U. S. Government Printing Office. • Irregular. $16.00 per year. Issued by the U.S. Bureau of the Census (http://www.census.gov). Each issue covers a special topic relating to household socioeconomic characteristics.

Current Population Reports: Population Characteristics, Special Studies, and Consumer Income, Series P-20, P-23, and P-60. Available from U. S. Government Printing Office. • Irregular. $39.00 per year. Issued by the U.S. Bureau of the Census (http://www.census.gov). Each issue covers a special topic relating to population or income. Series P-20, *Population Characteristics*, provides statistical studies on such items as mobility, fertility, education, and marital status. Series P-23, *Special Studies*, consists of occasional reports on methodology. Series P-60, *Consumer Income*, publishes reports on income in relation to age, sex, education, occupation, family size, etc.

Current Population Reports: Population Estimates and Projections, Series P-25. Available from U. S. Government Printing Office. • Irregular. $14.00 per year. Issued by the U.S. Bureau of the Census (http://www.census.gov). Provides monthly, mid-year, and annual population estimates, including data for states and Standard Metropolitan Statistical Areas. Projections are given for the U.S. population in future years.

Demographic Yearbook. United Nations, Dept. of Economic and Social Affairs. United Nations Publications. • Annual. $125.00. Text in English and French.

Demographics USA: County Edition. Market Statistics. • Annual. $435.00. Contains 200 statistical series for each of 3,000 counties. Includes population, household income, employment, retail sales, and consumer expenditures. Also provides Effective Buying Income, Buying Power Index, and data summaries by Metro Market, Media Market, and State. (CD-ROM version is available.).

Demographics USA: ZIP Edition. Market Statistics. • Annual. $435.00. Contains 50 statistical series for each of 40,000 ZIP codes. Includes population, household income, employment, retail sales, and consumer expenditures. Also provides Effective Buying Income, Business Characteristics, and data summaries by state, region, and the first three digits of ZIP codes. (CD-ROM version is available.).

European Marketing Forecasts 2001. Available from The Gale Group. • 2000. $1,190.00. Third edition. Published by Euromonitor. Contains demographic, economic, and market forecasts for the countries of Europe to the year 2010. Forecasts include market-size data for 15 consumer product sectors (food, clothing, automobiles, consumer electronics, etc.).

Gale City and Metro Rankings Reporter. The Gale Group. • 1996. $134.00. Second edition. Provides about 3,000 statistical ranking tables covering more than 1,500 U. S. cities and Metropolitan Statistical Areas. Covers economic, demographic, social, governmental, and cultural factors. Sources are private studies and government data.

Gale Country and World Rankings Reporter. The Gale Group. • 1997. $135.00. Second edition. Provides about 3,000 statistical ranking tables and charts covering more than 235 nations. Sources include the United Nations and various government publications.

Gale State Rankings Reporter. The Gale Group. • 1996. $110.00. Second edition Provides 3,000 ranked lists of states under 35 subject headings. Sources are newspapers, periodicals, books, research institute publications, and government publications.

Geographic Reference Report: Annual Report of Costs, Wages, salaries, and Human Resource Statistics for the United States and Canada. ERI. • Annual. $389.00. Provides demographic and other data for each of 298 North American metropolian areas, including local salaries, wage differentials, cost-of-living, housing costs, income taxation, employment, unemployment, population, major employers, crime rates, weather, etc.

Handbook of U. S. Labor Statistics: Employment, Earnings, Prices, Productivity, and Other Labor Data. Eva E. Jacobs, editor. Bernan Associates. • 1999. $74.00. Based on *Handbook of Labor Statistics*, formerly issued by the Bureau of Labor Statistics, U. S. Department of Labor. Includes the Bureau's projections of employment in the U. S. by industry and occupation. Provides a wide variety of data on the work force, prices, fringe benefits, and consumer expenditures.

International Marketing Forecasts 2001. Available from The Gale Group. • 2000. $1,090.00. Third edition. Published by Euromonitor. Contains demographic, economic, and market forecasts to the year 2010 for major, non-European countries, including the U. S. and Canada. Forecasts include market-size data for 15 consumer product sectors, such as food, clothing, and automobiles.

Labour Force Statistics, 1977/1997: 1998 Edition. Organization for Economic Cooperation and Development. Available from OECD Publications and Information Center. • 1999. $98.00. Provides 21 years of data for OECD member countries on population, employment, unemployment, civilian labor force, armed forces, and other labor factors.

Metropolitan Life Insurance Co. Statistical Bulletin SB. Metropolitan Life Insurance Co. • Quarterly. Individuals, $50.00 per year. Covers a wide range of social, economic and demographic health concerns.

Monthly Bulletin of Statistics. United Nations Publications. • Monthly. $295.00 per year. Provides current data for about 200 countries on a wide variety of economic, industrial, and demographic subjects. Compiled by United Nations Statistical Office.

Moving and Relocation Sourcebook and Directory: Reference Guide to the 100 Largest Metropolitan Areas in the United States. Kay Gill, editor. Omnigraphics, Inc. • 1998. $185.00. Second edition. Provides extensive statistical and other descriptive data for the 100 largest metropolitan areas in the U. S. Includes maps and a discussion of factors to be considered when relocating.

Places, Towns, and Townships, 1998. Deirdre A. Gaquin and Richard W. Dodge, editors. Bernan Press. • 1997. $89.00. Second edition. Presents demographic and economic statistics from the U. S. Census Bureau and other government sources for places, cities, towns, villages, census designated places, and minor civil divisions. Contains more than 60 data categories.

Population and Vital Statistics Report. United Nations Publications. • Quarterly. $40.00 per year. Contains worldwide demographic statistics.

Population of States and Counties of the United States: 1790-1990. Available from National Technical Information Service. • 1996. $35.00. Issued by the U. S. Census Bureau (http://www.census.gov). Provides data on the number of inhabitants of the U. S., states, territories, and counties according to 21 decennial censuses from 1790 to 1990. Includes descriptions of county origins and lists prior county names, where applicable.

Population Projections of the United States by Age, Sex, Race, and Hispanic Origin: 1995 to 2050. Available from U. S. Government Printing Office. •

1996. $8.50. Issued by the U. S. Bureau of the Census (http://www.census.gov). Contains charts and tables. Appendixes include detailed data on fertility rates by age, life expectancy, immigration, and armed forces population. (Current Population Reports, P25-1130.).

Quarterly Labour Force Statistics. Organization for Economic Cooperation and Development. Available from OECD Publications and Information Center. • Quarterly. $60.00 per year. Provides current data for OECD member countries on population, employment, unemployment, civilian labor force, armed forces, and other labor factors.

Social Statistics of the United States. Mark S. Littman, editor. Bernan Press. • 2000. $65.00. Includes statistical data on population growth, labor force, occupations, environmental trends, leisure time use, income, poverty, taxes, and other economic or demographic topics.

The Sourcebook of ZIP Code Demographics. Available from The Gale Group. • 2000. $495.00. 15th edition. Published by CACI Marketing Systems. Presents detailed statistical profiles of every ZIP code in America, based on the 1990 census. Each profile contains data on more than 70 variables.

State and Metropolitan Area Data Book. Available from U. S. Government Printing Office. • 1998. $31.00. Issued by the U. S. Bureau of the Census. Presents a wide variety of statistical data for U. S. regions, states, counties, metropolitan areas, and central cities, with ranking tables. Time period is 1970 to 1990.

State Profiles: The Population and Economy of Each U. S. State. Courtenay Slater and Martha Davis, editors. Bernan Press. • 1999. $74.00. Presents charts, tables, and text in an eight-page profile for each state. Covers population, labor force, income, poverty, employment, wages, industry, trade, housing, education, health, taxes, and government finances.

Statistical Abstract of the United States. Available from U. S. Government Printing Office. • Annual. $51.00. Issued by the U. S. Bureau of the Census.

Statistical Abstract of the World. The Gale Group. • 1997. $80.00. Third edition. Provides data on a wide variety of economic, social, and political topics for about 200 countries. Arranged by country.

Statistical Forecasts of the United States. The Gale Group. • 1995. $99.00. Second edition. Provides both long-term and short-term statistical forecasts relating to basic items in the U. S.: population, employment, labor, crime, education, and health care. Data in the form of charts, graphs, and tables has been taken from a wide variety of government and private sources. Includes a subject index and an "Index of Forecast by Year.".

Statistical Handbook on the American Family. Bruce A. Chadwick and Tim B. Heaton, editors. Oryx Press. • 1998. $65.00. Includes data on education, health, politics, employment, expenditures, social characteristics, the elderly, and women in the labor force. Historical statistics on marriage, birth, and divorce are shown from 1900 on. A list of sources and a subject index are provided. (Statistical Handbook Series).

Statistical Record of the Environment. The Gale Group. • 1996. $120.00. Third edition. Provides over 875 charts, tables, and graphs of major environmental statistics, arranged by subject. Covers population growth, hazardous waste, nuclear energy, acid rain, pesticides, and other subjects related to the environment. A keyword index is included.

Statistical Yearbook. United Nations Publications. • Annual. $125.00. Contains statistics for about 200 countries on a wide variety of economic, industrial, and demographic topics. Compiled by United Nations Statistical Office.

UNESCO Statistical Yearbook. Bernan Press. • Annual. $95.00. Co-published by Bernan Press and the United Nations Educational, Scientific, and Cultural Organization (http://www.unesco.org). Presents statistical data from more than 200 countries on education, technology, research, broadcasting, cinema, book publishing, newspapers, libraries, museums, and population. Includes charts, maps, and graphs.

United States Census of Population. Bureau of the Census, U.S. Department of Commerce. Available from U.S. Government Printing Office. • Quinquennial.

World Bank Atlas. The World Bank, Office of the Publisher. • Annual. Price on application. Contains "color maps, charts, and graphs representing the main social, economic, and environmental indicators for 209 countries and territories" (publisher).

World Development Indicators. World Bank, The Office of the Publisher. • Annual. $60.00. Provides data and information on the people, economy, environment, and markets of 148 countries. Emphasis is on statistics relating to major development issues.

World Factbook. U.S. National Technical Information Service. • Annual. $83.00. Prepared by the Central Intelligence Agency. For all countries of the world, provides current economic, demographic, geographic, communications, government, defense force, and illicit drug trade information (where applicable).

World Population Chart. United Nations Publications. • 1998. $5.95. Shows population, birth rate, death rate, etc., for all countries of the world, with forecasts to the year 2015 and to the year 2050.

World Population Data Sheet. Population Reference Bureau, Inc. • Annual. $3.50.

World Statistics Pocketbook. United Nations Publications. • Annual. $10.00. Presents basic economic, social, and environmental indicators for about 200 countries and areas. Covers more than 50 items relating to population, economic activity, labor force, agriculture, industry, energy, trade, transportation, communication, education, tourism, and the environment. Statistical sources are noted.

TRADE/PROFESSIONAL ASSOCIATIONS

Population Action International. 1120 19th St., N.W., Suite 550, Washington, DC 20036. Phone: (202)659-1833 Fax: (202)293-1795 • URL: http://www.populationaction.org.

Population Association of America. 721 Ellsworth Dr., Suite 303, Silver Spring, MD 20910. Phone: (301)565-6710 Fax: (301)565-7850 E-mail: info@popassoc.org • URL: http://www.popassoc.org.

Population Council. One Dag Hammerskjold Plaza, New York, NY 10017. Phone: (212)339-0500 Fax: (212)755-6052 E-mail: pubinfo@popcouncil.org • URL: http://www.popcouncil.org.

Population Reference Bureau. 1875 Connecticut Ave., N.W., Suite 520, Washington, DC 20009. Phone: 800-877-9881 or (202)483-1100 Fax: (202)328-3937 E-mail: popref@prb.org • URL: http://www.prb.org.

World Population Society. 1050 17th St., N.W., Suite 1000, Washington, DC 20036. Phone: (202)898-1303 Fax: (202)775-9694.

Zero Population Growth-Seattle Chapter. 4426 Burke Ave., N, Seattle, WA 98103. Phone: 800-767-1956 or (206)548-0152 Fax: (206)548-0152 E-mail: zpgseattle@earthlink.net • URL: http://www.cn.org/zpg.

OTHER SOURCES

MarketingClick Network: American Demographics. Intertec Publishing, a Primedia Co. • Web site provides full-text articles from *American Demographics*, *Marketing Tools*, and *Forecast*, with keyword searching. The *Marketing Tools Directory* can also be searched online, listing suppliers of products, information, and services for advertising, market research, and marketing. Fees: Free.

Omni Gazetteer of the United States of America: A Guide to 1,500,000 Place Names in the United States and Territories. Frank R. Abate, editor. Omnigraphics, Inc. • 1991. $3,025.00. 11 volumes. Comprehensive listing of cities, towns, suburbs, villages, boroughs, structures, facilities, locales, historic places, and named geographic features. Population is shown where applicable. Individual regional volumes are available at $275.00.

Trends in International Migration. Organization for Economic Cooperation and Development. • Annual. $59.00. Contains detailed data on population migration flows, channels of immigration, and migrant nationalities. Includes demographic analysis.

The World Economy: A Millennial Perspective. Angus Maddison. Organization for Economic Cooperation and Development. • 2001. $63.00. "...covers the development of the entire world economy over the past 2000 years," including data on world population and gross domestic product (GDP) since the year 1000, and exports since 1820. Focuses primarily on the disparity in economic performance among nations over the very long term. More than 200 statistical tables and figures are provided (detailed information available at http://www.theworldeconomy.org).

World Population Projections to 2150. United Nations Publications. • 1998. $15.00. Presents very long-range population projections for eight major areas of the world: Africa, Asia, China, Europe, India, Latin America, North America, and Oceania.

Zip Code Mapbook of Metropolitan Areas. CACI Marketing Systems. • 1992. $195.00. Second edition. Contains Zip Code two-color maps of 326 metropolitan areas. Includes summary statistical profiles of each area: population characteristics, employment, housing, and income.

PORCELAIN INDUSTRY

See: POTTERY INDUSTRY

PORK

See: SWINE INDUSTRY

PORT AUTHORITIES

See: PORTS

PORTABLE COMPUTERS

ABSTRACTS AND INDEXES

Business Periodicals Index. H. W. Wilson Co. • Monthly, except August, with quarterly and annual cumulations. Service basis for print edition; CD-ROM edition, $1,495.00 per year.

CompuMath Citation Index. Institute for Scientific Information. • Three times a year. $1,090.00 per year. Provides citations to the worldwide literature of computer science and mathematics.

Computer and Information Systems Abstracts Journal: An Abstract Journal Pertaining to the Theory, Design, Fabrication and Application of Computer and Information Systems. Cambridge Information Group. • Monthly. $1,045 per year.

Computer Literature Index: A Subject/Author Index to Computer and Data Processing Literature. Applied Computer Research, Inc. • Quarterly, with annual cumulation. $245.00 per year. Contains brief abstracts of book and periodical literature covering all phases of computing, including approximately 70 specific application areas.

Microcomputer Abstracts. Information Today, Inc. • Quarterly. $225.00 per year. Provides abstracts covering a wide variety of personal and business microcomputer literature. Formerly *Microcomputer Index.*

BIBLIOGRAPHIES

Computing Information Directory: Comprehensive Guide to the Computing and Computer Engineering Literature. Peter A. Hildebrandt, Inc. • Annual. $229.95. Describes computer journals, newsletters, handbooks, dictionaries, indexing services, review resources, directories, and other computer information sources. Includes a directory of publishers and a master subject index.

CD-ROM DATABASES

ABI/INFORM Global. Bell & Howell Information and Learning. • Monthly. $6,500.00 per year. Provides CD-ROM indexing and abstracting of worldwide business literature appearing in over 1,200 periodicals for the most recent five years. Archival discs are available from 1971. Formerly *ABI/INFORM OnDisc.*

Computer Select. The Gale Group. • Monthly. $1,250.00 per year. Provides one year of full-text on CD-ROM for 120 leading computer-related publications. Also includes 70,000 product specifications and brief profiles of 13,000 computer product vendors and manufacturers.

WILSONDISC: Wilson Business Abstracts. H. W. Wilson Co. • Monthly. $2,495.00 per year, including unlimited online access to *Wilson Business Abstracts* through WILSONLINE. Provides CD-ROM "cover-to-cover" abstracting and indexing of over 600 prominent business periodicals. Indexing is from 1982, abstracting from 1990. (*Business Periodicals Index* without abstracts is available on CD-ROM at $1,495 per year.).

DIRECTORIES

Data Sources: The Comprehensive Guide to the Data Processing Industry Hardware, Data Communications Products, Software, Company Profiles. The Gale Group. • Semiannual. $495.00 per year. Two volumes. Describes hardware and software for all computer operating sysems, including prices and technical details. Lists about 75,000 products from 14,000 suppliers. Industry-specific software applications are described.

Essential Business Buyer's Guide, from Cellular Services and Overnight Mail to Internet Access Providers, 401(k) Plans, and Desktop Computers: The Ultimate Guide to Buying Office Equipment, Products, and Services. Sourcebooks, Inc. • 1996. $18.95. Compiled by the staff of *Business Consumer Guide.* Lists recommended brands of office equipment.

Laptop Buyer's Guide and Handbook. Bedford Communications, Inc. • Monthly. $18.00 per year. Contains informative articles and critical reviews of laptop, notebook, subnotebook, and handheld computers. Includes portable peripheral equipment, such as printers and scanners. Directory information includes company profiles (major manufacturers), product comparison charts, street price guide, list of manufacturers, and list of dealers.

INTERNET DATABASES

InfoTech Trends. Data Analysis Group. Phone: (707)894-9100 Fax: (707)486-5618 E-mail: support@infotechtrends.com • URL: http://www.infotechtrends.com • Web site provides both free and fee-based market research data on the information technology industry, including computers, peripherals, telecommunications, the Internet, software, CD-ROM/DVD, e-commerce, and workstations. Fees: Free for current (most recent year) data; more extensive information has various fee structures. Formerly *Computer Industry Forecasts.*

Wired News. Wired Digital, Inc. Phone: (415)276-8400 Fax: (415)276-8499 E-mail: newsfeedback@wired.com • URL: http://www.wired.com • Provides summaries and full-text of "Top Stories" relating to the Internet, computers, multimedia, telecommunications, and the electronic information industry in general. These news stories are placed in the broad categories of Politics, Business, Culture, and Technology. Affiliated with *Wired* magazine. Fees: Free.

ONLINE DATABASES

ABI/INFORM. Bell & Howell Information and Learning. • Provides online indexing to business-related material occurring in over 1,000 periodicals from 1971 to the present. Inquire as to online cost and availability.

Computer Database. The Gale Group. • Provides online citations with abstracts to material appearing in about 150 trade journals and newsletters in the subject areas of computers, telecommunications, and electronics. Time period is 1983 to date, with weekly updates. Inquire as to online cost and availability.

Hard Sciences. Cambridge Scientific Abstracts. • Provides the online version of *Computer and Information Systems Abstracts, Electronics and Communications Abstracts, Health and Safety Science Abstracts, ISMEC: Mechanical Engineering Abstracts (Information Service in Mechanical Engineering)* and *Solid State and Superconductivity Abstracts.* Time period is 1981 to date, with monthly updates. Inquire as to online cost and availability.

Internet and Personal Computing Abstracts. Information Today, Inc. • Contains abstracts covering a wide variety of personal and business microcomputer literature appearing in more than 100 journals and popular magazines. Time period is 1981 to date, with monthly updates. Formerly *Microcomputer Index.* Inquire as to online cost and availability.

PROMT: Predicasts Overview of Markets and Technology. The Gale Group. • Companies, products, applied technologies and markets. U.S. and international literature coverage, 1972 to date. Inquire as to online cost and availability. Provides abstracts from more than 1,600 publications. Weekly updates.

Trade & Industry Index. The Gale Group. • Provides indexing of business periodicals, January 1981 to date. Daily updates. (Full text articles from some periodicals are available online, 1983 to date, in the companion database, *Trade & Industry ASAP.*) Inquire as to online cost and availability.

Wilson Business Abstracts Online. H. W. Wilson Co. • Indexes and abstracts 600 major business periodicals, plus the *Wall Street Journal* and the business section of the *New York Times.* Indexing is from 1982, abstracting from 1990, with the two newspapers included from 1993. Updated weekly. Inquire as to online cost and availability. (*Business Periodicals Index* without abstracts is also available online.).

PERIODICALS AND NEWSLETTERS

Mobile Computing and Communication. EMAP USA. • Monthly. $11.97 per year. Covers cellular phones, notebook computers, and other portable electronic items. New products are featured. Formerly *Mobile Office.*

STATISTICS SOURCES

U. S. Industry and Trade Outlook: The McGraw-Hill Companies and the U.S. Department of Commerce/ International Trade Administration. Datapso Research Corp. • Annual. $69.95. Produced by the International Trade Administration, U. S. Department of Commerce, in a "public-private" partnership with DRI/McGraw-Hill and Standard & Poor's. Provides basic data, outlook for the current year, and "Long-Term Prospects" (five-year projections) for a wide variety of products and services. Includes high technology industries. Formerly *U. S. Industrial Outlook.*

TRADE/PROFESSIONAL ASSOCIATIONS

Computing Technology Industry Association. 450 E. 22nd St., Suite 230, Lombard, IL 60148-6158. Phone: (630)268-1818 Fax: (630)268-1384 E-mail: info@comptia.org • URL: http://www.comptia.org • Members are resellers of various kinds of microcomputers and computer equipment.

Information Technology Industry Council. 1250 Eye St., N.W., Suite 200, Washington, DC 20005. Phone: (202)737-8888 Fax: (202)638-4922 E-mail: webmaster@itic.org • URL: http://www.itic.org.

OTHER SOURCES

Business & Company Resource Center. The Gale Group. • Fee-based Web site provides a wide range of business, industry, and specific company information. Access is offered to trade journal articles, market research data, insider trading activity, major shareholder data, corporate histories, emerging technology reports, corporate earnings estimates, press releases, and other sources. Provides detailed company profiles, industry overviews, and rankings. Offers integration of Predicasts PROMT, Newsletters ASAP, Investext Plus, Business Index ASAP, Brands and Their Companies, and other databases (many have full text).

PORTABLE DATABASES

See: OPTICAL DISK STORAGE DEVICES

PORTFOLIO MANAGEMENT

See: INSTITUTIONAL INVESTMENTS

PORTLAND CEMENT

See: CEMENT INDUSTRY

PORTS

GENERAL WORKS

Port Engineering. Per Bruun. Gulf Publishing Co. • 1989. Fourth edition. Two volumes. Vol. 1, $195.00; Volume 2, $195.00.

Port Planning and Development. Ernst G. Frankel. John Wiley and Sons, Inc. • 1987. $200.00.

BIBLIOGRAPHIES

Waterfront Revitalization. Eric J. Fournier. Sage Publications, Inc. • 1994. $10.00. (CPL Bibliographies Series, No. 310).

DIRECTORIES

U.S. Custom House Guide. Commonwealth Business Media. • Annual. $475.00. Quarterly supplements. List of ports having custom facilities, customs officials, port authorities, chambers of commerce, embassies and consulates, foreign trade zones, and other organizations; related trade services.

ENCYCLOPEDIAS AND DICTIONARIES

Exporters' Encyclopedia. Dun and Bradstreet Information Services. • 1995. $495.00. Lease basis.

HANDBOOKS AND MANUALS

Fairplay Ports Guide. Available from Fairplay Publications, Inc. • Annual. $425.00. Four volumes (CD-ROM is included). Published in the UK by Lloyd's Register-Fairplay Ltd. Provides detailed information about 6,500 worldwide ports and terminals. Includes more than 3,500 port plans and port photographs.

Maritime Guide. Available from Fairplay Publications, Inc. • Annual. $232.00. Published in the UK by Lloyd's Register-Fairplay Ltd. Serves as a worldwide directory of maritime services, equipment, builders, and manufacturers. Provides information on dry docks, ports, harbours, pontoons, docking installations, shipbuilders, marine engine builders, boilermakers, etc. Includes world maps and a gazetteer.

RESEARCH CENTERS AND INSTITUTES

National Ports and Waterways Institute. Louisiana State University, 2300 Claredon Blvd., Suite 300, Arlington, VA 22201. Phone: (703)276-7101 Fax: (703)276-7102 E-mail: npwi@seas.gwu.edu • URL: http://www.members.tripod.com/~npwi.

TRADE/PROFESSIONAL ASSOCIATIONS

American Association of Port Authorities. 1010 Duke St., Alexandria, VA 22314-3589. Phone: (703)684-5700 Fax: (703)684-6321 E-mail: info@aapa-ports.org • URL: http://www.aapa-ports.org.

International Association of Ports and Harbors. New Pier Takeshiba, N. Tower, 5th Fl., 1-11-1 Kaigan, Minato-ku, Tokyo 105-0022, Japan.

OTHER SOURCES

Lloyd's Maritime Atlas of World Ports and Shipping Places. Available from Informa Publishing Group Ltd. • Annual. $119.00. Published in the UK by Lloyd's List (http://www.lloydslist.com). Contains more than 70 pages of world, ocean, regional, and port maps in color. Provides additional information for the planning of world shipping routes, including data on distances, port facilities, recurring weather hazards at sea, international load line zones, and sailing times.

Lloyd's Port Management. Available from Informa Publishing Group Ltd. • Quarterly. $135.00 per year. Published in the UK by Lloyd's List (http://www.lloydslist.com). Covers port management issues for port operators and users.

Ports of the World. Available from Informa Publishing Group Ltd. • Annual. $399.00. Published in the UK by Lloyd's List (http://www.lloydslist.com). Provides detailed information on more than 2,600 ports worldwide.

POSITIONS

See: OCCUPATIONS

POST EXCHANGES

PERIODICALS AND NEWSLETTERS

Exchange and Commissary News. Executive Business Media, Inc. • Monthly. $95.00 per year.

Military Market: Magazine for the Military Retail System. Army Times Publishing Co. • Monthly. $79.00 per year. Aimed at officials who buy for and operate military base stores. *Buyers Guide* and *Almanac and Directory* available, $10.00 each.

Navy Supply Corps Newsletter. Available from U. S. Government Printing Office. • Bimonthly. $20.00 per year. Newsletter issued by U. S. Navy Supply Systems Command. Provides news of Navy supplies and stores activities.

POSTAL SERVICES

BIBLIOGRAPHIES

Postal Service. Available from U. S. Government Printing Office. • Annual. Free. Issued by the Superintendent of Documents. A list of government publications on mail services and the post office. (Subject Bibliography No. 169.).

DIRECTORIES

Better Buys for Business: The Independent Consumer Guide to Office Equipment. What to Buy for Business, Inc. • 10 times a year. $134.00 per year. Each issue is on a particular office product, with detailed evaluation of specific models: 1. Low-Volume Copier Guide, 2. Mid-Volume Copier Guide, 3. High-Volume Copier Guide, 4. Plain Paper Fax and Low-Volume Multifunctional Guide, 5. Mid/High-Volume Multifunctional Guide, 6. Laser Printer Guide, 7. Color Printer and Color Copier Guide, 8. Scan-to-File Guide, 9. Business Phone Systems Guide, 10. Postage Meter Guide, with a Short Guide to Shredders.

Direct Marketing List Source. SRDS. • Bimonthly. $542.00 per year. Provides detailed information and rates for business, farm, and consumer mailing lists (U. S., Canadian, and international). Includes current postal information and directories of list brokers, compilers, and managers. Formerly *Direct Mail List Rates and Data.*

National Five Digit Zip Code and Post Office Directory. U.S. Postal Service. • Annual. Two volumes. Formerly *National Zip Code and Post Office Directory-.*

HANDBOOKS AND MANUALS

Domestic Mail Manual. Available from U. S. Government Printing Office. • Loseleaf. $22.00 per year. Issued by U. S. Postal Service. Contains rates, regulations, classes of mail, special services, etc., for mail within the U. S.

International Mail Manual. Available from U. S. Government Printing Office. • Semiannual. $36.00 per year. Issued by U. S. Postal Service. Contains rates, regulations, classes of mail, special services, etc., for mail sent from the U. S. to foreign countries.

Mailing Services. Entrepreneur Media, Inc. • Looseleaf. $59.50. A practical guide to starting a mailing services business. Covers profit potential, start-up costs, market size evaluation, owner's time required, site selection, pricing, accounting, advertising, promotion, etc. (Start-Up Business Guide No. E1354.).

INTERNET DATABASES

United States Postal Service: Make Your Mark. U. S. Postal Service. Phone: (202)268-2000 E-mail: webmaster@email.usps.gov • URL: http://www.usps.gov • Web site contains detailed information on U. S. mail services and post offices, including ZIP codes, postage rates, stamps, addressing, Express Mail tracking, and consumer postal information in general. Links are provided to the State Department for passport procedures and to the IRS for tax forms.

PERIODICALS AND NEWSLETTERS

Postal Bulletin. Available from U. S. Government Printing Office. • Biweekly. $140.00 per year. Issued by the United States Postal Service. Contains orders, instructions, and information relating to U. S. mail service.

Postal World. United Communications Group. • Biweekly. $349.00 per year. Newsletter for mail users.

STATISTICS SOURCES

Annual Report of Postmaster General. U.S. Postal Service. • Annual.

U.S. Postal Service Revenue and Cost Analysis Report. U.S. Postal Service. • Annual.

TRADE/PROFESSIONAL ASSOCIATIONS

Advertising Mail Marketing Association. 1901 N. Fort Myer Dr., Ste. 401, Arlington, VA 22209-1609. Phone: (703)524-0096 Fax: (703)524-1871 E-mail: genedp@amma.org • URL: http://www.amma.org.

Association of Paid Circulation Publications. c/o Kim Scott, P.O. Box 10669, Rockville, MD 20849-0669. Phone: (301)260-1646 Fax: (301)424-1253.

Parcel Shippers Association. 1211 Connecticut Ave., N.W., Suite 610, Washington, DC 20036-2701. Phone: (202)296-3690 Fax: (202)296-0343.

OTHER SOURCES

Bullinger's Postal and Shippers Guide for the United States and Canada. Albery Leland Publishing. • Annual. $375.00. Approximately 260,000 communities in the United States and Canada.

Zip Code Mapbook of Metropolitan Areas. CACI Marketing Systems. • 1992. $195.00. Second edition. Contains Zip Code two-color maps of 326 metropolitan areas. Includes summary statistical profiles of each area: population characteristics, employment, housing, and income.

POSTERS

See also: ART IN INDUSTRY; COMMERCIAL ART; SIGNS AND SIGN BOARDS

RESEARCH CENTERS AND INSTITUTES

Design Research Unit. Massachusetts College of Art, 621 Huntington Ave., Boston, MA 02115. Phone: (617)232-1492 Fax: (617)566-4034 • Conducts research related to the design of printed matter, including annual reports, letterheads, posters, and brochures.

OTHER SOURCES

BBP's 3-in-1 Poster Programs. Bureau of Business Practice, Inc. • Monthly. $32.40 per year. Includes: customer awareness posters, productivity posters, safety posters. Quantity discounts available.

POTASH INDUSTRY

See also: FERTILIZER INDUSTRY

PRICE SOURCES

Green Markets. Pike and Fischer, Inc. • Weekly. $890.00 per year. Newsletter including prices for potash and other agricultural chemicals.

STATISTICS SOURCES

Mineral Commodity Summaries. Available from U. S. Government Printing Office. • Annual. Published by the U. S. Geological Survey, Department of the Interior (http://www.usgs.gov). Contains detailed, five-year data for about 90 nonfuel minerals. Covers a wide range of statistics, including production, imports, exports, consumption, reserves, prices, tariff information, and industry employment. (Two pages are devoted to each mineral.).

TRADE/PROFESSIONAL ASSOCIATIONS

Potash and Phosphate Institute. 655 Engineering Dr., No. 110, Norcross, GA 30092. Phone: (770)447-0335 Fax: (770)448-0439 E-mail: ppi@ppi-far.org • URL: http://www.ppi-far.org.

OTHER SOURCES

Major Chemical and Petrochemical Companies of the World. Available from The Gale Group. • 2001. $855.00. Third edition. Two volumes. Published by Graham & Whiteside. Contains profiles of more than 7,000 important chemical and petrochemical companies in various countries. Subject areas include general chemicals, specialty chemicals, agricultural chemicals, petrochemicals, industrial gases, and fertilizers.

POTATO CHIP INDUSTRY

See: POTATO INDUSTRY; SNACK FOOD INDUSTRY

POTATO INDUSTRY

See also: SWEET POTATO INDUSTRY; VEGETABLE INDUSTRY

ABSTRACTS AND INDEXES

Field Crop Abstracts: Monthly Abstract Journal on World Annual Cereal, Legume, Root, Oilseed and Fibre Crops. Available from CABI Publishing North America. • Monthly. $1,465.00 per year. Published in England by CABI Publishing, formerly Commonwealth Agricultural Bureaux. Provides worldwide coverage of the literature.

Potato Abstracts. Available from CABI Publishing North America. • Bimonthly. $435.00 per year. Published in England by CABI Publishing. Provides worldwide coverage of the literature.

CD-ROM DATABASES

Food Science and Technology Abstracts [CD-ROM]. Available from SilverPlatter Information, Inc. • Quarterly. $3,700 per year. Produced by International Food Information Service (home page is http://www.ifis.org). Provides worldwide coverage on CD-ROM of the literature of food technology and production. Various types of publications are indexed, with abstracts, including about 1,800 periodicals. Time period is 1969 to date.

INTERNET DATABASES

USDA. United States Department of Agriculture. Phone: (202)720-2791 E-mail: agsec@usda.gov • URL: http://www.usda.gov • The USDA home page has six sections: News and Information; What's New; About USDA; Agencies; Opportunities; Search and Help. Keyword searching is offered from the USDA home page and from various individual agency home pages. Agencies are the Economic Research Service, Agricultural Marketing Service, National Agricultural Statistics Service, National Agricultural Library, and about 12 others. Updating varies. Fees: Free.

ONLINE DATABASES

Biological and Agricultural Index Online. H. W. Wilson Co. • Indexes a wide variety of agricultural and biological periodicals, 1983 to date. Monthly updates. Inquire as to online cost and availability.

CAB Abstracts. CAB International North America. • Contains 46 specialized abstract collections covering over 10,000 journals and monographs in the areas of agriculture, horticulture, forest products, farm products, nutrition, dairy science, poultry, grains, animal health, entomology, etc. Time period is 1972 to date, with monthly updates. Inquire as to online cost and availability. *CAB Abstracts on CD-ROM* also available, with annual updating.

Food Science and Technology Abstracts [online]. IFIS North American Desk. • Produced by International Food Information Service. Provides about 500,000 online citations, with abstracts, to the international literature of food science, technology, commodities, engineering, and processing. Approximately 2,000 periodicals are covered. Time period is 1969 to date, with monthly updates. Inquire as to online cost and availability.

PERIODICALS AND NEWSLETTERS

American Journal of Potato Research. Potato Association of America. • Bimonthly. Individuals, $60.00 per year; libraries $75.00 per year.Information relating to production, marketing, processing, storage, disease control, insect control and new variety releases. Formerly *American Potato Journal.*

Potato Grower of Idaho. Potato Growers of Idaho, Inc. Harris Publishing, Inc. • Monthly. $15.95 per year.

STATISTICS SOURCES

Agricultural Statistics. Available from U. S. Government Printing Office. • Annual. Produced by the National Agricultural Statistics Service, U. S. Department of Agriculture. Provides a wide variety of statistical data relating to agricultural production, supplies, consumption, prices/price-supports, foreign trade, costs, and returns, as well as farm labor, loans, income, and population. In many cases, historical data is shown annually for 10 years. In addition to farm data, includes detailed fishery statistics.

Vegetables and Specialties Situation and Outlook. Available from U. S. Government Printing Office. • Three times a year. $15.00 per year. Issued by the Economic Research Service of the U. S. Department of Agriculture. Provides current statistical information on supply, demand, and prices.

TRADE/PROFESSIONAL ASSOCIATIONS

National Potato Council. 5690 DTC Blvd., Suite 230E, Englewood, CO 80111-3200. Phone: (303)773-9295 Fax: (303)773-9296 E-mail: npcspud@ix.netcom.com • URL: http://www.npcspud.com.

Potato Association of America. c/o University of Maine, 575 Coburn Hall, Rm. 6, Orono, ME 04469-5715. Phone: (207)581-3042 Fax: (207)581-3015 E-mail: umpotato@maine.edu • URL: http://www.potato.tamu.edu/variety-paa.htm.

Snack Food Association. 1711 King St., Suite 1, Alexandria, VA 22314. Phone: 800-628-1334 or (703)836-4500 Fax: (703)836-8262 E-mail: sfa@sfa.org • URL: http://www.snax.com.

OTHER SOURCES

Major Food and Drink Companies of the World. Available from The Gale Group. • 2001. $855.00. Fourth edition. Two volumes. Published by Graham & Whiteside. Contains profiles and trade names for more than 9,000 important food and beverage companies in various countries. In addition to foods, includes both alcoholic and nonalcoholic drink products.

The Market for Salted Snacks. MarketResearch.com. • 2000. $2,750.00. Market research report. Covers potato chips, corn chips, popcorn, nuts, pretzels, and other salted snacks. Market projections are provided to the year 2004.

Thomas Food and Beverage Market Place. Grey House Publishing. • Annual. $295.00. Three volumes. Contains more than 40,000 entries covering food companies, beverages, food equipment, warehouse companies, food brokers, wholesalers, importers, and exporters. Formerly *Thomas Food Industry Register.*

POTATOES, SWEET

See: SWEET POTATO INDUSTRY

POTTERY INDUSTRY

See also: CERAMICS INDUSTRY; GLASSWARE INDUSTRY

ENCYCLOPEDIAS AND DICTIONARIES

Potter's Dictionary of Materials and Techniques. Frank Hamer and Janet Hamer. University of Pennsylvania Press. • 1997. $49.95. Fourth edition.

HANDBOOKS AND MANUALS

Ceramics: A Potter's Handbook. Glenn C. Nelson. Harcourt Brace College Publishers. • 1998. $42.50. Sixth edition.

PERIODICALS AND NEWSLETTERS

Gift and Stationery Business. Miller Freeman, Inc. • Monthly. $45.00 per year. Products and services.

Giftware News: The International Magazine for Gifts, China and Glass, Stationery and Home Accessories. Talcott Communications Corp. • Monthly. $36.00 per year. Includes annual *Directory.*

TRADE/PROFESSIONAL ASSOCIATIONS

Associated Glass and Pottery Manufacturers. c/o Custom Deco, 1343 Miami St., Toledo, OH 43605. Phone: (419)698-2900 Fax: (419)698-9928.

POULTRY INDUSTRY

See also: TURKEY INDUSTRY

ABSTRACTS AND INDEXES

Food Science and Technology Abstracts. International Food Information Service Publishing. • Monthly. $1,780.00 per year. Provides worldwide coverage of the literature of food technology and food production.

Foods Adlibra: Key to the World's Food Literature. Foods Adlibra Publications. • Semimonthly.Provides journal citations and abstracts to the literature of food technology and packaging.

Poultry Abstracts. Available from CABI Publishing North America. • Monthly. $615.00 per year. Published in England by CABI Publishing. Provides worldwide coverage of the literature.

CD-ROM DATABASES

Food Science and Technology Abstracts [CD-ROM]. Available from SilverPlatter Information, Inc. • Quarterly. $3,700 per year. Produced by International Food Information Service (home page is http://www.ifis.org). Provides worldwide coverage on CD-ROM of the literature of food technology and production. Various types of publications are indexed, with abstracts, including about 1,800 periodicals. Time period is 1969 to date.

DIRECTORIES

Meat and Poultry Inspection Directory. U.S. Department of Agriculture. Available from U.S. Government Printing Office. • Semiannual. $42.00 per year.

Who's Who in the Egg and Poultry Industries. Watt Publishing Co. • Annual. $100.00. Producers, processors, and distributors of poultry meat and eggs in the United States; manufacturers of supplies and equipment for the poultry industry; breeders and hatcheries; refrigerated public warehouses;. food chain buyers of poultry meat and eggs; related government agencies; poultry associations.

FINANCIAL RATIOS

Annual Statement Studies. Robert Morris Associates: The Association of Lending and Credit Risk Professiona. • Annual. Free to members; non-members, $140.00. Median and quartile financial ratios are given for over 400 kinds of manufacturing, wholesale, retail, construction, and consumer finance establishments. Data is sorted by both asset size and sales volume. Includes a clearly written "Definition of Ratios" and an alphabetical industry index.

HANDBOOKS AND MANUALS

Commercial Chicken Production. Mack O. North. Chapman and Hall. • 1990. $79.95. Fourth edition.

Meat and Poultry Inspection Regulations. U.S. Department of Agriculture. Available from U.S. Government Printing Office. • Looseleaf. $297.00. Monthly updates included. Regulations for slaughter and processing of livestock and poultry as well as for certain voluntary services and humane slaughter.

Poultry Science. M. E. Ensminger. Interstate Publishers, Inc. • 1992. $69.95. Third edition.

INTERNET DATABASES

Fedstats. Federal Interagency Council on Statistical Policy. Phone: (202)395-7254 • URL: http://www.fedstats.gov • Web site features an efficient search facility for full-text statistics produced by more than 70 federal agencies, including the Census Bureau, the Bureau of Economic Analysis, and the Bureau of Labor Statistics. Boolean searches can be made within one agency or for all agencies combined. Links are offered to international statistical bureaus, including the UN, IMF, OECD, UNESCO, Eurostat, and 20 individual countries. Fees: Free.

USDA. United States Department of Agriculture. Phone: (202)720-2791 E-mail: agsec@usda.gov • URL: http://www.usda.gov • The USDA home page has six sections: News and Information; What's New; About USDA; Agencies; Opportunities; Search and Help. Keyword searching is offered from the USDA home page and from various individual agency home pages. Agencies are the Economic Research Service, Agricultural Marketing Service, National Agricultural Statistics Service, National Agricultural Library, and about 12 others. Updating varies. Fees: Free.

ONLINE DATABASES

Biological and Agricultural Index Online. H. W. Wilson Co. • Indexes a wide variety of agricultural and biological periodicals, 1983 to date. Monthly updates. Inquire as to online cost and availability.

CAB Abstracts. CAB International North America. • Contains 46 specialized abstract collections covering over 10,000 journals and monographs in the areas of agriculture, horticulture, forest products, farm products, nutrition, dairy science, poultry, grains, animal health, entomology, etc. Time period is 1972 to date, with monthly updates. Inquire as to online cost and availability. *CAB Abstracts on CD-ROM* also available, with annual updating.

DRI U.S. Central Database. Data Products Division. • Provides more than 23,000 business, financial, demographic, economic, foreign trade, and industry-related time series for the U.S. Includes national income, population, retail-wholesale trade, price indexes, labor data, housing, industrial production, banking, interest rates, money supply, etc. Time period is generally 1947 to date (some data back to 1929). Updating varies. Inquire as to online cost and availability.

Food Science and Technology Abstracts [online]. IFIS North American Desk. • Produced by International Food Information Service. Provides about 500,000 online citations, with abstracts, to the international literature of food science, technology, commodities, engineering, and processing. Approximately 2,000 periodicals are covered. Time period is 1969 to date, with monthly updates. Inquire as to online cost and availability.

FOODS ADLIBRA. General Mills, Inc. • Contains online citations, with abstracts, to the technical and business literature of food processing and packaging. New products and new ingredients are featured. Covers about 250 trade journals and 500 research journals from 1974 to date, with monthly updates. Inquire as to online cost and availability.

PERIODICALS AND NEWSLETTERS

Broiler Industry. Watt Publishing Co. • Monthly. Free to qualified personnel; others, $54.00 per year.

Egg Industry: Covering Egg Production, Processing and Marketing. Watt Publishing Co. • Monthly. $36.00 per year. Formerly *Poultry Tribune.*

Poultry and Egg Marketing: The Bi-Monthly News Magazine of the Poultry Marketing Industry. Poultry and Egg News. • Six times a year. Free to qualified personnel; others, $12.00 per year. Processing and marketing of eggs and poultry products.

Poultry Digest. Watt Publishing Co. • Bimonthly. Free to qualified personnel, others, $28.00 per year.

Poultry Science. Poultry Science Association, Inc. • Monthly. $180.00 per year.

Poultry Times. Poultry and Egg News. • Biweekly. $9.00 per year. Directed to grow-out operations for the egg and poultry business.

STATISTICS SOURCES

Agricultural Statistics. Available from U. S. Government Printing Office. • Annual. Produced by the National Agricultural Statistics Service, U. S. Department of Agriculture. Provides a wide variety of statistical data relating to agricultural production, supplies, consumption, prices/price-supports, foreign trade, costs, and returns, as well as farm labor, loans, income, and population. In many cases, historical data is shown annually for 10 years. In addition to farm data, includes detailed fishery statistics.

Annual Survey of Manufactures. Available from U. S. Government Printing Office. • Annual. Prices vary. Issued by the U. S. Census Bureau as an interim update to the *Census of Manufactures.* Includes data on number of manufacturing establishments in various industries, employment, labor costs, value of shipments, capital expenditures, inventories, energy costs, and assets. (See also Census Bureau home page, http://www.census.gov/.).

Business Statistics of the United States. Courtenay M. Slater, editor. Bernan Associates. • 1999. $74.00. Fifth edition. Based on *Business Statistics,* formerly issue by the Bureau of Economic Analysis, U. S. Department of Commerce. Provides basic data for a wide variety of U. S. industries, services, and economic indicators. Most statistics are shown annually for 29 years and monthly for the most recent four years.

Survey of Current Business. Available from U. S. Government Printing Office. • Monthly. $49.00 per year. Issued by Bureau of Economic Analysis, U. S. Department of Commerce. Presents a wide variety of business and economic data.

TRADE/PROFESSIONAL ASSOCIATIONS

American Egg Board. 1460 Renaissance Dr., Suite 301, Park Ridge, IL 60068. Phone: (708)296-7043 Fax: (708)296-7007 E-mail: aeb@aeb.org • URL: http://www.aeb.org.

American Poultry Association. 133 Milville St., Mendon, MA 01756. Phone: (508)473-8769 Fax: (508)473-8769 • URL: http://www.radiopark.com/apa.html.

National Chicken Council. 1015 15th St., N.W., Ste. 930, Washington, DC 20005. Phone: (202)296-2622 Fax: (202)293-4005 E-mail: wroenigk@chickenusa.org.

Poultry Science Association. 1111 N. Dunlap Ave., Savoy, IL 61874. Phone: (217)356-3182 Fax: (217)398-4119 E-mail: psa@assochq.org • URL: http://www.psa.uiuc.edu/.

OTHER SOURCES

Major Food and Drink Companies of the World. Available from The Gale Group. • 2001. $855.00. Fourth edition. Two volumes. Published by Graham & Whiteside. Contains profiles and trade names for more than 9,000 important food and beverage companies in various countries. In addition to foods, includes both alcoholic and nonalcoholic drink products.

Thomas Food and Beverage Market Place. Grey House Publishing. • Annual. $295.00. Three volumes. Contains more than 40,000 entries covering food companies, beverages, food equipment, warehouse companies, food brokers, wholesalers, importers, and exporters. Formerly *Thomas Food Industry Register.*

POVERTY

See: PUBLIC WELFARE

POWDER METALLURGY INDUSTRY

ABSTRACTS AND INDEXES

Metal Powder Report. Elsevier Science, Inc. • 11 times a year. $373.00. per year. Technical articles, company reports, up-to-date news and book reviews cover powder metallurgy worldwide.

Metalforming Digest. Cambridge Information Group. • Monthly. Provides abstracts of the international literature of metal forming, including powder metallurgy, stamping, extrusion, forging, etc.

ONLINE DATABASES

METADEX. Cambridge Scientific Abstracts. • Covers the worldwide literature of metals, metallurgy, and materials science, 1966 to date. Includes detailed alloys indexing from 1974. Biweekly updating. Inquire as to online cost and availability. (Formerly produced by ASM International.).

PERIODICALS AND NEWSLETTERS

International Journal of Powder Metallurgy. American Powder Metallurgy Institute. APMI International. • Eight times a year. Institutions, $175.00 per year. Formerly *PM Technology Newsletter.*

Powder Metallurgy. IOM Communications Ltd. • Quarterly. Members $233.25 per year; non-members, $495.00 per year.

STATISTICS SOURCES

Metal Statistics. Cahners Business Information. • Annual. $250.00. Provides statistical data on a wide variety of metals, metal products, ores, alloys, and scrap metal. Includes data on prices, production, consumption, shipments, imports, and exports.

TRADE/PROFESSIONAL ASSOCIATIONS

Metal Powder Industries Federation. 105 College Rd., E., Princeton, NJ 08540-6692. Phone: (609)452-7700 Fax: (609)987-8523 E-mail: info@mpif.org • URL: http://www.mpif.org.

POWER COMPANIES

See: ELECTRIC UTILITIES

POWER (MECHANICAL)

See also: FUEL; MECHANICAL ENGINEERING

DIRECTORIES

Design News OEM Directory. Cahners Business Information. • Annual. $60.00. About 6,000 manufacturers and suppliers of power transmission products, fluid power products and electrical/ electronic componets to the OEM (Original Equipment Manufacturers). Included with subscription to *Design News.* Formerly *Design News.*

HANDBOOKS AND MANUALS

Mechanical Engineer's Reference Book. E. H. Smith, editor. Society of Automotive Engineers, Inc. • 1994. $135.00. 12th edition. Covers mechanical engineering principles, computer integrated engineering systems, design standards, materials, power transmission, and many other engineering topics. (Authored Royalty Series).

PT Design Motion Systems Handbook (Power Transmission). Penton Media Inc. • Annual. $30.00. Formerly *Power Transmission Design Handbook.*

PERIODICALS AND NEWSLETTERS

IEEE Industry Applications Magazine. Institute of Electrical and Electronics Engineers. • Bimonthly. $190.00 per year. Covers new industrial applications of power conversion, drives, lighting, and control. Emphasis is on the petroleum, chemical, rubber, plastics, textile, and mining industries.

Journal of Turbomachinery. American Society of Mechanical Engineers. • Quarterly. Members, $40.00 per year; non-members, $215.00 per year. Series A of the *Transactions of the ASME.* Formerly *Journal of Gas Turbines.*

Power Engineering International. PennWell Corp., Industrial Div. • 10 times a year. $168.00 per year.

TRADE/PROFESSIONAL ASSOCIATIONS

Mechanical Power Transmission Association. 6724 Lone Oak Blvd., Naples, FL 34109. Phone: (941)514-3441 Fax: (941)514-3470 E-mail: mpta@mpta.org • URL: http://www.mpta.org.

National Association of Power Engineers. One Springfield St., Chicopee, MA 01013. Phone: (413)592-6273 Fax: (413)592-1998.

Power - Motion Technology Representatives Association. 330 S. Wells St., No. 1422, Chicago, IL 60606. Phone: 888-737-7872 or (312)360-0389 Fax: (312)360-0380 E-mail: info@ptra.org • URL: http://www.ptra.org.

Power Transmission Distributors Association. 6400 Shafer Court, Suite 670, Rosemont, IL 60018-4909. Phone: (847)825-2000 Fax: (847)825-0953 E-mail: ptda@ptda.org • URL: http://www.ptda.org.

POWER PLANTS, ELECTRIC

See: ELECTRIC POWER PLANTS

POWER TOOL INDUSTRY

See also: TOOL INDUSTRY

GENERAL WORKS

Portable Power Tools. Time-Life, Inc. • 1992. $14.95. Contains popular descriptions of power tools for woodworking. (Art of Woodworking Series).

ABSTRACTS AND INDEXES

Engineering Index Monthly: Abstracting and Indexing Services Covering Sources of the World's Engineering Literature. Engineering Information, Inc. • Monthly. $2,300.00 per year. Provides indexing and abstracting of the world's engineering and technical literature.

Mechanical Engineering Abstracts. Cambridge Information Group. • Bimonthly. $975.00 per year. Formerly *ISMEC - Mechanical Engineering Abstracts.*

NTIS Alerts: Manufacturing Technology. National Technical Information Service. • Semimonthly. $265.00 per year. Provides descriptions of government-sponsored research reports and software, with ordering information. Covers computer-aided design and manufacturing (CAD/CAM), engineering materials, quality control, machine tools, robots, lasers, productivity, and related subjects. Formerly *Abstract Newsletter.*

CD-ROM DATABASES

COMPENDEX PLUS [CD-ROM]. Engineering Information, Inc. • Quarterly. $3,450.00 per year. Provides CD-ROM indexing and abstracting of the world's engineering and technical information appearing in journals, reports, books, and proceedings, 1985 to date.

DIRECTORIES

Building Supply Home Centers Retail Giants Report. Cahners Business Information. • Annual. $30.00. Lists major retailers of a wide variety of building and home improvement materials, products, fixtures, accessories, equipment, and tools.

ProSales Buyer's Guide. Hanley-Wood, LLC. • Annual. $5.00. A directory of equipment for professional builders.

FINANCIAL RATIOS

Cost of Doing Business: Farm and Power Equipment Dealers, Industrial Dealers, and Outdoor Power Equipment Dealers. North American Equipment Dealers Association. • Annual. $50.00. Provides data on sales, profit margins, expenses, assets, and employee productivity.

HANDBOOKS AND MANUALS

Assembly Buyer's Guide. Cahners Business Information. • Annual. $25.00. Lists manufacturers and suppliers of equipment relating to assembly automation, fasteners, adhesives, robotics, and power tools.

ONLINE DATABASES

COMPENDEX PLUS. Engineering Information, Inc. • Provides online indexing and abstracting of the world's engineering and technical information appearing in journals, reports, books, and proceedings. Time period is 1970 to date, with weekly updates. Inquire as to online cost and availability.

Hard Sciences. Cambridge Scientific Abstracts. • Provides the online version of *Computer and Information Systems Abstracts, Electronics and Communications Abstracts, Health and Safety Science Abstracts, ISMEC: Mechanical Engineering Abstracts (Information Service in Mechanical Engineering)* and *Solid State and Superconductivity Abstracts.* Time period is 1981 to date, with monthly updates. Inquire as to online cost and availability.

PROMT: Predicasts Overview of Markets and Technology. The Gale Group. • Companies, products, applied technologies and markets. U.S. and international literature coverage, 1972 to date. Inquire as to online cost and availability. Provides abstracts from more than 1,600 publications. Weekly updates.

PERIODICALS AND NEWSLETTERS

Building Material Retailer. National Lumber and Building Material Dealers Association. • Monthly. $25.00 per year. Includes special feature issues on hand and power tools, lumber, roofing, kitchens, flooring, windows and doors, and insulation.

Hardware Age. Cahners Business Information. • Monthly. $75.00 per year.

National Home Center News: News and Analysis for the Home Improvement, Building, Material Industry. Lebhar-Friedman, Inc. • 22 times a year. $99.00 per year. Includes special feature issues on hardware and tools, building materials, millwork, electrical supplies, lighting, and kitchens.

ProSales: For Dealers and Distributors Serving the Professional Contractor. Hanley-Wood, LLC. • Monthly. $36.00 per year. Includes special feature issues on selling, credit, financing, and the marketing of power tools.

STATISTICS SOURCES

Annual Survey of Manufactures. Available from U. S. Government Printing Office. • Annual. Prices vary. Issued by the U. S. Census Bureau as an interim update to the *Census of Manufactures.* Includes data on number of manufacturing establishments in various industries, employment, labor costs, value of shipments, capital expenditures, inventories, energy costs, and assets. (See also Census Bureau home page, http://www.census.gov/.).

U. S. Industry and Trade Outlook: The McGraw-Hill Companies and the U.S. Department of Commerce/ International Trade Administration. Datapso Research Corp. • Annual. $69.95. Produced by the International Trade Administration, U. S. Department of Commerce, in a "public-private" partnership with DRI/McGraw-Hill and Standard & Poor's. Provides basic data, outlook for the current year, and "Long-Term Prospects" (five-year projections) for a wide variety of products and services. Includes high technology industries. Formerly *U. S. Industrial Outlook.*

TRADE/PROFESSIONAL ASSOCIATIONS

Portable Power Equipment Manufacturers Association. 4340 East West Highway, Suite 912, Bethesda, MD 20814. Phone: (301)652-0774 Fax: (301)654-6138 E-mail: ppemal@msn.com • URL: http://www.ppema.org.

Power Tool Institute. 1300 Sumner Ave., Cleveland, OH 44115-2851. Phone: (216)241-7333 Fax: (216)241-0105 E-mail: pti@taol.com • URL: http://www.taol.com/pti • Members are manufacturers of various kinds of portable and stationary power tools.

OTHER SOURCES

Assembly. Cahners Business Information. • Monthly. $68.00 per year. Covers assembly, fastening, and joining systems. Includes information on automation and robotics.

Business & Company Resource Center. The Gale Group. • Fee-based Web site provides a wide range of business, industry, and specific company information. Access is offered to trade journal articles, market research data, insider trading activity, major shareholder data, corporate histories, emerging technology reports, corporate earnings estimates, press releases, and other sources. Provides detailed company profiles, industry overviews, and rankings. Offers integration of Predicasts PROMT, Newsletters ASAP, Investext Plus, Business Index ASAP, Brands and Their Companies, and other databases (many have full text).

POWER TRANSMISSION (MECHANICAL)

See: POWER (MECHANICAL)

PRACTICE MANAGEMENT

See: MEDICAL ECONOMICS (PRACTICE MANAGEMENT)

PRECIOUS METALS

See: GOLD; METAL INDUSTRY; PLATINUM INDUSTRY; SILVER INDUSTRY

PRECIOUS STONES

See: GEMS AND GEMSTONES

PREFABRICATED HOUSE INDUSTRY

See also: BUILDING INDUSTRY; MOBILE HOME INDUSTRY

GENERAL WORKS

Manufactured Homes; Making Sense of a Housing Opportunity. Thomas E. Nutt-Powell. Greenwood Publishing Group, Inc. • 1982. $62.95.

DIRECTORIES

Automated Builder Annual Buyers' Guide. CMN Publications. • Annual. $12.00. Over 250 manufacturers and suppliers to the manufactured and pre-fabricated housing industry.

PERIODICALS AND NEWSLETTERS

Automated Builder: The No. 1 International Housing Technology Transfer Magazine for Manufacturing and Marketing. CMN Publications. • 11 times a year. Free to qualified personnel; others, $50.00 per year. Annual *Buyers' Guide* available.

STATISTICS SOURCES

U. S. Industry and Trade Outlook: The McGraw-Hill Companies and the U.S. Department of Commerce/ International Trade Administration. Datapso Research Corp. • Annual. $69.95. Produced by the International Trade Administration, U. S. Department of Commerce, in a "public-private" partnership with DRI/McGraw-Hill and Standard & Poor's. Provides basic data, outlook for the current year, and "Long-Term Prospects" (five-year projections) for a wide variety of products and services. Includes high technology industries. Formerly *U. S. Industrial Outlook.*

TRADE/PROFESSIONAL ASSOCIATIONS

Building Systems Councils of NAHB. 1201 15th St., N.W., Washington, DC 20005. Phone: 800-368-5242 or (202)822-0576 Fax: (202)861-2141.

Manufactured Housing Institute. 2101 Wilson Blvd., Suite 610, Arlington, VA 22201-3062. Phone: 800-505-5500 or (703)558-0400 Fax: (703)558-0401 E-mail: info@mfghome.org • URL: http://www.mfghome.org.

PREMIUMS

See also: ADVERTISING SPECIALTIES

DIRECTORIES

Creative's Illustrated Guide to P-O-P Exhibits and Promotion. Magazines Creative, Inc. • Annual. $25.00. Lists sources of point-of-purchase displays, signs, and exhibits and sources of other promotional materials and equipment. Available online.

Directory of Premium, Incentive, and Travel Buyers. Salesman's Guide. • Annual. $275.00. Provides information on about 19,000 buyers of premiums, incentive programs, and travel programs for motivation of sales personnel.

Incentive-Merchandise and Travel Directory. Bill Communications, Inc. • Annual. $5.00. A special issue of *Incentive* magazine.

PROMO Magazine's SourceBook: The Only Guide to the $70 Billion Promotion Industry. Intertec Publishing. • Annual. $49.95. Lists service and supply companies for the promotion industry. Includes annual salary survey and award winning campaigns.

The PROMO 100 Promotion Agency Ranking. Intertec Publishing Co. • Annual. $9.95. Provides information on 100 leading product promotion agencies.

HANDBOOKS AND MANUALS

Specialty Advertising. Entrepreneur Media, Inc. • Looseleaf. $59.50. A practical guide to starting a business dealing in advertising specialties. Covers profit potential, market size evaluation, start-up costs, pricing, accounting, advertising, promotion, etc. (Start-Up Business Guide No. E1292.).

PERIODICALS AND NEWSLETTERS

Creative: The Magazine of Promotion and Marketing. Magazines Creative, Inc. • Bimonthly. $30.00 per year. Covers promotional materials, including exhibits, incentives, point-of-purchase advertising, premiums, and specialty advertising.

Incentive: Managing and Marketing Through Motivation. Bill Communications, Inc. • Monthly. $55.00 per year.

Potentials: Ideas and Products that Motivate. Lakewood Publications, Inc. • 10 times a year. $24.00 per year. Covers incentives, premiums, awards, and gifts as related to promotional activities. Formerly *Potentials in Marketing.*

PROMO: Promotion Marketing Worldwide. Simba Information Inc. • Monthly. $65.00 per year. Edited for companies and agencies that utilize couponing, point-of-purchase advertising, special events, games, contests, premiums, product samples, and other unique promotional items.

STATISTICS SOURCES

Incentive-State of the Industry and Annual Facts Review. Bill Communications, Inc. • Annual. $5.00. A special issue of *Incentive* magazine.

TRADE/PROFESSIONAL ASSOCIATIONS

Incentive Manufacturers Representatives Association. 8201 Greenborrn Dr., Ste. 300, Mclean, VA 22102. Phone: (703)610-9005 Fax: (703)610-9005 • URL: http://www.imral.org.

OTHER SOURCES

Idea Source Guide; A Monthly Report to Executives in Advertising, Merchandising and Sales Promotion. Bramlee, Inc. • Monthly. $150.00 per year. Lists new premiums and novelty products.

PREPAID MEDICAL CARE

See: HEALTH INSURANCE; HEALTH MAINTENANCE ORGANIZATIONS

PREPARED FOODS

See: PROCESSED FOOD INDUSTRY

PRESIDENTS OF COMPANIES

See: EXECUTIVES

PRESS CLIPPINGS

See: CLIPPING SERVICES

PRESSURE GROUPS

ALMANACS AND YEARBOOKS

CQ Almanac. Congressional Quarterly, Inc. • Annual. $215.00.

CD-ROM DATABASES

Leadership Library on CD-ROM: Who's Who in the Leadership of the United States. Leadership Directories, Inc. • Quarterly. $2,641.00 per year, including access to Internet version (weekly updates). Contains all 14 *Yellow Book* personnel directories on CD-ROM, providing contact and brief biographical information for about 400,000 individuals. Covers business, government, financial institutions, news media, law firms, associations, foreign representatives, and nonprofit organizations. Includes photographs.

DIRECTORIES

Government Affairs Yellow Book: Who's Who in Government Affairs. Leadership Directories, Inc. • Semiannual. $235.00 per year. Includes in-house lobbyists of corporations and organizations, Political Action Committees (PACs), congressional liaisons, and independent lobbying firms.

Public Interest Profiles, 1998-1999. Available from Congressional Quarterly, Inc. • 1996. $175.00. Published by Foundation for Public Affairs. Provides detailed information on more than 250 influential public interest and public policy organizations (lobbyists) in the U.S. Includes e-mail addresses and Web sites where available.

Special Interest Group Profiles for Students. The Gale Group. • 1999. $99.00. Provides detailed descriptions for about 200 lobbies, political action committees, civic action groups, and political parties. Includes a glossary, chronology, and index.

Washington Representatives: Lobbyists, Foreign Agents, Consultants, Legal Advisors, Public Affairs, and Government Relations... Columbia Books, Inc. • Annual. $109.00. Over 14,000 individuals and law or public relations firms registered as lobbyists, foreign agents, or otherwise acting as representatives in Washington, DC, for companies, associations, labor unions, and special interest groups; legislative affairs personnel of federal government agencies and departments and the White House.

PERIODICALS AND NEWSLETTERS

Congressional Record. U.S. Congress. Available from U.S. Government Printing Office. • Daily. $357.00 per year. Indexes give names, subjects, and history of bills. Texts of bills not included.

TRADE/PROFESSIONAL ASSOCIATIONS

American League of Lobbyists. P.O. Box 30005, Alexandria, VA 22310. Phone: (703)960-3011 • URL: http://www.alldc.org.

OTHER SOURCES

CQ Weekly. Congressional Quarterly, Inc. • Weekly. $1,349.00 per year. Includes annual *Almanac.* Formerly *Congressional Quarterly Weekly Report.*

PRESSURE PACKAGING

See also: PACKAGING

DIRECTORIES

Spray Equipment Directory. American Business Directories. • Annual. Price on application.

ONLINE DATABASES

PIRA. Technical Centre for the Paper and Board, Printing and Packaging Industries. • Citations and abstracts pertaining to bookbinding and other pulp, paper, and packaging industries, 1975 to present. Weekly updates. Inquire as to online cost and availability.

PERIODICALS AND NEWSLETTERS

Spray Technology and Marketing: The Magazine of Spray Pressure Packaging. Industry Publications, Inc. • Monthly. $30.00 per year. Formerly *Aerosol Age.*

PRESSURE SENSITIVE TAPE INDUSTRY

See: ADHESIVES

PRETZEL INDUSTRY

See: SNACK FOOD INDUSTRY

PRICE CODING, ELECTRONIC

See: POINT-OF-SALE SYSTEMS (POS)

PRICES AND PRICING

See also: CONSUMER PRICE INDEXES; INFLATION

HANDBOOKS AND MANUALS

Marketing Manager's Handbook. Sidney J. Levy and others. Prentice Hall. • 2000. Price on application. Contains 71 chapters by various authors on a wide variety of marketing topics, including market segmentation, market research, international marketing, industrial marketing, survey methods, customer service, advertising, pricing, planning, strategy, and ethics.

Power Pricing: How Managing Price Transforms the Bottom Line. Robert J. Dolan and Hermann Simon. Free Press. • 1997. $40.00. Among topics included are pricing strategy, price customization, international pricing, nonlinear pricing, product-line pricing, and price bundling.

INTERNET DATABASES

Bureau of Economic Analysis (BEA). U. S. Department of Commerce, Bureau of Economic Analysis. Phone: (202)606-9900 Fax: (202)606-5310 E-mail: webmaster@bea.doc.gov • URL: http://www.bea.doc.gov • Web site includes "News Release Information" covering national, regional, and international economic estimates from the BEA. Highlights of releases appear online the same day, complete text and tables appear the next day. "Recent News Releases" section provides titles for past nine months, with links. "BEA Data and Methodology" includes "Frequently Requested NIPA Data" (national income and product accounts, such as gross domestic product and personal income). Other statistics are available. Fees: Free.

Bureau of Labor Statistics (BLS). U. S. Department of Labor, Bureau of Labor Statistics. Phone: (202)523-1092 E-mail: labstat.helpdesk@bls.gov • URL: http://www.bls.gov • Web site provides a great variety of employment, wage, price, and economic data. Some links are "Data," "Economy at a Glance," "Keyword Search of BLS Web Pages," "Regional Information," and "Other Statistical Sites." Fees: Free.

Fedstats. Federal Interagency Council on Statistical Policy. Phone: (202)395-7254 • URL: http://www.fedstats.gov • Web site features an efficient search facility for full-text statistics produced by more than 70 federal agencies, including the Census Bureau, the Bureau of Economic Analysis, and the Bureau of Labor Statistics. Boolean searches can be made within one agency or for all agencies combined. Links are offered to international statistical bureaus, including the UN, IMF, OECD, UNESCO, Eurostat, and 20 individual countries. Fees: Free.

ONLINE DATABASES

DRI U.S. Central Database. Data Products Division. • Provides more than 23,000 business, financial, demographic, economic, foreign trade, and industry-related time series for the U.S. Includes national income, population, retail-wholesale trade, price indexes, labor data, housing, industrial production, banking, interest rates, money supply, etc. Time period is generally 1947 to date (some data back to 1929). Updating varies. Inquire as to online cost and availability.

EconBase: Time Series and Forecasts. WEFA, Inc. • Presents online econometric data for business conditions, economics, demographics, industry, finance, employment, household income, interest rates, prices, etc. Includes two-year forecasts for a wide range of economic indicators. Time span is 1948 to date, with monthly updates. Inquire as to online cost and availability.

PRICE SOURCES

CPI Detailed Report: Consumer Price Index. Available from U.S. Government Printing Office. • Monthly. $45.00 per year. Cost of living data.

Monthly Commodity Price Bulletin. United Nations Publications. • Monthly. $125.00 per year. Provides monthly average prices for the previous 12 months for a wide variety of commodities traded internationally.

PPI Detailed Report. Bureau of Labor Statistics, U.S. Department of Labor. Available from U.S. Government Printing Office. • Monthly. $55.00 per year. Formerly *Producer Price Indexes.*

STATISTICS SOURCES

American Cost of Living Survey. The Gale Group. • 1995. $160.00. Second edition. Cost of living data is provided for 455 U.S. cities and metroploitan areas.

Bulletin of Labour Statistics: Supplementing the Annual Data Presented in the Year Book of Labour Statistics. International Labour Ofice. ILO Publications Center. • Quarterly. $84.00 per year. Includes five *Supplements.* A supplement to *Yearbook of Labour Statistics.* Provides current labor and price index statistics for over 130 countries. Generally includes data for the most recent four years. Text in English, French and Spanish.

Business Statistics of the United States. Courtenay M. Slater, editor. Bernan Associates. • 1999. $74.00. Fifth edition. Based on *Business Statistics*, formerly issue by the Bureau of Economic Analysis, U. S. Department of Commerce. Provides basic data for a wide variety of U. S. industries, services, and economic indicators. Most statistics are shown annually for 29 years and monthly for the most recent four years.

Economic Report of the President: Together with the Annual Report of the Council of Economic Advisors. Available from U. S. Government Printing Office. • Annual. $29.00. Includes about 130 pages of "Statistical Tables Relating to Income, Employment, and Production." Tables cover national income, employment, wages, productivity, manufacturing, prices, credit, finance (public and private), corporate profits, and foreign trade.

Handbook of U. S. Labor Statistics: Employment, Earnings, Prices, Productivity, and Other Labor Data. Eva E. Jacobs, editor. Bernan Associates. • 1999. $74.00. Based on *Handbook of Labor Statistics*, formerly issued by the Bureau of Labor Statistics, U. S. Department of Labor. Includes the Bureau's projections of employment in the U. S. by industry and occupation. Provides a wide variety of data on the work force, prices, fringe benefits, and consumer expenditures.

Monthly Bulletin of Statistics. United Nations Publications. • Monthly. $295.00 per year. Provides current data for about 200 countries on a wide variety of economic, industrial, and demographic subjects. Compiled by United Nations Statistical Office.

Monthly Labor Review. Available from U. S. Government Printing Office. • Monthly. $43.00 per year. Issued by the Bureau of Labor Statistics, U. S. Department of Labor. Contains data on the labor force, wages, work stoppages, price indexes, productivity, economic growth, and occupational injuries and illnesses.

Prices and Earnings Around the Globe. Union Bank of Switzerland. • Irregular. Free. Published in Zurich. Compares prices and purchasing power in 48 major cities of the world. Wages and hours are also compared. Text in English, French, German, and Italian.

Statistical Yearbook. United Nations Publications. • Annual. $125.00. Contains statistics for about 200 countries on a wide variety of economic, industrial, and demographic topics. Compiled by United Nations Statistical Office.

Survey of Current Business. Available from U. S. Government Printing Office. • Monthly. $49.00 per year. Issued by Bureau of Economic Analysis, U. S. Department of Commerce. Presents a wide variety of business and economic data.

The Value of a Dollar. Grey House Publishing, Inc. • 1999. $125.00.

World Cost of Living Survey. The Gale Group. • 1999. $255.00. Second edition. Arranged by country and then by city within each country. Provides cost of living data for many products and services. Includes indexes and an annotated bibliography.

Year Book of Labour Statistics. International Labour Office. • Annual. $168.00. Presents a wide range of labor and price data for most countries of the world. Supplement available *Sources and Methods. Labour Statistics.*

OTHER SOURCES

The Value of a Dollar: Millennium Edition, 1860-1999. Grey House Publishing. • 1999. $135.00. Second edition. Shows the actual prices of thousands of items available to consumers from the Civil War era to recent years. Includes selected data on consumer expenditures, investments, income, and jobs. (Universal Reference Publications.).

PRIME RATE

See: INTEREST

PRINTING AND PRINTING EQUIPMENT INDUSTRIES

See also: COPYING MACHINE INDUSTRY; GRAPHIC ARTS INDUSTRY; PHOTOENGRAVING; TYPESETTING

DIRECTORIES

Graphic Arts Monthly Sourcebook. Cahners. • Annual. $50.00. About 1,400 manufacturers and distributors of graphic arts equipment, supplies and services. Also includes list of corporate electronic publishers.

In-Plant Printer Buyer's Guide. Innes Publishing Co. • Annual. $10.00. Manufacturers of equipment for the in-plant and grahic arts industry. Formerly *In-*

Plant Printer and Electronic Publisher Buyer's Guide.

Print Media Production Source. SRDS. • Quarterly. $401.00 per year. Contains details of printing and mechanical production requirements for advertising in specific trade journals, consumer magazines, and newspapers. Formerly *Print Media Production Data.*

ENCYCLOPEDIAS AND DICTIONARIES

Graphically Speaking: An Illustrated Guide to the Working Language of Design and Publishing. Mark Beach. Coast to Coast Books. • 1992. $29.50. Provides practical definitions of 2,800 terms used in printing, graphic design, publishing, and desktop publishing. Over 300 illustrations are included, about 40 in color.

FINANCIAL RATIOS

Almanac of Business and Industrial Financial Ratios. Leo Troy. Prentice Hall. • Annual. $99.95. Contains financial ratios derived from federal tax returns. Ratios for each of about 200 industries are arranged according to company asset size.

PIA Financial Ratio Studies. Printing Industries of America, Inc. • Annual. Members, $650.00 set or $100.00 per volume; non-members, $995.00 set or $1,155.00 per volume. 14 volumes.

HANDBOOKS AND MANUALS

Getting It Printed: How to Work with Printers and Graphic Arts Services to Assure Quality, Stay on Schedule, and Control Costs. Mark Beach and Eric Kenly. F and W. Publications, Inc. • 1998. $32.99. Third edition.

Instant Print/Copy Shop. Entrepreneur Media, Inc. • Looseleaf. $59.50. A practical guide to starting a quick printing and copying business. Covers profit potential, start-up costs, market size evaluation, owner's time required, site selection, lease negotiation, pricing, accounting, advertising, promotion, etc. (Start-Up Business Guide No. E1298.).

INTERNET DATABASES

Fedstats. Federal Interagency Council on Statistical Policy. Phone: (202)395-7254 • URL: http://www.fedstats.gov • Web site features an efficient search facility for full-text statistics produced by more than 70 federal agencies, including the Census Bureau, the Bureau of Economic Analysis, and the Bureau of Labor Statistics. Boolean searches can be made within one agency or for all agencies combined. Links are offered to international statistical bureaus, including the UN, IMF, OECD, UNESCO, Eurostat, and 20 individual countries. Fees: Free.

ONLINE DATABASES

DRI U.S. Central Database. Data Products Division. • Provides more than 23,000 business, financial, demographic, economic, foreign trade, and industry-related time series for the U.S. Includes national income, population, retail-wholesale trade, price indexes, labor data, housing, industrial production, banking, interest rates, money supply, etc. Time period is generally 1947 to date (some data back to 1929). Updating varies. Inquire as to online cost and availability.

PERIODICALS AND NEWSLETTERS

American Printer. Intertec Publishing Corp. • Monthly. Free to qualified personnel; others, $65.00 per year. Serves the printing and lithographic industries and allied manufacturing and service segments.

Color Publishing. PennWell Corp., Advanced Technology Div. • Bimonthly. $29.70 per year.

Graphic Arts Monthly. Cahners Business Information. • Monthly. $110.00 per year.

In-Plant Printer: The In-Plant Management Magazine. Innes Publishing Co. • Bimonthly. $75.00 per year. Formerly *In-Plant Printer and Electronic Publisher.*

Printing Impressions. North American Publishing Co. • Monthly. Free to qualified personnel; others, $90.00 per year. Annual buyer's guide *Master Specifier.*

Quick Printing: The Information Source for Commercial Copyshops and Printshops. Cygnus Business Media. • Monthly. $48.00 per year.

RESEARCH CENTERS AND INSTITUTES

Technical and Educational Center of the Graphic Arts and Imaging. Rochester Institute of Technology, 67 Lomb Memorial Dr., Rochester, NY 14623-5603. Phone: 800-724-2536 or (716)475-2680 Fax: (716)475-7000 E-mail: webmail@rit.edu • URL: http://www.rit.edu/cime/te.

STATISTICS SOURCES

Annual Survey of Manufactures. Available from U. S. Government Printing Office. • Annual. Prices vary. Issued by the U. S. Census Bureau as an interim update to the *Census of Manufactures.* Includes data on number of manufacturing establishments in various industries, employment, labor costs, value of shipments, capital expenditures, inventories, energy costs, and assets. (See also Census Bureau home page, http://www.census.gov/.).

Business Statistics of the United States. Courtenay M. Slater, editor. Bernan Associates. • 1999. $74.00. Fifth edition. Based on *Business Statistics*, formerly issue by the Bureau of Economic Analysis, U. S. Department of Commerce. Provides basic data for a wide variety of U. S. industries, services, and economic indicators. Most statistics are shown annually for 29 years and monthly for the most recent four years.

Survey of Current Business. Available from U. S. Government Printing Office. • Monthly. $49.00 per year. Issued by Bureau of Economic Analysis, U. S. Department of Commerce. Presents a wide variety of business and economic data.

TRADE/PROFESSIONAL ASSOCIATIONS

Association for Suppliers of Printing and Publishing Technologies. 1899 Preston White Dr., Reston, VA 22091-4367. Phone: (703)264-7200 Fax: (703)620-0994 E-mail: npes@npes.org • URL: http://www.npes.org.

International Association of Printing House Craftsmen. 7042 Brooklyn Blvd., Minneapolis, MN 55429-1370. Phone: 800-466-4274 or (612)560-1620 Fax: (612)560-1350 E-mail: headquarters@iaphc.org • URL: http://www.iaphc.org.

National Association of Printers and Lithographers. 75 W. Century Rd., Paramus, NJ 07652-1408. Phone: 800-642-6275 or (201)634-9600 E-mail: info@napl.org • URL: http://www.napl.org.

Printimage International. 401 N. Michigan Ave., Ste. 2100, Chicago, IL 60611. Phone: 800-234-0040 or (312)321-6686 Fax: (312)527-6789 E-mail: printimage@printimage.org • URL: http://www.printimage.org.

Printing Industries of America. 100 Daingerfield Rd., Alexandria, VA 22314-2888. Phone: 800-742-2666 or (703)519-8100 Fax: (703)548-3227 E-mail: jsass@printing.org • URL: http://www.printing.org.

PRINTING INK INDUSTRY

ABSTRACTS AND INDEXES

CPI Digest: Key to World Literature Serving the Coatings, Plastics, Fibers, Adhesives, and Related Industries (Chemical Process Industries). CPI Information Services. • Monthly. $397.00 per year. Abstracts of business and technical articles for polymer-based, chemical process industries. Includes a monthly list of relevant U. S. patents. International coverage.

DIRECTORIES

American Inkmaker Buyers' Guide. Cygnus Business Media. • Annual. $20.00. Guide to suppliers of raw materials, equipment, and services for manufacturers of printing ink, pigments, varnishes, graphic chemicals, and similar products.

Rauch Guide to the U. S. Ink Industry. Impact Marketing Consultants. • $389.00. Looseleaf. 250 leading ink manufacturers with over $1 million in annual sales; and lists of activities, organizations, and sources of information in the ink industry. Formerly *Kline Guide to the U.S. Ink Industry.*

PERIODICALS AND NEWSLETTERS

American Inkmaker: For Manufacturers of Printing Inks and Related Graphic Arts Specialty Colors. Cygnus Business Media. • Monthly. $60.00 per year.

RESEARCH CENTERS AND INSTITUTES

Technical and Educational Center of the Graphic Arts and Imaging. Rochester Institute of Technology, 67 Lomb Memorial Dr., Rochester, NY 14623-5603. Phone: 800-724-2536 or (716)475-2680 Fax: (716)475-7000 E-mail: webmail@rit.edu • URL: http://www.rit.edu/cime/te.

STATISTICS SOURCES

Annual Survey of Manufactures. Available from U. S. Government Printing Office. • Annual. Prices vary. Issued by the U. S. Census Bureau as an interim update to the *Census of Manufactures.* Includes data on number of manufacturing establishments in various industries, employment, labor costs, value of shipments, capital expenditures, inventories, energy costs, and assets. (See also Census Bureau home page, http://www.census.gov/.).

TRADE/PROFESSIONAL ASSOCIATIONS

National Association of Printing Ink Manufacturers. 581 Main St., Woodbridge, NJ 07095-1104. Phone: (732)855-1525 Fax: (732)855-1838 E-mail: napim@napim.org • URL: http://www.napim.org.

PRINTING STYLE MANUALS

GENERAL WORKS

Style: Toward Clarity and Grace. Joseph M. Williams. University of Chicago Press. • 1990. $17.95. (Chicago Guides to Writing, Editing and Publishing Series).

HANDBOOKS AND MANUALS

ACS Style Guide: A Manual for Authors and Editors. Janet S. Dodd, editor. American Chemical Society Publications. • 1997. $39.95. Second edition. A style manual for scientific and technical writers. Includes the use of illustrations, tables, lists, numbers, and units of measure.

Associated Press Stylebook and Libel Manual. Addison-Wesley Longman, Inc. • 1996. $14.00. Sixth edition.

The Chicago Manual of Style: The Essential Guide for Authors, Editors, and Publishers. University of Chicago Press. • 1993. $40.00. 14th edition.

Electronic Styles: A Handbook for Citing Electronic Information. Xia Li and Nancy Crane. Information Today, Inc. • 1996. $19.99. Second edition. Covers the citing of text-based information, electronic journals, Web sites, CD-ROM items, multimedia products, and online documents.

Guide for Authors: Manuscript, Proof, and Illustration. Payne E. Thomas. Charles C. Thomas Publishers, Ltd. • 1993. $20.95. Fourth edition.

Handbook for Proofreading. Laura K. Anderson. NTC/Contemporary Publishing. • 1993. $24.95. (NTC Business Book Series).

The New York Public Library Writer's Guide to Style and Usage. Andrea Sutcliffe, editor. HarperCollins Publishers. • 1994. $40.00.

The New York Times Manual of Style and Usage. Allan M. Siegal and William G. Connolly, editors. Times Books. • 1999. $30.00. A revised and expanded version of the 1976 manual edited by Lewis Jordan.

United States Government Printing Office Style Manual. U. S. Government Printing Office. • 2000. $41.00. 29th edition. Supersedes the 1984 edition (28th). Designed to achieve uniformity in the style and form of government printing.

Words into Type. M. Skillen and R. Gay. Prentice Hall. • 1974. $39.95. Third edition.

PERIODICALS AND NEWSLETTERS

Copy Editor: Language News for the Publishing Profession. Mary Beth/Protomastro. • Bimonthly. $69.00 per year. Newsletter for professional copy editors and proofreaders. Includes such items as "Top Ten Resources for Copy Editors.".

PRISONS

See: LAW ENFORCEMENT INDUSTRIES

PRIVATE COMPANIES

See also: CLOSELY HELD CORPORATIONS

ABSTRACTS AND INDEXES

Business Periodicals Index. H. W. Wilson Co. • Monthly, except August, with quarterly and annual cumulations. Service basis for print edition; CD-ROM edition, $1,495.00 per year.

CD-ROM DATABASES

Corporate Affiliations Plus. National Register Publishing, Reed Reference Publishing. • Quarterly. $1,995.00 per year. Provides CD-ROM discs corresponding to *Directory of Corporate Affiliations* and *Corporate Finance Bluebook.* Contains corporate financial services information and worldwide data on subsidiaries and affiliates.

Hoover's Company Capsules on CD-ROM. Hoover's, Inc. • Quarterly. $349.95 per year (single-user). Provides the CD-ROM version of *Hoover's Handbook of American Business, Hoover's Handbook of Emerging Companies, Hoover's Handbook of World Business, Hoover's Guide to Computer Companies, Hoover's Guide to Media Companies, Hoover's Handbook of Private Companies,* and various regional guides. Includes more than 11,000 profiles of companies.

16 Million Businesses Phone Directory. Info USA. • Annual. $29.95. Provides more than 16 million yellow pages telephone directory listings on CD-ROM for all ZIP Code areas of the U. S.

DIRECTORIES

American Big Businesses Directory. American Business Directories. • Annual. $595.00. Lists 177,000 public and private U. S. companies in all fields having 100 or more employees. Includes sales volume, number of employees, and name of chief executive. Formerly *Big Businesses Directory.*

American Business Directory. InfoUSA, Inc. • Provides brief online information on more than 10 million U. S. companies, including individual plants and branches. Entries typically include address, phone number, industry classification code, and contact name. Updating is quarterly. Inquire as to online cost and availability.

American Manufacturers Directory. American Business Directories. • Annual. $595.00. Lists more than 150,000 public and private U. S. manufacturers having 20 or more employees. Includes sales volume, number of employees, and name of chief executive or owner.

Business Organizations, Agencies, and Publications Directory. The Gale Group. • 1999. $425.00. 12th edition. Over 40,000 entries describing 39 types of business information sources. Classified by type of organization, publication, or serviceIncludes state, national, and international agencies and organizations. Master index to names and keywords. Also includes e-mail addresses and web site URL's.

Directory of Corporate Affiliations. National Register Publishing. • Annual. $1,159.00. Five volumes. Volumes one and two: Master Index; volume three: U.S. Public Companies; volume four: U.S. Private Companies; volume five: International Public and Private Companies.

Hoover's Handbook of American Business: Profiles of Major U. S. Companies. Hoover's, Inc. • $149.95. 10th revised edition. Two volumes. Provides detailed profiles of more than 700 large public and private companies, including history, executives, brand names, key competitors, and up to 10 years of financial data. Includes indexes by industry, location, executive name, company name, and brand name.

Hoover's Handbook of Private Companies: Profiles of Major U. S. Private Enterprises. Hoover's, Inc. • Annual. $139.95. Contains profiles of 800 private companies and organizations. Includes indexes by industry, location, executive name, and product.

Hoover's Masterlist of Major U. S. Companies. Hoover's, Inc. • Biennial. $99.95. Provides brief information, including annual sales, number of employees, and chief executive, for about 5,100 U. S. companies, both public and private.

Inc.-The Inc. 500. Inc. Publishing Corp. • Annual. $3.50. Information on each of the 500 fastest-growing privately held companies in the U. S. Based on percentage increase in sales over the five year period prior to compilation of current year's list.

Job Seeker's Guide to Private and Public Companies. The Gale Group. • 1995. $365.00. Third edition. Four regional volumes: *The West, The Midwest, The Northeast,* and *The South.* Covers about 15,000 companies, providing information on personnel department contacts, corporate officials, company benefits, application procedures, etc. Regional volumes are available separately at $99.00.

Ward's Business Directory of U. S. Private and Public Companies. The Gale Group. • 2000. $2,590.00. Eight volumes. *Ward's* contains basic information on about 120,000 business firms, of which 90 percent are private companies. Includes mid-year *Supplement.* Volumes available individually. Prices vary.

Ward's Private Company Profiles: Excerpts and Articles on 150 Privately Held U. S. Companies. The Gale Group. • 1994. $139.00. Fourth edition. A collection of detailed information on 150 private companies.

HANDBOOKS AND MANUALS

How to Find Information About Private Companies. Washington Researchers. • Irregular. $145.00. Organizations, publications, and individuals that collect information on private companies.

INTERNET DATABASES

EBSCO Information Services. Ebsco Publishing. Phone: 800-871-8508 or (508)356-6500 Fax: (508)356-5640 E-mail: ep@epnet.com • URL: http://www.epnet.com • Fee-based Web site providing Internet access to a wide variety of databases, including business-related material. Full text is available for many periodical titles, with daily updates. Fees: Apply.

Hoover's Online. Hoover's, Inc. Phone: 800-486-8666 or (512)374-4500 Fax: (512)374-4501 • URL: http://www.hoovers.com • Web site provides stock quotes, lists of companies, and a variety of business information at no charge. In-depth company profiles are available at $29.95 per month.

ProQuest Direct. Bell & Howell Information and Learning. Phone: 800-521-0600 or (313)761-4700 Fax: (313)973-9145 • URL: http://www.umi.com/proquest • Fee-based Web site providing Internet access to more than 3,000 periodicals, newspapers, and other publications. Many items are available full-text, with daily updates. Includes extensive corporate and financial information from Disclosure, Inc. Fees: Apply.

Switchboard. Switchboard, Inc. Phone: (508)898-1000 Fax: (508)898-1755 E-mail: webmaster@switchboard.com • URL: http://www.switchboard.com • Web site provides telephone numbers and street addresses for more than 100 million business locations and residences in the U. S. Broad industry categories are available. Fees: Free.

ONLINE DATABASES

TRW Business Credit Profiles. TRW Inc., Business Credit Services Division. • Provides credit history (trade payments, payment trends, payment totals, payment history, etc.) for public and private U. S. companies. Key facts and banking information are also given. Updates are weekly. Inquire as to online cost and availability.

Wilson Business Abstracts Online. H. W. Wilson Co. • Indexes and abstracts 600 major business periodicals, plus the *Wall Street Journal* and the business section of the *New York Times.* Indexing is from 1982, abstracting from 1990, with the two newspapers included from 1993. Updated weekly. Inquire as to online cost and availability. (*Business Periodicals Index* without abstracts is also available online.).

PERIODICALS AND NEWSLETTERS

Inc.: The Magazine for Growing Companies. Goldhirsh Group, Inc. • 18 times a year. $19.00 per year. Edited for small office and office-in-the-home businesses with from one to 25 employees. Covers management, office technology, and lifestyle. Incorporates *Self-Employed Professional.*

RESEARCH CENTERS AND INSTITUTES

Center for Private Enterprise. Baylor University, Hankamer School of Business, P.O. Box 98003, Waco, TX 76798-8003. Phone: (254)710-2263 Fax: (254)710-1092 E-mail: jimtruitt@baylor.edu • URL: http://129.62.162.136/enterprise/ • Includes studies of entrepreneurship and women entrepreneurs.

TRADE/PROFESSIONAL ASSOCIATIONS

Center for Family Business. P.O. Box 24219, Cleveland, OH 44124. Phone: (440)442-0800 Fax: (440)442-0178 • Members are family-owned, independent, private, and closely-held businesses.

National Association of Private Enterprise. 7819 Shelburne Circle, Spring, TX 77379-4687. Phone: 800-223-6273 or (512)863-2699 Fax: (512)868-8037 E-mail: info@nape.org • URL: http://www.nape.org • Members are people involved in small businesses.

OTHER SOURCES

The Business Elite: Database of Corporate America. Donnelley Marketing. • Quarterly. $795.00. Formerly compiled by Database America. Provides current information on CD-ROM for about 850,000 businesses, comprising all U. S. private and public companies having more than 20 employees or sales of more than $1 million. Data for each firm includes detailed industry classification, year started, annual sales, name of top executive, and number of employees.

D & B Business Locator. Dun & Bradstreet, Inc. • Quarterly. $2,495.00 per year. CD-ROM provides concise information on more than 10 million U. S. companies or businesses. Includes data on number of employees.

Dun's Middle Market Disc. Dun & Bradstreet, Inc. • Quarterly. Price on application. CD-ROM provides information on more than 150,000 middle market U. S. private companies and their executives.

Dun's Million Dollar Disc. Dun & Bradstreet, Inc. • Quarterly. $3,800.00 per year to libraries; $5,500.00 per year to businesses. CD-ROM provides information on more than 240,000 public and private U. S. companies having sales volume of $5 million or more or 100 employees or more. Includes biographical data on more than 640,000 company executives.

Factiva. Dow Jones Reuters Business Interactive, LLC. • Fee-based Web site provides "global news and business information through Web sites and content integration solutions." Includes Dow Jones and Reuters newswires, The Wall Street Journal, and more than 7,000 other sources of current news, historical articles, market research reports, and investment analysis. Content includes 96 major U. S. newspapers, 900 non-English sources, trade publications, media transcripts, country profiles, news photos, etc.

InSite 2. Intelligence Data/Thomson Financial. • Fee-based Web site consolidates information in a "Base Pack" consisting of Business InSite, Market InSite, and Company InSite. Optional databases are Consumer InSite, Health and Wellness InSite, Newsletter InSite, and Computer InSite. Includes fulltext content from more than 2,500 trade publications, journals, newsletters, newspapers, analyst reports, and other sources. Continuous updating. Formerly produced by The Gale Group.

Nexis.com. Lexis-Nexis Group. • Fee-based Web site offers searching of about 2.8 billion documents in some 30,000 news, business, and legal information sources. Features include a subject directory covering 1,200 topics in 34 categories and a Company Dossier containing information on more than 500,000 public and private companies. Boolean searching is offered.

Standard & Poor's Corporations. Available from Dialog OnDisc. • Monthly. Price on application. Produced by Standard & Poor's. Contains three CD-ROM files: Executives, Private Companies, and Public Companies, providing detailed information on more than 70,000 business executives, 55,000 private companies, and 12,000 publicly-traded corporations.

PRIVATE LABEL PRODUCTS

ABSTRACTS AND INDEXES

Business Periodicals Index. H. W. Wilson Co. • Monthly, except August, with quarterly and annual cumulations. Service basis for print edition; CD-ROM edition, $1,495.00 per year.

CD-ROM DATABASES

ABI/INFORM Global. Bell & Howell Information and Learning. • Monthly. $6,500.00 per year. Provides CD-ROM indexing and abstracting of worldwide business literature appearing in over 1,200 periodicals for the most recent five years. Archival discs are available from 1971. Formerly *ABI/INFORM OnDisc.*

F & S Index Plus Text. The Gale Group. • Monthly. $7,575.00 per year. Provides CD-ROM citations to worldwide business, marketing, and industrial material appearing in a large assortment of trade journals, newspapers, and other publications. Time period is four years.

WILSONDISC: Wilson Business Abstracts. H. W. Wilson Co. • Monthly. $2,495.00 per year, including unlimited online access to *Wilson Business Abstracts* through WILSONLINE. Provides CD-ROM "cover-to-cover" abstracting and indexing of over 600 prominent business periodicals. Indexing is from 1982, abstracting from 1990. (*Business Periodicals Index* without abstracts is available on CD-ROM at $1,495 per year.).

DIRECTORIES

Household and Personal Products Industry - Buyers Guide. Rodman Publications. • Annual. $12.00. Lists of suppliers to manufacturers of cosmetics, toiletries, soaps, detergents, and related household and personal products.

Household and Personal Products Industry Contract Packaging and Private Label Directory. Rodman Publications. • Annual. $12.00. Provides information on about 450 companies offering private label or contract packaged household and personal care products, such as detergents, cosmetics, polishes, insecticides, and various aerosol items.

International Private Label Directory. E. W. Williams Publications Co. • Annual. $75.00. Provides information on over 2,000 suppliers of a wide variety of private label and generic products: food, over-the-counter health products, personal care items, and general merchandise. Formerly *Private Label Directory.*

ONLINE DATABASES

ABI/INFORM. Bell & Howell Information and Learning. • Provides online indexing to business-related material occurring in over 1,000 periodicals from 1971 to the present. Inquire as to online cost and availability.

F & S Index. The Gale Group. • Contains about four million citations to worldwide business, financial, and industrial or consumer product literature appearing from 1972 to date. Weekly updates. Inquire as to online cost and availability.

PROMT: Predicasts Overview of Markets and Technology. The Gale Group. • Companies, products, applied technologies and markets. U.S. and international literature coverage, 1972 to date. Inquire as to online cost and availability. Provides abstracts from more than 1,600 publications. Weekly updates.

Trade & Industry Index. The Gale Group. • Provides indexing of business periodicals, January 1981 to date. Daily updates. (Full text articles from some periodicals are available online, 1983 to date, in the companion database, *Trade & Industry ASAP.*) Inquire as to online cost and availability.

Wilson Business Abstracts Online. H. W. Wilson Co. • Indexes and abstracts 600 major business periodicals, plus the *Wall Street Journal* and the business section of the *New York Times*. Indexing is from 1982, abstracting from 1990, with the two newspapers included from 1993. Updated weekly. Inquire as to online cost and availability. (*Business Periodicals Index* without abstracts is also available online.).

PERIODICALS AND NEWSLETTERS

Household and Personal Products Industry: The Magazine for the Detergent, Soap, Cosmetic and Toiletry, Wax, Polish and Aerosol Industries. Rodman Publications. • Monthly. $48.00 per year. Covers marketing, packaging, production, technical innovations, private label developments, and aerosol packaging for soap, detergents, cosmetics, insecticides, and a variety of other household products.

Private Label International: The Magazine for Store Labels (Own Brands) and Generics. E. W. Williams Publications Co. • Semiannual. $20.00 per year. Edited for large chain store buyers and for manufacturers of private label products. Text in English; summaries in French and German.

Private Label News. Stagnito Communcitions, Inc. • Eight times a year. $75.00 per year. Covers new private label product developments for chain stores. Formerly *Private Label Product News.*

Private Label: The Magazine for House Brands and Generics. E. W. Williams Publications Co. • Bimonthly. $36.00 per year. Edited for buyers of private label, controlled packer, and generic-labeled products. Concentrates on food, health and beauty aids, and general merchandise.

TRADE/PROFESSIONAL ASSOCIATIONS

Private Label Manufacturers Association. 369 Lexington Ave., New York, NY 10017. Phone: (212)972-3131 Fax: (212)983-1382 • URL: http://www.plma.com • Members are manufacturers, wholesalers, and retailers of private brand products. Seeks to promote the private label industry.

OTHER SOURCES

Business & Company Resource Center. The Gale Group. • Fee-based Web site provides a wide range of business, industry, and specific company information. Access is offered to trade journal articles, market research data, insider trading activity, major shareholder data, corporate histories, emerging technology reports, corporate earnings estimates, press releases, and other sources. Provides detailed company profiles, industry overviews, and rankings. Offers integration of Predicasts PROMT, Newsletters ASAP, Investext Plus, Business Index ASAP, Brands and Their Companies, and other databases (many have full text).

PRIVATE SCHOOLS

See also: SCHOOLS

CD-ROM DATABASES

ERIC on SilverPlatter. Available from SilverPlatter Information, Inc. • Quarterly. $700.00 per year. Produced by the Office of Educational Research and Improvement, U. S. Dept. of Education. Provides CD-ROM indexing and abstracting of a wide variety of literature relating to education. Archival discs are available from 1966.

Leadership Library on CD-ROM: Who's Who in the Leadership of the United States. Leadership Directories, Inc. • Quarterly. $2,641.00 per year, including access to Internet version (weekly updates). Contains all 14 *Yellow Book* personnel directories on CD-ROM, providing contact and brief biographical information for about 400,000 individuals. Covers business, government, financial institutions, news media, law firms, associations, foreign representatives, and nonprofit organizations. Includes photographs.

DIRECTORIES

Handbook of Private Schools: An Annual Descriptive Survey of Independent Education. Porter Sargent Publishers, Inc. • Irregular. $93.00. Lists more than 1,600 elementary and secondary boarding and day schools in the United States.

Nonprofit Sector Yellow Book: Who's Who in the Management of the Leading Foundations, Universities, Museums, and Other Nonprofit Organizations. Leadership Directories, Inc. • Semiannual. $235.00 per year. Covers management personnel and board members of about 1,000 prominent, nonprofit organizations: foundations, colleges, museums, performing arts groups, medical institutions, libraries, private preparatory schools, and charitable service organizations.

Patterson's American Education. Educational Directories, Inc. • Annual. Individuals, $87.00; Schools and libraries, $75.00 schools in the U. S. Includes enrollment, grades offered, and name of principal. Geographical arrangement, with indexing by name of school and type of school.

Peterson's Private Secondary Schools. Peterson's. • Annual. $29.95. Provides information on more than 1,400 accredited private secondary schools in the U. S. Formerly *Peterson's Guide to Private Secondary Schools.*

Private Independent Schools: The Bunting and Lyon Blue Book. Bunting and Lyon, Inc. • Annual. $100.00. Over 1,200 elementary and secondary schools and summer programs in the United States and abroad.

HANDBOOKS AND MANUALS

How to Start Your Own School. Robert Love. Jameson Books, Inc. • 1973. $1.95.

ONLINE DATABASES

ERIC. Educational Resources Information Center. • Broad range of educational literature, 1966 to present. Monthly updates. Inquire as to online cost and availability.

PERIODICALS AND NEWSLETTERS

Independent School. National Association of Independent Schools. • Three times a year. $17.50 per year. An open forum for exchange of information about elementary and secondary education in general, and independent education in particular.

STATISTICS SOURCES

Digest of Education Statistics. Available from U. S. Government Printing Office. • Annual. $44.00. Covers all areas of education from kindergarten through graduate school. Includes data from both government and private sources. Compiled by National Center for Education Statistics, U. S. Department of Education.

TRADE/PROFESSIONAL ASSOCIATIONS

National Association of Independent Schools. 1620 L St., N.W., Ste. 1100, Washington, DC 20036-5605. Phone: (202)973-9700 Fax: (202)973-9790.

PRIVATIZATION

GENERAL WORKS

Does Privatization Deliver?: Highlights from a World Bank Conference. Ahmed Galal and Mary Shirley, editors. World Bank, The Office of the Publisher. • 1994. $22.00. Includes 12 international case studies on airlines, telecommunications, electric utilities, and other industries. Presents a favorable view of privatization. (EDI Development Studies Series).

Innovation and Entrepreneurship: Practice and Principles. Peter F. Drucker. HarperInformation. • 1986. $14.50.

ABSTRACTS AND INDEXES

Index to Legal Periodicals and Books. H. W. Wilson Co. • Monthly. Quarterly and annual cumulations. $270.00 per year. CD-ROM version available at $1,495.00 per year.

ONLINE DATABASES

Index to Legal Periodicals and Books (Online). H. W. Wilson Co. • Broad coverage of law journals and books 1981 to date. Monthly updates. Inquire as to online cost and availability.

Legal Resource Index. The Gale Group. • Broad coverage of law literature appearing in legal, business, and other periodicals, 1980 to date. Monthly updates. Inquire as to online cost and availability.

LEXIS. LEXIS-NEXIS. • The various LEXIS databases provide full text and indexing for a wide variety of legal cases, statutes, orders, and opinions.

TRADE/PROFESSIONAL ASSOCIATIONS

Citizens for a Sound Economy. 1250 H St., N.W., Suite 700, Washington, DC 20005-3908. Phone: 888-564-6273 or (202)783-3870 Fax: (202)783-4687 E-mail: cse@cse.org • URL: http://www.cse.org.

National Council for Public-Private Partnerships. 1010 Massachusetts Ave., N.W., Suite 350, Washington, DC 20001-5400. Phone: (202)467-6800 Fax: (202)467-6312 E-mail: ncppp@ncppp.org • URL: http://www.ncppp.org • Promotes private ownership of public services.

PRIZES

See: CONTESTS, PRIZES, AND AWARDS

PROCEDURE MANUALS

See also: TECHNICAL WRITING

GENERAL WORKS

Designing the User Interface: Strategies for Effective Human-Computer Interaction. Ben Shneiderman. Addison Wesley Longman, Inc. • 1997. $44.95. Third edition. Provides an introduction to computer user-interface design. Covers usability testing, dialog boxes, menus, command languages, interaction devices, tutorials, printed user manuals, and related subjects.

ENCYCLOPEDIAS AND DICTIONARIES

BLR Encyclopedia of Prewritten Job Descriptions. Business and Legal Reports, Inc. • $159.95. Looseleaf. Two volumes. Covers all levels "from president to mail clerk.".

HANDBOOKS AND MANUALS

Company Policy and Personnel Workbook. Ardella Ramey. PSI Research. • 1999. $29.95. Fourth edition. Contains about 50 model company personnel policies for use as examples in developing a personnel manual. Explains the basic laws governing employee-employer relationships. (Successful Business Library Series).

How to Develop an Employee Handbook. Joseph W. Lawson. AMACOM. • 1997. $75.00. Second edition. Includes sample handbooks, personnel policy statements, and forms.

How to Research, Write, and Package Administrative Manuals. Leo R. Lunine. AMACOM. • 1985. $75.00.

How to Write Usable User Documentation. Edmond H. Weiss. Oryx Press. • 1991. $24.95. Second edition. Shows how to explain a product, system, or procedure. Includes a glossary and a list of books and periodicals.

Office of Personnel Management Operating Manuals. Available from U. S. Government Printing Office. • Four looseleaf manuals at various prices ($25.00 to $190.00). Price of each manual includes updates for an indeterminate period. Manuals provides details of the federal wage system, the federal wage system "Nonappropriated Fund", personnel recordkeeping, personnel actions, qualification standards, and data reporting.

Writing and Designing Manuals: Operator's Manuals, Service Manuals, Manuals for International Markets. Gretchen H. Schoff and Patricia A. Robinson. Lewis Publishers. • 1991. $54.95. Includes planning, organization, format, visuals, writing strategies, and other topics.

PERIODICALS AND NEWSLETTERS

Technical Communication. Society for Technical Communication. • Quarterly. $60.00 per year. Production of technical literature.

TRADE/PROFESSIONAL ASSOCIATIONS

Society for Technical Communication. 901 N. Stuart St., Suite 904, Arlington, VA 22203-1854. Phone: (703)522-4114 Fax: (703)522-2075 E-mail: stc@stc-va.org • URL: http://www.stc-va.org.

Special Interest Group for Systems Documentation. Association for Computing Machinery, 1515 Broadway, New York, NY 10036. Phone: (212)626-7440 Fax: (212)302-5826 E-mail: sigs@acm.org • URL: http://www.acm.org • Members are individuals who write user manuals and other documentation for computer software applications and computer hardware.

PROCESS CONTROL EQUIPMENT

See: CONTROL EQUIPMENT INDUSTRY

PROCESSED FOOD INDUSTRY

See also: FOOD INDUSTRY

ABSTRACTS AND INDEXES

Food Science and Technology Abstracts. International Food Information Service Publishing. • Monthly. $1,780.00 per year. Provides worldwide coverage of the literature of food technology and food production.

Foods Adlibra: Key to the World's Food Literature. Foods Adlibra Publications. • Semimonthly.Provides journal citations and abstracts to the literature of food technology and packaging.

NTIS Alerts: Agriculture & Food. National Technical Information Service. • Semimonthly. $195.00 per year. Provides descriptions of government-sponsored research reports and software, with ordering information. Covers agricultural economics, horticulture, fisheries, veterinary medicine, food technology, and related subjects. Formerly *Abstract Newsletter.*

ALMANACS AND YEARBOOKS

Almanac of the Canning, Freezing, Preserving Industries, Vol. Two. Edward E. Judge and Sons, Inc. • Annual. $71.00. Contains U. S. food laws and regulations and detailed production statistics.

CD-ROM DATABASES

F & S Index Plus Text. The Gale Group. • Monthly. $7,575.00 per year. Provides CD-ROM citations to worldwide business, marketing, and industrial material appearing in a large assortment of trade journals, newspapers, and other publications. Time period is four years.

Food Science and Technology Abstracts [CD-ROM]. Available from SilverPlatter Information, Inc. • Quarterly. $3,700 per year. Produced by International Food Information Service (home page is http://www.ifis.org). Provides worldwide coverage on CD-ROM of the literature of food technology and production. Various types of publications are indexed, with abstracts, including about 1,800 periodicals. Time period is 1969 to date.

DIRECTORIES

BioScan: The Worldwide Biotech Industry Reporting Service. American Health Consultants, Inc. • Bimonthly. $1,395.00 per year. Looseleaf. Provides detailed information on over 900 U. S. and foreign companies broadly classified as biotechnological. In addition to medical technology and advanced pharmaceutical firms, includes firms doing research in food processing, waste management, agriculture, and veterinary science.

Directory of the Canning, Freezing, Preserving Industries. Edward E. Judge and Sons, Inc. • Biennial. $175.00. Provides information on about 2,950 packers of a wide variety of food products.

Food Processing Guide and Directory. Putman Publishing Co. • Annual. $75.00. Lists over 5,390 food ingredient and equipment manufacturers.

Prepared Foods Food Industry Sourcebook. Cahners Business Information. • Annual. $35.00. Provides information on more than 3,000 manufacturers and suppliers of products, ingredients, supplies, and equipment for the food processing industry.

World Food Marketing Directory. Available from The Gale Group. • 2001. $1,090.00. Second edition. Three volumes. Published by Euromonitor. Provides detailed information on the major food companies of the world, including specific brand data.

ENCYCLOPEDIAS AND DICTIONARIES

Encyclopedia of Food Science, Food Technology, and Nutrition. Robert Macrae and others, editors. Academic Press, Inc. • 1993. Eight volumes. $2,414.00.

Foods and Nutrition Encyclopedia. Audrey H. Ensminger and others. CRC Press, Inc. • 1993. $382.00. Second edition. Two volumes.

ONLINE DATABASES

F & S Index. The Gale Group. • Contains about four million citations to worldwide business, financial, and industrial or consumer product literature appearing from 1972 to date. Weekly updates. Inquire as to online cost and availability.

Food Science and Technology Abstracts [online]. IFIS North American Desk. • Produced by International Food Information Service. Provides about 500,000 online citations, with abstracts, to the international literature of food science, technology, commodities, engineering, and processing. Approximately 2,000 periodicals are covered. Time period is 1969 to date, with monthly updates. Inquire as to online cost and availability.

FOODS ADLIBRA. General Mills, Inc. • Contains online citations, with abstracts, to the technical and business literature of food processing and packaging. New products and new ingredients are featured. Covers about 250 trade journals and 500 research journals from 1974 to date, with monthly updates. Inquire as to online cost and availability.

PROMT: Predicasts Overview of Markets and Technology. The Gale Group. • Companies, products, applied technologies and markets. U.S. and international literature coverage, 1972 to date. Inquire as to online cost and availability. Provides abstracts from more than 1,600 publications. Weekly updates.

PERIODICALS AND NEWSLETTERS

Food Manufacturing. Cahners Business Information, New Product Information. • Monthly. $59.75 per year. Edited for food processing operations managers and food engineering managers. Includes end-of-year *Food Products and Equipment Literature Review.* Formerly *Food Products and Equipment.*

Food Processing. Putman Publishing Co. • Monthly. Free to qualified personnel; others, $98.00 per year. Edited for executive and operating personnel in the food processing industry.

Food Processing Newsletter. Putman Publishing Co. • Weekly. $100.00 per year. Covers food processing industry news and trends.

Journal of Food Products Marketing: Innovations in Food Advertising, Food Promotion, Food Publicity, Food Sales Promotion. Haworth Press, Inc. • Quarterly. Individuals, $60.00 per year; institutions, $95.00 per year; libraries, $175.00 per year.

National Packing News. Jack W. Soward. • Monthly. $25.00 per year. Newsletter for food processing executives. Covers production, marketing, new products, new processing plants, research news, news of personnel, etc. Formerly *Eastern Packing News* and *Western Packing News.*

Prepared Foods. Cahners Business Information. • Monthly. $99.90 per year. Edited for food manufacturing management, marketing, and operations personnel.

RESEARCH CENTERS AND INSTITUTES

Food Industries Center. Ohio State University, Howlett Hall, Suite 140, 2001 Fyffe Court, Columbus, OH 43210. Phone: (614)292-7004 Fax: (614)292-4233 E-mail: james.14@osu.edu • URL: http://www.osu.edu.

Institute for Food Law and Regulations. Michigan State University, 165C National Food Safety and Toxicology Bldg., East Lansing, MI 48224. Phone: 888-579-3663 or (517)355-8295 Fax: (517)432-1492 E-mail: vhegarty@pilot.msu.edu • URL: http://www.msu.edu • Conducts research on the food industry, including processing, packaging, marketing, and new products.

Institute of Food Science. Cornell University, 114 Stocking Hall, Ithaca, NY 14853. Phone: (607)255-7915 Fax: (607)254-4868 E-mail: mrm1@cornell.edu • URL: http://www.nysaes.cornell.edu/cifs/ • Research areas include the chemistry and processing of food commodities, food processing engineering, food packaging, and nutrition.

National Food Processors Association Research Foundation. 1350 Eye St., N.W., Suite 300, Washington, DC 20005. Phone: (202)639-5958 Fax: (202)639-5991 E-mail: rappleb@nfpa-food.org • URL: http://www.nfpa-food.org • Conducts research on food processing engineering, chemistry, microbiology, sanitation, preservation aspects, and public health factors.

TRADE/PROFESSIONAL ASSOCIATIONS

Food Processors Institute. 1401 New York Ave., N. W., Suite 400, Washington, DC 20005. Phone: (202)393-0890 or (202)639-5904 Fax: (202)639-5941 E-mail: fpi@nfpa-food.org • URL: http://www.nfpa-food.org • Provides education and training for the food processing industry through schools, seminars, and workshops. Affiliated with the National Food Processors Association.

National Food Processors Association. 1301 Eye St., N.W., Ste. 300, Washington, DC 20005. Phone: (202)639-5900 Fax: (202)639-5932 E-mail: nfpa@nfpa-food.org • URL: http://www.nfpa-food.org.

OTHER SOURCES

Business & Company Resource Center. The Gale Group. • Fee-based Web site provides a wide range of business, industry, and specific company information. Access is offered to trade journal articles, market research data, insider trading activity, major shareholder data, corporate histories, emerging technology reports, corporate earnings estimates, press releases, and other sources. Provides detailed company profiles, industry overviews, and rankings. Offers integration of Predicasts PROMT, Newsletters ASAP, Investext Plus, Business Index ASAP, Brands and Their Companies, and other databases (many have full text).

Major Food and Drink Companies of the World. Available from The Gale Group. • 2001. $855.00. Fourth edition. Two volumes. Published by Graham & Whiteside. Contains profiles and trade names for more than 9,000 important food and beverage companies in various countries. In addition to foods, includes both alcoholic and nonalcoholic drink products.

Thomas Food and Beverage Market Place. Grey House Publishing. • Annual. $295.00. Three volumes. Contains more than 40,000 entries covering food companies, beverages, food equipment, warehouse companies, food brokers, wholesalers, importers, and exporters. Formerly *Thomas Food Industry Register.*

PROCUREMENT, GOVERNMENT

See: GOVERNMENT PURCHASING

PRODUCE INDUSTRY

See: VEGETABLE INDUSTRY

PRODUCT CODING

See: POINT-OF-SALE SYSTEMS (POS)

PRODUCT DESIGN

See: DESIGN IN INDUSTRY

PRODUCT DEVELOPMENT

See: NEW PRODUCTS

PRODUCT LIABILITY

See: PRODUCT SAFETY AND LIABILITY

PRODUCT MANAGEMENT

See: MARKETING

PRODUCT QUALITY

See: QUALITY OF PRODUCTS

PRODUCT RATING RESEARCH

See: QUALITY OF PRODUCTS

PRODUCT SAFETY AND LIABILITY

GENERAL WORKS

Crisis Response: Inside Stories on Managing Image Under Siege. The Gale Group. • 1993. $60.00. Presents first-hand accounts by media relations professionals of major business crises and how they were handled. Topics include the following kinds of crises: environmental, governmental, corporate image, communications, and product.

ABSTRACTS AND INDEXES

Applied Science and Technology Index. H. W. Wilson Co. • 11 times a year. Quarterly and annual cumulations. Service basis for print edition; CD-

ROM edition, $1,495.00 per year. Indexes a wide variety of English language technical, industrial, and engineering periodicals.

Index to Legal Periodicals and Books. H. W. Wilson Co. • Monthly. Quarterly and annual cumulations. $270.00 per year. CD-ROM version available at $1,495.00 per year.

ALMANACS AND YEARBOOKS

Insurance Law Review. Pat Magarick. West Group. • 1990. $125.00. Provides review of legal topics within the casualty insurance area, including professional liability, product liability, and environmental issues.

CD-ROM DATABASES

Consumers Reference Disc. National Information Services Corp. • Quarterly. Provides the CD-ROM version of *Consumer Health and Nutrition Index* from Oryx Press and *Consumers Index to Product Evaluations and Information Sources* from Pierian Press. Contains citations to consumer health articles and consumer product evaluations, tests, warnings, and recalls.

DIRECTORIES

Directory of Certified Product Safety Managers. Board of Certified Product Safety Management. • Biennial. $15.00. Membership directory.

HANDBOOKS AND MANUALS

Fundamentals of Product Liability Law for Engineers. L. K. Enghagen. Industrial Press, Inc. • 1992. $39.95. Covers theories of liability, strategies for protection, defenses, and proving a case. Includes case histories.

ONLINE DATABASES

I.I.I. Data Base Search. Insurance Information Institute. • Provides online citations and abstracts of insurance-related literature in magazines, newspapers, trade journals, and books. Emphasis is on property and casualty insurance issues, including highway safety, product safety, and environmental liability. Inquire as to online cost and availability.

Index to Legal Periodicals and Books (Online). H. W. Wilson Co. • Broad coverage of law journals and books 1981 to date. Monthly updates. Inquire as to online cost and availability.

Legal Resource Index. The Gale Group. • Broad coverage of law literature appearing in legal, business, and other periodicals, 1980 to date. Monthly updates. Inquire as to online cost and availability.

LEXIS. LEXIS-NEXIS. • The various LEXIS databases provide full text and indexing for a wide variety of legal cases, statutes, orders, and opinions.

PERIODICALS AND NEWSLETTERS

Consumer Product Safety Review. Available from U. S. Government Printing Office. • Quarterly. $16.00 per year. Issued by the U. S. Consumer Product Safety Commission.

FDA Consumer. Available from U. S. Government Printing Office. • Bimonthly. $23.00 per year. Issued by the U. S. Food and Drug Administration. Provides consumer information about FDA regulations and product safety.

Product Liability Law and Strategy Newsletter. Leader Publications, Inc. • Monthly. $185.00 per year. Formerly *Product Liability Newsletter.*

Product Safety Letter. Washington Business Information, Inc. • Weekly. $967.00 per year. Newsletter on product safety regulation and legislation. *Supplement* available.

Product Safety News. National Safety Council. • Monthly. Members, $21.00 per year; non-members, $25.00 per year.

RESEARCH CENTERS AND INSTITUTES

Institute for Advanced Safety Studies. 5950 W. Touhy Ave., Niles, IL 60714. Phone: (847)647-1101 Fax: (847)647-2047.

Keystone Center. 1628 Saints John Rd., Keystone, CO 80435-7998. Phone: (970)513-5800 Fax: (970)262-0152 • URL: http://www.keystone.org • Research areas include product liability.

Law and Economics Center. University of Miami, Business School, P.O. Box 248000, Coral Gables, FL 33124. Phone: (305)284-6174 Fax: (305)662-9159 • Research areas include product liability law.

TRADE/PROFESSIONAL ASSOCIATIONS

Board of Certified Product Safety Management. 8009 Carita Court, Bethesda, MD 20817. Phone: (301)770-2540 • Evaluates qualifications of product safety managers.

Coalition for Uniform Product Liability Law. 1023 15th St., 7th Fl., Washington, DC 20005. Phone: (202)289-1780 Fax: (202)842-3275 • Lobbies for a uniform federal product liability law.

National Safety Council. 1121 Spring Lake Dr., Itasca, IL 60143-3201. Phone: 800-621-7615 or (630)285-1121 Fax: (630)285-1315 • URL: http://www.nsc.org.

The Product Liability Alliance. c/o National Association of Wholesaler-Distributors, 1725 K St., N. W., Suite 300, Washington, DC 20006. Phone: (202)872-0885 Fax: (202)296-5940 E-mail: naw@nawd.org • URL: http://www.nawd.org • Promotes reform of federal product liability laws.

Product Liability Prevention and Defense. 111 Park Place, Falls Church, VA 22046-4513. Phone: (703)538-1797 Fax: (703)241-5603 E-mail: plpdhq@aol.com • Purpose is to achieve more efficient product liability legal defense for machinery manufacturers.

OTHER SOURCES

Consumer Product Litigation Reporter. Andrews Publications. • Monthly. $725.00 per year. Provides reports on legislation and litigation relating to product liability.

Corporate Compliance Series. West Group. • Eleven looseleaf volumes, with periodic supplementation. $990.00. Covers criminal and civil liability problems for corporations. Includes employee safety, product liability, pension requirements, securities violations, equal employment opportunity issues, intellectual property, employee hiring and firing, and other corporate compliance topics.

Pharmaceutical Litigation Reporter: The National Journal of Record of Pharmaceutical Litigation. Andrews Publications. • Monthly. $775.00 per year. Reports on a wide variety of legal cases involving the pharmaceutical and medical device industries. Includes product liability lawsuits.

PRODUCT TESTING

See: QUALITY OF PRODUCTS

PRODUCTION CONTROL

See also: INVENTORY CONTROL; QUALITY CONTROL

ENCYCLOPEDIAS AND DICTIONARIES

Blackwell Encyclopedic Dictionary of Operations Management. Nigel Slack, editor. Blackwell Publishers. • 1997. $105.95. The editor is associated with the University of Warwick, England. Contains definitions of key terms combined with longer articles written by various U. S. and foreign business educators. Includes bibliographies and index. (Blackwell Encyclopedia of Management Series.).

HANDBOOKS AND MANUALS

Production and Inventory Control Handbook. James H. Greene. McGraw-Hill. • 1997. $95.00. Third edition.

Production and Operations Management: Total Quality and Responsiveness. Hamid Noori and Russell Radford. McGraw-Hill. • 1994. $70.25.

PERIODICALS AND NEWSLETTERS

Production. Gardner Publications, Inc. • Monthly. $48.00 per year. Covers the latest manufacturing management issues. Discusses the strategic and financial implications of various tecnologies as they impact factory management, quality and competitiveness.

Production and Inventory Management Journal. APICS: The Educational Society for Resource Management. • Quarterly. Members, $64.00 per year; non-members, $80.00 per year.

TRADE/PROFESSIONAL ASSOCIATIONS

APICS-The Educational Society for Resource Management. 5301 Shawnee Rd., Alexandria, VA 22312. Phone: 800-444-2742 or (703)354-8851 Fax: (703)354-8106 • URL: http://www.apics.org • Members are professional resource managers.

OTHER SOURCES

Federal Income Taxation of Inventories. Matthew Bender & Co., Inc. • $710.00. Three looseleaf volumes. Periodic supplementation.

PRODUCTION ENGINEERING

See: INDUSTRIAL ENGINEERING

PRODUCTION MANAGEMENT

See: OPERATIONS MANAGEMENT

PRODUCTIVITY

GENERAL WORKS

Chaos on the Shop Floor: A Worker's View of Quality, Productivity, and Management. Tom Juravich. Temple University Press. • 1988. $19.95. (Labor and Social Change Series).

Improving Public Productivity: Concepts and Practice. Ellen D. Rosen. Sage Publications, Inc. • 1993. $52.00. A discussion of strategies for improving service quality and client satisfaction in public agencies at the local, state, and national level. Methods for measuring public sector productivity are included.

Participative Management: An Analysis of Its Affect on Productivity. Michael H. Swearingen. Garland Publishing, Inc. • 1997. $35.00. (Garland Studies on Industrial Productivity).

People and Productivity. Robert A. Sutemeister. McGraw-Hill. • 1976. $24.95. Third edition. (Management Series).

Profit Sharing: Does It Make a Difference? The Productivity and Stability Effects of Profit Sharing Plans. Douglas L. Kruse. W. E. Upjohn Institute for Employment Research. • 1993. $27.00.

Reengineering Management: The Mandate for New Leadership. James Champy. DIANE Publishing Co. • 1998. $25.00.

Reengineering the Corporation: A Manifesto for Business Revolution. Michael Hammer and James Champy. HarperCollins Publishers, Inc. • 1999. $16.00. Revised edition.

ABSTRACTS AND INDEXES

NTIS Alerts: Manufacturing Technology. National Technical Information Service. • Semimonthly. $265.00 per year. Provides descriptions of government-sponsored research reports and software, with ordering information. Covers computer-aided design and manufacturing (CAD/CAM), engineering materials, quality control, machine tools, robots, lasers, productivity, and related subjects. Formerly *Abstract Newsletter.*

ENCYCLOPEDIAS AND DICTIONARIES

Blackwell Encyclopedic Dictionary of Organizational Behavior. Nigel Nicholson, editor. Blackwell Publishers. • 1995. $105.95. The editor is associated with the London Business School. Contains definitions of key terms combined with longer articles written by various U. S. and foreign business educators. Includes bibliographies and index. *Blackwell Encyclopedia of Management Series.*

HANDBOOKS AND MANUALS

AMA Management Handbook. John J. Hampton, editor. AMACOM. • 1994. $110.00. Third edition. Provides 200 chapters in 16 major subject areas. Covers a wide variety of business and industrial management topics.

Maximizing Employee Productivity: A Manager's Guide. Robert E. Sibson. AMACOM. • 1994. $22.95.

Reengineering Revolution: A Handbook. Michael Hammer and Steven Stanton. HarperInformation. • 1995. $16.00.

INTERNET DATABASES

Bureau of Labor Statistics (BLS). U. S. Department of Labor, Bureau of Labor Statistics. Phone: (202)523-1092 E-mail: labstat.helpdesk@bls.gov • URL: http://www.bls.gov • Web site provides a great variety of employment, wage, price, and economic data. Some links are "Data," "Economy at a Glance," "Keyword Search of BLS Web Pages," "Regional Information," and "Other Statistical Sites." Fees: Free.

ONLINE DATABASES

Business and Industry. Responsive Database Services, Inc. • Contains online citations, abstracts, and selected fulltext from more than 1,000 trade journals, newspapers, and other publications. Provides general coverage of both manufacturing and service industries, including marketing, production, industry trends, key events, and information on specific companies. Time span is 1994 to date. Daily updates. Inquire as to online cost and availability. (Also available in a CD-ROM version.).

Management Contents. The Gale Group. • Covers a wide range of management, financial, marketing, personnel, and administrative topics. About 150 leading business journals are indexed and abstracted from 1974 to date, with monthly updating. Inquire as to online cost and availability.

Tablebase. Responsive Database Services, Inc. • Provides online numerical tabular data from a wide variety of business, organization, and government sources, including 900 trade journals. Includes industry and individual company statistics relating to products, market share, sales forecasts, production, exports, market trends, etc. Time span is 1997 to date. Weekly updates. Inquire as to online cost and availability. (Also available in a CD-ROM version.).

PERIODICALS AND NEWSLETTERS

Lean Manufacturing Advisor: Techniques and Technologies Supporting Lean Manufacturing and TPM. Productivity, Inc. • Monthly. $167.00 per year. Formerly *Lean Marketing Advisor.*

The Motivational Manager: Strategies to Increase Morale and Productivity in the Workplace. Lawrence Ragan Communications, Inc. • Monthly. $119.00 per year. Newsletter. Emphasis is on participative management.

National Productivity Review: The Journal of Productivity Management. John Wiley and Sons, Inc. • Quarterly. Institutions, $345.00 per year.

RESEARCH CENTERS AND INSTITUTES

Center for Quality and Productivity. University of North Texas, College of Business Administration, Denton, TX 76203-3677. Phone: (940)565-4767 E-mail: prybutok@unt.edu • URL: http://www.coba.unt.edu:80/bcis.organize/cqp/cqp.htm • Fields of research include the management of quality systems and statistical methodology.

Center for Quality and Productivity Improvement. University of Wisconsin-Madison, 610 N. Walnut St., 575 WARF Bldg., Madison, WI 53705. Phone: (608)263-2520 Fax: (608)263-1425 E-mail: quality@engr.wisc.edu • URL: http://www.engr.wisc.edu/centers/cqpi • Research areas include quality management and industrial engineering.

W. E. Upjohn Institute for Employment Research. 300 S. Westnedge Ave., Kalamazoo, MI 49007-4686. Phone: (616)343-5541 Fax: (616)343-3308 E-mail: eberts@we.upjohninst.org • URL: http://www.upjohninst.org • Research fields include unemployment, unemployment insurance, worker's compensation, labor productivity, profit sharing, the labor market, economic development, earnings, training, and other areas related to employment.

STATISTICS SOURCES

Economic Report of the President: Together with the Annual Report of the Council of Economic Advisors. Available from U. S. Government Printing Office. • Annual. $29.00. Includes about 130 pages of "Statistical Tables Relating to Income, Employment, and Production." Tables cover national income, employment, wages, productivity, manufacturing, prices, credit, finance (public and private), corporate profits, and foreign trade.

Handbook of U. S. Labor Statistics: Employment, Earnings, Prices, Productivity, and Other Labor Data. Eva E. Jacobs, editor. Bernan Associates. • 1999. $74.00. Based on *Handbook of Labor Statistics*, formerly issued by the Bureau of Labor Statistics, U. S. Department of Labor. Includes the Bureau's projections of employment in the U. S. by industry and occupation. Provides a wide variety of data on the work force, prices, fringe benefits, and consumer expenditures.

Report on the American Workforce. Available from U. S. Government Printing Office. • Annual. $15.00. Issued by the U. S. Department of Labor (http://www.dol.gov). Appendix contains tabular statistics, including employment, unemployment, price indexes, consumer expenditures, employee benefits (retirement, insurance, vacation, etc.), wages, productivity, hours of work, and occupational injuries. Annual figures are shown for up to 50 years.

Services: Statistics on Value Added and Employment. Organization for Economic Cooperation and Development. • Annual. $67.00. Provides 10-year data on service industry employment and output (value added) for all OECD countries. Covers such industries as telecommunications, business services, and information technology services.

TRADE/PROFESSIONAL ASSOCIATIONS

National Association of Professional Organizers. 1033 La Posada Drive, Suite 220, Austin, TX 78752. Phone: (512)454-8626 Fax: (512)454-3036 E-mail: napo@assnmgmt.com • URL: http://www.napo.net • Members are concerned with time management, productivity, and the efficient organization of documents and activities.

PRODUCTS, NEW

See: NEW PRODUCTS

PRODUCTS, QUALITY OF

See: QUALITY OF PRODUCTS

PROFESSIONAL ASSOCIATIONS

See: ASSOCIATIONS

PROFESSIONAL CORPORATIONS

See also: CORPORATIONS

ABSTRACTS AND INDEXES

Index to Legal Periodicals and Books. H. W. Wilson Co. • Monthly. Quarterly and annual cumulations. $270.00 per year. CD-ROM version available at $1,495.00 per year.

HANDBOOKS AND MANUALS

How to Incorporate: A Handbook for Entrepreneurs and Professionals. Michael Diamond. John Wiley and Sons, Inc. • 1996. $49.95. Third edition.

Professional Corporations and Associations. Berrien C. Eaton. Matthew Bender & Co., Inc. • $1,140.00. Six looseleaf volumes. Periodic supplementation. Detailed information on forming, operating and changing a professional corporation or association.

Subchapter S Manual. P. L. Faber and Martin E. Holbrook. Prentice Hall. • Annual. Price on application.

Valuing Professional Practices: A Practitioner's Guide. Robert Reilly and Robert Schweihs. CCH, Inc. • 1997. $99.00. Provides a basic introduction to estimating the dollar value of practices in various professional fields.

ONLINE DATABASES

Legal Resource Index. The Gale Group. • Broad coverage of law literature appearing in legal, business, and other periodicals, 1980 to date. Monthly updates. Inquire as to online cost and availability.

PERIODICALS AND NEWSLETTERS

Business Strategies Bulletin. CCH, Inc. • Monthly. $166.00 per year. Newsletter.

OTHER SOURCES

Business Strategies. CCH, Inc. • Semimonthly. $819.00 per year. Four looseleaf volumes. Semimonthly updates. Legal, tax, and accounting aspects of business planning and decision-making. Provides information on start-ups, forms of ownership (partnerships, corporations), failing businesses, reorganizations, acquisitions, and so forth. Includes *Business Strategies Bulletin,* a monthly newsletter.

PROFESSIONAL LIABILITY

GENERAL WORKS

Professional Liability: An Economic Analysis. Roger Bowles and Philip Jones. Pearson Education and Technology. • 1989. $14.00. (David Hume Papers, No. 11).

ABSTRACTS AND INDEXES

Current Law Index: Multiple Access to Legal Periodicals. The Gale Group. • Monthly. $650.00 per year. Produced in cooperation with the American Association of Law Libraries. Indexes more than 900 law journals, legal newspapers, and specialty publications from the U.S., Canada, U.K., Ireland, Australia, and New Zealand.

Index to Legal Periodicals and Books. H. W. Wilson Co. • Monthly. Quarterly and annual cumulations. $270.00 per year. CD-ROM version available at $1,495.00 per year.

ALMANACS AND YEARBOOKS

Insurance Law Review. Pat Magarick. West Group. • 1990. $125.00. Provides review of legal topics within the casualty insurance area, including professional liability, product liability, and environmental issues.

BIBLIOGRAPHIES

Encyclopedia of Legal Information Sources. The Gale Group. • 1992. $180.00. Second edition. Lists more than 23,000 law-related information sources, including print, nonprint, and organizational.

CD-ROM DATABASES

LegalTrac. The Gale Group. • Monthly. $5,000.00 per year. Price includes workstation. Provides CD-ROM indexing of periodical literature relating to legal matters from 1980 to date. Corresponds to online *Legal Resource Index.*

WILSONDISC: Index to Legal Periodicals and Books. H. W. Wilson Co. • Monthly. Including unlimited online access to *Index to Legal Periodicals* through WILSONLINE. Contains CD-ROM indexing of more than 800 English language legal periodicals from 1981 to date and 2,500 books.

DIRECTORIES

Insurance Market Place: The Agents and Brokers Guide to Non-Standard and Specialty Lines, Aviation, Marine and International Insurance. Rough Notes Co., Inc. • Annual. $12.95. Lists specialty, excess, and surplus insurance lines.

Law and Legal Information Directory. The Gale Group. • 2000. $405.00. 11th edition. Two volumes. Contains a wide range of sources of legal information, such as associations, law schools, courts, federal agencies, referral services, libraries, publishers, and research centers. There is a separate chapter for each of 23 types of information source or service.

Physician Insurers Association of America: Membership Directory. Physician Insurers Association of America. • Annual. Lists 60 cooperative physicians' professional liability insurers affiliated with state medical societies. Formerly *Physician-Owned Medical-Society-Created Professional Liability Insurance Companies.*

HANDBOOKS AND MANUALS

Accountants' Liability. Practising Law Institute. • Looseleaf. $135.00. Annual revisions. Covers all aspects of accountants' professional liability issues, including depositions and court cases.

Codes of Professional Responsibility: Ethic Standards in Business, Health and Law. Rena Gorlin, editor. Bureau of National Affairs, Inc. • 1998. $95.00. Fourth edition. Contains full text or substantial excerpts of the official codes of ethics of major professional groups in the fields of law, business, and health care.

Directors' and Officers' Liability. Practising Law Institute. • Looseleaf. $125.00. Annual revisions. Covers all aspects of liability issues for corporate directors and executives. Indemnification, insurance, and dispute resolution are included as topics.

Directors' and Officers' Liability Insurance. Practising Law Institute. • 1992. $70.00. Legal handbook. (Commercial Law and Practice Course Handbook Series).

How to Avoid Liability: The Information Professionals' Guide to Negligence and Warrant Risks. T. R. Halvorson. Burwell Enterprises, Inc. • 1998. $24.50. Second edition. Provides legal advice, cases, and decisions relating to information brokers and others in the information business.

Legal Liability Problems in Cyberspace: Craters in the Information Highway. T. R. Halvorson. Burwell Enterprises, Inc. • 1998. $24.50. Covers the legal risks and liabilities involved in doing online research as a paid professional. Includes a table of cases.

Medical Malpractice. Thomas A. Moore and Daniel Kramer, editors. Practising Law Institute. • 1990. $25.00. Sixth edition. Legal handbook.

ONLINE DATABASES

Index to Legal Periodicals and Books (Online). H. W. Wilson Co. • Broad coverage of law journals and books 1981 to date. Monthly updates. Inquire as to online cost and availability.

Legal Resource Index. The Gale Group. • Broad coverage of law literature appearing in legal, business, and other periodicals, 1980 to date. Monthly updates. Inquire as to online cost and availability.

PERIODICALS AND NEWSLETTERS

Emergency Department Law: The Source for Comprehensive Coverage of Legal Trends in Emergency Medicine. Business Publishers, Inc. • Monthly. $355.00 per year. Newsletter for the medical profession. Formerly *Medical Liability Advisory Service.*

Life in Medicine: Business and Lifestyle Issues for New Physicians. Dynamic Graphics, Inc. • Bimonthly. $42.00 per year. Covers practice management and financial topics for new physicians.

Medical Economics. Medical Economics Co., Inc. • 25 times a year. $109.00 per year. Covers the financial, economic, insurance, administrative, and other non-clinical aspects of private medical practice. Provides investment and estate planning advice.

Medical Economics General Surgery-Orthopedic Surgery. Medical Economics Co., Inc. • Monthly. $65.00 per year. Provides information and advice on practice management (non-clinical) for surgeons. Formerly *Medical Economics for Surgeons.*

Professional Liability Reporter: Recent Decisions of National Significance. Shepard's. • Monthly. $305.00 per year.

Professional Negligence Law Reporter. Association of Trial Lawyers of America. • Monthly. Members $95.00 per year; non-members, $155.00 per year. Legal newsletter focusing on the liability of health care personnel, accountants, lawyers, engineers, insurance brokers, and real estate agents.

RESEARCH CENTERS AND INSTITUTES

Lexis.com Research System. Lexis-Nexis Group. Phone: 800-227-9597 or (937)865-6800 Fax: (937)865-6909 E-mail: webmaster@prod.lexis-nexis.com • URL: http://www.lexis.com • Fee-based Web site offers extensive searching of a wide variety of legal sources. Additional features include Daily Opinion Service, lexis.com Bookstore, Career Center, CLE Center, Law Schools, and Practice Pages ("Pages specific to areas of specialty").

TRADE/PROFESSIONAL ASSOCIATIONS

American Board of Professional Liability Attorneys. c/o Harvey F. Wachsman, 175 E. Shore Rd., Great Neck, NY 11023. Phone: 800-633-6255 or (516)487-1990 Fax: (516)487-4304 • Members are liability litigation lawyers who meet specific requirements as to experience and who pass written and oral Board examinations.

Defense Research International. 130 N. Michigan Ave., Chicago, IL 60601. Phone: 800-667-8108 or (312)795-1101 Fax: (312)795-0747 E-mail: custservice@dri.org • URL: http://www.dri.org • Members are attorneys, insurance companies, insurance adjusters, and others. Includes Product Liability and Professional Liability Committees.

Insurance Services Office. Seven World Trade Center, New York, NY 10048. Phone: (212)898-6000 Fax: (212)898-5525.

Physician Insurers Association of America. 2275 Research Blvd., Suite 250, Rockville, MD 20878. Phone: (301)947-9000 Fax: (301)947-9090 • URL: http://www.thepiaa.org • Members are cooperative physicians' professional liability insurers affiliated with state medical societies.

OTHER SOURCES

Andrews' Professional Liability Litigation Reporter. Andrews Publications. • Monthly. $550.00 per year. Provides reports on lawsuits against attorneys, accountants, and investment professionals.

Avoiding Tax Malpractice. Robert Feinschreiber and Margaret Kent. CCH, Inc. • 2000. $75.00. Covers malpractice considerations for professional tax practitioners.

Citation: Current Legal Developments Relating to Medicine and Allied Professions. American Medical Association, Health Law Div. Citation Publishing Corp. • Semimonthly. $130.00 per year. Contains summaries of lawsuits affecting medical personnel or hospitals.

Corporate Officers and Directors Liability Litigation Reporter: The Twice Monthly National Journal of Record of Litigation Based on Fiduciary Responsibility. Andrews Publications. • Semimonthly. $890.00 per year. Provides reports on lawsuits in the area of corporate officers' fiduciary responsibility.

PROFESSIONAL PRACTICE MANAGEMENT, MEDICAL

See: MEDICAL ECONOMICS (PRACTICE MANAGEMENT)

PROFESSIONS

See: OCCUPATIONS

PROFESSORS AND INSTRUCTORS

See: COLLEGE FACULTIES

PROFIT SHARING

See also: EMPLOYEE BENEFIT PLANS

GENERAL WORKS

Profit Sharing: Does It Make a Difference? The Productivity and Stability Effects of Profit Sharing Plans. Douglas L. Kruse. W. E. Upjohn Institute for Employment Research. • 1993. $27.00.

ENCYCLOPEDIAS AND DICTIONARIES

Dictionary of Finance and Investment Terms. John Downes and Jordan E. Goodman. Barron's Educational Series, Inc. • 1998. $12.95. Fifth revised edition. Provides clear explanations of more than

5,000 business, banking, financial, investment, and tax terms. Includes a separate list of financial abbreviations and acronyms.

HANDBOOKS AND MANUALS

Employee Stock Ownership Plans: A Practical Guide to ESOPs and Other Broad Ownership Programs. Scott Rodrick, editor. Harcourt Brace, Legal and Professional Publications, Inc. • 1996. $79.00. Contains 19 articles by various authors on ESOPs, 401(k) plans, profit sharing, executive stock option plans, and related subjects.

Guide to Pension and Profit Sharing Plans: Taxation, Selection, and Design. Donald S. Dunkle. Shepard's. • 1984. $115.00. (Commercial Law Publications).

Pension and Profit Sharing Plans. Matthew Bender & Co., Inc. • Six looseleaf volumes. Periodic supplementation. Price on application. Full treatment of pension and profit sharing plans, including forms and legal analysis.

Pension and Profit Sharing Plans for Small or Medium Size Businesses. Panel Publishers, Inc. • Monthly. $191.50 per year. Newsletter. Topics of interest and concern to professionals who serve small and medium size pension and profit sharing plans.

PERIODICALS AND NEWSLETTERS

Profit Sharing. Profit Sharing-401(K) Council of America. • Bimonthly. Membership.

RESEARCH CENTERS AND INSTITUTES

W. E. Upjohn Institute for Employment Research. 300 S. Westnedge Ave., Kalamazoo, MI 49007-4686. Phone: (616)343-5541 Fax: (616)343-3308 E-mail: eberts@we.upjohninst.org • URL: http://www.upjohninst.org • Research fields include unemployment, unemployment insurance, worker's compensation, labor productivity, profit sharing, the labor market, economic development, earnings, training, and other areas related to employment.

TRADE/PROFESSIONAL ASSOCIATIONS

Profit Sharing/401(K) Council of America. 10 S. Riverside Plaza, No. 1610, Chicago, IL 60606. Phone: (312)441-8550 Fax: (312)441-8559 E-mail: psca@psca.org • URL: http://www.psca.org • Members are business firms with profit sharing and/or 401(K) plans. Affiliated with the Profit Sharing/401(K) Education Foundation at the same address.

Profit Sharing/401(K) Education Foundation. 10 S. Riverside Plaza, No. 1610, Chicago, IL 60606. Phone: (312)441-8550 Fax: (312)441-8559 E-mail: psca@psca.org • URL: http://www.psca.org.

PROGRAM EVALUATION AND REVIEW TECHNIQUE

See: CRITICAL PATH METHOD/PERT (PROGRAM EVALUATION AND REVIEW TECHNIQUE)

PROGRAMMED LEARNING

PERIODICALS AND NEWSLETTERS

Educational Technology: The Magazine for Managers of Change in Education. Educational Technology Publications, Inc. • Bimonthly. $119.00 per year.

Innovations in Education and Training International. Association for Educational and Training Technology. • Quarterly. Individuals, $62.00 per year; libraries and other institutions, $190.00 per year. Provides up-to-date coverage of educational and training technologies. Formerly *Educational and Training Technology International.*

TRADE/PROFESSIONAL ASSOCIATIONS

International Society for Performance Improvement. 1300 L St., N.W., Suite 1250, Washington, DC 20005. Phone: (202)408-7969 Fax: (202)408-7972 E-mail: info@ispi.org • URL: http://www.ispi.org.

PROGRAMMING, COMPUTER

See: COMPUTER SOFTWARE INDUSTRY

PROGRAMMING, LINEAR

See: LINEAR PROGRAMMING

PROGRAMS, TELEVISION

See: TELEVISION PROGRAMS

PROJECT MANAGEMENT

See also: INDUSTRIAL MANAGEMENT

GENERAL WORKS

Essentials of Project Management. Dennis Lock. Ashgate Publishing Co. • 1996. $26.95. Published by Gower in England.

Fundamentals of Project Management. James P. Lewis. AMACOM. • 1995. $10.95. (Work Smart Series).

Project Management. Dennis Lock. John Wiley and Sons, Inc. • 1996. $69.95. Sixth edition.

Project Management Casebook. David I. Cleland and others, editors. Project Management Institute. • 1998. $69.95. Provides 50 case studies in various areas of project management.

CD-ROM DATABASES

Annotated Bibliography of Project and Team Management. Project Management Institute. • 1998. $119.95. Provides citations and annotations on CD-ROM for selected project management literature since 1956.

COMPENDEX PLUS [CD-ROM]. Engineering Information, Inc. • Quarterly. $3,450.00 per year. Provides CD-ROM indexing and abstracting of the world's engineering and technical information appearing in journals, reports, books, and proceedings, 1985 to date.

WILSONDISC: Business Periodicals Index. H. W. Wilson Co. • Monthly. $1,495.00 per year. Provides CD-ROM indexing of business periodicals from 1982 to date. Price includes online service.

HANDBOOKS AND MANUALS

AMA Management Handbook. John J. Hampton, editor. AMACOM. • 1994. $110.00. Third edition. Provides 200 chapters in 16 major subject areas. Covers a wide variety of business and industrial management topics.

Field Guide to Project Management. David I. Cleland, editor. John Wiley and Sons, Inc. • 1998. $39.95. Provides 38 articles by various authors on the major aspects of project management.

Gower Handbook of Project Management. Dennis Lock, editor. Ashgate Publishing Co. • 2000. $129.95. Second edition. Consists of 33 chapters written by various authors, with bibliographical references and index. Published by Gower in England.

Guide to the Project Management Body of Knowledge. Project Management Institute Standards Committee. Project Management Institute. • 1996. $32.95. Presents the fundamental tenets of project management. Covers the management of integration, scope, time, cost, quality, human resources, communications, risk, and procurement. Includes an extensive glossary.

Human Resource Skills for the Project Manager: The Human Aspects of Project Management, Volume Two. Vijay K. Verma. Project Management Institute. • 1996. $32.95. (Human Aspects of Project Management Series).

Little Black Book of Project Management. Michael C. Thomsett. AMACOM. • 1990. $14.95. Gives practical advice on the day-to-day management of new projects, including budgeting and scheduling. (Little Black Book Series).

Managing High-Technology Programs and Projects. Russell D. Archibald. John Wiley and Sons, Inc. • 1992. $107.50. Second edition. Written for senior executives, professional project managers, engineers, and information systems managers.

Managing the Project Team: The Human Aspects of Project Management, Volume Three. Vijay K. Verma. Project Management Institute. • 1997. $32.95. (Human Aspects of Project Management Series).

Organizing Projects for Success: The Human Aspects of Project Management, Volume One. Vijay K. Verma. Project Management Institute. • 1995. $32.95. (Human Aspects of Project Management Series).

PMI Book of Project Management Forms. Project Management Institute. • 1997. $49.95. Contains more than 100 sample forms for use in project management. Includes checklists, reports, charts, agreements, schedules, requisitions, order forms, and other documents.

Principles of Project Management: Collected Handbooks from the Project Management Institute. John R. Adams and others. Project Management Institute. • 1997. $59.95. Consists of reprints of eight "handbooks" by various authors, previously published by the Project Management Institute. Includes such topics as contract administration, conflict management, team building, and coping with stress.

Project Management: A Managerial Approach. Jack R. Meredith and Samuel J. Mantel. John Wiley and Sons, Inc. • 1995. $95.95. Third edition. (Productions-Operations Management Series).

Project Management: A Systems Approach to Planning, Scheduling, and Controlling. Harold Kerzner. John Wiley & Sons, Inc. • 1994. $65.00. Sixth edition. Includes chapters on time management, risk management, quality management, and program evaluation and review techniques (PERT). (Business Technology Series).

Project Management: How to Plan and Manage Successful Projects. Joan Knutson and Ira Bitz. AMACOM. • 1991. $55.00. Covers both technical and organizational skills.

Project Management: Strategic Design and Implementation. David I. Cleland. McGraw-Hill. • 1998. $64.95. Third edition.

ONLINE DATABASES

Management Contents. The Gale Group. • Covers a wide range of management, financial, marketing, personnel, and administrative topics. About 150 leading business journals are indexed and abstracted from 1974 to date, with monthly updating. Inquire as to online cost and availability.

Wilson Business Abstracts Online. H. W. Wilson Co. • Indexes and abstracts 600 major business periodicals, plus the *Wall Street Journal* and the business section of the *New York Times.* Indexing is from 1982, abstracting from 1990, with the two newspapers included from 1993. Updated weekly. Inquire as to online cost and availability. (*Business Periodicals Index* without abstracts is also available online.).

PERIODICALS AND NEWSLETTERS

Journal of Project Finance. Institutional Investor. • Quarterly. $290.00 per year. Covers the financing of large-scale construction projects, such as power plants and convention centers.

Project Management Journal. Project Management Institute. • Quarterly. $100.00 per year. Contains technical articles dealing with the interests of the field of project management.

STATISTICS SOURCES

Project Management Salary Survey. Project Management Institute. • Annual. $129.00. Gives compensation data for key project management positions in North America, according to job title, level of responsibility, number of employees supervised, and various other factors. Includes data on retirement plans and benefits.

TRADE/PROFESSIONAL ASSOCIATIONS

Project Management Institute. Four Campus Blvd., Newton Square, PA 19073-3200. Phone: (610)356-4600 Fax: (610)356-4647 E-mail: pmihq@pmi.org • URL: http://www.pmi.org.

OTHER SOURCES

Successful Project Management. American Management Association Extension Institute. • Looseleaf. $130.00. Self-study course. Emphasis is on practical explanations, examples, and problem solving. Quizzes and a case study are included.

PROMOTION

See: SALES PROMOTION

PROMOTIONAL MERCHANDISE

See: PREMIUMS

PROOFREADING

See: PRINTING STYLE MANUALS

PROPANE AND BUTANE GAS INDUSTRY

See also: NATURAL GAS; PETROLEUM INDUSTRY

ABSTRACTS AND INDEXES

Gas Abstracts. Institute of Gas Technology. • Monthly. $425.00 per year. Abstracts of gas and energy related articles from around the world.

CD-ROM DATABASES

Environment Abstracts on CD-ROM. Congressional Information Service, Inc. • Quarterly. $1,295.00 per year. Contains the following CD-ROM databases: *Environment Abstracts, Energy Abstracts,* and *Acid Rain Abstracts.* Length of coverage varies.

FINANCIAL RATIOS

Annual Statement Studies. Robert Morris Associates: The Association of Lending and Credit Risk Professiona. • Annual. Free to members; non-members, $140.00. Median and quartile financial ratios are given for over 400 kinds of manufacturing, wholesale, retail, construction, and consumer finance establishments. Data is sorted by both asset size and sales volume. Includes a clearly written "Definition of Ratios" and an alphabetical industry index.

ONLINE DATABASES

Energyline. Congressional Information Service, Inc. • Provides online citations and abstracts to the literature of all forms of energy: petroleum, natural gas, coal, nuclear power, solar energy, etc. Time period is 1971 to 1993 (closed file). Inquire as to online cost and availability.

Platt's Energy Prices. Data Products Division. • Contains daily high and low prices for crude oil and petroleum products, including gasoline, fuel oil, and liquefied petroleum gas (LPG). Coverage is international from 1983 to present, with daily updates. Inquire as to online cost and availability.

PERIODICALS AND NEWSLETTERS

Butane-Propane News. Butane-Propane News, Inc. • Monthly. $26.00 per year.

LP-GAS. Advanstar Communications, Inc. • Monthly. $30.00 per year. Covers the production, storage, utilization, and marketing of liquefied petroleum gas (propane). Gas appliances are included. Includes annual supplement.

Oil Daily: Daily Newspaper of the Petroleum Industry. Energy Intelligence Group. • Daily. $1,145.00 per year. Newspaper for the petroleum industry.

STATISTICS SOURCES

Gas Facts: A Statistical Record of the Gas Utility Industry. American Gas Association, Dept. of Statistics. • Annual. Members, $40.00; non-members, $80.00.

Petroleum Supply Annual. Available from U. S. Government Printing Office. • Annual. $78.00. Two volumes. Produced by the Energy Information Administration, U. S. Department of Energy. Contains worldwide data on the petroleum industry and petroleum products.

Petroleum Supply Monthly. Available from U. S. Government Printing Office. • Monthly. $100.00 per year. Produced by the Energy Information Administration, U. S. Department of Energy. Provides worldwide statistics on a wide variety of petroleum products. Covers production, supplies, exports and imports, transportation, refinery operations, and other aspects of the petroleum industry.

TRADE/PROFESSIONAL ASSOCIATIONS

Institute of Gas Technology. 1700 S. Mount Prospect Rd., Des Plaines, IL 60018-1804. Phone: (847)768-0500 Fax: (847)768-0516 • URL: http://www.igt.org.

National Propane Gas Association. 1600 Eisenhower Lane, Suite 100, Lisle, IL 60532. Phone: 800-457-4772 or (630)515-0600 Fax: (630)515-8774 E-mail: info@npga.org • URL: http://www.propanegas.com/npga.

PROPERTY AND LIABILITY INSURANCE

See also: CASUALTY INSURANCE; FIRE INSURANCE; INSURANCE; MARINE INSURANCE; PROFESSIONAL LIABILITY; RISK MANAGEMENT

GENERAL WORKS

Property and Liability Insurance. Solomon S. Huebner and others. Prentice Hall. • 1995. $96.00.

Smarter Insurance Solutions. Janet Bamford. Bloomberg Press. • 1996. $19.95. Provides practical advice to consumers, with separate chapters on the following kinds of insurance: automobile, homeowners, health, disability, and life. (Bloomberg Personal Bookshelf Series).

ABSTRACTS AND INDEXES

Insurance Periodicals Index. Specials Libraries Association, Insurance and Employees Benefits Div. CCH/NILS Publishing Co. • Annual. $250.00. Compiled by the Insurance and Employee Benefits Div., Special Libraries Association. A yearly index of over 15,000 articles from about 35 insurance periodicals. Arrangement is by subject, with an index to authors.

ALMANACS AND YEARBOOKS

Property and Casualty Insurance: Year in Review. CCH, Inc. • Annual. $75.00. Summarizes the year's significant legal and regulatory developments.

BIBLIOGRAPHIES

Insurance and Employee Benefits Literature. Special Libraries Association, Insurance and Employee Benefits Div. • Bimonthly. $15.00 per year.

CD-ROM DATABASES

U. S. Insurance: Property and Casualty. Sheshunoff Information Services, Inc. • Monthly. Price on application. CD-ROM provides detailed, current financial information on more than 3,200 property and casualty insurance companies.

DIRECTORIES

Best's Directory of Recommended Insurance Attorneys and Adjusters. A. M. Best Co. • Annual. $1130.00. Two volumes. More than 5,000 American, Canadian, and foreign insurance defense law firms; lists 1,200 national and international insurance adjusting firms. Formerly *Best's Directory of Recommended Insurance Adjusters.*

S & P's Insurance Book. Standard & Poor's Ratings Group, Insurance Rating Services. • Quarterly. Price on application. Contains detailed financial analyses and ratings of various kinds of insurance companies.

S & P's Insurance Digest: Property-Casualty and Reinsurance Edition. Standard & Poor's Ratings Group, Insurance Rating Services. • Quarterly. Contains concise financial analyses and ratings of property-casualty insurance companies.

ENCYCLOPEDIAS AND DICTIONARIES

Dictionary of Insurance. Lewis E. Davids. Rowman and Littlefield Publishers, Inc. • 1990. $17.95. Seventh revised edition.

Dictionary of Insurance Terms. Harvey W. Rubin. Barron's Educational Series, Inc. • 2000. $12.95. Fourth edition. Defines terms in a wide variety of insurance fields. Price on application.

Insurance Words and Their Meanings: A Dictionary of Insurance Terms. Diana Kowatch. The Rough Notes Co., Inc. • 1998. $38.50. 16th revised edition.

HANDBOOKS AND MANUALS

The Complete Book of Insurance: The Consumer's Guide to Insuring Your Life, Health, Property, and Income. Ben G. Baldwin. McGraw-Hill Professional. • 1996. $24.95. Revised edition. Provides basic information and advice on various kinds of insurance: life, health, property (fire), disability, long-term care, automobile, liability, and annuities.

ONLINE DATABASES

Best's Company Reports. A. M. Best Co. • Provides full financial data online for U. S. insurance companies (life, health, property, casualty), including balance sheet data, income statements, expenses, premium income, losses, and investments. Includes *Best's Company Reports, Best's Insurance News,* and Best's ratings of insuarance companies. Inquire as to online cost and availability.

I.I.I. Data Base Search. Insurance Information Institute. • Provides online citations and abstracts of insurance-related literature in magazines, newspapers, trade journals, and books. Emphasis is on property and casualty insurance issues, including highway safety, product safety, and environmental liability. Inquire as to online cost and availability.

PERIODICALS AND NEWSLETTERS

Best's Review: Insurance Issues and Analysis. A.M. Best Co. • Monthly. $25.00 per year. Editorial coverage of significant industry trends, developments, and important events. Formerly Best's Review: Property-Casualty Insurance.

CPCU Journal. Chartered Property and Casualty Underwriters Society. • Quarterly. $25.00 per year. Published by the Chartered Property and Casualty Underwriters Society (CPCU). Edited for professional insurance underwriters and agents.

Fire, Casualty and Surety Bulletin. The National Underwriter Co. • Monthly. $420.00 per year. Five base volumes. Monthly updates.

Insurance and Technology. Miller Freeman. • Monthly. $65.00 per year. Covers information technology and systems management as applied to the operation of life, health, casualty, and property insurance companies.

John Liner Letter. Standard Publishing Corp. • Monthly. $178.00 per year. Newsletter for users of business insurance.

National Underwriter, Property and Casualty Edition. The National Underwriter Co. • Weekly. $88.00 per year.

Professional Agent. National Association of Professional Insurance Agents. • Monthly. Members, $12,00 per year; non-members, $24.00 per year. Provides sales and marketing advice for independent agents in various fields of insurance, including life, health, property, and casualty.

Risk Management. Risk and Insurance Management Society. Risk Management Society Publishing, Inc. • Monthly. $54.00 per year.

Rough Notes: Property, Casualty, Surety. The Rough Notes Co., Inc. • Monthly. $27.50 per year.

RESEARCH CENTERS AND INSTITUTES

S. S. Huebner Foundation. University of Pennsylvania, Vance Hall, Room 430, Philadelphia, PA 19104-6301. Phone: (215)898-9631 Fax: (215)573-2218 E-mail: cummins@wharton.upenn.edu • URL: http://www.rider.wharton.upenn.edu/~sshuebne/ • Awards grants for research in various areas of insurance.

STATISTICS SOURCES

Property-Casualty Insurance Facts. Insurance Information Institute. • Annual. $22.50. Formerly *Insurance Facts.*

Standard & Poor's Industry Surveys. Standard & Poor's. • Semiannual. $1,800.00. Two looseleaf volumes. Includes monthly supplements. Provides detailed, individual surveys of 52 major industry groups. Each survey is revised on a semiannual basis. Also includes "Monthly Investment Review" (industry group investment analysis) and monthly "Trends & Projections" (economic analysis).

U. S. Industry and Trade Outlook: The McGraw-Hill Companies and the U.S. Department of Commerce/International Trade Administration. Datapso Research Corp. • Annual. $69.95. Produced by the International Trade Administration, U. S. Department of Commerce, in a "public-private" partnership with DRI/McGraw-Hill and Standard & Poor's. Provides basic data, outlook for the current year, and "Long-Term Prospects" (five-year projections) for a wide variety of products and services. Includes high technology industries. Formerly *U. S. Industrial Outlook.*

TRADE/PROFESSIONAL ASSOCIATIONS

American Institute for CPCU. P.O. Box 3016, Malvern, PA 19355-0716. Phone: 800-644-2101 or (610)644-2100 Fax: (610)640-9576 E-mail: cserv@cpuiia.org • URL: http://www.aicpcu.com.

American Insurance Association. 1130 Connecticut Ave., N.W., Suite 1000, Washington, DC 20036. Phone: 800-242-2302 or (202)828-7100 or (202)828-7183 Fax: (202)293-1219.

Insurance Information Institute. 110 William St., New York, NY 10038. Phone: 800-331-9146 Fax: (212)791-1807 E-mail: info@iii.org • URL: http://www.iii.org.

Insurance Services Office. Seven World Trade Center, New York, NY 10048. Phone: (212)898-6000 Fax: (212)898-5525.

National Association of Professional Insurance Agents. 400 N. Washington St., Alexandria, VA 22314. Phone: (703)836-9340 Fax: (703)836-1279 E-mail: piaweb@pianet.org • URL: http://www.pianet.com • Members are independent agents in various fields of insurance.

Risk and Insurance Management Society. 655 Third Ave., 2nd Fl., New York, NY 10017. Phone: (212)286-9292 Fax: (212)986-9716 • URL: http://www.rims.org.

OTHER SOURCES

Best's Insurance Reports: Property-Casualty. A.M. Best Co. • Annual. $745.00. Guide to over 1,750 major property/casualty companies.

Fire and Casualty Insurance Law Reports. CCH, Inc. • $870.00 per year. Looseleaf service. Semimonthly updates.

Insurance Day. Available from Informa Publishing Group Ltd. • Three times a week. $440.00 per year. Published in the UK by Lloyd's List (http://www.lloydslist.com). A newspaper providing international coverage of property/casualty/liability insurance, reinsurance, and risk, with an emphasis on marine insurance.

The Law of Liability Insurance. Matthew Bender & Co., Inc. • $1,230.00. Five looseleaf volumes. Periodic supplementation. Explains the terms and phases essential for a general understanding of liability insurance, and discusses injuries to both persons and property.

PROPERTY MANAGEMENT

See also: REAL ESTATE BUSINESS

ABSTRACTS AND INDEXES

Real Estate Index. National Association of Realtors. • 1987. $169.00 Two volumes. Vol. one, $99.00; vol. two, $99.00. Supplement available, 1988. $49.50.

DIRECTORIES

CRS Referral Directory. Council of Residential Specialists. • Annual. Membership. *CRB/CRS Referral Directory.*

U.S. Real Estate Register. Barry, Inc. • Annual. $87.50. Formerly *Industrial Real Estate Managers Directory.*

ENCYCLOPEDIAS AND DICTIONARIES

Dictionary of Real Estate. Jae K. Shim and others. John Wiley and Sons, Inc. • 1995. $80.00. Contains 3,000 definitions of commercial and residential real estate terms. Covers appraisal, escrow, investment, finance, mortgages, property management, construction, legal aspects, etc. Includes illustrations and formulas. (Business Dictionaries Series).

HANDBOOKS AND MANUALS

Every Landlord's Legal Guide. Marcia Stewart. Nolo.com. • 2000. $44.95. Fourth edition.

Every Tenant's Legal Guide. Janet Portman and Marcia Stewart. Nolo.com. • 1999. $26.95. Second edition.

PERIODICALS AND NEWSLETTERS

Building Operating Management: The National Magazine for Commercial and Institutional Buildings Construction, Renoration, Facility Management. Trade Press Publishing Corp. • Monthly. $55.00 per year.

Buildings: The Facilities Construction and Management Journal. Stamats Communications, Inc. • Monthly. $70.00 per year. Serves professional building ownership/management organizations.

Housing the Elderly Report. Community Development Services, Inc. CD Publications. • Monthly. $197.00 per year. Newsletter. Edited for retirement communities, apartment projects, and nursing homes. Covers news relative to business and property management issues.

Journal of Property Management. Institute of Real Estate Management. • Bimonthly. $43.95 per year.

Ledger Quarterly: A Financial Review for Community Association Practitioners. Community Associations Institute. • Quarterly. Members, $40.00 per year; non-members, $67.00 per year. Newsletter. Provides current information on issues affecting the finances of condominium, cooperative, homeowner, apartment, and other community housing associations.

Managing Housing Letter. Community Development Services, Inc. CD Publications. • Monthly. $225.00 per year. Newsletter for housing professionals. Provides property management advice and news relating to private and publicly-funded rental housing.

Properties. Properties Magazine, Inc. • Monthly. $15.00 per year. News and features of interest to income property owners managers and related industries in Northeastern Ohio.

Real Estate New York. • Ten times a year. $35.00 per year. Formerly *Better Bulidings.*

RESEARCH CENTERS AND INSTITUTES

Center for Finance and Real Estate. University of California, Los Angeles, John E. Anderson Graduate School of Management, P.O. Box 951481, Los Angeles, CA 90095-1481. Phone: (310)825-1953 Fax: (310)206-5455 E-mail: wtorous@anderson.ucla.edu • URL: http://www.agsm.ucla.edu/acadunit/finance/realestate.

TRADE/PROFESSIONAL ASSOCIATIONS

Building Owners and Managers Association International. 1201 New York Ave., N.W., Suite 300, Washington, DC 20005. Phone: (202)408-2662 Fax: (202)371-0181 E-mail: soppen@boma.org • URL: http://www.boma.org.

Community Associations Institute. 1630 Duke St., Alexandria, VA 22314. Phone: (703)548-8600 Fax: (703)684-1581 • URL: http://www.caionline.org • Members are condominium associations, homeowners associations, builders, property managers, developers, and others concerned with the common facilities and services in condominiums, townhouses, planned unit developments, and other planned communities.

Institute of Real Estate Management. 430 N. Michigan Ave., Chicago, IL 60611-4090. Phone: 800-837-0706 or (312)329-6000 Fax: (312)410-7960 E-mail: rvukas@irem.org • URL: http://www.irem.org.

National Apartment Association. 201 N. Union St., Suite 200, Alexandria, VA 22314. Phone: (703)513-6141 Fax: (703)513-6191 E-mail: membership@naahq.com • URL: http://www.naahq.com.

National Property Management Association. 1108 Pinehurst Rd., Dunedin, FL 34698. Phone: (727)736-3788 Fax: (727)736-6707 E-mail: npma@gte.net • URL: http://www.npma.org.

Property Management Association. 7900 Wisconsin Ave., Suite 204, Bethesda, MD 20814. Phone: (301)657-9200 Fax: (301)907-9326 E-mail: pma@erols.com • URL: http://www.pma-dc.org.

PROPERTY TAX

See also: INDUSTRIAL REAL ESTATE; TAX SHELTERS

GENERAL WORKS

Tips and Traps for Saving on All Your Real Estate Taxes. Robert Irwin and Norman Lane. McGraw-Hill. • 1992. $12.95.

ABSTRACTS AND INDEXES

Index to Legal Periodicals and Books. H. W. Wilson Co. • Monthly. Quarterly and annual cumulations. $270.00 per year. CD-ROM version available at $1,495.00 per year.

BIBLIOGRAPHIES

The Tax Reform Act of 1986 and Its Impact on the Real Estate Industry. Marilyn Hankel. Sage Publications, Inc. • 1993. $10.00.

DIRECTORIES

International Association of Assessing Officers: Membership Directory. International Association of Assessing Officers. • Annual. $400.00. Lists about 8,500 state and local officials concerned with valuation of property tax.

HANDBOOKS AND MANUALS

Real Estate Taxation: A Practitioner's Guide. David F. Windish. CCH, Inc. • 1998. $125.00. Second edition. Serves as a guide to the federal tax consequences of real estate ownership and operation. Covers mortgages, rental agreements, interest, landlord income, forms of ownership, and other tax-oriented topics.

U. S. Master Property Tax Guide. CCH, Inc. • Annual. $67.00. Provides state-by-state coverage of "key property tax issues and concepts," including exemptions, assessments, taxpayer remedies, and property tax calendars.

ONLINE DATABASES

Index to Legal Periodicals and Books (Online). H. W. Wilson Co. • Broad coverage of law journals and books 1981 to date. Monthly updates. Inquire as to online cost and availability.

Legal Resource Index. The Gale Group. • Broad coverage of law literature appearing in legal, business, and other periodicals, 1980 to date. Monthly updates. Inquire as to online cost and availability.

LEXIS. LEXIS-NEXIS. • The various LEXIS databases provide full text and indexing for a wide variety of legal cases, statutes, orders, and opinions.

PERIODICALS AND NEWSLETTERS

Assessment Journal. International Association of Assessing Officers. • Bimonthly. Free to members; non-members, $200.00 per year. Formed by merger of *Assessment* and *Valuation Legal Reporter and IAAO Update.*

The Journal of Taxation: A National Journal of Current Developments, Analysis and Commentary for Tax Professionals. Warren, Gorham & Lamont/RIA Group. • Monthly. $215.00 per year. Analysis of current tax developments for tax specialists.

Property Tax Alert. CCH, Inc. • Monthly. $197.00 per year. Newsletter. Covers trends in real estate valuation, assessment, and taxation.

Real Estate Finance. Institutional Investor. • Quarterly. $225.00 per year. Covers real estate for professional investors. Provides information on complex financing, legalities, and industry trends.

Real Estate Tax Ideas. Warren, Gorham & Lamont/RIA Group. • Monthly. $150.00 per year. Newsletter. Analysis of the current marketplace and regulatory agencies and new opportunities in real estate. Continuing coverage of recent and proposed tax developments.

RESEARCH CENTERS AND INSTITUTES

Center for Tax Policy Studies. Purdue University, 490 Krannert, West Lafayette, IN 47907-1310. Phone: (765)494-4442 Fax: (765)496-1778 E-mail: papke@mgmt.purdue.edu.

Institute for Real Estate Studies. Pennsylvania State University, Smeal College of Business Administration, 409 Business Administration Bldg., University Park, PA 16802. Phone: (814)865-4172 Fax: (814)865-6284 E-mail: ajj@psu.edu.

Office of Real Estate Research. University of Illinois at Urbana-Chamapign, 1407 E. Gregory Dr., 304 David Kinley Hall, Champaign, IL 61820. Phone: (217)244-0591 Fax: (217)244-9867 E-mail: orer@uiuc.edu • URL: http://www.cba.uiuc.edu/orer/orer.htm.

Tax Foundation. 1250 H St., N.W., Suite 750, Washington, DC 20005. Phone: (202)783-2760 Fax: (202)783-6868 E-mail: taxfnd@intr.net • URL: http://www.taxfoundation.org.

Urban Land Institute. 1025 Thomas Jefferson Ave. N.W., Suite 500W, Washington, DC 20004. Phone: (202)624-7000 Fax: (202)624-7140 E-mail: rlevitt@uli.org • URL: http://www.uli.org • Studies urban land planning and the growth and development of urbanized areas, including central city problems, industrial development, community development, residential development, taxation, shopping centers, and the effects of development on the environment.

TRADE/PROFESSIONAL ASSOCIATIONS

Institute for Professionals in Taxation. 3350 Peachtree Rd., N.E., Suite 280, Atlanta, GA 30326. Phone: (404)240-2300 Fax: (404)240-2315 E-mail: ipt@ipt.org • URL: http://www.ipt.org • Promotes education in the area of property taxation.

International Association of Assessing Officers. 130 E. Randolph St., Suite 850, Chicago, IL 60601. Phone: (312)819-6100 Fax: (312)819-6149 • URL: http://www.iaao.org.

OTHER SOURCES

Manufacturers' Tax Alert. CCH, Inc. • Monthly. $297.00 per year. Newsletter. Covers the major tax issues affecting manufacturing companies. Includes current developments in various kind of federal, state, and international taxes: sales, use, franchise, property, and corporate income.

PROPOSALS, BUSINESS

See: BUSINESS START-UP PLANS AND PROPOSALS

PROSTHETICS INDUSTRY

ABSTRACTS AND INDEXES

NTIS Alerts: Biomedical Technology & Human Factors Engineering. National Technical Information Service. • Semimonthly. $210.00 per year. Provides descriptions of government-sponsored research reports and software, with ordering information. Covers biotechnology, ergonomics, bionics, artificial intelligence, prosthetics, and related subjects. Formerly *Abstract Newsletter.*

FINANCIAL RATIOS

Annual Statement Studies. Robert Morris Associates: The Association of Lending and Credit Risk Professiona. • Annual. Free to members; non-members, $140.00. Median and quartile financial ratios are given for over 400 kinds of manufacturing, wholesale, retail, construction, and consumer finance establishments. Data is sorted by both asset size and sales volume. Includes a clearly written "Definition of Ratios" and an alphabetical industry index.

TRADE/PROFESSIONAL ASSOCIATIONS

American Orthotic and Prosthetic Association. 1650 King St., Suite 500, Alexandria, VA 22314. Phone: (703)836-7116 Fax: (703)836-0838 E-mail: generalinfo@opoffice.org • URL: http://www.opoffice.org/aopa.

PROTECTIVE SERVICES

See: INDUSTRIAL SECURITY PROGRAMS

PSYCHOLOGICAL TESTING

See also: INDUSTRIAL PSYCHOLOGY; RATING OF EMPLOYEES

GENERAL WORKS

Essentials of Psychological Testing. Lee J. Cronbach. Addison-Wesley Educational Publishers, Inc. • 1997. $113.00. Fifth edition.

Psychological Testing. Anne Anastasi. Prentice Hall. • 1996. $89.00. Seventh edition.

ABSTRACTS AND INDEXES

Psychological Abstracts. American Psychological Association. • Monthly. Members, $799.00 per year; individuals and institutions, $1,075.00 per year. Covers the international literature of psychology and the behavioral sciences. Includes journals, technical reports, dissertations, and other sources.

ALMANACS AND YEARBOOKS

Mental Measurements Yearbook. University of Nebraska-Lincoln Buros Institute of Mental Measurements. • Biennial. Price varies.

BIBLIOGRAPHIES

Tests in Print. Linda L. Murphy and others. University of Nebraska-Lincoln Buros Institute of Mental Measurements. • Quinquennial. Price varies. Two volumes. Lists over 4,000 testing instruments.

DIRECTORIES

The Human Resource Executive's Market Resource. LRP Publications. • Annual. $25.00. A directory of services and products of use to personnel departments. Includes 20 categories, such as training, outplacement, health benefits, recognition awards, testing, workers' compensation, temporary staffing, recruitment, and human resources software.

Test Critques. Pro-Ed. • 1998. 11 volumes. Prices vary. Presents detailed evaluations of the validity of tests in psychology, education, and business. Published by ProEd, Inc.

Tests: A Comprehensive Reference for Assessments in Psychology, Education and Business. Available from The Gale Group. • 1997. $99.00. Fourth edition. List nearly 500 publishers for over 3,000 tests. Published by Pro-Ed Inc.

ENCYCLOPEDIAS AND DICTIONARIES

The Gale Encyclopedia of Psychology. The Gale Group. • 1998. $130.00. Includes bibliographies arranged by topic and a glossary.

ONLINE DATABASES

Mental Health Abstracts. IFI/Plenum Data Corp. • Provides indexing and abstracting of mental health and mental illness literature appearing in more than 1,200 journals and other sources from 1969 to date. Monthly updates. Inquire as to online cost and availability.

PsycINFO. American Psychological Association. • Provides indexing and abstracting of the worldwide literature of psychology and the behavioral sciences. Time period is 1967 to date, with monthly updates. Inquire as to online cost and availability.

PERIODICALS AND NEWSLETTERS

Educational and Psychological Measurement: Devoted to the Development and Application of Measures of Individual Differences. Sage Publications, Inc. • Bimonthly. Individuals, $95.00 per year; institutions, $395.00 per year.

Journal of Business and Psychology. Business Psychology Research Institute. Kluwer Plenum Academic Publishers. • Quarterly. Institutions, $556.80 per year.

Measurement and Evaluation in Counseling and Development. Association for Measurement and Evaluation in Counseling and Development. American Counseling Association. • Quarterly. $50.00 per year.

TRADE/PROFESSIONAL ASSOCIATIONS

American Counseling Association. 5999 Stevenson Ave., Alexandria, VA 22304-3300. Phone: 800-347-6647 or (703)823-9800 Fax: (703)823-0252 • URL: http://www.counseling.org.

American Psychological Association: Industrial and Organizational Psychology Society. 750 First St., N.E., Washington, DC 20002-4242. Phone: 800-374-2721 or (202)336-5500 Fax: (202)336-5997 E-mail: executiveoffice@apa.org • URL: http://www.apa.org/.

PSYCHOLOGY

See: HUMAN RELATIONS; MENTAL HEALTH; MOTIVATION (PSYCHOLOGY)

PSYCHOLOGY, INDUSTRIAL

See: INDUSTRIAL PSYCHOLOGY

PUBLIC ACCOUNTANTS

See: CERTIFIED PUBLIC ACCOUNTANTS

PUBLIC ADMINISTRATION

See also: CIVIL SERVICE; COMPUTERS IN GOVERNMENT; MUNICIPAL GOVERNMENT; STATE GOVERNMENT

GENERAL WORKS

Improving Public Productivity: Concepts and Practice. Ellen D. Rosen. Sage Publications, Inc. • 1993. $52.00. A discussion of strategies for improving service quality and client satisfaction in public agencies at the local, state, and national level. Methods for measuring public sector productivity are included.

The Leader of the Future: New Essays by World-Class Leaders and Thinkers. Jossey-Bass, Inc., Publishers. • 1996. $25.00. Contains 32 articles on leadership by "executives, consultants, and commentators." (Management Series).

Performance Management in Government: Contemporary Illustrations. OECD Publications and Information Center. • 1996.

Public Administration and Public Affairs. Nicholas L. Henry. Prentice Hall. • 2000. $53.33. Eighth edition.

Public Administration: Design and Problem Solving. Jong S. Jun. Chatelaine Press. • 1986. $41.95.

Public Personnel Administration: Policies and Procedures for Personnel. Prentice Hall. • Looseleaf service. Price on application.

ABSTRACTS AND INDEXES

PAIS International in Print. Public Affairs Information Service, Inc. • Monthly. $650.00 per year; cumulations three times a year. Provides topical citations to the worldwide literature of public affairs, economics, demographics, sociology, and trade. Text in English; indexed materials in English, French, German, Italian, Portuguese and Spanish.

Sage Public Administration Abstracts. Sage Publications, Inc. • Quarterly. Individuals, $150.00 per year; institutions, $575.00 per year.

Social Sciences Citation Index. Institute for Scientific Information. • Three times a year. $6,900 per year. Annual cumulation. Includes *Source Index, Citation Index, Permuterm Subject Index,* and *Corporate Index.*

Social Sciences Index. H. W. Wilson Co. • Quarterly, with annual cumulation. Service basis for print edition; CD-ROM edition, $1,495 per year. Indexes more than 400 periodicals covering economics, environmental policy, government, insurance, labor, health care policy, plannning, public administration, public welfare, urban studies, women's issues, criminology, and related topics.

CD-ROM DATABASES

PAIS on CD-ROM. Public Affairs Information Service, Inc. • Quarterly. $1,995.00 per year. Provides a CD-ROM version of the online service, *PAIS International.* Contains over 400,000 citations to the literature of contemporary social, political, and economic issues.

Social Science Source. EBSCO Publishing. • Monthly. $1,495.00 per year. Provides CD-ROM citations and abstracts to social science articles in more than 600 periodicals, with full text from 125 periodicals. Covers economics, political science, public policy, international relations, psychology, and other topics. Time period is most recent five years.

Social Sciences Citation Index: Compact Disc Edition. Institute for Scientific Information. • Quarterly. Provides CD-ROM indexing of the world's social sciences literature, including economics, business, finance, management, communications, demographics, information and library science, political science, sociology, etc. Corresponds to online *Social Scisearch* and printed *Social Sciences Citation Index.*

Social Sciences Citation Index: Compact Disc Edition with Abstracts. Institute for Scientific Information. • Quarterly. Provides CD-ROM indexing and abstracting of "significant articles" from 1,400 social science journals worldwide, with additional selections from 3,200 other journals, 1986 to date. Includes economics, business, finance, management, communications, demographics, information and library science, political science, sociology, and many other subjects.

WILSONDISC: Wilson Social Sciences Abstracts. H. W. Wilson Co. • Monthly. Including unlimited online access to *Social Sciences Index* through WILSONLINE. Provides CD-ROM indexing from 1983 and abstracting from 1994 of more than 400 periodicals covering economics, area studies, community health, public administration, public welfare, urban studies, and many other topics related to the social sciences.

DIRECTORIES

CSG Directories II: Legislative Leadership. Committees and Staff by Function. Council of State Governments. • Annual. $45.00. Legislative leaders, committee members and staff, personnel of principal legislative staff offices. Formerly *Book of the States, Supplement Two: State Legislative Leadership, Committees, and Staff.*

ENCYCLOPEDIAS AND DICTIONARIES

International Encyclopedia of Public Policy and Administration. Jay M. Shafritz, editor. HarperCollins Publishers. • 1997. $550.00. Four volumes. Covers 20 major areas, such as public administration, government budgeting, industrial policy, nonprofit management, organizational theory, public finance, labor relations, and taxation. Includes a brief bibliography for each major entry and a comprehensive index.

HANDBOOKS AND MANUALS

The Federal Manager's Handbook: A Guide to Rehabilitating or Removing the Problem Employee. G. Jerry Shaw and William L. Bransford. FPMI Communications, Inc. • 1997. $24.95. Third revised edition.

ONLINE DATABASES

PAIS International. Public Affairs Information Service, Inc. • Corresponds to the former printed publications, *PAIS Bulletin* (1976-90) and *PAIS Foreign Language Index* (1972-90), and to the current *PAIS International in Print* (1991 to date). Covers economic, political, and sociological material appearing in periodicals, books, government documents, and other publications. Updating is monthly. Inquire as to online cost and availability.

Social Scisearch. Institute for Scientific Information. • Broad, multidisciplinary index to the literature of the social sciences, 1972 to present. Weekly updates. Worldwide coverage. Inquire as to online cost and availability.

Wilson Social Sciences Abstracts Online. H. W. Wilson Co. • Provides online abstracting and indexing of more than 415 periodicals covering area studies, community health, public administration, public welfare, urban studies, and many other social science topics. Time period is 1994 to date for abstracts and 1983 to date for indexing, with updates monthly. Inquire as to online cost and availability.

PERIODICALS AND NEWSLETTERS

Administration and Society. Sage Publications, Inc. • Bimonthly. Individuals, $85.00 per year; institutions, $420.00 per year. Scholarly journal concerned with public administration and the effects of bureaucracy.

Administrative Science Quarterly. Cornell University Press, Johnson Graduate School of Management. • Individuals: $55.00 per year; institutions, $100.00 per year.

Governing: The States and Localities. • Monthly. $39.95 per year. Edited for state and local government officials. Covers finance, office management, computers, telecommunications, environmental concerns, etc.

Journal of Nonprofit and Public Sector Marketing. Haworth Press, Inc. • Quarterly. Individuals, $60.00 per year; institutions, $120.00 per year; libraries, $225.00 per year. Subject matter has to do with the promotion or marketing of the services of nonprofit organizations and governmental agencies.

Leader to Leader. Peter F. Drucker Foundation for Nonprofit Management. Jossey-Bass Publishers. • Quarterly. Individuals, $149.00 per year; institutions, $149.00 per year. Contains articles on "management, leadership, and strategy" written by "leading executives, thinkers, and consultants." Covers both business and nonprofit issues.

Public Administration and Development: An International Journal of Training, Research and Practice. Available from John Wiley and Sons, Inc.,

Journals Div. • Five times a year. $760.00 per year. Focuses on administrative practice at the local, regional and national levels. International coverage. Published in England by John Wiley and Sons Ltd.

Public Administration Review. American Society for Public Administration. • Bimonthly. $80.00 per year.

Public Risk. Public Risk Management Association. • 10 times a year. $125.00 per year. Covers risk management for state and local governments, including various kinds of liabilities.

TRADE/PROFESSIONAL ASSOCIATIONS

American Society for Public Administration. 1120 G St., N.W., Suite 700, Washington, DC 20005-3885. Phone: (202)393-7878 Fax: (202)638-4952 E-mail: info@aspanet.org • URL: http://www.aspanet.org.

Institute of Public Administration. Luther Halsey Gulick Bldg., 411 Lafayette St., 3rd Fl., New York, NY 1003-7032. Phone: 800-258-1102 or (212)730-5480 Fax: (212)995-4876 E-mail: ipa@delphi.com • URL: http://www.theipa.org.

Public Administration Service. 7927 Jones Branch Dr., No. 1FL-S-WG, McLean, VA 22102-3322. Phone: (703)734-8970 Fax: (703)734-4965 E-mail: postmaster@pashq.org.

Public Risk Management Association. 1815 N. Fort Meyer Dr., Ste. 1020, Arlington, VA 22209-1805. Phone: (703)528-7701 Fax: (703)528-7966 E-mail: info@primacentral.org • URL: http://www.primacentral.org • Members are state and local government officials concerned with risk management and public liabilities.

Section for Women in Public Administration. 1120 G St., N.W., Suite 700, Washington, DC 20005-3885. Phone: (202)393-7878 Fax: (202)638-4952 E-mail: info@aspanet.org • URL: http://www.aspanet.org.

PUBLIC ASSISTANCE

See: PUBLIC WELFARE

PUBLIC DOCUMENTS

See: GOVERNMENT PUBLICATIONS

PUBLIC FINANCE

See also: COUNTY FINANCE; FEDERAL BUDGET; MUNICIPAL FINANCE; TAXATION

ABSTRACTS AND INDEXES

Banking Information Index. U M I Banking Information Index. • Monthly. Price on application. Covers a wide variety of banking, business, and financial subjects in periodicals. Formerly *Banking Literature Index.*

PAIS International in Print. Public Affairs Information Service, Inc. • Monthly. $650.00 per year; cumulations three times a year. Provides topical citations to the worldwide literature of public affairs, economics, demographics, sociology, and trade. Text in English; indexed materials in English, French, German, Italian, Portuguese and Spanish.

Social Sciences Index. H. W. Wilson Co. • Quarterly, with annual cumulation. Service basis for print edition; CD-ROM edition, $1,495 per year. Indexes more than 400 periodicals covering economics, environmental policy, government, insurance, labor, health care policy, plannning, public administration, public welfare, urban studies, women's issues, criminology, and related topics.

ALMANACS AND YEARBOOKS

State Budget Actions. Corina Eckl and Arturo Perez. National Conference of State Legislatures. • 1997. $35.00. Presents yearly summaries of state spending priorities and fiscal climates. Includes end-of-year general fund balances and other information on state funds.

CD-ROM DATABASES

PAIS on CD-ROM. Public Affairs Information Service, Inc. • Quarterly. $1,995.00 per year. Provides a CD-ROM version of the online service, *PAIS International.* Contains over 400,000 citations to the literature of contemporary social, political, and economic issues.

Social Science Source. EBSCO Publishing. • Monthly. $1,495.00 per year. Provides CD-ROM citations and abstracts to social science articles in more than 600 periodicals, with full text from 125 periodicals. Covers economics, political science, public policy, international relations, psychology, and other topics. Time period is most recent five years.

Social Sciences Citation Index: Compact Disc Edition with Abstracts. Institute for Scientific Information. • Quarterly. Provides CD-ROM indexing and abstracting of "significant articles" from 1,400 social science journals worldwide, with additional selections from 3,200 other journals, 1986 to date. Includes economics, business, finance, management, communications, demographics, information and library science, political science, sociology, and many other subjects.

WILSONDISC: Wilson Social Sciences Abstracts. H. W. Wilson Co. • Monthly. Including unlimited online access to *Social Sciences Index* through WILSONLINE. Provides CD-ROM indexing from 1983 and abstracting from 1994 of more than 400 periodicals covering economics, area studies, community health, public administration, public welfare, urban studies, and many other topics related to the social sciences.

DIRECTORIES

Bond Buyer's Municipal Marketplace. Thomson Financial Publishing. • Annual. $180.00 per year. Provides information on municipal bond professionals, such as dealers, underwriters, attorneys, arbitrage specialists, derivatives specialists, rating agencies, regulators, etc.

Book of the States. Council of State Governments. • Biennial. $99.00. Includes information on state constitutions, state-by-state voting in recent elections, data on state finances, and federal-state survey articles.

Municipal Issuer's Registry. The Bond Buyer's Municipal Marketplace. • Annual. $235.00. Provides contact information relating to 6,000 issuers of municipal debt, including individuals responsible for municipal bond assignments.

ENCYCLOPEDIAS AND DICTIONARIES

International Encyclopedia of Public Policy and Administration. Jay M. Shafritz, editor. HarperCollins Publishers. • 1997. $550.00. Four volumes. Covers 20 major areas, such as public administration, government budgeting, industrial policy, nonprofit management, organizational theory, public finance, labor relations, and taxation. Includes a brief bibliography for each major entry and a comprehensive index.

FINANCIAL RATIOS

Financial Report of the United States Government. Available from U. S. Government Printing Office. • Annual. $14.00. Issued by the U. S. Treasury Department (http://www.treas.gov). Presents information about the financial condition and operations of the federal government. Program accounting systems of various government agencies provide data for the report.

HANDBOOKS AND MANUALS

Government Auditing Standards. Available from U. S. Government Printing Office. • 1994. $6.50. Revised edition. Issued by the U. S. General Accounting Office (http://www.gao.gov). Contains standards for CPA firms to follow in financial and performance audits of federal government agencies and programs. Also known as the "Yellow Book.".

Handbook for Muni Bond Issuers. Joe Mysak. Bloomberg Press. • 1998. $40.00. Written primarily for the officers and attorneys of municipalities. Provides a practical explanation of the municipal bond market. (Bloomberg Professional Library.).

INTERNET DATABASES

Fedstats. Federal Interagency Council on Statistical Policy. Phone: (202)395-7254 • URL: http://www.fedstats.gov • Web site features an efficient search facility for full-text statistics produced by more than 70 federal agencies, including the Census Bureau, the Bureau of Economic Analysis, and the Bureau of Labor Statistics. Boolean searches can be made within one agency or for all agencies combined. Links are offered to international statistical bureaus, including the UN, IMF, OECD, UNESCO, Eurostat, and 20 individual countries. Fees: Free.

ONLINE DATABASES

DRI U.S. Central Database. Data Products Division. • Provides more than 23,000 business, financial, demographic, economic, foreign trade, and industry-related time series for the U.S. Includes national income, population, retail-wholesale trade, price indexes, labor data, housing, industrial production, banking, interest rates, money supply, etc. Time period is generally 1947 to date (some data back to 1929). Updating varies. Inquire as to online cost and availability.

EconLit. American Economic Association. • Covers the worldwide literature of economics as contained in selected monographs and about 550 journals. Subjects include microeconomics, macroeconomics, economic history, inflation, money, credit, finance, accounting theory, trade, natural resource economics, and regional economics. Time period is 1969 to present, with monthly updates. Inquire as to online cost and availability.

PAIS International. Public Affairs Information Service, Inc. • Corresponds to the former printed publications, *PAIS Bulletin* (1976-90) and *PAIS Foreign Language Index* (1972-90), and to the current *PAIS International in Print* (1991 to date). Covers economic, political, and sociological material appearing in periodicals, books, government documents, and other publications. Updating is monthly. Inquire as to online cost and availability.

Social Scisearch. Institute for Scientific Information. • Broad, multidisciplinary index to the literature of the social sciences, 1972 to present. Weekly updates. Worldwide coverage. Inquire as to online cost and availability.

Wilson Social Sciences Abstracts Online. H. W. Wilson Co. • Provides online abstracting and indexing of more than 415 periodicals covering area studies, community health, public administration, public welfare, urban studies, and many other social science topics. Time period is 1994 to date for abstracts and 1983 to date for indexing, with updates monthly. Inquire as to online cost and availability.

PERIODICALS AND NEWSLETTERS

Government Accountants Journal. Association of Government Accountants. • Quarterly. $60.00 per year.

Journal of Project Finance. Institutional Investor. • Quarterly. $290.00 per year. Covers the financing of large-scale construction projects, such as power plants and convention centers.

Project Finance: The Magazine for Global Development. Institutional Investor Journals. • Monthly. $635.00 per year. Provides articles on the financing of the infrastructure (transportation, utilities, communications, the environment, etc). Coverage is international. Supplements available *World Export Credit Guide* and *Project Finance Book of Lists.* Formed by the merger of *Infrastructure Finance* and *Project and Trade Finance.*

Public Finance Review. Sage Publications, Inc. • Quarterly. Individuals, $85.00 per year, institutions, $450.00 per year. Formerly *Public Finance Quarterly.*

RESEARCH CENTERS AND INSTITUTES

Government Finance Officers Center Association Research Center. 180 N. Michigan Ave., Suite 800, Chicago, IL 60601. Phone: (312)977-9700 Fax: (312)977-4806 E-mail: rmiranda@gfoa.org • URL: http://www.gfoa.org • Provides consulting and research services in state and local finance. Designs and produces microcomputer software packages for use in government finance functions.

STATISTICS SOURCES

Business Statistics of the United States. Courtenay M. Slater, editor. Bernan Associates. • 1999. $74.00. Fifth edition. Based on *Business Statistics*, formerly issue by the Bureau of Economic Analysis, U. S. Department of Commerce. Provides basic data for a wide variety of U. S. industries, services, and economic indicators. Most statistics are shown annually for 29 years and monthly for the most recent four years.

Daily Treasury Statement: Cash and Debt Operations of the United States Treasury. Available from U. S. Government Printing Office. • Daily, except Saturdays, Sundays, and holidays. $855.00 per year. (Financial Management Service, U. S. Treasury Department.).

Economic Report of the President: Together with the Annual Report of the Council of Economic Advisors. Available from U. S. Government Printing Office. • Annual. $29.00. Includes about 130 pages of "Statistical Tables Relating to Income, Employment, and Production." Tables cover national income, employment, wages, productivity, manufacturing, prices, credit, finance (public and private), corporate profits, and foreign trade.

Facts and Figures on Government Finance. Tax Foundation, Inc. • Annual. $60.00.

Global Development Finance: External Public Debt of Developing Countries. World Bank, The Office of the Publisher. • Irregular. Prices vary. Includes supplements. Contains detailed data from the International Bank for Reconstruction and Development (World Bank) on the external debt load of over 100 developing countries.

Monthly Statement of the Public Debt of the United States. U. S. Dept. of the Treasury, Public Debt Bureau. Available from U. S. Government Printing Office. • Monthly. $29.00 per year.

Monthly Treasury Statement of Receipts and Outlays of the United States Government. Available from U. S. Government Printing Office. • Monthly. $40.00 per year. Issued by the Financial Management Service, U. S. Treasury Department.

Revenue Statistics. OECD Publications and Information Center. • Annual. $65.00. Presents data on government revenues in OECD countries, classified by type of tax and level of government. Text in English and French.

State Profiles: The Population and Economy of Each U. S. State. Courtenay Slater and Martha Davis, editors. Bernan Press. • 1999. $74.00. Presents charts, tables, and text in an eight-page profile for each state. Covers population, labor force, income, poverty, employment, wages, industry, trade, housing, education, health, taxes, and government finances.

Statistical Information on the Financial Services Industry. American Bankers Association. • Annual. Members, $150.00; non-members, $275.00. Presents a wide variety of data relating to banking and financial services, including consumer economics, personal finance, credit, government loans, capital markets, and international banking.

Survey of Current Business. Available from U. S. Government Printing Office. • Monthly. $49.00 per year. Issued by Bureau of Economic Analysis, U. S. Department of Commerce. Presents a wide variety of business and economic data.

Treasury Bulletin. Available from U. S. Government Printing Office. • Quarterly. $39.00 per year. Issued by the Financial Management Service, U. S. Treasury Department. Provides data on the federal budget, government securities and yields, the national debt, and the financing of the federal government in general.

TRADE/PROFESSIONAL ASSOCIATIONS

Association of Government Accountants. 2208 Mount Vernon Ave., Alexandria, VA 22301-1314. Phone: 800-242-7211 or (703)684-6931 Fax: (703)548-9367 • URL: http://www.agacgfm.org • Members are employed by federal, state, county, and city government agencies. Includes accountants, auditors, budget officers, and other government finance administrators and officials.

Bond Market Association. 40 Broad St., 12th Fl., New York, NY 10004-2373. Phone: (212)809-7000 Fax: (212)440-5260 • URL: http://www.psa.com.

Citizens for a Sound Economy. 1250 H St., N.W., Suite 700, Washington, DC 20005-3908. Phone: 888-564-6273 or (202)783-3870 Fax: (202)783-4687 E-mail: cse@cse.org • URL: http://www.cse.org.

PUBLIC HOUSING

See: HOUSING

PUBLIC LIBRARIES

See: LIBRARIES

PUBLIC OPINION

GENERAL WORKS

Public Opinion: Politics, Communication and Social Process. Carroll J. Glyn and others. HarperCollins Publishers. • 1998. $75.00.

ABSTRACTS AND INDEXES

Business Periodicals Index. H. W. Wilson Co. • Monthly, except August, with quarterly and annual cumulations. Service basis for print edition; CD-ROM edition, $1,495.00 per year.

PAIS International in Print. Public Affairs Information Service, Inc. • Monthly. $650.00 per year; cumulations three times a year. Provides topical citations to the worldwide literature of public affairs, economics, demographics, sociology, and trade. Text in English; indexed materials in English, French, German, Italian, Portuguese and Spanish.

Social Sciences Index. H. W. Wilson Co. • Quarterly, with annual cumulation. Service basis for print edition; CD-ROM edition, $1,495 per year. Indexes more than 400 periodicals covering economics, environmental policy, government, insurance, labor, health care policy, plannning, public administration, public welfare, urban studies, women's issues, criminology, and related topics.

BIBLIOGRAPHIES

Public Opinion Polls and Survey Research: A Selected Annotated Bibliography of U.S. Guides and Studies from the 1980s. Graham R. Waldon. Garland Publishing, Inc. • 1990. $15.00. (Public Affairs and Administration Series, Vol. 24).

CD-ROM DATABASES

PAIS on CD-ROM. Public Affairs Information Service, Inc. • Quarterly. $1,995.00 per year. Provides a CD-ROM version of the online service, *PAIS International.* Contains over 400,000 citations to the literature of contemporary social, political, and economic issues.

Social Science Source. EBSCO Publishing. • Monthly. $1,495.00 per year. Provides CD-ROM citations and abstracts to social science articles in more than 600 periodicals, with full text from 125 periodicals. Covers economics, political science, public policy, international relations, psychology, and other topics. Time period is most recent five years.

Social Sciences Citation Index: Compact Disc Edition with Abstracts. Institute for Scientific Information. • Quarterly. Provides CD-ROM indexing and abstracting of "significant articles" from 1,400 social science journals worldwide, with additional selections from 3,200 other journals, 1986 to date. Includes economics, business, finance, management, communications, demographics, information and library science, political science, sociology, and many other subjects.

WILSONDISC: Wilson Social Sciences Abstracts. H. W. Wilson Co. • Monthly. Including unlimited online access to *Social Sciences Index* through WILSONLINE. Provides CD-ROM indexing from 1983 and abstracting from 1994 of more than 400 periodicals covering economics, area studies, community health, public administration, public welfare, urban studies, and many other topics related to the social sciences.

DIRECTORIES

Agencies and Organizations Represented in AAPOR/WAPOR Membership. American Association for Public Opinion Research. • Annual. Free. Lists over 220 firms engaged in public opinion research.

Business Organizations, Agencies, and Publications Directory. The Gale Group. • 1999. $425.00. 12th edition. Over 40,000 entries describing 39 types of business information sources. Classified by type of organization, publication, or serviceIncludes state, national, and international agencies and organizations. Master index to names and keywords. Also includes e-mail addresses and web site URL's.

HANDBOOKS AND MANUALS

An American Profile: Attitudes and Behaviors of the American People, 1972-1989. The Gale Group. • 1990. $89.50. A summary of responses to about 300 questions in the General Social Survey conducted annually by the National Opinion Research Center, covering family characteristics, social behavior, religion, political opinions, etc. Includes a chronology of significant world events from 1972 to 1989 and a subject-keyword index.

ONLINE DATABASES

PAIS International. Public Affairs Information Service, Inc. • Corresponds to the former printed publications, *PAIS Bulletin* (1976-90) and *PAIS Foreign Language Index* (1972-90), and to the current *PAIS International in Print* (1991 to date).

Covers economic, political, and sociological material appearing in periodicals, books, government documents, and other publications. Updating is monthly. Inquire as to online cost and availability.

Wilson Business Abstracts Online. H. W. Wilson Co. • Indexes and abstracts 600 major business periodicals, plus the *Wall Street Journal* and the business section of the *New York Times*. Indexing is from 1982, abstracting from 1990, with the two newspapers included from 1993. Updated weekly. Inquire as to online cost and availability. (*Business Periodicals Index* without abstracts is also available online.).

Wilson Social Sciences Abstracts Online. H. W. Wilson Co. • Provides online abstracting and indexing of more than 415 periodicals covering area studies, community health, public administration, public welfare, urban studies, and many other social science topics. Time period is 1994 to date for abstracts and 1983 to date for indexing, with updates monthly. Inquire as to online cost and availability.

PERIODICALS AND NEWSLETTERS

AAPOR News. American Association for Public Opinion Research. • Quarterly. Membership. Newsletter.

Polling Report: An Independent Survey of Trends Affecting Elections, Government, and Business. Polling Report, Inc. • Biweekly. Students and teachers, $78.00 per year; others, $195.00 per year. Newsletter. Reports on the results of a wide variety of public opinion polls.

Public Opinion Quarterly. American Association for Public Opinion Research. University of Chicago Press, Journals Div. • Quarterly. Individuals, $25.00 per year; institutions, $66.00 per year; students, $20.00 per year.

Public Pulse: Roper's Authoritative Report on What Americans are Thinking, D oing, and Buying. Roper Starch Worldwide. • Monthly. $297.00. Newsletter. Contains news of surveys of American attitudes, values, and behavior. Each issue includes a research supplement giving "complete facts and figures behind each survey question,".

World Opinion Update. Survey Research Consultants International, Inc. Hastings Publications. • Monthly. Individuals, $90.00 per year; educational libraries, $80.00 per year. Newsletter giving tabular results of recent public opinion polls around the world.

RESEARCH CENTERS AND INSTITUTES

Center for Public Interest Polling. Rutgers University, Eagleton Institute of Politics, New Brunswick, NJ 08901. Phone: (732)828-2210 Fax: (732)932-1551 E-mail: jballou@rci.rutgers.edu • URL: http://www.rci.rutgers.edu/~eaglepol • Provides survey research and program evaluation services.

Institute for Social Research. University of Michigan, P.O. Box 1248, Ann Arbor, MI 48106-1248. Phone: (734)764-8363 Fax: (734)764-2337 • URL: http://www.isr.umich.edu.

Institute for Survey Research. Temple University Center for Public Policy, 1601 N. Broad St., Philadelphia, PA 19122. Phone: 800-827-5477 or (215)204-8355 Fax: (215)204-3797 E-mail: lenlo@temss2.isr.temple.edu • URL: http://www.temple.edu/isr • Conducts methodological studies in various aspects of survey research.

TRADE/PROFESSIONAL ASSOCIATIONS

American Association for Public Opinion Research. P.O. Box 1248, Ann Arbor, MI 48106-1248. Phone: (313)764-1555 Fax: (313)764-3341 E-mail: aapor@umich.edu • URL: http://www.aapor.org • Members are individuals interested in methods and applications of opinion research.

International Survey Library Association. University of Connecticut, 341 Mansfield Rd., U-164, Storrs Mansfield, CT 06269. Phone: (860)486-4440 Fax: (860)486-2123 • Members are colleges, research organizations, and corporations. Holdings include basic data from over 10,000 public opinion surveys conducted since 1936.

National Council on Public Polls. 1375 Kings Highway East, Suite 300, Fairfield, CT 06430. Phone: 800-239-0909 Fax: (203)331-1750 • Members are public opinion polling organizations.

World Association for Public Opinion Research. University of North Carolina, School of Journalism and Mass, Communication, Howell Hall, No. CB-3365, Chapel Hill, NC 27599-3365. Phone: (919)962-6396 Fax: (919)962-4079 E-mail: wapor@unc.edu • URL: http://www.wapor.org • Members are opinion survey research experts, both academic and commercial. Promotes the use of objective, scientific, public opinion methodology and research. International emphasis.

PUBLIC RELATIONS AND PUBLICITY

See also: ADVERTISING

GENERAL WORKS

How to Promote, Publicize, and Advertise Your Growing Business: Getting the Word Out Without Spending a Fortune. Kim Baker and Sunny Baker. John Wiley and Sons, Inc. • 1992. $107.50.

PR News Casebook. The Gale Group. • 1993. $99.00. A collection of about 1,000 case studies covering major public relations campaigns and events, taken from the pages of *PR News*. Covers such issues as boycotts, new products, anniversaries, plant closings, downsizing, and stockholder relations.

Public Relations Practices: Managerial Case Studies and Problems. Allen H. Center. Prentice Hall. • 2000. $46.67. Sixth edition.

DIRECTORIES

Gale's Guide to the Media: A Gale Ready Reference Handbook. The Gale Group. • 2000. $125.00. Provides profiles of a wide variety of media-related organizations, publications, broadcasters, agencies, and databases, of interest to nonprofit groups. Contains three indexes and a glossary.

IEG Sponsorship Sourcebook. International Events Group, Inc. • Annual. $199.00. Provides information on about 3,000 festivals, celebrations, and sports events that are available for commercial sponsorship. Information is also given on public relations firms, sports marketing companies, fireworks suppliers, and other companies providing services for special events. Formerly *IEG Directory of Sponsorship Marketing*.

National Directory of Corporate Public Affairs. Columbia Books, Inc. • Annual. $109.00. Lists about 2,000 corporations that have foundations or other public affairs activities.

O'Dwyer's Directory of Corporate Communications. J. R. O'Dwyer Co., Inc. • Annual. $130.00. Public relations departments of major corporations.

O'Dwyer's Directory of Public Relations Firms. J. R. O'Dwyer Co., Inc. • Annual. $120.00. Over 2,200 public relations firms; international coverage.

Public Relations Tactics-Register The Blue Book. Public Relations Society of America. • Annual. $100.00. About 17,000 public relations practioners in business, government, education, etc. who are members. Formerly *Public Relations Journal-Register*.

ENCYCLOPEDIAS AND DICTIONARIES

NTC's Mass Media Dictionary. R. Terry Ellmore. NTC/Contemporary Publishing. • 1993. $24.95. Covers television, radio, newspapers, magazines, film, graphic arts, books, billboards, public relations, and advertising. Terms are related to production, research, audience measurement, audio-video engineering, printing, publishing, and other areas.

HANDBOOKS AND MANUALS

Complete Guide to Special Event Management: Business Insights, Financial Advice and Successful Strategies from Ernst and Young, Consultants to the Olympics, the Emmy Awards and the PGA Tour. Ernst and Young Staff. John Wiley and Sons, Inc. • 1992. $29.95. Covers the marketing, financing, and general management of special events in the fields of art, entertainment, and sports.

Dartnell's Public Relations Handbook. Robert L. Dilenschneider, editor. Dartnell Corp. • 1996. $69.95. Fourth revised edition. Covers press releases, media kits, media contacts, crisis management, and other topics.

Handbook for Public Relations Writing. Thomas Bivins. NTC/Contemporary Publishing. • 1999. $24.95. Third edition. (NTC Business Book Series).

Handbook of Public Relations. Robert L. Heath, editor. Sage Publications, Inc. • 2000. $89.95. Covers best practices, academic research, and theory. Contains articles by various advertising specialists.

International Public Relations: How to Establish Your Company's Product, Service, and Image in Foreign Markets. Joyce Wouters. Books on Demand. • 1991. $99.20.

Lesly's Handbook of Public Relations and Communications. Philip Lesly. NTC/Contemporary Publishing. • 1997. $100.00. Fifth edition.

Managing a Public Relations Firm for Growth and Profit. A. C. Croft. The Haworth Press, Inc. • 1995. $39.95.

The New Publicity Kit. Jeanette Smith. John Wiley and Sons, Inc. • 1995. $19.95 multi-media campaigns, and other forms of publicity.

Public Relations Writer's Handbook. Merry Aronson and Donald E. Spetner. Jossey-Bass, Inc., Publishers. • 1998. $20.95.

The Publicity Handbook: How to Maximize Publicity for Products, Services, and Organizations. David Yale. NTC/Contemporary Publishing. • 1994. $19.95. (NTC Business Books Series).

INTERNET DATABASES

EBSCO Information Services. Ebsco Publishing. Phone: 800-871-8508 or (508)356-6500 Fax: (508)356-5640 E-mail: ep@epnet.com • URL: http://www.epnet.com • Fee-based Web site providing Internet access to a wide variety of databases, including business-related material. Full text is available for many periodical titles, with daily updates. Fees: Apply.

ProQuest Direct. Bell & Howell Information and Learning. Phone: 800-521-0600 or (313)761-4700 Fax: (313)973-9145 • URL: http://www.umi.com/proquest • Fee-based Web site providing Internet access to more than 3,000 periodicals, newspapers, and other publications. Many items are available full-text, with daily updates. Includes extensive corporate and financial information from Disclosure, Inc. Fees: Apply.

PERIODICALS AND NEWSLETTERS

Communication Briefings: A Monthly Idea Source for Decision Makers. Briefings Publishing Group. • Monthly. $100.00 per year. Newsletter. Presents useful ideas for communication, public relations, customer service, human resources, and employee training.

Communication World: The Magazine for Communication Professionals. International Association of Business Communicators. • 10 times a year. Libraries, $95.00 per year. Emphasis is on public relations, media relations, corporate communication, and writing.

The Customer Communicator. Alexander Communications Group, Inc. • Monthly. $167.00 per year. Newsletter. Contains news and advice for business firms on how to improve customer relations and communications.

Healthcare PR and Marketing News. Phillips Business Information, Inc. • Biweekly. $497.00 per year. Newsletter on public relations and client communications for the healthcare industry.

Journal of Promotion Management: Innovations in Planning and Applied Research for Advertising, Sales Promotion, Personal Selling, Public Relations, and Re-Seller Support. Haworth Press, Inc. • Semiannual. Individuals, $40.00 per year; institutions, $65.00 per year; libraries, $95.00 per year.

Marketing Magazine. Maclean Hunter Business Publications. • Weekly. $60.00 per year. "Canada's national weekly publication dedicated to the businesses of marketing, advertising, and media." Includes annual Marketing Awards, quarterly Digital Marketing (emerging technology), Promo Marketing, and PR Quarterly (special issues on public relations).

Public Relations News. Phillips Business Information, Inc. • Weekly. $347.00 per year. Newsletter on public relations for business, government, and nonprofit organizations.

Public Relations Quarterly. • Quarterly. $49.00 per year. Opinion articles and case studies on the theory and practice of public relations for and by leading practitioners and academicians.

Public Relations Review: Journal of Research and Comment. JAI Press. • Quarterly. Individuals, $125.00 per year; institutions, $296.00 per year. Includes annual *Bibliography*.

Public Relations Strategist: Issues and Trends That Affect Management. Public Relations Society of America. • Quarterly. $48.00 per year. Provides public relations advice for corporate and government executives.

TRADE/PROFESSIONAL ASSOCIATIONS

Public Relations Society of America. 33 Irving Place, 3rd Fl., New York, NY 10003-2376. Phone: 800-937-7772 or (212)995-2230 Fax: (212)995-0757 E-mail: hq@prsa.org • URL: http://www.prsa.org.

OTHER SOURCES

InSite 2. Intelligence Data/Thomson Financial. • Fee-based Web site consolidates information in a "Base Pack" consisting of Business InSite, Market InSite, and Company InSite. Optional databases are Consumer InSite, Health and Wellness InSite, Newsletter InSite, and Computer InSite. Includes fulltext content from more than 2,500 trade publications, journals, newsletters, newspapers, analyst reports, and other sources. Continuous updating. Formerly produced by The Gale Group.

PUBLIC SERVICE CORPORATIONS

See: PUBLIC UTILITIES

PUBLIC SPEAKING

See also: DEBATES AND DEBATING; TOASTS

ABSTRACTS AND INDEXES

Speech Index: An Index to Collections of World Famous Orations and Speeches for Various Occasions, 1966-1980. Scarecrow Press, Inc. • 1982. $80.00. Fourth edition.

ENCYCLOPEDIAS AND DICTIONARIES

Dictionary of Business Quotations. Julia Vitullo-Martin and J. Robert Moskin. Oxford University Press, Inc. • 1993. $39.95.

HANDBOOKS AND MANUALS

American Speaker: Your Guide to Successful Speaking. Georgetown Publishing House. • Bimonthly. Price on application. Newsletter. Provides practical advice on public speaking.

Complete Speaker's and Toastmaster's Library. Jacob M. Braude. Prentice Hall. • 1992. $69.95. Second edition.

How to Be the Life of the Podium: Openers, Closers and Everything in Between to Keep Them Listening. Sylvia Simmons. AMACOM. • 1992. $15.95. A collection of 1,000 quips, quotes, analogies, stories, proverbs, and one-liners.

The Manager's Book of Quotations. Lewis D. Eigen and Jonathan P. Siegel. AMACOM. • 1991. $21.95. Reprint edition. Provides 5,000 modern and traditional quotations arranged by topics useful to business people for speeches and writing.

Persuasive Business Speaking. Elayne Snyder. AMACOM. • 1990. $17.95. Includes ready-to-use openers, sample speeches, anecdotes, and quotes.

Public Speaking. Thomas Farrell and Maureen M. Farrell. McGraw-Hill Higher Education. • 1996. $24.95. Third edition.

PERIODICALS AND NEWSLETTERS

Vital Speeches of the Day. City News Publishing Co., Inc. • Bimonthly. $45.00 per year.

TRADE/PROFESSIONAL ASSOCIATIONS

International Platform Association. P.O. Box 250, Winnetka, IL 60093. Phone: (219)483-7117 Fax: (219)483-6422.

International Training in Communication. 2519 Woodland Dr., Anaheim, CA 92801. Phone: (714)995-3660 Fax: (714)995-6974 E-mail: itcintl@itcintl.org • URL: http://www.itcintl.org.

National Speakers Association. 1500 S. Priest Dr., Tempe, AZ 85281. Phone: (480)968-2552 Fax: (480)968-0911 E-mail: information.nsaspeaker.org • URL: http://www.nsaspeaker.org.

Toastmasters International. P.O. Box 9052, Mission Viejo, CA 92690. Phone: (949)858-8255 Fax: (949)858-1207 E-mail: tminfo@toastmasters.org • URL: http://www.toastmasters.org.

PUBLIC TRANSPORTATION

See also: MOTOR BUSES; RAILROADS; TRANSPORTATION INDUSTRY

ABSTRACTS AND INDEXES

NTIS Alerts: Transportation. National Technical Information Service. • Semimonthly. $210.00 per year. Provides descriptions of government-sponsored research reports and software, with ordering information. Covers air, marine, highway, inland waterway, pipeline, and railroad transportation. Formerly *Abstract Newsletter.*

Readers' Guide to Periodical Literature. H. W. Wilson Co. • Monthly. $220.00 per year. CD-ROM edition, $1,495 per year, including annual cumulation. Indexes about 250 peridicals of general interest.

DIRECTORIES

Mass Transit: Consultants. Cygnus Publishing Co. • Annual. $40.00. Listings for over 300 urban transportation architects, designers, engineers, planners, consultants and other specialists serving the urban transportation industry.

Mass Transit: Supplier's Guide. Mass Transit. • Seven times a year. $48.00. Directory of over 800 manufacturers and distributors serving the urban transportation industry.

ENCYCLOPEDIAS AND DICTIONARIES

Macmillan Encyclopedia of Transportation. Available from The Gale Group. • 2000. $375.00. Six volumes. Published by Macmillan Reference USA. Covers the business, technology, and history of transportation on land, on water, in the air, and in space. Includes definitions, cross-references, and 200 color illustrations.

FINANCIAL RATIOS

Almanac of Business and Industrial Financial Ratios. Leo Troy. Prentice Hall. • Annual. $99.95. Contains financial ratios derived from federal tax returns. Ratios for each of about 200 industries are arranged according to company asset size.

HANDBOOKS AND MANUALS

Transportation Planning Handbook. John D. Edwards. Institute of Transportation Engineers Staff. • 1999. $110.00. Second edition.

INTERNET DATABASES

Fedstats. Federal Interagency Council on Statistical Policy. Phone: (202)395-7254 • URL: http://www.fedstats.gov • Web site features an efficient search facility for full-text statistics produced by more than 70 federal agencies, including the Census Bureau, the Bureau of Economic Analysis, and the Bureau of Labor Statistics. Boolean searches can be made within one agency or for all agencies combined. Links are offered to international statistical bureaus, including the UN, IMF, OECD, UNESCO, Eurostat, and 20 individual countries. Fees: Free.

ONLINE DATABASES

DRI U.S. Central Database. Data Products Division. • Provides more than 23,000 business, financial, demographic, economic, foreign trade, and industry-related time series for the U.S. Includes national income, population, retail-wholesale trade, price indexes, labor data, housing, industrial production, banking, interest rates, money supply, etc. Time period is generally 1947 to date (some data back to 1929). Updating varies. Inquire as to online cost and availability.

Readers' Guide Abstracts Online. H. W. Wilson Co. • Indexes and abstracts general interest periodicals, 1983 to date. Weekly updates. Inquire as to online cost and availability.

TRIS: Transportation Research Information Service. National Research Council. • Contains abstracts and citations to a wide range of transportation literature, 1968 to present, with monthly updates. Includes references to the literature of air transportation, highways, ships and shipping, railroads, trucking, and urban mass transportation. Formerly *TRIS-ON-LINE.* Inquire as to online cost and availability.

PERIODICALS AND NEWSLETTERS

Downtown Idea Exchange: Essential Information for Downtown Research and Development Center.

Downtown Research and Development Center. Alexander Communications Group, Inc. • Semimonthly. $157.00 per year. Newsletter for those concerned with central business districts. Provides news and other information on planning, development, parking, mass transit, traffic, funding, and other topics.

Mass Transit. Cygnus Publishing Co. • Bimonthly. 48.00 per year.

Metro. Bobit Publishing Co. • Bimonthly. $40.00 per year. Subject matter is the management of public transportationsystems. Includes *Factbook.*

Nation's Cities Weekly. National League of Cities. • Weekly. $96.00 per year. Topics covered by special issues include city budgets, surface transportation, water supply, economic development, finances, telecommunications, and computers.

Passenger Transport. American Public Transit Association. • Weekly. $65.00 per year. Covers current events and trends in mass transportation.

Urban Transport News: Management, Funding, Ridership, Technology. Business Publishers, Inc. • Biweekly. $407.00 per year. Provides current news from Capitol Hill, the White House, the Dept. of Transportation, as well as transit operations and industries across the country.

RESEARCH CENTERS AND INSTITUTES

Battelle Memorial Institute. 505 King Ave., Columbus, OH 43201-2693. Phone: 800-201-2011 or (614)424-6424 Fax: (614)424-3260 • URL: http://www.battelle.org • Multidisciplinary research facilities at various locations include: Microcomputer Applications and Technology Center; Battelle Industrial Technology Center; Technology and Society Research Center; Office of Transportation Systems and Planning; Office of Waste Technology Development; Materials Information Center; Office of Nuclear Waste Isolation.

Carnegie Mellon Research Institute. Carnegie Mellon University, 700 Technology Dr., Pittsburgh, PA 15219. Phone: (412)268-3190 Fax: (412)268-3101 E-mail: twillke@emu.edu • Multidisciplinary research activities include expert systems applications, minicomputer and microcomputer systems design, genetic engineering, and transportation systems analysis.

Center for Business and Industrial Studies. University of Missouri-St. Louis, School of Business Administration, 8001 Natural Bridge Rd., St. Louis, MO 63121. Phone: (314)516-5857 Fax: (314)516-6420 E-mail: ldsmith@.umsl.edu • URL: http://www.umsl.edu/~cbis/cbis.html • Research fields include inventory and management control. Specific projects also include development of computer software for operations in public transit systems.

Center for Transportation Studies. Massachusetts Institute of Technology. 77 Massachusetts Ave. Room 1-235, Cambridge, MA 02139. Phone: (617)253-5320 Fax: (617)253-4560 E-mail: ctsmail@mit.edu • URL: http://www.web.mit.edu/cts/www/.

Center for Urban Transportation Studies. University of Wisconsin at Milwaukee, College of Engineering and Applied Sciences, P.O. Box 784, Milwaukee, WI 53201-0784. Phone: (414)229-5787 Fax: (414)229-6958 E-mail: beimborn@uwm.edu • URL: http://www.uwm.edu/dept/cuts.

MPC Corporation. 5000 Forbes Ave., Pittsburgh, PA 15213. Phone: (412)268-2091 Fax: (412)268-5841 E-mail: te9b@andrew.cmu.edu • Research fields include mass rapid transit for metropolitan areas. Affiliated with Carnegie Mellon University and the University of Pittsburgh.

Texas Transportation Institute. Texas A & M University System, College Station, TX 77843-3135. Phone: (979)845-8552 Fax: (979)845-9356 E-mail: h.hrichardson@tamu.edu • URL: http://tti.tamu.edu • Concerned with all forms and modes of transportation. Research areas include transportation economics, highway construction, traffic safety, public transportation, and highway engineering.

Transportation Program. Princeton University Operations Research and Financial. E-407 Engineering Quadrangle, Princeton, NJ 08544. Phone: (609)258-1563 Fax: (609)683-0290 E-mail: alaink@princeton.edu.

Transportation Research Center. University of Florida. P.O. Box 116585, Gainesville, FL 32611-6585. Phone: 800-226-1013 or (352)392-7575 Fax: (352)392-3224 E-mail: uftrc@nervm.nerdc.ufl.edu • URL: http://www.uftrc.ce.ufl.edu.

Transportation Systems Institute. University of Central Florida, Dept. of Civil Engineering, 400 Central Florida Blvd., Orlando, FL 32816-2450. Phone: (407)823-2156 Fax: (407)823-3315 E-mail: haldeek@pegasus.cc.ucf.edu • Research areas include mass transportation systems.

STATISTICS SOURCES

Business Statistics of the United States. Courtenay M. Slater, editor. Bernan Associates. • 1999. $74.00. Fifth edition. Based on *Business Statistics*, formerly issue by the Bureau of Economic Analysis, U. S. Department of Commerce. Provides basic data for a wide variety of U. S. industries, services, and economic indicators. Most statistics are shown annually for 29 years and monthly for the most recent four years.

Gale City and Metro Rankings Reporter. The Gale Group. • 1996. $134.00. Second edition. Provides about 3,000 statistical ranking tables covering more than 1,500 U. S. cities and Metropolitan Statistical Areas. Covers economic, demographic, social, governmental, and cultural factors. Sources are private studies and government data.

Gale Country and World Rankings Reporter. The Gale Group. • 1997. $135.00. Second edition. Provides about 3,000 statistical ranking tables and charts covering more than 235 nations. Sources include the United Nations and various government publications.

Gale State Rankings Reporter. The Gale Group. • 1996. $110.00. Second edition Provides 3,000 ranked lists of states under 35 subject headings. Sources are newspapers, periodicals, books, research institute publications, and government publications.

Survey of Current Business. Available from U. S. Government Printing Office. • Monthly. $49.00 per year. Issued by Bureau of Economic Analysis, U. S. Department of Commerce. Presents a wide variety of business and economic data.

Transportation Statistics Annual Report. Available from U. S. Government Printing Office. • Annual. $21.00. Issued by Bureau of Transportation Statistics, U. S. Department of Transportation. Provides data on operating revenues, expenses, employees, passenger miles (where applicable), and other factors for airlines, automobiles, buses, local transit, pipelines, railroads, ships, and trucks.

TRADE/PROFESSIONAL ASSOCIATIONS

American Disabled for Attendant Program Today. 201 S. Cherokee St., Denver, CO 80223-1836. Phone: (303)733-9324 Fax: (303)738-6211 E-mail: adapt@adapt.org • Members are disabled individuals promoting wheelchair accessibility in all forms of public transportation.

American Public Transit Association. 1201 New York Ave., N.W., Suite 400, Washington, DC 20005. Phone: (202)898-4000 Fax: (202)898-4070 • URL: http://www.apta.com • Members are bus and rail urban transportation systems.

Institute of Transportation Engineers. 525 School St., S.W., Suite 410, Washington, DC 20024-2797. Phone: (202)554-8050 Fax: (202)863-5486 • URL: http://www.ite.org • Members are professionals in surface transportation, mass transit, and traffic engineering.

OTHER SOURCES

Infrastructure Industries USA. The Gale Group. • 2001. $240.00. Replaces *Agriculture, Forestry, Fishing, Mining, and Construction USA* and *Transportation and Public Utilities USA.* Presents statistics and projections relating to economic activity in a wide variety of natural resource and construction industries.

PUBLIC UTILITIES

See also: ELECTRIC UTILITIES; ENERGY SOURCES; GAS INDUSTRY; TELEPHONE INDUSTRY; WATER SUPPLY

CD-ROM DATABASES

Environment Abstracts on CD-ROM. Congressional Information Service, Inc. • Quarterly. $1,295.00 per year. Contains the following CD-ROM databases: *Environment Abstracts, Energy Abstracts*, and *Acid Rain Abstracts.* Length of coverage varies.

DIRECTORIES

Plunkett's Energy Industry Almanac: Complete Profiles on the Energy Industry 500 Companies. Plunkett Research Ltd. • Annual. $149.99. Includes major oil companies, utilities, pipelines, alternative energy companies, etc. Provides information on industry trends.

FINANCIAL RATIOS

Almanac of Business and Industrial Financial Ratios. Leo Troy. Prentice Hall. • Annual. $99.95. Contains financial ratios derived from federal tax returns. Ratios for each of about 200 industries are arranged according to company asset size.

HANDBOOKS AND MANUALS

Moody's Public Utility Manual. Financial Information Services. • Annual. $1,595.00. Two volumes. Supplemented twice weekly by *Moody's Public Utility News Reports.* Contains financial and other information concerning publicly-held utility companies (electric, gas, telephone, water).

INTERNET DATABASES

Bureau of Economic Analysis (BEA). U. S. Department of Commerce, Bureau of Economic Analysis. Phone: (202)606-9900 Fax: (202)606-5310 E-mail: webmaster@bea.doc.gov • URL: http://www.bea.doc.gov • Web site includes "News Release Information" covering national, regional, and international economic estimates from the BEA. Highlights of releases appear online the same day, complete text and tables appear the next day. "Recent News Releases" section provides titles for past nine months, with links. "BEA Data and Methodology" includes "Frequently Requested NIPA Data" (national income and product accounts, such as gross domestic product and personal income). Other statistics are available. Fees: Free.

Fedstats. Federal Interagency Council on Statistical Policy. Phone: (202)395-7254 • URL: http://www.fedstats.gov • Web site features an efficient search facility for full-text statistics produced by more than 70 federal agencies, including the Census Bureau, the Bureau of Economic Analysis, and the Bureau of Labor Statistics. Boolean searches can be made within one agency or for all agencies combined. Links are offered to international statistical bureaus, including the UN, IMF, OECD, UNESCO, Eurostat, and 20 individual countries. Fees: Free.

ONLINE DATABASES

DRI U.S. Central Database. Data Products Division. • Provides more than 23,000 business, financial, demographic, economic, foreign trade, and industry-related time series for the U.S. Includes national income, population, retail-wholesale trade, price indexes, labor data, housing, industrial production, banking, interest rates, money supply, etc. Time period is generally 1947 to date (some data back to 1929). Updating varies. Inquire as to online cost and availability.

Energyline. Congressional Information Service, Inc. • Provides online citations and abstracts to the literature of all forms of energy: petroleum, natural gas, coal, nuclear power, solar energy, etc. Time period is 1971 to 1993 (closed file). Inquire as to online cost and availability.

PERIODICALS AND NEWSLETTERS

Public Utilities Fortnightly. Public Utilities Reports, Inc. • 22 times a year. $129.00 per year. Management magazine for utility executives in electric, gas, telecommunications and water industries.

Utility Business. Intertec Publishing Corp. • Monthly. Controlled circulation. Edited for executives in various public utilities: electric, telephone, gas, and water. Covers a wide range of business issues affecting utilities.

RESEARCH CENTERS AND INSTITUTES

Public Utility Research Center. University of Florida. College of Business Administration, P.O. Box 117142, Gainesville, FL 32611-7142. Phone: (352)392-6148 Fax: (352)392-7796 E-mail: purcecon@dale.cba.ufl.edu • URL: http://www.cba.ufl.edu/eco/purc.

STATISTICS SOURCES

American Housing Survey for the United States in [year]. Available from U. S. Government Printing Office. • Biennial. Issued by the U. S. Census Bureau (http://www.census.gov). Covers both owner-occupied and renter-occupied housing. Includes data on such factors as condition of building, type of mortgage, utility costs, and housing occupied by minorities. (Current Housing Reports, H150.).

Business Statistics of the United States. Courtenay M. Slater, editor. Bernan Associates. • 1999. $74.00. Fifth edition. Based on *Business Statistics*, formerly issue by the Bureau of Economic Analysis, U. S. Department of Commerce. Provides basic data for a wide variety of U. S. industries, services, and economic indicators. Most statistics are shown annually for 29 years and monthly for the most recent four years.

Energy Balances of OECD Countries. Organization for Economic Cooperation and Development. Available from OECD Publications and Information Center. • Irregular. $110.00. Presents two-year data on the supply and consumption of solid fuels, oil, gas, and electricity, expressed in oil equivalency terms. Historical tables are also provided. Relates to OECD member countries.

Housing Statistics of the United States. Patrick A. Simmons, editor. Bernan Press. • 2000. $74.00. Third edition. (Bernan Press U.S. Data Book Series).

Survey of Current Business. Available from U. S. Government Printing Office. • Monthly. $49.00 per year. Issued by Bureau of Economic Analysis, U. S. Department of Commerce. Presents a wide variety of business and economic data.

WEFA Industrial Monitor. John Wiley and Sons, Inc. • Annual. $65.00. Prepared by industry analysts at WEFA, an economic forecasting and consulting firm (originally Wharton Econometric Forecasting Associates). Contains discussions of the outlook for major U. S. industries, with many 10-year forecasts (WEFA Web site is http://www.wefa.com).

TRADE/PROFESSIONAL ASSOCIATIONS

National Association of Regulatory Utility Commissioners. P.O. Box 684, Washington, DC 20044-0864. Phone: (202)898-2200 Fax: (202)898-2213 E-mail: pwelsh@naruc.com • URL: http://www.naruc.com.

Utility Communicators International. c/o Robert Janke, 5316 E. Grandview Rd., Scottsdale, AZ 85254. Phone: (602)971-1989 Fax: (602)971-2738 E-mail: bjanke@compuserve.com.

OTHER SOURCES

Infrastructure Industries USA. The Gale Group. • 2001. $240.00. Replaces *Agriculture, Forestry, Fishing, Mining, and Construction USA* and *Transportation and Public Utilities USA*. Presents statistics and projections relating to economic activity in a wide variety of natural resource and construction industries.

Utilities Industry Litigation Reporter: National Coverage of the Many Types of Litigation Stemming From the Transmission and Distribution of Energy By Publicly and Privately Owned Utilities. Andrews Publications. • Monthly. $775.00 per year. Reports on legal cases involving the generation or distribution of energy.

PUBLIC WELFARE

GENERAL WORKS

From Poor Law to Welfare State: A History of Social Welfare in America. Walter I. Trattner. Simon and Schuster Trade. • 1998. $16.95. Sixth edition.

Improving Poor People: The Welfare State, the "Underclass," and Urban Schools as History. Michael B. Katz. California Princeton Fulfillment Services. • 1995. $35.00.

Welfare: The Political Economy of Welfare Reform in the United States. Martin Anderson. Hoover Institution Press. • 1978. $6.78. (Publication Series, No. 181).

ABSTRACTS AND INDEXES

PAIS International in Print. Public Affairs Information Service, Inc. • Monthly. $650.00 per year; cumulations three times a year. Provides topical citations to the worldwide literature of public affairs, economics, demographics, sociology, and trade. Text in English; indexed materials in English, French, German, Italian, Portuguese and Spanish.

Social Sciences Citation Index. Institute for Scientific Information. • Three times a year. $6,900 per year. Annual cumulation. Includes *Source Index*, *Citation Index*, *Permuterm Subject Index*, and *Corporate Index*.

Social Sciences Index. H. W. Wilson Co. • Quarterly, with annual cumulation. Service basis for print edition; CD-ROM edition, $1,495 per year. Indexes more than 400 periodicals covering economics, environmental policy, government, insurance, labor, health care policy, plannning, public administration, public welfare, urban studies, women's issues, criminology, and related topics.

CD-ROM DATABASES

National Newspaper Index CD-ROM. The Gale Group. • Monthly. Provides comprehensive CD-ROM indexing of all material appearing in the late edition of the *New York Times*, the final edition of the *Washington Post*, the national edition of the *Christian Science Monitor*, the home edition of the *Los Angeles Times*, and the *Wall Street Journal*. Time period is four years. Also available online.

The New York Times Ondisc. New York Times Online Services. • Monthly. $2,650.00 per year. CD-ROM discs contain the full text of *The New York Times*, final edition. Inquire as to time period covered and availability of backfiles.

Newspaper Abstracts Ondisc. Bell & Howell Information and Learning. • Monthly. $2,950.00 per year (covers 1989 to date; archival discs are available for 1985-88). Provides cover-to-cover CD-ROM indexing and abstracting of 19 major newspapers, including the *New York Times, Wall Street Journal, Washington Post, Chicago Tribune,* and *Los Angeles Times*.

PAIS on CD-ROM. Public Affairs Information Service, Inc. • Quarterly. $1,995.00 per year. Provides a CD-ROM version of the online service, *PAIS International*. Contains over 400,000 citations to the literature of contemporary social, political, and economic issues.

Social Science Source. EBSCO Publishing. • Monthly. $1,495.00 per year. Provides CD-ROM citations and abstracts to social science articles in more than 600 periodicals, with full text from 125 periodicals. Covers economics, political science, public policy, international relations, psychology, and other topics. Time period is most recent five years.

Social Sciences Citation Index: Compact Disc Edition. Institute for Scientific Information. • Quarterly. Provides CD-ROM indexing of the world's social sciences literature, including economics, business, finance, management, communications, demographics, information and library science, political science, sociology, etc. Corresponds to online *Social Scisearch* and printed *Social Sciences Citation Index*.

Social Sciences Citation Index: Compact Disc Edition with Abstracts. Institute for Scientific Information. • Quarterly. Provides CD-ROM indexing and abstracting of "significant articles" from 1,400 social science journals worldwide, with additional selections from 3,200 other journals, 1986 to date. Includes economics, business, finance, management, communications, demographics, information and library science, political science, sociology, and many other subjects.

WILSONDISC: Readers' Guide to Periodical Literature. H. W. Wilson Co. • Monthly. $1,095.00 per year, including unlimited online access to *Readers' Guide to Periodical Literature* through WILSONLINE. Provides CD-ROM indexing of about 250 general interest periodicals. Covers 1983 to date. (*Readers' Guide Abstracts* also available on CD-ROM at $1,995 per year.).

WILSONDISC: Wilson Social Sciences Abstracts. H. W. Wilson Co. • Monthly. Including unlimited online access to *Social Sciences Index* through WILSONLINE. Provides CD-ROM indexing from 1983 and abstracting from 1994 of more than 400 periodicals covering economics, area studies, community health, public administration, public welfare, urban studies, and many other topics related to the social sciences.

DIRECTORIES

Catalog of Federal Domestic Assistance. U.S. Office of Management and Budget. Available from U.S. Government Printing Office. • Annual. $87.00. Looseleaf service. Includes up-dating service for indeterminate period. Summary of financial and nonfinanacial Federal programs, projects, services and activities that provide assistance or benefits to the American public.

Government Assistance Almanac: The Guide to Federal, Domestic, Financial and Other Programs Covering Grants, Loans, Insurance, Personal

Payments and Benefits. J. Robert Dumouchel, editor. Omnigraphics, Inc. • Annual. $190.00. Describes more than 1,300 federal assistance programs available from about 50 agencies. Includes statistics, a directory of 4,000 field offices, and comprehensive indexing.

Public Welfare Directory. American Public Welfare Association. • Annual. Members, $75.00; non-members, $80.00. Federal, state, territorial, county, and major municipal human service agencies.

HANDBOOKS AND MANUALS

Social Security Handbook. Available from U. S. Government Printing Office. • Annual. $45.00. Issued by the Social Security Administration (http://www.ssa.gov). Provides detailed information about social security programs, including Medicare, with brief descriptions of related programs administered by agencies other than the Social Security Administration.

INTERNET DATABASES

Social Security Online: The Official Web Site of the Social Security Administration. U. S. Social Security Administration. Phone: 800-772-1213 or (410)965-7700 • URL: http://www.ssa.gov • Web site provides a wide variety of online information relating to social security and Medicare. Topics include benefits, disability, employer wage reporting, personal earnings statements, statistics, government financing, social security law, and public welfare reform legislation.

U. S. Census Bureau: The Official Statistics. U. S. Bureau of the Census. Phone: (301)763-4100 Fax: (301)763-4794 • URL: http://www.census.gov • Web site is "Your Source for Social, Demographic, and Economic Information." Contains "Current U. S. Population Count," "Current Economic Indicators," and a wide variety of data under "Other Official Statistics." Keyword searching is provided. Fees: Free.

ONLINE DATABASES

Information Bank Abstracts. New York Times Index Dept. • Provides indexing and abstracting of current affairs, primarily from the final late edition of *The New York Times* and the Eastern edition of *The Wall Street Journal.* Time period is 1969 to present, with daily updates. Inquire as to online cost and availability.

Newspaper and Periodical Abstracts. Bell & Howell Information and Learning. • Provides online coverage (citations and abstracts) of 25 major newspapers, 1,600 perodicals, and 70 TV programs. Covers business, economics, current affairs, health, fitness, sports, education, technology, government, consumer affairs, psychology, the arts, and the social sciences. Time period is 1986 to date, with daily updates. Inquire as to online cost and availability.

PAIS International. Public Affairs Information Service, Inc. • Corresponds to the former printed publications, *PAIS Bulletin* (1976-90) and *PAIS Foreign Language Index* (1972-90), and to the current *PAIS International in Print* (1991 to date). Covers economic, political, and sociological material appearing in periodicals, books, government documents, and other publications. Updating is monthly. Inquire as to online cost and availability.

Readers' Guide Abstracts Online. H. W. Wilson Co. • Indexes and abstracts general interest periodicals, 1983 to date. Weekly updates. Inquire as to online cost and availability.

Social Scisearch. Institute for Scientific Information. • Broad, multidisciplinary index to the literature of the social sciences, 1972 to present. Weekly updates. Worldwide coverage. Inquire as to online cost and availability.

Wilson Social Sciences Abstracts Online. H. W. Wilson Co. • Provides online abstracting and indexing of more than 415 periodicals covering area studies, community health, public administration, public welfare, urban studies, and many other social science topics. Time period is 1994 to date for abstracts and 1983 to date for indexing, with updates monthly. Inquire as to online cost and availability.

PERIODICALS AND NEWSLETTERS

Journal of Human Resources: Education, Manpower and Welfare Economics. University of Wisconson at Madison, Industrial Relations Research Institute. University of Wisconsin Press. • Quarterly. Individuals, $54.00 per year; institutions, $124.00 per year. Articles on manpower, health and welfare policies as they relate to the labor market and to economic and social development.

Journal of Social Welfare and Family Law. Routledge Journals. • Quarterly. Individuals, $83.00 per year; institutions, $324.00 per year.

Public Assistance and Welfare Trends: State Capitals. Wakeman-Walworth, Inc. • Weekly. $245.00 per year. Newsletter. Formerly *From the State Capitals: Public Assistance and Welfare Trends.*

Public Welfare. American Public Welfare Association. • Quarterly. $35.00 per year.

Review of Social Economy. Association for Social Economics. Routledge Journals. • Quarterly. Individuals, $65.00 per year; institutions, $177.00 per year. Subject matter is concerned with the relationships between social values and economics. Includes articles on income distribution, poverty, labor, and class.

RESEARCH CENTERS AND INSTITUTES

Social Welfare Research Institute. Boston College. 140 Commonwealth Ave., 515 McGuinn Hall, Room 508, Chestnut Hill, MA 02167. Phone: (617)552-4070 Fax: (617)552-3903 E-mail: schervish@bc.edu • URL: http://www.bc.edu/swri.

STATISTICS SOURCES

County and City Extra: Annual Metro, City and County Data Book. Mark Littman and Deirdre A. Gaquin. Bernan Press. • 1999. $109.00. Updates and augments data published irregularly in print form by the U. S. Census Bureau in *County and City Data Book.* Covers "every state, county, metropolitan area, and congressional district in the United States, as well as all U. S. cities with a 1990 population of 25,000 or more." Contains a wide range tic maps.

Social Security Bulletin. Social Security Administration. Available from U.S. Government Printing Office. • Quarterly. $23.00 per year. Annual statistical supplement.

Social Statistics of the United States. Mark S. Littman, editor. Bernan Press. • 2000. $65.00. Includes statistical data on population growth, labor force, occupations, environmental trends, leisure time use, income, poverty, taxes, and other economic or demographic topics.

State Profiles: The Population and Economy of Each U. S. State. Courtenay Slater and Martha Davis, editors. Bernan Press. • 1999. $74.00. Presents charts, tables, and text in an eight-page profile for each state. Covers population, labor force, income, poverty, employment, wages, industry, trade, housing, education, health, taxes, and government finances.

Statistical Abstract of the United States. Available from U. S. Government Printing Office. • Annual. $51.00. Issued by the U. S. Bureau of the Census.

Statistical Handbook on Poverty in the Developing World. Chandrika Kaul. Oryx Press. • 1999. $65.00. Provides international coverage, including special sections on women and children, and on selected cities. (Statistical Handbook Series).

A Statistical Portrait of the United States: Social Conditions and Trends. Mark S. Littman, editor. Bernan Press. • 1998. $89.00. Covers "social, economic, and environmental trends in the United States over the past 25 years." Includes statistical tables, graphs, and analysis relating to such topics as population, income, poverty, wealth, labor, housing, education, healthcare, air/water quality, and government.

TRADE/PROFESSIONAL ASSOCIATIONS

American Public Human Services Association. 810 First St., N.E., Suite 500, Washington, DC 20002-4267. Phone: (202)682-0100 Fax: (202)289-6555 E-mail: pubs@aphsa.org • URL: http://www.aphsa.org.

OTHER SOURCES

FedWorld: A Program of the United States Department of Commerce. National Technical Information Service. • Web site offers "a comprehensive central access point for searching, locating, ordering, and acquiring government and business information." Emphasis is on searching the Web pages, databases, and government reports of a wide variety of federal agencies. Fees: Free.

FirstGov: Your First Click to the U. S. Government. General Services Administration. • Free Web site provides extensive links to federal agencies covering a wide variety of topics, such as agriculture, business, consumer safety, education, the environment, government jobs, grants, health, social security, statistics sources, taxes, technology, travel, and world affairs. Also provides links to federal forms, including IRS tax forms. Searching is offered, both keyword and advanced.

PUBLIC WORKS

See also: BUILDING CONTRACTS; BUILDING INDUSTRY

ABSTRACTS AND INDEXES

PAIS International in Print. Public Affairs Information Service, Inc. • Monthly. $650.00 per year; cumulations three times a year. Provides topical citations to the worldwide literature of public affairs, economics, demographics, sociology, and trade. Text in English; indexed materials in English, French, German, Italian, Portuguese and Spanish.

CD-ROM DATABASES

PAIS on CD-ROM. Public Affairs Information Service, Inc. • Quarterly. $1,995.00 per year. Provides a CD-ROM version of the online service, *PAIS International.* Contains over 400,000 citations to the literature of contemporary social, political, and economic issues.

DIRECTORIES

Public Works Manual. Public Works Journal Corp. • Annual. $45.00. Includes about 3,500 manufacturers and distributors of materials and equipment used in heavy construction. Special issue of (Public Works).

ONLINE DATABASES

PAIS International. Public Affairs Information Service, Inc. • Corresponds to the former printed publications, *PAIS Bulletin* (1976-90) and *PAIS Foreign Language Index* (1972-90), and to the current *PAIS International in Print* (1991 to date). Covers economic, political, and sociological material appearing in periodicals, books, government documents, and other publications. Updating is monthly. Inquire as to online cost and availability.

PERIODICALS AND NEWSLETTERS

APWA Reporter. American Public Works Association. • Monthly. Membership.

ENR Connecting the Industry Worldwide (Engineering News-Record). McGraw-Hill. • Weekly. $74.00 per year.

Project Finance: The Magazine for Global Development. Institutional Investor Journals. • Monthly. $635.00 per year. Provides articles on the financing of the infrastructure (transportation, utilities, communications, the environment, etc). Coverage is international. Supplements available *World Export Credit Guide* and *Project Finance Book of Lists.* Formed by the merger of *Infrastructure Finance* and *Project and Trade Finance.*

Public Works: City, County and State. Public Works Journal Corp. • 13 times a year. $60.00 per year. Includes *Public Works Manual.*

Public Works News. Reynolds Publishing Co., Inc. • Weekly. $520.00 per year.

RESEARCH CENTERS AND INSTITUTES

Municipal Technical Advisory Service Library. University of Tennessee, Knoxville, Conference Center Bldg.,, Suite 120, Knoxville, TN 37996-4105. Phone: (423)974-0411 Fax: (423)974-0423 E-mail: rschwartz@utk.edu • URL: http://www.mtas.utk.edu • Research areas include municipal finance, police administration, and public works.

STATISTICS SOURCES

United States Census of Construction Industries. U.S. Bureau of the Census. • Quinquennial. Results presented in reports, tape, and CD-ROM files.

TRADE/PROFESSIONAL ASSOCIATIONS

American Public Works Association. 2345 Grand Blvd., Suite 500, Kansas City, MO 64108. Phone: 800-595-2792 or (816)472-6100 Fax: (816)472-1610 E-mail: atatum@apwa.net.

OTHER SOURCES

Dodge Construction News. McGraw-Hill. • Daily. Los Angeles, $1,392.00 per year; Chicago, $1,245.00 per year.

PUBLICITY

See: PUBLIC RELATIONS AND PUBLICITY

PUBLISHERS, COLLEGE

See: UNIVERSITY PRESSES

PUBLISHING, DESKTOP

See: DESKTOP PUBLISHING

PUBLISHING, ELECTRONIC

See: ELECTRONIC PUBLISHING

PUBLISHING INDUSTRY

See also: BIBLIOGRAPHY; BOOK CATALOGS; BOOK INDUSTRY; BOOKSELLING; ELECTRONIC PUBLISHING; PAPERBOUND BOOK INDUSTRY; PERIODICALS; UNIVERSITY PRESSES

GENERAL WORKS

The Business of Publishing: How to Survive and Prosper in the Publishing and Bookselling Industry. Leonard Shatzkin. McGraw-Hill. • 1995. $24.95.

How to Get Happily Published: Complete and Candid Guide. Judith Appelbaum. HarperCollins Publishers. • 1998. $14.00. Fifth edition. Provides advice for writers on dealing with book and magazine publishers.

ABSTRACTS AND INDEXES

Book Review Digest: An Index to Reviews of Current Books. H.W. Wilson Co. • 10 times a year. Quarterly and annual cumulation. Service basis.

ALMANACS AND YEARBOOKS

Bowker Annual: Library and Book Trade Almanac. R. R. Bowker. • Annual. $175.00. Lists of accredited library schools; scholarships for education in library science; library organizations; major libraries; publishing and book sellers organizations. Includes statistics and news of the book business.

Trade Book Publishing: Review, Forecast, and Segment Analysis. SIMBA Information. • 1999. $1,495.00. Reviews current conditions in the book publishing industry, including analysis of market segments, retailing aspects, and profiles of major publishers.

BIBLIOGRAPHIES

American Book Publishing Record: Arranged by Dewey Decimal Classification and Indexed by Author, Title, and Subject. R. R. Bowker. • Monthly. $299.00. per year. Includes annual cumulation.

Booklist. American Library Association. • 22 times a year. $74.50. Reviews library materials for school and public libraries. Incorporates *Reference Books Bulletin.*

Books in Print. R. R. Bowker. • Annual. $595.00. Nine volumes. Annual supplement, $250.00 (three volumes).

Forthcoming Books. R. R. Bowker. • Bimonthly. $289.00 per year. Supplement to *Books in Print.*

Managing the Publishing Process: An Annotated Bibliography. Bruce W. Speck. Greenwood Publishing Group, Inc. • 1995. $75.00. (Bibliographies and Indexes in Mass Media and Communications Series, No. 9).

CD-ROM DATABASES

Books in Print On Disc: The Complete Books in Print System on Compact Laser Disc. Bowker Electronic Publishing. • Monthly. $1195.00 per year. The CD-ROM version of *Books in Print, Forthcoming Books*, and other Bowker bibliographic publications: lists the books of over 50,000 U.S. publishers. Includes books recently declared out-of-print. Also available with full text book reviews.

Books in Print with Book Reviews On Disc. Bowker Electronic Publishing. • Monthly. $1,755.00 per year. The CD-ROM version of *Books in Print, Forthcoming Books*,and other Bowker bibliographic publications, with the addition of full text book reviews from *Publishers Weekly, Library Journal, Booklist, Choice*, and other periodicals.

Bowker/Whitaker Global Books in Print On Disc. R. R. Bowker. • Monthly. $2,055.00 per year. Provides CD-ROM listing of English language books published throughout the world, including U. S., U. K., Canada, and Australia. Combines data from R. R. Bowker's *Books in Print Plus* and J. Whitaker & Sons Ltd.'s *Bookbank.* Includes more than two million titles.

Hoover's Company Capsules on CD-ROM. Hoover's, Inc. • Quarterly. $349.95 per year (single-user). Provides the CD-ROM version of *Hoover's Handbook of American Business, Hoover's Handbook of Emerging Companies, Hoover's Handbook of World Business, Hoover's Guide to Computer Companies, Hoover's Guide to Media Companies, Hoover's Handbook of Private Companies,* and various regional guides. Includes more than 11,000 profiles of companies.

LISA Plus: Library and Information Science Abstracts. Bowker-Saur, Reed Reference Publishing. • Quarterly. $1,450.00 per year. Provides CD-ROM abstracting and indexing of the world's library and information science literature. Covers a wide variety of topics.

DIRECTORIES

American Book Trade Directory. R. R. Bowker. • Annual. $255.00 More than 30,000 bookstores and other book outlets in the U.S. and Canada; 1,500 U.S. and Canadian book wholesalers and paperback distributors.

Cassell, Publishers Association and the Federation of European Publishers Association Directory of Publishing in Continental Europe. Cassell. • Biennial. $150.00. Published in London. Provides detailed profiles of United Kingdom and British Commonwealth publishers and agencies. Includes "publishers' turnover figures.".

International Literary Market Place: The Directory of the International Book Publishing Industry. R. R. Bowker. • Annual. $189.95. More than 10,370 publishers in over 180 countries outside the U.S.and Canada and about 1,150 trade and professional organizations related to publishing abroad.

Library Journal: Reference [year]: Print, CD-ROM, Online. Cahners Business Information. • Annual. Issued in November as supplement to *Library Journal.* Lists new and updated reference material, including general and trade print titles, directories, annuals, CD-ROM titles, and online sources. Includes material from more than 150 publishers, arranged by company name, with an index by subject. Addresses include e-mail and World Wide Web information, where available.

Literary Market Place: The Directory of the American Book Publishing Industry. R. R. Bowker. • Annual. $199.95. Two volumes. Over 16,000 firms or organizations offering services related to the publishing industry.

Marketer's Guide to Media. BPI Communications, Inc. • Quarterly. $105.00. Presents cost, circulation, and audience statistics for various mass media segments, including television, radio, magazines, newspapers, telephone yellow pages, and cinema. Formerly *Mediaweek's Guide to Media.*

Plunkett's Entertainment and Media Industry Almanac. Available from Plunkett Research, Ltd. • Biennial. $149.99. Provides profiles of leading firms in online information, films, radio, television, cable, multimedia, magazines, and book publishing. Includes World Wide Web sites, where available, plus information on careers and industry trends.

Publishers Directory: A Guide to New and Established Private and Special-Interest, Avant-Garde and Alternative, Organizational Association, Government and Institution Presses. The Gale Group. • 2000. $400.00. 23rd edition. Contains detailed information on more than 20,000 U.S. and Canadian publishers as well as small, independent presses.

Publishers, Distributors, and Wholesalers of the United States: A Directory of Publishers, Distributors, Associations, Wholesalers, Software Producers and Manufactureres Listing Editorial and Ordering Addresses, and and ISBN Publisher Prefi. R. R. Bowker. • Annual. $229.00. Two volumes. Lists more than 101,000 publishers, book distributors, and wholesalers. Includes museum and association imprints, inactive publishers, and publishers' fields of activity.

Publishers' International ISBN Directory. Available from The Gale Group. • Annual. $425.00. Three volumes. Compiled by the International ISBN Agency and published by K. G. Saur. Provides names and addresses of over 426,000 publishers in the United States and 210 other countries. Three sections: alphabetical, geographic, and ISBN number. Formerly *International ISBN Publishers' Directory*. Published by K. G. Saur.

Publishers' Trade List Annual: A Buying and Reference Guide to Books and Related Products. R. R. Bowker. • Annual. $315.00. Three volumes. About 1,000 publishers in the United States, with their catalogs.

Writer's Guide to Book Editors, Publishers, and Literary Agents, 2000-2001: Who They Are, What They Want, and How to Win Them Over. Jeff Herman. Prima Publishing. • Annual. $27.95; with CD-ROM, $49.95. Directory for authors includes information on publishers' response times and pay rates.

ENCYCLOPEDIAS AND DICTIONARIES

Dictionary of Bibliometrics. Virgil Diodato. Haworth Press, Inc. • 1994. $39.95. Contains detailed explanations of 225 terms, with references. (Bibliometrics is "the application of mathematical and statistical techniques to the study of publishing and professional communication.").

Graphically Speaking: An Illustrated Guide to the Working Language of Design and Publishing. Mark Beach. Coast to Coast Books. • 1992. $29.50. Provides practical definitions of 2,800 terms used in printing, graphic design, publishing, and desktop publishing. Over 300 illustrations are included, about 40 in color.

FINANCIAL RATIOS

Annual Statement Studies. Robert Morris Associates: The Association of Lending and Credit Risk Professiona. • Annual. Free to members; non-members, $140.00. Median and quartile financial ratios are given for over 400 kinds of manufacturing, wholesale, retail, construction, and consumer finance establishments. Data is sorted by both asset size and sales volume. Includes a clearly written "Definition of Ratios" and an alphabetical industry index.

HANDBOOKS AND MANUALS

Book Marketing Handbook: Tips and Techniques for the Sale and Promotion of Scientific, Technical, Professional, and Scholarly Books and Journals. Nat G. Bodian. R. R. Bowker. • Two volumes. $64.95 per volume. Volume one, 1980; volume two, 1983.

Directory Publishing: A Practical Guide. SIMBA Information. • 1996. $44.95. Fourth edition. Provides an overall review of the directory publishing industry, including types of directories, research, sales estimates, expenses, advertising, sales promotion, editorial content, and legal considerations.

Entertainment, Publishing, and the Arts Handbook. Robert Thorne and John D. Viera, editors. West Group. • Annual. $152.00. Presents recent legal cases, issues, developments, and trends.

Getting Your Book Published. Christine S. Smedley and Mitchell Allen. Sage Publications, Inc. • 1993. $37.00. A practical guide for academic and professional authors. Covers the initial book prospectus, contract negotiation, production procedures, and marketing. (Survival Skills for Scholars, vol. 10).

Rights and Liabilities of Publishers, Broadcasters, and Reporters. Slade R. Metcalf and Robin Bierstedt. Shepard's. • 1982. $200.00. Two volumes. A legal manual for the media.

INTERNET DATABASES

Amazon.com. Amazon.com, Inc. Phone: 800-201-7575 or (206)346-2992 Fax: (206)346-2950 E-mail: info@amazon.com • URL: http://www.amazon.com • "Welcome to Earth's Biggest Bookstore." Amazon.com claims to have more than 2.5 million titles that can be ordered online, but only through the Web site - no orders by mail, telephone, fax, or E-mail. Discounts are generally 30% for hardcovers and 20% for paperbacks. Efficient search facilities, including Boolean, make this Web site useful for reference (many titles have online reviews). Fees: Free.

GaleNet: Your Information Community. The Gale Group. Phone: 800-877-GALE or (248)699-GALE Fax: 800-414-5043 or (248)699-8069 E-mail: galenet@gale.com • URL: http://www.galenet.com • Web site provides a wide variety of full-text information from Gale databases, Taft, and other sources. Covers associations, biography, business directories, education, the information industry, literature, publishing, and science. Fee-based subscriptions are available for individual databases (free demonstration). Includes Boolean search features and the BRS/Search user interface.

Publishers' Catalogues Home Page. Northern Lights Internet Solutions Ltd. Phone: (306)931-0020 Fax: (306)931-7667 E-mail: info@lights.com • URL: http://www.lights.com/publisher • Provides links to the Web home pages of about 1,700 U. S. publishers (including about 80 University presses) and publishers in 48 foreign countries. "International/Multinational Publishers" are included, such as the International Monetary Fund, the World Bank, and the World Trade Organization. Publishers are arranged in convenient alphabetical lists. Searching is offered. Fees: Free.

ONLINE DATABASES

Book Review Index [Online]. The Gale Group. • Cites reviews of books and periodicals in journals, 1969 to present. Inquire as to online cost and availability.

Books in Print Online. Bowker Electronic Publishing. • The online version of *Books in Print*, *Forthcoming Books*, *Paperbound Books in Print*, and other Bowker bibliographic publications: lists the books of over 50,000 U. S. publishers. Includes books recently declared out-of-print. Updated monthly. Inquire as to online cost and availability.

LISA Online: Library and Information Science Abstracts. Bowker-Saur, Reed Reference Publishing. • Provides abstracting and indexing of the world's library and information science literature from 1969 to the present. Covers a wide variety of topics in over 550 journals from 60 countries, with biweekly updates. Inquire as to online cost and availability.

Wilson Publishers Directory Online. H. W. Wilson Co. • Provides names and addresses of more than 34,000 English-language book publishers and distributors appearing in *Cumulative Book Index* and other H. W. Wilson databases. Updated three times a week. Inquire as to online cost and availability.

PERIODICALS AND NEWSLETTERS

Book Publishing Report: Weekly News and Analysis of Events Shaping the Book Industry. SIMBA Information. • Weekly. $525.00 per year. Newsletter. Covers book publishing mergers, marketing, finance, personnel, and trends in general. Formerly *BP Report on the Business of Book Publishing*.

Choice: Current Reviews for Academic Libraries. Association of College Research Libraries. Choice. • 11 times a year. $200.00 per year. A publication of the Association of College and Research Libraries. Contains book reviews, primarily for college and university libraries.

Color Publishing. PennWell Corp., Advanced Technology Div. • Bimonthly. $29.70 per year.

Computer Publishing and Advertising Report: The Biweekly Newsletter for Publishing and Advertising Executives in the Computer Field. SIMBA Information, Inc. • Biweekly. $549.00 per year. Newsletter. Covers computer book publishing and computer-related advertising in periodicals and other media. Provides data on computer book sales and advertising in computer magazines.

Copy Editor: Language News for the Publishing Profession. Mary Beth/Protomastro. • Bimonthly. $69.00 per year. Newsletter for professional copy editors and proofreaders. Includes such items as "Top Ten Resources for Copy Editors.".

Digital Publishing Technologies: How to Implement New Media Publishing. Information Today, Inc. • Monthly. $196.00 per year. Covers online and CD-ROM publishing, including industry news, new applications, new products, electronic publishing technology, and descriptions of completed publishing projects.

Educational Marketer: The Educational Publishing Industry's Voice of Authority Since 1968. SIMBA Information. • Three times a month. $479.00 per year. Newsletter. Edited for suppliers of educational materials to schools and colleges at all levels. Covers print and electronic publishing, software, audiovisual items, and multimedia. Includes corporate news and educational statistics.

Independent Publisher: Leading the World of Book Selling in New Directions. Jenkins Group, Inc. • Bimonthly. $34.00 per year. Covers business, finance, production, marketing, and other management topics for small publishers, including college presses. Emphasis is on book publishing.

Innovative Publisher: Publishing Strategies for New Markets. Emmelle Publishing Co., Inc. • Biweekly. $69.00 per year. Provides articles and news on electronic publishing (CD-ROM or online) and desktop publishing.

Learned Publishing: ALPSP Bulletin. Association of Learned and Professional Society Publishers. • Quarterly. Free to members; non-members, $295.00 per year. Articles and news of interest to publishers of academic and learned society material.

Publishers Weekly: The International News Magazine of Book Publishing. Cahners Business Information, Broadcasting and Cables International Group. • Weekly. $189.00 per year. The international news magazine of book publishing.

The SIMBA Report on Directory Publishing. SIMBA Information. • Monthly. $59.00 per year. Newsletter.

STATISTICS SOURCES

By the Numbers: Electronic and Online Publishing. The Gale Group. • 1997. $385.00. Four volumes. $99.00 per volume. Covers "high-interest" industries: 1. *By the Numbers: Electronic and Online Publishing*; 2. *By the Numbers: Emerging Industries*; 3. *By the Numbers: Nonprofits*; 4. *By the Numbers: Publishing*. Each volume provides about 600 tabulations of industry data on revenues, market share, employment, trends, financial ratios, profits, salaries, and so forth. Citations to data sources are included.

Computer Publishing Market Forecast. SIMBA Information. • Annual. $1,995.00. Provides market data on computer-related books, magazines, newsletters, and other publications. Includes profiles of major publishers of computer-related material.

Librarian's Companion: A Handbook of Thousands of Facts on Libraries, Librarians, Books,

Newspapers, Publishers, Booksellers. Vladimir F. Wertsman. Greenwood Publishing Group, Inc. • 1996. $67.95. Second edition. Provides international statistics on libraries and publishing. Includes directory and biographical information.

Media Market Guide. Media Market Resources. • Quarterly. $675.00 per year. Presents circulation and cost data for television, radio, magazines, newspapers and outdoor markets.

Standard & Poor's Industry Surveys. Standard & Poor's. • Semiannual. $1,800.00. Two looseleaf volumes. Includes monthly supplements. Provides detailed, individual surveys of 52 major industry groups. Each survey is revised on a semiannual basis. Also includes "Monthly Investment Review" (industry group investment analysis) and monthly "Trends & Projections" (economic analysis).

U. S. Industry and Trade Outlook: The McGraw-Hill Companies and the U.S. Department of Commerce/ International Trade Administration. Datapso Research Corp. • Annual. $69.95. Produced by the International Trade Administration, U. S. Department of Commerce, in a "public-private" partnership with DRI/McGraw-Hill and Standard & Poor's. Provides basic data, outlook for the current year, and "Long-Term Prospects" (five-year projections) for a wide variety of products and services. Includes high technology industries. Formerly *U. S. Industrial Outlook.*

UNESCO Statistical Yearbook. Bernan Press. • Annual. $95.00. Co-published by Bernan Press and the United Nations Educational, Scientific, and Cultural Organization (http://www.unesco.org). Presents statistical data from more than 200 countries on education, technology, research, broadcasting, cinema, book publishing, newspapers, libraries, museums, and population. Includes charts, maps, and graphs.

TRADE/PROFESSIONAL ASSOCIATIONS

Association of American Publishers. 71 Fifth Ave., New York, NY 10003-3004. Phone: (212)255-0200 Fax: (212)255-7007 • URL: http://www.publishers.org.

Association of American University Presses. 71 W. 23rd St., Suite 901, New York, NY 10010-4102. Phone: (212)989-1010 Fax: (212)989-0275 E-mail: aaupny@aol.com • URL: http://www.aaupnet.org.

Association of Learned and Professional Society Publishers. Dovetail, Four Tintagel Crescent, London SE22 8HT, England. E-mail: andy.cawdell@alsiss.org.uk • URL: http://www.alsss.org.uk.

Book Industry Study Group. 160 Fifth Ave., New York, NY 10010. Phone: (212)929-1393 Fax: (212)989-7542 E-mail: sandy@booksinfo.org • URL: http://www.bisg.org.

Women's National Book Association. 160 Fifth Ave., Room 604, New York, NY 10010. Phone: (212)675-7805 Fax: (212)989-7542 E-mail: skpassoc@cwismail.com • URL: http://www.bookbuzz.com/wnba.htm.

OTHER SOURCES

Huenefeld Report: For Managers and Planners in Modest-Sized Book Publishing Houses. John Huenefeld. Huenefeld Co., Inc. • Biweekly. $88.00 per year.

Lindey on Entertainment, Publishing and the Arts: Agreements and the Law. Alexander Lindey, editor. West Group. • $673.00 per year. Looseleaf service. Periodic supplementation. Provides basic forms, applicable law, and guidance. (Entertainment and Communication Law Series).

Towards Electronic Journals: Realities for Scientists, Librarians, and Publishers. Carol Tenopir and Donald W. King. Special Libraries Association. • 2000. $59.00. Discusses journals in electronic form vs. traditional (paper) scholarly journals, including the impact of subscription prices.

PULPWOOD INDUSTRY

See: WOODPULP INDUSTRY

PUMPS AND COMPRESSORS

ABSTRACTS AND INDEXES

Applied Science and Technology Index. H. W. Wilson Co. • 11 times a year. Quarterly and annual cumulations. Service basis for print edition; CD-ROM edition, $1,495.00 per year. Indexes a wide variety of English language technical, industrial, and engineering periodicals.

Current Contents: Engineering, Computing and Technology. Institute for Scientific Information. • Weekly. $730.00 per year. Reproductions of contents pages of technical journals. Includes *Author Index, Address Directory, Current Book Contents* and *Title Word Index.* Formerly *Current Contents: Engineering, Technology and Applied Sciences.*

Fluid Abstracts: Process Engineering. Elsevier Science. • Monthly. $1,319.00 per year. Includes annual cumulation. Formerly *Pumps and Other Fluids Machinery: Abstracts.*

DIRECTORIES

Fluid Power Handbook and Directory. Penton Media Inc. • Biennial. $80.00 per year. Over 1,500 manufacturers and 3,000 distributors of fluid power products in the United States and Canada.

Macrae's Blue Book: Serving the Original Equipment Market. MacRae's Blue Book, Inc. • Annual. $170.00. Two volumes. Lists about 50,000 manufacturers of a wide variety of industrial equipment and supplies.

Thomas Register of American Manufacturers and Thomas Register Catalog File. Thomas Publishing Co., Inc. • Annual. $149.00. 34 volumes. A three-part system offering information on a wide variety of industrial equipment and supplies.

HANDBOOKS AND MANUALS

Pump Application Desk Book. Paul N. Garay. Prentice Hall. • 1996. $82.00. Third edition.

ONLINE DATABASES

Applied Science and Technology Index Online. H. W. Wilson Co. • Provides online indexing of 400 major scientific, technical, industrial, and engineering periodicals. Time period is 1983 to date. Monthly updates. Inquire as to online cost and availability.

FLUIDEX. Available from Elsevier Science, Inc., Secondary Publishing Division. • Produced in the Netherlands by Elsevier Science B.V. Provides indexing and abstracting of the international literature of fluid engineering and technology, 1973 to date, with monthly updates. Also known as *Fluid Engineering Abstracts.* Inquire as to online cost and availability.

PROMT: Predicasts Overview of Markets and Technology. The Gale Group. • Companies, products, applied technologies and markets. U.S. and international literature coverage, 1972 to date. Inquire as to online cost and availability. Provides abstracts from more than 1,600 publications. Weekly updates.

Thomas Register Online. Thomas Publishing Co., Inc. • Provides concise information on approximately 194,000 U. S. companies, mainly manufacturers, with over 50,000 product classifications. Indexes over 115,000 trade names. Information is updated semiannually. Inquire as to online cost and availability.

PERIODICALS AND NEWSLETTERS

Hydraulics and Pneumatics: The Magazine of Fluid Power and Motion Control Systems. Penton Media Inc. • Monthly. Free to qualified personnel; others, $55.00 per year.

Industrial Equipment News. Thomas Publishing Co. • Monthly. $95.00 per year. Free. What's new in equipment, parts and materials.

New Equipment Digest Market. Penton Media Inc. • Monthly. Free to qualified personnel; others, $55.00 per year. Formerly *Material Handling Engineering.*

New Equipment Reporter: New Products Industrial News. De Roche Publications. • Monthly. Controlled circulation.

Plant Engineering. Cahners Business Information. • 13 times a year. $135.90. per year. Includes *Plant Engineering Product Supplier Guide.*

Processing. Putman Media. • 14 times a year. $54.00 per year. Emphasis is on descriptions of new products for all areas of industrial processing, including valves, controls, filters, pumps, compressors, fluidics, and instrumentation.

World Pumps. Elsevier Science. • Monthly. $248.00 per year. Text in English, French and German.

RESEARCH CENTERS AND INSTITUTES

Ray W. Herrick Laboratories. Purdue University, School of Mechanical Engineering, West Lafayette, IN 47907-1077. Phone: (765)494-2132 Fax: (765)494-0787 E-mail: rhlab@ecn.purdue.edu.

STATISTICS SOURCES

Annual Survey of Manufactures. Available from U. S. Government Printing Office. • Annual. Prices vary. Issued by the U. S. Census Bureau as an interim update to the *Census of Manufactures.* Includes data on number of manufacturing establishments in various industries, employment, labor costs, value of shipments, capital expenditures, inventories, energy costs, and assets. (See also Census Bureau home page, http://www.census.gov/.).

Manufacturing Profiles. Available from U. S. Government Printing Office. • Annual. Issued by the U. S. Census Bureau. A printed consolidation of the entire *Current Industrial Report* series, presenting "all the data compiled." Contains statistics on production, shipments, inventories, consumption, exports, imports, and orders for a wide variety of manufactured products. (See also Census Bureau home page, http://www.census.gov/.).

Pumps and Compressors. U. S. Bureau of the Census. • Annual. Provides data on value of manufacturers' shipments, quantity, exports, imports, etc. (Current Industrial Reports, MA-35P.).

TRADE/PROFESSIONAL ASSOCIATIONS

Contractors Pump Bureau. 111 E. Wisconsin Ave., Suite 1000, Milwaukee, WI 53202. Phone: (414)272-0943 Fax: (414)272-1170 E-mail: cima@cimunet.com • URL: http://www.cimanet.com • Members are manufacturers of pumps for the construction industry.

Industrial Compressor Distributors Association. 412 Harbor View Lane, Largo, FL 33760-4009. Phone: (727)586-3693 Fax: (727)586-3573.

Submersible Wastewater Pump Association. 1866 Sheridan Rd., Ste. 210, Highland Park, IL 60035-2545. Phone: (847)681-1868 Fax: (847)681-1869 • URL: http://www.swpa.org.

Sump and Sewage Pump Manufacturers Association. P.O.Box 647, Northbrook, IL 60065-0647. Phone: (847)559-9233 Fax: (847)559-9235 E-mail: 103061.1063@compuserve.com • URL: http://www.sspma.org.

Water Systems Council. 800 Roosevelt Rd., Bldg. C, Suite 20, Glen Ellyn, IL 60137. Phone: (630)545-1762 Fax: (630)790-3095.

OTHER SOURCES

Industrial Pumps and Pumping Equipment. Available from MarketResearch.com. • 1997. $1,195.00. Market research report published by Specialists in Business Information. Covers centrifugal, rotary, turbine, reciprocating, and other types of pumps. Presents market data relative to sales growth, shipments, exports, imports, and end-use. Includes company profiles.

PURCHASING

GENERAL WORKS

Management of Retail Buying. R. Patrick Cash and others. John Wiley and Sons, Inc. • 1995. $110.00. Third edition.

Purchasing and Materials Management. Michiel R. Leenders and Harold E. Fearon. McGraw-Hill Professional. • 1996. $71.75. 11th edition.

Purchasing and Supply Management. P. J. Baily. Chapman and Hall. • 1987. $34.95. Fifth edition.

Strategic Supply Management: A Blueprint for Revitalizing the Manufacturer-Supplier Partnership. Keki R. Bhote. AMACOM. • 1989. $65.00. How to reduce the expense of supply management and improve quality, delivery time, and inventory control.

ABSTRACTS AND INDEXES

Business Periodicals Index. H. W. Wilson Co. • Monthly, except August, with quarterly and annual cumulations. Service basis for print edition; CD-ROM edition, $1,495.00 per year.

CD-ROM DATABASES

WILSONDISC: Wilson Business Abstracts. H. W. Wilson Co. • Monthly. $2,495.00 per year, including unlimited online access to *Wilson Business Abstracts* through WILSONLINE. Provides CD-ROM "cover-to-cover" abstracting and indexing of over 600 prominent business periodicals. Indexing is from 1982, abstracting from 1990. (*Business Periodicals Index* without abstracts is available on CD-ROM at $1,495 per year.).

DIRECTORIES

Macrae's Blue Book: Serving the Original Equipment Market. MacRae's Blue Book, Inc. • Annual. $170.00. Two volumes. Lists about 50,000 manufacturers of a wide variety of industrial equipment and supplies.

Nationwide Directory of Gift, Housewares and Home Textiles Buyers. Salesman's Guide. • Annual. $195.00.

Nationwide Directory of Major Mass Market Merchandisers. Salesman's Guide. • Annual. $179.95. Lists buyers of clothing for major retailers. (Does not include the metropolitan New York City area.).

Nationwide Directory of Men's and Boys' Wear Buyers. Salesman's Guide. • Annual. $229.00. About 6,000 retail stores selling men's and boys' clothing, sportswear, furnishings, and accessories; coverage does not include New York metropolitan area.

Nationwide Directory of Sporting Goods Buyers. Salesman's Guide. • Annual. $209.00. About 9,000 retail stores selling athletic and recreational equipment, footwear, apparel.

Nationwide Directory of Women's and Children's Wear Buyers. Salesman's Guide. • Annual. $229.00. About 7,200 retail stores selling women's dresses, coats, sportswear, intimate apparel, and women's accessories, infants' to teens wear, and accessories; coverage does not include New York metropolitan area.

Thomas Register of American Manufacturers and Thomas Register Catalog File. Thomas Publishing Co., Inc. • Annual. $149.00. 34 volumes. A three-part system offering information on a wide variety of industrial equipment and supplies.

ENCYCLOPEDIAS AND DICTIONARIES

Blackwell Encyclopedic Dictionary of Operations Management. Nigel Slack, editor. Blackwell Publishers. • 1997. $105.95. The editor is associated with the University of Warwick, England. Contains definitions of key terms combined with longer articles written by various U. S. and foreign business educators. Includes bibliographies and index. (Blackwell Encyclopedia of Management Series.).

Encyclopedia of Business. The Gale Group. • 2000. $425.00. Second edition. Two volumes. Contains more than 700 signed articles covering major business disciplines and concepts. International in scope.

HANDBOOKS AND MANUALS

Managing Purchasing: Making the Supply Team Work. John W. Kamauff and Kenneth H. Killen. McGraw-Hill Professional. • 1995. $45.00. (NAPM Professional Development Series: Vol. 2).

ONLINE DATABASES

ABI/INFORM. Bell & Howell Information and Learning. • Provides online indexing to business-related material occurring in over 1,000 periodicals from 1971 to the present. Inquire as to online cost and availability.

Thomas Register Online. Thomas Publishing Co., Inc. • Provides concise information on approximately 194,000 U. S. companies, mainly manufacturers, with over 50,000 product classifications. Indexes over 115,000 trade names. Information is updated semiannually. Inquire as to online cost and availability.

Wilson Business Abstracts Online. H. W. Wilson Co. • Indexes and abstracts 600 major business periodicals, plus the *Wall Street Journal* and the business section of the *New York Times.* Indexing is from 1982, abstracting from 1990, with the two newspapers included from 1993. Updated weekly. Inquire as to online cost and availability. (*Business Periodicals Index* without abstracts is also available online.).

PERIODICALS AND NEWSLETTERS

The Business Consumer's Advisor. Buyers Laboratory, Inc. • Monthly. $175.00 per year. Newsletter.

Healthcare Purchasing News: A Magazine for Hospital Materials Management Central Service, Infection Control Practitioners. McKnight Medical Communications. • Monthly. $44.00 per year. Edited for personnel responsible for the purchase of medical, surgical, and hospital equipment and supplies. Features new purchasing techniques and new products. Includes news of the activities of two major purchasing associations, Health Care Material Management Society and International Association of Healthcare Central Service Materiel Management.

Industrial Purchasing Agent. Publications for Industry. • Monthly. $25.00 per year. New product releases.

Journal of Supply Chain Management: A Global Review of Purchasing and Supply. National Association of Purchasing Management. • Quarterly. $59.00 per year. Formerly *International Journal of Purchasing and Materials Management.*

Purchasing: The Magazine of Total Supply Chain Management. Cahners Business Information. • 19 times a year. $99.90 per year.

Purchasing Today: For the Purchasing and Supply Professional. National Association of Purchasing Management. • Monthly. $24.00 per year to libraries. Includes special issues on logistics, transportation, cost management, and supply chain management.

TRADE/PROFESSIONAL ASSOCIATIONS

Association for Healthcare Resource and Materials Management. c/o American Hospital Association, One N. Franklin St ., Chicago, IL 60606. Phone: (312)422-3840 Fax: (312)422-3573 E-mail: ahrmm@aha.org • URL: http://www.ahrmm.org • Members are involved with the purchasing and distribution of supplies and equipment for hospitals and other healthcare establishments. Affiliated with the American Hospital Association.

Health Care Resource Management Society. P.O. Box 29253, Cincinnati, OH 45229-0253. Phone: (513)520-1058 or (513)872-6315 Fax: (513)872-6158 E-mail: hcrms@choice.net • URL: http://www.hcrms.com • Members are materials management (purchasing) personnel in hospitals and the healthcare industry. The Society is concerned with hospital costs, distribution, logistics, recycling, and inventory management.

International Association of Healthcare Central Service Materiel Management. 213 W. Institute Place, Suite 307, Chicago, IL 60610. Phone: 800-962-8274 or (312)440-0078 Fax: (312)440-9474 E-mail: mailbox@iahcsmm.com • URL: http://www.iahcsmm.com • Members are professional personnel responsible for management and distribution of supplies from a central service material management (purchasing) department of a hospital.

National Association of Purchasing Management. P.O. Box 22160, Tempe, AZ 85285-2160. Phone: 800-888-6276 or (480)752-6276 Fax: (480)752-7890 • URL: http://www.napm.org.

PURCHASING AGENTS

See: PURCHASING

PURCHASING POWER

See also: CONSUMER ECONOMICS; INCOME; MARKET STATISTICS

CD-ROM DATABASES

Sourcebook America. The Gale Group. • Annual. $995.00. Produced by CACI Marketing Systems. A combination on CD-ROM of *The Sourcebook of ZIP Code Demographics* and *The Sourcebook of County Demographics.* Provides detailed population and socio-economic data (about 75 items) for each of 3,141 U. S. counties and approximately 30,000 ZIP codes, plus states, metropolitan areas, and media market areas. Includes forecasts to the year 2004.

World Marketing Forecasts on CD-ROM. The Gale Group. • Annual. $2,500.00. Produced by Euromonitor. Provides detailed forecast data for the years to 2012 on CD-ROM for 54 countries in all parts of the world. Covers a wide range of social, demographic, economic, and market factors. Includes specific forecasts for many kinds of consumer products.

DIRECTORIES

Editor and Publisher Market Guide. Editor and Publisher Co., Inc. • Annual. $125.00. More than 1,700 newspaper markets in the Unite States and Canada.

INTERNET DATABASES

Bureau of Labor Statistics (BLS). U. S. Department of Labor, Bureau of Labor Statistics. Phone: (202)523-1092 E-mail: labstat.helpdesk@bls.gov • URL: http://www.bls.gov • Web site provides a great variety of employment, wage, price, and economic data. Some links are "Data," "Economy at a Glance," "Keyword Search of BLS Web Pages," "Regional Information," and "Other Statistical Sites." Fees: Free.

ONLINE DATABASES

Euromonitor Market Research. Euromonitor International. • Provides the complete text online of Euromonitor market analysis reports. Covers consumer goods market research data for all major countries, with emphasis on specific product categories. Time period is current. Continuous updating. Inquire as to online cost and availability.

STATISTICS SOURCES

The AIER Chart Book. AIER Research Staff. American Institute for Economic Research. • Annual. $3.00. A compact compilation of long-range charts ("Purchasing Power of the Dollar," for example, goes back to 1780) covering various aspects of the U. S. economy. Includes inflation, interest rates, debt, gold, taxation, stock prices, etc. (Economic Education Bulletin.).

Consumer Canada 1996. Available from The Gale Group. • 1996. $750.00. Published by Euromonitor. Provides consumer market, socioeconomic, and demographic data for Canada. Includes consumer market size (volume and value) for many specific kinds of products.

Consumer Expenditure Survey. Available from U. S. Government Printing Office. • Biennial. Issued by the Bureau of Labor Statistics, U. S. Department of Labor (http://www.bls.gov). Contains data on various kinds of consumer spending, according to household income, education, etc. (Bureau of Labor Statistics Bulletin.).

Consumer International 2000/2001. Available from The Gale Group. • 1998. $1,190.00. Seventh edition. Published by Euromonitor. Contains extensive consumer market, economic, and demographic data for 27 major, non-European countries, including the U. S. and Canada. Includes consumer market size (volume and value) for 150 product types in 14 categories (food, clothing, automobiles, cosmetics, appliances, etc.).

Consumer Power: How Americans Spend. Margaret Ambry. McGraw-Hill Professional. • 1992. $27.50. Contains detailed statistics on consumer income and spending. Nine major categories of products and services are covered, with spending data and dollar size of market for each item.

Consumer USA 2000. Available from The Gale Group. • 2000. $900.00. Fifth edition. Published by Euromonitor. Provides demographic and consumer market data for the United States. Forecasts to the year 2005.

Current Population Reports: Household Economic Studies, Series P-70. Available from U. S. Government Printing Office. • Irregular. $16.00 per year. Issued by the U.S. Bureau of the Census (http://www.census.gov). Each issue covers a special topic relating to household socioeconomic characteristics.

Demographics USA: County Edition. Market Statistics. • Annual. $435.00. Contains 200 statistical series for each of 3,000 counties. Includes population, household income, employment, retail sales, and consumer expenditures. Also provides Effective Buying Income, Buying Power Index, and data summaries by Metro Market, Media Market, and State. (CD-ROM version is available.).

Demographics USA: ZIP Edition. Market Statistics. • Annual. $435.00. Contains 50 statistical series for each of 40,000 ZIP codes. Includes population, household income, employment, retail sales, and consumer expenditures. Also provides Effective Buying Income, Business Characteristics, and data summaries by state, region, and the first three digits of ZIP codes. (CD-ROM version is available.).

European Marketing Forecasts 2001. Available from The Gale Group. • 2000. $1,190.00. Third edition. Published by Euromonitor. Contains demographic, economic, and market forecasts for the countries of Europe to the year 2010. Forecasts include market-size data for 15 consumer product sectors (food, clothing, automobiles, consumer electronics, etc.).

Handbook of U. S. Labor Statistics: Employment, Earnings, Prices, Productivity, and Other Labor Data. Eva E. Jacobs, editor. Bernan Associates. • 1999. $74.00. Based on *Handbook of Labor Statistics*, formerly issued by the Bureau of Labor Statistics, U. S. Department of Labor. Includes the Bureau's projections of employment in the U. S. by industry and occupation. Provides a wide variety of data on the work force, prices, fringe benefits, and consumer expenditures.

Household Spending: Who Spends How Much On What. Hoai Tran. New Strategist Publications, Inc. • 1999. $94.95. Fifth edition. Gives facts about the buying habits of U. S. consumers according to income, age, household type, and household size. Includes spending data for about 1,000 products and services.

International Marketing Forecasts 2001. Available from The Gale Group. • 2000. $1,090.00. Third edition. Published by Euromonitor. Contains demographic, economic, and market forecasts to the year 2010 for major, non-European countries, including the U. S. and Canada. Forecasts include market-size data for 15 consumer product sectors, such as food, clothing, and automobiles.

Money Income in the United States. Available from U. S. Government Printing Office. • Annual. $19.00. Issued by the U. S. Bureau of the Census. Presents data on consumer income in current and constant dollars, both totals and averages (means, medians, distributions). Includes figures for a wide variety of demographic and occupational characteristics. (Current Population Reports, P60-209.).

Prices and Earnings Around the Globe. Union Bank of Switzerland. • Irregular. Free. Published in Zurich. Compares prices and purchasing power in 48 major cities of the world. Wages and hours are also compared. Text in English, French, German, and Italian.

Sales and Marketing Management Survey of Buying Power. Bill Communications, Inc. • Annual. $150.00.

Sourcebook of Zip Code Demographics. CACI Marketing Systems. • 2000. $495.00. 15th revised edition. Published by CACI, Inc. Provides data on 75 demographic and socio-economic characteristics for each ZIP code in the U. S.

Statistical Handbook on Consumption and Wealth in the United States. Chandrika Kaul and Valerie Tomaselli-Moschovitis. Oryx Press. • 1999. $65.00. Provides more than 400 graphs, tables, and charts dealing with basic income levels, income inequalities, spending patterns, taxation, subsidies, etc. (Statistical Handbook Series).

World Consumer Income and Expenditure Patterns. Available from The Gale Group. • 2001. $650.00. Published by Euromonitor (http://www.euromonitor.com). Provides data on consumer income, earning power, and expenditures for 52 countries around the world.

OTHER SOURCES

MarketingClick Network: American Demographics. Intertec Publishing, a Primedia Co. • Web site provides full-text articles from *American Demographics*, *Marketing Tools*, and *Forecast*, with keyword searching. The *Marketing Tools Directory* can also be searched online, listing suppliers of products, information, and services for advertising, market research, and marketing. Fees: Free.

World Consumer Income and Expenditure Patterns. Available from The Gale Group. • 2001. $990.00. Second edition. Two volumes. Published by Euromonitor. Provides data for 52 countries on consumer income, earning power, spending patterns, and savings. Expenditures are detailed for 75 product or service categories.

PUTS AND CALLS

See: STOCK OPTION CONTRACTS

Q

QUALITY CONTROL

See also: PRODUCTION CONTROL; STANDARDIZATION; TOTAL QUALITY MANAGEMENT (TQM)

GENERAL WORKS

Chaos on the Shop Floor: A Worker's View of Quality, Productivity, and Management. Tom Juravich. Temple University Press. • 1988. $19.95. (Labor and Social Change Series).

Process Quality Control. Ellis R. Ott. McGraw-Hill. • 2000. $74.95. Third edition.

Quality Control. Dale H. Besterfield. Prentice Hall. • 2000. $78.67. Sixth edition. Covers basic quality control concepts and procedures, including statistical process control (SPC). Includes disk.

Quality Planning and Analysis. Joseph M. Juran. McGraw-Hill. • 1993. $90.63. Third edition.

ABSTRACTS AND INDEXES

NTIS Alerts: Manufacturing Technology. National Technical Information Service. • Semimonthly. $265.00 per year. Provides descriptions of government-sponsored research reports and software, with ordering information. Covers computer-aided design and manufacturing (CAD/CAM), engineering materials, quality control, machine tools, robots, lasers, productivity, and related subjects. Formerly *Abstract Newsletter.*

DIRECTORIES

Quality-Buyers Guide for; QA/QC Equipment. Cahners Business Information. • Annual. $15.00. List of manufacturers and distributors of quality control equipment for measurement, inspection, data analysis evaluation and destructive and nondestructive testing; also lists testing laboratories, consultants, software and training organizations. Formerly *Quality Buyers Guide for Test, Inspection, Measurement and Evaluation.*

ENCYCLOPEDIAS AND DICTIONARIES

Blackwell Encyclopedic Dictionary of Operations Management. Nigel Slack, editor. Blackwell Publishers. • 1997. $105.95. The editor is associated with the University of Warwick, England. Contains definitions of key terms combined with longer articles written by various U. S. and foreign business educators. Includes bibliographies and index. (Blackwell Encyclopedia of Management Series.).

HANDBOOKS AND MANUALS

Gower Handbook of Quality Management. Dennis Lock, editor. Ashgate Publishing Co. • 1994. $131.95. Second edition. Consists of 41 chapters written by various authors. Published by Gower in England.

Juran's Quality Control Handbook. Joseph M. Juran and Blandfor Godfrey, editors. McGraw-Hill. • 1999. $150.00. Fifth edition.

Management of Quality Assurance. Madhav N. Sinha and Walter O. Willborn. John Wiley and Sons, Inc. • 1985. $99.95.

Modern Methods for Quality Control and Improvement. Harrison M. Wadsworth and others. John Wiley and Sons, Inc. • 1986. $99.95.

Statistical Quality Control. Eugene L. Grant and Richard S. Leavenworth. McGraw-Hill. • 1996. $103.44. Seventh edition.

World Class Quality: Using Design of Experiments to Make It Happen. Keki R. Bhote. AMACOM. • 1999. $34.95. Second revised expanded edition. An explanation of seven Shainin techniques for quality control. Exercises and case studies are included.

PERIODICALS AND NEWSLETTERS

Journal of Quality Technology. American Society for Quality. • Quarterly. $30.00 per year.

Quality and Reliability Engineering International. Available from John Wiley and Sons, Inc., Journals Div. • Bimonthly. $1,145.00 per year. Designed to bridge the gap between existing theoretical methods and scientific research on the one hand, and current industrial practices on the other. Published in England by John Wiley and Sons Ltd.

Quality Management Journal. American Society for Quality. • Quarterly. Members, $50.00 per year; non-members, $60.00 per year. Emphasizes research in quality control and management.

Quality Progress. American Society for Quality. • Monthly. $50.00 per year. Covers developments in quality improvement throughout the world.

RESEARCH CENTERS AND INSTITUTES

Institute of Advanced Manufacturing Sciences, Inc. 1111 Edison Dr., Cincinnati, OH 45216. Phone: (513)948-2000 Fax: (513)948-2109 E-mail: conley@iams.org • URL: http://www.iams.org • Fields of research include quality improvement, computer-aided design, artificial intelligence, and employee training.

National Center for Manufacturing Sciences. 3025 Boardwalk, Ann Arbor, MI 48108. Phone: (734)995-0300 Fax: (734)995-4004 E-mail: johnd@ncms.org • URL: http://www.ncms.org • Research areas include process technology and control, machine mechanics, sensors, testing methods, and quality assurance.

TRADE/PROFESSIONAL ASSOCIATIONS

American Society for Quality. P.O. Box 3005, Milwaukee, WI 53201-3005. Phone: 800-248-1946 or (414)272-8575 Fax: (414)272-1734 E-mail: cs@asq.org • URL: http://www.asq.org.

Association for Quality and Participation. 2368 Victory Pkwy., Ste. 200, Cincinnati, OH 45206. Phone: 800-733-3310 or (513)381-1959 or (513)381-1979 Fax: (513)381-0070 E-mail: aqp@aqp.org • URL: http://www.aqp.org.

QUALITY OF PRODUCTS

See also: CONSUMER EDUCATION; STANDARDIZATION

CD-ROM DATABASES

Consumers Reference Disc. National Information Services Corp. • Quarterly. Provides the CD-ROM version of *Consumer Health and Nutrition Index* from Oryx Press and *Consumers Index to Product Evaluations and Information Sources* from Pierian Press. Contains citations to consumer health articles and consumer product evaluations, tests, warnings, and recalls.

ENCYCLOPEDIAS AND DICTIONARIES

Consumers' Guide to Product Grades and Terms: From Grade A to VSOP-Definitions of 8,000 Terms Describing Food Housewares and Other Everyday Terms. The Gale Group. • 1992. $75.00. Includes product grades and classifications defined by government agencies, such as the Food and Drug Administration (FDA), and by voluntary standards organizations, such as the American National Standards Institute (ANSI).

PERIODICALS AND NEWSLETTERS

Consumer Reports. Consumers Union of the United States, Inc. • Semimonthly. $24.00 per year. Includes *Annual Buying Guide.*

Consumers Digest: Best Buys, Best Prices, Best Reports for People Who Demand Value. Consumers Digest Inc. • Bimonthly. $15.97.

Consumer's Research Magazine: Analyzing Consumer Issues. Consumers' Research Inc. • Monthly. $24.00 per year.

NDT and E International; The Independent Journal of Non-Destructive Testing. Elsevier Science. • Eight times a year. $596.00 per year. Formerly *NDT International.*

TRADE/PROFESSIONAL ASSOCIATIONS

American National Standards Institute. 11 W. 42nd St., 13th Fl., New York, NY 10036. Phone: (212)642-4900 Fax: (212)398-0023 • URL: http://www.ansi.org.

Consumers Union of the United States. 101 Truman Ave., Yonkers, NY 10703. Phone: (914)378-2000 Fax: (914)378-2900.

QUARRYING

See also: CLAY INDUSTRY; LIMESTONE INDUSTRY; MARBLE

ABSTRACTS AND INDEXES

IMM Abstracts and Index: A Survey of World Literature on the Economic Geology and Mining of All Minerals (Except Coal), Mineral Processing, and Nonferrous Extraction Metallurgy. Institution of Mining and Metallurgy. • Bimonthly. Members, $142.00 per year; non-members, $215.00 per year. Provides international coverage of the literature of mining and nonferrous metallurgy. Includes mineral economics, tunnelling, and rock mechanics.

DIRECTORIES

Pit and Quarry Buyers' Guide. Advanstar Communications, Inc. • Annual. $25.00. Lists approximately 1,000 manufacturers and other suppliers of equipment products and services to the nonmetallic mining and quarrying industry. Absorbed: *Ready-Mix-Reference Manual.*

FINANCIAL RATIOS

Almanac of Business and Industrial Financial Ratios. Leo Troy. Prentice Hall. • Annual. $99.95. Contains financial ratios derived from federal tax returns. Ratios for each of about 200 industries are arranged according to company asset size.

Annual Statement Studies. Robert Morris Associates: The Association of Lending and Credit Risk Professiona. • Annual. Free to members; non-members, $140.00. Median and quartile financial ratios are given for over 400 kinds of manufacturing, wholesale, retail, construction, and consumer finance establishments. Data is sorted by both asset size and sales volume. Includes a clearly written "Definition of Ratios" and an alphabetical industry index.

ONLINE DATABASES

GEOARCHIVE. Geosystems. • Citations to literature on geoscience and water. 1974 to present. Monthly updates. Inquire as to online cost and availability.

GEOREF. American Geological Institute. • Bibliography and index of geology and geosciences literature, 1785 to present. Inquire as to online cost and availability.

PERIODICALS AND NEWSLETTERS

Building Stone Magazine. Building Stone Institute. • Bimonthly. $65.00 per year.

Pit and Quarry. Advanstar Communications, Inc. • Monthly. $49.00 per year. Covers crushed stone, sand and gravel, etc.

Rock Products: Industry's Recognized Authority. Intertec Publishing Corp. • Monthly. Price on application.

STATISTICS SOURCES

Annual Survey of Manufactures. Available from U. S. Government Printing Office. • Annual. Prices vary. Issued by the U. S. Census Bureau as an interim update to the *Census of Manufactures.* Includes data on number of manufacturing establishments in various industries, employment, labor costs, value of shipments, capital expenditures, inventories, energy costs, and assets. (See also Census Bureau home page, http://www.census.gov/.).

Mineral Commodity Summaries. Available from U. S. Government Printing Office. • Annual. Published by the U. S. Geological Survey, Department of the Interior (http://www.usgs.gov). Contains detailed, five-year data for about 90 nonfuel minerals. Covers a wide range of statistics, including production, imports, exports, consumption, reserves, prices, tariff information, and industry employment. (Two pages are devoted to each mineral.).

United States Census of Mineral Industries. Bureau of the Census, U.S. Department of Commerce. Available from U.S. Government Printing Office. • Quinquennial.

WEFA Industrial Monitor. John Wiley and Sons, Inc. • Annual. $65.00. Prepared by industry analysts at WEFA, an economic forecasting and consulting firm (originally Wharton Econometric Forecasting Associates). Contains discussions of the outlook for major U. S. industries, with many 10-year forecasts (WEFA Web site is http://www.wefa.com).

TRADE/PROFESSIONAL ASSOCIATIONS

Building Stone Institute. P.O. Box 5047, Purdys, NY 10578. Phone: (914)232-5725 Fax: (914)232-5259.

National Building Granite Quarries Association. 1220 L St., N.W., Suite 100-167, Washington, DC 20005. Phone: 800-557-2848 • URL: http://www.nbgqa.com.

National Stone Association. 1415 Elliot Place, N.W., Washington, DC 20007. Phone: 800-342-1415 or (202)342-1100 Fax: (202)342-0702 • URL: http://www.aggregates.org.

R

RACK JOBBERS

HANDBOOKS AND MANUALS

Trade Dimensions' Marketing Guidebook. Trade Dimensions. • Annual. $340.00. Over 850 major chain and independent food retailers and wholesalers in the United States and Canada; also includes food brokers, rack jobbers, candy and tobacco distributors, and magazine distributors. Formerly *Progressive Grocer's Marketing Guidebook.*

PERIODICALS AND NEWSLETTERS

Non-Foods Merchandising: For Sales and Disbribution of Non-Foods. Cardinal Business Media, Inc. • Monthly. Free to qualified personnel; others, $85.00 per year. Trade publication for supermarket merchandisers and retailers across the nation.

TRADE/PROFESSIONAL ASSOCIATIONS

National Association of Recording Merchandisers. Nine Eves Dr., Suite 120, Marlton, NJ 08053. Phone: (609)596-2221 Fax: (609)596-3268 • URL: http://www.narm.com.

RADIO AND TELEVISION ADVERTISING

See also: ADVERTISING; ADVERTISING MEDIA; RADIO BROADCASTING INDUSTRY; TELEVISION BROADCASTING INDUSTRY

GENERAL WORKS

Electronic Media Ratings. Karen Buzzard. Butterworth-Heinemann. • 1992. $22.95. Provides basic information about TV and radio audience-rating techniques. Includes glossary and bibliography. (Electronic Media Guide Series).

BIBLIOGRAPHIES

Topicator: Classified Guide to Articles in the Advertising/Communications/Marketing Periodical Press. • Bimonthly. $110.00 per year. An index of major articles appearing in 20 leading magazines in the advertising, communications, and marketing fields.

DIRECTORIES

Advertising Age-Leading National Advertisers. Crain Communications, Inc. • Annual. $5.00. List of the 100 leading advertisers in terms of the amount spent in national advertising and below-the-line forms of spending.

CARD The Media Information Network (Canadian Advertising Rates and Data). Available from SRDS. • Biennial. $225.00 per issue. Published by Maclean Hunter Publishing Ltd. (Toronto). Provides advertising rates and other information relating to Canadian media: daily newspapers, weekly community newspapers, consumer magazines, business publications, school publications, religious publications, radio, and television.

International Television and Video Almanac: Reference Tool of the Television and Home Video Industries. Quigley Publishing Co., Inc. • Annual. $119.00.

Marketer's Guide to Media. BPI Communications, Inc. • Quarterly. $105.00. Presents cost, circulation, and audience statistics for various mass media segments, including television, radio, magazines, newspapers, telephone yellow pages, and cinema. Formerly *Mediaweek's Guide to Media.*

Radio Co-op Directory. Radio Advertising Bureau. • Annual. $199.00. Lists over 5,000 manufacturers providing cooperative allowances for radio advertising.

The SHOOT Directory for Commercial Production and Postproduction. BPI Communications. • Annual. $79.00. Lists production companies, advertising agencies, and sources of professional television, motion picture, and audio equipment.

HANDBOOKS AND MANUALS

Do-It-Yourself Advertising: How to Produce Great Ads, Brochures, Catalogs, Direct Mail, and Much More!. Fred E. Hahn and Kenneth G. Mangun. John Wiley and Sons, Inc. • 1997. $45.00. Second edition. Covers magazines, newspapers, flyers, brochures, catalogs, direct mail, telemarketing, trade shows, and radio/TV promotions. Includes checklists. (Small Business Series).

Radio Advertising: The Authoritative Guide. Pete Schulberg. NTC/Contemporary Publishing. • 1994. $29.95. Second edition. (NTC Business Book Series).

Radio and Television Commercial. Albert C. Book and others. NTC/Contemporary Publishing. • 1995. $19.95. Third revised edition. How to guide showing how to create effective radio and television advertisements. (NTC Business Book Series).

ONLINE DATABASES

Arbitron Radio County Coverage. Arbitron Co. • Ratings of radio and TV stations plus audience measurement data, updated frequently. Inquire as to online cost and availability.

Nielsen Station Index. Nielsen Media Research. • Measures local television station audiences in about 220 U. S. geographic areas. Includes current and some historical data. Inquire as to online cost and availability.

Nielsen Television Index. Nielsen Media Research. • Measures national television program audiences by sampling approximately 4,000 U. S. households. Time period is 1970 to date, with weekly updates.

PERIODICALS AND NEWSLETTERS

Broadcasting and Cable. Cahners Business Information, Broadcasting and Cable's International Group. • 51 times a year. $149.00 per year. Formerly *Broadcasting.*

The Marketing Pulse: The Exclusive Insight Provider to the Entertainment, Marketing, Advertising and Media Industries. Unlimited Positive Communications, Inc. • Monthly. $300.00 per year. Newsletter concerned with advertising media forecasts and analyses. Emphasis is on TV and radio.

SHOOT: The Leading Newsweekly for Commercial Production and Postproduction. BPI Communications. • Weekly. $115.00 per year. Covers animation, music, sound design, computer graphics, visual effects, cinematography, and other aspects of television and motion picture production, with emphasis on TV commercials.

STATISTICS SOURCES

Cable TV Facts. Cabletelevision Advertising Bureau. • Annual. Free to members; non-members, $10.00. Provides statistics on cable TV and cable TV advertising in the U. S.

Media Market Guide. Media Market Resources. • Quarterly. $675.00 per year. Presents circulation and cost data for television, radio, magazines, newspapers and outdoor markets.

Radio Facts. Radio Advertising Bureau. • Annual. $50.00.

Television and Cable Factbook. Warren Publishing Inc. • Annual. $495.00. Three volumes. Commercial and noncommercial television stations and networks.

TRADE/PROFESSIONAL ASSOCIATIONS

Radio Advertising Bureau. 261 Madison Ave., 23rd Fl., New York, NY 10016. Phone: 800-232-3131 or (212)681-7200 Fax: (212)681-7223 • URL: http://www.rab.com.

Television Bureau of Advertising. Three E. 54th St., New York, NY 10022. Phone: (212)486-1111 Fax: (212)935-5631 E-mail: info@tvb.org • URL: http://www.tvb.org.

OTHER SOURCES

Radio Business Report. RBR. • Weekly. $220.00 per year. Covers radio advertising, FCC regulations, audience ratings, market research, station management, business conditions, and related topics.

RADIO AND TELEVISION REPAIR INDUSTRY

HANDBOOKS AND MANUALS

Color and Black and White Television Theory and Servicing. Alvin Liff and Sam Wilson. Prentice Hall. • 1993. $97.00. Third edition.

PERIODICALS AND NEWSLETTERS

Electronic Servicing & Technology: The How-To Magazine of Electronics. CQ Communications, Inc. • Monthly. $26.95 per year. Provides how-to technical information to technicians who service consumer electronics equipment.

Poptronics. Gernsback Publications, Inc. • Monthly. $19.99 per year. Incorporates *Electronics Now.*

STATISTICS SOURCES

United States Census of Service Industries. U.S. Bureau of the Census. • Quinquennial. Various reports available.

TRADE/PROFESSIONAL ASSOCIATIONS

National Electronics Service Dealers Association. 2708 W. Berry St., Fort Worth, TX 76109. Phone: 800-797-9197 or (817)921-9061 Fax: (817)921-3741 E-mail: clydenesda@aol.com • URL: http://www.nesda.com.

RADIO BROADCASTING INDUSTRY

See also: RADIO AND TELEVISION ADVERTISING; RADIO EQUIPMENT INDUSTRY; TELEVISION BROADCASTING INDUSTRY

GENERAL WORKS

Dissertations in Broadcasting. Christopher H. Sterling, editor. Ayer Co. Publishers, Inc. • 1979. $739.50. 26 volumes. Mainly reprints of historical, philosophical, political, and academic works.

Perspectives on Radio and Television: Telecommunication in the United States. F. Leslie Smith and others. Lawrence Erlbaum Associates. • 1998. Fourth edition. Price on application. (Communication Series).

ABSTRACTS AND INDEXES

Communication Abstracts. Sage Publications, Inc. • Bimonthly. Individuals, $185.00 per year; institutions, $805.00 per year. Provides broad coverage of the literature of communications, including broadcasting and advertising.

BIBLIOGRAPHIES

Topicator: Classified Guide to Articles in the Advertising/Communications/Marketing Periodical Press. • Bimonthly. $110.00 per year. An index of major articles appearing in 20 leading magazines in the advertising, communications, and marketing fields.

BIOGRAPHICAL SOURCES

Biographical Dictionary of American Journalism. Joseph P. McKerns, editor. Greenwood Publishing Group Inc. • 1989. $65.00. Covers major mass media: newspapers, radio, television, and magazines. Includes reporters, editors, columnists, cartoonists, commentators, etc.

CD-ROM DATABASES

Hoover's Company Capsules on CD-ROM. Hoover's, Inc. • Quarterly. $349.95 per year (single-user). Provides the CD-ROM version of *Hoover's Handbook of American Business, Hoover's Handbook of Emerging Companies, Hoover's Handbook of World Business, Hoover's Guide to Computer Companies, Hoover's Guide to Media Companies, Hoover's Handbook of Private Companies,* and various regional guides. Includes more than 11,000 profiles of companies.

DIRECTORIES

Bacon's Radio and TV Cable Directories. Bacon's Publishing Co. • Annual. $295.00. Two volumes. Includes educational and public broadcasters. Covers all United States broadcast media. Formerly *Bacon's Radio - TV Directory.*

Broadcasting and Cable Yearbook. R. R Bowker. • Annual. $179.95. Two volumes. Published in conjunction with *Broadcasting* magazine. Provides information on U. S. and Canadian TV stations, radio stations, cable TV companies, and radio-TV services of various kinds.

Burrelle's Media Directory: Broadcast Media. Burrelle's Information Services. • Annual. $275.00. Two volumes. *Radio* volume lists more than 12,000 radio stations in the U. S. and Canada. *Television and Cable* volume lists more than 1,700 television stations and cable systems. Provides detailed descriptions, including programming and key personnel.

Gale Directory of Publications and Broadcast Media. The Gale Group. • Annual. $650.00. Five volumes. A guide to publications and broadcasting stations in the U. S. and Canada, including newspapers, magazines, journals, radio stations, television stations, and cable systems. Geographic arrangement. Volume three consists of statistical tables, maps, subject indexes, and title index. Formerly *Ayer Directory of Publications.*

Plunkett's Entertainment and Media Industry Almanac. Available from Plunkett Research, Ltd. • Biennial. $149.99. Provides profiles of leading firms in online information, films, radio, television, cable, multimedia, magazines, and book publishing. Includes World Wide Web sites, where available, plus information on careers and industry trends.

Radio Advertising Source. SRDS. • Quarterly. $490.00 per year. Contains detailed information on U. S. radio stations, networks, and corporate owners, with maps of market areas. Includes key personnel.

Working Press of the Nation. R. R. Bowker. • Annual. $450.00. Three volumes: (1) *Newspaper Directory*; (2) *Magazine and Internal Publications Directory*; (3) *Radio and Television Directory.* Includes names of editors and other personnel. Individual volumes, $249.00.

ENCYCLOPEDIAS AND DICTIONARIES

Broadcast Communications Dictionary. Lincoln Diamant. Greenwood Publishing Group Inc. • 1989. $57.95. Third revised edition.

NTC's Mass Media Dictionary. R. Terry Ellmore. NTC/Contemporary Publishing. • 1993. $24.95. Covers television, radio, newspapers, magazines, film, graphic arts, books, billboards, public relations, and advertising. Terms are related to production, research, audience measurement, audio-video engineering, printing, publishing, and other areas.

FINANCIAL RATIOS

Almanac of Business and Industrial Financial Ratios. Leo Troy. Prentice Hall. • Annual. $99.95. Contains financial ratios derived from federal tax returns. Ratios for each of about 200 industries are arranged according to company asset size.

Annual Statement Studies. Robert Morris Associates: The Association of Lending and Credit Risk Professiona. • Annual. Free to members; non-members, $140.00. Median and quartile financial ratios are given for over 400 kinds of manufacturing, wholesale, retail, construction, and consumer finance establishments. Data is sorted by both asset size and sales volume. Includes a clearly written "Definition of Ratios" and an alphabetical industry index.

Radio Financial Report. National Association of Broadcasters. • 1993. $225.00.

HANDBOOKS AND MANUALS

Dun & Bradstreet/Gale Group Industry Handbooks. The Gale Group. • 2000. $630.00. Five volumes. $145.00 per volume. Each volume covers two or more major industries: 1. *Entertainment and Hospitality*; 2. *Construction and Agriculture*; 3. *Chemicals and Pharmaceuticals*; 4. *Computers & Software and Broadcasting & Telecommunications*; 5. *Insurance and Health & Medical Services.* The following are included for each industry: overview, statistics, financial ratios, rankings, merger information, company directory, directory of associations, and consultants directory.

Rights and Liabilities of Publishers, Broadcasters, and Reporters. Slade R. Metcalf and Robin Bierstedt. Shepard's. • 1982. $200.00. Two volumes. A legal manual for the media.

INTERNET DATABASES

GaleNet: Your Information Community. The Gale Group. Phone: 800-877-GALE or (248)699-GALE Fax: 800-414-5043 or (248)699-8069 E-mail: galenet@gale.com • URL: http://www.galenet.com • Web site provides a wide variety of full-text information from Gale databases, Taft, and other sources. Covers associations, biography, business directories, education, the information industry, literature, publishing, and science. Fee-based subscriptions are available for individual databases (free demonstration). Includes Boolean search features and the BRS/Search user interface.

ONLINE DATABASES

Gale Database of Publications and Broadcast Media. The Gale Group. • An online directory containing detailed information on over 67,000 periodicals, newspapers, broadcast stations, cable systems, directories, and newsletters. Corresponds to the following print sources: *Gale Directory of Publications and Broadcast Media; Directories in Print; City and State Directories in Print; Newsletters in Print.* Semiannual updates. Inquire as to online cost and availability.

PERIODICALS AND NEWSLETTERS

Broadcast Engineering: Journal of Broadcast Technology. Intertec Publishing Corp. • Monthly. Free to qualified personnel; others, $55.00 per year. Technical magazine for the broadcast industry.

Broadcast Investor: Newsletter on Radio-TV Station Finance. Paul Kagan Associates, Inc. • Monthly. $895.00 per year. Newsletter for investors in publicly held radio and television broadcasting companies.

Broadcasting and Cable. Cahners Business Information, Broadcasting and Cable's International Group. • 51 times a year. $149.00 per year. Formerly *Broadcasting.*

Entertainment Marketing Letter. EPM Communications, Inc. • 22 times a year. $319.00 per year. Newsletter. Covers the marketing of various entertainment products. Includes television broadcasting, videocassettes, celebrity tours and tie-ins, radio broadcasting, and the music business.

Journal of Broadcasting and Electronic Media. Broadcast Education Association. • Quarterly. $86.50 per year. Scholarly articles about developments, trends and research.

Radio World. IMAS Publishing. • Biweekly. $59.00 per year. Emphasis is on radio broadcast engineering and equipment. Text in English, Portuguese and Spanish.

Tuned In: Radio World's Management Magazine. IMAS Publishing. • Monthly. Price on application. Edited for radio broadcasting managers and producers, with an emphasis on marketing.

STATISTICS SOURCES

Standard & Poor's Industry Surveys. Standard & Poor's. • Semiannual. $1,800.00. Two looseleaf volumes. Includes monthly supplements. Provides detailed, individual surveys of 52 major industry groups. Each survey is revised on a semiannual basis. Also includes "Monthly Investment Review" (industry group investment analysis) and monthly "Trends & Projections" (economic analysis).

TRADE/PROFESSIONAL ASSOCIATIONS

American Sportscasters Association. Five Beekman St., Suite 814, New York, NY 10038. Phone: (212)227-8080 Fax: (212)571-0556 E-mail: asassn@juno.com • Members are radio and television sportscasters.

Broadcast Education Association. 1771 N St., N.W., Washington, DC 20036-2891. Phone: (202)429-5354 Fax: (202)775-2981 • URL: http://www.bea.web.net.

International Radio and Television Society Foundation. 420 Lexington Ave., Suite 1714, New York, NY 10170. Phone: (212)867-6650 Fax: (212)867-6653 • URL: http://www.irts.org.

National Association of Broadcasters. 1771 N. St., N.W., Washington, DC 20036. Phone: (202)429-5300 Fax: (202)429-5343 • URL: http://www.nab.org.

OTHER SOURCES

FCC Record. Available from U. S. Government Printing Office. • Biweekly. $535.00 per year. Produced by the Federal Communications Commission (http://www.fcc.gov). An inclusive compilation of decisions, reports, public notices, and other documents of the FCC.

Infrastructure Industries USA. The Gale Group. • 2001. $240.00. Replaces *Agriculture, Forestry, Fishing, Mining, and Construction USA* and *Transportation and Public Utilities USA.* Presents statistics and projections relating to economic activity in a wide variety of natural resource and construction industries.

Radio & Records. Radio & Records, Inc. • Weekly. $299.00 per year. Provides news and information relating to the record industry and to regional and national radio broadcasting. Special features cover specific types of programming, such as "classic rock," "adult alternative," "oldies," "country," and "news/talk." Radio station business and management topics are included.

Radio Business Report. RBR. • Weekly. $220.00 per year. Covers radio advertising, FCC regulations, audience ratings, market research, station management, business conditions, and related topics.

RADIO EQUIPMENT INDUSTRY

See also: COMMUNICATION SYSTEMS; HIGH FIDELITY/STEREO; TELEVISION APPARATUS INDUSTRY

ABSTRACTS AND INDEXES

NTIS Alerts: Communication. National Technical Information Service. • Semimonthly. $210.00 per year. . Provides descriptions of government-sponsored research reports and software, with ordering information. Covers common carriers, satellites, radio/TV equipment, telecommunication regulations, and related subjects.

DIRECTORIES

Broadcast Engineering: Equipment Reference Manual. Intertec Publishing Corp. • Annual. $20.00. Lists manufacturers and distributors of radio and TV broadcast and recording equipment. Included in subscription to *Broadcast Engineering.*

Directory of Computer and Consumer Electronics. Chain Store Age. • Annual. $290.00. Includes 2,900 "leading" retailers and over 200 "top" distributors. Formerly *Directory of Consumer Electronics Retails and Distributors.*

FINANCIAL RATIOS

Annual Statement Studies. Robert Morris Associates: The Association of Lending and Credit Risk Professiona. • Annual. Free to members; non-members, $140.00. Median and quartile financial ratios are given for over 400 kinds of manufacturing, wholesale, retail, construction, and consumer finance establishments. Data is sorted by both asset size and sales volume. Includes a clearly written "Definition of Ratios" and an alphabetical industry index.

PERIODICALS AND NEWSLETTERS

Broadcast Engineering: Journal of Broadcast Technology. Intertec Publishing Corp. • Monthly. Free to qualified personnel; others, $55.00 per year. Technical magazine for the broadcast industry.

Poptronics. Gernsback Publications, Inc. • Monthly. $19.99 per year. Incorporates *Electronics Now.*

RCR (Radio Communications Report): The Newspaper for the Wireless Communications Industry. RCR Publications/Crain Communications. • Weekly. $39.00 per year. Covers news of the wireless communications industry, including business and financial developments.

Sound and Communications. Testa Communications, Inc. • Monthly. $15.00 per year. A business, news and technical journal for contractors, consultants, engineers and system managers who design, install and purchase sound and communications equipment.

Wireless Week. Cahners Business Information. • 51 times a year. $59.00 per year. Covers news of cellular telephones, mobile radios, communications satellites, microwave transmission, and the wireless industry in general.

TRADE/PROFESSIONAL ASSOCIATIONS

Electronic Industries Association. 2500 Wilson Blvd., Arlington, VA 22201. Phone: (703)907-7500 Fax: (703)907-7501 • URL: http://www.eia.org • Includes a Solid State Products Committee.

North American Retail Dealers Association. 10 E. 22nd St., Suite 310, Lombard, IL 60148. Phone: 800-621-0298 or (630)953-8950 Fax: (630)953-8957 E-mail: nardahdq@aol.com • URL: http://www.narda.com.

RADIO STATIONS

See: RADIO BROADCASTING INDUSTRY

RADIOISOTOPES

See: ISOTOPES

RADIOLOGICAL EQUIPMENT

See: X-RAY EQUIPMENT INDUSTRY

RADIOS

See: RADIO EQUIPMENT INDUSTRY

RAILROAD EQUIPMENT INDUSTRY

DIRECTORIES

Thomas Register of American Manufacturers and Thomas Register Catalog File. Thomas Publishing Co., Inc. • Annual. $149.00. 34 volumes. A three-part system offering information on a wide variety of industrial equipment and supplies.

INTERNET DATABASES

Fedstats. Federal Interagency Council on Statistical Policy. Phone: (202)395-7254 • URL: http://www.fedstats.gov • Web site features an efficient search facility for full-text statistics produced by more than 70 federal agencies, including the Census Bureau, the Bureau of Economic Analysis, and the Bureau of Labor Statistics. Boolean searches can be made within one agency or for all agencies combined. Links are offered to international statistical bureaus, including the UN, IMF, OECD, UNESCO, Eurostat, and 20 individual countries. Fees: Free.

ONLINE DATABASES

DRI U.S. Central Database. Data Products Division. • Provides more than 23,000 business, financial, demographic, economic, foreign trade, and industry-related time series for the U.S. Includes national income, population, retail-wholesale trade, price indexes, labor data, housing, industrial production, banking, interest rates, money supply, etc. Time period is generally 1947 to date (some data back to 1929). Updating varies. Inquire as to online cost and availability.

Thomas Register Online. Thomas Publishing Co., Inc. • Provides concise information on approximately 194,000 U. S. companies, mainly manufacturers, with over 50,000 product classifications. Indexes over 115,000 trade names. Information is updated semiannually. Inquire as to online cost and availability.

PERIODICALS AND NEWSLETTERS

American Railway Engineering Association Bulletin. American Railway Engineering Association. • Five times a year. $78.00 per year.

Railway Track and Structures. Simmons-Boardman Publishing Corp. • Monthly. Qualified railroad personnel, $14.00 per year; others, $30.00 per year.

STATISTICS SOURCES

Annual Survey of Manufactures. Available from U. S. Government Printing Office. • Annual. Prices vary. Issued by the U. S. Census Bureau as an interim update to the *Census of Manufactures.* Includes data on number of manufacturing establishments in various industries, employment, labor costs, value of shipments, capital expenditures, inventories, energy costs, and assets. (See also Census Bureau home page, http://www.census.gov/.).

Business Statistics of the United States. Courtenay M. Slater, editor. Bernan Associates. • 1999. $74.00. Fifth edition. Based on *Business Statistics*, formerly issue by the Bureau of Economic Analysis, U. S. Department of Commerce. Provides basic data for a wide variety of U. S. industries, services, and economic indicators. Most statistics are shown annually for 29 years and monthly for the most recent four years.

Railroad Facts. Association of American Railroads. • Annual.

Survey of Current Business. Available from U. S. Government Printing Office. • Monthly. $49.00 per year. Issued by Bureau of Economic Analysis, U. S. Department of Commerce. Presents a wide variety of business and economic data.

WEFA Industrial Monitor. John Wiley and Sons, Inc. • Annual. $65.00. Prepared by industry analysts at WEFA, an economic forecasting and consulting firm (originally Wharton Econometric Forecasting Associates). Contains discussions of the outlook for major U. S. industries, with many 10-year forecasts (WEFA Web site is http://www.wefa.com).

TRADE/PROFESSIONAL ASSOCIATIONS

Air Brake Association. c/o Henry C. Christie, 2009 Oriole Trail, L.B., Michigan City, IN 46360-1423. Phone: (219)874-3129 Fax: (219)874-3121 E-mail: airbrake@niia.net.

American Railway Car Institute. 700 N. Fairfax St., Alexandria, VA 22314-2098. Phone: (703)549-5662 Fax: (703)548-0058 E-mail: ari@rpi.org.

American Railway Engineering and Maintenance Association. 8201 Corporate Dr., Suite 1125, Andover, MD 20785. Phone: (301)459-3200 Fax: (301)459-8077 • URL: http://www.arema.org.

Railway Engineering-Maintenance Suppliers Association. 210 Little Falls St., Suite 100, Falls Church, VA 22046. Phone: (703)241-8514 Fax:

(703)241-8589 E-mail: home@remsa.org • URL: http://www.remsa.org.

Railway Supply Association. 29 W. 140 Butterfield Rd., Suite 103A, Warrenville, IL 60555. Phone: (630)393-0106 or (630)393-0107 Fax: (630)393-0108 E-mail: rsainc@earthlink.net.

Railway Systems Suppliers, Inc. 9304 New LaGrange Rd., Ste. 200, Louisville, KY 40242-3671. Phone: (502)327-7774 Fax: (502)327-0541 E-mail: rssi@rssi.org • URL: http://www.rssi.org.

RAILROAD TIME TABLES

See: TIMETABLES

RAILROADS

See also: TRANSPORTATION INDUSTRY

ABSTRACTS AND INDEXES

NTIS Alerts: Transportation. National Technical Information Service. • Semimonthly. $210.00 per year. Provides descriptions of government-sponsored research reports and software, with ordering information. Covers air, marine, highway, inland waterway, pipeline, and railroad transportation. Formerly *Abstract Newsletter.*

BIOGRAPHICAL SOURCES

Pocket List of Railroad Officials. PRIMEDIA Information Group Inc. • Quarterly. $198.00 per year. Guide to over 30,000 officials in the freight railroad, rail transit and rail supply industries. Includes *Buyers' Guide.*

DIRECTORIES

Jane's World Railways. Jane's Information Group. • Annual. $390.00. Monthy updates. Lists nearly 1,400 railway industry manufacturers, 400 railway systems, and 200 rapid transit systems throughout 115 countries.

Official Railway Guide. Freight Service Edition. Commonwealth Business Media, Inc. • Bimonthly. $234.00 per year.

Railway Directory: A Railway Gazette Yearbook. Reed Business Information. • Annual. $255.00. Lists approximately 14,000 senior personnel from railroads worldwide and over 1,800 manufacturers, suppliers and consultants in the railroad industry.

Thomas Cook Overseas Timetable: Railway, Road and Shipping Services Outside Europe. Thomas Cook Publishing Co. • Bimonthly. $100.00. per year. International railroad passenger schedules. Text in English; summaries in French, German, Italian and Spanish.

ENCYCLOPEDIAS AND DICTIONARIES

Macmillan Encyclopedia of Transportation. Available from The Gale Group. • 2000. $375.00. Six volumes. Published by Macmillan Reference USA. Covers the business, technology, and history of transportation on land, on water, in the air, and in space. Includes definitions, cross-references, and 200 color illustrations.

FINANCIAL RATIOS

Almanac of Business and Industrial Financial Ratios. Leo Troy. Prentice Hall. • Annual. $99.95. Contains financial ratios derived from federal tax returns. Ratios for each of about 200 industries are arranged according to company asset size.

INTERNET DATABASES

Fedstats. Federal Interagency Council on Statistical Policy. Phone: (202)395-7254 • URL: http://www.fedstats.gov • Web site features an efficient search facility for full-text statistics produced by more than 70 federal agencies, including the Census Bureau, the Bureau of Economic Analysis, and the Bureau of Labor Statistics. Boolean searches can be made within one agency or for all agencies combined. Links are offered to international statistical bureaus, including the UN, IMF, OECD, UNESCO, Eurostat, and 20 individual countries. Fees: Free.

ONLINE DATABASES

DRI U.S. Central Database. Data Products Division. • Provides more than 23,000 business, financial, demographic, economic, foreign trade, and industry-related time series for the U.S. Includes national income, population, retail-wholesale trade, price indexes, labor data, housing, industrial production, banking, interest rates, money supply, etc. Time period is generally 1947 to date (some data back to 1929). Updating varies. Inquire as to online cost and availability.

TRIS: Transportation Research Information Service. National Research Council. • Contains abstracts and citations to a wide range of transportation literature, 1968 to present, with monthly updates. Includes references to the literature of air transportation, highways, ships and shipping, railroads, trucking, and urban mass transportation. Formerly *TRIS-ON-LINE.* Inquire as to online cost and availability.

PERIODICALS AND NEWSLETTERS

International Railway Journal: The First International Railway and Rapid Transit Journal. Simmons-Boardman Publishing Corp. • Monthly. $72.00 per year. Formerly *International Railway Journal and Rapid Transit Review.* Text in English; summaries in French, German and Spanish.

Progressive Railroading. Trade Press Publishing Corp. • Monthly. Free to qualified personnel; others, $50.00 per year. Provides feature articles, news, new product information, etc. Relative to the railroad and rail transit industry.

Railway Age. Simmons-Boardman Publishing Corp. • Monthly. $50.00 per year.

Trains; The Magazine of Railroading. Kalmbach Publishing Co. • Monthly. $39.95 per year.

United States Rail News. Business Publishers, Inc. • Biweekly. $499.00. Newsletter. Reports developments in all aspects of the rail transportation industry.

STATISTICS SOURCES

Business Statistics of the United States. Courtenay M. Slater, editor. Bernan Associates. • 1999. $74.00. Fifth edition. Based on *Business Statistics*, formerly issue by the Bureau of Economic Analysis, U. S. Department of Commerce. Provides basic data for a wide variety of U. S. industries, services, and economic indicators. Most statistics are shown annually for 29 years and monthly for the most recent four years.

Cars of Revenue Freight Loaded. Association of American Railroads. • Weekly.

Railroad Facts. Association of American Railroads. • Annual.

Survey of Current Business. Available from U. S. Government Printing Office. • Monthly. $49.00 per year. Issued by Bureau of Economic Analysis, U. S. Department of Commerce. Presents a wide variety of business and economic data.

Transportation Statistics Annual Report. Available from U. S. Government Printing Office. • Annual. $21.00. Issued by Bureau of Transportation Statistics, U. S. Department of Transportation. Provides data on operating revenues, expenses, employees, passenger miles (where applicable), and other factors for airlines, automobiles, buses, local transit, pipelines, railroads, ships, and trucks.

WEFA Industrial Monitor. John Wiley and Sons, Inc. • Annual. $65.00. Prepared by industry analysts at WEFA, an economic forecasting and consulting firm (originally Wharton Econometric Forecasting Associates). Contains discussions of the outlook for major U. S. industries, with many 10-year forecasts (WEFA Web site is http://www.wefa.com).

TRADE/PROFESSIONAL ASSOCIATIONS

Association of American Railroads. 50 F St., N.W., Washington, DC 20001. Phone: (202)639-2100 Fax: (202)639-2156 • URL: http://www.aar.org.

National Association of Railroad Passengers. 900 Second St., N.E., Suite 308, Washington, DC 20002. Phone: (202)408-8362 Fax: (202)408-8287 E-mail: narp@narprail.org • URL: http://www.narprail.org.

National Association of Railway Business Women. 6327 Wesleyan Rd., Jacksonville, FL 32217. Phone: 800-676-2729 E-mail: narbw@narbw.org • URL: http://www.narbw.org.

Railway Progress Institute. 700 N. Fairfax St., Alexandria, VA 22314. Phone: (703)836-2332 Fax: (703)548-0058 E-mail: rpi@rpi.org.

OTHER SOURCES

Infrastructure Industries USA. The Gale Group. • 2001. $240.00. Replaces *Agriculture, Forestry, Fishing, Mining, and Construction USA* and *Transportation and Public Utilities USA.* Presents statistics and projections relating to economic activity in a wide variety of natural resource and construction industries.

RAISIN INDUSTRY

See also: FRUIT INDUSTRY

TRADE/PROFESSIONAL ASSOCIATIONS

Diamond Walnut Growers. P.O. Box 1727, Stockton, CA 95201. Phone: (209)467-6000 Fax: (209)467-6257.

RARE BOOKS

See: BOOK COLLECTING

RARE EARTH METALS

ONLINE DATABASES

METADEX. Cambridge Scientific Abstracts. • Covers the worldwide literature of metals, metallurgy, and materials science, 1966 to date. Includes detailed alloys indexing from 1974. Biweekly updating. Inquire as to online cost and availability. (Formerly produced by ASM International.).

PERIODICALS AND NEWSLETTERS

Rare Earth Bulletin. Multi-Science Publishing Co. Ltd. • Bimonthly. $212.00 per year.

RIC News (Rare-Earth Information Center). Rare-Earth Information Center, Institute for Physical Research and Technology. • Quarterly. Free. Containing items of current interest concerning the science and technology of the rare earth.

STATISTICS SOURCES

Mineral Commodity Summaries. Available from U. S. Government Printing Office. • Annual. Published by the U. S. Geological Survey, Department of the Interior (http://www.usgs.gov). Contains detailed, five-year data for about 90 nonfuel minerals. Covers a wide range of statistics, including production, imports, exports, consumption, reserves, prices, tariff information, and industry employment. (Two pages are devoted to each mineral.).

TRADE/PROFESSIONAL ASSOCIATIONS

Rare Earth Research Conference. c/o Professor Larry Thomson. Argonne National Laboratory, Argonne, IL 60439. Phone: (630)252-4364 Fax: (630)252-9289.

RATING OF EMPLOYEES

See also: INDUSTRIAL PSYCHOLOGY; PERSONNEL MANAGEMENT; PSYCHOLOGICAL TESTING

ENCYCLOPEDIAS AND DICTIONARIES

Blackwell Encyclopedic Dictionary of Human Resource Management. Lawrence H. Peters and Charles R. Greer, editors. Blackwell Publishers. • 1996. $105.95. The editors are associated with Texas Christian University. Contains definitions of key terms combined with longer articles written by various U. S. and foreign business educators. Includes bibliographies and index. (Blackwell Encyclopedia of Management Series).

HANDBOOKS AND MANUALS

Complete Guide to Performance Standards for Library Personnel. Carol F. Goodson. Neal-Schuman Publishers, Inc. • 1997. $55.00. Provides specific job descriptions and performance standards for both professional and paraprofessional library personnel. Includes a bibliography of performance evaluation literature, with annotations.

Evaluating Library Staff: A Performance Appraisal System. Patricia Belcastro. American Library Association. • 1998. $35.00. Provides information on an appraisal system applicable to a wide variety of jobs in all types of libraries. Includes guidelines, performance appraisal forms, sample employee profiles, and a "Code of Service.".

Fair, Square, and Legal: Safe Hiring, Managing, and Firing Practices to Keep You and Your Company Out of Court. Donald Weiss. AMACOM. • 1999. $29.95. Third edition. Covers recruiting, interviewing, sexual discrimination, evaluation of employees, disipline, defamation charges, and wrongful discharge.

How to Design and Install Management Incentive Compensation Plans: A Practical Guide to Installing Performance Bonus Plans. Dale Arahood. Dale Arahood and Associates. • 1996. $129.00. Revised edition. "This book focuses on how pay should be determined rather than how much should be paid.".

How to Do a Performance Appraisal: A Guide for Managers and Professionals. William S. Swan. John Wiley and Sons, Inc. • 1991. $29.95. Contains advice on face-to-face discussions and offers guidelines on legal aspects.

Studying Your Workforce: Applied Research Methods and Tools for the Training and Development Practitioner. Alan Clardy. Sage Publications, Inc. • 1997. $45.00. Describes how to apply specific research methods to common training problems. Emphasis is on data collection methods: testing, observation, surveys, and interviews. Topics include performance problems and assessment.

RATIO ANALYSIS

See: FINANCIAL RATIOS

REAL ESTATE APPRAISAL

See: REAL PROPERTY VALUATION

REAL ESTATE BUSINESS

See also: APARTMENT HOUSES; BUILDING INDUSTRY; CONDOMINIUMS; HOUSING; MORTGAGES; OFFICE BUILDINGS; REAL ESTATE INVESTMENTS; REAL PROPERTY VALUATION; TAX SHELTERS

GENERAL WORKS

Modern Real Estate. Charles H. Wurtzebach and Mike E. Miles. John Wiley and Sons, Inc. • 1994. $92.95. Fifth edition.

Questions and Answers on Real Estate. Robert W. Semenow. Prentice Hall. • 1993. $24.95. Tenth edition.

Real Estate. Larry E. Wofford and Terrance M. Clauretie. John Wiley and Sons, Inc. • 1992. $81.95. Third edition.

ABSTRACTS AND INDEXES

Banking Information Index. U M I Banking Information Index. • Monthly. Price on application. Covers a wide variety of banking, business, and financial subjects in periodicals. Formerly *Banking Literature Index.*

Real Estate Index. National Association of Realtors. • 1987. $169.00 Two volumes. Vol. one, $99.00; vol. two, $99.00. Supplement available, 1988. $49.50.

BIBLIOGRAPHIES

Business Information Sources. Lorna M. Daniells. California Princeton Fulfillment Services. • 1993. $42.50. Third revised edition. Basic business sources, with discussion and full annotations.

The Tax Reform Act of 1986 and Its Impact on the Real Estate Industry. Marilyn Hankel. Sage Publications, Inc. • 1993. $10.00.

CD-ROM DATABASES

Business Source Plus. EBSCO Information Services. • Monthly. $1,495.00 per year. Provides CD-ROM citations and abstracts to articles in about 650 business periodicals and newspapers, including *The Wall Street Journal.* Full text is provided from 200 selected periodicals. Covers accounting, communications, economics, finance, management, marketing, and other business subjects.

DIRECTORIES

CRE Member Directory. The Counselors of Real Estate. • Annual. Free. Available online. Formerly *American Society of Real Estate Counselors Directory.*

National Real Estate Investor Sourcebook. Intertec Publishing Corp. • Annual. $79.95. List about 7,000 companies and individuals in eighteen real estate fields. Formerly *National Real Estate Investor Directory.*

National Referral Roster: The Nation's Directory of Residential Real Estate Firms. Stamats Communications, Inc. • Annual. $50.00. Formerly *National Roster of Realtors.*

ENCYCLOPEDIAS AND DICTIONARIES

Dictionary of Real Estate. Jae K. Shim and others. John Wiley and Sons, Inc. • 1995. $80.00. Contains 3,000 definitions of commercial and residential real estate terms. Covers appraisal, escrow, investment, finance, mortgages, property management, construction, legal aspects, etc. Includes illustrations and formulas. (Business Dictionaries Series).

Encyclopedia of Business. The Gale Group. • 2000. $425.00. Second edition. Two volumes. Contains more than 700 signed articles covering major business disciplines and concepts. International in scope.

Language of Real Estate. John Reilly. Dearborn, A Kaplan Professional Co. • 2000. Fith edition. Price on application. Encyclopedia of real estate terms.

New Encyclopedia of Real Estate Forms. Jerome S. Gross. Prentice Hall. • 1983. $59.95.

Real Estate Dictionary. Michael C. Thomsett. McFarland and Co., Inc., Publishers. • 1988. $38.50.

St. James Encyclopedia of Mortgage and Real Estate Finance. James Newell, editor. St. James Press. • 1991. $55.00. Defines over 1,000 terms related to the buying, selling, and financing of real estate. Includes charts and graphs.

FINANCIAL RATIOS

Almanac of Business and Industrial Financial Ratios. Leo Troy. Prentice Hall. • Annual. $99.95. Contains financial ratios derived from federal tax returns. Ratios for each of about 200 industries are arranged according to company asset size.

Annual Statement Studies. Robert Morris Associates: The Association of Lending and Credit Risk Professiona. • Annual. Free to members; non-members, $140.00. Median and quartile financial ratios are given for over 400 kinds of manufacturing, wholesale, retail, construction, and consumer finance establishments. Data is sorted by both asset size and sales volume. Includes a clearly written "Definition of Ratios" and an alphabetical industry index.

HANDBOOKS AND MANUALS

Essentials of Real Estate Investment. David Sirota. Dearborn , A Kaplan Professional Co. • 1997. $45.95. Sixth edition. Tax law revisions.

Every Landlord's Legal Guide. Marcia Stewart. Nolo.com. • 2000. $44.95. Fourth edition.

Every Tenant's Legal Guide. Janet Portman and Marcia Stewart. Nolo.com. • 1999. $26.95. Second edition.

Mastering Real Estate Mathematics. Ralph Tamper. Dearborn, Kaplan Professional Co. • 1995. $26.95. Sixth edition. Step-by-step workbook written to help sharpen real estate math skills.

Modern Real Estate and Mortgage Forms: Basic Forms and Agreements. Alvin L. Arnold. Warren, Gorham and Lamont/RIA Group. • Looseleaf. $130.00. Annual supplementation. Over 1,000 pages of forms.

Modern Real Estate Practice. Fillmore W. Galaty and others. Dearborn, Kaplan Professional Co. • 1997. $44.95. 15th edition. Provides essential up-to-date information to students preparing for a state licensing exam.

Real Estate Brokerage. John E. Cyr and others. Dearborn , A Kaplan Professional Co. • 1995. $37.95. Fourth edition. Covers the industry standard on opening and operation a real brokerage office.

Real Estate Handbook. Financial Publishing Co. • 1999. $20.00. Third revised edition.

Real Estate Marketing and Sales. Paddy Amyett. Prentice Hall. • 2000. $33.33.

Real Estate Taxation: A Practitioner's Guide. David F. Windish. CCH, Inc. • 1998. $125.00. Second edition. Serves as a guide to the federal tax consequences of real estate ownership and operation. Covers mortgages, rental agreements, interest, landlord income, forms of ownership, and other tax-oriented topics.

Real Estate Transactions, Tax Planning and Consequences. Mark L. Levine. West Publishing Co., College and School Div. • 1997. Periodic supplementation.

Taxation of Real Estate Transactions. Sanford M. Guerin. Shepard's. • 1988. $195.00. Second edition. Two volumes. Covers deferred payment sales, non-taxable exchanges, wraparound financing, defaults, foreclosures, and repossessions. Formerly *Taxation of Real Estate Dispositions.*

ONLINE DATABASES

Banking Information Source. Bell & Howell Information and Learning. • Provides indexing and abstracting of periodical and other literature from 1982 to date, with weekly updates. Covers the financial services industry: banks, savings institutions, investment houses, credit unions, insurance companies, and real estate organizations. Emphasis is on marketing and management. Inquire as to online cost and availability. (Formerly *FINIS: Financial Industry Information Service.*).

PERIODICALS AND NEWSLETTERS

Distressed Real Estate Law Alert. West Group. • Six times a year. $250.00 per year. Newsletter on such topics as default, bankruptcy, fraudulent conveyances, and foreclosure.

Journal of Property Management. Institute of Real Estate Management. • Bimonthly. $43.95 per year.

Journal of Real Estate Taxation. Warren, Gorham and Lamont/RIA Group. • Looseleaf service. $195.00 per year. Quarterly updates. Continuing coverage of the latest tax developments.

National Real Estate Investor. Intertec Publishing Corp. • Monthly. $85.00 per year. Includes annual *Directory.* Market surveys by city.

The Practical Real Estate Lawyer. American Law Institute-American Bar Association, Committee on Continuing Profess. • Bimonthly. $37.00 per year. Frequently includes legal forms for use in real estate practice.

Real Estate Forum. Real Estate Media, Inc. • Monthly. $55.00 per year. Emphasis on corporate and industrial real estate.

Real Estate Issues. The Counselors of Real Estate. • Semiannual. $48.00 per year.

Real Estate Law Journal. Warren, Gorham and Lamont/RIA Group. • Quarterly. $141.50 per year. Continuing practical concerns of real estate law professionals. Covers timely issues.

Real Estate Law Report. Warren, Gorham and Lamont/RIA Group. • Monthly. $123.75 per year. Provides complete, up-to-the-minute coverage of major developments in the field.

Real Estate Review. Warren, Gorham, and Lamont/ RIA Group. • Quarterly. $104.48 per year. Gives inside information on the latest ideas in real estate. Provides advice from the leaders of the real estate field.

Realtor Magazine. National Association of Realtors. • Monthly. Free to members; non-members, $54.00 per year. Provides industry news and trends for realtors. Special features include Annual Compensation Survey, Annual Technology Survey, Annual All Stars, and The Year in Real Estate.

Realty and Building. Realty and Building, Inc. • Biweekly. $48.00 per year.

Relocation Journal and Real Estate News. Mobility Services International. • Monthly. Free. Magazine for real estate, building, financing and investing. Formed by the merger of *Real Estate News* and *Relocation Journal.*

RESEARCH CENTERS AND INSTITUTES

Bureau of Economic and Business Research. University of Illinois at Urbana-Champaign, 1206 S. Sixth St., Champaign, IL 61820. Phone: (217)333-2330 Fax: (217)244-7410 E-mail: g-oldman@uiuc.edu • URL: http://www.cba.uiuc.edu/research.

Center for Finance and Real Estate. University of California, Los Angeles, John E. Anderson Graduate School of Management, P.O. Box 951481, Los Angeles, CA 90095-1481. Phone: (310)825-1953 Fax: (310)206-5455 E-mail: wtorous@anderson.ucla.edu • URL: http://www.agsm.ucla.edu/acadunit/finance/realestate.

Center for Real Estate Studies. Indiana University Bloomington, 1309 E. Tenth St., Suite 738, Bloomington, IN 47405. Phone: (812)855-7794 Fax: (812)855-9472 E-mail: cres@indiana.edu • URL: http://www.indiana.edu/~cres/.

Guthrie Center for Real Estate Research. J. L. Kellogg Graduate School of Management, Northwestern University, Evanston, IL 60208. Phone: (847)491-2673 Fax: (847)491-6459 • URL: http://www.kellogg.nwu.edu/research.

Real Estate Research Center. University of Florida. College of Business Administration, P.O. Box 117168, Gainesville, FL 32611-7168. Phone: (352)392-9307 Fax: (352)392-0381 E-mail: ling@dale.cba.ufl.edu • URL: http://www.bear.cba.ufl.edu/centers/ufrealestate/cres.htm.

Samuel Zell and Robert Lurie Real Estate Center at Wharton. University of Pennsylvania, Lauder-Fischer Hall, 3rd Fl., 256 S. 37th St., Philadelphia, PA 19104-6330. Phone: (215)898-9687 Fax: (215)573-2220 • URL: http://www.wharton.upenn.edu/faculty/gyourko.html.

STATISTICS SOURCES

New One-Family Houses Sold. Available from U. S. Government Printing Office. • Monthly. $45.00 per year. Bureau of the Census Construction Report, C25. Provides data on new, privately-owned, one-family homes sold during the month and for sale at the end of the month.

U. S. Housing Markets. Hanley-Wood, Inc. • Monthly. $345.00 per year. Includes eight interim reports. Provides data on residential building permits, apartment building completions, rental vacancy rates, sales of existing homes, average home prices, housing affordability, etc. All major U. S. cities and areas are covered.

ULI Market Profiles: North America. Urban Land Institute. • Annual. Members, $249.95; non-members, $299.95. Provides real estate marketing data for residential, retail, office, and industrial sectors. Covers 76 U. S. metropolitan areas and 13 major foreign metropolitan areas.

TRADE/PROFESSIONAL ASSOCIATIONS

Counselors of Real Estate. 430 N. Michigan Ave., Chicago, IL 60611-4089. Phone: (312)329-8427 Fax: (312)329-8881 E-mail: cre@interaccess.com • URL: http://www.cre.org.

Institute of Real Estate Management. 430 N. Michigan Ave., Chicago, IL 60611-4090. Phone: 800-837-0706 or (312)329-6000 Fax: (312)410-7960 E-mail: rvukas@irem.org • URL: http://www.irem.org.

National Association of Real Estate Brokers. 1629 K St., N.W., Suite 602, Washington, DC 20006. Phone: (202)785-4477 Fax: (202)785-1244.

National Association of Realtors. 430 N. Michigan Ave., Chicago, IL 60611. Phone: 800-874-6500 Fax: (312)329-5962 • URL: http://www.realtor.com.

Society of Industrial and Office Realtors. 700 11th St., N.W., Suite 510, Washington, DC 20001-4507. Phone: (202)737-1150 Fax: (202)737-8796 • URL: http://www.sior.com.

Women's Council of Realtors. 430 N. Michigan Ave., Chicago, IL 60611. Phone: (312)329-8483 Fax: (312)329-3290 E-mail: wcr@wcr.org • URL: http://www.wcr.org.

OTHER SOURCES

Information, Finance, and Services USA. The Gale Group. • 2001. $240.00. Replaces *Service Industries USA* and *Finance, Insurance, and Real Estate USA.* Presents statistics and projections relating to economic activity in a wide variety of non-manufacturing areas.

Law of Distressed Real Estate: Foreclosure, Workouts, and Procedures. Baxter Dunaway. West Group. • Four looseleaf volumes. $495.00. Periodic supplementation. (Real Property-ZoningSeries).

REAL ESTATE, INDUSTRIAL

See: INDUSTRIAL REAL ESTATE

REAL ESTATE INVESTMENT TRUSTS

See also: REAL ESTATE INVESTMENTS

GENERAL WORKS

Investing in REITs: Real Estate Investment Trusts. Ralph L. Block. Bloomberg Press. • 1998. $21.95. A basic guide to real estate investment trusts. (Bloomberg Personal Bookshelf.).

DIRECTORIES

Institutional Buyers of REIT Securities: A Targeted Directory. Investment Data Corp. • Semiannual. $995.00 per year. Provides detailed profiles of about 500 institutional buyers of REIT securities. Includes names of financial analysts and portfolio managers.

National Real Estate Investor Sourcebook. Intertec Publishing Corp. • Annual. $79.95. List about 7,000 companies and individuals in eighteen real estate fields. Formerly *National Real Estate Investor Directory.*

FINANCIAL RATIOS

Almanac of Business and Industrial Financial Ratios. Leo Troy. Prentice Hall. • Annual. $99.95. Contains financial ratios derived from federal tax returns. Ratios for each of about 200 industries are arranged according to company asset size.

HANDBOOKS AND MANUALS

Real Estate Investment Trusts Handbook: 1997. Peter M. Fass and others. West Group. • 1998. $92.00. Covers the legal and tax aspects of REITs. (Securities Law Series).

PERIODICALS AND NEWSLETTERS

Journal of Alternative Investments. Institutional Investor. • Quarterly. $380.00 per year. Covers such items as hedge funds, private equity financing, funds of funds, real estate investment trusts, natural resource investments, foreign exchange, and emerging markets.

National Real Estate Investor. Intertec Publishing Corp. • Monthly. $85.00 per year. Includes annual *Directory.* Market surveys by city.

STATISTICS SOURCES

Realty Stock Review: Market Analysis of Securities of REITS and Real Estate Companies. • Semimonthly. $325.00 per year.

TRADE/PROFESSIONAL ASSOCIATIONS

National Association of Real Estate Investment Trusts. 1875 Eye St., N.W. Ste. 600, Washington, DC 20006. Phone: 800-362-7348 or (202)739-9400 Fax: (202)739-9401 • URL: http://www.nareit.com.

REAL ESTATE INVESTMENTS

See also: REAL ESTATE BUSINESS; REAL ESTATE INVESTMENT TRUSTS

GENERAL WORKS

Fundamentals of Real Estate Investment. Austin J. Jaffe and C. F. Sirmans. Prentice Hall. • 1994. $72.00. Third edition.

Getting Started in Real Estate Investing. Michael C. Thomsett and Jean Thomsett. John Wiley and Sons,

Inc. • 1998. $18.95. Second edition. (Getting Started In... Series.).

How to Invest in Real Estate Using Free Money. Laurie Blum. John Wiley and Sons, Inc. • 1991. $89.95.

Real Estate Finance and Investments. William B. Brueggeman and Jeffrey Fisher. McGraw-Hill. • 1996. $68.25. 10th edition. Covers mortgage loans, financing, risk analysis, income properties, land development, real estate investment trusts, and related topics.

ABSTRACTS AND INDEXES

Real Estate Index. National Association of Realtors. • 1987. $169.00 Two volumes. Vol. one, $99.00; vol. two, $99.00. Supplement available, 1988. $49.50.

DIRECTORIES

Crittenden Directory of Real Estate Financing. Crittenden Research, Inc. • Semiannual. $399.00 per year. Included with subscription to weekly *Crittenden Report on Real Estate Financing.* Provides information on major U. S. real estate lenders.

National Real Estate Investor Sourcebook. Intertec Publishing Corp. • Annual. $79.95. List about 7,000 companies and individuals in eighteen real estate fields. Formerly *National Real Estate Investor Directory.*

Nelson's Directory of Institutional Real Estate. Wiesenberger/Thomson Financial. • Annual. $335.00. Includes real estate investment managers, service firms, consultants, real estate investment trusts (REITs), and various institutional investors in real estate.

ENCYCLOPEDIAS AND DICTIONARIES

Dictionary of Finance and Investment Terms. John Downes and Jordan E. Goodman. Barron's Educational Series, Inc. • 1998. $12.95. Fifth revised edition. Provides clear explanations of more than 5,000 business, banking, financial, investment, and tax terms. Includes a separate list of financial abbreviations and acronyms.

Dictionary of Real Estate. Jae K. Shim and others. John Wiley and Sons, Inc. • 1995. $80.00. Contains 3,000 definitions of commercial and residential real estate terms. Covers appraisal, escrow, investment, finance, mortgages, property management, construction, legal aspects, etc. Includes illustrations and formulas. (Business Dictionaries Series).

HANDBOOKS AND MANUALS

Profiting from Real Estate Rehab. Sandra M. Brassfield. John Wiley and Sons, Inc. • 1992. $39.95. How to fix up old houses and sell them at a profit.

Real Estate Finance and Investment Manual. Jack Cummings. Prentice Hall. • 1997. $34.95. Second edition.

Real Estate Investor's Answer Book. Jack Cummings. McGraw-Hill. • 1994. $17.95. Answers key questions relating to both residential and commercial real estate investments.

ONLINE DATABASES

Trade & Industry Index. The Gale Group. • Provides indexing of business periodicals, January 1981 to date. Daily updates. (Full text articles from some periodicals are available online, 1983 to date, in the companion database, *Trade & Industry ASAP.*) Inquire as to online cost and availability.

PERIODICALS AND NEWSLETTERS

Crittenden Report on Real Estate Financing: The Nation's Leading Weekly Newsletter on Real Estate Finance. Crittenden Research, Inc. • Weekly. $395.00 per year. Newsletter on real estate lending and mortgages. Includes semiannual *Crittenden Directory of Real Estate Financing.*

Marketscore. CB Richard Ellis. • Quarterly. Price on application. Newsletter. Provides proprietary forecasts of commercial real estate performance in metropolitan areas.

National Real Estate Investor. Intertec Publishing Corp. • Monthly. $85.00 per year. Includes annual *Directory.* Market surveys by city.

Quarterly Market Report. CB Richard Ellis. • Quarterly. Price on application. Newsletter. Reviews current prices, rents, capitalization rates, and occupancy trends for commercial real estate.

Real Estate Economics: Journal of the American Real Estate and Urban Economics Association. MIT Press. • Quarterly. Institutions, $165.00 per year.

Real Estate Finance. Institutional Investor. • Quarterly. $225.00 per year. Covers real estate for professional investors. Provides information on complex financing, legalities, and industry trends.

Real Estate Finance and Investment. Institutional Investor. • Weekly. $2,105.00 per year. Newsletter for professional investors in commercial real estate. Includes information on financing, restructuring, strategy, and regulation.

Real Estate Investing Letter. Orm Publishing Co., Inc. • Monthly. $96.00 per year.

Real Estate Tax Digest. Matthew Bender & Shepard. • Monthly. $295.00 per year. Newsletter.

Stanger Report: A Guide to Partnership Investing. Robert A. Stanger and Co. • Monthly. $447.00 per year. Newsletter providing analysis of limited partnership investments.

PRICE SOURCES

NAPEX Trade Price Reporter. National Partnership Exchange, Inc. • Quarterly. $160.00 per year. Provides high, low, and last-trade prices (resale prices) for about 500 limited partnerships, including many that have invested primarily in real estate.

National Real Estate Index. CB Richard Ellis. • Price and frequency on application. Provides reports on commercial real estate prices, rents, capitalization rates, and trends in more than 65 metropolitan areas. Time span is 12 years. Includes urban office buildings, suburban offices, warehouses, retail properties, and apartments.

RESEARCH CENTERS AND INSTITUTES

Rodney L. White Center for Financial Research. University of Pennsylvania, 3254 Steinberg Hall-Dietrich Hall, Philadelphia, PA 19104. Phone: (215)898-7616 Fax: (215)573-8084 E-mail: rlwtcr@finance.wharton.upenn.edu • URL: http://www.finance.wharton.upenn.edu/~rlwctr • Research areas include financial management, money markets, real estate finance, and international finance.

TRADE/PROFESSIONAL ASSOCIATIONS

American Real Estate and Urban Economics Association. Indiana University School of Business, 1309 E. 10th St., Suite 738, Bloomington, IN 47405-1701. Phone: (812)855-7794 Fax: (812)855-8679 E-mail: areuea@indiana.edu • URL: http://www.areuea.org • Members are real estate teachers, researchers, economists, and others concerned with urban real estate and investment.

Building Owners and Managers Association International. 1201 New York Ave., N.W., Suite 300, Washington, DC 20005. Phone: (202)408-2662 Fax: (202)371-0181 E-mail: soppen@boma.org • URL: http://www.boma.org.

OTHER SOURCES

Federal Taxes Affecting Real Estate. Matthew Bender & Co., Inc. • $215.00. Looseleaf service. Periodic supplementation. Explains and illustrates the most important federal tax principles applying to daily real estate transactions.

REAL ESTATE MANAGEMENT

See: PROPERTY MANAGEMENT

REAL ESTATE TAXES

See: PROPERTY TAX; TAX SHELTERS; TAXATION

REAL PROPERTY VALUATION

See also: REAL ESTATE BUSINESS; VALUATION

ALMANACS AND YEARBOOKS

Institute on Planning, Zoning and Eminent Domain, Southwestern Legal Foundation:Proceedings, 1971-1994. William S. Hein & Co., Inc. • 1971. $2,887.00. 24 volumes.

BIBLIOGRAPHIES

Real Estate Appraisal Bibliography, 1973-1980. Appraisal Institute. • 1981. $12.50. Several thousand articles published in major perodicals between 1973 and 1980.

ENCYCLOPEDIAS AND DICTIONARIES

Dictionary of Real Estate Appraisal. Jae Shim and others. Appraisal Institute. • 1996. $45.00. Second edition.

HANDBOOKS AND MANUALS

Appraisal of Real Estate. Appraisal Institute. • 1996. $49.50. 11th edition. Provides an in-depth discussion of the driving concept of market value; guildelines for market analysis projections and updated information throughout that addresses developments affecting the movement of investment capital.

Fundamentals of Real Estate Appraisal. William Ventolo and Martha Williams. Dearborn, A Kaplan Professional Co. • 1998. $46.95. Seventh edition. Explanation of real estate appraisal.

Real Estate Appraisal. Jack P. Friedman and others. Prentice Hall. • 1999. $25.00.

PERIODICALS AND NEWSLETTERS

Appraisal Journal. Appraisal Institute. • Quarterly. Free to members; non-members, $35.00 per year; students, $30.00 per year. Offers a broad variety of researched, documented articles.

Assessment Journal. International Association of Assessing Officers. • Bimonthly. Free to members; non-members, $200.00 per year. Formed by merger of *Assessment* and *Valuation Legal Reporter and IAAO Update.*

TRADE/PROFESSIONAL ASSOCIATIONS

American Society of Appraisers. 555 Herndon Pkwy, Ste. 125, Herndon, VA 20170. Phone: 800-272-8258 or (703)478-2228 Fax: (703)742-8471 E-mail: asainfo@appraisers.org • URL: http://www.appraisers.org.

Appraisal Institute. 875 N. Michigan Ave., Suite 2400, Chicago, IL 60611-1980. Phone: (312)335-4100 Fax: (312)335-4488 • URL: http://www.appraisalinstitute.org.

International Association of Assessing Officers. 130 E. Randolph St., Suite 850, Chicago, IL 60601. Phone: (312)819-6100 Fax: (312)819-6149 • URL: http://www.iaao.org.

National Association of Real Estate Appraisers. 1224 N. Nokomis N.E., Alexandria, MN 56308-5072. Phone: (320)763-7626 Fax: (320)763-9290 E-mail: narea@iami.org • URL: http://www.iami.org/narea.html.

RECESSIONS

See: BUSINESS CYCLES

RECORDING INDUSTRY

See: SOUND RECORDERS AND RECORDING; VIDEO RECORDING INDUSTRY

RECORDS MANAGEMENT

See also: FILES AND FILING (DOCUMENTS)

HANDBOOKS AND MANUALS

Business Records Control. Joseph S. Fosegan. South-Western Publishing Co. • 1995. $36.95. Seventh edition.

CCH Guide to Record Retention Requirements. CCH, Inc. • 1999. $49.95. Covers the record-keeping provisions of the Code of Federal Regulations. Explains which records must be kept and how long to keep them.

Financial Recordkeeping for Small Stores. Available from U. S. Government Printing Office. • 1986. Presents a basic record keeping system for the small retail owner-manager who does not have a trained bookkeeper. Produced by the Office of Business Development, Small Business Administration. (Small Business Management Series, 32.).

Guide to Record Retention Requirements. CCH, Inc. • Annual. $49.95. Explains federal recordkeeping regulations for individuals and businesses.

Preservation Microfilming: A Guide for Librarians and Archivists. Nancy E. Gwinn. Books on Demand. • 1995. $73.80. Second edition. Covers all aspects of planning and managing a microfilming operation.

Records Management: A Practical Guide. Susan Z. Diamond. AMACOM. • 1995. $29.95. Third edition. A guide to on-site and off- site storage of business documents, including a discussion of filing systems.

PERIODICALS AND NEWSLETTERS

The Infomation Management Journal. Association of Records Managers and Administrators. • Quarterly. Free to members; non-members, $60.00 per year; institutions and libraries, $53.00 per year. Formerly (Records management Quarterly).

Inform: The Magazine of Information and Image Management. Association for Information and Image Management. • Monthly. $85.00 per year. Covers technologies, applications, and trends.

TRADE/PROFESSIONAL ASSOCIATIONS

American Society of Corporate Secretaries. 521 Fifth Ave., New York, NY 10175-0003. Phone: (212)681-2000 Fax: (212)681-2005 • URL: http://www.ascs.org.

Association of Records Managers and Administrators. 4200 Somerset, Suite 215, Prairie Village, KS 66208. Phone: 800-422-2762 or (913)341-3808 Fax: (913)341-3742 E-mail: hq@arma.org • URL: http://www.arma.org/hq.

National Records Management Council. 60 E. 42nd St., New York, NY 10165. Phone: (212)697-0290 E-mail: info@naremco.com • URL: http://www.naremco.com.

OTHER SOURCES

Information and Image Management: The State of the Industry. Association for Information and Image Management. • Annual. $130.00. Market data with five-year forecasts. Covers electronic imaging, micrographics supplies and equipment, software, and records management services.

Keeping the Books: Basic Recordkeeping and Accounting for the Successful Small Business. Linda Pinson. Dearborn Financial Publishing. • 2000. $22.95. Fifth edition. Covers bookkeeping systems, financial statements, and IRS tax record requirements. Includes illustrations, worksheets, and forms.

RECORDS, PHONOGRAPH

See: PHONOGRAPH AND PHONOGRAPH RECORD INDUSTRIES

RECREATION, INDUSTRIAL

See: INDUSTRIAL RECREATION

RECREATION INDUSTRY

See also: AMUSEMENT INDUSTRY; INDUSTRIAL RECREATION; PARKS; SPORTING GOODS INDUSTRY; SPORTS BUSINESS

ABSTRACTS AND INDEXES

Leisure, Recreation, and Tourism Abstracts. Available from CABI Publishing North America. • Quarterly. $470.00 per year. Published in England by CABI Publishing. Provides coverage of the worldwide literature of travel, recreation, sports, and the hospitality industry. Emphasis is on research.

DIRECTORIES

Camp Directors Purchasing Guide. Klevens Publications, Inc. • Annual. $60.00. Suppliers of products and services used in the operation of children's summer camps.

Camping Magazine Buyer's Guide. American Camping Association. • Annual. $4.50. Over 200 firms listing camp supplies.

Guide to ACA Accredited Camps. American Camping Association. • Annual. $10.95. Lists over 2,200 summer camps. Included with subscription to *Camping Magazine.* Formerly *Guide to Accredited Camps.*

Guide to Summer Camps and Summer Schools. Porter Sargent Publishers, Inc. • Irregular. $35.00. Over 1,300 summer camping, recreational, pioneering, and academic programs in the United States and Canada, as well as travel programs worldwide.

Resorts and Parks Purchasing Guide. Klevens Publications, Inc. • Annual. $60.00. Lists suppliers of products and services for resorts and parks, including national parks, amusement parks, dude ranches, golf resorts, ski areas, and national monument areas.

Tenting Directory. Woodall Publishing Co. • Annual. $12.95. Campgrounds in the United States and Canada that have tent sites and tent rentals.

Tourist Attractions and Parks Magazine Buyers Guide. Kane Communications, Inc. • Annual. $10.00. Lists companies making products or services for leisure facilities.

Trailer Life Campground and RV Services Directory. Good Sam Club. Affinity Group Inc.,T L Enterprises. • Annual. Members, $9.95;non-members, $10.95. Describes and rates over 25,000 RV campgrounds, service centers and tourist attractions. Formerly *Good Sam Club's Recreational Vehicle Owners Directory.*

HANDBOOKS AND MANUALS

Club, Recreation, and Sport Management. Tom Sawyer and Owen Smith. Sagamore Publishing, Inc. • 1998. $44.95.

Resort Development Handbook. Dean Schwanke and others. Urban Land Institute. • 1997. $89.95. Covers a wide range of resort settings and amenities, with details of development, market analysis, financing, design, and operations. Includes color photographs and case studies. (ULI Development Handbook Series).

Sports, Convention, and Entertainment Facilities. David C. Petersen. Urban Land Institute. • 1996. $59.95. Provides advice and information on developing, financing, and operating amphitheaters, arenas, convention centers, and stadiums. Includes case studies of 70 projects.

PERIODICALS AND NEWSLETTERS

Campground Management: Business Publication for Profitable Outdoor Recreation. Woodall Publishing Co. • Monthly. $24.95 per year.

Campground Merchandising. Kane Communcations, Inc. • Quarterly. $5.00 per year.

Camping Magazine. American Camping Association. • Monthly. $34.55 per year.

Employee Services Management: The Journal of Employee Services, Recreation, Health and Education. National Employee Service and Recreation Association. • 10 times a year. $44.00 per year.

Journal of Hospitality and Leisure Marketing: The International Forum for Research, Theory and Practice. Haworth Press, Inc. • Quarterly. Individuals, $60.00 per year; institutions, $95.00 per year; libraries, $175.00 per year. An academic and practical journal covering various aspects of hotel, restaurant, and recreational marketing.

World Leisure and Recreation: Official Publication of the World Leisure and Recreation Association. World Leisure and Recreation Association. • Bimonthly. Libraries $80.00 per year. Formerly *World Leisure Review.*

STATISTICS SOURCES

Outlook for Travel and Tourism. Travel Industry Association of America. • Annual. Members, $100.00; non-members, $175.00. Contains forecasts of the performance of the U. S. travel industry, including air travel, business travel, recreation (attractions), and accomodations.

Social Statistics of the United States. Mark S. Littman, editor. Bernan Press. • 2000. $65.00. Includes statistical data on population growth, labor force, occupations, environmental trends, leisure time use, income, poverty, taxes, and other economic or demographic topics.

Statistical Abstract of the United States. Available from U. S. Government Printing Office. • Annual. $51.00. Issued by the U. S. Bureau of the Census.

TRADE/PROFESSIONAL ASSOCIATIONS

American Alliance for Health, Physical Education, Recreation, and Dance. 1900 Association Dr., Reston, VA 20191. Phone: 800-213-7193 or (703)476-3400 Fax: (703)476-9527 E-mail: evp@aahperd.org • URL: http://www.aahperd.org.

American Camping Association. 5000 State Rd., 67 N, Martinsville, IN 46151-7902. Phone: (765)342-8456 Fax: (765)342-2065 E-mail: aca@camps.org • URL: http://www.acacamps.org.

Amusement Industry Manufacturers and Suppliers International. P.O. Box 49947, Sarasota, FL 34320-6947. Phone: (941)954-3101 Fax: (941)954-3201 E-mail: aimsinterl@aol.com • URL: http://www.aimsintl.org.

National Association of RV Parks and Campgrounds. 113 Park Ave., Falls Church, VA 22046. Phone: (703)241-8801 Fax: (703)241-1004

E-mail: arvc@erols.com • URL: http://www.gocampingamerica.com.

National Employee Services and Recreation Association. 2211 York Rd., Suite 207, Oak Brook, IL 60521-2371. Phone: (630)368-1280 Fax: (630)368-1286 E-mail: nesrahq@aol.com • URL: http://www.nesra.org.

Society of Recreation Executives. P. O. Box 520, Gonzalez, FL 35260-0520. Phone: (850)944-7992 Fax: (850)944-0018 E-mail: nrvockws@spyder.net • Members are corporate executives employed in the recreation and leisure industries.

OTHER SOURCES

Superstudy of Sports Participation. Available from MarketResearch.com. • 1999. $650.00. Three volumes. Published by American Sports Data, Inc. Provides market research data on 102 sports and activities. Vol. 1: *Physical Fitness Activities.* Vol. 2: *Recreational Sports.* Vol. 3: *Outdoor Activities.* (Volumes are available separately at $275.00.).

RECREATIONAL VEHICLE INDUSTRY

See also: MOBILE HOME INDUSTRY

ABSTRACTS AND INDEXES

Trailer Life: RVing At Its Best. Good Sam Club. Affinity Group Inc., T L Enterprises. • Monthly. $22.00 per year.

DIRECTORIES

The R V D A Membership Directory. Recreation Vehicle Dealers Association of North America. • Annual. Members, $20.00; non-members, $100.00. Over 900 retail sales firms. Formerly *Recreation Vehicle Dealers Association Membership Directory.*

RV Buyer's Guide (Recreational Vehicle). Affinity Group, Inc.,T L Enterprises. • Annual. $7.95.

PERIODICALS AND NEWSLETTERS

Highways. Good Sam club. Affinity Group, Inc. T L Enterprises. • 11 times a year. Membership. Five regional editions. Formerly *Good Sam's Hi-Way Herald.*

MH/RV Builders News: The Magazine for Builders of Manufactured-Mobile-Modular-Marine Homes and Recreational Vehicles. Patrick Finn, editor. Dan Kamrow and Associates, Inc. • Bimonthly. $20.00 per year.

RV Business (Recreational Vehicle). Affinity Group Inc.,T L Enterprises. • Monthly. $48.00 per year. Includes annual *Directory.* News about the entire recreational vehicle industry in the U.S.

PRICE SOURCES

NADA Appraisal Guides. National Automobile Dealers Association. • Prices and frequencies vary. Guides to prices of used cars, old used cars, motorcycles, mobile homes, recreational vehicles, and mopeds.

STATISTICS SOURCES

Annual Survey of Manufactures. Available from U. S. Government Printing Office. • Annual. Prices vary. Issued by the U. S. Census Bureau as an interim update to the *Census of Manufactures.* Includes data on number of manufacturing establishments in various industries, employment, labor costs, value of shipments, capital expenditures, inventories, energy costs, and assets. (See also Census Bureau home page, http://www.census.gov/.).

TRADE/PROFESSIONAL ASSOCIATIONS

Good Sam Recreational Vehicle Club. P.O. Box 6888, Englewood, CO 80155-6888. Phone: 800-234-3450 or (805)667-4100 Fax: (805)667-4454 E-mail: goodsam@tl.com • URL: http://www.goodsamclub.com/.

Recreation Vehicle Dealers Association of North America. 3930 University Dr., No. 100, Fairfax, VA 22030-2515. Phone: (703)591-7130 Fax: (703)591-0734 E-mail: info@rvda.com.

Recreation Vehicle Industry Association. P.O. Box 2999, Reston, VA 20195. Phone: (703)620-6003 Fax: (703)620-5071 E-mail: dhomefrost@rvia.org • URL: http://www.rvia.com.

RECRUITMENT OF PERSONNEL

See also: COLLEGE PLACEMENT BUREAUS; PERSONNEL MANAGEMENT

BIBLIOGRAPHIES

Executive Search Books. Kennedy Information, LLC. • Annual. Free. Contains descriptions of selected books from various publishers on executive recruitment.

DIRECTORIES

Directory of Executive Recruiters. Kennedy Information, LLC. • Annual. $44.95. Contains profiles of more than 4,000 executive recruiting firms in the U. S., Canada, and Mexico.

50 Leading Retained Executive Search Firms in North America. Kennedy Information, LLC. • Annual. $15.00. Provides profiles of major search firms, including revenue data.

40 Largest Retained Executive Search Firms, U. S. & World. Kennedy Information, LLC. • Annual. $15.00. Rankings of search firms are by U. S. and world estimated revenues, with tables of staff sizes. Growth trends and market size estimates for the executive search industry are also provided.

The Human Resource Executive's Market Resource. LRP Publications. • Annual. $25.00. A directory of services and products of use to personnel departments. Includes 20 categories, such as training, outplacement, health benefits, recognition awards, testing, workers' compensation, temporary staffing, recruitment, and human resources software.

Kennedy's Directory of Executive Temporary Placement Firms. Kennedy Information, LLC. • 1995. $24.95. Eighth revised edition. Provides information on about 225 executive search firms that have temporary placement as a specialty.

Key European Executive Search Firms and Their U. S. Links. Kennedy Information, LLC. • 1995. Price on application. Includes 440 search offices in Europe and the U. S.

Key Women in Retained Executive Search. Kennedy Information, LLC. • 1994. Price on application. Lists about 600 women executives in 300 search firms in North America. Arranged by name of firm, with an index to names of individuals.

ENCYCLOPEDIAS AND DICTIONARIES

Blackwell Encyclopedic Dictionary of Human Resource Management. Lawrence H. Peters and Charles R. Greer, editors. Blackwell Publishers. • 1996. $105.95. The editors are associated with Texas Christian University. Contains definitions of key terms combined with longer articles written by various U. S. and foreign business educators. Includes bibliographies and index. (Blackwell Encyclopedia of Management Series).

HANDBOOKS AND MANUALS

Executive Recruiting Service. Entrepreneur Media, Inc. • Looseleaf. $59.50. A practical guide to starting an executive recruitment service. Covers profit potential, start-up costs, market size evaluation, owner's time required, pricing, accounting, advertising, promotion, etc. (Start-Up Business Guide No. E1228.).

Fair, Square, and Legal: Safe Hiring, Managing, and Firing Practices to Keep You and Your Company Out of Court. Donald Weiss. AMACOM. • 1999. $29.95. Third edition. Covers recruiting, interviewing, sexual discrimination, evaluation of employees, disipline, defamation charges, and wrongful discharge.

Hiring Right: A Practical Guide. Susan J. Herman. Sage Publications, Inc. • 1993. $46.00. A practical manual covering job definition, recruitment, interviewing, testing, and checking of references.

Hiring Winners. Richard J. Pinsker. AMACOM. • 1991. $19.95. Presents a practical system for finding and hiring people who will be ideal for a particular company or situation.

Kennedy's Pocket Guide to Working with Executive Recruiters. James H. Kennedy, editor. Kennedy Information, LLC. • 1996. $9.95. Second revised editon. Consists of 30 chapters written by various experts. Includes a glossary: "Lexicon of Executive Recruiting.".

Recruiter's Research Blue Book: A How-To Guide for Researchers, Search Consultants, Corporate Recruiters, Small Business Owners, Venture Capitalists, and Line Executives. Andrea A. Jupina. Kennedy Information. • 2000. $179.00. Second edition. Provides detailed coverage of the role that research plays in executive recruiting. Includes such practical items as "Telephone Interview Guide," "Legal Issues in Executive Search," and "How to Create an Execuive Search Library." Covers both person-to-person research and research using printed and online business information sources. Includes an extensive directory of recommended sources. Formerly *Handbook of Executive Search Research.*

Recruiting, Interviewing, Selecting, and Orienting New Employees. Diane Arthur. AMACOM. • 1998. $59.95. Third edition. A practical guide to the basics of hiring, including legal considerations and sample forms.

Recruiting Library Staff: A How-To-Do-It Manual for Librarians. Kathleen Low. Neal-Schuman Publishers, Inc. • 2000. $45.00. Includes position description forms, sample announcements, and checklists. Discusses job fairs and other career events.

Smart Hiring: The Complete Guide for Recruiting Employees. Robert W. Wendover. Leadership Resources, Inc. • 1989. $17.95.

PERIODICALS AND NEWSLETTERS

Affirmative Action Register: The E E O Recruitment Publication. Affirmative Action, Inc. • Monthly. Free to qualified personnel; others, $15.00 per year. "The *Affirmative Action Register* is the only nationwide publication that provides for systematic distribution to mandated minorities, females, handicapped, veterans, and Native Americans." Each issue consists of recruitment advertisements placed by equal opportunity employers (institutions and companies).

Executive Recruiter News. Kennedy Information, LLC. • Monthly. $187.00 per year. Newsletter. News and ideas for executive recruiters.

Human Resource Executive. LRP Publications, Inc. • Monthly. $89.95 per year. Edited for directors of corporate human resource departments. Special issues emphasize training, benefits, retirement planning, recruitment, outplacement, workers' compensation, legal pitfalls, and oes emphasize training, benefits, retirement planning, recruitment, outplacement, workers' compensation, legal pitfalls, and other personnel topics.

Human Resource Planning. Human Resource Planning Society. • Quarterly. $90.00 per year.

Recruiting Trends: The Monthly Newsletter for the Recruiting Executive. Kennedy Information LLC. • Monthly. $155.00 per year.

Workforce: The Business Magazine for Leaders in Human Resources. ACC Communications, Inc. • Monthly. $59.00 per year. Edited for human resources managers. Covers employee benefits, compensation, relocation, recruitment, training, personnel legalities, and related subjects. Supplements include bimonthly "New Product News" and semiannual "Recruitment/Staffing Sourcebook." Formerly *Personnel Journal.*

STATISTICS SOURCES

An Analysis of Executive Search in North America. Kennedy Information, LLC. • Annual. $59.00. Includes ranking of leading executive search firms and estimates of market share and total revenue.

TRADE/PROFESSIONAL ASSOCIATIONS

Association of Executive Search Consultants. 500 Fifth Ave., Suite 930, New York, NY 10110-0999. Phone: (212)398-9556 Fax: (212)398-9560 E-mail: aesc@aesc.org • URL: http://www.aesc.org.

Human Resource Planning Society. 317 Madison Ave., Suite 1509, New York, NY 10017. Phone: (212)490-6387 Fax: (212)682-6851 • Members are corporate human resource planning professionals and others concerned with employee recruitment, development, and utilization.

RECYCLING

See also: NATURAL RESOURCES; SURPLUS PRODUCTS; WASTE PRODUCTS

ABSTRACTS AND INDEXES

Environment Abstracts. Congressional Information Service. • Monthly. Price varies. Provides multidisciplinary coverage of the world's environmental literature. Incorporates *Acid Rain Abstracts.*

Environment Abstracts Annual: A Guide to the Key Environmental Literature of the Year. Congressional Information Service. • Annual. $495.00. A yearly cumulation of *Environment Abstracts.*

ALMANACS AND YEARBOOKS

Environmental Viewpoints. The Gale Group. • 1993. $195.00. Three volumes. $65.00 per volume. A compendium of excerpts of about 200 articles on a wide variety of environmental topics, selected from both popular and professional periodicals. Arranged alphabetically by topic, with a subject/keyword index.

Gale Environmental Almanac. The Gale Group. • 1994. $110.00. Contains 15 chapters, each on a broad topic related to the environment, such as "Waste and Recycling." Each chapter has a topical overview, charts, statistics, and illustrations. Includes a glossary of environmental terms and a bibliography.

CD-ROM DATABASES

Environment Abstracts on CD-ROM. Congressional Information Service, Inc. • Quarterly. $1,295.00 per year. Contains the following CD-ROM databases: *Environment Abstracts, Energy Abstracts,* and *Acid Rain Abstracts.* Length of coverage varies.

DIRECTORIES

Environmental Career Directory. Visible Ink Press. • 1993. $17.95. Includes career information relating to workers in conservation, recycling, wildlife management, pollution control, and other areas. Provides advice from "insiders," resume suggestions, a directory of companies that may offer entry-level positions, and a directory of career information sources. (Career Advisor Series.).

North American Scrap Metals Directory. G.I.E. Media, Inc. • Annual. $85.00. Lists more than 9,000 scrap metal processors, brokers, and dealers.

Recycling Sourcebook. The Gale Group. • 1992. $90.00. Provides information on organizations, agencies, recycling companies, and publications. Recycling methods and approaches are described, with case studies. (Environmental Library Series).

ENCYCLOPEDIAS AND DICTIONARIES

Environmental Encyclopedia. The Gale Group. • 1998. $235.00. Second edition. Provides over 1,300 articles on all aspects of the environment. Written in non-technical style.

ONLINE DATABASES

Enviroline. Congressional Information Service, Inc. • Provides online indexing and abstracting of worldwide environmental and natural resource literature from 1975 to date. Updated monthly. Inquire as to online cost and availability.

PERIODICALS AND NEWSLETTERS

Biocycle; Journal of Composting and Recycling. J.G. Press, Inc. • Monthly. $69.00 per year. Authoritative reports on the management of municipal sludge and solid wastes via recycling and composting.

EM: Environmental Solutions That Make Good Business Sense. Air and Waste Management Association. • Monthly. Individuals $99.00 per year; institutions, $130.00 per year. Newsletter. Provides news of regulations, legislation, and technology relating to the environment, recycling, and waste control. Formerly *Environmental Manager.*

Environmental Business Journal: Strategic Information for a Changing Industry. Environmental Business Publishing Co. • Monthly. $495.00 per year. Newsletter. Includes both industrial and financial information relating to individual companies and to the environmental industry in general. Covers air pollution, wat es, U. S. Department of Health and Human Services. Provides conference, workshop, and symposium proceedings, as well as extensive reviews of environmental prospects.

Recycling Today. Group Interest Enterprises. G.I.E., Media Inc. • Monthly. $30.00 per year. Serves the recycling industry in all areas.

Resources, Conservation and Recycling. Elsevier Science. • Monthly. $1,269.00 per year.

Reuse/Recycle. Technomic Publishing Co., Inc. • Monthly. $260.00 per year. Newsletter.

Scrap. Institute of Scrap Recycling Industries. • Bimonthly. Free to members; non-members, $32.95 per year. Formerly *Scrap Processing and Recycling.*

Solid Waste Report: Resource Recovery-Recycling-Collection-Disposal. Business Publishers, Inc. • Weekly. $627.00 per year. Newsletter. Covers regulation, business news, technology, and international events relating to solid waste management.

STATISTICS SOURCES

Health and Environment in America's Top-Rated Cities: A Statistical Profile. Grey House Publishing. • Biennial. $195.00. Covers 75 U. S. cities. Includes statistical and other data on a wide variety of topics, such as air quality, water quality, recycling, hospitals, physicians, health care costs, death rates, infant mortality, accidents, and suicides.

Statistical Handbook on Technology. Paula Berinstein, editor. Oryx Press. • 1999. $65.00. Provides statistical data on such items as the Internet, online services, computer technology, recycling, patents, prescription drug sales, telecommunications, and aerospace. Includes charts, tables, and graphs. Edited for the general reader. (Statistical Handbook Series).

U. S. Industry and Trade Outlook: The McGraw-Hill Companies and the U.S. Department of Commerce/ International Trade Administration. Datapso Research Corp. • Annual. $69.95. Produced by the International Trade Administration, U. S. Department of Commerce, in a "public-private" partnership with DRI/McGraw-Hill and Standard & Poor's. Provides basic data, outlook for the current year, and "Long-Term Prospects" (five-year projections) for a wide variety of products and services. Includes high technology industries. Formerly *U. S. Industrial Outlook.*

TRADE/PROFESSIONAL ASSOCIATIONS

Institute of Scrap Recycling Industries. 1325 G St., N.W., Suite 1000, Washington, DC 20005-3104. Phone: (202)737-1770 Fax: (202)626-0900 E-mail: isri@isri.com • URL: http://www.isri.org.

REDEVELOPMENT, URBAN

See: URBAN DEVELOPMENT

REFERENCE SOURCES

See: INFORMATION SOURCES

REFINERIES

See: PETROLEUM INDUSTRY

REFRACTORIES

See also: CERAMICS INDUSTRY; CLAY INDUSTRY

DIRECTORIES

Directory of the Refractories Industry. The Refractories Institute. • Irregular. Members, $45.00; non-members, $85.00.

RESEARCH CENTERS AND INSTITUTES

Edward Orton Jr. Ceramic Foundation-Refractories Testing and Research Center. 6991 Old 3C Highway, Westerville, OH 43082. Phone: (614)895-2663 Fax: (614)895-5610 E-mail: homeny@ortonceramic.com • URL: http://www.ortonceramic.com.

STATISTICS SOURCES

Annual Survey of Manufactures. Available from U. S. Government Printing Office. • Annual. Prices vary. Issued by the U. S. Census Bureau as an interim update to the *Census of Manufactures.* Includes data on number of manufacturing establishments in various industries, employment, labor costs, value of shipments, capital expenditures, inventories, energy costs, and assets. (See also Census Bureau home page, http://www.census.gov/.).

Manufacturing Profiles. Available from U. S. Government Printing Office. • Annual. Issued by the U. S. Census Bureau. A printed consolidation of the entire *Current Industrial Report* series, presenting "all the data compiled." Contains statistics on production, shipments, inventories, consumption, exports, imports, and orders for a wide variety of manufactured products. (See also Census Bureau home page, http://www.census.gov/.).

Refractories. U. S. Bureau of the Census. • Annual. Provides data on value of manufacturers' shipments, quantity, exports, imports, etc. (Current Industrial Reports, MA-32C.).

TRADE/PROFESSIONAL ASSOCIATIONS

Refractories Institute. 650 Smithfield St., Suite 1160, Pittsburgh, PA 15222-3907. Phone: (412)281-6787 Fax: (412)281-6881 E-mail: triassn@aol.com.

REFRIGERATION INDUSTRY

See also: AIR CONDITIONING INDUSTRY

GENERAL WORKS

Refrigeration and Air Conditioning. A.R. Trott and T. Welch. Butterworth-Heinemann. • 2000. $59.95. Third edition.

DIRECTORIES

Air Conditioning, Heating, and Refrigeration News-Directory. Business News Publishing Co. • Annual. $235.00.

Grocery Distribution Magazine Directory of Warehouse Equipment, Fixtures, and Services. Trend Publishing, Inc. • Annual. $7.50. Covers products related to food warehousing, distribution, and storage.

PERIODICALS AND NEWSLETTERS

Air Conditioning, Heating, and Refrigeration News. Business News Publishing Co. • Weekly. $87.00 per year. Includes *Annual Directory* and *Statistical Summary.*

ASHRAE Journal: Heating, Refrigeration, Air Conditioning, Ventilation. American Society of Heating, Refrigerating and Air Conditioning Engineers, Inc. • Monthly. Free to members; non-members, $59.00 per year.

International Journal of Refrigeration. Elsevier Science. • Eight times a year. $803.00 per year. Text in English or French.

Refrigeration. John W. Yopp Publications, Inc. • Monthly. $30.00 per year.

RESEARCH CENTERS AND INSTITUTES

Ray W. Herrick Laboratories. Purdue University, School of Mechanical Engineering, West Lafayette, IN 47907-1077. Phone: (765)494-2132 Fax: (765)494-0787 E-mail: rhlab@ecn.purdue.edu.

World Food Logistics Organization. 7315 Wisconsin Ave., Suite 1200 N, Bethesda, MD 20814. Phone: (301)652-5674 Fax: (301)652-7269 E-mail: email@iarw.org • URL: http://www.iarw.org • Concerned with food storage. Affiliated with the International Association of Refrigerated Warehouses and the University of Maryland.

STATISTICS SOURCES

Annual Survey of Manufactures. Available from U. S. Government Printing Office. • Annual. Prices vary. Issued by the U. S. Census Bureau as an interim update to the *Census of Manufactures.* Includes data on number of manufacturing establishments in various industries, employment, labor costs, value of shipments, capital expenditures, inventories, energy costs, and assets. (See also Census Bureau home page, http://www.census.gov/.).

Major Home Appliance Industry Fact Book: A Comprehensive Reference on the United States Major Home Appliance Industry. Association of Home Appliance Manufacturers. • Biennial. $35.00. Includes statistical data on manufacturing, industry shipments, distribution, and ownership.

Manufacturing Profiles. Available from U. S. Government Printing Office. • Annual. Issued by the U. S. Census Bureau. A printed consolidation of the entire *Current Industrial Report* series, presenting "all the data compiled." Contains statistics on production, shipments, inventories, consumption, exports, imports, and orders for a wide variety of manufactured products. (See also Census Bureau home page, http://www.census.gov/.).

Refrigeration, Air Conditioning, and Warm Air Heating Equipment. U. S. Bureau of the Census. • Annual. Provides data on quantity and value of shipments by manufacturers. Formerly *Air Conditioning and Refrigeration Equipment.* (Current Industrial Reports, MA-35M.).

U. S. Industry and Trade Outlook: The McGraw-Hill Companies and the U.S. Department of Commerce/ International Trade Administration. Datapso Research Corp. • Annual. $69.95. Produced by the International Trade Administration, U. S. Department of Commerce, in a "public-private" partnership with DRI/McGraw-Hill and Standard & Poor's. Provides basic data, outlook for the current year, and "Long-Term Prospects" (five-year projections) for a wide variety of products and services. Includes high technology industries. Formerly *U. S. Industrial Outlook.*

TRADE/PROFESSIONAL ASSOCIATIONS

Air-Conditioning and Refrigeration Institute. 4301 N. Fairfax Dr., Suite 425, Arlington, VA 22203. Phone: (703)524-8800 Fax: (703)528-3816 E-mail: ari@ari.org • URL: http://www.ari.org.

American Society of Heating, Refrigerating and Air Conditioning Engineers. 1791 Tullie Circle, N.E., Atlanta, GA 30329. Phone: 800-527-4723 or (404)636-8400 Fax: (404)321-5478 E-mail: ashrae@ashrae.org • URL: http://www.ashrae.org.

Commercial Refrigerator Manufacturers Association. 1200 19th St., Suite 300, Washington, DC 20036. Phone: (202)857-1145 Fax: (202)223-4579.

International Association of Refrigerated Warehouses. 7315 Wisconsin Ave., 1200N, Bethesda, MD 20814. Phone: (301)652-5674 Fax: (301)652-7269 E-mail: email@iarw.org • URL: http://www.iarw.org.

Refrigerating Engineers and Technicians Association. c/o Smith-Bucklin Associates, 4700 W. Lake Ave., Glenview, IL 60625-1485. Phone: (847)375-4738 • URL: http://www.reta.com/.

REFUSE DISPOSAL

See: SANITATION INDUSTRY

REGIONAL AIRLINES

See: AIRLINE INDUSTRY

REGIONAL PLANNING

See also: CITY PLANNING; PLANNING; ZONING

ABSTRACTS AND INDEXES

Journal of Planning Literature. Ohio State University, Dept. of City and Regional Planning. Sage Publications, Inc. • Quarterly. Individuals, $75.00 per year; institutions, $525.00 per year. Provides reviews and abstracts of city and regional planning lierature.

PAIS International in Print. Public Affairs Information Service, Inc. • Monthly. $650.00 per year; cumulations three times a year. Provides topical citations to the worldwide literature of public affairs, economics, demographics, sociology, and trade. Text in English; indexed materials in English, French, German, Italian, Portuguese and Spanish.

Social Sciences Citation Index. Institute for Scientific Information. • Three times a year. $6,900 per year. Annual cumulation. Includes *Source Index, Citation Index, Permuterm Subject Index,* and *Corporate Index.*

Social Sciences Index. H. W. Wilson Co. • Quarterly, with annual cumulation. Service basis for print edition; CD-ROM edition, $1,495 per year. Indexes more than 400 periodicals covering economics, environmental policy, government, insurance, labor, health care policy, plannning, public administration, public welfare, urban studies, women's issues, criminology, and related topics.

CD-ROM DATABASES

PAIS on CD-ROM. Public Affairs Information Service, Inc. • Quarterly. $1,995.00 per year. Provides a CD-ROM version of the online service, *PAIS International.* Contains over 400,000 citations to the literature of contemporary social, political, and economic issues.

Social Science Source. EBSCO Publishing. • Monthly. $1,495.00 per year. Provides CD-ROM citations and abstracts to social science articles in more than 600 periodicals, with full text from 125 periodicals. Covers economics, political science, public policy, international relations, psychology, and other topics. Time period is most recent five years.

Social Sciences Citation Index: Compact Disc Edition. Institute for Scientific Information. • Quarterly. Provides CD-ROM indexing of the world's social sciences literature, including economics, business, finance, management, communications, demographics, information and library science, political science, sociology, etc. Corresponds to online *Social Scisearch* and printed *Social Sciences Citation Index.*

Social Sciences Citation Index: Compact Disc Edition with Abstracts. Institute for Scientific Information. • Quarterly. Provides CD-ROM indexing and abstracting of "significant articles" from 1,400 social science journals worldwide, with additional selections from 3,200 other journals, 1986 to date. Includes economics, business, finance, management, communications, demographics, information and library science, political science, sociology, and many other subjects.

WILSONDISC: Wilson Social Sciences Abstracts. H. W. Wilson Co. • Monthly. Including unlimited online access to *Social Sciences Index* through WILSONLINE. Provides CD-ROM indexing from 1983 and abstracting from 1994 of more than 400 periodicals covering economics, area studies, community health, public administration, public welfare, urban studies, and many other topics related to the social sciences.

DIRECTORIES

AICP Roster. American Institute of Certified Planners. • Biennial. Members, $10.00 per year; non-members, $30.00 per year. Lists about 9,000 public and private planning agency officials, professional planners, planning educators and other persons who are members of the American Planning Association.

HANDBOOKS AND MANUALS

Zoning and Planning Deskbook. Douglas W. Kmiec. West Group. • $145.00. Looseleaf service. Periodic supplementation. Emphasis is on legal issues.

ONLINE DATABASES

PAIS International. Public Affairs Information Service, Inc. • Corresponds to the former printed publications, *PAIS Bulletin* (1976-90) and *PAIS Foreign Language Index* (1972-90), and to the current *PAIS International in Print* (1991 to date). Covers economic, political, and sociological material appearing in periodicals, books, government documents, and other publications. Updating is monthly. Inquire as to online cost and availability.

Social Scisearch. Institute for Scientific Information. • Broad, multidisciplinary index to the literature of the social sciences, 1972 to present. Weekly updates. Worldwide coverage. Inquire as to online cost and availability.

Wilson Social Sciences Abstracts Online. H. W. Wilson Co. • Provides online abstracting and indexing of more than 415 periodicals covering area studies, community health, public administration, public welfare, urban studies, and many other social science topics. Time period is 1994 to date for abstracts and 1983 to date for indexing, with updates monthly. Inquire as to online cost and availability.

PERIODICALS AND NEWSLETTERS

American Planning Association Journal. American Planning Association. • Quarterly. Members, $33.00 per year; non-members $65.00 per year.

Planning. American Planning Association. • Monthly. Free to members; non-members, $60.00 per year.

Planning and Zoning News. Planning and Zoning Center, Inc. • Monthly. $175.00 per year. Newsletter on planning and zoning issues in the United States.

TRADE/PROFESSIONAL ASSOCIATIONS

American Institute of Certified Planners. 1776 Massachusetts Ave., N.W., Suite 400, Washington, DC 20036. Phone: 800-954-1669 or (202)872-0611 Fax: (202)872-0643 E-mail: aicp@planning.org • URL: http://www.planning.org.

American Planning Association. 122 S. Michigan Ave., Suite. 1600, Chicago, IL 60603-6107. Phone: (312)431-9100 Fax: (312)431-9985 E-mail: research@planning.org • URL: http://www.planning.org.

American Society of Consulting Planners. 122 S. Michigan Ave., Suite 1600, Chicago, IL 60603. Phone: (312)431-9100 Fax: (312)431-9985.

Regional Science Association International. Univ of Illinois, 905 S. Goodwin Ave., Bevier Hall, Rm. 83, Urbana, IL 61801-3682. Phone: (217)333-8904 Fax: (217)333-3065 E-mail: rsai@ucic.edu.

REGISTRATION OF TRADEMARKS

See: TRADEMARKS AND TRADE NAMES

REGULATION OF INDUSTRY

See also: LAWS

GENERAL WORKS

Business, Government, and Society: A Managerial Perspective: Text and Cases. George A. Steiner and John F. Steiner. McGraw-Hill. • 1999. $82.19. Ninth edition. (Management Series).

Business, Government, and Society: Managing Competitiveness, Ethics, and Social Issues. Newman S. Perry. Prentice Hall. • 1994. $54.80.

Regulatory Policy and Practices: Regulating Better and Regulating Less. Fred Thompson. Greenwood Publishing Group, Inc. • 1982. $55.00.

Responsive Regulation: Transcending the Deregulation Debate. Ian Ayres and John Braithwaite. Oxford University Press, Inc. • 1992. $70.00. (Oxford Socio-Legal Studies).

ABSTRACTS AND INDEXES

Current Law Index: Multiple Access to Legal Periodicals. The Gale Group. • Monthly. $650.00 per year. Produced in cooperation with the American Association of Law Libraries. Indexes more than 900 law journals, legal newspapers, and specialty publications from the U.S., Canada, U.K., Ireland, Australia, and New Zealand.

Index to Legal Periodicals and Books. H. W. Wilson Co. • Monthly. Quarterly and annual cumulations. $270.00 per year. CD-ROM version available at $1,495.00 per year.

PAIS International in Print. Public Affairs Information Service, Inc. • Monthly. $650.00 per year; cumulations three times a year. Provides topical citations to the worldwide literature of public affairs, economics, demographics, sociology, and trade. Text in English; indexed materials in English, French, German, Italian, Portuguese and Spanish.

Social Sciences Index. H. W. Wilson Co. • Quarterly, with annual cumulation. Service basis for print edition; CD-ROM edition, $1,495 per year. Indexes more than 400 periodicals covering economics, environmental policy, government, insurance, labor, health care policy, plannning, public administration, public welfare, urban studies, women's issues, criminology, and related topics.

ALMANACS AND YEARBOOKS

Advertising Law: Year in Review. CCH, Inc. • Annual. $85.00. Summarizes the year's significant legal and regulatory developments.

American Law Yearbook. The Gale Group. • Annual. $155.00. Serves as a yearly supplement to *West's Encyclopedia of American Law.* Describes new legal developments in many subject areas.

Property and Casualty Insurance: Year in Review. CCH, Inc. • Annual. $75.00. Summarizes the year's significant legal and regulatory developments.

Securities, Commodities, and Banking: Year in Review. CCH, Inc. • Annual. $55.00. Summarizes the year's significant legal and regulatory developments.

CD-ROM DATABASES

National Newspaper Index CD-ROM. The Gale Group. • Monthly. Provides comprehensive CD-ROM indexing of all material appearing in the late edition of the *New York Times*, the final edition of the *Washington Post*, the national edition of the *Christian Science Monitor*, the home edition of the *Los Angeles Times*, and the *Wall Street Journal.* Time period is four years. Also available online.

The New York Times Ondisc. New York Times Online Services. • Monthly. $2,650.00 per year. CD-ROM discs contain the full text of *The New York Times*, final edition. Inquire as to time period covered and availability of backfiles.

Newspaper Abstracts Ondisc. Bell & Howell Information and Learning. • Monthly. $2,950.00 per year (covers 1989 to date; archival discs are available for 1985-88). Provides cover-to-cover CD-ROM indexing and abstracting of 19 major newspapers, including the *New York Times, Wall Street Journal, Washington Post, Chicago Tribune,* and *Los Angeles Times.*

PAIS on CD-ROM. Public Affairs Information Service, Inc. • Quarterly. $1,995.00 per year. Provides a CD-ROM version of the online service, *PAIS International.* Contains over 400,000 citations to the literature of contemporary social, political, and economic issues.

Social Science Source. EBSCO Publishing. • Monthly. $1,495.00 per year. Provides CD-ROM citations and abstracts to social science articles in more than 600 periodicals, with full text from 125 periodicals. Covers economics, political science, public policy, international relations, psychology, and other topics. Time period is most recent five years.

Social Sciences Citation Index: Compact Disc Edition with Abstracts. Institute for Scientific Information. • Quarterly. Provides CD-ROM indexing and abstracting of "significant articles" from 1,400 social science journals worldwide, with additional selections from 3,200 other journals, 1986 to date. Includes economics, business, finance, management, communications, demographics, information and library science, political science, sociology, and many other subjects.

WILSONDISC: Index to Legal Periodicals and Books. H. W. Wilson Co. • Monthly. Including unlimited online access to *Index to Legal Periodicals* through WILSONLINE. Contains CD-ROM indexing of more than 800 English language legal periodicals from 1981 to date and 2,500 books.

WILSONDISC: Wilson Business Abstracts. H. W. Wilson Co. • Monthly. $2,495.00 per year, including unlimited online access to *Wilson Business Abstracts* through WILSONLINE. Provides CD-ROM "cover-to-cover" abstracting and indexing of over 600 prominent business periodicals. Indexing is from 1982, abstracting from 1990. (*Business Periodicals Index* without abstracts is available on CD-ROM at $1,495 per year.).

WILSONDISC: Wilson Social Sciences Abstracts. H. W. Wilson Co. • Monthly. Including unlimited online access to *Social Sciences Index* through WILSONLINE. Provides CD-ROM indexing from 1983 and abstracting from 1994 of more than 400 periodicals covering economics, area studies, community health, public administration, public welfare, urban studies, and many other topics related to the social sciences.

DIRECTORIES

Federal Agency Profiles for Students. The Gale Group. • 1999. $99.00. Provides detailed descriptions of about 200 prominent U.S. government agencies, including major activities, organizational structure, political issues, budget, and history. Includes a glossary, chronology, and index.

Federal Regulatory Directory. Congressional Quarterly, Inc. • Biennial. $149.95. Published by Congressional Quarterly, Inc. Provides detailed profiles of government agency functions and duties, and describes the laws each agency enforces. Includes extensive directory information.

Federal Yellow Book: Who's Who in the Federal Departments and Agencies. Leadership Directories, Inc. • Quarterly. $305.00 per year. White House, Executive Office of the President and departments and agencies of the executive branch nationwide, plus 38,000 other personnel.

Public Interest Profiles, 1998-1999. Available from Congressional Quarterly, Inc. • 1996. $175.00. Published by Foundation for Public Affairs. Provides detailed information on more than 250 influential public interest and public policy organizations (lobbyists) in the U.S. Includes e-mail addresses and Web sites where available.

United States Government Manual. National Archives and Records Administration. Available from U.S. Government Printing Office. • Annual. $46.00.

ENCYCLOPEDIAS AND DICTIONARIES

Encyclopedia of Governmental Advisory Organizations. The Gale Group. • 2000. $615.00. 15th edition.

West's Encyclopedia of American Law. Available from The Gale Group. • 1997. $995.00. Second edition. 12 volumes. Published by West Group. Covers a wide variety of legal topics for the general reader. Formerly *Guide to American Law: Everyone's Legal Encyclopedia* (1985).

HANDBOOKS AND MANUALS

CCH Guide to Record Retention Requirements. CCH, Inc. • 1999. $49.95. Covers the record-keeping provisions of the Code of Federal Regulations. Explains which records must be kept and how long to keep them.

Code of Federal Regulations. Office of the Federal Register, U.S. General Services Administration. Available from U.S. Government Printing Office. • $1,094.00 per year. Complete service.

Corporate Counsellor's Deskbook. Dennis J. Block and Michael A. Epstein, editors. Panel Publishing. • 1999. $220.00. Fifth edition. Looseleaf. Annual supplementation. Covers a wide variety of corporate legal issues, including internal investigations, indemnification, insider trading, intellectual property, executive compensation, antitrust, export-import, real estate, environmental law, government contracts, and bankruptcy.

United States Export Administration Regulations. Available from U. S. Government Printing Office. • $116.00. Looseleaf. Includes basic manual and supplementary bulletins for one year. Issued by the Bureau of Export Administration, U. S. Department of Commerce (http://www.doc.gov). Consists of export licensing rules and regulations.

INTERNET DATABASES

GPO Access: Keeping America Informed Electronically. U. S. Government Printing Office Sales Program, Bibliographic Systems Branch. Phone: 888-293-6498 or (202)512-1530 Fax: (202)512-1262 E-mail: gpoaccess@gpo.gov • URL: http://www.access.gpo.gov • Web site provides searching of the GPO's Sales Product Catalog (SPC), also known as Publications Reference File (PRF). Covers all "Government information products currently offered for sale by the Superintendent of Documents." There are also specialized search pages for individual databases, such as the *Code of Federal Regulations*, the *Federal Register*, and *Commerce Business Daily*. Updated daily. Fees: Free.

ONLINE DATABASES

Index to Legal Periodicals and Books (Online). H. W. Wilson Co. • Broad coverage of law journals and books 1981 to date. Monthly updates. Inquire as to online cost and availability.

Information Bank Abstracts. New York Times Index Dept. • Provides indexing and abstracting of current affairs, primarily from the final late edition of *The New York Times* and the Eastern edition of *The Wall Street Journal*. Time period is 1969 to present, with daily updates. Inquire as to online cost and availability.

PAIS International. Public Affairs Information Service, Inc. • Corresponds to the former printed publications, *PAIS Bulletin* (1976-90) and *PAIS Foreign Language Index* (1972-90), and to the current *PAIS International in Print* (1991 to date). Covers economic, political, and sociological material appearing in periodicals, books, government documents, and other publications. Updating is monthly. Inquire as to online cost and availability.

Wilson Business Abstracts Online. H. W. Wilson Co. • Indexes and abstracts 600 major business periodicals, plus the *Wall Street Journal* and the business section of the *New York Times*. Indexing is from 1982, abstracting from 1990, with the two newspapers included from 1993. Updated weekly. Inquire as to online cost and availability. (*Business Periodicals Index* without abstracts is also available online.).

Wilson Social Sciences Abstracts Online. H. W. Wilson Co. • Provides online abstracting and indexing of more than 415 periodicals covering area studies, community health, public administration, public welfare, urban studies, and many other social science topics. Time period is 1994 to date for abstracts and 1983 to date for indexing, with updates monthly. Inquire as to online cost and availability.

PERIODICALS AND NEWSLETTERS

FCC Report: An Exclusive Report on Domestic and International Telecommunications Policy and Regulation. Warren Publishing Inc. • Semimonthly. $649.00 per year. Newsletter concerned principally with Federal Communications Commission reglations and policy.

Federal Register. Office of the Federal Register. Available from U.S. Government Printing Office. • Daily except Saturday and Sunday. $697.00 per year. Publishes regulations and legal notices issued by federal agencies, including executive orders and presidential proclamations. Issued by the National Archives and Records Administration (http://www.nara.gov).

Warren's Cable Regulation Monitor: The Authoritative Weekly News Service Covering Federal, State, and Local Cable Activities and Trends. Warren Publishing Inc. • Weekly. $594.00 per year. Newsletter. Emphasis is on Federal Communications Commission regulations affecting cable television systems. Covers rate increases made by local systems and cable subscriber complaints filed with the FCC.

RESEARCH CENTERS AND INSTITUTES

Lexis.com Research System. Lexis-Nexis Group. Phone: 800-227-9597 or (937)865-6800 Fax: (937)865-6909 E-mail: webmaster@prod.lexis-nexis.com • URL: http://www.lexis.com • Fee-based Web site offers extensive searching of a wide variety of legal sources. Additional features include Daily Opinion Service, lexis.com Bookstore, Career Center, CLE Center, Law Schools, and Practice Pages ("Pages specific to areas of specialty").

OTHER SOURCES

Chemical Regulation Reporter: A Weekly Review of Affecting Chemical Users and Manufacturers. Bureau of National Affairs, Inc. • Weekly. Price varies. Irregular supplements.

Corporate Compliance Series. West Group. • Eleven looseleaf volumes, with periodic supplementation. $990.00. Covers criminal and civil liability problems for corporations. Includes employee safety, product liability, pension requirements, securities violations, equal employment opportunity issues, intellectual property, employee hiring and firing, and other corporate compliance topics.

Factiva. Dow Jones Reuters Business Interactive, LLC. • Fee-based Web site provides "global news and business information through Web sites and content integration solutions." Includes Dow Jones and Reuters newswires, The Wall Street Journal, and more than 7,000 other sources of current news, historical articles, market research reports, and investment analysis. Content includes 96 major U. S. newspapers, 900 non-English sources, trade publications, media transcripts, country profiles, news photos, etc.

FCC Record. Available from U. S. Government Printing Office. • Biweekly. $535.00 per year. Produced by the Federal Communications Commission (http://www.fcc.gov). An inclusive compilation of decisions, reports, public notices, and other documents of the FCC.

Federal Trade Commission. Stephanie W. Kanwit. Shepard's. • 1979. $190.00. Two volumes. Discussion of regulations and procedures. (Regulatory Manual Series).

FedWorld: A Program of the United States Department of Commerce. National Technical Information Service. • Web site offers "a comprehensive central access point for searching, locating, ordering, and acquiring government and business information." Emphasis is on searching the Web pages, databases, and government reports of a wide variety of federal agencies. Fees: Free.

FirstGov: Your First Click to the U. S. Government. General Services Administration. • Free Web site provides extensive links to federal agencies covering a wide variety of topics, such as agriculture, business, consumer safety, education, the environment, government jobs, grants, health, social security, statistics sources, taxes, technology, travel, and world affairs. Also provides links to federal forms, including IRS tax forms. Searching is offered, both keyword and advanced.

Nexis.com. Lexis-Nexis Group. • Fee-based Web site offers searching of about 2.8 billion documents in some 30,000 news, business, and legal information sources. Features include a subject directory covering 1,200 topics in 34 categories and a Company Dossier containing information on more than 500,000 public and private companies. Boolean searching is offered.

U. S. Business Advisor. Small Business Administration. • Web site provides "a one-stop electronic link to all the information and services government provides for the business community." Covers about 60 federal agencies that exist to assist or regulate business. Detailed information is provided on financial assistance, workplace issues, taxes, regulations, international trade, and other business topics. Searching is offered. Fees: Free.

REGULATION OF SECURITIES

See: SECURITIES LAW AND REGULATION

REGULATIONS

See: LAWS; REGULATION OF INDUSTRY

REHABILITATION, VOCATIONAL

See: VOCATIONAL REHABILITATION

REIT'S

See: REAL ESTATE INVESTMENT TRUSTS

RELOCATION OF EMPLOYEES

ABSTRACTS AND INDEXES

Business Periodicals Index. H. W. Wilson Co. • Monthly, except August, with quarterly and annual cumulations. Service basis for print edition; CD-ROM edition, $1,495.00 per year.

Personnel Management Abstracts. • Quarterly. $190.00 per year. Includes annual cumulation.

DIRECTORIES

Craighead's International Business, Travel, and Relocation Guide to 81 Countries. Available from The Gale Group. • 2000. $725.00. Tenth edition. Four volumes. Compiled by Craighead Publications, Inc. Provides a wide range of business travel and relocation information for 78 different countries, including details on currency, customs regulations, visas, passports, healthcare, transportation, shopping, insurance, travel safety, etc. Formerly *International Business Travel and RelocatDirectory.*

HANDBOOKS AND MANUALS

Company Relocation Handbook: Making the Right Move. William G. Ward and Sharon K. Ward. PSI Research. • 1998. $19.95. A comprehensive guide to moving a business. (Successful Business Library Series).

A Guide to Employee Relocation and Relocation Policy Development. Employee Relocation Council. • 1987. $25.00. Second edition.

ONLINE DATABASES

Wilson Business Abstracts Online. H. W. Wilson Co. • Indexes and abstracts 600 major business periodicals, plus the *Wall Street Journal* and the business section of the *New York Times*. Indexing is from 1982, abstracting from 1990, with the two newspapers included from 1993. Updated weekly. Inquire as to online cost and availability. (*Business Periodicals Index* without abstracts is also available online.).

PERIODICALS AND NEWSLETTERS

Direction: For the Moving and Storage Industry. American Moving and Storage Association. • Monthly. $35.00 per year. Newsletter on developments affecting the household goods movingindustry. Formerly *American Mover.*

Insulation Outlook: Business Solutions for Expanding or Relocating Companies. National Insulation Association. • $45.00 per year. Covers site selection and related topics.

Mobility. Employee Relocation Council. • 12 times a year. $48.00 per year. Covers various aspects of the moving of corporate employees.

Office Relocation Magazine. ORM Group. • Bimonthly. $39.00 per year. Provides articles on the relocation of office facilities.

Runzheimer Reports on Relocation. Runzheimer International. • Monthly. $295.00 per year. Newsletter.

STATISTICS SOURCES

Moving and Relocation Sourcebook and Directory: Reference Guide to the 100 Largest Metropolitan Areas in the United States. Kay Gill, editor. Omnigraphics, Inc. • 1998. $185.00. Second edition. Provides extensive statistical and other descriptive data for the 100 largest metropolitan areas in the U. S. Includes maps and a discussion of factors to be considered when relocating.

Survey and Analysis of Employee Relocation Policies and Costs. Runzheimer International. • Annual. Based on surveys of relocation administrators.

TRADE/PROFESSIONAL ASSOCIATIONS

American Moving and Storage Association. c/o John Brewer. 1611 Duke St., Alexandria, VA 22314. Phone: (703)683-7410 Fax: (703)683-7527 • URL: http://www.amconf.org • Members are household goods movers, storage companies, and trucking firms.

Employee Relocation Council. 1720 N St., N.W., Washington, DC 20036. Phone: (202)857-0857 Fax: (202)467-4012 E-mail: info@erc.org • URL: http://www.erc.org • Members are major corporations seeking efficiency and minimum disruption when employee transfers take place.

REMODELING

See: HOME IMPROVEMENT INDUSTRY

RENTAL, EQUIPMENT

See: EQUIPMENT LEASING

RENTAL HOUSING

See: APARTMENT HOUSES; REAL ESTATE INVESTMENTS

RENTAL SERVICES

See also: AUTOMOBILE LEASE AND RENTAL SERVICES; EQUIPMENT LEASING

DIRECTORIES

Leasing Sourcebook: The Directory of the U. S. Capital Equipment Leasing Industry. Bibliotechnology Systems and Publishing Co. • Irregular. $135.00. Lists more than 5,200 capital equipment leasing companies.

Rental Equipment Register Buyer's Guide. Intertec Publishing Corp. • Annual. $39.95. Formerly *Rental Equipment Register Product Directory and Buyer's Guide.*

FINANCIAL RATIOS

Annual Statement Studies. Robert Morris Associates: The Association of Lending and Credit Risk Professiona. • Annual. Free to members; non-members, $140.00. Median and quartile financial ratios are given for over 400 kinds of manufacturing, wholesale, retail, construction, and consumer finance establishments. Data is sorted by both asset size and sales volume. Includes a clearly written "Definition of Ratios" and an alphabetical industry index.

NARDA's Cost of Doing Business Survey. North American Retail Dealers Association. • Annual. $250.00.

HANDBOOKS AND MANUALS

Handbook of Equipment Leasing: A Deal Maker's Guide. Richard M. Contino. AMACOM. • 1996. $65.00. Second edition.

PERIODICALS AND NEWSLETTERS

Equipment Leasing Today. Equipment Leasing Association. • 10 times a year. $100.00 per year. Edited for equipment leasing companies. Covers management, funding, marketing, etc.

Rental Equipment Register. Intertec Publishing Corp. • Monthly. $75.00 per year.

Rental Management. American Rental Association. • Monthly. Free to qualified personnel.

Rental Product News. Cygnus Publishing, Inc. • Bimonthly. $48.00 per year. Includes annual *Product* issue.

STATISTICS SOURCES

Survey of Industry Activity. Equipment Leasing Association of America. • Annual. $395.00. Provides financial and statistical data on the equipment leasing industry.

U. S. Industry and Trade Outlook: The McGraw-Hill Companies and the U.S. Department of Commerce/ International Trade Administration. Datapso Research Corp. • Annual. $69.95. Produced by the International Trade Administration, U. S. Department of Commerce, in a "public-private" partnership with DRI/McGraw-Hill and Standard & Poor's. Provides basic data, outlook for the current year, and "Long-Term Prospects" (five-year projections) for a wide variety of products and services. Includes high technology industries. Formerly *U. S. Industrial Outlook.*

TRADE/PROFESSIONAL ASSOCIATIONS

American Rental Association. 1900 19th St., Moline, IL 61265. Phone: 800-334-2177 or (309)764-2475 Fax: (309)764-2747 E-mail: ara@araental.org • URL: http://www.ararental.org.

Equipment Leasing Association. 4301 N. Fairfax Dr., Suite 550, Arlington, VA 22203. Phone: (703)527-8655 Fax: (703)527-2649 E-mail: ela@elamail.com • URL: http://www.elaonline.com.

OTHER SOURCES

How to Make the Right Leasing Decisions. American Management Association Extension Institute. • Looseleaf. $110.00. Self-study course. Emphasis is on practical explanations, examples, and problem solving. Quizzes and a case study are included.

RENTAL SERVICES, AUTOMOBILE

See: AUTOMOBILE LEASE AND RENTAL SERVICES

REPORT WRITING

See also: TECHNICAL WRITING

GENERAL WORKS

Business English. Mary E. Guffey. South-Western College Publishing. • 2001. $47.00. Seventh edition. (South-Western College-Busines Communications Series).

Improving Writing Skills: Memos, Letters, Reports, and Proposals. Arthur A. Berger. Sage Publications, Inc. • 1993. $37.00. Emphasis is on the business correspondence required of university professors and other academic personnel. (Survival Skills for Scholars, vol. 9).

HANDBOOKS AND MANUALS

Business Writing at Its Best. Minerva H. Neiditz. McGraw-Hill Professional. • 1993. $22.50.

Business Writing the Modular Way: How to Research, Organize and Compose Effective Memo Letters, Articles, Reports, Proposals, Manuals, Specifications and Books. Harley Bjelland. Books on Demand. • 1992. $80.70. Covers research and organization for various kinds of business writing, from simple to complex.

Business Writing with Style: Strategies for Success. John Tarrant. John Wiley and Sons, Inc. • 1991. $10.95. Second edition. Emphasizes the use of business writing styles that are creative or unusual.

Handbook for Business Writing. L. Sue Baugh. NTC/Contemporary Publishing. • 1993. $24.95. Second edition. Covers reports, letters, memos, and proposals. (Handbook for... Series).

Little Black Book of Business Reports. Michael C. Thomsett. AMACOM. • 1988. $14.95. How to write effective business reports. (Little Black Book Series).

Report Writing for Business. Raymond V. Lesikar and John Pettit. McGraw-Hill Professional. • 1998. $64.38. 10th edition.

PERIODICALS AND NEWSLETTERS

Harvard Management Communication Letter. Harvard Business School Press. • Monthly. $79.00 per year. Newsletter. Provides practical advice on both electronic and conventional business communication: e-mail, telephone, cell phones, memos, letters, written reports, speeches, meetings, and visual presentations (slides, flipcharts, easels, etc.). Also covers face-to-face communication, discussion, listening, and negotiation.

REPORTS

See: CORPORATION REPORTS; REPORT WRITING

RESEARCH, ADVERTISING

See: ADVERTISING RESEARCH

RESEARCH AND DEVELOPMENT

See also: BUSINESS RESEARCH; ECONOMIC RESEARCH; INDUSTRIAL RESEARCH; LABORATORIES; MARKET RESEARCH; SCIENTIFIC APPARATUS AND INSTRUMENT INDUSTRIES; TECHNOLOGY

GENERAL WORKS

The Innovator's Dilemma: When New Technologies Cause Great Firms to Fail. Clayton M. Christensen. Harvard Business School Press. • 1997. $27.50. Discusses management myths relating to innovation, change, and research and development. (Mangement of Innovation and Change Series).

Probable Tomorrows: How Science and Technology Will Transform Our Lives in the Next Twenty Years. Marvin J. Cetron and Owen L. Davies. St. Martin's Press. • 1997. $24.95. Predicts the developments in technological products, services, and "everyday conveniences" by the year 2017. Covers such items as personal computers, artificial intelligence, telecommunications, highspeed railroads, and healthcare.

ABSTRACTS AND INDEXES

Applied Science and Technology Index. H. W. Wilson Co. • 11 times a year. Quarterly and annual cumulations. Service basis for print edition; CD-ROM edition, $1,495.00 per year. Indexes a wide variety of English language technical, industrial, and engineering periodicals.

ALMANACS AND YEARBOOKS

Science and Technology Almanac. Oryx Press. • Annual. $65.00. Covers technological news, research, and statistics.

BIOGRAPHICAL SOURCES

American Men and Women of Science A Biographical Directory of Today's Leaders in Physical, Biological and Related Sciences. R. R. Bowker. • 1995. $900.00. Eight volumes. Over 119,600 United States and Canadian scientists active in the physical, biological, mathematical, computer science and engineering fields.

Who's Who in Science and Engineering. Marquis Who's Who. • Biennial. $269.00. Provides concise biographical information on 26,000 prominent engineers and scientists. International coverage, with geographical and professional indexes.

CD-ROM DATABASES

NTIS on SilverPlatter. Available from SilverPlatter Information, Inc. • Quarterly. $2,850.00 per year. Produced by the National Technical Information Service. Provides a CD-ROM guide to over 500,000 government reports on a wide variety of technical, industrial, and business topics.

Science Citation Index: Compact Disc Edition. Institute for Scientific Information. • Quarterly. Provides CD-ROM indexing of the world's scientific and technical literature. Corresponds to online *Scisearch* and printed *Science Citation Index.*

WILSONDISC: Applied Science and Technology Abstracts. H. W. Wilson Co. • Monthly. $1,495.00 per year, including unlimited access to the online version of *Applied Science and Technology Abstracts* through WILSONLINE. Provides CD-ROM indexing and abstracting of 400 prominent scientific, technical, engineering, and industrial periodicals. Indexing coverage is provided from 1983 to date and abstracting from 1993 to date.

DIRECTORIES

Directory of American Research and Technology: Organizations Active in Product Development for Business. R. R. Bowker. • Annual. $359.95. Lists over 13,000 publicly and privately owned research facilities. Formerly *Industrial Research Laboratories of the U.S.*

Government Research Directory. The Gale Group. • 2000. $530.00 14th edition. Lists more than 4,800 research facilities and programs of the United States and Canadian federal governments.

International Research Centers Directory. The Gale Group. • 2000. $515.00. 14th edition. Describes over 8,200 research centers in all countries of the world other than the U. S.

Materials Research Centres: A World Directory of Organizations and Programmes in Materials Science. Allyn and Bacon/Longman. • 1991. $475.00. Fourth edition. Profiles of research centers in 75 countries. Materials include plastics, metals, fibers, etc.

Medical Research Centres: A World Directory of Organizations and Programmes. Allyn and Bacon/Longman. • Irregular. $535.00. Two volumes. Contains profiles of about 7,000 medical research facilities around the world. Includes medical, dental, nursing, pharmaceutical, psychiatric, and surgical research centers.

New Research Centers. The Gale Group. • 2000. $395.00. A supplement to *Research Centers Directory.*

Plunkett's Engineering and Research Industry Almanac. Plunkett Research, Ltd. • Annual. $179.99. Contains detailed profiles of major engineering and technology corporations. Includes CD-ROM.

Research Centers Directory. The Gale Group. • Annual. $575.00. Two volumes. Lists more than 14,200 centers.

Research Services Directory: Commercial & Corporate Research Centers. Grey House Publishing. • 1999. $395.00. Seventh edition. Lists more than 6,200 independent commercial research centers and laboratories offering contract or fee-based services. Includes corporate research departments, market research companies, and information brokers.

Unique 3-in-1 Research and Development Directory. Government Data Publications, Inc. • Annual. $15.00. Government contractors in the research and development fields. Included with subscription to *R and D Contracts Monthly.* Formerly *Research and Development Directory.*

World Energy and Nuclear Directory. Allyn and Bacon/Longman. • 1996. Fifth edition. Price on application. Lists 5,000 public and private, international research and development organizations functioning in a wide variety of areas related to energy.

ENCYCLOPEDIAS AND DICTIONARIES

Encyclopedia of Emerging Industries. The Gale Group. • 2000. $295.00. Fourth edition. Provides detailed information on 90 "newly flourishing" industries. Includes historical background, organizational structure, significant individuals, current conditions, major companies, work force, technology trends, research developments, and other industry facts.

FINANCIAL RATIOS

Annual Statement Studies. Robert Morris Associates: The Association of Lending and Credit Risk Professiona. • Annual. Free to members; non-members, $140.00. Median and quartile financial ratios are given for over 400 kinds of manufacturing, wholesale, retail, construction, and consumer finance establishments. Data is sorted by both asset size and sales volume. Includes a clearly written "Definition of Ratios" and an alphabetical industry index.

HANDBOOKS AND MANUALS

Managing High-Technology Programs and Projects. Russell D. Archibald. John Wiley and Sons, Inc. • 1992. $107.50. Second edition. Written for senior executives, professional project managers, engineers, and information systems managers.

INTERNET DATABASES

GaleNet: Your Information Community. The Gale Group. Phone: 800-877-GALE or (248)699-GALE Fax: 800-414-5043 or (248)699-8069 E-mail: galenet@gale.com • URL: http://www.galenet.com • Web site provides a wide variety of full-text information from Gale databases, Taft, and other sources. Covers associations, biography, business directories, education, the information industry, literature, publishing, and science. Fee-based subscriptions are available for individual databases (free demonstration). Includes Boolean search features and the BRS/Search user interface.

ONLINE DATABASES

Applied Science and Technology Index Online. H. W. Wilson Co. • Provides online indexing of 400 major scientific, technical, industrial, and engineering periodicals. Time period is 1983 to date. Monthly updates. Inquire as to online cost and availability.

Current Contents Connect. Institute for Scientific Information. • Provides online abstracts of articles listed in the tables of contents of about 7,500 journals. Coverage is very broad, including science, social science, life science, technology, engineering, industry, agriculture, the environment, economics, and arts and humanities. Time period is two years, with weekly updates. Inquire as to online cost and availability.

New Product Announcements Plus. The Gale Group. • Contains the full text of new product and corporate activity press releases, with special emphasis on high technology and emerging industries. Covers 1985 to date. Weekly updates. Inquire as to online cost and availability.

NTIS Bibliographic Data Base. National Technical Information Service. • Contains citations and abstracts to unrestricted reports of government-sponsored research, 1964 to date. Covers a wide range of technical, engineering, business, and social science topics. Monthly updates. Inquire as to online cost and availability.

Research Centers and Services Directories. The Gale Group. • Contains profiles of about 30,000 research centers, organizations, laboratories, and agencies in 147 countries. Corresponds to the printed *Research Centers Directory, International Research Centers Directory, Government Research Directory,* and *Research Services Directory.* Updating is semiannual. Inquire as to online cost and availability.

Scisearch. Institute for Scientific Information. • Broad, multidisciplinary index to the literature of science and technology, 1974 to present. Inquire as to online cost and availability. Coverage of literature is worldwide, with weekly updates.

Who's Who in Technology [Online]. The Gale Group. • Provides online biographical profiles of over 25,000 American scientists, engineers, and others in technology-related occupations. Inquire as to online cost and availability.

PERIODICALS AND NEWSLETTERS

Inside R and D: A Weekly Report on Technical Innovation. Technical Insights. • Weekly. $840.00

per year. Concentrates on new and significant developments. Formerly *Technolog Transfer Week.*

Research and Development: The Voice of the Research and Development Community. Cahners Business Information. • 13 times a year. $81.90 per year.

The Scientist: The Newspaper for the Life Science Professionals. Information Science Institute. • Semimonthly. Individuals, $29.00 per year; institutions, $58.00 per year. Contains news for scientific, research, and technical personnel.

RESEARCH CENTERS AND INSTITUTES

Research-Technology Management. Industrial Research Institute, Inc. 1550 M St., N. W., Suite 1100, Washington, DC 20005-1712. Phone: (202)296-8811 Fax: (202)776-0756 • URL: http://www.iriinc.org • Bimonthly. $150.00 per year. Covers both theoretical and practical aspects of the management of industrial research and development.

SRI International. 333 Ravenswood Ave., Menlo Park, CA 94025-3493. Phone: (650)859-2000 Fax: (650)326-5512 E-mail: inquiryline@sri.com • URL: http://www.sri.com • Private research firm specializing in market research in high technology areas.

STATISTICS SOURCES

Main Science and Technology Indicators. OECD Publications and Information Center. • Semiannual. $75.00 per year. Provides latest available data on research and development expenditures in OECD countries.

UNESCO Statistical Yearbook. Bernan Press. • Annual. $95.00. Co-published by Bernan Press and the United Nations Educational, Scientific, and Cultural Organization (http://www.unesco.org). Presents statistical data from more than 200 countries on education, technology, research, broadcasting, cinema, book publishing, newspapers, libraries, museums, and population. Includes charts, maps, and graphs.

TRADE/PROFESSIONAL ASSOCIATIONS

Industrial Research Institute. 1550 M St., N.W., Suite 1100, Washington, DC 20005-1712. Phone: (202)296-8811 Fax: (202)776-0756.

National Research Council. 2101 Constitution Ave., N.W., Washington, DC 20418. Phone: (202)334-2000 • URL: http://www.nas.edu.

Society of Research Administrators. 1200 19th St., N.W., Ste. 300, Washington, DC 20036-2422. Phone: (202)857-1141 Fax: (202)828-6049 E-mail: sra@dc.sba.com • URL: http://www.sra.rams.com.

OTHER SOURCES

Army AL&T: Acquisitions, Logistics, and Technology Bulletin. Available from U. S. Government Printing Office. • Bimonthly. $20.00 per year. Produced by the U. S. Army Materiel Command (http://www.amc.army.mil). Reports on Army research, development, and acquisition. Formerly *Army RD&A.*

FedWorld: A Program of the United States Department of Commerce. National Technical Information Service. • Web site offers "a comprehensive central access point for searching, locating, ordering, and acquiring government and business information." Emphasis is on searching the Web pages, databases, and government reports of a wide variety of federal agencies. Fees: Free.

RESEARCH, BUSINESS

See: BUSINESS RESEARCH

RESEARCH, ECONOMIC

See: ECONOMIC RESEARCH

RESEARCH, INDUSTRIAL

See: INDUSTRIAL RESEARCH

RESEARCH, LIBRARY

See: LIBRARY RESEARCH

RESEARCH, MARKETING

See: MARKET RESEARCH

RESELLERS, COMPUTER

See: COMPUTER RETAILING

RESINS

See: NAVAL STORES; PLASTICS INDUSTRY

RESOURCES

See: NATURAL RESOURCES

RESTAURANTS, LUNCHROOMS, ETC.

See also: CATERERS AND CATERING; DRIVE-IN AND CURB SERVICES; EMPLOYEE LUNCHROOMS AND CAFETERIAS; FOOD SERVICE INDUSTRY

GENERAL WORKS

Fundamentals of Professional Food Preparation: A Laboratory Text-Workbook. Donald V. Laconi. John Wiley and Sons, Inc. • 1995. $54.95.

DIRECTORIES

Directory of Chain Restaurant Operators. Chain Store Guide. • Annual. $300.00. Includes fast food establishments, and leading chain hotel copanies operating foodservice unit.

Directory of Foodservice Distributors. Chain Store Guide. • Annual. $290.00. Covers distributors of food and equipment to restaurants and institutions.

Directory of High Volume Independent Restaurants. Chain Store Guide. • Annual. $300.00. Approximately 8,000 independently owned restaurants with minimum sales of greater than $1 million.

FINANCIAL RATIOS

Almanac of Business and Industrial Financial Ratios. Leo Troy. Prentice Hall. • Annual. $99.95. Contains financial ratios derived from federal tax returns. Ratios for each of about 200 industries are arranged according to company asset size.

Annual Statement Studies. Robert Morris Associates: The Association of Lending and Credit Risk Professiona. • Annual. Free to members; non-members, $140.00. Median and quartile financial ratios are given for over 400 kinds of manufacturing, wholesale, retail, construction, and consumer finance establishments. Data is sorted by both asset size and sales volume. Includes a clearly written "Definition of Ratios" and an alphabetical industry index.

Restaurant Industry Operations Report. National Restaurant Association. • Annual. Members, $44.95 per year; non-members, $89.95 per year.

HANDBOOKS AND MANUALS

Donut Shop. Entrepreneur Media, Inc. • Looseleaf. $59.50. A practical guide to starting a doughnut shop. Covers profit potential, start-up costs, market size evaluation, owner's time required, site selection, lease negotiation, pricing, accounting, advertising, promotion, etc. (Start-Up Business Guide No. E1126.).

Hotel and Restaurant Business. Donald E. Lundberg. John Wiley and Sons, Inc. • 1994. $54.95. Sixth edition. (Hospitality, Travel and Tourism Series).

Pizzeria. Entrepreneur Media, Inc. • Looseleaf. $59.50. A practical guide to starting a pizza shop. Covers profit potential, start-up costs, market size evaluation, owner's time required, site selection, lease negotiation, pricing, accounting, advertising, promotion, etc. (Start-Up Business Guide No. E1006.).

Profitable Restaurant Management. Kenneth L. Solomon and Norman Katz. Prentice Hall. • 1981. $60.00. Second edition.

Restaurant Start-Up. Entrepreneur Media, Inc. • Looseleaf. $59.50. A practical guide to starting a restaurant. Covers profit potential, start-up costs, market size evaluation, owner's time required, site selection, lease negotiation, pricing, accounting, advertising, promotion, etc. (Start-Up Business Guide No. E1279.).

Restaurant Start-Up Guide: A 12-Month Plan for Successfully Starting a Restaurant. Peter Rainsford and David H. Bangs. Dearborn Financial Publishing. • 2000. $22.95. Second edition. Emphasizes the importance of advance planning for restaurant startups.

Sandwich Shop/Deli. Entrepreneur Media, Inc. • Looseleaf. $59.50. A practical guide to starting a sandwich shop and delicatessen. Covers profit potential, start-up costs, market size evaluation, owner's time required, site selection, lease negotiation, pricing, accounting, advertising, promotion, etc. (Start-Up Business Guide No. E1156.).

INTERNET DATABASES

Fedstats. Federal Interagency Council on Statistical Policy. Phone: (202)395-7254 • URL: http://www.fedstats.gov • Web site features an efficient search facility for full-text statistics produced by more than 70 federal agencies, including the Census Bureau, the Bureau of Economic Analysis, and the Bureau of Labor Statistics. Boolean searches can be made within one agency or for all agencies combined. Links are offered to international statistical bureaus, including the UN, IMF, OECD, UNESCO, Eurostat, and 20 individual countries. Fees: Free.

ONLINE DATABASES

DRI U.S. Central Database. Data Products Division. • Provides more than 23,000 business, financial, demographic, economic, foreign trade, and industry-related time series for the U.S. Includes national income, population, retail-wholesale trade, price indexes, labor data, housing, industrial production, banking, interest rates, money supply, etc. Time period is generally 1947 to date (some data back to 1929). Updating varies. Inquire as to online cost and availability.

PERIODICALS AND NEWSLETTERS

The Bottomline. International Association of Hospitality Accountants. • Bimonthly. Free to members, educational institutions and libraries; others, $50.00 per year. Contains articles on accounting, finance, information technology, and management for hotels, resorts, casinos, clubs, and other hospitality businesses.

Chef. Talcott Communications Corp. • Monthly. $24.00 per year. Edited for executive chefs, food and beverage directors, caterers, banquet and club managers, and others responsible for food buying and food service. Special coverage of regional foods is provided.

Cooking for Profit. C P Publishing, Inc. • Monthly. $25.00 per year. The challenge of operations management in the food service industry.

The Cornell Hotel and Restaurant Administration Quarterly. Cornell University School of Hotel Administration. Elsevier Science. • Bimonthly. $258.00 per year.

Foodservice Equipment and Supplies. Cahners Business Information. • 13 times a year. $92.90 per year.

Hospitality Technology: Infosystems for Foodservice and Lodging. Edgell Communications, Inc. • Monthly. $36.00 per year. Covers information technology, computer communications, and software for foodservice and lodging enterprises.

International Journal of Hospitality and Tourism Administration: A Multinationaland Cross-Cultural Journal of Applied Research. Haworth Press, Inc. • Quarterly. Individuals, $36.00 per year; institutions, $48.00 per year; libraries, $85.00 per year. An academic journal with articles relating to lodging, food service, travel, tourism, and the hospitality/leisure industries in general. Formerly *Journal of International Hospitality, Leisure, and Tourism Management.*

Journal of Hospitality and Leisure Marketing: The International Forum for Research, Theory and Practice. Haworth Press, Inc. • Quarterly. Individuals, $60.00 per year; institutions, $95.00 per year; libraries, $175.00 per year. An academic and practical journal covering various aspects of hotel, restaurant, and recreational marketing.

Journal of Restaurant and Foodservice Marketing. Haworth Press, Inc. • Quarterly. Individuals, $50.00 per year; institutions, $60.00 per year; libraries, $75.00 per year.

Nation's Restaurant News: The Newspaper of the Food Service Industry. Lebhar-Friedman, Inc. • 50 times a year. $39.95 per year.

Nightclub & Bar Magazine: The Magazine for Nightclub and Bar Management. Oxford Publishing. • Monthly. $25.00 per year. Provides news and business advice for owners and managers of bars, nightclubs, and themed restaurants. Includes special issues on seasonal drinks, bar technology, beer trends, appetizers, food service, etc.

QSR: The Magazine of Quick Service Restaurant Success. Journalistic, Inc. • Nine times a year. $32.00 per year. Provides news and management advice for quick-service restaurants, including franchisors and franchisees.

Restaurant Business. Bill Communications, Inc. • 24 times a year. $110.00 per year.

Restaurant Hospitality. Penton Media Inc. • Monthly. Free to qualified personnel; others, $65.00 per year.

Restaurants and Institutions. Cahners Business Information. • Semimonthly. $136.90 per year. Features news, new products, recipes, menu concepts and merchandising ideas from the most successful foodservice operations around the U.S.

STATISTICS SOURCES

Business Statistics of the United States. Courtenay M. Slater, editor. Bernan Associates. • 1999. $74.00. Fifth edition. Based on *Business Statistics*, formerly issue by the Bureau of Economic Analysis, U. S. Department of Commerce. Provides basic data for a wide variety of U. S. industries, services, and economic indicators. Most statistics are shown annually for 29 years and monthly for the most recent four years.

Standard & Poor's Industry Surveys. Standard & Poor's. • Semiannual. $1,800.00. Two looseleaf volumes. Includes monthly supplements. Provides detailed, individual surveys of 52 major industry groups. Each survey is revised on a semiannual basis. Also includes "Monthly Investment Review" (industry group investment analysis) and monthly "Trends & Projections" (economic analysis).

Survey of Current Business. Available from U. S. Government Printing Office. • Monthly. $49.00 per year. Issued by Bureau of Economic Analysis, U. S. Department of Commerce. Presents a wide variety of business and economic data.

WEFA Industrial Monitor. John Wiley and Sons, Inc. • Annual. $65.00. Prepared by industry analysts at WEFA, an economic forecasting and consulting firm (originally Wharton Econometric Forecasting Associates). Contains discussions of the outlook for major U. S. industries, with many 10-year forecasts (WEFA Web site is http://www.wefa.com).

TRADE/PROFESSIONAL ASSOCIATIONS

Hospitality Financial and Technology Professionals. 11709 Boulder Lane, Suite 110, Austin, TX 78726. Phone: 800-646-4387 or (512)249-5333 Fax: (512)249-1533 E-mail: hftp@hftp.org • URL: http://www.hitecshow • Members are accounting and finance officers in the hotel, motel, casino, club, and other areas of the hospitality industry.

National Restaurant Association. 1200 17th St., N.W., Washington, DC 20036. Phone: (202)331-5900 Fax: (202)331-2429 E-mail: info@dineout.org • URL: http://www.restaurant.org.

RESTRAINT OF TRADE

See: ANTITRUST ACTIONS

RESUMES

See: JOB RESUMES

RETAIL AUTOMATION

See: POINT-OF-SALE SYSTEMS (POS)

RETAIL SECURITY

See: SHOPLIFTING

RETAIL SELLING

See: SALESMEN AND SALESMANSHIP

RETAIL TRADE

See also: CHAIN STORES; DEPARTMENT STORES; DISCOUNT HOUSES

GENERAL WORKS

Management of Retail Buying. R. Patrick Cash and others. John Wiley and Sons, Inc. • 1995. $110.00. Third edition.

Modern Retailing: Theory and Practice. Joseph B. Mason and others. McGraw-Hill Higher Education. • 1992. $69.95. Sixth edition.

Retailing Managment. Michael Levy. McGraw-Hill Professional. • 2000. $65.50. Fourth edition.

CD-ROM DATABASES

16 Million Businesses Phone Directory. Info USA. • Annual. $29.95. Provides more than 16 million yellow pages telephone directory listings on CD-ROM for all ZIP Code areas of the U. S.

DIRECTORIES

American Big Businesses Directory. American Business Directories. • Annual. $595.00. Lists 177,000 public and private U. S. companies in all fields having 100 or more employees. Includes sales volume, number of employees, and name of chief executive. Formerly *Big Businesses Directory.*

American Business Directory. InfoUSA, Inc. • Provides brief online information on more than 10 million U. S. companies, including individual plants and branches. Entries typically include address, phone number, industry classification code, and contact name. Updating is quarterly. Inquire as to online cost and availability.

American Manufacturers Directory. American Business Directories. • Annual. $595.00. Lists more than 150,000 public and private U. S. manufacturers having 20 or more employees. Includes sales volume, number of employees, and name of chief executive or owner.

Directory of Discount and General Merchandise Stores. Chain Store Guide. • Annual. $300.00. Includes retailers and wholesalers of housewares, giftwares, novelties, toys, hobby materials, crafts, and stationery. Formerly *Directory of Discount Stores Catalog Showrooms.*

European Directory of Retailers and Wholesalers. Available from The Gale Group. • 1997. $790.00. Second edition. Published by Euromonitor. Provides detailed information on more than 4,000 major retail and wholesale businesses in 17 countries of Western Europe. Contains 26 categories, such as supermarkets, superstores, department stores, discount stores, franchise operators, mail order, etc. Includes company, product, and geographic indexes.

Nationwide Directory of Major Mass Market Merchandisers. Salesman's Guide. • Annual. $179.95. Lists buyers of clothing for major retailers. (Does not include the metropolitan New York City area.).

Plunkett's Retail Industry Almanac: Complete Profiles on the Retail 500-The Leading Firms in Retail Stores, Services, Catalogs, and On-Line Sales. Available from Plunkett Research, Ltd. • Annual. $179.99. Provides detailed profiles of 500 major U. S. retailers. Industry trends are discussed.

Sheldon's Major Stores and Chains. Phelon Sheldon and Marsar, Inc. • Annual. $175.00. Lists department stores and chains in, women's specialty and chains, home furnishing chains and resident buying offices in the U.S. and Canada. Formerly *Sheldon's Retail Stores.*

World Retail Directory and Sourcebook 1999. Available from The Gale Group. • 1999. $590.00. Fourth edition. Published by Euromonitor. Provides information on more than 2,600 retailers around the world, with detailed profiles of the top 70. Information sources, conferences, trade fairs, and special libraries are also listed.

FINANCIAL RATIOS

Almanac of Business and Industrial Financial Ratios. Leo Troy. Prentice Hall. • Annual. $99.95. Contains financial ratios derived from federal tax returns. Ratios for each of about 200 industries are arranged according to company asset size.

Cost of Doing Business Survey for Retail Sporting Goods Stores. National Sporting Goods Association.

• Biennial. $125.00. Includes income statements, balance sheets, sales per employee, sales per square foot, inventory turnover, etc.

Financial and Operating Results of Department and Specialty Stores. National Retail Federation. John Wiley and Sons, Inc. • Annual. Members, $80.00; non-members, $100.00.

HANDBOOKS AND MANUALS

Financial Recordkeeping for Small Stores. Available from U. S. Government Printing Office. • 1986. Presents a basic record keeping system for the small retail owner-manager who does not have a trained bookkeeper. Produced by the Office of Business Development, Small Business Administration. (Small Business Management Series, 32.).

Retail Store Planning and Design Manual. Michael J. Lopez. John Wiley and Sons, Inc. • 1995. $190.00. Second edition. (NRF Publishing Program Series).

INTERNET DATABASES

Bureau of Economic Analysis (BEA). U. S. Department of Commerce, Bureau of Economic Analysis. Phone: (202)606-9900 Fax: (202)606-5310 E-mail: webmaster@bea.doc.gov • URL: http://www.bea.doc.gov • Web site includes "News Release Information" covering national, regional, and international economic estimates from the BEA. Highlights of releases appear online the same day, complete text and tables appear the next day. "Recent News Releases" section provides titles for past nine months, with links. "BEA Data and Methodology" includes "Frequently Requested NIPA Data" (national income and product accounts, such as gross domestic product and personal income). Other statistics are available. Fees: Free.

Fedstats. Federal Interagency Council on Statistical Policy. Phone: (202)395-7254 • URL: http://www.fedstats.gov • Web site features an efficient search facility for full-text statistics produced by more than 70 federal agencies, including the Census Bureau, the Bureau of Economic Analysis, and the Bureau of Labor Statistics. Boolean searches can be made within one agency or for all agencies combined. Links are offered to international statistical bureaus, including the UN, IMF, OECD, UNESCO, Eurostat, and 20 individual countries. Fees: Free.

ONLINE DATABASES

Business and Industry. Responsive Database Services, Inc. • Contains online citations, abstracts, and selected fulltext from more than 1,000 trade journals, newspapers, and other publications. Provides general coverage of both manufacturing and service industries, including marketing, production, industry trends, key events, and information on specific companies. Time span is 1994 to date. Daily updates. Inquire as to online cost and availability. (Also available in a CD-ROM version.).

DRI U.S. Central Database. Data Products Division. • Provides more than 23,000 business, financial, demographic, economic, foreign trade, and industry-related time series for the U.S. Includes national income, population, retail-wholesale trade, price indexes, labor data, housing, industrial production, banking, interest rates, money supply, etc. Time period is generally 1947 to date (some data back to 1929). Updating varies. Inquire as to online cost and availability.

Euromonitor Journals. Euromonitor International. • Contains full-text reports online from *Market Research Europe, Market Research Great Britain, Market Research International*, and *Retail Monitor International*. Time period is 1995 to date, with monthly updates. Inquire as to online cost and availability.

Tablebase. Responsive Database Services, Inc. • Provides online numerical tabular data from a wide variety of business, organization, and government sources, including 900 trade journals. Includes industry and individual company statistics relating to products, market share, sales forecasts, production, exports, market trends, etc. Time span is 1997 to date. Weekly updates. Inquire as to online cost and availability. (Also available in a CD-ROM version.).

PERIODICALS AND NEWSLETTERS

E-retailing World. Bill Communications, Inc. • Bimonthly. Controlled circulation. Covers various kinds of online retailing, including store-based, catalog-based, pure play, and "click-and-mortar." Includes both technology and management issues.

eShopper. Ziff-Davis. • Bimonthly. $9.97 per year. A consumer magazine providing advice and information for "shopping on the Web.".

Inside Retailing. Lebhar-Friedman Inc. • Biweekly. $229.00 per year. Newsletter.

Internet Retailer: Merchandising in an Age of Virtual Stores. Faulkner & Gray, Inc. • Bimonthly. $82.95. Covers the selling of retail merchandise through the Internet.

Journal of Retailing. New York University, Stern School of Business. JAI Press, Inc. • Quarterly. $287.00 per year.

NSGA Retail Focus. National Sporting Goods Association. • Bimonthy. Free to members; non-members, $50.00 per year. Covers news and marketing trends for sporting goods retailers. Formerly *NSGA Sports Retailer.*

Retail Monitor International. Euromonitor International. • Monthly. $1,050.00 per year. Covers many aspects of international retailing, with emphasis on market research data. Includes profiles of leading retail groups, country profiles, retail news, trends, consumer credit information, and "Retail Factfile" (statistics).

Retailing Today. Robert Kahn and Associates. • Monthly. $70.00 per year. Newsletter. Written for retail chief executive officers and other top retail management.

Stores. National Retail Federation. N R F Enterprises, Inc. • Monthly. $49.00 per year.

Value Retail News: The Journal of Outlet and Off-Price Retail and Development. Off-Price Specialists, Inc. Value Retail News. • Monthly. Members $99.00 per year; non-members, $144.00 per year. Provides news of the off-price and outlet store industry. Emphasis is on real estate for outlet store centers.

PRICE SOURCES

CPI Detailed Report: Consumer Price Index. Available from U.S. Government Printing Office. • Monthly. $45.00 per year. Cost of living data.

RESEARCH CENTERS AND INSTITUTES

Center for Retail Management. J. L. Kellogg Graduate School of Management, Northwestern University, Evanston, IL 60208. Phone: (847)467-3600 Fax: (847)467-3620 • URL: http://www.retailing-network.com • Conducts research related to retail marketing and management.

Center for Retailing Studies. Texas A & M University, Department of Marketing, 4112 Tamus, College Station, TX 77843-4112. Phone: (979)845-0325 Fax: (979)845-5230 E-mail: berryle@tamu.edu • URL: http://www.crstamu.org • Research areas include retailing issues and consumer economics.

STATISTICS SOURCES

Business Statistics of the United States. Courtenay M. Slater, editor. Bernan Associates. • 1999. $74.00. Fifth edition. Based on *Business Statistics*, formerly issue by the Bureau of Economic Analysis, U. S. Department of Commerce. Provides basic data for a wide variety of U. S. industries, services, and economic indicators. Most statistics are shown annually for 29 years and monthly for the most recent four years.

Demographics USA: County Edition. Market Statistics. • Annual. $435.00. Contains 200 statistical series for each of 3,000 counties. Includes population, household income, employment, retail sales, and consumer expenditures. Also provides Effective Buying Income, Buying Power Index, and data summaries by Metro Market, Media Market, and State. (CD-ROM version is available.).

Demographics USA: ZIP Edition. Market Statistics. • Annual. $435.00. Contains 50 statistical series for each of 40,000 ZIP codes. Includes population, household income, employment, retail sales, and consumer expenditures. Also provides Effective Buying Income, Business Characteristics, and data summaries by state, region, and the first three digits of ZIP codes. (CD-ROM version is available.).

Encyclopedia of American Industries. The Gale Group. • 1998. $560.00. Second edition. Two volumes. $280.00 per volume. Volume one is *Manufacturing Industries* and volume two is *Service and Non-Manufacturing Industries*. Provides the history, development, and recent status of approximately 1,000 industries. Includes statistical graphs, with industry and general indexes.

European Retail Statistics: 17 Countries. Available from European Business Publications, Inc. • Annual. $375.00. Published in London by Corporate Intelligence Research Publications Ltd. Presents national retail statistics for each of 17 major countries of Europe, including total sales, number of businesses, employment, the food sector, the non-food sector, and demographic data.

Retail Trade International. The Gale Group. • 2000. $1,990.00. Second edition. Six volumes. Presents comprehensive data on retail trends in 51 countries. Includes textual analysis and profiles of major retailers. Covers Europe, Asia, the Middle East, Africa and the Americas.

Standard & Poor's Industry Surveys. Standard & Poor's. • Semiannual. $1,800.00. Two looseleaf volumes. Includes monthly supplements. Provides detailed, individual surveys of 52 major industry groups. Each survey is revised on a semiannual basis. Also includes "Monthly Investment Review" (industry group investment analysis) and monthly "Trends & Projections" (economic analysis).

Survey of Current Business. Available from U. S. Government Printing Office. • Monthly. $49.00 per year. Issued by Bureau of Economic Analysis, U. S. Department of Commerce. Presents a wide variety of business and economic data.

U. S. Industry Profiles: The Leading 100. The Gale Group. • 1998. $120.00. Second edition. Contains detailed profiles, with statistics, of 100 industries in the areas of manufacturing, construction, transportation, wholesale trade, retail trade, and entertainment.

ULI Market Profiles: North America. Urban Land Institute. • Annual. Members, $249.95; non-members, $299.95. Provides real estate marketing data for residential, retail, office, and industrial sectors. Covers 76 U. S. metropolitan areas and 13 major foreign metropolitan areas.

United States Census of Retail Trade. U.S. Bureau of the Census. • Quinquennial.

WEFA Industrial Monitor. John Wiley and Sons, Inc. • Annual. $65.00. Prepared by industry analysts at WEFA, an economic forecasting and consulting firm (originally Wharton Econometric Forecasting Associates). Contains discussions of the outlook for major U. S. industries, with many 10-year forecasts (WEFA Web site is http://www.wefa.com).

World Retail Data and Statistics 1999/2000. Available from The Gale Group. • 2000. $1,190.00. Fourth edition. Published by Euromonitor. Provides detailed retail industry statistics for 51 countries.

TRADE/PROFESSIONAL ASSOCIATIONS

International Mass Retail Association. 1700 N. Moore St., Suite 2250, Arlington, VA 22209. Phone: (703)841-2300 Fax: (703)841-1184 • URL: http://www.imra.org.

National Retail Federation. 325 Seventh St., N.W., Suite 1000, Washington, DC 20004-2802. Phone: 800-673-4692 or (202)783-7971 Fax: (202)737-2849 E-mail: nrf@nrf.com • URL: http://www.nrf.com.

OTHER SOURCES

The Business Elite: Database of Corporate America. Donnelley Marketing. • Quarterly. $795.00. Formerly compiled by Database America. Provides current information on CD-ROM for about 850,000 businesses, comprising all U. S. private and public companies having more than 20 employees or sales of more than $1 million. Data for each firm includes detailed industry classification, year started, annual sales, name of top executive, and number of employees.

Key Note Market Report: Home Shopping. Jupiter Media Metrix. • Irregular. $365.00. Market research report. Covers "interactive retailing," mainly through the Internet and television, with predictions of future trends. Formerly *Key Note Report: Home Shopping.*

Manufacturing and Distribution USA. The Gale Group. • 2000. $375.00. Three volumes. Replaces *Manufacturing USA* and *Wholesale and Retail Trade USA.* Presents statistics and projections relating to economic activity in more than 500 business classifications.

RETAILERS, COMPUTER

See: COMPUTER RETAILING

RETAILERS, OFF-PRICE

See: DISCOUNT HOUSES

RETIREE MARKET

See: MATURE CONSUMER MARKET

RETIREMENT

See also: EMPLOYMENT OF OLDER WORKERS; MATURE CONSUMER MARKET; PENSIONS; RETIREMENT COMMUNITIES; SOCIAL SECURITY

GENERAL WORKS

Consumer Reports Money Book: How to Get It, Save It, and Spend It Wisely. Janet Bamford and others. Consumers Union of the United States, Inc. • 1997. $29.95. Revised edition. Covers budgeting, retirement planning, bank accounts, insurance, and other personal finance topics.

Don't Die Broke: How to Turn Your Retirement Savings into Lasting Income. Margaret A. Malaspina. Available from W.W. Norton and Co., Inc. • 1999. $21.95. Provides advice on such matters as retirement portfolio asset allocation and retirement spending accounts. (Bloomberg Personal Bookshelf.).

Financial Planning for the Utterly Confused. Joel Lerner. McGraw-Hill. • 1998. $12.00. Fifth edition. Covers annuities, certificates of deposit, bonds, mutual funds, insurance, home ownership, retirement, social security, wills, etc.

Fundamentals of Employee Benefit Programs. Employee Benefit Research Institute. • 1996. $49.95. Fifth edition. Provides basic explanation of employee benefit programs in both the private and public sectors, including health insurance, pension plans, retirement planning, social security, and long-term care insurance.

How to Plan Your Retirement Years. Kerry A. Lynch, editor. American Institute for Economic Research. • 1996. $6.00. Provides concise, conservative advice on retirement planning, savings, pensions, IRAs, Keogh plans, annuities, and making effective use of social security. (Economic Education Bulletin.).

Investing During Retirement: The Vanguard Guide to Managing Your Retirement Assets. Vanguard Group. McGraw-Hill Professional. • 1996. $17.95. A basic, general guide to investing after retirement. Covers pension plans, basic principles of investing, types of mutual funds, asset allocation, retirement income planning, social security, estate planning, and contingencies. Includes glossary and worksheets for net worth, budget, and income.

The Lifetime Book of Money Management. Grace W. Weinstein. Visible Ink Press. • 1993. $15.95. Third edition. Gives popularly-written advice on investments, life and health insurance, owning a home, credit, retirement, estate planning, and other personal finance topics.

Retirement Security: Understanding and Planning Your Financial Future. David M. Walker. John Wiley and Sons, Inc. • 1996. $29.95. Topics include investments, social security, Medicare, health insurance, and employer retirement plans.

Smart Questions to Ask Your Financial Advisers. Lynn Brenner. Bloomberg Press. • 1997. $19.95. Provides practical advice on how to deal with financial planners, stockbrokers, insurance agents, and lawyers. Some of the areas covered are investments, estate planning, tax planning, house buying, prenuptial agreements, divorce arrangements, loss of a job, and retirement. (Bloomberg Personal Bookshelf Series Library.).

Vanguard Retirement Investing Guide: Charting Your Course to a Secure Retirement. Vanguard Group. McGraw-Hill Professional. • 1995. $24.95. Second edition. Covers saving and investing for future retirement. Topics include goal setting, investment fundamentals, mutual funds, asset allocation, defined contribution retirement savings plans, social security, and retirement savings strategies. Includes glossary and worksheet for retirement saving.

ABSTRACTS AND INDEXES

Abstracts in Social Gerentology: Current Literature on Aging. National Council on the Aging. Sage Publications, Inc. • Quarterly. Individuals, $110.00 per year; institutions, $350.00 per year. Formerly *Current Literature on Aging.*

ALMANACS AND YEARBOOKS

Older Americans Information Directory. Group Grey House Publshing, Inc. • 2000. $190.00. Second edition. Presents articles (text) and sources of information on a wide variety of aging and retirement topics. Includes an index to personal names, organizations, and subjects.

CD-ROM DATABASES

Magazine Index Plus. The Gale Group. • Monthly. $4,000.00 per year (includes InfoTrac workstation). Provides full text on CD-ROM for about 100 popular, general interest magazines and indexing for 300 others. Includes special indexing of reviews and product evaluations. Time period is 1980 to date.

DIRECTORIES

Older Americans Information Directory. Laura Mars, editor. Grey House Publishing, Inc. • 1998. $160.00. First edition. Provides information on about 5,000 organizations and agencies concerned with the needs of older people in the U. S.

FINANCIAL RATIOS

Financial Planning for Older Clients. James E. Pearman. CCH, Inc. • 2000. $49.00. Covers income sources, social security, Medicare, Medicaid, investment planning, estate planning, and other retirement-related topics. Edited for accountants, attorneys, and other financial advisors.

HANDBOOKS AND MANUALS

ERISA: The Law and the Code (Employee Retirement Income Security Act). Bureau of National Affairs, Inc. • Irregular. $75.00. The Employee Retirement Income Security Act, as amended, withrelevant provisions of the Internal Revenue Code.

Estate and Retirement Planning Answer Book. William D. Mitchell. Aspen Publshers. • 1996. $118.00. Second edition. Basic questions and answers by a lawyer.

How to Build Wealth with Tax-Sheltered Investments. Kerry Anne Lynch. American Institute for Economic Research. • 2000. $6.00. Provides practical information on conservative tax shelters, including defined-contribution pension plans, individual retirement accounts, Keogh plans, U. S. savings bonds, municipal bonds, and various kinds of annuities: deferred, variable-rate, immediate, and foreign-currency. (Economic Education Bulletin.).

Individual Retirement Account Answer Book. Donald R. Levy and Steven G. Lockwood. Panel Publishers. • 1999. $136.00. Sixth edition. Periodic supplementation available. Questions and answers include information about contributions, distributions, rollovers, Roth IRAs, SIMPLE IRAs (Savings Incentive Match Plans for Employees), Education IRAs, and SEPs (Simplified Employee Pension plans). Chapters are provided on retirement planning, estate planning, and tax planning.

An Insurance Guide for Seniors. Insurance Forum, Inc. • 1997. $15.00. Provides concise advice and information on Medicare, Medicare supplement insurance, HMOs, long-term care insurance, automobile insurance, life insurance, annuities, and pensions. An appendix lists "Financially Strong Insurance Companies." (*The Insurance Forum*, vol. 24, no. 4.).

The New Working Woman's Guide to Retirement Planning. Martha P. Patterson. University of Pennsylvania Press. • 1999. $17.50. Second edition. Provides retirement advice for employed women, including information on various kinds of IRAs, cash balance and other pension plans, 401(k) plans, and social security. Four case studies are provided to illustrate retirement planning at specific life and career stages.

Planning for Your Retirement: IRA and Keogh Plans. CCH, Inc. • Annual.

Retirement Benefits Tax Guide. CCH, Inc. • Looseleaf. $199.00. Supplementation available.

Retirement Planning Guide. Sidney Kess and Barbara Weltman. CCH, Inc. • 1999. $49.00. Presents an overview for attorneys, accountants, and other professionals of the various concepts involved in retirement planning. Includes checklists, tables, forms, and study questions.

INTERNET DATABASES

InsWeb. InsWeb Corp. Phone: (650)372-2129 E-mail: info@insweb.com • URL: http://www.insweb.com • Web site offers a wide variety of advice and information on automobile, life, health, and "other" insurance. Includes glossaries of insurance terms, Standard & Poor's ratings of individual insurance companies, and "Financial Needs Estimators." Searching is available. Fees: Free.

Small Business Retirement Savings Advisor. U. S. Department of Labor, Pension and Welfare Benefits Administration. Phone: (202)219-8921 • URL: http://www.dol.gov/elaws/pwbaplan.htm • Web site provides "answers to a variety of commonly asked questions about retirement saving options for small business employers." Includes a comparison chart and detailed descriptions of various plans: 401(k), SEP-IRA, SIMPLE-IRA, Payroll Deduction IRA, Keogh Profit-Sharing, Keogh Money Purchase, and Defined Benefit. Searching is offered. Fees: Free.

ONLINE DATABASES

Ageline. American Association of Retired Persons. • Provides indexing and abstracting of the literature of social gerontology, including consumer aspects, financial planning, employment, housing, health care services, mental health, social security, and retirement. Time period is 1978 to date. Inquire as to online cost and availability.

PERIODICALS AND NEWSLETTERS

AARP Bulletin. American Association of Retired Persons. • 11 times a year. Membership.

Estate Planner's Alert. Research Institute of America, Inc. • Monthly. $140.00 per year. Newsletter. Covers the tax aspects of personal finance, including home ownership, investments, insurance, retirement planning, and charitable giving. Formerly *Estate and Financial Planners Alert.*

Financial Planning: The Magazine for Financial Service Professionals. Securities Data Publishing. • Monthly. $79.00 per year. Edited for independent financial planners and insurance agents. Covers retirement planning, estate planning, tax planning, and insurance, including long-term healthcare considerations. Special features include a Retirement Planning Issue, Mutual Fund Performance Survey, and Variable Life and Annuity Survey. (Securities Data Publishing is a unit of Thomson Financial.).

Jounal of Finacial Services Professionals. American Society of CLU and Ch F C. • Bimonthly. $38.00 per year. Provides information on life insurance and financial planning, including estate planning, retirement, tax planning, trusts, business insurance, long-term care insurance, disability insurance, and employee benefits. Formerly (American Society of CLU and Ch F C Journal).

Journal of Aging and Social Policy: A Journal Devoted to Aging and Social Policy. Haworth Press, Inc. • Quarterly. Individuals, $60.00 per year; institutions, $120.00 per year; libraries, $275.00 per year.

Journal of Retirement Planning. CCH, Inc. • Bimonthly. $169.00 per year. Emphasis is on retirement and estate planning advice provided by lawyers and accountants as part of their practices.

Kiplinger's Retirement Report. Kiplinger Washington Editors, Inc. • Bimonthly. $29.95 per year. Newsletter on various aspects of retirement, including finances, health, and leisure.

Modern Maturity. American Association of Retired Persons. • Bimonthly. Membership.

New Choices: Living Even Better After Fifty. Reader's Digest Association, Inc. • 10 times a year. $18.97 per year. Formerly *New Choices for Retirement Living.*

Older Americans Report. Business Publishers, Inc. • Weekly. $432.00 per year. Newsletter on health, economic, and social services for the aging, including social security, medicare, pensions, housing, nursing homes, and programs under the Older Americans Act. Edited for service providers.

ReCareering Newsletter: An Idea and Resource Guide to Second Career and Relocation Planning. Publications Plus, Inc. • Monthly. $59.00 per year. Edited for "downsized managers, early retirees, and others in career transition after leaving traditional employment." Offers advice on second careers, franchises, starting a business, finances, education, training, skills assessment, and other matters of interest to the newly unemployed.

Retirement Letter: The Money Newsletter for Mature People. Peter A. Dickinson, editor. Phillips Inc., Consumer Publishing. • Monthly. $49.00 per year.

Retirement Life. National Association of Retired Federal Employees. • Monthly. Free to members; non-members, $25.00 per year.

Retirement Plans Bulletin: Practical Explanations for the IRA and Retirement Plan Professional. Universal Pensions, Inc. • Monthly. $99.00 per year. Newsletter. Provides information on the rules and regulations governing qualified (tax-deferred) retirement plans.

RESEARCH CENTERS AND INSTITUTES

Center for Pension and Retirement Research. Miami University, Department of Economics, 109E Laws Hall, Oxford, OH 45056. Phone: (513)529-2850 Fax: (513)529-6992 E-mail: swilliamson@eh.net • URL: http://www.eh.net/~cprr • Research areas include pension economics, pension plans, and retirement decisions.

Employee Benefit Research Institute. 2121 K St., N. W., Suite 600, Washington, DC 20037-1896. Phone: (202)659-0670 Fax: (202)775-6312 E-mail: salisbury@ebri.org • URL: http://www.ebri.org • Conducts research on employee benefits, including various kinds of pensions, individual retirement accounts (IRAs), health insurance, social security, and long-term health care benefits.

Retirement Research Foundation. 8765 W. Higgins Rd., Suite 430, Chicago, IL 60631. Phone: (312)714-8080 Fax: (312)714-8089 E-mail: info@rrf • URL: http://www.fdncenter.org/grantmaker/rrf/index.html.

STATISTICS SOURCES

EBRI Databook on Employee Benefits. Employee Benefit Research Institute. • 1997 $99.00. Fourth edition. Contains more than 350 tables and charts presenting data on employee benefits in the U. S., including pensions, health insurance, social security, and medicare. Includes a glossary of employee benefit terms.

Income of the Population 55 and Older. Available from U. S. Government Printing Office. • Biennial. $19.00. Issued by the Social Security Administration (http://www.ssa.gov). Covers major sources and amounts of income for the 55 and older population in the U. S., "with special emphasis on some aspects of the income of the population 65 and older.".

Social Security Bulletin. Social Security Administration. Available from U.S. Government Printing Office. • Quarterly. $23.00 per year. Annual statistical supplement.

Statistical Handbook on Aging Americans. Renee Schick, editor. Oryx Press. • 1994. $65.00. Second edition. Provides data on demographics, social characteristics, health, employment, economic conditions, income, pensions, and social security. Includes bibliographic information and a glossary. (Statistical Handbook Series).

Statistical Handbook on the American Family. Bruce A. Chadwick and Tim B. Heaton, editors. Oryx Press. • 1998. $65.00. Includes data on education, health, politics, employment, expenditures, social characteristics, the elderly, and women in the labor force. Historical statistics on marriage, birth, and divorce are shown from 1900 on. A list of sources and a subject index are provided. (Statistical Handbook Series).

Statistical Record of Older Americans. The Gale Group. • 1996. $109.00. Second edition. Includes income and pension data.

TRADE/PROFESSIONAL ASSOCIATIONS

American Association of Retired Persons. 601 E St., N.W., Washington, DC 20049. Phone: 800-424-3410 Fax: (202)434-2320 E-mail: member@aarp.org • URL: http://www.aarp.org.

Institute for Retired Professionals. New School for Social Research, 66 W. 12th St., Room 502, New York, NY 10011. Phone: (212)229-5683 or (212)229-5682 Fax: (212)229-5872 E-mail: markowim@newschool.edu • URL: http://www.newsschool.edu/centers/irp.

Mature Outlook. P.O. Box 9390, Des Moines, IA 50306-9519. Phone: 800-336-6330 Fax: (515)334-9247.

National Association of Retired Federal Employees. 606 N. Washington St., Alexandria, VA 22314. Phone: 800-627-3394 or (703)838-7760 Fax: (703)838-7785 E-mail: natlhq@narfe.org.

National Council of Senior Citizens. 8403 Colesville Rd., Suite 1200, Silver Springs, MD 20910. Phone: (301)578-8800 Fax: (301)578-8999 • URL: http://www.ncscinc.org.

National Interfaith Coalition on Aging. 409 Third St., S.W., Suite 200, Washington, DC 20024. Phone: (202)479-1200 Fax: (202)479-0735 E-mail: info@ncoa.org • URL: http://www.ncoa.org.

Score Association. c/o Service Corps of Retired Executives Association, 409 Third St., S.W. 6th Fl., Washington, DC 20024. Phone: 800-634-0245 or (202)205-6762 Fax: (202)205-7636 • URL: http://www.score.org.

OTHER SOURCES

How to Plan for a Secure Retirement. Elias Zuckerman and others. Consumer Reports Books. • 2000. $29.95. Covers pension plans, health insurance, estate planning, retirement communities, and related topics. (Consumer Reports Money Guide.).

Individual Retirement Plans Guide. CCH, Inc. • $230.00 per year. Looseleaf service. Monthly updates. Covers IRA plans (Individual Retirement Accounts), SEP plans (Simplified Employee Pensions), and Keogh plans (self-employed retirement accounts).

RETIREMENT AGE

See: EMPLOYMENT OF OLDER WORKERS

RETIREMENT COMMUNITIES

See also: NURSING HOMES

GENERAL WORKS

Continuing Care Retirement Communities. Sylvia Sherwood and others. Johns Hopkins University Press. • 1996. $40.00. Presents research based on a study of continuing care retirement communities and 2,000 residents of the communities.

Long-Term Care and Its Alternatives. Charles B. Inlander. People's Medical Society. • 1996. $16.95. Provides practical advice on the financing of long-term health care. The author is a consumer advocate and president of the People's Medical Society.

ABSTRACTS AND INDEXES

PAIS International in Print. Public Affairs Information Service, Inc. • Monthly. $650.00 per year; cumulations three times a year. Provides topical citations to the worldwide literature of public affairs, economics, demographics, sociology, and trade. Text in English; indexed materials in English, French, German, Italian, Portuguese and Spanish.

Readers' Guide to Periodical Literature. H. W. Wilson Co. • Monthly. $220.00 per year. CD-ROM edition, $1,495 per year, including annual cumulation. Indexes about 250 peridicals of general interest.

BIBLIOGRAPHIES

AAHSA Resource Catalog. American Association of Homes and Services for the Aging. • Annual. Free. Provides descriptions of material relating to managed care, senior housing, assisted living, continuing care retirement communities (CCRCs), nursing facilities, and home health care. Publishers are AAHSA and others.

CD-ROM DATABASES

PAIS on CD-ROM. Public Affairs Information Service, Inc. • Quarterly. $1,995.00 per year. Provides a CD-ROM version of the online service, *PAIS International*. Contains over 400,000 citations to the literature of contemporary social, political, and economic issues.

WILSONDISC: Readers' Guide to Periodical Literature. H. W. Wilson Co. • Monthly. $1,095.00 per year, including unlimited online access to *Readers' Guide to Periodical Literature* through WILSONLINE. Provides CD-ROM indexing of about 250 general interest periodicals. Covers 1983 to date. (*Readers' Guide Abstracts* also available on CD-ROM at $1,995 per year.).

DIRECTORIES

Consumers' Directory of Continuing Care Retirement Communities. American Association of Homes and Services for the Aging. • 1997. $30.00. Contains information on fees, services, and accreditation of about 500 U. S. retirement facilities providing lifetime housing, meals, and health care. Introductory text discusses factors to be considered in selecting a continuing care community.

Contemporary Long Term Care Fax Directory. Bill Communications, Inc. • Annual. $10.50. Lists approximately 900 manufacturers and suppliers of equipment, products, and services for retirement communities and nursing homes. Formerly *Contemporary Administration for Long-Term Care Product Directory and Buyer's Guide.*

Directory of Retirement Facilities. Dorland Healthcare Information. • Annual. $249.00. Lists more than 18,500 assisted living, congregate care, independent living, and continuing care facilities.

McKnight's Long-Term Care News Industry Guide. McKnight Medical Communications Co. • Annual. $49.95. Lists suppliers of goods and services for retirement homes and nursing homes.

Provider: LTC Buyers' Guide. American Health Care Association. • Annual. $10.00. Lists several hundred manufacturers and suppliers of products and services for long term care (LTC) facilities.

Retirement Communities in Florida: A Consumer's Guide and Directory to Service-Oriented Facilities. Mary L. Brooks. Pineapple Press, Inc. • 1993. $12.95.

FINANCIAL RATIOS

Financial Ratios and Trend Analysis of CCAC Accredited Communities. American Association of Homes and Services for the Aging. • 1997. $115.00. A joint project of AAHSA, Ziegler Securities, KPMG Peat Marwick LLP, and the Continuing Care Accreditation Commission (CCAC). Provides analysis of 12 frequently used ratios applied to audited financial statements from 171 accredited retirement communities.

HANDBOOKS AND MANUALS

The Continuing Care Retirement Community, a Guidebook for Consumers. American Association of Homes and Services for the Aging. • 1984. $6.95. Provieds information for the evaluation of continuing care retirement communities and nursing facilities, including services and finances.

How to Cover the Gaps in Medicare: Health Insurance and Long-Term Care Options for the Retired. Robert A. Gilmour. American Institute for Economic Research. • 2000. $5.00. 12th revised edition. Four parts: "The Medicare Quandry," "How to Protect Yourself Against the Medigap," "Long-Term Care Options", and "End-of-Life Decisions" (living wills). Includes discussions of long-term care insurance, retirement communities, and HMO Medicare insurance, (Economic Education Bulletin Series, No. 10).

ONLINE DATABASES

Newspaper and Periodical Abstracts. Bell & Howell Information and Learning. • Provides online coverage (citations and abstracts) of 25 major newspapers, 1,600 perodicals, and 70 TV programs. Covers business, economics, current affairs, health, fitness, sports, education, technology, government, consumer affairs, psychology, the arts, and the social sciences. Time period is 1986 to date, with daily updates. Inquire as to online cost and availability.

PAIS International. Public Affairs Information Service, Inc. • Corresponds to the former printed publications, *PAIS Bulletin* (1976-90) and *PAIS Foreign Language Index* (1972-90), and to the current *PAIS International in Print* (1991 to date). Covers economic, political, and sociological material appearing in periodicals, books, government documents, and other publications. Updating is monthly. Inquire as to online cost and availability.

Readers' Guide Abstracts Online. H. W. Wilson Co. • Indexes and abstracts general interest periodicals, 1983 to date. Weekly updates. Inquire as to online cost and availability.

PERIODICALS AND NEWSLETTERS

American Health Care Association: Provider. American Health Care Association. • Monthly. $48.00 per year. Formerly *American Health Care Association Journal.*

Assisted Living Success. Virgo Publishing, Inc. • Monthly. $55.00 per year. Edited for owners, operators, and managers of assisted living facilities.

Assisted Living Today. Assisted Living Federation of America. • Nine times a year. $30.00 per year. Covers the management, marketing, and financing of assisted living residences.

Balance. American College of Health Care Administrators. • Eight times a year. Free to members; non-members, $80.00 per year. Includes research papers and articles on the administration of long term care facilities. Formerly*Continnum.*

Contemporary Long Term Care. Bill Communications, Inc. • Monthly. $72.00 per year. Edited for the long term health care industry, including retirement centers with life care, continuing care communities, and nursing homes.

Housing the Elderly Report. Community Development Services, Inc. CD Publications. • Monthly. $197.00 per year. Newsletter. Edited for retirement communities, apartment projects, and nursing homes. Covers news relative to business and property management issues.

Journal of Housing for the Elderly. Haworth Press, Inc. • Semiannual. Individuals, $60.00 per year; institutions, $150.00 per year; libraries, $275.00 per year. Covers a wide variety of topics related to retirement communities and housing conditions for the elderly.

Ledger Quarterly: A Financial Review for Community Association Practitioners. Community Associations Institute. • Quarterly. Members, $40.00 per year; non-members, $67.00 per year. Newsletter. Provides current information on issues affecting the finances of condominium, cooperative, homeowner, apartment, and other community housing associations.

McKnight's Long Term Care News. McKnight Medical Communications, Inc. • Monthly. $44.95 per year. Edited for retirement housing directors and nursing home administrators.

Retirement Community Business. Great River Publishing, Inc. • Quarterly. $15.00 per year. Contains articles on management, marketing, legal concerns, development, construction, and other business-related topics.

Retirement Housing Business Report. C D Publications. • Monthly. $149.00 per year. Newsletter. Contains practical information on designing, developing, financing, managing, and marketing residential facilities for the elderly.

RESEARCH CENTERS AND INSTITUTES

American Affordable Housing Institute. Rutgers University, 33 Livingston Ave., New Brunswick, NJ 08901-2009. Phone: (732)932-6812 Fax: (732)932-7974 • Conducts studies related to housing affordability and availability, especially for first-time homebuyers. Also does research on meeting the housing needs of America's senior citizens.

Urban Land Institute. 1025 Thomas Jefferson Ave. N.W., Suite 500W, Washington, DC 20004. Phone: (202)624-7000 Fax: (202)624-7140 E-mail: rlevitt@uli.org • URL: http://www.uli.org • Studies urban land planning and the growth and development of urbanized areas, including central city problems, industrial development, community development, residential development, taxation, shopping centers, and the effects of development on the environment.

STATISTICS SOURCES

The CCRC Industry: 1996 Profile. American Association of Homes and Services for the Aging. • 1996. $15.00. Includes tables and charts. Provides data on demographics, fees, contracts, finances, and other aspects of continuing care retirement communities.

TRADE/PROFESSIONAL ASSOCIATIONS

American Association of Homes and Services for the Aging. 901 E. St., N.W., Suite 500, Washington, DC 20004-2011. Phone: (202)783-2242 Fax: (202)783-2255 E-mail: info@aahsa.org • URL: http://www.aahsa.org.

American College of Health Care Administrators. 325 S. Patrick St., Alexandria, VA 22314. Phone: 888-882-2422 or (703)739-7900 Fax: (703)739-7901 E-mail: info@achca.org • URL: http://www.achca.org.

Community Associations Institute. 1630 Duke St., Alexandria, VA 22314. Phone: (703)548-8600 Fax: (703)684-1581 • URL: http://www.caionline.org • Members are condominium associations, homeowners associations, builders, property managers, developers, and others concerned with the common facilities and services in condominiums, townhouses, planned unit developments, and other planned communities.

National Institute of Senior Housing. c/o National Council on the Aging, 409 Third St. S.W., 2nd Fl., Washington, DC 20024. Phone: (202)479-6654 Fax: (202)479-0735 E-mail: info@ncoa.org • URL: http://www.ncoa.org • Members are organizations and individuals concerned with the housing needs of older persons. Provides information on the development and management of housing suitable for the elderly.

OTHER SOURCES

Business & Company Resource Center. The Gale Group. • Fee-based Web site provides a wide range of business, industry, and specific company information. Access is offered to trade journal articles, market research data, insider trading activity, major shareholder data, corporate histories, emerging technology reports, corporate earnings estimates, press releases, and other sources. Provides detailed company profiles, industry overviews, and rankings. Offers integration of Predicasts PROMT, Newsletters ASAP, Investext Plus, Business Index ASAP, Brands and Their Companies, and other databases (many have full text).

The U. S. Market for Assisted-Living Facilities. MarketResearch.com. • 1997. $1,125.00. Market research report. Includes market demographics and estimates of future revenues. Facility operators such as Emeritus, Manor Care, and Marriott Senior Living are profiled.

RETIREMENT INCOME PLANS

See: 401(K) RETIREMENT PLANS; INDIVIDUAL RETIREMENT ACCOUNTS

REVIEWS

See: BOOK REVIEWS

RICE INDUSTRY

ABSTRACTS AND INDEXES

Biological and Agricultural Index. H.W. Wilson Co. • 11 times a year. Annual and quarterly cumulations. Service basis.

Rice Abstracts. Available from CABI Publishing North America. • Quarterly. $485.00 per year. Published in England by CABI Publishing. Provides worldwide coverage of the literature.

CD-ROM DATABASES

Food Science and Technology Abstracts [CD-ROM]. Available from SilverPlatter Information, Inc. • Quarterly. $3,700 per year. Produced by International Food Information Service (home page is http://www.ifis.org). Provides worldwide coverage on CD-ROM of the literature of food technology and production. Various types of publications are indexed, with abstracts, including about 1,800 periodicals. Time period is 1969 to date.

INTERNET DATABASES

Fedstats. Federal Interagency Council on Statistical Policy. Phone: (202)395-7254 • URL: http://www.fedstats.gov • Web site features an efficient search facility for full-text statistics produced by more than 70 federal agencies, including the Census Bureau, the Bureau of Economic Analysis, and the Bureau of Labor Statistics. Boolean searches can be made within one agency or for all agencies combined. Links are offered to international statistical bureaus, including the UN, IMF, OECD, UNESCO, Eurostat, and 20 individual countries. Fees: Free.

USDA. United States Department of Agriculture. Phone: (202)720-2791 E-mail: agsec@usda.gov • URL: http://www.usda.gov • The USDA home page has six sections: News and Information; What's New; About USDA; Agencies; Opportunities; Search and Help. Keyword searching is offered from the USDA home page and from various individual agency home pages. Agencies are the Economic Research Service, Agricultural Marketing Service, National Agricultural Statistics Service, National Agricultural Library, and about 12 others. Updating varies. Fees: Free.

ONLINE DATABASES

Biological and Agricultural Index Online. H. W. Wilson Co. • Indexes a wide variety of agricultural and biological periodicals, 1983 to date. Monthly updates. Inquire as to online cost and availability.

CAB Abstracts. CAB International North America. • Contains 46 specialized abstract collections covering over 10,000 journals and monographs in the areas of agriculture, horticulture, forest products, farm products, nutrition, dairy science, poultry, grains, animal health, entomology, etc. Time period is 1972 to date, with monthly updates. Inquire as to online cost and availability. *CAB Abstracts on CD-ROM* also available, with annual updating.

DRI U.S. Central Database. Data Products Division. • Provides more than 23,000 business, financial, demographic, economic, foreign trade, and industry-related time series for the U.S. Includes national income, population, retail-wholesale trade, price indexes, labor data, housing, industrial production, banking, interest rates, money supply, etc. Time period is generally 1947 to date (some data back to 1929). Updating varies. Inquire as to online cost and availability.

Food Science and Technology Abstracts [online]. IFIS North American Desk. • Produced by International Food Information Service. Provides about 500,000 online citations, with abstracts, to the international literature of food science, technology, commodities, engineering, and processing. Approximately 2,000 periodicals are covered. Time period is 1969 to date, with monthly updates. Inquire as to online cost and availability.

PERIODICALS AND NEWSLETTERS

Rice Farming. Vance Publishing Corp. • Six times a year. $30.00 per year.

Rice Journal: For Commerical Growers of Rice and Related Agribusiness. SpecComm International, Inc. • Six times a year. $15.00 per year.

STATISTICS SOURCES

Agricultural Statistics. Available from U. S. Government Printing Office. • Annual. Produced by the National Agricultural Statistics Service, U. S. Department of Agriculture. Provides a wide variety of statistical data relating to agricultural production, supplies, consumption, prices/price-supports, foreign trade, costs, and returns, as well as farm labor, loans, income, and population. In many cases, historical data is shown annually for 10 years. In addition to farm data, includes detailed fishery statistics.

Business Statistics of the United States. Courtenay M. Slater, editor. Bernan Associates. • 1999. $74.00. Fifth edition. Based on *Business Statistics*, formerly issue by the Bureau of Economic Analysis, U. S. Department of Commerce. Provides basic data for a wide variety of U. S. industries, services, and economic indicators. Most statistics are shown annually for 29 years and monthly for the most recent four years.

FAO Quarterly Bulletin of Statistics. Food and Agriculture Organization of the United Nations. Available from UNIPUB. • Quarterly. $20.00 per year. Provides international data on agricultural production, trade, and prices, covering the major commodities of many countries. Text in English, French, and Spanish. Formerly *FAO Monthly Bulletin of Statistics*.

FAO Rice Report. Food and Agriculture Organization of the United Nations. • Annual.

Survey of Current Business. Available from U. S. Government Printing Office. • Monthly. $49.00 per year. Issued by Bureau of Economic Analysis, U. S. Department of Commerce. Presents a wide variety of business and economic data.

WEFA Industrial Monitor. John Wiley and Sons, Inc. • Annual. $65.00. Prepared by industry analysts at WEFA, an economic forecasting and consulting firm (originally Wharton Econometric Forecasting Associates). Contains discussions of the outlook for major U. S. industries, with many 10-year forecasts (WEFA Web site is http://www.wefa.com).

World Trade Annual. United Nations Statistical Office. Walker and Co. • Annual. Prices vary.

TRADE/PROFESSIONAL ASSOCIATIONS

Rice Millers' Association. 4301 N. Fairfax Dr., Suite 305, Arlington, VA 22203. Phone: (703)351-8161 E-mail: riceinfo@tx.usarice.com • URL: http://www.usarice.com.

OTHER SOURCES

Major Food and Drink Companies of the World. Available from The Gale Group. • 2001. $855.00. Fourth edition. Two volumes. Published by Graham & Whiteside. Contains profiles and trade names for more than 9,000 important food and beverage companies in various countries. In addition to foods, includes both alcoholic and nonalcoholic drink products.

Rice: Origin, History, Technology, and Production. C. Wayne Smith and Robert Dilday, editors. John Wiley and Sons, Inc. • 2001. $195.00. (Wiley Series in Crop Science.).

Thomas Food and Beverage Market Place. Grey House Publishing. • Annual. $295.00. Three volumes. Contains more than 40,000 entries covering food companies, beverages, food equipment, warehouse companies, food brokers, wholesalers, importers, and exporters. Formerly *Thomas Food Industry Register*.

RIFLES

See: FIREARMS INDUSTRY

RISK MANAGEMENT

See also: INSURANCE

GENERAL WORKS

Fundamentals of Risk and Insurance. Emmett J. Vaughan and Therese J. Vaughan. John Wiley and Sons, Inc. • 1999. $99.95. Eighth edition.

The New Face of Credit Risk Management: Balancing Growth and Credit Quality in an Integrated Risk Management Environment. Charles B. Wendel. Robert Morris Associates. • 1999. $65.00. Contains "In-depth interviews with senior credit officers from five major financial institutions." Coverage includes modeling, scoring, and other technology related to the management of credit risk.

ABSTRACTS AND INDEXES

Insurance Periodicals Index. Specials Libraries Association, Insurance and Employees Benefits Div.

CCH/NILS Publishing Co. • Annual. $250.00. Compiled by the Insurance and Employee Benefits Div., Special Libraries Association. A yearly index of over 15,000 articles from about 35 insurance periodicals. Arrangement is by subject, with an index to authors.

DIRECTORIES

Thomson Derivatives and Risk Management Directory. Thomson Learning. • 1998. $297.00. Lists "over 9,000 contacts at more than 4,000 institutions.".

Who's Who in Risk Management. Underwriter Printing and Publishing Co. • Annual. $75.00. Contains specialized biographies of insurance buyers for large business and industrial firms throughout the U.S.

ENCYCLOPEDIAS AND DICTIONARIES

Rupp's Insurance and Risk Management Glossary. Richard V. Rupp. Available from CCH, Inc. • 1996. $35.00. Second edition. Published by NILS Publishing Co. Provides definitions of 6,400 insurance words and phrases. Includes a guide to acronyms and abbreviations.

HANDBOOKS AND MANUALS

Advanced Strategies in Financial Risk Management. Robert J. Schwartz and Clifford W. Smith, editors. Prentice Hall. • 1993. $65.00. Includes technical discussions of financial swaps and derivatives.

Analyzing Banking Risk: A Framework for Assessing Corporate Governance and Financial Risk Management. Hennie van Greuning and Sonja Brajovic Bratanovic. The World Bank, Office of the Publisher. • 1999. $100.00. Provides a guide to the analysis of banking risk for bank executives, bank supervisors, and risk analysts. Includes a CD-ROM with spreadsheet-based tables to assist in the interpretation and analysis of a bank's financial risk.

Corporate Financial Risk Management: Practical Techniques of Financial Engineering. Diane B. Wunnicke and others. John Wiley and Sons, Inc. • 1992. $65.00. Discusses such financial risk items as interest rates, commodity prices, and foreign exchange. (Finance Series).

Credit Risk Management: A Guide to Sound Business Decisions. H. A. Schaeffer. John Wiley and Sons, Inc. • 2000. $69.95. Covers corporate credit policies, credit authorization procedures, and analysis of business credit applications. Includes 12 "real-life" case studies.

Derivatives Handbook: Risk Management and Control. Robert J. Schwartz and Clifford W. Smith. John Wiley and Sons, Inc. • 1997. $79.95. Some chapter topics are legal risk, risk measurement, and risk oversight. Includes "Derivatives Debacles: Case Studies of Losses in DerivativesMarkets." A glossary of derivatives terminology is provided. (Wiley Financial Engineering Series).

Handbook of Derivative Instruments: Investment Research, Analysis, and Portfolio Applications. Atsuo Konishi and Ravi E. Dattatreya, editors. McGraw-Hill Professional. • 1996. $80.00. Second revised edition. Contains 41 chapters by various authors on all aspects of derivative securities, including such esoterica as "Inverse Floaters," "Positive Convexity," "Exotic Options," and "How to Use the Holes in Black-Scholes.".

Handbook of Equity Derivatives. Jack C. Francis and others, editors. John Wiley and Sons, Inc. • 1999. $95.00. Contains 27 chapters by various authors. Covers options (puts and calls), stock index futures, warrants, convertibles, over-the-counter options, swaps, legal issues, taxation, etc. (Financial Engineering Series).

Interest Rate Risk Measurement and Management. Sanjay K. Nawalkha and Donald R. Chambers, editors. Institutional Investor, Inc. • 1999. $95.00. Provides interest rate risk models for fixed-income derivatives and for investments by various kinds of financial institutions.

International Guide to Foreign Currency Management. Gary Shoup, editor. Fitzroy Dearborn Publishers. • 1998. $65.00. Written for corporate financial managers. Covers the market for currencies, price forecasting, exposure of various kinds, and risk management.

McGill's Life Insurance. Edward E. Graves, editor. The American College. • 1998. $71.00. Second edition. Contains chapters by various authors on diverse kinds of life insurance, as well as annuities, disability insurance, long-term care insurance, risk management, reinsurance, and other insurance topics. Originally by Dan M. McGill.

Over-the-Counter Derivatives Products: A Guide to Legal Risk Management and Documentation. Robert M. McLaughlin. McGraw-Hill Professional. • 1998. $75.00.

Understanding Financial Derivatives: How to Protect Your Investments. Donald Strassheim. McGraw-Hill Professional. • 1996. $40.00. Covers three basic risk management instruments: options, futures, and swaps. Includes advice on equity index options, financial futures contracts, and over-the-counter derivatives markets.

ONLINE DATABASES

I.I.I. Data Base Search. Insurance Information Institute. • Provides online citations and abstracts of insurance-related literature in magazines, newspapers, trade journals, and books. Emphasis is on property and casualty insurance issues, including highway safety, product safety, and environmental liability. Inquire as to online cost and availability.

PERIODICALS AND NEWSLETTERS

Business Insurance: News Magazine for Corporate Risk, Employee Benefit and Financial Executives. Crain Communications, Inc. • Weekly. $89.00 per year. Covers a wide variety of business insurance topics, including risk management, employee benefits, workers compensation, marine insurance, and casualty insurance.

Claims. IW Publications, Inc. • Monthly. $42.00 per year. Edited for insurance adjusters, risk managers, and claims professionals. Covers investigation, fraud, insurance law, and other claims-related topics.

Collections and Credit Risk: The Monthly Magazine for Collections and Credit Policy Professionals. Faulkner & Gray, Inc. • Monthly. $95.00 per year. Contains articles on the technology and business management of credit and collection functions. Includes coverage of bad debts, bankruptcy, and credit risk management.

F W's Corporate Finance: The Magazine fo the Financing Strategist. Financial World Partners. • Quarterly. $50.00 per year. Edited for financial executives of U. S. corporations. Covers leveraged buyouts, mergers, insurance, pensions, risk management, and other corporate topics. Includes case studies. Formerly *Corporate Finance*.

Journal of Risk Finance: The Convergence of Financial Products and Insurance. Institutional Investor. • Quarterly. $395.00 per year. Covers the field of customized risk management, including securitization, insurance, hedging, derivatives, and credit arbitrage.

Public Risk. Public Risk Management Association. • 10 times a year. $125.00 per year. Covers risk management for state and local governments, including various kinds of liabilities.

Risk and Insurance. LRP Publications. • Monthly. Price on application. Topics include risk management, workers' compensation, reinsurance, employee benefits, and managed care.

Risk Management. Risk and Insurance Management Society. Risk Management Society Publishing, Inc. • Monthly. $54.00 per year.

Treasury and Risk Management. CFO Publishing Corp. • 10 times a year. $64.00 per year. Covers risk management tools and techniques. Incorporates *Corporate Risk Management*.

RESEARCH CENTERS AND INSTITUTES

Center for Risk Management and Insurance Research. Georgia State University, P.O. Box 4036, Atlanta, GA 30302-4036. Phone: (404)651-4250 Fax: (404)651-1897 E-mail: rwklein@gsu.edu • URL: http://www.rmi.gsu.edu/.

TRADE/PROFESSIONAL ASSOCIATIONS

American Risk and Insurance Association. P.O. Box 3028, Malvern, PA 19355-0728. Phone: (610)640-1997 Fax: (610)725-1007 E-mail: aria@cpcuiia.org • URL: http://www.aria.org • Promotes education and research in the science of risk and insurance.

American Society of Pension Actuaries. 4245 N. Fairfax Dr., Suite 750, Arlington, VA 22203. Phone: (703)516-9300 Fax: (703)516-9308 E-mail: aspa@aspa.org • URL: http://www.aspa.org • Members are involved in the pension and insurance aspects of employee benefits. Includes an Insurance and Risk Management Committee, and sponsors an annual 401(k) Workshop.

Public Risk Management Association. 1815 N. Fort Meyer Dr., Ste. 1020, Arlington, VA 22209-1805. Phone: (703)528-7701 Fax: (703)528-7966 E-mail: info@primacentral.org • URL: http://www.primacentral.org • Members are state and local government officials concerned with risk management and public liabilities.

Risk and Insurance Management Society. 655 Third Ave., 2nd Fl., New York, NY 10017. Phone: (212)286-9292 Fax: (212)986-9716 • URL: http://www.rims.org.

OTHER SOURCES

Insurance Day. Available from Informa Publishing Group Ltd. • Three times a week. $440.00 per year. Published in the UK by Lloyd's List (http://www.lloydslist.com). A newspaper providing international coverage of property/casualty/liability insurance, reinsurance, and risk, with an emphasis on marine insurance.

Managing Financial Risk with Forwards, Futures, Options, and Swaps. American Management Association Extension Institute. • Looseleaf. $130.00. Self-study course. Emphasis is on practical explanations, examples, and problem solving. Quizzes and a case study are included.

Quantitative Finance. Available from IOP Publishing, Inc. • Bimonthly. $199.00 per year. Published in the UK by the Institute of Physics. A technical journal on the use of quantitative tools and applications in financial analysis and financial engineering. Covers such topics as portfolio theory, derivatives, asset allocation, return on assets, risk management, price volatility, financial econometrics, market anomalies, and trading systems.

ROAD MAPS

See: MAPS

ROAD MATERIALS

See: ASPHALT INDUSTRY; CONCRETE INDUSTRY

ROAD SIGNS

See: SIGNS AND SIGN BOARDS

ROADS AND HIGHWAYS

See also: TOLL ROADS

GENERAL WORKS

Principles of Highway Engineering and Traffic Analysis. Fred L. Mannering and Walter P. Kilareski. John Wiley and Sons, Inc. • 1997. $64.95. Second edition.

Road Maintenance and Rehabilitation: Funding and Allocation Strategies. OECD Publications and Information Center. • 1995. Discusses the allocation of public funds for highway maintenance.

ABSTRACTS AND INDEXES

Current Literature in Traffic and Transportation. Northwestern University, Transportation Library. • Quarterly. $25.00 per year.

NTIS Alerts: Transportation. National Technical Information Service. • Semimonthly. $210.00 per year. Provides descriptions of government-sponsored research reports and software, with ordering information. Covers air, marine, highway, inland waterway, pipeline, and railroad transportation. Formerly *Abstract Newsletter*.

BIBLIOGRAPHIES

Road Construction and Safety. Available from U. S. Government Printing Office. • Annual. Free. Issued by the Superintendent of Documents. A list of government publications on highway construction and traffic safety. Formerly *Highway Construction, Safety and Traffic.* (Subject Bibliography No. 3.).

DIRECTORIES

American Road and Transportation Association Transportation Officials and Engineers Directory. American Road and Transportation Builders Association. • Annual. Members, $90.00; non-members, $120.00. Lists over 5,000 administrative engineers and officials in federal, state, and county transportation agencies.

Constructor-AGC Directory of Membership and Services. Associated General Contractors of America. AGC Information, Inc. • Annual. $250.00. Membership is made up of contractors and suppliers for general construction. Formerly *Associated General Contractors of America National Directory.*

Public Works Manual. Public Works Journal Corp. • Annual. $45.00. Includes about 3,500 manufacturers and distributors of materials and equipment used in heavy construction. Special issue of (Public Works).

ENCYCLOPEDIAS AND DICTIONARIES

Macmillan Encyclopedia of Transportation. Available from The Gale Group. • 2000. $375.00. Six volumes. Published by Macmillan Reference USA. Covers the business, technology, and history of transportation on land, on water, in the air, and in space. Includes definitions, cross-references, and 200 color illustrations.

HANDBOOKS AND MANUALS

Standard Highway Signs, as Specified in the Manual on Uniform Traffic Control Devices. Available from U. S. Government Printing Office. • Looseleaf. $70.00. Issued by the U. S. Department of Transportation (http://www.dot.gov). Includes basic manual, with updates for an indeterminate period. Contains illustrations of typical standard signs approved for use on streets and highways, and provides information on dimensions and placement of symbols.

INTERNET DATABASES

Fedstats. Federal Interagency Council on Statistical Policy. Phone: (202)395-7254 • URL: http://www.fedstats.gov • Web site features an efficient search facility for full-text statistics produced by more than 70 federal agencies, including the Census Bureau, the Bureau of Economic Analysis, and the Bureau of Labor Statistics. Boolean searches can be made within one agency or for all agencies combined. Links are offered to international statistical bureaus, including the UN, IMF, OECD, UNESCO, Eurostat, and 20 individual countries. Fees: Free.

ONLINE DATABASES

DRI U.S. Central Database. Data Products Division. • Provides more than 23,000 business, financial, demographic, economic, foreign trade, and industry-related time series for the U.S. Includes national income, population, retail-wholesale trade, price indexes, labor data, housing, industrial production, banking, interest rates, money supply, etc. Time period is generally 1947 to date (some data back to 1929). Updating varies. Inquire as to online cost and availability.

PAIS International. Public Affairs Information Service, Inc. • Corresponds to the former printed publications, *PAIS Bulletin* (1976-90) and *PAIS Foreign Language Index* (1972-90), and to the current *PAIS International in Print* (1991 to date). Covers economic, political, and sociological material appearing in periodicals, books, government documents, and other publications. Updating is monthly. Inquire as to online cost and availability.

TRIS: Transportation Research Information Service. National Research Council. • Contains abstracts and citations to a wide range of transportation literature, 1968 to present, with monthly updates. Includes references to the literature of air transportation, highways, ships and shipping, railroads, trucking, and urban mass transportation. Formerly *TRIS-ON-LINE.* Inquire as to online cost and availability.

PERIODICALS AND NEWSLETTERS

Better Roads. Gras Industries, Inc. • Monthly. $20.00 per year.

ENR Connecting the Industry Worldwide (Engineering News-Record). McGraw-Hill. • Weekly. $74.00 per year.

Highway Financing and Construction: State Capitals. Wakeman-Walworth, Inc. • Weekly. $345.00 per year. Newsletter. Formerly *From the State Capitals: Highway Financing and Construction.*

Public Roads: A Journal of Highway Research and Development. Available from U.S. Government Printing Office. • Bimonthly. $18.00 per year.

Roads and Bridges. Scranton Gillette Communications, Inc. • Monthly. $35.00 per year. Provides information on the planning/design, administration/management, engineering and contract execution for the road and bridge industry.

Transportation Builder. American Road and Transportation Builders Association. Heartland Custom Publishers Group. • Monthly. $50.00 per year.

RESEARCH CENTERS AND INSTITUTES

Center for Transportation Research. University of Texas at Austin, 3208 Red River, Suite 200, Austin, TX 78705-2650. Phone: (512)232-3100 Fax: (512)232-3151 E-mail: bfmccullough@mail.utexas.edu • URL: http://www.utexas.edu/depts/ctr/.

Center for Transportation Studies. Massachusetts Institute of Technology. 77 Massachusetts Ave. Room 1-235, Cambridge, MA 02139. Phone: (617)253-5320 Fax: (617)253-4560 E-mail: ctsmail@mit.edu • URL: http://www.web.mit.edu/cts/www/.

Texas Transportation Institute. Texas A & M University System, College Station, TX 77843-3135. Phone: (979)845-8552 Fax: (979)845-9356 E-mail: h.hrichardson@tamu.edu • URL: http://tti.tamu.edu • Concerned with all forms and modes of transportation. Research areas include transportation economics, highway construction, traffic safety, public transportation, and highway engineering.

Transportation Center. Northwestern University, 600 Foster, Evanston, IL 60208-4055. Phone: (847)491-7287 Fax: (847)491-3090 E-mail: a-gellman@northwestern.edu • URL: http://www.nutcweb.tpc.nwu.edu.

Transportation Research Institute. University of Michigan, 2901 Baxter Rd., Ann Arbor, MI 48109-2150. Phone: (734)764-6504 Fax: (734)936-1081 E-mail: umtri@umich.edu • URL: http://www.umtri.umich.edu • Research areas include highway safety, transportation systems, and shipbuilding.

STATISTICS SOURCES

Business Statistics of the United States. Courtenay M. Slater, editor. Bernan Associates. • 1999. $74.00. Fifth edition. Based on *Business Statistics*, formerly issue by the Bureau of Economic Analysis, U. S. Department of Commerce. Provides basic data for a wide variety of U. S. industries, services, and economic indicators. Most statistics are shown annually for 29 years and monthly for the most recent four years.

Highway Statistics. Federal Highway Administration, U.S. Department of Transportation. Available from U.S. Government Printing Office. • Annual. $26.00.

Survey of Current Business. Available from U. S. Government Printing Office. • Monthly. $49.00 per year. Issued by Bureau of Economic Analysis, U. S. Department of Commerce. Presents a wide variety of business and economic data.

Transportation Statistics Annual Report. Available from U. S. Government Printing Office. • Annual. $21.00. Issued by the U. S. Bureau of Transportation Statistics, Transportation Department (http://www.bts.gov). Summarizes national data for various forms of transportation, including airlines, railroads, and motor vehicles. Information on the use of roads and highways is included.

TRADE/PROFESSIONAL ASSOCIATIONS

American Association of State Highway and Transportation Officials. 444 N. Capitol St., N.W., Suite 249, Washington, DC 20001. Phone: (202)624-5800 Fax: (202)624-5806 • URL: http://www.aashto.org.

American Concrete Pavement Association. 5420 Old Orchard Rd., Suite A100, Skokie, IL 60077. Phone: (847)966-2272 Fax: (847)966-9970 E-mail: webmaster@pavement.com • URL: http://www.pavement.com.

American Highway Users Alliance. 1776 Massachusetts Ave., N.W., Washington, DC 20036. Phone: 888-499-8777 or (202)857-1200 Fax: (202)857-1220 E-mail: gohighway@aol.com • URL: http://www.highways.org.

American Road and Transportation Builders Association. The ARTBA Bldg., 1010 Massachusetts Ave., N.W., Washington, DC 20001. Phone: (202)289-4434 Fax: (202)289-4435 E-mail: artba@aol.com • URL: http://www.artba.org • Promotes on-the-job training programs.

Associated General Contractors of America: Highway Division. 333 John Carlyle St., Ste. 200, Alexandria, VA 22314. Phone: (703)548-3118 Fax: (703)548-3119 E-mail: info@aednet.org • URL: http://www.agc.org.

International Road Federation. 1010 Massachusetts Ave., N.W., Suite 410, Washington, DC 20001. Phone: (202)371-5544 Fax: (202)371-5565 E-mail: info@irfnet.org • A federation of associations promoting highway improvement.

National Asphalt Pavement Association. NAPA Bldg., 5100 Forbes Blvd., Lanham, MD 20706-4413. Phone: 888-468-6499 or (301)731-4748 Fax: (301)731-4621 E-mail: napa@hotmix.org • URL: http://www.hotmix.org.

The Road Information Program. 1726 M St., N.W., Ste. 401, Washington, DC 20036-4521. Phone: (202)466-6706 Fax: (202)785-4722 E-mail: trip@trip.org • URL: http://www.tripnet.org • Public relations for the highway construction industry.

ROADS, TOLL

See: TOLL ROADS

ROBOTS

See also: ARTIFICIAL INTELLIGENCE; AUTOMATION; MACHINE VISION

GENERAL WORKS

Foundations of Robotics: Analysis and Control. Tsuneo Yoshikawa. MIT Press. • 1990. $47.50.

Fundamentals of Robotics: Analysis and Control. Robert J. Schilling. Prentice Hall. • 1990. $60.00.

ABSTRACTS AND INDEXES

Applied Science and Technology Index. H. W. Wilson Co. • 11 times a year. Quarterly and annual cumulations. Service basis for print edition; CD-ROM edition, $1,495.00 per year. Indexes a wide variety of English language technical, industrial, and engineering periodicals.

Current Contents: Engineering, Computing and Technology. Institute for Scientific Information. • Weekly. $730.00 per year. Reproductions of contents pages of technical journals. Includes *Author Index, Address Directory, Current Book Contents* and *Title Word Index.* Formerly *Current Contents: Engineering, Technology and Applied Sciences.*

Engineering Index Monthly: Abstracting and Indexing Services Covering Sources of the World's Engineering Literature. Engineering Information, Inc. • Monthly. $2,300.00 per year. Provides indexing and abstracting of the world's engineering and technical literature.

Key Abstracts: Factory Automation. Available from INSPEC, Inc. • Monthly. $240.00 per year. Provides international coverage of journal and proceedings literature, including publications on CAD/CAM, materials handling, robotics, and factory management. Published in England by the Institution of Electrical Engineers (IEE).

Key Abstracts: Machine Vision. Available from INSPEC, Inc. • Monthly. $240.00 per year. Provides international coverage of journal and proceedings literature on optical noncontact sensing. Published in England by the Institution of Electrical Engineers (IEE).

Key Abstracts: Robotics and Control. Available from INSPEC, Inc. • Monthly. $240.00 per year. Provides international coverage of journal and proceedings literature. Published in England by the Institution of Electrical Engineers (IEE).

NTIS Alerts: Manufacturing Technology. National Technical Information Service. • Semimonthly. $265.00 per year. Provides descriptions of government-sponsored research reports and software, with ordering information. Covers computer-aided design and manufacturing (CAD/CAM), engineering materials, quality control, machine tools, robots, lasers, productivity, and related subjects. Formerly *Abstract Newsletter.*

Science Citation Index. Institute for Scientific Information. • Bimonthly. $15,020.00 per year. Annual cumulation. Includes *Source Index, Citation Index, Permuterm Subject Index,* and *Corporate Index.*

ALMANACS AND YEARBOOKS

Robots and Manufacturing: Recent Trends in Research, Education, and Applications. American Society of Mechanical Engineers. • Biennial. $189.00.

BIBLIOGRAPHIES

Automation. Available from U. S. Government Printing Office. • Annual. Free. Issued by the Superintendent of Documents. A list of government publications on automation, computers, and related topics. Formerly *Computers and Data Processing.* (Subject Bibliography No. 51.).

CD-ROM DATABASES

COMPENDEX PLUS [CD-ROM]. Engineering Information, Inc. • Quarterly. $3,450.00 per year. Provides CD-ROM indexing and abstracting of the world's engineering and technical information appearing in journals, reports, books, and proceedings, 1985 to date.

DIRECTORIES

Corptech Directory of Technology Companies. Corporate Technology Information Services, Inc. c/o Eileen Kennedy. • Annual. $795.00. Four volumes. Profiles of more than 45,000 manufacturers and developers of high technology products. Includes private companies, publicly-held corporations, and subsidiaries. Formerly *Corporate Technology Directory.*

ENCYCLOPEDIAS AND DICTIONARIES

Concise International Encyclopedia of Robotics: Applications and Automation. Richard C. Dorf and Shimon Y. Nof, editors. John Wiley and Sons, Inc. • 1990. $300.00.

HANDBOOKS AND MANUALS

Assembly Buyer's Guide. Cahners Business Information. • Annual. $25.00. Lists manufacturers and suppliers of equipment relating to assembly automation, fasteners, adhesives, robotics, and power tools.

Robot Technology and Applications. Ulrich Rembold, editor. Marcel Dekker, Inc. • 1990. $230.00. (Manufacturing Engineering Material Processing Series).

ONLINE DATABASES

Applied Science and Technology Index Online. H. W. Wilson Co. • Provides online indexing of 400 major scientific, technical, industrial, and engineering periodicals. Time period is 1983 to date. Monthly updates. Inquire as to online cost and availability.

COMPENDEX PLUS. Engineering Information, Inc. • Provides online indexing and abstracting of the world's engineering and technical information appearing in journals, reports, books, and proceedings. Time period is 1970 to date, with weekly updates. Inquire as to online cost and availability.

Globalbase. The Gale Group. • Provides more than one million online summaries of business, industrial, and economic news reports from more than 1,000 publications worldwide. Covers a wide range of material appearing in international trade journals, professional magazines, and newspapers. Time period is 1984 to date, with weekly updates. Inquire as to online cost and availability.

PROMT: Predicasts Overview of Markets and Technology. The Gale Group. • Companies, products, applied technologies and markets. U.S. and international literature coverage, 1972 to date. Inquire as to online cost and availability. Provides abstracts from more than 1,600 publications. Weekly updates.

Scisearch. Institute for Scientific Information. • Broad, multidisciplinary index to the literature of science and technology, 1974 to present. Inquire as to online cost and availability. Coverage of literature is worldwide, with weekly updates.

PERIODICALS AND NEWSLETTERS

Advanced Manufacturing Technology: Monthly Report. Technical Insights. • Monthly. $695.00 per year. Newsletter. Covers technological developments relating to robotics, computer graphics, automation, computer-integrated manufacturing, and machining.

International Journal of Robotics Research. Sage Publications, Inc. • Monthly. Individuals, $130.00 per year; institutions, $810.00 per year.

Journal of Robotic Systems. John Wiley and Sons, Inc., Journals Div. • Monthly. $1,920.00 per year. An international journal presenting high-level, scholarly discussions and case studies on automation, taskware design and implementation of robot systems. Text in English and Japanese; summaries in English and Japanese.

Robotics and Computer-Integrated Manufacturing: An International Journal. Elsevier Science. • Bimonthly. $900.00 per year.

RESEARCH CENTERS AND INSTITUTES

Center for Automation Research. University of Maryland, College Park, MD 20742-3275. Phone: (301)405-4526 Fax: (301)314-9115 E-mail: ar@cfar.umd.edu • URL: http://www.cfar.umd.edu/.

Center for Intelligent Machines and Robotics. University of Florida, 300 MEB, Gainesville, FL 32611. Phone: (352)392-0814 Fax: (352)392-1071 E-mail: cimar@cimar.me.ufl.edu • URL: http://ww.me.ufl.edu/cimar/.

Center for Research in Computing Technology. Harvard University, Pierce Hall, 29 Oxford St., Cambridge, MA 02138. Phone: (617)495-2832 Fax: (617)495-9837 E-mail: cheatham@das.harvard.edu • URL: http://www.das.harvard.edu/cs.grafs.html • Conducts research in computer vision, robotics, artificial intelligence, systems programming, programming languages, operating systems, networks, graphics, database management systems, and telecommunications.

General Robotics, Automation, Sensing and Perception (GRASP). University of Pennsylvania, 3401 Walnut St., GRASP Lab., Room 301C, Philadelphia, PA 19104-6228. Phone: (215)898-5814 Fax: (215)573-2048 E-mail: betsy@central.cis.upenn.edu • URL: http://www.cis.upenn.edu/~grasp/home.html.

Imaging and Computer Vision Center-Computer Vision Center for Vertebrate Brain Mapping. Drexel University, 32nd and Market Sts., Room 110-7, Philadelphia, PA 19104. Phone: (215)895-2279 Fax: (215)895-4987 • URL: http://www.drexel.icvc.com • Fields of research include computer vision, robot vision, and expert systems.

Robot Vision Laboratory. Purdue University, School of Electrical and Computer Engineering, West Lafayette, IN 47907-1285. Phone: (765)494-3456

Fax: (765)494-6440 E-mail: kak@ecn.purdue.edu • URL: http://www.ecn.purdue.edu.

Robotics and Automation Laboratory. University of Toronto, Department of Mechanical Engineering, Five King's College Rd., Toronto, ON, Canada M5S 3G8. Phone: (416)978-6808 Fax: (416)978-5745 E-mail: golden@mie.utoronto.ca.

Robotics Institute. Carnegie Mellon University, 500 Forbes Ave., Pittsburgh, PA 15213. Phone: (412)268-3818 Fax: (412)268-5570 E-mail: tk@cs.cmu.edu • URL: http://www.cs.cmu.edu.

Robotics Research Center. University of Rhode Island, Kirk Bldg., Kingston, RI 02881. Phone: (401)874-2514 Fax: (401)874-2355 E-mail: datseris@egr.uri.edu.

Stanford Integrated Manufacturing Association. Stanford University, Bldg. 02-530, Stanford, CA 94305-3036. Phone: (650)723-9038 Fax: (650)723-5034 E-mail: susan.hansen@stanford.edu • URL: http://www.sima.stanford.edu/ • Consists of four research centers: Center for Automation and Manufacturing Science, Center for Design Research, Center for Materials Formability and Processing Science, and Center for Teaching and Research in Integrated Manufacturing Systems. Research fields include automation, robotics, intelligent systems, computer vision, design in manufacturing, materials science, composite materials, and ceramics.

STATISTICS SOURCES

U. S. Industry and Trade Outlook: The McGraw-Hill Companies and the U.S. Department of Commerce/ International Trade Administration. Datapso Research Corp. • Annual. $69.95. Produced by the International Trade Administration, U. S. Department of Commerce, in a "public-private" partnership with DRI/McGraw-Hill and Standard & Poor's. Provides basic data, outlook for the current year, and "Long-Term Prospects" (five-year projections) for a wide variety of products and services. Includes high technology industries. Formerly *U. S. Industrial Outlook.*

World Robotics: Statistics, Market Analysis, Forecasts, Case Studies, and Profitability of Robot Investment. United Nations Publications. • Annual. $120.00. Presents international data on industrial robots and service robots. Statistical tables allow uniform comparison of numbers for 20 countries, broken down by type of application, type of robot, and other variables.

TRADE/PROFESSIONAL ASSOCIATIONS

American Automatic Control Council. Dept. of EECS, Northwestern University, 2145 Sheridan Rd., Evanston, IL 60208-3118. Phone: (847)491-8175 Fax: (847)491-4455 E-mail: acc@ece.nwu.edu.

Association for Unmanned Vehicle Systems. 1200 19th St., N.W., No. 300, Washington, DC 20036-2422. Phone: (202)857-1899 Fax: (202)223-4579 E-mail: auvsi@dc.erols.com • URL: http://www.auvsi.org/auvsicc • Concerned with the development of unmanned systems and robotics technologies.

IEEE Computer Society. 1730 Massachusetts Ave., N. W., Washington, DC 20036. Phone: (202)371-0101 Fax: (202)728-9614 E-mail: csinfo@computer.org • URL: http://www.computer.org • A society of the Institute of Electrical and Electronics Engineers. Said to be the world's largest organization of computer professionals. Some of the specific committees are: Computer Communications; Computer Graphics; Computers in Education; Design Automation; Office Automation; Personal Computing; Robotics; Security and Privacy; Software Engineering.

Robotic Industries Association. P.O. Box 3724, Ann Arbor, MI 48106. Phone: (734)994-6088 Fax: (734)994-3338 E-mail: ria@robotics.org • URL: http://www.robotics.org • Members are manufacturers and others concerned with the development and utilization of robot technology.

Robotics International of the Society of Manufacturing Engineers. P.O. Box 930, Dearborn, MI 48121-0930. Phone: (313)271-1500 Fax: (313)271-2861 • URL: http://www.sme.org/ri • Affiliated with the Society of Manufacturing Engineers.

OTHER SOURCES

Assembly. Cahners Business Information. • Monthly. $68.00 per year. Covers assembly, fastening, and joining systems. Includes information on automation and robotics.

ROCK PRODUCTS

See: QUARRYING

ROCKET INDUSTRY

See also: AEROSPACE INDUSTRY

GENERAL WORKS

History of Rocketry and Astronautics. American Astronautical Society. Available from Univelt, Inc. • Various volumes and prices. Covers the history of rocketry and astronautics since 1880. Prices vary. (AAS History Series).

ABSTRACTS AND INDEXES

International Aerospace Abstracts. American Institute of Aeronautics and Astronautics, Inc. • Monthly. $1,625.00 per year.

ALMANACS AND YEARBOOKS

Progress in Aerospace Sciences: An International Journal. Elsevier Science. • Bimonthly. $1,257.00 per year. Text in English, French and German.

DIRECTORIES

World Aviation Directory. McGraw-Hill Aviation Week Group. • Semiannual. $225.00 per year. Two volumes. Lists aviation, aerospace, and missile manufacturers. Includes *World Aviation Directory Buyer's Guide.*

HANDBOOKS AND MANUALS

Rocket Propulsion Elements: An Introduction to the Engineering of Rockets. George P. Sutton. John Wiley and Sons, Inc. • 2000. $89.95. Seventh edition.

PERIODICALS AND NEWSLETTERS

Aerospace Daily. Aviation Week Newsletter. McGraw-Hill. • Five times per week. $1,595.00 per year.

Aviation Week and Space Technology. McGraw-Hill Aviation Week Group. • Monthly. $89.00 per year.

Journal of Astronautical Sciences. American Astronautical Society. • Quarterly.Institutions, $155.00 per year.

Journal of Spacecraft and Rockets: Devoted to Astronautical Science and Technology. American Institute of Aeronautics and Astronautics, Inc. • Bimonthly. Members, $45.00 per year; non-members, $165.00 per year; institutions, $330.00 per year.

Space Times. American Astronautical Society. • Bimonthly. Institutions, $80.00 per year. Covers current developments in astronautics.

RESEARCH CENTERS AND INSTITUTES

Jet Propulsion Laboratory. 4800 Oak Grove Dr., Bldg. 180, Room 904, Pasadena, CA 91109. Phone: (818)354-3405 Fax: (818)393-4218.

Joint Institute for Advancement of Flight Sciences. George Washington University, NASA Langley Research Center, Mail Stop 269, Hampton, VA 23681-2199. Phone: (757)864-1982 Fax: (757)864-5894 E-mail: jiafs@seas.gwu.edu • URL: http://www.seas.gwu.edu/seas/jiafs • Conducts research in aeronautics, astronautics, and acoustics (flight-produced noise).

STATISTICS SOURCES

Aerospace Facts and Figures. Aerospace Industries Association of America. • Annual. $35.00. Includes financial data for the aerospace industries.

U. S. Industry and Trade Outlook: The McGraw-Hill Companies and the U.S. Department of Commerce/ International Trade Administration. Datapso Research Corp. • Annual. $69.95. Produced by the International Trade Administration, U. S. Department of Commerce, in a "public-private" partnership with DRI/McGraw-Hill and Standard & Poor's. Provides basic data, outlook for the current year, and "Long-Term Prospects" (five-year projections) for a wide variety of products and services. Includes high technology industries. Formerly *U. S. Industrial Outlook.*

TRADE/PROFESSIONAL ASSOCIATIONS

Aerospace Education Foundation. 1501 Lee Highway, Arlington, VA 22209-1198. Phone: 800-727-3337 or (703)247-5839 Fax: (703)247-5853 E-mail: aefstaff@aef.org • URL: http://www.aef.org.

Aerospace Industries Association of America. 1250 Eye St., N.W., Washington, DC 20005. Phone: (202)371-8400 Fax: (202)371-8470 E-mail: aia@aia-aerospace.org • URL: http://www.aia-aerospace.org.

American Astronautical Society. 6352 Rolling Mill Place, Suite 102, Springfield, VA 22152-2354. Phone: (703)866-0020 Fax: (703)866-3526 E-mail: aas@astronautical.org • URL: http://www.astronautical.org.

National Association of Rocketry. P.O. Box 177, Altoona, WI 54720. Phone: 800-262-4872 or (715)832-1946 Fax: (715)832-6432 E-mail: nar-hq@nar.org • URL: http://www.nar.org • Model rockets.

OTHER SOURCES

Advances in the Astronautical Sciences. American Astronautical Society. Available from Univelt, Inc. • Price varies. Volumes in this series cover the proceedings of various astronautical conferences and symposia.

ROLLER BEARINGS

See: BEARINGS AND BALL BEARINGS

ROOFING INDUSTRY

See also: BUILDING INDUSTRY; BUILDING MATERIALS INDUSTRY

DIRECTORIES

Building Supply Home Centers Retail Giants Report. Cahners Business Information. • Annual. $30.00. Lists major retailers of a wide variety of building and home improvement materials, products, fixtures, accessories, equipment, and tools.

FINANCIAL RATIOS

Annual Statement Studies. Robert Morris Associates: The Association of Lending and Credit Risk Professiona. • Annual. Free to members; non-members, $140.00. Median and quartile financial ratios are given for over 400 kinds of manufacturing, wholesale, retail, construction, and consumer finance establishments. Data is sorted by both asset size and sales volume. Includes a clearly written "Definition of Ratios" and an alphabetical industry index.

HANDBOOKS AND MANUALS

Roof Framing. Marshall Gross. Craftsman Book Co. • 1989. $22.00. Revised edition. (Home Craftsman Books).

PERIODICALS AND NEWSLETTERS

Building Material Retailer. National Lumber and Building Material Dealers Association. • Monthly. $25.00 per year. Includes special feature issues on hand and power tools, lumber, roofing, kitchens, flooring, windows and doors, and insulation.

RSI (Roofing, Siding, Insulation). Advanstar Communications, Inc. • Monthly. $39.00 per year.

STATISTICS SOURCES

Census of Construction Industries: Roofing Siding and Sheet Metal Work Special Trade Contractors. U.S. Bureau of the Census. • Quinquennial.

TRADE/PROFESSIONAL ASSOCIATIONS

Asphalt Roofing Manufacturers Association. 4041 Powder Mill Rd., Suite 404, Bettsville, MD 20705-3106. Phone: (301)348-2002 Fax: (301)348-2020.

National Roofing Contractors Association. 10255 W. Higgins Rd., Suite 600, Rosemont, IL 60018-5607. Phone: 800-323-9545 or (847)299-9070 Fax: (847)299-1183 E-mail: nrca@nrca.net • URL: http://www.nrca.net.

ROPE AND TWINE INDUSTRY

DIRECTORIES

Davison's Textile Blue Book. Davison Publishing Co. • Annual. $165.00. Over 8,400 companies in the textile industry in the United States, Canada, and Mexico, including about 4,400 textile plants.

TRADE/PROFESSIONAL ASSOCIATIONS

Cordage Institute. 994 Old Eagle School Rd., Ste. 109, Wayne, PA 19087-1866. Phone: (610)971-4854 Fax: (610)971-4859 E-mail: ropecord@aol.com • URL: http://www.ropecord.com/.

Hard Fibres Association. c/o Metcalf Agency, P.O. Box 250, Skaneateles, NY 13152. Phone: (315)685-5088 Fax: (315)685-5077 E-mail: pfmetcalf@aol.com.

RUBBER AND RUBBER GOODS INDUSTRIES

See also: PLASTICS INDUSTRY; TIRE INDUSTRY

GENERAL WORKS

Rubber Technology. Maurice Morton. Chapman and Hall. • 1987. $62.95. Third edition.

ABSTRACTS AND INDEXES

CPI Digest: Key to World Literature Serving the Coatings, Plastics, Fibers, Adhesives, and Related Industries (Chemical Process Industries). CPI Information Services. • Monthly. $397.00 per year. Abstracts of business and technical articles for polymer-based, chemical process industries. Includes a monthly list of relevant U. S. patents. International coverage.

RAPRA Abstracts. RAPRA Technology Ltd. • Monthly. $2,465.00 per year. Up-to-date survey of current international information relevant to the rubber, plastics and associated industries.

DIRECTORIES

Global Polyurethane Directory and Buyer's Guide. Crain Communications, Inc. • Annual. $30.00. List of over 1,000 rubber product manufacturers and 800 suppliers of equipment, services, and materials; list of trade associations. Formerly Rubber and Plastic News-Rubbicana Directory and Buyer's Guide.

Rubber Red Book: Directory of the Rubber Industry. Intertec Publishing. • Annual. $89.95. Lists manufacturers and suppliers of rubber goods in U.S., Puerto Rico and Canada.

Rubber World Blue Book of Materials, Compounding Ingredients and Machinery for Rubber. Don R. Smith, editor. Lippincott and Peto, Inc. • Annual. $111.00.

INTERNET DATABASES

Fedstats. Federal Interagency Council on Statistical Policy. Phone: (202)395-7254 • URL: http://www.fedstats.gov • Web site features an efficient search facility for full-text statistics produced by more than 70 federal agencies, including the Census Bureau, the Bureau of Economic Analysis, and the Bureau of Labor Statistics. Boolean searches can be made within one agency or for all agencies combined. Links are offered to international statistical bureaus, including the UN, IMF, OECD, UNESCO, Eurostat, and 20 individual countries. Fees: Free.

ONLINE DATABASES

Business and Industry. Responsive Database Services, Inc. • Contains online citations, abstracts, and selected fulltext from more than 1,000 trade journals, newspapers, and other publications. Provides general coverage of both manufacturing and service industries, including marketing, production, industry trends, key events, and information on specific companies. Time span is 1994 to date. Daily updates. Inquire as to online cost and availability. (Also available in a CD-ROM version.).

DRI U.S. Central Database. Data Products Division. • Provides more than 23,000 business, financial, demographic, economic, foreign trade, and industry-related time series for the U.S. Includes national income, population, retail-wholesale trade, price indexes, labor data, housing, industrial production, banking, interest rates, money supply, etc. Time period is generally 1947 to date (some data back to 1929). Updating varies. Inquire as to online cost and availability.

Tablebase. Responsive Database Services, Inc. • Provides online numerical tabular data from a wide variety of business, organization, and government sources, including 900 trade journals. Includes industry and individual company statistics relating to products, market share, sales forecasts, production, exports, market trends, etc. Time span is 1997 to date. Weekly updates. Inquire as to online cost and availability. (Also available in a CD-ROM version.).

PERIODICALS AND NEWSLETTERS

Rubber and Plastics News: The Rubber Industry's International Newspaper. Crain Communications, Inc. • Biweekly. $74.00 per year. Written for rubber product manufacturers.

Rubber Chemistry and Technology. American Chemical Society, Rubber Div. • Five times a year. $95.00 per year.

Rubber World. Lippincott and Peto, Inc. • 16 times a year. $29.00 per year.

RESEARCH CENTERS AND INSTITUTES

Tlargi Rubber Technology Foundation. University of Southern California. Los Angeles, CA 90089-1211. Phone: (213)740-2225 Fax: (213)740-8053 E-mail: salove@almaak.usc.edu.

STATISTICS SOURCES

Annual Survey of Manufactures. Available from U. S. Government Printing Office. • Annual. Prices vary. Issued by the U. S. Census Bureau as an interim update to the *Census of Manufactures.* Includes data on number of manufacturing establishments in various industries, employment, labor costs, value of shipments, capital expenditures, inventories, energy costs, and assets. (See also Census Bureau home page, http://www.census.gov/.).

Business Statistics of the United States. Courtenay M. Slater, editor. Bernan Associates. • 1999. $74.00. Fifth edition. Based on *Business Statistics*, formerly issue by the Bureau of Economic Analysis, U. S. Department of Commerce. Provides basic data for a wide variety of U. S. industries, services, and economic indicators. Most statistics are shown annually for 29 years and monthly for the most recent four years.

Encyclopedia of American Industries. The Gale Group. • 1998. $560.00. Second edition. Two volumes. $280.00 per volume. Volume one is *Manufacturing Industries* and volume two is *Service and Non-Manufacturing Industries.* Provides the history, development, and recent status of approximately 1,000 industries. Includes statistical graphs, with industry and general indexes.

Rubber Statistical Bulletin. International Rubber Study Group. • Monthly. Members, $346.00 per year; non-members, $327.00 per year.

Survey of Current Business. Available from U. S. Government Printing Office. • Monthly. $49.00 per year. Issued by Bureau of Economic Analysis, U. S. Department of Commerce. Presents a wide variety of business and economic data.

TRADE/PROFESSIONAL ASSOCIATIONS

International Institute of Synthetic Rubber Producers. 2077 S. Gessner Rd., Suite 133, Houston, TX 77063-1123. Phone: (713)783-7511 Fax: (713)783-7253 E-mail: info@iisrp.com • URL: http://www.iisrp.com.

Rubber Manufacturers Association. 1400 K St., N.W., Suite 900, Washington, DC 20005. Phone: (202)682-4800 Fax: (202)682-4854 • URL: http://www.rma.org.

RUG INDUSTRY

See: FLOOR COVERINGS

RUGS, ORIENTAL

See: ORIENTAL RUG INDUSTRY

RULES OF ORDER

See: PARLIAMENTARY PROCEDURE

RUM INDUSTRY

See: DISTILLING INDUSTRY

RURAL COMMUNITY DEVELOPMENT

See: COMMUNITY DEVELOPMENT

RURAL CREDIT

See: AGRICULTURAL CREDIT

RURAL ELECTRIFICATION

CD-ROM DATABASES

Environment Abstracts on CD-ROM. Congressional Information Service, Inc. • Quarterly. $1,295.00 per year. Contains the following CD-ROM databases: *Environment Abstracts, Energy Abstracts*, and *Acid Rain Abstracts.* Length of coverage varies.

ONLINE DATABASES

Energyline. Congressional Information Service, Inc. • Provides online citations and abstracts to the literature of all forms of energy: petroleum, natural gas, coal, nuclear power, solar energy, etc. Time period is 1971 to 1993 (closed file). Inquire as to online cost and availability.

PERIODICALS AND NEWSLETTERS

R E Magazine (Rural Electrification). National Rural Electric Cooperative Association. • Monthly. Free to members; non-members, $50.00 per year. News and information about the rural electric utility industry. Formerly *Rural Electrification*.

TRADE/PROFESSIONAL ASSOCIATIONS

National Rural Electric Cooperative Association. 4301 Wilson Blvd., Arlington, VA 22203-1860. Phone: (703)907-5500 Fax: (703)907-5511 E-mail: nreca@nreca.org • URL: http://www.nreca.org.

RYE INDUSTRY

See also: GRAIN INDUSTRY

ABSTRACTS AND INDEXES

Biological and Agricultural Index. H.W. Wilson Co. • 11 times a year. Annual and quarterly cumulations. Service basis.

Wheat, Barley, and Triticale Abstracts. Available from CABI Publishing North America. • Bimonthly. $895.00 per year. Published in England by CABI Publishing. Provides worldwide coverage of the literature of wheat, barley, and rye.

INTERNET DATABASES

Fedstats. Federal Interagency Council on Statistical Policy. Phone: (202)395-7254 • URL: http://www.fedstats.gov • Web site features an efficient search facility for full-text statistics produced by more than 70 federal agencies, including the Census Bureau, the Bureau of Economic Analysis, and the Bureau of Labor Statistics. Boolean searches can be made within one agency or for all agencies combined. Links are offered to international statistical bureaus, including the UN, IMF, OECD, UNESCO, Eurostat, and 20 individual countries. Fees: Free.

USDA. United States Department of Agriculture. Phone: (202)720-2791 E-mail: agsec@usda.gov • URL: http://www.usda.gov • The USDA home page has six sections: News and Information; What's New; About USDA; Agencies; Opportunities; Search and Help. Keyword searching is offered from the USDA home page and from various individual agency home pages. Agencies are the Economic Research Service, Agricultural Marketing Service, National Agricultural Statistics Service, National Agricultural Library, and about 12 others. Updating varies. Fees: Free.

ONLINE DATABASES

CAB Abstracts. CAB International North America. • Contains 46 specialized abstract collections covering over 10,000 journals and monographs in the areas of agriculture, horticulture, forest products, farm products, nutrition, dairy science, poultry, grains, animal health, entomology, etc. Time period is 1972 to date, with monthly updates. Inquire as to online cost and availability. *CAB Abstracts on CD-ROM* also available, with annual updating.

DRI U.S. Central Database. Data Products Division. • Provides more than 23,000 business, financial, demographic, economic, foreign trade, and industry-related time series for the U.S. Includes national income, population, retail-wholesale trade, price indexes, labor data, housing, industrial production, banking, interest rates, money supply, etc. Time period is generally 1947 to date (some data back to 1929). Updating varies. Inquire as to online cost and availability.

STATISTICS SOURCES

Agricultural Statistics. Available from U. S. Government Printing Office. • Annual. Produced by the National Agricultural Statistics Service, U. S. Department of Agriculture. Provides a wide variety of statistical data relating to agricultural production, supplies, consumption, prices/price-supports, foreign trade, costs, and returns, as well as farm labor, loans, income, and population. In many cases, historical data is shown annually for 10 years. In addition to farm data, includes detailed fishery statistics.

Business Statistics of the United States. Courtenay M. Slater, editor. Bernan Associates. • 1999. $74.00. Fifth edition. Based on *Business Statistics*, formerly issue by the Bureau of Economic Analysis, U. S. Department of Commerce. Provides basic data for a wide variety of U. S. industries, services, and economic indicators. Most statistics are shown annually for 29 years and monthly for the most recent four years.

Flour Milling Products. U. S. Bureau of the Census. • Monthly and annual. Covers production, mill stocks, exports, and imports of wheat and rye flour. (Current Industrial Reports, M20A.).

Survey of Current Business. Available from U. S. Government Printing Office. • Monthly. $49.00 per year. Issued by Bureau of Economic Analysis, U. S. Department of Commerce. Presents a wide variety of business and economic data.

S

SAFE DEPOSITS (BANKING)

See also: BANKS AND BANKING

PERIODICALS AND NEWSLETTERS

Bank Systems and Technology: For Senior-Level Executives in Operations and Technology. Miller Freeman, Inc. • 13 times a year. $65.00 per year. Focuses on strategic planning for banking executives. Formerly *Bank Systems and Equipment.*

Safe Deposit Bulletin. New York State Safe Deposit Association c/o Paul Sanchez. • Quarterly. Membership.

TRADE/PROFESSIONAL ASSOCIATIONS

American Safe Deposit Association. c/o Joyce A. McLin, P.O. Box 519, Franklin, IN 46131. Phone: (317)738-4432 Fax: (317)738-5267 E-mail: jmclin@aol.com.

SAFETY

See also: ACCIDENTS; FIRE PROTECTION; INDUSTRIAL HYGIENE; INDUSTRIAL SAFETY

ABSTRACTS AND INDEXES

Health and Safety Science Abstracts. Institute of Safety and Systems Management. Cambridge Information Group. • Quarterly. $775.00 per year. Formerly *Safety Science Abstracts Journal.*

CD-ROM DATABASES

OSH-ROM: Occupational Safety and Health Information on CD-ROM. Available from SilverPlatter Information, Inc. • Price and frequency on application. Produced in Geneva by the International Occupational Safety and Health Information Centre, International Labour Organization (http://www.ilo.org). Provides about two million citations and abstracts to the worldwide literature of industrial safety, industrial hygiene, hazardous materials, and accident prevention. Material is included from journals, technical reports, books, government publications, and other sources. Time span varies.

DIRECTORIES

Best's Safety and Security Directory: Safety-Industrial Hygiene-Security. A.M. Best Co. • Annual. $95.00. A manual of current industrial safety practices with a directory of manufacturers and distributors of plant safety, security and industrial hygiene products and services listed by hazard. Formerly *Best's Safety Directory.*

Safety and Health Safety Equipment Buyers' Guide. National Safety Council. • Annual. $5.00.

ENCYCLOPEDIAS AND DICTIONARIES

Unabridged Dictionary of Occupational and Environmental Safety and Health with CD-ROM. Jeffrey W. Vincoli and Kathryn L. Bazan. Lewis Publishers. • 1999. $89.95.

HANDBOOKS AND MANUALS

Handbook of Safety and Health Engineering. Roger L. Bauer and Jeffrey W. Vincoli. Lewis Publishers. • 1999. $89.95.

ONLINE DATABASES

Hard Sciences. Cambridge Scientific Abstracts. • Provides the online version of *Computer and Information Systems Abstracts, Electronics and Communications Abstracts, Health and Safety Science Abstracts, ISMEC: Mechanical Engineering Abstracts (Information Service in Mechanical Engineering)* and *Solid State and Superconductivity Abstracts.* Time period is 1981 to date, with monthly updates. Inquire as to online cost and availability.

NIOSHTIC: National Institute for Occupational Safety and Health Technical Information Center Database. National Institute for Occupational Safety and Health, Technical Information Bra. • Provides citations and abstracts of technical literature in the areas of industrial safety, industrial hygiene, and toxicology. Covers 1890 to date, but mostly 1973 to date. Monthly updates. (Database is also known as *Occupational Safety and Health.*) Inquire as to online cost and availability.

PERIODICALS AND NEWSLETTERS

Occupational Hazards: Magazine of Health and Environment. Penton Media Inc. • Monthly. $50.00 per year. Industrial safety and security management.

Professional Safety. American Society of Safety Engineers. • Monthly. $60.00 per year. Emphasis is on research and technology in the field of accident prevention.

Safety and Health: The International Safety Health and Environment Magazine. National Safety Council. • Monthly. Members, $80.00 per year; non-members, $91.00 per year. Formerly *National Safety and Health News.*

RESEARCH CENTERS AND INSTITUTES

Center for Health and Safety Studies. Indiana University Bloomington, Bloomington, IN 47405. Phone: (812)855-3627 Fax: (812)855-3936 E-mail: crowe@indiana.edu • URL: http://www.indiana.edu/~aphs/aphs.html.

STATISTICS SOURCES

Accident Facts. National Safety Council. • Annual. $37.95.

Metropolitan Life Insurance Co. Statistical Bulletin SB. Metropolitan Life Insurance Co. • Quarterly. Individuals, $50.00 per year. Covers a wide range of social, economic and demographic health concerns.

TRADE/PROFESSIONAL ASSOCIATIONS

American Society of Safety Engineers. 1800 E. Oakton St., Des Plaines, IL 60018-2187. Phone: (847)699-2929 Fax: (847)296-3769 E-mail: customerservice@asse.org • URL: http://www.asse.org.

National Child Safety Council. P.O. Box 1368, Jackson, MI 49204. Phone: (517)764-6070 Fax: (517)764-3068.

National Safety Council. 1121 Spring Lake Dr., Itasca, IL 60143-3201. Phone: 800-621-7615 or (630)285-1121 Fax: (630)285-1315 • URL: http://www.nsc.org.

OTHER SOURCES

Consumer Product Safety Guide. CCH, Inc. • Weekly. $1,122.00 per year. Looseleaf service. Three volumes. Periodic suplementation.

Employment Safety and Health Guide. CCH, Inc. • Weekly. $1,095.00 per year. Four looseleaf volumes.

SAFETY APPLIANCES

See: INDUSTRIAL SAFETY

SAFETY EDUCATION

See: SAFETY

SAFETY, INDUSTRIAL

See: INDUSTRIAL SAFETY

SAFETY, PRODUCT

See: PRODUCT SAFETY AND LIABILITY

SALAD OIL INDUSTRY

See: OIL AND FATS INDUSTRY

SALARIES

See: EXECUTIVE COMPENSATION; WAGES AND SALARIES

SALE OF BUSINESS ENTERPRISES

See: BUSINESS ENTERPRISES, SALE OF

SALES AUCTION

See: AUCTIONS

SALES CONTESTS

See: SALES PROMOTION

SALES CONVENTIONS

See also: CONFERENCES, WORKSHOPS, AND SEMINARS; CONVENTIONS; SALES MANAGEMENT

DIRECTORIES

Directory of Conventions Regional Editions. Bill Communications. • Annual. $155.00 per volume. Four volumes. Set $285.00. Over 14,000 meetings of North American national, regional, and state and local organizations.

Directory of Corporate Meeting Planners. Salesman's Guide. • Annual. $385.00. Lists about 18,000 planners of off-site meetings for over 11,000 U. S. and Canadian corporations. Provides information on number of attendees and professional speaker usage.

Trade Shows Worldwide: An International Directory of Events, Facilities and Suppliers. The Gale Group. • 2000. $299.00. 16th edition. Provides detailed information from over 75 countries on more than 8,400 trade shows and exhibitions. Separate sections are provided for trade shows/exhibitions, for sponsors/organizers, and for services, facilities, and information sources. Indexing is by date, location, subject, name, and keyword.

HANDBOOKS AND MANUALS

Big Meetings, Big Results. Tom McMahon. NTC/ Contemporary Publishing. • 1994. $19.95. Includes checklists and diagrams. (NTC Business Book Series).

Guerilla Trade Show Selling: New Unconventional Weapons and Tactics to Meet More People, Get More Leads, and Close More Sales. Jay C. Levinson and others. John Wiley and Sons, Inc. • 1997. $19.95.

INTERNET DATABASES

Trade Show Central: The Internet's Leading Trade Show Information Resource!. Trade Show Central. Phone: (781)235-8095 Fax: (781)416-4500 • URL: http://www.tscentral.com • Web site provides information on "more than 30,000 Trade Shows, Conferences, and Seminars, 5,000 service providers, and 5,000 venues and facilities around the world." Searching is offered by trade show name, industry category, date, and location. Results may be sorted by event name, city, country, or date. Includes a "Career Center" for trade show personnel. Continuous updating. Fees: Free.

PERIODICALS AND NEWSLETTERS

Successful Meetings: The Authority on Meetings and Incentive Travel Management. Bill Communications, Inc. • Monthly. $65.00 per year.

SALES FINANCE COMPANIES

See: FINANCE COMPANIES

SALES MANAGEMENT

See also: MARKETING; SALESMEN AND SALESMANSHIP

GENERAL WORKS

Contemporary Sales Force Management. Tony Carter. Haworth Press, Inc. • 1997. $49.95. Emphasis is on motivation of sales personnel. Includes case studies.

Management of a Sales Force. William J. Stanton and others. McGraw-Hill. • 1998. $85.00. 10th edition.

Managing Sales Professionals: The Reality of Profitability. Joseph P. Vaccaro. The Haworth Press, Inc. • 1995. $49.95.

Sales and Sales Management. Butterworth-Heinemann. • 1998. $34.95.

Sales Management. William C. Moncrief and Shannon Shipp. Addison-Wesley Longman, Inc. • 1997. $98.00. Includes chapters on personal selling, organization, training, motivation, compensation, evaluation, sales forecasting, and strategy. A glossary and case histories are provided.

Sales Management: Concepts and Cases. Douglas J. Dalyrmple and William J. Cron. John Wiley and Sons, Inc. • 1997. $95.95 Sixth edition.

ENCYCLOPEDIAS AND DICTIONARIES

Blackwell Encyclopedic Dictionary of Marketing. Barbara R. Lewis and Dale Littler, editors. Blackwell Publishers. • 1996. $105.95. The editors are associated with the Manchester School of Management. Contains definitions of key terms combined with longer articles written by various U. S. and foreign business educators. Includes bibliographies and index. (Blackwell Encyclopedia of Management series.).

HANDBOOKS AND MANUALS

AMA Management Handbook. John J. Hampton, editor. AMACOM. • 1994. $110.00. Third edition. Provides 200 chapters in 16 major subject areas. Covers a wide variety of business and industrial management topics.

The First-Time Sales Manager: A Survival Guide. Theodore Tyssen. Self-Counsel Press, Inc. • 1994. $8.95. Provides basic information and advice for beginning sales managers. (Business Series).

From Selling to Managing: Guidelines for the First-Time Sales Manager. Ronald Brown. AMACOM. • 1990. $17.95. Revised edition. A practical quide to the transformation of salesperson to sales manager.

Running an Effective Sales Office. Patrick Forsythe. John Wiley and Sons, Inc. • 1998. $35.95.

Sales Compensation Handbook. John K. Moynahan, editor. AMACOM. • 1998. $75.00. Second edition. Topics include salespeople compensation plans based on salary, commission, bonuses, and contests.

Sales Manager's Desk Book. Gene Garofalo. Prentice Hall. • 1996. $69.95. Second edition. A handbook covering many aspects of selling and sales management. Includes information on telemarketing, communications technology, voice mail, and teleconferencing.

Sales Manager's Handbook. John P. Steinbrink. Dartnell Corp. • 1989. $93.50. 14th edition.

Sales Manager's Model Letter Desk Book. Hal Fahner and Morris E. Miller. Prentice Hall. • 1988. $32.95. Second edition.

Sales Manager's Portable Answer Book. Gene Garofalo. Prentice Hall. • 1997. $59.95. Contains succinct information and advice on demonstrations, proposals, closing the sale, leadership, expenses, forecasting ("Crystal Balls, Tea Leaves, Palm Reading: Forecasting Sales"), compensation, sales meetings, trade shows, training, regional office management, and various other subjects.

What America's Small Companies Pay Their Sales Forces and How They Make It Pay Off. Christen P. Heide. Dartnell Corp. • 1997. $29.95. Provides advice on attracting, motivating, and retaining productive sales personnel. Includes sales position descriptions and "latest sales compensation figures for companies under $5 million in sales.".

ONLINE DATABASES

Management Contents. The Gale Group. • Covers a wide range of management, financial, marketing, personnel, and administrative topics. About 150 leading business journals are indexed and abstracted from 1974 to date, with monthly updating. Inquire as to online cost and availability.

PERIODICALS AND NEWSLETTERS

Marketing Management: Shaping the Profession of Marketing. American Marketing Association. • Quarterly. Members, $45.00 per year; non-members, $70.00 per year; institutions, $90.00 per year. Covers trends in the management of marketing, sales, and distribution.

Sales and Marketing Management. Bill Communications, Inc. • Monthly. $48.00 per year.

Sales & Marketing Report: Practical Ideas for Successful Selling. Lawence Ragan Communications, Inc. • Monthly. $119.00 per year. Newsletter. Emphasis is on sales training, staff morale, and marketing productivity.

Strategic Sales Management. Bureau of Business Practice, Inc. • Semimonthly. $187.80 per year. Newsletter. Provides advice and information for sales managers. Formerly *Sales Managers' Bulletin.*

TRADE/PROFESSIONAL ASSOCIATIONS

Sales and Marketing Executives. 5500 Interstate N. Parkway, No. 545, Atlanta, GA 30328. Phone: (770)661-8500 Fax: (770)661-8512 E-mail: smeihq@smel.org • URL: http://www.smei.org.

OTHER SOURCES

How to Be an Effective Sales Manager. American Management Association Extension Institute. • Looseleaf. $130.00. Self-study course. Emphasis is on practical explanations, examples, and problem solving. Quizzes and a case study are included.

Sales Forecasting. American Management Association Extension Institute. • Looseleaf. $110.00. Self-study course. Emphasis is on practical explanations, examples, and problem solving. Quizzes and a case study are included.

SALES MEETINGS

See: MEETING MANAGEMENT; SALES CONVENTIONS

SALES PROMOTION

See also: ADVERTISING; MARKETING; PREMIUMS; PUBLIC RELATIONS AND PUBLICITY; SALES MANAGEMENT

GENERAL WORKS

How to Promote, Publicize, and Advertise Your Growing Business: Getting the Word Out Without Spending a Fortune. Kim Baker and Sunny Baker. John Wiley and Sons, Inc. • 1992. $107.50.

Introduction to Advertising and Promotion: An Integrated Marketing Communications Perspective. George E. Belch and Michael A. Belch. McGraw-Hill Higher Education. • 1994. $69.94. Third edition.

Sales Promotion. Robert C. Blattberg. Prentice Hall. • 1995. $23.60.

ALMANACS AND YEARBOOKS

Major Marketing Campaigns Annual. The Gale Group. • Annual. $140.00. Describes in detail "100 major marketing initiatives of the previous calendar year." Includes illustrations.

DIRECTORIES

AMA International Member and Marketing Services Guide. American Marketing Association. • Annual. $150.00. Lists professional members of the American Marketing Association. Also contains information on providers of marketing support services and products, including software, communications, direct marketing, promotion, research, and consulting companies. Includes geographical and alphabetical indexes. Formerly *Marketing Yellow Pages and AMA International Membership Directory.*

Creative's Illustrated Guide to P-O-P Exhibits and Promotion. Magazines Creative, Inc. • Annual. $25.00. Lists sources of point-of-purchase displays, signs, and exhibits and sources of other promotional materials and equipment. Available online.

Directory of Premium, Incentive, and Travel Buyers. Salesman's Guide. • Annual. $275.00. Provides information on about 19,000 buyers of premiums, incentive programs, and travel programs for motivation of sales personnel.

Incentive-Merchandise and Travel Directory. Bill Communications, Inc. • Annual. $5.00. A special issue of *Incentive* magazine.

PROMO Magazine's SourceBook: The Only Guide to the $70 Billion Promotion Industry. Intertec Publishing. • Annual. $49.95. Lists service and supply companies for the promotion industry. Includes annual salary survey and award winning campaigns.

The PROMO 100 Promotion Agency Ranking. Intertec Publishing Co. • Annual. $9.95. Provides information on 100 leading product promotion agencies.

ENCYCLOPEDIAS AND DICTIONARIES

Encyclopedia of Major Marketing Campaigns. The Gale Group. • 2000. $265.00. Covers 500 major marketing and advertising campaigns "of the 20th century." Examines historical context, target market, expectations, competition, strategy, development, and outcomes. Includes illustrations.

HANDBOOKS AND MANUALS

Coupon Mailer Service. Entrepreneur Media, Inc. • Looseleaf. $59.50. A practical guide to starting a service for mailing business promotion discount coupons to consumers. Covers profit potential, start-up costs, market size evaluation, owner's time required, pricing, accounting, advertising, promotion, etc. (Start-Up Business Guide No. E1232.).

Online Marketing Handbook: How to Promote, Advertise and Sell, Your Products and Services on the Internet. Daniel S. Janal. John Wiley and Sons, Inc. • 1998. $29.95. Revised edition. Provides step-by-step instructions for utilizing online publicity, advertising, and sales promotion. Contains chapters on interactive marketing, online crisis communication, and Web home page promotion, with numerous examples and checklists.

The Only Sales Promotion Techniques You'll Ever Need: Proven Tactics and Expert Insights. Tamara Block, editor. Dartnell Corp. • 1996. $39.95. Covers sampling, sweepstakes, co-op advertising, event marketing, database management, and other topics.

The Perfect Sales Piece: A Complete Do-It-Yourself Guide to Creating Brochures, Catalogs, Fliers, and Pamphlets. Robert W. Bly. John Wiley and Sons, Inc. • 1994. $49.95. A guide to the use of various forms of printed literature for direct selling, sales promotion, and marketing. (Small Business Editions Series).

Promotional Marketing. Entrepreneur, Inc. • Looseleaf. $59.50. A practical guide to sales promotion and marketing for small businesses. (Start-Up Business Guide No. E1111.).

Sales Promotion Handbook. Tamara Brezen and William Robinson. Dartnell Corp. • 1994. $69.95. Eighth edition. Covers licensing, tie-ins, legal aspects, event marketing, database marketing, and other topics.

PERIODICALS AND NEWSLETTERS

Creative: The Magazine of Promotion and Marketing. Magazines Creative, Inc. • Bimonthly. $30.00 per year. Covers promotional materials, including exhibits, incentives, point-of-purchase advertising, premiums, and specialty advertising.

Database Marketer. Intertec Publishing Co. • Monthly. $329.00 per year.

Incentive: Managing and Marketing Through Motivation. Bill Communications, Inc. • Monthly. $55.00 per year.

Journal of Promotion Management: Innovations in Planning and Applied Research for Advertising, Sales Promotion, Personal Selling, Public Relations, and Re-Seller Support. Haworth Press, Inc. • Semiannual. Individuals, $40.00 per year; institutions, $65.00 per year; libraries, $95.00 per year.

The Licensing Letter. EPM Communications, Inc. • Monthly. $447.00 per year. Newsletter. Covers all aspects of licensed merchandising (compensation of a person or an organization for being associated with a product or service).

The Marketing Report: The Best Time-Saving Information Source for Marketing Execcutives. Progressive Business Publications. • Semimonthly. $264.00 per year. Newsletter. Covers marketing ideas, problem solving, and new product development. Includes case histories.

PROMO: Promotion Marketing Worldwide. Simba Information Inc. • Monthly. $65.00 per year. Edited for companies and agencies that utilize couponing, point-of-purchase advertising, special events, games, contests, premiums, product samples, and other unique promotional items.

TRADE/PROFESSIONAL ASSOCIATIONS

Association of Promotion Marketing Agencies Worldwide. 750 Summer St., Stamford, CT 06901. Phone: (203)325-3911 Fax: (203)969-1499 E-mail: apmaw@aol.com • URL: http://www.apmaw.org.

OTHER SOURCES

How to Develop Successful Sales Promotions. American Management Association Extension Institute. • Looseleaf. $130.00. Self-study course. Emphasis is on practical explanations, examples, and problem solving. Quizzes and a case study are included.

How to Write Successful Promotional Copy. American Management Association Extension Institute. • Looseleaf. $98.00. Self-study course. Emphasis is on practical explanations, examples, and problem solving. Quizzes are included.

Idea Source Guide; A Monthly Report to Executives in Advertising, Merchandising and Sales Promotion. Bramlee, Inc. • Monthly. $150.00 per year. Lists new premiums and novelty products.

SALES REPRESENTATIVES

See: MANUFACTURERS' AGENTS

SALES TAX

See also: STATE LAW

DIRECTORIES

National Sales Tax Rate Directory. Vertex Systems, Inc. • Looseleaf, with monthly updates. $585.00 Per year. Provides state, county, city, and special sales tax rates for all states.

HANDBOOKS AND MANUALS

Cybertaxation: The Taxation of E-Commerce. Karl A. Frieden. CCH, Inc. • 2000. $75.00. Includes state sales and use tax issues and corporate income tax rules, as related to doing business over the Internet.

U. S. Master Sales and Use Tax Guide. CCH, Inc. • Annual. $65.00. Contains concise information on sales and use taxes in all states and the District of Columbia.

Vertex National Sales Tax Manuals. Vertex Systems, Inc. • Six looseleaf regional volumes, $1,122.00 Monthly updates. $750.00 Price on application. Volumes include state by state charts of taxable goods and services, guides to exemptions, reporting requirements, a directory of taxing authorities, and other state and local sales tax information.

PERIODICALS AND NEWSLETTERS

E-Commerce Tax Alert. CCH, Inc. • Monthly. $397.00 per year. Newsletter. Edited for owners and managers of firms doing business through the Internet. Covers compliance with federal, state, local, and international tax regulations.

The Journal of Taxation: A National Journal of Current Developments, Analysis and Commentary for Tax Professionals. Warren, Gorham & Lamont/ RIA Group. • Monthly. $215.00 per year. Analysis of current tax developments for tax specialists.

Sales and Use Tax Alert. CCH, Inc. • Monthly. $197.00 per year. Newsletter. Provides nationwide coverage of new developments in sales tax laws and regulations.

RESEARCH CENTERS AND INSTITUTES

Center for Tax Policy Studies. Purdue University, 490 Krannert, West Lafayette, IN 47907-1310. Phone: (765)494-4442 Fax: (765)496-1778 E-mail: papke@mgmt.purdue.edu.

Tax Foundation. 1250 H St., N.W., Suite 750, Washington, DC 20005. Phone: (202)783-2760 Fax: (202)783-6868 E-mail: taxfnd@intr.net • URL: http://www.taxfoundation.org.

OTHER SOURCES

Manufacturers' Tax Alert. CCH, Inc. • Monthly. $297.00 per year. Newsletter. Covers the major tax issues affecting manufacturing companies. Includes current developments in various kind of federal, state, and international taxes: sales, use, franchise, property, and corporate income.

Multi-State Sales Tax Guide. CCH, Inc. • $1,160.00 per year. Looseleaf service. Nine volumes. Periodic supplementation. Formerly *All State Sales Tax Reports.*

Sales and Use Taxation of E-Commerce: State Tax Administrators' Current Thinking, with CCH Commentary. CCH, Inc. • 2000. $129.00. Provides advice and information on the impact of state sales taxes on e-commerce activity.

SALESMEN AND SALESMANSHIP

See also: SALES MANAGEMENT

GENERAL WORKS

Consultative Selling: The Hanan Formula for High-Margin Sales at High Levels. Mack Hanan. AMACOM. • 1999. $24.95. Sixth revised edition. How to treat customers as friends to be helped and not as foes to be overcome.

Fundamentals of Selling: Customers for Life. Charles Futrell. McGraw-Hill. • 1998. $67.50. Sixth edition. (Marketing Series).

High Efficiency Selling: How Superior Salespeople Get That Way. Stephan Schiffman. John Wiley and Sons, Inc. • 1997. $19.95.

I'll Get Back to You: 156 Ways to Get People to Return Your Calls and Other Helpful Sales Tips.

Robert L. Shook and Eric Yaverbaum. McGraw-Hill. • 1996. $9.95. Presents advice from business executives, celebrities, and others on how to make telephone calls seem important.

Personal Selling: A Relationship Approach. Ronald B. Marks. Prentice Hall. • 1996. $92.00. Sixth edition. Covers buying behavior, prospecting, presentation, objections, closing, selling as a career, and related topics. Includes a glossary.

Sales and Sales Management. Butterworth-Heinemann. • 1998. $34.95.

Sales Negotiation Skills That Sell. Robert E. Kellar. AMACOM. • 1996. $17.95. Covers negotiating objectives, risk assessment, planning, strategy, tactics, and face-to-face skills.

Secrets of Closing Sales. Charles B. Roth. Prentice Hall. • 1993. $16.95. Sixth edition.

Selling Today: Building Quality Partnerships. Gerald L. Manning and Barry L. Reece. Prentice Hall. • 2000. $84.00. Eighth edition.

CD-ROM DATABASES

WILSONDISC: Wilson Business Abstracts. H. W. Wilson Co. • Monthly. $2,495.00 per year, including unlimited online access to *Wilson Business Abstracts* through WILSONLINE. Provides CD-ROM "cover-to-cover" abstracting and indexing of over 600 prominent business periodicals. Indexing is from 1982, abstracting from 1990. (*Business Periodicals Index* without abstracts is available on CD-ROM at $1,495 per year.).

HANDBOOKS AND MANUALS

ABCs of Relationship Selling. Charles Futrell. McGraw-Hill Higher Education. • 1996. $51.45. Fifth revised edition.

Electronic Selling: Twenty-Three Steps to E-Selling Profits. Brian Jamison and others. McGraw-Hill. • 1997. $24.95. Covers selling on the World Wide Web, including security and payment issues. Provides a glossary and directory information. The authors are consultants specializing in Web site production.

Guerilla Trade Show Selling: New Unconventional Weapons and Tactics to Meet More People, Get More Leads, and Close More Sales. Jay C. Levinson and others. John Wiley and Sons, Inc. • 1997. $19.95.

How to Recruit and Select Successful Salesmen. Ashgate Publishing Co. • 1983. $78.95. Revised edition. Published by Gower in England.

Selling Through Independent Reps. Harold J. Novick. AMACOM. • 1999. $75.00. Third edition. Tells how to make good use of independent sales representatives.

Selling Through Negotiation: The Handbook of Sales Negotiation. Homer B. Smith. Marketing Education Associates. • 1988. $14.95.

Selling to the Affluent: The Professional's Guide to Closing the Sales That Count. Thomas Stanley. McGraw-Hill Professional. • 1990. $55.00.

Successful Cold Call Selling. Lee Boyan. AMACOM. • 1989. $16.95. Second edition.

ONLINE DATABASES

Wilson Business Abstracts Online. H. W. Wilson Co. • Indexes and abstracts 600 major business periodicals, plus the *Wall Street Journal* and the business section of the *New York Times*. Indexing is from 1982, abstracting from 1990, with the two newspapers included from 1993. Updated weekly. Inquire as to online cost and availability. (*Business Periodicals Index* without abstracts is also available online.).

PERIODICALS AND NEWSLETTERS

Pharmaceutical Representative. McKnight Medical Communications. • Monthly. $35.95 per year. Edited for drug company salespeople and sales managers.

Sales & Marketing Report: Practical Ideas for Successful Selling. Lawence Ragan Communications, Inc. • Monthly. $119.00 per year. Newsletter. Emphasis is on sales training, staff morale, and marketing productivity.

Success: For the Innovative Entrepreneur. Success Holdings LLC. • Monthly. $19.97 per year. Provides information to help individuals advance in business.

STATISTICS SOURCES

Dartnell's Sales Force Compensation Survey. Dartnell Corp. • Biennial. $159.00.

SALMON INDUSTRY

See also: FISH INDUSTRY; SEAFOOD INDUSTRY

ABSTRACTS AND INDEXES

Oceanic Abstracts. Cambridge Information Group. • Bimonthly. $1,045.00 per year. Covers oceanography, marine biology, ocean shipping, and a wide range of other marine-related subject areas.

ONLINE DATABASES

Oceanic Abstracts (Online). Cambridge Scientific Abstracts. • Oceanographic and other marine-related technical literature, 1981 to present.Monthly updates. Inquire as to online cost and availability.

STATISTICS SOURCES

Fisheries of the United States. Available from U. S. Government Printing Office. • Annual. $18.00. Issued by the National Marine Fisheries Service, National Oceanic and Atmospheric Administration, U. S. Department of Commerce.

TRADE/PROFESSIONAL ASSOCIATIONS

Pacific Salmon Commission. 1155 Robson St., Suite 600, Vancouver, BC, Canada V6E 1B5. Phone: (604)684-8081 Fax: (604)666-8707 E-mail: psc@psc.org • URL: http://www.psc.org.

SALT INDUSTRY

STATISTICS SOURCES

Mineral Commodity Summaries. Available from U. S. Government Printing Office. • Annual. Published by the U. S. Geological Survey, Department of the Interior (http://www.usgs.gov). Contains detailed, five-year data for about 90 nonfuel minerals. Covers a wide range of statistics, including production, imports, exports, consumption, reserves, prices, tariff information, and industry employment. (Two pages are devoted to each mineral.).

TRADE/PROFESSIONAL ASSOCIATIONS

Salt Institute. Fairfax Plaza, 700 N. Fairfax, Suite 600, Alexandria, VA 22314-2040. Phone: (703)549-4648 Fax: (703)548-2194 E-mail: info@saltinstitute.org • URL: http://www.saltinstitute.org.

OTHER SOURCES

Spices and Seasonings. Available from MarketResearch.com. • 1999. $2,250.00. Market research data. Published by Specialists in Business Information. Covers salt, pepper, garlic, salt substitutes, seasoning mixes, etc.

SAND AND GRAVEL INDUSTRY

See: QUARRYING

SANITATION INDUSTRY

See also: AIR POLLUTION; PUBLIC WORKS; RECYCLING; WASTE MANAGEMENT; WATER POLLUTION; WATER SUPPLY

ABSTRACTS AND INDEXES

Environment Abstracts. Congressional Information Service. • Monthly. Price varies. Provides multidisciplinary coverage of the world's environmental literature. Incorporates *Acid Rain Abstracts.*

Environment Abstracts Annual: A Guide to the Key Environmental Literature of the Year. Congressional Information Service. • Annual. $495.00. A yearly cumulation of *Environment Abstracts.*

Environmental Periodicals Bibliography: A Current Awareness Bibliography Featuring Citations of Scientific and Popular Articles in Serial Publications in the Area of the Environment. Environmental Studies Institute. International Academy at Santa Barbara. • Monthly. Price varies. An index to current environmental literature.

NTIS Alerts: Environmental Pollution & Control. National Technical Information Service. • Semimonthly. $245.00 per year. Provides descriptions of government-sponsored research reports and software, with ordering information. Covers the following categories of environmental pollution: air, water, solid wastes, radiation, pesticides, and noise. Formerly *Abstract Newsletter.*

Pollution Abstracts. Cambridge Information Group. • Monthly. $895.00 per year; with index, $985.00 per year.

CD-ROM DATABASES

Environment Abstracts on CD-ROM. Congressional Information Service, Inc. • Quarterly. $1,295.00 per year. Contains the following CD-ROM databases: *Environment Abstracts, Energy Abstracts*, and *Acid Rain Abstracts*. Length of coverage varies.

DIRECTORIES

Public Works Manual. Public Works Journal Corp. • Annual. $45.00. Includes about 3,500 manufacturers and distributors of materials and equipment used in heavy construction. Special issue of (Public Works).

Sanitary Maintenance Buyers' Guide. Trade Press Publishing Corp. • Annual. $20.00.

Waste Age Specification Guide. Intertec Publishing Corp. • Annual. $49.95. Lists manufacturers of refuse handling machinery and equipment in North America and Europe. Includes specifications and photographs of trucks and heavy equipment.

HANDBOOKS AND MANUALS

Solid Waste Handbook: A Practical Guide. William D. Robinson, editor. John Wiley and Sons, Inc. • 1986. $225.00.

Waste Treatment and Disposal. Paul T. Williams. John Wiley and Sons, Inc. • 1998. $165.00.

ONLINE DATABASES

Enviroline. Congressional Information Service, Inc. • Provides online indexing and abstracting of worldwide environmental and natural resource literature from 1975 to date. Updated monthly. Inquire as to online cost and availability.

PERIODICALS AND NEWSLETTERS

Environmental Regulation: State Capitals. Wakeman-Walworth, Inc. • Weekly. $245.00 per year. Newsletter. Formerly *From the State Capitals: Environmental Regulation.*

OSHA Required Safety Training for Supervisors. Occupational Safety and Health Administration. Business and Legal Reports, Inc. • Monthly. $99.00

per year. Newsletter. Formerly *Safetyworks for Supervisors.*

Public Works: City, County and State. Public Works Journal Corp. • 13 times a year. $60.00 per year. Includes *Public Works Manual.*

Sanitary Maintenance: The Journal of the Sanitary Supply Industry. Trade Press Publishing Corp. • Monthly. $55.00 per year.

Sludge Newsletter: The Newsletter on Municipal Wastewater and Biosolids. Business Publishers, Inc. • Biweekly. $409.00 per year. per year. Monitors sludge management developments in Washington and around the country.

Solid Waste Report: Resource Recovery-Recycling-Collection-Disposal. Business Publishers, Inc. • Weekly. $627.00 per year. Newsletter. Covers regulation, business news, technology, and international events relating to solid waste management.

Water and Wastes Digest. Scranton Gillette Communications, Inc. • 10 times a year. Free to qualified personnel; others, $40.00 per year. Exclusively designed to serve engineers, consultants, superintendents, managers and operators who are involved in water supply, waste water treatment and control.

World Wastes: The Independent Voice of the Industry. Intertec Publishing Corp. • Monthly. $52.00 per year. Includes annual catalog. Formerly *Management of World Wastes: The Independent Voice of the Industry.*

RESEARCH CENTERS AND INSTITUTES

Environmental Engineering Laboratory. Pennsylvania State University. 212 Sackett Bldg., University Park, PA 16802. Phone: (814)863-7908 Fax: (814)863-7304 E-mail: blogan@psu.edu • URL: http://www.engr.psu.edu/enve.

TRADE/PROFESSIONAL ASSOCIATIONS

American Public Works Association. 2345 Grand Blvd., Suite 500, Kansas City, MO 64108. Phone: 800-595-2792 or (816)472-6100 Fax: (816)472-1610 E-mail: atatum@apwa.net.

American Society of Sanitary Engineering. 28901 Clemens Rd., Suite. 100, Westlake, OH 44145-1166. Phone: (440)835-3040 Fax: (440)835-3488 E-mail: asse@ix.netcom.com.

International Sanitary Supply Association. 7373 N. Lincoln Ave., Lincolnwood, IL 60646-1799. Phone: 800-225-4772 or (847)982-0800 Fax: (847)982-1012 E-mail: info@issa.com • URL: http://www.issa.com.

NSF International. P.O. Box 130140, Ann Arbor, MI 48113-0140. Phone: 800-673-6275 or (734)769-8010 Fax: (734)769-0109 E-mail: info@nsf.org • URL: http://www.nsf.org.

OTHER SOURCES

Environment Reporter. Bureau of National Affairs, Inc. • Weekly. $2,844.00 per year. 18 volumes. Looseleaf. Covers legal aspects of wide variety of environmental concerns.

Infrastructure Industries USA. The Gale Group. • 2001. $240.00. Replaces *Agriculture, Forestry, Fishing, Mining, and Construction USA* and *Transportation and Public Utilities USA.* Presents statistics and projections relating to economic activity in a wide variety of natural resource and construction industries.

SATELLITE COMMUNICATIONS

See: COMMUNICATIONS SATELLITES

SAVINGS AND LOAN ASSOCIATIONS

See also: SAVINGS BANKS

GENERAL WORKS

The Greatest Ever Bank Robbery: The Collapse of the Savings and Loan Industry. Martin Mayer. Pearson Education and Technology. • 1992. $12.95. Reprint edition.

ABSTRACTS AND INDEXES

Banking Information Index. U M I Banking Information Index. • Monthly. Price on application. Covers a wide variety of banking, business, and financial subjects in periodicals. Formerly *Banking Literature Index.*

BIBLIOGRAPHIES

Financial Institutions. Available from U. S. Government Printing Office. • Annual. Free. Lists government publications. Formerly *Banks and Banking.* GPO Subject Bibliography No. 128.

The Savings and Loan Crisis: An Annotated Bibliography. Pat L. Talley, compiler. Greenwood Publishing Group, Inc. • 1993. $65.00. Includes 360 scholarly and popular titles (books and research papers). (Bibliographies and Indexes in Economic History, No. 14).

DIRECTORIES

Directory of the Savings and Community Bankers of America. American Community Bankers of America. • Annual. Members $55.00; non-members, $95.00. Includes about 2,000 savings banks and savings and loan associations, with assets, deposits, personnel, and other information. Formerly *Directory of Members of the United States League of Savings Institutions*; *National Council of Community Bankers.*

Institutional Buyers of Bank and Thrift Stocks: A Targeted Directory. Investment Data Corp. • Annual. $645.00. Provides detailed profiles of about 600 institutional buyers of bank and savings and loan stocks. Includes names of financial analysts and portfolio managers.

McFadden American Financial Directory. Thomson Financial Publishing. • Semiannual. $415.00 per year. Five volumes. Contains information on more than 23,000 banks, savings institutions, and credit unions in the U. S., Canada, and Mexico. Includes names of officers for key departments, financial statistics, hours of operation, branch information, and other data.

Polk Financial Institutions Directory. Thomson Financial Publishing. • Semiannual. $330.00 per semiannual volume. Provides detailed information on "virtually every bank, savings and loan, and major credit union in North America, including banks and branches in Canada, Mexico, the Caribbean, and Central America." Supersedes *Polk's Bank Directory.*

Thomson Savings Directory. Thomson Financial Publishing. • Semiannual. $169.00 per year. Contains information on nearly 2,000 U.S. savings institutions.

FINANCIAL RATIOS

Almanac of Business and Industrial Financial Ratios. Leo Troy. Prentice Hall. • Annual. $99.95. Contains financial ratios derived from federal tax returns. Ratios for each of about 200 industries are arranged according to company asset size.

INTERNET DATABASES

BanxQuote Banking, Mortgage, and Finance Center. BanxQuote, Inc. Phone: 800-765-3000 or (212)643-8000 Fax: (212)643-0020 E-mail: info@banx.com • URL: http://www.banx.com • Web site quotes interest rates paid by banks around the country on various savings products, as well as rates paid by consumers for automobile loans, mortgages, credit cards, home equity loans, and personal loans. Also provided: stock quotes, indexes, stock options, futures trading data, economic indicators, and links to many other financial sites. Daily updates. Fees: Free.

The Bauer Group: Reporting On and Analyzing the Performance of U. S. Banks, Thrifts, and Credit Unions. Bauer Financial Reports, Inc. Phone: 800-388-6686 or (305)445-9500 Fax: 800-230-9569 or (305)445-6775 • URL: http://www.bauerfinancial.com • Web site provides ratings (0 to 5 stars) of individual banks and credit unions, based on capital ratios and other financial criteria. Online searching for bank or credit union names is offered. Fees: Free.

Fedstats. Federal Interagency Council on Statistical Policy. Phone: (202)395-7254 • URL: http://www.fedstats.gov • Web site features an efficient search facility for full-text statistics produced by more than 70 federal agencies, including the Census Bureau, the Bureau of Economic Analysis, and the Bureau of Labor Statistics. Boolean searches can be made within one agency or for all agencies combined. Links are offered to international statistical bureaus, including the UN, IMF, OECD, UNESCO, Eurostat, and 20 individual countries. Fees: Free.

ONLINE DATABASES

Banking Information Source. Bell & Howell Information and Learning. • Provides indexing and abstracting of periodical and other literature from 1982 to date, with weekly updates. Covers the financial services industry: banks, savings institutions, investment houses, credit unions, insurance companies, and real estate organizations. Emphasis is on marketing and management. Inquire as to online cost and availability. (Formerly *FINIS: Financial Industry Information Service.*).

DRI U.S. Central Database. Data Products Division. • Provides more than 23,000 business, financial, demographic, economic, foreign trade, and industry-related time series for the U.S. Includes national income, population, retail-wholesale trade, price indexes, labor data, housing, industrial production, banking, interest rates, money supply, etc. Time period is generally 1947 to date (some data back to 1929). Updating varies. Inquire as to online cost and availability.

PERIODICALS AND NEWSLETTERS

America's Community Banker. America's Community Bankers. • Monthly. Members, $60.00 per year; non-members, $75.00 per year. Covers community banking operations and management. Formerly *Savings and Community Banker.*

Bank Rate Monitor: The Weekly Financial Rate Reporter. Advertising News Service, Inc. • Weekly. $895.00 per year. Newsletter. Includes online addition and monthly supplement. Provides detailed information on interest rates currently paid by U. S. banks and savings institutions.

Fee Income Growth Strategies. Siefer Consultants, Inc. • Monthly. $329.00 per year. Newsletter. Covers operations management for banks and other financial institutions. Formerly *Noninterest Income Growth Strategies.*

Guide to Banks and Thrifts: A Quarterly Compilation of Financial Institutions Ratings and Analysis. Weiss Ratings, Inc. • Quarterly. $438.00 per year. Emphasis is on rating of financial safety and relative risk. Includes annual summary.

Jumbo Rate News. Bauer Financial Newsletters, Inc. • Weekly. $445.00 per year. Newsletter. Lists more than 1,100 of the highest interest rates available for "jumbo" certificates of deposit ($100,000 or more).

One Hundred Highest Yields Among Federally-Insured Banks and Savings Institutions. Advertising News Service, Inc. • Weekly. $124.00 per year. Newsletter.

Recommended Bank and Thrift Report. Bauer Communications, Inc. • Quarterly. $585.00 per year. Newsletter provides information on "safe, financially sound" commercial banks, savings banks, and savings and loan institutions. Various factors are considered, including tangible capital ratios and total risk-based capital ratios. (Six regional editions are also available at $150.00 per edition per year.).

The Safe Money Report. Weiss Ratings, Inc. • Monthly. $148.00 per year. Newsletter. Provides financial advice and current safety ratings of various banks, savings and loan companies, insurance companies, and securities dealers.

Treasury Manager's Report: Strategic Information for the Financial Executive. Phillips Business Information, Inc. • Biweekly. $595.00. Newsletter reporting on legal developments affecting the operations of banks, savings institutions, and other financial service organizations. Formerly *Financial Services Law Report.*

Troubled and Problematic Bank and Thrift Report. Bauer Communications, Inc. • Quarterly. $225.00 per year. Newsletter provides information on seriously undercapitalized ("Troubled") banks and savings institutions, as defined by a federal Prompt Corrective Action Rule. "Problematic" banks and thrifts are those meeting regulatory capital levels, but showing negative trends.

STATISTICS SOURCES

Business Statistics of the United States. Courtenay M. Slater, editor. Bernan Associates. • 1999. $74.00. Fifth edition. Based on *Business Statistics*, formerly issue by the Bureau of Economic Analysis, U. S. Department of Commerce. Provides basic data for a wide variety of U. S. industries, services, and economic indicators. Most statistics are shown annually for 29 years and monthly for the most recent four years.

Economic Outlook: A Newsletter on Economic Issues for Financial Institutions. America's Community Bankers. • Monthly. Members, $106.00; non-members, $212.00 per year. Statistical profiles of the savings industry. Formerly *Economic Insight.*

Standard & Poor's Industry Surveys. Standard & Poor's. • Semiannual. $1,800.00. Two looseleaf volumes. Includes monthly supplements. Provides detailed, individual surveys of 52 major industry groups. Each survey is revised on a semiannual basis. Also includes "Monthly Investment Review" (industry group investment analysis) and monthly "Trends & Projections" (economic analysis).

Statistical Information on the Financial Services Industry. American Bankers Association. • Annual. Members, $150.00; non-members, $275.00. Presents a wide variety of data relating to banking and financial services, including consumer economics, personal finance, credit, government loans, capital markets, and international banking.

Survey of Current Business. Available from U. S. Government Printing Office. • Monthly. $49.00 per year. Issued by Bureau of Economic Analysis, U. S. Department of Commerce. Presents a wide variety of business and economic data.

OTHER SOURCES

Bank and Thrift Case Digest. West Group. • Three looseleaf volumes. Periodic supplementation. Provides court decisions involving claims against failed banks and savings institutions or on behalf of insured banks and savings institutions.

SAVINGS BANKS

See also: SAVINGS AND LOAN ASSOCIATIONS

BIBLIOGRAPHIES

Financial Institutions. Available from U. S. Government Printing Office. • Annual. Free. Lists government publications. Formerly *Banks and Banking.* GPO Subject Bibliography No. 128.

DIRECTORIES

Directory of the Savings and Community Bankers of America. American Community Bankers of America. • Annual. Members $55.00; non-members, $95.00. Includes about 2,000 savings banks and savings and loan associations, with assets, deposits, personnel, and other information. Formerly *Directory of Members of the United States League of Savings Institutions*; *National Council of Community Bankers.*

Thomson Savings Directory. Thomson Financial Publishing. • Semiannual. $169.00 per year. Contains information on nearly 2,000 U.S. savings institutions.

FINANCIAL RATIOS

Almanac of Business and Industrial Financial Ratios. Leo Troy. Prentice Hall. • Annual. $99.95. Contains financial ratios derived from federal tax returns. Ratios for each of about 200 industries are arranged according to company asset size.

HANDBOOKS AND MANUALS

Bank Tax Guide. CCH, Inc. • Annual. $195.00. Summarizes and explains federal tax rules affecting financial institutions.

INTERNET DATABASES

BanxQuote Banking, Mortgage, and Finance Center. BanxQuote, Inc. Phone: 800-765-3000 or (212)643-8000 Fax: (212)643-0020 E-mail: info@banx.com • URL: http://www.banx.com • Web site quotes interest rates paid by banks around the country on various savings products, as well as rates paid by consumers for automobile loans, mortgages, credit cards, home equity loans, and personal loans. Also provided: stock quotes, indexes, stock options, futures trading data, economic indicators, and links to many other financial sites. Daily updates. Fees: Free.

PERIODICALS AND NEWSLETTERS

America's Community Banker. America's Community Bankers. • Monthly. Members, $60.00 per year; non-members, $75.00 per year. Covers community banking operations and management. Formerly *Savings and Community Banker*,

Operations Alert. America's Community Bankers. • Biweekly. Free to members; non-members, $200.00 per year. Newsletter reporting on regulatory and new product developments that affect community banking operations.

Recommended Bank and Thrift Report. Bauer Communications, Inc. • Quarterly. $585.00 per year. Newsletter provides information on "safe, financially sound" commercial banks, savings banks, and savings and loan institutions. Various factors are considered, including tangible capital ratios and total risk-based capital ratios. (Six regional editions are also available at $150.00 per edition per year.).

STATISTICS SOURCES

Economic Outlook: A Newsletter on Economic Issues for Financial Institutions. America's Community Bankers. • Monthly. Members, $106.00; non-members, $212.00 per year. Statistical profiles of the savings industry. Formerly *Economic Insight.*

Federal Deposit Insurance Corporation; Annual Report. Federal Deposit Insurance Corp. • Annual.

SAVINGS BONDS

See: GOVERNMENT BONDS

SAW INDUSTRY

See also: HARDWARE INDUSTRY; TOOL INDUSTRY; WOODWORKING INDUSTRIES

DIRECTORIES

ProSales Buyer's Guide. Hanley-Wood, LLC. • Annual. $5.00. A directory of equipment for professional builders.

PERIODICALS AND NEWSLETTERS

Hardware Age. Cahners Business Information. • Monthly. $75.00 per year.

Power Equipment Trade. Hatton-Brown Publishers, Inc. • 10 times a year. $40.00 per year. Formerly *Chain Saw Age and Power Equipment Trade.*

TRADE/PROFESSIONAL ASSOCIATIONS

Hack and Band Saw Manufacturers Association of America. 1300 Sumner Ave., Cleveland, OH 44115-2851. Phone: (216)241-7333 Fax: (216)241-0105 E-mail: hbs@taol.com • URL: http://www.taol.com/hbs.

International Saw and Knife Association. 351 O St., Fresno, CA 93721. Phone: 800-275-4752 or (559)237-0809 Fax: (559)237-8879.

Portable Power Equipment Manufacturers Association. 4340 East West Highway, Suite 912, Bethesda, MD 20814. Phone: (301)652-0774 Fax: (301)654-6138 E-mail: ppemal@msn.com • URL: http://www.ppema.org.

SAWMILLS

See: LUMBER INDUSTRY

SCHEDULES, TRANSPORTATION

See: TIMETABLES

SCHOLARSHIPS AND STUDENT AID

See also: STUDY ABROAD

ABSTRACTS AND INDEXES

Readers' Guide to Periodical Literature. H. W. Wilson Co. • Monthly. $220.00 per year. CD-ROM edition, $1,495 per year, including annual cumulation. Indexes about 250 peridicals of general interest.

BIBLIOGRAPHIES

How to Find Out About Financial Aid: 1998-2000. Gail A. Schlachter. Reference Service Press. • 2001. $37.50. Annotated bibliography of student aid directories. Author, title, subject, and geographical indexes.

CD-ROM DATABASES

College Blue Book CD-ROM. Available from The Gale Group. • Annual. $250.00. Produced by Macmillan Reference USA. Serves as electronic version of printed *College Blue Book.* Provides detailed information on programs, degrees, and financial aid sources in the U.S. and Canada.

DIRECTORIES

Chronicle Financial Aid Guide. Chronicle Guidance Publications, Inc. • Annual. $24.98. Financial aid programs offered primarily by private organizations, independent and AFL-CIO affiliated labor unions and federal and state governments for undergraduate students. Formerly *Student Aid Annual.* Lists scholarship titles.

Government Assistance Almanac: The Guide to Federal, Domestic, Financial and Other Programs Covering Grants, Loans, Insurance, Personal Payments and Benefits. J. Robert Dumouchel, editor. Omnigraphics, Inc. • Annual. $190.00. Describes more than 1,300 federal assistance programs available from about 50 agencies. Includes statistics, a directory of 4,000 field offices, and comprehensive indexing.

Peterson's College Money Handbook: The Only Complete Guide to Scholarships, College Costs, and Financial Aid at U. S. Colleges. Peterson's Magazine Group. • Annual. $26.95. Provides information on more than 1,600 scholarships, loans, and financial aid programs.

Peterson's Scholarships, Grants, and Prizes: Your Complete Guide to College Aid from Private Sources. Peterson's. • 1998. $26.95. Second edition.

The Scholarship Book: The Complete Guide to Private Scholarships, Grants, and Loans for Undergraduates. Daniel J. Cassidy. Prentice Hall. • 2000. $35.95. Sixth edition.

Scholarships, Fellowships, and Loans. The Gale Group. • 1999. $190.00. 17th edition. Describes more than 3,700 scholarships, fellowships, loans, and other educational funding sources available to U. S. and Canadian undergraduate and graduate students.

HANDBOOKS AND MANUALS

Financing Graduate School: How to Get Money for Your Master's or Ph.D. Patricia McWade. Peterson's. • 1996. $16.95. Second revised edition. Discusses the practical aspects of various types of financial aid for graduate students. Includes bibliographic and directory information.

The Student Guide: Financial Aid. U.S. Dept. of Education, Federal Student Aid Information Center. • Annual. Describes financial aid for college and vocational school students. Available online.

ONLINE DATABASES

ERIC. Educational Resources Information Center. • Broad range of educational literature, 1966 to present. Monthly updates. Inquire as to online cost and availability.

Readers' Guide Abstracts Online. H. W. Wilson Co. • Indexes and abstracts general interest periodicals, 1983 to date. Weekly updates. Inquire as to online cost and availability.

PERIODICALS AND NEWSLETTERS

Student Aid News: The Independent Biweekly News Service on Student Financial Assistance Programs. Aspen Publishers, Inc. • Biweekly. $297.00 per year. Newsletter on federal student aid programs.

TRADE/PROFESSIONAL ASSOCIATIONS

Coalition of Higher Education Assistance Organizations. 1101 Vermont Ave., N.W., Suite 400, Washington, DC 20005. Phone: (202)289-3910 Fax: (202)371-0197 • URL: http://www.coheao.com • Purpose is to support student loan programs and monitor regulations.

National Association of Student Financial Aid Administrators. 1129 20th St., N.W. Ste 400, Washington, DC 20036-5020. Phone: (202)785-0453 Fax: (202)785-1487 E-mail: ask@nasfaa.org • URL: http://www.nsfaa.org • Serves as a national forum for matters related to student aid.

National Council of Higher Education Loan Programs. 1100 Connecticut Ave. N.W., 12th Fl., Washington, DC 20036. Phone: (202)822-2106 Fax: (202)822-2142 • Attempts to coordinate federal, state, and private functions in the student loan program.

USA Group. P.O. Box 7039, Indianapolis, IN 46207. Phone: 800-824-7044 or (317)849-6510 Fax: (317)951-5072 • USA Funds is a nonprofit corporation guaranteeing low-cost loans from about 10,000 lenders. Approximately 1,000 colleges participate.

SCHOOL COMPUTERS

See: COMPUTERS IN EDUCATION

SCHOOL JOURNALISM

See: COLLEGE AND SCHOOL NEWSPAPERS

SCHOOLS

See also: BUSINESS EDUCATION; COLLEGES AND UNIVERSITIES; PRIVATE SCHOOLS; STUDY ABROAD; VOCATIONAL EDUCATION

ABSTRACTS AND INDEXES

Education Index. H.W. Wilson Co. • 10 times a year. Service basis.

Educational Administration Abstracts. Corwin Press, Inc. • Quarterly. Indivduals, $110.00 per year; institutions, $475.00 per year.

ALMANACS AND YEARBOOKS

Educational Media and Technology Yearbook. Libraries Unlimited, Inc. • Annual. $65.00.

National Society for the Study of Education Yearbook. National Society for the Study of Education. University of Chicago Press, Journals Div. • Annual. Membership. Two volumes per year.

BIOGRAPHICAL SOURCES

Who's Who in American Education. Marquis Who's Who. • Biennial. $159.95. Contains over 27,000 concise biographies of teachers, administrators, and other individuals involved in all levels of American education.

CD-ROM DATABASES

ERIC on SilverPlatter. Available from SilverPlatter Information, Inc. • Quarterly. $700.00 per year. Produced by the Office of Educational Research and Improvement, U. S. Dept. of Education. Provides CD-ROM indexing and abstracting of a wide variety of literature relating to education. Archival discs are available from 1966.

Magazine Index Plus. The Gale Group. • Monthly. $4,000.00 per year (includes InfoTrac workstation). Provides full text on CD-ROM for about 100 popular, general interest magazines and indexing for 300 others. Includes special indexing of reviews and product evaluations. Time period is 1980 to date.

Newspaper Abstracts Ondisc. Bell & Howell Information and Learning. • Monthly. $2,950.00 per year (covers 1989 to date; archival discs are available for 1985-88). Provides cover-to-cover CD-ROM indexing and abstracting of 19 major newspapers, including the *New York Times, Wall Street Journal, Washington Post, Chicago Tribune,* and *Los Angeles Times.*

WILSONDISC: Education Index. H. W. Wilson Co. • Monthly. $1,295.00 per year. Provides CD-ROM indexing of education-related literature from 1983 to date. Price includes online service.

DIRECTORIES

American School and University-Who's Who Directory and Buyers' Guide. Intertec Publishing Co. • Annual. $10.00. List of companies supplying products and service for physical plants and business offices of schools, colleges and universities.

Educators Resource Directory. Grey House Publishing. • 2001. $145.00. Fourth edition. Listings include educational associations, conferences, trade shows, grants, research centers, library services, etc. (Sedgwick Press.) Also includes statistical data on elementary and secondary schools.

Guide to Federal Funding for Education. Education Funding Research Council. • Quarterly. $297.00 per year. Describes approximately 407 federal education programs that award grants and contracts. Includes semimonthly supplement: *Grant Updates.*

Internet Tools of the Profession: A Guide for Information Professionals. Hope N. Tillman, editor. Special Libraries Association. • 1997. $49.00. Second edition. Consists of 14 sections by various authors or compilers. After two introductory articles on searching the Internet, there are 12 annotated lists of useful Web sites, covering the SLA, business and finance, chemistry, education, food and agriculture, information technology, insurance and employee benefits, law, library management, metals and materials, pharmaceuticals, and telecommunications. An index is provided.

Patterson's American Education. Educational Directories, Inc. • Annual. Individuals, $87.00; Schools and libraries, $75.00 schools in the U. S. Includes enrollment, grades offered, and name of principal. Geographical arrangement, with indexing by name of school and type of school.

Patterson's Schools Classified. Educational Directories, Inc. • Annual. $15.00. Lists more than 7,000 accredited colleges, universities, junior colleges, and vocational schools. Includes brief descriptions. Classified arrangement, with index to name of school. Included in *Patterson's American Education.*

Peterson's Vocational and Technical Schools and Programs. Peterson's. • Annual. $34.95. Provides information on vocational schools in the eastern part of the U. S. Covers more than 370 career fields.

HANDBOOKS AND MANUALS

Comparative Guide to American Elementary & Secondary Schools. Grey House Publishing. • 1998. $85.00. Provides a "snapshot profile" of every public school district in the U. S. serving 2,500 or more students. Includes student-teacher ratios, expenditures per student, number of librarians, and socioeconomic indicators.

Handbook of Educational Technology: Practical Guide for Teachers. Fred Percival and others. Nichols Publishing Co. • 1993. $39.95. Third edition.

School Administrator's Complete Letter Book. Gerald Tomlinson. Prentice Hall. • 1984. $37.95.

INTERNET DATABASES

Internet Tools of the Profession. Special Libraries Association. Phone: (202)234-4700 Fax: (202)265-9317 E-mail: hope@tiac.net • URL: http://www.sla.org/pubs/itotp • Web site is designed to update the printed *Internet Tools of the Profession.* Provides links to a wide range of useful databases in business, finance, industry, information technology, insurance, law, library management, telecommunications, and other subject areas. Fees: Free.

U. S. Census Bureau: The Official Statistics. U. S. Bureau of the Census. Phone: (301)763-4100 Fax: (301)763-4794 • URL: http://www.census.gov • Web site is "Your Source for Social, Demographic, and Economic Information." Contains "Current U. S. Population Count," "Current Economic Indicators," and a wide variety of data under "Other Official Statistics." Keyword searching is provided. Fees: Free.

ONLINE DATABASES

Education Index Online. H. W. Wilson Co. • Indexes a wide variety of periodicals related to schools, colleges, and education, 1984 to date. Monthly updates. Inquire as to online cost and availability.

ERIC. Educational Resources Information Center. • Broad range of educational literature, 1966 to present. Monthly updates. Inquire as to online cost and availability.

Newspaper and Periodical Abstracts. Bell & Howell Information and Learning. • Provides online coverage (citations and abstracts) of 25 major newspapers, 1,600 perodicals, and 70 TV programs. Covers business, economics, current affairs, health, fitness, sports, education, technology, government, consumer affairs, psychology, the arts, and the social sciences. Time period is 1986 to date, with daily updates. Inquire as to online cost and availability.

PERIODICALS AND NEWSLETTERS

American School and University: Facilities, Purchasing, and Business Administration. Intertec Publishing Corp. • Monthly. Free to qualified personnel; others, $65.00 per year.

American School Board Journal. National School Boards Association. • Monthly. $54.00 per year. How to advice for community leaders who want to improve their schools.

Education Week: American Education's Newspaper of Record. Editorial Projects in Education, Inc. • 43 times a year. $79.94 per year.

Educational Administration Quarterly. University Council for Educational Administratiotion. Corwin Press, Inc. • Five times a year. Individuals, $85.00 per year; institutions, $308.00 per year.

Educational Marketer: The Educational Publishing Industry's Voice of Authority Since 1968. SIMBA Information. • Three times a month. $479.00 per year. Newsletter. Edited for suppliers of educational materials to schools and colleges at all levels. Covers print and electronic publishing, software, audiovisual items, and multimedia. Includes corporate news and educational statistics.

School Business Affairs. Association of School Business Officials. ASBO International. • Monthly. Free to members; non-members, $68.00 per year.

School Planning and Management. Peter Li, Inc. • Monthly. $48.00 per year. Formerly *School and College.*

Taxes-Property: State Capitals. Wakeman-Walworth, Inc. • Weekly. $345.00 per year. Formerly *From the State Capitals: Taxes-Property.*

STATISTICS SOURCES

Digest of Education Statistics. Available from U. S. Government Printing Office. • Annual. $44.00. Covers all areas of education from kindergarten through graduate school. Includes data from both government and private sources. Compiled by National Center for Education Statistics, U. S. Department of Education.

Education Statistics of the United States. Mark S. Littman and Deirdre A. Gaquin, editors. Bernan Press. • 2000. $74.00. Second edition. Provides detailed county and state data, includes enrollment, educational attainment, per pupil expenditure, teacher pay and class size.

Investing in Education: Analysis of the 1999 World Education Indicators. Organization for Economic Cooperation and Development. • 2000. $31.00. Compares educational performance data in various countries of the world, including the U. S., other OECD countries, and selected non-OECD nations.

School Enrollment, Social and Economic Characteristics of Students. Available from U. S. Government Printing Office. • Annual. Issued by the U. S. Bureau of the Census. Presents detailed tabulations of data on school enrollment of the civilian noninstitutional population three years old and over. Covers nursery school, kindergarten, elementary school, high school, college, and graduate school. Information is provided on age, race, sex, family income, marital status, employment, and other characteristics.

Social Statistics of the United States. Mark S. Littman, editor. Bernan Press. • 2000. $65.00. Includes statistical data on population growth, labor force, occupations, environmental trends, leisure time use, income, poverty, taxes, and other economic or demographic topics.

State Profiles: The Population and Economy of Each U. S. State. Courtenay Slater and Martha Davis, editors. Bernan Press. • 1999. $74.00. Presents charts, tables, and text in an eight-page profile for each state. Covers population, labor force, income, poverty, employment, wages, industry, trade, housing, education, health, taxes, and government finances.

Statistical Abstract of the United States. Available from U. S. Government Printing Office. • Annual. $51.00. Issued by the U. S. Bureau of the Census.

A Statistical Portrait of the United States: Social Conditions and Trends. Mark S. Littman, editor. Bernan Press. • 1998. $89.00. Covers "social, economic, and environmental trends in the United States over the past 25 years." Includes statistical tables, graphs, and analysis relating to such topics as population, income, poverty, wealth, labor, housing, education, healthcare, air/water quality, and government.

UNESCO Statistical Yearbook. Bernan Press. • Annual. $95.00. Co-published by Bernan Press and the United Nations Educational, Scientific, and Cultural Organization (http://www.unesco.org). Presents statistical data from more than 200 countries on education, technology, research, broadcasting, cinema, book publishing, newspapers, libraries, museums, and population. Includes charts, maps, and graphs.

World Statistics Pocketbook. United Nations Publications. • Annual. $10.00. Presents basic economic, social, and environmental indicators for about 200 countries and areas. Covers more than 50 items relating to population, economic activity, labor force, agriculture, industry, energy, trade, transportation, communication, education, tourism, and the environment. Statistical sources are noted.

TRADE/PROFESSIONAL ASSOCIATIONS

American Association of School Administrators. 1801 N. Moore St., Arlington, VA 22209. Phone: (703)528-0700 Fax: (703)841-1543 • URL: http://www.aasa.org.

Association of School Business Officials International. 11401 N. Shore Dr., Reston, VA 22190-4200. Phone: (703)478-0405 Fax: (703)478-0205 E-mail: ditharpe@sprynet.com.

National Education Association. 1201 16th St., N.W., Washington, DC 20036. Phone: (202)833-4000 Fax: (202)822-7767 • URL: http://www.nea.org.

National School Boards Association. 1680 Duke St., Alexandria, VA 22314-3493. Phone: (703)838-6722 Fax: (703)683-7590 • URL: http://www.nsba.org.

National School Supply and Equipment Association. 8300 Colesville Rd., Suite 250, Silver Spring, MD 20910. Phone: 800-395-5550 or (301)495-0240 Fax: (301)495-3330 E-mail: nssea@nssea.org • URL: http://www.nssea.org.

OTHER SOURCES

Education Law. Matthew Bender & Co., Inc. • $740.00. Four looseleaf volumes. Periodic supplementation. A reference for attorneys who represent persons having a grievance against educational institutions, and attorney representing such institutions, as well as school board members and administrators.

Educational Rankings Annual: A Compilation of Approximately 3,500 Published Rankings and Lists on Every Aspect of Education. The Gale Group. • 2000. $220.00. Provides national, regional, local, and international rankings of a wide variety of educational institutions, including business and professional schools.

FedWorld: A Program of the United States Department of Commerce. National Technical Information Service. • Web site offers "a comprehensive central access point for searching, locating, ordering, and acquiring government and business information." Emphasis is on searching the Web pages, databases, and government reports of a wide variety of federal agencies. Fees: Free.

FirstGov: Your First Click to the U. S. Government. General Services Administration. • Free Web site provides extensive links to federal agencies covering a wide variety of topics, such as agriculture, business, consumer safety, education, the environment, government jobs, grants, health, social security, statistics sources, taxes, technology, travel, and world affairs. Also provides links to federal forms, including IRS tax forms. Searching is offered, both keyword and advanced.

NetSavvy: Building Information Literacy in the Classroom. Ian Jukes and others. Phi Delta Kappa International. • 2000. $27.95. Second edition. Provides practical advice on the teaching of computer, Internet, and technological literacy. Includes sample lesson plans and grade-level objectives.

Using Technology to Increase Student Learning. Linda E. Reksten. Phi Delta Kappa International. • 2000. $34.95. Emphasis is on the use of computer technology in schools.

SCHOOLS, PRIVATE

See: PRIVATE SCHOOLS

SCIENTIFIC APPARATUS AND INSTRUMENT INDUSTRIES

See also: LABORATORIES; RESEARCH AND DEVELOPMENT

ABSTRACTS AND INDEXES

Applied Science and Technology Index. H. W. Wilson Co. • 11 times a year. Quarterly and annual cumulations. Service basis for print edition; CD-ROM edition, $1,495.00 per year. Indexes a wide variety of English language technical, industrial, and engineering periodicals.

Key Abstracts: Electronic Instrumentation. Available from INSPEC, Inc. • Monthly. $240.00 per year. Provides international coverage of journal and proceedings literature. Published in England by the Institution of Electrical Engineers (IEE).

ALMANACS AND YEARBOOKS

Advances in Instrumentation and Control. International Society for Measurement and Control. • Annual. Price on application. Consists of

Instrument Society of America International Conference Proceedings.

BIOGRAPHICAL SOURCES

Who's Who in Science and Engineering. Marquis Who's Who. • Biennial. $269.00. Provides concise biographical information on 26,000 prominent engineers and scientists. International coverage, with geographical and professional indexes.

CD-ROM DATABASES

Science Citation Index: Compact Disc Edition. Institute for Scientific Information. • Quarterly. Provides CD-ROM indexing of the world's scientific and technical literature. Corresponds to online *Scisearch* and printed *Science Citation Index.*

DIRECTORIES

ISA Directory of Instrumentation. Instrument Society of America. • Annual. $100.00. Over 2,400 manufacturers of control and instrumentation equipment, over 1,000 manufacturers' representatives, and several hundred service companies; coverage includes Canada.

ENCYCLOPEDIAS AND DICTIONARIES

Kirk-Othmer Encyclopedia of Chemical Technology. John Wiley and Sons, Inc. • 1991-97. $7,350.00, prepaid. 21 volumes. Fourth edition. Four volumes are scheduled to be published each year, with individual volumes available at $350.00.

FINANCIAL RATIOS

Almanac of Business and Industrial Financial Ratios. Leo Troy. Prentice Hall. • Annual. $99.95. Contains financial ratios derived from federal tax returns. Ratios for each of about 200 industries are arranged according to company asset size.

HANDBOOKS AND MANUALS

Electronic Instrument Handbook. Clyde F. Coombs. McGraw-Hill. • 1999. $125.00. Second edition. (Engineering Handbook Series).

ONLINE DATABASES

Applied Science and Technology Index Online. H. W. Wilson Co. • Provides online indexing of 400 major scientific, technical, industrial, and engineering periodicals. Time period is 1983 to date. Monthly updates. Inquire as to online cost and availability.

Scisearch. Institute for Scientific Information. • Broad, multidisciplinary index to the literature of science and technology, 1974 to present. Inquire as to online cost and availability. Coverage of literature is worldwide, with weekly updates.

PERIODICALS AND NEWSLETTERS

Control Engineering: Covering Control, Instrumentation and Automation Systems Worldwide. Cahners Business Information. • Monthly. $99.90 per year.

Instrumentation and Automation News: Instruments, Controls, Manufacturing Software, Electronics and Mechanical Components. Cahners Business Information. • Monthly. Price on application.

INTECH: The International Journal of Instrumentation and Control. ISA Services, Inc. • Monthly. $85.00 per year.

ISA Transactions. Instrument Society of America, United States. Elsevier Science. • Quarterly. $348.00 per year.

Measurement and Control. Measurements and Data Corp. • 10 times a year. $22.00 per year. Supplement available: *M & C: Measurement and Control News.*

Review of Scientific Instruments. American Institute of Physics. • Monthly. $1,125.00 per year.

Today's Chemist at Work. American Chemical Society. • Monthly. Institutions, $160.00 per year; others, price on application. Provide pracrtical information for chemists on day-to-day operations. Product coverage includes chemicals, equipment, apparatus, instruments, and supplies.

RESEARCH CENTERS AND INSTITUTES

Instrumentation and Control Laboratory. Princeton University. Department of MAE, Engineering Quadrangle, Princeton, NJ 08544. Phone: (609)452-5154 Fax: (609)452-6109 E-mail: enoch@princeton.edu.

STATISTICS SOURCES

Annual Survey of Manufactures. Available from U. S. Government Printing Office. • Annual. Prices vary. Issued by the U. S. Census Bureau as an interim update to the *Census of Manufactures.* Includes data on number of manufacturing establishments in various industries, employment, labor costs, value of shipments, capital expenditures, inventories, energy costs, and assets. (See also Census Bureau home page, http://www.census.gov/.).

Selected Instruments and Related Products. U.S. Bureau of the Census. • Annual. (Current Industrial Reports, MA-38B.).

U. S. Industry and Trade Outlook: The McGraw-Hill Companies and the U.S. Department of Commerce/ International Trade Administration. Datapso Research Corp. • Annual. $69.95. Produced by the International Trade Administration, U. S. Department of Commerce, in a "public-private" partnership with DRI/McGraw-Hill and Standard & Poor's. Provides basic data, outlook for the current year, and "Long-Term Prospects" (five-year projections) for a wide variety of products and services. Includes high technology industries. Formerly *U. S. Industrial Outlook.*

TRADE/PROFESSIONAL ASSOCIATIONS

SAMA Group of Associations. 225 Reinekers Ln., Ste. 625, Alexandria, VA 23314. Phone: (703)836-1360 Fax: (703)836-6644.

OTHER SOURCES

Biotechnology Instrumentation Markets. Theta Reports/PJB Medical Publications, Inc. • 1999. $1,495.00. Contains market research data, with projections through the year 2002. Covers such products as specialized analytical instruments, filters/membranes, and mass spectrometers. (Theta Report No. 960.).

SCIENTIFIC LABORATORIES

See: LABORATORIES

SCIENTIFIC RESEARCH

See: RESEARCH AND DEVELOPMENT

SCRAP

See: WASTE PRODUCTS

SCRAP METAL

See: IRON AND STEEL SCRAP METAL INDUSTRY

SCREW MACHINE INDUSTRY

See: MACHINE TOOL INDUSTRY

SEAFOOD INDUSTRY

See also: FISH INDUSTRY; OYSTER INDUSTRY; SHELLFISH INDUSTRY

ABSTRACTS AND INDEXES

Food Science and Technology Abstracts. International Food Information Service Publishing. • Monthly. $1,780.00 per year. Provides worldwide coverage of the literature of food technology and food production.

Foods Adlibra: Key to the World's Food Literature. Foods Adlibra Publications. • Semimonthly.Provides journal citations and abstracts to the literature of food technology and packaging.

NTIS Alerts: Agriculture & Food. National Technical Information Service. • Semimonthly. $195.00 per year. Provides descriptions of government-sponsored research reports and software, with ordering information. Covers agricultural economics, horticulture, fisheries, veterinary medicine, food technology, and related subjects. Formerly *Abstract Newsletter.*

Oceanic Abstracts. Cambridge Information Group. • Bimonthly. $1,045.00 per year. Covers oceanography, marine biology, ocean shipping, and a wide range of other marine-related subject areas.

CD-ROM DATABASES

Food Science and Technology Abstracts [CD-ROM]. Available from SilverPlatter Information, Inc. • Quarterly. $3,700 per year. Produced by International Food Information Service (home page is http://www.ifis.org). Provides worldwide coverage on CD-ROM of the literature of food technology and production. Various types of publications are indexed, with abstracts, including about 1,800 periodicals. Time period is 1969 to date.

ONLINE DATABASES

ASFA Aquaculture Abstracts [Online]. Cambridge Scientific Abstracts. • Indexing and abstracting of the literature of marine life, 1984 to present. Inquire as to online cost and availability.

Food Science and Technology Abstracts [online]. IFIS North American Desk. • Produced by International Food Information Service. Provides about 500,000 online citations, with abstracts, to the international literature of food science, technology, commodities, engineering, and processing. Approximately 2,000 periodicals are covered. Time period is 1969 to date, with monthly updates. Inquire as to online cost and availability.

FOODS ADLIBRA. General Mills, Inc. • Contains online citations, with abstracts, to the technical and business literature of food processing and packaging. New products and new ingredients are featured. Covers about 250 trade journals and 500 research journals from 1974 to date, with monthly updates. Inquire as to online cost and availability.

Oceanic Abstracts (Online). Cambridge Scientific Abstracts. • Oceanographic and other marine-related technical literature, 1981 to present.Monthly updates. Inquire as to online cost and availability.

PERIODICALS AND NEWSLETTERS

Fishermen's News. Fishermen's News, Inc. • Monthly. $15.00 per year.

National Fisherman. Diversified Business Communications. • Monthly. $22.95 per year. American fishing industry and boat building trade.

STATISTICS SOURCES

FAO Fishery Series. Food and Agriculture Organization of the United States. Available from Bernan Associates. • Irregular. Price varies. Text in English, French, and Spanish. Incorporates *Yearbook of Fishery Statistics.*

Fisheries of the United States. Available from U. S. Government Printing Office. • Annual. $18.00. Issued by the National Marine Fisheries Service, National Oceanic and Atmospheric Administration, U. S. Department of Commerce.

U. S. Industry and Trade Outlook: The McGraw-Hill Companies and the U.S. Department of Commerce/ International Trade Administration. Datapso Research Corp. • Annual. $69.95. Produced by the International Trade Administration, U. S. Department of Commerce, in a "public-private" partnership with DRI/McGraw-Hill and Standard & Poor's. Provides basic data, outlook for the current year, and "Long-Term Prospects" (five-year projections) for a wide variety of products and services. Includes high technology industries. Formerly *U. S. Industrial Outlook.*

TRADE/PROFESSIONAL ASSOCIATIONS

Board of Trade of the Wholesale Seafood Merchants. Seven Dey St., Suite 801, New York, NY 10007. Phone: (212)732-4340 Fax: (212)732-6644.

OTHER SOURCES

Major Food and Drink Companies of the World. Available from The Gale Group. • 2001. $855.00. Fourth edition. Two volumes. Published by Graham & Whiteside. Contains profiles and trade names for more than 9,000 important food and beverage companies in various countries. In addition to foods, includes both alcoholic and nonalcoholic drink products.

The Seafood Market. MarketResearch.com. • 1997. $595.00. Market research report. Covers fresh, frozen, and canned seafood. Market projections are provided to the year 2001.

Thomas Food and Beverage Market Place. Grey House Publishing. • Annual. $295.00. Three volumes. Contains more than 40,000 entries covering food companies, beverages, food equipment, warehouse companies, food brokers, wholesalers, importers, and exporters. Formerly *Thomas Food Industry Register.*

SEALANTS

See: ADHESIVES

SEAPORTS

See: PORTS

SECRETARIAL PRACTICE

See: OFFICE PRACTICE

SECRETARIES

See: OFFICE PRACTICE

SECURITIES

See also: BONDS; CONVERTIBLE SECURITIES; DERIVATIVE SECURITIES; DIVIDENDS; FINANCIAL ANALYSIS; GOVERNMENT BONDS; INVESTMENT COMPANIES; CLOSED-END FUNDS; INVESTMENTS; MUNICIPAL BONDS; OBSOLETE SECURITIES; OVER-THE-COUNTER SECURITIES INDUSTRY; REAL ESTATE INVESTMENT TRUSTS; SECURITIES LAW AND REGULATION

GENERAL WORKS

Buying Treasury Securities: Bills, Notes, Bonds, Offerings Schedule, Conversions. Federal Reserve Bank of Philadelphia. • Revised as required. Free pamphlet. Provides clear definitions, information, and instructions relating to U. S. Treasury securities: short-term (bills), medium-term (notes), and long-term (bonds).

Financial Markets and Institutions. Jeff Madura. South-Western College Publishing Co. • 2000. $91.95. Fifth edition. (SWC-Economics Series).

Investing in the Over-the-Counter Markets: Stocks, Bonds, IPOs. Alvin D. Hall. John Wiley and Sons, Inc. • 1995. $29.95. Provides advice and information on investing in "unlisted" or NASDAQ (National Association of Securities Dealers Automated Quotation System) stocks, bonds, and initial public offerings (IPOs).

Securities Markets. Kenneth D. Garbade. McGraw-Hill. • 1982. $66.25. (Finance Series).

Security Analysis and Portfolio Management. Donald E. Fischer and Ronald L. Jordan. Prentice Hall. • 1995. $87.00. Sixth edition.

ABSTRACTS AND INDEXES

Investment Statistics Locator. Linda H. Bentley and Jennifer J. Kiesl, editors. Oryx Press. • 1994. $69.95. Expanded revised edition. Provides detailed subject indexing of more than 50 of the most-used sources of financial and investment data. Includes an annotated bibliography.

ALMANACS AND YEARBOOKS

Irwin International Almanac: Business and Investments. McGraw-Hill Professional. • 1994. $95.00. Second edition. Covers trends in global business and summarizes trading in major foreign securities markets.

BIBLIOGRAPHIES

Business Library Review: An International Journal. International Publishers Distributor. • Quarterly. Academic institutions, $318.00 per year;corporations, $501.00 per year.Incorporates *The Wall Street Review of Books* and *Economics and Business: An Annotated Bibliography.* Publishes scholarly reviews of books on a wide variety of topics in business, economics, and finance. Text in French.

BIOGRAPHICAL SOURCES

Who's Who in the Securities Industry. Securities Industry Association. Economist Publishing Co. • Annual. Price on application about 1,000 investment bankers.

CD-ROM DATABASES

Business Source Plus. EBSCO Information Services. • Monthly. $1,495.00 per year. Provides CD-ROM citations and abstracts to articles in about 650 business periodicals and newspapers, including *The Wall Street Journal.* Full text is provided from 200 selected periodicals. Covers accounting, communications, economics, finance, management, marketing, and other business subjects.

DIRECTORIES

Association for Investment Management and Research-Membership Directory. Association for Investment Management and Research. • Annual. $150.00. Members are professional investment managers and securities analysts.

Corporate Finance Sourcebook: The Guide to Major Capital Investment Source and Related Financial Services. R. R. Bowker. • Annual. $625.00. Lists more than 3,550 sources of corporate capital: investment bankers, securities firms, pension management companies, trust companies, insurance companies, and private lenders. Includes the names of over 13,000 key personnel.

Directory of Companies Required to File Annual Reports with the Securities and Exchange Commission. Securities and Exchange Commission. Available from U.S. Government Printing Office. • Annual. $46.00.

Moody's International Manual. Financial Information Services. • Annual. $3,175.00 per year. Includes weekly *News Reports.* Financial and other information about 3,000 publicly-owned corporations in 95 countries.

Morningstar American Depositary Receipts. Morningstar, Inc. • Biweekly. $195.00 per year. Looseleaf. Provides detailed profiles of 700 foreign companies having shares traded in the U. S. through American Depositary Receipts (ADRs).

Mortgage & Asset-Based Desk Reference: U. S. Buyside and Sellside Profiles. Capital Access International. • Annual. $395.00. Provides "detailed buyside and sellside profiles and contacts" for the mortgage and asset-based securities market.

Securities Industry Yearbook. Securities Industry Association. • Annual. Members, $85.00; non-members, $125.00. Information about securities industry firms and capital markets.

Standard and Poor's Security Dealers of North America. Standard & Poor's. • Semiannual. $480.00 per year; with *Supplements* every six weeks, $590.00 per year. Geographical listing of over 12,000 stock, bond, and commodity dealers.

ENCYCLOPEDIAS AND DICTIONARIES

The A-Z Vocabulary for Investors. American Institute for Economic Research. • 1997. $7.00. Second half of book is a "General Glossary" of about 400 financial terms "most-commonly used" in investing. First half contains lengthier descriptions of types of banking institutions (commercial banks, thrift institutions, credit unions), followed by succinct explanations of various forms of investment: stocks, bonds, options, futures, commodities, and "Other Investments" (collectibles, currencies, mortgages, precious metals, real estate, charitable trusts). (Economic Education Bulletin.).

Blackwell Encyclopedic Dictionary of Finance. Dean Paxson and Douglas Wood, editors. Blackwell Publishers. • 1997. $110.00. The editors are associated with the University of Manchester. Contains definitions of key terms combined with longer articles written by various U. S. and foreign business educators. Includes bibliographies and index. (Blackwell Encyclopedia of Management Series).

Dictionary of Finance and Investment Terms. John Downes and Jordan E. Goodman. Barron's Educational Series, Inc. • 1998. $12.95. Fifth revised edition. Provides clear explanations of more than 5,000 business, banking, financial, investment, and tax terms. Includes a separate list of financial abbreviations and acronyms.

Dictionary of Investing. Jerry M. Rosenberg. John Wiley and Sons, Inc. • 1992. $79.95. (Business Dictionary Series).

Encyclopedia of Banking and Finance. Charles J. Woelfel. McGraw-Hill Professional. • 1996. $50.00. 10th revised edition.

Knowledge Exchange Business Encyclopedia: Your Complete Business Advisor. Lorraine Spurge, editor. Knowledge Exchange LLC. • 1997. $45.00. Provides definitions of business terms and financial expressions, profiles of leading industries, tables of economic statistics, biographies of business leaders, and other business information. Includes "A Chronology of Business from 3000 B.C. Through 1995." Contains illustrations and three indexes.

Wall Street Thesaurus. Paul Sarnoff. Astor-Honor, Inc. • 1963. $19.95.

Wall Street Words: The Basics and Beyond. Richard J. Maturi. McGraw-Hill Professional. • 1991. $14.95. (Investor's Quick Reference Series).

HANDBOOKS AND MANUALS

Econometric Analysis of Financial Markets. J. Kaehler and P. Kugler, editors. Springer-Verlag New York, Inc. • 1994. $71.95. (Studies in Empirical Economics Series).

Econometrics of Financial Markets. John Y. Campbell and others. California Princeton Fulfillment Services. • 1997. $49.50. Written for advanced students and industry professionals. Includes chapters on "The Predictability of Asset Returns," "Derivative Pricing Models," and "Fixed-Income Securities." Provides a discussion of the random walk theory of investing and tests of the theory.

Handbook of Fixed Income Securities. Frank J. Fabozzi. McGraw-Hill Higher Education. • 2000. $99.95. Sixth edition. Topics include risk measurement, valuation techniques, and portfolio strategy.

Handbook of Mortgage-Backed Securities. Frank J. Fabozzi, editor. McGraw-Hill Professional. • 1995. $85.00. Fourth edition.

Library of Investment Banking. Robert L. Kuhn, editor. McGraw-Hill Professional. • 1990. $475.00. Seven volumes: 1. Investing and Risk Management; 2. Capital Raising and Financial Structure; 3. Corporate and Municipal Securities; 4. Mergers, Acquisitions, and Leveraged Buyouts; 5. Mortgage and Asset Securitization; 6. International Finance and Investing; 7. Index.

Moody's Manuals. Bank and Finance Manual, Industrial Manual, Municipal and Government Manual, OTC Industrial Manual, Public Utility Manual, Transportation Manual. Financial Information Services. • Annual. Looseleaf supplements. Prices on application.

Moody's OTC Unlisted Manual (Over the Counter). Financial Information Services. • Annual, $1,550.00 per year. Includes supplement *Moody's OTC Unlisted News Report.*

Mortgage-Backed Securities: Developments and Trends in the Secondary Mortgage Market. Kenneth G. Lore. West Group. • Annual. $196.00.

Options, Futures, and Other Derivatives. John C. Hull. Prentice Hall. • 1999. $94.00. Fourth edition.

Securities: Public and Private Offerings. William W. Prifti. West Group. • $250.00. Two looseleaf volumes. Periodic supplementation. How to issue securities. (Securities Law Series).

INTERNET DATABASES

Business Week Online. McGraw-Hill. Phone: (212)512-2762 Fax: (212)512-6590 • URL: http://www.businessweek.com • Web site provides complete contents of current issue of *Business Week* plus "BW Daily" with additonal business news, financial market quotes, and corporate information from Standard & Poor's. Includes various features, such as "Banking Center" with mortgage and interest data, and "Interactive Computer Buying Guide." The "Business Week Archive" is fully searchable back to 1991. Fees: Mostly free, but full-text archive articles are $2.00 each.

Fedstats. Federal Interagency Council on Statistical Policy. Phone: (202)395-7254 • URL: http://www.fedstats.gov • Web site features an efficient search facility for full-text statistics produced by more than 70 federal agencies, including the Census Bureau, the Bureau of Economic Analysis, and the Bureau of Labor Statistics. Boolean searches can be made within one agency or for all agencies combined. Links are offered to international statistical bureaus, including the UN, IMF, OECD, UNESCO, Eurostat, and 20 individual countries. Fees: Free.

Wall Street Journal Interactive Edition. Dow Jones & Co., Inc. Phone: 800-369-2834 or (212)416-2000 Fax: (212)416-2658 E-mail: inquiries@interactive.wsj.com • URL: http://www.wsj.com • Fee-based Web site providing online searching of worldwide information from the *The Wall Street Journal.* Includes "Company Snapshots," "The Journal's Greatest Hits," "Index to Market Data," "14-Day Searchable Archive," "Journal Links," etc. Financial price quotes are available. Fees: $49.00 per year; $29.00 per year to print subscribers.

Web Finance: Covering the Electronic Evolution of Finance. Securities Data Publishing. Phone: (212)765-5311 or 800-455-5844 Fax: (212)321-2336 E-mail: webfinance@tfn.com • URL: http://www.webfinance.net • Bi-weekly print and daily web-site publication of financial services on the Web, including financial links, archives, brokerage stocks, deal financing, and other financial and investment news and information.

ONLINE DATABASES

DRI Financial and Credit Statistics. Data Products Division. • Contains U. S. and international statistical data relating to money markets, interest rates, foreign exchange, banking, and stock and bond indexes. Time period is 1973 to date, with continuous updating. Inquire as to online cost and availability.

DRI U.S. Central Database. Data Products Division. • Provides more than 23,000 business, financial, demographic, economic, foreign trade, and industry-related time series for the U.S. Includes national income, population, retail-wholesale trade, price indexes, labor data, housing, industrial production, banking, interest rates, money supply, etc. Time period is generally 1947 to date (some data back to 1929). Updating varies. Inquire as to online cost and availability.

F & S Index. The Gale Group. • Contains about four million citations to worldwide business, financial, and industrial or consumer product literature appearing from 1972 to date. Weekly updates. Inquire as to online cost and availability.

Fitch IBCA Ratings Delivery Service. Fitch IBCA, Inc. • Provides online delivery of Fitch financial ratings in three sectors: "Corporate Finance" (corporate bonds, insurance companies), "Structured Finance" (asset-backed securities), and "U.S. Public Finance" (municipal bonds). Daily updates. Inquire as to online cost and availability.

Standard and Poor's Daily News Online. Standard and Poor's Corp. • Full text of business news and other information, 1984 to present. Inquire as to online cost and availability.

Value Line Convertible Data Base. Value Line Publishing, Inc. • Provides online data for about 600 convertible bonds and other convertible securities: price, yield, premium, issue size, liquidity, and maturity. Information is current, with weekly updates. Inquire as to online cost and availability.

Vickers On-Line. Vickers Stock Research Corp. • Provides detailed online information relating to insider trading and the securities holdings of institutional investors. Daily updates. Inquire as to online cost and availability.

PERIODICALS AND NEWSLETTERS

Bank Credit Analyst. BCA Publications Ltd. • Monthly. $695.00 per year. "The independent monthly forecast and analysis of trends in business conditions and major investment markets based on a continuous appraisal of money and credit flows." Includes many charts and graphs relating to money, credit, and securities in the U. S.

Barron's: The Dow Jones Business and Financial Weekly. Dow Jones and Co., Inc. • Weekly. $145.00 per year.

Bloomberg: A Magazine for Market Professionals. Bloomberg L.P. • Monthly. Free to qualified personnel. Edited for securities dealers and investment managers.

Financial Analysts Journal. Association for Investment Management and Research. • Bimonthly. $175.00 per year.

Financial Markets, Institutions, and Instruments. New York University, Salomon Center. Blackwell Publishers. • Five times a year. $219.00 per year. Edited to "bridge the gap between the academic and professional finance communities." Special fifth issue each year provides surveys of developments in four areas: money and banking, derivative securities, corporate finance, and fixed-income securities.

Financial Times [London]. Available from FT Publications, Inc. • Daily, except Sunday. $184.00 per year. An international business and financial newspaper, featuring news from London, Paris, Frankfurt, New York, and Tokyo. Includes worldwide stock and bond market data, commodity market data, and monetary/currency exchange information.

Institutional Investor: The Magazine for Finance and Investment. Institutional Investor. • Monthly. $475.00 per year. Edited for portfolio managers and other investment professionals. Special feature issues include "Country Credit Ratings," "Fixed Income Trading Ranking," "All-America Research Team," and "Global Banking Ranking.".

International Bank Credit Analyst. BCA Publications Ltd. • Monthly. $795.00 per year. "A monthly forecast and analysis of currency movements, interest rates, and stock market developments in the principal countries, based on a continuous appraisal of money and credit trends worldwide." Includes many charts and graphs providing international coverage of money, credit, and securities.

Investment Dealers' Digest. Securities Data Publishing. • Weekly. $750.00 per year. Covers financial news, trends, new products, people, private placements, new issues of securities, and other aspects of the investment business. Includes feature stories. (Securities Data Publishing is a unit of Thomson Financial.).

Investor's Business Daily. Investor's Business Daily, Inc. • Daily. $169.00 per year. Newspaper.

Mortgage-Backed Securities Letter. Securities Data Publishing. • Weekly. $1,595.00 per year. Newsletter. Provides news and analysis of the mortgage-backed securities market, including performance reports. (Securities Data Publishing is a unit of Thomson Financial.).

Official Summary of Security Transactions and Holdings. U. S. Securities and Exchange Commission. Available from U. S. Government Printing Office. • Monthly. $166.00 per year. Lists buying or selling of each publicly held corporation's stock by its officers, directors, or other insiders.

Operations Management. Institutional Investor. • Weekly. $2,105.00 per year. Newsletter. Edited for managers of securities clearance and settlement at financial institutions. Covers new products, technology, legalities, management practices, and other topics related to securities processing.

SEC News Digest. U.S. Securities and Exchange Commission, Public Reference Room. • Daily.

Securities Industry News. American Banker. • Weekly. $275.00 per year. Covers securities dealing and processing, including regulatory compliance, shareholder services, human resources, transaction clearing, and technology.

Securities Week. McGraw-Hill. • Weekly. $1,325.00 per year.

The Wall Street Journal. Dow Jones & Co., Inc. • Daily. $175.00 per year. Covers news and trends relating to business, industry, finance, the economy, and international commerce. Provides extensive price and other data for the securities, commodity, options, futures, foreign exchange, and money markets.

Wall Street Transcript: A Professional Publication for the Business and Financial Community. Wall Street Transcript Corp. • Weekly. $1,890.00. per year. Provides reprints of investment research reports.

PRICE SOURCES

Bank and Quotation Record. William B. Dana Co. • Monthly. $130.00 per year.

National Bond Summary. National Quotation Bureau, Inc. • Monthly. $420.00 per year. Semiannual cumulations. Includes price quotes for both active and inactive issues.

National Stock Summary. National Quotation Bureau, Inc. • Monthly. $480.00 per year. Semiannual cumulations. Includes price quotes for both active and inactive issues, with transfer agents, market makers (brokers), and other information. (The National Quotation Bureau also provides daily and weekly stock price services.).

RESEARCH CENTERS AND INSTITUTES

Center for Research in Security Prices. University of Chicago, 725 S. Wells St., Suite 800, Chicago, IL 60607. Phone: (773)702-7467 Fax: (773)753-4797 E-mail: mail@crsp.uchicago.edu • URL: http://www.crsp.com.

Institute for Quantitative Research in Finance. Church Street Station, P.O. Box 6194, New York, NY 10249-6194. Phone: (212)744-6825 Fax: (212)517-2259 E-mail: daleberman@compuserve • Financial research areas include quantitative methods, securities analysis, and the financial structure of industries. Also known as the "Q Group.".

STATISTICS SOURCES

Business Statistics of the United States. Courtenay M. Slater, editor. Bernan Associates. • 1999. $74.00. Fifth edition. Based on *Business Statistics*, formerly issue by the Bureau of Economic Analysis, U. S. Department of Commerce. Provides basic data for a wide variety of U. S. industries, services, and economic indicators. Most statistics are shown annually for 29 years and monthly for the most recent four years.

International Guide to Securities Market Indices. Henry Shilling, editor. Fitzroy Dearborn Publishers. • 1996. $140.00. Describes 400 stock market, bond market, and other financial price indexes maintained in various countries of the world (300 of the indexes are described in detail, including graphs and 10-year data).

SBBI Monthly Market Reports. Ibbotson Associates. • Monthly. $995.00 per year. These reports provide current updating of stocks, bonds, bills, and inflation (SBBI) data. Each issue contains the most recent month's investment returns and index values for various kinds of securities, as well as monthly statistics for the past year. Analysis is included.

SBBI Quarterly Market Reports. Ibbotson Associates. • Quarterly. $495.00 per year. Each quarterly volume contains detailed updates to stocks, bonds, bills, and inflation (SBBI) data. Includes total and sector returns for the broad stock market, small company stocks, intermediate and long-term government bonds, long-term corporate bonds, and U. S. Treasury Bills. Analyses, tables, graphs, and market consensus forecasts are provided.

Standard & Poor's Stock Reports: American Stock Exchange. Standard & Poor's. • Irregular. $1,035.00 per year. Looseleaf service. Provides two pages of financial details and other information for each corporation listed on the American Stock Exchange.

Standard & Poor's Stock Reports: NASDAQ and Regional Exchanges. Standard & Poor's. • Irregular. $1,100.00 per year. Looseleaf service. Provides two pages of financial details and other information for each corporation included.

Standard & Poor's Stock Reports: New York Stock Exchange. Standard & Poor's. • Irregular. $1,295.00 per year. Looseleaf service. Provides two pages of financial details and other information for each corporation with stock listed on the N. Y. Stock Exchange.

Statistical Information on the Financial Services Industry. American Bankers Association. • Annual. Members, $150.00; non-members, $275.00. Presents a wide variety of data relating to banking and financial services, including consumer economics, personal finance, credit, government loans, capital markets, and international banking.

Stocks, Bonds, Bills, and Inflation Yearbook. Ibbotson Associates. • Annual. $92.00. Provides detailed data from 1926 to the present on inflation and the returns from various kinds of financial investments, such as small-cap stocks and long-term government bonds.

Survey of Current Business. Available from U. S. Government Printing Office. • Monthly. $49.00 per year. Issued by Bureau of Economic Analysis, U. S. Department of Commerce. Presents a wide variety of business and economic data.

United States Securities and Exchange Commission Annual Report. U.S. Government Printing Office. • Annual. The Commission maintains a Web site at http://www.sec.gov.

TRADE/PROFESSIONAL ASSOCIATIONS

Association for Investment Management and Research. 560 Ray C. Hunt Dr., Charlottesville, VA 22903-0668. Phone: 800-247-8132 or (804)951-5499 Fax: (804)951-5262 E-mail: info@aimr.org • URL: http://www.aimr.org.

National Association of Securities Dealers. 1735 K St., N.W., Washington, DC 20006-1506. Phone: (202)728-8000 Fax: (202)293-6260 • URL: http://www.nasdr.com/1000.asp.

Securities Industry Association. 120 Broadway, New York, NY 10271-0080. Phone: (212)608-1500 Fax: (212)608-1604 E-mail: info@sia.com • URL: http://www.sia.com.

Security Traders Association. One World Trade Center, Suite 4511, New York, NY 10048. Phone: (212)524-0484 Fax: (212)321-3449.

OTHER SOURCES

Capital Changes Reports. CCH, Inc. • Weekly. $1,310.00. Six looseleaf volumes. Arranged alphabetically by company. This service presents a chronological capital history that includes reorganizations, mergers and consolidations. Recent actions are found in Volume One - "New Matters.".

Factiva. Dow Jones Reuters Business Interactive, LLC. • Fee-based Web site provides "global news and business information through Web sites and content integration solutions." Includes Dow Jones and Reuters newswires, The Wall Street Journal, and more than 7,000 other sources of current news, historical articles, market research reports, and investment analysis. Content includes 96 major U. S. newspapers, 900 non-English sources, trade publications, media transcripts, country profiles, news photos, etc.

Fitch Insights. Fitch Investors Service, Inc. • Biweekly. $1,040.00 per year. Includes bond rating actions and explanation of actions. Provides commentary and Fitch's view of the financial markets.

Nexis.com. Lexis-Nexis Group. • Fee-based Web site offers searching of about 2.8 billion documents in some 30,000 news, business, and legal information sources. Features include a subject directory covering 1,200 topics in 34 categories and a Company Dossier containing information on more than 500,000 public and private companies. Boolean searching is offered.

SECURITIES AND EXCHANGE COMMISSION

See: SECURITIES LAW AND REGULATION

SECURITIES, CONVERTIBLE

See: CONVERTIBLE SECURITIES

SECURITIES, DERIVATIVE

See: DERIVATIVE SECURITIES

SECURITIES LAW AND REGULATION

GENERAL WORKS

Corporate Finance and the Securities Laws. Charles J. Johnson and Joseph McLaughlin. Panel Publishers. • 1997. $170.00. Second edition.

Federal Securities Laws: Legislative History, 1933-1982 and the 1987-90 Supplement. Federal Bar Association, Securities Law Committee. Books on Demand. • 1983. $1,150.40. Six volumes.

Securities Regulation. Louis Loss and Joel Seligman. Little, Brown and Co. • 1988. $240.00. Third edition. Three volumes. Includes 1969 supplement. Covers the fundamentals of government regulation of securities.

ABSTRACTS AND INDEXES

Current Law Index: Multiple Access to Legal Periodicals. The Gale Group. • Monthly. $650.00 per year. Produced in cooperation with the American Association of Law Libraries. Indexes more than 900 law journals, legal newspapers, and specialty publications from the U.S., Canada, U.K., Ireland, Australia, and New Zealand.

Index to Legal Periodicals and Books. H. W. Wilson Co. • Monthly. Quarterly and annual cumulations. $270.00 per year. CD-ROM version available at $1,495.00 per year.

ALMANACS AND YEARBOOKS

American Law Yearbook. The Gale Group. • Annual. $155.00. Serves as a yearly supplement to *West's Encyclopedia of American Law.* Describes new legal developments in many subject areas.

Emerging Trends in Securities Law. West Group. • Annual. $176.00. Presents a detailed chronicle of events and analysis of evolving trends.

Securities, Commodities, and Banking: Year in Review. CCH, Inc. • Annual. $55.00. Summarizes the year's significant legal and regulatory developments.

Securities Law Review. West Group. • Annual. $189.00. Current thinking in securities law.

CD-ROM DATABASES

Compact D/New Issues. Disclosure, Inc. • Monthly, $4,500.00 per year. Provides CD-ROM financial and other information relating to initial public offerings, spinoffs, recapitalizations, exchange offers, and other registrations filed with the Securities and Exchange Commission in compliance with the Securities Act of 1933. Time period is 1990 to date.

Compact D/SEC. Disclosure, Inc. • Monthly. Contains three CD-ROM files. (1) Disclosure: Provides Securities and Exchange Commission filings for over 12,500 publicly held corporations. (2) Disclosure/Spectrum Ownership Profiles: Provides detailed corporate descriptions and complete ownership information for over 6,000 public companies. (3) Zacks Earnings Estimates: Provides earnings per share forecasts for about 4,000 U. S. corporations.

SEC Online on SilverPlatter. Available from SilverPlatter Information, Inc. • Quarterly. $3,950.00 per year to nonprofit organizations; $6,950.00 per year to businesses. Produced by Disclosure, Inc. Provides complete text on CD-ROM of documents filed with the Securities and Exchange Commission by over 5,000 publicly held corporations, including 10K forms (annual), 10Q forms (quarterly), and proxies. Also includes annual reports to stockholders.

WILSONDISC: Index to Legal Periodicals and Books. H. W. Wilson Co. • Monthly. Including unlimited online access to *Index to Legal Periodicals* through WILSONLINE. Contains CD-ROM indexing of more than 800 English language legal periodicals from 1981 to date and 2,500 books.

DIRECTORIES

SEC Filing Companies. Disclosure Inc. • Semiannual. Free. A list of all public companies that file reports with the U.S. Securities and Exchange Commission.

ENCYCLOPEDIAS AND DICTIONARIES

West's Encyclopedia of American Law. Available from The Gale Group. • 1997. $995.00. Second edition. 12 volumes. Published by West Group. Covers a wide variety of legal topics for the general reader. Formerly *Guide to American Law: Everyone's Legal Encyclopedia* (1985).

HANDBOOKS AND MANUALS

Corporate Counsellor's Deskbook. Dennis J. Block and Michael A. Epstein, editors. Panel Publishing. • 1999. $220.00. Fifth edition. Looseleaf. Annual supplementation. Covers a wide variety of corporate legal issues, including internal investigations, indemnification, insider trading, intellectual property, executive compensation, antitrust, export-import, real estate, environmental law, government contracts, and bankruptcy.

Financing the Corporation. Richard A. Booth. West Group. • $110.00. Looseleaf service. Periodic supplementation. Covers a wide variety of corporate finance legal topics, from initial capital structure to public sale of securities.

Guide to Federal Regulation of Derivatives. CCH, Inc. • 1998. $99.00. Explains the complex derivatives regulations of the Securities and Exchange Commission. Covers swap agreements, third-party derivatives, credit derivatives, mutual fund liquidity, and other topics.

Law of Corporate Officers and Directors: Indemnification and Insurance. Joseph W. Bishop, Jr. West Group. • 1990. $130.00. Practical guidance for developing corporate policy, drafting agreements and litigation.

Publicly Traded Corporations: Governance, Operation, and Regulation. John H. Matheson. West Group. • 1993. $130.00. Covers a wide range of corporate legal problems and issues, including shareholder communications and "tender offers and change of control transactions." (Corporate Law Series).

Responsibilities of Corporate Officers and Directors Under Federal Securities Law. CCH, Inc. • Annual. $55.00. Includes discussions of indemnification, "D & O" insurance, corporate governance, and insider liability.

Responsibilities of Corporate Officers and Directors Under Federal Securities Laws. CCH, Inc. • 2000. $65.00.

SEC Accounting Rules, with Financial Reporting Releases, Codification of Financial Reporting Policies, Accounting and Auditing Enforcement Releases, and Staff Accounting Bulletins. CCH, Inc. • Looseleaf. $448.00.

SEC Financial Reporting: Annual Reports to Shareholders, Form 10-K, and Quarterly Financial Reporting. Matthew Bender & Co., Inc. • $215.00. Looseleaf service. Periodic supplementation. Coverage of aspects of financial reporting and disclosure under Regulations S-X and S-K, with step-by-step procedures for preparing information for Form 10-K and annual shareholders reports.

SEC Handbook: Rules and Forms for Financial Statements and Related Disclosures. CCH, Inc. • Annual. $54.00. Contains full text of rules and requirements set by the Securities and Exchange Commisssion for preparation of corporate financial statements.

Securities Counseling for New and Developing Companies. Stuart R. Cohn. West Group. • 1993. $130.00. Covers securities planning for new businesses, with an emphasis on the avoidance of legal violations and civil liabilities. (Corporate Law Series).

Securities Crimes. Marvin Pickholz. West Group. • $145.00. Looseleaf service. Periodic supplementation. Analyzes the enfo of federal securities laws from the viewpoint of the defendant. Discusses Securities and Exchange Commission (SEC) investigations and federal sentencing guidelines.

Securities Law Compliance: A Guide for Brokers, Dealers, and Investors. Allan H. Pessin. McGraw-Hill Professional. • 1989. $70.00.

Securities Law Handbook. Harold S. Bloomenthal. West Group. • Annual. $206.00.

Securities: Public and Private Offerings. William W. Prifti. West Group. • $250.00. Two looseleaf volumes. Periodic supplementation. How to issue securities. (Securities Law Series).

INTERNET DATABASES

DBC Online: America's Leading Provider of Real-Time Market Data to the Individual Investor. Data Broadcasting Corp. Phone: (415)571-1800 E-mail: dbcinfo@dbc.com • URL: http://www.dbc.com • Web site provides a wide variety of real-time securities market prices, data, and charts. Covers bonds ("BondVu"), stocks, commodities, options, mutual funds, major indexes, industry indexes, international markets, etc. Also includes news, SEC documents ("Smart-Edgar"), and various other features. Fees: Both free and fee-based, depending on level of information.

Rutgers Accounting Web (RAW). Rutgers University Accounting Research Center. Phone: (201)648-5172 Fax: (201)648-1233 • URL: http://www.rutgers.edu/accounting • RAW Web site provides extensive links to sources of national and international accounting information, such as the Big Six accounting firms, the Financial Accounting Standards Board (FASB), SEC filings (EDGAR), journals, publishers, software, the International Accounting Network, and "Internet's largest list of accounting firms in USA." Searching is offered. Fees: Free.

U. S. Securities and Exchange Commission. Phone: 800-732-0330 or (202)942-7040 Fax: (202)942-9634 E-mail: webmaster@sec.gov • URL: http://www.sec.gov • SEC Web site offers free access through EDGAR to text of official corporate filings, such as annual reports (10-K), quarterly reports (10-Q), and proxies. (EDGAR is "Electronic Data Gathering, Analysis, and Retrieval System.") An example is given of how to obtain executive compensation data from proxies. Text of the daily *SEC News Digest* is offered, as are links to other government sites, non-government market regulators, and U. S. stock exchanges. Search facilities are extensive. Fees: Free.

ONLINE DATABASES

EDGAR Plus. Disclosure, Inc. • Provides SEC corporate filings full-text, plus other information, such as Fortune and Forbes rankings. Time period is 1968 to date, with continuous updating. Inquire as to online cost and availability. (EDGAR is the SEC's Electronic Data Gathering, Analysis, and Retrieval system.).

Index to Legal Periodicals and Books (Online). H. W. Wilson Co. • Broad coverage of law journals and books 1981 to date. Monthly updates. Inquire as to online cost and availability.

LEXIS Financial Information Service. LEXIS-NEXIS. • Includes many business and financial files, including the full text of *SEC News Digest, Zacks Earnings Forecaster,* SEC filings, and brokerage house research reports. Various time spans and updating frequencies. Inquire as to online cost and availability.

SEC Online. Disclosure, Inc. • Provides complete text online of reports filed by over 5,000 public corporations with the U. S. Securities and Exchange Commission. Includes 10-K (official annual reports), 10-Q (quarterly), proxy statements, annual reports for stockholders, and other documents. Covers 1987 to date, with updates two or three times a week. Inquire as to online cost and availability.

PERIODICALS AND NEWSLETTERS

Compliance Reporter. Institutional Investor. • Biweekly. $2,105.00 per year. Newsletter for investment dealers and others on complying with securities laws and regulations.

Journal of Taxation of Financial Products. CCH, Inc. • Bimonthly. $249.00 per year.

Legal Times. American Lawyer Media, L.P. • Weekly. Individuals, $249.00 per year; institutions, $635.00 per year.

The Review of Securities and Commodities Regulations: An Analysis of Current Laws, Regulations Affecting the Securities and Futures Industries. Standard and Poor's. • 22 times a year. $350.00 per year.

SEC News Digest. U.S. Securities and Exchange Commission, Public Reference Room. • Daily.

SEC Today (Securities Exchange Commission). Washington Service Bureau, Inc. • Daily. $760.00 per year. Newsletter. Includes the official *SEC News Digest* from the Securities and Exchange Commission and reports on public company filing activity.

Securities and Federal Corporate Law Report. West Group. • 11 times a year. $308.00 per year. Newsletter.

Securities Arbitration Commentator: Covering Significant Issues and Events in Securities/ Commodities Arbitration. Richard P. Ryder. • Monthly. $348.00 per year. Newsletter. Edited for attorneys and other professionals concerned with securities arbitration.

Securities Regulation Law Journal. Warren, Gorham and Lamont/RIA Group. • Quarterly. $224.00 per year. Provides analysis and in-depth advice including regulations, SEC pronouncements, legislation and litigation. Shows how to comply with all the regulations affecting issuance and sale of securities and their transfer and trading.

Securities Week. McGraw-Hill. • Weekly. $1,325.00 per year.

Wall Street Letter: Newsweekly for Investment Banking and Brokerage Community. Institutional Investor. • Weekly. $2,665.00 per year. Newsletter for stock brokers and companies providing services for stock brokers. Emphasis is on regulatory matters.

RESEARCH CENTERS AND INSTITUTES

Lexis.com Research System. Lexis-Nexis Group. Phone: 800-227-9597 or (937)865-6800 Fax: (937)865-6909 E-mail: webmaster@prod.lexis-nexis.com • URL: http://www.lexis.com • Fee-based Web site offers extensive searching of a wide variety of legal sources. Additional features include Daily Opinion Service, lexis.com Bookstore, Career Center, CLE Center, Law Schools, and Practice Pages ("Pages specific to areas of specialty").

TRADE/PROFESSIONAL ASSOCIATIONS

North American Securities Administrators Association. 10 G St., N.E., Ste. 710, Washington, DC 20002. Phone: (202)737-0900 Fax: (202)783-3571 E-mail: info@nasaa.org • Members are state officials who administer "blue sky" securities laws.

OTHER SOURCES

Blue Sky Law. Joseph C. Long. West Group. • $250.00 per year. Two looseleaf volumes. Periodic supplementation. (Securities Law Series).

Blue Sky Law Reports. CCH, Inc. • Semimonthly. $1,214.00. Five looseleaf volumes. Covers state securities laws.

Blue Sky Regulation. Matthew Bender & Co., Inc. • $950.00. Four looseleaf volumes. Periodic supplementation. Covers state securities laws and regulations.

BNA's Banking Report: Legal and Regulatory Developments in the Financial Services Industry. Bureau of National Affairs, Inc. • Weekly. $1,221.00 per year. Two volumes. Looseleaf. Emphasis on federal regulations.

Commodity Futures Law Reports. CCH, Inc. • Semimonthly. $995.00 per year. Looseleaf service. Periodic supplementation. Includes legal aspects of financial futures and stock options trading.

Corporate Compliance Series. West Group. • Eleven looseleaf volumes, with periodic supplementation. $990.00. Covers criminal and civil liability problems for corporations. Includes employee safety, product liability, pension requirements, securities violations, equal employment opportunity issues, intellectual property, employee hiring and firing, and other corporate compliance topics.

Factiva. Dow Jones Reuters Business Interactive, LLC. • Fee-based Web site provides "global news and business information through Web sites and content integration solutions." Includes Dow Jones and Reuters newswires, The Wall Street Journal, and more than 7,000 other sources of current news, historical articles, market research reports, and investment analysis. Content includes 96 major U. S. newspapers, 900 non-English sources, trade publications, media transcripts, country profiles, news photos, etc.

Federal Securities Act of 1933-Treatise and Primary Source Material. A. A. Sommer. Matthew Bender & Co., Inc. • $660.00. Two looseleaf volumes. Covers application of the Federal Securities Act of 1933 and amendments.

Federal Securities Exchange Act of 1934. Edward N. Gadsby and A. A. Sommer. Matthew Bender & Co., Inc. • $660.00. Two looseleaf volumes. Periodic supplementation. Covers application of the Federal Securities Exchange Act of 1934 and amendments.

Federal Securities Law Reports. CCH, Inc. • Weekly. $1,600.00 per year. Looseleaf service. Seven volumes.

International Capital Markets and Securities Regulation. Harold S. Bloomenthal. West Group. • Six looseleaf volumes. $795.00. Periodic supplementation. Securities regulation in industrialized nations. (Securities Law Series).

Manual of Corporate Forms for Securities Practice. Arnold S. Jacobs. West Group. • $395.00. Three looseleaf volumes. Periodic supplementation. (Securitie Laws Series).

Nexis.com. Lexis-Nexis Group. • Fee-based Web site offers searching of about 2.8 billion documents in some 30,000 news, business, and legal information sources. Features include a subject directory covering 1,200 topics in 34 categories and a Company Dossier containing information on more than 500,000 public and private companies. Boolean searching is offered.

Taxation of Securities Transactions. Matthew Bender & Co., Inc. • $260.00. Looseleaf service.Periodic supplementation. Covers taxation of a wide variety of securities transactions, including those involving stocks, bonds, options, short sales, new issues, mutual funds, dividend distributions, foreign securities, and annuities.

SECURITIES, OBSOLETE

See: OBSOLETE SECURITIES

SECURITIES, TAX EXEMPT

See: MUNICIPAL BONDS

SECURITY ANALYSIS

See: FINANCIAL ANALYSIS

SECURITY, COMPUTER

See: COMPUTER CRIME AND SECURITY

SECURITY DEALERS

See: STOCK BROKERS

SECURITY, INDUSTRIAL

See: INDUSTRIAL SECURITY PROGRAMS

SECURITY SYSTEMS, ELECTRONIC

See: ELECTRONIC SECURITY SYSTEMS

SEED INDUSTRY

ABSTRACTS AND INDEXES

Biological and Agricultural Index. H.W. Wilson Co. • 11 times a year. Annual and quarterly cumulations. Service basis.

Seed Abstracts. Available from CABI Publishing North America. • Monthly. $540.00 per year. Published in England by CABI Publishing. Provides worldwide coverage of the literature.

FINANCIAL RATIOS

Annual Statement Studies. Robert Morris Associates: The Association of Lending and Credit Risk Professiona. • Annual. Free to members; non-members, $140.00. Median and quartile financial ratios are given for over 400 kinds of manufacturing, wholesale, retail, construction, and consumer finance establishments. Data is sorted by both asset size and sales volume. Includes a clearly written "Definition of Ratios" and an alphabetical industry index.

HANDBOOKS AND MANUALS

Global Seed Guide: World Reference Source for the Commercial Seed Industry. Ball Publishing. • Annual. $40.00. Edited by *Seed Trade News* (http://www.seedtradenews.com). Includes company listings, type of business, type of seed, research centers, industry data, events calendar, and associations.

ONLINE DATABASES

Biological and Agricultural Index Online. H. W. Wilson Co. • Indexes a wide variety of agricultural and biological periodicals, 1983 to date. Monthly updates. Inquire as to online cost and availability.

CAB Abstracts. CAB International North America. • Contains 46 specialized abstract collections covering over 10,000 journals and monographs in the areas of agriculture, horticulture, forest products, farm products, nutrition, dairy science, poultry, grains, animal health, entomology, etc. Time period is 1972 to date, with monthly updates. Inquire as to online cost and availability. *CAB Abstracts on CD-ROM* also available, with annual updating.

PERIODICALS AND NEWSLETTERS

The Seed Technologist Newsletter. Society of Commercial Seed Technologists. • Three times a year. $35.00 per year. Includes annual *Proceedings.*

Seed Trade News. Z M A G Publishing, Inc. • Monthly. $30.00 per year. Includes *International Seed Directory.*

Seed World. Scranton Gillette Communications, Inc. • Monthly. $30.00 per year. Provides information on the seed industry for buyers and sellers. Supplement available *Seed Trade Buyer's Guide.*

TRADE/PROFESSIONAL ASSOCIATIONS

American Seed Research Foundation. 601 13th St., N.W., Suite 570 S, Washington, DC 20005. Phone: (202)638-3128 Fax: (202)638-3171.

American Seed Trade Association. 601 13th St., N.W., Suite 570 S, Washington, DC 20005-3807. Phone: (202)638-3128 Fax: (202)638-3171 E-mail: amseed@amseed.com • URL: http://www.amseed.com.

Association of American Seed Control Officials. 50 Harry S. Truman Parkway, Annapolis, MD 21401. Phone: (410)841-5960 Fax: (410)841-5969 • URL: http://www.isco.purdue.edu/aasco/index_aasco.htm.

National Council of Commercial Plant Breeders. 601 13th St., N.W., Suite 570 S., Washington, DC 20005. Phone: (202)638-3128 Fax: (202)638-3171.

Society of Commercial Seed Technologists. c/o Andy Evans, 2021 Coffey Rd., 202 KH, Columbus, OH 43210. Phone: (614)292-8242 Fax: (614)292-

7162 E-mail: evans.223@osu.edu • URL: http://www.seedtechnology.net.

OTHER SOURCES

Global Seed Markets. Theta Reports/PJB Medical Publications, Inc. • 2000. $1,040.00. Market research data. Covers the major seed sectors, including cereal crops, legumes, oilseed crops, fibre crops, and beet crops. Provides analysis of biotechnology developments. (Theta Report No. DS208E.).

SELENIUM INDUSTRY

ABSTRACTS AND INDEXES

CA Selects: Selenium and Tellurium Chemistry. American Chemical Society. Chemical Abstracts Service. • Semiweekly. Members, $75.00 per year; non-members, $250.00 per year. Incorporates *Selenium and Tellurium Abstracts.*

DIRECTORIES

OPD Chemical Buyers Directory. Schnell Publishing Co., Inc. • Annual. $129.00. Included in subscription to *Chemical Marketing Reporter.* About 1,500 suppliers of chemical process materials and more than 300 companies which transport and store chemicals in the U.S.

ONLINE DATABASES

Globalbase. The Gale Group. • Provides more than one million online summaries of business, industrial, and economic news reports from more than 1,000 publications worldwide. Covers a wide range of material appearing in international trade journals, professional magazines, and newspapers. Time period is 1984 to date, with weekly updates. Inquire as to online cost and availability.

PRICE SOURCES

Chemical Market Reporter. Schnell Publishing Co., Inc. • Weekly. $139.00 per year. Quotes current prices for a wide range of chemicals. Formerly *Chemical Marketing Reporter.*

STATISTICS SOURCES

Mineral Commodity Summaries. Available from U. S. Government Printing Office. • Annual. Published by the U. S. Geological Survey, Department of the Interior (http://www.usgs.gov). Contains detailed, five-year data for about 90 nonfuel minerals. Covers a wide range of statistics, including production, imports, exports, consumption, reserves, prices, tariff information, and industry employment. (Two pages are devoted to each mineral.).

Non-Ferrous Metal Data Yearbook. American Bureau of Metal Statistics. • Annual. $395.00. Provides about 200 statistical tables covering many nonferrous metals. Includes production, consumption, inventories, exports, imports, and other data.

TRADE/PROFESSIONAL ASSOCIATIONS

American Bureau of Metal Statistics. P.O. Box 805, Chatham, NJ 07928. Phone: (973)701-2299 Fax: (973)701-2152 E-mail: info@abms.com • URL: http://www.abms.com • Members are metal companies. Compiles and publishes detailed statistical data on a wide variety of nonferrous metals: aluminum, copper, gold, lead, nickel, platinum, silver, tin, titanium, uranium, zinc, and others.

SELF-EMPLOYMENT

See also: ENTREPRENEURS AND INTRAPRENEURS; KEOGH PLANS; SMALL BUSINESS

GENERAL WORKS

Is It Too Late to Run Away and Join the Circus? Finding the Life You Really Want. Marti Smye. Simon and Schuster Trade. • 1998. $14.95. Provides philosophical and inspirational advice on leaving corporate life and becoming self-employed as a consultant or whatever. Central theme is dealing with major changes in life style and career objectives. (Macmillan Business Book.).

Working from Home: Everything You Need to Know About Living and Working Under the Same Roof. Paul Edwards and Sarah Edwards. Putnam Publishing Group. • 1999. $18.95. Fifth revised expanded edition.

ENCYCLOPEDIAS AND DICTIONARIES

Encyclopedia of Small Business. The Gale Group. • 1998. $395.00. Two volumes. Contains about 500 informative entries on a wide variety of topics affecting small business. Arrangement is alphabetical.

HANDBOOKS AND MANUALS

Accounting and Recordkeeping for the Self-Employed. Jack Fox. John Wiley and Sons, Inc. • 1994. Price on application.

CCH Guide to Car, Travel, Entertainment, and Home Office Deductions. CCH, Inc. • Annual. $42.00. Explains how to claim maximum tax deductions for common business expenses. Includes automobile depreciation tables, lease value tables, worksheets, and examples of filled-in tax forms.

Going Freelance: A Guide for Professionals. Robert Laurance. John Wiley and Sons, Inc. • 1995. $17.95. Third edition. Includes profiles of 150 professions using independent freelancers. Marketing, customer relations, and taxes are discussed.

Home Business Bible: Everything You Need to Know to Start and Run Your Home-Based Business. David R. Eyler. John Wiley and Sons, Inc. • 1994. $60.00. Includes CD-ROM.

Home Office Design: Everything You Need to Know about Planning, Organizing, and Furnishing Your Work Space. Neal Zimmerman. John Wiley and Sons, Inc. • 1996. $19.95. Covers furniture, seating, workstations, filing, storage, task lighting, etc.

Homemade Money: How to Select, Start, Manage, Market and Multiply the Profits of a Business at Home. Barbara Brabec. F and W Publications, Inc. • 1997. $21.99. Fifth revised edition. Covers sales, advertising, publicity, pricing, financing, legal issues, and other topics relating to businesses operated from home.

Legal Guide to Independent Contractor Status. Robert W. Wood. Panel Publishers. • 1999. $165.00. Third edition. A guide to the legal and tax-related differences between employers and independent contractors. Includes examples of both "safe" and "troublesome" independent contractor designations. Penalties and fines are discussed.

Start, Run, and Profit From Your Own Home-Based Business. Gregory Kishel and Patricia Kishel. John Wiley & Sons, Inc. • 1991. $37.95.

Tax Strategies for the Self-Employed. CCH, Inc. • Annual. $89.00 Covers tax-deferred retirement plans.

Telecom Made Easy: Money-Saving, Profit-Building Solutions for Home Businesses, Telecommuters, and Small Organizations. June Langhoff. Aegis Publishing Group Ltd. • 2000. $19.95. Fouth edition.

INTERNET DATABASES

Small Business Retirement Savings Advisor. U. S. Department of Labor, Pension and Welfare Benefits Administration. Phone: (202)219-8921 • URL: http://www.dol.gov/elaws/pwbaplan.htm • Web site provides "answers to a variety of commonly asked questions about retirement saving options for small business employers." Includes a comparison chart and detailed descriptions of various plans: 401(k), SEP-IRA, SIMPLE-IRA, Payroll Deduction IRA, Keogh Profit-Sharing, Keogh Money Purchase, and Defined Benefit. Searching is offered. Fees: Free.

SoHo Central. Home Office Association of America, Inc. Phone: 800-809-4622 Fax: 800-315-4622 E-mail: info@hoaa.com • URL: http://www.hoaa.com • Web site provides extensive lists of "Home Office Internet Resources" (links), including Business, Government, Continuing Education, Legal, Employment, Telecommunications, and Publishing. Includes an online newsletter. Fees: Free. (Membership in the Home Office Association of America is $49.00 per year.).

PERIODICALS AND NEWSLETTERS

Home Office Computing: Building Better Businesses with Technology. Freedom Technology Media Group. • Monthly. $16.97 per year. Office automation for the self-employed and small businesses. Formerly *Family and Home Office Computing.*

Home Office Connections: A Monthly Journal of News, Ideas, Opportunities, and Savings for Those Who Work at Home. Home Office Association of America, Inc. • Monthly. $49.00 per year. Newsletter. Includes membership in the Home Office Association of America.

HomeOffice: The Homebased Office Authority. Entrepreneur Media, Inc. • Bimonthly. $11.97 per year. Contains advice for operating a business in the home.

Inc.: The Magazine for Growing Companies. Goldhirsh Group, Inc. • 18 times a year. $19.00 per year. Edited for small office and office-in-the-home businesses with from one to 25 employees. Covers management, office technology, and lifestyle. Incorporates *Self-Employed Professional.*

ReCareering Newsletter: An Idea and Resource Guide to Second Career and Relocation Planning. Publications Plus, Inc. • Monthly. $59.00 per year. Edited for "downsized managers, early retirees, and others in career transition after leaving traditional employment." Offers advice on second careers, franchises, starting a business, finances, education, training, skills assessment, and other matters of interest to the newly unemployed.

Self-Employed America. National Association for the Self-Employed. • Controlled circulation. Provides articles on marketing, management, motivation, accounting, taxes, and other topics for businesses having fewer than 15 employees.

Small Business Tax News. Inside Mortgage Finance Publications. • Monthly. $175.00 per year. Newsletter. Formerly *Small Business Tax Control.*

Small Business Tax Review. A/N Group, Inc. • Monthly. $84.00 per year. Newsletter. Contains articles on Federal taxes and other issues affecting businesses.

SOHO Journal (Small Office Home Office). National Association for the Cottage Industry. • Members, $25.00 per year; libraries, $35.00 per year. Newsletter on business in thehome. Formerly *Mind Your Own Business at Home.*

TRADE/PROFESSIONAL ASSOCIATIONS

Home Office Association of America. 133 E. 5th St., Ste. 711, New York, NY 10022. Phone: 800-809-4622 or (212)588-9097 Fax: (212)588-9156 E-mail: hoaa@aol.com • URL: http://www.hoaa.com • A for-profit organization providing advice and information to home office workers and business owners.

National Association for the Self-Employed. P.O. Box 612067, Dallas, TX 75261-2067. Phone: 800-232-6273 Fax: 800-551-4446 • URL: http://www.nase.org • Members are very small businesses and the self-employed. Acts as an advocacy group at the state and federal levels.

National Association of Home-Based Businesses. P.O. Box 30220, Baltimore, MD 21270. Phone: (410)363-3698 • URL: http://www.usahomebusiness.com.

National Family Business Council. 1640 W. Kennedy Rd., Lake Forest, IL 60045. Phone: (847)295-1040 Fax: (847)295-1898 E-mail: lmsnfbc@email.msn.com • Seeks to ensure the survival of family-owned businesses.

National Federation of Independent Business. 53 Century Blvd., Suite 300, Nashville, TN 37214. Phone: 800-634-2669 or (615)872-5800 Fax: (615)872-5353 • URL: http://www.nfibonline.com • Members are independent business and professional people.

OTHER SOURCES

Home Business Magazine: The Home-Based Entrepreneur's Magazine. United Marketing and Research Co., Inc. • Bimonthly. $15.00 per year. Provides practical advice and ideas relating to the operation of a business in the home. Sections include "Marketing & Sales," "Money Corner" (financing), "Businesses & Opportunities," and "Home Office" (equipment, etc.). Includes an annual directory of more than 250 non-franchised home business opportunities, including start-up costs and information about providers.

Tax Strategies for the Self-Employed. CCH, Inc. • 2001. $89.00. Covers accounting methods, start-up expenses, transportation deductions, depreciation, pension deductions, tax penalties, and other topics related to tax planning for the self-employed.

SELLING

See: SALESMEN AND SALESMANSHIP

SELLING A BUSINESS

See: BUSINESS ENTERPRISES, SALE OF

SELLING BY TELEPHONE

See: TELEPHONE SELLING

SEMICONDUCTOR INDUSTRY

See also: MICROCOMPUTERS AND MINICOMPUTERS; SUPERCONDUCTORS

GENERAL WORKS

Crystal Fire: The Birth of the Information Age. Michael Riordan and Lillian Hoddeson. W. W. Norton & Co., Inc. • 1997. $27.50. A history of the transistor, from early electronic experiments to practical development at the former Bell Telephone Laboratories.

ABSTRACTS AND INDEXES

Applied Science and Technology Index. H. W. Wilson Co. • 11 times a year. Quarterly and annual cumulations. Service basis for print edition; CD-ROM edition, $1,495.00 per year. Indexes a wide variety of English language technical, industrial, and engineering periodicals.

Business Periodicals Index. H. W. Wilson Co. • Monthly, except August, with quarterly and annual cumulations. Service basis for print edition; CD-ROM edition, $1,495.00 per year.

Current Contents: Engineering, Computing and Technology. Institute for Scientific Information. • Weekly. $730.00 per year. Reproductions of contents pages of technical journals. Includes *Author Index, Address Directory, Current Book Contents* and *Title Word Index.* Formerly *Current Contents: Engineering, Technology and Applied Sciences.*

Key Abstracts: Semiconductor Devices. Available from INSPEC, Inc. • Monthly. $240.00 per year. Provides international coverage of journal and proceedings literature. Published in England by the Institution of Electrical Engineers (IEE).

NTIS Alerts: Electrotechnology. National Technical Information Service. • Semimonthly. $210.00 per year. Provides descriptions of government-sponsored research reports and software, with ordering information. Covers electronic components, semiconductors, antennas, circuits, optoelectronic devices, and related subjects. Formerly *Abstract Newsletter.*

Solid State and Superconductivity Abstracts. Cambridge Information Group. • Bimonthly. $1,045.00 per year. Formerly *Solid State Abstracts Journal.*

CD-ROM DATABASES

Electronic Strategies. Thomson Financial Securities Data. • Monthly. $2,995.00 per year. CD-ROM contains full text of investment analysts' reports on companies operating in the following fields: electronics, computers, semiconductors, and office products.

DIRECTORIES

Corptech Directory of Technology Companies. Corporate Technology Information Services, Inc. c/o Eileen Kennedy. • Annual. $795.00. Four volumes. Profiles of more than 45,000 manufacturers and developers of high technology products. Includes private companies, publicly-held corporations, and subsidiaries. Formerly *Corporate Technology Directory.*

IC Master (Integrated circuits). Hearst Business Communications, UTP Div. • Annual. $195.00. Semiannual supplements. List of over 1,500 manufacturers and distributors of integrated circuits.

Semiconductor International Product Data Source. Cahners Business Information. • Annual. $50.00. Products relating to the manufacture of semiconductors. Included in subscription to *Semiconductor International.* Formerly *Semiconductor International Technical Products Reference Source.*

SIA Status Report and Industry Directory. Semiconductor Industry Association. • Annual. Members, $105.00; non-members, $150.00. Provides information on key semiconductor issues. Formerly *Semiconductor Industry Association Yearbook/Directory.*

Solid State Technology Resource Guide. PennWell Corp., Advanced Technology Div. • 1998. $99.00. Lists suppliers of products and services related to the production and testing of solid state devices.

ENCYCLOPEDIAS AND DICTIONARIES

Wiley Encyclopedia of Electrical and Electronics Engineering. John G. Webster, editor. John Wiley and Sons, Inc. • 1999. $6,495.00. 24 volumes. Contains about 1,400 articles, each with bibliography. Arrangement is according to 64 categories.

FINANCIAL RATIOS

Industry Norms and Key Business Ratios. Desk Top Edition. Dun and Bradstreet Corp., Business Information Services. • Annual. Five volumes. $475.00 per volume. $1,890.00 per set. Covers over 800 kinds of businesses, arranged by Standard Industrial Classification number. More detailed editions covering longer periods of time are also available.

HANDBOOKS AND MANUALS

Solid State Electronic Devices. Prentice Hall. • 2000. Fifth edition. Price on application.

Solid State Electronics. George Rutkowski. Glencoe/McGraw-Hill. • Date not set. $104.25. Fourth edition.

ONLINE DATABASES

Applied Science and Technology Index Online. H. W. Wilson Co. • Provides online indexing of 400 major scientific, technical, industrial, and engineering periodicals. Time period is 1983 to date. Monthly updates. Inquire as to online cost and availability.

Computer Database. The Gale Group. • Provides online citations with abstracts to material appearing in about 150 trade journals and newsletters in the subject areas of computers, telecommunications, and electronics. Time period is 1983 to date, with weekly updates. Inquire as to online cost and availability.

Hard Sciences. Cambridge Scientific Abstracts. • Provides the online version of *Computer and Information Systems Abstracts, Electronics and Communications Abstracts, Health and Safety Science Abstracts, ISMEC: Mechanical Engineering Abstracts (Information Service in Mechanical Engineering)* and *Solid State and Superconductivity Abstracts.* Time period is 1981 to date, with monthly updates. Inquire as to online cost and availability.

PROMT: Predicasts Overview of Markets and Technology. The Gale Group. • Companies, products, applied technologies and markets. U.S. and international literature coverage, 1972 to date. Inquire as to online cost and availability. Provides abstracts from more than 1,600 publications. Weekly updates.

Scisearch. Institute for Scientific Information. • Broad, multidisciplinary index to the literature of science and technology, 1974 to present. Inquire as to online cost and availability. Coverage of literature is worldwide, with weekly updates.

Wilson Business Abstracts Online. H. W. Wilson Co. • Indexes and abstracts 600 major business periodicals, plus the *Wall Street Journal* and the business section of the *New York Times.* Indexing is from 1982, abstracting from 1990, with the two newspapers included from 1993. Updated weekly. Inquire as to online cost and availability. (*Business Periodicals Index* without abstracts is also available online.).

PERIODICALS AND NEWSLETTERS

Computer. Institute of Electrical and Electronic Engineers. • Monthly. $760.00 per year. Edited for computer technology professionals.

ECN Literature News (Electronic Component News). Cahners Business Information. • Bimonthly. Price on application.

IEEE Micro. Institute of Electrical and Electronics Engineers, Inc. • Bimonthly. Free to members; non members, $455.00 per year.

Inside Chips Ventures: The Global Report with Executive Perspective. HTE Research, Inc. • 12 times a year. $595.00 per year. Tracks the activities of semiconductor firms worldwide. Formerly *Semiconductor Industry and Business Survey Newsletter.*

Integrated Circuits International: An International Bulletin for Suppliers and Users of Integrated Circuits. Elsevier Science. • Monthly. $541.00 per year. For suppliers and users of integrated circuits.

Microprocessor Report: The Insiders' Guide to Microprocessor Hardware. Micro Design Resources. • 17 times a year. $695.00 per year. Newsletter. Covers the technical aspects of

For publishers addresses, refer to SOURCES CITED section at the back of the book.

microprocessors from Intel, IBM, Cyrix, Motorola, and others.

Semiconductor International. Cahners Business Information, Global Electronics Group. • Monthly. $99.90 per year. Devoted to processing, assembly and testing techniques.

Solid State Technology. PennWell Corp., Advanced Technology Div. • Monthly. $185.00 per year. Covers the technical and business aspects of semiconductor and integrated circuit production. Includes *Buyers Guide.*

WaferNews Confidential. PennWell Corp., Advanced Technology Div. • Semimonthly. $350.00 per year. Newsletter. Covers developments and trends in the semiconductor equipment industry.

RESEARCH CENTERS AND INSTITUTES

Center for Integrated Systems. Stanford University, 420 Vis Palou Mall, Stanford, CA 94305-4070. Phone: (650)725-3621 Fax: (650)725-0991 E-mail: rdasher@cis.stanford.edu • URL: http://www.cis.stanford.edu • Research programs include manufacturing science, design science, computer architecture, semiconductor technology, and telecommunications.

Center for Solid State Electronics Research. Arizona State University. College of Engineering and Applied Sciences, Tempe, AZ 85287-6206. Phone: (480)965-3708 Fax: (480)965-8118 E-mail: michael.kozicki@asu.edu • URL: http://www.ceaspub.eas.asu.edu/csser.

Electronic Materials and Processing Research Laboratory. Pennsylvania State University. 189 Materials Research Institute, University Park, PA 16802. Phone: (814)865-4931 Fax: (814)865-7173 E-mail: sfonash.empsu.edu • URL: http://www.emprl.psu.edu.

Lincoln Laboratory. Massachusetts Institute of Technology, 244 Wood St., Lexington, MA 02173. Phone: (781)863-5500 Fax: (781)862-9057 • URL: http://www.ll.mit.edu • Multidisciplinary off-campus research unit. Research fields include solid state devices.

Microelectronics Laboratory. Dept. of Electrical and Computer Engineering, University of Arizona, P.O. Box 210104, Tucson, AZ 85721-0104. Phone: (520)621-8237 Fax: (520)621-4698 E-mail: wells@ece.arizona.edu • URL: http://www.ece.arizona.edu.

Semiconductor Device Laboratory. University of Virginia, Thornton Hall, Dept. of Electrical Engineering, Charlottesville, VA 22903. Phone: (804)924-7693 Fax: (804)924-8818 E-mail: twc8u@virginia.edu • URL: http://www.ee.virginia.edu.

Semiconductor Research Laboratory. Duke University, P.O. Box 90291, Durham, NC 27708-0291. Phone: (919)660-5252 Fax: (919)660-5293 E-mail: massoud@ee.duke.edu • URL: http://www.ee.duke.edu.

Solid-State Device and Materials Research Laboratory. School of Electrical and Computer Engineering, Purdue University, West Lafayette, IN 47907-1285. Phone: (765)494-3461 Fax: (765)494-6441 E-mail: miller@ecn.purdue.edu • URL: http://www.ece.purdue.edu.

STATISTICS SOURCES

Annual Survey of Manufactures. Available from U. S. Government Printing Office. • Annual. Prices vary. Issued by the U. S. Census Bureau as an interim update to the *Census of Manufactures.* Includes data on number of manufacturing establishments in various industries, employment, labor costs, value of shipments, capital expenditures, inventories, energy costs, and assets. (See also Census Bureau home page, http://www.census.gov/.).

Manufacturing Profiles. Available from U. S. Government Printing Office. • Annual. Issued by the U. S. Census Bureau. A printed consolidation of the entire *Current Industrial Report* series, presenting "all the data compiled." Contains statistics on production, shipments, inventories, consumption, exports, imports, and orders for a wide variety of manufactured products. (See also Census Bureau home page, http://www.census.gov/.).

Semiconductors, Printed Circuit Boards, and Other Electronic Components. U. S. Bureau of the Census. • Annual. Provides data on shipments: value, quantity, imports, and exports. (Current Industrial Reports, MA-36Q.).

Standard & Poor's Industry Surveys. Standard & Poor's. • Semiannual. $1,800.00. Two looseleaf volumes. Includes monthly supplements. Provides detailed, individual surveys of 52 major industry groups. Each survey is revised on a semiannual basis. Also includes "Monthly Investment Review" (industry group investment analysis) and monthly "Trends & Projections" (economic analysis).

U. S. Industry and Trade Outlook: The McGraw-Hill Companies and the U.S. Department of Commerce/International Trade Administration. Datapso Research Corp. • Annual. $69.95. Produced by the International Trade Administration, U. S. Department of Commerce, in a "public-private" partnership with DRI/McGraw-Hill and Standard & Poor's. Provides basic data, outlook for the current year, and "Long-Term Prospects" (five-year projections) for a wide variety of products and services. Includes high technology industries. Formerly *U. S. Industrial Outlook.*

World Semiconductor Trade Statistics. SIA (Semiconductor Industry Association). • Monthly. $2,200 per year. Provides data on all world semiconductor markets including industry forecasts.

TRADE/PROFESSIONAL ASSOCIATIONS

Electronic Industries Association. 2500 Wilson Blvd., Arlington, VA 22201. Phone: (703)907-7500 Fax: (703)907-7501 • URL: http://www.eia.org • Includes a Solid State Products Committee.

IEEE Electron Devices Society. c/o IEEE Corporate Office, Three Park Ave., 17th Fl., New York, NY 10016-5997. Phone: (212)419-7900 • URL: http://www.ieee.org • A society of the Institute of Electrical and Electronics Engineers.

IEEE Solid State Circuits Council. c/o IEEE Corporate Office, Three Park Ave., 17th Fl., New York, NY 10016-5997. Phone: (212)419-7900 • URL: http://www.ieee.org • A council of the Institute of Electrical and Electronics Engineers.

Joint Electron Device Engineering Council. 2500 Wilson Blvd., Arlington, VA 22201-3834. Phone: (703)907-7534 Fax: (703)907-7583 • URL: http://www.jedec.org.

Semiconductor Industry Association. 181 Metro Dr., San Jose, CA 95110-1344. Phone: (408)436-6600 Fax: (408)246-6646 • URL: http://www.semichips.org • Members are producers of semiconductors and semiconductor products.

SEMINARS

See: CONFERENCES, WORKSHOPS, AND SEMINARS

SENATE

See: UNITED STATES CONGRESS

SENIOR CITIZENS

See: EMPLOYMENT OF OLDER WORKERS; MATURE CONSUMER MARKET; RETIREMENT

SENSORS, INDUSTRIAL

See: CONTROL EQUIPMENT INDUSTRY

SERIAL PUBLICATIONS

See: PERIODICALS

SERVICE, CUSTOMER

See: CUSTOMER SERVICE

SERVICE INDUSTRIES

GENERAL WORKS

Service Management: Strategy and Leadership in Service Business. Richard Normann. John Wiley and Sons, Inc. • 1991. $115.00. Second edition. Discusses the characteristics of successful service management.

CD-ROM DATABASES

16 Million Businesses Phone Directory. Info USA. • Annual. $29.95. Provides more than 16 million yellow pages telephone directory listings on CD-ROM for all ZIP Code areas of the U. S.

WILSONDISC: Wilson Business Abstracts. H. W. Wilson Co. • Monthly. $2,495.00 per year, including unlimited online access to *Wilson Business Abstracts* through WILSONLINE. Provides CD-ROM "cover-to-cover" abstracting and indexing of over 600 prominent business periodicals. Indexing is from 1982, abstracting from 1990. (*Business Periodicals Index* without abstracts is available on CD-ROM at $1,495 per year.).

DIRECTORIES

American Big Businesses Directory. American Business Directories. • Annual. $595.00. Lists 177,000 public and private U. S. companies in all fields having 100 or more employees. Includes sales volume, number of employees, and name of chief executive. Formerly *Big Businesses Directory.*

American Business Directory. InfoUSA, Inc. • Provides brief online information on more than 10 million U. S. companies, including individual plants and branches. Entries typically include address, phone number, industry classification code, and contact name. Updating is quarterly. Inquire as to online cost and availability.

American Business Locations Directory. The Gale Group. • 1999. $575.00. Second edition. (Four U. S. regional volumes and index volume). Provides 150,000 specific site locations for the 1,000 largest industrial and service companies in the U. S. Entries include the following for each location: address, senior officer, number of employees, sales volume, Standard Industrial Classification (SIC) codes, and name of parent company.

American Manufacturers Directory. American Business Directories. • Annual. $595.00. Lists more than 150,000 public and private U. S. manufacturers having 20 or more employees. Includes sales volume, number of employees, and name of chief executive or owner.

FINANCIAL RATIOS

Almanac of Business and Industrial Financial Ratios. Leo Troy. Prentice Hall. • Annual. $99.95.

Contains financial ratios derived from federal tax returns. Ratios for each of about 200 industries are arranged according to company asset size.

HANDBOOKS AND MANUALS

Service Quality Handbook. Eberhard E. Scheuing and William F. Christopher, editors. AMACOM. • 1993. $75.00. Contains articles by various authors on the management of service to customers.

INTERNET DATABASES

Fedstats. Federal Interagency Council on Statistical Policy. Phone: (202)395-7254 • URL: http://www.fedstats.gov • Web site features an efficient search facility for full-text statistics produced by more than 70 federal agencies, including the Census Bureau, the Bureau of Economic Analysis, and the Bureau of Labor Statistics. Boolean searches can be made within one agency or for all agencies combined. Links are offered to international statistical bureaus, including the UN, IMF, OECD, UNESCO, Eurostat, and 20 individual countries. Fees: Free.

ONLINE DATABASES

Business and Industry. Responsive Database Services, Inc. • Contains online citations, abstracts, and selected fulltext from more than 1,000 trade journals, newspapers, and other publications. Provides general coverage of both manufacturing and service industries, including marketing, production, industry trends, key events, and information on specific companies. Time span is 1994 to date. Daily updates. Inquire as to online cost and availability. (Also available in a CD-ROM version.).

DRI U.S. Central Database. Data Products Division. • Provides more than 23,000 business, financial, demographic, economic, foreign trade, and industry-related time series for the U.S. Includes national income, population, retail-wholesale trade, price indexes, labor data, housing, industrial production, banking, interest rates, money supply, etc. Time period is generally 1947 to date (some data back to 1929). Updating varies. Inquire as to online cost and availability.

Tablebase. Responsive Database Services, Inc. • Provides online numerical tabular data from a wide variety of business, organization, and government sources, including 900 trade journals. Includes industry and individual company statistics relating to products, market share, sales forecasts, production, exports, market trends, etc. Time span is 1997 to date. Weekly updates. Inquire as to online cost and availability. (Also available in a CD-ROM version.).

Wilson Business Abstracts Online. H. W. Wilson Co. • Indexes and abstracts 600 major business periodicals, plus the *Wall Street Journal* and the business section of the *New York Times*. Indexing is from 1982, abstracting from 1990, with the two newspapers included from 1993. Updated weekly. Inquire as to online cost and availability. (*Business Periodicals Index* without abstracts is also available online.).

PERIODICALS AND NEWSLETTERS

Cleaning Business: Published Monthly for the Self-Employed Cleaning and Maintenance Professionals. William R. Griffin, Publisher. • Monthly. $20.00 per year. Formerly *Service Business*.

Hotels. International Hotel Association. Cahners Business Information. • Monthly. Free to qualified personnel; others, $75.00 per year.

Service Reporter: The Magazine That Works for Contractors and In-Plant Engineers. Palmer Publishing Co. • Monthly. $12.00 per year.

STATISTICS SOURCES

Business Statistics of the United States. Courtenay M. Slater, editor. Bernan Associates. • 1999. $74.00. Fifth edition. Based on *Business Statistics*, formerly issue by the Bureau of Economic Analysis, U. S. Department of Commerce. Provides basic data for a wide variety of U. S. industries, services, and economic indicators. Most statistics are shown annually for 29 years and monthly for the most recent four years.

Encyclopedia of American Industries. The Gale Group. • 1998. $560.00. Second edition. Two volumes. $280.00 per volume. Volume one is *Manufacturing Industries* and volume two is *Service and Non-Manufacturing Industries*. Provides the history, development, and recent status of approximately 1,000 industries. Includes statistical graphs, with industry and general indexes.

Services: Statistics on International Transactions. Organization for Economic Cooperation and Development. Available from OECD Publications and Information Center. • Annual. $71.00. Presents a compilation and assessment of data on OECD member countries' international trade in services. Covers four major categories for 20 years: travel, transportation, government services, and other services.

Services: Statistics on Value Added and Employment. Organization for Economic Cooperation and Development. • Annual. $67.00. Provides 10-year data on service industry employment and output (value added) for all OECD countries. Covers such industries as telecommunications, business services, and information technology services.

Survey of Current Business. Available from U. S. Government Printing Office. • Monthly. $49.00 per year. Issued by Bureau of Economic Analysis, U. S. Department of Commerce. Presents a wide variety of business and economic data.

United States Census of Service Industries. U.S. Bureau of the Census. • Quinquennial. Various reports available.

TRADE/PROFESSIONAL ASSOCIATIONS

National Association of Service Managers. P.O. Box 712500, Santee, CA 92072-2500. Phone: 888-562-7004 or (619)562-7004 Fax: (619)562-7153 E-mail: nasm@nasm.com • URL: http://www.nasm.com.

National Technical Services Association. 325 S. Patrick St., Suite 104, Alexandria, VA 22314-3501. Phone: (703)684-4722 Fax: (703)684-7627.

OTHER SOURCES

Information, Finance, and Services USA. The Gale Group. • 2001. $240.00. Replaces *Service Industries USA* and *Finance, Insurance, and Real Estate USA*. Presents statistics and projections relating to economic activity in a wide variety of non-manufacturing areas.

SERVICE INDUSTRY, FOOD

See: FOOD SERVICE INDUSTRY

SERVICE MEN, DISCHARGED

See: VETERANS

SERVICE MERCHANDISERS

See: RACK JOBBERS

SERVICE STATIONS

See: GASOLINE SERVICE STATIONS

SEVERANCE PAY

See: WAGES AND SALARIES

SEWAGE DISPOSAL

See: SANITATION INDUSTRY

SEWING MACHINE INDUSTRY

See also: TEXTILE MACHINERY

TRADE/PROFESSIONAL ASSOCIATIONS

American Apparel Machinery Trade Association. c/o Richard Sussman, Sussman Automatic Products Corporation, 4320 34th St., Long Island City, NY 11101. Phone: (718)937-4500 Fax: (718)786-4051.

Home Sewing Association. 1350 Broadway, Suite 1601, New York, NY 10018. Phone: (212)714-1633 Fax: (212)714-1655 E-mail: info@sewing.com • URL: http://www.sewing.org.

SEXUAL HARASSMENT IN THE WORKPLACE

GENERAL WORKS

The 9 to 5 Guide to Combating Sexual Harassment: Candid Advice from 9 to 5, the National Association of Working Women. Ellen Bravo and Ellen Cassedy. John Wiley and Sons, Inc. • 1992. $12.95.

Sexual Harassment in the Workplace: How to Prevent, Investigate, and Resolve Problems in Your Organization. Ellen J. Wagner. AMACOM. • 1992. $17.95.

Sexual Harassment in the Workplace: Perspectives, Frontiers, and Response Strategies. Margaret S. Stockdale, editor. Sage Publications, Inc. • 1996. $55.00. Contains articles by various authors. (Women and Work Series, vol. 5).

Sexual Harassment on the Job: What It Is and How to Stop It. William Petrocelli and Barbara K. Repa. Nolo.com. • 1999. $18.95. Fourth edition.

ABSTRACTS AND INDEXES

Business Periodicals Index. H. W. Wilson Co. • Monthly, except August, with quarterly and annual cumulations. Service basis for print edition; CD-ROM edition, $1,495.00 per year.

Feminist Periodicals: A Current Listing of Contents. Women's Studies Librarian. • Quarterly. Individuals, $30.00 per year; institutions, $55.00 per year. Provides reproductions of the tables of contents of over 100 feminist periodicals. Includes *Feminist Collections* and *New Books on Women and Feminism*.

Index to Legal Periodicals and Books. H. W. Wilson Co. • Monthly. Quarterly and annual cumulations. $270.00 per year. CD-ROM version available at $1,495.00 per year.

PAIS International in Print. Public Affairs Information Service, Inc. • Monthly. $650.00 per year; cumulations three times a year. Provides topical citations to the worldwide literature of public affairs, economics, demographics, sociology, and trade. Text in English; indexed materials in English, French, German, Italian, Portuguese and Spanish.

Readers' Guide to Periodical Literature. H. W. Wilson Co. • Monthly. $220.00 per year. CD-ROM edition, $1,495 per year, including annual cumulation. Indexes about 250 peridicals of general interest.

Social Sciences Index. H. W. Wilson Co. • Quarterly, with annual cumulation. Service basis for print edition; CD-ROM edition, $1,495 per year. Indexes more than 400 periodicals covering economics, environmental policy, government, insurance, labor, health care policy, plannning, public administration, public welfare, urban studies, women's issues, criminology, and related topics.

BIBLIOGRAPHIES

Sexual Harassment: A Selected, Annotated Bibliography. Lynda J. Hartel and Helena M. VonVille. Greenwood Publishing Group, Inc. • 1995. $62.95. Includes articles and books on workplace sexual harassment. (Bibliographies and Indexes in Women's Studies, No. 23.).

CD-ROM DATABASES

ABI/INFORM Global. Bell & Howell Information and Learning. • Monthly. $6,500.00 per year. Provides CD-ROM indexing and abstracting of worldwide business literature appearing in over 1,200 periodicals for the most recent five years. Archival discs are available from 1971. Formerly *ABI/INFORM OnDisc.*

LegalTrac. The Gale Group. • Monthly. $5,000.00 per year. Price includes workstation. Provides CD-ROM indexing of periodical literature relating to legal matters from 1980 to date. Corresponds to online *Legal Resource Index.*

National Newspaper Index CD-ROM. The Gale Group. • Monthly. Provides comprehensive CD-ROM indexing of all material appearing in the late edition of the *New York Times*, the final edition of the *Washington Post*, the national edition of the *Christian Science Monitor*, the home edition of the *Los Angeles Times*, and the *Wall Street Journal.* Time period is four years. Also available online.

The New York Times Ondisc. New York Times Online Services. • Monthly. $2,650.00 per year. CD-ROM discs contain the full text of *The New York Times*, final edition. Inquire as to time period covered and availability of backfiles.

Newspaper Abstracts Ondisc. Bell & Howell Information and Learning. • Monthly. $2,950.00 per year (covers 1989 to date; archival discs are available for 1985-88). Provides cover-to-cover CD-ROM indexing and abstracting of 19 major newspapers, including the *New York Times, Wall Street Journal, Washington Post, Chicago Tribune,* and *Los Angeles Times.*

PAIS on CD-ROM. Public Affairs Information Service, Inc. • Quarterly. $1,995.00 per year. Provides a CD-ROM version of the online service, *PAIS International.* Contains over 400,000 citations to the literature of contemporary social, political, and economic issues.

Social Science Source. EBSCO Publishing. • Monthly. $1,495.00 per year. Provides CD-ROM citations and abstracts to social science articles in more than 600 periodicals, with full text from 125 periodicals. Covers economics, political science, public policy, international relations, psychology, and other topics. Time period is most recent five years.

Social Sciences Citation Index: Compact Disc Edition with Abstracts. Institute for Scientific Information. • Quarterly. Provides CD-ROM indexing and abstracting of "significant articles" from 1,400 social science journals worldwide, with additional selections from 3,200 other journals, 1986 to date. Includes economics, business, finance, management, communications, demographics, information and library science, political science, sociology, and many other subjects.

WILSONDISC: Index to Legal Periodicals and Books. H. W. Wilson Co. • Monthly. Including unlimited online access to *Index to Legal Periodicals* through WILSONLINE. Contains CD-ROM indexing of more than 800 English language legal periodicals from 1981 to date and 2,500 books.

WILSONDISC: Readers' Guide to Periodical Literature. H. W. Wilson Co. • Monthly. $1,095.00 per year, including unlimited online access to *Readers' Guide to Periodical Literature* through WILSONLINE. Provides CD-ROM indexing of about 250 general interest periodicals. Covers 1983 to date. (*Readers' Guide Abstracts* also available on CD-ROM at $1,995 per year.).

WILSONDISC: Wilson Business Abstracts. H. W. Wilson Co. • Monthly. $2,495.00 per year, including unlimited online access to *Wilson Business Abstracts* through WILSONLINE. Provides CD-ROM "cover-to-cover" abstracting and indexing of over 600 prominent business periodicals. Indexing is from 1982, abstracting from 1990. (*Business Periodicals Index* without abstracts is available on CD-ROM at $1,495 per year.).

WILSONDISC: Wilson Social Sciences Abstracts. H. W. Wilson Co. • Monthly. Including unlimited online access to *Social Sciences Index* through WILSONLINE. Provides CD-ROM indexing from 1983 and abstracting from 1994 of more than 400 periodicals covering economics, area studies, community health, public administration, public welfare, urban studies, and many other topics related to the social sciences.

DIRECTORIES

Encyclopedia of Women's Associations Worldwide. The Gale Group. • 1998. $85.00. Second edition. Provides detailed information for more than 3,400 organizations throughout the world that relate to women and women's issues.

Women's Information Directory. The Gale Group. • 1992. $75.00. A guide to approximately 6,000 organizations, agencies, institutions, programs, and publications concerned with women in the United States. Includes subject and title indexes.

HANDBOOKS AND MANUALS

Sex-Based Employment Discrimination. Susan M. Omilian. West Group. • 1990. $130.00. Covers the legal aspects of all areas of sexual discrimination, including compensation issues, harassment, sexual orientation, and pregnancy.

Sexual Harassment Awareness Training: 60 Practical Activities for Trainers. Andrea P. Baridon and David R. Eyler. McGraw-Hill. • 1996. $21.95. Discusses the kinds of sexual harassment, judging workplace behavior, application of the "reasonable person standard," employer liability, and related issues.

Sexual Harassment in Employment Law. Barbara Lindemann and David D. Kadue. BNA Books. • 1992. $165.00. Includes 1999 *Supplement.*

Sexual Harassment in the Workplace: A Guide to the Law and A Research Overview for Employers and Employees. Titus Aaron and Judith A. Isaksen. McFarland & Co., Inc., Publishers. • 1993. $32.50.

Sexual Harassment in the Workplace: Designing and Implementing a Successful Policy, Conducting the Investigation, Protecting the Rights of the Parties. Practising Law Institute. • 1992. $70.00. (Litigation and Administrative Practice Series).

Sexual Harassment: Investigator's Manual. Susan L. Webb. Pacific Resource Development Group, Inc. • 1996. $189.95. Revised edition. Looseleaf. Contains information relating to successfully investigating and resolving sexual harassment complaints in both private companies and public organizations.

Sexual Orientation in the Workplace: Gays, Lesbians, Bisexuals and Heterosexuals Working Together. Amy J. Zuckerman and George F. Simons. Sage Publications, Inc. • 1996. $18.95. A workbook containing "a variety of simple tools and exercises" to provide skills for "working realistically and effectively with diverse colleagues.".

Women and Sexual Harassment: A Guide to the Legal Protections of Title VII and the Hostile Environment Claim. Anja A. Chan. Haworth Press, Inc. • 1994. $29.95. Emphasis is on hostile environment claims under Title VII of the Civil Rights Act of 1964. Discusses employer liability, the statute of limitations, remedies, discovery and evidence, and related claims. Includes a research guide and lists of primary and secondary sources.

Women and the Law. Carol H. Lefcourt, editor. West Group. • $140.00. Looseleaf service. Periodic supplementation. Covers such topics as employment discrimination, pay equity (comparable worth), sexual harassment in the workplace, property rights, and child custody issues. (Civil Rights Series).

Workplace Sexual Harassment. Anne Levy. Simon and Schuster Trade. • 1996. $41.00. A management guide to confronting and preventing sexual harassment in organizations. Includes case studies and training materials.

ONLINE DATABASES

ABI/INFORM. Bell & Howell Information and Learning. • Provides online indexing to business-related material occurring in over 1,000 periodicals from 1971 to the present. Inquire as to online cost and availability.

Contemporary Women's Issues. Responsive Database Services, Inc. • Provides fulltext articles online from 150 periodicals and a wide variety of additional sources relating to economic, legal, social, political, education, health, and other women's issues. Time span is 1992 to date. Weekly updates. Inquire as to online cost and availability. (Also available in a CD-ROM version.).

Index to Legal Periodicals and Books (Online). H. W. Wilson Co. • Broad coverage of law journals and books 1981 to date. Monthly updates. Inquire as to online cost and availability.

Legal Resource Index. The Gale Group. • Broad coverage of law literature appearing in legal, business, and other periodicals, 1980 to date. Monthly updates. Inquire as to online cost and availability.

Newspaper and Periodical Abstracts. Bell & Howell Information and Learning. • Provides online coverage (citations and abstracts) of 25 major newspapers, 1,600 perodicals, and 70 TV programs. Covers business, economics, current affairs, health, fitness, sports, education, technology, government, consumer affairs, psychology, the arts, and the social sciences. Time period is 1986 to date, with daily updates. Inquire as to online cost and availability.

PAIS International. Public Affairs Information Service, Inc. • Corresponds to the former printed publications, *PAIS Bulletin* (1976-90) and *PAIS Foreign Language Index* (1972-90), and to the current *PAIS International in Print* (1991 to date). Covers economic, political, and sociological material appearing in periodicals, books, government documents, and other publications. Updating is monthly. Inquire as to online cost and availability.

Readers' Guide Abstracts Online. H. W. Wilson Co. • Indexes and abstracts general interest periodicals, 1983 to date. Weekly updates. Inquire as to online cost and availability.

Trade & Industry Index. The Gale Group. • Provides indexing of business periodicals, January 1981 to date. Daily updates. (Full text articles from some periodicals are available online, 1983 to date, in the companion database, *Trade & Industry ASAP*.) Inquire as to online cost and availability.

Wilson Business Abstracts Online. H. W. Wilson Co. • Indexes and abstracts 600 major business periodicals, plus the *Wall Street Journal* and the business section of the *New York Times*. Indexing is from 1982, abstracting from 1990, with the two newspapers included from 1993. Updated weekly. Inquire as to online cost and availability. (*Business Periodicals Index* without abstracts is also available online.).

Wilson Social Sciences Abstracts Online. H. W. Wilson Co. • Provides online abstracting and indexing of more than 415 periodicals covering area studies, community health, public administration, public welfare, urban studies, and many other social science topics. Time period is 1994 to date for abstracts and 1983 to date for indexing, with updates monthly. Inquire as to online cost and availability.

PERIODICALS AND NEWSLETTERS

Nine to Five Newsletter. National Association of Working Women. • Five times a year. Free to members; individuals, $25.00 per year. A newsletter dealing with the rights and concerns of women office workers.

The Webb Report: A Newsletter on Sexual Harassment. Susan L. Webb, editor. Pacific Resource Development Group, Inc. • Monthly. $96.00 per year. Contains news and information on sexual harassment issues and court cases. Provides guidelines for supervisors and employees as to what constitutes harassment.

Women's Rights Law Reporter. Rutgers University School of Law. • Three times a year. Individuals $20.00 per year; institutions, $40.00 per year; students, $15.00 per year. Provides analysis and commentary on legal issues affecting women, including gender-based discrimination.

RESEARCH CENTERS AND INSTITUTES

Center for Women Policy Studies. 1211 Connecticut Ave., N.W. Suite 312, Washington, DC 20036. Phone: (202)872-1770 Fax: (202)296-8962 E-mail: cwps@centerwomenpolicy.org • URL: http://www.centerwomenpolicy.org • Conducts research on the policy issues that affect the legal, economic, educational, and social status of women, including sexual harassment in the workplace, and women and AIDS.

Women Employed Institute. 22 W. Monroe St., Suite 1400, Chicago, IL 60603-2505. Phone: (312)782-3902 Fax: (312)782-5249 E-mail: info@womenemployed.org • URL: http://www.womenemployed.org • Research areas include the economic status of working women, sexual harassment in the workplace, equal employment opportunity, and career development.

TRADE/PROFESSIONAL ASSOCIATIONS

National Partnership for Women and Families. 1875 Connecticut Ave., N. W., Suite 710, Washington, DC 20009. Phone: (202)986-2600 Fax: (202)986-2539 E-mail: info@nationalpartnership.org • URL: http://www.nationalpartnership.org • Includes a Counseling on Employment Discrimination Committee. Offers telephone referral services.

National Women's Law Center. 11 Dupont Circle, N.W., Suite 800, Washington, DC 20036. Phone: (202)588-5180 Fax: (202)588-5185 E-mail: nwlcinfo@aol.com • Seeks protection and advancement of women's legal rights. Includes employment issues among areas of interest.

Nine to Five: National Association of Working Women. 231 W. Wisconsin Ave., Suite 900, Milwaukee, WI 53203. Phone: 800-522-0925 or (414)274-0925 Fax: (414)272-2870 E-mail: naww9to5@execpc.com • Members are women office workers. Strives for the improvement of office working conditions for women and the elimination of sex and race discrimination.

NOW Legal Defense and Education Fund. 395 Hudson St., 5th Fl., New York, NY 10014-3669. Phone: (212)925-6635 Fax: (212)226-1066 • URL: http://www.nowldef.org.

Women's Law Project. 125 S. Ninth St., Suite 401, Philadelphia, PA 19107. Phone: (215)928-9801 Fax: (215)928-9848 • URL: http://www.women'slawproject.org • Offers telephone counseling and referral services relating to women's legal rights in employment and other areas.

SHAREHOLDERS

See: STOCKHOLDERS

SHARES OF STOCK

See: STOCKS

SHEEP INDUSTRY

See also: LIVESTOCK INDUSTRY; WOOL AND WORSTED INDUSTRY

GENERAL WORKS

Sheep and Goat Science. M. E. Ensminger and Ronald B. Parker. Interstate Publishers. • 1998. $81.25. Fifth edition.

INTERNET DATABASES

USDA. United States Department of Agriculture. Phone: (202)720-2791 E-mail: agsec@usda.gov • URL: http://www.usda.gov • The USDA home page has six sections: News and Information; What's New; About USDA; Agencies; Opportunities; Search and Help. Keyword searching is offered from the USDA home page and from various individual agency home pages. Agencies are the Economic Research Service, Agricultural Marketing Service, National Agricultural Statistics Service, National Agricultural Library, and about 12 others. Updating varies. Fees: Free.

PERIODICALS AND NEWSLETTERS

Sheep Breeder and Sheepman. Mead Livestock Services. • Monthly. $18.00 per year.

PRICE SOURCES

The National Provisioner: Serving Meat, Poultry, and Seafood Processors. Stagnito Communications, Inc. • Monthly. Free to qualified personnel; others, $65.00 per year. Annual *Buyer's Guide* available. Meat, poultry and seafood newsletter.

STATISTICS SOURCES

Agricultural Statistics. Available from U. S. Government Printing Office. • Annual. Produced by the National Agricultural Statistics Service, U. S. Department of Agriculture. Provides a wide variety of statistical data relating to agricultural production, supplies, consumption, prices/price-supports, foreign trade, costs, and returns, as well as farm labor, loans, income, and population. In many cases, historical data is shown annually for 10 years. In addition to farm data, includes detailed fishery statistics.

Livestock, Meat, Wool, Market News. U.S. Department of Agriculture. • Weekly.

TRADE/PROFESSIONAL ASSOCIATIONS

American Sheep Industry Association. 6911 S. Yosemite St., Suite 200, Englewood, CO 80112-1414. Phone: (303)771-3500 Fax: (303)771-8200 E-mail: info@sheepusa.org • URL: http://www.sheepusa.org.

SHEET METAL INDUSTRY

See also: AIR CONDITIONING INDUSTRY; HEATING AND VENTILATION; ROOFING INDUSTRY

DIRECTORIES

FMA's Who's Who in Metal Forming and Fabricating (Fabricator's and ManufacturersAssociation). Fabricators and Manufacturers Association International. • Annual. Free to members; non-members, $200.00. Lists about 2,000 members of the Fabricators and Manufacturers Association (FMA), International; and 1,000 members of the Tube and Pipe Association. Includes five indexes. Formerly *FMA Member Resource Directory*.

Heating/Piping/Air Conditioning Info-Dex. Penton Media Inc. • Annual. $30.00. The HVAC/R industry's directory of products, manufacturers, and trade names and a composite of catalog data for mechanical systems engineering professionals.

FINANCIAL RATIOS

Annual Statement Studies. Robert Morris Associates: The Association of Lending and Credit Risk Professiona. • Annual. Free to members; non-members, $140.00. Median and quartile financial ratios are given for over 400 kinds of manufacturing, wholesale, retail, construction, and consumer finance establishments. Data is sorted by both asset size and sales volume. Includes a clearly written "Definition of Ratios" and an alphabetical industry index.

HANDBOOKS AND MANUALS

Sheet Metal Cutting: Collected Articles and Technical Papers. Amy Nickel, editor. Croyden Group, Ltd./FMA. • 1994. $33.00.

PERIODICALS AND NEWSLETTERS

The Fabricator. Fabricators and Manufacturers Association International. Croydon Group, Ltd. • Monthly. $75.00 per year. Covers the manufacture of sheet, coil, tube, pipe, and structural metal shapes.

Heating/Piping/Air Conditioning Engineering: The Magazine of Mechanical Systems Engineering. Penton Media Inc. • Monthly. Free to qualified personnel; others, $65.00 per year. Covers design, specification, installation, operation, and maintenance for systems in industrial, commercial, and institutional buildings. Formerly Heating, Piping and Air Conditioning.

Snips. Business News Publishing Co. • Monthly. $12.00 per year. Provides information for heating, air conditioning, sheet metal and ventilating contractors, wholesalers, manufacturers representatives and manufacturers.

TRADE/PROFESSIONAL ASSOCIATIONS

Fabricators and Manufacturers Association International. 833 Featherstone Rd., Rockford, IL 61107-6302. Phone: (815)399-8700 Fax: (815)399-7279 E-mail: info@fmametal.fab.org • URL: http://www.fmametalfab.org • Members are individuals concerned with metal forming, cutting, and fabricating. Includes a Sheet Metal Division and the Tube and Pipe Fabricators Association.

Sheet Metal and Air Conditioning Contractors' National Association. 4201 Lafayette Center Dr., Chantilly, VA 20151-1209. Phone: (703)803-2980 Fax: (703)803-3732 E-mail: info@smacna.org • URL: http://www.smacna.org.

Sheet Metal Industry Promotion Plan. 981 Keynote Circle, Suite 4, Cleveland, OH 44131. Phone: (216)398-5600 Fax: (216)398-5576.

SHELLFISH INDUSTRY

See also: FISH INDUSTRY; LOBSTER INDUSTRY; OYSTER INDUSTRY; SEAFOOD INDUSTRY

CD-ROM DATABASES

Food Science and Technology Abstracts [CD-ROM]. Available from SilverPlatter Information, Inc. • Quarterly. $3,700 per year. Produced by International Food Information Service (home page is http://www.ifis.org). Provides worldwide coverage on CD-ROM of the literature of food technology and production. Various types of publications are indexed, with abstracts, including about 1,800 periodicals. Time period is 1969 to date.

ONLINE DATABASES

Food Science and Technology Abstracts [online]. IFIS North American Desk. • Produced by International Food Information Service. Provides about 500,000 online citations, with abstracts, to the international literature of food science, technology, commodities, engineering, and processing. Approximately 2,000 periodicals are covered. Time period is 1969 to date, with monthly updates. Inquire as to online cost and availability.

STATISTICS SOURCES

Fisheries of the United States. Available from U. S. Government Printing Office. • Annual. $18.00. Issued by the National Marine Fisheries Service, National Oceanic and Atmospheric Administration, U. S. Department of Commerce.

TRADE/PROFESSIONAL ASSOCIATIONS

Molluscan Shellfish Institute. 1901 N. Fort Meyer Dr., Suite 700, Arlington, VA 22209. Phone: (703)524-8883 Fax: (703)524-4619 E-mail: office@nfi.org.

National Shellfisheries Association. c/o Nancy C. Lewis, P.O. Box 350, Wachapreague, VA 23480. Phone: (757)787-5816 Fax: (757)787-5831 E-mail: nlewis@vims.edu • URL: http://www.shellfish.org.

OTHER SOURCES

Major Food and Drink Companies of the World. Available from The Gale Group. • 2001. $855.00. Fourth edition. Two volumes. Published by Graham & Whiteside. Contains profiles and trade names for more than 9,000 important food and beverage companies in various countries. In addition to foods, includes both alcoholic and nonalcoholic drink products.

Thomas Food and Beverage Market Place. Grey House Publishing. • Annual. $295.00. Three volumes. Contains more than 40,000 entries covering food companies, beverages, food equipment, warehouse companies, food brokers, wholesalers, importers, and exporters. Formerly *Thomas Food Industry Register.*

SHELTERS, TAX

See: TAX SHELTERS

SHIPBUILDING

See: SHIPS, SHIPPING AND SHIPBUILDING

SHIPMENT OF GOODS

See: FREIGHT TRANSPORT; PACKAGING; POSTAL SERVICES; TRAFFIC MANAGEMENT (INDUSTRIAL); TRUCKING INDUSTRY

SHIPPING

See: SHIPS, SHIPPING AND SHIPBUILDING

SHIPS, SHIPPING AND SHIPBUILDING

See also: BOAT INDUSTRY; EXPORT-IMPORT TRADE; FREIGHT TRANSPORT; MARINE ENGINEERING; OCEANOGRAPHIC INDUSTRIES; PORTS; STEAMSHIP LINES; TANK SHIPS; TRANSPORTATION INDUSTRY

ABSTRACTS AND INDEXES

NTIS Alerts: Ocean Sciences and Technology. National Technical Information Service. • Semimonthly. $210.00 per year. Provides descriptions of government-sponsored research reports and software, with ordering information. Formerly *Abstract Newsletter.*

NTIS Alerts: Transportation. National Technical Information Service. • Semimonthly. $210.00 per year. Provides descriptions of government-sponsored research reports and software, with ordering information. Covers air, marine, highway, inland waterway, pipeline, and railroad transportation. Formerly *Abstract Newsletter.*

Oceanic Abstracts. Cambridge Information Group. • Bimonthly. $1,045.00 per year. Covers oceanography, marine biology, ocean shipping, and a wide range of other marine-related subject areas.

ALMANACS AND YEARBOOKS

American Bureau of Shipping Record. American Bureau of Shipping. • Annual. $520.00 per year. Quarterly supplements.

DIRECTORIES

Fairplay World Shipping Directory. Available from Fairplay Publications, Inc. • Annual. $360.00. Published in the UK by Lloyd's Register-Fairplay Ltd. Provides information on more than 64,000 companies providing maritime services and products, including 1,600 shipbuilders and data on 55,000 individual ships. Includes shipowners, shipbrokers, engine builders, salvage companies, marine insurance companies, maritime lawyers, consultants, maritime schools, etc. Five indexes cover a total of 170,000 entries.

Lloyd's Maritime Directory. Available from Informa Publishing Group Ltd. • Annual. $468.00. Two volumes. Published in the UK by Lloyd's List (http://www.lloydslist.com). Lists more than 5,500 shipowners, container companies, salvage firms, towing services, shipbuilders, ship repairers, marine engine builders, ship management services, maritime lawyers, consultants, etc.

ENCYCLOPEDIAS AND DICTIONARIES

Dictionary of Marine Technology. Cyril Hughes. Available from Informa Publishing Group Ltd. • 1997. $108.00. Published in the UK by Lloyd's List (http://www.lloydslist.com). Includes more than 1,000 terms and acronyms in the fields of ship operation, technology, marine construction, maritime safety, environmental issues, and government regulation of shipping.

Dictionary of Shipping Terms. Peter Brodie. Available from Informa Publishing Group Ltd. • 1997. $57.00. Third edition. Published in the UK by Lloyd's List (http://www.lloydslist.com). Defines more than 2,000 words, phrases, and abbreviations related to the shipping and maritime industries.

Exporters' Encyclopedia. Dun and Bradstreet Information Services. • 1995. $495.00. Lease basis.

Illustrated Dictionary of Cargo Handling. Peter Brodie. Available from Informa Publishing Group Ltd. • 1996. $100.00. Second edition. Published in the UK by Lloyd's List (http://www.lloydslist.com). Provides definitions of about 600 terms relating to "the vessels and equipment used in modern cargo handling and shipping," including containerization.

Macmillan Encyclopedia of Transportation. Available from The Gale Group. • 2000. $375.00. Six volumes. Published by Macmillan Reference USA. Covers the business, technology, and history of transportation on land, on water, in the air, and in space. Includes definitions, cross-references, and 200 color illustrations.

Marine Encyclopaedic Dictionary. Eric Sullivan. Available from Informa Publishing Group Ltd. • 1996. $110.00. Fifth edition. Published in the UK by Lloyd's List (http://www.lloydslist.com). Provides more than 20,000 marine-related definitions, including 2,000 technical terms. Covers all operational aspects of the shipping business: shipbroking, chartering, insurance, freight forwarding, maritime law, etc.

HANDBOOKS AND MANUALS

The Business of Shipping. Lane C. Kendall and James J. Buckley. Cornell Maritime Press, Inc. • 2000. $50.00. Seventh edition.

Guide to Shipbuilding, Repair, and Maintenance. Available from Informa Publishing Group Ltd. • Annual. $111.00. Published in the UK by Lloyd's List (http://www.lloydslist.com). Provides worldwide coverage of shipbuilding, repair, and maintenance facilities and marine equipment suppliers for the maritime industry. (Included with subscription to *Lloyd's Ship Manager.*).

Importers Manual U. S. A.: The Single Source Reference for Importing to the United States. Edward G. Hinkelman. World Trade Press. • 1997. $87.00. Second edition. Published by World Trade Press. Covers U. S. customs regulations, letters of credit, contracts, shipping, insurance, and other items relating to importing. Includes 60 essays on practical aspects of importing.

Lloyd's List Marine Equipment Buyers' Guide. Available from Informa Publishing Group Ltd. • Annual. $270.00. Published in the UK by Lloyd's List (http://www.lloydslist.com). Lists more than 6,000 companies worldwide supplying over 2,000 types of marine products and services, including offshore equipment.

Maritime Guide. Available from Fairplay Publications, Inc. • Annual. $232.00. Published in the UK by Lloyd's Register-Fairplay Ltd. Serves as a worldwide directory of maritime services, equipment, builders, and manufacturers. Provides information on dry docks, ports, harbours, pontoons, docking installations, shipbuilders, marine engine builders, boilermakers, etc. Includes world maps and a gazetteer.

INTERNET DATABASES

CDC Vessel Sanitation Program (VSP): Charting a Healthier Course. U. S. Centers for Disease Control and Prevention. Phone: (770)488-7333 Fax: 888-232-6789 E-mail: vsp@cdc.gov • URL: http://www.cdc.gov/nceh/vsp/vsp.htm • Web site provides details of unannounced sanitation inspections of individual cruise ships arriving at U. S. ports. Includes detailed results of the most recent inspection of each ship and results of inspections taking place in years past. There are lists of "Ships Inspected Past 2 Months" and "Ships with Not Satisfactory Scores" (passing grade is 85). CDC standards cover drinking water, food, and general cleanliness. Online searching is possible by ship name, inspection date, and numerical scores. Fees: Free.

ONLINE DATABASES

Globalbase. The Gale Group. • Provides more than one million online summaries of business, industrial, and economic news reports from more than 1,000 publications worldwide. Covers a wide range of material appearing in international trade journals, professional magazines, and newspapers. Time period is 1984 to date, with weekly updates. Inquire as to online cost and availability.

Oceanic Abstracts (Online). Cambridge Scientific Abstracts. • Oceanographic and other marine-related technical literature, 1981 to present.Monthly updates. Inquire as to online cost and availability.

TRIS: Transportation Research Information Service. National Research Council. • Contains abstracts and citations to a wide range of transportation literature, 1968 to present, with monthly updates. Includes references to the literature of air transportation, highways, ships and shipping, railroads, trucking, and urban mass transportation. Formerly *TRIS-ON-LINE.* Inquire as to online cost and availability.

PERIODICALS AND NEWSLETTERS

American Shipper: Ports, Transportation and Industry. Howard Publications, Inc. • Monthly. $48.00 per year.

International Trade Reporter Export Reference Manual. Bureau of National Affairs, Inc. • Weekly. $874.00 per year. Looseleaf. Formerly *Export Shipping Manual.*

Marine Digest. Newman-Burrows Publishing. • Monthly. $28.00 per year. Formerly *Marine Digest.*

Marine Engineers Review: Journal of the Institute of Marine Engineers. Available from Information Today, Inc. • Monthly. $140.00 per year. Published in London by the Institute of Marine Engineers. Covers marine engineering, offshore industries, and ocean shipping. Supplement available *Directory of Marine Diesel Engines.*

Marine Log. Simmons-Boardman Publishing Corp. • Monthly. $35.00 per year. Formerly *Marine Engineering-Log.*

Marine Management Holdings: Transactions. Available from Information Today, Inc. • Bimonthly. $220.00 per year. Published in London by Marine Management Holdings Ltd. Contains technical and regulatory material on a wide variety of marine and offshore topics. Formerly *Institute of Marine Engineers: Transactions.*

Maritime Reporter and Engineering News. Maritime Activity Reports, Inc. • Monthly. $44.00 per year.

Ocean Navigator: Marine Navigation and Ocean Voyaging. Navigator Publishing LLC. • Eight times a year. $26.00 per year.

Shipping Digest: For Export and Transportation Executives. Geyer-McAllister Publications, Inc. • Weekly. $57.00 per year.

RESEARCH CENTERS AND INSTITUTES

Transportation Research Institute. University of Michigan, 2901 Baxter Rd., Ann Arbor, MI 48109-2150. Phone: (734)764-6504 Fax: (734)936-1081 E-mail: umtri@umich.edu • URL: http://www.umtri.umich.edu • Research areas include highway safety, transportation systems, and shipbuilding.

STATISTICS SOURCES

Annual Survey of Manufactures. Available from U. S. Government Printing Office. • Annual. Prices vary. Issued by the U. S. Census Bureau as an interim update to the *Census of Manufactures.* Includes data on number of manufacturing establishments in various industries, employment, labor costs, value of shipments, capital expenditures, inventories, energy costs, and assets. (See also Census Bureau home page, http://www.census.gov/.).

Maritime Transport. Organization for Economic Cooperation and Development. • Annual. $36.00. Review of the maritime transport industry for OECD member countries. Includes statistical information.

Review of Maritime Transport. United Nations Conference on Trade and Development. United Nations Publications. • Annual. $55.00.

Transportation Statistics Annual Report. Available from U. S. Government Printing Office. • Annual. $21.00. Issued by Bureau of Transportation Statistics, U. S. Department of Transportation. Provides data on operating revenues, expenses, employees, passenger miles (where applicable), and other factors for airlines, automobiles, buses, local transit, pipelines, railroads, ships, and trucks.

U. S. Industry and Trade Outlook: The McGraw-Hill Companies and the U.S. Department of Commerce/International Trade Administration. Datapso Research Corp. • Annual. $69.95. Produced by the International Trade Administration, U. S. Department of Commerce, in a "public-private" partnership with DRI/McGraw-Hill and Standard & Poor's. Provides basic data, outlook for the current year, and "Long-Term Prospects" (five-year projections) for a wide variety of products and services. Includes high technology industries. Formerly *U. S. Industrial Outlook.*

World Fleet Statistics. Available from Fairplay Publications, Inc. • Annual. $142.00. Published in the UK by Lloyd's Register-Fairplay Ltd. Provides data on the "world fleet of propelled seagoing merchant ships of 100 gross tonnage and above." Includes five-year summaries.

World Shipbuilding Statistics. Available from Fairplay Publications, Inc. • Quarterly. $142.00 per year. Published in the UK by Lloyd's Register-Fairplay Ltd. Contains detailed, current data on shipbuilding orders placed and completions.

TRADE/PROFESSIONAL ASSOCIATIONS

American Bureau of Shipping. 16855 Northchase Dr., Houston, TX 77060. Phone: (281)877-6000 Fax: (281)877-6001 E-mail: abs-amer@eagle.org • URL: http://www.eagle.org.

American Maritime Association. 380 Madison Ave., New York, NY 10017. Phone: (212)557-9520 Fax: (212)557-9580.

Chamber of Shipping of America. 1730 M. St., N.W., Suite 407, Washington, DC 20036. Phone: (202)775-4399 Fax: (202)659-3795.

Institute of Marine Engineers. 76 Mark Lane, London EC3R 7JN, England. Phone: 44 207 3822600 Fax: 44 207 3822670 E-mail: mic@imare.org.uk • URL: http://www.imare.org.uk • An international organization of marine engineers, offshore engineers, and naval architects.

National Association of Marine Services. 5458 Wagonmaster Dr., Colorado Springs, CO 80917. Phone: (719)573-5946 Fax: (719)573-5952 E-mail: nams@citystar.com • URL: http://www.pcisys.net/~nams.

National Association of Waterfront Employers. 2011 Pennsylvania Ave., N.W., Suite 301, Washington, DC 20006. Phone: (202)296-2810 Fax: (202)331-7479.

Shipbuilders Council of America. 1600 Wilson Blvd., Ste. 100, Arlington, VA 22209. Phone: (703)351-6734 Fax: (703)351-6736 • URL: http://www.shipbuilders.org.

OTHER SOURCES

Capital for Shipping. Available from Informa Publishing Group Ltd. • Annual. $128.00. Published in the UK by Lloyd's List (http://www.lloydslist.com). Consists of a "Financial Directory" and a "Legal Directory," listing international ship finance providers and international law firms specializing in shipping. (Included with subscription to *Lloyd's Shipping Economist.*).

Fairplay: The International Shipping Weekly. Available from Fairplay Publications, Inc. • Weekly. $500.00 per year. Published in the UK by Lloyd's Register-Fairplay Ltd. Provides international shipping news, commentary, market reports, reports on shipbuilding activity, advice on operational problems, and other information.

Federal Carriers Reports. CCH, Inc. • Biweekly. $1,372.00 per year. Four looseleaf volumes. Periodic supplementation. Federal rules and regulations for motor carriers, water carriers, and freight forwarders.

Infrastructure Industries USA. The Gale Group. • 2001. $240.00. Replaces *Agriculture, Forestry, Fishing, Mining, and Construction USA* and *Transportation and Public Utilities USA.* Presents statistics and projections relating to economic activity in a wide variety of natural resource and construction industries.

List of Shipowners, Managers, and Managing Agents. Available from Fairplay Publications, Inc. • Annual. $270.00, including 10 updates per year. Published in the UK by Lloyd's Register-Fairplay Ltd. Lists 40,000 shipowners, managers, and agents worldwide. Cross-referenced with *Lloyd's Register of Ships.*

Lloyd's List. Available from Informa Publishing Group Ltd. • Daily. $1,665.00 per year. Published in the UK by Lloyd's List (http://www.lloydslist.com). Marine industry newspaper. Covers a wide variety of maritime topics, including global news, business/insurance, regulation, shipping markets, financial markets, shipping movements, freight logistics, and marine technology. (Also available weekly at $385.00 per year.).

Lloyd's Maritime Atlas of World Ports and Shipping Places. Available from Informa Publishing Group Ltd. • Annual. $119.00. Published in the UK by Lloyd's List (http://www.lloydslist.com). Contains more than 70 pages of world, ocean, regional, and port maps in color. Provides additional information for the planning of world shipping routes, including data on distances, port facilities, recurring weather hazards at sea, international load line zones, and sailing times.

Lloyd's Register of Ships. Available from Fairplay Publications, Inc. • Annual. $982.00. Three volumes and 10 cumulative supplements. Published in the UK by Lloyd's Register-Fairplay Ltd. Provides detailed information on more than 80,000 seagoing merchant ships of the world. Includes name, former names if any, date when built, owner, registration, tonnage, cargo capabilities, mechanical details, and other ship data.

Lloyd's Ship Manager. Available from Informa Publishing Group Ltd. • Monthly. $251.00 per year, including annual supplementary guides and directories. Published in the UK by Lloyd's List (http://www.lloydslist.com). Covers all management, technical, and operational aspects of ocean-going shipping.

Lloyd's Shipping Economist. Available from Informa Publishing Group Ltd. • Monthly. $1,446.00 per year. Published in the UK by Lloyd's List (http://www.lloydslist.com). Provides current analysis of world shipping markets, including coverage of the economics and costs of various kinds of ship operations. Statistical data and financial/legal directory listings are included.

Register of International Shipowning Groups. Available from Fairplay Publications, Inc. • Three times a year. $697.00 per year. Published in the UK by Lloyd's Register-Fairplay Ltd. "Provides intelligence on shipowners and managers, their subsidiary and associate companies, and owners' representatives." Includes detailed information on individual ships.

Ship Management. Malcolm Willingale and others. Available from Informa Publishing Group Ltd. • 1998. $105.00. Third edition. Published in the UK by Lloyd's List (http://www.lloydslist.com). Covers recruitment of personnel, training, quality control, liability, safety, responsibilities of ship managers, and other topics.

Shipcare. Available from Informa Publishing Group Ltd. • Quarterly. $188.00 per year. Published in the UK by Lloyd's List (http://www.lloydslist.com). Edited for the global ship repair, conversion, and maintenance industry. Provides news, market information, and technical analysis, including contract and pricing data.

SHOE INDUSTRY

See also: LEATHER INDUSTRY

DIRECTORIES

American Shoemaking Directory. Shoe Trades Publishing Co. • Annual. $54.00. Footwear manufacturers in the U.S., Puerto Rico and Canada.

Contemporary Fashion. Richard Martin, editor. St. James Press. • $140.00. Second edition. Date not set. Provides detailed information on more than 400 fashion designers, milliners, footwear designers, apparel companies, and textile houses. Includes black-and-white photographs, biographical information, and bibliographies.

Directory of Apparel Specialty Stores. Chain Store Guide. • Annual. $260.00. Lists over 5,000 women's, men's, family and sporting goods retailers.

Shoe Factory Buyer's Guide: Directory of Suppliers to the Shoe Manufacturing Industry. Shoe Trades Publishing Co. • Annual. $59.00. Lists over 750 suppliers and their representatives to the North American footwear industry.

FINANCIAL RATIOS

Almanac of Business and Industrial Financial Ratios. Leo Troy. Prentice Hall. • Annual. $99.95. Contains financial ratios derived from federal tax returns. Ratios for each of about 200 industries are arranged according to company asset size.

Annual Statement Studies. Robert Morris Associates: The Association of Lending and Credit Risk Professiona. • Annual. Free to members; non-members, $140.00. Median and quartile financial ratios are given for over 400 kinds of manufacturing, wholesale, retail, construction, and consumer finance establishments. Data is sorted by both asset size and sales volume. Includes a clearly written "Definition of Ratios" and an alphabetical industry index.

HANDBOOKS AND MANUALS

Shoe Stats. Footwear Industries of America. • Annual. Free to members; non-members, $350.00; libraries, $225.00. Includes *Statistical Reporter.*

INTERNET DATABASES

Fedstats. Federal Interagency Council on Statistical Policy. Phone: (202)395-7254 • URL: http://www.fedstats.gov • Web site features an efficient search facility for full-text statistics produced by more than 70 federal agencies, including the Census Bureau, the Bureau of Economic Analysis, and the Bureau of Labor Statistics. Boolean searches can be made within one agency or for all agencies combined. Links are offered to international statistical bureaus, including the UN, IMF, OECD, UNESCO, Eurostat, and 20 individual countries. Fees: Free.

ONLINE DATABASES

DRI U.S. Central Database. Data Products Division. • Provides more than 23,000 business, financial, demographic, economic, foreign trade, and industry-related time series for the U.S. Includes national income, population, retail-wholesale trade, price indexes, labor data, housing, industrial production, banking, interest rates, money supply, etc. Time period is generally 1947 to date (some data back to 1929). Updating varies. Inquire as to online cost and availability.

PERIODICALS AND NEWSLETTERS

American Shoemaking. James Sutton. Shoe Trades Publishing Co. • Monthly. $55.00 per year.

Footwear News. Fairchild Fashion and Merchandising Group. • Weekly. Retailers, $59.00 per year; mannufacturers and others, $72.00 per year.

STATISTICS SOURCES

Annual Survey of Manufactures. Available from U. S. Government Printing Office. • Annual. Prices vary. Issued by the U. S. Census Bureau as an interim update to the *Census of Manufactures.* Includes data on number of manufacturing establishments in various industries, employment, labor costs, value of shipments, capital expenditures, inventories, energy costs, and assets. (See also Census Bureau home page, http://www.census.gov/.).

Business Statistics of the United States. Courtenay M. Slater, editor. Bernan Associates. • 1999. $74.00. Fifth edition. Based on *Business Statistics*, formerly issue by the Bureau of Economic Analysis, U. S. Department of Commerce. Provides basic data for a wide variety of U. S. industries, services, and economic indicators. Most statistics are shown annually for 29 years and monthly for the most recent four years.

Footwear. U. S. Bureau of the Census. • Quarterly. Covers production and value of shipments of leather and rubber footwear. (Current Industrial Reports, MQ-31A.).

Manufacturing Profiles. Available from U. S. Government Printing Office. • Annual. Issued by the U. S. Census Bureau. A printed consolidation of the entire *Current Industrial Report* series, presenting "all the data compiled." Contains statistics on production, shipments, inventories, consumption, exports, imports, and orders for a wide variety of manufactured products. (See also Census Bureau home page, http://www.census.gov/.).

Standard & Poor's Industry Surveys. Standard & Poor's. • Semiannual. $1,800.00. Two looseleaf volumes. Includes monthly supplements. Provides detailed, individual surveys of 52 major industry groups. Each survey is revised on a semiannual basis. Also includes "Monthly Investment Review" (industry group investment analysis) and monthly "Trends & Projections" (economic analysis).

Survey of Current Business. Available from U. S. Government Printing Office. • Monthly. $49.00 per year. Issued by Bureau of Economic Analysis, U. S. Department of Commerce. Presents a wide variety of business and economic data.

TRADE/PROFESSIONAL ASSOCIATIONS

Footwear Distributors and Retailers of America. 1319 F St., N.W., 700, Washington, DC 20004. Phone: (202)737-5660 Fax: (202)638-2615.

Footwear Industries of America. 1420 K St., N.W. Suite 600, Washington, DC 20005. Phone: (202)789-1420 Fax: (202)789-4058 E-mail: info@fia.org • URL: http://www.fia.org.

National Shoe Retailers Association. 7150 Columbia Gateway Dr., Ste. G, Columbia, MD 21046-1151. Phone: 800-673-8446 or (410)381-8282 Fax: (410)381-1167 E-mail: info@nsra.org • URL: http://www.nsra.org.

OTHER SOURCES

Footwear Market. Available from MarketResearch.com. • 1998. $2,750.00. Published by Packaged Facts. Provides market data on shoes for walking, running, and specific sports.

SHOP PRACTICE

See: MACHINE SHOPS

SHOPLIFTING

See also: CRIME AND CRIMINALS

HANDBOOKS AND MANUALS

Security Applications in Industry and Institutions. Lawrence J. Fennelly, editor. Butterworth-Heinemann. • 1992. $46.95. Contains 19 chapters written by various security professionals in the U. S. Covers bank security, hotel security, shoplifting, college campus crime prevention, security in office buildings, hospitals, museums, libraries, etc.

SHOPPING

See: CONSUMER ECONOMICS; CONSUMER EDUCATION

SHOPPING CENTERS

See also: RETAIL TRADE

DIRECTORIES

Canadian Directory of Shopping Centres. Maclean Hunter Business Publications. • Annual. $400.00. Two volumes (Eastern Canada and Western Canada). Describes about 1,700 shopping centers and malls, including those under development.

Shopping Center Directory. National Research Bureau, Inc. • Annual. $655.00. Consists of four regional volumes. Individual volumes, $335.00 each. Provides detailed information on about 37,000 U. S. shopping centers. Includes *Top Contracts.*

Top Contacts: Major Owners, Leasing Agents, and Managers. National Research Bureau. • Annual. $305.00. Contains information on more than 1,300 owners, agents, and managers, each with control of three or more shopping centers.

HANDBOOKS AND MANUALS

Shopping Center and Store Leases. Emanuel B. Halper. New York Law Publishing Co. • Looseleaf service. $140.00. Two volumes.

Shopping Center Development Handbook. Michael D. Beyard and W. Paul O'Mara. Urban Land Institute. • 1998. $89.95. Third edition. (Development Handbook Series).

PERIODICALS AND NEWSLETTERS

Chain Store Age: The Newsmagazine for Retail Executives. Lebhar-Friedman, Inc. • Monthly. $105.00 per year. Formerly *Chain Store Age Executive with Shopping Center Age.*

Shopping Center World. Intertec Publishing Corp. • Monthly. $74.00 per year. Provides coverage of all phases of the shopping center industry. Includes annual *Directory.* Includes supplement *Outlet Retailer.*

Value Retail News: The Journal of Outlet and Off-Price Retail and Development. Off-Price Specialists, Inc. Value Retail News. • Monthly. Members $99.00 per year; non-members, $144.00 per year. Provides news of the off-price and outlet store industry. Emphasis is on real estate for outlet store centers.

RESEARCH CENTERS AND INSTITUTES
Urban Land Institute. 1025 Thomas Jefferson Ave. N.W., Suite 500W, Washington, DC 20004. Phone: (202)624-7000 Fax: (202)624-7140 E-mail: rlevitt@uli.org • URL: http://www.uli.org • Studies urban land planning and the growth and development of urbanized areas, including central city problems, industrial development, community development, residential development, taxation, shopping centers, and the effects of development on the environment.

STATISTICS SOURCES
Dollars and Cents of Shopping Centers. Urban Land Institute. • Triennial. Members, $29.95; non-members, $239.95. Supplemental *Special Report* available.

TRADE/PROFESSIONAL ASSOCIATIONS
International Council of Shopping Centers. 665 Fifth Ave., New York, NY 10022. Phone: (212)421-8181 Fax: (212)486-0849 E-mail: icsc@icsc.org • URL: http://www.icsc.org/.

SHORTHAND

See also: OFFICE PRACTICE

ENCYCLOPEDIAS AND DICTIONARIES
Gregg Shorthand Dictionary. John R. Gregg and others. McGraw-Hill. • 1974. $23.56. Second edition. (Diamond Jubilee Series).

HANDBOOKS AND MANUALS
Gregg Shorthand for Colleges. L. A. Leslie and others. McGraw-Hill. • Dates vary. Two volumes. Vol. 1, $96.20; Vol. 2, $101.40. (Series 90).

Gregg Shorthand Manual, Simplified. John R. Gregg and others. McGraw-Hill. • 1955. $23.96. Second edition.

SHORTHAND REPORTING

PERIODICALS AND NEWSLETTERS
Journal of Court Reporting. National Court Reporters Association. • 10 times a year. $49.00 per year. News and features about court reporting, reporter technology. Computer-aided transcription, real time translation captioning for the hearing-impaired, etc. Formerly *National Shorthand Reporter.*

TRADE/PROFESSIONAL ASSOCIATIONS
National Court Reporters Association. 8224 Old Courthouse Rd., Vienna, VA 22182. Phone: 800-272-6272 or (703)556-6272 Fax: (703)556-6291 E-mail: msic@ncrahq.org • URL: http://www.verbatimreporters.com.

SHOW BUSINESS

See also: AMUSEMENT INDUSTRY

ABSTRACTS AND INDEXES
Communication Abstracts. Sage Publications, Inc. • Bimonthly. Individuals, $185.00 per year; institutions, $805.00 per year. Provides broad coverage of the literature of communications, including broadcasting and advertising.

Readers' Guide to Periodical Literature. H. W. Wilson Co. • Monthly. $220.00 per year. CD-ROM edition, $1,495 per year, including annual cumulation. Indexes about 250 peridicals of general interest.

BIBLIOGRAPHIES
Entertainment and Sports Law Bibliography. American Bar Association. • 1986. $40.00.

Performing Arts: A Guide to the Reference Literature. Linda K. Simons. Libraries Unlimited, Inc. • 1994. $42.00. (Reference Sources in Humanities Series).

BIOGRAPHICAL SOURCES
Celebrity Register. The Gale Group. • 1989. $99.00. Fifth edition. Compiled by Celebrity Services International (Earl Blackwell). Contains profiles of 1,300 famous individuals in the performing arts, sports, politics, business, and other fields.

Contemporary Theatre, Film, and Television. The Gale Group. • 2000. 34 volumes in print. $165.00 per volume. Provides detailed biographical and career information on more than 11,000 currently popular performers, directors, writers, producers, designers, managers, choreographers, technicians, composers, executives, dancers, and critics.

CD-ROM DATABASES
Magazine Index Plus. The Gale Group. • Monthly. $4,000.00 per year (includes InfoTrac workstation). Provides full text on CD-ROM for about 100 popular, general interest magazines and indexing for 300 others. Includes special indexing of reviews and product evaluations. Time period is 1980 to date.

WILSONDISC: Readers' Guide to Periodical Literature. H. W. Wilson Co. • Monthly. $1,095.00 per year, including unlimited online access to *Readers' Guide to Periodical Literature* through WILSONLINE. Provides CD-ROM indexing of about 250 general interest periodicals. Covers 1983 to date. (*Readers' Guide Abstracts* also available on CD-ROM at $1,995 per year.).

DIRECTORIES
Billboard's International Talent and Touring Directory: The Music Industry's Worldwide Reference Source: Talent, Talent Management, Booking Agencies, Promoters, Venue Facilities, Venue Services and Products. BPI Communications, Inc. • Annual. $109.00. Lists entertainers, managers, booking agents, and others in the worldwide entertainment industry.

Cavalcade of Acts and Attractions. BPI Communications, Amusement Business Div. • Annual. $92.00. Directory of personal appearance artists, touring shows and other specialized entertainment. Lists promoters, producers, managers and booking agents.

Celebrity Directory: How to Reach Over 9,000 Movie, TV Stars and Other Famous Celebrities. Axiom Information Resources. • Annual. $39.95. Stars, agents, networks, studios, and other celebrities. Gives names and addresses.

Cyberhound's Guide to People on the Internet. The Gale Group. • 1997. $79.00. Second edition. Provides descriptions of about 5,500 Internet databases maintained by or for prominent individuals in business, the professions, entertainment, and sports. Indexed by name, subject, and keyword (master index).

Grey House Performing Arts Directory. Grey House Publishing. • 2001. $220.00. Contains more than 7,700 entries covering dance, instrumental music, vocal music, theatre, performance series, festivals, performance facilities, and media sources.

Hollywood Creative Directory. • Three times a year. $129.95 per year.$54.95 per issue. Lists more than 1,700 motion picture and television development and production companies in the U. S. (mainly California and New York). Includes names of studio and TV network executives.

Peterson's Professional Degree Programs in the Visual and Performing Arts. Peterson's. • Annual. $24.95. A directory of more than 900 degree programs in art, music, theater, and dance at 600 colleges and professional schools.

Protocol (Corporate Meetings, Entertainment, and Special Events). Protocol Directory, Inc. • Annual. $48.00. Provides information on about 4,000 suppliers of products and services for special events, shows (entertainment), and business meetings. Geographic arrangement.

Theatrical Index. Theatrical Index Ltd. • Weekly. $300.00 per year. (Lower rates available for biweekly or monthly service.) Lists pre-production theatrical presentations that are seeking investors.

ENCYCLOPEDIAS AND DICTIONARIES
Encyclopedia of Popular Music. Colin Larkin, editor. Groves Dictionaries, Inc. • 1998. $500.00. Third edition. Eight volumes. Covers a wide variety of music forms and pop culture. Includes bibliography and index.

HANDBOOKS AND MANUALS
Dun & Bradstreet/Gale Group Industry Handbooks. The Gale Group. • 2000. $630.00. Five volumes. $145.00 per volume. Each volume covers two or more major industries: 1. *Entertainment and Hospitality*; 2. *Construction and Agriculture*; 3. *Chemicals and Pharmaceuticals*; 4. *Computers & Software and Broadcasting & Telecommunications*; 5. *Insurance and Health & Medical Services.* The following are included for each industry: overview, statistics, financial ratios, rankings, merger information, company directory, directory of associations, and consultants directory.

Entertainment Industry Economics: A Guide for Financial Analysis. Harold Vogel. Cambridge University Press. • 1998. $39.95. Fourth revised edition.

Entertainment Law. Howard Siegel, editor. New York State Bar Association. • 1990. $60.00. Contains chapters by various authors on the legal aspects of television, motion pictures, theatre, music, phonograph records, and related topics.

Entertainment Law and Business, 1989-1993: A Guide to the Law and Business Prac Entertainment Industry. Harold Orenstein and David Sinacore-Guinn. LEXIS Publishing. • $180.00. Two volumes. Looseleaf. Periodic supplementation, $55.00.

Entertainment, Publishing, and the Arts Handbook. Robert Thorne and John D. Viera, editors. West Group. • Annual. $152.00. Presents recent legal cases, issues, developments, and trends.

Show Business Law: Motion Pictures, Television, Videos. Peter Muller. Greenwood Publishing Group, Inc. • 1990. $59.95.

ONLINE DATABASES
Readers' Guide Abstracts Online. H. W. Wilson Co. • Indexes and abstracts general interest periodicals, 1983 to date. Weekly updates. Inquire as to online cost and availability.

PERIODICALS AND NEWSLETTERS
Back Stage: The Performing Arts Weekly. BPI Communications, Inc. • Weekly. $95.00 per year. A theatre trade newspaper for show business professionals.

Daily Variety: News of the Entertainment Industry. Cahners Business Information. • Daily. $219.00 per year.

Entertainment Design: The Art and Technology of Show Business. Theatre Crafts International. • 11 times a year. $39.95 per year. Contains material on performing arts management, staging, scenery, costuming, etc. Formerly *TCI - Theatre Crafts International.*

Entertainment Marketing Letter. EPM Communications, Inc. • 22 times a year. $319.00 per year. Newsletter. Covers the marketing of various entertainment products. Includes television broadcasting, videocassettes, celebrity tours and tie-ins, radio broadcasting, and the music business.

The Hollywood Reporter. • Daily. $219.00 per year. Covers the latest news in film, TV, cable, multimedia, music, and theatre. Includes box office grosses and entertainment industry financial data.

Performing Arts Forum. International Society of Performing Arts Administrators. • 10 times a year. Free to members; non-members, $25.00 per year. Newsletter for performing arts managers, promoters, and talent representatives.

Theatre Journal. Association for Theatre in Higher Education. Johns Hopkins University Press. • Quarterly. Individuals $31.00 per year; institutions, $80.00 per year. Contains material on theatre history, theatre news, and reviews of books and plays.

Variety: The International Entertainment Weekly. Cahners Business Information, Broadcasting and Cable's International Group. • Weekly. $219.00 per year. Contains national and international news of show business, with emphasis on motion pictures and television.

RESEARCH CENTERS AND INSTITUTES

Wisconsin Center for Film and Theater Research. University of Wisconsin-Madison, 816 State St., Madison, WI 53706. Phone: (608)264-6466 Fax: (608)264-6472 E-mail: tbalio@facstaff.wisc.edu • URL: http://www.shsw.wisc.edu/archives/wcftr • Studies the performing arts in America, including theater, cinema, radio, and television.

STATISTICS SOURCES

United States Census of Service Industries. U.S. Bureau of the Census. • Quinquennial. Various reports available.

TRADE/PROFESSIONAL ASSOCIATIONS

International Society for the Performing Arts. P.O. Box 909, Rye, NY 10580-0909. Phone: (914)921-1550 Fax: (914)921-1593 E-mail: info@ispa.org • URL: http://www.ispa.org.

OTHER SOURCES

Sports and Entertainment Litigation Reporter: National Journal of Record Covering Crititcal Issues in Entertainment Law Field. Andrews Publications. • Monthly. $775.00 per year. Provides reports on lawsuits involving films, TV, cable broadcasting, stage productions, radio, and other areas of the entertainment business.Formerly *Entertainment Litigation Reporter.*

SHOW WINDOWS

See: DISPLAY OF MERCHANDISE

SICKNESS INSURANCE

See: HEALTH INSURANCE

SIGNS AND SIGN BOARDS

See also: COMMERCIAL ART; DISPLAY OF MERCHANDISE; OUTDOOR ADVERTISING; POSTERS

FINANCIAL RATIOS

Annual Statement Studies. Robert Morris Associates: The Association of Lending and Credit Risk Professiona. • Annual. Free to members; non-members, $140.00. Median and quartile financial ratios are given for over 400 kinds of manufacturing, wholesale, retail, construction, and consumer finance establishments. Data is sorted by both asset size and sales volume. Includes a clearly written "Definition of Ratios" and an alphabetical industry index.

HANDBOOKS AND MANUALS

Instant Sign Store. Entrepreneur Media, Inc. • Looseleaf. $59.50. A practical guide to starting an instant sign store. Covers profit potential, start-up costs, market size evaluation, owner's time required, site selection, lease negotiation, pricing, accounting, advertising, promotion, etc. (Start-Up Business Guide No. E1336.).

Practical Sign Shop Operations. Bob Fitzgerald. ST Publications, Inc. • 1992. $19.95. Seventh revised edition.

Standard Highway Signs, as Specified in the Manual on Uniform Traffic Control Devices. Available from U. S. Government Printing Office. • Looseleaf. $70.00. Issued by the U. S. Department of Transportation (http://www.dot.gov). Includes basic manual, with updates for an indeterminate period. Contains illustrations of typical standard signs approved for use on streets and highways, and provides information on dimensions and placement of symbols.

PERIODICALS AND NEWSLETTERS

Creative: The Magazine of Promotion and Marketing. Magazines Creative, Inc. • Bimonthly. $30.00 per year. Covers promotional materials, including exhibits, incentives, point-of-purchase advertising, premiums, and specialty advertising.

Signs of the Times: The National Journal of Signs and Advertising Displays. ST Publications, Inc. • 13 times a year. $36.00 per year. For designers and manufacturers of all types of signs. Features how-to-tips. Includes *Sign Erection, Maintenance Directory* and annual *Buyer's Guide.*

TRADE/PROFESSIONAL ASSOCIATIONS

International Sign Association. 707 N. Saint Asaph St., Alexandria, VA 22314-1911. Phone: (703)836-4012 Fax: (703)836-8353 • URL: http://www.signs.org.

SILK INDUSTRY

See also: TEXTILE INDUSTRY

ABSTRACTS AND INDEXES

Textile Technology Digest. Institute of Textile Technology. • Monthly. $535.00 per year. Provides indexing and abstracting of a wide variety of textile technology literature.

CD-ROM DATABASES

Textile Technology Digest [CD-ROM]. Textile Information Center, Institute of Textile Technology. • Quarterly. $1,700.00 per year. Provides CD-ROM indexing and abstracting of worldwide journals and monographs in various areas of textile technology, production, and management. Covers 1978 to date.

DIRECTORIES

Davison's Textile Blue Book. Davison Publishing Co. • Annual. $165.00. Over 8,400 companies in the textile industry in the United States, Canada, and Mexico, including about 4,400 textile plants.

ENCYCLOPEDIAS AND DICTIONARIES

Encyclopedia of Textiles. French and European Publications, Inc. • 1980. $39.95. Third edition.

Textile Terms and Definitions. J.E. McIntyre and Paul N. Daniels, editors. Available from State Mutual Book and Periodical Service Ltd., Trade Order Dept. • 1995. $110.00. 10th edition. Published by the Textile Insitute (UK). Includes more than 1,000 definitions of textile processes, fiber types, and end products. Illustrated.

ONLINE DATABASES

Globalbase. The Gale Group. • Provides more than one million online summaries of business, industrial, and economic news reports from more than 1,000 publications worldwide. Covers a wide range of material appearing in international trade journals, professional magazines, and newspapers. Time period is 1984 to date, with weekly updates. Inquire as to online cost and availability.

Textile Technology Digest [online]. Textile Information Center, Institute of Textile Technology. • Contains indexing and abstracting of more than 300 worldwide journals and monographs in various areas of textile technology, production, and management. Time period is 1978 to date, with monthly updating. Inquire as to online cost and availability.

World Textiles. Elsevier Science, Inc. • Provides abstracting and indexing from 1970 of worldwide textile literature (periodicals, books, pamphlets, and reports). Includes U. S., European, and British patent information. Updating is monthly. Inquire as to online cost and availability.

PERIODICALS AND NEWSLETTERS

Fiber Organon: Featuring Manufactured Fibers. Fiber Economics Bureau, Inc. • Monthly. $300.00 per year. Formerly *Textile Organon.*

TRADE/PROFESSIONAL ASSOCIATIONS

International Silk Association-U.S.A. c/o Seritex, One Madison St., East Rutherford, NJ 07073. Phone: (973)472-4200 Fax: (973)472-0222.

Textile Institute. Saint James Bldgs., 4th Fl., Oxford St., Manchester M1 6FQ, England. Phone: 44 161 2371188 Fax: 44 161 2361991 E-mail: tiihq@textileinst.org.uk • URL: http://www.texi.org • Members in 100 countries involved with textile industry management, marketing, science, and technology.

OTHER SOURCES

Textile Business Outlook. Statistikon Corp. • Quarterly. $985.00 per year. Analyzes current business, marketing, and financial conditions for the worldwide textile industry (fibers and fabrics). Includes statistical forecasts.

SILVER INDUSTRY

See also: COINS AS AN INVESTMENT; METAL INDUSTRY; MONEY

ABSTRACTS AND INDEXES

Nonferrous Metals Alert. Cambridge Information Group. • Monthly. $340.00 per year. Provides citations to the business and industrial literature of nonferrous metals. (Materials Business Information Series).

CD-ROM DATABASES

METADEX Materials Collection: Metals-Polymers-Ceramics. Cambridge Scientific Abstracts. • Quarterly. $6,950.00 per year. Provides CD-ROM citations to the worldwide literature of materials science and metallurgy. Corresponds to *Metals Abstracts, Alloys Index, Steels Alert, Nonferrous Alert, Polymers/Ceramics/Composites Alert,* and *Engineered Materials Abstracts.* (Formerly produced by ASM International.).

DIRECTORIES

Financial Times Energy Yearbook: Mining 2000. Available from The Gale Group. • Annual. $320.00. Published by Financial Times Energy. Provides production and financial details for more than 800 major mining companies worldwide. Includes coverage of reserves, operations, properties, and growth rates. Formerly *Financial Times International Yearbook: Mining.*

ENCYCLOPEDIAS AND DICTIONARIES

Encyclopedia of American Silver Manufacturers. Dorothy T. Rainwater and Judy Redfield, editors. Schiffer Publishing, Ltd. • 1998. $19.95. Fourth revised edition.

HANDBOOKS AND MANUALS

Jake Bernstein's New Guide to Investing in Metals. Jacob Bernstein. John Wiley and Sons, Inc. • 1991. $34.95. Covers bullion, coins, futures, options, mining stocks, and precious metal mutual funds. Includes the history of metals as an investment.

Silversmithing and Art Metal for Schools, Tradesmen, Craftsmen. Murray Bovin. Bovin Publishing. • 1977. $22.95. Revised edition.

ONLINE DATABASES

Materials Business File. Cambridge Scientific Abstracts. • Provides online abstracts and citations to worldwide materials literature, covering the business and industrial aspects of metals, plastics, ceramics, and composites. Corresponds to *Steels Alert, Nonferrous Metals Alert,* and *Polymers/Ceramics/ Composites Alert.* Time period is 1985 to date, with monthly updates. (Formerly produced by ASM International.) Inquire as to online cost and availability.

METADEX. Cambridge Scientific Abstracts. • Covers the worldwide literature of metals, metallurgy, and materials science, 1966 to date. Includes detailed alloys indexing from 1974. Biweekly updating. Inquire as to online cost and availability. (Formerly produced by ASM International.).

STATISTICS SOURCES

London Currency Report. World Reports Ltd. • 10 times a year. $950.00 per year. Formerly *Gold and Silver Survey.*

Mineral Commodity Summaries. Available from U. S. Government Printing Office. • Annual. Published by the U. S. Geological Survey, Department of the Interior (http://www.usgs.gov). Contains detailed, five-year data for about 90 nonfuel minerals. Covers a wide range of statistics, including production, imports, exports, consumption, reserves, prices, tariff information, and industry employment. (Two pages are devoted to each mineral.).

Minerals Yearbook. Available from U.S. Government Printing Office. • Annual. Three volumes.

Non-Ferrous Metal Data Yearbook. American Bureau of Metal Statistics. • Annual. $395.00. Provides about 200 statistical tables covering many nonferrous metals. Includes production, consumption, inventories, exports, imports, and other data.

Standard & Poor's Industry Surveys. Standard & Poor's. • Semiannual. $1,800.00. Two looseleaf volumes. Includes monthly supplements. Provides detailed, individual surveys of 52 major industry groups. Each survey is revised on a semiannual basis. Also includes "Monthly Investment Review" (industry group investment analysis) and monthly "Trends & Projections" (economic analysis).

Statistical Annual: Interest Rates, Metals, Stock Indices, Options on Financial Futures, Options on Metals Futures. Chicago Board of Trade. • Annual. Includes historical data on GNMA CDR Futures, Cash-Settled GNMA Futures, U. S. Treasury Bond Futures, U. S. Treasury Note Futures, Options on Treasury Note Futures, NASDAQ-100 Futures, Major Market Index Futures, Major Market Index MAXI Futures, Municipal Bond Index Futures, 1,000-Ounce Silver Futures, Options on Silver Futures, and Kilo Gold Futures.

United States Census of Mineral Industries. Bureau of the Census, U.S. Department of Commerce. Available from U.S. Government Printing Office. • Quinquennial.

TRADE/PROFESSIONAL ASSOCIATIONS

American Bureau of Metal Statistics. P.O. Box 805, Chatham, NJ 07928. Phone: (973)701-2299 Fax: (973)701-2152 E-mail: info@abms.com • URL: http://www.abms.com • Members are metal companies. Compiles and publishes detailed statistical data on a wide variety of nonferrous metals: aluminum, copper, gold, lead, nickel, platinum, silver, tin, titanium, uranium, zinc, and others.

Silver Institute. 1112 16th St., N.W., Suite 240, Washington, DC 20036. Phone: (202)835-0185 Fax: (202)835-0155 E-mail: info@silverinstitute.org • URL: http://www.silverinstitute.org.

Silver Users Association. 1730 M St., N.W., No. 911, Washington, DC 20036. Phone: (202)785-3050.

SILVERWARE

See: TABLEWARE

SKIP TRACERS

See: COLLECTING OF ACCOUNTS

SLOT MACHINES

See: VENDING MACHINES

SMALL ARMS

See: FIREARMS INDUSTRY

SMALL BUSINESS

See also: BUSINESS; BUSINESS ENTERPRISES, SALE OF; BUSINESS START-UP PLANS AND PROPOSALS; FRANCHISES; SELF-EMPLOYMENT; SMALL BUSINESS INVESTMENT COMPANIES; VENTURE CAPITAL

GENERAL WORKS

Managing the Small to Mid-Sized Company: Concepts and Cases. James C. Collins and William C. Lazier. McGraw-Hill Higher Education. • 1994. $68.95.

Net Income: Cut Costs, Boost Profits, and Enhance Operations Online. Wally Bock and Jeff Senne. John Wiley and Sons, Inc. • 1997. $29.95. "Net Income" in this case is hoped-for Internet income. Promotes the use of the Internet, intranet, and extranet to improve business operations or start new businesses. The authors take a nontechnical, business strategy approach.

Women Entrepreneurs: Moving Beyond the Glass Ceiling. Dorothy P. Moore and E. Holly Buttner. Sage Publications, Inc. • 1997. $46.00. Contains profiles of "129 successful female entrepreneurs who previously worked in corporate environments.".

BIBLIOGRAPHIES

Small Business Sourcebook. The Gale Group. • 2000. $335.00. 14th edtion. Two volumes. Information sources for about 100 kinds of small businesses.

BIOGRAPHICAL SOURCES

Contemporary Entrepreneurs: Profiles of Entrepreneurs and the Businesses They Started, Representing 74 Companies in 30 Industries. Craig E. Aronoff and John L. Ward, editors. Omnigraphics, Inc. • 1992. $95.00.

CD-ROM DATABASES

16 Million Businesses Phone Directory. Info USA. • Annual. $29.95. Provides more than 16 million yellow pages telephone directory listings on CD-ROM for all ZIP Code areas of the U. S.

DIRECTORIES

American Business Directory. InfoUSA, Inc. • Provides brief online information on more than 10 million U. S. companies, including individual plants and branches. Entries typically include address, phone number, industry classification code, and contact name. Updating is quarterly. Inquire as to online cost and availability.

Business Capital Sources. Tyler G. Hicks. International Wealth Success, Inc. • 2000. $15.00. 11th edition. Lists about 1,500 banks, insurance and mortgage companies, commerical finance, leasing and venture capital firms that lend money for business investment.

ENCYCLOPEDIAS AND DICTIONARIES

Encyclopedia of Small Business. The Gale Group. • 1998. $395.00. Two volumes. Contains about 500 informative entries on a wide variety of topics affecting small business. Arrangement is alphabetical.

FINANCIAL RATIOS

Business Profitability Data. John B. Walton. Weybridge Publishing Co. • 1996. $40.00. Sales and profitability ratios for 300 kinds of business.

HANDBOOKS AND MANUALS

Business Brokerage. Entrepreneur Media, Inc. • Looseleaf. $59.50. A practical guide to starting a brokerage service for the sale and purchase of small businesses. Covers profit potential, start-up costs, market size evaluation, owner's time required, pricing, accounting, advertising, promotion, etc. (Start-Up Business Guide No. E1317.).

Checklists and Operating Forms for Small Businesses. John C. Wisdom. John Wiley and Sons, Inc. • 1997. $125.00. 19th edition. Includes disk.

Complete Book of Small Business Legal Forms. Daniel Sitarz. Nova Publishing Co. • 1996. $29.95. Second revised edition. Includes basic forms and instructions for use by small businesses in routine legal situations. Forms are also available on IBM or MAC diskettes. (Small Business Library Series).

Computer Buying Guide. Consumer Guide Editors. Publications International Ltd. • Annual. $9.99.

Financial Management: How to Make a Go of Your Business. Available from U. S. Government Printing Office. • 1986. $3.50. Published by U. S. Small Business Administration. (Small Business Management Series, No. 44.).

Financial Management Techniques for Small Business. Art R. DeThomas. PSI Research. • 1991. $19.95. (Successful Business Library Series).

Financial Recordkeeping for Small Stores. Available from U. S. Government Printing Office. • 1986. Presents a basic record keeping system for the small retail owner-manager who does not have a trained bookkeeper. Produced by the Office of Business Development, Small Business Administration. (Small Business Management Series, 32.).

The Geek's Guide to Internet Business Success: The Definitive Business Blueprint for Internet Developers, Programmers, Consultants, Marketers, and Serivce Providers. Bob Schmidt. John Wiley and Sons, Inc. • 1997. $22.95. Written for beginning Internet entrepreneurs, especially those with technical expertise but little or no business experience. Covers fee or rate setting, developing new business, product mix, budgeting, partnerships, personnel, and planning. Includes checklists and worksheets.

How to Run a Small Business. Jacob K. Lasser. McGraw-Hill. • 1993. $27.95. Seventh edition.

Incorporate Your Business: The National Corporation Kit. Daniel Sitarz. Nova Publishing Co. • 1996. $29.95. Second revised edition. Includes basic forms and instructions for incorporating a small business in any state. Forms are also available on IBM or MAC diskettes. (Small Business Library Series).

Incorporation Kit. Entrepreneur Media, Inc. • Looseleaf. $59.50. A practical guide to incorporating a small business. Includes sample forms and information on how to construct bylaws and articles of incorporation. (Start-Up Business Guide No. E7100.).

Insuring Your Business: What You Need to Know to Get the Best Insurance Coverage for Your Business. Sean Mooney. Insurance Information Institute. • 1992. $22.50.

The Law in (Plain English) for Small Businesses. Leonard D. DuBoff. Allworth Press. • 1998. $19.95. Third revised edition. Discusses and explains legal issues relating to the organization, financing, and operation of a small business.

Marketing Without Advertising. Michael Phillips and Salli Rasberry. Nolo.com. • 1996. $19.00. Second revised edition. How to market a small business economically.

McGraw-Hill Guide to Starting Your Own Business: A Step-By-Step Blueprint for the First-Time Entrepreneur. Stephen C. Harper. McGraw-Hill. • 1992. $12.95. Places emphasis on the construction of an effective, realistic business plan.

Organizing Corporate and Other Business Enterprises. Matthew Bender & Co., Inc. • $240.00. Looseleaf service. Periodic supplementation. A guide to and tax factors to be considered in selecting a form of business organization for the attorney advising proposed or existing small businesses.

SBA Loan Guide. Entrepreneur Meida, Inc. • Looseleaf. $59.50. A practical guide to obtaining loans through the Small Business Administration. (Start-Up Business Guide No. E1315.).

Simplified Small Business Accounting. Daniel Sitarz. National Book Network. • 1998. $19.95. Second edition. Includes basic forms and instructions for small business accounting and bookkeeping. (Small Business Library Series).

Small Business Incorporation Kit. Robert L. Davidson. John Wiley and Sons, Inc. • 1992. $16.95.

Small Business Legal Smarts. Deborah L. Jacobs. Bloomberg Press. • 1998. $16.95. Discusses common legal problems encountered by small business owners. (Small Business Series Personal Bookshelf.).

Small Business Management. Justin Longenecker and others. South-Western Publishing Co. • 1996. $62.95. 10th edition. (GG-Small Business Management Series).

Small Business Management Fundamentals. Daniel Steinhoff and John Burgess. McGraw-Hill. • 1993. $62.50. Sixth edition.

Small Business Survival Guide: How to Manage Your Cash, Profits and Taxes. Robert E. Fleury. Sourcebooks, Inc. • 1995. $17.95. Third revised edition.

Small Time Operator: How to Start Your Own Small Business, Keep Your Books, Pay Your Taxes, and Stay Out of Trouble. Bernard Kamoroff. Bell Springs Publishing. • 1997. $16.95. Sixth edition. Concise, practical advice. Includes bookkeeping forms.

Standard Business Forms for the Entrepreneur. Entrepreneur Media, Inc. • Looseleaf. $59.50. A practical collection of forms useful to entrepreneurial small businesses. (Start-Up Business Guide No. E1319.).

Start-Up Business Guides. Entrepreneur Media, Inc. • Looseleaf. $59.50 each. Practical guides to starting a wide variety of small businesses.

Startup: An Entrepreneur's Guide to Launching and Managing a New Business. William J. Stolze. Rock Beach Press. • 1989. $24.95.

Successful Small Business Management: It's Your Business...Mind It!. David Siegel and Harold L. Goldman. Books on Demand. • $111.60. Reprint edition.

Telecom Made Easy: Money-Saving, Profit-Building Solutions for Home Businesses, Telecommuters, and Small Organizations. June Langhoff. Aegis Publishing Group Ltd. • 2000. $19.95. Fouth edition.

Ultimate Guide to Raising Money for Growing Companies. Michael C. Thomsett. McGraw-Hill Professional. • 1990. $45.00. Discusses the preparation of a practical business plan, how to manage cash flow, and debt vs. equity decisions.

Where to Go When the Bank Says No: Alternatives to Financing Your Business. David R. Evanson. Bloomberg Press. • 1998. $24.95. Emphasis is on obtaining business financing in the $250,000 to $15,000,000 range. Business plans are discussed. (Bloomberg Small Business Series).

INTERNET DATABASES

Deloitte & Touche Online. Deloitte & Touche LLP, Financial Consulting Services Center. Phone: (513)784-7100 E-mail: webmaster@dtonline.com • URL: http://www.dtonline.com • Web site provides concise, full-text articles on taxes, personal finance, and business from a leading accounting firm. Includes "Tax News and Views," "Personal Finance Advisor," "Business Advisor: A Resource for Small Business Owners," "Financial Tip of the Week," and "This Week Online: Top of the News." Weekly updates. Fees: Free.

MBEMAG. Minority Business Entrepreneur Magazine. Phone: (310)540-9398 Fax: (310)792-8263 E-mail: webmaster@mbemag.com • URL: http://www.mbemag.com • Web site's main feature is the "MBE Business Resources Directory." This provides complete mailing addresses, phone, fax, and Web site addresses (URL) for more than 40 organizations and government agencies having information or assistance for ethnic minority and women business owners. Some other links are "Current Events," "Calendar of Events," and "Business Opportunities." Updating is bimonthly. Fees: Free.

Small Business Retirement Savings Advisor. U. S. Department of Labor, Pension and Welfare Benefits Administration. Phone: (202)219-8921 • URL: http://www.dol.gov/elaws/pwbaplan.htm • Web site provides "answers to a variety of commonly asked questions about retirement saving options for small business employers." Includes a comparison chart and detailed descriptions of various plans: 401(k), SEP-IRA, SIMPLE-IRA, Payroll Deduction IRA, Keogh Profit-Sharing, Keogh Money Purchase, and Defined Benefit. Searching is offered. Fees: Free.

SoHo Central. Home Office Association of America, Inc. Phone: 800-809-4622 Fax: 800-315-4622 E-mail: info@hoaa.com • URL: http://www.hoaa.com • Web site provides extensive lists of "Home Office Internet Resources" (links), including Business, Government, Continuing Education, Legal, Employment, Telecommunications, and Publishing. Includes an online newsletter. Fees: Free. (Membership in the Home Office Association of America is $49.00 per year.).

Switchboard. Switchboard, Inc. Phone: (508)898-1000 Fax: (508)898-1755 E-mail: webmaster@switchboard.com • URL: http://www.switchboard.com • Web site provides telephone numbers and street addresses for more than 100 million business locations and residences in the U. S. Broad industry categories are available. Fees: Free.

PERIODICALS AND NEWSLETTERS

Business Start-Ups: Smart Ideas for Your Small Business. Entrepreneur Media, Inc. • Monthly. $14.97 per year. Provides advice for starting a small business. Includes business trends, new technology, E-commerce, and case histories ("real-life stories").

Entrepreneur: The Small Business Authority. Entrepreneur Media, Inc. • Monthly. $19.97 per year. Contains advice for small business owners and prospective owners. Includes numerous franchise advertisements.

Entrepreneurship: Theory and Practice. Baylor University, Hankamer School of Business. • Quarterly. Individuals, $55.00 per year; institutions, $90.00 per year. Formerly *American Journal of Small Business.*

Home Office Connections: A Monthly Journal of News, Ideas, Opportunities, and Savings for Those Who Work at Home. Home Office Association of America, Inc. • Monthly. $49.00 per year. Newsletter. Includes membership in the Home Office Association of America.

HomeOffice: The Homebased Office Authority. Entrepreneur Media, Inc. • Bimonthly. $11.97 per year. Contains advice for operating a business in the home.

In Business: The Magazine for Environmental Entrepreneuring. J G Press, Inc. • Bimonthly. $33.00 per year. Magazine for environmental entrepreneuring.

Inc.: The Magazine for Growing Companies. Goldhirsh Group, Inc. • 18 times a year. $19.00 per year. Edited for small office and office-in-the-home businesses with from one to 25 employees. Covers management, office technology, and lifestyle. Incorporates *Self-Employed Professional.*

International Wealth Success Newsletter: The Monthly Newsletter of Worldwide Wealth Opportunities. Tyler G. Hicks, editor. International Wealth Success, Inc. • Monthly. $24.00 per year. Newsletter. Provides information on a variety of small business topics, including financing, mail order, foreign opportunities, licensing, and franchises.

Journal of Small Business Management. West Virginia University Bureau of Business Research. • Quarterly. Individuals, $65.00 per year; institutions, $110.00 per year. Articles and features on small business and entrepreneurship.

Minority Business Entrepreneur. • Bimonthly. $16.00 per year. Reports on issues "critical to the growth and development of minority and women-owned firms." Provides information on relevant legislation and profiles successful women and minority entrepreneurs.

Smart Business for the New Economy. Ziff-Davis. • Monthly. $12.00 per year. Provides practical advice for doing business in an economy dominated by technology and electronic commerce.

Success: For the Innovative Entrepreneur. Success Holdings LLC. • Monthly. $19.97 per year. Provides information to help individuals advance in business.

Women's Business Exclusive: For Women Entrepreneurs. • Bimonthly. $39.00 per year. Newsletter. Reports news and information relating to financing, business procurement initiatives, technical assistance, and policy research. Provides advice on marketing, negotiating, and other management topics.

RESEARCH CENTERS AND INSTITUTES

Arthur M. Bank Center for Entrepreneurship. Babson College, Babson Park, MA 02157-0310. Phone: (617)239-4420 Fax: (617)239-4178 E-mail: spinelli@babson.edu • URL: http://www.babson.edu/entrep • Sponsors annual Babson College Entrepreneurship Research Conference.

Center for the Study of Entrepreneurship. Marquette University, College of Business Administration, Milwaukee, WI 53201-1881. Phone: (414)288-5100 Fax: (414)288-1660.

The Darla School of Business Administration-Research Division. University of South Carolina at Columbia, Columbia, SC 29208. Phone: 800-243-7232 or (803)777-2510 Fax: (803)777-9344 E-mail: woodward@darla.badm.sc.edu • URL: http://www.research.badm.sc.edu.

Small Business Development Center. Lehigh University, Rauch Business Center, 621 Taylor St., Bethlehem, PA 18015. Phone: (610)758-3980 Fax: (610)758-5205 E-mail: insbdc@lehigh.edu • URL: http://www.lehigh.edu/~insbdc/.

STATISTICS SOURCES

New Business Incorporations. Dun & Bradstreet, Economic Analysis Dept. • Monthly. $25.00 per year. Gives the number of new business incorporations in each of the 50 states. Includes commentary.

TRADE/PROFESSIONAL ASSOCIATIONS

Home Office Association of America. 133 E. 5th St., Ste. 711, New York, NY 10022. Phone: 800-809-4622 or (212)588-9097 Fax: (212)588-9156 E-mail: hoaa@aol.com • URL: http://www.hoaa.com • A for-profit organization providing advice and information to home office workers and business owners.

International Council for Small Business. c/o Jefferson Smurfit Center for Entrepreneurial Studies, St. Louis University, 3674 Lindell Blvd., St. Louis, MO 63108. Phone: (314)977-3628 Fax: (314)977-3627 E-mail: icsb@slu.edu • URL: http://www.icsb.org.

National Business Incubation Association. 20 E. Circle Dr., Suite 190, Athens, OH 45701. Phone: (740)593-4331 Fax: (740)593-1996 E-mail: info@nbia.org • URL: http://www.nbia.org • Members are business assistance professionals concerned with business startups, entrepreneurship, and effective small business management.

National Federation of Independent Business. 53 Century Blvd., Suite 300, Nashville, TN 37214. Phone: 800-634-2669 or (615)872-5800 Fax: (615)872-5353 • URL: http://www.nfibonline.com • Members are independent business and professional people.

National Small Business United. 1156 15th St., N.W., Suite 1100, Washington, DC 20005. Phone: 800-345-6728 or (202)293-8830 Fax: (202)872-8543 E-mail: nsbu@nsbu.org • URL: http://www.nsbu.org.

OTHER SOURCES

Keeping the Books: Basic Recordkeeping and Accounting for the Successful Small Business. Linda Pinson. Dearborn Financial Publishing. • 2000. $22.95. Fifth edition. Covers bookkeeping systems, financial statements, and IRS tax record requirements. Includes illustrations, worksheets, and forms.

Tax Planning for Individuals and Small Businesses. Sidney Kess. CCH, Inc. • 2000. $49.00. Includes illustrations, charts, and sample client letters. Edited primarily for accountants and lawyers.

U. S. Business Advisor. Small Business Administration. • Web site provides "a one-stop electronic link to all the information and services government provides for the business community." Covers about 60 federal agencies that exist to assist or regulate business. Detailed information is provided on financial assistance, workplace issues, taxes, regulations, international trade, and other business topics. Searching is offered. Fees: Free.

SMALL BUSINESS INVESTMENT COMPANIES

FINANCIAL RATIOS

Almanac of Business and Industrial Financial Ratios. Leo Troy. Prentice Hall. • Annual. $99.95. Contains financial ratios derived from federal tax returns. Ratios for each of about 200 industries are arranged according to company asset size.

HANDBOOKS AND MANUALS

Moody's Bank and Finance Manual. Moody's Investor Service. • Annual. $995.00 per year. Four volumes. Includes biweekly supplements in *Moody's Bank and Finance News Report.*

SBIC Directory and Handbook of Small Business Finance. International Wealth Success, Inc. • Annual. $15.00 per year. Includes small business investment companies.

STATISTICS SOURCES

Small Business Administration. Annual Report. U.S. Government Printing Office. • Annual. Two volumes.

TRADE/PROFESSIONAL ASSOCIATIONS

National Association of Small Business Investment Companies. 666 11th St., N.W., No. 750, Washington, DC 20001. Phone: (202)628-5055 Fax: (202)628-5080 E-mail: nasbic@nasbic.org • URL: http://www.nasbic.org.

SMALL LOAN COMPANIES

See: FINANCE COMPANIES

SMOKING POLICY

See also: TOBACCO AND TOBACCO INDUSTRY

GENERAL WORKS

Rise and Fall of the Cigarette: A Social and Cultural History of Smoking in the U. S. Allan Brandt. Basic Books. • 1997. $25.00.

Smoking and Politics: Policy Making and the Federal Bureaucracy. A. Lee Fritschler and James M. Hoepler. Prentice Hall. • 1995. $33.00. Fifth edition.

ABSTRACTS AND INDEXES

Readers' Guide to Periodical Literature. H. W. Wilson Co. • Monthly. $220.00 per year. CD-ROM edition, $1,495 per year, including annual cumulation. Indexes about 250 peridicals of general interest.

BIBLIOGRAPHIES

Smoking: The Health Consequences of Tobacco Use. Cecilia M. Schmitz and Richard A. Gray. Pierian Press. • 1995. $30.00. (Science and Social Responsibility Series).

DIRECTORIES

Evaluation Guide to Health and Wellness Programs. The Corporate University. • $189.00. Looseleaf service. Semiannual updates, $49.00 each. Provides detailed descriptions and evaluations of more than 200 employee wellness programs that are available nationally. Covers 15 major topics, such as stress management, substance abuse, occupational safety, smoking cessation, blood pressure management, exercise/fitness, diet, and mental health. Programs are available from both profit and non-profit organizations.

ONLINE DATABASES

Readers' Guide Abstracts Online. H. W. Wilson Co. • Indexes and abstracts general interest periodicals, 1983 to date. Weekly updates. Inquire as to online cost and availability.

RESEARCH CENTERS AND INSTITUTES

Tobacco and Health Research Institute. University of Kentucky. Cooper and University Drives, Lexington, KY 40546. Phone: (606)257-5798 Fax: (606)323-1077 E-mail: mdavies@pop.uky.edu • URL: http://www.uky.edu/~thri/homeweb.html.

STATISTICS SOURCES

Statistics on Alcohol, Drug, and Tobacco Use: A Selection of Statistical Charts, Graphs and Tables about Alcohol, Drug and Tobacco Use from a Variety of Published Sources with Explanatory Comments. The Gale Group. • 1995. $65.00. Includes graphs, charts, and tables arranged within subject chapters. Citations to data sources are provided.

TRADE/PROFESSIONAL ASSOCIATIONS

Action on Smoking and Health. 2013 H St., N. W., Washington, DC 20006. Phone: (202)659-4310 Fax: (202)833-3921 • URL: http://www.ash.org • Promotes national legal action against smoking.

Citizens for a Tobacco-Free Society. 8660 Lynnehaven Dr., Cincinnati, OH 45236. Phone: (513)677-6666 E-mail: antismoking@aol.com • Supports a ban on smoking in enclosed public places, including work places.

Group Against Smokers' Pollution. P.O. Box 632, College Park, MD 20741-0632. Phone: (301)459-4791 • Members are non-smokers seeking to regulate smoking in public places.

OTHER SOURCES

Cigarettes: Anatomy of an Industry, from Seed to Smoke. Available from W. W. Norton & Co., Inc. • 2001. $24.95. Published by The New Press. Covers the history, economic ramifications, marketing strategies, and legal problems of the cigarette industry. Popularly written.

SNACK FOOD INDUSTRY

See also: BAKING INDUSTRY; FOOD INDUSTRY

CD-ROM DATABASES

Food Science and Technology Abstracts [CD-ROM]. Available from SilverPlatter Information, Inc. • Quarterly. $3,700 per year. Produced by International Food Information Service (home page is http://www.ifis.org). Provides worldwide coverage on CD-ROM of the literature of food technology and production. Various types of publications are indexed, with abstracts, including about 1,800 periodicals. Time period is 1969 to date.

DIRECTORIES

Snack Food Buyer's Guide. Stagnito Publishing Co. • Annual. $55.00. Lists approximately 900 companies that provide supplies and services to the snack food industry.

Specialty Food Industry Directory. Phoenix Media Network, Inc. • Annual. Included in subscription to Food Distribution Magazine. Lists manufacturers and suppliers of specialty foods, and services and equipment for the specialty food industry. Featured food products include legumes, sauces, spices, upscale cheese, specialty beverages, snack foods, baked goods, ethnic foods, and specialty meats.

Who's Who in the Snack Food Industry. Snack Food Association. • Annual. $150.00. A directory of snack food manufacturers and suppliers to the industry.

HANDBOOKS AND MANUALS

Donut Shop. Entrepreneur Media, Inc. • Looseleaf. $59.50. A practical guide to starting a doughnut shop. Covers profit potential, start-up costs, market size evaluation, owner's time required, site selection, lease negotiation, pricing, accounting, advertising, promotion, etc. (Start-Up Business Guide No. E1126.).

Ice Cream Store. Entrepreneur Media, Inc. • Looseleaf. $59.50. A practical guide to starting an ice cream shop. Covers profit potential, start-up costs, market size evaluation, owner's time required, site selection, lease negotiation, pricing, accounting, advertising, promotion, etc. (Start-Up Business Guide No. E1187.).

ONLINE DATABASES

F & S Index. The Gale Group. • Contains about four million citations to worldwide business, financial, and industrial or consumer product literature appearing from 1972 to date. Weekly updates. Inquire as to online cost and availability.

Food Science and Technology Abstracts [online]. IFIS North American Desk. • Produced by International Food Information Service. Provides about 500,000 online citations, with abstracts, to the international literature of food science, technology, commodities, engineering, and processing. Approximately 2,000 periodicals are covered. Time period is 1969 to date, with monthly updates. Inquire as to online cost and availability.

Globalbase. The Gale Group. • Provides more than one million online summaries of business, industrial, and economic news reports from more than 1,000 publications worldwide. Covers a wide range of material appearing in international trade journals, professional magazines, and newspapers. Time period is 1984 to date, with weekly updates. Inquire as to online cost and availability.

PROMT: Predicasts Overview of Markets and Technology. The Gale Group. • Companies, products, applied technologies and markets. U.S. and international literature coverage, 1972 to date. Inquire as to online cost and availability. Provides abstracts from more than 1,600 publications. Weekly updates.

PERIODICALS AND NEWSLETTERS

Baking and Snack. Sosland Publishing Co. • Monthly. Free to qualified personnel; others, $30.00 per year. Covers manufacturing systems and ingredients for baked goods and snack foods.

Confectioner: Where Confectionery The Magazine. Stagnito Communcations, Inc. • Bimonthly. $30.00 per year. Covers a wide variety of topics relating to the distribution and retailing of candy and snacks.

Food Distribution Magazine. Phoenix Media Network, Inc. • Monthly. $49.00 per year. Edited for marketers and buyers of domestic and imported, specialty or gourmet food products, including ethnic foods, seasonings, and bakery items.

Snack Food and Wholesale Bakery: The Magazine That Defines the Snack Food Industry. Stagnito Publishing Co. • Monthly. Free to qualified personnel; others, $65.00 per year. Provides news and information for producers of pretzels, potato chips, cookies, crackers, nuts, and other snack foods. Includes *Annual Buyers Guide* and *State of Industry Report.*

TRADE/PROFESSIONAL ASSOCIATIONS

Biscuit and Cracker Distributors Association. 401 N. Michigan Ave., Chicago, IL 60611-4267. Phone: (312)644-6610 Fax: (312)321-6869 • Members are distributors and manufacturers of cookies, crackers, and related products.

Biscuit and Cracker Manufacturers Association. 8484 Georgia Ave., Suite 700, Silver Spring, MD 20910. Phone: (301)608-1552 Fax: (301)608-1557 E-mail: frooney@thebcma.org • URL: http://www.thebcma.org • Members are bakers of crackers and cookies.

Cookie and Snack Bakers Association. P.O. Box 37320, Cleveland, TN 37320. Phone: (423)472-1561 • Members are bakers of snacks and cookies.

Peanut and Tree Nut Processors Association. P.O. Box 59811, Potomac, MD 20859-9811. Phone: (301)365-2521 Fax: (301)365-7705 • URL: http://www.ptnpa.org.

Popcorn Institute. 401 N. Michigan Ave., Chicago, IL 60611-4267. Phone: (312)644-6610 Fax: (312)527-6658 • URL: http://www.popcorn.org • Members are popcorn companies.

Snack Food Association. 1711 King St., Suite 1, Alexandria, VA 22314. Phone: 800-628-1334 or (703)836-4500 Fax: (703)836-8262 E-mail: sfa@sfa.org • URL: http://www.snax.com.

OTHER SOURCES

Major Food and Drink Companies of the World. Available from The Gale Group. • 2001. $855.00. Fourth edition. Two volumes. Published by Graham & Whiteside. Contains profiles and trade names for more than 9,000 important food and beverage companies in various countries. In addition to foods, includes both alcoholic and nonalcoholic drink products.

Market for Healthy Snacks. MarketResearch.com. • 1996. $1,250.00. Provides market data on granola bars, dried fruit, trail mix, rice cakes, etc.

The Market for Salted Snacks. MarketResearch.com. • 2000. $2,750.00. Market research report. Covers potato chips, corn chips, popcorn, nuts, pretzels, and other salted snacks. Market projections are provided to the year 2004.

Thomas Food and Beverage Market Place. Grey House Publishing. • Annual. $295.00. Three volumes. Contains more than 40,000 entries covering food companies, beverages, food equipment, warehouse companies, food brokers, wholesalers, importers, and exporters. Formerly *Thomas Food Industry Register.*

SNUFF

See: TOBACCO AND TOBACCO INDUSTRY

SOAPS AND DETERGENTS

See: CLEANING PRODUCTS INDUSTRY

SOCIAL ACCOUNTING

See: NATIONAL ACCOUNTING

SOCIAL RESPONSIBILITY

See also: BUSINESS ETHICS; COMMUNITY RELATIONS

GENERAL WORKS

Business and Society: A Managerial Approach. Heidi Vernon. McGraw-Hill Professional. • 1997. Sixth edition. Price on application. Emphasizes ethics and social accountability.

Business, Government, and Society: A Managerial Perspective: Text and Cases. George A. Steiner and John F. Steiner. McGraw-Hill. • 1999. $82.19. Ninth edition. (Management Series).

Business, Government, and Society: Managing Competitiveness, Ethics, and Social Issues. Newman S. Perry. Prentice Hall. • 1994. $54.80.

Corporate Social Challenge: Cases and Commentaries. James E. Stacey and Frederick D. Sturdivant, editors. McGraw-Hill Professional. • 1994. $41.95. Fifth edition.

Up Against the Corporate Wall: Cases in Business and Society. S. Prakash Sethi and Paul Steidlmeier. Prentice Hall. • 1996. $57.00. Sixth edition.

Wired Neighborhood. Stephen Doheny-Farina. Yale University Press. • 1996. $32.00. The author examines both the hazards and the advantages of "making the computer the center of our public and private lives," as exemplified by the Internet and telecommuting.

ABSTRACTS AND INDEXES

PAIS International in Print. Public Affairs Information Service, Inc. • Monthly. $650.00 per year; cumulations three times a year. Provides topical citations to the worldwide literature of public affairs, economics, demographics, sociology, and trade. Text in English; indexed materials in English, French, German, Italian, Portuguese and Spanish.

Social Sciences Citation Index. Institute for Scientific Information. • Three times a year. $6,900 per year. Annual cumulation. Includes *Source Index, Citation Index, Permuterm Subject Index,* and *Corporate Index.*

Social Sciences Index. H. W. Wilson Co. • Quarterly, with annual cumulation. Service basis for print edition; CD-ROM edition, $1,495 per year. Indexes more than 400 periodicals covering economics, environmental policy, government, insurance, labor, health care policy, plannning, public administration, public welfare, urban studies, women's issues, criminology, and related topics.

ALMANACS AND YEARBOOKS

Research in Corporate Social Performance and Policy. JAI Press, Inc. • Irregular. $78.50.

CD-ROM DATABASES

National Newspaper Index CD-ROM. The Gale Group. • Monthly. Provides comprehensive CD-ROM indexing of all material appearing in the late edition of the *New York Times*, the final edition of the *Washington Post*, the national edition of the *Christian Science Monitor*, the home edition of the *Los Angeles Times*, and the *Wall Street Journal*. Time period is four years. Also available online.

The New York Times Ondisc. New York Times Online Services. • Monthly. $2,650.00 per year. CD-ROM discs contain the full text of *The New York Times*, final edition. Inquire as to time period covered and availability of backfiles.

Newspaper Abstracts Ondisc. Bell & Howell Information and Learning. • Monthly. $2,950.00 per year (covers 1989 to date; archival discs are available for 1985-88). Provides cover-to-cover CD-ROM indexing and abstracting of 19 major newspapers, including the *New York Times, Wall Street Journal, Washington Post, Chicago Tribune,* and *Los Angeles Times.*

PAIS on CD-ROM. Public Affairs Information Service, Inc. • Quarterly. $1,995.00 per year. Provides a CD-ROM version of the online service, *PAIS International*. Contains over 400,000 citations to the literature of contemporary social, political, and economic issues.

Social Science Source. EBSCO Publishing. • Monthly. $1,495.00 per year. Provides CD-ROM citations and abstracts to social science articles in more than 600 periodicals, with full text from 125 periodicals. Covers economics, political science, public policy, international relations, psychology, and other topics. Time period is most recent five years.

Social Sciences Citation Index: Compact Disc Edition. Institute for Scientific Information. • Quarterly. Provides CD-ROM indexing of the world's social sciences literature, including economics, business, finance, management, communications, demographics, information and library science, political science, sociology, etc. Corresponds to online *Social Scisearch* and printed *Social Sciences Citation Index.*

Social Sciences Citation Index: Compact Disc Edition with Abstracts. Institute for Scientific Information. • Quarterly. Provides CD-ROM indexing and abstracting of "significant articles" from 1,400 social science journals worldwide, with additional selections from 3,200 other journals, 1986 to date. Includes economics, business, finance, management, communications, demographics, information and library science, political science, sociology, and many other subjects.

WILSONDISC: Wilson Social Sciences Abstracts. H. W. Wilson Co. • Monthly. Including unlimited online access to *Social Sciences Index* through WILSONLINE. Provides CD-ROM indexing from 1983 and abstracting from 1994 of more than 400 periodicals covering economics, area studies, community health, public administration, public welfare, urban studies, and many other topics related to the social sciences.

DIRECTORIES

National Directory of Corporate Public Affairs. Columbia Books, Inc. • Annual. $109.00. Lists about 2,000 corporations that have foundations or other public affairs activities.

Shopping for a Better World: A Quick and Easy Guide to Socially Responsible Supermarket Shopping. Council on Economic Priorities. • Annual. $14.00. Rates 186 major corporations according to 10 social criteria: advancement of minorities, advancement of women, environmental concerns, South African investments, charity, community outreach, nuclear power, animal testing, military contracts, and social disclosure. Includes American, Japanese and British firms.

ENCYCLOPEDIAS AND DICTIONARIES

Blackwell Encyclopedic Dictionary of Business Ethics. Patricia H. Werhane and R. Edward Freeman, editors. Blackwell Publishers. • 1997. $105.95. The editors are associated with the University of Virginia. Contains definitions of key terms combined with longer articles written by various U. S. and foreign business educators. Includes bibliographies and index. (Blackwell Encyclopedia of Management Series).

HANDBOOKS AND MANUALS

Codes of Professional Responsibility: Ethic Standards in Business, Health and Law. Rena Gorlin, editor. Bureau of National Affairs, Inc. • 1998. $95.00. Fourth edition. Contains full text or substantial excerpts of the official codes of ethics of major professional groups in the fields of law, business, and health care.

ONLINE DATABASES

Information Bank Abstracts. New York Times Index Dept. • Provides indexing and abstracting of current affairs, primarily from the final late edition of *The New York Times* and the Eastern edition of *The Wall Street Journal.* Time period is 1969 to present, with daily updates. Inquire as to online cost and availability.

Newspaper and Periodical Abstracts. Bell & Howell Information and Learning. • Provides online coverage (citations and abstracts) of 25 major newspapers, 1,600 perodicals, and 70 TV programs. Covers business, economics, current affairs, health, fitness, sports, education, technology, government, consumer affairs, psychology, the arts, and the social sciences. Time period is 1986 to date, with daily updates. Inquire as to online cost and availability.

PAIS International. Public Affairs Information Service, Inc. • Corresponds to the former printed publications, *PAIS Bulletin* (1976-90) and *PAIS Foreign Language Index* (1972-90), and to the current *PAIS International in Print* (1991 to date). Covers economic, political, and sociological material appearing in periodicals, books, government documents, and other publications. Updating is monthly. Inquire as to online cost and availability.

Social Scisearch. Institute for Scientific Information. • Broad, multidisciplinary index to the literature of the social sciences, 1972 to present. Weekly updates. Worldwide coverage. Inquire as to online cost and availability.

Wilson Social Sciences Abstracts Online. H. W. Wilson Co. • Provides online abstracting and indexing of more than 415 periodicals covering area studies, community health, public administration, public welfare, urban studies, and many other social science topics. Time period is 1994 to date for abstracts and 1983 to date for indexing, with updates monthly. Inquire as to online cost and availability.

PERIODICALS AND NEWSLETTERS

Business and Society: A Journal of Interdisciplinary Exploration. International Association for Business and Society Research Committee. Sage Publications, Inc. • Quarterly. Individuals, $65.00 per year; institutions, $265.00 per year.

Business and Society Review: A Quarterly Forum on the Role of Business in a Free Society. Blackwell Publishers. • Quarterly. $120.00 per year.

Journal of Public Policy and Marketing. American Marketing Association. • Semiannual. Members, $50.00 per year; non-members, $70.00 per year; institutions, $100.00 per year. Devoted to the social and cultural impact of marketing activities.

Positive Leadership: Improving Performance Through Value-Centered Management. Lawence Ragan Communications, Inc. • Monthly. $119.00 per year. Newsletter. Emphasis is on employee motivation, family issues, ethics, and community relations.

Review of Social Economy. Association for Social Economics. Routledge Journals. • Quarterly. Individuals, $65.00 per year; institutions, $177.00 per year. Subject matter is concerned with the relationships between social values and economics. Includes articles on income distribution, poverty, labor, and class.

RESEARCH CENTERS AND INSTITUTES

Business, Government, and Society Research Institute. University of Pittsburgh. School of Business, Mervis Hall, Pittsburgh, PA 15260. Phone: (412)648-1555 Fax: (412)648-1693 E-mail: mitnick@pitt.edu.

Center for Corporate Community Relations. Boston College, 55 Lee Rd., Chestnut Hill, MA 02467. Phone: (617)552-4545 Fax: (617)552-8499 E-mail: cccr@bc.edu • URL: http://www.bc.edu/cccr • Areas of study include corporate images within local communities, corporate community relations, social vision, and philanthropy.

TRADE/PROFESSIONAL ASSOCIATIONS

Council on Economic Priorities. 30 Irving Place, New York, NY 10003. Phone: 800-729-4237 or (212)420-1133 Fax: (212)420-0988 E-mail: info@cepnyc.org • URL: http://www.cepnyc.org • Compiles and makes available information on the social responsibility of individual corporations.

Special Interest Group on Computers and Society. c/o Association for Computing Machinery, 1515 Broadway, 17th Fl., New York, NY 10036. Phone: (212)869-7440 Fax: (212)302-5826 E-mail: acmhelp@acm.org.

SOCIAL SECURITY

See also: MEDICARE

GENERAL WORKS

Fundamentals of Employee Benefit Programs. Employee Benefit Research Institute. • 1996. $49.95. Fifth edition. Provides basic explanation of employee benefit programs in both the private and public sectors, including health insurance, pension plans, retirement planning, social security, and long-term care insurance.

Retirement Security: Understanding and Planning Your Financial Future. David M. Walker. John Wiley and Sons, Inc. • 1996. $29.95. Topics include investments, social security, Medicare, health insurance, and employer retirement plans.

Social Insurance and Economic Security. George E. Rejda. Prentice Hall. • 1998. $92.00. Sixth edition.

Social Security, Medicare, and Pensions: Get the Most Out of Your Retirement and Medical Benefits. Joseph Matthews and Dorothy M. Berman. Nolo.com. • 1999. $21.95. Seventh edition. In addition to the basic topics, includes practical information on Supplemental Security Income (SSI), disability benefits, veterans benefits, 401(k) plans, Medicare HMOs, medigap insurance, Medicaid, and how to appeal decisions.

ABSTRACTS AND INDEXES

Social Sciences Index. H. W. Wilson Co. • Quarterly, with annual cumulation. Service basis for print edition; CD-ROM edition, $1,495 per year. Indexes more than 400 periodicals covering economics, environmental policy, government, insurance, labor, health care policy, plannning, public administration, public welfare, urban studies, women's issues, criminology, and related topics.

ALMANACS AND YEARBOOKS

Older Americans Information Directory. Group Grey House Publshing, Inc. • 2000. $190.00. Second edition. Presents articles (text) and sources of information on a wide variety of aging and retirement topics. Includes an index to personal names, organizations, and subjects.

CD-ROM DATABASES

Magazine Index Plus. The Gale Group. • Monthly. $4,000.00 per year (includes InfoTrac workstation). Provides full text on CD-ROM for about 100 popular, general interest magazines and indexing for 300 others. Includes special indexing of reviews and product evaluations. Time period is 1980 to date.

Social Science Source. EBSCO Publishing. • Monthly. $1,495.00 per year. Provides CD-ROM citations and abstracts to social science articles in more than 600 periodicals, with full text from 125 periodicals. Covers economics, political science, public policy, international relations, psychology, and other topics. Time period is most recent five years.

Social Sciences Citation Index: Compact Disc Edition with Abstracts. Institute for Scientific Information. • Quarterly. Provides CD-ROM

 For publishers addresses, refer to SOURCES CITED section at the back of the book.

indexing and abstracting of "significant articles" from 1,400 social science journals worldwide, with additional selections from 3,200 other journals, 1986 to date. Includes economics, business, finance, management, communications, demographics, information and library science, political science, sociology, and many other subjects.

SSA Publications on CD-ROM. Available from U. S. Government Printing Office. • Monthly. $238.00 per year. Provides updated text of three Social Security Administration publications: *Program Operations Manual; Social Security Handbook; Social Security Rulings.*

WILSONDISC: Readers' Guide to Periodical Literature. H. W. Wilson Co. • Monthly. $1,095.00 per year, including unlimited online access to *Readers' Guide to Periodical Literature* through WILSONLINE. Provides CD-ROM indexing of about 250 general interest periodicals. Covers 1983 to date. (*Readers' Guide Abstracts* also available on CD-ROM at $1,995 per year.).

WILSONDISC: Wilson Social Sciences Abstracts. H. W. Wilson Co. • Monthly. Including unlimited online access to *Social Sciences Index* through WILSONLINE. Provides CD-ROM indexing from 1983 and abstracting from 1994 of more than 400 periodicals covering economics, area studies, community health, public administration, public welfare, urban studies, and many other topics related to the social sciences.

DIRECTORIES

Government Assistance Almanac: The Guide to Federal, Domestic, Financial and Other Programs Covering Grants, Loans, Insurance, Personal Payments and Benefits. J. Robert Dumouchel, editor. Omnigraphics, Inc. • Annual. $190.00. Describes more than 1,300 federal assistance programs available from about 50 agencies. Includes statistics, a directory of 4,000 field offices, and comprehensive indexing.

FINANCIAL RATIOS

Financial Planning for Older Clients. James E. Pearman. CCH, Inc. • 2000. $49.00. Covers income sources, social security, Medicare, Medicaid, investment planning, estate planning, and other retirement-related topics. Edited for accountants, attorneys, and other financial advisors.

HANDBOOKS AND MANUALS

Complete and Easy Guide to Social Security and Medicare. Faustin Tehle. Fraser-Vance Publishing Co. • 1996. $12.95. 13th unabridged edition.

Medicare Explained. CCH, Inc. • Annual. $30.00.

The New Working Woman's Guide to Retirement Planning. Martha P. Patterson. University of Pennsylvania Press. • 1999. $17.50. Second edition. Provides retirement advice for employed women, including information on various kinds of IRAs, cash balance and other pension plans, 401(k) plans, and social security. Four case studies are provided to illustrate retirement planning at specific life and career stages.

Social Security Benefits, Including Medicare. CCH, Inc. • Annual.

Social Security Claims and Procedures. Harvey L. McCormick. West Publishing Co., College and School Div. • 1991. Two volumes. Fourth edition. Price on application. Periodic supplementation.

Social Security Explained. CCH, Inc. • Annual. $32.00.

Social Security Handbook. Available from U. S. Government Printing Office. • Annual. $45.00. Issued by the Social Security Administration (http://www.ssa.gov). Provides detailed information about social security programs, including Medicare, with brief descriptions of related programs administered by agencies other than the Social Security Administration.

Social Security Manual. The National Underwriter Co. • Annual. $17.50.

Social Security Practice Guide. Matthew Bender & Co., Inc. • $870.00. Five looseleaf volumes. Periodic supplementation. Complete, practical guide on all substantive and procedural aspects of social security practice. Prepared under the supervision of the National Organization of Social Security Claimants' Representatives (NOSSCR).

Social Security Programs Throughout the World. Available from U. S. Government Printing Office. • Annual. $43.00. Issued by the Social Security Administration (http://www.ssa.gov). Presents basic information on more than 170 social security systems around the world.

INTERNET DATABASES

Social Security Online: The Official Web Site of the Social Security Administration. U. S. Social Security Administration. Phone: 800-772-1213 or (410)965-7700 • URL: http://www.ssa.gov • Web site provides a wide variety of online information relating to social security and Medicare. Topics include benefits, disability, employer wage reporting, personal earnings statements, statistics, government financing, social security law, and public welfare reform legislation.

ONLINE DATABASES

Ageline. American Association of Retired Persons. • Provides indexing and abstracting of the literature of social gerontology, including consumer aspects, financial planning, employment, housing, health care services, mental health, social security, and retirement. Time period is 1978 to date. Inquire as to online cost and availability.

Newspaper and Periodical Abstracts. Bell & Howell Information and Learning. • Provides online coverage (citations and abstracts) of 25 major newspapers, 1,600 perodicals, and 70 TV programs. Covers business, economics, current affairs, health, fitness, sports, education, technology, government, consumer affairs, psychology, the arts, and the social sciences. Time period is 1986 to date, with daily updates. Inquire as to online cost and availability.

Readers' Guide Abstracts Online. H. W. Wilson Co. • Indexes and abstracts general interest periodicals, 1983 to date. Weekly updates. Inquire as to online cost and availability.

Wilson Social Sciences Abstracts Online. H. W. Wilson Co. • Provides online abstracting and indexing of more than 415 periodicals covering area studies, community health, public administration, public welfare, urban studies, and many other social science topics. Time period is 1994 to date for abstracts and 1983 to date for indexing, with updates monthly. Inquire as to online cost and availability.

PERIODICALS AND NEWSLETTERS

Journal of Aging and Social Policy: A Journal Devoted to Aging and Social Policy. Haworth Press, Inc. • Quarterly. Individuals, $60.00 per year; institutions, $120.00 per year; libraries, $275.00 per year.

Older Americans Report. Business Publishers, Inc. • Weekly. $432.00 per year. Newsletter on health, economic, and social services for the aging, including social security, medicare, pensions, housing, nursing homes, and programs under the Older Americans Act. Edited for service providers.

RESEARCH CENTERS AND INSTITUTES

Employee Benefit Research Institute. 2121 K St., N. W., Suite 600, Washington, DC 20037-1896. Phone: (202)659-0670 Fax: (202)775-6312 E-mail: salisbury@ebri.org • URL: http://www.ebri.org • Conducts research on employee benefits, including various kinds of pensions, individual retirement accounts (IRAs), health insurance, social security, and long-term health care benefits.

STATISTICS SOURCES

EBRI Databook on Employee Benefits. Employee Benefit Research Institute. • 1997 $99.00. Fourth edition. Contains more than 350 tables and charts presenting data on employee benefits in the U. S., including pensions, health insurance, social security, and medicare. Includes a glossary of employee benefit terms.

Fast Facts and Figures About Social Security. Available from U. S. Government Printing Office. • Annual. $4.50. Issued by the Social Security Administration (http://www.ssa.gov). Provides concise data and charts relating to social security benefits, beneficiaries, disability payments, supplemental security income, and income of the aged.

Income of the Population 55 and Older. Available from U. S. Government Printing Office. • Biennial. $19.00. Issued by the Social Security Administration (http://www.ssa.gov). Covers major sources and amounts of income for the 55 and older population in the U. S., "with special emphasis on some aspects of the income of the population 65 and older.".

Social Security Bulletin. Social Security Administration. Available from U.S. Government Printing Office. • Quarterly. $23.00 per year. Annual statistical supplement.

Statistical Abstract of the United States. Available from U. S. Government Printing Office. • Annual. $51.00. Issued by the U. S. Bureau of the Census.

Statistical Handbook on Aging Americans. Renee Schick, editor. Oryx Press. • 1994. $65.00. Second edition. Provides data on demographics, social characteristics, health, employment, economic conditions, income, pensions, and social security. Includes bibliographic information and a glossary. (Statistical Handbook Series).

TRADE/PROFESSIONAL ASSOCIATIONS

National Conference of State Social Security Administrators. Social Security Div. Two Northside 75, Suite 300, Atlanta, GA 30318. Phone: (404)352-6414 Fax: (404)352-6431.

SOCIAL WELFARE

See: PUBLIC WELFARE

SOCIETY AND BUSINESS

See: SOCIAL RESPONSIBILITY

SODIUM CHLORIDE INDUSTRY

See: SALT INDUSTRY

SOFT DRINK INDUSTRY

DIRECTORIES

Beverage Industry - Annual Manual. Stagnito Communications, Inc. • Annual. $55.00. Provides statistical information on multiple beverage markets. Includes an industry directory. Supplement to *Beverage Industry.*

The Beverage Marketing Directory. Beverage Marketing Corp. • Annual. $845.00. Provides information for approximately 11,000 beverage companies and suppliers to beverage companies. Includes sales volume and brand names. Formerly *National Beverage Marketing Directory.*

Beverage World Buyers Guide. Bill Communications, Inc. • Annual. $7.00. Lists suppliers to the beverage industry.

World Drinks Marketing Directory. Available from The Gale Group. • 2001. $1,090.00. Second edition. Published by Euromonitor. Provides detailed infromation on the leading beverage companies of the world, including specifi brand data.

FINANCIAL RATIOS

Almanac of Business and Industrial Financial Ratios. Leo Troy. Prentice Hall. • Annual. $99.95. Contains financial ratios derived from federal tax returns. Ratios for each of about 200 industries are arranged according to company asset size.

Annual Statement Studies. Robert Morris Associates: The Association of Lending and Credit Risk Professiona. • Annual. Free to members; non-members, $140.00. Median and quartile financial ratios are given for over 400 kinds of manufacturing, wholesale, retail, construction, and consumer finance establishments. Data is sorted by both asset size and sales volume. Includes a clearly written "Definition of Ratios" and an alphabetical industry index.

Industry Norms and Key Business Ratios. Desk Top Edition. Dun and Bradstreet Corp., Business Information Services. • Annual. Five volumes. $475.00 per volume. $1,890.00 per set. Covers over 800 kinds of businesses, arranged by Standard Industrial Classification number. More detailed editions covering longer periods of time are also available.

PERIODICALS AND NEWSLETTERS

Beverage Digest. Beverage Digest Co., LLC. • 22 times a year. $605.00 per year. Includes supplement. *Green Sheet.* News pertaining to the soft drink industry including new products, marketing territory changes, acquisitions, legal cases, etc. Supplement available *Green Sheet.*

Beverage Industry. Stagnito Communications, Inc. • Monthly. Free to qualified personnel; others, $65.00 per year. Supplement available *Beverage Industry-Annual Manual.*

Beverage World: Magazine of the Beverage Industry. Bill Communications, Inc. • Monthly. $55.00 per year.

Beverage World Periscope. Keller International Publishing Corp. • Monthly. $35.00 per year. Newsletter.

Soft Drink Letter. Whitaker Newsletter, Inc. • Biweekly. $299.00 per year. For owners and managers of bottling operations. Covers soft drinks, juices. Formerly *Leisure Beverage Insider Newsletter.*

STATISTICS SOURCES

Impact Beverage Trends in America. M. Shanken Communications, Inc. • Annual. $695.00. Detailed compilations of data for various segments of the liquor, beer, and soft drink industries.

U. S. Industry and Trade Outlook: The McGraw-Hill Companies and the U.S. Department of Commerce/ International Trade Administration. Datapso Research Corp. • Annual. $69.95. Produced by the International Trade Administration, U. S. Department of Commerce, in a "public-private" partnership with DRI/McGraw-Hill and Standard & Poor's. Provides basic data, outlook for the current year, and "Long-Term Prospects" (five-year projections) for a wide variety of products and services. Includes high technology industries. Formerly *U. S. Industrial Outlook.*

TRADE/PROFESSIONAL ASSOCIATIONS

International Society of Beverage Technologists. 8120 S. Suncoast Blvd., HomoSassa, FL 34446. Phone: (352)382-2008 Fax: (352)382-2018 E-mail: isbt@bevetch.org • URL: http://www.bevtech.org • Members are professionals engaged in the technical areas of soft drink production.

National Soft Drink Association. 1101 16th St., N.W., Washington, DC 20036. Phone: (202)463-6732 Fax: (202)463-8178 E-mail: info@nsda.org • URL: http://www.nsda.org.

OTHER SOURCES

Major Food and Drink Companies of the World. Available from The Gale Group. • 2001. $855.00. Fourth edition. Two volumes. Published by Graham & Whiteside. Contains profiles and trade names for more than 9,000 important food and beverage companies in various countries. In addition to foods, includes both alcoholic and nonalcoholic drink products.

Thomas Food and Beverage Market Place. Grey House Publishing. • Annual. $295.00. Three volumes. Contains more than 40,000 entries covering food companies, beverages, food equipment, warehouse companies, food brokers, wholesalers, importers, and exporters. Formerly *Thomas Food Industry Register.*

SOFTWARE INDUSTRY, COMPUTER

See: COMPUTER SOFTWARE INDUSTRY

SOFTWOOD INDUSTRY

See: FOREST PRODUCTS; LUMBER INDUSTRY

SOLAR ENERGY

GENERAL WORKS

Renewable Energy: Power for a Sustainable Future. Godfrey Boyle, editor. Available from Taylor & Francis. • 1996. $39.95. Published by Open University Press. Contains ten chapters, each on a particular renewable energy source, including solar, biomass, hydropower, wind, and geothermal.

ABSTRACTS AND INDEXES

Applied Science and Technology Index. H. W. Wilson Co. • 11 times a year. Quarterly and annual cumulations. Service basis for print edition; CD-ROM edition, $1,495.00 per year. Indexes a wide variety of English language technical, industrial, and engineering periodicals.

NTIS Alerts: Energy. National Technical Information Service. • Semimonthly. $245.00 per year. Provides descriptions of government-sponsored research reports and software, with ordering information. Covers electric power, batteries, fuels, geothermal energy, heating/cooling systems, nuclear technology, solar energy, energy policy, and related subjects. Formerly *Abstract Newsletter.*

Science Citation Index. Institute for Scientific Information. • Bimonthly. $15,020.00 per year. Annual cumulation. Includes *Source Index, Citation Index, Permuterm Subject Index,* and *Corporate Index.*

BIBLIOGRAPHIES

Solar Energy. Available from U. S. Government Printing Office. • Annual. Free. Lists government publications. GPO Subject Bibliography Number 9.

BIOGRAPHICAL SOURCES

Energy and Nuclear Sciences International Who's Who. Allyn and Bacon/Longman. • 1990. $310.00. Third edition.

CD-ROM DATABASES

Science Citation Index: Compact Disc Edition. Institute for Scientific Information. • Quarterly. Provides CD-ROM indexing of the world's scientific and technical literature. Corresponds to online *Scisearch* and printed *Science Citation Index.*

DIRECTORIES

Directory of SRCC Certified Collectors and Solar Water Heating Systems Ratings. Solar Rating and Certification Corp. • Irregular. $33.00. About 20 manufacturers of solar collectors and systems certified by the Organization. Includes technical information.

Energy User News: Energy Technology Buyers Guide. Cahners Business Information. • Annual. $10.00. List of about 400 manufacturers, manufacturers' representatives, dealers, and distributors of energy management equipment. *Annual Review* and *Forecast* issue.

The International Competitive Power Industry Directory. PennWell Corp. • Annual. $75.00. Lists suppliers of services, products, and equipment for the hydro, geothermal, solar, and wind power industries.

SYNERJY: A Directory of Renewable Energy. Synerjy. • Semiannual. Individuals, $30.00 per year; others, $62.00 per year. Includes organizations, publishers, and other resources. Lists articles, patents, government publications, research groups and facilities.

ENCYCLOPEDIAS AND DICTIONARIES

Macmillan Encyclopedia of Energy. Available from The Gale Group. • 2001. $350.00. Three volumes. Published by Macmillan Reference USA. Covers the business, technology, and history of a wide variety of energy sources.

Wiley Encyclopedia of Energy and the Environment. Frederick John Francis. John Wiley and Sons, Inc. • 1999. $1,500.00. Four volumes. Second edition. Covers a wide variety of energy and environmental topics, including legal and policy issues.

HANDBOOKS AND MANUALS

Practical Solar Energy Technology. Martin L. Greenwald and Thomas K. McHugh. Prentice Hall. • 1985. $45.00.

The Solar Home: How to Design and Build a House You Heat with the Sun. Mark Freeman. Stackpole Books, Inc. • 1994. $14.95.

ONLINE DATABASES

Energyline. Congressional Information Service, Inc. • Provides online citations and abstracts to the literature of all forms of energy: petroleum, natural gas, coal, nuclear power, solar energy, etc. Time period is 1971 to 1993 (closed file). Inquire as to online cost and availability.

Globalbase. The Gale Group. • Provides more than one million online summaries of business, industrial, and economic news reports from more than 1,000 publications worldwide. Covers a wide range of material appearing in international trade journals, professional magazines, and newspapers. Time period is 1984 to date, with weekly updates. Inquire as to online cost and availability.

PAIS International. Public Affairs Information Service, Inc. • Corresponds to the former printed publications, *PAIS Bulletin* (1976-90) and *PAIS Foreign Language Index* (1972-90), and to the current *PAIS International in Print* (1991 to date). Covers economic, political, and sociological material appearing in periodicals, books, government documents, and other publications. Updating is monthly. Inquire as to online cost and availability.

Scisearch. Institute for Scientific Information. • Broad, multidisciplinary index to the literature of science and technology, 1974 to present. Inquire as to online cost and availability. Coverage of literature is worldwide, with weekly updates.

PERIODICALS AND NEWSLETTERS

Alternative Energy Retailer. Zackin Publications, Inc. • Monthly. $32.00 per year.

Energy Conversion and Management. Elsevier Science. • 18 times a year. $2,835.00 per year. Presents a scholarly approach to alternative or renewable energy sources. Text in English, French and German.

Energy: The International Journal. Elsevier Science. • Monthly. $1,608.00 per year.

Independent Energy: The Power Industry's Business Magazine. PennWell Corp., Industrial Div. • 10 times a year. $127.00 per year. Covers non-utility electric power plants (cogeneration) and other alternative sources of electric energy.

National Energy Journal. c/o J. P. Dunlavey. National Wood Stove and Fireplace Journal, Inc. • Monthly. $21.00 per year.

Renewable Energy: An International Journal. Elsevier Science. • Monthly. $1,505.00 per year. Incorporates *Solar and Wind Technology.*

Renewable Energy News Digest. Sun Words. • Monthly. $60.00 per year. Newsletter. Covers geothermal, solar, wind, cogenerated, and other energy sources.

Solar Energy: International for Scientists, Engineers and Technologists in SolarEnergy and Its Application. International Solar Energy Society. Elsevier Science. • 18 times a year. $1,889.00 per year.

RESEARCH CENTERS AND INSTITUTES

Energy Laboratory. Massachusetts Institute of Technology. Bldg. E40-455, Cambridge, MA 02139-4307. Phone: (617)253-3401 Fax: (617)253-8013 E-mail: testerel@mit.edu • URL: http://www.web.mit.edu/energylab/www/.

Hawaii Natural Energy Institute. University of Hawaii at Manoa, 2540 Dole St., Holmes Hall 246, Honolulu, HI 96822. Phone: (808)956-8890 Fax: (808)956-2336 E-mail: hnei@hawaii.edu • URL: http://www.soest.hawaii.edu • Research areas include geothermal, wind, solar, hydroelectric, and other energy sources.

Solar Energy and Energy Conversion Laboratory. University of Florida, Dept. of Mechanical Engineering, P.O. Box 116300, Gainesville, FL 32611. Phone: (352)392-0812 Fax: (352)392-1071 E-mail: solar@cimar.me.ufl.edu • URL: http://www.me.ufl.edu/solar.

Solar Energy Center. University of Oregon, Depts. of Architecture and Physics, Eugene, OR 97403. Phone: (541)346-3656 Fax: (541)346-5861 E-mail: fevignola@darkwing.uoregon.edu.

STATISTICS SOURCES

Annual Energy Outlook [year], with Projections to [year]. Available from U. S. Government Printing Office. • Annual. Issued by the Energy Information Administration, U. S. Department of Energy (http://www.eia.doe.gov). Contains detailed statistics and 20-year projections for electricity, oil, natural gas, coal, and renewable energy. Text provides extensive discussion of energy issues and "Market Trends.".

International Energy Annual. Available from U. S. Government Printing Office. • Annual. $34.00. Issued by the Energy Information Administration, U. S. Department of Energy. Provides production, consumption, import, and export data for primary energy commodities in more than 200 countries and areas. In addition to petroleum products and alcohol, renewable energy sources are covered (hydroelectric, geothermal, solar, and wind).

U. S. Industry and Trade Outlook: The McGraw-Hill Companies and the U.S. Department of Commerce/International Trade Administration. Datapso Research Corp. • Annual. $69.95. Produced by the International Trade Administration, U. S. Department of Commerce, in a "public-private" partnership with DRI/McGraw-Hill and Standard & Poor's. Provides basic data, outlook for the current year, and "Long-Term Prospects" (five-year projections) for a wide variety of products and services. Includes high technology industries. Formerly *U. S. Industrial Outlook.*

TRADE/PROFESSIONAL ASSOCIATIONS

AERO. 25 S. Ewing St., Room 214, Helena, MT 59601. Phone: (406)443-7272 Fax: (406)442-9120 E-mail: aero@aeromt.org.

American Solar Energy Society. 2400 Central Ave., G-1, Boulder, CO 80301. Phone: (303)443-3130 Fax: (303)443-3212 E-mail: ases@ases.org • URL: http://www.ases.org/solar.

Passive Solar Industries Council. 1331 H St. N.W., Suite 1000, Washington, DC 20005. Phone: (202)628-7400 Fax: (202)393-5043 E-mail: psicouncil@aol.com.

Solar Energy Industries Association. 122 C St., N.W., 4th Fl., Washington, DC 20001. Phone: (202)383-2600 Fax: (202)383-2670 • URL: http://www.seia.org.

Solartherm. 1315 Apple Ave., Silver Spring, MD 20910. Phone: (301)587-8686 Fax: (301)587-8688 • Members are scientists engaged in the development of low-cost solar energy systems.

OTHER SOURCES

Major Energy Companies of the World. Available from The Gale Group. • 2001. $855.00. Fourth edition. Published by Graham & Whiteside. Contains detailed information on more than 3,300 important energy companies in various countries. Industries include electricity generation, coal, natural gas, nuclear energy, petroleum, fuel distribution, and equipment for energy production.

SOLE PROPRIETORSHIP

See: SELF-EMPLOYMENT

SOLID STATE DEVICES

See: SEMICONDUCTOR INDUSTRY

SOLID WASTE TREATMENT

See: SANITATION INDUSTRY

SOUND RECORDERS AND RECORDING

See also: HIGH FIDELITY/STEREO; PHONOGRAPH AND PHONOGRAPH RECORD INDUSTRIES

GENERAL WORKS

Sound and Recording: An Introduction. Francis Rumsey. Butterworth-Heinemann. • 1997. $39.95. Third edition. Covers the theory and principles of sound recording and reproduction, with chapters on amplifiers, microphones, mixers, and other components.

Sound Check: The Basics of Sound and Sound Systems. Tony Moscal. Hal Leonard Corp. • 1994. $14.95. Explains the fundamentals of sound and related electronics.

DIRECTORIES

Directory of Computer and Consumer Electronics. Chain Store Age. • Annual. $290.00. Includes 2,900 "leading" retailers and over 200 "top" distributors. Formerly *Directory of Consumer Electronics Retails and Distributors.*

International Tape/Disc Directory. Billboard. • Annual. $75.00. Tape/Audio/Video professional equipment manufacturers, audio/video duplicators; pre-recorded tape, tape service and supply companies; video music producers, production facilities, and video program suppliers. Primarily U.S. and Canadian coverage, with some international listings.

MixPlus: Music and Audio Resources for the U. S. and Canada. Intertec Publishing Corp. • Annual. $14.95 for each regional edition (East, West, Central). A professional directory for the recording and music businesses, listing concert promoters, rehearsal halls, consultants, record labels, recording studios, tape and disc mastering services, legal services, facility designers, music education programs, and other music and audio services.

Phonolog Reporter: All-in-One Reporter. i2 Technologies. • Weekly. $486.00 per year. Looseleaf. Contains over one million listings of recorded music (compact discs, cassette tapes, and phonograph records). Includes both popular and classical releases. Popular music is classified by title, artist, and album; classical performances are accessible by title, artist, and composer.

Recording Industry Sourcebook. Intertec Publishing. • Annual. $79.95. Provides more than 12,000 listings in 57 categories of record/tape/compact disc labels, producers, distributors, managers, equipment suppliers, and others.

Schwann Opus: The Classical Music Resource. Schwann Publications. • Annual. $27.45 per year. Lists classical music recordings by composer. Covers compact discs, minidiscs, and cassette tapes. Includes an extensive, alphabetical list of recording labels and distributors, with addresses and telephone numbers (many listings also include fax numbers and Internet addresses).

Schwann Spectrum: The Guide to Rock, Jazz, World...and Beyond. Schwann Publications. • Annual. $27.45 per year. Lists rock, jazz, country, folk, soundtrack, international, new age, religious, and other disc and tape popular recordings by performer. Includes an extensive, alphabetical list of recording labels and distributors, with addresses and telephone numbers (some listings also include fax numbers and Internet addresses).

The SHOOT Directory for Commercial Production and Postproduction. BPI Communications. • Annual. $79.00. Lists production companies, advertising agencies, and sources of professional television, motion picture, and audio equipment.

ENCYCLOPEDIAS AND DICTIONARIES

Encyclopedia of Acoustics. Malcolm J. Crocker. John Wiley and Sons, Inc. • 1997. $650.00. Four volumes.

HANDBOOKS AND MANUALS

Audio Recording and Reproduction: Practical Measures for Audio Enthusiasts. Michael Talbot-Smith. Butterworth-Heinemann. • 1994. $29.95.

CD-ROM Handbook. Chris Sherman. McGraw-Hill. • 1993. $70.50. Second edition. Covers technology (audio, video, and multimedia), design, production, and economics of the CD-ROM industry.

Compact Disc Handbook. Ken C. Pohlmann. A-R Editions, Inc. • 1992. $34.95. Second edition. A guide to compact disc technology, including player design and disc manufacturing. (Computer Music and Digital Audio Series).

Digital Audio and Compact Disk Technology. Luc Baert and others. Butterworth-Heinemann. • 1995. $57.95. Third edition.

Handbook for Sound Engineers: The New Audio Cyclopedia. Glen M. Ballou, editor. Butterworth-Heineman. • 1991. $120.00. Second edition. Covers fundamentals of sound, sound-system design, loudspeaker building, sound recording, audio circuits, and computer-generated music.

Handbook of Recording Engineering. John M. Eargle. Chapman and Hall. • 1996. $75.00. Third edition.

Music Technology Buyer's Guide. United Entertainment Media, Inc. • $7.95. Annual. Lists more than 4,000 hardware and software music production products from 350 manufacturers. Includes synthesizers, MIDI hardware and software, mixers, microphones, music notation software, etc. Produced by the editorial staffs of *Keyboard* and *EQ* magazines.

Studio Business Book: A Guide to Professional Recording Studio Business and Management. Jim Mandell. Intertec Publishing Corp. • 1995. $34.95. Second expanded edition. Includes information on business plans, studio equipment, financing, expenses, rate setting, and personnel.

PERIODICALS AND NEWSLETTERS

Audio. Hachette Filipacchi Magazines, Inc. • Monthly. $26.00 per year. Includes annual directory *Product Review.*

Computer Music Journal. MIT Press. • Quarterly. Individuals, $48.00 per year; instutitions, $158.00 per year. Covers digital sooound and the musical applications of computers.

Mix Magazine: Professional Recording, Sound, and Music Production. Intertec Publishing Corp. • Monthly. $34.95 per year.

SHOOT: The Leading Newsweekly for Commercial Production and Postproduction. BPI Communications. • Weekly. $115.00 per year. Covers animation, music, sound design, computer graphics, visual effects, cinematography, and other aspects of television and motion picture production, with emphasis on TV commercials.

Stereo Review's Sound & Vision: Home Theater-Audio- Video- MultimediaMovies- Music. Hachette Filipacchi Magazines, Inc. • 10 times a year. $24.00 per year. Popular magazine providing explanatory articles and critical reviews of equipment and media (CD-ROM, DVD, videocassettes, etc.). Supplement available *Stero Review's Sound and Vision Buyers Guide.* Replaces *Stereo Review* and *Video Magazine.*

PRICE SOURCES

Orion Audio Blue Book. Orion Research Corp. • Annual. $179.00. Quotes retail and wholesale prices of used audio equipment. Original list prices and years of manufacture are also shown.

Orion Guitars and Musical Instruments Blue Book. Orion Research Corp. • Annual. $179.00. List of manufacturers of guitars and musical instruments. Original list prices and years of manufacture are also shown. Formerly *Orion Professional Sound and Musical Instruments.*

RESEARCH CENTERS AND INSTITUTES

Computer Graphics Laboratory. New York Institute of Technology, Fine Arts, Old Westbury, NY 11568. Phone: (516)686-7542 Fax: (516)686-7428 E-mail: pvoci@nyit.edu • Research areas include computer graphics, computer animation, and digital sound.

Inter-Arts Center. San Francisco State University, School of Creative Arts, 1600 Holloway Ave., San Francisco, CA 94132. Phone: (415)338-1478 Fax: (415)338-6159 E-mail: jimdavis@sfsu.edu • URL: http://www.sfsu.edu/~iac • Research areas include multimedia, computerized experimental arts processes, and digital sound.

TRADE/PROFESSIONAL ASSOCIATIONS

Special Interest Group on Electronic Sound Technology. Association for Computing Machinery, 1515 Broadway, New York, NY 10036. Phone: (212)869-7440 Fax: (212)302-5826 E-mail: sigs@acm.org • URL: http://www.acm.org/sigsound • Concerned with software, algorithms, hardware, and applications relating to digitally generated audio.

OTHER SOURCES

EQ: The Project Recording and Sound Magazine. United Entertainment Media, Inc. • Monthly. $36.00 per year. Provides advice on professional music recording equipment and technique.

Keyboard: Making Music with Technology. United Entertainment Media, Inc. • Monthly. $36.00 per year. Emphasis is on recording systems, keyboard technique, and computer-assisted music (MIDI) systems.

Music and Sound Retailer. Testa Communications. • Monthly. $18.00 per year. Provides news and advice on the retailing of a wide range of music and sound products, including musical instruments, electronic keyboards, sound amplification systems, music software, and recording equipment.

Pro Sound News: The International News Magazine for the Professional Recording and Sound Production Industry. United Entertainment Media, Inc. • Monthly. $30.00 per year. Provides industry news for recording studios, audio contractors, sound engineers, and sound reinforcement specialists.

Schwann Inside: Jazz and Classical. Schwann Publications. • Monthly. $55.95 per year. Provides reviews and listings of new classical and jazz recordings. Includes "Billboard Charts" of top selling jazz, contemporary jazz, classical, classical crossover, classical midline, and classical budget albums.

SOUTH AMERICA

See: LATIN AMERICAN MARKETS

SOYBEAN INDUSTRY

See also: COMMODITY FUTURES TRADING; OIL AND FATS INDUSTRY

ABSTRACTS AND INDEXES

Field Crop Abstracts: Monthly Abstract Journal on World Annual Cereal, Legume, Root, Oilseed and Fibre Crops. Available from CABI Publishing North America. • Monthly. $1,465.00 per year. Published in England by CABI Publishing, formerly Commonwealth Agricultural Bureaux. Provides worldwide coverage of the literature.

Soyabean Abstracts. Available from CABI Publishing North America. • Bimonthly. $425.00 per year. Published in England by CABI Publishing. Provides worldwide coverage of the literature.

CD-ROM DATABASES

Food Science and Technology Abstracts [CD-ROM]. Available from SilverPlatter Information, Inc. • Quarterly. $3,700 per year. Produced by International Food Information Service (home page is http://www.ifis.org). Provides worldwide coverage on CD-ROM of the literature of food technology and production. Various types of publications are indexed, with abstracts, including about 1,800 periodicals. Time period is 1969 to date.

INTERNET DATABASES

USDA. United States Department of Agriculture. Phone: (202)720-2791 E-mail: agsec@usda.gov • URL: http://www.usda.gov • The USDA home page has six sections: News and Information; What's New; About USDA; Agencies; Opportunities; Search and Help. Keyword searching is offered from the USDA home page and from various individual agency home pages. Agencies are the Economic Research Service, Agricultural Marketing Service, National Agricultural Statistics Service, National Agricultural Library, and about 12 others. Updating varies. Fees: Free.

ONLINE DATABASES

Biological and Agricultural Index Online. H. W. Wilson Co. • Indexes a wide variety of agricultural and biological periodicals, 1983 to date. Monthly updates. Inquire as to online cost and availability.

CAB Abstracts. CAB International North America. • Contains 46 specialized abstract collections covering over 10,000 journals and monographs in the areas of agriculture, horticulture, forest products, farm products, nutrition, dairy science, poultry, grains, animal health, entomology, etc. Time period is 1972 to date, with monthly updates. Inquire as to online cost and availability. *CAB Abstracts on CD-ROM* also available, with annual updating.

Food Science and Technology Abstracts [online]. IFIS North American Desk. • Produced by International Food Information Service. Provides about 500,000 online citations, with abstracts, to the international literature of food science, technology, commodities, engineering, and processing. Approximately 2,000 periodicals are covered. Time period is 1969 to date, with monthly updates. Inquire as to online cost and availability.

PERIODICALS AND NEWSLETTERS

Barron's: The Dow Jones Business and Financial Weekly. Dow Jones and Co., Inc. • Weekly. $145.00 per year.

Consensus: National Futures and Financial Weekly. Consensus, Inc. • Weekly. $365.00 per year. Newspaper. Contains news, statistics, and special reports relating to agricultural, industrial, and financial futures markets. Features daily basis price charts, reprints of market advice, and "The Consensus Index of Bullish Market Opinion" (charts show percent bullish of advisors for various futures).

Soya and Oilseed Bluebook. Soyatech, Inc. • Annual. $70.00. Includes quarterly *Bluebook Update.* Formerly *Soya Bluebook Plus.*

Soybean Digest. American Soybean Association. Intertec Publishing Corp., Agribusiness Div. • 11 times a year. $25.00 per year. Provides high acreage farmers who grow soy beans in rotation with other crops timely production, marketing and management information.

STATISTICS SOURCES

Agricultural Statistics. Available from U. S. Government Printing Office. • Annual. Produced by the National Agricultural Statistics Service, U. S. Department of Agriculture. Provides a wide variety of statistical data relating to agricultural production, supplies, consumption, prices/price-supports, foreign trade, costs, and returns, as well as farm labor, loans, income, and population. In many cases, historical data is shown annually for 10 years. In addition to farm data, includes detailed fishery statistics.

Fats and Oils: Oilseed Crushings. U. S. Bureau of the Census. • Monthly and annual. Provides data on shipments of cottonseed oil and soybean oil: value, quantity, imports, and exports. (Current Industrial Reports, M20J.).

Fats and Oils: Production, Consumption, and Stocks. U. S. Bureau of the Census. • Monthly and annual. Covers the supply and distribution of cottonseed, soybean, and palm oils, and selected inedible products. (Current Industrial Reports, M20K.).

Statistical Annual: Grains, Options on Agricultural Futures. Chicago Board of Trade. • Annual. Includes historical data on Wheat Futures, Options on Wheat Futures, Corn Futures, Options on Corn Futures, Oats Futures, Soybean Futures, Options on Soybean Futures, Soybean Oil Futures, Soybean Meal Futures.

WEFA Industrial Monitor. John Wiley and Sons, Inc. • Annual. $65.00. Prepared by industry analysts at WEFA, an economic forecasting and consulting firm (originally Wharton Econometric Forecasting Associates). Contains discussions of the outlook for major U. S. industries, with many 10-year forecasts (WEFA Web site is http://www.wefa.com).

TRADE/PROFESSIONAL ASSOCIATIONS

American Soybean Association. 12125 Woodcrest Executive Dr., Suite 100, Saint Louis, MO 63141. Phone: 800-688-7692 or (314)576-1770 Fax: (314)576-2706 • URL: http://www.oilseeds.org.

National Oilseed Processors Association. 1255 23rd St., N.W., Suite 20, Washington, DC 20037. Phone: (202)452-8040 Fax: (202)835-0400 E-mail: nopa@nopa.org • URL: http://www.nopa.org.

OTHER SOURCES

Major Food and Drink Companies of the World. Available from The Gale Group. • 2001. $855.00. Fourth edition. Two volumes. Published by Graham & Whiteside. Contains profiles and trade names for more than 9,000 important food and beverage companies in various countries. In addition to foods, includes both alcoholic and nonalcoholic drink products.

Thomas Food and Beverage Market Place. Grey House Publishing. • Annual. $295.00. Three volumes. Contains more than 40,000 entries covering food companies, beverages, food equipment, warehouse companies, food brokers, wholesalers, importers, and exporters. Formerly *Thomas Food Industry Register.*

SPACE INDUSTRY

See: AEROSPACE INDUSTRY; ROCKET INDUSTRY

SPECIAL DAYS AND WEEKS

See: ANNIVERSARIES AND HOLIDAYS

SPECIAL EVENT PLANNING

GENERAL WORKS

PR News Casebook. The Gale Group. • 1993. $99.00. A collection of about 1,000 case studies covering major public relations campaigns and events, taken from the pages of *PR News.* Covers such issues as boycotts, new products, anniversaries, plant closings, downsizing, and stockholder relations.

DIRECTORIES

Chase's Calendar of Events: The Day-by-Day Directory. NTC/Contemporary Publishing. • Annual. $59.95. Provides information for over 10,000 special days and special events throughout the world. Chronological arrangement with an alphbetical index. Formerly *Chase's Annual Events.*

IEG Sponsorship Sourcebook. International Events Group, Inc. • Annual. $199.00. Provides information on about 3,000 festivals, celebrations, and sports events that are available for commercial sponsorship. Information is also given on public relations firms, sports marketing companies, fireworks suppliers, and other companies providing services for special events. Formerly *IEG Directory of Sponsorship Marketing.*

The PROMO 100 Promotion Agency Ranking. Intertec Publishing Co. • Annual. $9.95. Provides information on 100 leading product promotion agencies.

Protocol (Corporate Meetings, Entertainment, and Special Events). Protocol Directory, Inc. • Annual. $48.00. Provides information on about 4,000 suppliers of products and services for special events, shows (entertainment), and business meetings. Geographic arrangement.

HANDBOOKS AND MANUALS

Black Tie Optional: The Ultimate Guide to Planning and Producing Successful Special Events. Harry A. Freedman and Karen F. Smith. Fund Raising Institute. • 1994. $35.00. Includes checklists, flow charts, and worksheets.

The Business of Special Events: Fundraising Strategies for Changing Times. Harry A. Freedman and Karen Feldman. Pineapple Press, Inc. • 1998. $21.95.

Complete Guide to Special Event Management: Business Insights, Financial Advice and Successful Strategies from Ernst and Young, Consultants to the Olympics, the Emmy Awards and the PGA Tour. Ernst and Young Staff. John Wiley and Sons, Inc. • 1992. $29.95. Covers the marketing, financing, and general management of special events in the fields of art, entertainment, and sports.

Event Planning Service. Entrepreneur Media, Inc. • Looseleaf. $59.50. A practical guide to starting a social or corporate event planning service. Covers profit potential, start-up costs, market size evaluation, pricing, accounting, advertising, promotion, etc. (Start-Up Business Guide No. E1313.).

ONLINE DATABASES

Management Contents. The Gale Group. • Covers a wide range of management, financial, marketing, personnel, and administrative topics. About 150 leading business journals are indexed and abstracted from 1974 to date, with monthly updating. Inquire as to online cost and availability.

PERIODICALS AND NEWSLETTERS

IEG's Sponsorship Report: The International Newsletter of Event Sponsorship and Lifestyle Marketing. International Events Group, Inc. • Biweekly. $415.00 per year. Newsletter reporting on corporate sponsorship of special events: sports, music, festivals, and the arts. Edited for event producers, directors, and marketing personnel.

PROMO: Promotion Marketing Worldwide. Simba Information Inc. • Monthly. $65.00 per year. Edited for companies and agencies that utilize couponing, point-of-purchase advertising, special events, games, contests, premiums, product samples, and other unique promotional items.

Special Events Magazine. Intertec Publishing Corp. • Monthly. $39.00 per year. Edited for professionals concerned with parties, meetings, galas, and special events of all kinds and sizes. Provides practical ideas for the planning of special events. Formerly *Special Events.*

TRADE/PROFESSIONAL ASSOCIATIONS

International Special Events Society. 9202 N. Meridian St., Suite 200, Indianapolis, IN 46260. Phone: 800-688-4737 or (317)571-5601 Fax: (317)571-5603 E-mail: info@ises.com • URL: http://www.ises.com • Members are meeting planners, caterers, florists, and others involved in the conducting of special events. Promotes the art and science of special event planning and production.

SPECIAL LIBRARIES

See also: LIBRARIES

GENERAL WORKS

The Best of OPL, II: Selected Readings from the One-Person Library: 1990-1994. Guy St. Clair and Andrew Berner. Special Libraries Association. • 1996. $36.00. Contains reprints of useful material from *The One-Person Library: A Newsletter for Librarians and Management.*

Corporate Library Excellence. James M. Matarazzo. Special Libraries Association. • 1990. $28.00.

Expanding Technologies, Expanding Careers: Librarianship in Transition. Ellis Mount, editor. Special Libraries Association. • 1997. $45.00. Contains articles on alternative, non-traditional career paths for librarians, whether as entrepreneurs or employees. All the careers are related to computer-based, information retrieval and technology.

Extending the Librarian's Domain: A Survey of Emerging Occupational Opportunities for Librarians and Information Professionals. Forest W. Horton. Special Libraries Association. • 1994. $38.00. An examination of non-traditional career possibilities for special librarians. (Occasional Papers: No. 4).

Opening New Doors: Alternative Careers for Librarians. Ellis Mount, editor. Special Libraries Association. • 1992. $39.00. Information professionals in careers outside the library field discuss the nature of their work, qualifications, rewards, finding a job, etc.

Special Libraries: A Guide for Management. Cathy A. Porter and Elin B. Christianson. Special Libraries Association. • 1997. $42.00. Fourth edition. Provides basic information for the managers of business and other organizations on starting, staffing, and maintaining a special library.

Special Libraries and Information Centers: An Introductory Text. Ellis Mount and Renee Massoud. Special Libraries Association. • 1999. $49.00. Fourth edition. Includes descriptions of 13 outstanding libraries and information centers.

ABSTRACTS AND INDEXES

Library Literature and Information Science: An Index to Library and Information Science Publications. H. W. Wilson Co. • Bimonthly. Annual cumulation. Service basis. Formerly *Library Literature.*

Social Sciences Citation Index. Institute for Scientific Information. • Three times a year. $6,900 per year. Annual cumulation. Includes *Source Index, Citation Index, Permuterm Subject Index,* and *Corporate Index.*

ALMANACS AND YEARBOOKS

Bowker Annual: Library and Book Trade Almanac. R. R. Bowker. • Annual. $175.00. Lists of accredited library schools; scholarships for education in library science; library organizations; major libraries; publishing and book sellers organizations. Includes statistics and news of the book business.

BIBLIOGRAPHIES

The Basic Business Library: Core Resources. Bernard S. Schlessinger and June H. Schlessinger. Oryx Press. • 1994. $43.50. Third edition. Consists of three parts: (1) "Core List of Printed Business Reference Sources," (2) "The Literature of Business Reference and Business Libraries: 1976-1994," and (3) "Business Reference Sources and Services: Essays." Part one lists 200 basic titles, with annotations and evaluations.

CD-ROM DATABASES

Information Science Abstracts. Information Today, Inc. • Quarterly. $1,095.00 per year. Presents CD-ROM abstracts of worldwide information science and library science literature from 1966 to date.

LISA Plus: Library and Information Science Abstracts. Bowker-Saur, Reed Reference Publishing. • Quarterly. $1,450.00 per year. Provides CD-ROM abstracting and indexing of the world's library and information science literature. Covers a wide variety of topics.

Social Sciences Citation Index: Compact Disc Edition. Institute for Scientific Information. • Quarterly. Provides CD-ROM indexing of the world's social sciences literature, including economics, business, finance, management, communications, demographics, information and library science, political science, sociology, etc. Corresponds to online *Social Scisearch* and printed *Social Sciences Citation Index.*

Social Sciences Citation Index: Compact Disc Edition with Abstracts. Institute for Scientific Information. • Quarterly. Provides CD-ROM indexing and abstracting of "significant articles" from 1,400 social science journals worldwide, with additional selections from 3,200 other journals, 1986 to date. Includes economics, business, finance, management, communications, demographics, information and library science, political science, sociology, and many other subjects.

WILSONDISC: Library Literature and Information Science Index. H. W. Wilson Co. • Quarterly. Including unlimited access to the online version of *Library Literature.* Provides CD-ROM indexing of about 300 periodicals, covering a wide range of topics having to do with libraries, library management, and the information industry.

World Database of Business Information Sources on CD-ROM. The Gale Group. • Annual. Produced by Euromonitor. Presents Euromonitor's entire information source database on CD-ROM. Contains a worldwide total of about 35,000 publications, organizations, libraries, trade fairs, and online databases.

DIRECTORIES

American Library Directory. R. R. Bowker. • Annual. $269.95. Two volumes. Includes *Library Resource Guide.* Information on more than 36,000 public, academic, special and government libraries and library-related organizations in the U.S., Canada, and Mexico.

Directory of Federal Libraries. William R. Evinger, editor. Oryx Press. • 1997. $97.50. Third edition.

Directory of Special Libraries and Information Centers. The Gale Group. • 1999. $845.00. 25th edition. Three volumes. Two available separately: volume one,*Directory of Special Libraries and Information Centers,* $610.00; volume two *Geographic and Personnel Indexes,* $510.00. Contains 24,000 entries from the U.S., Canada, and 80 other countries. A detailed subject index is included in volume one.

Internet Tools of the Profession: A Guide for Information Professionals. Hope N. Tillman, editor. Special Libraries Association. • 1997. $49.00. Second edition. Consists of 14 sections by various authors or compilers. After two introductory articles on searching the Internet, there are 12 annotated lists of useful Web sites, covering the SLA, business and finance, chemistry, education, food and agriculture, information technology, insurance and employee benefits, law, library management, metals and materials, pharmaceuticals, and telecommunications. An index is provided.

Subject Collections: A Guide to Special Book Collections and Subject Emphasis in Libraries. Lee Ash and William G. Miller, editors. R. R. Bowker. • Irregular. $275.00. Two volumes. A guide to special book collections and subject emphases as reported by university, college, public and special libraries in th United States and Canada.

Subject Directory of Special Libraries and Information Centers. The Gale Group. • Annual. $845.00. Three volumes, available separately: volume one, *Business, Government, and Law Libraries,* $595.00; volume two, *Computer, Engineering, and Law Libraries,* $595.00; volume three, *Health Sciences Libraries,* $340.00. Altogether, 14,000 entries from the *Directory of Special Libraries and Information Centers* are arranged in 14 subject chapters.

Who's Who in Special Libraries. Special Libraries Association. • Annual. Free to members; non-members, $45.00. About 14,000 librarians of libraries and special collections having a specific subject focus.

World Directory of Business Information Libraries. Available from The Gale Group. • 2000. $590.00. Fourth edition. Published by Euromonitor. Provides detailed information on 2,000 major business libraries in 145 countries. Emphasis is on collections relevant to consumer goods and services markets.

World Directory of Marketing Information Sources. Available from The Gale Group. • 2001. $590.00. Third edition. Published by Euromonitor. Provides details on more than 6,000 sources of marketing information, including publications, libraries, associations, market research companies, online databases, and governmental organizations. Coverage is worldwide.

ENCYCLOPEDIAS AND DICTIONARIES

World Encyclopedia of Library and Information Services. Robert Wedgeworth, editor. American Library Association. • 1993. $200.00. Third edition. Contains about 340 articles from various contributors.

HANDBOOKS AND MANUALS

The Business Library and How to Use It: A Guide to Sources and Research Strategies for Information on Business and Management. Ernest L. Maier and others, editors. Omnigraphics, Inc. • 1996. $56.00. Explains library research methods and describes specific sources of business information. A revision of *How to Use the Business Library,* by H. Webster Johnson and others (fifth edition, 1984).

Control of Administrative and Financial Operations in Special Libraries. Madeline J. Daubert. Special Libraries Association. • 1996. $75.00. Self-study workbook.

Managing the Law Library 1999: Forging Effective Relationships in Today's Law Office. Practising Law Institute. • 1999. $99.00. Produced to provide background material for PLI seminars on the role of libraries and librarians in law firms.

Position Descriptions in Special Libraries. Del Sweeney and Karin Zilla, editors. Special Libraries Association. • 1996. $41.00. Third revised edition. Provides 87 descriptions of library and information management positions.

The SOLO Librarian's Sourcebook. Judith A. Siess. Information Today, Inc. • 1997. $39.50. Covers management and other aspects of one-librarian libraries.

Space Planning in the Special Library. Roberta Freifeld and Caryl Masyr. Special Libraries Association. • 1991. $23.00. Provides practical advice for planners of new libraries, renovations, and relocations.

University Science and Engineering Libraries. Ellis Mount. Greenwood Publishing Group, Inc. • 1985. $59.95. Second edition. (Contributions in Librarianship and Information Science Series, No 49).

World Guide to Special Libraries. Available from The Gale Group. • 2001. $400.00. Fifth edition. Two volumes. Published by K. G. Saur. Classifies more than 37,000 libraries in 183 countries under 750 subject headings.

INTERNET DATABASES

GaleNet: Your Information Community. The Gale Group. Phone: 800-877-GALE or (248)699-GALE Fax: 800-414-5043 or (248)699-8069 E-mail: galenet@gale.com • URL: http://www.galenet.com • Web site provides a wide variety of full-text information from Gale databases, Taft, and other sources. Covers associations, biography, business directories, education, the information industry, literature, publishing, and science. Fee-based subscriptions are available for individual databases (free demonstration). Includes Boolean search features and the BRS/Search user interface.

Internet Tools of the Profession. Special Libraries Association. Phone: (202)234-4700 Fax: (202)265-9317 E-mail: hope@tiac.net • URL: http://www.sla.org/pubs/itotp • Web site is designed to update the printed *Internet Tools of the Profession.* Provides links to a wide range of useful databases in business, finance, industry, information technology, insurance, law, library management, telecommunications, and other subject areas. Fees: Free.

ONLINE DATABASES

American Library Directory Online. R. R. Bowker. • Provides information on over 37,000 U. S. and Canadian libraries, including college, special, and public. Annual updates. Inquire as to online cost and availability.

Information Science Abstracts [online]. Information Today, Inc. • Provides indexing and abstracting of the international literature of information science, including library science, from 1966 to date. Monthly updates. Inquire as to online cost and availability.

Library Literature Online. H. W. Wilson Co. • Contains online indexing of a wide variety of library and information science literature from 1984 to date, with updating quarterly. Inquire as to online cost and availability.

LISA Online: Library and Information Science Abstracts. Bowker-Saur, Reed Reference Publishing. • Provides abstracting and indexing of the world's library and information science literature from 1969 to the present. Covers a wide variety of topics in over 550 journals from 60 countries, with biweekly updates. Inquire as to online cost and availability.

Social Scisearch. Institute for Scientific Information. • Broad, multidisciplinary index to the literature of the social sciences, 1972 to present. Weekly updates. Worldwide coverage. Inquire as to online cost and availability.

PERIODICALS AND NEWSLETTERS

Art Reference Services Quarterly. Haworth Press, Inc. • Quarterly. Individuals, $38.00 per year;

libraries and other institutions, $75.00 per year. A journal for art librarians.

Aslib Proceedings. Available from Information Today, Inc. • Ten times a year. Free to Members; non-members, $252.00 per year. Published in London by Aslib Covers a wide variety of information industry and library management topics.

Behavioral and Social Sciences Librarian. Haworth Press, Inc. • Semiannual. Individuals, $42.00 per year; institutions, $95.00 per year; libraries, $95.00 per year.

Business and Finance Division Bulletin. Special Libraries Association, Business and Finance Div. • Quarterly. $12.00 per year.

Corporate Library Update: News for Information Managers and Special Librarians. Cahners Business Information. • Biweekly. $95.00 per year. Newsletter. Covers information technology, management techniques, new products, trends, etc.

Information Outlook: The Monthly Magazine of the Special Libraries Association. Special Libraries Association. • Monthly. $65.00 per year. Topics include information technology, the Internet, copyright, research techniques, library management, and professional development. Replaces *Special Libraries* and *SpeciaList.*

Journal of Agricultural and Food Information. Haworth Press, Inc. • Quarterly. Individuals, $45.00 per year; libraries and other institutions, $85.00 per year. A journal for librarians and others concerned with the acquisition of information on food and agriculture.

Journal of Business and Finance Librarianship. Haworth Press, Inc. • Quarterly. Individuals, $40.00 per year; institutions, $85.00 per year; libraries, $85.00 per year.

Legal Reference Services Quarterly. Haworth Press, Inc. • Quarterly. Individuals, $60.00 per year; institutions and libraries, $135.00 per year.

Medical Reference Services Quarterly. Haworth Press, Inc. • Quarterly. Individuals, $50.00 per year; libraries and other institutions, $175.00 per year. An academic and practical journal for medical reference librarians.

Music Reference Services Quarterly. Haworth Press, Inc. • Quarterly. Individuals, $40.00 per year; libraries and other institutions, $75.00 per year. An academic journal for music librarians.

The One-Person Library: A Newsletter for Librarians and Management. Information Bridges International, Inc. • Monthly. $85.00 per year. Newsletter for librarians working alone or with minimal assistance. Contains reports on library literature, management advice, case studies, book reviews, and general information.

Science and Technology Libraries. Haworth Press, Inc. • Quarterly. Individuals, $45.00 per year; institutions, $160.00 per year; libraries, $160.00 per year.

STATISTICS SOURCES

Report on Corporate Library Spending. Primary Research. • 1995. $75.00. Provides market research data on corporate library expenditures for books, periodicals, and online/CD-ROM sources.

SLA Salary Survey. Special Libraries Association. • Annual. Members, $36.00; non-members, $45.00. Provides data on salaries for special librarians in the U. S. and Canada, according to location, job title, industry, budget, and years of experience.

TRADE/PROFESSIONAL ASSOCIATIONS

Special Libraries Association. 1700 18th St., N.W., Washington, DC 20009-2514. Phone: (202)234-4700 Fax: (202)265-9317 E-mail: sla@sla.org • URL: http://www.sla.org/.

OTHER SOURCES

Valuating Information Intangibles: Measuring the Bottom Line Contribution of Librarians and Information Professionals. Frank H. Portugal. Special Libraries Association. • 2000. $79.00. Focuses on the importance of the intangible aspects of appraising information resources and services.

SPECIALISTS

See: CONSULTANTS

SPECIALTY FOOD INDUSTRY

See also: FOOD INDUSTRY

ABSTRACTS AND INDEXES

Food Science and Technology Abstracts. International Food Information Service Publishing. • Monthly. $1,780.00 per year. Provides worldwide coverage of the literature of food technology and food production.

Foods Adlibra: Key to the World's Food Literature. Foods Adlibra Publications. • Semimonthly.Provides journal citations and abstracts to the literature of food technology and packaging.

CD-ROM DATABASES

F & S Index Plus Text. The Gale Group. • Monthly. $7,575.00 per year. Provides CD-ROM citations to worldwide business, marketing, and industrial material appearing in a large assortment of trade journals, newspapers, and other publications. Time period is four years.

Food Science and Technology Abstracts [CD-ROM]. Available from SilverPlatter Information, Inc. • Quarterly. $3,700 per year. Produced by International Food Information Service (home page is http://www.ifis.org). Provides worldwide coverage on CD-ROM of the literature of food technology and production. Various types of publications are indexed, with abstracts, including about 1,800 periodicals. Time period is 1969 to date.

DIRECTORIES

Directory of Delicatessen Products. Pacific Rim Publishing Co. • Annual. Included with February issue of *Deli News.* Lists suppliers of cheeses, lunch meats, packaged fresh meats, kosher foods, gourmet-specialty items, and bakery products.

Specialty Food Industry Directory. Phoenix Media Network, Inc. • Annual. Included in subscription to Food Distribution Magazine. Lists manufacturers and suppliers of specialty foods, and services and equipment for the specialty food industry. Featured food products include legumes, sauces, spices, upscale cheese, specialty beverages, snack foods, baked goods, ethnic foods, and specialty meats.

ONLINE DATABASES

F & S Index. The Gale Group. • Contains about four million citations to worldwide business, financial, and industrial or consumer product literature appearing from 1972 to date. Weekly updates. Inquire as to online cost and availability.

Food Science and Technology Abstracts [online]. IFIS North American Desk. • Produced by International Food Information Service. Provides about 500,000 online citations, with abstracts, to the international literature of food science, technology, commodities, engineering, and processing. Approximately 2,000 periodicals are covered. Time period is 1969 to date, with monthly updates. Inquire as to online cost and availability.

FOODS ADLIBRA. General Mills, Inc. • Contains online citations, with abstracts, to the technical and business literature of food processing and packaging. New products and new ingredients are featured. Covers about 250 trade journals and 500 research journals from 1974 to date, with monthly updates. Inquire as to online cost and availability.

PROMT: Predicasts Overview of Markets and Technology. The Gale Group. • Companies, products, applied technologies and markets. U.S. and international literature coverage, 1972 to date. Inquire as to online cost and availability. Provides abstracts from more than 1,600 publications. Weekly updates.

PERIODICALS AND NEWSLETTERS

Deli News. Delicatessen Council of Southern California, Inc. Pacific Rim Publishing Co. • Monthly. $25.00 per year. Includes product news and comment related to cheeses, lunch meats, packaged fresh meats, kosher foods, gourmet-specialty items, and bakery products.

Fancy Food. Talcott Communications Corp. • Monthly. $34.00 per year. Emphasizes new specialty food products and the business management aspects of the specialty food and confection industries. Includes special issues on wine, cheese, candy, "upscale" cookware, and gifts.

Food Distribution Magazine. Phoenix Media Network, Inc. • Monthly. $49.00 per year. Edited for marketers and buyers of domestic and imported, specialty or gourmet food products, including ethnic foods, seasonings, and bakery items.

Gourmet News: The Business Newspaper for the Gourmet Industry. United Publications, Inc. • Monthly. $55.00 per year. Provides news of the gourmet food industry, including specialty food stores, upscale cookware shops, and gift shops.

Gourmet Retailer. Bill Communications, Business Communications Group. • Monthly. $24.00 per year. Covers upscale food and housewares, including confectionery items, bakery operations, and coffee.

Pizza Today. National Association of Pizza Operators. • Monthly. $30.00 per year. Covers both practical business topics and food topics for pizza establishments.

TRADE/PROFESSIONAL ASSOCIATIONS

National Association for the Specialty Food Trade. 120 Wall St., 27th Fl., New York, NY 10005-4001. Phone: (212)482-6440 Fax: (212)482-6459 • URL: http://www.fancyfoodshows.com • Members are manufacturers, processors, importers, retailers, and brokers of specialty and gourmet food items.

National Association of Pizza Operators. P.O. Box 1347, New Albany, IN 47151-1347. Phone: (812)949-0909 Fax: (812)941-9711 • URL: http://www.pizzatoday.com • Members are pizza establishment operators, food suppliers, and equipment manufacturers.

OTHER SOURCES

Business & Company Resource Center. The Gale Group. • Fee-based Web site provides a wide range of business, industry, and specific company information. Access is offered to trade journal articles, market research data, insider trading activity, major shareholder data, corporate histories, emerging technology reports, corporate earnings estimates, press releases, and other sources. Provides detailed company profiles, industry overviews, and rankings. Offers integration of Predicasts PROMT, Newsletters ASAP, Investext Plus, Business Index ASAP, Brands and Their Companies, and other databases (many have full text).

From Kitchen to Market: Selling Your Gourmet Food Specialty. Stephen F. Hall. Dearborn Financial

Publishing. • 2000. $28.95. Third edition. Covers packaging, labeling, marketing, and distribution of specialty and gourmet food products. Includes charts, graphs, tables, guidelines, checklists, and industry examples.

The Gourmet/Specialty Foods Market. Available from MarketResearch.com. • 1998. $2,500.00. Market research data. Published by Packaged Facts. Discusses current trends, with projections to 2002.

Major Food and Drink Companies of the World. Available from The Gale Group. • 2001. $855.00. Fourth edition. Two volumes. Published by Graham & Whiteside. Contains profiles and trade names for more than 9,000 important food and beverage companies in various countries. In addition to foods, includes both alcoholic and nonalcoholic drink products.

The Market for Sweet Baked Goods. MarketResearch.com. • 2000. $2,750.00. Market research data. Covers both fresh and frozen, bakery products.

Thomas Food and Beverage Market Place. Grey House Publishing. • Annual. $295.00. Three volumes. Contains more than 40,000 entries covering food companies, beverages, food equipment, warehouse companies, food brokers, wholesalers, importers, and exporters. Formerly *Thomas Food Industry Register.*

SPECULATION

See also: TECHNICAL ANALYSIS (FINANCE)

GENERAL WORKS

Devil Take the Hindmost: A History of Financial Speculation. Edward Chancellor. Farrar, Straus & Giroux, LLC. • 1999. $25.00. Covers such events as the Dutch tulip mania of 1637, the South Sea bubble of 1720, and the Japanese real estate and stock market boom of the 1980's.

Dumb Money: Adventures of a Day Trader. Joey Anuff and Gary Wolf. Random House, Inc. • 2000. $23.95. An account of the day trading ordeals of one of the authors, Joey Anuff.

Education of a Speculator. Victor Niederhoffer. John Wiley and Sons, Inc. • 1997. $29.95. An autobiography providing basic advice on speculation, investment, and the commodity futures market.

Extraordinary Popular Delusions and the Madness of Crowds. Charles Mackay. Templeton Foundation Press. • 2000. $19.95. A classic work on speculation and crowd psychology, originally published in 1841.

Futures Markets. A. G. Malliaris, editor. Edward Elgar Publishing, Inc. • 1997. $450.00. Three volumes. Consists of reprints of 70 articles dating from 1959 to 1993, on futures market volatility, speculation, hedging, stock indexes, portfolio insurance, interest rates, and foreign currencies. (International Library of Critical Writings in Financial Economics.).

Money Madness: Strange Manias and Extraordinary Schemes On and Off Wall Street. John M. Waggoner. McGraw-Hill Professional. • 1990. $26.00.

Secrets of the Street: The Dark Side of Making Money. Gene Marcial. McGraw-Hill. • 1996. $10.95. Explains how the small, individual investor can be taken advantage of by Wall Street professionals.

A Short History of Financial Euphoria. John Kenneth Galbraith. Viking Penguin. • 1994. $10.95. An analysis of speculative euphoria and subsequent crashes, from the Holland tulip mania in 1637 to the 1987 unpleasantness in the U. S. stock market.

Stock Market Crashes and Speculative Manias. Eugene N. White, editor. Edward Elgar Publishing, Inc. • 1996. $230.00. Contains reprints of 23 articles dating from 1905 to 1994. (International Library of Macroeconomic and Financial History Series: No. 13).

Trading to Win: The Psychology of Mastering the Markets. Ari Kiev. John Wiley and Sons, Inc. • 1998. $34.95. A mental health guide for stock, bond, and commodity traders. Tells how to keep speculative emotions in check, overcome self-doubt, and focus on a winning strategy. (Trading Advantage Series).

ALMANACS AND YEARBOOKS

Supertrader's Almanac-Reference Manual: Reference Guide and Analytical Techniques for Investors. Market Movements, Inc. • 1991. $55.00. Explains technical methods for the trading of commodity futures, and includes data on seasonality, cycles, trends, contract characteristics, highs and lows, etc.

DIRECTORIES

Futures Guide to Computerized Trading. Futures Magazine, Inc. • Annual. $10.00. "A directory of products and services for the computerized trader." Provides information on computer software applications for commodity traders and money managers, including trading methods and technical analysis.

Futures Magazine SourceBook: The Most Complete List of Exchanges, Companies, Regulators, Organizations, etc., Offering Products and Services to the Futures and Options Industry. Futures Magazine, Inc. • Annual. $19.50. Provides information on commodity futures brokers, trading method services, publications, and other items of interest to futures traders and money managers.

National Directory of Investment Newsletters. GPS Co. • Biennial. $49.95. Describes about 800 investment newsletters, and their publishers.

Standard and Poor's Security Dealers of North America. Standard & Poor's. • Semiannual. $480.00 per year; with *Supplements* every six weeks, $590.00 per year. Geographical listing of over 12,000 stock, bond, and commodity dealers.

Walker's Manual of Unlisted Stocks. Harry K. Eisenberg, editor. Walker's Manual, LLC. • Annual. $85.00. Provides information on 500 over-the-counter stocks,including many "penny stocks" trading at less than $5.00 per share.

HANDBOOKS AND MANUALS

Day-Trader's Manual: Theory, Art, and Science of Profitable Short-Term Investing. William F. Eng. John Wiley and Sons, Inc. • 1992. $79.95. Covers short-term trading in stocks, futures, and options. Various technical trading systems are considered.

Derivatives: A Comprehensive Resource for Options, Futures, Interest Rate Swaps, and Mortgage Securities. Fred D. Arditti. Harvard Business School Press. • 1996. $60.00. Published by Harvard Business School Press. Provides detailed explanations of various kinds of financial derivatives (options, futures, swaps, etc.) and their trading tactics, uses, and risks. (Financial Management Association Survey and Synthesis Series).

Money Management Strategies for Futures Traders. Nauzer J. Balsara. John Wiley and Sons, Inc. • 1992. $69.95. How to limit risk and avoid catastrophic losses. (Financial Editions Series).

The Prudent Speculator: Al Frank on Investing. Al Frank. McGraw-Hill Professional. • 1989. $30.00. How to be a sensible investor or speculator. Includes advice on the use of margin accounts and stock market timing.

Swap Literacy. Elizabeth Ungar. Bloomberg Press. • 1996. $40.00. Written for corporate finance officers. Provides basic information on arbitrage, hedging, and speculation, involving interest rate, currency, and other types of financial swaps. (Bloomberg Professional Library.).

Trader Vic: Methods of a Wall Street Master. Victor Sperandeo. John Wiley and Sons, Inc. • 1993. $19.95.

Trading for a Living: Psychology, Trading Tactics, Money Management. Alexander Elder. John Wiley and Sons, Inc. • 1993. $59.95. Covers technical and chart methods of trading in commodity and financial futures, options, and stocks. Includes Elliott Wave Theory, oscillators, moving averages, point-and-figure, and other technical approaches. (Finance Editions Series).

INTERNET DATABASES

Futures Online. Oster Communications, Inc. Phone: 800-601-8907 or (319)277-1278 Fax: (319)277-7982 • URL: http://www.futuresmag.com • Web site presents updates of *Futures* magazine and links to other futures-related sites. Includes "Futures Industry News," "Technical Talk," "Today's Hot Markets," "Futures Talk" (forums), "Futures Library" (archives, 1993 to date), and other features. Keyword searching is available. Updating: daily. Fees: Free.

TheStreet.com: Your Insider's Look at Wall Street. TheStreet.com, Inc. Phone: 800-562-9571 or (212)321-5000 Fax: (212)321-5016 • URL: http://www.thestreet.com • Web site offers "Free Sections" and "Premium Sections" ($9.95 per month). Both sections offer iconoclastic advice and comment on the stock market, but premium service displays a more comprehensive selection of news and analysis. There are many by-lined articles. "Search the Site" is included.

PERIODICALS AND NEWSLETTERS

America's Fastest Growing Companies. Individual Investor Group, Inc. • Monthly. $165.00 per year. Newsletter. Provides investment information on about 150 publicly-held corporations that are showing rapidly expanding sales and earnings. Formerly *America's Fastest Growing Corporations.*

The Cheap Investor. Mathews and Associates, Inc. • Monthly. $98.00 per year. Newsletter. Gives three to six buy recommendations, updates on precious recommendations and investment tips on quality stock under $5.00. Free issue available upon request.

Financial Sentinel: Your Beacon to the World of Investing. Gulf Atlantic Publishing, Inc. • Monthly. $29.95 per year. Provides "The only complete listing of all OTC Bulletin Board stocks traded, with all issues listed on the Nasdaq SmallCap Market, the Toronto, and Vancouver Stock Exchanges." Also includes investment advice and recommendations of small capitalization stocks.

Futures: News, Analysis, and Strategies for Futures, Options, and Derivatives Traders. Futures Magazine, Inc. • Monthly. $39.00 per year. Edited for institutional money managers and traders, brokers, risk managers, and individual investors or speculators. Includes special feature issues on interest rates, technical indicators, currencies, charts, precious metals, hedge funds, and derivatives. Supplements available.

Individual Investor. Individual Investor Group. • Monthly. $22.95 per year. Emphasis is on stocks selling for less than ten dollars a share. Includes a "Guide to Insider Transactions" and "New Issue Alert.".

Low Priced Stock Survey. Horizon Publishing Co., LLC. • Monthly. $129.00 per year.

Managed Account Reports: The Clearing House for Commodity Money Management. Managed Account Reports, Inc. • Monthly. $425.00 per year. Newsletter. Reviews the performance and other characteristics of commodity trading advisors and their commodity futures funds or managed accounts. Includes tables and graphs.

Penny Fortune Newsletter. James M. Fortune, editor. • Monthly. $79.00 per year. Reports on special situations and low- priced stocks. Includes charts and graphs.

The Prudent Speculator. Al Frank Asset Management, Inc. • Monthly. $175.00 per year. Newsletter. Presents a fundamental approach to stock selection and buying strategies for long-term capital gains appreciation.

Special Situations Newsletter: In-depth Survey of Under-Valued Stocks. Charles Howard Kaplan. • Monthly. $75.00 per year. Newsletter. Principal content is "This Month's Recommendation," a detailed analysis of one special situation stock.

RESEARCH CENTERS AND INSTITUTES

Center for Research in Security Prices. University of Chicago, 725 S. Wells St., Suite 800, Chicago, IL 60607. Phone: (773)702-7467 Fax: (773)753-4797 E-mail: mail@crsp.uchicago.edu • URL: http://www.crsp.com.

Glucksman Institute. New York University. Salomon Center, Stern School of Business, 44 W. Fourth St., Room 9-65, New York, NY 10012-0267. Phone: (212)998-0714 Fax: (212)995-4220 E-mail: iwalter@stern.nyu.edu • URL: http://www.stern.nyu.edu/salomon.

Rodney L. White Center for Financial Research. University of Pennsylvania, 3254 Steinberg Hall-Dietrich Hall, Philadelphia, PA 19104. Phone: (215)898-7616 Fax: (215)573-8084 E-mail: rlwtcr@finance.wharton.upenn.edu • URL: http://www.finance.wharton.upenn.edu/~rlwctr • Research areas include financial management, money markets, real estate finance, and international finance.

OTHER SOURCES

The Options Workbook: Proven Strategies from a Market Wizard. Anthony J. Saliba. Dearborn Financial Publishing. • 2001. $40.00. Emphasis is on computerized trading on the Chicago Board Options Exchange. Includes information on specific trading strategies.

SPEECH RECOGNITION

See: VOICE RECOGNITION

SPEECHES

See: PUBLIC SPEAKING

SPICE INDUSTRY

GENERAL WORKS

Spices: Flavor Chemistry and Antioxidant Properties. Sara J. Risch and Chi-Tang Ho, editors. American Chemical Society. • 1997. $105.00. A review of spice chemistry "from both practical and historical perspectives." Covers antixidant properties of specific spices and potential health benefits. (ACS Symposium Series, No. 660.).

CD-ROM DATABASES

Food Science and Technology Abstracts [CD-ROM]. Available from SilverPlatter Information, Inc. • Quarterly. $3,700 per year. Produced by International Food Information Service (home page is http://www.ifis.org). Provides worldwide coverage on CD-ROM of the literature of food technology and production. Various types of publications are indexed, with abstracts, including about 1,800 periodicals. Time period is 1969 to date.

HANDBOOKS AND MANUALS

Spices: Their Botanical Origin, Their Chemical Composition, Their Commercial Use, Including Seeds, Herbs, and Leaves. Joseph K. Jank. Gordon Press Publishers. • 1980. $49.95.

ONLINE DATABASES

Food Science and Technology Abstracts [online]. IFIS North American Desk. • Produced by International Food Information Service. Provides about 500,000 online citations, with abstracts, to the international literature of food science, technology, commodities, engineering, and processing. Approximately 2,000 periodicals are covered. Time period is 1969 to date, with monthly updates. Inquire as to online cost and availability.

PERIODICALS AND NEWSLETTERS

Journal of Herbs, Spices and Medicinal Plants. Haworth Press, Inc. • Quarterly. Individuals, $45.00 per year; institutions, $65.00 per year; libraries, $175.00 per year. An academic and practical journal on production, marketing, and other aspects of herbs and spices.

Perfumer and Flavorist. Allured Publishing Corp. • Bimonthly. $135.00 per year. Provides information on the art and technology of flavors and fragrances, including essential oils, aroma chemicals, and spices.

TRADE/PROFESSIONAL ASSOCIATIONS

American Spice Trade Association. P.O. Box 1267, Englewood Cliffs, NJ 07632. Phone: (201)568-2163 Fax: (201)568-7318 • URL: http://www.astaspice.org.

OTHER SOURCES

Major Food and Drink Companies of the World. Available from The Gale Group. • 2001. $855.00. Fourth edition. Two volumes. Published by Graham & Whiteside. Contains profiles and trade names for more than 9,000 important food and beverage companies in various countries. In addition to foods, includes both alcoholic and nonalcoholic drink products.

Spices and Seasonings. Available from MarketResearch.com. • 1999. $2,250.00. Market research data. Published by Specialists in Business Information. Covers salt, pepper, garlic, salt substitutes, seasoning mixes, etc.

Thomas Food and Beverage Market Place. Grey House Publishing. • Annual. $295.00. Three volumes. Contains more than 40,000 entries covering food companies, beverages, food equipment, warehouse companies, food brokers, wholesalers, importers, and exporters. Formerly *Thomas Food Industry Register.*

SPORTING GOODS INDUSTRY

See also: RECREATION INDUSTRY

DIRECTORIES

Nationwide Directory of Sporting Goods Buyers. Salesman's Guide. • Annual. $209.00. About 9,000 retail stores selling athletic and recreational equipment, footwear, apparel.

FINANCIAL RATIOS

Annual Statement Studies. Robert Morris Associates: The Association of Lending and Credit Risk Professiona. • Annual. Free to members; non-members, $140.00. Median and quartile financial ratios are given for over 400 kinds of manufacturing, wholesale, retail, construction, and consumer finance establishments. Data is sorted by both asset size and sales volume. Includes a clearly written "Definition of Ratios" and an alphabetical industry index.

Cost of Doing Business Survey for Retail Sporting Goods Stores. National Sporting Goods Association. • Biennial. $125.00. Includes income statements, balance sheets, sales per employee, sales per square foot, inventory turnover, etc.

HANDBOOKS AND MANUALS

Sporting Goods Store. Entrepreneur Media, Inc. • Looseleaf. $59.50. A practical guide to starting a retail sporting goods business. Covers profit potential, start-up costs, market size evaluation, owner's time required, site selection, lease negotiation, pricing, accounting, advertising, promotion, etc. (Start-Up Business Guide No. E1286.).

PERIODICALS AND NEWSLETTERS

NSGA Retail Focus. National Sporting Goods Association. • Bimonthy. Free to members; non-members, $50.00 per year. Covers news and marketing trends for sporting goods retailers. Formerly *NSGA Sports Retailer.*

Sporting Goods Business: The National Newsmagazine of the Sporting Goods Industry. Miller Freeman, Inc. • Monthly. $65.00 per year. The national news magazine of the sporting goods industry.

Sporting Goods Dealer: The Voice of Team Dealers Since 1899. Shore-Varrone, Inc. • Quarterly. $38.00 per year.

Sports Trend. Shore-Varrone, Inc. • Monthly. $75.00 per year. Formerly *Sports Merchandiser.*

STATISTICS SOURCES

Annual Survey of Manufactures. Available from U. S. Government Printing Office. • Annual. Prices vary. Issued by the U. S. Census Bureau as an interim update to the *Census of Manufactures.* Includes data on number of manufacturing establishments in various industries, employment, labor costs, value of shipments, capital expenditures, inventories, energy costs, and assets. (See also Census Bureau home page, http://www.census.gov/.).

U. S. Industry and Trade Outlook: The McGraw-Hill Companies and the U.S. Department of Commerce/International Trade Administration. Datapso Research Corp. • Annual. $69.95. Produced by the International Trade Administration, U. S. Department of Commerce, in a "public-private" partnership with DRI/McGraw-Hill and Standard & Poor's. Provides basic data, outlook for the current year, and "Long-Term Prospects" (five-year projections) for a wide variety of products and services. Includes high technology industries. Formerly *U. S. Industrial Outlook.*

TRADE/PROFESSIONAL ASSOCIATIONS

National Association of Sporting Goods Wholesalers. 400 E. Randolph St., Suite 700, Chicago, IL 60601-7329. Phone: (312)565-0233 Fax: (312)565-2654.

National Sporting Goods Association. Lake Center Plaza Bldg., 1699 Wall St., Ste. 700, Mount Prospect, IL 60056-5780. Phone: (847)439-4000 Fax: (847)439-0111 E-mail: nsga1699@aol.com • URL: http://www.nsga.org.

Sporting Goods Manufacturers Association. 200 Castlewood Dr., North Palm Beach, FL 33408-5666. Phone: (561)842-4100 Fax: (561)863-8984 E-mail: sgma@ix.netcom.com • URL: http://www.sportlink.com.

OTHER SOURCES

American Sports Analysis. Available from MarketResearch.com. • 1998. $375.00. Published by

American Sports Data, Inc. Consumer market data. A study of participation in sports activities (golf, tennis, swimming, running, etc.) by American consumers.

Footwear Market. Available from MarketResearch.com. • 1998. $2,750.00. Published by Packaged Facts. Provides market data on shoes for walking, running, and specific sports.

SPORTS BUSINESS

See also: GOLF INDUSTRY; RECREATION INDUSTRY

GENERAL WORKS

Market Structure of Sports. Gerald W. Scully. University of Chicago Press. • 1995. $39.95.

Winning is the Only Thing: Sports in America Since 1945. Randy Roberts and James Olson. Johns Hopkins University Press. • 1989. $38.95.

ABSTRACTS AND INDEXES

Leisure, Recreation, and Tourism Abstracts. Available from CABI Publishing North America. • Quarterly. $470.00 per year. Published in England by CABI Publishing. Provides coverage of the worldwide literature of travel, recreation, sports, and the hospitality industry. Emphasis is on research.

Readers' Guide to Periodical Literature. H. W. Wilson Co. • Monthly. $220.00 per year. CD-ROM edition, $1,495 per year, including annual cumulation. Indexes about 250 peridicals of general interest.

ALMANACS AND YEARBOOKS

Sportbil. International Sport Summit. • Annual. Price on application. A yearly review of the business of sport.

BIBLIOGRAPHIES

Entertainment and Sports Law Bibliography. American Bar Association. • 1986. $40.00.

Information Sources in Sports and Leisure. Michele Shoebridge, editor. Bowker-Saur. • 1992. $95.00. (Guides to Information Sources Series).

BIOGRAPHICAL SOURCES

Celebrity Register. The Gale Group. • 1989. $99.00. Fifth edition. Compiled by Celebrity Services International (Earl Blackwell). Contains profiles of 1,300 famous individuals in the performing arts, sports, politics, business, and other fields.

CD-ROM DATABASES

WILSONDISC: Readers' Guide to Periodical Literature. H. W. Wilson Co. • Monthly. $1,095.00 per year, including unlimited online access to *Readers' Guide to Periodical Literature* through WILSONLINE. Provides CD-ROM indexing of about 250 general interest periodicals. Covers 1983 to date. (*Readers' Guide Abstracts* also available on CD-ROM at $1,995 per year.).

DIRECTORIES

Athletic Business: Professional Directory Section. Athletic Business Publications, Inc. • Monthly. $72.00 per year. Lists consultants in athletic facility planning, with architects, engineers, and contractors. Appears in each issue of *Athletic Business.*

Resorts and Parks Purchasing Guide. Klevens Publications, Inc. • Annual. $60.00. Lists suppliers of products and services for resorts and parks, including national parks, amusement parks, dude ranches, golf resorts, ski areas, and national monument areas.

Sports Market Place. Franklin Covey Co., Sports Div. • Annual. $199.00. Includes a wide variety of professional sports teams, marketing services, organizations, broadcasting services, syndicators, manufacturers, trade shows, and publications.

HANDBOOKS AND MANUALS

Club, Recreation, and Sport Management. Tom Sawyer and Owen Smith. Sagamore Publishing, Inc. • 1998. $44.95.

Complete Guide to Special Event Management: Business Insights, Financial Advice and Successful Strategies from Ernst and Young, Consultants to the Olympics, the Emmy Awards and the PGA Tour. Ernst and Young Staff. John Wiley and Sons, Inc. • 1992. $29.95. Covers the marketing, financing, and general management of special events in the fields of art, entertainment, and sports.

Financial Management of Sport-Related Organizations. Terry Haggerty and Garth Paton. Stipes Publishing L.L.C. • 1984. $4.80. (Sport and Physical Education Management Series).

Sports, Convention, and Entertainment Facilities. David C. Petersen. Urban Land Institute. • 1996. $59.95. Provides advice and information on developing, financing, and operating amphitheaters, arenas, convention centers, and stadiums. Includes case studies of 70 projects.

ONLINE DATABASES

Globalbase. The Gale Group. • Provides more than one million online summaries of business, industrial, and economic news reports from more than 1,000 publications worldwide. Covers a wide range of material appearing in international trade journals, professional magazines, and newspapers. Time period is 1984 to date, with weekly updates. Inquire as to online cost and availability.

Newspaper and Periodical Abstracts. Bell & Howell Information and Learning. • Provides online coverage (citations and abstracts) of 25 major newspapers, 1,600 perodicals, and 70 TV programs. Covers business, economics, current affairs, health, fitness, sports, education, technology, government, consumer affairs, psychology, the arts, and the social sciences. Time period is 1986 to date, with daily updates. Inquire as to online cost and availability.

PROMT: Predicasts Overview of Markets and Technology. The Gale Group. • Companies, products, applied technologies and markets. U.S. and international literature coverage, 1972 to date. Inquire as to online cost and availability. Provides abstracts from more than 1,600 publications. Weekly updates.

Readers' Guide Abstracts Online. H. W. Wilson Co. • Indexes and abstracts general interest periodicals, 1983 to date. Weekly updates. Inquire as to online cost and availability.

PERIODICALS AND NEWSLETTERS

Athletic Business. Athletic Business Publications, Inc. • Monthly. $50.00 per year. Published for those whose responsibility is the business of planning, financing and operating athletic/recreation/fitness programs and facilities.

Athletic Management. Momentum Media. • Bimonthly. $24.00 per year. Formerly *College Athletic Management.*

Media Sports Business. Paul Kagan Associates, Inc. • Monthly. $645.00. Newsletter. Primary subject is broadcasting of sports events by national and regional cable and pay television systems.

Sports Industry News: Management and Finance, Regulation and Litigation, Media and Marketing. Game Point Publishing. • Weekly. $244.00 per year. Newsletter. Covers ticket promotions, TV rights, player contracts, concessions, endorsements, etc.

RESEARCH CENTERS AND INSTITUTES

Center for the Study of Sport in Society. Northeastern University, 360 Huntington Ave., 161CP, Boston, MA 02115. Phone: (617)373-4025 Fax: (617)373-4566 • URL: http://www.sportinsociety.org • Research fields include sport sociology, sport journalism, and sport business.

National Sports Law Institute. Marquette University Law School, P.O. Box 1881, Milwaukee, WI 53201-1881. Phone: (414)288-5815 Fax: (414)288-5818 E-mail: anderson@vms.csd.mu.edu • URL: http://www.marquette.edu/law/sports/sports.htm • Promotes ethical practices in amateur and professional sports activities.

STATISTICS SOURCES

United States Census of Service Industries. U.S. Bureau of the Census. • Quinquennial. Various reports available.

TRADE/PROFESSIONAL ASSOCIATIONS

American Sportscasters Association. Five Beekman St., Suite 814, New York, NY 10038. Phone: (212)227-8080 Fax: (212)571-0556 E-mail: asassn@juno.com • Members are radio and television sportscasters.

National Sportscasters and Sportswriters Association. P.O. Box 559, Salisbury, NC 28144. Phone: (704)633-4275 Fax: (704)633-4275 • Members are sportswriters and radio/TV sportscasters.

Society of Recreation Executives. P. O. Box 520, Gonzalez, FL 35260-0520. Phone: (850)944-7992 Fax: (850)944-0018 E-mail: nrvockws@spyder.net • Members are corporate executives employed in the recreation and leisure industries.

Sports Foundation. 1699 Wall St., Mount Prospect, IL 60056-5780. Phone: (847)439-4000 Fax: (847)439-0111 • Seeks to stimulate interest in the development of new recreational activities and facilities through the promotion of sports and the sporting goods industry.

OTHER SOURCES

Infogate. Infogate, Inc. • Web site provides current news and information on seven "channels": News, Fun, Sports, Info, Finance, Shop, and Travel. Among the content partners are Business Wire, CBS MarketWatch, CNN, Morningstar, Standard & Poor's, and Thomson Investors Network. Fees: Free, but downloading of Infogate software is required (includes personalized news feature). Updating is continuous. Formerly Pointcast Network.

Law of Professional and Amateur Sports. Gary A. Uberstine. West Group. • $230.00 per year. Two looseleaf volumes. Periodic supplementation. Covers agent-player agreements, collective bargaining, negotiation of player contracts, taxation, and other topics. (Entertainment and Communication Law Series).

Superstudy of Sports Participation. Available from MarketResearch.com. • 1999. $650.00. Three volumes. Published by American Sports Data, Inc. Provides market research data on 102 sports and activities. Vol. 1: *Physical Fitness Activities.* Vol. 2: *Recreational Sports.* Vol. 3: *Outdoor Activities.* (Volumes are available separately at $275.00.).

SPORTSWEAR

See: CLOTHING INDUSTRY; WOMEN'S APPAREL

SPOT RADIO ADVERTISING

See: RADIO AND TELEVISION ADVERTISING

SPOT WELDING

See: WELDING

STAFF MAGAZINES

See: HOUSE ORGANS

STAINLESS STEEL

See: IRON AND STEEL INDUSTRY

STAMPS AS AN INVESTMENT

DIRECTORIES

Stamp Exchangers Annual Directory. Levine Publications. • Annual. $18.00. Lists over 500 people worldwide who are interested in exchanging stamps, coins, and other collectibles with Americans.

PERIODICALS AND NEWSLETTERS

Linn's Stamp News. Amos Press, Inc. • Weekly. $39.00 per year.

Scott Stamp Monthly: With Catalogue Update. Scott Publishing Co. • Monthly. $17.95 per year.

Stamp Collector. Krause Publications, Inc. • Biweekly. $31.98 per year. Newspaper.

Stamps: The Weekly Magazine of Philately. American Publishing Co. of New York. • Weekly. $23.50 per year.

TRADE/PROFESSIONAL ASSOCIATIONS

American Philatelic Society. P.O. Box 8000, State College, PA 16803-8000. Phone: (814)237-3803 Fax: (814)237-6128 E-mail: dmwilson@stamps.org • URL: http://www.stamps.org.

American Stamp Dealers Association. Three School St., Suite 205, Glen Cove, NY 11542. Phone: (516)759-7000 Fax: (516)759-7014.

Philatelic Foundation. 501 Fifth Ave., Suite 1901, New York, NY 10017. Phone: (212)867-3699 Fax: (212)867-3984.

Society of Philatelists and Numismatists. 1929 Millis St., Montebello, CA 90640-4533. 1929 Millis St.,.

STANDARD INDUSTRIAL CLASSIFICATION

See: INDUSTRY

STANDARD METROPOLITAN STATISTICAL AREAS

See: CITIES AND TOWNS; CITY PLANNING; URBAN DEVELOPMENT

STANDARDIZATION

See also: MATERIALS; QUALITY CONTROL

ABSTRACTS AND INDEXES

Index and Directory of Industry Standards. Information Handling Services. • Annual. Seven volumes. Price varies. Covers approximately 20,000 international and 35,000 U.S. industrial standards as well as 362 industrial organizations.

BIBLIOGRAPHIES

Publications of the National Institute of Standards and Technology. U.S. Government Printing Office. • Annual. Keyword and author indexes.

DIRECTORIES

Catalog of American National Standards. American National Standards Institute. • Annual. Price on application.

Directory of Standards Laboratories. National Conference of Standards Laboratories. • Biennial. Members, $30.00 per year; non-members, $120.00 per year. Lists about 1,500 measurement standards laboratories.

Standards Activities of Organizations in the United States. Available from U. S. Government Printing Office. • 1996. $70.00. Prepared by the Office of Standards Code and Information, National Institute of Standards and Technology, U. S. Dept. of Commerce. Describes the activities of over 750 U. S. organizations that develop and publish standards. Formerly *Directory of United States Standardization Activities.*

ENCYCLOPEDIAS AND DICTIONARIES

Consumers' Guide to Product Grades and Terms: From Grade A to VSOP-Definitions of 8,000 Terms Describing Food Housewares and Other Everyday Terms. The Gale Group. • 1992. $75.00. Includes product grades and classifications defined by government agencies, such as the Food and Drug Administration (FDA), and by voluntary standards organizations, such as the American National Standards Institute (ANSI).

HANDBOOKS AND MANUALS

Book of ASTM Standards. ASTM. • Annual.

Industry's Guide to ISO 9000. Adedeji B. Badiru. John Wiley and Sons, Inc. • 1995. $99.00. (Engineering and Technology Management Series).

International Standards Desk Reference: Your Passport to World Markets. Amy Zuckerman. AMACOM. • 1996. $35.00. Provides information on standards important in export-import trade, such as ISO 9000.

ISO 9000: Achieving Compliance and Certification. Maureen A. Dalfonso. John Wiley and Sons, Inc. • 1996. $155.00.

ISO 9000 and the Service Sector. James L. Lamprecht. American Society for Quality. • 1994. $38.00. A review of the ISO 9000 quality standards as they relate to service organizations. Includes examples of applications.

ISO 9000 Auditor's Companion. Kent A. Keeney and Joseph J. Tsiakals. American Society for Quality. • 1994. $30.00. Designed to help companies prepare for ISO 9000 quality management audits.

ISO 9000 Book: A Global Competitor's Guide to Compliance and Certification. John T. Rabbitt and Peter Bergh. AMACOM. • 1994. $26.95. Second edition.

ISO 9000 Handbook. Robert W. Peach, editor. McGraw-Hill Professional. • 1996. $80.00. Third edition. Includes detailed information for the ISO 9000 registration process.

ISO 9000 Made Easy: A Cost-Saving Guide to Documentation and Registration. Amy Zuckerman. AMACOM. • 1994. $75.00.

ONLINE DATABASES

Scisearch. Institute for Scientific Information. • Broad, multidisciplinary index to the literature of science and technology, 1974 to present. Inquire as to online cost and availability. Coverage of literature is worldwide, with weekly updates.

PERIODICALS AND NEWSLETTERS

ASTM Standardization News. American Society for Testing and Materials. • Monthly. $18.00 per year.

ISO 9000 and ISO 14000 News (International Organization for Standardization). Available from American National Standards Institute. • Bimonthly. Price on application. Newsletter on quality standards. Published by the International Organization for Standardization (ISO). Text in English. Formerly *ISO 9000 News.*

Journal of Research of the National Institute of Standards and Technology. Available from U. S. Government Printing Office. • Bimonthly. $31.00 per year. Formerly *Journal of Research of the National Bureau of Standards.*

Standards Action. American National Standards Institute. • Biweekly. Membership. Includes *ANSI Reporter.*

Standards Engineering. Standards Engineering Society. • Bimonthly. $45.00 per year.

TRADE/PROFESSIONAL ASSOCIATIONS

American National Standards Institute. 11 W. 42nd St., 13th Fl., New York, NY 10036. Phone: (212)642-4900 Fax: (212)398-0023 • URL: http://www.ansi.org.

International Organization for Standardization. One, rue de Varembe, CH-1211 Geneva 20, Switzerland. E-mail: central@iso.ch • URL: http://www.iso.ch/ • Members are national standards organizations. Develops and publishes international standards, including ISO 9000 quality management standards.

National Conference of Standards Laboratories. 1800 30th St., Suite 305B, Boulder, CO 80301. Phone: (303)440-3339 Fax: (303)440-3384 E-mail: ncsl-staff@ncsl-hq.org.

Standards Engineering Society. 13340 96th Ave. S.W., Miami, FL 33176-5799. Phone: (305)971-4798 Fax: (305)971-4799 E-mail: kearses@aol.com • URL: http://www.ses-standards.org.

START-UP PLANS

See: BUSINESS START-UP PLANS AND PROPOSALS

STATE EMPLOYEES

See: GOVERNMENT EMPLOYEES

STATE FINANCE

See: PUBLIC FINANCE

STATE GOVERNMENT

See also: PUBLIC ADMINISTRATION

GENERAL WORKS

Lawmaking and the Legislative Process: Committees, Connections, and Compromises. Tommy Neal. Oryx Press. • 1996. $26.50. Explains how bills are enacted into laws through the state legislative process. Provides step-by-step examples, using fictitious bills.

ABSTRACTS AND INDEXES

Current Law Index: Multiple Access to Legal Periodicals. The Gale Group. • Monthly. $650.00 per year. Produced in cooperation with the American Association of Law Libraries. Indexes more than 900 law journals, legal newspapers, and specialty publications from the U.S., Canada, U.K., Ireland, Australia, and New Zealand.

ALMANACS AND YEARBOOKS

State Budget Actions. Corina Eckl and Arturo Perez. National Conference of State Legislatures. • 1997. $35.00. Presents yearly summaries of state spending priorities and fiscal climates. Includes end-of-year general fund balances and other information on state funds.

Suggested State Legislation. Council of State Governments. • Annual. $59.00. A source of legislative ideas and drafting assistance for state government officials.

BIBLIOGRAPHIES

State Government Research Checklist. Council of State Governments. • Bimonthly. $24.99 per year. Lists reports by state legislative research agencies, study committees, commissions, and independent organizations.

State Reference Publications: A Bibliographic Guide to State Blue Books, Legislative Manuals and Other General Reference Sources. Government Research Service. • Biennial. $70.00. State government directories, blue books, legislative manuals, statistical abstracts, judicial direcrories, local government directories, and other general publications; state capitols.

BIOGRAPHICAL SOURCES

Who's Who in American Politics. Marquis Who's Who. • Biennial. $275.00. Two volumes. Contains about 27,000 biographical sketches of local, state, and national elected or appointed individuals.

CD-ROM DATABASES

Leadership Library on CD-ROM: Who's Who in the Leadership of the United States. Leadership Directories, Inc. • Quarterly. $2,641.00 per year, including access to Internet version (weekly updates). Contains all 14 *Yellow Book* personnel directories on CD-ROM, providing contact and brief biographical information for about 400,000 individuals. Covers business, government, financial institutions, news media, law firms, associations, foreign representatives, and nonprofit organizations. Includes photographs.

National Newspaper Index CD-ROM. The Gale Group. • Monthly. Provides comprehensive CD-ROM indexing of all material appearing in the late edition of the *New York Times*, the final edition of the *Washington Post*, the national edition of the *Christian Science Monitor*, the home edition of the *Los Angeles Times*, and the *Wall Street Journal*. Time period is four years. Also available online.

Newspaper Abstracts Ondisc. Bell & Howell Information and Learning. • Monthly. $2,950.00 per year (covers 1989 to date; archival discs are available for 1985-88). Provides cover-to-cover CD-ROM indexing and abstracting of 19 major newspapers, including the *New York Times, Wall Street Journal, Washington Post, Chicago Tribune,* and *Los Angeles Times.*

DIRECTORIES

Book of the States. Council of State Governments. • Biennial. $99.00. Includes information on state constitutions, state-by-state voting in recent elections, data on state finances, and federal-state survey articles.

Business Organizations, Agencies, and Publications Directory. The Gale Group. • 1999. $425.00. 12th edition. Over 40,000 entries describing 39 types of business information sources. Classified by type of organization, publication, or serviceIncludes state, national, and international agencies and organizations. Master index to names and keywords. Also includes e-mail addresses and web site URL's.

Carroll's State Directory. Carroll Publishing. • Three times a year. $300.00 per year. Lists about 42,000 individuals in executive, administrative, and legislative positions in 50 states, the District of Columbia, Puerto Rico, and the American Territories. Includes keyword and other indexing.

Carroll's State Directory: CD-ROM Edition. Carroll Publishing. • Three times a year. $600.00 per year. Provides CD-ROM listings of about 42,000 state officials, plus the text of all state constitutions and biographies of all governors. Also available online.

CSG Directories II: Legislative Leadership. Committees and Staff by Function. Council of State Governments. • Annual. $45.00. Legislative leaders, committee members and staff, personnel of principal legislative staff offices. Formerly *Book of the States, Supplement Two: State Legislative Leadership, Committees, and Staff.*

CSG State Directories: I State Elective Officials. Council of State Governments. • Annual. $45.00. Lists about 8,000 state legislators, state executive branch elected officials, and state supreme court judges. Formerly *Book of the States, Supplement One: State Elective Officials and the Legislatures.*

Directory of Legislative Leaders. National Conference of State Legislatures. • Annual. $20.00. Lists state presiding officers, majority and minority leaders, and key staff members. Preferred addresses, telephone numbers, and fax numbers are included.

Election Results Directory Supplement. National Conference of State Legislatures. • Annual. $35.00. Provides names, addresses, telephone numbers, and e-mail addresses of state legislators and executive officials.

Government Phone Book USA: Your Comprehensive Guide to Federal, State, County, and Local Government Offices in the United States. Omnigraphics, Inc. • Annual. $230.00. Contains more than 168,500 listings of federal, state, county, and local government offices and personnel, including legislatures. Formerly *Government Directory of Addresses and Phone Numbers.*

Governors' Staff Directory. National Governor's Association. Publications Fulfillment Service. • Semiannual. $9.95 per year. List of more than 1,000 key staff members and their titles in each of the 55 governor's offices.

Judicial Yellow Book: Who's Who in Federal and State Courts. Leadership Directories, Inc. • Semiannual. $235.00 per year. Lists more than 3,200 judges and staffs in various federal courts and 1,200 judges and staffs in state courts. Includes biographical profiles of judges.

State Yellow Book: Who's Who in the Executive and Legislative Branches of the 50 Governments. Leadership Directories, Inc. • Quarterly. $305.00 per year. Lists more than 37,000 elected and administrative officials by state, District of Columbia, and U. S. Territory. Includes state profiles, with historical and statistical data. County population and per capita income is also included.

HANDBOOKS AND MANUALS

Mason's Manual of Legislative Procedure. American Society of Legislative Clerks and Secretaries. National Conference of State Legislatures. • 1989. $40.00. Revised edition. Contains parliamentary law and rules, rules of debate, rules governing motions, how to conduct business, etc.

INTERNET DATABASES

Fedstats. Federal Interagency Council on Statistical Policy. Phone: (202)395-7254 • URL: http://www.fedstats.gov • Web site features an efficient search facility for full-text statistics produced by more than 70 federal agencies, including the Census Bureau, the Bureau of Economic Analysis, and the Bureau of Labor Statistics. Boolean searches can be made within one agency or for all agencies combined. Links are offered to international statistical bureaus, including the UN, IMF, OECD, UNESCO, Eurostat, and 20 individual countries. Fees: Free.

ONLINE DATABASES

DRI U.S. Central Database. Data Products Division. • Provides more than 23,000 business, financial, demographic, economic, foreign trade, and industry-related time series for the U.S. Includes national income, population, retail-wholesale trade, price indexes, labor data, housing, industrial production, banking, interest rates, money supply, etc. Time period is generally 1947 to date (some data back to 1929). Updating varies. Inquire as to online cost and availability.

Information Bank Abstracts. New York Times Index Dept. • Provides indexing and abstracting of current affairs, primarily from the final late edition of *The New York Times* and the Eastern edition of *The Wall Street Journal*. Time period is 1969 to present, with daily updates. Inquire as to online cost and availability.

PAIS International. Public Affairs Information Service, Inc. • Corresponds to the former printed publications, *PAIS Bulletin* (1976-90) and *PAIS Foreign Language Index* (1972-90), and to the current *PAIS International in Print* (1991 to date). Covers economic, political, and sociological material appearing in periodicals, books, government documents, and other publications. Updating is monthly. Inquire as to online cost and availability.

PERIODICALS AND NEWSLETTERS

Governing: The States and Localities. • Monthly. $39.95 per year. Edited for state and local government officials. Covers finance, office management, computers, telecommunications, environmental concerns, etc.

Government Technology: Solutions for State and Local Government in the Information Age. • Monthly. Free to qualified personnel.

Public Risk. Public Risk Management Association. • 10 times a year. $125.00 per year. Covers risk management for state and local governments, including various kinds of liabilities.

Spectrum: Journal of State Government. Council of State Governments. • Quarterly. $49.99 per year. Formerly *Journal of State Government.*

State Budget and Tax News. State Policy Research, Inc. • Semimonthly. $245.00 per year. Newsletter. Covers fiscal activities in the 50 states.

State Capitals. Wakeman-Walworth, Inc. • Irregular. Prices may vary. A group of 39 newsletters, with each publication having its own subtitle and topic of relevance to state government.

State Government News: The Monthly Magazine Covering All Facets of State Government. Council of State Governments. • Monthly. $39.00 per year.

State Legislative Report. National Conference of State Legislatures. • 12 to 16 times per year. $15.00 per issue. Discusses significant state legislation.

State Legislatures. National Conference of State Legislatures. • Monthly. $49.00 per year. Newsletter. Covers state legislative issues and politics.

RESEARCH CENTERS AND INSTITUTES

Academy for State and Local Government. 444 N. Capitol St., N.W., Suite 345, Washington, DC 20001. Phone: (202)434-4850 Fax: (202)434-4851.

Lexis.com Research System. Lexis-Nexis Group. Phone: 800-227-9597 or (937)865-6800 Fax: (937)865-6909 E-mail: webmaster@prod.lexis-nexis.com • URL: http://www.lexis.com • Fee-based Web site offers extensive searching of a wide variety of legal sources. Additional features include Daily Opinion Service, lexis.com Bookstore, Career Center, CLE Center, Law Schools, and Practice Pages ("Pages specific to areas of specialty").

STATISTICS SOURCES

Almanac of the Fifty States: Basic Data Profiles with Comparative Tables. Edith R. Hornor, editor. Information Publications. • Annual. $50.00. 14th revised edition.

Business Statistics of the United States. Courtenay M. Slater, editor. Bernan Associates. • 1999. $74.00.

Fifth edition. Based on *Business Statistics*, formerly issue by the Bureau of Economic Analysis, U. S. Department of Commerce. Provides basic data for a wide variety of U. S. industries, services, and economic indicators. Most statistics are shown annually for 29 years and monthly for the most recent four years.

Gale State Rankings Reporter. The Gale Group. • 1996. $110.00. Second edition Provides 3,000 ranked lists of states under 35 subject headings. Sources are newspapers, periodicals, books, research institute publications, and government publications.

State Profiles: The Population and Economy of Each U. S. State. Courtenay Slater and Martha Davis, editors. Bernan Press. • 1999. $74.00. Presents charts, tables, and text in an eight-page profile for each state. Covers population, labor force, income, poverty, employment, wages, industry, trade, housing, education, health, taxes, and government finances.

Survey of Current Business. Available from U. S. Government Printing Office. • Monthly. $49.00 per year. Issued by Bureau of Economic Analysis, U. S. Department of Commerce. Presents a wide variety of business and economic data.

TRADE/PROFESSIONAL ASSOCIATIONS

Council of State Governments. c/o Julia Nienaber, P.O. Box 11910, Lexington, KY 40578-1910. Phone: 800-800-1910 or (606)244-8000 or (606)244-8111 Fax: (606)244-8001 E-mail: info@csg.org • URL: http://www.csg.org.

National Association of State Budget Officers. Hall of States, 444 N. Capitol St., N.W., Ste. 642, Washington, DC 20001. Phone: (202)624-5382 Fax: (202)624-7745 • URL: http://www.nasbo.org.

National Association of State Procurement Officials. c/o Association Management Resources, 167 W. Main St., Suite 600, Lexington, KY 40507. Phone: (606)231-1877 or (606)231-1963 Fax: (606)231-1928 E-mail: croberts@amrinc.net • URL: http://www.naspo.org • Purchasing officials of the states and territories.

National Conference of State Legislatures. 1560 Broadway, Suite 700, Denver, CO 80202. Phone: (303)830-2200 Fax: (303)863-8003 • URL: http://www.ncsl.org.

National Governors' Association. Hall of States, 444 N. Capitol St., N.W., Suite 267, Washington, DC 20001-1512. Phone: (202)624-5300 Fax: (202)624-5313 • URL: http://www.nga.org.

Public Risk Management Association. 1815 N. Fort Meyer Dr., Ste. 1020, Arlington, VA 22209-1805. Phone: (703)528-7701 Fax: (703)528-7966 E-mail: info@primacentral.org • URL: http://www.primacentral.org • Members are state and local government officials concerned with risk management and public liabilities.

State Government Affairs Council. 1255 23rd St., N.W., Washington, DC 20037. Phone: (202)728-0500 Fax: (202)833-3636.

OTHER SOURCES

Government Discrimination: Equal Protection Law and Litigation. James A. Kushner. West Group. • $140.00 per year. Looseleaf service. Periodic supplementation. Covers discrimination in employment, housing, and other areas by local, state, and federal offices or agencies. (Civil Rights Series).

State Legislators' Occupations: 1994, A Survey. National Conference of State Legislatures. • 1994. $20.00. Presents survey results concerning the occupations of more than 7,000 state legislators. (Members of state legislatures usually combine government service with other occupations.).

STATE INCOME TAX

See: STATE TAXES

STATE LAW

See also: SALES TAX

ABSTRACTS AND INDEXES

Index to Legal Periodicals and Books. H. W. Wilson Co. • Monthly. Quarterly and annual cumulations. $270.00 per year. CD-ROM version available at $1,495.00 per year.

ALMANACS AND YEARBOOKS

Suggested State Legislation. Council of State Governments. • Annual. $59.00. A source of legislative ideas and drafting assistance for state government officials.

BIBLIOGRAPHIES

Encyclopedia of Legal Information Sources. The Gale Group. • 1992. $180.00. Second edition. Lists more than 23,000 law-related information sources, including print, nonprint, and organizational.

DIRECTORIES

Book of the States. Council of State Governments. • Biennial. $99.00. Includes information on state constitutions, state-by-state voting in recent elections, data on state finances, and federal-state survey articles.

Directory of Building Codes and Regulations. National Conference of States on Building Codes and Standards. • Annual, with quarterly updates. Two volumes. Members, $115.00; non-members, $150.00. In addition to information about residential and commerical building codes,includes a directory of state and majority administrators concerned with enforcement of the codes.

Law and Legal Information Directory. The Gale Group. • 2000. $405.00. 11th edition. Two volumes. Contains a wide range of sources of legal information, such as associations, law schools, courts, federal agencies, referral services, libraries, publishers, and research centers. There is a separate chapter for each of 23 types of information source or service.

Martindale-Hubbell Law Directory. Martindale-Hubbell. • Annual. $695.00. 25 volumes. Lists 800,000 lawyers in the U. S., Canada, and 150 other countries, with an index to areas of specialization. Three of the 25 volumes provide the *Martindale-Hubbell Law Digest*, summarizing the statutary laws of the U. S. (state and federal), Canada, and 61 other countries.

HANDBOOKS AND MANUALS

National Survey of State Laws. The Gale Group. • 1999. $85.00. Third edition. Provides concise state-by-state comparisons of current state laws on a wide variety of topics. Includes references to specific codes or statutes.

ONLINE DATABASES

Index to Legal Periodicals and Books (Online). H. W. Wilson Co. • Broad coverage of law journals and books 1981 to date. Monthly updates. Inquire as to online cost and availability.

Legal Resource Index. The Gale Group. • Broad coverage of law literature appearing in legal, business, and other periodicals, 1980 to date. Monthly updates. Inquire as to online cost and availability.

LEXIS. LEXIS-NEXIS. • The various LEXIS databases provide full text and indexing for a wide variety of legal cases, statutes, orders, and opinions.

PERIODICALS AND NEWSLETTERS

Land Use Law and Zoning Digest. American Planning Association. • Monthly. $275.00 per year. Covers judicial decisions and state laws affecting zoning and land use. Edited for city planners and lawyers. Monthly supplement available *Zoning News*.

State Legislative Report. National Conference of State Legislatures. • 12 to 16 times per year. $15.00 per issue. Discusses significant state legislation.

State Policy Reports. State Policy Research, Inc. • Semimonthly. $445.00 per year. Newsletter. Information about tax and budget activities in all states.

TRADE/PROFESSIONAL ASSOCIATIONS

Council of State Governments. c/o Julia Nienaber, P.O. Box 11910, Lexington, KY 40578-1910. Phone: 800-800-1910 or (606)244-8000 or (606)244-8111 Fax: (606)244-8001 E-mail: info@csg.org • URL: http://www.csg.org.

National Association of Attorneys General. 750 First St., N.E., Suite 1100, Washington, DC 20002. Phone: (202)326-6000 Fax: (202)408-7014 • URL: http://www.naag.org.

National Conference of Commissioners on Uniform State Laws. 211 E. Ontario St., Ste. 1300, Chicago, IL 60611. Phone: (312)915-0195 Fax: (312)915-0187 E-mail: nccusl@nccusl.org • URL: http://www.nccusl.org.

National Conference of State Legislatures. 1560 Broadway, Suite 700, Denver, CO 80202. Phone: (303)830-2200 Fax: (303)863-8003 • URL: http://www.ncsl.org.

North American Securities Administrators Association. 10 G St., N.E., Ste. 710, Washington, DC 20002. Phone: (202)737-0900 Fax: (202)783-3571 E-mail: info@nasaa.org • Members are state officials who administer "blue sky" securities laws.

OTHER SOURCES

Labor Law Reports. CCH, Inc. • 16 looseleaf volumes. $2,151.00 per year, including weekly updates. Covers laborrelations, wages and hours, state labor laws, and employment practices. Supplement available *Guide to Fair Employment Practices*.

STATE LEGISLATURES

See: LEGISLATURES; STATE GOVERNMENT

STATE TAXES

See also: TAXATION

CD-ROM DATABASES

Search Master Tax Library. Matthew Bender & Co., Inc. • Monthly. $1,200.00 per year. Provides current CD-ROM full text of *Bender's Federal Tax Service, Bender's Master Federal Tax Handbook,* and the current full text of Bender's state tax services for California, Florida, Illinois, New Jersey, New York, Ohio, Pennsylvania, and Texas.

The Tax Directory [CD-ROM]. Tax Analysts. • Quarterly. Provides *The Tax Directory* listings on CD-ROM, covering federal, state, and international tax officials, tax practitioners, and corporate tax executives.

DIRECTORIES

National Sales Tax Rate Directory. Vertex Systems, Inc. • Looseleaf, with monthly updates. $585.00 Per year. Provides state, county, city, and special sales tax rates for all states.

The Tax Directory. Tax Analysts. • Annual. $299.00. ($399.00 with quarterly CD-ROM updates.) Four volumes: *Government Officials Worldwide* (lists 15,000 state, federal, and international tax officials, with basic corporate and individual income tax rates for 100 countries); *Private Sector Professionals Worldwide* (lists 25,000 U.S. and foreign tax practitioners: accountants, lawyers, enrolled agents, and actuarial firms); *Corporate Tax Managers Worldwide* (lists 10,000 tax managers employed by U.S. and foreign companies).

HANDBOOKS AND MANUALS

All States Tax Handbook. Research Institute of America. • Annual. $30.00. Tax structures for fifty states.

Cybertaxation: The Taxation of E-Commerce. Karl A. Frieden. CCH, Inc. • 2000. $75.00. Includes state sales and use tax issues and corporate income tax rules, as related to doing business over the Internet.

State Tax Actions. Judy Zelio. National Conference of State Legislatures. • Annual. $35.00. Summarizes yearly tax changes by type and by state.

State Tax Handbook. CCH, Inc. • Annual. $41.95. Summarizes rates, deductions, exemptions, and reporting requirements for the 45 income tax states, the District of Columbia, and major cities.

U. S. Master Multistate Corporate Tax Guide. CCH, Inc. • Annual. $67.00. Provides corporate income tax information for 47 states, New York City, and the District of Columbia.

U. S. Master Property Tax Guide. CCH, Inc. • Annual. $67.00. Provides state-by-state coverage of "key property tax issues and concepts," including exemptions, assessments, taxpayer remedies, and property tax calendars.

U. S. Master Sales and Use Tax Guide. CCH, Inc. • Annual. $65.00. Contains concise information on sales and use taxes in all states and the District of Columbia.

Vertex National Sales Tax Manuals. Vertex Systems, Inc. • Six looseleaf regional volumes, $1,122.00 Monthly updates. $750.00 Price on application. Volumes include state by state charts of taxable goods and services, guides to exemptions, reporting requirements, a directory of taxing authorities, and other state and local sales tax information.

INTERNET DATABASES

Rutgers Accounting Web (RAW). Rutgers University Accounting Research Center. Phone: (201)648-5172 Fax: (201)648-1233 • URL: http://www.rutgers.edu/accounting • RAW Web site provides extensive links to sources of national and international accounting information, such as the Big Six accounting firms, the Financial Accounting Standards Board (FASB), SEC filings (EDGAR), journals, publishers, software, the International Accounting Network, and "Internet's largest list of accounting firms in USA." Searching is offered. Fees: Free.

ONLINE DATABASES

Accounting and Tax Database. Bell & Howell Information and Learning. • Provides indexing and abstracting of the literature of accounting, taxation, and financial management, 1971 to date. Updating is weekly. Especially covers accounting, auditing, banking, bankruptcy, employee compensation and benefits, cash management, financial planning, and credit. Inquire as to online cost and availability.

PERIODICALS AND NEWSLETTERS

E-Commerce Tax Alert. CCH, Inc. • Monthly. $397.00 per year. Newsletter. Edited for owners and managers of firms doing business through the Internet. Covers compliance with federal, state, local, and international tax regulations.

Highlights and Documents. Tax Analysts. • Daily. $2,249.00 per year, including monthly indexes. Newsletter. Provides daily coverage of IRS, congressional, judicial, state, and international tax developments. Includes abstracts and citations for "all tax documents released within the previous 24 to 48 hours." Annual compilation available *Highlights and Documents on Microfiche.*

Interstate Tax Insights. Interstate Tax Corp. • Monthly. $195.00 per year. Formerly *Interstate Tax Report.*

State Income Tax Alert. CCH, Inc. • Semimonthly. $247.00 per year. Newsletter. Provides nationwide coverage of latest state income tax laws, regulations, and court decisions.

State Tax Notes. Tax Analysts. • Weekly. $949.00 per year, including annual CD-ROM. Newsletter. Covers tax developments in all states. Provides state tax document summaries and citations.

State Tax Review. CCH, Inc. • Weekly. $129.00. per year.

RESEARCH CENTERS AND INSTITUTES

Center for Tax Policy Studies. Purdue University, 490 Krannert, West Lafayette, IN 47907-1310. Phone: (765)494-4442 Fax: (765)496-1778 E-mail: papke@mgmt.purdue.edu.

Tax Foundation. 1250 H St., N.W., Suite 750, Washington, DC 20005. Phone: (202)783-2760 Fax: (202)783-6868 E-mail: taxfnd@intr.net • URL: http://www.taxfoundation.org.

STATISTICS SOURCES

Gale State Rankings Reporter. The Gale Group. • 1996. $110.00. Second edition Provides 3,000 ranked lists of states under 35 subject headings. Sources are newspapers, periodicals, books, research institute publications, and government publications.

State Profiles: The Population and Economy of Each U. S. State. Courtenay Slater and Martha Davis, editors. Bernan Press. • 1999. $74.00. Presents charts, tables, and text in an eight-page profile for each state. Covers population, labor force, income, poverty, employment, wages, industry, trade, housing, education, health, taxes, and government finances.

Statistical Abstract of the United States. Available from U. S. Government Printing Office. • Annual. $51.00. Issued by the U. S. Bureau of the Census.

TRADE/PROFESSIONAL ASSOCIATIONS

Federation of Tax Administrators. 444 N. Capitol St., Suite 348, Washington, DC 20001. Phone: (202)624-5890 Fax: (202)624-7888 • URL: http://www.taxadmin.org.

OTHER SOURCES

All States Tax Guide. Prentice Hall. • Looseleaf. Periodic supplementation. Price on application. One volume summary of taxes for all states.

Manufacturers' Tax Alert. CCH, Inc. • Monthly. $297.00 per year. Newsletter. Covers the major tax issues affecting manufacturing companies. Includes current developments in various kind of federal, state, and international taxes: sales, use, franchise, property, and corporate income.

Multi-State Sales Tax Guide. CCH, Inc. • $1,160.00 per year. Looseleaf service. Nine volumes. Periodic supplementation. Formerly *All State Sales Tax Reports.*

Sales and Use Taxation of E-Commerce: State Tax Administrators' Current Thinking, with CCH Commentary. CCH, Inc. • 2000. $129.00. Provides advice and information on the impact of state sales taxes on e-commerce activity.

STATIONERY INDUSTRY

See: OFFICE EQUIPMENT AND SUPPLIES

STATISTICAL METHODS

See also: BUSINESS MATHEMATICS; BUSINESS STATISTICS; ECONOMIC STATISTICS; MARKET STATISTICS

GENERAL WORKS

Business Statistics: Contemporary Decision Making. Ken Black. South-Western Publishing Co. • 2000. $65.00. Third edition.

Business Statistics for Management and Economics. Wayne W. Daniel and James C. Terrell. Houghton Mifflin Co. • 2000. $19.47. Seventh edition.

Business Statistics for Quality and Productivity. John M. Levine. Prentice Hall. • 1994. $94.07. (Prentice Hall College Title Series).

Business Statistics Practice. Bruce L. Bowerman. McGraw-Hill. • 2000. $68.00. Second edition.

How to Lie with Statistics. Darrell Huff. W. W. Norton and Co., Inc. • 1993. $8.95.

The Visual Display of Quantitative Information. Edward R. Tufte. Graphics Press. • 1992. $40.00. A classic work on the graphic display of numerical data, including many illustrations. The two parts are "Graphical Practice," and "Theory of Data Graphics.".

ABSTRACTS AND INDEXES

Current Index to Statistics: Applications, Methods, and Theory. American Statistical Association. • Annual. Price on application. An index to journal articles on statistical applications and methodology.

Institute of Mathematical Statistics Bulletin. Institute of Mathematical Statistics, Business Office. • Bimonthly. $50.00 per year.

Statistical Theory and Method Abstracts. International Statistical Institute. • Quarterly. Members, $85.00 per year; non-members, $170.00 per year. Worldwide coverage of published papers on mathematical statistics and probability.

BIBLIOGRAPHIES

Business Information Sources. Lorna M. Daniells. California Princeton Fulfillment Services. • 1993. $42.50. Third revised edition. Basic business sources, with discussion and full annotations.

CD-ROM DATABASES

MathSci Disc. American Mathematical Society. • Semiannual. Price on application. Provides CD-ROM citations, with abstracts, to the literature of mathematics, statistics, and computer science, 1940 to date.

Science Citation Index: Compact Disc Edition. Institute for Scientific Information. • Quarterly. Provides CD-ROM indexing of the world's scientific and technical literature. Corresponds to online *Scisearch* and printed *Science Citation Index.*

ENCYCLOPEDIAS AND DICTIONARIES

A Dictionary of Statistical Terms. F.H. Marriott. Allyn and Bacon/Longman. • 1990. $76.65. Fifth edition.

Encyclopedia of Statistical Sciences. Samuel I. Kotz and others, editors. John Wiley and Sons, Inc. • 1988. $2,395.00. Nine volumes. Supplement available. Price vary for each individual volume.

HANDBOOKS AND MANUALS

Basic Statistics for Business and Economics. Douglas A. Lind and Robert D. Mason. McGraw-Hill Higher Education. • 1996. Second edition. Price on application.

Descriptive Statistical Techniques for Librarians. Arthur W. Hafner. American Library Association. • 1997. $55.00 Second edition.

General Statistics. Warren Chase and Fred Brown. John Wiley and Sons, Inc. • 1999. $90.95 Fourth edition.

The Numbers You Need. The Gale Group. • 1993. $55.00. Contains mathematical equations, formulas, charts, and graphs, including many that are related to business or finance. Explanations, step-by-step directions, and examples of use are provided.

Practical Business Statistics with StatPad. Andrew F. Siegel. McGraw-Hill Higher Education. • 1999. $87.81. Fourth edition. Includes CD-Rom.

Statistical Techniques in Business and Economics. Robert D. Mason and Douglas A. Lind. McGraw-Hill. • 1998. 10th edition. Price on application.

Statistics for the Environment: Statistical Aspects of Health and the Environment. Vic Barnett and K. Feridun Turkman, editors. John Wiley and Sons, Inc. • 1999. $180.00. Contains articles on the statistical analysis and interpretation of environmental monitoring and sampling data. Areas covered include meteorology, pollution of the environment, and forest resources.

ONLINE DATABASES

MathSci. American Mathematical Society. • Provides online citations, with abstracts, to the literature of mathematics, statistics, and computer science. Time period is 1940 to date, with monthly updates. Inquire as to online cost and availability.

Scisearch. Institute for Scientific Information. • Broad, multidisciplinary index to the literature of science and technology, 1974 to present. Inquire as to online cost and availability. Coverage of literature is worldwide, with weekly updates.

PERIODICALS AND NEWSLETTERS

American Statistician. American Statistical Association. • Quarterly. Individuals, $15.00 per year; libraries, $75.00 per year.

Annals of Probability. Institute of Mathematical Statistics, Business Office. • Quarterly. $160.00 per year.

Annals of Statistics. Institute of Mathematical Statistics, Business Office. • Bimonthly. $180.00 per year.

JASA (Journal of the American Statistical Association). American Statistical Association. • Quarterly. Members, $39.00 per year; non-members, $310.00 per year. Formerly *Amercan Statistical Association Journal.*

Journal of Business and Economic Statistics. American Statistical Association. • Quarterly. Libraries, $90.00 per year. Emphasis is on statistical measurement and applications for business and economics.

Mathematical Finance: An International Journal of Mathematics, Statistics, and Financial Economics. Blackwell Publishers. • Quarterly. $342.00 per year. Covers the use of sophisticated mathematical tools in financial research and practice.

The Review of Economics and Statistics. Harvard University, Economics Dept. MIT Press. • Quarterly. Individuals, $48.00 per year; institutions, $190.00 per year; students and retired persons, $25.00 per year.

RESEARCH CENTERS AND INSTITUTES

Center for Mathematical Studies in Economics and Management Sciences. Northwestern University, Leverone Hall, Room 317, 2001 Sheridan Rd., Evanston, IL 60208-2014. Phone: (847)491-3527 Fax: (847)491-2530 E-mail: sreiter@casbah.acns.nwu.edu • URL: http://www.kellogg.nwu.edu/research/math.

Center for Quality and Productivity. University of North Texas, College of Business Administration, Denton, TX 76203-3677. Phone: (940)565-4767 E-mail: prybutok@unt.edu • URL: http://www.coba.unt.edu:80/bcis.organize/cqp/cqp.htm • Fields of research include the management of quality systems and statistical methodology.

Center for Statistical Consultation and Research. University of Michigan. 3514 Rackham Bldg., Ann Arbor, MI 48109-1070. Phone: (734)764-7828 Fax: (734)647-2440 E-mail: cscar@umich.edu • URL: http://www.umich.edu/ncscar.

Cowles Foundation for Research in Economics. Yale University. 30 Hillhouse Ave., New Haven, CT 06520-8281. Phone: (203)432-3704 Fax: (203)432-6167 E-mail: john.geanakoplos@yale.edu • URL: http://www.econ.yale.edu.

TRADE/PROFESSIONAL ASSOCIATIONS

American Statistical Association. 1429 Duke St., Alexandria, VA 22314-3402. Phone: (703)684-1221 Fax: (703)684-2037 E-mail: asainfo@amstat.org • URL: http://www.amstat.org • A professional society concerned with statistical theory, methodology, and applications. Sections include Survey Research Methods, Government Statistics, and Business and Economic Statistics.

Institute of Mathematical Statistics. 3401 Investment Blvd., Suite 7, Hayward, CA 94545-3819. Phone: (510)783-8141 Fax: (510)783-4131 E-mail: ims@stat.org.

STATISTICS, BUSINESS

See: BUSINESS STATISTICS

STATISTICS, MATHEMATICAL

See: STATISTICAL METHODS

STATISTICS SOURCES

See also: BUSINESS STATISTICS; ECONOMIC STATISTICS; MARKET STATISTICS

GENERAL WORKS

Global Economic Prospects 2000. The World Bank, Office of the Publisher. • 1999. $25.00. "..offers an in-depth analysis of the economic prospects of developing countries.." Emphasis is on the impact of recessions and financial crises. Regional statistical data is included.

ABSTRACTS AND INDEXES

American Statistics Index: A Comprehensive Guide and Index to the Statistical Publications of the United States Government. Congressional Information Service, Inc. • Monthly. Quarterly and annual cumulations. Price varies.

Investment Statistics Locator. Linda H. Bentley and Jennifer J. Kiesl, editors. Oryx Press. • 1994. $69.95. Expanded revised edition. Provides detailed subject indexing of more than 50 of the most-used sources of financial and investment data. Includes an annotated bibliography.

Statistical Reference Index: A Selective Guide to American Statistical Publications from Sources Other than the United States Government. Congressional Information Service, Inc. • Monthly. Quarterly and annual cumulations. Price varies. Service basis.

ALMANACS AND YEARBOOKS

Irwin Business and Investment Almanac, 1996. Summer N. Levine and Caroline Levine. McGraw-Hill Professional. • 1995. $75.00. A review of last year's business activity. Covers a wide variety of business and economic data: stock market statistics, industrial information, commodity futures information, art market trends, comparative living costs for U. S. metropolitan areas, foreign stock market data, etc. Formerly *Business One Irwin Business and Investment Almanac.*

The Statesman's Yearbook: Statistical and Historical Annual of the States of the World. Stockton Press Direct Marketing. • Annual. $65.00.

World Almanac and Book of Facts. World Almanac Education Group, Inc. • Annual. $10.95.

World Development Report. The World Bank, Office of the Publisher. • Annual. $50.00. Covers history, conditions, and trends relating to economic globalization and localization. Includes selected data from *World Development Indicators* for 132 countries or economies. Key indicators are provided for 78 additional countries or economies.

BIBLIOGRAPHIES

Business Information Sources. Lorna M. Daniells. California Princeton Fulfillment Services. • 1993. $42.50. Third revised edition. Basic business sources, with discussion and full annotations.

Data Sources for Business and Market Analysis. John Ganly. Scarecrow Press, Inc. • 1994. $58.00. Fourth edition. Emphasis is on sources of statistics for market research, especially government sources. Relevant directories, periodicals, and research aids are included.

Global Data Locator. George T. Kurian. Bernan Associates. • 1997. $89.00. Provides detailed descriptions of international statistical sourcebooks and electronic databases. Covers a wide variety of trade, economic, and demographic topics.

Guide to Special Issues and Indexes of Periodicals. Miriam Uhlan and Doris B. Katz, editors. Special Libraries Association. • 1994. $59.00. Fourth edition. A listing, with prices, of the special issues of over 1700 U. S. and Canadian periodicals in business, industry, technology, science, and the arts. Includes a comprehensive subject index.

Statistics Sources: A Subject Guide to Data on Industrial, Business, Social, Educational, Financial and Other Topics for the U. S. and Selected Foreign Countries. The Gale Group. • 2000. $475.00. 25th edition. Two volumes. Lists sources of statistical information for more than 20,000 topics.

World Directory of Non-Official Statistical Sources. Gale Group, Inc. • 2001. $590.00. Provides detailed descriptions of more than 4,000 regularly published, non-governmental statistics sources. Includes surveys, studies, market research reports, trade journals, databank compilations, and other print sources. Coverage is international, with four indexes.

CD-ROM DATABASES

Sourcebook America. The Gale Group. • Annual. $995.00. Produced by CACI Marketing Systems. A combination on CD-ROM of *The Sourcebook of ZIP Code Demographics* and *The Sourcebook of County Demographics.* Provides detailed population and socio-economic data (about 75 items) for each of 3,141 U. S. counties and approximately 30,000 ZIP codes, plus states, metropolitan areas, and media market areas. Includes forecasts to the year 2004.

Statistical Abstract of the United States on CD-ROM. Hoover's, Inc. • Annual. $49.95. Provides all statistics from official print version, plus expanded historical data, greater detail, and keyword searching features.

Statistical Masterfile. Congressional Information Service. • Quarterly. Price varies. Provides CD-ROM versions of *American Statistics Index, Index to International Statistics,* and *Statistical Reference Index.* Contains indexing and abstracting of a wide variety of published statistics sources, both governmental and private.

World Development Report [CD-ROM]. The World Bank, Office of the Publisher. • Annual. Single-user, $375.00. Network version, $750.00. CD-ROM includes the current edition of *World Development Report* and 21 previous editions.

DIRECTORIES

The Internet Blue Pages: The Guide to Federal Government Web Sites. Information Today, Inc. • Annual. $34.95. Provides information on more than 900 Web sites used by various agencies of the federal government. Includes indexes to agencies and topics. Links to all Web sites listed are available at http://www.fedweb.com. (CyberAge Books.).

Marketing Know-How: Your Guide to the Best Marketing Tools and Sources. Intertec Publishing. • 1996. $49.95. Describes more than 700 public and private sources of consumer marketing data. Also discusses market trends and provides information on such marketing techniques as cluster analysis, focus groups, and geodemographic analysis.

HANDBOOKS AND MANUALS

Dun & Bradstreet/Gale Group Industry Handbooks. The Gale Group. • 2000. $630.00. Five volumes. $145.00 per volume. Each volume covers two or more major industries: 1. *Entertainment and Hospitality*; 2. *Construction and Agriculture*; 3. *Chemicals and Pharmaceuticals*; 4. *Computers & Software and Broadcasting & Telecommunications*; 5. *Insurance and Health & Medical Services*. The following are included for each industry: overview, statistics, financial ratios, rankings, merger information, company directory, directory of associations, and consultants directory.

Finding Statistics Online: How to Locate the Elusive Numbers You Need. Paula Berinstein. Information Today, Inc. • 1998. $29.95. Provides advice on efficient searching when looking for statistical data on the World Wide Web or from commercial online services and database producers. (CyberAge Books.).

Understanding the Census: A Guide for Marketers, Planners, Grant Writers, and Other Data Users. Michael R. Lavin. Epoch Books, Inc. • 1996. $49.95. Contains basic explanations of U. S. Census "concepts, methods, terminology, and data sources." Includes practical advice for locating and using Census data.

Using Government Information Sources, Print and Electronic. Jean L. Sears and Marilyn K. Moody. Oryx Press. • 1994. $115.00. Second edition. Contains detailed information in four sections on subject searches, agency searches, statistical searches, and special techniques for searching. Appendixes give selected agency and publisher addresses, telephone numbers, and computer communications numbers.

INTERNET DATABASES

Bureau of Labor Statistics (BLS). U. S. Department of Labor, Bureau of Labor Statistics. Phone: (202)523-1092 E-mail: labstat.helpdesk@bls.gov • URL: http://www.bls.gov • Web site provides a great variety of employment, wage, price, and economic data. Some links are "Data," "Economy at a Glance," "Keyword Search of BLS Web Pages," "Regional Information," and "Other Statistical Sites." Fees: Free.

Fedstats. Federal Interagency Council on Statistical Policy. Phone: (202)395-7254 • URL: http://www.fedstats.gov • Web site features an efficient search facility for full-text statistics produced by more than 70 federal agencies, including the Census Bureau, the Bureau of Economic Analysis, and the Bureau of Labor Statistics. Boolean searches can be made within one agency or for all agencies combined. Links are offered to international statistical bureaus, including the UN, IMF, OECD, UNESCO, Eurostat, and 20 individual countries. Fees: Free.

U. S. Census Bureau: The Official Statistics. U. S. Bureau of the Census. Phone: (301)763-4100 Fax: (301)763-4794 • URL: http://www.census.gov • Web site is "Your Source for Social, Demographic, and Economic Information." Contains "Current U. S. Population Count," "Current Economic Indicators," and a wide variety of data under "Other Official Statistics." Keyword searching is provided. Fees: Free.

ONLINE DATABASES

ASI (American Statistics Index). Congressional Information Service. • A comprehensive online index, with abstracts, to the statistical publications of over 500 federal government offices and agencies from 1973 to date. A wide variety of information is indexed, with emphasis on demographic, economic, social, and natural resources data. Updated monthly. Inquire as to online cost and availability.

DRI U.S. Central Database. Data Products Division. • Provides more than 23,000 business, financial, demographic, economic, foreign trade, and industry-related time series for the U.S. Includes national income, population, retail-wholesale trade, price indexes, labor data, housing, industrial production, banking, interest rates, money supply, etc. Time period is generally 1947 to date (some data back to 1929). Updating varies. Inquire as to online cost and availability.

Globalbase. The Gale Group. • Provides more than one million online summaries of business, industrial, and economic news reports from more than 1,000 publications worldwide. Covers a wide range of material appearing in international trade journals, professional magazines, and newspapers. Time period is 1984 to date, with weekly updates. Inquire as to online cost and availability.

GPO Monthly Catalog. U. S. Government Printing Office. • Contains over 375,000 online citations to U. S. government publications, 1976 to date, with monthly updates. Corresponds to the printed *Monthly Catalog of United States Government Publications*. Inquire as to online cost and availability.

GPO Publications Reference File. U. S. Government Printing Office. • An online guide to federal government publications in print (currently for sale), forthcoming, and recently out-of-print. Biweekly updates. Inquire as to online cost and availability.

Market Share Reporter (MSR) [online]. The Gale Group. • Provides online market share data for individual companies, products, and services, covering all industries. Sources include various publications, trade journals, associations, government agencies, corporate reports, investment research reports, etc. Time period is 1991 to date, with annual updates. Inquire as to online cost and availability.

Tablebase. Responsive Database Services, Inc. • Provides online numerical tabular data from a wide variety of business, organization, and government sources, including 900 trade journals. Includes industry and individual company statistics relating to products, market share, sales forecasts, production, exports, market trends, etc. Time span is 1997 to date. Weekly updates. Inquire as to online cost and availability. (Also available in a CD-ROM version.).

PERIODICALS AND NEWSLETTERS

Internet Connection: Your Guide to Government Resources. Glasser Legalworks. • 10 times a year. $89.00 per year. Newsletter (print) devoted to finding free or low-cost U. S. Government information on the Internet. Provides detailed descriptions of government Web sites.

STATISTICS SOURCES

Business Statistics of the United States. Courtenay M. Slater, editor. Bernan Associates. • 1999. $74.00. Fifth edition. Based on *Business Statistics*, formerly issue by the Bureau of Economic Analysis, U. S. Department of Commerce. Provides basic data for a wide variety of U. S. industries, services, and economic indicators. Most statistics are shown annually for 29 years and monthly for the most recent four years.

County and City Data Book, a Statistical Abstract Supplement. U.S. Bureau of the Census. Available from U.S. Government Printing Office. • 1994. $60.00.

County and City Extra: Annual Metro, City and County Data Book. Mark Littman and Deirdre A. Gaquin. Bernan Press. • 1999. $109.00. Updates and augments data published irregularly in print form by the U. S. Census Bureau in *County and City Data Book*. Covers "every state, county, metropolitan area, and congressional district in the United States, as well as all U. S. cities with a 1990 population of 25,000 or more." Contains a wide range tic maps.

County Business Patterns. Available from U. S. Government Printing Office. • Irregular. 52 issues containing annual data for each state, the District of Columbia, and a U. S. Summary. Produced by U.S. Bureau of the Census (http://www.census.gov). Provides local establishment and employment statistics by industry.

Gale Book of Averages. The Gale Group. • 1994. $70.00. Contains 1,100-1,200 statistical averages on a variety of topics, with references to published sources. Subjects include business, labor, consumption, crime, and other areas of contemporary society.

Historical Statistics of the United States, Colonial Times to 1970: A Statistical Abstract Supplement. U.S. Bureau of the Census. Available from U.S. Government Printing Office. • 1975. $79.00. Two volumes.

International Financial Statistics. International Monetary Fund, Publications Services. • Monthly. Individuals, $246.00 per year; libraries, $123.00 per year. Includes a wide variety of current data for individual countries in Europe and elsewhere. Annual issue available. Editions available in French and Spanish.

Main Economic Indicators. OECD Publication and Information Center. • Monthly. $450.00 per year. "The essential source of timely statistics for OECD member countries." Includes a wide variety of business, economic, and industrial data for the 29 OECD nations.

Main Economic Indicators: Historical Statistics. OECD Publications and Information Center. • Annual. $50.00.

Manufacturers' Shipments, Inventories, and Orders. Available from U. S. Government Printing Office. • Monthly. $70.00 per year. Issued by Bureau of the Census, U. S. Department of Commerce. Includes monthly *Advance Report on Durable Goods*. Provides data on production, value, shipments, and consumption for a wide variety of manufactured products. (Current Industrial Reports, M3-1.).

Metropolitan Life Insurance Co. Statistical Bulletin SB. Metropolitan Life Insurance Co. • Quarterly. Individuals, $50.00 per year. Covers a wide range of social, economic and demographic health concerns.

Monthly Bulletin of Statistics. United Nations Publications. • Monthly. $295.00 per year. Provides current data for about 200 countries on a wide variety of economic, industrial, and demographic subjects. Compiled by United Nations Statistical Office.

Places, Towns, and Townships, 1998. Deirdre A. Gaquin and Richard W. Dodge, editors. Bernan Press. • 1997. $89.00. Second edition. Presents demographic and economic statistics from the U. S. Census Bureau and other government sources for places, cities, towns, villages, census designated places, and minor civil divisions. Contains more than 60 data categories.

Social Indicators of Development. John Hopkins University Press. • 1996. $26.95. Provides social and economic statistics for over 170 countries. Includes population, labor force, income, poverty level, natural resources, medical care, education, the environment, and expenditures on living essentials. Covers a 30-year period. (World Bank Series).

Social Statistics of the United States. Mark S. Littman, editor. Bernan Press. • 2000. $65.00. Includes statistical data on population growth, labor force, occupations, environmental trends, leisure time use, income, poverty, taxes, and other economic or demographic topics.

The Sourcebook of ZIP Code Demographics. Available from The Gale Group. • 2000. $495.00. 15th edition. Published by CACI Marketing Systems. Presents detailed statistical profiles of every ZIP code in America, based on the 1990 census. Each profile contains data on more than 70 variables.

State and Metropolitan Area Data Book. Available from U. S. Government Printing Office. • 1998. $31.00. Issued by the U. S. Bureau of the Census. Presents a wide variety of statistical data for U. S. regions, states, counties, metropolitan areas, and central cities, with ranking tables. Time period is 1970 to 1990.

Statistical Abstract of the United States. Available from U. S. Government Printing Office. • Annual. $51.00. Issued by the U. S. Bureau of the Census.

Statistical Abstract of the World. The Gale Group. • 1997. $80.00. Third edition. Provides data on a wide variety of economic, social, and political topics for about 200 countries. Arranged by country.

Statistical Forecasts of the United States. The Gale Group. • 1995. $99.00. Second edition. Provides both long-term and short-term statistical forecasts relating to basic items in the U. S.: population, employment, labor, crime, education, and health care. Data in the form of charts, graphs, and tables has been taken from a wide variety of government and private sources. Includes a subject index and an "Index of Forecast by Year.".

Statistical Handbook on Women in America. Cynthia M. Taeuber, editor. Oryx Press. • 1996. $65.00. Includes data on demographics, employment, earnings, economic status, educational status, marriage, divorce, household units, health, and other topics. (Statistical Handbook Series).

A Statistical Portrait of the United States: Social Conditions and Trends. Mark S. Littman, editor. Bernan Press. • 1998. $89.00. Covers "social, economic, and environmental trends in the United States over the past 25 years." Includes statistical tables, graphs, and analysis relating to such topics as population, income, poverty, wealth, labor, housing, education, healthcare, air/water quality, and government.

Statistical Yearbook. United Nations Publications. • Annual. $125.00. Contains statistics for about 200 countries on a wide variety of economic, industrial, and demographic topics. Compiled by United Nations Statistical Office.

Survey of Current Business. Available from U. S. Government Printing Office. • Monthly. $49.00 per year. Issued by Bureau of Economic Analysis, U. S. Department of Commerce. Presents a wide variety of business and economic data.

World Bank Atlas. The World Bank, Office of the Publisher. • Annual. Price on application. Contains "color maps, charts, and graphs representing the main social, economic, and environmental indicators for 209 countries and territories" (publisher).

World Development Indicators. World Bank, The Office of the Publisher. • Annual. $60.00. Provides data and information on the people, economy, environment, and markets of 148 countries. Emphasis is on statistics relating to major development issues.

World Statistics Pocketbook. United Nations Publications. • Annual $10.00.

OTHER SOURCES

Business & Company Resource Center. The Gale Group. • Fee-based Web site provides a wide range of business, industry, and specific company information. Access is offered to trade journal articles, market research data, insider trading activity, major shareholder data, corporate histories, emerging technology reports, corporate earnings estimates, press releases, and other sources. Provides detailed company profiles, industry overviews, and rankings. Offers integration of Predicasts PROMT, Newsletters ASAP, Investext Plus, Business Index ASAP, Brands and Their Companies, and other databases (many have full text).

Business Rankings Annual. The Gale Group. • Annual. $305.00.Two volumes. Compiled by the Business Library Staff of the Brooklyn Public Library. This is a guide to lists and rankings appearing in major business publications. The top ten names are listed in each case.

Commercial Atlas and Marketing Guide. Rand McNally. • Annual. $395.00. Includes maps and marketing data: population, transportation, communication, and local area business statistics. Provides information on more than 128,000 U.S. locations.

FedWorld: A Program of the United States Department of Commerce. National Technical Information Service. • Web site offers "a comprehensive central access point for searching, locating, ordering, and acquiring government and business information." Emphasis is on searching the Web pages, databases, and government reports of a wide variety of federal agencies. Fees: Free.

FirstGov: Your First Click to the U. S. Government. General Services Administration. • Free Web site provides extensive links to federal agencies covering a wide variety of topics, such as agriculture, business, consumer safety, education, the environment, government jobs, grants, health, social security, statistics sources, taxes, technology, travel, and world affairs. Also provides links to federal forms, including IRS tax forms. Searching is offered, both keyword and advanced.

InSite 2. Intelligence Data/Thomson Financial. • Fee-based Web site consolidates information in a "Base Pack" consisting of Business InSite, Market InSite, and Company InSite. Optional databases are Consumer InSite, Health and Wellness InSite, Newsletter InSite, and Computer InSite. Includes fulltext content from more than 2,500 trade publications, journals, newsletters, newspapers, analyst reports, and other sources. Continuous updating. Formerly produced by The Gale Group.

MarketingClick Network: American Demographics. Intertec Publishing, a Primedia Co. • Web site provides full-text articles from *American Demographics*, *Marketing Tools*, and *Forecast*, with keyword searching. The *Marketing Tools Directory* can also be searched online, listing suppliers of products, information, and services for advertising, market research, and marketing. Fees: Free.

STATISTICS, VITAL

See: VITAL STATISTICS

STATUTES

See: LAWS

STEAM HEATING

See: HEATING AND VENTILATION

STEAMSHIP LINES

See also: SHIPS, SHIPPING AND SHIPBUILDING

DIRECTORIES

The Cruise Directory. Available from Informa Publishing Group Ltd. • Annual. $128.00. Published in the UK by Lloyd's List (http://www.lloydslist.com). Includes detailed information on cruise operators worldwide, individual cruise ship onboard facilities/features, ports capable of handling cruise ships, agents, ship builders/repairers, and equipment manufacturers.

Ford's Freighter Travel Guide and Waterways of the world. Ford's Travel Guides. • Semiannual. $24.00 per year. Describes freighters with passenger accommodations. Formerly *Ford's Freighter Travel Guide*.

Official Cruise Guide. Cahners Travel Group. • Annual. $85.00. Provides detailed information on more than 375 cruise ships and 150 cruise lines worldwide. Includes color coded deck plans, booking information, and fare schedules.

Star Service: The Critical Guide to Hotels and Cruise Ships. Cahners Travel Group. • $249.00. Looseleaf. Quarterly supplements. Provides "honest and unbiased descriptions of accommodations, facilities, amenities, ambience, appearance, and service" for more than 10,000 hotels worldwide and 150 cruise ships. Ship information includes history, passenger profiles, crew profiles, and other data.

ENCYCLOPEDIAS AND DICTIONARIES

Dictionary of Marine Technology. Cyril Hughes. Available from Informa Publishing Group Ltd. • 1997. $108.00. Published in the UK by Lloyd's List (http://www.lloydslist.com). Includes more than 1,000 terms and acronyms in the fields of ship operation, technology, marine construction, maritime safety, environmental issues, and government regulation of shipping.

Dictionary of Shipping Terms. Peter Brodie. Available from Informa Publishing Group Ltd. • 1997. $57.00. Third edition. Published in the UK by Lloyd's List (http://www.lloydslist.com). Defines more than 2,000 words, phrases, and abbreviations related to the shipping and maritime industries.

Macmillan Encyclopedia of Transportation. Available from The Gale Group. • 2000. $375.00. Six volumes. Published by Macmillan Reference USA. Covers the business, technology, and history of transportation on land, on water, in the air, and in space. Includes definitions, cross-references, and 200 color illustrations.

INTERNET DATABASES

CDC Vessel Sanitation Program (VSP): Charting a Healthier Course. U. S. Centers for Disease Control and Prevention. Phone: (770)488-7333 Fax: 888-232-6789 E-mail: vsp@cdc.gov • URL: http://www.cdc.gov/nceh/vsp/vsp.htm • Web site provides details of unannounced sanitation inspections of individual cruise ships arriving at U. S. ports. Includes detailed results of the most recent inspection of each ship and results of inspections taking place in years past. There are lists of "Ships Inspected Past 2 Months" and "Ships with Not Satisfactory Scores" (passing grade is 85). CDC standards cover drinking water, food, and general cleanliness. Online searching is possible by ship name, inspection date, and numerical scores. Fees: Free.

PERIODICALS AND NEWSLETTERS

Cruise Travel: Ships, Ports, Schedules, Prices. World Publishing Co. • Bimonthly. $23.94 per year.

Summary of Sanitation Inspections of International Cruise Ships. U. S. Public Health Service, Centers for Disease Control and Prevention (CDC). • Biweekly. Apply. "All passenger cruise ships arriving at U. S. ports are subject to unannounced inspection..to achieve levels of sanitation that will minimize the potential for gastrointestinal disease outbreaks on these ships." Individual ships are listed, with sanitation rating and date of inspection. (CDC Document No. 510051.).

Travel Weekly. Cahners Travel Group. • Weekly. $220.00 per year. Includes cruise guides, a weekly "Business Travel Update," and special issues devoted to particular destinations and areas. Edited mainly for travel agents and tour operators.

TRADE/PROFESSIONAL ASSOCIATIONS

Chamber of Shipping of America. 1730 M. St., N.W., Suite 407, Washington, DC 20036. Phone: (202)775-4399 Fax: (202)659-3795.

OTHER SOURCES

List of Shipowners, Managers, and Managing Agents. Available from Fairplay Publications, Inc. • Annual. $270.00, including 10 updates per year. Published in the UK by Lloyd's Register-Fairplay Ltd. Lists 40,000 shipowners, managers, and agents worldwide. Cross-referenced with *Lloyd's Register of Ships.*

Lloyd's Cruise International. Available from Informa Publishing Group Ltd. • Bimonthly. $198.00 per year. Published in the UK by Lloyd's List (http://www.lloydslist.com). Edited for management professionals in the cruise ship industry. Covers industry trends, technical/equipment developments, regulatory issues, new cruise ships, ship management, cruise marketing, and related topics.

Lloyd's Register of Ships. Available from Fairplay Publications, Inc. • Annual. $982.00. Three volumes and 10 cumulative supplements. Published in the UK by Lloyd's Register-Fairplay Ltd. Provides detailed information on more than 80,000 seagoing merchant ships of the world. Includes name, former names if any, date when built, owner, registration, tonnage, cargo capabilities, mechanical details, and other ship data.

Lloyd's Ship Manager. Available from Informa Publishing Group Ltd. • Monthly. $251.00 per year, including annual supplementary guides and directories. Published in the UK by Lloyd's List (http://www.lloydslist.com). Covers all management, technical, and operational aspects of ocean-going shipping.

Register of International Shipowning Groups. Available from Fairplay Publications, Inc. • Three times a year. $697.00 per year. Published in the UK by Lloyd's Register-Fairplay Ltd. "Provides intelligence on shipowners and managers, their subsidiary and associate companies, and owners' representatives." Includes detailed information on individual ships.

Ship Management. Malcolm Willingale and others. Available from Informa Publishing Group Ltd. • 1998. $105.00. Third edition. Published in the UK by Lloyd's List (http://www.lloydslist.com). Covers recruitment of personnel, training, quality control, liability, safety, responsibilities of ship managers, and other topics.

STEEL FOUNDRIES

See: FOUNDRIES

STEEL INDUSTRY

See: IRON AND STEEL INDUSTRY

STENOGRAPHERS

See: OFFICE PRACTICE

STENOGRAPHY

See: SHORTHAND

STEREOPHONIC SOUND

See: HIGH FIDELITY/STEREO

STOCK AND STOCK BREEDING

See: LIVESTOCK INDUSTRY

STOCK BROKERS

GENERAL WORKS

The Death of the Banker: The Decline and Fall of the Great Financial Dynasties and the Triumph of the Small Investor. Ron Chernow. Vintage Books. • 1997. $12.00. Contains three essays: "J. Pierpont Morgan," "The Warburgs," and "The Death of the Banker" (discusses the decline of banks in personal finance and the rise of mutual funds and stock brokers).

How to Avoid Financial Fraud. C. Edgar Murray. American Institute for Economic Research. • 1999. $3.00. Provides concise discussions of fraud victims, perpetrators, and sales tactics. Also includes practical advice on "Selecting a Financial Planner" and "Selecting a Broker." Contains a directory of state securities regulators and a glossary defining various fraudulant financial schemes. (Economic Education Bulletin.).

License to Steal: The Secret World of Wall Street and the Systematic Plundering of the American Investor. Anonymous and Timothy Harper. HarperCollins Publishers, Inc. • 1999. $26.00. A former stockbroker explains how brokers use persuavive and sometimes shady techniques to keep effective control of customers' accounts, regardless of losses. (HarperBusiness.).

Never Call Your Broker on Monday: And 300 Other Financial Lessons You Can't Afford Not to Know. Nancy Dunnan. HarperCollins Publishers. • 1996. $8.50. Presents a wide range of personal finance advice, covering investments, insurance, wills, credit, real estate, etc.

Secrets of the Street: The Dark Side of Making Money. Gene Marcial. McGraw-Hill. • 1996. $10.95. Explains how the small, individual investor can be taken advantage of by Wall Street professionals.

Smart Questions to Ask Your Financial Advisers. Lynn Brenner. Bloomberg Press. • 1997. $19.95. Provides practical advice on how to deal with financial planners, stockbrokers, insurance agents, and lawyers. Some of the areas covered are investments, estate planning, tax planning, house buying, prenuptial agreements, divorce arrangements, loss of a job, and retirement. (Bloomberg Personal Bookshelf Series Library.).

Women of the Street: Making It on Wall Street-the World's Toughest Business. Sue Herera. John Wiley and Sons, Inc. • 1997. $24.95. The author is a CNBC business television anchorperson.

BIOGRAPHICAL SOURCES

Who's Who in Finance and Industry. Marquis Who's Who. • Biennial. $295.00. Provides over 22,400 concise biographies of business leaders in all fields.

DIRECTORIES

Business and Finance Career Directory. Visible Ink Press. • 1992. $17.95.

Corporate Finance Sourcebook: The Guide to Major Capital Investment Source and Related Financial Services. R. R. Bowker. • Annual. $625.00. Lists more than 3,550 sources of corporate capital: investment bankers, securities firms, pension management companies, trust companies, insurance companies, and private lenders. Includes the names of over 13,000 key personnel.

The Discount Brokerage Directory. Mercer, Inc. • Annual. $34.95. Provides information on approximately 90 discount brokers and firms offering stocks and bonds options, commodities, precious metals and other investments at a discount.

Plunkett's Financial Services Industry Almanac: The Leading Firms in Investments, Banking, and Financial Information. Available from Plunkett Research, Ltd. • Annual. $245.00. Discusses important trends in various sectors of the financial industry. Five hundred major banking, credit card, investment, and financial services companies are profiled.

Plunkett's On-Line Trading, Finance, and Investment Web Sites Almanac. Plunkett Research, Ltd. • Annual. $149.99. Provides profiles and usefulness rankings of financial Web sites. Sites are rated from 1 to 5 for specific uses. Includes diskette.

Retail Broker-Dealer Directory. Securities Data Publishing. • Annual. $385.00. Provides detailed information on more than 1,300 retail stockbrokers, including key personnel, revenue, capital, and assets under management. (Securities Data Publishing is a unit of Thomson Financial.).

Standard and Poor's Security Dealers of North America. Standard & Poor's. • Semiannual. $480.00 per year; with *Supplements* every six weeks, $590.00 per year. Geographical listing of over 12,000 stock, bond, and commodity dealers.

Zacks Analyst Directory: Listed by Broker. Zacks Investment Research. • Quarterly. $395.00 per year. Lists stockbroker investment analysts and gives the names of major U. S. corporations covered by those analysts.

FINANCIAL RATIOS

Almanac of Business and Industrial Financial Ratios. Leo Troy. Prentice Hall. • Annual. $99.95. Contains financial ratios derived from federal tax returns. Ratios for each of about 200 industries are arranged according to company asset size.

The Financial Elite: Database of Financial Services Companies. Donnelley Marketing. • Quarterly. Price on application. Formerly compiled by Database America. Provides current information on CD-ROM for 500,000 major U. S. companies offering financial services. Data for each firm includes year started, type of financial service, annual revenues, name of top executive, and number of employees.

Major Financial Institutions of the World. Available from The Gale Group. • 2001. $855.00. Fourth edition. Two volumes. Published by Graham & Whiteside. Contains detailed information on more than 7,500 important financial institutions in various countries. Includes banks, investment companies, and insurance companies.

HANDBOOKS AND MANUALS

Audits of Brokers and Dealers in Securities. American Institute of Certified Public Accountants. • $33.00. Fourth edition.

Best Practices for Financial Advisors. Mary Rowland. • 1997. $40.00. Provides advice for professional financial advisors on practice management, ethics, marketing, and legal concerns. (Bloomberg Professional Library.).

Kiss Your Stockbroker Goodbye: A Guide to Independent Investing. John G. Wells. St. Martin's Press. • 1997. $25.95. The author believes that the small investor is throwing money away by using full-commission brokers when discount brokers and many sources of information are easily available. Contains separate chapters on stocks, bonds, mutual funds, asset allocation, financial planners, and related topics. Wells is a securities analyst (CFA) and portfolio manager.

NASD Manual. National Association of Securities Dealers, Inc. Available from CCH, Inc. • Quarterly. $430.00 per year.

Securities Crimes. Marvin Pickholz. West Group. • $145.00. Looseleaf service. Periodic supplementation. Analyzes the enfo of federal securities laws from the viewpoint of the defendant. Discusses Securities and Exchange Commission (SEC) investigations and federal sentencing guidelines.

Successful Cold Call Selling. Lee Boyan. AMACOM. • 1989. $16.95. Second edition.

INTERNET DATABASES

Web Finance: Covering the Electronic Evolution of Finance. Securities Data Publishing. Phone: (212)765-5311 or 800-455-5844 Fax: (212)321-2336 E-mail: webfinance@tfn.com • URL: http://www.webfinance.net • Bi-weekly print and daily web-site publication of financial services on the Web, including financial links, archives, brokerage stocks, deal financing, and other financial and investment news and information.

PERIODICALS AND NEWSLETTERS

Asset Management. Dow Jones Financial Publishing Corp. • Bimonthly. $345.00 per year. Covers the management of the assets of affluent, high net worth investors. Provides information on various financial products and services.

Bank Investment Product News. Institutional Investor, Newsletters Div. • Weekly. $1,195.00 per year. Newsletter. Edited for bank executives. Covers the marketing and regulation of financial products sold through banks, such as mutual funds, stock brokerage services, and insurance.

Bloomberg: A Magazine for Market Professionals. Bloomberg L.P. • Monthly. Free to qualified personnel. Edited for securities dealers and investment managers.

Financial Services Marketing: Finding, Keeping, and Profiting From the Right Customers. American Banker. • Bimonthly. Price on application. Covers marketing for a variety of financial institutions, including banks, investment companies, securities dealers, and credit unions.

Investment Advisor. Dow Jones Financial Publishing Corp. • Monthly. $79.00 per year. Edited for professional investment advisors, financial planners, stock brokers, bankers, and others concerned with the management of assets.

Investment Dealers' Digest. Securities Data Publishing. • Weekly. $750.00 per year. Covers financial news, trends, new products, people, private placements, new issues of securities, and other aspects of the investment business. Includes feature stories. (Securities Data Publishing is a unit of Thomson Financial.).

Investment Management Weekly. Securities Data Publishing. • Weekly. $1,370.00 per year. Newsletter. Edited for money managers and other investment professionals. Covers personnel news, investment strategies, and industry trends. (Securities Data Publishing is a unit of Thomson Financial.).

Investment News: The Weekly Newspaper for Financial Advisers. Crain Communications, Inc. • Weekly. $38.00 per year. Edited for both personal and institutional investment advisers, planners, and managers.

Journal of Private Portfolio Management. Institutional Investor. • Quarterly. $280.00 per year. Edited for managers of wealthy individuals' investment portfolios.

On Wall Street. Securities Data Publishing. • Monthly. $96.00 per year. Edited for securities dealers. Includes articles on financial planning, retirement planning, variable annuities, and money management, with special coverage of 401(k) plans and IRAs. (Securities Data Publishing is a unit of Thomson Financial.).

Operations Management. Institutional Investor. • Weekly. $2,105.00 per year. Newsletter. Edited for managers of securities clearance and settlement at financial institutions. Covers new products, technology, legalities, management practices, and other topics related to securities processing.

Registered Representative. Intertec Publishing Corp. • Monthly. $48.00 per year.

Research: All a Broker Needs to Succeed. Research Holdings, Ltd. • Monthly. $35.00 per year. Provides advice and information for full-service stockbrokers.

The Safe Money Report. Weiss Ratings, Inc. • Monthly. $148.00 per year. Newsletter. Provides financial advice and current safety ratings of various banks, savings and loan companies, insurance companies, and securities dealers.

Securities Arbitration Commentator: Covering Significant Issues and Events in Securities/ Commodities Arbitration. Richard P. Ryder. • Monthly. $348.00 per year. Newsletter. Edited for attorneys and other professionals concerned with securities arbitration.

Securities Industry News. American Banker. • Weekly. $275.00 per year. Covers securities dealing and processing, including regulatory compliance, shareholder services, human resources, transaction clearing, and technology.

Ticker: Tools for the Investment Professional. Individual Investor Group, Inc. • Bimonthly. Price on application. A trade journal for stockbrokers.

Traders Magazine. Securities Data Publishing. • Monthly. $60.00 per year. Edited for institutional buy side and sell side equity traders. Covers industry news, market trends, regulatory developments, and personnel news. Serves as the official publication of the Security Traders Association. (Securities Data Publishing is a unit of Thomson Financial.).

Wall Street and Technology: For Senior-Level Executives in Technology and Information Management in Securities and Invesment Firms. Miller Freeman, Inc. • Monthly. $99.00 per year. Includes material on the use of computers in technical investment strategies. Formerly *Wall Computer Review.*

Wall Street Letter: Newsweekly for Investment Banking and Brokerage Community. Institutional Investor. • Weekly. $2,665.00 per year. Newsletter for stock brokers and companies providing services for stock brokers. Emphasis is on regulatory matters.

PRICE SOURCES

The Discount Brokerage Survey: Stocks. Mercer, Inc. • 1994. Price on application. Quotes prices (commissions) charged by individual discount stockbrokers for 22 typical trades.

STATISTICS SOURCES

Standard & Poor's Industry Surveys. Standard & Poor's. • Semiannual. $1,800.00. Two looseleaf volumes. Includes monthly supplements. Provides detailed, individual surveys of 52 major industry groups. Each survey is revised on a semiannual basis. Also includes "Monthly Investment Review" (industry group investment analysis) and monthly "Trends & Projections" (economic analysis).

U. S. Industry and Trade Outlook: The McGraw-Hill Companies and the U.S. Department of Commerce/ International Trade Administration. Datapso Research Corp. • Annual. $69.95. Produced by the International Trade Administration, U. S. Department of Commerce, in a "public-private" partnership with DRI/McGraw-Hill and Standard & Poor's. Provides basic data, outlook for the current year, and "Long-Term Prospects" (five-year projections) for a wide variety of products and services. Includes high technology industries. Formerly *U. S. Industrial Outlook.*

United States Securities and Exchange Commission Annual Report. U.S. Government Printing Office. • Annual. The Commission maintains a Web site at http://www.sec.gov.

TRADE/PROFESSIONAL ASSOCIATIONS

National Association of Securities Dealers. 1735 K St., N.W., Washington, DC 20006-1506. Phone: (202)728-8000 Fax: (202)293-6260 • URL: http://www.nasdr.com/1000.asp.

Securities Industry Association. 120 Broadway, New York, NY 10271-0080. Phone: (212)608-1500 Fax: (212)608-1604 E-mail: info@sia.com • URL: http://www.sia.com.

Security Traders Association. One World Trade Center, Suite 4511, New York, NY 10048. Phone: (212)524-0484 Fax: (212)321-3449.

OTHER SOURCES

Andrews' Professional Liability Litigation Reporter. Andrews Publications. • Monthly. $550.00 per year. Provides reports on lawsuits against attorneys, accountants, and investment professionals.

Broker-Dealer Regulation. David A. Lipton. West Group. • $145.00 per year. Looseleaf service. Annual supplementation. Focuses on the basics of stockbroker license application procedure, registration, regulation, and responsibilities.

General Securities Registered Representative: Self-Study Course. New York Institute of Finance. • Looseleaf. Intended for candidates seeking to become licensed stockbrokers.

Information, Finance, and Services USA. The Gale Group. • 2001. $240.00. Replaces *Service Industries USA* and *Finance, Insurance, and Real Estate USA.* Presents statistics and projections relating to economic activity in a wide variety of non-manufacturing areas.

Thriving as a Broker in the 21st Century. Thomas J. Dorsey. Bloomberg Press. • 1999. $39.95. Provides advice for stockbrokers operating in today's rapidly changing financial environment.

STOCK DIVIDENDS

See: DIVIDENDS

STOCK EXCHANGES

See also: STOCKS

GENERAL WORKS

Financial Markets and Institutions. Jeff Madura. South-Western College Publishing Co. • 2000. $91.95. Fifth edition. (SWC-Economics Series).

It was a Very Good Year: Extraordinary Moments in Stock Market History. Martin S. Fridson. John Wiley and Sons, Inc. • 1997. $29.95. Provides details on what happened during each of the ten best years for the stock market since 1900.

ALMANACS AND YEARBOOKS

Emerging Markets Analyst. • Monthly. $895.00 per year. Provides an annual overview of the emerging financial markets in 24 countries of Latin America, Asia, and Europe. Includes data on international mutual funds and closed-end funds.

Irwin International Almanac: Business and Investments. McGraw-Hill Professional. • 1994. $95.00. Second edition. Covers trends in global business and summarizes trading in major foreign securities markets.

BIBLIOGRAPHIES

The American Stock Exchange: A Guide to Information Resources. Carol Z. Womack and Alice C. Littlejohn. Garland Publishing, Inc. • 1995. $15.00. (Research and Information Guides in Business, Industry, and Economic Institutions Series).

DIRECTORIES

American Stock Exchange Directory. CCH, Inc. • 2000. $30.00.

Asia Pacific Securities Handbook. Available from Hoover's, Inc. • Annual. $99.95. Published in Hong Kong. Provides detailed descriptions of stock exchanges in 17 Asia Pacific countries, including Australia, China, Hong Kong, India, Japan, and Singapore. Lists largest public companies and most active stock issues.

Brazil Company Handbook: Data on Major Listed Companies. Hoovers, Inc. • Annual. $49.95. Published by IMF Editora. Contains profiles of publicly traded companies in Brazil. Includes information on local stock exchanges and the nation's economic situation.

Business Organizations, Agencies, and Publications Directory. The Gale Group. • 1999. $425.00. 12th edition. Over 40,000 entries describing 39 types of business information sources. Classified by type of organization, publication, or serviceIncludes state, national, and international agencies and organizations. Master index to names and keywords. Also includes e-mail addresses and web site URL's.

Canada Company Handbook: The Globe and Mail Report on Business. Globe Information Services. • Annual. $49.95. Provides information on 400 Canadian companies. Detailed fiancncial data and rankings are presented for firms listed on the Toronto Stock Exchange.

Handbook of World Stock and Commodity Exchanges. Blackwell Publishers. • Annual. $265.00. Provides detailed information on over 200 stock and commodity exchanges in more than 50 countries.

Mexico Company Handbook: Data on Major Listed Companies. Available from Hoovers, Inc. • Annual. $29.95. Published by IMF Editora. Contains profiles of publicly traded companies in Mexico. Includes information on local stock exchanges and the nation's economic situation.

Trade Directory of Mexico. Mexican Foreign Trade Bank. • Annual. $100.00. Provides information on more than 4,200 Mexican companies involved in foreign trade. Lists forwarding agencies, customs brokers, consulting groups, transportation companies, and other trade-related Mexican organizations.

Venezuela Company Handbook: Data on Major Listed Companies. Hoovers, Inc. • Annual. $29.95. Published by IMF Editora. Contains profiles of publicly traded companies in Venezuela. Includes information on local stock exchanges and the nation's economic situation. Text in English.

ENCYCLOPEDIAS AND DICTIONARIES

Common Stock Newspaper Abbreviations and Trading Symbols. Howard R. Jarrell. Scarecrow Press, Inc. • 1989. $55.00. Gives the meanings of financial page company name abbreviations and stock symbols.

Common Stock Newspaper Abbreviations and Trading Symbols: Supplement One. Howard R. Jarrell. Scarecrow Press, Inc. • 1991. $35.00. Provides changes and new listings occurring since the publication of Jarrell's original volume in 1989.

International Encyclopedia of the Stock Market. Michael Sheimo and Andreas Loizou, editors. Fitzroy Dearborn Publishers. • 1999. $275.00. Two volumes. Covers the terminology of stock exchanges around the world. Individual country entries provide details of stock exchange conditions, practices, regulation, and brokers.

HANDBOOKS AND MANUALS

NASD Manual. National Association of Securities Dealers, Inc. Available from CCH, Inc. • Quarterly. $430.00 per year.

INTERNET DATABASES

U. S. Securities and Exchange Commission. Phone: 800-732-0330 or (202)942-7040 Fax: (202)942-9634 E-mail: webmaster@sec.gov • URL: http://www.sec.gov • SEC Web site offers free access through EDGAR to text of official corporate filings, such as annual reports (10-K), quarterly reports (10-Q), and proxies. (EDGAR is "Electronic Data Gathering, Analysis, and Retrieval System.") An example is given of how to obtain executive compensation data from proxies. Text of the daily *SEC News Digest* is offered, as are links to other government sites, non-government market regulators, and U. S. stock exchanges. Search facilities are extensive. Fees: Free.

Wall Street Journal Interactive Edition. Dow Jones & Co., Inc. Phone: 800-369-2834 or (212)416-2000 Fax: (212)416-2658 E-mail: inquiries@interactive.wsj.com • URL: http://www.wsj.com • Fee-based Web site providing online searching of worldwide information from the *The Wall Street Journal.* Includes "Company Snapshots," "The Journal's Greatest Hits," "Index to Market Data," "14-Day Searchable Archive," "Journal Links," etc. Financial price quotes are available. Fees: $49.00 per year; $29.00 per year to print subscribers.

PERIODICALS AND NEWSLETTERS

Financial History: Chronicling the History of America's Capital Markets. Museum of American Financial History. • Quarterly. Membership. Contains articles on early stock and bond markets and trading in the U. S., with photographs and other illustrations. Current trading in rare and unusual, obsolete stock and bond certificates is featured. Formerly *Friends or Financial History.*

Financial Sentinel: Your Beacon to the World of Investing. Gulf Atlantic Publishing, Inc. • Monthly. $29.95 per year. Provides "The only complete listing of all OTC Bulletin Board stocks traded, with all issues listed on the Nasdaq SmallCap Market, the Toronto, and Vancouver Stock Exchanges." Also includes investment advice and recommendations of small capitalization stocks.

The Wall Street Journal. Dow Jones & Co., Inc. • Daily. $175.00 per year. Covers news and trends relating to business, industry, finance, the economy, and international commerce. Provides extensive price and other data for the securities, commodity, options, futures, foreign exchange, and money markets.

STATISTICS SOURCES

American Stock Exchange Fact Book. NASD MediaSource. • Annual. $20.00. Published by the American Stock Exchange, Inc. Contains statistical data relating to the American Stock Exchange. Also provides the address and phone number for each company listed on the Exchange.

American Stock Exchange Weekly Bulletin. Nasdaq-AMEX Market Group. • Weekly. $20.00 per year. Looseleaf service.

Emerging Stock Markets Factbook. International Finance Corporation, Capital Market Dept. • Annual. $100.00. Published by the International Finance Corporation (IFC). Provides statistical profiles of more than 26 emerging stock markets in various countries of the world. Includes regional, composite, and industry indexes.

Financial Market Trends. Organization for Economic Cooperation and Development. • Three times a year. $100.00 per year. Provides analysis of developments and trends in international and national capital markets. Includes charts and graphs on interest rates, exchange rates, stock market indexes, bank stock indexes, trading volumes, and loans outstanding. Data from OECD countries includes international direct investment, bank profitability, institutional investment, and privatization.

International Guide to Securities Market Indices. Henry Shilling, editor. Fitzroy Dearborn Publishers. • 1996. $140.00. Describes 400 stock market, bond market, and other financial price indexes maintained in various countries of the world (300 of the indexes are described in detail, including graphs and 10-year data).

Nasdaq Fact Book and Company Directory. National Association of Security Dealers, Inc. Corporate Communications. • Annual. $20.00. Contains statistical data relating to the Nasdaq Stock Market. Also provides corporate address, phone, symbol, stock price, and trading volume information for more than 5,000 securities traded through the National Association of Securities Dealers Automated Quotation System (Nasdaq), including Small-Cap Issues. Includes indexing by Standard Industrial Classification (SIC) number.

New York Stock Exchange Fact Book. Available from Hoover's, Inc. • Annual. $9.95. Published by the New York Stock Exchange, Inc. Contains statistical data relating to the New York Stock

Exchange. Includes information on new listings and name changes.

SRC Green Book of 35-Year Charts. • Annual. $119.00. Chart book presents statistical information on the stocks of 400 leading companies over a 35-year period. Each full page chart is in semi-log format to avoid visual distortion. Also includes charts of 12 leading market averages or indexes and 39 major industry groups.

TRADE/PROFESSIONAL ASSOCIATIONS

Securities Industry Association. 120 Broadway, New York, NY 10271-0080. Phone: (212)608-1500 Fax: (212)608-1604 E-mail: info@sia.com • URL: http://www.sia.com.

OTHER SOURCES

American Stock Exchange Guide. CCH, Inc. • Monthly. $540.00 per year. Contains exchange rules and regulations, constitution, and a directory.

Factiva. Dow Jones Reuters Business Interactive, LLC. • Fee-based Web site provides "global news and business information through Web sites and content integration solutions." Includes Dow Jones and Reuters newswires, The Wall Street Journal, and more than 7,000 other sources of current news, historical articles, market research reports, and investment analysis. Content includes 96 major U. S. newspapers, 900 non-English sources, trade publications, media transcripts, country profiles, news photos, etc.

The Great Game: The Emergence of Wall Street as a World Power, 1653-2000. John S. Gordon. Scribner. • 1999. $25.00. Provides a history of U. S. financial markets, featuring such key figures as Alexander Hamilton, Commodore Vanderbilt, J. P. Morgan, Charles Merrill, and Michael Milken.

New York Stock Exchange Guide. CCH, Inc. • Monthly. $634.00 per year.

Nexis.com. Lexis-Nexis Group. • Fee-based Web site offers searching of about 2.8 billion documents in some 30,000 news, business, and legal information sources. Features include a subject directory covering 1,200 topics in 34 categories and a Company Dossier containing information on more than 500,000 public and private companies. Boolean searching is offered.

100 Years of Wall Street. Charles R. Geisst. McGraw-Hill. • 1999. $29.95. A popularly written, illustrated history of the American stock market. About 200 photographs, charts, cartoons, and reproductions of stock certificates are included.

Wall Street: A History. Charles R. Geisst. Oxford University Press. • 1997. $35.00. Presents the history of the U. S. stock market according to four distinct eras: 1790 to the Civil War, the Civil War to 1929, 1929 to 1954, and from 1954 to recent years.

STOCK INDEX TRADING

See also: FINANCIAL FUTURES TRADING

GENERAL WORKS

Futures Markets. A. G. Malliaris, editor. Edward Elgar Publishing, Inc. • 1997. $450.00. Three volumes. Consists of reprints of 70 articles dating from 1959 to 1993, on futures market volatility, speculation, hedging, stock indexes, portfolio insurance, interest rates, and foreign currencies. (International Library of Critical Writings in Financial Economics.).

Stock Index Options: How to Use and Profit from Indexed Options in Volatile and Uncertain Markets. Scot G. Barenblat and Donald T. Mesler. McGraw-Hill Professional. • 1991. $29.95. Revised editon.

ABSTRACTS AND INDEXES

Business Periodicals Index. H. W. Wilson Co. • Monthly, except August, with quarterly and annual cumulations. Service basis for print edition; CD-ROM edition, $1,495.00 per year.

DIRECTORIES

Futures Guide to Computerized Trading. Futures Magazine, Inc. • Annual. $10.00. "A directory of products and services for the computerized trader." Provides information on computer software applications for commodity traders and money managers, including trading methods and technical analysis.

Futures Magazine SourceBook: The Most Complete List of Exchanges, Companies, Regulators, Organizations, etc., Offering Products and Services to the Futures and Options Industry. Futures Magazine, Inc. • Annual. $19.50. Provides information on commodity futures brokers, trading method services, publications, and other items of interest to futures traders and money managers.

HANDBOOKS AND MANUALS

Derivatives: A Comprehensive Resource for Options, Futures, Interest Rate Swaps, and Mortgage Securities. Fred D. Arditti. Harvard Business School Press. • 1996. $60.00. Published by Harvard Business School Press. Provides detailed explanations of various kinds of financial derivatives (options, futures, swaps, etc.) and their trading tactics, uses, and risks. (Financial Management Association Survey and Synthesis Series).

Handbook of Derivative Instruments: Investment Research, Analysis, and Portfolio Applications. Atsuo Konishi and Ravi E. Dattatreya, editors. McGraw-Hill Professional. • 1996. $80.00. Second revised edition. Contains 41 chapters by various authors on all aspects of derivative securities, including such esoterica as "Inverse Floaters," "Positive Convexity," "Exotic Options," and "How to Use the Holes in Black-Scholes.".

Handbook of Equity Derivatives. Jack C. Francis and others, editors. John Wiley and Sons, Inc. • 1999. $95.00. Contains 27 chapters by various authors. Covers options (puts and calls), stock index futures, warrants, convertibles, over-the-counter options, swaps, legal issues, taxation, etc. (Financial Engineering Series).

Options: The International Guide to Valuation and Trading Strategies. Gordon Gemmill. McGraw-Hill. • 1993. $37.95. Covers valuation techniques for American, European, and Asian options. Trading strategies are discussed for options on currencies, stock indexes, interest rates, and commodities.

Stock Index Futures: Buying and Selling the Market Averages. Charles Sutcliffe. Thomson Learning. • 1998. $37.95. Third edition.

Understanding Financial Derivatives: How to Protect Your Investments. Donald Strassheim. McGraw-Hill Professional. • 1996. $40.00. Covers three basic risk management instruments: options, futures, and swaps. Includes advice on equity index options, financial futures contracts, and over-the-counter derivatives markets.

INTERNET DATABASES

BanxQuote Banking, Mortgage, and Finance Center. BanxQuote, Inc. Phone: 800-765-3000 or (212)643-8000 Fax: (212)643-0020 E-mail: info@banx.com • URL: http://www.banx.com • Web site quotes interest rates paid by banks around the country on various savings products, as well as rates paid by consumers for automobile loans, mortgages, credit cards, home equity loans, and personal loans. Also provided: stock quotes, indexes, stock options, futures trading data, economic indicators, and links to many other financial sites. Daily updates. Fees: Free.

Futures Online. Oster Communications, Inc. Phone: 800-601-8907 or (319)277-1278 Fax: (319)277-7982 • URL: http://www.futuresmag.com • Web site presents updates of *Futures* magazine and links to other futures-related sites. Includes "Futures Industry News," "Technical Talk," "Today's Hot Markets," "Futures Talk" (forums), "Futures Library" (archives, 1993 to date), and other features. Keyword searching is available. Updating: daily. Fees: Free.

ONLINE DATABASES

Wilson Business Abstracts Online. H. W. Wilson Co. • Indexes and abstracts 600 major business periodicals, plus the *Wall Street Journal* and the business section of the *New York Times*. Indexing is from 1982, abstracting from 1990, with the two newspapers included from 1993. Updated weekly. Inquire as to online cost and availability. (*Business Periodicals Index* without abstracts is also available online.).

PERIODICALS AND NEWSLETTERS

Barron's: The Dow Jones Business and Financial Weekly. Dow Jones and Co., Inc. • Weekly. $145.00 per year.

Futures: News, Analysis, and Strategies for Futures, Options, and Derivatives Traders. Futures Magazine, Inc. • Monthly. $39.00 per year. Edited for institutional money managers and traders, brokers, risk managers, and individual investors or speculators. Includes special feature issues on interest rates, technical indicators, currencies, charts, precious metals, hedge funds, and derivatives. Supplements available.

Technical Analysis of Stocks & Commodities: The Trader's Magazine. Technical Analysis, Inc. • 13 times a year. $49.95 per year. Covers use of personal computers for stock trading, price movement analysis by means of charts, and other technical trading methods.

RESEARCH CENTERS AND INSTITUTES

Center for Research in Security Prices. University of Chicago, 725 S. Wells St., Suite 800, Chicago, IL 60607. Phone: (773)702-7467 Fax: (773)753-4797 E-mail: mail@crsp.uchicago.edu • URL: http://www.crsp.com.

STATISTICS SOURCES

Statistical Annual: Interest Rates, Metals, Stock Indices, Options on Financial Futures, Options on Metals Futures. Chicago Board of Trade. • Annual. Includes historical data on GNMA CDR Futures, Cash-Settled GNMA Futures, U. S. Treasury Bond Futures, U. S. Treasury Note Futures, Options on Treasury Note Futures, NASDAQ-100 Futures, Major Market Index Futures, Major Market Index MAXI Futures, Municipal Bond Index Futures, 1,000-Ounce Silver Futures, Options on Silver Futures, and Kilo Gold Futures.

TRADE/PROFESSIONAL ASSOCIATIONS

National Association of Securities Dealers. 1735 K St., N.W., Washington, DC 20006-1506. Phone: (202)728-8000 Fax: (202)293-6260 • URL: http://www.nasdr.com/1000.asp.

Security Traders Association. One World Trade Center, Suite 4511, New York, NY 10048. Phone: (212)524-0484 Fax: (212)321-3449.

STOCK MARKET

See: STOCK EXCHANGES

STOCK MARKET CHARTS

See: TECHNICAL ANALYSIS (FINANCE)

STOCK OFFERINGS, INITIAL

See: NEW ISSUES (FINANCE)

STOCK OPTION CONTRACTS

GENERAL WORKS

Introduction to Futures and Options Markets. John C. Hull. Prentice Hall. • 1997. $94.00. Third edition.

DIRECTORIES

Futures Guide to Computerized Trading. Futures Magazine, Inc. • Annual. $10.00. "A directory of products and services for the computerized trader." Provides information on computer software applications for commodity traders and money managers, including trading methods and technical analysis.

Futures Magazine SourceBook: The Most Complete List of Exchanges, Companies, Regulators, Organizations, etc., Offering Products and Services to the Futures and Options Industry. Futures Magazine, Inc. • Annual. $19.50. Provides information on commodity futures brokers, trading method services, publications, and other items of interest to futures traders and money managers.

ENCYCLOPEDIAS AND DICTIONARIES

International Encyclopedia of Futures and Options. Michael R. Ryder, editor. Fitzroy Dearborn Publishers. • 2000. $275.00. Two volumes. Covers terminology, concepts, events, individuals, and markets.

HANDBOOKS AND MANUALS

Day-Trader's Manual: Theory, Art, and Science of Profitable Short-Term Investing. William F. Eng. John Wiley and Sons, Inc. • 1992. $79.95. Covers short-term trading in stocks, futures, and options. Various technical trading systems are considered.

Derivatives: A Comprehensive Resource for Options, Futures, Interest Rate Swaps, and Mortgage Securities. Fred D. Arditti. Harvard Business School Press. • 1996. $60.00. Published by Harvard Business School Press. Provides detailed explanations of various kinds of financial derivatives (options, futures, swaps, etc.) and their trading tactics, uses, and risks. (Financial Management Association Survey and Synthesis Series).

Handbook of Derivative Instruments: Investment Research, Analysis, and Portfolio Applications. Atsuo Konishi and Ravi E. Dattatreya, editors. McGraw-Hill Professional. • 1996. $80.00. Second revised edition. Contains 41 chapters by various authors on all aspects of derivative securities, including such esoterica as "Inverse Floaters," "Positive Convexity," "Exotic Options," and "How to Use the Holes in Black-Scholes.".

Handbook of Equity Derivatives. Jack C. Francis and others, editors. John Wiley and Sons, Inc. • 1999. $95.00. Contains 27 chapters by various authors. Covers options (puts and calls), stock index futures, warrants, convertibles, over-the-counter options, swaps, legal issues, taxation, etc. (Financial Engineering Series).

Investing in Call Options; An Alternative to Common Stock and Real Estate. James A. Willson. Greenwood Publishing Group, Inc. • 1982. $59.95.

Money Management Strategies for Futures Traders. Nauzer J. Balsara. John Wiley and Sons, Inc. • 1992. $69.95. How to limit risk and avoid catastrophic losses. (Financial Editions Series).

Options: Essential Concepts and Trading Strategies. Options Institute Staff. McGraw-Hill. • 1999. $55.00. Third edition.

Over-the-Counter Derivatives Products: A Guide to Legal Risk Management and Documentation. Robert M. McLaughlin. McGraw-Hill Professional. • 1998. $75.00.

Portfolio Management Formulas: Mathematical Trading Methods for the Futures, Options, and Stock Markets. Ralph Vince. John Wiley and Sons, Inc. • 1990. $85.00. Discusses optimization of trading systems by exploiting the rules of probability and making use of the principles of modern portfolio management theory. Computer programs are included.

Security Options Strategy. Albert I. Bookbinder. Programmed Press. • 1976. $15.00.

Understanding Financial Derivatives: How to Protect Your Investments. Donald Strassheim. McGraw-Hill Professional. • 1996. $40.00. Covers three basic risk management instruments: options, futures, and swaps. Includes advice on equity index options, financial futures contracts, and over-the-counter derivatives markets.

INTERNET DATABASES

BanxQuote Banking, Mortgage, and Finance Center. BanxQuote, Inc. Phone: 800-765-3000 or (212)643-8000 Fax: (212)643-0020 E-mail: info@banx.com • URL: http://www.banx.com • Web site quotes interest rates paid by banks around the country on various savings products, as well as rates paid by consumers for automobile loans, mortgages, credit cards, home equity loans, and personal loans. Also provided: stock quotes, indexes, stock options, futures trading data, economic indicators, and links to many other financial sites. Daily updates. Fees: Free.

Futures Online. Oster Communications, Inc. Phone: 800-601-8907 or (319)277-1278 Fax: (319)277-7982 • URL: http://www.futuresmag.com • Web site presents updates of *Futures* magazine and links to other futures-related sites. Includes "Futures Industry News," "Technical Talk," "Today's Hot Markets," "Futures Talk" (forums), "Futures Library" (archives, 1993 to date), and other features. Keyword searching is available. Updating: daily. Fees: Free.

Thomson Real Time Quotes: Real Fast...Real Free...Real Quotes...Real Time. Thomson Financial. Phone: (212)807-3800 • URL: http://www.thomsonfn.com/ • Web site provides continuous updating of prices for stocks, bonds, mutual funds, and options. Includes headline business news and market analysis. Fees: Free.

PERIODICALS AND NEWSLETTERS

Barron's: The Dow Jones Business and Financial Weekly. Dow Jones and Co., Inc. • Weekly. $145.00 per year.

Derivatives Tactics. Derivative Strategy and Tactics. • Semimonthly. $695.00 per year. Newsletter. Edited for institutional investors. Covers options, swaps, and other financial derivatives.

Financial Trader. Miller Freeman, Inc. • 11 times a year. $160.00 per year. Edited for professional traders. Covers fixed income securities, emerging markets, derivatives, options, futures, and equities.

Futures: News, Analysis, and Strategies for Futures, Options, and Derivatives Traders. Futures Magazine, Inc. • Monthly. $39.00 per year. Edited for institutional money managers and traders, brokers, risk managers, and individual investors or speculators. Includes special feature issues on interest rates, technical indicators, currencies, charts, precious metals, hedge funds, and derivatives. Supplements available.

Option Advisor. Investment Research Institute, Inc. • Monthly. $200.00 per year. Newsletter. Provides specific advice and recommendations for trading in stock option contracts (puts and calls).

Wall Street Transcript: A Professional Publication for the Business and Financial Community. Wall Street Transcript Corp. • Weekly. $1,890.00. per year. Provides reprints of investment research reports.

TRADE/PROFESSIONAL ASSOCIATIONS

Chicago Board Options Exchange. 400 S. LaSalle St., Chicago, IL 60605. Phone: 800-678-4667 or (312)786-5600 Fax: (312)786-7409 • URL: http://www.cboe.com • Members are individuals and firms engaged in the trading of listed options (puts and calls).

OTHER SOURCES

Chicago Board Options Exchange. CCH, Inc. • $539.00 per year. Looseleaf service. Periodic supplementation. Rules, regulations and legal aspects for the trading of puts and calls.

Commodity Futures Law Reports. CCH, Inc. • Semimonthly. $995.00 per year. Looseleaf service. Periodic supplementation. Includes legal aspects of financial futures and stock options trading.

Daily Graphs. Option Guide. Daily Graphs, Inc. • Weekly. $300.00 per year.

Managing Financial Risk with Forwards, Futures, Options, and Swaps. American Management Association Extension Institute. • Looseleaf. $130.00. Self-study course. Emphasis is on practical explanations, examples, and problem solving. Quizzes and a case study are included.

The Options Workbook: Proven Strategies from a Market Wizard. Anthony J. Saliba. Dearborn Financial Publishing. • 2001. $40.00. Emphasis is on computerized trading on the Chicago Board Options Exchange. Includes information on specific trading strategies.

STOCK OWNERSHIP PLANS

See: EMPLOYEE BENEFIT PLANS; EMPLOYEE STOCK OWNERSHIP PLANS; EXECUTIVE COMPENSATION

STOCKBROKERS

See: STOCK BROKERS

STOCKHOLDERS

See also: INSIDER TRADING

ABSTRACTS AND INDEXES

Business Periodicals Index. H. W. Wilson Co. • Monthly, except August, with quarterly and annual cumulations. Service basis for print edition; CD-ROM edition, $1,495.00 per year.

HANDBOOKS AND MANUALS

Federal Income Taxation of Corporations and Shareholders. Boris I. Bittker and James S. Eustice. Warren, Gorham and Lamont/RIA Group. • Looseleaf service. $235.00. Two volumes. Periodic supplementation. Provides details concerning best methods for structuring various corporation transactions. Actual forms used by top tax specialists covering a diverse range of tax situations are shown.

Publicly Traded Corporations: Governance, Operation, and Regulation. John H. Matheson. West Group. • 1993. $130.00. Covers a wide range of corporate legal problems and issues, including shareholder communications and "tender offers and change of control transactions." (Corporate Law Series).

INTERNET DATABASES

U. S. Securities and Exchange Commission. Phone: 800-732-0330 or (202)942-7040 Fax: (202)942-

9634 E-mail: webmaster@sec.gov • URL: http://www.sec.gov • SEC Web site offers free access through EDGAR to text of official corporate filings, such as annual reports (10-K), quarterly reports (10-Q), and proxies. (EDGAR is "Electronic Data Gathering, Analysis, and Retrieval System.") An example is given of how to obtain executive compensation data from proxies. Text of the daily *SEC News Digest* is offered, as are links to other government sites, non-government market regulators, and U. S. stock exchanges. Search facilities are extensive. Fees: Free.

ONLINE DATABASES

Wilson Business Abstracts Online. H. W. Wilson Co. • Indexes and abstracts 600 major business periodicals, plus the *Wall Street Journal* and the business section of the *New York Times*. Indexing is from 1982, abstracting from 1990, with the two newspapers included from 1993. Updated weekly. Inquire as to online cost and availability. (*Business Periodicals Index* without abstracts is also available online.).

PERIODICALS AND NEWSLETTERS

Barron's: The Dow Jones Business and Financial Weekly. Dow Jones and Co., Inc. • Weekly. $145.00 per year.

Investor Relations Business. Securities Data Publishing. • Semimonthly. $435.00 per year. Covers the issues affecting stockholder relations, corporate public relations, and institutional investor relations. (Securities Data Publishing is a unit of Thomson Financial.).

Pensions and Investments: The Newspaper of Corporate and Institutional Investing. Crain Communications, Inc. • Biweekly. $215.00 per year. Formerly *Pensions and Investment Age*.

Securities Industry News. American Banker. • Weekly. $275.00 per year. Covers securities dealing and processing, including regulatory compliance, shareholder services, human resources, transaction clearing, and technology.

Trusts and Estates. Intertec Publishing Corp. • Monthly. $129.00 per year. Includes annual *Directory*.

TRADE/PROFESSIONAL ASSOCIATIONS

Fund for Stockowners Rights. P.O. 65563, Washington, DC 20035. Phone: (703)241-3700 Fax: (818)223-8080 • Seeks to improve methods of electing corporate boards of directors and encourages the holding of annual meetings for stockholders.

OTHER SOURCES

Business & Company Resource Center. The Gale Group. • Fee-based Web site provides a wide range of business, industry, and specific company information. Access is offered to trade journal articles, market research data, insider trading activity, major shareholder data, corporate histories, emerging technology reports, corporate earnings estimates, press releases, and other sources. Provides detailed company profiles, industry overviews, and rankings. Offers integration of Predicasts PROMT, Newsletters ASAP, Investext Plus, Business Index ASAP, Brands and Their Companies, and other databases (many have full text).

STOCKINGS

See: HOSIERY INDUSTRY

STOCKS

See also: DIVIDENDS; INVESTMENT ADVISORY SERVICES; INVESTMENTS; OVER-THE-COUNTER SECURITIES INDUSTRY; SECURITIES; STOCK EXCHANGES

GENERAL WORKS

The Bear Book: Survive and Profit in Ferocious Markets. John Rothchild. John Wiley and Sons, Inc. • 1998. $24.95. Tells how to invest when the stock market is sinking.

Beating the Street: The Best-Selling Author of "One Up on Wall Street" Shows You How to Pick Winning Stocks and Mutual Funds. Peter Lynch and John Rothchild. Simon & Schuster Trade. • 1993. $23.00.

The Craft of Investing. John Train. • 1994. $22.00. Presents conservative discussions of a wide variety of investment topics, including market timing, growth vs. value stocks, mutual funds, emerging markets, retirement planning, and estate planning.

Dividend Investor: A Safe and Sure Way to Build Wealth with High-Yield Dividend Stocks. Harvey C. Knowles and Damon H. Petty. McGraw-Hill Professional. • 1992. $24.95.

Dow 40,000: Strategies for Profiting from the Greatest Bull Market in History. David Elias and Charles V. Moore. McGraw-Hill. • 1999. $24.95. Predicts continuing strong growth in the U. S. economy, low interest rates, and low inflation, resulting in a level of 40,000 for the Dow Jones Industrial Average in the year 2016.

Dow 100,000: Fact or Fiction. Charles W. Kadlec. Prentice Hall. • 1999. $25.00. Predicts a level of 100,000 for the Dow Jones Industrial Average in the year 2020, based mainly on a technological revolution.

Dow 36,000: The New Strategy for Profiting from the Coming Rise in the Stock Market. James K. Glassman and Kevin A. Hassett. Times Books. • 1999. $25.00. States that conventional measures of stock market value are obsolete.

Dumb Money: Adventures of a Day Trader. Joey Anuff and Gary Wolf. Random House, Inc. • 2000. $23.95. An account of the day trading ordeals of one of the authors, Joey Anuff.

Financial Institutions and Markets. Robert W. Kolb and Ricardo J. Rodriguez. Blackwell Publishers. • 1996. $77.95. Contains 40 articles (chapters) by various authors on U. S. financial markets and other topics. Includes separate chapters on the International Monetary Fund, inflation, monetary policy, the national debt, bank failures, derivatives, stock prices, initial public offerings, government bonds, pensions, foreign exchange, international markets, and other subjects.

Getting Started in Stocks, Bonds. Alvin D. Hall. John Wiley and Sons, Inc. • 1999. $56.85. (Getting Started In... Series).

How to Buy Stocks. Louis Engel and Henry L. Hecht. Little Brown and Co., Inc. • 1994. $16.00. Eighth edition.

How to Invest Wisely. Lawrence S. Pratt. American Institute for Economic Research. • 1998. $9.00. Presents a conservative policy of investing, with emphasis on dividend-paying common stocks. Gold and other inflation hedges are compared. Includes a reprint of *Toward an Optimal Stock Selection Strategy* (1997). (Economic Education Bulletin.).

The Individual Investor Revolution: Unlock the Secrets of Wall Street and Invest Like a Pro. Charles B. Carlson. McGraw-Hill. • 1998. $21.95. Emphasizes the growing importance of the individual investor, especially with regard to online trading (e-trading). Includes the author's favorite websites for investors and traders.

Intelligent Investor: The National Bestseller on Value Investing for Over 35 Years. Benjamin Graham. HarperInformation. • 2000. $30.00. Fifth edition.

The Internet Bubble: Inside the Overvalued World of High-Tech Stocks, and What You Should Know to Avoid the Coming Catastrophe. Tony Perkins and Michael C. Perkins. HarperCollins Publishers, Inc. • 1999. $27.00. The authors predict a shakeout in e-commerce stocks and other Internet-related investments. (HarperBusiness.).

Investing in Small-Cap Stocks. Christopher Graja and Elizabeth Ungar. Bloomberg Press. • 1999. $26.95. Second expanded revised edition. Provides a practical strategy for investing in small-capitalization stocks. (Bloomberg Personal Bookshelf Series.).

Investing in the Over-the-Counter Markets: Stocks, Bonds, IPOs. Alvin D. Hall. John Wiley and Sons, Inc. • 1995. $29.95. Provides advice and information on investing in "unlisted" or NASDAQ (National Association of Securities Dealers Automated Quotation System) stocks, bonds, and initial public offerings (IPOs).

Irrational Exuberance. Robert J. Shiller. Princeton University Press. • 2000. $27.95. States that below-average stock market returns occur in the years following very high price-earnings ratios and very low dividend yields. 1901, 1929, 1966, and 2000 are cited as portentous years.

It was a Very Good Year: Extraordinary Moments in Stock Market History. Martin S. Fridson. John Wiley and Sons, Inc. • 1997. $29.95. Provides details on what happened during each of the ten best years for the stock market since 1900.

Learn to Earn: An Introduction to the Basics of Investing and Business. Peter Lynch and John Rothchild. Simon & Schuster Trade. • 1996. $13.00.

Market Efficiency: Stock Market Behavior in Theory and Practice. Andrew W. Lo, editor. Edward Elgar Publishing, Inc. • 1997. $430.00. Two volumes. Consists of reprints of 49 articles dating from 1937 to 1993, in five sections: "Theoretical Foundations," "The Random Walk Hypothesis," "Variance Bounds Tests," "Overreaction and Underreaction," and "Anomalies." (International Library of Critical Writings in Financial Economics Series: No. 3).

One Up on Wall Street: How to Use What You Already Know to Make Money in the Market. Peter Lynch and John Rothchild. Viking Penguin. • 1990. $14.95.

A Random Walk Down Wall Street: Including a Life-Cycle Guide to Personal Investing. Burton G. Malkiel. W. W. Norton & Co., Inc. • 1999. $29.95. Seventh edition.

Relative Dividend Yield: Common Stock Investing for Income and Appreciation. Anthony E. Spare and Paul Ciotti. John Wiley and Sons, Inc. • 1999. $59.95. Second edition. (Frontiers in Finance Series).

Security Analysis. S. Cottle. McGraw-Hill. • 1988. $59.95. Fifth edition.

Stock Market Crashes and Speculative Manias. Eugene N. White, editor. Edward Elgar Publishing, Inc. • 1996. $230.00. Contains reprints of 23 articles dating from 1905 to 1994. (International Library of Macroeconomic and Financial History Series: No. 13).

Stocks for the Long Run: A Guide to Selecting Markets for Long-Term Growth. Jeremy J. Siegel.

McGraw-Hill. • 1998. $29.95. Second expanded edition. A favorable view of a buy-and-hold strategy for stock market investors. *Business Week Books.*

Toward an Optimal Stock Selection Strategy. Lawrence S. Pratt. American Institute for Economic Research. • 1997. $6.00. Second edition. Discusses the strategy of buying only the stocks in the Dow Jones Industrial Average that have the highest-yielding dividends. Includes detailed charts and tables. (Economic Education Bulletin.).

Trading to Win: The Psychology of Mastering the Markets. Ari Kiev. John Wiley and Sons, Inc. • 1998. $34.95. A mental health guide for stock, bond, and commodity traders. Tells how to keep speculative emotions in check, overcome self-doubt, and focus on a winning strategy. (Trading Advantage Series).

What Works on Wall Street: A Guide to the Best-Performing Investment Strategies of All Time. James P. O'Shaughnessy. McGraw-Hill. • 1998. $22.95. Second revised edition. Examines investment strategies over a 43-year period and concludes that large capitalization, high-dividend-yield stocks produce the best results.

The Witch Doctor of Wall Street: A Noted Financial Expert Guides You Through Today's Voodoo Economics. Robert H. Parks. Prometheus Books. • 1996. $25.95. The author, a professor of finance at Pace University, discusses "Practice and Malpractice" in relation to the following: business forecasting, economic theory, interest rates, monetary policy, the stock market, and corporate finance. Includes "A Short Primer on Derivatives," as an appendix.

ABSTRACTS AND INDEXES

Investment Statistics Locator. Linda H. Bentley and Jennifer J. Kiesl, editors. Oryx Press. • 1994. $69.95. Expanded revised edition. Provides detailed subject indexing of more than 50 of the most-used sources of financial and investment data. Includes an annotated bibliography.

CD-ROM DATABASES

BioMed Strategies. Thomson Financial Securities Data. • Monthly. $2,995.00 per year. CD-ROM contains full text of investment analysts' reports on companies operating in the following fields: biotechnology, pharmaceuticals, medical products, and health care.

Chemical Strategies. Thomson Financial Securities Data. • Monthly. $2,995.00 per year. CD-ROM contains full text of investment analysts' reports on companies active in the chemical industries.

Electronic Strategies. Thomson Financial Securities Data. • Monthly. $2,995.00 per year. CD-ROM contains full text of investment analysts' reports on companies operating in the following fields: electronics, computers, semiconductors, and office products.

Telecom Strategies. Thomson Financial Securities Data. • Monthly. $2,995.00 per year. CD-ROM contains full text of investment analysts' reports on companies operating in the following fields: telecommunications, broadcasting, and cable communications.

DIRECTORIES

Cyberstocks: An Investor's Guide to Internet Companies. Alan Chai. Hoover's, Inc. • 1996. $24.95. Provides detailed profiles of 101 publicly traded companies involved in one way or another with the Internet.

Dow Jones Guide to the Global Stock Market. Dow Jones & Co., Inc. • Annual. $34.95. Three volumes. Presents concise profiles and three-year financial performance data for each of 3,000 publicly held companies in 35 countries. (Includes all Dow Jones Global Index companies.).

FII Annual Guide to Stocks. Financial Information, Inc. • Annual. $2,250.00. Monthly supplements. Two volumes. Formerly *Financial Stock Guide Service: Directory of Active Stocks.*

Institutional Buyers of Small-Cap Stocks: A Targeted Directory. Investment Data Corp. • Annual. $295.00. Provides detailed profiles of more than 837 institutional buyers of small capitalization stocks. Includes names of financial analysts and portfolio managers.

Moneypaper's Guide to Dividend Reinvestment Plans. Moneypaper. • Annual. $9.00. Provides details on about 900 corporate dividend reinvestment plans that permit optional cash investments.

Morningstar American Depositary Receipts. Morningstar, Inc. • Biweekly. $195.00 per year. Looseleaf. Provides detailed profiles of 700 foreign companies having shares traded in the U. S. through American Depositary Receipts (ADRs).

National Directory of Investment Newsletters. GPS Co. • Biennial. $49.95. Describes about 800 investment newsletters, and their publishers.

Standard & Poor's 500 Guide. McGraw-Hill. • Annual. $24.95. Contains detailed profiles of the companies included in Standard & Poor's 500 Index of stock prices. Includes income and balance sheet data for up to 10 years, with growth and stability rankings for 500 major corporations.

Standard & Poor's MidCap 400 Guide. McGraw-Hill. • Annual. $24.95. Contains detailed profiles of the companies included in Standard & Poor's MidCap 400 Index of stock prices. Includes income and balance sheet data for up to 10 years, with growth and stability rankings for 400 midsized corporations.

Standard and Poor's Security Dealers of North America. Standard & Poor's. • Semiannual. $480.00 per year; with *Supplements* every six weeks, $590.00 per year. Geographical listing of over 12,000 stock, bond, and commodity dealers.

Standard & Poor's SmallCap 600 Guide. McGraw-Hill. • Annual. $24.95. Contains detailed profiles of the companies included in Standard & Poor's SmallCap 600 Index of stock prices. Includes income and balance sheet data for up to 10 years, with growth and stability rankings for 600 small capitalization corporations.

Walker's Manual of Unlisted Stocks. Harry K. Eisenberg, editor. Walker's Manual, LLC. • Annual. $85.00. Provides information on 500 over-the-counter stocks,including many "penny stocks" trading at less than $5.00 per share.

Zacks Analyst Directory: Listed by Broker. Zacks Investment Research. • Quarterly. $395.00 per year. Lists stockbroker investment analysts and gives the names of major U. S. corporations covered by those analysts.

Zacks Analyst Directory: Listed by Company. Zacks Investment Research. • Quarterly. $395.00 per year. Lists major U. S. corporations and gives the names of stockbroker investment analysts covering those companies.

Zacks EPS Calendar. Zacks Investment Research. • Biweekly. $1,250.00 per year. (Also available monthly at $895.00 per year.) Lists anticipated reporting dates of earnings per share for major U. S. corporations.

ENCYCLOPEDIAS AND DICTIONARIES

The A-Z Vocabulary for Investors. American Institute for Economic Research. • 1997. $7.00. Second half of book is a "General Glossary" of about 400 financial terms "most-commonly used" in investing. First half contains lengthier descriptions of types of banking institutions (commercial banks, thrift institutions, credit unions), followed by succinct explanations of various forms of investment: stocks, bonds, options, futures, commodities, and "Other Investments" (collectibles, currencies, mortgages, precious metals, real estate, charitable trusts). (Economic Education Bulletin.).

Common Stock Newspaper Abbreviations and Trading Symbols. Howard R. Jarrell. Scarecrow Press, Inc. • 1989. $55.00. Gives the meanings of financial page company name abbreviations and stock symbols.

Common Stock Newspaper Abbreviations and Trading Symbols: Supplement One. Howard R. Jarrell. Scarecrow Press, Inc. • 1991. $35.00. Provides changes and new listings occurring since the publication of Jarrell's original volume in 1989.

Dictionary of Finance and Investment Terms. John Downes and Jordan E. Goodman. Barron's Educational Series, Inc. • 1998. $12.95. Fifth revised edition. Provides clear explanations of more than 5,000 business, banking, financial, investment, and tax terms. Includes a separate list of financial abbreviations and acronyms.

Encyclopedia of Chart Patterns. Thomas N. Bulkowski. John Wiley and Sons, Inc. • 2000. $79.95. Provides explanations of the predictive value of various chart patterns formed by stock and commodity price movements.

Encyclopedia of Stock Market Techniques. Chartcraft, Inc. • 1963. $60.00.

Wall Street Words: The Basics and Beyond. Richard J. Maturi. McGraw-Hill Professional. • 1991. $14.95. (Investor's Quick Reference Series).

HANDBOOKS AND MANUALS

Dynamic Asset Allocation: Strategies for the Stock, Bond, and Money Markets. David A. Hammer. John Wiley and Sons, Inc. • 1991. $49.95. A practical guide to the distribution of investment portfolio funds among various kinds of assets. (Finance Editions Series).

Indexing for Maximum Investment Results. Albert S. Neuberg. Fitzroy Dearborn Publishers. • 1998. $65.00. Covers the Standard & Poor's 500 and other indexing strategies for both individual and institutional investors.

Kiss Your Stockbroker Goodbye: A Guide to Independent Investing. John G. Wells. St. Martin's Press. • 1997. $25.95. The author believes that the small investor is throwing money away by using full-commission brokers when discount brokers and many sources of information are easily available. Contains separate chapters on stocks, bonds, mutual funds, asset allocation, financial planners, and related topics. Wells is a securities analyst (CFA) and portfolio manager.

Moody's Handbook of Common Stocks. Financial Information Services. • Annual. $275.00 per year.

Technical Analysis of Stock Trends. Robert D. Edwards and John Magee. AMACOM. • 1998. $79.85. 7th revised edition. Standard manual of technical analysis.

Trading for a Living: Psychology, Trading Tactics, Money Management. Alexander Elder. John Wiley and Sons, Inc. • 1993. $59.95. Covers technical and chart methods of trading in commodity and financial futures, options, and stocks. Includes Elliott Wave Theory, oscillators, moving averages, point-and-figure, and other technical approaches. (Finance Editions Series).

INTERNET DATABASES

BanxQuote Banking, Mortgage, and Finance Center. BanxQuote, Inc. Phone: 800-765-3000 or (212)643-8000 Fax: (212)643-0020 E-mail: info@banx.com • URL: http://www.banx.com • Web site

For publishers addresses, refer to SOURCES CITED section at the back of the book.

quotes interest rates paid by banks around the country on various savings products, as well as rates paid by consumers for automobile loans, mortgages, credit cards, home equity loans, and personal loans. Also provided: stock quotes, indexes, stock options, futures trading data, economic indicators, and links to many other financial sites. Daily updates. Fees: Free.

Business Week Online. McGraw-Hill. Phone: (212)512-2762 Fax: (212)512-6590 • URL: http://www.businessweek.com • Web site provides complete contents of current issue of *Business Week* plus "BW Daily" with additonal business news, financial market quotes, and corporate information from Standard & Poor's. Includes various features, such as "Banking Center" with mortgage and interest data, and "Interactive Computer Buying Guide." The "Business Week Archive" is fully searchable back to 1991. Fees: Mostly free, but full-text archive articles are $2.00 each.

CANOE: Canadian Online Explorer. Canoe Limited Partnership. Phone: (416)947-2027 Fax: (416)947-2209 • URL: http://www.canoe.ca • Web site provides a wide variety of Canadian news and information, including business and financial data. Includes "Money," "Your Investment," "Technology," and "Stock Quotes." Allows keyword searching, with links to many other sites. Daily updating. Fees: Free.

DBC Online: America's Leading Provider of Real-Time Market Data to the Individual Investor. Data Broadcasting Corp. Phone: (415)571-1800 E-mail: dbcinfo@dbc.com • URL: http://www.dbc.com • Web site provides a wide variety of real-time securities market prices, data, and charts. Covers bonds ("BondVu"), stocks, commodities, options, mutual funds, major indexes, industry indexes, international markets, etc. Also includes news, SEC documents ("Smart-Edgar"), and various other features. Fees: Both free and fee-based, depending on level of information.

Fedstats. Federal Interagency Council on Statistical Policy. Phone: (202)395-7254 • URL: http://www.fedstats.gov • Web site features an efficient search facility for full-text statistics produced by more than 70 federal agencies, including the Census Bureau, the Bureau of Economic Analysis, and the Bureau of Labor Statistics. Boolean searches can be made within one agency or for all agencies combined. Links are offered to international statistical bureaus, including the UN, IMF, OECD, UNESCO, Eurostat, and 20 individual countries. Fees: Free.

The Financial Post (Web site). National Post Online (Hollinger/CanWest). Phone: (244)383-2300 Fax: (416)383-2443 • URL: http://www.nationalpost.com/financialpost/ • Provides a broad range of Canadian business news online, with daily updates. Includes news, opinion, and special reports, as well as "Investing," "Money Rates," "Market Watch," and "Daily Mutual Funds." Allows advanced searching (Boolean operators), with links to various other sites. Fees: Free.

FIS Online: The Preferred Source for Global Business and Financial Information. Mergent. Phone: 800-342-5647 or (212)413-7601 Fax: (212)413-7777 E-mail: fis@fisonline.com • URL: http://www.fisonline.com • Fee-based Web site provides detailed information on more than 10,000 publicly-owned corporations listed on the New York Stock Exchange, American Stock Exchange, NASDAQ, and U. S. regional exchanges. Searching is offered on eight financial variables and six text fields. Weekly updating. Fees: Rates on application. (Mergent is publisher of Moody's Manuals.).

Hoover's Online. Hoover's, Inc. Phone: 800-486-8666 or (512)374-4500 Fax: (512)374-4501 • URL: http://www.hoovers.com • Web site provides stock quotes, lists of companies, and a variety of business information at no charge. In-depth company profiles are available at $29.95 per month.

Morningstar.com: Your First Second Opinion. Morningstar, Inc. Phone: 800-735-0700 or (312)696-6000 Fax: (312)696-6001 E-mail: productsupport@morningstar.com • URL: http://www.morningstar.com • Web site provides a broad selection of information and advice on both mutual funds and individual stocks, including financial news and articles on investment fundamentals. Basic service is free, with "Premium Membership" available at $49.00 per year. Annual fee provides personal portfolio analysis, screening tools, and more extensive profiles of funds and stocks.

TheStreet.com: Your Insider's Look at Wall Street. TheStreet.com, Inc. Phone: 800-562-9571 or (212)321-5000 Fax: (212)321-5016 • URL: http://www.thestreet.com • Web site offers "Free Sections" and "Premium Sections" ($9.95 per month). Both sections offer iconoclastic advice and comment on the stock market, but premium service displays a more comprehensive selection of news and analysis. There are many by-lined articles. "Search the Site" is included.

Thomson Investors Network. Thomson Financial. Phone: (212)807-3800 • URL: http://thomsoninvest.net • Web site provides detailed data on insider trading, institutional portfolios, and "First Call" earnings estimates. Includes a stock screening (filtering) application, a search facility, and price quotes on stocks, bonds, and mutual funds. Continuous updating. Fees: $34.95 per year for general service. First Call earnings service is $19.95 per month or $199.00 per year.

Thomson Real Time Quotes: Real Fast...Real Free...Real Quotes...Real Time. Thomson Financial. Phone: (212)807-3800 • URL: http://www.thomsonfn.com/ • Web site provides continuous updating of prices for stocks, bonds, mutual funds, and options. Includes headline business news and market analysis. Fees: Free.

ONLINE DATABASES

DRI U.S. Central Database. Data Products Division. • Provides more than 23,000 business, financial, demographic, economic, foreign trade, and industry-related time series for the U.S. Includes national income, population, retail-wholesale trade, price indexes, labor data, housing, industrial production, banking, interest rates, money supply, etc. Time period is generally 1947 to date (some data back to 1929). Updating varies. Inquire as to online cost and availability.

F & S Index. The Gale Group. • Contains about four million citations to worldwide business, financial, and industrial or consumer product literature appearing from 1972 to date. Weekly updates. Inquire as to online cost and availability.

Standard and Poor's Daily News Online. Standard and Poor's Corp. • Full text of business news and other information, 1984 to present. Inquire as to online cost and availability.

Zacks Earnings Estimates. Zacks Investment Research. • Provides online earnings projections for about 6,000 U. S. corporations, based on investment analysts' reports. Data is mainly from 200 major brokerage firms. Time span varies according to online provider, with daily or weekly updates. Inquire as to online cost and availability.

PERIODICALS AND NEWSLETTERS

America's Fastest Growing Companies. Individual Investor Group, Inc. • Monthly. $165.00 per year. Newsletter. Provides investment information on about 150 publicly-held corporations that are showing rapidly expanding sales and earnings. Formerly *America's Fastest Growing Corporations.*

The Asian Wall Street Journal. Dow Jones & Co., Inc. • Daily. $610.00 per year (air mail). Published in Hong Kong. Also available in a weekly edition at $259.00 per year: *Asian Wall Street Journal Weekly.*

Barron's: The Dow Jones Business and Financial Weekly. Dow Jones and Co., Inc. • Weekly. $145.00 per year.

BI Research. Thomas Bishop, editor. BI Research, Inc. • Every six weeks. $156.00 per year. Newsletter. Five to eight in-depth investment recommendations per year.

Cabot Market Letter. Cabot Heritage Corp. • Semimonthly. $250.00 per year. Newsletter. Recommends various model portfolios.

Canadian Resources and PennyMines Analyst: The Canadian Newsletter for Penny-Mines Investors Who Insist on Geological Value. MPL Communication, Inc. • Weekly. $157.00 per year. Newsletter. Mainly on Canadian gold mine stocks. Formerly *Canadian PennyMines Analyst.*

Dick Davis Digest. Dick Davis Publishing, Inc. • Semimonthly. $180.00 per year. Newsletter. A digest of investment advisory services.

Dow Theory Forecasts: Business and Stock Market. Dow Theory Forecasts, Inc. • Weekly. $233.00 per year. Provides information and advice on blue chip and income stocks.

Dow Theory Letters. Dow Theory Letters, Inc. • Biweekly. $250.00 per year. Newsletter on stock market trends, investing, and economic conditions.

DRIP Investor: Your Guide to Buying Stocks Without a Broker. Horizon Publishing, Co., LLC. • Monthly. $89.00 per year. Newsletter covering the dividend reinvestment plans (DRIPs) of various publicly-owned corporations. Includes model portfolios and *Directory of Dividend Reinvestment Plans.*

The Financial Post: Canadian's Business Voice. Financial Post Datagroup. • Daily. $234.00 per year. Provides Canadian business, economic, financial, and investment news. Features extensive price quotes from all major Canadian markets: stocks, bonds, mutual funds, commodities, and currencies. Supplement available: *Financial Post 500.* Includes annual supplement.

Financial Sentinel: Your Beacon to the World of Investing. Gulf Atlantic Publishing, Inc. • Monthly. $29.95 per year. Provides "The only complete listing of all OTC Bulletin Board stocks traded, with all issues listed on the Nasdaq SmallCap Market, the Toronto, and Vancouver Stock Exchanges." Also includes investment advice and recommendations of small capitalization stocks.

Financial Times [London]. Available from FT Publications, Inc. • Daily, except Sunday. $184.00 per year. An international business and financial newspaper, featuring news from London, Paris, Frankfurt, New York, and Tokyo. Includes worldwide stock and bond market data, commodity market data, and monetary/currency exchange information.

Forbes. Forbes, Inc. • Biweekly. $59.95 per year. Includes supplements: *Forbes ASAP* and *Forbes FYI.*

Gilder Technology Report. George Gilder, editor. Gilder Technology Group, Inc. • Monthly. $295.00 per year. Newsletter. Makes specific recommendations for investing in technology stocks.

(A joint publication of Forbes Magazine and the Gilder Technology Group.).

Growth Stock Outlook. Charles Allmon, editor. Growth Stock Outlook, Inc. • Semimonthly. $195.00 per year. Newsletter. Provides data on stock earnings, sales, price-earnings ratios, dividends, book values, returns on shareholder equity and institutional holdings. Recommends specific companies for long-term investment. Subscription includes *Junior Growth Stocks, New Issues Digest,* and *Bank Stock Analyst.*

Individual Investor. Individual Investor Group. • Monthly. $22.95 per year. Emphasis is on stocks selling for less than ten dollars a share. Includes a "Guide to Insider Transactions" and "New Issue Alert.".

InvesTech Market Analyst: Technical and Monetary Investment Analysis. InvesTech Research. • Every three weeks. $190.00 per year. Newsletter. Provides interpretation of monetary statistics and Federal Reserve actions, especially as related to technical analysis of stock market price trends.

Investment Guide. American Investment Services. • Monthly. $49.00 per year. Newsletter. Emphasis is on blue-chip stocks with high dividend yields.

Investment Reporter. MPL Communication, Inc. • Weekly. $279.00 per year. Newsletter. Monthly supplement, *Investment Planning Guide.* Recommendations for Canadian investments. Formerly *Personal Wealth Reporter.*

Investor's Business Daily. Investor's Business Daily, Inc. • Daily. $169.00 per year. Newspaper.

Investors Intelligence. Michael Burke, editor. Chartcraft, Inc. • Biweekly. $184.00 per year. Monitors about 130 investment advisory services and prints summaries of advice from about half of them in each issue. Provides numerical index of bearish sentiment among services.

Low Priced Stock Survey. Horizon Publishing Co., LLC. • Monthly. $129.00 per year.

Market Logic. Norman Fosback, editor. Institute for Econometric Research. • Semimonthly. $200.00 per year. Newsletter. Forecasts of market prices.

Medical Technology Stock Letter. Piedmont Venture Group. • Semimonthly. $320.00 per year. Newsletter. Provides health care industry investment recommendations, including information on initial public offerings.

Moneypaper. • Monthly. $81.00 per year. Newsletter. Provides general investment advice, including summaries from other investment advisory services. Emphasis is on company-sponsored dividend reinvestment plans. Subscription includes annual directory: *The Moneypaper's Guide to Dividend Reinvestment Plans.*

Morningstar Stock Investor. Morningstar, Inc. • Monthly. $89.00 per year. Newsletter. Provides detailed information on the financial fundamentals of 450 selected, undervalued stocks. Estimated future worth of each stock is given, according to an "Intrinsic Value Measure.".

MPT Review; Specializing in Modern Portfolio Theory. Navellier and Associates, Inc. • Monthly. $275.00 per year. Newsletter. Provides specific stock selection and model portfolio advice (conservative, moderately aggressive, and aggressive) based on quantitative analysis and modern portfolio theory.

The Red Herring: The Business of Technology. Herring Communications, Inc. • Monthly. $49.00 per year. Contains ars on investing in high technology, especially within the computer, communications, and information industries. Initial public offerings (IPOs) are emphasized. Includes technology stock listings and the Red Herring "Tech 250" stock index.

Richard C. Young's Intelligence Report. Phillips Publishing International, Inc. • Monthly. $99.00 per year. Newsletter. Provides conservative advice for investing in stocks, fixed-income securities, and mutual funds.

Special Situations Newsletter: In-depth Survey of Under-Valued Stocks. Charles Howard Kaplan. • Monthly. $75.00 per year. Newsletter. Principal content is "This Month's Recommendation," a detailed analysis of one special situation stock.

Technology Investing. Michael Murphy, editor. Phillips Publishing International, Inc. • Monthly. $195.00 per year. Newsletter. Provides specific recommendations for investing in high technology companies.

Wall Street Digest. Wall Street Digest, Inc. • Monthly. $150.00 per year. Digest of investment advice from leading financial advisors.

The Wall Street Journal. Dow Jones & Co., Inc. • Daily. $175.00 per year. Covers news and trends relating to business, industry, finance, the economy, and international commerce. Provides extensive price and other data for the securities, commodity, options, futures, foreign exchange, and money markets.

Wall Street Journal/Europe. Dow Jones & Co., Inc. • Daily. $700.00 per year (air mail). Published in Europe. Text in English.

Wall Street Transcript: A Professional Publication for the Business and Financial Community. Wall Street Transcript Corp. • Weekly. $1,890.00. per year. Provides reprints of investment research reports.

Zacks Analyst Watch. Zacks Investment Research. • Biweekly. $250.00 per year. Provides the results of research by stockbroker investment analysts on major U. S. corporations.

Zacks Earnings Forecaster. Zacks Investment Research. • Biweekly. $495.00 per year. (Also available monthly at $375.00 per year.) Provides estimates by stockbroker investment analysts of earnings per share of individual U. S. companies.

Zacks Profit Guide. Zacks Investment Research. • Quarterly. $375.00 per year. Provides analysis of total return and stock price performance of major U. S. companies.

PRICE SOURCES

National Stock Summary. National Quotation Bureau, Inc. • Monthly. $480.00 per year. Semiannual cumulations. Includes price quotes for both active and inactive issues, with transfer agents, market makers (brokers), and other information. (The National Quotation Bureau also provides daily and weekly stock price services.).

Standard and Poor's Daily Stock Price Records. Standard and Poor's. • Quarterly. New York Stock Exchange, $420.00 per year; American Stock Exchange, $441.00 per year; NASDAQ, $530.00 per year.

Stock Market Values and Yields for 1997. Research Institute of America. • 1997. $20.00. Revised edition. Gives year-end prices and dividends for tax purposes.

Stock Values and Dividends for Tax Purposes. CCH, Inc. • Annual. Gives year-end prices and dividends for tax purposes.

RESEARCH CENTERS AND INSTITUTES

Center for Research in Security Prices. University of Chicago, 725 S. Wells St., Suite 800, Chicago, IL 60607. Phone: (773)702-7467 Fax: (773)753-4797 E-mail: mail@crsp.uchicago.edu • URL: http://www.crsp.com.

STATISTICS SOURCES

Advance-Decline Album. Dow Theory Letters, Inc. • Annual. Contains one page for each year since 1931. Includes charts of the New York Stock Exchange advance-decline ratio and the Dow Jones industrial average.

The AIER Chart Book. AIER Research Staff. American Institute for Economic Research. • Annual. $3.00. A compact compilation of long-range charts ("Purchasing Power of the Dollar," for example, goes back to 1780) covering various aspects of the U. S. economy. Includes inflation, interest rates, debt, gold, taxation, stock prices, etc. (Economic Education Bulletin.).

Business Statistics of the United States. Courtenay M. Slater, editor. Bernan Associates. • 1999. $74.00. Fifth edition. Based on *Business Statistics,* formerly issue by the Bureau of Economic Analysis, U. S. Department of Commerce. Provides basic data for a wide variety of U. S. industries, services, and economic indicators. Most statistics are shown annually for 29 years and monthly for the most recent four years.

Dow Jones Averages Chart Album. Dow Theory Letters, Inc. • Annual. Contains one page for each year since 1885. Includes line charts of the Dow Jones industrial, transportation, utilities, and bond averages. Important historical and economic dates are shown.

Dow Jones Averages 1885-1995. Phyllis S. Pierce, editor. McGraw-Hill. • 1996. $95.00. Fourth edition. Presents the daily Dow Jones stock price averages for more than 100 years.

Global Stock Guide. C I F A R Publications, Inc. • Monthly. $445.00 per year. Provides financial variables for 10,000 publicly traded companies in 48 countries.

SBBI Monthly Market Reports. Ibbotson Associates. • Monthly. $995.00 per year. These reports provide current updating of stocks, bonds, bills, and inflation (SBBI) data. Each issue contains the most recent month's investment returns and index values for various kinds of securities, as well as monthly statistics for the past year. Analysis is included.

SBBI Quarterly Market Reports. Ibbotson Associates. • Quarterly. $495.00 per year. Each quarterly volume contains detailed updates to stocks, bonds, bills, and inflation (SBBI) data. Includes total and sector returns for the broad stock market, small company stocks, intermediate and long-term government bonds, long-term corporate bonds, and U. S. Treasury Bills. Analyses, tables, graphs, and market consensus forecasts are provided.

Security Owner's Stock Guide. Standard and Poor's. • Monthly. $125.00 per year.

SRC Green Book of 35-Year Charts. • Annual. $119.00. Chart book presents statistical information on the stocks of 400 leading companies over a 35-year period. Each full page chart is in semi-log format to avoid visual distortion. Also includes charts of 12 leading market averages or indexes and 39 major industry groups.

Standard & Poor's Stock Reports: American Stock Exchange. Standard & Poor's. • Irregular. $1,035.00 per year. Looseleaf service. Provides two pages of financial details and other information for each corporation listed on the American Stock Exchange.

Standard & Poor's Stock Reports: NASDAQ and Regional Exchanges. Standard & Poor's. • Irregular. $1,100.00 per year. Looseleaf service. Provides two pages of financial details and other information for each corporation included.

Standard & Poor's Stock Reports: New York Stock Exchange. Standard & Poor's. • Irregular. $1,295.00 per year. Looseleaf service. Provides two pages of financial details and other information for each corporation with stock listed on the N. Y. Stock Exchange.

Stocks, Bonds, Bills, and Inflation Yearbook. Ibbotson Associates. • Annual. $92.00. Provides detailed data from 1926 to the present on inflation and the returns from various kinds of financial investments, such as small-cap stocks and long-term government bonds.

Survey of Current Business. Available from U. S. Government Printing Office. • Monthly. $49.00 per year. Issued by Bureau of Economic Analysis, U. S. Department of Commerce. Presents a wide variety of business and economic data.

TRADE/PROFESSIONAL ASSOCIATIONS

National Association of Securities Dealers. 1735 K St., N.W., Washington, DC 20006-1506. Phone: (202)728-8000 Fax: (202)293-6260 • URL: http://www.nasdr.com/1000.asp.

Securities Industry Association. 120 Broadway, New York, NY 10271-0080. Phone: (212)608-1500 Fax: (212)608-1604 E-mail: info@sia.com • URL: http://www.sia.com.

OTHER SOURCES

Blue Book of Stock Reports. MPL Communication Inc. • Biweekly. $260.00 per year. Canadian Business Service reports on over 250 Canadian companies.

Chartcraft Monthly NYSE and ASE Chartbook. Chartcraft, Inc. • Monthly. $402.00 per year. Includes all common stocks on New York and American Stock Exchanges.

Chartcraft Over-the-Counter Chartbook. Chartcraft, Inc. • Quarterly. $114.00 per year. Includes more than 1,000 unlisted stocks. Long term charts.

Daily Graphs. Daily Graphs, Inc. • New York Stock Exchange edition, $363.00 per year. American Stock Exchange edition, $363.00 per year. Both editions include the 200 leading over-the-counter stocks.

Elliott Wave Theorist. Robert Prechter, editor. Elliott Wave International. • Monthly. $233.00 per year. Newsletter Formerly *Elliott Wave Commodity Forecasts.*

Factiva. Dow Jones Reuters Business Interactive, LLC. • Fee-based Web site provides "global news and business information through Web sites and content integration solutions." Includes Dow Jones and Reuters newswires, The Wall Street Journal, and more than 7,000 other sources of current news, historical articles, market research reports, and investment analysis. Content includes 96 major U. S. newspapers, 900 non-English sources, trade publications, media transcripts, country profiles, news photos, etc.

Granville Market Letter. Joseph Granville, editor. • 46 times a year. $250.00 per year.

Mansfield Stock Chart Service. R.W. Mansfield Co., Inc. • Weekly. Price varies. Covers New York Stock Exchange, American Stock Exchange, OTC exchange, international stocks and industry groups. Partial subscriptions available.

Mergent Company Data. Mergent FIS, Inc. • Monthly. Price on application. CD-ROM provides detailed financial statement information for more than 10,000 New York Stock Exchange, American Stock Exchange, and NASDAQ corporations. Includes balance sheets, income statements, dividend history, annual price ranges, stock splits, Moody's debt ratings, etc. Formerly *Moody's Company Data.*

Nexis.com. Lexis-Nexis Group. • Fee-based Web site offers searching of about 2.8 billion documents in some 30,000 news, business, and legal information sources. Features include a subject directory covering 1,200 topics in 34 categories and a Company Dossier containing information on more than 500,000 public and private companies. Boolean searching is offered.

The Value Line Investment Survey. Value Line Publishing, Inc. • Weekly. $570.00 per year. Provides detailed information and ratings for 1,700 stocks actively-traded in the U. S.

STOCKYARDS

See: LIVESTOCK INDUSTRY; MEAT INDUSTRY

STONE INDUSTRY

See: QUARRYING

STORAGE

See: WAREHOUSES

STORE DISPLAYS

See: DISPLAY OF MERCHANDISE

STORES, CONVENIENCE

See: CONVENIENCE STORES

STORES, DEPARTMENT

See: DEPARTMENT STORES

STORES (RETAIL TRADE)

See: RETAIL TRADE

STRATEGIC PLANNING

See: PLANNING

STRATEGY, BUSINESS

See: BUSINESS STRATEGY

STREET LIGHTING

See: LIGHTING

STREET MAPS

See: MAPS

STRESS (ANXIETY)

See also: INDUSTRIAL PSYCHOLOGY; MENTAL HEALTH

GENERAL WORKS

Life After Stress. Martin Shaffer. Perseus Publishing. • 1982. $15.95.

Managing Stress: Subjectivity and Power in the Workplace. Tim Newton. Sage Publications, Inc. • 1995. $69.95.

Managing Workplace Stress. Susan Cartwright and Cary L. Cooper. Sage Publications, Inc. • 1996. $34.00. Includes references and indexes. *Advanced Topics in Organizational Behavior, vol. 1.*

Psychological Symptoms. Frank J. Bruno. John Wiley and Sons, Inc. • 1994. $24.95. Explains the meaning of common mental symptoms, what may cause them, and how to deal with them.

Stress and Burnout in Library Service. Janette S. Caputo. Oryx Press. • 1991. $24.95. Discusses symptoms of stress in library staff members and ways of dealing with stress. Includes self-help checklists and a list of references for further information.

Stress Management for Wellness. Walt Schafer. Harcourt Brace College Publishers. • 1995. $48.00. Third edition.

Stress Solution: An Action Plan to Manage the Stress in Your Life. Lyle H. Miller and others. Pocket Books. • 1993. $6.99.

ABSTRACTS AND INDEXES

Psychological Abstracts. American Psychological Association. • Monthly. Members, $799.00 per year; individuals and institutions, $1,075.00 per year. Covers the international literature of psychology and the behavioral sciences. Includes journals, technical reports, dissertations, and other sources.

CD-ROM DATABASES

Consumers Reference Disc. National Information Services Corp. • Quarterly. Provides the CD-ROM version of *Consumer Health and Nutrition Index* from Oryx Press and *Consumers Index to Product Evaluations and Information Sources* from Pierian Press. Contains citations to consumer health articles and consumer product evaluations, tests, warnings, and recalls.

Health Reference Center. The Gale Group. • Monthly. Provides CD-ROM citations, abstracts, and selected full-text articles on many health-related subjects. Includes references to medical journals, general periodicals, newsletters, newspapers, pamphlets, and medical reference books.

Magazine Index Plus. The Gale Group. • Monthly. $4,000.00 per year (includes InfoTrac workstation). Provides full text on CD-ROM for about 100 popular, general interest magazines and indexing for 300 others. Includes special indexing of reviews and product evaluations. Time period is 1980 to date.

ENCYCLOPEDIAS AND DICTIONARIES

The Gale Encyclopedia of Psychology. The Gale Group. • 1998. $130.00. Includes bibliographies arranged by topic and a glossary.

HANDBOOKS AND MANUALS

Personal Health Reporter. The Gale Group. • 1992. $105.00. Two volumes. Volume one, $105.00; volume two, $105.00. Presents a collection of professional and popular articles on 150 topics relating to physical and mental health conditions and treatments.

Stress and Well-Being at Work: Assessments and Interventions for Occupational Mental Health. James C. Quick and others, editors. American Psychological Association. • 1992. $19.95.

ONLINE DATABASES

Mental Health Abstracts. IFI/Plenum Data Corp. • Provides indexing and abstracting of mental health and mental illness literature appearing in more than 1,200 journals and other sources from 1969 to date. Monthly updates. Inquire as to online cost and availability.

PsycINFO. American Psychological Association. • Provides indexing and abstracting of the worldwide literature of psychology and the behavioral sciences.

Time period is 1967 to date, with monthly updates. Inquire as to online cost and availability.

PERIODICALS AND NEWSLETTERS

Behavioral Medicine: Investigations of Environmental Influences on Health and Behavior. Helen Dwight Reid Educational Foundation. Heldref Publications. • Quarterly. Individuals, $53.00 per year; institutions, $99.00 per year. An interdisciplinary journal of particular interest to physicians, psychologists, nurses, educators and all who are interested in behavorial and social influences on mental and physicial health. Formerly *Journal of Human Stress.*

Journal of Business and Psychology. Business Psychology Research Institute. Kluwer Plenum Academic Publishers. • Quarterly. Institutions, $556.80 per year.

Stress Medicine. Available from John Wiley and Sons, Inc., Journals Div. • Five times a year. Institutions, $870.00 per year. A forum for discussion of all aspects of stress which affect the individual in both health and disease. Provides international coverage.

RESEARCH CENTERS AND INSTITUTES

American Institute of Stress. 124 Park Ave., Yonkers, NY 10703. Phone: (914)963-1200 Fax: (914)965-6267 E-mail: stress124@earthlink.net • URL: http://www.stress.org • Explores personal and social consequences of stress. Compiles research data on occupational stress and executive stress or "burn out.".

OTHER SOURCES

The Market for Stress Management Products and Services. Available from MarketResearch.com. • 1996. $1,195.00. Market research report published by Marketdata Enterprises. Covers anti-anxiety drugs, stress management clinics, biofeedback centers, devices, seminars, workshops, spas, institutes, etc. Includes market size projections to the year 2000.

Personal Strategies for Managing Stress. American Management Association Extension Institute. • Looseleaf. $110.00. Self-study course. Emphasis is on practical explanations, examples, and problem solving. Quizzes and a case study are included.

STRIKES AND LOCKOUTS

See also: ARBITRATION; COLLECTIVE BARGAINING; LABOR; LABOR LAW AND REGULATION; LABOR UNIONS

GENERAL WORKS

Strike!. Jeremy Brecher. South End Press. • 1997. $40.00. Fourth revised edition. (Classics Series, volume one).

HANDBOOKS AND MANUALS

Labor-Management Relations: Strikes, Lockouts, and Boycotts. Douglas E. Ray and Emery W. Bartle. West Group. • Looseleaf. $110.00. Covers legal issues involved in labor-management confrontations. Includes recent decisions of the National Labor Relations Board (NLRB).

Operating During Strikes: Company Experience, NLRB Policies, and Governmental Regulations. Charles R. Perry and others. Univ. of Pennsylvania, Center for Human Resources, The Wharton School. • 1982. $20.00. (Labor Relations and Public Policy Series No. 23).

INTERNET DATABASES

Fedstats. Federal Interagency Council on Statistical Policy. Phone: (202)395-7254 • URL: http://www.fedstats.gov • Web site features an efficient search facility for full-text statistics produced by more than 70 federal agencies, including the Census Bureau, the Bureau of Economic Analysis, and the Bureau of Labor Statistics. Boolean searches can be made within one agency or for all agencies combined. Links are offered to international statistical bureaus, including the UN, IMF, OECD, UNESCO, Eurostat, and 20 individual countries. Fees: Free.

ONLINE DATABASES

DRI U.S. Central Database. Data Products Division. • Provides more than 23,000 business, financial, demographic, economic, foreign trade, and industry-related time series for the U.S. Includes national income, population, retail-wholesale trade, price indexes, labor data, housing, industrial production, banking, interest rates, money supply, etc. Time period is generally 1947 to date (some data back to 1929). Updating varies. Inquire as to online cost and availability.

PERIODICALS AND NEWSLETTERS

Union Labor Report. Bureau of National Affairs, Inc. • Biweekly. $848.00 per year.

STATISTICS SOURCES

Business Statistics of the United States. Courtenay M. Slater, editor. Bernan Associates. • 1999. $74.00. Fifth edition. Based on *Business Statistics*, formerly issue by the Bureau of Economic Analysis, U. S. Department of Commerce. Provides basic data for a wide variety of U. S. industries, services, and economic indicators. Most statistics are shown annually for 29 years and monthly for the most recent four years.

Monthly Labor Review. Available from U. S. Government Printing Office. • Monthly. $43.00 per year. Issued by the Bureau of Labor Statistics, U. S. Department of Labor. Contains data on the labor force, wages, work stoppages, price indexes, productivity, economic growth, and occupational injuries and illnesses.

Survey of Current Business. Available from U. S. Government Printing Office. • Monthly. $49.00 per year. Issued by Bureau of Economic Analysis, U. S. Department of Commerce. Presents a wide variety of business and economic data.

STRUCTURAL MATERIALS

See: BUILDING MATERIALS INDUSTRY

STUDENT AID

See: SCHOLARSHIPS AND STUDENT AID

STUDY ABROAD

GENERAL WORKS

Study Abroad: The Experience of American Undergraduates. Jerry S. Carlson and others. Greenwood Publishing Group, Inc. • 1990. $62.95. (Contributions to the Study of Education Series, No 37).

ABSTRACTS AND INDEXES

Education Index. H.W. Wilson Co. • 10 times a year. Service basis.

Readers' Guide to Periodical Literature. H. W. Wilson Co. • Monthly. $220.00 per year. CD-ROM edition, $1,495 per year, including annual cumulation. Indexes about 250 peridicals of general interest.

CD-ROM DATABASES

ERIC on SilverPlatter. Available from SilverPlatter Information, Inc. • Quarterly. $700.00 per year. Produced by the Office of Educational Research and Improvement, U. S. Dept. of Education. Provides CD-ROM indexing and abstracting of a wide variety of literature relating to education. Archival discs are available from 1966.

WILSONDISC: Education Index. H. W. Wilson Co. • Monthly. $1,295.00 per year. Provides CD-ROM indexing of education-related literature from 1983 to date. Price includes online service.

WILSONDISC: Readers' Guide to Periodical Literature. H. W. Wilson Co. • Monthly. $1,095.00 per year, including unlimited online access to *Readers' Guide to Periodical Literature* through WILSONLINE. Provides CD-ROM indexing of about 250 general interest periodicals. Covers 1983 to date. (*Readers' Guide Abstracts* also available on CD-ROM at $1,995 per year.).

DIRECTORIES

Academic Year Abroad. Institute of International Education. • Annual. $44.95. Lists over 2,700 undergraduate and graduate study abroad programs.

Academic Year and, Semester and Summer Programs Abroad. American Institute for Foreign Study. • Annual. Free. Formerly *Academic Year and Summer Programs Abroad.*

Bricker's International Directory: Long-Term University- Based Executive Programs. Peterson's. • Annual. $295.00. Presents detailed information about executive education programs offered by 85 universities and nonprofit organizations in the U. S. and around the world. Includes general management and function-specific programs.

Peterson's Guide to MBA Programs: The Most Comprehensive Guide to U. S., Canadian, and International Business Schools. Peterson's. • 1996. $21.95. Provides detailed information on about 850 graduate programs in business at 700 colleges and universities in the U. S., Canada, and other countries.

Peterson's Study Abroad: A Guide to Semester and Year Abroad Academic Programs. Peterson's. • Annual. $26.95. Describes about 1,300 academic programs available to U. S. students at 350 United States and foreign institutions.

Study Abroad: Scholarships and Higher Education Courses Worldwide. Available from Bernan Associates. • Biennial. Provides information on a wide variety of scholarships, fellowships, and educational exchange programs in over 100 countries. Text in English, French, and Spanish. Published by the United Nations Educational, Scientific, and Cultural Organization (UNESCO).

Vacation Study Abroad. Institute of International Education. • Annual. $36.95. Lists approximately 2,200 college-level and adult education summer courses sponsored by U. S. and foreign schools.

Work, Study, Travel Abroad; 1994-1995: The Whole World Handbook. Council on International Educational Exchange Staff. St. Martin's Press. • 1994. $13.95. 12th edition. Lists more than 1,000 employment, travel, and educational opportunities for the U. S. student abroad.

ONLINE DATABASES

Education Index Online. H. W. Wilson Co. • Indexes a wide variety of periodicals related to schools, colleges, and education, 1984 to date. Monthly updates. Inquire as to online cost and availability.

ERIC. Educational Resources Information Center. • Broad range of educational literature, 1966 to present. Monthly updates. Inquire as to online cost and availability.

Readers' Guide Abstracts Online. H. W. Wilson Co. • Indexes and abstracts general interest periodicals, 1983 to date. Weekly updates. Inquire as to online cost and availability.

PERIODICALS AND NEWSLETTERS

NAFSA Newsletter. National Association for Foreign Student Affairs, Association of International E. • Six times a year. Membership. Reports on international educational exchange. Formerly *National Association for Foreign Student Affairs.*

Transitions Abroad: The Guide to Learning, Living, and Working Overseas. Transitions Abroad Publishing, Inc. • Bimonthly. $28.00 per year, including annual directory of information sources. Provides practical information and advice on foreign education and employment. Supplement available *Overseas Travel Planner.*

STATISTICS SOURCES

Digest of Education Statistics. Available from U. S. Government Printing Office. • Annual. $44.00. Covers all areas of education from kindergarten through graduate school. Includes data from both government and private sources. Compiled by National Center for Education Statistics, U. S. Department of Education.

TRADE/PROFESSIONAL ASSOCIATIONS

The College Board. 45 Columbus Ave., New York, NY 10017. Phone: (212)713-8000 E-mail: mro@collegeboard.org • URL: http://www.collegeboard.org.

Council on International Educational Exchange - USA. 205 E. 42nd St., New York, NY 10017. Phone: (212)822-2600 Fax: (212)822-2699 • URL: http://www.ciee.org • Members are educational institutions and agencies that promote and sponsor international education exchange.

EF Foundation for Foreign Study. One Education St., Cambridge, MA 02141. Phone: 800-447-4273 or (617)619-1000 or (617)619-1400 Fax: (617)619-1401 E-mail: foundation@ef.com • URL: http://www.effoundation.org • Seeks to further international understanding through cultural and academic exchange. Sponsors academic homestay programs, such as High School Year in Europe.

Institute of International Education. 809 United Nations Plaza, New York, NY 10017-3580. Phone: (212)984-5200 Fax: (212)984-5452 E-mail: info@iie.org • URL: http://www.iie.org • Promotes international educational exchange programs. Administers scholarships, fellowships, and other grants provided by over 120 sponsors.

NAFSA/Association of International Educators. 1307 New York Ave., N.W., 8th Fl., Washington, DC 20005. Phone: (202)737-3699 Fax: (202)737-3657 E-mail: inbox@nafsa.org • URL: http://www.nafsa.org • Members are individuals, organizations, and institutions involved with international educational interchange, including foreign student advisors, overseas educational advisers, foreign student admission officers, and U. S. students abroad.

National Registration Center for Study Abroad. P.O. Box 1393, Milwaukee, WI 53201. Phone: (414)278-7410 Fax: (414)271-8884 E-mail: info@nrcsa.com • URL: http://www.nrcsa.com • Members are foreign universities, foreign language institutions, and other institutions or organizations offering foreign study programs designed for North Americans.

Youth for Understanding International Exchange. 3501 Newark St., N. W., Washington, DC 20016. Phone: 800-833-6243 or (202)966-6808 Fax: (202)895-1104 E-mail: pio@yfu.org • URL: http://www.youth.forunderstanding.org • Provides educational opportunities for young people and adults through international student exchange. Administers study abroad scholarship programs in cooperation with other governments, the U. S. Senate, the U. S. Information Agency, and various educational organizations.

STYLE MANUALS

See: PRINTING STYLE MANUALS

SUBCHAPTER "S" CORPORATIONS

See: CORPORATIONS; PROFESSIONAL CORPORATIONS

SUBJECT HEADINGS

See: INDEXING

SUBLIMINAL ADVERTISING

See: ADVERTISING

SUBSTANCE ABUSE

See: ALCOHOLISM; DRUG ABUSE AND TRAFFIC

SUBURBAN SHOPPING CENTERS

See: SHOPPING CENTERS

SUGAR INDUSTRY

CD-ROM DATABASES

Food Science and Technology Abstracts [CD-ROM]. Available from SilverPlatter Information, Inc. • Quarterly. $3,700 per year. Produced by International Food Information Service (home page is http://www.ifis.org). Provides worldwide coverage on CD-ROM of the literature of food technology and production. Various types of publications are indexed, with abstracts, including about 1,800 periodicals. Time period is 1969 to date.

DIRECTORIES

Sugar y Azucar Yearbook. Ruspam Communications, Inc. • Annual. $55.00. List of over 1,700 cane sugar mills and refineries-international coverage.

HANDBOOKS AND MANUALS

Cane Sugar Handbook: A Manual for Cane Sugar Manufacturers and Their Chemists. James C. Chen and Chung-Chi Chou. John Wiley and Sons, Inc. • 1993. $350.30. 2nd edition.

INTERNET DATABASES

Fedstats. Federal Interagency Council on Statistical Policy. Phone: (202)395-7254 • URL: http://www.fedstats.gov • Web site features an efficient search facility for full-text statistics produced by more than 70 federal agencies, including the Census Bureau, the Bureau of Economic Analysis, and the Bureau of Labor Statistics. Boolean searches can be made within one agency or for all agencies combined. Links are offered to international statistical bureaus, including the UN, IMF, OECD, UNESCO, Eurostat, and 20 individual countries. Fees: Free.

USDA. United States Department of Agriculture. Phone: (202)720-2791 E-mail: agsec@usda.gov • URL: http://www.usda.gov • The USDA home page has six sections: News and Information; What's New; About USDA; Agencies; Opportunities; Search and Help. Keyword searching is offered from the USDA home page and from various individual agency home pages. Agencies are the Economic Research Service, Agricultural Marketing Service, National Agricultural Statistics Service, National Agricultural Library, and about 12 others. Updating varies. Fees: Free.

ONLINE DATABASES

CAB Abstracts. CAB International North America. • Contains 46 specialized abstract collections covering over 10,000 journals and monographs in the areas of agriculture, horticulture, forest products, farm products, nutrition, dairy science, poultry, grains, animal health, entomology, etc. Time period is 1972 to date, with monthly updates. Inquire as to online cost and availability. *CAB Abstracts on CD-ROM* also available, with annual updating.

DRI U.S. Central Database. Data Products Division. • Provides more than 23,000 business, financial, demographic, economic, foreign trade, and industry-related time series for the U.S. Includes national income, population, retail-wholesale trade, price indexes, labor data, housing, industrial production, banking, interest rates, money supply, etc. Time period is generally 1947 to date (some data back to 1929). Updating varies. Inquire as to online cost and availability.

Food Science and Technology Abstracts [online]. IFIS North American Desk. • Produced by International Food Information Service. Provides about 500,000 online citations, with abstracts, to the international literature of food science, technology, commodities, engineering, and processing. Approximately 2,000 periodicals are covered. Time period is 1969 to date, with monthly updates. Inquire as to online cost and availability.

PERIODICALS AND NEWSLETTERS

Sugar Bulletin. American Sugar Cane League of the U.S.A. • Semimonthly. Free to members; non-members, $15.00 per year.

Sugar Journal: Covering the World's Sugar Industry. Kriedt Enterprises Ltd. • Monthly. $36.00 per year. A monthly technical publication designed to inform sugar beet and cane farms, factories, and refineries throughout the world about the latest developments in the sugar industry.

The Sugar Producer: Representing the Sugar Beet Industry in the United States. Harris Publishing, Inc. • Seven times a year. $10.95 per year. Supplies sugar beet growers with information to assist them in production of quality sugar beet crops.

Sugar y Azucar. Ruspam Communications, Inc. • Monthly. $75.00 per year. Text in English and Spanish.

STATISTICS SOURCES

Agricultural Statistics. Available from U. S. Government Printing Office. • Annual. Produced by the National Agricultural Statistics Service, U. S. Department of Agriculture. Provides a wide variety of statistical data relating to agricultural production, supplies, consumption, prices/price-supports, foreign trade, costs, and returns, as well as farm labor, loans, income, and population. In many cases, historical data is shown annually for 10 years. In addition to farm data, includes detailed fishery statistics.

Business Statistics of the United States. Courtenay M. Slater, editor. Bernan Associates. • 1999. $74.00. Fifth edition. Based on *Business Statistics*, formerly issue by the Bureau of Economic Analysis, U. S. Department of Commerce. Provides basic data for a wide variety of U. S. industries, services, and economic indicators. Most statistics are shown annually for 29 years and monthly for the most recent four years.

Sugar and Sweetener Situation and Outlook. Available from U. S. Government Printing Office. • Three times per year. $11.00 per year. Issued by

Economic Research Service, U. S. Department of Agriculture. Provides current statistical information on supply, demand, and prices.

Survey of Current Business. Available from U. S. Government Printing Office. • Monthly. $49.00 per year. Issued by Bureau of Economic Analysis, U. S. Department of Commerce. Presents a wide variety of business and economic data.

TRADE/PROFESSIONAL ASSOCIATIONS

American Sugar Alliance. 2111 Wilson Blvd., Ste. 700, Arlington, VA 22201. Phone: (703)351-5055 Fax: (703)351-6698 • URL: http://www.sugaralliance.org • Members are domestic producers of sugar beets, sugarcane, and corn for syrup.

American Sugar Cane League of the U.S.A. P.O. Drawer 938, Thibodaux, LA 70302. Phone: (504)448-3707 Fax: (504)448-3722.

Sugar Association. 1101 15th St., N.W., Suite 600, Washington, DC 20005. Phone: (202)785-1122 Fax: (202)785-5019 E-mail: sugar@sugar.com • URL: http://www.sugar.com.

Sweetener Users Association. 3231 Valley Lane, Falls Church, VA 22044. Phone: (703)532-2683 Fax: (703)532-9361 • Members are industrial users of sweeteners and companies in the sweetener industry.

United States Beet Sugar Association. 1156 15th St., N.W., Suite 1019, Washington, DC 20005. Phone: (202)296-4820 Fax: (202)331-2065.

OTHER SOURCES

Major Food and Drink Companies of the World. Available from The Gale Group. • 2001. $855.00. Fourth edition. Two volumes. Published by Graham & Whiteside. Contains profiles and trade names for more than 9,000 important food and beverage companies in various countries. In addition to foods, includes both alcoholic and nonalcoholic drink products.

Thomas Food and Beverage Market Place. Grey House Publishing. • Annual. $295.00. Three volumes. Contains more than 40,000 entries covering food companies, beverages, food equipment, warehouse companies, food brokers, wholesalers, importers, and exporters. Formerly *Thomas Food Industry Register.*

SUGGESTION SYSTEMS

DIRECTORIES

Employee Involvement Association Membership Directory. Employee Involvement Association. • Annual. Membership.

PERIODICALS AND NEWSLETTERS

New Horizons. Employee Involvement Association. • Quarterly. Membership. Newsletter.

STATISTICS SOURCES

Employee Involvement Association Statistical Report. Employee Involvement Association. • Annual. 150.00.

TRADE/PROFESSIONAL ASSOCIATIONS

Employee Involvement Association. 525 Fifth St., S.W., Ste. A, Des Moines, IA 50309-4501. Phone: (515)282-8192 Fax: (515)282-9117 E-mail: jbw@amg-inc.com • URL: http://www.eia.com • Members are business and government professionals dedicated to employee involvement processes, including suggestion systems.

SULPHUR INDUSTRY

See also: CHEMICAL INDUSTRIES

GENERAL WORKS

New Uses of Sulfur-II. Douglas Bourne, editor. American Chemical Society. • 1978. $32.95. (Advances in Chemistry Series: No. 165).

DIRECTORIES

OPD Chemical Buyers Directory. Schnell Publishing Co., Inc. • Annual. $129.00. Included in subscription to *Chemical Marketing Reporter.* About 1,500 suppliers of chemical process materials and more than 300 companies which transport and store chemicals in the U.S.

INTERNET DATABASES

Fedstats. Federal Interagency Council on Statistical Policy. Phone: (202)395-7254 • URL: http://www.fedstats.gov • Web site features an efficient search facility for full-text statistics produced by more than 70 federal agencies, including the Census Bureau, the Bureau of Economic Analysis, and the Bureau of Labor Statistics. Boolean searches can be made within one agency or for all agencies combined. Links are offered to international statistical bureaus, including the UN, IMF, OECD, UNESCO, Eurostat, and 20 individual countries. Fees: Free.

ONLINE DATABASES

DRI U.S. Central Database. Data Products Division. • Provides more than 23,000 business, financial, demographic, economic, foreign trade, and industry-related time series for the U.S. Includes national income, population, retail-wholesale trade, price indexes, labor data, housing, industrial production, banking, interest rates, money supply, etc. Time period is generally 1947 to date (some data back to 1929). Updating varies. Inquire as to online cost and availability.

Globalbase. The Gale Group. • Provides more than one million online summaries of business, industrial, and economic news reports from more than 1,000 publications worldwide. Covers a wide range of material appearing in international trade journals, professional magazines, and newspapers. Time period is 1984 to date, with weekly updates. Inquire as to online cost and availability.

PERIODICALS AND NEWSLETTERS

Sulphur: Covers All Aspects of World Sulphur and Sulphuric Acid Industry. British Sulphur Publishing. • Bimonthly. $520.00 per year.

RESEARCH CENTERS AND INSTITUTES

Sulphur Institute. 1140 Connecticut Ave., N.W., Suite. 612, Washington, DC 20036. Phone: (202)331-9660 Fax: (202)293-2940 E-mail: sulphur@sulphurinstitute.org • URL: http://www.sulphurinstitute.org.

STATISTICS SOURCES

Annual Survey of Manufactures. Available from U. S. Government Printing Office. • Annual. Prices vary. Issued by the U. S. Census Bureau as an interim update to the *Census of Manufactures.* Includes data on number of manufacturing establishments in various industries, employment, labor costs, value of shipments, capital expenditures, inventories, energy costs, and assets. (See also Census Bureau home page, http://www.census.gov/.).

Business Statistics of the United States. Courtenay M. Slater, editor. Bernan Associates. • 1999. $74.00. Fifth edition. Based on *Business Statistics,* formerly issue by the Bureau of Economic Analysis, U. S. Department of Commerce. Provides basic data for a wide variety of U. S. industries, services, and economic indicators. Most statistics are shown annually for 29 years and monthly for the most recent four years.

Mineral Commodity Summaries. Available from U. S. Government Printing Office. • Annual. Published by the U. S. Geological Survey, Department of the Interior (http://www.usgs.gov). Contains detailed, five-year data for about 90 nonfuel minerals. Covers a wide range of statistics, including production, imports, exports, consumption, reserves, prices, tariff information, and industry employment. (Two pages are devoted to each mineral.).

Survey of Current Business. Available from U. S. Government Printing Office. • Monthly. $49.00 per year. Issued by Bureau of Economic Analysis, U. S. Department of Commerce. Presents a wide variety of business and economic data.

OTHER SOURCES

Major Chemical and Petrochemical Companies of the World. Available from The Gale Group. • 2001. $855.00. Third edition. Two volumes. Published by Graham & Whiteside. Contains profiles of more than 7,000 important chemical and petrochemical companies in various countries. Subject areas include general chemicals, specialty chemicals, agricultural chemicals, petrochemicals, industrial gases, and fertilizers.

SULPHURIC ACID

See: SULPHUR INDUSTRY

SUN, ENERGY FROM

See: SOLAR ENERGY

SUPERCONDUCTORS

See also: SEMICONDUCTOR INDUSTRY

GENERAL WORKS

Superconductivity. Charles P. Poole and others. Academic Press, Inc. • 1995. $65.00.

Superconductivity: The Next Revolution?. Gianfranco Vidali. Cambridge University Press. • 1993. $21.95.

ABSTRACTS AND INDEXES

Applied Science and Technology Index. H. W. Wilson Co. • 11 times a year. Quarterly and annual cumulations. Service basis for print edition; CD-ROM edition, $1,495.00 per year. Indexes a wide variety of English language technical, industrial, and engineering periodicals.

Key Abstracts: High Temperature Superconductors. Available from INSPEC, Inc. • Monthly. $240.00 per year. Provides international coverage of journal and proceedings literature. Published in England by the Institution of Electrical Engineers (IEE).

Solid State and Superconductivity Abstracts. Cambridge Information Group. • Bimonthly. $1,045.00 per year. Formerly *Solid State Abstracts Journal.*

BIBLIOGRAPHIES

Superconductivity: An Annotated Bibliography with Abstracts. A. Bisarsh, editor. Nova Science Publishers, Inc. • 1998. $115.00.

DIRECTORIES

Corptech Directory of Technology Companies. Corporate Technology Information Services, Inc. c/o Eileen Kennedy. • Annual. $795.00. Four volumes. Profiles of more than 45,000 manufacturers and developers of high technology products. Includes private companies, publicly-held corporations, and subsidiaries. Formerly *Corporate Technology Directory.*

ONLINE DATABASES

Applied Science and Technology Index Online. H. W. Wilson Co. • Provides online indexing of 400 major scientific, technical, industrial, and engineering periodicals. Time period is 1983 to date. Monthly updates. Inquire as to online cost and availability.

Hard Sciences. Cambridge Scientific Abstracts. • Provides the online version of *Computer and Information Systems Abstracts, Electronics and Communications Abstracts, Health and Safety Science Abstracts, ISMEC: Mechanical Engineering Abstracts (Information Service in Mechanical Engineering)* and *Solid State and Superconductivity Abstracts.* Time period is 1981 to date, with monthly updates. Inquire as to online cost and availability.

PROMT: Predicasts Overview of Markets and Technology. The Gale Group. • Companies, products, applied technologies and markets. U.S. and international literature coverage, 1972 to date. Inquire as to online cost and availability. Provides abstracts from more than 1,600 publications. Weekly updates.

PERIODICALS AND NEWSLETTERS

Superconductivity Flash Report. Alan R. Lind. • Semimonthly. $295.00 per year. Newsletter.

Superconductor and Cyroelectronics. WestTech. • Quarterly. $22.00 per year.

RESEARCH CENTERS AND INSTITUTES

Edward L. Ginzton Laboratory. Stanford University, 450 Via Palou, Stanford, CA 94305-4085. Phone: (650)023-0111 Fax: (650)725-9355 E-mail: dabm@ee.stanford.edu • URL: http://www.stanford.edu/group/ginzton • Research fields include low-temperature physics and superconducting electronics.

Institute for Pure and Applied Physical Sciences. University of California, San Diego, 9500 Gilman Dr., La Jolla, CA 92093-0360. Phone: (858)534-3560 Fax: (858)534-7649 E-mail: mbmaple@uscd.edu • Areas of study include superconductivity.

Materials Processing Center. Massachusetts Institute of Technology, 77 Massachusetts Ave., Room 12-007, Cambridge, MA 02139-4307. Phone: (617)253-5179 Fax: (617)258-6900 E-mail: fmpage@.mit.edu • URL: http://www.web.mit.edu/mpc/www/ • Conducts processing, engineering, and economic research in ferrous and nonferrous metals, ceramics, polymers, photonic materials, superconductors, welding, composite materials, and other materials.

STATISTICS SOURCES

U. S. Industry and Trade Outlook: The McGraw-Hill Companies and the U.S. Department of Commerce/International Trade Administration. Datapso Research Corp. • Annual. $69.95. Produced by the International Trade Administration, U. S. Department of Commerce, in a "public-private" partnership with DRI/McGraw-Hill and Standard & Poor's. Provides basic data, outlook for the current year, and "Long-Term Prospects" (five-year projections) for a wide variety of products and services. Includes high technology industries. Formerly *U. S. Industrial Outlook.*

OTHER SOURCES

Superconductor Week. WestTech. • Weekly. $397.00 per year. Newsletter. Covers applications of superconductivity and cryogenics, including new markets and products.

SUPERMARKETS

See also: CHAIN STORES; GROCERY BUSINESS

ALMANACS AND YEARBOOKS

Facts About Supermarket Development. Food Marketing Institute. • Annual. Members, $20.00; non-members, $40.00.

DIRECTORIES

Directory of Single Unit Supermarket Operators. Chain Store Guide. • Annual. $290.00. Covers more than 7,100 one-store supermarket establishments with annual sales of at least $1,000,000. Includes names of primary wholesalers.

Directory of Supermarket, Grocery, and Convenience Store Chains. Chain Store Guide. • Annual. $300.00. Provides information on about 2,200 food store chains operating 30,000 individual stores. Store locations are given.

European Directory of Retailers and Wholesalers. Available from The Gale Group. • 1997. $790.00. Second edition. Published by Euromonitor. Provides detailed information on more than 4,000 major retail and wholesale businesses in 17 countries of Western Europe. Contains 26 categories, such as supermarkets, superstores, department stores, discount stores, franchise operators, mail order, etc. Includes company, product, and geographic indexes.

Grocery Distribution Magazine Directory of Warehouse Equipment, Fixtures, and Services. Trend Publishing, Inc. • Annual. $7.50. Covers products related to food warehousing, distribution, and storage.

Trade Dimensions' Market Scope. Trade Dimensions. • Annual. $325.00. Statistics of grocery distribution for 249 metropolitan areas. Formerly *Progressive Grocer's market Scope.*

FINANCIAL RATIOS

FMI Annual Financial Review. Food Marketing Institute. • Annual. Members, $30.00; non-members, $75.00. Provides financial data on the supermarket industry.

Food Marketing Industry Speaks. Food Marketing Institute. • Annual. Members, $30.00; non-members, $75.00. Provides data on overall food industry marketing performance, including retail distribution and store operations.

Operating Results of Independent Supermarkets. Food Marketing Institute. • Annual. Members, $30.00; non-members, $75.00. Includes data on gross margins, inventory turnover, expenses, etc.

Operations Review. Food Marketing Institute. • Quarterly. $50.00 per year. Includes operating ratios for food retailing companies.

HANDBOOKS AND MANUALS

Trade Dimensions' Marketing Guidebook. Trade Dimensions. • Annual. $340.00. Over 850 major chain and independent food retailers and wholesalers in the United States and Canada; also includes food brokers, rack jobbers, candy and tobacco distributors, and magazine distributors. Formerly *Progressive Grocer's Marketing Guidebook.*

ONLINE DATABASES

PROMT: Predicasts Overview of Markets and Technology. The Gale Group. • Companies, products, applied technologies and markets. U.S. and international literature coverage, 1972 to date. Inquire as to online cost and availability. Provides abstracts from more than 1,600 publications. Weekly updates.

PERIODICALS AND NEWSLETTERS

Grocery Headquarters: The Newspaper for the Food Industry. Trend Publishing, Inc. • Monthly. $100.00 per year. Covers the sale and distribution of food products and other items sold in supermarkets and grocery stores. Edited mainly for retailers and wholesalers. Formerly *Grocery Marketing.*

Military Grocer. Downey Communications, Inc. • Bimonthly. $40.00 per year. Edited for managers and employees of supermarkets on military bases. (These are supermarkets administered by the Defense Commissary Agency.).

Progressive Grocer: The Magazine of Supermarketing. Bill Communications, Inc. • Monthly. $99.00 per year.

Supermarket Business. Bill Communications, Inc. • Monthly. $85.00 per year.

PRICE SOURCES

Supermarket News: The Industry's Weekly Newspaper. Fairchild Publications. • Weekly. Individuals, $68.00 per year; instutions, $44.50 per year; corporations, $89.00 per year.

STATISTICS SOURCES

Standard & Poor's Industry Surveys. Standard & Poor's. • Semiannual. $1,800.00. Two looseleaf volumes. Includes monthly supplements. Provides detailed, individual surveys of 52 major industry groups. Each survey is revised on a semiannual basis. Also includes "Monthly Investment Review" (industry group investment analysis) and monthly "Trends & Projections" (economic analysis).

TRADE/PROFESSIONAL ASSOCIATIONS

Food Marketing Institute. 800 Connecticut Ave., N.W., Washington, DC 20006. Phone: (202)452-8444 Fax: (202)429-4519 E-mail: fmi@fmi.org • URL: http://www.fm.org.

National Grocers Association. 1825 Samuel Morse Dr., Reston, VA 22190-5317. Phone: (703)437-5300 Fax: (703)437-7768 E-mail: info@nationalgrocers.org • URL: http://www.nationalgrocers.org.

SUPERVISION

See: ADMINISTRATION; FACTORY MANAGEMENT; INDUSTRIAL MANAGEMENT

SUPPLY MANAGEMENT

See: INVENTORY CONTROL; PURCHASING

SURGICAL INSTRUMENTS INDUSTRY

See also: DENTAL SUPPLY INDUSTRY; HOSPITAL EQUIPMENT; MEDICAL TECHNOLOGY

ABSTRACTS AND INDEXES

Excerpta Medica: Biophysics, Bioengineering, and Medical Instrumentation. Elsevier Science. • 16 times a year. $2,207.00 per year. Section 27 of *Excerpta Medica.*

CD-ROM DATABASES

Health Devices Alerts [CD-ROM]. ECRI. • Weekly. $2,450.00 per year. Provides CD-ROM reports of medical equipment defects, problems, failures, misuses, and recalls.

DIRECTORIES

Health Devices Sourcebook. ECRI (Emergency Care Research Institute). • Annual. Lists over 6,000 manufacturers of a wide variety of medical equipment and supplies, including clinical laboratory equipment, testing instruments, surgical instruments, patient care equipment, etc.

Health Industry Buyers Guide. Spring House. • Annual. $195.00. About 4,000 manufacturers of hospital and physician's supplies and equipment. Formerly *Surgical Trade Buyers Guide.*

Medical Device Register. Medical Economics. • Annual. $325.00. Lists more than 12,000 suppliers of a wide variety of medical devices and clinical laboratory products.

OB/GYN Reference Guide. Access Publishing Co. • Annual. Price on application. Includes directory information for obstetrical/gynecological equipment, supplies, pharmaceuticals, services, organizations, and publications.

Surgeons' Desk Reference for Minimally Invasive Surgery Products. Medical Economics Co., Inc. • Annual. $125.00. A directory of products for laparoscopic surgery. Includes commentary.

FINANCIAL RATIOS

Annual Statement Studies. Robert Morris Associates: The Association of Lending and Credit Risk Professiona. • Annual. Free to members; non-members, $140.00. Median and quartile financial ratios are given for over 400 kinds of manufacturing, wholesale, retail, construction, and consumer finance establishments. Data is sorted by both asset size and sales volume. Includes a clearly written "Definition of Ratios" and an alphabetical industry index.

INTERNET DATABASES

National Library of Medicine (NLM). National Institutes of Health (NIH). Phone: 888-346-3656 or (301)496-1131 Fax: (301)480-3537 E-mail: access@nlm.nih.gov • URL: http://www.nlm.nih.gov • NLM Web site offers free access through MEDLINE ("PubMed") to about nine million references to articles appearing in some 3,800 biomedical journals, with abstracts. Search interfaces range from "simple keywords to advanced Boolean expressions." The NLM site offers many links to other sources of biomedical and technical information (the National Center for Biotechnology Information, for example). Fees: Free.

ONLINE DATABASES

Embase. Elsevier Science, Inc. • Worldwide medical literature, 1974 to present. Weekly updates. Inquire as to online cost and availability.

F-D-C Reports. FDC Reports, Inc. • An online version of "The Gray Sheet" (medical devices), "The Pink Sheet" (pharmaceuticals), "The Rose Sheet" (cosmetics), "The Blue Sheet" (biomedical), and "The Tan Sheet" (nonprescription). Contains full-text information on legal, technical, corporate, financial, and marketing developments from 1987 to date, with weekly updates. Inquire as to online cost and availability.

Health Devices Alerts [online]. ECRI. • Provides online reports of medical equipment defects, problems, failures, misuses, and recalls. Time period is 1977 to date, with weekly updates. Inquire as to online cost and availability.

PERIODICALS AND NEWSLETTERS

Biomedical Instrumentation and Technology. Association for the Advancement of Medical Instrumentation. Hanley and Belfus, Inc. • Bimonthly. Individuals, $106.00 per year; institutions, $136.00 per year.

Health Devices Alerts: A Summary of Reported Problems, Hazards, Recalls, and Updates. ECRI (Emergency Care Research Institute). • Weekly. Newsletter containing reviews of health equipment problems. Includes *Health Devices Alerts Action Items, Health Devices Alerts Abstracts, Health Devices Alerts FDA Data, Health Devices Alerts Implants, Health Devices Alerts Hazards Bulletin.*

Health Industry Today: The Market Letter for Health Care Industry Vendors. Business Word, Inc. • Monthly. $325.00 per year.

Healthcare Purchasing News: A Magazine for Hospital Materials Management Central Service, Infection Control Practitioners. McKnight Medical Communications. • Monthly. $44.00 per year. Edited for personnel responsible for the purchase of medical, surgical, and hospital equipment and supplies. Features new purchasing techniques and new products. Includes news of the activities of two major purchasing associations, Health Care Material Management Society and International Association of Healthcare Central Service Materiel Management.

Medical Devices, Diagnostics, and Instrumentation: The Gray Sheet Reports. F-D-C Reports, Inc. • Weekly. $955.00 per year. Newsletter. Provides industry and financial news, including a medical sector stock index. Monitors regulatory developments at the Center for Devices and Radiological Health of the U. S. Food and Drug Administration.

Medical Electronics and Equipment News. Reilly Publishing Co. • Bimonthly. Free to qualified personnel; others, $50.00 per year. Provides medical electronics industry news and new product information.

Medical Product Manufacturing News. Canon Communications LLC. • 10 times a year. Free to qualified personnel; others, $125.00 per year. Directed at manufacturers of medical devices and medical electronic equipment. Covers industry news, service news, and new products.

Medical Product Sales. Health Industry Distribution Association. Douglas Publications, Inc. • Monthly. $49.95 per year.

Surgical Products. Cahners Business Information. • 10 times a year. $24.00 per year. Covers new Technology and products for surgeons and operation rooms.

STATISTICS SOURCES

Annual Survey of Manufactures. Available from U. S. Government Printing Office. • Annual. Prices vary. Issued by the U. S. Census Bureau as an interim update to the *Census of Manufactures.* Includes data on number of manufacturing establishments in various industries, employment, labor costs, value of shipments, capital expenditures, inventories, energy costs, and assets. (See also Census Bureau home page, http://www.census.gov/.).

Standard & Poor's Industry Surveys. Standard & Poor's. • Semiannual. $1,800.00. Two looseleaf volumes. Includes monthly supplements. Provides detailed, individual surveys of 52 major industry groups. Each survey is revised on a semiannual basis. Also includes "Monthly Investment Review" (industry group investment analysis) and monthly "Trends & Projections" (economic analysis).

U. S. Industry and Trade Outlook: The McGraw-Hill Companies and the U.S. Department of Commerce/ International Trade Administration. Datapso Research Corp. • Annual. $69.95. Produced by the International Trade Administration, U. S. Department of Commerce, in a "public-private" partnership with DRI/McGraw-Hill and Standard & Poor's. Provides basic data, outlook for the current year, and "Long-Term Prospects" (five-year projections) for a wide variety of products and services. Includes high technology industries. Formerly *U. S. Industrial Outlook.*

TRADE/PROFESSIONAL ASSOCIATIONS

Association for Healthcare Resource and Materials Management. c/o American Hospital Association, One N. Franklin St ., Chicago, IL 60606. Phone: (312)422-3840 Fax: (312)422-3573 E-mail: ahrmm@aha.org • URL: http://www.ahrmm.org • Members are involved with the purchasing and distribution of supplies and equipment for hospitals and other healthcare establishments. Affiliated with the American Hospital Association.

Association for the Advancement of Medical Instrumentation. 3330 Washington Blvd., Suite 400, Arlington, VA 22201. Phone: 800-332-2264 or (703)525-4890 Fax: (703)276-0793 • Members are engineers, technicians, physicians, manufacturers, and others with an interest in medical instrumentation.

Health Care Resource Management Society. P.O. Box 29253, Cincinnati, OH 45229-0253. Phone: (513)520-1058 or (513)872-6315 Fax: (513)872-6158 E-mail: hcrms@choice.net • URL: http://www.hcrms.com • Members are materials management (purchasing) personnel in hospitals and the healthcare industry. The Society is concerned with hospital costs, distribution, logistics, recycling, and inventory management.

Health Industry Distributors Association. 66 Canal Center Plaza, Suite 520, Alexandria, VA 22314-1591. Phone: (703)549-4432 Fax: (703)549-6495 • URL: http://www.hida.org.

Health Industry Manufacturers Association. 1200 G St., N.W., Suite 400, Washington, DC 20005. Phone: (202)783-8700 Fax: (202)783-8750 • URL: http://www.himanet.com.

International Association of Healthcare Central Service Materiel Management. 213 W. Institute Place, Suite 307, Chicago, IL 60610. Phone: 800-962-8274 or (312)440-0078 Fax: (312)440-9474 E-mail: mailbox@iahcsmm.com • URL: http://www.iahcsmm.com • Members are professional personnel responsible for management and distribution of supplies from a central service material management (purchasing) department of a hospital.

OTHER SOURCES

Computer Assisted Surgery: Automation, Virtual Reality, Robotics, and Radiosurgery. Theta Reports/ PJB Medical Publications, Inc. • 2000. $2,295.00. Contains market research data relating to surgical systems technology. (Theta Report No. 1105.).

New and Breaking Technologies in the Pharmaceutical and Medical Device Industries. Theta Reports/PJB Medical Publications, Inc. • 1999. $1,695:00. Contains market research predictions of medical technology trends over the next 5 to 10 years (2004-2009), including developments in biotechnology, genetic engineering, medical device technology, therapeutic vaccines, non-invasive diagnostics, and minimally-invasive surgery. (Theta Report No. 931.).

New Ophthalmology: Treatments and Technologies. Theta Reports/PJB Medical Publications, Inc. • 2000. $1,695. Provides market research data relating to eye surgery, including LASIK, cataract surgery, and associated technology. (Theta Report No. 911.).

SURPLUS FARM PRODUCE

See: FARM PRODUCE

SURPLUS PRODUCTS

See also: RECYCLING; WASTE PRODUCTS

DIRECTORIES

Used Equipment Directory. Penton Media Inc. • Monthly. $30.00 per year. Lists of 800 dealers, in used metalworking, electrical power, process, and material handling equipment, machine tools, etc.

PERIODICALS AND NEWSLETTERS

Commerce Business Daily. Industry and Trade Administration, U.S. Department of Commerce. Available from U.S. Government Printing Office. • Daily. Priority, $324.00 per year; non-priority, $275.00 per year. Synopsis of *U.S. Government Proposed Procurement, Sales and Contract Awards.*

Surplus Record: Index of Available Capital Equipment. Surplus Record, Inc. • Monthly. $33.00 per year. Lists over 46,000 items of used and surplus machine tools, chemical processing and electrical equipment.

TRADE/PROFESSIONAL ASSOCIATIONS

Associated Surplus Dealers. 2950 31st St., Suite 100, Santa Monica, CA 90405-5201. Phone: 800-421-4511 or (310)396-6006 Fax: (310)399-2662.

Machinery Dealers National Association. 315 S. Patrick St., Alexandria, VA 22314-3501. Phone: 800-872-7807 or (703)836-9300 Fax: (703)836-9303 E-mail: office@mdna.com • URL: http://www.mdna.com.

SURVEY METHODS

See also: MARKET RESEARCH

ABSTRACTS AND INDEXES

Current Index to Statistics: Applications, Methods, and Theory. American Statistical Association. • Annual. Price on application. An index to journal articles on statistical applications and methodology.

DIRECTORIES

Focus Group Directory: International Directory of Focus Group Companies and Services. New York AMA-Green Book. • Annual. $80.00. Contains information on companies offering focus group facilities, including recruiting, moderating, and transcription services.

GreenBook: Worldwide Directory of Marketing Research Companies and Services. New York Ama-Green Book. • Annual. $145.00. Contains information in 300 categories on more than 2,500 market research companies, consultants, field services, computer services, survey research companies, etc. Indexed by specialty, industry, company, computer program, and personnel. Formerly (Greenbook Worldwide International Directory of Marketing Research Companies and Services).

Marketing Know-How: Your Guide to the Best Marketing Tools and Sources. Intertec Publishing. • 1996. $49.95. Describes more than 700 public and private sources of consumer marketing data. Also discusses market trends and provides information on such marketing techniques as cluster analysis, focus groups, and geodemographic analysis.

MRA Blue Book Research Services Directory. Marketing Research Association. • Annual. $169.95. Lists more than 1,200 international marketing research companies and survey services. Formerly *Directory of Research Services Provided by Members of the Marketing Research Association.*

HANDBOOKS AND MANUALS

Assessing Service Quality: Satisfying the Expectations of Library Customers. Peter Hernon and Ellen Altman. American Library Association. • 1998. $40.00. Discusses surveys, focus groups, and other data collection methods for measuring the quality of library service. Includes sample forms and an annotated bibliography.

Constructing Effective Questionnaires. Robert A. Peterson. Sage Publications, Inc. • 1999. $70.00. Covers the construction and wording of questionnaires for survey research.

Focus Group Kit. David L. Morgan and Richard A. Krueger, editors. Sage Publications, Inc. • 1997. $99.95. Six volumes. Various authors cover the basics of focus group research, including planning, developing questions, moderating, and analyzing results.

Focus Groups: A Practical Guide for Applied Research. Richard A. Krueger and Mary Anne Casey. Sage Publications, Inc. • 2000. $69.95. Third edition. A step-by-step guide to obtaining useful research data from a focus group.

Gower Handbook of Customer Service. Peter Murley, editor. Ashgate Publishing Co. • 1996. $113.95. Consists of 40 articles (chapters) written by various authors. Among the topics covered are benchmarking, customer surveys, focus groups, control groups, employee selection, incentives, training, teamwork, and telephone techniques. Published by Gower in England.

Handbook for Focus Group Research. Thomas L. Greenbaum. Sage Publications, Inc. • 1997. $49.95. Second edition. Includes glossary and index.

Marketing Manager's Handbook. Sidney J. Levy and others. Prentice Hall. • 2000. Price on application. Contains 71 chapters by various authors on a wide variety of marketing topics, including market segmentation, market research, international marketing, industrial marketing, survey methods, customer service, advertising, pricing, planning, strategy, and ethics.

Marketing Research Project Manual. Glen R. Jarboe. South-Western Publishing Co. • 1998. $27.95. Fourth edition. Covers the methodology of market research surveys.(SWC-Marketing Series).

Moderating Focus Groups: A Practical Guide for Group Facilitation. Thomas L. Greenbaum. Sage Publications, Inc. • 2000. $70.00. Covers participant recruitment, characteristics of successful moderators, moderating fundamentals, and related topics.

Studying Your Workforce: Applied Research Methods and Tools for the Training and Development Practitioner. Alan Clardy. Sage Publications, Inc. • 1997. $45.00. Describes how to apply specific research methods to common training problems. Emphasis is on data collection methods: testing, observation, surveys, and interviews. Topics include performance problems and assessment.

Survey Research Handbook: Guidelines and Strategies for Conducting a Survey. Pamela L. Alreck and Robert B. Settle. McGraw-Hill Higher Education. • 1994. $50.00. Second edition. Consists of four major parts: 1. Planning and Designing the Survey, 2. Developing Survey Instruments, 3. Collecting and Processing Data, 4. Interpreting and Reporting Results. Includes a glossary and index. (Marketing Series).

Workshops: Designing and Facilitating Experiential Learning. Jeff E. Brooks-Harris and Susan R. Stock-Ward. Sage Publications, Inc. • 1999. $55.00. Presents a practical approach to designing, running, and evaluating workshops in business, adult education, and other areas. Includes references.

PERIODICALS AND NEWSLETTERS

Journal of Business and Economic Statistics. American Statistical Association. • Quarterly. Libraries, $90.00 per year. Emphasis is on statistical measurement and applications for business and economics.

Survey Research. Survey Research Laboratory. • Three times a year. Individuals, $10.00 per year; institutions, $50.00-$500.00 per year. Includes information on current research and descriptions of recent methodological publications on survey research.

RESEARCH CENTERS AND INSTITUTES

Survey Research Center. University of California at Berkeley, 2538 Channing Way, Berkeley, CA 94720-5100. Phone: (510)642-6578 Fax: (510)643-8292 E-mail: hbrady@bravo.berkeley.edu • URL: http://www.grad.berkeley.edu:4229/ • Research areas include the utilization and development of survey methods.

Survey Research Laboratory. University of Illinois at Chicago, 410 S. Peoria St., Chicago, IL 60607. Phone: (312)996-5300 Fax: (312)996-3358 E-mail: info@srl.uic.edu • URL: http://www.srl.uic.edu • Research areas include survey methodology and sampling techniques.

TRADE/PROFESSIONAL ASSOCIATIONS

American Association for Public Opinion Research. P.O. Box 1248, Ann Arbor, MI 48106-1248. Phone: (313)764-1555 Fax: (313)764-3341 E-mail: aapor@umich.edu • URL: http://www.aapor.org • Members are individuals interested in methods and applications of opinion research.

American Statistical Association. 1429 Duke St., Alexandria, VA 22314-3402. Phone: (703)684-1221 Fax: (703)684-2037 E-mail: asainfo@amstat.org • URL: http://www.amstat.org • A professional society concerned with statistical theory, methodology, and applications. Sections include Survey Research Methods, Government Statistics, and Business and Economic Statistics.

Council of American Survey Research Organizations. Three Upper Devon Belle Terre, Port Jefferson, NY 11777. Phone: (516)928-6954 Fax: (516)928-6041 E-mail: dbowers@casro.org • URL: http://www.casro.org • Members are survey research companies. Various committees are concerned with standards, survey research quality, and technology.

World Association for Public Opinion Research. University of North Carolina, School of Journalism and Mass, Communication, Howell Hall, No. CB-3365, Chapel Hill, NC 27599-3365. Phone: (919)962-6396 Fax: (919)962-4079 E-mail: wapor@unc.edu • URL: http://www.wapor.org • Members are opinion survey research experts, both academic and commercial. Promotes the use of objective, scientific, public opinion methodology and research. International emphasis.

SURVEYS, CONSUMER

See: CONSUMER SURVEYS

SWEET POTATO INDUSTRY

See also: POTATO INDUSTRY

INTERNET DATABASES

USDA. United States Department of Agriculture. Phone: (202)720-2791 E-mail: agsec@usda.gov • URL: http://www.usda.gov • The USDA home page has six sections: News and Information; What's New; About USDA; Agencies; Opportunities; Search and Help. Keyword searching is offered from the USDA home page and from various individual agency home pages. Agencies are the Economic Research Service, Agricultural Marketing Service, National Agricultural Statistics Service, National Agricultural Library, and about 12 others. Updating varies. Fees: Free.

STATISTICS SOURCES

Agricultural Statistics. Available from U. S. Government Printing Office. • Annual. Produced by the National Agricultural Statistics Service, U. S.

Department of Agriculture. Provides a wide variety of statistical data relating to agricultural production, supplies, consumption, prices/price-supports, foreign trade, costs, and returns, as well as farm labor, loans, income, and population. In many cases, historical data is shown annually for 10 years. In addition to farm data, includes detailed fishery statistics.

Vegetables and Specialties Situation and Outlook. Available from U. S. Government Printing Office. • Three times a year. $15.00 per year. Issued by the Economic Research Service of the U. S. Department of Agriculture. Provides current statistical information on supply, demand, and prices.

SWEETENER INDUSTRY

See: SUGAR INDUSTRY

SWIMMING POOL INDUSTRY

DIRECTORIES

Pool and Spa News Directory. Leisure Publications. • Annual. $49.50. List of 1,500 manufacturers and distributors of pool, spa, and hot water equipment and supplies. Formerly *Pool and Spa News Source Book* .

Swimming Pool/Spa Age-Product Directory. Intertec Publishing Corp. • Annual. $44.95. About 2,000 manufacturers of swimming pool and spa equipment. Formerly *Swimming Pool and Spa Age-Data and Reference Annual.*

FINANCIAL RATIOS

Annual Statement Studies. Robert Morris Associates: The Association of Lending and Credit Risk Professiona. • Annual. Free to members; non-members, $140.00. Median and quartile financial ratios are given for over 400 kinds of manufacturing, wholesale, retail, construction, and consumer finance establishments. Data is sorted by both asset size and sales volume. Includes a clearly written "Definition of Ratios" and an alphabetical industry index.

PERIODICALS AND NEWSLETTERS

Pool and Spa News: The National Trade Magazine for the Swimming Poool & Spa Industry. Leisure Publications. • Semimonthly. $19.97 per year.

Swimming Pool-Spa Age. Intertec Publishing Corp. • Monthly. $48.00 per year. Includes annual *Data and Reference Directory*. Formerly *Swimming Pool Age and Swimming Pool Merchandiser.*

TRADE/PROFESSIONAL ASSOCIATIONS

National Spa and Pool Institute. 2111 Eisenhower Ave., Alexandria, VA 22314. Phone: (703)838-0083 Fax: (703)549-0493 E-mail: memberserviceinfo@nspi.org • URL: http://www.nspi.org • Members include a wide variety of business firms and individuals involved in some way with health spas, swimming pools, or hot tubs.

SWINDLERS AND SWINDLING

See: CRIME AND CRIMINALS; FRAUD AND EMBEZZLEMENT

SWINE INDUSTRY

See also: LIVESTOCK INDUSTRY; MEAT INDUSTRY

INTERNET DATABASES

USDA. United States Department of Agriculture. Phone: (202)720-2791 E-mail: agsec@usda.gov • URL: http://www.usda.gov • The USDA home page has six sections: News and Information; What's New; About USDA; Agencies; Opportunities; Search and Help. Keyword searching is offered from the USDA home page and from various individual agency home pages. Agencies are the Economic Research Service, Agricultural Marketing Service, National Agricultural Statistics Service, National Agricultural Library, and about 12 others. Updating varies. Fees: Free.

ONLINE DATABASES

CAB Abstracts. CAB International North America. • Contains 46 specialized abstract collections covering over 10,000 journals and monographs in the areas of agriculture, horticulture, forest products, farm products, nutrition, dairy science, poultry, grains, animal health, entomology, etc. Time period is 1972 to date, with monthly updates. Inquire as to online cost and availability. *CAB Abstracts on CD-ROM* also available, with annual updating.

PERIODICALS AND NEWSLETTERS

National Hog Farmer. Intertec Publishing Co., Agribusiness Div. • Monthly. $35.00 per year.

STATISTICS SOURCES

Agricultural Statistics. Available from U. S. Government Printing Office. • Annual. Produced by the National Agricultural Statistics Service, U. S. Department of Agriculture. Provides a wide variety of statistical data relating to agricultural production, supplies, consumption, prices/price-supports, foreign trade, costs, and returns, as well as farm labor, loans, income, and population. In many cases, historical data is shown annually for 10 years. In addition to farm data, includes detailed fishery statistics.

TRADE/PROFESSIONAL ASSOCIATIONS

National Association of Swine Records. P.O. Box 2417, West Lafayette, IN 47996-2417. Phone: (765)552-3988 Fax: (765)552-3989.

National Pork Producers Council. P.O. Box 10383, Des Moines, IA 50306. Phone: (515)223-2600 Fax: (515)223-2646 E-mail: pork@nppc.org • URL: http://www.nppc.org/.

SYNTHETIC FUELS

See also: FUEL

ABSTRACTS AND INDEXES

Applied Science and Technology Index. H. W. Wilson Co. • 11 times a year. Quarterly and annual cumulations. Service basis for print edition; CD-ROM edition, $1,495.00 per year. Indexes a wide variety of English language technical, industrial, and engineering periodicals.

NTIS Alerts: Energy. National Technical Information Service. • Semimonthly. $245.00 per year. Provides descriptions of government-sponsored research reports and software, with ordering information. Covers electric power, batteries, fuels, geothermal energy, heating/cooling systems, nuclear technology, solar energy, energy policy, and related subjects. Formerly *Abstract Newsletter.*

CD-ROM DATABASES

Environment Abstracts on CD-ROM. Congressional Information Service, Inc. • Quarterly. $1,295.00 per year. Contains the following CD-ROM databases: *Environment Abstracts, Energy Abstracts*, and *Acid Rain Abstracts.* Length of coverage varies.

DIRECTORIES

SYNERJY: A Directory of Renewable Energy. Synerjy. • Semiannual. Individuals, $30.00 per year; others, $62.00 per year. Includes organizations, publishers, and other resources. Lists articles, patents, government publications, research groups and facilities.

ENCYCLOPEDIAS AND DICTIONARIES

Macmillan Encyclopedia of Energy. Available from The Gale Group. • 2001. $350.00. Three volumes. Published by Macmillan Reference USA. Covers the business, technology, and history of a wide variety of energy sources.

ONLINE DATABASES

Energyline. Congressional Information Service, Inc. • Provides online citations and abstracts to the literature of all forms of energy: petroleum, natural gas, coal, nuclear power, solar energy, etc. Time period is 1971 to 1993 (closed file). Inquire as to online cost and availability.

PAIS International. Public Affairs Information Service, Inc. • Corresponds to the former printed publications, *PAIS Bulletin* (1976-90) and *PAIS Foreign Language Index* (1972-90), and to the current *PAIS International in Print* (1991 to date). Covers economic, political, and sociological material appearing in periodicals, books, government documents, and other publications. Updating is monthly. Inquire as to online cost and availability.

PROMT: Predicasts Overview of Markets and Technology. The Gale Group. • Companies, products, applied technologies and markets. U.S. and international literature coverage, 1972 to date. Inquire as to online cost and availability. Provides abstracts from more than 1,600 publications. Weekly updates.

PERIODICALS AND NEWSLETTERS

Clean Coal-Synfuels Letter. McGraw-Hill. • Weekly. $840.00 per year. Newsletter. Formerly *Synfuels.*

Coal Week International. McGraw-Hill, Chemical Engineering Div. • Weekly. $1,186.00 per year. Newsletter. Covers international trade in various types of coal, including prices, production, markets, regulation, research, and synthetic fuels. (Energy and Business Newsletters.).

Energy and Fuels. American Chemical Society. • Bimonthly. Institutions, $728.00 per year; others, price on application. an interdisciplinary technical journal covering non-nuclear energy sources: petroleum, gas, synthetic fuels, etc.

Energy: The International Journal. Elsevier Science. • Monthly. $1,608.00 per year.

Power Generation. Pasha Publishing. • Weekly. $790.00 per year. Newsletter. Formerly *Coals and Synfuels Technology.*

RESEARCH CENTERS AND INSTITUTES

Energy Center. University of Oklahoma, 100 E. Boyd, Suite 510, Norman, OK 73019. Phone: 800-523-7363 or (405)325-3821 Fax: (405)325-3180 E-mail: ggertsch@ou.edu • URL: http://www/ou.edu/sec.

Energy Laboratory. Massachusetts Institute of Technology. Bldg. E40-455, Cambridge, MA 02139-4307. Phone: (617)253-3401 Fax: (617)253-8013 E-mail: testerel@mit.edu • URL: http://www.web.mit.edu/energylab/www/.

TRADE/PROFESSIONAL ASSOCIATIONS

Institute of Gas Technology. 1700 S. Mount Prospect Rd., Des Plaines, IL 60018-1804. Phone: (847)768-0500 Fax: (847)768-0516 • URL: http://www.igt.org.

U.S. Energy Association; Research and Development Committee. 1620 Eye St., Suite 1000, Washington, DC 20006. Phone: (202)331-0415 Fax: (202)331-0418.

OTHER SOURCES

Major Energy Companies of the World. Available from The Gale Group. • 2001. $855.00. Fourth edition. Published by Graham & Whiteside. Contains detailed information on more than 3,300 important energy companies in various countries. Industries include electricity generation, coal, natural gas, nuclear energy, petroleum, fuel distribution, and equipment for energy production.

SYNTHETIC TEXTILE FIBER INDUSTRY

See also: FIBER INDUSTRY; TEXTILE INDUSTRY

ABSTRACTS AND INDEXES

CPI Digest: Key to World Literature Serving the Coatings, Plastics, Fibers, Adhesives, and Related Industries (Chemical Process Industries). CPI Information Services. • Monthly. $397.00 per year. Abstracts of business and technical articles for polymer-based, chemical process industries. Includes a monthly list of relevant U. S. patents. International coverage.

Textile Technology Digest. Institute of Textile Technology. • Monthly. $535.00 per year. Provides indexing and abstracting of a wide variety of textile technology literature.

World Textile Abstracts. Elsevier Science. • Monthly. $1,309.00 per year. Digests of articles published in the world's textile literature. Includes subscription to *World Textile Digest.*

CD-ROM DATABASES

Textile Technology Digest [CD-ROM]. Textile Information Center, Institute of Textile Technology. • Quarterly. $1,700.00 per year. Provides CD-ROM indexing and abstracting of worldwide journals and monographs in various areas of textile technology, production, and management. Covers 1978 to date.

DIRECTORIES

Davison's Textile Blue Book. Davison Publishing Co. • Annual. $165.00. Over 8,400 companies in the textle industry in the United States, Canada, and Mexico, including about 4,400 textile plants.

Manufactured Fiber Fact Book. American Fiber Manufactures Association, Inc. • Biennial $5.00. Provides information an production, characteristies, uses physical properties and history of manufactured fibers.

ENCYCLOPEDIAS AND DICTIONARIES

Encyclopedia of Textiles. French and European Publications, Inc. • 1980. $39.95. Third edition.

Textile Terms and Definitions. J.E. McIntyre and Paul N. Daniels, editors. Available from State Mutual Book and Periodical Service Ltd., Trade Order Dept. • 1995. $110.00. 10th edition. Published by the Textile Insitute (UK). Includes more than 1,000 definitions of textile processes, fiber types, and end products. Illustrated.

INTERNET DATABASES

Fedstats. Federal Interagency Council on Statistical Policy. Phone: (202)395-7254 • URL: http://www.fedstats.gov • Web site features an efficient search facility for full-text statistics produced by more than 70 federal agencies, including the Census Bureau, the Bureau of Economic Analysis, and the Bureau of Labor Statistics. Boolean searches can be made within one agency or for all agencies combined. Links are offered to international statistical bureaus, including the UN, IMF, OECD, UNESCO, Eurostat, and 20 individual countries. Fees: Free.

ONLINE DATABASES

DRI U.S. Central Database. Data Products Division. • Provides more than 23,000 business, financial, demographic, economic, foreign trade, and industry-related time series for the U.S. Includes national income, population, retail-wholesale trade, price indexes, labor data, housing, industrial production, banking, interest rates, money supply, etc. Time period is generally 1947 to date (some data back to 1929). Updating varies. Inquire as to online cost and availability.

Textile Technology Digest [online]. Textile Information Center, Institute of Textile Technology. • Contains indexing and abstracting of more than 300 worldwide journals and monographs in various areas of textile technology, production, and management. Time period is 1978 to date, with monthly updating. Inquire as to online cost and availability.

Textiles Information Treatment Users' Service (TITUS). Institut Textile de France. • Citations and abstracts of the worldwide literature on textiles, 1968 to present. Monthly updates. Inquire as to online cost and availability.

World Textiles. Elsevier Science, Inc. • Provides abstracting and indexing from 1970 of worldwide textile literature (periodicals, books, pamphlets, and reports). Includes U. S., European, and British patent information. Updating is monthly. Inquire as to online cost and availability.

PERIODICALS AND NEWSLETTERS

DNR: The Men's Fashion Retail Textile Authority. Fairchild Publications. • Daily. $85.00 per year. Formerly *Daily News Record.*

Fiber Organon: Featuring Manufactured Fibers. Fiber Economics Bureau, Inc. • Monthly. $300.00 per year. Formerly *Textile Organon.*

International Fiber Journal. International Media Group, Inc. • Bimonthly. $30.00 per year. Covers manmade fiber technology and manufacturing.

STATISTICS SOURCES

Business Statistics of the United States. Courtenay M. Slater, editor. Bernan Associates. • 1999. $74.00. Fifth edition. Based on *Business Statistics*, formerly issue by the Bureau of Economic Analysis, U. S. Department of Commerce. Provides basic data for a wide variety of U. S. industries, services, and economic indicators. Most statistics are shown annually for 29 years and monthly for the most recent four years.

Manufactured Fiber Handbook. Fiber Economics Bureau, Inc. • Looseleaf. Periodic supplementation. Contains extensive production, export, inventory, and other statistics. Formerly *Man-Made Fiber Producers' Handbook.*

Survey of Current Business. Available from U. S. Government Printing Office. • Monthly. $49.00 per year. Issued by Bureau of Economic Analysis, U. S. Department of Commerce. Presents a wide variety of business and economic data.

TRADE/PROFESSIONAL ASSOCIATIONS

American Fiber Manufacturers Association. 1150 17th St., N.W., Suite 310, Washington, DC 20036. Phone: (202)296-6508 Fax: (202)296-3052 • URL: http://www.fibersource.com.

Textile Institute. Saint James Bldgs., 4th Fl., Oxford St., Manchester M1 6FQ, England. Phone: 44 161 2371188 Fax: 44 161 2361991 E-mail: tiihq@textileinst.org.uk • URL: http://www.texi.org • Members in 100 countries involved with textile industry management, marketing, science, and technology.

OTHER SOURCES

Textile Business Outlook. Statistikon Corp. • Quarterly. $985.00 per year. Analyzes current business, marketing, and financial conditions for the worldwide textile industry (fibers and fabrics). Includes statistical forecasts.

SYRUP INDUSTRY

See: MOLASSES INDUSTRY; SUGAR INDUSTRY

SYSTEMS ENGINEERING

See: INDUSTRIAL ENGINEERING

SYSTEMS IN MANAGEMENT

See also: COMPUTERS; MANAGEMENT INFORMATION SYSTEMS; OFFICE MANAGEMENT; WORD PROCESSING

GENERAL WORKS

Information Systems Concepts for Management. Henry C. Lucas. McGraw-Hill. • 1994. $25.00. Fifth edition.

Systems Analysis and Design. Kenneth E. Kendall and Julie E. Kendall. Prentice Hall. • 1998. $90.67. Fourth edition.

Systems and Decision Making: A Management Science Approach. Hans G. Daellenbach. John Wiley and Sons, Inc. • 1994. $118.95.

ABSTRACTS AND INDEXES

Key Abstracts: Software Engineering. Available from INSPEC, Inc. • Monthly. $240.00 per year. Provides international coverage of journal and proceedings literature. Published in England by the Institution of Electrical Engineers (IEE).

ENCYCLOPEDIAS AND DICTIONARIES

Blackwell Encyclopedic Dictionary of Operations Management. Nigel Slack, editor. Blackwell Publishers. • 1997. $105.95. The editor is associated with the University of Warwick, England. Contains definitions of key terms combined with longer articles written by various U. S. and foreign business educators. Includes bibliographies and index. (Blackwell Encyclopedia of Management Series.).

ONLINE DATABASES

Management Contents. The Gale Group. • Covers a wide range of management, financial, marketing, personnel, and administrative topics. About 150 leading business journals are indexed and abstracted from 1974 to date, with monthly updating. Inquire as to online cost and availability.

PERIODICALS AND NEWSLETTERS

Computertalk: For Contemporary Pharmacy Management. Computertalk Associates, Inc. • Bimonthly. $50.00 per year. Provides detailed advice and information on computer systems for pharmacies, including a buyers' guide issue.

Insurance and Technology. Miller Freeman. • Monthly. $65.00 per year. Covers information technology and systems management as applied to the operation of life, health, casualty, and property insurance companies.

Journal of Systems Management. Association for Systems Management. • Monthly. $60.00 per year.

PlugIn Datamation: Profit and Value from Information Technology. Earth Web, Inc., Datamation. • Monthly. Price on application. Technical, semi-technical and general news covering EDP topics.

Software Economics Letter: Maximizing Your Return on Corporate Software. Computer Economics, Inc. • Monthly. $395.00 per year.

Newsletter for information systems managers. Contains data on business software trends, vendor licensing policies, and other corporate software management issues.

TRADE/PROFESSIONAL ASSOCIATIONS

Special Interest Group on Management of Data. Association for Computing Machinery, 1515 Broadway, New York, NY 10036. Phone: (212)869-7440 Fax: (212)302-5826 E-mail: sigs@acm.org • URL: http://www.acm.org/sigmod • Concerned with database management systems. Publishes the quarterly newsletter *SIGMOD Record*.

OTHER SOURCES

Darwin: Business Evolving in the Information Age. CXO Media Inc. • Monthly. $44.95 per year. Presents non-technical explanations of information technology (IT) to corporate business executives. Uses a case study format.

SYSTEMS INTEGRATION

ABSTRACTS AND INDEXES

Applied Science and Technology Index. H. W. Wilson Co. • 11 times a year. Quarterly and annual cumulations. Service basis for print edition; CD-ROM edition, $1,495.00 per year. Indexes a wide variety of English language technical, industrial, and engineering periodicals.

Business Periodicals Index. H. W. Wilson Co. • Monthly, except August, with quarterly and annual cumulations. Service basis for print edition; CD-ROM edition, $1,495.00 per year.

CompuMath Citation Index. Institute for Scientific Information. • Three times a year. $1,090.00 per year. Provides citations to the worldwide literature of computer science and mathematics.

Computer and Information Systems Abstracts Journal: An Abstract Journal Pertaining to the Theory, Design, Fabrication and Application of Computer and Information Systems. Cambridge Information Group. • Monthly. $1,045 per year.

Computer Literature Index: A Subject/Author Index to Computer and Data Processing Literature. Applied Computer Research, Inc. • Quarterly, with annual cumulation. $245.00 per year. Contains brief abstracts of book and periodical literature covering all phases of computing, including approximately 70 specific application areas.

Microcomputer Abstracts. Information Today, Inc. • Quarterly. $225.00 per year. Provides abstracts covering a wide variety of personal and business microcomputer literature. Formerly *Microcomputer Index*.

CD-ROM DATABASES

ABI/INFORM Global. Bell & Howell Information and Learning. • Monthly. $6,500.00 per year. Provides CD-ROM indexing and abstracting of worldwide business literature appearing in over 1,200 periodicals for the most recent five years. Archival discs are available from 1971. Formerly *ABI/INFORM OnDisc*.

Computer Select. The Gale Group. • Monthly. $1,250.00 per year. Provides one year of full-text on CD-ROM for 120 leading computer-related publications. Also includes 70,000 product specifications and brief profiles of 13,000 computer product vendors and manufacturers.

WILSONDISC: Applied Science and Technology Abstracts. H. W. Wilson Co. • Monthly. $1,495.00 per year, including unlimited access to the online version of *Applied Science and Technology Abstracts* through WILSONLINE. Provides CD-ROM indexing and abstracting of 400 prominent scientific, technical, engineering, and industrial periodicals. Indexing coverage is provided from 1983 to date and abstracting from 1993 to date.

WILSONDISC: Wilson Business Abstracts. H. W. Wilson Co. • Monthly. $2,495.00 per year, including unlimited online access to *Wilson Business Abstracts* through WILSONLINE. Provides CD-ROM "cover-to-cover" abstracting and indexing of over 600 prominent business periodicals. Indexing is from 1982, abstracting from 1990. (*Business Periodicals Index* without abstracts is available on CD-ROM at $1,495 per year.).

DIRECTORIES

Computing and Software Career Directory. The Gale Group. • 1993. $39.00. Includes career information relating to programmers, software engineers, technical writers, systems experts, and other computer specialists. Provides advice from "insiders," resume suggestions, a directory of companies that may offer entry-level positions, and a directory of career information sources. (Career Advisor Series.).

Data Sources: The Comprehensive Guide to the Data Processing Industry Hardware, Data Communications Products, Software, Company Profiles. The Gale Group. • Semiannual. $495.00 per year. Two volumes. Describes hardware and software for all computer operating sysems, including prices and technical details. Lists about 75,000 products from 14,000 suppliers. Industry-specific software applications are described.

Manufacturing Systems: Buyers Guide. Cahners Business Information. • Annual. Price on application. Contains information on companies manufacturing or supplying materials handling systems, CAD/CAM systems, specialized software for manufacturing, programmable controllers, machine vision systems, and automatic identification systems.

ENCYCLOPEDIAS AND DICTIONARIES

Encyclopedia of Emerging Industries. The Gale Group. • 2000. $295.00. Fourth edition. Provides detailed information on 90 "newly flourishing" industries. Includes historical background, organizational structure, significant individuals, current conditions, major companies, work force, technology trends, research developments, and other industry facts.

HANDBOOKS AND MANUALS

System Integration. Jeffrey O. Grady. CRC Press, Inc. • 1994. $99.95. (Systems Engineering Series).

System Integration with Corba. Thomas Mowbray and Ron Zahavi. John Wiley and Sons, Inc. • 1996. $49.95. Corba is "common object request broker architecture.".

INTERNET DATABASES

InfoTech Trends. Data Analysis Group. Phone: (707)894-9100 Fax: (707)486-5618 E-mail: support@infotechtrends.com • URL: http://www.infotechtrends.com • Web site provides both free and fee-based market research data on the information technology industry, including computers, peripherals, telecommunications, the Internet, software, CD-ROM/DVD, e-commerce, and workstations. Fees: Free for current (most recent year) data; more extensive information has various fee structures. Formerly *Computer Industry Forecasts*.

ONLINE DATABASES

ABI/INFORM. Bell & Howell Information and Learning. • Provides online indexing to business-related material occurring in over 1,000 periodicals from 1971 to the present. Inquire as to online cost and availability.

Applied Science and Technology Index Online. H. W. Wilson Co. • Provides online indexing of 400 major scientific, technical, industrial, and engineering periodicals. Time period is 1983 to date. Monthly updates. Inquire as to online cost and availability.

Computer Database. The Gale Group. • Provides online citations with abstracts to material appearing in about 150 trade journals and newsletters in the subject areas of computers, telecommunications, and electronics. Time period is 1983 to date, with weekly updates. Inquire as to online cost and availability.

Hard Sciences. Cambridge Scientific Abstracts. • Provides the online version of *Computer and Information Systems Abstracts, Electronics and Communications Abstracts, Health and Safety Science Abstracts, ISMEC: Mechanical Engineering Abstracts (Information Service in Mechanical Engineering)* and *Solid State and Superconductivity Abstracts*. Time period is 1981 to date, with monthly updates. Inquire as to online cost and availability.

Internet and Personal Computing Abstracts. Information Today, Inc. • Contains abstracts covering a wide variety of personal and business microcomputer literature appearing in more than 100 journals and popular magazines. Time period is 1981 to date, with monthly updates. Formerly *Microcomputer Index*. Inquire as to online cost and availability.

Management Contents. The Gale Group. • Covers a wide range of management, financial, marketing, personnel, and administrative topics. About 150 leading business journals are indexed and abstracted from 1974 to date, with monthly updating. Inquire as to online cost and availability.

Trade & Industry Index. The Gale Group. • Provides indexing of business periodicals, January 1981 to date. Daily updates. (Full text articles from some periodicals are available online, 1983 to date, in the companion database, *Trade & Industry ASAP*.) Inquire as to online cost and availability.

Wilson Business Abstracts Online. H. W. Wilson Co. • Indexes and abstracts 600 major business periodicals, plus the *Wall Street Journal* and the business section of the *New York Times*. Indexing is from 1982, abstracting from 1990, with the two newspapers included from 1993. Updated weekly. Inquire as to online cost and availability. (*Business Periodicals Index* without abstracts is also available online.).

PERIODICALS AND NEWSLETTERS

Advanced Manufacturing Technology: Monthly Report. Technical Insights. • Monthly. $695.00 per year. Newsletter. Covers technological developments relating to robotics, computer graphics, automation, computer-integrated manufacturing, and machining.

Industrial Computing. ISA Services, Inc. • Monthly. $50.00 per year. Published by the Instrument Society of America. Edited for engineering managers and systems integrators. Subject matter includes industrial software, programmable controllers, artificial intelligence systems, and industrial computer networking systems.

Journal of Systems Integration: An International Journal. Kluwer Academic Publishers. • Quarterly. $354.00 per year. Presents papers on systems integration research and applications. Online edition available.

Managing Automation. Thomas Publishing Co. • Monthly. Free to qualified personnel. Coverage includes software for manufacturing, systems planning, integration in process industry automation, computer integrated manufacturing (CIM), computer networks for manufacturing, management problems, industry news, and new products.

Manufacturing Computer Solutions. Hitchcock Publishing. • Monthly. Free to qualified personnel; others; $75.00 per year. Edited for managers of factory automation, emphasizing the integration of systems in manufacturing. Subjects include materials handling, CAD/CAM, specialized software for manufacturing, programmable controllers, machine vision, and automatic identification systems. Formerly *Manufacturing Systems.*

RESEARCH CENTERS AND INSTITUTES

Center for Integrated Systems. Stanford University, 420 Vis Palou Mall, Stanford, CA 94305-4070. Phone: (650)725-3621 Fax: (650)725-0991 E-mail: rdasher@cis.stanford.edu • URL: http://www.cis.stanford.edu • Research programs include manufacturing science, design science, computer architecture, semiconductor technology, and telecommunications.

Center for Research in Computing Technology. Harvard University, Pierce Hall, 29 Oxford St., Cambridge, MA 02138. Phone: (617)495-2832 Fax: (617)495-9837 E-mail: cheatham@das.harvard.edu • URL: http://www.das.harvard.edu/cs.grafs.html • Conducts research in computer vision, robotics, artificial intelligence, systems programming, programming languages, operating systems, networks, graphics, database management systems, and telecommunications.

Institute for Systems Research. University of Maryland, A. V. Williams Bldg., No. 115, College Park, MD 20742-3311. Phone: (301)405-6602 Fax: (301)314-9220 E-mail: isr@isr.umd.edu • URL: http://www.isr.umd.edu/ • A National Science Foundation Engineering Research Center. Areas of research include communication systems, manufacturing systems, chemical process systems, artificial intelligence, and systems integration.

Stanford Integrated Manufacturing Association. Stanford University, Bldg. 02-530, Stanford, CA 94305-3036. Phone: (650)723-9038 Fax: (650)723-5034 E-mail: susan.hansen@stanford.edu • URL: http://www.sima.stanford.edu/ • Consists of four research centers: Center for Automation and Manufacturing Science, Center for Design Research, Center for Materials Formability and Processing Science, and Center for Teaching and Research in Integrated Manufacturing Systems. Research fields include automation, robotics, intelligent systems, computer vision, design in manufacturing, materials science, composite materials, and ceramics.

TRADE/PROFESSIONAL ASSOCIATIONS

AIM U.S.A. 634 Alpha Dr., Pittsburgh, PA 15238-2802. Phone: 800-338-0206 or (412)963-8588 Fax: (412)963-8753 E-mail: info@aimglobal.org • URL: http://www.aimusa.org • Members are companies concerned with automatic identification and data capture, including bar code systems, magnetic stripes, machine vision, voice technology, optical character recognition, and systems integration technology.

Automatic Identification Manufacturers International. 623 Alpha Dr., Pittsburgh, PA 15238. Phone: (412)936-8009 Fax: (412)963-8753 • Members are automatic identification manufacturers and suppliers. Systems may utilize bar codes, magnetic stripes, radio frequencies, machine vision, voice technology, optical character recognition, or systems integration.

Information Technology Association of America. c/o ITAA, 1616 N. Fort Myer Dr., Suite 1300, Arlington, VA 22209-9998. Phone: (703)522-5055 Fax: (703)525-2279 • Members are computer software and services companies. Maintains an Information Systems Integration Services Section.

Instrument Society of America (ISA). P.O. Box 12277, Research Triangle Park, NC 27709. Phone: (919)549-8411 Fax: (919)549-8288 E-mail: info@isa.org • URL: http://www.isa.org • Members are engineers and others concerned with industrial instrumentation, systems, computers, and automation.

NASPA. 7044 S. 13th St., Milwaukee, WI 53154. Phone: (414)768-8000 Fax: (414)768-8001 E-mail: sherer@naspa.com • URL: http://www.naspa.net • Members are systems programmers, communications analysts, database administrators, and other technical management personnel.

Special Interest Group on Operating Systems. c/o Association for Computing Machinery, 1515 Broadway, 17th Fl., New York, NY 10036. Phone: (212)869-7440 Fax: (212)302-5826 E-mail: acmhelp@acm.org.

T

TABLEWARE

DIRECTORIES

Gift and Decorative Accessory Buyers Directory. Geyer-McAllister Publications, Inc. • Annual. Included in subscription to *Gifts and Decorative Accessories.* Manufacturers, importers, jobbers, and manufacturers' representatives of gifts, china and glass, lamps and home accessories, stationery, greeting cards, and related products.

Jewelers' Circular/Keystone-Jewelers' Directory. Cahners Business Information. • Annual. $33.95. About 8,500 manufacturers, importers and wholesale jewelers providing merchandise and supplies to the jewelry retailing industry; and related trade organizations. Included with subscription to *Jewelers' Circular Keystone.*

PERIODICALS AND NEWSLETTERS

Gift and Stationery Business. Miller Freeman, Inc. • Monthly. $45.00 per year. Products and services.

Gifts and Decorative Accessories: The International Business Magazine of Gifts, Tabletop, Gourmet, Home Accessories, Greeting Card and Social Stationery. Cahners Business Newspapers. • Monthly. $49.95 per year.

Giftware News: The International Magazine for Gifts, China and Glass, Stationery and Home Accessories. Talcott Communications Corp. • Monthly. $36.00 per year. Includes annual *Directory.*

Jewelers' Circular Keystone. Cahners Business Information. • Monthly. $90.00 per year.

TRADE/PROFESSIONAL ASSOCIATIONS

Associated Glass and Pottery Manufacturers. c/o Custom Deco, 1343 Miami St., Toledo, OH 43605. Phone: (419)698-2900 Fax: (419)698-9928.

OTHER SOURCES

The Tabletop Market. Available from MarketResearch.com. • 2000. $2,750.00. Published by Packaged Facts. Provides market data on dinnerware, glassware, and flatware, with projections to 2002.

TAILORING

See also: CLOTHING INDUSTRY; FASHION INDUSTRY; MEN'S CLOTHING INDUSTRY

PERIODICALS AND NEWSLETTERS

Custom Tailor. Custom Tailors and Designers Association of America. • Three times a year. $50.00 per year.

TRADE/PROFESSIONAL ASSOCIATIONS

Custom Tailors and Designers Association of America. P.O. Box 53052, Washington, DC 20009-9052. Phone: (202)387-7220 Fax: (202)387-7713 • URL: http://www.ctda.com.

TALL OIL INDUSTRY

See also: OIL AND FATS INDUSTRY

ALMANACS AND YEARBOOKS

CRB Commodity Yearbook. Commodity Research Bureau. CRB. • Annual. $99.95.

TRADE/PROFESSIONAL ASSOCIATIONS

Pine Chemicals Association. P.O. Box 105113, Atlanta, GA 30348. Phone: (770)446-1290 or (770)209-7237 Fax: (770)446-1487 • URL: http://www.pinechemicals.org.

TANK SHIPS

See also: SHIPS, SHIPPING AND SHIPBUILDING

DIRECTORIES

Fairplay World Shipping Directory. Available from Fairplay Publications, Inc. • Annual. $360.00. Published in the UK by Lloyd's Register-Fairplay Ltd. Provides information on more than 64,000 companies providing maritime services and products, including 1,600 shipbuilders and data on 55,000 individual ships. Includes shipowners, shipbrokers, engine builders, salvage companies, marine insurance companies, maritime lawyers, consultants, maritime schools, etc. Five indexes cover a total of 170,000 entries.

Lloyd's Maritime Directory. Available from Informa Publishing Group Ltd. • Annual. $468.00. Two volumes. Published in the UK by Lloyd's List (http://www.lloydslist.com). Lists more than 5,500 shipowners, container companies, salvage firms, towing services, shipbuilders, ship repairers, marine engine builders, ship management services, maritime lawyers, consultants, etc.

The Tanker Register. Clarkson Research Studies, Ltd. • Annual. $290.00. Details more than 3,300 tankers and combined carriers throughout the world having deadweight tonnage exceeding 10,000, and their owners and managers.

ENCYCLOPEDIAS AND DICTIONARIES

Dictionary of Shipping Terms. Peter Brodie. Available from Informa Publishing Group Ltd. • 1997. $57.00. Third edition. Published in the UK by Lloyd's List (http://www.lloydslist.com). Defines more than 2,000 words, phrases, and abbreviations related to the shipping and maritime industries.

Macmillan Encyclopedia of Transportation. Available from The Gale Group. • 2000. $375.00. Six volumes. Published by Macmillan Reference USA. Covers the business, technology, and history of transportation on land, on water, in the air, and in space. Includes definitions, cross-references, and 200 color illustrations.

HANDBOOKS AND MANUALS

Tanker Operations: A Handbook for the Ship's Officer. G. S. Marton. Cornell Maritime Press, Inc. • 2000. $45.00. Fourth edition.

PRICE SOURCES

American Tanker Rate Schedule. Association of Ship Brokers and Agents-USA. • Annual. $500.00. Contains tanker freight rates.

STATISTICS SOURCES

World Oil Tanker Trends. Jacobs and Partners Ltd. • Semiannual. $520.00 per year.

TRADE/PROFESSIONAL ASSOCIATIONS

Association of Ship Brokers and Agents-U.S.A. 75 Main St., Millburn, NJ 07041. Phone: (973)376-4144 Fax: (973)376-4145 • Includes a Tanker Committee.

OTHER SOURCES

List of Shipowners, Managers, and Managing Agents. Available from Fairplay Publications, Inc. • Annual. $270.00, including 10 updates per year. Published in the UK by Lloyd's Register-Fairplay Ltd. Lists 40,000 shipowners, managers, and agents worldwide. Cross-referenced with *Lloyd's Register of Ships.*

Lloyd's List. Available from Informa Publishing Group Ltd. • Daily. $1,665.00 per year. Published in the UK by Lloyd's List (http://www.lloydslist.com). Marine industry newspaper. Covers a wide variety of maritime topics, including global news, business/insurance, regulation, shipping markets, financial markets, shipping movements, freight logistics, and marine technology. (Also available weekly at $385.00 per year.).

Lloyd's Register of Ships. Available from Fairplay Publications, Inc. • Annual. $982.00. Three volumes and 10 cumulative supplements. Published in the UK by Lloyd's Register-Fairplay Ltd. Provides detailed information on more than 80,000 seagoing merchant ships of the world. Includes name, former names if any, date when built, owner, registration, tonnage, cargo capabilities, mechanical details, and other ship data.

Lloyd's Ship Manager. Available from Informa Publishing Group Ltd. • Monthly. $251.00 per year, including annual supplementary guides and directories. Published in the UK by Lloyd's List (http://www.lloydslist.com). Covers all management, technical, and operational aspects of ocean-going shipping.

Register of International Shipowning Groups. Available from Fairplay Publications, Inc. • Three times a year. $697.00 per year. Published in the UK by Lloyd's Register-Fairplay Ltd. "Provides intelligence on shipowners and managers, their subsidiary and associate companies, and owners' representatives." Includes detailed information on individual ships.

Tanker Market Quarterly. Available from Informa Publishing Group Ltd. • Quarterly. $495.00 per year. Published in the UK by Lloyd's List (http://www.lloydslist.com). Provides supply and demand information "required to make accurate market decisions." Includes detailed graphs and analytical commentary.

TANK TRUCKS

See: TRUCKING INDUSTRY

TANKERS

See: TANK SHIPS

TANNING INDUSTRY

See also: LEATHER INDUSTRY

DIRECTORIES

American Leather Chemists Association-Directory. American Leather Chemists Association. • Annual. $20.00. About 1,000 chemists, leather technologists, and educators concerned with the tanning and leather industry.

Leather Manufacturer Directory. Shoe Trades Publishing Co. • Annual. $55.00. Lists hide processors, tanners and leather finishers in the U.S. and Canada.

PERIODICALS AND NEWSLETTERS

American Leather Chemists Association Journal. American Leather Chemists Association. • Monthly. Free to members; non-members, $115.00 per year.

Leather Manufacturer. Shoe Trades Publishing Co. • Monthly. $52.00 per year. Edited for hide processors, tanners and leather finishers in the U.S. and Canada.

Newsbreak. Leather Industries of America. • Free to members and other qualified personnel. Reports on issues and events in the luggage industry.

Society of Leather Technologists and Chemists Journal. Society of Leather Technologies and Chemists. • Bimonthly. $65.00 per year. Scientific, technical, historical and commercial papers on leather and allied industries.

TRADE/PROFESSIONAL ASSOCIATIONS

American Leather Chemists Association. Texas Tech University, P.O. Box 41061, Lubbock, TX 79409-1061. Phone: (806)742-4138 Fax: (806)742-4139 E-mail: alca@leatherchemists.org • URL: http://www.leatherchemists.org.

Leather Industries of America. 1000 Thomas Jefferson St., N.W., Suite 515, Washington, DC 20007. Phone: (202)342-8086 Fax: (202)342-9063 E-mail: info@leatherusa.com • URL: http://www.leatherusa.com.

TAPE RECORDING

See: SOUND RECORDERS AND RECORDING; VIDEO RECORDING INDUSTRY

TARIFF

DIRECTORIES

U.S. Custom House Guide. Commonwealth Business Media. • Annual. $475.00. Quarterly supplements. List of ports having custom facilities, customs officials, port authorities, chambers of commerce, embassies and consulates, foreign trade zones, and other organizations; related trade services.

HANDBOOKS AND MANUALS

Harmonized Tariff Schedule of the United States, Annotated, Basic Manual. Available from U.S. Government Printing Office. • $67.00, including basic volumes and supplementary service for an indefinite period.

NAFTA: The North American Free Trade Agreement, A Guide to Customs Procedures. Available from U. S. Government Printing Office. • 1994. $7.00. Revised edition. Issued by the Customs Service, U. S. Treasury Department. Provides a summary of NAFTA customs requirements and benefits. (Customs Publication No. 571.).

PERIODICALS AND NEWSLETTERS

Customs Bulletin and Decisions. Available from U. S. Government Printing Office. • Weekly. $220.00 per year. Issued by U. S. Customs Service, Department of the Treasury. Contains regulations, rulings, decisions, and notices relating to customs laws.

TRADE/PROFESSIONAL ASSOCIATIONS

International Customs Tariffs Bureau. 38 Rue de l'Association, B-1000 Brussels, Belgium. Phone: 32 2 5018774 Fax: 32 2 5018779.

World Trade Organization. Centre William Rappard. 154 rue de Lausanne, CH-1211 Geneva 21, Switzerland. Phone: 41 22 739511 Fax: 41 22 7395007 E-mail: enquires@wto.org • URL: http://www.wto.org.

OTHER SOURCES

Customs Regulations of the United States. Available from U. S. Government Printing Office. • Looseleaf. $123.00. Issued by U. S. Customs Service, Department of the Treasury. Reprint of regulations published to carry out customs laws of the U. S. Includes supplementary material for an indeterminate period.

Worldtariff Guidebook on Customs Tariff Schedules of Import Duties. Worldtariff Division, Morse Agri-Energy Associates. • Looseleaf. Over 60 volumes. Prices vary. Consists generally of volumes for individual countries and volumes for broad classes of products, such as clothing. (Country volumes are typically $500.00 each.).

TAX ADMINISTRATION

See also: TAXATION

HANDBOOKS AND MANUALS

Federal Taxation Practice and Procedure. Robert E. Meldman and Richard J. Sideman. CCH, Inc. • 1998. $89.00. Fifth edition. Provides information on the administrative structure of the Internal Revenue Service. Includes discussions of penalties, ethical duties, statute of limitations, litigation, and IRS collection procedures. Contains IRS standardized letters and notices.

Tax Penalties and Interest Handbook. Howard Davidoff and David A. Minars. LEXIS Publishing. • $80.00. Looseleaf. Annual supplements.

ONLINE DATABASES

Accounting and Tax Database. Bell & Howell Information and Learning. • Provides indexing and abstracting of the literature of accounting, taxation, and financial management, 1971 to date. Updating is weekly. Especially covers accounting, auditing, banking, bankruptcy, employee compensation and benefits, cash management, financial planning, and credit. Inquire as to online cost and availability.

PERIODICALS AND NEWSLETTERS

The Journal of Taxation: A National Journal of Current Developments, Analysis and Commentary for Tax Professionals. Warren, Gorham & Lamont/ RIA Group. • Monthly. $215.00 per year. Analysis of current tax developments for tax specialists.

Tax Administrators News. Federation of Tax Administrators. • Monthly. $35.00 per year.

The Tax Executive. Tax Executives Institute. • Bimonthly. $115.00 per year. Professional journal for corporate tax executives.

RESEARCH CENTERS AND INSTITUTES

International Tax Program. Harvard University, Pound Hall, Room 400, Cambridge, MA 02138. Phone: (617)495-4406 Fax: (617)495-0423 • URL: http://www.law.harvard.edu/programs/itp • Studies the worldwide problems of taxation, including tax law and tax administration.

TRADE/PROFESSIONAL ASSOCIATIONS

Federation of Tax Administrators. 444 N. Capitol St., Suite 348, Washington, DC 20001. Phone: (202)624-5890 Fax: (202)624-7888 • URL: http://www.taxadmin.org.

Tax Executives Institute. 1200 G St., N.W., No. 300, Washington, DC 20005-3814. Phone: (202)638-5601 Fax: (202)638-5607 E-mail: askter@tei.org • URL: http://www.tei.org.

OTHER SOURCES

Internal Revenue Manual: Administration. CCH, Inc. • Six looseleaf volumes. Reproduces IRS tax administration provisions and procedures.

Internal Revenue Manual: Audit and Administration. CCH, Inc. • Irregular $1,156.00. Reproduces IRS audit provisions and procedures.

Partnerships and LLCs: Tax Practice and Analysis. Thomas G. Manolakas. CCH, Inc. • 2001. $99.00. Covers the taxation of partnerships and limited liability companies.

TAX, ESTATE

See: INHERITANCE TAX

TAX, EXCISE

See: EXCISE TAX

TAX EXEMPT SECURITIES

See: MUNICIPAL BONDS

TAX, GIFT

See: GIFT TAX

TAX, INCOME

See: INCOME TAX

TAX, INHERITANCE

See: INHERITANCE TAX

TAX LAW AND REGULATION

See also: INCOME TAX; STATE TAXES; TAXATION

GENERAL WORKS

Tax Policy and the Economy. MIT Press. • Annual. $30.00. Reviews "issues in the current tax debate." Produced by the National Bureau of Economic Research. (Tax Policy and the Economy Series).

ABSTRACTS AND INDEXES

Current Law Index: Multiple Access to Legal Periodicals. The Gale Group. • Monthly. $650.00 per year. Produced in cooperation with the American Association of Law Libraries. Indexes more than 900 law journals, legal newspapers, and specialty publications from the U.S., Canada, U.K., Ireland, Australia, and New Zealand.

Index to Legal Periodicals and Books. H. W. Wilson Co. • Monthly. Quarterly and annual cumulations. $270.00 per year. CD-ROM version available at $1,495.00 per year.

ALMANACS AND YEARBOOKS

Tax Year in Review. CCH, Inc. • Annual. Covers the year's "major new legislative and regulatory changes.".

CD-ROM DATABASES

Federal Tax Products. Available from U. S. Government Printing Office. • Annual. $20.00. CD-ROM issued by the Internal Revenue Service (http://www.irs.treas.gov/forms_pubs/). Provides current tax forms, instructions, and publications. Also includes older tax forms beginning with 1991.

WILSONDISC: Index to Legal Periodicals and Books. H. W. Wilson Co. • Monthly. Including unlimited online access to *Index to Legal Periodicals* through WILSONLINE. Contains CD-ROM indexing of more than 800 English language legal periodicals from 1981 to date and 2,500 books.

HANDBOOKS AND MANUALS

Bank Tax Guide. CCH, Inc. • Annual. $195.00. Summarizes and explains federal tax rules affecting financial institutions.

How to Practice Before the New IRS. Robert S. Schriebman. CCH, Inc. • 1999. $115.00. Reflects changes made by the IRS Restructuring and Reform Act of 1998. Covers audits, appeals, tax court basics, refunds, penalties, etc., for tax professionals.

Income Tax Regulations. CCH, Inc. • Annual. $95.00. Six volumes. Contains full text of official Internal Revenue Code regulations (approximately 11,000 pages).

Internal Revenue Code: Income, Estate, Gift, Employment, and Excise Taxes. CCH, Inc. • Annual. $69.00. Two volumes. Provides full text of the Internal Revenue Code (5,000 pages), including procedural and administrative provisions.

IRS Tax Collection Procedures. CCH, Inc. • Looseleaf. $189.00. Supplementation available. Covers IRS collection personnel, payment arrangements, penalties, abatements, summons, liens, etc.

Law of Federal Estate and Gift Taxation, 1978-1990. David T. Link and Larry D. Soderquist. West Group. • $100.00. Revised edition.

Practical Guide to Tax Issues in Employment. Julia K. Brazelton. CCH, Inc. • 1999. $95.00. Covers income taxation as related to labor law and tax law, including settlements and awards. Written for tax professionals.

RIA Federal Income Tax Regulations. Research Institute of America, Inc. • Annual. Contains the official U. S. Treasury Department interpretation of federal income tax law. Three volumes cover final and temporary regulations and one volume covers proposed regulations.

INTERNET DATABASES

CCH Essentials: An Internet Tax Research and Primary Source Library. CCH, Inc. Phone: 800-248-3248 or (773)866-6000 Fax: 800-224-8299 or (773)866-3608 E-mail: cust_serv@cch.com • URL: http://tax.cch.com/essentials • Fee-based Web site provides full-text coverage of federal tax law and regulations, including rulings, procedures, tax court decisions, and IRS publications, announcements, notices, and penalties. Includes explanation, analysis, tax planning guides, and a daily tax news service. Searching is offered, including citation search. Fee: $495.00 per year.

The Digital Daily. Internal Revenue Service. Phone: (202)622-5000 Fax: (202)622-5844 • URL: http://www.irs.ustreas.gov • Web site provides a wide variety of tax information, including IRS forms and publications. Includes "Highlights of New Tax Law." Searching is available. Fees: Free.

Rutgers Accounting Web (RAW). Rutgers University Accounting Research Center. Phone: (201)648-5172 Fax: (201)648-1233 • URL: http://www.rutgers.edu/accounting • RAW Web site provides extensive links to sources of national and international accounting information, such as the Big Six accounting firms, the Financial Accounting Standards Board (FASB), SEC filings (EDGAR), journals, publishers, software, the International Accounting Network, and "Internet's largest list of accounting firms in USA." Searching is offered. Fees: Free.

Tax Analysts [Web site]. Tax Analysts. Phone: 800-955-3444 or (703)533-4400 Fax: (703)533-4444 • URL: http://www.tax.org • The three main sections of Tax Analysts home page are "Tax News" (Today's Tax News, Feature of the Week, Tax Snapshots, Tax Calendar); "Products & Services" (Product Catalog, Press Releases); and "Public Interest" (Discussion Groups, Tax Clinic, Tax History Project). Fees: Free for coverage of current tax events; fee-based for comprehensive information. Daily updating.

ONLINE DATABASES

Auto-Cite. West Group. • Provides information concerning federal and state case law, administrative decisions, and taxation. Daily updates. Inquire as to online cost and availability.

Index to Legal Periodicals and Books (Online). H. W. Wilson Co. • Broad coverage of law journals and books 1981 to date. Monthly updates. Inquire as to online cost and availability.

PERIODICALS AND NEWSLETTERS

Daily Tax Report: From Today's Daily Report for Executives. Bureau of National Affairs, Inc. • Daily. $2,350.00 per year. Newsletter. Monitors tax legislation, hearings, rulings, and court decisions.

E-Commerce Tax Alert. CCH, Inc. • Monthly. $397.00 per year. Newsletter. Edited for owners and managers of firms doing business through the Internet. Covers compliance with federal, state, local, and international tax regulations.

Highlights and Documents. Tax Analysts. • Daily. $2,249.00 per year, including monthly indexes. Newsletter. Provides daily coverage of IRS, congressional, judicial, state, and international tax developments. Includes abstracts and citations for "all tax documents released within the previous 24 to 48 hours." Annual compilation available *Highlights and Documents on Microfiche.*

Internal Revenue Bulletin. Available from U. S. Government Printing Office. • Weekly. $230.00 per year. Issued by the Internal Revenue Service. Contains IRS rulings, Treasury Decisions, Executive Orders, tax legislation, and court decisions. (Semiannual *Cumulative Bulletins* are sold separately.).

Internal Revenue Cumulative Bulletin. Available from U. S. Government Printing Office. • Semiannual. Issued by the Internal Revenue Service. Cumulates all items of a "permanent nature" appearing in the weekly *Internal Revenue Bulletin.*

Journal of Tax Practice and Procedure. CCH, Inc. • Bimonthly. $195.00 per year. Covers the representation of taxpayers before the IRS, "from initial contact through litigation.".

Kiplinger Tax Letter. Kiplinger Washington Editors, Inc. • Biweekly. $59.00 per year.

The Practical Tax Lawyer. American Law Institute-American Bar Association. • Quarterly. Members, $27.50 per year; non-members, $35.00 per year.

Tax Law Review. New York University, School of Law. Warren, Gorham and Lamont/RIA Group. • Quarterly. $149.00 per year.

Tax Notes: The Weekly Tax Service. Tax Analysts. • Weekly. $1,699.00 per year. Includes an *Annual* and 1985-1996 compliations on CD-ROM. Newsletter. Covers "tax news from all federal sources," including congressional committees, tax courts, and the Internal Revenue Service. Each issue contains "summaries of every document that pertains to federal tax law," with citations. Commentary is provided.

Tax Practice. Tax Analysts. • Weekly. $199.00 per year. Newsletter. Covers news affecting tax practitioners and litigators, with emphasis on federal court decisions, rules and regulations, and tax petitions. Provides a guide to Internal Revenue Service audit issues.

Taxation and Revenue Policies: State Capitals. Wakeman-Walworth, Inc. • Weekly. $345.00 per year. Formerly *From the State Capitals: Taxation and Revenue Policies.*

Taxes-Property: State Capitals. Wakeman-Walworth, Inc. • Weekly. $345.00 per year. Formerly *From the State Capitals: Taxes-Property.*

Taxes: The Tax Magazine. CCH, Inc. • Monthly. $195.00. per year. Mainly for accountants and lawyers.

RESEARCH CENTERS AND INSTITUTES

Center for Tax Policy Studies. Purdue University, 490 Krannert, West Lafayette, IN 47907-1310. Phone: (765)494-4442 Fax: (765)496-1778 E-mail: papke@mgmt.purdue.edu.

International Tax Program. Harvard University, Pound Hall, Room 400, Cambridge, MA 02138. Phone: (617)495-4406 Fax: (617)495-0423 • URL: http://www.law.harvard.edu/programs/itp • Studies the worldwide problems of taxation, including tax law and tax administration.

Lexis.com Research System. Lexis-Nexis Group. Phone: 800-227-9597 or (937)865-6800 Fax: (937)865-6909 E-mail: webmaster@prod.lexis-nexis.com • URL: http://www.lexis.com • Fee-based Web site offers extensive searching of a wide variety of legal sources. Additional features include Daily Opinion Service, lexis.com Bookstore, Career Center, CLE Center, Law Schools, and Practice Pages ("Pages specific to areas of specialty").

Tax Foundation. 1250 H St., N.W., Suite 750, Washington, DC 20005. Phone: (202)783-2760 Fax: (202)783-6868 E-mail: taxfnd@intr.net • URL: http://www.taxfoundation.org.

TRADE/PROFESSIONAL ASSOCIATIONS

International Bureau of Fiscal Documentation. P.O. Box 20237, NL-1000 HE Amsterdam, Netherlands. P.O. Box 20237,.

Tax Analysts. 6830 N. Fairfax Dr., Arlington, VA 22213. Phone: 800-955-3444 or (703)533-4400 Fax: (703)533-4444 E-mail: webmaster@tax.org • URL: http://www.tax.org • An advocacy group reviewing U. S. and foreign income tax developments. Includes a Tax Policy Advisory Board.

OTHER SOURCES

Avoiding Tax Malpractice. Robert Feinschreiber and Margaret Kent. CCH, Inc. • 2000. $75.00. Covers malpractice considerations for professional tax practitioners.

Estate Planning Strategies After Estate Tax Reform: Insights and Analysis. CCH, Inc. • 2001. $45.00. Produced by the Estate Planning Department of Schiff, Hardin & Waite. Covers estate planning techniques and opportunities resulting from tax legislation of 2001.

Estate Planning Under the New Law: What You Need to Know. CCH, Inc. • 2001. $7.00. Booklet summarizes significant changes in estate planning brought about by tax legislation of 2001.

Factiva. Dow Jones Reuters Business Interactive, LLC. • Fee-based Web site provides "global news and business information through Web sites and content integration solutions." Includes Dow Jones and Reuters newswires, The Wall Street Journal, and more than 7,000 other sources of current news, historical articles, market research reports, and investment analysis. Content includes 96 major U. S. newspapers, 900 non-English sources, trade publications, media transcripts, country profiles, news photos, etc.

Federal Tax Coordinator 2D. Research Institute of America, Inc. • 35 looseleaf volumes. $1,375.00 per year. Weekly updates. Includes *Weekly Alert* newsletter and *Internal Revenue Bulletin.* Covers federal income, estate, gift, and excise taxes. Formerly *Federal Tax Coordinator.*

Foreign Tax and Trade Briefs. Matthew Bender & Co., Inc. • $470.00. Two looseleaf volumes. Periodic supplementation. The latest tax and trade information for over 100 foreign countries.

Nexis.com. Lexis-Nexis Group. • Fee-based Web site offers searching of about 2.8 billion documents in some 30,000 news, business, and legal information sources. Features include a subject directory covering 1,200 topics in 34 categories and a Company Dossier containing information on more than 500,000 public and private companies. Boolean searching is offered.

Tax Legislation 2001: Highlights. CCH, Inc. • 2001. $7.00. Booklet summarizes significant changes in U. S. tax law resulting from the legislation of 2001.

Tax Legislation 2001: Law, Explanation, and Analysis. CCH, Inc. • 2001. $42.50. Provides explanation and interpretation of federal tax legislation enacted in 2001.

TAX MANAGEMENT

See: TAXATION

TAX PLANNING

See also: ESTATE PLANNING; FINANCIAL PLANNING; INCOME TAX

GENERAL WORKS

Smart Questions to Ask Your Financial Advisers. Lynn Brenner. Bloomberg Press. • 1997. $19.95. Provides practical advice on how to deal with financial planners, stockbrokers, insurance agents, and lawyers. Some of the areas covered are investments, estate planning, tax planning, house buying, prenuptial agreements, divorce arrangements, loss of a job, and retirement. (Bloomberg Personal Bookshelf Series Library.).

ABSTRACTS AND INDEXES

Business Periodicals Index. H. W. Wilson Co. • Monthly, except August, with quarterly and annual cumulations. Service basis for print edition; CD-ROM edition, $1,495.00 per year.

DIRECTORIES

Business Organizations, Agencies, and Publications Directory. The Gale Group. • 1999. $425.00. 12th edition. Over 40,000 entries describing 39 types of business information sources. Classified by type of organization, publication, or serviceIncludes state, national, and international agencies and organizations. Master index to names and keywords. Also includes e-mail addresses and web site URL's.

HANDBOOKS AND MANUALS

Asset Protection Planning Guide: A State-of-the-Art Approach to Integrated Estate Planning. Barry S. Engel and others. CCH, Inc. • 2001. $99.00. Provides advice for attorneys, trust officers, accountants, and others engaged in financial planning for protection of assets.

CCH Analysis of Top Tax Issues: Return Preparation and Planning Guide. CCH, Inc. • Annual. $45.00. Covers yearly tax changes affecting business and personal transactions, planning, and returns.

CCH Financial and Estate Planning Guide [summary volume]. CCH, Inc. • Annual. $57.95. Contains four main parts: General Principles and Techniques, Special Situations, Building the Estate, and Planning Aids.

CCH Guide to Car, Travel, Entertainment, and Home Office Deductions. CCH, Inc. • Annual. $42.00. Explains how to claim maximum tax deductions for common business expenses. Includes automobile depreciation tables, lease value tables, worksheets, and examples of filled-in tax forms.

Charitable Planning Primer. Ralph G. Miller and Adam Smalley. CCH, Inc. • 1999. $99.00. Covers the legal and tax aspects of charitable giving and planned gifts. Includes annuity documents, tax forms, tables, and examples.

Ernst & Young's Personal Financial Planning Guide. John Wiley and Sons, Inc. • 1999. $19.95. Third edition.

Essentials of Federal Income Taxation for Individuals and Business. CCH, Inc. • Annual. $59.00. Covers basic tax planning and tax reduction strategies as affected by tax law changes and IRS interpretations. Includes sample filled-in forms.

Estate Plan Book 2000. William S. Moore. American Institute for Economic Research. • 2000. $10.00. Revision of 1997 edition. Part one: "Basic Estate Planning." Part two: "Reducing Taxes on the Disposition of Your Estate." Part three: "Putting it All Together: Examples of Estate Plans." Provides succinct information on wills, trusts, tax planning, and gifts. (Economic Education Bulletin.).

Family Tax Guide. Prentice Hall. • 1985. $44.95.

Individual Retirement Account Answer Book. Donald R. Levy and Steven G. Lockwood. Panel Publishers. • 1999. $136.00. Sixth edition. Periodic supplementation available. Questions and answers include information about contributions, distributions, rollovers, Roth IRAs, SIMPLE IRAs (Savings Incentive Match Plans for Employees), Education IRAs, and SEPs (Simplified Employee Pension plans). Chapters are provided on retirement planning, estate planning, and tax planning.

Retirement Benefits Tax Guide. CCH, Inc. • Looseleaf. $199.00. Supplementation available.

Tax Examples. John C. Wisdom. West Group. • 1993. $125.00. Presents yearly examples, with forms, of a wide variety of tax problems and issues. Subjects include taxable income, deductions, alternative minimum tax, dependents, gift taxes, partnerships, and other problem areas. Includesaccounting method considerations. (Tax Series).

Tax Planning and Compliance for Tax-Exempt Organizations: Forms, Checklists, Procedures. Jody Blazek. John Wiley and Sons, Inc. • 1999. $135.00. Third edition. Annual supplements available. (Wiley Nonprofit, Law, Finance, and Management Series).

Tax Planning for Highly Compensated Individuals. Robert E. Madden. Warren, Gorham & Lamont/RIA Group. • Looseleaf service. $160.00. Biennial supplementation.

INTERNET DATABASES

CCH Essentials: An Internet Tax Research and Primary Source Library. CCH, Inc. Phone: 800-248-3248 or (773)866-6000 Fax: 800-224-8299 or (773)866-3608 E-mail: cust_serv@cch.com • URL: http://tax.cch.com/essentials • Fee-based Web site provides full-text coverage of federal tax law and regulations, including rulings, procedures, tax court decisions, and IRS publications, announcements, notices, and penalties. Includes explanation, analysis, tax planning guides, and a daily tax news service. Searching is offered, including citation search. Fee: $495.00 per year.

Deloitte & Touche Online. Deloitte & Touche LLP, Financial Consulting Services Center. Phone: (513)784-7100 E-mail: webmaster@dtonline.com • URL: http://www.dtonline.com • Web site provides concise, full-text articles on taxes, personal finance, and business from a leading accounting firm. Includes "Tax News and Views," "Personal Finance Advisor," "Business Advisor: A Resource for Small Business Owners," "Financial Tip of the Week," and "This Week Online: Top of the News." Weekly updates. Fees: Free.

ONLINE DATABASES

Wilson Business Abstracts Online. H. W. Wilson Co. • Indexes and abstracts 600 major business periodicals, plus the *Wall Street Journal* and the business section of the *New York Times.* Indexing is from 1982, abstracting from 1990, with the two newspapers included from 1993. Updated weekly. Inquire as to online cost and availability. (*Business Periodicals Index* without abstracts is also available online.).

PERIODICALS AND NEWSLETTERS

Financial Planning: The Magazine for Financial Service Professionals. Securities Data Publishing. • Monthly. $79.00 per year. Edited for independent financial planners and insurance agents. Covers retirement planning, estate planning, tax planning, and insurance, including long-term healthcare considerations. Special features include a Retirement Planning Issue, Mutual Fund Performance Survey, and Variable Life and Annuity Survey. (Securities Data Publishing is a unit of Thomson Financial.).

Jounal of Finacial Services Professionals. American Society of CLU and Ch F C. • Bimonthly. $38.00 per year. Provides information on life insurance and financial planning, including estate planning, retirement, tax planning, trusts, business insurance, long-term care insurance, disability insurance, and employee benefits. Formerly (American Society of CLU and Ch F C Journal).

The Journal of Taxation: A National Journal of Current Developments, Analysis and Commentary for Tax Professionals. Warren, Gorham & Lamont/RIA Group. • Monthly. $215.00 per year. Analysis of current tax developments for tax specialists.

Money. Time Inc. • Monthly. $39.95 per year. Covers all aspects of family finance; investments, careers, shopping, taxes, insurance, consumerism, etc.

Practical Tax Strategies. Warren, Gorham & Lamont/RIA Group. • Monthly. $125.00 per year. Provides advice and information on tax planning for tax accountants, attorneys, and advisers.

Retirement Plans Bulletin: Practical Explanations for the IRA and Retirement Plan Professional. Universal Pensions, Inc. • Monthly. $99.00 per year. Newsletter. Provides information on the rules and regulations governing qualified (tax-deferred) retirement plans.

The Tax Adviser: A Magazine of Tax Planning, Trends and Techniques. American Institute of Certified Public Accountants. • Monthly. Members,

For publishers addresses, refer to SOURCES CITED section at the back of the book.

$71.00 per year; non-members, $98.00 per year. Newsletter.

Tax Management Weekly Report. Tax Management Inc. • Weekly. 1,073.00 per year. Newsletter.

Taxes: The Tax Magazine. CCH, Inc. • Monthly. $195.00. per year. Mainly for accountants and lawyers.

Worth: Financial Intelligence. Worth Media. • 10 times a year. $18.00 per year. Contains articles for affluent consumers on personal financial management, including investments, estate planning, and taxes.

RESEARCH CENTERS AND INSTITUTES

American Institute for Economic Research. P.O. Box 1000, Great Barrington, MA 01230. Phone: (413)528-1216 Fax: (413)528-0103 E-mail: info@aier.org • URL: http://www.aier.org.

TRADE/PROFESSIONAL ASSOCIATIONS

Institute of Tax Consultants. 7500 212th St., S.W., No. 205, Edmonds, WA 98026. Phone: (425)774-3521 Fax: (425)672-0461.

National Association of Tax Practitioners. 720 Association Dr., Appleton, WI 54914. Phone: (920)749-1040 Fax: (920)749-1062 • URL: http://www.natptax.com • Promotes high professional standards for tax practitioners.

Tax Executives Institute. 1200 G St., N.W., No. 300, Washington, DC 20005-3814. Phone: (202)638-5601 Fax: (202)638-5607 E-mail: askter@tei.org • URL: http://www.tei.org.

OTHER SOURCES

Business Transactions: Tax Analysis. Research Institute of America. • Three looseleaf volumes. Biweekly updates. Price on application. Analyzes the tax consequences of various business decisions for sole proprietorships, partnerships, S corporations, and other corporations.

Business Transactions: Tax Planning. Research Institute of America, Inc. • Four looseleaf volumes. Monthly updates. Price on application. Covers the tax planning aspects of business decisions for sole proprietorships, partnerships, S corporations, and other corporations.

Divorce and Taxes. CCH, Inc. • 2000. $39.00. Second edition. In addition to tax problems, topics include alimony, division of property, and divorce decrees.

Federal Tax Course. CCH, Inc. • Annual. $136.00. Looseleaf. Summarizes requirements of current federal income tax regulations, revenue codes, laws, and filing requirements.

Tax Planning for Individuals and Small Businesses. Sidney Kess. CCH, Inc. • 2000. $49.00. Includes illustrations, charts, and sample client letters. Edited primarily for accountants and lawyers.

Tax Strategies for the Self-Employed, CCH, Inc. • 2001. $89.00. Covers accounting methods, start-up expenses, transportation deductions, depreciation, pension deductions, tax penalties, and other topics related to tax planning for the self-employed.

TAX, PROPERTY

See: PROPERTY TAX

TAX, SALES

See: SALES TAX; STATE TAXES; TAXATION

TAX SHELTERS

See also: INCOME TAX; INDUSTRIAL REAL ESTATE; INTERNATIONAL TAXATION; KEOGH PLANS; PROPERTY TAX; REAL ESTATE INVESTMENTS; TAXATION

GENERAL WORKS

What the IRS Doesn't Want You to Know: A CPA Reveals the Tricks of the Trade. Martin Kaplan and Naomi Weiss. Villard Books. • 1999. $15.95. Sixth edition. Explains how to legally pay as little income tax as possible.

ABSTRACTS AND INDEXES

Business Periodicals Index. H. W. Wilson Co. • Monthly, except August, with quarterly and annual cumulations. Service basis for print edition; CD-ROM edition, $1,495.00 per year.

Index to Legal Periodicals and Books. H. W. Wilson Co. • Monthly. Quarterly and annual cumulations. $270.00 per year. CD-ROM version available at $1,495.00 per year.

HANDBOOKS AND MANUALS

Divorce Taxation. Warren, Gorham and Lamont/RIA Group. • Looseleaf service. $515.00 per year. Monthly *Report Bulletins* and updates.

How to Build Wealth with Tax-Sheltered Investments. Kerry Anne Lynch. American Institute for Economic Research. • 2000. $6.00. Provides practical information on conservative tax shelters, including defined-contribution pension plans, individual retirement accounts, Keogh plans, U. S. savings bonds, municipal bonds, and various kinds of annuities: deferred, variable-rate, immediate, and foreign-currency. (Economic Education Bulletin.).

Investment Limited Partnerships Handbook. Robert J. Haft and Peter M. Fass. West Group. • 1992. $97.50.

Practical Guide to Handling IRS Income Tax Audits. Ralph L. Guyette. Prentice Hall. • 1986. $39.95.

Real Estate Transactions, Tax Planning and Consequences. Mark L. Levine. West Publishing Co., College and School Div. • 1997. Periodic supplementation.

Tax Planning for Highly Compensated Individuals. Robert E. Madden. Warren, Gorham & Lamont/RIA Group. • Looseleaf service. $160.00. Biennial supplementation.

Taxation of Real Estate Transactions. Sanford M. Guerin. Shepard's. • 1988. $195.00. Second edition. Two volumes. Covers deferred payment sales, non-taxable exchanges, wraparound financing, defaults, foreclosures, and repossessions. Formerly *Taxation of Real Estate Dispositions.*

Working with Tax-Sheltered Annuities. CCH, Inc. • 1997. $69.00. Emphasis is on legal aspects of tax-deferred annuities.

ONLINE DATABASES

Index to Legal Periodicals and Books (Online). H. W. Wilson Co. • Broad coverage of law journals and books 1981 to date. Monthly updates. Inquire as to online cost and availability.

Legal Resource Index. The Gale Group. • Broad coverage of law literature appearing in legal, business, and other periodicals, 1980 to date. Monthly updates. Inquire as to online cost and availability.

LEXIS. LEXIS-NEXIS. • The various LEXIS databases provide full text and indexing for a wide variety of legal cases, statutes, orders, and opinions.

Wilson Business Abstracts Online. H. W. Wilson Co. • Indexes and abstracts 600 major business periodicals, plus the *Wall Street Journal* and the business section of the *New York Times.* Indexing is from 1982, abstracting from 1990, with the two newspapers included from 1993. Updated weekly. Inquire as to online cost and availability. (*Business Periodicals Index* without abstracts is also available online.).

PERIODICALS AND NEWSLETTERS

Bottom Line-Business. Boardroom, Inc. • Semimonthly. $36.00 per year. Newsletter. Formerly *Boardroom Reports.*

Bottom Line-Personal. Bottom Line Information, Inc. • Semimonthly. $29.95 per year. Provides information to help sophisticated people lead more productive lives.

The Journal of Taxation: A National Journal of Current Developments, Analysis and Commentary for Tax Professionals. Warren, Gorham & Lamont/RIA Group. • Monthly. $215.00 per year. Analysis of current tax developments for tax specialists.

Journal of Taxation of Financial Products. CCH, Inc. • Bimonthly. $249.00 per year.

Limited Partnership Investment Review. Limited Partnership Investment Review, Inc. • Monthly. $197.00 per year. Newsletter. Formerly *Tax Shelter Investment Review.*

Money. Time Inc. • Monthly. $39.95 per year. Covers all aspects of family finance; investments, careers, shopping, taxes, insurance, consumerism, etc.

Personal Finance. Kephart Communications, Inc. • Biweekly. $118.00 per year. Investment advisory newsletter.

Real Estate Tax Digest. Matthew Bender & Shepard. • Monthly. $295.00 per year. Newsletter.

Real Estate Tax Ideas. Warren, Gorham & Lamont/RIA Group. • Monthly. $150.00 per year. Newsletter. Analysis of the current marketplace and regulatory agencies and new opportunities in real estate. Continuing coverage of recent and proposed tax developments.

Stanger Report: A Guide to Partnership Investing. Robert A. Stanger and Co. • Monthly. $447.00 per year. Newsletter providing analysis of limited partnership investments.

Tax-Advantaged Securities. Robert J. Haft and Peter M. Fass, editors. West Group. • 10 times a year. $280.00 per year. Newsletter. Formerly *Investment Limited Partnerships Law Report.*

Tax Avoidance Digest. Agora, Inc. • Monthly. $71.00 per year. Includes digests of tax advice from other publications.

PRICE SOURCES

NAPEX Trade Price Reporter. National Partnership Exchange, Inc. • Quarterly. $160.00 per year. Provides high, low, and last-trade prices (resale prices) for about 500 limited partnerships, including many that have invested primarily in real estate.

RESEARCH CENTERS AND INSTITUTES

Center for Tax Policy Studies. Purdue University, 490 Krannert, West Lafayette, IN 47907-1310. Phone: (765)494-4442 Fax: (765)496-1778 E-mail: papke@mgmt.purdue.edu.

Tax Foundation. 1250 H St., N.W., Suite 750, Washington, DC 20005. Phone: (202)783-2760 Fax: (202)783-6868 E-mail: taxfnd@intr.net • URL: http://www.taxfoundation.org.

TRADE/PROFESSIONAL ASSOCIATIONS

Institute of Tax Consultants. 7500 212th St., S.W., No. 205, Edmonds, WA 98026. Phone: (425)774-3521 Fax: (425)672-0461.

OTHER SOURCES

Federal Taxes Affecting Real Estate. Matthew Bender & Co., Inc. • $215.00. Looseleaf service. Periodic supplementation. Explains and illustrates the most important federal tax principles applying to daily real estate transactions.

Investment Limited Partnerships. Robert J. Haft and Peter M. Fass. West Group. • Six looseleaf volumes. $795.00. Periodic supplementation. Provides extensive coverage of both the tax and securities law aspects of tax motivated investments. (Securities Law Series).

TAXATION

GENERAL WORKS

The Decline (and Fall?) of the Income Tax: How to Make Sense of the American Tax Mess and the Flat-Tax Cures That Are Supposed to Fix It. Michael J. Graetz. W. W. Norton & Co., Inc. • 1997. $27.50. The author, a former U. S. Treasury official, proposes a value-added tax (VAT) to augment federal income tax. He reviews recent tax history and provides entertaining tax anecdotes.

The Flat Tax. Robert E. Hall and Alvin Rabushka. Hoover Institution Press. • 1995. $14.95. Second edition. A favorable view of a flat tax as a replacement for the graduated federal income tax.

Politics of Taxation: Revenue Without Representation. Susan B. Hansen. Greenwood Publishing Group, Inc. • 1983. $55.00.

Tax Policy and the Economy. MIT Press. • Annual. $30.00. Reviews "issues in the current tax debate." Produced by the National Bureau of Economic Research. (Tax Policy and the Economy Series).

ABSTRACTS AND INDEXES

Accounting and Tax Index. UMI. • Quarterly. Price on application. Includes annual cumulative bound volume. Indexes accounting, auditing, and taxation literature appearing in journals, books, pamphlets, conference proceedings, and newsletters. (UMI is University Microfilms International, a Bell & Howell Co.).

Index to Federal Tax Articles. Warren, Gorham and Lamont/RIA Group. • $695.00 per year. Looseleaf service. Seven volumes. Quarterly supplementation. Bibliographic listing of every significant article on federal income, estate and gift taxation since 1913. Lists over 36,000 articles.

Monthly Digest of Tax Articles. Newkirk Products Inc. • Monthly. $60.00 per year.

ALMANACS AND YEARBOOKS

National Tax Association Proceedings of the Annual Conference. National Tax Association. • Annual. Members, $85.00; individuals, $70.00; libraries, $90.00.

New York University Annual Institute on Federal Taxation. Melvin Cornfield. Matthew Bender & Co., Inc. • Annual. Looseleaf service. Price on application. (New York University School of Continuing Education Series).

BIBLIOGRAPHIES

Business Information Sources. Lorna M. Daniells. California Princeton Fulfillment Services. • 1993. $42.50. Third revised edition. Basic business sources, with discussion and full annotations.

CD-ROM DATABASES

EconLit. Available from SilverPlatter Information, Inc. • Monthly. Single-user, $1,600.00 per year. Multi-user, $2,400.00 per year. Provides CD-ROM citations, with abstracts, to articles from more than 500 economics journals. Time period is 1969 to date. Produced by the American Economic Association.

National Newspaper Index CD-ROM. The Gale Group. • Monthly. Provides comprehensive CD-ROM indexing of all material appearing in the late edition of the *New York Times*, the final edition of the *Washington Post*, the national edition of the *Christian Science Monitor*, the home edition of the *Los Angeles Times*, and the *Wall Street Journal*. Time period is four years. Also available online.

The New York Times Ondisc. New York Times Online Services. • Monthly. $2,650.00 per year. CD-ROM discs contain the full text of *The New York Times*, final edition. Inquire as to time period covered and availability of backfiles.

Newspaper Abstracts Ondisc. Bell & Howell Information and Learning. • Monthly. $2,950.00 per year (covers 1989 to date; archival discs are available for 1985-88). Provides cover-to-cover CD-ROM indexing and abstracting of 19 major newspapers, including the *New York Times, Wall Street Journal, Washington Post, Chicago Tribune,* and *Los Angeles Times*.

Search Master Tax Library. Matthew Bender & Co., Inc. • Monthly. $1,200.00 per year. Provides current CD-ROM full text of *Bender's Federal Tax Service, Bender's Master Federal Tax Handbook,* and the current full text of Bender's state tax services for California, Florida, Illinois, New Jersey, New York, Ohio, Pennsylvania, and Texas.

The Tax Directory [CD-ROM]. Tax Analysts. • Quarterly. Provides *The Tax Directory* listings on CD-ROM, covering federal, state, and international tax officials, tax practitioners, and corporate tax executives.

U. S. Master Tax Guide on CD-ROM. CCH, Inc. • Annual. $97.95. CD-ROM version of the printed *U. S. Master Tax Guide*. Includes search commands, link commands, and on-screen prompts.

U. S. Master Tax Guide Plus: Federal CD. CCH, Inc. • Monthly. $199.00 per year. Includes *U. S. Master Tax Guide* on CD-ROM, plus the IRS Code, IRS Regulations, tax court opinions, tax cases, and other source material.

WILSONDISC: Wilson Business Abstracts. H. W. Wilson Co. • Monthly. $2,495.00 per year, including unlimited online access to *Wilson Business Abstracts* through WILSONLINE. Provides CD-ROM "cover-to-cover" abstracting and indexing of over 600 prominent business periodicals. Indexing is from 1982, abstracting from 1990. (*Business Periodicals Index* without abstracts is available on CD-ROM at $1,495 per year.).

DIRECTORIES

Property Tax Manual. Vertex Systems, Inc. • Annual. $1,060.00. Four regions. $265.00 per region. Monthly updates, $808.00 per year. Lists tax rates, assessment ratios, assessors, filing requirements, depreciation schedules, etc.

Sales Tax Rate Directory. Vertex Systems, Inc. • Annual. $670.00. Monthly updates. U.S. and Canadian sales/use tax rates in standardized format.

The Tax Directory. Tax Analysts. • Annual. $299.00. ($399.00 with quarterly CD-ROM updates.) Four volumes: *Government Officials Worldwide* (lists 15,000 state, federal, and international tax officials, with basic corporate and individual income tax rates for 100 countries); *Private Sector Professionals Worldwide* (lists 25,000 U.S. and foreign tax practitioners: accountants, lawyers, enrolled agents, and actuarial firms); *Corporate Tax Managers Worldwide* (lists 10,000 tax managers employed by U.S. and foreign companies).

ENCYCLOPEDIAS AND DICTIONARIES

Dictionary of Finance and Investment Terms. John Downes and Jordan E. Goodman. Barron's Educational Series, Inc. • 1998. $12.95. Fifth revised edition. Provides clear explanations of more than 5,000 business, banking, financial, investment, and tax terms. Includes a separate list of financial abbreviations and acronyms.

Dictionary of Taxation. Simon James. Edward Elgar Publishing, Inc. • 1998. $65.00. Provides detailed definitions of terms relating to "various aspects of taxes and tax systems throughout the world.".

International Encyclopedia of Public Policy and Administration. Jay M. Shafritz, editor. HarperCollins Publishers. • 1997. $550.00. Four volumes. Covers 20 major areas, such as public administration, government budgeting, industrial policy, nonprofit management, organizational theory, public finance, labor relations, and taxation. Includes a brief bibliography for each major entry and a comprehensive index.

HANDBOOKS AND MANUALS

Bender's Tax Return Manual. Ernest D. Fiore and others. Matthew Bender & Co., Inc. • Annual. Price on application. Includes all major federal tax forms and schedules.

CCH Analysis of Top Tax Issues: Return Preparation and Planning Guide. CCH, Inc. • Annual. $45.00. Covers yearly tax changes affecting business and personal transactions, planning, and returns.

Corporate, Partnership, Estate, and Gift Taxation 1997. James W. Pratt and William Kulsrud, editors. McGraw-Hill Higher Education. • 1996. $71.25. 10th edition.

Cybertaxation: The Taxation of E-Commerce. Karl A. Frieden. CCH, Inc. • 2000. $75.00. Includes state sales and use tax issues and corporate income tax rules, as related to doing business over the Internet.

Divorce Taxation. Warren, Gorham and Lamont/RIA Group. • Looseleaf service. $515.00 per year. Monthly *Report Bulletins* and updates.

Federal Tax Course: General Edition. CCH, Inc. • Annual. $123.00. Provides basic reference and training for various forms of federal taxation: individual, business, corporate, partnership, estate, gift, etc. Includes *Federal Taxation Study Manual*.

Federal Tax Handbook. Research Institute of America. • 2000. $45.00. Revised edition.

Federal Tax Manual. CCH, Inc. • Looseleaf. $175.00 per year. Covers "basic federal tax rules and forms affecting individuals and businesses." Includes a copy of *Annuity, Depreciation, and Withholding Tables*.

Individual Taxation. James W. Pratt and William N. Kulsrud. McGraw-Hill Higher Education. • 1996. $69.95. Tenth edition. Focuses on the federal income tax.

RIA Federal Tax Handbook. Research Institute of America, Inc. • Annual. $45.00. Formerly *Master Federal Tax Manual*.

Tax Guide for Small Business. U.S. Department of the Treasury, Internal Revenue Service. Available from U.S. Government Printing Office. • Annual. $5.00.

Taxation of Financially Distressed Businesses. David B. Newman. West Group. • 1993. $120.00. Covers bankruptcy, foreclosure, abandonment, legal reporting requirements, and other tax-related subjects. (Tax Series).

U. S. Master Estate and Gift Tax Guide. CCH, Inc. • Annual. $49.00. Covers federal estate and gift taxes, including generation-skipping transfer tax plans. Includes tax tables and sample filled-in tax return forms.

U. S. Master Tax Guide. CCH, Inc. • Annual. $46.00. Provides concise information on personal and business income tax, with cross-references to the Internal Revenue Code and Income Tax Regulations.

INTERNET DATABASES

CCH Essentials: An Internet Tax Research and Primary Source Library. CCH, Inc. Phone: 800-248-3248 or (773)866-6000 Fax: 800-224-8299 or (773)866-3608 E-mail: cust_serv@cch.com • URL: http://tax.cch.com/essentials • Fee-based Web site provides full-text coverage of federal tax law and regulations, including rulings, procedures, tax court decisions, and IRS publications, announcements, notices, and penalties. Includes explanation, analysis, tax planning guides, and a daily tax news service. Searching is offered, including citation search. Fee: $495.00 per year.

Fedstats. Federal Interagency Council on Statistical Policy. Phone: (202)395-7254 • URL: http://www.fedstats.gov • Web site features an efficient search facility for full-text statistics produced by more than 70 federal agencies, including the Census Bureau, the Bureau of Economic Analysis, and the Bureau of Labor Statistics. Boolean searches can be made within one agency or for all agencies combined. Links are offered to international statistical bureaus, including the UN, IMF, OECD, UNESCO, Eurostat, and 20 individual countries. Fees: Free.

Tax Analysts [Web site]. Tax Analysts. Phone: 800-955-3444 or (703)533-4400 Fax: (703)533-4444 • URL: http://www.tax.org • The three main sections of Tax Analysts home page are "Tax News" (Today's Tax News, Feature of the Week, Tax Snapshots, Tax Calendar); "Products & Services" (Product Catalog, Press Releases); and "Public Interest" (Discussion Groups, Tax Clinic, Tax History Project). Fees: Free for coverage of current tax events; fee-based for comprehensive information. Daily updating.

TAXNET. Carswell/Thomas Professional Publishing. Phone: 800-387-5164 or (416)609-3800 Fax: (416)298-5082 • URL: http://www.carswell.com/taxnet.htm • Fee-based Web site provides complete coverage of Canadian tax law and regulation, including income tax, provincial taxes, accounting, and payrolls. Daily updates. Base price varies according to product.

ONLINE DATABASES

Accounting and Tax Database. Bell & Howell Information and Learning. • Provides indexing and abstracting of the literature of accounting, taxation, and financial management, 1971 to date. Updating is weekly. Especially covers accounting, auditing, banking, bankruptcy, employee compensation and benefits, cash management, financial planning, and credit. Inquire as to online cost and availability.

DRI U.S. Central Database. Data Products Division. • Provides more than 23,000 business, financial, demographic, economic, foreign trade, and industry-related time series for the U.S. Includes national income, population, retail-wholesale trade, price indexes, labor data, housing, industrial production, banking, interest rates, money supply, etc. Time period is generally 1947 to date (some data back to 1929). Updating varies. Inquire as to online cost and availability.

EconLit. American Economic Association. • Covers the worldwide literature of economics as contained in selected monographs and about 550 journals. Subjects include microeconomics, macroeconomics, economic history, inflation, money, credit, finance, accounting theory, trade, natural resource economics, and regional economics. Time period is 1969 to present, with monthly updates. Inquire as to online cost and availability.

Information Bank Abstracts. New York Times Index Dept. • Provides indexing and abstracting of current affairs, primarily from the final late edition of *The New York Times* and the Eastern edition of *The Wall Street Journal*. Time period is 1969 to present, with daily updates. Inquire as to online cost and availability.

Wilson Business Abstracts Online. H. W. Wilson Co. • Indexes and abstracts 600 major business periodicals, plus the *Wall Street Journal* and the business section of the *New York Times*. Indexing is from 1982, abstracting from 1990, with the two newspapers included from 1993. Updated weekly. Inquire as to online cost and availability. (*Business Periodicals Index* without abstracts is also available online.).

PERIODICALS AND NEWSLETTERS

Bottom Line-Business. Boardroom, Inc. • Semimonthly. $36.00 per year. Newsletter. Formerly *Boardroom Reports*.

The Canadian Taxpayer. Carswell. • Semimonthly. $330.00 per year. Newsletter. Covers tax trends and policies in Canada.

Daily Tax Report: From Today's Daily Report for Executives. Bureau of National Affairs, Inc. • Daily. $2,350.00 per year. Newsletter. Monitors tax legislation, hearings, rulings, and court decisions.

E-Commerce Tax Alert. CCH, Inc. • Monthly. $397.00 per year. Newsletter. Edited for owners and managers of firms doing business through the Internet. Covers compliance with federal, state, local, and international tax regulations.

Highlights and Documents. Tax Analysts. • Daily. $2,249.00 per year, including monthly indexes. Newsletter. Provides daily coverage of IRS, congressional, judicial, state, and international tax developments. Includes abstracts and citations for "all tax documents released within the previous 24 to 48 hours." Annual compilation available *Highlights and Documents on Microfiche*.

International Tax Report: Maximizing Tax Opportunities Worldwide. I B C Donoghue Organization. • Monthly. $1,110.00 per year.

Journal of Corporate Taxation. Warren, Gorham, and Lamont/RIA Group. • Looseleaf service. $195.00 per year. Quarterly updates. Analysis and guidance for practitioners. Provides ongoing coverage of currently proposed tax reform bills.

The Journal of Taxation: A National Journal of Current Developments, Analysis and Commentary for Tax Professionals. Warren, Gorham & Lamont/RIA Group. • Monthly. $215.00 per year. Analysis of current tax developments for tax specialists.

Kiplinger Tax Letter. Kiplinger Washington Editors, Inc. • Biweekly. $59.00 per year.

National Tax Journal. National Tax Association - Tax Institute of America. • Quarterly. Members, $85.00 per year; membership libraries, $100.00 per year; membership corporations, $130.00 per year. Topics of current interest in the field of taxation and public finance in the U.S. and foreign countries.

The Practical Accountant: Accounting and Taxes in Everyday Practice. Faulkner and Gray, Inc. • Monthly. $60.00 per year. Covers tax planning, financial planning, practice management, client relationships, and related topics.

The Tax Adviser: A Magazine of Tax Planning, Trends and Techniques. American Institute of Certified Public Accountants. • Monthly. Members, $71.00 per year; non-members, $98.00 per year. Newsletter.

Tax Notes: The Weekly Tax Service. Tax Analysts. • Weekly. $1,699.00 per year. Includes an *Annual* and 1985-1996 compliations on CD-ROM. Newsletter. Covers "tax news from all federal sources," including congressional committees, tax courts, and the Internal Revenue Service. Each issue contains "summaries of every document that pertains to federal tax law," with citations. Commentary is provided.

Tax Practice. Tax Analysts. • Weekly. $199.00 per year. Newsletter. Covers news affecting tax practitioners and litigators, with emphasis on federal court decisions, rules and regulations, and tax petitions. Provides a guide to Internal Revenue Service audit issues.

Taxation for Accountants. Warren, Gorham & Lamont/RIA Group. • Monthly. $125.00. per year. Emphasis is on current tax developments as they affect accountants and their clients. Includes advice on tax software and computers.

Taxation for Lawyers. Warren, Gorham & Lamont/RIA Group. • Bimonthly. $114.98 per year. Edited for attorneys who are not tax specialists. Emphasis is on tax planning, estates, trusts, partnerships, and taxation of real estate.

Taxes on Parade. CCH, Inc. • Weekly. $113.00 per year. Newsletter.

Taxes: The Tax Magazine. CCH, Inc. • Monthly. $195.00. per year. Mainly for accountants and lawyers.

Weekly Alert. Research Institute of America, Inc. • Weekly. Newsletter. $175.00 per year. Federal tax trends and new legislation.

RESEARCH CENTERS AND INSTITUTES

Center for Tax Policy Studies. Purdue University, 490 Krannert, West Lafayette, IN 47907-1310. Phone: (765)494-4442 Fax: (765)496-1778 E-mail: papke@mgmt.purdue.edu.

International Tax Program. Harvard University, Pound Hall, Room 400, Cambridge, MA 02138. Phone: (617)495-4406 Fax: (617)495-0423 • URL: http://www.law.harvard.edu/programs/itp • Studies the worldwide problems of taxation, including tax law and tax administration.

Tax Foundation. 1250 H St., N.W., Suite 750, Washington, DC 20005. Phone: (202)783-2760 Fax: (202)783-6868 E-mail: taxfnd@intr.net • URL: http://www.taxfoundation.org.

STATISTICS SOURCES

The AIER Chart Book. AIER Research Staff. American Institute for Economic Research. • Annual. $3.00. A compact compilation of long-range charts ("Purchasing Power of the Dollar," for example, goes back to 1780) covering various aspects of the U. S. economy. Includes inflation, interest rates, debt, gold, taxation, stock prices, etc. (Economic Education Bulletin.).

Budget of the United States Government. U.S. Office of Management and Budget. Available from U.S. Government Printing Office. • Annual.

Business Statistics of the United States. Courtenay M. Slater, editor. Bernan Associates. • 1999. $74.00. Fifth edition. Based on *Business Statistics*, formerly issue by the Bureau of Economic Analysis, U. S. Department of Commerce. Provides basic data for a wide variety of U. S. industries, services, and economic indicators. Most statistics are shown annually for 29 years and monthly for the most recent four years.

Revenue Statistics. OECD Publications and Information Center. • Annual. $65.00. Presents data on government revenues in OECD countries, classified by type of tax and level of government. Text in English and French.

Social Statistics of the United States. Mark S. Littman, editor. Bernan Press. • 2000. $65.00. Includes statistical data on population growth, labor force, occupations, environmental trends, leisure time use, income, poverty, taxes, and other economic or demographic topics.

Statistical Handbook on Consumption and Wealth in the United States. Chandrika Kaul and Valerie Tomaselli-Moschovitis. Oryx Press. • 1999. $65.00. Provides more than 400 graphs, tables, and charts dealing with basic income levels, income inequalities, spending patterns, taxation, subsidies, etc. (Statistical Handbook Series).

Statistics of Income Bulletin. Available from U.S. Government Printing Office. • Quarterly. $35.00 per year. Current data compiled from tax returns relating to income, assets, and expenses of individuals and businesses. (U. S. Internal Revenue Service.).

Survey of Current Business. Available from U. S. Government Printing Office. • Monthly. $49.00 per year. Issued by Bureau of Economic Analysis, U. S. Department of Commerce. Presents a wide variety of business and economic data.

TRADE/PROFESSIONAL ASSOCIATIONS

Citizens for a Sound Economy. 1250 H St., N.W., Suite 700, Washington, DC 20005-3908. Phone: 888-564-6273 or (202)783-3870 Fax: (202)783-4687 E-mail: cse@cse.org • URL: http://www.cse.org.

National Tax Association. 725 15th St., N.W., No. 600, Washington, DC 20005-2109. Phone: (202)737-3325 Fax: (202)737-7308 E-mail: natltax@aol.com.

National Taxpayers Union. 108 N. Alfred St., Alexandria, VA 22314. Phone: 800-829-4258 or (703)683-5700 Fax: (703)683-5722 E-mail: ntu@ntu.org • URL: http://www.ntu.org.

OTHER SOURCES

All States Tax Guide. Prentice Hall. • Looseleaf. Periodic supplementation. Price on application. One volume summary of taxes for all states.

Factiva. Dow Jones Reuters Business Interactive, LLC. • Fee-based Web site provides "global news and business information through Web sites and content integration solutions." Includes Dow Jones and Reuters newswires, The Wall Street Journal, and more than 7,000 other sources of current news, historical articles, market research reports, and investment analysis. Content includes 96 major U. S. newspapers, 900 non-English sources, trade publications, media transcripts, country profiles, news photos, etc.

Federal Income, Gift and Estate Taxation. Matthew Bender & Co., Inc. • $1,070.00. Nine looseleaf volumes. Periodic supplementation.

Federal Tax Coordinator 2D. Research Institute of America, Inc. • 35 looseleaf volumes. $1,375.00 per year. Weekly updates. Includes *Weekly Alert* newsletter and *Internal Revenue Bulletin.* Covers federal income, estate, gift, and excise taxes. Formerly *Federal Tax Coordinator.*

Federal Taxation of Income, Estates and Gifts. Boris I. Bittker. Warren, Gorham and Lamont/RIA Group. • Looseleaf service. $465.00. Five volumes. Quarterly supplementation. Covers aspects of income taxation of individuals, corporations, partnerships, estates, and gifts. Clear analysis to exact answers to tax questions.

Federal Taxes Citator. MacMillan Publishing Co. • $550.00 per year. Two looseleaf volumes. Monthly supplements.

FedWorld: A Program of the United States Department of Commerce. National Technical Information Service. • Web site offers "a comprehensive central access point for searching, locating, ordering, and acquiring government and business information." Emphasis is on searching the Web pages, databases, and government reports of a wide variety of federal agencies. Fees: Free.

FirstGov: Your First Click to the U. S. Government. General Services Administration. • Free Web site provides extensive links to federal agencies covering a wide variety of topics, such as agriculture, business, consumer safety, education, the environment, government jobs, grants, health, social security, statistics sources, taxes, technology, travel, and world affairs. Also provides links to federal forms, including IRS tax forms. Searching is offered, both keyword and advanced.

Nexis.com. Lexis-Nexis Group. • Fee-based Web site offers searching of about 2.8 billion documents in some 30,000 news, business, and legal information sources. Features include a subject directory covering 1,200 topics in 34 categories and a Company Dossier containing information on more than 500,000 public and private companies. Boolean searching is offered.

Taxation of Securities Transactions. Matthew Bender & Co., Inc. • $260.00. Looseleaf service.Periodic supplementation. Covers taxation of a wide variety of securities transactions, including those involving stocks, bonds, options, short sales, new issues, mutual funds, dividend distributions, foreign securities, and annuities.

TAXATION, INTERNATIONAL

See: INTERNATIONAL TAXATION

TAXES, STATE

See: STATE TAXES

TAXICABS

DIRECTORIES

Taxicab and Transportation Service Directory. American Business Directories. • Annual. Price on application. Provides a geographical list for over 7,788 taxicab companies. Compiled from telephone company yellow pages. Formerly *Taxicab Directory.*

HANDBOOKS AND MANUALS

Limousine Service. Entrepreneur Media, Inc. • Looseleaf. $59.50. A practical guide to starting a limousine service. Covers profit potential, start-up costs, market size evaluation, owner's time required, site selection, lease negotiation, pricing, accounting, advertising, promotion, etc. (Start-Up Business Guide No. E1224.).

PERIODICALS AND NEWSLETTERS

Taxi and Livery Management. International Taxicab and Livery Association. • Quarterly. $16.00 per year.

TRADE/PROFESSIONAL ASSOCIATIONS

International Taxicab and Livery Association. 3849 Farragut Ave., Kensington, MD 20895. Phone: (301)946-5701 Fax: (301)946-4641 E-mail: itla@itla-info.org • URL: http://www.taxinetwork.com.

TAYLOR SYSTEM OF SHOP MANAGEMENT

See: TIME AND MOTION STUDY

TEA INDUSTRY

See also: COFFEE INDUSTRY

ALMANACS AND YEARBOOKS

CRB Commodity Yearbook. Commodity Research Bureau. CRB. • Annual. $99.95.

DIRECTORIES

Uker's International Tea and Coffee Directory and Buyers' Guide. Lockwood Trade Journal Co., Inc. • Annual. $40.00. Lists firms which export and import tea and coffee.

World Coffee and Tea OCS Buyer's Guide. GCI Publishing Co., Inc. • Annual. $5.00. Directory of manufacturers and suppliers of equipment and products for the office coffee service industry. Formerly *World Coffee and Tea-Office Coffee Service Red Book Directory.*

HANDBOOKS AND MANUALS

Coffee and Tea Store. Entrepreneur Media, Inc. • Looseleaf. $59.50. A practical guide to starting a coffee and tea store. Covers profit potential, start-up costs, market size evaluation, owner's time required, site selection, lease negotiation, pricing, accounting, advertising, promotion, etc. (Start-Up Business Guide No. E1202.).

INTERNET DATABASES

USDA. United States Department of Agriculture. Phone: (202)720-2791 E-mail: agsec@usda.gov • URL: http://www.usda.gov • The USDA home page has six sections: News and Information; What's New; About USDA; Agencies; Opportunities; Search and Help. Keyword searching is offered from the USDA home page and from various individual agency home pages. Agencies are the Economic Research Service, Agricultural Marketing Service, National Agricultural Statistics Service, National Agricultural Library, and about 12 others. Updating varies. Fees: Free.

ONLINE DATABASES

Globalbase. The Gale Group. • Provides more than one million online summaries of business, industrial, and economic news reports from more than 1,000 publications worldwide. Covers a wide range of material appearing in international trade journals, professional magazines, and newspapers. Time period is 1984 to date, with weekly updates. Inquire as to online cost and availability.

PERIODICALS AND NEWSLETTERS

Fancy Food. Talcott Communications Corp. • Monthly. $34.00 per year. Emphasizes new specialty food products and the business management aspects of the specialty food and confection industries. Includes special issues on wine, cheese, candy, "upscale" cookware, and gifts.

Sri Lanka Journal of Tea Science. Tea Research Institute of Sri Lanka. • Semiannual. $20.00 per year. Text in English. Formerly *Tea Quarterly.*

Tea and Coffee Trade Journal. Lockwood Trade Journal Co., Inc. • Monthly. $30.00 per year. Current trends in coffee roasting and tea packing industry.

World Coffee and Tea. GCI Publishing Co., Inc. • Monthly. $24.00.

STATISTICS SOURCES

Agricultural Statistics. Available from U. S. Government Printing Office. • Annual. Produced by the National Agricultural Statistics Service, U. S. Department of Agriculture. Provides a wide variety of statistical data relating to agricultural production, supplies, consumption, prices/price-supports, foreign trade, costs, and returns, as well as farm labor, loans, income, and population. In many cases, historical data is shown annually for 10 years. In addition to farm data, includes detailed fishery statistics.

TRADE/PROFESSIONAL ASSOCIATIONS

Tea Council of the United States of America. 420 Lexington Ave., Suite 825, New York, NY 10170. Phone: (212)986-6998 Fax: (212)697-8658 • Membership is international. Includes Tea Association of the U.S.A.

OTHER SOURCES

Coffee and Tea Market. MarketResearch.com. • 1999. $2,750.00. Market data with forecasts to 2004. Covers many types of coffee and tea.

TEA ROOMS

See: RESTAURANTS, LUNCHROOMS, ETC.

TECHNICAL ANALYSIS (FINANCE)

See also: COMPUTERS IN FINANCE; DOW THEORY; FINANCIAL ANALYSIS

GENERAL WORKS

Forecasting Financial Markets. Christian Dunis. John Wiley and Sons, Inc. • 1996. $110.00. Examines what are said to be the more reliable or "classic" theories of continuously recurring price patterns. Practical investment applications are discussed.

The New Science of Technical Analysis. Thomas R. DeMark. John Wiley and Sons, Inc. • 1994. $59.95. (Wiley Finance Editions Series).

ALMANACS AND YEARBOOKS

Don't Sell Stocks on Monday: An Almanac for Traders, Brokers, and Stock Market Watchers. Yale Hirsch. Books on Demand. • 1987. $74.40. Summarizes what are perceived as seasonal influences (day of the week, week of the month, month of the year, etc.) on stock prices.

Supertrader's Almanac-Reference Manual: Reference Guide and Analytical Techniques for Investors. Market Movements, Inc. • 1991. $55.00. Explains technical methods for the trading of commodity futures, and includes data on seasonality, cycles, trends, contract characteristics, highs and lows, etc.

DIRECTORIES

Association for Investment Management and Research-Membership Directory. Association for Investment Management and Research. • Annual. $150.00. Members are professional investment managers and securities analysts.

Futures Guide to Computerized Trading. Futures Magazine, Inc. • Annual. $10.00. "A directory of products and services for the computerized trader." Provides information on computer software applications for commodity traders and money managers, including trading methods and technical analysis.

Futures Magazine SourceBook: The Most Complete List of Exchanges, Companies, Regulators, Organizations, etc., Offering Products and Services to the Futures and Options Industry. Futures Magazine, Inc. • Annual. $19.50. Provides information on commodity futures brokers, trading method services, publications, and other items of interest to futures traders and money managers.

National Directory of Investment Newsletters. GPS Co. • Biennial. $49.95. Describes about 800 investment newsletters, and their publishers.

ENCYCLOPEDIAS AND DICTIONARIES

Encyclopedia of Chart Patterns. Thomas N. Bulkowski. John Wiley and Sons, Inc. • 2000. $79.95. Provides explanations of the predictive value of various chart patterns formed by stock and commodity price movements.

Encyclopedia of Technical Market Indicators. Robert W. Colby and Thomas A. Meyers. McGraw-Hill Professional. • 1988. $70.00.

Technical Analysis from A to Z: Covers Every Trading Tool from the Absolute Breadth Index to Zig Zag. Steven B. Achelis. McGraw-Hill Professional. • 2000. $39.95. Second edition. Provides definitions and explanations of more than 100 technical indicators used in attempts to predict stock and commodity price trends. Includes a general introduction to technical analysis.

HANDBOOKS AND MANUALS

Day-Trader's Manual: Theory, Art, and Science of Profitable Short-Term Investing. William F. Eng. John Wiley and Sons, Inc. • 1992. $79.95. Covers short-term trading in stocks, futures, and options. Various technical trading systems are considered.

Derivatives: A Comprehensive Resource for Options, Futures, Interest Rate Swaps, and Mortgage Securities. Fred D. Arditti. Harvard Business School Press. • 1996. $60.00. Published by Harvard Business School Press. Provides detailed explanations of various kinds of financial derivatives (options, futures, swaps, etc.) and their trading tactics, uses, and risks. (Financial Management Association Survey and Synthesis Series).

Fibonacci Applications and Strategies for Traders. Robert Fischer. John Wiley and Sons, Inc. • 1993. $49.95. Provides a new look at the Elliott Wave Theory and Fibonacci numbers as applied to commodity prices, business cycles, and interest rate movements. (Traders Library).

The New Technical Trader: Boost Your Profit by Plugging into the Latest Indicators. Tushar S. Chande and Stanley Kroll. John Wiley and Sons, Inc. • 1994. $64.95. (Finance Edition Series).

Portfolio Management Formulas: Mathematical Trading Methods for the Futures, Options, and Stock Markets. Ralph Vince. John Wiley and Sons, Inc. • 1990. $85.00. Discusses optimization of trading systems by exploiting the rules of probability and making use of the principles of modern portfolio management theory. Computer programs are included.

Stock Market Trading Systems. Gerald Appel and Fred Hitschler. Traders Press, Inc. • 1990. $45.00. Reprint of 1980 edition.

Technical Analysis Explained: The Successful Investor's Guide to Spotting Investment Trends and Turning Points. Martin J. Pring. McGraw-Hill. • 1991. $49.95. Third edition.

Technical Analysis of Stock Trends. Robert D. Edwards and John Magee. AMACOM. • 1998. $79.85. 7th revised edition. Standard manual of technical analysis.

Trading for a Living: Psychology, Trading Tactics, Money Management. Alexander Elder. John Wiley and Sons, Inc. • 1993. $59.95. Covers technical and chart methods of trading in commodity and financial futures, options, and stocks. Includes Elliott Wave Theory, oscillators, moving averages, point-and-figure, and other technical approaches. (Finance Editions Series).

Using Technical Analysis: A Step-by-Step Guide to Understanding and Applying Stock Market. Clifford Pistolese, editor. McGraw-Hill Professional. • 1994. $24.95. Revised edition.

INTERNET DATABASES

Futures Online. Oster Communications, Inc. Phone: 800-601-8907 or (319)277-1278 Fax: (319)277-7982 • URL: http://www.futuresmag.com • Web site presents updates of *Futures* magazine and links to other futures-related sites. Includes "Futures Industry News," "Technical Talk," "Today's Hot Markets," "Futures Talk" (forums), "Futures Library" (archives, 1993 to date), and other features. Keyword searching is available. Updating: daily. Fees: Free.

PERIODICALS AND NEWSLETTERS

Computerized Investing. American Association of Individual Investors. • Bimonthly. $40.00 per year. Newsletter on computer-aided investment analysis. Includes reviews of software.

Dow Theory Letters. Dow Theory Letters, Inc. • Biweekly. $250.00 per year. Newsletter on stock market trends, investing, and economic conditions.

Futures: News, Analysis, and Strategies for Futures, Options, and Derivatives Traders. Futures Magazine, Inc. • Monthly. $39.00 per year. Edited for institutional money managers and traders, brokers, risk managers, and individual investors or speculators. Includes special feature issues on interest rates, technical indicators, currencies, charts, precious metals, hedge funds, and derivatives. Supplements available.

InvesTech Market Analyst: Technical and Monetary Investment Analysis. InvesTech Research. • Every three weeks. $190.00 per year. Newsletter. Provides interpretation of monetary statistics and Federal Reserve actions, especially as related to technical analysis of stock market price trends.

Technical Analysis of Stocks & Commodities: The Trader's Magazine. Technical Analysis, Inc. • 13 times a year. $49.95 per year. Covers use of personal computers for stock trading, price movement analysis by means of charts, and other technical trading methods.

Technical Trends: The Indicator Accuracy Service. • 40 times a year. $147.00 per year. Technical investment newsletter.

Wall Street and Technology: For Senior-Level Executives in Technology and Information Management in Securities and Invesment Firms. Miller Freeman, Inc. • Monthly. $99.00 per year. Includes material on the use of computers in technical investment strategies. Formerly *Wall Computer Review.*

RESEARCH CENTERS AND INSTITUTES

Center for Research in Security Prices. University of Chicago, 725 S. Wells St., Suite 800, Chicago, IL 60607. Phone: (773)702-7467 Fax: (773)753-4797 E-mail: mail@crsp.uchicago.edu • URL: http://www.crsp.com.

Glucksman Institute. New York University. Salomon Center, Stern School of Business, 44 W. Fourth St., Room 9-65, New York, NY 10012-0267. Phone: (212)998-0714 Fax: (212)995-4220 E-mail: iwalter@stern.nyu.edu • URL: http://www.stern.nyu.edu/salomon.

Institute for Quantitative Research in Finance. Church Street Station, P.O. Box 6194, New York, NY 10249-6194. Phone: (212)744-6825 Fax: (212)517-2259 E-mail: daleberman@compuserve • Financial research areas include quantitative methods, securities analysis, and the financial structure of industries. Also known as the "Q Group.".

Research Foundation of AIMR (Association for Investment Management and Research). P.O. Box 3668, Charlottesville, VA 22903. Phone: (804)951-5390 Fax: (804)951-5370 E-mail: info@aimr.com • URL: http://www.aimr.org/aimr/knowledge/research • Affiliated with Financial Analysts Federation.

Rodney L. White Center for Financial Research. University of Pennsylvania, 3254 Steinberg Hall-

Dietrich Hall, Philadelphia, PA 19104. Phone: (215)898-7616 Fax: (215)573-8084 E-mail: rlwtcr@finance.wharton.upenn.edu • URL: http://www.finance.wharton.upenn.edu/~rlwctr • Research areas include financial management, money markets, real estate finance, and international finance.

STATISTICS SOURCES

Advance-Decline Album. Dow Theory Letters, Inc. • Annual. Contains one page for each year since 1931. Includes charts of the New York Stock Exchange advance-decline ratio and the Dow Jones industrial average.

Dow Jones Averages Chart Album. Dow Theory Letters, Inc. • Annual. Contains one page for each year since 1885. Includes line charts of the Dow Jones industrial, transportation, utilities, and bond averages. Important historical and economic dates are shown.

SRC Green Book of 35-Year Charts. • Annual. $119.00. Chart book presents statistical information on the stocks of 400 leading companies over a 35-year period. Each full page chart is in semi-log format to avoid visual distortion. Also includes charts of 12 leading market averages or indexes and 39 major industry groups.

TRADE/PROFESSIONAL ASSOCIATIONS

Association for Investment Management and Research. 560 Ray C. Hunt Dr., Charlottesville, VA 22903-0668. Phone: 800-247-8132 or (804)951-5499 Fax: (804)951-5262 E-mail: info@aimr.org • URL: http://www.aimr.org.

OTHER SOURCES

Daily Graphs. Daily Graphs, Inc. • New York Stock Exchange edition, $363.00 per year. American Stock Exchange edition, $363.00 per year. Both editions include the 200 leading over-the-counter stocks.

Mansfield Stock Chart Service. R.W. Mansfield Co., Inc. • Weekly. Price varies. Covers New York Stock Exchange, American Stock Exchange, OTC exchange, international stocks and industry groups. Partial subscriptions available.

The Options Workbook: Proven Strategies from a Market Wizard. Anthony J. Saliba. Dearborn Financial Publishing. • 2001. $40.00. Emphasis is on computerized trading on the Chicago Board Options Exchange. Includes information on specific trading strategies.

TECHNICAL ASSISTANCE

See also: DEVELOPING AREAS

GENERAL WORKS

Does Aid Work?. Robert Cassen. Oxford University Press, Inc. • 1994. $19.95. Second edition.

PERIODICALS AND NEWSLETTERS

Peace Corps Times. U. S. Peace Corps. • Quarterly. Presents news of the programs and activities of the Peace Corps.

TRADE/PROFESSIONAL ASSOCIATIONS

Volunteers in Technical Assistance. 1600 Wilson Blvd., Suite 710, Arlington, VA 22209. Phone: (703)276-1800 Fax: (703)243-1865 E-mail: vita@vita.org • URL: http://www.vita.org.

TECHNICAL BOOKS

See: TECHNOLOGY

TECHNICAL EDUCATION

See also: VOCATIONAL EDUCATION

ABSTRACTS AND INDEXES

Education Index. H.W. Wilson Co. • 10 times a year. Service basis.

Technical Education and Training Abstracts. Carfax Publishing Co. • Quarterly. Individuals, $238.00 per year; institutions, $754.00 per year. Published in England. Formerly *Technical Education Abstracts.*

CD-ROM DATABASES

ERIC on SilverPlatter. Available from SilverPlatter Information, Inc. • Quarterly. $700.00 per year. Produced by the Office of Educational Research and Improvement, U. S. Dept. of Education. Provides CD-ROM indexing and abstracting of a wide variety of literature relating to education. Archival discs are available from 1966.

DIRECTORIES

American Association of Community and Junior Colleges Directory. American Association of Community and Junior Colleges. • Annual. $35.00. Formerly *Community, Junior and Technical College Directory.*

American Trade Schools Directory. Croner Publications, Inc. • $120.00. Looseleaf service. Monthly updates. Directory of over 12,000 trade,technical and vocational schools arranged by state.

Peterson's Vocational and Technical Schools and Programs. Peterson's. • Annual. $34.95. Provides information on vocational schools in the eastern part of the U. S. Covers more than 370 career fields.

HANDBOOKS AND MANUALS

Specialty Occupational Outlook: Trade and Technical. The Gale Group. • 1996. $70.00. Provides information on 150 "high-interest" careers that do not require a bachelor's degree.

ONLINE DATABASES

Education Index Online. H. W. Wilson Co. • Indexes a wide variety of periodicals related to schools, colleges, and education, 1984 to date. Monthly updates. Inquire as to online cost and availability.

ERIC. Educational Resources Information Center. • Broad range of educational literature, 1966 to present. Monthly updates. Inquire as to online cost and availability.

PERIODICALS AND NEWSLETTERS

ATEA Journal. American Technical Education Association, Inc. • Four times a year. Individuals, $40.00 per year; institutions, $150.00; corporations, $200.00 per year.

Technical Education News. Glencoe-McGraw Hill. • Semiannual. Free to qualified personnel.

TRADE/PROFESSIONAL ASSOCIATIONS

American Technical Education Association. c/o North Dakota State College of Science. 800 N. Sixth St., Wahpeton, ND 58076. Phone: (701)671-2301 or (701)671-2240 Fax: (701)671-2660 E-mail: krump@plains.nodak.edu • URL: http://www.ndscs.nodak.edu/atea/.

Career College Association. 10 G St., N.W., Suite 750, Washington, DC 20002. Phone: (202)336-6700 Fax: (202)336-6828 E-mail: waltb@career.org • URL: http://www.career.org.

Special Interest Group for Computer Science Education. c/o Association for Computing Machinery, 1515 Broadway, New York, NY 10036-5701. Phone: (212)869-7440 Fax: (212)302-5826 E-mail: sigs@acm.org • URL: http://www.acm.org • Concerned with education relating to computer science and technology on various levels, ranging from secondary school to graduate degree programs.

TECHNICAL LITERATURE

See: TECHNOLOGY

TECHNICAL SOCIETIES

See: ASSOCIATIONS

TECHNICAL WRITING

See also: PROCEDURE MANUALS

HANDBOOKS AND MANUALS

ACS Style Guide: A Manual for Authors and Editors. Janet S. Dodd, editor. American Chemical Society Publications. • 1997. $39.95. Second edition. A style manual for scientific and technical writers. Includes the use of illustrations, tables, lists, numbers, and units of measure.

Effective Writing for Engineers, Managers, Scientists. H. J. Tichy and Sylvia Fourdrinier. John Wiley and Sons, Inc. • 1988. $104.95. Second edition.

Freelance Writing. Entrepreneur Media, Inc. • Looseleaf. $59.50. A practical guide to starting a freelance writing service. Covers profit potential, start-up costs, market size evaluation, pricing, accounting, advertising, promotion, etc. (Start-Up Business Guide No. E1258.).

How to Write and Present Technical Information. Charles H. Sides. Oryx Press. • 1998. $24.95. Third edition.

Technical Report Writing Today. Daniel Riordan. Houghton Mifflin Co. • 1995. $46.36. Sixth edition. Six volumes.

Technical Writing. John M. Lannon. Addison-Wesley Educational Publications, Inc. • 2000. Eighth edition. Price on application.

Writing and Designing Manuals: Operator's Manuals, Service Manuals, Manuals for International Markets. Gretchen H. Schoff and Patricia A. Robinson. Lewis Publishers. • 1991. $54.95. Includes planning, organization, format, visuals, writing strategies, and other topics.

PERIODICALS AND NEWSLETTERS

Journal of Business and Technical Communication. Sage Publications, Inc. • Individuals, $65.00 per year; institutions, $340.00 per year.

Journal of Computer Documentation. Special Interest Group for Documentation. • Quarterly. Members, $24.00 per year; non-members, $44.00 per year.

Journal of Technical Writing and Communication. Baywood Publishing Co., Inc. • Quarterly. $170.00 per year.

Technical Communication. Society for Technical Communication. • Quarterly. $60.00 per year. Production of technical literature.

TRADE/PROFESSIONAL ASSOCIATIONS

Society for Technical Communication. 901 N. Stuart St., Suite 904, Arlington, VA 22203-1854. Phone: (703)522-4114 Fax: (703)522-2075 E-mail: stc@stc-va.org • URL: http://www.stc-va.org.

Special Interest Group for Systems Documentation. Association for Computing Machinery, 1515 Broadway, New York, NY 10036. Phone: (212)626-7440 Fax: (212)302-5826 E-mail: sigs@acm.org • URL: http://www.acm.org • Members are individuals who write user manuals and other documentation for computer software applications and computer hardware.

TECHNOLOGICAL UNEMPLOYMENT

See: UNEMPLOYMENT

TECHNOLOGY

See also: RESEARCH AND DEVELOPMENT

GENERAL WORKS

Forecasting and Management of Technology. Alan L. Porter and others. John Wiley and Sons, Inc. • 1991. $140.00. Includes business aspects of technology. (Engineering and Management Technology Series).

How Products Are Made. The Gale Group. • Dates vary. Three volumes. $99.00 per volume. Provides easy-to-read, step-by-step descriptions of how approximately 100 different products are manufactured. Items are of all kinds, both mechanical and non-mechanical.

The Innovator's Dilemma: When New Technologies Cause Great Firms to Fail. Clayton M. Christensen. Harvard Business School Press. • 1997. $27.50. Discusses management myths relating to innovation, change, and research and development. (Mangement of Innovation and Change Series).

Interface Culture: How New Technology Transforms the Way We Create and Communicate. Steven Johnson. HarperCollins Publishers. • 1997. $24.00. A discussion of how computer interfaces and online technology ("cyberspace") affect society in general.

Probable Tomorrows: How Science and Technology Will Transform Our Lives in the Next Twenty Years. Marvin J. Cetron and Owen L. Davies. St. Martin's Press. • 1997. $24.95. Predicts the developments in technological products, services, and "everyday conveniences" by the year 2017. Covers such items as personal computers, artificial intelligence, telecommunications, highspeed railroads, and healthcare.

Science and Technology Desk Reference: Answers to Frequently Asked and Difficult to Answer Reference Questions in Science and Technology. Carnegie Library of Pittsburgh, Science and Technology Department Staff, editors. The Gale Group. • 1997. $70.00. Second edition. *The Handy Science Answer Book.* Covers a wide variety of subject areas, including biology, astronomy, chemistry, geology, the environment, and health.

When Technology Fails. The Gale Group. • 1994. $80.00. The stories of about 100 important technological disasters, accidents, and failures in the 20th century, caused by faults in design, construction, planning, and testing. Arranged in broad subject categories, with a keyword index.

ABSTRACTS AND INDEXES

Abstracts in New Technologies and Engineering. R. R. Bowker. • Bimonthly. $1,650.00 per year. Annual cumulation. Formerly *Current Technology Index.*

Applied Science and Technology Index. H. W. Wilson Co. • 11 times a year. Quarterly and annual cumulations. Service basis for print edition; CD-ROM edition, $1,495.00 per year. Indexes a wide variety of English language technical, industrial, and engineering periodicals.

Current Contents: Engineering, Computing and Technology. Institute for Scientific Information. • Weekly. $730.00 per year. Reproductions of contents pages of technical journals. Includes *Author Index, Address Directory, Current Book Contents* and *Title Word Index.* Formerly *Current Contents: Engineering, Technology and Applied Sciences.*

Engineering Index Monthly: Abstracting and Indexing Services Covering Sources of the World's Engineering Literature. Engineering Information, Inc. • Monthly. $2,300.00 per year. Provides indexing and abstracting of the world's engineering and technical literature.

NTIS Alerts: Manufacturing Technology. National Technical Information Service. • Semimonthly. $265.00 per year. Provides descriptions of government-sponsored research reports and software, with ordering information. Covers computer-aided design and manufacturing (CAD/CAM), engineering materials, quality control, machine tools, robots, lasers, productivity, and related subjects. Formerly *Abstract Newsletter.*

ALMANACS AND YEARBOOKS

McGraw-Hill Yearbook of Science and Technology. McGraw-Hill, Engineering and Science Group. • Annual. $125.00.

Research in Philosophy and Technology. Society for Philosophy and Technology. JAI Press, Inc. • Irregular. $78.50. Supplement available.

Research on Technological Innovation, Management and Policy. Richard S. Rosenbloom, editor. JAI Press, Inc. • Irregular. $73.25.

Science and Technology Almanac. Oryx Press. • Annual. $65.00. Covers technological news, research, and statistics.

BIBLIOGRAPHIES

Aslib Book Guide: A Monthly List of Recommended Scientific and Technical Books. Available from Information Today, Inc. • Monthly. Members, $164.00 per year; non-members, $204.00 per year. Published in London by Aslib: The Association for Information Management. Formerly *Aslib Book List.*

Bibliographic Guide to Technology. Available from The Gale Group. • Annual. $545.00. Two volumes. Published by G. K. Hall & Co. Lists technology publications cataloged by the New York Public Library and the Library of Congress.

Encyclopedia of Physical Science and Engineering Information. The Gale Group. • 1996. $160.00. Second edition. Includes print, electronic, and other information sources for a wide range of scientific, technical, and engineering topics.

New Technical Books: A Selective List With Descriptive Annotations. New York Public Library Science and Technology Research Center. • Bimonthly. $30.00 per year.

BIOGRAPHICAL SOURCES

American Men and Women of Science A Biographical Directory of Today's Leaders in Physical, Biological and Related Sciences. R. R. Bowker. • 1995. $900.00. Eight volumes. Over 119,600 United States and Canadian scientists active in the physical, biological, mathematical, computer science and engineering fields.

Who's Who in Science and Engineering. Marquis Who's Who. • Biennial. $269.00. Provides concise biographical information on 26,000 prominent engineers and scientists. International coverage, with geographical and professional indexes.

CD-ROM DATABASES

COMPENDEX PLUS [CD-ROM]. Engineering Information, Inc. • Quarterly. $3,450.00 per year. Provides CD-ROM indexing and abstracting of the world's engineering and technical information appearing in journals, reports, books, and proceedings, 1985 to date.

NTIS on SilverPlatter. Available from SilverPlatter Information, Inc. • Quarterly. $2,850.00 per year. Produced by the National Technical Information Service. Provides a CD-ROM guide to over 500,000 government reports on a wide variety of technical, industrial, and business topics.

WILSONDISC: Applied Science and Technology Abstracts. H. W. Wilson Co. • Monthly. $1,495.00 per year, including unlimited access to the online version of *Applied Science and Technology Abstracts* through WILSONLINE. Provides CD-ROM indexing and abstracting of 400 prominent scientific, technical, engineering, and industrial periodicals. Indexing coverage is provided from 1983 to date and abstracting from 1993 to date.

DIRECTORIES

Corptech Directory of Technology Companies. Corporate Technology Information Services, Inc. c/o Eileen Kennedy. • Annual. $795.00. Four volumes. Profiles of more than 45,000 manufacturers and developers of high technology products. Includes private companies, publicly-held corporations, and subsidiaries. Formerly *Corporate Technology Directory.*

Emerson's Directory of Leading U.S. Technology Consulting Firms. Available from Hoover's, Inc. • Biennial. $195.00. Published by the Emerson Company (http://www.emersoncompany.com). Provides information on 500 major consulting firms specializing in technology.

Peterson's Graduate and Professional Programs: Engineering and Applied Sciences. Peterson's. • Annual. $37.95. Provides details of more than 3,400 graduate and professional programs in engineering and related fields at colleges and universities. Formerly *Peterson's Guide to Graduate Programs in Engineering and Professional Sciences.*

Plunkett's Engineering and Research Industry Almanac. Plunkett Research, Ltd. • Annual. $179.99. Contains detailed profiles of major engineering and technology corporations. Includes CD-ROM.

Technology Media Source. SRDS. • Annual. $291.00. Contains detailed information on business publications, consumer magazines, and direct mail lists that may be of interest to "technology marketers." Emphasis is on aviation and telecommunications.

ENCYCLOPEDIAS AND DICTIONARIES

Concise Chemical and Technical Dictionary. Harry Bennett. Chemical Publishing Co., Inc. • 1986. $170.00. Fourth edition.

Encyclopedia of Emerging Industries. The Gale Group. • 2000. $295.00. Fourth edition. Provides detailed information on 90 "newly flourishing" industries. Includes historical background, organizational structure, significant individuals, current conditions, major companies, work force, technology trends, research developments, and other industry facts.

Every Manager's Guide to Information Technology: A Glossary of Key Terms and Concepts for Today's Business Leader. Peter G. W. Keen. Harvard Business School Press. • 1995. $18.95. Second edition. Provides definitions of terms related to computers, data communications, and information network systems. (Harvard Business Economist Reference Series).

Gale Five Language Dictionary of Technology: Simultaneous Translations of English, French, Spanish, German, and Italian. The Gale Group. • 1993. $75.00. Contains translations of frequently-used technological words and phrases.

McGraw-Hill Encyclopedia of Science & Technology. McGraw-Hill. • 1997. $1,995.00. Eighth edition. 20 volumes.

HANDBOOKS AND MANUALS

Dun & Bradstreet/Gale Group Industry Handbooks. The Gale Group. • 2000. $630.00. Five volumes.

$145.00 per volume. Each volume covers two or more major industries: 1. *Entertainment and Hospitality*; 2. *Construction and Agriculture*; 3. *Chemicals and Pharmaceuticals*; 4. *Computers & Software and Broadcasting & Telecommunications*; 5. *Insurance and Health & Medical Services*. The following are included for each industry: overview, statistics, financial ratios, rankings, merger information, company directory, directory of associations, and consultants directory.

Managing High-Technology Programs and Projects. Russell D. Archibald. John Wiley and Sons, Inc. • 1992. $107.50. Second edition. Written for senior executives, professional project managers, engineers, and information systems managers.

INTERNET DATABASES

WilsonWeb Periodicals Databases. H. W. Wilson. Phone: 800-367-6770 or (718)588-8400 Fax: 800-590-1617 or (718)992-8003 E-mail: custserv@hwwilson.com • URL: http://www.hwwilson.com/ • Web sites provide fee-based access to *Wilson Business Full Text, Applied Science & Technology Full Text, Biological & Agricultural Index, Library Literature & Information Science Full Text*, and *Readers' Guide Full Text, Mega Edition*. Daily updates.

ONLINE DATABASES

Aerospace/Defense Markets and Technology. The Gale Group. • Abstracts of commerical aerospace/defense related literature, 1982 to date. Also includes information about major defense contracts awarded by the U. S. Department of Defense. International coverage. Inquire as to online cost and availability.

Applied Science and Technology Index Online. H. W. Wilson Co. • Provides online indexing of 400 major scientific, technical, industrial, and engineering periodicals. Time period is 1983 to date. Monthly updates. Inquire as to online cost and availability.

Business and Industry. Responsive Database Services, Inc. • Contains online citations, abstracts, and selected fulltext from more than 1,000 trade journals, newspapers, and other publications. Provides general coverage of both manufacturing and service industries, including marketing, production, industry trends, key events, and information on specific companies. Time span is 1994 to date. Daily updates. Inquire as to online cost and availability. (Also available in a CD-ROM version.).

COMPENDEX PLUS. Engineering Information, Inc. • Provides online indexing and abstracting of the world's engineering and technical information appearing in journals, reports, books, and proceedings. Time period is 1970 to date, with weekly updates. Inquire as to online cost and availability.

Current Contents Connect. Institute for Scientific Information. • Provides online abstracts of articles listed in the tables of contents of about 7,500 journals. Coverage is very broad, including science, social science, life science, technology, engineering, industry, agriculture, the environment, economics, and arts and humanities. Time period is two years, with weekly updates. Inquire as to online cost and availability.

INSPEC. Institute of Electrical and Electronics Engineers (IEEE). • Provides indexing and abstracting of the worldwide literature of electrical engineering, electronics, physics, computer technology, information technology, and industrial controls. Time period is 1970 to date, with weekly updates. Inquire as to online cost and availability. (INSPEC is Information Services for the Physics and Engineering Communities.).

New Product Announcements Plus. The Gale Group. • Contains the full text of new product and corporate activity press releases, with special emphasis on high technology and emerging industries. Covers 1985 to date. Weekly updates. Inquire as to online cost and availability.

Newspaper and Periodical Abstracts. Bell & Howell Information and Learning. • Provides online coverage (citations and abstracts) of 25 major newspapers, 1,600 perodicals, and 70 TV programs. Covers business, economics, current affairs, health, fitness, sports, education, technology, government, consumer affairs, psychology, the arts, and the social sciences. Time period is 1986 to date, with daily updates. Inquire as to online cost and availability.

NTIS Bibliographic Data Base. National Technical Information Service. • Contains citations and abstracts to unrestricted reports of government-sponsored research, 1964 to date. Covers a wide range of technical, engineering, business, and social science topics. Monthly updates. Inquire as to online cost and availability.

Research Centers and Services Directories. The Gale Group. • Contains profiles of about 30,000 research centers, organizations, laboratories, and agencies in 147 countries. Corresponds to the printed *Research Centers Directory, International Research Centers Directory, Government Research Directory*, and *Research Services Directory*. Updating is semiannual. Inquire as to online cost and availability.

Tablebase. Responsive Database Services, Inc. • Provides online numerical tabular data from a wide variety of business, organization, and government sources, including 900 trade journals. Includes industry and individual company statistics relating to products, market share, sales forecasts, production, exports, market trends, etc. Time span is 1997 to date. Weekly updates. Inquire as to online cost and availability. (Also available in a CD-ROM version.).

Who's Who in Technology [Online]. The Gale Group. • Provides online biographical profiles of over 25,000 American scientists, engineers, and others in technology-related occupations. Inquire as to online cost and availability.

PERIODICALS AND NEWSLETTERS

CONTEXT: Business in a World Being Transformed by Technology. Diamond Technology Partners, Inc. • Quarterly. Price on application. Covers developments and trends in business and information technology for non-technical senior executives.

Futuretech. Technical Insights. • 18 times a year. $1,600.00 per year. Newsletter on newly emerging technologies and their markets.

Gilder Technology Report. George Gilder, editor. Gilder Technology Group, Inc. • Monthly. $295.00 per year. Newsletter. Makes specific recommendations for investing in technology stocks. (A joint publication of Forbes Magazine and the Gilder Technology Group.).

Internet Marketing and Technology Report: Advising Marketing, Sales, and Corporate Executives on Online Opportunities. Computer Economics, Inc. • Monthly. $387.00 per year. Newsletter. Covers strategic marketing, sales, advertising, public relations, and corporate communications, all in relation to the Internet. Includes information on "cutting-edge technology" for the Internet.

Journal of Research of the National Institute of Standards and Technology. Available from U. S. Government Printing Office. • Bimonthly. $31.00 per year. Formerly *Journal of Research of the National Bureau of Standards*.

MC: Technology Marketing Intelligence. BPI Communications, Inc. • Monthly. $47.00 per year. Edited for marketing executives in high technology industries. Covers both advertising and marketing.

The Red Herring: The Business of Technology. Herring Communications, Inc. • Monthly. $49.00 per year. Contains ars on investing in high technology, especially within the computer, communications, and information industries. Initial public offerings (IPOs) are emphasized. Includes technology stock listings and the Red Herring "Tech 250" stock index.

Technological Forecasting and Social Change. Elsevier Science. • Nine times a year. $688.00 per year. Three volumes.

Technology Business: The Magazine of Strategies for Innovation, Management, and Marketing. Technology Business LLC. • Bimonthly. Price on application. Edited for executives and managers of high technology firms.

Technology Forecasts and Technology Surveys. Technology Forecasts. • Monthly. $170.00 per year. Newsletter. Information on major breakthroughs in advanced technologies along with forecasts of effects on future applications and markets.

Technology in Society: An International Journal. Elsevier Science. • Quarterly. $804.00 per year.

Technology Investing. Michael Murphy, editor. Phillips Publishing International, Inc. • Monthly. $195.00 per year. Newsletter. Provides specific recommendations for investing in high technology companies.

Technology Review: MITs National Magazine of Technology and Policy. Massachusetts Institute of Technology. • Six times a year. $19.95 per year. Examines current technological issues facing society.

21.C: Scanning the Future: A Magazine of Culture, Technology, and Science. International Publishers Distributors. • Quarterly. $24.00 per year. Contains multidisciplinary articles relating to the 21st century.

Upside: People, Technology, Capital. Upside Publishing Co. • Monthly. $29.95 per year. Covers the business, investment, and entrepreneurial aspects of high technology.

RESEARCH CENTERS AND INSTITUTES

Center for the Study of Law, Science, and Technology. Arizona State University, College of Law, P.O. Box 877906, Tempe, AZ 85287-7906. Phone: (602)965-2554 Fax: (602)965-2427 E-mail: daniel.strouse@asu.edu • URL: http://www.law.asu.edu • Studies the legal problems created by technological advances.

Research-Technology Management. Industrial Research Institute, Inc. 1550 M St., N. W., Suite 1100, Washington, DC 20005-1712. Phone: (202)296-8811 Fax: (202)776-0756 • URL: http://www.iriinc.org • Bimonthly. $150.00 per year. Covers both theoretical and practical aspects of the management of industrial research and development.

SRI International. 333 Ravenswood Ave., Menlo Park, CA 94025-3493. Phone: (650)859-2000 Fax: (650)326-5512 E-mail: inquiryline@sri.com • URL: http://www.sri.com • Private research firm specializing in market research in high technology areas.

STATISTICS SOURCES

Encyclopedia of American Industries. The Gale Group. • 1998. $560.00. Second edition. Two volumes. $280.00 per volume. Volume one is *Manufacturing Industries* and volume two is *Service and Non-Manufacturing Industries*. Provides the history, development, and recent status of approximately 1,000 industries. Includes statistical graphs, with industry and general indexes.

Standard & Poor's Industry Surveys. Standard & Poor's. • Semiannual. $1,800.00. Two looseleaf volumes. Includes monthly supplements. Provides detailed, individual surveys of 52 major industry groups. Each survey is revised on a semiannual basis. Also includes "Monthly Investment Review" (industry group investment analysis) and monthly "Trends & Projections" (economic analysis).

Statistical Handbook on Technology. Paula Berinstein, editor. Oryx Press. • 1999. $65.00. Provides statistical data on such items as the Internet, online services, computer technology, recycling, patents, prescription drug sales, telecommunications, and aerospace. Includes charts, tables, and graphs. Edited for the general reader. (Statistical Handbook Series).

U. S. Industry and Trade Outlook: The McGraw-Hill Companies and the U.S. Department of Commerce/ International Trade Administration. Datapso Research Corp. • Annual. $69.95. Produced by the International Trade Administration, U. S. Department of Commerce, in a "public-private" partnership with DRI/McGraw-Hill and Standard & Poor's. Provides basic data, outlook for the current year, and "Long-Term Prospects" (five-year projections) for a wide variety of products and services. Includes high technology industries. Formerly *U. S. Industrial Outlook.*

UNESCO Statistical Yearbook. Bernan Press. • Annual. $95.00. Co-published by Bernan Press and the United Nations Educational, Scientific, and Cultural Organization (http://www.unesco.org). Presents statistical data from more than 200 countries on education, technology, research, broadcasting, cinema, book publishing, newspapers, libraries, museums, and population. Includes charts, maps, and graphs.

TRADE/PROFESSIONAL ASSOCIATIONS

Association for Science, Technology and Innovation. P.O. Box 1242, Arlington, VA 22210. Phone: (703)352-6567 Fax: (703)241-2850 E-mail: readams@erols.com.

Society for the History of Technology. John Hopkins University, Department of History, Science, Medicine and Technology, 216B Ames Hall, Baltimore, MD 21218. Phone: (410)516-7502 • URL: http://www.press.jhu.edu/associations/shot.

Technology Transfer Society. 230 E. Ohio St., Suite 400, Chicago, IL 60611. Phone: (312)644-0828 Fax: (312)644-8557 E-mail: bbecker@bostrom.com • Members are individuals and institutions involved in the process of technology transfer and utilization.

OTHER SOURCES

Aerospace America [online]. American Institute of Aeronautics and Astronautics. • Provides complete text of the periodical, *Aerospace America,* 1984 to date, with monthly updates. Also includes news from the *AIAA Bulletin.* Inquire as to online cost and availability.

Aerospace Database. American Institute of Aeronautics and Astronautics. • Contains abstracts of literature covering all aspects of the aerospace and aircraft in series 1983 to date. Semimonthly updates. Inquire as to online cost and availability.

Business & Company Resource Center. The Gale Group. • Fee-based Web site provides a wide range of business, industry, and specific company information. Access is offered to trade journal articles, market research data, insider trading activity, major shareholder data, corporate histories, emerging technology reports, corporate earnings estimates, press releases, and other sources. Provides detailed company profiles, industry overviews, and rankings. Offers integration of Predicasts PROMT, Newsletters ASAP, Investext Plus, Business Index ASAP, Brands and Their Companies, and other databases (many have full text).

FedWorld: A Program of the United States Department of Commerce. National Technical Information Service. • Web site offers "a comprehensive central access point for searching, locating, ordering, and acquiring government and business information." Emphasis is on searching the Web pages, databases, and government reports of a wide variety of federal agencies. Fees: Free.

InSite 2. Intelligence Data/Thomson Financial. • Fee-based Web site consolidates information in a "Base Pack" consisting of Business InSite, Market InSite, and Company InSite. Optional databases are Consumer InSite, Health and Wellness InSite, Newsletter InSite, and Computer InSite. Includes fulltext content from more than 2,500 trade publications, journals, newsletters, newspapers, analyst reports, and other sources. Continuous updating. Formerly produced by The Gale Group.

Survey of Advanced Technology. Computer Economics, Inc. • Annual. $795.00. Surveys the corporate use (or neglect) of advanced computer technology. Topics include major technology trends and emerging technologies.

World of Computer Science. The Gale Group. • 2001. $150.00. Alphabetical arrangement. Contains 650 entries covering discoveries, theories, concepts, issues, ethics, and people in the broad area of computer science and technology.

TECHNOLOGY TRANSFER

ABSTRACTS AND INDEXES

Business Periodicals Index. H. W. Wilson Co. • Monthly, except August, with quarterly and annual cumulations. Service basis for print edition; CD-ROM edition, $1,495.00 per year.

DIRECTORIES

Business Organizations, Agencies, and Publications Directory. The Gale Group. • 1999. $425.00. 12th edition. Over 40,000 entries describing 39 types of business information sources. Classified by type of organization, publication, or serviceIncludes state, national, and international agencies and organizations. Master index to names and keywords. Also includes e-mail addresses and web site URL's.

ONLINE DATABASES

Wilson Business Abstracts Online. H. W. Wilson Co. • Indexes and abstracts 600 major business periodicals, plus the *Wall Street Journal* and the business section of the *New York Times.* Indexing is from 1982, abstracting from 1990, with the two newspapers included from 1993. Updated weekly. Inquire as to online cost and availability. (*Business Periodicals Index* without abstracts is also available online.).

PERIODICALS AND NEWSLETTERS

Journal of Technology Transfer. Technology Transfer Society. Kluwer Academic Publishers. • Three times a year. $292.50 per year. Topics include technology transfer ventures, models, mechanisms, and case studies.

Technology Forecasts and Technology Surveys. Technology Forecasts. • Monthly. $170.00 per year. Newsletter. Information on major breakthroughs in advanced technologies along with forecasts of effects on future applications and markets.

Technology Transfer Highlights. Argonne National Laboratory, Industrial Technology Development Center. • Quarterly. Free. Newsletter on the transfer of federal technology.

RESEARCH CENTERS AND INSTITUTES

Argonne National Laboratory Industrial Technology Development Center. 9700 S. Cass Ave., Argonne, IL 60439-4832. Phone: 800-627-2596 Fax: (630)252-5230 E-mail: weso@anl.gov • URL: http://www.itd.anl.gov.

Battelle Memorial Institute. 505 King Ave., Columbus, OH 43201-2693. Phone: 800-201-2011 or (614)424-6424 Fax: (614)424-3260 • URL: http://www.battelle.org • Multidisciplinary research facilities at various locations include: Microcomputer Applications and Technology Center; Battelle Industrial Technology Center; Technology and Society Research Center; Office of Transportation Systems and Planning; Office of Waste Technology Development; Materials Information Center; Office of Nuclear Waste Isolation.

Center for International Science and Technology Policy. George Washington University, 2013 G St., N. W., Stuart Hall, Suite 201, Washington, DC 20052. Phone: (202)994-7292 Fax: (202)994-1639 E-mail: cistp@gwu.edu • URL: http://www.gwu.edu/~cistp • Research areas include technology transfer.

Office for Sponsored Research. Harvard University, Holyoke Center, Room 466, 1350 Massachusetts Ave., Cambridge, MA 02138. Phone: (617)495-1915 Fax: (617)495-2900 E-mail: elizabethmora@harvard.edu.

Office of Research Services. University of Pennsylvania, 133 S. 36th St., Mezzanine Fl., Philadelphia, PA 19104-3246. Phone: (215)898-7293 Fax: (215)898-9708 E-mail: abrud@pobox.upenn.edu • URL: http://www.upenn.edu/researchservices.

Office of Sponsored Programs. Massachusetts Institute of Technology, Bldg. E19, Room 750, Cambridge, MA 02139. Phone: (617)253-2492 Fax: (617)253-4734 E-mail: jnorris@mit.edu • URL: http://www.web.mit.edu/org/o/osp/www/.

Office of Sponsored Research. California Institute of Technology, Mail Code 213-6, Pasadena, CA 91125. Phone: (626)395-6357 Fax: (626)795-4571 E-mail: sponsoredresearch@sponsres.caltech.edu • URL: http://www.cco.caltech.edu/~tanyae.

Princeton Forrestal Center. Princeton University, 105 College Rd., E., Princeton, NJ 08540. Phone: (609)452-7720 Fax: (609)452-7485 E-mail: picus@picusassociates.com • Designed to create an interdependent mix of academia and business enterprise.

Progress Center: University of Florida Research and Technology Park. P.O. Box 10, Alachua, FL 32615. Phone: (904)462-4040 Fax: (904)462-3932 E-mail: sburgess@hawley-realply.com • Designed to transfer new technologies from the laboratory to the marketplace.

Rensselaer Polytechnic Institute. Rensselaer Technology Park, 100 Jordan Rd., Troy, NY 12180. Phone: (518)283-7102 Fax: (518)283-0695 E-mail: wachom@rpi.edu • URL: http://www.rpi.edu/dept/rtp • Serves as a conduit for research interactions between Rensselaer Polytechnic Institute and private companies.

Research Corporation Technologies. 101 N. Wilmot Rd., Suite 600, Tucson, AZ 85711-3335. Phone: (520)748-4400 Fax: (520)748-0025 • URL: http://www.rctech.com • Mainly concerned with the commercialization of technology from colleges, universities, medical research centers, and other nonprofit organizations.

Research Triangle Institute. P.O. Box 12194, Research Triangle Park, NC 27709-2194. Phone: (919)541-6000 Fax: (919)541-7004 E-mail: listen@rti.org • URL: http://www.rti.org • Affiliated with the

University of North Carolina, North Carolina State University, and Duke University.

Science Park Development Corporation. P.O. Box 35, New Haven, CT 06511. Phone: (203)786-5018 Fax: (203)786-5001 E-mail: dennis.lyndon@sciencepark.org • URL: http://www.sciencepark.org • Affiliated with Yale University.

Stanford Research Park. Stanford University, 2770 Sand Hill Rd., Menlo Park, CA 94025. Phone: (650)926-0211 Fax: (650)926-2000 • Links research resources of Stanford University with private enterprise.

TRADE/PROFESSIONAL ASSOCIATIONS

Industry Coalition on Technolgy Transfer. 1400 L St., N.W., 8th Fl., Washington, DC 20005-3502. Phone: (202)371-5994 Fax: (202)371-5950 • Members are computer industry associations concerned with federal regulations on technology transfer in the computer industry.

Technology Transfer Society. 230 E. Ohio St., Suite 400, Chicago, IL 60611. Phone: (312)644-0828 Fax: (312)644-8557 E-mail: bbecker@bostrom.com • Members are individuals and institutions involved in the process of technology transfer and utilization.

TEENAGE MARKET

See: YOUTH MARKET

TELECOMMUNICATIONS

See also: CABLE ADDRESSES; COMMUNICATION SYSTEMS; COMPUTER COMMUNICATIONS; TELEGRAPH; TELEPHONE INDUSTRY

GENERAL WORKS

Analog and Digital Communications. Hwei P. Hsu. McGraw-Hill. • 1997. $15.95.

Applying Telecommunications and Technology from a Global Business Perspective. Jay J. Zajas and Olive D. Church. Haworth Press, Inc. • 1996. $49.95. Provides an international, multicultural perspective.

Future Trends in Telecommunications. R. J. Horrocks and R.W. Scarr. John Wiley and Sons, Inc. • 1993. $235.00. Includes fiber optics technology, local area networks, and satellite communications. Discusses the future of telecommunications for the consumer and for industry. *Communication and Distributed Systems Series.*

Global Telecommunications: The Technology, Administration, and Policies. Raymond Akwule. Butterworth-Heinemann. • 1992. $46.95. Provides basic information on networks, satellite systems, socioeconomic impact, tariffs, government regulation, etc.

Managing to Communicate: Using Telecommunications for Increased Business Efficiency. M. P. Clark. John Wiley and Sons, Inc. • 1994. $79.95.

Telecommunications. Warren Hioki. Prentice Hall. • 2000. $95.00. Fourth edition.

ABSTRACTS AND INDEXES

Communication Abstracts. Sage Publications, Inc. • Bimonthly. Individuals, $185.00 per year; institutions, $805.00 per year. Provides broad coverage of the literature of communications, including broadcasting and advertising.

Electronics and Communications Abstracts Journal: Comprehensive Coverage of Essential Scientific Literature. Cambridge Information Group. • Monthly. $1,045.00 per year.

Key Abstracts: Telecommunications. Available from INSPEC, Inc. • Monthly. $240.00 per year. Provides international coverage of journal and proceedings literature. Published in England by the Institution of Electrical Engineers (IEE).

NTIS Alerts: Communication. National Technical Information Service. • Semimonthly. $210.00 per year. . Provides descriptions of government-sponsored research reports and software, with ordering information. Covers common carriers, satellites, radio/TV equipment, telecommunication regulations, and related subjects.

ALMANACS AND YEARBOOKS

Communication Technology Update. Butterworth-Heinemann. • Annual. $36.95. Reviews technological developments and statistical trends in five key areas: mass media, computers, consumer electronics, communications satellites, and telephony. Includes television, cellular phones, and the Internet. (Focal Press.).

Communications Outlook. OECD Publications and Information Center. • Annual. $65.00. Provides international coverage of yearly telecommunications activity. Includes charts, graphs, and maps.

BIOGRAPHICAL SOURCES

The Highwaymen: Warriors on the Information Superhighway. Ken Auletta. Harcourt Trade Publications. • 1998. $13.00. Revised expanded edition. Contains critical articles about Ted Turner, Rupert Murdoch, Barry Diller, Michael Eisner, and other key figures in electronic communications, entertainment, and information.

CD-ROM DATABASES

Business Source Plus. EBSCO Information Services. • Monthly. $1,495.00 per year. Provides CD-ROM citations and abstracts to articles in about 650 business periodicals and newspapers, including *The Wall Street Journal.* Full text is provided from 200 selected periodicals. Covers accounting, communications, economics, finance, management, marketing, and other business subjects.

Datapro on CD-ROM: Communications Analyst. Gartner Group, Inc. • Monthly. Price on application. Provides detailed information on products and services for communications systems, including local area networks and voice systems.

Hoover's Company Capsules on CD-ROM. Hoover's, Inc. • Quarterly. $349.95 per year (single-user). Provides the CD-ROM version of *Hoover's Handbook of American Business, Hoover's Handbook of Emerging Companies, Hoover's Handbook of World Business, Hoover's Guide to Computer Companies, Hoover's Guide to Media Companies, Hoover's Handbook of Private Companies,* and various regional guides. Includes more than 11,000 profiles of companies.

Telecom Strategies. Thomson Financial Securities Data. • Monthly. $2,995.00 per year. CD-ROM contains full text of investment analysts' reports on companies operating in the following fields: telecommunications, broadcasting, and cable communications.

DIRECTORIES

Essential Business Buyer's Guide, from Cellular Services and Overnight Mail to Internet Access Providers, 401(k) Plans, and Desktop Computers: The Ultimate Guide to Buying Office Equipment, Products, and Services. Sourcebooks, Inc. • 1996. $18.95. Compiled by the staff of *Business Consumer Guide.* Lists recommended brands of office equipment.

Internet Tools of the Profession: A Guide for Information Professionals. Hope N. Tillman, editor. Special Libraries Association. • 1997. $49.00. Second edition. Consists of 14 sections by various authors or compilers. After two introductory articles on searching the Internet, there are 12 annotated lists of useful Web sites, covering the SLA, business and finance, chemistry, education, food and agriculture, information technology, insurance and employee benefits, law, library management, metals and materials, pharmaceuticals, and telecommunications. An index is provided.

Marconi's International Register: Linking Buyers and Sellers Worldwide Through Fax and Business Listings. Telegraphic Cable and Radio Registrations, Inc. • Annual. $150.00. Lists more than 45,000 firms throughout the world in all lines of business. In four sections.

Plunkett's E-Commerce and Internet Business Almanac. Plunkett Research, Ltd. • Annual. $199.99. Contains detailed profiles of 250 large companies engaged in various areas of Internet commerce, including e-business Web sites, communications equipment manufacturers, and Internet service providers. Includes CD-ROM.

Plunkett's InfoTech Industry Almanac: Complete Profiles on the InfoTech 500-the Leading Firms in the Movement and Management of Voice, Data, and Video. Available from Plunkett Research, Ltd. • Annual. $149.99. Five hundred major information companies are profiled, with corporate culture aspects. Discusses major trends in various sectors of the computer and information industry, including data on careers and job growth. Includes several indexes.

Plunkett's Telecommunications Industry Almanac. Plunkett Research, Ltd. • Annual. $179.99. Provides detailed profiles of major telecommunications industry corporations. Includes CD-ROM.

Telecommunications Directory. The Gale Group. • 2000. $595.00. 12th edition. National and international voice, data, facsimile, and video communications services. Formerly *Telecommunications Systems and Services Directory.*

Telehealth Buyer's Guide. Miller Freeman. • Annual. $10.00. Lists sources of telecommunications and information technology products and services for the health care industry.

TIA-MMTA Directory and Desk Reference. Telecommunications Industry Association Multimedia Telecommunications Associatio. • Annual. $199.00. Lists manufacturers and suppliers of interconnect telephone equipment. Formerly *Multimedia Telecommunications Sourcebook.*

ENCYCLOPEDIAS AND DICTIONARIES

CyberDictionary: Your Guide to the Wired World. Knowledge Exchange LLC. • 1996. $17.95. Includes many illustrations.

Dictionary of PC Hardware and Data Communications Terms. Mitchell Shnier. Thomson Learning. • 1996. $19.95. (Online updates to print version available at http://www.ora.com/reference/dictionary.).

Encyclopedia of Communication and Information. Available from The Gale Group. • 2001. $325.00. Three volumes. Published by Macmillan Reference USA.

Encyclopedia of Emerging Industries. The Gale Group. • 2000. $295.00. Fourth edition. Provides detailed information on 90 "newly flourishing" industries. Includes historical background, organizational structure, significant individuals, current conditions, major companies, work force, technology trends, research developments, and other industry facts.

The Froehlich-Kent Encyclopedia of Telecommunications. Fritz E. Froehlich and Allen

Kent, editors. Marcel Dekker, Inc. • Dates vary. Five volumes. $975.00. $195.00 per volume. Contains scholarly articles written by telecommunications experts. Includes bibliographies.

Multimedia and the Web from A to Z. Patrick M. Dillon and David C. Leonard. Oryx Press. • 1998. $39.95. Second enlarged revised edition. Defines more than 1,500 terms relating to software and hardware in the areas of computing, online technology, telecommunications, audio, video, motion pictures, CD-ROM, and the Internet. Includes acronyms and an annotated bibliography. Formerly *Multimedia Technology from A to Z* (1994).

Telecom Lingo Guide. Warren Communication News. • 1996. $60.00. Eighth edition. Defines more than 1,000 words, phrases, and acronyms frequently used in the telecommunications industry.

Wiley Encyclopedia of Electrical and Electronics Engineering. John G. Webster, editor. John Wiley and Sons, Inc. • 1999. $6,495.00. 24 volumes. Contains about 1,400 articles, each with bibliography. Arrangement is according to 64 categories.

HANDBOOKS AND MANUALS

Digital Cellular Telecommunications Systems. Douglas A. Kerr. McGraw-Hill. • 1997. $50.00.

Dun & Bradstreet/Gale Group Industry Handbooks. The Gale Group. • 2000. $630.00. Five volumes. $145.00 per volume. Each volume covers two or more major industries: 1. *Entertainment and Hospitality*; 2. *Construction and Agriculture*; 3. *Chemicals and Pharmaceuticals*; 4. *Computers & Software and Broadcasting & Telecommunications*; 5. *Insurance and Health & Medical Services*. The following are included for each industry: overview, statistics, financial ratios, rankings, merger information, company directory, directory of associations, and consultants directory.

Irwin Handbook of Telecommunications. James H. Green. McGraw-Hill Professional. • 2000. $95.00. Fourth dition. Formerly *Dow Jones-Irwin Handbook of Telecommunications.*

Satellite-Based Cellular Communications. Bruno Pattan. McGraw-Hill. • 1997. $69.00. (Telecommunications Series).

Telecommunication Transmission Handbook. Roger L. Freeman. John Wiley and Sons, Inc. • 1998. $185.00. Fourth edition.

Telecommunications Engineer's Reference Book. Fraidoon Mazda, editor. Butterworth-Heinemann. • 1998. $150.00.

INTERNET DATABASES

InfoTech Trends. Data Analysis Group. Phone: (707)894-9100 Fax: (707)486-5618 E-mail: support@infotechtrends.com • URL: http://www.infotechtrends.com • Web site provides both free and fee-based market research data on the information technology industry, including computers, peripherals, telecommunications, the Internet, software, CD-ROM/DVD, e-commerce, and workstations. Fees: Free for current (most recent year) data; more extensive information has various fee structures. Formerly *Computer Industry Forecasts.*

Interactive Week: The Internet's Newspaper. Ziff Davis Media, Inc. 28 E. 28th St., New York, NY 10016. Phone: (212)503-3500 Fax: (212)503-5680 E-mail: iweekinfo@zd.com • URL: http://www.zd.com • Weekly. $99.00 per year. Covers news and trends relating to Internet commerce, computer communications, and telecommunications.

Internet Tools of the Profession. Special Libraries Association. Phone: (202)234-4700 Fax: (202)265-9317 E-mail: hope@tiac.net • URL: http://www.sla.org/pubs/itotp • Web site is designed to update the printed *Internet Tools of the Profession.* Provides links to a wide range of useful databases in business, finance, industry, information technology, insurance, law, library management, telecommunications, and other subject areas. Fees: Free.

Wired News. Wired Digital, Inc. Phone: (415)276-8400 Fax: (415)276-8499 E-mail: newsfeedback@wired.com • URL: http://www.wired.com • Provides summaries and full-text of "Top Stories" relating to the Internet, computers, multimedia, telecommunications, and the electronic information industry in general. These news stories are placed in the broad categories of Politics, Business, Culture, and Technology. Affiliated with *Wired* magazine. Fees: Free.

ONLINE DATABASES

Hard Sciences. Cambridge Scientific Abstracts. • Provides the online version of *Computer and Information Systems Abstracts, Electronics and Communications Abstracts, Health and Safety Science Abstracts, ISMEC: Mechanical Engineering Abstracts (Information Service in Mechanical Engineering)* and *Solid State and Superconductivity Abstracts*. Time period is 1981 to date, with monthly updates. Inquire as to online cost and availability.

PERIODICALS AND NEWSLETTERS

Business Communications Review. BCR Enterprises, Inc. • Bimonthly. $45.00 per year. Edited for communications managers in large end-user companies and institutions. Includes special feature issues on intranets and network management.

Communications Daily: The Authoritative News Service of Electronic Communications. Warren Publishing Inc. • Daily. $3,006.00 per year. Newsletter. Covers telecommunications, including the telephone industry, broadcasting, cable TV, satellites, data communications, and electronic publishing. Features corporate and industry news.

Communications News. American Society of Association Executives Communications Section. • Monthly. Membership.

Communications News: Solutions for Today's Networking Decision Managers. Nelson Publishing, Inc. • Monthly. Free to qualified personnel; others, $79.00 per year. Includes coverage of "Internetworking" and "Intrenetworking." Emphasis is on emerging telecommunications technologies.

Convergence: The Journal of Research Into New Media Technologies. Chilton Co. • Monthly. Individuals, $60,00 per year; institutions, $120.00 per year. Covers the merging of communications technologies. Includes telecommunications networks, interactive TV, multimedia, wireless phone service, and electronic information services.

Electronic Information Report: Empowering Industry Decision Makers Since 1979. SIMBA Information. • 46 times a year. $549.00 per year. Newsletter. Provides business and financial news and trends for online services, electronic publishing, storage media, multimedia, and voice services. Includes information on relevant IPOs (initial public offerings) and mergers. Formerly *Electronic Information Week.*

FCC Report: An Exclusive Report on Domestic and International Telecommunications Policy and Regulation. Warren Publishing Inc. • Semimonthly. $649.00 per year. Newsletter concerned principally with Federal Communications Commission reglations and policy.

Fiber Optics and Communications. Information Gatekeepers, Inc. • Monthly. $675.00. Emphasis on the use of fiber optics in telecommunications.

Harvard Management Communication Letter. Harvard Business School Press. • Monthly. $79.00 per year. Newsletter. Provides practical advice on both electronic and conventional business communication: e-mail, telephone, cell phones, memos, letters, written reports, speeches, meetings, and visual presentations (slides, flipcharts, easels, etc.). Also covers face-to-face communication, discussion, listening, and negotiation.

Healthcare Informatics: The Business of Healthcare Information Technology. McGraw-Hill. • Monthly. $40.00 per year. Covers various aspects of information and computer technology for the health care industry.

Interactive Home: Consumer Technology Monthly. Jupiter Media Metrix. • Monthly. $625.00 per year. Newsletter on devices to bring the Internet into the average American home. Covers TV set-top boxes, game devices, telephones with display screens, handheld computer communication devices, the usual PCs, etc.

International Journal of Communication Systems. Available from John Wiley and Sons, Inc., Journals Div. • Bimonthly. Institutions, $995.00 per year. Published in England by John Wiley and Sons Ltd. Formerly *International Journal of Digital and Analog Communication Systems.*

Internet Telephony Magazine: The Authority on Voice, Video, Fax, and Data Convergence. Technology Marketing Corp. • Monthly. $29.00 per year. Covers the business and technology of telephone and other communications service via the Internet.

PCS Systems and Technology: Personal Communications Services Technology of the Digital Wireless Age. Cahners Business Information. • Nine times a year. Price on application. Covers network management and other technical topics.

RCR (Radio Communications Report): The Newspaper for the Wireless Communications Industry. RCR Publications/Crain Communications. • Weekly. $39.00 per year. Covers news of the wireless communications industry, including business and financial developments.

State and Local Communications Report. Telecommunications Reports International, Inc. • Biweekly. $645.00 per year. Newsletter. Formerly *Telecommunications Week.*

Tele.com: Business and Technology for Public Network Service Providers. CMP Publications, Inc. • 14 times a year. $125.00 per year. Edited for executives and managers at both traditional telephone companies and wireless communications companies. Also provides news and information for Internet services providers and cable TV operators.

Telecom Business: Opportunities for Network Service Providers, Resellers, and Suppliers in the Competitive Telecom Industry. MultiMedia Publishing Corp. • Monthly. $56.95 per year. Provides business and technical information for telecommunications executives in various fields.

Telecommunications. Horizon-House Pubications, Inc. • Monthly. Free to qualified personnel; others, $75.00 per year. International coverage.

Telecommunications Policy. Elsevier Science. • 11 times a year. $883.00 per year.

Telecommunications Reports. Telecommunications Reports International, Inc. • Weekly. Institutions, $1,695.00 per year. Includes *TR Daily.* Regulatory newsletter.

Teleconference Magazine: The Magazine on Interactive Mulitmedia. Advanstar Communications, Inc. • Monthly. $60.00 per. year. Provides articles on new technology and the practical use of teleconferencing in business communications.

Telehealth Magazine. Miller Freeman. • Bimonthly. $50.00 per year. Covers Internet, wireless, and other telecommunications technologies for health care professionals.

Wireless Integration: Solutions for Enterprise Decision Makers. PennWell Corp., Advanced Technology Div. • Bimonthly. $48.00 per year. Edited for networking and communications managers. Special issues cover the wireless office, wireless intranet/Internet, mobile wireless, telemetry, and buyer's guide directory information.

Wireless Review: Intelligence for Competitive Providers. Intertec Publishing Corp. • Semimonthly. $48.00 per year. Covers business and technology developments for wireless service providers. Includes special issues on a wide variety of wireless topics. Formed by merger of *Cellular Business* and *Wireless World.*

X-Change. Virgo Publishing, Inc. • 18 times per year. $70.00 per year. Edited for local telecommunications exchange services, both wireline and wireless.

RESEARCH CENTERS AND INSTITUTES

Center for Integrated Systems. Stanford University, 420 Vis Palou Mall, Stanford, CA 94305-4070. Phone: (650)725-3621 Fax: (650)725-0991 E-mail: rdasher@cis.stanford.edu • URL: http://www.cis.stanford.edu • Research programs include manufacturing science, design science, computer architecture, semiconductor technology, and telecommunications.

Center for Research in Computing Technology. Harvard University, Pierce Hall, 29 Oxford St., Cambridge, MA 02138. Phone: (617)495-2832 Fax: (617)495-9837 E-mail: cheatham@das.harvard.edu • URL: http://www.das.harvard.edu/cs.grafs.html • Conducts research in computer vision, robotics, artificial intelligence, systems programming, programming languages, operating systems, networks, graphics, database management systems, and telecommunications.

International Data Corp. (IDC). Five Speen St., Framingham, MA 01701. Phone: (508)935-4389 Fax: (508)935-4789 • URL: http://www.idcresearch.com • Private research firm specializing in market research related to computers, multimedia, and telecommunications.

Studio for Creative Inquiry. Carnegie Mellon University, College of Fine Arts, Pittsburgh, PA 15213-3890. Phone: (412)268-3454 Fax: (412)268-2829 E-mail: mmbm@andrew.cmu.edu/ • URL: http://www.cmu.edu/studio/ • Research areas include artificial intelligence, virtual reality, hypermedia, multimedia, and telecommunications, in relation to the arts.

STATISTICS SOURCES

Communication Equipment, and Other Electronic Systems and Equipment. U. S. Bureau of the Census. • Annual. Provides data on shipments: value, quantity, imports, and exports. (Current Industrial Reports, MA-36P.).

OECD Information Technology Outlook 2000: ICTs, E-Commerce and the Information Economy. Organization for Economic Cooperation and Development. • 2000. $72.00. Provides data on information and communications technology (ICT) and electronic commerce in 11 OECD nations (includes U. S.). Coverage includes network infrastructure, electronic payment systems, financial transaction technologies, intelligent agents, global navigation systems, and portable flat panel display technologies.

Standard & Poor's Industry Surveys. Standard & Poor's. • Semiannual. $1,800.00. Two looseleaf volumes. Includes monthly supplements. Provides detailed, individual surveys of 52 major industry groups. Each survey is revised on a semiannual basis. Also includes "Monthly Investment Review" (industry group investment analysis) and monthly "Trends & Projections" (economic analysis).

Statistical Handbook on Technology. Paula Berinstein, editor. Oryx Press. • 1999. $65.00. Provides statistical data on such items as the Internet, online services, computer technology, recycling, patents, prescription drug sales, telecommunications, and aerospace. Includes charts, tables, and graphs. Edited for the general reader. (Statistical Handbook Series).

U. S. Industry and Trade Outlook: The McGraw-Hill Companies and the U.S. Department of Commerce/International Trade Administration. Datapso Research Corp. • Annual. $69.95. Produced by the International Trade Administration, U. S. Department of Commerce, in a "public-private" partnership with DRI/McGraw-Hill and Standard & Poor's. Provides basic data, outlook for the current year, and "Long-Term Prospects" (five-year projections) for a wide variety of products and services. Includes high technology industries. Formerly *U. S. Industrial Outlook.*

WEFA Industrial Monitor. John Wiley and Sons, Inc. • Annual. $65.00. Prepared by industry analysts at WEFA, an economic forecasting and consulting firm (originally Wharton Econometric Forecasting Associates). Contains discussions of the outlook for major U. S. industries, with many 10-year forecasts (WEFA Web site is http://www.wefa.com).

TRADE/PROFESSIONAL ASSOCIATIONS

Competitive Telecommunications Association. 1900 M. St., N.W., Suite 800, Washington, DC 20036. Phone: (202)296-6650 Fax: (202)296-7585 E-mail: ferguson@comptel.org • URL: http://www.comptel.org.

TCA-The Information Technology and Telecommunications Association. 74 New Montgomery St., Suite 230, San Francisco, CA 94105-3419. Phone: (415)777-4647 Fax: (415)777-5295.

OTHER SOURCES

Broadband Solutions. North American Publishing Co. • Monthly. Controlled circulation. Covers the high-bandwidth telecommunications industry, including new products and emerging technologies.

Broadband Week. Cahners Business Information. • Semimonthly. Controlled circulation. Provides news and trends for all parts of the evolving broadband industry, including operations, marketing, finance, and technology.

Consumer Internet Economy. Jupiter Media Metrix. • 1999. $3,495.00. Market research report. Provides data and forecasts relating to various hardware and software elements of the Internet, including browsers, provision of service, telephone line modems, cable modems, wireless access devices, online advertising, programming languages, and Internet chips. Includes company profiles.

Fat Pipe: The Business of Marketing Broadband Services. Dagda Mor Media, Inc. • Monthly. Controlled circulation. Edited for those who plan, develop, and market broadband Internet and telecommunications services.

Faulkner's Telecommunications World. Faulkner Information Services, Inc. • Three looseleaf volumes, with monthly updates. $1,260.00 per year. Contains product reports, technology overviews and management articles relating to all aspects of voice and data communications.

Fiber Systems International. Available from IOP Publishing, Inc. • Monthly. Controlled circulation. Published in the UK by the Institute of Physics. "Covering the optical communications marketplace within the Americas and Asia." *Fibre Systems Europe* is also available, covering the business and marketing aspects of fiber optics communications in Europe.

Infogate. Infogate, Inc. • Web site provides current news and information on seven "channels": News, Fun, Sports, Info, Finance, Shop, and Travel. Among the content partners are Business Wire, CBS MarketWatch, CNN, Morningstar, Standard & Poor's, and Thomson Investors Network. Fees: Free, but downloading of Infogate software is required (includes personalized news feature). Updating is continuous. Formerly Pointcast Network.

Major Telecommunications Companies of the World. Available from The Gale Group. • 2001. $855.00. Fourth edition. Published by Graham & Whiteside. Contains detailed information and trade names for more than 4,000 important telecommunications companies in various countries.

Telecommunications Regulation: Cable, Broadcasting, Satellite, and the Internet. Matthew Bender & Co., Inc. • Looseleaf. $700.00. Four volumes. Semiannual updates. Covers local, state, and federal regulation, with emphasis on the Telecommunications Act of 1996. Includes regulation of television, telephone, cable, satellite, computer communication, and online services. Formerly *Cable Television Law.*

Wireless Data Networks. Warren Publishing Inc. • 1998. $1,995.00. Fourth edition. Presents market research information relating to cellular data networks, paging networks, packet radio networks, satellite systems, and other areas of wireless communication. Contains "summaries of recent developments and trends in wireless markets.".

TELECOMMUTING

See also: COMPUTER COMMUNICATIONS

GENERAL WORKS

Data Smog: Surviving the Information Glut. David Shenk. HarperCollins Publishers. • 1997. $24.00. A critical view of both the electronic and print information industries. Emphasis is on information overload.

Making Telecommuting Happen: A Guide for Telemangers and Telecommuters. Jack M. Nilles. John Wiley and Sons, Inc. • 1994. $25.95. Includes tips for working productively in a home environment while maintaining good relationships with workers in the corporate office.

Telecommute! Go to Work Without Leaving Home. Lisa Shaw. John Wiley and Sons, Inc. • 1996. $14.95. Includes "Are You Right for Telecommuting?" and "How to Negotiate with Your Boss.".

What Will Be: How the New World of Information Will Change Our Lives. Michael L. Dertouzos. HarperSan Francisco. • 1997. $25.00. A discussion of the "information market place" of the future, including telecommuting, virtual reality, and computer recognition of speech. The author is director of the MIT Laboratory for Computer Science.

Wired Neighborhood. Stephen Doheny-Farina. Yale University Press. • 1996. $32.00. The author examines both the hazards and the advantages of "making the computer the center of our public and private lives," as exemplified by the Internet and telecommuting.

BIBLIOGRAPHIES

Telecommuters, the Workforce of the Twenty-First Century: An Annotated Bibliography. Teri R. Switzer. Scarecrow Press, Inc. • 1996. $34.00. Covers material published since 1970.

HANDBOOKS AND MANUALS

Manual of Remote Working. Kevin Curran and Geoff Williams. Ashgate Publishing Co. • 1997. $113.95. A British approach to telecommuting or "remote working." Among the chapters are "Planning a Remote Working Operation," "Human Resources," "Communication Systems," and "Project Management." Includes bibliographical references, glossary, and index. Published by Gower in England.

Telecom Made Easy: Money-Saving, Profit-Building Solutions for Home Businesses, Telecommuters, and Small Organizations. June Langhoff. Aegis Publishing Group Ltd. • 2000. $19.95. Fouth edition.

Telecommuting: A Manager's Guide to Flexible Work Arrangements. Joel Kugelmass. Jossey-Bass, Inc., Publishers. • 1995. $25.00. Part one is "Understanding Flexible Work" and part two is "Implementing Flexible Work." Includes bibliography and index.

Underground Guide to Telecommuting: Slightly Askew Advice on Leaving the Rat Race Behind. Woody Leonhard. Addison-Wesley Longman, Inc. • 1995. $24.95. Provides advice on hardware, software, telecommunications, zoning, taxes, mail, and other topics for telecommuters.

Virtual Office Survival Handbook: What Telecommuters and Entrepreneurs Need to Succeed in Today's Nontraditional Workplace. Alice Bredin. John Wiley and Sons, Inc. • 1996. $34.95. Presents broad coverage of telecommuting considerations, including workplace customizing and the evaluation of electronic office equipment. Coping with distractions and psychological issues are discussed.

INTERNET DATABASES

SoHo Central. Home Office Association of America, Inc. Phone: 800-809-4622 Fax: 800-315-4622 E-mail: info@hoaa.com • URL: http://www.hoaa.com • Web site provides extensive lists of "Home Office Internet Resources" (links), including Business, Government, Continuing Education, Legal, Employment, Telecommunications, and Publishing. Includes an online newsletter. Fees: Free. (Membership in the Home Office Association of America is $49.00 per year.).

Telecommuting, Teleworking, and Alternative Officing. Gil Gordon Associates. Phone: (732)329-2266 Fax: (732)329-2703 • URL: http://www.gilgordon.com • Web site includes "About Telecommuting" (questions and answers), "Worldwide Resources" (news groups, publications, conferences), and "Technology" (virtual office, intranets, groupware). Other features include monthly updates and an extensive list of telecommuting/telework related books. Fees: Free.

PERIODICALS AND NEWSLETTERS

Desktop Video Communications. BCR Enterprises, Inc,. • Bimonthly. $55.00 per year. Covers multimedia technologies, with emphasis on video conferencing and the "virtual office." Formerly *Virtual Workgroups.*

Home Office Connections: A Monthly Journal of News, Ideas, Opportunities, and Savings for Those Who Work at Home. Home Office Association of America, Inc. • Monthly. $49.00 per year. Newsletter. Includes membership in the Home Office Association of America.

InterActive Consumers. MarketResearch.com. • Monthly. $395.00 per year. Newsletter. Covers the emerging markets for digital content, products, and services. Includes market information on telecommuting, online services, the Internet, online investing, and other areas of electronic commerce.

Telecons. Applied Business Telecommunications. • Bimonthly. $30.00 per year. Topics include teleconferencing, videoconferencing, distance learning, telemedicine, and telecommuting.

TeleTrends. International Telework Association Council. • Quarterly. Price on application.

RESEARCH CENTERS AND INSTITUTES

Computerized Conferencing and Communications Center. New Jersey Institute of Technology, University Heights, Newark, NJ 07102. Phone: (973)596-3388 Fax: (973)596-5777 E-mail: 120@eies.njit.edu • URL: http://www.njit.edu/cccc • Research areas include computer conferencing software and computer-mediated communication systems.

TRADE/PROFESSIONAL ASSOCIATIONS

Home Office Association of America. 133 E. 5th St., Ste. 711, New York, NY 10022. Phone: 800-809-4622 or (212)588-9097 Fax: (212)588-9156 E-mail: hoaa@aol.com • URL: http://www.hoaa.com • A for-profit organization providing advice and information to home office workers and business owners.

International Teleconferencing Association. P.O. Box 906, Syosset, NY 11791-0079. Phone: (516)941-2020 Fax: (516)941-2015 E-mail: staff@itca.org • URL: http://www.itca.org • Members are vendors and users of teleconferencing equipment. Special Interest Groups include Telecommuting.

International Telework Association Council. 204 E St., N. E., Washington, DC 20002. Phone: (202)547-6157 Fax: (202)546-3289 • URL: http://www.telecommute.org • Members are individuals and organizations promoting the benefits of telecommuting and the "virtual office.".

TELEGRAPH

See also: CABLE ADDRESSES; TELECOMMUNICATIONS

DIRECTORIES

Marconi's International Register: Linking Buyers and Sellers Worldwide Through Fax and Business Listings. Telegraphic Cable and Radio Registrations, Inc. • Annual. $150.00. Lists more than 45,000 firms throughout the world in all lines of business. In four sections.

STATISTICS SOURCES

Communication Equipment, and Other Electronic Systems and Equipment. U. S. Bureau of the Census. • Annual. Provides data on shipments: value, quantity, imports, and exports. (Current Industrial Reports, MA-36P.).

TELEMARKETING

See also: TELEPHONE SELLING

GENERAL WORKS

Applying Telecommunications and Technology from a Global Business Perspective. Jay J. Zajas and Olive D. Church. Haworth Press, Inc. • 1996. $49.95. Provides an international, multicultural perspective.

ABSTRACTS AND INDEXES

Business Periodicals Index. H. W. Wilson Co. • Monthly, except August, with quarterly and annual cumulations. Service basis for print edition; CD-ROM edition, $1,495.00 per year.

DIRECTORIES

Call Center Solutions Buyer's Guide and Directory. Technology Marketing Corp. • Annual. $25.00. Over 1,100 domestic and foreign suppliers of equipment, products, and services to the telecommunications/telemarketing industry. Formerly *Telemarketing: Buyer's Guide and Directory.*

HANDBOOKS AND MANUALS

Successful Telemarketing: Opportunities and Techniques for Increasing Sales and Profits. Bob Stone and John Wyman. NTC/Contemporary Publishing. • 1993. $29.95. Second edition. Includes case histories and examples of effective telemarketing.

Total Telemarketing: Complete Guide to Increasing Sales and Profits. Robert J. McHatton. John Wiley and Sons, Inc. • 1988. $49.95.

ONLINE DATABASES

PROMT: Predicasts Overview of Markets and Technology. The Gale Group. • Companies, products, applied technologies and markets. U.S. and international literature coverage, 1972 to date. Inquire as to online cost and availability. Provides abstracts from more than 1,600 publications. Weekly updates.

Wilson Business Abstracts Online. H. W. Wilson Co. • Indexes and abstracts 600 major business periodicals, plus the *Wall Street Journal* and the business section of the *New York Times.* Indexing is from 1982, abstracting from 1990, with the two newspapers included from 1993. Updated weekly. Inquire as to online cost and availability. (*Business Periodicals Index* without abstracts is also available online.).

PERIODICALS AND NEWSLETTERS

Call Center Magazine. Miller Freeman. • Monthly. $14.00 per year. Covers telephone and online customer service, help desk, and marketing operations. Includes articles on communications technology.

CC News: The Business Newspaper for Call Center and Customer Care Professionals. United Publications, Inc. • Eight times a year. Price on application. Includes news of call center technical developments.

Call Center CMR Solutions: The Authority on Teleservices, Sales, and Support Since 1982. Technology Marketing Corp. • Monthly. $49.00 per year. Emphasis is on telemarketing, selling, and customer service. Formerly *Call Center Solutions.*

DM News: The Newspaper of Direct Marketing. DM News Corp. • Weekly. $75.00 per year. Includes special feature issues on catalog marketing, telephone marketing, database marketing, and fundraising. Includes monthly supplements. *DM News International, DRTV News,* and *TeleServices.*

Target Marketing: The Leading Magazine for Integrated Database Marketing. North American Publishing Co. • Monthly. $65.00 per year. Dedicated to direct marketing excellence. Formerly *Zip Target Marketing.*

The Telemarketer. Actel Marketing. • Semimonthly. $285.00 per year. Newsletter.

Telephone Selling Report: Providing Proven Sales Ideas You Can Use. Art Sobczak, editor. Business By Phone, Inc. • Monthly. $109.00 per year. Newsletter. How-to newsletter providing proven ideas, tips, and techniques for telephone prospecting and selling.

TRADE/PROFESSIONAL ASSOCIATIONS

American Teleservices Association. 1601 Eye St., N.W., Ste. 615, Washington, DC 20006. Phone: 877-779-3974 or (202)293-2452 Fax: (202)463-8498 E-mail: ata@moinc.com • URL: http://www.ataconnect.org • Members are businesses involved in telephone marketing.

TELEMETERING

PERIODICALS AND NEWSLETTERS

Wireless Integration: Solutions for Enterprise Decision Makers. PennWell Corp., Advanced Technology Div. • Bimonthly. $48.00 per year. Edited for networking and communications managers. Special issues cover the wireless office, wireless intranet/Internet, mobile wireless, telemetry, and buyer's guide directory information.

Wireless Review: Intelligence for Competitive Providers. Intertec Publishing Corp. • Semimonthly. $48.00 per year. Covers business and technology developments for wireless service providers. Includes special issues on a wide variety of wireless topics. Formed by merger of *Cellular Business* and *Wireless World.*

TRADE/PROFESSIONAL ASSOCIATIONS

International Foundation for Telemetering. 5959 Topanga Canyon Blvd., Suite 150, Woodland Hills, CA 91367. Phone: (818)884-9568 Fax: (818)884-9671.

TELEPHONE ANSWERING SERVICE

HANDBOOKS AND MANUALS

Telephone Answering Service. Entrepreneur Media, Inc. • Looseleaf. $59.50. A practical guide to starting a telephone answering service. Covers profit potential, start-up costs, market size evaluation, owner's time required, pricing, accounting, advertising, promotion, etc. (Start-Up Business Guide No. E1148).

PERIODICALS AND NEWSLETTERS

Answer. Association of Telemessaging Services International, Inc. • Bimonthly. Members, $30.00 per year; non-members, $50.00 per year.

Telecommunicator. Association of Telemessaging Services International, Inc. • Biweekly. Membership. Formerly *Telephone Secretary.*

STATISTICS SOURCES

United States Census of Service Industries. U.S. Bureau of the Census. • Quinquennial. Various reports available.

TRADE/PROFESSIONAL ASSOCIATIONS

Association of Telephone Answering Services. c/o Monte Engler, Phillips, Nizer, Krim and Ballon LLP, 666 Fifth Ave., New York, NY 10103-0084. Phone: (212)977-9700 Fax: (212)262-5152.

Association of Teleservices International. 1800 Diogonal Rd., Ste. 645, Alexandria, VA 22314. Phone: (703)684-4406 Fax: (703)684-2957 E-mail: atsi@dc.sba.com • URL: http://www.atsi.org • An organization of telephone answering and voice message services.

TELEPHONE EQUIPMENT INDUSTRY

ABSTRACTS AND INDEXES

Applied Science and Technology Index. H. W. Wilson Co. • 11 times a year. Quarterly and annual cumulations. Service basis for print edition; CD-ROM edition, $1,495.00 per year. Indexes a wide variety of English language technical, industrial, and engineering periodicals.

Science Citation Index. Institute for Scientific Information. • Bimonthly. $15,020.00 per year. Annual cumulation. Includes *Source Index, Citation Index, Permuterm Subject Index,* and *Corporate Index.*

DIRECTORIES

America's Network Directory and Buyers' Guide. Advanstar Communications, Inc. • Annual. $240.00. Independent telephone companies in the United States, regional Bell operating companies, cellular telephone system operators, foreign telephone companies, long distance carriers, and interconnects. Formerly *Telephone and Engineering Directory.*

Better Buys for Business: The Independent Consumer Guide to Office Equipment. What to Buy for Business, Inc. • 10 times a year. $134.00 per year. Each issue is on a particular office product, with detailed evaluation of specific models: 1. Low-Volume Copier Guide, 2. Mid-Volume Copier Guide, 3. High-Volume Copier Guide, 4. Plain Paper Fax and Low-Volume Multifunctional Guide, 5. Mid/High-Volume Multifunctional Guide, 6. Laser Printer Guide, 7. Color Printer and Color Copier Guide, 8. Scan-to-File Guide, 9. Business Phone Systems Guide, 10. Postage Meter Guide, with a Short Guide to Shredders.

Data Communications Production Selection Guide. McGraw-Hill. • Semiannual. $25.00. List of networking vendors. Formerly *Data Communications Buyer's Guide.*

Directory of Computer and Consumer Electronics. Chain Store Age. • Annual. $290.00. Includes 2,900 "leading" retailers and over 200 "top" distributors. Formerly *Directory of Consumer Electronics Retails and Distributors.*

Plunkett's Telecommunications Industry Almanac. Plunkett Research, Ltd. • Annual. $179.99. Provides detailed profiles of major telecommunications industry corporations. Includes CD-ROM.

Sound and Communications: The Blue Book. Testa Communications. • Annual. $15.00. Approximately 1,000 suppliers of sound and communications equipment; including audio/video products in the United States and Canada.

Telecommunications Directory. The Gale Group. • 2000. $595.00. 12th edition. National and international voice, data, facsimile, and video communications services. Formerly *Telecommunications Systems and Services Directory.*

TIA-MMTA Directory and Desk Reference. Telecommunications Industry Association Multimedia Telecommunications Associatio. • Annual. $199.00. Lists manufacturers and suppliers of interconnect telephone equipment. Formerly *Multimedia Telecommunications Sourcebook.*

FINANCIAL RATIOS

Annual Statement Studies. Robert Morris Associates: The Association of Lending and Credit Risk Professiona. • Annual. Free to members; non-members, $140.00. Median and quartile financial ratios are given for over 400 kinds of manufacturing, wholesale, retail, construction, and consumer finance establishments. Data is sorted by both asset size and sales volume. Includes a clearly written "Definition of Ratios" and an alphabetical industry index.

ONLINE DATABASES

Globalbase. The Gale Group. • Provides more than one million online summaries of business, industrial, and economic news reports from more than 1,000 publications worldwide. Covers a wide range of material appearing in international trade journals, professional magazines, and newspapers. Time period is 1984 to date, with weekly updates. Inquire as to online cost and availability.

PROMT: Predicasts Overview of Markets and Technology. The Gale Group. • Companies, products, applied technologies and markets. U.S. and international literature coverage, 1972 to date. Inquire as to online cost and availability. Provides abstracts from more than 1,600 publications. Weekly updates.

Scisearch. Institute for Scientific Information. • Broad, multidisciplinary index to the literature of science and technology, 1974 to present. Inquire as to online cost and availability. Coverage of literature is worldwide, with weekly updates.

PERIODICALS AND NEWSLETTERS

America's Network: A Telecommunications Magazine. Advanstar Communications, Inc. • Semimonthly. $85.00 per year. Formerly *Telephone Engineer and Management.*

Communications News. American Society of Association Executives Communications Section. • Monthly. Membership.

Communications/Systems Equipment Design. McGraw-Hill.

IEEE Communications Magazine. Institute of Electrical and Electronics Engineers. • Monthly. $190.00 per year.

PCS Systems and Technology: Personal Communications Services Technology of the Digital Wireless Age. Cahners Business Information. • Nine times a year. Price on application. Covers network management and other technical topics.

Teleconnect. Miller Freeman, Inc. • Monthly. Free to qualified personnel.

Telephony: For Today's Competing Network Market. Intertec Publishing Corp. • 51 times per year. $114.00 per year.

TWICE: This Week in Consumer Electronics. Cahners Business Information, Broadcasting and Cable's International Group. • 29 times a year. Free to qualified personnel; others, $99.90 per year. Contains marketing and manufacturing news relating to a wide variety of consumer electronic products, including video, audio, telephone, and home office equipment.

STATISTICS SOURCES

Annual Survey of Manufactures. Available from U. S. Government Printing Office. • Annual. Prices vary. Issued by the U. S. Census Bureau as an interim update to the *Census of Manufactures.* Includes data on number of manufacturing establishments in various industries, employment, labor costs, value of shipments, capital expenditures, inventories, energy costs, and assets. (See also Census Bureau home page, http://www.census.gov/.).

Communication Equipment, and Other Electronic Systems and Equipment. U. S. Bureau of the Census. • Annual. Provides data on shipments: value, quantity, imports, and exports. (Current Industrial Reports, MA-36P.).

Manufacturing Profiles. Available from U. S. Government Printing Office. • Annual. Issued by the U. S. Census Bureau. A printed consolidation of the entire *Current Industrial Report* series, presenting "all the data compiled." Contains statistics on production, shipments, inventories, consumption, exports, imports, and orders for a wide variety of manufactured products. (See also Census Bureau home page, http://www.census.gov/.).

Standard & Poor's Industry Surveys. Standard & Poor's. • Semiannual. $1,800.00. Two looseleaf volumes. Includes monthly supplements. Provides detailed, individual surveys of 52 major industry groups. Each survey is revised on a semiannual basis. Also includes "Monthly Investment Review" (industry group investment analysis) and monthly "Trends & Projections" (economic analysis).

TRADE/PROFESSIONAL ASSOCIATIONS

Multimedia Telecommunications Association. 2500 Wilson Blvd., Suite 300, Arlington, VA 22201-3834. Phone: 800-799-6682 or (703)907-7472 Fax: (703)907-7478 E-mail: info@mmta.org • URL: http:

For publishers addresses, refer to SOURCES CITED section at the back of the book.

//www.mmta.org • Members are manufacturers and suppliers of interconnect telephone equipment.

Telecommunications Industry Association. 2500 Wilson Blvd., Suite 300, Arlington, VA 22201-3834. Phone: (703)907-7700 Fax: (703)907-7728 E-mail: mlesso@tia.eia.org • URL: http://www.tiaonline.org.

OTHER SOURCES

Faulkner's Telecommunications World. Faulkner Information Services, Inc. • Three looseleaf volumes, with monthly updates. $1,260.00 per year. Contains product reports, technology overviews and management articles relating to all aspects of voice and data communications.

Major Telecommunications Companies of the World. Available from The Gale Group. • 2001. $855.00. Fourth edition. Published by Graham & Whiteside. Contains detailed information and trade names for more than 4,000 important telecommunications companies in various countries.

TELEPHONE INDUSTRY

See also: TELECOMMUNICATIONS

DIRECTORIES

America's Network Directory and Buyers' Guide. Advanstar Communications, Inc. • Annual. $240.00. Independent telephone companies in the United States, regional Bell operating companies, cellular telephone system operators, foreign telephone companies, long distance carriers, and interconnects. Formerly *Telephone and Engineering Directory.*

Association of Telemessaging Services International-Membership Directory. Association of Telemessaging Services International, Inc. • Annual. $100.00. Lists 825 telephone answering services.

AT & T Toll Free National Directory. AT&T Yellow Pages Directories. • Annual. Business edition, $24.99 per year; consumer edition, $14.99 per year. Formerly *AT&T Toll Free 800 Directory.*

Directory of Top Computer Executives. Applied Computer Research, Inc. • Semiannual. Price varies. Two volumes. Lists large companies and government agencies, with names of their data and systems executives.

Telecommunications Directory. The Gale Group. • 2000. $595.00. 12th edition. National and international voice, data, facsimile, and video communications services. Formerly *Telecommunications Systems and Services Directory.*

The Telephone Industry Directory. Phillips Publishing International, Inc. • Annual. $249.00. Lists telecommunications carriers, equipment manufacturers, distributors, agencies, and organizations.

ENCYCLOPEDIAS AND DICTIONARIES

Telecom Lingo Guide. Warren Communication News. • 1996. $60.00. Eighth edition. Defines more than 1,000 words, phrases, and acronyms frequently used in the telecommunications industry.

FINANCIAL RATIOS

Almanac of Business and Industrial Financial Ratios. Leo Troy. Prentice Hall. • Annual. $99.95. Contains financial ratios derived from federal tax returns. Ratios for each of about 200 industries are arranged according to company asset size.

Annual Statement Studies. Robert Morris Associates: The Association of Lending and Credit Risk Professiona. • Annual. Free to members; non-members, $140.00. Median and quartile financial ratios are given for over 400 kinds of manufacturing, wholesale, retail, construction, and consumer finance establishments. Data is sorted by both asset size and sales volume. Includes a clearly written "Definition of Ratios" and an alphabetical industry index.

Industry Norms and Key Business Ratios. Desk Top Edition. Dun and Bradstreet Corp., Business Information Services. • Annual. Five volumes. $475.00 per volume. $1,890.00 per set. Covers over 800 kinds of businesses, arranged by Standard Industrial Classification number. More detailed editions covering longer periods of time are also available.

HANDBOOKS AND MANUALS

Moody's Public Utility Manual. Financial Information Services. • Annual. $1,595.00. Two volumes. Supplemented twice weekly by *Moody's Public Utility News Reports.* Contains financial and other information concerning publicly-held utility companies (electric, gas, telephone, water).

INTERNET DATABASES

Switchboard. Switchboard, Inc. Phone: (508)898-1000 Fax: (508)898-1755 E-mail: webmaster@switchboard.com • URL: http://www.switchboard.com • Web site provides telephone numbers and street addresses for more than 100 million business locations and residences in the U. S. Broad industry categories are available. Fees: Free.

PERIODICALS AND NEWSLETTERS

America's Network: A Telecommunications Magazine. Advanstar Communications, Inc. • Semimonthly. $85.00 per year. Formerly *Telephone Engineer and Management.*

Communications News. American Society of Association Executives Communications Section. • Monthly. Membership.

FCC Report: An Exclusive Report on Domestic and International Telecommunications Policy and Regulation. Warren Publishing Inc. • Semimonthly. $649.00 per year. Newsletter concerned principally with Federal Communications Commission reglations and policy.

Internet Telephony Magazine: The Authority on Voice, Video, Fax, and Data Convergence. Technology Marketing Corp. • Monthly. $29.00 per year. Covers the business and technology of telephone and other communications service via the Internet.

Telco Business Report: Executive Briefings on the Bell Operating Companies and Independent Telcos. Capitol Publications Inc., Telecom Publishing Group. • Biweekly. $759.00 per year. Newsletter. Covers long-distance markets, emerging technologies, strategies of Bell operating companies, and other telephone business topics.

Tele.com: Business and Technology for Public Network Service Providers. CMP Publications, Inc. • 14 times a year. $125.00 per year. Edited for executives and managers at both traditional telephone companies and wireless communications companies. Also provides news and information for Internet services providers and cable TV operators.

Telecom Business: Opportunities for Network Service Providers, Resellers, and Suppliers in the Competitive Telecom Industry. MultiMedia Publishing Corp. • Monthly. $56.95 per year. Provides business and technical information for telecommunications executives in various fields.

Telecommunications. Horizon-House Pubications, Inc. • Monthly. Free to qualified personnel; others, $75.00 per year. International coverage.

Telecommunications Reports. Telecommunications Reports International, Inc. • Weekly. Institutions, $1,695.00 per year. Includes *TR Daily.* Regulatory newsletter.

Telephone Management Strategist. Buyers Laboratory, Inc. • Monthly. $125.00 per year. Newsletter. Information on business telecommunications.

Telephony: For Today's Competing Network Market. Intertec Publishing Corp. • 51 times per year. $114.00 per year.

X-Change. Virgo Publishing, Inc. • 18 times per year. $70.00 per year. Edited for local telecommunications exchange services, both wireline and wireless.

Yellow Pages and Directory Report: The Newsletter for the Yellow Page and Directory Publishing Industry. SIMBA Information. • 22 times a year. $579.00 per year. Newsletter. Covers the yellow pages publishing industry, including electronic directory publishing, directory advertising, and special interest directories.

Your Telephone Personality. Economics Press, Inc. • Biweekly. $33.00 per year. Telephone skills for office employees.

RESEARCH CENTERS AND INSTITUTES

National Regulatory Research Institute. Ohio State University, 1080 Carmack Rd., Columbus, OH 43210. Phone: (614)292-9404 Fax: (614)292-7196 E-mail: lawton.1@osu.edu • URL: http://www.nrri.ohio-state.edu.

STATISTICS SOURCES

Annual Statistical Reports of Independent Telephone Companies. Federal Communications Commission. • Annual.

Phonefacts. United States Telephone Association. • Annual. Members, $5.00; non-members, $10.00. Presents basic statistics on the independent telephone industry in the U. S.

Quarterly Operating Data of 68 Telephone Carriers. Federal Communications Commission. • Quarterly.

Standard & Poor's Statistical Service. Current Statistics. Standard & Poor's. • Monthly. $688.00 per year. Includes 10 *Basic Statistics* sections, *Current Statistics Supplements* and *Annual Security Price Index Record.*

TPG Briefing on Local Exchange Statistics. Warren Communication News. • Annual. $325.00. Contains statistics on local telephone companies: revenues, expenses, debt, income, advertising, access lines, network usage, etc. Provides "Current Information on Major Competitors.".

U. S. Industry and Trade Outlook: The McGraw-Hill Companies and the U.S. Department of Commerce/International Trade Administration. Datapso Research Corp. • Annual. $69.95. Produced by the International Trade Administration, U. S. Department of Commerce, in a "public-private" partnership with DRI/McGraw-Hill and Standard & Poor's. Provides basic data, outlook for the current year, and "Long-Term Prospects" (five-year projections) for a wide variety of products and services. Includes high technology industries. Formerly *U. S. Industrial Outlook.*

TRADE/PROFESSIONAL ASSOCIATIONS

Competitive Telecommunications Association. 1900 M. St., N.W., Suite 800, Washington, DC 20036. Phone: (202)296-6650 Fax: (202)296-7585 E-mail: ferguson@comptel.org • URL: http://www.comptel.org.

Multimedia Telecommunications Association. 2500 Wilson Blvd., Suite 300, Arlington, VA 22201-3834. Phone: 800-799-6682 or (703)907-7472 Fax: (703)907-7478 E-mail: info@mmta.org • URL: http:

//www.mmta.org • Members are manufacturers and suppliers of interconnect telephone equipment.

National Telephone Cooperative Association. 4121 Wilson Blvd., 10th Fl., Arlington, VA 22203. Phone: (703)351-2000 E-mail: frs@ntca.com • Members are telephone cooperatives and statewide associations.

Organization for the Promotion and Advancement of Small Telecommunications Companies. 21 Dupont Circle, N.W., Washington, DC 20036. Phone: (202)659-5990 Fax: (202)659-4619 E-mail: jnr@opastco.org • URL: http://www.opastco.org • Members are small telephone companies serving rural areas.

Power and Communication Contractors Association. 6301 Stevenson Ave., Suite 1, Alexandria, VA 22304. Phone: 800-542-7222 or (703)823-1555 Fax: (703)823-5064 • URL: http://www.pccaweb.org.

Telecommunications and Telephone Association. P.O. 2387, Arlington, VA 22202. Phone: (202)628-5696 or (202)521-1089 Fax: (202)521-1007 • Represents consumer interests in the areas of telephone communications, service, and equipment.

United States Telephone Association. 1401 H St., N. W., Suite 600, Washington, DC 20005-2164. Phone: (202)326-7300 Fax: (202)326-7333 • URL: http://www.usta.org • An association of independent telephone companies.

OTHER SOURCES

Infrastructure Industries USA. The Gale Group. • 2001. $240.00. Replaces *Agriculture, Forestry, Fishing, Mining, and Construction USA* and *Transportation and Public Utilities USA.* Presents statistics and projections relating to economic activity in a wide variety of natural resource and construction industries.

TELEPHONE SELLING

See also: TELEMARKETING

GENERAL WORKS

I'll Get Back to You: 156 Ways to Get People to Return Your Calls and Other Helpful Sales Tips. Robert L. Shook and Eric Yaverbaum. McGraw-Hill. • 1996. $9.95. Presents advice from business executives, celebrities, and others on how to make telephone calls seem important.

Selling by Phone: How to Reach and Sell to Customers. Linda Richardson. McGraw-Hill. • 1995. $14.95.

Teleselling Techniques That Close the Sale. Flyn L. Penoyer. AMACOM. • 1997. $19.95.

HANDBOOKS AND MANUALS

Making Money with the Telephone: The Complete Handbook of Telephone Marketing. M. T. Brown. Future Shop. • 1977. $12.95.

Teleselling: A Self-Teaching Guide. James D. Porterfield. John Wiley and Sons, Inc. • 1996. $19.95. Second revised edition. Provides practical information and advice on selling by telephone, including strategy, prospecting, script development, and performance evaluation.

PERIODICALS AND NEWSLETTERS

Call Center CMR Solutions: The Authority on Teleservices, Sales, and Support Since 1982. Technology Marketing Corp. • Monthly. $49.00 per year. Emphasis is on telemarketing, selling, and customer service. Formerly *Call Center Solutions.*

TELEPHONES

See: TELEPHONE EQUIPMENT INDUSTRY

TELEPHONES, MOBILE

See: MOBILE TELEPHONE INDUSTRY

TELESCOPES

See also: OPTICS INDUSTRY

HANDBOOKS AND MANUALS

How to Buy and Understand Refracting Telescopes. Jordan Levenson. Levenson Press. • 1991. $43.50. Third edition.

PERIODICALS AND NEWSLETTERS

Astronomy. Kalmbach Publishing Co. • Monthly. $39.95 per year.

Sky and Telescope: The Essential Magazine of Astronomy. Leif J. Robinson, editor. Sky Publishing Co. • Monthly. $39.95 per year. Reports astronomy and space science for amateurs and professionals. Many "how to" features.

TELETEXT

See: VIDEOTEX/TELETEXT

TELEVISION ADVERTISING

See: RADIO AND TELEVISION ADVERTISING

TELEVISION APPARATUS INDUSTRY

See also: TELEVISION ENGINEERING; VIDEO RECORDING INDUSTRY

DIRECTORIES

Broadcast Engineering: Equipment Reference Manual. Intertec Publishing Corp. • Annual. $20.00. Lists manufacturers and distributors of radio and TV broadcast and recording equipment. Included in subscription to *Broadcast Engineering.*

Directory of Computer and Consumer Electronics. Chain Store Age. • Annual. $290.00. Includes 2,900 "leading" retailers and over 200 "top" distributors. Formerly *Directory of Consumer Electronics Retails and Distributors.*

EIA Trade Directory and Membership List. Electronic Industries Association. • Annual. Members, $75.00; non-members, $150.00.

Interactive Television Buyer's Guide and Directory. Chilton Co. • Annual. Price on application. (A special issue of the periodical *Convergence.*).

The SHOOT Directory for Commercial Production and Postproduction. BPI Communications. • Annual. $79.00. Lists production companies, advertising agencies, and sources of professional television, motion picture, and audio equipment.

Video Systems: Equipment Buyer's Guide. Intertec Publishing Corp. • Annual. $10.00. Lists approximately 1,000 manufacturers and suppliers of professional video equipment.

ENCYCLOPEDIAS AND DICTIONARIES

Encyclopedia of Emerging Industries. The Gale Group. • 2000. $295.00. Fourth edition. Provides detailed information on 90 "newly flourishing" industries. Includes historical background, organizational structure, significant individuals, current conditions, major companies, work force, technology trends, research developments, and other industry facts.

FINANCIAL RATIOS

Annual Statement Studies. Robert Morris Associates: The Association of Lending and Credit Risk Professiona. • Annual. Free to members; non-members, $140.00. Median and quartile financial ratios are given for over 400 kinds of manufacturing, wholesale, retail, construction, and consumer finance establishments. Data is sorted by both asset size and sales volume. Includes a clearly written "Definition of Ratios" and an alphabetical industry index.

NARDA's Cost of Doing Business Survey. North American Retail Dealers Association. • Annual. $250.00.

HANDBOOKS AND MANUALS

Digital Video Buyer's Guide. CMP Media, Inc. • Annual. $10.00. A directory of professional video products, including digital cameras, monitors, editing systems, and software.

Home Entertainment Installation. Entrepreneur Media, Inc. • Looseleaf. $59.50. A practical guide to starting a home entertainment installation service. Covers profit potential, start-up costs, market size evaluation, owner's time required, pricing, accounting, advertising, promotion, etc. (Start-Up Business Guide No. E1349.).

PERIODICALS AND NEWSLETTERS

Convergence: The Journal of Research Into New Media Technologies. Chilton Co. • Monthly. Individuals, $60,00 per year; institutions, $120.00 per year. Covers the merging of communications technologies. Includes telecommunications networks, interactive TV, multimedia, wireless phone service, and electronic information services.

Dealerscope Consumer Electronics Marketplace: For CE,PC and Major Appliance Retailers. North American Publishing Co. • Monthly. Free to qualified personnel; others, $79.00 per year. Formerly *Dealerscope Merchandising.*

NARDA Independent Retailer. North American Retail Dealers Association. • Monthly. $78.00. Formerly *NARDA News.*

Smart TV: For Selective and Interactive Viewers. Videomaker, Inc. • Bimonthly. $14.97 per year. Consumer magazine covering WebTV, PC/TV appliances, DVD players, "Smart TV," advanced VCRs, and other topics relating to interactive television, the Internet, and multimedia.

Video Technology News. Phillips Business Information, Inc. • Biweekly. $697.00 per year. Newsletter. Covers developments relating to the introduction of high definition television technology and broadcasting. Formerly *H D T V Report.*

PRICE SOURCES

Orion Video and Television Blue Book. Orion Research Corp. • Annual. $144.00. Quotes retail and wholesale prices of used video and TV equipment. Original list prices and years of manufacture are also shown.

STATISTICS SOURCES

Annual Survey of Manufactures. Available from U. S. Government Printing Office. • Annual. Prices vary. Issued by the U. S. Census Bureau as an interim update to the *Census of Manufactures.* Includes data on number of manufacturing establishments in various industries, employment, labor costs, value of shipments, capital expenditures, inventories, energy costs, and assets. (See also Census Bureau home page, http://www.census.gov/.).

Electronic Market Data Book. Electronic Industries Association, Marketing Services Dept. • Annual. Members, $75.00; non-members, $125.00.

Manufacturing Profiles. Available from U. S. Government Printing Office. • Annual. Issued by the U. S. Census Bureau. A printed consolidation of the entire *Current Industrial Report* series, presenting "all the data compiled." Contains statistics on production, shipments, inventories, consumption, exports, imports, and orders for a wide variety of manufactured products. (See also Census Bureau home page, http://www.census.gov/.).

Standard & Poor's Industry Surveys. Standard & Poor's. • Semiannual. $1,800.00. Two looseleaf volumes. Includes monthly supplements. Provides detailed, individual surveys of 52 major industry groups. Each survey is revised on a semiannual basis. Also includes "Monthly Investment Review" (industry group investment analysis) and monthly "Trends & Projections" (economic analysis).

TRADE/PROFESSIONAL ASSOCIATIONS

Electronic Industries Association. 2500 Wilson Blvd., Arlington, VA 22201. Phone: (703)907-7500 Fax: (703)907-7501 • URL: http://www.eia.org • Includes a Solid State Products Committee.

North American Retail Dealers Association. 10 E. 22nd St., Suite 310, Lombard, IL 60148. Phone: 800-621-0298 or (630)953-8950 Fax: (630)953-8957 E-mail: nardahdq@aol.com • URL: http://www.narda.com.

OTHER SOURCES

Digital Video. CMP Media, Inc. • Monthly. $60.00 per year. Edited for professionals in the field of digital video production. Covers such topics as operating systems, videography, digital video cameras, audio, workstations, web video, software development, and interactive television.

New-Format Digital Television. Available from MarketResearch.com. • 1999. $3,995.00. Market research data. Published by Fuji- Keizai USA. Covers the developing U. S. market for digital TV.

U. S. Home Theater Market. Available from MarketResearch.com. • 1997. $2,,500.00. Market research report published by Packaged Facts. Covers big-screen TV, high definition TV, audio equipment, and video sources. Market projections are provided to the year 2001.

Videography. United Entertainment Media, Inc. • Monthly. $30.00 per year. Edited for the professional video production industry. Covers trends in technique and technology.

TELEVISION BROADCASTING INDUSTRY

See also: CABLE TELEVISION INDUSTRY; TELEVISION APPARATUS INDUSTRY; TELEVISION ENGINEERING

GENERAL WORKS

Dissertations in Broadcasting. Christopher H. Sterling, editor. Ayer Co. Publishers, Inc. • 1979. $739.50. 26 volumes. Mainly reprints of historical, philosophical, political, and academic works.

Perspectives on Radio and Television: Telecommunication in the United States. F. Leslie Smith and others. Lawrence Erlbaum Associates. • 1998. Fourth edition. Price on application. (Communication Series).

ABSTRACTS AND INDEXES

Communication Abstracts. Sage Publications, Inc. • Bimonthly. Individuals, $185.00 per year; institutions, $805.00 per year. Provides broad coverage of the literature of communications, including broadcasting and advertising.

BIOGRAPHICAL SOURCES

Biographical Dictionary of American Journalism. Joseph P. McKerns, editor. Greenwood Publishing Group Inc. • 1989. $65.00. Covers major mass media: newspapers, radio, television, and magazines. Includes reporters, editors, columnists, cartoonists, commentators, etc.

Celebrity Register. The Gale Group. • 1989. $99.00. Fifth edition. Compiled by Celebrity Services International (Earl Blackwell). Contains profiles of 1,300 famous individuals in the performing arts, sports, politics, business, and other fields.

Contemporary Theatre, Film, and Television. The Gale Group. • 2000. 34 volumes in print. $165.00 per volume. Provides detailed biographical and career information on more than 11,000 currently popular performers, directors, writers, producers, designers, managers, choreographers, technicians, composers, executives, dancers, and critics.

The Highwaymen: Warriors on the Information Superhighway. Ken Auletta. Harcourt Trade Publications. • 1998. $13.00. Revised expanded edition. Contains critical articles about Ted Turner, Rupert Murdoch, Barry Diller, Michael Eisner, and other key figures in electronic communications, entertainment, and information.

CD-ROM DATABASES

Hoover's Company Capsules on CD-ROM. Hoover's, Inc. • Quarterly. $349.95 per year (single-user). Provides the CD-ROM version of *Hoover's Handbook of American Business, Hoover's Handbook of Emerging Companies, Hoover's Handbook of World Business, Hoover's Guide to Computer Companies, Hoover's Guide to Media Companies, Hoover's Handbook of Private Companies,* and various regional guides. Includes more than 11,000 profiles of companies.

Magazine Index Plus. The Gale Group. • Monthly. $4,000.00 per year (includes InfoTrac workstation). Provides full text on CD-ROM for about 100 popular, general interest magazines and indexing for 300 others. Includes special indexing of reviews and product evaluations. Time period is 1980 to date.

Telecom Strategies. Thomson Financial Securities Data. • Monthly. $2,995.00 per year. CD-ROM contains full text of investment analysts' reports on companies operating in the following fields: telecommunications, broadcasting, and cable communications.

DIRECTORIES

Bacon's Radio and TV Cable Directories. Bacon's Publishing Co. • Annual. $295.00. Two volumes. Includes educational and public broadcasters. Covers all United States broadcast media. Formerly *Bacon's Radio - TV Directory.*

Broadcasting and Cable Yearbook. R. R Bowker. • Annual. $179.95. Two volumes. Published in conjunction with *Broadcasting* magazine. Provides information on U. S. and Canadian TV stations, radio stations, cable TV companies, and radio-TV services of various kinds.

Burrelle's Media Directory: Broadcast Media. Burrelle's Information Services. • Annual. $275.00. Two volumes. *Radio* volume lists more than 12,000 radio stations in the U. S. and Canada. *Television and Cable* volume lists more than 1,700 television stations and cable systems. Provides detailed descriptions, including programming and key personnel.

Gale Directory of Publications and Broadcast Media. The Gale Group. • Annual. $650.00. Five volumes. A guide to publications and broadcasting stations in the U. S. and Canada, including newspapers, magazines, journals, radio stations, television stations, and cable systems. Geographic arrangement. Volume three consists of statistical tables, maps, subject indexes, and title index. Formerly *Ayer Directory of Publications.*

Hollywood Creative Directory. • Three times a year. $129.95 per year.$54.95 per issue. Lists more than 1,700 motion picture and television development and production companies in the U. S. (mainly California and New York). Includes names of studio and TV network executives.

International Radio and Television Society: Foundation-Roster Yearbook. International Radio and Television Society, Inc. • Annual. Membership. A directory of approximately 1,600 members (persons involved professionally with radio or television).

International Television and Video Almanac: Reference Tool of the Television and Home Video Industries. Quigley Publishing Co., Inc. • Annual. $119.00.

NATPE International-Programmer's Guide. National Association of Television Program Executives. • Annual. $75.00 per copy. Lists production and distribution companies with titles of TV series or shows that each company provides. Includes categorized indexes of programs. Formerly *NATPE Programmer's Guide.*

NATPE: Pocket Guides Reps Groups Distributors. National Association of Television Program Executives. • Semiannual. Price on application. Includes station representatives, group owners (with stations owned), and program distributors.

News Media Yellow Book: Who's Who Among Reporters, Writers, Editors, and Producers in the Leading National News Media. Leadership Directories, Inc. • Quarterly. $305.00 per year. Lists the staffs of major newspapers and news magazines, TV and radio networks, news services and bureaus, and feature syndicates. Includes syndicated columnists and programs. Seven specialized indexes are provided.

Plunkett's Entertainment and Media Industry Almanac. Available from Plunkett Research, Ltd. • Biennial. $149.99. Provides profiles of leading firms in online information, films, radio, television, cable, multimedia, magazines, and book publishing. Includes World Wide Web sites, where available, plus information on careers and industry trends.

Pocket Station Listing Guide. National Association of Television Program Executives. • Quarterly. $15.00 per copy. Pocket-sized directory of all TV stations in the U. S. and Canada, and Latin America. Geographic arrangement. Includes major personnel.

Producer's Masterguide: The International Production Manual for Motion Pictures, Television, Commercials, Cable and Videotape Industries in the United States, Canada, the United Kingdom, Bermuda, the Caribbean Islands, Mexico, South America. • Annual. $125.00. A standard reference guide of the professional film, television, commercial and video tape industry throughout the U.S. and Canada. More than 30,000 listings.

Scriptwriters Market. Scriptwriters-Filmmakers Publishing Co. • Annual. $39.95. 450 literary agents, 375 film producers, over 3,000 actors and actresses, 325 directors, and 275 television producers.

TV and Cable Source. SRDS. • Quarterly. $464.00 per year. Provides detailed information on U. S. television stations, cable systems, networks, and group owners, with maps and market data. Includes key personnel.

Working Press of the Nation. R. R. Bowker. • Annual. $450.00. Three volumes: (1) *Newspaper Directory*; (2) *Magazine and Internal Publications Directory*; (3) *Radio and Television Directory.*

Includes names of editors and other personnel. Individual volumes, $249.00.

World Radio TV Handbook. BPI Communications, Inc. • Annual. $19.95. 25,000 radio and television stations worldwide.

ENCYCLOPEDIAS AND DICTIONARIES

Broadcast Communications Dictionary. Lincoln Diamant. Greenwood Publishing Group Inc. • 1989. $57.95. Third revised edition.

Encyclopedia of Television. Horace Newcomb, editor. Fitzroy Dearborn Publishers. • 1997. $300.00. Three volumes. Contains about 1,000 entries on TV performers, programs, organizations, social issues, technical aspects, and historical details.

International Film, Television, and Video Acronyms. Matthew Stevens, editor. Greenwood Publishing Group, Inc. • 1993. $85.00. A guide to 3,400 acronyms and 1,400 technical terms.

Multimedia and the Web from A to Z. Patrick M. Dillon and David C. Leonard. Oryx Press. • 1998. $39.95. Second enlarged revised edition. Defines more than 1,500 terms relating to software and hardware in the areas of computing, online technology, telecommunications, audio, video, motion pictures, CD-ROM, and the Internet. Includes acronyms and an annotated bibliography. Formerly *Multimedia Technology from A to Z* (1994).

NTC's Mass Media Dictionary. R. Terry Ellmore. NTC/Contemporary Publishing. • 1993. $24.95. Covers television, radio, newspapers, magazines, film, graphic arts, books, billboards, public relations, and advertising. Terms are related to production, research, audience measurement, audio-video engineering, printing, publishing, and other areas.

FINANCIAL RATIOS

Almanac of Business and Industrial Financial Ratios. Leo Troy. Prentice Hall. • Annual. $99.95. Contains financial ratios derived from federal tax returns. Ratios for each of about 200 industries are arranged according to company asset size.

Annual Statement Studies. Robert Morris Associates: The Association of Lending and Credit Risk Professiona. • Annual. Free to members; non-members, $140.00. Median and quartile financial ratios are given for over 400 kinds of manufacturing, wholesale, retail, construction, and consumer finance establishments. Data is sorted by both asset size and sales volume. Includes a clearly written "Definition of Ratios" and an alphabetical industry index.

Industry Norms and Key Business Ratios. Desk Top Edition. Dun and Bradstreet Corp., Business Information Services. • Annual. Five volumes. $475.00 per volume. $1,890.00 per set. Covers over 800 kinds of businesses, arranged by Standard Industrial Classification number. More detailed editions covering longer periods of time are also available.

Television Financial Report. National Association of Broadcasters. • Annual. Members, $100.00; non-members, $300.00. Provides data on the revenues, expenses, and profit margins of TV stations.

HANDBOOKS AND MANUALS

Contracts for the Film and Television Industry. Mark Litwak. Silman-James Press. • 1999. $35.95. Second expanded edition. Contains a wide variety of sample entertainment contracts. Includes material on rights, employment, joint ventures, music, financing, production, distribution, merchandising, and the retaining of attorneys.

Dun & Bradstreet/Gale Group Industry Handbooks. The Gale Group. • 2000. $630.00. Five volumes. $145.00 per volume. Each volume covers two or more major industries: 1. *Entertainment and Hospitality*; 2. *Construction and Agriculture*; 3. *Chemicals and Pharmaceuticals*; 4. *Computers & Software and Broadcasting & Telecommunications*; 5. *Insurance and Health & Medical Services.* The following are included for each industry: overview, statistics, financial ratios, rankings, merger information, company directory, directory of associations, and consultants directory.

Entertainment Law. Robert Fremlin. West Group. • $560.00. Looseleaf service. Includes updates. (Entertainment and Communicat Law Series).

Rights and Liabilities of Publishers, Broadcasters, and Reporters. Slade R. Metcalf and Robin Bierstedt. Shepard's. • 1982. $200.00. Two volumes. A legal manual for the media.

Television Production Handbook. Herbert Zettl. Wadsworth Publishing Co. • 1996. $64.95. Sixth edition. (Radio/TV/Film Series).

INTERNET DATABASES

GaleNet: Your Information Community. The Gale Group. Phone: 800-877-GALE or (248)699-GALE Fax: 800-414-5043 or (248)699-8069 E-mail: galenet@gale.com • URL: http://www.galenet.com • Web site provides a wide variety of full-text information from Gale databases, Taft, and other sources. Covers associations, biography, business directories, education, the information industry, literature, publishing, and science. Fee-based subscriptions are available for individual databases (free demonstration). Includes Boolean search features and the BRS/Search user interface.

ONLINE DATABASES

Gale Database of Publications and Broadcast Media. The Gale Group. • An online directory containing detailed information on over 67,000 periodicals, newspapers, broadcast stations, cable systems, directories, and newsletters. Corresponds to the following print sources: *Gale Directory of Publications and Broadcast Media; Directories in Print; City and State Directories in Print; Newsletters in Print.* Semiannual updates. Inquire as to online cost and availability.

Newspaper and Periodical Abstracts. Bell & Howell Information and Learning. • Provides online coverage (citations and abstracts) of 25 major newspapers, 1,600 perodicals, and 70 TV programs. Covers business, economics, current affairs, health, fitness, sports, education, technology, government, consumer affairs, psychology, the arts, and the social sciences. Time period is 1986 to date, with daily updates. Inquire as to online cost and availability.

PROMT: Predicasts Overview of Markets and Technology. The Gale Group. • Companies, products, applied technologies and markets. U.S. and international literature coverage, 1972 to date. Inquire as to online cost and availability. Provides abstracts from more than 1,600 publications. Weekly updates.

PERIODICALS AND NEWSLETTERS

Brill's Content: The Independent Voice of the Information Age. Brill Media Ventures, L.P. • Eight times a year. $19.95 per year. Presents a critical, iconoclastic view of various forms of news media, including TV, magazines, newspapers, and websites.

Broadcast Investor: Newsletter on Radio-TV Station Finance. Paul Kagan Associates, Inc. • Monthly. $895.00 per year. Newsletter for investors in publicly held radio and television broadcasting companies.

Broadcasting and Cable. Cahners Business Information, Broadcasting and Cable's International Group. • 51 times a year. $149.00 per year. Formerly *Broadcasting.*

Electronic Media. Crain Communications, Inc. • Weekly. $119.00 per year.

Entertainment Marketing Letter. EPM Communications, Inc. • 22 times a year. $319.00 per year. Newsletter. Covers the marketing of various entertainment products. Includes television broadcasting, videocassettes, celebrity tours and tie-ins, radio broadcasting, and the music business.

The Hollywood Reporter. • Daily. $219.00 per year. Covers the latest news in film, TV, cable, multimedia, music, and theatre. Includes box office grosses and entertainment industry financial data.

International Radio and Television Society Newsletter. International Radio and Television Society. • Quarterly.

Ross Reports Television and Film Casting, Production Scripts. BPI Communications, Inc. • Monthly. $50.00. per year. Directory, production and casting guide, designed for actors and writers. Formerly *Ross Reports Television.*

Television Digest with Consumer Electronics. Warren Communication News. • Weekly. $944.00 per year. Newsletter featuring new consumer entertainment products utilizing electronics. Also covers the television broadcasting and cable TV industries, with corporate and industry news.

Television Quarterly. National Academy of Television Arts and Sciences. • Quarterly. $30.00 per year.

TV Technology. IMAS Publishing Group. • Biweekly. $125.00 per year. International coverage available.

Variety: The International Entertainment Weekly. Cahners Business Information, Broadcasting and Cable's International Group. • Weekly. $219.00 per year. Contains national and international news of show business, with emphasis on motion pictures and television.

Video Week: Devoted to the Business of Program Sales and Distribution for Videocassettes, Disc, Pay TV and Allied News Media. Warren Publishing Inc. • Weekly. $907.00 per year. Newsletter. Covers video industry news and corporate developments.

RESEARCH CENTERS AND INSTITUTES

Center for Mass Media Research. Marquette University, 1131 W. Wisconsin Ave., Milwaukee, WI 53233. Phone: (414)288-3453 E-mail: griffinr@marquette.edu.

Institute for Telecommunications Studies. Ohio University, Nine S. College St., Athens, OH 45701. Phone: (740)593-4870 Fax: (740)593-9184 E-mail: korn@ohiou.edu • URL: http://www.ou.edu.

STATISTICS SOURCES

Circulation [year]. SRDS. • Annual. $256.00. Contains detailed statistical analysis of newspaper circulation by metropolitan area or county and data on television viewing by area. Includes maps.

Kagan Media Index. Paul Kagan Associates, Inc. • Monthly. $675.00 per year. Provides electronic and entertainment media industry statistics. Includes television, radio, motion pictures, and home video.

Standard & Poor's Industry Surveys. Standard & Poor's. • Semiannual. $1,800.00. Two looseleaf volumes. Includes monthly supplements. Provides detailed, individual surveys of 52 major industry groups. Each survey is revised on a semiannual basis. Also includes "Monthly Investment Review" (industry group investment analysis) and monthly "Trends & Projections" (economic analysis).

Television and Cable Factbook. Warren Publishing Inc. • Annual. $495.00. Three volumes. Commercial and noncommercial television stations and networks.

For publishers addresses, refer to SOURCES CITED section at the back of the book.

U. S. Industry Profiles: The Leading 100. The Gale Group. • 1998. $120.00. Second edition. Contains detailed profiles, with statistics, of 100 industries in the areas of manufacturing, construction, transportation, wholesale trade, retail trade, and entertainment.

United States Census of Service Industries. U.S. Bureau of the Census. • Quinquennial. Various reports available.

TRADE/PROFESSIONAL ASSOCIATIONS

Academy of Television Arts and Sciences. 5220 Lankershim Blvd., North Hollywood, CA 91601. Phone: (818)754-2800 Fax: (818)761-2827 E-mail: info@emmys.org • URL: http://www.emmys.org.

Alliance of Motion Picture and Television Producers. 15503 Ventura Blvd., Encino, CA 91436-3140. Phone: (818)995-3600 Fax: (818)382-1793.

American Federation of Television and Radio Artists. 260 Madison Ave., New York, NY 10016. Phone: (212)532-0800 Fax: (212)532-2242 E-mail: aftra@aftra.com • URL: http://www.aftra.com.

American Society of TV Cameramen and International Society of Videographers. 2520 Lotus Hill Dr., Las Vegas, NV 44145. Phone: (404)835-3040 Fax: (404)835-3488 E-mail: asse@ix.netcom.com • URL: http://www.asse-clemens.org.

American Sportscasters Association. Five Beekman St., Suite 814, New York, NY 10038. Phone: (212)227-8080 Fax: (212)571-0556 E-mail: asassn@juno.com • Members are radio and television sportscasters.

American Women in Radio and Television. 1650 Tysons Blvd., No. 200, McLean, VA 22102. Phone: (703)506-3290 Fax: (703)506-3266 E-mail: info@awrt.org • URL: http://www.awrt.org.

Association of America's Public Televised Stations. 1350 Connecticut Ave., N.W., Suite 200, Washington, DC 20036. Phone: (202)887-1700 Fax: (202)293-2422 E-mail: info@apts.org • URL: http://www.apts.org.

Association of Local Television Stations. 1320 19th St., N.W., Suite 300, Washington, DC 20036. Phone: (202)887-1970 Fax: (202)887-0950 E-mail: altv@aol.com • URL: http://www.altv.com • Members are TV stations not affiliated with a major network.

Broadcast Cable Financial Management Association. 701 Lee St., Suite 640, Des Plaines, IL 60016. Phone: (847)296-0200 Fax: (847)296-7510 E-mail: info@bcfm.com • URL: http://www.bcfm.com • Members are accountants and other financial personnel in the radio and television broadcasting industries.

Corporation for Public Broadcasting. 901 E St., N.W., Washington, DC 20004-2037. Phone: (202)879-9600 Fax: (202)783-1019 E-mail: comments@cpb.org • URL: http://www.cpb.org.

Institute of Electrical and Electronics Engineers; Consumer Electronics Society. Three Park Ave., 17th Fl., New York, NY 10016-5997. Phone: (212)419-7900 Fax: (212)752-4929 • URL: http://www.ieee.org.

International Radio and Television Society Foundation. 420 Lexington Ave., Suite 1714, New York, NY 10170. Phone: (212)867-6650 Fax: (212)867-6653 • URL: http://www.irts.org.

Media Rating Council. 200 W. 57th St., Suite 204, New York, NY 10019. Phone: (212)765-0200 Fax: (212)765-1868 • Purpose is to set standards for audience measurement services, such as A. C. Nielsen, Arbitron, and Statistical Research.

National Academy of Television Arts and Sciences. 111 W. 57th St., Suite 1020, New York, NY 10019. Phone: (212)586-8424 Fax: (212)246-8129.

National Association of Black Owned Broadcasters. 1155 Connecticut, N.W., 6th Fl., Washington, DC 20036. Phone: (202)463-8970 Fax: (202)429-0657 E-mail: nabob@abs.net.

National Association of Broadcasters. 1771 N. St., N.W., Washington, DC 20036. Phone: (202)429-5300 Fax: (202)429-5343 • URL: http://www.nab.org.

National Association of Television Program Executives. 2425 Olympic Blvd., Suite 550E, Santa Monica, CA 90404. Phone: (310)453-4440 Fax: (310)453-5258 E-mail: info@natpe.org • URL: http://www.natpe.org.

National Sportscasters and Sportswriters Association. P.O. Box 559, Salisbury, NC 28144. Phone: (704)633-4275 Fax: (704)633-4275 • Members are sportswriters and radio/TV sportscasters.

Promax International. 2029 Century Park E., Suite 555, Los Angeles, CA 90067-3283. Phone: (310)788-7600 Fax: (310)788-7616 • URL: http://www.promax.org • Members are advertising and public relations personnel in the radio and television broadcasting industries.

Society for the Eradication of Television. P.O. Box 10491, Oakland, CA 94610. Phone: (510)763-8712 • Encourages the removal of television sets from homes.

Society of Broadcast Engineers. 8445 Keystone Crossing, Suite 140, Indianapolis, IN 46240. Phone: (317)253-1640 Fax: (317)253-0418 E-mail: jporay@sbe.org • URL: http://www.sbe.org.

Society of Motion Picture and Television Engineers. 595 W. Hartsdale Ave., White Plains, NY 10607. Phone: (914)761-1100 Fax: (914)761-3115 E-mail: smpte@smpte.org • URL: http://www.smpte.org.

Station Representatives Association. 16 W. 77th St., No. 9-E, New York, NY 10024-5126. Phone: (212)362-8868 Fax: (212)362-4999 E-mail: srajerry@aol.com • Members are sales representatives concerned with the sale of radio and television "spot" advertising.

Television Bureau of Advertising. Three E. 54th St., New York, NY 10022. Phone: (212)486-1111 Fax: (212)935-5631 E-mail: info@tvb.org • URL: http://www.tvb.org.

OTHER SOURCES

FCC Record. Available from U. S. Government Printing Office. • Biweekly. $535.00 per year. Produced by the Federal Communications Commission (http://www.fcc.gov). An inclusive compilation of decisions, reports, public notices, and other documents of the FCC.

Infrastructure Industries USA. The Gale Group. • 2001. $240.00. Replaces *Agriculture, Forestry, Fishing, Mining, and Construction USA* and *Transportation and Public Utilities USA.* Presents statistics and projections relating to economic activity in a wide variety of natural resource and construction industries.

The Market for Interactive Television. MarketResearch.com. • 2000. $995.00. Market research data.

North American Interactive Television Markets. Available from MarketResearch.com. • 1999. $3,450.00. Published by Frost & Sullivan. Contains market research data on growth, end-user trends, and market strategies. Company profiles are included.

Sports and Entertainment Litigation Reporter: National Journal of Record Covering Crititcal Issues in Entertainment Law Field. Andrews Publications. • Monthly. $775.00 per year. Provides reports on lawsuits involving films, TV, cable broadcasting, stage productions, radio, and other areas of the entertainment business.Formerly *Entertainment Litigation Reporter.*

Telecommunications Regulation: Cable, Broadcasting, Satellite, and the Internet. Matthew Bender & Co., Inc. • Looseleaf. $700.00. Four volumes. Semiannual updates. Covers local, state, and federal regulation, with emphasis on the Telecommunications Act of 1996. Includes regulation of television, telephone, cable, satellite, computer communication, and online services. Formerly *Cable Television Law.*

Television Broadcast. United Entertainment Media, Inc. • Monthly. $40.00 per year. Contains articles on management, production, and technology for TV stations.

TELEVISION, CABLE

See: CABLE TELEVISION INDUSTRY

TELEVISION ENGINEERING

See also: TELEVISION APPARATUS INDUSTRY

ALMANACS AND YEARBOOKS

Communication Technology Update. Butterworth-Heinemann. • Annual. $36.95. Reviews technological developments and statistical trends in five key areas: mass media, computers, consumer electronics, communications satellites, and telephony. Includes television, cellular phones, and the Internet. (Focal Press.).

DIRECTORIES

Broadcast Engineering: Equipment Reference Manual. Intertec Publishing Corp. • Annual. $20.00. Lists manufacturers and distributors of radio and TV broadcast and recording equipment. Included in subscription to *Broadcast Engineering.*

Society of Motion Picture and Television Engineers Directory for Members. Society of Motion Picture and Television Engineers. • Annual. Membership.

Video Systems: Equipment Buyer's Guide. Intertec Publishing Corp. • Annual. $10.00. Lists approximately 1,000 manufacturers and suppliers of professional video equipment.

PERIODICALS AND NEWSLETTERS

Broadcast Engineering: Journal of Broadcast Technology. Intertec Publishing Corp. • Monthly. Free to qualified personnel; others, $55.00 per year. Technical magazine for the broadcast industry.

SHOOT: The Leading Newsweekly for Commercial Production and Postproduction. BPI Communications. • Weekly. $115.00 per year. Covers animation, music, sound design, computer graphics, visual effects, cinematography, and other aspects of television and motion picture production, with emphasis on TV commercials.

SMPTE Journal. Society of Motion Picture and Television Engineers. • Monthly. $125.00 per year.

Video Systems: The Magazine for Video Professionals. Intertec Publishing Corp. • Monthly. Price on application.

Video Technology News. Phillips Business Information, Inc. • Biweekly. $697.00 per year. Newsletter. Covers developments relating to the introduction of high definition television technology and broadcasting. Formerly *H D T V Report.*

TRADE/PROFESSIONAL ASSOCIATIONS
Society of Motion Picture and Television Engineers. 595 W. Hartsdale Ave., White Plains, NY 10607. Phone: (914)761-1100 Fax: (914)761-3115 E-mail: smpte@smpte.org • URL: http://www.smpte.org.

OTHER SOURCES
Videography. United Entertainment Media, Inc. • Monthly. $30.00 per year. Edited for the professional video production industry. Covers trends in technique and technology.

TELEVISION, FOREIGN

See: FOREIGN RADIO AND TELEVISION

TELEVISION PROGRAMS

DIRECTORIES
NATPE International-Programmer's Guide. National Association of Television Program Executives. • Annual. $75.00 per copy. Lists production and distribution companies with titles of TV series or shows that each company provides. Includes categorized indexes of programs. Formerly *NATPE Programmer's Guide.*

ENCYCLOPEDIAS AND DICTIONARIES
Film-Video Terms and Concepts: A Focal Handbook. Steven Browne. Butterworth-Heinemann. • 1992. $31.95. Defines production terms, techniques, and jargon relating to motion pictures, television, and the video industry. (Focal Handbook).

PERIODICALS AND NEWSLETTERS
Better Radio and Television. National Association for Better Broadcasting. • Quarterly. $6.00 per year.

Multichannel News. Cahners Business Information. • Weekly. $119.00 per year. Covers the business, programming, marketing, and technology concerns of cable television operators and their suppliers.

TV Guide. News America Publications, Inc. • Weekly. $52.00 per year.

STATISTICS SOURCES
Nielsen Report on Television. Nielsen Media Research. • Annual. $25.00. General statistics on television programming, plus ranking of the year's most popular shows. Pamphlet.

TRADE/PROFESSIONAL ASSOCIATIONS
National Association of Television Program Executives. 2425 Olympic Blvd., Suite 550E, Santa Monica, CA 90404. Phone: (310)453-4440 Fax: (310)453-5258 E-mail: info@natpe.org • URL: http://www.natpe.org.

OTHER SOURCES
Creativity Rules! A Writer's Workbook. John Vorhaus. Silman-James Press. • 2000. $15.95. Covers the practical process of conceiving, outlining, and developing a story, especially for TV or film scripts. Includes "tactics and exercises.".

Television Broadcast. United Entertainment Media, Inc. • Monthly. $40.00 per year. Contains articles on management, production, and technology for TV stations.

TELEVISION RECORDING

See: VIDEO RECORDING INDUSTRY

TELEVISION REPAIR INDUSTRY

See: RADIO AND TELEVISION REPAIR INDUSTRY

TELEVISION, SATELLITE

See: COMMUNICATIONS SATELLITES

TELEVISION STATIONS

See: TELEVISION BROADCASTING INDUSTRY

TELLER MACHINES

See: BANK AUTOMATION

TEMPERATURE (CLIMATE)

See: CLIMATE; WEATHER AND WEATHER FORECASTING

TEMPORARY EMPLOYEES

GENERAL WORKS
Flesh Peddlers and Warm Bodies: The Temporary Help Industry and Its Workers. Robert E. Parker. Rutgers University Press. • 1994. $40.00. A critical view of temporary work. (Arnold and Caroline Rose Monograph Series of the American Sociological Association).

How to Choose and Use Temporary Services. Bill Lewis and Nancy H. Molloy. Books on Demand. • 1991. $80.60. Tells what to expect from temporary services and their workers.

Managing Contingent Workers: How to Reap the Benefits and Reduce the Risk. Stanley Nollen and Helen Axel. AMACOM. • 1995. $55.00.

ABSTRACTS AND INDEXES
Business Periodicals Index. H. W. Wilson Co. • Monthly, except August, with quarterly and annual cumulations. Service basis for print edition; CD-ROM edition, $1,495.00 per year.

Personnel Management Abstracts. • Quarterly. $190.00 per year. Includes annual cumulation.

DIRECTORIES
The Human Resource Executive's Market Resource. LRP Publications. • Annual. $25.00. A directory of services and products of use to personnel departments. Includes 20 categories, such as training, outplacement, health benefits, recognition awards, testing, workers' compensation, temporary staffing, recruitment, and human resources software.

Kennedy's Directory of Executive Temporary Placement Firms. Kennedy Information, LLC. • 1995. $24.95. Eighth revised edition. Provides information on about 225 executive search firms that have temporary placement as a specialty.

FINANCIAL RATIOS
Annual Statement Studies. Robert Morris Associates: The Association of Lending and Credit Risk Professiona. • Annual. Free to members; non-members, $140.00. Median and quartile financial ratios are given for over 400 kinds of manufacturing, wholesale, retail, construction, and consumer finance establishments. Data is sorted by both asset size and sales volume. Includes a clearly written "Definition of Ratios" and an alphabetical industry index.

HANDBOOKS AND MANUALS
Legal Guide to Independent Contractor Status. Robert W. Wood. Panel Publishers. • 1999. $165.00. Third edition. A guide to the legal and tax-related differences between employers and independent contractors. Includes examples of both "safe" and "troublesome" independent contractor designations. Penalties and fines are discussed.

Temporary Help Service. Entrepreneur Media, Inc. • Looseleaf. $59.50. A practical guide to starting an employment agency for temporary workers. Covers profit potential, start-up costs, market size evaluation, owner's time required, site selection, lease negotiation, pricing, accounting, advertising, promotion, etc. (Start-Up Business Guide No. E1189.).

ONLINE DATABASES
PROMT: Predicasts Overview of Markets and Technology. The Gale Group. • Companies, products, applied technologies and markets. U.S. and international literature coverage, 1972 to date. Inquire as to online cost and availability. Provides abstracts from more than 1,600 publications. Weekly updates.

Wilson Business Abstracts Online. H. W. Wilson Co. • Indexes and abstracts 600 major business periodicals, plus the *Wall Street Journal* and the business section of the *New York Times*. Indexing is from 1982, abstracting from 1990, with the two newspapers included from 1993. Updated weekly. Inquire as to online cost and availability. (*Business Periodicals Index* without abstracts is also available online.).

PERIODICALS AND NEWSLETTERS
Contemporary Times. National Association of Temporary Staffing Services, Inc. • Quarterly. Members, $60.00 per year; non-members, $240.00 per year; non-profit, $80.00 per year. Management support articles for the temporary help industry and current information on industry activities. Formerly *National Association of Temporary Services, Inc.*

Working Options. Association of Part-Time Professionals. • Bimonthly. Members in the Washington Metropolitan Area, $45.00 per year; other members, $20.00 per year. Formerly *The Part-Time Professional.*

TRADE/PROFESSIONAL ASSOCIATIONS
American Staffing Association. 277 S. Washington St., Ste. 200, Alexandria, VA 22314-3119. Phone: (703)549-6287 Fax: (703)549-4808 E-mail: asa@staffingtoday.net • URL: http://www.staffingtoday.net • An association of private employment agencies for temporary workers.

TENNIS INDUSTRY

DIRECTORIES
Tennis Buyer's Guide Buying Directory. Golf Digest/Tennis, Inc. • Annual $5.00. Lists more than 200 manufacturers of tennis rackets, apparel, shoes, equipment, and accessories.

PERIODICALS AND NEWSLETTERS
Tennis Industry. Miller Publishing Group. • 11 times a year. $22.00 per year. Edited for retailers serving the "serious tennis enthusiast." Provides news of apparel, rackets, equipment, and court construction.

TRADE/PROFESSIONAL ASSOCIATIONS
United States Professional Tennis Association. 3535 Briarpark Dr., Ste. 1, Houston, TX 77042. Phone: 800-877-8248 or (713)978-7782 Fax: (713)978-7780 E-mail: uspta@uspta.org • URL: http://www.uspta.org • Members are professional tennis instructors and college coaches.

United States Tennis Association. 70 W. Red Oak Lane, White Plains, NY 10604. Phone: (914)696-7000 Fax: (914)696-7167 • URL: http://www.usta.com • Members are individuals, institutions, and groups interested in the promotion of tennis as a recreational and healthful sport.

OTHER SOURCES
Superstudy of Sports Participation. Available from MarketResearch.com. • 1999. $650.00. Three volumes. Published by American Sports Data, Inc.

Provides market research data on 102 sports and activities. Vol. 1: *Physical Fitness Activities*. Vol. 2: *Recreational Sports*. Vol. 3: *Outdoor Activities*. (Volumes are available separately at $275.00.).

TERMINATION OF EMPLOYMENT

See: DISMISSAL OF EMPLOYEES

TESTING OF MATERIALS

See: MATERIALS; STANDARDIZATION

TESTING OF PERSONNEL

See: PSYCHOLOGICAL TESTING; RATING OF EMPLOYEES

TESTING OF PRODUCTS

See: QUALITY OF PRODUCTS

TEXTBOOKS

See: BOOK INDUSTRY; PUBLISHING INDUSTRY

TEXTILE DESIGN

See also: TEXTILE INDUSTRY

ABSTRACTS AND INDEXES

Textile Technology Digest. Institute of Textile Technology. • Monthly. $535.00 per year. Provides indexing and abstracting of a wide variety of textile technology literature.

CD-ROM DATABASES

Textile Technology Digest [CD-ROM]. Textile Information Center, Institute of Textile Technology. • Quarterly. $1,700.00 per year. Provides CD-ROM indexing and abstracting of worldwide journals and monographs in various areas of textile technology, production, and management. Covers 1978 to date.

ENCYCLOPEDIAS AND DICTIONARIES

Encyclopedia of Textiles. French and European Publications, Inc. • 1980. $39.95. Third edition.

Textile Terms and Definitions. J.E. McIntyre and Paul N. Daniels, editors. Available from State Mutual Book and Periodical Service Ltd., Trade Order Dept. • 1995. $110.00. 10th edition. Published by the Textile Insitute (UK). Includes more than 1,000 definitions of textile processes, fiber types, and end products. Illustrated.

ONLINE DATABASES

Textile Technology Digest [online]. Textile Information Center, Institute of Textile Technology. • Contains indexing and abstracting of more than 300 worldwide journals and monographs in various areas of textile technology, production, and management. Time period is 1978 to date, with monthly updating. Inquire as to online cost and availability.

World Textiles. Elsevier Science, Inc. • Provides abstracting and indexing from 1970 of worldwide textile literature (periodicals, books, pamphlets, and reports). Includes U. S., European, and British patent information. Updating is monthly. Inquire as to online cost and availability.

TRADE/PROFESSIONAL ASSOCIATIONS

American Printed Fabrics Council. 45 W. 36th St., 3rd Fl., New York, NY 10018. 45 W. 36th St., 3rd Fl.,.

Textile Institute. Saint James Bldgs., 4th Fl., Oxford St., Manchester M1 6FQ, England. Phone: 44 161 2371188 Fax: 44 161 2361991 E-mail: tiihq@textileinst.org.uk • URL: http://www.texi.org • Members in 100 countries involved with textile industry management, marketing, science, and technology.

OTHER SOURCES

Textile Business Outlook. Statistikon Corp. • Quarterly. $985.00 per year. Analyzes current business, marketing, and financial conditions for the worldwide textile industry (fibers and fabrics). Includes statistical forecasts.

TEXTILE FIBERS

See: FIBER INDUSTRY; SYNTHETIC TEXTILE FIBER INDUSTRY

TEXTILE FIBERS, SYNTHETIC

See: SYNTHETIC TEXTILE FIBER INDUSTRY

TEXTILE INDUSTRY

ABSTRACTS AND INDEXES

Textile Chemist and Colorist. American Association of Textile Chemists and Colorists. • Monthly. Free to members; non-members, $60.00 per year. Annual *Buyer's Guide* available.

Textile Technology Digest. Institute of Textile Technology. • Monthly. $535.00 per year. Provides indexing and abstracting of a wide variety of textile technology literature.

World Textile Abstracts. Elsevier Science. • Monthly. $1,309.00 per year. Digests of articles published in the world's textile literature. Includes subscription to *World Textile Digest*.

CD-ROM DATABASES

Textile Technology Digest [CD-ROM]. Textile Information Center, Institute of Textile Technology. • Quarterly. $1,700.00 per year. Provides CD-ROM indexing and abstracting of worldwide journals and monographs in various areas of textile technology, production, and management. Covers 1978 to date.

DIRECTORIES

America's Textiles International-The Textile Redbook. Billian Publishing, Inc. • Annual. $145.00. Formerly *America's Textiles International Directory*.

Davison's Gold Book. Davison Publishing Co. • Annual. $80.00. Textile mill supplies, products, services, equipment and machinery.Formerly *Davison's Textile Buyers*.

Davison's Textile Blue Book. Davison Publishing Co. • Annual. $165.00. Over 8,400 companies in the textle industry in the United States, Canada, and Mexico, including about 4,400 textile plants.

Garment Manufacturer's Index. Klevens Publications, Inc. • Annual. $60.00. A directory of about 8,000 manufacturers and suppliers of products and services used in the making of men's, women's, and children's clothing. Includes fabrics, trimmings, factory equipment, and other supplies.

LDB Interior Textiles Buyer's Guide. E.W. Williams Publications Co. • Annual. $40.00. Includes over 2,000 manufacturers, distributors, and importers of curtains, draperies, hard window treatments, bedspreads, pillows, etc. Formerly *LDB Interior Textiles Directory*.

ENCYCLOPEDIAS AND DICTIONARIES

Encyclopedia of Textiles. French and European Publications, Inc. • 1980. $39.95. Third edition.

Fairchild's Dictionary of Textiles. Phyllis B. Tortora, editor. Fairchild Books. • 1996. $75.00. Seventh edition.

Textile Terms and Definitions. J.E. McIntyre and Paul N. Daniels, editors. Available from State Mutual Book and Periodical Service Ltd., Trade Order Dept. • 1995. $110.00. 10th edition. Published by the Textile Insitute (UK). Includes more than 1,000 definitions of textile processes, fiber types, and end products. Illustrated.

FINANCIAL RATIOS

Almanac of Business and Industrial Financial Ratios. Leo Troy. Prentice Hall. • Annual. $99.95. Contains financial ratios derived from federal tax returns. Ratios for each of about 200 industries are arranged according to company asset size.

Quarterly Financial Report for Manufacturing, Mining, and Trade Corporations. U.S. Federal Trade Commission and U.S. Securities and Exchange Commission. Available from U.S. Government Printing Office. • Quarterly. $39.00 per year.

HANDBOOKS AND MANUALS

American Association of Textile Chemists and Colorists Technical Manual. American Association of Textile Chemists and Colorists. • Annual. Members, $75.00; non-members, $117.00.

Fabric Science. Arhtur Price and others. Fairchild Books. • 1999. $52.00. Looseleaf Service. Includes swatch kit.

INTERNET DATABASES

Fedstats. Federal Interagency Council on Statistical Policy. Phone: (202)395-7254 • URL: http://www.fedstats.gov • Web site features an efficient search facility for full-text statistics produced by more than 70 federal agencies, including the Census Bureau, the Bureau of Economic Analysis, and the Bureau of Labor Statistics. Boolean searches can be made within one agency or for all agencies combined. Links are offered to international statistical bureaus, including the UN, IMF, OECD, UNESCO, Eurostat, and 20 individual countries. Fees: Free.

ONLINE DATABASES

Business and Industry. Responsive Database Services, Inc. • Contains online citations, abstracts, and selected fulltext from more than 1,000 trade journals, newspapers, and other publications. Provides general coverage of both manufacturing and service industries, including marketing, production, industry trends, key events, and information on specific companies. Time span is 1994 to date. Daily updates. Inquire as to online cost and availability. (Also available in a CD-ROM version.).

DRI U.S. Central Database. Data Products Division. • Provides more than 23,000 business, financial, demographic, economic, foreign trade, and industry-related time series for the U.S. Includes national income, population, retail-wholesale trade, price indexes, labor data, housing, industrial production, banking, interest rates, money supply, etc. Time period is generally 1947 to date (some data back to 1929). Updating varies. Inquire as to online cost and availability.

Tablebase. Responsive Database Services, Inc. • Provides online numerical tabular data from a wide variety of business, organization, and government sources, including 900 trade journals. Includes industry and individual company statistics relating to products, market share, sales forecasts, production, exports, market trends, etc. Time span is 1997 to date. Weekly updates. Inquire as to online cost and availability. (Also available in a CD-ROM version.).

Textile Technology Digest [online]. Textile Information Center, Institute of Textile Technology.

• Contains indexing and abstracting of more than 300 worldwide journals and monographs in various areas of textile technology, production, and management. Time period is 1978 to date, with monthly updating. Inquire as to online cost and availability.

Textiles Information Treatment Users' Service (TITUS). Institut Textile de France. • Citations and abstracts of the worldwide literature on textiles, 1968 to present. Monthly updates. Inquire as to online cost and availability.

World Textiles. Elsevier Science, Inc. • Provides abstracting and indexing from 1970 of worldwide textile literature (periodicals, books, pamphlets, and reports). Includes U. S., European, and British patent information. Updating is monthly. Inquire as to online cost and availability.

PERIODICALS AND NEWSLETTERS

America's Textiles International. Billian Publishing Inc. • Monthly. $43.00 per year. Formerly *America's Textiles.*

DNR: The Men's Fashion Retail Textile Authority. Fairchild Publications. • Daily. $85.00 per year. Formerly *Daily News Record.*

International Dyer. World Textile Publications Ltd. • Monthly. $120.00 per year.

International Textile Bulletin: Dyeing-Printing-Finishing Edition. ITS Publishing, International Textile Service. • Quarterly. $170.00 per year. Editions in Chinese, English, French, German, Italian and Spanish.

International Textile Bulletin: Nonwovens and Industrial Textiles Edition. ITS Publishing, International Textile Service. • Quarterly. $170.00 per year. Editions in Chinese, English, French, German, Italian and Spanish.

International Textile Bulletin: Yarn and Fabric Forming Edition. ITS Publishing, International Textile Service. • Quarterly. $170.00 per year. Editions in Chinese, English, French, German, Italian and Spanish.

International Textiles: Information and Inspiration. Textile Institute. Benjamin Dent and Co., Ltd. • 10 times a year. $445.00 per year. Text in English, French and German; supplement in Japanese.

LDB Interior Textiles. E.W. Williams Publications Co. • Monthly. $66.00 per year. Supplement available *Linens, Domestics and Baths-Interior Textile Annual Buyer's Guide.* Formerly *Interior Textiles.*

Textile Horizons: Providing Essential Reading for All Present and Future Decision Makers in Textiles and Fashion Worldwide. Textile Institute. Benjamin Dent and Co. Ltd. • Bimonthly. $180.00 per year.

Textile Research Journal. Textile Research Institute. • Monthly. $265.00 per year.

Textile World. Intertec Publishing Corp., Textile Publications. • Monthly. Price on application.

RESEARCH CENTERS AND INSTITUTES

Institute of Textile Technology. 2551 Ivy Rd., Charlottesville, VA 22903-4614. Phone: (804)296-5511 Fax: (804)296-2957 E-mail: library@itt.edu • URL: http://www.itt.edu.

Textiles and Materials. Philadelphia University, Schoolhouse Lane and Henry Ave., Philadelphia, PA 19144. Phone: (215)951-2751 Fax: (215)951-2651 E-mail: brooksteind@philau.edu • URL: http://www.philau.edu • Many research areas, including industrial and nonwoven textiles.

TRI/Princeton. P.O. Box 625, Princeton, NJ 08542. Phone: (609)924-3150 Fax: (609)683-7149 E-mail: info@triprinceton.org • URL: http://www.triprinceton.org.

STATISTICS SOURCES

Annual Survey of Manufactures. Available from U. S. Government Printing Office. • Annual. Prices vary. Issued by the U. S. Census Bureau as an interim update to the *Census of Manufactures.* Includes data on number of manufacturing establishments in various industries, employment, labor costs, value of shipments, capital expenditures, inventories, energy costs, and assets. (See also Census Bureau home page, http://www.census.gov/.).

Broadwoven Fabrics (Gray). U.S. Bureau of the Census. • Quarterly. Provides statistical data on production, value, shipments, and consumption. Includes woolen and worsted fabrics, tire fabrics, cotton broadwoven fabrics, etc. (Current Industrial Reports, MQ-22T.).

Business Statistics of the United States. Courtenay M. Slater, editor. Bernan Associates. • 1999. $74.00. Fifth edition. Based on *Business Statistics,* formerly issue by the Bureau of Economic Analysis, U. S. Department of Commerce. Provides basic data for a wide variety of U. S. industries, services, and economic indicators. Most statistics are shown annually for 29 years and monthly for the most recent four years.

Consumption on the Woolen System and Worsted Combing. U. S. Bureau of the Census. • Quarterly and annual. Provides data on consumption of fibers in woolen and worsted spinning mills, by class of fibers and end use. (Current Industrial Reports, MQ-22D.).

Encyclopedia of American Industries. The Gale Group. • 1998. $560.00. Second edition. Two volumes. $280.00 per volume. Volume one is *Manufacturing Industries* and volume two is *Service and Non-Manufacturing Industries.* Provides the history, development, and recent status of approximately 1,000 industries. Includes statistical graphs, with industry and general indexes.

Manufacturing Profiles. Available from U. S. Government Printing Office. • Annual. Issued by the U. S. Census Bureau. A printed consolidation of the entire *Current Industrial Report* series, presenting "all the data compiled." Contains statistics on production, shipments, inventories, consumption, exports, imports, and orders for a wide variety of manufactured products. (See also Census Bureau home page, http://www.census.gov/.).

Survey of Current Business. Available from U. S. Government Printing Office. • Monthly. $49.00 per year. Issued by Bureau of Economic Analysis, U. S. Department of Commerce. Presents a wide variety of business and economic data.

WEFA Industrial Monitor. John Wiley and Sons, Inc. • Annual. $65.00. Prepared by industry analysts at WEFA, an economic forecasting and consulting firm (originally Wharton Econometric Forecasting Associates). Contains discussions of the outlook for major U. S. industries, with many 10-year forecasts (WEFA Web site is http://www.wefa.com).

TRADE/PROFESSIONAL ASSOCIATIONS

American Association of Textile Chemists and Colorists. P.O. Box 12215, Research Triangle Park, NC 27709-2215. Phone: (919)549-8141 Fax: (919)549-8933 • URL: http://www.aatcc.org.

American Textile Manufacturers Institute. 1130 Connecticut Ave., N.W., Ste. 1200, Washington, DC 20036. Phone: (202)862-0500 Fax: (202)862-0570 • URL: http://www.atmi.org.

Textile Distributors Association. 104 W. 40th St., 18th Fl., New York, NY 10018-3617. 104 W. 40th St., 18th Fl.,.

Textile Institute. Saint James Bldgs., 4th Fl., Oxford St., Manchester M1 6FQ, England. Phone: 44 161 2371188 Fax: 44 161 2361991 E-mail: tiihq@textileinst.org.uk • URL: http://www.texi.org • Members in 100 countries involved with textile industry management, marketing, science, and technology.

OTHER SOURCES

Textile Business Outlook. Statistikon Corp. • Quarterly. $985.00 per year. Analyzes current business, marketing, and financial conditions for the worldwide textile industry (fibers and fabrics). Includes statistical forecasts.

TEXTILE MACHINERY

See also: MACHINERY; TEXTILE INDUSTRY

DIRECTORIES

Davison's Gold Book. Davison Publishing Co. • Annual. $80.00. Textile mill supplies, products, services, equipment and machinery.Formerly *Davison's Textile Buyers.*

RESEARCH CENTERS AND INSTITUTES

Institute of Textile Technology. 2551 Ivy Rd., Charlottesville, VA 22903-4614. Phone: (804)296-5511 Fax: (804)296-2957 E-mail: library@itt.edu • URL: http://www.itt.edu.

STATISTICS SOURCES

U. S. Industry and Trade Outlook: The McGraw-Hill Companies and the U.S. Department of Commerce/ International Trade Administration. Datapso Research Corp. • Annual. $69.95. Produced by the International Trade Administration, U. S. Department of Commerce, in a "public-private" partnership with DRI/McGraw-Hill and Standard & Poor's. Provides basic data, outlook for the current year, and "Long-Term Prospects" (five-year projections) for a wide variety of products and services. Includes high technology industries. Formerly *U. S. Industrial Outlook.*

TRADE/PROFESSIONAL ASSOCIATIONS

American Textile Machinery Association. 111 Park Place, Falls Church, VA 22046. Phone: (703)538-1789 Fax: (703)241-5603 E-mail: atmahq@aol.com • URL: http://www.webmasters.net/atma/.

TEXTILE MILLS

See: TEXTILE INDUSTRY

TEXTILES, HOME

See: LINEN INDUSTRY

TEXTILES, INDUSTRIAL

See: INDUSTRIAL FABRICS INDUSTRY

TEXTILES, NONWOVEN

See: NONWOVEN FABRICS INDUSTRY

THEATER MANAGEMENT

DIRECTORIES

Grey House Performing Arts Directory. Grey House Publishing. • 2001. $220.00. Contains more than 7,700 entries covering dance, instrumental music, vocal music, theatre, performance series, festivals, performance facilities, and media sources.

Peterson's Professional Degree Programs in the Visual and Performing Arts. Peterson's. • Annual.

$24.95. A directory of more than 900 degree programs in art, music, theater, and dance at 600 colleges and professional schools.

Theatrical Index. Theatrical Index Ltd. • Weekly. $300.00 per year. (Lower rates available for biweekly or monthly service.) Lists pre-production theatrical presentations that are seeking investors.

HANDBOOKS AND MANUALS

Handbook for Theatrical Production Managers. Robert S. Telford. Samuel French, Inc. • 1983. $8.95.

Small Theatre Handbook: A Guide to Management and Production. Joann Green. Harvard Common Press. • 1981. $9.95.

PERIODICALS AND NEWSLETTERS

Entertainment Design: The Art and Technology of Show Business. Theatre Crafts International. • 11 times a year. $39.95 per year. Contains material on performing arts management, staging, scenery, costuming, etc. Formerly *TCI - Theatre Crafts International.*

Facility Manager. International Association of Auditorium Managers. • Quarterly. Free to members; non-members, $45.00 per year.

NATO News. National Association of Theatre Owners. • Monthly. $65.00 per year. Newsletter. Highlights industry trends and activities. Formerly *NATO News and Views.*

Theatre Design and Technology. U. S. Institute for Theatre Technology. • Quarterly. $48.00 per year. Covers developments in theatre lighting, sound, scenic design, costuming, and safety.

RESEARCH CENTERS AND INSTITUTES

International Theatre Studies Center. University of Kansas, 339 Murphy Hall, Lawrence, KS 66045. Phone: (913)864-3534 Fax: (913)864-5251 E-mail: atsubaki@falcon.cc.ukans.edu.

Jerome Lawrence and Robert E. Lee Theatre Research Institute. Ohio State University, 1430 Lincoln Tower, 1800 Cannon Dr., Columbus, OH 43210-1230. Phone: (614)292-6614 Fax: (614)688-8417 E-mail: woods1@osu.edu • URL: http://www.lib.ohio-state.edu/osuprofile/triweb.

Martin E. Segal Theatre Center. City University of New York, 33 W. 42nd St., New York, NY 10036. Phone: (212)642-2225 Fax: (212)642-1977 E-mail: casta@email.gc.cuny.edu.

Wisconsin Center for Film and Theater Research. University of Wisconsin-Madison, 816 State St., Madison, WI 53706. Phone: (608)264-6466 Fax: (608)264-6472 E-mail: tbalio@facstaff.wisc.edu • URL: http://www.shsw.wisc.edu/archives/wcftr • Studies the performing arts in America, including theater, cinema, radio, and television.

TRADE/PROFESSIONAL ASSOCIATIONS

Association of Theatrical Press Agents and Managers. 1560 Broadway, Suite 700, New York, NY 10036. Phone: (212)719-3666 Fax: (212)302-1585 E-mail: atpam@erols.com • A labor union for theater managers and press agents.

International Association of Assembly Managers. 4425 W. Airport Freeway, Suite 590, Irving, TX 75062. Phone: 800-935-4226 or (972)255-8020 Fax: (972)255-9582 E-mail: iaam.info@iaam.org • URL: http://www.iaam.org • Members are auditorium, theater, exhibit hall, and other facility managers.

The International Ticketing Association. 250 W. 57th St., Suite 722, New York, NY 10107. Phone: (212)264-0600 Fax: (212)581-0885 E-mail: info@intix.org • URL: http://www.itea.com • Members are box office managers, theater marketing managers, and other entertainment management personnel.

League of American Theatres and Producers. 226 W. 47th St., New York, NY 10036. Phone: (212)764-1122 or (212)703-0200 Fax: (212)719-4389 E-mail: league@broadway.org • URL: http://www.broadway.org • Members are legitimate theater producers and owners and operators of legitimate theaters.

National Association of Theatre Owners. 4605 Lankershim Blvd., Suite 340, North Hollywood, CA 91602. Phone: (818)506-1778 Fax: (818)506-0269 E-mail: nato@chq.com • URL: http://www.hollywood.com/nato.

United States Institute for Theatre Technology. 6443 Ridings Rd., Syracuse, NY 13206-1111. Phone: 800-938-7488 or (315)463-6463 Fax: (315)463-6525 E-mail: info@office.usitt.com • URL: http://www.usitt.com • Members include acousticians, architects, costumers, educators, engineers, lighting designers, and others.

THEATERS, MOTION PICTURE

See: MOTION PICTURE THEATERS

THEFT

See: CRIME AND CRIMINALS; SHOPLIFTING

THESES

See: DISSERTATIONS

THIRD WORLD NATIONS

See: DEVELOPING AREAS

TILE INDUSTRY

DIRECTORIES

Tile and Decorative Surfaces: Directory and Purchasing Guide. Tile and Stone, Inc. • Annual. $12.00. List of over 2,000 manufacturers and distributors of the products and tile setting materials.

FINANCIAL RATIOS

Industry Norms and Key Business Ratios. Desk Top Edition. Dun and Bradstreet Corp., Business Information Services. • Annual. Five volumes. $475.00 per volume. $1,890.00 per set. Covers over 800 kinds of businesses, arranged by Standard Industrial Classification number. More detailed editions covering longer periods of time are also available.

PERIODICALS AND NEWSLETTERS

Tile and Decorative Surfaces: The Voice of America's Tile Market. Tile and Stone, Inc. • Monthly. $50.00 per year.

Tile Design and Installation. Business News Publishing Co. • Quarterly. $55.00 per year. Formerly *Tile World.*

STATISTICS SOURCES

U. S. Industry and Trade Outlook: The McGraw-Hill Companies and the U.S. Department of Commerce/ International Trade Administration. Datapso Research Corp. • Annual. $69.95. Produced by the International Trade Administration, U. S. Department of Commerce, in a "public-private" partnership with DRI/McGraw-Hill and Standard & Poor's. Provides basic data, outlook for the current year, and "Long-Term Prospects" (five-year projections) for a wide variety of products and services. Includes high technology industries. Formerly *U. S. Industrial Outlook.*

TRADE/PROFESSIONAL ASSOCIATIONS

Ceramic Tile Distributors Association. 800 Roosevelt Rd., Bldg. C., Ste. 20, Glen Ellyn, IL 60137. Phone: 800-938-2382 or (630)545-9415 Fax: (630)790-3095 • URL: http://www.ctdahome.org • Members include wholesalers and manufacturers of ceramic tile and related products.

Facing Tile Institute. P.O. Box 8880, Canton, OH 44711. Phone: (330)488-1211 Fax: (330)488-0333 • Members are manufacturers of glazed and unglazed structural facing tile.

Italian Trade Commission. 499 Park Ave., New York, NY 10022. Phone: (212)980-1500 Fax: (212)758-1050 E-mail: newyork@italtrade.com • URL: http://www.italtrade.com • Promotes the use of Italian ceramic tile in the U. S.

National Tile Roofing Manufacturers Association. P.O. Box 40337, Eugene, OR 97404-0049. Phone: (541)689-0366 Fax: (541)689-5530 E-mail: rolson@ntrma.org • URL: http://www.ntrma.org • Members are producers of clay and concrete tile roofing.

Resilient Floor Covering Institute. 401 E. Jefferson St., Ste. 102, Rockville, MD 20805-2617. Phone: (301)340-8580 Fax: (301)340-7283 • Members include manufacturers of solid vinyl tile and vinyl composition tile.

OTHER SOURCES

Ceramic Tile. Available from MarketResearch.com. • 1998. $1295.00. Market research report published by Specialists in Business Information. Presents market data relative to demographics, sales growth, shipments, exports, imports, price trends, and end-use. Includes company profiles.

U. S. Floor Coverings Industry. Available from MarketResearch.com. • 1999. $1,795.00. Market research report published by Specialists in Business Information. Covers carpets, hardwood flooring, and tile. Presents market data relative to demographics, sales growth, shipments, exports, imports, price trends, and end-use. Includes company profiles.

Vinyl Sheet and Floor Tile. Available from MarketResearch.com. • 1997. $495.00. Market research report published by Specialists in Business Information. Presents vinyl flooring market data relative to demographics, sales growth, shipments, exports, imports, price trends, and end-use. Includes company profiles.

TIMBER INDUSTRY

See: LUMBER INDUSTRY

TIME AND MOTION STUDY

ENCYCLOPEDIAS AND DICTIONARIES

Blackwell Encyclopedic Dictionary of Operations Management. Nigel Slack, editor. Blackwell Publishers. • 1997. $105.95. The editor is associated with the University of Warwick, England. Contains definitions of key terms combined with longer articles written by various U. S. and foreign business educators. Includes bibliographies and index. (Blackwell Encyclopedia of Management Series.).

HANDBOOKS AND MANUALS

Motion and Time Study: Design and Management of Work. Ralph M. Barnes. John Wiley and Sons, Inc. • 1980. $103.95. Seventh edition.

Work Simplification: An Analyst's Handbook. Pierre Theriault. Engineering and Management Press. • 1996. $25.00. A basic guide to work simplification as an industrial management technique.

PERIODICALS AND NEWSLETTERS

Work Study. MCB University Press Ltd. • Seven times a year. $3,199.00 per year. Provides information on management services and industrial engineering.

TRADE/PROFESSIONAL ASSOCIATIONS
MTM Association for Standards and Research. 1111 E. Touhy Ave., Des Plaines, IL 60018. Phone: (847)299-1111 Fax: (847)299-3509 E-mail: mtm@mtm.org • URL: http://www.mtm.org.

TIMETABLES

DIRECTORIES
OAG Desktop Flight Guide, North American Edition. OAG Worldwide. • Biweekly. $285.00 per year. Provides detailed airline travel schedules for the U. S., Canada, Mexico, and the Caribbean. Includes aircraft seat charts and airport diagrams. Formerly *Official Airline Guide, North American Edition*.

OAG Flight Guide. OAG Worldwide. • Monthly. $399.00 per year. Provides detailed airline schedules for international travel (travel within North America not included).

OAG Pocket Flight Guide. OAG Worldwide. • Monthly. $96.00 per year. Regional editions available for international areas.

Official Railway Guide. Freight Service Edition. Commonwealth Business Media, Inc. • Bimonthly. $234.00 per year.

Russell's Official National Motor Coach Guide: Official Publications of Bus Lines for the United States and Canada. Russell's Guides, Inc. • Monthly. $100.35 per year. Publications of bus lines for the U.S., Canada, and Mexico.

Thomas Cook Overseas Timetable: Railway, Road and Shipping Services Outside Europe. Thomas Cook Publishing Co. • Bimonthly. $100.00. per year. International railroad passenger schedules. Text in English; summaries in French, German, Italian and Spanish.

TRADE/PROFESSIONAL ASSOCIATIONS
Forum Train Europe. c/o Swiss Federal Railways. Hochschulstrase 6, CH-3030 Berne, Switzerland. Phone: 41 512 201111 Fax: 41 512 202302 • URL: http://www.sbb.ch/.

TIN INDUSTRY

GENERAL WORKS
Tin: Its Production and Marketing. William Robertson. Greenwood Publishing Group, Inc. • 1982. $55.00. (Contributions in Economics and Economic History Series, No. 51).

ABSTRACTS AND INDEXES
IMM Abstracts and Index: A Survey of World Literature on the Economic Geology and Mining of All Minerals (Except Coal), Mineral Processing, and Nonferrous Extraction Metallurgy. Institution of Mining and Metallurgy. • Bimonthly. Members, $142.00 per year; non-members, $215.00 per year. Provides international coverage of the literature of mining and nonferrous metallurgy. Includes mineral economics, tunnelling, and rock mechanics.

ALMANACS AND YEARBOOKS
CRB Commodity Yearbook. Commodity Research Bureau. CRB. • Annual. $99.95.

DIRECTORIES
Dun's Industrial Guide: The Metalworking Directory. Dun and Bradstreet Information Services Dun & Bradstreet Corp. • Annual. Libraries, $485; commercial institutions, $795.00. Lease basis. Three volumes. Lists about 65,000 U. S. manufacturing plants using metal and suppliers of metalworking equipment and materials. Includes names and titles of key personnel. Products, purchases, and processes are indicated.

HANDBOOKS AND MANUALS
Tin. J. W. Price and R. Smith. Springer-Verlag New York, Inc. • 1978. $117.95. (Handbook of Analytical Chemistry Series: Vol. 4, Part 3, Section A,Y).

INTERNET DATABASES
Fedstats. Federal Interagency Council on Statistical Policy. Phone: (202)395-7254 • URL: http://www.fedstats.gov • Web site features an efficient search facility for full-text statistics produced by more than 70 federal agencies, including the Census Bureau, the Bureau of Economic Analysis, and the Bureau of Labor Statistics. Boolean searches can be made within one agency or for all agencies combined. Links are offered to international statistical bureaus, including the UN, IMF, OECD, UNESCO, Eurostat, and 20 individual countries. Fees: Free.

ONLINE DATABASES
DRI U.S. Central Database. Data Products Division. • Provides more than 23,000 business, financial, demographic, economic, foreign trade, and industry-related time series for the U.S. Includes national income, population, retail-wholesale trade, price indexes, labor data, housing, industrial production, banking, interest rates, money supply, etc. Time period is generally 1947 to date (some data back to 1929). Updating varies. Inquire as to online cost and availability.

Globalbase. The Gale Group. • Provides more than one million online summaries of business, industrial, and economic news reports from more than 1,000 publications worldwide. Covers a wide range of material appearing in international trade journals, professional magazines, and newspapers. Time period is 1984 to date, with weekly updates. Inquire as to online cost and availability.

METADEX. Cambridge Scientific Abstracts. • Covers the worldwide literature of metals, metallurgy, and materials science, 1966 to date. Includes detailed alloys indexing from 1974. Biweekly updating. Inquire as to online cost and availability. (Formerly produced by ASM International.).

PERIODICALS AND NEWSLETTERS
The Northern Miner: Devoted to the Mineral Resources Industry of Canada. Southam Magazine Group. • Weekly. $87.00 per year.

Tin International. Tin Magazines Ltd. • Monthly. $215.00 per year. News and analysis for the international tin industry.

PRICE SOURCES
Metals Week. McGraw-Hill Commodity Services Group. • Weekly. $770.00 per year.

STATISTICS SOURCES
Business Statistics of the United States. Courtenay M. Slater, editor. Bernan Associates. • 1999. $74.00. Fifth edition. Based on *Business Statistics*, formerly issue by the Bureau of Economic Analysis, U. S. Department of Commerce. Provides basic data for a wide variety of U. S. industries, services, and economic indicators. Most statistics are shown annually for 29 years and monthly for the most recent four years.

International Tin Council. Quarterly Statistical Bulletin. International Tin Council. • Quarterly. $100.00 per year. Includes eight monthly statistical summaries.

Mineral Commodity Summaries. Available from U. S. Government Printing Office. • Annual. Published by the U. S. Geological Survey, Department of the Interior (http://www.usgs.gov). Contains detailed, five-year data for about 90 nonfuel minerals. Covers a wide range of statistics, including production, imports, exports, consumption, reserves, prices, tariff information, and industry employment. (Two pages are devoted to each mineral.).

Non-Ferrous Metal Data Yearbook. American Bureau of Metal Statistics. • Annual. $395.00. Provides about 200 statistical tables covering many nonferrous metals. Includes production, consumption, inventories, exports, imports, and other data.

Survey of Current Business. Available from U. S. Government Printing Office. • Monthly. $49.00 per year. Issued by Bureau of Economic Analysis, U. S. Department of Commerce. Presents a wide variety of business and economic data.

TRADE/PROFESSIONAL ASSOCIATIONS
American Bureau of Metal Statistics. P.O. Box 805, Chatham, NJ 07928. Phone: (973)701-2299 Fax: (973)701-2152 E-mail: info@abms.com • URL: http://www.abms.com • Members are metal companies. Compiles and publishes detailed statistical data on a wide variety of nonferrous metals: aluminum, copper, gold, lead, nickel, platinum, silver, tin, titanium, uranium, zinc, and others.

TIRE INDUSTRY

See also: RUBBER AND RUBBER GOODS INDUSTRIES

ABSTRACTS AND INDEXES
RAPRA Abstracts. RAPRA Technology Ltd. • Monthly. $2,465.00 per year. Up-to-date survey of current international information relevant to the rubber, plastics and associated industries.

ALMANACS AND YEARBOOKS
Tire and Rim Association Year Book. Tire and Rim Association, Inc. • Annual. $50.00.

DIRECTORIES
Modern Tire Dealer: Facts/Directory. Bill Communications, Inc. • Annual. $30.00. Directories of tire and car service suppliers, tire shop jobbers, and national state associations.

INTERNET DATABASES
Fedstats. Federal Interagency Council on Statistical Policy. Phone: (202)395-7254 • URL: http://www.fedstats.gov • Web site features an efficient search facility for full-text statistics produced by more than 70 federal agencies, including the Census Bureau, the Bureau of Economic Analysis, and the Bureau of Labor Statistics. Boolean searches can be made within one agency or for all agencies combined. Links are offered to international statistical bureaus, including the UN, IMF, OECD, UNESCO, Eurostat, and 20 individual countries. Fees: Free.

ONLINE DATABASES
DRI U.S. Central Database. Data Products Division. • Provides more than 23,000 business, financial, demographic, economic, foreign trade, and industry-related time series for the U.S. Includes national income, population, retail-wholesale trade, price indexes, labor data, housing, industrial production, banking, interest rates, money supply, etc. Time period is generally 1947 to date (some data back to 1929). Updating varies. Inquire as to online cost and availability.

PERIODICALS AND NEWSLETTERS
Dealernews: The Voice of the Powersports Vehicle Industry. Advanstar Communications, Inc. • Monthly. Free to qualified personnel; others, $40.00 per year. News concerning the power sports motor vehicle industry.

Modern Tire Dealer: Covering Tire Sales and Car Service. Bill Communications, Inc. • Monthly. $60.00 per year. Serves independent tire dealers.

Cover automotive service and dealership management topics.

Tire Business. Crain Communications, Inc. • Biweekly. $62.00 per year. Edited for independent tire retailers and wholesalers.

Tire Review: The Authority on Tire Dealer Profitability. Babcox Publications, Inc. • Monthly. $64.00. Includes*LiftGuide, Custom Wheel and Tire Style Guide, Sourcebook and Directory and NTDRA Show.*

STATISTICS SOURCES

Annual Survey of Manufactures. Available from U. S. Government Printing Office. • Annual. Prices vary. Issued by the U. S. Census Bureau as an interim update to the *Census of Manufactures.* Includes data on number of manufacturing establishments in various industries, employment, labor costs, value of shipments, capital expenditures, inventories, energy costs, and assets. (See also Census Bureau home page, http://www.census.gov/.).

Business Statistics of the United States. Courtenay M. Slater, editor. Bernan Associates. • 1999. $74.00. Fifth edition. Based on *Business Statistics*, formerly issue by the Bureau of Economic Analysis, U. S. Department of Commerce. Provides basic data for a wide variety of U. S. industries, services, and economic indicators. Most statistics are shown annually for 29 years and monthly for the most recent four years.

Survey of Current Business. Available from U. S. Government Printing Office. • Monthly. $49.00 per year. Issued by Bureau of Economic Analysis, U. S. Department of Commerce. Presents a wide variety of business and economic data.

TRADE/PROFESSIONAL ASSOCIATIONS

International Tire and Rubber Association. P.O. Box 37203, Louisville, KY 40233-7203. Phone: 800-426-8835 or (502)968-8900 Fax: (502)964-7859 E-mail: itra@itra.com • URL: http://www.itra.com.

Tire and Rim Association. 175 Montrose Ave., W., Copley, OH 44321. Phone: (330)666-8121 Fax: (330)666-8340 E-mail: tireandrim@aol.com.

Tire Association of North America. 11921 Freedom Dr., Suite 550, Reston, VA 20190-5608. Phone: 800-876-8372 or (703)736-8082 Fax: (703)904-4339 E-mail: members@tana.net • URL: http://www.tana.net • Members are tire dealers and retreaders.

Tire Industry Safety Council. P.O. Box 3147, Medina, OH 44258. URL: http://www.tisc.org.

TITANIUM INDUSTRY

See also: METAL INDUSTRY; MINES AND MINERAL RESOURCES

ABSTRACTS AND INDEXES

IMM Abstracts and Index: A Survey of World Literature on the Economic Geology and Mining of All Minerals (Except Coal), Mineral Processing, and Nonferrous Extraction Metallurgy. Institution of Mining and Metallurgy. • Bimonthly. Members, $142.00 per year; non-members, $215.00 per year. Provides international coverage of the literature of mining and nonferrous metallurgy. Includes mineral economics, tunnelling, and rock mechanics.

ALMANACS AND YEARBOOKS

CRB Commodity Yearbook. Commodity Research Bureau. CRB. • Annual. $99.95.

DIRECTORIES

Guide to Products and Services of Member Companies. International Titanium Association. • Annual. Free. Lists about 130 titanium metal industry companies.

International Titanium Association Buyers Guide. International Titanium Association. • Annual. Members, $5.00; non-members, $20.00.

HANDBOOKS AND MANUALS

Materials Properties Handbook: Titanium Alloys. E.W. Collings and others, editors. ASM International. • 1994. $290.00. Covers titanium alloy applications, fabrication, properties, specifications, effects of processing, corrosion, etc.

Titanium: A Technical Guide. Matthew J. Donachie, editor. ASM International. • 2000. Second edition. Provides coverage of all major, technical aspects of titanium and titanium alloys. Price on application.

ONLINE DATABASES

CA Search. Chemical Abstracts Service. • Guide to chemical literature, 1967 to present. Inquire as to online cost and availability.

Globalbase. The Gale Group. • Provides more than one million online summaries of business, industrial, and economic news reports from more than 1,000 publications worldwide. Covers a wide range of material appearing in international trade journals, professional magazines, and newspapers. Time period is 1984 to date, with weekly updates. Inquire as to online cost and availability.

PERIODICALS AND NEWSLETTERS

Light Metal Age. Fellom Publishing Co. • Bimonthly. $40.00 per year. Edited for production and engineering executives of the aluminum industry and other nonferrous light metal industries.

New Steel: Mini and Integrated Mill Management and Technologies. Cahners Business Information. • Monthly. $89.00 per year. Covers the primary metals industry, both ferrous and nonferrous. Includes technical, marketing, and product development articles. Formerly *Iron Age.*

33 Metalproducing: For Primary Producers of Steel, Aluminum, and Copper-Base Alloys. Penton Media, Inc. • Monthly. $65.00 per year. Covers metal production technology and methods and industry news. Includes a bimonthly *Nonferrous Supplement.*

Titanium Newsletter. International Titanium Association. • Quarterly. $42.00 per year. Formerly Titanium Development Association.

Titanium Technology: Present Status and Future Trends. F. H. Froes and others. International Titanium Association. • 1985. $19.95.

PRICE SOURCES

Metals Week. McGraw-Hill Commodity Services Group. • Weekly. $770.00 per year.

STATISTICS SOURCES

Mineral Commodity Summaries. Available from U. S. Government Printing Office. • Annual. Published by the U. S. Geological Survey, Department of the Interior (http://www.usgs.gov). Contains detailed, five-year data for about 90 nonfuel minerals. Covers a wide range of statistics, including production, imports, exports, consumption, reserves, prices, tariff information, and industry employment. (Two pages are devoted to each mineral.).

Non-Ferrous Metal Data Yearbook. American Bureau of Metal Statistics. • Annual. $395.00. Provides about 200 statistical tables covering many nonferrous metals. Includes production, consumption, inventories, exports, imports, and other data.

Titanium: A Statistical Review. International Titanium Association. • Annual. Free to members; non-members, $100.00.

U. S. Industry and Trade Outlook: The McGraw-Hill Companies and the U.S. Department of Commerce/International Trade Administration. Datapso Research Corp. • Annual. $69.95. Produced by the International Trade Administration, U. S. Department of Commerce, in a "public-private" partnership with DRI/McGraw-Hill and Standard & Poor's. Provides basic data, outlook for the current year, and "Long-Term Prospects" (five-year projections) for a wide variety of products and services. Includes high technology industries. Formerly *U. S. Industrial Outlook.*

TRADE/PROFESSIONAL ASSOCIATIONS

American Bureau of Metal Statistics. P.O. Box 805, Chatham, NJ 07928. Phone: (973)701-2299 Fax: (973)701-2152 E-mail: info@abms.com • URL: http://www.abms.com • Members are metal companies. Compiles and publishes detailed statistical data on a wide variety of nonferrous metals: aluminum, copper, gold, lead, nickel, platinum, silver, tin, titanium, uranium, zinc, and others.

International Titanium Association. 350 Interlocken Blvd., Suite 390, Broomfield, CO 80021-3485. Phone: (303)404-2221 Fax: (303)404-9111 E-mail: info@titanium.org • URL: http://www.titanium.org • Members are producers, fabricators, and users of titanium and titanium alloys.

TITLE INSURANCE

ENCYCLOPEDIAS AND DICTIONARIES

Title Insurance and Real Estate Securities Terminology. Real Estate Publishing Co. • 1980. $6.95.

HANDBOOKS AND MANUALS

Clearing Land Titles. West Publishing Co., College and School Div. • Second edition. Price on application.

PERIODICALS AND NEWSLETTERS

Capital Comment. American Land Title Association. • Monthly. Price application.

Title News. American Land Title Association. • Bimonthly. $48.00 per year.

TRADE/PROFESSIONAL ASSOCIATIONS

American Land Title Association - Sections: Abstractors and Title Insurance AgenTitle Insurance and Underwriters. 1828 L St., N.W., Suite 705, Washington, DC 20036. Phone: 800-787-2582 or (202)296-3671 Fax: (202)223-5843 E-mail: service@alta.org • URL: http://www.alta.org.

TITLES OF DEGREES

See: ACADEMIC DEGREES

TOASTS

See also: PUBLIC SPEAKING

DIRECTORIES

Roster of Clubs. International Training in Communication. • Annual. Price on application.

Toastmasters International Club Directory. Toastmasters International. • Annual. Price on application. Lists toastmasters clubs across the world.

PERIODICALS AND NEWSLETTERS

The Toastmaster: For Better Listening, Thinking, Speaking. Suzanne Frey, editor. Toastmasters International. • Monthly. Membership. Provides information and "how-to" articles on communication and leadership.

TRADE/PROFESSIONAL ASSOCIATIONS

International Training in Communication. 2519 Woodland Dr., Anaheim, CA 92801. Phone:

(714)995-3660 Fax: (714)995-6974 E-mail: itcintl@itcintl.org • URL: http://www.itcintl.org.

Toastmasters International. P.O. Box 9052, Mission Viejo, CA 92690. Phone: (949)858-8255 Fax: (949)858-1207 E-mail: tminfo@toastmasters.org • URL: http://www.toastmasters.org.

TOBACCO AND TOBACCO INDUSTRY

See also: CIGAR AND CIGARETTE INDUSTRY; SMOKING POLICY

ABSTRACTS AND INDEXES

Tobacco Abstracts: World Literature on Nicotiana. Tobacco Literature Service. • Bimonthly. $39.50 per year.

ALMANACS AND YEARBOOKS

Tobacco Retailers Almanac. Retail Tobacco Dealers of America. • Annual. Price on application.

Tobacco Science Yearbook. Lockwood Trade Journal Co., Inc. • Annual. $26.00.

BIBLIOGRAPHIES

Smoking: The Health Consequences of Tobacco Use. Cecilia M. Schmitz and Richard A. Gray. Pierian Press. • 1995. $30.00. (Science and Social Responsibility Series).

CD-ROM DATABASES

World Marketing Forecasts on CD-ROM. The Gale Group. • Annual. $2,500.00. Produced by Euromonitor. Provides detailed forecast data for the years to 2012 on CD-ROM for 54 countries in all parts of the world. Covers a wide range of social, demographic, economic, and market factors. Includes specific forecasts for many kinds of consumer products.

DIRECTORIES

Tobacco International Buyers' Guide and Directory. Lockwood Trade Journal Co., Inc. • Annual. $40.00. Formerly*Tobacco Internatonal Directory and Buyers' Guide.*

United States Distribution Journal-Source Book. Bill Communications. • Annual. $95.00. Formerly *United States Distribution Journal Buyers Guide.*

ENCYCLOPEDIAS AND DICTIONARIES

Encyclopedia of Smoking and Tobacco. Arlene B. Hirschfelder. Oryx Press. • 1999. $65.00. Includes information on the economics of the tobacco industry, health issues, tobacco history, advertising, legal issues, government subsidies, etc. Provides illustrations, charts, and statistical data.

FINANCIAL RATIOS

Almanac of Business and Industrial Financial Ratios. Leo Troy. Prentice Hall. • Annual. $99.95. Contains financial ratios derived from federal tax returns. Ratios for each of about 200 industries are arranged according to company asset size.

Quarterly Financial Report for Manufacturing, Mining, and Trade Corporations. U.S. Federal Trade Commission and U.S. Securities and Exchange Commission. Available from U.S. Government Printing Office. • Quarterly. $39.00 per year.

INTERNET DATABASES

Fedstats. Federal Interagency Council on Statistical Policy. Phone: (202)395-7254 • URL: http://www.fedstats.gov • Web site features an efficient search facility for full-text statistics produced by more than 70 federal agencies, including the Census Bureau, the Bureau of Economic Analysis, and the Bureau of Labor Statistics. Boolean searches can be made within one agency or for all agencies combined. Links are offered to international statistical bureaus, including the UN, IMF, OECD, UNESCO, Eurostat, and 20 individual countries. Fees: Free.

USDA. United States Department of Agriculture. Phone: (202)720-2791 E-mail: agsec@usda.gov • URL: http://www.usda.gov • The USDA home page has six sections: News and Information; What's New; About USDA; Agencies; Opportunities; Search and Help. Keyword searching is offered from the USDA home page and from various individual agency home pages. Agencies are the Economic Research Service, Agricultural Marketing Service, National Agricultural Statistics Service, National Agricultural Library, and about 12 others. Updating varies. Fees: Free.

ONLINE DATABASES

DRI U.S. Central Database. Data Products Division. • Provides more than 23,000 business, financial, demographic, economic, foreign trade, and industry-related time series for the U.S. Includes national income, population, retail-wholesale trade, price indexes, labor data, housing, industrial production, banking, interest rates, money supply, etc. Time period is generally 1947 to date (some data back to 1929). Updating varies. Inquire as to online cost and availability.

Euromonitor Market Research. Euromonitor International. • Provides the complete text online of Euromonitor market analysis reports. Covers consumer goods market research data for all major countries, with emphasis on specific product categories. Time period is current. Continuous updating. Inquire as to online cost and availability.

PERIODICALS AND NEWSLETTERS

Bureau of Alcohol, Tobacco, and Firearms Quarterly Bulletin. Bureau of Alcohol, Tobacco, and Firearms, U.S. Department of the Treasury. Available from U.S. Government Printing Office. • Quarterly. $18.00 per year. Laws and regulations.

Smokeshop. Lockwood Publications. • Bimonthly. $32.00 per year.

Tobacco Barometer: Cigars, Cigarettes. Tobacco Merchants Association of the United States, Inc. • Monthly. Free. Guide to manufactured production, taxable removals, and tax-exempt removals for cigarettes, large cigars, little cigars, chewing tobacco, snuff, and pipe tobacco.

Tobacco International. Lockwood Trade Journal Co., Inc. • Weekly. $32.00 per year.

Tobacco Reporter: Devoted to All Segments of the International Tobacco Trade Processing, Trading, Manufacturing. SpecComm International, Inc. • Monthly. $36.00 per year. Two supplements. Formerly *TR: Tobacco Reporter.*

World Tobacco. DMG World Media. • Six times a year. $230.00 per year.

RESEARCH CENTERS AND INSTITUTES

Tobacco and Health Research Institute. University of Kentucky. Cooper and University Drives, Lexington, KY 40546. Phone: (606)257-5798 Fax: (606)323-1077 E-mail: mdavies@pop.uky.edu • URL: http://www.uky.edu/~thri/homeweb.html.

STATISTICS SOURCES

Agricultural Statistics. Available from U. S. Government Printing Office. • Annual. Produced by the National Agricultural Statistics Service, U. S. Department of Agriculture. Provides a wide variety of statistical data relating to agricultural production, supplies, consumption, prices/price-supports, foreign trade, costs, and returns, as well as farm labor, loans, income, and population. In many cases, historical data is shown annually for 10 years. In addition to farm data, includes detailed fishery statistics.

Annual Survey of Manufactures. Available from U. S. Government Printing Office. • Annual. Prices vary. Issued by the U. S. Census Bureau as an interim update to the *Census of Manufactures.* Includes data on number of manufacturing establishments in various industries, employment, labor costs, value of shipments, capital expenditures, inventories, energy costs, and assets. (See also Census Bureau home page, http://www.census.gov/.).

Business Statistics of the United States. Courtenay M. Slater, editor. Bernan Associates. • 1999. $74.00. Fifth edition. Based on *Business Statistics*, formerly issue by the Bureau of Economic Analysis, U. S. Department of Commerce. Provides basic data for a wide variety of U. S. industries, services, and economic indicators. Most statistics are shown annually for 29 years and monthly for the most recent four years.

Consumer Canada 1996. Available from The Gale Group. • 1996. $750.00. Published by Euromonitor. Provides consumer market, socioeconomic, and demographic data for Canada. Includes consumer market size (volume and value) for many specific kinds of products.

Consumer International 2000/2001. Available from The Gale Group. • 1998. $1,190.00. Seventh edition. Published by Euromonitor. Contains extensive consumer market, economic, and demographic data for 27 major, non-European countries, including the U. S. and Canada. Includes consumer market size (volume and value) for 150 product types in 14 categories (food, clothing, automobiles, cosmetics, appliances, etc.).

European Marketing Forecasts 2001. Available from The Gale Group. • 2000. $1,190.00. Third edition. Published by Euromonitor. Contains demographic, economic, and market forecasts for the countries of Europe to the year 2010. Forecasts include market-size data for 15 consumer product sectors (food, clothing, automobiles, consumer electronics, etc.).

International Marketing Forecasts 2001. Available from The Gale Group. • 2000. $1,090.00. Third edition. Published by Euromonitor. Contains demographic, economic, and market forecasts to the year 2010 for major, non-European countries, including the U. S. and Canada. Forecasts include market-size data for 15 consumer product sectors, such as food, clothing, and automobiles.

Monthly Statistical Release: Tobacco Products. U.S. Bureau of Alcohol, Tobacco, and Firearms. • Monthly.

Standard & Poor's Industry Surveys. Standard & Poor's. • Semiannual. $1,800.00. Two looseleaf volumes. Includes monthly supplements. Provides detailed, individual surveys of 52 major industry groups. Each survey is revised on a semiannual basis. Also includes "Monthly Investment Review" (industry group investment analysis) and monthly "Trends & Projections" (economic analysis).

Statistics on Alcohol, Drug, and Tobacco Use: A Selection of Statistical Charts, Graphs and Tables about Alcohol, Drug and Tobacco Use from a Variety of Published Sources with Explanatory Comments. The Gale Group. • 1995. $65.00. Includes graphs, charts, and tables arranged within subject chapters. Citations to data sources are provided.

Survey of Current Business. Available from U. S. Government Printing Office. • Monthly. $49.00 per year. Issued by Bureau of Economic Analysis, U. S. Department of Commerce. Presents a wide variety of business and economic data.

Tobacco Situation and Outlook. Available from U. S. Government Printing Office. • Three times per year. $11.00 per year. Issued by the Economic Research Service of the U. S. Department of Agriculture. Provides current statistical information on supply, demand, and prices.

WEFA Industrial Monitor. John Wiley and Sons, Inc. • Annual. $65.00. Prepared by industry analysts at WEFA, an economic forecasting and consulting firm (originally Wharton Econometric Forecasting Associates). Contains discussions of the outlook for major U. S. industries, with many 10-year forecasts (WEFA Web site is http://www.wefa.com).

TRADE/PROFESSIONAL ASSOCIATIONS

American Wholesale Marketers Association. 1128 16th St., Washington, DC 20036. Phone: 800-482-2962 or (202)463-2124 Fax: (202)463-6456 E-mail: davids@awmanet.org • URL: http://www.awmanet.org.

Retail Tobacco Dealers of America. 12 Galloway Ave., Ste. 1B, Cockeysville, MD 21030. Phone: (410)628-1674 Fax: (410)628-1679 E-mail: rtda@msn.com • URL: http://www.rtda.org.

Tobacco Associates. 1725 K St., N.W., Suite 512, Washington, DC 20006. Phone: (202)828-9144 Fax: (202)828-9149.

Tobacco Association of the U.S. 3716 National Dr., Suite 114, Raleigh, NC 27612. Phone: (919)782-5151 Fax: (919)781-0915.

Tobacco Merchants Association. 231 Clarksville Rd., Lawrence, NJ 08648. Phone: (609)275-4900 Fax: (609)275-8379 E-mail: tma@tma.org.

OTHER SOURCES

Tobacco Industry Litigation Reporter: The National Journal of Record of Litigation Affecting the Tobacco Industry. Andrews Publications. • Monthly. $725.00 per year. Reports on major lawsuits brought against tobacco companies.

TOILETRIES

See: COSMETICS INDUSTRY; PERFUME INDUSTRY

TOLL ROADS

See also: ROADS AND HIGHWAYS

BIBLIOGRAPHIES

Road Construction and Safety. Available from U. S. Government Printing Office. • Annual. Free. Issued by the Superintendent of Documents. A list of government publications on highway construction and traffic safety. Formerly *Highway Construction, Safety and Traffic*. (Subject Bibliography No. 3.).

ENCYCLOPEDIAS AND DICTIONARIES

Macmillan Encyclopedia of Transportation. Available from The Gale Group. • 2000. $375.00. Six volumes. Published by Macmillan Reference USA. Covers the business, technology, and history of transportation on land, on water, in the air, and in space. Includes definitions, cross-references, and 200 color illustrations.

ONLINE DATABASES

TRIS: Transportation Research Information Service. National Research Council. • Contains abstracts and citations to a wide range of transportation literature, 1968 to present, with monthly updates. Includes references to the literature of air transportation, highways, ships and shipping, railroads, trucking, and urban mass transportation. Formerly *TRIS-ON-LINE.* Inquire as to online cost and availability.

PERIODICALS AND NEWSLETTERS

Tollways. International Bridge, Tunnel and Turnpike Association. • Monthly. Membership. Newsletter.

STATISTICS SOURCES

Highway Statistics. Federal Highway Administration, U.S. Department of Transportation. Available from U.S. Government Printing Office. • Annual. $26.00.

Transportation Statistics Annual Report. Available from U. S. Government Printing Office. • Annual. $21.00. Issued by the U. S. Bureau of Transportation Statistics, Transportation Department (http://www.bts.gov). Summarizes national data for various forms of transportation, including airlines, railroads, and motor vehicles. Information on the use of roads and highways is included.

TRADE/PROFESSIONAL ASSOCIATIONS

International Bridge, Tunnel and Turnpike Association. 2120 L St., N.W., Suite 305, Washington, DC 20037-1527. Phone: (202)659-4620 Fax: (202)659-0500 E-mail: ibtta@ibtta.org • URL: http://www.ibtta.org.

TOMATO INDUSTRY

See also: VEGETABLE INDUSTRY

CD-ROM DATABASES

Food Science and Technology Abstracts [CD-ROM]. Available from SilverPlatter Information, Inc. • Quarterly. $3,700 per year. Produced by International Food Information Service (home page is http://www.ifis.org). Provides worldwide coverage on CD-ROM of the literature of food technology and production. Various types of publications are indexed, with abstracts, including about 1,800 periodicals. Time period is 1969 to date.

INTERNET DATABASES

USDA. United States Department of Agriculture. Phone: (202)720-2791 E-mail: agsec@usda.gov • URL: http://www.usda.gov • The USDA home page has six sections: News and Information; What's New; About USDA; Agencies; Opportunities; Search and Help. Keyword searching is offered from the USDA home page and from various individual agency home pages. Agencies are the Economic Research Service, Agricultural Marketing Service, National Agricultural Statistics Service, National Agricultural Library, and about 12 others. Updating varies. Fees: Free.

ONLINE DATABASES

Food Science and Technology Abstracts [online]. IFIS North American Desk. • Produced by International Food Information Service. Provides about 500,000 online citations, with abstracts, to the international literature of food science, technology, commodities, engineering, and processing. Approximately 2,000 periodicals are covered. Time period is 1969 to date, with monthly updates. Inquire as to online cost and availability.

STATISTICS SOURCES

Agricultural Statistics. Available from U. S. Government Printing Office. • Annual. Produced by the National Agricultural Statistics Service, U. S. Department of Agriculture. Provides a wide variety of statistical data relating to agricultural production, supplies, consumption, prices/price-supports, foreign trade, costs, and returns, as well as farm labor, loans, income, and population. In many cases, historical data is shown annually for 10 years. In addition to farm data, includes detailed fishery statistics.

Vegetables and Specialties Situation and Outlook. Available from U. S. Government Printing Office. • Three times a year. $15.00 per year. Issued by the Economic Research Service of the U. S. Department of Agriculture. Provides current statistical information on supply, demand, and prices.

OTHER SOURCES

Major Food and Drink Companies of the World. Available from The Gale Group. • 2001. $855.00. Fourth edition. Two volumes. Published by Graham & Whiteside. Contains profiles and trade names for more than 9,000 important food and beverage companies in various countries. In addition to foods, includes both alcoholic and nonalcoholic drink products.

Thomas Food and Beverage Market Place. Grey House Publishing. • Annual. $295.00. Three volumes. Contains more than 40,000 entries covering food companies, beverages, food equipment, warehouse companies, food brokers, wholesalers, importers, and exporters. Formerly *Thomas Food Industry Register.*

TOOL INDUSTRY

See also: HARDWARE INDUSTRY; MACHINE TOOL INDUSTRY; POWER TOOL INDUSTRY

ABSTRACTS AND INDEXES

Engineering Index Monthly: Abstracting and Indexing Services Covering Sources of the World's Engineering Literature. Engineering Information, Inc. • Monthly. $2,300.00 per year. Provides indexing and abstracting of the world's engineering and technical literature.

Mechanical Engineering Abstracts. Cambridge Information Group. • Bimonthly. $975.00 per year. Formerly *ISMEC - Mechanical Engineering Abstracts.*

CD-ROM DATABASES

COMPENDEX PLUS [CD-ROM]. Engineering Information, Inc. • Quarterly. $3,450.00 per year. Provides CD-ROM indexing and abstracting of the world's engineering and technical information appearing in journals, reports, books, and proceedings, 1985 to date.

DIRECTORIES

Dun's Industrial Guide: The Metalworking Directory. Dun and Bradstreet Information Services Dun & Bradstreet Corp. • Annual. Libraries, $485; commercial institutions, $795.00. Lease basis. Three volumes. Lists about 65,000 U. S. manufacturing plants using metal and suppliers of metalworking equipment and materials. Includes names and titles of key personnel. Products, purchases, and processes are indicated.

Thomas Register of American Manufacturers and Thomas Register Catalog File. Thomas Publishing Co., Inc. • Annual. $149.00. 34 volumes. A three-part system offering information on a wide variety of industrial equipment and supplies.

ONLINE DATABASES

COMPENDEX PLUS. Engineering Information, Inc. • Provides online indexing and abstracting of the world's engineering and technical information appearing in journals, reports, books, and proceedings. Time period is 1970 to date, with weekly updates. Inquire as to online cost and availability.

Hard Sciences. Cambridge Scientific Abstracts. • Provides the online version of *Computer and Information Systems Abstracts, Electronics and Communications Abstracts, Health and Safety Science Abstracts, ISMEC: Mechanical Engineering Abstracts (Information Service in Mechanical Engineering)* and *Solid State and Superconductivity Abstracts.* Time period is 1981 to date, with monthly updates. Inquire as to online cost and availability.

Thomas Register Online. Thomas Publishing Co., Inc. • Provides concise information on approximately 194,000 U. S. companies, mainly manufacturers, with over 50,000 product classifications. Indexes over 115,000 trade names. Information is updated semiannually. Inquire as to online cost and availability.

PERIODICALS AND NEWSLETTERS

American Tool, Die and Stamping News. Eagle Publications, Inc. • Bimonthly. Controlled circulation.

Cutting Tool Engineering. CTE Publications, Inc. • Nine times a year. $30.00 per year.

Die Casting Engineer. North American Die Casting Association. • Bimonthly. Free to members; non-members, $55.00 per year.

STATISTICS SOURCES

U. S. Industry and Trade Outlook: The McGraw-Hill Companies and the U.S. Department of Commerce/ International Trade Administration. Datapso Research Corp. • Annual. $69.95. Produced by the International Trade Administration, U. S. Department of Commerce, in a "public-private" partnership with DRI/McGraw-Hill and Standard & Poor's. Provides basic data, outlook for the current year, and "Long-Term Prospects" (five-year projections) for a wide variety of products and services. Includes high technology industries. Formerly *U. S. Industrial Outlook.*

TRADE/PROFESSIONAL ASSOCIATIONS

National Tooling and Machining Association. 9300 Livingston Rd., Fort Washington, MD 20744. Phone: 800-248-6862 or (301)248-6200 Fax: (301)248-7104 • URL: http://www.ntma.org.

North American Die Casting Association. 9701 W. Higgins Rd., Suite 880, Rosemont, IL 60018. Phone: (847)292-3600 Fax: (847)292-3620.

TOOLS, POWER

See: POWER TOOL INDUSTRY

TOTAL QUALITY MANAGEMENT (TQM)

See also: QUALITY CONTROL

GENERAL WORKS

Cases in Total Quality Management. Jay H. Heizer. Course Technology, Inc. • 1997. $45.95. (GC Principles in Management Series.).

Managing Quality in America's Most Admired Companies. Jay W. Spechler. Engineering and Management Press. • 1993. $49.95. Part one provides "Guidelines for Implementing Quality Management," including detailed information on the Malcolm Baldridge National Quality Award. Part two contains 30 "Case Studies of Quality Management in Leading Companies.".

Principles and Practices of TQM. Thomas J. Cartin. American Society for Quality. • 1993. $28.00.

Putting Total Quality Management to Work: What TQM Means, How to Use It, and How to Sustain It Over the Long Run. Marshall Sashkin and Kenneth J. Kiser. Berrett-Koehler Publications, Inc. • 1993. $19.95. Includes control charts, flow charts, scatter diagrams, and criteria for the Baldridge Quality Award.

Quality Movement: What Total Quality Management is All About. Helga Drummond. Nichols Publishing Co. • 1992. $14.95.

Taking the Mystery Out of TQM: A Practical Guide to Total Quality Management. Peter Capezio and Debra Morehouse. Career Press, Inc. • 1995. $16.99. Second edition. A step-by-step guide for managers, executives, and entrepreneurs.

Total Quality Management in Action. Gopal K. Kanji. Chapman and Hall. • 1996. $129.95.

TQM: Leadership for the Quality Transformation. Richard S. Johnson. American Society for Quality. • 1993. $37.95. Covers leadership styles and the creation of a quality environment. *Johnson TQM Series: volume one.*

ABSTRACTS AND INDEXES

Business Periodicals Index. H. W. Wilson Co. • Monthly, except August, with quarterly and annual cumulations. Service basis for print edition; CD-ROM edition, $1,495.00 per year.

CD-ROM DATABASES

ABI/INFORM Global. Bell & Howell Information and Learning. • Monthly. $6,500.00 per year. Provides CD-ROM indexing and abstracting of worldwide business literature appearing in over 1,200 periodicals for the most recent five years. Archival discs are available from 1971. Formerly *ABI/INFORM OnDisc.*

WILSONDISC: Wilson Business Abstracts. H. W. Wilson Co. • Monthly. $2,495.00 per year, including unlimited online access to *Wilson Business Abstracts* through WILSONLINE. Provides CD-ROM "cover-to-cover" abstracting and indexing of over 600 prominent business periodicals. Indexing is from 1982, abstracting from 1990. (*Business Periodicals Index* without abstracts is available on CD-ROM at $1,495 per year.).

DIRECTORIES

Quality Progress: QA/QC Services Directory. American Society for Quality. • Annual. $12.00. Provides information on companies offering services related to quality management, such as consulting, inspection, auditing, calibrating, and training.

Quality Progress: Quality Assurance and Quality Control Software Directory. American Society for Quality. • Annual. Price on application. Covers computer software application packages related to quality management. Includes information about software companies and descriptions of programs offered. Formerly *Quality Progress Directory of Software for Quality Assurance and Quality Contol.*

HANDBOOKS AND MANUALS

Industry's Guide to ISO 9000. Adedeji B. Badiru. John Wiley and Sons, Inc. • 1995. $99.00. (Engineering and Technology Management Series).

International Standards Desk Reference: Your Passport to World Markets. Amy Zuckerman. AMACOM. • 1996. $35.00. Provides information on standards important in export-import trade, such as ISO 9000.

ISO 9000: Achieving Compliance and Certification. Maureen A. Dalfonso. John Wiley and Sons, Inc. • 1996. $155.00.

ISO 9000 and the Service Sector. James L. Lamprecht. American Society for Quality. • 1994. $38.00. A review of the ISO 9000 quality standards as they relate to service organizations. Includes examples of applications.

ISO 9000 Auditor's Companion. Kent A. Keeney and Joseph J. Tsiakals. American Society for Quality. • 1994. $30.00. Designed to help companies prepare for ISO 9000 quality management audits.

ISO 9000 Book: A Global Competitor's Guide to Compliance and Certification. John T. Rabbitt and Peter Bergh. AMACOM. • 1994. $26.95. Second edition.

ISO 9000 Handbook. Robert W. Peach, editor. McGraw-Hill Professional. • 1996. $80.00. Third edition. Includes detailed information for the ISO 9000 registration process.

ISO 9000 Made Easy: A Cost-Saving Guide to Documentation and Registration. Amy Zuckerman. AMACOM. • 1994. $75.00.

Production and Operations Management: Total Quality and Responsiveness. Hamid Noori and Russell Radford. McGraw-Hill. • 1994. $70.25.

Quality Manager's Complete Guide to ISO 9000. Richard B. Clements. Prentice Hall. • 1996. $39.95. Third edition.

Quality Manager's Complete Guide to ISO 9000: 2000 Edition. Richard B. Clements. Prentice Hall. • 2000. $39.95. Supplement to *Quality Manager's Complete Guide to ISO 9000* (third edition).

Teambuilding and Total Quality: A Guidebook to TQM Success. Gene Milas. Engineering and Management Press. • 1997. $29.95. A practical, how-to-do-it guide to total quality management in industry. The importance of employee involvement is stressed.

Total Quality Management Handbook. John L. Hradesky. McGraw-Hill. • 1994. $74.50.

TQM: Management Processes for Quality Operations. Richard S. Johnson. American Society for Quality. • 1993. $45.00. Topics include management systems, planning, hiring, performance management, procedure manuals, and time managment. ASQC Total Quality Control Management Series: volume. 12.

TQM: Quality Training Practices. Richard S. Johnson. American Society for Quality. • 1993. $45.00. An industrial quality training manual, with samples of checklists, charts, surveys, comparisons, and questionnaires. (Johnson TQM Series: volume 4.).

ONLINE DATABASES

ABI/INFORM. Bell & Howell Information and Learning. • Provides online indexing to business-related material occurring in over 1,000 periodicals from 1971 to the present. Inquire as to online cost and availability.

Management Contents. The Gale Group. • Covers a wide range of management, financial, marketing, personnel, and administrative topics. About 150 leading business journals are indexed and abstracted from 1974 to date, with monthly updating. Inquire as to online cost and availability.

Trade & Industry Index. The Gale Group. • Provides indexing of business periodicals, January 1981 to date. Daily updates. (Full text articles from some periodicals are available online, 1983 to date, in the companion database, *Trade & Industry ASAP.*) Inquire as to online cost and availability.

Wilson Business Abstracts Online. H. W. Wilson Co. • Indexes and abstracts 600 major business periodicals, plus the *Wall Street Journal* and the business section of the *New York Times.* Indexing is from 1982, abstracting from 1990, with the two newspapers included from 1993. Updated weekly. Inquire as to online cost and availability. (*Business Periodicals Index* without abstracts is also available online.).

PERIODICALS AND NEWSLETTERS

ISO 9000 and ISO 14000 News (International Organization for Standardization). Available from American National Standards Institute. • Bimonthly. Price on application. Newsletter on quality standards. Published by the International Organization for Standardization (ISO). Text in English. Formerly *ISO 9000 News.*

Lakewood Report on Positive Employee Practices. Lakewood Publications, Inc. • Monthly. $128.00 per year. Newsletter. Provides news for quality improvement managers. Includes columns entitled "Eye on Quality" and "Quality Movement News." Formerly *Total Quality*.

Quality Management. Bureau of Business Practice, Inc. • Semimonthly. $167.00 per year. Newsletter. Covers news of quality management issues and trends. Formerly *Quality Assurance Bulletin*.

Quality Management Journal. American Society for Quality. • Quarterly. Members, $50.00 per year; non-members, $60.00 per year. Emphasizes research in quality control and management.

Quality Progress. American Society for Quality. • Monthly. $50.00 per year. Covers developments in quality improvement throughout the world.

RESEARCH CENTERS AND INSTITUTES

Center for Quality and Productivity. University of North Texas, College of Business Administration, Denton, TX 76203-3677. Phone: (940)565-4767 E-mail: prybutok@unt.edu • URL: http://www.coba.unt.edu:80/bcis.organize/cqp/cqp.htm • Fields of research include the management of quality systems and statistical methodology.

Center for Quality and Productivity Improvement. University of Wisconsin-Madison, 610 N. Walnut St., 575 WARF Bldg., Madison, WI 53705. Phone: (608)263-2520 Fax: (608)263-1425 E-mail: quality@engr.wisc.edu • URL: http://www.engr.wisc.edu/centers/cqpi • Research areas include quality management and industrial engineering.

TRADE/PROFESSIONAL ASSOCIATIONS

American Society for Quality. P.O. Box 3005, Milwaukee, WI 53201-3005. Phone: 800-248-1946 or (414)272-8575 Fax: (414)272-1734 E-mail: cs@asq.org • URL: http://www.asq.org.

International Organization for Standardization. One, rue de Varembe, CH-1211 Geneva 20, Switzerland. E-mail: central@iso.ch • URL: http://www.iso.ch/ • Members are national standards organizations. Develops and publishes international standards, including ISO 9000 quality management standards.

TOURIST INDUSTRY

See: TRAVEL INDUSTRY

TOWN GOVERNMENT

See: MUNICIPAL GOVERNMENT

TOWN PLANNING

See: CITY PLANNING

TOWNS AND CITIES

See: CITIES AND TOWNS

TOXIC SUBSTANCES

See: HAZARDOUS MATERIALS

TOXICOLOGY, INDUSTRIAL

See: INDUSTRIAL HYGIENE

TOY INDUSTRY

CD-ROM DATABASES

World Marketing Forecasts on CD-ROM. The Gale Group. • Annual. $2,500.00. Produced by Euromonitor. Provides detailed forecast data for the years to 2012 on CD-ROM for 54 countries in all parts of the world. Covers a wide range of social, demographic, economic, and market factors. Includes specific forecasts for many kinds of consumer products.

DIRECTORIES

Directory of Discount and General Merchandise Stores. Chain Store Guide. • Annual. $300.00. Includes retailers and wholesalers of housewares, giftwares, novelties, toys, hobby materials, crafts, and stationery. Formerly *Directory of Discount Stores Catalog Showrooms*.

Playthings Buyers Guide. Geyer-McAllister Publications, Inc. • Annual. Included in subscription to *Playthings*. Lists of toy manufacturers and their suppliers, designers and inventors, manufacturers' representatives, licensor, importers. Formerly *Playthings. Who Makes It*.

FINANCIAL RATIOS

Annual Statement Studies. Robert Morris Associates: The Association of Lending and Credit Risk Professiona. • Annual. Free to members; non-members, $140.00. Median and quartile financial ratios are given for over 400 kinds of manufacturing, wholesale, retail, construction, and consumer finance establishments. Data is sorted by both asset size and sales volume. Includes a clearly written "Definition of Ratios" and an alphabetical industry index.

ONLINE DATABASES

Euromonitor Market Research. Euromonitor International. • Provides the complete text online of Euromonitor market analysis reports. Covers consumer goods market research data for all major countries, with emphasis on specific product categories. Time period is current. Continuous updating. Inquire as to online cost and availability.

PERIODICALS AND NEWSLETTERS

Playthings: For Today's Merchandiser of Toys, Hobbies and Crafts. Frank Reysen, editor. Cahners Business Newspapers. • Monthly. $32.00 per year. Covers the major toy and hobby categories, industry news and news products.

STATISTICS SOURCES

Annual Survey of Manufactures. Available from U. S. Government Printing Office. • Annual. Prices vary. Issued by the U. S. Census Bureau as an interim update to the *Census of Manufactures*. Includes data on number of manufacturing establishments in various industries, employment, labor costs, value of shipments, capital expenditures, inventories, energy costs, and assets. (See also Census Bureau home page, http://www.census.gov/.).

Consumer Canada 1996. Available from The Gale Group. • 1996. $750.00. Published by Euromonitor. Provides consumer market, socioeconomic, and demographic data for Canada. Includes consumer market size (volume and value) for many specific kinds of products.

Consumer International 2000/2001. Available from The Gale Group. • 1998. $1,190.00. Seventh edition. Published by Euromonitor. Contains extensive consumer market, economic, and demographic data for 27 major, non-European countries, including the U. S. and Canada. Includes consumer market size (volume and value) for 150 product types in 14 categories (food, clothing, automobiles, cosmetics, appliances, etc.).

European Marketing Forecasts 2001. Available from The Gale Group. • 2000. $1,190.00. Third edition. Published by Euromonitor. Contains demographic, economic, and market forecasts for the countries of Europe to the year 2010. Forecasts include market-size data for 15 consumer product sectors (food, clothing, automobiles, consumer electronics, etc.).

International Marketing Forecasts 2001. Available from The Gale Group. • 2000. $1,090.00. Third edition. Published by Euromonitor. Contains demographic, economic, and market forecasts to the year 2010 for major, non-European countries, including the U. S. and Canada. Forecasts include market-size data for 15 consumer product sectors, such as food, clothing, and automobiles.

TRADE/PROFESSIONAL ASSOCIATIONS

Official International Toy Center Directory. P.O. Box 173, Old Greenwich, CT 06870-0173. Fax: (203)637-8549 E-mail: robtoy1@aol.com.

Toy Manufacturers of America. 1115 Broadway, Suite 400, New York, NY 10010. Phone: (212)675-1141 Fax: (212)633-1429 E-mail: info@toy-tma.org • URL: http://www.toy-tma.com.

TRACTORS

See: AGRICULTURAL MACHINERY

TRADE

See: BUSINESS; FOREIGN TRADE

TRADE ASSOCIATIONS

See: ASSOCIATIONS

TRADE, BOARDS OF

See: CHAMBERS OF COMMERCE

TRADE CATALOGS

See: CATALOGS AND DIRECTORIES

TRADE DIRECTORIES

See: CATALOGS AND DIRECTORIES

TRADE EXHIBITS

See: CONVENTIONS; FAIRS; TRADE SHOWS

TRADE FAIRS

See: CONVENTIONS; FAIRS; TRADE SHOWS

TRADE JOURNALS

See also: PERIODICALS

GENERAL WORKS

Business Journals of the United States: Historical Guides to the World's Periodicals and Newspapers. William Fisher, editor. Greenwood Publishing Group, Inc. • 1991. $75.00. Contains historical and descriptive essays covering over 100 leading business publications.

ABSTRACTS AND INDEXES

Abstracts in New Technologies and Engineering. R. R. Bowker. • Bimonthly. $1,650.00 per year. Annual cumulation. Formerly *Current Technology Index.*

Business Periodicals Index. H. W. Wilson Co. • Monthly, except August, with quarterly and annual cumulations. Service basis for print edition; CD-ROM edition, $1,495.00 per year.

Canadian Index. Micromedia Ltd. • Monthly, with annual cumulation. Price varies. Indexes approximately 500 Canadian periodicals of all kinds, including business magazines and trade journals. Ten daily Canadian newspapers are also indexed.

Canadian Periodical Index. The Gale Group. • Monthly. $515.00 per year. Annual cumulation. Indexes more than 400 English and French language periodicals.

BIBLIOGRAPHIES

Guide to Special Issues and Indexes of Periodicals. Miriam Uhlan and Doris B. Katz, editors. Special Libraries Association. • 1994. $59.00. Fourth edition. A listing, with prices, of the special issues of over 1700 U. S. and Canadian periodicals in business, industry, technology, science, and the arts. Includes a comprehensive subject index.

CD-ROM DATABASES

Business Source Plus. EBSCO Information Services. • Monthly. $1,495.00 per year. Provides CD-ROM citations and abstracts to articles in about 650 business periodicals and newspapers, including *The Wall Street Journal.* Full text is provided from 200 selected periodicals. Covers accounting, communications, economics, finance, management, marketing, and other business subjects.

CPI.Q: The Canadian Periodical Index Full-Text on CD-ROM. The Gale Group. • Bimonthly. Provides CD-ROM citations from 1988 to date for more than 400 English and French language periodicals. Contains full-text coverage from 1995 to date for 150 periodicals.

MediaFinder CD-ROM: Oxbridge Directories of Print Media and Catalogs. Oxbridge Communications, Inc. • Quarterly. $1,695.00 per year. CD-ROM includes about 100,000 listings from *Standard Periodical Directory, National Directory of Catalogs, National Directory of British Mail Order Catalogs, National Directory of German Mail Order Catalogs, Oxbridge Directory of Newsletters, National Directory of Mailing Lists, College Media Directory,* and *National Directory of Magazines.*

DIRECTORIES

Books and Periodicals Online: The Guide to Business and Legal Information on Databases and CD-ROM's. Nuchine Nobari, editor. Library Technology Alliance, Inc. • Annual. $365.00 per year. 97,000 periodicals available as part of online and CD-ROM databases; international coverage.

Burrelle's Media Directory: Magazines and Newsletters. Burrelle's Information Services. • Annual. $275.00. Provides detailed descriptions of more than 13,500 magazines and newsletters published in the U. S., Canada, and Mexico. Categories are professional, consumer, trade, and college.

Business Publication Advertising Source. SRDS. • Monthly. $682.00 per year. Issued in three parts: (1) U. S. Business Publications, (2) U. S. Healthcare Publications, and (3) International Publications. Provides detailed advertising rates, profiles of editorial content, management names, "Multiple Publications Publishers," circulation data, and other trade journal information. Formerly *Business Publication Rates and Data.*

Cabell's Directory of Publishing Opportunities in Economics, and Finance. Cabell Publishing Co. • 1997. $89.95. Provides editorial policies of commercial and scholarly periodicals in the areas of business and economics. Formerly *Cabell's Directory of Publishing Opportunities in Accounting, Economics, and Finance.*

Cabell's Directory of Publishing Opportunities in Management. Cabell Publishing Co. • 1997. $89.95. Provides editorial policies of more than 300 management periodicals. Emphasis is on publishing opportunities for college faculty members. Formerly *Cabell's Directory of Publishing Opportunities Business and Economics.*

CARD The Media Information Network (Canadian Advertising Rates and Data). Available from SRDS. • Biennial. $225.00 per issue. Published by Maclean Hunter Publishing Ltd. (Toronto). Provides advertising rates and other information relating to Canadian media: daily newspapers, weekly community newspapers, consumer magazines, business publications, school publications, religious publications, radio, and television.

Cyberhound's Guide to Publications on the Internet. The Gale Group. • 1996. $79.00. First edition. Presents critical descriptions and ratings of more than 3,400 Internet databases of journals, newspapers, newsletters, and other publications. Includes a glossary of Internet terms, a bibliography, and three indexes.

Fulltext Sources Online. Information Today, Inc. • Semiannual. $199.00 per year; $119.50 per issue. Lists more than 8,000 journals, newspapers, magazines, newsletters, and newswires found online in fulltext through DIALOG, LEXIS-NEXIS, Dow Jones, Westlaw, etc. Includes journals that have free Internet archives. (Formerly published by BiblioData.).

Gale Directory of Publications and Broadcast Media. The Gale Group. • Annual. $650.00. Five volumes. A guide to publications and broadcasting stations in the U. S. and Canada, including newspapers, magazines, journals, radio stations, television stations, and cable systems. Geographic arrangement. Volume three consists of statistical tables, maps, subject indexes, and title index. Formerly *Ayer Directory of Publications.*

Grey House Directory of Special Issues: A Guide to Business Magazines' Buyer's Guides & Directory Issues. Grey House Publishing. • 2001. $105.00. Provides information on more than 4,000 specialized directories issued by trade journals, arranged according to 90 industry groups.

International Media Guide: Business Professional Publications: Asia Pacific/Middle East/Africa. International Media Guides, Inc. • Annual. $285.00. Provides information on 3,000 trade journals "from Africa to the Pacific Rim," including advertising rates and circulation data.

International Media Guide: Business Professional Publications: Europe. International Media Guides, Inc. • Annual. $285.00. Describes 6,000 trade journals from Eastern and Western Europe, with advertising rates and circulation data.

International Media Guide: Business/Professional Publications: The Americas. International Media Guides, Inc. • Annual. $285.00. Describes trade journals from North, South, and Central America, with advertising rates and circulation data.

Magazines Careers Directory: A Practical One-Stop Guide to Getting a Job in Publc Relations. Visible Ink Press. • 1993. $17.95. Fifth edition. Includes information on magazine publishing careers in art, editing, sales, and business management. Provides advice from "insiders," resume suggestions, a directory of companies that may offer entry-level positions, and a directory of career information sources. *Career Advisor Series.*

Print Media Production Source. SRDS. • Quarterly. $401.00 per year. Contains details of printing and mechanical production requirements for advertising in specific trade journals, consumer magazines, and newspapers. Formerly *Print Media Production Data.*

Technology Media Source. SRDS. • Annual. $291.00. Contains detailed information on business publications, consumer magazines, and direct mail lists that may be of interest to "technology marketers." Emphasis is on aviation and telecommunications.

INTERNET DATABASES

EBSCO Information Services. Ebsco Publishing. Phone: 800-871-8508 or (508)356-6500 Fax: (508)356-5640 E-mail: ep@epnet.com • URL: http://www.epnet.com • Fee-based Web site providing Internet access to a wide variety of databases, including business-related material. Full text is available for many periodical titles, with daily updates. Fees: Apply.

ProQuest Direct. Bell & Howell Information and Learning. Phone: 800-521-0600 or (313)761-4700 Fax: (313)973-9145 • URL: http://www.umi.com/proquest • Fee-based Web site providing Internet access to more than 3,000 periodicals, newspapers, and other publications. Many items are available full-text, with daily updates. Includes extensive corporate and financial information from Disclosure, Inc. Fees: Apply.

PubList.com: The Internet Directory of Publications. Bowes & Associates, Inc. Phone: (781)792-0999 Fax: (781)792-0988 E-mail: info@publist.com • URL: http://www.publist.com • "The premier online global resource for information about print and electronic publications." Provides online searching for information on more than 150,000 magazines, journals, newsletters, e-journals, and monographs. Database entries generally include title, publisher, format, address, editor, circulation, subject, and International Standard Serial Number (ISSN). Fees: Free.

Ulrichsweb.com. R. R. Bowker. Phone: 888-269-5372 or (908)464-6800 Fax: (908)464-3553 E-mail: info@bowker.com • URL: http://www.ulrichsweb.com • Web site provides fee-based access to about 250,000 serials records from the *Ulrich's International Periodicals Directory* database. Includes periodical evaluations from *Library Journal* and *Magazines for Libraries.* Monthly updates.

WilsonWeb Periodicals Databases. H. W. Wilson. Phone: 800-367-6770 or (718)588-8400 Fax: 800-590-1617 or (718)992-8003 E-mail: custserv@hwwilson.com • URL: http://www.hwwilson.com/ • Web sites provide fee-based access to *Wilson Business Full Text, Applied Science & Technology Full Text, Biological & Agricultural Index, Library Literature & Information Science Full Text,* and *Readers' Guide Full Text, Mega Edition.* Daily updates.

ONLINE DATABASES

ABI/INFORM. Bell & Howell Information and Learning. • Provides online indexing to business-related material occurring in over 1,000 periodicals from 1971 to the present. Inquire as to online cost and availability.

Gale Database of Publications and Broadcast Media. The Gale Group. • An online directory containing detailed information on over 67,000 periodicals, newspapers, broadcast stations, cable systems, directories, and newsletters. Corresponds to the following print sources: *Gale Directory of Publications and Broadcast Media; Directories in*

Print; City and State Directories in Print; Newsletters in Print. Semiannual updates. Inquire as to online cost and availability.

Trade & Industry Index. The Gale Group. • Provides indexing of business periodicals, January 1981 to date. Daily updates. (Full text articles from some periodicals are available online, 1983 to date, in the companion database, *Trade & Industry ASAP.*) Inquire as to online cost and availability.

PERIODICALS AND NEWSLETTERS

Computer Publishing and Advertising Report: The Biweekly Newsletter for Publishing and Advertising Executives in the Computer Field. SIMBA Information, Inc. • Biweekly. $549.00 per year. Newsletter. Covers computer book publishing and computer-related advertising in periodicals and other media. Provides data on computer book sales and advertising in computer magazines.

Folio: The Magazine for Magazine Management. Intertec Publishing Co. • 17 times a year. $96.00 per year.

SI: Special Issues. Trip Wyckoff, editor. Hoover's, Inc. • Bimonthly. $149.95 per year. Newsletter. Serves as a supplement to *Directory of Business Periodical Special Issues.* Provides current information on trade journal special issues and editorial calendars.

RESEARCH CENTERS AND INSTITUTES

Knight Center for Specialized Journalism. University of Maryland, 290 University College, College Park, MD 20742-1645. Phone: (301)985-7279 Fax: (301)985-7840 E-mail: knight@umail.umd.edu • URL: http://www.inform.umd.edu/knight • Research area is media coverage of complex subjects, such as economics, law, science, and medicine.

STATISTICS SOURCES

Computer Publishing Market Forecast. SIMBA Information. • Annual. $1,995.00. Provides market data on computer-related books, magazines, newsletters, and other publications. Includes profiles of major publishers of computer-related material.

TRADE/PROFESSIONAL ASSOCIATIONS

American Society of Business Press Editors. 107 W. Ogden Ave., LaGrange, IL 60525-2022. Phone: (708)352-6950 Fax: (708)352-3780 E-mail: 7114.34@compuserve.com • URL: http://www.asbpe.com.

BPA International. 270 Madison Ave., New York, NY 10016-0699. Phone: (212)779-3200 Fax: (212)779-3615 • URL: http://www.bpai.com • Verifies business and consumer periodical circulation statements. Includes a Circulation Managers Committee. *Formerly Business Publications Audit of Circulation.*

OTHER SOURCES

Bizlink. Rogers Media. • Web site provides news and information from 30 Canadian business and industrial publications issued by Rogers Media (formerly Maclean Hunter). Keyword searching is available for "all of the Bizlink archive" or for each of seven areas: Industry, Financial, Construction, Retailing, Marketing, Media, and Agriculture. Updates are daily. Fees: Free.

Business & Company Resource Center. The Gale Group. • Fee-based Web site provides a wide range of business, industry, and specific company information. Access is offered to trade journal articles, market research data, insider trading activity, major shareholder data, corporate histories, emerging technology reports, corporate earnings estimates, press releases, and other sources. Provides detailed company profiles, industry overviews, and rankings. Offers integration of Predicasts PROMT, Newsletters ASAP, Investext Plus, Business Index ASAP, Brands and Their Companies, and other databases (many have full text).

InSite 2. Intelligence Data/Thomson Financial. • Fee-based Web site consolidates information in a "Base Pack" consisting of Business InSite, Market InSite, and Company InSite. Optional databases are Consumer InSite, Health and Wellness InSite, Newsletter InSite, and Computer InSite. Includes fulltext content from more than 2,500 trade publications, journals, newsletters, newspapers, analyst reports, and other sources. Continuous updating. Formerly produced by The Gale Group.

TRADE NAMES

See: TRADEMARKS AND TRADE NAMES

TRADE SECRETS

See also: INTELLECTUAL PROPERTY

ABSTRACTS AND INDEXES

Business Periodicals Index. H. W. Wilson Co. • Monthly, except August, with quarterly and annual cumulations. Service basis for print edition; CD-ROM edition, $1,495.00 per year.

Index to Legal Periodicals and Books. H. W. Wilson Co. • Monthly. Quarterly and annual cumulations. $270.00 per year. CD-ROM version available at $1,495.00 per year.

HANDBOOKS AND MANUALS

Protecting Trade Secrets, Patents, Copyrights, and Trademarks. Robert C. Dorr and Christopher H. Munch. Panel Publishers. • Looseleaf service. $165.00.

Trade Secret Protection in an Information Age. Gale R. Peterson. Glasser Legalworks. • Looseleaf. $149.00, including sample forms on disk. Periodic supplementation available. Covers trade secret law relating to computer software, online databases, and multimedia products. Explanations are based on more than 1,000 legal cases. Sample forms on disk include work-for-hire examples and covenants not to compete.

Worldwide Trade Secrets Law. Terrence F. MacLaren, editor. West Group. • $425.00. Looseleaf service. Periodic supplementation.

ONLINE DATABASES

Index to Legal Periodicals and Books (Online). H. W. Wilson Co. • Broad coverage of law journals and books 1981 to date. Monthly updates. Inquire as to online cost and availability.

Legal Resource Index. The Gale Group. • Broad coverage of law literature appearing in legal, business, and other periodicals, 1980 to date. Monthly updates. Inquire as to online cost and availability.

LEXIS. LEXIS-NEXIS. • The various LEXIS databases provide full text and indexing for a wide variety of legal cases, statutes, orders, and opinions.

Wilson Business Abstracts Online. H. W. Wilson Co. • Indexes and abstracts 600 major business periodicals, plus the *Wall Street Journal* and the business section of the *New York Times.* Indexing is from 1982, abstracting from 1990, with the two newspapers included from 1993. Updated weekly. Inquire as to online cost and availability. (*Business Periodicals Index* without abstracts is also available online.).

PERIODICALS AND NEWSLETTERS

Security Management. American Society for Industrial Security. • Monthly. Free to members; non-members, $48.00 per year. Articles cover the protection of corporate assets, including personnel property and information security.

TRADE/PROFESSIONAL ASSOCIATIONS

ASIS International (American Society for Industrial Security). 1625 Prince St., Alexandria, VA 22314-2818. Phone: (703)519-6200 Fax: (703)519-6299 • URL: http://www.asisonline.org.

TRADE SHOWS

See also: CONVENTIONS

ABSTRACTS AND INDEXES

Business Periodicals Index. H. W. Wilson Co. • Monthly, except August, with quarterly and annual cumulations. Service basis for print edition; CD-ROM edition, $1,495.00 per year.

CD-ROM DATABASES

World Database of Business Information Sources on CD-ROM. The Gale Group. • Annual. Produced by Euromonitor. Presents Euromonitor's entire information source database on CD-ROM. Contains a worldwide total of about 35,000 publications, organizations, libraries, trade fairs, and online databases.

DIRECTORIES

Business Organizations, Agencies, and Publications Directory. The Gale Group. • 1999. $425.00. 12th edition. Over 40,000 entries describing 39 types of business information sources. Classified by type of organization, publication, or serviceIncludes state, national, and international agencies and organizations. Master index to names and keywords. Also includes e-mail addresses and web site URL's.

The Directory of Business Information Resources: Associations, Newsletters, Magazine Trade Shows. Grey House Publishing, Inc. • Annual. $195.00. Provides concise information on associations, newsletters, magazines, and trade shows for each of 90 major industry groups. An "Entry & Company Index" serves as a guide to titles, publishers, and organizations.

Directory of Conventions Regional Editions. Bill Communications. • Annual. $155.00 per volume. Four volumes. Set $285.00. Over 14,000 meetings of North American national, regional, and state and local organizations.

Encyclopedia of Associations. The Gale Group. • Annual. $1,425.00. Three volumes. Volume 1, National Organizations, $545.00; Volume 2, Geographic and Executive Indexes, $425.00; Volume 3, supplement, $455.00.

Exhibitor Magazine Buyer's Guide to Trade Show Exhibits. Exhibitor Magazine Group, Inc. • Annual. $42.00. Covers manufacturers of trade show exhibit equipment. Formerly *Buyer's Guide to Trade Show Displays.*

International Tradeshow Directory: The Annual Statistical Directory of U.S. and Canadian Tradeshows and Public Shows. Tradeshow Week. • Annual. $450.00. Provides detailed information for more than 9,000 U. S. and Canadian trade shows of 5,000 square feet or more scheduled for the next four years.

Trade Show Exhibitors Association Membership Directory and Product/Service Guide. Trade Show Exhibitors Association. • Annual. 55.00. Provides listings and details for approximately 2,300 exhibit professionals. Formerly *International Exhibitors Association-Membership Directory and Product/Service Guide.*

Trade Shows Worldwide: An International Directory of Events, Facilities and Suppliers. The Gale Group. • 2000. $299.00. 16th edition. Provides detailed information from over 75 countries on more than 8,400 trade shows and exhibitions. Separate sections are provided for trade shows/exhibitions, for sponsors/organizers, and for services, facilities, and information sources. Indexing is by date, location, subject, name, and keyword.

TradeShow and Convention Guide. BPI Communications. • Annual. $115.00. Dates and data for convention and trade shows for the next five years; local companies that supply services such as photograpy, exhibit design etc.; halls and hotels catering to conventions and shows.

Tradeshow and Exhibit Manager Buyer's Guide. Goldstein and Associates. • Annual. $10.00. Lists about 1,000 suppliers providing products and services for exhibits and tradeshows.

HANDBOOKS AND MANUALS

Guerilla Trade Show Selling: New Unconventional Weapons and Tactics to Meet More People, Get More Leads, and Close More Sales. Jay C. Levinson and others. John Wiley and Sons, Inc. • 1997. $19.95.

How to Get the Most Out of Trade Shows. Steve Miller. NTC/Contemporary Publishing. • 1999. $29.95. Third revised edition. (NTC Business Book Series).

Show and Sell: 133 Business Building Ways to Promote Your Trade Show Exhibit. Margit B. Weisgal. AMACOM. • 1996. $55.00. Contains information and advice on pre-show advertising and promotion, booth management, literature distribution, customer dialogue, "damage control," follow-up, evaluation, and other exhibit topics. Includes bibliography, checklists, worksheets, and index.

The Successful Exhibitor's Handbook: Trade Show Techniques for Beginners and Pros. Barry Siskind. Self-Counsel Press, Inc. • 1996. $14.95. Third edition.

INTERNET DATABASES

Trade Show Central: The Internet's Leading Trade Show Information Resource!. Trade Show Central. Phone: (781)235-8095 Fax: (781)416-4500 • URL: http://www.tscentral.com • Web site provides information on "more than 30,000 Trade Shows, Conferences, and Seminars, 5,000 service providers, and 5,000 venues and facilities around the world." Searching is offered by trade show name, industry category, date, and location. Results may be sorted by event name, city, country, or date. Includes a "Career Center" for trade show personnel. Continuous updating. Fees: Free.

ONLINE DATABASES

Wilson Business Abstracts Online. H. W. Wilson Co. • Indexes and abstracts 600 major business periodicals, plus the *Wall Street Journal* and the business section of the *New York Times*. Indexing is from 1982, abstracting from 1990, with the two newspapers included from 1993. Updated weekly. Inquire as to online cost and availability. (*Business Periodicals Index* without abstracts is also available online.).

PERIODICALS AND NEWSLETTERS

Exhibit Builder. Exhibit Builder, Inc. • Bimonthly. $25.00 per year. For designers and builders of trade show exhibits.

Facility Manager. International Association of Auditorium Managers. • Quarterly. Free to members; non-members, $45.00 per year.

Journal of Convention and Exhibition Management. Haworth Press, Inc. • Quarterly. Individuals $50.00 per year; institutions, $85.00 per year; libraries, $95.00 per year.

Successful Meetings: The Authority on Meetings and Incentive Travel Management. Bill Communications, Inc. • Monthly. $65.00 per year.

Tradeshow and Exhibit Manager. Goldstein and Associates. • Bimonthly. $80.00 per year. Edited for exhibit, tradeshow, and exposition managers. Covers design trends, site selection, shipping problems, industry news, etc. Supplement available *Tradeshow Directory*.

Tradeshow Week: Since 1971, the Only Weekly Source of News and Statistics on the Tradeshow Industry. Tradeshow Week, Inc. • 49 times a year. $389.00 per year. Edited for corporate and association trade show and exhibit managers. Includes show calendars and labor rates.

TRADE/PROFESSIONAL ASSOCIATIONS

Center for Exhibition Industry Research. 2301 S. Lake Shore Dr., Suite E1002, Chicago, IL 60616. Phone: (312)808-2347 Fax: (312)949-3472 • URL: http://www.ceir.org • Promotes the trade show as a marketing device.

Exhibit Designers and Producers Association. 5775 Peachtree-Dunwoody Rd., N.E., Suite 500-G, Atlanta, GA 30342. Phone: (404)303-7310 Fax: (404)252-0774 E-mail: edpa@asshq.com • URL: http://www.edpa.com • Members are firms that design and build displays for trade shows.

Exposition Service Contractors Association. Dobson/Simmons Associates, 400 S. Houston St., Suite 210, Dallas, TX 75202. Phone: (214)742-9217 Fax: (214)741-2519 E-mail: esca@airmail.net • URL: http://www.esca.org • Members are companies providing supplies and services for trade shows and conventions.

International Association of Assembly Managers. 4425 W. Airport Freeway, Suite 590, Irving, TX 75062. Phone: 800-935-4226 or (972)255-8020 Fax: (972)255-9582 E-mail: iaam.info@iaam.org • URL: http://www.iaam.org • Members are auditorium, theater, exhibit hall, and other facility managers.

International Association of Exposition Management. 5001 LBJ Freeway, Suite 350, Dallas, TX 75244-6120. Phone: (972)458-8002 Fax: (972)458-8119 • URL: http://www.iaem.org.

Trade Show Exhibitors Association. 5501 Backlick Rd., Suite 105, Springfield, VA 22151. Phone: (703)941-3725 Fax: (703)941-8275 E-mail: tsea@tsea.org • Promotes the use of trade shows for marketing products and services.

TRADE UNIONS

See: LABOR UNIONS

TRADEMARKS AND TRADE NAMES

See also: COPYRIGHT; PATENTS

GENERAL WORKS

Basic Facts About Trademarks. Available from U. S. Government Printing Office. • 1996. $4.25. Issued by the Patent and Trademark Office, U. S. Department of Commerce. Includes filing requirements and sample applications.

Living Logos: How U. S. Corporations Revitalize Their Trademarks. David E. Carter, editor. Art Direction Book Co. • 1993. $22.95. Traces the history and evolution of 70 famous U. S. company logos.

The 22 Immutable Laws of Branding: How to Build a Product or Service Into a World-Class Brand. Al Ries and Laura Ries. HarperInformation. • 1999. $23.00. Provides advice on attaining positive brand recognition.

ABSTRACTS AND INDEXES

Index of Trademarks Issued from the United States Patent and Trademark Office. Available from U. S. Government Printing Office. • Annual. Arranged alphabetically by name of registrant. The caption title is "List of Trademark Registrants.".

ALMANACS AND YEARBOOKS

Intellectual Property Law Review. W. Bryan Forney, editor. West Group. • 1992. $115.00. Patent, trademark, and copyright practices.

CD-ROM DATABASES

CASSIS (Trademarks). U. S. Patent and Trademark Office, Office of Electronic Information Products. • CD-ROM products include *Trademarks ASSIGN* (assignment deeds, bimonthly), *Trademarks ASSIST* (search tools, single- disc), *Trademarks PENDING* (applications on file, bimonthly), *Trademarks REGISTERED* (active trademarks, 1884 to date).

TRADEMARKSCAN: U. S. Federal [CD-ROM]. Thomson & Thomson. • Monthly. $7,500.00 per year. Contains information on CD-ROM for more than two million trademarks from the U. S. Patent and Trademark Office. For active trademarks, time period is 1884 to date. Graphic images are shown for many of the records.

TRADEMARKSCAN: U. S. State [CD-ROM]. Thomson & Thomson. • Monthly. $3,500.00 per year. Provides information on CD-ROM for more than one million trademarks registered with the Office of the Secretary of State in all 50 states and in Puerto Rico. For active trademarks, time period is 1900 to date.

World Database of Consumer Brands and Their Owners on CD-ROM. The Gale Group. • Annual. $3,190.00. Produced by Euromonitor. Provides detailed information on CD-ROM for about 10,000 companies and 80,000 brands around the world. Covers 1,000 product sectors.

DIRECTORIES

Alphaphonetic Directory of International Trademarks. Available from Thomson & Thomson. • Annual, with three cumulative updates during the year. $1,914.00 per year. 15 volumes. Published in Belgium by Compu-Mark. Provides owner, registration, and classification information for more than one million trademarks registered with the World Intellectual Property Organization (WIPO).

Brands and Their Companies. The Gale Group. • 2001. $805.00. 22nd edition. Three volumes. Includes mid-year *Supplement*. Provides over 365,000 entries ontrade names, trademarks, and brand names of consumer-oriented products and their 80,000 manufacturers, importers, marketers, or distributors. Formerly *Trade Names Dictionary*.

Companies and Their Brands. The Gale Group. • 2001. $570.00. 22nd edition. Two volumes. Lists companies alphabetically, with their names. (A rearrangment of the data in *Brands and Their Companies*.).

Directory of Canadian Trademarks. Thomson & Thomson. • Annual. Price on application. Provides owner, registration, and classification information for Canadian trademarks registered with the Canadian Intellectual Property Office (CIPO).

Directory of Consumer Brands and Their Owners: Asia Pacific. Available from The Gale Group. • 1998. $990.00. Published by Euromonitor. Provides information about brands available from major Asia Pacific companies. Descriptions of companies are also included.

Directory of Consumer Brands and Their Owners: Eastern Europe. Available from The Gale Group. •

1998. $990.00. Published by Euromonitor. Provides information about brands available from major Eastern European companies. Descriptions of companies are also included.

Directory of Consumer Brands and Their Owners: Europe. Available from The Gale Group. • 1998. $990.00. Two volumes. Third edition. Published by Euromonitor. Provides information about brands available from major European companies. Descriptions of companies are also included.

Directory of Consumer Brands and Their Owners: Latin America. Available from The Gale Group. • 1999. $990.00. Published by Euromonitor. Provides information about brands available from major Latin American companies. Descriptions of companies are also included.

The Directory of U. S. Trademarks. Thomson & Thomson. • Annual, with three cumulative updates during the year. $1,295.00 per year. 12 volumes. Provides owner, registration, and classification information for about 1.5 million active and pending trademarks filed with the U. S. Patent and Trademark Office.

International Brands and Their Companies. The Gale Group. • 1998. $295.00. Fifth edition. Contains about 84,000 worldwide (non-U. S.) entries for trade names, trademarks, and brand names of consumer-oriented products and their manufacturers, importers, distributors, or marketers. Formerly *International Trade Names Dictionary.*

International Directory of Consumer Brands and Their Owners. Available from The Gale Group. • 1997. $450.00. Published by Euromonitor. Contains detailed information on more than 38,000 consumer product brands and their companies in 62 countries of the world, excluding Europe.

Macrae's Blue Book: Serving the Original Equipment Market. MacRae's Blue Book, Inc. • Annual. $170.00. Two volumes. Lists about 50,000 manufacturers of a wide variety of industrial equipment and supplies.

Thomas Register of American Manufacturers and Thomas Register Catalog File. Thomas Publishing Co., Inc. • Annual. $149.00. 34 volumes. A three-part system offering information on a wide variety of industrial equipment and supplies.

Trademark Register of the United States. Trademark Register. • Annual. $435.00. Lists all trademarks currently registered and renewed trademarks in the U.S. Patent and Trademark Office.

World Drinks Marketing Directory. Available from The Gale Group. • 2001. $1,090.00. Second edition. Published by Euromonitor. Provides detailed infromation on the leading beverage companies of the world, including specifi brand data.

World Food Marketing Directory. Available from The Gale Group. • 2001. $1,090.00. Second edition. Three volumes. Published by Euromonitor. Provides detailed information on the major food companies of the world, including specific brand data.

World's Greatest Brands: An International Review by Interbrand. John Wiley and Sons, Inc. • 1992. $49.95. Compiled by Interbrand. Provides details on 330 of the most successful international brand names and trademarks. Includes color illustrations.

ENCYCLOPEDIAS AND DICTIONARIES

Dictionary of Trade Name Origins. Adrian Room. NTC/Contemporary Publishing. • 1994. $39.95. Revised edition.

McCarthy's Desk Encyclopedia of Intellectual Property. J. Thomas McCarthy. BNA Books. • 1995. $75.00.Second edition. Defines legal terms relating to patents, trademarks, copyrights, trade secrets, entertainment, and the computer industry.

HANDBOOKS AND MANUALS

Copyrights, Patents, and Trademarks: Protect Your Rights Worldwide. Hoyt L. Barber. McGraw-Hill. • 1996. $32.95. Second edition.

Intellectual Property Infringement Damages: A Litigation Support Handbook. Russell L. Parr. John Wiley and Sons, Inc. • 1999. $145.00. Annual supplement, $60.00. Describes how to calculate damages for patent, trademark, and copyright infringement. (Intellectual Property Series).

Inventors Desktop Companion: A Guide to Successfully Marketing and Protecting Your Ideas. Richard C. Levy. Visible Ink Press. • 1998. $24.95. Second edition. Explains how to patent, trademark, or copyright an idea. Includes a listing of 2,000 associations and services for inventors.

Patent, Copyright, and Trademark: A Desk Reference to Intellectual Property Law. Stephen Elias. Nolo.com. • 1999. $24.95. Third revised edition. Contains practical explanations of the legalities of patents, copyrights, trademarks, and trade secrets. Includes examples of relevant legal forms. A 1985 version was called *Nolo's Intellectual Property Law Dictionary.* (Nolo Press Self-Help Law Series).

Patent, Trademark, and Copyright Laws, 2000. Jeffrey Samuels. BNA Books. • $95.00. Date not set. Contains text of "all pertinent intellectual property legislation to date.".

Trademark Law Handbook. United States Trademark Association. West Group. • Annual. $65.00.

Trademark Manual of Examining Procedure. Available from U. S. Government Printing Office. • $51.00 for basic manual and semiannual changes for an indeterminate period. Covers "practices and procedures" relating to the processing of applications to register trademarks in the U. S. Patent and Trademark Office.

Trademark Protection and Practice. Jerome Gilson. Matthew Bender & Co., Inc. • $1,160.00. 11 looseleaf volumes. Periodic supplementation. Covers U. S. trademark practice.

World Trademark Law and Practice. Matthew Bender & Co., Inc. • $720.00. Four looseleaf volumes. Periodic Supplementation. A guide to international trademark practice with detailed coverage of 35 major jurisdictions and summary coverage for over 100.

INTERNET DATABASES

SAEGIS Internet Search. Thomson & Thomson. Phone: 800-692-8833 or (617)479-1600 Fax: (617)786-8273 E-mail: support@thomson-thomson.com • URL: http://www.thomson-thomson.com • Fee-based Web site provides extensive, common law screening of the World Wide Web for trademarks. Searches are performed offline, with final report delivered to user's "SAEGIS Inbox." Context of trademark within each relevant Web site is indicated, and links are provided.

ONLINE DATABASES

Brands and Their Companies Database. The Gale Group. • An online directory of about 382,000 domestic and international trade names, with a primary focus on consumer goods. Semiannual updates. Inquire as to online cost and availability.

Thomas Register Online. Thomas Publishing Co., Inc. • Provides concise information on approximately 194,000 U. S. companies, mainly manufacturers, with over 50,000 product classifications. Indexes over 115,000 trade names. Information is updated semiannually. Inquire as to online cost and availability.

TRADEMARKSCAN: International Register. Thomson & Thomson. • Supplies current information on more than 400,000 trademarks registered with the World Intellectual Property Organization. Updates are monthly. Inquire as to online cost and availability. (TRADEMARKSCAN also maintains extensive databases for individual countries: Canada, U. K., Germany, Italy, France, and others.).

TRADEMARKSCAN: U. S. Federal. Thomson & Thomson. • Provides information on more than two million trademarks registered and pending at the U. S. Patent and Trademark Office. Time period is 1884 to date for active trademarks, with updates twice a week. Graphic images are shown for approximately 40% of the records. Inquire as to online cost and availability.

TRADEMARKSCAN: U. S. State. Thomson & Thomson. • Contains information on more than 970,000 trademarks registered with the Office of the Secretary of State in all 50 states and in Puerto Rico. Time period is 1900 to date for active trademarks, with weekly updates. Inquire as to online cost and availability.

PERIODICALS AND NEWSLETTERS

BNA's Patent, Trademark and Copyright Journal. Bureau of National Affairs, Inc. • Weekly. $1,366.00 per year.

Intellectual Property Today. Omega Communications. • Monthly. $48.00 per year. Covers legal developments in copyright, patents, trademarks, and licensing. Emphasizes the effect of new technology on intellectual property. Formerly *Law Works.*

LES Nouvelles. Licensing Executives Society. • Quarterly. Free to members; libraries, $35.00 per year. Concerned with licensing agreements, patents, and trademarks.

Official Gazette of the United States Patent and Trademark Office: Trademarks. Available from U. S. Government Printing Office. • Weekly. $980.00 per year by first class mail. Contains Trademarks, Trademark Notices, Marks Published for Opposition, Trademark Registrations Issued, and Index of Registrants (http://www.uspto.gov).

Remarks: Trademark News for Business. International Trademark Association. • Quarterly. Newsletter.

Trademark Alert. Thomson & Thomson. • Weekly. $1,075.00 per year. Contains information on new trademark applications filed with the U. S. Patent and Trademark Office. Arranged by International Class and indexed by significant word or character.

Trademark Reporter. International Trademark Association. • Bimonthly. Membership. Contains articles on trademark developments, trademark law, and the use of trademarks.

TRADE/PROFESSIONAL ASSOCIATIONS

International Intellectual Property Association. 1255 23rd St. N.W., Suite 850, Washington, DC 20037. Phone: (202)785-1814 Fax: (202)466-2893.

International Trademark Association. 1133 Ave. of the Americas, New York, NY 10036. Phone: (212)768-9887 Fax: (212)768-7796 • URL: http://www.inta.org • Members are trademark owners, lawyers, designers, and others concerned with the proper use of trademarks and trade names.

OTHER SOURCES

Business & Company Resource Center. The Gale Group. • Fee-based Web site provides a wide range of business, industry, and specific company information. Access is offered to trade journal articles, market research data, insider trading activity, major shareholder data, corporate histories, emerging technology reports, corporate earnings estimates, press releases, and other sources. Provides detailed company profiles, industry overviews, and rankings. Offers integration of Predicasts PROMT, Newsletters ASAP, Investext Plus, Business Index ASAP, Brands and Their Companies, and other databases (many have full text).

Callmann Unfair Competition, Trademarks & Monopolies: 1981-1989. Rudolf Callmann and Louis Altman. West Group. • Nine looseleaf volumes. $1,195.00. Periodic supplementation. Covers various aspects of anti-competitive behavior.

Intellectual Property and Antitrust Law. William C. Holmes. West Group. • Looseleaf. $145.00. Periodic supplementation. Includes patent, trademark, and copyright practices.

TRADES

See: OCCUPATIONS

TRADING

See: BARTER AND COUNTERTRADE

TRAFFIC ACCIDENTS AND TRAFFIC SAFETY

See also: ACCIDENTS

GENERAL WORKS

Highway and Traffic Safety and Accident Research, Management, and Issues. Norman Solomon, editor. Transportation Research Board. • 1993. $28.00. (Transportation Research Record Series).

ABSTRACTS AND INDEXES

Highway Safety Literature. • Annual. $80.00.

Transportation Research Information Services (TRIS). Transportation Research Board, Highway Research Information. • Monthly. Price on application. Formerly *Highway Research Abstracts.*

BIBLIOGRAPHIES

Road Construction and Safety. Available from U. S. Government Printing Office. • Annual. Free. Issued by the Superintendent of Documents. A list of government publications on highway construction and traffic safety. Formerly *Highway Construction, Safety and Traffic.* (Subject Bibliography No. 3.).

ONLINE DATABASES

I.I.I. Data Base Search. Insurance Information Institute. • Provides online citations and abstracts of insurance-related literature in magazines, newspapers, trade journals, and books. Emphasis is on property and casualty insurance issues, including highway safety, product safety, and environmental liability. Inquire as to online cost and availability.

TRIS: Transportation Research Information Service. National Research Council. • Contains abstracts and citations to a wide range of transportation literature, 1968 to present, with monthly updates. Includes references to the literature of air transportation, highways, ships and shipping, railroads, trucking, and urban mass transportation. Formerly *TRIS-ON-LINE.* Inquire as to online cost and availability.

PERIODICALS AND NEWSLETTERS

Insurance Institute for Highway Safety, Status Report. Insurance Institute for Highway Safety. • Monthly. Free.

Journal of Safety Research. National Safety Council. Elsevier Science. • Quarterly. $564.00 per year.

Journal of Traffic Safety Education. California Association for Safety Education. • Quarterly. $8.00 per year.

Traffic Safety: The Magazine for Traffic Safety Professionals. National Safety Council. • Bimonthly. Members, $33.00 per year; non-members, $44.00 per year.

RESEARCH CENTERS AND INSTITUTES

Insurance Institute for Highway Safety. 1005 N. Glebe Rd., Arlington, VA 22201-4751. Phone: (703)247-1500 Fax: (703)247-1678 E-mail: iihs@hwysafety.org • URL: http://www.hwysafety.org • Studies highway safety, including seat belt use, air bags, property damage, vehicle recalls, and the role of alcohol and drugs.

Texas Transportation Institute. Texas A & M University System, College Station, TX 77843-3135. Phone: (979)845-8552 Fax: (979)845-9356 E-mail: h.hrichardson@tamu.edu • URL: http://tti.tamu.edu • Concerned with all forms and modes of transportation. Research areas include transportation economics, highway construction, traffic safety, public transportation, and highway engineering.

Transportation Research Institute. University of Michigan, 2901 Baxter Rd., Ann Arbor, MI 48109-2150. Phone: (734)764-6504 Fax: (734)936-1081 E-mail: umtri@umich.edu • URL: http://www.umtri.umich.edu • Research areas include highway safety, transportation systems, and shipbuilding.

STATISTICS SOURCES

Accident Facts. National Safety Council. • Annual. $37.95.

TRADE/PROFESSIONAL ASSOCIATIONS

American Driver and Traffic Safety Education Association. Highway Safety Center, IUP, Indiana, PA 15705. Phone: (724)357-4051 Fax: (724)357-7595.

American Highway Users Alliance. 1776 Massachusetts Ave., N.W., Washington, DC 20036. Phone: 888-499-8777 or (202)857-1200 Fax: (202)857-1220 E-mail: gohighway@aol.com • URL: http://www.highways.org.

Center for Auto Safety. 1825 Connecticut Ave., 330, Washington, DC 20009-1160. Phone: (202)328-7700 • URL: http://www.autosafety.org.

National Safety Council. 1121 Spring Lake Dr., Itasca, IL 60143-3201. Phone: 800-621-7615 or (630)285-1121 Fax: (630)285-1315 • URL: http://www.nsc.org.

TRAFFIC ENGINEERING

See also: TOLL ROADS; TRAFFIC MANAGEMENT (STREETS AND HIGHWAYS); TRANSPORTATION INDUSTRY

GENERAL WORKS

Principles of Highway Engineering and Traffic Analysis. Fred L. Mannering and Walter P. Kilareski. John Wiley and Sons, Inc. • 1997. $64.95. Second edition.

ABSTRACTS AND INDEXES

Transportation Research Information Services (TRIS). Transportation Research Board, Highway Research Information. • Monthly. Price on application. Formerly *Highway Research Abstracts.*

ENCYCLOPEDIAS AND DICTIONARIES

Macmillan Encyclopedia of Transportation. Available from The Gale Group. • 2000. $375.00. Six volumes. Published by Macmillan Reference USA. Covers the business, technology, and history of transportation on land, on water, in the air, and in space. Includes definitions, cross-references, and 200 color illustrations.

HANDBOOKS AND MANUALS

Transportation Engineering and Planning. C. S. Papacostas and Panos D. Prevedouros. Prentice Hall. • 2000. $105.00. Third edition.

Transportation Planning Handbook. John D. Edwards. Institute of Transportation Engineers Staff. • 1999. $110.00. Second edition.

PERIODICALS AND NEWSLETTERS

ITE Journal. Institute of Transportation Engineers. • Monthly. $60.00 per year. Formerly *Transportation Engineering.*

Traffic Engineering and Control. Printerhall Ltd. • Monthly. $120.00 per year. Provides authoritative articles on planning, engineering and management of highways for safe and efficient operation.

Traffic World: The Weekly Newsmagazine of Transportation and Distribution. Journal of Commerce, Inc. • Weekly. $174.00 per year.

Transportation Quarterly. Eno Transportation Foundation. • Quarterly. $55.00 per year. To qualify a written request must be submitted.

TRADE/PROFESSIONAL ASSOCIATIONS

American Road and Transportation Builders Association. The ARTBA Bldg., 1010 Massachusetts Ave., N.W., Washington, DC 20001. Phone: (202)289-4434 Fax: (202)289-4435 E-mail: artba@aol.com • URL: http://www.artba.org • Promotes on-the-job training programs.

ENO Transportation Foundation. One Farragut Square, S., Ste. 500, Washington, District of Columbia, 20006-4003. Phone: (202)879-4700 Fax: (202)879-4719 • URL: http://www.enotrans.com.

Institute of Transportation Engineers. 525 School St., S.W., Suite 410, Washington, DC 20024-2797. Phone: (202)554-8050 Fax: (202)863-5486 • URL: http://www.ite.org • Members are professionals in surface transportation, mass transit, and traffic engineering.

TRAFFIC MANAGEMENT (INDUSTRIAL)

See also: DISTRIBUTION; TRANSPORTATION INDUSTRY

BIBLIOGRAPHIES

Business Information Sources. Lorna M. Daniells. California Princeton Fulfillment Services. • 1993. $42.50. Third revised edition. Basic business sources, with discussion and full annotations.

ENCYCLOPEDIAS AND DICTIONARIES

Blackwell Encyclopedic Dictionary of Operations Management. Nigel Slack, editor. Blackwell Publishers. • 1997. $105.95. The editor is associated with the University of Warwick, England. Contains definitions of key terms combined with longer articles written by various U. S. and foreign business educators. Includes bibliographies and index. (Blackwell Encyclopedia of Management Series.).

PERIODICALS AND NEWSLETTERS

Chilton's Distribution: The Transportation and Business Logistics Magazine. Cahners Business Information. • Monthly. $65.00 per year.

Logistics Management and Distribution Report: For Buyers of Logistics, Transportation Services, Logistic Technology and Related Equipment. Cahners Publishing Co. • Monthly. $92.90 per year. Includes *International Shipping* and *Warehousing and Distribution.* Formerly *Logistics Management.*

Traffic World: The Weekly Newsmagazine of Transportation and Distribution. Journal of Commerce, Inc. • Weekly. $174.00 per year.

Transportation and Distribution. Penton Media Inc. • Monthly. Free to qualified personnel; others, $50.00 per year. Essential information on transportation and distribution practices in domestic and international trade.

Transportation Journal. American Society of Transportation and Logistics, Inc. • Quarterly. $55.00 per year.

TRADE/PROFESSIONAL ASSOCIATIONS

American Society of Transportation and Logistics. 320 E. Water St., Lock Haven, PA 17745-1419. Phone: (570)748-8515 Fax: (570)748-9118 E-mail: info@astl.org • URL: http://www.astl.org.

National Industrial Transportation League. 1700 N. Moore St., Suite 1900, Arlington, VA 22209-1904. Phone: (703)524-5011 Fax: (703)524-5017 E-mail: info@nitl.org • URL: http://www.nitl.org.

TRAFFIC MANAGEMENT (STREETS AND HIGHWAYS)

See also: TRAFFIC ENGINEERING; TRANSPORTATION INDUSTRY

GENERAL WORKS

Moving Beyond Gridlock: Traffic and Development. Robert T. Dunphy. Urban Land Institute. • 1996. $45.95. Describes how various regions have dealt with traffic growth. Includes case studies from seven cities.

ABSTRACTS AND INDEXES

Current Literature in Traffic and Transportation. Northwestern University, Transportation Library. • Quarterly. $25.00 per year.

Transportation Research Information Services (TRIS). Transportation Research Board, Highway Research Information. • Monthly. Price on application. Formerly *Highway Research Abstracts.*

BIBLIOGRAPHIES

Road Construction and Safety. Available from U. S. Government Printing Office. • Annual. Free. Issued by the Superintendent of Documents. A list of government publications on highway construction and traffic safety. Formerly *Highway Construction, Safety and Traffic.* (Subject Bibliography No. 3.).

DIRECTORIES

Jane's Road Traffic Management. Jane's Information Group, Inc. • Annual. $375.00. A directory of traffic control equipment and services. Includes detailed product descriptions.

HANDBOOKS AND MANUALS

Standard Highway Signs, as Specified in the Manual on Uniform Traffic Control Devices. Available from U. S. Government Printing Office. • Looseleaf. $70.00. Issued by the U. S. Department of Transportation (http://www.dot.gov). Includes basic manual, with updates for an indeterminate period. Contains illustrations of typical standard signs approved for use on streets and highways, and provides information on dimensions and placement of symbols.

ONLINE DATABASES

TRIS: Transportation Research Information Service. National Research Council. • Contains abstracts and citations to a wide range of transportation literature, 1968 to present, with monthly updates. Includes references to the literature of air transportation, highways, ships and shipping, railroads, trucking, and urban mass transportation. Formerly *TRIS-ON-LINE.* Inquire as to online cost and availability.

PERIODICALS AND NEWSLETTERS

Downtown Idea Exchange: Essential Information for Downtown Research and Development Center. Downtown Research and Development Center. Alexander Communications Group, Inc. • Semimonthly. $157.00 per year. Newsletter for those concerned with central business districts. Provides news and other information on planning, development, parking, mass transit, traffic, funding, and other topics.

Public Roads: A Journal of Highway Research and Development. Available from U.S. Government Printing Office. • Bimonthly. $18.00 per year.

Transportation Journal. American Society of Transportation and Logistics, Inc. • Quarterly. $55.00 per year.

World Highways. International Road Federation. • Eight times a year. $165.00 per year. Text in English, French, German and Spanish.

RESEARCH CENTERS AND INSTITUTES

Center for Public Safety. Northwestern University. P.O. Box 1409, Evanston, IL 60204-1409. Phone: 800-323-4011 or (847)491-5476 Fax: (847)491-5270 E-mail: alweiss@nwu.edu • URL: http://www.nwu.edu/traffic.

STATISTICS SOURCES

Highway Statistics. Federal Highway Administration, U.S. Department of Transportation. Available from U.S. Government Printing Office. • Annual. $26.00.

TRADE/PROFESSIONAL ASSOCIATIONS

American Association of Motor Vehicle Administrators. 4301 Wilson Blvd. Suite 400, Arlington, VA 22203-1800. Phone: (703)522-4200 Fax: (703)522-1553 • URL: http://www.aamva.org.

American Society of Transportation and Logistics. 320 E. Water St., Lock Haven, PA 17745-1419. Phone: (570)748-8515 Fax: (570)748-9118 E-mail: info@astl.org • URL: http://www.astl.org.

TRAILERS

See: MOBILE HOME INDUSTRY; RECREATIONAL VEHICLE INDUSTRY; TRUCK TRAILERS

TRAINING OF EMPLOYEES

See also: EXECUTIVE TRAINING AND DEVELOPMENT

ALMANACS AND YEARBOOKS

Training and Development Yearbook. Carolyn Nilson. Prentice Hall. • Annual. $79.95. Includes reprints of journal articles on employee training and development.

DIRECTORIES

The Human Resource Executive's Market Resource. LRP Publications. • Annual. $25.00. A directory of services and products of use to personnel departments. Includes 20 categories, such as training, outplacement, health benefits, recognition awards, testing, workers' compensation, temporary staffing, recruitment, and human resources software.

Training and Development Organizations Directory. The Gale Group. • 1994. $385.00. Sixth edition.

ENCYCLOPEDIAS AND DICTIONARIES

Dictionary of HRD. Angus Reynolds and others. • 1997. $67.95. Provides definitions of more than 3,000 terms related to human resource development. Includes acronyms, abbreviations, and a list of "100 Essential HRD Terms." Published by Gower in England.

HANDBOOKS AND MANUALS

Career Guide to Industries. Available from U. S. Government Printing Office. • 1998. $17.00. Issued by the Bureau of Labor Statistics, U. S. Department of Labor (http://www.bls.gov). Presents background career information (text) and statistics for the 40 industries that account for 70 percent of wage and salary jobs in the U. S. Includes nature of the industry, employment data, working conditions, training, earnings, rate of job growth, outlook, and other career factors. (BLS Bulletin 2503.).

Equality in the Workplace: An Equal Opportunities Handbook for Trainers. Helen Collins. Blackwell Publishers. • 1995. $43.95. (Human Resource Management in Action Series).

Gower Handbook of Training and Development. John Prior, editor. Ashgate Publishing Co. • 1994. $109.95. Second edition. Consists of 40 chapters written by various authors. Includes glossary and index. Published by Gower in England.

Handbook of Training Evaluation and Measurement Methods. Jack J. Phillips. Gulf Publishing Co. • 1997. $55.00. Third edition. (Improving Human Performance Series).

How to Develop a Personnel Policy Manual. Joseph Lawson. AMACOM. • 1998. $75.00. Sixth edition.

How to Manage Training: A Guide to Administration, Design and Delivery. Carolyn Nilson. AMACOM. • 1991. $69.95. Looseleaf service. Presents ideas and techniques for cost-effective training.

Sexual Harassment Awareness Training: 60 Practical Activities for Trainers. Andrea P. Baridon and David R. Eyler. McGraw-Hill. • 1996. $21.95. Discusses the kinds of sexual harassment, judging workplace behavior, application of the "reasonable person standard," employer liability, and related issues.

Studying Your Workforce: Applied Research Methods and Tools for the Training and Development Practitioner. Alan Clardy. Sage Publications, Inc. • 1997. $45.00. Describes how to apply specific research methods to common training problems. Emphasis is on data collection methods: testing, observation, surveys, and interviews. Topics include performance problems and assessment.

Training for Non-Trainers: A Do-It-Yourself Guide for Managers. Carolyn Nilson. AMACOM. • 1990. $16.95.

PERIODICALS AND NEWSLETTERS

Human Resource Executive. LRP Publications, Inc. • Monthly. $89.95 per year. Edited for directors of corporate human resource departments. Special issues emphasize training, benefits, retirement planning, recruitment, outplacement, workers' compensation, legal pitfalls, and oes emphasize training, benefits, retirement planning, recruitment, outplacement, workers' compensation, legal pitfalls, and other personnel topics.

Team Leader. Dartnell Corp. • Biweekly. $76.70 per year. Newsletter. Includes coverage of self-directed work groups.

Training and Development. American Society for Training and Development. • Monthly. Free to members; non-members, $85.00 per year.

Training: The Magazine of Covering the Human Side of Business. Lakewood Publications, Inc. • Monthly. $78.00 per year.

Vocational Training News: The Independent Weekly Report on Employment, Training, and Vocational Education. Aspen Publishers, Inc. • Weekly. $319.00 per year. Newsletter. Emphasis is on federal job training and vocational education programs. Formerly *Manpower and Vocational Education Weekly.*

Workforce: The Business Magazine for Leaders in Human Resources. ACC Communications, Inc. •

Monthly. $59.00 per year. Edited for human resources managers. Covers employee benefits, compensation, relocation, recruitment, training, personnel legalities, and related subjects. Supplements include bimonthly "New Product News" and semiannual "Recruitment/Staffing Sourcebook." Formerly *Personnel Journal.*

RESEARCH CENTERS AND INSTITUTES

Industrial Relations Section. Princeton University, Firestone Library, Pinceton, NJ 08544. Phone: (609)258-4040 Fax: (609)258-2907 • URL: http://www.irs.princeton.edu/ • Fields of research include labor supply, manpower training, unemployment, and equal employment opportunity.

Institute of Advanced Manufacturing Sciences, Inc. 1111 Edison Dr., Cincinnati, OH 45216. Phone: (513)948-2000 Fax: (513)948-2109 E-mail: conley@iams.org • URL: http://www.iams.org • Fields of research include quality improvement, computer-aided design, artificial intelligence, and employee training.

National Institute for Work and Learning. Academy for Educational Development, 1875 Connecticut Ave., N.W., Washington, DC 20009. Phone: (202)884-8187 Fax: (202)884-8422 E-mail: ichaner@aed.org • URL: http://www.niwl.org • Research areas include adult education, training, unemployment insurance, and career development.

W. E. Upjohn Institute for Employment Research. 300 S. Westnedge Ave., Kalamazoo, MI 49007-4686. Phone: (616)343-5541 Fax: (616)343-3308 E-mail: eberts@we.upjohninst.org • URL: http://www.upjohninst.org • Research fields include unemployment, unemployment insurance, worker's compensation, labor productivity, profit sharing, the labor market, economic development, earnings, training, and other areas related to employment.

STATISTICS SOURCES

Occupational Projections and Training Data. Available from U. S. Government Printing Office. • Biennial. $7.00. Issued by Bureau of Labor Statistics, U. S. Department of Labor. Contains projections of employment change and job openings over the next 15 years for about 500 specific occupations. Also includes the number of associate, bachelor's, master's, doctoral, and professional degrees awarded in a recent year for about 900 specific fields of study.

TRADE/PROFESSIONAL ASSOCIATIONS

Adult Workforce Education Organization. 2815 25th St., Meridian, MS 39305. Phone: (601)484-5165 Fax: (601)484-4999 • Members are concerned with employee training and vocational education. Formerly National Employment and Training Association.

American Institute, Inc. 4301 Fairfax Dr., Suite 630, Arlington, VA 22203-1627. 4301 Fairfax Dr., Suite 630,.

American Society for Training and Development. P.O. Box 1443, Alexandria, VA 22313-2043. Phone: (703)683-8100 Fax: (703)683-8103 E-mail: csc4@astd.org • URL: http://www.astd.org.

American Technical Education Association. c/o North Dakota State College of Science. 800 N. Sixth St., Wahpeton, ND 58076. Phone: (701)671-2301 or (701)671-2240 Fax: (701)671-2660 E-mail: krump@plains.nodak.edu • URL: http://www.ndscs.nodak.edu/atea/.

Center on Education and Training for Employment. Ohio State University. 1900 Kenny Rd., Columbus, OH 43210. Phone: 800-848-4815 or (614)292-4353 Fax: (614)292-1260 • URL: http://www.cete.org/products/.

Manpower Education Institute. 715 Ladd Rd., Bronx, NY 10471. Phone: (718)548-4200 Fax: (718)548-4202 E-mail: meiready@aol.com • URL: http://www.manpower.education.org.

National Association for Industry-Education Cooperation. 235 Hendricks Blvd., Buffalo, NY 14226. Phone: (716)834-7047 Fax: (716)834-7047 E-mail: naiec@pcom.net • URL: http://www.pcom.net/naiec.

National Association of State Supervisors of Trade and Industrial Education. c/o Ralph Green, Division of Technical and Adult Education, Capital Complex Bldg. 6, 1900 Kanawha Blvd., E., Room 243, Charleston, WV 25305. Phone: (304)558-6314 or (304)558-6313 Fax: (304)558-1149 E-mail: rgreen@access.kiz.wv.us.

OTHER SOURCES

Employment and Training Reporter. MII Publications, Inc. • $747.00 per year. Looseleaf service. Weekly reports. Two volumes.

TRAINS

See: RAILROADS

TRANSDUCERS, INDUSTRIAL

See: CONTROL EQUIPMENT INDUSTRY

TRANSISTORS

See: SEMICONDUCTOR INDUSTRY

TRANSLATING MACHINES

See: MACHINE TRANSLATING

TRANSLATIONS AND TRANSLATORS

See also: MACHINE TRANSLATING

ABSTRACTS AND INDEXES

Transdex Index. UMI. • Monthly. Price on application.

DIRECTORIES

ATA Translation Services Directory. American Translators Association. • Avalible online. Over 3,700 member translators and interpreters. Formerly *Professional Services Directory of the American Translators Association.*

ENCYCLOPEDIAS AND DICTIONARIES

Lexique General; A General Lexicon of Terms-United Nations as Well as General-Used by Translators, Interpreters, etc. United Nations Publications. • 1991. Fourth edition.

HANDBOOKS AND MANUALS

Language Translation Service. Entrepreneur Media, Inc. • Looseleaf. $59.50. A practical guide to starting a language translation service. Covers profit potential, start-up costs, market size evaluation, pricing, accounting, advertising, promotion, etc. (Start-Up Business Guide No. E1353.).

PERIODICALS AND NEWSLETTERS

ATA Chronicle. American Translators Association. • Monthly. $50.00.

TRADE/PROFESSIONAL ASSOCIATIONS

American Translators Association. 225 Reinekers Ln., Ste. 590, Alexandria, VA 22314. Phone: (703)683-6100 Fax: (703)683-6122 E-mail: ata@atanet.org • URL: http://www.atanet.org.

International Association of Conference Translators. 15, route des Morillons, CH-1218 Grand-Saconnex, Switzerland. Phone: 41 22 7910666 Fax: 41 22 7885644 E-mail: aitc@atge.automail.com.

Society of Federal Linguists. P.O. Box 7765, Washington, DC 20044. Phone: (202)707-5397 E-mail: president@federal-linguists.org • URL: http://www.federal-linguists.org.

TRANSPORTATION EQUIPMENT INDUSTRY

FINANCIAL RATIOS

Almanac of Business and Industrial Financial Ratios. Leo Troy. Prentice Hall. • Annual. $99.95. Contains financial ratios derived from federal tax returns. Ratios for each of about 200 industries are arranged according to company asset size.

Industry Norms and Key Business Ratios. Desk Top Edition. Dun and Bradstreet Corp., Business Information Services. • Annual. Five volumes. $475.00 per volume. $1,890.00 per set. Covers over 800 kinds of businesses, arranged by Standard Industrial Classification number. More detailed editions covering longer periods of time are also available.

Quarterly Financial Report for Manufacturing, Mining, and Trade Corporations. U.S. Federal Trade Commission and U.S. Securities and Exchange Commission. Available from U.S. Government Printing Office. • Quarterly. $39.00 per year.

ONLINE DATABASES

TRIS: Transportation Research Information Service. National Research Council. • Contains abstracts and citations to a wide range of transportation literature, 1968 to present, with monthly updates. Includes references to the literature of air transportation, highways, ships and shipping, railroads, trucking, and urban mass transportation. Formerly *TRIS-ON-LINE.* Inquire as to online cost and availability.

PERIODICALS AND NEWSLETTERS

ITE Journal. Institute of Transportation Engineers. • Monthly. $60.00 per year. Formerly *Transportation Engineering.*

STATISTICS SOURCES

Annual Survey of Manufactures. Available from U. S. Government Printing Office. • Annual. Prices vary. Issued by the U. S. Census Bureau as an interim update to the *Census of Manufactures.* Includes data on number of manufacturing establishments in various industries, employment, labor costs, value of shipments, capital expenditures, inventories, energy costs, and assets. (See also Census Bureau home page, http://www.census.gov/.).

WEFA Industrial Monitor. John Wiley and Sons, Inc. • Annual. $65.00. Prepared by industry analysts at WEFA, an economic forecasting and consulting firm (originally Wharton Econometric Forecasting Associates). Contains discussions of the outlook for major U. S. industries, with many 10-year forecasts (WEFA Web site is http://www.wefa.com).

TRANSPORTATION INDUSTRY

GENERAL WORKS

Transportation. Time-Life, Inc. • 1999. $16.95. Revised edition. (Understanding Computers Series.).

ABSTRACTS AND INDEXES

Current Literature in Traffic and Transportation. Northwestern University, Transportation Library. • Quarterly. $25.00 per year.

NTIS Alerts: Transportation. National Technical Information Service. • Semimonthly. $210.00 per year. Provides descriptions of government-sponsored research reports and software, with ordering information. Covers air, marine, highway, inland waterway, pipeline, and railroad transportation. Formerly *Abstract Newsletter*.

ALMANACS AND YEARBOOKS

Research in Transportation Economics. JAI Press, Inc. • Irregular. $78.50.

CD-ROM DATABASES

WILSONDISC: Wilson Business Abstracts. H. W. Wilson Co. • Monthly. $2,495.00 per year, including unlimited online access to *Wilson Business Abstracts* through WILSONLINE. Provides CD-ROM "cover-to-cover" abstracting and indexing of over 600 prominent business periodicals. Indexing is from 1982, abstracting from 1990. (*Business Periodicals Index* without abstracts is available on CD-ROM at $1,495 per year.).

DIRECTORIES

Jane's Urban Transport Systems. Jane's Information Group, Inc. • Annual. $352.00; CD-Rom edition, $650.00. Operating bus, metro, light rail, tram, ferry, and trolley bus transport systems. Includes manufacturers of equipment for urban systems.

Transportation Telephone Tickler. Journal of Commerce, Inc. • Annual. $99.95. Four volumes. National edition. Directory of freight services and facilities in all U.S. and Canadian ports. Eleven regional editions are also available. $15.00 per volume.

ENCYCLOPEDIAS AND DICTIONARIES

Dictionary of Shipping Terms. Peter Brodie. Available from Informa Publishing Group Ltd. • 1997. $57.00. Third edition. Published in the UK by Lloyd's List (http://www.lloydslist.com). Defines more than 2,000 words, phrases, and abbreviations related to the shipping and maritime industries.

Macmillan Encyclopedia of Transportation. Available from The Gale Group. • 2000. $375.00. Six volumes. Published by Macmillan Reference USA. Covers the business, technology, and history of transportation on land, on water, in the air, and in space. Includes definitions, cross-references, and 200 color illustrations.

FINANCIAL RATIOS

Almanac of Business and Industrial Financial Ratios. Leo Troy. Prentice Hall. • Annual. $99.95. Contains financial ratios derived from federal tax returns. Ratios for each of about 200 industries are arranged according to company asset size.

HANDBOOKS AND MANUALS

Recommendations on the Transport of Dangerous Goods. United Nations Publications. • 1999. $120.00. 11th edition. Covers regulations imposed by various governments and international organizations.

Transportation Engineering and Planning. C. S. Papacostas and Panos D. Prevedouros. Prentice Hall. • 2000. $105.00. Third edition.

Transportation Planning Handbook. John D. Edwards. Institute of Transportation Engineers Staff. • 1999. $110.00. Second edition.

INTERNET DATABASES

Bureau of Economic Analysis (BEA). U. S. Department of Commerce, Bureau of Economic Analysis. Phone: (202)606-9900 Fax: (202)606-5310 E-mail: webmaster@bea.doc.gov • URL: http://www.bea.doc.gov • Web site includes "News Release Information" covering national, regional, and international economic estimates from the BEA. Highlights of releases appear online the same day, complete text and tables appear the next day. "Recent News Releases" section provides titles for past nine months, with links. "BEA Data and Methodology" includes "Frequently Requested NIPA Data" (national income and product accounts, such as gross domestic product and personal income). Other statistics are available. Fees: Free.

Fedstats. Federal Interagency Council on Statistical Policy. Phone: (202)395-7254 • URL: http://www.fedstats.gov • Web site features an efficient search facility for full-text statistics produced by more than 70 federal agencies, including the Census Bureau, the Bureau of Economic Analysis, and the Bureau of Labor Statistics. Boolean searches can be made within one agency or for all agencies combined. Links are offered to international statistical bureaus, including the UN, IMF, OECD, UNESCO, Eurostat, and 20 individual countries. Fees: Free.

ONLINE DATABASES

Business and Industry. Responsive Database Services, Inc. • Contains online citations, abstracts, and selected fulltext from more than 1,000 trade journals, newspapers, and other publications. Provides general coverage of both manufacturing and service industries, including marketing, production, industry trends, key events, and information on specific companies. Time span is 1994 to date. Daily updates. Inquire as to online cost and availability. (Also available in a CD-ROM version.).

DRI U.S. Central Database. Data Products Division. • Provides more than 23,000 business, financial, demographic, economic, foreign trade, and industry-related time series for the U.S. Includes national income, population, retail-wholesale trade, price indexes, labor data, housing, industrial production, banking, interest rates, money supply, etc. Time period is generally 1947 to date (some data back to 1929). Updating varies. Inquire as to online cost and availability.

Tablebase. Responsive Database Services, Inc. • Provides online numerical tabular data from a wide variety of business, organization, and government sources, including 900 trade journals. Includes industry and individual company statistics relating to products, market share, sales forecasts, production, exports, market trends, etc. Time span is 1997 to date. Weekly updates. Inquire as to online cost and availability. (Also available in a CD-ROM version.).

TRIS: Transportation Research Information Service. National Research Council. • Contains abstracts and citations to a wide range of transportation literature, 1968 to present, with monthly updates. Includes references to the literature of air transportation, highways, ships and shipping, railroads, trucking, and urban mass transportation. Formerly *TRIS-ON-LINE*. Inquire as to online cost and availability.

Wilson Business Abstracts Online. H. W. Wilson Co. • Indexes and abstracts 600 major business periodicals, plus the *Wall Street Journal* and the business section of the *New York Times*. Indexing is from 1982, abstracting from 1990, with the two newspapers included from 1993. Updated weekly. Inquire as to online cost and availability. (*Business Periodicals Index* without abstracts is also available online.).

PERIODICALS AND NEWSLETTERS

Defense Transportation Journal: Magazine of International Defense Transportation and Logistics. National Defense Transportation Association. • Bimonthly. Free to members; non-members, $35.00 per year.

Hazardous Materials Transportation. Washington Business Information, Inc. • Biweekly. $797.00 per year. Looseleaf service. Newsletter on the responsibilities of shippers and carriers for the safe transportation of hazardous materials.

ITE Journal. Institute of Transportation Engineers. • Monthly. $60.00 per year. Formerly *Transportation Engineering*.

Journal of Transport Economics and Policy. University of Bath. • Three times a year. Individuals, $54.00 per year; institutions, $120.00 per year; students, $20.00 per year. Text in English, French, German and Spanish.

Modern Bulk Transporter. Intertec Publishing Corp. • Monthly. Price on application.

Passenger Transport. American Public Transit Association. • Weekly. $65.00 per year. Covers current events and trends in mass transportation.

Research on Transport Economics. OECD Publications and Information Center. • Annual. $98.00.

Transport 2000 and Intermodal World. BuenaVentura Publishing Co. • Bimonthly. $15.00 per year.

Transportation: An International Journal Devoted to the Improvement of Transportation Planning and Practice. Kluwer Academic Publishers. • Quarterly. $370.00 per year.

Transportation Journal. American Society of Transportation and Logistics, Inc. • Quarterly. $55.00 per year.

Transportation Review Part E: Logistics and Transportation Review. University of British Columbia Centre for Transportation Studies. Available from Elsevier Science Inc. • Bimonthly. $735.00 per year.

Transportation Science. • Quarterly. $69.00 per year.

Urban Transport News: Management, Funding, Ridership, Technology. Business Publishers, Inc. • Biweekly. $407.00 per year. Provides current news from Capitol Hill, the White House, the Dept. of Transportation, as well as transit operations and industries across the country.

RESEARCH CENTERS AND INSTITUTES

Center for Transportation Studies. Massachusetts Institute of Technology. 77 Massachusetts Ave. Room 1-235, Cambridge, MA 02139. Phone: (617)253-5320 Fax: (617)253-4560 E-mail: ctsmail@mit.edu • URL: http://www.web.mit.edu/cts/www/.

Institute of Transportation Studies. University of California at Berkeley. 109 McLaughlin Hall, Berkeley, CA 94720. Phone: (510)642-3585 Fax: (510)642-1246 E-mail: its@its.berkeley.edu • URL: http://www.its.berkeley.edu.

Texas Transportation Institute. Texas A & M University System, College Station, TX 77843-3135. Phone: (979)845-8552 Fax: (979)845-9356 E-mail: h.hrichardson@tamu.edu • URL: http://tti.tamu.edu • Concerned with all forms and modes of transportation. Research areas include transportation economics, highway construction, traffic safety, public transportation, and highway engineering.

Transportation Center. Northwestern University, 600 Foster, Evanston, IL 60208-4055. Phone: (847)491-7287 Fax: (847)491-3090 E-mail: a-gellman@northwestern.edu • URL: http://www.nutcweb.tpc.nwu.edu.

Transportation Program. Princeton University Operations Research and Financial. E-407 Engineering Quadrangle, Princeton, NJ 08544. Phone: (609)258-1563 Fax: (609)683-0290 E-mail: alaink@princeton.edu.

Transportation Research Center. University of Florida. P.O. Box 116585, Gainesville, FL 32611-6585. Phone: 800-226-1013 or (352)392-7575 Fax:

(352)392-3224 E-mail: uftrc@nervm.nerdc.ufl.edu • URL: http://www.uftrc.ce.ufl.edu.

Transportation Research Institute. University of Michigan, 2901 Baxter Rd., Ann Arbor, MI 48109-2150. Phone: (734)764-6504 Fax: (734)936-1081 E-mail: umtri@umich.edu • URL: http://www.umtri.umich.edu • Research areas include highway safety, transportation systems, and shipbuilding.

STATISTICS SOURCES

Business Statistics of the United States. Courtenay M. Slater, editor. Bernan Associates. • 1999. $74.00. Fifth edition. Based on *Business Statistics*, formerly issue by the Bureau of Economic Analysis, U. S. Department of Commerce. Provides basic data for a wide variety of U. S. industries, services, and economic indicators. Most statistics are shown annually for 29 years and monthly for the most recent four years.

Encyclopedia of American Industries. The Gale Group. • 1998. $560.00. Second edition. Two volumes. $280.00 per volume. Volume one is *Manufacturing Industries* and volume two is *Service and Non-Manufacturing Industries*. Provides the history, development, and recent status of approximately 1,000 industries. Includes statistical graphs, with industry and general indexes.

Monthly Bulletin of Statistics. United Nations Publications. • Monthly. $295.00 per year. Provides current data for about 200 countries on a wide variety of economic, industrial, and demographic subjects. Compiled by United Nations Statistical Office.

Standard & Poor's Industry Surveys. Standard & Poor's. • Semiannual. $1,800.00. Two looseleaf volumes. Includes monthly supplements. Provides detailed, individual surveys of 52 major industry groups. Each survey is revised on a semiannual basis. Also includes "Monthly Investment Review" (industry group investment analysis) and monthly "Trends & Projections" (economic analysis).

Statistical Yearbook. United Nations Publications. • Annual. $125.00. Contains statistics for about 200 countries on a wide variety of economic, industrial, and demographic topics. Compiled by United Nations Statistical Office.

Survey of Current Business. Available from U. S. Government Printing Office. • Monthly. $49.00 per year. Issued by Bureau of Economic Analysis, U. S. Department of Commerce. Presents a wide variety of business and economic data.

Transportation Statistics Annual Report. Available from U. S. Government Printing Office. • Annual. $21.00. Issued by the U. S. Bureau of Transportation Statistics, Transportation Department (http://www.bts.gov). Summarizes national data for various forms of transportation, including airlines, railroads, and motor vehicles. Information on the use of roads and highways is included.

U. S. Industry and Trade Outlook: The McGraw-Hill Companies and the U.S. Department of Commerce/International Trade Administration. Datapso Research Corp. • Annual. $69.95. Produced by the International Trade Administration, U. S. Department of Commerce, in a "public-private" partnership with DRI/McGraw-Hill and Standard & Poor's. Provides basic data, outlook for the current year, and "Long-Term Prospects" (five-year projections) for a wide variety of products and services. Includes high technology industries. Formerly *U. S. Industrial Outlook.*

U. S. Industry Profiles: The Leading 100. The Gale Group. • 1998. $120.00. Second edition. Contains detailed profiles, with statistics, of 100 industries in the areas of manufacturing, construction, transportation, wholesale trade, retail trade, and entertainment.

United States Census of Transportation. Bureau of the Census, U.S. Department of Commerce. Available from U.S. Government Printing Office. • Quinquennial.

World Statistics Pocketbook. United Nations Publications. • Annual. $10.00. Presents basic economic, social, and environmental indicators for about 200 countries and areas. Covers more than 50 items relating to population, economic activity, labor force, agriculture, industry, energy, trade, transportation, communication, education, tourism, and the environment. Statistical sources are noted.

TRADE/PROFESSIONAL ASSOCIATIONS

American Public Transit Association. 1201 New York Ave., N.W., Suite 400, Washington, DC 20005. Phone: (202)898-4000 Fax: (202)898-4070 • URL: http://www.apta.com • Members are bus and rail urban transportation systems.

American Society of Transportation and Logistics. 320 E. Water St., Lock Haven, PA 17745-1419. Phone: (570)748-8515 Fax: (570)748-9118 E-mail: info@astl.org • URL: http://www.astl.org.

Institute of Transportation Engineers. 525 School St., S.W., Suite 410, Washington, DC 20024-2797. Phone: (202)554-8050 Fax: (202)863-5486 • URL: http://www.ite.org • Members are professionals in surface transportation, mass transit, and traffic engineering.

National Defense Transportation Association. 50 S. Pickett St., Suite 220, Alexandria, VA 22304-7296. Phone: (703)751-5011 Fax: (703)823-8761 E-mail: ndta@ndtahq.com • URL: http://www.web2volpe.dot.gov/ndta.

Transportation Clubs International. 7116 Stinson Ave., No. B-221, Gig Harbor, WA 98335-1100. E-mail: firstchoicesuc@sprintmail.com • URL: http://www.trans-club.com.

OTHER SOURCES

Federal Carriers Reports. CCH, Inc. • Biweekly. $1,372.00 per year. Four looseleaf volumes. Periodic supplementation. Federal rules and regulations for motor carriers, water carriers, and freight forwarders.

Infrastructure Industries USA. The Gale Group. • 2001. $240.00. Replaces *Agriculture, Forestry, Fishing, Mining, and Construction USA* and *Transportation and Public Utilities USA*. Presents statistics and projections relating to economic activity in a wide variety of natural resource and construction industries.

TRANSPORTATION, PUBLIC

See: PUBLIC TRANSPORTATION

TRANSPORTATION TIME TABLES

See: TIMETABLES

TRAVEL AGENCIES

See also: TRAVEL INDUSTRY

BIBLIOGRAPHIES

Travel and Tourism. Available from U. S. Government Printing Office. • Annual. Free. Issued by the Superintendent of Documents. A list of government publications on the travel industry and tourism. Formerly *Mass Transit, Travel and Tourism.* (Subject Bibliography No. 302.).

DIRECTORIES

American Society of Travel Agents-Membership Directory. American Society of Travel Agents. • Annual. $195.00. Listings of over 13,500 worldwide members of ASTA.

Travel Industry Personnel Directory. Fairchild Books. • Annual. $25.00. Air and steamship lines, tour operators, bus lines, hotel representatives, foreign and domestic railroads, foreign and domestic tourist information offices, travel trade associations, etc. Includes names of personnel.

FINANCIAL RATIOS

Annual Statement Studies. Robert Morris Associates: The Association of Lending and Credit Risk Professiona. • Annual. Free to members; non-members, $140.00. Median and quartile financial ratios are given for over 400 kinds of manufacturing, wholesale, retail, construction, and consumer finance establishments. Data is sorted by both asset size and sales volume. Includes a clearly written "Definition of Ratios" and an alphabetical industry index.

HANDBOOKS AND MANUALS

Travel Agency. Entrepreneur Media, Inc. • Looseleaf. $59.50. A practical guide to starting a travel agency. Covers profit potential, start-up costs, market size evaluation, owner's time required, site selection, lease negotiation, pricing, accounting, advertising, promotion, etc. (Start-Up Business Guide No. E1154.).

PERIODICALS AND NEWSLETTERS

ASTA Agency Management: Official Publication of American Society of Travel Agents, Inc. Pace Communications. • Monthly. $36.00 per year.

Travel Agent: The National Newsweekly Magazine of the Travel Industry. Advanstar Communications Inc. • 54 times a year. 250.00 per. year.

TRADE/PROFESSIONAL ASSOCIATIONS

American Society of Travel Agents. 1101 King St., Suite 200, Alexandria, VA 22314. Phone: (703)739-2782 Fax: (703)549-7987 • URL: http://www.astanet.com.

Association of Retail Travel Agents. 2692 Richmond Rd., Ste. 202, Lexington, KY 40509-1542. Phone: 800-969-6069 or (606)269-9739 Fax: (606)266-9396 E-mail: info@artahdq.com • URL: http://www.artaonline.com.

Institute of Certified Travel Agents. P.O. Box 812059, Wellesley, MA 02482. Phone: 800-542-4282 or (781)237-0280 Fax: (781)237-3860 E-mail: icta-info@icta.com • URL: http://www.icta.com.

OTHER SOURCES

ICTA Travel Management Text Series. Institute of Certified Travel Agents. • Four volumes. Volume one, *Business Management for Travel Agents*; volume two, *Personnel Management for Travel Agents*; volume three, *Marketing for Travel Agents*; volume four, *Domestic Leisure and International Tourism.*

TRAVEL, AIR

See: AIR TRAVEL

TRAVEL, BUSINESS

See: BUSINESS TRAVEL

TRAVEL INDUSTRY

See also: AIR TRAVEL; BUSINESS TRAVEL; HOTEL AND MOTEL INDUSTRY; TIMETABLES; TRAVEL AGENCIES

GENERAL WORKS

International Travel and Tourism. Donald E. Lundberg. John Wiley and Sons, Inc. • 1993. $59.50. Second edition. Provides an overview of the international travel business.

Tourism: Principles, Practices, Philosophies. Robert W. McIntosh and others. John Wiley and Sons, Inc. • 1999. $64.95. Eighth edition. General review of the travel industry.

ABSTRACTS AND INDEXES

Leisure, Recreation, and Tourism Abstracts. Available from CABI Publishing North America. • Quarterly. $470.00 per year. Published in England by CABI Publishing. Provides coverage of the worldwide literature of travel, recreation, sports, and the hospitality industry. Emphasis is on research.

BIBLIOGRAPHIES

Tourism Planning. David Marcouiller. Sage Publications, Inc. • 1995. $10.00. (CPL Bibliographies Series).

Travel and Tourism. Available from U. S. Government Printing Office. • Annual. Free. Issued by the Superintendent of Documents. A list of government publications on the travel industry and tourism. Formerly *Mass Transit, Travel and Tourism.* (Subject Bibliography No. 302.).

DIRECTORIES

The Cruise Directory. Available from Informa Publishing Group Ltd. • Annual. $128.00. Published in the UK by Lloyd's List (http://www.lloydslist.com). Includes detailed information on cruise operators worldwide, individual cruise ship onboard facilities/features, ports capable of handling cruise ships, agents, ship builders/repairers, and equipment manufacturers.

Golf Index. Ingledue Travel Publications. • Semiannual. $40.00 per year. Provides directory listings of golf courses and resorts around the world. Contains information on golf travel packages, tour operators, and tournaments.

Resorts and Parks Purchasing Guide. Klevens Publications, Inc. • Annual. $60.00. Lists suppliers of products and services for resorts and parks, including national parks, amusement parks, dude ranches, golf resorts, ski areas, and national monument areas.

Travel Industry Personnel Directory. Fairchild Books. • Annual. $25.00. Air and steamship lines, tour operators, bus lines, hotel representatives, foreign and domestic railroads, foreign and domestic tourist information offices, travel trade associations, etc. Includes names of personnel.

HANDBOOKS AND MANUALS

Health Information for International Travel. Available from U. S. Government Printing Office. • Annual. Issued by Centers for Disease Control, U. S. Department of Health and Human Services. Discusses potential health risks of international travel and specifies vaccinations required by different countries.

Marketing in Travel and Tourism. Victor Middleton. Butterworth-Heinemann. • 2000. $37.95. Third edition. Explains, with examples, the application of marketing concepts and principles to the travel industry.

Resort Development Handbook. Dean Schwanke and others. Urban Land Institute. • 1997. $89.95. Covers a wide range of resort settings and amenities, with details of development, market analysis, financing, design, and operations. Includes color photographs and case studies. (ULI Development Handbook Series).

INTERNET DATABASES

Fedstats. Federal Interagency Council on Statistical Policy. Phone: (202)395-7254 • URL: http://www.fedstats.gov • Web site features an efficient search facility for full-text statistics produced by more than 70 federal agencies, including the Census Bureau, the Bureau of Economic Analysis, and the Bureau of Labor Statistics. Boolean searches can be made within one agency or for all agencies combined. Links are offered to international statistical bureaus, including the UN, IMF, OECD, UNESCO, Eurostat, and 20 individual countries. Fees: Free.

ONLINE DATABASES

DRI U.S. Central Database. Data Products Division. • Provides more than 23,000 business, financial, demographic, economic, foreign trade, and industry-related time series for the U.S. Includes national income, population, retail-wholesale trade, price indexes, labor data, housing, industrial production, banking, interest rates, money supply, etc. Time period is generally 1947 to date (some data back to 1929). Updating varies. Inquire as to online cost and availability.

United States International Air Travel Statistics. U. S. Department of Transportation, Center for Transportation Information. • Provides detailed statistics on air passenger travel between the U. S. and foreign countries for both scheduled and charter flights. Time period is 1975 to date, with monthly updates. Inquire as to online cost and availability.

PERIODICALS AND NEWSLETTERS

ASTA Agency Management: Official Publication of American Society of Travel Agents, Inc. Pace Communications. • Monthly. $36.00 per year.

Consumer Reports Travel Letter. Consumers Union of the United States, Inc. • Monthly. $39.00 per year. Newsletter with information on air fares, travel discounts, special hotel rates, etc.

Cruise Travel: Ships, Ports, Schedules, Prices. World Publishing Co. • Bimonthly. $23.94 per year.

International Journal of Hospitality and Tourism Administration: A Multinationaland Cross-Cultural Journal of Applied Research. Haworth Press, Inc. • Quarterly. Individuals, $36.00 per year; institutions, $48.00 per year; libraries, $85.00 per year. An academic journal with articles relating to lodging, food service, travel, tourism, and the hospitality/leisure industries in general. Formerly *Journal of International Hospitality, Leisure, and Tourism Management.*

Journal of Travel and Tourism Marketing. Haworth Press, Inc. • Quarterly. Individuals, $45.00 per year; institutions, $95.00 per year; libraries, $175.00 per year.

Journal of Travel Research. University of Colorado, Business Research Div. Sage Publications, Inc. • Quarterly. Individuals, $150.00 per year; institutions, $195.00 per year. Includes *Travel Research Bookshelf* which abstracts current literature in the field.

Newsline: Research News from the U. S. Travel Data Center. Travel Industry Association of America. • Monthly. $55.00 per year. Newsletter. Covers trends in the U. S. travel industry.

Passport Newsletter. Remy Publishing Co. • Monthly. $89.00 per year. Formerly *Passport.*

Resort Management and Operations: The Resort Resource. Finan Publishing Co., Inc. • Quarterly. $21.95 per year. Edited for hospitality professionals at both large and small resort facilities.

Summary of Health Information for International Travel. U. S. Department of Health and Human Services. • Biweekly. Formerly *Weekly Summary of Health Information for International Travel.*

Travel and Leisure. American Express Publishing Corp. • Monthly. $39.00 per year. In three regional editions and one demographic edition.

Travel Holiday. Hachette Filipacchi Magazines, Inc. • 10 times a year. $17.94 per year.

Travel Management Daily. Cahners Travel Group. • Daily. $797.00 per year. Newsletter for travel industry professionals.

Travel Smart: Pay Less, Enjoy More. Communications House, Inc. • Monthly. $44.00 per year. Newsletter. Provides information and recommendations for travelers. Emphasis is on travel value and opportunities for bargains.

Travel Trade News Edition: The Business Paper of the Travel Industry. Travel Trade Publications. • Weekly. $10.00 per year. Formerly *Travel Trade.*

Travel Weekly. Cahners Travel Group. • Weekly. $220.00 per year. Includes cruise guides, a weekly "Business Travel Update," and special issues devoted to particular destinations and areas. Edited mainly for travel agents and tour operators.

STATISTICS SOURCES

Business Statistics of the United States. Courtenay M. Slater, editor. Bernan Associates. • 1999. $74.00. Fifth edition. Based on *Business Statistics,* formerly issue by the Bureau of Economic Analysis, U. S. Department of Commerce. Provides basic data for a wide variety of U. S. industries, services, and economic indicators. Most statistics are shown annually for 29 years and monthly for the most recent four years.

Economic Review of Travel in America. Travel Industry Association of America. • Annual. Members, $75.00; non-members, $125.00. Presents a statistical summary of travel in the U.S., including travel expenditures, travel industry employment, tax data, international visitors, etc.

Outlook for Travel and Tourism. Travel Industry Association of America. • Annual. Members, $100.00; non-members, $175.00. Contains forecasts of the performance of the U. S. travel industry, including air travel, business travel, recreation (attractions), and accomodations.

Services: Statistics on International Transactions. Organization for Economic Cooperation and Development. Available from OECD Publications and Information Center. • Annual. $71.00. Presents a compilation and assessment of data on OECD member countries' international trade in services. Covers four major categories for 20 years: travel, transportation, government services, and other services.

Summary of International Travel to the United States. International Trade Administration, Tourism Industries. U.S. Dept. of Commerce. • Monthly. Quarterly and annual versions available. Provides statistics on air travel to the U.S. from each of 90 countries. Formerly *Summary and Analysis of International Travel to the United States.*

Survey of Current Business. Available from U. S. Government Printing Office. • Monthly. $49.00 per year. Issued by Bureau of Economic Analysis, U. S. Department of Commerce. Presents a wide variety of business and economic data.

Tourism Policy and International Tourism in OECD Member Countries. Available from OECD Publications and Information Center. • Annual.

$50.00. Reviews developments in the international tourism industry in OECD member countries. Includes statistical information.

World Statistics Pocketbook. United Nations Publications. • Annual. $10.00. Presents basic economic, social, and environmental indicators for about 200 countries and areas. Covers more than 50 items relating to population, economic activity, labor force, agriculture, industry, energy, trade, transportation, communication, education, tourism, and the environment. Statistical sources are noted.

TRADE/PROFESSIONAL ASSOCIATIONS

National Tour Association. 546 E. Main St., Lexington, KY 40508-2300. Phone: 800-682-8886 Fax: (606)226-4414 E-mail: ntawebmaster@ntastaff.com • URL: http://www,ntaonline.com.

Travel and Tourism Research Association. P.O. Box 2133, Boise, ID 83701-2133. Phone: (208)429-9511 Fax: (208)429-9512 E-mail: ttr@uswest.net • URL: http://www.ttra.com • Members are travel directors, airline officials, hotels, government agencies, and others interested in the travel field.

Travel Industry Association of America. 1100 New York Ave., N.W., Suite 450, Washington, DC 20005. Phone: (202)408-8422 Fax: (202)408-1255 E-mail: membership@tia.org.

OTHER SOURCES

Lloyd's Cruise International. Available from Informa Publishing Group Ltd. • Bimonthly. $198.00 per year. Published in the UK by Lloyd's List (http://www.lloydslist.com). Edited for management professionals in the cruise ship industry. Covers industry trends, technical/equipment developments, regulatory issues, new cruise ships, ship management, cruise marketing, and related topics.

TRAVEL TRAILERS

See: RECREATIONAL VEHICLE INDUSTRY

TREASURERS

See: CORPORATE DIRECTORS AND OFFICERS

TREASURY BONDS

See: GOVERNMENT BONDS

TREES

See: FOREST PRODUCTS; LUMBER INDUSTRY

TRENDS, BUSINESS

See: BUSINESS CYCLES; BUSINESS FORECASTING

TRIALS AND JURIES

See also: STATE LAW

GENERAL WORKS

Great American Trials. The Gale Group. • 1994. $80.00. Contains discussions and details of momentous American trials from 1637 to 1993.

Inside the Juror: The Psychology of Juror Decision Making. Reid Hastie, editor. Cambridge University Press. • 1994. $22.95. (Judgement and Decision Making Series).

ABSTRACTS AND INDEXES

Index to Legal Periodicals and Books. H. W. Wilson Co. • Monthly. Quarterly and annual cumulations. $270.00 per year. CD-ROM version available at $1,495.00 per year.

DIRECTORIES

National Board of Trial Advocacy: Directory of Board Members and Certified Diplomates. National Board of Trial Advocacy. • Biennial. Free. More than 2,400 trial lawyers board certified in civil and criminal trial advocacy; members of the board.

HANDBOOKS AND MANUALS

Jury Manual: A Guide for Prospective Jurors. William R. Pabst. Metro Publishing. • 1985. $19.95.

ONLINE DATABASES

Index to Legal Periodicals and Books (Online). H. W. Wilson Co. • Broad coverage of law journals and books 1981 to date. Monthly updates. Inquire as to online cost and availability.

Legal Resource Index. The Gale Group. • Broad coverage of law literature appearing in legal, business, and other periodicals, 1980 to date. Monthly updates. Inquire as to online cost and availability.

LEXIS. LEXIS-NEXIS. • The various LEXIS databases provide full text and indexing for a wide variety of legal cases, statutes, orders, and opinions.

PERIODICALS AND NEWSLETTERS

Champion. National Association of Criminal Defense Lawyers. • 10 times a year. $25.00 per year.

Judges' Journal. American Bar Association, Judicial Administration Div. • Quarterly. Free to members; non-members, $25.00 per year. Focuses on the court.

Judicature. American Judicature Society. • Bimonthly. $66.00 per year.

Trial. Association of Trial Lawyers of America. • Monthly. $79.00 per year.

Trial Lawyer's Guide. West Group. • Quarterly. $100.00 per year.

Trial Lawyers Quarterly. New York State Trial Lawyers Association. • Quarterly. $50.00 per year.

TRADE/PROFESSIONAL ASSOCIATIONS

American Judges Association. 300 Newport Ave., Williamsburg, VA 23187-8798. Phone: (757)259-1841 Fax: (757)259-1520 • URL: http://www.theaja.org.

American Judicature Society. 180 N. Michigan Ave., Suite 600, Chicago, IL 60601-7401. Phone: (312)558-6900 Fax: (312)558-9175 E-mail: members@ajs.org • URL: http://www.ajs.org.

American Society of Trial Consultants. Towson State University, Dept. of Mass Communication and Community Studies, Towson, MD 21252. Phone: (410)830-2448 Fax: (410)830-3656 • Concerned with the behavioral aspects of litigation.

Association of Trial Lawyers of America. 1050 31st St., N. W., Washington, DC 20007. Phone: 800-424-2725 or (202)965-3500 Fax: (202)625-7312.

Council for Court Excellence. 1150 Connecticut Ave., Suite 620, Washington, DC 20036. Phone: (202)785-5917 Fax: (202)785-5922 E-mail: office@courtexcellence.org • URL: http://www.courtexcellence.org.

Institute of Judicial Administration. New York School of Law, 40 Washington Square S., New York, NY 10012. Phone: (212)998-6196 or (212)998-6149 Fax: (212)995-4036 E-mail: forrestj@turing.law.nyu.edu • URL: http://www.nyu.law.edu.

National Association for Court Management. P.O. Box 8798, Williamsburg, VA 23187-8798. Phone: 800-616-6165 or (757)259-1841 or (757)253-2000 Fax: (757)259-1520 • URL: http://www.ncsc.dni.us/nacm/nacm.htm.

National Association of Criminal Defense Lawyers. 1025 Connecticut Ave., N.W., Suite 901, Washington, DC 20036. Phone: (202)872-8600 Fax: (202)872-8690 E-mail: assist@nacdl.com • URL: http://www.criminaljustice.com.

National Center for State Courts. 300 Newport Ave., Williamsburg, VA 23185. Phone: (757)253-2000 Fax: (757)220-0449.

TRUCK TRAILERS

See also: AUTOMOTIVE INDUSTRY; TRUCKING INDUSTRY

DIRECTORIES

Truck Trailer Manufacturers Association Membership Directory. Truck Trailer Manufacturers Association. • Annual. $135.00. About 100 trucks and tank trailer manufacturers and 120 suppliers to the industry.

FINANCIAL RATIOS

Annual Statement Studies. Robert Morris Associates: The Association of Lending and Credit Risk Professiona. • Annual. Free to members; non-members, $140.00. Median and quartile financial ratios are given for over 400 kinds of manufacturing, wholesale, retail, construction, and consumer finance establishments. Data is sorted by both asset size and sales volume. Includes a clearly written "Definition of Ratios" and an alphabetical industry index.

INTERNET DATABASES

Fedstats. Federal Interagency Council on Statistical Policy. Phone: (202)395-7254 • URL: http://www.fedstats.gov • Web site features an efficient search facility for full-text statistics produced by more than 70 federal agencies, including the Census Bureau, the Bureau of Economic Analysis, and the Bureau of Labor Statistics. Boolean searches can be made within one agency or for all agencies combined. Links are offered to international statistical bureaus, including the UN, IMF, OECD, UNESCO, Eurostat, and 20 individual countries. Fees: Free.

ONLINE DATABASES

DRI U.S. Central Database. Data Products Division. • Provides more than 23,000 business, financial, demographic, economic, foreign trade, and industry-related time series for the U.S. Includes national income, population, retail-wholesale trade, price indexes, labor data, housing, industrial production, banking, interest rates, money supply, etc. Time period is generally 1947 to date (some data back to 1929). Updating varies. Inquire as to online cost and availability.

PERIODICALS AND NEWSLETTERS

Trailer Body Builders Buyers Guide. Tunnell Publications, Inc. • Annual. Controlled circulation. List of 8,000 products used by original equipment manufacturers of truck trailers and truck bodies.

STATISTICS SOURCES

Annual Survey of Manufactures. Available from U. S. Government Printing Office. • Annual. Prices vary. Issued by the U. S. Census Bureau as an interim update to the *Census of Manufactures.* Includes data on number of manufacturing establishments in various industries, employment, labor costs, value of shipments, capital expenditures, inventories, energy costs, and assets. (See also Census Bureau home page, http://www.census.gov/.).

Business Statistics of the United States. Courtenay M. Slater, editor. Bernan Associates. • 1999. $74.00.

Fifth edition. Based on *Business Statistics*, formerly issue by the Bureau of Economic Analysis, U. S. Department of Commerce. Provides basic data for a wide variety of U. S. industries, services, and economic indicators. Most statistics are shown annually for 29 years and monthly for the most recent four years.

Manufacturing Profiles. Available from U. S. Government Printing Office. • Annual. Issued by the U. S. Census Bureau. A printed consolidation of the entire *Current Industrial Report* series, presenting "all the data compiled." Contains statistics on production, shipments, inventories, consumption, exports, imports, and orders for a wide variety of manufactured products. (See also Census Bureau home page, http://www.census.gov/.).

Survey of Current Business. Available from U. S. Government Printing Office. • Monthly. $49.00 per year. Issued by Bureau of Economic Analysis, U. S. Department of Commerce. Presents a wide variety of business and economic data.

Truck Trailers. U. S. Bureau of the Census. • Monthly and annual. Provides data on shipments of truck trailers and truck trailer vans: value, quantity, imports, and exports. (Current Industrial Reports, M37L.).

TRADE/PROFESSIONAL ASSOCIATIONS

Truck Trailer Manufacturers Association. 1020 Princess St., Alexandria, VA 22314. • Phone: (703)549-3010 Fax: (703)549-3014.

TRUCKING INDUSTRY

ALMANACS AND YEARBOOKS

Ward's Automotive Yearbook. Ward's Communications, Inc. • Annual. $385.00. Comprehensive statistical information on automotive production, sales, truck data and suppliers. Included with subscription to *Ward's Automotive Reports*.

BIBLIOGRAPHIES

Trucksource: Sources of Trucking Industry Information. American Trucking Associations, Inc. • Annual. $55.00. Lists various kinds of hard copy and electronic information sources on the subject of trucking.

DIRECTORIES

American Motor Carrier Directory. Commonwealth Business Media. • Annual. $517.00 per year. Lists all licensed Less Than Truckload (LTL) general commodity carriers in the U. S., including specialized motor carriers and related services. Formerly *American Motor Carrier Directory*.

Modern Bulk Transporter Buyers Guide. Tunnell Publications, Inc. • Annual. Controlled circulation. Suppliers of products or services for companies operating tank trucks.

Motor Carrier Permit and Tax Bulletin. J.J. Keller and Associates, Inc. • Monthly. $125.00 per year. Formerly *Trucking Permit and Tax Bulletin*.

My Little Salesman Truck Catalog. MSL, Inc. • Monthly. $18.00 per year. Products serving the trucking industry. Central and Western editions.

National Tank Truck Carrier Directory. National Tank Truck Carriers, Inc. • Annual. Members, $54.00; non-members, $80.00. For-hire tank truck carriers.

Official Motor Shippers Guide. Official Motor Freight Guide, Inc. • $60.50 per year. 17 regional editions. Includes one update. Formerly *Offical Shippers Guide*.

ENCYCLOPEDIAS AND DICTIONARIES

Macmillan Encyclopedia of Transportation. Available from The Gale Group. • 2000. $375.00. Six volumes. Published by Macmillan Reference USA. Covers the business, technology, and history of transportation on land, on water, in the air, and in space. Includes definitions, cross-references, and 200 color illustrations.

FINANCIAL RATIOS

Almanac of Business and Industrial Financial Ratios. Leo Troy. Prentice Hall. • Annual. $99.95. Contains financial ratios derived from federal tax returns. Ratios for each of about 200 industries are arranged according to company asset size.

Annual Statement Studies. Robert Morris Associates: The Association of Lending and Credit Risk Professiona. • Annual. Free to members; non-members, $140.00. Median and quartile financial ratios are given for over 400 kinds of manufacturing, wholesale, retail, construction, and consumer finance establishments. Data is sorted by both asset size and sales volume. Includes a clearly written "Definition of Ratios" and an alphabetical industry index.

ONLINE DATABASES

TRIS: Transportation Research Information Service. National Research Council. • Contains abstracts and citations to a wide range of transportation literature, 1968 to present, with monthly updates. Includes references to the literature of air transportation, highways, ships and shipping, railroads, trucking, and urban mass transportation. Formerly *TRIS-ON-LINE*. Inquire as to online cost and availability.

PERIODICALS AND NEWSLETTERS

Commercial Carrier Journal: For Fleet Management. Cahners Business Information. • Monthly. $45.00 per year. Formerly *Chilton's CCJ*.

Fleet Owner. Intertec Publishing Corp. • Monthly. $45.00 per year.

Heavy Duty Trucking: The Business Magazine of Trucking. Newport Communications. • Monthly. $65.00 per year.

Lifting and Transportation International. Specialized Carriers and Rigging Association. Douglas Publications, Inc. • Nine times a year.$65.00 per year. Covers specialized trucking, including oversized loads, cranes, hauling steel, heavy rigging, etc. Serves as the official publication of the Specialized Carriers and Rigging Association.

Modern Bulk Transporter. Intertec Publishing Corp. • Monthly. Price on application.

Private Carrier. National Private Truck Council. • Monthly. Free to qualified personnel.

Transport Topics: National Newspaper of the Trucking Industry. American Trucking Associations. • Weekly. $79.00 per year.

STATISTICS SOURCES

American Trucking Trends. American Trucking Associations. Trucking Information Services, Inc. • Annual. $45.00.

F and OS Motor Carrier Annual Report: Results of Operations Class I & II Motor Carriers of Property. American Trucking Associations. Trucking Information Services, Inc. • Annual. $400.00.

F and OS Motor Carrier Quarterly Report. American Trucking Associations. Trucking Information Services, Inc. • Quarterly. $150.00 per number. Includes *Motor Carrier Annual Report*.

Monthly Truck Tonnage Report. American Trucking Associations. Trucking Information Services, Inc. • Monthly. $50.00 per year.

Transportation Statistics Annual Report. Available from U. S. Government Printing Office. • Annual. $21.00. Issued by Bureau of Transportation Statistics, U. S. Department of Transportation. Provides data on operating revenues, expenses, employees, passenger miles (where applicable), and other factors for airlines, automobiles, buses, local transit, pipelines, railroads, ships, and trucks.

U. S. Industry and Trade Outlook: The McGraw-Hill Companies and the U.S. Department of Commerce/ International Trade Administration. Datapso Research Corp. • Annual. $69.95. Produced by the International Trade Administration, U. S. Department of Commerce, in a "public-private" partnership with DRI/McGraw-Hill and Standard & Poor's. Provides basic data, outlook for the current year, and "Long-Term Prospects" (five-year projections) for a wide variety of products and services. Includes high technology industries. Formerly *U. S. Industrial Outlook*.

WEFA Industrial Monitor. John Wiley and Sons, Inc. • Annual. $65.00. Prepared by industry analysts at WEFA, an economic forecasting and consulting firm (originally Wharton Econometric Forecasting Associates). Contains discussions of the outlook for major U. S. industries, with many 10-year forecasts (WEFA Web site is http://www.wefa.com).

TRADE/PROFESSIONAL ASSOCIATIONS

American Moving and Storage Association. c/o John Brewer. 1611 Duke St., Alexandria, VA 22314. Phone: (703)683-7410 Fax: (703)683-7527 • URL: http://www.amconf.org • Members are household goods movers, storage companies, and trucking firms.

American Trucking Associations. 2200 Mill Rd., Alexandria, VA 22314-4677. Phone: 800-282-5463 or (703)838-1700 Fax: (703)684-5720 E-mail: ata-infocenter@trucking.org • URL: http://www.truckline.org.

Distribution and LTL Carriers Association. 2200 Mill Rd., Alexandria, VA 22314. Phone: (703)838-1806 Fax: (703)684-8143 E-mail: dltlca@aol.com.

National Motor Freight Traffic Association. 2200 Mill Rd., Alexandria, VA 22314. Phone: (703)838-1810 or (703)838-1811 Fax: (703)683-1094 E-mail: nmfta@erols.com • URL: http://www.erols.com/nmfta.

National Private Truck Council. 66 Canal Center Plaza, Suite 600, Alexandria, VA 22314. Phone: (703)683-1300 Fax: (703)683-1217 E-mail: gmundell@erols.com • URL: http://www.nptc.org.

National Tank Truck Carriers. 2200 Mill Rd., Alexandria, VA 22314. Phone: (703)838-1960 Fax: (703)684-5753 E-mail: nttc@juno.com.

OTHER SOURCES

Federal Carriers Reports. CCH, Inc. • Biweekly. $1,372.00 per year. Four looseleaf volumes. Periodic supplementation. Federal rules and regulations for motor carriers, water carriers, and freight forwarders.

Infrastructure Industries USA. The Gale Group. • 2001. $240.00. Replaces *Agriculture, Forestry, Fishing, Mining, and Construction USA* and *Transportation and Public Utilities USA*. Presents statistics and projections relating to economic activity in a wide variety of natural resource and construction industries.

TRUCKS (MANUFACTURING)

See also: AUTOMOTIVE INDUSTRY; TRANSPORTATION INDUSTRY; TRUCK TRAILERS; TRUCKING INDUSTRY

DIRECTORIES

National Truck Equipment Association Membership Roster and Product Directory. National Truck Equipment Association. • Annual. $50.00. Provides company information and products for over 850 of the nation's commercial truck body and equipment manufacturers and distributors.

Truck Trailer Manufacturers Association Membership Directory. Truck Trailer Manufacturers Association. • Annual. $135.00. About 100 trucks and tank trailer manufacturers and 120 suppliers to the industry.

INTERNET DATABASES

Fedstats. Federal Interagency Council on Statistical Policy. Phone: (202)395-7254 • URL: http://www.fedstats.gov • Web site features an efficient search facility for full-text statistics produced by more than 70 federal agencies, including the Census Bureau, the Bureau of Economic Analysis, and the Bureau of Labor Statistics. Boolean searches can be made within one agency or for all agencies combined. Links are offered to international statistical bureaus, including the UN, IMF, OECD, UNESCO, Eurostat, and 20 individual countries. Fees: Free.

ONLINE DATABASES

DRI U.S. Central Database. Data Products Division. • Provides more than 23,000 business, financial, demographic, economic, foreign trade, and industry-related time series for the U.S. Includes national income, population, retail-wholesale trade, price indexes, labor data, housing, industrial production, banking, interest rates, money supply, etc. Time period is generally 1947 to date (some data back to 1929). Updating varies. Inquire as to online cost and availability.

Ward's AutoInfoBank. Ward's Communications, Inc. • Provides weekly, monthly, quarterly, and annual statistical data drom 1965 to date for U. S. and imported cars and trucks. Covers production, shipments, sales, inventories, optional equipment, etc. Updating varies by series. Inquire as to online cost and availability.

PERIODICALS AND NEWSLETTERS

Successful Dealer. Kona Communications, Inc. • Bimonthly. $50.00 per year. For truck and heavy duty equipment dealers.

STATISTICS SOURCES

Business Statistics of the United States. Courtenay M. Slater, editor. Bernan Associates. • 1999. $74.00. Fifth edition. Based on *Business Statistics*, formerly issue by the Bureau of Economic Analysis, U. S. Department of Commerce. Provides basic data for a wide variety of U. S. industries, services, and economic indicators. Most statistics are shown annually for 29 years and monthly for the most recent four years.

Survey of Current Business. Available from U. S. Government Printing Office. • Monthly. $49.00 per year. Issued by Bureau of Economic Analysis, U. S. Department of Commerce. Presents a wide variety of business and economic data.

TRADE/PROFESSIONAL ASSOCIATIONS

National Truck Equipment Association. 37400 Hills Tech Dr., Farmington Hills, MI 48331-3414. Phone: 800-441-6832 or (248)489-7090 Fax: (248)489-8590 E-mail: info@ntea.com • URL: http://www.ntea.com.

TRUST COMPANIES

See: BANKS AND BANKING; TRUSTS AND TRUSTEES

TRUSTS AND TRUSTEES

See also: ESTATE PLANNING; FOUNDATIONS; INSTITUTIONAL INVESTMENTS; INVESTMENT COMPANIES

GENERAL WORKS

Staying Wealthy: Strategies for Protecting Your Assets. Brian H. Breuel. Bloomberg Press. • 1998. $21.95. Presents ideas for estate planning and personal wealth preservation. Includes case studies. (Bloomberg Personal Bookshelf Series).

ABSTRACTS AND INDEXES

Accounting and Tax Index. UMI. • Quarterly. Price on application. Includes annual cumulative bound volume. Indexes accounting, auditing, and taxation literature appearing in journals, books, pamphlets, conference proceedings, and newsletters. (UMI is University Microfilms International, a Bell & Howell Co.).

Banking Information Index. U M I Banking Information Index. • Monthly. Price on application. Covers a wide variety of banking, business, and financial subjects in periodicals. Formerly *Banking Literature Index.*

Current Law Index: Multiple Access to Legal Periodicals. The Gale Group. • Monthly. $650.00 per year. Produced in cooperation with the American Association of Law Libraries. Indexes more than 900 law journals, legal newspapers, and specialty publications from the U.S., Canada, U.K., Ireland, Australia, and New Zealand.

Index to Legal Periodicals and Books. H. W. Wilson Co. • Monthly. Quarterly and annual cumulations. $270.00 per year. CD-ROM version available at $1,495.00 per year.

ALMANACS AND YEARBOOKS

American Law Yearbook. The Gale Group. • Annual. $155.00. Serves as a yearly supplement to *West's Encyclopedia of American Law.* Describes new legal developments in many subject areas.

CD-ROM DATABASES

WILSONDISC: Index to Legal Periodicals and Books. H. W. Wilson Co. • Monthly. Including unlimited online access to *Index to Legal Periodicals* through WILSONLINE. Contains CD-ROM indexing of more than 800 English language legal periodicals from 1981 to date and 2,500 books.

DIRECTORIES

Corporate Finance Sourcebook: The Guide to Major Capital Investment Source and Related Financial Services. R. R. Bowker. • Annual. $625.00. Lists more than 3,550 sources of corporate capital: investment bankers, securities firms, pension management companies, trust companies, insurance companies, and private lenders. Includes the names of over 13,000 key personnel.

Directory of Trust Banking. Thomson Financial Publishing. • Annual. $315.00. Contains profiles of bank affiliated trust companies, independent trust companies, trust investment advisors, and trust fund managers. Provides contact information for professional personnel at more than 3,000 banking and other financial institutions.

Foundation Directory. The Foundation Center. • Annual. $215.00. Over 37,700 of the largest foundations in the United States, all having 2,000,000.00 or more assets or awarding $200,000 or more in grants in a recent year.

Money Market Directory of Pension Funds and Their Investment Managers. Money Market Directories, Inc. • Annual. $995.00. Institutional funds and managers.

Plunkett's Financial Services Industry Almanac: The Leading Firms in Investments, Banking, and Financial Information. Available from Plunkett Research, Ltd. • Annual. $245.00. Discusses important trends in various sectors of the financial industry. Five hundred major banking, credit card, investment, and financial services companies are profiled.

Trusts and Estates - Directory of Trust Institutions. Intertec Publishing Corp. • Annual. $79.95. Lists approximately 5,000 trust departments in U.S. and Canadian banks.

Vickers Directory of Institutional Investors. Vickers Stock Research Corp. • Semiannual. $195.00 per year. Detailed alphabetical listing of more than 4,000 U. S., Canadian, and foreign institutional investors. Includes insurance companies, banks, endowment funds, and investment companies. Formerly *Directory of Institutional Investors.*

ENCYCLOPEDIAS AND DICTIONARIES

Dictionary of Finance and Investment Terms. John Downes and Jordan E. Goodman. Barron's Educational Series, Inc. • 1998. $12.95. Fifth revised edition. Provides clear explanations of more than 5,000 business, banking, financial, investment, and tax terms. Includes a separate list of financial abbreviations and acronyms.

West's Encyclopedia of American Law. Available from The Gale Group. • 1997. $995.00. Second edition. 12 volumes. Published by West Group. Covers a wide variety of legal topics for the general reader. Formerly *Guide to American Law: Everyone's Legal Encyclopedia* (1985).

FINANCIAL RATIOS

The Financial Elite: Database of Financial Services Companies. Donnelley Marketing. • Quarterly. Price on application. Formerly compiled by Database America. Provides current information on CD-ROM for 500,000 major U. S. companies offering financial services. Data for each firm includes year started, type of financial service, annual revenues, name of top executive, and number of employees.

HANDBOOKS AND MANUALS

Best Practices for Financial Advisors. Mary Rowland. • 1997. $40.00. Provides advice for professional financial advisors on practice management, ethics, marketing, and legal concerns. (Bloomberg Professional Library.).

Corporation-Partnership-Fiduciary Filled-in Tax Return Forms, 1999. CCH, Inc. • 1999. $21.50.

Federal Income Taxes of Decedents, Estates, and Trusts. CCH, Inc. • Annual. $45.00. Provides rules for preparing a decedent's final income tax return. Includes discussions of fiduciary duties, grantor trusts, and bankruptcy estates.

Federal Taxation of Trusts, Grantors, and Beneficiaries. John L. Peschel and Edward D. Spurgeon. Warren, Gorham and Lamont/RIA Group. • Looseleaf. $160.00. Annual supplementation.

Fiduciary Tax Return Guide 1992. Research Institute of America, Inc. • 1992. $10.00.

How to Save Time and Taxes Preparing Fiduciary Income Tax Returns: Federal and State. Matthew Bender & Co., Inc. • $230.00. Looseleaf service. Periodic supplementation. (How to Save Time and Taxes Series).

Inheritor's Handbook: A Definitive Guide for Beneficiaries. Dan Rottenberg. Bloomberg Press. • 1998. $23.95. Covers both financial and emotional issues faced by beneficiaries. (Bloomberg Personal Bookshelf Series.).

Revocable Trusts. George M. Turner. Shepard's. • 1995. Third edition. Price on application.

Trust Administration and Taxation. Matthew Bender & Co., Inc. • $830.00. Four looseleaf volumes.

Periodic supplementation. Text on establishment, administration, and taxation of trusts.

Trust Department Administration and Operations. Matthew Bender & Co., Inc. • $305.00. Two looseleaf volumes. Periodic supplementation. A procedural manual, training guide and idea source.

ONLINE DATABASES

Banking Information Source. Bell & Howell Information and Learning. • Provides indexing and abstracting of periodical and other literature from 1982 to date, with weekly updates. Covers the financial services industry: banks, savings institutions, investment houses, credit unions, insurance companies, and real estate organizations. Emphasis is on marketing and management. Inquire as to online cost and availability. (Formerly *FINIS: Financial Industry Information Service.*).

Index to Legal Periodicals and Books (Online). H. W. Wilson Co. • Broad coverage of law journals and books 1981 to date. Monthly updates. Inquire as to online cost and availability.

PERIODICALS AND NEWSLETTERS

Asset Management. Dow Jones Financial Publishing Corp. • Bimonthly. $345.00 per year. Covers the management of the assets of affluent, high net worth investors. Provides information on various financial products and services.

Investment Advisor. Dow Jones Financial Publishing Corp. • Monthly. $79.00 per year. Edited for professional investment advisors, financial planners, stock brokers, bankers, and others concerned with the management of assets.

Investment Management Weekly. Securities Data Publishing. • Weekly. $1,370.00 per year. Newsletter. Edited for money managers and other investment professionals. Covers personnel news, investment strategies, and industry trends. (Securities Data Publishing is a unit of Thomson Financial.).

Investment News: The Weekly Newspaper for Financial Advisers. Crain Communications, Inc. • Weekly. $38.00 per year. Edited for both personal and institutional investment advisers, planners, and managers.

Jounal of Finacial Services Professionals. American Society of CLU and Ch F C. • Bimonthly. $38.00 per year. Provides information on life insurance and financial planning, including estate planning, retirement, tax planning, trusts, business insurance, long-term care insurance, disability insurance, and employee benefits. Formerly (American Society of CLU and Ch F C Journal).

Journal of Private Portfolio Management. Institutional Investor. • Quarterly. $280.00 per year. Edited for managers of wealthy individuals' investment portfolios.

Private Asset Management. Institutional Investor. • Biweekly. $2,105.00 per year. Newsletter. Edited for managers investing the private assets of wealthy ("high-net-worth") individuals. Includes marketing, taxation, regulation, and fee topics.

Trust Letter. American Bankers Association. • Members $140.00 per year, non-members, $210.00 per year. Current information on national liegislation and regulation that impacts the trust and investment businesses.

Trust Management Update. American Bankers Association. • Bimonthly. $95.00 per year.

Trusts and Estates. Intertec Publishing Corp. • Monthly. $129.00 per year. Includes annual *Directory.*

RESEARCH CENTERS AND INSTITUTES

Lexis.com Research System. Lexis-Nexis Group. Phone: 800-227-9597 or (937)865-6800 Fax: (937)865-6909 E-mail: webmaster@prod.lexis-nexis.com • URL: http://www.lexis.com • Fee-based Web site offers extensive searching of a wide variety of legal sources. Additional features include Daily Opinion Service, lexis.com Bookstore, Career Center, CLE Center, Law Schools, and Practice Pages ("Pages specific to areas of specialty").

STATISTICS SOURCES

Quarterly Pension Investment Report. Employee Benefit Research Institute. • Quarterly. $1,500.00 per year. $400.00 per year to nonprofit organizations. Provides aggregate financial asset data for U. S. private and public pension systems. Statistics are given for both defined contribution and defined benefit plans, including investment mixes (stocks, bonds, cash, other). Contains historical data for private trust, life insurance, and state and local government funds.

TRADE/PROFESSIONAL ASSOCIATIONS

American Bankers Association. 1120 Connecticut Ave., N.W., Washington, DC 20036. Phone: 800-226-5377 or (202)663-5000 Fax: (202)663-7543 • URL: http://www.aba.com.

OTHER SOURCES

Estate Planning: Wills, Trusts and Forms. Research Institute of America. • Looseleaf service. Includes bimonthly *Report Bulletins* and updates.

Fiduciary Tax Guide. CCH, Inc. • Monthly. $439.00 per year, Includes looseleaf monthly updates. Covers federal income taxation of estates, trusts, and beneficiaries. Provides information on gift and generation- skipping taxation.

Pension Fund Litigation Reporter. Andrews Publications. • Monthly. $750.00 per year. Contains reports on legal cases involving pension fund fiduciaries (trustees).

TRUSTS, INVESTMENT

See: INVESTMENT COMPANIES

TUNA FISH INDUSTRY

See also: FISH INDUSTRY

ABSTRACTS AND INDEXES

Oceanic Abstracts. Cambridge Information Group. • Bimonthly. $1,045.00 per year. Covers oceanography, marine biology, ocean shipping, and a wide range of other marine-related subject areas.

ALMANACS AND YEARBOOKS

Inter-American Tropical Tuna Commission Annual Report. William H. Bayliff, editor. • Annual. Price varies. Summary of scientific research carried on during the year. Includes financial statements. Text in English and Spanish.

ONLINE DATABASES

Oceanic Abstracts (Online). Cambridge Scientific Abstracts. • Oceanographic and other marine-related technical literature, 1981 to present.Monthly updates. Inquire as to online cost and availability.

PERIODICALS AND NEWSLETTERS

Inter-American Tropical Tuna Commission Bulletin. Inter-American Tropical Tuna Commission. • Irregular. Price varies. Description of results of scientific studies. Text in English and Spanish.

STATISTICS SOURCES

Fisheries of the United States. Available from U. S. Government Printing Office. • Annual. $18.00. Issued by the National Marine Fisheries Service, National Oceanic and Atmospheric Administration, U. S. Department of Commerce.

TRADE/PROFESSIONAL ASSOCIATIONS

American Tunaboat Association. One Tuna Lane, San Diego, CA 92101. Phone: (619)233-6405.

Inter-American Tropical Tuna Commission. c/o Scripps Institution of Oceanography, 8604 La Jolla Shores Dr., La Jolla, CA 92037. Phone: (858)546-7100 Fax: (858)546-7133 E-mail: rallen@iattc.ucsd.edu.

United States Tuna Foundation. 1101 17th St., N.W., Suite 609, Washington, DC 20036. Phone: (202)857-0610 Fax: (202)331-9686.

TURKEY INDUSTRY

See also: POULTRY INDUSTRY

ALMANACS AND YEARBOOKS

CRB Commodity Yearbook. Commodity Research Bureau. CRB. • Annual. $99.95.

INTERNET DATABASES

USDA. United States Department of Agriculture. Phone: (202)720-2791 E-mail: agsec@usda.gov • URL: http://www.usda.gov • The USDA home page has six sections: News and Information; What's New; About USDA; Agencies; Opportunities; Search and Help. Keyword searching is offered from the USDA home page and from various individual agency home pages. Agencies are the Economic Research Service, Agricultural Marketing Service, National Agricultural Statistics Service, National Agricultural Library, and about 12 others. Updating varies. Fees: Free.

PERIODICALS AND NEWSLETTERS

Turkey World. Watt Publishing. • Bimonthly. $28.00 per year.

PRICE SOURCES

PPI Detailed Report. Bureau of Labor Statistics, U.S. Department of Labor. Available from U.S. Government Printing Office. • Monthly. $55.00 per year. Formerly *Producer Price Indexes.*

STATISTICS SOURCES

Agricultural Statistics. Available from U. S. Government Printing Office. • Annual. Produced by the National Agricultural Statistics Service, U. S. Department of Agriculture. Provides a wide variety of statistical data relating to agricultural production, supplies, consumption, prices/price-supports, foreign trade, costs, and returns, as well as farm labor, loans, income, and population. In many cases, historical data is shown annually for 10 years. In addition to farm data, includes detailed fishery statistics.

TRADE/PROFESSIONAL ASSOCIATIONS

National Turkey Federation. 1225 New York Ave., N.W., Suite 400, Washington, DC 20005. Phone: (202)898-0100 Fax: (202)898-0203 E-mail: info@turkeyfed.org • URL: http://www.turkeyfed.org.

TURNPIKES

See: TOLL ROADS

TURPENTINES AND RESINS

See: NAVAL STORES

TWINE INDUSTRY

See: ROPE AND TWINE INDUSTRY

TWO-INCOME FAMILIES

See: EMPLOYMENT OF WOMEN; WOMEN IN THE WORK FORCE

TYPE AND TYPE FOUNDING

See also: PRINTING AND PRINTING EQUIPMENT INDUSTRIES; TYPESETTING

TRADE/PROFESSIONAL ASSOCIATIONS

Type Directors Club. 60 E. 42nd St., Suite 721, New York, NY 10165. Phone: (212)983-6042 Fax: (212)983-6043 E-mail: director@tdc.org • URL: http://www.tdc.org.

TYPESETTING

FINANCIAL RATIOS

Annual Statement Studies. Robert Morris Associates: The Association of Lending and Credit Risk Professiona. • Annual. Free to members; non-members, $140.00. Median and quartile financial ratios are given for over 400 kinds of manufacturing, wholesale, retail, construction, and consumer finance establishments. Data is sorted by both asset size and sales volume. Includes a clearly written "Definition of Ratios" and an alphabetical industry index.

TRADE/PROFESSIONAL ASSOCIATIONS

American Center for Design. 325 W. Huron St., Suite 711, Chicago, IL 60610-3617. Phone: (312)787-2018 Fax: (312)649-9518 E-mail: members@ac4d.org • URL: http://www.ac4d.org.

International Digital Imaging Association. 203 Towne Centre Dr., Somerville, NJ 08876. Phone: (908)359-3924 Fax: (908)359-7619 E-mail: idia@blast.net.

TYPEWRITER INDUSTRY

See: OFFICE EQUIPMENT AND SUPPLIES; WORD PROCESSING

TYPOGRAPHY

See: PRINTING AND PRINTING EQUIPMENT INDUSTRIES; TYPESETTING

U

ULTRASONICS

ABSTRACTS AND INDEXES

Acoustics Abstracts. Multi-Science Publishing Co., Ltd. • Monthly. $416.00. per year. Parts A and B.

DIRECTORIES

Sensors Buyers Guide. Advanstar Communications. • Annual. Price on application. Provides information on over 1,400 manufacturers of high technology sensors.

ENCYCLOPEDIAS AND DICTIONARIES

Encyclopedia of Acoustics. Malcolm J. Crocker. John Wiley and Sons, Inc. • 1997. $650.00. Four volumes.

PERIODICALS AND NEWSLETTERS

Journal of Clinical Ultrasound. John Wiley and Sons, Inc., Journals Div. • Nine times a year. Institutions, $680.00 per year. Devoted exclusively to the clinical application of ultrasound in medicine.

Russian Ultrasonics. Multi-Science Publishing Co. Ltd. • Bimonthly. $303.00 per year.

Seminars in Ultrasound, CT, and MR (Computerized Tomography and Magnetic Resonance. Harcourt Health Sciences. • Bimonthly. $169.00 per year.

Sensors: The Journal of Applied Sensing Technology. Advanstar Communications. • Monthly. $62.00 per year. Edited for design, production, and manufacturing engineers involved with sensing systems. Emphasis is on emerging technology.

Ultrasonic Imaging, An International Journal. Dynamedia, Inc. • Quarterly. $182.00 per year.

Ultrasonics: The World's Leading Journal Covering the Science and Technology of Ultrasound. Elsevier Science. • 10 times a year. $1,198.00 per year. Text in English.

Ultrasound in Medicine and Biology. Elsevier Science. • Monthly. $1,041.00 per year.

TRADE/PROFESSIONAL ASSOCIATIONS

Ultrasonic Industry Association. 1250 Arthur E. Adams Dr., Columbus, OH 43221. Phone: (614)688-5111 Fax: (614)688-5001 E-mail: uia@ultrasonics.org • URL: http://www.ultrasonics.org.

UNDERDEVELOPED AREAS AND COUNTRIES

See: DEVELOPING AREAS; ECONOMIC DEVELOPMENT; TECHNICAL ASSISTANCE

UNDERTAKERS AND UNDERTAKING

See: FUNERAL HOMES AND DIRECTORS

UNDERWEAR INDUSTRY

See also: KNIT GOODS INDUSTRY

DIRECTORIES

BFIA Annual Direcotry (Body Fashions - Intimate Apparel). Advanstar Communications, Inc. • Annual. $20.00. Sections listing manufacturers of women's intimate apparel and bodywear along with their suppliers; trade associations; industry clubs; schools of design; New York buying offices.

HANDBOOKS AND MANUALS

Lingerie Shop. Entrepreneur Media, Inc. • Looseleaf. $59.50. A practical guide to starting a lingerie store. Covers profit potential, start-up costs, market size evaluation, owner's time required, site selection, lease negotiation, pricing, accounting, advertising, promotion, etc. (Start-Up Business Guide No. E1152.).

PERIODICALS AND NEWSLETTERS

Body Fashions: Intimate Apparel. Advanstar Communications, Inc. • Monthly. $39.00 per year.

Intimate Fashion News. MacKay Publishing Corp. • Semimonthly. $30.00 per year. Provides essential information on the intimate apparel industry. Includes *Fashion Merchandiser*.

WWD (Women's Wear Daily): The Retailer's Daily Newspaper. Fairchild Publications. • Daily. Institutions, $75.00 per year; corporations $195.00 per year.

TRADE/PROFESSIONAL ASSOCIATIONS

Associated Corset and Brassiere Manufacturers. 1430 Broadway, Suite 1603, New York, NY 10018. Phone: (212)354-0707 Fax: (212)221-3540.

Intimate Apparel Manufacturers Association. 1430 Broadway, Suite 1603, New York, NY 10018-3308. Phone: (212)354-0707 Fax: (212)221-3540.

OTHER SOURCES

Women's Undergarments. Available from MarketResearch.com. • 1997. $995.00. Published by Specialists in Business Information, Inc. Provides market data with forecasts of sales to the year 2005 for various kinds of women's underwear.

UNDERWRITERS

See: INSURANCE UNDERWRITERS

UNEMPLOYMENT

See also: DISMISSAL OF EMPLOYEES; EMPLOYMENT; UNEMPLOYMENT INSURANCE

GENERAL WORKS

Unemployment and Inflation: Institutional and Structuralist Views: A Reader in Labor Economics. Michael J. Piore, editor. M. E. Sharpe, Inc. • 1980. $32.95.

ABSTRACTS AND INDEXES

Human Resources Abstracts: An International Information Service. Sage Publications, Inc. • Quarterly. Individuals, $150.00 per year; institutions, $610.00 per year.

CD-ROM DATABASES

Sourcebooks America CD-ROM. CACI Marketing Systems. • Annual. $1,250.00. Provides the CD-ROM version of *The Sourcebook of ZIP Code Demographics: Census Edition* and *The Sourcebook of County Demographics: Census Edition.*

INTERNET DATABASES

Bureau of Economic Analysis (BEA). U. S. Department of Commerce, Bureau of Economic Analysis. Phone: (202)606-9900 Fax: (202)606-5310 E-mail: webmaster@bea.doc.gov • URL: http://www.bea.doc.gov • Web site includes "News Release Information" covering national, regional, and international economic estimates from the BEA. Highlights of releases appear online the same day, complete text and tables appear the next day. "Recent News Releases" section provides titles for past nine months, with links. "BEA Data and Methodology" includes "Frequently Requested NIPA Data" (national income and product accounts, such as gross domestic product and personal income). Other statistics are available. Fees: Free.

Bureau of Labor Statistics (BLS). U. S. Department of Labor, Bureau of Labor Statistics. Phone: (202)523-1092 E-mail: labstat.helpdesk@bls.gov • URL: http://www.bls.gov • Web site provides a great variety of employment, wage, price, and economic data. Some links are "Data," "Economy at a Glance," "Keyword Search of BLS Web Pages," "Regional Information," and "Other Statistical Sites." Fees: Free.

Fedstats. Federal Interagency Council on Statistical Policy. Phone: (202)395-7254 • URL: http://www.fedstats.gov • Web site features an efficient search facility for full-text statistics produced by more than 70 federal agencies, including the Census Bureau, the Bureau of Economic Analysis, and the Bureau of Labor Statistics. Boolean searches can be made within one agency or for all agencies combined. Links are offered to international statistical bureaus, including the UN, IMF, OECD, UNESCO, Eurostat, and 20 individual countries. Fees: Free.

ONLINE DATABASES

DRI U.S. Central Database. Data Products Division. • Provides more than 23,000 business, financial, demographic, economic, foreign trade, and industry-related time series for the U.S. Includes national income, population, retail-wholesale trade, price indexes, labor data, housing, industrial production, banking, interest rates, money supply, etc. Time period is generally 1947 to date (some data back to 1929). Updating varies. Inquire as to online cost and availability.

RESEARCH CENTERS AND INSTITUTES

Industrial Relations Section. Princeton University, Firestone Library, Pinceton, NJ 08544. Phone: (609)258-4040 Fax: (609)258-2907 • URL: http://www.irs.princeton.edu/ • Fields of research include labor supply, manpower training, unemployment, and equal employment opportunity.

W. E. Upjohn Institute for Employment Research. 300 S. Westnedge Ave., Kalamazoo, MI 49007-4686. Phone: (616)343-5541 Fax: (616)343-3308 E-mail: eberts@we.upjohninst.org • URL: http://www.upjohninst.org • Research fields include unemployment, unemployment insurance, worker's compensation, labor productivity, profit sharing, the labor market, economic development, earnings, training, and other areas related to employment.

STATISTICS SOURCES

Area Trends in Employment and Unemployment. Available from U. S. Government Printing Office. • Monthly. $60.00 per year. Issued by the U. S. Department of Labor (http://www.dol.gov). Includes a listing of labor surplus areas in the U. S.

Bulletin of Labour Statistics: Supplementing the Annual Data Presented in the Year Book of Labour Statistics. International Labour Ofice. ILO Publications Center. • Quarterly. $84.00 per year. Includes five *Supplements.* A supplement to *Yearbook of Labour Statistics.* Provides current labor and price index statistics for over 130 countries. Generally includes data for the most recent four years. Text in English, French and Spanish.

Business Statistics of the United States. Courtenay M. Slater, editor. Bernan Associates. • 1999. $74.00. Fifth edition. Based on *Business Statistics*, formerly issue by the Bureau of Economic Analysis, U. S. Department of Commerce. Provides basic data for a wide variety of U. S. industries, services, and economic indicators. Most statistics are shown annually for 29 years and monthly for the most recent four years.

County and City Extra: Annual Metro, City and County Data Book. Mark Littman and Deirdre A. Gaquin. Bernan Press. • 1999. $109.00. Updates and augments data published irregularly in print form by the U. S. Census Bureau in *County and City Data Book.* Covers "every state, county, metropolitan area, and congressional district in the United States, as well as all U. S. cities with a 1990 population of 25,000 or more." Contains a wide range tic maps.

Economic Report of the President: Together with the Annual Report of the Council of Economic Advisors. Available from U. S. Government Printing Office. • Annual. $29.00. Includes about 130 pages of "Statistical Tables Relating to Income, Employment, and Production." Tables cover national income, employment, wages, productivity, manufacturing, prices, credit, finance (public and private), corporate profits, and foreign trade.

Employment and Earnings. Available from U. S. Government Printing Office. • Monthly. $50.00 per year, including annual supplement. Produced by the Bureau of Labor Statistics, U. S. Department of Labor. Provides current data on employment, hours, and earnings for the U. S. as a whole, for states, and for more than 200 local areas.

Geographic Profile of Employment and Unemployment. Available from U. S. Government Printing Office. • Annual. Issued by Bureau of Labor Statistics, U. S. Department of Labor. Presents detailed, annual average employment, unemployment, and labor force data for regions, states, and metropolitan areas. Characteristics include sex, age, race, Hispanic origin, marital status, occupation, and type of industry.

Geographic Reference Report: Annual Report of Costs, Wages, salaries, and Human Resource Statistics for the United States and Canada. ERI. • Annual. $389.00. Provides demographic and other data for each of 298 North American metropolian areas, including local salaries, wage differentials, cost-of-living, housing costs, income taxation, employment, unemployment, population, major employers, crime rates, weather, etc.

Handbook of U. S. Labor Statistics: Employment, Earnings, Prices, Productivity, and Other Labor Data. Eva E. Jacobs, editor. Bernan Associates. • 1999. $74.00. Based on *Handbook of Labor Statistics*, formerly issued by the Bureau of Labor Statistics, U. S. Department of Labor. Includes the Bureau's projections of employment in the U. S. by industry and occupation. Provides a wide variety of data on the work force, prices, fringe benefits, and consumer expenditures.

Labour Force Statistics, 1977/1997: 1998 Edition. Organization for Economic Cooperation and Development. Available from OECD Publications and Information Center. • 1999. $98.00. Provides 21 years of data for OECD member countries on population, employment, unemployment, civilian labor force, armed forces, and other labor factors.

Monthly Labor Review. Available from U. S. Government Printing Office. • Monthly. $43.00 per year. Issued by the Bureau of Labor Statistics, U. S. Department of Labor. Contains data on the labor force, wages, work stoppages, price indexes, productivity, economic growth, and occupational injuries and illnesses.

Quarterly Labour Force Statistics. Organization for Economic Cooperation and Development. Available from OECD Publications and Information Center. • Quarterly. $60.00 per year. Provides current data for OECD member countries on population, employment, unemployment, civilian labor force, armed forces, and other labor factors.

Report on the American Workforce. Available from U. S. Government Printing Office. • Annual. $15.00. Issued by the U. S. Department of Labor (http://www.dol.gov). Appendix contains tabular statistics, including employment, unemployment, price indexes, consumer expenditures, employee benefits (retirement, insurance, vacation, etc.), wages, productivity, hours of work, and occupational injuries. Annual figures are shown for up to 50 years.

Survey of Current Business. Available from U. S. Government Printing Office. • Monthly. $49.00 per year. Issued by Bureau of Economic Analysis, U. S. Department of Commerce. Presents a wide variety of business and economic data.

Year Book of Labour Statistics. International Labour Office. • Annual. $168.00. Presents a wide range of labor and price data for most countries of the world. Supplement available *Sources and Methods. Labour Statistics.*

OTHER SOURCES

Foreign Labor Trends. Available from U. S. Government Printing Office. • Irregular (50 to 60 issues per year, each on an individual country). $38.00 per year. Prepared by various American Embassies. Issued by the Bureau of International Labor Affairs, U. S. Department of Labor. Covers labor developments in important foreign countries, including trends in wages, working conditions, labor supply, employment, and unemployment.

UNEMPLOYMENT INSURANCE

HANDBOOKS AND MANUALS

U. S. Master Payroll Guide. CCH, Inc. • Annual. $75.00. Covers the basics of payroll management, including employer obligations, recordkeeping, taxation, unemployment insurance, processing of new employees, and government penalties.

INTERNET DATABASES

Fedstats. Federal Interagency Council on Statistical Policy. Phone: (202)395-7254 • URL: http://www.fedstats.gov • Web site features an efficient search facility for full-text statistics produced by more than 70 federal agencies, including the Census Bureau, the Bureau of Economic Analysis, and the Bureau of Labor Statistics. Boolean searches can be made within one agency or for all agencies combined. Links are offered to international statistical bureaus, including the UN, IMF, OECD, UNESCO, Eurostat, and 20 individual countries. Fees: Free.

ONLINE DATABASES

DRI U.S. Central Database. Data Products Division. • Provides more than 23,000 business, financial, demographic, economic, foreign trade, and industry-related time series for the U.S. Includes national income, population, retail-wholesale trade, price indexes, labor data, housing, industrial production, banking, interest rates, money supply, etc. Time period is generally 1947 to date (some data back to 1929). Updating varies. Inquire as to online cost and availability.

I.I.I. Data Base Search. Insurance Information Institute. • Provides online citations and abstracts of insurance-related literature in magazines, newspapers, trade journals, and books. Emphasis is on property and casualty insurance issues, including highway safety, product safety, and environmental liability. Inquire as to online cost and availability.

RESEARCH CENTERS AND INSTITUTES

National Institute for Work and Learning. Academy for Educational Development, 1875 Connecticut Ave., N.W., Washington, DC 20009. Phone: (202)884-8187 Fax: (202)884-8422 E-mail: ichaner@aed.org • URL: http://www.niwl.org • Research areas include adult education, training, unemployment insurance, and career development.

STATISTICS SOURCES

Business Statistics of the United States. Courtenay M. Slater, editor. Bernan Associates. • 1999. $74.00. Fifth edition. Based on *Business Statistics*, formerly issue by the Bureau of Economic Analysis, U. S. Department of Commerce. Provides basic data for a wide variety of U. S. industries, services, and economic indicators. Most statistics are shown annually for 29 years and monthly for the most recent four years.

Survey of Current Business. Available from U. S. Government Printing Office. • Monthly. $49.00 per year. Issued by Bureau of Economic Analysis, U. S. Department of Commerce. Presents a wide variety of business and economic data.

Unemployment Insurance Claims Weekly Report. U.S. Department of Labor, Employment and Training Administration. • Weekly.

UNIFORM COMMERCIAL CODE

See: BUSINESS LAW

UNIFORMS

DIRECTORIES

Law and Order Magazine Police Equipment Buyer's Guide. Hendon, Inc. • Annual. $15.00. Lists manufacturers, dealers, and distributors of equipment and services for police departments.

Law Enforcement Technology Directory. Cygnus Business Media. • Annual. $60.00 per year. $6.00

per issue; a directory of products, equipment, services, and technology for police professionals. Includes weapons, uniforms, communications equipment, and software.

PERIODICALS AND NEWSLETTERS

Law and Order Magazine: The Magazine for Police Management. Hendon Publishing Co. • Monthly. $22.00 per year. Edited for law enforcement officials. Includes special issues on communications, technology, weapons, and uniforms and equipment.

Law Enforcement Technology. Cygnus Business Media. • Monthly. $60.00 per year. Covers new products and technologies for police professionals. Includes special issues on weapons, uniforms, communications equipment, computers (hardware-software), vehicles, and enforcement of drug laws.

Made to Measure. Halper Publishing Co. • Semiannual. Controlled circulation.

NAUMD News. National Association of Uniform Manufacturers and Distributors. • Three times a year. Price on application.

TRADE/PROFESSIONAL ASSOCIATIONS

National Association of Uniform Manufacturers and Distributors. 1156 Ave. of the Americas, Room 700, New York, NY 10036. Phone: (212)869-0670 Fax: (212)575-2847 E-mail: nyoffice@naumd.com • URL: http://www.naumd.com.

UNIONS

See: LABOR UNIONS

UNITED FUNDS

See: COMMUNITY FUNDS

UNITED NATIONS

See also: INTERNATIONAL AGENCIES

ABSTRACTS AND INDEXES

Index to Proceedings of the Economic and Social Council. United Nations Publications. • Irregular.

UNDOC: Current Index (United Nations Documents). United Nations Publications. • Quarterly. $150.00. Annual cumulation on microfiche. Text in English.

ALMANACS AND YEARBOOKS

Annual Review of United Nations Affairs: Covering Years from 1961 Through 1997. Oceana Publications, Inc. • Annual. 53 volumes. Price varies.

National Accounts Statistics: Main Aggregates and Detailed Tables. United Nations Publications. • Annual. $160.00.

BIBLIOGRAPHIES

Monthly Bibliography. United Nations Publications. • Monthly. $125.00 per year. Text in English and French.

DIRECTORIES

Directory of United Nations Databases and Information Systems. United Nations Publications. • Annual. $35.00. Nearly 38 United Nations organizations maintaining over 615 databases and information systems.

ENCYCLOPEDIAS AND DICTIONARIES

Lexique General; A General Lexicon of Terms-United Nations as Well as General-Used by Translators, Interpreters, etc. United Nations Publications. • 1991. Fourth edition.

HANDBOOKS AND MANUALS

Basic Facts About the United Nations. United Nations Publications. • 1998. $10.00.

PERIODICALS AND NEWSLETTERS

UN Chronicle. United Nations Pulications. • 11 times a year. $20.00 per year. Editions in English, French and Spanish.

STATISTICS SOURCES

Demographic Yearbook. United Nations, Dept. of Economic and Social Affairs. United Nations Publications. • Annual. $125.00. Text in English and French.

Industrial Commodity Statistics Yearbook. United Nations Dept. of Economic and Social Affairs. United Nations Publications. • Annual.

International Trade Statistics Yearbook. United Nations Statistical Office. United Nations Publications. • Annual. $135.00. Two volumes.

Monthly Bulletin of Statistics. United Nations Publications. • Monthly. $295.00 per year. Provides current data for about 200 countries on a wide variety of economic, industrial, and demographic subjects. Compiled by United Nations Statistical Office.

Statistical Yearbook. United Nations Publications. • Annual. $125.00. Contains statistics for about 200 countries on a wide variety of economic, industrial, and demographic topics. Compiled by United Nations Statistical Office.

World Statistics Pocketbook. United Nations Publications. • Annual $10.00.

TRADE/PROFESSIONAL ASSOCIATIONS

United Nations Association of the United States of America. 801 Second Ave., New York, NY 10017. Phone: (212)907-1300 Fax: (212)682-9185 E-mail: unahq@unausa.org • URL: http://www.unausa.org.

OTHER SOURCES

International Standard Industrial Classification of All Economic Activities. United Nations Publications. • 1992. Third revised edition.

UNITED STATES CONGRESS

See also: LAWS

GENERAL WORKS

Congressional Investigations: Law and Practice. John C. Grabow. Aspen Law and Business. • 1988. $95.00. Looseleaf service.

Guide to Congress; Origins, History and Procedure. Congressional Quarterly, Inc. • 1999. $259.00. Fifth edition.

ABSTRACTS AND INDEXES

Congressional Index. CCH, Inc. • Weekly when Congress is in session. $1,283.00 per year. Index to action on Public Bills from introduction to final disposition. Subject, author, and bill number indexes.

Current Law Index: Multiple Access to Legal Periodicals. The Gale Group. • Monthly. $650.00 per year. Produced in cooperation with the American Association of Law Libraries. Indexes more than 900 law journals, legal newspapers, and specialty publications from the U.S., Canada, U.K., Ireland, Australia, and New Zealand.

ALMANACS AND YEARBOOKS

CQ Almanac. Congressional Quarterly, Inc. • Annual. $215.00.

BIBLIOGRAPHIES

Congress in Print: The Weekly Catalog of Congressional Documents. Congressional Quarterly, Inc. • 48 times a year. $198.00 per year.

BIOGRAPHICAL SOURCES

Almanac of American Politics. National Journal Group, Inc. • Biennial. $54.95. Includes biographies of U.S. senators and representatives, with group ratings, key votes, and election results.

Biographical Directory of the American Congress, 1774-1996. CQ Staff Directories, Inc. • 1996. $295.00. Provides detailed biographies of members of the Continental Congress (1774-1789) and the U. S. Congress (1789-1996). Includes presidential Cabinet members.

Who's Who in American Politics. Marquis Who's Who. • Biennial. $275.00. Two volumes. Contains about 27,000 biographical sketches of local, state, and national elected or appointed individuals.

CD-ROM DATABASES

National Newspaper Index CD-ROM. The Gale Group. • Monthly. Provides comprehensive CD-ROM indexing of all material appearing in the late edition of the *New York Times*, the final edition of the *Washington Post*, the national edition of the *Christian Science Monitor*, the home edition of the *Los Angeles Times*, and the *Wall Street Journal*. Time period is four years. Also available online.

The New York Times Ondisc. New York Times Online Services. • Monthly. $2,650.00 per year. CD-ROM discs contain the full text of *The New York Times*, final edition. Inquire as to time period covered and availability of backfiles.

Newspaper Abstracts Ondisc. Bell & Howell Information and Learning. • Monthly. $2,950.00 per year (covers 1989 to date; archival discs are available for 1985-88). Provides cover-to-cover CD-ROM indexing and abstracting of 19 major newspapers, including the *New York Times, Wall Street Journal, Washington Post, Chicago Tribune,* and *Los Angeles Times.*

Staff Directories on CD-ROM. CQ Staff Directories, Inc. • Three times a year. $495.00 per year. Provides the contents on CD-ROM of *Congressional Staff Directory, Federal Staff Directory*, and *Judicial Staff Directory.* Includes photographs and maps.

DIRECTORIES

Almanac of the Unelected: Staff of the U. S. Congress. Bernan Press. • Annual. $275.00. Provides detailed information on key staff members of the legislative branch of the federal government. Includes educational background, previous employment, job responsibilities, etc.

Carroll's Federal & Federal Regional Directory: CD-ROM Edition. Carroll Publishing. • Bimonthly. $800.00 per year. Provides CD-ROM listings of more than 120,000 (55,000 high-level and 65,000 mid-level) U. S. government officials in Washington and throughout the country, including in military installations. Also available online.

Carroll's Federal Directory. Carroll Publishing. • Bimonthly. $325.00 per year. Lists 40,000 key U. S. officials, including members of Congress, Cabinet members, federal judges, Executive Office of the President personnel, and a wide variety of administrators.

Congressional Directory. U.S. Government Printing Office. • Biennial. $45.00.

Congressional Staff Directory: With Biographical Information on Members and Key Congressional Staff. CQ Staff Directories, Inc. • Three times a year. $227.00 per year. Single copies, $89.00. Contains more than 3,200 detailed biographies of members of Congress and their staffs. Includes committees and subcommittees. Keyword and name indexes are provided.

Congressional Yellow Book: Who's Who in Congress, Including Committees and Key Staff. Leadership Directories, Inc. • Quarterly. $305.00 per year. Looseleaf. A directory of members of congress, including their committees and their key aides.

Washington Information Directory. Congressional Quarterly, Inc. • Annual. $119.00. Published by

Congressional Quarterly, Inc. Lists names, addresses, phone numbers, fax numbers, and some Internet addresses for Congress, federal agencies, and nonprofit organizations in Washington, DC. Includes brief descriptions of each group and a subject index.

HANDBOOKS AND MANUALS

Constitution, Jefferson's Manual and Rules of the House of Representatives. U.S. Government Printing Office. • Biennial. $58.00.

Senate Manual. U.S. Government Printing Office. • Biennial. $57.00.

ONLINE DATABASES

CIS. Congressional Information Service, Inc. • Indexes publications of the United States Congress, 1970 to present. Inquire as to online cost and availability.

Information Bank Abstracts. New York Times Index Dept. • Provides indexing and abstracting of current affairs, primarily from the final late edition of *The New York Times* and the Eastern edition of *The Wall Street Journal*. Time period is 1969 to present, with daily updates. Inquire as to online cost and availability.

Newspaper and Periodical Abstracts. Bell & Howell Information and Learning. • Provides online coverage (citations and abstracts) of 25 major newspapers, 1,600 perodicals, and 70 TV programs. Covers business, economics, current affairs, health, fitness, sports, education, technology, government, consumer affairs, psychology, the arts, and the social sciences. Time period is 1986 to date, with daily updates. Inquire as to online cost and availability.

PERIODICALS AND NEWSLETTERS

Congressional Monitor: Daily Listing of All Scheduled Congressional Committee Hearings with Witnesses. Congressional Quarterly. Inc. • Daily. $1,349.00 per year. Weekly supplements.

Congressional Record. U.S. Congress. Available from U.S. Government Printing Office. • Daily. $357.00 per year. Indexes give names, subjects, and history of bills. Texts of bills not included.

Congressional Record Scanner. Congressional Quarterly, Inc. • 180 times a year. $395.00 per year. Abstract of each day's Congressional Record.

National Journal: The Weekly on Politics and Government. National Journal Group, Inc. • Semiweekly. $1,197.00 per year. Includes semiannual supplement *Capital Source*. A non-partisan weekly magazine on politics and government.

RESEARCH CENTERS AND INSTITUTES

Lexis.com Research System. Lexis-Nexis Group. Phone: 800-227-9597 or (937)865-6800 Fax: (937)865-6909 E-mail: webmaster@prod.lexis-nexis.com • URL: http://www.lexis.com • Fee-based Web site offers extensive searching of a wide variety of legal sources. Additional features include Daily Opinion Service, lexis.com Bookstore, Career Center, CLE Center, Law Schools, and Practice Pages ("Pages specific to areas of specialty").

TRADE/PROFESSIONAL ASSOCIATIONS

National Committee for an Effective Congress. 10 E. 39th St., Suite 601, New York, NY 10016. Phone: (212)686-4905 Fax: (212)686-4908.

United States Association of Former Members of Congress. 330 A St., N.E., Washington, DC 20002. Phone: (202)543-8676 Fax: (202)543-7145 E-mail: usafmc@erols.com • URL: http://www.usafmc.org.

OTHER SOURCES

CIS Microfiche Library. Congressional Information Service, Inc. • Monthly. Price varies. Prearranged retrospective files. An optional companion to *CIS Index*.

CQ Weekly. Congressional Quarterly, Inc. • Weekly. $1,349.00 per year. Includes annual *Almanac*. Formerly *Congressional Quarterly Weekly Report*.

FedWorld: A Program of the United States Department of Commerce. National Technical Information Service. • Web site offers "a comprehensive central access point for searching, locating, ordering, and acquiring government and business information." Emphasis is on searching the Web pages, databases, and government reports of a wide variety of federal agencies. Fees: Free.

FirstGov: Your First Click to the U. S. Government. General Services Administration. • Free Web site provides extensive links to federal agencies covering a wide variety of topics, such as agriculture, business, consumer safety, education, the environment, government jobs, grants, health, social security, statistics sources, taxes, technology, travel, and world affairs. Also provides links to federal forms, including IRS tax forms. Searching is offered, both keyword and advanced.

Major Legislation of the Congress. Available from U. S. Government Printing Office. • Irregular. Issued by the Legislative Reference Service, Library of Congress. Usually consists of five or six issues per session of Congress. Provides summaries of topical congressional concerns and major legislation introduced in response to those concerns.

UNITED STATES CUSTOMS SERVICE

See: CUSTOMS HOUSE, U.S. CUSTOMS SERVICE

UNITED STATES GOVERNMENT BONDS

See: GOVERNMENT BONDS

UNITED STATES GOVERNMENT PUBLICATIONS

See: GOVERNMENT PUBLICATIONS

UNIVERSAL PRODUCT CODE (UPC)

See: POINT-OF-SALE SYSTEMS (POS)

UNIVERSITIES

See: COLLEGES AND UNIVERSITIES

UNIVERSITY DEGREES

See: ACADEMIC DEGREES

UNIVERSITY LIBRARIES

See: COLLEGE AND UNIVERSITY LIBRARIES

UNIVERSITY PRESSES

See also: PUBLISHING INDUSTRY

CD-ROM DATABASES

ERIC on SilverPlatter. Available from SilverPlatter Information, Inc. • Quarterly. $700.00 per year. Produced by the Office of Educational Research and Improvement, U. S. Dept. of Education. Provides CD-ROM indexing and abstracting of a wide variety of literature relating to education. Archival discs are available from 1966.

INTERNET DATABASES

Amazon.com. Amazon.com, Inc. Phone: 800-201-7575 or (206)346-2992 Fax: (206)346-2950 E-mail: info@amazon.com • URL: http://www.amazon.com • "Welcome to Earth's Biggest Bookstore." Amazon.com claims to have more than 2.5 million titles that can be ordered online, but only through the Web site - no orders by mail, telephone, fax, or E-mail. Discounts are generally 30% for hardcovers and 20% for paperbacks. Efficient search facilities, including Boolean, make this Web site useful for reference (many titles have online reviews). Fees: Free.

Publishers' Catalogues Home Page. Northern Lights Internet Solutions Ltd. Phone: (306)931-0020 Fax: (306)931-7667 E-mail: info@lights.com • URL: http://www.lights.com/publisher • Provides links to the Web home pages of about 1,700 U. S. publishers (including about 80 University presses) and publishers in 48 foreign countries. "International/Multinational Publishers" are included, such as the International Monetary Fund, the World Bank, and the World Trade Organization. Publishers are arranged in convenient alphabetical lists. Searching is offered. Fees: Free.

ONLINE DATABASES

ERIC. Educational Resources Information Center. • Broad range of educational literature, 1966 to present. Monthly updates. Inquire as to online cost and availability.

PERIODICALS AND NEWSLETTERS

Independent Publisher: Leading the World of Book Selling in New Directions. Jenkins Group, Inc. • Bimonthly. $34.00 per year. Covers business, finance, production, marketing, and other management topics for small publishers, including college presses. Emphasis is on book publishing.

Learned Publishing: ALPSP Bulletin. Association of Learned and Professional Society Publishers. • Quarterly. Free to members; non-members, $295.00 per year. Articles and news of interest to publishers of academic and learned society material.

TRADE/PROFESSIONAL ASSOCIATIONS

Association of American University Presses. 71 W. 23rd St., Suite 901, New York, NY 10010-4102. Phone: (212)989-1010 Fax: (212)989-0275 E-mail: aaupny@aol.com • URL: http://www.aaupnet.org.

Association of Learned and Professional Society Publishers. Dovetail, Four Tintagel Crescent, London SE22 8HT, England. E-mail: andy.cawdell@alsiss.org.uk • URL: http://www.alsss.org.uk.

UNIX

See also: COMPUTER SOFTWARE INDUSTRY

ABSTRACTS AND INDEXES

Computer Literature Index: A Subject/Author Index to Computer and Data Processing Literature. Applied Computer Research, Inc. • Quarterly, with annual cumulation. $245.00 per year. Contains brief abstracts of book and periodical literature covering all phases of computing, including approximately 70 specific application areas.

Key Abstracts: Software Engineering. Available from INSPEC, Inc. • Monthly. $240.00 per year. Provides international coverage of journal and proceedings literature. Published in England by the Institution of Electrical Engineers (IEE).

Microcomputer Abstracts. Information Today, Inc. • Quarterly. $225.00 per year. Provides abstracts covering a wide variety of personal and business microcomputer literature. Formerly *Microcomputer Index.*

CD-ROM DATABASES

Computer Select. The Gale Group. • Monthly. $1,250.00 per year. Provides one year of full-text on CD-ROM for 120 leading computer-related publications. Also includes 70,000 product specifications and brief profiles of 13,000 computer product vendors and manufacturers.

Datapro on CD-ROM: Computer Systems Analyst. Gartner Group, Inc. • Monthly. Price on application. Includes detailed information on specific computer hardware and software products, such as peripherals, security systems, document imaging systems, and UNIX-related products.

DIRECTORIES

Data Sources: The Comprehensive Guide to the Data Processing Industry Hardware, Data Communications Products, Software, Company Profiles. The Gale Group. • Semiannual. $495.00 per year. Two volumes. Describes hardware and software for all computer operating sysems, including prices and technical details. Lists about 75,000 products from 14,000 suppliers. Industry-specific software applications are described.

Open Systems Products Directory. UniForum. • Annual. $50.00. A guide to Unix and open systems products from about 2,100 vendors. Lists software, hardware, systems, tools, peripherals, services, and publications.

The Software Encyclopedia: A Guide for Personal, Professional, and Business Users. R. R. Bowker. • Annual. $255.00. Two volumes. Volume one lists software programs by title and producer. Volume two provides information on programs according to application and operating system. Includes prices and requirements for hardware and memory.

ENCYCLOPEDIAS AND DICTIONARIES

Every Manager's Guide to Information Technology: A Glossary of Key Terms and Concepts for Today's Business Leader. Peter G. W. Keen. Harvard Business School Press. • 1995. $18.95. Second edition. Provides definitions of terms related to computers, data communications, and information network systems. (Harvard Business Economist Reference Series).

UNIX Dictionary of Commands, Terms, and Acronyms. John Levine and Margaret L. Young. McGraw-Hill. • 1996. $39.50.

HANDBOOKS AND MANUALS

Applied UNIX Programming 4.2. Bharat Kurani. Prentice Hall. • 1996. $90.00. Volume two.

Halting the Hacker: A Guide to Computer Security. Donald A. Pipkin. Prentice Hall. • 1996. $44.95.

Schaum's Outline of Unix. Harley Hahn. McGraw-Hill. • 1995. $7.38. (Schaum's Outline Series).

UNIX and Windows 2000 Integration Toolkit: A Complete Guide for System Administrators and Developers. Rawn Shah. John Wiley and Sons, Inc. • 2000. $49.99. Includes CD-ROM.

UNIX and Windows 2000: Interoperability Guide. Alan Roberts. Prentice Hall. • 2000. $44.99.

UNIX System Administration Handbook. Evi Nemeth. Prentice Hall. • 1995. $74.00. Second edition. Includes CD-Rom.

UNIX Unbounded: A Beginning Approach. Amir Afzal. Prentice Hall. • 1999. $85.00. Third edition.

INTERNET DATABASES

InfoTech Trends. Data Analysis Group. Phone: (707)894-9100 Fax: (707)486-5618 E-mail: support@infotechtrends.com • URL: http://www.infotechtrends.com • Web site provides both free and fee-based market research data on the information technology industry, including computers, peripherals, telecommunications, the Internet, software, CD-ROM/DVD, e-commerce, and workstations. Fees: Free for current (most recent year) data; more extensive information has various fee structures. Formerly *Computer Industry Forecasts.*

ONLINE DATABASES

Globalbase. The Gale Group. • Provides more than one million online summaries of business, industrial, and economic news reports from more than 1,000 publications worldwide. Covers a wide range of material appearing in international trade journals, professional magazines, and newspapers. Time period is 1984 to date, with weekly updates. Inquire as to online cost and availability.

Internet and Personal Computing Abstracts. Information Today, Inc. • Contains abstracts covering a wide variety of personal and business microcomputer literature appearing in more than 100 journals and popular magazines. Time period is 1981 to date, with monthly updates. Formerly *Microcomputer Index.* Inquire as to online cost and availability.

Microcomputer Software Guide Online. R. R. Bowker. • Provides information on more than 30,000 microcomputer software applications from more than 4,000 producers. Corresponds to printed *Software Encyclopedia*, but with monthly updates. Inquire as to online cost and availability.

PROMT: Predicasts Overview of Markets and Technology. The Gale Group. • Companies, products, applied technologies and markets. U.S. and international literature coverage, 1972 to date. Inquire as to online cost and availability. Provides abstracts from more than 1,600 publications. Weekly updates.

PERIODICALS AND NEWSLETTERS

Dr. Dobb's Journal: Software Tools for the Professional Programmer. • Monthly. $34.95 per year. A technical publication covering software development, languages, operating systems, and applications.

Information Week: For Business and Technology Managers. CMP Publications, Inc. • Weekly. $149.00 per year. The magazine for information systems management.

Interoperability. Miller Freeman, Inc. • Quarterly. Price on application. Covers the operation of wide-area networks, including UNIX systems.

SysAdmin: The Journal for Unix System Administrators. Miller Freeman, Inc. • Monthly. $39.00 per year. Provides technical information for managers of Unix systems.

TRADE/PROFESSIONAL ASSOCIATIONS

Usenix Association. 2560 Ninth St., Suite 215, Berkeley, CA 94710. Phone: (510)528-8649 Fax: (510)548-5738 E-mail: office@usenix.org • URL: http://www.usenix.org • Members are professional and technical users of UNIX computer operating systems.

UNLISTED SECURITIES

See: OVER-THE-COUNTER SECURITIES INDUSTRY

UPHOLSTERY

HANDBOOKS AND MANUALS

Practical Upholstery: And the Cutting of Slip Covers. Frederick Palmer. Madison Books, Inc., USA. • 1982. $11.95.

Upholstering Methods. Fred W. Zimmerman. Goodheart - Willcox Publishers. • 1992. $26.60.

TRADE/PROFESSIONAL ASSOCIATIONS

National Association of Decorative Fabric Distributors. 3008 Millwood Ave., Columbia, SC 29205. Phone: 800-445-8629 Fax: (803)765-0860 E-mail: info@nadfd.com • URL: http://www.nadfd.com.

Upholstered Furniture Action Council. P.O. Box 2436, High Point, NC 27261. Phone: (919)885-5065 Fax: (919)884-5303.

URANIUM INDUSTRY

See also: MINES AND MINERAL RESOURCES

ALMANACS AND YEARBOOKS

CRB Commodity Yearbook. Commodity Research Bureau. CRB. • Annual. $99.95.

CD-ROM DATABASES

Environment Abstracts on CD-ROM. Congressional Information Service, Inc. • Quarterly. $1,295.00 per year. Contains the following CD-ROM databases: *Environment Abstracts, Energy Abstracts*, and *Acid Rain Abstracts.* Length of coverage varies.

ONLINE DATABASES

Energyline. Congressional Information Service, Inc. • Provides online citations and abstracts to the literature of all forms of energy: petroleum, natural gas, coal, nuclear power, solar energy, etc. Time period is 1971 to 1993 (closed file). Inquire as to online cost and availability.

GEOARCHIVE. Geosystems. • Citations to literature on geoscience and water. 1974 to present. Monthly updates. Inquire as to online cost and availability.

GEOREF. American Geological Institute. • Bibliography and index of geology and geosciences literature, 1785 to present. Inquire as to online cost and availability.

PERIODICALS AND NEWSLETTERS

Nuclear Fuel. McGraw-Hill. • Biweekly. $1,035.00 per year. Newsletter.

STATISTICS SOURCES

Non-Ferrous Metal Data Yearbook. American Bureau of Metal Statistics. • Annual. $395.00. Provides about 200 statistical tables covering many nonferrous metals. Includes production, consumption, inventories, exports, imports, and other data.

TRADE/PROFESSIONAL ASSOCIATIONS

American Bureau of Metal Statistics. P.O. Box 805, Chatham, NJ 07928. Phone: (973)701-2299 Fax: (973)701-2152 E-mail: info@abms.com • URL: http://www.abms.com • Members are metal companies. Compiles and publishes detailed statistical data on a wide variety of nonferrous metals: aluminum, copper, gold, lead, nickel, platinum, silver, tin, titanium, uranium, zinc, and others.

URBAN AREAS

See: CITIES AND TOWNS

URBAN DEVELOPMENT

See also: CITY PLANNING; COMMUNITY DEVELOPMENT; HOUSING

GENERAL WORKS

Cities for the 21st Century. OECD Publications and Information Center. • 1994. $39.00. Contains discussions of the economic, social, and environmental problems of today's cities.

Moving Beyond Gridlock: Traffic and Development. Robert T. Dunphy. Urban Land Institute. • 1996. $45.95. Describes how various regions have dealt with traffic growth. Includes case studies from seven cities.

Urban Revitalization: Policies and Practices. Fritz W. Wagner and others. Sage Publications, Inc. • 1995. $48.00.

ABSTRACTS AND INDEXES

Index to Current Urban Documents. Greenwood Publishing Group, Inc., Subscription Publications. • Quarterly. $425.00 per year. Annual cumulation.

Sage Urban Studies Abstracts. Sage Publications, Inc. • Quarterly. Individuals, $150.00 per year; institutions, $560.00 per year.

Social Sciences Index. H. W. Wilson Co. • Quarterly, with annual cumulation. Service basis for print edition; CD-ROM edition, $1,495 per year. Indexes more than 400 periodicals covering economics, environmental policy, government, insurance, labor, health care policy, plannning, public administration, public welfare, urban studies, women's issues, criminology, and related topics.

ALMANACS AND YEARBOOKS

Institute on Planning, Zoning and Eminent Domain, Southwestern Legal Foundation:Proceedings, 1971-1994. William S. Hein & Co., Inc. • 1971. $2,887.00. 24 volumes.

BIBLIOGRAPHIES

Waterfront Revitalization. Eric J. Fournier. Sage Publications, Inc. • 1994. $10.00. (CPL Bibliographies Series, No. 310).

CD-ROM DATABASES

National Newspaper Index CD-ROM. The Gale Group. • Monthly. Provides comprehensive CD-ROM indexing of all material appearing in the late edition of the *New York Times*, the final edition of the *Washington Post*, the national edition of the *Christian Science Monitor*, the home edition of the *Los Angeles Times*, and the *Wall Street Journal*. Time period is four years. Also available online.

The New York Times Ondisc. New York Times Online Services. • Monthly. $2,650.00 per year. CD-ROM discs contain the full text of *The New York Times*, final edition. Inquire as to time period covered and availability of backfiles.

Newspaper Abstracts Ondisc. Bell & Howell Information and Learning. • Monthly. $2,950.00 per year (covers 1989 to date; archival discs are available for 1985-88). Provides cover-to-cover CD-ROM indexing and abstracting of 19 major newspapers, including the *New York Times, Wall Street Journal, Washington Post, Chicago Tribune,* and *Los Angeles Times.*

Social Science Source. EBSCO Publishing. • Monthly. $1,495.00 per year. Provides CD-ROM citations and abstracts to social science articles in more than 600 periodicals, with full text from 125 periodicals. Covers economics, political science, public policy, international relations, psychology, and other topics. Time period is most recent five years.

Social Sciences Citation Index: Compact Disc Edition with Abstracts. Institute for Scientific Information. • Quarterly. Provides CD-ROM indexing and abstracting of "significant articles" from 1,400 social science journals worldwide, with additional selections from 3,200 other journals, 1986 to date. Includes economics, business, finance, management, communications, demographics, information and library science, political science, sociology, and many other subjects.

WILSONDISC: Wilson Social Sciences Abstracts. H. W. Wilson Co. • Monthly. Including unlimited online access to *Social Sciences Index* through WILSONLINE. Provides CD-ROM indexing from 1983 and abstracting from 1994 of more than 400 periodicals covering economics, area studies, community health, public administration, public welfare, urban studies, and many other topics related to the social sciences.

DIRECTORIES

Funding Sources for Community and Economic Development: A Guide to Current Sources for Local Programs and Projects. Oryx Press. • 2000. $64.95. Sixth edition. Provides information on 2,600 funding sources. Includes "A Guide to Proposal Planning.".

HANDBOOKS AND MANUALS

Hotel Development. Urban Land Institute. • 1996. $59.95. Provides practical information on developing, acquiring, and renovating hotels in urban areas. Covers market analysis, financing, construction, and management. Includes case studies.

New Uses for Obsolete Buildings. Urban Land Institute. • 1996. $64.95. Covers various aspects of redevelopment: zoning, building codes, environment, economics, financing, and marketing. Includes eight case studies and 75 descriptions of completed "adaptive use projects.".

Resort Development Handbook. Dean Schwanke and others. Urban Land Institute. • 1997. $89.95. Covers a wide range of resort settings and amenities, with details of development, market analysis, financing, design, and operations. Includes color photographs and case studies. (ULI Development Handbook Series).

Sports, Convention, and Entertainment Facilities. David C. Petersen. Urban Land Institute. • 1996. $59.95. Provides advice and information on developing, financing, and operating amphitheaters, arenas, convention centers, and stadiums. Includes case studies of 70 projects.

Urban Parks and Open Space. Gayle L. Berens and others. Urban Land Institute. • 1997. Price on application. Covers financing, design, management, and public-private partnerships relative to the development of open space for new urban parks. Includes color illustrations and the history of urban parks.

Zoning and Planning Law Handbook. West Group. • 1996. Price on application. (Real Property-Zoning Series).

ONLINE DATABASES

Information Bank Abstracts. New York Times Index Dept. • Provides indexing and abstracting of current affairs, primarily from the final late edition of *The New York Times* and the Eastern edition of *The Wall Street Journal.* Time period is 1969 to present, with daily updates. Inquire as to online cost and availability.

Wilson Social Sciences Abstracts Online. H. W. Wilson Co. • Provides online abstracting and indexing of more than 415 periodicals covering area studies, community health, public administration, public welfare, urban studies, and many other social science topics. Time period is 1994 to date for abstracts and 1983 to date for indexing, with updates monthly. Inquire as to online cost and availability.

PERIODICALS AND NEWSLETTERS

Downtown Idea Exchange: Essential Information for Downtown Research and Development Center. Downtown Research and Development Center. Alexander Communications Group, Inc. • Semimonthly. $157.00 per year. Newsletter for those concerned with central business districts. Provides news and other information on planning, development, parking, mass transit, traffic, funding, and other topics.

Downtown Promotion Reporter. Downtown Research and Development Center. Alexander Communications Group, Inc. • Monthly. $157.00 per year. Newsletter. Provides information on public relations, market research, advertising, budgeting, etc. Edited for promoters of downtown areas in cities and towns.

Journal of Housing and Community Development. National Association of Housing and Redevelopment Officials (NAHRO). • Bimonthly. $24.00 per year. Formerly *Journal of Housing.*

Land Use Law and Zoning Digest. American Planning Association. • Monthly. $275.00 per year. Covers judicial decisions and state laws affecting zoning and land use. Edited for city planners and lawyers. Monthly supplement available *Zoning News.*

Real Estate Economics: Journal of the American Real Estate and Urban Economics Association. MIT Press. • Quarterly. Institutions, $165.00 per year.

Urban Affairs Review. Sage Publications, Inc. • Bimonthly. Individuals, $80.00 per year; institutions, $410.00 per year. Formerly *Urban Affairs Quarterly.*

Urban Land: News and Trends in Land Development. Urban Land Institute. • Monthly. Membership.

Zoning and Planning Law Report. West Group. • 11 times a year. $283.00 per year. Newsletter.

RESEARCH CENTERS AND INSTITUTES

Institute of Urban and Regional Development. University of California at Berkeley, 316 Wurster Hall, Berkeley, CA 94720-1870. Phone: (510)642-4874 Fax: (510)643-9576 E-mail: iurd@uclink.berkeley.edu • URL: http://www.ced.berkeley.edu/iurd • Research topics include the effects of changing economic trends in urban areas.

Urban Institute. 2100 M St., N. W., Washington, DC 20037. Phone: (202)833-7200 Fax: (202)728-0232 E-mail: paffairs@ui.urban.org • URL: http://www.urban.org • Research activities include the study of urban economic affairs, development, housing, productivity, and municipal finance.

Urban Land Institute. 1025 Thomas Jefferson Ave. N.W., Suite 500W, Washington, DC 20004. Phone: (202)624-7000 Fax: (202)624-7140 E-mail: rlevitt@uli.org • URL: http://www.uli.org • Studies urban land planning and the growth and development of urbanized areas, including central city problems, industrial development, community development, residential development, taxation, shopping centers, and the effects of development on the environment.

STATISTICS SOURCES

Budget of the United States Government. U.S. Office of Management and Budget. Available from U.S. Government Printing Office. • Annual.

Facts About the Cities. Allan Carpenter and Carl Provorse. H. W. Wilson Co. • 1996. $65.00. Second edition. Contains a wide variety of information on 300 American cities, including cities in Puerto Rico, Guam, and the U. S. Virgin Islands. Data is provided on the workplace, taxes, revenues, cost of living, population, climate, housing, transportation, etc.

Housing and Urban Development Trends: Annual Summary. U.S. Department of Housing and Urban Development. • Annual.

TRADE/PROFESSIONAL ASSOCIATIONS

American Planning Association. 122 S. Michigan Ave., Suite. 1600, Chicago, IL 60603-6107. Phone: (312)431-9100 Fax: (312)431-9985 E-mail: research@planning.org • URL: http://www.planning.org.

American Real Estate and Urban Economics Association. Indiana University School of Business, 1309 E. 10th St., Suite 738, Bloomington, IN 47405-1701. Phone: (812)855-7794 Fax: (812)855-8679 E-mail: areuea@indiana.edu • URL: http://www.areuea.org • Members are real estate teachers, researchers, economists, and others concerned with urban real estate and investment.

Council for Urban Economic Development. 1730 K St., N.W., Suite 700, Washington, DC 20006. Phone: (202)223-4735 Fax: (202)223-4745 E-mail: mail@urbandevelopment.com • URL: http://www.cued.org.

National Association of Housing and Redevelopment Officials. 630 Eye St., N.W., Washington, DC 20001. Phone: (202)289-3500 Fax: (202)289-8181 E-mail: nahro@nahro.org • URL: http://www.nahro.org.

OTHER SOURCES

American Land Planning Law. Norman Williams, and John Taylor. West Group. • $750.00. Eight volumes. Periodic supplementation. (Real Property and Zoning Series).

URBAN MANAGEMENT

See: MUNICIPAL GOVERNMENT

URBAN PLANNING

See: CITY PLANNING

URBAN TRANSPORTATION

See: PUBLIC TRANSPORTATION; TRANSPORTATION INDUSTRY

USED CAR INDUSTRY

See also: AUTOMOBILE DEALERS

GENERAL WORKS

What Your Car Really Costs: How to Keep a Financially Safe Driving Record. American Institute for Economic Research. • 1999. $6.00. Contains "Should You Buy or Lease?," "Should You Buy New or Used?," "Dealer Trade-in or Private Sale?," "Lemon Laws," and other car buying information. Includes rankings of specific models for resale value, 1992 to 1998. (Economic Education Bulletin.).

HANDBOOKS AND MANUALS

Used-Car Rental Agency. Entrepreneur Media, Inc. • Looseleaf. $59.50. A practical guide to starting a used-car rental business. Covers profit potential, start-up costs, market size evaluation, owner's time required, site selection, lease negotiation pricing, accounting, advertising, promotion, etc. (Start-Up Business Guide No. E1108.).

Used Car Sales. Entrepreneur Media, Inc. • Looseleaf. $59.50. A practical guide to getting started in the business of selling used cars. Covers profit potential, start-up costs, market size evaluation, owner's time required, site selection, lease negotiation, pricing, accounting, advertising, etc. (Start-Up Business Guide No. E2330.).

PERIODICALS AND NEWSLETTERS

Used Car Dealer. National Independent Automobile Dealers Association. • Monthly. Members, $36.00 per year; non-members, $120.00 per year.

PRICE SOURCES

Automobile Red Book Used Car Valuations. National Market Reports, Inc. • Eight times per year. $49.50 per year. Formerly *Automobile Red Book.*

Automotive Market Report. Automotive Auction Publishing, Inc. • Biweekly. $130.00 Per Year. Current wholesale values of used vehicles.

Edmund's Used Car Prices. Edmund Publications Corp. • Four times a year. $20.00 per year. Lists American and foreign used car prices for the past 10 years. Also lists van, pickup and sports utility used prices for the past 8 years.

NADA Appraisal Guides. National Automobile Dealers Association. • Prices and frequencies vary. Guides to prices of used cars, old used cars, motorcycles, mobile homes, recreational vehicles, and mopeds.

TRADE/PROFESSIONAL ASSOCIATIONS

NAtional Auto Auction Association. 5320-D Spectrum Dr., Frederick, MD 21703-7337. Phone: (301)696-0400 Fax: (301)631-1359 E-mail: naaa@earthlink.net • URL: http://www.naaa.com.

National Independent Automobile Dealers Association. 2521 Brown Blvd., Arlington, TX 76006-5203. Phone: (817)640-3838 Fax: (817)649-5866 E-mail: rb@niada.com • URL: http://www.niada.com.

USED PRODUCTS

See: SURPLUS PRODUCTS

UTENSILS, COOKING

See: HOUSEWARES INDUSTRY

UTILITIES, PUBLIC

See: PUBLIC UTILITIES

V

VACUUM CLEANERS

INTERNET DATABASES

Fedstats. Federal Interagency Council on Statistical Policy. Phone: (202)395-7254 • URL: http://www.fedstats.gov • Web site features an efficient search facility for full-text statistics produced by more than 70 federal agencies, including the Census Bureau, the Bureau of Economic Analysis, and the Bureau of Labor Statistics. Boolean searches can be made within one agency or for all agencies combined. Links are offered to international statistical bureaus, including the UN, IMF, OECD, UNESCO, Eurostat, and 20 individual countries. Fees: Free.

ONLINE DATABASES

DRI U.S. Central Database. Data Products Division. • Provides more than 23,000 business, financial, demographic, economic, foreign trade, and industry-related time series for the U.S. Includes national income, population, retail-wholesale trade, price indexes, labor data, housing, industrial production, banking, interest rates, money supply, etc. Time period is generally 1947 to date (some data back to 1929). Updating varies. Inquire as to online cost and availability.

STATISTICS SOURCES

Business Statistics of the United States. Courtenay M. Slater, editor. Bernan Associates. • 1999. $74.00. Fifth edition. Based on *Business Statistics*, formerly issue by the Bureau of Economic Analysis, U. S. Department of Commerce. Provides basic data for a wide variety of U. S. industries, services, and economic indicators. Most statistics are shown annually for 29 years and monthly for the most recent four years.

Survey of Current Business. Available from U. S. Government Printing Office. • Monthly. $49.00 per year. Issued by Bureau of Economic Analysis, U. S. Department of Commerce. Presents a wide variety of business and economic data.

TRADE/PROFESSIONAL ASSOCIATIONS

Vacuum Cleaner Manufacturers Association. P.O. Box 2642, North Canton, OH 44720. Phone: (330)499-5998 Fax: (330)499-5292.

VALUATION

See also: REAL PROPERTY VALUATION

HANDBOOKS AND MANUALS

CCH Guide to Business Valuation. CCH, Inc. • Looseleaf. $295.00 per year, including quarterly newsletter. Covers latest developments and trends in the evaluation of businesses.

Corporate Valuation: Tools for Effective Appraisal and Decision Making. Randolph W. Westerfield and others. McGraw-Hill Professional. • 1993. $65.00. Discusses the four most widely-used corporate appraisal methods.

Handbook of Business Valuation. Thomas L. West and Jeffrey D. Jones. John Wiley and Sons, Inc. • 1999. $125.00. Second edition. A collection of articles, worksheets, and appraisal techniques.

Manager's Guide to Financial Statement Analysis. Stephen F. Jablonsky and Noah P. Barsky. John Wiley and Sons, Inc. • 1998. $67.95. The two main sections are "Financial Statements and Business Strategy" and "Market Valuation and Business Strategy.".

Valuation: Measuring and Managing the Value of Companies. Tom Copeland and others. John Wiley and Sons, Inc. • 2000. $75.00. Second editon. A practical guide to economic value analysis for bankers, accountants, financial analysts, and others concerned with company valuation. (Frontiers in Finance Series).

Valuing a Business: Analysis and Appraisal of Closely Held Companies. Shannon P. Pratt and others. McGraw-Hill. • 2000. $95.00. Fourth edition. Includes information on how to appraise partial interests and how to write a valuation report.

Valuing Professional Practices: A Practitioner's Guide. Robert Reilly and Robert Schweihs. CCH, Inc. • 1997. $99.00. Provides a basic introduction to estimating the dollar value of practices in various professional fields.

PERIODICALS AND NEWSLETTERS

ASA Newsletter. American Studies Association. • Quarterly. Membership.

Journal of Corporate Accounting and Finance. John Wiley and Sons, Inc., Subscription Dept. • Bimonthly. $263.00 per year. Topics include government regulation, corporate taxation, financial risk, business valuation, and strategic planning.

TRADE/PROFESSIONAL ASSOCIATIONS

American Society of Appraisers. 555 Herndon Pkwy, Ste. 125, Herndon, VA 20170. Phone: 800-272-8258 or (703)478-2228 Fax: (703)742-8471 E-mail: asainfo@appraisers.org • URL: http://www.appraisers.org.

Appraisers Association of America. 386 Park Ave., S., Suite 2000, New York, NY 10016. Phone: (212)889-5404 Fax: (212)889-5503 E-mail: aaal@rcn.com.

VALVES

FINANCIAL RATIOS

Annual Statement Studies. Robert Morris Associates: The Association of Lending and Credit Risk Professiona. • Annual. Free to members; non-members, $140.00. Median and quartile financial ratios are given for over 400 kinds of manufacturing, wholesale, retail, construction, and consumer finance establishments. Data is sorted by both asset size and sales volume. Includes a clearly written "Definition of Ratios" and an alphabetical industry index.

PERIODICALS AND NEWSLETTERS

Processing. Putman Media. • 14 times a year. $54.00 per year. Emphasis is on descriptions of new products for all areas of industrial processing, including valves, controls, filters, pumps, compressors, fluidics, and instrumentation.

STATISTICS SOURCES

Annual Survey of Manufactures. Available from U. S. Government Printing Office. • Annual. Prices vary. Issued by the U. S. Census Bureau as an interim update to the *Census of Manufactures.* Includes data on number of manufacturing establishments in various industries, employment, labor costs, value of shipments, capital expenditures, inventories, energy costs, and assets. (See also Census Bureau home page, http://www.census.gov/.).

Manufacturing Profiles. Available from U. S. Government Printing Office. • Annual. Issued by the U. S. Census Bureau. A printed consolidation of the entire *Current Industrial Report* series, presenting "all the data compiled." Contains statistics on production, shipments, inventories, consumption, exports, imports, and orders for a wide variety of manufactured products. (See also Census Bureau home page, http://www.census.gov/.).

U. S. Industry and Trade Outlook: The McGraw-Hill Companies and the U.S. Department of Commerce/International Trade Administration. Datapso Research Corp. • Annual. $69.95. Produced by the International Trade Administration, U. S. Department of Commerce, in a "public-private" partnership with DRI/McGraw-Hill and Standard & Poor's. Provides basic data, outlook for the current year, and "Long-Term Prospects" (five-year projections) for a wide variety of products and services. Includes high technology industries. Formerly *U. S. Industrial Outlook.*

TRADE/PROFESSIONAL ASSOCIATIONS

Manufacturers Standardization Society of the Valve and Fittings Industry. 127 Park St., N. E., Vienna, VA 22180. Phone: (703)281-6613 Fax: (703)281-6671 E-mail: info@mss-hq.com • URL: http://www.mss-hq.com • Members are valve and fitting companies. Publishes standards and specifications.

Valve Manufacturers Association of America. 1050 17th St., N.W., Suite 280, Washington, DC 20036. Phone: (202)331-8105 Fax: (202)296-0378 E-mail: vma@vma.org • URL: http://www.vma.org.

VARIABLE ANNUITIES

See: ANNUITIES

VARIETY STORES

See also: RETAIL TRADE

DIRECTORIES

Directory of Discount and General Merchandise Stores. Chain Store Guide. • Annual. $300.00. Includes retailers and wholesalers of housewares, giftwares, novelties, toys, hobby materials, crafts, and stationery. Formerly *Directory of Discount Stores Catalog Showrooms.*

European Directory of Retailers and Wholesalers. Available from The Gale Group. • 1997. $790.00. Second edition. Published by Euromonitor. Provides detailed information on more than 4,000 major retail and wholesale businesses in 17 countries of Western Europe. Contains 26 categories, such as supermarkets, superstores, department stores, discount stores, franchise operators, mail order, etc. Includes company, product, and geographic indexes.

FINANCIAL RATIOS

Annual Statement Studies. Robert Morris Associates: The Association of Lending and Credit Risk Professiona. • Annual. Free to members; non-members, $140.00. Median and quartile financial ratios are given for over 400 kinds of manufacturing, wholesale, retail, construction, and consumer finance establishments. Data is sorted by both asset size and sales volume. Includes a clearly written "Definition of Ratios" and an alphabetical industry index.

INTERNET DATABASES

Fedstats. Federal Interagency Council on Statistical Policy. Phone: (202)395-7254 • URL: http://www.fedstats.gov • Web site features an efficient search facility for full-text statistics produced by more than 70 federal agencies, including the Census Bureau, the Bureau of Economic Analysis, and the Bureau of Labor Statistics. Boolean searches can be made within one agency or for all agencies combined. Links are offered to international statistical bureaus, including the UN, IMF, OECD, UNESCO, Eurostat, and 20 individual countries. Fees: Free.

ONLINE DATABASES

DRI U.S. Central Database. Data Products Division. • Provides more than 23,000 business, financial, demographic, economic, foreign trade, and industry-related time series for the U.S. Includes national income, population, retail-wholesale trade, price indexes, labor data, housing, industrial production, banking, interest rates, money supply, etc. Time period is generally 1947 to date (some data back to 1929). Updating varies. Inquire as to online cost and availability.

STATISTICS SOURCES

Business Statistics of the United States. Courtenay M. Slater, editor. Bernan Associates. • 1999. $74.00. Fifth edition. Based on *Business Statistics*, formerly issue by the Bureau of Economic Analysis, U. S. Department of Commerce. Provides basic data for a wide variety of U. S. industries, services, and economic indicators. Most statistics are shown annually for 29 years and monthly for the most recent four years.

Survey of Current Business. Available from U. S. Government Printing Office. • Monthly. $49.00 per year. Issued by Bureau of Economic Analysis, U. S. Department of Commerce. Presents a wide variety of business and economic data.

TRADE/PROFESSIONAL ASSOCIATIONS

International Mass Retail Association. 1700 N. Moore St., Suite 2250, Arlington, VA 22209. Phone: (703)841-2300 Fax: (703)841-1184 • URL: http://www.imra.org.

VARNISH AND VARNISHING

See also: PAINT AND PAINTING

DIRECTORIES

Paint Red Book. PTN Publishing Co. • Annual. $53.00. Lists manufacturers of paint, varnish, lacquer, and specialized coatings. Suppliers of raw materials, chemicals, and equipment are included.

ONLINE DATABASES

World Surface Coatings Abstracts [Online]. Paint Research Association of Great Britain. • Indexing and abstracting of the literature of paint and surface coatings, 1976 to present. Monthly updates. Inquire as to online cost and availability.

PERIODICALS AND NEWSLETTERS

Modern Paint and Coatings. Chemical Week Associates. • Monthly. $52.00 per year.

STATISTICS SOURCES

Annual Survey of Manufactures. Available from U. S. Government Printing Office. • Annual. Prices vary. Issued by the U. S. Census Bureau as an interim update to the *Census of Manufactures.* Includes data on number of manufacturing establishments in various industries, employment, labor costs, value of shipments, capital expenditures, inventories, energy costs, and assets. (See also Census Bureau home page, http://www.census.gov/.).

Manufacturing Profiles. Available from U. S. Government Printing Office. • Annual. Issued by the U. S. Census Bureau. A printed consolidation of the entire *Current Industrial Report* series, presenting "all the data compiled." Contains statistics on production, shipments, inventories, consumption, exports, imports, and orders for a wide variety of manufactured products. (See also Census Bureau home page, http://www.census.gov/.).

Paint, Varnish, and Lacquer. U. S. Bureau of the Census. • Quarterly and annual. Provides data on shipments: value, quantity, imports, and exports. Includes paint, varnish, lacquer, product finishes, and special purpose coatings. (Current Industrial Reports, MQ-28F.).

TRADE/PROFESSIONAL ASSOCIATIONS

National Paint and Coatings Association. 1500 Rhode Island Ave., N.W., Washington, DC 20005-5597. Phone: (202)462-6272 Fax: (202)462-8549 E-mail: npca@paint.org • URL: http://www.paint.org.

VCR

See: VIDEO RECORDING INDUSTRY

VEGETABLE INDUSTRY

ABSTRACTS AND INDEXES

Field Crop Abstracts: Monthly Abstract Journal on World Annual Cereal, Legume, Root, Oilseed and Fibre Crops. Available from CABI Publishing North America. • Monthly. $1,465.00 per year. Published in England by CABI Publishing, formerly Commonwealth Agricultural Bureaux. Provides worldwide coverage of the literature.

Food Science and Technology Abstracts. International Food Information Service Publishing. • Monthly. $1,780.00 per year. Provides worldwide coverage of the literature of food technology and food production.

Foods Adlibra: Key to the World's Food Literature. Foods Adlibra Publications. • Semimonthly.Provides journal citations and abstracts to the literature of food technology and packaging.

Horticultural Abstracts: Compiled from World Literature on Temperate and Tropical Fruits, Vegetables, Ornaments, Plantation Crops. Available from CABI Publishing North America. • Monthly. $1,605.00 per year. Published in England by CABI Publishing. Provides worldwide coverage of the literature of fruits, vegetables, flowers, plants, and all aspects of gardens and gardening.

CD-ROM DATABASES

AGRICOLA on SilverPlatter. Available from SilverPlatter Information, Inc. • Quarterly. $825.00 per year. Produced by the National Agricultural Library. Provides about three million citations on CD-ROM to the literature of agriculture, agricultural economics, animal sciences, entomology, fertilizer, food, forestry, nutrition, pesticides, plant science, water resources, and other topics. Each quarterly disc covers the past ten years, with archival discs available from 1970.

Food Science and Technology Abstracts [CD-ROM]. Available from SilverPlatter Information, Inc. • Quarterly. $3,700 per year. Produced by International Food Information Service (home page is http://www.ifis.org). Provides worldwide coverage on CD-ROM of the literature of food technology and production. Various types of publications are indexed, with abstracts, including about 1,800 periodicals. Time period is 1969 to date.

DIRECTORIES

American Vegetable Grower Source Book. Meister Publishing Co. • Annual. $2.75. Formerly *American Vegetable Grower Buyers' Guide.*

Packer Produce Availability and Merchandising Guide. Vance Publishing Corp. • Annual. $35.00. A buyer's directory giving sources of fresh fruits and vegetables. Shippers are listed by location for each commodity.

Specialty Food Industry Directory. Phoenix Media Network, Inc. • Annual. Included in subscription to Food Distribution Magazine. Lists manufacturers and suppliers of specialty foods, and services and equipment for the specialty food industry. Featured food products include legumes, sauces, spices, upscale cheese, specialty beverages, snack foods, baked goods, ethnic foods, and specialty meats.

Western Growers Association-Membership Directory. Western Growers Association. • Annual. Membership.

ENCYCLOPEDIAS AND DICTIONARIES

Encyclopedia of Agriculture Science. Charles J. Arntzen and Ellen M. Ritter, editors. Academic Press, Inc. • 1994. $625.00. Four volumes.

Foods and Nutrition Encyclopedia. Audrey H. Ensminger and others. CRC Press, Inc. • 1993. $382.00. Second edition. Two volumes.

HANDBOOKS AND MANUALS

Vegetable Growing: Traditional Methods. Arthur Billitt. State Mutual Book and Periodical Service, Ltd. • 1988. $55.00. Third edition.

INTERNET DATABASES

USDA. United States Department of Agriculture. Phone: (202)720-2791 E-mail: agsec@usda.gov • URL: http://www.usda.gov • The USDA home page has six sections: News and Information; What's New; About USDA; Agencies; Opportunities; Search and Help. Keyword searching is offered from the USDA home page and from various individual agency home pages. Agencies are the Economic Research Service, Agricultural Marketing Service, National Agricultural Statistics Service, National Agricultural Library, and about 12 others. Updating varies. Fees: Free.

ONLINE DATABASES

Agricola. U.S. National Agricultural Library. • Covers worldwide agricultural literature. Over 2.8 million citations, 1970 to present, with monthly updates. Inquire as to online cost and availability.

Food Science and Technology Abstracts [online]. IFIS North American Desk. • Produced by International Food Information Service. Provides about 500,000 online citations, with abstracts, to the international literature of food science, technology, commodities, engineering, and processing. Approximately 2,000 periodicals are covered. Time period is 1969 to date, with monthly updates. Inquire as to online cost and availability.

FOODS ADLIBRA. General Mills, Inc. • Contains online citations, with abstracts, to the technical and business literature of food processing and packaging. New products and new ingredients are featured. Covers about 250 trade journals and 500 research journals from 1974 to date, with monthly updates. Inquire as to online cost and availability.

PERIODICALS AND NEWSLETTERS

American Vegetable Grower. Meister Publishing Co. • Monthly. $27.47 per year.

Food Distribution Magazine. Phoenix Media Network, Inc. • Monthly. $49.00 per year. Edited for marketers and buyers of domestic and imported, specialty or gourmet food products, including ethnic foods, seasonings, and bakery items.

Journal of Vegetable Crop Production. Haworth Press, Inc. • Semiannual. Individuals, $50.00 per year; institutions, $85.00 per year; libraries, $125.00 per year. Covers the production and marketing of vegetables.

The Packer: Devoted to the Interest of Commericial Growers, Packers, Shippers, Receivers and Retailers of Fruits, Vegetables and Other Products. Vance Publishing Corp., Produce Div. • Weekly. $65.00 per year. Supplments available, *Brand Directory* and *Fresh Trends, Packer's Produce Availiability and Merchandising Guide* and *Produce Services Sourcebooks.*

Produce Merchandising: The Packer's Retailing and Merchandising Magazine. Vance Publishing Corp., Produce Div. • Monthly. $35.00 per year. Provides information and advice on the retail marketing and promotion of fresh fruits and vegetalbe.

Produce News. Zim-Mer Trade Publications, Inc. • Weekly. $35.00 per year.

Western Grower and Shipper: The Business Magazine of the Western Product Industry. Western Growers Association. Western Grower and Shipper Publishing Co. • Monthly. $18.00 per year.

STATISTICS SOURCES

Agricultural Statistics. Available from U. S. Government Printing Office. • Annual. Produced by the National Agricultural Statistics Service, U. S. Department of Agriculture. Provides a wide variety of statistical data relating to agricultural production, supplies, consumption, prices/price-supports, foreign trade, costs, and returns, as well as farm labor, loans, income, and population. In many cases, historical data is shown annually for 10 years. In addition to farm data, includes detailed fishery statistics.

FAO Quarterly Bulletin of Statistics. Food and Agriculture Organization of the United Nations. Available from UNIPUB. • Quarterly. $20.00 per year. Provides international data on agricultural production, trade, and prices, covering the major commodities of many countries. Text in English, French, and Spanish. Formerly *FAO Monthly Bulletin of Statistics.*

Foreign Agricultural Trade of the United States. Available from U. S. Government Printing Office. • Monthly. $50.00 per year. Issued by the Economic Research Service of the U. S. Department of Agriculture. Provides data on U. S. exports and imports of agricultural commodities.

Vegetables and Specialties Situation and Outlook. Available from U. S. Government Printing Office. • Three times a year. $15.00 per year. Issued by the Economic Research Service of the U. S. Department of Agriculture. Provides current statistical information on supply, demand, and prices.

World Agricultural Supply and Demand Estimates. Available from U. S. Government Printing Office. • Monthly. $38.00 per year. Issued by the Economics and Statistics Service and the Foreign Agricultural Service of the U. S. Department of Agriculture. Consists mainly of statistical data and tables.

TRADE/PROFESSIONAL ASSOCIATIONS

United Fresh Fruit and Vegetable Association. 727 N. Washington St., Alexandria, VA 22314. Phone: (703)836-3410 Fax: (703)836-7745 E-mail: uffva@uffva.org.

OTHER SOURCES

Major Food and Drink Companies of the World. Available from The Gale Group. • 2001. $855.00. Fourth edition. Two volumes. Published by Graham & Whiteside. Contains profiles and trade names for more than 9,000 important food and beverage companies in various countries. In addition to foods, includes both alcoholic and nonalcoholic drink products.

The Market for Value-Added Fresh Produce. MarketResearch.com. • 1999. $2,750.00. Market research report. Covers packaged salad mixes, bulk salad mixes, pre-cut fruits, and pre-cut vegetables. Market projections are provided to the year 2003.

Thomas Food and Beverage Market Place. Grey House Publishing. • Annual. $295.00. Three volumes. Contains more than 40,000 entries covering food companies, beverages, food equipment, warehouse companies, food brokers, wholesalers, importers, and exporters. Formerly *Thomas Food Industry Register.*

VEGETABLE OIL INDUSTRY

See: OIL AND FATS INDUSTRY

VENDING MACHINES

DIRECTORIES

American Automatic Merchandiser Blue Book Buyer's Guide. Cygnus Publishing. • Annual. $35.00. Suppliers of products, services, and equipment to the merchandise vending, contract food services, and office coffee service industries.

National Automatic Merchandising Association-Directory of Members. National Automatic Merchandising Association. • Annual. $150.00. Lists 2,300 vending and food service management firms, along with vending machine manufacturers and distributors and producers of other equipment and food items.

Vending Times Buyers Guide and Directory. Vending Times Inc. • Annual. $35.00. Formerly *Vending Times International Buyers Guide and Directory.*

FINANCIAL RATIOS

Annual Statement Studies. Robert Morris Associates: The Association of Lending and Credit Risk Professiona. • Annual. Free to members; non-members, $140.00. Median and quartile financial ratios are given for over 400 kinds of manufacturing, wholesale, retail, construction, and consumer finance establishments. Data is sorted by both asset size and sales volume. Includes a clearly written "Definition of Ratios" and an alphabetical industry index.

Cost and Profit Ratios for Vending Operators. National Automatic Merchandising Association. • Annual. $100.00 to members; $250.00 to nonmembers. Provides data on profits and operating expenses.

HANDBOOKS AND MANUALS

Making Money with Vending Machines. Billy Mason. Kelso Manufacturing Co. • 1995. $7.00.

PERIODICALS AND NEWSLETTERS

Automatic Merchandiser. Cygnus Publishing, Inc., Johnson Hill Press. • 11 times a year. $60.00 per year. Includes annual *Product* issue. Formerly *American Automatic Merchandiser.*

Cash Box: The International Music-Record Weekly. Cash Box Publishing Co., Inc. • Weekly. $185.00 per year.

Vending Times: Vending-Feeding-Coffee Service-Music and Games. Vending Times, Inc. • Monthly. $35.00 per year. Incorporates *V-T Music and Games.*

STATISTICS SOURCES

Annual Survey of Manufactures. Available from U. S. Government Printing Office. • Annual. Prices vary. Issued by the U. S. Census Bureau as an interim update to the *Census of Manufactures.* Includes data on number of manufacturing establishments in various industries, employment, labor costs, value of shipments, capital expenditures, inventories, energy costs, and assets. (See also Census Bureau home page, http://www.census.gov/.).

Manufacturing Profiles. Available from U. S. Government Printing Office. • Annual. Issued by the U. S. Census Bureau. A printed consolidation of the entire *Current Industrial Report* series, presenting "all the data compiled." Contains statistics on production, shipments, inventories, consumption, exports, imports, and orders for a wide variety of manufactured products. (See also Census Bureau home page, http://www.census.gov/.).

Vending Machines. U. S. Bureau of the Census. • Annual. Provides data on value of manufacturers' shipments, quantity, exports, imports, etc. (Current Industrial Reports, MA-35U.).

Vending Times Census of the Industry. Vending Times, Inc. • Annual. $25.00.

TRADE/PROFESSIONAL ASSOCIATIONS

National Automatic Merchandising Association. 20 N. Wacker Dr., Suite 350, Chicago, IL 60606. Phone: (312)346-0370 Fax: (312)704-4140 • URL: http://www.vending.org.

National Bulk Vendors Association. 200 N. La Salle St., Room 2100, Chicago, IL 60601. Phone: (312)621-1400 Fax: (312)621-1718 E-mail: nbva@muchlaw.com • URL: http://www.nbva.org.

VENEERS AND VENEERING

See also: LUMBER INDUSTRY; PLYWOOD INDUSTRY

DIRECTORIES

Directory of the Wood Products Industry. Miller Freeman, Inc. • Biennial. $295.00. Lists sawmills, panelmills, logging operations, plywood products, wood products, distributors, etc. Geographic arrangement, with an index to lumber specialities. Formerly *Directory of the Forest Products Industry.*

Where to Buy Hardwood Plywood and Veneer. Hardwood Plywood Manufacturers Association. • Annual. $20.00. Lists about 190 member manufacturers, prefinishers, and suppliers of hardwood veneer and plywood.

PERIODICALS AND NEWSLETTERS

Wood and Wood Products: Furniture, Cabinets, Woodworking and Allied Products Management and

Operations. Vance Publishing Corp. • 13 times a year. $50.00 per year.

TRADE/PROFESSIONAL ASSOCIATIONS

American Walnut Manufacturers Association. P.O. Box 5046, Zionsville, IN 46077. Phone: (317)873-8780 Fax: (317)873-8788 E-mail: larryfrye@compuserve.com.

VENTURE CAPITAL

GENERAL WORKS

The Leap: A Memoir of Love and Madness in the Internet Gold Rush. Tom Ashbrook. Houghton Mifflin Co. • 2000. $25.00. The author relates his personal and family tribulations while attempting to obtain financing for an eventually successful e-business startup, HomePortfolio.com.

DIRECTORIES

Business Capital Sources. Tyler G. Hicks. International Wealth Success, Inc. • 2000. $15.00. 11th edition. Lists about 1,500 banks, insurance and mortgage companies, commerical finance, leasing and venture capital firms that lend money for business investment.

Corporate Finance Sourcebook: The Guide to Major Capital Investment Source and Related Financial Services. R. R. Bowker. • Annual. $625.00. Lists more than 3,550 sources of corporate capital: investment bankers, securities firms, pension management companies, trust companies, insurance companies, and private lenders. Includes the names of over 13,000 key personnel.

Directory of Venture Capital Firms: Domestic & International. Grey House Publishing. • 2001. $350.00. Fifth edition. Provides detailed information on more than 2,500 U. S. and foreign sources of venture capital. Includes five indexes.

Fitzroy Dearborn International Directory of Venture Capital Funds. Jennifer Schellinger, editor. Fitzroy Dearborn Publishers, Inc. • 1998. $175.00. Third edition. Provides detailed information on more than 1,000 sources of venture capital, with articles on entrepreneurship.

Pratt's Guide to Venture Capital Sources. Securities Data Publishing. • Annual. $575.00. Describes about 1,400 venture capital firms, including key personnel, capital under management, and recent investments. Company, personnel, and industry indexes are provided. (Securities Data Publishing is a unit of Thomson Financial.).

Venture Capital Directory (Small Business Administation). Forum Publishing Co. • Annual. $12.95. Over 500 members of the Small Business Administration and the Small Business Investment. Companies that provide funding for small and minority businesses.

Venture Capital Report Guide to Venture Capital in Europe. Pitman Publishing. • 1991. $125.00. Provides information on more than 500 European venture capital firms. Lists current investments.

HANDBOOKS AND MANUALS

Handbook of Alternative Investment Strategies. Thomas Schneeweis and Joseph F. Pescatore, editors. Institutional Investor. • 1999. $95.00. Covers various forms of alternative investment, including hedge funds, managed futures, derivatives, venture capital, and natural resource financing.

New Venture Creation: Entrepreneurship for the 21st Century. Jeffrey A. Timmons and others. McGraw-Hill Professional. • 1998. Fifth edition. Price on application.

SBIC Directory and Handbook of Small Business Finance. International Wealth Success, Inc. • Annual. $15.00 per year. Includes small business investment companies.

Starting on a Shoestring: Building a Business Without a Bankroll. Arnold S. Goldstein. John Wiley and Sons, Inc. • 1995. $29.95. Third edition. Includes chapters on venture capital and Small Business Administration (SBA) loans.

Venture Capital: An Authoritative Guide for Investors, Entrepreneurs, and Managers. Douglas A. Lindgren. McGraw-Hill Professional. • 1998. $65.00.

Where to Go When the Bank Says No: Alternatives to Financing Your Business. David R. Evanson. Bloomberg Press. • 1998. $24.95. Emphasis is on obtaining business financing in the $250,000 to $15,000,000 range. Business plans are discussed. (Bloomberg Small Business Series).

PERIODICALS AND NEWSLETTERS

Black Enterprise. Earl G. Graves Publishing Co. • Monthly. $21.95 per year. Covers careers, personal finances and leisure.

Corporate Financing Week: The Newsweekly of Corporate Finance, Investment Banking and M and A. Institutional Investor. • Weekly. $2,550.00 per year. Newsletter for corporate finance officers. Emphasis is on debt and equity financing, mergers, leveraged buyouts, investment banking, and venture capital.

Inc.: The Magazine for Growing Companies. Goldhirsh Group, Inc. • 18 times a year. $19.00 per year. Edited for small office and office-in-the-home businesses with from one to 25 employees. Covers management, office technology, and lifestyle. Incorporates *Self-Employed Professional.*

Journal of Business Venturing. Elsevier Science. • Bimonthly. $545.00 per year.

Journal of Private Equity: Strategies and Techniques for Venture Investing. Institutional Investor. • Quarterly. $355.00 per year. Includes venture capital case histories, financial applications, foreign opportunities, industry analysis, management methods, etc.

Venture Capital Journal. Securities Data Publishing. • Monthly. $1,165.00 per year. Provides information and analysis concerning the venture capital and private equity markets. (Securities Data Publishing is a unit of Thomson Financial.).

RESEARCH CENTERS AND INSTITUTES

Center for the Study of Entrepreneurship. Marquette University, College of Business Administration, Milwaukee, WI 53201-1881. Phone: (414)288-5100 Fax: (414)288-1660.

STATISTICS SOURCES

U. S. Industry and Trade Outlook: The McGraw-Hill Companies and the U.S. Department of Commerce/International Trade Administration. Datapso Research Corp. • Annual. $69.95. Produced by the International Trade Administration, U. S. Department of Commerce, in a "public-private" partnership with DRI/McGraw-Hill and Standard & Poor's. Provides basic data, outlook for the current year, and "Long-Term Prospects" (five-year projections) for a wide variety of products and services. Includes high technology industries. Formerly *U. S. Industrial Outlook.*

TRADE/PROFESSIONAL ASSOCIATIONS

American Council for Capital Formation. 1750 K St., N.W., Suite 400, Washington, DC 20006. Phone: (202)293-5811 Fax: (202)785-8165 E-mail: info@accf.org • URL: http://www.accf.org • Supports capital formation as a general concept.

Chief Executive Officers Club. 180 Varick St., Penthouse Suite, New York, NY 10014. Phone: (212)633-0060 or (212)633-0061 Fax: (212)633-0063 E-mail: ceoclubs@bway.net • URL: http://www.ceo-clubs.org • Serves as an information resource for small business owners and managers.

International Venture Capital Institute. P.O. Box 1333, Stamford, CT 06904. Phone: (203)323-3143 Fax: (203)348-0622.

Interracial Council for Business Opportunity. 550 Fifth Ave., Suite 2202, New York, NY 10118-2202. Phone: (212)779-4360 Fax: (212)779-4365 • Provides technical and financial assistance to minority business people.

National Association of Investment Companies. 733 15th St., N.W., Suite 700, Washington, DC 20005. Phone: (202)289-4336 Fax: (202)289-4329.

National Association of Small Business Investment Companies. 666 11th St., N.W., No. 750, Washington, DC 20001. Phone: (202)628-5055 Fax: (202)628-5080 E-mail: nasbic@nasbic.org • URL: http://www.nasbic.org.

National Business Incubation Association. 20 E. Circle Dr., Suite 190, Athens, OH 45701. Phone: (740)593-4331 Fax: (740)593-1996 E-mail: info@nbia.org • URL: http://www.nbia.org • Members are business assistance professionals concerned with business startups, entrepreneurship, and effective small business management.

National Development Council. 51 E. 42nd St., Suite 300, New York, NY 10017. Phone: (212)682-1106 Fax: (212)573-6118 • Provides technical and financial assistance to minority business people.

National Venture Capital Association. 1655 N. Fort Myer Dr., Suite 850, Arlington, VA 22209. Phone: (703)524-2549 Fax: (703)524-3940 • URL: http://www.nvca.org • Members are providers of venture capital.

OTHER SOURCES

Cyberfinance: Raising Capital for the E-Business. Martin B. Robins. CCH, Inc. • 2001. $79.00. Covers the taxation, financial, and legal aspects of raising money for new Internet-based ("dot.com") companies, including the three stages of startup, growth, and initial public offering.

VETERANS

GENERAL WORKS

Social Security, Medicare, and Pensions: Get the Most Out of Your Retirement and Medical Benefits. Joseph Matthews and Dorothy M. Berman. Nolo.com. • 1999. $21.95. Seventh edition. In addition to the basic topics, includes practical information on Supplemental Security Income (SSI), disability benefits, veterans benefits, 401(k) plans, Medicare HMOs, medigap insurance, Medicaid, and how to appeal decisions.

HANDBOOKS AND MANUALS

Federal Benefits for Veterans and Dependents (Veterans Administration). U.S. Government Printing Office. • Annual. $5.00.

INTERNET DATABASES

U. S. Census Bureau: The Official Statistics. U. S. Bureau of the Census. Phone: (301)763-4100 Fax: (301)763-4794 • URL: http://www.census.gov • Web site is "Your Source for Social, Demographic, and Economic Information." Contains "Current U. S. Population Count," "Current Economic Indicators," and a wide variety of data under "Other Official Statistics." Keyword searching is provided. Fees: Free.

PERIODICALS AND NEWSLETTERS

American Legion Magazine. • Monthly. Free to members; non-members, $15.00 per year.

The Retired Officer. Retired Officers' Association. • Monthly. $20.00 per year.

VFW Magazine. Veterans of Foreign Wars of the United States. • 11 times a year. Free to members; non-members,$10.00 per year. Events and general features.

STATISTICS SOURCES

Annual Report of the Secretary of Veterans Affairs. U.S. Department of Veterans Affairs. • Annual. Shows monies distributed and received by the Dept. of Veterans Affairs. Describes the activities of the Department during the fiscal year.

Budget of the United States Government. U.S. Office of Management and Budget. Available from U.S. Government Printing Office. • Annual.

Social Statistics of the United States. Mark S. Littman, editor. Bernan Press. • 2000. $65.00. Includes statistical data on population growth, labor force, occupations, environmental trends, leisure time use, income, poverty, taxes, and other economic or demographic topics.

Statistical Abstract of the United States. Available from U. S. Government Printing Office. • Annual. $51.00. Issued by the U. S. Bureau of the Census.

A Statistical Portrait of the United States: Social Conditions and Trends. Mark S. Littman, editor. Bernan Press. • 1998. $89.00. Covers "social, economic, and environmental trends in the United States over the past 25 years." Includes statistical tables, graphs, and analysis relating to such topics as population, income, poverty, wealth, labor, housing, education, healthcare, air/water quality, and government.

TRADE/PROFESSIONAL ASSOCIATIONS

American Legion. c/o Public Relations Division, 700 N. Pennsylvania St., Indianapolis, IN 46204. Phone: 800-433-3318 or (317)630-1200 Fax: (317)630-1223 E-mail: natlcmdr@legion.org • URL: http://www.legion.org.

American Veterans Committee. 6309 Bannockburn Dr., Bethesda, MD 20817. Phone: (301)320-6490 Fax: (301)320-6490 E-mail: willenzj@mindspring.com.

National Association of State Directors of Veterans Affairs. 500 E. Capitol Ave., Pierre, SD 57501-5070. Phone: (605)773-3269 Fax: (605)773-5380 • URL: http://www.naasdva.com.

The Retired Officers Association. 201 N. Washington St., Alexandria, VA 22314-2539. Phone: 800-245-8762 or (703)549-2311 Fax: (703)838-8173 E-mail: pr@troa.org • URL: http://www.troa.org.

Veterans of Foreign Wars of the United States. 406 W. 34th St., Kansas, MO 64111. Phone: (816)756-3390 Fax: (816)968-1157 E-mail: vfw@vfwdc.org • URL: http://www.vfw.org.

Women's Army Corps Veterans Association. 1340 Bayonne Ave., Whiting, NJ 08759. Phone: (732)350-8176.

VETERINARY PRODUCTS

See also: PET INDUSTRY

ABSTRACTS AND INDEXES

Index Veterinarius: Comprehensive Monthly and Author Index to the World's Veterinary Literature. Availabe in Print and on the Internet. Available from CABI Publishing North America. • Monthly. $1,450.00 per year. Published in England by CABI Publishing. Provides worldwide coverage of the literature.

NTIS Alerts: Agriculture & Food. National Technical Information Service. • Semimonthly. $195.00 per year. Provides descriptions of government-sponsored research reports and software, with ordering information. Covers agricultural economics, horticulture, fisheries, veterinary medicine, food technology, and related subjects. Formerly *Abstract Newsletter.*

Review of Medical and Veterinary Entomology. Available from CABI Publishing North America. • Monthly. $710.00 per year. Provides worldwide coverage of the literature. Formerly *Review of Applied Entomology, Series B: Medical and Veterinary.*

ALMANACS AND YEARBOOKS

Advances in Veterinary Medicine. Academic Press, Inc., Journal Div. • Annual. Prices vary.

BIOGRAPHICAL SOURCES

AVMA Directory. American Veterinary Medical Association. • Annual. $90.00. 62,500 veterinarians; not limited to AVMA members. Formerly *American Veterinary Medical Association Directory.*

CD-ROM DATABASES

AGRICOLA on SilverPlatter. Available from SilverPlatter Information, Inc. • Quarterly. $825.00 per year. Produced by the National Agricultural Library. Provides about three million citations on CD-ROM to the literature of agriculture, agricultural economics, animal sciences, entomology, fertilizer, food, forestry, nutrition, pesticides, plant science, water resources, and other topics. Each quarterly disc covers the past ten years, with archival discs available from 1970.

DIRECTORIES

BioScan: The Worldwide Biotech Industry Reporting Service. American Health Consultants, Inc. • Bimonthly. $1,395.00 per year. Looseleaf. Provides detailed information on over 900 U. S. and foreign companies broadly classified as biotechnological. In addition to medical technology and advanced pharmaceutical firms, includes firms doing research in food processing, waste management, agriculture, and veterinary science.

ENCYCLOPEDIAS AND DICTIONARIES

Encyclopedia of Agriculture Science. Charles J. Arntzen and Ellen M. Ritter, editors. Academic Press, Inc. • 1994. $625.00. Four volumes.

HANDBOOKS AND MANUALS

Merck Veterinary Manual: A Handbook of Diagnosis and Therapy for the Veterinarian. Merck Publishing Group. • 1998. $32.00. 8th edidion.

ONLINE DATABASES

CAB Abstracts. CAB International North America. • Contains 46 specialized abstract collections covering over 10,000 journals and monographs in the areas of agriculture, horticulture, forest products, farm products, nutrition, dairy science, poultry, grains, animal health, entomology, etc. Time period is 1972 to date, with monthly updates. Inquire as to online cost and availability. *CAB Abstracts on CD-ROM* also available, with annual updating.

Derwent Veterinary Drug File. Derwent, Inc. • Provides indexing and abstracting of the world's veterinary drug literature since 1968, with monthly updates. Formerly *VETDOC.* Inquire as to online cost and availability.

PERIODICALS AND NEWSLETTERS

American Veterinary Medical Association Journal. American Veterinary Medical Association. • Semimonthly. $120.00 per year.

DVM: The Newsmagazine of Veterinary Medicine. Advanstar Communications, Inc., Healthcare Group. • Monthly. $39.00 per year. Includes new drugs and new products.

Veterinary Economics: Business Solutions for Practicing Veterinarians. Veterinary Medicine Publishing Group. • Monthly. $42.00 per year. Provides business management and financial articles for veterinarians.

TRADE/PROFESSIONAL ASSOCIATIONS

American Veterinary Exhibitors Association. 4800 Lamar Ave., Mission, KS 66202-1775. Phone: (913)286-2996 Fax: (913)286-2996.

American Veterinary Medical Association. 1931 N. Meacham Rd., Suite 100, Schaumburg, IL 60173-4360. Phone: 800-248-2862 or (847)925-8070 Fax: (847)925-1329 E-mail: avmainfo@avma.org • URL: http://www.avma.org.

OTHER SOURCES

World Animal Health Markets. Theta Reports/PJB Medical Publications, Inc. • 2000. $830.00. Market research data. Covers the market for animal health products in 15 major countries, including the U.S. (Theta Report No. SR198E.).

VICE

See: CRIME AND CRIMINALS

VIDEO CAMERAS

See: VIDEO RECORDING INDUSTRY

VIDEO RECORDING INDUSTRY

ABSTRACTS AND INDEXES

Applied Science and Technology Index. H. W. Wilson Co. • 11 times a year. Quarterly and annual cumulations. Service basis for print edition; CD-ROM edition, $1,495.00 per year. Indexes a wide variety of English language technical, industrial, and engineering periodicals.

Business Periodicals Index. H. W. Wilson Co. • Monthly, except August, with quarterly and annual cumulations. Service basis for print edition; CD-ROM edition, $1,495.00 per year.

Communication Abstracts. Sage Publications, Inc. • Bimonthly. Individuals, $185.00 per year; institutions, $805.00 per year. Provides broad coverage of the literature of communications, including broadcasting and advertising.

Current Contents: Engineering, Computing and Technology. Institute for Scientific Information. • Weekly. $730.00 per year. Reproductions of contents pages of technical journals. Includes *Author Index, Address Directory, Current Book Contents* and *Title Word Index.* Formerly *Current Contents: Engineering, Technology and Applied Sciences.*

Electronics and Communications Abstracts Journal: Comprehensive Coverage of Essential Scientific Literature. Cambridge Information Group. • Monthly. $1,045.00 per year.

BIBLIOGRAPHIES

Films and Audiovisual Information. Available from U. S. Government Printing Office. • Annual. Free. Issued by the Superintendent of Documents. A list of government publications on motion picture and audiovisual topics. Formerly *Motion Pictures, Films and Audiovisual Information.* (Subject Bibliography No. 73.).

CD-ROM DATABASES

Bowker's Complete Video Directory on Disc. Bowker Electronic Publishing. • Quarterly. $520.00 per year. An extensive CD-ROM directory of video tapes and laserdisks. Includes film reviews from *Variety.*

DIRECTORIES

AV Market Place: The Complete Business Directory of: Audio, Audio Visual, Computer Systems, Film,

Video, Programming - with industry yellow pages. R. R. Bowker. • Annual. $165.00. Lists over 7,000 producers and distributors of a wide variety of audiovisual and video equipment, computer systems, films, and tapes. Includes many application-specific listings.

Bowker's Complete Video Directory. R. R. Bowker. • Annual. $249.95. Four volumes. Lists over 151,000 theatrical and nontheatrical videocassette titles.

Broadcast Engineering: Equipment Reference Manual. Intertec Publishing Corp. • Annual. $20.00. Lists manufacturers and distributors of radio and TV broadcast and recording equipment. Included in subscription to *Broadcast Engineering.*

Directory of Computer and Consumer Electronics. Chain Store Age. • Annual. $290.00. Includes 2,900 "leading" retailers and over 200 "top" distributors. Formerly *Directory of Consumer Electronics Retails and Distributors.*

Directory of Video, Computer, and Audio-Visual Products. International Communications Industries Association. • Annual. $65.00. Contains detailed descriptions and photographs of specific items of equipment. Includes video cameras, overhead projectors, LCD panels, computer projection systems, film recording equipment, etc. A "Glossary of Terms" is also provided.

Film and Video Finder. National Information Center for Educational Media. Plexus Publishing, Inc. • Biennial. $295.00. Contains 92,000 listings of film and video educational, technical and vocational children's programs and literary materials.

International Television and Video Almanac: Reference Tool of the Television and Home Video Industries. Quigley Publishing Co., Inc. • Annual. $119.00.

Plunkett's InfoTech Industry Almanac: Complete Profiles on the InfoTech 500-the Leading Firms in the Movement and Management of Voice, Data, and Video. Available from Plunkett Research, Ltd. • Annual. $149.99. Five hundred major information companies are profiled, with corporate culture aspects. Discusses major trends in various sectors of the computer and information industry, including data on careers and job growth. Includes several indexes.

Producer's Masterguide: The International Production Manual for Motion Pictures, Television, Commercials, Cable and Videotape Industries in the United States, Canada, the United Kingdom, Bermuda, the Caribbean Islands, Mexico, South America. • Annual. $125.00. A standard reference guide of the professional film, television, commercial and video tape industry throughout the U.S. and Canada. More than 30,000 listings.

The SHOOT Directory for Commercial Production and Postproduction. BPI Communications. • Annual. $79.00. Lists production companies, advertising agencies, and sources of professional television, motion picture, and audio equipment.

Telecommunications Directory. The Gale Group. • 2000. $595.00. 12th edition. National and international voice, data, facsimile, and video communications services. Formerly *Telecommunications Systems and Services Directory.*

Video Recorder Dealers Directory. American Business Directories. • Annual. Price on application. Lists over 1,106 dealers. Compiled from U.S. yellow pages.

The Video Source Book. The Gale Group. • 2000. $345.00. 26th edition. Two volumes. Describes 160,000 video programs currently available on tape and disc. Includes Subject Category Index, Videodisc Index, Captioned Index (for hearing impaired), and Credits Index (actors, directors, etc.).

Video Systems: Guide to Production Services. Intertec Publishing Corp. • Annual. $10.00. Lists of about 1,000 firms offering services to videotape production companies.

Videolog. Trade Service Corp. • Weekly. $252.00 per year. Looseleaf. Contains over 30,000 descriptive listings of videocassettes and videodiscs arranged by title, director, and "Stars." Titles are grouped also by genre (15 sections).

ENCYCLOPEDIAS AND DICTIONARIES

Film-Video Terms and Concepts: A Focal Handbook. Steven Browne. Butterworth-Heinemann. • 1992. $31.95. Defines production terms, techniques, and jargon relating to motion pictures, television, and the video industry. (Focal Handbook).

International Film, Television, and Video Acronyms. Matthew Stevens, editor. Greenwood Publishing Group, Inc. • 1993. $85.00. A guide to 3,400 acronyms and 1,400 technical terms.

Multimedia and the Web from A to Z. Patrick M. Dillon and David C. Leonard. Oryx Press. • 1998. $39.95. Second enlarged revised edition. Defines more than 1,500 terms relating to software and hardware in the areas of computing, online technology, telecommunications, audio, video, motion pictures, CD-ROM, and the Internet. Includes acronyms and an annotated bibliography. Formerly *Multimedia Technology from A to Z* (1994).

HANDBOOKS AND MANUALS

Digital Video Buyer's Guide. CMP Media, Inc. • Annual. $10.00. A directory of professional video products, including digital cameras, monitors, editing systems, and software.

Today's Video: Equipment, Setup, and Production. Peter Utz. Prentice Hall. • 1998. $89.00. Third edition.

Videocassette Rental Store. Entrepreneur Media, Inc. • Looseleaf. $59.50. A practical guide to starting a videocassette rental store. Covers profit potential, start-up costs, market size evaluation, owner's time required, site selection, lease negotiation, pricing, accounting, advertising, promotion, etc. (Start-Up Business Guide No. E1192.).

ONLINE DATABASES

Applied Science and Technology Index Online. H. W. Wilson Co. • Provides online indexing of 400 major scientific, technical, industrial, and engineering periodicals. Time period is 1983 to date. Monthly updates. Inquire as to online cost and availability.

Marketing and Advertising Reference Service (MARS). The Gale Group. • Provides abstracts of literature relating to consumer marketing and advertising, including all forms of advertising media. Time period is 1984 to date. Daily updates. Inquire as to online cost and availability.

PROMT: Predicasts Overview of Markets and Technology. The Gale Group. • Companies, products, applied technologies and markets. U.S. and international literature coverage, 1972 to date. Inquire as to online cost and availability. Provides abstracts from more than 1,600 publications. Weekly updates.

Wilson Business Abstracts Online. H. W. Wilson Co. • Indexes and abstracts 600 major business periodicals, plus the *Wall Street Journal* and the business section of the *New York Times.* Indexing is from 1982, abstracting from 1990, with the two newspapers included from 1993. Updated weekly. Inquire as to online cost and availability. (*Business Periodicals Index* without abstracts is also available online.).

PERIODICALS AND NEWSLETTERS

DV: Digital Video. Miller Freeman, Inc. • Monthly. $29.97 per year. Edited for producers and creators of digital media. Includes topics relating to video, audio, animation, multimedia, interactive design, and special effects. Covers both hardware and software, with product reviews. Formerly *Digital Video Magazine.*

Electronic Media. Crain Communications, Inc. • Weekly. $119.00 per year.

Entertainment Marketing Letter. EPM Communications, Inc. • 22 times a year. $319.00 per year. Newsletter. Covers the marketing of various entertainment products. Includes television broadcasting, videocassettes, celebrity tours and tie-ins, radio broadcasting, and the music business.

Presentations: Technology and Techniques for Effective Communication. Lakewood Publications, Inc. • Monthly. $50.00 per year. Covers the use of presentation hardware and software, including audiovisual equipment and computerized display systems. Includes an annual *"Buyers Guide to Presentation Products.".*

SHOOT: The Leading Newsweekly for Commercial Production and Postproduction. BPI Communications. • Weekly. $115.00 per year. Covers animation, music, sound design, computer graphics, visual effects, cinematography, and other aspects of television and motion picture production, with emphasis on TV commercials.

Smart TV: For Selective and Interactive Viewers. Videomaker, Inc. • Bimonthly. $14.97 per year. Consumer magazine covering WebTV, PC/TV appliances, DVD players, "Smart TV," advanced VCRs, and other topics relating to interactive television, the Internet, and multimedia.

Stereo Review's Sound & Vision: Home Theater-Audio- Video- MultimediaMovies- Music. Hachette Filipacchi Magazines, Inc. • 10 times a year. $24.00 per year. Popular magazine providing explanatory articles and critical reviews of equipment and media (CD-ROM, DVD, videocassettes, etc.). Supplement available *Stero Review's Sound and Vision Buyers Guide.* Replaces *Stereo Review* and *Video Magazine.*

Television Digest with Consumer Electronics. Warren Communication News. • Weekly. $944.00 per year. Newsletter featuring new consumer entertainment products utilizing electronics. Also covers the television broadcasting and cable TV industries, with corporate and industry news.

TWICE: This Week in Consumer Electronics. Cahners Business Information, Broadcasting and Cable's International Group. • 29 times a year. Free to qualified personnel; others, $99.90 per year. Contains marketing and manufacturing news relating to a wide variety of consumer electronic products, including video, audio, telephone, and home office equipment.

Video Investor. Paul Kagan Associates, Inc. • Monthly. $695.00 per year. Newsletter on the pre-recorded videocassette industry. Includes statistics and forecasts. Formerly *VCR Letter.*

Video Store: News, Research, Trends, Analysis. Advanstar Communications, Inc. • Monthly. $85.00 per year.

Video Systems: The Magazine for Video Professionals. Intertec Publishing Corp. • Monthly. Price on application.

Video Week: Devoted to the Business of Program Sales and Distribution for Videocassettes, Disc, Pay TV and Allied News Media. Warren Publishing Inc.

• Weekly. $907.00 per year. Newsletter. Covers video industry news and corporate developments.

PRICE SOURCES
Orion Video and Television Blue Book. Orion Research Corp. • Annual. $144.00. Quotes retail and wholesale prices of used video and TV equipment. Original list prices and years of manufacture are also shown.

RESEARCH CENTERS AND INSTITUTES
American Video Institute. Rochester Institute of Technology, P.O. Box 9887, Rochester, NY 14623-0887. Phone: (716)475-6969 Fax: (716)475-5804 • Conducts research relating to videodiscs and interactive media.

STATISTICS SOURCES
Standard & Poor's Industry Surveys. Standard & Poor's. • Semiannual. $1,800.00. Two looseleaf volumes. Includes monthly supplements. Provides detailed, individual surveys of 52 major industry groups. Each survey is revised on a semiannual basis. Also includes "Monthly Investment Review" (industry group investment analysis) and monthly "Trends & Projections" (economic analysis).

U. S. Industry and Trade Outlook: The McGraw-Hill Companies and the U.S. Department of Commerce/ International Trade Administration. Datapso Research Corp. • Annual. $69.95. Produced by the International Trade Administration, U. S. Department of Commerce, in a "public-private" partnership with DRI/McGraw-Hill and Standard & Poor's. Provides basic data, outlook for the current year, and "Long-Term Prospects" (five-year projections) for a wide variety of products and services. Includes high technology industries. Formerly *U. S. Industrial Outlook.*

TRADE/PROFESSIONAL ASSOCIATIONS
Association of Cinema and Video Laboratories. c/o Frank Ricotta, Technicolor, Inc., 4050 Lankershin Blvd., North Hollywood, CA 91608. Phone: (818)769-8500 Fax: (818)761-4835.

Home Recording Rights Coalition. 1341 G St., N.W., Suite 200, Washington, DC 20005-3105. Phone: 800-282-8273 or (202)628-9212 Fax: (202)628-9227 • URL: http://www.hrrc.work.org • Opposes efforts to restrict or tax audiovideo recording by consumers.

Institute of Electrical and Electronics Engineers; Consumer Electronics Society. Three Park Ave., 17th Fl., New York, NY 10016-5997. Phone: (212)419-7900 Fax: (212)752-4929 • URL: http://www.ieee.org.

Interactive Digital Software Association. 1775 Eye St., N.W., Ste. 420, Washington, DC 20005. E-mail: info@idsa.com • URL: http://www.e3expo.com • Members are interactive entertainment software publishers concerned with rating systems, software piracy, government relations, and other industry issues.

International Communications Industries Association. 11242 Waples Mill Rd., Suite 200, Fairfax, VA 22030-6079. Phone: 800-659-7469 or (703)273-2700 Fax: (703)278-8082 E-mail: icia@icia.org • Members are manufacturers and suppliers of audio-visual, video, and computer graphics equipment and materials.

International Recording Media Association. 182 Nassau St., Suite 204, Princeton, NJ 08542. Phone: (609)279-1700 Fax: (609)279-1999 E-mail: info@recordingmedia.org • URL: http://www.recordingmedia.org • Members are manufacturers and distributors of audiotape, videotape, and associated equipment.

International Television Association. 9202 N. Meridian St., Suite 200, Indianapois, IN 46260-1810. Phone: 888-879-4882 or (317)816-6269 Fax: 800-801-8926 E-mail: chris@itva.org • URL: http://www.itva.org • Concerned with non-broadcast industrial television recording for business training and corporate communications.

ITS-The Association of Imaging Technology and Sound. 527 Maple Ave., E., Suite 204, Vienna, VA 22180. Phone: (703)319-0800 Fax: (703)319-1120 • URL: http://www.itsnet.org • Members are individuals interested in various aspects of prerecorded videotape production. Acts as a source of general information about videotape.

National Association of Video Distributors. 700 Frederica St., Suite 205, Owensboro, KY 42301. Phone: (502)926-6002 Fax: (502)685-6080 • Members are wholesalers of home video software, both tapes and discs.

Professional Audiovideo Retailers Association. 10 E. 22nd St., Suite 310, Lombard, IL 60148. Phone: (630)268-1500 Fax: (630)953-8957 E-mail: parahdq@aol.com • URL: http://www.paralink.org • Members are retailers of high quality equipment.

Semiconductor Industry Association. 181 Metro Dr., San Jose, CA 95110-1344. Phone: (408)436-6600 Fax: (408)246-6646 • URL: http://www.semichips.org • Members are producers of semiconductors and semiconductor products.

Video Software Dealers Association. 16530 Ventura Blvd., Suite 400, Encino, CA 91436. Phone: (818)385-1500 Fax: (818)385-0567 E-mail: vsdaoffice@usda.org • URL: http://www.vsda.org • Members are retailers and wholesalers of videocassettes and videodiscs.

OTHER SOURCES
Digital Video. CMP Media, Inc. • Monthly. $60.00 per year. Edited for professionals in the field of digital video production. Covers such topics as operating systems, videography, digital video cameras, audio, workstations, web video, software development, and interactive television.

DVD Assessment, No. 3. Julie B. Schwerin and Theodore A. Pine, editors. InfoTech, Inc. • 1998. $1,295.00. Third edition. Provides detailed market research data on Digital Video Discs (also known as Digital Versatile Discs). Includes history of DVD, technical specifications, DVD publishing outlook, "Industry Overview," "Market Context," "Infrastructure Analysis," "Long-Range Forecast to 2005," and emerging technologies.

Optical Publishing Industry Assessment. Julie B. Schwerin and Theodore A. Pine, editors. InfoTech, Inc. • 1998. $1,295.00. Ninth edition. Provides market research data and forecasts to 2005 for DVD-ROM, "Hybrid ROM/Online Media," and other segments of the interactive entertainment, digital information, and consumer electronics industries. Covers both software (content) and hardware. Includes Video-CD, DVD- Video, CD-Audio, DVD-Audio, DVD-ROM, PC-Desktop, TV Set-Top, CD-R, CD-RW, DVD-R and DVD-RAM.

U. S. Home Theater Market. Available from MarketResearch.com. • 1997. $2,,500.00. Market research report published by Packaged Facts. Covers big-screen TV, high definition TV, audio equipment, and video sources. Market projections are provided to the year 2001.

Videography. United Entertainment Media, Inc. • Monthly. $30.00 per year. Edited for the professional video production industry. Covers trends in technique and technology.

VIDEOCASSETTES

See: VIDEO RECORDING INDUSTRY

VIDEODISCS

See: VIDEO RECORDING INDUSTRY

VIDEOTAPE

See: VIDEO RECORDING INDUSTRY

VIDEOTEX/TELETEXT

ALMANACS AND YEARBOOKS
Communication Technology Update. Butterworth-Heinemann. • Annual. $36.95. Reviews technological developments and statistical trends in five key areas: mass media, computers, consumer electronics, communications satellites, and telephony. Includes television, cellular phones, and the Internet. (Focal Press.).

Interactive Television: Profiles and Analysis. Arlen Communications, Inc. • Annual. $2,295.00. Provides current information on interactive-TV applications and technical developments. Includes forecasts.

New Media Market Place and New Media Titles. Waterlow New Media Information. • 1996. $155.00. Provides a wide variety of information on multimedia industries, including CD-ROM publishing, digital video, interactive TV, portable information products, and video CD. Includes industry review articles, interviews, market data, profiles of 2,000 multimedia companies, product directories, and a bibliography.

CD-ROM DATABASES
LISA Plus: Library and Information Science Abstracts. Bowker-Saur, Reed Reference Publishing. • Quarterly. $1,450.00 per year. Provides CD-ROM abstracting and indexing of the world's library and information science literature. Covers a wide variety of topics.

DIRECTORIES
Information Marketplace Directory. SIMBA Information. • 1996. $295.00. Second edition. Lists computer-based information processing and multimedia companies, including those engaged in animation, audio, video, and interactive video.

Interactive Advertising Source. SRDS. • Quarterly. $561.00 per year. Provides descriptive profiles, rates, audience, personnel, etc., for producers of various forms of interactive or multimedia advertising: online/Internet, CD-ROM, interactive TV, interactive cable, interactive telephone, interactive kiosk, and others. Includes online supplement *SRDS' URlink.*

Interactive Television Buyer's Guide and Directory. Chilton Co. • Annual. Price on application. (A special issue of the periodical *Convergence.*).

Telecommunications Directory. The Gale Group. • 2000. $595.00. 12th edition. National and international voice, data, facsimile, and video communications services. Formerly *Telecommunications Systems and Services Directory.*

ENCYCLOPEDIAS AND DICTIONARIES
Multimedia and the Web from A to Z. Patrick M. Dillon and David C. Leonard. Oryx Press. • 1998. $39.95. Second enlarged revised edition. Defines more than 1,500 terms relating to software and hardware in the areas of computing, online technology, telecommunications, audio, video, motion pictures, CD-ROM, and the Internet. Includes acronyms and an annotated bibliography. Formerly *Multimedia Technology from A to Z* (1994).

HANDBOOKS AND MANUALS

Digital Video Buyer's Guide. CMP Media, Inc. • Annual. $10.00. A directory of professional video products, including digital cameras, monitors, editing systems, and software.

Interactive Computer Systems: Videotex and Multimedia. Antone F. Alber. Perseus Publishing. • 1993. $79.50.

INTERNET DATABASES

Interactive Week: The Internet's Newspaper. Ziff Davis Media, Inc. 28 E. 28th St., New York, NY 10016. Phone: (212)503-3500 Fax: (212)503-5680 E-mail: iweekinfo@zd.com • URL: http://www.zd.com • Weekly. $99.00 per year. Covers news and trends relating to Internet commerce, computer communications, and telecommunications.

ONLINE DATABASES

Computer Database. The Gale Group. • Provides online citations with abstracts to material appearing in about 150 trade journals and newsletters in the subject areas of computers, telecommunications, and electronics. Time period is 1983 to date, with weekly updates. Inquire as to online cost and availability.

LISA Online: Library and Information Science Abstracts. Bowker-Saur, Reed Reference Publishing. • Provides abstracting and indexing of the world's library and information science literature from 1969 to the present. Covers a wide variety of topics in over 550 journals from 60 countries, with biweekly updates. Inquire as to online cost and availability.

PROMT: Predicasts Overview of Markets and Technology. The Gale Group. • Companies, products, applied technologies and markets. U.S. and international literature coverage, 1972 to date. Inquire as to online cost and availability. Provides abstracts from more than 1,600 publications. Weekly updates.

PERIODICALS AND NEWSLETTERS

Computer Video. IMAS Publishing, Inc. • Bimonthly. $50.00 per year.

Convergence: The Journal of Research Into New Media Technologies. Chilton Co. • Monthly. Individuals, $60,00 per year; institutions, $120.00 per year. Covers the merging of communications technologies. Includes telecommunications networks, interactive TV, multimedia, wireless phone service, and electronic information services.

Electronic Media. Crain Communications, Inc. • Weekly. $119.00 per year.

Interactive Home: Consumer Technology Monthly. Jupiter Media Metrix. • Monthly. $625.00 per year. Newsletter on devices to bring the Internet into the average American home. Covers TV set-top boxes, game devices, telephones with display screens, handheld computer communication devices, the usual PCs, etc.

Link-Up: The Newsmagazine for Users of Online Services, CD-Rom, and the Internet. Information Today, Inc. • Bimonthly. $29.95 per year.

Micropublishing News: The Newsmonthly for Electronic Designers and Publishers. Cygnus Business Media. • Monthly. Free to qualified personnel. Price on application. Edited for business and professional users of electronic publishing products and services. Topics covered include document imaging, CD-ROM publishing, digital video, and multimedia services. Available in four regional editions.

NewMedia: The Magazine for Creators of the Digital Future. HyperMedia Communications, Inc. • Monthly. $29.95 per year. Edited for multimedia professionals, with emphasis on digital video and Internet graphics, including animation. Contains reviews of new products. Formerly *NewMedia Age.*

Report on Electronic Commerce: Online Business, Financial and Consumer Strategies and Trends. Telecommunications Reports International, Inc. • 23 times a year. $745.00 per year. Newsletter. Includes *Daily Multimedia News Service.* Incorporates *Interactive Services Report.*

Silicon Alley Reporter. Rising Tide Studios. • Monthly. $29.95 per year. Covers the latest trends in e-commerce, multimedia, and the Internet.

Smart TV: For Selective and Interactive Viewers. Videomaker, Inc. • Bimonthly. $14.97 per year. Consumer magazine covering WebTV, PC/TV appliances, DVD players, "Smart TV," advanced VCRs, and other topics relating to interactive television, the Internet, and multimedia.

Telecons. Applied Business Telecommunications. • Bimonthly. $30.00 per year. Topics include teleconferencing, videoconferencing, distance learning, telemedicine, and telecommuting.

Telematics and Informatics: An International Journal. Elsevier Science. • Quarterly. $713.00 per year.

Video Systems: The Magazine for Video Professionals. Intertec Publishing Corp. • Monthly. Price on application.

Wired. Wired Ventures Ltd. • Monthly. $24.00 per year. Edited for creators and managers in various areas of electronic information and entertainment, including multimedia, the Internet, and video. Often considered to be the primary publication of the "digital generation.".

PRICE SOURCES

Opportunities in Interactive TV Applications & Services: An Analysis of Market Interest & Price Sensitivity. Available from MarketResearch.com. • 2001. $1,395. Published by TechTrends, Inc. Market research data. Includes an analysis of how much consumers are willing to pay per month for each application.

RESEARCH CENTERS AND INSTITUTES

Media Laboratory. Massachusetts Institute of Technology, 20 Ames St., Room E-15, Cambridge, MA 02139. Phone: (617)253-0338 Fax: (617)258-6264 E-mail: casr@media.mit.edu • URL: http://www.media.mit.edu • Research areas include electronic publishing, spatial imaging, human-machine interface, computer vision, and advanced television.

TRADE/PROFESSIONAL ASSOCIATIONS

Association for Interactive Media. 1301 Connecticut Ave. N.W., 5th Fl., Washington, DC 20036-5105. Phone: (202)408-0008 Fax: (202)408-0111 E-mail: info@interactivehg.org • URL: http://www.interactivehg.org • Members are companies engaged in various interactive enterprises, utilizing the Internet, interactive television, computer communications, and multimedia.

International Interactive Communications Society. 4840 McKnight Rd., Suite A, Pittsburgh, PA 15237. Phone: (412)734-1928 Fax: (412)369-3507 E-mail: worldhq@iics.org • URL: http://www.iics.org • Members are interactive media professionals concerned with intetractive arts and technologies.

OTHER SOURCES

Cable Television and Other Nonbroadcast Media: Law and Policy. Daniel J. Brenner and others. West Group. • $145.00 per year. Looseleaf service. Periodic supplementation. (Entertainment and Communications Law Series).

Digital Video. CMP Media, Inc. • Monthly. $60.00 per year. Edited for professionals in the field of digital video production. Covers such topics as operating systems, videography, digital video cameras, audio, workstations, web video, software development, and interactive television.

Key Note Market Report: Home Shopping. Jupiter Media Metrix. • Irregular. $365.00. Market research report. Covers "interactive retailing," mainly through the Internet and television, with predictions of future trends. Formerly *Key Note Report: Home Shopping.*

The Market for Interactive Television. MarketResearch.com. • 2000. $995.00. Market research data.

North American Interactive Television Markets. Available from MarketResearch.com. • 1999. $3,450.00. Published by Frost & Sullivan. Contains market research data on growth, end-user trends, and market strategies. Company profiles are included.

Videography. United Entertainment Media, Inc. • Monthly. $30.00 per year. Edited for the professional video production industry. Covers trends in technique and technology.

World Interactive Television and Video Transmission Overview. Primary Research. • 1994. Contains market research data. Price on application.

VIEWTEXT

See: VIDEOTEX/TELETEXT

VIRTUAL REALITY

See also: COMPUTER ANIMATION

GENERAL WORKS

Data Smog: Surviving the Information Glut. David Shenk. HarperCollins Publishers. • 1997. $24.00. A critical view of both the electronic and print information industries. Emphasis is on information overload.

Virtual Realism. Michael Heim. Oxford University Press, Inc. • 1998. $26.00. Discusses computer simulation and human/computer interaction.

Virtual Reality: Computers Mimic the Physical World. Sean M. Grady. Facts on File, Inc. • 1998. $19.95. (Facts on File Science Sourcebooks Series.).

What Will Be: How the New World of Information Will Change Our Lives. Michael L. Dertouzos. HarperSan Francisco. • 1997. $25.00. A discussion of the "information market place" of the future, including telecommuting, virtual reality, and computer recognition of speech. The author is director of the MIT Laboratory for Computer Science.

ALMANACS AND YEARBOOKS

Virtual Reality Annual International Symposium. IEEE Computer Society. • Annual. $70.00.

CD-ROM DATABASES

Computer Select. The Gale Group. • Monthly. $1,250.00 per year. Provides one year of full-text on CD-ROM for 120 leading computer-related publications. Also includes 70,000 product specifications and brief profiles of 13,000 computer product vendors and manufacturers.

DIRECTORIES

Data Sources: The Comprehensive Guide to the Data Processing Industry Hardware, Data Communications Products, Software, Company Profiles. The Gale Group. • Semiannual. $495.00 per year. Two volumes. Describes hardware and software for all computer operating sysems, including prices and technical details. Lists about 75,000 products from 14,000 suppliers. Industry-specific software applications are described.

ENCYCLOPEDIAS AND DICTIONARIES

Cyberspeak: An Online Dictionary. Andy Ihnatko. Random House, Inc. • 1996. $12.95. An informal guide to the language of computers, multimedia, and the Internet.

Encyclopedia of Emerging Industries. The Gale Group. • 2000. $295.00. Fourth edition. Provides detailed information on 90 "newly flourishing" industries. Includes historical background, organizational structure, significant individuals, current conditions, major companies, work force, technology trends, research developments, and other industry facts.

New Hacker's Dictionary. Eric S. Raymond. MIT Press. • 1996. $39.00. Third edition. Includes three classifications of hacker communication: slang, jargon, and "techspeak.".

INTERNET DATABASES

InfoTech Trends. Data Analysis Group. Phone: (707)894-9100 Fax: (707)486-5618 E-mail: support@infotechtrends.com • URL: http://www.infotechtrends.com • Web site provides both free and fee-based market research data on the information technology industry, including computers, peripherals, telecommunications, the Internet, software, CD-ROM/DVD, e-commerce, and workstations. Fees: Free for current (most recent year) data; more extensive information has various fee structures. Formerly *Computer Industry Forecasts.*

Wired News. Wired Digital, Inc. Phone: (415)276-8400 Fax: (415)276-8499 E-mail: newsfeedback@wired.com • URL: http://www.wired.com • Provides summaries and full-text of "Top Stories" relating to the Internet, computers, multimedia, telecommunications, and the electronic information industry in general. These news stories are placed in the broad categories of Politics, Business, Culture, and Technology. Affiliated with *Wired* magazine. Fees: Free.

PERIODICALS AND NEWSLETTERS

IMAGES. IMAGE Society. • Semiannual. $25.00 per year. Provides news of virtual reality developments and the IMAGE Society.

RESEARCH CENTERS AND INSTITUTES

Electronic Visualization Laboratory. University of Illinois at Chicago, Engineering Research Facility, 842 W. Taylor St., Room 2032, Chicago, IL 60607-7053. Phone: (312)996-3002 Fax: (312)413-7585 E-mail: tom@eecs.uic.edu • URL: http://www.evl.uic.edu • Research areas include computer graphics, virtual reality, multimedia, and interactive techniques.

Graphics, Visualization, and Usability Center. Georgia Institute of Technology, Mail Code 0280, Atlanta, GA 30332-0280. Phone: (404)894-4488 Fax: (404)894-0673 E-mail: jarek@cc.gatech.edu • URL: http://www.cc.gatech.edu/gvu/ • Research areas include computer graphics, multimedia, image recognition, interactive graphics systems, animation, and virtual realities.

Studio for Creative Inquiry. Carnegie Mellon University, College of Fine Arts, Pittsburgh, PA 15213-3890. Phone: (412)268-3454 Fax: (412)268-2829 E-mail: mmbm@andrew.cmu.edu/ • URL: http://www.cmu.edu/studio/ • Research areas include artificial intelligence, virtual reality, hypermedia, multimedia, and telecommunications, in relation to the arts.

TRADE/PROFESSIONAL ASSOCIATIONS

IMAGE Society. P.O. Box 6221, Chandler, AZ 85246-6221. Phone: (602)839-8709 E-mail: image@asu.edu • URL: http://www.public.asu.edu/~image • Promotes the technical advancement and application of real-time visual simulation. Special Interest Groups include Computer Image Generation, Virtual Reality Ancillary Technologies, and Virtual Reality in Education and Training.

VIRUSES, COMPUTER

See: COMPUTER CRIME AND SECURITY

VISUAL EDUCATION

See: AUDIOVISUAL AIDS IN EDUCATION

VITAL STATISTICS

See also: CENSUS REPORTS; POPULATION

ABSTRACTS AND INDEXES

Index to Health Information. Congressional Information Service, Inc. • Quarterly. $945.00 per year, including two-volume annual cumulation. Provides index and abstracts covering the medical and health field in general, with emphasis on statistical sources and government documents. Service with microfiche source documents, $4,995.00 per year.

BIBLIOGRAPHIES

Vital and Health Statistics. Available from U. S. Government Printing Office. • Annual. Free. Lists government publications. (GPO Subject Bibliography Number 121).

CD-ROM DATABASES

Statistical Abstract of the United States on CD-ROM. Hoover's, Inc. • Annual. $49.95. Provides all statistics from official print version, plus expanded historical data, greater detail, and keyword searching features.

DIRECTORIES

Where to Write for Vital Records: Births, Deaths, Marriages, and Divorces. Available from U. S. Government Printing Office. • 1999. $3.00. Issued by the National Center for Health Statistics, U. S. Department of Health and Human Services. Arranged by state. Provides addresses, telephone numbers, and cost of copies for various kinds of vital records or certificates. (DHHS Publication No. PHS 93-1142.).

HANDBOOKS AND MANUALS

International Vital Records Handbook. Thomas J. Kemp. Genealogical Publishing Co., Inc. • Triennial. $29.95. Provides procedures and copies of forms for obtaining birth, marriage, divorce, and death records from 67 countries and territories in North America, the British Isles and other English-speaking countries and Europe.

INTERNET DATABASES

Fedstats. Federal Interagency Council on Statistical Policy. Phone: (202)395-7254 • URL: http://www.fedstats.gov • Web site features an efficient search facility for full-text statistics produced by more than 70 federal agencies, including the Census Bureau, the Bureau of Economic Analysis, and the Bureau of Labor Statistics. Boolean searches can be made within one agency or for all agencies combined. Links are offered to international statistical bureaus, including the UN, IMF, OECD, UNESCO, Eurostat, and 20 individual countries. Fees: Free.

National Center for Health Statistics: Monitoring the Nation's Health. National Center for Health Statistics, Centers for Disease Control and Preventio. Phone: (301)458-4636 E-mail: nchsquery@cdc.gov • URL: http://www.cdc.gov/nchswww • Web site provides detailed data on diseases, vital statistics, and health care in the U. S. Includes a search facility and links to many other health-related Web sites. "Fastats A to Z" offers quick data on hundreds of topics from Accidents to Work-Loss Days, with links to Comprehensive Data and related sources. Frequent updates. Fees: Free.

U. S. Census Bureau: The Official Statistics. U. S. Bureau of the Census. Phone: (301)763-4100 Fax: (301)763-4794 • URL: http://www.census.gov • Web site is "Your Source for Social, Demographic, and Economic Information." Contains "Current U. S. Population Count," "Current Economic Indicators," and a wide variety of data under "Other Official Statistics." Keyword searching is provided. Fees: Free.

STATISTICS SOURCES

County and City Extra: Annual Metro, City and County Data Book. Mark Littman and Deirdre A. Gaquin. Bernan Press. • 1999. $109.00. Updates and augments data published irregularly in print form by the U. S. Census Bureau in *County and City Data Book.* Covers "every state, county, metropolitan area, and congressional district in the United States, as well as all U. S. cities with a 1990 population of 25,000 or more." Contains a wide range tic maps.

Current Population Reports: Population Characteristics, Special Studies, and Consumer Income, Series P-20, P-23, and P-60. Available from U. S. Government Printing Office. • Irregular. $39.00 per year. Issued by the U.S. Bureau of the Census (http://www.census.gov). Each issue covers a special topic relating to population or income. Series P-20, *Population Characteristics,* provides statistical studies on such items as mobility, fertility, education, and marital status. Series P-23, *Special Studies,* consists of occasional reports on methodology. Series P-60, *Consumer Income,* publishes reports on income in relation to age, sex, education, occupation, family size, etc.

Gale City and Metro Rankings Reporter. The Gale Group. • 1996. $134.00. Second edition. Provides about 3,000 statistical ranking tables covering more than 1,500 U. S. cities and Metropolitan Statistical Areas. Covers economic, demographic, social, governmental, and cultural factors. Sources are private studies and government data.

Gale Country and World Rankings Reporter. The Gale Group. • 1997. $135.00. Second edition. Provides about 3,000 statistical ranking tables and charts covering more than 235 nations. Sources include the United Nations and various government publications.

Gale State Rankings Reporter. The Gale Group. • 1996. $110.00. Second edition Provides 3,000 ranked lists of states under 35 subject headings. Sources are newspapers, periodicals, books, research institute publications, and government publications.

Health and Environment in America's Top-Rated Cities: A Statistical Profile. Grey House Publishing. • Biennial. $195.00. Covers 75 U. S. cities. Includes statistical and other data on a wide variety of topics, such as air quality, water quality, recycling, hospitals, physicians, health care costs, death rates, infant mortality, accidents, and suicides.

Health, United States, 1999: Health and Aging Chartbook. Available from U. S. Government Printing Office. • 1999. $37.00. Issued by the National Center for Health Statistics, U. S. Department of Health and Human Services. Contains 34 bar charts in color, with related statistical tables. Provides detailed data on persons over 65 years of age, including population, living arrangements, life expectancy, nursing home residence, poverty, health status, assistive devices, health insurance, and health care expenditures.

Monthly Bulletin of Statistics. United Nations Publications. • Monthly. $295.00 per year. Provides current data for about 200 countries on a wide variety of economic, industrial, and demographic subjects. Compiled by United Nations Statistical Office.

Monthly Vital Statistics Report. U. S. Department of Health and Human Services, Data Dissemination Branch. • Monthly. Provides data on births, deaths, cause of death, marriage, and divorce.

Morbidity and Mortality Weekly Report. Available from U. S. Government Printing Office. • Weekly. $255.00 per year (priority mail). Issued by the Center for Disease Control (Atlanta), U. S. Department of Health and Human Services. Provides analysis and statistics on the occurrence of disease and death from all causes in the U. S.

Population and Vital Statistics Report. United Nations Publications. • Quarterly. $40.00 per year. Contains worldwide demographic statistics.

Social Statistics of the United States. Mark S. Littman, editor. Bernan Press. • 2000. $65.00. Includes statistical data on population growth, labor force, occupations, environmental trends, leisure time use, income, poverty, taxes, and other economic or demographic topics.

Statistical Abstract of the United States. Available from U. S. Government Printing Office. • Annual. $51.00. Issued by the U. S. Bureau of the Census.

Statistical Abstract of the World. The Gale Group. • 1997. $80.00. Third edition. Provides data on a wide variety of economic, social, and political topics for about 200 countries. Arranged by country.

Statistical Handbook on the American Family. Bruce A. Chadwick and Tim B. Heaton, editors. Oryx Press. • 1998. $65.00. Includes data on education, health, politics, employment, expenditures, social characteristics, the elderly, and women in the labor force. Historical statistics on marriage, birth, and divorce are shown from 1900 on. A list of sources and a subject index are provided. (Statistical Handbook Series).

A Statistical Portrait of the United States: Social Conditions and Trends. Mark S. Littman, editor. Bernan Press. • 1998. $89.00. Covers "social, economic, and environmental trends in the United States over the past 25 years." Includes statistical tables, graphs, and analysis relating to such topics as population, income, poverty, wealth, labor, housing, education, healthcare, air/water quality, and government.

Statistical Yearbook. United Nations Publications. • Annual. $125.00. Contains statistics for about 200 countries on a wide variety of economic, industrial, and demographic topics. Compiled by United Nations Statistical Office.

Universal Healthcare Almanac: A Complete Guide for the Healthcare Professional - Facts, Figures, Analysis. Silver & Cherner, Ltd. • Looseleaf service. $195.00 per year. Quarterly updates. Includes a wide variety of health care statistics: national expenditures, hospital data, health insurance, health professionals, vital statistics, demographics, etc. Years of coverage vary, with long range forecasts provided in some cases.

Vital Statistics of the United States. Public Health Service, U.S. Dept. of Health and Human Services. Available from U.S. Government Printing Office. • Annual. Two volumes.

Vital Statistics of the United States: Life Tables. Available from U. S. Government Printing Office. • Annual. $2.25. Produced by the National Center for Health Statistics, Public Health Service, U. S. Department of Health and Human Services. Provides detailed data on expectation of life by age, race, and sex. Historical data is shown annually from the year 1900. (Vital Statistics, volume 2, section 6.).

World Statistics Pocketbook. United Nations Publications. • Annual. $10.00. Presents basic economic, social, and environmental indicators for about 200 countries and areas. Covers more than 50 items relating to population, economic activity, labor force, agriculture, industry, energy, trade, transportation, communication, education, tourism, and the environment. Statistical sources are noted.

TRADE/PROFESSIONAL ASSOCIATIONS

National Association for Public Health Statistics and Information Systems. 1220 19th St., N. W., Ste. 802, Washington, DC 20036. Phone: (202)463-8851 Fax: (202)463-4870 E-mail: tme.nq@naphsis.org • URL: http://www.naphsis.org • Members are officials of state and local health agencies.

VITAMINS

See also: DIET; HEALTH FOOD INDUSTRY

ABSTRACTS AND INDEXES

Nutrition Abstracts and Reviews, Series A: Human and Experimental. Available from CABI Publishing North America. • Monthly. $1,385.00 per year. Published in England by CABI Publishing. Provides worldwide coverage of the literature.

ALMANACS AND YEARBOOKS

Vitamins and Hormones: Advances in Research and Applications. Academic Press. • Irregular. Price on applications.

CD-ROM DATABASES

International Pharmaceutical Abstracts [CD-ROM]. American Society of Health-System Pharmacists. • Quarterly. $1,795.00 per year. Contains CD-ROM indexing and abstracting of international pharmaceutical literature from 1970 to date.

ENCYCLOPEDIAS AND DICTIONARIES

CRC Desk Reference for Nutrition. Carolyn D. Berdanier. CRC Press, Inc. • 1998. $69.95. Encyclopedic, alphabetical arrangement of topics.

Encyclopedia of Food Science, Food Technology, and Nutrition. Robert Macrae and others, editors. Academic Press, Inc. • 1993. Eight volumes. $2,414.00.

Foods and Nutrition Encyclopedia. Audrey H. Ensminger and others. CRC Press, Inc. • 1993. $382.00. Second edition. Two volumes.

HANDBOOKS AND MANUALS

Advanced Nutrition: Micronutrients. Carolyn D. Berdanier and Mark L. Failla. CRC Press, Inc. • 2000. $99.95. Provides detailed coverage of essential vitamins and minerals. Written for professional dietitions and nutritionists. (Modern Nutrition Series).

Health Food/Vitamin Store. Entrepreneur Media, Inc. • Looseleaf. $59.50. A practical guide to starting a health food store. Covers profit potential, start-up costs, market size evaluation, owner's time required, site selection, lease negotiation, pricing, accounting, advertising, promotion, etc. (Start-Up Business Guide No. E1296.).

PDR Family Guide to Nutrition and Health: The Facts to Remember...The Claims to Forget. Medical Economics Co., Inc. • 1995. $25.95. Provides advice on diet, vitamins, minerals, fat, salt, cholesterol, and other topics related to nutrition.

Vitamin Book. Consumer Guide editors. Simon and Schuster Trade. • 1979. $5.95.

INTERNET DATABASES

National Library of Medicine (NLM). National Institutes of Health (NIH). Phone: 888-346-3656 or (301)496-1131 Fax: (301)480-3537 E-mail: access@nlm.nih.gov • URL: http://www.nlm.nih.gov • NLM Web site offers free access through MEDLINE ("PubMed") to about nine million references to articles appearing in some 3,800 biomedical journals, with abstracts. Search interfaces range from "simple keywords to advanced Boolean expressions." The NLM site offers many links to other sources of biomedical and technical information (the National Center for Biotechnology Information, for example). Fees: Free.

ONLINE DATABASES

Embase. Elsevier Science, Inc. • Worldwide medical literature, 1974 to present. Weekly updates. Inquire as to online cost and availability.

International Pharmaceutical Abstracts [online]. American Society of Health-System Pharmacists. • Provides online indexing and abstracting of the world's pharmaceutical literature from 1970 to date. Monthly updates. Inquire as to online cost and availability.

PERIODICALS AND NEWSLETTERS

Health Supplement Retailer. Virgo Publishing, Inc. • Monthly. $38.00 per year. Covers all aspects of the vitamin and health supplement market, including new products. Includes an annual buyer's guide, an annual compilation of industry statistics, and annual guides to vitamins and herbs.

International Journal for Vitamin and Nutrition Research. Hogrefe & Huber Publishers. • Quarterly. $198.00 per year.

Journal of Nutritional Science and Vitaminology. Japanese Society of Nutrition and Food Science. Center for Academic Pulbications. • Bimonthly. $145.00 per year.

Nonprescription Pharmaceuticals and Nutritionals: The Tan Sheet. F-D-C Reports, Inc. • Weekly. $860.00 per year. Newsletter covering over-the-counter drugs and vitamin supplements. Emphasis is on regulatory activities of the U. S. Food and Drug Administration (FDA).

Prevention; The Magazine for Better Health. Rodale Press, Inc. • Monthly $21.97. per year.

Supplement Industry Executive. Vitamin Retailer Magazine, Inc. • Bimonthly. $25.00 per year. Edited for manufacturers of vitamins and other dietary supplements. Covers marketing, new products, industry trends, regulations, manufacturing procedures, and related topics. Includes a directory of suppliers to the industry.

Vitamin Retailer. Vitamin Retailer Magazine, Inc. • Monthly. $45.00 per year. Edited for retailers of vitamins, herbal remedies, minerals, antioxidants, essential fatty acids, and other food supplements.

TRADE/PROFESSIONAL ASSOCIATIONS

National Nutritional Foods Association. 3931 MacArthur Blvd., No. 101, Newport Beach, CA 92660-3021. Phone: (949)622-6272 Fax: (949)622-6266 E-mail: nnfa@aol.com • URL: http://www.nnfa.org.

OTHER SOURCES

Health Care Products and Remedies. Available from MarketResearch.com. • 1997. $600.00 each. Consists of market reports published by Simmons Market Research Bureau on each of about 25 health care product categories. Examples are cold remedies, contraceptives, hearing aids, bandages, headache remedies, eyeglasses, contact lenses, and vitamins. Each report covers buying patterns and demographics.

Pharmacopeia of Herbs. CME, Inc. • $149.00. Frequently updated CD-ROM provides searchable data on a wide variety of herbal medicines, vitamins, and amino acids. Includes information on clinical studies, contraindications, side-effects, phytoactivity, and 534 therapeutic use categories. Contains a 1,000 word glossary.

The U. S. Market for Vitamins, Supplements, and Minerals. Available from MarketResearch.com. • 2000. $2,750.00. Market research report published by Packaged Facts. Includes company profiles and sales forecasts to the year 2003.

VOCABULARY

ENCYCLOPEDIAS AND DICTIONARIES

Oxford English Dictionary. J. A. Simpson and Edmund S. Weiner. Oxford University Press, Inc. • 1989. $3,000.00. Second edition. 20 volumes.

Roget's International Thesaurus. Robert L. Chapman, editor. HarperCollins Publishers. • 1992. $19.95. Fifth edition.

HANDBOOKS AND MANUALS

Gaining Word Power. Dorothy Rubin. Allyn and Bacon, Inc. • 1999. $41.00. Fifth edition. Purpose of book is to help students and others build a "college-level" vocabulary, including information-age words.

NTC's Dictionary of Tricky Words: With Complete Examples of Correct Usage. Deborah K. Williams. NTC/Contemporary Publishing. • 1996. $19.95. Focuses on words that commonly cause confusion in everyday usage (can & may, shall & will, infer & imply, disinterested & uninterested, and so forth).

VOCATIONAL EDUCATION

See also: TECHNICAL EDUCATION; TRAINING OF EMPLOYEES

ABSTRACTS AND INDEXES

Education Index. H.W. Wilson Co. • 10 times a year. Service basis.

BIBLIOGRAPHIES

Materials for Occupational Education: An Annotated Source Guide. Patricia Glass Schuman, editor'. Neal-Schuman Publishers, Inc. • 1983. $39.95. Second edition. (Neal-Schuman Sourcebook Series).

CD-ROM DATABASES

ERIC on SilverPlatter. Available from SilverPlatter Information, Inc. • Quarterly. $700.00 per year. Produced by the Office of Educational Research and Improvement, U. S. Dept. of Education. Provides CD-ROM indexing and abstracting of a wide variety of literature relating to education. Archival discs are available from 1966.

DIRECTORIES

American Trade Schools Directory. Croner Publications, Inc. • $120.00. Looseleaf service. Monthly updates. Directory of over 12,000 trade,technical and vocational schools arranged by state.

Patterson's Schools Classified. Educational Directories, Inc. • Annual. $15.00. Lists more than 7,000 accredited colleges, universities, junior colleges, and vocational schools. Includes brief descriptions. Classified arrangement, with index to name of school. Included in *Patterson's American Education.*

Peterson's Vocational and Technical Schools and Programs. Peterson's. • Annual. $34.95. Provides information on vocational schools in the eastern part of the U. S. Covers more than 370 career fields.

HANDBOOKS AND MANUALS

Resume Writing and Career Counseling. Entrepreneur Media, Inc. • Looseleaf. $59.50. A practical guide to starting a resume writing and career counseling service. Covers profit potential, start-up costs, market size evaluation, owner's time required, site selection, pricing, accounting, advertising, promotion, etc. (Start-Up Business Guide No. E1260.).

ONLINE DATABASES

Education Index Online. H. W. Wilson Co. • Indexes a wide variety of periodicals related to schools, colleges, and education, 1984 to date. Monthly updates. Inquire as to online cost and availability.

ERIC. Educational Resources Information Center. • Broad range of educational literature, 1966 to present. Monthly updates. Inquire as to online cost and availability.

PERIODICALS AND NEWSLETTERS

Techniques. Association for Career and Technical Education. • Eight times a year. Free to members; non-members, $39.00 per year. Formerly *Vocational Educational Journal.*

Vocational Training News: The Independent Weekly Report on Employment, Training, and Vocational Education. Aspen Publishers, Inc. • Weekly. $319.00 per year. Newsletter. Emphasis is on federal job training and vocational education programs. Formerly *Manpower and Vocational Education Weekly.*

TRADE/PROFESSIONAL ASSOCIATIONS

Adult Workforce Education Organization. 2815 25th St., Meridian, MS 39305. Phone: (601)484-5165 Fax: (601)484-4999 • Members are concerned with employee training and vocational education. Formerly National Employment and Training Association.

American Vocational Educational Research Association. c/o Hollie B. Thomas, Florida State University, College of Education, 113 Stone Bldg., Tallahassee, FL 32306. Phone: (850)644-7078 Fax: (850)644-1258 E-mail: hthomas@garnet.acns.fsu.edu.

Association for Career and Technical Education. 1410 King St., Alexandria, VA 22314. Phone: 800-826-9772 or (703)683-3111 Fax: (703)683-7424 E-mail: acte@acteonline.org • URL: http://www.acteonline.org.

Center on Education and Training for Employment. Ohio State University. 1900 Kenny Rd., Columbus, OH 43210. Phone: 800-848-4815 or (614)292-4353 Fax: (614)292-1260 • URL: http://www.cete.org/products/.

VOCATIONAL GUIDANCE

See also: COUNSELING; JOB HUNTING; OCCUPATIONS

GENERAL WORKS

Encyclopedia of Careers and Vocational Guidance. Holli Cosgrove. Ferguson Publishing Co. • 2000. $159.95. 11th edition.

Is It Too Late to Run Away and Join the Circus? Finding the Life You Really Want. Marti Smye. Simon and Schuster Trade. • 1998. $14.95. Provides philosophical and inspirational advice on leaving corporate life and becoming self-employed as a consultant or whatever. Central theme is dealing with major changes in life style and career objectives. (Macmillan Business Book.).

BIBLIOGRAPHIES

Educators Guide to Free Guidance Materials. Educators Progress Service, Inc. • Annual. $34.95. Lists free-loan films, filmstrips, audiotapes, videotapes and free printed materials on guidance.

Job & Career Books. Kennedy Information, LLC. • Annual. Free. Contains descriptions of selected books from various publishers on job searching and choice of career.

Professional Careers Sourcebook. The Gale Group. • 1999. $105.00. Sixth edition. Includes information sources for 122 professions or occupations.

Vocational Careers Sourcebook. The Gale Group. • 1999. $110.00. Fourth edition. A companion volume to *Professional Careers Sourcebook.* Includes information sources for 1345 occupations that typically do not require a four-year college degree. Compiled in cooperation with InfoPLACE of the Cuyahoga County Public Library, Ohio.

DIRECTORIES

Business and Finance Career Directory. Visible Ink Press. • 1992. $17.95.

Computing and Software Career Directory. The Gale Group. • 1993. $39.00. Includes career information relating to programmers, software engineers, technical writers, systems experts, and other computer specialists. Provides advice from "insiders," resume suggestions, a directory of companies that may offer entry-level positions, and a directory of career information sources. (Career Advisor Series.).

Directory of Counseling Services. International Association of Counseling Services. • Annual. $50.00. About 200 accredited services in the United States and Canada concerned with psychological educational, and vocational counseling, including those at colleges and universities and public and private agencies.

Environmental Career Directory. Visible Ink Press. • 1993. $17.95. Includes career information relating to workers in conservation, recycling, wildlife management, pollution control, and other areas. Provides advice from "insiders," resume suggestions, a directory of companies that may offer entry-level positions, and a directory of career information sources. (Career Advisor Series.).

Healthcare Career Directory: Nurses and Physicians: A Practical One-Stop Guide to Getting a Job in Public Relations. The Gale Group. • 1993. $17.95. Second edition. Includes information on careers in nursing, family medicine, surgery, and other medical areas. Provides advice from "insiders," resume suggestions, a directory of companies that may offer entry-level positions, and a directory of career information sources. *Career Advisor Series.*

Magazines Careers Directory: A Practical One-Stop Guide to Getting a Job in Publc Relations. Visible Ink Press. • 1993. $17.95. Fifth edition. Includes information on magazine publishing careers in art, editing, sales, and business management. Provides advice from "insiders," resume suggestions, a directory of companies that may offer entry-level positions, and a directory of career information sources. *Career Advisor Series.*

HANDBOOKS AND MANUALS

Career Guide to Industries. Available from U. S. Government Printing Office. • 1998. $17.00. Issued by the Bureau of Labor Statistics, U. S. Department of Labor (http://www.bls.gov). Presents background career information (text) and statistics for the 40 industries that account for 70 percent of wage and salary jobs in the U. S. Includes nature of the industry, employment data, working conditions, training, earnings, rate of job growth, outlook, and other career factors. (BLS Bulletin 2503.).

Occupational Outlook Handbook. Bureau of Labor Statistics, U.S. Department of Labor. Available from U.S. Government Printing Office. • Biennial. $53.00. Issued as one of the Bureau's *Bulletin* series and kept up to date by *Occupational Outlook Quarterly.*

Peterson's Guide to Colleges for Careers in Computing: The Only Combined Career and College

Guide for Future Computer Professionals. Peterson's. • 1996. $14.95. Describes career possibilities in various fields related to computers.

Specialty Occupational Outlook: Professions. The Gale Group. • 1995. $70.00. Provides information on 150 professional occupations.

Specialty Occupational Outlook: Trade and Technical. The Gale Group. • 1996. $70.00. Provides information on 150 "high-interest" careers that do not require a bachelor's degree.

Standard Occupational Classification Manual. Available from Bernan Associates. • 2000. $38.00. Replaces the *Dictionary of Occupational Titles.* Produced by the federal Office of Management and Budget, Executive Office of the President. "Occupations are classified based on the work performed, and on the required skills, education, training, and credentials for each one." Six-digit codes contain elements for 23 Major Groups, 96 Minor Groups, 451 Broad Occupations, and 820 Detailed Occupations. Designed to reflect the occupational structure currently existing in the U. S.

PERIODICALS AND NEWSLETTERS

Black Careers. Emory W. Washington, editor. Project Magazine, Inc. • Bimonthly. $20.00 per year. Provides information on career preparation and advancement to working professionals in industry, business, and technology.

The Career Development Quarterly. National Career Development Association. ACPA. • Quarterly. Individuals, $45.00 per year; institutions, $67.00 per year.

Counseling and Values. Association for Religious and Value Issues in Counseling. American Counseling Association. • Three times a year. Individuals, $18.00 per year; institutions, $29.00 per year.

Counseling Today. Jennifer Sacks, editor. American Counseling Association. • Monthly. $66.00 per year. Articles and information pertaining to the counseling profession. Formerly *GuidePost.*

Journal of Counseling and Development. American Counseling Association. • Bimonthly. Individuals, $60.00 per year; institutions, $128.00 per year. Contains authoritative in-depth articles on professional and scientific issues. Formerly *Personnel and Guidance Journal.*

Journal of Employment Counseling. National Employment Counsel Association. American Counseling Association. • Quarterly. Institutions, $38.00 Per year.

Occupational Outlook Quarterly. U.S. Department of Labor. Available from U.S. Government Printing Office. • Quarterly. $9.50 per year.

RESEARCH CENTERS AND INSTITUTES

National Institute for Work and Learning. Academy for Educational Development, 1875 Connecticut Ave., N.W., Washington, DC 20009. Phone: (202)884-8187 Fax: (202)884-8422 E-mail: ichaner@aed.org • URL: http://www.niwl.org • Research areas include adult education, training, unemployment insurance, and career development.

STATISTICS SOURCES

Statistical Handbook of Working America. The Gale Group. • 1997. $125.00. Second edition. Provides statistics, rankings, and forecasts relating to a wide variety of careers, occupations, and working conditions.

TRADE/PROFESSIONAL ASSOCIATIONS

American Counseling Association. 5999 Stevenson Ave., Alexandria, VA 22304-3300. Phone: 800-347-6647 or (703)823-9800 Fax: (703)823-0252 • URL: http://www.counseling.org.

National Career Development Association. 4700 Reed Rd., Suite M, Columbus, OH 43220. Phone: 888-326-1750 or (614)326-1750 Fax: (614)326-1760 E-mail: jmiller@ncda.org • URL: http://www.ncda.org.

VOCATIONAL REHABILITATION

DIRECTORIES

Complete Directory for People with Disabilities. Grey House Publishing. • Annual. $165.00. Provides information on a wide variety of products, goods, services, and facilities, including job training programs, rehabilitation services, and funding sources. Indexed by organization name, disability/need, and location.

Encyclopedia of Medical Organizations and Agencies. The Gale Group. • 2000. $285.00. 11th edition. Information on over 14,000 public and private organizations in medicine and related fields.

Medical and Health Information Directory. The Gale Group. • 1999. $630.00. Three volumes. 12th edition. Vol. one covers medical organizations, agencies, and institutions; vol. two includes bibliographic, library, and database information; vol. three is a guide to services available for various medical and health problems.

PERIODICALS AND NEWSLETTERS

American Rehabilitation: AR. U. S. Dept. of Health, Education, and Welfare; Rehabilitation Services Administr. Available from U. S. Government Printing Office. • Quarterly. $10.00 per year. Official publication of the Rehabilitation Services Administration. Comments on all aspects of life affecting handicapped people.

International Journal of Rehabilitation and Health. Plenum Publishing Corp. • Quarterly. $239.50 per year.

International Rehabilitation Review. Rehabilitation International. • Three times a year. $30.00 per year.

RESEARCH CENTERS AND INSTITUTES

Vocational and Rehabilitation Research Institute. 3304 33rd St., N.W., Calgary, AB, Canada T2L 2A6. Phone: (403)284-1121 Fax: (403)289-6427 E-mail: vrri@cadvision.com • URL: http://www.vrri.org • Associated with University of Calgary.

TRADE/PROFESSIONAL ASSOCIATIONS

American Medical Rehabilitation Providers Association. 1606 20th St., N.W., Washington, DC 20009. Phone: (202)265-4404 Fax: (202)833-9168.

CARF, The Rehabilitation Accreditation Commission. 4891 E. Grant Rd., Tucson, AZ 85712. Phone: (520)325-1044 Fax: (520)318-1129 E-mail: webmaster@carf.org • URL: http://www.carf.org.

Council of State Administrators of Vocational Rehabilitation. P.O. Box 3776, Washington, DC 20007. Phone: (202)638-4634.

International Association of Jewish Vocational Services. 1845 Walnut St., 6th Fl., Philadelphia, PA 19103. Phone: (215)854-0233 Fax: (215)854-0212 E-mail: iajvs@iajvs.org • URL: http://www.iajvs.org.

National Rehabilitation Information Center. 1010 Wayne Ave., Ste. 800, Silver Spring, MD 20910. Phone: 800-346-2742 or (301)562-2400 Fax: (301)562-2401 E-mail: naricinfo@kra.com • URL: http://www.naric.com/naric.

Rehabilitation International; Vocational Commission. 25 E. 21st St., New York, NY 10010. Phone: (212)420-1500 Fax: (212)505-0871.

Vocational Evaluation and Work Adjustment Association. 202 E. Cheyenne Mountain Blvd., Suite N, Colorado Spings, CO 80906. Phone: (719)527-1800 Fax: (719)576-1818 E-mail: info@vewaa.org • URL: http://www.vewaa.org.

OTHER SOURCES

Disability and Rehabilitation Products Markets. Theta Reports/PJB Medical Publications, Inc. • 1999. $1,295.00. Market research data. Covers the market for products designed to help differently-abled people lead more active lives. Includes such items as adaptive computers, augmentative communication devices, lifts/vans, and bath/home products. Profiles of leading suppliers are included. (Theta Report No. 800.).

VOCATIONS

See: OCCUPATIONS

VOICE RECOGNITION

See also: COMPUTER COMMUNICATIONS; MICROCOMPUTERS AND MINICOMPUTERS

GENERAL WORKS

Data Smog: Surviving the Information Glut. David Shenk. HarperCollins Publishers. • 1997. $24.00. A critical view of both the electronic and print information industries. Emphasis is on information overload.

What Will Be: How the New World of Information Will Change Our Lives. Michael L. Dertouzos. HarperSan Francisco. • 1997. $25.00. A discussion of the "information market place" of the future, including telecommuting, virtual reality, and computer recognition of speech. The author is director of the MIT Laboratory for Computer Science.

ABSTRACTS AND INDEXES

Applied Science and Technology Index. H. W. Wilson Co. • 11 times a year. Quarterly and annual cumulations. Service basis for print edition; CD-ROM edition, $1,495.00 per year. Indexes a wide variety of English language technical, industrial, and engineering periodicals.

Business Periodicals Index. H. W. Wilson Co. • Monthly, except August, with quarterly and annual cumulations. Service basis for print edition; CD-ROM edition, $1,495.00 per year.

Communication Abstracts. Sage Publications, Inc. • Bimonthly. Individuals, $185.00 per year; institutions, $805.00 per year. Provides broad coverage of the literature of communications, including broadcasting and advertising.

Computer and Control Abstracts. Available from INSPEC, Inc. • Monthly. $2,160.00 per year. Section C of *Science Abstracts.*

Computer and Information Systems Abstracts Journal: An Abstract Journal Pertaining to the Theory, Design, Fabrication and Application of Computer and Information Systems. Cambridge Information Group. • Monthly. $1,045 per year.

Computer Literature Index: A Subject/Author Index to Computer and Data Processing Literature. Applied Computer Research, Inc. • Quarterly, with annual cumulation. $245.00 per year. Contains brief abstracts of book and periodical literature covering all phases of computing, including approximately 70 specific application areas.

Current Contents: Engineering, Computing and Technology. Institute for Scientific Information. • Weekly. $730.00 per year. Reproductions of contents pages of technical journals. Includes *Author Index, Address Directory, Current Book Contents*

and *Title Word Index*. Formerly *Current Contents: Engineering, Technology and Applied Sciences*.

Electronics and Communications Abstracts Journal: Comprehensive Coverage of Essential Scientific Literature. Cambridge Information Group. • Monthly. $1,045.00 per year.

Microcomputer Abstracts. Information Today, Inc. • Quarterly. $225.00 per year. Provides abstracts covering a wide variety of personal and business microcomputer literature. Formerly *Microcomputer Index*.

DIRECTORIES

Audiotex Directory and Buyer's Guide. ADBG Publishing. • Annual. $55.00. Lists about 1,200 voice processing product and service companies. Includes speech synthesis and recognition products.

Faulkner Information Service. Faulkner Information Services, Inc. • Looseleaf. Monthly updates. Many titles and volumes, covering virtually all aspects of computer software and hardware. Gives descriptions and technical data for specific products, including producers' names and addresses. Prices and details on request. Formerly (The Auerbach Series).

Frontline Solutions Buyer's Guide. Advanstar Communications, Inc. • Annual. $34.95. Provides information on manufacturers and suppliers of bar code, magnetic stripe, machine vision, optical character recognition, voice data, smart card, radio frequency, and other automatic identification systems. Formerly (Automatic I.D. News Buyer's Guide).

Telecommunications Directory. The Gale Group. • 2000. $595.00. 12th edition. National and international voice, data, facsimile, and video communications services. Formerly *Telecommunications Systems and Services Directory*.

ENCYCLOPEDIAS AND DICTIONARIES

Dictionary of Computing. Valerie Illingworth, editor. Oxford University Press, Inc. • 1996. $49.95. Fourth edition.

Dictionary of Information Technology and Computer Science. Tony Gunton. Blackwell Publishers. • 1994. $50.95. Second edition. Covers key words, phrases, abbreviations, and acronyms used in computing and data communications.

HANDBOOKS AND MANUALS

Speech Synthesis and Recognition. J.N. Holmes. Chapman and Hall. • 1987. $56.95.

ONLINE DATABASES

Applied Science and Technology Index Online. H. W. Wilson Co. • Provides online indexing of 400 major scientific, technical, industrial, and engineering periodicals. Time period is 1983 to date. Monthly updates. Inquire as to online cost and availability.

Computer Database. The Gale Group. • Provides online citations with abstracts to material appearing in about 150 trade journals and newsletters in the subject areas of computers, telecommunications, and electronics. Time period is 1983 to date, with weekly updates. Inquire as to online cost and availability.

Internet and Personal Computing Abstracts. Information Today, Inc. • Contains abstracts covering a wide variety of personal and business microcomputer literature appearing in more than 100 journals and popular magazines. Time period is 1981 to date, with monthly updates. Formerly *Microcomputer Index*. Inquire as to online cost and availability.

PROMT: Predicasts Overview of Markets and Technology. The Gale Group. • Companies, products, applied technologies and markets. U.S. and international literature coverage, 1972 to date. Inquire as to online cost and availability. Provides abstracts from more than 1,600 publications. Weekly updates.

Wilson Business Abstracts Online. H. W. Wilson Co. • Indexes and abstracts 600 major business periodicals, plus the *Wall Street Journal* and the business section of the *New York Times*. Indexing is from 1982, abstracting from 1990, with the two newspapers included from 1993. Updated weekly. Inquire as to online cost and availability. (*Business Periodicals Index* without abstracts is also available online.).

PERIODICALS AND NEWSLETTERS

Computer Industry Report. International Data Corp. • Semimonthly. $495.00 per year. Newsletter. Annual supplement. Also known as "The Gray Sheet." Formerly *EDP Industry Report and Market Review*.

EDP Weekly: The Leading Weekly Computer News Summary. Computer Age and E D P News Services. • Weekly. $495.00 per year. Newsletter. Summarizes news from all areas of the computer and microcomputer industries.

Frontline Solutions. Advanstar Communications, Inc. • Monthly. $41.00 per year. Provides news and information about the applications and technology of automated data capture systems. Formerly (Automatic I.D. News).

RESEARCH CENTERS AND INSTITUTES

Artificial Language Laboratory. Michigan State University, 405 Computer Center, East Lansing, MI 48824-1042. Phone: (517)353-5399 Fax: (517)353-4766 E-mail: artlang@pilot.msu.edu • URL: http://www.msu.edu/unit/artlang/ • Research areas include speech analysis and synthesis by computer.

Center for Intelligent Systems, Controls, and Signal Processing. Marquette University, Haggerty Hall, P.O. Box 1881, Milwaukee, WI 53201-1881. Phone: (414)288-3500 Fax: (414)288-5579 E-mail: james.heinen@marquette.edu • URL: http://www.eng.mu.edu/~eece/html/research.html.

Communications and Information Processing Group. Rensselaer Polytechnic Institute, Electrical, Computer, and Systems Engineering Dept., Troy, NY 12180-3590. Phone: (518)276-6823 Fax: (518)276-6261 E-mail: modestino@ipl.rpi.edu • URL: http://www.rpi.edu • Includes Optical Signal Processing Laboratory and Speech Processing Laboratory.

Computer Vision Laboratory. University of Arizona, Department of Electrical and Computer Engineering, ECE Bldg. 404, Room 230, Tucson, AZ 85721. Phone: (520)621-6191 Fax: (520)621-8076 E-mail: strickland@ece.arizona.edu • URL: http://www.ece.arizona.edu • Research areas include computer vision and speech synthesis.

Information Systems Laboratory. Stanford University, Stanford, CA 94305-9510. Phone: (650)723-4539 Fax: (650)723-8473 E-mail: char@isl.stanford.edu • URL: http://www-isl.stanford.edu • Research fields include speech coding and recognition.

Laboratory for Computer Science. Massachusetts Institute of Technology, 545 Technology Square, Bldg. NE43, Cambridge, MA 02139. Phone: (617)253-5851 Fax: (617)258-8682 E-mail: mld@hq.lcs.mit.edu • URL: http://www.lcs.mit.edu/ • Research is in four areas: Intelligent Systems; Parallel Systems; Systems, Languages, and Networks; and Theory. Emphasis is on the application of online computing.

Mind-Machine Interaction Research Center. University of Florida, Electrical and Computer Engineering Department, P.O. Box 116130, Gainesville, FL 32611-6130. Phone: (352)392-2633 Fax: (352)392-0044 E-mail: childers@ece.ufl.edu.

TRADE/PROFESSIONAL ASSOCIATIONS

AIM U.S.A. 634 Alpha Dr., Pittsburgh, PA 15238-2802. Phone: 800-338-0206 or (412)963-8588 Fax: (412)963-8753 E-mail: info@aimglobal.org • URL: http://www.aimusa.org • Members are companies concerned with automatic identification and data capture, including bar code systems, magnetic stripes, machine vision, voice technology, optical character recognition, and systems integration technology.

The Association for Work Process Improvement. 185 Devonshire St., Suite 770, Boston, MA 02110-1407. Phone: 800-998-2974 or (617)426-1167 Fax: (617)521-8675 E-mail: Info@tawpi.org • URL: http://www.tawpi.org • Members are companies that use or supply various recognition technologies equipment.

OTHER SOURCES

DataWorld. Faulkner Information Services, Inc. • Four looseleaf volumes, with monthly supplements. $1,395.00 per year. Describes and evaluates both hardware and software relating to midrange, micro, and mainframe computers. Available on CD-ROM.

VOLUME FEEDING

See: FOOD SERVICE INDUSTRY

WAGE DIFFERENTIALS

See: WAGES AND SALARIES

WAGE INCENTIVES

See: WAGES AND SALARIES

WAGE NEGOTIATIONS

See: COLLECTIVE BARGAINING

WAGES AND SALARIES

See also: EXECUTIVE COMPENSATION; INCOME

GENERAL WORKS

Compensation. George T. Milkovich. McGraw-Hill Professional. • 1998. $87.81. Sixth edition.

BIBLIOGRAPHIES

Available Pay Survey Reports: An Annotated Bibliography. Abbott, Langer and Associates. • 1995. U.S. volume, $450.00; international volume, $160.00. Fourth edition.

CD-ROM DATABASES

Sourcebooks America CD-ROM. CACI Marketing Systems. • Annual. $1,250.00. Provides the CD-ROM version of *The Sourcebook of ZIP Code Demographics: Census Edition* and *The Sourcebook of County Demographics: Census Edition.*

WILSONDISC: Wilson Business Abstracts. H. W. Wilson Co. • Monthly. $2,495.00 per year, including unlimited online access to *Wilson Business Abstracts* through WILSONLINE. Provides CD-ROM "cover-to-cover" abstracting and indexing of over 600 prominent business periodicals. Indexing is from 1982, abstracting from 1990. (*Business Periodicals Index* without abstracts is available on CD-ROM at $1,495 per year.).

DIRECTORIES

American Compensation Association-Membership Directory. American Compensation Association. • Annual. Free to members; non-members, $150.00. Covers 20,000 member benefits and compensation professionals in Canada and United States.

ENCYCLOPEDIAS AND DICTIONARIES

Blackwell Encyclopedic Dictionary of Human Resource Management. Lawrence H. Peters and Charles R. Greer, editors. Blackwell Publishers. • 1996. $105.95. The editors are associated with Texas Christian University. Contains definitions of key terms combined with longer articles written by various U. S. and foreign business educators. Includes bibliographies and index. (Blackwell Encyclopedia of Management Series).

HANDBOOKS AND MANUALS

Bender's Payroll Tax Guide. Matthew Bender & Co., Inc. • Annual. $117.00. Guide to payroll tax planning. Includes procedures, forms, and examples.

Career Guide to Industries. Available from U. S. Government Printing Office. • 1998. $17.00. Issued by the Bureau of Labor Statistics, U. S. Department of Labor (http://www.bls.gov). Presents background career information (text) and statistics for the 40 industries that account for 70 percent of wage and salary jobs in the U. S. Includes nature of the industry, employment data, working conditions, training, earnings, rate of job growth, outlook, and other career factors. (BLS Bulletin 2503.).

Personnel Management: Compensation. Prentice Hall. • Looseleaf. Periodic supplementation. Price on application.

Practical Guide to Tax Issues in Employment. Julia K. Brazelton. CCH, Inc. • 1999. $95.00. Covers income taxation as related to labor law and tax law, including settlements and awards. Written for tax professionals.

Sales Compensation Handbook. John K. Moynahan, editor. AMACOM. • 1998. $75.00. Second edition. Topics include salespeople compensation plans based on salary, commission, bonuses, and contests.

U. S. Master Compensation Tax Guide. CCH, Inc. • Annual. $54.95. Provides concise coverage of taxes on salaries, bonuses, fringe benefits, other current compensation, and deferred compensation (qualified and nonqualified).

U. S. Master Payroll Guide. CCH, Inc. • Annual. $75.00. Covers the basics of payroll management, including employer obligations, recordkeeping, taxation, unemployment insurance, processing of new employees, and government penalties.

INTERNET DATABASES

Bureau of Economic Analysis (BEA). U. S. Department of Commerce, Bureau of Economic Analysis. Phone: (202)606-9900 Fax: (202)606-5310 E-mail: webmaster@bea.doc.gov • URL: http://www.bea.doc.gov • Web site includes "News Release Information" covering national, regional, and international economic estimates from the BEA. Highlights of releases appear online the same day, complete text and tables appear the next day. "Recent News Releases" section provides titles for past nine months, with links. "BEA Data and Methodology" includes "Frequently Requested NIPA Data" (national income and product accounts, such as gross domestic product and personal income). Other statistics are available. Fees: Free.

Bureau of Labor Statistics (BLS). U. S. Department of Labor, Bureau of Labor Statistics. Phone: (202)523-1092 E-mail: labstat.helpdesk@bls.gov • URL: http://www.bls.gov • Web site provides a great variety of employment, wage, price, and economic data. Some links are "Data," "Economy at a Glance," "Keyword Search of BLS Web Pages," "Regional Information," and "Other Statistical Sites." Fees: Free.

EBSCO Information Services. Ebsco Publishing. Phone: 800-871-8508 or (508)356-6500 Fax: (508)356-5640 E-mail: ep@epnet.com • URL: http://www.epnet.com • Fee-based Web site providing Internet access to a wide variety of databases, including business-related material. Full text is available for many periodical titles, with daily updates. Fees: Apply.

Fedstats. Federal Interagency Council on Statistical Policy. Phone: (202)395-7254 • URL: http://www.fedstats.gov • Web site features an efficient search facility for full-text statistics produced by more than 70 federal agencies, including the Census Bureau, the Bureau of Economic Analysis, and the Bureau of Labor Statistics. Boolean searches can be made within one agency or for all agencies combined. Links are offered to international statistical bureaus, including the UN, IMF, OECD, UNESCO, Eurostat, and 20 individual countries. Fees: Free.

ProQuest Direct. Bell & Howell Information and Learning. Phone: 800-521-0600 or (313)761-4700 Fax: (313)973-9145 • URL: http://www.umi.com/proquest • Fee-based Web site providing Internet access to more than 3,000 periodicals, newspapers, and other publications. Many items are available full-text, with daily updates. Includes extensive corporate and financial information from Disclosure, Inc. Fees: Apply.

Wageweb: Salary Survey Data On-Line. HRPDI: Human Resources Programs Development and Improvement. Phone: (609)254-5893 Fax: (856)232-6989 E-mail: salaries@wageweb.com • URL: http://www.wageweb.com • Web site provides salary information for more than 170 benchmark positions, including (for example) 29 information management jobs. Data shows average minimum, median, and average maximum compensation for each position, based on salary surveys. Fees: Free for national salary data; $169.00 per year for more detailed information (geographic, organization size, specific industries).

ONLINE DATABASES

Accounting and Tax Database. Bell & Howell Information and Learning. • Provides indexing and abstracting of the literature of accounting, taxation, and financial management, 1971 to date. Updating is weekly. Especially covers accounting, auditing, banking, bankruptcy, employee compensation and benefits, cash management, financial planning, and credit. Inquire as to online cost and availability.

DRI U.S. Central Database. Data Products Division. • Provides more than 23,000 business, financial, demographic, economic, foreign trade, and industry-related time series for the U.S. Includes national income, population, retail-wholesale trade, price indexes, labor data, housing, industrial production, banking, interest rates, money supply, etc. Time period is generally 1947 to date (some data back to

1929). Updating varies. Inquire as to online cost and availability.

Wilson Business Abstracts Online. H. W. Wilson Co. • Indexes and abstracts 600 major business periodicals, plus the *Wall Street Journal* and the business section of the *New York Times.* Indexing is from 1982, abstracting from 1990, with the two newspapers included from 1993. Updated weekly. Inquire as to online cost and availability. (*Business Periodicals Index* without abstracts is also available online.).

PERIODICALS AND NEWSLETTERS

ACA Conference Proceedings. American Compensation Association. • Annual.

ACA News. American Compensation Association. • 10 times a year. Free to members; non-members; $60.00 per year.

Compensation and Benefits Review. Sage Publications, Inc. • Individuals, $240.00 per year; institutions, $240.00 per year.

Paytech. American Payroll Association. • Bimonthly. Membership. Covers the details and technology of payroll administration.

RESEARCH CENTERS AND INSTITUTES

W. E. Upjohn Institute for Employment Research. 300 S. Westnedge Ave., Kalamazoo, MI 49007-4686. Phone: (616)343-5541 Fax: (616)343-3308 E-mail: eberts@we.upjohninst.org • URL: http://www.upjohninst.org • Research fields include unemployment, unemployment insurance, worker's compensation, labor productivity, profit sharing, the labor market, economic development, earnings, training, and other areas related to employment.

STATISTICS SOURCES

ALA Survey of Librarian Salaries. American Library Association. • Annual. $55.00. Provides data on salaries paid to librarians in academic and public libraries. Position categories range from beginning librarian to director.

American Salaries and Wages Survey. The Gale Group. • 2001. $135.00. Sixth edition. Arranged alphabetically by 4,402 occupational classifications. Provides salary data for different experience levels and in specific areas of the U.S. Includes cost of living data for metropolitan areas.

Bulletin of Labour Statistics: Supplementing the Annual Data Presented in the Year Book of Labour Statistics. International Labour Office. ILO Publications Center. • Quarterly. $84.00 per year. Includes five *Supplements.* A supplement to *Yearbook of Labour Statistics.* Provides current labor and price index statistics for over 130 countries. Generally includes data for the most recent four years. Text in English, French and Spanish.

Business Statistics of the United States. Courtenay M. Slater, editor. Bernan Associates. • 1999. $74.00. Fifth edition. Based on *Business Statistics,* formerly issue by the Bureau of Economic Analysis, U. S. Department of Commerce. Provides basic data for a wide variety of U. S. industries, services, and economic indicators. Most statistics are shown annually for 29 years and monthly for the most recent four years.

Compensation and Working Conditions. Available from U. S. Government Printing Office. • Quarterly. $18.00 per year. Issued by the Bureau of Labor Statistics, U. S. Department of Labor. Presents wage and benefit changes that result from collective bargaining settlements and unilateral management decisions. Includes statistical summaries and special reports on wage trends. Formerly *Current Wage Developments.*

Compensation Benchmarks for Private Practice Attorneys. Altman Weil Publications, Inc. • Annual. $295.00. Provides legal-office compensation standards arranged by region, firm size, legal specialty, and various other factors. Covers attorneys, paralegals, and other personnel.

Dartnell's Sales Force Compensation Survey. Dartnell Corp. • Biennial. $159.00.

Economic Report of the President: Together with the Annual Report of the Council of Economic Advisors. Available from U. S. Government Printing Office. • Annual. $29.00. Includes about 130 pages of "Statistical Tables Relating to Income, Employment, and Production." Tables cover national income, employment, wages, productivity, manufacturing, prices, credit, finance (public and private), corporate profits, and foreign trade.

Employment and Earnings. Available from U. S. Government Printing Office. • Monthly. $50.00 per year, including annual supplement. Produced by the Bureau of Labor Statistics, U. S. Department of Labor. Provides current data on employment, hours, and earnings for the U. S. as a whole, for states, and for more than 200 local areas.

Employment and Wages: Annual Averages. Available from U. S. Government Printing Office. • Annual. $48.00. Issued by the Bureau of Labor Statistics, U. S. Department of Labor. Presents a wide variety of data arranged by state and industry.

Executive Compensation Survey Report. Mid Atlantic Employees' Association. • Annual. $400.00. Looseleaf service.

Geographic Reference Report: Annual Report of Costs, Wages, salaries, and Human Resource Statistics for the United States and Canada. ERI. • Annual. $389.00. Provides demographic and other data for each of 298 North American metropolitan areas, including local salaries, wage differentials, cost-of-living, housing costs, income taxation, employment, unemployment, population, major employers, crime rates, weather, etc.

Handbook of U. S. Labor Statistics: Employment, Earnings, Prices, Productivity, and Other Labor Data. Eva E. Jacobs, editor. Bernan Associates. • 1999. $74.00. Based on *Handbook of Labor Statistics,* formerly issued by the Bureau of Labor Statistics, U. S. Department of Labor. Includes the Bureau's projections of employment in the U. S. by industry and occupation. Provides a wide variety of data on the work force, prices, fringe benefits, and consumer expenditures.

Monthly Labor Review. Available from U. S. Government Printing Office. • Monthly. $43.00 per year. Issued by the Bureau of Labor Statistics, U. S. Department of Labor. Contains data on the labor force, wages, work stoppages, price indexes, productivity, economic growth, and occupational injuries and illnesses.

National Compensation Survey. Available from U. S. Government Printing Office. • Irregular. $300.00 per year. Consists of bulletins reporting on earnings for jobs in clerical, professional, technical, and other fields in 70 major metropolitan areas. Formerly *Occupational Compensation Survey.*

Occupational Earnings and Wage Trends in Metropolitan Areas. U.S. Bureau of Labor Statistics. • Three times a year.

Prices and Earnings Around the Globe. Union Bank of Switzerland. • Irregular. Free. Published in Zurich. Compares prices and purchasing power in 48 major cities of the world. Wages and hours are also compared. Text in English, French, German, and Italian.

Project Management Salary Survey. Project Management Institute. • Annual. $129.00. Gives compensation data for key project management positions in North America, according to job title, level of responsibility, number of employees supervised, and various other factors. Includes data on retirement plans and benefits.

Report on the American Workforce. Available from U. S. Government Printing Office. • Annual. $15.00. Issued by the U. S. Department of Labor (http://www.dol.gov). Appendix contains tabular statistics, including employment, unemployment, price indexes, consumer expenditures, employee benefits (retirement, insurance, vacation, etc.), wages, productivity, hours of work, and occupational injuries. Annual figures are shown for up to 50 years.

State Profiles: The Population and Economy of Each U. S. State. Courtenay Slater and Martha Davis, editors. Bernan Press. • 1999. $74.00. Presents charts, tables, and text in an eight-page profile for each state. Covers population, labor force, income, poverty, employment, wages, industry, trade, housing, education, health, taxes, and government finances.

Survey of Current Business. Available from U. S. Government Printing Office. • Monthly. $49.00 per year. Issued by Bureau of Economic Analysis, U. S. Department of Commerce. Presents a wide variety of business and economic data.

The Value of a Dollar. Grey House Publishing, Inc. • 1999. $125.00.

Year Book of Labour Statistics. International Labour Office. • Annual. $168.00. Presents a wide range of labor and price data for most countries of the world. Supplement available *Sources and Methods. Labour Statistics.*

TRADE/PROFESSIONAL ASSOCIATIONS

American Compensation Association. 14040 N. Northsight Blvd., Scottsdale, AZ 85260. Phone: 877-951-9191 or (480)951-9191 Fax: (480)483-8352 E-mail: aca@acaonline.org • URL: http://www.acaonline.org.

American Payroll Association. 30 E. 33rd St., 5th Fl., New York, NY 10016. Phone: (212)686-2030 Fax: (212)686-4080 E-mail: apa@apa-ed.com • URL: http://www.americanpayroll.org • Members are payroll administrators and personnel managers.

OTHER SOURCES

BNA Policy and Practice Series: Wages and Hours. Bureau of National Affairs, Inc. • Biweekly. $835.00 per year. Three volumes. Looseleaf.

Business Rankings Annual. The Gale Group. • Annual. $305.00.Two volumes. Compiled by the Business Library Staff of the Brooklyn Public Library. This is a guide to lists and rankings appearing in major business publications. The top ten names are listed in each case.

Compensation. Bureau of National Affairs, Inc. • Weekly. $533.00 per year. Three volumes. Looseleaf. (BNA Policy and Practice Series.).

Foreign Labor Trends. Available from U. S. Government Printing Office. • Irregular (50 to 60 issues per year, each on an individual country). $38.00 per year. Prepared by various American Embassies. Issued by the Bureau of International Labor Affairs, U. S. Department of Labor. Covers labor developments in important foreign countries, including trends in wages, working conditions, labor supply, employment, and unemployment.

InSite 2. Intelligence Data/Thomson Financial. • Fee-based Web site consolidates information in a "Base Pack" consisting of Business InSite, Market InSite, and Company InSite. Optional databases are Consumer InSite, Health and Wellness InSite,

Newsletter InSite, and Computer InSite. Includes fulltext content from more than 2,500 trade publications, journals, newsletters, newspapers, analyst reports, and other sources. Continuous updating. Formerly produced by The Gale Group.

Labor Law Reports. CCH, Inc. • 16 looseleaf volumes. $2,151.00 per year, including weekly updates. Covers laborrelations, wages and hours, state labor laws, and employment practices. Supplement available *Guide to Fair Employment Practices.*

WALLPAPER INDUSTRY

DIRECTORIES

Building Supply Home Centers Retail Giants Report. Cahners Business Information. • Annual. $30.00. Lists major retailers of a wide variety of building and home improvement materials, products, fixtures, accessories, equipment, and tools.

Directory of Home Center Operators and Hardware Chains. Chain Store Age. • Annual. $300.00. Nearly 5,400 home center operators, paint and home decorating chains, and lumber and building materials companies.

Paint and Decorating Retailer's Directory of the Wallcoverings Industry: The Gold Book. Paint and Decorating Retailers Association. • Annual. $25.00. Formerly *Decorating Retailer's Directory of the Wallcovering Industry.*

PERIODICALS AND NEWSLETTERS

Paint and Decorating Retailer. Paint and Decorating Retailers Association. • Monthly. $45.00 per year. Formerly *Decorating Retailer.*

Waland Window Trends. Cygnus Business Media. • Monthly $36.00 per year. Edited for retailers of interior decoration products, with an emphasis on wallcoverings. Formerly *Wallcoverings, Windows and Interior Fashion.*

The Wall Paper: The Only Monthly Journal Serving the Wallcovering Trade Exclusively. G & W McNamara Publishing, Inc. • Monthly. $25.00 per year. News, events, trends, marketing, and merchandising covering the wallcovering industry.

TRADE/PROFESSIONAL ASSOCIATIONS

Painting and Decorating Contractors of America. 3913 Old Lee Highway, Suite 33B, Fairfax, VA 22030-2433. Phone: 800-332-7322 or (703)359-0826 Fax: (703)359-2576 • URL: http://www.pdca.org.

Wallcoverings Association. 401 N. Michigan Ave., Chicago, IL 60611-4267. Phone: (312)644-6610 Fax: (312)527-6705 • URL: http://www.wallcoverings.org.

WAREHOUSES

DIRECTORIES

American Chain of Warehouses-Membership Directory. American Chain of Warehouses. • Annual. Free. Controlled circulation. About 45 member public warehouses in the United States.

Grocery Distribution Magazine Directory of Warehouse Equipment, Fixtures, and Services. Trend Publishing, Inc. • Annual. $7.50. Covers products related to food warehousing, distribution, and storage.

International Directory of Public Refrigerated Warehouses and Distribution Centers. International Association of Refrigerated Warehouses. • Annual. Free to qualified personnel; others, $150.00 per year. Lists locations/services of 1,000 public refrigerated warehouses in 30 countries.

International Warehouse Logistics Association Membership Directory and Resource Guide. International Warehouse Logistics Association. • Annual. Free to members, manufacturers, and distributors. Detailed listing of 700 public merchandise warehousing firms located throughout the U.S., Canada, Mexico, Costa Rica, Dominacan Republic, Panama, Venezuela, and Russia. Formerly *American Warehouse Association and Canadian Association of Warehousing and Distribution Services Membership Directory and Resource Guide.*

Warehouse Management's Guide to Public Warehousing. Cahners Business Information. • Annual. $55.00. List of general merchandise,contract and refrigerated warehouses. Formerly *Distribution Guide to Public Warehousing.*

Warehousing Distribution Directory. Commonwealth Business Media. • Semiannual. $63.00. Lists about 800 warehousing and consolidation companies and firms offering trucking, trailer on flatcar, container on flatcar, and piggyback carriers services.

FINANCIAL RATIOS

Annual Statement Studies. Robert Morris Associates: The Association of Lending and Credit Risk Professiona. • Annual. Free to members; non-members, $140.00. Median and quartile financial ratios are given for over 400 kinds of manufacturing, wholesale, retail, construction, and consumer finance establishments. Data is sorted by both asset size and sales volume. Includes a clearly written "Definition of Ratios" and an alphabetical industry index.

HANDBOOKS AND MANUALS

Warehouse Management Handbook. James A. Tompkins. McGraw-Hill. • 1997. $89.95. Second edition. Covers site selection, order fulfillment, inventory control systems, storage space determination, equipment maintenance programs, and other warehousing topics.

PERIODICALS AND NEWSLETTERS

Chilton's Distribution: The Transportation and Business Logistics Magazine. Cahners Business Information. • Monthly. $65.00 per year.

Distribution Center Management. Alexander Communications Group, Inc. • Monthly. $139.00 per year.

Transportation and Distribution. Penton Media Inc. • Monthly. Free to qualified personnel; others, $50.00 per year. Essential information on transportation and distribution practices in domestic and international trade.

RESEARCH CENTERS AND INSTITUTES

World Food Logistics Organization. 7315 Wisconsin Ave., Suite 1200 N, Bethesda, MD 20814. Phone: (301)652-5674 Fax: (301)652-7269 E-mail: email@iarw.org • URL: http://www.iarw.org • Concerned with food storage. Affiliated with the International Association of Refrigerated Warehouses and the University of Maryland.

STATISTICS SOURCES

Capacity of Refrigerated Warehouses. U.S. Department of Agriculture. • Annual.

TRADE/PROFESSIONAL ASSOCIATIONS

American Chain of Warehouses. 20500 S. LaGrange Rd., Frankfort, IL 60423. Phone: (815)469-4354 or (815)469-4570 Fax: (815)469-2941 E-mail: don@acwiwarehouses.com • URL: http://www.acwiwarehouses.com.

American Moving and Storage Association. c/o John Brewer. 1611 Duke St., Alexandria, VA 22314. Phone: (703)683-7410 Fax: (703)683-7527 • URL: http://www.amconf.org • Members are household goods movers, storage companies, and trucking firms.

International Association of Refrigerated Warehouses. 7315 Wisconsin Ave., 1200N, Bethesda, MD 20814. Phone: (301)652-5674 Fax: (301)652-7269 E-mail: email@iarw.org • URL: http://www.iarw.org.

International Warehouse Logistics Association. 1300 W. Higgins, Suite 111, Park Ridge, IL 60068. Phone: (847)292-1891 Fax: (847)292-1896 E-mail: bstephens@warehouselogistics.org • URL: http://www.warehouselogistics.org.

OTHER SOURCES

How to Plan and Manage Warehouse Operations. American Management Association Extension Institute. • Looseleaf. $130.00. Self-study course. Emphasis is on practical explanations, examples, and problem solving. Quizzes and a case study are included.

WARM AIR HEATING

See: HEATING AND VENTILATION

WASHING MACHINE INDUSTRY

See: ELECTRIC APPLIANCE INDUSTRY

WASTE DISPOSAL

See: SANITATION INDUSTRY

WASTE MANAGEMENT

See also: HAZARDOUS MATERIALS

GENERAL WORKS

Hazardous Waste Management. McGraw-Hill. • 2000. $85.63. Second edition.

ABSTRACTS AND INDEXES

Applied Science and Technology Index. H. W. Wilson Co. • 11 times a year. Quarterly and annual cumulations. Service basis for print edition; CD-ROM edition, $1,495.00 per year. Indexes a wide variety of English language technical, industrial, and engineering periodicals.

DIRECTORIES

BioScan: The Worldwide Biotech Industry Reporting Service. American Health Consultants, Inc. • Bimonthly. $1,395.00 per year. Looseleaf. Provides detailed information on over 900 U. S. and foreign companies broadly classified as biotechnological. In addition to medical technology and advanced pharmaceutical firms, includes firms doing research in food processing, waste management, agriculture, and veterinary science.

EI Environmental Services Directory. Environmental Information Ltd. • Biennial. $1,250.00. Over 620 waste-handling facilities, 600 transportation firms, 500 spill response firms, 2,100 consultants, 470 laboratories, 450 soil boring/well drilling firms, incineration services, asbestos services, etc. Formerly *Industrial and Hazardous Waste Management Firms.*

Hazardous Waste Consultant Directory of Commercial Hazardous Waste Management Facilities. Elsevier Science. • Annual. $115.00. List of 170 facilities that process, store, and dispose of hazardous waste materials.

National Solid Waste Management Association Directory of Professional Services. National Solid

Wastes Management Association. • Annual. Lists waste management consulting firms.

Waste Age Buyers' Guide. Intertec Publishing Corp. • Annual. $39.95. Manufacturers of equipment and supplies for the waste management industry.

Waste Age Specification Guide. Intertec Publishing Corp. • Annual. $49.95. Lists manufacturers of refuse handling machinery and equipment in North America and Europe. Includes specifications and photographs of trucks and heavy equipment.

HANDBOOKS AND MANUALS

Hazardous Waste Management in Small Businesses: Regulating and Assisting the Small Generator. Robert E. Deyle. Greenwood Publishing Group, Inc. • 1989. $59.95. Emphasis on legal aspects.

Waste Treatment and Disposal. Paul T. Williams. John Wiley and Sons, Inc. • 1998. $165.00.

PERIODICALS AND NEWSLETTERS

Air and Waste Management Association Journal. Association Journal. • Monthly. Individuals, $110.00 per year; nonprofit institutions, $130.00 per year; others, $240.00 per year. Includes annual *Directory of Governmental Air Pollution Agencies.*

EM: Environmental Solutions That Make Good Business Sense. Air and Waste Management Association. • Monthly. Individuals $99.00 per year; institutions, $130.00 per year. Newsletter. Provides news of regulations, legislation, and technology relating to the environment, recycling, and waste control. Formerly *Environmental Manager.*

Environmental Regulation: State Capitals. Wakeman-Walworth, Inc. • Weekly. $245.00 per year. Newsletter. Formerly *From the State Capitals: Environmental Regulation.*

Hazardous Waste Business. McGraw-Hill, Energy and Business Newsletter. • Biweekly. $695.00 per year. Newsletter on the control and cleanup of hazardous waste from a business viewpoint. Covers regulation, new technology, corporate activities, and industry trends.

Sludge Newsletter: The Newsletter on Municipal Wastewater and Biosolids. Business Publishers, Inc. • Biweekly. $409.00 per year. per year. Monitors sludge management developments in Washington and around the country.

Solid Waste Report: Resource Recovery-Recycling-Collection-Disposal. Business Publishers, Inc. • Weekly. $627.00 per year. Newsletter. Covers regulation, business news, technology, and international events relating to solid waste management.

Waste Age. Environmental Industry Association. Intertec Publishing Corp. • Monthly. Price on application.

Waste Management: Industrial-Radioactive-Hazardous. Elsevier Science. • Eight times a year. $1,350.00 per year. Formerly *Nuclear and Chemical Waste Management.*

Waste Treatment Technology News. Business Communications Co., Inc. • Monthly. $395.00 per year. Newsletter.

World Wastes: The Independent Voice of the Industry. Intertec Publishing Corp. • Monthly. $52.00 per year. Includes annual catalog. Formerly *Management of World Wastes: The Independent Voice of the Industry.*

RESEARCH CENTERS AND INSTITUTES

Battelle Memorial Institute. 505 King Ave., Columbus, OH 43201-2693. Phone: 800-201-2011 or (614)424-6424 Fax: (614)424-3260 • URL: http://www.battelle.org • Multidisciplinary research facilities at various locations include: Microcomputer Applications and Technology Center; Battelle Industrial Technology Center; Technology and Society Research Center; Office of Transportation Systems and Planning; Office of Waste Technology Development; Materials Information Center; Office of Nuclear Waste Isolation.

Center for the Environment. Cornell University, 200 Rice Hall, Ithaca, NY 14853-5601. Phone: (607)255-7535 Fax: (607)255-0238 E-mail: cucfe@cornell.edu • URL: http://www.cfe.cornell.edu • Includes Waste Management Institute and New York State Solid Waste Combustion Institute.

Environmental Engineering Center. Michigan Technological University, 1400 Townsend Dr., Houghton, MI 49931. Phone: (906)487-2520 Fax: (906)487-2943 E-mail: baillod@mtu.edu • URL: http://www.bigmac.civil.mtu.edu/enveng.html • Applies biotechnological research to waste management and resource recovery.

Waste Management Research and Education Institute. University of Tennessee, Knoxville, 600 Henley St., Suite 311, Knoxville, TN 37996-4134. Phone: (865)674-4251 Fax: (865)974-1838 E-mail: kdavis17@utk.edu • URL: http://www.eerc.ra.utk.edu/wmrei • Research fields include chemical, nuclear, and solid waste management, especially waste policy and environmental biotechnology studies.

TRADE/PROFESSIONAL ASSOCIATIONS

Air and Waste Management Association. One Gateway Center, 3rd Fl., Pittsburgh, PA 15222. Phone: 800-270-3444 or (412)232-3444 Fax: (412)232-3450 E-mail: info@awma.org • URL: http://www.awma.org.

Solid Waste Association of North America. P.O. Box 7219, Silver Spring, MD 20907. Phone: 800-467-9262 or (301)585-2898 Fax: (301)589-7068 E-mail: info@swana.org • URL: http://www.swana.org • Members are officials from both public agencies and private companies. Attempts to improve waste management services to the public and industry.

OTHER SOURCES

Hazardous Waste Litigation Reporter: The National Journal of Record of Hazardous Waste-Related Litigation. Andrews Publications. • Semimonthly. $875.00 per year. Reports on hazardous waste legal cases.

WASTE PRODUCTS

See also: IRON AND STEEL SCRAP METAL INDUSTRY; RECYCLING; SANITATION INDUSTRY

ABSTRACTS AND INDEXES

Environment Abstracts. Congressional Information Service. • Monthly. Price varies. Provides multidisciplinary coverage of the world's environmental literature. Incorporates *Acid Rain Abstracts.*

Environment Abstracts Annual: A Guide to the Key Environmental Literature of the Year. Congressional Information Service. • Annual. $495.00. A yearly cumulation of *Environment Abstracts.*

Environmental Periodicals Bibliography: A Current Awareness Bibliography Featuring Citations of Scientific and Popular Articles in Serial Publications in the Area of the Environment. Environmental Studies Institute. International Academy at Santa Barbara. • Monthly. Price varies. An index to current environmental literature.

Pollution Abstracts. Cambridge Information Group. • Monthly. $895.00 per year; with index, $985.00 per year.

CD-ROM DATABASES

Environment Abstracts on CD-ROM. Congressional Information Service, Inc. • Quarterly. $1,295.00 per year. Contains the following CD-ROM databases: *Environment Abstracts, Energy Abstracts,* and *Acid Rain Abstracts.* Length of coverage varies.

ONLINE DATABASES

Enviroline. Congressional Information Service, Inc. • Provides online indexing and abstracting of worldwide environmental and natural resource literature from 1975 to date. Updated monthly. Inquire as to online cost and availability.

PERIODICALS AND NEWSLETTERS

Scrap. Institute of Scrap Recycling Industries. • Bimonthly. Free to members; non-members, $32.95 per year. Formerly *Scrap Processing and Recycling.*

Waste Age. Environmental Industry Association. Intertec Publishing Corp. • Monthly. Price on application.

Waste Treatment Technology News. Business Communications Co., Inc. • Monthly. $395.00 per year. Newsletter.

World Wastes: The Independent Voice of the Industry. Intertec Publishing Corp. • Monthly. $52.00 per year. Includes annual catalog. Formerly *Management of World Wastes: The Independent Voice of the Industry.*

TRADE/PROFESSIONAL ASSOCIATIONS

Institute of Scrap Recycling Industries. 1325 G St., N.W., Suite 1000, Washington, DC 20005-3104. Phone: (202)737-1770 Fax: (202)626-0900 E-mail: isri@isri.com • URL: http://www.isri.org.

WATCH INDUSTRY

See: CLOCK AND WATCH INDUSTRY

WATER POLLUTION

See also: SANITATION INDUSTRY; WATER SUPPLY

GENERAL WORKS

Pollution: Causes, Effects, and Control. R. M. Harrison, editor. American Chemical Society. • 1996. $71.00. Third edition. Published by The Royal Society of Chemistry. A basic introduction to pollution of air, water, and land. Includes discussions of pollution control technologies.

ABSTRACTS AND INDEXES

Environment Abstracts. Congressional Information Service. • Monthly. Price varies. Provides multidisciplinary coverage of the world's environmental literature. Incorporates *Acid Rain Abstracts.*

Environment Abstracts Annual: A Guide to the Key Environmental Literature of the Year. Congressional Information Service. • Annual. $495.00. A yearly cumulation of *Environment Abstracts.*

Environmental Periodicals Bibliography: A Current Awareness Bibliography Featuring Citations of Scientific and Popular Articles in Serial Publications in the Area of the Environment. Environmental Studies Institute. International Academy at Santa Barbara. • Monthly. Price varies. An index to current environmental literature.

Excerpta Medica: Environmental Health and Pollution Control. Elsevier Science. • 16 times a year. 2,506.00 per year. Section 46 of *Excerpta Medica.* Covers air, water, and land pollution and noise control.

NTIS Alerts: Environmental Pollution & Control. National Technical Information Service. •

Semimonthly. $245.00 per year. Provides descriptions of government-sponsored research reports and software, with ordering information. Covers the following categories of environmental pollution: air, water, solid wastes, radiation, pesticides, and noise. Formerly *Abstract Newsletter*.

Pollution Abstracts. Cambridge Information Group. • Monthly. $895.00 per year; with index, $985.00 per year.

ALMANACS AND YEARBOOKS

Environmental Viewpoints. The Gale Group. • 1993. $195.00. Three volumes. $65.00 per volume. A compendium of excerpts of about 200 articles on a wide variety of environmental topics, selected from both popular and professional periodicals. Arranged alphabetically by topic, with a subject/keyword index.

Gale Environmental Almanac. The Gale Group. • 1994. $110.00. Contains 15 chapters, each on a broad topic related to the environment, such as "Waste and Recycling." Each chapter has a topical overview, charts, statistics, and illustrations. Includes a glossary of environmental terms and a bibliography.

BIBLIOGRAPHIES

Literature Review. Water Environment Federation. • Annual. Price on application.

CD-ROM DATABASES

Environment Abstracts on CD-ROM. Congressional Information Service, Inc. • Quarterly. $1,295.00 per year. Contains the following CD-ROM databases: *Environment Abstracts, Energy Abstracts*, and *Acid Rain Abstracts*. Length of coverage varies.

DIRECTORIES

Environmental Career Directory. Visible Ink Press. • 1993. $17.95. Includes career information relating to workers in conservation, recycling, wildlife management, pollution control, and other areas. Provides advice from "insiders," resume suggestions, a directory of companies that may offer entry-level positions, and a directory of career information sources. (Career Advisor Series.).

Gale Environmental Sourcebook: A Guide to Organizations, Agencies, and Publications. The Gale Group. • 1993. $95.00. Second edition. A directory of print and non-print information sources on a wide variety of environmental topics.

Pollution Equipment News Buyer's Guide. Rimbach Publishing, Inc. • Annual. $100.00. Over 3,000 manufacturers of pollution control equipment and products.

ENCYCLOPEDIAS AND DICTIONARIES

Encyclopedia of Environmental Science. John Mongillo and Linda Zierdt-Warshaw. Oryx Press. • 2000. $95.00. Provides information on more than 1,000 topics relating to the environment. Includes graphs, tables, maps, illustrations, and 400 Web site addresses.

Environmental Encyclopedia. The Gale Group. • 1998. $235.00. Second edition. Provides over 1,300 articles on all aspects of the environment. Written in non-technical style.

HANDBOOKS AND MANUALS

Industrial Pollution Prevention Handbook. Harry M. Freeman. McGraw-Hill. • 1992. $115.00.

Statistics for the Environment: Statistical Aspects of Health and the Environment. Vic Barnett and K. Feridun Turkman, editors. John Wiley and Sons, Inc. • 1999. $180.00. Contains articles on the statistical analysis and interpretation of environmental monitoring and sampling data. Areas covered include meteorology, pollution of the environment, and forest resources.

ONLINE DATABASES

Aqualine. Water Research Centre. • Citations and abstracts of literature on aquatic environment, 1960 to present. Inquire as to online cost and availability.

Enviroline. Congressional Information Service, Inc. • Provides online indexing and abstracting of worldwide environmental and natural resource literature from 1975 to date. Updated monthly. Inquire as to online cost and availability.

Pollution Abstracts [online]. Cambridge Scientific Abstracts. • Provides indexing and abstracting of international, environmentally related literature, 1970 to date. Monthly updates. Inquire as to online cost and availability.

PERIODICALS AND NEWSLETTERS

Air-Water Pollution Report: The Weekly Report on Environmental Executives. Business Publishers, Inc. • Weekly. $667.00 per year. Newsletter covering legislation, regulation, business news, research news, etc. Formed by merger of *Environment Week* and *Air-Water Pollution Report.*

Chartered Institution of Water and Environmental Management Journal. Terence Dalton Ltd. • Bimonthly. $255.00 per year.

Environmental Business Journal: Strategic Information for a Changing Industry. Environmental Business Publishing Co. • Monthly. $495.00 per year. Newsletter. Includes both industrial and financial information relating to individual companies and to the environmental industry in general. Covers air pollution, wat es, U. S. Department of Health and Human Services. Provides conference, workshop, and symposium proceedings, as well as extensive reviews of environmental prospects.

Environmental Regulation: State Capitals. Wakeman-Walworth, Inc. • Weekly. $245.00 per year. Newsletter. Formerly *From the State Capitals: Environmental Regulation.*

Marine Pollution Bulletin: The International Journal for Marine Environmentalists, Scientists, Engineers, Administrators, Politicians, and Lawyers. Elsevier Science. • Semimonthly. $942.00 per year.

Municipal and Industrial Water and Pollution Control. Zanny Publications Ltd. • Bimonthly. $65.00 per year. Formerly *Water and Pollution Control.*

Pollution Engineering: Magazine of Environmental Control. Cahners Business Information. • 13 times a year. $85.90 per year. Includes *Product-Service Locater.*

Water, Air and Soil Pollution: An International Journal of Environmental Pollution. Kluwer Academic Publishers. • 32 times a year. $2,813.00 per year. Includes online edition.

Water and Wastes Digest. Scranton Gillette Communications, Inc. • 10 times a year. Free to qualified personnel; others, $40.00 per year. Exclusively designed to serve engineers, consultants, superintendents, managers and operators who are involved in water supply, waste water treatment and control.

Water Engineering and Management. Scranton Gillette Communications, Inc. • Monthly. $40.00 per year.

Water Environment Research. Water Environment Federation. • Bimonthly. Members, $158.00 per year; non-members, $404.00 per year. Formerly *Water Pollution Control Federation. Research Journal.*

Water Research. International Association on Water Quality. Elsevier Science. • 18 times a year. $3,721.00 per year.

Water Science and Technology. International Association on Water Quality. Elsevier Science. • 24 times a year. $3,514.00 per year.

STATISTICS SOURCES

Health and Environment in America's Top-Rated Cities: A Statistical Profile. Grey House Publishing. • Biennial. $195.00. Covers 75 U. S. cities. Includes statistical and other data on a wide variety of topics, such as air quality, water quality, recycling, hospitals, physicians, health care costs, death rates, infant mortality, accidents, and suicides.

Standard & Poor's Industry Surveys. Standard & Poor's. • Semiannual. $1,800.00. Two looseleaf volumes. Includes monthly supplements. Provides detailed, individual surveys of 52 major industry groups. Each survey is revised on a semiannual basis. Also includes "Monthly Investment Review" (industry group investment analysis) and monthly "Trends & Projections" (economic analysis).

Statistical Record of the Environment. The Gale Group. • 1996. $120.00. Third edition. Provides over 875 charts, tables, and graphs of major environmental statistics, arranged by subject. Covers population growth, hazardous waste, nuclear energy, acid rain, pesticides, and other subjects related to the environment. A keyword index is included.

U. S. Industry and Trade Outlook: The McGraw-Hill Companies and the U.S. Department of Commerce/ International Trade Administration. Datapso Research Corp. • Annual. $69.95. Produced by the International Trade Administration, U. S. Department of Commerce, in a "public-private" partnership with DRI/McGraw-Hill and Standard & Poor's. Provides basic data, outlook for the current year, and "Long-Term Prospects" (five-year projections) for a wide variety of products and services. Includes high technology industries. Formerly *U. S. Industrial Outlook.*

TRADE/PROFESSIONAL ASSOCIATIONS

Association of State and Interstate Water Pollution Control Administrators. 750 First St., N.E., Suite 910, Washington, DC 20002. Phone: (202)898-0905 Fax: (202)898-0929 E-mail: admin1@asiwpca.org • URL: http://www.asiwpca.org.

United Kingdom National Committee of International Association on Water Quality. c/o J.M. Tyson, 45 Riverside Close, Warrington, Cheshire WA1 2JO, England. Phone: 44 192 5368226.

Water Environment Federation. 601 Wythe St., Alexandria, VA 22314-1994. Phone: 800-666-0206 or (703)684-2400 Fax: (703)684-2492 E-mail: csc@wef.org • URL: http://www.wef.org.

Water Quality Association. 4151 Naperville Rd., Lisle, IL 60532. Phone: (630)505-0160 Fax: (630)505-9637 • URL: http://www.wqa.org.

OTHER SOURCES

BNA Policy and Practice Series: Water Pollution Control. Bureau of National Affairs. • Biweekly. $1,136.00 per year. Looseleaf.

Environment Reporter. Bureau of National Affairs, Inc. • Weekly. $2,844.00 per year. 18 volumes. Looseleaf. Covers legal aspects of wide variety of environmental concerns.

WATER POWER

See: HYDROELECTRIC INDUSTRY

WATER SUPPLY

See also: DESALINATION INDUSTRY; SANITATION INDUSTRY; WATER POLLUTION

GENERAL WORKS

Recent Advances and Issues in Environmental Science. John R. Callahan. Oryx Press. • 2000. $44.95. Includes environmental economic problems, such as saving jobs vs. protecting the environment. (Oryx Frontiers of Science Series.).

ABSTRACTS AND INDEXES

Environmental Periodicals Bibliography: A Current Awareness Bibliography Featuring Citations of Scientific and Popular Articles in Serial Publications in the Area of the Environment. Environmental Studies Institute. International Academy at Santa Barbara. • Monthly. Price varies. An index to current environmental literature.

Pollution Abstracts. Cambridge Information Group. • Monthly. $895.00 per year; with index, $985.00 per year.

ALMANACS AND YEARBOOKS

Earth Almanac: An Annual Geophysical Review of the State of the Planet. Natalie Goldstein. Oryx Press. • Annual. $65.00. Provides background information, statistics, and a summary of major events relating to the atmosphere, oceans, land, and fresh water.

BIBLIOGRAPHIES

Planning for Water Source Protection. Philip M. Kappen. Sage Publications, Inc. • 1993. $10.00.

Protecting Stream Corridors. Lee Nellis. Sage Publications, Inc. • 1993. $10.00.

CD-ROM DATABASES

AGRICOLA on SilverPlatter. Available from SilverPlatter Information, Inc. • Quarterly. $825.00 per year. Produced by the National Agricultural Library. Provides about three million citations on CD-ROM to the literature of agriculture, agricultural economics, animal sciences, entomology, fertilizer, food, forestry, nutrition, pesticides, plant science, water resources, and other topics. Each quarterly disc covers the past ten years, with archival discs available from 1970.

DIRECTORIES

American Water Works Sourcebook. American Water Works Association. • Annual. Membership. Products and services of interest to the water industry. Formerly American Water Resources Association.

National Ground Water Association - Membership Directory. National Ground Water Association. • Triennial. Membership.

ENCYCLOPEDIAS AND DICTIONARIES

Encyclopedia of Agriculture Science. Charles J. Arntzen and Ellen M. Ritter, editors. Academic Press, Inc. • 1994. $625.00. Four volumes.

Water Encyclopedia. Frits Von Der Leeden and others, editors. Lewis Publishers. • 1990. $179.00. Second edition. Covers a wide variety of topics relating to water. (Geraghty and Miller Ground Water Series).

FINANCIAL RATIOS

Almanac of Business and Industrial Financial Ratios. Leo Troy. Prentice Hall. • Annual. $99.95. Contains financial ratios derived from federal tax returns. Ratios for each of about 200 industries are arranged according to company asset size.

HANDBOOKS AND MANUALS

Water Resources: Distribution, Use and Management. John R. Mather. John Wiley and Sons, Inc. • 1983. $150.00. (Environmental Science and Technology Series).

ONLINE DATABASES

Aqualine. Water Research Centre. • Citations and abstracts of literature on aquatic environment, 1960 to present. Inquire as to online cost and availability.

GEOARCHIVE. Geosystems. • Citations to literature on geoscience and water. 1974 to present. Monthly updates. Inquire as to online cost and availability.

PERIODICALS AND NEWSLETTERS

American Water Works Association Journal. American Water Works Association. • Monthly. Free to members; libraries and governmental agencies only, 85.00 per year.

Environmental Regulation: State Capitals. Wakeman-Walworth, Inc. • Weekly. $245.00 per year. Newsletter. Formerly *From the State Capitals: Environmental Regulation.*

Ground Water. National Ground Water Association. Ground Water Publishing Co. • Bimonthly. $150.00 per year.

National Water Conditions. U.S. Geological Survey. • Monthly. Free.

Water Engineering and Management. Scranton Gillette Communications, Inc. • Monthly. $40.00 per year.

Water Operation and Maintenance Bulletin. • Quarterly.

Water Well Journal. Ground Water Publishing Co. • Monthly. $39.00 per year.

RESEARCH CENTERS AND INSTITUTES

Water Resources Center. University of Illinois, Urbana-Chapaign. 1101 W. Peabody Dr., Urbana, IL 61801. Phone: (217)333-0536 Fax: (217)244-8583 E-mail: iwrc@uiuc.edu • URL: http://www.w3.aces.uiuc.edu/lwrc/.

TRADE/PROFESSIONAL ASSOCIATIONS

American Water Resources Association. P.O. Box 1626, Middleburg, VA 20118-1626. Phone: (540)687-8390 Fax: (540)687-8395 E-mail: info@awra.org • URL: http://www.awra.org.

American Water Works Association. 6666 W. Quincy Ave., Denver, CO 80235. Phone: 800-926-7337 or (303)794-7711 • URL: http://www.awwa.org.

International Association of Theoretical and Applied Limnology. c/o Dr. Robert G. Wetzel, University of Alabama, Dept. of Biology, Tuscaloosa, AL 35487-0206. Phone: (205)348-1793 or (205)348-1787 Fax: (205)348-1403 E-mail: rwetzel@biology.as.ua.edu.

National Ground Water Association. 601 Dempsey Rd., Westerville, OH 43081. Phone: 800-551-7379 or (614)898-7791 Fax: (614)898-7786 E-mail: ngwa@ngwa.org • URL: http://www.ngwa.org.

Water and Wastewater Equipment Manufacturers Association. P.O. Box 17402, Washington, DC 20041. Phone: (703)444-1777 Fax: (703)444-1779 • URL: http://www.ema.org.

OTHER SOURCES

Infrastructure Industries USA. The Gale Group. • 2001. $240.00. Replaces *Agriculture, Forestry, Fishing, Mining, and Construction USA* and *Transportation and Public Utilities USA.* Presents statistics and projections relating to economic activity in a wide variety of natural resource and construction industries.

WATERFRONTS

See: PORTS

WATERWAYS

ABSTRACTS AND INDEXES

NTIS Alerts: Transportation. National Technical Information Service. • Semimonthly. $210.00 per year. Provides descriptions of government-sponsored research reports and software, with ordering information. Covers air, marine, highway, inland waterway, pipeline, and railroad transportation. Formerly *Abstract Newsletter.*

Oceanic Abstracts. Cambridge Information Group. • Bimonthly. $1,045.00 per year. Covers oceanography, marine biology, ocean shipping, and a wide range of other marine-related subject areas.

DIRECTORIES

Inland River Guide. Waterways Journal, Inc. • Annual. $60.00. Covers domestic barge and towing industry.

Waterway Guide: The Yachtman's Bible. Intertec Publishing Corp. • Annual. $33.95 per edition. Three regional editions: Northern, and Middle Atlantic, Southern. Provides detailed information concerning marinas on inland and coastal waterways.

ENCYCLOPEDIAS AND DICTIONARIES

Macmillan Encyclopedia of Transportation. Available from The Gale Group. • 2000. $375.00. Six volumes. Published by Macmillan Reference USA. Covers the business, technology, and history of transportation on land, on water, in the air, and in space. Includes definitions, cross-references, and 200 color illustrations.

ONLINE DATABASES

Oceanic Abstracts (Online). Cambridge Scientific Abstracts. • Oceanographic and other marine-related technical literature, 1981 to present.Monthly updates. Inquire as to online cost and availability.

PERIODICALS AND NEWSLETTERS

AWO Letter. American Waterways Operators. • Biweekly. $75.00 per year. Formerly *AWO Weekly Letter.*

Waterways Journal: Devoted to the Marine Profession and Commercial Interest of All Inland Waterways. Waterways Journal, Inc. • Weekly. $32.00 per year. Weekly business journal serving nation's inland marine industry. Supplement available *Annual Review Number.*

TRADE/PROFESSIONAL ASSOCIATIONS

National Waterways Conference. 1130 17th St., N.W., Suite 200, Washington, DC 20036. Phone: (202)296-4415 Fax: (202)835-3861 E-mail: hcook@waterways.org • URL: http://www.waterways.org.

WATERWORKS

See: WATER SUPPLY

WEALTHY CONSUMERS

See: AFFLUENT MARKET

WEAPONS MARKET

See: DEFENSE INDUSTRIES; MILITARY MARKET

 For publishers addresses, refer to SOURCES CITED section at the back of the book.

WEATHER AND WEATHER FORECASTING

See also: CLIMATE

ABSTRACTS AND INDEXES

Meteorological and Geoastrophysical Abstracts. American Meteorological Society. • Monthly. $1.120.00 per year.

ALMANACS AND YEARBOOKS

AMS Conference Proceedings. American Meteorological Society. • Annual.

The Weather Almanac: A Reference Guide to Weather, Climate, and Air Quality in the United States and Its Key Cities, Comprising Statistics, Principles, and Terminology. The Gale Group. • 1999. $145.00. Ninth edition. Weather reports for 108 major U.S. cities and a climatic overview of the country.

ENCYCLOPEDIAS AND DICTIONARIES

Macmillan Encyclopedia of Weather. Available from The Gale Group. • 2001. $125.00. Published by Macmillan Reference USA. Contains 150 entries covering the basics of weather and weather forecasting. Includes illustrations in color.

HANDBOOKS AND MANUALS

Climates of the States. The Gale Group. • 1998. $245.00. Fourth edition. Two volumes. State-by-state summaries of climatebased on first order weather reporting stations.

USA Today Weather Book. Jack Williams. Random House, Inc. • 1997. $20.00. Contains a state-by-state guide to U. S. climate, with color illustrations. Author (weather editor of *USA Today*) includes discussions of weather patterns and computerized forecasting.

Weather of U.S. Cities. The Gale Group. • 1996. $225.00. Fifth edition.

ONLINE DATABASES

Accu-Data. Accu-Weather, Inc. • Provides detailed, current weather conditions and weather forecasts for many U. S. and foreign cities and regions. Updating is continuous. Inquire as to online cost and availability.

PERIODICALS AND NEWSLETTERS

Daily Weather Maps (Weekly Series). U.S. Dept. of Commerce.

Hourly Precipitation Data. U.S. National Climatic Data Center. • Monthly. Published separately for 41 states.

Journal of Applied Meteorology. American Meteorological Society. • Monthly. $335.00 per year.

Journal of the Atmospheric Sciences. American Meteorological Society. • Semimonthly. $495.00 per year.

Monthly Climatic Data for the World. U.S. National Climatic Data Center. • Monthly.

Monthly Weather Review. American Meteorological Society. • Monthly. $445.00 per year.

Storm Data. U.S. National Climatic Data Center. • Monthly.

Weather and Climate Report. Nautilus Press, Inc. • Monthly. $95.00 per year.

Weatherwise: The Magazine About the Weather. Helen Dwight Reid Educational Foundation. Heldref Publications. • Bimonthly. Individuals, $29.00 per year; institutions, $62.00 per year. Popular magazine devoted to weather.

Weekly Weather and Crop Bulletin. Available from U.S. Department of Agriculture, Agricultural Weather Facility. • Weekly.

STATISTICS SOURCES

Weather America: A Thirty-Year Summary of Statistical Data and Weather Trends. Grey House Publishing. • 2000. $175.00. Second edition. Contains detailed climatological data for 4,000 national and cooperative weather stations in the U. S. Organized by state, with an index to cities. (Universal Reference Publications.).

TRADE/PROFESSIONAL ASSOCIATIONS

American Meteorological Society. 45 Beacon St., Boston, MA 02108-3693. Phone: (617)227-2425 Fax: (617)742-8718 E-mail: webadmin@ametsoc.org • URL: http://www.ametsoc.org/ams.

Weather Modification Association. P.O. Box 26926, Fresno, CA 93729-6926. Phone: (209)434-3486 Fax: (209)434-3486 E-mail: wxmod@ix.netcom.com.

OTHER SOURCES

Infogate. Infogate, Inc. • Web site provides current news and information on seven "channels": News, Fun, Sports, Info, Finance, Shop, and Travel. Among the content partners are Business Wire, CBS MarketWatch, CNN, Morningstar, Standard & Poor's, and Thomson Investors Network. Fees: Free, but downloading of Infogate software is required (includes personalized news feature). Updating is continuous. Formerly Pointcast Network.

Lloyd's Maritime Atlas of World Ports and Shipping Places. Available from Informa Publishing Group Ltd. • Annual. $119.00. Published in the UK by Lloyd's List (http://www.lloydslist.com). Contains more than 70 pages of world, ocean, regional, and port maps in color. Provides additional information for the planning of world shipping routes, including data on distances, port facilities, recurring weather hazards at sea, international load line zones, and sailing times.

WEAVING

See also: TEXTILE INDUSTRY

ABSTRACTS AND INDEXES

Textile Technology Digest. Institute of Textile Technology. • Monthly. $535.00 per year. Provides indexing and abstracting of a wide variety of textile technology literature.

CD-ROM DATABASES

Textile Technology Digest [CD-ROM]. Textile Information Center, Institute of Textile Technology. • Quarterly. $1,700.00 per year. Provides CD-ROM indexing and abstracting of worldwide journals and monographs in various areas of textile technology, production, and management. Covers 1978 to date.

ENCYCLOPEDIAS AND DICTIONARIES

Encyclopedia of Textiles. French and European Publications, Inc. • 1980. $39.95. Third edition.

Textile Terms and Definitions. J.E. McIntyre and Paul N. Daniels, editors. Available from State Mutual Book and Periodical Service Ltd., Trade Order Dept. • 1995. $110.00. 10th edition. Published by the Textile Insitute (UK). Includes more than 1,000 definitions of textile processes, fiber types, and end products. Illustrated.

HANDBOOKS AND MANUALS

The Art of Weaving. Else Regensteiner. Schiffer Publishing, Ltd. • 1986. $29.95.

ONLINE DATABASES

Textile Technology Digest [online]. Textile Information Center, Institute of Textile Technology. • Contains indexing and abstracting of more than 300 worldwide journals and monographs in various areas of textile technology, production, and management. Time period is 1978 to date, with monthly updating. Inquire as to online cost and availability.

World Textiles. Elsevier Science, Inc. • Provides abstracting and indexing from 1970 of worldwide textile literature (periodicals, books, pamphlets, and reports). Includes U. S., European, and British patent information. Updating is monthly. Inquire as to online cost and availability.

PERIODICALS AND NEWSLETTERS

International Textile Bulletin: Yarn and Fabric Forming Edition. ITS Publishing, International Textile Service. • Quarterly. $170.00 per year. Editions in Chinese, English, French, German, Italian and Spanish.

Shuttle, Spindle, and Dyepot. Handweavers Guild of America. • Quarterly. $25.00 per year.

STATISTICS SOURCES

Consumption on the Woolen System and Worsted Combing. U. S. Bureau of the Census. • Quarterly and annual. Provides data on consumption of fibers in woolen and worsted spinning mills, by class of fibers and end use. (Current Industrial Reports, MQ-22D.).

TRADE/PROFESSIONAL ASSOCIATIONS

Handweavers Guild of America. 3327 Deluth Highway, Suite 201, Duluth, GA 30096-3383. Phone: (770)495-7702 Fax: (770)495-7706 E-mail: weavespindye@compuserve.com.

Textile Institute. Saint James Bldgs., 4th Fl., Oxford St., Manchester M1 6FQ, England. Phone: 44 161 2371188 Fax: 44 161 2361991 E-mail: tiihq@textileinst.org.uk • URL: http://www.texi.org • Members in 100 countries involved with textile industry management, marketing, science, and technology.

OTHER SOURCES

Textile Business Outlook. Statistikon Corp. • Quarterly. $985.00 per year. Analyzes current business, marketing, and financial conditions for the worldwide textile industry (fibers and fabrics). Includes statistical forecasts.

WEEKLY NEWSPAPERS

See: NEWSPAPERS

WEIGHT CONTROL

See: DIET

WEIGHTS AND MEASURES

ALMANACS AND YEARBOOKS

International Society of Weighing and Measurement Membership Directory and Product Guide. International Society of Weighing and Measurement. • Annual. Free to members; non-members, $50.00.

HANDBOOKS AND MANUALS

Conversion Factors and Tables. O. T. Zimmerman. Industrial Research Service, Inc. • 1961. $30.00.

ONLINE DATABASES

Scisearch. Institute for Scientific Information. • Broad, multidisciplinary index to the literature of science and technology, 1974 to present. Inquire as to online cost and availability. Coverage of literature is worldwide, with weekly updates.

PERIODICALS AND NEWSLETTERS

ISWM News. International Society of Weighing and Measurement. • Quarterly.

Metric Reporter. American National Metric Council. • Bimonthly. Membership. Updates and developments in the progress of voluntary implementation of the metric system of measurement.

Metric Today. U.S. Metric Association, Inc. • Bimonthly. Individuals, $30.00 per year; institutions, $150.00 per year. Formerly *USMA Newsletter*.

Weighing and Measurement. Key Markets Publishing Co. • Bimonthly. $30.00 per year. Provides information relating to industrial weighing methods.

TRADE/PROFESSIONAL ASSOCIATIONS

American National Metric Council. 4340 East-West Highway, Suite 401, Bethesda, MD 20814-4408. Phone: (301)718-6508 Fax: (301)656-0989.

International Bureau of Weights and Measures. Pavillon de Breteuil, F-92312 Sevres Cedex, France. Phone: 33 1 45077070 Fax: 33 1 45342021 E-mail: info@bipm.fr • URL: http://www.bipm.fr • Works for the establishment of international weights and measures standards, including international time standards.

International Society of Weighing and Measurement. 10 W. Kimball St., Windsor, GA 30680. Phone: (770)868-5300 Fax: (770)868-5301 E-mail: staff@iswm.org • URL: http://www.iswm.org.

National Conference on Weights and Measures. 15245 Shady Grove Rd., Suite 130, Rockville, MD 20850-3222. Phone: (301)258-9210 Fax: (301)990-9771 E-mail: ncwm@mgmtsol.com • URL: http://www.nist.gov/ncwm.

Scale Manufacturers Association. 6724 Lone Oak Blvd., Naples, FL 34109. Phone: (941)514-3441 Fax: (941)514-3470 E-mail: staff@scalemanufacturers.org • URL: http://www.scalemanufacturers.org.

U.S. Metric Association. 10245 Andasol Ave., Northridge, CA 91325-1504. Phone: (818)363-5606 E-mail: hillger@cira.colostate.edu • URL: http://www.lamar.colostate.edu/hillger/.

United Weighers Association. P.O. Box 1027, Floral Park, NY 11002. Phone: (516)352-2673 Fax: (516)352-3569.

WELDING

GENERAL WORKS

Science and Practice of Welding. A. C. Davies. Cambridge University Press. • 1993. 10th edition. Two volumes. Vol. 1, *Welding Science and Technology, $29.95; volume two, The Practice of Welding*, $39.95.

Welding Technology. Gower A. Kennedy. Pearson Education and Technology. • 1982. $52.94.

ABSTRACTS AND INDEXES

Applied Science and Technology Index. H. W. Wilson Co. • 11 times a year. Quarterly and annual cumulations. Service basis for print edition; CD-ROM edition, $1,495.00 per year. Indexes a wide variety of English language technical, industrial, and engineering periodicals.

ALMANACS AND YEARBOOKS

Welding Research Council Yearbook. Welding Research Council. • Annual. Membership.

DIRECTORIES

Welding and Fabricating Data Book. Penton Media Inc. • Biennial. $30.00. List of over 1,500 manufacturers and suppliers of products and equipment for the welding and fabricating industry.

ENCYCLOPEDIAS AND DICTIONARIES

The Welding Encyclopedia. Ted B. Jefferson and Don Jefferson, editors. Jefferson Publications, Inc. • 1988. $27.50. 18th edition.

FINANCIAL RATIOS

Annual Statement Studies. Robert Morris Associates: The Association of Lending and Credit Risk Professiona. • Annual. Free to members; non-members, $140.00. Median and quartile financial ratios are given for over 400 kinds of manufacturing, wholesale, retail, construction, and consumer finance establishments. Data is sorted by both asset size and sales volume. Includes a clearly written "Definition of Ratios" and an alphabetical industry index.

ONLINE DATABASES

Applied Science and Technology Index Online. H. W. Wilson Co. • Provides online indexing of 400 major scientific, technical, industrial, and engineering periodicals. Time period is 1983 to date. Monthly updates. Inquire as to online cost and availability.

METADEX. Cambridge Scientific Abstracts. • Covers the worldwide literature of metals, metallurgy, and materials science, 1966 to date. Includes detailed alloys indexing from 1974. Biweekly updating. Inquire as to online cost and availability. (Formerly produced by ASM International.).

Weldasearch. The Welding Institute. • Contains abstracts of international welding literature, 1967 to date. Inquire as to online cost and availability.

PERIODICALS AND NEWSLETTERS

The Gases and Welding Distributor. Penton Media Inc. • Bimonthly. Free to qualified personnel; others, $45.00 Per year. Formerly *Welding Distributor*.

Welding and Metal Fabrication. DMG World Media. • 10 times a year. $293.00 per year.

Welding Design and Fabrication. Penton Media Inc. • Monthly. Free to qualified personnel; others, $70.00 per year.

Welding in the World. International Institute of Welding. Elsevier Science. • Semiannual. $449.00 per year. Text in English and French.

Welding Journal. American Welding Society. • Monthly. Membership.

Welding Research Abroad. Welding Research Council. • 10 times a year. $1,100.00. Includes *Progress Reports, WRC Bulletins, WRC News* and *Welding Journal.*

WRC Progress Reports. Welding Research Council. • Bimonthly. $1,100 per year. Includes *Welding Research Abroad; WRC Bulletins, WRC News* and *Welding Journal.*

RESEARCH CENTERS AND INSTITUTES

Materials Processing Center. Massachusetts Institute of Technology, 77 Massachusetts Ave., Room 12-007, Cambridge, MA 02139-4307. Phone: (617)253-5179 Fax: (617)258-6900 E-mail: fmpage@.mit.edu • URL: http://www.web.mit.edu/mpc/www/ • Conducts processing, engineering, and economic research in ferrous and nonferrous metals, ceramics, polymers, photonic materials, superconductors, welding, composite materials, and other materials.

STATISTICS SOURCES

U. S. Industry and Trade Outlook: The McGraw-Hill Companies and the U.S. Department of Commerce/International Trade Administration. Datapso Research Corp. • Annual. $69.95. Produced by the International Trade Administration, U. S. Department of Commerce, in a "public-private" partnership with DRI/McGraw-Hill and Standard & Poor's. Provides basic data, outlook for the current year, and "Long-Term Prospects" (five-year projections) for a wide variety of products and services. Includes high technology industries. Formerly *U. S. Industrial Outlook*.

United States Census of Service Industries. U.S. Bureau of the Census. • Quinquennial. Various reports available.

TRADE/PROFESSIONAL ASSOCIATIONS

American Council of the International Institute of Welding. 550 N.W. LeJeune Rd., Miami, FL 33126. Phone: 800-443-9353 or (305)443-9353 Fax: (305)443-7559 E-mail: aciiw@amweld.org • URL: http://www.iiw-iis.org.

American Welding Society. 550 N.W. Le Jeune Rd., Miami, FL 33126. Phone: 800-443-9353 or (305)443-9353 Fax: (305)443-7559 E-mail: info@aws.org • URL: http://www.aws.org.

National Welding Supply Association. 1900 Arch St., Philadelphia, PA 19103. Phone: (215)564-3484 Fax: (215)564-2175 E-mail: nwsa@nwsa.com • URL: http://www.nwsa.com.

Resistance Welder Manufacturers' Association. 1900 Arch St., Philadelphia, PA 19103-1498. Phone: (215)564-3484 Fax: (215)963-9785 E-mail: rwma@fernley.com • URL: http://www.rwma.org.

Welding Research Council. Three Park Ave., 27th Fl., New York, NY 10016-5902. Phone: (212)591-7956 Fax: (212)591-7183 • URL: http://www.forengineers.org/wrc.

WELFARE, PUBLIC

See: PUBLIC WELFARE

WELLNESS PROGRAMS

See: EMPLOYEE WELLNESS PROGRAMS

WHARVES

See: PORTS

WHEAT INDUSTRY

See also: COMMODITY FUTURES TRADING; FLOUR INDUSTRY; GRAIN INDUSTRY

ABSTRACTS AND INDEXES

Wheat, Barley, and Triticale Abstracts. Available from CABI Publishing North America. • Bimonthly. $895.00 per year. Published in England by CABI Publishing. Provides worldwide coverage of the literature of wheat, barley, and rye.

ALMANACS AND YEARBOOKS

CRB Commodity Yearbook. Commodity Research Bureau. CRB. • Annual. $99.95.

INTERNET DATABASES

Fedstats. Federal Interagency Council on Statistical Policy. Phone: (202)395-7254 • URL: http://www.fedstats.gov • Web site features an efficient search facility for full-text statistics produced by more than 70 federal agencies, including the Census Bureau, the Bureau of Economic Analysis, and the Bureau of Labor Statistics. Boolean searches can be made within one agency or for all agencies combined. Links are offered to international statistical bureaus, including the UN, IMF, OECD, UNESCO, Eurostat, and 20 individual countries. Fees: Free.

USDA. United States Department of Agriculture. Phone: (202)720-2791 E-mail: agsec@usda.gov • URL: http://www.usda.gov • The USDA home page has six sections: News and Information; What's New; About USDA; Agencies; Opportunities; Search and Help. Keyword searching is offered from the USDA home page and from various individual agency home pages. Agencies are the Economic Research Service, Agricultural Marketing Service, National Agricultural Statistics Service, National Agricultural Library, and about 12 others. Updating varies. Fees: Free.

ONLINE DATABASES

Biological and Agricultural Index Online. H. W. Wilson Co. • Indexes a wide variety of agricultural and biological periodicals, 1983 to date. Monthly updates. Inquire as to online cost and availability.

CAB Abstracts. CAB International North America. • Contains 46 specialized abstract collections covering over 10,000 journals and monographs in the areas of agriculture, horticulture, forest products, farm products, nutrition, dairy science, poultry, grains, animal health, entomology, etc. Time period is 1972 to date, with monthly updates. Inquire as to online cost and availability. *CAB Abstracts on CD-ROM* also available, with annual updating.

DRI U.S. Central Database. Data Products Division. • Provides more than 23,000 business, financial, demographic, economic, foreign trade, and industry-related time series for the U.S. Includes national income, population, retail-wholesale trade, price indexes, labor data, housing, industrial production, banking, interest rates, money supply, etc. Time period is generally 1947 to date (some data back to 1929). Updating varies. Inquire as to online cost and availability.

PERIODICALS AND NEWSLETTERS

Kansas Farmer. Farm Progress Cos. • 15 times a year. $19.95 per year.

Montana Farmer. Western Farmer-Stockman Magazines. • Monthly. $15.00. per year.

Oregon Wheat. Oregon Wheat Growers League. • Monthly. Free to members; non-members, $15.00 per year. Deals with planting, weeds, and disease warnings, storage and marketing of wheat and barley. Specifically for Oregon growers.

Wheat Life. Washington Association of Wheat Growers. • 11 times a year. $12.00 per year. Covers research, marketing information, and legislative and regulatory news pertinent to the wheat and barley industries of the Pacific Northwest.

PRICE SOURCES

Nebraska Farmer. Nebraska Farmer Co. Farm Progress Cos. • 15 times a year. $19.95 per year.

STATISTICS SOURCES

Agricultural Statistics. Available from U. S. Government Printing Office. • Annual. Produced by the National Agricultural Statistics Service, U. S. Department of Agriculture. Provides a wide variety of statistical data relating to agricultural production, supplies, consumption, prices/price-supports, foreign trade, costs, and returns, as well as farm labor, loans, income, and population. In many cases, historical data is shown annually for 10 years. In addition to farm data, includes detailed fishery statistics.

Business Statistics of the United States. Courtenay M. Slater, editor. Bernan Associates. • 1999. $74.00. Fifth edition. Based on *Business Statistics*, formerly issue by the Bureau of Economic Analysis, U. S. Department of Commerce. Provides basic data for a wide variety of U. S. industries, services, and economic indicators. Most statistics are shown annually for 29 years and monthly for the most recent four years.

Chicago Board of Trade Statistical Annual. Board of Trade of the City of Chicago. • Annual.

FAO Quarterly Bulletin of Statistics. Food and Agriculture Organization of the United Nations. Available from UNIPUB. • Quarterly. $20.00 per year. Provides international data on agricultural production, trade, and prices, covering the major commodities of many countries. Text in English, French, and Spanish. Formerly *FAO Monthly Bulletin of Statistics.*

Flour Milling Products. U. S. Bureau of the Census. • Monthly and annual. Covers production, mill stocks, exports, and imports of wheat and rye flour. (Current Industrial Reports, M20A.).

International Grains Council. World Grain Statistics. International Grains Council. • Annual. $125.00. Text in English, French, Russian and Spanish. Formerly *International Wheat Council. World Grain Statistics.*

Statistical Annual: Grains, Options on Agricultural Futures. Chicago Board of Trade. • Annual. Includes historical data on Wheat Futures, Options on Wheat Futures, Corn Futures, Options on Corn Futures, Oats Futures, Soybean Futures, Options on Soybean Futures, Soybean Oil Futures, Soybean Meal Futures.

Survey of Current Business. Available from U. S. Government Printing Office. • Monthly. $49.00 per year. Issued by Bureau of Economic Analysis, U. S. Department of Commerce. Presents a wide variety of business and economic data.

WEFA Industrial Monitor. John Wiley and Sons, Inc. • Annual. $65.00. Prepared by industry analysts at WEFA, an economic forecasting and consulting firm (originally Wharton Econometric Forecasting Associates). Contains discussions of the outlook for major U. S. industries, with many 10-year forecasts (WEFA Web site is http://www.wefa.com).

Wheat Facts. National Association of Wheat Growers. • Annual. Price on application.

World Trade Annual. United Nations Statistical Office. Walker and Co. • Annual. Prices vary.

TRADE/PROFESSIONAL ASSOCIATIONS

National Association of Wheat Growers. 415 Second St., N.E., Suite 300, Washington, DC 20002. Phone: (202)547-7800 Fax: (202)546-2638 E-mail: wheatworld@wheatworld.org • URL: http://www.wheatworld.org.

North American Millers' Association. 600 Maryland Ave., S.W., Suite 305-W, Washington, DC 20024-2573. Phone: (202)484-2200 Fax: (202)488-7416.

United States Durum Growers Association. c/o Diane Scheflo, 824 Thompson St., Bottineau, ND 58318. Phone: (701)228-3057 Fax: (701)228-3057 • URL: http://www.durumgrowers.com.

U.S. Wheat Associates. 1620 Eye St., N.W., Suite 801, Washington, DC 20006. Phone: (202)463-0999 Fax: (202)785-1052 • URL: http://www.uswheat.org.

OTHER SOURCES

Grains: Production, Processing, Marketing. Chicago Board of Trade. • 1992. $12.00. Revised edition.

WHISKEY INDUSTRY

See: DISTILLING INDUSTRY

WHITE COLLAR CRIME

See: CRIME AND CRIMINALS; FRAUD AND EMBEZZLEMENT

WHOLESALE TRADE

See also: DISTRIBUTION; RACK JOBBERS

CD-ROM DATABASES

16 Million Businesses Phone Directory. Info USA. • Annual. $29.95. Provides more than 16 million yellow pages telephone directory listings on CD-ROM for all ZIP Code areas of the U. S.

DIRECTORIES

American Big Businesses Directory. American Business Directories. • Annual. $595.00. Lists 177,000 public and private U. S. companies in all fields having 100 or more employees. Includes sales volume, number of employees, and name of chief executive. Formerly *Big Businesses Directory.*

American Business Directory. InfoUSA, Inc. • Provides brief online information on more than 10 million U. S. companies, including individual plants and branches. Entries typically include address, phone number, industry classification code, and contact name. Updating is quarterly. Inquire as to online cost and availability.

American Manufacturers Directory. American Business Directories. • Annual. $595.00. Lists more than 150,000 public and private U. S. manufacturers having 20 or more employees. Includes sales volume, number of employees, and name of chief executive or owner.

American Wholesalers and Distributors Directory. The Gale Group. • 2000. $215.00. Eighth edition. Lists more than 27,000 national, regional, state, and local wholesalesrs.

Directory of Automotive Aftermarket Suppliers. Chain Store Guide. • Annual. $300.00. Covers auto supply store chains. Includes distributors.

Directory of Building Products and Hardlines Distributors. Chain Store Guide. • Annual. $280.00. Includes hardware, houseware, and building supply distributors. Formerly *Directory of Hardline Distributors.*

Directory of Computer and Consumer Electronics. Chain Store Age. • Annual. $290.00. Includes 2,900 "leading" retailers and over 200 "top" distributors. Formerly *Directory of Consumer Electronics Retails and Distributors.*

Directory of Discount and General Merchandise Stores. Chain Store Guide. • Annual. $300.00. Includes retailers and wholesalers of housewares, giftwares, novelties, toys, hobby materials, crafts, and stationery. Formerly *Directory of Discount Stores Catalog Showrooms.*

Directory of Foodservice Distributors. Chain Store Guide. • Annual. $290.00. Covers distributors of food and equipment to restaurants and institutions.

Directory of Home Furnishings Retailers. Chain Store Guide. • Annual. $290.00. Includes more than 4,800 furniture retailers and wholesalers.

Directory of Single Unit Supermarket Operators. Chain Store Guide. • Annual. $290.00. Covers more than 7,100 one-store supermarket establishments with annual sales of at least $1,000,000. Includes names of primary wholesalers.

Directory of Wholesale Grocers: Service Merchandisers. Chain Store Age. • Annual. $300.00. Profiles over 2,000 cooperatives, voluntaries, non-sponsoring wholesalers, cash and carry warehouses, and nearly 220 service merchandisers. Formerly *Directory of Cooperatives, Voluntaries, and Wholesale Grocers.*

European Directory of Retailers and Wholesalers. Available from The Gale Group. • 1997. $790.00. Second edition. Published by Euromonitor. Provides detailed information on more than 4,000 major retail and wholesale businesses in 17 countries of Western Europe. Contains 26 categories, such as supermarkets, superstores, department stores, discount stores, franchise operators, mail order, etc. Includes company, product, and geographic indexes.

Grocery Distribution Magazine Directory of Warehouse Equipment, Fixtures, and Services. Trend Publishing, Inc. • Annual. $7.50. Covers products related to food warehousing, distribution, and storage.

The Wholesaler "Wholesaling 100". TMB Publishing, Inc. • Annual. $25.00. Provides information on the 100 leading wholesalers of plumbing, piping, heating, and air conditioning equipment.

FINANCIAL RATIOS

Almanac of Business and Industrial Financial Ratios. Leo Troy. Prentice Hall. • Annual. $99.95. Contains financial ratios derived from federal tax returns. Ratios for each of about 200 industries are arranged according to company asset size.

INTERNET DATABASES

Bureau of Economic Analysis (BEA). U. S. Department of Commerce, Bureau of Economic Analysis. Phone: (202)606-9900 Fax: (202)606-5310 E-mail: webmaster@bea.doc.gov • URL: http://www.bea.doc.gov • Web site includes "News Release Information" covering national, regional, and international economic estimates from the BEA. Highlights of releases appear online the same day, complete text and tables appear the next day. "Recent News Releases" section provides titles for past nine months, with links. "BEA Data and Methodology" includes "Frequently Requested NIPA Data" (national income and product accounts, such as gross domestic product and personal income). Other statistics are available. Fees: Free.

Fedstats. Federal Interagency Council on Statistical Policy. Phone: (202)395-7254 • URL: http://www.fedstats.gov • Web site features an efficient search facility for full-text statistics produced by more than 70 federal agencies, including the Census Bureau, the Bureau of Economic Analysis, and the Bureau of Labor Statistics. Boolean searches can be made within one agency or for all agencies combined. Links are offered to international statistical bureaus, including the UN, IMF, OECD, UNESCO, Eurostat, and 20 individual countries. Fees: Free.

ONLINE DATABASES

Business and Industry. Responsive Database Services, Inc. • Contains online citations, abstracts, and selected fulltext from more than 1,000 trade journals, newspapers, and other publications. Provides general coverage of both manufacturing and service industries, including marketing, production, industry trends, key events, and information on specific companies. Time span is 1994 to date. Daily updates. Inquire as to online cost and availability. (Also available in a CD-ROM version.).

DRI U.S. Central Database. Data Products Division. • Provides more than 23,000 business, financial, demographic, economic, foreign trade, and industry-related time series for the U.S. Includes national income, population, retail-wholesale trade, price indexes, labor data, housing, industrial production, banking, interest rates, money supply, etc. Time period is generally 1947 to date (some data back to 1929). Updating varies. Inquire as to online cost and availability.

Tablebase. Responsive Database Services, Inc. • Provides online numerical tabular data from a wide variety of business, organization, and government sources, including 900 trade journals. Includes industry and individual company statistics relating to products, market share, sales forecasts, production, exports, market trends, etc. Time span is 1997 to date. Weekly updates. Inquire as to online cost and availability. (Also available in a CD-ROM version.).

PERIODICALS AND NEWSLETTERS

Grocery Headquarters: The Newspaper for the Food Industry. Trend Publishing, Inc. • Monthly. $100.00 per year. Covers the sale and distribution of food products and other items sold in supermarkets and grocery stores. Edited mainly for retailers and wholesalers. Formerly *Grocery Marketing.*

The Wholesaler. TMB Publishing, Inc. • Monthly. $75.00 per year. Edited for wholesalers and distributors of plumbing, piping, heating, and air conditioning equipment.

PRICE SOURCES

PPI Detailed Report. Bureau of Labor Statistics, U.S. Department of Labor. Available from U.S. Government Printing Office. • Monthly. $55.00 per year. Formerly *Producer Price Indexes.*

STATISTICS SOURCES

Business Statistics of the United States. Courtenay M. Slater, editor. Bernan Associates. • 1999. $74.00. Fifth edition. Based on *Business Statistics*, formerly issue by the Bureau of Economic Analysis, U. S. Department of Commerce. Provides basic data for a wide variety of U. S. industries, services, and economic indicators. Most statistics are shown annually for 29 years and monthly for the most recent four years.

Encyclopedia of American Industries. The Gale Group. • 1998. $560.00. Second edition. Two volumes. $280.00 per volume. Volume one is *Manufacturing Industries* and volume two is *Service and Non-Manufacturing Industries.* Provides the history, development, and recent status of approximately 1,000 industries. Includes statistical graphs, with industry and general indexes.

Survey of Current Business. Available from U. S. Government Printing Office. • Monthly. $49.00 per year. Issued by Bureau of Economic Analysis, U. S. Department of Commerce. Presents a wide variety of business and economic data.

U. S. Industry Profiles: The Leading 100. The Gale Group. • 1998. $120.00. Second edition. Contains detailed profiles, with statistics, of 100 industries in the areas of manufacturing, construction, transportation, wholesale trade, retail trade, and entertainment.

United States Census of Wholesale Trade. Bureau of the Census, U.S. Department of Commerce. Available from U.S. Government Printing Office. • Quinquennial.

WEFA Industrial Monitor. John Wiley and Sons, Inc. • Annual. $65.00. Prepared by industry analysts at WEFA, an economic forecasting and consulting firm (originally Wharton Econometric Forecasting Associates). Contains discussions of the outlook for major U. S. industries, with many 10-year forecasts (WEFA Web site is http://www.wefa.com).

TRADE/PROFESSIONAL ASSOCIATIONS

National Association of Wholesaler-Distributors. 1725 K St., N.W., Washington, DC 20006. Phone: (202)872-0885 Fax: (202)785-0586 E-mail: meetings@nawd.org • URL: http://www.nawmeetings.org.

OTHER SOURCES

The Business Elite: Database of Corporate America. Donnelley Marketing. • Quarterly. $795.00. Formerly compiled by Database America. Provides current information on CD-ROM for about 850,000 businesses, comprising all U. S. private and public companies having more than 20 employees or sales of more than $1 million. Data for each firm includes detailed industry classification, year started, annual sales, name of top executive, and number of employees.

Manufacturing and Distribution USA. The Gale Group. • 2000. $375.00. Three volumes. Replaces *Manufacturing USA* and *Wholesale and Retail Trade USA.* Presents statistics and projections relating to economic activity in more than 500 business classifications.

Product Distribution Law Guide. CCH, Inc. • Looseleaf. $199.00. Annual updates available. Covers the legal aspects of various methods of product distribution, including franchising.

WILLS

See also: ESTATE PLANNING

HANDBOOKS AND MANUALS

The Complete Probate Kit. Jen C. Appel and F. Bruce Gentry. John Wiley and Sons, Inc. • 1991. $29.95. A practical guide to settling estates. Provides summaries of the applicable state laws and definitions of relevant terms.

Inheritor's Handbook: A Definitive Guide for Beneficiaries. Dan Rottenberg. Bloomberg Press. • 1998. $23.95. Covers both financial and emotional issues faced by beneficiaries. (Bloomberg Personal Bookshelf Series.).

Murphy's Will Clauses: Annotations and Forms with Tax Effects. Matthew Bender & Co., Inc. • $928.00. Four looseleaf volumes. Periodic supplementation. Over 1,400 framed will clauses.

TRADE/PROFESSIONAL ASSOCIATIONS

American College of Trust and Estate Counsel. 3415 S. Sepulveda Blvd., Suite 330, Los Angeles, CA 90034. Phone: (310)398-1888 Fax: (310)572-7280 E-mail: info@actec.org • URL: http://www.actec.org.

OTHER SOURCES

Estate Planning: Wills, Trusts and Forms. Research Institute of America. • Looseleaf service. Includes bimonthly *Report Bulletins* and updates.

WIND ENERGY

See: COGENERATION OF ENERGY

WINDOW COVERING INDUSTRY

See also: INTERIOR DECORATION

GENERAL WORKS

Curtains, Blinds and Valances. Yvonne Rees. F & W Publications, Inc. • 1998. $18.99. (Sew in a Weekend Series).

Window Treatments. Karla J. Nielson. John Wiley and Sons, Inc. • 1989. $75.00.

ABSTRACTS AND INDEXES

Art Index. H. W. Wilson Co. • Quarterly. Annual cumulations. Service basis for print edition; CD-ROM edition, $1,495.00 per year. Subject and author index to periodicals in art, architecture, industrial design, city planning, photography, and various related topics.

BIOGRAPHICAL SOURCES

Who's Who in Interior Design. Baron's Who's Who. • Annual. $280.00. Contains biographical data for over 3,500 interior designers worldwide.

CD-ROM DATABASES

WILSONDISC: Art Index. H. W. Wilson Co. • Monthly. $1,495.00 per year. Provides CD-ROM indexing of art-related literature from 1982 to date. Price includes online service.

DIRECTORIES

Directory of the Decorating Products Industry. Painting and Decorating Retailers Association. • Annual. $595.00. Lists nearly 2,800 retailers of window treatments, wall coverings, floor coverings, etc. Formerly *Directory of Decorating Products Retailers.* Formerly National Decorating Products Association.

Draperies and Window Coverings: Directory and Buyer's Guide. L. C. Clark Publishing Co., Inc. • Annual. $15.00. Includes about 2,000 manufacturers and distributors of window coverings and related products.

Home Fashions: Buyer's Guide. Fairchild Publications. • Annual. $10.00. Lists manufacturers, importers, and regional sales representatives supplying bed, bath, kitchen, and table linens; window treatments; wall coverings; and fibers and fabrics.

LDB Interior Textiles Buyer's Guide. E.W. Williams Publications Co. • Annual. $40.00. Includes over 2,000 manufacturers, distributors, and importers of curtains, draperies, hard window treatments, bedspreads, pillows, etc. Formerly *LDB Interior Textiles Directory.*

Window Fashions Magazine. G & W McNamara Publishing, Inc. • Monthly. $39.00 per year. A directory of suppliers, manufacturers, and fabricators of vertical blinds, soft shades, curtains, draperies, and other window treatment items. Appears as a regular feature of *Window Fashions Magazine* and covers a different product category each month.

FINANCIAL RATIOS

Annual Statement Studies. Robert Morris Associates: The Association of Lending and Credit Risk Professiona. • Annual. Free to members; non-members, $140.00. Median and quartile financial ratios are given for over 400 kinds of manufacturing, wholesale, retail, construction, and consumer finance establishments. Data is sorted by both asset size and sales volume. Includes a clearly written "Definition of Ratios" and an alphabetical industry index.

HANDBOOKS AND MANUALS

Custom Draperies in Interior Design. M. Neal. Prentice Hall. • 1982. $40.25.

ONLINE DATABASES

Art Index Online. H. W. Wilson Co. • Indexes a wide variety of art-related periodicals, 1984 to date. Monthly updates. Inquire as to online cost and availability.

Avery Architecture Index. Avery Architectural and Fine Arts Library. • Indexes a wide range of periodicals related to architecture and design. Subjects include building design, building materials, interior design, housing, land use, and city planning. Time span: 1977 to date. *bul* URL: http://www-rlg.stanford.edu/cit-ave.html.

Globalbase. The Gale Group. • Provides more than one million online summaries of business, industrial, and economic news reports from more than 1,000 publications worldwide. Covers a wide range of material appearing in international trade journals, professional magazines, and newspapers. Time period is 1984 to date, with weekly updates. Inquire as to online cost and availability.

PROMT: Predicasts Overview of Markets and Technology. The Gale Group. • Companies, products, applied technologies and markets. U.S. and international literature coverage, 1972 to date. Inquire as to online cost and availability. Provides abstracts from more than 1,600 publications. Weekly updates.

PERIODICALS AND NEWSLETTERS

Draperies and Window Coverings. L. C. Clark Publishing Co., Inc. • 13 times a year. $33.00 per year. Published for retailers, designers, manufacturers, and distributors of window coverings.

Home Fashions Magazine. Fairchild Fashion and Merchandising Group. • Monthly. $30.00 per year.

LDB Interior Textiles. E.W. Williams Publications Co. • Monthly. $66.00 per year. Supplement available *Linens, Domestics and Baths-Interior Textile Annual Buyer's Guide.* Formerly *Interior Textiles.*

Waland Window Trends. Cygnus Business Media. • Monthly $36.00 per year. Edited for retailers of interior decoration products, with an emphasis on wallcoverings. Formerly *Wallcoverings, Windows and Interior Fashion.*

Window Fashions. G & W McNamara Publishing, Inc. • Monthly. $39.00 per year. Published for designers and retailers of draperies, blinds, and shades.

RESEARCH CENTERS AND INSTITUTES

Interior Design Laboratory. Lambuth University, P.O. Box 431, Jackson, TN 38301. Phone: (901)425-3275 Fax: (901)425-3497.

TRADE/PROFESSIONAL ASSOCIATIONS

Contractors Co-Op Council. 7077 Orangewood Ave., Suite 120, Garden Grove, CA 92641. Phone: (714)898-0583 Fax: (714)891-5616 • Members are custom drapery merchants.

Home Fashions Products Association. 355 Lexington Ave., 17th Fl., New York, NY 10017-6603. Phone: (212)297-2122 Fax: (212)370-9047 • Members are manufacturers of curtains and draperies.

Window Covering Manufacturers Association. 355 Lexington Ave., 17th Fl., New York, NY 10017. Phone: (212)661-4261 Fax: (212)370-9047 E-mail: assocmgmt@aol.com • Members are manufacturers of venetian blinds, vertical blinds, and pleated shades.

WINDOW DISPLAYS

See: DISPLAY OF MERCHANDISE

WINDOWS (SOFTWARE)

See also: COMPUTER SOFTWARE INDUSTRY

GENERAL WORKS

Computing Essentials: Introducing Windows 95. Don Cassel. Prentice Hall. • 1997. $7.77. A Windows primer.

Introducing Windows 95: The Next Generation of Microsoft Windows. Microsoft Press. • 1995. $12.95. An introductory description of features. (Professional Editions Series).

The Mother of All Windows 98 Books. Woody Leonhard and Barry Simon. Addison-Wesley Longman, Inc. • 1999. $39.95.

Windows 98 for Dummies. IDG Books Worldwide. • 1999. $19.99.

Windows 98 in a Nutshell. Tim O'Reilly and Troy Mott. O'Reilly & Associates, Inc. • 1999. $24.95. (Nutshell Handbooks.).

Windows 95 for Busy People. Ron Mansfield. Osborne/McGraw-Hill. • 1997. $24.99. Second edition. A basic guide to Windows, featuring many illustrations.

Windows 95 is Driving Me Crazy! A Practical Guide to Windows 95 Headaches, Hassles, Bugs, Potholes, and Installation Problems. Kay Y. Nelson. Peachpit Press. • 1996. $24.95. Includes many illustrations.

ABSTRACTS AND INDEXES

CompuMath Citation Index. Institute for Scientific Information. • Three times a year. $1,090.00 per year. Provides citations to the worldwide literature of computer science and mathematics.

Computer and Information Systems Abstracts Journal: An Abstract Journal Pertaining to the Theory, Design, Fabrication and Application of Computer and Information Systems. Cambridge Information Group. • Monthly. $1,045 per year.

Computer Literature Index: A Subject/Author Index to Computer and Data Processing Literature. Applied Computer Research, Inc. • Quarterly, with annual cumulation. $245.00 per year. Contains brief abstracts of book and periodical literature covering all phases of computing, including approximately 70 specific application areas.

CD-ROM DATABASES

Computer Select. The Gale Group. • Monthly. $1,250.00 per year. Provides one year of full-text on CD-ROM for 120 leading computer-related publications. Also includes 70,000 product specifications and brief profiles of 13,000 computer product vendors and manufacturers.

DIRECTORIES

Data Sources: The Comprehensive Guide to the Data Processing Industry Hardware, Data Communications Products, Software, Company Profiles. The Gale Group. • Semiannual. $495.00 per year. Two volumes. Describes hardware and software for all computer operating sysems, including prices and technical details. Lists about 75,000 products from 14,000 suppliers. Industry-specific software applications are described.

The Software Encyclopedia: A Guide for Personal, Professional, and Business Users. R. R. Bowker. • Annual. $255.00. Two volumes. Volume one lists software programs by title and producer. Volume two provides information on programs according to application and operating system. Includes prices and requirements for hardware and memory.

HANDBOOKS AND MANUALS

Networking Windows for Workgroups. Barry Nance. John Wiley and Sons, Inc. • 1993. $22.95. Designed for small businesses or small groups. Covers the installation and troubleshooting of local area networks using Microsoft's Windows for Workgroups.

System Administrator's Guide to Windows NT Server 5. Robin Burke. Simon And Schuster Trade. • 1999. $49.99.

UNIX and Windows 2000 Integration Toolkit: A Complete Guide for System Administrators and Developers. Rawn Shah. John Wiley and Sons, Inc. • 2000. $49.99. Includes CD-ROM.

UNIX and Windows 2000: Interoperability Guide. Alan Roberts. Prentice Hall. • 2000. $44.99.

Unix Secrets. James Armstrong. IDG Books Worldwide. • 1999. $49.99. Second edition.

Windows Internet Tour Guide: Cruising the Internet the Easy Way. Michael Fraase and Phil James. Ventana Communications Group, Inc. • 1995. $29.95. Second edition., An introduction to the Internet via Windows software.

Windows Millennium: The Missing Manual - The Book That Should Have Been in the Box. David Pogue. O'Reilly & Associates, Inc. • 2000. $19.95. Popularly written explanation of Windows ME features. (Pogue Press.).

Windows 98 Bible. Fred Davis and Kip Crosby. Available from Addison-Wesley Longman, Inc. • 1998. $34.95. Published by Peachpit Press (http://www.peachpit.com).

Windows 98 Unleashed. Paul McFedries. Pearson Education and Technology. • 1998. $34.99.

Windows 98: Visual Quick-Start Guide. Steve Sagman. Available from Addison-Wesley Longman,

Inc. • 1998. Price on application. Published by Peachpit Press (http://www.peachpit.com).

Windows 95: The Complete Reference. John Levine and Margaret L. Young. Osborne/McGraw-Hill. • 1997. $39.99. Provides detailed coverage of the various Windows attributes.

Windows 97 Professional Reference. Joe Casad. Pearson Education and Technology. • 1999. $59.99.

Windows NT Administrators Handbook. Mark Graham and Becky Campbell. Simon and Schuster Trade. • 1997. $24.99.

Windows NT Server Concise. Jerry Dixon and J. Scott Reeves. Pearson Education and Technology. • Date not set. $19.99.

Windows NT System Administration. Pearson Education and Technology. • 1999. Price on application.

Windows 2000 Performance Guide: Help for Windows 2000 Administrators. Mark Friedman. O'Reilly & Associates, Inc. • 2001. $39.95.

Windows 2000 Professional Reference. Karanjit Siyan. Pearson Education and Technology. • 2000. $75.00. Third edition.

Windows 2000 System Administration Handbook. David Watts and others. Prentice Hall. • 2000. $59.99.

INTERNET DATABASES

InfoTech Trends. Data Analysis Group. Phone: (707)894-9100 Fax: (707)486-5618 E-mail: support@infotechtrends.com • URL: http://www.infotechtrends.com • Web site provides both free and fee-based market research data on the information technology industry, including computers, peripherals, telecommunications, the Internet, software, CD-ROM/DVD, e-commerce, and workstations. Fees: Free for current (most recent year) data; more extensive information has various fee structures. Formerly *Computer Industry Forecasts.*

ONLINE DATABASES

Computer Database. The Gale Group. • Provides online citations with abstracts to material appearing in about 150 trade journals and newsletters in the subject areas of computers, telecommunications, and electronics. Time period is 1983 to date, with weekly updates. Inquire as to online cost and availability.

Hard Sciences. Cambridge Scientific Abstracts. • Provides the online version of *Computer and Information Systems Abstracts, Electronics and Communications Abstracts, Health and Safety Science Abstracts, ISMEC: Mechanical Engineering Abstracts (Information Service in Mechanical Engineering)* and *Solid State and Superconductivity Abstracts.* Time period is 1981 to date, with monthly updates. Inquire as to online cost and availability.

Internet and Personal Computing Abstracts. Information Today, Inc. • Contains abstracts covering a wide variety of personal and business microcomputer literature appearing in more than 100 journals and popular magazines. Time period is 1981 to date, with monthly updates. Formerly *Microcomputer Index.* Inquire as to online cost and availability.

Microcomputer Software Guide Online. R. R. Bowker. • Provides information on more than 30,000 microcomputer software applications from more than 4,000 producers. Corresponds to printed *Software Encyclopedia*, but with monthly updates. Inquire as to online cost and availability.

PERIODICALS AND NEWSLETTERS

Exploring Windows NT: Tips & Techniques for Microsoft Windows NT Professionals. Z-D Journals. • Monthly. $99.00 per year. Newsletter on the Windows operating system for networks.

MSDN Magazine (Microsoft Systems for Developers). • Monthly. $84.95 per year. Produced for professional software developers using Windows, MS-DOS, Visual Basic, and other Microsoft Corporation products. Incorporates *Microsoft Systems Journal.*

Windows Developer's Journal. Miller Freeman, Inc. • Monthly. $34.99 per year. Edited for advanced programming developers working under DOS and Windows. Formerly *Windows-DOS Developer's Journal.*

Windows NT Systems: The Magazine for Windows NT Systems Management and Administration. Miller Freeman. • Monthly. $39.95 per year. Provides articles on Windows NT administration, communications, and performance.

Windows 2000 Magazine. Duke Communications International. • Monthly. $39.95 per year. Edited for information systems personnel developing business applications for Windows NT software.

RESEARCH CENTERS AND INSTITUTES

Center for Research in Computing Technology. Harvard University, Pierce Hall, 29 Oxford St., Cambridge, MA 02138. Phone: (617)495-2832 Fax: (617)495-9837 E-mail: cheatham@das.harvard.edu • URL: http://www.das.harvard.edu/cs.grafs.html • Conducts research in computer vision, robotics, artificial intelligence, systems programming, programming languages, operating systems, networks, graphics, database management systems, and telecommunications.

OTHER SOURCES

Windows ME Annoyances. David Karp. O'Reilly & Associates, Inc. • 2001. $29.95. A critical but helpful view of Windows Millennium Edition.

Windows Millennium Edition: The Complete Reference. John R. Levine and Margaret L. Young. Osborne-McGraw. • 2000. $39.99. Includes CD-ROM.

Windows NT Administration and Security. Richard O. Hudson. Prentice Hall. • 2001. $79.00.

Windows 2000 Commands Pocket Reference. Aeleen Frisch. O'Reilly & Associates, Inc. • 2001. $9.95.

Windows 2000 Quick Fixes. Jim Boyce. O'Reilly & Associates, Inc. • 2000. $29.95. Covers troubleshooting for Windows 2000, both Professional Edition and Server Edition.

WINE INDUSTRY

See also: DISTILLING INDUSTRY

GENERAL WORKS

Wine: Nutritional and Therapeutic Benefits. Thomas R. Watkins, editor. American Chemical Society Publications. • 1997. $95.95. A review of wine chemistry, agronomic practice at vineyards, and the potential health benefits of wine drinking. (ACS Symposium Series, No. 661.).

ABSTRACTS AND INDEXES

VITIS: Viticulture and Enology Abstracts. Bundesanstalt fuer Zuechtungsforschungan an Kulturpflanzen Institut fuer Rebenzu. • Quarterly. $65.00 per year. Provides abstracts of journal and other literature relating to wine technology and the cultivation of grapes.

ALMANACS AND YEARBOOKS

The U.S. Wine Market: Impact Databank Review and Forecast. M. Shanken Communications, Inc. • Annual. $845.00. Includes industry commentary and statistics.

DIRECTORIES

The Beverage Marketing Directory. Beverage Marketing Corp. • Annual. $845.00. Provides information for approximately 11,000 beverage companies and suppliers to beverage companies. Includes sales volume and brand names. Formerly *National Beverage Marketing Directory.*

Wines and Vines: Directory of the Wine Industry in North America. Hiaring Co. • Annual. $65.00. List of wineries and wine bottlers in the United States, Canada, and Mexico; also lists industry suppliers.

ENCYCLOPEDIAS AND DICTIONARIES

Larousse Encyclopedia of Wine. Christopher Foulkes, editor. Larousse Kingfisher Chambers, Inc. • 1994. $40.00. Provides information on major wine producers of the world, with emphasis on French vineyards. Includes statistics and a glossary.

Oxford Companion to Wine. Jancis Robinson, editor. Oxford University Press, Inc. • 1999. $65.00. Second edition. Contains approximately 3,000 entries explaining the making of wine, varieties of wine, and characteristics of vineyards.

FINANCIAL RATIOS

Annual Statement Studies. Robert Morris Associates: The Association of Lending and Credit Risk Professiona. • Annual. Free to members; non-members, $140.00. Median and quartile financial ratios are given for over 400 kinds of manufacturing, wholesale, retail, construction, and consumer finance establishments. Data is sorted by both asset size and sales volume. Includes a clearly written "Definition of Ratios" and an alphabetical industry index.

HANDBOOKS AND MANUALS

Winemaking Basics. Cornelius S. Ough. Haworth Press, Inc. • 1992. $59.95. Covers all practical aspects of commercial winemaking from harvesting grapes to bottling and storage.

Winery Technology and Operations: A Handbook for Small Wineries. Yair Margalit. Wine Appreciation Guild. • 1990. $29.95. Covers a wide variety of topics from grape harvest to wine bottling, including aging and quality control.

INTERNET DATABASES

Fedstats. Federal Interagency Council on Statistical Policy. Phone: (202)395-7254 • URL: http://www.fedstats.gov • Web site features an efficient search facility for full-text statistics produced by more than 70 federal agencies, including the Census Bureau, the Bureau of Economic Analysis, and the Bureau of Labor Statistics. Boolean searches can be made within one agency or for all agencies combined. Links are offered to international statistical bureaus, including the UN, IMF, OECD, UNESCO, Eurostat, and 20 individual countries. Fees: Free.

ONLINE DATABASES

DRI U.S. Central Database. Data Products Division. • Provides more than 23,000 business, financial, demographic, economic, foreign trade, and industry-related time series for the U.S. Includes national income, population, retail-wholesale trade, price indexes, labor data, housing, industrial production, banking, interest rates, money supply, etc. Time period is generally 1947 to date (some data back to 1929). Updating varies. Inquire as to online cost and availability.

PERIODICALS AND NEWSLETTERS

American Journal of Enology and Viticulture. American Society for Enology and Viticulture. • Quarterly. $155.00 per year.

Fancy Food. Talcott Communications Corp. • Monthly. $34.00 per year. Emphasizes new specialty food products and the business management aspects of the specialty food and confection industries.

Includes special issues on wine, cheese, candy, "upscale" cookware, and gifts.

Impact: U.S. News and Research for the Wine, Spirits, and Beer Industries. M. Shanken Communications, Inc. • Biweekly. $375.00 per year. Newsletter covering the marketing, economic, and financial aspects of alcoholic beverages.

Kane's Beverage Week: The Newsletter of Beverage Marketing. Whitaker Newsletters, Inc. • Weekly. $449.00 per year. Newsletter. Covers news relating to the alcoholic beverage industries, including social, health, and legal issues.

Wine Business Monthly and Grower and Seller News. SmartWired Inc. • Monthly. $69.00 per year; students, $24.00 per year. Edited for executives in the North American wine making industry. Covers marketing, finance, export-import, management, new technology, etc.

Wine Enthusiast. • 13 times a year. $32.95 per year. Covers domestic and world wine. Formerly *Wine Times.*

The Wine Spectator. M. Shanken Communications, Inc. • 20 times a year. $40.00 per year. Wine ratings.

Wines and Vines: The Authoritative Voice of the Grape and Wine Industry. Hiaring Co. • Monthly. $32.50 per year.

PRICE SOURCES

Beverage Media. Beverage Media, Ltd. • Monthly. $78.00 per year. Wholesale prices.

Wine Price File. Wine Appreciation Guild. • Annual. $45.00. Lists prices of more than 90,000 "good to great" wines for collectors, wholesalers, retailers, and appraisers.

STATISTICS SOURCES

Business Statistics of the United States. Courtenay M. Slater, editor. Bernan Associates. • 1999. $74.00. Fifth edition. Based on *Business Statistics*, formerly issue by the Bureau of Economic Analysis, U. S. Department of Commerce. Provides basic data for a wide variety of U. S. industries, services, and economic indicators. Most statistics are shown annually for 29 years and monthly for the most recent four years.

Impact Beverage Trends in America. M. Shanken Communications, Inc. • Annual. $695.00. Detailed compilations of data for various segments of the liquor, beer, and soft drink industries.

Monthly Statistical Release: Wines. U.S. Bureau of Alcohol, Tobacco, and Firearms. • Monthly.

Survey of Current Business. Available from U. S. Government Printing Office. • Monthly. $49.00 per year. Issued by Bureau of Economic Analysis, U. S. Department of Commerce. Presents a wide variety of business and economic data.

TRADE/PROFESSIONAL ASSOCIATIONS

American Society for Enology and Viticulture. P.O. Box 1855, Davis, CA 95617. Phone: (530)753-3142 Fax: (530)753-3318 E-mail: society@asev.org • URL: http://www.asev.com.

American Wine Society. 3006 Latta Rd., Rochester, NY 14612. Phone: (716)225-7613 Fax: (716)225-7613 E-mail: aws@vicon.net • URL: http://www.vicon.net/~aws.

Society of Wine Educators. 1200 G St., N.W., Ste. 360, Washington, DC 20005. Phone: (202)347-5677 Fax: (202)347-5667 E-mail: vintage@erols.com.

Wine and Spirits Guild of America. c/o James Newberry. 30 W. 39th Ave., Ste. 106, San Mateo, CA 94403. Phone: (415)577-9800 Fax: (415)577-9805.

Wine and Spirits Wholesalers of America. 805 15th St., N.W., Suite 430, Washington, DC 20005. Phone: (202)371-9792 Fax: (202)789-2405 E-mail: juanita.duggan@wswa.org • URL: http://www.wswa.org.

Wine Institute. c/o Librarian, 425 Market St., Suite 1000, San Francisco, CA 94105. Phone: (415)512-0151 Fax: (415)442-0742 • URL: http://www.wineinstitute.org.

OTHER SOURCES

Concepts in Wine Chemistry. Yair Margalit. Wine Appreciation Guild. • 1997. $79.95. Explains wine chemical changes in fermentation, aging, cellaring, and shipping.

Liquor Control Law Reports: Federal and All States. CCH, Inc. • $3,338.00 per year. Nine looseleaf volumes. Biweekly updates. Federal and state regulation and taxation of alcoholic beverages.

Major Food and Drink Companies of the World. Available from The Gale Group. • 2001. $855.00. Fourth edition. Two volumes. Published by Graham & Whiteside. Contains profiles and trade names for more than 9,000 important food and beverage companies in various countries. In addition to foods, includes both alcoholic and nonalcoholic drink products.

Thomas Food and Beverage Market Place. Grey House Publishing. • Annual. $295.00. Three volumes. Contains more than 40,000 entries covering food companies, beverages, food equipment, warehouse companies, food brokers, wholesalers, importers, and exporters. Formerly *Thomas Food Industry Register.*

WIRE INDUSTRY

DIRECTORIES

Directory of Wire Companies of North America. CRU International. • Annual. $119.00. Profiles approximately 950 companies in the wire industry in North America. Also profiles fiber optic companies having to do with fiber optic cables and a supplier section profiling supplier companies.

Dun's Industrial Guide: The Metalworking Directory. Dun and Bradstreet Information Services Dun & Bradstreet Corp. • Annual. Libraries, $485; commercial institutions, $795.00. Lease basis. Three volumes. Lists about 65,000 U. S. manufacturing plants using metal and suppliers of metalworking equipment and materials. Includes names and titles of key personnel. Products, purchases, and processes are indicated.

Wire and Cable Technology International Buyers' Guide. Initial Publications, Inc. • Annual. $35.00. About 2,000 companies listed by product categories. Formerly *Wire Technology International Buyers' Guide.*

Wire Journal International Reference Guide. Wire Association International. Wire Journal, Inc. • Annual. Free to members; non-members, $125.00. Manufacturers and suppliers of steel and nonferrous rods, strip, wire, wire products, electrical wire and cable, fiber optics, and machinery and equipment to the industry.

FINANCIAL RATIOS

Annual Statement Studies. Robert Morris Associates: The Association of Lending and Credit Risk Professiona. • Annual. Free to members; non-members, $140.00. Median and quartile financial ratios are given for over 400 kinds of manufacturing, wholesale, retail, construction, and consumer finance establishments. Data is sorted by both asset size and sales volume. Includes a clearly written "Definition of Ratios" and an alphabetical industry index.

INTERNET DATABASES

Fedstats. Federal Interagency Council on Statistical Policy. Phone: (202)395-7254 • URL: http://www.fedstats.gov • Web site features an efficient search facility for full-text statistics produced by more than 70 federal agencies, including the Census Bureau, the Bureau of Economic Analysis, and the Bureau of Labor Statistics. Boolean searches can be made within one agency or for all agencies combined. Links are offered to international statistical bureaus, including the UN, IMF, OECD, UNESCO, Eurostat, and 20 individual countries. Fees: Free.

ONLINE DATABASES

DRI U.S. Central Database. Data Products Division. • Provides more than 23,000 business, financial, demographic, economic, foreign trade, and industry-related time series for the U.S. Includes national income, population, retail-wholesale trade, price indexes, labor data, housing, industrial production, banking, interest rates, money supply, etc. Time period is generally 1947 to date (some data back to 1929). Updating varies. Inquire as to online cost and availability.

PERIODICALS AND NEWSLETTERS

Wire Industry: International Monthly Journal. Publex International Ltd. • Monthly. $151.00 per year. News, information and technical articles on manufacture of wire, wire products and cable. International coverage.

Wire: International Technical Journal for the Wire and Cable Industries and All Areas of Wire Processing. Meisenbach GMBH. • Bimonthly. $70.00 per year. (English edition of *Draht-Welt.*).

Wire Journal International. Wire Association International. Wire Journal, Inc. • Monthly. $75.00 per year.

STATISTICS SOURCES

Annual Survey of Manufactures. Available from U. S. Government Printing Office. • Annual. Prices vary. Issued by the U. S. Census Bureau as an interim update to the *Census of Manufactures.* Includes data on number of manufacturing establishments in various industries, employment, labor costs, value of shipments, capital expenditures, inventories, energy costs, and assets. (See also Census Bureau home page, http://www.census.gov/.).

Business Statistics of the United States. Courtenay M. Slater, editor. Bernan Associates. • 1999. $74.00. Fifth edition. Based on *Business Statistics*, formerly issue by the Bureau of Economic Analysis, U. S. Department of Commerce. Provides basic data for a wide variety of U. S. industries, services, and economic indicators. Most statistics are shown annually for 29 years and monthly for the most recent four years.

Manufacturing Profiles. Available from U. S. Government Printing Office. • Annual. Issued by the U. S. Census Bureau. A printed consolidation of the entire *Current Industrial Report* series, presenting "all the data compiled." Contains statistics on production, shipments, inventories, consumption, exports, imports, and orders for a wide variety of manufactured products. (See also Census Bureau home page, http://www.census.gov/.).

Survey of Current Business. Available from U. S. Government Printing Office. • Monthly. $49.00 per year. Issued by Bureau of Economic Analysis, U. S. Department of Commerce. Presents a wide variety of business and economic data.

TRADE/PROFESSIONAL ASSOCIATIONS

American Wire Producers Association. 515 King St., Suite 420, Alexandria, VA 22314-3137. Phone: (703)549-6003 Fax: (703)684-6048 E-mail: info@awpa.org • URL: http://www.awpa.org.

Wire Association International. P.O. Box 578, Guilford, CT 06437. Phone: (203)453-2777 Fax: (203)453-8384 E-mail: jcoer@wirenet.org • URL: http://www.wirenet.org.

Wire Industry Suppliers Association. 111 Park Place, Falls Church, VA 22046-4513. Phone: (703)533-9530 Fax: (703)241-5603.

Wire Reinforcement Institute. P.O. Box 450, Findlay, OH 45839-0450. Phone: (419)425-9473 Fax: (419)425-5741 E-mail: wwri@bright.net • URL: http://www.bright.net/~rreiter.

WIRING, ELECTRIC

See: ELECTRICAL CONSTRUCTION INDUSTRY

WOMEN ACCOUNTANTS

ABSTRACTS AND INDEXES

Accounting and Tax Index. UMI. • Quarterly. Price on application. Includes annual cumulative bound volume. Indexes accounting, auditing, and taxation literature appearing in journals, books, pamphlets, conference proceedings, and newsletters. (UMI is University Microfilms International, a Bell & Howell Co.).

BIOGRAPHICAL SOURCES

Who's Who of American Women. Marquis Who's Who. • Biennial. $259.00. Provides over 27,000 biographical profiles of important women, including individuals prominent in business, finance, and industry.

INTERNET DATABASES

Rutgers Accounting Web (RAW). Rutgers University Accounting Research Center. Phone: (201)648-5172 Fax: (201)648-1233 • URL: http://www.rutgers.edu/accounting • RAW Web site provides extensive links to sources of national and international accounting information, such as the Big Six accounting firms, the Financial Accounting Standards Board (FASB), SEC filings (EDGAR), journals, publishers, software, the International Accounting Network, and "Internet's largest list of accounting firms in USA." Searching is offered. Fees: Free.

TRADE/PROFESSIONAL ASSOCIATIONS

American Society of Women Accountants. 60 Revere Dr., Suite 500, Northbrook, IL 60062. Phone: 800-326-2163 or (847)205-1029 Fax: (847)480-9282 E-mail: aswa@aswa.org • URL: http://www.aswa.org.

American Woman's Society of Certified Public Accountants. 401 N. Michigan Ave., Chicago, IL 60611. Phone: 800-297-2721 or (312)644-6610 Fax: (312)321-6869 E-mail: awscpa__hq@sba.com.

WOMEN ENGINEERS

BIOGRAPHICAL SOURCES

Who's Who of American Women. Marquis Who's Who. • Biennial. $259.00. Provides over 27,000 biographical profiles of important women, including individuals prominent in business, finance, and industry.

PERIODICALS AND NEWSLETTERS

SWE. Anne Perusek, editor. Society of Women Engineers. • Bimonthly. Members, $10.00 per year; non-members, $20.00 per year. Covers technical articles, continuing development, career guidance and recruitment and product advertising. Formerly *U.S. Woman Engineer.*

TRADE/PROFESSIONAL ASSOCIATIONS

Society of Women Engineers. 120 Wall St., 11th Fl., New York, NY 10005. Phone: (212)509-9577 Fax: (212)509-0224 • URL: http://www.swe.org.

WOMEN EXECUTIVES

See also: ENTREPRENEURS AND INTRAPRENEURS

GENERAL WORKS

Advancing Women in Business: The Catalyst Guide to Best Practices from the Corporate Leaders. Catalyst Staff. Available from Jossey-Bass, Inc., Publishers. • 1998. $26.00. Explains the human resources practices of corporations providing a favorable climate for the advancement of female employees.

Women Breaking Through: Overcoming the Final 10 Obstacles at Work. Deborah J. Swiss. Peterson's. • 1996. $24.95. Discusses specific strategies for women to use to advance beyond the middle management level. Based on a survey of 300 women "on the leading edge of change.".

Women Entrepreneurs: Moving Beyond the Glass Ceiling. Dorothy P. Moore and E. Holly Buttner. Sage Publications, Inc. • 1997. $46.00. Contains profiles of "129 successful female entrepreneurs who previously worked in corporate environments.".

Women in Management: Trends, Issues, and Challenges in Managerial Diversity. Ellen A. Fagenson, editor. Sage Publications, Inc. • 1993. $55.00. Includes material from 22 contributors on topics related to the experiences of women managers. (Women and Work Series, Vol. 4).

Women of the Street: Making It on Wall Street-the World's Toughest Business. Sue Herera. John Wiley and Sons, Inc. • 1997. $24.95. The author is a CNBC business television anchorperson.

ABSTRACTS AND INDEXES

Women Studies Abstracts. Transaction Publishers. • Quarterly. Individuals, $102.00 per year; institutions, $216.00 per year.

BIOGRAPHICAL SOURCES

Who's Who of American Women. Marquis Who's Who. • Biennial. $259.00. Provides over 27,000 biographical profiles of important women, including individuals prominent in business, finance, and industry.

DIRECTORIES

American Women Managers and Administrators: A Selective Biographical Dictionary of Twentieth Century Leaders in Business, Education, and Government. Greenwood Publishing Group Inc. • 1985. $75.00. A directory of 20th-century women who hold or have held administrative, managerial, or leadership positions in business, education, or government.

D & B Women-Owned Business Directory. Dun & Bradstreet Information Services. • 2000. Price on application.

National Association for Women in Education: Member Directory. NAWE: Advancing Women in Higher Education. • Membership. 2,000 American and foreign members.

National Directory of Women-Owned Business Firms. The Gale Group. • 2000. $285.00. 11th edition. Published by Business Research Services. Includes more than 28,000 businesses owned by women.

Regional Directory of Minority-and Women-Owned Business Firms. Business Research Services, Inc. • Annual. Three volumes. $175.00 per volume. Regional editions are Eastern, Central,and Western.

INTERNET DATABASES

MBEMAG. Minority Business Entrepreneur Magazine. Phone: (310)540-9398 Fax: (310)792-8263 E-mail: webmaster@mbemag.com • URL: http://www.mbemag.com • Web site's main feature is the "MBE Business Resources Directory." This provides complete mailing addresses, phone, fax, and Web site addresses (URL) for more than 40 organizations and government agencies having information or assistance for ethnic minority and women business owners. Some other links are "Current Events," "Calendar of Events," and "Business Opportunities." Updating is bimonthly. Fees: Free.

ONLINE DATABASES

Management Contents. The Gale Group. • Covers a wide range of management, financial, marketing, personnel, and administrative topics. About 150 leading business journals are indexed and abstracted from 1974 to date, with monthly updating. Inquire as to online cost and availability.

PERIODICALS AND NEWSLETTERS

Minority Business Entrepreneur. • Bimonthly. $16.00 per year. Reports on issues "critical to the growth and development of minority and women-owned firms." Provides information on relevant legislation and profiles successful women and minority entrepreneurs.

Perspective. Catalyst, Inc. • Monthly. $60.00 per year. Newsletter. Covers leadership, mentoring, work/family programs, success stories, and other topics for women in the corporate world.

Self. Conde Nast Publications, Inc. • Monthly. $16.00 per year. Written for business women.

Today's Insurance Woman. National Association of Insurance Women. • Quarterly. $15.00 per year. Provides advice on professional and personal development for women in the insurance business.

WIN News: All the News that is Fit to Print By, For and About Women. Women's International Network. • Quarterly. Individuals $35.00 per year; institutions, $48.00 per year. World-wide communication system by, for and about women of all backgrounds, beliefs, nationalities and age-groups.

Women as Managers: Strategies for Success. Economics Press, Inc. • Biweekly. $69.00 per year. Newsletter. Covers management skills and techniques leading to higher career levels. Discusses problems women face on the job.

Women's Business Exclusive: For Women Entrepreneurs. • Bimonthly. $39.00 per year. Newsletter. Reports news and information relating to financing, business procurement initiatives, technical assistance, and policy research. Provides advice on marketing, negotiating, and other management topics.

Working Mother. MacDonald Communications Corp. • 10 times a year. $12.97 per year.

RESEARCH CENTERS AND INSTITUTES

Business and Professional Women's Foundation. 2012 Massachusetts Ave., N.W., Washington, DC 20036. Phone: (202)293-1200 Fax: (202)861-0298 E-mail: gshaffer@bpwusa.org • URL: http://www.bpwusa.org.

Center for Private Enterprise. Baylor University, Hankamer School of Business, P.O. Box 98003, Waco, TX 76798-8003. Phone: (254)710-2263 Fax: (254)710-1092 E-mail: jimtruitt@baylor.edu • URL: http://129.62.162.136/enterprise/ • Includes studies of entrepreneurship and women entrepreneurs.

Institute for Case Development and Research. Simmons College, Graduate School of Management, 409 Commonwealth Ave., Boston, MA 02215. Phone: (617)521-3800 Fax: (617)521-3880 E-mail: jennifer.bruce@simmons.edu • Studies issues and problems confronting women in management.

National Association of Women Business Owners. 1100 Wayne Ave., Suite 830, Silver Spring, MD 20910-5603. Phone: (301)608-2590 Fax: (301)608-

For publishers addresses, refer to SOURCES CITED section at the back of the book.

2596 E-mail: nawbohq@aol.com • URL: http://www.nfwbo.org • Provides research reports and statistical studies relating to various aspects of women-owned business enterprises. Affiliated with the National Association of Women Business Owners.

National Council for Research on Women. 11 Hanover Square, 20th Fl., New York, NY 10005. Phone: (212)785-7335 Fax: (212)785-7350 E-mail: lbasch@ncrw.org • URL: http://www.ncrw.org.

Women Employed Institute. 22 W. Monroe St., Suite 1400, Chicago, IL 60603-2505. Phone: (312)782-3902 Fax: (312)782-5249 E-mail: info@womenemployed.org • URL: http://www.womenemployed.org • Research areas include the economic status of working women, sexual harassment in the workplace, equal employment opportunity, and career development.

TRADE/PROFESSIONAL ASSOCIATIONS

American Business Women's Association. P.O. Box 8728, Kansas City, MO 64114-0728. Phone: 800-228-0007 or (816)361-6621 Fax: (816)361-4991 E-mail: info@abwa.org • URL: http://www.abwahq.org.

Association of African-American Women Business Owners. c/o Brenda Alford, P.O. Box 13858, Silver Spring, MD 20911-0858. Phone: (301)585-8051.

Catalyst. 120 Wall St., 5th Fl., New York, NY 10005-3904. Phone: (212)514-7600 Fax: (212)514-8470 E-mail: info@catalystwomen.org • URL: http://www.catalystwomen.org • Provides information, research, and publications relating to women's workplace issues. Promotes corporate leadership for women.

Cosmetic Executive Women. 109 E. 73rd St., Apt. 5C, New York, NY 10021-3559. Phone: (212)717-2415 Fax: (212)717-2419 E-mail: cexecutive@aol.com • Members are women executives in the cosmetics industry.

Executive Women International. 515 S. 700 East, Suite 2E, Salt Lake City, UT 84102. Phone: 888-394-1229 or (801)355-2800 Fax: (801)355-2852 E-mail: ewi@executivewomen.org • URL: http://www.executivewomen.org • Members are executive secretaries or administrators.

Financial Women's Association of New York. 215 Park Ave. S., Suite 1713, New York, NY 10003. Phone: (212)533-2141 Fax: (212)982-3008 E-mail: info@fwa.org • URL: http://www.fwa.org • Members are professional women in finance.

The International Alliance, An Association of Executive and Professional Women. P.O. Box 1119, Baltimore, MD 21203-1119. Phone: (410)472-4221 Fax: (410)472-2920 E-mail: info@t-i-a.com • URL: http://www.t-i-a.com • Facilitates communication (networking) among women executives.

National Association for Female Executives. 135 W. 50th St., 16th Fl., New York, NY 10020. Phone: 800-634-6233 or (212)445-6233 or (212)445-6235 Fax: (212)445-6228 E-mail: nafe@nafe.com • URL: http://www.nafe.com.

National Association of Women Business Owners. 1411 K St., N.W., Washington, DC 20005. Phone: 800-556-2926 or (202)347-8686 Fax: (202)347-9210 E-mail: national@nawbo.org • URL: http://www.nawbo.org.

National Council of Administrative Women in Education. One Potbelly Beach Rd., Aptos, CA 95003-3579. One Potbelly Beach Rd.,.

National Women's Economic Alliance Foundation. 1001 D St., No. 1000, Washington, DC 20003-1830. Phone: (202)863-8689 • Promotes dialogue between executive level women and men.

NAWE: Advancing Women in Higher Education. 1325 18th St., N.W., Suite 210, Washington, DC 20036-6511. Phone: (202)659-9330 Fax: (202)457-0946 E-mail: webweaver@ncwe.org • URL: http://www.nawe.org.

Women Executives in Public Relations. WEPR FDR Station, P.O. Box 7657, New York, NY 10150-7657. Phone: (212)750-7373 Fax: (212)750-7375 • URL: http://www.wepr.org.

WOMEN IN INDUSTRY

See: EMPLOYMENT OF WOMEN; WOMEN IN THE WORK FORCE

WOMEN IN THE WORK FORCE

See also: EMPLOYMENT OF WOMEN

GENERAL WORKS

The Managerial Woman. Margaret Henning and Anne Jardim. Pocket Books. • 1983. $5.99.

When Work Doesn't Work Anymore: Women, Work, and Identity. Elizabeth P. McKenna. Doubleday. • 1997. $12.95. A popularly written discussion of the conflict between corporate culture and the traditional, family roles of women.

Women and Careers: Issues, Pressures, and Challenges. Carol W. Konek and Sally L. Kitch, editors. Sage Publications, Inc. • 1993. $49.95. Based on a major survey assessing women's experiences in the workplace.

Women and Work: Exploring Race, Ethnicity, and Class. Elizabeth Higginbotham and Mary Romero, editors. Sage Publications, Inc. • 1997. $55.00. Contains articles by various authors, including material on the historical and economic background of women in the workplace. (Women and Work, vol. 6.).

ABSTRACTS AND INDEXES

Social Sciences Index. H. W. Wilson Co. • Quarterly, with annual cumulation. Service basis for print edition; CD-ROM edition, $1,495 per year. Indexes more than 400 periodicals covering economics, environmental policy, government, insurance, labor, health care policy, plannning, public administration, public welfare, urban studies, women's issues, criminology, and related topics.

Sociological Abstracts. Cambridge Information Group. • Bimonthly. $635.00 per year. A compendium of non-evaluative abstracts covering the field of sociology and related disciplines. Includes an annual *Index*.

CD-ROM DATABASES

Magazine Index Plus. The Gale Group. • Monthly. $4,000.00 per year (includes InfoTrac workstation). Provides full text on CD-ROM for about 100 popular, general interest magazines and indexing for 300 others. Includes special indexing of reviews and product evaluations. Time period is 1980 to date.

Social Science Source. EBSCO Publishing. • Monthly. $1,495.00 per year. Provides CD-ROM citations and abstracts to social science articles in more than 600 periodicals, with full text from 125 periodicals. Covers economics, political science, public policy, international relations, psychology, and other topics. Time period is most recent five years.

Social Sciences Citation Index: Compact Disc Edition with Abstracts. Institute for Scientific Information. • Quarterly. Provides CD-ROM indexing and abstracting of "significant articles" from 1,400 social science journals worldwide, with additional selections from 3,200 other journals, 1986 to date. Includes economics, business, finance, management, communications, demographics, information and library science, political science, sociology, and many other subjects.

WILSONDISC: Wilson Social Sciences Abstracts. H. W. Wilson Co. • Monthly. Including unlimited online access to *Social Sciences Index* through WILSONLINE. Provides CD-ROM indexing from 1983 and abstracting from 1994 of more than 400 periodicals covering economics, area studies, community health, public administration, public welfare, urban studies, and many other topics related to the social sciences.

DIRECTORIES

Encyclopedia of Women's Associations Worldwide. The Gale Group. • 1998. $85.00. Second edition. Provides detailed information for more than 3,400 organizations throughout the world that relate to women and women's issues.

Women's Information Directory. The Gale Group. • 1992. $75.00. A guide to approximately 6,000 organizations, agencies, institutions, programs, and publications concerned with women in the United States. Includes subject and title indexes.

HANDBOOKS AND MANUALS

The New Working Woman's Guide to Retirement Planning. Martha P. Patterson. University of Pennsylvania Press. • 1999. $17.50. Second edition. Provides retirement advice for employed women, including information on various kinds of IRAs, cash balance and other pension plans, 401(k) plans, and social security. Four case studies are provided to illustrate retirement planning at specific life and career stages.

Women and the Law. Carol H. Lefcourt, editor. West Group. • $140.00. Looseleaf service. Periodic supplementation. Covers such topics as employment discrimination, pay equity (comparable worth), sexual harassment in the workplace, property rights, and child custody issues. (Civil Rights Series).

INTERNET DATABASES

Bureau of Labor Statistics (BLS). U. S. Department of Labor, Bureau of Labor Statistics. Phone: (202)523-1092 E-mail: labstat.helpdesk@bls.gov • URL: http://www.bls.gov • Web site provides a great variety of employment, wage, price, and economic data. Some links are "Data," "Economy at a Glance," "Keyword Search of BLS Web Pages," "Regional Information," and "Other Statistical Sites." Fees: Free.

U. S. Census Bureau: The Official Statistics. U. S. Bureau of the Census. Phone: (301)763-4100 Fax: (301)763-4794 • URL: http://www.census.gov • Web site is "Your Source for Social, Demographic, and Economic Information." Contains "Current U. S. Population Count," "Current Economic Indicators," and a wide variety of data under "Other Official Statistics." Keyword searching is provided. Fees: Free.

ONLINE DATABASES

Contemporary Women's Issues. Responsive Database Services, Inc. • Provides fulltext articles online from 150 periodicals and a wide variety of additional sources relating to economic, legal, social, political, education, health, and other women's issues. Time span is 1992 to date. Weekly updates. Inquire as to online cost and availability. (Also available in a CD-ROM version.).

Wilson Social Sciences Abstracts Online. H. W. Wilson Co. • Provides online abstracting and indexing of more than 415 periodicals covering area studies, community health, public administration, public welfare, urban studies, and many other social science topics. Time period is 1994 to date for abstracts and 1983 to date for indexing, with updates monthly. Inquire as to online cost and availability.

PERIODICALS AND NEWSLETTERS

Feminist Economics. International Association for Feminist Economics. Routledge Journals. • Three times a year. Individuals, $50.00 per year; institutions, $150.00 per year. Includes articles on issues relating to the employment and economic opportunities of women.

Nine to Five Newsletter. National Association of Working Women. • Five times a year. Free to members; individuals, $25.00 per year. A newsletter dealing with the rights and concerns of women office workers.

Perspective. Catalyst, Inc. • Monthly. $60.00 per year. Newsletter. Covers leadership, mentoring, work/family programs, success stories, and other topics for women in the corporate world.

RESEARCH CENTERS AND INSTITUTES

Consumer Research Center. The Conference Board, Inc., 845 Third Ave., New York, NY 10022. Phone: (212)759-0900 Fax: (212)980-7014 E-mail: franco@conference-board.org • URL: http://www.crc-conquest.org • Conducts research on the consumer market, including elderly and working women segments.

Women Employed Institute. 22 W. Monroe St., Suite 1400, Chicago, IL 60603-2505. Phone: (312)782-3902 Fax: (312)782-5249 E-mail: info@womenemployed.org • URL: http://www.womenemployed.org • Research areas include the economic status of working women, sexual harassment in the workplace, equal employment opportunity, and career development.

STATISTICS SOURCES

Handbook of U. S. Labor Statistics: Employment, Earnings, Prices, Productivity, and Other Labor Data. Eva E. Jacobs, editor. Bernan Associates. • 1999. $74.00. Based on *Handbook of Labor Statistics*, formerly issued by the Bureau of Labor Statistics, U. S. Department of Labor. Includes the Bureau's projections of employment in the U. S. by industry and occupation. Provides a wide variety of data on the work force, prices, fringe benefits, and consumer expenditures.

Social Statistics of the United States. Mark S. Littman, editor. Bernan Press. • 2000. $65.00. Includes statistical data on population growth, labor force, occupations, environmental trends, leisure time use, income, poverty, taxes, and other economic or demographic topics.

Statistical Abstract of the United States. Available from U. S. Government Printing Office. • Annual. $51.00. Issued by the U. S. Bureau of the Census.

Statistical Handbook on the American Family. Bruce A. Chadwick and Tim B. Heaton, editors. Oryx Press. • 1998. $65.00. Includes data on education, health, politics, employment, expenditures, social characteristics, the elderly, and women in the labor force. Historical statistics on marriage, birth, and divorce are shown from 1900 on. A list of sources and a subject index are provided. (Statistical Handbook Series).

Statistical Handbook on Women in America. Cynthia M. Taeuber, editor. Oryx Press. • 1996. $65.00. Includes data on demographics, employment, earnings, economic status, educational status, marriage, divorce, household units, health, and other topics. (Statistical Handbook Series).

A Statistical Portrait of the United States: Social Conditions and Trends. Mark S. Littman, editor. Bernan Press. • 1998. $89.00. Covers "social, economic, and environmental trends in the United States over the past 25 years." Includes statistical tables, graphs, and analysis relating to such topics as population, income, poverty, wealth, labor, housing, education, healthcare, air/water quality, and government.

Statistical Record of Women Worldwide. The Gale Group. • 1996. $125.00. Second edition. Includes employment data and other economic statistics relating to women in the U. S. and internationally.

Women in the World of Work: Statistical Analysis and Projections to the Year 2000. Shirley Nuss and others. International Labour Office. • 1989. $18.00. (Women, Work, and Development Series, No. 18).

TRADE/PROFESSIONAL ASSOCIATIONS

Catalyst. 120 Wall St., 5th Fl., New York, NY 10005-3904. Phone: (212)514-7600 Fax: (212)514-8470 E-mail: info@catalystwomen.org • URL: http://www.catalystwomen.org • Provides information, research, and publications relating to women's workplace issues. Promotes corporate leadership for women.

International Association for Feminist Economics. c/o Jean Schackleford, Dept. of Economics, Bucknell University, Lewisburg, PA 17837. Phone: (570)524-3441 Fax: (570)524-3451 E-mail: jshackle@bucknell.edu • Members are economists having a feminist viewpoint. Promotes greater economic opportunities for women.

Nine to Five: National Association of Working Women. 231 W. Wisconsin Ave., Suite 900, Milwaukee, WI 53203. Phone: 800-522-0925 or (414)274-0925 Fax: (414)272-2870 E-mail: naww9to5@execpc.com • Members are women office workers. Strives for the improvement of office working conditions for women and the elimination of sex and race discrimination.

WOMEN LAWYERS

See also: LAWYERS

BIOGRAPHICAL SOURCES

Who's Who in American Law. Marquis Who's Who. • Biennial. $285.00. Contains over 22,000 concise biographies of American lawyers, judges, and others in the legal field.

Who's Who of American Women. Marquis Who's Who. • Biennial. $259.00. Provides over 27,000 biographical profiles of important women, including individuals prominent in business, finance, and industry.

PERIODICALS AND NEWSLETTERS

National Association of Women Lawyers. President's Newsletter. National Association of Women Lawyers. • Quarterly.

Women Lawyers Journal. National Association of Women Lawyers. • Quarterly. $16.00 per year.

TRADE/PROFESSIONAL ASSOCIATIONS

National Association of Women Lawyers. 750 N. Lake Shore Dr., Chicago, IL 60611. Phone: (312)988-6186 Fax: (312)988-6281 E-mail: nawl@staff.abanet.org • URL: http://www.kentlaw.edu/nawl.

WOMEN MANAGERS

See: WOMEN EXECUTIVES

WOMEN PHYSICIANS

BIOGRAPHICAL SOURCES

Who's Who of American Women. Marquis Who's Who. • Biennial. $259.00. Provides over 27,000 biographical profiles of important women, including individuals prominent in business, finance, and industry.

ONLINE DATABASES

Embase. Elsevier Science, Inc. • Worldwide medical literature, 1974 to present. Weekly updates. Inquire as to online cost and availability.

Medline. Medlars Management Section. • Provides indexing and abstracting of worldwide medical literature, 1966 to date. Weekly updates. Inquire as to online cost and availability.

PERIODICALS AND NEWSLETTERS

AMWA Journal. American Medical Writers Association. • Quarterly. $35.00 per year.

TRADE/PROFESSIONAL ASSOCIATIONS

American Medical Women's Association. 801 N. Fairfax St., Suite 400, Alexandria, VA 22314. Phone: (703)838-0500 Fax: (703)549-3864 E-mail: info@amwa.doc.org • URL: http://www.amwa-foc.org.

WOMEN'S APPAREL

See also: CLOTHING INDUSTRY; FASHION INDUSTRY; MILLINERY INDUSTRY; UNDERWEAR INDUSTRY

ABSTRACTS AND INDEXES

Textile Technology Digest. Institute of Textile Technology. • Monthly. $535.00 per year. Provides indexing and abstracting of a wide variety of textile technology literature.

CD-ROM DATABASES

Textile Technology Digest [CD-ROM]. Textile Information Center, Institute of Textile Technology. • Quarterly. $1,700.00 per year. Provides CD-ROM indexing and abstracting of worldwide journals and monographs in various areas of textile technology, production, and management. Covers 1978 to date.

DIRECTORIES

Contemporary Fashion. Richard Martin, editor. St. James Press. • $140.00. Second edition. Date not set. Provides detailed information on more than 400 fashion designers, milliners, footwear designers, apparel companies, and textile houses. Includes black-and-white photographs, biographical information, and bibliographies.

Directory of Apparel Specialty Stores. Chain Store Guide. • Annual. $260.00. Lists over 5,000 women's, men's, family and sporting goods retailers.

Garment Manufacturer's Index. Klevens Publications, Inc. • Annual. $60.00. A directory of about 8,000 manufacturers and suppliers of products and services used in the making of men's, women's, and children's clothing. Includes fabrics, trimmings, factory equipment, and other supplies.

Nationwide Directory of Women's and Children's Wear Buyers. Salesman's Guide. • Annual. $229.00. About 7,200 retail stores selling women's dresses, coats, sportswear, intimate apparel, and women's accessories, infants' to teens wear, and accessories; coverage does not include New York metropolitan area.

Phelon's Women's Apparel and Accessory Shops. Kenneth W. Phelon, Jr., editor. Phelon, Sheldon and Marsar, Inc. • Biennial. $175.00. Lists ladies boutiques from popular to higher priced clothing and accessories throughout the U.S. Formerly *Phelon's Women's Apparel Shops.*

ENCYCLOPEDIAS AND DICTIONARIES

Encyclopedia of Textiles. French and European Publications, Inc. • 1980. $39.95. Third edition.

Fashion Production Terms. Debbie Ann Gioello and Beverly Berke. Fairchild Books. • 1979. $50.00. (Language of Fashion Series).

Textile Terms and Definitions. J.E. McIntyre and Paul N. Daniels, editors. Available from State Mutual Book and Periodical Service Ltd., Trade Order Dept. • 1995. $110.00. 10th edition. Published by the Textile Insitute (UK). Includes more than 1,000 definitions of textile processes, fiber types, and end products. Illustrated.

FINANCIAL RATIOS

Annual Statement Studies. Robert Morris Associates: The Association of Lending and Credit Risk Professiona. • Annual. Free to members; non-members, $140.00. Median and quartile financial ratios are given for over 400 kinds of manufacturing, wholesale, retail, construction, and consumer finance establishments. Data is sorted by both asset size and sales volume. Includes a clearly written "Definition of Ratios" and an alphabetical industry index.

HANDBOOKS AND MANUALS

Lingerie Shop. Entrepreneur Media, Inc. • Looseleaf. $59.50. A practical guide to starting a lingerie store. Covers profit potential, start-up costs, market size evaluation, owner's time required, site selection, lease negotiation, pricing, accounting, advertising, promotion, etc. (Start-Up Business Guide No. E1152.).

Women's Accessories Store. Entrepreneur Media, Inc. • Looseleaf. $59.50. A practical guide to starting a women's clothing accessories shop. Covers profit potential, start-up costs, market size evaluation, owner's time required, site selection, lease negotiation, pricing, accounting, advertising, promotion, etc. (Start-Up Business Guide No. E1333.).

Women's Apparel Shop. Entrepreneur Media, Inc. • Looseleaf. $59.50. A practical guide to starting a women's clothing store. Covers profit potential, start-up costs, market size evaluation, owner's time required, site selection, lease negotiation, pricing, accounting, advertising, promotion, etc. (Start-Up Business Guide No. E1107.).

INTERNET DATABASES

Fedstats. Federal Interagency Council on Statistical Policy. Phone: (202)395-7254 • URL: http://www.fedstats.gov • Web site features an efficient search facility for full-text statistics produced by more than 70 federal agencies, including the Census Bureau, the Bureau of Economic Analysis, and the Bureau of Labor Statistics. Boolean searches can be made within one agency or for all agencies combined. Links are offered to international statistical bureaus, including the UN, IMF, OECD, UNESCO, Eurostat, and 20 individual countries. Fees: Free.

ONLINE DATABASES

DRI U.S. Central Database. Data Products Division. • Provides more than 23,000 business, financial, demographic, economic, foreign trade, and industry-related time series for the U.S. Includes national income, population, retail-wholesale trade, price indexes, labor data, housing, industrial production, banking, interest rates, money supply, etc. Time period is generally 1947 to date (some data back to 1929). Updating varies. Inquire as to online cost and availability.

F & S Index. The Gale Group. • Contains about four million citations to worldwide business, financial, and industrial or consumer product literature appearing from 1972 to date. Weekly updates. Inquire as to online cost and availability.

PROMT: Predicasts Overview of Markets and Technology. The Gale Group. • Companies, products, applied technologies and markets. U.S. and international literature coverage, 1972 to date. Inquire as to online cost and availability. Provides abstracts from more than 1,600 publications. Weekly updates.

Textile Technology Digest [online]. Textile Information Center, Institute of Textile Technology. • Contains indexing and abstracting of more than 300 worldwide journals and monographs in various areas of textile technology, production, and management. Time period is 1978 to date, with monthly updating. Inquire as to online cost and availability.

World Textiles. Elsevier Science, Inc. • Provides abstracting and indexing from 1970 of worldwide textile literature (periodicals, books, pamphlets, and reports). Includes U. S., European, and British patent information. Updating is monthly. Inquire as to online cost and availability.

PERIODICALS AND NEWSLETTERS

Apparel Industry Magazine. Shore-Varrone, Inc. • Monthly. $65.00 per year.

Bobbin. Bobbin Blenheim Media Corp. • Monthly. Free to qualified personnel. For management in the sewing products industry. Covers problem solving, technology and legislation.

Fashion Showcase Retailer. Fashion Retailer Publishing. • Bimonthly. $12.00 per year.

Femme-Lines. Earl Barron Publications, Inc. • Bimonthly. $8.00 per year.

Harper's Bazaar. Hearst Corp. • Monthly. $10.00 per year.

Mademoiselle. Conde Nast Publications, Inc.,. • Monthly. $16.00 per year.

Vogue. Conde Nast Publications, Inc. • Monthly. $28.00 per year.

WWD (Women's Wear Daily): The Retailer's Daily Newspaper. Fairchild Publications. • Daily. Institutions, $75.00 per year; corporations $195.00 per year.

STATISTICS SOURCES

Annual Survey of Manufactures. Available from U. S. Government Printing Office. • Annual. Prices vary. Issued by the U. S. Census Bureau as an interim update to the *Census of Manufactures.* Includes data on number of manufacturing establishments in various industries, employment, labor costs, value of shipments, capital expenditures, inventories, energy costs, and assets. (See also Census Bureau home page, http://www.census.gov/.).

Business Statistics of the United States. Courtenay M. Slater, editor. Bernan Associates. • 1999. $74.00. Fifth edition. Based on *Business Statistics,* formerly issue by the Bureau of Economic Analysis, U. S. Department of Commerce. Provides basic data for a wide variety of U. S. industries, services, and economic indicators. Most statistics are shown annually for 29 years and monthly for the most recent four years.

Manufacturing Profiles. Available from U. S. Government Printing Office. • Annual. Issued by the U. S. Census Bureau. A printed consolidation of the entire *Current Industrial Report* series, presenting "all the data compiled." Contains statistics on production, shipments, inventories, consumption, exports, imports, and orders for a wide variety of manufactured products. (See also Census Bureau home page, http://www.census.gov/.).

Survey of Current Business. Available from U. S. Government Printing Office. • Monthly. $49.00 per year. Issued by Bureau of Economic Analysis, U. S. Department of Commerce. Presents a wide variety of business and economic data.

TRADE/PROFESSIONAL ASSOCIATIONS

Affiliated Dress Manufacturers. 500 Seventh Ave., New York, NY 10018. Phone: (212)819-1011.

American Cloak and Suit Manufacturers Association. 450 Seventh Ave., New York, NY 10123. Phone: (212)244-7300.

Textile Institute. Saint James Bldgs., 4th Fl., Oxford St., Manchester M1 6FQ, England. Phone: 44 161 2371188 Fax: 44 161 2361991 E-mail: tiihq@textileinst.org.uk • URL: http://www.texi.org • Members in 100 countries involved with textile industry management, marketing, science, and technology.

OTHER SOURCES

Textile Business Outlook. Statistikon Corp. • Quarterly. $985.00 per year. Analyzes current business, marketing, and financial conditions for the worldwide textile industry (fibers and fabrics). Includes statistical forecasts.

WOMEN'S CLUBS

PERIODICALS AND NEWSLETTERS

GFWC Clubwoman. General Federation of Women's Clubs. • Bimonthly. $6.00 per year.

TRADE/PROFESSIONAL ASSOCIATIONS

Business and Professional Women USA. 2012 Massachusetts Ave., N.W., Washington, DC 20036. Phone: (202)293-1100 Fax: (202)861-0298 • URL: http://www.bpwusa.org.

General Federation of Women's Clubs. 1734 N St., N.W., Washington, DC 20036-2990. Phone: 800-443-4392 or (202)347-3168 Fax: (202)835-0246 E-mail: gfwc@gfwc.org • URL: http://www.gfwc.org.

National Council of Women of the United States. 777 United Nations Plaza, New York, NY 10017. Phone: (212)697-1278 Fax: (212)972-0164.

WOOD

See: FOREST PRODUCTS; LUMBER INDUSTRY

WOOD FINISHING

See: WOODWORKING INDUSTRIES

WOODPULP INDUSTRY

See also: PAPER INDUSTRY; TALL OIL INDUSTRY

DIRECTORIES

International Pulp and Paper Directory. Miller Freeman Books. • Biennial. $317.00.

Lockwood-Post's Directory of the Pulp, Paper and Allied Trades. Miller Freeman, Inc. • Annual. $277.00. Formerly *Lockwood's Directory of the Paper and Allied Trades.*

PIMA Directory. Paper Industry Management Association. • Annual. $140.00. Manufacturers and distributors of chemicals, equipment, supplies, and services used in the manufacture of paper. Formerly *PIMA Catalog.*

Pulp and Paper Buyer's Guide. Miller Freeman, Inc. • Annual. $155.00. Supplies and equipment.

INTERNET DATABASES

Fedstats. Federal Interagency Council on Statistical Policy. Phone: (202)395-7254 • URL: http://www.fedstats.gov • Web site features an efficient search facility for full-text statistics produced by more than 70 federal agencies, including the Census

Bureau, the Bureau of Economic Analysis, and the Bureau of Labor Statistics. Boolean searches can be made within one agency or for all agencies combined. Links are offered to international statistical bureaus, including the UN, IMF, OECD, UNESCO, Eurostat, and 20 individual countries. Fees: Free.

ONLINE DATABASES

DRI U.S. Central Database. Data Products Division. • Provides more than 23,000 business, financial, demographic, economic, foreign trade, and industry-related time series for the U.S. Includes national income, population, retail-wholesale trade, price indexes, labor data, housing, industrial production, banking, interest rates, money supply, etc. Time period is generally 1947 to date (some data back to 1929). Updating varies. Inquire as to online cost and availability.

PaperChem Database. Information Services Div. • Worldwide coverage of the scientific and technical paper industry chemical literature, including patents, 1967 to present. Weekly updates. Inquire as to online cost and availability.

PERIODICALS AND NEWSLETTERS

Pulp and Paper. Miller Freeman, Inc. • Monthly. $135.00 per year.

Pulp and Paper Canada. Pulp and Paper Technical Association of Canada. Southam Magazine Group. • Monthly. $73.00 per year.

Pulp and Paper International. Miller Freeman, Inc. • Monthly. Free to qualified personnel; others, $130.00 per year.

Southern Pulp and Paper. Ernest H. Abernathy Publishing Co. • Monthly. $18.00 per year.

TAPPI Journal. Technical Association of the Pulp and Paper Industry, Inc. • Monthly. Membership.

PRICE SOURCES

Official Board Markets: "The Yellow Sheet". Mark Arzoumanian. Advanstar Communications, Inc. • Weekly. $150.00 per year. Covers the corrugated container, folding carton, rigid box and waste paper industries.

RESEARCH CENTERS AND INSTITUTES

Pulp and Paper Laboratory. North Carolina State University. Dept. of Wood and Paper Science, P.O. 8005, Raleigh, NC 27695. Phone: (919)515-5807 Fax: (919)515-6302 E-mail: mikekocurek@ncsu.edu • URL: http://www.cfr.ncsu.edu/wps/.

STATISTICS SOURCES

Business Statistics of the United States. Courtenay M. Slater, editor. Bernan Associates. • 1999. $74.00. Fifth edition. Based on *Business Statistics*, formerly issue by the Bureau of Economic Analysis, U. S. Department of Commerce. Provides basic data for a wide variety of U. S. industries, services, and economic indicators. Most statistics are shown annually for 29 years and monthly for the most recent four years.

The Pulp and Paper Industry in the OECD Member Countries. Organization for Economic Cooperation and Development. Available from OECD Publications and Information Center. • Annual. $31.00. Presents annual data on production, consumption, capacity, utilization, and foreign trade. Covers 33 pulp and paper products in OECD countries. Text in English and French.

Survey of Current Business. Available from U. S. Government Printing Office. • Monthly. $49.00 per year. Issued by Bureau of Economic Analysis, U. S. Department of Commerce. Presents a wide variety of business and economic data.

TRADE/PROFESSIONAL ASSOCIATIONS

Forest Resources Association. 600 Jefferson Dr., Suite 350, Rockville, MD 20852-1157. Phone: (301)838-9385 Fax: (301)838-9481 E-mail: nward@apulpa.org • URL: http://www.apulpa.org.

TAPPI. P.O. Box 105113, Atlanta, GA 30348-5113. Phone: 800-332-8686 or (770)446-1400 Fax: (770)446-6947 E-mail: serviceline@tappi.org • URL: http://www.tappi.org.

WOODWORKING INDUSTRIES

See also: CARPENTRY; FOREST PRODUCTS; FURNITURE INDUSTRY; VENEERS AND VENEERING

DIRECTORIES

FDM-The Source-Woodworking Industry Directory. Cahners Business Information. • Annual. $25.00. A product-classified listing of more than 1,800 suppliers to the furniture and cabinet industries. Includes Canada.

Wood Digest Showcase. Cygnus Publishing, Inc., Johnson Hill Press, Inc. • Annual. Controlled circulation. Formerly *Furniture Wood/Digest-Showcase*.

ENCYCLOPEDIAS AND DICTIONARIES

Illustrated Dictionary of Building Materials and Techniques: An Invaluable Sourcebook to the Tools, Terms, Materials, and Techniques Used by Building Professionals. Paul Bianchina. John Wiley and Sons, Inc. • 1993. $49.95. Contains 4,000 definitions of building and building materials terms, with 500 illustrations. Includes materials grades, measurements, and specifications.

FINANCIAL RATIOS

Annual Statement Studies. Robert Morris Associates: The Association of Lending and Credit Risk Professiona. • Annual. Free to members; non-members, $140.00. Median and quartile financial ratios are given for over 400 kinds of manufacturing, wholesale, retail, construction, and consumer finance establishments. Data is sorted by both asset size and sales volume. Includes a clearly written "Definition of Ratios" and an alphabetical industry index.

HANDBOOKS AND MANUALS

Advanced Woodwork and Furniture Making. John L. Feirer and Gilbert R. Hutchings. Glencoe/McGraw-Hill. • 1982. $43.56. Fourth revised edition.

Woodturner's Bible. Percy Blandford. McGraw-Hill Professional. • 1990. $26.95. Third edition.

Woodworking Factbook: Basic Information on Wood for Wood Carvers, Home Woodshop Craftsmen, Tradesmen and Instructors. Donald G. Coleman. Robert Speller and Sons Publishers, Inc. • 1996. $22.50.

Woodworking for Industry: Technology and Practice. John L. Feirer and Gilbert R. Hutchings. Glencoe/McGraw-Hill. • 1979. $23.72.

PERIODICALS AND NEWSLETTERS

FDM: Furniture Design and Manufacturing: Serving the Upholstered Furniture Industry. Chartwell Communications, Inc. • Monthly. Free to qualified personnel. Edited for furniture executives, production managers, and designers. Covers the manufacturing of household, office, and institutional furniture, store fixtures, and kitchen and bathroom cabinets.

Forest Products Journal. Forest Products Society. • 10 times a year. $135.00 per year.

National Home Center News: News and Analysis for the Home Improvement, Building, Material Industry. Lebhar-Friedman, Inc. • 22 times a year. $99.00 per year. Includes special feature issues on hardware and tools, building materials, millwork, electrical supplies, lighting, and kitchens.

Wood and Wood Products: Furniture, Cabinets, Woodworking and Allied Products Management and Operations. Vance Publishing Corp. • 13 times a year. $50.00 per year.

Wood Digest. Cygnus Publishing, Inc. • Monthly. $60.00 per year. Formerly *Furniture Wood Digest*.

RESEARCH CENTERS AND INSTITUTES

Wood and Paper Science. North Carolina State University, P.O. Box 8005, Raleigh, NC 27695. Phone: (919)515-5807 Fax: (919)515-6302 E-mail: mikekocurek@ncsu.edu • URL: http://www.cfr.ncsu.edu/wps/ • Studies the mechanical and engineering properties of wood, wood finishing, wood anatomy, wood chemistry, etc.

Wood Research Laboratory. Purdue University, Department of Forestry and Natural Resources, West Lafayette, IN 47907-1200. Phone: (765)494-3615 Fax: (765)496-1344 E-mail: mhunt@fnr.purdue.edu • URL: http://www.fnr.purdue.edu.

STATISTICS SOURCES

Annual Survey of Manufactures. Available from U. S. Government Printing Office. • Annual. Prices vary. Issued by the U. S. Census Bureau as an interim update to the *Census of Manufactures*. Includes data on number of manufacturing establishments in various industries, employment, labor costs, value of shipments, capital expenditures, inventories, energy costs, and assets. (See also Census Bureau home page, http://www.census.gov/.).

U. S. Industry and Trade Outlook: The McGraw-Hill Companies and the U.S. Department of Commerce/ International Trade Administration. Datapso Research Corp. • Annual. $69.95. Produced by the International Trade Administration, U. S. Department of Commerce, in a "public-private" partnership with DRI/McGraw-Hill and Standard & Poor's. Provides basic data, outlook for the current year, and "Long-Term Prospects" (five-year projections) for a wide variety of products and services. Includes high technology industries. Formerly *U. S. Industrial Outlook*.

TRADE/PROFESSIONAL ASSOCIATIONS

Architectural Woodwork Institute. 1952 Isaac Newton Square, W., Reston, VA 20190. Phone: (703)733-0600 Fax: (703)733-0584 E-mail: jdurham@awinet.org • URL: http://www.awinet.org.

Wood Machinery Manufacturers of America. 1900 Arch St., Philadelphia, PA 19103-1498. Phone: 800-289-9662 or (215)564-3484 Fax: (215)963-9785 E-mail: wmma@fernley.com • URL: http://www.wmma.org.

OTHER SOURCES

Kitchen Cabinets and Countertops. Available from MarketResearch.com. • 1999. $2,250.00. Market research report published by Specialists in Business Information. Covers both custom and stock cabinets. Presents market data relative to demographics, sales growth, shipments, exports, imports, price trends, and end-use. Includes company profiles.

WOOL AND WORSTED INDUSTRY

See also: SHEEP INDUSTRY; TEXTILE INDUSTRY; YARN

ABSTRACTS AND INDEXES

Textile Technology Digest. Institute of Textile Technology. • Monthly. $535.00 per year. Provides indexing and abstracting of a wide variety of textile technology literature.

ALMANACS AND YEARBOOKS

CRB Commodity Yearbook. Commodity Research Bureau. CRB. • Annual. $99.95.

CD-ROM DATABASES

Textile Technology Digest [CD-ROM]. Textile Information Center, Institute of Textile Technology. • Quarterly. $1,700.00 per year. Provides CD-ROM indexing and abstracting of worldwide journals and monographs in various areas of textile technology, production, and management. Covers 1978 to date.

ENCYCLOPEDIAS AND DICTIONARIES

Encyclopedia of Textiles. French and European Publications, Inc. • 1980. $39.95. Third edition.

Textile Terms and Definitions. J.E. McIntyre and Paul N. Daniels, editors. Available from State Mutual Book and Periodical Service Ltd., Trade Order Dept. • 1995. $110.00. 10th edition. Published by the Textile Insitute (UK). Includes more than 1,000 definitions of textile processes, fiber types, and end products. Illustrated.

INTERNET DATABASES

Fedstats. Federal Interagency Council on Statistical Policy. Phone: (202)395-7254 • URL: http://www.fedstats.gov • Web site features an efficient search facility for full-text statistics produced by more than 70 federal agencies, including the Census Bureau, the Bureau of Economic Analysis, and the Bureau of Labor Statistics. Boolean searches can be made within one agency or for all agencies combined. Links are offered to international statistical bureaus, including the UN, IMF, OECD, UNESCO, Eurostat, and 20 individual countries. Fees: Free.

USDA. United States Department of Agriculture. Phone: (202)720-2791 E-mail: agsec@usda.gov • URL: http://www.usda.gov • The USDA home page has six sections: News and Information; What's New; About USDA; Agencies; Opportunities; Search and Help. Keyword searching is offered from the USDA home page and from various individual agency home pages. Agencies are the Economic Research Service, Agricultural Marketing Service, National Agricultural Statistics Service, National Agricultural Library, and about 12 others. Updating varies. Fees: Free.

ONLINE DATABASES

DRI U.S. Central Database. Data Products Division. • Provides more than 23,000 business, financial, demographic, economic, foreign trade, and industry-related time series for the U.S. Includes national income, population, retail-wholesale trade, price indexes, labor data, housing, industrial production, banking, interest rates, money supply, etc. Time period is generally 1947 to date (some data back to 1929). Updating varies. Inquire as to online cost and availability.

Globalbase. The Gale Group. • Provides more than one million online summaries of business, industrial, and economic news reports from more than 1,000 publications worldwide. Covers a wide range of material appearing in international trade journals, professional magazines, and newspapers. Time period is 1984 to date, with weekly updates. Inquire as to online cost and availability.

Textile Technology Digest [online]. Textile Information Center, Institute of Textile Technology. • Contains indexing and abstracting of more than 300 worldwide journals and monographs in various areas of textile technology, production, and management. Time period is 1978 to date, with monthly updating. Inquire as to online cost and availability.

World Textiles. Elsevier Science, Inc. • Provides abstracting and indexing from 1970 of worldwide textile literature (periodicals, books, pamphlets, and reports). Includes U. S., European, and British patent information. Updating is monthly. Inquire as to online cost and availability.

PERIODICALS AND NEWSLETTERS

Canadian Co-Operative Wool Growers Magazine. Canadian Cooperative Wool Growers, Ltd. • Annual. Free to members; non-members, $3.00.

Wool Record. World Textile Publications Ltd. • Monthly. $120.00 per year.

Wool Research Organization of New Zealand, Inc. • Irregular. Individuals, $75.00 per year; institutions, $115.00 per year.

The Wool Sack. Mid-States Wool Growers Cooperative. • Semiannual. Free. Information on lamb production and the wool industry.

RESEARCH CENTERS AND INSTITUTES

Montana Wool Laboratory. Montana State University-Bozeman. Bozeman, MT 59717. Phone: (406)994-2100 Fax: (406)994-5589 E-mail: woollab@montana.campus.mci.net.

STATISTICS SOURCES

Agricultural Statistics. Available from U. S. Government Printing Office. • Annual. Produced by the National Agricultural Statistics Service, U. S. Department of Agriculture. Provides a wide variety of statistical data relating to agricultural production, supplies, consumption, prices/price-supports, foreign trade, costs, and returns, as well as farm labor, loans, income, and population. In many cases, historical data is shown annually for 10 years. In addition to farm data, includes detailed fishery statistics.

Annual Survey of Manufactures. Available from U. S. Government Printing Office. • Annual. Prices vary. Issued by the U. S. Census Bureau as an interim update to the *Census of Manufactures.* Includes data on number of manufacturing establishments in various industries, employment, labor costs, value of shipments, capital expenditures, inventories, energy costs, and assets. (See also Census Bureau home page, http://www.census.gov/.).

Broadwoven Fabrics (Gray). U.S. Bureau of the Census. • Quarterly. Provides statistical data on production, value, shipments, and consumption. Includes woolen and worsted fabrics, tire fabrics, cotton broadwoven fabrics, etc. (Current Industrial Reports, MQ-22T.).

Business Statistics of the United States. Courtenay M. Slater, editor. Bernan Associates. • 1999. $74.00. Fifth edition. Based on *Business Statistics,* formerly issue by the Bureau of Economic Analysis, U. S. Department of Commerce. Provides basic data for a wide variety of U. S. industries, services, and economic indicators. Most statistics are shown annually for 29 years and monthly for the most recent four years.

Consumption on the Woolen System and Worsted Combing. U. S. Bureau of the Census. • Quarterly and annual. Provides data on consumption of fibers in woolen and worsted spinning mills, by class of fibers and end use. (Current Industrial Reports, MQ-22D.).

Livestock, Meat, Wool, Market News. U.S. Department of Agriculture. • Weekly.

Manufacturing Profiles. Available from U. S. Government Printing Office. • Annual. Issued by the U. S. Census Bureau. A printed consolidation of the entire *Current Industrial Report* series, presenting "all the data compiled." Contains statistics on production, shipments, inventories, consumption, exports, imports, and orders for a wide variety of manufactured products. (See also Census Bureau home page, http://www.census.gov/.).

Survey of Current Business. Available from U. S. Government Printing Office. • Monthly. $49.00 per year. Issued by Bureau of Economic Analysis, U. S. Department of Commerce. Presents a wide variety of business and economic data.

World Trade Annual. United Nations Statistical Office. Walker and Co. • Annual. Prices vary.

TRADE/PROFESSIONAL ASSOCIATIONS

American Sheep Industry Association. 6911 S. Yosemite St., Suite 200, Englewood, CO 80112-1414. Phone: (303)771-3500 Fax: (303)771-8200 E-mail: info@sheepusa.org • URL: http://www.sheepusa.org.

National Wool Marketing Corporation. 9449 Basil Western Rd., Canal Winchester, OH 43110. Phone: (614)834-1957 Fax: (614)834-2008.

Textile Institute. Saint James Bldgs., 4th Fl., Oxford St., Manchester M1 6FQ, England. Phone: 44 161 2371188 Fax: 44 161 2361991 E-mail: tiihq@textileinst.org.uk • URL: http://www.texi.org • Members in 100 countries involved with textile industry management, marketing, science, and technology.

Woolmark Company. 330 Madison Ave., New York, NY 10017. Phone: 800-986-9665 or (212)986-6222 Fax: (212)557-5985 • URL: http://www.woolmark.com.

OTHER SOURCES

Textile Business Outlook. Statistikon Corp. • Quarterly. $985.00 per year. Analyzes current business, marketing, and financial conditions for the worldwide textile industry (fibers and fabrics). Includes statistical forecasts.

WORD PROCESSING

See also: COMPUTERS; DESKTOP PUBLISHING; MICROCOMPUTERS AND MINICOMPUTERS; OFFICE AUTOMATION; OFFICE EQUIPMENT AND SUPPLIES; OFFICE MANAGEMENT

ABSTRACTS AND INDEXES

Computer and Information Systems Abstracts Journal: An Abstract Journal Pertaining to the Theory, Design, Fabrication and Application of Computer and Information Systems. Cambridge Information Group. • Monthly. $1,045 per year.

Computer Literature Index: A Subject/Author Index to Computer and Data Processing Literature. Applied Computer Research, Inc. • Quarterly, with annual cumulation. $245.00 per year. Contains brief abstracts of book and periodical literature covering all phases of computing, including approximately 70 specific application areas.

LAMP (Literature Analysis of Microcomputer Publications). Soft Images. • Bimonthly. $89.95 per year. Annual cumulation.

BIBLIOGRAPHIES

Computer Book Review. • Quarterly. $30.00 per year. Includes annual index. Reviews new computer books. Back issues available.

CD-ROM DATABASES

Computer Select. The Gale Group. • Monthly. $1,250.00 per year. Provides one year of full-text on CD-ROM for 120 leading computer-related publications. Also includes 70,000 product specifications and brief profiles of 13,000 computer product vendors and manufacturers.

DIRECTORIES

Data Sources: The Comprehensive Guide to the Data Processing Industry Hardware, Data Communications Products, Software, Company Profiles. The Gale Group. • Semiannual. $495.00 per year. Two volumes. Describes hardware and software for all computer operating sysems, including prices and technical details. Lists about 75,000 products from 14,000 suppliers. Industry-specific software applications are described.

MicroLeads Vendor Directory on Disk (Personal Computer Industry). Chromatic Communications Enterprises, Inc. • Annual. $495.00. Includes computer hardware manufacturers, software producers, book-periodical publishers, and franchised or company-owned chains of personal computer equipment retailers, support services and accessory manufacturers. Formerly *MicroLeads U.S. Vender Directory.*

ENCYCLOPEDIAS AND DICTIONARIES

Dictionary of Computing. Valerie Illingworth, editor. Oxford University Press, Inc. • 1996. $49.95. Fourth edition.

Dictionary of Information Technology and Computer Science. Tony Gunton. Blackwell Publishers. • 1994. $50.95. Second edition. Covers key words, phrases, abbreviations, and acronyms used in computing and data communications.

HANDBOOKS AND MANUALS

Secretarial/Word Processing Service. Entrepreneur Media, Inc. • Looseleaf. $59.50. A practical guide to starting a secretarial and word processing business. Covers profit potential, start-up costs, market size evaluation, owner's time required, site selection, pricing, accounting, advertising, promotion, etc. (Start-Up Business Guide No. E1136.).

The Word Processor Book. Peter McWilliams. Putnam Publishing Group. • 1997. $14.95.

ONLINE DATABASES

Computer Database. The Gale Group. • Provides online citations with abstracts to material appearing in about 150 trade journals and newsletters in the subject areas of computers, telecommunications, and electronics. Time period is 1983 to date, with weekly updates. Inquire as to online cost and availability.

Internet and Personal Computing Abstracts. Information Today, Inc. • Contains abstracts covering a wide variety of personal and business microcomputer literature appearing in more than 100 journals and popular magazines. Time period is 1981 to date, with monthly updates. Formerly *Microcomputer Index.* Inquire as to online cost and availability.

PROMT: Predicasts Overview of Markets and Technology. The Gale Group. • Companies, products, applied technologies and markets. U.S. and international literature coverage, 1972 to date. Inquire as to online cost and availability. Provides abstracts from more than 1,600 publications. Weekly updates.

PERIODICALS AND NEWSLETTERS

Computer Industry Report. International Data Corp. • Semimonthly. $495.00 per year. Newsletter. Annual supplement. Also known as "The Gray Sheet." Formerly *EDP Industry Report and Market Review.*

Distributed Computing Monitor. Patricia Seybold Group. • Monthly. $595.00 per year. Newsletter. Formerly *Distributed Computing.*

In Command! A Series of Messages About Getting the Most From Your Word Processor. Economics Press, Inc. • Weekly. $146.00 per year. Quantity prices available. A newsletter for word processing operators.

Inside Microsoft Word: Tips and Techniques for Microsoft Windows. Z-D Journals. • Monthly. $49.00 per year. Newsletter on word processing with Microsoft Word for Windows. Covers applications and problem-solving.

Inside Wordperfect for Windows. Z-D Journals. • Monthly. $59.00 per year. Newsletter on word processing with Wordperfect software. Includes tips and techniques for both beginners and experts.

The Page. Z-D Journals. • 10 times a year. $59.00 per year. Newsletter on the use of MacIntosh computers for desktop publishing.

Prompt. Pasadena IBM User Group. • Monthly. Membership. Helps users of IBM compatibles understand their system.

OTHER SOURCES

Electronic Office: Management and Technology. Faulkner Information Services, Inc. • Two looseleaf volumes, with monthly updates. $990.00 per year. Contains product reports and other information relating to automated office and integrated services.

WORDS

See: VOCABULARY

WORK CLOTHES

See: UNIFORMS

WORK FORCE

See: LABOR SUPPLY

WORK MEASUREMENT

See: TIME AND MOTION STUDY

WORK SCHEDULES

See: FACTORY MANAGEMENT; INDUSTRIAL MANAGEMENT

WORK SIMPLIFICATION

See: TIME AND MOTION STUDY

WORK STOPPAGES

See: STRIKES AND LOCKOUTS

WORK STUDY

See: TIME AND MOTION STUDY

WORKERS' COMPENSATION

ABSTRACTS AND INDEXES

Current Law Index: Multiple Access to Legal Periodicals. The Gale Group. • Monthly. $650.00 per year. Produced in cooperation with the American Association of Law Libraries. Indexes more than 900 law journals, legal newspapers, and specialty publications from the U.S., Canada, U.K., Ireland, Australia, and New Zealand.

Index to Legal Periodicals and Books. H. W. Wilson Co. • Monthly. Quarterly and annual cumulations. $270.00 per year. CD-ROM version available at $1,495.00 per year.

Insurance Periodicals Index. Specials Libraries Association, Insurance and Employees Benefits Div. CCH/NILS Publishing Co. • Annual. $250.00. Compiled by the Insurance and Employee Benefits Div., Special Libraries Association. A yearly index of over 15,000 articles from about 35 insurance periodicals. Arrangement is by subject, with an index to authors.

Personnel Management Abstracts. • Quarterly. $190.00 per year. Includes annual cumulation.

DIRECTORIES

The Human Resource Executive's Market Resource. LRP Publications. • Annual. $25.00. A directory of services and products of use to personnel departments. Includes 20 categories, such as training, outplacement, health benefits, recognition awards, testing, workers' compensation, temporary staffing, recruitment, and human resources software.

HANDBOOKS AND MANUALS

Managing Worker's Compensation: A Guide to Injury Reduction and Effective Claim Management. Keith Wertz and C. Bradley Layton. Lewis Publishers. • Date not set. $59.95. (Occupation Safety and Health Guide Series).

Modern Workers Compensation. West Group. • $395.00. Three looseleaf volumes. Periodic supplementation. Provides detailed coverage of workers' compensation law and procedure, including medical benefits, rehabilitation benefits, compensation costs, noncompensable injuries, etc.

U. S. Master Employee Benefits Guide. CCH, Inc. • Annual. $49.00. Explains federal tax and labor laws relating to health care benefits, disability benefits, workers' compensation, employee assistance plans, etc.

INTERNET DATABASES

National Center for Health Statistics: Monitoring the Nation's Health. National Center for Health Statistics, Centers for Disease Control and Preventio. Phone: (301)458-4636 E-mail: nchsquery@cdc.gov • URL: http://www.cdc.gov/nchswww • Web site provides detailed data on diseases, vital statistics, and health care in the U. S. Includes a search facility and links to many other health-related Web sites. "Fastats A to Z" offers quick data on hundreds of topics from Accidents to Work-Loss Days, with links to Comprehensive Data and related sources. Frequent updates. Fees: Free.

ONLINE DATABASES

I.I.I. Data Base Search. Insurance Information Institute. • Provides online citations and abstracts of insurance-related literature in magazines, newspapers, trade journals, and books. Emphasis is on property and casualty insurance issues, including highway safety, product safety, and environmental liability. Inquire as to online cost and availability.

Index to Legal Periodicals and Books (Online). H. W. Wilson Co. • Broad coverage of law journals and books 1981 to date. Monthly updates. Inquire as to online cost and availability.

Legal Resource Index. The Gale Group. • Broad coverage of law literature appearing in legal, business, and other periodicals, 1980 to date. Monthly updates. Inquire as to online cost and availability.

LEXIS. LEXIS-NEXIS. • The various LEXIS databases provide full text and indexing for a wide variety of legal cases, statutes, orders, and opinions.

PERIODICALS AND NEWSLETTERS

Business Insurance: News Magazine for Corporate Risk, Employee Benefit and Financial Executives. Crain Communications, Inc. • Weekly. $89.00 per year. Covers a wide variety of business insurance topics, including risk management, employee benefits, workers compensation, marine insurance, and casualty insurance.

Human Resource Executive. LRP Publications, Inc. • Monthly. $89.95 per year. Edited for directors of corporate human resource departments. Special issues emphasize training, benefits, retirement planning, recruitment, outplacement, workers' compensation, legal pitfalls, and oes emphasize training, benefits, retirement planning, recruitment, outplacement, workers' compensation, legal pitfalls, and other personnel topics.

Journal of Workers Compensation. John Liner Organization. Standard Publishing Corp. • Quarterly. $130.00 per year. Compensation topics include legal considerations, cost control, worker coverage, appropriate medical treatment, and managed care.

Risk and Insurance. LRP Publications. • Monthly. Price on application. Topics include risk management, workers' compensation, reinsurance, employee benefits, and managed care.

Workers' Compensation Law Bulletin. Quinlan Publishing Co., Inc. • Monthly, $79.00 per year; semimonthly, $129.00 per year.

Workers' Compensation Monitor. LRP Publications. • Monthly. $175.00 per year. Newsletter. Covers workers' compensation legislation, regulations, and publications. Formerly *John Burton's Workers' Compensation.*

RESEARCH CENTERS AND INSTITUTES

Center for Human Resources. Brandeis University, Heller Graduate School, 60 Turner St., Waltham, MA 02453. Phone: (781)736-3770 Fax: (781)736-3773 E-mail: curnan@brandeis.org • URL: http://www.heller.brandeis.edu/chr.

Lexis.com Research System. Lexis-Nexis Group. Phone: 800-227-9597 or (937)865-6800 Fax: (937)865-6909 E-mail: webmaster@prod.lexis-nexis.com • URL: http://www.lexis.com • Fee-based Web site offers extensive searching of a wide variety of legal sources. Additional features include Daily Opinion Service, lexis.com Bookstore, Career Center, CLE Center, Law Schools, and Practice Pages ("Pages specific to areas of specialty").

W. E. Upjohn Institute for Employment Research. 300 S. Westnedge Ave., Kalamazoo, MI 49007-4686. Phone: (616)343-5541 Fax: (616)343-3308 E-mail: eberts@we.upjohninst.org • URL: http://www.upjohninst.org • Research fields include unemployment, unemployment insurance, worker's compensation, labor productivity, profit sharing, the labor market, economic development, earnings, training, and other areas related to employment.

TRADE/PROFESSIONAL ASSOCIATIONS

International Association of Industrial Accident Boards and Commissions. 1201 Wakarusa Dr., Lawrence, KS 66049. Phone: (785)840-9103 Fax: (785)840-9107 E-mail: workcomp@iaiabc.org • URL: http://www.iaiabc.org • Members are government agencies, insurance companies, lawyers, unions, self-insurers, and others with an interest in industrial safety and the administration of workers' compensation laws.

National Council on Compensation Insurance. 750 Park of Commerce Dr., Boca Raton, FL 33487. Phone: 800-622-4123 • URL: http://www.5ncci.com/ncciweb/ • Members are insurance companies.

National Foundation for Unemployment Compensation and Workers Compensation. 1201 New York Ave., N.W., Suite 750, Washington, DC 20005-6143. Phone: (202)682-1517 Fax: (202)842-2556 E-mail: info@uwcstrategy.org • URL: http://www.uwcstrategy.org.

OTHER SOURCES

BNA's Workers' Compensation Report. Bureau of National Affairs, Inc. • Biweekly. $570.00 per year. Looseleaf business and legal service.

WORKING CLASS

See: LABOR

WORKING MOTHERS

See: EMPLOYMENT OF WOMEN; WOMEN IN THE WORK FORCE

WORKING WOMEN

See: EMPLOYMENT OF WOMEN; WOMEN IN THE WORK FORCE

WORKMEN'S COMPENSATION

See: WORKERS' COMPENSATION

WORKSHOPS

See: CONFERENCES, WORKSHOPS, AND SEMINARS

WORLD BANKING

See: INTERNATIONAL FINANCE

WORLD LAW

See: INTERNATIONAL LAW AND REGULATION

WORLD TRADE

See: FOREIGN TRADE

WORLD WIDE WEB

See: INTERNET

WORSTED INDUSTRY

See: WOOL AND WORSTED INDUSTRY

WORTHLESS SECURITIES

See: OBSOLETE SECURITIES

WRITERS AND WRITING

See also: REPORT WRITING; TECHNICAL WRITING

GENERAL WORKS

Business English. Mary E. Guffey. South-Western College Publishing. • 2001. $47.00. Seventh edition. (South-Western College-Busines Communications Series).

How to Get Happily Published: Complete and Candid Guide. Judith Appelbaum. HarperCollins Publishers. • 1998. $14.00. Fifth edition. Provides advice for writers on dealing with book and magazine publishers.

How to Take the Fog Out of Business Writing. Robert Gunning and Richard A. Kallan. Dartnell Corp. • 1994. $12.95. Includes "The 10 Principles of Clear Statement.".

Improving Writing Skills: Memos, Letters, Reports, and Proposals. Arthur A. Berger. Sage Publications, Inc. • 1993. $37.00. Emphasis is on the business correspondence required of university professors and other academic personnel. (Survival Skills for Scholars, vol. 9).

ABSTRACTS AND INDEXES

Author Biographies Master Index. The Gale Group. • 1997. $290.00. Fith edition. Two volumes. Contains over 1,140,000 references tobiographies of 550,000 different authors.

ALMANACS AND YEARBOOKS

Sage Series in Written Communication: An International Survey of Research and Theory. Sage Publications, Inc. • Irregular. $22.95.

BIOGRAPHICAL SOURCES

Contemporary Authors. The Gale Group. • 189 volumes in print. Prices vary. Provides biographical information on over 100,000 modern authors, including novelists, nonfiction writers, poets, play wrights, journalists, and scriptwriters.

International Authors and Writers Who's Who. Available from Taylor & Francis, Inc. • Biennial. $155.00. About 8,000 authors, writers, and poets, primarily American and British but including writers from nearly 40 countries in the English-speaking world. Published by Melrose Press Ltd.

Major 20th-Century Writers: A Selection of Sketches from Contemporary Authors. The Gale Group. • 1999. $314.00. Second edition. Five volumes. Includes important nonfiction writers and journalists.

CD-ROM DATABASES

Contemporary Authors on CD-ROM. The Gale Group. • Semiannual. $795.00 per year. Provides CD-ROM biographical and bibliographical information on about 100,000 modern authors. Includes novelists, nonfiction writers, poets, playwrights, screenwriters, editors, and journalists.

Leadership Library on CD-ROM: Who's Who in the Leadership of the United States. Leadership Directories, Inc. • Quarterly. $2,641.00 per year, including access to Internet version (weekly updates). Contains all 14 *Yellow Book* personnel directories on CD-ROM, providing contact and brief biographical information for about 400,000 individuals. Covers business, government, financial institutions, news media, law firms, associations, foreign representatives, and nonprofit organizations. Includes photographs.

DIRECTORIES

American Society of Journalists and Authors-Directory. American Society of Journalists and Authors. • Annual. $75.00. Lists 900 freelance nonfiction writers. Formerly *American Society of Journalists and Authors Directory of Professional Writers.*

BPI Syndicated Columnists Contacts. BPI Communications, Inc. • Annual. $120.00. Contains information needed to contact over 1500 major columinists covering four different subjects. Formerly *Syndicated Colmnists Directory.*

Cabell's Directory of Publishing Opportunities in Economics, and Finance. Cabell Publishing Co. • 1997. $89.95. Provides editorial policies of commercial and scholarly periodicals in the areas of business and economics. Formerly *Cabell's Directory of Publishing Opportunities in Accounting, Economics, and Finance.*

Cabell's Directory of Publishing Opportunities in Education. Cabell Publishing Co. • 1998. $89.95. Over 430 journals in education which will consider manuscripts forpublication.

Cabell's Directory of Publishing Opportunities in Management. Cabell Publishing Co. • 1997. $89.95. Provides editorial policies of more than 300 management periodicals. Emphasis is on publishing opportunities for college faculty members. Formerly *Cabell's Directory of Publishing Opportunities Business and Economics*.

Editor and Publisher Syndicate Directory: Annual Directory of Syndicate Services. Editor and Publisher Co., Inc. • Annual. $8.00. Directory of several hundred syndicates serving newspapers in the United States and abroad with news, columns, features, comic strips, editorial cartoons, etc.

International Literary Market Place: The Directory of the International Book Publishing Industry. R. R. Bowker. • Annual. $189.95. More than 10,370 publishers in over 180 countries outside the U.S.and Canada and about 1,150 trade and professional organizations related to publishing abroad.

Literary Market Place: The Directory of the American Book Publishing Industry. R. R. Bowker. • Annual. $199.95. Two volumes. Over 16,000 firms or organizations offering services related to the publishing industry.

News Media Yellow Book: Who's Who Among Reporters, Writers, Editors, and Producers in the Leading National News Media. Leadership Directories, Inc. • Quarterly. $305.00 per year. Lists the staffs of major newspapers and news magazines, TV and radio networks, news services and bureaus, and feature syndicates. Includes syndicated columnists and programs. Seven specialized indexes are provided.

Novel and Short Story Writer's Market: 2000 Places to Sell Your Fiction. F & W Publications, Inc. • Annual. $22.99. List of more than 2,000 literary magazines, general periodicals, small presses, book publishers, and authors' agents; contests awards; and writers' organizations.

Scriptwriters Market. Scriptwriters-Filmmakers Publishing Co. • Annual. $39.95. 450 literary agents, 375 film producers, over 3,000 actors and actresses, 325 directors, and 275 television producers.

Working Press of the Nation. R. R. Bowker. • Annual. $450.00. Three volumes: (1) *Newspaper Directory*; (2) *Magazine and Internal Publications Directory*; (3) *Radio and Television Directory*. Includes names of editors and other personnel. Individual volumes, $249.00.

Writers' and Artists' Yearbook: A Directory for Writers, Artists, Playwrights, Writers for Film, Radio and Television, Photographers and Composers. MidPoint Trade Books. • Annual. $20.00. A worldwide guide to markets for various kinds of writing and artwork. Formerly*International Writers' and Artists' Yearbook.*

The Writers Directory 2001. Available from The Gale Group. • 2000. $165.00. 15th edition. Lists more than 17,500 authors from English-Speaking countries. Includes classification by writing category.

Writer's Guide to Book Editors, Publishers, and Literary Agents, 2000-2001: Who They Are, What They Want, and How to Win Them Over. Jeff Herman. Prima Publishing. • Annual. $27.95; with CD-ROM, $49.95. Directory for authors includes information on publishers' response times and pay rates.

The Writer's Handbook. Writer, Inc. • Annual. $32.95. List of 3,000 markets for writer's work.

Writer's Market: 8000 Editors Who Buy What You Write. F & W Publications, Inc. • Annual. $27.99. More than 4,000 buyers of books, articles, short stories, plays, gags, verses, fillers, and other original written material. Includes book and periodical publishers, greeting card publishers, play producers and publishers, audiovisual material producers, syndicates, and contests, and awards. Formerly *Writer's Market: Where and How to Sell What You Write.*

ENCYCLOPEDIAS AND DICTIONARIES

Dictionary of Business Quotations. Julia Vitullo-Martin and J. Robert Moskin. Oxford University Press, Inc. • 1993. $39.95.

HANDBOOKS AND MANUALS

Business Writing at Its Best. Minerva H. Neiditz. McGraw-Hill Professional. • 1993. $22.50.

Business Writing the Modular Way: How to Research, Organize and Compose Effective Memo Letters, Articles, Reports, Proposals, Manuals, Specifications and Books. Harley Bjelland. Books on Demand. • 1992. $80.70. Covers research and organization for various kinds of business writing, from simple to complex.

Business Writing with Style: Strategies for Success. John Tarrant. John Wiley and Sons, Inc. • 1991. $10.95. Second edition. Emphasizes the use of business writing styles that are creative or unusual.

Effective Writing for Engineers, Managers, Scientists. H. J. Tichy and Sylvia Fourdrinier. John Wiley and Sons, Inc. • 1988. $104.95. Second edition.

Freelance Writing. Entrepreneur Media, Inc. • Looseleaf. $59.50. A practical guide to starting a freelance writing service. Covers profit potential, start-up costs, market size evaluation, pricing, accounting, advertising, promotion, etc. (Start-Up Business Guide No. E1258.).

Getting Your Book Published. Christine S. Smedley and Mitchell Allen. Sage Publications, Inc. • 1993. $37.00. A practical guide for academic and professional authors. Covers the initial book prospectus, contract negotiation, production procedures, and marketing. (Survival Skills for Scholars, vol. 10).

Handbook for Business Writing. L. Sue Baugh. NTC/Contemporary Publishing. • 1993. $24.95. Second edition. Covers reports, letters, memos, and proposals. (Handbook for... Series).

Handbook for Memo Writing. L. Sue Baugh. NTC/Contemporary Publishing. • 1995. $32.95. (NTC Business Book Series).

Handbook for Practical Letter Writing. L. Sue Baugh. NTC/Contemporary Publishing. • 1993. $29.95.

Handbook for Proofreading. Laura K. Anderson. NTC/Contemporary Publishing. • 1993. $24.95. (NTC Business Book Series).

Handbook for Public Relations Writing. Thomas Bivins. NTC/Contemporary Publishing. • 1999. $24.95. Third edition. (NTC Business Book Series).

How to Produce Creative Advertising: Traditional Techniques and Computer Applications. Thomas Bivins and Ann Keding. NTC/Contemporary Publishing. • 1993. $37.95. Covers copywriting, advertising design, and the use of desktop publishing techniques in advertising. (NTC Business Book Series).

How to Produce Creative Publications: Traditional Techniques and Computer Applications. Thomas Bivins and William E. Ryan. NTC/Contemporary Publishing. • 1994. $32.95. A practical guide to the writing, designing, and production of magazines, annual reports, brochures, and newsletters by traditional methods and by desktop publishing.

Librarian-Author: A Practical Guide on How to Get Published. Betty Carol Sellen, editor. Neal-Schuman Publishers, Inc. • 1985. $38.50.

The Manager's Book of Quotations. Lewis D. Eigen and Jonathan P. Siegel. AMACOM. • 1991. $21.95. Reprint edition. Provides 5,000 modern and traditional quotations arranged by topics useful to business people for speeches and writing.

NTC's Business Writer's Handbook. Arthur H. Bell. NTC/Contemporary Publishing. • 1995. $35.00. (NTC Business Book Series).

Personnel Management: Communications. Prentice Hall. • Looseleaf. Periodic supplementation. Price on application. Includes how to write effectively and how to prepare employee publications.

Public Relations Writer's Handbook. Merry Aronson and Donald E. Spetner. Jossey-Bass, Inc., Publishers. • 1998. $20.95.

Writer's Handbook for Editing and Revision. Rick Wilber. NTC/Contemporary Publishing. • 1996. $19.95. Discusses rewrites and before-and-after drafts.

INTERNET DATABASES

GaleNet: Your Information Community. The Gale Group. Phone: 800-877-GALE or (248)699-GALE Fax: 800-414-5043 or (248)699-8069 E-mail: galenet@gale.com • URL: http://www.galenet.com • Web site provides a wide variety of full-text information from Gale databases, Taft, and other sources. Covers associations, biography, business directories, education, the information industry, literature, publishing, and science. Fee-based subscriptions are available for individual databases (free demonstration). Includes Boolean search features and the BRS/Search user interface.

PERIODICALS AND NEWSLETTERS

Copy Editor: Language News for the Publishing Profession. Mary Beth/Protomastro. • Bimonthly. $69.00 per year. Newsletter for professional copy editors and proofreaders. Includes such items as "Top Ten Resources for Copy Editors.".

Freelance Writer's Report. Dana K. Cassell, editor. CNW Publishing. • Monthly. $39.00 per year. Newsletter. Provides marketing tips and information on new markets for freelance writers. Includes interviews with editors and advice on taxation and legalities.

Publishers Weekly: The International News Magazine of Book Publishing. Cahners Business Information, Broadcasting and Cables International Group. • Weekly. $189.00 per year. The international news magazine of book publishing.

Quill: The Magazine for Journalists. Society of Professional Journalists. • Monthly. $29.00 per year. A magazine for journalists.

The Writer. Writer, Inc. • Monthly. $29.00 per year. Freelance writers.

Writer's Digest. F and W Publications. • Monthly. $27.00 per year.

Written Communication: A Quarterly Journal of Research, Theory, and Application. Sage Publications, Inc. • Quarterly. Individuals, $70.00 per year; institutions, $320.00 per year.

TRADE/PROFESSIONAL ASSOCIATIONS

American Society of Business Press Editors. 107 W. Ogden Ave., LaGrange, IL 60525-2022. Phone: (708)352-6950 Fax: (708)352-3780 E-mail: 7114.34@compuserve.com • URL: http://www.asbpe.com.

American Society of Journalists and Authors. 1501 Broadway, Suite 302, New York, NY 10036. Phone: (212)997-0947 Fax: (212)768-7414.

Associated Writing Programs. George Mason University, Tallwood House, Mail Stop 1E3, Fairfax, VA 22030. Phone: (703)933-4301 Fax: (703)933-4302 E-mail: awp@gmu.edu • URL: http://www.web.gmu.edu/departments/awp • Purpose is to help writers get published or get jobs.

Association for Business Communication. Baruch College, 17 Lexington Ave., New York, NY 10010. Phone: (212)387-1340 Fax: (212)387-1655 E-mail: myersabc@compuserve.com • URL: http://www.theabc.org.

Association of Authors' Representatives. Ansonia Station, P.O. Box 237201, New York, NY 10023. Phone: (212)252-3695 E-mail: aarinc@mindspring.com • URL: http://www.aar-online.org.

Authors Guild. 330 W. 42nd St., New York, NY 10036. Phone: (212)563-5904 Fax: (212)564-8363 E-mail: staff@authorsguild.org • URL: http://www.authorsguild.org.

Authors League of America. 330 W. 42nd St., 29th Fl., New York, NY 10036. Phone: (212)564-8350 Fax: (212)564-8363 E-mail: staff@authorguild.org • URL: http://www.authorguild.org.

Council of Writers Organizations. 12724 Sagamore Rd., Leawood, KS 66209. Phone: (913)451-9023 Fax: (913)451-4866 E-mail: hurleypr@sound.net • URL: http://www.councilofwriters.com.

Editorial Freelancers Association. 71 W. 23rd St., Suite 1504, New York, NY 10010. Phone: (212)929-5400 Fax: (212)929-5439 • URL: http://www.the-efa.org.

International Black Writers. P.O. Box 1030, Chicago, IL 60690. Phone: (312)458-9254.

International Women's Writing Guild. Gracie Station, P.O. Box 810, New York, NY 10028-0082. Phone: (212)737-7536 Fax: (212)737-9469 E-mail: iwwg@iwwgh.com • URL: http://www.iwwg.com.

National Sportscasters and Sportswriters Association. P.O. Box 559, Salisbury, NC 28144. Phone: (704)633-4275 Fax: (704)633-4275 • Members are sportswriters and radio/TV sportscasters.

National Writers Association. 3140 S. Peoria St., Ste. 295, Aurora, CO 80014-3155. Phone: (303)841-0246 Fax: (303)841-2607 E-mail: sandywrter@aol.com • URL: http://www.nationalwriters.com.

Society of American Business Editors and Writers. c/o University of Missouri,, School of Journalism, 76 Gannet Hall, Columbia, MO 65211. Phone: (573)882-7862 or (573)882-8985 Fax: (573)884-1372 E-mail: carolyn-guniss@jmail.jour.missouri.edu • URL: http://www.sabew.org.

Society of Professional Journalists. 16 S. Jackson, Greencastle, IN 46135. Phone: (765)653-3333 Fax: (765)653-4631 E-mail: spj@spjhq.org • URL: http://www.spj.org.

OTHER SOURCES

Creativity Rules! A Writer's Workbook. John Vorhaus. Silman-James Press. • 2000. $15.95. Covers the practical process of conceiving, outlining, and developing a story, especially for TV or film scripts. Includes "tactics and exercises.".

Lindey on Entertainment, Publishing and the Arts: Agreements and the Law. Alexander Lindey, editor. West Group. • $673.00 per year. Looseleaf service. Periodic supplementation. Provides basic forms, applicable law, and guidance. (Entertainment and Communication Law Series).

WRITING, BUSINESS

See: BUSINESS CORRESPONDENCE; REPORT WRITING; WRITERS AND WRITING

WRITING INSTRUMENTS

See also: OFFICE EQUIPMENT AND SUPPLIES

CD-ROM DATABASES

World Marketing Forecasts on CD-ROM. The Gale Group. • Annual. $2,500.00. Produced by Euromonitor. Provides detailed forecast data for the years to 2012 on CD-ROM for 54 countries in all parts of the world. Covers a wide range of social, demographic, economic, and market factors. Includes specific forecasts for many kinds of consumer products.

DIRECTORIES

Directory of Manufacturers Supporting the Writing and Marking Instrument Industry. Writing Instrument Manufacturers Association. • Biennial. $50.00. About 200 manufacturers; includes non-members. Formerly *Directory of Manufacturers and Products of the Handwriting Instrument Manufacturing Industry.*

ONLINE DATABASES

Euromonitor Market Research. Euromonitor International. • Provides the complete text online of Euromonitor market analysis reports. Covers consumer goods market research data for all major countries, with emphasis on specific product categories. Time period is current. Continuous updating. Inquire as to online cost and availability.

PERIODICALS AND NEWSLETTERS

WIMA Bulletin. Writing Instrument Manufacturers Association. • 50 times a year. Price on application.

WIMA Directory. Writing Instrument Manufacturers Association. • Biennial. $50.00. Lists manufacturers, suppliers and products of the writing industry.

STATISTICS SOURCES

Annual Survey of Manufactures. Available from U. S. Government Printing Office. • Annual. Prices vary. Issued by the U. S. Census Bureau as an interim update to the *Census of Manufactures.* Includes data on number of manufacturing establishments in various industries, employment, labor costs, value of shipments, capital expenditures, inventories, energy costs, and assets. (See also Census Bureau home page, http://www.census.gov/.).

Consumer Canada 1996. Available from The Gale Group. • 1996. $750.00. Published by Euromonitor. Provides consumer market, socioeconomic, and demographic data for Canada. Includes consumer market size (volume and value) for many specific kinds of products.

Consumer International 2000/2001. Available from The Gale Group. • 1998. $1,190.00. Seventh edition. Published by Euromonitor. Contains extensive consumer market, economic, and demographic data for 27 major, non-European countries, including the U. S. and Canada. Includes consumer market size (volume and value) for 150 product types in 14 categories (food, clothing, automobiles, cosmetics, appliances, etc.).

European Marketing Forecasts 2001. Available from The Gale Group. • 2000. $1,190.00. Third edition. Published by Euromonitor. Contains demographic, economic, and market forecasts for the countries of Europe to the year 2010. Forecasts include market-size data for 15 consumer product sectors (food, clothing, automobiles, consumer electronics, etc.).

International Marketing Forecasts 2001. Available from The Gale Group. • 2000. $1,090.00. Third edition. Published by Euromonitor. Contains demographic, economic, and market forecasts to the year 2010 for major, non-European countries, including the U. S. and Canada. Forecasts include market-size data for 15 consumer product sectors, such as food, clothing, and automobiles.

TRADE/PROFESSIONAL ASSOCIATIONS

Writing Instrument Manufacturers Association. 236 Route 38 W., Suite 100, Moorestown, NJ 08057. Phone: (856)231-8500 Fax: (856)231-4664 E-mail: wima@ahint.com.

WRITING, TECHNICAL

See: TECHNICAL WRITING

X

X-RAY EQUIPMENT INDUSTRY

See also: HOSPITAL EQUIPMENT; MEDICAL TECHNOLOGY

ABSTRACTS AND INDEXES

Applied Science and Technology Index. H. W. Wilson Co. • 11 times a year. Quarterly and annual cumulations. Service basis for print edition; CD-ROM edition, $1,495.00 per year. Indexes a wide variety of English language technical, industrial, and engineering periodicals.

CD-ROM DATABASES

WILSONDISC: Applied Science and Technology Abstracts. H. W. Wilson Co. • Monthly. $1,495.00 per year, including unlimited access to the online version of *Applied Science and Technology Abstracts* through WILSONLINE. Provides CD-ROM indexing and abstracting of 400 prominent scientific, technical, engineering, and industrial periodicals. Indexing coverage is provided from 1983 to date and abstracting from 1993 to date.

DIRECTORIES

Health Industry Buyers Guide. Spring House. • Annual. $195.00. About 4,000 manufacturers of hospital and physician's supplies and equipment. Formerly *Surgical Trade Buyers Guide.*

Radiology Reference Guide. Access Publishing Co. • Annual. Price on application. Includes directory information for radiological equipment, supplies, services, organizations, and publications.

ONLINE DATABASES

Applied Science and Technology Index Online. H. W. Wilson Co. • Provides online indexing of 400 major scientific, technical, industrial, and engineering periodicals. Time period is 1983 to date. Monthly updates. Inquire as to online cost and availability.

Globalbase. The Gale Group. • Provides more than one million online summaries of business, industrial, and economic news reports from more than 1,000 publications worldwide. Covers a wide range of material appearing in international trade journals, professional magazines, and newspapers. Time period is 1984 to date, with weekly updates. Inquire as to online cost and availability.

Health Devices Alerts [online]. ECRI. • Provides online reports of medical equipment defects, problems, failures, misuses, and recalls. Time period is 1977 to date, with weekly updates. Inquire as to online cost and availability.

PROMT: Predicasts Overview of Markets and Technology. The Gale Group. • Companies, products, applied technologies and markets. U.S. and international literature coverage, 1972 to date. Inquire as to online cost and availability. Provides abstracts from more than 1,600 publications. Weekly updates.

Trade & Industry Index. The Gale Group. • Provides indexing of business periodicals, January 1981 to date. Daily updates. (Full text articles from some periodicals are available online, 1983 to date, in the companion database, *Trade & Industry ASAP.*) Inquire as to online cost and availability.

PERIODICALS AND NEWSLETTERS

Decisions in Imaging Economics: The Journal of Imaging Technology Management. Curant Communications, Inc. • Bimonthly. Controlled circulation. Edited for health care executives and radiologists concerned with the purchase and management of imaging technology.

Healthcare Purchasing News: A Magazine for Hospital Materials Management Central Service, Infection Control Practitioners. McKnight Medical Communications. • Monthly. $44.00 per year. Edited for personnel responsible for the purchase of medical, surgical, and hospital equipment and supplies. Features new purchasing techniques and new products. Includes news of the activities of two major purchasing associations, Health Care Material Management Society and International Association of Healthcare Central Service Materiel Management.

Medical Devices, Diagnostics, and Instrumentation: The Gray Sheet Reports. F-D-C Reports, Inc. • Weekly. $955.00 per year. Newsletter. Provides industry and financial news, including a medical sector stock index. Monitors regulatory developments at the Center for Devices and Radiological Health of the U. S. Food and Drug Administration.

Radiology and Imaging Letter. Lippincott Williams and Wilkins Publishers. • 22 times a year. Individuals, $363.00 per year; institutions, $425.00 per year. Edited for radiologists, technicians, hospital administrators, and medical equipment manufacturers. Provides imformation on advances in medical imaging technology.

RESEARCH CENTERS AND INSTITUTES

Mallinckrodt Institute of Radiology - Hyperthermia Service. Washington University in Saint Louis, Radiation Oncology Center, 4939 Children's Place, Suite 5500, St. Louis, MO 63110. Phone: (314)362-8503 Fax: (314)362-8521 E-mail: moros@castor.wustl.edu • URL: http://www.mir.wustl.edu/ • Maintains laboratories for research pertaining to various kinds of radiological equipment.

STATISTICS SOURCES

Annual Survey of Manufactures. Available from U. S. Government Printing Office. • Annual. Prices vary. Issued by the U. S. Census Bureau as an interim update to the *Census of Manufactures.* Includes data on number of manufacturing establishments in various industries, employment, labor costs, value of shipments, capital expenditures, inventories, energy costs, and assets. (See also Census Bureau home page, http://www.census.gov/.).

Electromedical Equipment and Irradiation Equipment, Including X-Ray. U. S. Bureau of the Census. • Annual. Contains shipment quantity, value of shipment, export, and import data. (Current Industrial Report No. MA-38R.).

Manufacturing Profiles. Available from U. S. Government Printing Office. • Annual. Issued by the U. S. Census Bureau. A printed consolidation of the entire *Current Industrial Report* series, presenting "all the data compiled." Contains statistics on production, shipments, inventories, consumption, exports, imports, and orders for a wide variety of manufactured products. (See also Census Bureau home page, http://www.census.gov/.).

TRADE/PROFESSIONAL ASSOCIATIONS

American College of Radiology. 1891 Preston White Dr., Reston, VA 22091. Phone: 800-227-5463 or (703)648-8900 Fax: (703)648-9176 • URL: http://www.acr.org • A professional society of physicians.

Association for Healthcare Resource and Materials Management. c/o American Hospital Association, One N. Franklin St ., Chicago, IL 60606. Phone: (312)422-3840 Fax: (312)422-3573 E-mail: ahrmm@aha.org • URL: http://www.ahrmm.org • Members are involved with the purchasing and distribution of supplies and equipment for hospitals and other healthcare establishments. Affiliated with the American Hospital Association.

Health Care Resource Management Society. P.O. Box 29253, Cincinnati, OH 45229-0253. Phone: (513)520-1058 or (513)872-6315 Fax: (513)872-6158 E-mail: hcrms@choice.net • URL: http://www.hcrms.com • Members are materials management (purchasing) personnel in hospitals and the healthcare industry. The Society is concerned with hospital costs, distribution, logistics, recycling, and inventory management.

International Association of Healthcare Central Service Materiel Management. 213 W. Institute Place, Suite 307, Chicago, IL 60610. Phone: 800-962-8274 or (312)440-0078 Fax: (312)440-9474 E-mail: mailbox@iahcsmm.com • URL: http://www.iahcsmm.com • Members are professional personnel responsible for management and distribution of supplies from a central service material management (purchasing) department of a hospital.

Radiological Society of North America. 820 Jorie Blvd., Oak Brook, IL 60523-2251. Phone: (630)571-2670 Fax: (630)571-7837 • URL: http://www.rsna.org • Members are radiologists and scientists. Includes a Technical Exhibits Committee and a Scientific Exhibits Committee.

Radiology Business Management Association. 1550 S. Coast Highway, Suite 201, Laguna Beach, CA 92651. Phone: 888-224-7262 Fax: (949)376-2246 • URL: http://www.rbma.org • Members include vendors of X-ray equipment, services, and supplies.

OTHER SOURCES

Digital X-Ray Markets: Imaging in the 21st Century. Theta Reports/PJB Medical Publications, Inc. • 2000. $1,995.00. Market research data. Covers digital filmless radiography as a replacement for traditional x-ray technology. (Theta Report No. 1027.).

Y

YACHTS

See: BOAT INDUSTRY

YARN

See also: COTTON INDUSTRY; SILK INDUSTRY; TEXTILE INDUSTRY; WEAVING; WOOL AND WORSTED INDUSTRY

ABSTRACTS AND INDEXES

Textile Technology Digest. Institute of Textile Technology. • Monthly. $535.00 per year. Provides indexing and abstracting of a wide variety of textile technology literature.

CD-ROM DATABASES

Textile Technology Digest [CD-ROM]. Textile Information Center, Institute of Textile Technology. • Quarterly. $1,700.00 per year. Provides CD-ROM indexing and abstracting of worldwide journals and monographs in various areas of textile technology, production, and management. Covers 1978 to date.

DIRECTORIES

America's Textiles International-Buyer's Guide. Billian Publishing, Inc. • Annual. $25.00. List of 2,800 suppliers for the textile industry.

ENCYCLOPEDIAS AND DICTIONARIES

Encyclopedia of Textiles. French and European Publications, Inc. • 1980. $39.95. Third edition.

Textile Terms and Definitions. J.E. McIntyre and Paul N. Daniels, editors. Available from State Mutual Book and Periodical Service Ltd., Trade Order Dept. • 1995. $110.00. 10th edition. Published by the Textile Insitute (UK). Includes more than 1,000 definitions of textile processes, fiber types, and end products. Illustrated.

FINANCIAL RATIOS

Annual Statement Studies. Robert Morris Associates: The Association of Lending and Credit Risk Professiona. • Annual. Free to members; non-members, $140.00. Median and quartile financial ratios are given for over 400 kinds of manufacturing, wholesale, retail, construction, and consumer finance establishments. Data is sorted by both asset size and sales volume. Includes a clearly written "Definition of Ratios" and an alphabetical industry index.

INTERNET DATABASES

Fedstats. Federal Interagency Council on Statistical Policy. Phone: (202)395-7254 • URL: http://www.fedstats.gov • Web site features an efficient search facility for full-text statistics produced by more than 70 federal agencies, including the Census Bureau, the Bureau of Economic Analysis, and the Bureau of Labor Statistics. Boolean searches can be made within one agency or for all agencies combined. Links are offered to international statistical bureaus, including the UN, IMF, OECD, UNESCO, Eurostat, and 20 individual countries. Fees: Free.

ONLINE DATABASES

DRI U.S. Central Database. Data Products Division. • Provides more than 23,000 business, financial, demographic, economic, foreign trade, and industry-related time series for the U.S. Includes national income, population, retail-wholesale trade, price indexes, labor data, housing, industrial production, banking, interest rates, money supply, etc. Time period is generally 1947 to date (some data back to 1929). Updating varies. Inquire as to online cost and availability.

Textile Technology Digest [online]. Textile Information Center, Institute of Textile Technology. • Contains indexing and abstracting of more than 300 worldwide journals and monographs in various areas of textile technology, production, and management. Time period is 1978 to date, with monthly updating. Inquire as to online cost and availability.

World Textiles. Elsevier Science, Inc. • Provides abstracting and indexing from 1970 of worldwide textile literature (periodicals, books, pamphlets, and reports). Includes U. S., European, and British patent information. Updating is monthly. Inquire as to online cost and availability.

PERIODICALS AND NEWSLETTERS

American Sportswear and Knitting Times. National Knitwear and Sportswear Association. • Monthly. $40.00 per year. Includes *American Sportswear and Knitting Times Buyer's Guide.* Formerly *Knitting Times.*

DNR: The Men's Fashion Retail Textile Authority. Fairchild Publications. • Daily. $85.00 per year. Formerly *Daily News Record.*

International Textile Bulletin: Yarn and Fabric Forming Edition. ITS Publishing, International Textile Service. • Quarterly. $170.00 per year. Editions in Chinese, English, French, German, Italian and Spanish.

STATISTICS SOURCES

Annual Survey of Manufactures. Available from U. S. Government Printing Office. • Annual. Prices vary. Issued by the U. S. Census Bureau as an interim update to the *Census of Manufactures.* Includes data on number of manufacturing establishments in various industries, employment, labor costs, value of shipments, capital expenditures, inventories, energy costs, and assets. (See also Census Bureau home page, http://www.census.gov/.).

Business Statistics of the United States. Courtenay M. Slater, editor. Bernan Associates. • 1999. $74.00. Fifth edition. Based on *Business Statistics*, formerly issue by the Bureau of Economic Analysis, U. S. Department of Commerce. Provides basic data for a wide variety of U. S. industries, services, and economic indicators. Most statistics are shown annually for 29 years and monthly for the most recent four years.

Consumption on the Woolen System and Worsted Combing. U. S. Bureau of the Census. • Quarterly and annual. Provides data on consumption of fibers in woolen and worsted spinning mills, by class of fibers and end use. (Current Industrial Reports, MQ-22D.).

Manufacturing Profiles. Available from U. S. Government Printing Office. • Annual. Issued by the U. S. Census Bureau. A printed consolidation of the entire *Current Industrial Report* series, presenting "all the data compiled." Contains statistics on production, shipments, inventories, consumption, exports, imports, and orders for a wide variety of manufactured products. (See also Census Bureau home page, http://www.census.gov/.).

Survey of Current Business. Available from U. S. Government Printing Office. • Monthly. $49.00 per year. Issued by Bureau of Economic Analysis, U. S. Department of Commerce. Presents a wide variety of business and economic data.

TRADE/PROFESSIONAL ASSOCIATIONS

American Yarn Spinners Association. P.O. Box 99, Gastonia, NC 28053. Phone: (704)824-3522 Fax: (704)824-0630 • URL: http://www.aysa.org.

Textile Institute. Saint James Bldgs., 4th Fl., Oxford St., Manchester M1 6FQ, England. Phone: 44 161 2371188 Fax: 44 161 2361991 E-mail: tiihq@textileinst.org.uk • URL: http://www.texi.org • Members in 100 countries involved with textile industry management, marketing, science, and technology.

OTHER SOURCES

Textile Business Outlook. Statistikon Corp. • Quarterly. $985.00 per year. Analyzes current business, marketing, and financial conditions for the worldwide textile industry (fibers and fabrics). Includes statistical forecasts.

YOUTH MARKET

See also: CHILDREN'S APPAREL INDUSTRY

ALMANACS AND YEARBOOKS

Research Alert Yearbook: Vital Facts on Consumer Behavior and Attitudes. EPM Communications, Inc. • Annual. $295.00. Provides summaries of consumer market research from the newsletters *Research Alert, Youth Markets Alert, and Minority Markets Alert.* Includes tables, charts, graphs, and textual summaries for 41 subject categories. Sources include reports, studies, polls, and focus groups.

CD-ROM DATABASES

Magazine Index Plus. The Gale Group. • Monthly. $4,000.00 per year (includes InfoTrac workstation). Provides full text on CD-ROM for about 100 popular, general interest magazines and indexing for 300 others. Includes special indexing of reviews and product evaluations. Time period is 1980 to date.

PERIODICALS AND NEWSLETTERS

KidTrends Newsletter. Available from MarketResearch.com. • Monthly. $199.00 per year.

Published by Children's Market Research, Inc. Market data newsletter.

Selling to Kids: News and Practical Advice on Successfully Marketing to Children. Available from MarketResearch.com. • Biweekly. $495.00 per year. Newsletter. Published by Phillips Business Information.

Targeting Teens Newsletter. Available from MarketResearch.com. • Monthly. $199.00 per year. Published by Children's Market Research, Inc. Provides current data and information for marketing to the 12 to 18 age group.

Youth Markets Alert. EPM Communications, Inc. • Monthly. $295.00 per year. Newsletter on youth market research. Covers age groups from elementary school to college years.

OTHER SOURCES

KidTrends Report: Trends, Buying Patterns, and Lifestyles. Available from MarketResearch.com. • 1998. $2595.00 Market research report published by Children's Market Research, Inc. Covers computer software, video games, music, books, electronic equipment, and toys for children and pre-teens.

Teenage Economic Power. Available from MarketResearch.com. • 1998. $1,200.00. Published by Rand Youth Poll. Provides consumer market data on the 13-year to 19-year age group. Gives results of an extensive survey of teenage attitudes toward shopping and spending.

The U. S. College Market. Available from MarketResearch.com. • 2001. $2,799.00. Published by Packaged Facts. Market research report on college students as consumers.

The U. S. Tweens Market. Available from MarketResearch.com. • 2001. $2,750.00. Published by Packaged Facts. Market research report on American consumers aged 8 to 14.

Z

ZERO-BASE BUDGETING

See: BUDGETING, BUSINESS

ZERO DEFECTS

See: QUALITY CONTROL

ZINC INDUSTRY

See also: METAL INDUSTRY; MINES AND MINERAL RESOURCES

ABSTRACTS AND INDEXES

IMM Abstracts and Index: A Survey of World Literature on the Economic Geology and Mining of All Minerals (Except Coal), Mineral Processing, and Nonferrous Extraction Metallurgy. Institution of Mining and Metallurgy. • Bimonthly. Members, $142.00 per year; non-members, $215.00 per year. Provides international coverage of the literature of mining and nonferrous metallurgy. Includes mineral economics, tunnelling, and rock mechanics.

Nonferrous Metals Alert. Cambridge Information Group. • Monthly. $340.00 per year. Provides citations to the business and industrial literature of nonferrous metals. (Materials Business Information Series).

Zincscan: A Review of Recent Technical Literature On the Use of Zinc and Its Products. C & C Associates. • Quarterly. $125.00. per year. Provides technical articles and abstracts of recent technical and market related literature on zinc. Formerly *Zinc Abstracts.*

ALMANACS AND YEARBOOKS

CRB Commodity Yearbook. Commodity Research Bureau. CRB. • Annual. $99.95.

CD-ROM DATABASES

METADEX Materials Collection: Metals-Polymers-Ceramics. Cambridge Scientific Abstracts. • Quarterly. $6,950.00 per year. Provides CD-ROM citations to the worldwide literature of materials science and metallurgy. Corresponds to *Metals Abstracts, Alloys Index, Steels Alert, Nonferrous Alert, Polymers/Ceramics/Composites Alert,* and *Engineered Materials Abstracts.* (Formerly produced by ASM International.).

INTERNET DATABASES

Fedstats. Federal Interagency Council on Statistical Policy. Phone: (202)395-7254 • URL: http://www.fedstats.gov • Web site features an efficient search facility for full-text statistics produced by more than 70 federal agencies, including the Census Bureau, the Bureau of Economic Analysis, and the Bureau of Labor Statistics. Boolean searches can be made within one agency or for all agencies combined. Links are offered to international statistical bureaus, including the UN, IMF, OECD, UNESCO, Eurostat, and 20 individual countries. Fees: Free.

ONLINE DATABASES

DRI U.S. Central Database. Data Products Division. • Provides more than 23,000 business, financial, demographic, economic, foreign trade, and industry-related time series for the U.S. Includes national income, population, retail-wholesale trade, price indexes, labor data, housing, industrial production, banking, interest rates, money supply, etc. Time period is generally 1947 to date (some data back to 1929). Updating varies. Inquire as to online cost and availability.

GEOARCHIVE. Geosystems. • Citations to literature on geoscience and water. 1974 to present. Monthly updates. Inquire as to online cost and availability.

GEOREF. American Geological Institute. • Bibliography and index of geology and geosciences literature, 1785 to present. Inquire as to online cost and availability.

Materials Business File. Cambridge Scientific Abstracts. • Provides online abstracts and citations to worldwide materials literature, covering the business and industrial aspects of metals, plastics, ceramics, and composites. Corresponds to *Steels Alert, Nonferrous Metals Alert,* and *Polymers/Ceramics/Composites Alert.* Time period is 1985 to date, with monthly updates. (Formerly produced by ASM International.) Inquire as to online cost and availability.

METADEX. Cambridge Scientific Abstracts. • Covers the worldwide literature of metals, metallurgy, and materials science, 1966 to date. Includes detailed alloys indexing from 1974. Biweekly updating. Inquire as to online cost and availability. (Formerly produced by ASM International.).

PERIODICALS AND NEWSLETTERS

The Mining Record. Howell International Enterprises. • Weekly. $45.00 per year.

PRICE SOURCES

Metals Week. McGraw-Hill Commodity Services Group. • Weekly. $770.00 per year.

STATISTICS SOURCES

Business Statistics of the United States. Courtenay M. Slater, editor. Bernan Associates. • 1999. $74.00. Fifth edition. Based on *Business Statistics*, formerly issue by the Bureau of Economic Analysis, U. S. Department of Commerce. Provides basic data for a wide variety of U. S. industries, services, and economic indicators. Most statistics are shown annually for 29 years and monthly for the most recent four years.

Lead and Zinc Statistics. International Lead and Zinc Study Group. • Monthly. $370.00 per year. Supplement available *Advance Data Service.* Text in English and French.

Mineral Commodity Summaries. Available from U. S. Government Printing Office. • Annual. Published by the U. S. Geological Survey, Department of the Interior (http://www.usgs.gov). Contains detailed, five-year data for about 90 nonfuel minerals. Covers a wide range of statistics, including production, imports, exports, consumption, reserves, prices, tariff information, and industry employment. (Two pages are devoted to each mineral.).

Non-Ferrous Metal Data Yearbook. American Bureau of Metal Statistics. • Annual. $395.00. Provides about 200 statistical tables covering many nonferrous metals. Includes production, consumption, inventories, exports, imports, and other data.

Survey of Current Business. Available from U. S. Government Printing Office. • Monthly. $49.00 per year. Issued by Bureau of Economic Analysis, U. S. Department of Commerce. Presents a wide variety of business and economic data.

WEFA Industrial Monitor. John Wiley and Sons, Inc. • Annual. $65.00. Prepared by industry analysts at WEFA, an economic forecasting and consulting firm (originally Wharton Econometric Forecasting Associates). Contains discussions of the outlook for major U. S. industries, with many 10-year forecasts (WEFA Web site is http://www.wefa.com).

World Trade Annual. United Nations Statistical Office. Walker and Co. • Annual. Prices vary.

TRADE/PROFESSIONAL ASSOCIATIONS

American Bureau of Metal Statistics. P.O. Box 805, Chatham, NJ 07928. Phone: (973)701-2299 Fax: (973)701-2152 E-mail: info@abms.com • URL: http://www.abms.com • Members are metal companies. Compiles and publishes detailed statistical data on a wide variety of nonferrous metals: aluminum, copper, gold, lead, nickel, platinum, silver, tin, titanium, uranium, zinc, and others.

International Lead Zinc Research Organization. P.O. Box 12036, Research Triangle Park, NC 27709. Phone: (919)361-4647 Fax: (919)361-1957 E-mail: jcole@ilzro.org • URL: http://www.ilzro.com.

Non-Ferrous Metals Producers Committee. c/o Kenneth Button, Economic Consulting Service, 2030 M. St., N.W., Suite 800, Washington, DC 20036. Phone: (202)466-7720 Fax: (202)466-2710 • Members are copper, lead, and zinc producers. Promotes the copper, lead, and zinc mining and metal industries.

ZIP CODE

See: POSTAL SERVICES

ZONING

See also: CITY PLANNING; REGIONAL PLANNING

ABSTRACTS AND INDEXES

Current Law Index: Multiple Access to Legal Periodicals. The Gale Group. • Monthly. $650.00 per year. Produced in cooperation with the American

Association of Law Libraries. Indexes more than 900 law journals, legal newspapers, and specialty publications from the U.S., Canada, U.K., Ireland, Australia, and New Zealand.

Index to Legal Periodicals and Books. H. W. Wilson Co. • Monthly. Quarterly and annual cumulations. $270.00 per year. CD-ROM version available at $1,495.00 per year.

PAIS International in Print. Public Affairs Information Service, Inc. • Monthly. $650.00 per year; cumulations three times a year. Provides topical citations to the worldwide literature of public affairs, economics, demographics, sociology, and trade. Text in English; indexed materials in English, French, German, Italian, Portuguese and Spanish.

ALMANACS AND YEARBOOKS

American Law Yearbook. The Gale Group. • Annual. $155.00. Serves as a yearly supplement to *West's Encyclopedia of American Law.* Describes new legal developments in many subject areas.

BIBLIOGRAPHIES

NIMBYS and LULUs (Not-in-My-Back-Yard and Locally-Unwanted-Land-Uses). Jan Horah and Heather Scott. Sage Publications, Inc. • 1993. $10.00.

CD-ROM DATABASES

PAIS on CD-ROM. Public Affairs Information Service, Inc. • Quarterly. $1,995.00 per year. Provides a CD-ROM version of the online service, *PAIS International.* Contains over 400,000 citations to the literature of contemporary social, political, and economic issues.

WILSONDISC: Index to Legal Periodicals and Books. H. W. Wilson Co. • Monthly. Including unlimited online access to *Index to Legal Periodicals* through WILSONLINE. Contains CD-ROM indexing of more than 800 English language legal periodicals from 1981 to date and 2,500 books.

ENCYCLOPEDIAS AND DICTIONARIES

Encyclopedia of Housing. Willem van Vliet, editor. Sage Publications, Inc. • 1998. $169.95. Contains 500 entries covering all aspects of housing. Includes index of names and subjects.

West's Encyclopedia of American Law. Available from The Gale Group. • 1997. $995.00. Second edition. 12 volumes. Published by West Group. Covers a wide variety of legal topics for the general reader. Formerly *Guide to American Law: Everyone's Legal Encyclopedia* (1985).

HANDBOOKS AND MANUALS

New Uses for Obsolete Buildings. Urban Land Institute. • 1996. $64.95. Covers various aspects of redevelopment: zoning, building codes, environment, economics, financing, and marketing. Includes eight case studies and 75 descriptions of completed "adaptive use projects.".

Zoning and Planning Deskbook. Douglas W. Kmiec. West Group. • $145.00. Looseleaf service. Periodic supplementation. Emphasis is on legal issues.

Zoning and Planning Law Handbook. West Group. • 1996. Price on application. (Real Property-Zoning Series).

ONLINE DATABASES

Index to Legal Periodicals and Books (Online). H. W. Wilson Co. • Broad coverage of law journals and books 1981 to date. Monthly updates. Inquire as to online cost and availability.

PAIS International. Public Affairs Information Service, Inc. • Corresponds to the former printed publications, *PAIS Bulletin* (1976-90) and *PAIS Foreign Language Index* (1972-90), and to the current *PAIS International in Print* (1991 to date). Covers economic, political, and sociological material appearing in periodicals, books, government documents, and other publications. Updating is monthly. Inquire as to online cost and availability.

PERIODICALS AND NEWSLETTERS

Land Use Law and Zoning Digest. American Planning Association. • Monthly. $275.00 per year. Covers judicial decisions and state laws affecting zoning and land use. Edited for city planners and lawyers. Monthly supplement available *Zoning News.*

Planning and Zoning News. Planning and Zoning Center, Inc. • Monthly. $175.00 per year. Newsletter on planning and zoning issues in the United States.

Zoning and Planning Law Report. West Group. • 11 times a year. $283.00 per year. Newsletter.

Zoning Bulletin. Quinlan Publishing Co., Inc. • Semimonthly. $89.00 per year. Newsletter dealing with zoning legal issues.

Zoning News. American Planning Association. • Monthly. $55.00 per year. Newsletter on local community zoning.

RESEARCH CENTERS AND INSTITUTES

Institute of State and Regional Affairs. Pennsylvania State University at Harrisburg, 777 W. Harrisburg Pike, Middletown, PA 17057-4898. Phone: (717)948-6178 Fax: (717)948-6306 E-mail: xvc@psu.edu • URL: http://www.psdc.hbg.psu.edu/isra • Conducts research in environmental, general, and socioeconomic planning. Zoning is included.

Lexis.com Research System. Lexis-Nexis Group. Phone: 800-227-9597 or (937)865-6800 Fax: (937)865-6909 E-mail: webmaster@prod.lexis-nexis.com • URL: http://www.lexis.com • Fee-based Web site offers extensive searching of a wide variety of legal sources. Additional features include Daily Opinion Service, lexis.com Bookstore, Career Center, CLE Center, Law Schools, and Practice Pages ("Pages specific to areas of specialty").

For publishers addresses, refer to SOURCES CITED section at the back of the book.

Sources Cited

SOURCES CITED

A/C Flyer: Best Read Resale Magazine Worldwide. McGraw-Hill, 1221 Ave. of the Americas New York, NY 10020. Phone: 800-722-4726 or (212)904-2000 Fax: (212)904-2072 E-mail: customer.service@mcgraw-hill.com • URL: http://www.mcgraw-hill.com • Monthly. $28.00 per year. Lists used airplanes for sale by dealers, brokers, and private owners. Provides news and trends relating to the aircraft resale industry. Special issues include "Product & Service Buyer's Guide" and "Dealer/Broker Directory."

A-V Online. Access Innovations, Inc., National Information Center for Educational Media, P. O. Box 8640 Albuquerque, NM 87198. Phone: 800-926-8328 or (505)265-3591 Fax: (505)256-1080 Provides online descriptions of non-print educational materials for all levels, kindergarten to graduate school. Includes all types of audio, film, and video media. Updated quarterly. Inquire as to online cost and availability.

A-V Online (CD-ROM). Access Innovations, Inc., National Information Center for Educational Media, P. O. Box 8640 Albuquerque, NM 87198. Phone: 800-926-8328 or (505)998-0800 Fax: (505)998-3372 Annual. $795.00 per year. Provides CD-ROM descriptions of all types of non-print educational materials, covering all learning levels.

The A-Z Vocabulary for Investors. American Institute for Economic Research, Division St. Great Barrington, MA 01230-1000. Phone: (413)528-1216 Fax: (413)528-0103 E-mail: info@aier.org • URL: http://www.aier.org • 1997. $7.00. Second half of book is a "General Glossary" of about 400 financial terms "most-commonly used" in investing. First half contains lengthier descriptions of types of banking institutions (commercial banks, thrift institutions, credit unions), followed by succinct explanations of various forms of investment: stocks, bonds, options, futures, commodities, and "Other Investments" (collectibles, currencies, mortgages, precious metals, real estate, charitable trusts). (Economic Education Bulletin.)

A.A.A. Offices to Serve You-Names and Addresses of Affiliated Motor Clubs and Associations. American Automobile Association, 1000 AAA Dr. Heathrow, FL 32746. Phone: (407)444-7000 Fax: (404)444-7380 Annual.

AAA Rated: Unscrambling the Bond Market. Lydia LaFaro. Reference & User Services Association (RUSA), c/o American Library Association, 50 E. Huron St. Chicago, IL 60611-2795. Phone: 800-545-2433 or (312)944-6780 Fax: (312)944-8085 E-mail: rusa@ala.org • URL: http://www.ala.org/rusa • 1997. $20.00. Provides basic information on various kinds of bonds and their ratings. Includes a "comprehensive glossary of terms related to the bond market." (RUSA Occasional Papers Series, No. 22.)

AACE International-Directory of Members. AACE International, 209 Prairie Ave., Suite 100 Morgantown, WV 26505. Phone: 800-858-2678 or (304)296-8444 Fax: (304)291-5728 E-mail: info@aacei.org • URL: http://www.aacei.com • Annual. $10.00 per year. 6,000 cost engineers, estimators, and cost management professionals worldwide.

AACE International. Transactions of the Annual Meetings. American Association of Cost Engineers. AACE International, 209 Prairie Ave., Suite 100 Morgantown, WV 26505. Phone: 800-858-2678 or (304)296-8444 Fax: (304)291-5728 E-mail: info@aacei.org • URL: http://www.aacei.org • Annual. Price varies. Contains texts of papers presented at AACE meetings.

AACSB Newsline. American Assembly of Collegiate Schools of Business, The International Association for Management Education, 600 Emerson Rd., Suite 300 Saint Louis, MO 63141-6762. Phone: (314)872-8481 Fax: (314)872-8495 URL: http://www.aacsb.edu • Quarterly. $15.00 per yer. Contains news of AACSB activities and developments i higher education for business and management.

AACSB: The International Association for Management Education. American Assembly of Collegiate Schools of Business, 600 Emerson Rd., Suite 300 Saint Louis, MO 63141-6762. Phone: (314)872-8481 Fax: (314)872-8495 URL: http://www.aacsb.edu • Annual. $15.00. Lists over 800 member institutions offering instructional programs in business administration at the college level. Formerly (American Assembley of Collegiate Schools of Business Membership Directory)

AACSB - The International Association for Management Education.

AAHP/Dorland Directory of Health Plans. Dorland Healthcare Information, 1500 Walnut St., Suite 1000 Philadelphia, PA 19102. Phone: 800-784-2332 or (215)875-1212 Fax: (215)735-3966 E-mail: info@dorlandhealth.com • URL: http://www.dorlandhealth.com • Annual. $215.00. Published in association with the American Association of Health Plans (http://www.aahp.org). Lists more than 2,400 health plans, including Health Maintenance Organizations (HMOs), Preferred Provider Organizations (PPOs), and Point of Service plans (POS). Includes the names of about 9,000 health plan executives. Formerly *Managed Health Care Directory*.

AAHSA Resource Catalog. American Association of Homes and Services for the Aging, 901 E St., N. W., Suite 500 Washington, DC 20004-2011. Phone: 800-508-9442 or (202)783-2242 Fax: (202)783-2255 E-mail: info@aahsa.org • URL: http://www.aahsa.org • Annual. Free. Provides descriptions of material relating to managed care, senior housing, assisted living, continuing care retirement communities (CCRCs), nursing facilities, and home health care. Publishers are AAHSA and others.

AAII Journal. American Association of Individual Investors, 625 N. Michigan Ave., Suite No. 1900 Chicago, IL 60611. Phone: (312)280-0170 Fax: (312)280-1625 E-mail: members@aaii.com • URL: http://www.aii.org • 10 times a year. $49.00 per year. Covers strategy and investment techniques.

AAMVA Bulletin. American Association of Motor Vehicle Administrators, 4301 Wilson Blvd., Suite 400 Arlington, VA 22203-1800. Phone: (703)522-4200 Fax: (703)522-1553 Monthly. $25.00.

AAPOR News. American Association for Public Opinion Research, P.O. Box 1248 Ann Arbor, MI 48106-1248. Phone: (313)764-1555 Fax: (313)764-3341 E-mail: aapor@umich.edu • URL: http://www.aapor.org • Quarterly. Membership. Newsletter.

AARP Bulletin. American Association of Retired Persons, 601 E. St., N.W. Washington, DC 20049. Phone: (202)434-2277 Fax: (202)434-6881 URL: http://www.aarp.org • 11 times a year. Membership.

AAUW Outlook. American Association of University Women, 1111 16th St., N.W. Washington, DC 20036. Phone: (202)785-7734 Fax: (202)872-1425 URL: http://www.aauw.org • Quarterly. Free to members; non-members, $15.00 per year. Formerly *Graduate Woman*.

AB Bookman's Weekly: For the Specialist Book World (Antiquarian Bookman)., P.O. Box AB Clifton, NJ 07015. Phone: (973)772-0020 Fax: (973)772-9281 E-mail: abbookman@aol.com • URL: http://www.abbookman.com • Weekly. $125.00 per year. Includes *A B Bookman's Yearbook*.

AB Bookman's Yearbook: Specialist Book Trade Annual (Antiquarian Bookman)., P.O. Box AB Clifton, NJ 07015. Phone: (973)772-0020 Fax: (973)772-9281 E-mail: abbookman@aol.com • URL: http://www.bookman.com • Annual.

ABA Bankers News. American Bankers Association, Member Communications, 1120 Connecticut Ave., N.W. Washington, DC 20036-3971. Phone: 800-338-0626 or (202)663-5000 Fax: (202)663-7543 URL: http://www.aba.com • Biweekly. Members, $48.00 per year; non-members, $96.00 per year. Formerly *ABA Banker News Weekly*. Incorporating *Agricultural Banker*.

ABA Banking Journal. American Bankers Association, Member Communications. Simmons-Boardman Publishing Corp., 345 Hudson St. New York, NY 10014-4502. Phone: (212)620-7200 Fax: (212)633-1165 URL: http://www.banking.com/aba • Monthly. Free to qualified personnel; others, $25.00 per year.

ABA/BNA Lawyer's Manual on Professional Conduct. American Bar Association. Bureau of National Affairs, Inc., 1231 25th St., N.W. Washington, DC 20037-1197. Phone: 800-372-1033 or (202)452-4200 Fax: (202)822-8092 E-mail: books@bna.com • URL: http://www.bna.com • Biweekly. $845.00 per year. Looseleaf. Covers American Bar Association's model rules governing ethical practice of law.

ABA Book Buyer's Handbook. American Booksellers Association, 828 S. Broadway Tarrytown, NY 10591-5112. Phone: 800-637-0037 or (914)591-2665 Fax: (914)591-2720 E-mail: ab-info@bookweb.org • URL: http://www.bookweb.org • Annual. Membership. Trade policies. Formerly *Book Buyer's Handbook*.

ABA Journal: The Lawyers Magazine. American Bar Association, 750 N. Lake Shore Dr. Chicago, IL 60611-3314. Phone: 800-285-2221 or (312)988-5000 Fax: (312)988-6014 E-mail: abajournal@attmail.com • URL: http://www.abanet.org/journal/home.html • Monthly. Free to members; non-members, $66.00 per year. Includes five regular sections: news affecting lawyers, practical applications of court decisions, pratice management advice, feature articles, and lifestyle stories.

ABC Today-Associated Builders and Contractors National Membership Directory. Associated Builders and Contractors, Inc. ABC Publications, 1300 N. 17th St. Rosslyn, VA 22209. Phone: (703)812-2000 Fax: (703)812-8203 E-mail: info@abc.org • Annual. $150.00. List of approximately 19,000 member construction contractors and suppliers. Formerly *Builder and Contractor-Associated Builders and Contractors Membership Directory*.

ABCs of Relationship Selling. Charles Futrell. McGraw-Hill Higher Education, 1221 Ave. of the Americas New York, NY 10020. Phone: 800-722-4726 or (212)904-2000 Fax: (212)904-2072 E-mail: customer.service@mcgraw-hill.com • URL: http://www.mcgraw-hill.com • 1996. $51.45. Fifth revised edition.

The Aberdeen's Concrete Construction. Aberdeen Group, 426 S. Westgate St. Addison, IL 60101. Phone: 800-837-0870 or (630)543-0870 Fax: (630)543-3112 E-mail: creditor@wocnet.com • URL: http://www.wocnet.com/mags.cc.htm • Monthly. $30.00 per year. Covers methods of building with precast, prestressed, and other forms of concrete. Emphasis is on technology and new products or construction procedures.

Aberdeen's Concrete Construction Buyers' Guide. The Aberdeen Group, 426 S. Westgate St. Addison, IL 60101-4546. Phone: 800-837-0870 or (630)543-0870 Fax: (630)543-3112 E-mail: aberdeen@wocnet.com • URL: http://www.worldofconcrete.com • Annual. $5.00. Lists sources of products and services related to building with concrete.

The Aberdeen's Magazine of Masonry Construction. Aberdeen Group, 426 S. Westgate St. Addison, IL 60101-4546. Phone: 800-837-0870 or (630)543-0870 Fax: (630)543-3112 E-mail: aberdeen@wocnet.com • URL: http://www.wocnet.com/mags.mc.htm • Monthly. $30.00 per year. Covers the business, production, and marketing aspects of various kind of masonry construction: brick, concrete block, glass block, etc.

ABG Division United Steel Worker.

ABI/INFORM. Bell & Howell Information and Learning, 300 N. Zeeb Rd. Ann Arbor, MI 48103. Phone: 800-521-0600 or (734)761-4700 Fax: 800-864-0019 URL: http://

www.umi.com • Provides online indexing to business-related material occurring in over 1,000 periodicals from 1971 to the present. Inquire as to online cost and availability.

ABI/INFORM Global. Bell & Howell Information and Learning, 300 N. Zeeb Rd. Ann Arbor, MI 48103. Phone: (734)761-4700 or 800-521-0600 Fax: 800-864-0019 URL: http://www.umi.com • Monthly. $6,500.00 per year. Provides CD-ROM indexing and abstracting of worldwide business literature appearing in over 1,200 periodicals for the most recent five years. Archival discs are available from 1971. Formerly *ABI/INFORM OnDisc*.

Abrasive Ages. William G. Pinkstone. Sutter House, P.O. Box 212 Lititz, PA 17543. Phone: (717)626-0800 Fax: (717)627-2772 1975. $16.95.

Abrasive Engineering Society.

Abrasive Engineering Society Conference Proceedings. Abrasive Engineering Society, Meadowlark Technical Services, P.O. Box 3157 Butler, PA 16003-3157. Phone: (724)282-6210 Fax: (724)282-6210 Annual. Price varies.

Abrasives Magazine. Abrasive Magazine, Inc., P.O. Box 101 Ellenton, FL 34222. Phone: (941)722-0356 Fax: (941)721-9691 E-mail: rose@abrasivemag.com • URL: http://www.abrasivemag.com • Eight times a year. $27.00 per year.

Abridged Biography and Genealogy Master Index. The Gale Group, 27500 Drake Rd. Farmington Hills, MI 48331-3535. Phone: 800-877-GALE or (248)699-GALE Fax: 800-414-5043 or (248)699-8069 E-mail: galeord@galegroup.com • URL: http://www.galegroup.com • 1995. $475.00. Second edition. Three volumes. Indexes 266 widely held biographical reference sources, with approximately 2.2 million citations. Based on the larger *Biography and Genealogy Master Index*.

The Absolute Sound: The High End Journal of Audio and Music. Harry Pearson, editor. Absolute Multimedia Inc., 7035 Bee Caves Rd., Ste. 203 Austin, TX 78746. Phone: 800-222-3201 or (512)306-8780 Fax: (512)328-7528 E-mail: paturner@isat.com • URL: http://www.theabsolutesound.com/ • Six times a year. $42.00 per year.

Abstract of Previous Meetings. Society for the Investigation of Recurring Events, c/o John Wood, P.O. Box 1020 Downingtown, PA 19335. Phone: (610)269-5900 Fax: (610)269-5901 E-mail: sirecycles@aol.com • Monthly. Price on application.

Abstracts in New Technologies and Engineering. R. R. Bowker, 121 Chanlon Rd. New Providence, NJ 07974. Phone: 888-269-5372 or (908)464-6800 Fax: (908)771-7704 E-mail: info@bowker.com • URL: http://www.bowker.com • Bimonthly. $1,650.00 per year. Annual cumulation. Formerly *Current Technology Index*.

Abstracts in Social Gerentology: Current Literature on Aging. National Council on the Aging. Sage Publications, Inc., 2455 Teller Rd. Thousand Oaks, CA 91320. Phone: (805)499-0721 Fax: (805)499-0871 E-mail: info@sagepub.com • URL: http://www.sagepub.com • Quarterly. Individuals, $110.00 per year; institutions, $350.00 per year. Formerly *Current Literature on Aging*.

Abstracts on Tropical Agriculture. Koninklijk Instituut voor de Tropen/Royal Tropical Institute, Mauritskade 63, NL-1092 AD Amsterdam, Netherlands. Phone: (613)568-8298 Fax: (312)0120-6654423 Abstracts of journals, articles, monographs, conferences, reports, 1975 to present. Inquire as to online cost and availability.

ACA Conference Proceedings. American Compensation Association, 14040 N. Northsight Blvd. Scottsdale, AZ 85260. Phone: 800-800-0341 or (480)951-9191 Fax: (480)483-8352 Annual.

ACA News. American Compensation Association, 14040 N. Northsight Blvd. Scottsdale, AZ 85260. Phone: 800-800-0341 or (480)951-9191 Fax: (480)483-8352 10 times a year. Free to members; non-members; $60.00 per year.

ACADEME. American Association of University Professors, 1012 14th St., N.W., Suite 500 Washington, DC 20005-3465. Phone: (202)737-5900 Fax: (202)737-5526 E-mail: aaup@aaup.org • URL: http://www.aaup.org • Bimonthly. $62.00 per year.

The Academic Library in Transition: Planning for the 1990s. Beverly P. Lynch, editor. Neal-Schuman Publishers, Inc., 100 Varick St. New York, NY 10013. Phone: (212)925-8650 Fax: 800-584-2414 or (212)219-8916 E-mail: info@neal-schuman.com • URL: http://www.neal-schuman.com • 1989. $49.95.

Academic Year Abroad. Institute of International Education, P.O. Box 371 Annapolis, MD 20701-0371. Phone: 800-445-0443 or (301)617-7804 Fax: (301)953-2838 E-mail: iiebooks@iie.org • URL: http://www.iie.org/ • Annual. $44.95. Lists over 2,700 undergraduate and graduate study abroad programs.

Academic Year and, Semester and Summer Programs Abroad. American Institute for Foreign Study, College Div., River Plaza, 9 W. Broad St. Stamford, CT 06902-3788. Phone: 800-727-2437 or (203)399-5000 Fax: (203)399-5597 Annual. Free. Formerly *Academic Year and Summer Programs Abroad*.

Academy for Educational Development.

Academy for State and Local Government.

Academy of Arts and Sciences of the Americas., 9450 Old Cutler Rd. Miami, FL 33156. Phone: (305)663-9897 Fax: (305)667-8426 Seeks an interdisciplinary approach to the 21st century.

Academy of Family Mediators.

Academy of Food Marketing. Saint Joseph's University

Academy of Legal Studies in Business.

Academy of Management., P.O. Box 3020 Briarcliff Manor, NY 10510-3020. Phone: (914)923-2607 Fax: (914)923-2615 E-mail: aom@academy.pace.edu • URL: http://www.aom.pace.edu • Members are university professors of management and selected business executives.

The Academy of Management Executive. Oxford University Press, Journals, 2001 Evans Rd. Cary, NC 27513. Phone: 800-852-7323 Fax: (919)677-1714 E-mail: jnl.info@oup.co.uk • URL: http://www.aom.pace.edu/publications • Quarterly. $135.00 per year. Contains articles relating to the practical application of management principles and theory.

Academy of Management Journal. Academy of Management, P.O. Box 3020 Briarcliff, NY 10510-8020. Phone: (914)923-2607 Fax: (914)923-2615 URL: http://www.aom.pace.edu • Bimonthly. $95.00 per year. Presents research papers on management-related topics.

Academy of Management Review. Academy of Management, P.O. Box 3020 Briarcliff, NY 10510-8020. Phone: (914)923-2607 Fax: (914)923-2615 URL: http://www.aom/pace.edu • Quarterly. $80.00 per year. A scholarly journal concerned with the theory of management and organizations.

Academy of Motion Picture Arts and Sciences.

Academy of Television Arts and Sciences.

Access Reports: Freedom of Information. Access Reports, Inc., 1624 Dogwood Lane Lynchburg, VA 24503. Phone: (804)384-5334 Fax: (804)384-8272 Biweekly. $325.00 per year. Newsletter.

Access to European Union: Law, Economics, Policies. Euroconfidentiel S. A., Rue de Rixensart 18 B-1332 Genval, Belgium. Phone: (32)02 653 01 25 Fax: (32)02 653 01 80 E-mail: nigel.hunt@euronet.be • Annual. $62.00. Covers EU legislation and policy in major industrial and commercial sectors. Includes customs policy, the common market, monetary union, taxation, competition, "The EU in the World," and related topics. Contains more than 300 bibliographical references.

Accessories Resources Directory. Business Journals, Inc., P.O. Box 5550 Norwalk, CT 06856. Phone: 800-521-0227 or (203)853-6015 Fax: (203)852-8175 Annual. $30.00. 1,600 manufacturers, importers, and sales representatives producing or handling belts, gloves, handbags, scarves, hosiery, jewelry, sunglasses and umbrellas. Formerly *Accessories Directory*.

Accident Analysis and Prevention. Elsevier Science, 655 Ave. of the Americas New York, NY 10010. Phone: 888-437-4636 or (212)989-5800 Fax: (212)633-3680 E-mail: usinfo@elsevier.com • URL: http://www.elsevier.com • Bimonthly. $1123.00 per year.

Accident Facts. National Safety Council, Statistics Dept., 1121 Spring Lake Dr. Itasca, IL 60143. Phone: 800-621-7619 or (630)285-1121 Fax: (630)285-1315 URL: http://www.nsc.org • Annual. $37.95.

Accident Prevention. Flight Safety Foundation, Inc., 601 Madison St., Suite 300 Alexandria, VA 22314-1756. Phone: (703)739-6700 Fax: (703)739-6708 E-mail: fsf@radix.net • Monthly. Memebers, $120.00 per year; non-members, $240.00 per year. Covers airline safety. Formerly *Accident Prevention Bulletin*.

Accountant's Guide to Employee Benefits. Paul Rosenfield. Warren, Gorham and Lamont/RIA Group, 395 Hudson St. New York, NY 10014. Phone: 800-950-1207 or (212)367-6300 Fax: (651)687-7000 E-mail: customer_services@riag.com • URL: http://www.riahome.com • $205.00. Periodic supplementation. Formerly *Accounting and Auditing for Employee Benefits*.

Accountants' Handbook. Douglas R. Carmichael and others, editors. John Wiley and Sons, Inc., 605 Third Ave. New York, NY 10158-0012. Phone: 800-225-5945 or (212)850-6000 Fax: (212)850-6088 E-mail: info@wiley.com • URL: http://www.wiley.com • 1999. $135.00. Ninth edition. Chapters are written by various accounting and auditing specialists.

Accountant's Handbook of Fraud and Commercial Crime. G. Jack Bologna and others. John Wiley and Sons, Inc., 605 Third Ave. New York, NY 10158-0012. Phone: 800-225-5945 or (212)850-6000 Fax: (212)850-6088 E-mail: info@wiley.com • URL: http://www.wiley.com • 1992. $155.00. *1996 Supplement*, $65.00.

Accountant's Handbook of Information Technology. G. Jack Bologna and Anthony M. Walsh. John Wiley and Sons, Inc., 605 Third Ave. New York, NY 10158-0012. Phone: 800-225-5945 or (212)850-6000 Fax: (212)850-6088 E-mail: info@wiley.com • 1997. $125.00.

Accountants' Liability. Practising Law Institute, 810 Seventh Ave. New York, NY 10019-5818. Phone: 800-260-4754 or (212)824-5700 Fax: (212)265-4742 E-mail: info@pli.edu • URL: http://www.pli.edu • Looseleaf. $135.00. Annual revisions. Covers all aspects of accountants' professional liability issues, including depositions and court cases.

Accounting and Budgeting in Public and Non-profit Organizations: A Manager's Guide. C. William Garner. Jossey-Bass, Inc. Publishers, 350 Sansome St. San Francisco, CA 94104. Phone: 888-378-2537 or (415)433-1740 Fax: (415)433-0499 E-mail: webperson@jbp.com • URL: http://www.josseybass.comm • Date not set. $39.95. An accounting primer for non-profit executives with no formal training in accounting. Includes an explanation of Generally Accepted Accounting Principles (GAAP) as applied to non-profit organizations. (Public Administration-Non Profit Sector Series).

Accounting and Finance for Non-Specialists. Peter Atrill and Eddie McLaney. Prentice Hall, 240 Frisch Court Paramus, NJ 07652-5240. Phone: 800-947-7700 or (201)909-6200 Fax: 800-445-6991 or (201)909-6361 URL: http://www.prenhall.com • 2000. Third edition. Price on application. Includes the measurement and reporting of financial performance and cash flow.

Accounting and Recordkeeping for the Self-Employed. Jack Fox. John Wiley and Sons, Inc., 605 Third Ave. New York, NY 10158-0012. Phone: 800-225-5945 or (212)850-6000 Fax: (212)850-6088 E-mail: info@wiley.com • URL: http://www.wiley.com • 1994. Price on application.

Accounting and Tax Database. Bell & Howell Information and Learning, 300 N. Zeeb Rd. Ann Arbor, MI 48103. Phone: 800-521-0600 or (734)761-4700 Fax: 800-864-0019 URL: http://www.umi.com • Provides indexing and abstracting of the literature of accounting, taxation, and financial management, 1971 to date. Updating is weekly. Especially covers accounting, auditing, banking, bankruptcy, employee compensation and benefits, cash management, financial planning, and credit. Inquire as to online cost and availability.

Accounting and Tax Index. UMI, 300 N. Zeeb Rd. Ann Arbor, MI 48106-1346. Phone: 800-521-0600 or (313)761-4700 Fax: 800-864-0019 or (313)761-1203 URL: http://www.umi.com • Quarterly. Price on application. Includes annual cumulative bound volume. Indexes accounting, auditing, and taxation literature appearing in journals, books, pamphlets, conference proceedings, and newsletters. (UMI is University Microfilms International, a Bell & Howell Co.)

Accounting Articles. CCH, Inc., 4025 W. Peterson Ave. Chicago, IL 60646-6085. Phone: 800-248-3248 or (773)866-6000 Fax: 800-224-8299 or (773)866-3608 URL: http://www.cch.com • Monthly. $594.00 per year. Looseleaf service.

Accounting Deskbook: The Accountant's Everyday Instant Answer Book. Douglas L. Blensly and Tom M. Plank. Prentice Hall, 240 Frisch Court Paramus, NJ 07652-5240. Phone: 800-947-7700 or (201)909-6200 Fax: 800-445-6991 or (201)909-6361 URL: http://www.prenhall.com • 1995. $69.95. 10th edition. 2000 *Supplement*, $39.95. Covers more than 230 accounting topics with examples, checklists, worksheets, and tables.

Accounting for Governmental and Non-Profit Entities. Earl R. Wilson and others. McGraw-Hill, 1221 Ave. of the Americas New York, NY 10020. Phone: 800-722-4726 or (212)904-2000 Fax: (212)904-2072 E-mail: customer.service@mcgraw-hill.com • URL: http://www.mcgraw-hill.com • 2000. 12th edition. Price on application.

Accounting for Libraries and Other Not-for-Profit Organizations. G. Stevenson Smith. American Library Association, 50 E. Huron St. Chicago, IL 60611-2795. Phone: 800-545-2433 or (312)944-6780 Fax: (312)440-9374 E-mail: ala@ala.org • URL: http://www.ala.org • 1999. $82.00. Second edition. Covers accounting fundamentals for nonprofit organizations. Includes a glossary.

Accounting Research Directory. John C. Gardner and others, editors. Markus Wiener Publishing, Inc., 231 Nassau St. Princeton, NJ 08542. Phone: (609)921-1141 Fax: (908)921-1141 E-mail: wiener95@aol.com • Irregular. $69.95. Contains lists and evaluations of all publications in seven leading accounting, journals.

Accounting Research Program.

Accounting Research Studies. American Institute of Certified Public Accountants, 1211 Ave. of the Americas New York, NY 10036-8775. Phone: 800-862-4272 or (212)596-6200 Fax: (212)596-6213 E-mail: journal@aicpa.org • URL: http://www.aicpa.org/pubs • Irregular.

Accounting Review. American Accounting Association, 5717 Bessie Dr. Sarasota, FL 34233. Phone: (914)921-7747 Fax: (914)923-4093 URL: http://www.rutgers.edu/ • Quarterly. Free to members; non-members, $125.00 per year.

Accounting Software Guide. Anderson McLean, Inc., Five Town and Country Village, Suite 508 San Jose, CA 95128. Phone: (408)972-0401 Fax: (408)371-6242 Annual. $29.95. Lists accounting software by type of application and by name of dealer or producer.

Accounting Systems for Law Offices. William J. Burke and Carl W. Bradbury. Matthew Bender & Co., Inc., Two Park Ave.

New York, NY 10016. Phone: 800-223-1940 or (212)448-2000 Fax: (212)244-3188 E-mail: international@bender.com • URL: http://www.bender.com • Looseleaf Service. $220.00. Periodic supplementation.

Accounting Technology. Faulkner & Gray, Inc., 11 Penn Plaza, 17th Fl. New York, NY 10001. Phone: 800-535-8403 or (212)967-7000 Fax: (212)967-7155 E-mail: orders@faulknergray.com • URL: http://www.faulknergray.com • Nine times a year. $58.00 per year. Provides advice and information on computers and software for accountants. Formerly *Computers in Accounting*.

Accounting: The Basis for Business Decisions. Robert F. Meigs and Mary A. Meigs. McGraw-Hill, 1221 Ave. of the Americas New York, NY 10020-1095. Phone: 800-722-4726 or (212)904-2000 Fax: (212)904-2072 E-mail: customer.service@mcgraw-hill.com • URL: http://www.mcgraw-hill.com • 1995. $68.75. 10th edition.

Accounting Theory. Ahmed Riahi-Belkaoui. Thomson Learning, 7625 Empire Dr. Florence, KY 41042. Phone: 800-347-7707 or (606)525-6620 Fax: (606)647-5023 E-mail: findit@thomsonlearning.com • URL: http://www.thomsonlearning.com • 2000. $77.99. Fourth edition. (ITBP Textbook Series.)

Accounting Today: The Newspaper for the Accounting Professional. Faulkner & Gray, Inc., 11 Penn Plaza, 17th Fl. New York, NY 10001. Phone: 800-535-8403 or (212)967-7000 Fax: (212)967-7155 E-mail: orders@faulknergray.com • URL: http://www.faulknergray.com • Biweekly. $84.00 per year. Provides news of accounting and taxes.

Accounting Trends and Techniques in Published Corporate Annual Reports. American Institute of Certified Public Accountants, 1211 Ave. of the Americas New York, NY 10036-8775. Phone: 800-862-4272 or (212)596-6200 Fax: (212)596-6213 E-mail: journal@aicpa.org • URL: http://www.aicpa.org/pubs • Annual. $50.00.

ACCRA Cost of Living Index (Association for Applied Community Reseach). ACCRA, PO Box 407 Arlington, VA 22210-0407. Phone: (703)522-4980 Fax: (703)522-4985 E-mail: sam@acura.org • URL: http://www.accra.org • Quarterly. $130.00 per year. Compares price levels for 280-310 U.S. cities.

Accredited Institutions of Postsecondary Education. Allison Anaya, editor. Oryx Press, 4041 N. Central Ave., Suite 700 Phoenix, AZ 85012-3397. Phone: 800-279-6799 or (602)265-2651 Fax: 800-279-4663 Annual. $39.95. Lists more than 5,500 accredited institutions and programs.

Accredited Journalism and Mass Communication Education. School of Journalism. Accrediting Council on Education for Journalism and Mass Communications, University of Kansas, Stauffer-Flint Hall Lawrence, KS 66045. Phone: (913)864-3973 Fax: (913)864-5225 URL: http://www.ukans.edu/~acejmc • Annual. Free. Lists about 109 accredited schools.

Accredited Programs in Architecture; And Professional Degrees Conferred on Completion of Their Curricula in Architecture. National Architectural Accrediting Board, 1735 New York Ave., N.W. Washington, DC 20006. Phone: (202)783-2007 Fax: (202)783-2822 E-mail: info@naab.org • URL: http://www.naab.org • Annual. Free.

Accrediting Council on Education in Journalism and Mass Communications. University of Kansas

Accu-Data. Accu-Weather, Inc., 385 Science Rark Rd. State College, PA 16803. Phone: 800-566-6606 or (814)234-9601 Fax: (814)238-1339 Provides detailed, current weather conditions and weather forecasts for many U. S. and foreign cities and regions. Updating is continuous. Inquire as to online cost and availability.

Accuracy in Media., 4455 Connecticut Ave., N.W.,, Suite 330 Washington, DC 20008. Phone: 800-787-0044 or (202)364-4401 Fax: (202)371-4098 E-mail: ar@aim.org • URL: http://www.aim.org • A nonpartisan organization that receives and researches complaints from the public relating to factual errors made by the news media.

Achieving the Competitive Edge with Customer Service. American Management Association Extension Institute, P.O. Box 1026 Saranac Lake, NY 12983-9957. Phone: 800-262-9699 or (518)891-1500 Fax: (518)891-0368 E-mail: amapubs@aol.com • URL: http://www.amanet.org • Looseleaf. $110.00. Self-study course. Emphasis is on practical explanations, examples, and problem solving. Quizzes and a case study are included.

ACI Manual of Concrete Practice. American Concrete Institute, P.O. Box 9094 Farmington Hills, MI 48333-9040. Phone: (248)848-3700 Fax: (248)848-3701 E-mail: webmaster@aci-int.org • URL: http://www.aci-int.org • Free to members; non-members, $595.00 per set. Five volumes.

ACIL.

ACM Computing Surveys: The Survey and Tutorial Journal of the ACM. Association for Computing Machinery, 1515 Broadway, 17th Fl. New York, NY 10036-5701. Phone: (212)626-0500 Fax: (212)944-1318 URL: http://www.acm.org • Quarterly. Free to members; non-members, $100.00 per year.

ACM Electronic Guide to Computing Literature: Bibliographic Listing, Author IndeIndex, Category Index, Proper Noun Subject Index, Reviewer Index, Source Index. Association for Computing Machinery, 1515 Broadway, 17th Fl. New York, NY 10036-5701. Phone: (212)626-0500 Fax: (212)944-1318 URL: http://www.acm.org • Quarterly. Members, $175.00; non-members, $499.00 per year. A comprehensive guide to each year's computer literature (books, proceedings, journals, etc.), with an emphasis on technical material. Indexed by author, keyword, category, proper noun, reviewer, and source. Formerly *ACM Guide to Computing Literature*.

ACM Transactions on Graphics. Association for Computing Machinery, 1515 Broadway, 17th Fl. New York, NY 10036-5701. Phone: (212)626-0500 Fax: (212)944-1318 E-mail: holly@watson.ibm.com • URL: http://www.acm.org • Semiannual. Free to members; non-members, $110.00 per year.

Acoustical Society of America.

Acoustical Society of America Journal. American Institute of Physics, One Physics Ellipse College Park, MD 20740-3843. Phone: (301)209-3100 Fax: (301)209-0843 E-mail: ojsed@aip.org • URL: http://www.asa.aip.org/jasa • Monthly. $1,020.00 per year.

Acoustics Abstracts. Multi-Science Publishing Co., Ltd, P.O. Box 176 Avenel, NJ 07001. E-mail: sciencem@hotmail.com • Monthly. $416.00. per year. Parts A and B.

Acquiring or Selling the Privately Held Company. Practising Law Institute, 810 Seventh Ave. New York, NY 10019-5818. Phone: 800-260-4754 or (212)824-5700 Fax: (212)265-4742 E-mail: info@pli.edu • URL: http://www.pli.edu • 1995. $149.00. Two volumes. (Corporate Law and Practice Series).

Acquisitions and Mergers: Negotiated and Contested Transactions. Simon M. Lorne. West Group, 610 Opperman Dr. Eagan, MN 55123. Phone: 800-328-4880 or (651)687-7000 Fax: 800-213-2323 or (651)687-5827 URL: http://www.westgroup.com • Four looseleaf volumes. $445.00. Periodic supplementation. Includes legal forms and documents. (Securities Law Series).

Acronyms, Initialisms, and Abbreviations Dictionary. The Gale Group, 27500 Drake Rd. Farmington Hills, MI 48331-3535. Phone: 800-877-GALE or (248)699-GALE Fax: 800-414-5043 or (248)699-8069 E-mail: galeord@galegroup.com • URL: http://www.galegroup.com • Annual. $650.00. Three volumes. Provides more than 586,000 definitions in all subject areas.

ACS Style Guide: A Manual for Authors and Editors. Janet S. Dodd, editor. American Chemical Society Publications, Available from Oxford University Press, 198 Madison Ave. New York, NY 10016-4314. Phone: 800-445-9714 or (212)726-6000 Fax: (212)726-6446 E-mail: egt@oup.usa.org • URL: http://www.oup-usa.orgorg • 1997. $39.95. Second edition. A style manual for scientific and technical writers. Includes the use of illustrations, tables, lists, numbers, and units of measure.

ACT-American College Testing.

ACTA Materialia: An International Journal for the Science of Materials. Elsevier Science, 655 Ave. of the Americas New York, NY 10010. Phone: 888-437-4636 or (212)989-5800 Fax: (212)633-3680 E-mail: usinfo@elsevier.com • URL: http://www.elsevier.com • Monthly. $1,135.00 per year. Formerly *ACTA Metallutgical et Materalia*.

Action on Smoking and Health., 2013 H St., N. W. Washington, DC 20006. Phone: (202)659-4310 Fax: (202)833-3921 URL: http://www.ash.org • Promotes national legal action against smoking.

Active Portfolio Management: Quantitative Theory and Applications. Richard C. Grinold. McGraw-Hill, 1221 Ave. of the Americas New York, NY 10020. Phone: 800-722-4726 or (212)904-2000 Fax: (212)904-2072 E-mail: customer.service@mcgraw-hill.com • URL: http://www.mcgraw-hill.com • 1999. $70.00. Second edition.

The Actuary. Society of Actuaries, 475 N. Martingale Rd., Suite 800 Schaumburg, IL 60173-2226. Phone: (847)706-3500 Fax: (847)706-3599 E-mail: cgreen@soa.org • URL: http://www.soa.org • 10 times a year. $25.00 per year.

The Ad Men and Women: A Biographical Dictionary of Advertising. Edd Applegate, editor. Greenwood Publishing Group, Inc., 88 Post Rd., W. Westport, CT 06881-5007. Phone: 800-225-5800 or (203)226-3571 Fax: (203)222-2540 E-mail: bookinfo@greenwood.com • URL: http://www.greenwood.com • 1994. $85.00. Provides extended biographical profiles of "54 men and women who have shaped advertising from the nineteenth century to the present." Includes bibliographies.

ADA Compliance Guide (Americans with Disabilities Act). Thompson Publishing Group, 1725 K St., N. W., Suite 200 Washington, DC 20006. Phone: 800-424-2959 or (202)872-1766 Fax: (202)296-1091 Looseleaf, with monthly updates and monthly news bulletin. $287.00 per year. Provides detailed information for employers and local governments on the requirements of the Americans with Disabilities Act.

Addiction Research Foundation Journal: Addiction News for Professionals. Addiction Research Foundation of Ontario, Subscription-Marketing Dept., 33 Russell St. Toronto, ON, Canada M5S 2S1. Phone: (416)595-6059 Fax: (416)593-4694 E-mail: adubey@arf.org • URL: http://www.intropage.html • Six times a year. $19.00 per year. News and opinions from the drug and alcohol field around th world. Formerly *Alcoholism and Drug Addiction Research Foundation Journal*.

Adhesion Science. J. Comyn. American Chemical Society, 1155 16th St., N. W. Washington, DC 20036. Phone: 800-333-9511 or (202)872-4600 Fax: (202)872-4615 E-mail: service@acs.org • URL: http://www.pubs.acs.org • 1997. Published by The Royal Society of Chemistry. Provides basic scientific and technical information on "common adhesives." (RSC Paperback Series).

Adhesive and Sealant Council.

Adhesives Age. Chemical Week Associates, 110 Williams St., 11th Fl. New York, NY 10038. Phone: 800-308-6397 or (212)621-4900 Fax: (212)621-4949 E-mail: webmaster@chemweek.com • URL: http://www.adhesiveage.com • Monthly. $60.00 per year. Includes annual *Directory*.

Adhesives Age Directory. Intertec Publishing Corp., 6151 Powers Ferry Rd., N.W., Suite 200 Atlantic, GA 30339-2941. Phone: 800-621-9907 or (770)955-2500 Fax: (770)955-0476 E-mail: subs@intertec.com • URL: http://www.intertec.com • Annual. $59.95. Formerly *Adhesives Red Book*.

Adhesives and Sealants. ASM International, 6939 Kinsman Rd. Materials Park, OH 44073-0002. Phone: 800-336-5152 or (440)338-5151 Fax: (440)338-4634 E-mail: cust.serv@po.asm-intl.org • URL: http://www.asm-intl.org • 1990. $186.00. Volume three. (Engineered Materials Handbook Series).

Adhesives Manufacturers Association.

Adhesives Technology Handbook. Arthur H. Landrock. Noyes Data Corp., 169 Kinderkamack Rd., Ste. 5 Park Ridge, NJ 07676-1338. Phone: (201)505-4965 1986. $64.00.

Adjuntas Substation. University of Puerto Rico

Administering Successful Programs for Adults: Promoting Excellence in Adult, Community, and Continuing Education. Michael W. Galbraith and others. Krieger Publishing Co., P.O. Box 9542 Melbourne, FL 32902-9542. Phone: 800-724-0025 or (321)724-9542 Fax: (321)951-3671 E-mail: info@krieger-publishing.com • URL: http://www.krieger-publishing.com • 1996. $24.50. Provides practical advice on the "day-to-day duties and responsibilities of organizing and administering successful programs in adult, community, and continuing education settings." (Professional Practices in Adult Education and Human Resource Development Series).

Administration and Society. Sage Publications, Inc., 2455 Teller Rd. Thousand Oaks, CA 91320. Phone: (805)499-0721 Fax: (805)499-0871 E-mail: info@sagepub.com • URL: http://www.sagepub.com • Bimonthly. Individuals, $85.00 per year; institutions, $420.00 per year. Scholarly journal concerned with public administration and the effects of bureaucracy.

Administration of the Public Library. Alice Gertzog and Edwin Beckerman. Scarecrow Press, Inc., 4720 Boston Way Lanham, MD 20706-4310. Phone: 800-462-6420 or (301)459-3366 Fax: 800-338-4550 or (301)459-1705 E-mail: orders@scarecrowpress.com • URL: http://www.scarecrowpress.com • 1994. $62.50.

Administrative Assistant's Update. Carswell Thomson Professional Publishing, 2075 Kennedy Rd. Scarborough, ON, Canada MIT 3V4. Phone: (416)609-8000 Fax: (416)869-0456 Monthly. $139.00 per year. Newsletter. Advice and information for secretaries and office workers. Formerly *Secretary's Update*.

Administrative Law. Matthew Bender & Co., Inc., Two Park Ave. New York, NY 10016. Phone: 800-223-1940 or (212)448-2000 Fax: (212)244-3188 E-mail: international@bender.com • URL: http://www.bender.com • $1,200.00 per year. Six looseleaf volumes. Periodic supplementation. Covers investigations, adjudications, hearings, licenses, judicial review, and so forth.

Administrative Law. Steven J. Cann. Sage Publications, Inc., 2455 Teller Rd. Thousand Oaks, CA 91320. Phone: (805)499-0721 Fax: (805)499-0871 E-mail: info@sagepub.com • URL: http://www.sagepub.com • 1998. $55.00. Second edition.

Administrative Law Review. American University, Washington College of Law, 4801 Massachusetts Ave., N.W., Suite 621 Washington, DC 20016. Phone: (202)274-4481 Fax: ((20)2)274-0802 E-mail: air-editor-in-chief@wcl.american.edu • URL: http://www.wcl.american.edu/pub/journals/air/ • Quarterly. Members; $35.00 per year; non-members, $40.00 per year. Scholarly legal journal on developments in the field of administrative law.

Administrative Office Management: An Introduction. Zane B. Quible. Prentice Hall, 240 Frisch Court Paramus, NJ 07652-5240. Phone: 800-947-7700 or (201)909-6200 Fax: 800-445-6991 URL: http://www.prenhall.com • 2000. $52.00. 7th edition. (KU-Office Procedures Series).

Administrative Science Quarterly. Cornell University Press, Johnson Graduate School of Management, 20 Thornwood Dr., Suite 100 Ithaca, NY 14850-1265. Phone: 800-666-2211 or (607)254-7143 Fax: (607)254-7100 E-mail: orderbook@cupserv.org • URL: http://

www.cornellpress.cornell.edu • Individuals: $55.00 per year; institutions, $100.00 per year.

Administrator's Handbook for Community Health and Home Care Services. Anne S. Smith. National League for Nursing Press, 61 Broadway, 33rd Fl. New York, NY 10006-2701. Phone: 800-669-1656 or (212)989-9393 Fax: (212)989-3710 E-mail: commentsnlweb@nln.org • URL: http://www.nln.org • 1988. $175.00.

Adult and Continuing Education Today. Learning Resources Network, 1554 Hayes Dr. Manhattan, KS 66502. Phone: (913)539-5376 BiWeekly. $95.00 per year.

Adult Education Quarterly. American Association for Adult and Continuing Education, 1200 19th St., N.W., Suite 300 Washington, DC 20036. Phone: (202)429-5131 Quarterly. $50.00 per year.

Adult Learning. American Association for Adult and Continuing Education, 1200 19th St., N.W., Suite 300 Washington, DC 20036. Phone: (202)429-5131 10 times a year. $58.00 per year.

Adult Workforce Education Organization., 2815 25th St. Meridian, MS 39305. Phone: (601)484-5165 Fax: (601)484-4999 Members are concerned with employee training and vocational education. Formerly National Employment and Training Association.

Adults as Learners: Increasing Participation and Facilities Learning. Kathryn P. Cross. Jossey-Bass Inc., Publishers, 350 Sansome St. San Francisco, CA 94104. Phone: 888-378-2537 or (415)433-1740 Fax: (415)433-0499 E-mail: webperson@jbp.com • URL: http://www.josseybass.com • 1981. $28.95. (Classic Series).

Advance-Decline Album. Dow Theory Letters, Inc., P.O. Box 1759 La Jolla, CA 92038-1759. Phone: (619)454-0481 E-mail: dowtheory@hotmail.com • URL: http://www.dowtheoryletters.com • Annual. Contains one page for each year since 1931. Includes charts of the New York Stock Exchange advance-decline ratio and the Dow Jones industrial average.

Advanced Accounting. Debra Jeter and others. John Wiley and Sons, Inc., 605 Third Ave. New York, NY 10158-0012. Phone: 800-225-5945 or (212)850-6000 Fax: (212)850-6088 E-mail: info@wiley.com • URL: http://www.wiley.com • 2000. $107.95. Seventh edition. Reflects recent pronouncements of the Financial Accounting Standards Board (FASB) and the Governmental Accounting Standards Board (GASB).

Advanced Battery Technology. Seven Mountains Scientific, Inc., P.O. Box 650 Boalsburg, PA 16827. Phone: (814)466-6559 Fax: (814)466-2777 E-mail: sevmtnsci@srlink.net • Monthly. $165.00 per year. Newsletter. Provides technical and marketing information for the international battery industry.

Advanced Coatings and Surface Technology. Technical Insights, 605 Third Ave. New York, NY 10158-0012. Phone: (212)850-8600 Fax: (212)850-8800 E-mail: insights@wiley.com • URL: http://www.wiley.com/ • Monthly. $650.00 per year. Newsletter on technical developments relating to industrial coatings.

Advanced Composites Monthly. Composite Market Reports, Inc., 459 N. Gilbert Rd., Suite A-150 Gilbert, AZ 85234-4592. Phone: (480)507-6882 Fax: (480)507-6986 Monthly. $2,325.00 per year. Newsletter. Quarterly calenders and updates. Emphasizes aerospace applications of advanced composite materials throughout the world. Includes industry news, research news, and case histories of applications. Supplement available *GraFiber*.

Advanced Imaging Buyers Guide: The Most Comprehensive Worldwide Directory of Imaging Product and Equipment Vendors. Cygnus Business Media, 445 Broad Hollow Rd. Melville, NY 11747-3601. Phone: 800-308-6397 or (631)845-2700 Fax: (631)845-2736 E-mail: rich.reiff@cygnuspub.com • URL: http://www.cygnuspub.com • Annual. $19.95. List of about 800 electronic imaging companies and their products.

Advanced Imaging: Solutions for the Electronic Imaging Professional. Cygnus Business Media, 445 Broad Hollow Rd. Melville, NY 11747. Phone: 800-308-6397 or (516)845-2700 Fax: (631)845-2798 E-mail: rich.reiff@cygnuspub.com • URL: http://www.cygnuspub.com • Monthly. Free to qualified personnel; others, $60.00 per year Covers document-based imaging technologies, products, systems, and services. Coverage is also devoted to multimedia and electronic printing and publishing.

Advanced Manufacturing Engineering Institute.

Advanced Manufacturing Technology: Monthly Report. Technical Insights, 605 Third Ave. New York, NY 10158-0012. Phone: (212)850-8600 Fax: (212)850-8800 E-mail: insights@wiley.com • URL: http://www.wiley.com/ • Monthly. $695.00 per year. Newsletter. Covers technological developments relating to robotics, computer graphics, automation, computer-integrated manufacturing, and machining.

Advanced Materials and Processes. ASM International, 9639 Kinsman Rd. Materials Park, OH 44073-0002. Phone: 800-336-5152 or (440)338-5151 Fax: (440)338-4634 E-mail: custserv@po.asm-intl.org • URL: http://www.asm-intl.org • Monthly. Free to members; non-members $250.00 per year; institutions, $250.00 per year. Incorporates *Metal Progress*.Technical information and reports on new developments in the technology of engineered materials and manufacturing processes.

Advanced Networking Research Group., Washington University, Campus Box 1045 St. Louis, MO 63130-4899. Phone: (314)935-8552 Fax: (314)935-7302 E-mail: jst@cs.wustl.edu • Research fields include the design of high speed internetworks and the design of host interfaces.

Advanced Nutrition: Micronutrients. Carolyn D. Berdanier and Mark L. Failla. CRC Press, Inc., 2000 Corporate Blvd., N. W. Boca Raton, FL 33431. Phone: 800-272-7737 or (561)994-0555 Fax: (561)241-7856 E-mail: orders@crcpress.com • URL: http://www.crcpress.com • 2000. $99.95. Provides detailed coverage of essential vitamins and minerals. Written for professional dietitions and nutritionists. (Modern Nutrition Series).

Advanced Polymer Composites: Principles and Applications. Bor Z. Jang. ASM International, 9639 Kinsman Rd. Materials Park, OH 44073-0002. Phone: 800-336-5152 or (440)338-5151 Fax: (440)338-4634 E-mail: custserv@po.asm-intl.org • URL: http://www.asm-intl.org • 1994. $93.00.

Advanced Strategies in Financial Risk Management. Robert J. Schwartz and Clifford W. Smith, editors. Prentice Hall, 240 Frisch Court Paramus, NJ 07652-5240. Phone: 800-947-7700 or (201)909-6200 Fax: 800-445-6991 or (201)909-6361 URL: http://www.prenhall.com • 1993. $65.00. Includes technical discussions of financial swaps and derivatives.

Advanced Techniques for Java Developers. Daniel J. Berg and J. Steven Fritzinger. John Wiley and Sons, Inc., 605 Third Ave. New York, NY 10158-0012. Phone: 800-225-5945 or (212)850-6000 Fax: (212)850-6088 E-mail: info@jwiley.com • URL: http://www.wiley.com • 1998. $49.99. Second revised edition. Written for experienced Java programmers. CD-ROM included.

Advanced Woodwork and Furniture Making. John L. Feirer and Gilbert R. Hutchings. Glencoe/McGraw-Hill, 8787 Orion Place Columbus, OH 43240-4027. Phone: 800-848-1567 or (614)430-4000 Fax: (614)860-1877 E-mail: customer.service@mcgraw-hill.com • URL: http://www.mcgraw.hill.com • 1982. $43.56. Fourth revised edition.

Advances and Innovations in the Bond and Mortgage Markets. Frank J. Fabozzi, editor. McGraw-Hill Professional, 1221 Ave. of the Americas New York, NY 10020. Phone: 800-722-4726 or (212)904-2000 Fax: (212)904-2072 E-mail: customer.service@mcgraw-hill.com • URL: http://www.mcgraw-hill.com • 1989. $65.00.

Advances in Agronomy. Academic Press, Inc., Journal Div., 525 B St., Suite 1900 San Diego, CA 92101-4495. Phone: 800-321-5068 or (619)230-1840 Fax: (619)699-6715 E-mail: ap@acad.com • URL: http://www.academicpress.com • Annual. Prices vary.

Advances in Chemical Engineering. Academic Press, Inc., Journal Div., 525 B St., Suite 1900 San Diego, CA 92101-4495. Phone: 800-321-5068 or (619)230-1840 Fax: (619)699-6715 E-mail: ap@acad.com • URL: http://www.academicpress.com • Annual. Prices vary.

Advances in Computer Vision and Image Processing. JAI Press, Inc., P.O. Box 811 Stamford, CT 06904-0811. Phone: (203)323-9606 Fax: (203)357-8446 E-mail: order@jaipress.com • URL: http://www.jaipress.com • Dates vary. $270.75. Three volumes. Volume one, $90.25; volume two, $90.25; volume three,$90.25.

Advances in Computers. Academic Press, Inc., Journal Div., 525 B St., Suite 1900 San Diego, CA 92101-4495. Phone: 800-321-5068 or (619)230-1809 Fax: (619)699-6715 E-mail: ap@acad.com • URL: http://www.academicpress.com • Annual. Prices vary.

Advances in Cryogenic Engineering. Plenum Publishing Corp., 233 Spring St. New York, NY 10013-1578. Phone: 800-221-9369 or (212)620-8000 Fax: (212)463-0742 E-mail: info@plenum.com • URL: http://www.plenum.com • Irregular. Price varies. Represents *Cryogenic Engineering Conference Proceedings*.

Advances in Econometrics and Quantitative Economics. Morris H. DeGroot and others. Blackwell Publishers, 350 Main St., 6th Fl. Malden, MA 02148-5018. Phone: 800-216-2522 or (781)388-8200 Fax: (781)388-8210 E-mail: books@blackwellpub.com • URL: http://www.blackwellpub.com • 1995. $99.95.

Advances in Health Economics and Health Services Research. JAI Press, Inc., P.O. Box 811 Stamford, CT 06904-0811. Phone: (203)323-9606 Fax: (203)357-8446 E-mail: order@jaipress.com • URL: http://www.jaipress.com • Irregular. $73.25.

Advances in Industrial and Labor Relations. David B. Lipsky and David Levin, editors. JAI Press, Inc., P.O. Box 811 Stamford, CT 06904-0811. Phone: (203)323-9606 Fax: (203)357-8446 E-mail: order@jaipress.com • URL: http://www.jaipress.com • Irregular. $78.50. *Supplement* available.

Advances in Instrumentation and Control. International Society for Measurement and Control, P.O. Box 12277 Research Triangle Park, NC 27709. Phone: (919)549-8411 Fax: (919)549-8288 E-mail: info@isa.org • URL: http://www.isa.org • Annual. Price on application. Consists of Instrument Society of America International Conference Proceedings.

Advances in Investment Analysis and Portfolio Management. Chung-Few Lee, editor. JAI Press, Inc., P.O. Box 811 Stamford, CT 06904-0811. Phone: (203)323-9606 Fax: (203)357-8446 E-mail: order@jaipress.com • URL: http://www.jaipress.com • 1999. $78.50.

Advances in Librarianship. Academic Press, Inc., Journal Div., 525 B St., Suite 1900 San Diego, CA 92101-4495. Phone: 800-321-5068 or (619)230-1840 Fax: (619)699-6715 E-mail: ap@acad.com • URL: http://www.academicpress.com • Annual. Prices vary.

Advances in Library Administration and Organization. JAI Press, Inc., P.O. Box 811 Stamford, CT 06904-811. Phone: (203)323-9606 Fax: (203)357-8446 E-mail: order@jaipress.com • URL: http://www.jaipress.com • Annual. $78.50.

Advances in Library Automation and Networking. JAI Press, Inc., P.O. Box 811 Stamford, CT 06904-0811. Phone: (203)323-9606 Fax: (203)357-8446 E-mail: order@jaipress.com • URL: http://www.jaipress.com • Annual. $73.25.

Advances in Optotronics and Avionics Technologies. M. Garcia, editor. John Wiley and Sons, Inc., 605 Third Ave. New York, NY 10158-0012. Phone: 800-225-5945 or (212)850-6000 Fax: (212)850-6088 E-mail: info@wiley.com • URL: http://www.wiley.com • 1996. $90.00.

Advances in Polymer Technology. Polymer Processing Institute. John Wiley and Sons, Inc., Journals Div., 605 Third Ave. New York, NY 10158-0012. Phone: 800-225-5945 or (212)850-6000 Fax: (212)850-6088 E-mail: info@wiley.com • URL: http://www.wiley.com • Quarterly. Institutions, $765.00 per year.

Advances in the Astronautical Sciences. American Astronautical Society. Available from Univelt, Inc., P. O. Box 28130 San Diego, CA 92128-0198. Phone: (760)746-4005 Fax: (760)746-3139 E-mail: 76121.1532@compuserve.com • URL: http://www.univelt.staigerland.com • Price varies. Volumes in this series cover the proceedings of various astronautical conferences and symposia.

Advances in Veterinary Medicine. Academic Press, Inc., Journal Div., 525 B St., Suite 1900 San Diego, CA 92101-4495. Phone: 800-321-5068 or (619)230-1840 Fax: (619)699-6715 E-mail: ap@acad.com • URL: http://www.academicpress.com • Annual. Prices vary.

Advancing Women in Business: The Catalyst Guide to Best Practices from the Corporate Leaders. Catalyst Staff. Available from Jossey-Bass, Inc., Publishers, 350 Sansome St. San Francisco, CA 94101. Phone: 888-378-2537 or (415)433-1740 Fax: (212)514-8470 E-mail: webperson@jbp.com • URL: http://www.josseybass.com • 1998. $26.00. Explains the human resources practices of corporations providing a favorable climate for the advancement of female employees.

Advertiser and Agency Red Books Plus. National Register Publishing, Reed Reference Publishing, 121 Chanlon Rd. New Providence, NJ 07974. Phone: 800-323-3288 or (908)464-6800 Fax: (908)508-7671 Quarterly. $1,295.00 per year. The CD-ROM version of *Standard Directory of Advertisers, Standard Directory of Advertising Agencies*, and *Standard Directory of International Advertisers and Agencies*.

Advertisers Annual. Hollis Directories Ltd., Harlequin House, Seven High St. Teddington, Middlesex TW11 8EL 4, England. E-mail: orders@hollis-pr.co.uk • URL: http://www.hollis-pr.co.uk • Annual. $420.00. About 2,700 advertising and media agencies in the United Kingdom, Ireland and abroad, relevant to all forms of advertising.

Advertising. Ray Wright. Trans-Atlantic Publications, Inc., 311 Bainbridge St. Philadelphia, PA 19147. Phone: 800-775-1500 or (215)925-2762 Fax: (215)925-1912 E-mail: order@transatlanticpub.com • URL: http://www.transatlanticpub.com • 2000. $49.50.

Advertising Age-Leading National Advertisers. Crain Communications, Inc., 740 N. Rush St. Chicago, IL 60611-2590. Phone: 800-678-9595 or (312)649-5200 Fax: (312)649-5360 URL: http://www.adage.com • Annual. $5.00. List of the 100 leading advertisers in terms of the amount spent in national advertising and below-the-line forms of spending.

Advertising Age: National Expenditures in Newspapers. Crain Communications, Inc., 711 Third Ave. New York, NY 10017-5806. Phone: 800-678-9595 or (212)210-0100 Fax: (212)210-0111 URL: http://www.crain.com • Annual.

Advertising Age: The International Newspaper of Marketing. Crain Communications, Inc., 740 N. Rush St. Chicago, IL 60611-2590. Phone: 800-678-9595 or (312)649-5200 Fax: (312)280-3174 URL: http://www.adage.com • Weekly. $109.00 per year. Includes supplement *Creativity*.

Advertising Agency. Entrepreneur Media, Inc., 2445 McCabe Way Irvine, CA 92614. Phone: 800-421-2300 or (949)261-2325 Fax: (949)261-0234 E-mail: entmag@entrepreneur.com • URL: http://www.entrepreneur.com •

Looseleaf. $59.50. A practical guide to starting a small advertising agency. Covers profit potential, start-up costs, market size evaluation, pricing, accounting, advertising, promotion, etc. (Start-Up Business Guide No. E1223.)

Advertising Age's B to B: News Monthly Concerning the How-To Strategic and Tact ical Marketing, Sales and Advertising of Business-to-Business Products and Services. Crain Communications, Inc., 740 N. Rush St. Chicago, IL 60611-2590. Phone: 800-678-9595 or (312)649-5200 Fax: (312)649-5228 E-mail: ckosek@crain.com • URL: http://www.crain.com • Monthly. $49.00 per year. Formerly Business Marketing.

Advertising Age's Euromarketing. Crain Communications, Inc., 740 N. Bush St. Chicago, IL 60611-2590. Phone: 800-678-9595 Fax: (312)649-5443 URL: http://www.crain.com • Weekly. $295.00 per year. Newsletter on European advertising and marketing.

Advertising and Marketing International Network.

The Advertising Business: Operations, Creativity, Media Planning, Integrated Communications. John P. Jones, editor. Sage Publications, Inc., 2455 Teller Rd. Thousand Oaks, CA 91320. Phone: (805)499-0721 Fax: (805)499-0871 E-mail: info@sagepub.com • URL: http://www.sagepub.com • 1999. $85.00. Contains articles by professionals in various fields of advertising.

Advertising Compliance Service Newsletter. John Lichtenberger, 26 Hawthorn Dr. Roxbury, NJ 07876-2112. Phone: (973)252-7552 Fax: (973)252-7552 E-mail: lawpublish@aol.com • Bimonthly. $495.00 per year.

Advertising Copywriting. Philip W. Burton. NTC/Contemporary Publishing, P.O. Box 545 Blacklick, OH 43004. Phone: 800-338-3987 or (614)755-4151 Fax: (614)755-5645 E-mail: ntcpub@mcgraw-hill.com • URL: http://www.ntc-cb.com • 1996. $44.95. Seventh edition. (NTC Business Book Series).

Advertising Council.

Advertising Handbook for Health Care Services. William J. Winston, editor. The Haworth Press, Inc., 10 Alice St. Binghamton, NY 13904-1580. Phone: 800-429-6784 or (607)722-5857 Fax: 800-895-0582 or (607)722-1424 E-mail: getinfo@haworthpressinc.com • URL: http://www.haworthpressinc.com • 1986. $8.95. (Health Marketing Quarterly Series: Supplement No. 1).

Advertising Law: Year in Review. CCH, Inc., 4025 W. Peterson Ave. Chicago, IL 60646-6085. Phone: 800-248-3248 or (773)866-6000 Fax: 800-224-8299 or (773)866-3608 URL: http://www.cch.com • Annual. $85.00. Summarizes the year's significant legal and regulatory developments.

Advertising Mail Marketing Association.

Advertising Management. Rajeev Batra. Prentice Hall, 240 Frisch Court Paramus, NJ 07652-5240. Phone: 800-947-7700 or (201)909-6200 Fax: 800-445-6991 or (201)909-6361 URL: http://www.prenhall.com • 1995. $99.00. Fifth edition.

Advertising Manager's Handbook. Robert W. Bly. Prentice Hall, 240 Frisch Court Paramus, NJ 07652-5240. Phone: 800-947-7700 or (201)909-6200 Fax: 800-445-6991 or (201)909-6361 URL: http://www.prenhall.com • 1998. $79.95. Second edition.

Advertising Media Planning. Jack Z. Sissors. NTC/Contemporary Publishing, P.O. Box 545 Blacklick, OH 43004. Phone: 800-338-3987 or (614)755-4151 Fax: (614)755-5645 E-mail: ntcpub@mcgraw-hill.com • URL: http://www.ntc-cb.com • 1995. $52.95. Fifth edition. Introduction to media planning.

Advertising Organizations and Publications: A Resource Guide. John P. Jones, editor. Sage Publications, Inc., 2455 Teller Rd. Thousand Oaks, CA 91320. Phone: (805)499-0721 Fax: (805)499-0871 E-mail: info@sagepub.com • URL: http://www.sagepub.com • 2000. $70.00. Describes advertising associations, books, periodicals, etc.

Advertising: Principles and Practice. William Wells and John Burnett. Prentice Hall, 240 Frisch Court Paramus, NJ 07652-5240. Phone: 800-947-7700 or (201)909-6200 Fax: 800-445-6991 or (201)909-6361 URL: http://www.prenhall.com • 2000. Fifth edition. Price on application.

Advertising Research Foundation.

Advertising: What It Is and How to Do It. Roderick White. McGraw-Hill, 1221 Ave. of the Americas New York, NY 10020. Phone: 800-722-4726 or (212)512-2000 Fax: (212)512-2821 1993. $16.95. Third edition.

Advisory Today. National Association of insurance and Finacial Advisors, 1922 F St., N. W. Washington, DC 20006-4387. Phone: 800-247-4074 or (202)331-6070 Fax: (202)835-9068 E-mail: jkosnett@nalu.org • URL: http://www.advisorytoday.com • Monthly. Free to members; non-members, $7.00 per year. Edited for individual life and health insurance agents. Among the topics included are disability insurance and long-term care insurance. Formerly Life Association News.

ADWEEK. BPI Communications, Inc., 770 Broadway New York, NY 10003-9595. Phone: 800-344-7119 or (646)654-5500 Fax: (646)654-5835 E-mail: info@bpi.com • URL: http://www.bpicomm.com • Weekly. Price varies. Covers local, national, and international advertising news and trends. Includes critiques of advertising campaigns.

ADWEEK Agency Directory. BPI Communications, Inc., 770 Broadway New York, NY 10003-9595. Phone: 800-344-7119 or (646)654-5500 Fax: (646)654-5835 E-mail: info@bpi.com • URL: http://www.bpicomm.com • Annual. $340.00. Over 5,200 advertising agencies, public relations firms, and media buying services, and related organizations in the U.S. Supplement to *Client-Brand Directory* and *Major Media Directory*.

ADWEEK Asia. BPI Communications, Inc., 770 Broadway New York, NY 10003-9595. Phone: 800-344-7119 or (646)654-5500 Fax: (646)654-5835 E-mail: info@bpi.com • URL: http://www.bpicomm.com • Bimonthly. $99.00 per year. Covers advertising and marketing across the Asia-Pacific area. Published in Hong Kong.

AERO.

Aerobics and Fitness Association of America., 15250 Ventura Blvd., Suite 200 Sherman Oaks, CA 91403. Phone: 800-446-2322 or (818)905-0040 Fax: (818)990-5468 E-mail: afaa@pop3.com • URL: http://www.afaa.com • Members are fitness professionals and aerobic exercise instructors.

Aeronautical Repair Station Association.

Aerospace America. American Institute of Aeronautics and Astronautics, Inc., 1801 Alexander Dr., Suite 500 Reston, VA 20191-4344. Phone: 800-639-2422 or (703)264-7500 Fax: (202)264-7551 E-mail: custserv@aiaa.org • URL: http://www.aiaa.org/publications/ • Monthly. Free to members; non-members, $75.00 per year. Provides coverage of key issues affecting the aerospace field.

Aerospace America Ïonline. American Institute of Aeronautics and Astronautics, 1801 Alexander Bell Drive, Suite 500 Reston, VA 20191-4344. Phone: (703)264-7500 Fax: (703)264-7551 E-mail: access@aiaa.org • URL: http://www.aiaa.org • Provides complete text of the periodical, *Aerospace America*, 1984 to date, with monthly updates. Also includes news from the *AIAA Bulletin*. Inquire as to online cost and availability.

Aerospace and Defense Science. Aerospace and Defense Science, Inc., P.O. Box 033619 Indialantic, FL 32903-3619. Fax: (407)773-0286 Quarterly. $24.00 per year. Provides executive overviews and insights into defense and aerospace technologies and future applications.

Aerospace Daily. Aviation Week Newsletter. McGraw-Hill, 1200 G St., N.W., Suite 200 Washington, DC 20005. Phone: (202)383-2350 Fax: (202)383-2442 Five times per week. $1,595.00 per year.

Aerospace Database. American Institute of Aeronautics and Astronautics, 1801 Alexander Bell Drive, Suite 500 Reston, VA 20191-4344. Phone: (703)264-7500 Fax: (703)264-7551 E-mail: access@aiaa.org • URL: http://www.aiaa.org • Contains abstracts of literature covering all aspects of the aerospace and aircraft in series 1983 to date. Semimonthly updates. Inquire as to online cost and availability.

Aerospace/Defense Markets and Technology. The Gale Group, 27500 Drake Rd. Farmington Hills, MI 48331-3535. Phone: 800-877-GALE or (248)699-GALE Fax: 800-414-5043 or (248)699-8069 E-mail: galeord@gale.com • URL: http://www.gale.com • Abstracts of commerical aerospace/defense related literature, 1982 to date. Also includes information about major defense contracts awarded by the U. S. Department of Defense. International coverage. Inquire as to online cost and availability.

Aerospace Education Foundation.

Aerospace Electrical Society.

Aerospace Engineering Magazine. Society of Automotive Engineers, 400 Commonwealth Dr. Warrendale, PA 15096-0001. Phone: 800-832-6723 or (724)776-4841 Fax: (724)776-5960 E-mail: sae@sae.org • URL: http://www.sae.org/ • Monthly. $66.00 per year. Provides technical information that can be used in the design of new and improved aerospace systems.

Aerospace Facts and Figures. Aerospace Industries Association of America, 1250 Eye St., N. W. Washington, DC 20005. Phone: (202)371-8561 Fax: (202)371-8470 URL: http://www.aia-aerospace.org • Annual. $35.00. Includes financial data for the aerospace industries.

Aerospace Industries Association of America.

Aerospace Journal. Available from U.S. Government Printing Office, Washington, DC 20402. Phone: (202)512-1800 Fax: (202)512-2250 E-mail: gpoaccess@gpo.gov • URL: http://www.access.gpo.gov • Quarterly. $29.00 per year. Published to stimulate professional thought concerning aerospace doctrines, strategy, tactics and related techniques. Formerly *Air University Review*.

AESF Shop Guide-A Directory of Surface Finishing Shops. American Electroplaters' and Surface Finishers Society, 12644 Research Parkway Orlando, FL 32826-3298. Phone: 800-334-2052 or (407)281-6441 Fax: (407)281-6446 E-mail: editor@aesf.org • URL: http://www.aesf.org • Annual. Price on application. List of over 1,700 electroplating, coating, and other surface finishing firms.

AF and PA Statistical Roundup. American Forest and Paper Association, 1119 19th St., N. W., Suite 200 Washington, DC 20036. Phone: (202)463-2700 Fax: (202)463-2785 Monthly. Members, $57.00 per year; non-members, $157.00 per year. Contains monthly statistical data for hardwood and softwood products. Formerly *NFPA Statistical Roundup*.

AFE Newsline. Association for Facilities Engineering, 8180 Corporate Park Dr., Suite 305 Cincinnati, OH 45242-3309. Phone: (513)489-2473 Fax: (513)247-7422 Bimonthly. Members, $7.00; non-members, $14.00. Covers national, regional and local chapter activities of the Association for Facilities Engineering. Formerly *AIPE Newsline*.

Affiliated Dress Manufacturers.

Affirmative Action. Lynne Eisaguirre. ABC-CLIO, Inc., 1130 Cremona Dr. Santa Barbara, CA 93117. Phone: 800-368-6868 or (805)968-1911 Fax: (805)685-9685 E-mail: sales@abc-clio.com • URL: http://www.abc-clio.com • 1999. $45.00. Provides an impartial survey and analysis of affirmative action controversies, including historical background and statistical data. (Contemporary World Issues.)

Affirmative Action Compliance Manual for Federal Contractors. Bureau of National Affairs, Inc., 1231 25th St., N.W. Washington, DC 20037-1197. Phone: 800-372-1033 or (202)452-4200 Fax: (202)822-8092 E-mail: books@bna.com • URL: http://www.bna.com • Two looseleaf volumes. $410.00 per year. Monthly updates.

Affirmative Action Register: The E E O Recruitment Publication. Affirmative Action, Inc., 8356 Olive Blvd. St. Louis, MO 63132. Phone: (314)991-1335 Fax: (314)997-1788 URL: http://www.aar-eeo.com • Monthly. Free to qualified personnel; others, $15.00 per year. "The *Affirmative Action Register* is the only nationwide publication that provides for systematic distribution to mandated minorities, females, handicapped, veterans, and Native Americans." Each issue consists of recruitment advertisements placed by equal opportunity employers (institutions and companies).

The Affluent Market. MarketResearch.com, 641 Ave. of the Americas, Third Fl. New York, NY 10011. Phone: 800-298-5699 or (212)807-2629 Fax: (212)807-2716 E-mail: order@marketresearch.com • URL: http://www.marketresearch.com • 1998. $2,250.00 Consumer market data. Includes demographics of affluent house holds and the expenditures of the affluent on 250 types of products.

Affordable Housing Finance. Alexander & Edwards Publishing, 657 Mission St., Suite 502 San Francisco, CA 94105-4118. Phone: (415)546-7255 Fax: (415)546-0954 E-mail: ahf@housingfinance.com • URL: http://www.housingfinance.com • Ten times a year. $119.00 per year. Provides advice and information on obtaining financing for lower-cost housing. Covers both government and private sources.

AFL-CIO.

African-American Business Leaders: A Biographical Dictionary. John N. Ingham and Lynne B. Feldman. Greenwood Publishing Group, Inc., 88 Post Rd. W. Westport, CT 06881-5007. Phone: 800-225-5800 or (203)226-3571 Fax: (203)222-2540 E-mail: bookinfo@greenwood.com • URL: http://www.greenwood.com • 1993. $115.00. Contains extended biographical profiles of 123 African-American individuals prominent in business, from early days in America to recent times.

The African American Market. Available from MarketResearch.com, 641 Ave. of the Americas, 3rd Fl. New York, NY 10011. Phone: 800-298-5699 or (212)807-2629 Fax: (212)807-2716 E-mail: order@marketresearch.com • URL: http://www.marketresearch.com • 2000. $2,750.00. Published by Packaged Facts. Provides consumer market data and demographics, with projections to 2004.

AFSCME Public Employee. American Federation of State, County, and Municipal Employees, AFL-CIO, 1625 L St., N.W. Washington, DC 20036-5687. Phone: (202)429-1144 Fax: (202)429-1120 URL: http://www.afscme.org • Bimonthly. Membership; free to libraries. Formerly *Public Employee Magazine*.

Aftermarket Business. Advanstar Communications, Inc., One Park Ave., 2nd Fl. New York, NY 10016-5802. Phone: 800-346-0085 or (212)951-6600 Fax: (212)951-6693 E-mail: information@advanstar.com • URL: http://www.advanstar.comom • Monthly. $45.00 per year. Automobile aftermarket, including batteries.

Ag Executive. Ag Executive, Inc., 115 E. Twyman Bushnell, IL 61422. Phone: (309)772-2168 Fax: (309)772-2167 E-mail: darrellld@aol.com • Monthly. $84.00 per year. Newsletter. Topics include farm taxes, accounting, real estate, and financial planning.

Ag Lender. Doane Agricultural Services, 11701 Borman Dr., Suite 100 St. Louis, MO 63146-4199. Phone: (314)569-2700 Fax: (314)569-1083 E-mail: info@agrimarketing.com • Nine times a year. Price on application. Formerly *Agri Finance*.

Ag Retailer Magazine. Doane Agricultural Service Co., 11701 Borman Dr., Suite 100 St. Louis, MO 63146-4199. Phone: 800-535-2342 or (314)569-2700 Fax: (314)569-1083 E-mail: info@agrimarketing.com • Nine times a year. Free. Published to meet the business needs of the retail fertilizer and agrichemical dealer industry.

AGA American Gas. American Gas Association, 444 N. Capitol St., N.W. Washington, DC 20001-1511. Phone: (202)824-7000 Fax: (202)824-7115 E-mail: amgas@aga.com • URL: http://www.aga.org • 11 times a year. $39.00 per year. Formerly *American Gas Association Monthly*.

AGA Publications. Abrasive Grain Association, 712 Lakewood Center N., 30200 Detroit Rd. Cleveland, OH 44145. Phone: (216)899-0010 Series of booklets on uses of abrasive grains.

The AGA Rate Service. American Gas Association, 444 N. Capitol St., N.W., 4th Fl. Washington, DC 20001-1511. Phone: (202)824-7000 Fax: (202)824-7115 E-mail: amgas@aga.com • URL: http://www.aga.org • Semiannual. Members, $175.00 per year; non-members, $300.00 per year.

Age Discrimination. Shepard's, 555 Middle Creek Parkway Colorado Springs, CO 80921. Phone: 800-743-7393 or (719)481-7371 Fax: 800-525-0053 or (719)488-7031 E-mail: customer_service@shepards.com • URL: http://www.shepards.com • Three looseleaf volumes. $300.00. Annual supplementation. Emphasis on the Age Discrimination Act, the Age Discrimination in Employment Act, and the Equal Credit Opportunity Act.

Age of Diminished Expectations: U. S. Economic Policy in the 1990s. Paul Krugman. MIT Press, Five Cambridge Center Cambridge, MA 02142-1493. Phone: 800-356-0343 or (617)253-2864 Fax: (617)253-6779 E-mail: mitpress-orders@mit.edu • URL: http://www.mitpress.mit.edu • 1997. $30.00. Third edition. States that the big problem is slow growth in productivity.

Age of Giant Corporations: A Microeconomic History of American Business, 1914-1984. Robert Sobel. Greenwood Publishing Group Inc., 88 Post Rd. W. Westport, CT 06881-5007. Phone: 800-225-5800 or (203)226-3571 Fax: (203)222-2540 E-mail: bookinfo@greenwood.com • URL: http://www.greenwood.com • 1993. $55.00. Third edition. (Contributions in Economics and Economic History Series, No.46).

The Age of Spiritual Machines: When Computers Exceed Human Intelligence. Ray Kurzweil. Viking Penguin, 375 Hudson St. New York, NY 10014-3657. Phone: 800-331-4624 or (212)366-2000 Fax: 800-227-9604 or (212)366-2666 E-mail: customer.servicepennsylvaniaguin.co.uk • URL: http://www.penguin.com • 1999. $25.95. Provides speculation on the future of artificial intelligence and "computer consciousness."

Ageline. American Association of Retired Persons, Research Information Center, 601 E. St., N. W. Washington, DC 20049. Phone: (202)434-6231 Fax: (202)434-6408 Provides indexing and abstracting of the literature of social gerontology, including consumer aspects, financial planning, employment, housing, health care services, mental health, social security, and retirement. Time period is 1978 to date. Inquire as to online cost and availability.

Agencies and Organizations Represented in AAPOR/WAPOR Membership. American Association for Public Opinion Research, P.O. Box 1248 Ann Arbor, MI 48106-1248. Phone: (313)764-1555 Fax: (313)764-3341 E-mail: aapor@umich.edu • URL: http://www.aapor.org • Annual. Free. Lists over 220 firms engaged in public opinion research.

Agency Sales: The Marketing Magazine for Manufacturers' Agencies and Their Principals. Manufacturers' Agents National Association, P.O. Box 3467 Laguna Hills, CA 92654-3467. Phone: (714)859-4040 Fax: (714)855-2973 E-mail: mana@manonline.org • URL: http://www.manaonline.org • Monthly. $49.00 per year.

AgExporter. Available from U. S. Government Printing Office, Washington, DC 20402. Phone: (202)512-1800 Fax: (202)512-2250 E-mail: gpoaccess@gpo.gov • URL: http://www.access.gpo.gov • Monthly. $44.00 per year. Issued by the Foreign Agricultural Service, U. S. Department of Agriculture. Edited for U. S. exporters of farm products. Provides practical information on exporting, including overseas trade opportunities.

Aggregate Reserves of Depository Institutions and the Monetary Base. U.S. Federal Reserve System, Publications Servicesm Room MS-138 Washington, DC 20551. Phone: (202)452-3244 Fax: (202)728-5886 Weekly.

Agri Marketing: Marketing Services Guide. Doane Agricultural Services, 11701 Borman Dr., Suite 100 St. Louis, MO 63146-4199. Phone: 800-353-2342 or (314)569-2700 Fax: (314)569-1083 E-mail: info.@agrimarketing.com • Annual. $30.00. Wide range of listings related to agricultural marketing.

Agri Marketing: The Magazine for Professionals Selling to the Farm Market. Doane Agricultural Services, 11701 Borman Dr., Suite 100 St. Louis, MO 63146-4199. Phone: 800-535-2342 or (314)569-2700 Fax: (314)564-1083 E-mail: info@agrimarketing.com • 11 times a year. $30.00 per year.

Agribusiness: An International Journal. John Wiley and Sons, Inc., Journals Div., 605 Third Ave. New York, NY 10158-0012. Phone: 800-225-5945 or (212)850-6000 Fax: (212)850-6088 E-mail: info@wiley.com • URL: http://www.wiley.com • Bimonthly. Institutions, $845.00 per year.

Agribusiness Council.

Agribusiness Fieldman. Western Agricultural Publishing Co., Inc., 4969 E. Clinton Way, Suite 119 Fresno, CA 93727-1549. Phone: (559)252-7000 Fax: (559)252-7387 Monthly. $19.95 per year.

Agribusiness Management. David Downey and Steven Erickson. McGraw-Hill, 1221 Ave. of the Americas New York, NY 10020. Phone: 800-722-4276 or (212)904-2000 Fax: (212)904-2072 E-mail: customer.service@mcgraw-hill.com • URL: http://www.mcgraw-hill.com • 1987. $81.56. Second edition.

Agricola. U.S. National Agricultural Library, Beltsville, MD 20705. Phone: (301)504-6813 Fax: (301)504-7473 Covers worldwide agricultural literature. Over 2.8 million citations, 1970 to present, with monthly updates. Inquire as to online cost and availability.

AGRICOLA on SilverPlatter. Available from SilverPlatter Information, Inc., 100 River Ridge Rd. Norwood, MA 02062-5026. Phone: 800-343-0064 or (781)769-2599 Fax: (781)769-8763 Quarterly. $825.00 per year. Produced by the National Agricultural Library. Provides about three million citations on CD-ROM to the literature of agriculture, agricultural economics, animal sciences, entomology, fertilizer, food, forestry, nutrition, pesticides, plant science, water resources, and other topics. Each quarterly disc covers the past ten years, with archival discs available from 1970.

Agricultural and Environmental Biotechnology Abstracts. Cambridge Information Group, 7200 Wisconsin Ave., 6th Fl. Bethesda, MD 20814. Phone: 800-843-7751 or (301)961-6700 Fax: (301)961-6720 E-mail: market@csa.com • Bimonthly. $345.00 per year. Formerly *Biotechnology Research Abstracts*.

Agricultural Communicators in Education.

Agricultural Credit and Related Data. American Bankers Association, 1120 Connecticut Ave., N.W. Washington, DC 20036-3971. Phone: 800-338-0626 or (202)663-5000 Fax: (202)663-7543 URL: http://www.aba.com • Annual.

Agricultural Economics and Agribusiness. Gail L. Cramer and others. John Wiley and Sons, Inc., 605 Third Ave. New York, NY 10158-0012. Phone: 800-225-5945 or (212)850-6000 Fax: (212)850-6088 E-mail: info@wiley.com • URL: http://www.wiley.com • 2000. Eighth edition. Price on application.

Agricultural Engineering Abstracts. Available from CABI Publishing North America, 10 E. 40th St. New York, NY 10016. Phone: 800-528-4841 or (212)481-7018 Fax: (212)686-7993 E-mail: cabi@cabi.org • URL: http://www.cabi.org • Monthly. $735.00 per year. Published in England by CABI Publishing.

Agricultural Engineering Research Center.

Agricultural Experiment Station. Cornell University

Agricultural Finance. Warren F. Lee and others. Iowa State University Press, 2121 S. State Ave. Ames, IA 50014-8300. Phone: 800-862-6657 or (515)292-0140 Fax: (515)292-3348 E-mail: orders@isupress.edu • URL: http://www.isupress.edu • 1988. $44.95. Eighth revised edition.

Agricultural Finance Databook. U. S. Federal Reserve System, Board of Governors, Publications Services, MS-127 Washington, DC 20551. Phone: (202)452-3244 Fax: (202)728-5886 URL: http://www.federalreserve.gov • Quarterly. $5.00 per year. (Federal Reserve Statistical Release, E.15.)

Agricultural Guide to Washington: Whom to Contact and Where. Dow Elunco, 9002 Purdue Rd., Quad IV Indianapolis, IN 46268. Phone: (317)871-8216 Biennial. Free. Heads of congressional committees and subcommittees in Washington, D.C. that deal with agricultural matters, and members of federal agencies and trade associations concerned with agribusiness.

Agricultural Law. Matthew Bender & Co., Inc., Two Park Ave. New York, NY 10016. Phone: 800-223-1940 or (212)448-2000 Fax: (212)244-3188 E-mail: international@bender.com • URL: http://www.bender.com • $2,120.00 per year. 15 looseleaf volumes. Periodic supplementation. Covers all aspects of state and federal law relating to farms, ranches and other agricultural interests. Includes five volumes dealing with agricultural estate, tax and business planning.

Agricultural Letter. Federal Reserve Bank of Chicago, Public Information Center, P.O. Box 834 Chicago, IL 60690. Phone: (312)322-5112 Quarterly. Free.

Agricultural Options: Trading, Risk Management, and Hedging. Christopher A. Bobin. John Wiley and Sons, Inc., 605 Third Ave. New York, NY 10158-0012. Phone: 800-225-5945 or (212)850-6000 Fax: (212)850-6088 E-mail: info@wiley.com • URL: http://www.wiley.com • 1990. $49.95. Practical advice on trading commodity futures options (puts and calls).

Agricultural Outlook. Available from U. S. Government Printing Office, Washington, DC 20402. Phone: (202)512-1800 Fax: (202)512-2250 E-mail: gpoaccess@gpo.gov • URL: http://www.access.gpo.gov • Monthly. $60.00 per year. Issued by the Economic Research Service of the U. S. Department of Agriculture. Provides analysis of agriculture and the economy.

Agricultural Policies, Markets, and Trade: Monitoring and Evaluation. Organization for Economic Cooperation and Development. Available from OECD Publications and Information Center, 2001 L St., N. W., Suite 650 Washington, DC 20036-4922. Phone: 800-456-6323 or (202)785-6323 Fax: (202)785-0350 E-mail: washington.contact@oecd.org • URL: http://www.oecd.org • Annual. $62.00. A yearly report on agricultural and trade policy developments in OECD member countries.

Agricultural Product Prices. William G. Tomek and Kenneth L. Robinson. Cornell University Press, Sage House, 512 E. State St. Ithaca, NY 14851. Phone: 800-666-2211 or (607)257-2338 Fax: 800-688-2877 E-mail: orderbook@cupserv.org • URL: http://www.cornellpress.cornell.edu • 1990. $35.00. Third edition.

Agricultural Research. Available from U. S. Government Printing Office, Washington, DC 20402. Phone: (202)512-1800 Fax: (202)512-2250 E-mail: gpoaccess@gpo.gov • URL: http://www.access.gpo.gov • Monthly. $45.00 per year. Issued by the Agricultural Research Service of the U. S. Department of Agriculture. Presents results of research projects related to a wide variety of farm crops and products.

Agricultural Research and Extension Center at Uvalde. Texas A & M University

Agricultural Research Division. University of Nebraska - Lincoln

Agricultural Research Institute.

Agricultural Retailers Association.

Agricultural Statistics. Available from U. S. Government Printing Office, Washington, DC 20402. Phone: (202)512-1800 Fax: (202)512-2250 E-mail: gpoaccess@gpo.gov • URL: http://www.access.gpo.gov • Annual. Produced by the National Agricultural Statistics Service, U. S. Department of Agriculture. Provides a wide variety of statistical data relating to agricultural production, supplies, consumption, prices/price-supports, foreign trade, costs, and returns, as well as farm labor, loans, income, and population. In many cases, historical data is shown annually for 10 years. In addition to farm data, includes detailed fishery statistics.

Agriculture Council of America.

Agriculture, Economics and Resource Management. Milton M. Snodgrass and Luther T. Wallace. Prentice Hall, 240 Frisch Court Paramus, NJ 07652. Phone: 800-947-7700 or (201)909-6200 Fax: 800-445-6991 or (201)909-6361 URL: http://www.prenhall.com • 1980. $48.20. Second edition.

Agriculture Fact Book. Available from U. S. Government Printing Office, Washington, DC 20402. Phone: (202)512-1800 Fax: (202)512-2250 E-mail: gpoaccess@gpo.gov • URL: http://www.access.gpo.gov • Annual. Issued by the Office of Communications, U. S. Department of Agriculture. Includes data on U. S. agriculture, farmers, food, nutrition, and rural America. Programs of the Department of Agriculture in six areas are described: rural economic development, foreign trade, nutrition, the environment, inspection, and education.

Agrindex: International Information System for the Agricultural Sciences and Technology. Food and Agriculture Organization of the United Nations. UNIPUB, 4611-F Assembly Dr. Lanham, MD 20706-4391. Phone: 800-274-4888 or (301)459-2255 Fax: 800-865-3450 or (301)459-0056 URL: http://www.unesco.org/publications • Monthly. $500.00 per year. Text in English, French, and Spanish.

Agrochemical Companies Fact File. Theta Reports/PJB Medical Publications, Inc., 1775 Broadway, Suite 511 New York, NY 10019. Phone: (212)262-8230 Fax: (212)262-8234 E-mail: customerservice@thetareports.com • URL: http://www.thetareports.com • Annual. $1,460.00. Provides detailed profiles of more than 360 crop protection companies worldwide, including manufacturers of agrochemicals and biopesticides. Coverage includes finances, products, and joint ventures. Major agrochemical trading companies are also profiled. (Theta Report No. DS190E.)

Agronomy Journal. American Society of Agronomy, Inc., 677 S. Segoe Rd. Madison, WI 53711. Phone: (608)273-8080 Fax: (608)273-2021 E-mail: journal@agronomy.org • URL: http://www.agronomy.org/journals • Bimonthly. Free to members; non-members, $171.00 per year.

AGS Quarterly. American Golf Sponsors, Four Sawgrass Village, Suite 220-A Ponte Vedra Beach, FL 32083. Phone: (904)285-4222 Fax: (904)273-5726 Quarterly. Membership newsletter for sponsors of major golf tournaments.

AH & MA Buyers Guide. American Hotel and Motel Association, 1201 New York Ave., N. W., Suite 600 Washington, DC 20005-3931. Phone: (202)289-3100 Fax: (202)289-3199 E-mail: info@ahma.com • URL: http://www.ahma.com • Annual. $50.00. Contains more than 3,500 listings of suppliers of products and services for the lodging industry.

AHA Guide to the Health Care Field. American Hospital Association. American Hospital Publishing, Inc., One N. Franklin., 27th Fl. Chicago, IL 60606-3421. Phone: 800-242-2626 or (312)422-3000 Fax: (312)422-4796 URL:

http://www.aha.org • Annual. $280.00. A directory of hospitals and health care systems.

AHA Hospital Statistics. American Hospital Association. American Hospital Publishing, Inc., One N. Franklin St., 27th Fl. Chicago, IL 60606-3421. Phone: 800-242-2626 or (312)422-3000 Fax: (312)422-4505 URL: http://www.aha.org • Annual. Members, $59.00 per year; non-members $139.00 per year. Provides detailed statistical data on the nation's hospitals, including revenues, expenses, utilization, and personnel. Formerly *Hospital Statistics*.

AHA News. Health Forum, Inc., One North Franklin St., 27th Floor Chicago, IL 60606. Phone: 800-621-6902 or (312)893-6800 Fax: (312)422-4600 URL: http://www.healthforum.com or http://www.ahanews • Weekly. $147.00 per year. Edited for hospital and health care industry administrators. Covers health care news events and legislative activity. An American Hospital Association publication (http://www.aha.org).

AHFS Drug Information. American Hospital Formulary Service. American Society of Health-System Pharmacists, 7272 Wisconsin Ave. Bethesda, MD 20814. Phone: (301)657-3000 Fax: (301)657-1641 $162.95 per year. Looseleaf service. Detailed information about drugs and groups of drugs.

AI Magazine (Artificial Intelligence). American Association for Artificial Intelligence. AAAI Press, 445 Burgess Dr. Menlo Park, CA 94025-3442. Phone: (650)328-3123 Fax: (650)321-4457 E-mail: aimagazine@aaai.org • URL: http://www.aaai.org • Quarterly. $50.00 per year. Information on artificial intelligence research and innovative applications of the science.

AI Trends: Newsletter. Relayer Group, 8232 E. Buckskin Trail, 2nd Fl. Scottsdale, AZ 85255-2132. Phone: (602)945-9620 or (602)585-8587 Fax: (602)585-3067 Monthly. $295.00 per year.

AIAA Journal: Devoted to Aerospace Research and Development. American Institute of Aeronautics and Astronautics, Inc., 1801 Alexander Bell Dr., Suite 500 Reston, VA 20191-4344. Phone: 800-639-2422 or (703)264-7500 Fax: (703)264-7551 E-mail: custserv@aiaa.org • URL: http://www.aiaa.org/publications/ • Monthly. Members, $65.00 per year; non-members, $185.00 per year; institutions, $645.00 per year.

AICHE Journal. American Institute of Chemical Engineers, Three Park Ave. New York, NY 10016-5901. Phone: 800-242-4363 or (212)591-8100 Fax: (212)591-8888 E-mail: xpress@aiche.org • URL: http://www.aiche.org • Monthly. Members, $95.00 per year; non-members, $765.00 per year; students, $35.00 per year. Devoted to research and technological developments in chemical engineering and allied fields. Available online.

AICP Roster. American Institute of Certified Planners, 1776 Massachusetts Ave., N.W. Washington, DC 20036. Phone: (202)872-0611 Fax: (202)872-0643 E-mail: rjones@planning.org • Biennial. Members, $10.00 per year; non-members, $30.00 per year. Lists about 9,000 public and private planning agency officials, professional planners, planning educators and other persons who are members of the American Planning Association.

AICPA Audit and Accounting Manual. American Institute of Certified Public Accountants, 1211 Ave. of the Americas New York, NY 10036-8775. Phone: 800-862-4272 or (212)596-6200 Fax: (212)596-6213 URL: http://www.aicpa.org • 1999. $99.00. Covers working papers, internal control, audit approach, etc.

AICPA Codification of Statements on Auditing Standards. American Institute of Certified Public Accountants, 1211 Ave. of the Americas New York, NY 10036-8775. Phone: 800-862-4272 or (212)596-6200 Fax: (212)596-6213 URL: http://www.aicpa.org • 1999. $81.25. Includes *Auditing Interpretations* and *International Auditing Guidelines*.

AICPA Codification of Statements on Standards for New Accounting and Review Services. American Institute of Certified Public Accountants, 1211 Ave. of the Americas Ney York, NY 10036-8775. Phone: 800-862-4272 or (212)596-6200 Fax: (212)596-6213 URL: http://www.aicpa.org • 1998. $19.00.

AICPA Professional Standards, U. S. Auditing Standards, Accounting and Review Services, Ethics, Bylaws, International Accounting, International Auditing, Management Advisory Services, Quality Control, and Tax Practice. American Institute of Certified Public Accountants, 1211 Ave. of the Americas New York, NY 10036-8775. Phone: 800-862-4272 or (212)569-6200 Fax: (212)569-6213 URL: http://www.aicpa.org • Annual. $180.00. Two volumes. Updates. Looseleaf. Three parts: Accounting, Ethics, Auditing.

AICPA Technical Practice Aids. American Institute of Certified Public Accountants, 1211 Ave. of the Americas New York, NY 10036-8775. Phone: 800-862-4272 or (212)596-6200 Fax: (212)596-6213 E-mail: journals@aicpa.org • URL: http://www.aicpa.org • $180.00 per year. Looseleaf service. Periodic supplementation. Advisory opinions, statements of position, and other material.

AIDS: Abstracts of the Psychological and Behavioral Literature, 1983-1991. John Anderson and others, editors. American Psychological Association, 750 First St., N.E. Washington, DC 20002-4242. Phone: 800-374-2721 or (202)366-5500 Fax: (202)336-5630 E-mail: ach.apa@email.org • URL: http://www.apa.org/books • 1991. $19.95. Third edition. (Bibliographies in Psychology Series: No.6).

AIDS Action Council., 1875 Connecticut Ave., N.W., Suite 700 Washington, DC 20009. Phone: 800-644-2437 or (202)986-1300 Fax: (202)986-1345 E-mail: aidsaction@aidsaction.org • URL: http://www.aidsaction.org • Political action organization.

AIDS and Drug Abuse in the Workplace: Resolving the Thorny Legal-Medical Issues. Charles G. Bakaly and Saul G. Kramer. Harcourt Brace and Co., 525 B St., Suite 1900 San Diego, CA 92101-4495. Phone: 800-543-1918 or (619)699-6707 Fax: 800-876-0186 URL: http://www.harcourt.com • 1991. $40.00.

AIDS and Public Policy Journal. Andrews Publications, 175 Strafford Ave., Bldg. 4, Suite 140 Wayne, PA 19087. Phone: (610)225-0510 Fax: (610)225-0501 URL: http://www.andrewspub.com • Quarterly. Individuals, $59.00 per year; institutions, $115.00 per year.

AIDS and the Law. David W. Webber, editor. John Wiley and Sons, Inc., 605 Third Ave. New York, NY 10158-0012. Phone: 800-225-5945 or (212)850-6000 Fax: (212)850-6088 E-mail: info@wiley.com • URL: http://www.wiley.com • 1997. $150.00. Third edition. (Civil Rights Library Series).

AIDS Benefits Handbook: Everything You Need to Know to Get Social Security, Welfare, Medicaid, Medicare, Food Stamps, Housing, Drugs, and Other Benefits. Thomas P. McCormack. Yale University Press, 302 Temple St. New Haven, CT 06511. Phone: 800-987-7323 or (203)432-0960 Fax: (203)432-0948 E-mail: yupmkt@yale.edu • URL: http://www.yale.edu/yup/ • 1990. $37.50.

AIDS Issues in the Workplace: A Response Model for Human Resource Management. Dale A. Masi. Greenwood Publishing Group, Inc., 88 Post Rd., W. Westport, CT 06881-5007. Phone: 800-225-5800 or (203)226-3571 Fax: (203)222-2540 E-mail: bookinfo@greenwood.com • URL: http://www.greenwood.com • 1990. $59.95.

AIDS Law. Margaret C. Jasper. Oceana Publications, Inc., 75 Main St. Dobbs Ferry, NY 10522-1601. Phone: 800-831-0758 or (914)693-8100 Fax: (914)693-0402 E-mail: orders@oceanalaw.com • URL: http://www.oceanalaw.com • 1996. $22.50. (Legal Almanac Series).

AIDS Law and Litigation Reporter: The National Journal of Record of AIDS-Related Litigation. Andrews Publications, 175 St. Strafford Ave., Bdg. 4, Suite 140 Wayne, PA 19087. Phone: (610)225-0510 Fax: (610)225-0501 URL: http://www.andrewspub.com • Semimonthly. $2,975.00 per year.

AIDS Law Today: A New Guide for the Public. Yale AIDS Law Project Staff. Yale University Press, 302 Temple St. New Haven, CT 06511. Phone: 800-987-7323 or (203)432-0960 Fax: (203)432-0948 E-mail: yupmkt@yale.edu • URL: http://www.yale.edu/yup/ • 1993. $52.00. Second edition.

AIDS Literature and Law Review. University Publishing Group, Inc., 17100 Cole Rd., Suite 312 Hagerstown, MD 31740. Phone: 800-654-8188 Fax: (301)582-2406 E-mail: orders@upgbooks.com • Monthly. $225.00 per year. Contains abstracts of journal and newspaper articles. Formerly *AIDS Literature and News Review*.

AIDS Litigation Reporter (Acquired Immune Deficiency Syndrome): The National Journal of Record of AIDS-Related Litigation. Andrews Publications, 175 Strafford Ave., Bldg. 4, Suite 140 Wayne, PA 19087. Phone: 800-345-1101 or (610)622-0510 Fax: (610)622-0501 URL: http://www.andrewspub.com • Semimonthly. $775.00 per year. Provides reports on a wide variety of legal cases in which AIDS is a factor.

AIDS Policy and Law: The Biweekly Newsletter on Legislation, Regulation, and Litigation Concerning AIDS. LRP Publications, P.O. Box 980 Horsham, PA 19044-0980. Phone: 800-341-7874 or (215)784-0941 Fax: (215)784-9639 E-mail: custserv@lrp.com • URL: http://www.lrp.com • Biweekly. $487.00 per year. Newsletter for personnel managers, lawyers, and others.

AIDS Reference Guide: A Sourcebook for Planners and Decision Makers. Atlantic Information Services, Inc., 1100 17th St., N. W., Suite 300 Washington, DC 20036-4601. Phone: 800-521-4323 or (202)775-9008 Fax: (202)331-9542 URL: http://www.aispub.com • $335.00 Looseleaf. Two volumes. Includes twelve updates and twelve newsletters. Covers a wide range of AIDS topics, including "Employment Policies and Issues," "Legal Issues," "Financing Issues," "Impact on Healthcare Providers," "Global Issues," and "Legislative, Regulatory, and Governance Issues."

AIDSLINE. U. S. National Library of Medicine, MEDLARS Management Section, 8600 Rockville Pike Bethesda, MD 20894. Phone: 800-638-8480 or (301)496-3147 Fax: (301)496-0822 URL: http://www.nlm.nih.gov • Provides about 200,000 online citations (some abstracts) to the worldwide literature of Acquired Immune Deficiency Syndrome, compiled from MEDLINE and Health Planning and Administration databases. Coverage includes social and health policy issues. Time span is 1980 to date, with weekly updates. Inquire as to online cost and availability.

AIDSLINE CD-ROM. Available from SilverPlatter Information, Inc., 100 River Ridge Rd. Norwood, MA 02062-5026. Phone: 800-343-0064 or (781)769-2599 Fax: (781)769-8763 E-mail: info@silverplatter.com • URL: http://www.silverplatter.com • Quarterly. $595.00 per year. Produced by the National Library of Medicine (http://www.nlm.nih.gov). In addition to medical citations, CD-ROM database includes references to social, behavioral, and health policy issues. Time period is 1980 to date.

The AIER Chart Book. AIER Research Staff. American Institute for Economic Research, Division St. Great Barrington, MA 01230-1000. Phone: (413)528-1216 Fax: (413)528-0103 E-mail: info@aier.org • URL: http://www.aier.org • Annual. $3.00. A compact compilation of long-range charts ("Purchasing Power of the Dollar," for example, goes back to 1780) covering various aspects of the U. S. economy. Includes inflation, interest rates, debt, gold, taxation, stock prices, etc. (Economic Education Bulletin.)

AIIM Buying Guide. Association for Information and Image Management, 1100 Wayne Ave., Suite 1100 Silver Spring, MD 20910-5603. Phone: 800-477-2446 or (301)587-8202 Fax: (301)587-2711 E-mail: aiim@aiim.org • URL: http://www.aiim.org • Annual. $64.00. 460 manufacturers, suppliers, service companies and consultants in the information management industry. Formerly *Buyer's Guide to Micrographic Equipment, Products and Services*.

AIM U.S.A., 634 Alpha Dr. Pittsburgh, PA 15238-2802. Phone: 800-338-0206 or (412)963-8588 Fax: (412)963-8753 E-mail: info@aimglobal.org • URL: http://www.aimusa.org • Members are companies concerned with automatic identification and data capture, including bar code systems, magnetic stripes, machine vision, voice technology, optical character recognition, and systems integration technology.

Air and Expedited Motor Carriers Conference.

Air and Waste Management Association.

Air and Waste Management Association Journal. Association Journal, One Gateway Center, 3rd Fl. Pittsburgh, PA 15222. Phone: (412)232-3444 Fax: (412)232-3450 URL: http://www.awma.org • Monthly. Individuals, $110.00 per year; nonprofit institutions, $130.00 per year; others, $240.00 per year. Includes annual *Directory of Governmental Air Pollution Agencies*.

Air Brake Association.

Air Cargo News. Air Cargo News, Inc., Borough Hall Station Jamaica, NY 11424. Phone: (718)651-3591 Monthly. $36.00 per year.

Air Cargo World. Intertec Publishing Corp., 6151 Powers Ferry Rd., N.W., Suite 200 Atlanta, GA 30339. Phone: 800-400-5945 or (770)955-2500 Fax: (770)955-0400 E-mail: subs@intertec.com • URL: http://www.intertec.com • Monthly. $58.00 per year.

Air Carrier Financial Statistics. U. S. Department of Transportation, Bureau of Transportation Statistics Washington, DC 20590. Phone: (202)366-3282 Fax: (202)366-3640 E-mail: info@bts.gov • URL: http://www.bts.gov • Quarterly. Contains profit and loss and asset information for specific airlines.

Air Carrier Industry Scheduled Service Traffic Statistics. U. S. Department of Transportation, John A. Volpe National Transportation Systems Center, Center for Transportation Information, Kendall Square Cambridge, MA 02142. Phone: (617)494-2224 Fax: (617)494-3064 Quarterly. Includes data for commuter airlines.

Air Carrier Traffic Statistics Monthly. U. S. Department of Transportation, John A. Volpe National Transportation Systems Center, Center for Transportation Information, Kendall Square Cambridge, MA 02142. Phone: (617)494-2224 Fax: (617)494-3064 Monthly. Provides passenger traffic data for large airlines.

Air-Conditioning and Refrigeration Institute.

Air Conditioning Contractors of America.

Air Conditioning, Heating, and Refrigeration News. Business News Publishing Co., 755 W. Big Beaver Rd., Suite 1000 Troy, MI 48084. Phone: 800-837-7370 or (248)362-3700 Fax: (248)362-0317 URL: http://www.acsnews.com • Weekly. $87.00 per year. Includes *Annual Directory* and *Statistical Summary*.

Air Conditioning, Heating, and Refrigeration News-Directory. Business News Publishing Co., 755 W. Big Beaver Rd., Suite 1000 Troy, MI 48084. Phone: 800-837-7370 or (248)362-3700 Fax: (248)362-0317 URL: http://www.bnp.com • Annual. $235.00.

Air Conditioning Testing-Adjusting-Balancing: A Field Practice Manual. John Gladstone. Engineers Press, P.O. Box 141651 Coral Gables, FL 33114-1651. Phone: (305)856-0031 1991. $44.95. Second edition.

Air Force Aid Society.

Air Force Association.

Air Force Historical Foundation.

Air Force Journal of Logistics. Available from U. S. Government Printing Office, Washington, DC 20402. Phone: (202)512-1800 Fax: (202)512-2250 E-mail: gpoaccess@gpo.gov • URL: http://www.access.gpo.gov • Quarterly.

$15.00 per year. Issued by the Air Force Logistics Management Center, Air Force Department, Defense Department. Presents research and information of interest to professional Air Force logisticians.

Air Force Magazine: The Force Behind the Force. Air Force Association, 1501 Lee Highway Arlington, VA 22209-1198. Phone: (703)247-5800 Fax: (703)247-5855 URL: http://www.afa.org • Monthly. $30.00 per year.

Air Force Sergeants Association.

Air Force Times. Army Times Publishing Co., 6883 Commercial Dr. Springfield, VA 22159. Phone: 800-368-5718 or (703)750-8646 Fax: (703)750-8622 URL: http://www.armytimes.com • Weekly. $52.00 per year. In two editions: Domestic and International.

Air Freight Directory. Air Cargo, Inc., 1819 Bay Ridge Ave. Annapolis, MD 21403. Phone: (410)280-8911 Fax: (410)268-3154 Bimonthly. $84.00 per year. Air freight motor carriers.

Air Line Pilot; The Magazine of Professional Flight Deck Crews. Air Line Pilots Association, AFL-CIO, P.O. Box 1169 Herndon, VA 20172. Phone: (703)481-4460 Fax: (703)689-4370 E-mail: magazine@alpa.org • URL: http://www.alpa.org • Monthly. $26.00 per year.

Air Line Pilots Association International.

Air Market News. General Publications Co., P.O. Box 480 Hatch, NM 87937-0408. Phone: (505)267-1030 Fax: (505)267-1920 Bimonthly. Free to qualified personnel. Subject matter is news of aircraft products and services.

Air Pollution. O. Hutzinger, editor. Springer-Verlag New York, Inc., 175 Fifth Ave. New York, NY 10010. Phone: 800-777-4643 or (212)460-1500 Fax: (212)473-6272 E-mail: orders@springer.ny.com • URL: http://www.springer.ny.com • 1989. $154.95. Two volumes. Vol. 4, Part B, $190.95; Vol. 4, Part C, $154.95. (Handbook of Environmental Chemistry Series).

Air Pollution Control. Bureau of National Affairs, 1231 25th St., N.W. Washington, DC 20037-1197. Phone: 800-372-1033 or (202)452-4200 Fax: (202)822-8092 E-mail: books@bna.com • URL: http://www.bna.com • Biweekly. $798.00 per year. Newsletter.

Air Pollution: Federal Law and Analysis. David P. Currie. West Group, 610 Opperman Dr. Eagan, MN 55123. Phone: 800-328-4880 or (651)687-7000 Fax: 800-213-2323 or (651)687-5827 URL: http://www.westgroup.com • $110.00. Periodic supplementation. Explains Clean Air Act and related laws, rules and regulations.

Air Pollution Research Center. University of California, Riverside

Air Pollution Research Laboratory. University of Florida

Air Quality Data. U.S. Environmental Protection Agency, Washington, DC 20460. Phone: 888-372-8255 or (202)564-9828 Annual.

Air Traffic Control Association.

Air Transport. Air Transport Association of America, 1301 Pennsylvania Ave., N.W., Suite 100 Washington, DC 20004-1707. Phone: 800-497-3326 or (202)626-4000 Fax: (202)626-4081 Annual. $20.00.

Air Transport Association of America.

Air Transport World. Penton Media Inc., 1300 E. Ninth St. Cleveland, OH 44114. Phone: (216)696-7000 Fax: (216)696-0836 E-mail: corpcomm@penton.com • URL: http://www.penton.com • Monthly. Free to qualified personnel, others, $55.00 per year. Includes supplement *World Airline Reports*.

Air Transportation: A Management Perspective. Alexander Wells. Wadsworth Publishing, 10 Davis Dr. Belmont, CA 94002. Phone: 800-354-9706 or (650)595-2350 Fax: (650)637-9955 URL: http://www./wadsworth.com • 1998. $69.95. Fourth edition.

Air University Library Index to Military Periodicals. U.S. Air Force, Air University Library Maxwell Air Force Base, AL 36112-6424. Phone: (334)953-2504 Fax: (334)953-1192 E-mail: mstewart@max1.au.af.mil • URL: http://www.au.af.mil/au/aul/aul.htm • Quarterly. Free to qualified personnel. Annual cumulation.

Air-Water Pollution Report: The Weekly Report on Environmental Executives. Business Publishers, Inc., 8737 Colesville Rd., Suite 1100 Silver Spring, MD 20910-3928. Phone: 800-274-6737 or (301)587-6300 Fax: (301)587-1081 E-mail: bpinews@bpinews.com • URL: http://www.bpinews.com • Weekly. $667.00 per year. Newsletter covering legislation, regulation, business news, research news, etc. Formed by merger of *Environment Week* and *Air-Water Pollution Report*.

Aircraft Electronics Association.

Aircraft Owners and Pilots Association.

Airline Financial News. Phillips Business Information, Inc., 1201 Seven Locks Rd., Suite 300 Potomac, MD 20854. Phone: 800-777-5006 or (301)340-1520 Fax: (301)309-3847 E-mail: pbi@phillips.com • URL: http://www.phillips.com/marketplaces.htm • Weekly. $697.00 per year. Newsletter on the financial situation of airlines.

Airline Handbook. AeroTravel Research, P.O. Box 3694 Cranston, RI 02910. Annual. $16.00. Directory of commercial airlines, both scheduled and chartered.

Airman: Official Magazine of the U.S. Air Force. Available from U.S. Government Printing Office, Washington, DC 20204. Phone: (202)512-1800 Fax: (202)512-2250 E-mail: gpoaccess@gpo.gov • URL: http://www.access.gpo.gov • Monthly. $41.00 per year.

Airport Activity Statistics of Certificated Route Air Carriers. U. S. Department of Transportation. Available from U. S. Government Printing Office, Washington, DC 20402. Phone: (202)512-1800 Fax: (202)512-2250 E-mail: gpoaccess@gpo.gov • URL: http://www.access.gpo.gov • Annual $47.00.

Airport Business. Cygnus Publishing, Inc., Johnson Hill Press, 1233 Janesville Ave. Fort Atkinson, WI 53538-0460. Phone: 800-547-7377 or (920)563-6388 Fax: (920)563-1707 E-mail: rich.reiff@cygnuspub.com • URL: http://www.cygnuspub.com • Nine times a year. $54.00 per year.

Airport/Facility Directory. U. S. National Ocean Service, 1305 East West Highway Silver Spring, MD 20910. Phone: (301)713-3074 URL: http://www.nos.noaa.gov • Bimonthly. $140.00 per year, complete. Issued in seven regional volumes (single region, $20.00 per year). Provides detailed non-military airport information for pilots, including control center and navigational data.

Airport Press., J.F.K. Station, P.O. Box 300879 Jamaica, NY 11430. Phone: 800-982-5832 or (718)244-6788 Fax: (718)995-3432 Monthly. $32.00 per year.

Airports Council International - North America.

Airports USA. Aircraft Owners and Pilots Association, 421 Aviation Way Frederick, MD 21701. Phone: 800-942-4269 or (301)695-2350 Fax: (301)695-2180 URL: http://www.aopa.org • Annual. $24.95. Primarily for pilots.

Al-Anon Family Group Headquarters, World Service Office.

ALA Handbook of Organization. American Library Association, 50 E. Huron St. Chicago, IL 60611-2795. Phone: 800-545-2433 or (312)944-6780 Fax: (312)440-9374 E-mail: ala@ala.org • URL: http://www.ala.org • Annual. $30.00. Includes information on ALA officers, committees, divisions, sections, round tables, and state chapters. (Issued as a supplement to *American Libraries*.)

ALA Survey of Librarian Salaries. American Library Association, 50 E. Huron St. Chicago, IL 60611-2795. Phone: 800-545-2433 or (312)944-6780 Fax: (312)440-9374 E-mail: ala@ala.org • URL: http://www.ala.org • Annual. $55.00. Provides data on salaries paid to librarians in academic and public libraries. Position categories range from beginning librarian to director.

Alabama Law Institute. University of Alabama

Alabama State Data Center. University of Alabama

Alberta Research Council.

Alcohol Education Materials: An Annotated Bibliography. Gail Gleason Milgram. Rutgers Center of Alcohol Studies Publications, Rutgers State University of New Jersey, 607 Alison Rd. Piscataway, NJ 08854-8001. Phone: (732)445-2190 Fax: (732)445-5944 E-mail: chrouse@rci.rutgers.edu • URL: http://www.rci.rutgers.edu/ • 1981. $70.00. Five volumes, 1950-1981. Volumes 1 and 2, $20.00 per volume; volumes 3, 4, and 5, $10.00 per volume. Price on application.

Alcohol Research and Health. Available from U. S. Government Printing Office, Washington, DC 20402. Phone: (202)512-1800 Fax: (202)512-2250 E-mail: gpoaccess@gpo.gov • URL: http://www.access.gpo.gov • Quarterly. $22.00 per year. Issued by the National Institute on Alcohol Abuse and Alcoholism. Presents alcohol-related research findings and descriptions of alcoholism prevention and treatment programs.

Alcoholic Beverage Control: State Capitals. Wakeman-Walworth Inc., 300 N. Washington St. Alexandria, VA 22314. Phone: (703)549-8606 Fax: (703)549-1372 E-mail: newsletters@statecapitals.com • URL: http://www.statecapitals.com • Weekly. $245.00 per year. Formerly *From the State Capitals: Alcoholic Beverage Control*.

Alcoholics Anonymous World Services.

Alcoholism: Causes, Effect and Treatment. Joseph F. Perez. Accelerated Development, 1900 Frost Rd., Suite 101 Bristol, PA 19007-1598. Phone: 800-821-8312 or (215)785-5800 Fax: (215)785-5515 URL: http://www.mosby.com • 1992. $23.95. Third edition.

Alcoholism: Clinical and Experimental Research. Research Society on Alcoholism. Williams & Wilkins Co., 351 W. Camden St. Baltimore, MD 21201-2436. Phone: 800-527-5597 or (410)528-4000 Fax: (410)528-4422 E-mail: custserv@wilkins.com • URL: http://www.wwilkins.com • Monthly. Individuals, $251.00 per year; institutions, $484.00 per year.

Alcoholism Digest Annual. Information Planning Associates, Inc., 5205 Leesburg Pike Falls Church, VA. Phone: (202)820-6100 Annual. Price on application.

Alcoholism Treatment Quarterly: The Practitioner's Quarterly for Individual, Group, and Family Therapy. Haworth Press, Inc., 10 Alice St. Binghamton, NY 13904-1580. Phone: 800-429-6784 or (607)722-5857 Fax: 800-895-0582 or (607)722-1424 E-mail: getinfo@haworthpressinc.com • URL: http://www.haworthpressinc.com • Quarterly. Individuals, $50.00 per year; institutions, $120.00 per year; libraries, $350.00 per year. Edited for professionals working with alcoholics and their families. Formerly *Alcoholism Counseling and Treatment*.

All About Medicare. The National Underwriter Co., 505 Gest St. Cincinnati, OH 45203-1716. Phone: 800-543-0874 or (513)721-2140 Fax: (513)721-0126 URL: http://www.nauo.com • Annual. $12.25.

All Hands: Magazine of the United States Navy. Available from U. S. Government Printing Office, Washington, DC 20402. Phone: (202)512-1800 Fax: (202)512-2250 E-mail: gpoaccess@gpo.gov • URL: http://www.access.gpo.gov • Monthly. $42.00 per year. Contains articles of general interest concerning the U. S. Navy (http://www.navy.mil).

All States Tax Guide. Prentice Hall, 240 Frisch Court Paramus, NJ 07652-5240. Phone: 800-947-7700 or (201)909-6200 Fax: 800-445-6991 or (201)909-6361 URL: http://www.prenhall.com • Looseleaf. Periodic supplementation. Price on application. One volume summary of taxes for all states.

All States Tax Handbook. Research Institute of America, 90 Fifth Ave. New York, NY 10011. Phone: 800-431-9025 or (212)645-4800 Fax: (201)816-3581 Annual. $30.00. Tax structures for fifty states.

All You Need to Know About the Music Business: Revised and Updated for the 21st Century. Donald S. Passman. Simon & Schuster Trade, 1230 Ave. of the Americas New York, NY 10020. Phone: 800-223-2336 or (212)698-7000 Fax: 800-943-9831 or (212)698-7007 E-mail: sson-line_feedback@simonsays.com • URL: http://www.simonsays.com • 2000. Price on application. Covers the practical and legal aspects of record contracts, music publishing, management agreements, touring, and other music business topics.

Alliance for Community Media.

Alliance for Nonprofit Management.

Alliance of American Insurers.

Alliance of Manufacturers and Exporters of Canada.

Alliance of Motion Picture and Television Producers.

Alliance of Nonprofit Mailers.

Allied Artists of America.

Allied Finance Adjusters Conference.

Allied Pilots Association.

Allied Trades of the Baking Industry.

Alloys Index. Cambridge Information Group, 7200 Wisconsin Ave., 6th Fl. Bethesda, MD 20814. Phone: 800-843-7751 or (301)961-6700 Fax: (301)961-6720 E-mail: market@csa.com • URL: http://www.csa.com • Monthly. $445.00 per year. Annual cumulation, $760.00 per year. Auxiliary publication to *Metals Abstracts* and *Metals Abstracts Index*.

Almanac. Penton Media Inc., 1300 E. Ninth St. Cleveland, OH 44114. Phone: (216)696-7000 Fax: (216)696-0836 E-mail: corpcomm@penton.com • URL: http://www.penton.com • Annual. $50.00. Lists equipment, products, and services for the hotel and motel industry.

The Almanac of American Employers: The Only Complete Guide to the Hottest, Fastest-Growing Major Corporations. Plunkett Research, Ltd., P.O. Drawer 541737 Houston, TX 77254-1737. Phone: (713)932-0000 Fax: (713)932-7080 E-mail: info@plunkettresearch.com • URL: http://www.plunkettresearch.com • Annual. $149.99. Provides descriptions of 500 large corporations, including salaries/benefits ratings, corporate culture profiles, types of employment, and other company information for job-seekers. Includes four indexes.

Almanac of American Politics. National Journal Group, Inc., 1501 M St., N.W., Suite 300 Washington, DC 20005. Phone: 800-424-2921 or (202)739-8400 Fax: (202)739-8511 Biennial. $54.95. Includes biographies of U.S. senators and representatives, with group ratings, key votes, and election results.

Almanac of Business and Industrial Financial Ratios. Leo Troy. Prentice Hall, 240 Frisch Court Paramus, NJ 07652-5240. Phone: 800-947-7700 or (201)909-6200 Fax: 800-445-6991 or (201)909-6361 URL: http://www.prenhall.com • Annual. $99.95. Contains financial ratios derived from federal tax returns. Ratios for each of about 200 industries are arranged according to company asset size.

Almanac of Famous People. The Gale Group, 27500 Drake Rd. Farmington Hills, MI 48331-3535. Phone: 800-877-GALE or (248)699-GALE Fax: 800-414-5043 or (248)699-8069 E-mail: galeord@galegroup.com • URL: http://www.galegroup.com • 2001. $140.00. Two volumes. Seventh edition. Contains about 30,000 short biographies, with bibliographic citations. Chronological, geographic, and occupational indexes. Formerly *Biography Almanac*.

Almanac of the Canning, Freezing, Preserving Industries, Vol. Two. Edward E. Judge and Sons, Inc., P.O. Box 866 Westminster, MD 21158. Phone: (410)876-2052 Fax: (410)848-2034 E-mail: info@eejudge.com • URL: http://www.eejudge.com • Annual. $71.00. Contains U. S. food laws and regulations and detailed production statistics.

The Almanac of the Executive Branch. Maximov Publications, 200 E. 32nd St., Suite 13 B New York, NY 10016. Phone: (212)251-0819 Fax: (212)251-1042 E-mail: maximov@

usa.net • Annual. $149.00. Provides detailed information on more than 830 key staff memebers of the executive branch of the federal government. Includes educational background, previous employment, job responsibilities, etc.

Almanac of the Federal Judiciary. Publishers, Inc., 1185 Ave. of the Americas, 37th Fl. New York, NY 10036. Phone: 800-444-1717 or (212)597-0200 Fax: (212)597-0339 E-mail: customer.service@aspenpubl.com • URL: http://www.aspenpub.com • Annual. $295.00 per set. Two volumes. Volume one provides information on federal district judges; volume two relates to federal circuit judges.

Almanac of the Fifty States: Basic Data Profiles with Comparative Tables. Edith R. Hornor, editor. Information Publications, 3790 El Camino Real Palo Alto, CA 94306. Phone: (650)965-4449 Fax: (650)965-3801 E-mail: infopubs@wenet.net • URL: http://www.wenet.net/users/infopubs • Annual. $50.00. 14th revised edition.

Almanac of the Unelected: Staff of the U. S. Congress. Bernan Press, 4611-F Assembly Dr. Lanham, MD 20706-4391. Phone: 800-274-4447 or (301)459-7666 Fax: 800-865-3450 or (301)459-0056 E-mail: info@bernan.com • URL: http://www.bernan.com • Annual. $275.00. Provides detailed information on key staff members of the legislative branch of the federal government. Includes educational background, previous employment, job responsibilities, etc.

Alphaphonetic Directory of International Trademarks. Available from Thomson & Thomson, 500 Victory Rd. North Quincy, MA 02171-3145. Phone: 800-692-8833 or (617)479-1600 Fax: (617)786-8273 E-mail: support@thomson-thomson.com • URL: http://www.thomson-thomson.com • Annual, with three cumulative updates during the year. $1,914.00 per year. 15 volumes. Published in Belgium by Compu-Mark. Provides owner, registration, and classification information for more than one million trademarks registered with the World Intellectual Property Organization (WIPO).

Altered Fates: The Genetic Re-Engineering of Human Life. Jeff Lyon and Peter Gorner. W. W. Norton & Co., Inc., 500 Fifth Ave. New York, NY 10110. Phone: 800-223-2584 or (212)354-5500 Fax: (212)869-0856 E-mail: webmaster@wwnorton.com • URL: http://www.norton.com • 1995. $27.50. A discussion of recent progress in genetic engineering.

Alternative Energy Retailer. Zackin Publications, Inc., P.O. Box 2180 Waterbury, CT 06722. Phone: (203)755-0158 Monthly. $32.00 per year.

Aluminum Association.

Aluminum Extruders Council.

Aluminum Industry Abstracts: A Monthly Review of the World's Technical Literature on Aluminum. Aluminum Association, 900 19th St. N.W. Washington, DC 44073. Phone: (202)862-5100 Fax: (202)862-5164 E-mail: dbartel@po.asm-intl.org • URL: http://www.aluminum.org • Monthly. $595.00 per year. Formerly *World Aluminum Abstracts*.

Aluminum Standards and Data. Aluminum Association Inc., 900 19th St., N.W., Suite 300 Washington, DC 20006. Phone: (202)862-5100 Fax: (202)862-5164 URL: http://www.aluminum.org • Biennial. $25.00.

Aluminum Statistical Review. Aluminum Association Inc., 900 19th St., N.W., Suite 300 Washington, DC 20006. Phone: (202)862-5100 Fax: (202)862-5164 URL: http://www.aluminum.org • Annual. $50.00.

AM/FM Broadcast Financial Data/TV Broadcast Financial Data. U.S. Federal Communications Commission, Washington, DC 20554. Phone: 888-225-5322 or (202)418-0500 URL: http://www.fcc.gov • Annual. Free.

AMA Handbook of Business Letters. Jeffrey L. Seglin. AMACOM, 1601 Broadway, 12th Fl. New York, NY 10019. Phone: 800-262-9699 or (212)586-8100 Fax: (212)903-8168 E-mail: custmserv@amanet.org • URL: http://www.amanet.org • 1996. $69.95. Second edition. Contains 300 sample letters, with advice on business correspondence.

AMA International Member and Marketing Services Guide. American Marketing Association, 311 S. Wacker Dr., Suite 5800 Chicago, IL 60606-5819. Phone: 800-262-1150 or (312)542-9000 Fax: (312)542-9001 E-mail: info@ama.org • URL: http://www.ama.org • Annual. $150.00. Lists professional members of the American Marketing Association. Also contains information on providers of marketing support services and products, including software, communications, direct marketing, promotion, research, and consulting companies. Includes geographical and alphabetical indexes. Formerly *Marketing Yellow Pages and AMA International Membership Directory*.

AMA Management Handbook. John J. Hampton, editor. AMACOM, 1601 Broadway, 8th Fl. New York, NY 10019-7420. Phone: 800-262-9699 or (212)586-8100 Fax: (212)903-8168 E-mail: custmserv@amanet.org • URL: http://www.amanet.org • 1994. $110.00. Third edition. Provides 200 chapters in 16 major subject areas. Covers a wide variety of business and industrial management topics.

Amalgamated Clothing and Textile Workers Union.

The Amazing Internet Challenge: How Leading Projects Use Library Skills to Organize the Web. Amy T. Wells and others. American Library Association, 50 E. Huron St. Chicago, IL 60611-2795. Phone: 800-545-2433 or (312)944-6780 Fax: (312)440-9374 E-mail: ala@ala.org • URL: http://www.ala.org • 1999. $45.00. Presents profiles of 12 digital libraries, such as the Agriculture Network Information Center and the Social Science Information Gateway. Emphasis is on how online indexes were created.

Amazon.com. Amazon.com, Inc.Phone: 800-201-7575 or (206)346-2992 Fax: (206)346-2950 E-mail: info@amazon.com • URL: http://www.amazon.com • "Welcome to Earth's Biggest Bookstore." Amazon.com claims to have more than 2.5 million titles that can be ordered online, but only through the Web site - no orders by mail, telephone, fax, or E-mail. Discounts are generally 30% for hardcovers and 20% for paperbacks. Efficient search facilities, including Boolean, make this Web site useful for reference (many titles have online reviews). Fees: Free.

AMCA Directory of Licensed Products. Air Movement and Control Association, 30 W. University Dr. Arlington Heights, IL 60004. Phone: (708)394-0150 Fax: (708)253-0088 Annual. Free. Lists member manufacturers of equipment and supplies for the air and movement control industry.

America at Work. AFL-CIO, Public Affairs Dept., 815 16th St., N.W. Washington, DC 20006. Phone: (202)637-5010 Fax: (202)637-5058 E-mail: atwork@aflcio.org • URL: http://www.aflcio.org • Monthly. $10.00 per year. Formerly *AFL-CIO News*.

America on Record: A History of Recorded Sound. Andre Millard. Cambridge University Press, 40 W. 20th St. New York, NY 10011-4211. Phone: 800-221-4512 or (212)924-3900 Fax: (212)691-3239 E-mail: info@cup.org • URL: http://www.cup.org • 1995. $18.95.

American Academy of Actuaries.

American Academy of Actuaries Yearbook. American Academy of Actuaries, 1100 17th St., N.W., Suite 700 Washington, DC 20036. Phone: (202)223-8196 Fax: (202)872-1948 E-mail: info@actuary.org • URL: http://www.actuary.org • Annual. $25.00

American Academy of Advertising.

American Academy of Dental Group Practice.

American Academy of Dental Practice Administration.

American Academy of Family Physicians.

American Academy of Matrimonial Lawyers., 150 N. Michigan Ave., Suite 2040 Chicago, IL 60601. Phone: (312)263-6477 Fax: (312)263-7682 URL: http://www.aaml.org • Members are attorneys specializing in family law.

American Academy of Matrimonial Lawyers: List of Certified Fellows. American Academy of Matrimonial Lawyers, 150 N. Michigan Ave., Suite 2040 Chicago, IL 60601. Phone: (312)263-6477 Annual. Membership.

American Academy of Medical Administrators., 701 Lee St., Ste. 600 Des Plaines, IL 60016. Phone: (847)759-8601 Fax: (847)759-8602 E-mail: info@aameda.org • URL: http://www.aameda.org • Members are executives and middle managers in health care administration.

American Academy of Optometry.

American Accounting Association.

American Advertising. American Advertising Federation, 1101 Vermont Ave., N.W., Suite 500 Washington, DC 20005. Phone: (202)898-0089 Fax: (202)898-0159 E-mail: acroot@aaf.org • Quarterly. Membership.

American Advertising Federation.

American Affordable Housing Institute., Rutgers University, 33 Livingston Ave. New Brunswick, NJ 08901-2009. Phone: (732)932-6812 Fax: (732)932-7974 Conducts studies related to housing affordability and availability, especially for first-time homebuyers. Also does research on meeting the housing needs of America's senior citizens.

American Agricultural Economics Association.

American Agricultural Editor's Association.

American Agricultural Marketing Association.

American Alliance for Health, Physical Education, Recreation, and Dance.

American Amusement Machine Association.

American Apparel Machinery Trade Association.

American Apparel Manufacturers Association.

American Apparel Manufacturers Association Directory of Members and Associate Members. American Apparel Manufacturers Association, 2500 Wilson Blvd., Suite 301 Arlington, VA 22201-3816. Phone: 800-520-2262 or (703)524-1864 Fax: (703)522-6741 E-mail: jmorgan@americanapparel.org • Annual. $100.00. Lists 900 clothing manufacturers and suppliers of goods and services to apparel manufacturers.

American Arbitration Association.

American Architectural Manufacturers Association., 1827 Walden Office Square, Suite 104 Schamburg, IL 60173. Phone: (847)303-5664 Fax: (847)303-5774 E-mail: webmaster@aamanet.org • URL: http://www.aamanet.org • Members are manufacturers of a wide variety of architectural products. Includes a Residential/Commercial Window and Door Committee.

American Art Directory. National Register Publishing Co., 121 Chanlon Rd. New Providence, NJ 07974. Phone: 800-521-8110 or (908)464-6800 Fax: (908)771-7704 E-mail: info@bowker.com • URL: http://www.bowker.com • Biennial. $165.00. About 7,000 museums, art libraries and art organizations; also includes, 1,700 art schools.

American Artists Professional League.

American Association for Adult and Continuing Education.

American Association for Adult and Continuing Education: Membership Directory. American Association for Adult and Continuing Education, 1200 19th St., N.W., Suite 300 Washington, DC 20036. Phone: (202)429-5131 Fax: (202)223-4579 URL: http://www.albany.edu/aaace • Irregular.

American Association for Affirmative Action.

American Association for Artificial Intelligence.

American Association for Continuity of Care., P.O. Box 7073 North Brunswick, NJ 08902. Phone: 800-816-1575 Fax: (301)352-7086 URL: http://www.continuitycare.com • Members are professionals concerned with continuity of care, health care after hospital discharge, and home health care.

American Association for Public Opinion Research., P.O. Box 1248 Ann Arbor, MI 48106-1248. Phone: (313)764-1555 Fax: (313)764-3341 E-mail: aapor@umich.edu • URL: http://www.aapor.org • Members are individuals interested in methods and applications of opinion research.

American Association of Advertising Agencies.

American Association of Airport Executives.

American Association of Bioanalysts., 917 Locust St., Suite 1100 St. Louis, MO 63101-1413. Phone: (314)241-1445 Fax: (314)241-1449 E-mail: aab1445@primary.net • URL: http://www.aab.org • Members are owners and managers of bioanalytical clinical laboratories.

American Association of Collegiate Registrars and Admissions Officers.

American Association of Community and Junior Colleges Directory. American Association of Community and Junior Colleges, One Dupont Circle, N.W. Suite 410 Washington, DC 20036-1176. Phone: (202)728-0200 Fax: (202))833-2467 E-mail: mlatif@aacc.nche.edu • URL: http://www.aacc.nche.edu • Annual. $35.00. Formerly *Community, Junior and Technical College Directory*.

American Association of Community Colleges. National Center for Higher Education

American Association of Cosmetology Schools/Cosmetology Educators of America.

American Association of Exporters and Importers.

American Association of Fund-Raising Counsel.

American Association of Handwriting Analysts.

American Association of Health Plans., 1129 20th St., N.W., Suite 600 Washington, DC 20036-3421. Phone: (202)728-3200 Fax: (202)331-7487 URL: http://www.aahp.org • Members are alternate health care organizations, including HMOs.

American Association of Healthcare Consultants., 11208 Waples Mill Rd., Suite 109 Fairfax, VA 22030. Phone: 800-362-4674 or (703)691-2242 Fax: (703)691-2247 E-mail: consultahc@aol.com • URL: http://www.aahc.net • Members are professional consultants who specialize in the health care industry.

American Association of Homes and Services for the Aging.

American Association of Individual Investors.

American Association of Industrial Management.

American Association of Managing General Agents.

American Association of Meat Processors.

American Association of Motor Vehicle Administrators.

American Association of Motor Vehicle Administrators: Membership Directory. American Association of Motor Vehicle Administrators, 4301 Wilson Blvd., Suite 400 Arlington, VA 22203-1800. Phone: (703)522-4200 Fax: (703)522-1553 Annual. $100.00.

American Association of Port Authorities.

American Association of Preferred Provider Organizations.

American Association of Retired Persons.

American Association of School Administrators.

American Association of School Librarians., 50 E. Huron St. Chicago, IL 60611. Phone: 800-545-2433 or (312)280-4386 Fax: (312)664-7459 E-mail: aasl@ala.org • URL: http://www.ala.org/aasl • A division of the American Library Association.

American Association of State Highway and Transportation Officials.

American Association of Textile Chemists and Colorists.

American Association of Textile Chemists and Colorists Technical Manual. American Association of Textile Chemists and Colorists, P.O. Box 12215 Research Triangle Park, NC 27709-2215. Phone: (919)549-8141 Fax: (919)549-8933 URL: http://www.aatcc.org • Annual. Members, $75.00; non-members, $117.00.

American Association of University Administrators.

American Association of University Professors.

American Association of University Women.

American Astronautical Society.

American Automatic Control Council.

American Automatic Merchandiser Blue Book Buyer's Guide. Cygnus Publishing, 1233 Jonwsville Ave. Fort Atkinson, WI 53538. Phone: 800-547-7377 or (920)563-6388 Fax: (920)563-1707 E-mail: rich.reiff@cygnuspub.com • URL: http://www.cygnuspub.com • Annual. $35.00. Suppliers of products, services, and equipment to the merchandise vending, contract food services, and office coffee service industries.

American Automobile Association.

American Automotive Leasing Association.

American Bakers Association.

American Banker. Thomson Financial Media, One State St. Place New York, NY 10004-1549. Phone: 800-733-4371 or (212)803-8345 Fax: (212)843-9600 URL: http://www.americanbanker.com • Daily. $825.00 per year. Includes*Future Banker*.

American Banker Full Text. American Banker-Bond Buyer, Database Services, One State St. Plaza New York, NY 10004. Phone: 800-356-4763 or (212)803-8366 Fax: (212)843-9605 Provides complete text online of the daily *American Banker*. Inquire as to online cost and availability.

American Bankers Association.

American Bankers Association Key to Routing Numbers. Thomas Financial Information, 4709 Golf Rd., 6th Fl. Skokie, IL 60076-1253. Phone: 800-321-3373 or (847)676-9600 Fax: (847)933-8101 Semiannual. $125.00. per year. Lists over 30,000 finanical institutions in the U.S. and their routing members.

American Bankruptcy Institute., 44 Canal Center Plaza, Suite 404 Alexandria, VA 22314. Phone: (703)739-0800 Fax: (703)739-1060 E-mail: info@abiworld.org • URL: http://www.abiworld.org • Members are accountants, lawyers, bankers, and other interested individuals. Promotes the exchange of information on bankruptcy and insolvency issues and compiles statistics.

American Bankruptcy Law Journal. National Conference of Bankruptcy Judges, 235 Secret Cove Dr. Lexington, SC 29072. Phone: (803)957-6225 Quarterly. $65.00.

American Bar Association.

American Bar Association Directory. American Bar Association, 750 N. Lake Shore Dr. Chicago, IL 60611-4497. Phone: 800-285-2221 or (312)988-5000 Fax: (312)988-5528 E-mail: abajournal@abanet.org • URL: http://www.abanet.org • Annual. $14.95. Lists about 7,500 lawyers.

American Bearing Manufacturers Association.

American Bee Journal. Dadant and Sons, Inc., Hamilton, IL 62341. Phone: (217)847-3324 Fax: (217)847-3660 E-mail: abj@dadant.com • URL: http://www.dadant.com • Monthly. $19.25 per year. Magazine for hobbyist and professional beekeepers.

American Beekeeping Federation.

American Beekeeping Federation Newsletter. American Beekeeping Federation, P.O. Box 1038 Jesup, GA 31545. Phone: (912)427-4233 Fax: (912)427-8447 E-mail: info@abfnet.org • URL: http://www.abfnet.org • Bimonthly. $25.00 per year. Newsletter.

American Behavioral Scientist. Sage Publications, Inc., 2455 Teller Rd. Thousand Oaks, CA 91320. Phone: (805)499-0721 Fax: (805)499-0871 E-mail: info@sagepub.com • URL: http://www.sagepub.com • Monthly. Individuals, $125.00 per year; institutions, $775.00 per year.

American Bench: Judges of the Nation. Forster-Long, Inc., 3280 Ramos Circle Sacramento, CA 95827. Phone: 800-328-5091 or (916)362-3276 Fax: (916)362-5643 E-mail: clientrelations@forster-long.com • Annual. $360.00. Features biographies of 18,000 members of the U.S. Judiciary at federal, state and local levels.

American Bicyclist. Willow Publishing Co., 400 Skokie Blvd. Northbrook, IL 60062-2816. Phone: (847)291-1117 Fax: (847)559-4444 Monthly. Free to qualified personnel; others, $35.00 per year. Trade journal edited for bicycle retailers and wholesalers. Includes product reviews.

American Big Businesses Directory. American Business Directories, P.O. Box 27347 Omaha, NE 68127. Phone: 800-555-6124 or (402)593-4600 Fax: (402)331-5481 E-mail: jerry.verner@abii.com • URL: http://www.abii.com • Annual. $595.00. Lists 177,000 public and private U. S. companies in all fields having 100 or more employees. Includes sales volume, number of employees, and name of chief executive. Formerly *Big Businesses Directory*.

The American Blue Book of Funeral Directors. Kates-Bolyston Publications, Inc., 100 Wood Ave. S. Iselin, NJ 08830-2716. Phone: 800-500-4585 or (732)767-9300 Fax: (732)767-9741 E-mail: americanfd@aol.com • URL: http://www.kates-boylston.com • Biennial. $75.00. About 22,000 funeral homes primarily in the United States and Canada.

American Board of Medical Specialties., 1007 Church St., Suite 404 Evanston, IL 60201-5913. Phone: (847)491-9091 Fax: (847)328-3596 URL: http://www.abms.org/abms • Functions as the parent organization for U. S. medical specialty boards.

American Board of Ophthalmology.

American Board of Professional Liability Attorneys., c/o Harvey F. Wachsman, 175 E. Shore Rd. Great Neck, NY 11023. Phone: 800-633-6255 or (516)487-1990 Fax: (516)487-4304 Members are liability litigation lawyers who meet specific requirements as to experience and who pass written and oral Board examinations.

American Boat and Yacht Council.

American Boat Builders and Repairers Association.

American Book-Prices Current. Bancroft-Parkman, Inc., P.O. Box 1236 Washington, CT 06793. Phone: (860)868-7408 Fax: (860)868-0080 E-mail: abpc@snet.net • Annual. $109.95.

American Book Publishing Record: Arranged by Dewey Decimal Classification and Indexed by Author, Title, and Subject. R. R. Bowker, 121 Chanlon Rd. New Providence, NJ 07974. Phone: 888-269-5372 or (908)464-6800 Fax: (908)771-7704 E-mail: info@bowker.com • URL: http://www.bowker.com • Monthly. $299.00. per year. Includes annual cumulation.

American Book Trade Directory. R. R. Bowker, 121 Chanlon Rd. New Providence, NJ 07974. Phone: 888-269-5372 or (908)464-6800 Fax: (908)771-7704 E-mail: info@bowker.com • URL: http://www.bowker.com • Annual. $255.00 More than 30,000 bookstores and other book outlets in the U.S. and Canada; 1,500 U.S. and Canadian book wholesalers and paperback distributors.

American Booksellers Association.

American Bureau of Metal Statistics., P.O. Box 805 Chatham, NJ 07928. Phone: (973)701-2299 Fax: (973)701-2152 E-mail: info@abms.com • URL: http://www.abms.com • Members are metal companies. Compiles and publishes detailed statistical data on a wide variety of nonferrous metals: aluminum, copper, gold, lead, nickel, platinum, silver, tin, titanium, uranium, zinc, and others.

American Bureau of Shipping.

American Bureau of Shipping Record. American Bureau of Shipping, One World Trade Center, 9165 New York, NY 10048-9165. Phone: (212)839-5100 Fax: (212)839-5130 Annual. $520.00 per year. Quarterly supplements.

American Bus Association.

American Business Climate and Economic Profiles. The Gale Group, 27500 Drake Rd. Farmington Hills, MI 48331-3535. Phone: 800-877-GALE or (248)699-GALE Fax: 800-414-5043 E-mail: galeord@galegroup.com • URL: http://www.galegroup.com • 1993. $135.00. Provides business, industrial, demographic, and economic figures for all states and 300 metropolitan areas. Includes production, taxation, population, growth rates, labor force data, incomes, total sales, etc.

American Business Directory. InfoUSA, Inc., 378 Vintage Park Drive Foster City, CA 94404. Phone: 800-321-0869 or (650)389-0700 Fax: (650)389-0707 E-mail: help@infousa.com • URL: http://www.infousa.com • Provides brief online information on more than 10 million U. S. companies, including individual plants and branches. Entries typically include address, phone number, industry classification code, and contact name. Updating is quarterly. Inquire as to online cost and availability.

American Business Leaders: From Colonial Times to the Present. Neil A. Hamilton. ABC-CLIO, Inc., 1130 Cremona Drive Santa Barbara, CA 93117. Phone: 800-368-6868 or (805)968-1911 Fax: (805)685-9685 E-mail: sales@abc-clio.com • URL: http://www.abc-clio.com • 1999. $150.00. Two volumes. Contains biographies of 413 notable business figures. Historical coverage is from the 17th century to the 1990s.

American Business Locations Directory. The Gale Group, 27500 Drake Rd. Farmington Hills, MI 48331-3535. Phone: 800-877-GALE or (248)699-GALE Fax: 800-414-5043 E-mail: galeord@galegroup.com • URL: http://www.galegroup.com • 1999. $575.00. Second edition. (Four U. S. regional volumes and index volume). Provides 150,000 specific site locations for the 1,000 largest industrial and service companies in the U. S. Entries include the following for each location: address, senior officer, number of employees, sales volume, Standard Industrial Classification (SIC) codes, and name of parent company.

American Business Press., 675 Third Ave., Suite 415 New York, NY 10017. Phone: (212)661-6360 Fax: (212)370-0736 E-mail: abp@abp2.com • URL: http://www.americanbusinesspress.com • Members are publishers of business and technical periodicals with audited circulation. Includes a Publishing Management Committee.

American Business Values. Gerald F. Cavanaugh. Prentice Hall, 240 Frisch Court Paramus, NJ 07652-5240. Phone: 800-947-7700 or (201)909-6200 Fax: 800-445-6991 or (201)909-6361 URL: http://www.prenhall.com • 1997. $38.60. Fourth edition.

American Business Women's Association.

American Butter Institute.

American Camping Association.

American Car Rental Association.

American Cement Directory: Directory of Cement Companies and Personnel. Bradley Pulverizer Co., P.O. Box 1318 Allentown, PA 18105-1318. Phone: 800-355-1186 or (610)434-5191 Fax: (610)770-9400 URL: http://www.bradleypulv.com • Annual. $71.00. About 200 cement manufacturing plants in the United States, Canada,Mexico, Central and South America.

American Center for Design.

American Ceramic Society.

American Ceramic Society Bulletin. American Ceramic Society, P.O. Box 6136 Westerville, OH 43081-6136. Phone: (614)890-4700 Fax: (614)899-6109 E-mail: customersrvc@acers.org • URL: http://www.acers.org • Monthly. Free to members; non-members, $50.00 per year.

American Ceramic Society Journal. American Ceramic Society, P.O. Box 6136 Westerville, OH 43081. Phone: (614)890-4700 Fax: (614)899-6109 E-mail: customersrvc@acers.org • URL: http://www.acers.org • Monthly. Members, $125.00 per year; non-members, $625.00 per year. Includes subscription to *Ceramic Bulletin and Abstracts*.

American Chain of Warehouses.

American Chain of Warehouses-Membership Directory. American Chain of Warehouses, 20500 S. LaGrange Rd. Frankfort, IL 60423. Phone: (815)469-4354 Fax: (815)469-2941 E-mail: don@acwiwarehouses.com • URL: http://www.aciwarehouses.com • Annual. Free. Controlled circulation. About 45 member public warehouses in the United States.

American Chamber of Commerce Executives.

American Chemical Society.

American Cinematographer: International Journal of Motion Picture Production Techniques. American Society of Cinematographers. ASC Holding Corp., P.O. Box 2230 Los Angeles, CA 90078. Phone: 800-448-0145 or (213)969-4333 Fax: (213)876-4973 E-mail: ascmag@aol.com • URL: http://www.cinematographers.com • Monthly. $40.00 per year.

American Cinematographer Manual. Rod Ryan, editor. ASC Holding Corp., P.O. Box 2230 Los Angles, CA 90078. Phone: 800-448-0145 or (213)969-4333 Fax: (213)876-4973 E-mail: ascmag@aol.com • URL: http://www.cinematographers.com • 1993. $49.95. Seventh edition. A pocket size encyclopedia of practical information about cameras, lenses, films, exposure, depth of field, lighting, special effects, etc.

American City and County: Administration, Engineering and Operations in Relation to Local Government. Intertec Publishing Corp., 6151 Powers Ferry Rd., N.W., Suite 200 Atlanta, GA 30339. Phone: 800-400-5945 or (770)955-2500 Fax: (770)955-0400 E-mail: subs@intertec.com • URL: http://www.intertec.com • Monthly. $58.00 per year. Edited for mayors, city managers, and other local officials. Emphasis is on equipment and basic services.

American City and County Municipal Index: Purchasing Guide for City, Township, County Officials and Consulting Engineers. Intertec Publishing Corp., 6151 Powers Ferry Rd., N. W., Suite 200 Atlanta, GA 30339. Phone: 800-400-5945 or (770)955-2500 Fax: (770)955-0400 E-mail: subs@intertec.com • URL: http://www.intertec.com • Annual. $61.95. Includes a directory of city and county governments with populations of 10,000 or more. Names and telephone numbers of municipal purchasing officials are listed. Also includes a directory of manufacturers and suppliers of materials, equipment, and services for municipalities.

American Civil Liberties Union.

American Clean Car. Crain Communications, Inc., 500 N. Dearborn St. Chicago, IL 60610. Phone: (312)337-7700 Fax: (312))337-8654 Bimonthly. $35.00 per year. Provides articles on new products and management for the carwash industry.

American Clinical Laboratory Association., 1250 H St., N. W., Suite 880 Washington, DC 20005. Phone: (202)637-9466 Fax: (202)637-2050 E-mail: acla@erols.com • Members are owners of clinical laboratories operating for a profit.

American Cloak and Suit Manufacturers Association.

American Cocoa Research Institute.

American Coin-Op: The Magazine for Coin-Operated Laundry and Drycleaning Businessmen. Crain Communications, Inc., 500 N. Dearborn St. Chicago, IL 60610. Phone: (312)337-7700 Fax: (312)337-8654 Monthly. $35.00 per year.

American Coke and Coal Chemicals Institute.

American Collectors Association.

American Collectors Association - Membership Roster. American Collectors Association, Inc., P.O. Box 39106 Minneapolis, MN 55435. Phone: (612)926-6547 Fax: (612)926-1624 E-mail: aca@collector.com • Annual. Membership.

American College of Apothecaries., P.O. Box 341266 Memphis, TN 38184-1266. Phone: (901)383-8119 Fax: (901)383-8882 A professional society of pharmacists.

American College of Counselors.

American College of Health Care Administrators.

American College of Healthcare Executives.

American College of Medical Practice Executives.

American College of Occupational and Environmental Medicine-Membership Directory., 1114 N. Arlington Heights Rd. Arlington Heights, IL 60004. Phone: (847)818-1800 Fax: (847)818-9266 Annual. $150.00. Lists 6,500 medical directories and plant physicians specializing in occupational medicine and surgery; coverage includes Canada and other foreign countries. Geographically arranged.

American College of Radiology., 1891 Preston White Dr. Reston, VA 22091. Phone: 800-227-5463 or (703)648-8900 Fax: (703)648-9176 URL: http://www.acr.org • A professional society of physicians.

American College of Trial Lawyers.

American College of Trust and Estate Counsel.

American Compensation Association.

American Compensation Association-Membership Directory. American Compensation Association, 14040 N. Northsight Blvd. Scottsdale, AZ 85260. Phone: (602)951-9191 Fax: (602)483-8352 Annual. Free to members; non-members, $150.00. Covers 20,000 member benefits and compensation professionals in Canada and United States.

American Concrete Institute.

American Concrete Pavement Association.

American Conference of Governmental Industrial Hygienists., 1330 Kemper Meadow Dr. Cincinnati, OH 45240. Phone: (513)742-2020 Fax: (513)742-3355 E-mail: mail@acgih.org • URL: http://www.acgih.org • Members are government employees.

American Congress on Surveying and Mapping.

American Consultants League., 30466 Prince William St. Prince Anne, MD 21853. Phone: (410)651-4869 Members are part-time and full-time consultants in various fields. Offers marketing and legal advice.

American Consulting Engineers Council.

American Consulting Engineers Council-Membership Directory. American Consulting Engineers Council, 1015 15th St., N.W., Suite 802 Washington, DC 20005. Phone: (202)347-7474 Fax: (202)898-0068 Annual. $140.00. A state-by-state listing of ACEC's 5,200 consulting engineering firms with a total of over 180,000 employees.

American Consumers Association., 2633 Flossmoor Rd. Flossmoor, IL 60422. Phone: (708)957-2900 E-mail: tuetall@aol.com • Promotes the interests and well-being of consumers.

American Corn Millers' Federation.

American Correctional Association., 4380 Forbes Blvd. Lanham, MD 20706-4322. Phone: 800-222-5646 or (301)918-1800 Fax: (301)918-1900 URL: http://www.corrections.com/aca • Members are correctional administrators, prison wardens, parole boards, educators, and others with an interest in correctional institutions. Various departments are concerned with conventions, corporate relations, finance, administration, communications, and standards.

American Correctional Food Service Association., 4248 Park Glen Rd. Minneapolis, MN 55416. Phone: (612)928-4658 Fax: (612)929-1318 E-mail: acfsa@corrections.com • URL: http://www.corrections.com/acfsa • Members are employees of food service operations at correctional institutions.

American Cost of Living Survey. The Gale Group, 27500 Drake Rd. Farmington Hills, MI 48331-3535. Phone: 800-877-GALE or (248)699-GALE Fax: 800-414-5043 or (248)699-8069 E-mail: galeord@galegroup.com • URL: http://www.galegroup.com • 1995. $160.00. Second edition. Cost of living data is provided for 455 U.S. cities and metroploitan areas.

American Cotton Shippers Association.

American Council for an Energy-Efficient Economy., 1001 Connecticut Ave., N. W., Suite 801 Washington, DC 20036. Phone: (202)429-0063 Fax: (202)429-0193 E-mail: info@aceee.org • URL: http://www.aceee.org • Promotes energy efficiency as a means of enhancing both economic prosperity and environmental protection. Publishes books, proceedings, and reports.

American Council for Capital Formation., 1750 K St., N.W., Suite 400 Washington, DC 20006. Phone: (202)293-5811 Fax: (202)785-8165 E-mail: info@accf.org • URL: http://www.accf.org • Supports capital formation as a general concept.

American Council of Life Insurance.

American Council of State Savings Supervisors., P.O. Box 34175 Washington, DC 20043-4175. Phone: (202)922-5153 Fax: (202)922-6237 Members are state savings and loan supervisors. Includes a Joint Committee on Examinations and Education.

American Council of the International Institute of Welding.

American Council on Alcohol Problems.

American Council on Consumer Awareness, Inc.

American Council on Consumer Interests.

American Council on Education.

American Counseling Association.

The American Country Club: Its Origins and Development. James M. Mayo. Rutgers University Press, 100 Joyce Kilmer Ave. New Brunswick, NJ 08854-8099. Phone: 800-446-9323 or (732)445-7762 Fax: 888-471-9014 or (732)445-7039 E-mail: ccapps@rci.rutgers.edu • URL: http://www.rutgerspress.rutgers.edu • 1998. $25.00.

American Crop Protection Association.

American Dairy Science Association.

American Dairy Science Association.

American Decades. The Gale Group, 27500 Drake Rd. Farmington Hills, MI 48331-3535. Phone: 800-877-GALE or (248)699-GALE Fax: 800-414-5043 or (248)699-8069 E-mail: galeord@galegroup.com • URL: http://www.galegroup.com • 1996. $890.00. $99.00 per volume. Consists of 10 volumes, each covering a decade during the period 1900-1989. ''Each volume begins with an overview and chronology covering the entire decade. Subject chapters follow, each including an overview, subject-specific timeline and alphabetically arranged entries.''

American Demographics: Consumer Trends for Business Leaders. Intertec Publishing Co., 11 Riverbend Dr., S. Stamford, CT 06907-2524. Phone: 800-795-5445 or (203)358-9900 Fax: (203)358-5811 E-mail: subs@intertec.com • URL: http://www.intertec.com • Monthly. $69.00 per year.

American Dental Association.

American Dental Association Journal. American Dental Association, 211 E. Chicago Ave. Chicago, IL 60611. Phone: 800-947-4746 or (312)440-2500 Fax: (312)440-3538 URL: http://www.ada.org • Monthly. Free to members; non-members, $100.00 per year; institutions, $121.00 per year.

American Dental Directory. American Dental Association, 211 E. Chicago Ave. Chicago, IL 60611. Phone: 800-947-4746 or (312)440-2500 Fax: (312)440-9970 URL: http://www.ada.org • Annual. $187.50. Contains brief information for over 170,000 dentists.

American Dental Trade Association.

American Design Drafting Association.

American Dietetic Association.

American Dietetic Association Journal. American Dietetic Association, 216 W. Jackson Blvd., Suite 800 Chicago, IL 60606-6995. Phone: (312)899-0040 Fax: (312)899-1757 E-mail: journal@eatright.org • URL: http://www.eatright.org/journaloc.html • Monthly. $125.00 per year.

American Disabled for Attendant Program Today., 201 S. Cherokee St. Denver, CO 80223-1836. Phone: (303)733-9324 Fax: (303)738-6211 E-mail: adapt@adapt.org • Members are disabled individuals promoting wheelchair accessibility in all forms of public transportation.

American Doctoral Dissertations. Association of Research Libraries. UMI, 300 N. Zeeb Rd. Ann Arbor, MI 48106-1346. Phone: 800-521-0600 or (313)761-4700 Fax: 800-864-0019 URL: http://www.umi.com • Annual. Price on application.

American Driver and Traffic Safety Education Association.

American Drug Index. Facts and Comparison, 111 W. Port Plaza, Suite 300 St. Louis, MO 6314-3098. Phone: 800-223-0554 or (314)878-2515 Fax: (314)878-5563 Annual. $49.95. Lists over 20,000 drug entries in dictionary style.

American Druggist. Press Corps, Inc., 444 Park Ave., S., Ste. 402 New York, NY 10016-7321. Phone: (212)686-8584 Fax: (212)686-9098 E-mail: amdruggist@aol.com • Monthly. $44.00 per year. Provides news and analysis of major trends affecting pharmacists. Includes an annual ''Generic Survey'' (September).

American Drycleaner. Crain Communications, Inc., 500 N. Dearborn St. Chicago, IL 60610. Phone: (312)337-7700 Fax: (312)337-8654 Monthly. $35.00 per year.

American Economic Association.

American Economic Development Council.

American Economic Development Council News. American Economic Development Council, 1030 W. Higgins Rd., No 301 Park Ridge, IL 60068-5726. Phone: (847)692-9944 Fax: (847)696-2990 E-mail: aedc@interaccess.com • URL: http://www.aedc.org/hqtrs • Six times per year. Membership.

American Economic Review. American Economic Association, 2014 Broadway, Suite 305 Nashville, TN 37203-2418. Phone: (615)322-2595 Fax: (615)343-7590 E-mail: aeainfo@ctrvax.vanderbilt.edu • URL: http://www.vanderbilt.edu/aea • Quarterly. Free to members; non-members, $135.00 per year. (Includes *Journal of Economic Literature* and *Journal of Economic Persepective*).

American Editor. American Society of Newspaper Editors, 11690 Sunrise Valley Dr., No. B Reston, VA 20191-1490. Phone: (703)453-1122 Fax: (703)453-1133 E-mail: asne@asne.org • URL: http://www.asne.org/ • Nine times a year. $29.00 per year. Formerly *American Society of Newspaper Editors Bulletin*.

American Egg Board.

American Electronics Association.

American Electroplaters' and Surface Finishers Society.

American Enterprise Institute.

American Entomological Society.

American Entomologist: Entomological Articles of General Interest. Entomological Society of America, 9301 Annopolis Rd. Lanham, MD 20706. Phone: (301)731-4535 Fax: (301)731-4538 Quarterly. Members, $15.00 per year; non-members, $36.00 per year, institutions, $64.00 per year. Formerly *Entomological Society of America Bulletin*.

American Export Register. Available from Thomas Publishing Co., International Div, Five Penn Plaza New York, NY 10001. Phone: 800-699-9822 or (212)695-0500 Fax: (212)629-1140 URL: http://www.thomaspublishing.com • Annual. $120.00. Two volumes. Supplement available *American Export Products*. Lists over 44,000 American firms with exporting programs. Includes *American Export Products*. Formerly *American Register of Exporters and Importers*.

American Farm Bureau Federation.

American Federation of Government Employees.

American Federation of Home Health Agencies., 1320 Fenwick Lane,, Suite 100 Silver Spring, MD 20910. Phone: 800-234-4211 Fax: (301)588-4732 E-mail: afhha@his.com • URL: http://www.his.com/~afhha/usa.html • Promotes home health care.

American Federation of Mineralogical Societies.

American Federation of State, County and Municipal Employees.

American Federation of Television and Radio Artists.

American Feed Industry Association.

American Fiber Manufacturers Association.

American Finance Association., c/o Professor David Pyle, University of California Berkeley, Haas School of Business, 545 Student Services Bldg. Berkeley, CA 94720-1900. Phone: (510)642-4417 E-mail: pyle@haas.berkeley.edu • URL: http://www.afajof.org • Members are business educators and financial executives.

American Financial Services Association.

American Firearms Industry. National Association of Federally Licensed Firearms Dealers. AFI Communications Group, Inc., 2455 E. Sunrise Blvd., 9th Fl. Fort Lauderdale, FL 33304-3118. Phone: (954)561-3505 Fax: (954)561-4129 URL: http://www.amfire.com • Monthly. $35.00 per year.

American Fisheries Society.

American Fitness Association., 1945 Palo Verde Ave., Suite 202 Long Beach, CA 90815. Phone: (562)799-8333 Fax: (562)799-3355 E-mail: staff@nsfa-online.com • URL: http://www.nsfa-online.com • Members are health and fitness professionals.

American Flint Glass Workers Union.

American Foreign Service Association.

American Forensic Association.

American Forensic Association Newsletter - Directory. American Forensic Association, P.O. Box 256 River Falls, WI 54022-0256. Phone: 800-228-5424 or (715)425-3198 Fax: (715)429-9533 Annual. Free with subscription; non-subscription, $7.50. List of 1,500 member teachers of argumentation and debate.

American Forest and Paper Association.

American Foundation for AIDS Research., 120 Wall St., 13th Fl. New York, NY 10005. Phone: 800-392-6327 or (212)806-1600 Fax: (212)806-1601 E-mail: donors@amfar.org • URL: http://www.amfar.org • Purpose is to raise funds to support AIDS research.

American Foundrymen's Society.

American Frozen Food Institute.

American Frozen Food Institute-Membership Directory and Buyers Guide. American Frozen Food Institute, 2000 Corporate Ridge, Suite 1000 McLean, VA 22102. Phone: (703)821-0770 Fax: (703)821-1350 URL: http://www.affi.com • Annual. $100.00. 550 member frozen food processors, suppliers, brokers, and distributors.

American Fruit Grower. Meister Publishing Co., 37733 Euclid Ave. Willoughby, OH 44094-5992. Phone: 800-572-7740 or (440)942-2000 Fax: (440)942-0662 E-mail: info@meisternet.com • Monthly. $27.47 per year.

American Fruit Grower Source Book. Meister Publishing Co., 37733 Euclid Ave Willoughby, OH 44094. Phone: 800-572-7740 or (440)942-2000 Fax: (440)942-0662 E-mail: info@meisternet.com • Annual. $5.00.

American Funeral Director. Kates-Bolyston Publications, Inc., 100 Wood Ave. S. Iselin, NJ 08830-2716. Phone: 800-500-4585 or (732)767-9300 Fax: (732)767-9741 E-mail: americanfd@aol.com • URL: http://www.kates-boylston.com • Monthly. $28.00 per year.

American Fur Merchants' Association.

American Furniture Manufacturers Association.

American Gas. American Gas Association, 444 N. Capitol St., N.W. Washington, DC 20001-1511. Phone: (202)824-7000 Fax: (202)824-7115 E-mail: amgas@aga.com • URL: http://www.aga.org • 11 times a year. $59.00 per year. Formerly *AGA Monthly*.

American Gas Association.

American Gear Manufacturers Association., 1500 King St., Suite 201 Alexandria, VA 22314-2730. Phone: (703)684-0211 Fax: (703)684-0242 E-mail: webmaster@agma.org • URL: http://www.agma.org • Members are manufacturers of gears and gear-cutting equipment.

American Gear Manufacturers Association News Digest. American Gear Manufacturers Association, 1500 King St., Suite 201 Alexandria, VA 22314-2730. Phone: (703)684-0211 Fax: (703)684-0242 Bimonthly. $50.00 per year. Newsletter. Covers business and research news relating to the gear industry.

American Gem and Mineral Suppliers Association.

American Gem Society.

American Gem Trade Association.

American Genetic Association., P.O. Box 257 Buckeystown, MD 21717-0257. Phone: (301)695-9292 Fax: (301)695-9292 Members are scientists engaged in genetics research.

American Glass Review. Doctorow Communications, Inc., 1011 Clifton Ave., Suite B1 Clifton, NJ 07013-3518. Phone: (973)779-1600 Fax: (973)779-3242 Seven times a year. $25.00 per year. Covers the manufacture, distribution and processing of flat glass, industrial glass, scientific and optical glass, etc. Includes *American Glass Review Glass Factory Directory*.

American Gold News and Western Prospector. DeServices, Inc., P.O. Box 35048 Las Vegas, NV 89133-5048. Phone: (801)628-7771 Monthly. $18.00 per year. Provides news about gold mining. Incorporates *Western Prospector*. Formerly *American Gold News*.

American Government: Readings and Cases. Peter Woll. Addison-Wesley Longman, Inc., One Jacob Way Reading, MA 08167. Phone: 800-447-2226 or (781)944-3700 Fax: (781)944-9351 URL: http://www.awl.com • 1998. $36.00. 13th edition.

American Hardware Export Council.

American Hardware Manufacturers Association.

American Health Care Association.

American Health Care Association: Provider. American Health Care Association, 1201 L St., N.W. Washington, DC 20005-4046. Phone: (202)842-4444 Fax: (202)842-3860 URL: http://www.ahca.org • Monthly. $48.00 per year. Formerly *American Health Care Association Journal*.

American Helicopter Society.

American Helicopter Society Journal. American Helicopter Society, Inc., 217 N. Washington St. Alexandria, VA 22314. Phone: (703)684-6777 Fax: (703)739-9279 URL: http://www.vtol.org/journal • Quarterly. $60.00 per year.

American Highway Users Alliance.

American Hospital Association.

American Hotel and Motel Association.

American Hotel Foundation.

*American Housing Survey for the United States in Îyear*l. Available from U. S. Government Printing Office, Washington, DC 20402. Phone: (202)512-1800 Fax: (202)512-2250 E-mail: gpoaccess@gpo.gov • URL: http://www.access.gpo.gov • Biennial. Issued by the U. S. Census Bureau (http://www.census.gov). Covers both owner-occupied and renter-occupied housing. Includes data on such factors as condition of building, type of mortgage, utility costs, and housing occupied by minorities. (Current Housing Reports, H150.)

American Humor Studies Association.

American Immigration Lawyers Association.

American Independent Refiners Association.

American Indonesian Chamber of Commerce.

American Industrial Health Council.

American Industrial Hygiene Association.

American Industrial Hygiene Association Journal: A Publication for the Science of Occupational and Environmental Health. American Industrial Hygiene Association, 2700 Prosperity Ave., Suite 250 Fairfax, VA 22031-4307. Phone: (703)849-8888 Fax: (703)207-3561 E-mail: infonet@aiha.org • URL: http://www.aiha.org • Monthly. Institutions, $160.00 per year.

American Industrial Real Estate Association.

American Industry. Publications for Industry, 21 Russell Woods Rd. Great Neck, NY 11021. Phone: (516)487-0990 Fax: (516)487-0809 Monthly. $25.00 per year.

American Industry-Structure, Conduct, Performance. Richard E. Caves. Prentice Hall, 240 Frisch Court Paramus, NJ 07652-5240. Phone: 800-947-7700 or (201)909-6200 Fax: 800-445-6991 or (201)909-6361 URL: http://www.prenhall.com • 1992. $51.93. Seventh edition.

American Inkmaker Buyers' Guide. Cygnus Business Media, 445 Broad Hollow Rd. Melville, NY 11747. Phone: 800-308-6397 or (631)845-2700 Fax: (631)845-2798 E-mail: rich.reiff@cygnuspub.com • URL: http://wwww.cygnuspub.com • Annual. $20.00. Guide to suppliers of raw materials, equipment, and services for manufacturers of printing ink, pigments, varnishes, graphic chemicals, and similar products.

American Inkmaker: For Manufacturers of Printing Inks and Related Graphic Arts Specialty Colors. Cygnus Business Media, 445 Broad Hollow Rd. Melville, NY 11747. Phone: 800-308-6397 or (631)845-2700 Fax: (631)845-2736 E-mail: rich.reiff@cygnuspub.com • URL: http://www.cygnuspub.com • Monthly. $60.00 per year.

American Institute for CPCU.

American Institute for Economic Research.

American Institute for Medical and Biological Engineering.

American Institute, Inc.

American Institute of Aeronautics and Astronautics.

American Institute of Architects.

American Institute of Baking.

American Institute of Biological Sciences.

American Institute of Biomedical Climatology.

American Institute of Building Design.

American Institute of Certified Planners.

American Institute of Certified Public Accountants.

American Institute of Chemical Engineers.

American Institute of Constructors.

American Institute of Food Distribution.

American Institute of Graphic Arts.

American Institute of Marine Underwriters.

American Institute of Parliamentarians.

American Institute of Stress., 124 Park Ave. Yonkers, NY 10703. Phone: (914)963-1200 Fax: (914)965-6267 E-mail: stress124@earthlink.net • URL: http://www.stress.org • Explores personal and social consequences of stress. Compiles research data on occupational stress and executive stress or "burn out."

American Insurance Association.

American Insurers Highway Safety Alliance.

American Intellectual Property Law Association.

American International Automobile Dealers Association.

American Iron and Steel Annual Statistical Report. American Iron and Steel Institute, 1101 17th St., N.W., Suite 1300 Washington, DC 20036-4700. Phone: (202)463-6573 Fax: (202)463-6573 Annual. $100.00 per year.

American Iron and Steel Institute.

American Jewelry Manufacturer. Manufacturing Jewelers and Silversmiths of America, Inc., One State St., 6th Fl. Porvidence, RI 02908-5035. Monthly. $36.00 per year.

American Jobs Abroad. The Gale Group, 27500 Drake Rd. Farmington Hills, MI 48331-3535. Phone: 800-877-GALE or (248)699-GALE Fax: 800-414-5043 or (248)699-8069 E-mail: galeord@galegroup.com • URL: http://www.galegroup.com • 1996. $65.00. Provides information on more than 800 U. S. companies and 110 government agencies, associations, and other organizations that employ Americans overseas. (American Jobs Abroad Series).

American Journal of Agricultural Economics. American Agricultural Economics Association Blackwell Publishers, Inc., 350 Main St. Malden, MA 02148. Phone: 800-835-6770 or (781)388-8200 Fax: (781)388-8232 E-mail: subscript@blackwellpub.com • URL: http://www.aaea.org • Five times a year. $123.00 per year. Provides a forum for creative and scholarly work in agriculture economics.

American Journal of Botany: Devoted to All Branches of Plant Sciences. Botanical Society of America, Inc., Business Office, 1735 Neil Ave. Columbus, OH 43210-1293. Phone: (614)292-3519 Fax: (614)292-3519 E-mail: orders@allenpress.com • URL: http://www.botany.org • Monthly. $195.00 per year. Includes *Plant Science Bulletin*.

American Journal of Clinical Nutrition: A Journal Reporting the Practical Application of Our World-Wide Knowledge of Nutrition. American Society for Clinical Nutrition, Inc., 9650 Rockville Pike, Room L-2310 Bethesda, MD 20814-3998. Phone: 800-433-1863 or (301)530-7110 Fax: (301)571-8303 E-mail: journal@ascn.faseb.org • URL: http://www.ajcn.org • Monthly. Individuals, $133.00 per year; institutions, $209.00 per year.

American Journal of Comparative Law. University of California, 394 Boalt Hall Berkeley, CA 94720. Phone: (510)643-6115 Fax: (510)643-2698 URL: http://www.acls.org/ascomlaw.htm • Quarterly. $30.00 per year.

American Journal of Drug and Alcohol Abuse. Marcel Dekker Journals, 270 Madison Ave. New York, NY 10016. Phone: 800-228-1160 or (212)696-9000 Fax: (212)685-4540 E-mail: bookorders@dekker.com • URL: http://www.dekker.com • Quarterly. $750.00 per year.

American Journal of Enology and Viticulture. American Society for Enology and Viticulture, P.O. Box 1855 Davis, CA 95617. Phone: (916)753-3142 Fax: (916)753-3318 Quarterly. $155.00 per year.

American Journal of Health System Pharmacy. American Society of Health-System Pharmacists, 7272 Wisconsin Ave. Bethesda, MD 20814. Phone: (301)657-3000 Fax: (301)657-1258 Semimonthly. $165.00 per year. Formerly American Society of Hospital Pharmacists. Formerly *American Journal of Hospital Pharmacy*.

American Journal of Industrial Medicine. John Wiley and Sons, Inc., Journals Div., 605 Third Ave. New York, NY 10158-0012. Phone: 800-225-5945 or (212)850-6000 Fax: (212)850-6088 E-mail: info@wiley.com • URL: http://www.wiley.com • Monthly. Institutions, $2,620.00 per year.

American Journal of International Law. American Society of International Law, 2223 Massachusetts Ave., N.W. Washington, DC 20008-2864. Phone: (202)939-6000 Fax: (202)797-7133 URL: http://www.asil.org • Quarterly. $140.00 per year.

American Journal of Nursing. American Nurses Association. Lippincott Williams and Wilkins, 530 Walnut St. Philadelphia, PA 19106-3780. Phone: 800-638-3030 or (215)521-8300 Fax: (215)521-8902 E-mail: custserv@lww.com • URL: http://www.lww.com • Monthly. Individuals, $29.95 per year; institutions, $79.95 per year. For registered nurses. Emphasis on the latest technological advances affecting nursing care.

American Journal of Occupational Therapy. American Occupational Therapy Association, P.O. Box 31220 Bethesda, MD 20824-1220. Phone: (301)652-2682 Fax: (301)652-7711 URL: http://www.aota.org • Six times a year. $120.00 per year.

American Journal of Ophthalmology. Elsevier Science Inc., 655 Ave. of the Americas New York, NY 10010. Phone: 888-437-4636 or (212)989-5800 Fax: (212)633-3680 E-mail: usinfo@selsevier.com • URL: http://www.elsevier.com • Monthly. $324.00 per year.

American Journal of Potato Research. Potato Association of America, University of Maine, 5715 Coburn Hall, Room 6 Orono, ME 04469-5715. Phone: (207)581-3042 Fax: (207)581-3015 E-mail: umpotato@maine.edu • URL: http://www.ume.maine.edu • Bimonthly. Individuals, $60.00 per year; libraries $75.00 per year.Information relating to production, marketing, processing, storage, disease control, insect control and new variety releases. Formerly *American Potato Journal*.

American Judges Association.

American Judicature Society.

American Laboratory. International Scientific Communications, Inc., P.O. Box 870 Shelton, CT 06484-0870. Phone: (203)926-9300 Fax: (203)926-9310 E-mail: iscpubs@iscpubs.com • URL: http://www.iscpubs.com • Monthly. $235.00 per year. Includes annual *Buyers' Guide*.

American Laboratory Buyers' Guide. International Scientific Communications, Inc., P.O. Box 870 Shelton, CT 06484-0870. Phone: (203)926-9300 Fax: (203)926-9310 E-mail: iscpubs@iscpubs.com • URL: http://www.iscpubs.com • Annual. $25.00. Manufacturers of and dealers in scientific instruments, equipment, apparatus, and chemicals worldwide.

American Land Planning Law. Norman Williams, and John Taylor. West Group, 610 Opperman Dr. Eagan, MN 55123. Phone: 800-328-4880 or (651)687-7000 Fax: 800-213-2323 or (651)687-5827 URL: http://www.westgroup.com • $750.00. Eight volumes. Periodic supplementation. (Real Property and Zoning Series).

American Land Title Association - Sections: Abstractors and Title Insurance AgenTitle Insurance and Underwriters.

American Laundry News. Crain Communications, Inc., 500 N. Dearborn St. Chicago, IL 60610. Phone: (312)337-7700 Fax: (312)337-8654 Monthly. $35.00 per year. Formerly *Laundry News*.

American Law Institute.

American Law of Mining: The Rocky Mountain Mineral Law Foundation. Matthew Bender & Co., Inc., Two Park Ave. New York, NY 10016. Phone: 800-223-1940 or (212)448-2000 Fax: (212)244-3188 E-mail: international@bender.com • URL: http://www.bender.com • $650.00. Six looseleaf volumes. Annual update.

American Law Yearbook. The Gale Group, 27500 Drake Rd. Farmington Hills, MI 48331-3535. Phone: 800-877-GALE or (248)699-GALE Fax: 800-414-5043 or (248)699-8069 E-mail: galeord@galegroup.com • URL: http://www.galegroup.com • Annual. $155.00. Serves as a yearly supplement to *West's Encyclopedia of American Law*. Describes new legal developments in many subject areas.

The American Lawyer. American Lawyer Media L.P., 345 Park Ave., S. New York, NY 10010-1707. Phone: 800-888-8300 or (212)779-9200 E-mail: catalog@amlaw.com • URL: http://www.americanlawyermedia.com • 10 times a year. $149.00 per year. General information for American attorneys.

American League for Exports and Security Assistance.

American League of Lobbyists.

American Leather Chemists Association.

American Leather Chemists Association-Directory. American Leather Chemists Association, Campus Station, P.O. Box 210014 Cincinnati, OH 45221-0014. Phone: (513)556-1197 Fax: (513)556-2377 E-mail: alca@usa.net • Annual. $20.00. About 1,000 chemists, leather technologists, and educators concerned with the tanning and leather industry.

American Leather Chemists Association Journal. American Leather Chemists Association, Campus Station, P.O. Box 210014 Cincinnati, OH 45221-0014. Phone: (513)556-1197 Fax: (513)556-2377 E-mail: alca@leatherchemists.org • URL: http://www.leatherchemists.org • Monthly. Free to members; non-members, $115.00 per year.

American Legion.

American Legion Magazine., P.O. Box 1055 Indianapolis, IN 46206. Phone: (317)630-1200 Fax: (317)630-1280 URL: http://www.legion.org • Monthly. Free to members; non-members, $15.00 per year.

American Legislative Process: Congress and the States. William J. Keefe and Morris Ogul, editors, Prentice Hall, 240 Frisch Court Paramus, NJ 07652-5240. Phone: 800-947-7700 or (201)909-6452 Fax: 800-445-6991 URL: http://www.prenhall.com • 2000. $44.00. 10th edition.

American Libraries. American Library Association, 50 E. Huron St. Chicago, IL 60611-2795. Phone: 800-545-2433 or (312)280-4216 Fax: (312)440-9374 E-mail: ala@ala.org • URL: http://www.ala.org • 11 times a year. Institutions and libraries only, $60.00 per year. Current news and information concerning the library industry.

American Library Association.

American Library Association Handbook of Organization. American Library Association, 50 E. Huron St. Chicago, IL 60611-2795. Phone: 800-545-2433 or (312)280-5038 Fax: (312)440-9374 E-mail: ala@ala.org • URL: http://

www.ala.org • Annual. $30.00. Lists about 52,000 librarians. Formerly *American Library Association Membership Directory*.

American Library Association Social Responsibilities Round-Table/Gay, Lesbian and Bisexual Task Force., 50 E. Huron St. Chicago, IL 60611. Phone: 800-545-2433 or (312)280-4294 Fax: (312)280-3256 URL: http://www.ala.org • A division of the Social Responsibilities Round Table of the American Library Association.

American Library Directory. R. R. Bowker, 121 Chanlon Rd. New Providence, NJ 07974. Phone: 888-269-5372 or (908)464-6800 Fax: (908)771-7704 E-mail: info@bowker.com • URL: http://www.bowker.com • Annual. $269.95. Two volumes. Includes *Library Resource Guide*. Information on more than 36,000 public, academic, special and government libraries and library-related organizations in the U.S., Canada, and Mexico.

American Library Directory Online. R. R. Bowker, 121 Chanlon Rd. New Providence, NJ 07974. Phone: 800-521-8110 or (908)464-6800 Fax: (908)665-6688 Provides information on over 37,000 U. S. and Canadian libraries, including college, special, and public. Annual updates. Inquire as to online cost and availability.

American Lighting Association.

American Logistics Association., 1133 15th St., N.W., Suite 640 Washington, DC 20005. Phone: (202)466-2520 Fax: (202)296-4419 URL: http://www.ala-national.org • Members are armed forces purchasing agencies and commercial firms.

American Lumber Standards Committee.

American Machine Tool Distributors' Association.

American Machinist. Penton Media Inc., 1300 E. Ninth St. Cleveland, OH 44114. Phone: (216)696-7000 Fax: (216)696-0836 E-mail: corpcomm@penton.com • URL: http://www.penton.com • Monthly. Free to qualified personnel; others, $75.00 per year.

American Management Association.

American Manufacturers Directory. American Business Directories, P.O. Box 27347 Omaha, NE 68127. Phone: 800-555-6124 or (402)593-4600 Fax: (402)331-5481 E-mail: jerry.verner@abii.com • Annual. $595.00. Lists more than 150,000 public and private U. S. manufacturers having 20 or more employees. Includes sales volume, number of employees, and name of chief executive or owner.

American Maritime Association.

American Maritime Cases. American Maritime Cases, Inc., 28 E. 21st St. Baltimore, MD 21218-5932. Phone: (410)752-2939 Fax: (410)625-1174 E-mail: amcrptr@clark.net • 10 times a year. $637.50 per year.

American Marketing Association.

American Meat Institute.

American Medical Association., 515 N. State St. Chicago, IL 60610. Phone: (312)464-5000 Fax: (312)464-4184 URL: http://www.ama-assn.org/ • Concerned with retirement planning and other financial planning for physicians 55 years of age or older.

American Medical Group Association.

American Medical Group Association Directory. American Group Practice Association, 1422 Duke St. Alexandria, VA 22314-3430. Phone: (703)838-5476 Fax: 800-284-3291 or (703)549-7837 E-mail: amga@va.amga.org • URL: http://www.amga.org • Annual. $399.00. Lists about 250 private group medical practices and their professional staffs, totaling about 25,000 physicians and administrators. Formerly *American Group Practice Association Directory*.

American Medical Group Association-Executive News Service. American Medical Group Association, 1422 Duke St Alexandria, VA 22314-3430. Phone: (703)838-0033 Fax: (703)548-1890 Monthly. Membership. Newsletter. Formerly *American Group Practice Association-Executive News Service*.

American Medical News. American Medical Association, 515 N. State St. Chicago, IL 60610. Phone: 800-262-2350 or (312)464-5000 Fax: (312)464-4184 E-mail: amaa@ama-assn.org • URL: http://www.ama-assn.org • 48 times a year. Individuals, $145.00 per year, institutions, $245.00 per year. Economic and legal news for the medical profession.

American Medical Rehabilitation Providers Association.

American Medical Technologists., 710 Higgins Rd. Park Ridge, IL 60068. Phone: 800-275-1268 or (847)823-5169 Fax: (847)823-0458 E-mail: amtmail@aol.com • National professional registry of medical laboratory technicians and medical assistants.

American Medical Women's Association.

American Men and Women of Science A Biographical Directory of Today's Leaders in Physical, Biological and Related Sciences. R. R. Bowker, 121 Chanlon Rd. New Providence, NJ 07974. Phone: 888-269-5372 or (908)464-6800 Fax: (908)771-7704 E-mail: info@bowker.com • URL: http://www.bowker.com • 1995. $900.00. Eight volumes. Over 119,600 United States and Canadian scientists active in the physical, biological, mathematical, computer science and engineering fields.

American Mental Health Counselors Association.

American Meteorological Society.

American Mineralogist. Mineralogical Society of America, 1015 18th St., N.W., Suite 601 Washington, DC 20036-5274. Phone: (202)775-4344 Fax: (202)775-0018 E-mail: business@minsocam.org • URL: http://www.minsocam.org • Bimonthly. $430.00 per year.

American Motor Carrier Directory. Commonwealth Business Media, 10 Lake Dr. Hightstown, NJ 08520-5397. Phone: 800-221-5488 or (609)371-7700 Fax: (609)371-7879 E-mail: pcoleman@primediainfo.com • URL: http://www.primediainfo.com • Annual. $517.00 per year. Lists all licensed Less Than Truckload (LTL) general commodity carriers in the U. S., including specialized motor carriers and related services. Formerly *American Motor Carrier Directory*.

American Motorcyclist. American Motorcyclist Association, 13515 Yarmouth Dr. Pickerington, OK 43147-8214. Phone: (614)891-2425 Fax: (614)891-5012 URL: http://www.amacycle.org/magazine • Monthly. $12.50 per year.

American Motorcyclist Association.

American Moving and Storage Association. c/o John Brewer, 1611 Duke St. Alexandria, VA 22314. Phone: (703)683-7410 Fax: (703)683-7527 URL: http://www.amconf.org • Members are household goods movers, storage companies, and trucking firms.

American Mushroom Institute.

American Music Conference.

American National Metric Council.

American National Standards Institute.

American Notary. American Society of Notaries, P.O. Box 5707 Tallahassee, FL 32314-5707. Phone: 800-522-3392 or (850)671-5164 Fax: (850)671-5165 E-mail: mail@notaries.org • URL: http://www.notaries.org • Quarterly. $26.00 per year. Provides information on new legislation, court decisions and other matters of interest to notaries public.

American Nuclear Insurers., 29 S. Main St., Suite 300-S West Hartford, CT 06107-2445. Phone: (860)561-3443 Fax: (860)561-4655 URL: http://www.amnucins.com • Member companies provide property and liability insurance to the nuclear energy industry.

American Nuclear Society., 555 N. Kensington Ave. La Grange Park, IL 60526. Phone: (708)352-6611 Fax: (708)352-0499 URL: http://www.ans.org • Purpose is to advance science and engineering in the nuclear power industry.

American Nuclear Society Transactions. American Nuclear Society, 555 N. Kensington Ave. La Grange Park, IL 60525. Phone: 800-682-6397 or (708)352-6611 Fax: (708)352-0499 URL: http://www.ans.org • Two times a year. $450.00 per year. Supplement available.

American Numismatic Association.

American Numismatic Society.

American Nursery and Landscape Association.

American Nursery and Landscape Association Membership Directory. American Nursery and Landscape Association, 1250 Eye St., N.W., Suite 500 Washington, DC 20005. Phone: (202)789-2900 Fax: (202)789-1893 E-mail: aanpubs@aol.com • URL: http://www.anyla.org • Annual. Free to members; non-members, $250.00 per year. Lists 2,200 member firms. Formerly *American Association of Nurserymen Membership Directory*.

American Nurseryman. American Nurseryman Publishing Co., 77 Washington St., Suite 2100 Chicago, IL 60602-2904. Phone: 800-621-5727 or (312)782-5505 Fax: (312)782-3232 E-mail: subscriptions@amerinursery.com • URL: http://www.allenpress.com • Semimonthly. $45.00 per year.

American Nurses Association.

American Occupational Therapy Association.

American Oil Chemists' Society.

American Oil Chemists' Society Journal. American Oil Chemists' Society. AOCS Press, P.O. Box 3489 Champaign, IL 61821-3489. Phone: (217)359-2344 Fax: (217)351-8091 E-mail: publications@aocs.org • URL: http://www.aocs.org • Monthly. Individuals, $145.00 per year; institutions, $195.00 per year. Includes *INFORM: International News on Fats, Oils and Related Materials*.

American Optometric Association.

American Optometric Association; Contact Lens Section.

American Optometric Association News. American Optometric Association, 243 N. Lindbergh Blvd. St. Louis, MO 63141. Phone: (314)991-4100 Fax: (314)991-4101 E-mail: almiller@theaoa.org • URL: http://www.aoanet.org • Semimonthly. Free to members; non-members, $76.00 per year.

American Optometric Foundation.

American Orthotic and Prosthetic Association.

American Painting Contractor. Douglas Publications, Inc., 2807 N. Parham Rd., Suite 200 Richmond, VA 23294. Phone: (804)762-9600 Fax: (804)217-8999 E-mail: ajdwyer1@aol.com • URL: http://www.douglaspublications.com • Nine times a year. $30.00 per year.

American Payroll Association., 30 E. 33rd St., 5th Fl. New York, NY 10016. Phone: (212)686-2030 Fax: (212)686-4080 E-mail: apa@apa-ed.com • URL: http://www.americanpayroll.org • Members are payroll administrators and personnel managers.

American Peanut Council.

American Peanut Council-Membership Directory. National Peanut Council, Inc., 1500 King St.,, Suite 301 Alexandria, VA 22314-2737. Phone: (703)838-9500 Fax: (703)838-9508 E-mail: peanutsusa@aol.com • URL: http://www.peanutsusa.com • Annual. $100.00. About 250 growers, shellers, processors, manufacturers, brokes and allied businesses providing goods and services to the peanut industry.

American Peanut Research and Education Society.

American Pet Products Manufacturers Association.

American Petroleum Institute.

American Petroleum Institute. Division of Statistics. Weekly Statistical Bulletin. American Petroleum Institute, Publications Dept., 1220 L St., N. W. Washington, DC 20005. Phone: (202)682-8375 Fax: (202)962-4776 URL: http://www.api.org • Weekly. $115.00 per year. Includes *Monthly Statistical Report*.

American Pharmaceutical Association/Academy of Pharmacy Practice and Management.

American Philatelic Society.

American Places Dictionary: A Guide to 45,000 Populated Places, Natural Features, and Other United States Places. Frank R. Abate, editor. Omnigraphics, Inc., Penobscot Bldg. Detroit, MI 48226. Phone: 800-234-1340 or (313)961-1340 Fax: 800-875-1340 or (313)961-1383 E-mail: info@omnigraphics.com • URL: http://www.omnigraphics.com • 1994. $400.00. Four regional volumes: Northeast, South, Midwest, and West. Provides statistical data and other information on 45,000 U. S. cities, towns, townships, boroughs, and villages. Includes detailed state profiles, county profiles, and more than 10,000 name origins. Arranged by state, then by county. (Individual regional volumes are available at $100.00.)

American Planning Association.

American Planning Association Journal. American Planning Association, 122 S. Michigan Ave., Suite 1600 Chicago, IL 60603-6107. Phone: (312)431-9100 Fax: (312)431-9985 URL: http://www.planning.org • Quarterly. Members, $33.00 per year; non-members $65.00 per year.

American Poultry Association.

American Printed Fabrics Council.

American Printer. Intertec Publishing Corp., P.O. Box 12901 Overland Park, KS 66282-2901. Phone: 800-400-5945 or (913)341-1300 Fax: (913)967-1901 E-mail: subs@intertec.com • URL: http://www.americanprinter.com • Monthly. Free to qualified personnel; others, $65.00 per year. Serves the printing and lithographic industries and allied manufacturing and service segments.

American Professional Practice Association., Hillsboro Executive Center N., 350 Fairway Dr., Suite 200 Deerfield Park, FL 33441-1834. Phone: 800-221-2168 or (954)571-1877 Fax: (954)571-8582 E-mail: membership@assnservices.com • URL: http://www.appa-assn.com • Concerned with financial planning for physicians and dentists.

An American Profile: Attitudes and Behaviors of the American People, 1972-1989. The Gale Group, 27500 Drake Rd. Farmington Hills, MI 48331-3535. Phone: 800-877-GALE or (248)699-GALE Fax: 800-414-5043 or (248)699-8069 E-mail: galeord@galegroup.com • URL: http://www.galegroup.com • 1990. $89.50. A summary of responses to about 300 questions in the General Social Survey conducted annually by the National Opinion Research Center, covering family characteristics, social behavior, religion, political opinions, etc. Includes a chronology of significant world events from 1972 to 1989 and a subject-keyword index.

American Psychological Association: Industrial and Organizational Psychology Society.

American Public Gas Association.

American Public Gas Association-Directory. American Public Gas Association, 11094-D Lee Highway, Suite 102 Fairfax, VA 22030-5014. Phone: (703)352-3890 Fax: (703)352-1271 Annual. $17.00. About 1,000 municipally owned gas systems throughout the United States.

American Public Gas Association Public Gas News. American Public Gas Association, 11094-D Lee Highway, Suite 102 Fairfax, VA 22030. Phone: (703)352-3890 Fax: (703)352-1271 Biweekly. $45.00 per year. Formerly, *American Public Gas Association Newsletter*.

American Public Human Services Association.

American Public Power Association.

American Public Transit Association., 1201 New York Ave., N.W., Suite 400 Washington, DC 20005. Phone: (202)898-4000 Fax: (202)898-4070 URL: http://www.apta.com • Members are bus and rail urban transportation systems.

American Public Works Association.

American Railway Car Institute.

American Railway Engineering and Maintenance Association.

American Railway Engineering Association Bulletin. American Railway Engineering Association, 50 F St., N.W. Suite 7702 Washington, DC 20001. Phone: (202)639-2190 Five times a year. $78.00 per year.

American Real Estate and Urban Economics Association., Indiana University School of Business, 1309 E. 10th St., Suite 738 Bloomington, IN 47405-1701. Phone: (812)855-7794 Fax: (812)855-8679 E-mail: areuea@indiana.edu • URL: http://www.areuea.org • Members are real estate teachers, researchers, economists, and others concerned with urban real estate and investment.

American Recreational Golf Association., P.O. Box 35189 Chicago, IL 60707-0189. Phone: (708)453-0080 Fax: (708)453-0083 Evaluates golf equipment and offers equipment certification.

American Reference Books Annual. Bohdan S. Wynar others, editors. Libraries Unlimited, Inc., P.O. Box 6633 Englewood, CO 80155-6633. Phone: 800-237-6124 or (303)770-1220 Fax: (303)220-8843 E-mail: lubooks@lu.com • URL: http://www.lu.com • Annual. $110.00.

American Rehabilitation: AR. U. S. Dept. of Health, Education, and Welfare; Rehabilitation Services Administr. Available from U. S. Government Printing Office, Washington, DC 20402. Phone: (202)512-1800 Fax: (202)512-1800 E-mail: gpoaccess@gpo.gov • URL: http://www.access.gpo.gov • Quarterly. $10.00 per year. Official publication of the Rehabilitation Services Administration. Comments on all aspects of life affecting handicapped people.

American Rehabilitation Counseling Association.

American Rental Association.

American Rifleman. National Rifle Association of America. NRA Publications, 11250 Waples Mill Rd. Fairfax, VA 22030-9400. Phone: 800-672-3888 or (703)267-1316 Fax: (703)267-3800 E-mail: membership@nrahq.org • URL: http://www.nra.org • Monthly. $35.00 per year.

American Risk and Insurance Association., P.O. Box 3028 Malvern, PA 19355-0728. Phone: (610)640-1997 Fax: (610)725-1007 E-mail: aria@cpcuiia.org • URL: http://www.aria.org • Promotes education and research in the science of risk and insurance.

American Road and Transportation Association Transportation Officials and Engineers Directory. American Road and Transportation Builders Association, The ARTBA, 1010 Massachusetts Ave., N.W. Washington, DC 20001. Phone: (202)289-4434 Fax: (202)289-4435 E-mail: artbadc@aol.com • Annual. Members, $90.00; non-members, $120.00. Lists over 5,000 administrative engineers and officials in federal, state, and county transportation agencies.

American Road and Transportation Builders Association., The ARTBA Bldg., 1010 Massachusetts Ave., N.W. Washington, DC 20001. Phone: (202)289-4434 Fax: (202)289-4435 E-mail: artba@aol.com • URL: http://www.artba.org • Promotes on-the-job training programs.

American Safe Deposit Association.

American Salaries and Wages Survey. The Gale Group, 27500 Drake Rd. Farmington Hills, MI 48331-3535. Phone: 800-877-GALE or (248)699-GALE Fax: 800-414-5043 or (248)699-8069 E-mail: galeord@galegroup.com • URL: http://www.galegroup.com • 2001. $135.00. Sixth edition. Arranged alphabetically by 4,402 occupational classifications. Provides salary data for different experience levels and in specific areas of the U.S. Includes cost of living data for metropolitan areas.

American Salon. National Hairdressers and Cosmetologists Association. Advanstar Communications, Inc., One Park Ave., 2nd Fl. New York, NY 10016-5802. Phone: 800-346-0085 or (212)951-6600 Fax: (212)951-6693 E-mail: information@advanstar.com • URL: http://www.advanstar.com • Monthly. $24.00 per year. Supplement available*American Salon Distributor-Manufacturer News.*

American School and University: Facilities, Purchasing, and Business Administration. Intertec Publishing Corp., P.O. Box 12901 Overland Park, KS 66282-2901. Phone: 800-400-5945 or (913)341-1300 Fax: (913)967-1898 E-mail: subs@intertec.com • URL: http://www.asumag.com • Monthly. Free to qualified personnel; others, $65.00 per year.

American School and University-Who's Who Directory and Buyers' Guide. Intertec Publishing Co., P.O. Box 12901 Overland Park, KS 66282-2901. Phone: 800-400-5945 or (913)341-1300 Fax: (913)967-1898 E-mail: subs@intertec.com • URL: http://www.intertec.com • Annual. $10.00. List of companies supplying products and service for physical plants and business offices of schools, colleges and universities.

American School Board Journal. National School Boards Association, 1680 Duke St. Alexandria, VA 22314. Phone: (703)838-6722 URL: http://www.nsba.com • Monthly. $54.00 per year. How to advice for community leaders who want to improve their schools.

American School Food Service Association.

American Scientific Glassblowers Society.

American Seed Research Foundation.

American Seed Trade Association.

American Sheep Industry Association.

American Shipper: Ports, Transportation and Industry. Howard Publications, Inc., 300 W. Adams St., Suite 600 Jacksonville, FL 32202-4304. Phone: (904)355-2601 Fax: (904)791-8836 URL: http://www.tradecompass.com/asplus/ • Monthly. $48.00 per year.

American Shoemaking. James Sutton. Shoe Trades Publishing Co., P.O. Box 198 Cambridge, MA 02140. Phone: (781)648-8160 Fax: (781)646-9832 Monthly. $55.00 per year.

American Shoemaking Directory. Shoe Trades Publishing Co., P.O. Box 198 Cambridge, MA 02140. Phone: (781)648-8160 Fax: (781)646-9832 E-mail: info@shoetrades.com • Annual. $54.00. Footwear manufacturers in the U.S., Puerto Rico and Canada.

American Society for Clinical Laboratory Science., 7910 Woodmont Ave., Suite 530 Bethesda, MD 20814. Phone: (301)657-2768 Fax: (301)657-2909 E-mail: ascls@ascls.org • URL: http://www.ascls.org • Seeks to promote high standards in clincal laboratory methods.

American Society for Enology and Viticulture.

American Society for Healthcare Food Service Administrators.

American Society for Information Science., 8720 Georgia Ave., Suite 501 Silver Spring, MD 20910-3602. Phone: (301)495-0900 Fax: (301)495-0810 E-mail: asis@asis.org • URL: http://www.asis.org • Members are information managers, scientists, librarians, and others who are interested in the storage, retrieval, and use of information.

American Society for Information Science Journal. John Wiley and Sons, Inc., Journals Div., 605 Third Ave. New York, NY 10158-0012. Phone: 800-225-5945 or (212)850-6000 Fax: (212)850-6088 E-mail: info@wiley.com • URL: http://www.wiley.com • 14 times a year. $1,259.00 per year.

American Society for Nutritional Sciences.

American Society for Public Administration.

American Society for Quality.

American Society for Training and Development.

American Society of Access Professionals., 1441 Eye St. N.W., 7th Fl. Washington, DC 20005-2210. Phone: (202)712-9054 Fax: (202)216-9646 E-mail: asap@7bostromdc.com • URL: http://www.podi.com/asap • Members are individuals concerned with safeguarding freedom of information, privacy, open meetings, and fair credit reporting laws.

American Society of Access Professionals-Membership Directory. American Society of Access Professionals, 1444 Eye St., N.W., Suite 700 Washington, DC 20005. Phone: (202)712-9054 Fax: (202)216-9646 E-mail: asap@bostromdc.com • URL: http://www.podi.com/asap • Annual. Membership.

American Society of Agricultural Consultants.

American Society of Agricultural Engineers.

American Society of Agronomy.

American Society of Animal Science.

American Society of Appraisers.

American Society of Association Executives.

American Society of Baking.

American Society of Baking. American Society of Bakery Engineers, 1200 Cental Ave., Suite 360 Wilmette, IL 60691-2087. Phone: (312)332-2246 Fax: (312)332-6560 E-mail: asbe@asbe.org • URL: http://www.asbe.org • Annual. Free to members.

American Society of Bariatric Physicians - Directory. American Society of Bariatric Physicians, 5600 S. Quebec St., Suite 109-A Englewood, CO 80111. Phone: (303)770-2526 Fax: (303)779-4834 E-mail: bariatric@asbp.org • Annual. $50.00. Lists 1300 physicians concerned with obesity.

American Society of Brewing Chemists.

American Society of Brewing Chemists Journal. American Society of Brewing Chemists, 3340 Pilot Knob Rd. Saint Paul, MN 55121-2097. Phone: (612)454-7250 Fax: (612)454-0766 URL: http://www.scisoc.org/asbc • Quarterly. Members, $95.00 per year; non-members, $137.00 per year; corporate members, $195.00 per year; student members, $25.00 per year.

American Society of Business Press Editors.

American Society of Cataract and Refractive Surgery.

American Society of Cinematographers.

American Society of Civil Engineers.

American Society of Civil Engineers-Official Register. American Society of Civil Engineers, 1801 Alexander Graham Bell Dr. Reston, VA 20191-4400. Phone: 800-548-2723 or (703)295-6300 Fax: (703)295-6222 URL: http://www.asce.org • Annual. Free.

American Society of Civil Engineers. Proceedings. American Society of Civil Engineers, 1801 Alexander Graham Bell Dr. Reston, VA 20191-4400. Phone: 800-548-2723 or (703)295-6300 Fax: (703)295-6222 URL: http://www.asce.org • Monthly. $2,289.00 per year. Consists of the Journals of the various Divisions of the Society.

American Society of Civil Engineers: Transactions. American Society of Civil Engineers, 1801 Alexander Graham Bell Dr. Reston, VA 20191-4400. Phone: 800-548-2723 or (703)295-6300 Fax: (703)295-6222 URL: http://www.asce.org • Annual. $230.00.

American Society of Comparative Law.

American Society of Composers, Authors and Publishers.

American Society of Consulting Planners.

American Society of Contemporary Ophthalmology.

American Society of Corporate Secretaries.

American Society of Criminology.

American Society of Farm Managers and Rural Appraisers.

American Society of Gas Engineers.

American Society of Golf Course Architects., 221 N. LaSalle St. Chicago, IL 60601. Phone: (312)372-7090 Fax: (312)372-6160 E-mail: asgca@selz.com • URL: http://www.golfdesign.org • Members are professional designers and architects of golf courses.

American Society of Health System Pharmacists.

American Society of Heating, Refrigerating and Air Conditioning Engineers.

American Society of Indexers., 11250 Roger Bacon Dr., Ste. 8 Reston, VA 20190. Phone: (703)234-4147 Fax: (703)435-4390 E-mail: info@asindexing.org • URL: http://www.asindexing.org • Affiliated with the American Library Association, the American Society for Information Science, and other organizations.

American Society of Interior Designers.

American Society of Interior Designers - Membership List. American Society of Interior Designers, 1430 Broadway New York, NY 10018. Phone: (212)944-9220 Annual. Membership.

American Society of International Law.

American Society of Inventors.

American Society of Journalists and Authors.

American Society of Journalists and Authors-Directory. American Society of Journalists and Authors, 1501 Broadway, Suite 302 New York, NY 10036. Phone: (212)997-0947 Fax: (212)768-7414 E-mail: asja@compuserve.com • Annual. $75.00. Lists 900 freelance nonfiction writers. Formerly *American Society of Journalists and Authors Directory of Professional Writers.*

American Society of Landscape Architects.

American Society of Magazine Editors.

American Society of Mechanical Engineers.

American Society of Media Photographers.

American Society of Naval Engineers.

American Society of Newspaper Editors.

American Society of Notaries.

American Society of Pension Actuaries., 4245 N. Fairfax Dr., Suite 750 Arlington, VA 22203. Phone: (703)516-9300 Fax: (703)516-9308 E-mail: aspa@aspa.org • URL: http://www.aspa.org • Members are involved in the pension and insurance aspects of employee benefits. Includes an Insurance and Risk Management Committee, and sponsors an annual 401(k) Workshop.

American Society of Photographers - Membership Directory. American Society of Photographers, Inc., P.O. Box 316 Williamantic, CT 06226. Phone: 800-638-9609 or (860)423-1402 Fax: (860)423-9402 Annual. Price on application.

American Society of Plumbing Engineers.

American Society of Professional Estimators., 11141 Georgia Ave., Suite 412 Wheaton, MD 20902. Phone: (301)929-8848 Fax: (301)929-0231 E-mail: info@aspenational.com • URL: http://www.aspenational.com • Members are construction cost estimators and construction educators.

American Society of Safety Engineers.

American Society of Sanitary Engineering.

American Society of Transportation and Logistics.

American Society of Travel Agents.

American Society of Travel Agents-Membership Directory. American Society of Travel Agents, 1101 King St. Alexandria, VA 22314. Phone: (703)739-2782 Fax: (703)684-8319 Annual. $195.00. Listings of over 13,500 worldwide members of ASTA.

American Society of Trial Consultants., Towson State University, Dept. of Mass Communication and Community Studies Towson, MD 21252. Phone: (410)830-2448 Fax: (410)830-3656 Concerned with the behavioral aspects of litigation.

American Society of TV Cameramen and International Society of Videographers.

American Society of Women Accountants.

American Solar Energy Society.

American Soybean Association.

American Spa and Health Resort Association., P.O. Box 585 Lake Forest, IL 60045. Phone: (847)234-8851 Fax: (847)295-7790 Members are owners and operators of health spas.

American Speaker: Your Guide to Successful Speaking. Georgetown Publishing House, 1101 30th St., N. W., Suite 130 Washington, DC 20007. Phone: 800-915-0022 or (202)337-8096 Fax: (202)337-1512 E-mail: cs@gphinc.com • URL: http://www.gphinc.com • Bimonthly. Price on application. Newsletter. Provides practical advice on public speaking.

American Spice Trade Association.

American Sports Analysis. Available from MarketResearch.com, 641 Ave. of the Americas, 3rd Fl. New York, NY 10011. Phone: 800-298-5699 or (212)807-2629 Fax: (212)807-2716 E-mail: order@marketresearch.com • URL: http://www.marketresearch.com • 1998. $375.00. Published by American Sports Data, Inc. Consumer market data. A study of participation in sports activities (golf, tennis, swimming, running, etc.) by American consumers.

American Sportscasters Association., Five Beekman St., Suite 814 New York, NY 10038. Phone: (212)227-8080 Fax: (212)571-0556 E-mail: asassn@juno.com • Members are radio and television sportscasters.

American Sportswear and Knitting Times. National Knitwear and Sportswear Association, 307 Seventh Ave., Room 1601 New York, NY 10001-6007. Phone: (212)683-7520 Fax: (212)532-0766 E-mail: askted@pop.interport.net • URL: http://www.asktmag.com • Monthly. $40.00 per year. Includes *American Sportswear and Knitting Times Buyer's Guide*. Formerly *Knitting Times*.

American Sportswear and Knitting Times Buyers' Guide. National Knitwear and Sportswear Association, 307 Seventh Ave., Room 1601 New York, NY 10001-6007. Phone: (212)683-7520 Fax: (212)532-0766 E-mail: askted@pop.interport.net • URL: http://www.asktmag.com • Annual. $25.00. Formerly *Knitting Times Buyers' Guide*.

American Staffing Association., 277 S. Washington St., Ste. 200 Alexandria, VA 22314-3119. Phone: (703)549-6287 Fax: (703)549-4808 E-mail: asa@staffingtoday.net • URL: http://www.staffingtoday.net • An association of private employment agencies for temporary workers.

American Stamp Dealers Association.

American Statistical Association., 1429 Duke St. Alexandria, VA 22314-3402. Phone: (703)684-1221 Fax: (703)684-2037 E-mail: asainfo@amstat.org • URL: http://www.amstat.org • A professional society concerned with statistical theory, methodology, and applications. Sections include Survey Research Methods, Government Statistics, and Business and Economic Statistics.

American Statistician. American Statistical Association, 1429 Duke St. Alexandria, VA 22314-3415. Phone: (703)684-1221 Fax: (703)684-2037 E-mail: asainfo@amstat.org • URL: http://www.amstat.org/ • Quarterly. Individuals, $15.00 per year; libraries, $75.00 per year.

American Statistics Index: A Comprehensive Guide and Index to the Statistical Publications of the United States Government. Congressional Information Service, Inc., 4520 East-West Highway, Suite 800 Bethesda, MD 20814-3389. Phone: 800-638-8380 or (301)654-1550 Fax: (301)654-4033 E-mail: cisinfo@lexis-nexis.com • URL: http://www.cispubs.com/ • Monthly. Quarterly and annual cumulations. Price varies.

American Statistics Index: A Comprehensive Guide and Index to the Statistical Publications of the United States Government Îonlinel. Congressional Information Service, Inc., 4520 East-West Highway Bethesda, MD 20814-3389. Phone: 800-638-8380 or (301)654-1550 Fax: (301)654-4033 URL: http://www.cispubs.com • Indexes and abstracts, 1973 to date. Inquire as to online cost and availability.

American Stock Exchange.

The American Stock Exchange: A Guide to Information Resources. Carol Z. Womack and Alice C. Littlejohn. Garland Publishing, Inc., 19 Union Square West, 8th Fl. New York, NY 10003-3382. Phone: 800-627-6273 or (212)414-0650 Fax: (212)414-0659 E-mail: info@garland.com • URL: http://www.garlandpub.com • 1995. $15.00. (Research and Information Guides in Business, Industry, and Economic Institutions Series).

American Stock Exchange Directory. CCH, Inc., 4025 W. Peterson Ave. Chicago, IL 60646-6085. Phone: 800-248-3248 or (773)866-6000 Fax: 800-224-8299 or (773)866-3608 URL: http://www.cch.com • 2000. $30.00.

American Stock Exchange Fact Book. NASD MediaSource, P.O. Box 9403 Gaithersburg, MD 20890-9403. Phone: (301)590-6142 Annual. $20.00. Published by the American Stock Exchange, Inc. Contains statistical data relating to the American Stock Exchange. Also provides the address and phone number for each company listed on the Exchange.

American Stock Exchange Guide. CCH, Inc., 4025 W. Peterson Ave. Chicago, IL 60646-6085. Phone: 800-248-3248 or (773)583-8500 Fax: 800-224-8299 or (773)866-3608 URL: http://www.cch.com • Monthly. $540.00 per year. Contains exchange rules and regulations, constitution, and a directory.

American Stock Exchange Weekly Bulletin. Nasdaq-AMEX Market Group, 86 Trinity Place New York, NY 10006-1872. Phone: (212)306-1442 Weekly. $20.00 per year. Looseleaf service.

American Subcontractors Association.

American Sugar Alliance., 2111 Wilson Blvd., Ste. 700 Arlington, VA 22201. Phone: (703)351-5055 Fax: (703)351-6698 URL: http://www.sugaralliance.org • Members are domestic producers of sugar beets, sugarcane, and corn for syrup.

American Sugar Cane League of the U.S.A.

American Supply and Machinery Manufacturers Association.

American Supply Association.

American Supply Association Operating Performance Report. American Supply Association, 222 Merchandise Mart Place, Suite 1360 Chicago, IL 60654-1202. Phone: (312)464-0090 Fax: (312)464-0091 E-mail: asaemail@interserv.com • URL: http://www.asa.net • Annual. Members, $45.00; non-members, $150.00.

American Tanker Rate Schedule. Association of Ship Brokers and Agents-USA, c/o Thomas Allegretti, 1600 Wilson Blvd., Suite 1000 Arlington, VA 22209. Phone: (703)841-9300 Fax: (703)841-0389 Annual. $500.00. Contains tanker freight rates.

American Technical Education Association. c/o North Dakota State College of Science

American Teleservices Association., 1601 Eye St., N.W., Ste. 615 Washington, DC 20006. Phone: 877-779-3974 or (202)293-2452 Fax: (202)463-8498 E-mail: ata@moinc.com • URL: http://www.ataconnect.org • Members are businesses involved in telephone marketing.

American Textile Machinery Association.

American Textile Manufacturers Institute.

American Tool, Die and Stamping News. Eagle Publications, Inc., 42400 Grand River Ave., Suite 103 Novi, MI 48375-2572. Phone: 800-783-3491 or (248)347-3486 Fax: (248)347-3492 Bimonthly. Controlled circulation.

American Trade Schools Directory. Croner Publications, Inc., 10951 Sorrento Valley Rd., Suite 1-D San Diego, CA 92121-1613. Phone: 800-441-4033 or (619)546-1894 Fax: (619)546-1855 URL: http://www.sdic.net/croner • $120.00. Looseleaf service. Monthly updates. Directory of over 12,000 trade,technical and vocational schools arranged by state.

American Translators Association.

American Trucking Associations.

American Trucking Trends. American Trucking Associations. Trucking Information Services, Inc., 2200 Mill Rd. Alexandria, VA 22314-4677. Phone: 800-282-5463 or (703)838-1700 Fax: (703)684-5720 E-mail: ata-infocenter@trucking.org • URL: http://www.trucking.org • Annual. $45.00

American Tunaboat Association.

American Universities and Colleges. Walter de Gruyter, Inc., 200 Saw Mill River Rd. Hawthorne, NY 10532. Phone: (914)747-0110 Fax: (914)747-1326 E-mail: cs@degruyter.com • URL: http://www.degruyter.com • 2001. $249.50. 16th edition. Two volumes. Produced in collaboration with the American Council on Education. Provides full descriptions of more than 1,900 institutions of higher learning, including details of graduate and professional programs.

American Vegetable Grower. Meister Publishing Co., 37733 Euclid Ave. Willoughby, OH 44094. Phone: 800-572-7740 or (440)942-2000 Fax: (440)975-3447 E-mail: avgcirc@meisternet.com • Monthly. $27.47 per year.

American Vegetable Grower Source Book. Meister Publishing Co., 37733 Euclid Ave. Willoughby, OH 44094. Phone: 800-572-7740 or (440)942-2000 Fax: (440)942-0662 E-mail: info@meisternet.com • URL: http://www.meisterpro.com • Annual. $2.75. Formerly *American Vegetable Grower Buyers' Guide*.

American Veterans Committee.

American Veterinary Exhibitors Association.

American Veterinary Medical Association.

American Veterinary Medical Association Journal. American Veterinary Medical Association, 1931 N. Meacham Rd., Suite 100 Schaumburg, IL 60173-4360. Phone: (847)925-8070 Fax: (847)925-1329 URL: http://www.avma.org/home.html • Semimonthly. $120.00 per year.

American Video Institute., Rochester Institute of Technology, P.O. Box 9887 Rochester, NY 14623-0887. Phone: (716)475-6969 Fax: (716)475-5804 Conducts research relating to videodiscs and interactive media.

American Visions Non-Profit Center. American Visions Society/American Visions MagazinePhone: (202)462-1779 Fax: (202)462-3997 URL: http://www.americanvisions.com • Web site "Created by African Americans for African Americans..enables non-profit professionals to share ideas, provide assistance, seek funding, Îandl browse for information." Includes "Black Endowment," a monthly online newsletter covering people, grants, non-profit seminars, and non-profit news. Registration required, with two options: "Grantseeker" or "Grantmaker." Free 30-day trial available.

American Vocational Educational Research Association.

American Walnut Manufacturers Association.

American Watch Association.

American Watchmakers Institute.

American Water Resources Association.

American Water Works Association.

American Water Works Association Journal. American Water Works Association, 6666 W. Quincy Ave Denver, CO 80235. Phone: 800-926-7337 or (303)794-7711 Fax: (303)794-7310 URL: http://www.awwa.org/journal • Monthly. Free to members; libraries and governmental agencies only, 85.00 per year.

American Water Works Sourcebook. American Water Works Association, 6666 W. Quincy Ave. Denver, CO 80235. Phone: 800-926-7337 or (303)794-7711 Fax: (303)794-7310 URL: http://www.awwa.org • Annual. Membership. Products and services of interest to the water industry. Formerly American Water Resources Association.

American Welding Society.

American Wholesale Marketers Association.

American Wholesalers and Distributors Directory. The Gale Group, 27500 Drake Rd. Farmington Hills, MI 48331-3535. Phone: 800-877-GALE or (248)699-GALE Fax: 800-414-5043 or (248)699-8069 E-mail: galeord@galegroup.com • URL: http://www.galegroup.com • 2000. $215.00. Eighth edition. Lists more than 27,000 national, regional, state, and local wholesalesrs.

American Wind Energy Association.

American Wine Society.

American Wire Producers Association.

American Woman's Society of Certified Public Accountants.

American Women in Radio and Television.

American Women Managers and Administrators: A Selective Biographical Dictionary of Twentieth Century Leaders in Business, Education, and Government. Greenwood Publishing Group Inc., 88 Post Rd. W. Westport, CT 06881-5007. Phone: 800-225-5800 or (203)226-3571 Fax: (203)222-2540 1985. $75.00. A directory of 20th-century women who hold or have held administrative, managerial, or leadership positions in business, education, or government.

American Wood Preservers Institute.

American Yarn Spinners Association.

Americana Annual. Grolier Inc., Sherman Turnpike Danbury, CT 06816. Phone: (203)797-3500 Annual. $29.95.

Americans for the Arts., 1000 Vermont Ave., N.W., 12th Fl. Washington, DC 20005. Phone: 800-321-4510 or (202)371-2830 Fax: (202)371-0424 URL: http://www.artsusa.org • Members are arts organizations and interested individuals. Conducts research and provides information and clearinghouse services relating to the visual arts.

Americans with Disabilities Act: A Practical and Legal Guide to Impact, Enforcement, and Compliance. BNA Plus, 1231 25th St., N.W. Washington, DC 20037. Phone: 800-372-1033 or (202)452-4323 Fax: (202)822-8092 E-mail: bnaplus@bna.com • URL: http://www.bna.com • 1990. $95.00. (Special Report Series).

Americans with Disabilities Act Handbook. Henry H. Perritt. John Wiley and Sons, Inc., 605 Third Ave. New York, NY 10158-0012. Phone: 800-225-5945 or (212)850-6000 Fax: (212)850-6088 E-mail: info@wiley.com • URL: http://www.wiley.com • 1997. $360.00. Third edition. Two volumes. 1996 Cumulative Supplement, $78.00. Two Volumes. Provides analysis of the 1990 Americans with Disabilities Act (ADA). Discusses employment provisions and the requirements for physical access to public accommodations. An appendix contains the complete ADA text.

America's Community Banker. America's Community Bankers, 900 19th St., N.W., Suite 400 Washington, DC 20006. Phone: (202)857-3100 Fax: (202)857-5581 URL: http://www.acbankers.org • Monthly. Members, $60.00 per year; non-members, $75.00 per year. Covers community banking operations and management. Formerly *Savings and Community Banker*.

America's Corporate Families and International Affliates. Dun and Bradstreet Information Services, Three Sylvan Way Parsippany, NJ 07054-3896. Phone: 800-526-0651 or (973)455-0900 Fax: (973)254-4063 E-mail: customerservice@dnb.com • URL: http://www.dnb.com • Annual. Libraries, $895.00; corporations, $1,020.00. Lease basis. Three Volumes U.S. parent companies with foreign affiliates and foreign parent companies with U.S. affiliates.

America's Corporate Finance Directory. National Register Publishing, 121 Chanlon Rd. New Providence, NJ 07974. Phone: 800-521-8110 or (908)464-6800 Fax: (908)790-5405 E-mail: info@reedref.com • URL: http://www.reedref.com • Annual. $699.00. A directory of financial executives employed at over 5,000 U. S. corporations. Includes a listing of the outside financial services (banks, pension managers, insurance firms, auditors) used by each corporation.

America's Fastest Growing Companies. Individual Investor Group, Inc., 125 Broad Street, 14th Fl. New York, NY 10004. Phone: 800-888-4741 or (212)742-0747 E-mail: letters@individualinvestor.com • URL: http://www.iionline.com • Monthly. $165.00 per year. Newsletter. Provides investment information on about 150 publicly-held corporations that are showing rapidly expanding sales and earnings. Formerly *America's Fastest Growing Corporations*.

America's Network: A Telecommunications Magazine. Advanstar Communications, Inc., 201 E. Sandpointe Ave,. Suite 600 Santa Ana, CA 92700-8700. Phone: 800-346-0085 or (714)513-8400 Fax: (714)513-8632 E-mail: information@advanstar.com • URL: http://www.advanstar.com • Semimonthly. $85.00 per year. Formerly *Telephone Engineer and Management*.

America's Network Directory and Buyers' Guide. Advanstar Communications, Inc., One Park Ave., 2nd Fl. New York, NY 10016-5802. Phone: 800-346-0085 or (212)951-6600 Fax: (212)951-6693 E-mail: information@advanstar.com • URL: http://www.advanstar.com • Annual. $240.00. Independent telephone companies in the United States, regional Bell operating companies, cellular telephone system operators, foreign telephone companies, long distance carriers, and interconnects. Formerly *Telephone and Engineering Directory*.

America's Pharmacist. National Community Pharmacists Association, 205 Daingerfield Rd. Alexandria, VA 22314-2885. Phone: (703)683-8200 Fax: (703)683-3619 E-mail: info@ncpanet.org • URL: http://www.ncpanet.org • Monthly. $50.00 per year. Formerly *N A R D Journal*.

America's Textiles International. Billian Publishing Inc., 2100 Powers Ferry Rd., Suite 300 Atlanta, GA 30339. Phone: 800-533-8484 or (770)955-5656 Fax: (770)952-0669 E-mail: ati@billian.com • Monthly. $43.00 per year. Formerly *America's Textiles*.

America's Textiles International-Buyer's Guide. Billian Publishing, Inc., 2100 Powers Ferry Rd. Atlanta, GA 30339. Phone: 800-533-8484 or (770)955-5656 Fax: (770)955-8485 URL: http://www.billian.com • Annual. $25.00. List of 2,800 suppliers for the textile industry.

America's Textiles International-The Textile Redbook. Billian Publishing, Inc., 2100 Powers Ferry Rd. Atlanta, GA 30339. Phone: 800-533-8484 or (770)955-5656 Fax: (770)952-0669 E-mail: ati@billian.com • Annual. $145.00. Formerly *America's Textiles International Directory*.

America's Top Rated Cities: A Statistical Handbook. Grey House Publishing, P.O. Box 1866 Lakeville, CT 06039. Phone: 800-562-2139 or (860)435-0868 Fax: (860)435-0867 E-mail: books@greyhouse.com • URL: http://www.citystats.com • Annual. $195.00. Four volumes. Each volume covers major cities in a region of the U. S.: Northeastern, Eastern, Southern, Central, and Western. Volumes are available individually at $49.00. City statistics cover the "Business Environment" (finances, employment, taxes, utilities, etc.) and the "Living Environment" (cost of living, housing, education, health care, climate, etc.).

America's Top-Rated Smaller Cities: A Statistical Handbook. Grey House Publishing, P.O. Box 1866 Lakeville, Connecticut, 06039. Phone: 800-562-2139 or (860)435-0868 Fax: (860)435-0867 E-mail: books@greyhouse.com • URL: http://www.citystats.com • Biennial. $125.00. Provides detailed profiles of 60 U. S. cities ranging in population from 25,000 to 100,000. Includes data on cost of living, employment, income, taxes, climate, media, and many other factors.

America's Western Boating Magazine. Sailing Co., PO Box 3400 Newport, RI 02840-0992. Phone: (401)847-1588 Fax: (401)848-5448 E-mail: editor@sailingworld.com • URL: http://www.sailingworld.com • 10 times a year. $28.00 per year. Covers the thirteen Western United States; British Columbia, Canada, and the West Coast of Mexico.

AMS Conference Proceedings. American Meteorological Society, 45 Beacon St. Boston, MA 02108. Phone: (617)227-2425 Fax: (617)742-8718 E-mail: rhallgren.@amet.soc/org/ams • URL: http://www.ametsoc.org/ams • Annual.

Amusement Business: International Live Entertainment and Amusement Industry Newsletter. BPI Communications, Inc., Amusement Business Div., P.O. Box 24970 Nashville, TN 37202. Phone: 800-344-7119 or (615)321-4250 Fax: (615)321-1575 E-mail: info@bpi.com • URL: http://www.bpicomm.com • Weekly. $159.00 per year.

Amusement Industry Manufacturers and Suppliers International.

AMWA Journal. American Medical Writers Association, 40 W. Gude Dr., No. 101 Bethesda, MD 20850-1192. Phone: (301)493-0003 E-mail: amspubs@ametsoc.org/ams • URL: http://www.amwa.org • Quarterly. $35.00 per year.

Amy Vanderbilt's Complete Book of Etiquette. Nancy Tuckerman and Nancy Dunnan. Doubleday, 1540 Broadway New York, NY 10036-4094. Phone: 800-223-6834 or (212)354-6500 Fax: (212)492-9700 URL: http://www.doubledaybookclub.com • 1995. $32.00. Revised edition.

Analog and Digital Communications. Hwei P. Hsu. McGraw-Hill, 1221 Ave. of the Americas New York, NY 10020. Phone: 800-722-4726 or (212)904-2000 Fax: (212)904-2072 E-mail: customer.service@mcgraw-hill.com • URL: http://www.mcgraw-hill.com • 1997. $15.95.

Analysis and Use of Financial Statements. Gerald I. White and others. John Wiley and Sons, Inc., 605 Third Ave. New York, NY 10158-0012. Phone: 800-225-5945 or (212)850-6000 Fax: (212)850-6088 E-mail: info@jwiley.com • URL: http://www.wiley.com • 1997. $112.95. Second edition. Includes analysis of financial ratios, cash flow, inventories, assets, debt, etc. Also covered are employee benefits, corporate investments, multinational operations, financial derivatives, and hedging activities

Analysis for Financial Management. Robert C. Higgins. McGraw-Hill, 1221 Ave. of the Americas New York, NY 10020. Phone: 800-722-4726 or (212)904-2000 Fax: (212)904-2072 E-mail: customer.service@mcgraw-hill.com • URL: http://www.mcgraw-hill.com • 2000. $55.94. Sixth edition.

An Analysis of Executive Search in North America. Kennedy Information, LLC, One Kennedy Place, Route 12, S. Fitzwilliam, NH 03447. Phone: 800-531-1026 or (603)585-3101 Fax: (603)585-9555 E-mail: office@kennedypub.com • URL: http://www.kennedyinfo.com • Annual. $59.00. Includes ranking of leading executive search firms and estimates of market share and total revenue.

Analysis of Financial Statements. Leopold A. Bernstein and John J. Wild. McGraw-Hill, 1221 Ave. of the Americas New York, NY 10020-1095. Phone: 800-722-4726 or (212)904-2000 Fax: (212)904-2072 E-mail: customer.service@mcgraw-hill.com • URL: http://www.mcgraw-hill.com • 1999. $60.00. Fifth edition. Includes practical examples of analysis.

An Analysis of Outplacement Consulting in North America. Kennedy Information, LLC, One Kennedy Place, Route 12, S. Fitzwilliam, NH 03447. Phone: 800-531-1026 or (603)585-3101 Fax: (603)585-9555 E-mail: office@kennedypub.com • URL: http://www.kennedyinfo.com • 1995. $35.00. Fourth edition. Includes ranking of leading outplacement consulting firms and estimates of market share and total revenue.

An Analysis of the Management Consulting Business in the U. S. Today. Kennedy Information, LLC, One Kennedy Pl., Route 12, S. Fitzwilliam, NH 03447. Phone: 800-531-1026 or (603)585-3101 Fax: (603)585-9555 E-mail: office@kennedypub.com • URL: http://www.kennedyinfo.com • Annual. $35.00. Includes ranking of leading management consulting firms and estimates of market share and total revenue.

Analyst's Handbook: Composite Corporate Per Share Data by Industry. Standard and Poor's, 55 Water St. New York, NY 10041. Phone: 800-221-5277 or (212)438-2000 Fax: (212)438-0040 E-mail: questions@standardandpoors.com • URL: http://www.standardandpoors.com • Annual. $795.00. Monthly updates.

Analyzing Banking Risk: A Framework for Assessing Corporate Governance and Financial Risk Management. Hennie van Greuning and Sonja Brajovic Bratanovic. The World Bank, Office of the Publisher, 1818 H St., N. W. Washington, DC 20433. Phone: 800-645-7247 or (202)477-1234 Fax: (202)477-6391 E-mail: books@worldbank.org • URL: http://www.worldbank.org • 1999. $100.00. Provides a guide to the analysis of banking risk for bank executives, bank supervisors, and risk analysts. Includes a CD-ROM with spreadsheet-based tables to assist in the interpretation and analysis of a bank's financial risk.

Analyzing Your Competition: Simple, Low-Cost Techniques for Intelligence Gathering. Michael Strenges. MarketResearch.com, 641 Ave. of the Americas, 3rd Fl. New York, NY 10011. Phone: 800-298-5699 or (212)807-2629 Fax: (212)807-2716 E-mail: order@marketresearch.com • URL: http://www.marketresearch.com • 1997. $95.00. Third edition. Mainly an annotated listing of specific, business information sources, but also contains concise discussions of information-gathering techniques. Indexed by publisher and title.

Anatomy of a Business Plan: A Step-by-Step Guide to Start Smart, Building the Business and Securing Your Companies Future. Linda J. Pinson. Dearborn, A Kaplan Professional Co., 155 N. Wacker Dr. Chicago, IL 60606-1719. Phone: 800-621-9621 or (312)836-4400 Fax: (312)836-1021 1999. $21.95. Fourth edition.

Anderson's Manual for Notaries Public: A Complete Guide for Notaries Public and Commissioners. Anderson Publishing Co., 2035 Reading Rd. Cincinnati, OH 45202-1416. Phone: 800-582-7295 or (513)421-4142 Fax: (513)562-8110 E-mail: mail@adnersonpublishing.com • URL: http://www.andersonpublishing.com • 1999. $25.00. Eighth edition.

Andrew Seybold's Outlook: A Monthly Perspective of Issues Affecting the Mobile Computer and Communications Industries. Andrew Seybold's Outlook, P.O. Box 2460 Boulder Creek, CA 95006. Phone: (831)338-7701 Fax: (831)338-7806 E-mail: andys@outlook.com • URL: http://www.outlook.com • Monthly. $395.00 per year. Newsletter. Provides analysis of the computer industry to corporate buyers and to end users. Reports on hardware, software trends and future products. Formerly *Andrew Seybold's Outlook on Communications and Computing*.

Andrews' Professional Liability Litigation Reporter. Andrews Publications, 175 Strafford Ave., Bldg. 4, Suite 140 Wayne, PA 19087. Phone: 800-345-1101 or (610)622-0510 Fax: (610)622-0501 URL: http://www.andrewspub.com • Monthly. $550.00 per year. Provides reports on lawsuits against attorneys, accountants, and investment professionals.

Animal Breeding Abstracts: A Monthly Abstract of World Literature. Available from CABI Publishing North America, 10 E. 40th St. New York, NY 10016. Phone: 800-528-4841 or (212)481-7018 Fax: (212)686-7993 E-mail: cabi@cabi.org • URL: http://www.cabi.org • Monthly. $1095.00 per year. Published in England by CABI Publishing. Provides worldwide coverage of the literature.

Annals of Nuclear Energy. Elsevier Science, 655 Ave. of the Americas New York, NY 10010. Phone: 888-437-4636 or (212)989-5800 Fax: (212)633-3680 E-mail: usinfo@elsevier.com • URL: http://www.elsevier.com • 18 times a year. $2,709 per year. Text and summaries in English, French and German.

Annals of Probability. Institute of Mathematical Statistics, Business Office, 3401 Investment Blvd., Suite 7 Hayward, CA 94545-3819. Phone: (510)783-8141 Fax: (510)783-4131 E-mail: ims@imstat.org • URL: http://www.jstor.org • Quarterly. $160.00 per year.

Annals of Statistics. Institute of Mathematical Statistics, Business Office, 3401 Investment Blvd., Suite 7 Hayward, CA 94545-3819. Phone: (510)783-8141 Fax: (510)783-4131 E-mail: ims@imstat.org • URL: http://www.jstor.org • Bimonthly. $180.00 per year.

Anniversaries and Holidays. Bernard Trawicky. American Library Association, 50 E. Huron St. Chicago, IL 60611-2795. Phone: 800-545-2433 or (312)944-6780 Fax: (312)440-9374 E-mail: ala@ala.org • URL: http://www.ala.org • 1997. $45.00. Fifth edition. Provides information on 3,500 holidays and anniversaries.

Annotated Bibliography of Project and Team Management. Project Management Institute, Four Campus Blvd. Newtown Square, PA 19073-3299. Phone: (610)356-4600 Fax: (610)356-4647 URL: http://www.pmibookstore.org • 1998. $119.95. Provides citations and annotations on CD-ROM for selected project management literature since 1956.

Annual Bulletin of Trade in Chemical Products. Economic Commission for Europe. United Nations Publications, United Nations Concourse Level, First Ave. and 46th St. New York, NY 10017. Phone: 800-553-3210 or (212)963-7680 Fax: (212)963-4910 E-mail: bookstore@un.org • URL: http://www.un.org/publications • Annual. $47.00.

Annual Business Survey. Menswear Retailers of America, 2011 Eye St., N.W., Suite 600 Washington, DC 20006. Phone: (202)347-1932 Annual. $35.00.

Annual Embroidery and Laces Directory. I. Leonard Seiler, editor. Schiffli Lace and Embroidery Manufacturers Association, 596 Anderson Ave., Ste. 203 Cliffside Park, NJ 07510-1831. Phone: (201)943-7757 Fax: (201)943-7793 Annual. $5.00. Embroidery and lace product merchandisers, producers, and industry service providers in the United States with limited international coverage. Formerly *Embroidery Directory*.

Annual Energy Outlook Îyearl, with Projections to Îyearl. Available from U. S. Government Printing Office, Washington, DC 20402. Phone: (202)512-1800 Fax: (202)512-2250 E-mail: gpoaccess@gpo.gov • URL: http://www.access.gpo.gov • Annual. Issued by the Energy Information Administration, U. S. Department of Energy (http://www.eia.doe.gov). Contains detailed statistics and 20-year projections for electricity, oil, natural gas, coal, and renewable energy. Text provides extensive discussion of energy issues and "Market Trends."

Annual Energy Review. Available from U. S. Government Printing Office, Washington, DC 20402. Phone: (202)512-1800 Fax: (202)512-2250 E-mail: gpoaccess@gpo.gov • URL: http://www.access.gpo.gov • Annual Issued by the Energy Information Administration, Office of Energy Markets and End Use, U. S. Department of Energy. Presents long-term historical as well as recent data on production, consumption, stocks, imports, exports, and prices of the principal energy commodities in the U. S.

Annual Index to Motion Picture Credits. Academy of Motion Picture Arts and Sciences, 8949 Wilshire Blvd. Beverly Hills, CA 90211-1972. Phone: (310)274-3000 Fax: (310)859-9619 URL: http://www.oscars.org • Annual. $50.00.

Annual Institute on Oil and Gas Law and Taxation. Matthew Bender & Co., Inc., Two Park Ave. New York, NY 10016. Phone: 800-223-1940 or (212)448-2000 Fax: (212)244-3188 E-mail: international@bender.com • URL: http://www.bender.com • Annual. Price on application. Answers to current legal and tax problems, including cases and regulations implementing tax reduction and tax form.

The Annual Register: A Record of World Events. Keesing's Worldwide, LLC, P.O. Box 5590 Washington, DC 20016-1190. Phone: (301)718-8770 Fax: (301)718-8494 E-mail: info@keesings.com • URL: http://www.keesings.com • Annual. $185.00. Published by Keesings Worldwide. Lists major economic, social, and cultural events of the past year. International coverage.

Annual Report of Postmaster General. U.S. Postal Service, Washington, DC 20260. Phone: (202)268-2000 Annual.

Annual Report of the Commuter Regional Airline Industry. Regional Airline Association, 1200 19th St., N.W., Suite 300 Washington, DC 20036-2401. Phone: (202)857-1170 Fax: (202)429-5113 E-mail: raa@dc.sba.com • URL: http://www.raa.org • Annual. $75.00. Lists commuter and regional airlines and gives statistical information.

Annual Report of the Director. Administrative Office of the United States Courts, U.S. Supreme Court Bldg., One First St. N.W. Washington, DC 20544. Phone: (202)479-3000 Annual.

Annual Report of the Secretary of Defense. U.S. Department of Defense, Office of the Secretary, The Pentagon Washington, DC 20301. Phone: (703)545-6700 Annual.

Annual Report of the Secretary of Veterans Affairs. U.S. Department of Veterans Affairs, Washington, DC 20420. Phone: (202)273-5700 Annual. Shows monies distributed and received by the Dept. of Veterans Affairs. Describes the activities of the Department during the fiscal year.

The Annual Report on the Economic Status of the Profession. American Association of University Professors, 1012 14th St., N.W., Suite 500 Washington, DC 20005-3465. Phone: (202)737-5900 Fax: (202)737-5526 E-mail: aaup@aaup.org • URL: http://www.aaup.org • Special annual issue of *ACADEME*.

Annual Review of Biophysics and Biomolecular Structure. Annual Reviews, Inc., P.O. Box 10139 Palo Alto, CA 94303-0139. Phone: 800-523-8635 or (650)493-4400 Fax: (650)424-0910 E-mail: service @annurev.org • URL: http://www.annualreviews.org • Annual. $70.00. Formerly *Annual Review of Biophysics and Bioengineering*.

Annual Review of Energy and the Environment. Annual Reviews, Inc., P.O. Box 10139 Palo Alto, CA 94303-0139. Phone: 800-523-8635 or (650)493-4400 Fax: (650)855-9815 E-mail: service@annurev.org • URL: http://www.annualreviews.org • Annual. Individuals, $76.00; institutions, $152.00. Formerly *Annual Review of Energy*.

Annual Review of Entomology. Annual Reviews, Inc., P.O. Box 10139 Palo Alto, CA 94303-0139. Phone: 800-523-8635 or (650)493-4400 Fax: (650)424-0910 E-mail: service@annurev.org • URL: http://www.annualreviews.org • Annual. Individuals, $60.00, institutions, $120.00.

Annual Review of Information Science and Technology. Martha E. Williams, editor. Information Today, Inc., 143 Old Marlton Pike Medford, NJ 08055-8750. Phone: 800-300-9868 or (609)654-6266 Fax: (609)654-4309 E-mail: custserv@infotoday.com • URL: http://www.infotoday.com • Annual. Members, $79.95; non-members, $99.95. Published on behalf of the American Society for Information Science (ASIS). Covers trends in planning, basic techniques, applications, and the information profession in general.

Annual Review of Medicine: Selected Topics in the Clinical Sciences. Annual Reviews, Inc., P.O. Box 10139 Palo Alto, CA 94303-0139. Phone: 800-523-8635 or (650)493-4400 Fax: (650)424-0910 E-mail: service@annurev.org • URL: http://www.annualreviews.org • Annual. Individuals, $60.00; institutions, $120.00.

Annual Review of Nuclear and Particle Science. Annual Reviews, Inc., P.O. Box 10139 Palo Alto, CA 94303-0139. Phone: 800-523-8635 or (650)493-4400 Fax: (650)424-0910 E-mail: service@annurev.org • URL: http://www.annualreviews.org • Annual. Individuals, $70.00; institutions, $140.00.

Annual Review of Pharmacology and Toxicology. Annual Reviews, Inc., P.O. Box 10139 Palo Alto, CA 94303-0139. Phone: 800-523-8635 or (650)493-4400 Fax: (650)424-0910 E-mail: service@annurev.org • URL: http://www.annualreviews.org • Annual. Individuals, $60.00; institutions, $120.00.

Annual Review of Public Health. Annual Reviews, Inc., P.O. Box 10139 Palo Alto, CA 94303-0139. Phone: 800-523-8635 or (650)493-4400 Fax: (650)855-9815 E-mail: service@annurev.org • URL: http://www.annualreviews.org • Annual. Individuals, $64.00; institutions, $128.00.

Annual Review of the Chemical Industry. United Nations Publications, United Nations Concourse Level, First Ave. and 46th St. New York, NY 10017. Phone: 800-553-3210 or (212)963-7680 Fax: (212)963-4910 E-mail: bookstore@un.org • URL: http://www.un.org/publications • Annual. $100.00.

Annual Review of United Nations Affairs: Covering Years from 1961 Through 1997. Oceana Publications, Inc., 75 Main St. Dobbs Ferry, NY 10522-1601. Phone: 800-831-0758 or (914)693-8100 Fax: (914)693-0402 E-mail: orders@oceanalaw.com • URL: http://www.oceanalaw.com • Annual. 53 volumes. Price varies.

Annual Reviews in Control. Elsevier Science, 655 Ave. of the Americas New York, NY 10010. Phone: 888-437-4636 or (212)989-5800 Fax: (212)633-3680 E-mail: usinfo@elsevier.com • URL: http://www.elsevier.com • Annual. $329.00 per year. Formerly*Annual Review in Automatic Programming*.

Annual Statement Studies. Robert Morris Associates: The Association of Lending and Credit Risk Professiona, One Liberty Place, 1650 Market St. Philadelphia, PA 19103-7398. Phone: 800-677-7621 or (215)446-4000 Fax: (215)446-4100 E-mail: info@rmahq.org • URL: http://www.rmahq.org • Annual. Free to members; non-members, $140.00. Median and quartile financial ratios are given for over 400 kinds of manufacturing, wholesale, retail, construction, and consumer finance establishments. Data is sorted by both asset size and sales volume. Includes a clearly written "Definition of Ratios" and an alphabetical industry index.

Annual Statistical Reports of Independent Telephone Companies. Federal Communications Commission, 1919 M St., N.W. Washington, DC 20554. Phone: (202)418-0200 Annual.

Annual Survey of American Law, 1942-1995. New York University Law Publications. Oceana Publications, Inc., 75 Main St. Dobbs Ferry, NY 10522-1601. Phone: 800-831-0758 or (914)693-8100 Fax: (914)693-0402 E-mail: orders@oceanalaw.com • URL: http://www.oceanalaw.com • 1943. $2,367.50. 62 volumes.

Annual Survey of Bankruptcy. William L. Norton, Jr. and others. West Group, 610 Opperman Dr. Eagan, MN 55123. Phone: 800-328-4880 or (651)687-7000 Fax: 800-213-2323 or (651)687-5827 URL: http://www.westgroup.com • 1979. $145.00.

Annual Survey of Manufactures. Available from U. S. Government Printing Office, Washington, DC 20402. Phone: (202)512-1800 Fax: (202)512-2250 E-mail: gpoaccess@gpo.gov • URL: http://www.access.gpo.gov • Annual. Prices vary. Issued by the U. S. Census Bureau as an interim update to the *Census of Manufactures*. Includes data on number of manufacturing establishments in various industries, employment, labor costs, value of shipments, capital expenditures, inventories, energy costs, and assets. (See also Census Bureau home page, http://www.census.gov/.)

Annuity and Life Insurance Shopper. United States Annuities, Eight Talmadge Rd. Jamesburg, NJ 08831-2910. Phone: 800-872-6684 or (908)521-5110 Fax: (908)521-5113 Quarterly. $65.00 per year. Provides information on rates and performance for fixed annuities, variable annuities, and term life policies issued by more than 250 insurance companies.

Annuity Market News. Securities Data Publishing, 40 West 57th St. New York, NY 10019. Phone: 800-455-5844 or (212)765-5311 Fax: (212)956-0112 E-mail: sdp@tfn.com • URL: http://www.sdponline.com • Monthly. $625.00 per year. Newsletter. Edited for investment and insurance professionals. Covers the marketing, management, and servicing of variable and fixed annuity products. (Securities Data Publishing is a unit of Thomson Financial.)

Answer. Association of Telemessaging Services International, Inc., 1200 19th St. N.W. Washington, DC 20036-2412. Phone: (202)429-5151 URL: http://www.206.69.91.109/icenter • Bimonthly. Members, $30.00 per year; non-members, $50.00 per year.

Anti-Friction Bearings. U.S. Bureau of the Census, Washington, DC 20233-0800. Phone: (301)457-4100 Fax: (301)457-3842 URL: http://www.census.gov • Annual.

Antiquarian Booksellers Association of America.

Antiquarian Booksellers' Association of America-Membership List. Antiquarian Booksellers' Association of America, 20 W. 44th St. New York, NY 10036. Phone: (212)944-8291 Fax: (212)944-8293 E-mail: abaa@panix.com • URL: http://www.abaa-booknet.com • Annual. Free. Lists about 470 rare book dealers. Send self-addressed business-size envelope with $1.43 postage.

Antiquarian, Specialty, and Used Book Sellers: A Subject Guide and Directory. James M. Ethridge and Karen Ethridge, editors. Omnigraphics, Inc., Penobscot Bldg. Detroit, MI 48226. Phone: 800-234-1340 or (313)961-1340 Fax: 800-875-1340 or (313)961-1383 E-mail: info@omnigraphics.com • URL: http://www.omnigraphics.com • 1997. $85.00. Second edition. Provides information on more than 3,000 specialized book dealers. Indexed by store name, store owner, and subject specialty.

Antique Appraisal Association of America.

Antique Automobile. Antique Automobile Club of America, 501 W. Governor Rd. Hershey, PA 17033. Phone: (717)534-1910 Fax: (717)534-9101 Membership.

Antique Dealer and Collector's Guide. Statuscourt Ltd., P.O. Box 805 London SE1O 8TD, England. E-mail: antiquedealercollectorsguide@ukbusiness.com • URL: http://www.ukbusiness.com/antiquedealercollectorsguide • Monthly. $66.00 per year. Incorporates *Art and Antiques*.

Antique Shop Guide-Central Edition. Mayhill Publications, P.O. Box 90 Knightstown, IN 46148. Phone: 800-876-5133 or (317)345-5133 Fax: 800-695-8153 E-mail: antiquewk@aol.com • Annual. $3.50. Covers 10 midwestern states, western Pennsylvania, and West Virginia.

Antiques and Collecting Magazine. Frances L. Graham, editor. Lightner Publishing Corp., 1006 S. Michigan Ave. Chicago, IL 60605. Phone: 800-762-7576 or (312)939-4767 Fax: (312)939-0053 E-mail: lightnerpb@aol.com • URL: http://www.antiqueweek.com • Monthly. $32.00 per year.

Antitrust Adviser. Shepard's, 555 Middle CreeK Parkway Colorado Springs, CO 80921. Phone: 800-743-7393 or (719)481-7371 Fax: 800-525-0053 or (719)481-7621 E-mail: customer_service@shepards.com • URL: http://www.shepards.com • 1985. $105.00. Third edition. General overview of the Sherman Act, the Clayton Act, the Robinson-Patman Act, and the Federal Trade Commission Act.

Antitrust and Trade Regulation Report. Bureau of National Affairs, Inc., 1231 25th St., N.W. Washington, DC 20037-1197. Phone: 800-372-1033 or (202)452-4200 Fax: (202)822-8092 E-mail: books@bna.com • URL: http://www.bna.com • Weekly. $1,277.00 per year. Looseleaf service.

The Antitrust Bulletin. Federal Legal Publications, Inc., 335 Route 312 Brewster, NY 10509. Phone: (914)279-0362 Fax: (914)279-0259 E-mail: flp@bestweb.com • Quarterly. Institutions, $85.00 per year.

Antitrust Counseling and Litigation Techniques. Matthew Bender & Co., Inc., Two Park Ave. New York, NY 10016. Phone: 800-223-1940 or (212)448-2000 Fax: (212)244-3188 E-mail: international@bender.com • URL: http://www.bender.com • Five looseleaf volumes. Annual supplement. Price on application.

Antitrust Division Manual. Available from U. S. Government Printing Office, Washington, DC 20402. Phone: (202)512-1800 Fax: (202)512-2250 E-mail: gpoaccess@gpo.gov • URL: http://www.access.gpo.gov • Looseleaf. $60.00. Includes basic manual, with supplementary material for an indeterminate period. Serves as a guide to the operating policies and procedures of the Antitrust Division of the U. S. Department of Justice (http://www.usdoj.gov). Covers suggested methods of conducting investigations and litigation.

Antitrust Law and Economics Review. Charles E. Mueller, editor. Antitrust Law and Economics Review, Inc., P.O. Box 3532 Vero Beach, FL 32964-3532. Fax: (561)461-6007 URL: http://www.home.mpinet.net • Quarterly. $129.50 per year.

Antitrust Law and Practice. West Publishing Co., College and School Div., 610 Opperman Dr. Eagan, MN 55123. Phone: 800-328-4880 or (651)687-7000 Fax: 800-213-2323 or (651)687-5827 E-mail: legal_ed@westgroup.com • URL: http://www.westgroup.com • Periodic supplementation. Price on application.

Antitrust Law Handbook, 1993. William C. Holmes. West Group, 610 Opperman Dr. Eagan, MN 55123. Phone: 800-328-4880 or (651)687-7000 Fax: 800-213-2323 or (651)687-5827 URL: http://www.westgroup.com • 1991. $85.00 (Antitrust Series).

Antitrust Law Journal. American Bar Association, Antitrust Law Section, 750 N. Lake Shore Dr. Chicago, IL 60611-4497. Phone: 800-285-2221 or (312)988-5000 Fax: (312)988-5528 E-mail: abajournal@abanet.org/antitrust • URL: http://www.abanet.org • Three times a year. Free to members; non-members, $40.00 per year.

Antitrust Laws and Trade Regulation. Matthew Bender & Co., Inc., Two Park Ave. New York, NY 10016. Phone: 800-223-1940 or (212)448-2000 Fax: (212)244-3188 E-mail: international@bender.com • URL: http://www.bender.com • 16 looseleaf volumes. $1,650.00. Periodic supplementation. Covers provisions and applications of the Sherman, Clayton, Robinson-Patman, and Federal Trade Commission Acts. Also covers state antitrust laws. Issued with *Antitrust Laws and Trade Regulation Newsletter*.

Antitrust Laws and Trade Regulation: Desk Edition. Matthew Bender & Co., Inc., Two Park Ave. New York, NY 10016. Phone: 800-223-1940 or (212)448-2000 Fax: (212)244-3188 E-mail: international@bender.com • URL: http://www.bender.com • $600.00. Two looseleaf volumes. Periodic supplementation. The history and organization of the antitrust laws.

Antitrust Litigation Reporter: The National Journal of Record on Antitrust Litigation. Andrews Publications, 175 Strafford Ave., Bldg. 4, Suite 140 Wayne, PA 19087. Phone: 800-345-1101 or (610)622-0510 Fax: (610)622-0501 URL: http://www.andrewspub.com • Monthly. $775.00 per year. Provides reports on federal and state antitrust statutes.

AOAC International.

AOAC International Journal. AOAC International, 481 N. Frederick Ave., Suite 500 Gaithersberg, MD 20877-2917. Phone: (301)924-7077 Fax: (301)924-7089 Bimonthly. Members $176.00 per year; non-members, $242.00 per year; institutions, $262.00 per year. Formerly *Association of Official Analytical Chemist Journal*.

AOMA Newsletter: Profile of the Multi-Family Housing Industry. Apartment Owners and Managers Association of America, 65 Cherry Plaza, 65 Cherry Ave. Watertown, CT 06735-2836. Phone: (203)274-2589 Fax: (203)274-2580 Monthly. Free to members; non-members, $125.00 per year.

AOPA Pilot. Aircraft Owners and Pilots Association, 421 Aviation Way Frederick, MD 21701. Phone: 800-942-4269 or (301)695-2350 Fax: (301)695-2180 URL: http://www.aopa.org/pilot/pwelcome.html • Monthly. Membership.

APA: The Engineered Wood Association.

Apartment Building Income-Expense Analysis. Institute of Real Estate Management, P.O. Box 109025 Chicago, IL 60610-4090. Phone: 800-837-0706 or (312)329-6000 Fax: (312)329-6039 E-mail: custserv@irem.org • URL: http://www.irem.org • Annual.

Apartment Finance Today. Alexander & Edwards Publishing, 657 Mission St., Suite 502 San Francisco, CA 94105-4118. Phone: (415)546-7255 Fax: (415)546-0954 E-mail: ahe@housingfinance.com • URL: http://www.housingfinance.com • Bimonthly. $29.00 per year. Covers mortgages and financial services for apartment developers, builders, and owners.

Apartment Management Magazine. Apartment News Publications, Inc., 15502 Graham St. Huntington Beach, CA

92649-1609. Phone: (714)893-3971 Fax: (714)893-6484 Monthly. $24.00 per year. In four Los Angeles area editions.

Apartment Management Newsletter: Wealth Building Techniques for Apartment Owners and Their Managers. Apartment Management Publishing Co., Inc., 2095 Broadway, No. 404 New York, NY 10023. Phone: (212)787-6931 Monthly. $95.00 per year.

Apartment Management Report: For Managers of Apartments. Apartment Owners and Managers Association of America, 65 Cherry Plaza, 65 Cherry Ave. Watertown, CT 06795-2836. Phone: (203)274-2589 Fax: (203)274-2580 Monthly. $85.00 per year.

APEC.

APICS-The Educational Society for Resource Management., 5301 Shawnee Rd. Alexandria, VA 22312. Phone: 800-444-2742 or (703)354-8851 Fax: (703)354-8106 URL: http://www.apics.org • Members are professional resource managers.

Apicultural Abstracts. International Bee Research Association, 18 North Rd. Cardiff CF1 3DY Wales, Wales. E-mail: ibra@cardiff.ac.uk • Quarterly. $295.00 per year. Up-to-date summary of world literature on bees and beekeeping.

Appalachian Hardwood Manufacturers, Inc., P.O. Box 427 High Point, NC 27261. Phone: (336)885-8315 Fax: (336)886-8865 E-mail: applumber@aol.com • Members are manufacturers interested in promoting the use of Appalachian hardwood.

Apparel Industry Magazine. Shore-Varrone, Inc., 6225 Barfield Rd., N.E., Suite 200 Atlanta, GA 30328-4300. Phone: 800-241-9034 or (404)252-8831 Fax: (404)252-4436 E-mail: sbaker@svi-atl.com • URL: http://www.aimagazine.com • Monthly. $65.00 per year.

Apple News. International Apple Institute, 6707 Old Dominion Dr., Suite 320 McLean, VA 22101. Phone: (703)442-8850 Fax: (703)790-0845 Biweekly. Newsletter. Price on application.

Appliance. Dana Chase Publications, Inc., 1110 Jorie Blvd., Suite 203 Oakbrook, IL 60522-9019. Phone: (630)990-3484 Fax: (630)990-0078 URL: http://www.appliance.com • Monthly. $75.00 per year.

Appliance - Appliance Industry Purchasing Directory. Dana Chase Publications, Inc., 1110 Jorie Blvd., Suite 203 Oakbrook, IL 60522-9019. Phone: (630)990-3484 Fax: (630)990-0078 E-mail: scot@appliance.com • URL: http://www.appliance.com • Annual. $40.00. Suppliers to manufacturers of consumer, commercial, and business appliances.

Appliance Manufacturer. Business News Publishing Co., 755 W. Big Beaver, Suite 1000 Troy, MI 48084. Phone: 800-837-7370 or (248)362-3700 Fax: (248)362-0317 E-mail: amjoe@now-online.com • URL: http://www.bpn.com • Monthly. $55.00 per year.

Appliance Manufacturer Buyers Guide. Business News Publishing Co., 755 W. Big Beaver, Suite 1000 Troy, MI 48084. Phone: 800-837-7370 or (248)362-3700 Fax: (248)362-0317 URL: http://www.bnp.com • Annual. $25.00.

Appliance Parts Distributors Association.

Appliance Service News. Gamit Enterprises, Inc., P.O. Box 789 Lombard, IL 60148-0789. Phone: (708)932-9550 Fax: (708)932-9552 E-mail: asnews@cin.net • URL: http://www.asnews.com • Monthly. $34.95.

Applied Economics. Routledge Journals, 29 W. 35th St. New York, NY 10001-2299. Phone: 800-634-7064 or (212)216-7800 Fax: 800-248-4724 or (212)564-7854 E-mail: journals@routledge.com • URL: http://www.thomson.com/routledge/ • Monthly. $2,120.00 per year. Emphasizes quantitative studies having results of practical use. Supplements available, *Applied Financial Economics* and *Applied Economics Letters*.

Applied Economics Letters. Routledge Journals, 29 W. 35th St. New York, NY 10001-2299. Phone: 800-634-7064 or (212)216-7800 Fax: 800-248-4724 or (212)564-7854 E-mail: journals@routledge.com • URL: http://www.routledge.com/routledge/ • Monthly. $554.00 per year. Provides short accounts of new, original research in practical economics. Supplement to *Applied Economics*.

Applied Ergonomics: Human Factors in Technology and Society. Elsevier Science, 655 Ave. of the Americas New York, NY 10010. Phone: 888-437-4636 or (212)989-5800 Fax: (212)633-3680 E-mail: usinfo@elsevier.com • URL: http://www.elsevier.com • Bimonthly $772.00 per year.

Applied Financial Economics. Routledge Journals, 29 W. 35th St. New York, NY 10001-2299. Phone: 800-634-7064 or (212)216-7800 Fax: 800-248-4724 or (212)564-7854 E-mail: journals@routledge.com • URL: http://www.routledge.com/routledge/ • Bimonthly. Individuals, $648.00 per year; institutions, $1,053.00 per year. Covers practical aspects of financial economics, banking, and monetary economics. Supplement to *Applied Economics*.

Applied Genetics News. Business Communications Co., Inc., 25 Van Zant St., Suite 13 Norwalk, CT 06855. Phone: (203)853-4266 Fax: (203)853-0348 Monthly. $415.00 per year. Newsletter on research developments.

Applied Mechanics Reviews: An Assessment of World Literature in Engineering Sciences. American Society of Mechanical Engineers, 22 Law Dr. Fairfield, NJ 07007-2900. Phone: 800-843-2763 or (973)882-1167 Fax: (973)882-1717 E-mail: infocentral@asme.org • URL: http://www.asme.org • Monthly. Members, $126.00 per year; non-members, $663.00 per year.

Applied Optics. Optical Society of America, Inc., 2010 Massachusetts Ave., N.W. Washington, DC 20036-1023. Phone: (202)416-1907 Fax: (202)416-6140 E-mail: info@osa.org • URL: http://www.osa.org • 36 times a year. $1,910.00 per year.

Applied Photonics. Chai Yeh, editor. Academic Press, Inc., 525 B St., Suite 1900 San Diego, CA 92101-4495. Phone: 800-321-5068 or (619)230-1840 Fax: (619)699-6715 E-mail: ap@acad.comm • URL: http://www.academicpress.com • 1994. $73.00.

Applied Research Laboratories. University of Texas at Austin

Applied Research Laboratory. Pennsylvania State University

Applied Science and Technology Index. H. W. Wilson Co., 950 University Ave. Bronx, NY 10452. Phone: 800-367-6770 or (718)588-8400 Fax: (718)590-1617 E-mail: custserv@hwwilson.com • URL: http://www.hwwilson.com • 11 times a year. Quarterly and annual cumulations. Service basis for print edition; CD-ROM edition, $1,495.00 per year. Indexes a wide variety of English language technical, industrial, and engineering periodicals.

Applied Science and Technology Index Online. H. W. Wilson Co., 950 University Ave. Bronx, NY 10452. Phone: 800-367-6770 or (718)588-8400 Fax: (718)590-1617 E-mail: hwwmsg@info.hwwilson.com • URL: http://www.hwwilson.com • Provides online indexing of 400 major scientific, technical, industrial, and engineering periodicals. Time period is 1983 to date. Monthly updates. Inquire as to online cost and availability.

Applied UNIX Programming 4.2. Bharat Kurani. Prentice Hall, 240 Frisch Court Paramus, NJ 07652-5240. Phone: 800-947-7700 or (201)909-6200 Fax: 800-445-6991 or (201)909-6361 URL: http://www.prenhall.com • 1996. $90.00. Volume two.

Applying GAAP and GAAS. Matthew Bender & Co., Inc., Two Park Ave. New York, NY 10016. Phone: 800-223-1940 or (212)448-2000 Fax: (212)244-3188 E-mail: international@bender.com • URL: http://www.bender.com • Two looseleaf volumes. Periodic supplementation. Price on application. In-depth explanations of generally accepted accounting principles (GAAP) and generally accepted auditing standards (GAAS).

Applying Telecommunications and Technology from a Global Business Perspective. Jay J. Zajas and Olive D. Church. Haworth Press, Inc., 10 Alice St. Binghamton, NY 13904-1580. Phone: 800-429-6784 or (607)722-5857 Fax: 800-895-0582 or (607)722-1424 E-mail: getinfo@haworthpressinc.com • URL: http://www.haworthpressinc.com • 1996. $49.95. Provides an international, multicultural perspective.

Appraisal Institute.

Appraisal Journal. Appraisal Institute, 875 N. Michigan Ave., Suite 2400 Chicago, IL 60611-1980. Phone: (312)335-4100 Fax: (312)335-4400 Quarterly. Free to members; non-members, $35.00 per year; students, $30.00 per year. Offers a broad variety of researched, documented articles.

Appraisal of Real Estate. Appraisal Institute, 875 N. Michigan Ave., Suite 2400 Chicago, IL 60611-1980. Phone: (312)335-4100 Fax: (312)819-2360 1996. $49.50. 11th edition. Provides an in-depth discussion of the driving concept of market value; guildelines for market analysis projections and updated information throughout that addresses developments affecting the movement of investment capital.

Appraisers Association of America.

Approved Drug Products, with Therapeutic Equivalence Evaluations. Available from U. S. Government Printing Office, Washington, DC 20402. Phone: (202)512-1800 Fax: (202)512-2250 E-mail: gpoaccess@gpo.gov • URL: http://www.access.gpo.gov • $101.00 for basic manual and supplemental material for an indeterminate period. Issued by the Food and Drug Administration, U. S. Department of Health and Human Services. Lists prescription drugs that have been approved by the FDA. Includes therapeutic equivalents to aid in containment of health costs and to serve State drug selection laws.

APWA Reporter. American Public Works Association, 106 W. 11th St. Kansas City, MO 64105-1806. Phone: (816)472-6100 or (312)667-2200 Fax: (816)472-1610 Monthly. Membership.

Aquacultural Research and Teaching Facility.

Aquaculture-Buyers Guide. Achill River Corp., P.O. Box 2329 Asheville, NC 28802. Phone: (828)254-7344 Fax: (828)253-0677 E-mail: aquamag@ioa.com • URL: http://www.aquaculturemag.com • Annual. $20.00. Lists about 1,400 sources of supplies and services.

Aquaculture; An International Journal Devoted to Fundamental Aquatic Food Resources. Elsevier Science, 655 Ave. of the Americas, New York, NY 10010 New York, NY 10010. Phone: 888-437-4636 or (212)989-5800 Fax: (212)633-3680 E-mail: usinfo@elsevier.com • URL: http://www.elsevier.com • 44 times a year. $2,704.00 per year. Text in English.

Aquaculture Magazine. Achill River Corp., P.O. Box 2329 Asheville, NC 28802. Phone: (704)254-7344 Fax: (704)253-0677 URL: http://www.aquaculturemag.com • Bimonthly. $15.00 per year.

Aqualine. Water Research Centre, Frankland Road Blagrove, Swindon, Wilts SN5 8YF, England. Phone: (079)3-511711 Fax: (079)3-511712 Citations and abstracts of literature on aquatic environment, 1960 to present. Inquire as to online cost and availability.

Aquatic Research Institute.

Aquatic Sciences and Fisheries Abstracts. Food and Agriculture Organization of the United Nations. Cambridge Information Group, 7200 Wisconsin Ave., 6th Fl. Bethesda, MD 20814. Phone: 800-843-7751 or (301)961-6700 Fax: (301)961-6720 E-mail: market@csa.com • URL: http://www.csa.com • Monthly. Part one, $1,045.00 per year; part two, $815.00 per year.

Arbitron Radio County Coverage. Arbitron Co., 142 W. 57th St. New York, NY 10019. Phone: (212)887-1300 Fax: (212)887-1390 Ratings of radio and TV stations plus audience measurement data, updated frequently. Inquire as to online cost and availability.

Architects and Engineers: Their Professional Responsibilities. James Acret. McGraw-Hill, 1221 Ave. of the Americas New York, NY 10020. Phone: 800-722-4726 or (212)904-2000 Fax: (212)904-2000 E-mail: customer.service@mcgraw-hill.com • URL: http://www/mcgraw-hill.com • 1977. $95.00. Second edition. Covers legal responsibilities, liabilities, and malpractice.

Architects Handbook of Professional Practice. David Haviland. American Institute of Architects Press, 1735 New York Ave., N.W. Washington, DC 20006. Phone: 800-365-2724 or (202)626-7575 1994. $225.00. 12th edition.

Architectural Graphic Standards. C.G. Ramsey and others. John Wiley and Sons, Inc., 605 Third Ave. New York, NY 10158-0012. Phone: 800-225-5945 or (212)850-6000 Fax: (212)850-6088 E-mail: info@wiley.com • URL: http://www.wiley.com • 2000. $600.00. Tenth edition.

Architectural Publications Index. British Architectural Library. RIBA Publications Ltd., Finsbury Mission, 39 Moreland St. London EC1V 8BB, England. Phone: 44 171 2510791 Fax: 44 171 6082375 URL: http://www.ribac.co.uk • Quarterly. Individuals, $270.00 per year. Formerly *Architectural Periodicals Index*.

Architectural Record. American Institute of Architects. McGraw-Hill Construction Information Group, 1221 Ave. of the Americas New York, NY 10020-1095. Phone: 800-722-4726 or (212)904-2000 Fax: (212)904-2072 E-mail: customer.service@mcgraw-hill.com • URL: http://www.mcgraw-hill.com • Monthly $59.00 per year. Includes supplements *Record Interiors*. and *Record Houses*.

Architectural Review. Fenner, Reed and Jackson, P.O.Box 754 Manhasset, NY 11030-0754. Monthly. Individuals, $100.00 per year; students, $60.00 per year. Visits innovative buildings around the world.

Architectural Woodwork Institute.

Architecture. BPI Communications, Inc., 770 Broadway New York, NY 10003-9595. Phone: 800-344-7119 or (646)654-5500 Fax: (646)654-5835 E-mail: info@bpi.com • URL: http://wwwbpicomm.com • Monthly. $55.00 per year. Incorporates *Building Renovation*.

Archives of Environmental Health. Helen Dwight Reid Educational Foundation. Heldref Publications, 1319 18th St., N.W. Washington, DC 20036-1802. Phone: 800-296-5149 or (202)296-6267 Fax: (202)296-5149 E-mail: aeh@heldref.org • URL: http://www/helderf.org • Bimonthly. $137.00 per year. Objective documentation of the effects of environmental agents on human health.

Area Development Sites and Facility Planning: The Executive Magazine of Sites and Facility Planning. S H Publications, Inc., 400 Post Ave. Westbury, NY 11590. Phone: (516)338-0900 Fax: (516)338-0100 Monthly. $65.00 per year. Site selection, facility planning, and plant relocation. Formerly *Area Development Magazines*.

Area Trends in Employment and Unemployment. Available from U. S. Government Printing Office, Washington, DC 20402. Phone: (202)512-1800 Fax: (202)512-2250 E-mail: gpoaccess@gpo.gov • URL: http://www.access.gpo.gov • Monthly. $60.00 per year. Issued by the U. S. Department of Labor (http://www.dol.gov). Includes a listing of labor surplus areas in the U. S.

Argonne National Laboratory.

Argonne National Laboratory Industrial Technology Development Center.

Argumentation and Advocacy. American Forensic Association, P.O. Box 256 River Falls, WI 54022-0256. Phone: 800-228-5424 or (715)425-3198 Fax: (715)425-9533 Quarterly. $55.00 per year. Formerly *American Forensic Association Journal*.

ARL: A Bimonthly Newsletter of Research Library Issues and Actions. Association of Research Libraries, 21 Dupont Circle, Suite 800 Washington, DC 20036. Phone: (202)296-2296 Fax: (202)296-2296 E-mail: pubs@arl.rog

• URL: http://www.arl.org • Bimonthly. Members, $25.00; non-members, $50.00 per year.

ARL Annual Salary Survey. Association of Research Libraries, 21 Dupont Circle, Suite 800 Washington, DC 20036. Phone: (202)296-2296 Fax: (202)872-0884 E-mail: pubs@arl.org • URL: http://www.arl.org/stats/salary • Annual. Members, $39.00; non-members, $79.00. Statistics on salaries by institution, region, position, sex/race and other data for the 119 research libraries in ARL.

ARL Statistics. Association of Research Libraries, 21 Dupont Circle, Suite 800 Washington, DC 20036. Phone: (202)232-2466 Fax: (202)872-0884 E-mail: pubs@arl.org • URL: http://www.arl.org/stats/arlstat • Annual. Members, $39.00; non-members, $79.00. Presents a variety of statistics for about 120 university and other major research libraries.

Armed Forces Communications and Electronics Association.

Armed Forces Comptroller. American Society of Military Comptrollers, 2034 Eisenhower Ave., Suite 145 Alexandria, VA 22314. Phone: (703)549-0360 Fax: (703)549-3181 Quarterly. $15.00 per year.

Armed Forces Journal International. Armed Forces Journal International, Inc., 8201 Greenboro Dr., Suite 611 McLean, VA 22102-3810. Phone: (703)848-0490 Fax: (703)848-0480 E-mail: afji@aol.com • URL: http://www.afji.com • Monthly. $45.00 per year. A defense magazine for career military officers and industry executives. Covers defense events, plans, policies, budgets, and innovations.

Army AL&T: Acquisitions, Logistics, and Technology Bulletin. Available from U. S. Government Printing Office, Washington, DC 20402. Phone: (202)512-1800 Fax: (202)512-2250 E-mail: gpoaccess@gpo.gov • URL: http://www.access.gpo.gov • Bimonthly. $20.00 per year. Produced by the U. S. Army Materiel Command (http://www.amc.army.mil). Reports on Army research, development, and acquisition. Formerly *Army RD&A*.

Army and Air Force Mutual Aid Association.

Army Aviation Association of America.

Army Emergency Relief.

Army Logistician: The Professional Bulletin of United States Army Logistics. United States Army Logistics Management College. Available from U.S. Government Printing Office, Washington, DC 20401. Phone: (202)512-1800 Fax: (202)512-2250 E-mail: gpoaccess@gpo.gov • URL: http://www.access.gpo.gov • Bimonthly. $21.00 per year.

The Army Officer's Guide. Keith E. Bonn. Stackpole Books, 5067 Ritter Rd. Mechanicsburg, PA 17055. Phone: 800-732-3669 or (717)769-0411 Fax: (717)796-0412 E-mail: sales@stackpolebooks.com • URL: http://www.stackpolebooks.com • 1999. $22.95. 48th edition.

Army Reserve Magazine. Available from U. S. Government Printing Office, Washington, DC 20402. Phone: (202)512-1800 Fax: (202)512-2250 E-mail: gpoaccess@gpo.gov • URL: http://www.access.gpo.gov • Quarterly. $14.00 per year. Issued by the Army Reserve, U. S. Department of Defense.

Army Times. Army Times Publishing Co., 6883 Commercial Dr. Springfield, VA 22159. Phone: 800-368-5718 or (703)750-8646 Fax: (703)750-8699 URL: http://www.armytimes.com • Weekly. $52.00 per year. In two editions: Domestic and International.

Art and Antique Dealers League of America.

Art and Antiques. Trans World Publishing Co., 2100 Powers Ferry Rd., Suite 300 Atlanta, GA 30339. Phone: (770)955-5656 Fax: (770)952-0669 E-mail: service@billian.com • URL: http://www.artantiquesmag.com • 11 times a year. $36.00 per year. Formerly *Antique Monthly*.

Art and Auction. Auction Guild, 11 E. 36th St., 9th Fl. New York, NY 10016-3318. Phone: (212)582-5633 Fax: (212)246-3891 11 times a year. $42.00 per year.

Art and Creative Materials Institute., 100 Boylston St., Suite 1050 Boston, MA 02116. Phone: (781)293-4100 Fax: (781)293-0808 E-mail: acmi@fanningnet.com • URL: http://www.creative-industries.com/acmi • Members are manufacturers of school and professional art and craft materials.

The Art and Science of Leadership. Afsaneh Nahavandi. Prentice Hall, 240 Frisch Court Paramus, NJ 07652-5240. Phone: 800-947-7700 or (201)909-6200 Fax: 800-445-6991 or (201)909-6361 URL: http://www.prenhall.com • 1999. $55.00. Second edition. Includes a discussion of participative management. Emphasis is on strategic leadership.

Art Business Encyclopedia. Leonard DuBoff. Allworth Press, 10 E. 23rd St., Suite 210 New York, NY 10010. Phone: 800-491-2808 or (212)777-8395 Fax: (212)777-8261 E-mail: jbarager@allworth.com • URL: http://www.allworth.com • 1994. $18.95. Defines words, phrases, and concepts relating to the business of art, with emphasis on legal matters. Includes relevant statutes, arranged by state. Published in cooperation with the American Council for the Arts.

Art Business News. Advanstar Communications, Inc., One Park Ave., 2nd Fl. New York, NY 10016-5802. Phone: 800-346-0085 or (212)951-6600 Fax: (212)951-6793 E-mail: information@advanstar.com • URL: http://www.advanstar.com • Monthly. $43.00 per year.

Art Business News Buyer's Guide. Advanstar Communications, Inc., One Park Ave. New York, NY 10016-5802. Phone: 800-346-0085 or (212)951-6600 Fax: (212)951-6793 E-mail: information@advanstar.com • URL: http://www.advanstar.com • Annual. $25.00. Lists companies furnishing supplies and services to art dealers and framers. Includes art by subject and media.

Art Dealers Association of America.

Art Direction: The Magazine of Visual Communication. Advertising Trade Publications, Inc., c/o Dan Barron, 456 Glenbrook Rd. Stamford, CT 06906-1800. Phone: (212)889-6500 Fax: (212)889-6504 Monthly. $29.97 per year. Current advertising in art, photography, design, type, etc.

Art Directors Annual. Art Directors Club Inc. Rotovision, S.A., 250 Park Ave. S. New York, NY 10003-1402. Phone: (212)420-8798 Fax: (212)460-8506 E-mail: mdavis@adcny.orgnet • URL: http://www.adcny.org • Annual. $70.00. Formerly *Annual of Advertising, Editorial and Television Art and Design with the Annual Copy Awards.*

Art Directors Club.

Art in America. Brant Publications, Inc., 575 Broadway, 5th Fl. New York, NY 10012. Phone: 800-925-9271 or (212)941-2800 Fax: (212)941-2870 Monthly. $39.95 per year. Comprehensive reviews of U.S. and worldwide exhibits.

Art Index. H. W. Wilson Co., 950 University Ave. Bronx, NY 10452. Phone: 800-367-6770 or (718)558-8400 Fax: (718)590-1617 URL: http://www.hwwilson.com • Quarterly. Annual cumulations. Service basis for print edition; CD-ROM edition, $1,495.00 per year. Subject and author index to periodicals in art, architecture, industrial design, city planning, photography, and various related topics.

Art Index Online. H. W. Wilson Co., 950 University Ave. Bronx, NY 10452. Phone: 800-367-6770 or (718)558-8400 Fax: (718)590-1617 Indexes a wide variety of art-related periodicals, 1984 to date. Monthly updates. Inquire as to online cost and availability.

Art Information Center., 55 Mercer St., 3rd Fl. New York, NY 10013. Phone: (212)966-3443 For contemporary art.

Art Law: The Guide for Collectors, Investors, Dealers, and Artists. Ralph E. Lerner and Judith Bresler. Practising Law Institute, 810 Seventh Ave. New York, NY 10019-5818. Phone: 800-260-4754 or (212)824-5700 Fax: (212)265-4742 E-mail: info@pli.edu • URL: http://www.pli.edu • 1997. $125.00. Two volumes. Second edition. Covers artist/dealer relationships, artists' rights, appraisals, museum law, tax aspects, estate planning issues, and other legal topics relating to visual art. There are six main headings: Dealers, Artwork Transactions, Artists' Rights, Collectors, Taxes and Estate Planning, and Museums and Multimedia.

Art Marketing Handbook: Marketing Art in the Nineties. Calvin J. Goodman. Gee Tee Bee, 11901 Sunset Blvd., No. 102 Los Angeles, CA 90049. Phone: (310)476-2622 Fax: (310)472-8785 E-mail: geteebee@aol.com • 1991. $60.00. Sixth revised edition. A complete guide to all aspects of the art market.

Art Marketing Sourcebook. ArtNetwork Press, P.O. Box 1360 Penn Valley, CA 95959-1360. Phone: (530)470-0862 Fax: (530)470-0256 Biennial. $23.95. Over 2,000 representatives, consultants, galleries, critics, architects, interior designers, corporations, museum curators, and art organizations. Formerly *Directory of Art Associations and Exhibition Space.*

Art Now Gallery Guides. Art Now, Inc., P.O. Box 5541 Clinton, NJ 08809. Phone: (908)638-5255 Fax: (908)638-8737 URL: http://www.gallery-guide.com • 10 times a year. In eight regional editions. International coverage. Prices vary.Lists current exhibitions in over 1,800 art galleries and museums.

The Art of Asking: How to Solicit Philanthropic Gifts. Paul H. Schneiter. Fund Raising Institute, 27500 Drake Rd. Farmington Hills, MI 48331-3535. Phone: 800-877-GALE or (248)699-GALE Fax: 800-414-5043 or (248)699-8069 E-mail: galeord@gale.com • URL: http://www.gale.com • 1985. $25.00.

The Art of Commercial Lending. Edward Morsman. Robert Morris Associates, One Liberty Place, 1650 Market St., Suite 2300 Philadelphia, PA 19103. Phone: 800-677-7621 or (215)446-4000 Fax: (215)446-4100 E-mail: info@rmahq.org • URL: http://www.rmahq.org • 1997. $64.00. Describes the diverse skills required for success as a commercial lender. Covers both personal and institutional aspects.

The Art of Editing. Floyd K. Baskette and Jack Z. Sissors. Allyn and Bacon, Inc., 160 Gould St. Needham Heights, MA 02194-2310. Phone: 800-278-3525 or (781)455-1250 Fax: (781)455-1294 E-mail: ab_webmaster@abacon.com • URL: http://www.abacon.com • 2000. 7th edition. Price on applications.

The Art of Electronic Publishing: The Internet and Beyond. Sanford Ressler. Prentice Hall, 240 Frisch Court Paramus, NJ 07652-5240. Phone: 800-947-7700 or (201)909-6200 Fax: 800-445-6991 or (201)909-6361 URL: http://www.prenhall.com • 1996. $39.95. Places emphasis on the World Wide Web. Includes information on document processors, standards, integration and management, with case studies.

The Art of Fund Raising. Irving R. Warner. Fund Raising Institute, 27500 Drake Rd. Farmington Hills, MI 48331-3535. Phone: 800-877-GALE or (248)699-GALE Fax: 800-414-5043 or (248)699-8069 E-mail: galeord@gale.com • URL: http://www.galegroup.com • 1991. $19.95. Third edition. Includes case histories.

The Art of M & A: A Merger-Acquisition-Buyout Guide. Stanley F. Reed and Aleandra R. Lajoux. McGraw-Hill Professional, 1221 Ave. of the Americas New York, NY 10020. Phone: 800-722-4726 or (212)904-2000 Fax: (212)904-2072 E-mail: customer.service@mcgraw-hill.com • URL: http://www.mcgraw-hill.com • 1998. $179.95. Second edition. A how-to-do-it guide for merger and acquisition ventures. Emphasis is on legal issues.

The Art of the Long View: Planning for the Future in an Uncertain World. Peter Schwartz. Doubleday, 1540 Broadway New York, NY 10036-4094. Phone: 800-223-6834 or (212)354-6500 Fax: (212)492-9700 URL: http://www.doubledaybookclub.com • 1991. $15.95. Covers strategic planning for corporations and smaller firms. Includes "The World in 2005: Three Scenarios."

The Art of 3-D Computer Animation and Imaging. Isaac V. Kerlow. John Wiley and Sons, Inc., 605 Third Ave. New York, NY 10158-0012. Phone: 800-225-5945 or (212)850-6000 Fax: (212)850-6088 E-mail: info@jwiley.com • URL: http://www.wiley.com • 2000. $59.95. Second edition. Covers special effects, hypermedia formats, video output, the post-production process, etc. Includes full-color illustrations and step-by-step examples. (Design and Graphic Design Series).

The Art of Weaving. Else Regensteiner. Schiffer Publishing, Ltd., 4880 Lower Valley Rd. Atglen, PA 19310. Phone: (610)593-1777 Fax: (610)593-2002 1986. $29.95.

Art Reference Services Quarterly. Haworth Press, Inc., 10 Alice St. Binghamton, NY 13904-1580. Phone: 800-429-6784 or (607)722-5857 Fax: 800-895-0582 or (607)722-1424 E-mail: getinfo@haworthpressinc.com • URL: http://www.haworthpressinc.com • Quarterly. Individuals, $38.00 per year; libraries and other institutions, $75.00 per year. A journal for art librarians.

Art Sources Directory. Art Marketing Institute, P.O. Box 4564 North Hollywood, CA 91607. Phone: (818)879-0339 Fax: (818)879-9326 Irregular. $95.00. Lists buyers and suppliers of art and art materials. Includes artists' grants, competitions, shows, associations, and publications.

ARTbibliographies Modern. ABC-CLIO, Inc., P.O. Box 1911 Santa Barbara, CA 93116-1911. Phone: 800-422-2546 or (805)968-1911 Fax: (805)685-9685 Covers the literature of contemporary art and related subjects from 1974 to date, including art collecting, exhibitions, galleries, graphic design, photography, etc. Inquire as to online cost and availability.

Arthur Andersen North American Business Sourcebook: The Most Comprehensive, Authoritative Reference Guide to Expanding Trade in the North American Market. Triumph Books, 644 S. Clark St., Suite 2000 Chicago, IL 60605-9808. Phone: 800-335-5323 or (312)939-3330 Fax: (312)663-3557 E-mail: triumphbooks@aol.com • 1993. $195.00. Includes statistical, regulatory, economic, and directory information relating to North American trade, including information on the North American Free Trade Agreement (NAFTA). Emphasis is on exporting to Mexico and Canada.

Arthur M. Bank Center for Entrepreneurship., Babson College Babson Park, MA 02157-0310. Phone: (617)239-4420 Fax: (617)239-4178 E-mail: spinelli@babson.edu • URL: http://www.babson.edu/entrep • Sponsors annual Babson College Entrepreneurship Research Conference.

Artificial Intelligence. P. Henry. Addison-Wesley Longman, Inc., One Jacob Way Reading, MA 01867. Phone: 800-447-2226 or (781)944-3700 Fax: (781)944-9351 URL: http://www.awl.com • 2001. Fourth edition. Price on application.

Artificial Intelligence and Computer Vision Laboratory., University of Cincinnati, Dept. of Electrical, Computer Engineering and Computer Scien, 802 Rhodes Hall Cincinnati, OH 45221-0030. Phone: (513)556-4778 Fax: (513)556-7326 E-mail: william.wee@uc.edu • Fields of research include computer vision, computer graphics, and artificial intelligence.

Artificial Intelligence and Software Engineering. Darek Partridge. Fitzroy Dearborn Publishers, Inc., 919 N. Michigan Ave., Suite 760 Chicago, IL 60611. Phone: 800-850-8102 or (312)587-0131 Fax: (312)587-1049 E-mail: website@fitzroydearborn.com • URL: http://www.fitzroydearborn.com • 1998. $55.00. Includes applications of artificial intelligence software to banking and financial services.

Artificial Intelligence: Concepts and Applications. A.R. Mirzai, editor. MIT Press, Five Cambridge Center Cambridge, MA 02142-1493. Phone: 800-356-0343 or (617)253-5646 Fax:

(617)253-6779 E-mail: mitpress-orders@mit.edu • URL: http://www.mitpress.mit.edu • 1990. $42.00. (Artificial Intelligence Series).

Artificial Intelligence Dictionary: A Dictionary Specifically for Artificial Intelligence Users and Specialists. Ellen Thro. Slawson Communications, Inc., P.O. Box 28459 San Diego, CA 92198-0459. 1991. $24.95. Includes common lay words that lead to correct medical terms. (Lance A. Levanthal Microtrend Series).

Artificial Intelligence in Perspective. Daniel G. Bobrow, editor. MIT Press, Five Cambridge Center Cambridge, MA 02142-1493. Phone: 800-356-0343 or (617)253-5646 Fax: (617)253-6779 E-mail: mitpress-orders@mit.edu • URL: http://www.mitpress.mit.edu • 1994. $42.50. (Artificial Intelligence Series).

Artificial Intelligence in the Capital Markets: State-of-the-Art Applications. Roy A Freedman and Robert A. Klein. McGraw-Hill Professional, 1221 Ave. of the Americas New York, NY 10020-1095. Phone: 800-722-4726 or (212)904-2000 Fax: (212)904-2072 E-mail: customer.service@mcgraw-hill.com • URL: http://www.mcgraw-hill.com • 1994. $85.00.

Artificial Intelligence: Its Role in the Information Industry. Peter Davies. Information Today, Inc., 143 Old Marlton Pike Medford, NJ 08055-8750. Phone: 800-300-9868 or (609)654-6266 Fax: (609)654-4309 E-mail: custserv@infotoday.com • URL: http://www.infotoday.com • 1991. $39.50.

Artificial Intelligence: Its Scope and Limits. Kluwer Academic Publishers, 101 Philip Dr. Norwell, MA 02061. Phone: (781)871-6600 Fax: (781)871-6528 E-mail: kluwer@wkap.nl • URL: http://www.wkap.nl • 1990. $137.50.

Artificial Intelligence Laboratory.

Artificial Intelligence Laboratory.

Artificial Intelligence: Reality or Fantasy? Leslie Chase and Robert Landers, editors. Software and Information Industry Association, 1730 M St., N.W., Suite 700 Washington, DC 20036-4510. Phone: (202)452-1600 Fax: (202)223-8756 URL: http://www.siia.net • 1984. $59.95. General information and market considerations.

Artificial Language Laboratory., Michigan State University, 405 Computer Center East Lansing, MI 48824-1042. Phone: (517)353-5399 Fax: (517)353-4766 E-mail: artlang@pilot.msu.edu • URL: http://www.msu.edu/unit/artlang/ • Research areas include speech analysis and synthesis by computer.

Artist's and Graphic Designer's Market: 2,500 Places to Sell Your Art and Design. F and W. Publications, Inc., 1507 Dana Ave. Cincinnati, OH 45207-1005. Phone: 800-289-0963 or (513)531-2222 Fax: 888-590-4082 Annual. $24.99. Lists art galleries, advertising agencies, TV producers, publishers, and other buyers of free-lance art work. Formerly *Artist's Market*.

Artist's Resource Handbook. Daniel Grant. Allworth Press, 10 E. 23rd St., Suite 210 New York, NY 10010. Phone: 800-491-2808 or (212)777-8395 Fax: (212)777-8261 E-mail: jbarager@allworth.com • URL: http://www.allworth.com • 1997. $18.95. Second revised edition. A directory of organizations and services that may be helpful to artists. Published in cooperation with the American Council for the Arts.

ARTnews. Artnews LLC, 48 W. 38th St. New York, NY 10018. Phone: 800-284-4625 or (212)398-1690 Fax: (212)819-0394 URL: http://www.artnewsonline.com • 11 times a year. $39.95 per year.

The ARTnewsletter: The International Biweekly Business Report on the Art Market. ARTnews LLC, 48 W. 38th St. New York, NY 10018. Phone: 800-227-7585 or (212)398-1690 Fax: (212)819-0394 Biweekly. $249.00 per year. Newsletter on forthcoming auctions, price trends, ownership squabbles, criminal cases, etc.

The Arts and the World of Business: A Selected Bibliography. Charlotte Georgi. Scarecrow Press, Inc., 4720 Boston Way Lanham, MD 20706-4310. Phone: 800-462-6420 or (301)459-3366 Fax: 800-338-4550 or (301)459-1705 E-mail: orders@scarecrowpress.com • URL: http://www.scarecrowpress.com • 1979. $24.00. Second edition.

Arts Management. Radius Group Inc., 110 Riverside Dr., No. 4E New York, NY 10024. Phone: (212)579-2039 Fax: (212)579-2049 Five times a year. $22.00 per year. National news service for those who finance, manage and communicate the arts.

Arts Management: A Guide to Finding Funds and Winning Audiences. Alvin H. Reiss. Fund Raising Institute, 27500 Drake Rd. Farmington Hills, MI 48331-3535. Phone: 800-877-8238 or (248)699-GALE Fax: 800-414-5043 or (248)699-8069 E-mail: galeord@gale.com • URL: http://www.galegroup.com • 1992. $45.00.

Arts Management Reader. Alvin H. Reiss. Marcel Dekker, Inc., 270 Madison Ave. New York, NY 10016. Phone: 800-228-1160 or (212)696-9000 Fax: (212)685-4540 E-mail: bookorders@dekker.com • URL: http://www.dekker.com • 1979. $55.00.

ASA Newsletter. American Studies Association, 1120 19th St., N.W., Suite 301 Washington, DC 20036. Phone: (202)467-4783 Fax: (202)467-4786 E-mail: asastaff@erols.com • URL: http://www.georgetown.edu/crossroads • Quarterly. Membership.

ASBC Newsletter. American Society of Brewing Chemists, 3340 Pilot Knob Rd. Saint Paul, MN 55121-2097. Phone: (612)454-7250 Fax: (612)454-0766 URL: http://www.scisoc.org/asbc • Quarterly. Members, $95.00 per year; non-members, $130.00 per year; corporate members, $195.00 per year; student members, $26.00 per year.

Asbestos and Lead Abatement Report: Inspection, Analysis, Removal, Maintenance, Alternatives. Business Publishers, Inc., 8737 Colesville Rd., Suite 1100 Silver Spring, MD 20910-3928. Phone: 800-274-6737 or (301)587-6300 Fax: (301)587-1081 E-mail: bpinews@bpinews.com • URL: http://www.bpinews.com • Biweekly. $357.00 per year. Newsletter on legal issues relating to the removal or containment of asbestos and lead. Includes news of research activities.

Asbestos Information Association/North America.

Asbestos Institute.

Asbestos Litigation Reporter: The National Journal of Record of Asbestos Litigation. Andrews Publications, 175 Strafford Ave., Bldg 4, Suite 140 Wayne, PA 19087. Phone: 800-345-1101 or (610)622-0510 Fax: (610)622-0501 URL: http://www.andrewspub.com • Semimonthly. $995.00 per year. Provides reports on legal cases involving asbestos as a health hazard.

ASCE News. American Society of Civil Engineers, 1801 Alexander Graham Bell Dr. Reston, VA 20191-4400. Phone: 800-548-2723 or (703)295-6300 Fax: (703)295-6222 E-mail: webmaster@asce.org • URL: http://www.asce.org • Monthly. $42.00 per year. Newsletter.

*ASFA Aquaculture Abstracts ÎOnline*l. Cambridge Scientific Abstracts, 7200 Wisconsin Ave., 6th Fl. Bethesda, MD 20814. Phone: 800-843-7751 or (301)961-6700 Fax: (301)961-6720 Indexing and abstracting of the literature of marine life, 1984 to present. Inquire as to online cost and availability.

ASHRAE Handbook. American Society of Heating, Refrigerating, and Air Conditioning Engineers, Inc., 1791 Tullie Circle, N.E. Atlanta, GA 30329. Phone: (404)636-8400 Fax: (404)321-5478 E-mail: orders@ashrae.org • URL: http://www.ashrae.org • Annual. Members, $98.00; non-members, $248.00. Four volumes.

ASHRAE Journal: Heating, Refrigeration, Air Conditioning, Ventilation. American Society of Heating, Refrigerating and Air Conditioning Engineers, Inc., 1791 Tullie Circle, N.E. Atlanta, GA 30329. Phone: (404)636-8400 Fax: (404)321-5478 E-mail: orders@ashrae.org • URL: http://www.ashrae.org • Monthly. Free to members; non-members, $59.00 per year.

ASHRAE Transactions. American Society of Heating, Refrigerating, and Air Conditioning Engineers, Inc., 1791 Tullie Circle, N.E. Atlanta, GA 30329. Phone: (404)636-8400 Fax: (404)321-5478 E-mail: orders@ashrae.org • URL: http://wwwe.ashrae.org • Semiannual. Members, $126.00 per year; non-members, $187.00 per year.

ASI (American Statistics Index). Congressional Information Service, 4250 East-West Highway Bethesda, MD 20814-3389. Phone: 800-638-8380 or (301)654-1550 Fax: (301)654-4033 A comprehensive online index, with abstracts, to the statistical publications of over 500 federal government offices and agencies from 1973 to date. A wide variety of information is indexed, with emphasis on demographic, economic, social, and natural resources data. Updated monthly. Inquire as to online cost and availability.

Asia: A Directory and Sourcebook. Available from The Gale Group, 27500 Drake Rd. Farmington Hills, MI 48331-3535. Phone: 800-877-GALE or (248)699-GALE Fax: 800-414-5043 or (248)699-8069 E-mail: galeord@galegroup.com • URL: http://www.galegroup.com • Irregular. $430.00. Published by Euromonitor. Lists official and unofficial sources of information for Hong Kong, China, Singapore, Taiwan, India, Indonesia, Malaysia, Pakistan, the Philippines, South Korea, Sri Lanka, and Thailand. Includes profiles of leading companies and assessments of consumer markets.

Asia, Inc. Online. Manager Media Group, Hong KongPhone: (852)581-8088 Fax: (852)851-0962 E-mail: marketing@manager.com • URL: http://www.asia-inc.com • Web site provides Asian business news and information. Includes "Today's Financial News" (commentary and Asian stock prices), "This Week's Special Items," "Feature Stories," "Net Resources," "Archive," and other contents. Includes a search facility. Fees: Free.

Asia Inc.: The Region's Business Magazine. Asia, Inc., Ltd., 8/F Kinwick Centre, 32 Hollywood Rd. Central, Hong Kong, Hong Kong. Phone: 852 2581 8088 Fax: 852 2851 0302 E-mail: adsales@asia-inc.com • URL: http://www.asia-inc.com • Monthly. $79.00 per year. Contains business, financial, and other news and commentary from various countries in Asia. Main sections are "At Work," "Asia Abroad: A World of Business," and "After Hours: Travel and Leisure." Text in English.

Asia Pacific Economic Review: Bridging Pacific Rim Business and Society. Zencore, Inc., P.O. Box 14089 Seattle, WA 98119. Phone: (206)860-4970 Fax: (206)860-4895 URL: http://www.asialinks.com • Monthly. $35.00 per year. Includes special issues on individual countries: Taiwan, Malayasia, China/Hong Kong, Japan, and Korea.

Asia Pacific Kompass on Disc. Available from Kompass USA, Inc., 1255 Route 70, Suite 25-S Lakewood, NJ 08701. Phone: 877-566-7277 or (732)730-0340 Fax: (732)730-0342 E-mail: mail@kompass-usa.com • URL: http://www.kompass.com • Annual. $2,190.00. CD-ROM provides information on more than 280,000 companies in Australia, China, Hong Kong, India, Korea, Malaysia, New Zealand, Philippines, Singapore, Thailand, and Taiwan. Classification system covers approximately 50,000 products and services.

Asia Pacific Securities Handbook. Available from Hoover's, Inc., 1033 La Posada Dr., Suite 250 Austin, TX 78752. Phone: 800-486-8666 or (512)374-4500 Fax: (512)374-4501 E-mail: orders@hoovers.com • URL: http://www.hoovers.com • Annual. $99.95. Published in Hong Kong. Provides detailed descriptions of stock exchanges in 17 Asia Pacific countries, including Australia, China, Hong Kong, India, Japan, and Singapore. Lists largest public companies and most active stock issues.

Asia Times: The Voice of Asia. Available from Asia Times Circulation Dept., 918 Glenhaven Dr. Pacific Palisades, CA 90272. Phone: 888-234-2742 or (310)459-5336 Fax: (310)454-2203 E-mail: editor@asiatimes.com • URL: http://www.asiatimes.com • Daily. $392.00 per year. Published in Thailand by Asia Network Publication Co. Ltd. A business newspaper presenting trade, financial, and general news from most Asian countries. Includes 100 high volume, large capitalization stock price quotes from each of nine markets: Tokyo, Hong Kong, Seoul, Taipei, Bangkok, Manila, Kuala Lumpur, Singapore, and Jakarta. (A Manager Media Group publication.)

Asian Business. TPL Corp Ltd, 10/F, Block C, Seaview Estate, 2-8 Watson Rd. North Point, Hong Kong. Phone: (852)2566 8381 Fax: (852)2508 0197 Monthly. $105.00 per year. Covers Asian business, investment, and franchise opportunities, especially in Hong Kong, Singapore, and Taiwan.

Asian Company Handbook. Available from Hoover's, Inc., 1033 La Posada Drive, Suite 250 Austin, TX 78752. Phone: 800-486-8666 or (512)374-4500 Fax: (512)374-4505 E-mail: orders@hoovers.com • URL: http://www.hoovers.com • 1998. $79.95. Published by Toyo Keizai, Japan. Text in English. Provides detailed profiles of 1,060 publicly-traded companies listed on stock exchanges in Hong Kong, Indonesia, Malaysia, the Republic of Korea, Singapore, Taiwan, and Thailand.

Asian/Pacific American Librarians Association.

Asian Pacific Markets: A Guide to Company and Industry Information Sources. Washington Researchers Ltd., 1655 N. Fort Myer Dr., Suite 800 Arlington, VA 22209. Phone: (703)527-4585 Fax: (703)312-2863 E-mail: research@researchers.com • URL: http://www.researchers.com/pub • Irregular. $335.00. A directory of government offices, "experts," publications, and databases related to Asian markets and companies. Includes individual chapters on "the 11 most important nations in Asia." Formerly *Asian Markets*.

The Asian Wall Street Journal. Dow Jones & Co., Inc., 200 Liberty St. New York, NY 10281. Phone: 800-568-7625 or (212)416-2700 Fax: (212)416-2658 URL: http://www.dowjones.com • Daily. $610.00 per year (air mail). Published in Hong Kong. Also available in a weekly edition at $259.00 per year: *Asian Wall Street Journal Weekly*.

Asia's 7,500 Largest Companies. Dun & Bradstreet Information Services, Three Sylvan Way Parsippany, NJ 07054-3896. Phone: 800-526-0651 or (973)455-0900 Fax: (973)254-4063 E-mail: customerservice@dng.com • URL: http://www.dnb.com • Annual. $250.00. Published in London by ELC Publishing Ltd. Provides information on the top 7,500 companies in Hong Kong, Indonesia, Japan, South Korea, Malaysia, the Philippines, Singapore, Taiwan, Thailand, and China.

ASIS Handbook and Directory. American Society for Information Science, 8700 Georgia Ave., Suite 501 Silver Spring, MD 20910. Phone: (301)495-0900 Fax: (301)495-0810 E-mail: asis@asis.org • URL: http://www.asis.org • Annual. Members, $25.00; non-members, $100.00.

ASIS International (American Society for Industrial Security).

ASLA Members Handbook. American Society of Landscape Architects, 636 Eye St., N.W. Washington, DC 20001-3736. Phone: (202)216-2320 Fax: (202)898-1115 E-mail: scahill@asla.org • URL: http://www.asla.org • Annual. Members $25.00; non-members, $195.00.

Aslib Book Guide: A Monthly List of Recommended Scientific and Technical Books. Available from Information Today, Inc., 143 Old Marlton Pike Medford, NJ 08055-8750. Phone: 800-300-9868 or (609)654-6266 Fax: (609)654-4309 E-mail: custserv@infotoday.com • URL: http://www.infotoday.com • Monthly. Members, $164.00 per year; non-members, $204.00 per year. Published in London by Aslib: The Association for Information Management. Formerly *Aslib Book List*.

Aslib Proceedings. Available from Information Today, Inc., 143 Old Marlton Pike Medford, NJ 08055-8750. Phone: 800-300-9868 or (609)654-6266 Fax: (609)654-4309 E-mail: custserv@infotoday.com • URL: http://www.infotoday.com • Ten times a year. Free to Members; non-members, $252.00 per year. Published in London by Aslib Covers a wide variety of information industry and library management topics.

ASM Engineered Materials Reference Book. Michael L. Bauccio. ASM International, 9639 Kinsman Rd. Materials Park, OH 44073-0002. Phone: 800-336-5152 or (440)338-5151 Fax: (440)338-4634 E-mail: memserv@po.asm-intl.org • URL: http://www.asm-intl.org • 1994. $139.00. Second edition. Provides information on a wide range of materials, with special sections on ceramics, industrial glass products, and plastics.

ASM International., 9639 Kinsman Rd. Materials Park, OH 44073. Phone: 800-336-5152 or (216)338-5151 Fax: (216)338-4634 E-mail: memserv@po.asm-intl.org • URL: http://www.asm-intl.org • Members are materials engineers, metallurgists, industry executives, educators, and others concerned with a wide range of materials and metals. Divisions include Aerospace, Composites, Electronic Materials and Processing, Energy, Highway/Off-Highway Vehicle, Joining, Materials Testing and Quality Control, Society of Carbide and Tool Engineers, and Surface Engineering.

ASM Materials Engineering Dictionary. Joseph R. Davis, editor. ASM International, 9639 Kinsman Rd. Materials Park, OH 44073-0002. Phone: 800-336-5152 or (440)338-5151 Fax: (440)338-4634 E-mail: cust.serv@po.asm-intl.org • URL: http://www.asm.intl.org • 1992. $146.00. Contains 10,000 entries, 700 illustrations, and 150 tables relating to metals, plastics, ceramics, composites, and adhesives. Includes "Technical Briefs" on 64 key material groups.

ASM Metals Reference Book. Michael L. Bauccio, editor. ASM International, 9639 Kinsman Rd. Materials Park, OH 44073-0002. Phone: 800-336-5152 or (440)338-5151 Fax: (440)338-4634 E-mail: cust-serv@po.sm-intl.org • URL: http://www.asm-intl.org • 1993. $144.00. Third edition. Includes glossary, tables, formulas, and diagrams. Covers a wide range of ferrous and nonferrous metals.

Asphalt. Asphalt Institute, P.O. Box 14052 Lexington, KY 40512-4052. Phone: (606)288-4960 Fax: (606)288-4999 URL: http://www.asphaltinstitute.org • Three times a year. Free.

Asphalt Emulsion Manufacturers Association.

Asphalt Institute.

Asphalt Products and Markets. Available from MarketResearch.com, 641 Ave. of the Americas, 3rd Fl. New York, NY 10011. Phone: 800-298-5699 or (212)807-2629 Fax: (212)807-2716 E-mail: order@marketresearch.com • URL: http://www.marketresearch.com • 1998. $3,200.00. Published by the Freedonia Group. Market data with forecasts to 2002 and 2007. Includes information on paving, coating, and roofing asphalt products.

Asphalt Roofing Manufacturers Association.

Assembly. Cahners Business Information, 2000 Clearwater Drive Oak Brook, IL 60523. Phone: 800-826-6270 or (630)320-7000 Fax: (630)320-7101 URL: http://www.cahners.com • Monthly. $68.00 per year. Covers assembly, fastening, and joining systems. Includes information on automation and robotics.

Assembly Buyer's Guide. Cahners Business Information, 2000 Clearwater Drive Oak Brook, IL 60523. Phone: 800-826-6270 or (630)320-7000 Fax: (630)320-7101 URL: http://www.cahners.com • Annual. $25.00. Lists manufacturers and suppliers of equipment relating to assembly automation, fasteners, adhesives, robotics, and power tools.

Assessing Service Quality: Satisfying the Expectations of Library Customers. Peter Hernon and Ellen Altman. American Library Association, 50 E. Huron St. Chicago, IL 60611-2795. Phone: 800-545-2433 or (312)944-6780 Fax: (312)440-9374 URL: http://www.ala.org • 1998. $40.00. Discusses surveys, focus groups, and other data collection methods for measuring the quality of library service. Includes sample forms and an annotated bibliography.

Assessment Journal. International Association of Assessing Officers, 130 E. Randolph St., Suite 850 Chicago, IL 60601-6217. Phone: (312)819-6100 Fax: (312)819-6149 E-mail: webmaster@iaao.org • URL: http://www.iaao.org • Bimonthly. Free to members; non-members, $200.00 per year. Formed by merger of *Assessment* and *Valuation Legal Reporter and IAAO Update*.

Asset Allocation and Financial Market Timing: Techniques for Investment Professionals. Carroll D. Aby and Donald E. Vaughn. Greenwood Publishing Group, Inc., 88 Post Rd., W. Westport, CT 06881-5007. Phone: 800-225-5800 or (203)226-3571 Fax: (203)222-2540 E-mail: bookinfo@greenwood.com • URL: http://www.greenwood.com • 1995. $77.50.

Asset Management. Dow Jones Financial Publishing Corp., 170 Ave. at the Common Shrewsbury, NJ 07002. Phone: (732)389-8700 Fax: (732)389-6065 URL: http://www.djfpc.com • Bimonthly. $345.00 per year. Covers the management of the assets of affluent, high net worth investors. Provides information on various financial products and services.

Asset Protection Planning Guide: A State-of-the-Art Approach to Integrated Estate Planning. Barry S. Engel and others. CCH, Inc., 4025 West Peterson Ave. Chicago, IL 60646-6085. Phone: 800-248-3248 or (773)866-6000 Fax: 800-224-8299 or (773)866-3608 E-mail: cust_serv@cch.com • URL: http://www.cch.com • 2001. $99.00. Provides advice for attorneys, trust officers, accountants, and others engaged in financial planning for protection of assets.

Assets and Liabilities of Commercial Banks in the United States. U. S. Federal Reserve System, Board of Governors, Publications Services, MS-127 Washington, DC 20551. Phone: (202)452-3244 Fax: (202)728-5886 URL: http://www.federalreserve.gov • Weekly. $30.00 per year. (Federal Reserve Statistical Release, H.8.)

Assisted Living Success. Virgo Publishing, Inc., 3300 N. Central Ave., Suite 2500 Phoenix, AZ 85012. Phone: (480)990-1101 Fax: (480)675-8109 URL: http://www.alsuccess.com • Monthly. $55.00 per year. Edited for owners, operators, and managers of assisted living facilities.

Assisted Living Today. Assisted Living Federation of America, 10300 Eaton Place, Suite 400 Fairfax, VA 22030-2239. Phone: (703)691-8100 Fax: (703)691-8106 E-mail: altoday@strattonpub.com • URL: http://www.alfa.org • Nine times a year. $30.00 per year. Covers the management, marketing, and financing of assisted living residences.

Associated Builders and Contractors.

Associated Collegiate Press. University of Minnesota

Associated Cooperage Industries of America.

Associated Corset and Brassiere Manufacturers.

Associated Equipment Distributors.

Associated General Contractors of America.

Associated General Contractors of America: Highway Division.

Associated Glass and Pottery Manufacturers.

Associated Locksmiths of America.

Associated Press Managing Editors.

Associated Press Stylebook and Libel Manual. Addison-Wesley Longman, Inc., One Jacob Way Reading, MA 01867. Phone: 800-447-2226 or (781)944-3700 Fax: (781)944-9351 URL: http://www.awl.com • 1996. $14.00. Sixth edition.

Associated Specialty Contractors.

Associated Surplus Dealers.

Associated Writing Programs., George Mason University, Tallwood House, Mail Stop 1E3 Fairfax, VA 22030. Phone: (703)933-4301 Fax: (703)933-4302 E-mail: awp@gmu.edu • URL: http://www.web.gmu.edu/departments/awp • Purpose is to help writers get published or get jobs.

Association Executive Compensation Study. American Society of Association Executives, 1575 Eye St., N.W. Washington, DC 20005-1168. Phone: (202)626-2723 or (202)626-2742 Fax: (202)371-8825 E-mail: books@asaenet.org • URL: http://www.asaenet.org • 1999. $150.00. A salary survey.

Association for Accounting Administration., 136 S. Keowee St. Dayton, OH 45402. Phone: (937)222-0030 Fax: (937)222-5794 E-mail: aaainfo@cpaadmin.org • URL: http://www.cpaadmin.org • Members are accounting and office systems executives. Includes an Information Management Committee.

Association for Advanced Life Underwriting.

Association for Business Communication.

Association for Business Simulation and Experiential Learning.

Association for Career and Technical Education.

Association for Computational Linguistics.

Association for Computing Machinery., 1515 Broadway, 17th Fl. New York, NY 10036. Phone: (212)626-0500 Fax: (212)944-1318 E-mail: acmhelp@acm.org • URL: http://www.acm.org • Includes many Special Interest Groups.

Association for Computing Machinery Communications. Association for Computing Machinery, 1515 Broadway, 17th Fl. New York, NY 10036-5701. Phone: (212)626-0500 Fax: (212)944-1318 E-mail: crawford_d@acm.org • URL: http://www.acm.org • Monthly. Free to members; non-members, $114.00 per year.

Association for Computing Machinery Journal. Association for Computing Machinery, 1515 Broadway, 17th Fl. New York, NY 10036-5701. Phone: (212)869-7440 Fax: (212)944-1318 URL: http://www.acm.org • Quarterly. Members, $45.00 per year; non-members, $200.00 per year.

Association for Continuing Higher Education.

Association for Corporate Growth.

Association for Correctional Research and Information Management., 1129 Rivara Court Sacramento, CA 95864-3720. Phone: (916)487-9334 Fax: (916)487-9929 E-mail: ajipres@aol.com • Research areas include the statistics of prisons and jails.

Association for Data Center, Networking and Enterprise Systems., 742 E. Chapman Ave. Orange, CA 92666. Phone: (714)997-7966 Fax: (714)997-9743 E-mail: afcom@afcom.com • URL: http://www.afcom.com • Members are data processing operations management professionals.

Association for Education in Journalism and Mass Communication.

Association for Educational Communications and Technology.

Association for Facilities Engineering.

Association for Financial Counseling and Planning Education., 2121 Arlington Ave., Suite 5 Upper Arlington, OH 43221. Phone: (614)485-9650 Fax: (614)485-9621 E-mail: sburns@finsolve.com • URL: http://www.afcpe.org • Members are professional financial planners and academics.

Association for Financial Professionals., 7315 Wisconsin Ave., Suite 600-W Bethesda, MD 20814-3211. Phone: (301)907-2862 Fax: (301)907-2864 E-mail: afp@afponline.org • URL: http://www.afponline.org • Members are corporate treasurers and other managers of business finance. Formerly Treasury Management Association.

Association for Financial Technology., Blendonview Office Park, 5008-2 Pine Creek Dr. Westerville, OH 43081-4899. Phone: (614)895-1208 Fax: (614)895-3466 E-mail: aft@fitech.org • URL: http://www.fitech.org • Concerned with bank computer technology.

Association for Finishing Processes of the Society of Manufacturing Engineers., P.O. Box 930 Dearborn, MI 48121-0930. Phone: 800-733-4863 or (313)271-1500 Fax: (313)271-2861 URL: http://www.sme.org • Sponsored by the Society of Manufacturing Engineers.

Association for Healthcare Resource and Materials Management., c/o American Hospital Association, One N. Franklin St . Chicago, IL 60606. Phone: (312)422-3840 Fax: (312)422-3573 E-mail: ahrmm@aha.org • URL: http://www.ahrmm.org • Members are involved with the purchasing and distribution of supplies and equipment for hospitals and other healthcare establishments. Affiliated with the American Hospital Association.

Association for Information and Image Management., 1100 Wayne Ave., Suite 1100 Silver Spring, MD 20910-5603. Phone: (301)587-8202 Fax: (301)587-2711 E-mail: aiim@aiim.org • URL: http://www.aiim.org • Members are producers and users of image management equipment.

Association for Interactive Media., 1301 Connecticut Ave. N.W., 5th Fl. Washington, DC 20036-5105. Phone: (202)408-0008 Fax: (202)408-0111 E-mail: info@interactivehg.org • URL: http://www.interactivehg.org • Members are companies engaged in various interactive enterprises, utilizing the Internet, interactive television, computer communications, and multimedia.

Association for Investment Management and Research.

Association for Investment Management and Research-Membership Directory. Association for Investment Management and Research, P.O. Box 3668 Charlottesville, VA 22903-0668. Phone: 800-247-8132 or (804)951-5499 Fax: (804)951-5262 E-mail: info@aimr.org • URL: http://www.aimr.org • Annual. $150.00. Members are professional investment managers and securities analysts.

Association for Library Collections and Technical Services.

Association for Management Information in Financial Services., 7950 E. La Junta Rd. Scottsdale, AZ 85255-2798. Phone: (602)515-2160 Fax: (602)515-2101 E-mail: ami@amifs.org • URL: http://www.amifs.org • Members are financial institution employees interested in management accounting and cost analysis.

Association for Quality and Participation.

Association for Science, Technology and Innovation.

Association for Suppliers of Printing and Publishing Technologies.

Association for the Advancement of Medical Instrumentation., 3330 Washington Blvd., Suite 400 Arlington, VA 22201. Phone: 800-332-2264 or (703)525-4890 Fax: (703)276-0793 Members are engineers, technicians, physicians, manufacturers, and others with an interest in medical instrumentation.

Association for the Advancement of Medical Instrumentation Membership Directory. Association for the Advancement of Medical Instrumentation, 3330 Washington Blvd., Suite 400 Arlington, VA 22201-4598. Phone: 800-332-2264 or (703)525-4890 Fax: (703)276-0793 E-mail: publications@aami.org • URL: http://www.aami.org • Annual. Membership. List 6,500 physicians, clinical engineers, biomedical engineersand technicians and nurses, researchers, and medical equipment manufacturers.

Association for Transportation Law, Logistics, and Policy.

Association for University Business and Economic Research Membership Directory. Association for University Business and Economic Research, 801 W. Michigan St. Indianapolis, IN 46202-5151. Phone: (317)274-2204 Fax: (317)274-3312 Annual. $10.00. Member institutions in the United States and abroad with centers, bureaus, departments, etc., concerned with business and economic research.

Association for Unmanned Vehicle Systems., 1200 19th St., N.W., No. 300 Washington, DC 20036-2422. Phone: (202)857-1899 Fax: (202)223-4579 E-mail: auvsi@dc.erols.com • URL: http://www.auvsi.org/auvsicc • Concerned with the development of unmanned systems and robotics technologies.

The Association for Work Process Improvement., 185 Devonshire St., Suite 770 Boston, MA 02110-1407. Phone: 800-998-2974 or (617)426-1167 Fax: (617)521-8675

E-mail: Info@tawpi.org • URL: http://www.tawpi.org • Members are companies that use or supply various recognition technologies equipment.

Association for Worksite Health Promotion., 60 Revere Dr., Suite 500 Northbrook, IL 60062-1577. Phone: (847)480-9574 Fax: (847)480-9282 E-mail: awhp@awhp.com • URL: http://www.awhp.com • Members are physical fitness professionals hired by major corporations to conduct health and fitness programs.

Association Management. American Society of Association Executives, 1575 Eye St., N.W. Washington, DC 20005-1168. Phone: (202)626-2723 Fax: (202)371-8825 E-mail: asea@asaenet.org • URL: http://www.asaenet.org • Monthly. $30.00.

Association Meeting Trends. American Society of Association Executives, 1575 Eye St., N. W. Washington, DC 20005-1168. Phone: (202)626-2723 Fax: (202)371-8825 E-mail: asea@asaenet.org • URL: http://www.asaenet.org • 1999. $90.00.

Association of African-American Women Business Owners.

Association of American Chambers of Commerce in Latin America.

Association of American Colleges and Universities.

Association of American Pesticide Control Officials.

Association of American Plant Food Control Officials.

Association of American Plant Food Control Officials Official Publication. Association of American Plant Food Control Officials, Inc. University of Kentucky, Div. of Regulatory Services Lexington, KY 40546. Phone: (606)257-2668 Fax: (606)257-7351 E-mail: dterry@ca.uky.edu • URL: http://www.uky.edu/agriculture/regulatorservices/aapfco • Annual. $25.00.

Association of American Publishers.

Association of American Railroads.

Association of American Seed Control Officials.

Association of American Universities.

Association of American University Presses.

Association of America's Public Televised Stations.

Association of Artist-Run Galleries.

Association of Asphalt Paving Technologists.

Association of Authors' Representatives.

Association of Career Management Consulting Firms International., 204 E. St., N.E. Washington, DC 20002. Phone: (202)857-1185 Fax: (202)547-6348 URL: http://www.aocfi.org • Promotes professional standards of competence, objectivity, and integrity in the service of clients.

Association of Cinema and Video Laboratories.

Association of College and Research Libraries.

Association of Consulting Chemists and Chemical Engineers.

Association of Container Reconditioners-Membership and Industrial Supply Directory. Association of Container Reconditioners, 8401 Corporate Dr., Suite 140 Landover, MD 20785. Phone: 800-533-3786 or (301)577-3786 Fax: (301)577-6476 E-mail: prankin@igc.apc.org • Annual. $30.00. Lists approximately 215 container reconditioners and dealers, worldwide. Also lists suppliers of machinery and accessories.

Association of Defense Trial Attorneys.

Association of Diesel Specialists.

Association of Directory Publishers.

Association of Edison Illuminating Companies.

Association of Energy Engineers., 4025 Pleasantdale Rd., Suite 420 Atlanta, GA 30340. Phone: (770)447-5083 Fax: (770)446-3969 E-mail: info@aeecenter.org • URL: http://www.aeecenter.org • Members are engineers and other professionals concerned with energy management and cogeneration.

Association of Executive Search Consultants.

Association of Family and Conciliation Courts., c/o Ann Milne, 329 W. Wilson Madison, WI 53703. Phone: (608)251-4001 Fax: (608)251-2231 E-mail: afcc@afccnet.org • Members are judges, attorneys, and family counselors. Promotes conciliation counseling as a complement to legal procedures.

Association of Food Industries.

Association of Free Community Papers.

Association of Golf Merchandisers., P.O. Box 19899 Fountain Hills, AZ 85269. Phone: (480)373-8564 Fax: (480)373-8518 Members are vendors of gold equipment and merchandise.

Association of Governing Boards of Universities and Colleges.

Association of Government Accountants., 2208 Mount Vernon Ave. Alexandria, VA 22301-1314. Phone: 800-242-7211 or (703)684-6931 Fax: (703)548-9367 URL: http://www.agacgfm.org • Members are employed by federal, state, county, and city government agencies. Includes accountants, auditors, budget officers, and other government finance administrators and officials.

Association of Graduate Schools in the Association of American Universities.

Association of Home Appliance Manufacturers.

Association of Independent Information Professionals., 10290 Monroe Dr. Dallas, TX 75229. Phone: (609)730-8759 E-mail: aiipinfo@aiip.org • URL: http://www.aiip.org • Members are information brokers, document providers, librarians, consultants, database designers, webmasters, and other information professionals. Formerly International Association of Independent Information Brokers.

Association of Industrial Metallizers, Coaters and Laminators.

Association of Information and Dissemination Centers.

Association of Information Technology Professionals.

Association of Insolvency Accountants.

Association of International Automobile Manufacturers.

Association of International Marketing., P.O. Box 70 London E13 8BQ, England. Phone: 44 181 9867539 Fax: 44 181 9867539 A multinational organization. Promotes the advancement and exchange of information and ideas in international marketing.

Association of Iron and Steel Engineers.

Association of Knitted Fabrics Manufacturers.

Association of Learned and Professional Society Publishers.

Association of Life Insurance Counsel., c/o J. Michael Keefer, 200 E. Berry St. Fort Wayne, IN 46802. Phone: (219)455-5582 Fax: (219)455-5403 Members are attorneys for life insurance companies.

Association of Local Air Pollution Control Officials.

Association of Local Television Stations., 1320 19th St., N.W., Suite 300 Washington, DC 20036. Phone: (202)887-1970 Fax: (202)887-0950 E-mail: altv@aol.com • URL: http://www.altv.com • Members are TV stations not affiliated with a major network.

Association of Management Consulting Firms., 380 Lexington Ave., No. 1699 New York, NY 10168-0002. Phone: (212)697-9693 Fax: (212)949-6571 E-mail: info@amcf.org • URL: http://www.amcf.org • Members are management consultants. One of the two divisions of the Council of Consulting Organizations.

Association of Marine Engine Manufacturers.

Association of Master of Business Administration Executives.

Association of Minicomputer Users.

Association of National Advertisers.

Association of Oil Pipe Lines.

Association of Operative Millers.

Association of Paid Circulation Publications.

Association of Performing Arts Presenters.

Association of Private Pension and Welfare Plans., 1212 New York Ave., N. W., Suite 1250 Washington, DC 20005-3987. Phone: (202)289-6700 Fax: (202)289-4582 URL: http://www.appwp.org • Members are large and small business firms offering pension and other benefit plans for their employees.

Association of Professional Material Handling Consultants.

Association of Promotion Marketing Agencies Worldwide.

Association of Publicly Traded Companies.

Association of Records Managers and Administrators.

Association of Research Libraries.

Association of Retail Travel Agents.

Association of School Business Officials International.

Association of Schools of Journalism and Mass Communication.

Association of Ship Brokers and Agents-U.S.A., 75 Main St. Millburn, NJ 07041. Phone: (973)376-4144 Fax: (973)376-4145 Includes a Tanker Committee.

Association of State and Interstate Water Pollution Control Administrators.

Association of Steel Distributors.

Association of Telemessaging Services International-Membership Directory. Association of Telemessaging Services International, Inc., 1200 19th St. N.W., Suite 300 Washington, DC 20036-2422. Phone: (202)429-5151 Fax: (202)223-4579 E-mail: atsi@dc.sba.com • Annual. $100.00. Lists 825 telephone answering services.

Association of Telephone Answering Services.

Association of Teleservices International., 1800 Diogonal Rd., Ste. 645 Alexandria, VA 22314. Phone: (703)684-4406 Fax: (703)684-2957 E-mail: atsi@dc.sba.com • URL: http://www.atsi.org • An organization of telephone answering and voice message services.

Association of the United States Army.

Association of Theatrical Press Agents and Managers., 1560 Broadway, Suite 700 New York, NY 10036. Phone: (212)719-3666 Fax: (212)302-1585 E-mail: atpam@erols.com • A labor union for theater managers and press agents.

Association of Trial Lawyers of America.

Association of Wall and Ceiling Industries - International.

Association Operating Ratio Report. American Society of Association Executives, 1575 Eye St., N. W. Washington, DC 20005-1168. Phone: (202)626-2723 Fax: (202)371-8825 E-mail: asea@aseanet.org • URL: http://www.asaenet.org • 1997. $165.00. Contains comparison data from associations.

Association Sales and Marketing Companies.

Association Trends. Martineau Corporation, 7910 Woodmont Ave., No. 1150 Bethesda, MD 20814. Phone: (301)652-8666 Fax: (301)656-8654 Weekly. $95.00 per year. For staff executives of national, local, regional trade and professional associations. Contains news and information on association management and related issues.

Associations Canada: The Directory of Associations in Canada. Micromedia, 20 Victoria St. Toronto, ON, Canada M5C 2N8. Phone: 800-387-2689 or (416)362-5211 Fax: (416)362-6161 E-mail: info@micromedia.on.ca • URL: http://www.circ.micromedia.on.ca • Annual. $299.00. Provides detailed information in English and French on 20,000 active Canadian associations. Includes subject, keyword, personal name, and other indexes. Formerly *Directory of Associations in Canada*.

Associations Unlimited. The Gale Group, 27500 Drake Rd. Farmington Hills, MI 48331-3535. Phone: 800-877-GALE or (248)699-GALE Fax: 800-414-5043 or (248)699-8069 E-mail: galeord@gale.com • URL: http://www.gale.com • Semiannual. Includes all information on CD-ROM from all of the Gale *Encyclopedia of Associations* directories, plus association materials from about 2,500 of the associations-full-text documents and membership applications.

Associations Yellow Book: Who's Who at the Leading U. S. Trade and Professional Associations. Leadership Directories, Inc., 104 Fifth Ave., 2nd Fl. New York, NY 10011. Phone: (212)627-4140 Fax: (212)645-0931 E-mail: info@leadershipdirectories.com • URL: http://www.leadershipdirectories.com • Semiannual. $235.00 per year. Gives the names and titles of over 43,000 staff members in about 1,100 major associations. Six indexes are included: association name, individual name, industry, budget, acronym, and political action committee (PAC).

ASTA Agency Management: Official Publication of American Society of Travel Agents, Inc. Pace Communications, 1301 Carolina St. Greensboro, NC 27401. Phone: (910)378-6065 Fax: (910)378-6828 Monthly. $36.00 per year.

ASTM List of Publications. American Society for Testing and Materials (ASTM), 100 Barr Harbor Dr. W. Conshohocken, PA 19428-2959. Phone: (610)832-9500 Fax: (610)832-9555 E-mail: service@astm.org • URL: http://www.astm.org • Annual.

ASTM Standardization News. American Society for Testing and Materials, 100 Barr Harbor Dr., W. Conshohocken, PA 19428-2959. Phone: (610)832-9500 Fax: (610)832-9555 E-mail: service@astm.org • URL: http://www.astm.org • Monthly. $18.00 per year.

Astronomy. Kalmbach Publishing Co., P.O. Box 1612 Waukesha, WI 53187-1612. Phone: 800-558-1544 or (262)796-8776 Fax: (262)798-6468 E-mail: webmaster@kalmbach.com • URL: http://www.kalmbach.com • Monthly. $39.95 per year.

ASU Travel Guide: The Airline Employee's Discount Directory. Christopher Gil, editor. A S U Travel Guide, Inc., 1525 Francisco Blvd., E. San Rafael, CA 94901. Phone: (415)459-0300 Fax: (415)459-0494 URL: http://www.asuguide.com • Quarterly. $34.95. Lists air travel discounts available to airline employees.

AT & T Toll Free National Directory. AT&T Yellow Pages Directories, PO Box 414991 Kansas City, MO 64141-4991. Phone: 800-562-2255 or (908)658-2255 URL: http://www.tollfree.att.net • Annual. Business edition, $24.99 per year; consumer edition, $14.99 per year. Formerly *AT&T Toll Free 800 Directory*.

ATA Chronicle. American Translators Association, 225 Reinekers Lane, Suite 590 Alexandria, VA 22314-2875. Phone: (703)683-6100 Fax: (703)683-6122 URL: http://www.atanet.org • Monthly. $50.00.

ATA Translation Services Directory. American Translators Association, 225 Reinkers Lane, Suite 590 Alexandria, VA 22314. Phone: (703)683-6100 Fax: (703)683-6122 E-mail: ata@atanet.org • URL: http://www.ata.org • Avalible online. Over 3,700 member translators and interpreters. Formerly *Professional Services Directory of the American Translators Association*.

ATEA Journal. American Technical Education Association, Inc., North Dakota State College of Science, 800 N. Sixth St. Wahpeton, ND 58076. Phone: (701)671-2240 Fax: (701)671-2260 E-mail: krump@plains.nodak.edu • URL: http://www.ndscs.nodak.edu/atea • Four times a year. Individuals, $40.00 per year; institutions, $150.00; corporations, $200.00 per year.

Athletic Business. Athletic Business Publications, Inc., 4130 Lien Rd. Madison, WI 53704-3602. Phone: 800-722-8764 or (608)249-0186 Fax: (608)249-1153 E-mail: editors@athleticbusiness.com • Monthly. $50.00 per year. Published for those whose responsibility is the business of planning, financing and operating athletic/recreation/fitness programs and facilities.

Athletic Business: Professional Directory Section. Athletic Business Publications, Inc., 4130 Lien Rd. Madison, WI 53704-3602. Phone: 800-722-8764 or (608)249-0186 Fax: (608)249-1153 E-mail: abmag@aol.com • Monthly. $72.00 per year. Lists consultants in athletic facility planning, with architects, engineers, and contractors. Appears in each issue of *Athletic Business*.

Athletic Management. Momentum Media, 2488 N. Triphammer Rd. Ithaca, NY 14850-1014. Phone: (607)257-6970 Fax: (607)257-7328 E-mail: inform@mementummedia.com •

Bimonthly. $24.00 per year. Formerly *College Athletic Management*.

Atlas & Gazetteer Series. DeLorme Mapping Co., Two DeLorme Dr. Yarmouth, ME 04096. Phone: 800-569-8313 or (207)865-4171 Fax: 800-575-2244 or (207)865-7080 URL: http://www.delorme.com/reference • Dates vary. $649.95 complete ($74.95 per region). Consists of 50 volumes covering all areas of the U. S. Includes detailed maps, as well as descriptions of attractions, natural areas, and historic sites. (CD-ROM versions available.)

Atmospheric Environment. Elsevier Science, 655 Ave. of the Americas New York, NY 10010. Phone: 888-437-4636 or (212)989-5800 Fax: (212)633-3680 E-mail: usinfo@elsevier.com • URL: http://www.elsevier.com • 36 times a year. $4,402.00 per year. Text in English, French and German.

Atmospheric Sciences Research Center. University of Albany, State University of New York

Atomic Energy. Russian Academy of Sciences, RU. Plenum Publishing Corp., Consultants Bureau, 233 Spring St. New York, NY 10013-1578. Phone: 800-221-9369 or (212)620-8000 Fax: (212)463-0742 E-mail: info@plenum.com • URL: http://www.plenum.com • Monthly. $2,286.00 per year. Formerly *Soviet Atomic Energy*.

ATP-FAR 135, Airline Transport Pilot: A Comprehensive Text and Workbook for the en Exam. K.T. Boyd. Iowa State University Press, 2121 S. State Ave. Ames, IA 50014-8300. Phone: 800-862-6657 or (515)292-0140 Fax: (515)292-3348 E-mail: orders@isupress.edu • URL: http://www.isupress.edu • 1994. $29.95. Third edition.

Attorneys and Agents Registered to Practice Before United States Patent and Trademark Office. U.S. Patent and Trademark Office. Available from U.S. Government Printing Office, Washington, DC 20402. Phone: (202)512-1800 Fax: (202)512-2250 E-mail: gpoaccess@gpo.gov • URL: http://www.access.gpo.gov • Annual. $56.00.

Attorneys' Dictionary of Medicine. J. E. Schmidt. Matthew Bender & Shepherd, Two Park Ave. New York, NY 10016. Phone: 800-223-1940 or (212)448-2000 Fax: (212)244-3188 E-mail: international@bender.com • URL: http://www.bender.com • $570.00. Looseleaf service. Six volumes. Periodic supplementation. Includes common lay words that lead to correct medical terms.

Attorney's Dictionary of Patent Claims: Legal Materials and Practice Commentaries. Irwin M. Aisenberg. Matthew Bender & Co., Inc., Two Park Ave. New York, NY 10016. Phone: 800-223-1940 or (212)448-2000 Fax: (212)244-3188 E-mail: international@bender.com • URL: http://www.bender.com • Looseleaf service. Two volumes. $470.00. Periodic supplementation. Operational guidance for bank officers, with analysis of statutory law and agency regulations.

Attorneys' Textbook of Medicine. Matthew Bender & Co., Inc., Two Park Ave. New York, NY 10016. Phone: 800-223-1940 or (212)448-2000 Fax: (212)244-3188 E-mail: international@bender.com • URL: http://www.bender.com • Annual. $2,760.00. 23 looseleaf volumes. Quarterly updates. Periodic supplementation. Medico-legal material.

The Auctioneer. National Auctioneers Association, 8880 Ballentine Overland Park, KS 66214-1985. Phone: (913)541-8084 Fax: (913)894-5281 E-mail: naahq@aol.com • Monthly. Membership. News of interest to auctioneers.

AudArena Stadium International Guide and Facility Buyers Guide. BPI Communications, Amusement Business Div., P.O. Box 24970 Nashville, TN 37202. Phone: 800-407-6874 or (615)321-4250 Fax: (615)327-1575 URL: http://www.amusementbusiness.com • Annual. $95.00. More than 4,400 arenas, auditoriums, stadiums, exhibit halls, and coliseums in U.S., Canada and in less depth, Europe and South America. Formerly *Audarena Stadium International Guide*.

Audio. Hachette Filipacchi Magazines, Inc., 1633 Broadway, 43rd Fl. New York, NY 10019. Phone: 800-274-4027 or (212)767-6000 Fax: (212)767-5619 Monthly. $26.00 per year. Includes annual directory *Product Review*.

Audio Annual Product Review Directory. Hachette Filipacchi Magazines, Inc., 1633 Broadway New York, NY 10019. Phone: 800-274-4027 or (212)767-6000 Fax: (212)767-5633 Annual. $3.95.

Audio Electronics. John L. Hood. Butterworth-Heinemann, 225 Wildwood Ave. Woburn, MA 01801. Phone: 800-366-2665 or (781)904-2500 Fax: 800-446-6520 E-mail: orders@bhusa.com • URL: http://www.bh.com • 1999. $47.95. Second edition.

Audio Engineer's Reference Book. Michael Talbot-Smith, editor. Butterworth-Heinemann, 225 Wildwood Ave. Woburn, MA 01801. Phone: 800-366-2665 or (781)904-2500 Fax: 800-446-6520 E-mail: orders@bhusa.com • URL: http://www.bh.com • 1994. $165.00. Second edition.

Audio Recording and Reproduction: Practical Measures for Audio Enthusiasts. Michael Talbot-Smith. Butterworth-Heinemann, 225 Wildwood Ave. Woburn, MA 01801. Phone: 800-366-2665 or (781)904-2500 Fax: 800-446-6520 E-mail: orders@bhusa.com • URL: http://www.bh.com • 1994. $29.95.

Audio Week: The Authoritative News Service of the Audio Consumer Electronics Industry., 2115 Ward Court, N. W. Washington, DC 20037-1209. Phone: 800-771-9202 or (202)872-9200 Fax: (202)293-3435 E-mail: customerservice@warren-news.com • URL: http://www.telecommunications.com • Weekly. $617.00. Newsletter. Provdies audio industry news, company news, and new product information.

Audiotex Directory and Buyer's Guide. ADBG Publishing, P.O. Box 25929 Los Angeles, CA 90025. Phone: (310)479-3533 Fax: (310)479-0654 Annual. $55.00. Lists about 1,200 voice processing product and service companies. Includes speech synthesis and recognition products.

Audit Bureau of Circulations., 900 N. Meacham Rd. Schaumburg, IL 60173-4968. Phone: (847)605-0909 Fax: (847)605-0483 URL: http://www.accessabvs.com • Verifies newspaper and periodical circulation statements. Includes a Business Publications Industry Committee and a Magazine Directors Advisory Committee.

Auditing. Jack C. Robertson and Timothy J. Louwers. McGraw-Hill, 1221 Ave. of the Americas New York, NY 10020. Phone: 800-722-4726 or (212)904-2000 Fax: (212)904-2076 E-mail: customer.service@mcgraw-hill.com • URL: http://www.mcgraw-hill.com • 1998. $91.43. Ninth edition.

Auditing: Integrated Approach. Alvin A. Arens. Simon and Schuster Trade Prentice Hall, 1230 Ave. of the Americas, 240 Frisch Court Paramus, NJ 07652-5240. Phone: 800-922-0579 or (212)698-7000 Fax: 800-445-6991 URL: http://www.simonsays.com • 1999. $98.00. Eighth edition.

Auditing Research Monographs. American Institute of Certified Public Accountants, 1211 Ave. of the Americas New York, NY 10036-8775. Phone: 800-862-4272 or (212)596-6200 Fax: (212)596-6213 E-mail: journal@aicpa.org • URL: http://www.aicpa.org/pubs • Irregular. Price varies.

Audits of Brokers and Dealers in Securities. American Institute of Certified Public Accountants, 1211 Ave. of the Americas New York, NY 10036-8775. Phone: 800-862-4272 or (212)596-6200 Fax: (212)596-6213 E-mail: journal@aicpa.org • URL: http://www.aicpa.org/pubs • $33.00. Fourth edition.

Author Biographies Master Index. The Gale Group, 27500 Drake Rd. Farmington Hills, MI 48331-3535. Phone: 800-877-GALE or (248)699-GALE Fax: 800-414-5043 or (248)699-8069 E-mail: galeord@galegroup.com • URL: http://www.galegroup.com • 1997. $290.00. Fith edition. Two volumes. Contains over 1,140,000 references tobiographies of 550,000 different authors.

Authors Guild.

Authors League of America.

Auto-Cite. West Group, 610 Opperman Dr. Eagan, MN 55123. Phone: 800-328-4880 or (651)687-7000 Fax: (651)687-5827 URL: http://www.westgroup.com • Provides information concerning federal and state case law, administrative decisions, and taxation. Daily updates. Inquire as to online cost and availability.

Auto Industries of Europe, U.S. and Japan. Richard Phillps and others. HarperInformation, 10 E. 53rd St. New York, NY 10022-5299. Phone: 800-242-7737 or (212)207-7000 Fax: 800-822-4090 or (212)207-7145 URL: http://www.harpercollins.com • 1982. $32.00. (Economist Intelligence Series).

Auto Laundry News: The Voice of the Car Care Industry. E.W. Williams Publications Co., 2125 Center Ave., Suite 305 Fort Lee, NJ 07024. Phone: (201)532-9290 Fax: (201)779-8345 Monthly. $48.00 per year. Covers management, technical information, trends, and marketing for the vehicle cleaning industry. Edited for owners, operators, managers, and investors.

Autocar. Haymarket Publishing, Ltd., 38-42 Hampton Rd. Teddington TW11 OJE, England. Monthly. $230.00 per year. Formerly *Autocar and Motor*.

Automated Builder Annual Buyers' Guide. CMN Publications, 1445 Donlon St., Suite 16 Ventura, CA 93003-5640. Phone: 800-344-2537 or (805)642-9735 Fax: (805)642-8820 E-mail: automatedbuilder.com • URL: http://www.autbldrmag.com/ • Annual. $12.00. Over 250 manufacturers and suppliers to the manufactured and pre-fabricated housing industry.

Automated Builder: The No. 1 International Housing Technology Transfer Magazine for Manufacturing and Marketing. CMN Publications, 1445 Donlon St., Suite 16 Ventura, CA 93003-5640. Phone: 800-344-2537 or (805)642-9735 Fax: (805)642-8820 E-mail: bob@automatedbuilders.com • URL: http://www.automatedbuilders.com • 11 times a year. Free to qualified personnel; others, $50.00 per year. Annual *Buyers' Guide* available.

Automated Imaging Association., P.O. Box 3724 Ann Arbor, MI 48106. Phone: (313)994-6088 Fax: (313)994-3338 E-mail: aia@automated-imaging.org • URL: http://www.automated-imaging.org • Promotes the use of machine vision technology.

Automatic Control Systems. Benjamin C. Kuo. Simon and Schuster Trade, 1230 Ave. of the Americas New York, NY 10020. Phone: 800-223-2336 or (212)698-7000 Fax: (212)698-7007 E-mail: ssonline_feedback@simonsays.com • URL: http://www.simonsays.com • 1999. $95.00. Seventh edition.

Automatic Fire Alarm Association.

Automatic Identification Manufacturers International., 623 Alpha Dr. Pittsburgh, PA 15238. Phone: (412)936-8009 Fax: (412)963-8753 Members are automatic identification manufacturers and suppliers. Systems may utilize bar codes, magnetic stripes, radio frequencies, machine vision, voice technology, optical character recognition, or systems integration.

Automatic Merchandiser. Cygnus Publishing, Inc., Johnson Hill Press, 1233 Janesville Ave. Fort Atkinson, WI 53538-0460. Phone: 800-547-7377 or (920)563-6388 Fax: (920)563-1707 E-mail: rich.reiff@cygnuspub.com • URL: http://www.cygnuspub.com • 11 times a year. $60.00 per year. Includes annual *Product* issue. Formerly *American Automatic Merchandiser*.

Automatica. Elsevier Science, 655 Ave. of the Americas New York, NY 10010. Phone: 888-437-4636 or (212)989-5800 Fax: (212)633-3680 E-mail: usinfo@elsevier.com • URL: http://www.elsevier.com • Bimonthly. $1,792.00 per year. Text in English, French, German, and Russian.

Automating the Small Library. William Saffady. American Library Association, 50 E. Huron St. Chicago, IL 60611-2795. Phone: 800-545-2433 or (312)944-6780 Fax: (312)440-9374 E-mail: ala@ala.org • URL: http://www.ala.org • 1991. $8.00. A concise overview of computer applications appropriate to small libraries. Covers circulation, cataloging, reference, acquisitions, and administration.

Automation. Available from U. S. Government Printing Office, Washington, DC 20402. Phone: (202)512-1800 Fax: (202)512-2250 E-mail: gpoaccess@gpo.gov • URL: http://www.access.gpo.gov • Annual. Free. Issued by the Superintendent of Documents. A list of government publications on automation, computers, and related topics. Formerly *Computers and Data Processing*. (Subject Bibliography No. 51.)

Automobile Insurance Losses, Collision Coverages, Variations by Make and Series. Highway Loss Data Institute, c/o Stephen L. Oesch, 1005 N. Glebe Rd., Suite 800 Arlington, VA 22201. Phone: (703)247-1600 Fax: (703)247-1678 E-mail: iihs@highwaysafety.org • URL: http://www.carsafety.com • Semiannual. Membership.

Automobile Liability Insurance. Irvin E. Schermer. West Group, 610 Opperman Dr. Eagan, MN 55123. Phone: 800-328-4880 or (651)687-7000 Fax: 800-213-2323 or (651)687-5827 URL: http://www.westgroup.com • Three looseleaf volumes. $395.00. Periodic supplementation.

Automobile Quarterly: The Connoisseur's Magazine of Motoring Today, Yesterday and Tomorrow. Automobile Quarterly, Inc., P.O. Box 348 Kutztown, PA 19530. Phone: 800-523-0236 or (610)683-3169 Fax: (610)683-3287 E-mail: agspec@fast.net • URL: http://www.autoquarterly.com • Five times a year. $89.95 per year.

Automobile Red Book Used Car Valuations. National Market Reports, Inc., 29 N. Wacker Dr. Chicago, IL 60606-3297. Phone: (312)726-2802 Fax: (312)855-0137 Eight times per year. $49.50 per year. Formerly *Automobile Red Book*.

Automotive Aftermarket Industry Association., 4600 East-West Highway, Suite 300 Bethesda, MD 20814-3415. Phone: (301)654-6664 Fax: (301)654-3299 E-mail: aia@aftermarket.org • URL: http://www.aftermarket.org • Retailers, distributors, and manufacturers.

Automotive Burglary Protection and Mechanical Equipment Directory. Underwriters Laboratories, Inc., 333 Pfingsten Rd. Northbrook, IL 60062-2096. Phone: (847)272-8800 Fax: (847)272-0472 E-mail: northbrook@ul.com • Annual. $10.00. Lists manufacturers authorized to use UL label.

Automotive Engine Rebuilders Association.

Automotive Engineering Magazine. Society of Automotive Engineers, 400 Commonwealth Dr. Warrendale, PA 15096-0001. Phone: 800-832-6723 or (724)776-4841 Fax: (724)776-5944 E-mail: sae@sae.org • URL: http://www.sae.org • Monthly. $96.00 per year. Provides 86,000 automotive product planners and engineers with state-of-the-art technology that can be applied to the development of new and improved vehicles. Supplement available *Off-Highway Engineering*.

Automotive Industries. Cahners Business Information, 301 Gibraltar Dr. Morris Plains, NJ 07950-0650. Phone: 800-662-7776 or (973)292-5100 E-mail: corporatecommunications@cahners.com • URL: http://www.cahners.com • Monthly. $74.00 per year.

Automotive Market Report. Automotive Auction Publishing, Inc., 1713 Ardmore Blvd. Pittsburgh, PA 15221-4405. Phone: (412)242-3900 Biweekly. $130.00 Per Year. Current wholesale values of used vehicles.

Automotive Market Research Council.

Automotive News: Engineering, Financial, Manufacturing, Sales, Marketing, Servicing. Crain Communications, Inc., 1400 Woodbridge Ave. Detroit, MI 48207-3187. Phone: 800-678-9595 Fax: (313)446-0383 URL: http://www.crain.com • Weekly. $114.00 per year. Business news coverage of the automobile industry at the retail, wholesale, and manufacturing levels. Includes statistics.

Automotive News Market Data Book. Crain Communications, Inc., 1400 Woodbridge Ave. Detroit, MI 48207-3187. Phone: 800-678-9595 or (313)446-6000 Fax: (313)446-0383 URL: http://www.crain.com • Annual. $19.95. Directory of automotive vendors and worldwide vehicle manufacturing. Formerly *Automotive News Almanac*.

Automotive Recycling. Automotive Recyclers Association, 3975 Fair Ridge Dr., Suite 20N Fairfax, VA 22033-2924. Phone: (703)385-1001 Bimonthly. Free to members; non-members, $40.00 per year. Foremrly *Dismantl ers Digest*.

Automotive Service Association., P.O. Box 929 Bedford, TX 76095-0929. Phone: 800-272-7467 or (817)283-6205 Fax: (817)685-0225 E-mail: asainfo@asashop.org • URL: http://www.asashop.org • Members are body, paint, radiator, transmission, brake, and other shops or garages doing automotive repair work.

Automotive Service Industry Association., 25 Northwest Point Elk Grove Village, IL 60007-1035. Phone: (847)228-1310 Fax: (847)228-1510 Members are distributors and manufacturers of automotive replacement parts.

Automotive Trade Association Executives.

Automotive Troubleshooting: Glossary. William Carroll. Coda Publication, P.O. Box 711 San Marcos, CA 92069-0711. Phone: (760)727-0100 E-mail: sdbooks@adnc.com • URL: http://www.sandiego-books.com • 1973. $5.00.

Automotive Warehouse Distributors Association.

Automotive Warehouse Distributors Association-Membership Directory. Automotive Warehouse Distributors Association, PO Box 13966 Research Triangle Park, NC 27709-3966. Phone: (919)549-4800 Fax: (919)549-4824 Annual. $100.00. Over 500 automotive parts distributors, 200 manufacturers of automotive parts, and 8 marketing associations,17 manufacturer representatives, and 15 affiliate members.

AV Guide: The Learning Media Newsletter. Educational Screen, Inc., 380 E. Northwest Highway Des Plaines, IL 60016-2282. Phone: (847)391-1024 Fax: (847)390-0408 Monthly. $15.00 per year. Provides information on audiovisual aids. Formerly *AV Guide Newsletter*.

AV Market Place: The Complete Business Directory of: Audio, Audio Visual, Computer Systems, Film, Video, Programming - with industry yellow pages. R. R. Bowker, 121 Chanlon Rd. New Providence, NJ 07974. Phone: 888-269-5372 or (908)464-6800 Fax: (908)771-7704 E-mail: info@bowker.com • URL: http://www.bowker.com • Annual. $165.00. Lists over 7,000 producers and distributors of a wide variety of audiovisual and video equipment, computer systems, films, and tapes. Includes many application-specific listings.

AV Presentation Buyer's Guide. Cygnus Business Media, 445 Broad Hollow Rd. Melville, NY 11747. Phone: 800-308-6397 or (631)845-2700 Fax: (631)845-2798 E-mail: rich.reiff@cygnuspub.com • URL: http://wwww.cygnuspub.com • Annual. $6.00. Lists of film and slide laboratory services and manufacturers of media production and presentation equipment and audiovisual supplies. Formerly *Audio Visual Communications Buyer's Guide*.

Available Pay Survey Reports: An Annotated Bibliography. Abbott, Langer and Associates, 548 First St. Crete, IL 60417. Phone: (708)672-4200 Fax: (708)672-4674 1995. U.S. volume, $450.00; international volume, $160.00. Fourth edition.

Avery Architecture Index. Avery Architectural and Fine Arts Library, Columbia University New York, NY 10027. Phone: (212)854-8407 Fax: (212)854-8904 Indexes a wide range of periodicals related to architecture and design. Subjects include building design, building materials, interior design, housing, land use, and city planning. Time span: 1977 to date. *bul* URL: http://www-rlg.stanford.edu/cit-ave.html

Avery Index to Architectural Periodicals. Columbia University, Avery Architectural Library. Available from G.K. Hall Co., Macmillan Library Reference, PO Box 159 Thorndike, ME 04986. Phone: 800-223-6121 or (212)654-8275 Fax: (212)698-7336 URL: http://www.mlr.com • Annual. $995.00.

Aviation. Available from U. S. Government Printing Office, Washington, DC 20402. Phone: (202)512-1800 Fax: (202)512-2250 E-mail: gpoaccess@gpo.gov • URL: http://www.access.gpo.gov • Annual. Free. Lists government publications. (GPO Subject Bibliography Number 18).

Aviation Buyer's Directory. Air Service Directory, Inc., 105 Calvert St. Harrison, NY 10528-3138. Phone: (914)835-7200 Quarterly. $45.00 per year. Lists aircraft for sale and sources of parts and supplies.

Aviation Consumer Action Project.

Aviation Daily. Aviation Week Newsletter. McGraw-Hill, 1200 G St., N.W., Suite 200, Washington, DC 20005 New York, NY 10020. Phone: (202)383-2350 Fax: (202)383-2442 E-mail: customer.service@mcgraw-hill.com • URL: http://www.mcgraw-hill.com • Daily. $1,595.00 per year. Newsletter. Covers current developments in air transportation and aviation manufacturing.

Aviation Development Council.

Aviation Distributors and Manufacturers Association International.

Aviation Law Reports. CCH, Inc., 4025 W. Peterson Ave. Chicago, IL 60646-6085. Phone: 800-248-3248 or (773)583-8500 Fax: 800-224-8299 or(773)866- URL: http://www.cch.com • $2,419.00 per year. Four looseleaf volumes. Semimonthly updates.

Aviation Maintenance. Phillips Business Information, Inc., 1201 Seven Locks Rd., Suite 300 Potomac, MD 20854. Phone: 800-777-5006 or (301)340-1520 Fax: (301)309-3487 E-mail: pbi@phillips.com • URL: http://www.phillips.com/marketplaces.htm • Monthly. Free to qualified personnel. Formerly *Aviation Equipment Maintenance*.

Aviation Safety Institute.

Aviation Week and Space Technology. McGraw-Hill Aviation Week Group, 1200 G St., N.W., Ste. 922 Washington, DC 20005. Phone: 800-722-4726 or (202)383-2484 Fax: (202)383-2446 E-mail: avweek@mgh.com • URL: http://www.aviationnow.com • Monthly. $89.00 per year.

Avionics.

Avionics Engineering Center. Ohio University

Avionics Maintenance Conference.

Avis Licensee Directory. Avis Licensee Association, 300 Old Country Rd., Suite 341 Mineola, NY 11501. Phone: (516)747-4951 Fax: (516)747-0195 Irregular. Membership.

AVMA Directory. American Veterinary Medical Association, 1931 N Meacham Rd., Suite 100 Schaumburg, IL 60173-4360. Phone: 800-248-2862 or (847)925-8070 Fax: (847)925-1329 URL: http://www.avma.org/home.html • Annual. $90.00. 62,500 veterinarians; not limited to AVMA members. Formerly *American Veterinary Medical Association Directory*.

Avoiding Tax Malpractice. Robert Feinschreiber and Margaret Kent. CCH, Inc., 4025 West Peterson Ave. Chicago, IL 60646-6085. Phone: 800-248-3248 or (773)866-6000 Fax: 800-224-8299 or (773)866-3608 E-mail: cust_serv@cch.com • URL: http://www.cch.com • 2000. $75.00. Covers malpractice considerations for professional tax practitioners.

Awards and Recognition Association.

Awards, Honors, and Prizes. The Gale Group, 27500 Drake Rd. Farmington Hills, MI 48331-3535. Phone: 800-877-GALE or (248)699-GALE Fax: 800-414-5043 or (248)699-8069 E-mail: galeord@galegroup.com • URL: http://www.galegroup.com • 2001. 18th edition. Two volumes. Domestic volume, $245.00. International volume, $275.00.

AWO Letter. American Waterways Operators, 1600 Wilson Blvd., Suite 1000 Arlington, VA 22209. Phone: (703)841-9300 Fax: (703)841-0389 Biweekly. $75.00 per year. Formerly *AWO Weekly Letter*.

B to B Marketing: Creating and Implementing a Successful Business-to-Business Marketing Program. Philip G. Duffy. McGraw-Hill Professional, 1221 Ave. of the Americas New York, NY 10020. Phone: 800-722-4726 or (212)904-2000 Fax: (212)904-2072 E-mail: customer.service@mcgraw-hill.com • URL: http://www.mcgraw-hill.com • 1992. $29.95.

Baby and Junior: International Trade Magazine for Children's and Youth Fashions and Supplies. Meisenbach GmbH, Franz-Ludwig-Str.7A 96047 Bamberg, Germany. Phone: 49 951 861126 10 times a year. 60.00 per year. Text in German.

The Babysitter's Handbook. Dorling Kindersley Publishing, Inc., 95 Madison Ave., 10th Fl. New York, NY 10016. Phone: 888-342-5357 or (212)213-4800 Fax: (212)213-5240 URL: http://www.dk.com • 1995. $12.95.

Back Stage: The Performing Arts Weekly. BPI Communications, Inc., 770 Broadway New York, NY 10003-9595. Phone: 800-344-7119 or (646)654-5500 Fax: (646)654-5835 E-mail: info@bpi.com • URL: http://www.bpicomm.com • Weekly. $95.00 per year. A theatre trade newspaper for show business professionals.

Bacon's International Media Directory. Bacon's Publishing Co., Inc., 332 S. Michigan Ave. Chicago, IL 60604-4434. Phone: 800-621-0561 or (312)922-2400 Fax: (312)922-3127 E-mail: directories@baconsinfo.com • URL: http://www.baconsinfo.com • Annual. $295.00. Covers print media in Western Europe. Formerly *Bacon's International Publicity Checker*.

Bacon's Newspaper/Magazine Directories. Bacon's Publishing Co., 332 S. Michigan Ave. Chicago, IL 60604-4434. Phone: 800-621-0561 or (312)922-2400 Fax: (312)922-3127 E-mail: directories@baconsinfo.com • URL: http://www.baconsinfo.com • Annual. $295.00 per year. Quarterly update. Two volumes: Magazines and Newspapers. Covers print media in the United States and Canada. Formerly *Bacon's Publicity Checker*.

Bacon's Radio and TV Cable Directories. Bacon's Publishing Co., 332 S. Michigan Ave. Chicago, IL 60604-4434. Phone: 800-621-0561 or (312)922-2400 Fax: (312)922-3127 E-mail: directories@baconsinfo.com • URL: http://www.baconsinfo.com • Annual. $295.00. Two volumes. Includes educational and public broadcasters. Covers all United States broadcast media. Formerly *Bacon's Radio - TV Directory*.

Bailey's Industrial Oil and Fat Products. Alton E. Bailey. John Wiley and Sons, Inc., 605 Third Ave. New York, NY 10158-0012. Phone: 800-225-5945 or (212)850-6000 Fax: (212)850-6088 E-mail: info@wiley.comm • URL: http://www.wiley.com • 1996. $610.00. Five volumes. Fifth edition.

Baker's Manual. Joseph Amendola. John Wiley and Sons, Inc., 605 Third Ave. New York, NY 10158-0012. Phone: 800-842-3636 or (212)850-6000 Fax: (212)850-6088 E-mail: info@wiley.com • URL: http://www.wiley.com • 1993. $32.95. Fourth edition.

Bakery. Entrepreneur Media, Inc., 2445 McCabe Way Irvine, CA 92614. Phone: 800-421-2300 or (949)261-2325 Fax: (949)261-0234 E-mail: entmag@entrepreneur.com • URL: http://www.entrepreneur.com • Looseleaf. $59.50. A practical guide to starting a retail bakery. Covers profit potential, start-up costs, market size evaluation, owner's time required, site selection, lease negotiation, pricing, accounting, advertising, promotion, etc. (Start-Up Business Guide No. E1158.)

Bakery, Confectionery and Tobacco Workers International Union.

Baking and Snack. Sosland Publishing Co., 4800 Main St., Suite 100 Kansas City, MO 64112-2513. Phone: (816)756-1000 Fax: (816)756-0494 E-mail: bakesnack@sosland.com • Monthly. Free to qualified personnel; others, $30.00 per year. Covers manufacturing systems and ingredients for baked goods and snack foods.

Baking Industry Sanitation Standards Committee.

Balance. American College of Health Care Administrators, 325 S. Patrick St. Alexandria, VA 22314. Phone: 888-882-2422 or (703)739-7900 Fax: (703)739-7901 E-mail: info@achca.org • URL: http://www.achca.org • Eight times a year. Free to members; non-members, $80.00 per year. Includes research papers and articles on the administration of long term care facilities. Formerly*Continnum*.

The Balance of Payments in a Monetary Economy. John F. Kyle. Books on Demand, 300 Zeeb Rd. Ann Arbor, MI 48106-1346. Phone: 800-521-0600 or (734)761-4700 Fax: (734)665-5022 E-mail: info@umi.com • URL: http://www.lib.umi.com • 1976. $64.50. (Irving Fisher Award Series).

Balance of Payments Statistics. International Monetary Fund, 700 19th St., N.W. Washington, DC 20431-0001. Phone: (202)623-6180 Fax: (202)623-7201 Time series compiled by IMF, mid-1960's to present. Inquire as to online cost and availability.

Balanced Budgets and American Politics. James D. Savage. Cornell University Press, Sage House, 512 E. State St. Ithaca, NY 14851. Phone: 800-666-2211 or (607)257-2338 Fax: 800-688-2877 E-mail: orderbook@cupserv.org • URL: http://www.cornellpress.cornell.edu • 1988. $45.00. States the case for economic growth being more important than a balanced federal budget.

Baltia Kompass Business Disc. Available from Kompass USA, Inc., 1255 Route 70, Suite 25-S Lakewood, NJ 08701. Phone: 877-566-7277 or (732)730-0340 Fax: (732)730-0342 E-mail: mail@kompass-usa.com • URL: http://www.kompass.com • Annual. $360.00. CD-ROM provides information on more than 22,000 companies in Estonia, Latvia, and Lithuania. Classification system covers approximately 50,000 products and services.

The Banana: Its History, and Cultivation. Philip Keep Reynolds. Gordon Press Publishers, P.O. Box 459 New York, NY 10004. Phone: (212)969-8419 Fax: (718)624-8419 1981. $250.00. Reprint of 1977 edition.

Bank Accounting and Finance. Institutional Investor, 488 Madison Ave. New York, NY 10022. Phone: (212)224-3300 Fax: (212)224-3527 E-mail: info@iijournals.com • URL: http://www.iijournals.com • Quarterly. $250.00 per year. Emphasis is on the practical aspects of bank accounting and bank financial management.

Bank Administration Institute., One N. Franklin St., Suite 1000 Chicago, IL 60606. Phone: 800-224-9889 or (312)653-2464 Fax: (312)683-2373 E-mail: info@bai.org • URL: http://www.bai.org • Provides educational and advisory services to bank managers. Includes Audit Commission and Accounting and Finance Commission.

Bank Administration Institute; Operations and Technology Commission.

Bank and Lender Litigation Reporter: The Nationwide Litigation Report of Failed National and State Banks and Savings and Loan Associations, including FDIC and FSLIC Complaints and Related Actions Among Shareholders, Officers, Directors, Ins. Andrews Publications, 175 Strafford Ave., Bldg. 4, Suite 140 Wayne, PA 19087. Phone: 800-345-1101 or (610)622-0510 Fax: (610)622-0501 URL: http://www.andrewspub.com • Semimonthly. $875.00 per year. Provides summaries of significant litigation and regulatory agency complaints. Formerly *Lender Liability Litigation Reporter*.

Bank and Quotation Record. William B. Dana Co., P.O. Box 1839 Daytona Beach, FL 32115-1839. Phone: (904)252-0230 Monthly. $130.00 per year.

Bank and Thrift Case Digest. West Group, 610 Opperman Dr. Eagan, MN 55123. Phone: 800-328-4880 or (651)687-7000

Fax: 800-213-2323 or (651)687-5827 URL: http://www.westgroup.com • Three looseleaf volumes. Periodic supplementation. Provides court decisions involving claims against failed banks and savings institutions or on behalf of insured banks and savings institutions.

Bank Asset/Liability Management. Warren, Gorham & Lamont/RIA Group, 395 Hudson St. New York, NY 10014. Phone: 800-950-1215 or (212)367-6300 Fax: (212)367-6718 E-mail: customer_services@riag.com • URL: http://www.riahome.com • Monthly. $193.75 per year. Newsletter. For bankers concerned with balancing an asset and liability portfolio.

Bank Auditing and Accounting Report. Warren, Gorham and Lamont/RIA Group, 395 Hudson St. New York, NY 10014. Phone: 800-950-1215 or (212)367-6300 Fax: (212)367-6718 E-mail: customer_services@riag.com • URL: http://www.riahome.com • Monthly. $199.00 per year. Newsletter covering bank regulations, accounting techniques, and audit controls.

Bank Automation News., 1201 Seven Locks Rd., Suite 300 Potomac, MD 20854. Phone: 800-777-5006 or (301)309-3487 Fax: (301)424-4297 E-mail: pbi@phillips.com • URL: http://www.phillips.com/marketplaces.htm • Biweekly. $595.00 per year. Newsletter.

Bank Credit Analyst. BCA Publications Ltd., 1002 Sherbrooke St., W., 16th Fl. Montreal PQ, QC, Canada H3A 3L6. Phone: (514)499-9706 Fax: (514)499-9709 Monthly. $695.00 per year. ''The independent monthly forecast and analysis of trends in business conditions and major investment markets based on a continuous appraisal of money and credit flows.'' Includes many charts and graphs relating to money, credit, and securities in the U. S.

The Bank Director's Handbook. Edwin B Cox and others. Greenwood Publishing Group, Inc., 88 Post Rd., W. Westport, CT 06881-5007. Phone: 800-225-5800 or (203)226-3571 Fax: (203)222-2540 E-mail: bookinfo@greenwood.com • URL: http://www.greenwood.com • 1986. $65.00. Second edition.

Bank Investment Product News. Institutional Investor, Newsletters Div., 488 Madison Ave. New York, NY 10022. Phone: (212)224-3300 Fax: (212)224-3353 E-mail: info@iijournals.com • URL: http://www.iijournals.com • Weekly. $1,195.00 per year. Newsletter. Edited for bank executives. Covers the marketing and regulation of financial products sold through banks, such as mutual funds, stock brokerage services, and insurance.

Bank Investments and Funds Management. Gerald O. Hatler. American Bankers Association, 1120 Connecticut Ave., N. W. Washington, DC 20036-3971. Phone: 800-338-0626 or (202)663-5000 Fax: (202)663-7543 URL: http://www.aba.com • 1991. $49.00. Second edition. Focuses on portfolio management, risk analysis, and investment strategy.

Bank Letter: Newsletter of Commercial and Institutional Banking. Institutional Investor, Newsletters Div., 488 Madison Ave. New York, NY 10022. Phone: (212)224-3300 Fax: (212)224-3353 E-mail: info@iijournals.com • URL: http://www.iijournals.com • Weekly. $2,220.00 per year. Newsletter. Covers retail banking, commercial lending, foreign loans, bank technology, government regulations, and other topics related to banking.

Bank Loan Report. Securities Data Publishing, 40 West 57th St. New York, NY 10019. Phone: 800-455-5844 or (212)765-5311 Fax: (212)956-0112 E-mail: sdp@tfn.com • URL: http://www.sdponline.com • Weekly. $3,600.00 per year. Newsletter. Covers the syndicated loan marketplace for corporate finance professionals. (Securities Data Publishing is a unit of Thomson Financial.)

Bank Management: Text and Cases. George H. Hempel and Donald G. Simonson. John Wiley and Sons, Inc., 605 Third Ave. New York, NY 10158-0012. Phone: 800-225-5945 or (212)850-6000 Fax: (212)850-6088 E-mail: info@wiley.com • URL: http://www.wiley.com • 1998. $106.95. Fifth edition.

Bank Marketing. Bank Marketing Association, 1120 Connecticut Ave., N.W. Washington, DC 20036-3902. Phone: 800-338-0626 or (202)663-5278 Fax: (202)828-4540 Monthly. Members, $80.00 per year; non-members, $120.00 per year. Includes a Buyer's Guide.

Bank Marketing Annual Buyer's Guide. Bank Marketing Association, 1120 Connecticut Ave., N.W. Washington, DC 20036-3902. Phone: 800-433-9013 or (202)663-5278 Fax: (202)828-4540 Annual. $20.00

Bank Marketing Association.

Bank Marketing for the 90's: New Ideas from 55 of the Best Marketers in Banking. Don Wright. John Wiley and Sons, Inc., 605 Third Ave. New York, NY 10158-0012. Phone: 800-225-5945 or (212)850-6000 Fax: (212)850-6088 E-mail: info@wiley.com • URL: http://www.wiley.com • 1991. $99.95.

Bank Mergers & Acquisitions: The Authoritative Newsletter Providing In-Depth Analysis of the Restructuring of American Banking. SNL Securities, P.O. Box 2124 Charlottesville, VA 22902-2124. Phone: (804)977-1600 Fax: (804)977-4466 E-mail: subscriptions@snlnet.com • URL: http://www.snlnet.com • Monthly. $795.00 per year. Newsletter. Includes information on transactions assisted by the Federal Deposit Insurance Corporation (FDIC) for commercial banks or by the Resolution Trust Corporation (RTC) for savings and loan institutions.

Bank Network News; News and Analysis of Shared EFT Networks. Faulkner & Gray, Inc., 300 S. Wacker Dr., 18th Fl. Chicago, IL 60606. Phone: 800-535-8403 or (312)913-1334 Fax: (312)913-1959 E-mail: orders@faulknergray.com • URL: http://www.faulkner.gray.com • Semimonthly. $395.00 per year. Newsletter.

Bank Operating Statistics. Federal Deposit Insurance Corp., 550 17th St., N.W. Washington, DC 20429. Phone: (202)393-8400 Annual. Price on application. Based on Reports of Condition and Reports of Income.

Bank Profitability: Financial Statements of Banks. Organization for Economic Cooperation and Development. Available from OECD Publications and Information Center, 2001 L St., N. W., Suite 650 Washington, DC 20036-4922. Phone: 800-456-6323 or (202)785-6323 Fax: (202)785-0350 E-mail: washington.contact@oecd.org • URL: http://www.oecd.wash.org • Annual. $60.00. Presents data for 10 years on bank profitability in OECD member countries.

Bank Rate Monitor: The Weekly Financial Rate Reporter. Advertising News Service, Inc., P.O. Box 88888 North Palm Beach, FL 33408-8888. Phone: (407)627-7330 Fax: (407)627-7335 E-mail: webmaster@bankrate.com • URL: http://www.bankrate.com • Weekly. $895.00 per year. Newsletter. Includes online addition and monthly supplement. Provides detailed information on interest rates currently paid by U. S. banks and savings institutions.

Bank Strategies. Bank Administration Institute, One N. Franklin St. Chicago, IL 60606. Phone: (312)683-2248 Fax: (312)312-2373 Monthly. $59.00 per year. Formerly *Bank Management.*

Bank Systems and Technology-Directory and Buyer's Guide. Miller Freeman, Inc., 600 Harrison St. San Francisco, CA 94107. Phone: 800-227-4675 or (415)905-2200 Fax: (415)905-2232 E-mail: techlearning_editors@mfi.com • URL: http://www.mfi.com • Annual. $25.00. List of more than 1,800 manufacturers, distributors, and other suppliers of equipment and materials to the banking industry.

Bank Systems and Technology: For Senior-Level Executives in Operations and Technology. Miller Freeman, Inc., One Penn Plaza New York, NY 10119-1198. Phone: 800-950-1314 or (212)714-1300 Fax: (212)302-6273 URL: http://www.mfi.com • 13 times a year. $65.00 per year. Focuses on strategic planning for banking executives. Formerly *Bank Systems and Equipment.*

Bank Systems Management: The Project Management Guide to Planning and Implementing Systems. Kent S. Belasco. McGraw-Hill Professional, 1221 Ave. of the Americas New York, NY 10020. Phone: 800-772-4726 or (212)904-2000 Fax: (212)904-2072 E-mail: customer.service@mcgraw-hill.com • URL: http://www.mcgraw-hill.com • 1993. $62.50.

Bank Tax Guide. CCH, Inc., 4025 W. Peterson Ave. Chicago, IL 60646-6085. Phone: 800-248-3248 or (773)866-6000 Fax: 800-224-8299 or (773)866-3608 URL: http://www.cch.com • Annual. $195.00. Summarizes and explains federal tax rules affecting financial institutions.

Bank Technology News: Banking's Information Source for Systems Purchasing. Faulkner & Gray, Inc., 11 Penn Plaza, 17th Fl. New York, NY 10001. Phone: 800-535-8403 or (212)967-7000 Fax: (212)967-7155 E-mail: order@faulknergray.com • URL: http://www.faulknergray.com • Monthly. $48.00 per year.

Bank Technology Review: A Bank Manager's Guide to New Technology Products, Systems, and Applications. Tom Groenfeldt. McGraw-Hill Professional, 1221 Ave. of the Americas New York, NY 10020. Phone: 800-772-4726 or (212)904-2000 Fax: (212)904-2072 E-mail: customer.service@mcgraw-hill.com • URL: http://www.mcgraw-hill.com • 1995. $37.50.

Bankcard Consumer News. Bankcard Holders of America, 333 Maple Ave., E., No. 2005 Vienna, VA 22180-4717. Phone: (703)389-5445 Fax: (703)481-6037 Bimonthly. $24.00 per year. Newsletter for consumers.

Bankcard Holders of America., 333 Maple Ave. E., No. 2005 Vienna, VA 22180-4717. Promotes the ''wise and careful'' use of credit cards. A consumer organization.

The Banker. Financial Times, 14 E. 60th St. New York, NY 10022. Phone: (212)752-4500 Monthly. $197.00 per year. Includes supplement. Published in England.

The Bankers' Almanac. Reed Business Information, East Grinstead House, Windsor Court, East Grinstead W. Sussex RH19 1XA, England. Phone: 01342 335819 Fax: 01342 335998 E-mail: bankersalmanac@reedinfo.co.uk • URL: http://www.bankersalmanac.com • Semiannual. $730.00. Six volumes. Lists more than 4,500 banks; international coverage. Lists more than 4,500 banks; international coverage. Formerly *Bankers' Almanac and Yearbook.*

Bankers' Association for Foreign Trade.

Bankers in the Selling Role: A Consultative Guide to Cross Selling Financial Services. Linda Richardson. John Wiley and Sons, Inc., 605 Third Ave. New York, NY 10158-0012. Phone: 800-225-5945 or (212)850-6000 Fax: (212)850-6088 E-mail: info@wiley.com • URL: http://www.wiley.com • 1992. $22.50. Second edition.

The Bankers: The Next Generation: The New Worlds of Money, Credit, and Banking in an Electronic Age. Martin Mayer. NAL-Dutton, 375 Hudson St. New York, NY 10014-3657. Phone: 800-526-0275 or (212)366-2000 Fax: (212)366-2666 E-mail: online@penguinputnam.com • URL: http://www.penguinputnam.com • 1998. $16.95. A popularly written discussion of the future of banks, bankers, and banking.

Banking and Finance on the Internet. Mary J. Cronin, editor. John Wiley and Sons, Inc., 605 Third Ave. New York, NY 10158-0012. Phone: 800-842-3636 or (212)850-6000 Fax: (212)850-6088 E-mail: info@wiley.com • URL: http://www.wiley.com • 1997. $45.00. Contains articles on Internet services, written by bankers, money mangers, investment analysts, and stockbrokers. Emphasis is on operations management. (Communications Series).

Banking Crimes: Fraud, Money Laundering, Embezzlement. John K. Villa. West Group, 610 Opperman Dr. Eagan, MN 55123. Phone: 800-328-4880 or (651)687-7000 Fax: 800-213-2323 or (651)687-5827 URL: http://www.westgroup.com • Annual. $125.00. Covers fraud and embezzlement. Looseleaf.

Banking in the U. S.: An Annotated Bibliography. Jean Deuss. Scarecrow Press, Inc., 4720 Boston Way Lanham, MD 20706-4310. Phone: 800-462-6420 or (301)459-3366 Fax: 800-338-4550 or (301)459-1705 E-mail: orders@scarecrowpress.com • URL: http://www.scarecrowpress.com • 1990. $26.50.

Banking Information Index. U M I Banking Information Index, 620 S. Third St. Louisville, KY 40202-2475. Phone: 800-626-2823 or (502)583-4110 URL: http://www.aba.com • Monthly. Price on application. Covers a wide variety of banking, business, and financial subjects in periodicals. Formerly *Banking Literature Index.*

Banking Information Source. Bell & Howell Information and Learning, 300 N. Zeeb Rd. Ann Arbor, MI 48103. Phone: 800-521-0600 or (734)761-4700 Fax: 800-864-0019 URL: http://www.umi.com • Provides indexing and abstracting of periodical and other literature from 1982 to date, with weekly updates. Covers the financial services industry: banks, savings institutions, investment houses, credit unions, insurance companies, and real estate organizations. Emphasis is on marketing and management. Inquire as to online cost and availability. (Formerly *FINIS: Financial Industry Information Service.*)

Banking Law. Matthew Bender & Co., Inc., Two Park Ave. New York, NY 10016. Phone: 800-223-1940 or (212)448-2000 Fax: (212)244-3188 E-mail: international@bender.com • URL: http://www.bender.com • $1,970.00. 20 volumes. Periodic supplementation. Operational guidance for bank officers, with analysis of statutory law and agency regulations. Includes *Checks, Drafts* and *Notes* as volumes 7, 7a, 8, 8a.

Banking Law Journal. Warren, Gorham and Lamont, Inc/RIA Group, 395 Hudson St. New York, NY 10014. Phone: 800-950-1215 or (212)367-6300 Fax: (212)924-0460 URL: http://www.wgl.com • Monthly. $135.98 per year. Latest developments in banking law.

Banking Law Manual: Legal Guide to Commercial Banks, Thrift Institutions, and Credit Unions. Matthew Bender & Co., Inc., Two Park Ave. New York, NY 10016. Phone: 800-233-1940 or (212)448-2000 Fax: (212)244-3188 E-mail: international@bender.com • URL: http://www.bender.com • $215.00. Looseleaf service. Periodic supplementation. Desk reference, procedural guide, or training and management tool for the banking professional.

Banking Research Center., Northwestern University, 401 Anderson Hall, 2001 Sheridan Rd. Evanston, IL 60208. Phone: (847)491-3562 Fax: (847)491-5719 E-mail: m-fishman@nwu.edu • Does research in the management and public regulation of financial institutions. A unit of the J. L. Kellogg Graduate School of Management.

BANKPAC., c/o Heather Harrell, American Bankers Association, 1120 Connecticut Ave., N.W. Washington, DC 20036. Phone: (202)663-5117 or (202)663-5113 Fax: (202)663-7544 Serves as the political action committee of the American Bankers Association.

Bankruptcy and Insolvency Accounting. Grant Newton. John Wiley and Sons, Inc., 605 Third Ave. New York, NY 10158-0012. Phone: 800-225-5945 or (212)850-6000 Fax: (212)850-6088 E-mail: info@wiley.com • URL: http://www.wiley.com • 2000. $330.00. Three volumes.

Bankruptcy and Insolvency Taxation. Grant W. Newton and Gilbert D. Bloom. John Wiley and Sons, Inc., 605 Third Ave. New York, NY 10158-0012. Phone: 800-225-5945 or (212)850-6000 Fax: (212)850-6088 E-mail: info@wiley.com • URL: http://www.wiley.com • 1993. $180.00. Second edition. 2000 cumulative supplement, $85.00.

Bankruptcy Basics. Available from U. S. Government Printing Office, Washington, DC 20402. Phone: (202)512-1800 Fax: (202)512-2250 E-mail: gpoaccess@gpo.gov • URL: http://www.access.gpo.gov • 1998. $3.50. Second edition. Issued by the Bankruptcy Judges Division, Administrative Office of the United States Courts. Provides concise explanation of five Chapters of the U.S. Bankruptcy Code: Chapter 7 (Liquidation), Chapter 9 (Municipal), Chapter 11 (Reorganization), Chapter 12 (Family Farmer), and Chapter 13 (Debt Adjustment). Includes a seven-page glossary, ''Bankruptcy Terminology.'' (Public Information Series.)

Bankruptcy Concepts: A Desk Reference for Lenders. Bonnie K. Donahue. Robert Morris Associates, One Liberty Place, 1650 Market St., Suite 2300 Philadelphia, PA 19103. Phone: 800-677-7621 or (215)446-4000 Fax: (215)446-4100 E-mail: info@rmahq.org • URL: http://www.rmahq.org • 1994. $55.00. Designed to help loan officers deal with the intricacies of bankruptcy law. Chapters include a brief history of bankruptcy law, basic bankruptcy principles, and ''Adjustments of Debts.''

Bankruptcy Law Fundamentals. Richard I. Aaron. West Group, 610 Opperman Dr. Eagan, MN 55123. Phone: 800-328-4880 or (651)687-7000 Fax: 800-213-2323 or (651)687-5827 URL: http://www.westgroup.com • Looseleaf. $145.00. Periodic supplementation.

Bankruptcy Law Manual. Benjamin Weintraub and Alan N. Resnick. West Group, 610 Opperman Dr. Eagan, MN 55123. Phone: 800-328-4880 or (651)687-7000 Fax: (651)687-5827 URL: http://www.westgroup.com • $210.00. Looseleaf service. Periodic supplementation. Complete, practical to modern bankruptcy practice and procedure.

Bankruptcy Law Reports. CCH, Inc., 4025 W. Peterson Ave. Chicago, IL 60646-6085. Phone: 800-248-3248 or (773)583-8500 Fax: 800-224-8299 or (773)866-3608 URL: http://www.cch.com • Biweekly. $1,208.00 per year. Three looseleaf volumes.

Bankruptcy Practice Handbook. Rosemary E. Williams. West Group, 610 Opperman Dr. Eagan, MN 55123. Phone: 800-328-4880 or (651)687-7000 Fax: 800-213-2323 or (651)687-5827 URL: http://www.westgroup.com • Looseleaf. $145.00. Periodic supplementation.

Bankruptcy Reorganization. Martin J. Bienenstock. Practising Law Institute, 810 Seventh Ave. New York, NY 10019-5818. Phone: 800-260-4754 or (212)824-5700 Fax: (212)265-4742 E-mail: info@pli.edu • URL: http://www.pli.edu • 1987. $108.00.

Bankruptcy Yearbook and Almanac. New Generation Research, Inc., 225 Friend St., Suite 801 Boston, MA 02114. Phone: 800-468-3810 or (617)573-9550 Fax: (617)573-9554 Annual. Price on application.

Banksearch. Thomas Financial Media, 505 Barton Springs Rd., Suite 1101 Austin, TX 78704. Phone: 800-456-2340 or (512)472-2244 Quarterly. $275.00 per year. Rates banks as to loan exposure, capital adequacy, asset quality, liquidity, and other factors. Arranged geographically. Formerly *Sheshunoff Bank Quarterly Ratings and Analysis*.

BanxQuote Banking, Mortgage, and Finance Center. BanxQuote, Inc.Phone: 800-765-3000 or (212)643-8000 Fax: (212)643-0020 E-mail: info@banx.com • URL: http://www.banx.com • Web site quotes interest rates paid by banks around the country on various savings products, as well as rates paid by consumers for automobile loans, mortgages, credit cards, home equity loans, and personal loans. Also provided: stock quotes, indexes, stock options, futures trading data, economic indicators, and links to many other financial sites. Daily updates. Fees: Free.

Bargaining Across Borders: How to Conduct Business Successfully Anywhere in th e World. Dean A. Foster. McGraw-Hill, 1221 Ave. of the Americas New York, NY 10020-1095. Phone: 800-722-4726 or (212)904-2000 Fax: (212)904-2072 E-mail: customer.service@mcgraw-hill.com • URL: http://www.mcgraw-hill.com • 1992. $14.95. Includes a consideration of non-negotiable cultural differences.

Barometer of Business. Harris Trust and Savings Bank, 111 W. Monroe St. Chicago, IL 60690. Phone: (312)461-5322 Bimonthly. Free.

Barron's: The Dow Jones Business and Financial Weekly. Dow Jones and Co., Inc., 200 Liberty St. New York, NY 10281. Phone: 800-568-7625 or (212)416-2000 Fax: (212)416-2829 URL: http://www.barrons.com • Weekly. $145.00 per year.

Barter Communique. Full Circle Marketing Corp., P.O. Box 2527 Sarasota, FL 34230-2527. Phone: (941)394-3300 Fax: (941)365-6642 Quarterly. $30.00 per year. Lists barter businesses and publications.

Barter Update. Ed A. Doyle, editor. Update Publicare Co. c/o Prosperity and Profits Unlimited, Distribution Services, P.O. Box 416 Denver, CO 80201-0416. Phone: (303)575-5676 Annual. $4.00 per year.

Basic Accounting for the Small Business: Simple, Foolproof Techniques for Keeping Your Books Straight and Staying Out of Trouble. Clive C. Cornish. Self-Counsel Press, Inc., 1704 N. State St. Bellingham, WA 98225. Phone: 877-877-6490 or (360)676-4530 Fax: (360)676-4530 E-mail: service@self-counsel.com • URL: http://www.self-counsel.com • 1993. $8.95. Ninth revised edition. (Business Series).

The Basic Business Library: Core Resources. Bernard S. Schlessinger and June H. Schlessinger. Oryx Press, 4041 N. Central Ave., Ste. 700 Phoenix, AZ 85012-3397. Phone: 800-279-6799 or (602)265-2651 Fax: 800-279-4663 or (602)265-6250 E-mail: info@oryxpress.com • URL: http://www.oryxpress.com • 1994. $43.50. Third edition. Consists of three parts: (1) ''Core List of Printed Business Reference Sources,'' (2) ''The Literature of Business Reference and Business Libraries: 1976-1994,'' and (3) ''Business Reference Sources and Services: Essays.'' Part one lists 200 basic titles, with annotations and evaluations.

Basic Computer Concepts. Que Staff. Que Education & Training, Macmillan Computer Publishing, 201 W. 103rd St. Indianapolis, IN 46290-1094. Phone: 800-428-5331 or 800-858-7674 Fax: (317)581-4675 URL: http://www.mcp.com/que • 1997. $16.99.

Basic Construction Material. Charles Herubin and Theodore Marotta. Prentice-Hall, 240 Frisch Court Paramus, NJ 07652-5240. Phone: 800-947-7700 or (201)909-6200 Fax: 800-445-6991 or (201)909-6361 URL: http://www.prenhall.com • 1996. $77.00. Fifth edition.

Basic Documents in International Law. Ian Brownlie. Oxford University Press, Inc., 198 Madison Ave. New York, NY 10016-4314. Phone: 800-451-7556 or (212)726-6000 Fax: (212)726-6446 E-mail: custserv@oup-usa.org • URL: http://www.oup-usa.org • 1995. $85.00. Fourth edition.

Basic Electronics. Bernard Grob. Pearson Education and Technology, 201 W. 103rd St. Indianapolis, IN 46290-1097. Phone: 800-858-7674 or (317)581-3500 Fax: (317)581-4670 URL: http://www.mcp.com • 1996. $84.75. Eight edition.

Basic Estimating for Construction. James A. S. Fatzinger. Prentice Hall, 240 Frisch Court Paramus, NJ 07652-5240. Phone: 800-947-7700 or (201)909-6200 Fax: 800-445-6991 or (201)909-6361 URL: http://www.prenhall.com • 2000. $69.95. Covers electrical, plumbing, concrete, masonry, framing, etc. Includes a glossary and typical bid forms.

Basic Facts About the United Nations. United Nations Publications, United Nations Concourse Level, First Ave., 46th St. New York, NY 10017. Phone: 800-553-3210 or (212)963-7680 Fax: (212)963-4910 E-mail: bookstore@un.org • URL: http://www.un.org/publications • 1998. $10.00.

Basic Facts About Trademarks. Available from U. S. Government Printing Office, Washington, DC 20402. Phone: (202)512-1800 Fax: (202)512-2250 E-mail: gpoaccess@gpo.gov • URL: http://www.access.gpo.gov • 1996. $4.25. Issued by the Patent and Trademark Office, U. S. Department of Commerce. Includes filing requirements and sample applications.

Basic Guide to Exporting. Available from U. S. Government Printing Office, Washington, DC 20402. Phone: (202)512-1800 Fax: (202)512-2250 E-mail: gpoaccess@gpo.gov • URL: http://www.access.gpo.gov • 1999. $16.00. Issued by the International Trade Administration, U. S. Department of Commerce. Discusses the costs, risks, and strategy of exporting. Includes sources of assistance and a glossary of terms used in the export business.

Basic Hospital Financial Management. Donald F. Beck. Aspen Publishers, Inc., 200 Orchard Ridge Dr., Suite 200 Gaithersburg, MD 20878. Phone: 800-638-8437 or (301)417-7500 Fax: (301)417-7550 URL: http://www.aspenpub.com • 1989. $62.00. Second edition.

Basic Internet for Busy Librarians: A Quick Course for Catching Up. Laura K. Murray. American Library Association, 50 E. Huron St. Chicago, IL 60611-2795. Phone: 800-545-2433 or (312)944-6780 Fax: (312)440-9374 E-mail: ala@ala.org • URL: http://www.ala.org • 1998. $26.00. A ''practical crash-course primer'' for learning how to effectively navigate the Internet and the World Wide Web.

Basic Legal Forms with Commentary. Marvin Hyman. Warren, Gorham and Lamont/RIA Group, 395 Hudson St. New York, NY 10014. Phone: 800-950-1215 or (212)367-6300 Fax: (914)749-5300 E-mail: customer_services@riag.com • URL: http://www.riahome.com • Looseleaf. $105.00. Periodic supplementation. Forms for any type of legal transaction. Includes commentary.

Basic Metals Processing Research Institute.

Basic Petroleum Data Book. American Petroleum Institute, Publications Section, 1220 L St., N. W. Washington, DC 20005. Phone: (202)682-8375 Fax: (202)962-4776 E-mail: info@apiencompass.org • URL: http://www.api.org • Three times a year. $230.00 per year.

Basic Statistics for Business and Economics. Douglas A. Lind and Robert D. Mason. McGraw-Hill Higher Education, 1221 Ave. of the Americas New York, NY 10020. Phone: 800-722-4726 or (212)904-2000 Fax: (212)904-2072 E-mail: customer.service@mcgraw-hill.com • URL: http://www.mcgraw-hill.com • 1996. Second edition. Price on application.

Basic Statistics of the European Union. Statistical Office of the European Communities. Available from Bernan Associates, 4611-F Assembly Dr. Lanham, MD 20706-4391. Phone: 800-274-4447 or (301)459-7666 Fax: 800-865-3450 or (301)459-0056 E-mail: info@bernan.com • URL: http://www.bernan.com • Annual. Provides European demographic, economic, and other basic data. The U. S., Canada, Japan, and the Soviet Union are included for comparative purposes. Text in Dutch, English, French, and German. Formerly *Basic Statistics of the European Community*.

Basics of Budgeting. Robert G. Finney. AMACOM, 1601 Broadway, 12th Fl. New York, NY 10019. Phone: 800-262-9699 or (212)586-8100 Fax: (212)903-8168 E-mail: custmserv@amanet.org • URL: http://www.amanet.org • 1993. $19.95

Battelle Memorial Institute., 505 King Ave. Columbus, OH 43201-2693. Phone: 800-201-2011 or (614)424-6424 Fax: (614)424-3260 URL: http://www.battelle.org • Multidisciplinary research facilities at various locations include: Microcomputer Applications and Technology Center; Battelle Industrial Technology Center; Technology and Society Research Center; Office of Transportation Systems and Planning; Office of Waste Technology Development; Materials Information Center; Office of Nuclear Waste Isolation.

Battery and EV Technology News. Business Communications Co., Inc., 25 Van Zant St., Suite 13 Norwalk, CT 06855. Phone: (203)853-4266 Fax: (203)853-0348 Monthly. $450.00 per year. Newsletter. Technical and economic studies of electric vehicles and battery technology.

Battery Council International., 401 N. Michigan Ave. Chicago, IL 60611. Phone: (312)644-6610 Fax: (312)321-6869 E-mail: info@batterycouncil.org • URL: http://www.batterycouncil.org • Manufacturers of lead-acid storage batteries.

The Battery Man: International Journal for Starting, Lighting, Ignition and Generating Systems. Independent Battery Manufacturers Association, 100 Larchwood Dr. Largo, FL 34640. Phone: 800-237-6126 or (813)586-1408 Fax: (813)586-1400 Monthly. $22.00 per year.

The Bauer Group: Reporting On and Analyzing the Performance of U. S. Banks, Thrifts, and Credit Unions. Bauer Financial Reports, Inc.Phone: 800-388-6686 or (305)445-9500 Fax: 800-230-9569 or (305)445-6775 URL: http://www.bauerfinancial.com • Web site provides ratings (0 to 5 stars) of individual banks and credit unions, based on capital ratios and other financial criteria. Online searching for bank or credit union names is offered. Fees: Free.

Baxter's Environmental Compliance Manual: Procedures, Checklists, and Forms for Effective Compliance. West Group, 610 Opperman Dr. Eagan, MN 55123. Phone: 800-328-4880 or (651)687-7000 Fax: 800-213-2323 or (651)687-5827 URL: http://www.westgroup.com • Three looseleaf volumes. $475.00. Periodic supplementation. Covers the creation, implementation, and management of corporate environmental compliance programs, so that liability exposure will be reduced. (Environmental Law Series).

BBC World Glossary of Current Affairs. Available from St. James Press, 27500 Drake Rd. Farmington Hills, MI 48331-3535. Phone: 800-877-GALE or (248)699-GALE Fax: 800-414-5043 or (248)699-8063 E-mail: galeord@galegroup.com • URL: http://www.galegroup.com • 1991. $85.00. Published by Longman Group Ltd. Provides definitions of 7,000 terms used in world affairs. Arranged by country, with an alphabetical index.

The BBI Newsletter: A Perceptive Analysis of the Healthcare Industry and Marketplace Focusing on New Technology, Strategic Planning, and Marketshare Projections. American Health Consultants, 3525 Piedmont Rd., N.E., Bldg. 6, Suite 400 Atlanta, GA 30305-5278. Phone: 800-284-3291 or (404)262-7436 Fax: (404)262-5447 E-mail: custserv@ahcpub.com • URL: http://www.ahcpub.org • Monthly. $827.00 per year.

BBP's 3-in-1 Poster Programs. Bureau of Business Practice, Inc., 24 Rope Ferry Rd. Waterford, CT 06386. Phone: 800-243-0876 or (860)442-4365 Fax: (860)437-3555 URL: http://www.bbpnews.com • Monthly. $32.40 per year. Includes: customer awareness posters, productivity posters, safety posters. Quantity discounts available.

BCA Interest Rate Forecast: A Monthly Analysis and Forecast of U.S. Bond and Money Market Trades. BCA Publications, 1002 Sherbrooke St., W., 16th Fl. Montreal, PQ, Canada H3A 3L6. Phone: (514)499-9706 Fax: (514)499-9709 Monthly. $695.00 per year. Formerly *Interest Rate Forecast*.

The Bear Book: Survive and Profit in Ferocious Markets. John Rothchild. John Wiley and Sons, Inc., 605 Third Ave. New York, NY 10158-0012. Phone: 800-225-5945 or (212)850-6000 Fax: (212)850-6088 E-mail: info@jwiley.com • URL: http://www.wiley.com • 1998. $24.95. Tells how to invest when the stock market is sinking.

Bearing Specialists Association.

Beating the Street: The Best-Selling Author of ''One Up on Wall Street'' Shows You How to Pick Winning Stocks and Mutual Funds. Peter Lynch and John Rothchild. Simon & Schuster Trade, 1230 Ave. of the Americas New York, NY 10020. Phone: 800-223-2336 or (212)698-7000 Fax: 800-943-9831 or (212)698-7007 E-mail: sson-line_feedback@simonsays.com • URL: http://www.simonsays.com • 1993. $23.00.

Beauty and Barber Supply Institute.

Beauty Salons. Available from MarketResearch.com, 641 Ave. of the Americas, 3rd Fl. New York, NY 10011. Phone:

800-298-5699 or (212)807-2629 Fax: (212)807-2716 E-mail: order@marketresearch.com • URL: http://www.marketresearch.com • 1997. $995.00. Market research report published by Specialists in Business Information. Covers beauty salon revenues, as well as sales of supplies and equipment for beauty salons and barber shops.

Beauty Supply Store. Entrepreneur Media, Inc., 2445 McCabe Way Irvine, CA 92614. Phone: 800-421-2300 or (949)261-2325 Fax: (949)261-0234 E-mail: entman@entrepreneur.com • URL: http://www.entrepreneur.com • Looseleaf. $59.50. A practical guide to starting a store for professional beauty supplies. Covers profit potential, start-up costs, market size evaluation, owner's time required, site selection, lease negotiation, pricing, accounting, advertising, promotion, etc. (Start-Up Business Guide No. E1277.)

Becker the Counterfeiter. G. F. Hill. Obol International, 63 S. Broadway Aurora, IL 60505. Phone: (630)844-0590 Fax: (630)844-0591 1979. $20.00.

Bee Biology and Systematics Laboratory. Utah State University

Bee Craft: The Official Journal of the British BeeKeepers' Association. Bee Craft Ltd., The Secretary, 24 Dogger Lane, Wells-Next-to-the-Sea Norfolk NR23 1BE, England. Phone: 44 1328 711681 Monthly. $35.00 per year.

Bee Culture. A. I. Root Co., P.O. Box 706 Medina, OH 44258-0706. Phone: (330)725-6677 Fax: (330)725-5624 E-mail: beeculture@airoot.com • URL: http://www.airoot.com • Monthly. $20.00 per year. Articles, reports and stories about beekeeping market. Latest industry news. Formerly *Gleanings in Bee Culture*.

Bee World. International Bee Research Association, 18 North Rd. Cardiff CF1 3DY Wales, Wales. E-mail: ibra@cardiff.ac.uk • Quarterly. $70.00 per year. Authoritative articles and reviews about recent scientific and technological developments.

Beef. Intertec Publishing Co., Agribusiness Div., 7900 International Dr., 3rd Fl. Minneapolis, MN 55425. Phone: 800-400-5945 or (612)851-9329 Fax: (612)851-4601 E-mail: beef@intertec.com • URL: http://www.intertec.com • 13 times a year. $35.00 per year.

BEEF. National Cattlemen's Beef AssociationPhone: (303)694-0305 Fax: (303)694-2851 E-mail: cows@beef.org • URL: http://www.beef.org • Web site provides detailed information from the "Cattle and Beef Handbook," including "Beef Economics" (production, sales, consumption, retail value, foreign competition, etc.). Text of monthly newsletter is also available: "The Beef Brief-Issues & Trends in the Cattle Industry." Keyword searching is offered. Fees: Free.

Beef Cattle and Sheep Research Center. Pennsylvania State University

Beekeeping. Devon Beekeepers Association, c/o Brian Gant, Leaf Orchard, Grange Rd. Buckfast, Devon TQ11 OEH, England. Phone: 44 1364 642233 Fax: 44 1364 342233 E-mail: 106213.3313@compuserve.com • Ten times a year. Free to members; non-members, $15.00 per year.

Beer Institute.

Beer Marketer's Insights. Beer Marketer's Insights, Inc., P.O. Box 264 West Nyack, NY 10994. Phone: (914)624-2337 23 times a year. $435.00 per year. Newsletter for brewers and wholesalers.

Beer Statistics News. Beer Marketer's Insights, Inc., P.O. Box 264 West Nyack, NY 10994. Phone: (914)624-2337 24 times a year. $360.00 per year. Market share and shipments by region and brewer.

Behavioral and Social Sciences Librarian. Haworth Press, Inc., 10 Alice St. Binghamton, NY 13904-1580. Phone: 800-429-6784 or (607)722-5857 Fax: 800-895-0582 or (607)722-1424 E-mail: getinfo@haworthpressinc.com • URL: http://www.haworthpressinc.com • Semiannual. Individuals, $42.00 per year; institutions, $95.00 per year; libraries, $95.00 per year.

Behavioral Medicine: Investigations of Environmental Influences on Health and Behavior. Helen Dwight Reid Educational Foundation. Heldref Publications, 1319 18th St., N.W. Washington, DC 20016-1802. Phone: 800-296-5149 or (202)296-6267 Fax: (202)296-5149 E-mail: bmed@helderf.org • URL: http://www.helderf.org • Quarterly. Individuals, $53.00 per year; institutions, $99.00 per year. An interdisciplinary journal of particular interest to physicians, psychologists, nurses, educators and all who are interested in behavorial and social influences on mental and physicial health. Formerly *Journal of Human Stress*.

Behind the Veil of Economics: Essays in the Worldly Philosophy. Robert L. Heilbroner. W. W. Norton Co., Inc., 500 Fifth Ave. New York, NY 10110. Phone: 800-223-2584 or (212)354-5500 Fax: (212)869-0856 E-mail: webmaster@wwnorton.com • URL: http://www.norton.com • 1989. $7.95.

Being Digital. Nicholas Negroponte. Vintage Books, 299 Park Ave., 7th Fl. New York, NY 10171. Phone: 800-726-0600 or (212)751-2600 Fax: 800-659-2436 URL: http://www.vintagebooks.com • 1995. $28.00. A kind of history of multimedia, with visions of future technology and public participation. Predicts how computers will affect society in years to come.

BEMA (Bakery Equipment Manufacturers Association).

Bender's Payroll Tax Guide. Matthew Bender & Co., Inc., Two Park Ave. New York, NY 10016. Phone: 800-223-1940 or (212)448-2000 Fax: (212)244-3188 E-mail: international@bender.com • URL: http://www.bender.com • Annual. $117.00. Guide to payroll tax planning. Includes procedures, forms, and examples.

Bender's Tax Return Manual. Ernest D. Fiore and others. Matthew Bender & Co., Inc., Two Park Ave. New York, NY 10016. Phone: 800-223-1940 or (212)448-2000 Fax: (212)244-3188 E-mail: international@bender.com • URL: http://www.bender.com • Annual. Price on application. Includes all major federal tax forms and schedules.

Benedict on Admiralty. Matthew Bender & Co., Inc., Two Park Ave. New York, NY 10016. Phone: 800-223-1940 or (212)448-2000 Fax: (212)244-3188 E-mail: international@bender.com • URL: http://www.bender.com • $2,660.00. 25 looseleaf volumes. Periodic supplementation. Covers American law of the sea and shipping.

Benefits News Analysis. Benefits News Analysis, Inc., P.O. Box 4033 New Haven, CT 06525. Phone: (203)393-2272 Bimonthly. $89.00. Analysis of corporate employee benefit practices. Includes review of benefit program changes at a number of large corporations.

Benelux Kompass Business Disc. Available from Kompass USA, Inc., 1255 Route 70, Suite 25-S Lakewood, NJ 08701. Phone: 877-566-7277 or (732)730-0340 Fax: (732)730-0342 E-mail: mail@kompass-usa.com • URL: http://www.kompass.com • Annual. $560.00. CD-ROM provides information on more than 54,000 companies in Belgium, Netherlands, and Luxembourg. Classification system covers approximately 50,000 products and services.

Benn's Media Directories. Nichols Publishing Co., 155 W. 72nd St. New York, NY 10023. Phone: (212)580-8079 URL: http://www.mfinfo.com • Annual. $620.00. Three volumes. Over 47,000 daily and weekly newspapers, free newspapers, periodicals directories, major publishers, in-house periodicals, television and broadcasting stations, media associations and suppliers of services to the publishing and broadcasting industry. Formerly *Benn's Press Directory*.

Berkeley Journal of Employment and Labor Law. University of California at Berkeley. University of California Press, Journals Div., Berkeley, CA 94720-5812. Phone: 800-822-6657 or (510)642-7154 Fax: (510)642-9917 E-mail: journal@ucop.edu • URL: http://www.ucpress/edu/journals • Semiannual. Individuals, $34.00 per year; institutions, $43.00 per year. Formerly *Industrial Relations Law Journal*.

Berkley Center for Entrepreneurial Studies.

Best Bet Internet: Reference and Research When You Don't Have Time to Mess Around. Shirley D. Kennedy. American Library Association, 50 E. Huron St. Chicago, IL 60611-2795. Phone: 800-545-2433 or (312)944-6780 Fax: (312)440-9374 E-mail: ala@ala.org • URL: http://www.ala.org • 1997. $35.00. Provides advice for librarians and others on the effective use of World Wide Web information sources.

The Best of OPL, II: Selected Readings from the One-Person Library: 1990-1994. Guy St. Clair and Andrew Berner. Special Libraries Association, 1700 18th St., N. W., 17th Fl. Washington, DC 20009-2514. Phone: (202)234-4700 Fax: 888-411-2856 or (202)234-2442 E-mail: books@sla.org • URL: http://www.sla.org • 1996. $36.00. Contains reprints of useful material from *The One-Person Library: A Newsletter for Librarians and Management*.

The Best of Times: A Personal and Occupational Odyssey. Paul Wasserman. Omnigraphics, Inc., Penobscot Bldg. Detroit, MI 48226. Phone: 800-234-1340 or (313)961-1340 Fax: 800-875-1340 or (313)961-1383 E-mail: info@omnigraphics.com • URL: http://www.omnigraphics.com • 2000. $35.00. Autobiography of a well known librarian, educator, and reference book editor. Foreward by Frederick G. Ruffner.

Best Practices for Financial Advisors. Mary Rowland., 500 Fifth Ave. New York, NY 10110-0017. Phone: 800-223-2584 or (212)354-5500 Fax: (212)869-0856 E-mail: webmaster@wwnorton.com • URL: http://norton.com • 1997. $40.00. Provides advice for professional financial advisors on practice management, ethics, marketing, and legal concerns. (Bloomberg Professional Library.)

Best's Aggregates and Averages: Property-Casualty. A.M. Best Co., Ambest Rd. Oldwick, NJ 08858. Phone: (908)439-2200 Fax: (908)439-3296 URL: http://www.ambest.com • Annual. $335.00. Statistical summary of composite property casualty business. 400 pages of historical data, underwriting expenses and underwriting experience by line.

Best's Casualty Loss Reserve Development. A.M. Best Co., Ambest Rd. Oldwick, NJ 08858. Phone: (908)439-2200 Fax: (908)439-3296 URL: http://www.ambest.com • Annual. $600.00. Looseleaf. Provides ten years of reserving patterns for the largest companies in the major casualty line.

Best's Company Reports. A. M. Best Co., Ambest Rd. Oldwick, NJ 08858. Phone: (908)439-2200 Fax: (908)439-3296 URL: http://www.ambest.com • Provides full financial data online for U. S. insurance companies (life, health, property, casualty), including balance sheet data, income statements, expenses, premium income, losses, and investments. Includes *Best's Company Reports*, *Best's Insurance News*, and Best's ratings of insuarance companies. Inquire as to online cost and availability.

Best's Directory of Recommended Insurance Attorneys and Adjusters. A. M. Best Co., Oldwick, NJ 08858. Phone: (908)439-2200 Fax: (908)534-1506 E-mail: legal_claims@ambest.com • URL: http://www.ambest.com • Annual. $1130.00. Two volumes. More than 5,000 American, Canadian, and foreign insurance defense law firms; lists 1,200 national and international insurance adjusting firms. Formerly *Best's Directory of Recommended Insurance Adjusters*.

Best's Insurance Reports. A.M. Best Co., Ambest Rd. Oldwick, NJ 08858. Phone: (908)439-2200 Fax: (908)439-3296 URL: http://www.ambest.com • Annual. $745.00 per edition. Two editions, Life-health insurance covering about 1,750 companies, and property-casualty insurance covering over 2,500 companies. Includes one year subscription to both *Best's Review* and *Best's Insurance Management Reports*.

Best's Insurance Reports: Property-Casualty. A.M. Best Co., Ambest Rd. Oldwick, NJ 08858. Phone: (908)439-2200 Fax: (908)439-3296 URL: http://www.ambest.com • Annual. $745.00. Guide to over 1,750 major property/casualty companies.

Best's Key Rating Guide. A.M. Best Co., Ambest Rd. Oldwick, NJ 08858. Phone: (908)439-2200 Fax: (908)439-3296 URL: http://www.ambest.com • Annual. $95.00. Financial information and ratings on over 2,000 property/casualty insurers.

Best's Review: Inurance Issues and Analysis. A.M. Best Co., Ambest Rd. Oldwick, NJ 08858. Phone: (908)439-2200 Fax: (908)439-3296 URL: http://www.ambest.com • Monthly. $25.00 per year. Editorial coverage of significant industry trends, developments, and important events. Formerly Best's Review: Property-Casualty Insurance.

Best's Safety and Security Directory: Safety-Industrial Hygiene-Security. A.M. Best Co., Ambest Rd. Oldwick, NJ 08858. Phone: (908)439-2200 Fax: (908)439-3296 URL: http://www.ambest.com • Annual. $95.00. A manual of current industrial safety practices with a directory of manufacturers and distributors of plant safety, security and industrial hygiene products and services listed by hazard. Formerly *Best's Safety Directory*.

BestWeek: Property-Casualty. A.M. Best Co., Ambest Rd. Oldwick, NJ 08858. Phone: (908)439-2200 Fax: (908)439-3296 URL: http://www.ambest.com • Weekly. $495.00 per year. Newsletter. Focuses on key areas of the insurance industry. Formerly *Best's Insurance Management Reports: Property-Casualty*.

The Betrayed Profession: Lawyering at the End of the Twentieth Century. Sol M. Linowitz and Martin Mayer. John Hopkins University Press, 2715 N. Charles St. Baltimore, MD 21218-4319. Phone: 800-537-5487 or (410)516-6900 Fax: (410)516-6998 E-mail: bkinfo@chaos.press.jhu.edu • URL: http://www.muse.jhu.edu/ • 1996. $15.95. Reprint edition. A critical view of present-day lawyers and law firms.

Better Buys for Business: The Independent Consumer Guide to Office Equipment. What to Buy for Business, Inc., 370 Technology Dr. Malvern, PA 19355. Phone: 800-247-2185 E-mail: orders@betterbuys.com • URL: http://www.betterbuys.com • 10 times a year. $134.00 per year. Each issue is on a particular office product, with detailed evaluation of specific models: 1. Low-Volume Copier Guide, 2. Mid-Volume Copier Guide, 3. High-Volume Copier Guide, 4. Plain Paper Fax and Low-Volume Multifunctional Guide, 5. Mid/High-Volume Multifunctional Guide, 6. Laser Printer Guide, 7. Color Printer and Color Copier Guide, 8. Scan-to-File Guide, 9. Business Phone Systems Guide, 10. Postage Meter Guide, with a Short Guide to Shredders.

Better Crops With Plant Food. Potash and Phosphate Institute, 655 Engineering Dr., Suite 110 Norcross, GA 30092-2843. Phone: (770)447-0335 Fax: (770)448-0439 Quarterly. $8.00.

Better Investing. National Association of Investors Corp., P.O. Box 220 Royal Oak, MI 48067. Phone: (248)583-6242 Fax: (248)583-4880 URL: http://www.better-investing.org • Monthly. $24.00 per year. Provides stock study ideas and information for do-it-yourself common stock investors.

Better Radio and Television. National Association for Better Broadcasting, 1100 Graynold Ave. Glendale, CA 91202-2019. Phone: (213)641-4903 Quarterly. $6.00 per year.

Better Roads. Gras Industries, Inc., P.O. Box 558 Park Ridge, IL 60068. Phone: (312)693-7710 Fax: (847)696-3445 E-mail: theeditors@worldnet.att.net • Monthly. $20.00 per year.

Better Supervision; Some Old Ideas and a Few New Ones about How to be a Better Boss. Economics Press, Inc., 12 Daniel Rd. Fairfield, NJ 07006. Phone: 800-526-2554 or (973)227-1224 Fax: (973)227-9742 E-mail: edit@epinc.com • Biweekly. $35.00 per year. Motivational pamphlets for supervisors.

Better Vision Institute.

Beverage Digest. Beverage Digest Co., LLC, P.O. Box 621 Bedford Hills, NY 10507-0621. E-mail: bevnews@beverage-digest.com • URL: http://www.beverage-digest.com • 22 times a year. $605.00 per year. Includes supplement. *Green Sheet*. News pertaining to the soft drink industry including new products, marketing territory changes, acquisitions, legal cases, etc. Supplement available *Green Sheet*.

Beverage Industry. Stagnito Communications, Inc., 1935 Shermer Rd., Suite 100 Northbrook, IL 60062. Phone: (847)205-5660 Fax: (847)205-5680 E-mail: info@stagnito.com • URL: http://www.stagnito.com • Monthly. Free to qualified personnel; others, $65.00 per year. Supplement available *Beverage Industry-Annual Manual*.

Beverage Industry - Annual Manual. Stagnito Communications, Inc., 1935 Shermer Rd., Suite 100 Northbrook, IL 60062. Phone: (847)205-5660 Fax: (847)205-5680 E-mail: info@stagnito.com • URL: http://www.stagnito.com • Annual. $55.00. Provides statistical information on multiple beverage markets. Includes an industry directory. Supplement to *Beverage Industry*.

Beverage Industry News. BIN Publications, 171 Mayhew Way, Suite 202 Pleasant Hill, CA 94523-4348. Phone: (925)932-4999 Fax: (925)932-4966 E-mail: binmagqa.com • Monthly. $49.00 per year. Incorporates *Beverage Industry News Merchandiser*.

The Beverage Marketing Directory. Beverage Marketing Corp., 2670 Commercial Ave. Mingo Junction, OH 43938. Phone: 800-332-6222 or (740)598-4133 Fax: (740)598-3977 Annual. $845.00. Provides information for approximately 11,000 beverage companies and suppliers to beverage companies. Includes sales volume and brand names. Formerly *National Beverage Marketing Directory*.

Beverage Media. Beverage Media, Ltd., 161 Ave. of the Americas New York, NY 10013. Phone: (212)734-0322 Fax: (212)620-0473 Monthly. $78.00 per year. Wholesale prices.

Beverage World Buyers Guide. Bill Communications, Inc., 770 Broadway New York, NY 10003-9595. Phone: 800-266-4712 or (646)654-5400 Fax: (646)654-7212 E-mail: info@bpi.com • URL: http://www.billcom.com • Annual. $7.00. Lists suppliers to the beverage industry.

Beverage World: Magazine of the Beverage Industry. Bill Communications, Inc., 770 Broadway New York, NY 10003-9595. Phone: 800-266-4712 or (646)654-7212 Fax: (646)654-5835 URL: http://www.billcom.com • Monthly. $55.00 per year.

Beverage World Periscope. Keller International Publishing Corp., 150 Great Neck Rd. Great Neck, NY 11021. Phone: (516)829-9210 Fax: (516)829-5414 Monthly. $35.00 per year. Newsletter.

Beyond Book Indexing: How to Get Started in Web Indexing, Embedded Indexing, and Other Computer-Based Media. Diane Brenner and Marilyn Rowland, editors. Information Today, Inc., 143 Old Marlton Pike Medford, NJ 08055-8750. Phone: 800-300-9868 or (609)654-6266 Fax: (609)654-4309 E-mail: custserv@infotoday.com • URL: http://www.infotoday.com • 2000. $31.25. Published for the American Society of Indexers. Contains 12 chapters written by professional indexers. Part one discusses making an index by marking items in an electronic document (embedded indexing); part two is on indexing to make Web pages more accessible; part three covers CD-ROM and multimedia indexing; part four provides career and promotional advice for professionals in the field. Includes an index by Janet Perlman and a glossary.

BFIA Annual Direcotry (Body Fashions - Intimate Apparel). Advanstar Communications, Inc., One Park Ave., 2nd Fl. New York, NY 10016-5802. Phone: 800-346-0085 or (212)951-6600 Fax: (212)951-6793 E-mail: information@advanstar.com • URL: http://www.advanstar.com • Annual. $20.00. Sections listing manufacturers of women's intimate apparel and bodywear along with their suppliers; trade associations; industry clubs; schools of design; New York buying offices.

BGF Bulletin. Banana Growers Federation Co-Operative Ltd., P.O. Box 31 Murwillumbah, NSW 2484, Australia. Phone: (066)-72-2488 Fax: (066)-72-4868 Monthly. $35.00 per year. Formerly *Banana Bulletin*.

BI Research. Thomas Bishop, editor. BI Research, Inc., P.O. Box 133 Redding, CT 06875. Phone: (203)270-9244 E-mail: birstocks@aol.com • URL: http://www.biresearch.com • Every six weeks. $156.00 per year. Newsletter. Five to eight in-depth investment recommendations per year.

BiblioData's Price Watcher: The Researcher's Guide to Online Prices. BiblioData, P.O. Box 61 Needham Heights, MA 02194. Phone: (781)444-1154 Fax: (781)449-4584 E-mail: lindacooper@erols.com • URL: http://www.bibliodata.com • Semimonthly. Individuals $129.00 per year; institutions, $169.00 per year; nonprofit organizations, $129.00 per year. Newsletter. Provides detailed analysis and reviews of pricing schemes used by Internet and other online information providers.

A Bibliographic Guide to American Colleges and Universities from Colonial Times to the Present. Mark Beach. Greenwood Publishing Group Inc., 88 Post Rd. W. Westport, CT 06881. Phone: 800-225-5800 or (203)226-3571 Fax: (203)222-1502 E-mail: bookinfo@greenwood.com • URL: http://www.greenwood.com • 1975. $55.00.

Bibliographic Guide to Business and Economics. Available from The Gale Group, 27500 Drake Rd. Farmington Hills, MI 48331-3535. Phone: 800-877-GALE or (248)699-GALE Fax: 800-414-5043 or (248)699-8069 E-mail: galeord@galegroup.com • URL: http://www.galegroup.com • Annual. $795.00. Three volumes. Published by G. K. Hall & Co. Lists business and economics publications cataloged by the New York Public Library and the Library of Congress.

Bibliographic Guide to Conference Publications. Available from The Gale Group, 27500 Drake Rd. Farmington Hills, MI 48331-3535. Phone: 800-877-GALE or (248)699-GALE Fax: 800-414-5043 or (248)699-8069 E-mail: galeord@galegroup.com • URL: http://www.galegroup.com • Annual. $545.00. Two volumes. Published by G. K. Hall & Co., Lists a wide range of conference publications cataloged by the New York Public Library and the Library of Congress.

Bibliographic Guide to Government Publications: Foreign. Available from The Gale Group, 27500 Drake Rd. Farmington Hills, MI 48331-3535. Phone: 800-877-GALE or (248)699-GALE Fax: 800-414-5043 or (248)699-8069 E-mail: galeord@galegroup.com • URL: http://www.galegroup.com • Annual. $720.00. Two volumes. Published by G. K. Hall & Co. Lists government publications from countries other than the U. S.

Bibliographic Guide to Government Publications: U. S. Available from The Gale Group, 27500 Drake Rd. Farmington Hills, MI 48331-3535. Phone: 800-877-GALE or (248)699-GALE Fax: 800-414-5043 or (248)699-8069 E-mail: galeord@galegroup.com • URL: http://www.galegroup.com • Annual. $620.00. Two volumes. Published by G. K. Hall & Co. Lists U. S. government publications.

Bibliographic Guide to Law. Available from The Gale Group, 27500 Drake Rd. Farmington Hills, MI 48331-3535. Phone: 800-877-GALE or (248)699-GALE Fax: 800-414-5043 or (248)699-8069 E-mail: galeord@galegroup.com • URL: http://www.galegroup.com • Annual. $545.00. Two volumes. Published by G. K. Hall & Co. Lists legal publications cataloged by the New York Public Library and the Library of Congress.

Bibliographic Guide to Maps and Atlases. Available from The Gale Group, 27500 Drake Rd. Farmington Hills, MI 48331-3535. Phone: 800-877-GALE or (248)699-GALE Fax: 800-414-5043 or (248)699-8069 E-mail: galeord@galegroup.com • URL: http://www.galegroup.com • Annual. $295.00. Published by G. K. Hall & Co. Lists maps and atlases cataloged by the New York Public Library and the Library of Congress.

Bibliographic Guide to Psychology. Available from The Gale Group, 27500 Drake Rd. Farmington Hills, MI 48331-3535. Phone: 800-877-GALE or (248)699-GALE Fax: 800-414-5043 or (248)699-8069 E-mail: galeord@galegroup.com • URL: http://www.galegroup.com • Annual. $295.00. Published by G. K. Hall & Co. Lists psychology publications cataloged by the New York Public Library and the Library of Congress.

Bibliographic Guide to Technology. Available from The Gale Group, 27500 Drake Rd. Farmington Hills, MI 48331-3535. Phone: 800-877-GALE or (248)699-GALE Fax: 800-414-5043 or (248)699-8069 E-mail: galeord@galegroup.com • URL: http://www.galegroup.com • Annual. $545.00. Two volumes. Published by G. K. Hall & Co. Lists technology publications cataloged by the New York Public Library and the Library of Congress.

Bibliographic Index: A Subject List of Bibliographies in English and Foreign Languages. H.W. Wilson Co., 950 University Ave. Bronx, NY 10452. Phone: 800-367-6770 or (718)588-8400 Fax: (718)590-1617 E-mail: custserv@hwwilson.com • URL: http://www.hwwilson.com • Three issues a year. Third issues cumulates all three issues. Service basis.

Bibliographical Center for Research, Inc., Rocky Mountain Region., 14394 E. Evans Ave. Aurora, CO 80014-1478. Phone: 800-397-1552 or (303)751-6277 Fax: (303)751-9787 E-mail: admin@bec.org • URL: http://www.ber.org • Fields of research include information retrieval systems, Internet technology, CD-ROM technology, document delivery, and library automation.

Bibliographical Society of America.

Bibliographical Society of the University of Virginia.

Bibliography of Agriculture. U.S. National Agricultural Libary, Technical Information Systems. Oryx Press, 4041 N. Central Ave., Ste. 700 Phoenix, AZ 85012-3397. Phone: 800-279-6799 or (602)265-2651 Fax: 800-279-4663 or (602)265-6250 E-mail: infor@oryxpress.com • URL: http://www.oryxpress.com • Monthly. $695.00. Annual cumulation.

A Bibliography of Business Ethics, 1981-1985: University of Virginia. Donald G. Jones and Patricia Bennett, editors. The Edwin Mellen Press, P.O. Box 250 Lewiston, NY 14092-0450. Phone: (716)754-2788 Fax: (716)754-4056 E-mail: mellen@ag.net • URL: http://www.mellen.com • 1986. $99.95. (Mellen Studies in Business Series: volume two).

Bibliography of Fund Raising and Philanthropy. National Catholic Development Conference, 86 Front St. Hempstead, NY 11550. Phone: (516)481-6000 1982. $22.50. Second edition.

Bibliography Without Footnotes. Herbert H. Hoffman. Headway Publications, 1700 Port Manleigh Circle Newport Beach, CA 92660. Phone: (714)644-9126 1978. $4.00. Second edition.

Bicycle Dealer Showcase Buyers Guide. Skies America Publishing Co., 9655 S.W. Sunshine, Suite 500 Beaverton, OR 97005. Phone: (503)520-1955 Fax: (503)520-1275 Annual. Free to qualified personnel.

Bicycle Product Suppliers Association.

Bicycles. Available from MarketResearch.com, 641 Ave. of the Americas, 3rd Fl. New York, NY 10011. Phone: 800-298-5699 or (212)807-2629 Fax: (212)807-2716 E-mail: order@marketresearch.com • URL: http://www.marketresearch.com • 1999. $1,295.00 Published by Specialists in Business Information, Inc. ProvidesU.S. and international market data for bicycles and bicycle parts. Gives profiles of major manufacturers.

Bicycling. Rodale Press, Inc., 33 E. Minor St. Emmaus, PA 18098-0099. Phone: 800-666-2806 or (610)967-5171 Fax: (610)967-8963 E-mail: bicycling@rodale.com • URL: http://www.bicycling.com • 11 times a year. $19.97 per year. Information on buying and repairing bicycles.

Biennial Survey of Education in the United States. U.S. Department of Education, Washington, DC 20202. Phone: 800-872-5327 Biennial.

Big Meetings, Big Results. Tom McMahon. NTC/Contemporary Publishing, P.O. Box 545 Blacklick, OH 43004. Phone: 800-323-4900 or (614)755-4151 Fax: (614)755-5645 E-mail: ntcpub@mcgraw-hill.com • URL: http://www.ntc-cb.com • 1994. $19.95. Includes checklists and diagrams. (NTC Business Book Series).

Billboard: The International Newsweekly of Music, Video, and Home Entertainment. BPI Communications, Inc., 1515 Broadway New York, NY 10003-9595. Phone: 800-344-7119 or (646)654-5500 Fax: (646)654-5835 E-mail: info@bpi.com • URL: http://www.bpicomm.com • 51 times a year. $289.00 per year. Newsweekly for the music and home entertainment industries.

Billboard's International Buyer's Guide. Billboard Books, 1515 Broadway New York, NY 10036. Phone: 800-344-7119 or (212)764-7300 Fax: (212)382-6090 URL: http://www.billboard.com • Annual. $141.00. Record companies; music publishers; record and tape wholesalers; services and supplies for the music-record-tape-video industry; record and tape dealer accessories, fixtures, and merchandising products; includes United States and over 65 countries.

Billboard's International Talent and Touring Directory: The Music Industry's Worldwide Reference Source: Talent, Talent Management, Booking Agencies, Promoters, Venue Facilities, Venue Services and Products. BPI Communications, Inc., 770 Broadway New York, NY 10003-9595. Phone: 800-344-7119 or (646)654-5500 Fax: (646)654-5835 E-mail: info@bpi.com • URL: http://www.bpicomm.com • Annual. $109.00. Lists entertainers, managers, booking agents, and others in the worldwide entertainment industry.

BIN Number Directory of all Visa and Mastercard Issuing Banks. Fraud and Theft Information Bureau, P.O. Box 400 Boynton Beach, FL 33425. Phone: (561)737-8700 Fax: (561)737-5800 E-mail: sales@fraudandtheftinfo.com • Annual. $1,175.00. Base edition. Semiannual updates, $360.00 per year. Numerical arrangement of about 30,000 banks worldwide. BIN numbers (also called ISO or prefix numbers) identify a credit card holder's issuing bank.

Binding Industries of America.

Binding of Books. Herbert P. Horne. M.S.G. Haskell House, P.O. Box 190420 Brooklyn, NY 11219-0009. Phone: (718)435-7878 Fax: (718)633-7050 1969. $75.00. Reprint of 1894 edition. (Reference Series No. 44).

Bio-Base: A Master Index on Microfiche to Biographical Sketches Found in Current and Retrospective Biographical Dictionaries. The Gale Group, 27500 Drake Rd. Farmington Hills, MI 48331-3535. Phone: 800-877-GALE or (248)699-GALE Fax: 800-414-5043 or (248)699-8069 E-mail: galeord@galegroup.com • URL: http://www.galegroup.com • Annual. $1,095.00; update, $295.00. Indexes more than 12 million biographical sketches.

BioCommerce Abstracts. Biocommerce Data, Ltd., 18-20 Hill Rise Richmond, Surrey TW10 64A, England. E-mail: biocom@dial.pipex.com • URL: http://www.pjbpubs.co.uk/

bcd • Semimonthly. $2,715 per year. Quarterly cumulation. Includes CD-Rom. Emphasis is on commercial biotechnology.

Biocycle; Journal of Composting and Recycling. J.G. Press, Inc., 419 State Ave. Emmaus, PA 18049. Phone: (610)967-4135 E-mail: biocycle@jgress.com • URL: http://www.jgress.com • Monthly. $69.00 per year. Authoritative reports on the management of municipal sludge and solid wastes via recycling and composting.

Biofuels. OECD Publications and Information Center, 2001 L St., N.W., Ste. 650 Washington, DC 20036-4922. Phone: 800-456-6323 or (202)785-6323 Fax: (202)785-0350 E-mail: washington.contact@oecd.org • URL: http://www.oecdwash.org • 1994. $28.00. Produced by the International Energy Agency (IEA). Analyzes costs and greenhouse gas emissions resulting from the production and use of ethanol fuel. In addition to ethanol from corn, wheat, and sugar beets, consideration is given to diesel fuel from rapeseed oil and methanol from wood.

Biographical Dictionary of American Journalism. Joseph P. McKerns, editor. Greenwood Publishing Group Inc., 88 Post Rd., W. Westport, CT 06881-5001. Phone: 800-225-5800 or (203)226-3571 Fax: (203)222-2540 E-mail: bookinfo@greenwood.com • URL: http://www.greenwood.com • 1989. $65.00. Covers major mass media: newspapers, radio, television, and magazines. Includes reporters, editors, columnists, cartoonists, commentators, etc.

Biographical Dictionary of American Labor. Gary M. Fink, editor. Greenwood Publishing Group Inc., 88 Post Rd., W. Westport, CT 06881-5007. Phone: 800-225-5800 or (203)226-3571 Fax: (203)222-2540 E-mail: bookinfo@greenwood.com • URL: http://www.greenwood.com • 1984. $115.00.

Biographical Directory of the American Congress, 1774-1996. CQ Staff Directories, Inc., 815 Slaters Lane Alexandria, VA 22314. Phone: 800-252-1722 or (703)739-0900 Fax: (703)739-0234 E-mail: staffdir@staffdirectories.com • URL: http://www.staffdirectories.com • 1996. $295.00. Provides detailed biographies of members of the Continental Congress (1774-1789) and the U. S. Congress (1789-1996). Includes presidential Cabinet members.

Biography: An Interdisciplinary Quarterly. Biographical Research Center. University of Hawaii Press Journals Dept., 2840 Kolowalu St. Honolulu, HI 96822. Phone: (808)956-8833 Fax: (808)988-6052 E-mail: biography@hawaii.edu • URL: http://www.hawaii.edu • Quarterly. Individuals, $28.00 per year; institutions, $40.00 per year.

Biography and Genealogy Master Index. The Gale Group, 27500 Drake Rd. Farmington Hills, MI 48331-3535. Phone: 800-877-GALE or (248)699-GALE Fax: 800-414-5043 or (248)699-8069 E-mail: galeord@galegroup.com • URL: http://www.galegroup.com • Annual. $270.00. Three volumes. Previous editions available.

Biography Index. H.W. Wilson Co., 950 University Ave, Bronx, NY 10452. Phone: 800-367-6770 or (718)588-8400 Fax: (718)590-1617 E-mail: custserv@hwwilson.com • URL: http://www.hwwilson.com • Quarterly. $215.00 per year. Annual and biennial cumulations.

Biography Index Online. H. W. Wilson Co., 950 University Ave. Bronx, NY 10452. Phone: 800-367-6770 or (718)588-8400 Fax: (718)590-1617 An index to biographies appearing in periodicals, newspapers, current books, and other sources. Covers 1984 to date. Inquire as to online cost and availability.

Biography Master Index ÎOnlineI. The Gale Group, 27500 Drake Rd. Farmington Hills, MI 48331-3535. Phone: 800-877-GALE or (248)699-GALE Fax: 800-414-5043 or (248)699-8069 E-mail: galeord@gale.com • URL: http://www.gale.com • An index to biographies appearing in hundreds of biographical reference volumes, both historical and current. Inquire as to online cost and availability.

Biological and Agricultural Index. H.W. Wilson Co., 950 University Ave. Bronx, NY 10452. Phone: 800-367-6770 or (718)588-8400 Fax: (718)590-1617 E-mail: custserv@hwwilson.com • URL: http://www.hwwilson.com • 11 times a year. Annual and quarterly cumulations. Service basis.

Biological and Agricultural Index Online. H. W. Wilson Co., 950 University Ave. Bronx, NY 10452. Phone: 800-367-6770 or (718)588-8400 Fax: (718)590-1617 Indexes a wide variety of agricultural and biological periodicals, 1983 to date. Monthly updates. Inquire as to online cost and availability.

BioMed Strategies. Thomson Financial Securities Data, Two Gateway Center Newark, NJ 07102. Phone: 888-989-8373 or (973)622-3100 Fax: (973)622-1421 E-mail: tfsd.cs@tfn.com • URL: http://www.tfsd.com • Monthly. $2,995.00 per year. CD-ROM contains full text of investment analysts' reports on companies operating in the following fields: biotechnology, pharmaceuticals, medical products, and health care.

Biomedical Engineering Society.

Biomedical Instrumentation and Technology. Association for the Advancement of Medical Instrumentation. Hanley and Belfus, Inc., 210 S. 13th St. Philadelphia, PA 19107. Phone: (215)546-7293 Fax: (215)790-9330 Bimonthly. Individuals, $106.00 per year; institutions, $136.00 per year.

Biomedical Products. Cahners Business Information, New Product Information, 301 Gibraltar Dr. Morris Plains, NJ 07950. Phone: 800-622-7776 or (973)292-5100 or (973)292-0650 Fax: (973)605-1220 E-mail: corporatecommunications@cahners.com • URL: http://www.cahners.com • Monthly. $43.90 per year. Features new products and services.

Biomedical Technology Information Service. Aspen Publishers, Inc., 200 Orchard Ridge Dr. Gaithersburg, MD 20878. Phone: 800-638-8437 or (301)417-7500 Fax: (301)417-7650 E-mail: customer.service@aspenpubl.com • URL: http://www.aspenpub.com • Semimonthly. Individuals, $335.00 per year; institutions, $385.00 per year. Newsletter on developments in medical devices and medical electronics.

BioScan: The Worldwide Biotech Industry Reporting Service. American Health Consultants, Inc., 3525 Piedmont Ave., N.E. Bldg. 6, Suite 400 Atlanta, GA 30305. Phone: 800-688-2421 or (404)262-5476 Fax: 800-284-3291 E-mail: custserv@ahcpub.com • URL: http://www.ahcpub.com • Bimonthly. $1,395.00 per year. Looseleaf. Provides detailed information on over 900 U. S. and foreign companies broadly classified as biotechnological. In addition to medical technology and advanced pharmaceutical firms, includes firms doing research in food processing, waste management, agriculture, and veterinary science.

Bioscience. American Institute of Biological Sciences, 1444 Eye St. N. W., Suite 200 Washington, DC 20005. Phone: (202)628-1500 Fax: (202)628-1509 E-mail: bioscience@aibs.org • URL: http://www.aibs.org/bioscience.html • Monthly. Members, $70.00 per year; institutions, $190.00 per year.

BioTechniques: The Journal of Laboratory Technology for Bioresearch. Eaton Publishing, 154 E. Central St. Natick, MA 01760. Phone: (508)655-8282 Fax: (508)655-9910 12 times a year. $110.00 per year.

Biotechnology. John E. Smith. Cambridge University Press, 40 W. 20th St. New York, NY 10011-4211. Phone: 800-221-4512 or (212)924-3900 Fax: (212)691-3239 E-mail: info@cup.org • URL: http://www.cup.org • 1996. $59.95. Third edition. Provides discussions of biotechnology in relation to medicine, agriculture, food, the environment, biological fuel generation, genetics, ethics, safety, etc. Includes a glossary and bibliography. (Studies in Biology Series).

Biotechnology Abstracts on CD-ROM. Derwent, Inc., 1725 Duke St., Suite 250 Alexandria, VA 22314. Phone: 800-337-9368 or (703)706-4220 Fax: (703)519-5838 E-mail: info@derwent.com • URL: http://www.derwent.com • Quarterly. Price on application. Provides CD-ROM indexing and abstracting of the world's biotechnology journal literature since 1982, including genetic engineering topics.

Biotechnology and the Law. Iver P. Cooper. West Group, 610 Opperman Dr. Eagan, MN 55123. Phone: 800-328-4880 or (651)687-7000 Fax: 800-213-2323 or (651)687-5827 URL: http://www.westgroup.com • Two looseleaf volumes. $260.00. per year. Periodic supplementation.

Biotechnology Directory. Grove's Dictionaries Inc., 345 Park Ave. S. New York, NY 10010-1707. Phone: 800-221-2123 or (212)689-9200 Fax: (212)689-9711 E-mail: grove@grovereference.com • URL: http://www.grovereference.com • Annual. $295.00. Provides information on more than 10,000 biotechnology-related companies and organizations. Geographical arrangement, with name and product indexes.

Biotechnology from A to Z. William Bains. Oxford University Press, Inc., 198 Madison Ave. New York, NY 10016-4314. Phone: 800-451-7556 or (212)726-6000 Fax: (212)726-6446 E-mail: custserv@oup-usa.org • URL: http://www.oup-usa.org • 1998. $27.95. Second edition. Covers the terminology of biotechnology for non-specialists.

Biotechnology Industry Organization.

Biotechnology Instrumentation Markets. Theta Reports/PJB Medical Publications, Inc., 1775 Broadway, Suite 511 New York, NY 10019. Phone: (212)262-8230 Fax: (212)262-8234 E-mail: customerservice@thetareports.com • URL: http://www.thetareports.com • 1999. $1,495.00. Contains market research data, with projections through the year 2002. Covers such products as specialized analytical instruments, filters/membranes, and mass spectrometers. (Theta Report No. 960.)

Biotechnology Process Engineering Center., Massachusetts Institute of Technology, 77 Massachusetts Ave., Room 16-429 Cambridge, MA 02139-4307. Phone: (617)253-0805 Fax: (617)253-2400 E-mail: childs@mit.edu • URL: http://www.web.mit.edu/bpec/ • Includes an Industrial Advisory Board and a Biotechnology Industrial Consortium.

BioWorld Today: The Daily Biotechnology Newspaper. American Health Consultants, Inc., BioWorld Publishing Group, 3525 Piedmont Rd., N.E., Bldg. 6, Suite 400 Atlanta, GA 30305-5278. Phone: 800-688-2421 or (404)262-7436 Fax: (404)814-0759 E-mail: custserv@ahcpub.com • URL: http://www.ahcpub.com • Daily. $1,897.00 per year. Covers news of the biotechnology and genetic engineering industries, with emphasis on finance, investments, and marketing.

BioWorld Week: The Weekly Biotechnology Report. American Health Consultants, Inc., BioWorld Publishing Group, 3525 Piedmont Rd., N.E., Bldg. 6, Suite 400 Atlanta, GA 30305-5278. Phone: 800-688-2421 or (404)262-7436 Fax: (404)814-0759 E-mail: custserv@ahcpub.com • URL: http://www.achpub.com • Weekly. $747.00 per year. Provides a weekly summary of business and financial news relating to the biotechnology and genetic engineering industries.

Biscuit and Cracker Distributors Association., 401 N. Michigan Ave. Chicago, IL 60611-4267. Phone: (312)644-6610 Fax: (312)321-6869 Members are distributors and manufacturers of cookies, crackers, and related products.

Biscuit and Cracker Manufacturers Association., 8484 Georgia Ave., Suite 700 Silver Spring, MD 20910. Phone: (301)608-1552 Fax: (301)608-1557 E-mail: frooney@thebcma.org • URL: http://www.thebcma.org • Members are bakers of crackers and cookies.

Bits and Pieces: A Monthly Mixture of Horse Sense and Common Sense About Working with People. Economics Press, Inc., 12 Daniel Rd. Fairfield, NJ 07006. Phone: 800-526-2554 or (973)227-1224 Fax: (973)227-9742 E-mail: info@epinc.com • URL: http://www.epinc.com • Monthly. $22.00 per year. Quantity rates available. Pamphlets contain inspirational humor for employees.

Bituminous Research Laboratory. Iowa State University of Science and Technology

The Biz: The Basic Business, Legal, and Financial Aspects of the Film Industry. Schuyler M. Moore. Silman-James Press, 3624 Shannon Rd. Los Angeles, CA 90027. Phone: 800-729-6423 or (323)661-9922 Fax: (323)661-9933 E-mail: silmanjamespress@earthlink.net • 2000. $26.95. Provides information for independent filmmakers on raising money, business structure, budgeting, loans, legalities, taxation, industry jargon, and other topics. The author is an entertainment industry lawyer.

Bizlink. Rogers MediaPhone: (416)596-5702 Fax: (416)596-5912 URL: http://www.bizlink.com • Web site provides news and information from 30 Canadian business and industrial publications issued by Rogers Media (formerly Maclean Hunter). Keyword searching is available for "all of the Bizlink archive" or for each of seven areas: Industry, Financial, Construction, Retailing, Marketing, Media, and Agriculture. Updates are daily. Fees: Free.

Black and White Photography: A Basic Manual. Henry Horenstein. Little, Brown and Co., Time and Life Bldg., 1271 Ave. of the Americas New York, NY 10020. Phone: 800-343-9204 or (212)522-8700 Fax: 800-286-9741 or (212)522-2067 E-mail: cust.service@littlebrown.com • URL: http://www.littlebrown.com • 1983. $24.95. Revised edition.

Black Careers. Emory W. Washington, editor. Project Magazine, Inc., P.O. Box 8214 Philadelphia, PA 19101. Phone: (215)387-1600 Bimonthly. $20.00 per year. Provides information on career preparation and advancement to working professionals in industry, business, and technology.

Black Caucus of the American Library Association.

Black Diamond. Black Diamond Co., Inc., 159 Pierce Rd. Highland Park, IL 60035-5326. Phone: (708)922-8031 Monthly. $36.00 per year.

Black Enterprise. Earl G. Graves Publishing Co., 130 Fifth Ave. New York, NY 10011. Phone: 800-727-7777 or (212)242-8000 Fax: (212)886-9610 E-mail: beeditor@aol.com • URL: http://www.blackenterprise.com • Monthly. $21.95 per year. Covers careers, personal finances and leisure.

Black Enterprise: Top Black Businesses. Earl G. Graves Publishing Co., 130 Fifth Ave., 10th Fl. New York, NY 10011. Phone: 800-727-7777 or (212)242-8000 Fax: (212)886-9610 E-mail: beeditor@aol.com • URL: http://www.blackenterprise.com • Annual. $3.95. Lists of 100 black-owned businesses, banks, savings and loan associations, and insurance companies.

The Black Manager: Making It in the Corporate World. Floyd Dickens and Jacqueline B. Dickens. AMACOM, 1601 Broadway, 12th Fl. New York, NY 10019. Phone: 800-262-9699 or (212)586-8100 Fax: (212)903-8168 E-mail: custmserv@amanet.org • URL: http://www.amanet.org • 1991. $22.95. Revised edition. Covers the four following career phases: entry, adjusting, planned growth, and success. Advice on personal and professional development is included.

Black Tie Optional: The Ultimate Guide to Planning and Producing Successful Special Events. Harry A. Freedman and Karen F. Smith. Fund Raising Institute, 27500 Drake Rd. Farmington Hills, MI 48331-3535. Phone: 800-877-8238 or (248)699-GALE Fax: 800-414-5043 or (248)699-8069 E-mail: galeord@gale.com • URL: http://www.galegroup.com • 1994. $35.00. Includes checklists, flow charts, and worksheets.

Black's Law Dictionary. Bryan A. Garner, editor. West Group, 610 Opperman Dr. Eagan, MN 55123. Phone: 800-328-4880 or (651)687-7000 Fax: 800-213-2323 or (651)687-5827 URL: http://www.westgroup.com • 1999. $39.00. Seventh edition. Contains a total of 30,000 legal definitions, including 5,000 new terms, 2,200 legal maxims, and 2,000 illustrative quotations from scholarly works.

Black's Law Dictionary. Henry Campbell and Henry Black. West Publishing Co., College and School Div., 610 Opperman Dr. Saint Paul, MN 55164-1396. Phone: 800-328-9352 or (612)687-8000 Fax: 800-213-2323 or (612)687-5388 E-mail: legal_ed@westgroup.com • URL: http://www.lawschool.westgroup.com • 1999. $69.90. Seventh edition. Definitions of the terms and phrases of American and English jurisprudence, ancient and modern.

Blackwell Encyclopedic Dictionary of Accounting. Rashad Abdel-khalik. Blackwell Publishers, 350 Main St., 6th Fl. Malden, MA 02148-5018. Phone: 800-216-2522 or (617)388-8200 Fax: (781)388-8210 E-mail: books@blackwellpub.com • URL: http://www.blackwellpub.com • 1997. $105.95. The editor is associated with the University of Florida. Contains definitions of key terms combined with longer articles written by various U. S. and foreign business educators. Includes bibliographies and index. (Blackwell Encyclopedia of Management Series).

Blackwell Encyclopedic Dictionary of Business Ethics. Patricia H. Werhane and R. Edward Freeman, editors. Blackwell Publishers, 350 Main St., 6th Fl. Malden, MA 02148-5018. Phone: 800-216-2522 or (781)388-8200 Fax: (781)388-8210 E-mail: books@blackwellpub.com • URL: http://www.blackwellpub.com • 1997. $105.95. The editors are associated with the University of Virginia. Contains definitions of key terms combined with longer articles written by various U. S. and foreign business educators. Includes bibliographies and index. (Blackwell Encyclopedia of Management Series).

Blackwell Encyclopedic Dictionary of Finance. Dean Paxson and Douglas Wood, editors. Blackwell Publishers, 350 Main St., 6th Fl. Malden, MA 02148-5018. Phone: 800-216-2522 or (781)388-8200 Fax: (781)388-8210 E-mail: books@blackwellpub.com • URL: http://www.blackwellpub.com • 1997. $110.00. The editors are associated with the University of Manchester. Contains definitions of key terms combined with longer articles written by various U. S. and foreign business educators. Includes bibliographies and index. (Blackwell Encyclopedia of Management Series).

Blackwell Encyclopedic Dictionary of Human Resource Management. Lawrence H. Peters and Charles R. Greer, editors. Blackwell Publishers, 350 Main St., 6th Fl. Malden, MA 02148-5018. Phone: 800-216-2522 or (781)388-8200 Fax: (781)388-8210 E-mail: books@blackwellpub.com • URL: http://www.blackwellpub.com • 1996. $105.95. The editors are associated with Texas Christian University. Contains definitions of key terms combined with longer articles written by various U. S. and foreign business educators. Includes bibliographies and index. (Blackwell Encyclopedia of Management Series).

Blackwell Encyclopedic Dictionary of International Management. John J. O'Connell, editor. Blackwell Publishers, 350 Main St., 6th Fl. Malden, MA 02148-5018. Phone: 800-216-2522 or (781)388-8200 Fax: (781)388-8210 E-mail: books@blackwellpub.com • URL: http://www.blackwellpub.com • 1997. $105.95. The editor is associated with the American Graduate School of International Management. Contains definitions of key terms combined with longer articles written by various U. S. and foreign business educators. Includes bibliographies and index. (Blackwell Encyclopedia of Management Series).

Blackwell Encyclopedic Dictionary of Management Information Systems. Gordon B. Davis, editor. Blackwell Publishers, 350 Main St., 6th Fl. Malden, MA 02148-5018. Phone: 800-216-2522 or (781)388-8200 Fax: (781)388-8210 E-mail: books@blackwellpub.com • URL: http://www.blackwellpub.com • 1996. $110.00. The editor is associated with the University of Minnesota. Contains definitions of key terms combined with longer articles written by various U. S. and foreign business educators. Includes bibliographies and index. *Blackwell Encyclopedia of Management Series*.

Blackwell Encyclopedic Dictionary of Managerial Economics. Robert McAuliffe, editor. Blackwell Publishers, 350 Main St., 6th Fl. Malden, MA 02148-5018. Phone: 800-216-2522 or (781)388-8200 Fax: (781)388-8210 E-mail: books@blackwellpub.com • URL: http://www.blackwellpub.com • 1997. $105.95. The editor is associated with Boston College. Contains definitions of key terms combined with longer articles written by various U. S. and foreign business educators. Includes bibliographies and index. *Blackwell Encyclopedia of Management Series*.

Blackwell Encyclopedic Dictionary of Marketing. Barbara R. Lewis and Dale Littler, editors. Blackwell Publishers, 350 Main St., 6th Fl. Malden, MA 02148-5018. Phone: 800-216-2522 or (781)388-8200 Fax: (781)388-8210 E-mail: books@blackwellpub.com • URL: http://www.blackwellpub.com • 1996. $105.95. The editors are associated with the Manchester School of Management. Contains definitions of key terms combined with longer articles written by various U. S. and foreign business educators. Includes bibliographies and index. (Blackwell Encyclopedia of Management series.)

Blackwell Encyclopedic Dictionary of Operations Management. Nigel Slack, editor. Blackwell Publishers, 350 Main St., 6th Fl. Malden, MA 02148-5018. Phone: 800-216-2522 or (781)388-8200 Fax: (781)388-8210 E-mail: books@blackwellpub.com • URL: http://www.blackwellpub.com • 1997. $105.95. The editor is associated with the University of Warwick, England. Contains definitions of key terms combined with longer articles written by various U. S. and foreign business educators. Includes bibliographies and index. (Blackwell Encyclopedia of Management Series.)

Blackwell Encyclopedic Dictionary of Organizational Behavior. Nigel Nicholson, editor. Blackwell Publishers, 350 Main St., 6th Fl. Malden, MA 02148-5018. Phone: 800-216-2522 or (781)388-8200 Fax: (781)388-8210 E-mail: books@blackwellpub.com • URL: http://www.blackwellpub.com • 1995. $105.95. The editor is associated with the London Business School. Contains definitions of key terms combined with longer articles written by various U. S. and foreign business educators. Includes bibliographies and index. *Blackwell Encyclopedia of Management Series*.

Blackwell Encyclopedic Dictionary of Strategic Management. Derek F. Channon, editor. Blackwell Publishers, 350 Main St., 6th Fl. Malden, MA 02148-5018. Phone: 800-216-2522 or (781)388-8200 Fax: (781)388-8210 E-mail: books@blackwellpub.com • URL: http://www.blackwellpub.com • 1997. $110.00. The editor is associated with Imperial College, London. Contains definitions of key terms combined with longer articles written by various U. S. and foreign business educators. Includes bibliographies and index. (Blackwell Encyclopedia of Management Series.)

Bloomberg: A Magazine for Market Professionals. Bloomberg L.P., 499 Park Ave. New York, NY 10022. Phone: 800-388-2749 or (212)318-2000 Fax: (212)980-4585 E-mail: magazine@bloomberg.com • URL: http://www.bloomberg.com • Monthly. Free to qualified personnel. Edited for securities dealers and investment managers.

Bloomberg Personal Finance. Bloomberg L.P., 499 Park Ave. New York, NY 10022. Phone: 800-388-2749 or (212)318-2000 Fax: (212)980-4585 E-mail: personal@bloomberg.com • URL: http://www.bloomberg.com • Monthly. $24.95 per year. Provides advice on personal finance, investments, travel, real estate, and maintaining an ''upscale life style.'' Formerly *Bloomberg Personal*.

BLR Encyclopedia of Prewritten Job Descriptions. Business and Legal Reports, Inc., P.O. Box 6001 Old Saybrook, CT 06475-6001. Phone: 800-727-5257 or (203)318-0000 Fax: (203)245-2559 $159.95. Looseleaf. Two volumes. Covers all levels ''from president to mail clerk.''

Blue Book of Building and Construction. Blue Book of Building and Construction, P.O. Box 500 Jefferson Valley, NY 10535. Phone: 800-431-2584 or (914)245-0200 Fax: (914)245-5781 Annual. Controlled circulation. 11 regional editions. Lists architects, contractors, subcontractors, manufacturers and suppliers of constructions materials and equipment.

Blue Book of Commercial Collection. International Association Commercial Collectors, 4040 W. 70th St. Minneapolis, MN 55435-4199. Phone: (612)925-0760 Fax: (612)926-1624 E-mail: smitht@collector.com • URL: http://www.collector.com • Annual. $25.00.

Blue Book of Fur Farming. Becker Publishing, PO Box 655 Hopkins, MN 55343. Phone: (952)949-2159 Fax: (952)934-3668 URL: http://www.beckerpublishing.com • Annual. $20.00. Lists manufacturers and suppliers of equipment and materials used in the raising of fur-bearing animals for the fur industry.

Blue Book of Stock Reports. MPL Communication Inc., 133 Richmond St., W., Suite 700 Toronto, ON, Canada M5H 3M8. Phone: (416)869-1177 Fax: (416)869-0456 Biweekly. $260.00 per year. Canadian Business Service reports on over 250 Canadian companies.

Blue Chip Economic Indicators: What Top Economists Are Saying About the U.S. Outlook for the Year Ahead. Aspen Publishers, Inc., 200 Orchard Ridge Dr. Gaithersburg, MD 20878. Phone: 800-638-8437 or (301)417-7500 Fax: (301)695-7931 E-mail: customer.service@aspenpubl.com • URL: http://www.aspenpub.com • Monthly. $654.00 per year. Newsletter containing U. S. economic consensus forecasts.

Blue Chip Financial Forecasts: What Top Analysts are Saying About U. S. and Foreign Interest Rates, Monetary Policy, Inflation, and Economic Growth. Aspen Publishers, Inc., 200 Orchard Ridge Dr. Gaithersburg, MD 20878. Phone: 800-638-8437 or (301)417-7500 Fax: (301)695-7931 E-mail: customer.service@aspenpubl.com • URL: http://www.aspenpub.com • Monthly. $654.00 per year. Newsletter. Gives forecasts about a year in advance for interest rates, inflation, currency exchange rates, monetary policy, and economic growth rates.

Blue Cross and Blue Shield Association.

Blue List of Current Municipal and Corporate Bond Offerings. Standard and Poor's, 55 Water St. New York, NY 10041. Phone: 800-221-5277 or (212)438-2000 Fax: (212)438-0040 E-mail: questions@standardandpoors.com • URL: http://www.standardandpoors.com • Daily. $940.00 per year. Compendium of municipal and corporate bond offers.

Blue Sky Law. Joseph C. Long. West Group, 610 Opperman Dr. Eagan, MN 55123. Phone: 800-328-4880 or (651)687-7000 Fax: 800-213-2323 or (651)687-5827 URL: http://www.westgroup.com • $250.00 per year. Two looseleaf volumes. Periodic supplementation. (Securities Law Series).

Blue Sky Law Reports. CCH, Inc., 4025 W. Peterson Ave. Chicago, IL 60646-6085. Phone: 800-248-3248 or (773)583-8500 Fax: 800-224-8299 or (773)866-3608 URL: http://www.cch.com • Semimonthly. $1,214.00. Five looseleaf volumes. Covers state securities laws.

Blue Sky Regulation. Matthew Bender & Co., Inc., Two Park Ave. New York, NY 10016. Phone: 800-223-1940 or (212)448-2000 Fax: (212)244-3188 E-mail: international@bender.com • URL: http://www.bender.com • $950.00. Four looseleaf volumes. Periodic supplementation. Covers state securities laws and regulations.

Blueprint for Franchising a Business. Steven S. Raab and Gregory Matusky. John Wiley and Sons, Inc., 605 Third Ave. New York, NY 10158-0012. Phone: 800-225-5945 or (212)850-6000 Fax: (212)850-6088 E-mail: info@wiley.com • URL: http://www.wiley.com • 1987. $45.00.

BMA Membership Directory and Resource Guide. Business Marketing Association, 400 N. Michigan Ave., 15th Fl. Chicago, IL 60611-4104. Phone: (312)409-4262 Fax: (312)409-4266 E-mail: bma@marketing.org • URL: http://www.marketing.org • Annual. Academic, $75.00; business, $150.00. Lists professionals in business and industrial advertising and marketing. Formerly *BMA Membership Directory and Yellow Pages*.

BMI: Music World. Broadcast Music, Inc., 320 W. 57th St. New York, NY 10019. Phone: (212)586-2000 Quarterly. Free to qualified personnel. Formerly *BMI: The Many Worlds of Music*.

BNA Fair Employment Practice Service. Bureau of National Affairs, Inc., 1231 25th St. Washington, DC 20037-1197. Phone: 800-372-1033 or (202)452-4200 Fax: (202)822-8092 E-mail: books@bna.com • URL: http://www.bna.com • Weekly. $501.00 per year. Three volumes. Looseleaf.

BNA Pension and Benefits Reporter. Bureau of National Affairs, Inc., 1231 25th St., N.W. Washington, DC 20037-1197. Phone: 800-372-1033 or (202)452-4200 Fax: (202)822-8092 E-mail: books@bna.com • URL: http://www.bna.com • Weekly. $996.00 per year. Three looseleaf volumes. Legal developments affecting pensions. Formerly *BNA Pension Reporter*.

BNA Policy and Practice Series. Bureau of National Affairs, Inc., 1231 25th St., N.W. Washington, DC 20037-1197. Phone: 800-371-1033 or (202)452-4200 Fax: (202)822-8092 E-mail: books@bna.com • URL: http://www.bna.com • Weekly. $1,749.00 per year. Five volumes. Looseleaf. Includes personnel management, labor relations, fair employment practice, compensation, and wage-hour laws.

BNA Policy and Practice Series: Wages and Hours. Bureau of National Affairs, Inc., 1231 25th St., N.W. Washington, DC 20037. Phone: 800-372-1033 or (202)452-4200 Fax: (202)822-8092 E-mail: books@bna.com • URL: http://www.bna.com • Biweekly. $835.00 per year. Three volumes. Looseleaf.

BNA Policy and Practice Series: Water Pollution Control. Bureau of National Affairs, 1231 25th St., N.W. Washington, DC 20037-1197. Phone: 800-372-1033 or (202)452-4200 Fax: (202)822-8092 E-mail: books@bna.com • URL: http://www.bna.com • Biweekly. $1,136.00 per year. Looseleaf.

BNA's Banking Report: Legal and Regulatory Developments in the Financial Services Industry. Bureau of National Affairs, Inc., 1231 25th St., N.W. Washington, DC 20037-1197. Phone: 800-372-1033 or (202)452-4200 Fax: (202)822-8092 E-mail: books@bna.com • URL: http://www.bna.com • Weekly. $1,221.00 per year. Two volumes. Looseleaf. Emphasis on federal regulations.

BNA's Patent, Trademark and Copyright Journal. Bureau of National Affairs, Inc., 1231 25th St., N.W. Washington, DC 20037-1197. Phone: 800-372-1033 or (202)452-4200 Fax: (202)822-8092 E-mail: books@bna.com • URL: http://www.bna.com • Weekly. $1,366.00 per year.

BNA's Safetynet. Bureau of National Affairs, Inc., 1231 25th St., N.W. Washington, DC 20037-1197. Phone: 800-372-1033 or (202)452-4200 Fax: (202)822-8092 E-mail: books@bna.com • URL: http://www.bna.com • Biweekly. $680.00 per year. Looseleaf. Formerly *Job Safety and Health*.

BNA's Workers' Compensation Report. Bureau of National Affairs, Inc., 1231 25th St., N. W. Washington, DC 2003-1197. Phone: 800-372-1033 or (202)452-4200 Fax: (202)822-8092 URL: http://www.bna.com • Biweekly. $570.00 per year. Looseleaf business and legal service.

Board Member: The Periodical for Members of the National Center for Nonprofit Boards. National Center for Nonprofit Boards, 2000 L St., N. W., Suite 510 Washington, DC 20036-4907. Phone: 800-883-6262 or (202)452-6262 Fax: (202)452-6299 E-mail: ncnb@ncnb.org • URL: http://

www.ncnb.org • 10 times a year. Membership. Newsletter for trustees of nonprofit organizations.

Board of Certified Product Safety Management., 8009 Carita Court Bethesda, MD 20817. Phone: (301)770-2540 Evaluates qualifications of product safety managers.

Board of Immigration Appeals Interim Decisions. U.S. Immigration and Naturalization Service. Available from U.S. Government Printing Office, Washington, DC 20402. Phone: (202)512-1800 Fax: (202)512-2250 E-mail: gpoaccess@gpo.gov • URL: http://www.access.gpo.gov • Irregular.

Board of Research., Babson College Babson Park, MA 02457. Phone: (718)239-5339 Fax: (718)239-6416 URL: http://www.babson.edu/bor • Research areas include management, entrepreneurial characteristics, and multi-product inventory analysis.

Board of Trade of the Wholesale Seafood Merchants.

Boardwatch Magazine Directory of Internet Service Providers. Penton Media Inc., 1300 E. Ninth St. Cleveland, OH 44114. Phone: (216)696-7000 Fax: (216)696-0836 E-mail: corpcomm@penton.com • URL: http://www.penton.com • Monthly. $36.00 per year. Lists thousands of Internet service providers by state and telephone area code, with monthly fees, ISDN availability, and other information. Includes a ''Glossary of Internet Terms'' and detailed technical articles on accessing the Internet.

Boardwatch Magazine: Guide to the Internet, World Wide Web, and BBS. Penton Media Inc., 1300 E. Ninth St. Cleveland, OH 44114. Phone: (216)696-7000 Fax: (216)696-0836 E-mail: corpcomm@penton.com • URL: http://www.penton.com • Monthly. $72.00 per year. Covers World Wide Web publishing, Internet technology, educational aspects of online communication, Internet legalities, and other computer communication topics.

Boat and Motor Dealer. Preston Publications, Inc., 6600 W. Touhy Ave. Niles, IL 60714. Phone: (847)647-2900 Fax: (847)965-7639 URL: http://www.boatdealer.marina.info.com • Monthly. $48.00. Boat retailing.

Boat Owners Association of the United States.

Boating. Hachette Filipacchi Magazines, Inc., 1633 Broadway, 43rd Fl. New York, NY 10019. Phone: 800-274-4027 or (212)767-6000 Fax: (212)767-5600 Monthly. $28.00 per year.

Boating Industry: The Management Magazine of the Boating Industry. Intertec Publishing Corp., 6151 Powers Ferry Rd., N.W., Suite 200 Atlanta, GA 30339. Phone: 800-400-5945 or (770)955-2500 Fax: (404)955-0400 E-mail: subs@intertec.com • URL: http://www.intertec.com • Monthly. $38.00 per year. Supplement available: *Boating Industry Marine Buyer's Guide.*

Bobbin. Bobbin Blenheim Media Corp., P.O. Box 1986 Columbia, SC 29202. Phone: (803)771-7500 Fax: (803)799-1461 URL: http://www.bobbin.com • Monthly. Free to qualified personnel. For management in the sewing products industry. Covers problem solving, technology and legislation.

Body Fashions: Intimate Apparel. Advanstar Communications, Inc., One Park Ave., 2nd Fl. New York, NY 10016-5802. Phone: 800-346-0085 or (212)951-6600 Fax: (212)951-6793 E-mail: information@advanstar.com • URL: http://www.advanstar.com • Monthly. $39.00 per year.

Bogle on Mutual Funds: New Perspectives for the Intelligent Investor. John C. Bogle. McGraw-Hill Professional, 1221 Ave. of the Americas New York, NY 10020. Phone: 800-722-4726 or (212)904-2000 Fax: (212)904-2072 E-mail: customer.service@mcgraw-hill.com • URL: http://www.mcgraw-hill.com • 1993. $25.00.

The Bond Buyer. American Banker Newsletter, Thomson Financial Media, One State St. Place New York, NY 10004-1549. Phone: 800-733-4371 or (212)803-8345 Fax: (212)843-9600 URL: http://www.americanbanker.com • Daily edition, $1,897 per year. Weekly edition, $525.00 per year. Reports on new municipal bond issues.

Bond Buyer's Municipal Marketplace. Thomson Financial Publishing, 4709 W. Golf Rd. Skokie, IL 60076-1253. Phone: 800-321-3373 or (847)676-9600 Fax: (847)933-8101 E-mail: customerservice@tfp.com • URL: http://www.tfp.com • Annual. $180.00 per year. Provides information on municipal bond professionals, such as dealers, underwriters, attorneys, arbitrage specialists, derivatives specialists, rating agencies, regulators, etc.

Bond Market Association.

Bond Markets: Analysis and Stratgies. Frank J. Fabozzi. Prentice Hall, 240 Frisch Court Paramus, NJ 07652-5240. Phone: 800-947-7700 or (201)909-6200 Fax: 800-445-6991 or (201)909-6361 URL: http://www.prenhall.com • 1999. $96.00. Fourth edition.

Bond's Franchise Guide. Robert Bond. Sourcebook Publications, 1814 Franklin St., Suite 820 Oakland, CA 94612. Phone: (510)839-5471 Fax: (510)547-3245 Annual. $29.95. Contains listings of more than 2,300 franchises in 54 categories, with detailed profiles of over 1,000 major franchise companies. Profiles include information on services provided by franchisers and financing needed by franchisees. Formerly *Source Book of Franchise Opportunities.*

Bondweek: The Newsweekly of Fixed Income and Credit Markets. Institutional Investor, 488 Madison Ave. New York, NY 10022. Phone: (212)224-3300 Fax: (212)224-3353 E-mail: info@iijournals.com • URL: http://www.iijournals.com • Weekly. $2,220.00 per year. Newsletter. Covers taxable, fixed-income securities for professional investors, including corporate, government, foreign, mortgage, and high-yield.

Book Auction Records. Dawson UK Ltd., Cannon House, Farm Rd., Folkestone Kent CT19 5EE, England. Phone: 44 1303 850101 Fax: 44 1303 850440 Annual. $200.00.

Book Collecting: A Comprehensive Guide. Allen Ahearn and Patricia Ahearn. Penguin Putnam Book for Young Readers, 375 Hudson St. New York, NY 10014. Phone: 800-526-0275 or (212)366-2000 Fax: 800-227-9604 E-mail: online@penguinputnam.com • URL: http://www.penguinputnam.com • 2000. $45.00.

Book Collector. Nicolas J. Barker. Collector Ltd., P.O. Box 12426 London W11 3GW, England. Phone: 44 171 7923492 Fax: 44 171 7923492 Quarterly. $62.00 per year. Subscription.

Book Industry Study Group.

Book Industry Trends. Book Industry Study Group, Inc., 160 Fifth Ave. New York, NY 10010-7000. Phone: (212)929-1393 Fax: (212)989-7542 E-mail: bill@bookinfo.org • URL: http://www.bisg.org • Annual. $650.00.

Book Manufacturers Institute.

The Book Market: How to Write, Publish, and Market Your Book. Aron M. Mathieu. Andover Press, 516 W. 34th St. New York, NY 10001. Phone: (212)594-3556 Fax: (212)736-2273 1981. $19.95.

Book Marketing Handbook: Tips and Techniques for the Sale and Promotion of Scientific, Technical, Professional, and Scholarly Books and Journals. Nat G. Bodian. R. R. Bowker, 121 Chanlon Rd. New Providence, NJ 07974. Phone: 888-269-5372 or (908)464-6800 Fax: (908)771-7704 E-mail: info@bowker.com • URL: http://www.bowker.com • Two volumes. $64.95 per volume. Volume one, 1980; volume two, 1983.

Book Marketing Update. Open Horizons Publishing, P.O. Box 205 Fairfield, IA 52556-0205. Phone: (641)472-6130 Fax: (641)472-1560 E-mail: johnkremer@bookmarket.com • URL: http://www.bookmarket.com • Monthly. $60.00 per year. Newsletter for book publishers.

Book of ASTM Standards. ASTM, 1916 Race St. Philadelphia, PA 19103. Phone: (610)832-9500 Annual.

The Book of Coffee and Tea: A Guide to the Appreciation of Fine Coffees, Teas and Herbal Beverages. Joel Schapira and others. St. Martin's Press, 175 Fifth Ave. New York, NY 10010. Phone: 800-221-7945 or (212)674-5151 Fax: 800-672-2054 or (212)529-0594 URL: http://www.stmartins.com • 1996. $14.95. Second edition.

The Book of European Forecasts. Available from The Gale Group, 27500 Drake Rd. Farmington Hills, MI 48331-3535. Phone: 800-877-GALE or (248)699-GALE Fax: 800-414-5043 or (248)699-8069 E-mail: galeord@galegroup.com • URL: http://www.galegroup.com • 1996. $320.00. Second edition. Published by Euromonitor. Presents economic, commercial, demographic, and social forecasts for Europe, with statistical data and commentary.

The Book of European Regions. Available from The Gale Group, 27500 Drake Rd. Farmington Hills, MI 48331-3535. Phone: 800-877-GALE or (248)699-GALE Fax: 800-414-5043 or (248)699-8069 E-mail: galeord@galegroup.com • URL: http://www.galegroup.com • 1992. $290.00. Second edition. Published by Euromonitor. Contains economic and demographic data for over 220 European regions. Maps and regional rankings are included.

Book of the States. Council of State Governments, P.O. Box 11910 Lexington, KY 40578-1910. Phone: 800-800-1910 or (606)244-8000 Fax: (606)244-8001 E-mail: info@csg.org • URL: http://www.csg.org • Biennial. $99.00. Includes information on state constitutions, state-by-state voting in recent elections, data on state finances, and federal-state survey articles.

Book Publishing Report: Weekly News and Analysis of Events Shaping the Book Industry. SIMBA Information, P.O. Box 4234 Stamford, CT 06907-0234. Phone: 800-307-2529 or (203)358-4100 Fax: (203)358-5824 E-mail: info@simbanet.com • URL: http://www.simbanet.com • Weekly. $525.00 per year. Newsletter. Covers book publishing mergers, marketing, finance, personnel, and trends in general. Formerly *BP Report on the Business of Book Publishing.*

Book Repair: A How-To-Do-It Manual for Librarians. Kenneth Lavender and Scott Stockton. Neal-Schuman Publishers, Inc., 100 Varick St. New York, NY 10013. Phone: (212)925-8650 Fax: 800-584-2414 or (212)219-8916 E-mail: info@neal-schuman.com • URL: http://www.neal-schuman.com • 1992. $45.00. Covers basic book repair and conservation techniques.

Book Review Digest: An Index to Reviews of Current Books. H.W. Wilson Co., 950 University Ave. Bronx, NY 10452. Phone: 800-367-6770 or (718)588-8400 Fax: (718)590-1617 E-mail: custserv@hwwilson.com • URL: http://www.hwwilson.com • 10 times a year. Quarterly and annual cumulation. Service basis.

Book Review Index. The Gale Group, 27500 Drake Rd. Farmington Hills, MI 48331-3535. Phone: 800-877-GALE or (248)699-GALE Fax: 800-414-5043 or (248)699-8069 E-mail: galeord@galegroup.com • URL: http://www.galegroup.com • Annual. $295.00. Three yearly issues. An index to reviews appearing in hundreds of periodicals. Back volumes available.

Book Review Index [Online]. The Gale Group, 27500 Drake Rd. Farmington Hills, MI 48331-3535. Phone: 800-877-GALE or (248)699-GALE Fax: 800-414-5043 E-mail: galeord@gale.com • URL: http://www.gale.com • Cites reviews of books and periodicals in journals, 1969 to present. Inquire as to online cost and availability.

Bookkeeping Service. Entrepreneur Media, Inc., 2445 McCabe Way Irvine, CA 92614. Phone: 800-421-2300 or (949)261-2325 Fax: (949)261-0234 E-mail: entmag@entrepreneur.com • URL: http://www.entrepreneur.com • Looseleaf. $59.50. A practical guide to starting a computer-oriented bookkeeping business. Covers profit potential, start-up costs, market size evaluation, pricing, accounting, advertising, promotion, etc. (Start-Up Business Guide No. E2335.)

Booklist. American Library Association, 50 E. Huron St. Chicago, IL 60611-2795. Phone: 800-545-2433 or (312)944-6780 Fax: (312)440-9374 E-mail: bsegedin@ala.org • URL: http://www.ala.org • 22 times a year. $74.50. Reviews library materials for school and public libraries. Incorporates *Reference Books Bulletin.*

Bookman's Price Index. The Gale Group, 27500 Drake Rd. Farmington Hills, MI 48331-3535. Phone: 800-877-GALE or (248)699-GALE Fax: 800-414-5043 or (248)699-8069 E-mail: galeord@galegroup.com • URL: http://www.galegroup.com • Annual. 65 volumes. $320.00 per volume. Price guide to out more than 17,000 out-of-print and rare books.

Books and Periodicals Online: The Guide to Business and Legal Information on Databases and CD-ROM's. Nuchine Nobari, editor. Library Technology Alliance, Inc., P.O. Box 77232 Washington, DC 20013-8232. Phone: (202)789-2099 Fax: (202)789-2474 E-mail: lta@bellatlantic.net • Annual. $365.00 per year. 97,000 periodicals available as part of online and CD-ROM databases; international coverage.

Books for the Millions: A History of the Men Whose Methods and Machines Packaged the Printed Word. Frank E. Comparato. Labyrinthos, 3064 Holline Court Lancaster, CA 93535-4910. Phone: (661)946-2726 1971. $12.50.

Books in Print. R. R. Bowker, 121 Chanlon Rd. New Providence, NJ 07974. Phone: 888-269-5372 or (908)464-6800 Fax: (908)771-7704 E-mail: info@bowker.com • URL: http://www.bowker.com • Annual. $595.00. Nine volumes. Annual supplement, $250.00 (three volumes).

Books in Print On Disc: The Complete Books in Print System on Compact Laser Disc. Bowker Electronic Publishing, 121 Chanlon Rd. New Providence, NJ 07974. Phone: 800-323-3288 or (908)464-6800 Fax: (908)665-6688 Monthly. $1195.00 per year. The CD-ROM version of *Books in Print, Forthcoming Books,* and other Bowker bibliographic publications: lists the books of over 50,000 U.S. publishers. Includes books recently declared out-of-print. Also available with full text book reviews.

Books in Print Online. Bowker Electronic Publishing, 121 Chanlon Rd. New Providence, NJ 07974. Phone: 800-323-3288 or (908)464-6800 Fax: (908)665-3528 The online version of *Books in Print, Forthcoming Books, Paperbound Books in Print,* and other Bowker bibliographic publications: lists the books of over 50,000 U. S. publishers. Includes books recently declared out-of-print. Updated monthly. Inquire as to online cost and availability.

Books in Print with Book Reviews On Disc. Bowker Electronic Publishing, 121 Chanlon Rd. New Providence, NJ 07974. Phone: 800-323-3288 or (908)464-6800 Fax: (908)665-6688 Monthly. $1,755.00 per year. The CD-ROM version of *Books in Print, Forthcoming Books,*and other Bowker bibliographic publications, with the addition of full text book reviews from *Publishers Weekly, Library Journal, Booklist, Choice,* and other periodicals.

Books: Their Care and Repair. H. W. Wilson Co., 950 University Ave. Bronx, NY 10452. Phone: 800-367-6770 or (718)588-8400 Fax: (718)590-1617 1984. $42.00. Covers the repair of books, maps, and documents and the various kinds of pamphlet binding.

The Bookseller: The Organ of the Book Trade. J. Whitaker and Sons, Ltd., 12 Dyott St. London WC1A 1DF, England. E-mail: letters.to.editor@bookseller.co.uk • URL: http://www.thebookseller.com • Weekly. $178.00 per year. Provides international book trade news.

Bookselling This Week. American Booksellers Association, 828 S. Broadway Tarrytown, NY 10591-5112. Phone: 800-637-0037 or (914)591-2665 Fax: (914)591-2720 E-mail: ab-info@bookweb.org • URL: http://www.bookweb.org • Weekly. Members, $30.00 per year; non-members, $60.00 per year. Newsletter. Formerly *ABA Newswire.*

SOURCES CITED

Bookstore Journal. Christian Booksellers Association. C B A Service Corp., P.O. Box 200 Colorado Springs, CO 80901. Phone: (719)576-7880 Fax: (719)576-0795 Monthly. $45.00 per year. Edited for religious book stores.

BookWeb. American Booksellers AssociationPhone: 800-637-0037 or (914)591-2665 Fax: (914)591-2720 E-mail: info@bookweb.org • URL: http://www.bookweb.org/bookstores • Web site provides descriptions of more than 4,500 independent bookstores, searchable by name, specialty, or zip code. Fees: Free.

The Boomer Report: The Insights You Need to Reach America's Most Influential Consumer Group. Age Wave Communications Corp., 2000 Powell St., 15th Fl. Emeryville, CA 94608. Phone: (510)652-9099 Monthly. $195.00 per year. Newsletter. Presents market research relating to the ''baby boomers,'' an age group generally defined as having been born between 1950 and 1970.

Border Belt Tobacco Research Station.

The Botanical Review: Interpreting Botanical Progress. Society for Economic Botany. New York Botanical Garden Press, Bronx, NY 10458-5126. Phone: (718)817-8721 Fax: (718)817-8842 E-mail: nygbpress@nygb.org • URL: http://www.nybg.org • Quarterly. $82.00 per year. Reviews articles in all fields of botany.

Botanical Society of America.

The Bottom Line: A Financial Magazine for Librarians. Neal-Schuman Publishers, Inc., 100 Varick St. New York, NY 10013. Phone: (212)925-8650 Fax: 800-584-2414 or (212)219-8916 E-mail: info@neal-schuman.com • URL: http://www.neal-schuman.com • Quarterly. $49.95 per year. Provides articles on the financial management of libraries: budgeting, funding, cost analysis, etc.

Bottom Line-Business. Boardroom, Inc., P.O. Box 2614 Greenwich, CT 06836-2614. Phone: 800-234-3834 or (203)625-5900 Fax: (203)861-7443 Semimonthly. $36.00 per year. Newsletter. Formerly *Boardroom Reports*.

Bottom Line-Personal. Bottom Line Information, Inc., P.O. Box 2614 Greenwich, CT. Phone: 800-274-5611 or (203)861-7443 URL: http://www.boardroom.com • Semimonthly. $29.95 per year. Provides information to help sophisticated people lead more productive lives.

The Bottomline. International Association of Hospitality Accountants, 11709 Boulder Lane, Suite 110 Austin, TX 78726-1832. Phone: (512)346-5680 Fax: (512)346-5760 E-mail: hftp@hftp.org • URL: http://www.hftp.org • Bimonthly. Free to members, educational institutions and libraries; others, $50.00 per year. Contains articles on accounting, finance, information technology, and management for hotels, resorts, casinos, clubs, and other hospitality businesses.

Bowker Annual: Library and Book Trade Almanac. R. R. Bowker, 121 Chanlon Rd. New Providence, NJ 07974. Phone: 888-269-5372 or (908)464-6800 Fax: (908)771-7704 E-mail: info@bowker.com • URL: http://www.bowker.com • Annual. $175.00. Lists of accredited library schools; scholarships for education in library science; library organizations; major libraries; publishing and book sellers organizations. Includes statistics and news of the book business.

Bowker/Whitaker Global Books in Print On Disc. R. R. Bowker, 121 Chanlon Rd. New Providence, NJ 07974. Phone: 800-521-8110 or (908)464-6800 Fax: (908)665-6688 Monthly. $2,055.00 per year. Provides CD-ROM listing of English language books published throughout the world, including U. S., U. K., Canada, and Australia. Combines data from R. R. Bowker's *Books in Print Plus* and J. Whitaker & Sons Ltd.'s *Bookbank*. Includes more than two million titles.

Bowker's Complete Video Directory. R. R. Bowker, 121 Chanlon Rd. New Providence, NJ 07974. Phone: 888-269-5372 or (908)464-6800 Fax: (908)771-7704 E-mail: info@bowker.com • URL: http://www.bowker.com • Annual. $249.95. Four volumes. Lists over 151,000 theatrical and nontheatrical videocassette titles.

Bowker's Complete Video Directory on Disc. Bowker Electronic Publishing, 121 Chanlon Rd. New Providence, NJ 07974. Phone: 800-323-3288 or (908)464-6800 Fax: (908)665-6688 Quarterly. $520.00 per year. An extensive CD-ROM directory of video tapes and laserdisks. Includes film reviews from *Variety*.

Bowker's Law Books and Serials in Print: A Multimedia Sourcebook. R. R. Bowker, 121 Chanlon Rd. New Providence, NJ 07974. Phone: 800-521-8110 or (908)464-6800 Fax: (908)665-3502 E-mail: info@bowker.com • URL: http://www.bowker.com • Annual $725.00. Three volumes. Includes supplement.

Bowman's Accounting Report. Hudson Sawyer Professional Services Marketing, Inc., 3445 Peachtree Rd., N.E., Suite 600 Atlanta, GA 30326-1234. Phone: (404)264-9977 Fax: (404)264-9968 E-mail: awbowman@cris.com • Monthly. $275.00 per year. Newsletter. Provides information and news relating to the accounting profession, with emphasis on certified public accounting firms.

Boxboard Containers International. Intertec Publishing Corp., 29 N. Wacker Dr. Chicago, IL 60606. Phone: 800-621-9907 or (312)609-4254 Fax: (312)726-2574 E-mail: subs@intertec.com • URL: http://www.worldwastes.com • Monthly. $28.00 per year. Formerly *Boxboard Containers*.

Boxoffice: The Business Magazine of the Global Motion Picture Industry. RLD Communication, 1555 S. El Molino Ave., Ste. 100 Pasadena, CA 91101-2563. Phone: (626)396-0250 Fax: (626)396-0248 E-mail: boxoffice@earthlink.net • URL: http://www.boxoffice.com • Monthly. $40.00 per year.

BPA International., 270 Madison Ave. New York, NY 10016-0699. Phone: (212)779-3200 Fax: (212)779-3615 URL: http://www.bpai.com • Verifies business and consumer periodical circulation statements. Includes a Circulation Managers Committee. *Formerly Business Publications Audit of Circulation*.

BPI Syndicated Columnists Contacts. BPI Communications, Inc., 770 Broadway New York, NY 10003-9595. Phone: 800-344-7119 or (646)654-5500 Fax: (646)654-5835 E-mail: info@bpi.com • URL: http://www.bpi.com • Annual. $120.00. Contains information needed to contact over 1500 major columinists covering four different subjects. Formerly *Syndicated Colmnists Directory*.

Bradford's International Directory of Marketing Research Agencies n the United States and the World. Business Research Services, Inc., 4201 Connecticut Ave., N.W., Suite 610 Washington, DC 20008. Phone: 800-845-8420 or (202)364-6947 Fax: (202)686-3228 E-mail: brspubs@sba8a.com • Annual. $90.00. Over 1,800 marketing research agencies and management consultants in market research. Formerly *Bradford's Directory of Marketing Research Agencies and Management Consultants*.

Bradley Policy Research Center., University of Rochester, William E. Simon Graduate School of Business Administration Rochester, NY 14627. Phone: (716)275-0834 Fax: (716)461-3309 E-mail: mullen@ssb.rochester.edu • Corporate control and corporate takeovers are among the research areas covered.

Brake and Frontend: The Complete Car Undercar Service Magazine. Babcox Publications, 11 S. Forge St. Akron, OH 44304. Phone: (330)535-6117 Fax: (330)535-0874 Monthly. $64.00 per year.

Brandeis Law Journal. Louis D. Brandeis School of Law. University of Louisville, 2301 S. Third St. Louisville, KY 40292. Phone: (502)852-6396 Fax: (502)852-0862 URL: http://www.louisville.edu/law • Quarterly. $30.00 per year. Formerly *Journal of Family Law*.

Brands and Their Companies. The Gale Group, 27500 Drake Rd. Farmington Hills, MI 48331-3535. Phone: 800-877-GALE or (248)699-GALE Fax: 800-414-5043 or (248)699-8069 E-mail: galeord@galegroup.com • URL: http://www.galegroup.com • 2001. $805.00. 22nd edition. Three volumes. Includes mid-year *Supplement*. Provides over 365,000 entries ontrade names, trademarks, and brand names of consumer-oriented products and their 80,000 manufacturers, importers, marketers, or distributors. Formerly *Trade Names Dictionary*.

Brands and Their Companies Database. The Gale Group, 27500 Drake Rd. Farmington Hills, MI 48331-3535. Phone: 800-877-GALE or (248)699-GALE Fax: 800-414-5043 or (248)699-8069 E-mail: galeord@gale.com • URL: http://www.gale.com • An online directory of about 382,000 domestic and international trade names, with a primary focus on consumer goods. Semiannual updates. Inquire as to online cost and availability.

Brandweek. BPI Communications, Inc., 770 Broadway New York, NY 10003-9595. Phone: 800-344-7119 or (646)654-5500 Fax: (646)654-5835 E-mail: info@bpi.com • URL: http://www.bpicomm.com • 47 times a year. $145.00 per year. Includes articles and case studies on mass marketing and mass media. Formerly *Adweek's Marketing Week*.

Brassey's Defence Yearbook. Brassey's, 22883 Quicksilver Dr., Suite 100 Dulles, VA 20166. Phone: (703)661-1500 Fax: (703)661-1501 E-mail: dmckeon@batsfordbrassey.com • URL: http://www.batsford.com • 1997. $55.00. Formerly *RUSI*.

Brazil Company Handbook: Data on Major Listed Companies. Hoovers, Inc., 1033 La Posada Dr., Suite 250 Austin, TX 78752. Phone: 800-486-8666 or (512)374-4500 Fax: (512)374-4501 E-mail: orders@hoovers.com • Annual. $49.95. Published by IMF Editora. Contains profiles of publicly traded companies in Brazil. Includes information on local stock exchanges and the nation's economic situation.

Brazilian-American Chamber of Commerce., 509 W. Madison Ave., Suite 304 New York, NY 10022. Phone: (212)751-4691 Fax: (212)751-7692 E-mail: info@brazilcham.com • URL: http://www.brazilcham.com • Promotes trade between Brazil and the U. S.

Brazilian Government Trade Bureau., 1185 Ave. of the Americas, 21st Fl. New York, NY 10036-2601. Phone: (212)916-3200 Fax: (212)573-9406 E-mail: info@braziltradeny.com • URL: http://www.braziltradeny.com • Offers assistance to American firms wishing to purchase Brazilian products, and promotes Brazilian firms and their exports.

The Bread Market. Available from MarketResearch.com, 641 Ave. of the Americas, Third Floor New York, NY 10011. Phone: 800-298-5699 or (212)807-2629 Fax: (212)807-2716 E-mail: order@marketresearch.com • URL: http://www.marketresearch.com • 2000. $3,250.00. Published by Packaged Facts. Provides market data on a wide variety of packaged, frozen, and fresh- baked bread products.

Breaking Up America: Advertisers and the New Media World. Joseph Turow. University of Chicago Press, 5801 Ellis Ave., 4th Fl. Chicago, IL 60637. Phone: 800-621-2736 or (773)702-7700 Fax: (773)702-9756 E-mail: marketing@press.uchicago.edu • URL: http://www.press.uchicago.edu • 1997. $22.50. A social criticism of target marketing, market segmentation, and customized media.

Bretton Woods Committee., 1990 M St., N.W., Suite 450 Washington, DC 20036. Phone: (202)331-1616 Fax: (202)785-9423 E-mail: info@brettonwoods.org • URL: http://www.brettonwoods.org • Members are corporate executives, government officials, college administrators, bankers, and other ''National Leaders.'' Seeks to inform and educate the public as to the activities of the International Monetary Fund, the World Bank, and other multinational development banking organizations. Promotes U. S. participation in multinational banking.

Brewers Almanac. Beer Institute, 122 C St., Suite 750 Washington, DC 20001-2109. Phone: (202)737-2337 Fax: (202)737-7004 URL: http://www.beerinst.org • Annual. $170.00.

Brewers' Association of America.

Brewers Digest. Siebel Publishing Co., Inc., P.O. Box 677 Thiensville, WI 53092. Phone: (312)463-3401 Monthly. $25.00 per year. Covers all aspects of brewing. Annual *Buyers' Guide* and *Directory* available.

Brewers Digest Annual Buyers Guide and Brewery Directory. Siebel Publishing Co., Inc., PO Box 677 Thiensville, WI 53092. Phone: (312)463-3401 Annual. $50.00. Lists breweries throughout the western hemisphere.

Brewery and Soft Drink Workers Conference-U.S.A. and Canada.

Brewing and Distilling International. Brewery Traders Publications, Ltd., 52 Glenhouse Rd. Eltham SE19 1JQ, England. Monthly. $160.00 per year.

Brick Industry Association.

Bricker's International Directory: Long-Term University-Based Executive Programs. Peterson's, Princeton Pike Dr. Lawrenceville, NJ 08648. Phone: 800-338-3282 or (609)896-1800 E-mail: info@petersons.com • URL: http://www.petersons.com • Annual. $295.00. Presents detailed information about executive education programs offered by 85 universities and nonprofit organizations in the U. S. and around the world. Includes general management and function-specific programs.

A Brief History of Cocaine. Steven B. Karch. CRC Press, Inc., 2000 Corporate Blvd., N. W. Boca Raton, FL 33431. Phone: 800-272-7737 or (561)994-0555 Fax: (561)241-7856 E-mail: orders@crcpress.com • URL: http://www.crcpress.com • 1997. $24.95. Emphasizes the societal effects of cocaine abuse in various regions of the world.

Brill's Content: The Independent Voice of the Information Age. Brill Media Ventures, L.P., 521 Fifth Ave., 11th Fl. New York, NY 10175. Phone: (212)824-1900 Fax: (212)824-1950 E-mail: customerservice@brillscontent.com • URL: http://www.brillscontent.com • Eight times a year. $19.95 per year. Presents a critical, iconoclastic view of various forms of news media, including TV, magazines, newspapers, and websites.

British Year Book of International Law. Royal Institute of International Affairs. Oxford University Press, Inc., 198 Madison Ave. New York, NY 10016-4314. Phone: 800-451-7556 or (212)726-6000 Fax: (212)726-6446 E-mail: custserv@oup-usa.org • URL: http://www.oup-usa.org • Annual. Price varies.

Broadband Solutions. North American Publishing Co., 401 North Broad St. Philadelphia, PA 19108. Phone: (215)238-5300 Fax: (215)238-5457 URL: http://www.broadbandsolution.com • Monthly. Controlled circulation. Covers the high-bandwidth telecommunications industry, including new products and emerging technologies.

Broadband Week. Cahners Business Information, 8878 South Barron Blvd. Highlands Ranch, CO 80129. Phone: (303)470-4800 Fax: (303)470-4892 URL: http://www.broadbandweek.com • Semimonthly. Controlled circulation. Provides news and trends for all parts of the evolving broadband industry, including operations, marketing, finance, and technology.

Broadcast Cable Financial Management Association., 701 Lee St., Suite 640 Des Plaines, IL 60016. Phone: (847)296-0200 Fax: (847)296-7510 E-mail: info@bcfm.com • URL: http://www.bcfm.com • Members are accountants and other financial personnel in the radio and television broadcasting industries.

Broadcast Communications Dictionary. Lincoln Diamant. Greenwood Publishing Group Inc., 88 Post Rd., W. Westport, CT 06881-5007. Phone: 800-225-5800 or (203)226-3571 Fax: (203)222-2540 E-mail: bookinfo@greenwood.com • URL: http://www.greenwood.com • 1989. $57.95. Third revised edition.

Broadcast Education Association.

Broadcast Engineering: Equipment Reference Manual. Intertec Publishing Corp., P.O. Box 12901 Overland Park, KS 66282-2901. Phone: 800-400-5945 or (913)341-1300 Fax: (913)967-1898 E-mail: subs@intertec.com • URL: http://www.intertec.com • Annual. $20.00. Lists manufacturers and distributors of radio and TV broadcast and recording equipment. Included in subscription to *Broadcast Engineering*.

Broadcast Engineering: Journal of Broadcast Technology. Intertec Publishing Corp., P.O. Box 12901 Overland Park, KS 66282-2901. Phone: 800-400-5945 or (913)341-1300 Fax: (913)967-1898 E-mail: subs@intertec.com • URL: http://www.broadcastengineering.com • Monthly. Free to qualified personnel; others, $55.00 per year. Technical magazine for the broadcast industry.

Broadcast Investor: Newsletter on Radio-TV Station Finance. Paul Kagan Associates, Inc., 126 Clock Tower Place Carmel, CA 93923. Phone: (831)624-1536 Fax: (831)625-3225 E-mail: info@kagan.com • Monthly. $895.00 per year. Newsletter for investors in publicly held radio and television broadcasting companies.

Broadcast Music, Inc.

Broadcasting and Cable. Cahners Business Information, Broadcasting and Cable's International Group, 245 W. 17th St. New York, NY 10011-5300. Phone: 800-662-7776 or (212)645-0067 Fax: (212)337-6948 E-mail: corporatecommunications@cahners.com • URL: http://www.cahners.com • 51 times a year. $149.00 per year. Formerly *Broadcasting*.

Broadcasting and Cable Yearbook. R. R Bowker, 121 Chanlon Rd. New Providence, NJ 07974. Phone: 888-269-5372 or (908)464-6800 Fax: (908)771-7704 E-mail: info@bowker.com • URL: http://www.bowker.com • Annual. $179.95. Two volumes. Published in conjunction with *Broadcasting* magazine. Provides information on U. S. and Canadian TV stations, radio stations, cable TV companies, and radio-TV services of various kinds.

Broadwoven Fabrics (Gray). U.S. Bureau of the Census, Washington, DC 20233-0800. Phone: (301)457-4100 Fax: (301)457-3842 URL: http://www.census.gov • Quarterly. Provides statistical data on production, value, shipments, and consumption. Includes woolen and worsted fabrics, tire fabrics, cotton broadwoven fabrics, etc. (Current Industrial Reports, MQ-22T.)

Broiler Industry. Watt Publishing Co., 122 S. Wesley Ave. Mount Morris, IL 61054-4197. Phone: (815)734-4171 Fax: (815)734-4201 URL: http://www.wattnet.com • Monthly. Free to qualified personnel; others, $54.00 per year.

Broker-Dealer Regulation. David A. Lipton. West Group, 610 Opperman Dr. Eagan, MN 55123. Phone: 800-328-4880 or (651)687-7000 Fax: 800-213-2323 or (651)687-5827 URL: http://www.westgroup.com • $145.00 per year. Looseleaf service. Annual supplementation. Focuses on the basics of stockbroker license application procedure, registration, regulation, and responsibilities.

Broker World. Insurance Publications, Inc., 9404 Reeds Rd. Shawnee Mission, KS 66207-2500. Phone: 800-762-3387 or (913)383-9191 Fax: (913)383-1247 Monthly. $6.00 per year. Edited for independent insurance agents and brokers. Special feature issue topics include annuities, disability insurance, estate planning, and life insurance.

Brookings Institution.

Brown's Directory. Advanstar Communications, Inc., One Park Ave., 2nd Fl. New York, NY 10016-5802. Phone: 800-346-0085 or (212)951-6600 Fax: (212)951-6793 E-mail: information@advanstar.com • URL: http://www.advanstar.com • Annual. $335.00.

Budget of the United States Government. U.S. Office of Management and Budget. Available from U.S. Government Printing Office, Washington, DC 20402. Phone: (202)512-1800 Fax: (202)512-2250 E-mail: gpoaccess@gpo.gov • URL: http://www.access.gpo.gov • Annual.

Budgeting: A How-to-Do-it Manual for Librarians. Alice S. Warner. Neal-Schuman Publishers, Inc., 100 Varick St. New York, NY 10013. Phone: (212)925-8650 Fax: 800-584-2414 or (212)219-8916 E-mail: info@neal-schuman.com • URL: http://www.neal-schuman.com • 1998. $49.95. Explains six forms of budgeting suitable for various kinds of libraries. Includes a bibliography. (How-to-Do-It Series).

Build a World Wide Web Commerce Center: Plan, Program, and Manage Internet Commerce for Your Company. Net-Genesis Staff. John Wiley and Sons, Inc., 605 Third Ave. New York, NY 10158-0012. Phone: 800-225-5945 or (212)850-6000 Fax: (212)850-6088 E-mail: info@jwiley.com • URL: http://www.wiley.com • 1996. $29.95. Covers business and marketing applications of the World Wide Web.

Builder: Buyer's Guide. Hanley-Wood, LLC., One Thomas Circle, Suite 600 Washington, DC 20005. Phone: 888-269-8410 or (212)452-0800 Fax: (202)785-1974 URL: http://www.hanleywood.com • Annual. $10.00. A directory of products and services for the home building and remodeling industry.

Builder: Official Publication of the National Association of Home Builders. National Association of Home Builders of the United States. Hanley-Wood, LLC., One Thomas Circle, Suite 600 Washington, DC 20005-5811. Phone: 888-269-8410 or (202)452-0800 Fax: (202)785-1974 E-mail: johnbutter@builderonline.com • URL: http://www.builderonline.com • Monthly. $29.95 per year. Covers the home building and remodeling industry in general, including design, construction, and marketing.

Builders' Hardware Manufacturers Association.

Building a Mail Order Business: A Complete Manual for Success. William A. Cohen. John Wiley and Sons, Inc., 605 Third Ave. New York, NY 10158-0012. Phone: 800-225-5945 or (212)850-6000 Fax: (212)850-6088 E-mail: info@wiley.com • URL: http://www.wiley.com • 1996. $42.95. Fourth edition.

Building and Construction Trades Department - AFL-CIO.

Building and Managing the Corporate Intranet. Ronald L. Wagner and others. McGraw-Hill, 1221 Ave. of the Americas New York, NY 10020. Phone: 800-722-4726 or (212)904-2000 Fax: (212)904-2072 E-mail: customer.service@mcgraw-hill.com • URL: http://www.mcgraw-hill.com • 1997. $34.95.

Building Construction Cost Data. R.S. Means Co., Inc., 100 Construction Plaza Kingston, MA 02364-0800. Phone: 800-334-3509 or (781)422-5000 Fax: 800-632-6732 E-mail: meanscustserv@rsmeans.com • URL: http://www.rsmeans.com • Annual. $76.95. Lists over 20,000 entries for estimating.

Building Construction Handbook. Ray Chudley. Butterworth-Heinemann, 225 Wildwood Ave. Woburn, MA 01081. Phone: 800-366-2665 or (781)904-2500 Fax: 800-446-6520 E-mail: orders@bhusa.com • URL: http://www.bh.com • 1998. $34.95. Third edition.

Building Design and Construction. Cahners Publishing Inc., 1350 E. Touhy Ave. Des Plaines, IL 60018-3358. Phone: 800-662-7776 or (847)635-8800 Fax: (847)390-2769 E-mail: corporatecommunications@cahners.com • URL: http://www.cahners.com • Monthly. $108.90 per year. For non-residential building owners, contractors, engineers and architects.

Building Material Retailer. National Lumber and Building Material Dealers Association, 40 Ivy St., S.E. Washington, DC 20003. Phone: 800-328-9125 or (202)547-2230 Fax: (202)547-8645 Monthly. $25.00 per year. Includes special feature issues on hand and power tools, lumber, roofing, kitchens, flooring, windows and doors, and insulation.

Building Officials and Code Administrators International.

Building Officials and Code Administrators International-Membership Directory. Building Officials and Code Administrators International BOCA, 4051 W. Flossmoor Rd. Country Club Hills, IL 60478. Phone: (708)799-2300 Fax: (708)799-4981 E-mail: boca@bocai.org • Annual. $16.00. Approximately 14,000 construction code officials, architects, engineers, trade associations, and manufacturers.

Building Operating Management: The National Magazine for Commercial and Institutional Buildings Construction, Renoration, Facility Management. Trade Press Publishing Corp., 2100 W. Florist Ave. Milwaukee, WI 53209. Phone: 800-727-7995 or (414)228-7701 Fax: (414)228-1134 URL: http://www.tradepress.com • Monthly. $55.00 per year.

Building Owners and Managers Association International.

Building Research. Building Research Publications Board, 2101 Constitution Ave., N.W. Washington, DC 20418. Phone: (202)339-3376 Membership.

Building Service Contractors Association International.

Building Stone Institute.

Building Stone Magazine. Building Stone Institute, P.O.Box 507 Purdys, NY 10578-0507. Phone: (914)232-5725 Fax: (914)232-5259 Bimonthly. $65.00 per year.

Building Supply Home Centers Retail Giants Report. Cahners Business Information, 1350 E. Touhy Ave. Des Plaines, IL 60018-3358. Phone: 800-662-7776 or (847)635-8800 Fax: (847)390-2690 E-mail: corporatecommunications@cahners.com • URL: http://www.cahners.com • Annual. $30.00. Lists major retailers of a wide variety of building and home improvement materials, products, fixtures, accessories, equipment, and tools.

Building Systems Councils of NAHB.

Building Technology Center.

Building the Reference Collection: A How-To-Do-It Manual for School and Public Librarians. Neal-Schuman Publishers, Inc., 100 Varick St. New York, NY 10013. Phone: (212)925-8650 Fax: 800-584-2414 or (212)219-8916 E-mail: info@neal-schuman.com • URL: http://www.neal-schuman.com • 1992. $38.50. Includes a list of 300 basic reference sources. (How-to-Do-It Series).

Building the Service-Based Library Web Site: A Step-by-Step Guide to Design and Options. Kristen L. Garlock and Sherry Piontek. American Library Association, 50 E. Huron St. Chicago, IL 60611-2795. Phone: 800-545-2433 or (312)944-6780 Fax: (312)280-3255 E-mail: ala@ala.org • URL: http://www.ala.org • 1996. $30.00. Provides practical information for libraries planning a World Wide Web home page.

Buildings: The Facilities Construction and Management Journal. Stamats Communications, Inc., 615 5th St., S.E. Cedar Rapids, IA 52406-1888. Phone: 800-553-8878 or (319)364-6167 Fax: (319)364-4278 E-mail: inforequest@stamats.com • URL: http://www.stamats.com • Monthly. $70.00 per year. Serves professional building ownership/management organizations.

Bull and Bear Financial Newspaper., P. O. Box 917179 Longwood, FL 32791. Phone: 800-336-2855 or (407)682-6170 Fax: (407)682-6170 URL: http://www.thebullandbear.com • Monthly. $29.00 per year. Each issue includes a digest of advice from investment advisory newsletters.

The Bullet. SRDS, 1700 Higgins Rd. Des Plaines, IL 60018. Phone: 800-851-7737 or (847)375-5000 Fax: (847)375-5001 URL: http://www.srds.com • Bimonthly. Included with subscription to *Direct Marketing List Source*. Newsletter on direct mail advertising and mailing lists. Includes list updates and management changes.

Bulletin of Bibliography. Greenwood Publishing Group, Inc., 88 Post Rd., W. Westport, CT 06881-5007. Phone: 800-225-5800 or (203)226-3571 Fax: (203)222-1502 E-mail: bookinfo@greenwood.com • URL: http://www.greenwood.com • Quarterly. $115.00 per year.

Bulletin of Labour Statistics: Supplementing the Annual Data Presented in the Year Book of Labour Statistics. International Labour Office. ILO Publications Center, 49 Sheridan Ave. Albany, NY 12210. Phone: (518)436-9686 Fax: (518)436-7433 URL: http://www.us.ilo.org • Quarterly. $84.00 per year. Includes five *Supplements*. A supplement to *Yearbook of Labour Statistics*. Provides current labor and price index statistics for over 130 countries. Generally includes data for the most recent four years. Text in English, French and Spanish.

Bulletin of the Atomic Scientists: Magazine of Science and World Affairs. Educational Foundation for Nuclear Science, 6042 S. Kimbark Ave. Chicago, IL 60637. Phone: (312)702-2555 Fax: (312)702-0275 E-mail: bulletin@bullatomsci.org • URL: http://www.bullatomsci.org • Bimonthly. $36.00 per year.

Bulletin of the European Union. Commision of the European Communities. Bernan Associates, 4611-F Assembly Dr. Lanham, MD 20706-4391. Phone: 800-274-4447 or (301)459-7666 Fax: 800-865-3450 or (301)459-2255 E-mail: info@bernan.com • URL: http://www.bernan.com • 11 times a year. $210.00 per year. Published by the Office of Official Publications of the European Communities. Covers all main events within the Union. Supplement available. Text in Danish, Dutch, English, French, German, Greek, Italian, Spanish, Portuguese. Formerly *Bulletin of the European Communities*.

Bulletin on Narcotics. United Nations Publications, United Nations Concourse Level, First Ave., 46th St. New York, NY 10017. Phone: 800-553-3210 or (212)963-7680 Fax: (212)963-4910 E-mail: bookstore@un.org • URL: http://www.un.org/publications • Quarterly. $10.00 per issue. Editions in Chinese, French, Russian and Spanish.

Bullinger's Postal and Shippers Guide for the United States and Canada. Albery Leland Publishing, 500 N. Skinker Blvd. Saint Luis, MO 63130. Annual. $375.00. Approximately 260,000 communities in the United States and Canada.

Bullion Report. Investor Metals Services, Inc., 201-B E. 82nd St. New York, NY 10028-2701. Phone: (212)628-9780 Semimonthly. $90.00 per year.

Bureau of Alcohol, Tobacco, and Firearms Quarterly Bulletin. Bureau of Alcohol, Tobacco, and Firearms, U.S. Department of the Treasury. Available from U.S. Government Printing Office, Washington, DC 20402. Phone: (202)512-1800 Fax: (202)512-2250 Quarterly. $18.00 per year. Laws and regulations.

Bureau of Economic Analysis (BEA). U. S. Department of Commerce, Bureau of Economic AnalysisPhone: (202)606-9900 Fax: (202)606-5310 E-mail: webmaster@bea.doc.gov • URL: http://www.bea.doc.gov • Web site includes "News Release Information" covering national, regional, and international economic estimates from the BEA. Highlights of releases appear online the same day, complete text and tables appear the next day. "Recent News Releases" section provides titles for past nine months, with links. "BEA Data and Methodology" includes "Frequently Requested NIPA Data" (national income and product accounts, such as gross domestic product and personal income). Other statistics are available. Fees: Free.

Bureau of Economic and Business Research.

Bureau of Economic and Business Research. University of Florida

Bureau of Economic Geology. University of Texas at Austin

Bureau of Economic Research. Rutgers University

Bureau of Educational Research and Evaluation. Mississippi State University

Bureau of Governmental Research. University of Maryland

Bureau of Labor Statistics (BLS). U. S. Department of Labor, Bureau of Labor StatisticsPhone: (202)523-1092 E-mail: labstat.helpdesk@bls.gov • URL: http://www.bls.gov • Web site provides a great variety of employment, wage, price, and economic data. Some links are "Data," "Economy at a Glance,'' ''Keyword Search of BLS Web Pages,'' ''Regional Information,'' and ''Other Statistical Sites.'' Fees: Free.

Bureau of Wholesale Sales Representatives.

Bureaucracy: What Government Agencies Do and Why They Do It. James Q. Wilson. Basic Books, 10 E. 53rd St. New York, NY 10022-5299. Phone: 800-386-5656 or (212)207-7057 Fax: (212)207-7703 E-mail: westview.orders@perseusbooks.com • URL: http://www.perseusbooksgroup.com • 1991. $23.00.

Burglar Alarm Sales and Installation. Entrepreneur Media, Inc., 2445 McCabe Way Irvine, CA 92614. Phone: 800-421-2300 or (949)261-2325 Fax: (949)261-0234 E-mail: entmag@entrepreneur.com • URL: http://www.entrepreneur.com • Looseleaf. $59.50. A practical guide to starting a burglar alarm service. Covers profit potential, start-up costs, market size evaluation, owner's time required, pricing, accounting, advertising, promotion, etc. (Start-Up Business Guide No. E1091.)

Burlap and Jute Association.

Burley Auction Warehouse Association.

Burrelle's Media Directory: Broadcast Media. Burrelle's Information Services, 589 Eighth Ave., 16th Floor New York, NY 10018. Phone: 800-766-5114 or (212)227-5570 Fax: (212)279-4275 E-mail: directorysales@burrelles.com • URL: http://www.burrelles.com/mediadirectory • Annual. $275.00. Two volumes. *Radio* volume lists more than 12,000 radio stations in the U. S. and Canada. *Television and Cable* volume lists more than 1,700 television stations and cable systems. Provides detailed descriptions, including programming and key personnel.

Burrelle's Media Directory: Magazines and Newsletters. Burrelle's Information Services, 589 Eighth Ave., 16th Floor New York, NY 10018. Phone: 800-766-5114 or (212)227-5570 Fax: (212)279-4275 E-mail: directorysales@burrelles.com • URL: http://www.burrelles.com/mediadirectory • Annual. $275.00. Provides detailed descriptions of more than 13,500 magazines and newsletters published in the U. S., Canada, and Mexico. Categories are professional, consumer, trade, and college.

Burrelle's Media Directory: Newspapers and Related Media. Burrelle's Information Services, 589 Eighth Ave., 16th Floor New York, NY 10018. Phone: 800-766-5114 or (212)227-5570 Fax: (212)279-4275 E-mail: directorysales@burrelles.com • URL: http://www.burrelles.com/mediadirectory • Annual. $275.00. Two volumes. *Daily Newspapers* volume lists more than 2,000 daily publications in the U. S., Canada, and Mexico. *Non-Daily Newspapers* volume lists more than 10,000 items published no more than three times a week. Provides detailed descriptions, including key personnel.

Burwell World Directory of Information Brokers. Helen P. Burwell, editor. Burwell Enterprises, Inc., 5619 Plumtree Dr. Dallas, TX 75252-4928. Phone: (281)537-9051 Fax: (281)537-8332 E-mail: burwellinfo@burwellinc.com • URL: http://www.burwellinc.com • Annual. $59.50. Lists nearly 1,800 information brokers, document delivery firms, free-lance librarians, and fee-based library services. Provides U. S. and international coverage (46 countries). Formerly *Directory of Fee-Based Information Services*.

Bus Ride. Friendship Publications, Inc., 1550 E. Missouri Ave., Suite 100 Phoenix, AZ 85014-2455. Phone: (602)265-7600 10 times a year. $35.00 per year.

Business and Acquisition Newsletter. Newsletters International, Inc., 2600 S. Gessner Rd. Houston, TX 77063. Phone: (713)783-0100 Monthly. $300.00 per year. Information about firms that want to buy or sell companies, divisions, subsidiaries, product lines, patents, etc.

Business and Administrative Communication. Kitty O. Locker. McGraw-Hill, 1221 Ave.of the Americas New York, NY 10020. Phone: 800-722-4726 or (212)904-2000 Fax: (212)904-2072 E-mail: customer.service@mcgraw-hill.com • URL: http://www.mcgraw-hill.com • 2000. Fifth edition. Price on application.

Business and Commercial Aviation. McGraw-Hill, Aviation Week Group, 1221 Ave. of the Americas New York, NY 10020. Phone: 800-722-4726 or (212)904-2000 Fax: (212)904-2072 E-mail: customer.service@mcgraw-hill.com • URL: http://www.aviationnow.com • Monthly. $52.00 per year. Supplement available: *Annual Planning Purchasing Handbook*.

Business & Company Resource Center. The Gale GroupPhone: 800-877-GALE or (248)699-GALE Fax: 800-414-5043 or (248)699-8069 E-mail: galeord@galegroup.com • URL: http://www.galegroup.com/BusinessRC/ • Fee-based Web site provides a wide range of business, industry, and specific company information. Access is offered to trade journal articles, market research data, insider trading activity, major shareholder data, corporate histories, emerging technology reports, corporate earnings estimates, press releases, and other sources. Provides detailed company profiles, industry overviews, and rankings. Offers integration of Predicasts PROMT, Newsletters ASAP, Investext Plus, Business Index ASAP, Brands and Their Companies, and other databases (many have full text).

Business and Finance Career Directory. Visible Ink Press, 27500 Drake Rd. Farmington Hills, MI 48331-3535. Phone: 800-877-GALE or (248)699-GALE Fax: 800-414-5043 or (248)699-8069 E-mail: galeord@galegroup.com • URL: http://www.visibleink.com • 1992. $17.95.

Business and Finance Division Bulletin. Special Libraries Association, Business and Finance Div., 1700 18th St., N.W., 17th Fl. Washington, DC 20009-2514. Phone: (202)234-4700 Fax: 888-411-2856 URL: http://www.sla.org • Quarterly. $12.00 per year.

Business and Health. Medical Economics Co., Inc., Five Paragon Dr. Montvale, NJ 07645-1742. Phone: 800-232-7379 or (201)358-7200 Fax: (201)573-8999 E-mail: customerservice@medec.com • URL: http://www.medec.com • Monthly. $99.00 per year. Edited for business, government, and other buyers of employee healthcare insurance or HMO coverage.

Business and Industry. Responsive Database Services, Inc., 23611 Chagrin Blvd., Suite 320 Beachwood, OH 44122. Phone: 800-313-2212 or (216)292-9620 Fax: (216)292-9621 E-mail: customer_service@rdsinc.com • URL: http://www.rdsinc.com • Contains online citations, abstracts, and selected fulltext from more than 1,000 trade journals, newspapers, and other publications. Provides general coverage of both manufacturing and service industries, including marketing, production, industry trends, key events, and information on specific companies. Time span is 1994 to date. Daily updates. Inquire as to online cost and availability. (Also available in a CD-ROM version.)

Business and Institutional Furniture Manufacturers Association.

Business and Management Practices. Responsive Database Services, Inc., 23611 Chagrin Blvd., Suite 320 Beachwood, OH 44122. Phone: 800-313-2212 or (216)292-9620 Fax: (216)292-9621 E-mail: customer_service@rdsinc.com • URL: http://www.rdsinc.com • Provides fulltext of management articles appearing in more than 350 relevant publications. Emphasis is on ''the processes, methods, and strategies of managing a business.'' Time span is 1995 to date. Inquire as to online cost and availability. (Also available in a CD-ROM version.)

Business and Professional Women USA.

Business and Professional Women's Foundation.

Business and Society: A Journal of Interdisciplinary Exploration. International Association for Business and Society Research Committee. Sage Publications, Inc., 2455 Teller Rd. Thousand Oaks, CA 91320. Phone: (805)499-0721 Fax: (805)499-0871 E-mail: info@sagepub.com • URL: http://www.sagepub.com • Quarterly. Individuals, $65.00 per year; institutions, $265.00 per year.

Business and Society: A Managerial Approach. Heidi Vernon. McGraw-Hill Professional, 1221 Ave. of the Americas New York, NY 10020. Phone: 800-772-4726 or (212)904-2000 Fax: (212)904-2072 E-mail: customer.service@mcgraw-hill.com • URL: http://www.mcgraw-hill.com • 1997. Sixth edition. Price on application. Emphasizes ethics and social accountability.

Business and Society Review: A Quarterly Forum on the Role of Business in a Free Society. Blackwell Publishers, 350 Main St., 6th Fl. Malden, MA 02148-5018. Phone: 800-216-2522 or (781)388-8200 Fax: (781)388-8232 E-mail: subscript@blackwellpub.com • URL: http://www.blackwellpub.com • Quarterly. $120.00 per year.

Business and Technical Writing: An Annotated Bibliography of Books 1880-1980. Gerald J. Alred and others. Scarecrow Press, Inc., 4720 Boston Way Lanham, MD 20706-4310. Phone: 800-462-6420 or (301)459-3366 Fax: 800-338-4550 or (301)459-1705 E-mail: orders@scarecrowpress.com • URL: http://www.scarecrowpress.com • 1981. $21.00.

Business Arbitration-What You Need to Know. Robert Coulson. American Arbitration Association, 355 Madison Ave. New York, NY 10017-4605. Phone: 800-778-7879 or (212)716-5800 Fax: (212)716-5905 URL: http://www.adr.org • 1991. $10.00 Fourth edition. Alternatives to the courts in settling business disputes.

Business Automation Reference Service: Office Equipment. Alltech Publishing Co., 212 Cooper Center, North Park Dr. and Browning Rd. Pennsauken, NJ 08109. Monthly. $100.00 per year. Looseleaf service.

Business Brokerage. Entrepreneur Media, Inc., 2445 McCabe Way Irvine, CA 92614. Phone: 800-421-2300 or (949)261-2325 Fax: (949)261-0234 E-mail: entmag@entrepreneur.com • URL: http://www.entrepreneur.com • Looseleaf. $59.50. A practical guide to starting a brokerage service for the sale and purchase of small businesses. Covers profit potential, start-up costs, market size evaluation, owner's time required, pricing, accounting, advertising, promotion, etc. (Start-Up Business Guide No. E1317.)

Business Brokers Directory. American Business Directories, P.O. Box 27347 Omaha, NE 68127. Phone: 800-555-6124 or (402)593-4600 Fax: (402)331-5481 E-mail: internet@infousa.com • URL: http://www.abii.com • Annual. Price on application. Lists about 3,383 U. S. business brokers. Information is derived from telephone yellow page directories.

Business Capital Sources. Tyler G. Hicks. International Wealth Success, Inc., 24 Canterbury Rd. Rockville Center, NY 11570. Phone: 800-323-0548 or (516)766-5850 Fax: (516)766-5919 2000. $15.00. 11th edition. Lists about 1,500 banks, insurance and mortgage companies, commerical finance, leasing and venture capital firms that lend money for business investment.

Business Committee for the Arts.

Business Communication. John M. Penrose and James M. Lahiff. Prentice Hall, 240 Frisch Court Paramus, NJ 07652-5240. Phone: 800-947-7700 or (201)909-6200 Fax: 800-445-6991 or (201)909-6361 URL: http://www.prenhall.com • 1996. $70.00. Fifth edition.

Business Communication Quarterly. Association for Business Communication, c/o Dr. Robert Myers, Baruch College, Dept. of Speech Communication, 17 Lexington Ave. New York, NY 10010. Phone: (212)387-1620 Fax: (212)387-1655 E-mail: abcrjm@compuserve.com • URL: http://www.theabc.org • Quarterly. Memebers, $65.00 per year; non-memebers, $150.00 per year. Features articles about teaching and writing course outlines. Description of training programs, problems, soutions, etc. Includes *Journal of Business Communcation*.

Business Communications. Carol M. Lehman and others. South-Western Publishing Co., 5101 Madison Rd. Cincinnati, OH 45227. Phone: 800-543-0487 or (513)271-8811 Fax: 800-437-8488 E-mail: billhendee@itped.com • URL: http://www.swcollege.com • 1995. $67.95. 11th edition.

Business Communications. Carol M. Lehman and others. South-Western Publishing Co., 5101 Madison Rd. Cincinnati, OH 45227. Phone: (513)271-8811 or 800-354-9706 E-mail: billhendee@itped.com • URL: http://www.swcollege.com • 1995. $67.95. 11th edition.

Business Communications Made Simple. Butterworth-Heinemann, 225 Wildwood Ave. Woburn, MA 01801. Phone: 800-366-2665 or (781)904-2500 Fax: 800-446-6520 Date not set. $19.95.

Business Communications Review. BCR Enterprises, Inc., 999 Oakmont Plaza Dr., Suite 100 Westmont, IL 60559-1381. Phone: 800-227-1234 or (630)986-1432 Fax: (630)323-5324 E-mail: fknight@bcr.com • URL: http://www.bcr.com/bcrmag • Bimonthly. $45.00 per year. Edited for communications managers in large end-user companies and institutions. Includes special feature issues on intranets and network management.

The Business Consumer's Advisor. Buyers Laboratory, Inc., 108 John St. Hackensack, NJ 07601. Phone: (201)489-6439 Fax: (201)489-9365 E-mail: ctd@buyerslaboratory.com • URL: http://www.buyers-lab.com • Monthly. $175.00 per year. Newsletter.

Business Consumers's Network. Buyers Laboratory Inc., 108 John St. Hackensack, NJ 07601. Phone: (201)489-6439 Fax: (201)489-9365 E-mail: ctd@buyerslaboratory.com • URL: http://www.buyers-lab.com • Monthly. $795.00 per year. Looseleaf service. Tests office equipment and issues reports. Formerly *Buyers Laboratory Report on Office Products*.

Business Council.

Business Counsel: A Quarterly Update of the Litigation Activities of the U.S. Chambers of Commerce. National Chamber Litigation Center (NCLC), 1615 H St., N.W. Washington, DC 20062. Phone: (202)463-5337 Fax: (202)463-5346 Quarterly. Free to members; non-member legal libraries, $15.00 per year.

Business Credit. National Association of Credit Management, 8840 Columbia 100 Parkway Columbia, MD 21045. Phone: (410)740-5560 Fax: (410)740-5574 E-mail: info@nacm.org • URL: http://www.nacm.org • Monthly. $34.00 per year. Formerly *Credit and Financial Management*.

Business Crime: Criminal Liability of the Business Community. Matthew Bender & Co., Inc., Two Park Ave. New York, NY 10016. Phone: 800-223-1940 or (212)448-2000 Fax: (212)244-3188 E-mail: international@bender.com • URL: http://www.bender.com • $1,380.00. Seven looseleaf volumes. Periodic supplementation. Guide to the many criminal problems that can arise in modern business practice. Provides how-to guidance.

Business Cycle Indicators. Conference Board, Inc., 845 Third Ave. New York, NY 10022-6679. Phone: (212)759-0900 Fax: (212)980-7014 E-mail: lei@conference-board.org • URL: http://www.tcb-indicators.org • Monthly. $120.00 per year. Contains detailed business and economic statistics in tables that were formerly published by the U. S. Department of Commerce in *Survey of Current Business*, and before that, in the discontinued *Business Conditions Digest*. Includes composite indexes of leading economic indicators, coincident indicators, and lagging indicators.

Business Cycles: A Theoretical, Historical and Statistical Analysis of the Capitalist Process. Joseph A. Schumpeter. Porcupine Press, Inc., 310 S. Juniper St. Philadelphia, PA 19107-5818. Phone: (215)735-0101 Fax: (215)546-0664 1989. $24.95.

Business Cycles and Depressions: An Encyclopedia. David Glasner, editor. Garland Publishing, Inc., 29 W. 35th St., 10th Fl. New York, NY 10001-2299. Phone: 800-627-6273 or (212)414-0650 Fax: (212)308-9399 E-mail: info@

garland.com • URL: http://www.garlandpub.com • 1997. $100.00. Contains 327 alphabetical entries by various contributors. Defines and reviews all significant depressions, recessions, and financial crises in the U. S. and Europe since 1790. Includes chronologies, bibliographies, and indexes.

Business Cycles and Forecasting. Howard J. Sherman and David X. Kolk. Addison-Wesley Educational Publications, Inc., One Jacob Way Redding, MA 01867. Phone: 800-447-2226 or (781)944-3700 Fax: (781)942-1117 URL: http://www.awl.com • 1997. $101.00.

Business Cycles: Theory, History, Indicators, and Forecasting. Victor Zarnowitz. University of Chicago Press, 5801 Ellis Ave., 4th Fl. Chicago, IL 60637. Phone: 800-621-2736 or (773)702-7700 Fax: (773)702-9756 E-mail: marketing@press.uchicago.edu • URL: http://www.press.uchicago.edu • 1992. $77.00.

Business Dictionary of Computers. Jerry M. Rosenberg. John Wiley and Sons, Inc., 605 Third Ave. New York, NY 10158-0012. Phone: 800-225-5945 or (212)850-6000 Fax: (212)850-6088 E-mail: info@wiley.com • URL: http://www.wiley.com • 1993. $14.95. Third edition. Provides concise definitions of over 7,500 computer terms, including slang terms, abbreviations, acronyms, and technical jargon. (Business Dictionary Series).

Business Directory of Hong Kong. Available from Estrin & Diamond Publications, 20832 Roscoe Blvd. Canoga Park, CA 91306. Phone: (818)700-6920 Fax: (818)700-6921 Annual. $160.00. Published in Hong Kong by Current Publications Ltd. Provides information on more than 12,300 Hong Kong businesses in various fields, including manufacturing, finance, services, construction, transportation, and foreign trade.

Business Economics: Designed to Serve the Needs of People Who Use Economics in Their Work. National Association for Business Economics, 1233 20th St., N.W. Suite 505 Washington, DC 20036-2304. Phone: (202)463-6223 Fax: (202)463-6239 E-mail: nabe@nabe.com • URL: http://www.nabe.com • Quarterly. Individuals, $60.00 per year; institution, $54.00 per year. Features articles on applied economics.

Business Education Forum. National Business Education Association, 1914 Association Dr. Reston, VA 20191-1596. Phone: (703)860-8300 Fax: (703)620-4483 E-mail: nbea@nbea.org • URL: http://www.nbea.org/nbea.html • Four times a year. Libraries, $70.00 per year. Includes *Yearbook* and *Keying In*, a newsletter.

Business Education Index of Business Education Articles, Research Studies and Textbooks Compiled from a Selected List of Periodicals, Publishers and Yearbooks Published During the Calendar Year. Delta Pi Epsilon Graduate Business Education Society, National Office, P.O. Box 4340 Little Rock, AR 72214. Phone: (501)562-1233 Fax: (501)562-1293 Annual. $25.00.

The Business Elite: Database of Corporate America. Donnelley Marketing, 5711 S. 86th Circle Omaha, NE 68127. Phone: (402)537-7788 Fax: (402)537-7785 URL: http://www.donnelleymarketing.com • Quarterly. $795.00. Formerly compiled by Database America. Provides current information on CD-ROM for about 850,000 businesses, comprising all U. S. private and public companies having more than 20 employees or sales of more than $1 million. Data for each firm includes detailed industry classification, year started, annual sales, name of top executive, and number of employees.

Business English. Jeanne Reed. McGraw-Hill, 1221 Ave. of the Americas New York, NY 10020-1095. Phone: 800-722-4726 or (212)904-2000 Fax: (212)904-2072 E-mail: customer.service@mcgraw-hill.com • URL: http://www.mcgraw-hill.com • 1986. $61.64. Fourth edition.

Business English. Mary E. Guffey. South-Western College Publishing, 5101 Madison Rd. Cincinnati, OH 45227. Phone: 800-543-0487 or (513)527-1989 Fax: (513)527-6137 URL: http://www.thomson.com • 2001. $47.00. Seventh edition. (South-Western College-Busines Communications Series).

Business Essentials. Prentice Hall, 240 Frisch Court Paramus, NJ 07652-5240. Phone: 800-947-7700 or (201)909-6200 Fax: 800-445-6991 or (201)909-6361 URL: http://www.prenhall.com • 2000. Third edition. Price on application.

Business Ethics. J. Michael Hoffman. McGraw-Hill, 1221 Ave. of the Americas New York, NY 10020-1095. Phone: 800-722-4726 or (212)904-2000 Fax: (212)904-2072 E-mail: customer.service@mcgraw-hill.com • URL: http://www.mcgraw-hill.com • 2000. $39.25. Fourth edition.

Business Ethics: Roles and Responsibilities. Joseph Badaracco. McGraw-Hill Higher Education, 1221 Ave. of the Americas New York, NY 10020. Phone: 800-722-4726 or (212)904-2000 Fax: (212)904-2072 E-mail: customer.service@mcgraw-hill.com • URL: http://www.mcgraw-hill.com • 1994. $63.50.

Business Etiquette. Marjorie Brody and Barbara Pachter. McGraw-Hill Professional, 1221 Ave. of the Americas New York, NY 10020. Phone: 800-722-4726 or (212)904-2000 Fax: (212)904-2072 E-mail: customer.service@mcgraw-hill.com • URL: http://www.mcgraw-hill.com • 1994. $10.95.

Business Facilities. Group C Communications, P.O. Box 2060 Red Bank, NJ 07701. Phone: 800-524-0337 or (732)842-7433 E-mail: jcarzon@group.com • URL: http://www.busfac.com • Monthly. $30.00 per year. Facility planning and site selection.

Business Failure Record. Dun & Bradstreet, Economic Analysis Dept., Three Sylvan Way Parippany, NJ 07054-3896. Phone: 800-526-0651 or (973)455-0900 Fax: (973)254-4063 E-mail: customerservice@dnb.com • URL: http://www.dnb.com • Annual. Free upon request. Provides historical business failure data.

Business Finance. Duke Communications International, 221 E. 29th St. Loveland, CO 80538. Phone: 800-621-1544 or (970)663-4700 Fax: (970)663-3285 E-mail: info@businessfinancemag.com • URL: http://www.businessfinancemag.com • Monthly. $59.00 per year. Covers trends in finance, technology, and economics for corporate financial executives.

Business Forecasting. Holton J. Wilson. McGraw-Hill Professional, 1221 Ave of the Americas New York, NY 10020. Phone: 800-722-4726 or (212)904-2000 Fax: (212)904-2072 E-mail: customer.service@mcgraw-hill.com • URL: http://www.mcgraw-hill.com • 2001. $67.50. Fourth edition.

Business Forecasting. John E. Hanke and Arthur G. Reitsch. Prentice Hall, 240 Frisch Court Paramus, NJ 07652-5240. Phone: 800-947-7700 or (201)909-6200 Fax: 800-445-6991 or (201)909-6361 URL: http://www.prenhall.com • 1997. $90.00. Sixth edition.

Business Forecasting for Management. Branko Pecar. McGraw-Hill, 1221 Ave. of the Americas New York, NY 10020-1095. Phone: 800-722-4726 or (212)904-2000 Fax: (212)904-2072 E-mail: customer.service@mcgraw-hill.com • URL: http://www.mcgraw-hill.com • 1994. $14.95.

Business Forecasting Project. University of California, Los Angeles

Business Forms, Labels and Systems. North American Publishing Co., 401 N. Broad St. Philadelphia, PA 19108-9988. Phone: 800-627-2689 or (215)238-5300 Fax: (215)238-5457 E-mail: dbrennan@napco.com • URL: http://www.napco.com • Semimonthly. $95.00 per year. Formerly *Business Forms and Systems*.

Business Forms, Labels, and Systems: Who's Who of Manufacturers and Suppliers. North American Publishing Co., 401 N. Broad St. Philadelphia, PA 19108-9988. Phone: 800-627-2689 or (215)238-5300 Fax: (215)238-5457 E-mail: napco@napco.com • URL: http://www.napco.com • Annual. $20.00. Lists more than 800 suppliers and manufacturers of business forms, labels, and related equipment.

Business Forms Management Association.

Business Forms on File Collection. Facts on File Staff. Facts on File, Inc., 11 Penn Plaza, 15th Fl. New York, NY 10001-2006. Phone: 800-322-8755 or (212)967-8800 Fax: (212)967-9196 E-mail: lharris@factsonfile.com • URL: http://www/factsonfile.com • Annual. $125.00.

Business, Government, and Society: A Managerial Perspective: Text and Cases. George A. Steiner and John F. Steiner. McGraw-Hill, 1221 Ave. of the Americas New York, NY 10020-1095. Phone: 800-722-4726 or (212)904-2000 Fax: (212)904-2072 E-mail: customer.service@mcgraw-hill.com • URL: http://www.mcgraw-hill.com • 1999. $82.19. Ninth edition. (Management Series).

Business, Government, and Society: Managing Competitiveness, Ethics, and Social Issues. Newman S. Perry. Prentice Hall, 240 Frisch Court Paramus, NJ 07652-5240. Phone: 800-947-7700 or (201)909-6200 Fax: 800-445-6991 or (201)909-6361 URL: http://www.prenhall.com • 1994. $54.80.

Business, Government, and Society Research Institute. University of Pittsburgh

Business Guide to Modern China. Jon P. Alston and Yongxin He. Michigan State University Press, 1405 S. Harrison Rd., Suite 25 East Lansing, MI 48823-5202. Phone: (517)355-9543 Fax: (517)432-2611 E-mail: mspos@msu.edu • URL: http://www.msu.edu/press • 1996. $29.95. (International Business Series).

Business History. ISBS, 5804 N.E. Hassalo St. Portland, OR 97213-3644. Phone: 800-944-6190 or (503)280-8832 Fax: (503)280-8832 Quarterly. Individuals, $58.00 per year; institutions, $265.00 per year.

Business History Conference.

Business History of the World: A Chronology. Richard B. Robinson, compiler. Greenwood Publishing Group, Inc., 88 Post Rd., W. Westport, CT 06881-5007. Phone: 800-225-5800 or (203)226-3571 Fax: (203)222-2540 E-mail: bookinfo@greenwood.com • URL: http://www.greenwood.com • 1993. $79.50. Provides "a basic chronology of the business world outside the United States from prehistory through the 1980s."

Business History Review. Harvard Business School Publishing, 60 Harvard Way Boston, MA 02163. Phone: (617)495-6154 Fax: (617)496-5985 E-mail: custserv@cchbspub.harvard.edu • URL: http://www.hpsp.harvard.edu • Quarterly. Individuals, $35.00 per year; institutions, $75.00 per year; students, $20.00 per year.

Business Indexes. Board of Governors of the Federal Reserve System, 20th and C Sts. N.W. Washington, DC 20551. Phone: (202)452-3000 Fax: (202)452-3819 Monthly.

Business Information Alert: Sources, Strategies and Signposts for Information Professionals. Donna T. Heroy, editor. Alert Publications, Inc., 401 W. Fullerton Parkway, Suite 1403E Chicago, IL 60614-3857. Phone: (773)525-7594 Fax: (773)525-7015 E-mail: alertpub@compuserve.com • URL: http://www.alertpub.com • 10 times per year. $152.00 per year. Newsletter for business librarians and information specialists.

Business Information Desk Reference: Where to Find Answers to Your Business Questions. Melvyn N. Freed and Virgil P. Diodato. Prentice Hall, 240 Frisch Court Paramus, NJ 07652-5240. Phone: 800-947-7700 or (201)909-6200 Fax: 800-445-6991 or (201)909-6361 URL: http://www.prenhall.com • 1992. $20.00. Offers a unique, question and answer approach to business information sources. Covers print sources, online databases, trade associations, and government agencies.

Business Information: How to Find It, How to Use It. Michael R. Lavin. Oryx Press, 4041 N. Central Ave., Ste. 700 Phoenix, AZ 85012-3397. Phone: 800-279-6799 or (602)265-2651 Fax: 800-279-4663 or (602)265-6250 E-mail: info@oryxpress.com • URL: http://www.oryxpress.com • 2001. $61.00. Third edition. Combines discussions of business research techniques with detailed descriptions of major business publications and databases. Includes title and subject indexes.

Business Information Sources. Lorna M. Daniells. California Princeton Fulfillment Services, 1445 Lower Ferry Rd. Ewing, NJ 08618. Phone: 800-777-4726 or (609)883-1759 E-mail: donnaw@cpfs.pupress.princeton.edu • URL: http://www.ucpress.edu • 1993. $42.50. Third revised edition. Basic business sources, with discussion and full annotations.

Business Insurance Directory of Corporate Buyers of Insurance, Benefit Plans and Risk Management Services. Crain Communications, Inc., 740 N. Rush St. Chicago, IL 60611-2590. Phone: 800-678-9595 or (312)649-5200 Fax: (312)649-5443 URL: http://www.crain.com • Annual. $95.00. More than 2,600 corporations. Includes names of corporate employee benefits managers.

Business Insurance: Directory of 401(k) Plan Administrators. Crain Communications, Inc., 740 N. Rush St. Chicago, IL 60611-2590. Phone: 800-678-9595 or (312)649-5200 Fax: (312)649-5360 URL: http://www.crain.com • Annual. $4.00. Provides information on approximately 75 companies that administer 401(k) retirement plans.

Business Insurance: Employee Benefit Consultants. Crain Communications, Inc., 740 N. Rush St. Chicago, IL 60611-2590. Phone: 800-678-9595 or (312)649-5200 Fax: (312)649-5360 URL: http://www.crain.com • Annual. $4.00. List of about 130 firms that offer empolyee benefit counseling services.

Business Insurance Guide: How to Purchase the Best and Most Affordable Insurance. Jamie McLeroy. Summers Press, Inc., 950 Westbank Dr., Suite 204 Austin, TX 78746-6684. Phone: 800-743-6491 or (512)329-9140 Fax: (512)367-2029 E-mail: getlegd@summerspress.com • URL: http://www.summerpress.com • Looseleaf service. $96.50.

Business Insurance: News Magazine for Corporate Risk, Employee Benefit and Financial Executives. Crain Communications, Inc., 740 N. Rush St. Chicago, IL 60611-2590. Phone: 800-678-9595 or (312)649-5200 Fax: (312)649-7937 URL: http://www.businessinsurance.com • Weekly. $89.00 per year. Covers a wide variety of business insurance topics, including risk management, employee benefits, workers compensation, marine insurance, and casualty insurance.

Business Internet and Intranets: A Manager's Guide to Key Terms and Concepts. Peter G. W. Keen and others. Harvard Business School Press, 60 Harvard Way Boston, MA 02163. Phone: 800-545-7685 or (617)783-7440 E-mail: custserv@cchbspub.harvard.edu • URL: http://www.hbsp.harvard.edu • 1998. $39.95. Defines more than 100 words and phrases relating to the Internet or corporate intranets.

Business Interruption Coverage. American Bar Association, 750 N. Lake Shore Dr. Chicago, IL 60611-4497. Phone: 800-285-2221 or (312)988-5000 Fax: (312)988-5528 E-mail: abajournal@abanet.org • URL: http://www.abanet.org • 1987. $29.95. Produced by ABA Tort and Insurance Practice Section. Covers legal aspects of business interruption insurance.

Business Journals of the United States: Historical Guides to the World's Periodicals and Newspapers. William Fisher, editor. Greenwood Publishing Group, Inc., 88 Post Rd., W. Westport, CT 06881-5007. Phone: 800-225-5800 or (203)226-3571 Fax: (203)222-2540 E-mail: bookinfo@greenwood.com • URL: http://www.greenwood.com • 1991. $75.00. Contains historical and descriptive essays covering over 100 leading business publications.

Business Latin America: Weekly Report to Managers of Latin American Operations. Economist Intelligence Unit, 111 W. 57th St. New York, NY 10019. Phone: 800-938-4685 or (212)554-0600 Fax: (212)586-1182 URL: http://www.eiu.com • Weekly. $1,195.00 per year. Newsletter covering Latin American business trends, politics, regulations, exchange rates, economics, and finance. Provides statistical data on foreign debt, taxes, labor costs, gross domestic product (GDP), and inflation rates.

Business Law. S.B. Marsh and J. Soulsby. Trans-Atlantic Publications, Inc., 311 Bainbridge St. Philadelphia, PA 19147. Phone: (215)925-2762 Fax: (215)925-1912 E-mail: order@transatlanticpub.com • URL: http://www.transatlanticpub.com • 1999. Seventh. $48.00. Seventh edition.

Business Law and the Regulatory Environment: Concepts and Cases. Jane Mallor and A. James Barnes. McGraw-Hill Higher Education, 1221 Ave. of the Americas New York, NY 10020. Phone: 800-722-4726 or (212)904-2000 Fax: (212)904-2072 E-mail: customer.service@mcgraw-hill.com • URL: http://www.mcgraw-hill.com • 1997. $101.25. 10th edition.

Business Law Made Simple. Stephen G. Christianson. Doubleday, 1540 Broadway New York, NY 10036-4094. Phone: 800-223-6834 or (212)354-6500 Fax: (212)492-9700 URL: http://www.doubledaybookclub.com • 1995. $12.00.

Business Law Monographs. Matthew Bender & Co., Inc., Two Park Ave. New York, NY 10016. Phone: 800-223-1940 or (212)448-2000 Fax: (212)244-3188 E-mail: international@bender.com • URL: http://www.bender.com • $1,450.00. 36 looseleaf volumes. Quarterly updates. Intended for in-house and outside corporate counsel. Each monograph concentrates on a particular subject.

Business Law: Principles and Cases in the Legal Environment. Daniel V. Davidson and Brenda E. Knowles. South-Western Publishing Co., 5101 Madison Rd. Cincinnati, OH 45227. Phone: 800-543-0487 or (513)271-8811 E-mail: billhendee@itped.com • URL: http://www.swcollege.com • 1997. $107.95. Sixth edition. (Miscellaneous/Catalogs Series).

Business Law: Principles and Practices. Arnold J. Goldman. Houghton Mifflin Co., 215 Park Ave. South New York, NY 10003. Phone: 800-225-3362 or (212)420-5800 Fax: (212)420-5855 URL: http://www.hmco.com • 2000. $60.45. Fifth edition.

Business Law: The Legal, Ethical, and International Environment. Henry R. Cheesman. Prentice Hall, 240 Frisch Court Paramus, NJ 07652-5240. Phone: 800-947-7700 or (201)909-6200 Fax: 800-445-6991 or (201)909-6361 URL: http://www.prenhall.com • 1997. $105.00. Third edition.

Business Lawyer. American Bar Association, 750 N. Lake Shore Dr. Chicago, IL 60611-4497. Phone: 800-285-2221 or (312)988-5000 Fax: (312)988-5528 E-mail: abajournal@abanet.org • URL: http://www.lexis-nexis.com/incc/sources/libcont/aba.html • Quarterly. Memebers $99.00 per year; non-memebers, $149.00 per year.

Business Letter Writing. Sheryl Lindsell-Roberts. Pearson Education and Technology, 201 W. 103rd. St. Indianapolis, IN 46290-1097. Phone: 800-858-7674 or (317)581-3500 Fax: 800-822-8583 or (317)581-4670 1994. $12.00.

Business Letters for Busy People: More Than 200 Timesaving, Ready-to-Use Business Letters for Any Occasion. Jim Dugger. Career Press, Inc., P.O. Box 687 Franklin Lakes, NJ 07417-1322. Phone: 800-227-3371 or (201)848-0310 Fax: (201)848-1727 E-mail: contact@careerpress.com • URL: http://www.careerpress.com • 1995. $15.99. Third edition.

The Business Library and How to Use It: A Guide to Sources and Research Strategies for Information on Business and Management. Ernest L. Maier and others, editors. Omnigraphics, Inc., Penobscot Bldg. Detroit, MI 48226. Phone: 800-234-1340 or (313)961-1340 Fax: 800-875-1340 or (313)961-1383 E-mail: info@omnigraphics.com • URL: http://www.omnigraphics.com • 1996. $56.00. Explains library research methods and describes specific sources of business information. A revision of *How to Use the Business Library*, by H. Webster Johnson and others (fifth edition, 1984).

Business Library Review: An International Journal. International Publishers Distributor, P.O. Box 32160 Newark, NJ 07102. Phone: 800-545-8398 Fax: (215)750-6343 URL: http://www.21c.com • Quarterly. Academic institutions, $318.00 per year;corporations, $501.00 per year.Incorporates *The Wall Street Review of Books* and *Economics and Business: An Annotated Bibliography*. Publishes scholarly reviews of books on a wide variety of topics in business, economics, and finance. Text in French.

Business Marketing: A Global Approach. Robert W. Haas. McGraw-Hill Higher Education, 1221 Ave. of the Americas New York, NY 10020. Phone: 800-722-4726 or (212)904-2000 Fax: (212)904-2072 E-mail: customer.service@mcgraw-hill.com • URL: http://www.mcgraw-hill.com • 1996. $68.95. Sixth revised edition.

Business Marketing Association., 400 N. Michigan Ave., 15th Fl. Chicago, IL 60611. Phone: 800-664-4262 or (312)409-4262 Fax: (312)409-4266 E-mail: bma@marketing.org • URL: http://www.marketing.org • Members are professionals in business and industrial advertising and marketing. Formerly known as Business/Professional Advertising Association.

Business Marketing Management. Frank G. Bingham. NTC/Contemporary Publishing, P.O. Box 545 Blacklick, OH 43004. Phone: 800-338-3987 or (614)755-4151 Fax: (614)755-5645 E-mail: ntcpub@mcgraw-hill.com • URL: http://www.net-cb.com • 1997. $71.95.

Business Math: Practical Applications. Cheryl Cleaves and others. Prentice Hall, 240 Frisch Court Paramus, NJ 07652-5240. Phone: 800-947-7700 or (201)909-6200 Fax: 800-445-6991 or (201)909-6361 URL: http://www.prenhall.com • 1993. Third annotated edition. Price on application.

Business Mathematics. Charles D. Miller and others. Addison Wesley Educational Publications, Inc., One Jacob Way Reading, MA 01867. Phone: 800-447-2226 or (781)944-3700 Fax: (781)942-1117 URL: http://www.awl.com • 1999. $78.00. Eighth edition.

Business Mathematics. South-Western College Publishing, 5101 Madison Rd. Cincinnati, OH 45227. Phone: 800-543-0487 or (513)527-1989 Fax: (513)523-6137 1998. $76.95. (Miscellaneous Catalog Series).

Business Mathematics for Colleges. James Dietz. South-Western Publishing Co., 5101 Madison Rd. Cincinnati, OH 45227. Phone: 800-543-0487 or (513)271-8811 Fax: 800-437-8488 E-mail: billhendee@itped.com • URL: http://www.swcollege.com • 1995. $59.95. 11th edition. (MB-Business/Vocational Math Series).

Business Multimedia Explained: A Manager's Guide to Key Terms and Concepts. Peter G. W. Keen. Harvard Business School Press, 60 Harvard Way Boston, MA 02163. Phone: 800-545-7685 or (617)783-7440 E-mail: custserv@cchbspub.harvard.edu • URL: http://www.hbsp.harvard.edu • 1997. $39.95.

Business Negotiating Basics. Peter Economy. McGraw-Hill Higher Education, 1221 Ave. of the Americas New York, NY 10020. Phone: 800-722-4726 or (212)512-2000 Fax: (212)512-2072 E-mail: customer.service@mcgraw-hill.com • URL: http://www.mcgraw-hill.com • 1993. $19.95.

The Business of Banking for Bank Directors. George K. Darling and James F. Chaston. Robert Morris Associates, One Liberty Place, 1650 Market St., Suite 2300 Philadelphia, PA 19103. Phone: 800-677-7621 or (215)446-4000 Fax: (215)446-4100 E-mail: info@rmahq.org • URL: http://www.rmahq.org • 1995. $33.00. Presents basic banking concepts and issues for new directors of financial institutions. Emphasis is on the specific duties of directors.

The Business of Law: A Handbook on How to Manage Law Firms. Aspen Law and Business, 1185 Ave. of the Americas New York, NY 10036. Phone: 800-638-8437 or (212)597-0200 Fax: 800-597-0338 or (212)597-0338 URL: http://www.aspenpub.com • $95.00. 1990. Looseleaf service.

The Business of Publishing: How to Survive and Prosper in the Publishing and Bookselling Industry. Leonard Shatzkin. McGraw-Hill, 1221 Ave. of the Americas New York, NY 10020. Phone: 800-722-4726 or (212)904-2000 Fax: (212)904-2072 E-mail: customer.service@mcgraw-hill.com • URL: http://www.mcgraw-hill.com • 1995. $24.95.

The Business of Shipping. Lane C. Kendall and James J. Buckley. Cornell Maritime Press, Inc., P.O. Box 456 Centreville, MD 21617. Phone: 800-638-7641 or (410)758-1075 Fax: (410)758-2478 E-mail: cornell@crosslink.net • 2000. $50.00. Seventh edition.

The Business of Special Events: Fundraising Strategies for Changing Times. Harry A. Freedman and Karen Feldman. Pineapple Press, Inc., PO Box 3899 Sarasota, FL 34230-3899. Phone: 800-746-3275 or (941)359-0886 Fax: (941)351-9988 E-mail: info@pineapplepress.com • URL: http://www.pineapplepress.com • 1998. $21.95.

Business Organizations, Agencies, and Publications Directory. The Gale Group, 27500 Drake Rd. Farmington Hills, MI 48331-3535. Phone: 800-877-GALE or (248)699-GALE Fax: 800-414-5043 or (248)699-8069 E-mail: galeord@galegroup.com • URL: http://www.galegroup.com • 1999. $425.00. 12th edition. Over 40,000 entries describing 39 types of business information sources. Classified by type of organization, publication, or serviceIncludes state, national, and international agencies and organizations. Master index to names and keywords. Also includes e-mail addresses and web site URL's.

Business Organizations with Tax Planning. Zolman Cavitch. Matthew Bender & Co., Inc., Two Park Ave. New York, NY 10016. Phone: 800-223-1940 or (212)448-2000 Fax: (212)244-3188 E-mail: international@bender.com • URL: http://www.bender.com • $2,570.00. 16 looseleaf volumes. Periodic supplementation. In-depth analytical coverage of corporation law and all relevant aspects of federal corporation taxation.

Business Periodicals Index. H. W. Wilson Co., 950 University Ave. Bronx, NY 10452. Phone: 800-367-6770 or (718)588-8400 Fax: (718)590-1617 URL: http://www.hwwilson.com • Monthly, except August, with quarterly and annual cumulations. Service basis for print edition; CD-ROM edition, $1,495.00 per year.

Business Plan Guide for Independent Consultants. Herman Holtz. John Wiley and Sons, Inc., 605 Third Ave. New York, NY 10158-0012. Phone: 800-225-5945 or (212)850-6000 Fax: (212)850-6088 E-mail: info@wiley.com • URL: http://www.wiley.com • 1994. $115.00.

Business Plan: Planning for the Small Business. Alan West. Nichols Publishing Co., P.O. Box 6036 East Brunswick, NJ 08816-6036. Phone: (732)297-2862 Fax: (732)940-0549 1988. $21.95.

Business Plans Handbook. The Gale Group, 27500 Drake Rd. Farmington Hills, MI 48331-3535. Phone: 800-877-GALE or (248)699-GALE Fax: 800-414-5043 or (248)699-8069 E-mail: galeord@galegroup.com • URL: http://www.galegroup.com • 2001. $135.00. Contains examples of detailed plans for starting or developing various kinds of businesses. Categories within plans include statement of purpose, market description, personnel requirements, financial needs, etc.

Business Policy Game: An International Simulation: Player's Manual. Richard V. Cotter and David J. Fritzsche. Prentice Hall, 240 Frisch Court Paramus, NJ 07652-5240. Phone: 800-947-7700 or (201)909-6200 Fax: 800-445-6991 or (201)909-6361 URL: http://www.prenhall.com • 1995. $42.00. Fourth edition.

Business Policy: Managing Strategic Processes. Joseph L. Bower and others. McGraw-Hill Higher Education, 1221 Ave. of the Americas New York, NY 10020. Phone: 800-722-4726 or (212)904-2000 Fax: (212)904-2072 E-mail: customer.service@mcgraw-hill.com • URL: http://www.mcgraw-hill.com • 1995. $72.75. Eighth edition.

Business Products Industry Association.

Business Products Industry Association Membership Directory and Buyer's Guide. Business Products Industry Association, 301 N. Fairfax St. Alexandria, VA 22314. Phone: 800-542-6672 or (703)549-9040 Fax: (703)683-7552 URL: http://www.bpia.org • Annual. Members, $20.00; Free to members; non-members, $80.00. 9,000 manufacturers, wholesalers, retailers and sales and marketing representatives in the office products industry.

Business-Professional Online Services: Review, Trends, and Forecast. SIMBA Information, Inc., P.O. Box 4234 Stamford, CT 06907-0234. Phone: 800-307-2529 or (203)358-4100 Fax: (203)358-5824 E-mail: info@simbanet.com • URL: http://www.simbanet.com • Annual. $1,295.00 Provides a review of current conditions in the online information industry. Profiles of major database producers and online services are included. Formerly*Online Services: Review, Trends and Forecast*.

Business Profitability Data. John B. Walton. Weybridge Publishing Co., 16911 Brushfield Dr. Dallas, TX 75248. Phone: (214)931-7770 1996. $40.00. Sales and profitability ratios for 300 kinds of business.

Business Publication Advertising Source. SRDS, 1700 Higgins Rd. Des Plaines, IL 60018. Phone: 800-851-7737 or (847)375-5000 Fax: (847)375-5001 E-mail: lalbr@srds.com • URL: http://www.srds.com • Monthly. $682.00 per year. Issued in three parts: (1) U. S. Business Publications, (2) U. S. Healthcare Publications, and (3) International Publications. Provides detailed advertising rates, profiles of editorial content, management names, "Multiple Publications Publishers," circulation data, and other trade journal information. Formerly *Business Publication Rates and Data*.

Business Rankings Annual. The Gale Group, 27500 Drake Rd. Farmington Hills, MI 48331-3535. Phone: 800-877-GALE or (248)699-GALE Fax: 800-414-5043 or (248)699-8069 E-mail: galeord@galegroup.com • URL: http://www.galegroup.com • Annual. $305.00.Two volumes. Compiled by the Business Library Staff of the Brooklyn Public Library. This is a guide to lists and rankings appearing in major business publications. The top ten names are listed in each case.

Business Records Control. Joseph S. Fosegan. South-Western Publishing Co., 5101 Madison Rd. Cincinnati, OH 45227. Phone: 800-543-0487 or (513)271-8811 Fax: 800-437-8480 E-mail: billhendee@itped.com • URL: http://www.swcollege.com • 1995. $36.95. Seventh edition.

Business Research for Decision Making. Duane Davis. Wadsworth Publishing Co., 10 Davis Dr. Belmont, CA 94002. Phone: 800-354-9706 or (650)595-2350 Fax: (650)637-9955 URL: http://www.wadsworth • 1999. $62.00. Fifth edition. (Business Statistics Series).

Business Research Handbook: Methods and Sources for Lawyers and Business Professionals. Kathy E. Shimpock. Aspen Law and Business, 1185 Ave. of the Americas New York, NY 10036. Phone: 800-447-1717 or (212)597-0200 Fax: 800-901-9075 or (212)597-0338 E-mail: customer.service@aspenpubl.com • URL: http://www.aspenpub.com • $145.00. Looseleaf. Periodic supplementation. Provides detailed advice on how to find business information. Describes a wide variety of data sources, both private and government.

Business Source Plus. EBSCO Information Services, 10 Estes St. Ipswich, MA 01938. Phone: 800-653-2726 or (978)356-6500 Fax: (978)356-6565 E-mail: ep@epnet.com • URL: http://www.epnet.com • Monthly. $1,495.00 per year. Provides CD-ROM citations and abstracts to articles in about 650 business periodicals and newspapers, including *The Wall Street Journal*. Full text is provided from 200 selected periodicals. Covers accounting, communications, economics, finance, management, marketing, and other business subjects.

Business Start-Ups: Smart Ideas for Your Small Business. Entrepreneur Media, Inc., 2445 McCabe Way Irvine, CA 92614. Phone: 800-421-2300 or (949)261-2325 Fax: (949)261-0234 E-mail: entmag@entrepreneur.com • URL: http://www.entrepreneur.com • Monthly. $14.97 per year. Provides advice for starting a small business. Includes business trends, new technology, E-commerce, and case histories (''real-life stories'').

Business Statistics: A Decision-Making Approach. David F. Groebner and Patrick W. Shannon. Prentice Hall, 240 Frisch Court Paramus, NJ 07652-5240. Phone: 800-947-7700 or (201)909-6200 Fax: 800-445-6991 or (201)909-6361 URL: http://www.prenhall.com • 1993. $72.80. Fourth edition.

Business Statistics by Example. Terry Sincich. Prentice Hall, 240 Frisch Court Paramus, NJ 07652. Phone: 800-947-7700 or (201)909-6452 Fax: 800-445-6991 URL: http://www.prenhall.com • 1995. $86.00. Fifth edition. Includes disk.

Business Statistics: Contemporary Decision Making. Ken Black. South-Western Publishing Co., 5101 Madison Rd. Cincinnati, OH 45227. Phone: 800-543-0487 or (513)271-8811 Fax: 800-487-8488 or (513)527-6956 E-mail: billhendee@itped.com • URL: http://www.swcollege.com • 2000. $65.00. Third edition.

Business Statistics for Management and Economics. Wayne W. Daniel and James C. Terrell. Houghton Mifflin Co., 215 Park Ave. S. New York, NY 10003. Phone: 800-225-3362 or (212)420-5800 Fax: (212)420-5855 URL: http://www.hmco.com • 2000. $19.47. Seventh edition.

Business Statistics for Quality and Productivity. John M. Levine. Prentice Hall, 240 Frisch Court Paramus, NJ 07652-5240. Phone: 800-947-7700 or (201)909-6200 Fax: 800-445-6991 or (201)909-6361 URL: http://www.prenhall.com • 1994. $94.07. (Prentice Hall College Title Series).

Business Statistics of the United States. Courtenay M. Slater, editor. Bernan Associates, 4611-F Assembly Dr. Lanham, MD 20706-4391. Phone: 800-274-4447 or (301)459-7666 Fax: 800-865-3450 or (301)459-0056 E-mail: info@bernan.com • URL: http://www.bernan.com • 1999. $74.00. Fifth edition. Based on *Business Statistics*, formerly issue by the Bureau of Economic Analysis, U. S. Department of Commerce. Provides basic data for a wide variety of U. S. industries, services, and economic indicators. Most statistics are shown annually for 29 years and monthly for the most recent four years.

Business Statistics Practice. Bruce L. Bowerman. McGraw-Hill, 1221 Ave. of the Americas New York, NY 10020. Phone: 800-722-4726 or (212)904-2000 Fax: (212)904-2072 E-mail: customer.service@mcgraw-hill.com • URL: http://www.mcgraw-hill.com • 2000. $68.00. Second edition.

Business Strategies. CCH, Inc., 4025 W. Peterson Ave. Chicago, IL 60646-6085. Phone: 800-248-3248 or (773)583-8500 Fax: 800-224-8299 or (773)866-3608 URL: http://www.cch.com • Semimonthly. $819.00 per year. Four looseleaf volumes. Semimonthly updates. Legal, tax, and accounting aspects of business planning and decision-making. Provides information on start-ups, forms of ownership (partnerships, corporations), failing businesses, reorganizations, acquisitions, and so forth. Includes *Business Strategies Bulletin*, a monthly newsletter.

Business Strategies Bulletin. CCH, Inc., 4025 W. Peterson Ave. Chicago, IL 60646-6085. Phone: 800-248-3248 or (773)583-8500 Fax: 800-224-8299 or (773)866-3608 URL: http://www.cch.com • Monthly. $166.00 per year. Newsletter.

Business Strategy and Policy. Danny R. Arnold and others. Houghton Mifflin Software, School and College Div., 222 Berkeley St. Boston, MA 02116-3764. Phone: 800-225-3362 or (617)351-5000 Fax: (617)227-5409 URL: http://www.hmco.com • 1991. Third edition. Three volumes. Price on application.

Business Technology Association.

Business to Business Advertising: A Marketing Management Approach. Charles Patti and others. NTC/Contemporary Publishing, P.O. Box 545 Blacklick, OH 43004. Phone: 800-338-3987 or (614)755-4151 Fax: (614)755-5645 E-mail: ntcpub@mcgraw-hill.com • URL: http://www.ntc-cb.com • 1994. $39.95. (NTC Business Book Series).

Business Transactions: Tax Analysis. Research Institute of America, 90 Fifth Ave. New York, NY 10011. Phone: 800-431-9025 or (212)645-4800 Fax: (201)816-3581 Three looseleaf volumes. Biweekly updates. Price on application. Analyzes the tax consequences of various business decisions for sole proprietorships, partnerships, S corporations, and other corporations.

Business Transactions: Tax Planning. Research Institute of America, Inc., 90 Fifth Ave. New York, NY 10011. Phone: 800-431-9025 or (212)645-4800 Fax: (201)816-3581 Four looseleaf volumes. Monthly updates. Price on application. Covers the tax planning aspects of business decisions for sole proprietorships, partnerships, S corporations, and other corporations.

Business Travel News: News and Ideas for Business Travel Management. Miller Freeman, Inc., One Penn Plaza New York, NY 10119-1198. Phone: 800-950-1314 or (212)714-1300 Fax: (212)279-3945 URL: http://www.mfi.com • 29 times a year. $115.00 per year. Includes annual directory of travel sources. Formerly *Corporate Travel*.

Business 2.0. Imagine Media, Inc., 150 North Hill Dr. Brisbane, CA 94005. Phone: 800-234-0804 or (415)468-4684 Fax: (415)468-4686 E-mail: forwardslash@business2.com • URL: http://www.business2.com • Monthly. $12.00 per year. General business magazine emphasizing ideas and innovation.

Business Week. McGraw-Hill, 1221 Ave. of the Americas New York, NY 10020-1095. Phone: 800-722-4726 or (212)904-2000 Fax: (212)904-2072 E-mail: customer.service@mcgraw-hill.com • URL: http://www.mcgraw-hill.com • Weekly. $54.95 per year. Last volume is a double issue.

Business Week China. Ministry of Foreign Economic Relations and Trade, Institute of International Tra. McGraw-Hill, 1221 Ave. of the Americas New York, NY 10020-1095. Phone: 800-722-4726 or (212)904-2000 Fax: (212)904-2072 E-mail: customer.service@mcgraw-hill.com • URL: http://www.mcgraw-hill.com • Bimonthly. Price on application. Edited for business and government officials in the People's Republic of China. Selected Chinese translation of *Business Week*.

Business Week International: The World's Only International Newsweekly of Business. McGraw-Hill, 1221 Ave. of the Americas New York, NY 10020-1095. Phone: 800-722-4726 or (212)904-2000 Fax: (212)904-2072 E-mail: customer.service@mcgraw-hill.com • URL: http://www.mcgraw-hill.com • Weekly. $105.00 per year.

Business Week Online. McGraw-HillPhone: (212)512-2762 Fax: (212)512-6590 URL: http://www.businessweek.com • Web site provides complete contents of current issue of *Business Week* plus ''BW Daily'' with additonal business news, financial market quotes, and corporate information from Standard & Poor's. Includes various features, such as ''Banking Center'' with mortgage and interest data, and ''Interactive Computer Buying Guide.'' The ''Business Week Archive'' is fully searchable back to 1991. Fees: Mostly free, but full-text archive articles are $2.00 each.

Business Week's Guide to Mutual Funds. Jeffrey M. Laderman. McGraw-Hill, 1221 Ave. of the Americas New York, NY 10020-1095. Phone: 800-722-4726 or (212)904-2000 Fax: (212)904-2072 E-mail: customer.service@mcgraw-hill.com • URL: http://www.mcgraw-hill.com • 2000. $14.95. 10th edition. Includes basic information, ratings, and performance data.

Business Week's Guide to the Best Business Schools. John A. Byrne. McGraw-Hill, 1221 Ave. of the Americas New York, NY 10020-1095. Phone: 800-722-4726 or (212)904-2000 Fax: (212)904-2072 E-mail: customer.service@mcgraw-hill.com • URL: http://www.mcgraw-hill.com • 1997. $16.95. Fifth edition. Includes the best regional business schools.

Business Writing at Its Best. Minerva H. Neiditz. McGraw-Hill Professional, 1221 Ave. of the Americas New York, NY 10020. Phone: 800-722-4726 or (212)904-2000 Fax: (212)904-2072 E-mail: customer.service@mcgraw-hill.com • URL: http://www.mcgraw-hill.com • 1993. $22.50.

Business Writing the Modular Way: How to Research, Organize and Compose Effective Memo Letters, Articles, Reports, Proposals, Manuals, Specifications and Books. Harley Bjelland. Books on Demand, 300 N. Zeeb Rd. Ann Arbor, MI 48106-1346. Phone: 800-521-0600 or (734)761-4700 Fax: (734)665-5022 E-mail: info@umi.com • URL: http://www.lib.umi.com • 1992. $80.70. Covers research and organization for various kinds of business writing, from simple to complex.

Business Writing with Style: Strategies for Success. John Tarrant. John Wiley and Sons, Inc., 605 Third Ave. New York, NY 10158-0012. Phone: 800-225-5945 or (212)850-6000 Fax: (212)850-6088 E-mail: info@jwiley.com • URL: http://www.wiley.com • 1991. $10.95. Second edition. Emphasizes the use of business writing styles that are creative or unusual.

Butane-Propane News. Butane-Propane News, Inc., P.O. Box 660698 Arcadia, CA 91006-0698. Phone: (818)357-2168 Fax: (818)303-2854 Monthly. $26.00 per year.

Buyers' Guide for the Health Care Market: A Directory of Products and Services for Health Care Institutions. American Hospital Association. Health Forum, Inc., One N. Franklin St., 27th Fl. Chicago, IL 60606-3421. Phone: (312)422-2626 Fax: (312)422-4600 URL: http://www.healthforum.com • Annual. $17.95. Lists 1,200 suppliers and manufacturers of health care products and services for hospitals, nursing homes, and related organizations.

Buyers Guide to Outdoor Advertising. Competitive Media Reporting, 11 W. 42nd St., 11th Fl. New York, NY 10036. Phone: (212)789-1400 Fax: (212)789-1450 Semiannual. $425.00 per year. Lists more than 800 outdoor advertising companies and their market rates, etc.

Buyer's Guide to the New York Market. Earnshaw Publications, Inc., 225 W. 34th St., Suite 1212 New York, NY 10001. Phone: (212)563-2742 Fax: (212)629-3249 Annual. Included with *Earnshaw's Magazine*.

Buying and Maintaining Personal Computers: A How-To-Do-It Manual for Librarians. Norman Howden. Neal-Schuman Publishers, Inc., 100 Varick St. New York, NY 10013. Phone: (212)925-8650 Fax: 800-584-2414 or (212)219-8916 E-mail: info@neal-schuman.com • URL: http://www.neal-schuman.com • 2000. $45.00. Covers various aspects of buying PCs or MACs for library use, including choice of hardware, software selection, warranties, backup systems, staffing, and dealing with vendors.

Buying and Selling a Business. Ralph Warner, editor. Nolo.com, 950 Parker St. Berkeley, CA 94710. Phone: 800-992-6656 or (510)549-1976 Fax: (510)548-5902 E-mail: cs@nolo.com • URL: http://www.nolo.com • 1998. Price on application.

Buying and Selling a Small Business: A Complete Guide to a Successful Deal. Ernest J. Honigmann. CCH, Inc., 2700 Lake Cook Rd. Riverwoods, IL 60015. Phone: 800-248-3248 or (360)676-4530 URL: http://www.cch.com • 1999. $91.95.

Buying Books: A How-To-Do-It Manual for Librarians. Audrey Eaglen. Neal-Schuman Publishers, Inc., 100 Varick St. New York, NY 10013. Phone: (212)925-8650 Fax: 800-584-2414 or (212)219-8916 E-mail: info@neal-schuman.com • URL: http://www.neal-schuman.com • 2000. $45.00. Second edition. Discusses vendor selection and book ordering in the age of electronic commerce. Covers both print and electronic bibliographic sources. (How-to-Do-It Manual for Librarians Series).

Buying Serials: A How-To-Do-It Manual for Librarians. N. Bernard Basch and Judy McQueen. Neal-Schuman Publishers, Inc., 100 Varick St. New York, NY 10013. Phone: (212)925-8650 Fax: 800-584-2414 or (212)219-8916 E-mail: info@neal-schuman.com • URL: http://www.neal-schuman.com • 1990. $49.95. (How-to-Do-It Series).

Buying Treasury Securities: Bills, Notes, Bonds, Offerings Schedule, Conversions. Federal Reserve Bank of Philadelphia, P.O. Box 66 Philadelphia, PA 19105-0066. Phone: (215)574-6000 Fax: (212)574-4364 URL: http://www.libertynet.org/fedreserv/whats/welcome.html • Revised as required. Free pamphlet. Provides clear definitions, information, and instructions relating to U. S. Treasury securities: short-term (bills), medium-term (notes), and long-term (bonds).

Buyout Financing Sources/M & A Intermediaries. Securities Data Publishing, 40 West 57th St. New York, NY 10019. Phone: 800-455-5844 or (212)765-5311 Fax: (212)956-0112 E-mail: sdp@tfn.com • URL: http://www.sdponline.com • Annual. $895.00. Provides the CD-ROM combination of *Directory of Buyout Financing Sources* and *Directory of M & A Intermediaries*. Contains information on more than 1,000 financing sources (banks, insurance companies, venture capital firms, etc.) and 850 intermediaries (corporate acquirers, valuation firms, lawyers, accountants, etc.). Also includes back issues of *Buyouts Newsletter* and *Mergers & Acquisitions Report*. Fully searchable. (Securities Data Publishing is a unit of Thomson Financial.)

Buyouts: The Newsletter for Management Buyouts, Leveraged Aquisitions, and Special Situations. Securities Data Publishing, 40 West 57th St. New York, NY 10019. Phone: 800-455-5844 or (212)765-5311 Fax: (212)956-0112 E-mail: sdp@tfn.com • URL: http://www.sdponline.com • Biweekly. $1,265.00 per year. Newsletter. Covers news and trends for the buyout industry. Provides information on deal makers and current buyout activity. (Securities Data Publishing is a unit of Thomson Financial.)

By the Numbers: Electronic and Online Publishing. The Gale Group, 27500 Drake Rd. Farmington Hills, MI 48331-3535. Phone: 800-877-GALE or (248)699-GALE Fax: 800-414-5043 or (248)699-8069 E-mail: galeord@galegroup.com • URL: http://www.galegroup.com • 1997. $385.00. Four volumes. $99.00 per volume. Covers ''high-interest'' industries: 1. *By the Numbers: Electronic and Online Publishing*; 2. *By the Numbers: Emerging Industries*; 3. *By the Numbers: Nonprofits*; 4. *By the Numbers: Publishing*. Each volume provides about 600 tabulations of industry data on revenues, market share, employment, trends, financial ratios, profits, salaries, and so forth. Citations to data sources are included.

Byline., c/o Marcia Preston, P.O. Box 130596 Edmond, OK 73013-0001. Phone: (405)348-5591 E-mail: bylinemp@

aol.com • URL: http://www.bylinemp@aol.com • 11 times a year. $22.00 per year.

C E D: The Premier Magazine of Broadband Communications. Cahners Business Information, P.O. Box 266008 Highlands Ranch, CO 80163-6008. Phone: 800-662-7776 or (303)470-4800 Fax: (303)393-6654 E-mail: corporatecommunications@cahners.com • URL: http://www.cahners.com • Monthly. $75.00 per year. Formerly *Communications Engineering and Design*.

CA Search. Chemical Abstracts Service, 2540 Olentangy River Rd. Columbus, OH 43210. Phone: 800-753-4227 or (614)447-3731 Fax: (614)447-3751 Guide to chemical literature, 1967 to present. Inquire as to online cost and availability.

CA Selects: Fiber Optics and Optical Communication. Chemical Abstracts Service, P.O. Box 3012 Columbus, OH 43210-0012. Phone: 800-753-4227 or (614)447-3600 Fax: (614)447-3751 URL: http://www.acs.org • Semiweekly. $275.00 per year.

CA Selects: Selenium and Tellurium Chemistry. American Chemical Society. Chemical Abstracts Service, P.O. Box 3012 Columbus, OH 43210-0012. Phone: 800-753-4227 or (614)447-3600 Fax: (614)447-3713 URL: http://www.acs/org • Semiweekly. Members, $75.00 per year; non-members, $250.00 per year. Incorporates *Selenium and Tellurium Abstracts*.

CAB Abstracts. CAB International North America, 10 E. 40th St. New York, NY 10016. Phone: 800-528-4842 or (212)481-7018 Fax: (212)686-7993 E-mail: cabi-nao@cabi.org • URL: http://www.cabi.org • Contains 46 specialized abstract collections covering over 10,000 journals and monographs in the areas of agriculture, horticulture, forest products, farm products, nutrition, dairy science, poultry, grains, animal health, entomology, etc. Time period is 1972 to date, with monthly updates. Inquire as to online cost and availability. *CAB Abstracts on CD-ROM* also available, with annual updating.

Cabell's Directory of Publishing Opportunities in Economics, and Finance. Cabell Publishing Co., Tobe Hahn Station, P.O. Box 5428 Beaumont, TX 77726-5428. Phone: (409)898-0575 Fax: (409)866-9554 E-mail: publish@cabells.com • 1997. $89.95. Provides editorial policies of commercial and scholarly periodicals in the areas of business and economics. Formerly *Cabell's Directory of Publishing Opportunities in Accounting, Economics, and Finance*.

Cabell's Directory of Publishing Opportunities in Education. Cabell Publishing Co., Tobe Hahn Station, P.O. Box 5428 Beaumont, TX 77726-5428. Phone: (409)898-0575 Fax: (409)866-9554 E-mail: publish@cabells.com • 1998. $89.95. Over 430 journals in education which will consider manuscripts forpublication.

Cabell's Directory of Publishing Opportunities in Management. Cabell Publishing Co., Tobe Hahn Station, P.O. Box 5428 Beaumont, TX 77726-5428. Phone: (409)898-0575 Fax: (409)866-9554 E-mail: publisher@cabells.com • 1997. $89.95. Provides editorial policies of more than 300 management periodicals. Emphasis is on publishing opportunities for college faculty members. Formerly *Cabell's Directory of Publishing Opportunities Business and Economics*.

Cable and Station Coverage Atlas. Warren Publishing Inc., 2115 Ward Court, N.W. Washington, DC 20037-1209. Phone: 800-771-9202 or (202)872-9200 Fax: (202)293-3435 E-mail: customer service@warren-news.com • URL: http://www.warren-news.com • Annual. $474.00.

Cable Communications-Products Directory and Buyers' Guide. Udo Salewsky, editor. Ter-Sat Media Publications, Ltd., 57 Peachwood Court Kitchener, ON, Canada N2B 1S7. Phone: (519)744-4411 Fax: (519)744-1261 Annual. $20.00. Lists about 300 manufacturers and distributors of cable television-specific equipment and services; primarily covers United States and Canada.

Cable Television and Other Nonbroadcast Media: Law and Policy. Daniel J. Brenner and others. West Group, 610 Opperman Dr. Eagan, MN 55123. Phone: 800-328-4880 or (651)687-7000 Fax: (651)687-5827 URL: http://www.westgroup.com • $145.00 per year. Looseleaf service. Periodic supplementation. (Entertainment and Communications Law Series).

Cable Television Revenues. U.S. Federal Communications Commission, Washington, DC 20554. Phone: 888-225-5322 or (202)418-0500 URL: http://www.fcc.gov • Annual.

Cable TV Facts. Cabletelevision Advertising Bureau, 830 Third Ave., Frnt. 2 New York, NY 10022-7522. Phone: (212)508-1200 Fax: (212)832-3268 Annual. Free to members; non-members, $10.00. Provides statistics on cable TV and cable TV advertising in the U. S.

Cable TV Financial Databook: Sourcebook for All Key Financial Data on Cable TV. Paul Kagan Associates, Inc., 126 Clock Tower Place Carmel, CA 93923. Phone: (831)624-1536 Fax: (831)625-3225 E-mail: info@kagan.com • Annual. $495.00. Includes analysis of operating results of private and public cable television companies, historical data and projections.

Cable TV Investor: Newsletter on Investments in Cable TV Systems and Publicly Held Cable TV Stocks. Paul Kagan Associates, Inc., 126 Clock Tower Place Carmel, CA 93923. Phone: (831)624-1536 Fax: (831)625-3225 E-mail: info@kagan.com • Monthly. $895.00 per year.

Cable TV Programming: Newsletter on Programs for Pay Cable TV and Analysis of Basic Cable Networks. Paul Kagan Associates, Inc., 126 Clock Tower Place Carmel, CA 93923. Phone: (831)624-1536 Fax: (831)625-3225 E-mail: info@kagan.com • Monthly. $745.00 per year.

Cable TV Technology: Newsletter on Technical Advances, Construction of New Systems and Rebuild of Existing Systems. Paul Kagan Associates, Inc., 126 Clock Tower Place Carmel, CA 93923. Phone: (831)624-1536 Fax: (831)625-3225 E-mail: info@kagan.com • Monthly. $695.00 per year. Newsletter. Contains news of cable TV technical advances.

Cabletelevision Advertising Bureau.

Cablevision: The Analysis and Features Bi-Weekly of the Cable Television Industry. Cahners Business Information, Broadcasting and Cable's International Group, 245 W. 17th St. New York, NY 10011-5300. Phone: 800-662-7776 or (212)645-0067 Fax: (212)463-6703 E-mail: corporatecommunications@cahners.com • URL: http://www.cahners.com • Semimonthly. $65.00 per year.

Cabot Market Letter. Cabot Heritage Corp., P.O. Box 3044 Salem, MA 01970-6344. Phone: 800-777-2658 or (508)745-5532 Fax: (508)745-1283 Semimonthly. $250.00 per year. Newsletter. Recommends various model portfolios.

Cabot's Mutual Fund Navigator: Your Guide to Investing for Profits and Safety in the Best Mutual Funds. Cabot Heritage Corp., P.O. Box 3044 Salem, MA 01970-6344. Phone: 800-777-2658 or (508)745-5532 Fax: (508)745-1283 Monthly. $125.00 per year. Newsletter. Recommends various mutual fund portfolios.

CAD/CAM,CAE: Survey, Review and Buyers' Guide. Daratech, Inc., 225 Bent St. Cambridge, MA 02141-2081. Phone: (617)354-2339 Fax: (617)354-7822 E-mail: daratech@daratech.com • $972.00 per year. Looseleaf service. Includes computer-aided engineering (CAE). (Daratech Series in CAD-CAM, CAE).

Caine Dairy Center. Utah State University

California Agricultural Experiment Station. University of California at Berkeley

California Farmer: The Business Magazine for Commercial Agriculture. Farm Progress Cos., 191 S. Gary Ave. Carol Stream, IL 60188. Phone: (630)690-5600 Fax: (630)462-2869 15 times a year. $21.95 per year. Three editions: Northern, Southern and Central Valley.

California Management Review. University of California at Berkeley, S549 Haas School of Business, Suite 1900 Berkeley, CA 94720-1900. Phone: 800-777-4726 or (510)642-7159 Fax: (510)642-1318 E-mail: cmr@haas.berkeley.edu • URL: http://www.haas.berkeley.edu • Quarterly. Individuals, $50.00 per year; institutions, $65.00 per year; students, $24.00 per year.

Call Center CMR Solutions: The Authority on Teleservices, Sales, and Support Since 1982. Technology Marketing Corp., One Technology Plaza Norwalk, CT 06854. Phone: 800-243-6002 or (203)852-6800 Fax: (203)853-2845 E-mail: tmc@tmcnet.com • URL: http://www.ccsmag.com • Monthly. $49.00 per year. Emphasis is on telemarketing, selling, and customer service. Formerly *Call Center Solutions*.

Call Center Magazine. Miller Freeman, 12 W. 21st St. New York, NY 10012. Phone: (212)691-8215 Fax: (212)691-1191 URL: http://www.telecomlibrary.com • Monthly. $14.00 per year. Covers telephone and online customer service, help desk, and marketing operations. Includes articles on communications technology.

Call Center Solutions Buyer's Guide and Directory. Technology Marketing Corp., One Technology Plaza Norwalk, CT 06854. Phone: 800-243-6002 or (203)852-6800 Fax: (203)853-2845 E-mail: tmc@tmcnet.com • URL: http://www.tmcnet.com • Annual. $25.00. Over 1,100 domestic and foreign suppliers of equipment, products, and services to the telecommunications/telemarketing industry. Formerly *Telemarketing: Buyer's Guide and Directory*.

Callahan's Credit Union Directory. Callahan & Associates, Inc., 1001 Connecticut Ave., N.W., Suite 1001 Washington, DC 20036. Phone: 800-446-7453 or (202)223-3920 Fax: (202)223-1311 E-mail: callahan@callahan.com • URL: http://www.callahan.com • Annual. $135.00. Covers 11,843 state, federal, and United States credit unions; regulators, organizations, and leagues.Includes financial data.

Callmann Unfair Competition, Trademarks & Monopolies: 1981-1989. Rudolf Callmann and Louis Altman. West Group, 610 Opperman Dr. Eagan, MN 55123. Phone: 800-328-4880 or (651)687-7000 Fax: 800-213-2323 or (651)687-5827 URL: http://www.westgroup.com • Nine looseleaf volumes. $1,195.00. Periodic supplementation. Covers various aspects of anti-competitive behavior.

Calories and Carbohydrates. Barbara Kraus. NAL, 375 Hudson St. New York, NY 10014-3657. Phone: 800-331-4624 or (212)366-2000 Fax: (212)366-2666 E-mail: online@penguinputnam.com • URL: http://www.penguinputnam.com • 1999. $6.99. Revised edition.

Camp Directors Purchasing Guide. Klevens Publications, Inc., 7600 Ave.V Littlerock, CA 93543. Phone: (805)944-4111 Fax: (805)944-1800 E-mail: klevenspub@aol.com • URL: http://www.garmentindex.com • Annual. $60.00. Suppliers of products and services used in the operation of children's summer camps.

Campbell's List: A Directory of Selected Lawyers and Includes Court Reporters and Process Servers. Campbell's List, Inc., P.O. Box 428 Maitland, FL 32751. Phone: 800-249-6934 or (407)644-8298 Fax: (407)740-6494 Annual. $10.00. September supplement. About 1,000 selected out-of-town lawyers in the United States, Canada, and foreign countries who are willing to handle correspondent work for other lawyers and businesses.

Campground Management: Business Publication for Profitable Outdoor Recreation. Woodall Publishing Co., 13975 W. Polo Trail Dr. Lake Forest, IL 60045. Phone: 800-323-9076 or (847)362-6700 Fax: (847)362-8776 URL: http://www.woodall's.com • Monthly. $24.95 per year.

Campground Merchandising. Kane Communcations, Inc., 7000 Terminal Square, No. 210 Upper Darby, PA 19082-2310. Phone: (215)925-9744 or (215)734-2420 Quarterly. $5.00 per year.

Camping Magazine. American Camping Association, 5000 State Rd., 67 N. Martinsville, IN 46151-7902. Phone: 800-428-2267 or (317)342-8456 Fax: (317)342-2065 E-mail: scameron@aca.-camps.org • URL: http://www.acacamps.org • Monthly. $34.55 per year.

Camping Magazine Buyer's Guide. American Camping Association, 5000 State Rd., 67 N. Martinsville, IN 46151-7902. Phone: 800-428-2267 or (765)342-8456 Fax: (765)342-2065 E-mail: acaacademy-camps.org • URL: http://www.aca.-camps.org • Annual. $4.50. Over 200 firms listing camp supplies.

Can Ethics Be Taught? Perspectives, Challenges, and Approaches at the Harvard Business School. Thomas R. Piper and others. Harvard Business School Press, 60 Harvard Way Boston, MA 02163. Phone: 888-500-1016 or (617)783-7440 E-mail: custserv@hbsp.harvard.edu • URL: http://www.hbsp.harvard.edu • 1993. $24.95.

Can Manufacturers Institute.

Can You Recommend a Good Book on Indexing? Bella H. Weinberg. Information Today, Inc., 143 Old Marlton Pike Medford, NJ 08055-8750. Phone: 800-300-9868 or (609)654-6266 Fax: (609)654-4309 E-mail: custserv@infotoday.com • URL: http://www.infotoday.com • 1998. $39.50. Contains reviews of books on indexing, classified of general works, theory, book indexing, databases, thesauri, and computer-assisted (automatic) indexing. (CyberAge Books.)

Canada Company Handbook: The Globe and Mail Report on Business. Globe Information Services, 444 Front St., W. Toronto, ON, Canada M5V 259. Phone: 800-268-9128 or (416)585-5163 Fax: (416)585-5249 URL: http://www.globeandmail.ca • Annual. $49.95. Provides information on 400 Canadian companies. Detailed fianncial data and rankings are presented for firms listed on the Toronto Stock Exchange.

Canada NewsWire. Canada NewsWire Ltd., 10 Bay St., Suite 914 Toronto, ON, Canada M5J 2R8. Phone: (416)863-9350 Fax: (416)863-4825 Provides the complete online text of currrent press releases from more than 5,000 Canadian companies, institutions, and government agencies, including stock exchanges and the Ontario Securities Commission. Emphasis is on mining, petroleum, technology, and pharmaceuticals. Time span is 1996 to date, with daily updates. Inquire as to online cost and availability.

Canada-U. S. Trade. Carswell, 2075 Kennedy Rd. Scarborough, ON, Canada M1T 3V4. Phone: 800-387-5164 or (416)609-8000 Fax: (416)298-5094 Monthly. $185.00 per year. Newsletter on all current aspects of trade between the U. S. and Canada.

Canada-United States Business Association., 600 Renaissance Center, Suite 1100 Detroit, MI 48243. Phone: (313)567-2208 Fax: (313)567-2164 Promotes business and trade between the U. S. and Canada.

Canada Year Book. Statistics Canada, Operations and Integration Div., Circulation Management, Jean Talon Bldg., 2 C-12, Tunney's Pasture Ottawa, ON, Canada K1A OT6. Phone: 800-267-6677 or (613)951-7277 Fax: 800-899-9734 or (613)951-1582 URL: http://www.statcan.ca • Annual. $66.00. Contains "sixteen chapters on the social, economic, demographic and cultural life of Canada," with more than 300 tables, charts and graphs.

Canada Year Book on CD-ROM. Statistics Canada, Publications Division, Ottawa, ON, Canada K1A OT6. Phone: 800-267-6677 or (613)951-7277 Fax: 800-899-9734 or (613)951-1582 URL: http://www.statcan.ca • Annual. $90.00. CD-ROM in English and French provides basic statistical and other information on Canada. Contains multimedia features and search capabilities.

Canadian Almanac and Directory. Available from The Gale Group, 27500 Drake Rd. Farmington Hills, MI 48331-3535. Phone: 800-877-GALE or (248)699-GALE Fax:

800-414-5043 or (248)699-8069 E-mail: galeord@galegroup.com • URL: http://www.galegroup.com • Annual. $259.00. Published by Micromedia. Contains general information and statistical data relating to Canadian and provides information on about 60,000 Canadian agencies, associations, institutions, museums, libraries, etc.

Canadian-American Business Council., 1629 K St., N. W., Suite 1100 Washington, DC 20006. Phone: (202)785-6717 Fax: (202)331-4212 E-mail: canambusco@aol.com • Promotes trade between Canada and the United States.

Canadian-American Center., University of Maine - Canada House, 154 College Ave. Orono, ME 04473. Phone: (207)581-4220 Fax: (207)581-4223 E-mail: hornsby@maine.edu • URL: http://www.ume.maine.edu/canam • Research areas include Canadian-American business, economics, and trade.

Canadian American Trade Site: Promoting Trade Between Canada and the Southeastern United States. Small Business Development Center of South CarolinaPhone: 800-243-7232 or (803)777-4909 Fax: (803)777-4403 E-mail: canamtr@darla.badm.sc.edu • URL: http://canamtrade.badm.sc.edu • Web site provides information about trade between the U. S. and Canada. Includes links to other trade-related Web sites. Fees: Free.

Canadian Business. Canadian Business Media, 777 Bay St., 5th Fl. Toronto, ON, Canada M5W 1A7. Phone: (416)596-5100 Fax: (416)596-5152 E-mail: letters@cbmedia.ca • 21 times a year. $34.70 per year. Edited for corporate managers and executives, this is a major periodical in Canada covering a variety of business, economic, and financial topics. Emphasis is on the top 500 Canadian corporations.

Canadian Business and Current Affairs Fulltext. Micromedia Ltd., 20 Victoria St. Toronto, ON, Canada M5C 2N8. Phone: 800-387-2689 or (416)362-5211 Fax: (416)362-2689 E-mail: info@mmltd.com • URL: http://www.mmltd.com • Provides full-text of eight Canadian daily newspapers and more than 100 Canadian business magazines and trade journals. Indexing is 1982 to date, with selected full text from 1993. Updates are twice a month. Inquire as to online cost and availability.

Canadian Co-Operative Wool Growers Magazine. Canadian Cooperative Wool Growers, Ltd., P.O. Box 130 Carleton Place, ON, Canada K7C 3P3. Fax: (613)257-8896 Annual. Free to members; non-members, $3.00.

Canadian Directory of Shopping Centres. Maclean Hunter Business Publications, 777 Bay St. Toronto, ON, Canada M5W 1A7. Phone: (416)596-5000 Fax: (416)596-5553 URL: http://www.mhbizlink.com • Annual. $400.00. Two volumes (Eastern Canada and Western Canada). Describes about 1,700 shopping centers and malls, including those under development.

Canadian Dun's Enhanced Market Identifiers. Dun & Bradstreet Canada, 5770 Hurontario St. Mississauga, ON, Canada L5R 3G5. Phone: 800-234-3867 or (905)568-6000 Fax: (905)568-6279 URL: http://www.dnb.com • Contains descriptive and sales information for more than 900,000 Canadian companies and branch offices. Quarterly updates. Inquire as to online cost and availability.

The Canadian Employer. Carswell, 2075 Kennedy Rd. Scarborough, ON, Canada M1T 3V4. Phone: 800-387-5164 or (416)609-8000 Fax: (416)298-5094 Monthly. $185.00 per year. Newsletter. Provides current information on Canadian employment and labor laws.

Canadian Energy Research Institute., 3512 33rd St., N. W., Suite 150 Calgary, AB, Canada T2L 2A6. Phone: (403)282-1231 Fax: (403)284-4181 E-mail: ceri@ceri.ca • URL: http://www.ceri.ca • Conducts research on the economic aspects of various forms of energy, including petroleum, natural gas, coal, nuclear, and water power (hydroelectric).

Canadian Index. Micromedia Ltd., 20 Victoria St. Toronto, ON, Canada M5C 2N8. Phone: 800-387-2689 or (416)362-5211 Fax: (416)362-6161 E-mail: info@micromedia.on.ca • URL: http://www.mmltd.com • Monthly, with annual cumulation. Price varies. Indexes approximately 500 Canadian periodicals of all kinds, including business magazines and trade journals. Ten daily Canadian newspapers are also indexed.

Canadian Industrial Equipment News: Reader Service On New, Improved and Redesigned Industrial Equipment and Supplies. Southam Magazine Group, 1450 Don Mills Rd. Don Mills, ON, Canada M3B 2X7. Phone: 800-387-0273 or (416)445-6641 Fax: (416)442-2214 Monthly. $62.95 per year. Supplement available. Formerly *Electrical Equipment News*.

Canadian Key Business Directory. Available from Dun & Bradstreet Information Services, Three Sylvan Way Parsippany, NJ 07054. Phone: 800-526-0651 or (973)455-0900 Fax: (973)605-6920 URL: http://www.dnb.com • Annual. $450.00. Published by Dun & Bradstreet Canada Ltd. Provides information in English and French on 20,000 leading Canadian business firms.

Canadian Market Outlook. DRI Canck, PO Box 193 Tornto, ON, Canada M5X 1A6. Phone: (416)360-8885 Fax: (416)360-0088 Quarterly. Price on application. Presents detailed forecasts of Canadian business and economic data.

Canadian Mines Handbook. Southam Magazine Group, 1450 Don Mills Rd. Don Mills, ON, Canada M3B 2X7. Phone: 800-387-0273 or (416)510-6772 Fax: (416)442-2272 E-mail: kcollins@southam.ca • Annual. $65.00. About 2,000 mining companies in Canada; also includes smelters, refineries, trade associations, related government agencies and similar organizations.

Canadian News Facts: The Indexed Digest of Canadian Current Events. MPL Communication, Inc., 133 Richmond St., W., Suite 700 Toronto, ON, Canada M5H 3M8. Phone: (416)869-1177 Fax: (416)869-0456 Bimonthly. $200.00 per year. Monthly and quarterly indexes. A summary of current events in Canada.

Canadian Periodical Index. The Gale Group, 27500 Drake Rd. Farmington Hills, MI 48331-3535. Phone: 800-877-GALE or (248)699-GALE Fax: 800-414-5043 or (248)699-8069 E-mail: galeord@galegroup.com • URL: http://www.galegroup.com • Monthly. $515.00 per year. Annual cumulation. Indexes more than 400 English and French language periodicals.

Canadian Resources and PennyMines Analyst: The Canadian Newsletter for Penny-Mines Investors Who Insist on Geological Value. MPL Communication, Inc., 133 Richmond St., W., Suite 700 Toronto, ON, Canada M5H 3M8. Phone: (416)869-1177 Fax: (416)869-0456 Weekly. $157.00 per year. Newsletter. Mainly on Canadian gold mine stocks. Formerly *Canadian PennyMines Analyst*.

Canadian Studies Program., University of Vermont, 589 Main St. Burlington, VT 05401. Phone: (802)656-3062 Fax: (802)656-8518 E-mail: canada@zoo.uvm.edu • URL: http://www.uvm.edu/~canada • Research areas include Canadian corporate strategies, telecommunications, and natural resources.

The Canadian Taxpayer. Carswell, 2075 Kennedy Rd. Scarborough, ON, Canada M1T 3V4. Phone: 800-387-5164 or (416)609-8000 Fax: (416)298-5094 Semimonthly. $330.00 per year. Newsletter. Covers tax trends and policies in Canada.

Canadian Trade Index. Alliance of Manufacturers Exporters and Importers Canada, 75 International Blvd., Suite 400 Toronto, ON, Canada M9W 6L9. Phone: (416)798-8000 Fax: (416)798-8050 Annual. $190.00. Provides information on about 15,000 manufacturers in Canada, including key personnel. Indexed by trade name, product, and location.

Canadian Who's Who. University of Toronto Press, Reverence Div., 10 Saint Mary St., Suite 700 Toronto, ON, Canada M4Y 2W8. Phone: 800-565-9523 or (416)978-2239 Fax: (416)978-4738 E-mail: utpbooks@utpress.utoronto.ca • URL: http://www.utpress.utoronto.ca • Annual. $165.00. Provides concise biographical information in English and French on 15,000 prominent Canadians.

CanCorp Plus Canadian Financial Database. Micromedia Ltd., 20 Victoria St. Toronto, ON, Canada M5C 2N8. Phone: 800-387-2689 or (416)362-5211 Fax: (416)362-2689 E-mail: info@mmltd.com • URL: http://www.mmltd.com • Monthly. $3,600.00 per year. Also available quarterly at $2,975.00 per year. Provides comprehensive information on CD-ROM for more than 11,000 public and private Canadian corporations. Emphasis is on detailed financial data for up to seven years.

CanCorp Plus Canadian Financial Database. Micromedia Ltd., 20 Victoria St. Toronto, ON, Canada M5C 2N8. Phone: 800-387-2689 or (416)362-5211 Fax: (416)362-2689 E-mail: info@mmltd.com • URL: http://www.mmltd.com • Provides detailed information, including descriptive, marketing, personnel, and financial data, for more than 11,000 public and private Canadian corporations. Weekly updates. Inquire as to online cost and availability.

Candy Buyers' Directory. Manufacturing Confectioner Publishing Co., 175 Rock Rd. Glen Rock, NJ 07452. Phone: (201)652-2655 Fax: (201)652-3419 E-mail: themc@gomc.com • Annual. $65.00. Lists confectionary and snack manufacturers by category and brand name. Includes *Directory of Candy Brokers*.

The Candy Dish. National Candy Brokers Association, 710 East Ogden Ave., Suite 600 Naperville, IL 60563-8603. Phone: (630)369-2406 Fax: (630)369-2488 E-mail: ncba@b-online.com • URL: http://www.candynet.com • Quarterly. Apply. Provides industry news and event information for candy brokers and distributors.

Candy Industry Buying Guide. Stagnito Publishing Co., 1935 Shermer Rd., Ste. 100 Northbrook, IL 60062. Phone: (847)205-5660 Fax: (847)205-5680 E-mail: info@stagnito.com • URL: http:/.www.stagnito.com • Annual. $25.00. List of approximately 600 suppliers of ingredients, equipment, services, and supplies to the candy industry.

Candy Industry: The Global Magazine of Chocolate and Confectionary. Stagnito Publishing Co., 1935 Shermer Rd., Ste. 100 Northbrook, IL 60062. Phone: (847)205-5660 Fax: (847)205-5680 E-mail: info@stagnito.com • URL: http://www.stagnito.com • Monthly $39.00 per year

The Candy Market. Available from MarketResearch.com, 641 Ave. of the Americas, Third Floor New York, NY 10011. Phone: 800-298-5699 or (212)807-2629 Fax: (212)807-2716 E-mail: order@markerresearch.com • URL: http://www.marketresearch.com • 1998. $2,500.00. Published by Packaged Facts. Provides market data on chocolate and non-chocolate candy, with sales projections to 2002.

Cane Sugar Handbook: A Manual for Cane Sugar Manufacturers and Their Chemists. James C. Chen and Chung-Chi Chou. John Wiley and Sons, Inc., 605 Third Ave. New York, NY 10158-0012. Phone: 800-225-5945 or (212)850-6000 Fax: (212)850-6088 E-mail: info@wiley.com • URL: http://www.wiley.com • 1993. $350.30. 2nd edition.

CANOE: Canadian Online Explorer. Canoe Limited PartnershipPhone: (416)947-2027 Fax: (416)947-2209 URL: http://www.canoe.ca • Web site provides a wide variety of Canadian news and information, including business and financial data. Includes "Money," "Your Investment," "Technology," and "Stock Quotes." Allows keyword searching, with links to many other sites. Daily updating. Fees: Free.

CANSIM Time Series Database. Statistics Canada, Statistical Reference Center, R. H. Coats Bldg., Holland Ave. Ottawa, ON, Canada K1A OT6. Phone: 800-263-1136 or (613)951-8116 Fax: (613)951-0581 E-mail: infostats@statcan.ca • URL: http://www.statcan.ca • CANSIM is the Canadian Socio-Economic Information Management System. Contains more than 700,000 statistical time series relating to Canadian business, industry, trade, economics, finance, labor, health, welfare, and demographics. Time period is mainly 1946 to date, with daily updating. Inquire as to online cost and availability.

Cantech International. Trend Publishing, 625 N. Michigan Ave., Suite 2500 Chicago, IL 60611. Phone: (312)654-2300 Fax: (312)654-2323 Bimonthly. $70.00 per year. Covers metal can manufacturing, tooling, and decorating.

Capacity of Refrigerated Warehouses. U.S. Department of Agriculture, Washington, DC 20250. Phone: (202)720-2791 Annual.

Capital Changes Reports. CCH, Inc., 4025 W. Peterson Ave. Chicago, IL 60646-6085. Phone: 800-248-3248 or (773)583-8500 Fax: 800-224-8299 or (773)866-3608 URL: http://www.cch.com • Weekly. $1,310.00. Six looseleaf volumes. Arranged alphabetically by company. This service presents a chronological capital history that includes reorganizations, mergers and consolidations. Recent actions are found in Volume One - "New Matters."

Capital Comment. American Land Title Association, 1828 L St., N.W. Washington, DC 20036. Phone: 800-787-2582 or (202)296-3671 Fax: (202)223-5843 E-mail: service@alta.org • URL: http://www.alta.org • Monthly. Price application.

Capital for Shipping. Available from Informa Publishing Group Ltd., PO Box 1017 Westborough, MA 01581-6017. Phone: 800-493-4080 Fax: (508)231-0856 E-mail: enquiries@informa.com • URL: http://www.informa.com • Annual. $128.00. Published in the UK by Lloyd's List (http://www.lloydslist.com). Consists of a "Financial Directory" and a "Legal Directory," listing international ship finance providers and international law firms specializing in shipping. (Included with subscription to *Lloyd's Shipping Economist*.)

Car and Driver. Hachette Filipacchi Magazines, Inc., 2002 Hogback Rd. Ann Arbor, MI 48105. Phone: 800-274-4027 or (734)971-3600 Fax: (734)971-9188 E-mail: feedback@caranddriver.com • URL: http://www.caranddriver.com • Monthly. $21.94 per year.

Car Dealer Insider. United Communications Group, 11300 Rockville Pike, Suite 1100 Rockville, MD 20852-3030. Phone: (301)816-8950 Fax: (301)287-2049 URL: http://www.ucg.com • Weekly. $275.00. per year. Newsletter covering management trends and industry news.

Car Dealer Insider: Profit Making Secrets for the Competitive Dealer. United Communications Group (UCG), 11300 Rockville Pike, Suite 1100 Rockville, MD 20852-3030. Phone: 800-287-2223 or (301)287-2700 Fax: (301)816-8945 E-mail: webmaster@ucg.com • URL: http://www.ucg.com • Weekly. $295.00 per year. Newsletter. Provides automotive industry news, with ideas and advice for car dealers on advertising, marketing, and management. Formerly *Car and Truck Dealer Insider Newsletter*.

Car Ownership Forecasting. E.W. Allanson, editor. Gordon and Breach Publishing Group, Two Gateway Center Newark, NJ 07102-0301. Phone: 800-545-8398 or (973)643-7500 Fax: (973)643-7676 E-mail: book.orders@aidcvt.com • URL: http://www.gbhap.com • 1982. $173.00. Volume one.

Car Rental Insider. United Communications Group (UCG), 11300 Rockville Pike, Suite 1100 Rockville, MD 20852-3030. Phone: 800-287-2223 or (301)287-2700 Fax: (301)816-8945 E-mail: webmaster@ucg.com • URL: http://www.ucg.com • Biweekly. $235.00 per year. Newsletter. Contains news of the automobile leasing and renting industry, including information on legislation, insurance, consumer trends, and rental management.

Car Wash Owners and Suppliers Association.

Card Industry Directory. Faulkner & Gray, Inc., 11 Penn Plaza, 17th Fl. New York, NY 10001. Phone: 800-535-8403 or (212)967-7000 Fax: (212)967-7155 E-mail: orders@

faulknergray.com • URL: http://www.faulknergray.com • Annual. $425.00.

Card Marketing. Faulkner & Gray, Inc., 300 S. Wacker Dr., 18th Fl. Chicago, IL 60606. Phone: 800-535-8403 Fax: (312)913-1959 E-mail: orders@faulknergray.com • URL: http://www.cardmarketing.faulknergray.com • Monthly. $73.95. Edited for payment card marketing executives: credit cards, debit cards, phone cards, ''loyalty'' cards, and smart cards.

Card Marketing Buyer's Guide. Faulkner & Gray, Inc., 300 S. Wacker Dr., 18th Fl. Chicago, IL 60606. Phone: 800-535-8403 or (312)913-1334 Fax: (312)913-1959 E-mail: orders@faulknergray.com • URL: http://www.cardmarketing.faulknergray.com • Annual. Price on application. Lists companies concerned with the marketing of credit cards and other forms of payment cards.

Card News: The Executive Report on the Transaction Card Marketplace. Phillips Business Information, Inc., 1201 Seven Locks Rd., Suite 300 Potomac, MD 20854. Phone: 800-777-5006 or (301)340-1520 Fax: (301)309-3487 E-mail: pbi@phillips.com • URL: http://www.phillips.com/marketplaces.com • Biweekly. $695.00 per year. Newsletter on transaction cards, debit and credit cards, automatic teller machines, etc.

Card Technology. Faulkner & Gray, Inc., 300 S. Wacker Drive, 18th Floor Chicago, IL 60606. Phone: (312)913-1334 Fax: (312)913-1369 URL: http://www.faulknergray.com • Monthly. $79.00 per year. Covers advanced technology for credit, debit, and other cards. Topics include smart cards, optical recognition, and card design.

CARD The Media Information Network (Canadian Advertising Rates and Data). Available from SRDS, 1700 Higgins Rd. Des Plaines, IL 60018. Phone: 800-851-7737 or (847)375-5000 Fax: (847)375-5001 URL: http://www.srds.com • Biennial. $225.00 per issue. Published by Maclean Hunter Publishing Ltd. (Toronto). Provides advertising rates and other information relating to Canadian media: daily newspapers, weekly community newspapers, consumer magazines, business publications, school publications, religious publications, radio, and television.

Career College Association.

The Career Development Quarterly. National Career Development Association. ACPA, One Dupont Circle, N.W., Suite 300 Washington, DC 20036. Phone: 800-347-6647 Quarterly. Individuals, $45.00 per year; institutions, $67.00 per year.

Career Guide to Industries. Available from U. S. Government Printing Office, Washington, DC 20402. Phone: (202)512-1800 Fax: (202)512-2250 E-mail: gpoaccess@gpo.gov • URL: http://www.access.gpo.gov • 1998. $17.00. Issued by the Bureau of Labor Statistics, U. S. Department of Labor (http://www.bls.gov). Presents background career information (text) and statistics for the 40 industries that account for 70 percent of wage and salary jobs in the U. S. Includes nature of the industry, employment data, working conditions, training, earnings, rate of job growth, outlook, and other career factors. (BLS Bulletin 2503.)

Career Legal Secretary. National Association of Legal Secretaries. West Publishing Co., College and School Div., 610 Opperman Dr. Eagan, MN 55123. Phone: 800-328-4880 or (651)687-7000 Fax: 800-213-2323 or (651)687-5827 E-mail: legal_ed@westgroup.com • URL: http://www.lawschool.westgroup.com • 1997. $35.50. Fourth edition.

Career World. Weekly Reader Corp., 200 First Stamford Place Stamford, CT 06912-0023. Phone: 800-446-3355 Fax: (609)786-3360 URL: http://www.weeklyreader.com • Six times a year. $9.25. per year. Up-to-the-minute, important career and vocational news for students in grades 7 thru 12.

CARF, The Rehabilitation Accreditation Commission.

Cargo Airline Association.

Cargo Facts., 1501 Fourth Ave., No.1620 Seattle, WA 98101-1662. Phone: (206)587-6537 Fax: (206)587-6540 Monthly. $345.00 per year. Newsletter. Provides analysis of developments in the air freight and express industry.

Caribbean Business. Casiano Communications, 1700 Fernandez Juncos Ave., Stop 25 San Juan 00909-2999, Puerto Rico. Phone: (787)728-3000 Fax: (787)768-7325 Weekly. $45.00 per year. Text in English.

Caring. National Association for Home Care, 228 Seventh St., S. E. Washington, DC 20003-4306. Phone: (202)547-7424 Fax: (202)547-3540 E-mail: webmaster@nahc.org • URL: http://www.nahc.org • Monthly. $45.00 per year. Provides articles on the business of home health care

Caring for Frail Elderly People: New Directions in Care. OECD Publications and Information Center, 2001 L St., N.W., Ste. 650 Washington, DC 20036-4922. Phone: 800-456-6323 or (202)785-6323 Fax: (202)785-0350 E-mail: wasington.contact@oecd.org • URL: http://www.oecdwash.org • 1994. $27.00. Discusses the problem in OECD countries of providing good quality care to the elderly at manageable cost. Includes trends in family care, housing policies, and private financing.

Carnegie Mellon Research Institute., Carnegie Mellon University, 700 Technology Dr. Pittsburgh, PA 15219. Phone: (412)268-3190 Fax: (412)268-3101 E-mail: twillke@emu.edu • Multidisciplinary research activities include expert systems applications, minicomputer and microcomputer systems design, genetic engineering, and transportation systems analysis.

The Carpenter. United Brotherhood of Carpenters and Joiners of America, 101 Constitution Ave., N.W. Washington, DC 20001. Phone: (202)546-6206 Fax: (202)547-8979 Bimonthly. Free to members; non-members, $10.00 per year.

Carpenters and Builders Library. John E. Ball. Pearson Education and Technology, 201 W. 103rd St. Indianapolis, IN 46290-1097. Phone: 800-858-7674 or (317)581-3500 Fax: 800-822-8583 or (317)581-4670 1991. Four volumes. $21.95 per volume. Sixth edition.

Carpentry and Building Construction. John Feirer and Gilbert Hutchings. Glencoe/McGraw-Hill, 8787 Orion Place Columbus, OH 43240-4027. Phone: 800-848-1567 or (614)430-4000 Fax: (614)860-1877 E-mail: customer.service@mcgraw-hill.com • URL: http://www.glencoe.com • 1999. $53.25. Fifth edition.

Carpet and Floorcoverings Review. Miller Freeman PLC, Sovereign Way Tonbridge, Kent TN9 1RW, England. Phone: 44 173 2364422 Fax: 44 173 2361534 Biweekly. $140.00 per year.

Carpet and Rug Industry. Rodman Publications, 17 S. Franklin Parkway Ramsey, NJ 07446. Phone: (201)825-2552 Fax: (201)825-0553 Monthly. $42.00 per year. Edited for manufacturers and distributors of carpets and rugs.

Carpet and Rug Institute.

Carpet Cleaning Service. Entrepreneur Media, Inc., 2445 McCabe Way Irvine, CA 92614. Phone: 800-421-2300 or (949)261-2325 Fax: (949)261-0234 E-mail: entmag@entrepreneur.com • URL: http://www.entrepreneur.com • Looseleaf. $59.50. A practical guide to starting a carpet cleaning business. Covers profit potential, start-up costs, market size evaluation, owner's time required, pricing, accounting, advertising, promotion, etc. (Start-Up Business Guide No. E1053.)

Carpet Cushion Council.

Carpets and Rugs. Available from MarketResearch.com, 641 Ave. of the Americas, Third Floor New York, NY 10011. Phone: 800-298-5699 or (212)807-2629 Fax: (212)807-2716 E-mail: order@marketresearch.com • URL: http://www.marketresearch.com • 1999. $3,300.00. Market research data. Published by the Freedonia Group. Provides both historical data and forecasts to 2007 for various kinds of carpeting.

Carroll's County Directory. Carroll Publishing, 4701 Sangamore Rd., Suite S-155 Bethesda, MD 20816. Phone: 800-336-4240 or (301)263-9800 Fax: (301)263-9801 E-mail: custsvc@carrollpub.com • URL: http://www.carrollpub.com • Semiannual. $255.00 per year. Lists about 42,000 officials in 3,100 U. S. counties, with expanded listings for counties having a population of over 50,000. Includes state maps.

Carroll's Defense Industry Charts. Carroll Publishing, 4701 Sangamore Rd., Suite S-155 Bethesda, MD 20816. Phone: 800-336-4240 or (301)263-9800 Fax: (301)263-9801 E-mail: custsvc@carrollpub.com • URL: http://www.carrollpub.com • Quarterly. $1,150.00 per year. Provides 180 large, fold-out paper charts showing personnel relationships at more than 100 major U. S. defense contractors. Charts are also available online and on CD-ROM.

Carroll's Defense Organization Charts. Carroll Publishing, 4701 Sangamore Rd., Suite S-155 Bethesda, MD 20816. Phone: 800-336-4240 or (301)263-9800 Fax: (301)263-9801 E-mail: custsvc@carrollpub.com • URL: http://www.carrollpub.com • Quarterly. $1,470.00 per year. Provides more than 200 large, fold-out paper charts showing personnel relationships in 2,400 U. S. military offices. Charts are also available online and on CD-ROM.

Carroll's Federal & Federal Regional Directory: CD-ROM Edition. Carroll Publishing, 4701 Sangamore Rd., Suite S-155 Bethesda, MD 20816. Phone: 800-336-4240 or (301)263-9800 Fax: (301)263-9801 E-mail: custsvc@carrollpub.com • URL: http://www.carrollpub.com • Bimonthly. $800.00 per year. Provides CD-ROM listings of more than 120,000 (55,000 high-level and 65,000 mid-level) U. S. government officials in Washington and throughout the country, including in military installations. Also available online.

Carroll's Federal Assistance Directory. Carroll Publishing-Phone: 800-336-4240 or (301)263-9800 Fax: (301)263-9801 E-mail: custsvc@carrollpub.com • URL: http://www.carrollpub.com/cfad/ • Free Web site provides detailed information on more than 1,500 federal programs ''disbursing financial and technical support to individuals and organizations.'' Simple or advanced searching is offered by popular name, federal agency, or keyword.

Carroll's Federal Directory. Carroll Publishing, 4701 Sangamore Rd., Suite S-155 Bethesda, MD 20816. Phone: 800-336-4240 or (301)263-9800 Fax: (301)263-9801 E-mail: custsvc@carrollpub.com • URL: http://www.carrollpub.com • Bimonthly. $325.00 per year. Lists 40,000 key U. S. officials, including members of Congress, Cabinet members, federal judges, Executive Office of the President personnel, and a wide variety of administrators.

Carroll's Federal Organization Charts. Carroll Publishing, 4701 Sangamore Rd., Suite S-155 Bethesda, MD 20816. Phone: 800-336-4240 or (301)263-9800 Fax: (301)263-9801 E-mail: custsvc@carrollpub.com • URL: http://www.carrollpub.com • Quarterly. $950.00 per year. Provides 200 large, fold-out paper charts showing personnel relationships in 2,100 federal departments and agencies. Charts are also available online and on CD-ROM.

Carroll's Federal Regional Directory. Carroll Publishing, 4701 Sangamore Rd., Suite S-155 Bethesda, MD 20816. Phone: 800-336-4240 or (301)263-9800 Fax: (301)263-9801 E-mail: custsvc@carrollpub.com • URL: http://www.carrollpub.com • Semiannual. $255.00 per year. Lists more than 28,000 non-Washington based federal executives in administrative agencies, the courts, and military bases. Arranged in four sections: Alphabetical (last names), Organizational, Geographical, and Keyword. Includes maps.

Carroll's Municipal/County Directory: CD-ROM Edition. Carroll Publishing, 4701 Sangamore Rd., Suite S-155 Bethesda, MD 20816. Phone: 800-336-4240 or (301)263-9800 Fax: (301)263-9801 E-mail: custsvc@carrollpub.com • URL: http://www.carrollpub.com • Semiannual. $750.00 per year. Provides CD-ROM listings of about 99,000 city, town, and county officials in the U. S. Also available online.

Carroll's Municipal Directory. Carroll Publishing, 4701 Sangamore Rd., Suite S-155 Bethesda, MD 20816. Phone: 800-336-4240 or (301)263-9800 Fax: (301)263-9801 E-mail: custsvc@carrollpub.com • URL: http://www.carrollpub.com • Semiannual. $255.00 per year. Lists about 50,000 officials in 7,900 U. S. towns and cities, with expanded listings for cities having a population of over 25,000. Top 100 cities are ranked by population and size.

Carroll's State Directory. Carroll Publishing, 4701 Sangamore Rd., Suite S-155 Bethesda, MD 20816. Phone: 800-336-4240 or (301)263-9800 Fax: (301)263-9801 E-mail: custsvc@carrollpub.com • URL: http://www.carrollpub.com • Three times a year. $300.00 per year. Lists about 42,000 individuals in executive, administrative, and legislative positions in 50 states, the District of Columbia, Puerto Rico, and the American Territories. Includes keyword and other indexing.

Carroll's State Directory: CD-ROM Edition. Carroll Publishing, 4701 Sangamore Rd., Suite S-155 Bethesda, MD 20816. Phone: 800-336-4240 or (301)263-9800 Fax: (301)263-9801 E-mail: custsvc@carrollpub.com • URL: http://www.carrollpub.com • Three times a year. $600.00 per year. Provides CD-ROM listings of about 42,000 state officials, plus the text of all state constitutions and biographies of all governors. Also available online.

Cars of Revenue Freight Loaded. Association of American Railroads, American Railroads Bldg., 50 F St., N.W. Washington, DC 20001. Phone: (202)639-2100 Fax: (202)639-2156 URL: http://www.aar.org • Weekly.

Cartography and Geographic Information Science. American Congress on Surveying and Mapping, 5410 Grosvenor Lane, Suite 100 Bethesda, MD 20814. Phone: (301)493-0200 Fax: (301)493-8245 E-mail: infoacsm@mindspring.com • URL: http://www.survmap.org • Quarterly. Free to members; non-members, $90.00 per year.

Case Studies in Business Ethics. Thomas Donaldson and Al Gini, editors. Prentice-Hall, 240 Frisch Court Paramus, NJ 07652-5240. Phone: 800-947-7700 or (201)909-6200 Fax: 800-445-6991 or (201)909-6361 URL: http://www.prenhall.com • 1995. $36.20. Fourth edition.

Case Studies in Business, Society, and Ethics. Thomas L. Beauchamp, editor. Prentice Hall, 240 Frisch Court Paramus, NJ 07652-5240. Phone: 800-947-7700 or (201)909-6200 Fax: 800-445-6991 or (201)909-6361 URL: http://www.prenhall.com • 1997. $31.80. Fourth edition.

Case Studies in Finance: Managing for Corporate Value Creation. Robert Bruner. McGraw-Hill Professional, 1221 Ave. of the Americas New York, NY 10020. Phone: 800-722-4726 or (212)904-2000 Fax: (212)904-2072 E-mail: customer.service@mcgraw-hill.com • URL: http://www.mcgraw-hill.com • 1998. Third edition. Price on application.

Case Studies in Financial Decision Making. Diana R. Harrington and Kenneth M. Eades. Dryden Press, 301 Commerce St., Suite 3700 Fort Worth, TX 32887-1437. Phone: 800-447-9479 or (817)334-7500 Fax: (817)334-7844 URL: http://www.little@harbrace.com • 1993. $63.50. Third edition.

A Casebook of Grant Proposals in the Humanities. William Coleman and others, editors. Neal-Schuman Publishers, Inc., 100 Varick St. New York, NY 10013. Phone: (212)925-8650 Fax: 800-584-2414 or (212)219-8916 E-mail: info@neal-schuman.com • URL: http://www.neal-schuman.com • 1982. $45.00.

Cases and Materials on Corporations-Including Partnerships and Limited Partnerships. Robert W. Hamilton. West Publishing Co., College and School Div., 610 Opperman Dr. Eagan, MN 55123. Phone: 800-328-2209 or (651)687-7000 Fax: 800-213-2323 or (651)687-5827 E-mail: legal_ed@westgroup.com • URL: http://

www.lawschool.westgroup.com • 1998. $68.50. Sixth edition. American Case book Series

Cases in Advertising Communication Management. Stephen A. Greyser. Prentice Hall, 240 Frisch Court Paramus, NJ 07652-5240. Phone: 800-947-7700 or (201)909-6200 Fax: 800-445-6991 or (201)909-6361 URL: http://www.prenhall.com • 1991. $30.00. Third edition.

Cases in Agribusiness Management. George J. Seperich and others. Holcomb Hathaway, Inc., 6207 N. Cattle Track Rd., Suite 1 Scottsdale, AZ 85250. Phone: (602)991-7881 Fax: (602)991-4770 1995. $27.95. Second edition.

Cases in Corporate Acquisitions, Buyouts, Mergers, and Takeovers. The Gale Group, 27500 Drake Rd. Farmington Hills, MI 48331-3535. Phone: 800-877-GALE or (248)699-GALE Fax: 800-414-5043 or (248)699-8069 E-mail: galeord@galegroup.com • URL: http://www.galegroup.com • 1999. $310.00. Reviews and analyzes about 300 cases of both success and failure in corporate acquisitiveness.

Cases in Corporate Innovation. The Gale Group, 27500 Drake Rd. Farmington Hills, MI 48331-3535. Phone: 800-877-GALE or (248)699-GALE Fax: 800-414-5043 or (248)699-8069 E-mail: galeord@galegroup.com • URL: http://www.galegroup.com • 1999. $295.00. Reviews and analyzes about 300 cases to illustrate both successful and failed management of innovation.

Cases in Financial Mangement: Directed Versions. Eugene Brigham and Louis Gapenski. Dryden Press, 301 Commerce St., Suite 3700 Fort Worth, TX 76102-4137. Phone: 800-447-9479 or (817)334-7500 Fax: (817)334-7844 URL: http://www.little@harbrace.com • 1993. $32.00.

Cases in Financial Statement Reporting and Analysis. Leopold A. Bernstein and Mostafa M. Maksy. McGraw-Hill Higher Education, 1221 Ave. of the Americas New York, NY 10020. Phone: 800-722-4726 or (212)904-2000 Fax: (212)904-2072 E-mail: customer.service@mcgraw-hill.com • URL: http://www.mcgraw-hill.com • 1985. $36.95. Second edition.

Cases in International Finance. Gunter Duffey. Addison-Wesley Longman, Inc., One Jacob Way Reading, MA 01867. Phone: 800-447-2226 or (781)944-3700 Fax: (781)944-9351 E-mail: info@wiley.com • URL: http://www.wiley.com • 2001. Price on application.

Cases in Marketing Management. Kenneth L. Bernhardt and Thomas C. Kinnear. McGraw-Hill Higher Education, 1221 Ave. of the Americas New York, NY 10020. Phone: 800-722-4726 or (212)904-2000 Fax: (212)904-2072 E-mail: customer.service@mcgraw-hill.com • URL: http://www.mcgraw-hill.com • 1997. Ninth edition. Price on application.

Cases in Portfolio Management. John A. Quelch. McGraw-Hill Higher Education, 1221 Ave. of the Americas New York, NY 10020. Phone: 800-722-4726 or (212)904-2000 Fax: (212)904-2072 E-mail: customer.service@mcgraw-hill.com • URL: http://www.mcgraw-hill.com • 1994. $52.99.

Cases in Strategic Management. Thomas J. Wheelen and J. David Hunger. Addison-Wesley Longman, Inc., One Jacob Way Reading, MA 01867. Phone: 800-447-2226 or (781)944-3700 Fax: (781)944-9351 URL: http://www.awl.com • 1999. $59.00. Seventh edition.

Cases in Strategic Management. A.J. Strickland. McGraw-Hill, 1221 Ave. of the Americas New York, NY 10020-1095. Phone: 800-722-4726 or (212)904-2000 Fax: (212)904-2072 E-mail: customer.service@mcgraw-hill.com • URL: http://www.mcgraw-hill.com • 2000. $41.25. 12th edition.

Cases in Strategic Marketing: An Integrated Approach. William J. McDonald. Pearson Education and Technology, 201 W. 103rd St. Indianapolis, IN 46290-1097. Phone: 800-858-7674 or (317)581-3500 Fax: (317)581-4670 URL: http://www.mcp.com • 1997. $53.00. Second edition.

Cases in the Management of Information Systems and Information Technology. Richard Lorette and Howard Walton. McGraw-Hill Higher Education, 1221 Ave. of the Americas New York, NY 10020-1095. Phone: 800-722-4726 or (212)904-2000 Fax: (212)904-2072 E-mail: customer.service@mcgraw-hill.com • URL: http://www.mcgraw-hill.com • 1994. $40.95.

Cases in Total Quality Management. Jay H. Heizer. Course Technology, Inc., One Main St. Cambridge, MA 02142. Phone: 800-648-7450 or (617)225-2595 Fax: (617)621-3078 E-mail: laura-hildebrand@course.com • URL: http://www.course.com • 1997. $45.95. (GC Principles in Management Series.)

Cash Box: The International Music-Record Weekly. Cash Box Publishing Co., Inc., 51 E. Eighth St., Suite 155 New York, NY 10003-6494. Phone: (212)586-2640 Weekly. $185.00 per year.

Casino and Gaming Market Research Handbook. Available from MarketResearch.com, 641 Ave. of the Americas, Third Floor New York, NY 10011. Phone: 800-298-5699 or (212)807-2629 Fax: (212)807-2642 E-mail: order@marketresearch.com • URL: http://www.marketresearch.com • 2001. $375.00. Fifth edition. Published by Richard K. Miller & Associates. Includes analysis and statistical data on casinos, lotteries, table games, electronic gaming machines, bingo, and online gambling.

Casino Chronicle. Casino Chronicle, Inc. Ben Borowsky, PO Box 740465 Boynton Beach, FL 33474-0465. Phone: (561)732-6117 48 times a year. $175.00 per year. Newsletter focusing on the Atlantic City gambling industry.

Cassell, Publishers Association and the Federation of European Publishers Association Directory of Publishing in Continental Europe. Cassell, PCS Data Processing, Inc., 360 W. 31st St. New York, NY 10001. Biennial. $150.00. Published in London. Provides detailed profiles of United Kingdom and British Commonwealth publishers and agencies. Includes ''publishers' turnover figures.''

CASSIS (Patents). U. S. Patent and Trademark Office, Office of Electronic Information Products, Crystal Park 3, Suite 441 Washington, DC 20231. Phone: (703)306-2600 Fax: (703)306-2737 E-mail: oeip@uspto.gov • URL: http://www.uspto.gov • A series of CD-ROM products, including *Patents ASSIGN* (assignment deeds, quarterly), *Patents ASSIST* (search tools, quarterly), *Patents BIB* (abstracts and search information, bimonthly), *Patents CLASS* (classifications, 1790 to date, bimonthly), *Patents SNAP* (serial number concordance, annual).

CASSIS (Trademarks). U. S. Patent and Trademark Office, Office of Electronic Information Products, Crystal Park 3, Suite 441 Washington, DC 20231. Phone: (703)306-2600 Fax: (703)306-2737 E-mail: oeip@uspto.gov • URL: http://www.uspto.gov • CD-ROM products include *Trademarks ASSIGN* (assignment deeds, bimonthly), *Trademarks ASSIST* (search tools, single- disc), *Trademarks PENDING* (applications on file, bimonthly), *Trademarks REGISTERED* (active trademarks, 1884 to date).

Cast Metals Laboratory.

Casting Digest. ASM International, 9639 Kinsman Rd. Materials Park, OH 44073-0002. Phone: 800-336-5152 or (440)338-5151 Fax: (440)338-4634 E-mail: memserv@po.asm-intl.org • URL: http://www.asm-intl.org • Bimonthly. $165.00 per year. Provides abstracts of the international literature of metal casting, forming, and molding.

Casting Industry Suppliers Association.

Casualty Actuarial Society.

Casualty Actuarial Society Yearbook. Casualty Actuarial Society, 1100 N. Glebe Rd., No. 600 Arlington, VA 22201-4714. Phone: (703)276-3100 Fax: (703)276-3108 E-mail: office@cassct.org • URL: http://www.cassact.org • Annual. $40.00. Approximately 2,500 actuaries working in insurance other than life insurance.

Casualty Insurance Claims: Coverage-Investigation-Law. Pat Magarick. West Group, 610 Opperman Dr. Eagan, MN 55123. Phone: 800-328-4880 or (651)687-7000 Fax: 800-213-2323 or (651)687-5827 URL: http://www.westgroup.com • Two looseleaf volumes. $215.00. Annual supplementation.

Catalog Age. Cowles Business Media, Inc., PO Box 4225 Stamford, CT 06907-0225. Phone: 800-795-5445 or (203)358-9900 Fax: (203)358-5811 E-mail: subs@intertec.com • URL: http://www.catalogagemag.com • Monthly. $72.00 per year. Edited for catalog marketing and management personnel.

Catalog Age/Direct Sourcebook. Intertec Publishing Co., 11 Riverbend Dr., S. Stamford, CT 06907-2524. Phone: 800-795-5445 or (203)358-9900 Fax: (203)358-5831 E-mail: subs@intertec.com • URL: http://www.intertec.com • Annual. $35.00. Lists of approximately 300 suppliers of products and services for direct marketing, especially catalog marketing.

The Catalog Marketer. Maxwell Sroge Publishing, Inc., 522 Forest Ave. Evanston, IL 60202-3005. Phone: (847)866-1890 Fax: (847)866-1899 Biweekly. $199.00 per year. Newsletter. ''How-to'' for catalog producers.

Catalog of American National Standards. American National Standards Institute, 11 W. 42nd St., 13th Fl. New York, NY 10036. Phone: (212)642-4900 Fax: (212)398-1286 URL: http://www.ansi.org • Annual. Price on application.

Catalog of Asphalt Institute Publications. Asphalt Institute, Research Park Dr., P.O. Box 14052 Lexington, KY 40512-4052. Phone: (606)288-4960 Fax: (608)288-4699 URL: http://www.asphaltinstitute.org • Annual. Free.

Catalog of Catalogs: The Complete Mail-Order Directory. Edward L. Palder. Woodbine House, 6510 Bells Mill Rd. Bethesda, MD 20817. Phone: 800-843-7323 or (301)897-3570 Fax: (301)897-5838 E-mail: info@woodbinehouse.com • Biennial. $25.95. Provides information on more than 14,000 U. S. and Canadian companies that issue catalogs and sell through the mail. Arrangement is by product, with an index to company names.

Catalog of Copyright Entries. U.S. Library of Congress, Copyright Office. Available from U.S. Government Printing Office, Washington, DC 20402. Phone: (202)512-1800 Fax: (202)512-2250 Frequency and prices vary.

Catalog of Federal Domestic Assistance. U.S. Office of Management and Budget. Available from U.S. Government Printing Office, Washington, DC 20402. Phone: (202)512-1800 Fax: (202)512-2250 Annual. $87.00. Looseleaf service. Includes up-dating service for indeterminate period. Summary of financial and nonfinanacial Federal programs, projects, services and activities that provide assistance or benefits to the American public.

Catalogue of Statistical Materials of Developing Countries. Institute of Developing Economies/Ajia Keizai Kenkyusho., 42 Ichigaya-Hommura-cho, Shinjuku-ku Tokyo 162-8442 8, Japan. Phone: 81 3 3353 4231 Fax: 81 3 3226 8475 E-mail: info@ide.go.jp • URL: http://www.ide.go.jp • Semiannual. Price varies. Text in English and Japanese.

Catalyst., 120 Wall St., 5th Fl. New York, NY 10005-3904. Phone: (212)514-7600 Fax: (212)514-8470 E-mail: info@catalystwomen.org • URL: http://www.catalystwomen.org • Provides information, research, and publications relating to women's workplace issues. Promotes corporate leadership for women.

Catalyst Institute., 33 N. LaSalle St., Suite 1900 Chicago, IL 60602-2604. Phone: (312)541-5400 Fax: (312)541-5401 E-mail: postmaster@catalystinstitute.org • URL: http://www.dstcatalyst.com • Investigates the financial services industry, including bank failures and the domino effect, the liability crisis, and regulations designed to prevent bank failures.

Catering Handbook. Hal Weiss and Edith Weiss. John Wiley and Sons, Inc., 605 Third Ave. New York, NY 10158-0012. Phone: 800-842-3636 or (212)850-6000 Fax: (212)850-6088 E-mail: info@wiley.com • URL: http://www.wiley.com • 1990. $42.95.

Catering Industry Employee. Hotel Employees and Restaurant Employees International Union, AFLO-CIO, 1219 28th St., N.W. Washington, DC 20007-3316. Phone: (202)393-4373 Fax: (202)965-2958 URL: http://www.hereunion.org • Bimonthly. $5.00.

Catering Magazine: The Magazine for Off-Premise Caterers. MiniCo., Inc., 2531 W. Dunlap Ave. Phoenix, AZ 85021. Phone: 800-528-1056 or (602)870-1711 Fax: (602)861-1094 E-mail: catering@minico.com • URL: http://www.minico.com • Bimonthly. Price on application. Covers the marketing and management aspects of the catering business.

Catering Service. Entrepreneur Media, Inc., 2445 McCabe Way Irvine, CA 92614. Phone: 800-421-2300 or (949)261-2325 Fax: (949)261-0234 E-mail: entmag@entrepreneur.com • URL: http://www.entrepreneur.com • Looseleaf. $59.50. A practical guide to starting a food and beverage catering business. Covers profit potential, start-up costs, market size evaluation, owner's time required, site selection, pricing, accounting, advertising, promotion, etc. (Start-Up Business Guide No. E1215.)

Catholic Library Association.

Cattle Fever Tick Research Laboratory.

Cattleman. Texas and Southwestern Cattle Raisers Association, Inc., 1301 W. Seventh Ave. Fort Worth, TX 76102. Phone: (817)332-7155 Monthly. $40.00 per year.

Cavalcade of Acts and Attractions. BPI Communications, Amusement Business Div., P.O. Box 24970 Nashville, TN 37202. Phone: 800-407-6874 or (615)321-4250 Fax: (615)327-1575 URL: http://www.amusementbusiness.com • Annual. $92.00. Directory of personal appearance artists, touring shows and other specialized entertainment. Lists promoters, producers, managers and booking agents.

CBA-Christian Booksellers Association.

CC News: The Business Newspaper for Call Center and Customer Care Professionals. United Publications, Inc., P.O. Box 997 Yarmouth, ME 04096. Phone: 800-441-6982 or (207)846-0600 Fax: (207)846-0657 URL: http://www.ccnews.com • Eight times a year. Price on application. Includes news of call center technical developments.

CCH Analysis of Top Tax Issues: Return Preparation and Planning Guide. CCH, Inc., 4025 West Peterson Ave. Chicago, IL 60646-6085. Phone: 800-248-3248 or (773)866-6000 Fax: 800-224-8299 or (773)866-3608 E-mail: cust_serv@cch.com • URL: http://www.cch.com • Annual. $45.00. Covers yearly tax changes affecting business and personal transactions, planning, and returns.

CCH Essentials: An Internet Tax Research and Primary Source Library. CCH, Inc.Phone: 800-248-3248 or (773)866-6000 Fax: 800-224-8299 or (773)866-3608 E-mail: cust_serv@cch.com • URL: http://tax.cch.com/essentials • Fee-based Web site provides full-text coverage of federal tax law and regulations, including rulings, procedures, tax court decisions, and IRS publications, announcements, notices, and penalties. Includes explanation, analysis, tax planning guides, and a daily tax news service. Searching is offered, including citation search. Fee: $495.00 per year.

CCH Financial and Estate Planning. CCH, Inc., 4025 W. Peterson Ave. Chicago, IL 60646-6085. Phone: 800-248-3248 or (773)583-8500 Fax: 800-224-8299 or (773)866-3608 URL: http://www.cch.com • Semimonthly. $845.00 per year. Four looseleaf volumes.

CCH Financial and Estate Planning Guide Îsummary volumel. CCH, Inc., 4025 W. Peterson Ave. Chicago, IL 60646-6085. Phone: 800-248-3248 or (773)866-6000 Fax: 800-224-8299 or (773)866-3608 URL: http://www.cch.com • Annual. $57.95. Contains four main parts: General Principles and Techniques, Special Situations, Building the Estate, and Planning Aids.

CCH Guide to Business Valuation. CCH, Inc., 4025 W. Peterson Ave. Chicago, IL 60646-6085. Phone: 800-248-3248 or (773)866-6000 Fax: 800-224-8299 or (773)866-3608 URL: http://www.cch.com • Looseleaf. $295.00 per year, including quarterly newsletter. Covers latest developments and trends in the evaluation of businesses.

CCH Guide to Car, Travel, Entertainment, and Home Office Deductions. CCH, Inc., 4025 West Peterson Ave. Chicago, IL 60646-6085. Phone: 800-248-3248 or (773)866-6000 Fax: 800-224-8299 or (773)866-3608 URL: http://www.cch.com • Annual. $42.00. Explains how to claim maximum tax deductions for common business expenses. Includes automobile depreciation tables, lease value tables, worksheets, and examples of filled-in tax forms.

CCH Guide to Record Retention Requirements. CCH, Inc., 4025 West Peterson Ave. Chicago, IL 60646-6085. Phone: 800-248-3248 or (773)866-6000 Fax: 800-224-8299 or (773)866-3608 URL: http://www.cch.com • 1999. $49.95. Covers the record-keeping provisions of the Code of Federal Regulations. Explains which records must be kept and how long to keep them.

CCIA Newsletter. Consumer Credit Insurance Association, 542 S. Dearborn St., Suite 400 Chicago, IL 60605. Phone: (312)939-2242 Fax: (312)929-8287 Monthly. Membership.

The CCRC Industry: 1996 Profile. American Association of Homes and Services for the Aging, 901 E St., N. W., Suite 500 Washington, DC 20004-2011. Phone: 800-508-9442 or (202)783-2242 Fax: (202)783-2255 E-mail: info@aahsa.org • URL: http://www.aahsa.org • 1996. $15.00. Includes tables and charts. Provides data on demographics, fees, contracts, finances, and other aspects of continuing care retirement communities.

CD-ROM Finder. Information Today, Inc., 143 Old Marlton Pike Medford, NJ 08055-8750. Phone: 800-300-9868 or (609)654-6266 Fax: (609)654-4309 E-mail: custserv@infotoday.com • URL: http://www.infotoday.com • Irregular. $69.50. Describes over 2,300 CD-ROM titles. Formerly *Optical Electronic Publishing Directory*.

CD-ROM Handbook. Chris Sherman. McGraw-Hill, 1221 Ave. of the Americas New York, NY 10020-1095. Phone: 800-722-4726 or (212)904-2000 Fax: (212)904-2072 E-mail: customer.service@mcgraw-hill.com • URL: http://www.mcgraw-hill.com • 1993. $70.50. Second edition. Covers technology (audio, video, and multimedia), design, production, and economics of the CD-ROM industry.

CD-ROM Information Products: The Evaluative Guide. Ashgate Publishing Co., Old Post Rd. Brookfield, VT 05036-9704. Phone: 800-535-9544 or (802)276-3162 Fax: (802)276-3837 E-mail: info@ashgate.com • URL: http://www.ashgate.com • Quarterly. $110.00 per year. Provides detailed evaluations of new CD-ROM information products.

CD-ROM Primer: The ABCs of CD-ROM. Cheryl LaGuardia. Neal-Schuman Publishers, Inc., 100 Varick St. New York, NY 10013. Phone: (212)925-8650 Fax: 800-584-2414 or (212)219-8916 E-mail: info@neal-schuman.com • URL: http://www.neal-schuman.com • 1994. $49.95. Provides advice for librarians and others on CD-ROM equipment, selection, collecting, and maintenance. Includes a glossary, bibliography, and directory of suppliers.

CD-ROM World: The Magazine and Review for CD-ROM Users. PC World Communications, Inc., 501 Second St., Ste. 600 San Francisco, CA 94107. Phone: 800-234-3498 or (415)234-3498 Fax: (415)442-1891 E-mail: letters@pcworld.com • URL: http://www.pcworld.com • 10 times a year. $29.00 per year.

CD-ROMS in Print. The Gale Group, 27500 Drake Rd. Farmington Hills, MI 48331-3535. Phone: 800-877-GALE or (248)699-GALE Fax: 800-414-5043 or (248)699-8069 E-mail: galeord@galegroup.com • URL: http://www.galegroup.com • Annual. $175.00. Describes more than 13,000 currrently available reference and multimedia CD-ROM titles and provides contact information for about 4,000 CD-ROM publishing and distribution companies. Includes several indexes.

CDC Vessel Sanitation Program (VSP): Charting a Healthier Course. U. S. Centers for Disease Control and Prevention-Phone: (770)488-7333 Fax: 888-232-6789 E-mail: vsp@cdc.gov • URL: http://www.cdc.gov/nceh/vsp/vsp.htm • Web site provides details of unannounced sanitation inspections of individual cruise ships arriving at U. S. ports. Includes detailed results of the most recent inspection of each ship and results of inspections taking place in years past. There are lists of "Ships Inspected Past 2 Months" and "Ships with Not Satisfactory Scores" (passing grade is 85). CDC standards cover drinking water, food, and general cleanliness. Online searching is possible by ship name, inspection date, and numerical scores. Fees: Free.

CDLA, The Computer Leasing and Remarketing Association.

CDMARC: Bibliographic. U. S. Library of Congress, Cataloging Distribution Service Washington, DC 20541-4912. Phone: (202)707-6100 Fax: (202)707-1334 URL: http://www.loc.gov/cds • Quarterly. $1,340.00 per year. Provides bibliographic records on CD-ROM for over five million books cataloged by the Library of Congress since 1968. (MARC is Machine Readable Cataloging.)

CEC Chemical Equipment Catalog: Equipment for the Process Industries. Cahners Business Information, 301 Gibraltar Dr. Morris Plains, NJ 07950-0650. Phone: 800-662-7776 or (973)292-5100 Fax: (973)539-3476 E-mail: corporatecommunications@cahners.com • URL: http://www.cahners.com • Annual. $60.00. Provides catalog descriptions of chemical processing equipment in 12 major product or service categories.

CEC Communications (Chemical Engineering Communications). IPD (International Publishers Distributors), P.O. Box 321609 Newark, NJ 07102. Phone: 800-545-8398 Fax: (215)750-6343 Bimonthly. Institutions, $87.00 per year; corporations, $135.00 per year. Formerly *Chemical Engineering Communications*.

CEE News. Intertec Publishing Corp., P.O. Box 12901 Overland Park, KS 66212. Phone: 800-400-5945 or (913)341-1300 Fax: (913)967-1898 E-mail: subs@intertec.com • URL: http://www.ceenews.com • Monthly. $30.00 per year. Formerly *Electrical Construction Technology*.

CEE News Buyers' Guide. Intertec Publishing Corp., P.O. Box 12901 Overland Park, KS 66282-2901. Phone: 800-400-5945 or (913)341-1300 Fax: (913)967-1898 E-mail: subs@intertec.com • URL: http://www.intertec.com • Annual. $25.00. List of approximately 1,900 manufacturers of products used in the electrical construction industry; coverage includes Canada.

Celebrity Directory: How to Reach Over 9,000 Movie, TV Stars and Other Famous Celebrities. Axiom Information Resources, P.O. Box 8015 Ann Arbor, MI 48107. Phone: (734)761-4842 Fax: (734)761-3276 E-mail: axiominfo@celebritylocator.com • Annual. $39.95. Stars, agents, networks, studios, and other celebrities. Gives names and addresses.

Celebrity Register. The Gale Group, 27500 Drake Rd. Farmington Hills, MI 48331-3535. Phone: 800-877-GALE or (248)699-GALE Fax: 800-414-5043 or (248)699-8069 E-mail: galeord@galegroup.com • URL: http://www.galegroup.com • 1989. $99.00. Fifth edition. Compiled by Celebrity Services International (Earl Blackwell). Contains profiles of 1,300 famous individuals in the performing arts, sports, politics, business, and other fields.

Cellular Phone Service. Entrepreneur Media, Inc., 2445 McCabe Way Irvine, CA 92614. Phone: 800-421-2300 or (959)261-2325 Fax: (949)261-0234 E-mail: entmag@entrepreneur.com • URL: http://www.entrepreneur.com • Looseleaf. $59.50. A practical guide to starting a business for the servicing of cellular (mobile) telephones. Covers profit potential, start-up costs, market size evaluation, owner's time required, site selection, lease negotiation, pricing, accounting, advertising, promotion, etc. (Start-Up Business Guide No. E1268.)

Cellular Telecommunications Industry Association., 1250 Connecticut Ave., N.W., Suite 200 Washington, DC 20036. Phone: (202)785-0081 Fax: (202)785-0721 Promotes the commercial development of cellular radiotelephone communications.

CEMA Bulletin. Conveyor Equipment Manufacturers Association, 6724 Lone Oak Blvd. Naples, FL 34109-6834. Phone: (703)330-7079 Fax: (703)330-7984 E-mail: cema@cemanet.org • URL: http://www.cemanet.org • Quarterly. Controlled circulation.

Cement and Concrete Research. Elsevier Science, 655 Ave. of the Americas New York, NY 10010. Phone: 888-437-4636 or (212)989-5800 Fax: (212)633-3680 E-mail: usinfo@elsevier.com • URL: http://www.elsevier.com • Monthly. $1,761.00 per year. Text in English, French, German and Russian.

Cement and Concrete Terminology. American Concrete Institute, 38800 Country Club Rd. Farmington Hills, MI 48331. Phone: (248)848-3700 Fax: (248)848-3701 E-mail: webmaster@aci-int.org • URL: http://www.aci-int.org • 1990. $54.50.

Cement Data Book: International Process Engineering in the Cement Industry. Walter H. Duda. French and European Publications, Inc., Rockefelle Center Promenade, 610 Fifth Ave. New York, NY 10020-2479. Phone: (212)581-8810 Fax: (212)265-1094 E-mail: livresny@aol.com • URL: http://www.frencheuropean.com • 1985. $950.00. Third edition. Three volumes. Vol.1, $375.00; vol.2, $325.00; vol.3, $250.00. Text in English and German.

Cement Employers Association.

Cement, Lime, Gypsum, and Allied Workers Division.

Cement, Quarry and Mineral Aggregates Newsletter. National Safety Council, Periodicals Dept., 1121 Spring Lake Dr. Itasca, IL 60143-3201. Phone: 800-621-7619 or (630)285-1121 Fax: (630)285-1315 URL: http://www.nsc.org • Bimonthly. Members, $15.00 per year; non-members, $19.00 per year.

Census Catalog and Guide. U. S. Government Printing Office, Washington, DC 20402. Phone: (202)512-1800 Fax: (202)512-2250 E-mail: gpoaccess@gpo.gov • URL: http://www.access.gpo.gov • Annual. Lists publications and electronic media products currently available from the U. S. Bureau of the Census, along with some out of print items. Includes comprehensive title and subject indexes. Formerly *Bureau of the Census Catalog*.

Census of Construction Industries: Roofing Siding and Sheet Metal Work Special Trade Contractors. U.S. Bureau of the Census, Washington, DC 20233-0800. Phone: (301)457-4100 Fax: (301)457-3842 URL: http://www.census.gov • Quinquennial.

Census of Construction: Subject Bibliography No. 157. Available from U. S. Government Printing Office, Washington, DC 20402. Phone: (202)512-1800 Fax: (202)512-2250 E-mail: gpoaccess@gpo.gov • URL: http://www.access.gpo.gov • Annual. Free. Lists government publications.

Census of Governments: Subject Bibliography No. 156. Available from U. S. Government Printing Office, Washington, DC 20402. Phone: (202)512-1800 Fax: (202)512-2250 E-mail: gpoaccess@gpo.gov • URL: http://www.access.gpo.gov • Annual. Free. Lists government publications.

Center Court. National Center for State Courts, 300 Newport Ave. Williamsburg, VA 23187-8798. Phone: (757)259-1838 Fax: (757)259-1520 Quarterly. Free. Formerly *State Court Report*.

Center for Acoustics and Vibration. Pennsylvania State University

Center for Adult Education. Columbia University

Center for Advanced Materials Research. Brown University

Center for Advanced Phototonic and Electronic Materials., State University of New York at Buffalo, 217 C Bonner Hall Buffalo, NY 14260. Phone: (716)645-2422 Fax: (716)645-5964 E-mail: waanders@eng.buffalo.edu • URL: http://www.ee.buffalo.edu • Does integrated optics research, including photonic circuitry.

Center for Advanced Technology in Computers and Information Systems.

Center for Advanced Technology in Telecommunications., Polytechnic University, Five Metrotech Center Brooklyn, NY 11201. Phone: (718)260-3050 Fax: (718)260-3074 E-mail: panwar@poly.edu • URL: http://www.catt.poly.edu • Research fields include active media for optical communication.

Center for Aeromechanics Research. University of Texas at Austin

Center for Applied Energy Research.

Center for Applied Thermodynamics.

Center for Artificial Intelligence.

Center for Arts Administration Program. Florida State University

Center for Auto Safety.

Center for Automation Research.

Center for Business and Industrial Studies., University of Missouri-St. Louis, School of Business Administration, 8001 Natural Bridge Rd. St. Louis, MO 63121. Phone: (314)516-5857 Fax: (314)516-6420 E-mail: ldsmith@.umsl.edu • URL: http://www.umsl.edu/~cbis/cbis.html • Research fields include inventory and management control. Specific projects also include development of computer software for operations in public transit systems.

Center for Canadian-American Studies., Western Washington University, Canada House, Room 201 Bellingham, WA 98225-9110. Phone: (360)650-3728 Fax: (360)650-3995 E-mail: canam@cc.edu • URL: http://www.wwu.edu/~canam • Research areas include Canadian business and economics.

Center for Cement Composite Materials. University of Illinois at Urbana-Champaign

Center for Climatic Research. University of Wisconsin - Madison

Center for Communication Research.

Center for Composite Materials.

Center for Composite Materials and Structures.

Center for Consumer Research.

Center for Corporate Community Relations., Boston College, 55 Lee Rd. Chestnut Hill, MA 02467. Phone: (617)552-4545 Fax: (617)552-8499 E-mail: cccr@bc.edu • URL: http://www.bc.edu/cccr • Areas of study include corporate images within local communities, corporate community relations, social vision, and philanthropy.

Center for Decision Research. University of Chicago Graduate School of Business

Center for Defense Information.

Center for Energy and Combustion Research. University of California, San Diego

Center for Energy and Environmental Studies. Carnegie Mellon University Department of Engineering and Public Policy

Center for Entrepreneurial Studies and Development, Inc., West Virginia University, College of Engineering and Mineral Resources, P.O. Box 6107 Morgantown, WV 26506-6107. Phone: (304)293-3612 Fax: (304)293-6707 E-mail: byrd@cemr.wvu.edu • URL: http://www.cesd.wvu.edu • Inventory control systems included as a research field.

Center for Environmental Design Research. University of California at Berkeley

Center for Exercise Science., University of Florida, 27 Florida Gym Gainesville, FL 32611. Phone: (352)392-9575 Fax: (352)392-0316 E-mail: spowers@hhp.ufl.edu • Studies fitness as it relates to the general population and as it relates to athletic performance.

Center for Exhibition Industry Research., 2301 S. Lake Shore Dr., Suite E1002 Chicago, IL 60616. Phone: (312)808-2347 Fax: (312)949-3472 URL: http://www.ceir.org • Promotes the trade show as a marketing device.

Center for Family Business., P.O. Box 24219 Cleveland, OH 44124. Phone: (440)442-0800 Fax: (440)442-0178 Members are family-owned, independent, private, and closely-held businesses.

Center for Finance and Real Estate.

Center for Geoenvironmental Science and Technology.

Center for Governmental Responsibility., University of Florida, College of Law, P.O. Box 117629 Gainesville, FL 32611-7629. Phone: (352)392-2237 Fax: (352)392-1457 E-mail: jlmills@law.ufl.edu • URL: http://www.law.ufl.edu/college/cgr • Research fields include family law.

Center for Health Administration Studies.

Center for Health and Safety Studies.

Center for Health Economics Research., Waverly Oaks Rd., Suite 330 Waltham, MA 02452. Phone: (781)788-8100 Fax: (781)788-8101 E-mail: jmitchell@cher.org • URL: http://www.her-cher.org • Studies the financing of Medicare.

Center for Health Policy Law and Management.

Center for Health Promotion Research and Development., University of Texas, Houston Health Science Center, P.O. Box 20186 Houston, TX 77225. Phone: (713)500-9601 Fax: (713)500-9602 E-mail: guy@utsph.sph.uth.tmc.edu • URL: http://www.utsph.sph.uth.tmc.edu • Fields of study include worksite health promotion.

Center for Health Research., Wayne State University, College of Nursing, 5557 Cass Ave. Detroit, MI 48202. Phone: (313)577-4134 Fax: (313)577-5777 E-mail: ajacox@wayne.edu • URL: http://www.comm.wayne.edu/nursing/nursing.html • Studies innovation in health care organization and financing.

Center for Human Resources.

Center for Human Resources.

Center for Imaging Science., Rochester Institute of Technology, 54 Lomb Memorial Dr. Rochester, NY 14623. Phone: (716)475-5994 Fax: (716)475-5988 E-mail: gatley@cis.rit.edu • URL: http://www.cis.rit.edu • Activities include research in color science and digital image processing.

Center for Industrial Research and Service. Iowa State University of Science and Technology

Center for Information Systems Research. Massachusetts Institute of Technology

Center for Integrated Manufacturing Studies., Rochester Institute of Technology, 111 Lomb Memorial Dr. Rochester, NY 14623-5608. Phone: (716)475-5101 Fax: (716)475-5250 E-mail: wjsasp@rit.edu • URL: http://www.cims.rit.edu • Research areas include electronics, imaging, printing, and publishing.

Center for Integrated Plant Systems. Michigan State University

Center for Integrated Systems., Stanford University, 420 Vis Palou Mall Stanford, CA 94305-4070. Phone: (650)725-3621 Fax: (650)725-0991 E-mail: rdasher@cis.stanford.edu • URL: http://www.cis.stanford.edu • Research programs include manufacturing science, design science, computer architecture, semiconductor technology, and telecommunications.

Center for Intelligent Machines and Robotics.

Center for Intelligent Systems, Controls, and Signal Processing.

Center for International Education and Research in Accounting. University of Illinois at Urbana-Champaign

Center for International Policy., 1755 Massachusetts Ave., N. W., Suite 312 Washington, DC 20036. Phone: (202)232-3317 Fax: (202)232-3440 E-mail: cip@ciponline.org • URL: http://www.ciponline.org • Research subjects include the International Monetary Fund, the World Bank, and other international financial institutions. Analyzes the impact of policies on social and economic conditions in developing countries.

Center for International Science and Technology Policy., George Washington University, 2013 G St., N. W., Stuart Hall, Suite 201 Washington, DC 20052. Phone: (202)994-7292 Fax: (202)994-1639 E-mail: cistp@gwu.edu • URL: http://www.gwu.edu/~cistp • Research areas include technology transfer.

Center for Labor and Human Resource Studies., Temple University, School of Business and Management, Speakman Hall, Room 366 Philadelphia, PA 19122. Phone: (215)204-8029 Fax: (215)204-5698 Investigates factors affecting labor market success.

Center for Labor Education and Research. University of Alabama at Birmingham

Center for Laser Applications., UT Space Institute Research Park, University of Tennessee Tullahoma, TN 37388. Phone: (931)393-7485 Fax: (931)454-2271 E-mail: jlewis@utsi.edu • URL: http://view.utsi.edu/cla • In addition to research, provides technical assistance relating to the industrial use of lasers.

Center for Laser Studies., University of Southern California, Denney Research Bldg., University Park Los Angeles, CA 90089-1112. Phone: (213)740-4235 Fax: (213)740-8158 Concerned with commercial and military laser applications.

Center for Latin American Studies., University of Chicago, 5848 S. University Ave., K308 Chicago, IL 60637. Phone: (773)702-8420 Fax: (773)702-1755 E-mail: clas@uchicago.edu • URL: http://www.uchicago.edu • Includes economic inquiry on Latin America.

Center for Latin American Studies., University of Florida, P.O. Box 115530 Gainesville, FL 32611-5530. Phone: (352)392-0375 Fax: (352)392-7682 E-mail: cwood@latam.ufl.edu • URL: http://www.latam.ufl.edu • Research areas include Latin American business, with emphasis on the Caribbean and South America.

Center for Latin American Studies., Stanford University, Bolivar House, 582 Alvarado Row Stanford, CA 94305-8545. Phone: (650)723-4444 Fax: (650)723-9822 E-mail: clas-boho@lists.stanford.edu • URL: http://www.stanford.edu/group/las • Areas of research include Latin American trade, finance, and economic integration.

Center for Leadership Development. c/o American Council on Education

Center for Mass Media Research.

Center for Mathematical Studies in Economics and Management Sciences.

Center for Mature Consumer Studies., Georgia State University, Broad St. Atlanta, GA 30303. Phone: (404)651-4177 Fax: (404)651-4198 E-mail: gmoschis@gsu.edu • URL: http://www.gsu.edu/~mkteer/cmcs.html • Serves as an information resource, assisting in strategy development for reaching the mature consumer market.

Center for Media and Public Affairs.

Center for Medical Economics Studies. Northeastern University

Center for Microelectronic and Computer Engineering., Rochester Institute of Technology, 82 Lomb Memorial Dr. Rochester, NY 14623-5604. Phone: (716)475-2035 Fax: (716)475-5041 E-mail: lffeee@rit.edu • URL: http://www.microe.rit.edu • Facilities include digital computer organization/microcomputer laboratory.

Center for Migration Studies., 209 Flagg Place Staten Island, NY 10304-1199. Phone: (718)351-8800 Fax: (718)667-4598 E-mail: cmslft@aol.com • URL: http://www.cmsny.org • A nonprofit institute "committed to encourage and facilitate the study of sociodemographic, economic, political..aspects of human migration and refugee movement."

Center for National Policy.

Center for Negotiation and Conflict Resolution.

Center for Pension and Retirement Research., Miami University, Department of Economics, 109E Laws Hall Oxford, OH 45056. Phone: (513)529-2850 Fax: (513)529-6992 E-mail: swilliamson@eh.net • URL: http://www.eh.net/~cprr • Research areas include pension economics, pension plans, and retirement decisions.

Center for Photonics and Optoelectronic Materials.

Center for Population and Development Studies. Harvard University

Center for Private Enterprise., Baylor University, Hankamer School of Business, P.O. Box 98003 Waco, TX 76798-8003. Phone: (254)710-2263 Fax: (254)710-1092 E-mail: jimtruitt@baylor.edu • URL: http://129.62.162.136/enterprise/ • Includes studies of entrepreneurship and women entrepreneurs.

Center for Public Interest Polling., Rutgers University, Eagleton Institute of Politics New Brunswick, NJ 08901. Phone: (732)828-2210 Fax: (732)932-1551 E-mail: jballou@rci.rutgers.edu • URL: http://www.rci.rutgers.edu/~eaglepol • Provides survey research and program evaluation services.

Center for Public-Private Sector Cooperation.

Center for Public Safety. Northwestern University

Center for Quality and Productivity., University of North Texas, College of Business Administration Denton, TX 76203-3677. Phone: (940)565-4767 E-mail: prybutok@unt.edu • URL: http://www.coba.unt.edu:80/bcis.organize/cqp/cqp.htm • Fields of research include the management of quality systems and statistical methodology.

Center for Quality and Productivity Improvement., University of Wisconsin-Madison, 610 N. Walnut St., 575 WARF Bldg. Madison, WI 53705. Phone: (608)263-2520 Fax: (608)263-1425 E-mail: quality@engr.wisc.edu • URL: http://www.engr.wisc.edu/centers/cqpi • Research areas include quality management and industrial engineering.

Center for Real Estate Studies.

Center for Research and Education in Optics and Lasers.

Center for Research and Management Services. Indiana State University

Center for Research in Ambulatory Health Care Administration., 104 Inverness Terrace E. Englewood, CO 80112-5306. Phone: (303)397-7879 Fax: (303)397-1827 E-mail: npiland@mgma.com • URL: http://www.mgma.com/research • Fields of research include medical group practice management.

Center for Research in Computing Technology., Harvard University, Pierce Hall, 29 Oxford St. Cambridge, MA 02138. Phone: (617)495-2832 Fax: (617)495-9837 E-mail: cheatham@das.harvard.edu • URL: http://www.das.harvard.edu/cs.grafs.html • Conducts research in computer vision, robotics, artificial intelligence, systems programming, programming languages, operating systems, networks, graphics, database management systems, and telecommunications.

Center for Research in Economic Development. San Diego State University

Center for Research in Regulated Industries. Rutgers University

Center for Research in Security Prices.

Center for Retail Management., J. L. Kellogg Graduate School of Management, Northwestern University Evanston, IL 60208. Phone: (847)467-3600 Fax: (847)467-3620 URL: http://www.retailing-network.com • Conducts research related to retail marketing and management.

Center for Retailing Studies., Texas A & M University, Department of Marketing, 4112 Tamus College Station, TX 77843-4112. Phone: (979)845-0325 Fax: (979)845-5230 E-mail: berryle@tamu.edu • URL: http://www.crstamu.org • Research areas include retailing issues and consumer economics.

Center for Risk Management and Insurance Research.

Center for Solid State Electronics Research. Arizona State University

Center for Space Research. Massachusetts Institute of Technology

Center for Statistical Consultation and Research. University of Michigan

Center for Studies in Creativity. State University of New York College at Buffalo

Center for Study of Librarianship.

Center for Study of Responsive Law., P.O. Box 19367 Washington, DC 20036. Phone: (202)387-8030 Fax: (202)234-5176 E-mail: csrl@csrl.org • URL: http://www.csrl.org • A consumer-oriented research group.

Center for Tax Policy Studies.

Center for the Environment., Cornell University, 200 Rice Hall Ithaca, NY 14853-5601. Phone: (607)255-7535 Fax: (607)255-0238 E-mail: cucfe@cornell.edu • URL: http://www.cfe.cornell.edu • Includes Waste Management Institute and New York State Solid Waste Combustion Institute.

Center for the Study of Aging., University of Bridgeport, Division of Counseling and Human Services, Carlson Hall, 303 University Ave. Bridgeport, CT 06601. Phone: (203)576-4175 Fax: (203)576-4200 Research activities include the study of Medicare and Medicaid.

Center for the Study of American Business. Washington University in Saint Louis, Campus Box 1027 St. Louis, MO 63130-4899. Phone: (314)935-5630 Fax: (314)935-5688 URL: http://csab.wustl.edu • Research activity includes the study of corporate takeovers.

Center for the Study of Entrepreneurship.

Center for the Study of Higher Education. Pennsylvania State University

Center for the Study of Law, Science, and Technology., Arizona State University, College of Law, P.O. Box 877906 Tempe, AZ 85287-7906. Phone: (602)965-2554 Fax: (602)965-2427 E-mail: daniel.strouse@asu.edu • URL: http://www.law.asu.edu • Studies the legal problems created by technological advances.

Center for the Study of Services., 733 15th St., N.W., Suite 820 Washington, DC 20005. Phone: 800-475-7283 or (202)347-9612 Fax: (202)347-4000 E-mail: editors@checkbook.org • URL: http://www.checkbook.org • Evaluates consumer services.

Center for the Study of Sport in Society., Northeastern University, 360 Huntington Ave., 161CP Boston, MA 02115. Phone: (617)373-4025 Fax: (617)373-4566 URL: http://www.sportinsociety.org • Research fields include sport sociology, sport journalism, and sport business.

Center for the Study of the Presidency.

Center for Transportation Research.

Center for Transportation Studies. Massachusetts Institute of Technology

Center for Urban and Industrial Pest Management., Purdue University, 1158 Entomology Hall West Lafayette, IN 47907. Phone: (765)494-4564 Fax: (765)494-2152 E-mail: gbennett@entm.purdue.edu • URL: http://www.purdue.edu/entomology/urbancenter/home.html • Conducts research on the control of household and structural insect pests.

Center for Urban and Regional Studies. University of North Carolina at Chapel Hill

Center for Urban Transportation Studies.

Center for Women Policy Studies., 1211 Connecticut Ave., N.W. Suite 312 Washington, DC 20036. Phone: (202)872-1770 Fax: (202)296-8962 E-mail: cwps@centerwomenpolicy.org • URL: http://www.centerwomenpolicy.org • Conducts research on the policy issues that affect the legal, economic, educational, and social status of women, including sexual harassment in the workplace, and women and AIDS.

Center for Worksite Health Enhancement., Pennsylvania State University, One White Bldg. University Park, PA 16802. Phone: (814)863-0435 Fax: (814)863-8586 E-mail: ryr@psuvm.psu.edu • Evaluates health and fitness programs.

Center of International Studies. Princeton University

Center on Education and Training for Employment. Ohio State University

Center on Japanese Economy and Business., Columbia University, 521 Uris Hall, 3022 Broadway New York, NY 10027-6902. Phone: (212)854-3976 Fax: (212)678-6958 E-mail: hpatrick@claven.gsb.colombia.edu • URL: http://www.gsb.columbia.edu/japan/ • Research areas include Pacific Basin trade policy.

Central Banking Directory. Available from European Business Publications, Inc., P.O. Box 891 Darien, CT 06820-9859. Phone: (203)656-2701 Fax: (203)655-8332 E-mail: centralbank@easynet.co.uk • URL: http://www.easyweb.co.uk/centralbank • Biennial. Published in England by Central Banking Publications. Provides detailed information on over 160 central banks around the world. A full page is devoted to each country included. Included in subscription to *Central Banking*.

Central Banking: Policy, Markets, Supervision. Available from European Business Publications, Inc., P.O. Box 891 Darien, CT 06820-9859. Phone: (203)656-2701 Fax: (203)655-8332 E-mail: centralbank@easynet.co.uk • URL: http://www.easyweb.co.uk/centralbank • Quarterly. $350.00 per year, including annual *Central Banking Directory*. Published in England by Central Banking Publications. Reports and comments on the activities of central banks around the world. Also provides discussions of the International Monetary Fund (IMF), the Organization for Economic Cooperation and Development (OECD), the Bank for International Settlements (BIS), and the World Bank.

Central Station Alarm Association.

Centre for Building Science. University of Toronto Department of Engineering

A Century of Cameras. Eaton S. Lothrop. Morgan and Morgan, Inc., P.O. Box 595 Keene Valley, NY 12943-0595. Phone: (518)576-9277 Fax: (518)576-9282 E-mail: sales@morganmorgan.com • URL: http://www.morganmorgan.com • 1982. $24.00. Revised edition.

The CEO Report. United Communications Group (UCG), 11300 Rockville Pike, Suite 1100 Rockville, MD 20852-3030. Phone: 800-287-2223 or (301)287-2700 Fax: (301)816-8945 E-mail: webmaster@ucg.com • URL: http://www.ucg.com • Biweekly. $287.00 per year. Newsletter for credit union executives. Formerly *Credit Union Information Service*.

Ceramic Industries International. Turret RAI plc, Armstrong House, 38 Market Square Uxbridge UB8 1TG Middlesex, England. Phone: 44 1895 454545 Fax: 44 1895 454647 Bimonthly. $115.00. per year.

Ceramic Industry Data Book Buyer's Guide. Business News Publishing Co., 755 Big Beaver, Suite 1000 Troy, MI 48084. Phone: 800-837-7370 or (248)362-3700 Fax: (248)362-0317 URL: http://www.bnp.com • Annual. $25.00. Included with subscription to *Ceramic Industry*. Formerly *Ceramic Data Book*.

Ceramic Industry: The Magazine for Refractories, Traditional and Advanced Ceramic Manufacturers. Business News Publishing Co., 755 W. Big Beaver Rd., Suite 1000 Troy, MI 48084. Phone: 800-837-7370 or (248)362-3700 Fax: (248)362-0317 URL: http://www.bnp.com • 13 times a year. $65.00 per year. Includes *Data Buyers Guide, Materials Handbook, Economic Forecast*, and *Giants in Ceramic*.

Ceramic Tile. Available from MarketResearch.com, 641 Ave. of the Americas, Third Floor New York, NY 10011. Phone: 800-298-5699 or (212)807-2629 Fax: (212)807-2716 E-mail: order@marketresearch.com • URL: http://www.marketresearch.com • 1998. $1295.00. Market research report published by Specialists in Business Information. Presents market data relative to demographics, sales growth, shipments, exports, imports, price trends, and end-use. Includes company profiles.

Ceramic Tile Distributors Association., 800 Roosevelt Rd., Bldg. C., Ste. 20 Glen Ellyn, IL 60137. Phone: 800-938-2382 or (630)545-9415 Fax: (630)790-3095 URL: http://www.ctdahome.org • Members include wholesalers and manufacturers of ceramic tile and related products.

Ceramics: A Potter's Handbook. Glenn C. Nelson. Harcourt Brace College Publishers, 301 Commerce St., Suite 3700 Fort Worth, TX 76102-4137. Phone: 800-245-8774 or (817)334-8060 Fax: (817)334-8060 E-mail: wlittle@harbrace.com • 1998. $42.50. Sixth edition.

Ceramics Monthly. American Ceramic Society, P.O. Box 6136 Westerville, OH 43286-6136. Phone: (614)890-4700 Fax: (614)899-6100 E-mail: customersrvc@acers.org • URL: http://www.acers.org • 10 times a year. $28.00 per year.

Cereal Crops Research Unit U.S. Department of Agricultural Research Service.

Cereal Disease Laboratory U.S. Department of Agricultural Research Service.

Certified Milk Producers Association of America.

CFMA Building Profits. Construction Financial Management Association, 29 Emmons Dr., Suite F-50 Princeton, NJ 08540-1413. Phone: (609)452-8000 Fax: (609)452-0474 E-mail: info@cfma.org • URL: http://www.cfma.org • Bimonthly. Controlled circulation. Covers the financial side of the construction industry.

CFO: The Magazine for Senior Financial Executives. CFO Publishing Corp., The Economist Group, 253 Summer St. Boston, MA 02210. Phone: 800-877-5416 or (617)345-9700 Fax: (617)951-4090 E-mail: juliahomer@cfopub.com • URL: http://www.cfonet.com • Monthly. Free to qualified subscribers; others, $50.00 per year.

Chain Drug Review: The Reporter for the Chain Drug Store Industry. Racher Press, Inc., 220 Fifth Ave., 18th Fl. New York, NY 10001. Phone: (212)213-6000 Fax: (212)213-6106 Biweekly. $136.00 per year. Covers news and trends of concern to the chain drug store industry. Includes special articles on OTC (over-the-counter) drugs.

Chain Store Age: The Newsmagazine for Retail Executives. Lebhar-Friedman, Inc., 425 Park Ave. New York, NY 10022. Phone: 800-766-6999 or (212)756-5000 Fax: (212)756-5250 E-mail: info@lf.com • URL: http://www.lf.com • Monthly. $105.00 per year. Formerly *Chain Store Age Executive with Shopping Center Age*.

Challenge: The Magazine of Economic Affairs. M. E. Sharpe, Inc., 80 Business Park Dr. Armonk, NY 10504. Phone: 800-541-6543 or (914)273-1800 Fax: (914)273-2106 E-mail: mesinfo@usa.net • URL: http://www.mesharpe.com/ • Bimonthly. Individuals, $45.00 per year; institutions, $146.00 per year. A nontechnical journal on current economic policy and economic trends.

Chamber Executive. American Chamber of Commerce Executives, 4232 King St. Alexandria, VA 22302-9950. Phone: (703)998-0072 Fax: (703)931-5624 URL: http://www.acce.org • Monthly. $187.00 per year. Edited for local chamber of commerce managers.

Chamber of Commerce of the Apparel Industry.

Chamber of Shipping of America.

Champion. National Association of Criminal Defense Lawyers, 1025 Connecticut Ave., N.W., Suite 901 Washington, DC 20036. Fax: (202)331-8269 10 times a year. $25.00 per year.

Change: The Magazine of Higher Learning. American Association of Higher Education. Helderf Publications, 1319 18th St. N.W. Washington, DC 20036-1802. Phone: (202)296-6267 Fax: (202)296-5149 E-mail: ch@helderf.org • URL: http://www.helderf.com • Bimonthly. Individuals, $40.00 per year; institutions, $82.00 per year.

Changing Medical Markets: The Monthly Newsletter for Executives in the Healthcare and Biotechnology Industries. Theta Reports/PJB Medical Publications, Inc., 1775 Broadway, Suite 511 New York, NY 10019. Phone: (212)262-8230 Fax: (212)262-8234 E-mail: customerservice@thetareports.com • URL: http://www.thetareports.com • Monthly. $295.00 per year. Newsletter. Covers developments in medical technology, new products, corporate trends, medical market research, mergers, personnel, and other healthcare topics.

Chaos on the Shop Floor: A Worker's View of Quality, Productivity, and Management. Tom Juravich. Temple University Press, 1601 N. Broad St., University Services Bldg., Room 305 Philadelphia, PA 19122-6099. Phone: 800-447-1656 or (215)204-8787 Fax: (215)204-4719 E-mail: tempress@astro.ocis.temple.edu • URL: http://www.temple.edu/tempress • 1988. $19.95. (Labor and Social Change Series).

Chapter 11: Reorganizations. Shepard's, 555 Middle Creek Parkway Colorado Springs, CO 80921. Phone: 800-743-7393 or (719)481-7371 Fax: 800-525-0053 or (719)481-7621 E-mail: customer_service@shepards.com • URL: http://www.shepards.com • 1983. $105.00. Annual supplementation.

Chapter 11 Update: Monitors All Major Developments in Today's Corporate Bankruptcies and Examines Pertinent Court Decisions Related to Chapter 11 Filings. Andrews Publications, 175 Strafford Ave., Bldg. 4, Suite 140 Wayne, PA 19087. Phone: 800-345-1101 or (610)622-0510 Fax: (610)622-0501 URL: http://www.andrewspub.com • Semimonthly. $500.00 per year. Newsletter on corporate Chapter 11 bankruptcy filings.

Chapter 13: Practice and Procedure. William Drake and Jeffrey W. Morris. Shepard's, 555 Middle Creek Parkway Colorado Springs, CO 80921. Phone: 800-743-7393 or (719)481-7371 Fax: 800-525-0053 or (719)481-7621 E-mail: customer_service@shepards.com • URL: http://www.shepards.com • Looseleaf service. $105.00. Annual supplementation.

The Character of a Corporation: How Your Company's Culture Can Make or Break Your Business. Rob Goffee and Gareth Jones. HarperCollins Publishers, Inc., 10 E. 53rd St. New York, NY 10022-5299. Phone: 800-242-7737 or (212)207-7000 Fax: 800-822-4090 or (212)207-7145 URL: http://www.harpercollins.com • 1998. $25.00. Provides advice on establishing a positive business environment.

Characteristics of Apartments Completed. U.S. Bureau of the Census. Available from U.S. Government Printing Office, Washington, DC 20402. Phone: (202)512-1800 Fax: (202)512-2250 E-mail: gpoaccess@gpo.gov • URL: http://www.access.gpo.gov • Annual.

Charitable Giving and Solicitation. Warren Gorham and Lamont/RIA Group, 395 Hudson St. New York, NY 10014. Phone: 800-950-1215 or (212)367-6300 Fax: (212)337-4280 E-mail: customer_services@riag.com • URL: http://www.riahome.com • $495.00 per year. Looseleaf service. Monthly bulletin discusses federal tax rules pertaining to charitable contributions.

Charitable Organizations of the U. S.: A Descriptive and Financial Information Guide. The Gale Group, 27500 Drake Rd. Farmington Hills, MI 48331-3535. Phone: 800-877-GALE or (248)699-GALE Fax: 800-414-5043 or (248)699-8069 E-mail: galeord@galegroup.com • URL: http://www.galegroup.com • 1991. $150.00. Second edition. Describes nearly 800 nonprofit groups active in soliciting funds from the American public. Includes nearly 800 data on sources of income, administrative expenses, and payout.

Charitable Planning Primer. Ralph G. Miller and Adam Smalley. CCH, Inc., 4025 W. Peterson Ave. Chicago, IL 60646-6085. Phone: 800-248-3248 or (773)866-6000 Fax: 800-224-8299 or (773)866-3608 URL: http://www.cch.com • 1999. $99.00. Covers the legal and tax aspects of charitable giving and planned gifts. Includes annuity documents, tax forms, tables, and examples.

Chartcraft Monthly NYSE and ASE Chartbook. Chartcraft, Inc., P.O. Box 2046 New Rochelle, NY 10801. Phone: (914)632-0422 Fax: (914)632-0335 Monthly. $402.00 per year. Includes all common stocks on New York and American Stock Exchanges.

Chartcraft Over-the-Counter Chartbook. Chartcraft, Inc., P.O. Box 2046 New Rochelle, NY 10801. Phone: (914)632-0422 Fax: (914)632-0335 Quarterly. $114.00 per year. Includes more than 1,000 unlisted stocks. Long term charts.

Chartered Institution of Water and Environmental Management Journal. Terence Dalton Ltd., Arbons House, Water St. Lavenham, Suffolk CO10 9RN, England. E-mail: postmaster@lavenhambroup.co.uk • Bimonthly. $255.00 per year.

Chase's Calendar of Events: The Day-by-Day Directory. NTC/Contemporary Publishing, P.O. Box 545 Blacklick, OH 43004. Phone: 800-338-3987 or (614)755-4151 Fax: (614)755-5645 E-mail: ntcpub@mcgraw-hill.com • URL: http://www.ntc-cb.com • Annual. $59.95. Provides information for over 10,000 special days and special events throughout the world. Chronological arrangement with an alphbetical index. Formerly *Chase's Annual Events*.

The Cheap Investor. Mathews and Associates, Inc., 2549 W. Golf Rd., Suite 350 Hoffman Estates, IL 60164. Phone: (847)697-5666 Fax: (847)697-5699 Monthly. $98.00 per year. Newsletter. Gives three to six buy recommendations, updates on precious recommendations and investment tips on quality stock under $5.00. Free issue available upon request.

Check-In-Check-Out. Principles of Effective Front Office Management. Gary K. Vallen and Jerome J. Vallen. Brown and Benchmark, 25 Kessel Court Madison, WI 53711. Phone: 800-338-5578 or (608)273-0040 Fax: 800-346-2372 E-mail: customer.service@mcgraw-hill.com • URL: http://www.mhhe.com • $44.75. Looseleaf service.

The Check is Not in the Mail: How to Get Paid More, in Full, on Time, at Less Cost, and Without Losing Valued Customers. Leonard Sklar. Baroque Publishing, 783 Mediterranean Lane Redwood City, CA 94065-1758. Phone: (415)654-9138 Fax: (415)654-9139 E-mail: lenwriter@aol.com • 1995. $19.95. Explains how to establish the right collection cycle, what is harassment, choosing a collection agency, and collection procedures in general.

Checklists and Operating Forms for Small Businesses. John C. Wisdom. John Wiley and Sons, Inc., 605 Third Ave. New York, NY 10158-0012. Phone: 800-225-5945 or (212)850-6000 Fax: (212)850-6088 E-mail: info@wiley.com • URL: http://www.wiley.com • 1997. $125.00. 19th edition. Includes disk.

The Cheese Handbook: A Guide to the World's Best Cheese. T.A. Layton. Dover Publications, Inc., 31 E. Second St. Mineola, NY 11501. Phone: 800-223-3130 or (516)294-7000 Fax: (516)742-5049 1973. $4.50. Revised edition.

Cheese Importers Association of America.

Cheese Importers Association of America Bulletin. Cheese Importers Association of America, 460 Park Ave., 11th Fl. New York, NY 10022. Phone: (212)753-7500 Fax: (212)688-2870 Irregular. Membership.

Cheese Market News. Quarne Publishing L.L.C., P. O. Box 620244 Middleton, WI 53562-0244. Phone: (608)831-6002 Fax: (608)831-1004 E-mail: chmarknews@aol.com • URL: http://www.cahners.com • Weekly. $85.00 per year. Covers market trends, legislation, and new products.

Cheese Market News Market Directory. Quarne Publishing LLC, P. O. Box 620244 Middleton, WI 53562-0244. Phone: (608)831-6002 Fax: (608)831-1004 E-mail: chmarknews@

aol.com • URL: http://www.cahners.com • Annual. $40.00. Lists suppliers of equipment, services, and ingredients for the cheese industry.

Cheese Reporter. Richard Groves, editor. Cheese Reporter Publishing Co., Inc., 4210 E. Washington Ave. Madison, WI 53704-3742. Phone: (608)246-8430 Fax: (608)246-8431 E-mail: info@cheesereporter.com • URL: http://www.cheesereporter.com • Weekly. $80.00 per year. Reports technology, production, sales, merchandising, promotion, research and general industry news of and pertaining to the manufacture and marketing of cheese.

Chef. Talcott Communications Corp., 20 N. Wacker Dr., Suite 1865 Chicago, IL 60606. Phone: (312)849-2220 Fax: (312)849-4994 Monthly. $24.00 per year. Edited for executive chefs, food and beverage directors, caterers, banquet and club managers, and others responsible for food buying and food service. Special coverage of regional foods is provided.

Chem-Bank. SilverPlatter Information, Inc., 100 River Ridge Rd. Norwood, MA 02062. Phone: 800-343-0064 or (781)769-2599 Fax: (781)769-8763 Quarterly. $1,595.00 per year. Provides CD-ROM information on hazardous substances, including 140,000 chemicals in the *Registry of Toxic Effects of Chemical Substances* and 60,000 materials covered by the *Toxic Substances Control Act Initial Inventory*.

Chem Sources International. Chemical Sources International, Inc., P.O. Box 1824 Clemson, SC 29633-1824. Phone: 800-222-4531 or (864)646-7840 Fax: (864)646-9938 E-mail: info@chemsources.com • URL: http://www.chemssources.com • Semiannual. $875.00. List of 2,500 chemical producers and distributors in 80 countries;lists agents and representatives of 7,400 industry firms.

Chem Sources USA. Chemical Sources International, Inc., P.O. Box 1824 Clemson, SC 29633-1824. Phone: 800-222-4531 or (864)646-7840 Fax: (864)646-9938 E-mail: info@chemsources.com • URL: http://www.chemssources.com • Annual. $395.00. List of 100 chemical producers and distributors in the U. S.

Chemcyclopedia. American Chemical Society, 1155 16th St., N. W. Washington, DC 20036. Phone: 800-333-9511 or (202)872-4600 Fax: (202)872-4615 E-mail: service@acs.org • URL: http://www.chemcenter.org • Annual. $60.00. Lists 10,000 chemicals in 12 product groups, produced by 900 manufacturers. Includes chemical characteristics, trade names, and indexes.

Chemical Abstracts. Chemical Abstracts Service, P.O. Box 3012 Columbus, OH 43210-0012. Phone: 800-753-4227 or (614)447-3600 Fax: (614)447-3751 URL: http://www.cas.org • Weekly. $22,600.00 per year.

Chemical and Engineering News-Career Opportunities Issue. American Chemical Society, 1155 16th St., N.W. Washington, DC 20036. Phone: 800-333-9511 or (202)872-4600 Fax: (202)872-4615 E-mail: acsbooks@acs.org • URL: http://www.pubs.acs.org • Annual. $9.00.

Chemical and Engineering News: Facts and Figures. American Chemical Society, Microforms and Back Issues Office, 1155 16th St., N. W. Washington, DC 20036. Phone: 800-333-9511 or (202)872-4600 Fax: (202)872-4615 E-mail: service@acs.org • URL: http://www.pubs.acs.org • Annual. $20.00. List of 100 largest chemical producers by total chemical sales.

Chemical and Engineering News: The Newsmagazine of the Chemical World. American Chemical Society, 1155 16th St., N.W. Washington, DC 20036. Phone: 800-333-9511 or (202)872-4600 Fax: (202)872-4615 E-mail: service@acs.org • URL: http://www.pubs.acs.org/cen/index.html • Weekly. Institutions, $181.00 per year; others, price on application.

Chemical Coaters Association International., P.O. Box 54316 Cincinnati, OH 45254. Phone: (513)624-6767 Fax: (513)624-0601 E-mail: aygoyer@one.net • URL: http://www.finishing.com/ccai • Members are industrial users of organic finishing systems.

Chemical Engineering. McGraw-Hill Chemical Week Associates, 888 Seventh Ave., 26th Fl. New York, NY 10106. Phone: 800-722-4726 or (212)621-4900 Fax: (212)621-4949 E-mail: customer.service@mcgraw-hill.com • URL: http://www.mcgraw-hill.com • Monthly. $29.50 per year. Includes annual *Chemical Engineering Buyers Guide*.

Chemical Engineering-Buyer's Guide. McGraw-Hill Chemical Week Associates, 888 7th Ave., 26th Fl. New York, NY 10106. Phone: 800-722-4726 or (212)621-4900 Fax: (212)621-4949 E-mail: email@che.com • URL: http://www.mcgraw-hill.com • Annual. Included with subscription to Chemical Engineering. Over 4,000 firms supplying equipment and machinery to the chemical processing industry. Formerly *Chemical Engineering-Equipment Buyer's Guide*.

Chemical Engineering for Chemists. Richard G. Griskey. American Chemical Society, Available from Oxford University Press, Inc., 198 Madison Ave. New York, NY 10016-4314. Phone: 800-445-9714 or (212)726-6000 Fax: (212)726-6446 E-mail: custserv@oup-usa.org • URL: http://www.oup-usa.org • 1997. $130.00. Provides basic knowledge of chemical engineering and engineering economics.

Chemical Engineering Progress. American Institute of Chemical Engineers, Three Park Ave. New York, NY 10016-5901. Phone: 800-242-4363 or (212)591-8100 Fax: (212)591-8888 E-mail: orders@allenpress.com • URL: http://www.aiche.org • Monthly. $85.00 per year. Covers current advances and trends in the chemical process and related industries. Supplement available *AICh Extra*.

Chemical Equipment. Cahners Business Information, New Product Information Unit, 301 Gibraltar Drive Morris Plains, NJ 07950-0650. Phone: 800-662-7776 or (973)292-5100 Fax: (973)539-3476 E-mail: corporatecommunications@cahners.com • URL: http://www.cahners.com • Monthly. $39.95 per year. Covers the design, building, and operation of chemical process plants. Includes end-of-year *Chemical Equipment Literature Review*

Chemical Industry Europe. State Mutual Book and Periodical Service, Ltd., 521 Fifth Ave., 17th Fl. New York, NY 10175. Phone: (718)261-1704 Fax: (516)537-0412 Annual. $150.00. About 10,500 companies within the chemical industry. Available in English, French, German, Italian and Spanish. Formerly *Chemical Industry Directory*.

Chemical Industry Notes. Chemical Abstracts Service, P.O. Box 3012 Columbus, OH 43210-0012. Phone: 800-753-4227 or (614)447-3600 Fax: (614)447-3751 URL: http://www.cas.org • Weekly. $1,135.00 per year.

Chemical Management and Resources Association., 60 Bay St., Suite 702 Staten Island, NY 10301. Phone: (718)876-8800 Members are individuals engaged in chemical market research.

Chemical Manufacturers Association.

Chemical Market Reporter. Schnell Publishing Co., Inc., Two Rector St., 26th Fl. New York, NY 10006-1819. Phone: (212)791-4200 Fax: (212)791-4313 URL: http://www.chemexpo.com • Weekly. $139.00 per year. Quotes current prices for a wide range of chemicals. Formerly *Chemical Marketing Reporter*.

Chemical Processing. Putman Media, 555 W. Pierce Rd., Suite 301 Itasca, IL 60143-2649. Phone: (630)467-1300 Fax: (630)467-1109 E-mail: ckappel@putnam.net • URL: http://www.chemicalprocessing.com • Monthly. Free to qualified personnel; others, $67.00 per year.

Chemical Regulation Reporter: A Weekly Review of Affecting Chemical Users and Manufacturers. Bureau of National Affairs, Inc., 1231 25th St., N.W. Washington, DC 20037-1197. Phone: 800-372-1033 or (202)452-4200 Fax: (202)822-8092 E-mail: books@bna.com • URL: http://www.bna.com • Weekly. Price varies. Irregular supplements.

Chemical Sources Association., P.O. Box 3189 Secaucus, NJ 07096-3189. Phone: (201)392-8900 Fax: (201)348-3877 E-mail: chemsources@nilegalink.com • URL: http://www.chemsources.org • Rare chemicals and oils for flavors.

Chemical Specialties Manufacturers Association.

Chemical Strategies. Thomson Financial Securities Data, Two Gateway Center Newark, NJ 07102. Phone: 888-989-8373 or (973)622-3100 Fax: (973)622-1421 E-mail: tfsd.cs@tfn.com • URL: http://www.tfsd.com • Monthly. $2,995.00 per year. CD-ROM contains full text of investment analysts' reports on companies active in the chemical industries.

Chemical Week. Chemical Week Associates, 110 Sillimas St., 11th Fl. New York, NY 10038. Phone: (212)621-4900 Fax: (212)621-4949 E-mail: webmaster@chemweek.com • URL: http://www.chemweek.com • 49 times a year. $139.00 per year. Includes annual *Buyers' Guide*.

Chemical Week-Buyers Guide. Chemical Week Associates, 110 Williams St., 11th Fl. New York, NY 10038. Phone: 800-308-6397 or (212)621-4900 Fax: (212)621-4949 E-mail: webmaster@chemweek.com • URL: http://www.chemweek.com • Annual. $115.00. Included in subscription to *Chemical Week*.

Chemical Week: Financial Survey of the 300 Largest Companies in the U. S. Chemical Process Industries. Chemical Week Associates, 110 Williams St., 11th Fl. New York, NY 10038. Phone: 800-308-6397 or (212)621-4900 Fax: (212)621-4949 E-mail: webmaster@chemweek.com • URL: http://www.chemweek.com • Annual. $8.00. Supersedes *Chemical Week-Chemical Week 300*.

Chemical Wholesalers Directory. American Business Directories, P.O. Box 27347 Omaha, NE 68127. Phone: 800-555-6124 or (402)593-4600 Fax: (402)331-5481 E-mail: internet@infousa.com • URL: http://www.abii.com • Annual. Price on application. Lists 8,082 United States wholesalers and 1,199 Canadian wholesalers. Compiled from telephone company yellow pages.

The Chemistry and Physics of Coatings. Alastair R. Marrion, editor. CRC Press, Inc., 200 Corporate Blvd., N.W. Boca Raton, FL 33431. Phone: 800-272-7737 or (561)994-0555 Fax: 800-374-3401 or (561)241-7856 E-mail: orders@crcpress.com • URL: http://www.crcpress.com • 1994. $42.00. Published by The Royal Society of Chemistry. Provides an overview of paint science and technology, including environmental considerations.

Chemistry Laboratories. Rensselaer Polytechnic Institute

The Chemistry of Fragrances. D. Pybus and C. Sell. Available from American Chemical Society, 1155 16th St., N. W. Washington, DC 20036. Phone: 800-333-9511 or (202)872-4600 Fax: (202)872-4615 E-mail: service@acs.org • URL: http://www.pubs.acs.org/books • 1998. $39.00. Published by The Royal Society of Chemistry.

The Chemistry of Mind-Altering Drugs: History, Pharmacology, and Cultural Context. Daniel M. Perrine. American Chemical Society, Oxford University Press, Inc., 198 Madison Ave. New York, NY 10016-4314. Phone: 800-333-9511 or (212)726-6000 Fax: (212)726-6446 E-mail: service@acs.org • URL: http://www.pubs.acs.org • 1996. $42.00. Contains detailed descriptions of the pharmacological and psychological effects of a wide variety of drugs, "from alcohol to zopiclone."

Chemistry Today and Tomorrow: The Central, Useful, and Creative Science. Ronald Breslow. American Chemical Society, 1155 16th St., N. W. Washington, DC 20036. Phone: 800-333-9511 or (202)872-4600 Fax: (202)872-4615 E-mail: service@acs.org • URL: http://www.pubs.acs.org • 1996. $19.95. Written in nontechnical language for the general reader. Discusses the various disciplines of chemistry, such as medicinal, environmental, and industrial.

CHF Newsbriefs. Cooperative Housing Foundation, 8300 Colesville Rd., Suite 420 Silver Spring, MD 20910-3243. Phone: (301)587-4700 Fax: (301)587-2626 E-mail: mailbox@chfhq.com • URL: http://www.chfhq.com • Quarterly. Single issue free.

Chicago Board of Trade Statistical Annual. Board of Trade of the City of Chicago, 141 W. Jackson Blvd. Chicago, IL 60604. Phone: (312)435-3500 Annual.

Chicago Board of Trade: The World's Leading Futures Exchange. Chicago Board of TradePhone: (312)345-3500 Fax: (312)341-3027 E-mail: comments@cbot.com • URL: http://www.cbot.com • Web site provides a wide variety of statistics, commentary, charts, and news relating to both agricultural and financial futures trading. For example, Web page "MarketPlex: Information MarketPlace to the World" offers prices & volume, contract specifications & margins, government reports, etc. The CBOT *Statistical Annual*, in book form for 109 years, is now offered online. Searching is available, with daily updates for current data. Fees: Mostly free (some specialized services are fee-based).

Chicago Board Options Exchange., 400 S. LaSalle St. Chicago, IL 60605. Phone: 800-678-4667 or (312)786-5600 Fax: (312)786-7409 URL: http://www.cboe.com • Members are individuals and firms engaged in the trading of listed options (puts and calls).

Chicago Board Options Exchange. CCH, Inc., 4025 W. Peterson Ave. Chicago, IL 60646-6085. Phone: 800-248-3248 or (773)583-8500 Fax: 800-224-8299 or (773)866-3608 URL: http://www.cch.com • $539.00 per year. Looseleaf service. Periodic supplementation. Rules, regulations and legal aspects for the trading of puts and calls.

The Chicago Manual of Style: The Essential Guide for Authors, Editors, and Publishers. University of Chicago Press, 5801 S. Ellis Ave., 4th Fl. Chicago, IL 60637. Phone: 800-621-2736 or (773)702-7700 Fax: (773)702-9756 E-mail: marketing@press.uchicago.edu • URL: http://www.press.uchicago.edu • 1993. $40.00. 14th edition.

Chief Executive Magazine. Chief Executive Group, Inc., 733 Third Ave., 24th Fl. New York, NY 10017. Phone: (212)687-8288 Fax: (212)687-8456 10 times a year. $95.00 per year.

Chief Executive Officers Club., 180 Varick St., Penthouse Suite New York, NY 10014. Phone: (212)633-0060 or (212)633-0061 Fax: (212)633-0063 E-mail: ceoclubs@bway.net • URL: http://www.ceo-clubs.org • Serves as an information resource for small business owners and managers.

Chief Executive Officers Newsletter: For the Entrepreneurial Manager and the Pr ofessionals Who Advise Him. Center for Entrepreneurial Management, Inc., Penthouse, 180 Varick St. New York, NY 10014. Phone: (212)633-0060 Fax: (212)633-0063 Monthly. $96.00 per year. Formerly *Entrepreneurial Manager's Newsletter*.

Chief Executives Organization.

Child Care Service. Entrepreneur Media, Inc., 2445 McCabe Way Irvine, CA 92614. Phone: 800-421-2300 or (949)261-2325 Fax: (949)261-0234 E-mail: entmag@entrepreneur.com • URL: http://www.entrepreneur.com • Looseleaf. $59.50. A practical guide to starting a day care center for children. Covers profit potential, start-up costs, market size evaluation, owner's time required, site selection, pricing, accounting, advertising, promotion, etc. (Start-Up Business Guide No. E1058.)

Children's Book Review Index. The Gale Group, 27500 Drake Rd. Farmington Hills, MI 48331-3535. Phone: 800-877-GALE or (248)699-GALE Fax: 800-414-5043 or (248)699-8069 E-mail: galeord@galegroup.com • URL: http://www.galegroup.com • Annual. $155.00. Back volumes available. Contains more than 25,000 review citations.

Children's Book Review Service. Ann L. Kalkhoff, editor. Children's Book Review Service Inc., 220 Berkeley Place, No. 1-D Brooklyn, NY 11217. Fax: (718)622-4036 Monthly. $40.00 per year. Includes two Supplements.

Children's Bookstore. Entrepreneur Media, Inc., 2445 McCabe Way Irvine, CA 92614. Phone: 800-421-2300 or (949)261-2325 Fax: (949)261-0234 E-mail: entmag@entrepreneur.com • URL: http://www.entrepreneur.com • Looseleaf. $59.50. A practical guide to starting a children's bookstore. Covers profit potential, start-up costs, market size evaluation, owner's time required, site selection, lease negotiation, pricing, accounting, advertising, promotion, etc. (Start-Up Business Guide No. E1293.)

Children's Clothing Store. Entrepreneur Media, Inc., 2445 McCabe Way Irvine, CA 92614. Phone: 800-421-2300 or (949)261-2325 Fax: (949)261-0234 E-mail: entmag@entrepreneur.com • URL: http://www.entrepreneur.com • Looseleaf. $59.50. A practical guide to starting a children's clothing shop. Covers profit potential, start-up costs, market size evaluation, owner's time required, site selection, lease negotiation, pricing, accounting, advertising, promotion, etc. (Start-Up Business Guide No. E1161.)

Children's Fitness Center. Entrepreneur Media, Inc., 2445 McCabe Way Irvine, CA 92614. Phone: 800-421-2300 or (949)261-2325 Fax: (949)261-0234 E-mail: entmag@entrepreneur.com • URL: http://www.entrepreneur.com • Looseleaf. $59.50. A practical guide to starting a physical fitness center for children. Covers profit potential, start-up costs, market size evaluation, owner's time required, site selection, lease negotiation, pricing, accounting, advertising, promotion, etc. (Start-Up Business Guide No. E1351.)

Chilton's Automotive Marketing: A Monthly Publication for the Retail Jobber and Distributor of Automotive Aftermarket. Cahners Business Information, Valley Forge Park Place, 1018 W. 9th Ave. King of Prussia, PA 19406. Phone: 800-695-1214 or (610)205-1000 Fax: (610)964-4981 E-mail: corporatecommunications@cahners.com • URL: http://www.cahners.com • Monthly. Free to qualified personnel; others, $48.00 per year. Includes marketing of automobile batteries. Formerly *Automotive Aftermarket News*.

Chilton's Distribution: The Transportation and Business Logistics Magazine. Cahners Business Information, Valley Forge Park Place, 1018 W. 9th Ave. King of Prussia, PA 19406. Phone: 800-695-1214 or (610)205-1000 Fax: (610)964-4745 URL: http://www.cahners.com • Monthly. $65.00 per year.

Chilton's Product Design and Development. Cahners Business Information, Valley Forge Park Place, 1018 W. 9th Ave. King of Prussia, PA 19406. Phone: 800-695-1214 or (610)205-1000 Fax: (610)964-4947 E-mail: corporatecommunications@cahners.com • URL: http://www.cahners.com • Monthly. $80.00 per year.

China: A Directory and Sourcebook. Available from The Gale Group, 27500 Drake Rd. Farmington Hills, MI 48331-3535. Phone: 800-877-GALE or (248)699-GALE Fax: 800-414-5043 or (248)699-8069 E-mail: galeord@galegroup.com • URL: http://www.galegroup.com • 1998. $590.00. Second edition. Published by Euromonitor. Describes about 800 companies in both China and Hong Kong. Sourcebook section provides 500 information sources.

China Business and Trade. Welt Publishing, LLC, 1524 18th St., N.W. Washington, DC 20036-1333. Phone: 800-898-4685 or (202)371-0555 Fax: (202)408-9369 Semimonthly. Institutions, $367.20 per year; corporations, $459.00 per year. Newsletter. Covers business and trade developments in the People's Republic of China.

China Business Review. United States-China Business Council, 1818 N St., N. W., Suite 200 Washington, DC 20036-2406. Phone: (202)429-0340 Fax: (202)833-9027 E-mail: info@uschina.org • URL: http://www.uschinabusinessreview.com/r • Bimonthly. $99.00 per year. Covers trends and issues affecting U. S. investment and trade with China and Hong Kong.

China Business: The Portable Encyclopedia for Doing Business with China. Christine Genzberger and others. World Trade Press, 1450 Grant Ave., Suite 204 Novato, CA 94945-3142. Phone: 800-833-8586 or (415)454-9934 Fax: (415)453-7980 E-mail: worldpress@aol.com • URL: http://www.worldtradepress.com • 1994. $24.95. Covers economic data, import/export possibilities, basic tax and trade laws, travel information, and other useful facts for doing business with the People's Republic of China. (Country Business Guides Series).

China: Foreign Trade Reform. World Bank, The Office of the Publisher, 1818 H St., N. W. Washington, DC 20433. Phone: 800-645-7247 or (202)477-1234 Fax: (202)477-6391 E-mail: books@worldbank.org • URL: http://www.worldbank.org • 1994. $30.00. Makes recommendations for trade liberalization and the reduction of export-import bureaucracy in China. (World Bank Country Study.)

China Marketing Data and Statistics. Available from The Gale Group, 27500 Drake Rd. Farmington Hills, MI 48331-3535. Phone: 800-877-GALE or (248)699-GALE Fax: 800-414-5043 or (248)699-8069 E-mail: galeord@galegroup.com • URL: http://www.galegroup.com • 2000. $430.00. Second edition. Two volumes. Published by Euromonitor. In addition to national statistics, includes data for 30 cities and 400 administrative areas. Major source is the Chinese State Statistical Bureau.

Chinese American Association of Commerce., 778 Clay St., Suite C San Francisco, CA 94108. Phone: (415)362-4306 Fax: (415)362-1478 Members are individuals interested in improving trade between the U. S. and the People's Republic of China.

Chinese-American Librarians Association.

Chocolate Fads, Folklore, and Fantasies: 1,000 Chunks of Chocolate Information. Linda K. Fuller. The Haworth Press, Inc., 10 Alice St. Binghamton, NY 13904-1580. Phone: 800-429-6784 or (607)722-5857 Fax: 800-895-0582 or (607)722-1424 E-mail: getinfo@haworthpressinc.com • URL: http://www.haworthpressinc.com • 1994. $49.95. Includes "Choco-Marketing-Mania Survey," "Media Citations: Chocolate 1979-1992," "Choco-References," and addresses of chocolate companies. (Original Book Series).

Chocolate Manufacturers Association of the U.S.A.

Choice: Current Reviews for Academic Libraries. Association of College Research Libraries. Choice, 100 Riverview Center Middletown, CT 06457-3445. Phone: (860)347-6933 Fax: (860)704-0465 E-mail: choicemag@ala-choice.org • URL: http://www.ala/org/acrl/choice • 11 times a year. $200.00 per year. A publication of the Association of College and Research Libraries. Contains book reviews, primarily for college and university libraries.

Choosing and Using an HMO. Ellyn Spragins., 500 Fifth Ave. New York, NY 10110-0017. Phone: 800-223-2584 or (212)354-5500 Fax: (212)869-0856 E-mail: webmaster@wwnorton.com • URL: http://www.norton.com • 1997. $19.95. Includes advice on finding a doctor, going outside the plan, and avoiding excess costs. (Bloomberg Personal Bookshelf Series.)

Chromatographia: An International Journal for Rapid Communication in Chromatography and Associated Techniques. Elsevier Science, 655 Ave. of the Americas New York, NY 10010. Phone: 888-437-4636 or (212)989-5800 Fax: (212)633-3680 E-mail: usinfo@elsevier.com • URL: http://www.chromatographia.com • 24 times a year. $1,245.00 per year. Text in English; summaries in English, French and German.

Chronicle Financial Aid Guide. Chronicle Guidance Publications, Inc., P.O. Box 1190 Moravia, NY 13118-1190. Phone: 800-622-7284 or (315)497-0330 Fax: (315)497-3359 E-mail: customerservice@chronicleguidance.com • URL: http://wwwchronicleguide.com • Annual. $24.98. Financial aid programs offered primarily by private organizations, independent and AFL-CIO affiliated labor unions and federal and state governments for undergraduate students. Formerly *Student Aid Annual*. Lists scholarship titles.

Chronicle Four-Year College Databook, 1996-97. Chronicle Guidance Publications, Inc., P.O. Box 1190 Moravia, NY 13118. Phone: 800-622-7284 or (315)497-0330 Fax: (315)497-3359 1996. $24.99. Revised edition. More than 790 baccalaureate, master's, doctoral, and first professional programs offered by more than 2,130 colleges and universities in the United States. Formerly *Chronicle Buide to Four-Year College Majors*.

Chronicle Occupational Briefs. Chronicle Guidance Publications, Inc., P.O. Box 1190 Moravia, NY 13118. Phone: 800-622-7284 or (315)497-0330 Fax: (315)497-3359 Pamphlets about various occupations.

The Chronicle of Higher Education. Chronicle of Higher Education, Inc., 1255 23rd St., N.W., Suite 700 Washington, DC 20037. Phone: 800-728-2819 or (202)466-1032 Fax: (202)659-2236 E-mail: editor@chronicle.com • URL: http://www.chronicle.com • 49 times a year. $75.00 per year. Includes *Almanac*. Provides news, book reviews and job listings for college professors and administrators. Suplement available: *Chronicle of Higher Education Almanac*.

Chronicle of Latin American Economic Affairs Îonlinel. Latin America Data Base, Latin American Institute, University of New Mexico, 801 Yale Blvd., N. E. Albuquerque, NM 87131-1016. Phone: 800-472-0888 or (505)277-6839 Fax: (505)277-5989 Contains the complete text online of the weekly newsletter, *Chronicle of Latin American Economic Affairs*. Provides news and analysis of trade and economic developments in Latin America, including Caribbean countries. Time period is 1986 to date, with weekly updates. Inquire as to online cost and availability.

Chronicle of Philanthropy:The Newspaper of the Non-Profit World. Chronicle of Higher Education, Inc., 1255 23rd St., N.W., Suite 700 Washington, DC 20037. Phone: 800-728-2819 or (202)466-1032 Fax: (202)659-2236 E-mail: editor@chronicle.com • URL: http://www.chronicle.com • Biweekly. $67.50 per year.

CIES: Food Business Forum.

Cigar Association of America.

The Cigar Market. Available from MarketResearch.com, 641 Ave. of the Americas, 3rd Fl. New York, NY 10011. Phone: 800-298-5699 or (212)807-2629 Fax: (212)807-2716 E-mail: order@marketresearch.com • URL: http://www.marketresearch.com • 1997. $1,230.00. Market research report published by Packaged Facts. Who smokes cigars? Why are they smoking? Are they likely to continue? Sales projections are provided to the year 2001.

Cigarettes: Anatomy of an Industry, from Seed to Smoke. Available from W. W. Norton & Co., Inc., 500 Fifth Ave. New York, NY 10110. Phone: 800-223-4830 or (212)354-5500 Fax: (212)869-0856 URL: http://www.wwnorton.com • 2001. $24.95. Published by The New Press. Covers the history, economic ramifications, marketing strategies, and legal problems of the cigarette industry. Popularly written.

CIMA Marketing Communications Council.

CIO: The Magazine for Information Executives. CIO Communications, P.O. Box 9208 Framingham, MA 01701-9208. Phone: 800-788-4605 or (508)872-0080 Fax: (508)879-7784 E-mail: bob@automatedbuilders.com • URL: http://www.automatedbuilders.com • Semimonthly. $89.00 per year. Edited for chief information officers. Includes a monthly "Web Business" section (incorporates the former *WebMaster* periodical) and a monthly "Enterprise" section for company executives other than CIOs.

Circulation Council of DMA., 1120 Ave. of the Americas New York, NY 10036. Phone: (212)768-7277 Fax: (212)768-4546 URL: http://www.the-dma.org • A division of the Direct Marketing Association. Members include publishers and circulation directors.

Circulation Management. Intertec Publishing Co., 11 Riverbend Dr., S. Stamford, CT 06907-2524. Phone: 800-795-5445 or (203)358-9900 Fax: (203)358-5824 E-mail: subs@intertec.com • URL: http://www.intertec.com • Monthly. $39.00 per year. Edited for circulation professionals in the magazine and newsletter publishing industry. Covers marketing, planning, promotion, management, budgeting, and related topics.

Circulation Îyearl. SRDS, 1700 Higgins Rd. Des Plaines, IL 60018-5605. Phone: 800-851-7737 or (847)375-5000 Fax: (847)375-5001 E-mail: srobe@srds.com • URL: http://www.srds.com • Annual. $256.00. Contains detailed statistical analysis of newspaper circulation by metropolitan area or county and data on television viewing by area. Includes maps.

CIS. Congressional Information Service, Inc., 4520 East-West Highway Bethesda, MD 20814. Phone: 800-638-8380 or (301)654-1550 Fax: (301)657-3203 Indexes publications of the United States Congress, 1970 to present. Inquire as to online cost and availability.

CIS Microfiche Library. Congressional Information Service, Inc., 4520 East-West Highway, Suite 800 Bethesda, MD 20814-3389. Phone: 800-638-8380 or (301)654-1550 Fax: (301)657-3203 E-mail: infocispubs.co • URL: http://www.cispubs.com • Monthly. Price varies. Prearranged retrospective files. An optional companion to *CIS Index*.

Citation: Current Legal Developments Relating to Medicine and Allied Professions. American Medical Association, Health Law Div. Citation Publishing Corp., P.O. Box 3538 RFD Long Grove, IL 60047. Phone: (847)438-2020 Fax: (847)438-2299 Semimonthly. $130.00 per year. Contains summaries of lawsuits affecting medical personnel or hospitals.

Cities for the 21st Century. OECD Publications and Information Center, 2001 L St., N.W., Ste. 650 Washington, DC 20036-4922. Phone: 800-456-6323 or (202)785-6323 Fax: (202)785-0350 E-mail: washington.contact@oecd.org • URL: http://www.oecdwash.org • 1994. $39.00. Contains discussions of the economic, social, and environmental problems of today's cities.

Cities of the United States. The Gale Group, 27500 Drake Rd. Farmington Hills, MI 48331-3535. Phone: 800-877-GALE or (248)699-GALE Fax: 800-414-5043 or (248)699-8069 E-mail: galeord@galegroup.com • URL: http://www.galegroup.com • 2001. $425.00. Fourth edition. Four regional volumes. $125.00 per volume. Detailed information is provided on 164 U. S. cities. Includes economic data, climate, geography, government, and history, with maps and photographs.

Cities of the World. The Gale Group, 27500 Drake Rd. Farmington Hills, MI 48331-3535. Phone: 800-877-GALE or (248)699-GALE Fax: 800-414-5043 or (248)699-8069 E-mail: galeord@galegroup.com • URL: http://www.galegroup.com • 1998. $350.00. Fifth edition. Four regional volumes. $99.00 per volume. Detailed information is provided for more than 3,407 cities in 177 countries (excluding U.S.) Includes maps and photographs. Based in U.S. State Department reports.

Citizen's Energy Council., P.O. Box U Hewitt, NJ 07421. Phone: (201)728-2322 Fax: (201)728-7664 E-mail: nonukes@canoemail.com • Concerned with hazards of nuclear power.

Citizens for a Sound Economy.

Citizens for a Tobacco-Free Society., 8660 Lynnehaven Dr. Cincinnati, OH 45236. Phone: (513)677-6666 E-mail: antismoking@aol.com • Supports a ban on smoking in enclosed public places, including work places.

Citizens for Public Action on Blood Pressure and Cholesterol.

Citizen's Guide on Using the Freedom of Information Act and the Privacy Act of 1974 to Request Government Records. U. S. Government Printing Office, Washington, DC 20402. Phone: (202)512-1800 Fax: (202)512-2250 E-mail: gpoaccess@gpo.gov • URL: http://www.access.gpo.gov • 1997. $5.00.

Citizen's Guide to the Federal Budget. Available from U. S. Government Printing Office, Washington, DC 20402. Phone: (202)512-1800 Fax: (202)512-2250 E-mail: gpoaccess@gpo.gov • URL: http://www.access.gpo.gov • Annual. $3.25. Issued by the Office of Management and Budget, Executive Office of the President (http://www.whitehouse.gov). Provides basic data for the general public about the budget of the U. S. government.

Citizens League Research Institute.

Citrograph: Magazine of the Citrus Industry. Western Agricultural Publishing Co., Inc., 4969 E. Clinton Way, Suite 119 Fresno, CA 93727-1549. Phone: (209)252-7000 Fax: (209)252-7387 E-mail: westag2@psnw.com • Monthly. $19.95 per year. Gives produce growing tips.

Citrus Center. Texas A & M University at Kingsville

Citrus Industry Magazine. Association Publications Corp., P.O. Box 89 Bartow, FL 33831. Phone: (813)533-4114 Monthly. $20.00 per year. Gives food growing tips.

Citrus Research and Education Center, Lake Alfred. University of Florida

Citrus Research Center and Agricultural Experiment Station. University of California

City & Country Club Life: The Social Magazine for South Florida. Club Publications, Inc., 665 La Villa Dr. Miami, FL 33166. Phone: (305)887-1701 Fax: (305)885-1923 Bimonthly. $15.00 per year.

City Planning in America: Between Promise and Despair. Mary E. Hommann. Greenwood Publishing Group, Inc., 88 Post Rd., West Westport, CT 06881-5007. Phone: 800-225-5800 or (203)226-3571 Fax: (203)222-2540 E-mail: bookinfo@greenwood.com • URL: http://www.greenwood.com • 1993. $49.95.

City Profiles USA: A Traveler's Guide to Major U. S. and Canadian Cities. Darren L. Smith, editor. Omnigraphics, Inc., Penobscot Bldg. Detroit, MI 48226. Phone: 800-234-1340 or (313)961-1340 Fax: 800-875-1340 or (313)961-1383 E-mail: info@omnigraphics.com • URL: http://www.omnigraphics.com • Annual. $110.00. A directory of information useful to business and other travelers in major cities. Includes services, facilities, attractions, and events. Arranged by city.

Civil Engineering Database (CEDB). American Society of Civil Engineers, 1801 Alexander Bell Drive Reston, VA 20191-4400. Phone: 800-548-2723 or (703)295-6240 Fax: (703)295-6278 Provides abstracts of the U. S. and international literature of civil engineering, 1975 to date. Inquire as to online cost and availability.

Civil Engineering: Engineered Design and Construction. American Society of Civil Engineers, 1801 Alexander Graham Bell Dr. Reston, VA 20191-4400. Phone: 800-548-2723 or (703)295-6300 Fax: (703)295-6222 URL: http://www.asce.org • Monthly. $125.00 per year.

Civil Engineering Practice: Engineering Success By Analysis of Failure. David D. Piesold. McGraw-Hill, 1221 Ave. of the Americas New York, NY 10020-1095. Phone: 800-722-4726 or (212)904-2000 Fax: (212)904-2072 E-mail: customer.service@mcgraw-hill.com • URL: http://www.mcgraw-hill.com • 1991. $52.00.

Civil Liberties. American Civil Liberties Union, 125 Broad St., 18th Fl. New York, NY 10004. Phone: 800-775-2258 or (212)549-2500 Fax: (212)549-2646 URL: http://www.aclu.org • Annual. Membership.

Civil Liberties Under the Constitution. M. Glenn Abernathy and A. Perry Barbara. University of South Carolina Press, Carolina Plaza, 937 Assembly St., 8th Fl. Columbia, SC 29208. Phone: 800-768-2500 or (803)777-5243 Fax: (803)777-0160 E-mail: carolynm@sc.edu • URL: http://www.sc.edu.uscpress • 1993. $34.95. Sixth edition.

Civil Rights Actions. Matthew Bender & Co., Inc., Two Park Ave. New York, NY 10016. Phone: 800-223-1940 or (212)448-2000 Fax: (212)244-3188 E-mail: international@bender.com • URL: http://www.bender.com • $980.00. Seven looseleaf volumes. Semiannual updates, $661.00. Contains legal analysis of civil rights activities.

Civil Rights: State Capitals. Wakeman-Walworth, Inc., P.O. Box 7376 Alexandria, VA 22307-0376. Phone: 800-876-2545 or (703)549-8606 Fax: (703)549-1372 E-mail: newsletters@statecapitals.com • URL: http://www.statecapitals.com • Weekly. $245.00 per year. Newsletter. Includes coverage of state affirmative action programs. Formerly *From the State Capitals: Civil Rights.*

Civil Service Employees Association.

Civil Service Handbook: How to Get a Civil Service Job. Pearson Education and Technology, 201 W. 103rd St. Indianapolis, IN 46290-1094. Phone: 800-858-7674 or (317)581-3500 Fax: (317)581-4670 URL: http://www.mcp.com • 1999. $12.95. 14th edition. (Arco Civil Service Series).

CLAIMS. IFI/Plenum Data Corp., 3202 Kirkwood Hwy., Ste. 203 Wilmington, DE 19808. Phone: 800-331-4955 or (302)998-0478 Fax: (302)998-0733 URL: http://www.ifiplenum.com • Includes seven separate databases: *CLAIMS/Citation, CLAIMS/Compound Registry, CLAIMS/Comprehensive Data Base, CLAIMS/Reassignment & Reexamination, CLAIMS/Reference, CLAIMS/U. S. Patent Abstracts*, and *CLAIMS/Uniterm*. Provides extensive current and historical information on U. S. Patents. Inquire as to online cost and availability.

Claims. IW Publications, Inc., 1001 Fourth Ave. Plaza, Suite 3320 Seattle, WA 98154. Phone: (206)624-6965 Fax: (206)624-5021 URL: http://www.claimsmag.com • Monthly. $42.00 per year. Edited for insurance adjusters, risk managers, and claims professionals. Covers investigation, fraud, insurance law, and other claims-related topics.

CLAO Journal. Contact Lens Association of Ophthalmologists. Kellner/McCaffery Associates, Inc., 150 Fifth Ave. New York, NY 10011. Phone: (212)741-0280 Quarterly. $76.00 per year. Formerly *Contact and Intraocular Lens Medical Journal*. Provides scientific reports on contact lenses and cornea.

Classified Directory of Artists' Signatures, Symbols, and Monograms. H. H. Caplan, editor. Dealer's Choice Books, Inc., P.O. Box 710 Land O' Lakes, FL 34639. Phone: 800-238-8288 or (813)996-6599 Fax: (813)996-5226 E-mail: booksales@art-amer.com • URL: http://www.art-amer.copy.com • 1982. $125.00. Second edition. American artists.

Clay Mineralogy. M. J. Wilson. John Wiley and Sons, Inc., 605 Third Ave. New York, NY 10158-0012. Phone: 800-842-3636 or (212)850-6000 Fax: (212)850-6088 E-mail: info@wiley.com • URL: http://www.wiley.com • 1992. $105.00.

Clay Minerals Society.

Clays and Clay Minerals. Clay Minerals Society, P.O. Box 460130 Aurora, CO 80046. Phone: (303)444-6405 E-mail: orders@allenpress.com • URL: http://www.shadow.agry.purdue.edu • Bimonthly. $195.00 per year.

Clean Coal-Synfuels Letter. McGraw-Hill, 1221 Ave. of the Americas New York, NY 10020-1095. Phone: 800-722-4726 or (212)904-2000 Fax: (212)904-2072 E-mail: customer.service@mcgraw-hill.com • URL: http://www.mcgraw-hill.com • Weekly. $840.00 per year. Newsletter. Formerly *Synfuels*.

Cleaning Business: Published Monthly for the Self-Employed Cleaning and Maintenance Professionals. William R. Griffin, Publisher, P.O. Box 1273 Seattle, WA 98111-1273. Phone: (206)622-4241 Fax: (206)622-6876 E-mail: wgriffin@cleaningconsultants.com • URL: http://www.cleaningconsultants.com • Monthly. $20.00 per year. Formerly *Service Business*

CLEAR News. Council on Licensure, Enforcement, and Regulation, Council of State Governments, P.O. Box 11910 Lexington, KY 40578-1910. Phone: 800-800-1910 or (606)244-8000 Fax: (606)244-8001 E-mail: info@csg.org • URL: http://www.csg.com • Quarterly. Price on application. Newsletter on occupational and professional licenses and licensing.

Clearance and Copyright: Everything the Independent Filmmaker Needs to Know. Michael C. Donaldson. Silman-James Press, 3624 Shannon Rd. Los Angeles, CA 90027. Phone: (323)661-9922 Fax: (323)661-9933 E-mail: ghfeldman@earthlink.net • 1996. $26.95. Covers film rights problems in pre-production, production, post-production, and final release. Includes sample contracts and forms.

Clearing Land Titles. West Publishing Co., College and School Div., 610 Opperman Dr. Eagan, MN 55123. Phone: 800-328-4880 or (651)687-7000 Fax: 800-213-2323 or (651)687-5827 E-mail: legal_ed@westgroup.com • URL: http://www.lawschool.westgroup.com • Second edition. Price on application.

Click Here! Internet Advertising: How the Pros Attract, Design, Price, Place, and Measure Ads Online. Eugene Marlow. John Wiley and Sons, Inc., 605 Third Ave. New York, NY 10158-0012. Phone: 800-842-3636 or (212)850-6000 Fax: (212)850-6088 E-mail: info@wiley.com • URL: http://www.wiley.com • 1997. $29.95. Covers pricing, effectiveness, Web site selection, content, and other aspects of Internet advertising. (Business Technology Series).

Climates of the States. The Gale Group, 27500 Drake Rd. Farmington Hills, MI 48331-3535. Phone: 800-877-GALE or (248)699-GALE Fax: 800-414-5043 or (248)699-8069 E-mail: galeord@galegroup.com • URL: http://www.galegroup.com • 1998. $245.00. Fourth edition. Two volumes. State-by-state summaries of climatebased on first order weather reporting stations.

Clin-Alert. Technomic Publishing Co. Inc., 851 New Holland Ave. Lancaster, PA 17604. Phone: 800-223-9936 or (717)291-5609 Fax: (717)295-4538 E-mail: marketing@techpub.com • URL: http://www.techpub.com • 24 times a year. $155.00 per year for print or electronic edition; $175.00 per year for print and electronics edition. Newsletter. Contains current abstracts of drug adverse reactions and interactions reported in over 600 medical journals. Includes quarterly cumulative indexes.

Clinical Lab Letter. Lippincott Williams and Wilkins, Publishers, 227 E. Washington Square Philadelphia, PA 19106-3780. Phone: 800-777-2295 or (215)238-4200 Fax: (215)238-4227 URL: http://www.lrpub.com • 22 times a year. Individuals, $327.00 per year; institutions, $409.00 per year. Newsletter on clinical laboratory management, safety, and technology.

Clinical Laboratory Management Association., 989 Old Eagle School Rd., Suite 815 Wayne, PA 19087. Phone: (610)995-9580 Fax: (610)995-9568 URL: http://www.clma.org • Members are individuals who manage or supervise clinical laboratories.

Clinical Laboratory Management Review. Clinical Laboratory Management Association. Williams & Wilkins, 351 W. Camden St. Baltimore, MD 21201-2436. Phone: 800-572-5597 or (410)528-4000 Fax: (410)528-4422 E-mail: custserv@wilkins.com • URL: http://www.wwilkins.com • Bimonthly. Individuals, $106.00 per year; institutions, $143.00 per year.

Close Corporations: Law and Practice. Little, Brown and Co., Time and Life Bldg., 1271 Ave. of the Americas New York, NY 10020. Phone: 800-343-9024 or 800-522-8700 Fax: 800-286-9741 or (212)522-2067 E-mail: cust.service@littlebrown.com • URL: http://www.littlebrown.com • $350.00. Two volumes. Volume one $175.00; volume two, $175.00. Periodic supplementation. Covers family and other closely held corporations.

Closed-End Fund Digest. Morningstar, Inc., 225 W. Walker Dr., Ste. 400 Chicago, IL 60606. Phone: (312)696-6000 Fax: (312)696-6001 Monthly. $195.00 per year. Newsletter. Provides news and statistical information for approximately 500 closed-end investment funds. Includes recommendations of specific funds.

Clothing Manufacturers of the U.S.A.

CLR (Clinical Laboratory Reference). Medical Laboratory Observer. Medical Economics Co., Inc., Five Paragon Dr. Montvale, NJ 07645-1742. Phone: 800-232-7379 or (201)358-7200 Fax: (201)573-8999 E-mail: customerservice@medec.com • URL: http://www.medec.com • Annual. $32.00. Describes diagnostic reagents, test systems, instruments, equipment, and services for medical laboratories. Includes ''Directory of Diagnostic Marketers'' and ''Index of Tests, Equipment, and Services.''

Club Director. National Club Association, One Lafayette Center, 1120 20th St., N.W., Suite 725 Washington, DC 20036. Phone: (202)822-9822 Fax: (202)822-9808 URL: http://www.natlclub.org • Six times a year. $18.00 per year. Magazine for directors, owners and managers of private clubs.

Club Industry: Buyers Guide. Intertec Publishing Corp., Sport/Fitness Div., 1300 Virginia Dr., Suite 400 Fort Washington, PA 19034-3221. Phone: 800-400-5945 or (215)643-8000 Fax: (215)643-8099 E-mail: subs@intertec.com • URL: http://www.intertec.com • Annual. $25.00. A directory of over 1,000 companies furnishing equipment, supplies, and services to health and fitness clubs.

Club Management: The Resource for Successful Club Operations. Club Managers Association of America. Finan Publishing Co., 8730 Big Bend Blvd. Saint Louis, MO 63119. Phone: (314)961-6644 Fax: (314)961-4809 E-mail: teri@finan.com • URL: http://www.club-mgmt.com • Bimonthly. $21.95 per year.

Club Managers Association of America.

Club Manager's Guide to Private Parties and Club Functions. Joe Perdue and others. John Wiley and Sons, Inc., 605 Third Ave. New York, NY 10158-0012. Phone: 800-225-5945 or (212)850-6000 Fax: (212)850-6088 E-mail: info@jwiley.com • URL: http://www.wiley.com • 1998. $49.95. Covers on-premises catering at clubs, including member relations, meal functions, beverage functions, room setup, staffing, etc.

Club, Recreation, and Sport Management. Tom Sawyer and Owen Smith. Sagamore Publishing, Inc., 804 N. Neil St., Suite 100 Champaign, IL 61820-3015. Phone: 800-327-5557 or (217)359-5940 Fax: (217)359-5975 E-mail: sagamore@prairienet.org • URL: http://www.sportspublishinginc.com • 1998. $44.95.

Clubs in Town and Country. Pannell Kerr Forster, 5845 Richmond Highway Alexandria, VA 22303. Phone: (703)329-1952 URL: http://www.pkf.com • Annual. $50.00. Provides financial statistics and other information relating to city clubs and country clubs of different sizes in various areas of the U. S.

CMAA Yearbook. Club Managers Association of America, 1733 King St. Alexandria, VA 22314. Phone: (703)739-9500 Fax: (703)739-0124 E-mail: cmaa@cmaa.org • URL: http://www.cmaa.org • Annual. Membership directory

Co-op Advertising Programs Sourcebook. R. R. Bowker, 121 Chanlon Rd. New Providence, NJ 07974. Phone: 800-521-8110 or (908)464-6800 Fax: (908)771-7704 E-mail: info@bowker.com • URL: http://www.reedref.com • Semiannual. $499.00 per year. Lists 5,000 cooperative advertising programs offered by manufacturers. Formerly *Co-op Source Directory*.

Coal Age. Intertec Publishing Corp., P.O. Box 12901 Overland Park, KS 66282-2901. Phone: 800-400-5945 or (913)341-1300 Fax: (913)967-1898 E-mail: subs@

intertec.com • URL: http://www.coalage.com • Monthly. Free to qualified personnel; others, $36.00 per year. Formerly *Coal*.

Coal and Modern Coal Processing: An Introduction. G.J. Pitt and G.R. Milward, editors. Academic Press, Inc., 525 B St., Suite 1900 San Diego, CA 92101-4495. Phone: 800-321-5068 or (619)230-1840 Fax: (619)699-6715 E-mail: ap@acad.com • URL: http://www.academicpress.com • 1979. $73.00.

Coal Facts. National Mining Association, 1130 17th St., N.W. Washington, DC 20036-4677. Phone: (202)463-2625 Fax: (202)463-6152 E-mail: rlawson@nma.org • URL: http://www.nma.org • Annual. $15.00.

The Coal Industry in America: Bibliography and Guide to Studies. Robert F. Munn. West Virginia University Press, P.O. Box 6069 Morgantown, WV 26506. Phone: (304)293-5267 Fax: (304)293-6638 E-mail: vlinger@wvu.edu • 1977. $12.50. Second edition.

Coal Information. OECD Publications and Information Center, OECD Washington Center, 2001 L St., N.W.,Suite 650 Washington, DC 20036-4922. Phone: 800-456-6323 or (202)785-6323 Fax: (202)785-0350 E-mail: washington.contact@oecd.org • URL: http://www.oecd.org • Annual. $200.00. A yearly report on world coal market trends and prospects.

The Coal Leader: Dedicated to Public Awareness and Understanding in the Mine Industry. National Independent Coal Operators Association, P.O. Box 858 Richlands, VA 24641-0858. Phone: (540)963-2779 URL: http://www.coalleader.com • Monthly. $18.00 per year. Formerly *National Coal Leader*.

Coal Liquefaction Fundamentals. Darrell Duayne Whitehurst, editor. American Chemical Society, 1155 16th St., N.W. Washington, DC 20036. Phone: 800-333-9511 or (202)872-4600 Fax: (202)872-4615 E-mail: service@acs.org • URL: http://www.pubs.acs.org • 1980. $49.95. (ACS Symposium Series: No. 139).

Coal Outlook. Pasha Publishing, 1600 Wilson Blvd. Arlington, VA 22209. Phone: 800-424-2908 or (703)528-1244 Fax: (703)528-4926 Weekly. $1,097.00 per year.

Coal Research Center. Southern Illinois University at Carbondale

Coal Transportation Statistics. National Mining Association, 1130 17th St. N.W. Washington, DC 20036-4677. Phone: (202)463-2625 Fax: (202)463-6152 E-mail: rlawson@nma.org • URL: http://www.nma.org • Annual. Non-profit organizations, $25.00; others, $35.00. Formerly *Coal Traffic Annual*.

Coal Week. McGraw-Hill Energy and Business Newsletter, 1221 Ave. of the Americas New York, NY 10020-1095. Phone: 800-722-4726 or (212)904-2000 Fax: (212)904-2072 E-mail: customer.service@mcgraw-hill.com • URL: http://www.mcgraw-hill.com • Weekly. $912.00 per year. Newsletter. Edited as "a weekly intelligence report for executives in the coal industry and peripheral operations." Covers prices, markets, politics, and coal economics.

Coal Week International. McGraw-Hill, Chemical Engineering Div., 1221 Ave. of the Americas New York, NY 10020-1095. Phone: 800-722-4726 or (212)904-2000 Fax: (212)904-2000 E-mail: customer.service@mcgraw-hill.com • URL: http://www.mcgraw-hill.com • Weekly. $1,186.00 per year. Newsletter. Covers international trade in various types of coal, including prices, production, markets, regulation, research, and synthetic fuels. (Energy and Business Newsletters.)

Coalition for Uniform Product Liability Law., 1023 15th St., 7th Fl. Washington, DC 20005. Phone: (202)289-1780 Fax: (202)842-3275 Lobbies for a uniform federal product liability law.

Coalition of Higher Education Assistance Organizations., 1101 Vermont Ave., N.W., Suite 400 Washington, DC 20005. Phone: (202)289-3910 Fax: (202)371-0197 URL: http://www.coheao.com • Purpose is to support student loan programs and monitor regulations.

Coalition of Labor Union Women.

Coast Guard Reservist. Commandant, U.S. Coast Guard, 400 7th St., S.W. Washington, DC 20590. Phone: (202)267-1991 Fax: (202)267-4553 Monthly. Free.

Coast Guardsman's Manual. George E. Krietmeyer. Naval Institute Press, Beach Hall, 291 Wood Rd. Annapolis, MD 21402. Phone: 800-223-8764 or (410)268-6110 Fax: (410)295-1084 E-mail: customer@usni.org • URL: http://www.nip.org • 2000. $21.95. Ninth edition.

Coatings. National Paint and Coatings Association, 1500 Rhode Island Ave, N.W. Washington, DC 20005. Phone: (202)462-6272 Fax: (202)462-8549 E-mail: npca@paint.org • URL: http://www.paint.org • 10 times a year. $62.00 per year.

Coatings. Roger Media Publishing Ltd., Magazine Div., 777 Bay St., 6th Fl. Tronto, ON, Canada M5W 1A7. Phone: (905)844-9773 Fax: (905)844-5672 URL: http://www.coatingsmagazine.com • Bimonthly. $75.00 per year.

Coatings-Protective Directory. American Business Directories, P.O. Box 27347 Omaha, NE 68127. Phone: 800-555-6124 or (402)593-4600 Fax: (402)331-5481 E-mail: internet@infousa.com • URL: http://www.abii.com • Annual. Price on application. Lists about 3,095 sources of corrosion control protective coatings. Includes number of employees and name of manager or owner.

Cocoa Merchants' Association of America.

Code of Federal Regulations. Office of the Federal Register, U.S. General Services Administration. Available from U.S. Government Printing Office, Washington, DC 20402. Phone: (202)512-1800 Fax: (202)512-2250 E-mail: gpoaccess@gpo.gov • URL: http://www.access.gpo.gov • $1,094.00 per year. Complete service.

Codes of Professional Responsibility: Ethic Standards in Business, Health and Law. Rena Gorlin, editor. Bureau of National Affairs, Inc., 1231 25th St., N. W. Washington, DC 20037-1197. Phone: 800-372-1033 or (202)452-4200 Fax: (202)452-4062 E-mail: books@bna.com • URL: http://www.bna.com • 1998. $95.00. Fourth edition. Contains full text or substantial excerpts of the official codes of ethics of major professional groups in the fields of law, business, and health care.

Coffee and Cocoa International. DMG Business Media Ltd. International Trade Publications Ltd., Queensway House, Two Queensway, Redhill Redhill, Surrey RH1 1QS, England. Phone: (44-)1737-855485 Fax: (44-)1737-855470 URL: http://www.dmg.co.uk • Seven times a year. $185.00 per year.

Coffee and Tea Market. MarketResearch.com, 641 Ave. of the Americas, Third Floor New York, NY 10011. Phone: 800-298-5699 or (212)807-2629 Fax: (212)807-2716 E-mail: order@marketresearch.com • URL: http://www.marketresearch.com • 1999. $2,750.00. Market data with forecasts to 2004. Covers many types of coffee and tea.

Coffee and Tea Store. Entrepreneur Media, Inc., 2445 McCabe Way Irvine, CA 92614. Phone: 800-421-2300 or (949)261-2325 Fax: (949)261-0234 E-mail: entmag@entrepreneur.com • URL: http://www.entrepreneur.com • Looseleaf. $59.50. A practical guide to starting a coffee and tea store. Covers profit potential, start-up costs, market size evaluation, owner's time required, site selection, lease negotiation, pricing, accounting, advertising, promotion, etc. (Start-Up Business Guide No. E1202.)

Coffee Intelligence. Coffee Publications, P.O. Box 1315 Stamford, CT 06904. Phone: (203)969-2107 Fax: (203)327-5343 Monthly. $95.00 per year. Provides trade information for the coffee industry.

The Coffee Reporter. National Coffee Association of U.S.A Inc., 15 Maiden Lane, Suite 1405 New York, NY 10038-4003. Phone: (212)344-5596 Weekly. $65.00 per year.

Coffee, Sugar and Cocoa Exchange.

Cognitive Science Society.

Coin Dealer Newsletter., P.O. Box 7939 Torrance, CA 90504. Phone: (310)515-7369 Fax: (310)515-7534 Weekly. $98.00 per year. Newsletter for dealers and investors covering U. S. coins from 1793 to the present. Provides current prices, information, and market analysis.

Coin Launderer and Cleaner. Sheidko Corp., 4512 Lindenwood Lane Northbrook, IL 60062-1034. Phone: (708)272-8490 Monthly. $25.00 per year.

Coin Laundry Association.

The Coin Laundry Association Supplier Directory. Coin Laundry Association, 1315 Butterfield Rd., Suite 212 Downers Grove, IL 60515. Phone: 877-252-4332 or (630)963-5547 Fax: (630)963-5864 E-mail: info@coinlaundry.org • URL: http://www.coinlaundry.org • Annual. $30.00. Lists sources of equipment, supplies, and services for coin-operated laundries.

Coin Prices. Krause Publications, Inc., 700 E. State St. Iola, WI 54990. Phone: 800-258-0929 or (715)445-2214 Fax: (715)445-4087 E-mail: info@krause.com • URL: http://www.krause.com/ • Bimonthly. $18.95 per year. Gives current values of U. S. coins.

Coin World. Amos Press, Inc., P.O. Box 150 Sidney, OH 45365. Phone: 800-253-4555 or (937)498-0800 Fax: (937)498-0812 E-mail: cweditor@amospress.com • URL: http://www.coinworld.com • Weekly. $29.95 per year.

Coin Yearbook. Numismatic Publishing Co., Sovereign House, Brentwood Essex CM14 4SE, England. Annual. Price on application.

Coinage. Miller Magazines, Inc., 4880 Market St. Ventura, CA 93003-2888. Phone: (805)644-3824 Monthly. $23.00 per year.

Coins. Krause Publications, Inc., 700 E. State St. Iola, WI 54990. Phone: 800-258-0929 or (715)445-2214 Fax: (715)445-4087 E-mail: info@krause.com • URL: http://www.krause.com/ • Monthly. $25.98 per year.

Collaboratory for Research on Electronic Work., University of Michigan, 1075 Beal Ave. Ann Arbor, MI 48109-2112. Phone: (734)647-4948 Fax: (734)936-3168 E-mail: finholt@umich.edu • URL: http://crew.umich.edu/ • Concerned with the design and use of computer-based tools for thinking and planning in the professional office.

Collaboratory for Research on Electronic Work., University of Michigan, 1075 Beal Ave. Ann Arbor, MI 48109-2112. Phone: (734)647-4948 Fax: (734)936-3168 E-mail: finholt@umich.edu • URL: http://crew.umich.edu/ • Concerned with the design and use of computer-based tools for thinking and planning in the professional office.

Collectibles Broker. Entrepreneur Media, Inc., 2445 McCabe Way Irvine, CA 92614. Phone: 800-421-2300 or (949)261-2325 Fax: (949)261-0234 E-mail: entmag@entrepreneur.com • URL: http://www.entrepreneur.com • Looseleaf. $59.50. A practical guide to starting a brokerage service for collectibles. Covers profit potential, start-up costs, market size evaluation, owner's time required, pricing, accounting, advertising, promotion, etc. (Start-Up Business Guide No. E1360.)

Collection Agency. Entrepreneur Media, Inc., 2445 McCabe Way Irvine, CA 92614. Phone: 800-421-2300 or (949)261-2325 Fax: (949)261-0234 E-mail: entmag@entrepreneur.com • URL: http://www.entrepreneur.com • Looseleaf. $59.50. A practical guide to starting a collection agency. Covers profit potential, start-up costs, market size evaluation, owner's time required, pricing, accounting, advertising, promotion, etc. (Start-Up Business Guide No. E1207.)

Collection Management: A Quarterly Journal Devoted to the Management of Library Collections. Haworth Press, Inc., 10 Alice St. Binghamton, NY 13904-1580. Phone: 800-429-6784 or (607)722-5857 Fax: 800-895-0582 or (607)722-1424 E-mail: getinfo@haworthpressinc.com • URL: http://www.haworthpressinc.com • Quarterly. Individuals, $60.00 per year; institutions, $150.00 per year; libraries, $150.00 per year.

Collections and Credit Risk: The Monthly Magazine for Collections and Credit Policy Professionals. Faulkner & Gray, Inc., 300 S. Wacker Dr., 18th Fl. Chicago, IL 60606. Phone: 800-535-8403 or (312)913-1334 Fax: (312)913-1959 E-mail: order@faulknergray.com • URL: http://www.ccr.faulknergray.com • Monthly. $95.00 per year. Contains articles on the technology and business management of credit and collection functions. Includes coverage of bad debts, bankruptcy, and credit risk management.

Collective Bargaining and Labor. Terry L. Leap. Prentice Hall, 240 Frisch Court Paramus, NJ 07652-5240. Phone: 800-947-7700 or (201)909-6200 Fax: 800-445-6991 or (201)909-6361 URL: http://www.prenhall.com • 1994. $90.00. Second edition.

Collective Bargaining and Labor Relations. E. Edward Herman. Prentice Hall, 240 Frisch Court Paramus, NJ 07652-5240. Phone: 800-947-7700 or (201)909-6200 Fax: 800-445-6991 or (201)909-6361 URL: http://www.prenhall.com • 1997. $87.00. Fourth edition.

Collective Bargaining by Objectives: A Positive Approach. Reed C. Richardson. Prentice Hall, 240 Frisch Court Paramus, NJ 07652-5240. Phone: 800-947-7700 or (201)909-6200 Fax: 800-445-6991 or (201)909-6361 URL: http://www.prenhall.com • 1977. $18.95. Second edition.

Collective Bargaining Negotiations and Contracts. Bureau of National Affairs, Inc., 1231 25th St., N.W. Washington, DC 20037-1197. Phone: 800-372-1033 or (202)452-4200 Fax: (202)822-8092 E-mail: books@bna.com • URL: http://www.bna.com • Biweekly. $1,056.00. Two volumes. Looseleaf.

Collector. American Collectors Association, Inc., P.O. Box 39106 Minneapolis, MN 55435. Phone: (612)926-6547 Fax: (612)926-1624 E-mail: aca@collector.com • Monthly. Members, $30.00 per year; non-members, $60.00 per year. Provides news and education in the field of credit and collections.

College Admissions: A Selected Annotated Bibliography. Linda Sparks, compiler. Greenwood Publishing Group, Inc., 88 Post Rd., W. Westport, CT 06881-5007. Phone: 800-225-5800 or (203)226-3571 Fax: (203)222-2540 E-mail: bookinfo@greenwood.com • URL: http://www.greenwood.com • 1993. $55.00. Describes about 1,000 professional or academic items relating to undergraduate college admissions in the United States. Topics include marketing and recruitment. (Popular guides are not included.) (Bibliographic and Indexes in Education Series, No.11).

College Admissions Data Handbook. Riverside Publishing, 425 Spring Lake Dr. Itasca, IL 60143-2079. Phone: 800-323-9540 or (630)467-7000 Fax: (630)467-6069 E-mail: rpcwebmaster@hmco.com • Annual. $195.00. Four volumes. Gives detailed admissions data for approximately $1,650.00 four year accredited colleges in the U.S. Four volumes. Looseleaf service. Single regional books are available.

College and Research Libraries (CRL). Association of College and Research Libraries. American Library Association, 50 E. Huron St. Chicago, IL 60611-2795. Phone: 800-545-2433 or (312)944-6780 Fax: (312)440-9374 E-mail: acrl@ala.org • URL: http://www.ala.org • Bimonthly. $60.00 per year. Supplement available *C and R L News*.

College and Research Libraries News. Association of College and Research Libraries. American Library Association, 50 E. Huron St. Chicago, IL 60611-2795. Phone: 800-545-2433 or (312)944-6780 Fax: (312)440-9374 E-mail: acrl@ala.org • URL: http://www.ala.org • 11 times per year. Free to members; non-members, $35.00 per year. Supplement to *College and Research Libraries*.

College and Undergraduate Libraries. Haworth Press, Inc., 10 Alice St. Binghamton, NY 13904-1580. Phone: 800-429-6784 or (607)722-5857 Fax: 800-895-0582 or (607)722-1424 E-mail: getinfo@haworthpressinc.com • URL: http://www.haworthpressinc.com • Semiannual. Individuals, $30.00 per year; libraries and other institutions, $90.00 per year. A practical journal dealing with everyday library problems.

College and University. American Association of Collegiate Registrars and Admissions Officers, One Dupont Circle, N.W., Suite 520 Washington, DC 20036-1135. Phone: (202)293-9161 Fax: (202)872-8857 E-mail: pubs@aacrao.nche.org • URL: http://www.aacrao.com • Quarterly. Free to members; non-members, $50.00 per year. Addresses issues in higher education; looks at new procedures, policies, technology; reviews new publications.

College Blue Book. Pearson Education and Technology, 201 W. 103rd St. Indianapolis, IN 46290. Phone: 800-858-7674 or (317)581-3520 Fax: (317)581-4670 URL: http://www.mcp.com • Biennial. $625.00. Five volumes. Covers 3,000 two and four year colleges and universities, professional schools in medicine, law, etc.; over 7,500 trade technical, and business schools, and community colleges; over 2,000 public and private sources of financial aid; coverage includes Canada.

College Blue Book CD-ROM. Available from The Gale Group, 27500 Drake Rd. Farmington Hills, MI 48331-3535. Phone: 800-877-GALE or (248)699-GALE Fax: 800-414-5043 or (248)699-8069 E-mail: galeord@galegroup.com • URL: http://www.galegroup.com • Annual. $250.00. Produced by Macmillan Reference USA. Serves as electronic version of printed *College Blue Book*. Provides detailed information on programs, degrees, and financial aid sources in the U.S. and Canada

The College Board.

College Board Review. College Board Publications, 45 Columbus Ave. New York, NY 10023. Phone: 800-323-7155 or (212)713-8000 Fax: (212)713-8143 URL: http://www.collegeboard.org • Quarterly. $25.00 per year.

College Facts Chart. National Beta Club, 151 W. Lee St. Spartanburg, SC 29306-3012. Phone: 800-845-8281 or (864)583-4553 Fax: (864)542-9300 E-mail: betaclub@betaclub.org • URL: http://www.betaclub.org • Annual. $7.00. Reference guide to American colleges and universities. Charts locate tuition and fee costs, telephone numbers and school size.

The College Handbook. The College Board Publications, 45 Columbus Ave. New York, NY 10023-6992. Phone: 800-323-7155 or (212)713-8000 Fax: (212)713-8309 URL: http://www.collegeboard.org • Annual. $25.95. Over 3,200 undergraduate schools.

College Media Advisors. University of Memphis

College Media Directory. Oxbridge Communications, Inc., 150 Fifth Ave., Suite 302 New York, NY 10011. Phone: 800-955-0231 or (212)741-0231 Fax: (212)633-2938 E-mail: info@mediafinder.com • URL: http://www.mediafinder.com • 1997. $245.00. Lists more than 6,000 publications from about 3,500 colleges and universities.

College Media Review. College Media Advisors. University of Memphis, c/o Dept. of Journalism Memphis, TN 38152. Phone: (901)678-2403 E-mail: rspelbrgr@cc.memphis.edu • URL: http://www.spub.ksu.edu • Quarterly. Free to members; non-members, $15.00 per year.

College Press Service.

The College Store. National Association of College Stores, 500 E. Lorain St. Oberlin, OH 44074-1298. Phone: (216)775-7777 Fax: (216)775-4769 E-mail: info@nacs.org • URL: http://www.nacs.org • Six times a year. Members, $54.00 per year; non-members, $64.00 per year. Formerly *College Store Journal*

College Store Executive. Executive Business Media, Inc., P.O.Box 1500 Westbury, NY 11590. Phone: (516)334-3030 Fax: (516)334-8958 URL: http://www.cconline.com • 10 times a year. $40.00 per year.

College Teaching: International Quarterly Journal. Helen Dwight Reid Educational Foundation. Heldref Publications, 1319 18th St., N.W. Washington, DC 20036-1802. Phone: 800-296-5149 or (202)296-6267 Fax: (202)296-5149 E-mail: orders@allenpress.com • URL: http://www.helderf.org • Quarterly. Individuals, $36.00 per year; institutions, $66.00 per year. Practical ideas, successful methods, and new programs for faculty development.

Collier Bankruptcy Practice Guide. Matthew Bender & Co., Inc., Two Park Ave. New York, NY 10016. Phone: 800-223-1940 or (212)448-2000 Fax: (212)244-3188 E-mail: international@bender.com • URL: http://www.bender.com • $1,180.00. Six looseleaf volumes. Periodic supplementation. Strategic and procedural guide for all cases instituted under the code.

Collier on Bankruptcy. Lawrence P. King and others. Matthew Bender & Co., Inc., Two Park Ave. New York, NY 10016. Phone: 800-223-1940 or (212)448-2000 Fax: (212)244-3188 E-mail: international@bender.com • URL: http://www.bender.com • $2,570.00. 16 looseleaf volumes. Periodic supplementation. Detailed discussion, by the leading bankruptcy authorities, of the Bankruptcy Code as amended.

Colombian American Association., 30 Vesey St., Rm. 506 New York, NY 10007. Phone: (212)233-7776 Fax: (212)233-7779 E-mail: andean@nyct.net • Seeks to facilitate trade and commerce between the Republic of Colombia and the U. S.

Colombian Government Trade Bureau., 277 Park Ave., 47th Fl. New York, NY 10172-4797. Phone: (212)223-1120 Fax: (212)223-1325 E-mail: proexpny@nyct.net • URL: http://www.proexport.com.co • Promotes Colombian exports to the U. S.

Color and Black and White Television Theory and Servicing. Alvin Liff and Sam Wilson. Prentice Hall, 240 Frisch Court Paramus, NJ 07652-5240. Phone: 800-947-7700 or (201)909-6200 Fax: 800-445-6991 or (201)990-6361 URL: http://wwww.prenhall.com • 1993. $97.00. Third edition.

Color Association of the United States.

Color in Business, Science, and Industry. Deane B. Judd and Gunter Wyszecki. John Wiley and Sons, Inc., 605 Third Ave. New York, NY 10158-0012. Phone: 800-225-5945 or (212)850-6000 Fax: (212)850-6088 E-mail: info@wiley.com • URL: http://www.wiley.com • 1975. $195.00. Third edition. (Pure and Applied Optics Series).

Color in the Office: Design Trends from 1950 to 1990 and Beyond. Sara O. Marberry. John Wiley & Sons, Inc., 605 Third Ave., 4th Fl. New York, NY 10158-0012. Phone: 800-225-5945 or (212)850-6000 Fax: (212)850-6088 E-mail: info@wiley.com • URL: http://www.wiley.com • 1993. $75.00. Presents past, present, and future color trends in corporate office design. Features color photographs of traditional, postmodern, and neoclassical office designs. (Architecture Series).

Color Marketing Group.

Color Pigments Manufacturers Association.

Color Publishing. PennWell Corp., Advanced Technology Div., 98 Spit Brook Rd. Nashua, NH 03062-5737. Phone: 800-331-4463 or (603)891-0123 Fax: (603)891-0539 E-mail: webmaster@pennwell.com • URL: http://www.pennwell.com • Bimonthly. $29.70 per year.

Color Research and Application. John Wiley and Sons, Inc., Journals Div., 605 Third Ave. New York, NY 10158-0012. Phone: 800-225-5945 or (212)850-6645 Fax: (212)850-6021 E-mail: info@wiley.com • URL: http://www.wiley.com • Bimonthly. Institutions, $645 per year. International coverage.

Color Science: Concepts and Methods, Quantitative Data and Formulae. Gunter Wyszecki and W.S. Stiles. John Wiley and Sons, Inc., 605 Third Ave. New York, NY 10158-0012. Phone: 800-225-5945 or (212)850-6000 Fax: (212)850-6088 E-mail: info@wiley.com • URL: http://www.wiley.com • 1982. $270.00. Second edition. (Pure and Applied Optics Series).

Colorado School of Mines.

Colorado School of Mines Quarterly Review. Colorado School of Mines Press, 1500 Illinois Golden, CO 80401-1887. Phone: (303)273-3595 Fax: (303)273-3199 E-mail: lpang@mines.edu • Quarterly. $65.00 per year. Formerly *Colorado School of Mines Quarterly*.

Columbia Gazetteer of North America. Saul B. Cohen, editor. Columbia University Press, 562 W. 113th St. New York, NY 10025. Phone: 800-944-8648 or (212)666-1000 Fax: 800-944-1844 or (212)316-9422 URL: http://www.columbiabooks.com • 2000. $250.00. Contains information on 50,000 places within the U. S., Canada, Mexico, and the Caribbean. Includes 24 pages of color maps. Provides brief descriptions of natural resources and industrial activities.

Columbia Gazetteer of the World. Saul B. Cohen, editor. Columbia University Press, 562 W. 113th St. New York, NY 10025. Phone: 800-944-8648 or (212)666-1000 Fax: 800-944-1844 or (212)316-9422 URL: http://www.columbiabooks.com • 1998. $750.00. Three volumes. Also available online (http://www.columbiagazetteer.org) and on CD-ROM.

Columbia Institute for Tele-Information., Columbia University, Columbia Business School, 3022 Broadway, Uris Hall, Suite 1A New York, NY 10027. Phone: (212)854-4222 Fax: (212)932-1471 E-mail: noam@columbia.edu • URL: http://www.vii.org • Areas of research include private and public networking, the economics of networks, pricing of network access, and economics of technology adoption in the public network.

Columbia Journalism Review. Columbia University, Graduate School of Journalism, 2950 Broadway, Journalism Bldg. New York, NY 10027. Phone: (212)854-3958 Fax: (212)854-8580 URL: http://www.cjr.org • Bimonthly. $19.95 per year. Critical review of news media.

Columbia Scholastic Press Advisors Association. Columbia University

Commerce Business Daily. Industry and Trade Administration, U.S. Department of Commerce. Available from U.S. Government Printing Office, Washington, DC 20402. Phone: (202)512-1800 Fax: (202)512-2250 Daily. Priority, $324.00 per year; non-priority, $275.00 per year. Synopsis of *U.S. Government Proposed Procurement, Sales and Contract Awards*.

Commercial and Financial Chronicle. William B. Dana Co., P.O. Box 1839 Daytona Beach, FL 32115-1839. Phone: (904)252-0230 Weekly. $140.00. per year.

Commercial Atlas and Marketing Guide. Rand McNally, 8255 N. Central Park Ave. Skokie, IL 60076-2970. Phone: 800-726-0600 or (847)329-8100 Fax: (847)673-0813 URL: http://www.randmcnally.com • Annual. $395.00. Includes maps and marketing data: population, transportation, communication, and local area business statistics. Provides information on more than 128,000 U.S. locations.

Commercial Bank Management: Producing and Selling Financial Services. Peter S. Rose. McGraw-Hill, 1221 Ave. of the Americas New York, NY 10020-1095. Phone: 800-722-4726 or (212)904-2000 Fax: (212)904-2072 E-mail: customer.service@mcgraw-hill.com • URL: http://www.mcgraw-hill.com • 1998. $88.44. Fourth edition.

Commercial Building: Tranforming Plans into Buildings. Stamats Communications, 615 5th St., S.E. Cedar Rapids, IA 52406-1888. Phone: 800-553-8878 or (319)364-6167 Fax: (319)364-4278 E-mail: inforequest@stamats.com • URL: http://www.buildings.com • Bimonthly. $48.00 per year. Edited for building contractors, engineers, and architects. Includes special features on new products, climate control, plumbing, and vertical transportation.

Commercial Carrier Journal: For Fleet Management. Cahners Business Information, Valley Forge Park Place, 1018 W. 9th Ave. King of Prussia, PA 19406. Phone: 800-695-1214 or (610)205-1000 Fax: (610)964-4512 E-mail: corporate-communications@cahners.com • URL: http://www.cahners.com • Monthly. $45.00 per year. Formerly *Chilton's CCJ*.

Commercial Chicken Production. Mack O. North. Chapman and Hall, 115 Fifth Ave., 4th Fl. New York, NY 10003-1004. Phone: 800-842-3636 or (212)260-1354 Fax: (212)260-1730 E-mail: info@chapall.com • URL: http://www.chapall.com • 1990. $79.95. Fourth edition.

Commercial Development and Marketing Association.

Commercial Finance Association.

Commercial Food Equipment Service Association.

Commercial Law Journal. Commercial Law League of America, 150 North Michigan Ave. Chicago, IL 60601. Phone: (312)781-2000 Fax: (312)782-2010 URL: http://www.clla.org • 10 times a year. $99.00 per year.

Commercial Law League of America.

Commercial Lending. George E. Ruth. American Bankers Association, 1120 Connecticut Ave., N. W. Washington, DC 20036-3971. Phone: 800-338-0626 or (202)663-5000 Fax: (202)663-7543 URL: http://www.aba.com • 1990. $57.00. Second edition. Discusses the practical aspects of commercial lending.

Commercial Lending Litigation News. LRP Publications, P.O. Box 980 Horsham, PA 19044-0980. Phone: 800-341-7874 or (215)784-9014 Fax: (215)784-9639 E-mail: custserve@lrp.com • URL: http://www.lrp.com • Biweekly. $597.00 per year. Newsletter on court decisions, settlements, significant new cases, legislation, regulation, and industry trends. Formerly *Lender Liability News*.

Commercial Lending Review. Institutional Investor, 488 Madison Ave. New York, NY 10022. Phone: (212)224-3300 Fax: (212)224-3527 E-mail: info@iijournals.com • URL: http://www.iijournals.com • Quarterly. $195.00 per year. Edited for senior-level lending officers. Includes specialized lending techniques, management issues, legal developments, and reviews of specific industries.

Commercial Refrigerator Manufacturers Association.

Commercial Review. Oregon Feed and Grain Association. Commercial Review, Inc., 2380 N.W. Roosevelt St. Portland, OR 97210-2323. Phone: (503)226-2758 Fax: (503)244-0947 Weekly. $30.00 per year.

Commission on International Affairs.

Commissioner of Patents Annual Report. U.S. Patent Office. Available from U.S. Government Printing Office, Washington, DC 20402. Phone: (202)512-1800 Fax: (202)512-2250 Annual.

Commitment-Plus Newsletter. Quality and Productivity Management Association. Pride Publications, 300 Martingdale Rd., Suite 230 Schaumburg, IL 60173. Phone: (708)619-2909 Monthly. $97.00 per year. The latest trends and developments in the behavorial sciences as they apply to business and industry. Formerly *Behavioral Sciences Newsletter*.

Committee for a Responsible Federal Budget., 220 1/2 E St., N. E. Washington, DC 20002. Phone: (202)547-4484 Fax: (202)547-4476 E-mail: crfb@aol.com • Members are corporations and others seeking to improve the federal budget process.

Committee for Economic Development.

Committee on Human Development. University of Chicago

Commline. Numeridex, Inc., P.O. Box 11000 Wheeling, IL 60090. Phone: (312)541-8840 Bimonthly. Free to qualified personnel; others, $20.00 per year. Emphasizes NC/CNC (numerically controlled and computer numerically controlled machinery).

Commodities Regulation: Fraud, Manipulation, and Other Claims. Jerry W. Markham. West Group, 610 Opperman Dr. Eagan, MN 55123. Phone: 800-328-4880 or (651)687-7000 Fax: 800-213-2323 or (651)687-5827 URL: http://www.westgroup.com • Two looseleaf volumes. $250.00. Periodic supplementation. Covers the commodity futures trading prohibitions of the Commodity Exchange Act.

Commodity Futures Law Reports. CCH, Inc., 4025 W. Peterson Ave. Chicago, IL 60646-6085. Phone: 800-248-3248 or (773)866-6000 Fax: 800-224-8299 or (773)866-3608 URL: http://www.cch.com • Semimonthly. $995.00 per year. Looseleaf service. Periodic supplementation. Includes legal aspects of financial futures and stock options trading.

Commodity Review and Outlook: 1993-94. Available from Bernan Associates, 4611-F Assembly Dr. Lanham, MD 20706-4391. Phone: 800-274-4888 or (301)459-7666 Fax: 800-865-3450 or (301)459-0056 E-mail: info@bernan.com • URL: http://www.bernan.com • Annual. Published by the Food and Agriculture Organization of the United Nations (FAO). Reviews the global outlook for over 20 commodity groups.

Commodity Trading Manual. Patrick J. Catania and others. Chicago Board of Trade, 141 W. Jackson Blvd., Suite 2210 Chicago, IL 60604-2994. Phone: 800-572-3276 or (312)435-3542 Fax: (312)341-3168 E-mail: bw0050@cbot.com • URL: http://www.cbot.com • 1993. $45.95. Revised edition. Textbook and reference manual.

Common Market Reporter. CCH, Inc., 4025 W. Peterson Ave. Chicago, IL 60646-6085. Phone: 800-248-3248 or (773)583-8500 Fax: 800-224-8299 or (773)866-3608 URL: http://www.cch.com • $1,070.00 per year, including weekly *Euromarket News*. Looseleaf service. Four volumes. Periodic supplementation.

Common Sense on Mutual Funds: New Imperatives for the Intelligent Investor. John C. Bogle. John Wiley and Sons, Inc., 605 Third Ave. New York, NY 10158-0012. Phone: 800-225-5945 or (212)850-6000 Fax: (212)850-6088 E-mail: info@jwiley.com • URL: http://www.wiley.com • 1999. $24.95. Provides practical, conservative advice for the average investor. Topics include asset allocation, index funds, global investing, fund selection, and taxes.

Common Stock Newspaper Abbreviations and Trading Symbols. Howard R. Jarrell. Scarecrow Press, Inc., 4720 Boston Way Lanham, MD 20706-4310. Phone: 800-462-6420 or (301)459-3366 Fax: 800-338-4550 or (301)459-1705 E-mail: orders@scarecrowpress.com • URL: http://www.scarecrowpress.com • 1989. $55.00. Gives the meanings of financial page company name abbreviations and stock symbols.

Common Stock Newspaper Abbreviations and Trading Symbols: Supplement One. Howard R. Jarrell. Scarecrow Press, Inc., 4720 Boston Way Lanham, MD 20706. Phone: 800-462-6420 or (301)459-3366 Fax: 800-338-4550 or (301)459-1705 E-mail: orders@scarecrowpress.com • URL: http://www.scarecrowpress.com • 1991. $35.00. Provides changes and new listings occurring since the publication of Jarrell's original volume in 1989.

A Commonsense Guide to Your 401(k). Mary Rowland. Available from W.W. Norton and Co., Inc., 500 Fifth Ave. New York, NY 10110-0017. Phone: 800-223-2584 or (212)354-5500 Fax: (212)869-0856 E-mail: webmaster@wwnorton.com • URL: http://www.norton.com • 1997. $19.95. Explains how to use a 401(k) plan as a foundation for financial planning. (Bloomberg Personal Bookshelf Series.)

Communicating with Legal Databases: Terms and Abbreviations for the Legal Researcher. Anne L. McDonald. Neal-Schuman Publishers, Inc., 100 Varick St. New York, NY 10013. Phone: (212)925-8650 Fax: 800-584-2414 or (212)219-8916 E-mail: info@neal-schuman.com • URL: http://www.neal-schuman.com • 1987. $82.50.

Communication Abstracts. Sage Publications, Inc., 2455 Teller Rd. Thousand Oaks, CA 91320. Phone: (805)499-0721 Fax: (805)499-0871 E-mail: info@sagepub.com • URL: http://www.sagepub.com • Bimonthly. Individuals, $185.00 per year; institutions, $805.00 per year. Provides broad coverage of the literature of communications, including broadcasting and advertising.

Communication Booknotes Quarlterly : Recent Titles in Telecommunications, Informmation, and Media. Lawrence Erlbaum Associates, Inc., 10 Industrial Ave. Mahwah, NJ 07430-2262. Phone: 800-926-6579 or (201)236-9500 Fax: (201)236-0072 E-mail: journals@erlbaum.com • URL: http://www.members.icsi.berkeley.edu • Bimonthly. Individuals, $45.00 per year; institutions, $95.00 per year. Contains descriptive reviews of new publications. Formerly *Mass Media Booknotes*.

Communication Briefings: A Monthly Idea Source for Decision Makers. Briefings Publishing Group, 1101 King St., Suite 110 Alexandria, VA 22314. Phone: 800-888-2084 or (703)548-3800 Fax: (703)648-2136 E-mail: customerservice@briefings.com • URL: http://www.briefings.com • Monthly. $100.00 per year. Newsletter. Presents useful ideas for communication, public relations, customer service, human resources, and employee training.

Communication Equipment, and Other Electronic Systems and Equipment. U. S. Bureau of the Census, Washington, DC 20233-0800. Phone: (301)457-4100 Fax: (301)457-3842 URL: http://www.census.gov • Annual. Provides data on shipments: value, quantity, imports, and exports. (Current Industrial Reports, MA-36P.)

Communication Research. Sage Publications, Inc., 2455 Teller Rd. Thousand Oaks, CA 91320. Phone: (805)499-0721 Fax: (805)499-0871 E-mail: info@sagepub.com • URL: http://www.sagepub • Bimonthly. Individuals, $85.00 per year; institutions, $450.00 per year.

Communication Technology Update. Butterworth-Heinemann, 225 Wildwood Ave. Woburn, MA 01801. Phone: 800-366-2665 or (781)904-2500 Fax: 800-446-6520 E-mail: orders@bhusa.com • URL: http://www.bh.com • Annual. $36.95. Reviews technological developments and statistical trends in five key areas: mass media, computers, consumer electronics, communications satellites, and telephony. Includes television, cellular phones, and the Internet. (Focal Press.)

Communication Technology Update. Focal Press, 313 Washington St. Newton, MA 02158. Phone: 800-366-2665 or (617)928-2500 Fax: 800-446-6520 or (617)933-6333 E-mail: orders@repp.com • URL: http://www.bh.com/fp • Annual. $32.95. A yearly review of developments in electronic media, telecommunications, and the Internet.

Communication World: The Magazine for Communication Professionals. International Association of Business Communicators, One Hallidie Plaza, Suite 600 San Francisco, CA 94102. Phone: (415)544-4700 Fax: (415)544-4747 E-mail: ggordon@iabc.com • URL: http://www.iabc.com • 10 times a year. Libraries, $95.00 per year. Emphasis is on public relations, media relations, corporate communication, and writing.

Communication Yearbook. International Communication Association, P.O. Box 9589 Austin, TX 78766. Phone: (512)454-8299 Fax: (512)451-6270 E-mail: icahdq@uts.cc.utexas.edu • URL: http://www.icahdq.org • Annual. $49.95.

Communications and Information Processing Group., Rensselaer Polytechnic Institute, Electrical, Computer, and Systems Engineering Dept. Troy, NY 12180-3590. Phone: (518)276-6823 Fax: (518)276-6261 E-mail: modestino@ipl.rpi.edu • URL: http://www.rpi.edu • Includes Optical Signal Processing Laboratory and Speech Processing Laboratory.

Communications and Signal Processing Laboratory. University of Michigan

Communications Daily: The Authoritative News Service of Electronic Communications. Warren Publishing Inc., 2115 Ward Court, N. W. Washington, DC 20037-1209. Phone: 800-771-9202 or (202)872-9200 Fax: (202)293-3435 E-mail: customerservice@warren-news.com • URL: http://www.telecommunications.com • Daily. $3,006.00 per year. Newsletter. Covers telecommunications, including the telephone industry, broadcasting, cable TV, satellites, data communications, and electronic publishing. Features corporate and industry news.

Communications Industries Report. International Communications Industries Association, 11242 Waples Mill Rd., Suite 200 Fairfax, VA 22030-6079. Phone: 800-659-7469 or (703)273-7200 Fax: (703)278-8082 Monthly. Free.

Communications Media Management Association.

Communications News. American Society of Association Executives Communications Section, 1575 Eye St., N.W. Washington, DC 20005-1168. Phone: (202)626-2723 Fax: (202)371-8825 E-mail: asea@aseanet.org • URL: http://www.asaenet.org • Monthly. Membership.

Communications News: Solutions for Today's Networking Decision Managers. Nelson Publishing, Inc., 2500 Tamiami Trail N. Nokomis, FL 34275. Phone: (941)966-9521 Fax: (941)966-2590 E-mail: cn@nelsonpub.com • URL: http://www.comnews.com • Monthly. Free to qualified personnel; others, $79.00 per year. Includes coverage of "Internetworking" and "Intrenetworking." Emphasis is on emerging telecommunications technologies.

Communications Outlook. OECD Publications and Information Center, 2001 L St., N.W., Ste. 650 Washington, DC 20036-4922. Phone: 800-456-6323 or (202)785-6323 Fax: (202)785-0350 E-mail: washington.contact@oecd.org • URL: http://www.oecdwash.org • Annual. $65.00. Provides international coverage of yearly telecommunications activity. Includes charts, graphs, and maps.

Communications/Systems Equipment Design. McGraw-Hill

Communities: Journal of Cooperative Living. Fellowship for International Communities, PO Box 155 Rutledge, MO 63563. E-mail: communities@ic.org • URL: http://www.ic.org • Monthly. $18.00 per year.

Community and Junior College Libraries: The Journal for Learning Resources Centers. Haworth Press, Inc., 10 Alice St. Binghamton, NY 13904-1580. Phone: 800-429-6784 or (607)722-5857 Fax: 800-895-0582 or (607)722-1424 E-mail: getinfo@haworthpressinc.com • URL: http://www.haworthpressinc.com • Semiannual. Individuals, $34.00 per year; institutions, $60.00 per year.

Community Associations Institute., 1630 Duke St. Alexandria, VA 22314. Phone: (703)548-8600 Fax: (703)684-1581 URL: http://www.caionline.org • Members are condominium associations, homeowners associations, builders, property managers, developers, and others concerned with the common facilities and services in condominiums, townhouses, planned unit developments, and other planned communities.

The Community Bank President. Siefer Consultants, Inc., P.O. Box 1384 Storm Lake, IA 50588. Phone: (712)732-7340 Fax: (712)732-7906 E-mail: siefer@ncn.net • Monthly. $329.00 per year.

Community College Journal. American Association of Community and Junior Colleges, One Dupont Circle, N.W., Suite 410 Washington, DC 20036-1176. Phone: (202)728-0200 Fax: (202)223-9390 E-mail: cgamble@aacc.nche.edu • URL: http://www.aacc.nche.edu • Bimonthly. $28.00 per year. Formerly *Community, Technical and Junior College Journal*.

Community College Review. Dept. of Adult and Community College Education. North Carolina State University, P.O. Box 7801 Raleigh, NC 27695-7801. Phone: (919)515-6248 Fax: (919)515-4039 E-mail: barbara__scott@nscu.edu • URL: http://www.ncsu.edu/ • Quarterly. $55.00 per year.

Community College Week: The Independent Voice Serving Community, Technical and Junior Colleges. Cox, Matthews & Associates, 10520 Warwick Ave., Suite B-8 Fairfax, VA 22030. Phone: (703)385-2981 Fax: (703)385-1839 URL: http://www.ccw.com • Biweekly. $40.00 per year. Covers a wide variety of current topics relating to the administration and operation of community colleges.

Community Development Digest: Semimonthly Development, Planning, Infrastructure, Financing. Community Services Development, Inc. C D Publications, 8204 Fenton St. Silver Springs, MD 20910-2889. Phone: (301)588-6380 Fax: (301)588-6385 E-mail: cdpubs@clark.net • Semimonthly. $423.00 per year. Newsletter.

Community Development Society.

Community Journal. Community Service, Inc., P.O. Box 243 Yellow Springs, OH 45387. Phone: (937)767-2161 Fax: (937)767-2826 E-mail: communityservice@usa.net • Quarterly. $25.00 per year.

The Community Orchestra: A Handbook for Conductors, Managers and Boards. James Van Horn. Greenwood Publishing Group Inc., 88 Post Rd., W. Westport, CT 06881-5007. Phone: 800-225-5800 or (203)226-3571 Fax: (203)222-2540 E-mail: bookinfo@greenwood.com • URL: http://www.greenwood.com • 1979. $49.95.

Community Pharmacist: Meeting the Professional and Educational Needs of Today's Practitioner. ELF Publicatons, Inc., 5285 W. Louisiana Ave., Suite 112 Lakewood, CO 80232. Phone: 800-922-8513 or (303)975-0075 Fax: (303)975-0132 Bimonthly. $25.00 per year. Edited for retail pharmacists in various settings, whether independent or chain-operated. Covers both pharmaceutical and business topics.

Community Publication Advertising Source. SRDS, 1700 Higgins Rd. Des Plaines, IL 60018. Phone: 800-851-7737 or (847)375-5000 Fax: (847)375-5001 E-mail: srobe@srds.com • URL: http://www.srds.com • Semiannual. $161.00 per issue. Provides advertising rates for weekly community newspapers, shopping guides, and religious newspapers, with circulation data and other information. Formerly *Community Publication Rates and Data*.

Community Relations Report. Joe Williams Communications, P.O. Box 924 Bartlesville, OK 74005. Phone: (918)336-2267 Monthly. $160.00 per year. Newsletter on corporate community relations.

Community Service.

Commuter Airlines. Alexander T. Wells and Franklin D. Richey. Krieger Publishing Co., P.O. Box 9542 Melbourne, FL 32902-9542. Phone: 800-724-0025 or (321)724-9542 Fax: (321)951-3671 E-mail: info@krieger-publishing.com • URL: http://www.krieger-publishing.com • 1996. $46.50. Provides an overview of the commuter airline industry, including operating and management functions.

Compact D/New Issues. Disclosure, Inc., 5161 River Rd. Bethesda, MD 20816. Phone: 800-843-7747 or (301)951-1300 Fax: (301)951-1753 Monthly, $4,500.00 per year. Provides CD-ROM financial and other information relating to initial public offerings, spinoffs, recapitalizations, exchange offers, and other registrations filed with the Securities and Exchange Commission in compliance with the Securities Act of 1933. Time period is 1990 to date.

Compact D/SEC. Disclosure, Inc., 5161 River Rd. Bethesda, MD 20816. Phone: 800-843-7747 or (301)951-1300 Fax: (301)951-1753 Monthly. Contains three CD-ROM files. (1) Disclosure: Provides Securities and Exchange Commission filings for over 12,500 publicly held corporations. (2) Disclosure/Spectrum Ownership Profiles: Provides detailed corporate descriptions and complete ownership information for over 6,000 public companies. (3) Zacks Earnings Estimates: Provides earnings per share forecasts for about 4,000 U. S. corporations.

Compact Disc Handbook. Ken C. Pohlmann. A-R Editions, Inc., 801 Deming Way Madison, WI 53717. Phone:

800-736-0070 or (608)836-9000 Fax: (608)831-8200 E-mail: info@areditions.com • URL: http://www.areditions.com • 1992. $34.95. Second edition. A guide to compact disc technology, including player design and disc manufacturing. (Computer Music and Digital Audio Series).

Companies and Their Brands. The Gale Group, 27500 Drake Rd. Farmington Hills, MI 48331-3535. Phone: 800-877-GALE or (248)699-GALE Fax: 800-414-5043 or (248)699-8069 E-mail: galeord@galegroup.com • URL: http://www.galegroup.com • 2001. $570.00. 22nd edition. Two volumes. Lists companies alphabetically, with their names. (A rearrangment of the data in *Brands and Their Companies*.)

Companies Holding Nuclear Certificates of Authorization. Boiler and Pressure Vessel Control Committee, American Society of Mechanical Engineers, 22 Law Dr. Fairfield, NJ 07004. Phone: 800-843-2763 or (201)882-1170 Fax: (201)882-1717 Bimonthly. $65.00 per year. Lists about 700 manufacturers certified for production of nuclear pressure vessels.

Company Policy and Personnel Workbook. Ardella Ramey. PSI Research, P.O. Box 3727 Central Point, OR 97502-0032. Phone: 800-228-2275 or (541)479-9464 Fax: (541)476-1479 E-mail: info@psi-research.com • URL: http://www.psiresearch.com • 1999. $29.95. Fourth edition. Contains about 50 model company personnel policies for use as examples in developing a personnel manual. Explains the basic laws governing employee-employer relationships. (Successful Business Library Series).

Company Relocation Handbook: Making the Right Move. William G. Ward and Sharon K. Ward. PSI Research, P.O. Box 3727 Central Point, OR 97502-0032. Phone: 800-228-2275 or (541)479-9464 Fax: (541)476-1479 E-mail: info@psi-research.com • URL: http://www.psiresearch.com • 1998. $19.95. A comprehensive guide to moving a business. (Successful Business Library Series).

Comparative Guide to American Elementary & Secondary Schools. Grey House Publishing, 185 Millerton Rd. Millerton, NY 12546. Phone: 800-562-2139 or (518)789-8700 Fax: (518)789-0556 E-mail: books@greyhouse.com • URL: http://www.greyhouse.com • 1998. $85.00. Provides a "snapshot profile" of every public school district in the U. S. serving 2,500 or more students. Includes student-teacher ratios, expenditures per student, number of librarians, and socioeconomic indicators.

Comparative Guide to American Suburbs. Grey House Publishing, 185 Millerton Rd. Millerton, NY 12546. Phone: 800-562-2139 or (518)789-8700 Fax: (518)789-0556 E-mail: books@greyhouse.com • URL: http://www.greyhouse.com • 2001. $130.00. Second edition. Contains detailed profiles of 1,800 suburban communities having a population of 10,000 or more and located within the 50 largest metropolitan areas. Includes ranking tables for income, unemployment, new housing permits, home prices, and crime, as well as information on school districts. (Universal Reference Publications.)

Comparative Statistics of Industrial Office Real Estate Markets. Society of Industrial and Office Realtors, 700 11th St., N. W.,, Suite 510 Washington, DC 20001-4511. Phone: (202)737-1150 Fax: (202)737-8796 E-mail: lnasvaderani@mail.sior.com • URL: http://www.sior.com • Annual. $100.00. Includes review and forecast section. Formerly *Guide to Industrial and Office Real Estate Markets*.

COMPENDEX PLUS. Engineering Information, Inc., Castle Point on the Hudson Hoboken, NJ 07030. Phone: 800-221-1044 or (201)216-8500 Fax: (201)216-8532 Provides online indexing and abstracting of the world's engineering and technical information appearing in journals, reports, books, and proceedings. Time period is 1970 to date, with weekly updates. Inquire as to online cost and availability.

COMPENDEX PLUS ÎCD-ROMl. Engineering Information, Inc., Castle Point on the Hudson Hoboken, NJ 07030. Phone: 800-221-1044 or (201)216-8500 Fax: (201)216-8532 Quarterly. $3,450.00 per year. Provides CD-ROM indexing and abstracting of the world's engineering and technical information appearing in journals, reports, books, and proceedings, 1985 to date.

Compendium of Education and Training Facilities for Meteorology and Operational Hydrology. American Meteorological Society, 45 Beacon St. Boston, MA 02108-3693. Phone: (617)227-2425 Fax: (617)742-8718 E-mail: amspubs@ametsoc.org/ams • URL: http://www.ametsoc.org/ams • 1996. $50.00. Approximately 233 training institutions for meteorology and operational hydrology in nearly 100 countries. Formerly *Compendium of Training Facilities for Meteorology and Operational Hydrology*.

Compensating Executives. Arthur H. Kroll. CCH, Inc., 4025 W. Peterson Ave. Chicago, IL 60646-6085. Phone: 800-248-3248 or (773)866-6000 Fax: 800-224-8299 or (773)866-3608 URL: http://www.cch.com • 1998. $115.00. Covers the creation and implementation of executive compensation programs. Includes sample forms, plans, and checklists.

Compensation. Robert E. Sibson. AMACOM, 1601 Broadway, 12th Fl. New York, NY 10019. Phone: 800-262-9699 or (212)586-8100 Fax: (212)903-8168 E-mail: custmserv@amanet.org • URL: http://www.amanet.org • 1990. $69.95. Fifth edition. Discusses planning, implementing, and managing employee compensation.

Compensation. Bureau of National Affairs, Inc., 1231 25th St., N.W. Washington, DC 20037-1197. Phone: 800-372-1033 or (202)452-4200 Fax: (202)822-8092 E-mail: books@bna.com • URL: http://www.bna.com • Weekly. $533.00 per year. Three volumes. Looseleaf. (BNA Policy and Practice Series.)

Compensation. George T. Milkovich. McGraw-Hill Professional, 1221 Ave. of the Americas New York, NY 10020. Phone: 800-722-4267 or (212)904-2000 Fax: (212)904-2072 E-mail: customer.service@mcgraw-hill.com • URL: http://www.mcgraw-hill.com • 1998. $87.81. Sixth edition.

Compensation and Benefits Management. Panel Publishers, 1185 Ave. of the Americas New York, NY 10036. Phone: 800-447-1717 or (212)597-0200 Fax: 800-901-9075 or (212)597-0334 E-mail: customer.service@aspenpubl.com • URL: http://www.panelpublishers.com • Quarterly. $164.00 per year. Timely articles and regular columns directed to the executive, manager or professional responsible for design, implementation and management of compensation programs.

Compensation and Benefits Review. Sage Publications, Inc., 2455 Teller Rd. Thousand Oaks, CA 91320. Phone: 800-313-8650 or (805)499-0721 Fax: (805)499-0871 E-mail: info@sage.com • URL: http://www.sagepub.com • Individuals, $240.00 per year; institutions, $240.00 per year.

Compensation and Benefits Update. Warren, Gorham and Lamont/RIA Group, 395 Hudson St. New York, NY 10014. Phone: 800-950-1215 or (212)367-6300 Fax: (651)687-5827 E-mail: customer_services@riag.com • URL: http://www.westgroup.com • Monthly. $149.00 per year. Provides information on the latest ideas and developments in the field of employee benefits. In-depth exploration of popular benefits programs. Formerly *Benefits and Compensation Update*.

Compensation and Working Conditions. Available from U. S. Government Printing Office, Washington, DC 20402. Phone: (202)512-1800 Fax: (202)512-2250 E-mail: gpoaccess@gpo.gov • URL: http://www.access.gpo.gov • Quarterly. $18.00 per year. Issued by the Bureau of Labor Statistics, U. S. Department of Labor. Presents wage and benefit changes that result from collective bargaining settlements and unilateral management decisions. Includes statistical summaries and special reports on wage trends. Formerly *Current Wage Developments*.

Compensation Benchmarks for Private Practice Attorneys. Altman Weil Publications, Inc., Two Campus Blvd. Newtown Square, PA 19073. Phone: 888-782-7297 or (610)359-9900 Fax: (610)359-0467 E-mail: info@altmanweil.com • URL: http://www.altmanweil.com • Annual. $295.00. Provides legal-office compensation standards arranged by region, firm size, legal specialty, and various other factors. Covers attorneys, paralegals, and other personnel.

Compensation Management in a Knowledge-Based World. Richard I. Henderson. Prentice Hall, 240 Frisch Court Paramus, NJ 07652-5240. Phone: 800-947-7700 or (201)909-6200 Fax: 800-445-6991 or (201)990-6361 URL: http://www.prenhall.com • 1999. $93.00. Eighth edition.

The Competitive Edge. InterStudy Publications, P.O. Box 4366 St. Paul, MN 55104. Phone: 800-844-3351 or (612)858-9291 Fax: (612)584-5698 Semiannual. Price on application. Provides highly detailed statistical, directory, and market information on U. S. health maintenance organizations. Consists of three parts: *The HMO Directory, The HMO Industry Report*, and *The Regional Market Analysis*. (Emphasis is on market research. http://www.dresources.com/)

Competitive Intelligence From Black Ops to Boardrooms: How Businesses Gather, Analyze, and Use Information to Succeed in the Global Marketplace. Larry Kahaner. Simon & Schuster Trade, 1230 Ave. of the Americas New York, NY 10020. Phone: 800-223-2336 or (212)698-7000 Fax: 800-943-9831 or (212)698-7007 E-mail: ssonline_feedback@simonsays.com • URL: http://www.simonsays.com • 1996. $24.00. Emphasizes corporate espionage as opposed to more traditional information gathering (the author is a former licensed private investigator). Includes a "Glossary of Competitive Intelligence."

Competitive Intelligence Guide. Fuld & Co.Phone: (617)492-5900 Fax: (617)492-7108 E-mail: info@fuld.com • URL: http://www.fuld.com • Web site includes "Intelligence Index" (links to Internet sites), "Strategic Intelligence Organizer" (game-board format), "Intelligence Pyramid" (graphics), "Thoughtleaders" (expert commentary), "Intelligence System Evaluator" (interactive questionnaire), and "Reference Resource" (book excerpts from *New Competitor Intelligence*). Fees: information provided by Web site is free, but Fuld & Co. offers fee-based research and consulting services.

Competitive Intelligence Review. Society of Competitive Intelligence Professionals. John Wiley and Sons, Inc. Journals Div., 605 Third Ave. New York, NY 10158-0012. Phone: 800-225-5945 or (212)850-6000 Fax: (212)850-6088 E-mail: info@wiley.com • URL: http://www.wiley.com • Quarterly. Institutions, $345.00 per year.

Competitive Telecommunications Association.

Complete and Easy Guide to Social Security and Medicare. Faustin Tehle. Fraser-Vance Publishing Co., P.O. Box 34056 Peterborough, NH 03458-3056. Phone: 800-234-8791 or (603)924-3030 Fax: (603)924-7049 1996. $12.95. 13th unabridged edition.

The Complete Book of Insurance: The Consumer's Guide to Insuring Your Life, Health, Property, and Income. Ben G. Baldwin. McGraw-Hill Professional, 1221 Ave. of the Americas New York, NY 10020-1095. Phone: 800-722-4726 or (212)904-2000 Fax: (212)904-2072 E-mail: customer.service@mcgraw-hill.com • URL: http://www.mcgraw-hill.com • 1996. $24.95. Revised edition. Provides basic information and advice on various kinds of insurance: life, health, property (fire), disability, long-term care, automobile, liability, and annuities.

Complete Book of Model Business Letters. Jack Griffin. Prentice Hall, 240 Frisch Court Paramus, NJ 07652-5240. Phone: 800-947-7700 or (201)909-6200 Fax: 800-445-6991 or (201)909-6361 URL: http://www.prenhall.com • 1997. $34.95.

Complete Book of Personal Legal Forms. Daniel Sitarz. Nova Publishing Co., 1103 W. College St. Carbondale, IL 62901. Phone: 800-748-1175 or (618)457-3521 Fax: (618)457-2541 E-mail: dansitarz@earthlink.net • URL: http://www.novapublishing.com • 1996. $29.95. Second revised edition. Provides more than 100 forms, including contracts, bills of sale, promissory notes, leases, deeds, receipts, and wills. Forms are also available on IBM or MAC diskettes. (Legal Self-Help Series).

Complete Book of Small Business Legal Forms. Daniel Sitarz. Nova Publishing Co., 1103 W. College St. Carbondale, IL 62901. Phone: 800-748-1175 or (618)457-3521 Fax: (618)457-2541 E-mail: dansitarz@earthllink.net • URL: http://www.novapublishing.com • 1996. $29.95. Second revised edition. Includes basic forms and instructions for use by small businesses in routine legal situations. Forms are also available on IBM or MAC diskettes. (Small Business Library Series).

Complete Building Equipment Maintenance Desk Book. Sheldon J. Fuchs, editor. Prentice Hall, 240 Frisch Court Paramus, NJ 07652-5240. Phone: 800-947-7700 or (201)909-6200 Fax: 800-445-6991 or (201)909-6361 URL: http://www.prenhall.com • 1992. $69.95. Second edition.

Complete Business Statistics. Amir D. Aczel. McGraw-Hill, 1221 Ave. of the Americas New York, NY 10020. Phone: 800-722-4267 or (212)904-2000 Fax: (212)904-2072 E-mail: customer.service@mcgraw-hill.com • URL: http://www.mcgraw-hill.com • 1998. $90.95. Fourth edition. (Irwin/McGraw-Hill Operations and Decision Sciences Series).

Complete Course in Professional Locksmithing. Robert L. Robinson. Burnham, Inc., 111 N. Canal St., Ste. 399 Chicago, IL 60606. Phone: (312)930-9446 Fax: (312)930-5903 E-mail: publishers@burnhaminc.com • URL: http://www.burnhaminc.com • 1973. $68.95.

Complete Direct Marketing Sourcebook: A Step-by-Step Guide to Organizing and Managing a Successful Direct Marketing Program. John Kremer. John Wiley and Sons, Inc., 605 Third Ave. New York, NY 10158-0012. Phone: 800-225-5945 or (212)850-6000 Fax: (212)850-6088 E-mail: info@wiley.com • URL: http://www.wiley.com • 1992. $27.95. Includes checklists, sample direct mail letters, and the calculation of break-even points. (Small Business Editions Series).

Complete Directory for People with Disabilities. Grey House Publishing, Pocket Knife Square Lakeville, CT 06039. Phone: 800-562-2139 or (860)435-0868 Fax: 800-248-0115 or (860)435-3004 E-mail: books@greyhouse.com • URL: http://www.greyhouse.com • Annual. $165.00. Provides information on a wide variety of products, goods, services, and facilities, including job training programs, rehabilitation services, and funding sources. Indexed by organization name, disability/need, and location.

Complete Federal Tax Forms. Research Institute of America, Inc., 90 Fifth Ave. New York, NY 10011. Phone: 800-431-9025 or (212)645-4800 Fax: (201)816-3581 Three looseleaf volumes. Periodic supplementations. Price on application. Contains more than 650 reprints of blank Internal Revenue Service forms, with instructions.

Complete Guide to Becoming a U. S. Citizen. Eve P. Steinberg. Pearson Education and Technology, 201 W. 103rd St. Indianapolis, IN 46290-1097. Phone: 800-858-7674 or (317)581-3500 Fax: (317)581-4670 URL: http://www.mcp.com • 1994. $11.95.

Complete Guide to Corporate Fund Raising. Joseph Dermer and Stephen Wertheimer, editors. Fund Raising Institute, 27500 Drake Rd. Farmington Hills, MI 48331-3535. Phone: 800-877-8238 or (248)699-GALE Fax: 800-414-5043 or (248)699-8069 E-mail: galeord@gale.com • URL: http://

www.galegroup.com • 1991. $19.95. Discusses the art of obtaining grants from corporate sources. Written by nine fund raising counselors.

Complete Guide to Performance Standards for Library Personnel. Carol F. Goodson. Neal-Schuman Publishers, Inc., 100 Varick St. New York, NY 10013. Phone: (212)925-8650 Fax: 800-584-2414 or (212)219-8916 E-mail: info@neal-schuman.com • URL: http://www.neal-schuman.com • 1997. $55.00. Provides specific job descriptions and performance standards for both professional and paraprofessional library personnel. Includes a bibliography of performance evaluation literature, with annotations.

Complete Guide to Prescription and Non-Prescription Drugs: Side Effects, Warnings, and Vital Data for Safe Use. H. Winter Griffith. Berkley Publishing Group, 375 Madison Ave. New York, NY 10014. Phone: 800-631-8571 or (212)366-2000 Fax: (212)213-6706 E-mail: online@penguinputnam.com • URL: http://www.penguinputnam.com • Annual. $16.95. A guide for consumers.

Complete Guide to Special Event Management: Business Insights, Financial Advice and Successful Strategies from Ernst and Young, Consultants to the Olympics, the Emmy Awards and the PGA Tour. Ernst and Young Staff. John Wiley and Sons, Inc., 605 Third Ave. New York, NY 10158-0012. Phone: 800-225-5945 or (212)850-6000 Fax: (212)850-6088 E-mail: info@wiley.com • URL: http://www.wiley.com • 1992. $29.95. Covers the marketing, financing, and general management of special events in the fields of art, entertainment, and sports.

Complete Marquis Who's Who. Marquis Who's Who, Reed Reference Publishing, 121 Chanlon Rd. New Providence, NJ 07974. Phone: 800-521-8110 or (908)464-6800 Fax: (908)665-3528 Frequency and price on application. Contains CD-ROM biographical profiles of over 800,000 notable individuals. Includes *Who's Who in America*, *Who Was Who in America*, and 14 regional and professional directories.

Complete Mental Health Directory. Grey House Publishing, 185 Millerton Rd. Millerton, NY 12546. Phone: 800-562-2139 or (518)789-8700 Fax: (518)789-0556 E-mail: books@greyhouse.com • URL: http://www.greyhouse.com • 2001. $165.00. Second edition. Listings include mental health associations, support groups, facilities, media, HMOs, and government agencies. Includes basic descriptions of 25 mental health disorders. (Sedgwick Press.)

Complete Multilingual Dictionary of Advertising, Marketing, and Communications. Hans W. Paetzel, editor. NTC/Contemporary Publishing, P.O. Box 545 Blacklick, OH 43004. Phone: 800-338-3987 or (614)755-4151 Fax: (614)755-5645 E-mail: ntcpub@mcgraw-hill.com • URL: http://www.ntc-cb.com • 1994. $49.95. Provides translations of about 8,000 technical and general terms. English, French and German terms.

The Complete Probate Kit. Jen C. Appel and F. Bruce Gentry. John Wiley and Sons, Inc., 605 Third Ave. New York, NY 10158-0012. Phone: 800-225-5945 or (212)850-6000 Fax: (212)850-6088 E-mail: info@wiley.com • URL: http://www.wiley.com • 1991. $29.95. A practical guide to settling estates. Provides summaries of the applicable state laws and definitions of relevant terms.

Complete Secretary's Handbook. Mary A. De Vries. Prentice Hall, 240 Frisch Court Paramus, NJ 07652-5240. Phone: 800-947-7700 or (201)909-6200 Fax: 800-445-6991 or (201)909-6361 URL: http://www.prenhall.com • 1993. $24.95. Seventh edition.

Complete Speaker's and Toastmaster's Library. Jacob M. Braude. Prentice Hall, 240 Frisch Court Paramus, NJ 07652-5240. Phone: 800-947-7700 or (201)909-6200 Fax: 800-445-6991 or (201)909-6361 URL: http://www.prenhall.com • 1992. $69.95. Second edition.

Compliance Reporter. Institutional Investor, 488 Madison Ave. New York, NY 10022. Phone: (212)224-3300 Fax: (212)224-3353 E-mail: info@iijournals.com • URL: http://www.iijournals.com • Biweekly. $2,105.00 per year. Newsletter for investment dealers and others on complying with securities laws and regulations.

Composite Catalog of Oil Field Equipment and Services. Gulf Publishing Co., P.O. Box 2608 Houston, TX 77252-2608. Phone: 800-231-6275 or (713)529-4301 Fax: (713)520-4433 E-mail: ezorder@gulfpub.com • URL: http://www.gpcbooks.com • Biennial. Price on application.

Composite Materials and Structures Center., Michigan State University, College of Engineering, 2100 Engineering Bldg. East Lansing, MI 48824-1226. Phone: (517)353-5466 Fax: (517)432-1634 E-mail: cmsc@engr.smsu.edu • URL: http://www.cmscsun.egr.msu.edu/index/html • Studies polymer, metal, and ceramic based composites.

Composite Materials Research Group.

The Composites and Adhesives Newsletter. T-C Press, P.O. Box 36006 Los Angeles, CA 90036-0006. Phone: (213)938-6923 Fax: (213)938-6923 E-mail: geps222@aol.com • Quarterly. $190.00. Presents news of the composite materials and adhesives industries, with particular coverage of new products and applications.

Composites Industry Monthly. Composite Market Reports, Inc., 459 N. Gilbert Rd., Suite A-150 Gilbert, AZ 85234-4592. Phone: (480)507-6882 Fax: (480)507-6986 Monthly. $1,495.00 per year. Newsletter. Supplement to *ACM Monthly*. Emphasizes non-aerospace applications of composite materials. Includes quarterly calendars, meetings and other periodic supplements and indexes.

Composites Manufacturing Association of the Society of Manufacturing Engineers., P.O. Box 930 Dearborn, MI 48121-0930. Phone: 800-733-4763 or (313)271-1500 Fax: (313)271-2861 URL: http://www.sme.org • Members are composites manufacturing professionals and students.

Comprehensive Catalog of United States Paper Money. Gene Hessler. BNR Press, 132 E. Second St. Port Clinton, OH 43452. Phone: 800-793-0683 or (419)732-6683 E-mail: bnrpress@aol.com • 1992. $42.50. Fifth edtion.

Comprehensive Composite Materials. Anthony Kelly and Carl Zweben, editors-in-chief. Elsevier Science, 655 Ave. of the Americas New York, NY 10010. Phone: 888-437-4636 or (212)989-5800 Fax: (212)633-3680 E-mail: usinfo@elsevier.com • URL: http://www.elsevier.com • 2000. $3,250.00. Six volumes. Provides detailed information on a wide variety of materials used in composites, including metals, polymers, cements, concrete, carbon, ceramics, and fibers. (Pergamon Press.)

Comprehensive Day Care Programs. Stevens Administrative Center

Comprehensive Guide to the Hazardous Properties of Chemical Substances. Pradyot Patnaik. John Wiley and Sons, Inc., 605 Third Ave. New York, NY 10158-0012. Phone: 800-842-3636 or (212)850-6000 Fax: (212)850-6088 E-mail: info@wiley.com • URL: http://www.wiley.com • 1998. $130.00. Second edition.

Compulsory Health Insurance: The Continuing American Debate. Ronald L. Numbers, editor. Greenwood Publishing Group Inc., 88 Post Rd., W. Westport, CT 06881-5007. Phone: 800-225-5800 or (203)226-3571 Fax: (203)222-2540 E-mail: bookinfo@greenwood.com • URL: http://www.greenwood.com • 1982. $49.95. (Contributions in Medical History Series, No.11).

CompuMath Citation Index. Institute for Scientific Information, 3501 Market St. Philadelphia, PA 19104. Phone: 800-336-4474 or (215)386-0100 Fax: (215)386-2991 URL: http://www.isinet.com • Three times a year. $1,090.00 per year. Provides citations to the worldwide literature of computer science and mathematics.

Compuserve Internet Tour Guide. Richard Wagner. Ventana Communications Group, Inc., P.O. Box 13964 Research Triangle Park, NC 27709-3964. Phone: 800-777-7955 or (919)544-9404 Fax: (919)942-9472 E-mail: contact@vmedia.com • URL: http://www.vmedia.com • 1996. $34.95. A detailed guide to accessing various features of the Internet by way of the Compuserve online service.

Compustat. Standard and Poor's, 7400 S. Alton Court, Englewood, CO 80112. Phone: 800-525-8640 or (303)771-6510 Fax: (303)740-4687 Financial data on publicly held U.S. and some foreign corporations; data held for 20 years. Inquire as to online cost and availability.

Computation Center. University of Texas at Austin

Computational Linguistics. Association for Computational Linguistics. MIT Press, Five Cambridge Center Cambridge, MA 02142-1493. Phone: 800-356-0343 or (617)253-5646 Fax: (617)253-1545 E-mail: mitpress-orders@mit.edu • URL: http://www.mitpress.mit.edu • Quarterly. Institutions, $128.00 per year. Covers developments in research and applications of natural language processing.

Computer. Institute of Electrical and Electronic Engineers, Three Park Ave., 17th Fl. New York, NY 10017-5997. Phone: 800-678-4333 E-mail: customerservice@ieee.org • URL: http://www.ieee.org • Monthly. $760.00 per year. Edited for computer technology professionals.

Computer Abstracts. Anbar Electronic Intelligence. MCB University Press Ltd., 60-62 Toller Lane Bradford West Yorkshire BD8 9BY, England. Phone: 44 1274 777700 Fax: 44 1274 785204 E-mail: ithoreymcb.co.uk • URL: http://www.mcb.co.uk • Bimonthly. $3,799.00 per year.

Computer Aided Design. Robert Becker and Carmo J. Pereira, editors. Marcel Dekker, Inc., 270 Madison Ave. New York, NY 10016. Phone: 800-228-1160 or (212)696-9000 Fax: (212)685-4540 E-mail: bookorders@dekker.com • URL: http://www.dekker.com • 1993. $235.00.

Computer-Aided Engineering; Data Base Applications in Design and Manufacturing. Penton Media Inc., 1300 E. Ninth St. Cleveland, OH 44114. Phone: (216)696-7000 Fax: (216)696-0836 E-mail: corpcomm@penton.com • URL: http://www.penton.com • Monthly. $55.00 per year.

Computer Aided Manufacturing International.

Computer and Automated Systems Association of Society of Manufacturing Engineers., P.O. Box 930 Dearborn, MI 48121-0930. Phone: (313)271-1500 Fax: (313)271-2861 URL: http://www.sme.org/casa • Sponsored by the Society of Manufacturing Engineers.

Computer and Communications Industry Association.

Computer and Control Abstracts. Available from INSPEC, Inc., 379 Thornall St. Edison, NJ 08337-2225. Phone: (732)321-5575 Fax: (732)321-5702 E-mail: inspec@iee.org • URL: http://www.iee.org • Monthly. $2,160.00 per year. Section C of *Science Abstracts*.

Computer and Information Science Research Center. Ohio State University

Computer and Information Systems Abstracts Journal: An Abstract Journal Pertaining to the Theory, Design, Fabrication and Application of Computer and Information Systems. Cambridge Information Group, 7200 Wisconsin Ave., 6th Fl. Bethesda, MD 20814. Phone: 800-843-7751 or (301)961-6700 Fax: (301)961-6720 E-mail: market@csa.com • URL: http://www.csa.com • Monthly. $1,045 per year.

Computer and Online Industry Litigation Reporter: The National Journal of Record of Computer Online Industry. Andrews Publications, Inc., 175 Strafford Ave., Bldg 4, Suite 140 Wayne, PA 19087. Phone: 800-345-1101 or (610)622-0510 Fax: (610)622-0501 URL: http://www.andrewspub.com • Semimonthly. $875.00 per year. Provides complete text of key decisions relating to copyright, patents, trademarks, breach of contract, etc. Formerly *Computer Industry Litigation Reporter*.

Computer Animation Techniques. Pearson Education and Technology, 201 W. 103rd St. Indianapolis, IN 46290. Phone: 800-428-5331 or (317)581-3500 Fax: (317)581-4670 URL: http://www.mcp.com • 1996. $50.00.

Computer Animation Îyearl. Institute of Electrical and Electronic Engineers, Three Park Ave., 17th Fl. New York, NY 10016-5997. Phone: 800-678-4333 or (212)419-7900 Fax: (212)752-4929 E-mail: customerservice@ieee.org • URL: http://www.ieee.org • Annual. $110.00.

Computer Assisted Surgery: Automation, Virtual Reality, Robotics, and Radiosurgery. Theta Reports/PJB Medical Publications, Inc., 1775 Broadway, Suite 511 New York, NY 10019. Phone: (212)262-8230 Fax: (212)262-8234 E-mail: customerservice@thetareports.com • URL: http://www.thetareports.com • 2000. $2,295.00. Contains market research data relating to surgical systems technology. (Theta Report No. 1105.)

Computer-Based Education and Instructional Design Project. Temple University

Computer Book Review., P.O. Box 61067 Honolulu, HI 96839. E-mail: cbr@bookwire.com • URL: http://www/bookwire.com/cbr • Quarterly. $30.00 per year. Includes annual index. Reviews new computer books. Back issues available.

Computer Buying Guide. Consumer Guide Editors. Publications International Ltd, 7373 N. Cicero Ave. Lincolnwood, IL 60646. Phone: 800-745-9299 or (847)676-3470 Fax: (847)676-3671 URL: http://www.consumerguide.com • Annual. $9.99.

Computer Communications Review. Association for Computing Machinery, Special Interest Group on Data Communicatio, 1515 Broadway, 17th Fl. New York, NY 10036. Phone: (212)869-7440 Fax: (212)869-0481 Quarterly. $37.00 per year.

Computer Crime Law. Jay J. Bloombecker. West Group, 610 Opperman Dr. Eagan, MN 55123. Phone: 800-328-4880 or (651)687-7000 Fax: 800-213-2323 or (651)687-5827 URL: http://www.westgroup.com • $125.00 per year. Looseleaf service. Provides analysis of recent case law and emerging trends in computer-related crime. Includes current information on the technical aspects of computer crime.

Computer Database. The Gale Group, 27500 Drake Rd. Farmington Hills, MI 48331-3535. Phone: 800-877-GALE or (248)699-GALE Fax: 800-414-5043 or (248)699-8069 E-mail: galeord@gale.com • URL: http://www.gale.com • Provides online citations with abstracts to material appearing in about 150 trade journals and newsletters in the subject areas of computers, telecommunications, and electronics. Time period is 1983 to date, with weekly updates. Inquire as to online cost and availability.

Computer Dealers Directory. American Business Directories, P.O. Box 27347 Omaha, NE 68127. Phone: 800-555-6124 or (402)593-4600 Fax: (402)331-5481 E-mail: internet@infousa.com • Annual. Price on application. Lists over 30,847 computer dealers. Brand names are indicated. Compiled from telephone company yellow pages. Regional editions and franchise editions available.

Computer Dictionary. Donald D. Spencer. Camelot Publishing Co., P.O. Box 1357 Ormond Beach, FL 32175-1357. Phone: (904)672-5672 1993. $24.95. Fourth edition.

Computer Economics Report: The Financial Advisor of Data Processing Users. Computer Economics, Inc., 5841 Edison Place Carlsbad, CA 92008-6519. Phone: 800-326-8100 or (760)438-8100 Fax: (760)431-1126 E-mail: custserv@compecon.com • URL: http://www.computereconomics.com • Monthly. $595.00 per year. Newsletter on lease/purchase decisions, prices, discounts, residual value forecasts, personnel allocation, cost control, and other corporate computer topics. Edited for information technology (IT) executives.

Computer Fraud and Security. Elsevier Science, 655 Ave. of the Americas New York, NY 10010. Phone: 888-437-4636 or (212)989-5800 Fax: (212)633-3680 E-mail: usinfo@elsevier.com • URL: http://www.elsevier.com • Monthly.

$710.00 per year. Newsletter. Formerly *Computer Fraud and Security Bulletin*.

Computer Glossary: The Complete Illustrated Desk Reference. Alan Freedman. AMACOM, 1601 Broadway, 12th Fl. New York, NY 10019. Phone: 800-262-9699 or (212)586-8100 Fax: (212)903-8168 E-mail: custmserv@amanet.org • URL: http://www.amanet.org • 1998. $29.95. Eighth edition.

Computer Graphics. Donald Hearn and M. Pauline Baker. Prentice Hall, 240 Frisch Court Paramus, NJ 07652-5240. Phone: 800-947-7700 or (201)909-6200 Fax: 800-445-6991 or (201)909-6361 URL: http://www.prenhall.com • 2000. Price on application.

Computer Graphics. Special Interest Group on Computer Graphics, Association for Computing Machinery, 1515 Broadway, 17th Fl. New York, NY 10036. Phone: (212)869-7440 Fax: (212)869-0481 Quarterly. Members, $59.00 per year; non-members, $95.00 per year; students, $50.00 per year.

Computer Graphics Laboratory., New York Institute of Technology, Fine Arts Old Westbury, NY 11568. Phone: (516)686-7542 Fax: (516)686-7428 E-mail: pvoci@nyit.edu • Research areas include computer graphics, computer animation, and digital sound.

Computer Graphics World. PennWell Corp., Advanced Technology Div., 98 Spit Brook Rd. Nashua, NH 03062-5737. Phone: 800-331-4463 or (603)891-0123 Fax: (603)891-0539 E-mail: webmaster@pennwell.com • URL: http://www.penton.com • Monthly. $55.00 per year.

Computer Industry Almanac. Egil Juliussen and Karen Petska. Computer Industry Almanac, Inc., 1013 S. Belmont Ave. Arlington Heights, IL 60005. Phone: 800-718-6810 E-mail: mail@c-i-a.com • URL: http://www.c-i-a.com • Annual. $63.00. Analyzes recent trends in various segments of the computer industry, with forecasts, employment data and industry salary information. Includes directories of computer companies, industry organizations, and publications.

Computer Industry Report. International Data Corp., Five Speen St. Framingham, MA 01701. Phone: (508)935-4530 URL: http://www.idcresearch • Semimonthly. $495.00 per year. Newsletter. Annual supplement. Also known as "The Gray Sheet." Formerly *EDP Industry Report and Market Review*.

Computer Languages. Elsevier Science, 655 Ave. of the Americas New York, NY 10010. Phone: 888-437-4636 or (212)989-5800 Fax: (212)633-3680 E-mail: usinfo@elsevier.com • URL: http://www.elsevier.com • Quarterly. $778.00 per year.

Computer Law and Tax Report: Monthly Newsletter Covering Computer-Related Law and Tax Issues. Roditti Reports Corp., P.O. Box 2066 New York, NY 10021-5013. Phone: (212)879-3325 Fax: (212)879-4496 URL: http://www.computerlawandtax.com • Monthly. $297.00 per year. Newsletter.

Computer Law Association., 3028 Javier Rd., Suite 402 Fairfax, VA 22031. Phone: (703)560-7747 Fax: (703)207-7028 E-mail: clanet@aol.com • URL: http://www.cla.org • Members are lawyers and others concerned with the legal problems affecting computer-telecommunications technology.

Computer Law: Cases, Comments, Questions. Peter B. Maggs and others. West Publishing Co., College and School Div., 610 Opperman Dr. Saint Paul, MN 55164-0526. Phone: 800-338-9424 or (612)687-8000 Fax: 800-213-2323 or (612)687-5388 E-mail: legal_ed@westgroup.com • URL: http://www.lawschool.westgroup.com • 1992. Price on application. (Amrican Casebook Series).

Computer Law: Evidence and Procedures. David Bender. Matthew Bender & Co., Inc., Two Park Ave. New York, NY 10016. Phone: 800-223-1940 or (212)448-2000 Fax: (212)244-3188 E-mail: international@bender.com • URL: http://www.bender.com • $580.00. Three looseleaf volumes. Periodic supplementation. Covers the concepts and techniques of evidence and discovery procedures as they apply to computer-based information, and to the protection of computer software under intellectual property.

Computer Law Forms Handbook: A Legal Guide to Drafting and Negotiating. Laurens R. Schwartz. West Group, 610 Opperman Dr. Eagan, MN 55123. Phone: 800-328-4880 or (651)687-7000 Fax: 800-213-2323 or (651)687-5827 URL: http://www.westgroup.com • Annual. $162.00.

Computer-Law Journal: International Journal of Computer, Communication and Information Law. Center for Computer Law, P.O. Box 3549 Manhattan Beach, CA 90266. Phone: (310)544-7372 Quarterly. $97.50 per year.

Computer Law Reporter: A Monthly Journal of Computer Law and Practice, Intellectual Property, Copyright and Trademark Law. Computer Law Reporter, Inc., 1601 Connecticut Ave., N. W., Suite 602 Washington, DC 20009. Phone: (202)462-5755 Fax: (202)328-2430 Monthly. $1,650.00 per year.

Computer Law Strategist. American Lawyer Media, L.P., 345 Park Ave., S. New York, NY 10010-1707. Phone: 800-888-8300 or (212)545-6170 Fax: (212)696-1848 E-mail: catalog@amlaw.com • URL: http://www.americanlawyermedia.com • Monthly. $265.00 per year.

Computer Letter: Business Issues in Technology. Technologic Partners, Inc., 120 Wooster St., 6th Fl. New York, NY 10012. Phone: (212)343-1900 Fax: (212)343-1915 E-mail: klein@technoglogicp.com • 40 times a year. $595.00 per year. Computer industry newsletter with emphasis on information for investors.

Computer Literature Index: A Subject/Author Index to Computer and Data Processing Literature. Applied Computer Research, Inc., P.O. Box 82266 Phoenix, AZ 85071-2266. Phone: 800-234-2227 or (602)995-5929 Fax: (602)995-0905 URL: http://www.archq.com • Quarterly, with annual cumulation. $245.00 per year. Contains brief abstracts of book and periodical literature covering all phases of computing, including approximately 70 specific application areas.

Computer Music Journal. MIT Press, Five Cambridge Center Cambridge, MA 02142-1493. Phone: 800-356-0343 or (617)253-2864 Fax: (617)253-1545 E-mail: mitpress-orders@mit.edu • URL: http://www.mitpress.mit.edu • Quarterly. Individuals, $48.00 per year; instutitions, $158.00 per year. Covers digital soound and the musical applications of computers.

Computer Network Center.

Computer Networks. Andrew S. Tanenbaum. Prentice Hall, 240 Frisch Court Paramus, NJ 07652-5240. Phone: 800-947-7700 or (201)909-6200 Fax: 800-445-6991 or (201)909-6361 URL: http://www.prenhall.com • 1996. $85.00. Third edition.

Computer Parts and Supplies Directory. American Business Directories, P.O. Box 27347 Omaha, NE 68127. Phone: 800-555-6124 or (402)593-4600 Fax: (402)331-5481 E-mail: internet@infousa.com • Annual. Price on application. Lists 8,347 companies. Compiled from telephone company yellow pages.

Computer Price Guide: The Blue Book of Used IBM Computer Prices. Computer Economics, Inc., 5841 Edison Place Carlsbad, CA 92008-6519. Phone: 800-326-8100 or (760)438-8100 Fax: (760)431-1126 E-mail: custserv@compecon.com • URL: http://www.computereconomics.com • Quarterly. $140.00 per year. Provides average prices of used IBM computer equipment, including "complete lists of obsolete IBM equipment." Includes a newsletter on trends in the used computer market. Edited for dealers, leasing firms, and business computer buyers.

Computer Publishing and Advertising Report: The Biweekly Newsletter for Publishing and Advertising Executives in the Computer Field. SIMBA Information, Inc., P.O. Box 4234 Stamford, CT 06907-0234. Phone: 800-307-2529 or (203)358-4100 Fax: (203)358-5824 E-mail: info@simbanet.com • URL: http://www.simbanet.com • Biweekly. $549.00 per year. Newsletter. Covers computer book publishing and computer-related advertising in periodicals and other media. Provides data on computer book sales and advertising in computer magazines.

Computer Publishing Market Forecast. SIMBA Information, P.O.Box 4234 Stamford, CT 06907-0234. Phone: 800-307-2529 or (203)358-4100 Fax: (203)358-5824 E-mail: info@simbanet.com • URL: http://www.simbanet.com • Annual. $1,995.00. Provides market data on computer-related books, magazines, newsletters, and other publications. Includes profiles of major publishers of computer-related material.

Computer Repair Service. Entrepreneur Media, Inc., 2445 McCabe Way Irvine, CA 92614. Phone: 800-421-2300 or (949)261-2325 Fax: (949)261-0234 E-mail: entmag@entrepreneur.com • URL: http://www.entrepreneur.com • Looseleaf. $59.50. A practical guide to starting a computer repair service. Covers profit potential, start-up costs, market size evaluation, owner's time required, site selection, lease negotiation, pricing, accounting, advertising, promotion, etc. (Start-Up Business Guide No. E1256.)

Computer Reseller News: The Newspaper for Microcomputer Reselling. CMP Publications, Inc., 600 Community Dr. Manhasset, NY 11030. Phone: 800-577-5356 or (516)562-5000 Fax: (516)733-6916 URL: http://www.crn.com • Weekly. $209.00 per year. Includes bimonthly supplement. Incorporates *Computer Reseller Sources and Macintosh News*. Formerly *Computer Retailer News*.

Computer Review., P.O. Box 260 Gloucester, MA 01930. Phone: (978)283-2100 Fax: (978)281-3125 E-mail: info@computerreview.com • URL: http://www.computerreview.com • Semiannual. $425.00 per year; renewal subscription, $355.00 per year. A complete reference to the global internet market. Covers top 1,000 information technology companies.

Computer Security Basics. Deborah F. Russell and G. T. Gangemi. Thomson Learning, 7625 Empire Dr. Florence, KY 41042. Phone: 800-347-7707 or (606)525-6620 Fax: (606)525-0978 URL: http://www.thomsonlearning.com • 1991. $29.95. (Computer Science Series).

Computer Security Buyer's Guide. Computer Security Institute, 600 Harrison St. San Francisco, CA 94107. Phone: 800-227-4675 or (415)905-2370 Fax: (415)905-2234 E-mail: csi@cmp.com • URL: http://www.gocsi.com • Annual. $95.00. About 650 suppliers and consultants of computer security products.

Computer Security Digest. Jack Bologna. Computer Protection Systems, Inc., 12275 Appletree Dr. Plymouth, MI 48170-3739. Phone: (313)459-8787 Fax: (313)459-2720 Monthly. $125.00 per year. Newsletter. Abstracts of news events that involve computer crimes and security.

Computer Security Institute.

Computer Security Journal. Computer Security Institute. Miller Freeman, Inc., 600 Harrison St. San Francisco, CA 94107. Phone: 800-227-4675 or (415)905-2200 Fax: (415)905-2232 URL: http://www.mfi.com • Semiannual. $100.00 per year.

Computer Select. The Gale Group, 27500 Drake Rd. Farmington Hills, MI 48331-3535. Phone: 800-877-GALE or (248)699-GALE Fax: 800-414-5043 or (248)699-8069 E-mail: galeord@gale.com • URL: http://www.gale.com • Monthly. $1,250.00 per year. Provides one year of full-text on CD-ROM for 120 leading computer-related publications. Also includes 70,000 product specifications and brief profiles of 13,000 computer product vendors and manufacturers.

Computer Shopper: The Computer Magazine for Direct Buyers. Ziff-Davis Publishing Co., 28 E. 28th St. New York, NY 10016. Phone: 800-999-7467 or (212)503-3500 Fax: (212)503-3995 E-mail: john_blackford@zd.com • URL: http://www.computershopper.com • Monthly. $24.97 per year. Nationwide marketplace for computer equipment.

Computer Software: Protection, Liability, Forms. L. J. Kutten. West Group, 610 Opperman Dr. Eagan, MN 55123. Phone: 800-328-4880 or (651)687-7000 Fax: 800-213-2323 or (651)687-5827 URL: http://www.westgroup.com • Three looseleaf volumes. $350.00. Periodic supplementation. Covers copyright law, patents, trade secrets, licensing, publishing contracts, and other legal topics related to computer software.

Computer Studies: Computers in Education. John Hirschbuhl and Loretta Wilkinson. McGraw-Hill, 1221 Ave. of the Americas New York, NY 10020. Phone: 800-722-4726 or (212)904-2000 Fax: (212)904-2072 E-mail: customer.service@mcgraw-hill.com • URL: http://www.mcgraw-hill.com • 1997. $11.64. Eighth edition.

Computer Video. IMAS Publishing, Inc., 5827 Columbia Pike, Suite 310 Falls Church, VA 22041. Phone: 800-336-3045 or (703)998-7600 Fax: (703)998-2966 E-mail: http://www.imaspub.com • Bimonthly. $50.00 per year.

Computer Virus Crisis. Philip E. Fites and others. DIANE Publishing Co., 330 Pusey Ave., Suite 3 Collingdale, PA 19023. Phone: (610)461-6200 Fax: (610)461-6130 E-mail: dianepub@erols.com • URL: http://www.dianepublishing.com • 1999. $15.00. Second reprint edition.

Computer Vision Laboratory.

Computer Vision Laboratory., University of Arizona, Department of Electrical and Computer Engineering, ECE Bldg. 404, Room 230 Tucson, AZ 85721. Phone: (520)621-6191 Fax: (520)621-8076 E-mail: strickland@ece.arizona.edu • URL: http://www.ece.arizona.edu • Research areas include computer vision and speech synthesis.

Computerized Conferencing and Communications Center., New Jersey Institute of Technology, University Heights Newark, NJ 07102. Phone: (973)596-3388 Fax: (973)596-5777 E-mail: 120@eies.njit.edu • URL: http://www.njit.edu/cccc • Research areas include computer conferencing software and computer-mediated communication systems.

Computerized Investing. American Association of Individual Investors, 625 N. Michigan Ave., Suite 1900 Chicago, IL 60611. Phone: (312)280-0170 Fax: (312)280-1625 E-mail: members@aaii.com • URL: http://www.aii.org • Bimonthly. $40.00 per year. Newsletter on computer-aided investment analysis. Includes reviews of software.

Computers. Timothy Trainor and Diane Krasnewich. McGraw-Hill, 1221 Ave. of the Americas New York, NY 10020. Phone: 800-722-4726 or (212)904-2000 Fax: (212)904-2072 E-mail: customer.service@mcgraw-hill.com • URL: http://www.mcgraw-hill.com • 1996. $52.50. Fifth edition.

Computers and Graphics: International Journal of Systems Applications in Computer Graphic. Elsevier Science, 655 Ave. of the Americas New York, NY 10010. Phone: 888-437-4636 or (212)989-5800 Fax: (212)633-3680 E-mail: usinfo@elsevier.com • URL: http://www.elsevier.com • Bimonthly. $1,444.00 per year.

Computers and Industrial Engineering: An International Journal. Elsevier Science, 655 Ave. of the Americas New York, NY 10010. Phone: 888-437-4636 or (212)989-5800 Fax: (212)633-3680 E-mail: usinfo@elsevier.com • URL: http://www.elsevier.com • Eight times a year. $2,113.00 per year.

Computers and Information Processing. South-Western Publishing Co., 5101 Madison Rd. Cincinnati, OH 45227. Phone: 800-271-8811 or (513)271-8811 Fax: 800-354-9706 or (201)909-6361 E-mail: billhendee@itped.com • URL: http://www.swcollege.com • 1998. $29.95. Seventh edition.

Computers and Office and Accounting Machines. U. S. Bureau of the Census, Washington, DC 20233-0800. Phone: (301)457-4100 Fax: (301)457-3842 URL: http://www.census.gov • Annual. Provides data on shipments: value, quantity, imports, and exports. (Current Industrial Reports, MA-35R.)

Computers and Security: The International Journal Devoted to the Study of the Technical and Financial Aspects of Computer Security. International Federation for Information Processing on Computer Security. Elsevier Science, 655 Ave. of the Americas New York, NY 10010. Phone: 888-437-4636 or (212)989-5800 Fax: (212)633-3680 E-mail: usinfo@elsevier.com • URL: http://www.elsevier.com • Eight times a year. $648.00 per year.

Computers in Education. Paul F. Merrill and others. Allyn and Bacon, Inc., 160 Gould St. Needham Heights, MA 02194-2310. Phone: 800-278-3525 or (781)455-1250 Fax: (781)455-1294 E-mail: ab_webmaster@abacon.com • URL: http://www.abacon.com • 1995. $59.00. Third edition.

Computers in Human Behavior. Elsevier Science, 655 Ave. of the Americas New York, NY 10010. Phone: 888-437-4636 or (212)989-5800 Fax: (212)633-4680 E-mail: usinfo@elsevier.com • URL: http://www.elsevier.com • Bimonthly. $902.00 per year.

Computers in Libraries. Information Today, Inc., 143 Old Marlton Pike Medford, NJ 08055-8750. Phone: 800-300-9868 or (609)654-6266 Fax: (609)654-4309 E-mail: custserv@infotoday.com • URL: http://www.infotoday.com • 10 times a year. $89.95 per year.

Computers in Libraries: Buyer's Guide and Consultant Directory. Information Today, Inc., 143 Marlton Pike Medford, NJ 08055-8750. Phone: 800-632-5597 or (609)654-6266 Fax: (609)654-4309 Annual. $30.00. Price on application.

Computers in the Schools: The Interdisciplinary Journal of Practice, Theory, and Applied Research. Haworth Press, Inc., 10 Alice St. Binghamton, NY 13904-1580. Phone: 800-429-6784 or (607)722-5857 Fax: 800-895-0582 or (607)722-1424 E-mail: getinfo@haworth.com • URL: http://www.haworth.com • Quarterly. Individuals, $60.00 per year; institutions, $90.00 per year; libraries, $300.00 per year.

Computers: The User Perspective. Sarah E. Hutchinson and Stacey C. Sawyer. McGraw-Hill Higher Education, 1221 Ave. of the Americas New York, NY 10020. Phone: 800-722-4726 or (212)904-2000 Fax: (212)904-2072 E-mail: customer. service@mcgraw-hill.com • URL: http://www.mcgraw-hill.com • 1991. $41.95. Third edition.

Computertalk: For Contemporary Pharmacy Management. Computertalk Associates, Inc., 492 Norristown Rd., Suite 160 Blue Bell, PA 19422-2355. Phone: (610)825-7686 Fax: (610)825-7641 E-mail: maggie@computertalk.com • URL: http://www.computertalk.com • Bimonthly. $50.00 per year. Provides detailed advice and information on computer systems for pharmacies, including a buyers' guide issue.

Computerworld: Newsweekly for Information Technology Leaders. Computerworld, Inc., P.O. Box 9171 Framingham, MA 01701-9171. Phone: 800-669-1002 or (508)879-0700 Fax: (508)875-8931 URL: http://www.computerworld.com • Weekly. $39.95 per year.

Computing and Software Career Directory. The Gale Group, 27500 Drake Rd. Farmington Hills, MI 48331-3535. Phone: 800-877-GALE or (248)699-GALE Fax: 800-414-5043 or (248)699-8069 E-mail: galeord@galegroup.com • URL: http://www.galegroup.com • 1993. $39.00. Includes career information relating to programmers, software engineers, technical writers, systems experts, and other computer specialists. Provides advice from ''insiders,'' resume suggestions, a directory of companies that may offer entry-level positions, and a directory of career information sources. (Career Advisor Series.)

Computing Essentials: Introducing Windows 95. Don Cassel. Prentice Hall, 240 Frisch Court Paramus, NJ 07652-5240. Phone: 800-947-7700 or (201)909-6200 Fax: 800-445-6991 or (201)909-6361 URL: http://www.prenhall.com • 1997. $7.77. A Windows primer.

Computing Information Directory: Comprehensive Guide to the Computing and Computer Engineering Literature. Peter A. Hildebrandt, Inc., 3876 Swallows Nest Court Clarkston, WA 99403-1740. Phone: (509)243-3393 Annual. $229.95. Describes computer journals, newsletters, handbooks, dictionaries, indexing services, review resources, directories, and other computer information sources. Includes a directory of publishers and a master subject index.

Computing Reviews. Association for Computing Machinery, 1515 Broadway, 17th Fl. New York, NY 10036-5701. Phone: (212)626-0500 Fax: (212)944-1318 URL: http://www.acm.org • Monthly. Free to members; non-members, $130.00 per year.

Computing Technology Industry Association., 450 E. 22nd St., Suite 230 Lombard, IL 60148-6158. Phone: (630)268-1818 Fax: (630)268-1384 E-mail: info@comptia.org • URL: http://www.comptia.org • Members are resellers of various kinds of microcomputers and computer equipment.

Concepts in Wine Chemistry. Yair Margalit. Wine Appreciation Guild, 360 Swift Ave. San Francisco, CA 94080. Phone: 800-231-9463 or (650)866-3020 Fax: (650)866-3513 E-mail: info@wineappreciation.com • URL: http://www.wineappreciation.com • 1997. $79.95. Explains wine chemical changes in fermentation, aging, cellaring, and shipping.

Concession Profession. National Association of Concessionaires, 35 E. Wacker Dr., Suite 1816 Chicago, IL 60601. Phone: (312)236-3858 Fax: (312)236-7809 Biennial. Membership. Advertising vehicle serving the concession industry. Formerly *Insite*.

Concise Chemical and Technical Dictionary. Harry Bennett. Chemical Publishing Co., Inc., 192 Lexington Ave., No. 1201 New York, NY 10016. Phone: 800-786-3659 or (212)799-0090 Fax: (212)889-1537 E-mail: chempub@aol.com • URL: http://www.chemicalpublishing.com • 1986. $170.00. Fourth edition.

Concise International Encyclopedia of Robotics:Applications and Automation. Richard C. Dorf and Shimon Y. Nof, editors. John Wiley and Sons, Inc., 605 Third Ave. New York, NY 10158-0012. Phone: 800-225-5945 or (212)850-6000 Fax: (212)850-6088 E-mail: info@wiley.com • URL: http://www.wiley.com • 1990. $300.00.

Concord Consortium, Inc., 37 Thoreau St. Concord, MA 01742. Phone: (978)369-4367 Fax: (978)371-0696 E-mail: shea@concord.org • URL: http://www.concord.org • Research areas include educational applications of computers and computer networks.

Concrete International. American Concrete Institute, 38800 Country Club Rd. Farmington Hills, MI 48331. Phone: (248)848-3700 Fax: (248)848-3701 E-mail: bsemioli@aci-int.org • URL: http://www.aci-int.org • Monthly. $122.00 per year. Covers practical technology, industry news, and business management relating to the concrete construction industry.

Concrete Journal Buyers' Guide. The Aberdeen Group, 426 S. Westgate St. Addison, IL 60101-4546. Phone: 800-837-0870 or (630)543-0870 Fax: (630)543-3112 E-mail: aberdeen@wocnet.com • URL: http://www.wocnet.com • Annual. $3.00. Lists manufacturers or suppliers of concrete-related products and services.

The Concrete Producer. The Aberdeen Group, 426 S. Westgate St. Addison, IL 60101-4546. Phone: 800-837-0870 or (630)543-0870 Fax: (630)543-3112 E-mail: aberdeen@wocnet.com • URL: http://www.wocnet.com • Monthly. $27.00 per year. Covers the production and marketing of various concrete products, including precast and prestressed concrete. Formerly *Aberdeen's Concrete Journal*.

Concrete Products. Intertec Publishing Corp., 29 N. Wacker Dr. Chicago, IL 60606-3298. Phone: 800-400-5945 or (312)726-2802 Fax: (312)726-0241 E-mail: subs@intertec.com • URL: http://www.intertec.com • Monthly. $36.00 per year.

Concrete Repair Digest Buyers' Guide. The Aberdeen Group, 426 S. Westgate St. Addison, IL 60101-4546. Phone: 800-837-0870 or (630)543-0870 Fax: (630)543-3112 E-mail: aberdeen@wocnet.com • URL: http://www.wocnet.com • Annual. $3.00. Lists sources of products and services for concrete repair and maintenance specialists.

The Concrete Yearbook. EMAP Construction, 151 Roseberry Ave. London EC1R 4GB, England. Phone: 44 171 505 8600 Fax: 44 171 505 6610 URL: http://www.emapcontructco.uk • Annual. $115.00.

Concurrent Technology Corporation.

Conditions in Occupational Therapy: Effect on Occupational Performance. Ruth Hansen and Ben Atchison. Lippincott Williams & Wilkins, 530 Walnut St. Philadelphia, PA 19106-3780. Phone: 800-638-3030 or (215)521-8300 Fax: (215)521-8902 E-mail: custserv@ww.com • URL: http://www.lww.com • 1999. $42.00. Second edition. Each chapter ''describes a major condition that occupational therapists frequently treat.'' Includes case studies.

Condo Business. Shelter Pubications, 36 Toronto St., Suite 720 Toronto, ON, Canada M5C 2C5. Phone: (416)585-2552 Fax: (416)585-9741 Monthly. $65.00 per year. Covers condominium development and administration industries.

Condominium Law and Practice Forms. Patrick J. Rohan and Melvin A. Reskin. Matthew Bender & Co., Inc., Two Park Ave. New York, NY 10016. Phone: 800-223-1940 or (212)448-2000 Fax: (212)244-3188 E-mail: international@bender.com • URL: http://www.bender.com • $1,400.00. Eight looseleaf volumes. Periodic supplementation. Guide for handling condominium transactions. (Real Estate Transaction Series).

Condominiums, The Effects of Conversion on a Community. John R. Dinkelspiel and others. Greenwood Publishing Group, Inc, 88 Post Rd., W. Westport, CT 06881-5007. Phone: 800-225-5800 or (203)226-3571 Fax: (203)222-2540 E-mail: bookinfo@greenwood.com • URL: http://www.greenwood.com • 1981. $55.00.

Conducting a Successful Capital Campaign: A Comprehensive Fundraising Guide for Nonprofit Organizations. Kent E. Dove. Jossey-Bass, Inc., Publishers, 350 Sansome St. San Francisco, CA 94104. Phone: 888-378-2537 or (415)433-1740 Fax: (415)433-0499 E-mail: webperson@jbp.com • URL: http://www.josseybass.com • 1988. $38.95. (Nonprofit Sector-Public Administration Series).

Confectioner: Where Confectionery The Magazine. Stagnito Communcations, Inc., 1935 Shemer Rd., Suite 100 Northbrook, IL 60062. Phone: (847)205-5660 Fax: (847)205-5680 E-mail: info@stagnito.com • URL: http://www.stagnito.com • Bimonthly. $30.00 per year. Covers a wide variety of topics relating to the distribution and retailing of candy and snacks.

Conference Board, Inc.

Conference Board of Canada., 255 Smyth Rd. Ottawa, ON, Canada K1H 8M7. Phone: 800-267-0666 or (613)526-3280 Fax: (613)526-4857 URL: http://www.conferenceboard.ca • Research areas include economics, finance, international business, and consumer buying intentions.

Conference of Casualty Insurance Companies.

Conference of Consulting Actuaries.

Conference of State Bank Supervisors., 1015 18th St., N. W., Suite 1100 Washington, DC 20036-5275. Phone: 800-886-2727 or (202)296-2840 Fax: (202)296-1928 E-mail: nmilner@csbsdc.org • URL: http://www.csbsdc.org/index.html • Members are state officials responsible for supervision of state-chartered banking institutions.

Conference on Consumer Finance Law.

Conference on Safe Transportation of Hazardous Articles., 7811 Carrleigh Parkway Springfield, VA 22152. Phone: (703)451-4031 Fax: (703)451-4207 E-mail: mail@costha.com • URL: http://www.costha.org • Members are shipper associations concerned with the legal aspects of transporting hazardous materials.

Conference Papers Index. Cambridge Scientific Abstracts, 7200 Wisconsin Ave., 6th Fl. Bethesda, MD 20814. Phone: 800-843-7751 or (301)961-6700 Fax: (301)961-6720 Citations to scientific and technical papers presented at meetings, 1973 to present. Inquire as to online cost and availability.

Conference Terminology in English, Spanish, Russian, Italian, German and Hungarian. J. Herbert. Elsevier Science, 655 Ave. of the Americas New York, NY 10010. Phone: 888-437-4636 or (212)989-5800 Fax: (212)633-3680 E-mail: usinfo@elsevier.com • URL: http://www.elsevier.com • 1976. $130.25. Second revised edition.

Confidential Reference Book of the Jewelers Board of Trade. Jewelers Board of Trade, 70 Catamore Blvd. East Providence, RI 02914. Phone: (401)438-0750 Supplied on loan basis only to members of the Jewelers Board of Trade. Jewelry and allied product manufacturers, wholesalers and retailers; complete address, phone number and credit rating.

Congress in Print: The Weekly Catalog of Congressional Documents. Congressional Quarterly, Inc., 1414 22nd St., N.W. Washington, DC 20037. Phone: 800-432-2250 or (202)887-8500 E-mail: bookhelp@cq.com • URL: http://www.cq.com • 48 times a year. $198.00 per year.

Congressional Directory. U.S. Government Printing Office, Washington, DC 20402. Phone: (202)512-1800 Fax: (202)512-2250 Biennial. $45.00.

Congressional Index. CCH, Inc., 4025 W. Peterson Ave. Chicago, IL 60646-6085. Phone: 800-248-3248 or (773)583-8500 Fax: 800-224-8299 or (773)866-3608 URL: http://www.cch.com • Weekly when Congress is in session. $1,283.00 per year. Index to action on Public Bills from introduction to final disposition. Subject, author, and bill number indexes.

Congressional Investigations: Law and Practice. John C. Grabow. Aspen Law and Business, 1185 Ave. of the Americas New York, NY 10036. Phone: 800-444-1717 or (212)597-0200 Fax: 800-901-9075 or (212)597-0338 E-mail: customer.service@aspenpubl.com • URL: http://www.aspenpub.com • 1988. $95.00. Looseleaf service.

Congressional Monitor: Daily Listing of All Scheduled Congressional Committee Hearings with Witnesses. Congressional Quarterly. Inc., 1414 22nd St., N.W. Washington, DC 20037. Phone: 800-432-2250 or (202)887-8500 Fax: (202)887-6706 E-mail: bookhelp@cq.com • URL: http://www.cq.com • Daily. $1,349.00 per year. Weekly supplements.

Congressional Record. U.S. Congress. Available from U.S. Government Printing Office, Washington, DC 20402. Phone: (202)512-1800 Fax: (202)512-2250 Daily. $357.00 per year. Indexes give names, subjects, and history of bills. Texts of bills not included.

Congressional Record Scanner. Congressional Quarterly, Inc., 1414 22nd St., N.W. Washington, DC 20037. Phone: 800-432-2250 or (202)887-8500 Fax: (202)887-6706 E-mail: bookhelp@cq.com • URL: http://www.cq.com • 180 times a year. $395.00 per year. Abstract of each day's Congressional Record.

Congressional Staff Directory: With Biographical Information on Members and Key Congressional Staff. CQ Staff Directories, Inc., 815 Slaters Lane Alexandria, VA 22314. Phone: 800-252-1722 or (703)739-0900 Fax: (703)739-0234

E-mail: staffdir@staffdirectories.com • URL: http://www.staffdirectories.com • Three times a year. $227.00 per year. Single copies, $89.00. Contains more than 3,200 detailed biographies of members of Congress and their staffs. Includes committees and subcommittees. Keyword and name indexes are provided.

Congressional Yellow Book: Who's Who in Congress, Including Committees and Key Staff. Leadership Directories, Inc., 104 Fifth Ave., 2nd Fl. New York, NY 10011. Phone: (212)627-4140 Fax: (212)645-0931 E-mail: info@leadershipdirectories.com • URL: http://www.leadershipdirectories.com • Quarterly. $305.00 per year. Looseleaf. A directory of members of congress, including their committees and their key aides.

Consensus Forecasts: A Digest of International Economic Forecasts. Consensus Economics Inc., 53 Upper Brook St. London W1K 2LT, England. Phone: (44)20 7491 3211 Fax: (44)20 7409 2331 URL: http://www.consensuseconomics.com • Monthly. $565.00 per year. Provides a survey of more than 200 "prominent" financial and economic forecasters, covering 20 major countries. Two-year forecasts for each country include future growth, inflation, interest rates, and exchange rates. Each issue contains analysis of business conditions in various countries.

Consensus: National Futures and Financial Weekly. Consensus, Inc., 1737 McGee St., Suite 401 Kansas City, MO 64108. Phone: 800-383-1441 or (816)471-3862 Fax: (816)221-2045 E-mail: rsalva@aol.com • URL: http://www.consensus-inc.com • Weekly. $365.00 per year. Newspaper. Contains news, statistics, and special reports relating to agricultural, industrial, and financial futures markets. Features daily basis price charts, reprints of market advice, and "The Consensus Index of Bullish Market Opinion" (charts show percent bullish of advisors for various futures).

Conservation Directory: A Listing of Organizations, Agencies and Officials Concerned with Natural Resource Use and Management. Rue Gordon, editor. National Wildlife Federation, 8925 Leesburg Pike Vienna, VA 22184-0001. Phone: 800-477-5560 or (703)790-4000 Fax: (703)790-4468 E-mail: gordon@nwf.org • URL: http://www.nwf.org • Annual. Members, $54.90; non-members, $61.00. Lists agencies and private organizations in U.S. and Canada concerned with conservation and natural resource management.

Conservation of Library Materials: A Manual and Bibliography on the Care, Repair and Restoration of Library Materials. George M. Cunha and Dorothy G. Cunha. Scarecrow Press, Inc., 4720 Boston Way Lanham, MD 20706-4310. Phone: 800-462-6420 or (301)459-3366 Fax: 800-338-4550 or (301)459-1705 E-mail: orders@scarecrowpress.com • URL: http://www.scarecrowpress.com • 1972. Two volumes. Volume one, $47.50; volume two, $50.00.

Consortium for Graduate Study in Management.

Constitution, Jefferson's Manual and Rules of the House of Representatives. U.S. Government Printing Office, Washington, DC 20402. Phone: (202)512-1800 Fax: (202)512-2250 E-mail: gpoaccess@gpo.gov. • URL: http://www.accessgpo.gov • Biennial. $58.00.

Constructing Effective Questionnaires. Robert A. Peterson. Sage Publications, Inc., 2455 Teller Rd. Thousand Oaks, CA 91320. Phone: (805)499-0721 Fax: (805)499-0871 E-mail: info@sagepub.com • URL: http://www.sagepub.com • 1999. $70.00. Covers the construction and wording of questionnaires for survey research.

Construction Arbitration Handbook. James Acret. Shepard's, 555 Middle Creek Parkway Colorado Springs, CO 80921. Phone: 800-743-7393 or (719)481-7371 Fax: 800-525-0053 or (719)481-7621 E-mail: customer_service@shepards.com • URL: http://www.shepards.com • 1985. $110.00. Explains the arbitration of disputes involving builders.

Construction Contracting. Richard H. Clough and Glenn A. Sears. John Wiley and Sons, Inc., 605 Third Ave. New York, NY 10158-0012. Phone: 800-225-5945 or (212)850-6000 Fax: (212)850-6088 E-mail: info@wiley.com • URL: http://www.wiley.com • 1994. $99.00. Sixth edition.

Construction Contractors' Survival Guide. Thomas C. Schleifer. John Wiley and Sons, Inc., 605 Third Ave. New York, NY 10158-0012. Phone: 800-225-5945 or (212)850-6000 Fax: (212)850-6088 E-mail: info@wiley.com • URL: http://www.wiley.com • 1990. $80.00. (Practical Construction Guides Series).

Construction Equipment Buyers' Guide. Cahners Business Information, 1350 E. Touhy Ave. Des Plaines, IL 60018-5080. Phone: 800-662-7776 or (847)635-8800 Fax: (847)390-2690 E-mail: corporatecommunications@cahners.com • URL: http://www.cahners.com • Annual. Included in subscription to *Construction Equipment*.

Construction Equipment Distribution. Associated Equipment Distributors, 615 W. 22nd St. Oak Brook, IL 60521. Phone: 800-338-0650 or (630)574-0650 Fax: (630)574-0132 Monthly. Members, $20.00 per year; non-members, $40.00 per year.

Construction Equipment Distribution-Directory. Associated Equipment Distributors, 615 W. 22nd St. Oak Brook, IL 60521. Phone: 800-388-0650 or (630)574-0650 Fax: (630)574-0132 E-mail: info@aednet.org • URL: http://www.aednet.org • Annual. $100.00 per year. Lists about 1,300 members of the association.

Construction Equipment Operation and Maintenance. Construction Publications Inc., P.O. Box 1689 Cedar Rapids, IA 52406. Phone: (319)366-1597 Fax: (319)362-8808 Bi-monthly. $12.00 per year. Information for users of construction equipment and industry news.

Construction Financial Management Association., 29 Emmons Dr., Suite F-50 Princeton, NJ 08540. Phone: (609)452-8000 Fax: (609)452-0474 E-mail: info@cfma.org • URL: http://www.cfma.org • Members are accountants and other financial managers in the construction industry.

Construction Industry Annual Financial Survey. Construction Financial Management Association, 29 Emmons Dr., Suite F-50 Princeton, NJ 08540-1413. Phone: (609)452-8000 Fax: (609)452-0474 Annual. $149.00. Contains key financial ratios for various kinds and sizes of construction contractors.

Construction Industry Institute., University of Texas at Austin, 3208 Red River, Suite 300 Austin, TX 78705-2697. Phone: (512)232-3000 Fax: (512)499-8101 E-mail: k.eickman@mail.utexas.edu • URL: http://www.construction-institution.org • Research activities are related to the management, planning, and design aspects of construction project execution.

Construction Industry Manufacturers Association.

Construction Labor Report. Bureau of National Affairs, Inc., 1231 25th St., N.W. Washington, DC 20037-1197. Phone: 800-372-1033 or (202)452-4200 Fax: (202)822-8092 E-mail: books@bna.com • URL: http://www.bna.com. • Weekly. $1,039.00 per year. Two volumes. Looseleaf.

Construction Law Adviser: Monthly Practical Advice for Lawyers and Construction Professionals. West Group, 610 Opperman Dr. Eagan, MN 55123. Phone: 800-328-4880 or (651)687-7000 Fax: 800-213-2323 or (651)687-5827 URL: http://www.westgroup.com • Monthly. $295.00 per year. Newsletter.

Construction Materials and Processes. Donald A. Watson. McGraw-Hill, 1221 Ave. of the Americas New York, NY 10020. Phone: 800-722-4726 or (212)904-2000 Fax: (212)904-2072 E-mail: customer.service@mcgraw-hill.com • URL: http://www.mcgraw-hill.com • 1986. $83.34. Third edition.

Construction Materials: Types, Uses, and Applications. Caleb Hornbostel. John Wiley and Sons, Inc., 605 Third Ave. New York, NY 10158-0012. Phone: 800-225-5945 or (212)850-6000 Fax: (212)850-6088 E-mail: info@wiley.com • URL: http://www.wiley.com • 1991. $225.00. Second edition. (Practical Construction Guides Series).

Construction Research Center., Georgia Institute of Technology Atlanta, GA 30332-0245. Phone: (404)894-3013 Fax: (404)894-9140 E-mail: steve.johnson@mse.gatech.edu • URL: http://www.arch.gatech.edu/crc/ • Conducts interdisciplinary research in all aspects of construction, including planning, design, cost estimating, and management.

Construction Sealants and Adhesives. Julian R. Panek and John P. Cook. John Wiley and Sons, Inc., 605 Third Ave. New York, NY 10158-0012. Phone: 800-526-5945 or (212)850-6000 Fax: (212)850-6088 E-mail: info@wiley.com • URL: http://www.wiley.com • 1991. $120.00. Third edition. (Practical Construction Guides Series).

Construction Specifier: For Commercial and Industrial Construction. Construction Specifications Institute, 99 Canal Center Plaza, Suite 300 Alexandria, VA 22314-1588. Phone: 800-689-2900 or (703)684-0300 Fax: (703)684-0465 E-mail: csimail@csinet.org • URL: http://www.csinet.org • Monthly. Free to members; non-members, $36.00 per year; universities, $30.00 per year. Technical aspects of the construction industry.

Construction Specifier - Member Directory. Construction Specifications Institute, 601 Madison St. Alexandria, VA 22314-1741. Phone: 800-689-2900 or (703)684-0300 Fax: (703)684-0465 E-mail: csimail@csinet.org • URL: http://www.csinet.org • Annual. $30.00. Roster of construction specifers by the institute, and 17,200 members.

Constructor-AGC Directory of Membership and Services. Associated General Contractors of America. AGC Information, Inc., 333 John Carley St., Suite 200 Alecandria, VA 22314-5745. Phone: (703)837-5355 Fax: (703)837-5402 URL: http://www.agc.org • Annual. $250.00. Membership is made up of contractors and suppliers for general construction. Formerly *Associated General Contractors of America National Directory*.

Constructor: The Management Magazine of the Construction Industry. Associated General Contractors of America. AGC Information, Inc., 333 John Carlye St., 2nd Fl. Alexandria, VA 22314-5745. Phone: (703)837-5355 Fax: (703)837-5402 URL: http://www.agc.org • Monthly. Free to members; non-members, $250.00 per year. Includes *Directory*.

Consultants and Consulting Organizations Directory. The Gale Group, 27500 Drake Rd. Farmington Hills, MI 48331-3535. Phone: 800-877-GALE or (248)699-GALE Fax: 800-414-5043 or (248)699-8069 E-mail: galeord@galegroup.com • URL: http://www.galegroup.com • 2001. $795.00. 23rd edition. Three volumes. Includes mid-year *Supplement*.

Consultants News. Kennedy Information, LLC, One Kennedy Place, Route 12 S. Fitzwilliam, NH 03447. Phone: 800-531-1026 or (603)585-3101 Fax: (603)585-9555 E-mail: office@kennedypub.com • URL: http://www.kennedyinfo.com • Monthly. $229.00 per year. Newsletter. News and ideas for management consultants.

The Consultant's Proposal, Fee, and Contract Problem-Solver. Ronald Tepper. John Wiley and Sons, Inc., 605 Third Ave. New York, NY 10158-0012. Phone: 800-225-5945 or (212)850-6000 Fax: (212)850-6088 E-mail: info@wiley.com • URL: http://www.wiley.com • 1993. $24.95. Provides advice for consultants on fees, contracts, proposals, and client communications. Includes case histories in 10 specific fields, such as finance, marketing, engineering, and management.

Consultative Selling: The Hanan Formula for High-Margin Sales at High Levels. Mack Hanan. AMACOM, 1601 Broadway, 12th Fl. New York, NY 10019. Phone: 800-262-9699 or (212)586-8100 Fax: (212)903-8168 E-mail: custmserv@amanet.org • URL: http://www.amanet.org • 1999. $24.95. Sixth revised edition. How to treat customers as friends to be helped and not as foes to be overcome.

Consulting Business. Entrepreneur Media, Inc., 2445 McCabe Way Irvine, CA 92614. Phone: 800-421-2300 or (949)261-2325 Fax: (949)261-0234 E-mail: entmag@entrepreneur.com • URL: http://www.entrepreneur.com • Looseleaf. $59.50. A practical guide to becoming a business consultant. Covers profit potential, start-up costs, market size evaluation, pricing, accounting, advertising, promotion, etc. (Start-Up Business Guide No. E1151.)

Consulting Services. Association of Consulting Chemists and Chemical Engineers, Inc., PO Box 297 Sparta, NJ 07871. Phone: (973)729-6671 Fax: (973)729-7088 E-mail: accce@chemconsult.org • URL: http://www.chemconsult.org • Biennial. $30.00. Directory containing one-page "scope sheet" for each member and an extensive classified directory.

Consulting-Specifiying Engineer. Cahners Business Information, 1350 E. Touhy Ave. Des Plains, IL 60018-5080. Phone: 800-662-7776 or (847)390-2730 Fax: (847)390-2769 E-mail: corporatecommunications@cahners.com • URL: http://www.cahners.com • 13 times a year. $86.90 per year. Formerly *Consulting Engineer*.

Consumer Affairs Letter: Monthly Report to Management on Issue Activities, Strategies, etc. of Consumer Groups. George Idelson, P.O. Box 65313 Washington, DC 20035. Phone: (202)362-4279 Monthly. Non-profit institutions, $125.00 per year; corporations, $247.00 per year.

Consumer and Commercial Credit: Installment Sales. Prentice Hall, 240 Frisch Court Paramus, NJ 07652-5240. Phone: 800-947-7700 or (201)909-6200 Fax: 800-445-6991 or (201)909-6361 URL: http://www.prenhall.com • Three looseleaf volumes. Periodic supplementation. Price on application. Covers secured transactions under the Uniform Commercial Code and the Uniform Consumer Credit Code. Includes retail installment sales, home improvement loans, higher education loans, and other kinds of installment loans.

Consumer and Commercial Credit Management. Robert H. Cole and Lon Mishler. McGraw-Hill Professional, 1221 Ave. of the Americas New York, NY 10020. Phone: 800-772-4267 or (212)904-2000 Fax: (212)904-2072 E-mail: customer.service@mcgraw-hill.com • URL: http://www.mcgraw-hill.com • 1997. 11th edition. Price on application.

Consumer Asia 2001. Available from The Gale Group, 27500 Drake Rd. Farmington Hills, MI 48331-3535. Phone: 800-877-GALE or (248)699-GALE Fax: 800-414-5043 or (248)699-8069 E-mail: galeord@galegroup.com • URL: http://www.galegroup.com • 2001. $970.00. Eighth edition. Published by Euromonitor. Provides statistical andanalytical surveys of factors affecting Asian consumer markets: energy, labor, population, finance, debt, tourism, consumer expenditures, household characteristics, etc. Emphasis is on Hong Kong, Singapore, Taiwan, South Korea, Indonesia, and Malaysia.

Consumer Attitudes Toward Physical Fitness and Health Clubs. Available from MarketResearch.com, 641 Ave. of the Americas, Third Floor New York, NY 10011. Phone: 800-298-5699 or (212)807-2629 Fax: (212)807-2716 E-mail: order@marketresearch.com • URL: http://www.marketresearch.com • 1999. $795.00. Published by American Sports Data, Inc. Contains market research information.

Consumer Bankers Association.

Consumer Bankruptcy. Allyn Buzzell, editor. American Bankers Association, 1120 Connecticut Ave., N. W. Washington, DC 20036-3971. Phone: 800-338-0626 or (202)663-5000 Fax: (202)663-7543 URL: http://www.aba.com • 1991. $39.00. Second edition. Includes a step-by-step guide for banks on responding to a consumer bankruptcy filing.

Consumer Behavior. Robert D. Blackwell and others. Dryden Press, 301 Commerce St., Suite 3700 Fort Worth, TX

32887-1437. Phone: 800-447-9479 or (817)334-7500 Fax: (817)334-7844 URL: http://www.little@harbrace.com • 1994. $102.50. Eighth edition.

Consumer Canada 1996. Available from The Gale Group, 27500 Drake Rd. Farmington Hills, MI 48331-3535. Phone: 800-877-GALE or (248)699-GALE Fax: 800-414-5043 or (248)699-8069 E-mail: galeord@galegroup.com • URL: http://www.galegroup.com • 1996. $750.00. Published by Euromonitor. Provides consumer market, socioeconomic, and demographic data for Canada. Includes consumer market size (volume and value) for many specific kinds of products.

Consumer China 2001. Available from The Gale Group, 27500 Drake Rd. Farmington Hills, MI 48331-3535. Phone: 800-877-GALE or (248)699-GALE Fax: 800-414-5043 or (248)699-8069 E-mail: galeord@galegroup.com • URL: http://www.galegroup.com • 2001. $970.00. Seventh edition. Published by Euromonitor. Provides demographic and consumer market data for China.

Consumer Confidence Survey. Conference Board, Inc., 845 Third Ave. New York, NY 10022-6679. Phone: (212)759-0900 Fax: (212)980-7014 E-mail: lei@conference-board.org • URL: http://www.tcb-indicators.org • Monthly. Members, $95.00 per year; non-members, $195.00 per year. Attitudes toward business conditions and employment, plans to buy major durable goods, and intended vacations. Formerly *Consumer Attitudes and Buying Plans*.

Consumer Credit. U. S. Federal Reserve System, Board of Governors, Publications Services, MS-127 Washington, DC 20551. Phone: (202)452-3244 Fax: (202)728-5886 URL: http://www.federalreserve.gov • Monthly. $5.00 per year. (Federal Reserve Statistical Release, G.19.)

Consumer Credit and Compliance Guide with Annual Percentage Rate Tables. David Thorndike. Warren, Gorham and Lamont/RIA Group, 395 Hudson St. New York, NY 10014. Phone: 800-950-1215 or (212)367-6300 Fax: (651)687-5827 E-mail: customer_services@riag.com • URL: http://www.westgroup.com • $88.00. Periodic supplementation.

Consumer Credit and the Law. Dee Pridgen. West Group, 610 Opperman Dr. Eagan, MN 55123. Phone: 800-328-4880 or (651)687-7000 Fax: 800-213-2323 or (651)687-5827 URL: http://www.westgroup.com • Looseleaf. $135.00.

Consumer Credit and Truth-in-Lending Compliance Report. Warren, Gorham and Lamont/RIA Group, 395 Hudson St. New York, NY 10014. Phone: 800-950-1215 or (212)367-6300 Fax: (651)687-7000 E-mail: customer_services@riag.com • URL: http://www.westgroup.com • Monthly. $183.75 per year. Newsletter. Focuses on the latest regulatory rulings and findings involving consumer lending and credit activity. Formerly *Bank Installment Lending Newsletter*.

Consumer Credit Compliance Manual. John R. Fonseca. West Group, 610 Opperman Dr. Eagan, MN 55123. Phone: 800-328-4880 or (651)687-7000 Fax: 800-213-2323 or (651)687-5827 URL: http://www.westgroup.com • 1984. $135.00. Second edition. Interprets current consumer credit laws and regulations.

Consumer Credit Guide. CCH, Inc., 4025 W. Peterson Ave. Chicago, IL 60646-6085. Phone: 800-248-3248 Fax: 800-224-8299 or (773)866-3608 URL: http://www.cch.com • Biweekly. $1,206.00 per year. Looseleaf service.

Consumer Credit Insurance Association.

Consumer Credit Laws: Transaction and Forms. Matthew Bender & Co., Inc., Two Park Ave. New York, NY 10016. Phone: 800-223-1940 or (212)448-2000 Fax: (212)244-3188 E-mail: international@bender.com • URL: http://www.bender.com • $720.00. Four looseleaf volumes. Periodic supplementation. Detailed treatment of the law with practical step-by-step guidance for every stage of a consumer credit transaction.

Consumer Eastern Europe. Available from The Gale Group, 27500 Drake Rd. Farmington Hills, MI 48331-3535. Phone: 800-877-GALE or (248)699-GALE Fax: 800-414-5043 or (248)699-8069 E-mail: galeord@galegroup.com • URL: http://www.galegroup.com • 2001. $1,090.00. Eighth edition. Published by Euromonitor. Provides demographic and consumer market data for the countries of Eastern Europe.

Consumer Education Research Center.

The Consumer Electronics Industry and the Future of American Manufacturing: How the U. S. Lost the Lead and Why We Must Get Back in the Game. Susan W. Sanderson. Economic Policy Institute, 1660 L St., N.W., Suite 1200 Washington, DC 20036. Phone: (202)775-8810 Fax: (202)775-0819 E-mail: economic@capcon.net • 1990. $12.00.

Consumer Europe 2000/2001. Available from The Gale Group, 27500 Drake Rd. Farmington Hills, MI 48331-3535. Phone: 800-877-GALE or (248)699-GALE Fax: 800-414-5043 or (248)699-8069 E-mail: galeord@galegroup.com • URL: http://www.galegroup.com • 2000. $1,190.00. 16th edition. Published by Euromonitor. Detailed statistical tables furnish five-year data on the production, sales, distribution, consumption, and other aspects of more than 240 consumer product categories. Thirteen countries of Western Europe are included.

Consumer Expenditure Survey. Available from U. S. Government Printing Office, Washington, DC 20402. Phone: (202)512-1800 Fax: (202)512-2250 E-mail: gpoaccess@gpo.gov • URL: http://www.access.gpo.gov • Biennial. Issued by the Bureau of Labor Statistics, U. S. Department of Labor (http://www.bls.gov). Contains data on various kinds of consumer spending, according to household income, education, etc. (Bureau of Labor Statistics Bulletin.)

Consumer Federation of America., 1424 16th St., N. W., Suite 604 Washington, DC 20036. Phone: (202)387-6121 Members are national, regional, state, and local consumer groups.

Consumer Finance Bulletin. American Financial Services Association, 919 18th St., N.W., 3rd Fl. Washington, DC 20006. Phone: (202)296-5544 Fax: (202)223-0321 Monthly. $126.00 per year.

Consumer Finance Newsletter. Financial Publishing Co., P.O. Box 15698 Boston, MA 02215. Phone: 800-247-3214 or (617)262-4040 Fax: (617)247-0136 Monthly. $24.50 per year. Covers changes in state and federal consumer lending regulations.

The Consumer Health Information Source Book. Alan Rees, editor. Oryx Press, 4041 N. Central Ave., Ste. 700 Phoenix, AZ 85012-3397. Phone: 800-279-6799 or (602)265-2651 Fax: 800-279-4663 or (602)265-6250 E-mail: info@oryxpress.com • URL: http://www.oryxpress.com • 2000. $59.50. Sixth edition. Bibliography of current literature and guide to organizations.

Consumer Health Product Association., 1150 Connecticut Ave., N. W. Washington, DC 20036. Phone: (202)429-9260 Fax: (202)233-6835 Members are over-the-counter drug manufacturers and suppliers.

Consumer Information Center., 18th and F St., N.W., Room G-142 Washington, DC 20405. Phone: 888-878-3256 Fax: (202)501-4281 E-mail: cic.info@pueblo.gsa.gov • URL: http://www.pueblo.gsa.gov • Develops, promotes, and distributes information of interest to consumers.

Consumer Installment Credit. Board of Governors, U.S. Federal Reserve System, Publications Services, Room MS-138 Washington, DC 20551. Phone: (202)452-3244 Fax: (202)728-5886 Monthly. $5.00 per year.

Consumer International 2000/2001. Available from The Gale Group, 27500 Drake Rd. Farmington Hills, MI 48331-3535. Phone: 800-877-GALE or (248)699-GALE Fax: 800-414-5043 or (248)699-8069 E-mail: galeord@galegroup.com • URL: http://www.galegroup.com • 1998. $1,190.00. Seventh edition. Published by Euromonitor. Contains extensive consumer market, economic, and demographic data for 27 major, non-European countries, including the U. S. and Canada. Includes consumer market size (volume and value) for 150 product types in 14 categories (food, clothing, automobiles, cosmetics, appliances, etc.).

Consumer Internet Economy. Jupiter Media Metrix, 21 Asor Place New York, NY 10003. Phone: 800-488-4345 or (212)780-6060 Fax: (212)780-6075 E-mail: jupiter@jup.com • URL: http://www.jmm.com • 1999. $3,495.00. Market research report. Provides data and forecasts relating to various hardware and software elements of the Internet, including browsers, provision of service, telephone line modems, cable modems, wireless access devices, online advertising, programming languages, and Internet chips. Includes company profiles.

Consumer Latin America. Available from The Gale Group, 27500 Drake Rd. Farmington Hills, MI 48331-3535. Phone: 800-877-GALE or (248)699-GALE Fax: 800-414-5043 or (248)699-8069 E-mail: galeord@galegroup.com • URL: http://www.galegroup.com • 2001. $970.00. Eighth edition. Published by Euromonitor. Contains a wide variety of consumer market data relating to the countries of Latin America. Includes market forecasts.

Consumer Magazine and Advertising Source. SRDS, 1700 Higgins Rd. Des Plaines, IL 60018. Phone: 800-851-7737 or (847)375-5000 Fax: (847)375-5001 E-mail: krizz@srds.com • URL: http://www.srds.com • Monthly. $661.00 per year. Contains advertising rates and other data for U. S. consumer magazines and agricultural publications. Also provides consumer market data for population, households, income, and retail sales. Formerly *Consumer Magazine and Agri-Media Source*.

Consumer Mexico, 1996. Available from The Gale Group, 27500 Drake Rd. Farmington Hills, MI 48331-3535. Phone: 800-877-GALE or (248)699-GALE Fax: 800-414-5043 or (248)699-8069 E-mail: galeord@galegroup.com • URL: http://www.galegroup.com • 1996. $750.00. Published by Euromonitor. Provides demographic and consumer market data for Mexico.

Consumer Online Services Report. Jupiter Media Metrix, 21 Asor Place New York, NY 10003. Phone: 800-488-4345 or (212)780-6060 Fax: (212)780-6075 E-mail: jupiter@jup.com • URL: http://www.jmm.com • Annual. $1,895.00. Market research report. Provides analysis of trends in the online information industry, with projections of growth in future years (five-year forecasts). Contains profiles of electronic media companies.

Consumer Power: How Americans Spend. Margaret Ambry. McGraw-Hill Professional, 1221 Ave. of the Americas New York, NY 10020-1095. Phone: 800-772-4726 or (212)904-2000 Fax: (212)904-2072 E-mail: customer.service@mcgraw-hill.com • URL: http://www.mcgraw-hill.com • 1992. $27.50. Contains detailed statistics on consumer income and spending. Nine major categories of products and services are covered, with spending data and dollar size of market for each item.

Consumer Price Indices: An ILO Manual. Ralph Turvey and others. International Labour Office, 1828 L St., N.W., Suite 801 Washington, DC 20036. Phone: (202)653-7652 Fax: (202)653-7687 E-mail: ilopubs@tascol.com • URL: http://www.ilo.org/pubns • 1990. $24.75.

Consumer Product Litigation Reporter. Andrews Publications, 175 Strafford Ave., Bldg 4, Suite 140 Wayne, PA 19087. Phone: 800-345-1101 or (610)622-0510 Fax: (610)622-0501 URL: http://www.andrewspub.com • Monthly. $725.00 per year. Provides reports on legislation and litigation relating to product liability.

Consumer Product Safety Guide. CCH, Inc., 4025 W. Peterson Ave. Chicago, IL 60646-6085. Phone: 800-248-3248 or (773)583-8500 Fax: 800-224-8299 or (773)866-3608 URL: http://www.cch.com • Weekly. $1,122.00 per year. Looseleaf service. Three volumes. Periodic suplementation.

Consumer Product Safety Review. Available from U. S. Government Printing Office, Washington, DC 20402. Phone: (202)512-1800 Fax: (202)512-2250 E-mail: gpoaccess@gpo.gov • URL: http://www.access.gpo.gov • Quarterly. $16.00 per year. Issued by the U. S. Consumer Product Safety Commission.

Consumer Protection and the Law. Dee Pridgen. West Group, 610 Opperman Dr. Eagan, MN 55123. Phone: 800-328-4880 or (651)687-7000 Fax: 800-213-2323 or (651)687-5827 URL: http://www.westgroup.com • Looseleaf. $135.00. Periodic supplementation. Covers advertising, sales practices, unfair trade practices, consumer fraud, and product warranties.

Consumer Reports. Consumers Union of the United States, Inc., 101 Truman Ave. Yonkers, NY 10703-1057. Phone: 800-234-1645 or (914)378-2000 Fax: (914)378-2900 URL: http://www/consumerreports.org • Semimonthly. $24.00 per year. Includes *Annual Buying Guide*.

Consumer Reports Money Book: How to Get It, Save It, and Spend It Wisely. Janet Bamford and others. Consumers Union of the United States, Inc., 101 Truman Ave. Yonkers, NY 10703-1057. Phone: 800-234-1645 or (914)378-2000 Fax: (914)378-2904 URL: http://www.consumerreports.org • 1997. $29.95. Revised edition. Covers budgeting, retirement planning, bank accounts, insurance, and other personal finance topics.

Consumer Reports Travel Letter. Consumers Union of the United States, Inc., 101 Truman Ave. Yonkers, NY 10703-1057. Phone: 800-234-1645 or (914)378-2000 Fax: (914)378-2906 URL: http://www.consumerreports.org • Monthly. $39.00 per year. Newsletter with information on air fares, travel discounts, special hotel rates, etc.

Consumer Research Center., The Conference Board, Inc., 845 Third Ave. New York, NY 10022. Phone: (212)759-0900 Fax: (212)980-7014 E-mail: franco@conference-board.org • URL: http://www.crc-conquest.org • Conducts research on the consumer market, including elderly and working women segments.

Consumer Sourcebook: A Directory and Guide. The Gale Group, 27500 Drake Rd. Farmington Hills, MI 48331-3535. Phone: 800-877-GALE or (248)699-GALE Fax: 800-414-5043 or (248)699-8069 E-mail: galeord@galegroup.com • URL: http://www.galegroup.com • 2001. $290.00. 14th edition. Consumer-oriented agencies, associations, institutes, centers, etc.

Consumer Trends: An Independent Newsletter on Credit Issues and Financial Affairs. International Credit Association, P.O. Box 15945-314 Lenexa, KS 66284-5945. Phone: (913)307-9432 Fax: (913)541-0156 E-mail: ica@ica-credit.org • URL: http://www.ica-credit.org • Monthly. $100.00 per year.

Consumer USA 2000. Available from The Gale Group, 27500 Drake Rd. Farmington Hills, MI 48331-3535. Phone: 800-877-GALE or (248)699-GALE Fax: 800-414-5043 or (248)699-8069 E-mail: galeord@galegroup.com • URL: http://www.galegroup.com • 2000. $900.00. Fifth edition. Published by Euromonitor. Provides demographic and consumer market data for the United States. Forecasts to the year 2005.

The Consumer's Dictionary of Cosmetic Ingredients. Ruth Winter. Crown Publishers Group, Inc., 201 E. 50th St. New York, NY 10022. Phone: 800-726-0600 or (212)751-2600 Fax: (301)857-9460 1999. $16.00. Fifth edition.

Consumers Digest: Best Buys, Best Prices, Best Reports for People Who Demand Value. Consumers Digest Inc., 8001 N. Lincoln Ave., 6th Fl. Skokie, IL 60077-3657. Phone: 800-777-0025 or (847)763-9200 Fax: (847)763-0200 URL: http://www.consumersdigest.com • Bimonthly. $15.97.

Consumers' Directory of Continuing Care Retirement Communities. American Association of Homes and Services for the Aging, 901 E St., N. W., Suite 500 Washington, DC

20004-2037. Phone: 800-508-9442 or (202)783-2242 Fax: (202)783-2255 E-mail: info@aahsa.org • URL: http://www.aahsa.org • 1997. $30.00. Contains information on fees, services, and accreditation of about 500 U. S. retirement facilities providing lifetime housing, meals, and health care. Introductory text discusses factors to be considered in selecting a continuing care community.

Consumers Education and Protective Association International.

Consumers' Guide to Health Plans. Center for the Study of Services, 733 15th St., N. W., Suite 820 Washington, DC 20005. Phone: 800-213-7283 or (202)347-7283 Fax: (202)347-4000 URL: http://www.checkbook.org • 1996. $12.00. Revised edition. Presents the results of a consumer survey on satisfaction with specific managed care health insurance plans, and related information. Includes "Top-Rated Plans," "Health Plans That Chose Not to Have Their Members Surveyed," and other lists. General advice is provided on choosing a plan, finding a good doctor, getting good care, etc.

Consumers' Guide to Product Grades and Terms: From Grade A to VSOP-Definitions of 8,000 Terms Describing Food Housewares and Other Everyday Terms. The Gale Group, 27500 Drake Rd. Farmington Hills, MI 48331-3535. Phone: 800-877-GALE or (248)699-GALE Fax: 800-414-5043 or (248)699-8069 E-mail: galeord@galegroup.com • URL: http://www.galegroup.com • 1992. $75.00. Includes product grades and classifications defined by government agencies, such as the Food and Drug Administration (FDA), and by voluntary standards organizations, such as the American National Standards Institute (ANSI).

Consumers Reference Disc. National Information Services Corp., Wyman Towers, Suite 6, 3100 Saint Paul St. Baltimore, MD 21218. Phone: (410)243-0797 Fax: (410)243-0982 Quarterly. Provides the CD-ROM version of *Consumer Health and Nutrition Index* from Oryx Press and *Consumers Index to Product Evaluations and Information Sources* from Pierian Press. Contains citations to consumer health articles and consumer product evaluations, tests, warnings, and recalls.

Consumers' Research.

Consumer's Research Magazine: Analyzing Consumer Issues. Consumers' Research Inc., 800 Maryland Ave., N.E. Washington, DC 20002. Phone: (202)546-1713 Fax: (202)546-1638 Monthly. $24.00 per year.

Consumers Union of the United States.

Consumption on the Woolen System and Worsted Combing. U. S. Bureau of the Census, Washington, DC 20233-0800. Phone: (301)457-4100 Fax: (301)457-3842 URL: http://www.census.gov • Quarterly and annual. Provides data on consumption of fibers in woolen and worsted spinning mills, by class of fibers and end use. (Current Industrial Reports, MQ-22D.)

Contact Lens Association of Ophthalmologists.

Contact Lens Manufacturers Association.

Contact Lens Manufacturers Association: Directory of Members. Contact Lens Manufacturers Association, 4400 East-West Highway 33 Bethesda, MD 20814. Phone: 800-343-5367 or (301)654-2229 Annual. Membership.

Contact Lens Society of America.

Contact Lens Spectrum. Boucher Communications, Inc., 1300 Virginia Dr. Suite 400 Fort Washington, PA 19034-3221. Phone: 800-306-6332 or (215)643-8000 Fax: (215)643-8099 20 times a year. $43.00 per year. Provides news and information on clinical issues and the contact lens industry. Incorporates *Contact Lens Forum*.

Containerization and Intermodal Institute.

Contemporary Advertising. William F. Arens. McGraw-Hill, 1221 Ave. of the Americas New York, NY 10020. Phone: 800-722-4726 or (212)904-2000 Fax: (212)904-2072 E-mail: customer.service@mcgraw-hill.com • URL: http://www.mcgraw-hill.com • 1998. $83.13. Seventh edition.

Contemporary Architects. Available from The Gale Group, 27500 Drake Rd. Farmington Hills, MI 48331-3535. Phone: 800-877-GALE or (248)699-GALE Fax: 800-414-5043 or (248)699-8069 E-mail: galeord@galegroup.com • URL: http://www.galegroup.com • 1994. $175.00. Third edition. Published by St. James Press. Living architects of the world and influential architects of earlier times.

Contemporary Artists. Available from The Gale Group, 27500 Drake Rd. Farmington Hills, MI 48331-3535. Phone: 800-877-GALE or (248)699-GALE Fax: 800-414-5043 or (248)699-8069 E-mail: galeord@galegroup.com • URL: http://www.galegroup.com • 1996. $170.00. Fourth edition. Published by St. James Press. International coverage.

Contemporary Authors. The Gale Group, 27500 Drake Rd. Farmington Hills, MI 48331-3535. Phone: 800-877-GALE or (248)699-GALE Fax: 800-414-5043 or (248)699-8069 E-mail: galeord@galegroup.com • URL: http://www.galegroup.com • 189 volumes in print. Prices vary. Provides biographical information on over 100,000 modern authors, including novelists, nonfiction writers, poets, play wrights, journalists, and scriptwriters.

Contemporary Authors on CD-ROM. The Gale Group, 27500 Drake Rd. Farmington, MI 48331-3535. Phone: 800-877-GALE or (248)699-GALE Fax: 800-414-5043 or (248)699-8069 E-mail: galeord@gale.com • URL: http://www.gale.com • Semiannual. $795.00 per year. Provides CD-ROM biographical and bibliographical information on about 100,000 modern authors. Includes novelists, nonfiction writers, poets, playwrights, screenwriters, editors, and journalists.

Contemporary Business: Alternate Study Guide. Louis E. Boone. Dryden Press, 301 Commerce St., Suite 3700 Fort Worth, TX 32887-1437. Phone: 800-447-9479 or (817)334-7500 Fax: (817)334-7844 URL: http://www.little@harbrace.com • 1998. $88.50. Ninth edition.

Contemporary Business Communication. Louis E. Boone and others. Prentice Hall, 240 Frisch Court Paramus, NJ 07652-5240. Phone: 800-947-7700 or (201)909-6200 Fax: 800-445-6991 or (201)909-6361 URL: http://www.prenhall.com • 1996. $80.00. Second edition.

Contemporary Business Law and the Legal Environment: Principles and Cases. J. David Reitzel and others. McGraw-Hill, 1221 Ave. of the Americas New York, NY 10020. Phone: 800-722-4726 or (212)904-2000 Fax: (212)904-2072 E-mail: customer.service@mcgraw-hill.com • URL: http://www.mcgraw-hill.com • 1994. $72.74. Fifth revised edition.

Contemporary Business Mathematics. John Webber. McGraw-Hill Higher Education, 1221 Ave. of the Americas New York, NY 10020-1095. Phone: 800-772-4726 or (212)904-2000 Fax: (212)904-2072 E-mail: customer.service@mcgraw-hill.com • URL: http://www.mcgraw-hill.com • 1994. $61.50.

Contemporary Designers. The Gale Group, 27500 Drake Rd. Farmington Hills, MI 48331-3535. Phone: 800-877-GALE or (248)699-GALE Fax: 800-414-5043 or (248)699-8069 E-mail: galeord@galegroup.com • URL: http://www.galegroup.com • 1997. $175.00. Third edition. Profiles the careers and accomplishments of 685 designers from throughout the world.

Contemporary Drug Problems. Federal Legal Publications, Inc., 335 Route 312 Brewster, NY 10509. Phone: (914)279-0362 Fax: (914)279-0259 E-mail: flp@bestweb.com • Quarterly. $45.00 per year.

Contemporary Entrepreneurs: Profiles of Entrepreneurs and the Businesses They Started, Representing 74 Companies in 30 Industries. Craig E. Aronoff and John L. Ward, editors. Omnigraphics, Inc., Penobscot Bldg. Detroit, MI 48226. Phone: 800-234-1340 or (313)961-1340 Fax: 800-875-1340 or (313)961-1383 E-mail: info@omnigraphics.com • URL: http://www.omnigraphics.com • 1992. $95.00.

Contemporary Fashion. Richard Martin, editor. St. James Press, 27500 Drake Rd. Farmington Hills, MI 48331-3535. Phone: 800-877-GALE or (248)699-GALE Fax: 800-414-5043 or (248)699-8063 E-mail: galeord@galegroup.com • URL: http://www.galegroup.com • $140.00. Second edition. Date not set. Provides detailed information on more than 400 fashion designers, milliners, footwear designers, apparel companies, and textile houses. Includes black-and-white photographs, biographical information, and bibliographies.

Contemporary Long Term Care. Bill Communications, Inc., 770 Broadway New York, NY 10003-9595. Phone: 800-266-4712 or (646)654-5400 Fax: (646)654-7212 E-mail: info@bpi.com • URL: http://www.billcom.com • Monthly. $72.00 per year. Edited for the long term health care industry, including retirement centers with life care, continuing care communities, and nursing homes.

Contemporary Long Term Care Fax Directory. Bill Communications, Inc., 770 Broadway New York, NY 10003-9595. Phone: 800-266-4712 or (646)654-4500 Fax: (646)654-7212 URL: http://www.billcom.com • Annual. $10.50. Lists approximately 900 manufacturers and suppliers of equipment, products, and services for retirement communities and nursing homes. Formerly *Contemporary Administration for Long-Term Care Product Directory and Buyer's Guide*.

Contemporary Musicians: Profiles of the People in Music. Available from The Gale Group, 27500 Drake Rd. Farmington Hills, MI 48331-3535. Phone: 800-877-GALE or (248)699-GALE Fax: 800-414-5043 or (248)699-8069 E-mail: galeord@galegroup.com • URL: http://www.galegroup.com • 2001. $2,880.00. 32 volumes in print. $81.00 per volume.

Contemporary Photographers. Available from The Gale Group, 27500 Drake Rd. Farmington Hills, MI 48331-3535. Phone: 800-877-GALE or (248)699-GALE Fax: 800-414-5043 or (248)699-8069 E-mail: galeord@galegroup.com • URL: http://www.galegroup.com • 1995. $175.00. Provides biographical and critical information on more than 850 international photographers.

Contemporary Sales Force Management. Tony Carter. Haworth Press, Inc., 10 Alice St. Binghamton, NY 13904-1580. Phone: 800-429-6784 or (607)722-5857 Fax: 800-895-0582 or (607)722-1424 E-mail: getinfo@haworthpressinc.com • URL: http://www.haworthpressinc.com • 1997. $49.95. Emphasis is on motivation of sales personnel. Includes case studies.

Contemporary Supervision: Managing People and Technology. Betty R. Ricks. McGraw-Hill, 1221 Ave. of the Americas New York, NY 10020. Phone: 800-722-4726 or (212)904-2000 Fax: (212)904-2072 E-mail: customer.service@mcgraw-hill.com • URL: http://www.mcgraw-hill.com • 1994. $68.75.

Contemporary Theatre, Film, and Television. The Gale Group, 27500 Drake Rd. Farmington Hills, MI 48331-3535. Phone: 800-877-GALE or (248)699-GALE Fax: 800-414-5043 or (248)699-8069 E-mail: galeord@galegroup.com • URL: http://www.galegroup.com • 2000. 34 volumes in print. $165.00 per volume. Provides detailed biographical and career information on more than 11,000 currently popular performers, directors, writers, producers, designers, managers, choreographers, technicians, composers, executives, dancers, and critics.

Contemporary Times. National Association of Temporary Staffing Services, Inc., 119 S. Saint Asaph St. Alexandria, VA 22314. Phone: (703)549-6287 Fax: (703)549-4808 Quarterly. Members, $60.00 per year; non-members, $240.00 per year; non-profit, $80.00 per year. Management support articles for the temporary help industry and current information on industry activities. Formerly *National Association of Temporary Services, Inc.*

Contemporary Women's Issues. Responsive Database Services, Inc., 23611 Chagrin Blvd., Suite 320 Beachwood, OH 44122. Phone: 800-313-2212 or (216)292-9620 Fax: (216)292-9621 E-mail: customer_service@rdsinc.com • URL: http://www.rdsinc.com • Provides fulltext articles online from 150 periodicals and a wide variety of additional sources relating to economic, legal, social, political, education, health, and other women's issues. Time span is 1992 to date. Weekly updates. Inquire as to online cost and availability. (Also available in a CD-ROM version.)

Contests for Students: All You Need to Know to Enter and Win 600 Contests. The Gale Group, 27500 Drake Rd. Farmington Hills, MI 48331-3535. Phone: 800-877-GALE or (248)699-GALE Fax: 800-414-5043 or (248)699-8069 E-mail: galeord@galegroup.com • URL: http://www.galegroup.com • 1999. $45.00. Second edition. details 600 regional, national, and international contests for elementary, junior high, and high school students.

CONTEXT: Business in a World Being Transformed by Technology. Diamond Technology Partners, Inc., 875 N. Michigan Ave., Suite 3000 Chicago, IL 60611. Phone: (312)255-5550 Fax: (312)255-6550 E-mail: info@contextmag.com • URL: http://www.contextmag.com • Quarterly. Price on application. Covers developments and trends in business and information technology for non-technical senior executives.

Continental Europe Market Guide. Dun and Bradstreet Information Services, Dun and Bradstreet Corp., Three Sylvan Way Parsippany, NJ 07054-3896. Phone: 800-526-0651 or (973)455-0900 Fax: (973)254-4063 E-mail: customerservice@dnb.com • URL: http://www.dnb.com • Semiannual. $1,600.00 per two volume set. Lists about 220,000 firms in 21 European countries. Includes financial strength and credit ratings. Geographic arrangement.

Contingencies: The Magazine of the Actuarial Profession. American Academy of Actuaries, 1100 17th St., N. W., Suite 700 Washington, DC 20036. Phone: (202)223-8196 Fax: (202)872-1948 E-mail: info@actuary.org • URL: http://www.actuary.org • Bimonthly. $30.00 per year. Provides non-technical articles on the actuarial aspects of insurance, employee benefits, and pensions.

Continuing Care Retirement Communities. Sylvia Sherwood and others. Johns Hopkins University Press, 2715 N. Charles St. Baltimore, MD 21218. Phone: 800-548-1784 or (410)516-6900 Fax: (410)516-6998 URL: http://www.jhu.edu • 1996. $40.00. Presents research based on a study of continuing care retirement communities and 2,000 residents of the communities.

The Continuing Care Retirement Community, a Guidebook for Consumers. American Association of Homes and Services for the Aging, 901 E St., N. W., Suite 500 Washington, DC 20004-2037. Phone: 800-508-9442 or (202)783-2242 Fax: (202)783-2255 E-mail: info@aahsa.org • URL: http://www.aahsa.org • 1984. $6.95. Provieds information for the evaluation of continuing care retirement communities and nursing facilities, including services and finances.

Continuing Care: Supporting the Transition into Post Hospital Care. Stevenson Publishing Corp., 5151 Beltline Rd., 10th Fl. Dallas, TX 75240-6738. Phone: (972)687-6700 Fax: (972)687-6769 Monthly. $99.00 per year. Topics include insurance, legal issues, health business news, ethics, and case management. Includes annual *Buyer's Guide*.

The Contract and Fee-Setting Guide for Consultants and Professionals. Howard L. Shenson. John Wiley and Sons, Inc., 605 Third Ave. New York, NY 10158-0012. Phone: 800-225-5945 or (212)850-6000 Fax: (212)850-6088 E-mail: info@wiley.com • URL: http://www.wiley.com • 1990. $108.95.

Contract Design: The Business Magazine of Commercial and Institutional Interior Design, and Architecture, Planning and Construction. Miller Freeman, Inc., One Penn Plaza New York, NY 10119. Phone: 800-950-1314 or (212)714-1300 Fax: (212)714-1313 URL: http://www.mfi.com • Monthly. $65.00 per year. Firms engaged in specifying furniture and furnishings for commercial installations. Formerly *Contract*.

Contract Management. National Contract Management Association, 1912 Woodford Rd. Vienna, VA 22182-3728. Phone: 800-344-8096 or (703)448-9231 Fax: (703)448-0939 URL: http://www.ncmahq.org • Monthly. $72.00 per year.

Contract Services Association of America.

Contracting with the Federal Government. Margaret M. Worhtingotn and Louis P. Goldman. John Wiley and Sons, Inc., 605 Third Ave. New York, NY 10158-0012. Phone: 800-225-5945 or (212)850-6000 Fax: (212)850-6088 E-mail: info@wiley.com • URL: http://www.wiley.com • 1998. $115.00. Fourth edition. Tells how to acquire federal contracts and execute them profitably.

Contractors Co-Op Council., 7077 Orangewood Ave., Suite 120 Garden Grove, CA 92641. Phone: (714)898-0583 Fax: (714)891-5616 Members are custom drapery merchants.

Contractor's Guide: The Guide to the Roofing, Insulation, Siding, Solar, and Window Industries. Century Communications Corp., 6201 W. Howard St. Niles, IL 60714-3435. Phone: (847)647-1200 Fax: (847)647-7055 Monthly. $26.00 per year. For roofing and insulation contractors.

Contractors Pump Bureau., 111 E. Wisconsin Ave., Suite 1000 Milwaukee, WI 53202. Phone: (414)272-0943 Fax: (414)272-1170 E-mail: cima@cimunet.com • URL: http://www.cimanet.com • Members are manufacturers of pumps for the construction industry.

Contracts for the Film and Television Industry. Mark Litwak. Silman-James Press, 3624 Shannon Rd. Los Angeles, CA 90027. Phone: (323)661-9922 Fax: (323)661-9933 E-mail: ghfeldman@earthlink.net • 1999. $35.95. Second expanded edition. Contains a wide variety of sample entertainment contracts. Includes material on rights, employment, joint ventures, music, financing, production, distribution, merchandising, and the retaining of attorneys.

Control Engineering Buyers Guide. Cahners Business Information, 200 Clearwater Dr. Oak Brook, IL 60523. Phone: 800-662-7776 or (630)320-3730 Fax: (630)320-7132 E-mail: corporatecommunications@cahners.com • URL: http://www.cahners.com • Annual. Free to qualified personnel. Contains specifications, prices, and manufacturers' listings for computer software, as related to control engineering.

Control Engineering: Covering Control, Instrumentation and Automation Systems Worldwide. Cahners Business Information, 200 Clearwater Dr. Oak Brook, IL 60523. Phone: 800-662-7776 or (630)320-7118 Fax: (630)320-7132 E-mail: corporatecommunications@cahners.com • URL: http://www.cahners.com • Monthly. $99.90 per year.

Control Handbook. William S. Levine, editor. CRC Press, Inc., 2000 Corporate Blvd., N. W. Boca Raton, FL 33431. Phone: 800-272-7737 or (561)994-0555 Fax: 800-374-3401 or (561)241-7856 E-mail: orders@crcpress.com • URL: http://www.crcpress.com • 1996. $159.95. Contains about 140 articles by various authors on automatic control, control theory, and control engineering. (Electrical Engineering Handbook Series).

Control of Administrative and Financial Operations in Special Libraries. Madeline J. Daubert. Special Libraries Association, 1700 18th St., N. W., 17th Fl. Washington, DC 20009-2514. Phone: (202)234-4700 Fax: 888-411-2856 or (202)234-2442 E-mail: books@sla.org • URL: http://www.sla.org • 1996. $75.00. Self-study workbook.

Control of Banking. Prentice Hall, 240 Frisch Court Paramus, NJ 07652-5240. Phone: 800-947-7700 or (201)909-6200 Fax: 800-445-6991 or (201)909-6361 URL: http://www.prenhall.com • Two looseleaf volumes. $465.00 per year. Periodic supplementation. Banking rules and regulations affecting day-to-day operations and financial practices of banks.

Controllership: The Work of the Managerial Accountant. James D. Wilson and others. John Wiley and Sons, Inc., 605 Third Ave. New York, NY 10158-0012. Phone: 800-225-5945 or (212)850-6000 E-mail: info@wiley.com • URL: http://www.wiley.com • 1999. $170.00. Sixth edition. 2000 Supplement, $60.00.

Convenience Food Store. Entrepreneur Media, Inc., 2445 McCabe Way Irvine, CA 92614. Phone: 800-421-2300 or (949)261-2325 Fax: (949)261-0234 E-mail: entmag@entrepreneur.com • URL: http://www.entrepreneur.com • Looseleaf. $59.50. A practical guide to starting a convenience food store. Covers profit potential, start-up costs, market size evaluation, owner's time required, site selection, lease negotiation, pricing, accounting, advertising, promotion, etc. (Start-Up Business Guide No. E1173.)

Convenience Store Decisions. Meehan Publishing Co., Two Greenwood Square, Suite 410, 3331 Street Rd. Bensalem, PA 19020-2023. Phone: (215)245-4555 Fax: (215)245-4060 Monthly. $60.00 per year. Edited for headquarters and regional management personnel of convenience store chains.

Convenience Store News Buyers Guide. Bill Communications, 770 Broadway New York, NY 10003. Phone: 800-266-4712 or (646)654-4500 Fax: (646)654-7212 URL: http://www.billcom.com • Annual. $200.00. Provides information on convenience store chains, including service station stores, and suppliers of products, equipment, and services to convenience stores.

Convenience Store News: The Information Source for the Industry. Bill Communications, Business Communications Group, 770 Broadway New York, NY 10003. Phone: 800-266-4712 or (646)654-4500 Fax: (646)654-7212 URL: http://www.billcom.com • 15 times a year. Free to qualified personnel; others, $85.00 per year. Contains news of industry trends and merchandising techniques.

Convergence: The Journal of Research Into New Media Technologies. Chilton Co., 600 S. Cherry St., Suite 400 Denver, CO 80222. Phone: 800-695-1214 or (303)393-7449 Fax: (303)329-3453 URL: http://www.chilton.net • Monthly. Individuals, $60,00 per year; institutions, $120.00 per year. Covers the merging of communications technologies. Includes telecommunications networks, interactive TV, multimedia, wireless phone service, and electronic information services.

Conversion Factors and Tables. O. T. Zimmerman. Industrial Research Service, Inc., 26 Strafford Ave. Durham, NC 03824. Phone: (603)868-2593 1961. $30.00.

Converted Flexible Packaging. Available from MarketResearch.com, 641 Ave. of the Americas, Third Floor New York, NY 10011. Phone: 800-298-5699 or (212)807-2629 Fax: (212)807-2716 E-mail: order@marketresearch.com • URL: http://www.marketresearch.com • 1998. $3,400.00. Published by the Freedonia Group. Market data with forecasts to the year 2006. Covers plastic, paper, and foil packaging for food and non-food products.

Convertible Securities: The Latest Instruments, Portfolio Strategies, and Valuation Analysis. John P. Calamos. McGraw-Hill Professional, 1221 Ave. of the Americas New York, NY 10020-1095. Phone: 800-772-4726 or (212)904-2000 Fax: (212)904-2072 E-mail: customer.service@mcgraw-hill.com • URL: http://www.mcgraw-hill.com • 1998. $65.00. Second edition.

Conveyor Equipment Manufacturers Association.

Cookie and Snack Bakers Association., P.O. Box 37320 Cleveland, TN 37320. Phone: (423)472-1561 Members are bakers of snacks and cookies.

Cooking for Fifty: The Complete Reference and Cookbook. Chet Holden. John Wiley and Sons, Inc., 605 Third Ave. New York, NY 10158-0012. Phone: 800-225-5945 or (212)850-6000 Fax: (212)850-6088 E-mail: info@wiley.com • URL: http://www.wiley.com • 1993. $90.00. Discusses commercial cooking techniques and includes 300 "contemporary" recipes for institutional and commercial cooks.

Cooking for Profit. C P Publishing, Inc., P.O. Box 267 Fond du Lac, WI 54936-0267. Phone: (920)923-3700 Fax: (920)923-6805 Monthly. $25.00 per year. The challenge of operations management in the food service industry.

Cookware Manufacturers Association., c/o Hugh J. Rushing, P.O. Box 531335 Mountain Brook, AL 35253. Phone: (205)802-7600 Fax: (205)802-7610 E-mail: hrushing@cookware.org • URL: http://www.cookware.org • Members are manufacturers of cooking utensils and accessories.

Cooperative Housing Bulletin. National Association of Housing Cooperatives, 1401 New York Ave., N.W., Ste. 1100 Washington, DC 20005. Phone: (202)737-0797 Fax: (202)783-7869 Bimonthly. $50.00 per year. Includes *Cooperative Housing Journal*.

Cooperative Housing Law and Practice-Forms. Patrick J. Rohan and Melvin A. Reskin. Matthew Bender & Co., Inc., Two Park Ave. New York, NY 10016. Phone: 800-223-1940 or (212)448-2000 Fax: (212)244-3188 E-mail: international@bender.com • URL: http://www.bender.com • $860.00. Six looseleaf volumes. Periodic supplementation. Covers every aspect of the creation, financing, operation, sale and tax consequences of cooperatives. (Real Estate Transaction Series).

Cooperative Program in Metallurgy.

Coordinated Science Laboratory. University of Illinois at Urbana-Champaign

Coping with Difficult People. Robert N. Bramson. Dell Publishing, 1540 Broadway New York, NY 10036-4094. Phone: 800-223-6834 or (212)354-6500 Fax: (212)492-9698 1981. $17.50.

Copper and Brass Fabricators Council.

Copper and Brass Servicenter Association.

Copper Development Association.

Copy Editor: Language News for the Publishing Profession. Mary Beth/Protomastro, Ansonia Station, P.O. Box 604 New York, NY 10023-0604. Phone: (212)995-0112 Fax: (212)995-2147 E-mail: barpan@interportinet • URL: http://www.copyeditor.com • Bimonthly. $69.00 per year. Newsletter for professional copy editors and proofreaders. Includes such items as "Top Ten Resources for Copy Editors."

The Copyright Book: A Practical Guide. William S. Strong. MIT Press, Five Cambridge Center Cambridge, MA 02142-1493. Phone: 800-356-0343 or (617)253-2864 Fax: (617)253-6779 E-mail: mitpress-orders@mit.edu • URL: http://www.mitpress.mit.edu • 1999. $34.95. Fifth edition.

Copyright Bulletin: Quarterly Review. Available from Bernan Associates, 4611-F Assembly Dr. Lanham, MD 20706-4391. Phone: 800-274-4447 or (301)459-7666 Fax: 800-865-3450 or (301)459-0056 E-mail: info@bernan.com • URL: http://www.bernan.com • Quarterly. $30.00 per year.

Copyright Clearance Center.

Copyright for the Nineties: 1997 Supplement and Appendix. Robert A. Gorman and Jane C. Ginsburg. LEXIS Publishing, 701 E. Water St. Charlottesville, VA 22902. Phone: 800-446-3410 or (804)972-7600 Fax: 800-643-1280 or (804)972-7686 E-mail: custserv@michie.com • URL: http://www.lexislaw.publishing • 1998. $52.00.

Copyright Handbook: How to Protect and Use Written Words. Stephen Fishman. Nolo.com, 950 Parker St. Berkeley, CA 94710. Phone: 800-992-6656 or (510)549-1976 Fax: (510)548-5902 E-mail: cs@nolo.com • URL: http://www.nolo.com • 1997. $24.95. Fourth revised edition. Includes sample forms and copyright agreements.

Copyright Handbook: How to Protect and Use Written Works. Stephen Fishman. Nolo.com, 950 Parker St. Berkeley, CA 94710. Phone: 800-992-6656 or (510)549-1976 Fax: (510)548-5902 E-mail: cs@nolo.com • URL: http://www.nolo.com • 1999. $34.95. Fifth edition.

Copyright Law in Business and Practice. John W. Hazard. West Group, 90 Fifth Ave. Saint Paul, MN 55164-0526. Phone: 800-328-9352 or (615)687-7000 Fax: (615)687-5664 URL: http://www.westgroup.com • 1998. $160.00.

Copyright Law '99 and Beyond Handbook. Glasser Legalworks, 150 Clove Rd. Little Falls, NJ 07424. Phone: 800-308-1700 or (973)890-0008 Fax: (973)890-0042 E-mail: legalwks@aol.com • URL: http://www.legalwks.com • 1999. $95.00. Examines current trends in copyright litigation. Based on a 1999 seminar held in cooperation with the U. S. Copyright Office.

Copyright Law of the United States of America. Available from U. S. Government Printing Office, Washington, DC 20402. Phone: (202)512-1800 Fax: (202)512-2250 E-mail: gpoaccess@gpo.gov • URL: http://www.access.gpo.gov • Annual. $4.75. Issued by U. S. Copyright Office, Library of Congress. Provides the text of copyright law contained in Title 17 of the U. S. Code.

Copyright Law Reports. CCH, Inc., 4025 W. Peterson Ave. Chicago, IL 60646-6085. Phone: 800-248-3248 or (773)583-8500 Fax: 800-224-8299 or (773)866-3608 URL: http://www.cch.com • $703.00 per year. Two looseleaf volumes. Monthly updates.

Copyright Laws and Treaties of the World. Bureau of National Affairs, Inc., 1231 25th St., N.W. Washington, DC 20037-1197. Phone: 800-372-1033 or (202)452-4226 Fax: (202)822-8092 E-mail: books@bna.com • URL: http://www.bna.com • Looseleaf. $695.00. Three volumes. Periodic supplementation.

Copyright, Patent, Trademark and Related State Doctrines; Cases and Materials on the Law of Intellectual Property. Paul Goldstein. Foundation Press, Inc., 11 Penn Plaza New York, NY 10001. Phone: 877-888-1330 or (212)760-8700 Fax: (212)760-8740 E-mail: gerry.gelke@westgroup.com • URL: http://www.fdpress.com • 1999. $43.50. Fourth edition.

Copyright Primer for Librarians and Educators. Janis H. Bruwelheide. American Library Association, 50 E. Huron St. Chicago, IL 60611-2795. Phone: 800-545-2433 or (312)944-6780 Fax: (312)440-9374 URL: http://www.ala.org • 1995. $25.00. Second edition.

Copyright Principles, Law, and Practice. Paul Goldstein. Aspen Books, 2961 W. California Ave., Suite E Salt Lake City, UT 84104. Phone: 800-748-4850 or (801)974-0414 Fax: (801)886-1603 E-mail: prawlins@aspenbook.com • 1989. $375.00. Three volumes.

Copyright Society of the United States of America Journal. Copyright Society of the U.S.A., 1133 Ave. of the America, 33rd Fl. New York, NY 10036. Phone: (212)354-6401 Fax: (212)354-2847 URL: http://www.csusa.org • Quarterly. Individuals, $125.00 per year; nonprofit organizations, $50.00 per year; corporations, $500.00 per year.

Copyright Society of the U.S.A.

Copyrights, Patents, and Trademarks: Protect Your Rights Worldwide. Hoyt L. Barber. McGraw-Hill, 1221 Ave. of the Americas New York, NY 10020-1095. Phone: 800-722-4726 or (212)904-2000 Fax: (212)904-2072 E-mail: customer.service@mcgraw-hill.com • URL: http://www.mcgraw-hill.com • 1996. $32.95. Second edition.

Copywriter's Handbook. Robert W. Bly. Henry Holt & Co., LLC, 115 W. 18th St., 5th Fl. New York, NY 10011. Phone: (212)886-9200 Fax: (212)633-0748 E-mail: info@hholt.com • URL: http://www.henryholt.com • 1995. $13.95.

Copywriting Secrets and Tactics: How to Put More Sell into All Your Copy. Herschell G. Lewis. Dartnell Corp., 360 Hiatt Dr. Palm Beach, FL 33418. Phone: 800-621-5463 or (561)622-6520 Fax: 800-327-8635 or (561)622-2423 E-mail: cusserv@lrp.com • URL: http://www.dartnell.corp.com • $91.50. Looseleaf service.

Corbin on Contracts. Arthur L. Corbin. West Publishing Co., College and School Div., 610 Opperman Dr. Eagan, MN 55123. Phone: 800-328-4880 or (651)687-7000 Fax: 800-213-2323 or (651)687-5827 E-mail: legal_ed@

westgroup.com • URL: http://www.lawschool.westgroup.com • 14 volumes. Price on application.

Cordage Institute.

CORE Magazine. Congress of Racial Equality. CORE Publications, 30 Cooper Square, No. 9 New York, NY 10003-7151. Phone: (212)598-4000 Fax: (212)982-0184 Quarterly. $10.00 per year.

Corn Annual. Corn Refiners Association, Inc., 1701 Pennsylvania Ave., N.W., Suite 950 Washington, DC 20006. Phone: (202)331-1634 Fax: (202)331-2054 E-mail: details@corn.org • URL: http://www.corn.org • Annual. Single copies free.

Corn: Origin, History, Technology, and Production. C. Wayne Smith and others, editors. John Wiley and Sons, Inc., 605 Third Ave. New York, NY 10158-0012. Phone: 800-225-5945 or (212)850-6000 Fax: (212)850-6088 E-mail: info@wiley.com • URL: http://www.wiley.com • 2002. $250.00. (Wiley Series in Crop Science.)

Corn Refiners Association.

The Cornell Hotel and Restaurant Administration Quarterly. Cornell University School of Hotel Administration. Elsevier Science, 655 Ave. of the Americas New York, NY 10010. Phone: 888-437-4636 or (212)989-5800 Fax: (212)633-3680 E-mail: usinfo@elsevier.com • URL: http://www.elsevier.com • Bimonthly. $258.00 per year.

Corporate Acquisitions. A R C H Group, 55 Main St. Tiburon, CA 94920-2507. Phone: (415)435-2175 Fax: (415)435-6310 E-mail: ncra@acquisitionresource.com • Weekly. $425.00 per year. Newsletter.

Corporate Acquisitions and Mergers. Byron E. Fox and Eleanor M. Fox. Kluwer Law International, 675 Massachusets Ave. Cambridge, MA 02139. Phone: (617)354-0140 Fax: (617)354-8595 E-mail: kluwer@wkap.nl • URL: http://www.wkap.nl • $405.00. Two looseleaf volumes. Quarterly supplements. A guide to the antiturst, tax, corporate, securities and financial aspects of business combinations. Includes extensive forms, charts and tables.

Corporate Acquisitions, Mergers, and Divestitures. Lewis D. Solomon. Prentice Hall, 240 Frisch Court Paramus, NJ 07652-5240. Phone: 800-947-7700 or (201)909-6452 Fax: 800-445-6991 URL: http://www.prenhall.com • Looseleaf. Periodic supplementation. Price on application. Includes how to buy a company with its own assets or earnings.

Corporate Affiliations Plus. National Register Publishing, Reed Reference Publishing, 121 Chanlon Rd. New Providence, NJ 07974. Phone: 800-323-3288 or (908)464-6800 Fax: (908)665-6688 Quarterly. $1,995.00 per year. Provides CD-ROM discs corresponding to *Directory of Corporate Affiliations* and *Corporate Finance Bluebook*. Contains corporate financial services information and worldwide data on subsidiaries and affiliates.

Corporate and Tax Aspects of Closely Held Corporations. William H. Painter. Aspen Books, 2961 W. California Ave., Suite E Salt Lake City, UT 84104. Phone: 800-748-4850 or 800-748-4850 Fax: (801)886-1603 E-mail: prawlins@aspenbook.com • 1981. $80.00. Second edition.

Corporate Bond Desk Reference: U. S. Buyside and Sellside Profiles. Capital Access International, 430 Mountain Ave. Murray Hill, NJ 07974-2732. Phone: 800-866-5987 or (908)771-0800 Fax: (908)771-0330 E-mail: rlongo@capital-access.com • URL: http://www.capital-access.com • Annual. $395.00. Provides "detailed buyside and sellside profiles and contacts" for the the corporate bond market. (Desk Reference Series, volume one.)

Corporate Cashflow: The Magazine of Treasury Management. Intertec Publishing Corp., 6151 Powers Ferry Rd., N.W., Suite 200 Atlanta, GA 30339-2941. Phone: 800-400-5945 or (770)955-2500 Fax: (770)955-0400 E-mail: subs@intertec.com • URL: http://www.intertec.com • Monthly. $78.00 per year. Published for chief financial officers of corporations. Includes annual *Directory*.

Corporate Compliance Series. West Group, 610 Opperman Dr. Eagan, MN 55123. Phone: 800-328-4880 or (651)687-7000 Fax: 800-213-2323 or (651)687-5827 URL: http://www.westgroup.com • Eleven looseleaf volumes, with periodic supplementation. $990.00. Covers criminal and civil liability problems for corporations. Includes employee safety, product liability, pension requirements, securities violations, equal employment opportunity issues, intellectual property, employee hiring and firing, and other corporate compliance topics.

Corporate Contributions Handbook: Devoting Private Means to Public Needs. James P. Shannon, editor. Jossey-Bass, Inc., Publishers, 350 Sansome St. San Francisco, CA 94104. Phone: 888-378-2537 or (415)433-1740 Fax: (415)433-0499 E-mail: webperson@jbp.com • URL: http://www.jossey.com • 1991. $48.95. Published jointly with the Council on Foundations. Provides practical management and legal advice for corporate philanthropic units. (Nonprofit Sector-Public Administration Series).

Corporate Control Alert; A Report on Current Changes for Corporate Control. American Lawyer Media, L.P., 345 Park Ave., S. New York, NY 10010-1707. Phone: 800-888-8300 or (212)545-6170 Fax: (212)696-1848 E-mail: catalog@amlaw.com • URL: http://www.americanlawyermedia.com • Monthly. $1,595 per year. A monthly mergers and acquisitions newsletter.

Corporate Controller. Faulkner and Gray, Inc., 11 Penn Plaza, 17th Fl. New York, NY 10001. Phone: 800-535-8403 or (212)967-7000 Fax: (212)967-7155 E-mail: order@faulknergray.com • URL: http://www.faulknergay.com • Bimonthly. $115.00 per year.

Corporate Controller. Paul J. Wendell. Warren, Gorham and Lamont/RIA Group, 395 Hudson St. New York, NY 10014. Phone: 800-950-1215 or (212)367-6300 Fax: (651)367-6718 E-mail: customer_services@riag.com • URL: http://www.riahome.com • Bimonthly. $130.00. Covers every aspect of a controller's responsibilities.

Corporate Counsellor's Deskbook. Dennis J. Block and Michael A. Epstein, editors. Panel Publishing, 1185 Ave. of the Americas New York, NY 10036. Phone: 800-447-1717 or (212)597-0200 Fax: (212)597-0334 1999. $220.00. Fifth edition. Looseleaf. Annual supplementation. Covers a wide variety of corporate legal issues, including internal investigations, indemnification, insider trading, intellectual property, executive compensation, antitrust, export-import, real estate, environmental law, government contracts, and bankruptcy.

Corporate Creativity: How Innovation and Improvement Actually Happen. Alan G. Robinson and Sam Stern. Berrett-Koehler Pulishers, Inc., 450 Sansome St., Suite 1200 San Francisco, CA 94111-3320. Phone: 800-929-2929 or (415)288-0260 Fax: (415)362-2512 E-mail: bkpub@aol.com • URL: http://www.bkconnection.com • 1997. $29.95. Describes the six "essential elements" of business creativity.

Corporate Criminal Liability. Kathleen F. Brickley. West Group, 610 Opperman Dr. Eagan, MN 55123. Phone: 800-328-4880 or (651)687-7000 Fax: 800-213-2323 or (651)687-5827 URL: http://www.westgroup.com • $335.00 per year. Three looseleaf volumes. Periodic supplementation. Discusses how the general principles of criminal law apply to the corporate world. Provides a detailed analysis of liability under major federal crime statutes.

Corporate Culture and Organizational Effectiveness. Daniel R. Denison. Aviat, Inc., 10101 Wexford Court South Lyon, MI 48178. Phone: 800-421-5323 or (313)663-2386 Fax: (313)663-3670 E-mail: aviat@chamber.branch.com • URL: http://www.aviatchamber.com • 1990. Includes five case studies. Price on application.

Corporate Cultures: The Rites and Rituals of Corporate Life. Terrance E. Deal and Allan Kennedy. Perseus Publishing, 11 Cambridge Center Cambridge, MA 02142. Phone: 800-447-2226 or (617)252-5200 Fax: (617)252-5285 URL: http://www.awl.com • 1982. $15.00.

Corporate Directors' Compensation. Conference Board, Inc., 845 Third Ave. New York, NY 10022-6679. Phone: (212)759-0900 Fax: (212)980-7014 E-mail: lei@conference-board.org • URL: http://www.tcb-indicators.org • Irregular.

The Corporate Directory of U.S. Public Companies. Walker's Western Research, 1650 Borel Place, No. 130 San Mateo, CA 94402-3506. Phone: 800-258-5737 or (415)341-1110 Fax: (415)341-2351 E-mail: walkersres@aol.com • URL: http://www.walkersresearch.com • Annual. $360.00. Two volumes. Contains information on more than 10,000 publicly-traded companies, including names of executives and major subsidiaries. Includes financial and stock data.

Corporate Dividends and Stock Repurchases. Barbara Black. West Group, 610 Opperman Dr. Eagan, MN 55123. Phone: 800-328-4880 or (651)687-7000 Fax: 800-213-2323 or (651)687-5827 URL: http://www.westgroup.com • $130.00. Looseleaf service. Periodic supplementation. Covers the law relating to dividends in general, illegal dividends, stock splits, stock dividends, corporate repurchases, and other dividend topics.

Corporate EFT Report (Electronic Funds Tranfer). Phillips Business Information, Inc., 1201 Seven Locks Rd., Suite 300 Potomac, MD 20854. Phone: 800-777-5006 or (301)340-1520 Fax: (301)309-3487 E-mail: pbi@phillips.com • URL: http://www.phillips.com/marketplaces.htm • Biweekly. $595.00 per year. Newsletter on subject of electronic funds transfer.

Corporate Executions: The Ugly Truth About Layoffs. How Corporate Greed Is Shattering lives, Companies and Communities. Alan Downs. AMACOM, 1601 Broadway, 12th Fl. New York, NY 10019. Phone: 800-262-9699 or (212)586-8100 Fax: (212)903-8168 E-mail: custmserv.@amanet.org • URL: http://www.amanet.org • 1995. $22.95. States that management layoffs are usually unnecessary and a detriment to the corporation.

Corporate Finance. Stephen A. Ross and others. McGraw-Hill Professional, 1221 Ave. of the Americas New York, NY 10020-1095. Phone: 800-722-4726 or (212)904-2000 Fax: (212)904-2072 E-mail: customer.service@mcgraw-hill.com • URL: http://www.mcgraw-hill.com • 1998. Fifth edition. Price on application. *Irwin-McGraw Hill Finance, Insurance and Real Estate Series*.

Corporate Finance and the Securities Laws. Charles J. Johnson and Joseph McLaughlin. Panel Publishers, 1185 Ave. of the Americas New York, NY 10036. Phone: 800-447-1717 or (212)597-0200 Fax: 800-901-9075 or (212)597-0334 E-mail: customer.service@aspenpubl.com • URL: http://www.panelpublishers.com • 1997. $170.00. Second edition.

Corporate Finance Sourcebook: The Guide to Major Capital Investment Source and Related Financial Services. R. R. Bowker, 121 Chanlon Rd. New Providence, NJ 07974. Phone: 888-269-5372 or (908)464-6800 Fax: (908)771-7704 E-mail: info@bowker.com • URL: http://www.bowker.com • Annual. $625.00. Lists more than 3,550 sources of corporate capital: investment bankers, securities firms, pension management companies, trust companies, insurance companies, and private lenders. Includes the names of over 13,000 key personnel.

Corporate Financial Analysis: Decisions in a Global Environment. Diana R. Harrington and Brent D. Wilson. McGraw-Hill Professional, 1221 Ave. of the Americas New York, NY 10020. Phone: 800-722-4726 or (212)904-2000 Fax: (202)904-2072 E-mail: customer.service@mcgraw-hill.com • URL: http://www.mcgraw-hill.com • 1993. $50.00. Fourth edition.

Corporate Financial Distress and Bankruptcy: A Complete Guide to Predicting and Avoiding Distress and Profiting from Bankruptcy. Edward I. Altman. John Wiley and Sons, Inc., 605 Third Ave. New York, NY 10158-0012. Phone: 800-225-5945 or (212)850-6000 Fax: (212)850-6088 E-mail: info@wiley.com • URL: http://www.wiley.com • 1993. $99.95. Second edition. Provides practical advice on analyzing the financial position of a corporation, with case studies. Includes a discussion of the junk bond market.

Corporate Financial Reporting: Text and Cases. E. Richard Brownlee and others. McGraw-Hill Professional, 1221 Ave. of the Americas New York, NY 10020-1095. Phone: 800-772-4726 or (212)904-2000 Fax: (212)904-2072 E-mail: customer.service@mcgraw-hill.com • URL: http://www.mcgraw-hill.com • 1997. Third edition. Price on application.

Corporate Financial Risk Management: Practical Techniques of Financial Engineering. Diane B. Wunnicke and others. John Wiley and Sons, Inc., 605 Third Ave. New York, NY 10158-0012. Phone: 800-225-5945 or (212)850-6000 Fax: (212)850-6088 E-mail: info@wiley.com • URL: http://www.wiley.com • 1992. $65.00. Discusses such financial risk items as interest rates, commodity prices, and foreign exchange. (Finance Series).

Corporate Financing Week: The Newsweekly of Corporate Finance, Investment Banking and M and A. Institutional Investor, 488 Madison Ave. New York, NY 10022. Phone: (212)224-3300 Fax: (212)224-3353 E-mail: info@iijournals.com • URL: http://www.iijournals.com • Weekly. $2,550.00 per year. Newsletter for corporate finance officers. Emphasis is on debt and equity financing, mergers, leveraged buyouts, investment banking, and venture capital.

Corporate Foundation Profiles. The Foundation Center, 79 Fifth Ave. New York, NY 10003-3076. Phone: 800-424-9836 or (212)620-4230 Fax: (212)807-3677 E-mail: mfn@fdncenter.org • URL: http://www.fdncenter.org • Biennial. $155.00 per year.

Corporate Fraud. Michael J. Comer. Available from Ashgate Publishing Co., Old Post Rd. Brookfield, VT 05036-9704. Phone: 800-535-9544 or (802)276-3162 Fax: (802)276-3837 E-mail: info@ashgate.com • URL: http://www.ashgate.com • 1997. $113.95. Third edition. Examines new risks of corporate fraud related to "electronic commerce, derivatives, computerization, empowerment, downsizing, and other recent developments." Covers fraud detection, prevention, and internal control systems. Published by Gower in England.

Corporate Giving Directory: Comprehensive Profiles of America's Major Corporate Foundations and Corporate Charitable Giving Programs. The Gale Group, 27500 Drake Rd. Farmington Hills, MI 48331-3535. Phone: 800-877-8238 or (248)699-GALE Fax: 800-414-5043 or (248)699-8069 E-mail: galeord@galegroup.com • URL: http://www.galegroup.com • Annual. $485.00. Contains detailed descriptions of the philanthropic foundations of over 1,000 major U. S. corporations. Includes grant types, priorities for giving, recent grants, and advice on approaching corporate givers.

Corporate Giving Watch: News and Ideas for Nonprofit Organizations Seeking Corporate Funds. Available from The Gale Group, 27500 Drake Rd. Farmington Hills, MI 48331-3535. Phone: 800-877-GALE or (248)699-GALE Fax: 800-414-5043 or (248)699-8069 E-mail: galeord@galegroup.com • URL: http://www.taftgroup.com • Monthly. $149.00 per year. Newsletter. Published by The Taft Group. Includes news, trends, and statistics related to corporate giving programs. "Corporate Profiles" insert contains profiles of individual programs.

Corporate Growth. Princeton Research Institute, Western Management Center, P.O. Box 2702 Scottsdale, AZ 85252-2702. Phone: (609)396-0305 Monthly. $198.00 per year.

Corporate Growth Report. Quality Services Co., 5290 Overpass Rd., Suite 126 Santa Barbara, CA 93111-9950. Phone: (805)964-7841 Fax: (805)964-1073 Weekly. $895.00 per year. Newsletter. Gives details of current merger and buy-out transactions or negotiations. Includes lists of companies wishing to buy and companies wishing to be bought. Formerly *Acquisition-Divestiture Weekly Report*.

Corporate Identity: Making Business Strategy Visible Through Design. Wally Olins. McGraw-Hill, 1221 Ave. of the Americas New York, NY 10020. Phone: 800-722-4726 or (212)904-2000 Fax: (212)904-2072 E-mail: customer.service@mcgraw-hill.com • URL: http://www.mcgraw-hill.com • 1990. $50.00.

Corporate Image: A Practical Guide to the Implementation of a Corporate Identity Program. Nicholas Ind. Beekman Publishers, Inc., P.O. Box 888 Woodstock, NY 12498. Phone: 800-233-5626 or (914)679-2300 Fax: (914)679-2301 E-mail: manager@beekman.net • URL: http://www.beekman.net • 1990. $44.95.

Corporate Image: Communicating Visions and Values. Allyson LaBorde, editor. Conference Board, Inc., 845 Third Ave., 3rd. Fl. New York, NY 10022-6679. Phone: (212)759-0900 Fax: (212)980-7014 E-mail: info@conference-board.org • URL: http://www.conference-board.org • 1993. $100.00.

Corporate Internet Planning Guide: Aligning Internet Strategy with Business Goals. Richard J. Gascoyne and Koray Ozcubucku. John Wiley and Sons, Inc., 605 Third Ave. New York, NY 10158-0012. Phone: 800-225-5945 or (212)850-6000 Fax: (212)850-6088 E-mail: info@wiley.com • URL: http://www.wiley.com • 1996. $34.95. Provides administrative advice on planning, developing, and managing corporate Internet or intranet functions. Emphasis is on strategic planning. (Business, Commerce, Management Series).

The Corporate Intranet: Create and Manage an Internal Web for your Organization. Ryan Bernard. John Wiley and Sons, Inc., 605 Third Ave. New York, NY 10158-0012. Phone: 800-225-5945 or (212)850-6000 Fax: (212)850-6088 E-mail: info@jwiley.com • URL: http://www.wiley.com • 1997. $29.99. Second edition.

Corporate Jobs Outlook! Plunkett Research, Ltd., P. O. Drawer 541737 Houston, TX 77254-1737. Phone: (713)932-0000 Fax: (713)932-7080 E-mail: info@plunkettresearch.com • URL: http://www.plunkettresearch.com • Bimonthly. $179.99 per year. Newsletter. Presents data on job possibilities at fast-growing, mid-sized corporations. Supplement available *Almanac of American Employers*.

Corporate Library Excellence. James M. Matarazzo. Special Libraries Association, 1700 18th St., N. W., 17th Fl. Washington, DC 20009-2514. Phone: (202)234-4700 Fax: 888-411-2856 or (202)234-2442 E-mail: books@sla.org • URL: http://www.sla.org • 1990. $28.00.

Corporate Library Update: News for Information Managers and Special Librarians. Cahners Business Information, Broadcasting and Cable's International Group, 245 W. 17th St. New York, NY 10011-5300. Phone: 800-662-7776 or (212)645-0067 Fax: (212)463-6734 E-mail: corporatecommunications@cahners.com • URL: http://www.cahners.com • Biweekly. $95.00 per year. Newsletter. Covers information technology, management techniques, new products, trends, etc.

Corporate Liquidity: Management and Measurement. Kenneth L. Parkinson and Jarl G. Kallberg. McGraw-Hill Higher Education, 1221 Ave. of the Americas New York, NY 10020-1095. Phone: 800-722-4726 or (212)904-2000 Fax: (212)904-2072 E-mail: customer.service@mcgraw-hill.com • URL: http://www.mcgraw-hill.com • 1992. $67.95. Topics include cash management and risk.

Corporate Officers and Directors Liability Litigation Reporter: The Twice Monthly National Journal of Record of Litigation Based on Fiduciary Responsibility. Andrews Publications, 175 Strafford Ave., Bldg 4, Suite 140 Wayne, PA 19087. Phone: 800-345-1101 or (215)622-0510 Fax: (215)622-0501 URL: http://www.andrewspub.com • Semimonthly. $890.00 per year. Provides reports on lawsuits in the area of corporate officers' fiduciary responsibility.

Corporate, Partnership, Estate, and Gift Taxation 1997. James W. Pratt and William Kulsrud, editors. McGraw-Hill Higher Education, 1221 Ave. of the Americas New York, NY 10020-1095. Phone: 800-772-4726 or (212)904-2000 Fax: (212)904-2072 E-mail: customer.service@mcgraw-hill.com • URL: http://www.mcgraw-hill.com • 1996. $71.25. 10th edition.

Corporate Philanthropy Report. Capitol Publications, Inc., 1101 King St., Suite 444 Alexandria, VA 22314. Phone: (703)683-4100 Fax: (703)739-6501 Monthly. $229.00 per year. Newsletter. Reports on trends in corporate giving and provides information on potential sources of corporate philanthropy.

Corporate Practice Series. Bureau of National Affairs, Inc., 1231 25th St., N.W. Washington, DC 20037-1197. Phone: 800-372-1033 or (202)452-4200 Fax: (202)822-8092 E-mail: books@bna.com • URL: http://www.bna.com. • Weekly. $795.00 per year. Series of about 30 ''portfolios'' on various aspects of corporate law. Includes BNA's *Corporate Counsel Weekly*.

Corporate Public Issues and Their Management: The Executive Systems Approach to Public Policy Formation. Issue Action Publications, Inc., 207 Loudoun St. S.E. Leesburg, VA 22075-3115. Phone: (703)777-8450 Semimonthly. $195.00 per year. Newsletter.

Corporate Secretary. American Society of Corporate Secretaries, 521 Fifth Ave. New York, NY 10175. Phone: (212)681-2000 Fax: (212)681-2005 Quarterly. Free to members; non-members, $95.00 per year.

Corporate Secretary's Guide. CCH, Inc., 4025 W. Peterson Ave. Chicago, IL 60646-6085. Phone: 800-248-3248 or (773)583-8500 Fax: 800-224-8299 or (773)866-3608 URL: http://www.cch.com • Monthly. $590.00 per year. Includes newsletter and semimonthly updates. Published in consultation with the American Society of Corporate Secretaries. Covers the duties of corporate secretaries, especially as related to taxation and securities.

Corporate Social Challenge: Cases and Commentaries. James E. Stacey and Frederick D. Sturdivant, editors. McGraw-Hill Professional, 1221 Ave. of the Americas New York, NY 10020-1095. Phone: 800-772-4726 or (212)904-2000 Fax: (212)904-2072 E-mail: customer.service@mcgraw-hill.com • URL: http://www.mcgraw-hill.com • 1994. $41.95. Fifth edition.

Corporate Taxes: Worldwide Summaries. Price Waterhouse Coopers. John Wiley and Sons, Inc., 605 Third Ave. New York, NY 10158-0012. Phone: 800-225-5945 or (212)850-6000 Fax: (212)850-6088 E-mail: info@jwiley.com • URL: http://www.wiley.com • 1999. $95.00. Summarizes the corporate tax regulations of more than 125 countries. Provides information useful for international tax planning and foreign investments.

Corporate Travel's Blackbook. Miller Freeman Books, 6600 Silacci Way Gilroy, CA 95020. Phone: 800-848-5594 or (408)848-5296 Fax: (408)848-5784 E-mail: mfi@rushorder.com • URL: http://www.books.mfi.com/ • Annual. $15.00. Included with subscription to *Corporate Travel*. Gives sources of corporate travel packages. Formerly *Corporate Travel-Directory ''Blackbook''*.

Corporate Valuation: Tools for Effective Appraisal and Decision Making. Randolph W. Westerfield and others. McGraw-Hill Professional, 1221 Ave. of the Americas New York, NY 10020-1095. Phone: 800-772-4726 or (212)904-2000 Fax: (212)904-2072 E-mail: customer.service@mcgraw-hill.com • URL: http://www.mcgraw-hill.com • 1993. $65.00. Discusses the four most widely-used corporate appraisal methods.

Corporate Yellow Book: Who's Who at the Leading U.S. Companies. Leadership Directions, Inc., 104 Fifth Ave., 2nd Fl. New York, NY 10011. Phone: (212)627-4140 Fax: (212)645-0931 E-mail: info@leadershipdirectories.com • URL: http://www.leadershipdirectories.com • Quarterly. $305.00 per year. Lists names and titles of over 51,000 key executives in major U. S. corporations. Includes four indexes: industry, personnel, geographic by state, and company/subsidiary. Companion volume to *Financial Yellow Book*.

Corporation and Partnership Tax Return Guide. Research Institute of America Inc., 90 Fifth Ave. New York, NY 10011. Phone: 800-431-9025 or (212)645-4800 Fax: (201)816-3581 2000. $16.50. Revised edition.

Corporation for Public Broadcasting.

Corporation Forms. Prentice Hall, 240 Frisch Court Paramus, NJ 07652-5240. Phone: 800-947-7700 or (201)909-6200 Fax: 800-445-6991 or (201)909-6361 URL: http://www.prenhall.com • Looseleaf. Periodic supplementation. Price on application.

Corporation-Partnership-Fiduciary Filled-in Tax Return Forms, 1999. CCH, Inc., 4025 W. Peterson Ave. Chicago, IL 60646-6085. Phone: 800-248-3248 or (773)866-6000 Fax: 800-224-8299 or (773)866-3608 URL: http://www.cch.com • 1999. $21.50.

Corptech Directory of Technology Companies. Corporate Technology Information Services, Inc. c/o Eileen Kennedy, 12 Alfred St., Suite 200 Woburn, MA 01801-1915. Phone: 800-333-8036 or (781)932-3100 Fax: (617)932-6335 E-mail: sales@corptech.com • URL: http://www.corptech.com • Annual. $795.00. Four volumes. Profiles of more than 45,000 manufacturers and developers of high technology products. Includes private companies, publicly-held corporations, and subsidiaries. Formerly *Corporate Technology Directory*.

Corpus Juris Secundum: Criminal Law. West Publishing Co., College and School Div., 610 Opperman Dr. Eagan, MN 55123. Phone: 800-328-4880 or (651)687-7000 Fax: 800-213-2323 or (651)687-5827 E-mail: legal_ed@westgroup.com • URL: http://www.lawschool.westgroup.com • Seven volumes. Price on application. Periodic supplementation. A complete restatement of the entire body of American law based on all reported cases from 1658 to date. Encyclopedic arrangement.

Correctional Building News. Emlen Publications, Inc., 969-A Beachland Blvd. Vero Beach, FL 32963. Phone: (407)231-1400 Fax: (407)231-4183 Bimonthly. Controlled circulation. Edited for designers and builders of prisons.

Correctional Industries Association., 1420 N. Charles St., Ste. CH415 Baltimore, MD 21201. Phone: (410)837-5036 Fax: (410)837-5039 E-mail: ciahq@worldnet.att.net • URL: http://www.corrections.com/industries • Members are managers and supervisors in prison-operated industries.

The Corrections Market. Available from FIND/SVP, Inc., 625 Ave. of the Americas New York, NY 10011-2002. Phone: 800-346-3787 or (212)645-4500 Fax: (212)807-2716 E-mail: catalog@findsvp.com • URL: http://www.findsvp.com • 1996. $2,150.00. Market research report published by Packaged Facts. Covers the markets for prison food service, health care, private management, and telecommunications. Includes market growth projections to the year 2000.

Corrections Today. American Correctional Association, 4380 Forbes Blvd. Lanham, MD 20706-4322. Phone: 800-222-5646 or (301)918-1800 Fax: (301)918-1900 E-mail: admin@aca.com • Bimonthly. $25.00 per year. Includes ''Annual Architecture, Construction, and Design Issue'' on prisons and other correctional facilities.

Corrosion Abstracts: Abstracts of the World's Literature on Corrosion and Corrosion Mitigation. National Association of Corrosion Engineers. Cambridge Information Group, 7200 Wisconsin Ave., 6th Fl. Bethesda, MD 20814. Phone: 800-843-7751 or (301)961-6700 Fax: (301)961-6720 E-mail: market@csa.com • URL: http://www.csa.com • Bimonthly. Members, $215.00 per year; non-members, $250.00 per year. Provides abstracts of the worldwide literature of corrosion and corrosion control. Also available on CD-ROM.

Corrosion Control. Samuel A. Bradford. Chapman and Hall, 115 Fifth Ave., 4th Fl. New York, NY 10003-1004. Phone: 800-842-3636 or (212)260-1354 Fax: (212)260-1730 E-mail: info@chapall.com • URL: http://www.chapall.com • 1992. $80.50. Discusses basic corrosion theory, corrosion causes, coatings, plastics, metals, and many other highly detailed, technical topics. (Chapman & Hall.)

Corrosion Engineering Laboratory., Texas A & M University, Mechanical Engineering Dept. 3123 College Station, TX 77843. Phone: (409)845-9779 Fax: (409)862-2418 E-mail: rgriffin@mengr.tamu.edu • URL: http://www.mengr.tamu.edu/researchgroups/corrosion.html • Research areas include various types of corrosion, including atmospheric, seawater, and stress-related.

Corrosion: Journal of Science and Engineering. National Association of Corrosion Engineers. NACE International, P.O. Box 218340 Houston, TX 77218. Phone: (281)228-6200 Fax: (281)228-6300 E-mail: pubs@mail.nace.org • URL: http://www.nace.org • Monthly. Members, $95.00 per year; non-members, $160.00 per year. Covers corrosion control science, theory, engineering, and practice.

Corrosion of Stainless Steels. A. John Sedriks. John Wiley and Sons, Inc., 605 Third Ave. New York, NY 10158-0012. Phone: 800-225-5945 or (212)850-6000 Fax: (212)850-6088 E-mail: info@wiley.com • URL: http://www.wiley.com • 1996. $86.50. Second edition. Covers the corrosion and corrosion control of stainless steels used in a variety of applications. (Corrosion Monograph Series).

Corrosion Research Center., University of Minnesota, 221 Church St., S. E. Minneapolis, MN 55455. Phone: (612)625-4048 Fax: (612)626-7246 E-mail: dshores@maroon.tc.umn.edu • URL: http://www.cems.umn.edu • Research areas include the effect of corrosion on high technology materials and devices.

Cosmetic Executive Women., 109 E. 73rd St., Apt. 5C New York, NY 10021-3559. Phone: (212)717-2415 Fax: (212)717-2419 E-mail: cexecutive@aol.com • Members are women executives in the cosmetics industry.

Cosmetic, Toiletry and Fragrance Association.

Cosmetic World News: The International News Magazine of the Perfumery, Cosemetics and Toiletries Industry. World News Publications, 130 Wigmore St. London W1H 0AT, England. Fax: 44 171 4875436 Bimonthly. $192.00 per year.

Cosmetics and Toiletries: The International Journal of Cosmetic Technology. Allured Publishing Corp., 362 S. Schmale Rd. Carol Stream, IL 60188-2787. Phone: (630)653-2155 Fax: (630)653-2192 E-mail: allured@allured.com • URL: http://www.allured.com • Monthly. $98.00 per year.

Cosmetics: Science and Technology. M.S. Balsam and Edward Sagarin, editors. Krieger Publishing Co., P.O. Box 9542 Melbourne, FL 32902-9542. Phone: 800-724-0025 or (321)724-9542 Fax: (321)951-3671 E-mail: info@krieger-publishing.com • URL: http://www.krieger-publishing.com • 1992. $375.00. Second edition. Three volumes. Vol. one, $135.00; vol. two, $143.50; vol. three, $163.50.

Cosmetology. Jack Rudman. National Learning Corp., 212 Michael Dr. Syosset, NY 11791. Phone: 800-645-6337 or (516)921-8888 Fax: (516)921-8743 $43.95. (Occupational Competency Examination Series: OCE-13).

Cost Accounting. Prentice Hall, 240 Frisch Court Paramus, NJ 07652-5240. Phone: 800-922-0579 Fax: 800-445-6991 E-mail: info@wiley.com • URL: http://www.wiley.com • 1999. $105.00. 10th edition.

Cost Accounting: Managerial Emphasis. Prentice Hall, 240 Frisch Court Paramus, NJ 07652-5240. Phone: 800-947-7700 or (201)909-6200 Fax: 800-445-6991 or

(201)909-6361 URL: http://www.prenhall.com • 2000. 10th edition. Price on application.

Cost Accounting Standards Board Regulations. CCH, Inc., 4025 W. Peterson Ave. Chicago, IL 60646-6085. Phone: 800-248-3248 or (773)866-6000 Fax: 800-224-8299 or (773)866-3608 URL: http://www.cch.com • 1999. $24.00. Covers Federal Acquisition Regulation (FAR) cost accounting standards for both defense and civilian government contracts. Provides the rules for estimating and reporting costs for contracts of more than $500,000.

Cost Accounting Standards Guide. CCH, Inc., 4025 W. Peterson Ave. Chicago, IL 60646-6085. Phone: 800-248-3248 or (773)583-8500 Fax: 800-224-8299 or (773)866-3608 URL: http://www.cch.com • Monthly. $350.00 per year. Looseleaf serivce. Periodic supplementation.

Cost and Profit Ratios for Vending Operators. National Automatic Merchandising Association, 20 N. Wacker Dr., Suite 3500 Chicago, IL 60606. Phone: 888-337-8363 or (312)346-0370 Fax: (312)704-4140 URL: http://www.vending.org • Annual. $100.00 to members; $250.00 to nonmembers. Provides data on profits and operating expenses.

Cost Control Handbook. R. M. Wilson. Ashgate Publishing Co., Old Post Rd. Brookfield, VT 05036. Phone: 800-535-9544 or (802)276-3162 Fax: (802)276-3837 E-mail: info@ashgate.com • URL: http://www.ashgate.com • 1983. $102.95. Second edition.

Cost Control Strategies for Managers, Controllers and Finance Executives. Siefer Consultants, Inc., P.O. Box 1384 Storm Lake, IA 50588. Phone: (712)732-7340 Fax: (712)732-7906 E-mail: siefer@ncn.net • Monthly. $259.00 per year. Newsletter. Provides a variety of ideas on business budgeting and controlling company expenses. Formerly *Cost Control Strategies for Financial Institutions*.

Cost Engineering: The Journal of Cost Estimating, Cost Control, and Project Management. American Association of Cost Engineers, AACE International, 209 Prairie Ave., Suite 100 Morgantown, WV 26505. Phone: 800-858-2678 or (304)296-8444 Fax: (304)291-5728 E-mail: info@aacei.org • URL: http://www.aacei.org • Monthly. $57.00 per year. Subjects include cost estimation and cost control.

Cost Estimating. Rodney D. Stewart. John Wiley and Sons, Inc., 605 Third Ave. New York, NY 10158-0012. Phone: 800-225-5945 or (212)850-6000 Fax: (212)850-6088 E-mail: info@wiley.com • URL: http://www.wiley.com • 1991. $130.00. Second edition. Discusses high technology engineering cost forecasting, including the estimation of software costs.

Cost Management Handbook. Barry J. Brinker. John Wiley and Sons, Inc., 605 Third Ave. New York, NY 10158-0012. Phone: 800-225-5945 or (212)850-6000 Fax: (212)850-6088 E-mail: info@jwiley.com • URL: http://www.wiley.com • 2000. $140.00.

Cost of Doing Business and Financial Position Survey of the Retail Lumber and Building Material Dealers of the Northeastern States. Northeastern Retail Lumber Association, 585 N. Greenbush Rd. Rensselaer, NY 12144-9453. Phone: 800-292-6752 or (518)286-1010 Fax: (518)286-1755 E-mail: rfnrla@aol.com • URL: http://www.nrla.org • Annual. Free to members; non-members, $300.00. Includes sales figures, profit margins, pricing methods, rates of return, and other financial data for retailers of lumber and building supplies in the Northeast.

Cost of Doing Business: Farm and Power Equipment Dealers, Industrial Dealers, and Outdoor Power Equipment Dealers. North American Equipment Dealers Association, 1195 Smizer Mill Rd. Fenton, MO 63026-3480. Phone: (636)349-5000 E-mail: naeda@ataneda.com • URL: http://www.naeda.com • Annual. $50.00. Provides data on sales, profit margins, expenses, assets, and employee productivity.

Cost of Doing Business Survey. Photo Marketing Association International, 3000 Picture Place Jackson, MI 49201. Phone: (517)788-8100 Fax: (517)788-8371 E-mail: gpageau@pmai.org • URL: http://www.pmai.org • Biennial. $225.00. Emphasis is on photographic retailing.

Cost of Doing Business Survey for Retail Sporting Goods Stores. National Sporting Goods Association, 1601 Feehanville Dr., Ste. 300 Mt. Prospect, IL 60056-6305. Phone: 800-815-5422 or (847)296-6742 Fax: (847)391-9827 E-mail: nsga1699@aol.com • URL: http://www.nsga.org • Biennial. $125.00. Includes income statements, balance sheets, sales per employee, sales per square foot, inventory turnover, etc.

Cost of Personal Borrowing in the United States. Financial Publishing Co., 3975 William Richardson. Dr. South Bend, IN 46628. Phone: 800-247-3214 or (219)243-6040 Fax: (219)243-6060 E-mail: www.financial-publishing.com • Annual. $175.00.

Cotton Council International.

Cotton Digest International. Cotton Digest Co., Inc., P.O. Box 820768 Houston, TX 77282-0768. Phone: (713)977-1644 Fax: (713)783-8658 E-mail: cottonabb@aol.com • Monthly. $40.00 per year. Formerly *Cotton Digest*.

Cotton Farming. Vance Publishing Corp., 400 Knightsbridge Parkway Lincolnshire, IL 60069-1414. Phone: 800-621-2845 or (847)634-2600 Fax: (847)634-4379 URL: http://www.vancepublishing.com • Nine times a year. $35.00 per year.

Cotton Grower. Meister Publishing Co., 37733 Euclid Ave. Willoughby, OH 44094-5992. Phone: 800-572-7740 or (440)942-2000 Fax: (440)942-0662 E-mail: info@meisternet.com • URL: http://www.meisterpro.com • 10 times a year. $32.10 per year.

Cotton Incorporated.

Cotton International. Meister Publishing Co., 37733 Euclid Ave. Willoughby, OH 44094-5992. Phone: 800-572-7740 or (440)942-2000 Fax: (440)942-0662 E-mail: info@meisternet.com • URL: http://www.meisterpro.com • Annual. $30.00.

Cotton: Origin, History, Technology, and Production. C. Wayne Smith and J. Tom Cothren, editors. John Wiley and Sons, Inc., 605 Third Ave. New York, NY 10158-0012. Phone: 800-225-5945 or (212)850-6000 Fax: (212)850-6088 E-mail: info@wiley.com • URL: http://www.wiley.com • 1999. $250.00. (Wiley Series in Crop Science.)

Cotton Price Statistics. U.S. Department of Agriculture, Washington, DC 20250. Phone: (202)720-2791 Monthly.

Cotton Production Prospects for the Decade to 2002: A Global Review. Hamdy M. Eisa and others. World Bank, The Office of the Publisher, 1818 H St., N. W. Washington, DC 20433. Phone: (202)477-1234 Fax: (202)477-6391 E-mail: books@worldbank.org • URL: http://www.worldbank.org • 1994. $22.00. Provides information on cotton's key technologies, marketing, consumption, production trends, and price prospects. (Technical Paper Series, No. 231).

Cotton: Review of the World Situation. International Cotton Advisory Committee, 1629 K St., N.W., Suite 702 Washington, DC 20006-1197. Phone: (202)463-6660 Fax: (202)463-6950 E-mail: publications@icac.org • URL: http://wwwicac.org • Bimonthly. $135.00 per year. Monthly updates available by fax. Editions in English, French, and Spanish.

Cotton's Week. National Cotton Council of America, P.O. Box 820285 Memphis, TN 38182-0285. Phone: (901)274-9030 Fax: (901)725-0510 E-mail: info@cotton.org • URL: http://www.cotton.org/ncc • Weekly. Free to members; non-members, $250.00 per year. Newsletter.

Cottonwood Range and Livestock Research Station. South Dakota State University

Couch on Insurance. Ronald Anderson. West Group, 610 Opperman Dr. Eagan, MN 55123. Phone: 800-328-4880 or (651)687-7000 Fax: 800-213-2323 or (651)687-5827 URL: http://www.westgroup.com • 1984. $2,900.00. Second edition. 33 volumes. An encyclopedic statement of all phases of insurance law.

Council for Advancement and Support of Education.

Council for Aid to Education.

Council for Court Excellence.

Council for Responsible Genetics., Five Upland Rd., Suite 3 Cambridge, MA 02140. Phone: (617)868-0870 Fax: (617)491-5344 E-mail: crg@gene-watch.org • URL: http://www.gene-watch.org • Concerned with the social implications of genetic engineering.

Council for Urban Economic Development.

Council of American Survey Research Organizations., Three Upper Devon Belle Terre Port Jefferson, NY 11777. Phone: (516)928-6954 Fax: (516)928-6041 E-mail: dbowers@casro.org • URL: http://www.casro.org • Members are survey research companies. Various committees are concerned with standards, survey research quality, and technology.

Council of Better Business Bureaus.

Council of Chemical Association Executives.

Council of Communication Management.

Council of Fashion Designers of America.

Council of Graduate Schools.

Council of Institutional Investors., 1730 Rhode Island Ave., N. W., Suite 512 Washington, DC 20036. Phone: (202)822-0800 Fax: (202)822-0801 E-mail: info@cii.org • URL: http://www.cii.org • Members are nonprofit organization pension plans and other nonprofit institutional investors.

Council of Insurance Agents and Brokers.

Council of Logistics Management.

Council of Planning Librarians., 101 N. Wacker Dr., No. CM-190 Chicago, IL 60606. Phone: (312)409-3349 Fax: (312)263-7417 E-mail: dahm@concentric.net • Members are libraries, librarians, and professional planners concerned with urban and regional planning. Affiliated with the American Planning Association.

Council of State Administrators of Vocational Rehabilitation.

Council of State Chambers of Commerce.

Council of State Governments.

Council of the Americas., 680 Park Ave. New York, NY 10021. Phone: (212)628-3200 Fax: (212)249-1880 URL: http://www.counciloftheamericas.org • Members are U. S. corporations with business interests in Latin America.

Council of Writers Organizations.

Council on Career Development for Minorities., 1341 W. Mockingbird Lane, Suite 722-E Dallas, TX 75247. Phone: (214)631-3677 Fax: (214)905-2046 E-mail: ccdm35@aol.com • URL: http://www.ccdm.org • Seeks to improve career counseling and placement services for minority college students.

Council on Economic Priorities., 30 Irving Place New York, NY 10003. Phone: 800-729-4237 or (212)420-1133 Fax: (212)420-0988 E-mail: info@cepnyc.org • URL: http://www.cepnyc.org • Compiles and makes available information on the social responsibility of individual corporations.

Council on Employee Benefits.

Council on Employee Relations. University of Pennsylvania

Council on Family Health., 1155 Connecticut Ave., Suite 400 Washington, DC 20036. Phone: (202)429-6600 E-mail: sdibartolo@chpa-info.org • URL: http://www.cfhinfo.org • Members are drug manufacturers. Concerned with proper use of medications.

Council on Foundations.

Council on International Educational Exchange - USA., 205 E. 42nd St. New York, NY 10017. Phone: (212)822-2600 Fax: (212)822-2699 URL: http://www.ciee.org • Members are educational institutions and agencies that promote and sponsor international education exchange.

Council on Licensure, Enforcement and Regulation., 403 Marquis Ave., Suite 100 Lexington, KY 40502. Phone: (606)269-1289 E-mail: clear@uky.compuscw.net • URL: http://www.clearhq.org • Members are state government occupational and professional licensing officials.

Counseling and Values. Association for Religious and Value Issues in Counseling. American Counseling Association, 5999 Stevenson Ave. Alexandria, VA 22304-3300. Phone: 800-347-6647 or (703)823-9800 Fax: (703)823-0252 URL: http://www.counseling.org • Three times a year. Individuals, $18.00 per year; institutions, $29.00 per year.

The Counseling Psychologist. American Psychological Association. Sage Publications, Inc., 2455 Teller Rd. Thousand Oaks, CA 91320. Phone: (805)499-0721 Fax: (805)499-0871 E-mail: info@sagepub.com • URL: http://www.sagepub • Bimonthly. Individuals, $75.00 per year; institutions, $395.00 per year.

Counseling Services: IACS Newsletter. International Association of Counseling Services, 101 S. Whiting, Suite 211 Alexandria, VA 22304. Phone: (703)823-9840 Fax: (703)823-9843 E-mail: iacs@gmu.edu • Three times a year. Membership.

Counseling Today. Jennifer Sacks, editor. American Counseling Association, 5999 Stevenson Ave. Alexandria, VA 22304-3300. Phone: 800-347-6647 or (703)823-9800 Fax: (703)823-0252 URL: http://www.counseling.org • Monthly. $66.00 per year. Articles and information pertaining to the counseling profession. Formerly *GuidePost*.

Counselors of Real Estate.

Counterfeiting and Forgery: A Practical Guide to the Law. Roland Rowell. LEXIS Publishing, 701 E. Water St. Charlottesville, VA 22902. Phone: 800-446-3210 or (804)972-7600 Fax: 800-643-1280 or (804)972-7686 E-mail: custserv@michie.com • URL: http://www.lexislaw.publishing • 1986. $100.00

Countertrade and Offset: Weekly Intelligence on Unconventional and Reciprocal International Trade. CTO Data Services, Fairfax Station, P.O. Box 7130 Fairfax Station, VA 22039. Phone: (703)383-5816 Fax: (703)383-5815 24 times a year. $688.00 per year. Newsletter. Intelligence on reciprocal international trade and unconventional trade finance. Covers developments and trends in the directory publishing industry, including publisher profiles, start-ups, corporate acquisitions, and business opportunities. Includes *Directory of Countertrade Services*. Formerly *Countertrade Outlook*. itions, and business opportunities. Formerly *Cowles-Simba Report on Directory Publishing*.

Countries of the World and Their Leaders Yearbook. The Gale Group, 27500 Drake Rd. Farmington Hills, MI 48331-3535. Phone: 800-877-GALE or (248)699-GALE Fax: 800-414-5043 or (248)699-8069 E-mail: galeord@galegroup.com • URL: http://www.galegroup.com • 2000. $235.00. Two volumes. Interedition supplement,$105.00. Based on U. S. State Department data covering nearly 170 countries. Features ''Background Notes on countries of the World.'' Also includes the CIA's list of ''Chiefs of State and Cabinet Members of Foreign Governments,'' as well as key officers at U.S. embassies and other information.

Country Data Forecasts. Bank of America, World Information Services, Dept. 3015, 555 California St. San Francisco, CA 94104. Phone: 800-645-6667 or (415)622-1446 Fax: (415)622-0909 Looseleaf, with semiannual updates. $495.00 per year. Provides detailed statistical tables for 80 countries, showing historical data and five-year forecasts of 23 key economic series. Includes population, inflation figures, debt, per capita income, foreign trade, exchange rates, and other data.

Country Finance. Economist Intelligence Unit, 111 W. 57th St. New York, NY 10019. Phone: 800-938-4685 or (212)554-0600 Fax: (212)586-1181 URL: http://www.eiu.com • Semiannual (quarterly for ''fast-changing countries''). $395.00 per year for each country. Discusses banking and financial conditions in each of 47 countries. Includes foreign exchange regulations, the currency outlook, sources of capital, financing techniques, and tax considerations. Formerly Financing Foreign Operations.

Country Forecasts. Economist Intelligence Unit, 111 W. 57th St. New York, NY 10019. Phone: 800-938-4685 or (212)554-0600 Fax: (212)586-1182 URL: http://www.eiu.com • Quarterly. $845.00 per year per country. Five-year forecasts are provided for each of 62 countries. Analyzes economic, political, and business prospects.

Country Outlooks. Bank of America, World Information Services, Dept. 3015, 555 California St. San Francisco, CA 94104. Phone: (415)622-3456 Fax: (415)622-0909 Looseleaf. $495.00 per year. Covers 30 major countries, with each country updated twice a year (60 issues per year). Provides detailed economic data and financial forecasts, including tables of key economic indicators.

Country Profile: Annual Survey of Political and Economic Background. Economist Intelligence Unit, 111 57th St. New York, NY 10019. Phone: 800-938-4685 or (212)554-0600 Fax: (212)586-1182 URL: http://www.eiu.com • Annual. $225.00 per country or country group. Contains statistical tables "showing the last 6 year run of macro-economic indicators, and an overview of a country's politics, economy and industry." Covers 180 countries in 115 annual editions.

Country Report Services. The PRS Group, Post Office Box 248 East Syracuse, NY 13057-0248. Phone: (315)431-0511 Fax: (315)431-0200 Provides full text of reports describing the business risks and opportunities currently existing in more than 150 countries of the world. Contains a wide variety of statistics and forecasts relating to economics political and social conditions. Also includes demographics, tax, and currency information. Updated monthly. Inquire as to online cost and availability.

Country Reports. Economist Intelligence Unit, 111 W. 57th St. New York, NY 10019. Phone: 800-938-4685 or (212)554-0600 Fax: (212)586-1182 URL: http://www.eiu.com • Quarterly. $425.00 per year per country or country group. Comprehensive economic and political information is presented for 180 countries in 99 *Country Reports*, with 12 to 18 month forecasts. Each subscription includes an annual *Country Profile* containing statistical tables.

Country Risk Monitor. Bank of America, World Information Services, Dept. 3015, 555 California St. San Francisco, CA 94104. Phone: (415)622-3456 Fax: (415)622-0909 Looseleaf, with semiannual updates. $495.00 per year. Provides rankings of 80 countries according to current and future business risk. Utilizes key economic ratios and benchmarks for countries in a manner similar to financial ratio analysis for industries.

Country Risk Service. Economist Intelligence Unit, 111 W. 57th St. New York, NY 10019. Phone: 800-938-4685 or (212)554-0600 Fax: (212)586-1182 URL: http://www.eiu.com • Quarterly. $625.00 per year per country. Two-year risk forecasts are provided for each of 82 countries. Business, political, economic, and credit risks are analyzed.

County Agents Directory: The Reference Book for Agricultural Extension Workers. Doane Agricultural Services, 11701 Borman Dr., Suite 100 St. Louis, MO 63146-4199. Phone: 800-535-2342 or (314)569-2700 Fax: (314)564-1083 E-mail: info@agrimartketing.com • Biennial. $23.95. About 17,000 county agents and university agricultural extension workers.

County and City Data Book, a Statistical Abstract Supplement. U.S. Bureau of the Census. Available from U.S. Government Printing Office, Washington, DC 20402. Phone: (202)512-1800 Fax: (202)512-2250 1994. $60.00.

County and City Extra: Annual Metro, City and County Data Book. Mark Littman and Deirdre A. Gaquin. Bernan Press, 4611-F Assembly Dr. Lanham, MD 20706-4391. Phone: 800-274-4447 or (301)459-7666 Fax: 800-865-3450 or (301)459-0056 E-mail: order@bernan.com • URL: http://www.bernan.com • 1999. $109.00. Updates and augments data published irregularly in print form by the U. S. Census Bureau in *County and City Data Book*. Covers "every state, county, metropolitan area, and congressional district in the United States, as well as all U. S. cities with a 1990 population of 25,000 or more." Contains a wide range tic maps.

County Business Patterns. Available from U. S. Government Printing Office, Washington, DC 20402. Phone: (202)512-1800 Fax: (202)512-2250 E-mail: gpoaccess@gpo.gov • URL: http://www.access.gpo.gov • Irregular. 52 issues containing annual data for each state, the District of Columbia, and a U. S. Summary. Produced by U.S. Bureau of the Census (http://www.census.gov). Provides local establishment and employment statistics by industry.

County News. National Association of Counties

Coupon Mailer Service. Entrepreneur Media, Inc., 2445 McCabe Way Irvine, CA 92614. Phone: 800-421-2300 or (949)261-2325 Fax: (949)261-0234 E-mail: entmag@entrepreneur.com • URL: http://www.entrepreneur.com • Looseleaf. $59.50. A practical guide to starting a service for mailing business promotion discount coupons to consumers. Covers profit potential, start-up costs, market size evaluation, owner's time required, pricing, accounting, advertising, promotion, etc. (Start-Up Business Guide No. E1232.)

Court Review. American Judges Association. National Center for State Courts, 300 Newport Ave. Williamsburg, VA 23187-8798. Phone: (757)259-1838 Fax: (757)259-1520 Quarterly. Free to members; non-members, $25.00 per year.

Courts, Judges and Politics: An Introduction to the Judicial Process. Walter Murphy and Charles H. Pritchett. McGraw-Hill, 1221 Ave. of the Americas New York, NY 10020-1095. Phone: 800-722-4726 or (212)904-2000 Fax: (212)904-2072 E-mail: customer.service@mcgraw-hill.com • URL: http://www.mcgraw-hill.com • 1986. $56.88. Fourth edition.

Cowans Bankruptcy Law and Practice. West Publishing Co., College and School Div., 610 Opperman Dr. Eagan, MN 55123. Phone: 800-328-4880 or (651)687-7000 Fax: 800-213-2323 or (651)687-5827 E-mail: legal_ed@westgroup.com • URL: http://www.lawschool.westgroup.com • 1986. $180.00.

Cowles Foundation for Research in Economics. Yale University

Coyle's Information Highway Handbook: A Practical File on the New Information Order. Karen Coyle. American Library Association, 50 E. Huron St. Chicago, IL 60611-2795. Phone: 800-545-2433 or (312)944-6780 Fax: (312)440-9374 E-mail: ala@ala.org • URL: http://www.ala.org • 1997. $30.00. Provides useful "essays on copyright, access, privacy, censorship, and the information marketplace."

CPA Examination Review Business Law and Professional Responibilities. Patrick R. Delaney. John Wiley and Sons, Inc., 605 Third Ave. New York, NY 10158. Phone: 800-225-5945 or (212)850-6000 Fax: (212)850-6088 E-mail: info@wiley.com • URL: http://www.wiley.com • 1996. $109.00.

The CPA Journal. New York State Society of Certified Public Accountants, 530 Fifth Ave., 5th Fl. New York, NY 10036-5101. Phone: (212)719-8300 Fax: (212)719-4755 Monthly. $42.00 per year.

The CPA Letter: A News Report to Members. American Institute of Certified Public Accountants - Communications, 1211 Ave. of the Americas New York, NY 10036-8775. Phone: 800-862-4272 or (212)596-6200 Fax: (212)596-6213 E-mail: journal@aicpa.org • URL: http://www.aicpa.org • 8 times a year. Free to members; non-members, $40.00 per year.

CPA Managing Partner Report: Management News for Accounting Executives. Strafford Publications, Inc., Specialized Information Services, 590 Dutch Valley Rd., N.E. Atlanta, GA 30324. Phone: 800-926-7926 or (404)881-1141 Fax: (404)881-0074 E-mail: custserv@straffordpub.com • URL: http://www.straffordpubs.com • Monthly. $297.00 per year. Newsletter. Covers practice management and professional relationships.

CPA Marketing Report. Strafford Publications, Inc., Specialized Information Services, 590 Dutch Valley Rd., N.E. Atlanta, GA 30324. Phone: 800-926-7926 or (404)881-1141 Fax: (404)881-0074 E-mail: custserv@straffordpub.com • URL: http://www.straffordpubs.com • Monthly. $287.00 per year. Newsletter. Contains strategies for practice development.

CPA Personnel Report. Strafford Publications, Inc., Specialized Information Services, 590 Dutch Valley Rd., N.E. Atlanta, GA 30324. Phone: 800-926-7926 or (404)881-1141 Fax: (404)881-0074 E-mail: custserv@straffordpub.com • URL: http://www.straffordpubs.com • Monthly. $287.00 per year. Newsletter. Provides advice on human relations and personnel procedures for accounting firms.

CPA Software News. Cygnus Business Media, 445 Broad Hollow Rd. Melville, NY 11747-3601. Phone: 800-308-6397 or (631)845-2700 Fax: (631)845-2798 Eight times a year. $39.95 per year. Provides articles and reviews relating to computer technology and software for accountants.

CPA Technology Advisor (Certified Public Accountant): Profitable Strategies and Practical Solutions for Managing. Harcourt Brace Professional Publishing, 525 B St., Suite 1900 San Diego, CA 92101-4495. Phone: 800-782-1272 or (312)782-7853 Fax: (312)782-2378 Monthly. $237.00 per year. Newsletter. Describes hardware and software products and makes recommendations. Formerly *C P A Technology Report*.

CPB's Directory of Limited Partnerships. American Partnership Board, Inc., 10 S. Riverside Plaza, Suite 1100 Chicago, IL 60606-3708. Phone: 800-272-6273 or (312)332-4100 Fax: (312)332-3171 Published periodically. Free booklet listing the names of more than 1,000 limited partnerships in which the Chicago Partnership Board "typically maintains trading information and auctioneering services."

CPB's Partnership Trade Prices. American Partnership Board, Inc., 10 S. Riverside Plaza, Suite 1100 Chicago, IL 60606-3708. Phone: 800-272-6273 or (312)332-4100 Fax: (312)332-3171 Quarterly. $299.00 per year. Provides actual high, low, and last auction trade prices for more than 800 limited partnerships. Valuations by general partners are also shown where available.

CPCU Journal. Chartered Property and Casualty Underwriters Society, P.O. Box 3009 Malvern, PA 19355. Phone: 800-932-2728 or (610)251-2728 Fax: (610)251-2761 URL: http://www.cpcusociety.org • Quarterly. $25.00 per year. Published by the Chartered Property and Casualty Underwriters Society (CPCU). Edited for professional insurance underwriters and agents.

CPCU Society.

CPI Detailed Report: Consumer Price Index. Available from U.S. Government Printing Office, Washington, DC 20402. Phone: (202)512-1800 Fax: (202)512-2250 Monthly. $45.00 per year. Cost of living data.

CPI Digest: Key to World Literature Serving the Coatings, Plastics, Fibers, Adhesives, and Related Industries (Chemical Process Industries). CPI Information Services, 2117 Cherokee Parkway Louisville, KY 40204. Phone: (502)456-6288 Fax: (502)454-4808 E-mail: cpidigest@mindspring.com • Monthly. $397.00 per year. Abstracts of business and technical articles for polymer-based, chemical process industries. Includes a monthly list of relevant U. S. patents. International coverage.

CPI.Q: The Canadian Periodical Index Full-Text on CD-ROM. The Gale Group, 27500 Drake Rd. Farmington Hills, MI 48331-3535. Phone: 800-877-GALE or (248)699-GALE Fax: 800-414-5043 or (248)699-8069 E-mail: galeord@gale.com • URL: http://www.gale.com • Bimonthly. Provides CD-ROM citations from 1988 to date for more than 400 English and French language periodicals. Contains full-text coverage from 1995 to date for 150 periodicals.

CQ Almanac. Congressional Quarterly, Inc., 1414 22nd St., N.W. Washington, DC 20037. Phone: 800-638-1710 or (202)887-8500 Fax: (202)887-6706 E-mail: bookhelp@cq.com • URL: http://www.cq.com • Annual. $215.00.

CQ Weekly. Congressional Quarterly, Inc., 1414 22nd St., N.W. Washington, DC 20037. Phone: 800-432-2250 or (202)887-8500 Fax: (202)887-6706 E-mail: bookhelp@cq.com • URL: http://www.cq.com • Weekly. $1,349.00 per year. Includes annual *Almanac*. Formerly *Congressional Quarterly Weekly Report*.

Craft and Needlework Age Trade Directory. Krause Publications, Inc., 700 E. State St. Iola, WI 54990. Phone: 800-258-0929 or (715)445-2214 Fax: (715)445-4087 E-mail: info@krause.com • URL: http://www.krause.com/ • Annual. $35.00. Lists of about 300 manufacturers and 50 publishers of books and periodicals in the craft and needlework industry.

Craft Businesses. Entrepreneur Media, Inc., 2445 McCabe Way Irvine, CA 92614. Phone: 800-421-2300 or (949)261-2325 Fax: (949)261-0234 E-mail: entmag@entrepreneur.com • URL: http://www.entrepreneur.com • Looseleaf. $59.50. A practical guide to starting a handicrafts-related business. Covers profit potential, start-up costs, market size evaluation, owner's time required, site selection, lease negotiation, pricing, accounting, advertising, promotion, etc. (Start-Up Business Guide No. E1304.)

The Craft of Investing. John Train., 10 E. 53rd St. New York, NY 10022-5299. Phone: 800-242-7737 or (212)207-7000 Fax: (617)661-3281 URL: http://www.harpercollins.com • 1994. $22.00. Presents conservative discussions of a wide variety of investment topics, including market timing, growth vs. value stocks, mutual funds, emerging markets, retirement planning, and estate planning.

Craighead's International Business, Travel, and Relocation Guide to 81 Countries. Available from The Gale Group, 27500 Drake Rd. Farmington Hills, MI 48331-3535. Phone: 800-877-GALE or (248)699-GALE Fax: 800-414-5043 or (248)699-8069 E-mail: galeord@galegroup.com • URL: http://www.galegroup.com • 2000. $725.00. Tenth edition. Four volumes. Compiled by Craighead Publications, Inc. Provides a wide range of business travel and relocation information for 78 different countries, including details on currency, customs regulations, visas, passports, healthcare, transportation, shopping, insurance, travel safety, etc. Formerly *International Business Travel and RelocatDirectory*.

Crawford Perspectives. Arch Crawford, 6890 E. Sunrise Dr., No.70 Tuscon, AZ 85718. Phone: (520)577-1158 E-mail: astromoney@worldnet.att.net • Monthly. $250.00 per year.

CRB Commodity Index Report. Commodity Research Bureau. Bridge-CRB, CRB, 30 S. Wacker Dr., Suite 1810 Chicago, IL 60606. Phone: 800-621-5271 or (312)454-1801 Fax: (312)454-0239 E-mail: crbinfo@bridge.com • URL: http://www.crbindex.com • Weekly. $295.00 per year. Quotes the CRB Futures Price Index and the CRB Spot Market Index for the last five business days, plus the previous week, month, and year. Includes tables and graphs.

CRB Commodity Yearbook. Commodity Research Bureau. CRB, 30 S. Wacker Dr., Suite 1810 Chicago, IL 60606. Phone: 800-621-5271 or (312)454-1801 Fax: (312)454-0239 E-mail: crbinfo@bridge.com • URL: http://www.crbindex.com • Annual. $99.95.

CRB Futures Chart Service. Bridge Publishing, 30 S. Wacker Dr., Suite 1820 Chicago, IL 60606. Phone: 800-621-5271 or (312)454-1801 Fax: (312)454-0239 Weekly. $425.00 per year. Formerly *CRB Futures Chart Service*.

CRC Desk Reference for Nutrition. Carolyn D. Berdanier. CRC Press, Inc., 2000 Corporate Blvd., N. W. Boca Raton, FL 33431. Phone: 800-272-7737 or (561)994-0555 Fax: (561)241-7856 E-mail: orders@crcpress.com • URL: http://www.crcpress.com • 1998. $69.95. Encyclopedic, alphabetical arrangement of topics.

CRE Member Directory. The Counselors of Real Estate, 430 N. Michigan Ave. Chicago, IL 60611. Phone: (312)329-8427 Fax: (312)329-8881 E-mail: cre@interaccess.com • URL: http://www.cre.org • Annual. Free. Available online. Formerly *American Society of Real Estate Counselors Directory*.

Creating a Culture of Competence. Michael Zwell. John Wiley and Sons, Inc., 605 Third Ave. New York, NY 10158-0012. Phone: 800-225-5945 or (212)850-6000 Fax: (212)850-6088 E-mail: business@jwiley.com • URL: http://www.wiley.com • 2000. $35.95. Emphasizes employee participation to arrive at a desired change in organizational culture.

Creating a Financial Plan: A How-To-Do-It Manual for Librarians. Betty J. Turock amd Andrea Pedolsky. Neal-Schuman Publishers, Inc., 100 Varick St. New York, NY 10013. Phone: (212)925-8650 Fax: 800-584-2414 or (212)219-8916 E-mail: info@neal-schuman.com • URL: http://www.neal-schuman.com • 1992. $49.95. (How-to-Do-It Series).

Creating a Flexible Workplace: How to Select and Manage Alternative Work Options. Barry Olmsted and Suzanne Smith. AMACOM, 1601 Broadway, 12th Fl. New York, NY 10019. Phone: 800-262-9699 or (212)586-8100 Fax: (212)903-8168 E-mail: custmserv@amanet.org • URL: http://www.amanet.org • 1994. $59.95. Covers ten work options, such as flextime, job sharing, and permanent part-time employment.

Creating Newsletters, Brochures, and Pamphlets: A How-To-Do-It Manual for Librarians. Barbara A. Radke and Barbara Stein. Neal-Schuman Publishers, Inc., 100 Varick St. New York, NY 10013. Phone: (212)925-8650 Fax: 800-584-2414 or (212)219-8916 E-mail: info@neal-schuman.com • URL: http://www.neal-schuman.com • 1992. $39.95. Includes desktop publishing. (How-to-Do-It Series).

Creating Winning Marketing Plans: What Today's Managers Must Do to Succeed. Sidney J. Levy, editor. Dartnell Corp., 360 Hiatt Dr. Palm Beach, FL 33418. Phone: 800-621-5463 or (561)622-6520 Fax: (561)622-2423 E-mail: custserv@lrp.com • URL: http://www.dartnellcorp.com • 1996. $39.95. Consists of articles by 25 "Top Experts." Covers marketing objectives, customer needs, market segmentation, database marketing, consumer scanning, and other topics.

Creative Management. Jane Henry. Sage Publications, Inc., 2455 Teller Rd. Thousand Oaks, CA 91320-2218. Phone: 800-323-4900 or (805)499-0721 Fax: (805)499-0871 E-mail: info@sagepub.com • URL: http://www.sagepub.com • 1991. $60.00.

Creative Strategy in Advertising; What the Copywriter Should Know About the Creative Side of the Business. A. Jerome Jewler. Wadsworth Publishing, 10 Davis Dr. Belmont, CA 94002. Phone: 800-354-9706 or (650)595-2350 Fax: (650)637-9955 URL: http://www.thomson.com/wadsworth • 2000. $52.00. Seventh edition. (Mass Communication Series).

Creative Strategy in Direct Marketing. Susan K. Jones. NTC/Contemporary Publishing, P.O. Box 545 Blacklick, OH 43004. Phone: 800-338-3987 or (614)755-4151 Fax: (614)755-5645 E-mail: ntcpub@mcgraw-hill.com • URL: http://www.ntc-cb.com • 1997. $39.95. Second edition.

Creative: The Magazine of Promotion and Marketing. Magazines Creative, Inc., 42 W. 38th St., Rm. 601 New York, NY 10016-6210. Phone: (212)840-0160 Fax: (212)819-0945 Bimonthly. $30.00 per year. Covers promotional materials, including exhibits, incentives, point-of-purchase advertising, premiums, and specialty advertising.

Creative's Illustrated Guide to P-O-P Exhibits and Promotion. Magazines Creative, Inc., 42 W. 38th St., Rm. 601 New York, NY 10016-6210. Phone: (212)840-0160 Fax: (212)819-0945 Annual. $25.00. Lists sources of point-of-purchase displays, signs, and exhibits and sources of other promotional materials and equipment. Available online.

Creativity. Art Direction Magazine. Art Directon Book Co., Inc, 456 Glenbrook Rd. Glenbrook, CT 06906-1800. Phone: (203)353-1441 Fax: (203)353-1371 Annual. $62.95.

Creativity Rules! A Writer's Workbook. John Vorhaus. Silman-James Press, 3624 Shannon Rd. Los Angeles, CA 90027. Phone: 800-729-6423 or (323)661-9922 Fax: (323)661-9933 E-mail: silmanjamespress@earthlink.net • 2000. $15.95. Covers the practical process of conceiving, outlining, and developing a story, especially for TV or film scripts. Includes "tactics and exercises."

Credit. American Financial Services Association, 919 18th St., N.W., Suite 300 Washington, DC 20006. Phone: (202)296-5544 Fax: (202)223-0321 Bimonthly. Members, $12.00 per year; non-members, $22.00 per year.

Credit & Collections News. Faulkner & Gray, Inc., 300 S. Wacker Drive, 18th Floor Chicago, IL 60606. Phone: (312)913-1334 Fax: (312)913-1369 URL: http://www.faulknergray.com • Weekly. $425.00 per year. Newsletter. Covers trends and new developments in credit and collections, including technology.

Credit and Lending Dictionary. Daphne Smith and Shelley W. Geehr, editors. Robert Morris Associates, One Liberty Place, 1650 Market St., Suite 2300 Philadelphia, PA 19103. Phone: 800-677-7621 or (215)446-4000 Fax: (215)446-4100 E-mail: info@rmahq.org • URL: http://www.rmahq.org • 1994. $25.00.

Credit Card Management. Faulkner & Gray, Inc., 300 S. Wacker Dr., 18th Fl. Chicago, IL 60606. Phone: 800-535-8403 or (312)913-1334 Fax: (312)913-1959 E-mail: order@faulknergray.com • URL: http://www.faulkner.gray.com • Monthly. $98.00 per year. Edited for bankers and other credit card managers. Supplements available: *Card Technology Review* and *Debit Card Directory*.

Credit Card Management Buyer's Guide. Faulkner & Gray, Inc., 300 S. Wacker Dr. Chicago, IL 60606. Phone: 800-535-8403 or (312)913-1334 Fax: (312)913-1959 E-mail: order@faulknergray.com • URL: http://www.ccm.faulknergray.com • Annual. Free. Lists companies related to the management of credit cards and debit cards.

Credit Card Marketing Sourcebook. Faulkner & Gray, Inc., 300 S. Wacker Dr., 18th Fl. Chicago, IL 60606. Phone: 800-535-8403 Fax: (312)913-1959 E-mail: order@faulknergray.com • URL: http://www.ccm.faulknergray.com • Annual. Price on application.

Credit Card News. Faulkner & Gray, Inc., 300 S. Wacker Drive, 18th Floor Chicago, IL 60606. Phone: (312)913-1334 Fax: (312)913-1369 URL: http://www.faulknergray.com • Semimonthly. $465.00 per year. Newsletter. Covers the latest trends in credit card marketing. Includes the effects of government regulation and court decisions.

Credit Card Users of America., P.O. Box 7100 Beverly Hills, CA 90212. Phone: (818)343-4434 Supports the rights of credit card users.

Credit Consulting. Entrepreneur Media, Inc., 2445 McCabe Way Irvine, CA 92614. Phone: 800-421-2300 or (949)261-2325 Fax: (949)261-0234 E-mail: entmag@entrepreneur.com • URL: http://www.entrepreneur.com • Looseleaf. $59.50. A practical guide to starting a consumer credit and debt counseling and consulting service. Covers profit potential, start-up costs, market size evaluation, owner's time required, pricing, accounting, advertising, promotion, etc. (Start-Up Business Guide No. E1321.)

Credit Department Management. D. Laurence Blackstone. Robert Morris Associates, One Liberty Place, Suite 2300, 1650 Market St. Philadelphia, PA 19103. Phone: 800-677-7621 or (949)446-4000 Fax: (949)446-4100 E-mail: info@rmahq.org • URL: http://www.rmahq.org • 1992. $65.00. Second edition.

Credit Management Handbook. Burt Edwards and others. Ashgate Publishing Co., Old Post Rd. Brookfield, VT 05036. Phone: 800-535-9544 or (802)276-1362 Fax: (802)276-3837 E-mail: info@ashgate.com • URL: http://www.ashgate.com • 1997. $96.95. Fourth edition. Published by Gower in England.

The Credit Memo. New York Credit and Financial Management Association, 49 W. 45th St., 5th Fl. New York, NY 10036-4603. Phone: (212)944-2400 Fax: (212)944-2663 Bimonthly. Membership. Formerly *Credit Executive*.

Credit Research Center. Georgetown University

Credit Research Foundation.

Credit Risk Management. Phillips Business Information, Inc., 1201 Seven Locks Rd., Suite 300 Potomac, MD 20854. Phone: 800-777-5006 or (301)340-1520 Fax: (301)309-3847 E-mail: pbi@phillips.com • URL: http://www.phillips.com/marketplaces.htm • Biweekly. $695.00 per year. Newsletter on consumer credit, including delinquency aspects.

Credit Risk Management: A Guide to Sound Business Decisions. H. A. Schaeffer. John Wiley and Sons, Inc., 605 Third Ave. New York, NY 10158-0012. Phone: 800-225-5945 or (212)850-6000 Fax: (212)850-6088 E-mail: info@jwiley.com • URL: http://www.wiley.com • 2000. $69.95. Covers corporate credit policies, credit authorization procedures, and analysis of business credit applications. Includes 12 "real-life" case studies.

Credit Union Executive Journal: For Active Leaders and Managers of Credit Unions. Credit Union National Association, Communications Div. CUNA Publications, P.O. Box 431 Madison, WI 53701. Phone: 800-356-8010 or (608)231-4000 Fax: (608)231-4370 URL: http://www.cuna.org • Bimonthly. $99.00 per year. A management journal for credit union CEOs and senior executives.

Credit Union Executives Society.

Credit Union Guide. Credit Union National Association. Prentice Hall, 240 Frisch Court Paramus, NJ 07652-5240. Phone: 800-947-7700 or (201)909-6200 Fax: 800-445-6991 or (201)909-6361 URL: http://www.prenhall.com • Four looseleaf volumes. Periodic supplementation. Price on application. Laws, regulations, and developments affecting credit unions.

Credit Union Magazine: For Credit Union Elected Officials, Managers and Employees. Credit Union National Association, Communications Div. CUNA Publications, P.O. Box 431 Madison, WI 53701. Phone: 800-356-8010 or (608)231-4000 Fax: (608)231-4370 URL: http://www.cuna.org • Monthly. $38.00 per year. News analysis and operational information for credit union management, staff, directors, and committee executives.

Credit Union National Association.

Credit Union Report. Credit Union National Association, P.O. Box 431 Madison, WI 53701. Phone: 800-356-9655 or (608)231-4043 Fax: (608)231-4858 Annual. $25.00. Credit union leagues, associations, for each of the 50 states and the District of Columbia.

Credit World. International Credit Association, P.O. Box 15945-314 Lenexa, KS 66284-5945. Phone: (913)307-9432 Fax: (913)541-0156 E-mail: ica@ica-credit.org • URL: http://www.ica-credit.org • Bimonthly. Free to members; non-members, $60.00 per year.

CreditWeek. Standard and Poor's, 55 Water St. New York, NY 10041. Phone: 800-221-5277 or (212)438-2000 Fax: (212)438-0040 E-mail: questions@standardandpoors.com • URL: http://www.standardandpoors.com • Weekly. $1,695.00 per year.

CreditWeek Municipal Edition. Standard & Poor's, 55 Water St. New York, NY 10041. Phone: 800-221-5277 or (212)438-2000 Fax: (212)438-0040 E-mail: questions@standardandpoors.com • URL: http://www.standardandpoors.com • Weekly. $2,200.00 per year. Newsletter. Provides news and analysis of the municipal bond market, including information on new issues.

Crime, Criminals, and Corrections. Donal E. Macnamara and Lloyd McCorkle. John Jay Press, 899 Tenth Ave. New York, NY 10019. Phone: (212)237-8442 Fax: (212)237-8486 1982. $17.00.

Crime in America's Top-Rated Cities: A Statistical Profile. Grey House Publishing, Pocketknife Square Lakeville, CT 06039. Phone: 800-562-2139 or (860)435-0868 Fax: 800-248-0115 or (860)435-3004 E-mail: books@greyhouse.com • URL: http://www.greyhouse.com • Biennial. $125.00. Contains 20-year data for major crime categories in 75 cities, suburbs, metropolitan areas, and the U. S. Also includes statistics on correctional facilities, inmates, hate crimes, illegal drugs, and other crime-related matters.

Crimes Against Business: A Practical Guide to the Prevention and Detection of Business Crime. Jules B. Kroll, editor. Ayer Co. Publishers, Inc., Six Rd., C/O IDS, 195 McGregor St. Manchester, NH 03102. Phone: 888-267-7323 Fax: (603)922-3348 URL: http://www.scry.com/ayer • 1980. $102.95 per volume. Two volumes.

Criminal Defense Technique. Matthew Bender & Co., Inc., Two Park Ave. New York, NY 10016. Phone: 800-223-1940 or (212)448-2000 Fax: (212)244-3188 $1,900.00. 10 looseleaf volumes. Periodic supplementation.

Criminal Justice Information: How to Find It, How to Use It. Dennis C. Benamati and others. Oryx Press, 4041 North Central Ave., Suite 700 Phoenix, AZ 85012-3397. Phone: 800-279-6799 or (602)265-2651 Fax: 800-279-4663 or (602)265-6250 E-mail: info@oryxpress.com • URL: http://www.oryxpress.com • 1997. $59.95. A guide to print, electronic, and online criminal justice information resources. Includes statistical reports, directories, periodicals, monographs, databases, and other sources.

Criminal Law Advocacy Reporter. Matthew Bender and Co., Inc., Two Park Ave. New York, NY 10016. Phone: 800-223-1940 or (212)448-2000 Fax: (212)244-3188 E-mail: international@bender.com • URL: http://www.bender.com • Monthly. $310.00 per year. Analysis of the latest cases and trends in criminal law and procedure.

Criminal Law Deskbook. Patrick McCloskey and Ronald Schoenberg. Matthew Bender and Co., Inc., Two Park Ave. New York, NY 10016. Phone: 800-223-1940 or (212)448-2000 Fax: (212)244-3188 E-mail: international@bender.com • URL: http://www.bender.com • Irregular. $205.00. Discussions of the basic principles of criminal procedure, substantive law, and criminal trial strategy and tactics.

Criminal Law Reporter. Bureau of National Affairs, Inc., 1231 25th St., N.W. Washington, DC 20037-1197. Phone: 800-372-1033 or (202)452-4200 Fax: (202)822-8092 E-mail: books@bna.com • URL: http://www.bna.com • Weekly. $519.00 per year. Includes full text of U. S. Supreme Court criminal law decisions.

Criminal Procedure Handbook. Tertius Geldenhuys and J.J. Joubert, editors. Gaunt, Inc., 3011 Gulf Dr. Holmes Beach, FL 34217-2199. Phone: 800-942-8683 or (914)778-5211 Fax: (914)778-5252 E-mail: info@gaunt.com • URL: http://www.gaunt.com • 1999. $42.50. Fourth edition.

Criminology; An Interdisciplinary Journal. American Society of Criminology, 1314 Kinnear Rd. Columbus, OH 43212. Phone: (614)292-9207 URL: http://www.bsos.umd.edu/asc/ • Quarterly. Individuals, $50.00 per year; institutions, $90.00 per year.

Crisis Response: Inside Stories on Managing Image Under Siege. The Gale Group, 27500 Drake Rd. Farmington Hills, MI 48331-3535. Phone: 800-877-GALE or (248)699-GALE Fax: 800-414-5043 or (248)699-8069 E-mail: galeord@galegroup.com • URL: http://www.galegroup.com • 1993. $60.00. Presents first-hand accounts by media relations professionals of major business crises and how they were handled. Topics include the following kinds of crises: environmental, governmental, corporate image, communications, and product.

Critical Path Methods in Construction Practice. James M. Antill and Ronald Woodhead. John Wiley and Sons, Inc., 605 Third Ave. New York, NY 10158-0012. Phone: 800-225-5368 or (212)850-6000 Fax: (212)850-6088 E-mail: info@wiley.com • URL: http://www.wiley.com • 1990. $120.00. Fourth edition.

Crittenden Directory of Real Estate Financing. Crittenden Research, Inc., P.O. Box 1150 Novato, CA 94948. Phone: 800-421-3483 or (415)382-2400 Fax: (415)382-2476 E-mail: webmaster@crittendenonline.com • Semiannual. $399.00 per year. Included with subscription to weekly *Crittenden Report on Real Estate Financing*. Provides information on major U. S. real estate lenders.

Crittenden Report on Real Estate Financing: The Nation's Leading Weekly Newsletter on Real Estate Finance. Crittenden Research, Inc., P.O. Box 1150 Novato, CA 94948. Phone: 800-421-3483 or (415)382-2400 Fax: (415)382-2476 Weekly. $395.00 per year. Newsletter on real estate lending and mortgages. Includes semiannual *Crittenden Directory of Real Estate Financing*.

Crop Protection Chemicals Reference. Chemical and Pharmaceutical Press, Inc., 110 Williams St., 11th Fl. New York, NY 10038. Phone: 800-544-7377 or (212)399-0126 Fax: (212)399-1122 1994. $130.00. 10th edition. Contains the complete text of product labels. Indexed by manufacturer, product category, pest use, crop use, chemical name, and brand name.

Crop Science. Crop Science Society of America, 677 S. Segoe Rd. Madison, WI 53711. Phone: (608)273-8080 Fax: (608)273-2021 URL: http://www.crops.org/ • Bimonthly. Free to members, non-members, $241.00 per year.

Crop Science - Soil Science - Agronomy News. American Society of Agronomy, Inc., 677 S. Segoe Rd. Madison, WI 53711. Phone: (608)273-8080 Fax: (608)273-2021 E-mail: journal@agronomy.org • URL: http://www.agronomy.org/journals • Monthly. Free to members; non-members, $12.00 per year. Formerly *Agronomy News*.

CRS Referral Directory. Council of Residential Specialists, 430 N. Michigan Ave. Suite 500 Chicago, IL 60611-4092. Phone: (312)321-4400 Fax: (312)329-8882 E-mail: products@rscouncil.com • URL: http://www.rscouncil.com • Annual. Membership. *CRB/CRS Referral Directory*.

The Cruise Directory. Available from Informa Publishing Group Ltd., PO Box 1017 Westborough, MA 01581-6017. Phone: 800-493-4080 Fax: (508)231-0856 E-mail: enquiries@informa.com • URL: http://www.informa.com • Annual. $128.00. Published in the UK by Lloyd's List (http://www.lloydslist.com). Includes detailed information on cruise operators worldwide, individual cruise ship onboard facilities/features, ports capable of handling cruise ships, agents, ship builders/repairers, and equipment manufacturers.

Cruise Travel: Ships, Ports, Schedules, Prices. World Publishing Co., 990 Grove St. Evanston, IL 60201. Phone: (847)491-6440 Fax: (847)491-0459 E-mail: cs@sports.net • URL: http://www.travel.org/cruisetravel • Bimonthly. $23.94 per year.

CryoGas International: The Source of Timely and Relevant Information for the Industrial Gas and Cyrogenics Industries. J. R. Campbell & Associates, Inc., Five Militia Dr. Lexington, MA 02173. Phone: (781)862-0624 Fax: (781)863-9411 E-mail: cryogas@cyrogas.com • URL: http://www.cryogas.com • 11 times a year. $150.00 per year. Reports developments in technology market development and new products for the industrial gases and cryogenic equipment industries. Formerly *Cryogenic Information Report*.

Cryogenic Engineering Conference., c/o Dr. J. Theilacker, P.O. Box 500 Batavia, IL 60510. Phone: (630)840-3238 Fax: (630)840-4989 Members are researchers and managers concerned with the science and technology of extreme cold. Subjects of interest include superconductivity, liquefied gases, and cryobiology.

Cryogenic Society of America., c/o Laurie Huget, Huget Advertising, 1033 South Blvd. Oak Park, IL 60302. Phone: (708)383-6220 Fax: (708)383-9337 E-mail: csa@huget.com • URL: http://www.-csa.fnal.gov • Seeks to encourage the dissemination of information on low temperature industrial technology.

Cryogenics: The International Journal of Low Temperature Engineering and Research. Elsevier Science, 655 Ave. of the Americas New York, NY 10010. Phone: 888-437-4636 or (212)989-5800 Fax: (212)633-3680 E-mail: usinfo@elsevier.com • URL: http://www.elsevier.com • Monthly. $1,779.00 per year.

Crystal Fire: The Birth of the Information Age. Michael Riordan and Lillian Hoddeson. W. W. Norton & Co., Inc., 500 Fifth Ave. New York, NY 10110. Phone: 800-223-2584 or (212)354-5500 Fax: (212)869-0856 E-mail: webmaster@wwnorton.com • URL: http://www.wwnorton.com • 1997. $27.50. A history of the transistor, from early electronic experiments to practical development at the former Bell Telephone Laboratories.

CSA Life Sciences Collection. Cambridge Scientific Abstracts, 7200 Wisconsin Ave., Suite 601 Bethesda, MD 20814. Phone: 800-843-7751 or (301)961-6700 Fax: (301)961-6720 Includes online versions of *Biotechnology Research Abstracts, Entomology Abstracts, Genetics Abstracts*, and about 20 other abstract collections. Time period is 1978 to date, with monthly updates. Inquire as to online cost and availability.

CSA Life Sciences Collection ÎCD-ROMÌ. Cambridge Scientific Abstracts, 7200 Wisconsin Ave., Suite 601 Bethesda, MD 20814. Phone: 800-843-7751 or (301)961-6750 Fax: (301)961-6720 Quarterly. Includes CD-ROM versions of *Biotechnology Research Abstracts, Entomology Abstracts, Genetics Abstracts*, and about 20 other abstract collections.

CSG Directories II: Legislative Leadership. Committees and Staff by Function. Council of State Governments, P.O. Box 11910 Lexington, KY 40578-1910. Phone: 800-800-1910 or (606)244-8000 Fax: (606)244-8001 E-mail: info@csg.org • URL: http://www.csg.org • Annual. $45.00. Legislative leaders, committee members and staff, personnel of principal legislative staff offices. Formerly *Book of the States, Supplement Two: State Legislative Leadership, Committees, and Staff*.

CSG State Directories: I State Elective Officials. Council of State Governments, P.O. Box 11910 Lexington, KY 40578-1910. Phone: 800-800-1910 or (606)244-8000 Fax: (606)244-8001 E-mail: info@csg.org • URL: http://www.csg.org • Annual. $45.00. Lists about 8,000 state legislators, state executive branch elected officials, and state supreme court judges. Formerly *Book of the States, Supplement One: State Elective Officials and the Legislatures*.

CSM. CSM Marketing, Inc., 195 Smithtown Blvd. Nesconset, NY 11767-1849. Monthly. $30.00 per year. Formerly *Catalog Showroom Merchandiser*.

CSP: The Magazine for C-Store People. CSP Information Group, 1100 Jorie Blvd., Suite 314 Oak Brook, IL 60523-4433. Phone: (212)965-8800 Fax: (212)965-8811 Monthly. $48.00 per year. Emphasizes the influence of people (both store personnel and consumers) on the C-store industry.

CTFA News. Cosmetic, Toiletry, and Fragrance Association, 1101 17th St., N. W., Suite 300 Washington, DC 20036. Phone: (202)331-1770 Fax: (202)331-1969 E-mail: membership@ctfa.org • URL: http://www.ctfa.org • Bimonthly. Newsletter.

CTMA, The Marketing Society for the Cable and Telecommunications Industry.

CUIS (Credit Union Information Service). United Communications Group, 11300 Rockville Ave., Suite 1100 Rockville, MD 20852-3030. Phone: (301)816-8950 Fax: (301)816-8945 E-mail: cdonoghue@ucg.com • URL: http://www.ucg.com • Biweekly. $277.00 per year. Newsletter. Supplement available *CUIS Special Reoprt*.

Cumulative Index to Nursing and Allied Health Literature. CINAHL Information Systems, 1509 Wilson Terrace Glendale, CA 91209-0871. Phone: 800-959-7167 or (818)409-8005 Fax: (818)546-5679 E-mail: cinahl@cinahl.com • URL: http://www.cinahl.com • Quarterly. $365.00 per year. Annual cumulation.

Cumulative List of Organizations Described in Section 170(c) of the Internal Revenue Code of 1986. Available from U. S. Government Printing Office, Washington, DC 20402. Phone: (202)512-1800 Fax: (202)512-2250 E-mail: gpoaccess@gpo.gov • URL: http://www.access.gpo.gov • Annual. $114.00 per year, including quarterly supplements. Lists about 300,000 organizations eligible for contributions deductible for federal income tax purposes. Provides name of each organization and city, but not complete address information. Arranged alphabetically by name of institution. (Office of Employee Plans and Exempt Organizations, Internal Revenue Service.)

Currency and Interest Rate Hedging: A User's Guide to Options, Futures, Swaps, and Forward Contracts. Torben J. Andersen. New York Institute of Finance, Two World Trade Center, 17th Fl. New York, NY 10048-0203. Phone: (212)344-2900 Fax: (212)514-8423 1993. $49.95. Second edition.

Currency Options: Hedging and Trading Strategies. Henry Clasing. McGraw-Hill Professional, 1221 Ave. of the Americas New York, NY 10020-1095. Phone: 800-772-4726 or (212)904-2000 Fax: (212)904-2072 E-mail: customer.service@mcgraw-hill.com • URL: http://www.mcgraw-hill.com • 1992. $70.00.

Currency Risk Management. Gary Shoup, editor. Fitzroy Dearborn Publishers Inc, 919 N. Michigan Ave., Suite 760 Chicago, IL 60611. Phone: 800-850-8102 or (312)587-0131 Fax: (312)587-1049 E-mail: website@fitzroydearborn.com • URL: http://www.fitzroydearborn.com • 1998. $55.00.

Current Biography. H. W. Wilson Co., 950 University Ave. Bronx, NY 10452. Phone: 800-367-6770 or (718)588-8400 Fax: (718)590-1617 E-mail: custserv@hwwilson.com • Monthly, except December. $78.00 per year. Includes profiles of business people and economists who have been prominent in the news.

Current Biography on WILSONDISC. H. W. Wilson Co., 950 University Ave. Bronx, NY 10452. Phone: 800-367-6770 or (718)588-8400 Fax: 800-590-1617 Annual. $189.00 ($129.00 renewal). Provides the most recent 12 years of *Current Biography* on CD-ROM.

Current Biography Yearbook. H. W. Wilson Co., 950 University Ave. Bronx, NY 10452. Phone: 800-367-6770 or (718)588-8400 Fax: (718)590-1617 E-mail: custserv@hwwilson.com • URL: http://www.hwwilson.com • Annual. $69.00. The yearly cumulation of *Current Biography*.

Current Biotechnology. The Royal Society of Chemistry. Publications Expediting, Inc., 200 Meacham Ave. Elmont, NY 11003. Monthly. $1,229.00 per year. Reports on the latest scientific, technical and commercial advances in the field of technology. Formerly *Current Biotechnology Abstracts*.

Current Contents Connect. Institute for Scientific Information, 3501 Market St. Philadelphia, PA 19104. Phone: 800-386-4474 or (215)386-0100 Fax: (215)386-2911 URL: http://www.isinet.com • Provides online abstracts of articles listed in the tables of contents of about 7,500 journals. Coverage is very broad, including science, social science, life science, technology, engineering, industry, agriculture, the environment, economics, and arts and humanities. Time period is two years, with weekly updates. Inquire as to online cost and availability.

Current Contents: Engineering, Computing and Technology. Institute for Scientific Information, 3501 Market St. Philadelphia, PA 19104. Phone: 800-336-4474 or (215)386-0100 Fax: (215)386-2911 URL: http://www.isinet.com • Weekly. $730.00 per year. Reproductions of contents pages of technical journals. Includes *Author Index, Address Directory, Current Book Contents* and *Title Word Index*. Formerly *Current Contents: Engineering, Technology and Applied Sciences*.

Current Contents: Social and Behavioral Sciences. Institute for Scientific Information, 3501 Market St. Philadelphia, PA 19104. Phone: 800-336-4474 or (215)386-0100 Fax: (215)386-2911 URL: http://www.isinet.com • Weekly. $730.00 per year. Includes *Author Index*.

Current Index to Journals in Education (CIJE). Oryx Press, 4041 N. Central Ave., Ste. 700 Phoenix, AZ 85012-3397. Phone: 800-279-6799 or (602)265-2651 Fax: 800-279-4663 or (602)265-6250 E-mail: info@oryxpress.com • URL: http://www.oryxpress.com • Monthly. $245.00 per year. Semiannual cumulations, $475.00.

Current Index to Statistics: Applications, Methods, and Theory. American Statistical Association, 1429 Duke St. Alexandria, VA 22314-3415. Phone: (703)684-1221 Fax: (703)684-2036 E-mail: asainfo@amstat.org • URL: http://www.amstat.org • Annual. Price on application. An index to journal articles on statistical applications and methodology.

Current Law Index: Multiple Access to Legal Periodicals. The Gale Group, 27500 Drake Rd. Farmington Hills, MI 48331-3535. Phone: 800-877-GALE or (248)699-GALE Fax: 800-414-5043 or (248)699-8069 E-mail: galeord@galegroup.com • URL: http://www.galegroup.com • Monthly. $650.00 per year. Produced in cooperation with the American Association of Law Libraries. Indexes more than 900 law journals, legal newspapers, and specialty publications from the U.S., Canada, U.K., Ireland, Australia, and New Zealand.

Current Legal Forms with Tax Analysis. Matthew Bender and Co., Inc., Two Park Ave. New York, NY 10016. Phone: 800-223-1940 or (212)448-2000 Fax: (212)244-3188 E-mail: international@bender.com • URL: http://www.bender.com • Quarterly. $730.00 per year. 23 looseleaf volumes. Periodic supplementation, $1,685.00.

Current Literature in Traffic and Transportation. Northwestern University, Transportation Library, Evanston, IL 60208-2300. Phone: (847)491-5275 Fax: (847)491-8601 E-mail: b-simms@nwu.edu/transportation/ • URL: http://www.library.nwu.edu • Quarterly. $25.00 per year.

Current Municipal Problems. West Group, 610 Opperman Dr. Eagan, MN 55123. Phone: 800-328-4880 or (651)687-7000 Fax: 800-213-2323 or (651)687-5827 URL: http://www.westgroup.com • Quarterly. $153.50 per year. Annual cumulation. Full text journal articles on municipal law and administration. Indexing included.

Current Population Reports: Household Economic Studies, Series P-70. Available from U. S. Government Printing Office, Washington, DC 20402. Phone: (202)512-1800 Fax: (202)512-2250 E-mail: gpoaccess@gpo.gov • URL: http://www.access.gpo.gov • Irregular. $16.00 per year. Issued by the U.S. Bureau of the Census (http://www.census.gov). Each issue covers a special topic relating to household socioeconomic characteristics.

Current Population Reports: Population Characteristics, Special Studies, and Consumer Income, Series P-20, P-23, and P-60. Available from U. S. Government Printing Office, Washington, DC 20402. Phone: (202)512-1800 Fax: (202)512-2250 E-mail: gpoaccess@gpo.gov • URL: http://www.access.gpo.gov • Irregular. $39.00 per year. Issued by the U.S. Bureau of the Census (http://www.census.gov). Each issue covers a special topic relating to population or income. Series P-20, *Population Characteristics*, provides statistical studies on such items as mobility, fertility, education, and marital status. Series P-23, *Special Studies*, consists of occasional reports on methodology. Series P-60, *Consumer Income*, publishes reports on income in relation to age, sex, education, occupation, family size, etc.

Current Population Reports: Population Estimates and Projections, Series P-25. Available from U. S. Government Printing Office, Washington, DC 20402. Phone: (202)512-1800 Fax: (202)512-2250 E-mail: gpoaccess@gpo.gov • URL: http://www.access.gpo.gov • Irregular. $14.00 per year. Issued by the U.S. Bureau of the Census (http://www.census.gov). Provides monthly, mid-year, and annual population estimates, including data for states and Standard Metropolitan Statistical Areas. Projections are given for the U.S. population in future years.

Current Publications in Legal and Related Fields. American Association of Law Libraries. Fred B. Rothman and Co., 10368 W. Centennial Rd. Littleton, CO 80127. Phone: 800-457-1986 or (303)979-5657 Fax: (303)978-1457 Nine times a year. $185.00 per year. Annual cumulation.

Current Trends in Information: Research and Theory. Bill Katz and Robin Kinder, editors. The Haworth Press, Inc., 10 Alice St. Binghamton, NY 13940-1580. Phone: 800-429-6784 or (607)722-5857 Fax: 800-895-0582 or (607)722-1424 E-mail: getinfo@haworthpressinc.com • URL: http://www.haworthpressinc.com • 1987. $49.95. (Reference Librarian Series, No. 18).

Curricula in the Atmospheric Oceanic, Hydrologic and Related Sciences. American Meteorological Society, 45 Beacon St. Boston, MA 02108-3693. Phone: (617)227-2425 Fax: (617)742-8718 E-mail: amspubs@ametsoc.org/ams • URL: http://www.ametsoc.org/ams • Biennial. $40.00. Formerly *Curricula in the Atmospheric and Oceanographic Sciences-Colleges and Universities in the U.S. and Canada*.

Curtains, Blinds and Valances. Yvonne Rees. F & W Publications, Inc., 1507 Dana Ave. Cincinnati, OH 45207. Phone: 800-289-0963 or (513)531-2690 Fax: (513)531-4082 1998. $18.99. (Sew in a Weekend Series).

Custom Draperies in Interior Design. M. Neal. Prentice Hall, 240 Frisch Ct. Paramus, NJ 07652-5240. Phone: 800-947-7700 or (201)909-6452 Fax: 800-445-6991 URL: http://www.prenhall.com • 1982. $40.25.

Custom Tailor. Custom Tailors and Designers Association of America, P.O. Box 53052 Washington, DC 20009-9052. Phone: (202)387-7220 Three times a year. $50.00 per year.

Custom Tailors and Designers Association of America.

The Customer Communicator. Alexander Communications Group, Inc., 215 Park Ave. S, Suite 1301 New York, NY 10003. Phone: (212)228-0246 Fax: (212)228-0376 Monthly. $167.00 per year. Newsletter. Contains news and advice for business firms on how to improve customer relations and communications.

Customer Service: A Practical Approach. Elaine K. Harris. Prentice Hall, 240 Frisch Court Paramus, NJ 07652-5240. Phone: 800-947-7700 or (201)909-6200 Fax: 800-445-6991 or (201)909-6361 URL: http://www.prenhall.com • 1995. $43.33. Covers various topics in relation to providing good customer service: problem solving; strategy; planning; communication; coping with difficult customers; motivation; leadership. Glossary, information sources, and index are included.

Customer Service Excellence: A Concise Guide for Librarians. Darlene E. Weingand. American Library Association, 50 E. Huron St. Chicago, IL 60611-2795. Phone: 800-545-2433 or (312)944-6780 Fax: (312)440-9374 E-mail: ala@ala.org • URL: http://www.ala.org • 1997. $30.00. Includes information on quality of service benchmarks, teamwork, patron-librarian conflict management, ''customer service language,'' and other library service topics.

Customer Service Newsletter. Alexander Communications Group, Inc., 215 Park Ave. S, Suite 1301 New York, NY 10003. Phone: (212)228-0246 Fax: (212)228-0376 Monthly. $167.00 per year. Newsletter. Contains news and ideas for customer service managers

Customer Service Operations: The Complete Guide. Warren Blanding. AMACOM, 1601 Broadway, 12th Fl. New York, NY 10019. Phone: 800-262-9699 or (212)586-8100 Fax: (212)903-8168 E-mail: custmserv@amanet.org • URL: http://www.amanet.org • 1991. $75.00. Covers standards, procedures, customer satisfaction, complaint policies, and other customer service topics.

Customs Bulletin and Decisions. Available from U. S. Government Printing Office, Washington, DC 20402. Phone: (202)512-1800 Fax: (202)512-2250 E-mail: gpoaccess@gpo.gov • URL: http://www.access.gpo.gov • Weekly. $220.00 per year. Issued by U. S. Customs Service, Department of the Treasury. Contains regulations, rulings, decisions, and notices relating to customs laws.

Customs Law and Administration: Including Treaties and International Agreements and Customs Law and Administration Statutes. Oceana Publications, Inc., 75 Main St. Dobbs Ferry, NY 10522-1601. Phone: 800-831-0758 or (914)693-8100 Fax: (914)693-0402 E-mail: orders@oceanalaw.com • URL: http://www.oceanalaw.com • Looseleaf service. $400.00. Two volumes.

Customs Regulations of the United States. Available from U. S. Government Printing Office, Washington, DC 20402. Phone: (202)512-1800 Fax: (202)512-2250 E-mail: gpoaccess@gpo.gov • URL: http://www.access.gpo.gov • Looseleaf. $123.00. Issued by U. S. Customs Service, Department of the Treasury. Reprint of regulations published to carry out customs laws of the U. S. Includes supplementary material for an indeterminate period.

Cutting Technology. Penton Media, Inc., 1300 E. Ninth St. Cleveland, OH 44114-1503. Phone: (216)696-7000 Fax: (216)931-9524 URL: http://www.penton.com • Monthly. Controlled circulation. Provides abstracts of the international literature of metal cutting and machining. Formerly *Cutting Tool-Mchine Digest*.

Cutting Tool Engineering. CTE Publications, Inc., 400 Skokie Blvd., Suite 395 Northbrook, IL 60062-7903. Phone: (708)441-7520 Fax: (708)441-8740 Nine times a year. $30.00 per year.

C.V. Starr Center for Applied Economics.

CyberDictionary: Your Guide to the Wired World. Knowledge Exchange LLC, 16350 Ventura Blvd., Suite 364 Encino, CA 91436. Phone: (818)705-3740 Fax: (818)708-8764 E-mail: kex@kex.com • URL: http://www.kex.com • 1996. $17.95. Includes many illustrations.

Cyberfinance: Raising Capital for the E-Business. Martin B. Robins. CCH, Inc., 4025 West Peterson Ave. Chicago, IL 60646-6085. Phone: 800-248-3248 or (773)866-6000 Fax: 800-224-8299 or (773)866-3608 E-mail: cust_serv@cch.com • URL: http://www.cch.com • 2001. $79.00. Covers the taxation, financial, and legal aspects of raising money for new Internet-based (''dot.com'') companies, including the three stages of startup, growth, and initial public offering.

Cyberhound's Guide to Companies on the Internet. The Gale Group, 27500 Drake Rd. Farmington Hills, MI 48331-3535. Phone: 800-877-GALE or (248)699-GALE Fax: 800-414-5043 or (248)699-8069 E-mail: galeord@galegroup.com • URL: http://www.galegroup.com • 1996. $79.00. Presents critical descriptions and ratings of more than 2,000 company or corporate Internet databases. Includes a glossary of Internet terms, a bibliography, and indexes.

Cyberhound's Guide to International Discussion Groups. Visible Ink Press, 27500 Drake Rd. Farmington Hills, MI 48331-3535. Phone: 800-877-GALE or (248)699-GALE Fax: 800-414-5043 or (248)699-8069 E-mail: galeord@galegroup.com • URL: http://www.galegroup.com • 1996. $79.00 Second edition. Presents critical descriptions and ratings of more tha 4,400 Internet discussion groups (newsgroups) covering a wide variety of topics.

Cyberhound's Guide to Internet Libraries. The Gale Group, 27500 Drake Rd. Farmington Hills, MI 48331-3535. Phone: 800-877-GALE or (248)699-GALE Fax: 800-414-5043 or (248)699-8069 E-mail: galeord@galegroup.com • URL: http://www.galegroup.com • 1996. 79.00. Presents critical descriptions and ratings of more than 2,000 library Internet databases. Includes a glossary of Internet terms, a bibliography, and indexes.

Cyberhound's Guide to People on the Internet. The Gale Group, 27500 Drake Rd. Farmington Hills, MI 48331-3535. Phone: 800-877-GALE or (248)699-GALE Fax: 800-414-5043 or (248)699-8069 E-mail: galeord@galegroup.com • URL: http://www.galegroup.com • 1997. $79.00. Second edition. Provides descriptions of about 5,500 Internet databases maintained by or for prominent individuals in business, the professions, entertainment, and sports. Indexed by name, subject, and keyword (master index).

Cyberhound's Guide to Publications on the Internet. The Gale Group, 27500 Drake Rd. Farmington Hills, MI 48331-3535. Phone: 800-877-GALE or (248)699-GALE Fax: 800-414-5043 or (248)699-8069 E-mail: galeord@galegroup.com • URL: http://www.galegroup.com • 1996. $79.00. First edition. Presents critical descriptions and ratings of more than 3,400 Internet databases of journals, newspapers, newsletters, and other publications. Includes a glossary of Internet terms, a bibliography, and three indexes.

Cyberquake: How the Internet will Erase Profits, Topple Market Leaders, and Shatter Business Models. Michael Sullivan-Trainor. John Wiley & Sons, Inc., 605 Third Ave., 4th Fl. New York, NY 10158-0012. Phone: 800-225-5945 or (212)850-6000 Fax: (212)850-6088 E-mail: info@wiley.com • URL: http://www.wiley.com • 1997. $26.95. Predicts that the Internet will cause ''an overwhelming shift in control of the worldwide marketplace'' in the early 21st century. (Business Technology Series).

The CyberSkeptic's Guide to Internet Research. BiblioData, P.O. Box 61 Needham Heights, MA 02192. Phone: (781)444-1154 Fax: (781)449-4584 E-mail: ina@bibliodata.com • URL: http://www.bibliodata.com • 10 times a year. $104.00 per year; nonprofit organizations, $159.00 per year. Newsletter. Presents critical reviews of World Wide Web sites and databases, written by information professionals. Includes ''Late Breaking News'' of Web sites.

Cyberspace Lexicon: An Illustrated Dictionary of Terms from Multimedia to Virtual Reality. Bob Cotton and Richard Oliver. Phaidon Press, Inc., 180 Varick St., 12th Fl. New York, NY 10014. Phone: 877-742-4366 or (212)209-1185 Fax: (212)209-1192 E-mail: ussales@phaidon.com • 1994. $29.95. Defines more than 800 terms, with manyillustrations. Includes a bibliography.

Cyberspeak: An Online Dictionary. Andy Ihnatko. Random House, Inc., 201 E. 50th St. New York, NY 10022. Phone: 800-726-0600 or (212)751-2600 Fax: 800-659-2436 or (212)572-8700 URL: http://www.randomhouse.com • 1996. $12.95. An informal guide to the language of computers, multimedia, and the Internet.

Cyberstocks: An Investor's Guide to Internet Companies. Alan Chai. Hoover's, Inc., 1033 La Posada Dr., Suite 250 Austin, TX 78752. Phone: 800-486-8666 or (512)374-4500 Fax: (512)374-4501 E-mail: orders@hoovers.com • URL: http://www.hoovers.com • 1996. $24.95. Provides detailed profiles of 101 publicly traded companies involved in one way or another with the Internet.

Cybertaxation: The Taxation of E-Commerce. Karl A. Frieden. CCH, Inc., 4025 West Peterson Ave. Chicago, IL 60646-6085. Phone: 800-248-3248 or (773)866-6000 Fax: 800-224-8299 or (773)866-3608 URL: http://www.cch.com • 2000. $75.00. Includes state sales and use tax issues and corporate income tax rules, as related to doing business over the Internet.

CyberTools for Business: Practical Web Sites that will Save You Time and Money. Wayne Harris. Hoover's, Inc., 1033 La Posada Dr., Suite 250 Austin, TX 78752. Phone: 800-486-8666 or (512)374-4500 Fax: (512)374-4501 E-mail: orders@hoovers.com • URL: http://www.hoovers.com • 1997. $19.95. Describes 100 World Wide Web sites that are useful for business, investing, and job hunting. Also lists Web addresses for about 4,500 public and private companies.

The Cybrarian's Manual. Pat Ensor, editor. American Library Association, 50 E. Huron St. Chicago, IL 60611-2795. Phone: 800-545-2433 or (312)944-6780 Fax: (312)440-9374 E-mail: ala@ala.org • URL: http://www.ala.org • 1996. $35.00. Provides information for librarians concerning the Internet, expert systems, computer networks, client/server architecture, Web pages, multimedia, information industry careers, and other ''cyberspace'' topics.

Cycle Projections. Foundation for the Study of Cycles, 900 W. Valley Rd., Suite 502 Wayne, PA 19087. Phone: (610)995-2120 Fax: (610)995-2130 E-mail: cycles@cycles.org • URL: http://www.cycles.org/~cycles • Monthly. $125.00 per year. Newsletter includes trend projections for stocks, commodities, real estate, and the economy. Short, intermediate, and long-term cycles are covered.

Cycle World. Hachette Filipacchi Magazines, Inc., 1499 Monravia Ave. Newport Beach, CA 92663. Phone: 800-274-4027 or (949)720-5300 Fax: (949)631-0651 Monthly. $19.94 per year. Incorporates *Cycle*.

Cycles. Foundation for the Study of Cycles, 900 W. Valley Rd., Suite 502 Wayne, PA 19087. Phone: (610)995-2120 Fax: (610)995-2130 E-mail: cycles@cycles.org • URL: http://www.cycles.org/~cycles • Bimonthly. Membership. Provides information on cycle research in economic and other areas.

D & B Business Locator. Dun & Bradstreet, Inc., One Diamond Hill Rd. Murray Hill, NJ 07974-1218. Phone: 800-234-3867 or (908)665-5000 Fax: (908)665-5803 URL: http://www.dnb.com • Quarterly. $2,495.00 per year. CD-ROM provides concise information on more than 10 million U. S. companies or businesses. Includes data on number of employees.

D and B Employment Opportunities Directory Career Guide. Dun and Bradstreet Information Services, Dun and Bradstreet Corp., Three Sylvan Way Parsippany, NJ 07054-3896. Phone: 800-526-0651 or (973)455-0900 Fax: (973)254-4063 E-mail: customerservice@dnb.com • URL: http://www.dnb.com • Annual. Libraries, $495.00. Lists more than 5,000 companies that have career opportunities in various fields. A Dun & Bradstreet publication.

D and B Million Dollar Directory. Dun and Bradstreet Information Services, Dun and Bradstreet Corp., Three Sylvan Way Parsippany, NJ 07054-3896. Phone: 800-526-0521 or (973)455-0900 Fax: (973)254-4063 E-mail: customerservice@dnb.com • URL: http://www.dnb.com • Annual. Commercial institutions, $1,395.00; libraries, $1,275.00. Lease basis.

D & B Minority-Owned Business Directory. Dun & Bradstreet Information Services, Three Sylvan Way Parsippany, NJ 07054-3896. Phone: 800-526-0651 or (973)455-0900 Fax: (973)254-4063 E-mail: customerservice@dnb.com • URL: http://www.dnb.com • 2000. Price on application. Regional editions.

D & B Women-Owned Business Directory. Dun & Bradstreet Information Services, Three Sylvan Way Parsippany, NJ 07054-3896. Phone: 800-526-0651 or (973)455-0900 Fax: (973)254-4063 E-mail: customerservice@dnb.com • URL: http://www.dnb.com • 2000. Price on application.

Daily Graphs. Daily Graphs, Inc, P.O. Box 66919 Los Angeles, CA 90066-0919. Phone: 800-472-7479 or (310)448-6843 New York Stock Exchange edition, $363.00 per year. American Stock Exchange edition, $363.00 per year. Both editions include the 200 leading over-the-counter stocks.

Daily Graphs. Option Guide. Daily Graphs, Inc., P.O. Box 66919 Los Angeles, CA 90066-0919. Phone: 800-472-7479 or (310)448-6843 Weekly. $300.00 per year.

Daily Labor Report. Bureau of National Affairs, Inc., 1231 25th St., N.W. Washington, DC 20037-1197. Phone: 800-372-1033 or (202)452-4200 Fax: (202)822-8092 E-mail: books@bna.com • URL: http://www.bna.com • Daily. $6,530.00 per year. Comprehensive newsletter reporting on national labor developments. Includes full text of many official documents and decisions.

Daily Market Report. Coffee, Sugar and Coca Exchange, Inc., Four World Trade Center New York, NY 10048. Phone: (212)938-2800 Fax: (212)524-9863 Daily except Saturday and Sunday. $110.00 per year.

Daily Report for Executives. Bureau of National Affairs, Inc., 1231 25th St., N.W. Washington, DC 20037-1197. Phone: 800-372-1033 or (202)452-4200 Fax: (202)822-8092 E-mail: books@bna.com • URL: http://www.bna.com • Daily. $6,927.00 per year. Newsletter. Covers legal, regulatory, economic, and tax developments affecting corporations.

Daily Tax Report: From Today's Daily Report for Executives. Bureau of National Affairs, Inc., 1231 25th St., N.W. Washington, DC 20037-1197. Phone: 800-372-1033 or (202)452-4200 Fax: (202)822-8092 E-mail: books@bna.com • URL: http://www.bna.com • Daily. $2,350.00 per year. Newsletter. Monitors tax legislation, hearings, rulings, and court decisions.

Daily Treasury Statement: Cash and Debt Operations of the United States Treasury. Available from U. S. Government Printing Office, Washington, DC 20402. Phone: (202)512-1800 Fax: (202)512-2250 E-mail: gpoaccess@gpo.gov • URL: http://www.access.gpo.gov • Daily, except Saturdays, Sundays, and holidays. $855.00 per year. (Financial Management Service, U. S. Treasury Department.)

Daily Variety: News of the Entertainment Industry. Cahners Business Information, Entertainment Div., 245 W. 17th St. New York, NY 10011-5300. Phone: 800-662-7776 or (212)645-0067 Fax: (212)337-6974 E-mail: corporatecommunications@cahners.com • URL: http://www.cahners.com • Daily. $219.00 per year.

Daily Weather Maps (Weekly Series). U.S. Dept. of Commerce

Dairy Field Buyer's Guide. Stagnito Publishing Co., 1935 Shermer Rd., Suite 100 Northbrook, IL 60062-5354. Phone: (847)205-5660 Fax: (847)205-5680 E-mail: info@stagnito.com • Annual. $55.00. Lists more than 500 suppliers of equipment and services and distributors for the dairy processing industry.

Dairy Field: Helping Processors Manage the Changing Industry. Stagnito Publishing Co., 1935 Shermer Rd., Ste. 100 Northwood, IL 60062-5354. Phone: (847)205-5660 Fax: (847)205-5680 E-mail: info@stagnito.com • URL: http://www.stagnito.com • Monthly. $65.00 per year. Annual *Buyers Guide* availble.

Dairy Foods: Innovative Ideas and Technologies for Dairy Processors. Cahners Business Information, 1350 E. Touhy Ave. Des Plaines, IL 60018-3358. Phone: 800-662-7776 or (847)635-8800 Fax: (847)390-2445 E-mail: corporatecommunications@cahners.com • URL: http://www.cahners.com • Monthly. $99.90 per year. Provides broad coverage of new developments in the dairy industry, including cheese and ice cream products. Includes an annual *Supplement*.

Dairy Foods Market Directory. Cahners Business Information, 200 Clearwater Dr. Des Plaines, IL 60523. Phone: 800-662-7776 or (847)635-8800 Fax: (847)390-2445 E-mail: corporatecommunications@cahners.com • URL: http://www.cahners.com • Annual. $99.90. Lists a wide variety of suppliers to the dairy industry.

Dairy Industry Committee.

Dairy Market Statistics. U.S. Department of Agriculture, Agricultural Marketing Service, Washington, DC 20250. Phone: (202)720-2791 Annual.

Dairy Research and Education Center. Pennsylvania State University

Dairy Science Abstracts. Available from CABI Publishing North America, 10 E. 40th St. New York, NY 10016. Phone: 800-528-4841 or (212)481-7018 Fax: (212)686-7993 E-mail: cabi@cabi.org • URL: http://www.cabi.org • Monthly. $1095.00 per year. Published in England by CABI Publishing. Provides worldwide coverage of the literature.

Dairy Society International.

Dalton Carpet Journal. Daily Citizen-News, P.O. Box 1167 Dalton, GA 30722-1167. Phone: (404)278-1011 Monthly. $12.00. Covers the international tufted carpet market.

Dangerous Company: The Secret Story of the Consulting Powerhouses and the Corporations They Save and Ruin. James O'Shea and Charles Madigan. Random House, Inc., 201 E. 50th St. New York, NY 10022. Phone: 800-726-0600 or (212)751-2600 Fax: 800-659-2436 URL: http://www.randomhouse.com • 1997. $27.50. A critical view of the major consulting firms in the U. S. and how they influence large corporations.

The Darla School of Business Administration-Research Division.

Darling Marine Center., University of Maine, 193 Clarks Cove Rd. Walpole, ME 04573. Phone: (207)563-3146 Fax: (207)563-3119 E-mail: kevin@maine.maine.edu • URL: http://server.dmc.maine.edu • *Formerly Ira C. Darling Center for Research, Teaching, and Service*.

Dartnell's Advertising Manager's Handbook. David Bushko, editor. Dartnell Corp., 360 Hiatt Dr. Palm Beach, FL 33418. Phone: 800-621-5463 or (561)622-6520 Fax: (561)622-2423 E-mail: custserv@lrp.com • URL: http://www.dartnellcorp.com • 1997. $69.95. Fourth revised edition.

Dartnell's Public Relations Handbook. Robert L. Dilenschneider, editor. Dartnell Corp., 360 Hiatt Dr. Palm Beach, FL 33418. Phone: 800-621-5463 or (561)622-6520 Fax: (561)622-2423 E-mail: custserv@lrp.com • URL: http://www.dartnellcorp.com • 1996. $69.95. Fourth revised edition. Covers press releases, media kits, media contacts, crisis management, and other topics.

Dartnell's Sales Force Compensation Survey. Dartnell Corp., 360 Hiatt Dr. Palm Beach, FL 33418. Phone: 800-621-5463 or (561)622-6520 Fax: (561)622-2423 E-mail: custserv@lrp.com • URL: http://www.dartnellcorp.com • Biennial. $159.00.

Darwin: Business Evolving in the Information Age. CXO Media Inc., 492 Old Connecticut Path Framingham, MA 01701. Phone: (508)872-0080 Fax: (508)872-0618 URL: http://www.darwinmag.com • Monthly. $44.95 per year. Presents non-technical explanations of information technology (IT) to corporate business executives. Uses a case study format.

Data Communications. CMP Media, Inc., CMP Media, Inc., 600 Community Dr. Manhasset, NY 11030. Phone: 800-577-5356 or (516)562-5000 Fax: (516)562-5049 URL: http://www.data.com • 18 times a year. $125.00 per year.

Data Communications Production Selection Guide. McGraw-Hill, 1221 Ave. of the Americas Two Penn Plaza New York, NY 10020-1095. Phone: 800-722-4726 or (212)904-2000 Fax: (212)904-2072 E-mail: customer.service@mcgraw-hill.com • URL: http://www.mcgraw-hill.com • Semiannual. $25.00. List of networking vendors. Formerly *Data Communications Buyer's Guide*.

Data Smog: Surviving the Information Glut. David Shenk. HarperCollins Publishers, 10 E. 53rd St. New York, NY 10022-7000. Phone: 800-242-7737 or (212)207-7000 Fax: 800-822-4090 URL: http://www.harpercollins.com • 1997. $24.00. A critical view of both the electronic and print information industries. Emphasis is on information overload.

Data Sources for Business and Market Analysis. John Ganly. Scarecrow Press, Inc., 4720 Boston Way Lanham, MD 20706-4310. Phone: 800-462-6420 or (301)459-3366 Fax: 800-338-4550 or (301)459-1705 E-mail: orders@scarecrowpress.com • URL: http://www.scarecrowpress.com • 1994. $58.00. Fourth edition. Emphasis is on sources of statistics for market research, especially government sources. Relevant directories, periodicals, and research aids are included.

Data Sources: The Comprehensive Guide to the Data Processing Industry Hardware, Data Communications Products, Software, Company Profiles. The Gale Group, 27500 Drake Rd. Farmington Hills, MI 48331-3535. Phone: 800-877-GALE or (248)699-GALE Fax: 800-414-5043 or (248)699-8069 E-mail: galeord@galegroup.com • URL: http://www.galegroup.com • Semiannual. $495.00 per year. Two volumes. Describes hardware and software for all computer operating sysems, including prices and technical details. Lists about 75,000 products from 14,000 suppliers. Industry-specific software applications are described.

Database Marketer. Intertec Publishing Co., 11 Riverbend Dr., S. Stamford, CT 06907-2524. Phone: 800-795-5445 or (203)358-9900 Fax: (203)358-5824 E-mail: subs@intertec.com • URL: http://www.intertec.com • Monthly. $329.00 per year.

Datapro on CD-ROM: Communications Analyst. Gartner Group, Inc., 56 Top Gallant Rd. Stamford, CT 06904. Phone: (203)316-1111 Fax: (203)316-6300 E-mail: info@gartner.com • URL: http://www.gartner.com • Monthly, Price on application. Provides detailed information on products and services for communications systems, including local area networks and voice systems.

Datapro on CD-ROM: Computer Systems Analyst. Gartner Group, Inc., 56 Top Gallant Rd. Stamford, CT 06904. Phone: (203)316-1111 Fax: (203)316-6300 E-mail: info@gartner.com • URL: http://www.gartner.com • Monthly. Price on application. Includes detailed information on specific computer hardware and software products, such as peripherals, security systems, document imaging systems, and UNIX-related products.

Datapro on CD-ROM: Computer Systems Hardware and Software. Gartner Group, Inc., 56 Top Gallant Rd. Stamford, CT 06904. Phone: (203)316-1111 Fax: (203)316-6300 E-mail: info@gartner.com • URL: http://www.gartner.com • Monthly. Price on application. CD-ROM provides product specifications, product reports, user surveys, and market forecasts for a wide range of computer hardware and software.

Datapro Software Finder. Gartner Group, Inc., 56 Top Gallant Rd. Stamford, CT 06904. Phone: (203)316-1111 Fax: (203)316-6300 E-mail: info@gartner.com • URL: http://www.gartner.com • Quarterly. $1,770.00 per year. CD-ROM provides detailed information on more than 18,000 software products for a wide variety of computers, personal to mainframe. Covers software for 130 types of business, finance, and industry. (Editions limited to either microcomputer or mainframe software are available at $995.00 per year.)

DataWorld. Faulkner Information Services, Inc., 114 Cooper Center, 7905 Browning Rd. Pennsauken, NJ 08109-4319. Phone: (856)662-2070 Fax: (856)662-3380 Four looseleaf volumes, with monthly supplements. $1,395.00 per year. Describes and evaluates both hardware and software relating to midrange, micro, and mainframe computers. Available on CD-ROM.

Davidson Laboratory. Stevens Institute of Technology

Davison's Gold Book. Davison Publishing Co., P.O. Box 1289 Concord, NC 28026-1289. Phone: 800-328-4766 or (704)785-8700 Fax: (704)785-8701 E-mail: textiles@davisonbluebook.com • URL: http://www.davisonbluebook.com • Annual. $80.00. Textile mill supplies, products, services, equipment and machinery.Formerly *Davison's Textile Buyers*.

Davison's Textile Blue Book. Davison Publishing Co., P.O. Box 1289 Concord, NC 28026-1289. Phone: 800-328-4766 or (704)785-8700 Fax: (704)785-8701 E-mail: textiles@davisonbluebook.com • URL: http://www.davisonbluebook.com • Annual. $165.00. Over 8,400 companies in the textile industry in the United States, Canada, and Mexico, including about 4,400 textile plants.

Day Care USA Newsletter: The Independent Biweekly Newsletter of Day Care Information Service. United Communications Group (UCG), 11300 Rockville Pike, Suite 1100 Rockville, MD 20852-3030. Phone: 800-287-2223 or (301)287-2700 Fax: (301)816-8945 E-mail: webmaster@ucg.com • URL: http://www.ucg.com • Biweekly. $294.00 per year. Newsletter. Provides current information on child day care center funding, legislation, and regulation.

Day-Trader's Manual: Theory, Art, and Science of Profitable Short-Term Investing. William F. Eng. John Wiley and Sons, Inc., 605 Third Ave. New York, NY 10158-0012. Phone: 800-225-5945 or (212)850-6000 Fax: (212)850-6088 E-mail: info@wiley.com • URL: http://www.wiley.com • 1992. $79.95. Covers short-term trading in stocks, futures, and options. Various technical trading systems are considered.

DBC Online: America's Leading Provider of Real-Time Market Data to the Individual Investor. Data Broadcasting Corp.Phone: (415)571-1800 E-mail: dbcinfo@dbc.com • URL: http://www.dbc.com • Web site provides a wide variety of real-time securities market prices, data, and charts. Covers bonds (''BondVu''), stocks, commodities, options, mutual funds, major indexes, industry indexes, international markets, etc. Also includes news, SEC documents (''Smart-Edgar''), and various other features. Fees: Both free and fee-based, depending on level of information.

Dealer and Applicator. Vance Publishing Corp., 400 Knightsbridge Parkway Lincolnshire, IL 60069-1414. Phone: 800-621-2845 or (847)634-2600 Fax: (847)634-4379 URL: http://www.vancepublishing.com • Nine times a year. $35.00 per year. Formerly *Custom Applicator*.

Dealer Business. Ward's Communications, 3000 Town Center, Suite 2750 Southfield, MI 48075-1212. Phone: (248)357-0800 Fax: (248)357-0810 E-mail: mike_arnholt@intertec.com • URL: http://www.wardsauto.com • Monthly. $36.00 per year. Formerly *Auto Age*.

Dealer Operating Analysis. Beauty and Barber Supply Institute, 271 Route 46 West, Suite F-209 Fairfield, NJ 07004. Phone: (201)808-7444 Annual.

Dealer Progress: How Smart Agribusiness is Growing. Clear Window, Inc., 15444 Clayton Rd., Suite 314 Ballwin, MO 63011. Phone: (314)527-4001 Fax: (314)527-4010 URL: http://www.precisionag.com • Bimonthly. $40.00 per year. Published in association with the Fertilizer Institute. Includes information on fertilizers and agricultural chemicals, including farm pesticides. Formerly *Progress*.

Dealernews Buyers Guide. Advnastar Communications, Inc., One Park Ave., 2nd Fl. New York, NY 10016-5802. Phone: 800-346-0085 or (212)951-6600 Fax: (212)951-6623 E-mail: information@advanstar.com • URL: http://www.advanstar.com • Annual. $25.00. List of manufacturers, distributors, OEMs, and service organizations serving the motorcycle, all-terrain vehicle, and watercraft industries.

Dealernews: The Voice of the Powersports Vehicle Industry. Advanstar Communications, Inc., One Park Ave., 2nd Fl. New York, NY 10016-5802. Phone: 800-346-0085 or (212)951-6600 Fax: (212)951-6623 E-mail: information@advanstar.com • URL: http://www.advanstar.com • Monthly. Free to qualified personnel; others, $40.00 per year. News concerning the power sports motor vehicle industry.

Dealerscope Consumer Electronics Marketplace: For CE,PC and Major Appliance Retailers. North American Publishing Co., 401 N. Broad St. Philadelphia, PA 19108-9988. Phone: 800-627-2689 or (215)238-5300 Fax: (215)238-5457 E-mail: dbrennan@napco.com • URL: http://www.dealerscope.com • Monthly. Free to qualified personnel; others, $79.00 per year. Formerly *Dealerscope Merchandising*.

Dealing Creatively with Death: A Manual of Death Education and Simple Burial. Ernest Morgan and Jennifer Morgan. Upper Access, Inc., 87 Upper Access Rd. Hinesburg, VT 05460. Phone: 800-310-8320 E-mail: info@upperaccess.com • 2001. $12.95. 14th revised edition. A humanistic approach to dying and grieving; pursuing economy, simplicity and greater sensitivity in funeral practices.

The Death of the Banker: The Decline and Fall of the Great Financial Dynasties and the Triumph of the Small Investor. Ron Chernow. Vintage Books, 201 E. 50th St. New York, NY 10022. Phone: 800-726-0600 or (212)751-2600 Fax: 800-659-2436 or (212)572-8700 URL: http://www.randomhouse.com • 1997. $12.00. Contains three essays: "J. Pierpont Morgan," "The Warburgs," and "The Death of the Banker" (discusses the decline of banks in personal finance and the rise of mutual funds and stock brokers).

Debit Card News: Newsletter for Retail Electronic Payments. Faulkner & Gray, Inc., 300 S. Wacker Dr., 18th Fl. Chicago, IL 60606. Phone: 800-535-8403 or (312)913-1334 Fax: (312)913-1959 E-mail: order@faulknergray.com • URL: http://www.faulknergray.com • Monthly. $245.00 per year. Includes three special issues. Formerly *POS News*.

Debits and Deposit Turnover at Commercial Banks. Board of Governors, U.S. Federal Reserve System, Publications Services, Room MS-138 Washington, DC 20551. Phone: (202)452-3244 Fax: (202)728-5886 Monthly. $5.00 per year.

Debt Free: The National Bankruptcy Kit. Daniel Sitarz. National Book Network, 15200 NBN Way Blue Ridge Summit, PA 17214. Phone: 800-462-6420 or (717)794-3800 Fax: 800-338-4550 URL: http://www.nbnbooks.com • 1998. $19.95. Second edition. Includes basic forms and instructions for use in uncomplicated personal bankruptcy situations. (Small Business Library Series).

Debtor-Creditor Law. Matthew Bender & Co., Inc., Two Park Ave. New York, NY 10016. Phone: 800-223-1940 or (212)448-2000 Fax: (212)244-3188 E-mail: international@bender.com • URL: http://www.bender.com • $1,595.00. 10 looseleaf volumes. Periodic supplementation. Covers all aspects of the creation and enforcement of the debtor-creditor relationship.

Decision Line. Decision Sciences Institute, University Plaza Atlanta, GA 30303. Phone: (404)651-4073 URL: http://www.dsi.gsu.edu • Five times a year. Free to members; non-members, $6.00 per year.

Decision Making: Alternatives to Rational Choice Models. Mary Zey. Sage Publications, Inc., 2455 Teller Rd. Thousand Oaks, CA 91320. Phone: (805)499-0721 Fax: (805)499-0871 E-mail: info@sagepub.com • URL: http://www.sagepub.com • 1992. $58.00. Eighteen contributors provide material on decision-making theory.

Decision Making and Forecasting: With Emphasis on Model Building and Policy Analysis. Kneale T. Marshall and Robert M. Oliver. McGraw-Hill, 1221 Ave. of the Americas New York, NY 10020. Phone: 800-722-4726 or (212)904-2000 Fax: (212)904-2072 E-mail: customer.service@mcgraw-hill.com • URL: http://www.mcgraw-hill.com • 1995. $86.88.

Decision-Making in Forest Management. M. R. Williams. State Mutual Book and Periodical Service, Ltd., 521 Fifth Ave., 17th Fl. New York, NY 10175. Phone: (718)261-1704 Fax: (516)537-0412 1988. $270.00.

Decision Sciences. Decision Sciences Institute, University Plaza Atlanta, GA 30303. Phone: (404)651-4073 URL: http://www.dsi.gsu.edu • Bimonthly. $59.00 per year.

Decision Sciences Institute.

Decisions in Imaging Economics: The Journal of Imaging Technology Management. Curant Communications, Inc., 4676 Admiralty Way, Suite 202 Marina Del Rey, CA 90292-6603. Phone: (310)306-2206 Fax: (310)306-9548 Bimonthly. Controlled circulation. Edited for health care executives and radiologists concerned with the purchase and management of imaging technology.

The Decline (and Fall?) of the Income Tax: How to Make Sense of the American Tax Mess and the Flat-Tax Cures That Are Supposed to Fix It. Michael J. Graetz. W. W. Norton & Co., Inc., 500 Fifth Ave. New York, NY 10110. Phone: 800-223-2584 or (212)354-5500 Fax: (212)869-0856 E-mail: webmaster@wwnorton.com • URL: http://www.norton.com • 1997. $27.50. The author, a former U. S. Treasury official, proposes a value-added tax (VAT) to augment federal income tax. He reviews recent tax history and provides entertaining tax anecdotes.

Decorators Club.

Defense and Security. Available from U. S. Government Printing Office, Washington, DC 20402. Phone: (202)512-1800 Fax: (202)512-2250 E-mail: gpoaccess@gpo.gov • URL: http://www.access.gpo.gov • Annual. Free. Issued by the Superintendent of Documents. A list of government publications on defense and related topics. Formerly *Defense Supply and Logistics*. (Subject Bibliography No. 153.)

Defense Counsel Journal. International Association of Defense Counsel, One N. Franklin St., Suite 2400 Chicago, IL 60606-3401. Phone: (312)368-1494 Fax: (312)368-1854 Quarterly. $65.00 per year. Scholarly and practical articles dealing with defense of civil cases, particularly those involving insurance.

Defense Credit Union Council.

Defense Daily: The Daily of Aerospace and Defense. Phillips Business Information, Inc., 1201 Seven Locks Rd., Suite 300 Potomac, MD 20854. Phone: 800-777-5006 or (301)340-1520 Fax: (301)309-3847 E-mail: pbi@phillips.com • URL: http://www.phillips.com • Daily (five times a week). $1,697.00 per year. Newsletter.

Defense Electronics. Intertec Publishing Corp., 6151 Powers Ferry Rd., N.W., Suite 200 Atlanta, GA 30339. Phone: 800-400-5945 Fax: (770)955-0400 E-mail: subs@intertec.com • URL: http://www.intertec.com • Monthly. $52.00 per year.

Defense Industry Report. Phillips Publishing, Inc., 1201 Seven Locks Rd, Ste. 300 Potomac, MD 20854. Phone: 800-777-5006 or (301)340-2100 Fax: (301)309-3847 E-mail: pbi@phillips.com • URL: http://www.phillips.com/marketplaces.htm • Biweekly. $795.00 per year. Newsletter.

Defense Monitor. Center for Defense Information, 1779 Massachusetts Ave., N.W. Washington, DC 20036-2109. Phone: (202)332-0600 Fax: (202)462-4559 E-mail: cdi@igc.apc.org • URL: http://www.cdi.org • Ten times a year. $35.00 per year.

Defense of Equal Employment Claims. William L. Diedrich and William Gaus. Shepard's, 555 Middle Creek Parkway Colorado Springs, CO 80921. Phone: 800-743-7393 or (719)481-7371 Fax: 800-525-0053 or (719)481-7621 E-mail: customer_service@shepards.com • URL: http://www.shepards.com • 1982. $105.00 per year. (Individual Rights Series).

Defense of Narcotics Cases. David Bernheim. Matthew Bender & Co., Inc., Two Park Ave. New York, NY 10016. Phone: 800-223-1940 or (212)448-2000 Fax: (212)244-3188 E-mail: international@bender.com • URL: http://www.bender.com • $590.00. Three looseleaf volumes. Periodic supplementation. Up-to-date coverage of all aspects of narcotics cases and related matters.

Defense Research International., 130 N. Michigan Ave. Chicago, IL 60601. Phone: 800-667-8108 or (312)795-1101 Fax: (312)795-0747 E-mail: custservice@dri.org • URL: http://www.dri.org • Members are attorneys, insurance companies, insurance adjusters, and others. Includes Product Liability and Professional Liability Committees.

Defense Systems Review and Military Communications. Cosgriff-Martin Publishing Group, Inc., 2595 Solano Ave. Napa, CA 94558. Phone: (707)257-8480 Monthly. $35.00 per year.

Defense Transportation Journal: Magazine of International Defense Transportation and Logistics. National Defense Transportation Association, 50 S. Pickett St., No 220 Alexandria, VA 22304-3008. Phone: (703)751-5011 Fax: (703)823-8761 URL: http://www.brf.volpe-dot.gov/ndta/index.htm • Bimonthly. Free to members; non-members, $35.00 per year.

Defined Contribution News. Institutional Investor, 488 Madison Ave. New York, NY 10022. Phone: (212)224-3300 Fax: (212)224-3353 E-mail: info@iijournals.com • URL: http://www.iijournals.com • Biweekly. $2,330.00 per year. Newsletter. Edited for financial institutions and others offering defined contribution pension plans.

Defining Your Market: Winning Strategies for High-Tech, Industrial, and Service Firms. Art Weinstein. Haworth Press, Inc., 10 Alice St. Binghamton, NY 13904-1580. Phone: 800-429-6784 or (607)722-5857 Fax: 800-895-0582 or (607)722-1424 E-mail: getinfo@haworthpressinc.com • URL: http://www.haworthpressinc.com • 1998. $39.95. Includes "models, frameworks, and processes" for effective industrial marketing.

Degrees and Other Awards Conferred by Institutions of Higher Education. Available from U. S. Government Printing Office, Washington, DC 20402. Phone: (202)512-1800 Fax: (202)512-2250 E-mail: gpoaccess@gpo.gov • URL: http://www.access.gpo.gov • Annual. Issued by the National Center for Education Statistics, U. S. Department of Education. Provides data on the number of degrees awarded at the associate's, bachelor's, master's, and doctor's levels. Includes fields of study and racial-ethnic-sex data by major field or discipline.

Deli News. Delicatessen Council of Southern California, Inc. Pacific Rim Publishing Co., P.O. Box 4533 Huntington Beach, CA 92605-4533. Phone: (714)375-3904 Fax: (714)375-3906 Monthly. $25.00 per year. Includes product news and comment related to cheeses, lunch meats, packaged fresh meats, kosher foods, gourmet-specialty items, and bakery products.

Deloitte & Touche Online. Deloitte & Touche LLP, Financial Consulting Services CenterPhone: (513)784-7100 E-mail: webmaster@dtonline.com • URL: http://www.dtonline.com • Web site provides concise, full-text articles on taxes, personal finance, and business from a leading accounting firm. Includes "Tax News and Views," "Personal Finance Advisor," "Business Advisor: A Resource for Small Business Owners," "Financial Tip of the Week," and "This Week Online: Top of the News." Weekly updates. Fees: Free.

Delta Pi Epsilon., P.O. Box 4340 Little Rock, AR 72214. Phone: (501)562-1233 Fax: (501)562-1293 E-mail: dpe@ipa.net • URL: http://www.dpe.org • A professional society for teachers of business subjects.

Delta Sigma Pi., P.O. 230 Oxford, OH 45056-0230. Phone: (513)523-1907 Fax: (513)523-7292 E-mail: centraloffice@dspnet.org • URL: http://www.dspnet.org • A professional fraternity related to education in business administration.

Demographic Yearbook. United Nations, Dept. of Economic and Social Affairs. United Nations Publications, Concourse Level, First Ave., 46th St. New York, NY 10017. Phone: 800-553-3210 or (212)963-7680 Fax: (212)963-4910 E-mail: bookstore@un.org • URL: http://www.un.org/publications • Annual. $125.00. Text in English and French.

Demographics USA: County Edition. Market Statistics, 45 Danbury Rd. Wilton, CT 06897. Phone: (203)563-3100 Fax: (203)563-3131 Annual. $435.00. Contains 200 statistical series for each of 3,000 counties. Includes population, household income, employment, retail sales, and consumer expenditures. Also provides Effective Buying Income, Buying Power Index, and data summaries by Metro Market, Media Market, and State. (CD-ROM version is available.)

Demographics USA: ZIP Edition. Market Statistics, 45 Danbury Rd. Wilton, CT 06897. Phone: (203)563-3100 Fax: (203)563-3131 Annual. $435.00. Contains 50 statistical series for each of 40,000 ZIP codes. Includes population, household income, employment, retail sales, and consumer expenditures. Also provides Effective Buying Income, Business Characteristics, and data summaries by state, region, and the first three digits of ZIP codes. (CD-ROM version is available.)

Demography. Population Association of America, 721 Ellsworth Dr., Suite 303 Silver Spring, MD 20910-4436. Phone: (301)565-6710 Fax: (301)565-7850 E-mail: info@popassoc.org • URL: http://www.popassoc.org • Quarterly. $85.00 per year.

Dental Dealers of America.

Dental Economics. Pennwell Publishing Co., Dental Economics Div., P.O. Box 3408 Tulsa, OK 74101. Phone: 800-331-4463 or (918)831-9421 Fax: (918)831-9295 E-mail: webmaster@pennwell.com • Monthly. $78.00 per year.

Dental Lab Products. MEDEC Dental Communications, Two Northfield Plaza, Ste. 300 Northfield, IL 60093-1219. Phone: (847)441-3700 Bimonthly. $35.00 per year. Edited for dental laboratory managers. Covers new products and technical developments.

Dental Manufacturers of America.

Dental Practice and Finance. MEDEC Dental Communications, Two Northfield Plaza, Suite 300 Northfield, IL 60093-1219. Phone: (847)441-3700 Bimonthly. $55.00 per year. Covers practice management and financial topics for dentists. Includes investment advice.

Dental Products Report Europe. MEDEC Dental Communications, Two Northfield Plaza, Ste. 300 Northfield, IL 60093-1219. Phone: (847)441-3700 Bimonthly. $40.00 per year. Covers new dental products for the European market.

Dental Products Report: Trends in Industry. MEDEC Dental Communications, Two Northfield Plaza, Ste. 300 Northfield, IL 60093-1219. Phone: (847)441-3700 11 times a year. $90.00 per year. Provides information on new dental products, technology, and trends in dentistry.

Dental Trade Newsletter. American Dental Trade Association, 4222 King St. Alexandria, VA 22302. Phone: (703)379-7755 Bimonthly. Price on application.

Dentistry Today: Equipment Buyers' Guide. Dentistry Today, Inc., 26 Park St. Montclair, NJ 07042. Phone: (973)783-3935 Fax: (973)783-7112 Annual. Price on application. Provides purchasing information for more than 500 dental products.

Department of Defense Telephone Directory. Available from U. S. Government Printing Office, Washington, DC 20402. Phone: (202)512-1800 Fax: (202)512-2250 E-mail: gpoaccess@gpo.gov • URL: http://www.access.gpo.gov • Three times a year. $44.00 per year. An alphabetical directory of U. S. Department of Defense personnel, including Departments of the Army, Navy, and Air Force.

Department of Fisheries and Allied Aquacultures.

Department of Molecular and Human Genetics.

Department of the Navy Annual Report to the Congress. U.S. Department of the Navy, Washington, DC 20350. Phone: (703)697-7391 Annual.

Deposit Account Operations. Institute of Financial Education, 55 W. Monroe St., Suite 2800 Chicago, IL 60603-5014. Phone: 800-946-0488 or (312)364-0100 Fax: (312)364-0190 E-mail: ystoffregen@bai.org • URL: http://www.theinstitute.com • 1997. $49.95.

Deposit Accounts Regulation Manual. Kenneth F. Hall. West Group, 610 Opperman Dr. Eagan, MN 55123. Phone: 800-328-4880 or (651)687-7000 Fax: 800-213-2323 or (651)687-5827 URL: http://www.westgroup.com • 1993. $135.00. Provides yearly coverage of federal laws and regulations governing bank deposit accounts, including Truth-in-Savings, Federal Deposit Insurance, Electronic Funds Transfers, fee disclosure, privacy issues, and reserve requirements. (Commercial Law Series).

Deposit Operations. David H. Friedman. American Bankers Association, 1120 Connecticut Ave., N. W. Washington, DC 20036-3971. Phone: 800-338-0626 or (202)663-5000 Fax: (202)663-7543 URL: http://www.aba.com • 1992. Price on application.

Depreciation and Investment Credit Manual. Prentice Hall, 240 Frisch Court Paramus, NJ 07652-5240. Phone: 800-947-7700 or (201)909-6200 Fax: 800-445-6991 or (201)909-6361 URL: http://www.prenhall.com • Annual. Price on application.

Depreciation Handbook. Matthew Bender & Co., Inc., Two Park Ave. New York, NY 10016. Phone: 800-223-1940 or (212)448-2000 Fax: (212)244-3188 E-mail: international@bender.com • URL: http://www.bender.com • $180.00. Looseleaf service. Periodic supplementation. Treatment of depreciation in one volume.

Derivatives. Derivatives Strategy and TacticsPhone: (212)366-9578 Fax: (212)366-0551 E-mail: office@derivatives.com • URL: http://www.derivatives.com • Web site provides articles from *Derivatives Strategy* magazine (three-month delay). Also includes ''Derivatives Comix,'' explaining complex topics in comic book form. An example is ''Boovis and Beethead Play the Yield Curve Game.'' Links to useful derivatives Web sites and descriptions of recommended books are provided. Fees: Free.

Derivatives: A Comprehensive Resource for Options, Futures, Interest Rate Swaps, and Mortgage Securities. Fred D. Arditti. Harvard Business School Press, 60 Harvard Way Boston, MA 02163. Phone: 888-500-1016 or (617)783-7440 E-mail: custserv@hbsp.harvard.edu • URL: http://www.hbsp.harvard.edu • 1996. $60.00. Published by Harvard Business School Press. Provides detailed explanations of various kinds of financial derivatives (options, futures, swaps, etc.) and their trading tactics, uses, and risks. (Financial Management Association Survey and Synthesis Series).

Derivatives Desk Reference: Buyside and Sellside Profiles. Capital Access International, 430 Mountain Ave. Murray Hill, NJ 07974. Phone: 800-866-5987 or (908)771-0800 Fax: (908)771-0330 E-mail: info@capital-access.com • URL: http://www.capital-access.com • Annual. $295.00. A directory of about 900 firms active in the use of such derivatives as options, futures, currency swaps, interest rate swaps, and structured notes. Includes names of derivatives specialists in each firm.

Derivatives Handbook: Risk Management and Control. Robert J. Schwartz and Clifford W. Smith. John Wiley and Sons, Inc., 605 Third Ave. New York, NY 10158-0012. Phone: 800-225-5945 or (212)850-6000 Fax: (212)850-6088 E-mail: info@jwiley.com • URL: http://www.wiley.com • 1997. $79.95. Some chapter topics are legal risk, risk measurement, and risk oversight. Includes ''Derivatives Debacles: Case Studies of Losses in DerivativesMarkets.'' A glossary of derivatives terminology is provided. (Wiley Financial Engineering Series).

Derivatives Quarterly. Institutional Investor, 488 Madison Ave. New York, NY 10022. Phone: (212)224-3300 Fax: (212)224-3527 E-mail: info@iijournals.com • URL: http://www.iijournals.com • Quarterly. $280.00 per year. Emphasis is on the practical use of derivatives. Includes case studies to demonstrate ''real-life'' risks and benefits.

Derivatives Strategy. Derivatives Strategy and Tactics, 153 Waverly Place, Suite 1200 New York, NY 10014. Phone: (212)366-9578 Fax: (212)366-0551 E-mail: office@derivatives.com • URL: http://www.derivatives.com • Monthly. $245.00 per year. Provides practical explanations of financial derivatives for institutional investors, corporate treasury officers, dealers, and others.

Derivatives Tactics. Derivative Strategy and Tactics, 153 Waverly Place, Suite 1200 New York, NY 10014. Phone: (212)366-9578 Fax: (212)366-0551 E-mail: office@derivatives.com • URL: http://www.derivatires.com • Semimonthly. $695.00 per year. Newsletter. Edited for institutional investors. Covers options, swaps, and other financial derivatives.

Derivatives Week: The Newsweekly on Derivatives Worldwide. Institutional Investor, 488 Madison Ave. New York, NY 10022. Phone: (212)224-3300 Fax: (212)224-3353 E-mail: info@iijournals.com • URL: http://iijournals.com • Weekly. $2,330.00 per year. Newsletter on financial derivatives linked to equities, interest rates, commodities, and currencies. Covers new products, investment opportunities, legalities, etc.

Derwent Biotechnology Abstracts. Derwent, Inc., 1725 Duke St., Suite 250 Alexandria, VA 22314. Phone: 800-451-3551 or (703)706-4220 Fax: (703)519-5829 E-mail: info@derwent.com • URL: http://www.derwent.com • Provides indexing and abstracting of the world's biotechnology journal literature since 1982, including genetic engineering topics. Monthly updates. Inquire as to online cost and availability.

Derwent Crop Protection File. Derwent, Inc., 1725 Duke St., Suite 250 Alexandria, VA 22314. Phone: 800-451-3551 or (703)706-4220 Fax: (703)519-5829 E-mail: info@derwent.com • URL: http://www.derwent.com • Provides citations to the international journal literature of agricultural chemicals and pesticides from 1968 to date, with updating eight times per year. Formerly *PESTDOC*. Inquire as to online cost and availability.

Derwent Drug File. Derwent, Inc., 1725 Duke St., Suite 250 Alexandria, VA 22314. Phone: 800-451-3551 or (703)706-4220 Fax: (703)519-5829 E-mail: info@derwent.com • URL: http://www.derwent.com • Provides indexing and abstracting of the world's pharmaceutical journal literature since 1964, with weekly updates. Formerly *RINGDOC*. Inquire as to online cost and availability.

Derwent U. S. Patents. Derwent, Inc., 1725 Duke St., Suite 250 Alexandria, VA 22314. Phone: 800-451-3551 or (703)706-4220 Fax: (703)519-5829 E-mail: info@derwent.com • URL: http://www.derwent.com • Provides citations and abstracts for more then one million U. S. patents issued since 1971. Weekly updates. Inquire as to online cost and availability.

Derwent Veterinary Drug File. Derwent, Inc., 1725 Duke St., Suite 250 Alexandria, VA 22314. Phone: 800-451-3551 or (703)706-4220 Fax: (703)519-5829 E-mail: info@derwent.com • URL: http://www.derwent.com • Provides indexing and abstracting of the world's veterinary drug literature since 1968, with monthly updates. Formerly *VETDOC*. Inquire as to online cost and availability.

Derwent World Patents Index. Derwent, Inc., 1725 Duke St., Suite 250 Alexandria, VA 22314. Phone: 800-451-3551 or (703)706-4220 Fax: (703)519-5829 E-mail: info@derwent.com • URL: http://www.derwent.com • Contains abstracts of more than 20 million patent documents from many countries. Time span varies. Weekly updates. Inquire as to online cost and availability.

Desalination Directory: Desalination and Water Reuse. Elsevier Scientific, 655 Ave. of the Americas New York, NY 10010. Phone: 888-437-4636 or (212)989-5800 Fax: (212)633-3680 E-mail: usinfo@elsevier.com • URL: http://www.elsevier.com • Annual. Members, $160.00; non-members, $250.00. Lists business firms, institutes, associations, government agencies, and individuals involved in some way with desalination. International coverage. Published in Italy by the School of Scientific Communication. Text in English.

Desalination Technology: Developments and Practice. Andrew Porteous, editor. Elsevier Science, 655 Ave. of the Americas New York, NY 10010. Phone: 888-437-4636 or (212)989-5800 Fax: (212)633-3680 E-mail: usinfo@elsevier.com • URL: http://www.elsevier.com • 1983. $74.00.

Descriptive Statistical Techniques for Librarians. Arthur W. Hafner. American Library Association, 50 E. Huron St. Chicago, IL 60611-2795. Phone: 800-545-2433 or (312)944-6780 Fax: (312)440-9374 E-mail: ala@ala.org • URL: http://www.ala.org • 1997. $55.00 Second edition.

Design and Marketing of New Products. Glen L. Urban and John R. Hauser. Simon and Schuster Trade, 1230 Ave. of the Americas New York, NY 10020. Phone: 800-223-2336 or (212)698-7000 Fax: 800-943-9831 or (212)698-7007 E-mail: ssonline_feedback@simonsays.com • URL: http://www.simonsays.com • 1993. $97.00. Second edition.

Design Cost Data: The Cost Estimating Magazine for Architects, Builders and Specifiers. L. M. Rector Corp., 8602 N. 40th St. Tampa, FL 33604. Phone: (813)989-9300 Fax: (813)980-3982 Bimonthly. $64.80 per year. Provides a preliminary cost estimating system for architects, contractors, builders, and developers, utilizing historical data. Includes case studies of actual costs. Formerly *Design Cost and Data*.

Design Drafting News. American Design Drafting Association, P.O. Box 11937 Columbia, SC 29211-1937. Phone: (803)771-0008 Fax: (803)771-4272 Bimonthly. Membership. Newsletter.

Design Firm Directory: A Listing of Firms and Consultants in Grap hic Design in the United States. Wefler & Associates, Inc., P.O. Box 1167 Evanston, IL 60204. Phone: (847)475-1866 Annual. $145.00. Three volumes. Provides information on more than 2,600 commercial, private, and consulting design firms. Includes graphic, interior, landscape, and environmental designers.

Design Management Institute., 29 Temple Place, 2nd Fl. Boston, MA 02111. Phone: (617)338-6380 Fax: (617)338-6570 E-mail: dmistaff@dmi.org • URL: http://www.dmi.org • Membership includes firms concerned with various kinds of commercial design, including product, graphic, interior, exhibit, package, and architectural.

Design Management Journal. Design Management Institute, 29 Temple Place, 2nd Fl. Boston, MA 02111-1350. Phone: (617)338-6380 Fax: (617)338-6570 E-mail: dmistaff@dmiorg • URL: http://www.dmi.org • Quarterly. $96.00 per year. Covers the management of product-related design.

Design News OEM Directory. Cahners Business Information, Design News, 275 Washington St. Newton, MA 02158-1630. Phone: 800-662-7776 or (617)964-3030 Fax: (617)558-4402 E-mail: corporatecommunications@cahners.com • URL: http://www.cahners.com • Annual. $60.00. About 6,000 manufacturers and suppliers of power transmission products, fluid power products and electrical/electronic componets to the OEM (Original Equipment Manufacturers). Included with subscription to *Design News*. Formerly *Design News*.

The Design of Advertising. Roy Paul Nelson. Brown and Benchmark, 25 Kessel Court Madison, WI 53711. Phone: 800-338-5578 or (608)273-0040 Fax: 800-346-2377 E-mail: customer.service@mcgraw-hill.com • URL: http://www.mhhe.com • 1996. Seventh edition. Price on application.

Design of Concrete Structures. Arthur H. Nilson and David Darwin. McGraw-Hill, 1221 Ave. of the Americas New York, NY 10020-1095. Phone: 800-722-4726 or (212)904-2000 Fax: (212)904-2072 E-mail: customer.service@mcgraw-hill.com • URL: http://www.mcgraw-hill.com • 1997. $95.31. 12th edition. (Construction Engineering and Project Management Series).

Design of Machine Elements. Merhyle F. Spotts and Terry E. Shoup. Prentice Hall, 240 Frisch Court Paramus, NJ 07458-5240. Phone: 800-947-7700 or (201)909-6200 Fax: 800-445-6991 or (201)909-6361 URL: http://www.prenhall.com • 1997. $105.00. Seventh edition.

Design Perspectives. Industrial Designers Society of America, 1142 E. Walker Rd. Great Falls, VA 22066. Phone: (703)759-0100 Fax: (703)759-7679 10 times a year. $32.00 per year.

Design Research Unit., Massachusetts College of Art, 621 Huntington Ave. Boston, MA 02115. Phone: (617)232-1492 Fax: (617)566-4034 Conducts research related to the design of printed matter, including annual reports, letterheads, posters, and brochures.

Designing Infographics. Eric K. Meyer. Hayden, 201 W. 103rd St. Indianapolis, IN 46290-1094. Phone: 800-858-7674 or (317)581-3718 URL: http://www.macmillan.com • 1997. $39.99. A basic handbook on the design and presentation of computer-generated charts, graphs, tables, maps, diagrams, etc.

Designing the User Interface: Strategies for Effective Human-Computer Interaction. Ben Shneiderman. Addison Wesley Longman, Inc., One Jacob Way Reading, MA 01867. Phone: 800-447-2226 or (781)944-3700 Fax: (781)944-9351 URL: http://www.awl.com • 1997. $44.95. Third edition. Provides an introduction to computer user-interface design. Covers usability testing, dialog boxes, menus, command languages, interaction devices, tutorials, printed user manuals, and related subjects.

Desktop Communications. International Desktop Communications, Ltd., 342 Madison Ave., Suite 622 New York, NY 10173-0002. Phone: (212)768-7666 Fax: (212)768-0288 Bimonthly. $24.00 per year. Emphasis on typeface selection and page layout. Formerly *ITC Desktop*.

The Desktop Designer's Illustration Handbook. Marcelle L. Toor. John Wiley and Sons, Inc., 605 Third Ave. New York, NY 10158-0012. Phone: 800-842-3636 or (212)850-6000 Fax: (212)850-6088 E-mail: info@wiley.com • URL: http://www.wiley.com • 1996. $29.95. Serves as a guide to locating, selecting, and using illustrations for desktop publications. (ITCP-U.S. Computer Science Series).

Desktop Publishers Journal. Business Media Group LLC, 462 Boston St. Topsfield, MA 01983-1232. Phone: (978)887-7900 Fax: (978)887-6117 URL: http://www.dtpjournal.com • Ten times a year. $49.00 per year. Edited for professional publishers, graphic designers, and industry service providers. Covers new products and emerging technologies for the electronic publishing industry.

Desktop Publishing. Entrepreneur Media, Inc., 2445 McCabe Way Irvine, CA 92614. Phone: 800-421-2300 or (949)261-2325 Fax: (949)261-0234 E-mail: entmag@entrepreneur.com • URL: http://www.entrepreneur.com • Looseleaf. $59.50. A practical guide to starting a desktop publishing service. Covers profit potential, start-up costs, market size evaluation, pricing, accounting, advertising, promotion, etc. (Start-Up Business Guide No. E1288.)

Desktop Publishing by Design: Everyone's Guide to Pagemaker 6. Ronnie Shushan and others. Microsoft Press, One Microsoft Way Redmond, WA 98052-6399. Phone: 800-677-7377 or (425)882-8080 Fax: (425)936-7329 URL: http://www.microsoft.com/mspress • 1996. $39.95. Fourth edition. (By Design Series).

Desktop Video Communications. BCR Enterprises, Inc., 950 York Rd. Hinsdale, IL 60521. Phone: 800-227-1234 or

(630)986-1432 Fax: (630)323-5324 E-mail: jwillet@bcr • URL: http://www.bcr.com/ • Bimonthly. $55.00 per year. Covers multimedia technologies, with emphasis on video conferencing and the "virtual office." Formerly *Virtual Workgroups*.

DETC News. Distance Education and Training Council, 1601 18th St. N.W. Washington, DC 20009. Phone: (202)234-5100 Fax: (202)332-1386 E-mail: detc@detc.org • Semiannual. Free. Items of interest to correspondence educators. Formerly *NHSC News*.

Detwiler's Directory of Health and Medical Resources. Dorland Healthcare Information, 1500 Walnut St., Suite 1000 Philadelphia, PA 19102. Phone: 800-784-2332 or (215)875-1212 Fax: (215)735-3966 E-mail: info@dorlandhealth.com • URL: http://www.dorlandhealth.com • Annual. $195.00. Lists a wide range of healthcare information resources, including more than 2,000 corporations, associations, government agencies, publishers, licensure organizations, market research firms, foundations, and institutes, as well as 6,000 publications. Indexed by type of information, publication, acronym, and 600 subject categories.

Detwiler's Directory of Health and Medical Resources. S. M. Detwiler and Associates. Hatherleigh Co., Ltd., P.O. Box 15308 Fort Wayne, IN 46885. Phone: 800-367-2550 or (219)749-6534 Fax: (219)493-6717 Annual. $220.00. Lists sources of information relating to the healthcare industry, including government agencies, medical experts, directories, newsletters, research groups, associations, and mailing list producers. Four indexes are provided: subject, publication, service, and acronym.

Developing a Consulting Practice. Robert O. Metzger. Sage Publications, Inc., 2455 Teller Rd. Thousand Oaks, CA 91320. Phone: (805)499-0721 Fax: (805)499-0871 E-mail: info@sagepub.com • URL: http://www.sagepub.com • 1993. $37.00. Aimed at university professors and other academic personnel who wish to go into the consulting business. Contains practical advice on identifying skills, finding clients, making proposals, and management details. (Survival Skills for Scholars, vol. 3).

Developing and Managing E-Journal Collections: A How-To-DoIt Manual for Librarians. Donnelyn Curtis and others. Neal-Schuman Publishers, Inc., 100 Varick St. New York, NY 10013. Phone: (212)925-8650 Fax: 800-584-2414 or (212)219-8916 E-mail: info@neal-schuman.com • URL: http://www.neal-schuman.com • 2000. $55.00. Covers the acquisition, management, and integration of journals published in electronic form.

Developing Business Strategies. David A. Adler. John Wiley and Sons, Inc., 605 Third Ave. New York, NY 10158-0012. Phone: 800-225-5945 or (212)850-6000 Fax: (212)850-6088 E-mail: info@wiley.com • URL: http://www.wiley.com • 1998. $39.95. Fifth edition.

Developing E-Business Architectures: A Manager's Guide. Paul Harmon and others. Academic Press, 525 B St., Suite 1900 San Diego, CA 92101. Phone: 800-321-5068 or (619)699-6719 Fax: 800-336-7377 or (619)699-6380 E-mail: ap@acad.com • URL: http://www.academicpress.com • 2000. $34.95.

Developing Java Software. Russel Winder. John Wiley and Sons, Inc., 605 Third Ave. New York, NY 10158-0012. Phone: 800-225-5945 or (212)850-6000 Fax: (212)850-6088 E-mail: info@jwiley.com • URL: http://www.wiley.com • 2000. $49.99. Second edition.

Developing Reference Collections and Services in an Electronic Age: A How-To-Do-It Manual for Librarians. Kay A. Cassell. Neal-Schuman Publishers, Inc., 100 Varick St. New York, NY 10013. Phone: (212)925-8650 Fax: 800-584-2414 or (212)219-8916 E-mail: info@neal-schuman.com • URL: http://www.neal-schuman.com • 1999. $55.00. Discusses print vs. electronic media for library reference services.

Development. National Association of Industrial and Office Properties, Woodland Park, 2201 Cooperative Way Herndon, VA 22071-3024. Phone: 800-666-6780 or (703)904-7100 Fax: (703)904-7942 Quarterly. Free to members; non-members, $65.00 per year. Focuses on issues, trends and new ideas affecting the commercial and industrial real estate development industry.

Development Business. United Nations Publications, Concourse Level, First Ave., 46th St. New York, NY 10017. Phone: 800-553-3210 or (212)963-7680 Fax: (212)963-4910 E-mail: dbusiness@un.org • URL: http://www.devbusiness.com • Semimonthly. $495.00 per year. Provides leads on contract opportunities worldwide for engineering firms and multinational corporations. Text in English, French, Portuguese, and Spanish.

The Development of Plastics. S. Mossman and P. Morris, editors. CRC Press, Inc., 200 Corporate Blvd., N.W. Boca Raton, FL 33431-7372. Phone: 800-272-7737 or (561)994-0555 E-mail: orders@crcpress.com • URL: http://www.crcpress.com • 1994. $68.00. Published by The Royal Society of Chemistry. Covers the history of plastics from the Victorian era to the present. Includes technical, scientific, and cultural perspectives.

Devil Take the Hindmost: A History of Financial Speculation. Edward Chancellor. Farrar, Straus & Giroux, LLC, 19 Union Square New York, NY 10003. Phone: 800-788-6262 or (212)741-6900 Fax: (212)633-9385 1999. $25.00. Covers such events as the Dutch tulip mania of 1637, the South Sea bubble of 1720, and the Japanese real estate and stock market boom of the 1980's.

DFISA Reporter. Dairy and Food Industries Supply Association, Inc., 6245 Executive Blvd. Rockville, MD 20852-3906. Phone: (301)984-1444 Fax: (301)881-7832 Monthly. Free. Provides industry and association news to manufacturers of equipment products and services to the dairy and food industry.

Di Yiddishe Heim/Jewish Home. Kehot Publication Society, 770 Eastern Parkway Brooklyn, NY 11213. Phone: (718)493-9571 Quarterly. $8.00 per year. Text in English and Yiddishe.

Dial Up! Gale's Bulletin Board Locator. The Gale Group, 27500 Drake Rd. Farmington Hills, MI 48331-3535. Phone: 800-877-GALE or (248)699-GALE Fax: 800-414-5043 or (248)699-8069 E-mail: galeord@galegroup.com • URL: http://www.galegroup.com • 1996. $49.00. Contains access and other information for 10,000 computer bulletin boards in the U. S. Arranged geographically, with indexes to bulletin board names, organizations, and topics.

Diamond Council of America.

Diamond Dealers Club.

Diamond Manufacturers and Importers Association of America Yearbook., c/o Ben Kinzler, P.O. Box 5297 New York, NY 10185-5297. Phone: (212)944-2066 Annual.

Diamond Walnut Growers.

Diamond World Review. World Federation of Diamond Bourses. International Diamond Publications, Ltd., 54 Bezalel St. 52131 972 Ramat Gon, Israel. Phone: 972 3 7512165 Fax: 972 3 5752201 E-mail: rshor@chilton.net • Bimonthly. $78.00 per year. Text in English.

Diamonds. Fred Ware. Gem Book Publishers, 7106 Saunders Court Bethesda, MD 20817. Phone: 800-345-0096 or (301)983-1990 Fax: (301)983-3980 E-mail: fward@erols.com • URL: http://www.erols.com/fward/ • 1998. $14.95. Revised edition. (Fred Ware Gem Book Series).

Diamonds and Precious Stones. Harry Emmanuel. Gordon Press Publishers, P.O. Box 459 New York, NY 10004. Phone: (212)969-8419 Fax: (718)624-8419 1977. $79.95.

Diaper Delivery Service. Entrepreneur Media, Inc., 2445 McCabe Way Irvine, CA 92614. Phone: 800-421-2300 or (949)261-2325 Fax: (949)261-0234 E-mail: entmag@entrepreneur.com • URL: http://www.entrepreneur.com • Looseleaf. $59.50. A practical guide to starting a service for the laundering and delivery of all-cotton diapers. Covers profit potential, start-up costs, market size evaluation, owner's time required, site selection, pricing, accounting, advertising, promotion, etc. (Start-Up Business Guide No. E1364.)

Dick Davis Digest. Dick Davis Publishing, Inc., 2881 E. Oakland Park Blvd. Fort Lauderdale, FL 33306-1824. Phone: (954)733-3996 URL: http://www.dickdavis.com • Semimonthly. $180.00 per year. Newsletter. A digest of investment advisory services.

Dictionary of Accounting. Ralph Estes. MIT Press, Five Cambridge Center Cambridge, MA 02142-1399. Phone: 800-356-0343 or (617)253-5646 Fax: (617)253-6779 E-mail: mitpress-orders@mit.edu • URL: http://www.mitpress.mit.edu • 1985. $11.95. Second edition.

Dictionary of Accounting Terms. Joel G. Siegel and Jae K. Shim. Barron's Educational Series, Inc., 250 Wireless Blvd. Hauppauge, NY 11788-3917. Phone: 800-645-3476 or (516)434-3311 Fax: (516)434-3723 E-mail: barrons@barronseduc.com • URL: http://www.barronseduc.com • 1995. $11.95. Second edition.

Dictionary of Agriculture: From Abaca to Zoonosis. Kathryn L. Lipton. Lynne Rienner Publishers, Inc., 1800 30th St., Suite 314 Boulder, CO 80301-1026. Phone: (303)444-6684 Fax: (303)444-0824 E-mail: cservice@rienner.com • URL: http://www.rienner.com • 1995. $75.00. Emphasis is on agricultural economics.

Dictionary of American Medical Biography. Martin Kaufman and others. Greenwood Publishing Group Inc., 88 Post Rd., W. Westport, CT 06881-5007. Phone: 800-225-5800 or (203)226-3571 Fax: (203)222-2540 E-mail: bookinfo@greenwood.com • URL: http://www.greenwood.com • 1984. $195.00. Two volumes. Vol. one, $100.00; vol. two, $100.00.

A Dictionary of Architecture. Henry Saylor. John Wiley and Sons, Inc., 605 Third Ave. New York, NY 10158-0012. Phone: 800-225-5945 or (212)850-6000 Fax: (212)850-6088 E-mail: info@wiley.com • URL: http://www.wiley.com • 1994. $39.95.

Dictionary of Architecture and Construction. Cyril M. Harris. McGraw-Hill Professional, 1221 Ave. of the Americas New York, NY 10020-1095. Phone: 800-722-4726 or (212)904-2000 Fax: (212)904-2072 E-mail: customer.service@mcgraw-hill.com • URL: http://www.mcgraw-hill.com • 2000. $69.95. Third edition.

Dictionary of Architecture, Building, Construction and Materials. Herbert Bucksch. French and European Publishers, Inc., Rockefelle Center Promenade, 610 Fifth Ave. New York, NY 10020-2479. Phone: (212)581-8810 Fax: (212)265-1094 E-mail: liversny@aol.com • URL: http://www.frencheuropean.com • 1983. Second edition. Two volumes. $295.00 per volume. Text in English and German.

Dictionary of Aviation. R. J. Hall and R. D. Campbell. Available from St. James Press, 27500 Drake Rd. Farmington Hills, MI 48331-3535. Phone: 800-877-GALE or (248)699-GALE Fax: 800-414-5043 or (248)699-8063 E-mail: galeord@galegroup.com • URL: http://www.galegroup.com • 1991. $50.00. Published by Blackwell Scientific. Includes aeronautical words, phrases, acronyms, and abbreviations.

Dictionary of Banking. Jerry M. Rosenberg. John Wiley and Sons, Inc., 605 Third Ave. New York, NY 10158-0012. Phone: 800-225-5945 or (212)850-6000 Fax: (212)850-6088 E-mail: info@wiley.com • URL: http://www.wiley.com • 1992. $19.95. Third edition. (Business Dictionary Series).

Dictionary of Banking and Finance Terms: 'AAA to Zloty'. John Clark. State Mutual Book and Periodical Services Ltd., 521 Fifth Ave., 17th Fl. New York, NY 10175. Phone: (718)261-1704 Fax: (516)537-0412 1998. $60.00.

Dictionary of Banking: Over 4,000 Terms Defined and Explained. Charles J. Woelfel. McGraw-Hill Professional, 1221 Ave. of the Americas New York, NY 10020-1095. Phone: 800-722-4726 or (212)904-2000 Fax: (212)904-2072 E-mail: customer.service@mcgraw-hill.com • URL: http://www.mcgraw-hill.com • 1994. $24.95. Contains brief definitions of more than 4,000 banking terms.

Dictionary of Banking Terms. Thomas P. Fitch. Barron's Educational Series, Inc., 250 Wireless Blvd. Hauppauge, NY 11788. Phone: 800-645-3476 or (516)434-3311 Fax: (516)434-3723 E-mail: barrons@barronseduc.com • URL: http://www.barronseduc.com • 2000. Fifth edition. Price on application.

Dictionary of Bibliometrics. Virgil Diodato. Haworth Press, Inc., 10 Alice St. Binghamton, NY 13904-1580. Phone: 800-429-6784 or (607)722-5857 Fax: 800-895-0582 or (607)722-1424 E-mail: getinfo@haworthpressinc.com • URL: http://www.haworthpressinc.com • 1994. $39.95. Contains detailed explanations of 225 terms, with references. (Bibliometrics is "the application of mathematical and statistical techniques to the study of publishing and professional communication.")

Dictionary of Building. Randall McMullan. G P Courseware, 324 S. Main St., Suite 600 Tulsa, OK 74103-3682. Phone: (918)492-3338 Fax: (918)599-8316 1991. $59.50.

Dictionary of Business and Management. Jerry M. Rosenberg. John Wiley and Sons, Inc., 605 Third Ave. New York, NY 10158-0012. Phone: 800-225-5945 or (212)850-6000 Fax: (212)850-6088 E-mail: info@wiley.com • URL: http://www.wiley.com • 1992. $14.95. Third edition. (Business Dictionary Series).

Dictionary of Business Quotations. Julia Vitullo-Martin and J. Robert Moskin. Oxford University Press, Inc., 198 Madison Ave. New York, NY 10016-4314. Phone: 800-451-7556 or (212)726-6000 Fax: (212)726-6446 E-mail: custserv@oup-usa.org • URL: http://www.oup-usa.org • 1993. $39.95.

Dictionary of Chemical Terminology. Dobromila Kryt. Elsevier Science, 655 Ave. of the Americas New York, NY 10010. Phone: 888-437-4636 or (212)989-5800 Fax: (212)633-3680 E-mail: usinfo@elsevier.com • URL: http://www.elsevier.com • 1980. $190.75. Text in English, French, German, Polish, and Russian.

Dictionary of Civil Engineering and Construction Machinery and Equipment. Herbert Bucksch. French and European Publishers, Inc., Rockefelle Center Promenade, 610 Fifth Ave. New York, NY 10020-2479. Phone: (212)581-8810 Fax: (212)265-1094 E-mail: liversny@aol.com • URL: http://www.frencheuropean.com • 1976. $275.00. Two volumes. Vol. 1, $225.00; vol. 2, $225.00. Text in English and French.

Dictionary of Commercial, Financial and Legal Terms in Two Languages. R. Herbst. Adlers Foreign Books, Inc., 915 Foster St. Evanston, IL 60201. Phone: 800-235-3771 or (847)864-0664 Fax: (847)864-0804 E-mail: info@afb-adlers.com • URL: http://www.adlers.com • Two volumes. Vol. A, $179.50; vol. B $179.50. Text in English and German.

Dictionary of Computer Graphics Technology and Application. Roy Lanham. Springer-Verlag New York, Inc., 175 Fifth Ave. New York, NY 10010. Phone: 800-777-4643 or (212)460-1500 Fax: (212)473-6272 E-mail: orders@springer.ny.com • URL: http://www.springer.ny.com • 1995. $21.95. Second edition.

Dictionary of Computer Terms. Brian Phaffenberger. Pearson Education and Technology, 201 W. 103rd St. Indianapolis, IN 46290-1097. Phone: 800-858-7674 or (317)581-3500 Fax: (317)581-4670 URL: http://www.mcp.com • 1997. $10.95. Sixth edition.

Dictionary of Computing. Valerie Illingworth, editor. Oxford University Press, Inc., 198 Madison Ave. New York, NY 10016-4314. Phone: 800-451-7556 or (212)726-6000 Fax: (212)726-6446 E-mail: custserv@oup-usa.org • URL: http://www.oup-usa.org • 1996. $49.95. Fourth edition.

Dictionary of Econometrics. Adrian C. Darnell. Edward Elgar Publishing, Inc., 136 West St., Suite 202 Northampton, MA 01060. Phone: 800-390-3149 or (413)584-5551 Fax: (413)584-9933 E-mail: eep.orders@aidcvt.com • URL: http://www.e-elgar.co.uk • 1994. $150.00. Published by Edward Elgar Publishing Co. (UK).

Dictionary of Economic Plants. J.C. Uphof. Lubrecht and Cramer, Ltd., P.O. Box 3110 Port Jervis, NY 12771. Phone: 800-920-9334 or (914)856-5990 E-mail: lubrecht@ny.frontiernet.net • URL: http://www.lubrechtcramer.com • 1968. $49.00. Second enlarged revised edition.

Dictionary of Economics. Jae K. Shim and Joel G. Siegel. John Wiley and Sons, Inc., 605 Third Ave. New York, NY 10158-0012. Phone: 800-225-5945 or (212)850-6000 Fax: (212)850-6088 E-mail: info@jwiley.com • URL: http://www.wiley.com • 1995. $79.95. Contains 2,200 definitions of economic terms. Includes graphs, charts, tables, and economic formulas. (Business Dictionary Series).

Dictionary of Electronics. S.W. Amos and Roger Amos. Butterworth-Heinemann, 225 Wildwood Ave. Woburn, MA 01081. Phone: 800-366-2665 or (781)904-2500 Fax: 800-446-6520 E-mail: orders@bhusa.com • URL: http://www.bh.com • 1996. $34.95. Third edition.

Dictionary of Finance and Investment Terms. John Downes and Jordan E. Goodman. Barron's Educational Series, Inc., 250 Wireless Blvd. Hauppauge, NY 11788. Phone: 800-645-3476 or (516)434-3311 Fax: (516)434-3723 E-mail: barrons@barronseduc.com • URL: http://www.barronseduc.com • 1998. $12.95. Fifth revised edition. Provides clear explanations of more than 5,000 business, banking, financial, investment, and tax terms. Includes a separate list of financial abbreviations and acronyms.

Dictionary of Food and Ingredients. Robert S. Igoe and Y.H. Hui. Aspen Publishers, Inc., 200 Orchard Ridge Dr. Gaithersburg, MD 20878. Phone: 800-638-8437 or (301)417-7500 Fax: (301)695-7931 E-mail: customer.service@aspenpubl.com • URL: http://www.aspenpub.com • 1995. $30.00. Third edition.

Dictionary of Gambling and Gaming. Thomas L. Clark. Lexik House Publishers, P.O. Box 247 Cold Spring, NY 10516. Phone: (914)424-4115 E-mail: lexik@highlands.com • URL: http://www.highlands.com • 1988. $48.00.

Dictionary of HRD. Angus Reynolds and others., Old Post Rd. Brookfield, VT 05036-9704. Phone: 800-535-9544 or (802)276-3162 Fax: (802)276-3837 1997. $67.95. Provides definitions of more than 3,000 terms related to human resource development. Includes acronyms, abbreviations, and a list of ''100 Essential HRD Terms.'' Published by Gower in England.

Dictionary of Hydraulic Machinery. A. T. Troskolanski. Elsevier Science, 655 Ave. of the Americas New York, NY 10010. Phone: 888-437-4636 or (212)989-5800 Fax: (212)633-3680 E-mail: usinfo@elsevier.com • URL: http://www.elsevier.com • 1986. $289.00. Text in English, French, German, Italian, and Russian.

Dictionary of Information Technology and Computer Science. Tony Gunton. Blackwell Publishers, 350 Main St., 6th Fl. Malden, MA 02148-5018. Phone: 800-216-2522 or (781)388-8200 Fax: (781)388-8210 E-mail: books@blackwellpub.com • URL: http://www.blackwellpub.com • 1994. $50.95. Second edition. Covers key words, phrases, abbreviations, and acronyms used in computing and data communications.

Dictionary of Insurance. Lewis E. Davids. Rowman and Littlefield Publishers, Inc., 4720 Boston Way Lanham, MD 20706. Phone: 800-462-6420 or (301)459-3366 Fax: (301)459-2118 E-mail: rogers@univpress.com • URL: http://www.rowmanlittlefield.com • 1990. $17.95. Seventh revised edition.

Dictionary of Insurance Terms. Harvey W. Rubin. Barron's Educational Series, Inc., 250 Wireless Blvd. Hauppauge, NY 11788. Phone: 800-645-3476 or (516)434-3311 Fax: (516)434-3723 E-mail: barrons@barronseduc.com • URL: http://www.barronseduc.com • 2000. $12.95. Fourth edition. Defines terms in a wide variety of insurance fields. Price on application.

Dictionary of International Biography. Taylor & Francis, Inc., 325 Chestnut St., 8th Fl. Philadelphia, PA 19106. Phone: 800-821-8312 or (215)625-8900 Fax: (215)625-2940 E-mail: webmaster@taylorand francis.com • URL: http://www.tandfdc.com/ • 1996. $199.00. 24th edition.

Dictionary of International Business Terms. Jae K. Shim and others, editors. Fitzroy Dearborn Publishers, 919 N. Michigan Ave., Suite 760 Chicago, IL 60611. Phone: 800-850-8102 or (312)587-0131 Fax: (312)587-1049 E-mail: website@firzroydearborn.com • URL: http://www.fitzroydearborn.com • 1998. $45.00. Defines more than 2,000 terms currently used in international business.

Dictionary of Investing. Jerry M. Rosenberg. John Wiley and Sons, Inc., 605 Third Ave. New York, NY 10158-0012. Phone: 800-225-5945 or (212)850-6000 Fax: (212)850-6088 E-mail: info@wiley.com • URL: http://www.wiley.com • 1992. $79.95. (Business Dictionary Series).

Dictionary of Marine Technology. Cyril Hughes. Available from Informa Publishing Group Ltd., PO Box 1017 Westborough, MA 01581-6017. Phone: 800-493-4080 Fax: (508)231-0856 E-mail: enquiries@informa.com • URL: http://www.informa.com • 1997. $108.00. Published in the UK by Lloyd's List (http://www.lloydslist.com). Includes more than 1,000 terms and acronyms in the fields of ship operation, technology, marine construction, maritime safety, environmental issues, and government regulation of shipping.

Dictionary of Marketing and Advertising. Jerry M. Rosenberg. John Wiley and Sons, Inc., 605 Third Ave. New York, NY 10158-0012. Phone: 800-225-5945 or (212)850-6000 Fax: (212)850-6088 E-mail: info@wiley.com • URL: http://www.wiley.com • 1995. $79.95. (Business Dictionary Series).

Dictionary of Marketing Terms. Betsy-Ann Toffler. Barron's Educational Series, Inc., 250 Wireless Blvd. Hauppauge, NY 11788-3917. Phone: 800-645-3476 or (516)434-3311 Fax: (516)434-3217 E-mail: barreons@barronseduc.com • URL: http://www.barronseduc.com • 2000. $12.95. Third edition. Business Dictionaries Series.

Dictionary of Multimedia: Terms and Acronyms. Brad Hansen, editor. Fitzroy Dearborn Publishers, 919 N. Michigan Ave., Suite 760 Chicago, IL 60611. Phone: 800-850-8102 or (312)587-0131 Fax: (312)587-1049 E-mail: website@fitzroydearborn.com • URL: http://www.fitzroydearborn.com • 1998. $55.00. Second edition.

Dictionary of 1040 Deductions. Matthew Bender & Co., Inc., Two Park Ave. New York, NY 10016. Phone: 800-223-1940 or (212)448-2000 Fax: (212)244-3188 E-mail: international@bender.com • URL: http://www.bender.com • Annual. Price on application. Organized by schedule and supported by thousands of citations. Designed to quickly answer all questions about deductions.

Dictionary of PC Hardware and Data Communications Terms. Mitchell Shnier. Thomson Learning, 7625 Empire Dr. Florence, KY 41042. Phone: 800-347-7707 or (606)525-6620 Fax: (606)525-0978 URL: http://www.thomsonlearning.com • 1996. $19.95. (Online updates to print version available at http://www.ora.com/reference/dictionary.)

Dictionary of Personal Finance. Joel G. Siegel and others. Pearson Education and Technology, 201 W. 103rd St. Indianapolis, IN 46290-1097. Phone: 800-858-7674 or (317)581-3520 URL: http://www.mcp.com • 1993. $20.00.

Dictionary of Plastics Technology. H. D. Junge. John Wiley and Sons, Inc., 605 Third Ave. New York, NY 10158-0012. Phone: 800-225-5945 or (212)850-0662 Fax: (212)850-6088 E-mail: info@wiley.com • URL: http://www.wiley.com • 1987. $150.00.

The Dictionary of Practical Law. Charles F. Hemphill, Jr. and Phyllis Hemphill. Pearson Eduation and Technology, 201 W. 103rd St. Indianapolis, IN 46290-1097. Phone: 800-858-7674 or (317)581-3500 Fax: (317)581-4670 URL: http://www.mcp.com • 1979. $12.95.

Dictionary of Real Estate. Jae K. Shim and others. John Wiley and Sons, Inc., 605 Third Ave. New York, NY 10158-0012. Phone: 800-225-5945 or (212)850-6000 Fax: (212)850-6088 E-mail: info@jwiley.com • URL: http://www.wiley.com • 1995. $80.00. Contains 3,000 definitions of commercial and residential real estate terms. Covers appraisal, escrow, investment, finance, mortgages, property management, construction, legal aspects, etc. Includes illustrations and formulas. (Business Dictionaries Series).

Dictionary of Real Estate Appraisal. Jae Shim and others. Appraisal Institute, 875 N. Michigan Ave., Suite 2400 Chicago, IL 60611-1980. Phone: (312)335-4100 Fax: (312)819-2360 1996. $45.00. Second edition.

Dictionary of Shipping Terms. Peter Brodie. Available from Informa Publishing Group Ltd., PO Box 1017 Westborough, MA 01581-6017. Phone: 800-493-4080 Fax: (508)231-0856 E-mail: enquiries@informa.com • URL: http://www.informa.com • 1997. $57.00. Third edition. Published in the UK by Lloyd's List (http://www.lloydslist.com). Defines more than 2,000 words, phrases, and abbreviations related to the shipping and maritime industries.

A Dictionary of Statistical Terms. F.H. Marriott. Allyn and Bacon/Longman, 1185 Ave. of the Americas New York, NY 10036. Phone: 800-922-0579 E-mail: the.webmaster@ablongman.com • URL: http://www.ablongman.com • 1990. $76.65. Fifth edition.

Dictionary of Taxation. Simon James. Edward Elgar Publishing, Inc., 136 West St., Suite 202 Northampton, MA 01060. Phone: 800-390-3149 or (413)584-5551 Fax: (413)584-9933 E-mail: eep.orders@aidcvt.com • URL: http://www.e-elgar.co.uk • 1998. $65.00. Provides detailed definitions of terms relating to ''various aspects of taxes and tax systems throughout the world.''

Dictionary of the Graphic Arts Industry. Wolfgang Muller. Elsevier Science, 655 Ave. of the Americas New York, NY 10010. Phone: 888-437-4636 or (212)989-5800 Fax: (212)633-3680 E-mail: usinfo@elsevier.com • URL: http://www.elsevier.com • 1981. $240.75. Text in English, French, German, Hungarian, and Polish.

Dictionary of the History of the American Brewing and Distilling Industries. William L. Downard. Greenwood Publishing Group Inc., 88 Post Rd., W. Westport, CT 06881-5007. Phone: 800-225-5800 or (203)226-3571 Fax: (203)222-2540 E-mail: bookinfo@greenwood.com • URL: http://www.greenwood.com • 1980. $69.50.

Dictionary of Trade Name Origins. Adrian Room. NTC/Contemporary Publishing, P.O. Box 545 Blacklick, OH 43004. Phone: 800-338-3987 or (614)755-4151 Fax: (614)755-5645 E-mail: ntcpub@mcgraw-hill.com • URL: http://www.ntc-cb.com • 1994. $39.95. Revised edition.

Die Casting Engineer. North American Die Casting Association, 9701 W. Higgins Rd., No. 880 Rosemont, IL 60018-4721. Phone: (847)292-3600 Fax: (847)292-3620 E-mail: bralower@diecasting.org • URL: http://www.diecasting.org • Bimonthly. Free to members; non-members, $55.00 per year.

Diesel and Gas Turbine Worldwide: The International Engine Power Systems Magazine. Joseph M. Kane, editor. Diesel & Gas Turbine Publications, 20855 Watertown Rd. No.220 Waukesra, WI 53186-1873. Phone: (414)784-9177 Fax: (414)784-8133 10 times a year. $65.00 per year.

Diesel Progress North American Edition: For Engine, Drive and Hydraulic System Enginneering and Equipment Management. Diesel and Gas Turbine Publications, 20855 Watertown Rd., No.220 Waukesra, WI 53186-1873. Phone: (414)784-9177 Fax: (414)784-8133 Monthly. $75.00 per year. List of over 1,500 factory-authorized engine distributors and independent service keepers. Formerly *Diesel Progress Engines and Drives?*.

Diet and Meal Planning. Entrepreneur Media, Inc., 2445 McCabe Way Irvine, CA 92614. Phone: 800-421-2300 or (949)261-2325 Fax: (949)261-0234 E-mail: entmag@entrepreneur.com • URL: http://www.entrepreneur.com • Looseleaf. $59.50. A practical guide to starting a diet and meal planning service. Covers profit potential, start-up costs, market size evaluation, pricing, accounting, advertising, promotion, etc. (Start-Up Business Guide No. E2333.)

Dietary Managers Association.

Digest of Commercial Laws of the World. Paul E. Comeau and N. Stephan Kinsella. Oceana Publications, Inc., 75 Main St. Dobbs Ferry, NY 10522-1601. Phone: 800-831-0758 or (914)693-1733 Fax: (914)693-0402 E-mail: orders@oceanalaw.com • URL: http://www.oceanalaw.com • Looseleaf service. $295.00.

Digest of Education Statistics. Available from U. S. Government Printing Office, Washington, DC 20402. Phone: (202)512-1800 Fax: (202)512-2250 E-mail: gpoaccess@gpo.gov • URL: http://www.access.gpo.gov • Annual. $44.00. Covers all areas of education from kindergarten through graduate school. Includes data from both government and private sources. Compiled by National Center for Education Statistics, U. S. Department of Education.

Digital Audio and Compact Disk Technology. Luc Baert and others. Butterworth-Heinemann, 225 Wildwood Ave. Woburn, MA 01801. Phone: 800-366-2665 or (781)904-2500 Fax: 800-446-6520 E-mail: orders@bhusa.com • URL: http://www.bh.com • 1995. $57.95. Third edition.

Digital Cellular Telecommunications Systems. Douglas A. Kerr. McGraw-Hill, 1221 Ave. of the Americas New York, NY 10020. Phone: 800-722-4726 or (212)904-2000 Fax: (212)904-2072 E-mail: customer.service@mcgraw-hill.com • URL: http://www.mcgraw-hill.com • 1997. $50.00.

The Digital Daily. Internal Revenue ServicePhone: (202)622-5000 Fax: (202)622-5844 URL: http://www.irs.ustreas.gov • Web site provides a wide variety of tax information, including IRS forms and publications. Includes ''Highlights of New Tax Law.'' Searching is available. Fees: Free.

Digital Image Analysis Laboratory., University of Arizona, Dept. of Electrical and Computer Engineering Tucson, AZ 85721. Phone: (520)621-4554 Fax: (520)621-8076 E-mail: schowengerdt@ece.arizona.edu • URL: http://www.ece.arizona.edu/~dial • Research fields include image processing, computer vision, and artificial intelligence.

Digital Information Network. Buyers Laboratory, Inc., 108 John St. Hackensack, NJ 07601. Phone: (201)489-6439 Fax: (201)489-9365 E-mail: ctd@buyerslaboratory.com • URL: http://www/buyers-lab.com • Monthly. $725.00 per year. Newsletter. Information on the copier industry, including test reports on individual machines. Formerly *Digital Information Network*.

Digital Literacy: Personal Preparation for the Internet Age. Paul Gilster. John Wiley and Sons, Inc., 605 Third Ave. New York, NY 10158-0012. Phone: 800-225-5945 or (212)850-6000 Fax: (212)850-6088 E-mail: info@jwiley.com • URL: http://www.wiley.com • 1997. $22.95. Provides practical advice for the online consumer on how to evaluate various aspects of the Internet (''digital literacy'' is required, as well as ''print literacy'').

Digital Publishing Technologies: How to Implement New Media Publishing. Information Today, Inc., 143 Old Marlton Pike Medford, NJ 08055-8750. Phone: 800-300-9868 or (609)654-6266 Fax: (609)654-4309 E-mail: custserv@infotoday.com • URL: http://www.infotoday.com • Monthly. $196.00 per year. Covers online and CD-ROM publishing, including industry news, new applications, new products, electronic publishing technology, and descriptions of completed publishing projects.

Digital Video. CMP Media, Inc., 600 Harrison St., Fourth Floor San Francisco, CA 94107. Phone: (415)905-2200 Fax: (415)947-6050 E-mail: letters@dv.com • URL: http://www.dv.com • Monthly. $60.00 per year. Edited for professionals in the field of digital video production. Covers such topics as operating systems, videography, digital video cameras, audio, workstations, web video, software development, and interactive television.

Digital Video Buyer's Guide. CMP Media, Inc., 600 Harrison St., Fourth Floor San Francisco, CA 94107. Phone: (415)905-2200 Fax: (415)947-6050 E-mail: letters@dv.com • URL: http://www.dv.com • Annual. $10.00. A directory of professional video products, including digital cameras, monitors, editing systems, and software.

Digital X-Ray Markets: Imaging in the 21st Century. Theta Reports/PJB Medical Publications, Inc., 1775 Broadway, Suite 511 New York, NY 10019. Phone: (212)262-8230 Fax: (212)262-8234 E-mail: customerservice@thetareports.com • URL: http://www.thetareports.com • 2000. $1,995.00. Market research data. Covers digital filmless radiography as a replacement for traditional x-ray technology. (Theta Report No. 1027.)

Dinosaur Brains: Dealing with All Those Impossible People at Work. Albert J. Bernstein and Sydney C. Rozen. John Wiley and Sons, Inc., 605 Third Ave. New York, NY 10158-0012. Phone: 800-225-5945 or (212)850-6000 Fax: (212)850-6088 E-mail: info@wiley.com • URL: http://www.wiley.com • 1989. $29.95. How to cope with ''lizard logic'' and overcome the ''reptile response.'' That is, how to deal with irrational, impulsive, and self-destructive work behavior. Covers problem bosses, manipulators, self-promoters, the old boy network, etc.

Diplomatic and Consular Officers, Retired.

Diplomatic Bookshelf and Review. Arthur H. Thrower, Ltd., 44-46 S. Ealing Rd. London W5, England. Monthly.

Diplomatic History. Society for Historians of American Foreign Relations. Blackwell Publishers, 350 Main St., 6th Fl. Malden, MA 02148-5018. Phone: 800-216-2522 or (781)388-8200 Fax: (781)388-8210 E-mail: subscript@blackwell.pub • URL: http://www.blackwellpub.com • Quarterly. $109.00 per year.

Diplomatic List. U.S. Department of State. Available from U.S. Government Printing Office, Washington, DC 20402. Phone: (202)512-1800 Fax: (202)512-2250 Quarterly. $16.00 per year. List of foreign diplomats in and around Washington, D.C.

Diplomatic Observer. Institute for International Sociological Research, 50858 Weiner Weg Six Cologne, Germany. Monthly. $16.50 per year.

Diplomatic World Bulletin and Delegates World Bulletin: Dedicated to Serving the United Nations and the International Community. Diplomatic World Bulletin Publications, Inc., 307 E. 44th St., Suite A New York, NY 10017. Phone: (212)747-9500 Biweekly. $45.00 per year.

Direct: Magazine for Direct Marketing Management. Intertec Publinshing Co., 11 Riverbend Dr., S. Stamford, CT 06907-2524. Phone: 800-795-5445 or (203)358-9900 Fax: (203)358-5824 URL: http://www.intertec.com • Monthly. Free to qualified personnel; others, $74.00 per year.

Direct Marketing Association.

Direct Marketing, Direct Selling, and the Mature Consumer: A Research Study. James R. Lumpkin and others. Greenwood Publishing Group, Inc., 88 Post Rd., W. Westport, CT 06881-5007. Phone: (203)225-5800 or (203)226-3571 Fax: (203)222-2540 E-mail: bookinfo@greenwood.com • URL: http://www.greenwood.com • 1989. $62.95. A study of older consumers and their use of mail order, telephone shopping, party-plans, etc.

Direct Marketing Educational Foundation.

Direct Marketing List Source. SRDS, 1700 Higgins Rd. Des Plaines, IL 60018. Phone: 800-851-7737 or (847)375-5000 Fax: (847)375-5001 URL: http://www.srds.com • Bimonthly. $542.00 per year. Provides detailed information and rates for business, farm, and consumer mailing lists (U. S., Canadian, and international). Includes current postal information and directories of list brokers, compilers, and managers. Formerly *Direct Mail List Rates and Data*.

Direct Marketing Market Place: The Networking Source of the Direct Marketing Industry. National Register Publishing, 121 Chanlon Rd. New Providence, NJ 07974. Phone: 800-521-8110 or (908)464-6800 Fax: (908)790-5405 URL: http://www.reedref.com • Annual. $269.00. Lists direct marketers, service companies, creative sources, professional groups, photographers, paper suppliers, etc.

Direct Marketing Success: What Works and Why. Freeman F. Gosden. John Wiley and Sons, Inc., 605 Third Ave. New York, NY 10158-0012. Phone: 800-526-5368 or (212)850-6000 Fax: (212)850-6088 E-mail: info@wiley.com • URL: http://www.wiley.com • 1989. $24.95.

Direct Marketing: Using Direct Response Advertising to Enhance Marketing Database. Hoke Communications, Inc., 224 Seventh St. Garden City, NY 11530. Phone: 800-229-6700 or (516)746-6700 Fax: (516)294-8141 E-mail: 71410.2423@compuserve.com • Monthly. $65.00 per year. Direct marketing to consumers and business.

Direct Selling Association.

Direct Selling Association World Federation News. Direct Selling Association. World Federation of Direct Selling Associations, 1666 K St., N.W., Suite 1010 Washington, DC 20006-2808. Phone: (202)293-5760 Fax: (202)463-4569 E-mail: info@wfdsa.org • URL: http://www.wfdsa.org • Six times a year. Membership.

Direction: For the Moving and Storage Industry. American Moving and Storage Association, 1611 Duke St. Alexandria, VA 22314. Phone: (703)683-7410 Fax: (703)548-1845 E-mail: amc1@erols.com • Monthly. $35.00 per year. Newsletter on developments affecting the household goods movingindustry. Formerly *American Mover*.

Direction of Trade Statistics. International Monetary Fund. International Monetary Fund Publications Services, 700 19th St., N.W., Suite 12-607 Washington, DC 20431-0001. Phone: (202)623-7430 Fax: (202)623-7201 URL: http://www.imf.org • Quarterly. $110.00 per year. Includes *Yearbook*.

The Director. National Funeral Directors Association. NFDA Publications, Inc., 13625 Bishops Dr. Brookfield, WI 53005-6607. Phone: 800-228-6332 or (262)789-1880 Fax: (262)789-6977 E-mail: nfda@nfda.org • URL: http://www.nfda.org • Monthly $30.00 per year.

Directories in Print. The Gale Group, 27500 Drake Rd. Farmington Hills, MI 48331-3535. Phone: 800-877-GALE or (248)699-GALE Fax: 800-414-5043 or (248)699-8069 E-mail: galeord@galegroup.com • URL: http://www.galegroup.com • Annual. $530.00. Three volumes. Includes interedition *Supplement*. An annotated guide to approximately 15,500 business, industrial, professional, and scientific directories. Formerly *Directory of Directories*.

Directors & Boards., 1845 Walnut St., 9th Fl. Philadelphia, PA 19103-4709. Phone: (215)567-3200 Fax: (215)450-6078 Quarterly. $295.00 per year. Edited for corporate board members and senior executive officers.

Directors' and Officers' Liability. Practising Law Institute, 810 Seventh Ave. New York, NY 10019-5818. Phone: 800-260-4754 or (212)824-5700 Fax: (212)265-4742 E-mail: info@pli.edu • URL: http://www.pli.edu • Looseleaf. $125.00. Annual revisions. Covers all aspects of liability issues for corporate directors and executives. Indemnification, insurance, and dispute resolution are included as topics.

Directors' and Officers' Liability Insurance. Practising Law Institute, 810 Seventh Ave. New York, NY 10019-5818. Phone: 800-260-4754 or (212)824-5700 Fax: (212)265-4742 E-mail: info@pli.edu • URL: http://www.pli.edu • 1992. $70.00. Legal handbook. (Commercial Law and Practice Course Handbook Series).

Directors Guild of America.

Directors Guild of America Directory of Members. Directors Guild of America, 7920 Sunset Blvd. Hollywood, CA 90046. Phone: (310)289-2000 Fax: (310)289-2029 URL: http://www.dga.org • Annual. $25.00.

Director's Monthly. National Association of Corporate Directors, 1707 L St., N.W. Suite 560 Washington, DC 20036. Phone: (202)775-0509 Fax: (202)775-4857 Monthly. $350.00 per year. Newsletter.

Directory of Accredited Home Study Schools. National Home Study, 1601 18th St. N.W. Washington, DC 20009. Phone: (202)234-5100 Fax: (202)332-1386 E-mail: detc@detc.org • Annual. Free. Lists more than 70 accredited home study schools and the subjects they offer.

Directory of American Firms Operating in Foreign Countries. Uniworld Business Publications Inc., 257 Central Park W., Suite 10A New York, NY 10024-4110. Phone: (212)496-2448 Fax: (212)769-0413 E-mail: uniworldbp@aol.com • URL: http://www.uniworldbp.com • Biennial. $275.00. Three volumes. Lists approximately 2,450 American companies with more than 29,500 subsidiaries and affiliates in 138 foreign countries.

Directory of American Research and Technology: Organizations Active in Product Development for Business. R. R. Bowker, 121 Chanlon Rd. New Providence, NJ 07974. Phone: 888-269-5372 or (908)464-6800 Fax: (908)771-7704 E-mail: info@bowker.com • URL: http://www.bowker.com • Annual. $359.95. Lists over 13,000 publicly and privately owned research facilities. Formerly *Industrial Research Laboratories of the U.S.*

Directory of American Scholars. The Gale Group, 27500 Drake Rd. Farmington Hills, MI 48331-3535. Phone: 800-877-GALE or (248)699-GALE Fax: 800-414-5043 or (248)699-8069 E-mail: galeord@galegroup.com • URL: http://www.galegroup.com • 1999. $495.00. Ninth edition. Five volumes. Provides biographical information and publication history for more than 24,000 scholars in the humanities. Previously published (1942-1982) by R. R. Bowker.

Directory of Apparel Specialty Stores. Chain Store Age, 3922 Coconut Palm Dr. Tampa, FL 33619. Phone: 800-925-2288 or (813)664-6800 Fax: (813)664-6882 E-mail: info@csgis.com • URL: http://www.csgis.com • Annual. $260.00. Over 5,000 companies that own over 55,500 women's and 474 children's apparel specialty companies operating over 2,200 stores. Generally includes product lines, sales volume, year founded, key personnel, and related information.

Directory of Apparel Specialty Stores. Chain Store Guide, 3922 Coconut Palm Dr. Tampa, FL 33619. Phone: 800-778-9794 or (813)664-6800 Fax: (813)664-6882 URL: http://www.csgis.com • Annual. $260.00. Lists over 5,000 women's, men's, family and sporting goods retailers.

Directory of Association Meeting Planners and Conference/Convention Directors. Salesman's Guide, 2807 Parham Rd., Ste. 200 Richmond, VA 23294. Phone: 800-223-1797 or (804)762-4455 Fax: (804)935-0271 Annual. $259.95. Lists about 13,600 planners of meetings for over 8,100 national associations. Provides past and future convention locations, dates held, number of attendees, exhibit space required, and other convention information. Formerly *Association Meeting Planners*.

Directory of Automotive Aftermarket Suppliers. Chain Store Guide, 3922 Coconut Palm Dr. Tampa, FL 33619. Phone: 800-778-9794 or (813)664-6800 Fax: (813)664-6882 URL: http://www.csgis.com • Annual. $300.00. Covers auto supply store chains. Includes distributors.

Directory of Better Business Bureaus. Council of Better Business Bureaus, Inc., 4200 Wilson Blvd. No. 800 Arlington, VA 22203-1838. Phone: (703)276-0100 Fax: (703)525-8277 URL: http://www.bbb.org • Annual. Free. Send stamped, self-addressed envelope. Lists about 185 Better Business Bureaus in the United States and Canada.

Directory of British Associations and Associations in Ireland. CBD Research Research Ltd., 15 Wickham Rd. Beckenham, Kent BR3 5JS, England. Phone: 0208 650 7745 Fax: 0208 650 0768 E-mail: cbdresearch@compuserve.com • Biennial. $320.00. Lists about 7,000 national organizations of England Wales, Scotland, Northern Ireland, and the Irish Republic. Published by CBD Research.

Directory of Building Codes and Regulations. National Conference of States on Building Codes and Standards, 505 Huntmar Park Dr., Suite 210 Herndon, VA 20170. Phone: 800-362-2633 or (703)437-0100 Fax: (703)481-3596 E-mail: membership@ncsbcs.org • URL: http://www.ncsbcs.org • Annual, with quarterly updates. Two volumes. Members, $115.00; non-members, $150.00. In addition to information about residential and commerical building codes,includes a directory of state and majority administrators concerned with enforcement of the codes.

Directory of Building Products and Hardlines Distributors. Chain Store Guide, 3922 Coconut Palm Dr. Tampa, FL 33619. Phone: 800-778-9794 or (813)664-6800 Fax: (813)664-6882 URL: http://www.csgis.com • Annual. $280.00. Includes hardware, houseware, and building supply distributors. Formerly *Directory of Hardline Distributors*.

The Directory of Business Information Resources: Associations, Newsletters, Magazine Trade Shows. Grey House Publishing, Inc., Pocket Knife Square Lakeville, CT 06039. Phone: 800-562-2139 or (860)435-0868 Fax: 800-248-0115 or (860)435-3004 E-mail: books@greyhouse.com • URL: http://www.greyhouse.com • Annual. $195.00. Provides concise information on associations, newsletters, magazines, and trade shows for each of 90 major industry groups. An ''Entry & Company Index'' serves as a guide to titles, publishers, and organizations.

Directory of Business-to-Business Catalogs. Grey House Publishing, Pocket Knife Square Lakeville, CT 06039. Phone: 800-562-2139 or (860)435-0868 Fax: 800-248-0115 or (860)435-3004 E-mail: books@greyhouse.com • URL: http://www.greyhouse.com • Annual. $190.00. Provides over 6,000 listings of U. S. mail order companies selling business or industrial products and services.

Directory of Buyout Financing Sources. Securities Data Publishing, 40 West 57th St. New York, NY 10019. Phone: 800-455-5844 or (212)765-5311 Fax: (212)956-0112 E-mail: sdp@tfn.com • URL: http://www.sdponline.com • Annual. $395.00. Describes more than 1,000 U. S. and foreign sources of financing for buyout deals. Indexed by personnel, company, industry, and location. (Securities Data Publishing is a unit of Thomson Financial.)

Directory of Canadian Trademarks. Thomson & Thomson, 500 Victory Rd. North Quincy, MA 02171-3145. Phone: 800-692-8833 or (617)479-1600 Fax: (617)786-8273 E-mail: support@thomson-thomson.com • URL: http://www.thomson-thomson.com • Annual. Price on application. Provides owner, registration, and classification information for Canadian trademarks registered with the Canadian Intellectual Property Office (CIPO).

Directory of Certified Product Safety Managers. Board of Certified Product Safety Management, 8009 Carita Court Bethesda, MD 20817. Phone: (301)770-2540 Fax: (301)770-2540 E-mail: bchcm@juno.com • Biennial. $15.00. Membership directory.

Directory of Chain Restaurant Operators. Chain Store Guide, 3922 Coconut Palm Dr. Tampa, FL 33619. Phone: 800-778-9794 or (813)664-6800 Fax: (813)664-6882 URL: http://www.cagis.com • Annual. $300.00. Includes fast food establishments, and leading chain hotel copanies operating foodservice unit.

Directory of Chemical Producers - United States. SRI Consulting, 333 Ravenswood Ave. Menlo Park, CA 94025-3493. Phone: (650)859-3627 Fax: (650)859-4623 E-mail: inquiry_line@sri.com • URL: http://www.cbrd.sriconsulting.com • Annual. $2,030.00. Information on over 1,200 United States basic chemical producers, manufacturing nearly 8,000 chemicals in commercial quantities at 3,500 plant locations.

Directory of College Stores. B. Klein Publications, Inc., P.O. Box 6578 Delray Beach, FL 33482. Phone: (407)496-3316 Fax: (407)496-5546 Irregular. $75.00. Covers about 4,400 stores selling books, stationery, personal care items, gifts, etc., which serve primarily a college student population.

Directory of Companies Required to File Annual Reports with the Securities and Exchange Commission. Securities and Exchange Commission. Available from U.S. Government Printing Office, Washington, DC 20402. Phone: (202)512-1800 Fax: (202)512-2250 Annual. $46.00.

Directory of Composites Manufacturers, Suppliers, and Services. Society of Manufacturing Engineers, P.O. Box 930 Dearborn, MI 48121-0930. Phone: 800-733-4763 or (313)271-1500 Fax: (313)271-2861 URL: http://www.sme.org • Biennial. $25.00 per year. Provides information for more than 500 firms involved in the production of composite materials: composite manufacturers, material suppliers, service companies, consultants, etc.

Directory of Computer and Consumer Electronics. Chain Store Age, 3922 Coconut Palm Dr. Tampa, FL 33619. Phone: 800-925-2288 or (813)664-6800 Fax: (813)664-6882 E-mail: info@csgis.com • URL: http://www.csgis.com • Annual. $290.00. Includes 2,900 ''leading'' retailers and over 200 ''top'' distributors. Formerly *Directory of Consumer Electronics Retails and Distributors*.

Directory of Computer Consumer Electronics Retailers. Chain Store Guide, 425 Park Ave. New York, NY 10022. Phone: 800-778-9794 or (813)664-6800 Fax: (813)664-6882 URL: http://www.csigis.com • Annual. $290.00. Detailed information about companies operating computer and/or computer software stores. Formerly *Directory of Computer Dealers and Distributors Retailers*.

Directory of Computer V A R's and System Integrators. Chain Store Guide, 3922 Coconut Palm Dr. Tampa, FL 33619. Phone: 800-778-9794 or (813)664-6800 Fax: (813)664-6882 URL: http://www.csgis.com • Annual. $290.00. Provides information on computer companies that modify, enhance, or customize hardware or software. Includes systems houses, systems integrators, turnkey systems specialists, original equipment manufacturers, and value added retailers. Formerly *Directory of Value Added Resellers*.

Directory of Consumer Brands and Their Owners: Asia Pacific. Available from The Gale Group, 27500 Drake Rd. Farmington Hills, MI 48331-3535. Phone: 800-877-GALE or (248)699-GALE Fax: 800-414-5043 or (248)699-8069 E-mail: cbdresearch@compuserve.com • 1998. $990.00. Published by Euromonitor. Provides information about brands available from major Asia Pacific companies. Descriptions of companies are also included.

Directory of Consumer Brands and Their Owners: Eastern Europe. Available from The Gale Group, 27500 Drake Rd. Farmington Hills, MI 48331-3535. Phone: 800-877-GALE or (248)699-GALE Fax: 800-414-5043 or (248)699-8063 E-mail: cbdresearch@compuserve.com • URL: http://www.galegroup.com • 1998. $990.00. Published by Euromonitor. Provides information about brands available from major Eastern European companies. Descriptions of companies are also included.

Directory of Consumer Brands and Their Owners: Europe. Available from The Gale Group, 27500 Drake Rd. Farmington Hills, MI 48331-3535. Phone: 800-877-GALE or (248)699-GALE Fax: 800-414-5043 or (248)699-8069 URL: http://www.galegroup.com • 1998. $990.00. Two volumes. Third edition. Published by Euromonitor. Provides information about brands available from major European companies. Descriptions of companies are also included.

Directory of Consumer Brands and Their Owners: Latin America. Available from The Gale Group, 27500 Drake Rd. Farmington Hills, MI 48331-3535. Phone: 800-877-GALE or (248)699-GALE Fax: 800-414-5043 or (248)699-8069 URL: http://www.galegroup.com • 1999. $990.00. Published by Euromonitor. Provides information about brands available from major Latin American companies. Descriptions of companies are also included.

Directory of Conventions Regional Editions. Bill Communications, 770 Broadway New York, NY 10003. Phone: 800-266-4712 or (646)654-4500 Fax: (646)654-7212 URL: http://www.billcom.com • Annual. $155.00 per volume. Four volumes. Set $285.00. Over 14,000 meetings of North American national, regional, and state and local organizations.

Directory of Corporate Affiliations. National Register Publishing, 121 Chanlon Rd. New Providence, NJ 07974. Phone: 800-521-8110 or (908)464-6800 Fax: (908)790-5405 E-mail: info@reedref.com • URL: http://www.reedref.com • Annual. $1,159.00. Five volumes. Volumes one and two: Master Index; volume three: U.S. Public Companies; volume four: U.S. Private Companies; volume five: International Public and Private Companies.

Directory of Corporate Meeting Planners. Salesman's Guide, 2807 Parham Rd., Ste. 200 Richmond, VA 23294. Phone: 800-223-1797 or (804)762-4455 Fax: (804)935-0271 E-mail: eblank@douglaspublications.com • URL: http://www.salesmanguide.com • Annual. $385.00. Lists about 18,000 planners of off-site meetings for over 11,000 U. S. and Canadian corporations. Provides information on number of attendees and professional speaker usage.

Directory of Counseling Services. International Association of Counseling Services, 101 S. Whiting, Suite 211 Alexandria, VA 22304-3416. Phone: (703)823-9840 Fax: (703)823-9843 E-mail: iacs@gmu.edu • Annual. $50.00. About 200 accredited services in the United States and Canada concerned with psychological educational, and vocational counseling, including those at colleges and universities and public and private agencies.

Directory of Delicatessen Products. Pacific Rim Publishing Co., P.O. Box 4533 Huntington Beach, CA 92605-4533. Phone: (714)375-3904 Fax: (714)375-3906 Annual. Included with February issue of *Deli News*. Lists suppliers of cheeses, lunch meats, packaged fresh meats, kosher foods, gourmet-specialty items, and bakery products.

Directory of Department Stores. Chain Store Guide, 3922 Coconut Palm Dr. Tampa, FL 33619. Phone: 800-778-9794 or (813)664-6800 Fax: (813)664-6882 URL: http://www.csgis.com • Annual. $290.00. Lists over 350 department stores and 1,100 mail order firms.

Directory of Discount and General Merchandise Stores. Chain Store Guide, 3922 Coconut Palm Dr. Tampa, FL 33619. Phone: 800-778-9794 or (813)664-6800 Fax: (813)664-6882 URL: http://www.csgis.com • Annual. $300.00. Includes retailers and wholesalers of housewares, giftwares, novelties, toys, hobby materials, crafts, and stationery. Formerly *Directory of Discount Stores Catalog Showrooms*.

Directory of Electrical Wholesale Distributors. Intertec Publishing Corp., P.O. Box 12901 Overland Park, KS 66282-2901. Phone: 800-400-5945 or (913)341-1300 Fax: (913)967-1898 E-mail: subs@intertec.com • URL: http://www.intertec.com • Biennial. $695.00. Over 2,800 companies with over 9,000 locations.

Directory of Environmental Attorneys. Aspen Law and Business, 1185 Ave. of the Americas New York, NY 10036. Phone: 800-444-1717 or (212)597-0200 Fax: 800-901-9075 or (212)597-0338 URL: http://www.aspenpub.com • 1994. $195.00.

Directory of EU Information Sources. Euroconfidentiel S. A., Rue de Rixensart 18 B-1332 Genval, Belgium. Phone: (32)02 653 01 25 Fax: (32)02 653 01 80 E-mail: nigel.hunt@euronet.be • Annual. $250.00. Lists more than 12,500 publications, associations, consultants, law firms, diplomats, jounalists, and other sources of information about Europe and the European Union.

Directory of Executive Compensation Consultants. Kennedy Information, LLC, One Kennedy Place, Route 12, S. Fitzwilliam, NH 03447. Phone: 800-531-1026 or (603)585-3101 Fax: (603)585-9555 E-mail: office@kennedypub.com • URL: http://www.kennedyinfo.com • 1993. $47.50. Includes over 250 office locations maintained by about 65 executive compensation consulting firms.

Directory of Executive Recruiters. Kennedy Information, LLC, One Kennedy Place, Route 12, S. Fitzwilliam, NH 03447. Phone: 800-531-1026 or (603)585-3101 Fax: (603)585-9555 E-mail: office@kennedypub.com • URL: http://www.kennedyinfo.com • Annual. $44.95. Contains profiles of more than 4,000 executive recruiting firms in the U. S., Canada, and Mexico.

Directory of Federal Libraries. William R. Evinger, editor. Oryx Press, 4041 N. Central Ave., Ste. 700 Phoenix, AZ 85012-3397. Phone: 800-279-6799 or (602)265-2651 Fax: 800-279-4663 or (602)265-6250 E-mail: info@oryxpress.com • URL: http://www.oryxpress.com • 1997. $97.50. Third edition.

Directory of Foodservice Distributors. Chain Store Guide, 3922 Coconut Store Guide Tampa, FL 33619. Phone: 800-778-9794 or (813)664-6800 Fax: (813)664-6882 URL: http://www.csgis.com • Annual. $290.00. Covers distributors of food and equipment to restaurants and institutions.

Directory of Foreign Firms Operating in the United States. Uniworld Business Publications, Inc., 257 Central Park W., Suite 10-A New York, NY 10024-4110. Phone: (212)496-2448 Fax: (212)769-0413 E-mail: uniworldbp@aol.com • URL: http://www.uniworldbp.com • Biennial. $225.00. Lists about 2,400 foreign companies and 5,700 American affiliates. 75 countries are represented.

Directory of Franchising Organizations. Pilot Books, P.O. Box 2102 Greenport, NY 11944-1439. Phone: (516)477-1094 Fax: (516)477-0978 E-mail: feedback@pilotbooks.com • URL: http://www.pilotbooks.com • Annual. $12.95. Lists the nation's top franchises with description and cost of investment.

Directory of Funparks and Attractions: International Guide to Amusement Parks, Family Entertainment Centers, Waterparks, and Attractions. BPI Communications, Amusement Business Div., P.O. Box 24970 Nashville, TN 37202. Phone: 800-999-3322 or (615)321-4250 Fax: (615)327-1575 E-mail: info@bpi.com • URL: http://www.bpicomm.com • Annual. $60.00. Over 2,100, amusement parks, theme parks, family entertainment centers, water parks, zoos, kiddielands and other tourist attractions in U.S., Canada and overseas. Formerly *Amusement Business Directory of Funparks and Attractions*.

Directory of Golf. National Golf Foundation, 1150 S. U.S. Highway 1, Suite 401 Jupiter, FL 33477. Phone: 800-733-6006 or (561)744-6006 Fax: (561)744-6107 E-mail: ngf@ngf.org • URL: http://www.ngf.org • Annual $60.00. Lists golf course architects, contractors, builders, appraisers, and consulting firms. Golf equipment manufacturers are also included.

Directory of Government Document Collections and Librarians. Government Documents Round Table. American Library Association, Washington Office, 1301 Pennsylvania Ave., N.W., Suite 403 Washington, DC 20002. Phone: (202)628-8410 Fax: (202)629-8419 Seventh edition. Price on application. A guide to federal, state, local, foreign, and international document collections in the U.S. Includes name of libratians and other government document professionals.

Directory of Graduate Programs. Educational Testing Service, Princeton, NJ 08541-0001. Phone: (609)921-9000 Irregular. $80.00. Four volumes. $20.00 per volume. 15th edition. Accredited institutions that offer advanced deree in 84 graduate program areas. Degrees not included are J.D., D.D.S., M.D. and some other professional degrees.

Directory of Grants for Organizations Serving People with Disabilities: A Guide to Sources of Funding in the United States for Programs and Services for Personswith Disabilities. Richard M. Eckstein. Research Grant Guides, P.O. Box 1214 Loxahatchee, FL 33470. Phone: (561)795-6129 Fax: (561)795-7794 URL: http://www.researchgrant.com • Biennial. $59.50. Lists over 800 foundations, associations, and government agencies that grant funds to non-profit organizations for projects related to handicapped persons. Formerly *Handicapped Funding Directory*.

Directory of Health Care Professionals. Dorland Healthcare Information, 1500 Walnut St., Suite 1000 Philadelphia, PA 19102. Phone: 800-784-2332 or (215)875-1212 Fax: (215)735-3966 E-mail: info@dorlandhealth.com • URL: http://www.dorlandhealth.com • Annual. $299.00. Lists about 175,000 professional staff members at 7,000 U. S. hospitals and health systems.

Directory of High Volume Independent Restaurants. Chain Store Guide, 3922 Coconut Palm Dr. Tampa, FL 33619. Phone: 800-778-9794 or (813)664-6800 Fax: (813)664-6882 URL: http://www.csgis.com • Annual. $300.00. Approximately 8,000 independently owned restaurants with minimum sales of greater than $1 million.

Directory of Home Center Operators and Hardware Chains. Chain Store Age, 3922 Coconut Palm Dr. Tampa, FL 33619. Phone: 800-925-2288 or (813)664-6800 Fax: (813)664-6882 E-mail: info@csgis.com • URL: http://www.csgis.com • Annual. $300.00. Nearly 5,400 home center operators, paint and home decorating chains, and lumber and building materials companies.

Directory of Home Furnishings Retailers. Chain Store Guide, 3922 Coconut Palm Dr. Tampa, FL 33619. Phone: 800-778-9794 or (813)664-6800 Fax: (813)664-6882 URL: http://www.csgis.com • Annual. $290.00. Includes more than 4,800 furniture retailers and wholesalers.

Directory of Hospital Personnel. Medical Economics Co., Inc., Five Paragon Dr Montvale, NJ 07645-1742. Phone: 800-745-2601 or (201)358-7200 Fax: (201)573-8999 E-mail: customerservice@medec.com • URL: http://www.medec.com • Annual. $325.00. Lists over 200,000 healthcare professionals in 7,000 U. S. hospitals. Geographic arrangement, with indexes by personnel, hospital name, and bed size.

Directory of Hotel and Motel Companies. American Hotel and Motel Association, 1201 New York Ave., N.W., Suite 600 Washington, DC 20005-3917. Phone: 800-621-6902 or (202)289-3157 Fax: (202)289-3199 E-mail: rturner.ahma.com • Annual. $79.00 per year. International coverage.

Directory of Intellectual Property Attorneys. Aspen Law and Business, 1185 Ave. of the Americas New York, NY 10036. Phone: 800-444-1717 or (212)597-0200 Fax: 800-901-9075 or (212)597-0338 E-mail: customer.service@aspenpubl.com • URL: http://www.aspenpub.com • Annual. Price on application.

Directory of International Corporate Giving in America and Abroad. Available from The Gale Group, 27500 Drake Rd. Farmington Hills, MI 48331-3535. Phone: 800-877-GALE or (248)699-GALE Fax: 800-414-5043 or (248)699-8069 E-mail: galeord@galegroup.com • URL: http://www.galegroup.com • 1997. $205.00. Contains details of the philanthropic activities of over 650 major foreign corporations with operations in the U. S. Includes 18 indexes.

Directory of Iron and Steel Plants (The Black Book). Association of Iron and Steel Engineers, Three Gateway Center,

Suite 1900 Pittsburgh, PA 15222-1004. Phone: (412)281-6323 Fax: (412)281-6216 E-mail: directory@aise.org • Annual. $50.00. Lists executives and officials in the United States and selected overseas steel companies and plants.

Directory of Japanese-Affiliated Companies in the USA and Canada. Available from The Gale Group, 27500 Drake Rd. Farmington Hills, MI 48331-3535. Phone: 800-877-GALE or (248)699-GALE Fax: 800-414-5043 or (248)699-8069 E-mail: galeord@galegroup.com • URL: http://www.galegroup.com • Annual. $375.00. Published by the Japanese External Trade Organization (JETRO). Provides data on more than 5,000 Japanese-affiliated companies located in the U. S. and Canada. (CD-ROM version included with printed directory.)

Directory of Judges with Juvenile/Family Law Jurisdiction. National Council of Juvenile and Family Court Judges, P.O. Box 8970 Reno, NV 89507. Phone: (702)784-6012 Fax: (702)784-1084 Irregular. $25.00. 1,400 judges who have juvenile, family, or domestic relations jurisdiction.

Directory of Juvenile and Adult Correctional Departments, Institutions, Agencies, and Paroling Authorities. American Correctional Association, 4380 Forbes Blvd. Lanham, MD 20706-4322. Phone: 800-222-5646 or (301)918-1800 Fax: (301)918-1900 E-mail: admin@aca.com • URL: http://www.aca.org • Annual. $80.00. Provides information on approximately 4,000 correctional agencies and institutions in the U. S. and Canada.

Directory of Legislative Leaders. National Conference of State Legislatures, 1560 Broadway, No. 700 Denver, CO 80202-5140. Phone: (303)830-2200 Fax: (303)863-8003 E-mail: books@ncsl.org • URL: http://www.ncsl.org • Annual. $20.00. Lists state presiding officers, majority and minority leaders, and key staff members. Preferred addresses, telephone numbers, and fax numbers are included.

Directory of Library Automation Software, Systems, and Services. Information Today, Inc., 143 Old Marlton Pike Medford, NJ 08055-8750. Phone: 800-300-9868 or (609)654-6266 Fax: (609)654-4309 E-mail: custserv@infotoday.com • URL: http://www.infotoday.com • Biennial. $89.00. Provides detailed descriptions of about 330 software programs and software services for libraries.

Directory of Litigation Attorneys. Aspen Law and Business, 1185 Ave. of the Americas New York, NY 10036. Phone: 800-444-1717 or (212)597-0200 Fax: 800-901-9075 or (212)597-0338 URL: http://www.aspenpub.com • 1993. $450.00. Two volumes. Includes about 40,000 attorneys, 15,000 law firms, and 100 areas of litigation specialization.

Directory of M & A Intermediaries. Securities Data Publishing, 40 West 57th St. New York, NY 10019. Phone: 800-455-5844 or (212)765-5311 Fax: (212)956-0112 E-mail: sdp@tfn.com • URL: http://www.sdponline.com • Annual. $360.00. Lists more than 850 dealmakers for mergers and acquisitions, including investment banks, business brokers, and commercial banks. (Securities Data Publishing is a unit of Thomson Financial.)

Directory of Mail Order Catalogs. Grey House Publishing, Pocket Knife Square Lakeville, CT 06039. Phone: 800-562-2139 or (860)435-0868 Fax: 800-248-0115 or (860)435-3004 E-mail: books@greyhouse.com • URL: http://www.greyhouse.com • Annual. $275.00. Contains 11,000 entries for mail order companies selling consumer products throughout the U.S.

Directory of Mailing List Companies. Todd Publications, P.O. Box 635 West Nyack, NY 10960-0635. Phone: 800-747-1056 or (914)358-6213 Fax: (914)358-1059 E-mail: toddpub@aol.com • URL: http://www.toddpublications.com • Biennial. $50.00. Lists and describes approximately 1,100 of the most active list brokers, owners, managers and compilers.

Directory of Management Consultants. Kennedy Information, LLC, One Kennedy Place, Route 12, S. Fitzwilliam, NH 03447. Phone: 800-531-1026 or (603)585-3101 Fax: (603)585-9555 E-mail: office@kennedypub.com • URL: http://www.kennedyinfo.com • Annual. $149.00. Contains profiles of more than 1,800 general and specialty management consulting firms in the U. S., Canada, and Mexico.

Directory of Manufacturers Supporting the Writing and Marking Instrument Industry. Writing Instrument Manufacturers Association, 236 Route 38 W., Suite 100 Moorestown, NJ 08057. Phone: (609)231-8500 Fax: (609)231-4664 E-mail: wima@ahint.com • Biennial. $50.00. About 200 manufacturers; includes non-members. Formerly *Directory of Manufacturers and Products of the Handwriting Instrument Manufacturing Industry*.

Directory of Marketing Information Companies. American Demographics, Inc., P.O. Box 4949 Stamford, CT 06907. Phone: 800-828-1133 E-mail: editors@demographics.com • URL: http://www.marketingtools.com • Annual. $10.00. Lists companies offering market research and information services, with a selection of the ''Best 100 Sources of Marketing Information.''

Directory of Minority-Owned Professional and Personnel Services Consultants. San Francisco Redevelopment Agency, 770 Golden Gate Ave. San Francisco, CA 94101-3120. Phone: (415)749-2423 Fax: (415)749-2590 Annual. Free. About 650 minority firms in Northern California.

Directory of Multinationals. Available from The Gale Group, 27500 Drake Rd. Farmington Hills, MI 48331-3535. Phone: 800-877-GALE or (248)699-GALE Fax: 800-414-5043 or (248)699-8069 URL: http://www.galegroup.com • 1998. $695.00. Two volumes. Fifth edition. Published by Waterlow Specialist Information Publishing. Provides detailed information on multinational firms with total annual sales in excess of one billion dollars and overseas sales in excess of $500 million. Includes narrative company descriptions and statistical data.

Directory of North American Fairs, Festivals and Expositions. BPI Communications, Amusement Business Div., P.O. Box 24970 Nashville, TN 37202. Phone: 800-344-7119 or (615)321-4250 Fax: (615)327-1575 E-mail: info@bpi.com • URL: http://www.amusementbusiness.com • Annual. $65.00. Lists over 5,000 fairs, festivals and expositions in the U.S. and Canada which run three days or more. Formerly *Calvacade and Directory of Fairs*.

Directory of Nursing Homes. Dorland Healthcare Information, 1500 Walnut St., Suite 1000 Philadelphia, PA 19102. Phone: 800-784-2332 or (215)875-1212 Fax: (215)735-3966 E-mail: info@dorlandhealth.com • URL: http://www.dorlandhealth.com • Annual. $249.00. Provides information on admission requirements, resident facilities, and staff at more than 16,500 nursing homes.

Directory of Obsolete Securities. Financial Information, Inc., 30 Montgomery St. Jersey City, NJ 07302-0473. Phone: 800-367-3441 or (201)332-5400 Fax: 800-344-3292 Annual. Qualified personnel, $595.00.

Directory of Operating Grants. Research Grant Guides, P.O. Box 1214 Loxahatchee, FL 33470. Phone: (561)795-6129 Fax: (561)795-7794 URL: http://www.researchgrant.com • Annual. $59.50. Contains profiles for approximately 800 foundations that award grants to nonprofit organizations for such operating expenses as salaries, rent, and utilities. Geographical arrangement, with indexes.

Directory of Outplacement and Career Management Firms. Kennedy Information, LLC, One Kennedy Place, Route 12 S. Fitzwilliam, NH 03447. Phone: 800-531-1026 or (603)585-3101 Fax: (603)585-9555 E-mail: office@kennedypub.com • URL: http://www.kennedyinfo.com • Annual. $129.95. Contains profiles of more than 320 firms specialize in helping ''downsized'' executives find new employment.

Directory of Partnership Sponsors. American Partnership Board, Inc., 10 S. Riverside Plaza, Suite 1100 Chicago, IL 60606-3708. Phone: 800-272-6273 or (312)332-4100 Fax: (312)332-3171 Annual. $199.00. A directory of more than 400 major sponsors of publicly registered and private placement limited partnerships.

Directory of Physician Groups and Networks. Dorland Healthcare Information, 1500 Walnut St., Suite 1000 Philadelphia, PA 19102. Phone: 800-784-2332 or (215)875-1212 Fax: (215)735-3966 E-mail: info@dorlandhealth.com • URL: http://www.dorlandhealth.com • Annual. $345.00. Lists more than 4,200 independent practice associations (IPAs), physician hospital organizations (PHOs), management service organizations (MSOs), physician practice management companies (PPMCs), and group practices having 20 or more physicians.

Directory of Physicians in the United States. American Medical Association, 515 N. State St. Chicago, IL 60610-4377. Phone: 800-262-2350 or (312)464-5000 Fax: (312)464-4184 E-mail: amaa@ama-assn.org • URL: http://www.ama-assn.org • Biennial. $595.00. Four volumes. Brief information for more than 686,000 physicians. Formerly*American Medical Directory*.

Directory of Premium, Incentive, and Travel Buyers. Salesman's Guide, 2807 N. Parham Rd., Ste. 200 Richmond, NJ 23294. Phone: 800-223-1797 or (804)762-4455 Fax: (804)935-0271 E-mail: eblank@douglaspublications.com • URL: http://www.salesmansguide.com • Annual. $275.00. Provides information on about 19,000 buyers of premiums, incentive programs, and travel programs for motivation of sales personnel.

Directory of Privately-Owned Hospitals,Residential Treatment Facilities and Centers, Hospital Management Companies, and Health Systems. Federation of American Health Systems, 1405 N. Pierce St., Suite 311 Little Rock, AR 72207. Phone: (501)661-9555 Fax: (501)663-4903 Annual. $125.00

Directory of Regional Councils. National Association of Regional Councils, 1700 K St. N.W., Suite 1300 Washington, DC 20006. Phone: (202)457-0710 Fax: (202)296-9353 Annual. $100.00. Lists about 535 regional councils within U.S., including contacts and counties they serve. Formerly *National Association of Regional Councils-Directory of Regional Councils*.

Directory of Registered Investment Advisors. Money Market Directories, Inc., P.O. Box 1608 Charlottesville, VA 22902. Phone: 800-446-2810 or (804)997-1450 Fax: (804)979-9962 URL: http://www.mmdaccess.com • Annual. $450.00. Lists over 14,000 investment advisors and advisory firms. Indicates services offered, personnel, and amount of assets being managed. Formerly *Directory of Registered Investment Advisors with the Securities and Exchange Commission*.

Directory of Research Grants. Oryx Press, 4041 N. Central Ave., Ste. 700 Phoenix, AZ 85012-3379. Phone: 800-279-6799 or (602)265-2651 Fax: 800-279-4663 or (602)265-6250 E-mail: info@oryxpress.com • URL: http://www.oryxpress.com • Annual. $135.00. More than 6,000 research grants available from government, business, foundation and private sources.

Directory of Retail Chains in Canada. Maclean Hunter Business Publications, 777 Bay St. Toronto, ON, Canada M5W 1A7. Phone: (416)596-5000 Fax: (416)596-5553 URL: http://www.mhbizlink.com • Annual. $340.00. Provides detailed information on approximately 1,600 retail chains of all sizes in Canada.

Directory of Retirement Facilities. Dorland Healthcare Information, 1500 Walnut St., Suite 1000 Philadelphia, PA 19102. Phone: 800-784-2332 or (215)875-1212 Fax: (215)735-3966 E-mail: info@dorlandhealth.com • URL: http://www.dorlandhealth.com • Annual. $249.00. Lists more than 18,500 assisted living, congregate care, independent living, and continuing care facilities.

Directory of Single Unit Supermarket Operators. Chain Store Guide, 33619 Coconut Palm Dr. Tampa, FL 33619. Phone: 800-778-9794 or (813)664-6800 Fax: (813)664-6882 URL: http://www.csgis.com • Annual. $290.00. Covers more than 7,100 one-store supermarket establishments with annual sales of at least $1,000,000. Includes names of primary wholesalers.

Directory of Special Libraries and Information Centers. The Gale Group, 27500 Drake Rd. Farmington Hills, MI 48331-3535. Phone: 800-877-GALE or (248)699-GALE Fax: 800-414-5043 or (248)699-8069 E-mail: galeord@galegroup.com • URL: http://www.galegroup.com • 1999. $845.00. 25th edition. Three volumes. Two available separately: volume one,*Directory of Special Libraries and Information Centers*, $610.00; volume two *Geographic and Personnel Indexes*, $510.00. Contains 24,000 entries from the U.S., Canada, and 80 other countries. A detailed subject index is included in volume one.

Directory of SRCC Certified Collectors and Solar Water Heating Systems Ratings. Solar Rating and Certification Corp., c/o FSEC, 1697 Clearlake Rd. Cocoa, FL 32927-5703. Phone: (407)638-1537 Fax: (407)638-1010 E-mail: srcc@fsec.ucf.edu • Irregular. $33.00. About 20 manufacturers of solar collectors and systems certified by the Organization. Includes technical information.

Directory of Standards Laboratories. National Conference of Standards Laboratories, 1800 30th St., Suite 305B Boulder, CO 80301. Phone: (303)440-3339 Fax: (303)440-3384 E-mail: ncsl-staff@ncsl-hq.org • Biennial. Members, $30.00 per year; non-members, $120.00 per year. Lists about 1,500 measurement standards laboratories.

Directory of State and Local Mortgage Bankers Association. Mortgage Bankers Association of America, c/o Janice Stango, 1125 15th St., N.W. Washington, DC 20005. Phone: 800-793-6222 or (202)861-6500 Fax: (202)785-2967 E-mail: info@mbaa.org • URL: http://www.mbaa.org • Irregular. $50.00.

Directory of Statisticians. American Statistical Association, 1429 Duke St. Alexandria, VA 22314-3415. Phone: (703)684-1211 Fax: (703)684-2037 E-mail: asainfo@amstat.org • URL: http://www.amstat.org • Triennial. Free to members; non-members, $125.00. List more than 25,000 memebers.

Directory of Steel Foundries and Buyers Guide. Steel Founders' Society of America, 205 Park Ave. Barrington, IL 60010. Phone: (847)382-8240 Fax: (847)382-8287 E-mail: monroe@scra.org • URL: http://www.sfsa.org • Biennial. $95.00. Formerly *Directory of Steel Foundries in the United States, Canada, and Mexico*.

Directory of Supermarket, Grocery, and Convenience Store Chains. Chain Store Guide, 3922 Coconut Palm Dr. Tampa, FL 33619. Phone: 800-927-9292 or (813)664-6800 Fax: (813)664-6882 URL: http://www.csgis.com • Annual. $300.00. Provides information on about 2,200 food store chains operating 30,000 individual stores. Store locations are given.

Directory of the Canning, Freezing, Preserving Industries. Edward E. Judge and Sons, Inc., P.O. Box 866 Westminster, MD 21158. Phone: (410)876-2052 Fax: (410)848-2034 E-mail: info@ejudge.com • URL: http://www.eejudge.com • Biennial. $175.00. Provides information on about 2,950 packers of a wide variety of food products.

Directory of the Decorating Products Industry. Painting and Decorating Retailers Association, 403 Axminster Dr. Fenton, MO 63026. Phone: 800-737-0107 or (314)326-2636 Fax: (314)326-1823 E-mail: info@pdra.org • URL: http://www.pdra.org • Annual. $595.00. Lists nearly 2,800 retailers of window treatments, wall coverings, floor coverings, etc. Formerly *Directory of Decorating Products Retailers*. Formerly National Decorating Products Association.

Directory of the Refractories Industry. The Refractories Institute, 650 Smithfield St., Suite 1160 Pittsburgh, PA 15222-3907. Phone: (412)281-6787 Fax: (412)281-6881

E-mail: triassn@aol.com • Irregular. Members, $45.00; non-members, $85.00.

Directory of the Savings and Community Bankers of America. American Community Bankers of America, 900 19th St., N.W., Suite 400 Washington, DC 20006-5002. Phone: 800-321-3373 or (202)857-3100 Fax: (202)296-8716 Annual. Members $55.00; non-members, $95.00. Includes about 2,000 savings banks and savings and loan associations, with assets, deposits, personnel, and other information. Formerly *Directory of Members of the United States League of Savings Institutions*; *National Council of Community Bankers*.

Directory of the Wood Products Industry. Miller Freeman, Inc., 600 Harrison St. San Francisco, CA 94107. Phone: 800-227-4675 or (415)905-2200 Fax: (415)905-2191 E-mail: techlearning_editors@mfi.com • URL: http://www.mfi.com • Biennial. $295.00. Lists sawmills, panelmills, logging operations, plywood products, wood products, distributors, etc. Geographic arrangement, with an index to lumber specialities. Formerly *Directory of the Forest Products Industry*.

Directory of Top Computer Executives. Applied Computer Research, Inc., P.O. Box 82266 Phoenix, AZ 85071-2266. Phone: 800-234-2227 or (602)995-5929 Fax: (602)995-0905 URL: http://www.archq.com • Semiannual. Price varies. Two volumes. Lists large companies and government agencies, with names of their data and systems executives.

Directory of Trade and Professional Associations in the European Union. Euroconfidentiel S. A., Rue de Rixensart 18 B-1332 Genval, Belgium. Phone: (32)02 653 01 25 Fax: (32)02 653 01 80 E-mail: nigel.hunt@euronet.be • Annual. $160.00. Includes more than 9,000 EU-related associations.

Directory of Trust Banking. Thomson Financial Publishing, 4709 West Golf Rd. Skokie, IL 60076-1253. Phone: 800-321-3373 or (847)676-9600 Fax: (847)933-8101 E-mail: support@bankinfo.com • URL: http://www.tfp.com • Annual. $315.00. Contains profiles of bank affiliated trust companies, independent trust companies, trust investment advisors, and trust fund managers. Provides contact information for professional personnel at more than 3,000 banking and other financial institutions.

The Directory of U. S. Trademarks. Thomson & Thomson, 500 Victory Rd. North Quincy, MA 02171-3145. Phone: 800-692-8833 or (617)479-1600 Fax: (617)786-8273 E-mail: support@thomson-thomson.com • URL: http://www.thomson-thomson.com • Annual, with three cumulative updates during the year. $1,295.00 per year. 12 volumes. Provides owner, registration, and classification information for about 1.5 million active and pending trademarks filed with the U. S. Patent and Trademark Office.

Directory of United Nations Databases and Information Systems. United Nations Publications, Available from Bernan Associates, 4611-F Assembly Dr. Lanham, MD 20706-4391. Phone: 800-274-4447 or (301)459-2255 Fax: (301)459-0056 Annual. $35.00. Nearly 38 United Nations organizations maintaining over 615 databases and information systems.

Directory of United States Importers/Directory of United States Exporters. Journal of Commerce, Inc., Two World Trade Center, 27th Fl. New York, NY 10048-0203. Phone: 800-222-0356 or (212)837-7000 Fax: (212)837-7130 E-mail: editor@mail.joc.com • URL: http://www.joc.com • Annual. Two volumes. $450.00 per volume. Approximately 55,000 firms with import and export interests; export and import managers, agents, and merchants in the United States; World ports; consulates and embassies. Formerly *United States Importers and Exporters Directories*.

Directory of U.S. Military Bases Worldwide. William R. Evinger, editor. Oryx Press, 4041 N. Central Ave., Ste. 700 Phoenix, AZ 85012-3397. Phone: 800-279-6799 or (602)265-2651 Fax: 800-279-4663 or (602)265-6250 E-mail: info@oryxpress.com • URL: http://www.oryxpress.com • 1998. $125.00. Third edition.

Directory of Venture Capital Firms: Domestic & International. Grey House Publishing, 185 Millerton Rd. Millerton, NY 12546. Phone: 800-562-2139 or (518)789-8700 Fax: (518)789-0556 E-mail: books@greyhouse.com • URL: http://www.greyhouse.com • 2001. $350.00. Fifth edition. Provides detailed information on more than 2,500 U. S. and foreign sources of venture capital. Includes five indexes.

Directory of Video, Computer, and Audio-Visual Products. International Communications Industries Association, 11242 Waples Mill Rd., Suite 200 Fairfax, VA 22030-6079. Phone: 800-659-7469 or (703)273-7200 Fax: (703)278-8082 Annual. $65.00. Contains detailed descriptions and photographs of specific items of equipment. Includes video cameras, overhead projectors, LCD panels, computer projection systems, film recording equipment, etc. A ''Glossary of Terms'' is also provided.

Directory of Wholesale Grocers: Service Merchandisers. Chain Store Age, 3922 Coconut Palm Dr. Tampa, FL 33619. Phone: 800-925-2288 or (813)664-6800 Fax: (813)664-6882 E-mail: info@csgis.com • URL: http://www.csgis.com • Annual. $300.00. Profiles over 2,000 cooperatives, voluntaries, non-sponsoring wholesalers, cash and carry warehouses, and nearly 220 service merchandisers. Formerly *Directory of Cooperatives, Voluntaries, and Wholesale Grocers*.

Directory of Wire Companies of North America. CRU International, 7474 Greenway Center Dr., Ste. 480 Greenbelt, MD 20770. Phone: (301)441-8997 Fax: (301)441-9091 Annual. $119.00. Profiles approximately 950 companies in the wire industry in North America. Also profiles fiber optic companies having to do with fiber optic cables and a supplier section profiling supplier companies.

Directory Publishing: A Practical Guide. SIMBA Information, P.O. Box 4234 Stamford, CT 06907-0234. Phone: 800-307-2529 or (203)358-4100 Fax: (203)358-5824 E-mail: info@simbanet.com • URL: http://www.simbanet.com • 1996. $44.95. Fourth edition. Provides an overall review of the directory publishing industry, including types of directories, research, sales estimates, expenses, advertising, sales promotion, editorial content, and legal considerations.

Dirty Business: Exploring Corporate Misconduct: Analysis and Cases. Maurice Punch. Sage Publications, Inc., 2455 Teller Rd. Thousand Oaks, CA 91320. Phone: (805)499-0721 Fax: (805)499-0871 E-mail: info@sagepub.com • URL: http://www.sagepub.com • 1996. $79.95. Covers organizational misbehavior and white-collar crime. Includes ''Ten Cases of Corporate Deviance.''

Disability and Rehabilitation Products Markets. Theta Reports/PJB Medical Publications, Inc., 1775 Broadway, Suite 511 New York, NY 10019. Phone: (212)262-8230 Fax: (212)262-8234 E-mail: customerservice@thetareports.com • URL: http://www.thetareports.com • 1999. $1,295.00. Market research data. Covers the market for products designed to help differently-abled people lead more active lives. Includes such items as adaptive computers, augmentative communication devices, lifts/vans, and bath/home products. Profiles of leading suppliers are included. (Theta Report No. 800.)

Disability Rights Center.

Disclosure SEC Database. Disclosure, Inc., 5161 River Rd. Bethesda, MD 20816. Phone: (301)951-1300 Fax: (301)657-1962 Provides information from records filed with the Securities and Exchange Commission by publicly owned corporations, 1977 to present. Weekly updates. Inquire as to online cost and availability.

The Discount Brokerage Directory. Mercer, Inc., 379 W. Broadway, Suite 400 New York, NY 10012. Phone: 800-582-9854 or (212)334-6212 Fax: (212)334-6434 URL: http://www.mercer.inc.com • Annual. $34.95. Provides information on approximately 90 discount brokers and firms offering stocks and bonds options, commodities, precious metals and other investments at a discount.

The Discount Brokerage Survey: Stocks. Mercer, Inc., 379 W. Broadway, Suite 400 New York, NY 10012. Phone: 800-582-9854 or (212)334-6212 Fax: (212)334-6434 URL: http://www.mercer.inc.com • 1994. Price on application. Quotes prices (commissions) charged by individual discount stockbrokers for 22 typical trades.

Discount Store News - Top Chains. Chain Store Guide, 3922 Coconut Palm Dr. Tampa, FL 33619. Phone: (813)664-68000 Fax: (813)664-6882 E-mail: info@lf.com • URL: http://www.lf.com • Annual. $79.00.

The Dismal Scientist. Dismal Sciences, Inc.Phone: (610)241-1000 Fax: (610)696-3836 E-mail: webmaster@dismal.com • URL: http://www.dismal.com • Web site contains a wide variety of economic data and rankings. A search feature provides detailed economic profiles of local areas by ZIP code. Major divisions of the site are Economy, Data, Thoughts, Forecasts, and Toolkit, with many specially written articles and currrent analysis by ''recognized economists.'' Fees: Free.

Disposable Medical Supplies. Available from MarketResearch.com, 641 Ave. of the Americas, Third Floor New York, NY 10011. Phone: 800-298-5699 or (212)807-2629 Fax: (212)807-2716 E-mail: order@marketresearch.com • URL: http://www.marketresearch.com • 1998. $3,500.00. Published by the Freedonia Group. Market data with forecasts to 2002 and 2007. Includes disposable syringes, catheters, kits, trays, etc.

Disposable Paper Products. Available from MarketResearch.com, 641 Ave. of the Americas, Third Floor New York, NY 10011. Phone: 800-298-5699 or (212)807-2629 Fax: (212)807-2716 E-mail: order@marketresearch.com • URL: http://www.marketresearch.com • 1998. $5,900.00. Published by Euromonitor Publications Ltd. Provides consumer market data and forecasts to 2001 for the United States, the United Kingdom, Germany, France, and Italy.

Dispute Resolution Journal. American Arbitration Association, 355 Madison Ave. New York, NY 10017-4605. Phone: 800-778-7879 or (212)716-5800 Fax: (212)716-5905 URL: http://www.adr.org • Quarterly. $55.00 per year. Formerly *Arbitration Journal*.

Dissertation Abstracts International. UMI, 300 N. Zeeb Rd. Ann Arbor, MI 48106-1346. Phone: 800-521-0600 or (313)761-4700 Fax: 800-864-0019 URL: http://www.umi.com • Monthly. Price on application. Section A: Humanities and Social Sciences. Author-written summaries of current doctoral dissertations from over 500 educational institutions.

Dissertation Abstracts Online. Bell & Howell Information and Learning, 300 N. Zeeb Rd. Ann Arbor, MI 48106. Phone: 800-521-0600 or (734)761-4700 Fax: 800-864-0019 Citations to all dissertations accepted for doctoral degrees by accredited U.S. educational institutions, 1861 to date. Includes British theses, 1988 to date. Inquire as to online cost and availability.

Dissertations in Broadcasting. Christopher H. Sterling, editor. Ayer Co. Publishers, Inc., Six Rd., C/O IDS, 195 McGregor St. Manchester, NH 03102. Phone: 888-267-7323 Fax: (603)922-3348 URL: http://www.scry.com/ayer • 1979. $739.50. 26 volumes. Mainly reprints of historical, philosophical, political, and academic works.

Distance Education and Training Council.

Distilled Spirits Council of the United States.

Distressed Hospital Quarterly. Health Care Investment Analysts, 300 E. Lombard St., Suite 750 Baltimore, MD 21202. Phone: 800-568-3282 or (410)576-9600 Fax: (410)783-0575 Quarterly. $500.00 per year. Names and provides information on specific distressed hospitals, which are defined as those ''exhibiting substantial adverse changes'' in such factors as capital structure, profitability, liquidity, payor mix, and utilization.

Distressed Real Estate Law Alert. West Group, 610 Opperman Dr. Eagan, MN 55123. Phone: 800-328-4880 or (651)687-7000 Fax: 800-213-2323 or (651)687-5827 URL: http://www.westgroup.com • Six times a year. $250.00 per year. Newsletter on such topics as default, bankruptcy, fraudulent conveyances, and foreclosure.

Distributed Computing Monitor. Patricia Seybold Group, 85 Devonshire St., 5th Fl. Boston, MA 02109-3504. Phone: 800-826-2424 or (617)742-5200 Fax: (617)742-1028 E-mail: info@psgroup.com • URL: http://www.psgroup.com • Monthly. $595.00 per year. Newsletter. Formerly *Distributed Computing*.

Distribution and LTL Carriers Association.

Distribution Center Management. Alexander Communications Group, Inc., 215 Park Ave., S, Suite 1301 New York, NY 10003. Phone: (212)228-0246 Fax: (212)228-0376 Monthly. $139.00 per year.

Distribution Channels: The Magazine for Candy, Tobacco, Grocery and General Merchandise Distributors. American Wholesalers Marketers Association, 1128 16th St. N.W. Washington, DC 20036. Phone: (202)463-2124 Fax: (202)467-0559 10 times a year. $46.00 per year. Formerly *Candy Wholesaler*.

Dividend Investor: A Safe and Sure Way to Build Wealth with High-Yield Dividend Stocks. Harvey C. Knowles and Damon H. Petty. McGraw-Hill Professional, 1221 Ave. of the Americas New York, NY 10020-1095. Phone: 800-722-4726 or (212)904-2000 Fax: (212)904-2072 E-mail: customer.service@mcgraw-hill.com • URL: http://www.mcgraw-hill.com • 1992. $24.95.

Division of Business and Economic Research. University of New Orleans

Division of Educational Research and Service. Louisiana Tech University

Division of Engineering Research. Michigan State University

Division of Government Research. University of New Mexico

Division of Health Services Research and Policy., University of Minnesota, P.O. Box 729 Minneapolis, MN 55455. Phone: (612)624-6151 Fax: (612)624-2196 E-mail: foote003@tc.umn.edu • URL: http://www.hsr.umn.edu • Fields of research include health insurance, consumer choice of health plans, quality of care, and long-term care.

Division of Hypertension. University of Michigan

Division Officer's Guide. James Stavridis. Naval Institute Press, Beach Hall, 291 Wood Rd. Annapolis, MD 21402. Phone: 800-223-8764 or (410)268-6110 Fax: (410)295-1084 E-mail: customer@usni.org • URL: http://www.nip.org • 1995. $19.95. 10th revised edition.

Divorce and Taxes. CCH, Inc., 4025 West Peterson Ave. Chicago, IL 60646-6085. Phone: 800-248-3248 or (773)866-6000 Fax: 800-224-8299 or (773)866-3608 E-mail: cust_serv@cch.com • URL: http://www.cch.com • 2000. $39.00. Second edition. In addition to tax problems, topics include alimony, division of property, and divorce decrees.

Divorce Decisions Workbook: A Planning and Action Guide. Marjorie L. Engel and Diana D. Gould. McGraw-Hill, 1221 Ave. of the Americas New York, NY 10020. Phone: 800-722-4726 or (212)904-2000 Fax: (212)904-2072 E-mail: customer.service@mcgraw-hill.com • URL: http://www.mcgraw-hill.com • 1992. $27.95. Covers the business, financial, legal, and tax aspects of divorce.

Divorce Taxation. Warren, Gorham and Lamont/RIA Group, 395 Hudson St. New York, NY 10014. Phone: 800-950-1215 or (212)367-6300 Fax: (212)924-0460 E-mail: customer_services@riag.com • URL: http://www.westgroup.com • Looseleaf service. $515.00 per year. Monthly *Report Bulletins* and updates.

Divorce Yourself: The National No-Fault Divorce Kit. Daniel Sitarz. Nova Publishing Co., 1103 W. College St. Carbondale, IL 62901. Phone: 800-748-1175 or (618)457-3521 Fax: (618)457-2541 E-mail: dansitarz@earthlink.net •

URL: http://www.novapublishing.com • 1996. $34.95. Third edition. Provides instructions, checklists, questionnaires, worksheets, and forms for use in uncomplicated divorce proceedings. Forms are also available on IBM or MAC diskettes. (Legal Self-Help Series).

DM News: The Newspaper of Direct Marketing. DM News Corp., 100 Ave. of the Americas, 6th Fl. New York, NY 10013-1689. Phone: (212)925-7300 Fax: (212)925-8752 E-mail: editor@dmnews.com • URL: http://www.dmnews.com • Weekly. $75.00 per year. Includes special feature issues on catalog marketing, telephone marketing, database marketing, and fundraising. Includes monthly supplements. *DM News International*, *DRTV News*, and *TeleServices*.

DMA Direct and Interactive Marketing Buying Practices Study. Direct Marketing Association, Inc., 1120 Ave. of the Americas New York, NY 10036-6700. Phone: (212)768-7277 Fax: (212)398-6725 E-mail: dma@the-dma.org • URL: http://www.the-dma.org • 2000. $1,295.00. Provides marketing research data relating to consumer purchasing from catalogs. "Incidence and profile of Internet buying" is also included. (Research conducted by Elrick & Lavidge.)

DMA State of the Catalog Industry Report. Direct Marketing Association, Inc., 1120 Ave. of the Americas New York, NY 10036-6700. Phone: (212)768-7277 Fax: (212)398-6725 E-mail: dma@the-dma.org • URL: http://www.the-dma.org • Annual. $495.00. Provides merchandising, operating, and financial statistics on consumer and business-to-business marketing through both print and electronic (interactive) catalogs. (Produced in association with W. A. Dean & Associates.)

DMA Statistical Fact Book. Direct Marketing Association, Inc., 1120 Ave. of the Americas New York, NY 10036-6700. Phone: (212)768-7277 Fax: (212)398-6725 E-mail: dma@the-dma.org • URL: http://www.the-dma.org • Annual. $165.95 to non-members; $105.95 to members. Provides data in five sections covering direct response advertising, media, mailing lists, market applications, and "Practical Management Information." Includes material on interactive/online marketing. (Cover title: *Direct Marketing Association's Statistical Fact Book*.)

DMA Washington Report: Federal and State Regulatory Issues of Concern. Direct Marketing Association, 1120 Ave. of the Americas New York, NY 10036-6700. Phone: (212)768-7277 Fax: (212)768-6725 E-mail: dma@the-dma.org • URL: http://www.the-dma.org • Monthly. Membership.

dNET. dNET Online Services, Inc.Phone: 800-378-3638 or (215)569-0100 Fax: (215)569-0101 E-mail: booksales@d-net.com • URL: http://www.d-net.com • "Where the World Goes for Directory Information." Web site provides ordering information for more than 3,200 U. S. and foreign directories, with brief descriptions of content. Searching is by keyword, title, topic, or publisher. There is also an extensive listing of products and services for directory publishers. Fees: Free. Frequent updates.

DNR: The Men's Fashion Retail Textile Authority. Fairchild Publications, Seven W. 34th St. New York, NY 10001. Phone: 800-932-4724 or (212)630-4000 Fax: (212)630-2602 URL: http://www.dailynewsrecord.com • Daily. $85.00 per year. Formerly *Daily News Record*.

Do-It-Yourself Advertising: How to Produce Great Ads, Brochures, Catalogs, Direct Mail, and Much More! Fred E. Hahn and Kenneth G. Mangun. John Wiley and Sons, Inc., 605 Third Ave. New York, NY 10158-0012. Phone: 800-225-5945 or (212)850-6000 Fax: (212)850-6088 E-mail: info@wiley.com • URL: http://www.wiley.com • 1997. $45.00. Second edition. Covers magazines, newspapers, flyers, brochures, catalogs, direct mail, telemarketing, trade shows, and radio/TV promotions. Includes checklists. (Small Business Series).

Do-It-Yourself Direct Marketing: Secrets for Small Business. Mark S. Bacon. John Wiley and Sons, Inc., 605 Third Ave. New York, NY 10158-0012. Phone: 800-225-5945 or (212)850-6000 Fax: (212)850-6088 E-mail: info@wiley.com • URL: http://www.wiley.com • 1997. $16.95. Second edition.

Do-it-Yourself Marketing Research. George Breen and Albert B. Blankenship. Replica Books, 1200 U.S. Highway E. Bridgewater, NJ 08807. Phone: 800-775-1800 or (908)429-4045 E-mail: btinfo@baker_taylor.com • URL: http://www.replicabooks.com • 1998. $44.95. Third edition.

Do-it-Yourself Retailing: Serving Hardware, Home Center and Building Material Retailers. National Retail Hardware Association, 5822 W. 74th St. Indianapolis, IN 46278-1756. Phone: 800-772-4424 or (317)290-0338 Fax: (317)328-4354 E-mail: nrha@quest.net • URL: http://www.nrha.org • Monthly. $50.00 per year. Formerly *Hardware Retailing*.

Doane's Agricultural Report. Doane Agricultural Services, 11701 Borman Dr. Saint Louis, MO 63146. Phone: (314)569-2700 Fax: (314)569-1083 E-mail: info@agrimarketing.com • Weekly. $98.00 per year. Edited for "high volume document printing" professionals. Covers imaging, printing, and mailing.

Dr. Dobb's Journal: Software Tools for the Professional Programmer., 2800 Campus Dr. San Mateo, CA 94403. Phone: 800-227-4675 E-mail: editors@ddj.com • URL: http://www.ddj.com • Monthly. $34.95 per year. A technical publication covering software development, languages, operating systems, and applications.

Document Imaging Report. Corry Publishing, Inc., 2840 W. 21st St. Erie, PA 16506-9945. Phone: (814)838-0025 Fax: (814)835-0441 E-mail: edm@corrypub.com • URL: http://www.corrypub.com • Biweekly. $597.00 per year. Newsletter.

Document Management Industries Association.

Document Processing Technology. RB Publishing Co., 2424 American Lane Madison, WI 53704-3102. Phone: (608)241-8777 Fax: (608)241-8666 URL: http://www.rbpub.com • Five times a year. Controlled circulation. Edited for "high volume document printing" professionals. Covers imaging, printing, and mailing.

Documents of Title Under the Uniform Commercial Code. American Law Institute-American Bar Association, 4025 Chestnut St. Philadelphia, PA 19104-3099. Phone: 800-253-6397 or (215)243-1600 Fax: (215)243-1664 URL: http://www.ali-aba.org • 1990. $90.00. Second edition.

Documents to the People. Government Documents Round Table. American Library Association, 50 E. Huron St. Chicago, IL 60611-2795. Phone: 800-545-2433 or (312)944-6780 Fax: (312)440-9374 E-mail: ala@ala.org • Quarterly. $20.00 per year.

Dodge Construction News. McGraw-Hill, 1221 Ave of the Americas New York, NY 10020. Phone: 800-722-4726 or (212)904-2000 Fax: (212)904-2072 E-mail: customer.service@mcgraw-hill.com • URL: http://www.mcgraw.hill.com • Daily. Los Angeles, $1,392.00 per year; Chicago, $1,245.00 per year.

Dodge Reports. F. W. Dodge Group, McGraw-Hill Information Systems Co., 1221 Ave. of the Americas New York, NY 10020. Phone: (212)512-2000 Daily. Price on application. Individual reports on new construction jobs.

Dodge/SCAN. F. W. Dodge Group, McGraw-Hill Information Systems Co., 1221 Ave. of the Americas New York, NY 10020. Phone: (212)512-2000 Price on application. Provides plans and specifications of new construction jobs.

Does Aid Work? Robert Cassen. Oxford University Press, Inc., 198 Madison Ave. New York, NY 10016-4314. Phone: 800-451-7556 or (212)726-6000 Fax: (212)726-6446 E-mail: custserv@oup-usa.org • URL: http://www.oup-usa.org • 1994. $19.95. Second edition.

Does Financial Deregulation Work? A Critique of Free Market Approaches. Bruce Coggins. Edward Elgar Publishing, Inc., 136 West St., Suite 202 Northampton, MA 01060. Phone: 800-390-3149 or (413)584-5551 Fax: (413)584-9933 E-mail: eep.orders@aidcvt.com • URL: http://www.e-elgar.co.uk • 1998. $85.00. Provides a critique of bank deregulation in the United States. Includes suggestions for more effective financial regulation. (New Directions in Modern Economics Series).

Does Privatization Deliver?: Highlights from a World Bank Conference. Ahmed Galal and Mary Shirley, editors. World Bank, The Office of the Publisher, 1818 H St., N. W. Washington, DC 20433. Phone: (202)477-1234 Fax: (202)477-6391 E-mail: books@worldbank.org • URL: http://www.worldbank.org • 1994. $22.00. Includes 12 international case studies on airlines, telecommunications, electric utilities, and other industries. Presents a favorable view of privatization. (EDI Development Studies Series).

Doing Business in China: The Last Great Market. Geoffrey Murray. St. Martin's Press, 175 Fifth Ave. New York, NY 10010. Phone: 800-221-7945 or (212)674-5151 Fax: 800-672-2054 or (212)529-0594 URL: http://www.stmartins.com • 1994. $80.00.

Doing Business in the United States: Legal Opportunities and Pitfalls. Lawrence B. Landman. John Wiley and Sons, Inc., 605 Third Ave. New York, NY 10158-0012. Phone: 800-225-5945 or (212)850-6000 Fax: (212)850-6088 E-mail: info@wiley.com • URL: http://www.wiley.com • 1997. $35.00.

Doing Business Internationally: The Guide to Cross Cultural Success. Terence Brake. McGraw-Hill Professional, 1221 Ave. of the Americas New York, NY 10020-1095. Phone: 800-722-4726 or (212)904-2000 Fax: (212)904-2072 E-mail: customer.service@mcgraw-hill.com • URL: http://www.mcgraw-hill.com • 1994. $27.50.

Doing Exemplary Research. Peter J. Frost and Ralph E. Stablein, editors. Sage Publications, Inc., 2455 Teller Rd. Thousand Oaks, CA 91320. Phone: (805)499-0721 Fax: (805)499-0871 E-mail: info@sagepub.com • URL: http://www.sagepub.com • 1992. $48.00. Contains discussions of research methodologies.

Dollars and Cents of Shopping Centers. Urban Land Institute, 1025 Thomas Jefferson St., N.W., Suite 500 W. Washington, DC 20007-5201. Phone: 800-321-5011 or (202)624-7000 Fax: (202)624-7140 E-mail: bookstore@uli.org • URL: http://www.uli.org • Triennial. Members, $29.95; non-members, $239.95. Supplemental *Special Report* available.

Domestic Mail Manual. Available from U. S. Government Printing Office, Washington, DC 20402. Phone: (202)512-1800 Fax: (202)512-2250 E-mail: gpoaccess@gpo.gov • URL: http://www.access.gpo.gov • Loseleaf. $22.00 per year. Issued by U. S. Postal Service. Contains rates, regulations, classes of mail, special services, etc., for mail within the U. S.

Domke on Commercial Arbitration; The Law and Practice of Commercial Arbitration. Gabriel Wilner and Rudolphe De-Seife. West Group, 610 Opperman Dr. Eagan, MN 55123. Phone: 800-328-4880 or (651)687-7000 Fax: 800-213-2323 or (651)687-5827 URL: http://www.westgroup.com • 1992. $225.00. Two volumes. Revised edition.

Don Kramer's Nonprofit Issues. Don Kramer Publisher, PO Box 482 Dresher, PA 19025-9215. Phone: 888-674-7783 Fax: (215)542-7548 URL: http://www.nonprofitissues.com • Monthly. $129.00 per year. Newsletter with legal emphasis. Covers the laws, rules, regulations, and taxes affecting nonprofit organizations.

DIrectory of U. S. Labor Organizations. BNA Books. Bureau of National Affairs, Inc., 1231 25th St., N.W. Washington, DC 20037-1197. Phone: 800-372-1033 or (202)452-4200 Fax: (202)822-8092 E-mail: books@bna.com • URL: http://www.bna.com • Biennial. $85.00. More than 200 national unions and professional and state employees associations engaged in labor representation.

Don't Die Broke: How to Turn Your Retirement Savings into Lasting Income. Margaret A. Malaspina. Available from W.W. Norton and Co., Inc., 500 Fifth Ave. New York, NY 10110-0017. Phone: 800-223-2584 or (212)354-5500 Fax: (212)869-0856 E-mail: webmaster@wwnorton.com • URL: http://www.norton.com • 1999. $21.95. Provides advice on such matters as retirement portfolio asset allocation and retirement spending accounts. (Bloomberg Personal Bookshelf.)

Don't Sell Stocks on Monday: An Almanac for Traders, Brokers, and Stock Market Watchers. Yale Hirsch. Books on Demand, 300 N. Zeeb Rd. Ann Arbor, MI 48106-1346. Phone: 800-521-0600 or (734)761-4700 Fax: (734)665-5022 1987. $74.40. Summarizes what are perceived as seasonal influences (day of the week, week of the month, month of the year, etc.) on stock prices.

Donut Shop. Entrepreneur Media, Inc., 2445 McCabe Way Irvine, CA 92614. Phone: 800-421-2300 or (949)261-2325 Fax: (949)261-0234 E-mail: entmag@entrepreneur.com • URL: http://www.entrepreneur.com • Looseleaf. $59.50. A practical guide to starting a doughnut shop. Covers profit potential, start-up costs, market size evaluation, owner's time required, site selection, lease negotiation, pricing, accounting, advertising, promotion, etc. (Start-Up Business Guide No. E1126.)

Door and Access Systems Manufacturers Association International., 1300 Sumner Ave. Cleveland, OH 44115-2851. Phone: (216)241-7333 Fax: (216)241-0105 E-mail: dasma@taol.com • URL: http://www.dasma.com • Members are manufacturers of "upward-acting" garage doors and related products, both residential and commercial.

Door and Hardware Institute.

Door and Operator Industry. International Door Association, P.O. Box 246 West Milton, OH 45383-0117. Phone: (513)698-4186 Bimonthly. Free. Edited for garage door and opener dealers.

Door and Window Retailing. Jervis & Associates, 11300 US Highway 1,Suite 400 North Palm Beach, FL 33401-4322. Phone: (908)850-8100 Fax: (908)850-6464 Bimonthly. $15.00 per year. Edited for door and window retailers. Formerly *Door and Window Business*.

Door Hardware. Available from MarketResearch.com, 641 Ave. of the Americas, Third Floor New York, NY 10011. Phone: 800-298-5699 or (212)807-2629 Fax: (212)807-2716 E-mail: order@marketresearch.com • URL: http://www.marketresearch.com • 1997. $495.00. Market research report published by Specialists in Business Information. Covers locks, closers, doorknobs, security devices, and other door hardware. Presents market data relative to demographics, sales growth, shipments, exports, imports, price trends, and end-use. Includes company profiles.

Doors. Available from MarketResearch.com, 641 Ave. of the Americas, Third Floor New York, NY 10011. Phone: 800-298-5699 or (212)807-2629 Fax: (212)807-2716 E-mail: order@marketreseach.com • URL: http://www.marketreseach.com • 1999. $2,250.00. Market research report published by Specialists in Business Information. Covers residential doors, including garage doors. Presents market data relative to demographics, sales growth, shipments, exports, imports, price trends, and end-use. Includes company profiles.

Doors and Hardware. Door and Hardware Institute, 14170 Newbrook Dr., Suite 200 Chantilly, VA 20151-2232. Phone: (703)222-2010 Fax: (703)222-2410 E-mail: publications@dhi.org • URL: http://www.dhi.org • Monthly. $49.00 per year.

Dow 40,000: Strategies for Profiting from the Greatest Bull Market in History. David Elias and Charles V. Moore.

McGraw-Hill, 1221 Ave. of the Americas New York, NY 10020. Phone: 800-722-4726 or (212)904-2000 Fax: (212)904-2072 E-mail: customer.service@mcgraw-hill.com • URL: http://www.mcgraw-hill.com • 1999. $24.95. Predicts continuing strong growth in the U. S. economy, low interest rates, and low inflation, resulting in a level of 40,000 for the Dow Jones Industrial Average in the year 2016.

Dow Jones Averages Chart Album. Dow Theory Letters, Inc., P.O. Box 1759 La Jolla, CA 92038-1759. Phone: (619)454-0481 Annual. Contains one page for each year since 1885. Includes line charts of the Dow Jones industrial, transportation, utilities, and bond averages. Important historical and economic dates are shown.

Dow Jones Averages 1885-1995. Phyllis S. Pierce, editor. McGraw-Hill, 1221 Ave. of the Americas New York, NY 10020. Phone: 800-722-4726 or (212)904-2000 Fax: (212)904-2072 E-mail: customer.service@mcgraw-hill.com • URL: http://www.mcgraw-hill.com • 1996. $95.00. Fourth edition. Presents the daily Dow Jones stock price averages for more than 100 years.

Dow Jones Guide to the Global Stock Market. Dow Jones & Co., Inc., 200 Liberty St. New York, NY 10281. Phone: 800-832-1234 or (212)416-2000 Fax: (212)416-2658 URL: http://www.dowjones.com • Annual. $34.95. Three volumes. Presents concise profiles and three-year financial performance data for each of 3,000 publicly held companies in 35 countries. (Includes all Dow Jones Global Index companies.)

Dow Jones Text Library. Dow Jones and Co., Inc., Post Office Box 300 Princeton, NJ 08543-0300. Phone: (609)520-4000 Fax: (609)520-4660 Full text and edited news stories and articles on business affairs; 1984 to date. Inquire as to online cost and availability.

Dow 100,000: Fact or Fiction. Charles W. Kadlec. Prentice Hall, 240 Frisch Ct. Paramus, NJ 07652-5240. Phone: 800-947-7700 or (201)909-6452 Fax: 800-445-6991 URL: http://www.prenhall.com • 1999. $25.00. Predicts a level of 100,000 for the Dow Jones Industrial Average in the year 2020, based mainly on a technological revolution.

Dow Theory Forecasts: Business and Stock Market. Dow Theory Forecasts, Inc., 7412 Calumet Ave. Hammond, IN 46324-2692. Phone: (219)931-6480 Fax: (219)931-6487 Weekly. $233.00 per year. Provides information and advice on blue chip and income stocks.

Dow Theory Letters. Dow Theory Letters, Inc., P.O. Box 1759 La Jolla, CA 92038-1759. Phone: (619)454-0481 E-mail: dowtheory@hotmail.com • URL: http://www.dowtheoryletter.som • Biweekly. $250.00 per year. Newsletter on stock market trends, investing, and economic conditions.

Dow Theory Today. Richard Russell. Fraser Publishing Co., 309 S. Willard St. Burlington, VT 05401. Phone: 800-253-0900 or (802)658-0324 Fax: (802)658-0260 E-mail: info@fraserbooks.com • URL: http://www.fraserbooks.com • 1981. $12.00. Reprint of 1958 edition.

Dow 36,000: The New Strategy for Profiting from the Coming Rise in the Stock Market. James K. Glassman and Kevin A. Hassett. Times Books, 201 E. 50th St. New York, NY 10022. Phone: 800-726-0600 or (212)751-2600 Fax: (212)572-8797 URL: http://www.randomhouse.com • 1999. $25.00. States that conventional measures of stock market value are obsolete.

Down Beat: Jazz, Blues and Beyond. Maher Publications, Inc., 102 N. Haven Rd. Elmhurst, IL 60126. Phone: 800-535-7496 or (630)941-2030 Fax: (630)941-3210 E-mail: downbeat@worldnet.att.net • URL: http://www.downbeatjazz.com • Monthly. $35.00 per year. Contemporary music.

Downtown Idea Exchange: Essential Information for Downtown Research and Development Center. Downtown Research and Development Center. Alexander Communications Group, Inc., 215 Park Ave. S., Suite 1301 New York, NY 10003. Phone: (212)228-0246 Fax: (212)228-0376 Semimonthly. $157.00 per year. Newsletter for those concerned with central business districts. Provides news and other information on planning, development, parking, mass transit, traffic, funding, and other topics.

Downtown Promotion Reporter. Downtown Research and Development Center. Alexander Communications Group, Inc., 215 Park Ave. S., Suite 1301 New York, NY 10003. Phone: (212)228-0246 Fax: (212)228-0376 Monthly. $157.00 per year. Newsletter. Provides information on public relations, market research, advertising, budgeting, etc. Edited for promoters of downtown areas in cities and towns.

Drafting Patent License Agreements, 1992-1993. Brian G. Brunsvold. Bureau of National Affairs, Inc., 1231 25th St., N.W. Washington, DC 20037-1197. Phone: 800-372-1033 or (202)452-4200 Fax: (202)822-8092 E-mail: books@bna.com • URL: http://www.bna.com • 1998. $125.00. Fourth edition.

Draperies and Window Coverings. L. C. Clark Publishing Co., Inc., 666 Dundee Rd., Suite 807 Northbrook, IL 60062-2769. Phone: (407)627-3993 Fax: (407)627-3447 13 times a year. $33.00 per year. Published for retailers, designers, manufacturers, and distributors of window coverings.

Draperies and Window Coverings: Directory and Buyer's Guide. L. C. Clark Publishing Co., Inc., 840 U.S. Hwy., Ste. 330 North Palm Beach, FL 33408. Phone: 800-833-9056 or (407)627-3993 Fax: (407)627-3447 E-mail: info@dwc.designet.com • URL: http://www.dwcdesignet.com • Annual. $15.00. Includes about 2,000 manufacturers and distributors of window coverings and related products.

DRG Handbook: Comparative Clinical and Financial Standards (Diagnosis Related Group). HCIA, Inc. (Health Care Investment Analysts), 300 E. Lombard St., Suite 750 Baltimore, MD 21202. Phone: 800-568-3282 or (410)576-9600 Fax: (410)752-6309 URL: http://www.hcia.com • Annual. $399.00. Presents summary data for all 477 DRGs (diagnosis-related groups) and the 23 MDCs (major diagnostic categories), based on information from more than 11 million Medicare patients. Ranks DRG information for 100 hospital groups according to number of beds, payor mix, case-mix, system affiliation, and profitability. Emphasis is financial. Formerly *Medicare DRG Handbook*.

DRI Financial and Credit Statistics. Data Products Division, 24 Hartwell Ave. Lexington, MA 02173. Phone: (781)863-5100 Fax: (781)860-6332 Contains U. S. and international statistical data relating to money markets, interest rates, foreign exchange, banking, and stock and bond indexes. Time period is 1973 to date, with continuous updating. Inquire as to online cost and availability.

DRI U.S. Central Database. Data Products Division, 24 Hartwell Ave. Lexington, MA 02173-3154. Phone: 800-933-3374 or (781)863-5100 Fax: (781)860-6332 URL: http://www.dri.mcgraw-hill.com • Provides more than 23,000 business, financial, demographic, economic, foreign trade, and industry-related time series for the U.S. Includes national income, population, retail-wholesale trade, price indexes, labor data, housing, industrial production, banking, interest rates, money supply, etc. Time period is generally 1947 to date (some data back to 1929). Updating varies. Inquire as to online cost and availability.

DRIP Investor: Your Guide to Buying Stocks Without a Broker. Horizon Publishing, Co., LLC, 7412 Calumet Ave., Suite 200 Hammond, IN 46324-2692. Phone: (219)852-3200 Fax: (219)931-6487 Monthly. $89.00 per year. Newsletter covering the dividend reinvestment plans (DRIPs) of various publicly-owned corporations. Includes model portfolios and *Directory of Dividend Reinvestment Plans*.

Driving Range Directory. National Golf Foundation, 1150 S. U.S. Highway. 1, Suite 401 Jupiter, FL 33477. Phone: 800-733-6006 or (561)744-6006 Fax: (561)744-6107 E-mail: ngf@ngf.org • URL: http://www.ngf.org • 1998. $99.00. Lists about 1,700 golf driving ranges in the U. S.

Drop Shipping as a Marketing Function: A Handbook of Methods and Policies. Nicholas T. Scheel. Greenwood Publishing Group, Inc., 88 Post Rd., W. Westport, CT 06881-5007. Phone: 800-225-5800 or (203)226-3571 Fax: (203)222-2540 E-mail: bookinfo@greenwood.com • URL: http://www.greenwood.com • 1990. $59.95.

Drop Shipping News., P.O. Box 7838 New York, NY 10150. Phone: (212)688-8797 Monthly. Price on application. Newsletter.

Drop Shipping Source Directory of Major Consumer Product Lines. Drop Shipping News, P.O. Box 7838 New York, NY 10150. Phone: (212)688-8797 Annual. $15.00. Lists over 700 firms of a wide variety of consumer products that can be drop shipped.

Drug Abuse and the Law Sourcebook. Gerald F. Uelmen and Victor G. Haddox. West Group, 610 Opperman Dr. Eagan, MN 55123. Phone: 800-328-4880 or (651)687-7000 Fax: 800-213-2323 or (651)687-5827 URL: http://www.westgroup.com • $240.00 per year. Two looseleaf volumes. Periodic supplementation. Covers drugs of abuse, criminal responsibility, possessory offenses, trafficking offenses, and related topics. (Criminal Law Series).

Drug Abuse Handbook. Steven B. Karch, editor. CRC Press, Inc., 2000 Corporate Blvd., N. W. Boca Raton, FL 33431. Phone: 800-272-7737 or (561)994-0555 Fax: 800-374-3401 or (561)241-7856 E-mail: orders@crcpress.com • URL: http://www.crcpress.com • 1997. $99.95. Provides comprehensive coverage of drug abuse issues and trends. Edited for healthcare professionals.

Drug Abuse in Society: A Reference Handbook. Geraldine Woods. ABC-CLIO, Inc., P.O. Box 1911 Santa Barbara, CA 93116-1911. Phone: 800-368-6868 or (805)968-1911 Fax: (805)685-9685 E-mail: sales@abc-clio.com • URL: http://www.abc-clio.com • 1993. $39.50. (Contemporary World Issues Series).

Drug and Alcohol Abuse Education. Editorial Resources, Inc., P.O. Box 21129 Washington, DC 20009. Phone: (202)783-2929 Monthly. $84.00 per year. Newsletter covering education, prevention, and treatment relating to abuse of drugs and alcohol.

Drug Benefit Trends: For Pharmacy Managers and Managed Healthcare Professionals. SCP Communications, Inc., 134 W. 29th St. New York, NY 10001-5399. Phone: (212)631-1600 E-mail: subs@scp.com • URL: http://www.medscape.com • Monthly. Individuals, $72.00 per year; institutions, $120.00 per year. Covers the business of managed care drug benefits.

Drug, Chemical and Allied Trades Association.

Drug Development Research. John Wiley and Sons, Inc., Journals Div., 605 Third Ave. New York, NY 10158-0012. Phone: 800-225-5945 or (212)850-6000 Fax: (212)850-6088 E-mail: info@wiley.com • URL: http://www.wiley.com • Monthly. $3,395.00 per year.

Drug Information Association., 501 Office Center Dr., Suite 450 Fort Washington, PA 19034-3211. Phone: (215)628-2288 Fax: (215)641-1229 E-mail: dia@diahome.org • URL: http://www.diahome.org • Concerned with the technology of drug information processing.

Drug Information Fulltext. American Society of Health-System Pharmacists, 7272 Wisconsin Ave. Bethesda, MD 20814. Phone: (301)657-3000 Fax: (301)657-1641 Provides full text monographs from the *American Hospital Formulary Service* and the *Handbook On Injectable Drugs*. Inquire as to online cost and availability.

Drug Product Liability. Matthew Bender & Co., Inc., Two Park Ave. New York, NY 10016. Phone: 800-223-1940 or (212)448-2000 Fax: (212)244-3188 E-mail: international@bender.com • URL: http://www.bender.com • $680.00. Three looseleaf volumes. Periodic supplementation. All aspects of drugs: manufacturing, marketing, distribution, quality control, multiple prescription problems, drug identification, FDA coverage, etc.

Drug Store News. Lebhar-Friedman Inc., 425 Park Ave. New York, NY 10022. Phone: 800-766-6999 or (212)756-5000 Fax: (212)486-1180 E-mail: info@lf.com • URL: http://www.drugstorenews.com • Biweekly. $95.00 per year.

Drug Store News. Chain Pharmacy. Lebhar-Friedman, Inc., 425 Park Ave. New York, NY 10022. Phone: 800-766-6999 or (212)756-5000 Fax: (212)756-5250 Monthly. $36.00 per year. Formerly *Drug Store News for the Pharmacists*.

Drug Testing Legal Manual. Kevin B. Zeese. West Group, 610 Opperman Dr. Eagan, MN 55123. Phone: 800-328-4880 or (651)687-7000 Fax: 800-213-2323 or (651)687-5827 URL: http://www.westgroup.com • Two looseleaf volumes. $210.00. Periodic supplementation. Covers methods of testing for illegal drugs, pre-employment drug testing, technological problems, testing of school students, and related topics. (Criminal Law Series).

Drug Topics. Medical Economics Co., Inc., Five Paragon Dr. Montvale, NJ 07645-1742. Phone: 800-526-4870 or (201)358-7200 Fax: (201)573-8999 E-mail: customer-service@medec.com • URL: http://www.drugtopics.com • 23 times a year. $61.00 per year. Edited for retail pharmacists, hospital pharmacists, pharmacy chain store executives, wholesalers, buyers, and others concerned with drug dispensing and drug store management. Provides information on new products, including personal care items and cosmetics.

Drugs and Society: A Journal of Contemporary Issues. Haworth Press, Inc., 10 Alice St. Binghamton, NY 13904-1580. Phone: 800-429-6784 or (607)722-5857 Fax: 800-895-0582 or (607)722-1424 E-mail: getinfo@haworthpressinc.com • URL: http://www.haworthpressinc.com • Quarterly. Individuals, $42.00 per year; institutions, $90.00 per year;libraries, $200.00 per year. Edited for researchers and practitioners. Covers various areas of susbstance abuse, including alcoholism.

Drugs of Abuse. Available from U. S. Government Printing Office, Washington, DC 20402. Phone: (202)512-1800 Fax: (202)512-2250 E-mail: gpoaccess@gpo.gov • URL: http://www.access.gpo.gov • 1997. $15.00. Issued by the Drug Enforcement Administration, U. S. Department of Justice (http://www.usdoj.gov). Provides detailed information on various kinds of narcotics, depressants, stimulants, hallucinogens, cannabis, steroids, and inhalants. Contains many color illustrations and a detailed summary of the Controlled Substances Act.

Dry Cleaning Shop. Entrepreneur Media, Inc., 2445 McCabe Way Irvine, CA 92614. Phone: 800-421-2300 or (949)261-2325 Fax: (949)851-9088 E-mail: entmag@entrepreneurmag.com • URL: http://www.entrepreneurmag.com • Looseleaf. $59.50. A practical guide to starting a dry cleaning business. Covers profit potential, start-up costs, market size evaluation, owner's time required, site selection, lease negotiation, pricing, accounting, advertising, promotion, etc. (Start-Up Business Guide No. E1037.)

Drycleaners News. Zackin Publications, Inc., P.O. Box 2180 Waterbury, CT 66722. Phone: (203)755-0158 Monthly. $36.00.

DSN Retailing Today (Discount Store News). Lebhar-Friedman, Inc., 425 Park Ave. New York, NY 10022. Phone: 800-766-6999 or (212)756-5000 Fax: (212)756-5123 E-mail: info@lf.com • URL: http://www.discountstorenews.com • Biweekly. $119.00 per year. Includes supplement *Apparel Merchandising*. Formerly Discount Store News.

Ductile Iron Pipe Research Association.

Dumb Money: Adventures of a Day Trader. Joey Anuff and Gary Wolf. Random House, Inc., 201 E. 50th St. New York,

NY 10022. Phone: 800-726-0600 or (212)751-2600 Fax: 800-659-2436 or (212)572-8700 URL: http://www.randomhouse.com • 2000. $23.95. An account of the day trading ordeals of one of the authors, Joey Anuff.

Dun & Bradstreet/Gale Group Industry Handbooks. The Gale Group, 27500 Drake Rd. Farmington Hills, MI 48331-3535. Phone: 800-877-GALE or (248)699-GALE Fax: 800-414-5043 or (248)699-8069 E-mail: galeord@galegroup.com • URL: http://www.galegroup.com • 2000. $630.00. Five volumes. $145.00 per volume. Each volume covers two or more major industries: 1. *Entertainment and Hospitality*; 2. *Construction and Agriculture*; 3. *Chemicals and Pharmaceuticals*; 4. *Computers & Software and Broadcasting & Telecommunications*; 5. *Insurance and Health & Medical Services*. The following are included for each industry: overview, statistics, financial ratios, rankings, merger information, company directory, directory of associations, and consultants directory.

Dun and Bradstreet Guide to Your Investments: The Year-Round Investment Sourc ebook for Managing Your Personal Finances. Nancy Dunnan, editor. HarperSan Francisco, 353 Sacramento St., Suite 500 San Francisco, CA 94111. Phone: 800-242-7737 or (415)477-4400 Fax: 800-822-4090 or (415)477-4444 URL: http://www.harpercollins.com • 1996. $35.00.

Dun's Asia Pacific Key Business Enterprises. Dun and Bradstreet Information Services, Dun and Bradstreet Corp., Three Sylvan Way Parsippany, NJ 07054-3896. Phone: 800-526-0651 or (973)605-6000 Fax: (973)254-4063 E-mail: customerservice@dnb.com • URL: http://www.dnb.com • Annual. Price on application. Provides information on 30,000 companies in 14 Pacific Rim countries. Firms have sales of ten million dollars or over, or have 500 or more employees.

Dun's Census of American Business. Dun and Bradstreet, Economic Analysis Dept., Three Sylvan Way Parsippany, NJ 10017-4717. Phone: 800-526-0651 or (973)455-0900 Fax: (973)254-4063 E-mail: customerservice@dnb.com • URL: http://www.dnb.com • Annual. $325.00.

Dun's Consultants Directory. Dun and Bradstreet Information Services, Three Sylvan Way Parsippany, NJ 07054-3896. Phone: 800-526-0651 or (973)455-0900 Fax: (973)254-4063 E-mail: customerservice@dnb.com • URL: http://www.dnb.com • 1996. $425.00. Lease basis. Lists about 25,000 top consulting firms in more than 200 fields.

Dun's Industrial Guide: The Metalworking Directory. Dun and Bradstreet Information Services Dun & Bradstreet Corp., Three Sylvan Way Parsippany, NJ 07054-3896. Phone: 800-526-0651 or (973)455-0900 Fax: (973)254-4063 E-mail: customerservice@dnb.com • URL: http://www.dnb.com • Annual. Libraries, $485; commercial institutions, $795.00. Lease basis. Three volumes. Lists about 65,000 U. S. manufacturing plants using metal and suppliers of metalworking equipment and materials. Includes names and titles of key personnel. Products, purchases, and processes are indicated.

Dun's Key Decision-Makers in Hong Kong Business. Dun and Bradstreet Information Services, Dun and Bradstreet Corp., Three Sylvan Way Parsippany, NJ 07054-3896. Phone: 800-526-0651 or (973)455-0900 Fax: (973)254-4063 E-mail: customerservice@dnb.com • URL: http://www.dnb.com • Annual. $380.00. Provides information on over 8,000 major Hong Kong companies.

Dun's Middle Market Disc. Dun & Bradstreet, Inc., One Diamond Hill Rd. Murray Hill, NJ 07974-1218. Phone: 800-234-3867 or (908)665-5000 Fax: (908)665-5803 URL: http://www.dnb.com • Quarterly. Price on application. CD-ROM provides information on more than 150,000 middle market U. S. private companies and their executives.

Dun's Million Dollar Disc. Dun & Bradstreet, Inc., One Diamond Hill Rd. Murray Hill, NJ 07974-1218. Phone: 800-234-3867 or (908)665-5000 Fax: (908)665-5803 URL: http://www.dnb.com • Quarterly. $3,800.00 per year to libraries; $5,500.00 per year to businesses. CD-ROM provides information on more than 240,000 public and private U. S. companies having sales volume of $5 million or more or 100 employees or more. Includes biographical data on more than 640,000 company executives.

DV: Digital Video. Miller Freeman, Inc., 411 Borel Ave., Suite 100 San Mateo, CA 94402. Phone: 800-227-4675 or (415)358-9500 Fax: (415)358-9966 E-mail: letters@dv.com • URL: http://www.mfi.com • Monthly. $29.97 per year. Edited for producers and creators of digital media. Includes topics relating to video, audio, animation, multimedia, interactive design, and special effects. Covers both hardware and software, with product reviews. Formerly *Digital Video Magazine*.

DVD Assessment, No. 3. Julie B. Schwerin and Theodore A. Pine, editors. InfoTech, Inc., P.O. Box 1563 Norwich, VT 05055-1563. Phone: (802)649-8700 Fax: (802)649-8877 E-mail: info@infotechresearch.com • URL: http://www.infotechresearch.com • 1998. $1,295.00. Third edition. Provides detailed market research data on Digital Video Discs (also known as Digital Versatile Discs). Includes history of DVD, technical specifications, DVD publishing outlook, ''Industry Overview,'' ''Market Context,'' ''Infrastructure Analysis,'' ''Long-Range Forecast to 2005,'' and emerging technologies.

DVM: The Newsmagazine of Veterinary Medicine. Advanstar Communications, Inc., Healthcare Group, 7500 Old Oak Blvd. Cleveland, OH 44130-3369. Phone: 800-346-0085 or (440)826-2833 Fax: (440)891-2740 E-mail: information@advanstar.com • Monthly. $39.00 per year. Includes new drugs and new products.

Dynamic Asset Allocation: Strategies for the Stock, Bond, and Money Markets. David A. Hammer. John Wiley and Sons, Inc., 605 Third Ave. New York, NY 10158-0012. Phone: 800-225-5945 or (212)850-6000 Fax: (212)850-6088 E-mail: info@wiley.com • URL: http://www.wiley.com • 1991. $49.95. A practical guide to the distribution of investment portfolio funds among various kinds of assets. (Finance Editions Series).

The Dynamic Decision Maker: Five Decision Styles for Executive and Business Success. Michael J. Driver and others. HarperInformation, 10 E. 53rd St. New York, NY 10022-5299. Phone: 800-242-7737 or (212)207-7000 Fax: (212)207-7826 URL: http://www.harpercollins.com • 1993. $24.95. The five styles are decisive, flexible, hierarchial, integrative, and systemic.

Dynamic E-Business Implementation Management: How to Effectively Manage E-Business Implementation. Bennet P. Lientz and Kathryn P. Rea. Academic Press, 525 B St., Suite 1900 San Diego, CA 92101. Phone: 800-321-5068 or (619)699-6719 Fax: 800-336-7377 or (619)699-6380 E-mail: ap@acad.com • URL: http://www.academicpress.com • 2000. $44.95.

E & M J International Directory of Mining. Intertec Publishing Corp., Mining Information Services, 29 N. Wacker Dr. Chicago, IL 60606-3298. Phone: 800-400-5945 or (312)726-2802 Fax: (312)726-0241 E-mail: subs@intertec.com • URL: http://www.intertec.com • Annual. $140.00. Lists 2,100 companies and 3,000 mines and plants producing metals and nonmetallic minerals worldwide.

e-Business Advisor: Technology Strategies for Business Innovators. Advisor Media, Inc., 5675 Ruffin Rd., Suite 200 San Diego, CA 92123. Phone: 800-336-6060 or (858)278-5600 Fax: (858)278-0300 URL: http://www.advisor.com • Monthly. $39.00 per year. Covers electronic commerce management and technology, including payment technology, Web development, knowledge management, and e-business market research.

The E-Commerce Book: Building the E-Empire. Steffano Korper and Juanita Ellis. Academic Press, 525 B St., Suite 1900 San Diego, CA 92101-4495. Phone: 800-321-5068 or (619)230-1840 Fax: (619)699-6715 E-mail: ap@acad.com • URL: http://www.academicpress.com • 1999. $39.95. Covers the practical aspects of Internet commerce, including sales, marketing, advertising, payment systems, and security. Written for a general audience.

E-Commerce Tax Alert. CCH, Inc., 4025 West Peterson Ave. Chicago, IL 60646-6085. Phone: 800-248-3248 or (773)866-6000 Fax: 800-224-8299 or (773)866-3608 URL: http://www.cch.com • Monthly. $397.00 per year. Newsletter. Edited for owners and managers of firms doing business through the Internet. Covers compliance with federal, state, local, and international tax regulations.

E Media. Online, Inc., 462 Danbury Rd. Wilton, CT 06897-4006. Phone: 800-248-8466 or (203)761-1466 Fax: (203)761-1444 E-mail: emedia@onlineinc.com • URL: http://www.emediapro.net • Bimonthly. Individuals, $55.00 per year; institutions, $98.00 per year. Contains ''how-to'' articles and reviews of CD-ROMs and equipment. Formerly *E Media Professional*.

E-retailing World. Bill Communications, Inc., 770 Broadway New York, NY 10003-9595. Phone: 800-266-4712 or (646)654-4500 Fax: (646)654-7212 URL: http://www.billcom.com • Bimonthly. Controlled circulation. Covers various kinds of online retailing, including store-based, catalog-based, pure play, and ''click-and-mortar.'' Includes both technology and management issues.

E: The Environment Magazine. Earth Action Network, Inc., 28 Knight St. Norwalk, CT 06851. Phone: (203)854-5559 Fax: (203)866-0602 E-mail: jimm@magazine.com • URL: http://www.emagazine.com • Bimonthly. $20.00 per year. A popular, consumer magazine providing news, information, and commentary on a wide range of environmental issues.

E: The Environmental Magazine [online]. Earth Action Network, Inc.Phone: (203)854-5559 Fax: (203)866-0602 URL: http://www.emagazine.com • Web site provides full-text articles from *E: The Environmental Magazine* for a period of about two years. Searching is provided. Alphabetical and subject links are shown for a wide variety of environmental Web sites. Fees: Free.

Earl Warren Legal Institute. University of California at Berkeley

Early American Bookbindings from the Collection of Michael Papantonio. Michael Papantonio. Oak Knoll Press, 310 Delaware St. New Castle, DE 19720. Phone: 800-996-2556 or (302)328-7232 Fax: (302)328-7274 E-mail: oakknoll@oakknoll.com • URL: http://www.oakknoll.com • 1985. $27.50. Second edition.

Earnshaw's Infants, Girls and Boys Wear Review. Earnshaw Publications, Inc., 225 W. 34th St., Suite 1212 New York, NY 10001. Phone: (212)563-2742 Fax: (212)629-3249 Annual. $24.00.

Earth Almanac: An Annual Geophysical Review of the State of the Planet. Natalie Goldstein. Oryx Press, 4041 North Central Ave., Suite 700 Phoenix, AZ 85012-3397. Phone: 800-279-6799 or (602)265-2651 Fax: 800-279-4663 or (602)265-6250 E-mail: info@oryxpress.com • URL: http://www.oryxpress.com • Annual. $65.00. Provides background information, statistics, and a summary of major events relating to the atmosphere, oceans, land, and fresh water.

Earth and Mineral Sciences. College of Earth and Mineral Sciences. Pennsylvania State University, 116 Deike Bldg. University Park, PA 16802. Phone: (814)863-4667 Fax: (814)863-7708 Semiannual. Free. Current research in material science, mineral engineering, geosciences, meteorology, geography and mineral economics.

Earth Data Analysis. University of New Mexico

East Asian Executive Reports. International Executive Reports Ltd., 717 D St., N. W., Suite 300 Washington, DC 20004-2807. Phone: (202)628-6900 Fax: (202)628-6618 Monthly. $455.00 per year. Newsletter. Covers the legal, financial, and practical aspects of doing business in East Asia, including importing, joint ventures, and licensing.

East European Kompass on Disc. Available from Kompass USA, Inc., 1255 Route 70, Suite 25-S Lakewood, NJ 08701. Phone: 877-566-7277 or (732)730-0340 Fax: (732)730-0342 E-mail: mail@kompass-usa.com • URL: http://www.kompass.com • Annual. $1,280.00. CD-ROM provides information on more than 294,000 companies in Austria, Azerbaijan, Belarus, Croatia, Czech Republic, Estonia, Hungary, Latvia, Lithuania, Moldova, Poland, Romania, Russia, Slovakia, Slovenia, Ukraine, and Yugoslavia. Classification system covers approximately 50,000 products and services.

East-West Center.

Eastern Europe: A Directory and Sourcebook. Available from The Gale Group, 27500 Drake Rd. Farmington Hills, MI 48331-3535. Phone: 800-877-GALE or (248)699-GALE Fax: 800-414-5043 or (248)699-8069 E-mail: cbdresearch@compuserve.com • URL: http://www.galegroup.com • 1999. $590.00. Second edition. Published by Euromonitor. Describes major companies in Eastern Europe. Sourcebook section provides marketing and business information sources.

EBN Benefits Sourcebook. Securities Data Publishing, 40 West 57th St. New York, NY 10019. Phone: 800-455-5844 or (212)765-5311 Fax: (212)956-0112 E-mail: sdp@tfn.com • URL: http://www.sdponline.com • Annual. $36.95. Lists vendors of products and services for the employee benefits industry. Includes industry trends and statistics. (Securities Data Publishing is a unit of Thomson Financial.)

eBrands: Building an Internet Business at Breakneck Speed. Phil Carpenter. Harvard Business School Press, 60 Harvard Way Boston, MA 02163. Phone: 888-500-1016 or (617)783-7440 E-mail: custserv@hbsp.harvard.edu • URL: http://www.hbsp.harvard.edu • 2000. $25.95. Emphasis is on the marketing aspects of electronic commerce.

EBRI Databook on Employee Benefits. Employee Benefit Research Institute, 2121 K St., N. W., Suite 600 Washington, DC 20037-1986. Phone: (202)659-0670 Fax: (202)775-6312 E-mail: info@ebri.org • URL: http://www.ebri.org • 1997 $99.00. Fourth edition. Contains more than 350 tables and charts presenting data on employee benefits in the U. S., including pensions, health insurance, social security, and medicare. Includes a glossary of employee benefit terms.

Ebsco Bulletin of Serials Changes. EBSCO Industries, Inc.,Title Information Dept., 5724 Highway 280 East Birmingham, AL 35242. Phone: 800-633-6088 or (205)991-6600 Fax: (205)995-1518 Bimonthly. $20.00 per year. New titles, discontinuations, title changes, mergers, etc.

EBSCO Information Services. Ebsco PublishingPhone: 800-871-8508 or (508)356-6500 Fax: (508)356-5640 E-mail: ep@epnet.com • URL: http://www.epnet.com • Fee-based Web site providing Internet access to a wide variety of databases, including business-related material. Full text is available for many periodical titles, with daily updates. Fees: Apply.

Ebusiness Forum: Global Business Intelligence for the Digital Age. Economist Intelligence Unit (EIU), Economist GroupPhone: 800-938-4685 or (212)554-0600 Fax: (212)586-0248 E-mail: newyork@eiu.com • URL: http://www.ebusinessforum.com • Web site provides information relating to multinational business, with an emphasis on activities in specific countries. Includes rankings of countries for ''e-business readiness,'' additional data on the political, economic, and business environment in 180 nations (''Doing Business in.''), and ''Today's News Analysis.'' Fees: Free, but registration is required for access to all content. Daily updates.

EC Software News. Faulkner & Gray, Inc., 300 S. Wacker Drive, 18th Floor Chicago, IL 60606. Phone: (312)913-1334 Fax:

(312)913-1369 URL: http://www.faulknergray.com • Monthly. $59.95 per year. Newsletter. Covers the latest developments in e-commerce software, both business-to-business and business-to-consumer.

EC&M's Electrical Products Yearbook (Electrical Construction and Maintenance). Intertec Publishing Corp., P.O. Box 12901 Overland Park, KS 66282-2901. Phone: 800-400-5945 or (913)341-1300 Fax: (913)967-1898 E-mail: subs@intertec.com • URL: http://www.intertec.com • Annual. Free to qualified personnel; others, $10.00.

EC.COM Magazine: The Magazine for Electronic Commerce Management. Electronic Commerce Media, Inc., 14407 Big Basin Way Saratoga, CA 95070. Phone: (408)867-6300 Fax: (408)867-9800 URL: http://www.ecmedia.com • Monthly. $48.00 per year. Covers both technical and business issues relating to e-commerce. information

Eckstrom's Licensing Law Library. Lawrence J. Eckstrom. West Group, 610 Opperman Dr. Eagan, MN 55123. Phone: 800-328-4880 or (651)687-7000 Fax: 800-213-2323 or (651)687-5827 URL: http://www.westgroup.com • 12 looseleaf volumes. $1,570.00. Periodic supplementation. Covers foreign and domestic operations and joint ventures, with forms and agreements.

ECN Literature News (Electronic Component News). Cahners Business Information, 1018 W. 9th Ave. King of Prussia, PA 19406. Phone: 800-662-7776 or (610)205-1000 Fax: (610)964-4273 E-mail: corporatecommunications@cahners.com • URL: http://www.cahner.com • Bimonthly. Price on application.

ECN's Electronic Industry Telephone Directory. Cahners Business Information, 1018 W. 9th Ave. King of Prussia, PA 19406. Phone: 800-662-7776 or (610)205-1000 Fax: (610)964-2915 E-mail: corporatecommunications@cahners.com • URL: http://www.cahners.com • Annual. $55.00. Information on 30,000 electronic manufacturers, distributors, and representatives. Formerly *Electronic Industry Telephone Directory*.

EcoCentral. Latin America Data Base, Latin American Institute, University of New Mexico, 801 Yale Blvd., N. E. Albuquerque, NM 87131-1016. Phone: 800-472-0888 or (505)277-6839 Fax: (505)277-5989 An online newsletter covering economic, trade, political, and social issues in Central America, especially in Nicaragua and El Salvador. Time period is 1986 to date, with weekly updates. Inquire as to online cost and availability.

Ecology. Ecological Society of America, 2010 Massachusetts Ave., N.W., Suite 400 Washington, DC 20036. Phone: (202)833-8773 Fax: (202)833-8775 E-mail: esahq@esa.org • URL: http://www.sdsc.edu • Eight times a year. $350.00 per year. All forms of life in relation to environment.

Ecology Law Quarterly. University of California at Berkeley, Boalt Hall School of Law. University of California Press, Journals Div., 2000 Center St., Suite 303 Berkeley, CA 94704-1223. Phone: 800-822-6657 or (510)643-7154 Fax: 800-999-1958 or (510)642-9917 E-mail: journal@ucop.edu • URL: http://www.ucpress.edu/journals • Quarterly. Individuals, $30.00 per year; institutions, $54.00 per year; students, $22.00 per year.

The Ecology of Land Use: A Bibliographic Guide. Graham Trelstad. Sage Publications, Inc., 2455 Teller Rd. Thousand Oaks, CA 91320. Phone: (805)499-0721 Fax: (805)499-0871 E-mail: info@sagepub.com • URL: http://www.sagepub.com • 1994. $10.00.

Ecology USA. Business Publishers, Inc., 8737 Colesville Rd., Suite 1100 Silver Spring, MD 20910-3928. Phone: 800-274-6737 or (301)587-6300 Fax: (301)587-1081 E-mail: bpinews@bpinews.com • URL: http://www.bpinews.com • Biweekly. $135.00 per year.

EconBase: Time Series and Forecasts. WEFA, Inc., 800 Baldwin Tower Eddystone, PA 19022. Phone: (610)490-4000 Fax: (610)490-2770 URL: http://www.wefa.com • Presents online econometric data for business conditions, economics, demographics, industry, finance, employment, household income, interest rates, prices, etc. Includes two-year forecasts for a wide range of economic indicators. Time span is 1948 to date, with monthly updates. Inquire as to online cost and availability.

EconLit. American Economic Association, 2014 Broadway, Suite 305 Nashville, TN 37203-2418. Phone: (615)322-2595 Fax: (615)343-7590 E-mail: info@econlit.org • URL: http://www.econlit.org • Covers the worldwide literature of economics as contained in selected monographs and about 550 journals. Subjects include microeconomics, macroeconomics, economic history, inflation, money, credit, finance, accounting theory, trade, natural resource economics, and regional economics. Time period is 1969 to present, with monthly updates. Inquire as to online cost and availability.

EconLit. Available from SilverPlatter Information, Inc., 100 River Ridge Rd. Norwood, MA 02062-5026. Phone: 800-343-0064 or (781)769-2599 Fax: (781)769-8763 Monthly. Single-user, $1,600.00 per year. Multi-user, $2,400.00 per year. Provides CD-ROM citations, with abstracts, to articles from more than 500 economics journals. Time period is 1969 to date. Produced by the American Economic Association.

Econometric Analysis. William H. Greene. Prentice Hall, 240 Frisch Court Paramus, NJ 07652-5240. Phone: 800-947-7700 or (201)909-6200 Fax: 800-445-6991 or (201)909-6361 URL: http://www.prenhall.com • 2000. Fourth edition. Price on application. Includes bibliographical references.

Econometric Analysis of Financial Markets. J. Kaehler and P. Kugler, editors. Springer-Verlag New York, Inc., 175 Fifth Ave. New York, NY 10010. Phone: 800-777-4643 or (212)460-1500 Fax: (212)473-6272 E-mail: orders@springer.ny.com • URL: http://www.springer.ny.com • 1994. $71.95. (Studies in Empirical Economics Series).

Econometric Methods. John Johnston. McGraw-Hill, 1221 Ave. of the Americas New York, NY 10020. Phone: 800-722-4726 or (212)904-2000 Fax: (212)904-2072 E-mail: customer.service@mcgraw-hill.com • URL: http://www.mcgraw-hill.com • 1996. $85.63. Fourth edition. Covers various models, equations, variables, relationships, and ''A Smorgasbord of Computationally Intense Methods.''

Econometric Models and Economic Forecasts. Robert S. Pindyck and Daniel L. Rubinfield. McGraw-Hill, 1221 Ave. of the Americas New York, NY 10020-1095. Phone: 800-722-4726 or (212)904-2000 Fax: (212)904-2072 E-mail: customer.service@mcgraw-hill.com • URL: http://www.mcgraw-hill.com • 1997. $86.88. Fourth edition.

Econometric Research Program. Princeton University

Econometric Society.

Econometric Theory. Cambridge University Press, Journals Dept., 40 W. 20th St. New York, NY 10011. Phone: 800-221-4512 or (212)924-3900 Fax: (212)691-3239 E-mail: info@cup.org • URL: http://www.cup.org • Bimonthly. $280.00 Per year. Devoted to the advancement of theoretical research in econometrics.

Econometrica. Blackwell Publishers, 350 Main St., 6th Fl Malden, MA 02148-5018. Phone: 800-216-2522 or (781)388-8200 Fax: (781)388-8210 E-mail: subscript@blackwell.pub • URL: http://www.blackwellpub.com • Bimonthly. $350.00 per year. Published in England by Basil Blackwell Ltd.

Econometrics of Financial Markets. John Y. Campbell and others. California Princeton Fulfillment Services, 1445 Lower Ferry Rd. Ewing, NJ 08618. Phone: 800-777-4726 or (609)883-1759 E-mail: donnaw@cpfs.pupress.princeton.edu • 1997. $49.50. Written for advanced students and industry professionals. Includes chapters on ''The Predictability of Asset Returns,'' ''Derivative Pricing Models,'' and ''Fixed-Income Securities.'' Provides a discussion of the random walk theory of investing and tests of the theory.

Economic Accounts for Agriculture. Organization for Economic Cooperation and Development. Available from OECD Publications and Information Center, 2001 L St., N. W., Suite 650 Washington, DC 20036-4922. Phone: 800-456-6323 or (202)785-6323 Fax: (202)785-0350 E-mail: washington.contact@oecd.org • URL: http://www.oecd.org • Annual. $51.00. Provides data for 14 years on agricultural output and its components, intermediate consumption, and gross value added to net income and capital formation. Relates to various commodities produced by OECD member countries.

Economic and Budget Outlook: Fiscal Years 2000-2009. Available from U. S. Government Printing Office, Washington, DC 20402. Phone: (202)512-1800 Fax: (202)512-2250 E-mail: gpoaccess@gpo.gov • URL: http://www.access.gpo.gov • 1999. $15.00. Issued by the Congressional Budget Office (http://www.cbo.gov). Contains CBO economic projections and federal budget projections annually to 2009 in billions of dollars. An appendix contains ''Historical Budget Data'' annually from 1962 to 1998, including revenues, outlays, deficits, surpluses, and debt held by the public.

Economic and Social Progress in Latin America Report. Inter-American Development Bank, 1300 New York Ave., N. W. Washington, DC 20577. Phone: (202)623-1000 Fax: (202)623-3096 E-mail: webmaster@iadb.org • URL: http://www.iadb.org • Annual. $24.95. Includes surveys of economic conditions in individual Latin American countries. Text in English.

Economic Botany: Devoted to Applied Botany and Plant Utilization. Society for Economic Botany. New York Botanical Garden Press, Bronx, NY 10458-5126. Phone: (718)817-8721 Fax: (718)817-8842 E-mail: nygbpress@nygb.org • URL: http://www.nybg.org • Quarterly. $88.00 per year. Includes *Plants and People*. Newsletter. Original research and review articles on the uses of plants.

Economic Development. Jan S. Hogendorn. Addison-Wesley Educational Publishers, Inc., One Jacob Way Reading, MA 01867. Phone: 800-447-2226 or (781)944-3706 Fax: (781)942-1117 1997. $81.00.

Economic Development. Michael P. Todaro. Addison-Wesley Longman, Inc., One Jacob Way Reading, MA 01867. Phone: 800-447-2226 or (781)944-3700 Fax: (781)944-9351 URL: http://www.awl.com • 2000. Seventh edition. Price on application.

Economic Development and Cultural Change. University of Chicago Press, Journals Div., P.O. Box 37005 Chicago, IL 60637. Phone: 800-621-2736 or (773)753-3347 Fax: (773)753-0811 E-mail: subscriptions@journals.uchicago.edu • URL: http://www.journals.uchicago.edu • Quarterly. Individuals, $44.00 per year; institutions, $138.00 per year. Examines the economic and social forces that affect development and the impact of development on culture.

Economic Development Monitor. Whitaker Newsletters, Inc., 313 South Ave. Fanwood, NJ 07023. Phone: (908)889-6336 Fax: (908)889-6339 Biweekly. $247.00 per year. Newsletter. Covers the news of U. S. economic and industrial development, including legislation, regulation, planning, and financing.

Economic Development Quarterly: The Journal of American Revitalization. Sage Publications, Inc., 2455 Teller Rd. Thousand Oaks, CA 91320. Phone: (805)499-0721 Fax: (805)499-0871 E-mail: info@sagepub.com • URL: http://www.sagepub.com • Quarterly. Individuals, $75.00 per year; institutions, $325.00 per year.

Economic Development Review. American Economic Development Council, 9801 W. Higgins Rd., Suite 540 Rosemont, IL 60018-4726. Phone: (847)692-9944 Fax: (847)696-2990 E-mail: aedc@interaccess.com • URL: http://www.aedc.org/hqtrs • Quarterly. Individuals, $60.00 per year; institutions, $48.00 per year.

Economic Forecasting Center., Georgia State University, College of Business Administration, University Plaza, 35 Broad St. Atlanta, GA 30303-3083. Phone: (404)651-3282 Fax: (404)651-3299 E-mail: efcdon@langate.gsu.edu • URL: http://www-ecfor.gsu.edu • Concerned with national and regional economic analysis and forecasting.

Economic Geology and the Bulletin of the Society of Economic Geologists. Society of Economic Geologist. Economic Geology Publishing Co., 7811 Shaffer Parkway Littleton, CO 80127. Phone: (720)981-7882 Fax: (720)981-7874 E-mail: seg@segweb.org • URL: http://www.segweb.org • Irregular. Individuals, $75.00 per year; institutions, $145.00 per year

Economic Growth Center. Yale University

Economic History Association., University of Kansas, Department of Economics, 213 Summerfield Hall Lawrence, KS 66045. Phone: (785)864-3501 or (785)864-2847 Fax: (785)864-5270 E-mail: eha@falcon.cc.ukans.edu • URL: http://www.eh.net/eha • Members are teachers and students of economic history.

Economic History of the United States. M.E. Sharpe, Inc., 80 Business Park Dr. Armonk, NY 10504. Phone: 800-541-6563 or (914)273-1800 Fax: (914)273-2106 E-mail: mesinfo@usa.net • 1977. Seven volumes.

Economic Impact of the Arts: A Sourcebook. Anthony Radich. National Conference of State Legislatures, 1560 Broadway, Suite 700 Denver, CO 80202-5140. Phone: (303)830-2200 Fax: (303)863-8003 E-mail: name.name@ncsl.org • URL: http://www.ncsl.org • 1987. $15.00. A collection of writings and studies on the economic impact of the arts.

Economic Indicators. Council of Economic Advisors, Executive Office of the President. Available from U.S. Government Printing Office, Washington, DC 20402. Phone: (202)512-1800 Fax: (202)512-2250 E-mail: gpoaccess@gpo.gov • URL: http://www.access.gpo.gov • Monthly. $55.00 per year.

Economic Indicators Handbook: Time Series, Conversions, Documentation. The Gale Group, 27500 Drake Rd. Farmington Hills, MI 48331-3535. Phone: 800-877-GALE Fax: 800-414-5043 or (248)699-8069 E-mail: galeord@galegroup.com • URL: http://www.galegroup.com • 2000. $195.00. Sixth edition. Provides data for about 175 U. S. economic indicators, such as the consumer price index (CPI), gross national product (GNP), and the rate of inflation. Values for series are given since inception, in both original form and adjusted for inflation. A bibliography of sources is included.

Economic Justice Report: Global Issues of Economic Justice. Ecumenical Coalition for Economic Justice, 947 Queen St., E., Suite 208 Toronto, ON, Canada M4M1J9. Phone: (416)462-1613 Fax: (416)463-5569 E-mail: ecej@accessv.com • URL: http://www.ecej.org • Quarterly. Individuals, $30.00 per year; institutions, $40.00 per year. Reports on economic fairness in foreign trade. Formerly *Gatt-Fly Report*.

Economic Outlook. Available from Basil Blackwell, Inc., 350 Main St., 6th Fl. Cambridge, MA 02148-5018. Phone: 800-216-2522 or (617)388-8200 Fax: (617)388-8210 E-mail: subscript@blackwellpub.com • URL: http://www.blackwellpub.com • Quarterly. $658.00 per year. Published by the London Business School. Includes country and global forecasts of over 170 economic and business variables. Actual data is shown for two years, with forecasts up to ten years.

Economic Outlook: A Newsletter on Economic Issues for Financial Institutions. America's Community Bankers, 900 19th St., N.W., Suite 400 Washington, DC 20006. Phone:

(202)857-3100 Fax: (202)296-8716 URL: http://www.acbankers.org • Monthly. Members, $106.00; non-members, $212.00 per year. Statistical profiles of the savings industry. Formerly *Economic Insight*.

Economic Perspectives (Chicago). Federal Reserve Bank of Chicago, Public Information Center, P.O. Box 834 Chicago, IL 60690. Phone: (312)322-5111 Quarterly. Free.

Economic Policy, Financial Markets, and Economic Growth. Benjamin Zycher and Lewis C. Solmon, editors. HarperCollins Publishers, 10 E. 53rd St. New York, NY 10022-5299. Phone: 800-242-7737 or (212)207-7000 Fax: 800-822-4090 or (212)207-7145 URL: http://www.harpercollins.com • 1993. $63.00.

Economic Report of the President: Together with the Annual Report of the Council of Economic Advisors. Available from U. S. Government Printing Office, Washington, DC 20402. Phone: (202)512-1800 Fax: (202)512-2250 E-mail: gpoaccess@gpo.gov • URL: http://www.access.gpo.gov • Annual. $29.00. Includes about 130 pages of "Statistical Tables Relating to Income, Employment, and Production." Tables cover national income, employment, wages, productivity, manufacturing, prices, credit, finance (public and private), corporate profits, and foreign trade.

Economic Review of Travel in America. Travel Industry Association of America, 1100 New York Ave., N.W., Suite 240 Washington, DC 20005-3934. Phone: (202)408-8422 Fax: (202)408-1255 E-mail: rmcclur@tia.org • URL: http://www.tia.org • Annual. Members, $75.00; non-members, $125.00. Presents a statistical summary of travel in the U.S., including travel expenditures, travel industry employment, tax data, international visitors, etc.

Economic Survey of Europe. United Nations Publications, Concourse Level, First Ave., 46th St. New York, NY 10017. Phone: 800-553-3210 or (212)963-7680 Fax: (212)963-4910 E-mail: bookstore@un.org • URL: http://www.un.org/publications • Three times a year. Price varies. Provides yearly analysis and review of the European economy, including Eastern Europe and the USSR. Text in English.

Economic Trends. American Hospital Association. American Hospital Publishing, Inc., One N. Franklin St., 27th Fl. Chicago, IL 60606-3421. Phone: 800-242-2626 or (312)422-3000 Fax: (312)422-4505 URL: http://www.aha.org • Quarterly. Members, $85.00 per year; non-members $135.00 per year. Provides statistical data on the nation's hospitals, including revenues, expenses.

Economics. Paul A. Samuelson and William D. Nordhaus. McGraw-Hill, 1221 Ave. of the Americas New York, NY 10020. Phone: 800-722-4726 or (212)904-2000 Fax: (212)904-2072 E-mail: customer.service@mcgraw-hill.com • URL: http://www.mcgraw-hill.com • 2000. $68.00. 17th edition.

Economics Explained: Everything You Need to Know About How the Economy Works and Where It's Going. Robert L. Heilbroner. Simon & Schuster Trade, 1230 Ave. of the Americas New York, NY 10020. Phone: 800-223-2336 or (212)698-7000 Fax: 800-445-6991 or (212)698-7007 URL: http://www.simonandschuster.com • 1994. $12.00. Fourth revised edition.

Economics of Corporation Law and Securities Regulation. Richard A. Posner and Kenneth E. Scott, editors. Aspen Books, 2961 W. California Ave., Suite E Salt Lake City, UT 84104. Phone: 800-748-4850 or (801)974-0414 Fax: (801)886-1603 E-mail: prawlins@aspenbook.com • URL: http://www.littlebrown.com • 1981. $20.95.

Economics of Development. Malcolm Gillis and others. W. W. Norton and Co., Inc., 500 Fifth Ave. New York, NY 10110. Phone: 800-223-2584 or (212)354-5500 Fax: (212)869-0856 E-mail: webmaster@wwnorton.com • URL: http://www.norton.com • 2000. Fifth edition. Price on application.

Economics of Divorce: The Effect on Parents and Children. Craig A. Everett. Haworth Press, Inc., 10 Alice St. Binghamton, NY 13904-1580. Phone: 800-429-6784 or (607)722-5857 Fax: 800-895-0582 or (607)722-1424 E-mail: getinfo@haworthpressinc.com • URL: http://www.haworthpressinc.com • 1994. $39.95. (Journal of Divorce and Remarriage Series).

Economics of Information: A Guide to Economic and Cost-Benefit Analysis for Information Professionals. Bruce R. Kingma. Libraries Unlimited, Inc., P.O. Box 6633 Englewood, CO 80155-6633. Phone: 800-237-6124 or (303)770-1220 Fax: (303)220-8843 E-mail: lu-books@lu.com • URL: http://www.lu.com • 2000. $45.00. Second edition. A technical discussion of market forces affecting the information industry. (Library and Information Science Text Series).

The Economics of Money, Banking and Financial Markets. Frederic S. Miskin. Addison Wesley Longman, Inc., One Jacob Way Reading, MA 01867. Phone: 800-447-2226 or (781)944-3700 Fax: (781)944-9351 URL: http://www.awl.com • 1999. $98.00. Fifth edition. (Economics Series).

Economics on Trial: Lies, Myths, and Realities. Mark Skousen. McGraw-Hill, 1221 Ave. of the Americas New York, NY 10020. Phone: 800-722-4726 or (212)904-2000 Fax: (212)904-2072 E-mail: customer.service@mcgraw-hill.com • URL: http://www.mcgraw-hill.com • 1993. $17.50.

Economics: Principles, Problems, and Policies. Campbell R. McConnell and Stanley Lee Brue. McGraw-Hill, 1221 Ave. of the Americas New York, NY 10020. Phone: 800-722-4726 or (212)904-2000 Fax: (212)904-2072 E-mail: customer.service@mcgraw-hill.com • URL: http://www.mcgraw-hill.com • 1998. $92.50. 13th edition.

Economics Today. Roger L. Miller. Addison-Wesley Longman, Inc., One Jacob Way Reading, MA 08167. Phone: 800-447-2226 or (781)944-3700 Fax: (781)944-9351 URL: http://www.awl.com • 2000. 11th edition. Price on application.

The Economist. Economist Intelligence Unit, 111 W. 57th St. New York, NY 10019-2211. Phone: 800-938-4685 or (212)554-0600 Fax: (212)586-1182 URL: http://www.eiu.com • 51 times a year. Individuals, $130.00 per year; institutions, $125.00 per year.

EContent. Online, Inc., 462 Danbury Rd. Wilton, CT 06897-2126. Phone: 800-248-8466 or (203)761-1466 Fax: (203)761-1444 E-mail: info@onlineinc.com • URL: http://www.onlineinc.com • Bimonthly. $55.00 per year. Directed at professional online information searchers. Formerly *Database*.

ECRI: Emergency Care Research Institute., 5200 Butler Pike Plymouth Meeting, PA 19462. Phone: (610)825-6000 Fax: (610)834-1275 E-mail: ecri@hslc.org • URL: http://www.ecri.org • Major research area is health care technology.

EDGAR Plus. Disclosure, Inc., 5161 River Rd. Bethesda, MD 20816. Phone: (301)951-1300 Fax: (301)657-1962 Provides SEC corporate filings full-text, plus other information, such as Fortune and Forbes rankings. Time period is 1968 to date, with continuous updating. Inquire as to online cost and availability. (EDGAR is the SEC's Electronic Data Gathering, Analysis, and Retrieval system.)

Edison Electric Institute.

Editing: An Annotated Bibliography. Bruce W. Speck. Greenwood Publishing Group, Inc., 88 Post Rd., W. Westport, CT 06881-5007. Phone: 800-225-5800 or (203)226-3571 Fax: (203)222-2540 E-mail: bookinfo@greenwood.com • URL: http://www.greenwood.com • 1991. $67.95. (Bibliographies and Indexes in Mass Media and Communications Series, No. 47).

Editing Your Newsletter: How to Produce an Effective Publication Using Traditional Tools and Computers. Mark Beach. F and W Publications, Inc., 1507 Dana Ave. Cincinnati, OH 45207-1005. Phone: 800-289-0963 or (513)531-2690 Fax: 888-590-4082 1995. $22.99. Fourth edition. Covers design, writing, editing, production and distribution. Emphasis on in-house publications.

Editor and Publisher International Yearbook: Encyclopedia of the Newspaper Industry. Editor and Publisher Co., Inc., 11 W. 19th St. New York, NY 10011-4234. Phone: (212)675-4380 Fax: (212)691-6939 E-mail: edpub@mediainfo.com • URL: http://www.mediainfo.com • Annual. $125.00. Daily and Sunday newspapers in the United States and Canada.

Editor and Publisher Journalism Awards and Fellowship Directory. Editor and Publisher Co., Inc., 11 W. 19th St. New York, NY 10011-4234. Phone: (212)675-4380 Fax: (212)691-6939 E-mail: edpub@mediainfo.com • URL: http://www.mediainfo.com • Annual. Price on application. Over 500 cash prizes scholarships, fellowships, and grants available to journalists and students for work on special subjects or in specific fields.

Editor and Publisher Market Guide. Editor and Publisher Co., Inc., 11 W. 19th St. New York, NY 10011-4234. Phone: (212)675-4380 Fax: (212)691-6939 E-mail: edpub@mediainfo.com • URL: http://www.mediainfo.com • Annual. $125.00. More than 1,700 newspaper markets in the Unite States and Canada.

Editor and Publisher Syndicate Directory: Annual Directory of Syndicate Services. Editor and Publisher Co., Inc., 11 W. 19th St. New York, NY 10011-4234. Phone: (212)675-4380 Fax: (212)691-6939 E-mail: edpub@mediainfo.com • URL: http://www.mediainfo.com • Annual. $8.00. Directory of several hundred syndicates serving newspapers in the United States and abroad with news, columns, features, comic strips, editorial cartoons, etc.

Editor and Publisher - The Fourth Estate: Spot News and Features About Newspapers, Advertisers and Agencies. Editor and Publisher Co., Inc., 11 W. 19th St. New York, NY 10011-4234. Phone: (212)675-4380 Fax: (212)691-6939 E-mail: edpub@mediainfo.com • URL: http://www.mediainfo.com • Weekly. $75.00 per year. Trade journal of the newspaper industry.

Editorial Freelancers Association.

Edmunds New Car Prices-Domestic and Import. Edmund Publications Corp., P.O. Box 18827 Beverly Hills, CA 90209-4827. Phone: (310)640-7840 Fax: (310)640-2456 Three times a year. $15.00 per year. Wholesale and retail prices for all American and import models and accessories. Includes federal crash reports, leasing facts, and accident report forms. Formerly *Edmund's New Car Prices*. Incorporates *Edmund's Foreign Car Prices*.

Edmund's Used Car Prices. Edmund Publications Corp., P.O. Box 18827 Beverly Hills, CA 90209-4827. Phone: (310)640-7840 Fax: (310)640-2456 Four times a year. $20.00 per year. Lists American and foreign used car prices for the past 10 years. Also lists van, pickup and sports utility used prices for the past 8 years.

EDP Weekly: The Leading Weekly Computer News Summary. Computer Age and E D P News Services, 714 Church St. Alexandria, VA 22314-4202. Phone: (703)739-8500 Fax: (703)739-8505 E-mail: millin@erols.com • URL: http://www.millimpubs.com • Weekly. $495.00 per year. Newsletter. Summarizes news from all areas of the computer and microcomputer industries.

Education for Older Adult Learning: A Selected, Annotated Bibliography. Reva M. Greenberg. Greenwood Publishing Group, Inc., 88 Post Rd., W. Westport, CT 06881-5007. Phone: 800-225-5800 or (203)226-3571 Fax: (203)222-2540 E-mail: bookinfo@greenwood.com • URL: http://www.greenwood.com • 1993. $75.00. Describes more than 700 books, articles, and other items relating to formal and informal education for older adults. (Bibliographies and Indexes in Gerontology Series, No. 20).

Education Index. H.W. Wilson Co., 950 University Ave. Bronx, NY 10452. Phone: 800-367-6770 or (718)588-8400 Fax: (718)590-1617 E-mail: custserv@hwwilson.com • URL: http://www.hwwilson.com • 10 times a year. Service basis.

Education Index Online. H. W. Wilson Co., 950 University Ave. Bronx, NY 10452. Phone: 800-367-6770 or (718)558-8400 Fax: (718)590-1617 Indexes a wide variety of periodicals related to schools, colleges, and education, 1984 to date. Monthly updates. Inquire as to online cost and availability.

Education Law. Matthew Bender & Co., Inc., Two Park Ave. New York, NY 10016. Phone: 800-223-1940 or (212)448-2000 Fax: (212)244-3188 E-mail: international@bender.com • URL: http://www.bender.com • $740.00. Four looseleaf volumes. Periodic supplementation. A reference for attorneys who represent persons having a grievance against educational institutions, and attorney representing such institutions, as well as school board members and administrators.

Education of a Speculator. Victor Niederhoffer. John Wiley and Sons, Inc., 605 Third Ave. New York, NY 10158-0012. Phone: 800-225-5945 or (212)850-6000 Fax: (212)850-6088 E-mail: info@jwiley.com • URL: http://www.wiley.com • 1997. $29.95. An autobiography providing basic advice on speculation, investment, and the commodity futures market.

Education Statistics of the United States. Mark S. Littman and Deirdre A. Gaquin, editors. Bernan Press, 4611-F Assembly Dr. Lanham, MD 20706-4391. Phone: 800-274-4447 or (301)459-7666 Fax: 800-865-3450 or (301)459-0056 E-mail: info@bernan.com • URL: http://www.bernan.com • 2000. $74.00. Second edition. Provides detailed county and state data, includes enrollment, educational attainment, per pupil expenditure, teacher pay and class size.

Education Week: American Education's Newspaper of Record. Editorial Projects in Education, Inc., 6935 Arlington Rd., Suite. 100 Bethesda, MD 20814. Phone: (301)280-3100 URL: http://www.edweek.org • 43 times a year. $79.94 per year.

Educational Administration Abstracts. Corwin Press, Inc., c/o Elizabeth Dix, 2455 Teller Rd. Thousand Oaks, CA 91320. Phone: (805)499-9734 Fax: (805)499-0871 E-mail: order@corwin.sagepub.com • URL: http://www.sagepub.com • Quarterly. Indivduals, $110.00 per year; institutions, $475.00 per year.

Educational Administration Quarterly. University Council for Educational Administratiotion. Corwin Press, Inc., c/o Elizabeth Dix, 2455 Teller Rd. Thousand Oaks, CA 91320. Phone: (805)499-9734 Fax: (805)499-5323 E-mail: order@corwin.sagepub.com • URL: http://www.sage.pub.com • Five times a year. Individuals, $85.00 per year; institutions, $308.00 per year.

Educational and Psychological Measurement: Devoted to the Development and Application of Measures of Individual Differences. Sage Publications, Inc., 2455 Teller Rd. Thousand Oaks, CA 91320. Phone: (805)499-0721 Fax: (805)499-0871 E-mail: info@sagepub.com • URL: http://www.sagepub • Bimonthly. Individuals, $95.00 per year; institutions, $395.00 per year.

Educational Foundation for Nuclear Science.

Educational Marketer: The Educational Publishing Industry's Voice of Authority Since 1968. SIMBA Information, P.O. Box 4234 Stamford, CT 06907-0234. Phone: 800-307-2529 or (203)358-4100 Fax: (203)358-5824 E-mail: info@simbanet.com • URL: http://www.simbanet.com • Three times a month. $479.00 per year. Newsletter. Edited for suppliers of educational materials to schools and colleges at all levels. Covers print and electronic publishing, software, audiovisual items, and multimedia. Includes corporate news and educational statistics.

Educational Media and Technology Yearbook. Libraries Unlimited, Inc., P.O. Box 6633 Englewood, CO 80155-6633.

Phone: 800-237-6124 or (303)770-1220 Fax: (303)220-8843 E-mail: lu-books@lu.com • Annual. $65.00.

Educational Rankings Annual: A Compilation of Approximately 3,500 Published Rankings and Lists on Every Aspect of Education. The Gale Group, 27500 Drake Rd. Farmington Hills, MI 48331-3535. Phone: 800-877-GALE or (248)699-GALE Fax: 800-414-5043 or (248)699-8069 E-mail: galeord@galegroup.com • URL: http://www.galegroup.com • 2000. $220.00. Provides national, regional, local, and international rankings of a wide variety of educational institutions, including business and professional schools.

Educational Technology News. Business Publishers, Inc., 8737 Colesville Rd., Suite 1100 Silver Spring, MD 20910-3928. Phone: 800-274-6737 or (301)587-6300 Fax: (301)587-1081 E-mail: bpinews@bpinews.com • URL: http://www.bpinews.com • Biweekly. $318.00 per year. Newsletter. Formerly *Education Computer News*.

Educational Technology Research and Development. Association for Educational Communications and Technology, 1800 N. Stonelake Dr., Suite 2 Bloomington, IN 47404-1517. Phone: (812)335-7675 Fax: (812)335-7675 URL: http://www.aect.org • Quarterly. $55.00 per year.

Educational Technology: The Magazine for Managers of Change in Education. Educational Technology Publications, Inc., 700 Palisade Ave. Englewood Cliffs, NJ 07632. Phone: 800-952-2665 or (201)871-4007 Fax: (201)871-4009 E-mail: ettecpubs@aol.com • Bimonthly. $119.00 per year.

Educational Testing Service.

Educators Guide to Free Films, Filmstrips and Slides. Educators Progress Service, Inc., 214 Center St. Randolph, WI 53956. Phone: 888-951-4469 or (920)326-3126 Fax: (920)326-3127 E-mail: epsinc@centurytel.net • Annual. $34.95. Lists more than 978 educational and recreational films in all subject areas for free use by teachers and other educators. Formerly *Educators Guide to Free Filmstrips and Slides*.

Educators Guide to Free Guidance Materials. Educators Progress Service, Inc., 214 Center St. Randolph, WI 53956. Phone: 888-951-4469 or (920)326-3126 Fax: (920)326-3127 E-mail: epsinc@centurytel.net • Annual. $34.95. Lists free-loan films, filmstrips, audiotapes, videotapes and free printed materials on guidance.

Educators Guide to Free Videotapes. James Berger, editor. Educators Progress Service, Inc., 214 Center St. Randolph, WI 53956. Phone: 888-951-4469 or (920)326-3126 Fax: (920)326-3127 E-mail: epsince@centurytel.net • Annual. $34.95. Lists free-loan audiotapes, videotapes and records. Formerly *Educators Guide to Free Audio and Video Materials*.

Educators Resource Directory. Grey House Publishing, 185 Millerton Rd. Millerton, NY 12546. Phone: 800-562-2139 or (518)789-8700 Fax: (518)789-0556 E-mail: books@greyhouse.com • URL: http://www.greyhouse.com • 2001. $145.00. Fourth edition. Listings include educational associations, conferences, trade shows, grants, research centers, library services, etc. (Sedgwick Press.) Also includes statistical data on elementary and secondary schools.

Edward L. Ginzton Laboratory., Stanford University, 450 Via Palou Stanford, CA 94305-4085. Phone: (650)023-0111 Fax: (650)725-9355 E-mail: dabm@ee.stanford.edu • URL: http://www.stanford.edu/group/ginzton • Research fields include low-temperature physics and superconducting electronics.

Edward Orton, Jr. Ceramic Foundation.

Edward Orton Jr. Ceramic Foundation-Refractories Testing and Research Center.

EE Product News (Electronics-Electrical). Penton Media Inc., 611 Route 46 W. Hasbrouck Heights, NJ 07604. Phone: (201)393-6060 Fax: (201)393-6043 E-mail: corpcomm@penton.com • URL: http://www.penton.com • Monthly. Free to qualified personnel; others, $55.00 per year.

EEO Law and Personnel Practices. Arthur Gutman. Sage Publications, Inc., 2455 Teller Rd. Thousand Oaks, CA 91320. Phone: (805)499-0721 Fax: (805)499-0871 E-mail: info@sagepub.com • URL: http://www.sagepub • 1993. $58.00. Discusses the practical effect of federal regulations dealing with race, color, religion, sex, national origin, age, and disability. Explains administrative procedures, litigation actions, and penalties.

EEOC Compliance Manual (Equal Employment Opportunity Commission). Bureau of National Affairs, Inc., 1231 25th St., N.W. Washington, DC 20037-1197. Phone: 800-372-1033 or (202)452-4200 Fax: (202)822-8092 E-mail: books@bna.com • URL: http://www.bna.com • Irregular. $263.00 per year, including periodic updates. Two volumes. Looseleaf.Guide to federal Equal Employment Opportunity Commission activities.

EF Foundation for Foreign Study., One Education St. Cambridge, MA 02141. Phone: 800-447-4273 or (617)619-1000 or (617)619-1400 Fax: (617)619-1401 E-mail: foundation@ef.com • URL: http://www.effoundation.org • Seeks to further international understanding through cultural and academic exchange. Sponsors academic homestay programs, such as High School Year in Europe.

Effective Clinical Practice. American College of Physicians, American Society of Internal Medicine, 190 N. Independence Mall West Philadelphia, PA 19106-1572. Phone: 800-523-1546 or (215)351-2400 Fax: (215)351-2799 E-mail: custserve@mail.acpooline.org • URL: http://www.acpoline.org • Bimonthly. Individuals, $54.00 per year; institutions, $70.00 per year. Formerly *HMO Practice*.

Effective Physical Security: Design, Equipment, and Operations. Lawrence J. Fennelly, editor. Butterworth-Heinemann, 225 Wildwood Ave. Woburn, MA 01081. Phone: 800-366-2665 or (781)904-2500 Fax: 800-446-6520 E-mail: orders@bhusa.com • URL: http://www.bh.com • 1996. $36.95. Second edition. Contains chapters written by various U. S. security equipment specialists. Covers architectural considerations, locks, safes, alarms, intrusion detection systems, closed circuit television, identification systems, etc.

Effective Supervisor's Handbook. Louis V. Imundo. AMACOM, 1601 Broadway, 12th Fl. New York, NY 10019-7406. Phone: 800-262-9699 or (212)586-8100 Fax: (518)891-2372 E-mail: custmserv.@amanet.org • URL: http://www.amanet.org • 1992. $16.95. Second edition.

Effective Writing for Engineers, Managers, Scientists. H. J. Tichy and Sylvia Fourdrinier. John Wiley and Sons, Inc., 605 Third Ave. New York, NY 10158-0012. Phone: 800-526-5368 or (212)850-6000 Fax: (212)850-6088 E-mail: info@wiley.com • URL: http://www.wiley.com • 1988. $104.95. Second edition.

EFT Report (Electronic Funds Transfer). Phillips Business Information, Inc., 1201 Seven Locks Rd., Suite 300 Potomac, MD 20854. Phone: 800-777-5006 or (301)340-1520 Fax: (301)309-3847 E-mail: pbi@phillips.com • URL: http://www.phillips.com/marketplaces.htm • Biweekly. $695.00 per year. Newsletter on subject of electronic funds transfer.

Egg Industry: Covering Egg Production, Processing and Marketing. Watt Publishing Co., 122 S. Wesley Ave. Mount Morris, IL 61054-1497. Phone: (815)734-4171 Fax: (815)734-4201 URL: http://www.wattnet.com • Monthly. $36.00 per year. Formerly *Poultry Tribune*.

EI Environmental Services Directory. Environmental Information Ltd., 7301 Ohms Lane, Suite 460 Minneapolis, MN 55439. Phone: (953)831-2473 Fax: (953)831-6550 E-mail: ei@mr.net • URL: http://www.envirobiz.com • Biennial. $1,250.00. Over 620 waste-handling facilities, 600 transportation firms, 500 spill response firms, 2,100 consultants, 470 laboratories, 450 soil boring/well drilling firms, incineration services, asbestos services, etc. Formerly *Industrial and Hazardous Waste Management Firms*.

EIA Residential Electric Bills in Major Cities. Energy Information Administration. U.S. Department of Energy, Washington, DC 20585. Phone: (202)586-4940 Annual.

EIA Trade Directory and Membership List. Electronic Industries Association, 2500 Wilson Blvd. Arlington, VA 22201. Phone: (703)907-7500 Fax: (703)907-7501 URL: http://www.eia.org • Annual. Members, $75.00; non-members, $150.00.

Election Results Directory Supplement. National Conference of State Legislatures, 1560 Broadway, Suite 700 Denver, CO 80202-5140. Phone: (303)830-2200 Fax: (303)863-8003 E-mail: name.name@ncsl.org • URL: http://www.ncsl.org • Annual. $35.00. Provides names, addresses, telephone numbers, and e-mail addresses of state legislators and executive officials.

Electric Lamps. U. S. Bureau of the Census, Washington, DC 20233-0800. Phone: (301)457-4100 Fax: (301)457-3842 URL: http://www.census.gov • Quarterly and annual. Provides data on shipments: value, quantity, imports, and exports. (Current Industrial Reports, MQ-36B.)

Electric Perspectives. Edison Electric Institute, 701 Pennsylvania Ave., N. W. Washington, DC 20004-2696. Phone: 800-334-5453 or (202)508-5000 Fax: 800-525-5562 or (202)508-5360 E-mail: vickyjcm@eei.org • URL: http://www.eei.org • Bimonthly. $50.00 per year. Covers business, financial, and operational aspects of the investor-owned electric utility industry. Edited for utility executives and managers.

Electric Power Monthly. Available from U. S. Government Printing Office, Washington, DC 20402. Phone: (202)512-1800 Fax: (202)512-2250 E-mail: gpoaccess@gpo.gov • URL: http://www.access.gpo.gov • Monthly. $115.00 per year. Issued by the Office of Coal and Electric Power Statistics, Energy Information Administration, U. S. Department of Energy. Contains statistical data relating to electric utility operation, capability, fuel use, and prices.

Electric Power Supply Association., 1401 H St., N. W., Suite 760 Washington, DC 20005. Phone: (202)789-7200 Fax: (202)789-7201 URL: http://www.epsa.org • Members are independent power producers.

Electric Utility Week: The Electric Utility Industry Newsletter. McGraw-Hill, Chemical Engineering Div., 1221 Ave. of the Americas New York, NY 10020. Phone: 800-722-4726 or (212)904-2000 Fax: (212)904-2072 E-mail: customer.service@mcgraw-hill.com • URL: http://www.mcgraw-hill.com • Weekly. $1,475.00 per year. Newsletter. Formerly *Electric Week*.

Electrical and Computer Engineering Industrial Institute. Purdue University School of Electrical and Computer Engineering

Electrical and Electronic Abstracts. INSPEC, Inc., 379 Thornall St. Edison, NJ 08837-2225. Phone: (732)321-5575 Fax: (732)321-5702 E-mail: inspec@iee.org • URL: http://www.iee.com • Monthly. $3,435.00 per year, with annual cumulation. *Science Abstracts. Section B*.

Electrical Apparatus: Magazine of Electromechanical Operation and Maintenance. Barks Publications, Inc., 400 N. Michigan Ave., Suite 900 Chicago, IL 60611-4104. Phone: (312)321-9440 Fax: (312)321-1288 E-mail: eamagazine@aol.com • Monthly. $45.00. Lists 3,000 manufacturers and distributors of electrical and electronic products.

Electrical Construction and Maintenance (EC&M). Intertec Publishing Corp., P.O. Box 12901 Overland Park, KS 66282-2901. Phone: 800-400-5945 or (913)341-1300 Fax: (913)967-1898 E-mail: subs@intertec.com • URL: http://www.intertec.com • Monthly. Free to qualified personnel; individuals, $30.00 per year; libraries, $25.00 per year.

Electrical Construction Materials Directory. Underwriters Laboratories, Inc., 333 Pfingsten Rd. Northbrook, IL 60062-2096. Phone: (847)272-8800 Fax: (847)272-0472 E-mail: northbrook@ul.com • Annual. $22.00. Lists construction materials manufacturers authorized to use UL label.

Electrical Contractor. National Electrical Contractors Association, Three Bethesda Metro Center, Suite 1100 Bethesda, MD 20814. Phone: (301)657-3110 Fax: (301)961-6495 Monthly. Membership.

Electrical Engineering Research Laboratory. University of Texas at Austin

Electrical Equipment Representatives Association.

Electrical Generating Systems Association.

Electrical Wholesaling. Intertec Publishing Corp., P.O. Box 12901 Overland Park, KS 66282-2901. Phone: 800-400-5945 or (913)341-1300 Fax: (913)967-1898 E-mail: subs@intertec.com • URL: http://www.ewweb.com • Monthly. $20.00 per year.

Electrical World. McGraw-Hill, 1221 Ave. of the Americas New York, NY 10020-1095. Phone: 800-722-4726 or (212)904-2000 Fax: (212)904-2072 E-mail: customer.service@mcgraw-hill.com • URL: http://www.mcgraw-hill.com • Monthly. $99.00 per year.

Electrical World Directory of Electric Power Producers and Distributors., 1200 G St., Suite 250 Washington, DC 20005. Phone: 800-486-3660 or (202)942-8788 Fax: (202)942-8789 E-mail: info@udidata.com • URL: http://www.infostore.mhenergy-com • Annual. $395.00. Over 3,500 investor-owned, municipal, rural cooperative and government electric utility systems in the U.S. and Canada. Formerly *Electrical World-Directory of Electric Power Producers*.

Electricity Information. OECD Publications and Information Center, 2001 L St., N.W., Ste. 650 Washington, DC 20036-4922. Phone: 800-456-6323 or (202)785-6323 Fax: (202)785-0350 E-mail: washinton.contact@oecd.org • URL: http://www.oecdwash.org • Annual. $130.00. Compiled by the International Energy Agency (IEA). Provides detailed electric power statistics for each OECD country, including data on prices, production, and consumption.

Electricity Supply Industry: Structure, Ownership, and Regulation. OECD Publications and Information Center, 2001 L St., N.W., Ste. 650 Washington, DC 20036-4922. Phone: 800-456-6323 or (202)785-6323 Fax: (202)785-0350 E-mail: washington.contact@oecd.org • URL: http://www.oecdwash.org • 1994. $113.00. Discusses the "extensive reform" of the electric utility industry that is underway worldwide. Includes profiles of the electricity supply industry.

Electrochemical Analysis and Diagnostic Laboratory.

Electromedical Equipment and Irradiation Equipment, Including X-Ray. U. S. Bureau of the Census, Washington, DC 20233-0800. Phone: (301)457-4100 Fax: (301)457-3842 URL: http://www.census.gov • Annual. Contains shipment quantity, value of shipment, export, and import data. (Current Industrial Report No. MA-38R.)

Electronic Business. Cahners Business Information, 275 Washington St. Newton, MA 02158-1630. Phone: 800-662-7776 or (617)964-3030 Fax: (617)558-4470 E-mail: corporate-communications@cahners.com • URL: http://www.cahners.com • Monthly. $83.90 per year. For the non-technical manager and executive in the electronics industry. Offers news, trends, figures and forecasts. Formerly *Electronic Business Today*.

Electronic Commerce World. Faulkner & Gray, Inc., 300 S. Wacker Drive, 18th Floor Chicago, IL 60606. Phone: (312)913-1334 Fax: (312)913-1369 URL: http://www.faulknergray.com • Monthly. $45.00 per year. Provides practical information on the application of electronic commerce technology. Also covers such items as taxation of e-business, cash management, copyright, and legal issues.

Electronic Design. Penton Media Inc., 611 Route 46 W. Hasbrouck Heights, NJ 07604-0823. Phone: (201)393-6060 Fax: (201)393-0204 E-mail: corpcomm@penton.com • URL: http://www.elecdesign.com • Biweekly. $100.00 per year. Provides technical information for U.S. design engineers and managers.

Electronic Design and Publishing: Business Practices. Liane Sebastian. Allworth Press, 10 E. 23rd St., Suite 210 New York, NY 10010. Phone: 800-491-2808 or (212)777-8395 Fax: (212)777-8261 E-mail: jbarager@allworth.com • URL: http://www.allworth.com • 1995. $19.95. Second edition.

Electronic Document Management Systems: A Practical Guide for Evaluators and Users. Thomas M. Koulopoulos. McGraw-Hill, 1221 Ave. of the Americas New York, NY 10020-1095. Phone: 800-722-4726 or (212)904-2000 Fax: (212)904-2072 E-mail: customer.service@mcgraw-hill.com • URL: http://www.mcgraw-hill.com • 1995. $45.00.

Electronic Engineering Times: The Industry Newspaper for Engineers and Technical Management. CMP Publications, Inc., 600 Community Dr. Manhasset, NY 11030. Phone: 800-577-5356 or (516)562-5000 Fax: (516)562-5325 URL: http://www.eetimes.com • Weekly. $199.00 per year.

Electronic Frontier Foundation., 1550 Bryant St., Suite 725 San Francisco, CA 94103. Phone: (415)436-9333 Fax: (415)436-9993 E-mail: info@eff.org • URL: http://www.eff.org • Members are individuals with an interest in computer-based communications. Promotes electronic communication civil liberties and First Amendment rights.

Electronic Funds Transfer Association.

Electronic Industries Association., 2500 Wilson Blvd. Arlington, VA 22201. Phone: (703)907-7500 Fax: (703)907-7501 URL: http://www.eia.org • Includes a Solid State Products Committee.

Electronic Industries Association's - Executive Report. Eletronic Industries Association, 2500 Wilson Blvd. Arlington, VA 22201. Phone: (703)907-7500 Fax: (703)907-7501 URL: http://www.eia.org • Bimonthly. Free to members; non-members, $50.00 per year.

Electronic Information Report: Empowering Industry Decision Makers Since 1979. SIMBA Information, P.O. Box 4234 Stamford, CT 06907-0234. Phone: 800-307-2529 or (203)358-4100 Fax: (203)358-5824 E-mail: info@simbanet.com • URL: http://www.simbanet.com • 46 times a year. $549.00 per year. Newsletter. Provides business and financial news and trends for online services, electronic publishing, storage media, multimedia, and voice services. Includes information on relevant IPOs (initial public offerings) and mergers. Formerly *Electronic Information Week*.

Electronic Instrument Handbook. Clyde F. Coombs. McGraw-Hill, 1221 Ave. of the Americas New York, NY 10020. Phone: 800-722-4726 or (212)904-2000 Fax: (212)904-2072 E-mail: customer.service@mcgraw-hill.com • URL: http://www.mcgraw-hill.com • 1999. $125.00. Second edition. (Engineering Handbook Series).

Electronic Learning in Your Classroom. Scholastic, Inc., 555 Broadway New York, NY 10012-3999. Phone: 800-724-6527 or (212)343-6100 Fax: (212)343-4535 URL: http://www.scholastic.com • Four times a year. $19.95 per year. Includes classroom applications for computers. For teachers of grades K-12. Formerly *Electronic Learning*.

The Electronic Library. Information Today, Inc., 143 Old Marlton Pike Medford, NJ 08055-8750. Phone: 800-300-9868 or (609)654-6266 Fax: (609)654-4309 E-mail: custserv@infotoday.com • URL: http://www.infotoday.com • Bimonthly. $269.00 per year.

Electronic Library: The Promise and the Process. Kenneth E. Dowlin. Neal-Schuman Publishers, Inc., 100 Varick St. New York, NY 10013. Phone: (212)925-8650 Fax: 800-584-2414 or (212)219-8916 E-mail: info@neal-schuman.com • URL: http://www.neal-schuman.com • 1984. $45.00. (Applications in Information Management and Technology Series).

Electronic Market Data Book. Electronic Industries Association, Marketing Services Dept., 2500 Wilson Blvd. Arlington, VA 22201. Phone: (703)907-7500 Fax: (703)907-7501 URL: http://www.eia.org • Annual. Members, $75.00; non-members, $125.00.

Electronic Market Trends. Electronic Industries Association, Marketing Services Dept., 2500 Wilson Blvd. Arlington, VA 22201. Phone: (703)907-7500 Fax: (703)907-7501 URL: http://www.eia.org • Monthly. Members, $100.00 per year; non-members, $150.00 per year.

Electronic Materials and Processing Research Laboratory. Pennsylvania State University

Electronic Media. Crain Communications, Inc., 740 N. Rush St. Chicago, IL 60611-2590. Phone: 800-678-9595 or (312)649-5200 Fax: (312)649-5465 URL: http://www.crain.com • Weekly. $119.00 per year.

Electronic Media Management. Peter K. Pringle and others. Butterworth-Heinemann, 225 Wildwood Ave. Woburn, MA 01801. Phone: 800-366-2665 or (781)904-2500 Fax: 800-446-6520 E-mail: orders@bhusa.com • URL: http://www.bh.com • 1999. $44.95. Fourth edition. (Focal Press).

Electronic Media Ratings. Karen Buzzard. Butterworth-Heinemann, 225 Wildwood Ave. Woburn, MA 01081. Phone: 800-366-2665 or (781)904-2500 Fax: 800-446-6520 E-mail: orders@bhusa.com • URL: http://www.bh.com • 1992. $22.95. Provides basic information about TV and radio audience-rating techniques. Includes glossary and bibliography. (Electronic Media Guide Series).

Electronic Messaging News: Strategies, Applications, and Standards. Phillips Business Information, Inc., 1201 Seven Locks Rd., Suite 300 Potomac, MD 20854. Phone: 800-777-5006 or (301)340-1520 Fax: (301)309-3847 E-mail: pbi@phillips.com • URL: http://www.phillips.com/marketplaces.htm • Biweekly. $597.00 per year. Newsletter.

Electronic Musician. Intertec Publishing Corp., 6400 Hollis St., Suite 12 Emeryville, CA 94608. Phone: 800-400-5945 or (510)653-3307 Fax: (510)653-5142 E-mail: subs@intertec.com • URL: http://www.intertec.com • Monthly. $23.95 per year.

Electronic News. Cahners Business Information, 345 Hudson St., 4th Fl. New York, NY 10014-4502. Phone: 800-662-7776 or (212)519-7200 Fax: (212)519-7675 E-mail: corporatecommunications@cahners.com • URL: http://www.cahners.com • 51 times a year. $119.00 per year.

Electronic Office Machines. William R. Pasewark. South-Western Publishing Co., 5101 Madison Rd. Cincinnati, OH 45227. Phone: 800-543-0487 or (513)271-8811 Fax: 800-437-8488 E-mail: billhendee@itped.com • URL: http://www.swcollege.com • 1995. $14.25. Seventh edition.

Electronic Office: Management and Technology. Faulkner Information Services, Inc., 114 Cooper Center, 7905 Browning Rd. Pennsauken, NJ 08109-4319. Phone: (856)662-2070 Fax: (856)662-3380 Two looseleaf volumes, with monthly updates. $990.00 per year. Contains product reports and other information relating to automated office and integrated services.

Electronic Products. Hearst Business Communications, Inc. UTP Div., 645 Stewart Ave. Garden City, NY 11530. Phone: (516)227-1300 Fax: (516)227-1444 URL: http://www.electronicproducts.com • Monthly. $50.00 per year.

Electronic Publishing: Applications and Implications. Elisabeth Logan and Myke Gluck, editors. Information Today, Inc., 143 Old Marlton Pike Medford, NJ 08055-8750. Phone: 800-300-9868 or (609)654-6266 Fax: (609)654-4309 E-mail: custserv@infotoday.com • URL: http://www.infotoday.com • 1997. $34.95. Provides information on copyright, preservation, standards, and other issues relating to the substitution of electronic media for paper-based print.

Electronic Publishing: For the Business Leaders Who Buy Technology. PennWell Corp., Advanced Technology Div., 98 Spit Brook Rd. Nashua, NH 03062-5737. Phone: 800-331-4463 or (603)891-0123 Fax: (603)891-0539 E-mail: webmaster@pennwell.com • URL: http://www.pennwell.com • Monthly. $45.00 per year. Edited for digital publishing professionals. New products are featured.

Electronic Selling: Twenty-Three Steps to E-Selling Profits. Brian Jamison and others. McGraw-Hill, 1221 Ave. of the Americas New York, NY 10020. Phone: 800-722-4726 or (212)904-2000 Fax: (212)904-2072 E-mail: customer.service@mcgraw-hill.com • URL: http://www.mcgraw-hill.com • 1997. $24.95. Covers selling on the World Wide Web, including security and payment issues. Provides a glossary and directory information. The authors are consultants specializing in Web site production.

Electronic Servicing & Technology: The How-To Magazine of Electronics. CQ Communications, Inc., 25 Newbridge Rd. Hicksville, NY 11801-2805. Phone: 800-853-9797 or (516)681-2922 Fax: (516)681-2926 E-mail: cq@cq-amateur-radio.com • URL: http://www.electronic-servicing.com • Monthly. $26.95 per year. Provides how-to technical information to technicians who service consumer electronics equipment.

Electronic Strategies. Thomson Financial Securities Data, Two Gateway Center Newark, NJ 07102. Phone: 888-989-8373 or (973)622-3100 Fax: (973)622-1421 E-mail: tfsd.cs@tfn.com • URL: http://www.tfsd.com • Monthly. $2,995.00 per year. CD-ROM contains full text of investment analysts' reports on companies operating in the following fields: electronics, computers, semiconductors, and office products.

Electronic Styles: A Handbook for Citing Electronic Information. Xia Li and Nancy Crane. Information Today, Inc., 143 Old Marlton Pike Medford, NJ 08055-8750. Phone: 800-300-9868 or (609)654-6266 Fax: (609)654-4309 E-mail: custserv@infotoday.com • URL: http://www.infotoday.com • 1996. $19.99. Second edition. Covers the citing of text-based information, electronic journals, Web sites, CD-ROM items, multimedia products, and online documents.

Electronic Visualization Laboratory., University of Illinois at Chicago, Engineering Research Facility, 842 W. Taylor St., Room 2032 Chicago, IL 60607-7053. Phone: (312)996-3002 Fax: (312)413-7585 E-mail: tom@eecs.uic.edu • URL: http://www.evl.uic.edu • Research areas include computer graphics, virtual reality, multimedia, and interactive techniques.

Electronics and Communications Abstracts Journal: Comprehensive Coverage of Essential Scientific Literature. Cambridge Information Group, 7200 Wisconsin Ave., 6th Fl. Bethesda, MD 20814. Phone: 800-843-7751 or (301)961-6700 Fax: (301)961-6720 Monthly. $1,045.00 per year.

Electronics Fundamentals: Circuits, Devices, and Applications. Thomas L. Floyd. Prentice Hall, 240 Frisch Court Paramus, NJ 07652-5240. Phone: 800-947-7700 or (201)909-6200 Fax: 800-445-6991 or (201)909-6361 URL: http://www.prenhall.com • 2000. $90.67. Fifth edition.

Electronics Laboratory. Oklahoma State University

Electronics Representatives Association., 444 N. Michigan Ave., Suite 1960 Chicago, IL 60611. Phone: 800-776-7377 or (312)527-3050 Fax: (312)527-3783 E-mail: info@era.org • URL: http://www.era.org • Includes a Consumer Products Division. Members are manufacturers' representatives.

Electronics Research Laboratory. University of California at Berkeley

Elements of Bibliography: A Guide to Information Sources and Practical Applications. Robert B. Harmon. Scarecrow Press, Inc., 4720 Boston Way Lanham, MD 20706-4310. Phone: 800-462-6420 or (301)459-3366 Fax: 800-338-4550 or (301)459-1705 1998. $49.50. Third edition.

Elements of Bibliography: A Simplified Approach. Robert B. Harmon. Scarecrow Press, Inc., 4720 Boston Way Lanham, MD 20706-4310. Phone: 800-462-6420 or (301)459-3366 Fax: 800-338-4550 or (301)459-1705 E-mail: orders@scarecrowpress.com • URL: http://www.scarecrowpress.com • 1989. $37.00. Revised edition.

The Elements of Editing: A Modern Guide for Editors and Journalists. Arthur Plotnik. Pearson Education and Technology, 201 W. 103rd St. Indianapolis, IN 46290-1097. Phone: 800-858-7674 or (317)581-3500 Fax: (317)581-4670 URL: http://www.mcp.com • 1986. $9.95.

Elevator World. Elevator World, Inc., P.O. Box 6507 Mobile, AL 36660. Phone: 800-730-5093 or (334)479-4514 Fax: (334)479-7403 E-mail: sales@elevator-world.com • URL: http://www.elevator-world.com • Monthly. $67.00 per year.

Elevator World-Source Issue. Elevator World, Inc., 356 Morgan Ave. Mobile, AL 36606. Phone: 800-730-5093 or (334)479-4514 Fax: (334)479-7403 E-mail: sales@elevator-world.com • URL: http://www.elevator-world.com • Annual. $35.00. Lists about 450 elevator manufacturers and suppliers to the industry; consultants and 109 trade associations; international coverage.

Elliott Wave Theorist. Robert Prechter, editor. Elliott Wave International, P.O. Box 1618 Gainesville, GA 30503. Phone: (770)536-0309 Monthly. $233.00 per year. Newsletter Formerly *Elliott Wave Commodity Forecasts*.

Elsevier's Dictionary of Automotive Engineering. A. Schellings. Elsevier Science, 655 Ave. of the Americas New York, NY 10010. Phone: 888-437-4636 or (212)989-5800 Fax: (212)633-3680 E-mail: usinfo@elsevier.com • URL: http://www.elsevier.com • 1998. Price on application.

EM: Environmental Solutions That Make Good Business Sense. Air and Waste Management Association, One Gateway Center, 3rd Fl. Pittsburgh, PA 15222. Phone: 800-270-3444 or (412)232-3444 Fax: (412)232-3450 URL: http://www.awma.org • Monthly. Individuals $99.00 per year; institutions, $130.00 per year. Newsletter. Provides news of regulations, legislation, and technology relating to the environment, recycling, and waste control. Formerly *Environmental Manager*.

eMarketer's eAdvertising Report. Available from MarketResearch.com, 641 Ave. of the Americas, Third Floor New York, NY 10011. Phone: 800-298-5699 or (212)807-2629 Fax: (212)807-2716 E-mail: order@marketresearch.com • URL: http://www.marketresearch.com • 1999. $795.00. Market research data published by eMarketer. Covers the growth of the Internet online advertising market. Includes future trends and Internet users' attitudes.

Embase. Elsevier Science, Inc., 655 Ave. of the Americas New York, NY 10010. Phone: (212)633-3730 Fax: (212)633-3680 Worldwide medical literature, 1974 to present. Weekly updates. Inquire as to online cost and availability.

Embroidery News. I. Leonard Seiler, editor. Schiffli Lace and Embroidery Manufacturers Association, 596 Anderson Ave., Ste. 203 Cliffside Park, NJ 07010-1831. Phone: (201)943-7757 Fax: (201)943-7793 Bimonthly. Free to qualified personnel; others, $10.00.

Emergency Department Law: The Source for Comprehensive Coverage of Legal Trends in Emergency Medicine. Business Publishers, Inc., 8737 Colesville Rd., Suite 1100 Silver Spring, MD 20910-3928. Phone: 800-274-6737 or (301)587-6300 Fax: (301)587-1081 E-mail: bpinews@bpinews.com • URL: http://www.bpinews.com • Monthly.

$355.00 per year. Newsletter for the medical profession. Formerly *Medical Liability Advisory Service*.

Emergency Response Directory for Hazardous Materials Accidents. Odin Press, P.O. Box 536 New York, NY 10021. Phone: (212)744-2538 Biennial. $36.00. Provides resources for the containment and cleanup of toxic spills. Lists government agencies, spill response contractors, chemical manufacturers, hot lines, etc.

Emerging and Special Situations. Standard & Poor's, 55 Water St. New York, NY 10041. Phone: 800-221-5277 or (212)438-2000 Fax: (212)438-0040 E-mail: questions@standardandpoor.com • URL: http://www.standardandpoors.com • Monthly. $210.00 per year. Newsletter.

Emerging Markets Analyst., P.O. Box 238 Chazy, NY 12921. Phone: (514)499-9706 Fax: (514)499-9709 Monthly. $895.00 per year. Provides an annual overview of the emerging financial markets in 24 countries of Latin America, Asia, and Europe. Includes data on international mutual funds and closed-end funds.

Emerging Markets Debt Report. Securities Data Publishing, 40 West 57th St. New York, NY 10019. Phone: 800-455-5844 or (212)765-5311 Fax: (212)956-0112 E-mail: sdp@tfn.com • URL: http://www.sdponline.com • Weekly. $895.00 per year. Newsletter. Provides information on new and prospective sovereign and corporate bond issues from developing countries. Includes an emerging market bond index and pricing data. (Securities Data Publishing is a unit of Thomson Financial.)

Emerging Markets Quarterly. Institutional Investor, 488 Madison Ave. New York, NY 10022. Phone: (212)224-3300 Fax: (212)224-3353 E-mail: info@iijournals.com • URL: http://www.iijournals.com • Quarterly. $325.00 per year. Newsletter on financial markets in developing areas, such as Africa, Latin America, Southeast Asia, and Eastern Europe. Topics include institutional investment opportunities and regulatory matters. Formerly *Emerging Markets Weekly*.

Emerging Markets Traders Association., 63 Wall St., 20th Fl. New York, NY 10005. Phone: (212)293-5000 URL: http://www.emta.org • Promotes orderly trading markets for emerging market instruments. Includes Options/Derivatives Working Group.

Emerging Stock Markets Factbook. International Finance Corporation, Capital Market Dept., 2121 Pennsylvania Ave., N.W. Washington, DC 20433. Phone: (202)473-9520 Fax: (202)974-4805 E-mail: emdb@ifc.org • URL: http://www.ifc.org • Annual. $100.00. Published by the International Finance Corporation (IFC). Provides statistical profiles of more than 26 emerging stock markets in various countries of the world. Includes regional, composite, and industry indexes.

Emerging Trends in Securities Law. West Group, 610 Opperman Dr. Eagan, MN 55123. Phone: 800-328-4880 or (651)687-7000 Fax: 800-213-2323 or (651)687-5827 URL: http://www.westgroup.com • Annual. $176.00. Presents a detailed chronicle of events and analysis of evolving trends.

Emerson's Directory of Leading U.S. Accounting Firms. Available from Hoover's, Inc., 1033 La Posada Drive, Suite 250 Austin, TX 78752. Phone: 800-486-8666 or (512)374-4500 Fax: (512)374-4505 E-mail: orders@hoovers.com • URL: http://www.hoovers.com • Biennial. $195.00. Published by the Emerson Company (http://www.emersoncompany.com). Provides information on 500 major CPA firms.

Emerson's Directory of Leading U.S. Law Firms. Available from Hoover's, Inc., 1033 La Posada Drive, Suite 250 Austin, TX 78752. Phone: 800-486-8666 or (512)374-4500 Fax: (512)374-4505 E-mail: orders@hoovers.com • URL: http://www.hoovers.com • Biennial. $195.00. Published by the Emerson Company (http://www.emersoncompany.com). Provides information on 500 major law firms.

Emerson's Directory of Leading U.S. Technology Consulting Firms. Available from Hoover's, Inc., 1033 La Posada Drive, Suite 250 Austin, TX 78752. Phone: 800-486-8666 or (512)374-4500 Fax: (512)374-4505 E-mail: orders@hoovers.com • URL: http://www.hoovers.com • Biennial. $195.00. Published by the Emerson Company (http://www.emersoncompany.com). Provides information on 500 major consulting firms specializing in technology.

The Emperor's Virtual Clothes: The Naked Truth About Internet Culture. Dinty Moore. Algonquin Books of Chapel Hill, P.O. Box 2225 Chapel Hill, NC 27515-2225. Phone: (919)967-0108 Fax: (919))933-0272 1995. $17.95. A readable consideration of both positive and negative aspects of the Internet.

Employee and Union Member Guide to Labor Law. National Lawyers Guild. West Group, 610 Opperman Dr. Eagan, MN 55123. Phone: 800-328-4880 or (651)687-7000 Fax: 800-213-2323 or (651)687-5827 URL: http://www.westgroup.com • Two looseleaf volumes. $235.00. Periodic supplementation. Labor law for union members.

Employee Assistance Programs: An Annotated Bibliography. Donna Kemp. Garland Publishing, Inc., 19 Union Square West, 8th Fl. New York, NY 10003-3382. Phone: 800-627-6273 or (212)414-0650 Fax: (212)414-0659 E-mail: info@garland.com • URL: http://www.garlandpub.com • 1989. $15.00. (Public Affairs and Administration Series).

Employee Assistance Quarterly. Haworth Press, Inc., 10 Alice St. Binghamton, NY 13904-1580. Phone: 800-429-6784 or (607)722-5857 Fax: 800-895-0582 or (607)722-1424 E-mail: getinfo@haworthpressinc.com • URL: http://www.haworthpressinc.com • Quarterly. Individuals, $40.00 per year; institutions. $80.00 per year; libraries, $375.00 per year. An academic and practical journal focusing on employee alcoholism and mental health problems. Formerly *Labor-Management Alcoholism Journal*.

Employee Benefit Cases. Bureau of National Affairs, Inc., 1231 25th St., N.W. Washington, DC 20037-1197. Phone: 800-372-1033 or (202)452-4200 Fax: (202)822-8092 E-mail: books@bna.com • URL: http://www.bna.com • 50 times a year. $1,141.00 per year. Looseleaf.

Employee Benefit News: The News Magazine for Employee Benefit Management. Securities Data Publishing, 40 West 57th St. New York, NY 10019. Phone: 800-455-5844 or (212)765-5311 Fax: (212)956-0112 E-mail: sdp@tfn.com • URL: http://www.sdponline.com • Monthly. $94.00 per year. Edited for human relations directors and other managers of employee benefits. (Securities Data Publishing is a unit of Thomson Financial.)

Employee Benefit Plan Review. Charles D. Spencer and Associates, Inc., 250 S. Wacker Dr., Suite 600 Chicago, IL 60606-5834. Phone: (312)993-7900 Monthly. $75.00 per year. (Also *Spencer's Research Reports on Employee Benefits*. Looseleaf service. $585.00 per year). Provides a review of recent events affecting the administration of employee benefit programs.

Employee Benefit Plans: A Glossary of Terms. Judith A. Sankey, editor. International Foundation of Employee Benefit Plans, P.O. Box 69 Brookfield, WI 53008-0069. Phone: 888-334-3327 or (414)786-6700 Fax: (414)786-8670 E-mail: books@ifebp.org • URL: http://www.ifebp.org • 1997. $32.00. Ninth edition. Contains updated and new definitions derived from all aspects of the employee benefits field in the U.S. and Canada.

Employee Benefit Research Institute., 2121 K St., N. W., Suite 600 Washington, DC 20037-1896. Phone: (202)659-0670 Fax: (202)775-6312 E-mail: salisbury@ebri.org • URL: http://www.ebri.org • Conducts research on employee benefits, including various kinds of pensions, individual retirement accounts (IRAs), health insurance, social security, and long-term health care benefits.

Employee Benefits Digest. International Foundation of Employee Benefit Plans, P.O. Box 69 Brookfield, WI 53008-0069. Phone: 888-334-3327 or (262)786-6700 Fax: (262)786-8670 E-mail: journals@ifebp.org • URL: http://www.ifebp.org • Monthly. $190.00 per year. Articles on timely topics and information on current employee benefits literature.

Employee Benefits Handbook. Warren, Gorham and Lamont/RIA Group, 395 Hudson St. New York, NY 10014. Phone: 800-950-1215 or (212)367-6300 Fax: (212)924-0460 E-mail: customer_services@riag.com • URL: http://www.westgroup.com • Looseleaf service. $195.00. Semiannual updates.

Employee Benefits in Medium and Large Private Establishments. Available from U. S. Government Printing Office, Washington, DC 20402. Phone: (202)512-1800 Fax: (202)512-2250 E-mail: gpoaccess@gpo.gov • URL: http://www.access.gpo.gov • Biennial. Issued by Bureau of Labor Statistics, U. S. Department of Labor. Provides data on benefits provided by companies with 100 or more employees. Covers benefits for both full-time and part-time workers, including health insurance, pensions, a wide variety of paid time-off policies (holidays, vacations, personal leave, maternity leave, etc.), and other fringe benefits.

Employee Benefits in Small Private Establishments. Available from U. S. Government Printing Office, Washington, DC 20402. Phone: (202)512-1800 Fax: (202)512-2250 E-mail: gpoaccess@gpo.gov • URL: http://www.access.gpo.gov • Biennial. Issued by Bureau of Labor Statistics, U. S. Department of Labor. Supplies data on a wide variety of benefits provided by companies with fewer than 100 employees. Includes statistics for both full-time and part-time workers.

Employee Benefits Infosource. International Foundation of Employee Benefit Plans, P.O. Box 69 Brookfield, WI 53008-0069. Phone: (262)786-6710 Fax: (262)786-8780 Provides citations and abstracts to the literature of employee benefits, 1986 to present. Monthly updates. Inquire as to online cost and availability.

Employee Benefits Journal. International Foundation of Employee Benefit Plans, P.O. Box 69 Brookfield, WI 53008-0069. Phone: 888-334-3327 or (262)786-6700 Fax: (262)786-8670 E-mail: pr@ifebp.org • URL: http://www.ifebp.org • Quarterly. $70.00 per year. Selected articles on timely and important benefit subjects.

Employee Benefits Management. CCH, Inc., 4025 W. Peterson Ave. Chicago, IL 60646-6085. Phone: 800-248-3248 or (773)583-8500 Fax: 800-224-8299 URL: http://www.cch.com • Five looseleaf volumes. Newsletter and semimonthly updates. Emphasis on pension plans.

Employee Health and Fitness: The Executive Update on Health Improvement Programs. American Health Consultants, Inc., 3525 Piedmont Rd., N.E., Bldg. 6, Suite 400 Atlanta, GA 30305-5278. Phone: 800-688-2421 or (404)262-7436 Fax: 800-284-3291 or (404)262-7837 E-mail: custserv@ahcpub.com • URL: http://www.ahcpub.com • Monthly. $499.00 per year. Newsletter. Executive update on health improvement programs.

Employee Involvement Association., 525 Fifth St., S.W., Ste. A Des Moines, IA 50309-4501. Phone: (515)282-8192 Fax: (515)282-9117 E-mail: jbw@amg-inc.com • URL: http://www.eia.com • Members are business and government professionals dedicated to employee involvement processes, including suggestion systems.

Employee Involvement Association Membership Directory. Employee Involvement Association, 525 S.W. Fifth St., Suite A Des Moines, IA 50309. Phone: (515)282-8192 Fax: (515)282-9117 E-mail: eia@assoc-mgmt.com • URL: http://www.eia.com • Annual. Membership.

Employee Involvement Association Statistical Report. Employee Involvement Association, 525 S.W. Fifth St., Suite A Des Moines, IA 50309. Phone: (515)282-8192 Fax: (515)282-9117 E-mail: eia@assoc-mgmt.com • URL: http://www.eia.com • Annual. 150.00.

Employee Ownership Report. National Center for Employee Ownership, Inc., 1736 Franklin St., 8th Fl. Oakland, CA 94612. Phone: (510)208-1300 Fax: (510)272-9510 E-mail: nceo@nceo.org • URL: http://www.nceo.org • Bimonthly. Membership. Formerly *Employee Ownership*.

Employee Policy for the Private and Public Sector: State Capitals. Wakeman-Walworth, Inc., P.O. Box 7376 Alexandria, VA 22307-0376. Phone: 800-876-2545 or (703)549-8606 Fax: (703)549-1372 E-mail: newsletters@statecapitals.com • URL: http://www.statecapitals.com • Weekly. $245.00 per year. Newsletter. Formerly *From the State Capitals: Employee Policy for the Private and Public Sector*.

Employee Relations Bulletin. Bureau of Business Practice, Inc., 24 Rope Ferry Rd. Waterford, CT 06386. Phone: 800-243-0876 or (860)442-4365 Fax: (860)437-3555 E-mail: rebecca_armitage@prenhall.com • URL: http://www.bbpnews.com • Semimonthly. $199.00 per year. Newsletter. Formerly *Employee Relations and Human Resources Bulletin*.

Employee Relocation Council., 1720 N St., N.W. Washington, DC 20036. Phone: (202)857-0857 Fax: (202)467-4012 E-mail: info@erc.org • URL: http://www.erc.org • Members are major corporations seeking efficiency and minimum disruption when employee transfers take place.

Employee Representation: Alternatives and Future Directions. Bruce E. Kaufman and Morris Kleiner, editors. University of Wisconsin, Industrial Realtions Research Assoc., 4233 Social Science Bldg., 1180 Observatory Dr. Madison, WI 53706-1393. Phone: (608)262-2762 Fax: (608)265-4591 E-mail: irra@macc.wisc.edu • URL: http://www.ilr.cornell.edu/irra • 1993. $28.00.

Employee Services Management: The Journal of Employee Services, Recreation, Health and Education. National Employee Service and Recreation Association, 2211 S. York Rd., Suite 207 Oak Brook, IL 60523. Phone: (630)368-1280 Fax: (630)368-1286 E-mail: nesrahq@nesra.org • URL: http://www.nesra.org • 10 times a year. $44.00 per year.

Employee Stock Ownership Plans: A Practical Guide to ESOPs and Other Broad Ownership Programs. Scott Rodrick, editor. Harcourt Brace, Legal and Professional Publications, Inc., 111 W. Jackson Blvd., 7th Fl. Chicago, IL 60604-3502. Phone: 800-782-1272 or (312)853-3662 Fax: (312)782-2378 E-mail: cszillage@harcourtbrace.com • 1996. $79.00. Contains 19 articles by various authors on ESOPs, 401(k) plans, profit sharing, executive stock option plans, and related subjects.

Employee Terminations Law Bulletin. Quinlan Publishing Co., Inc., 23 Drydock Ave., 2nd Fl. Boston, MA 02110-2387. Phone: 800-229-2084 or (617)542-0048 Fax: (617)345-9646 Monthly. $89.00 per year. Newsletter.

Employers Council on Flexible Compensation., 927 15th St., N.W., Suite 1000 Washington, DC 20005. Phone: (202)659-4300 E-mail: infoefc@ecfc.org • URL: http://www.ecfc.org • Promotes flexible or "cafeteria" plans for employee compensation and benefits.

Employment Agency. Entrepreneur Media, Inc., 2445 McCabe Way Irvine, CA 92614. Phone: 800-421-2300 or (949)261-2325 Fax: (949)261-0234 E-mail: entmag@entrepreneur.com • URL: http://www.entrepreneur.com • Looseleaf. $59.50. A practical guide to starting an employment agency. Covers profit potential, start-up costs, market size evaluation, owner's time required, site selection, lease negotiation, pricing, accounting, advertising, promotion, etc. (Start-Up Business Guide No. E1051.)

Employment and Earnings. Available from U. S. Government Printing Office, Washington, DC 20402. Phone: (202)512-1800 Fax: (202)512-2250 E-mail: gpoaccess@gpo.gov • URL: http://www.access.gpo.gov • Monthly. $50.00 per year, including annual supplement. Produced by the Bureau of Labor Statistics, U. S. Department of Labor.

Provides current data on employment, hours, and earnings for the U. S. as a whole, for states, and for more than 200 local areas.

Employment and Training Reporter. MII Publications, Inc., 733 15th St., N.W., Suite 900 Washington, DC 20005-2112. Phone: (202)347-4822 Fax: (202)347-4893 $747.00 per year. Looseleaf service. Weekly reports. Two volumes.

Employment and Wages: Annual Averages. Available from U. S. Government Printing Office, Washington, DC 20402. Phone: (202)512-1800 Fax: (202)512-2250 E-mail: gpoaccess@gpo.gov • URL: http://www.access.gpo.gov • Annual. $48.00. Issued by the Bureau of Labor Statistics, U. S. Department of Labor. Presents a wide variety of data arranged by state and industry.

Employment Discrimination. Matthew Bender & Co., Inc., Two Park Ave. New York, NY 10016. Phone: 800-223-1940 or (212)448-2000 Fax: (212)244-3188 E-mail: international@bender.com • URL: http://www.bender.com • $1,260.00. Nine looseleaf volumes. Periodic supplementation, $849.00. Treatise on both substantive and procedural law governing employment discrimination based on sex, age, race, religion, national origin, etc.

Employment Discrimination: Law and Litigation. Merrick T. Rossein. West Group, 610 Opperman Dr. Eagan, MN 55123. Phone: 800-328-4880 or (651)687-7000 Fax: 800-213-2323 or (651)687-5827 URL: http://www.westgroup.com • $220.00 per year. Looseleaf service. Periodic supplementation. Covers employment provisions of the Civil Rights Act, the Equal Pay Act, and related topics.

Employment Law Guide to the Americans with Disabilities Act. Mark Daniels. Prentice Hall, 240 Frisch Court Paramus, NJ 07652-5240. Phone: 800-947-7700 or (201)909-6200 Fax: 800-445-6991 or (201)909-6361 URL: http://www.prenhall.com • 1992. $95.00.

Employment Litigation Reporter: The National Journal of Record for Termination Lawsuits Alleging Tort and Contract Claims Against Employers. Andrews Publications, 175 Strafford Ave., Bldg. 4, Suite 140 Wayne, PA 19087. Phone: 800-345-1101 or (610)622-0510 Fax: (610)622-0501 URL: http://www.andrewspub.com • Semimonthly. $825.00 per year. Provides reports on wrongful dismissal lawsuits.

Employment Outlook. OECD Publications and Information Center, 2001 L St., N.W., Ste. 650 Washington, DC 20036-4922. Phone: 800-456-6323 or (202)785-6323 Fax: (202)785-0350 E-mail: washington.contact@oecd.org • URL: http://www.oecdwash.org • Annual. $50.00. Outlines the employment prospects for the coming year in OECD countries. Also discusses labor force growth, job creation, labor standards, and collective bargaining.

Employment Outlook, 1996-2006: A Summary of BLS Projections. Available from U. S. Government Printing Office, Washington, DC 20402. Phone: (202)512-1800 Fax: (202)512-2250 E-mail: gpoaccess@gpo.gov • URL: http://www.access.gpo.gov • 1998. $10.00. Issued by the Bureau of Labor Statistics, U. S. Department of Labor (http://www.bls.gov). Provides 1996 employment data and 2006 projections for a wide variety of managerial, professional, technical, marketing, clerical, service, agricultural, and production occupations. Includes factors affecting the employment growth of various industries. (Bureau of Labor Statistics Bulletin 2502.)

Employment Practice Guide. CCH, Inc., 4025 W. Peterson Ave. Chicago, IL 60646-6085. Phone: 800-248-3248 or (773)583-8500 Fax: 800-224-8299 URL: http://www.cch.com • Weekly. $999.00 per year. Four looseleaf volumes.

Employment Practices Update. West Group, 610 Opperman Dr. Eagan, MN 55123. Phone: 800-328-4880 or (651)687-7000 Fax: 800-213-2323 or (651)687-5827 URL: http://www.westgroup.com • Monthly. $275.00 per year. Newsletter. Formerly *Equal Employment Compliance Update*.

Employment Safety and Health Guide. CCH, Inc., 4025 W. Peterson Ave. Chicago, IL 60646-6085. Phone: 800-248-3248 or (773)583-8500 Fax: 800-224-8299 URL: http://www.cch.com • Weekly. $1,095.00 per year. Four looseleaf volumes.

Employment Termination: Rights and Remedies. William J. Holloway and Michael J. Leech. BNA Books, Bureau of National Affairs, Inc., 1231 25th St., N.W. Washington, DC 20037. Phone: 800-960-1220 or (202)833-7490 Fax: (202)833-7490 E-mail: books@bna.com • URL: http://www.bna.com/bnabooks • 1993. $145.00. Second edition. Discusses employment contracts and wrongful-discharge claims.

Emulsion Polymers Institute., Lehigh University, Iacocca Hall, 111 Research Dr. Bethlehem, PA 18015. Phone: (610)758-3590 Fax: (610)758-5880 E-mail: mse0@lehigh.edu • URL: http://www.lehigh.edu/~esd0/epihome.html • Includes latex paint research.

Encyclopedia of Accounting Systems. Tom M. Plank and Lois R. Plank. Prentice Hall, 240 Frisch Court Paramus, NJ 07652-5240. Phone: 800-947-7700 or (201)909-6200 Fax: 800-445-6991 or (201)909-6361 URL: http://www.prenhall.com • 1994. $110.00. Three volumes.

Encyclopedia of Acoustics. Malcolm J. Crocker. John Wiley and Sons, Inc., 605 Third Ave. New York, NY 10158-0012. Phone: 800-225-5945 or (212)850-6000 Fax: (212)850-6088 E-mail: info@wiley.com • URL: http://www.wiley.com • 1997. $650.00. Four volumes.

Encyclopedia of Advanced Materials. David Bloor and others. Elsevier Science, 655 Ave. of the Americas New York, NY 10010. Phone: 888-437-4636 or (212)989-5800 Fax: (212)633-3680 E-mail: usinfo@elsevier.com • URL: http://www.elsevier.com • 1994. $1,811.25. Four volumes.

Encyclopedia of Agriculture Science. Charles J. Arntzen and Ellen M. Ritter, editors. Academic Press, Inc., 525 B St., Suite 1900 San Diego, CA 92101-4495. Phone: 800-321-5068 or (619)230-1840 Fax: (619)699-6715 E-mail: ap@acad.com • URL: http://www.academicpress.com • 1994. $625.00. Four volumes.

Encyclopedia of AIDS: A Social, Political, Cultural, and Scientific Record of the HIV Epidemic. Raymond A. Smith, editor. Fitzroy Dearborn Publishers, 70 E. Walton St. Chicago, IL 60611. Phone: 800-850-8102 or (312)587-0131 Fax: (312)587-1049 E-mail: website@fitzroydearborn.com • URL: http://www.fitzroydearborn.com • 1998. $125.00. Emphasis is historical, covering the years 1981 to 1996. Includes information on AIDS law, policy, and activism.

Encyclopedia of American Economic History. Glenn Porter. Available from Gale Group, 27500 Drake Rd. Farmington Hills, MI 48331-3535. Phone: 800-877-4253 or (248)699-4253 Fax: 800-414-5043 E-mail: galeord@galegroup.com • URL: http://www.galegroup.com • 1980. $350.00. Three volumes. Individual volumes, $120.00.

Encyclopedia of American Facts and Dates. Gorton Carruth. HarperCollins Publishers, 10 E. 53rd St. New York, NY 10022-5299. Phone: 800-242-7737 or (212)207-7000 Fax: 800-822-4090 or (212)207-7145 URL: http://www.harpercollins.com • 1997. $45.00. 10th edition.

Encyclopedia of American Industries. The Gale Group, 27500 Drake Rd. Farmington Hills, MI 48331-3535. Phone: 800-877-GALE or (248)699-GALE Fax: 800-414-5043 or (248)699-8069 E-mail: galeord@galegroup.com • URL: http://www.galegroup.com • 1998. $560.00. Second edition. Two volumes. $280.00 per volume. Volume one is *Manufacturing Industries* and volume two is *Service and Non-Manufacturing Industries*. Provides the history, development, and recent status of approximately 1,000 industries. Includes statistical graphs, with industry and general indexes.

Encyclopedia of American Prisons. Marilyn D. McShane and Frank P. Williams, editors. Garland Publishing, Inc., 19 Union Square West, 8th Fl. New York, NY 10003-3382. Phone: 800-627-6273 or (212)414-0650 Fax: (212)414-0659 E-mail: info@garland.com • URL: http://www.garlandpub.com • 1996. $100.00. (Reference Library of the Humanities Series, Volume 17487).

Encyclopedia of American Silver Manufacturers. Dorothy T. Rainwater and Judy Redfield, editors. Schiffer Publishing, Ltd., 4880 Lower Valley Rd. Atglen, PA 19310. Phone: (610)593-1777 Fax: (610)593-2002 1998. $19.95. Fourth revised edition.

Encyclopedia of Architecture: Design, Engineering and Construction. Joseph A. Wilkes and R. T. Packard, editors. John Wiley and Sons, Inc., 605 Third Ave. New York, NY 10158-0012. Phone: 800-526-5368 or (212)850-6000 Fax: (212)850-6088 E-mail: info@wiley.com • URL: http://www.wiley.com • 1990. $1,440.00. Five volumes.

Encyclopedia of Associations. The Gale Group, 27500 Drake Rd. Farmington Hills, MI 48331-3535. Phone: 800-877-GALE or (248)699-GALE Fax: 800-414-5043 or (248)699-8069 E-mail: galeord@galegroup.com • URL: http://www.galegroup.com • Annual. $1,425.00. Three volumes. Volume 1, National Organizations, $545.00; Volume 2, Geographic and Executive Indexes, $425.00; Volume 3, supplement, $455.00.

Encyclopedia of Associations CD-ROM. The Gale Group, 27500 Drake Rd. Farmington Hills, MI 48331-3535. Phone: 800-877-GALE or (248)699-GALE Fax: 800-414-5043 or (248)699-8069 E-mail: galeord@gale.com • URL: http://www.gale.com • Semiannual. $1,095.00 per year, single user; $1,895.00 per year, network. Available for IBM or MAC. Provides detailed CD-ROM information on over 160,000 international, national, regional, state, and local organizations. Corresponds to the various volumes and supplements that make up the Gale *Encyclopedia of Associations* series.

Encyclopedia of Associations: International Organizations. The Gale Group, 27500 Drake Rd. Farmington Hills, MI 48331-3535. Phone: 800-877-GALE or (248)699-GALE Fax: 800-414-5043 or (248)699-8069 E-mail: galeord@galegroup.com • URL: http://www.galegroup.com • Annual. $615.00. Two volumes. Includes detailed information on more than 20,600 international nonprofit membership organizations.

Encyclopedia of Associations ÎOnlinel. The Gale Group, 27500 Drake Rd. Farmington Hills, MI 48331-3535. Phone: 800-877-GALE or (248)669-GALE Fax: 800-414-5043 or (248)699-8069 E-mail: galeord@gale.com • URL: http://www.gale.com • Provides detailed information on about 160,000 U. S. and International non-profit organizations. Semiannual updates. Inquire as to online cost and availability.

Encyclopedia of Associations: Regional, State, and Local Organizations. The Gale Group, 27500 Drake Rd. Farmington Hills, MI 48331-3535. Phone: 800-877-GALE or (248)699-GALE Fax: 800-414-5043 or (248)699-8069 E-mail: galeord@galegroup.com • URL: http://www.galegroup.com • Annual. $600.00. Five volumes. $140.00 per volume. Each volume covers a particular region of the U. S.

Encyclopedia of Banking and Finance. Charles J. Woelfel. McGraw-Hill Professional, 1221 Ave. of the Americas New York, NY 10020-1095. Phone: 800-722-4726 or (212)904-2000 Fax: (212)904-2072 E-mail: customer-service@mcgraw-hill.com • URL: http://www.mcgraw-hill.com • 1996. $50.00. 10th revised edition.

Encyclopedia of Business. The Gale Group, 27500 Drake Rd. Farmington Hills, MI 48331-3535. Phone: 800-877-GALE or (248)699-GALE Fax: 800-414-5043 or (248)699-8069 E-mail: galeord@galegroup.com • URL: http://www.galegroup.com • 2000. $425.00. Second edition. Two volumes. Contains more than 700 signed articles covering major business disciplines and concepts. International in scope.

Encyclopedia of Business and Finance. Burton Kaliski, editor. Available from The Gale Group, 27500 Drake Rd. Farmington Hills, MI 48331-3535. Phone: 800-877-GALE or (248)699-GALE Fax: 800-414-5043 or (248)699-8069 E-mail: galeord@galegroup.com • URL: http://www.galegroup.com • 2001. $240.00. Two volumes. Published by Macmillan Reference USA. Contains articles by various contributors on accounting, business administration, banking, finance, management information systems, and marketing.

Encyclopedia of Careers and Vocational Guidance. Holli Cosgrove. Ferguson Publishing Co., 200 W. Madison St., Suite 300 Chicago, IL 60606. Phone: 800-306-9941 or (312)580-5480 Fax: 800-580-4948 E-mail: fergpub@aol.com • URL: http://www.fergpubco.com • 2000. $159.95. 11th edition.

Encyclopedia of Chart Patterns. Thomas N. Bulkowski. John Wiley and Sons, Inc., 605 Third Ave. New York, NY 10158-0012. Phone: 800-225-5945 or (212)850-6000 Fax: (212)850-6088 E-mail: info@jwiley.com • URL: http://www.wiley.com • 2000. $79.95. Provides explanations of the predictive value of various chart patterns formed by stock and commodity price movements.

Encyclopedia of Communication and Information. Available from The Gale Group, 27500 Drake Rd. Farmington Hills, MI 48331-3535. Phone: 800-877-GALE or (248)699-GALE Fax: 800-414-5043 or (248)699-8069 E-mail: galeord@galegroup.com • URL: http://www.galegroup.com • 2001. $325.00. Three volumes. Published by Macmillan Reference USA.

Encyclopedia of Computer Science and Technology. Marcel Dekker, Inc., 270 Madison Ave. New York, NY 10016. Phone: 800-228-1160 or (212)696-9000 Fax: (212)685-4540 E-mail: bookorders@dekker.com • URL: http://www.dekker.com • Dates vary. 39 volumes. $7,605.00. $195.00 per volume. Contains scholarly articles written by computer experts. Includes bibliographies.

Encyclopedia of Corporate Meetings, Minutes and Resolutions. William Sardell, editor. Prentice Hall, 240 Frisch Court Paramus, NJ 07652-5240. Phone: 800-947-7700 or (201)909-6200 Fax: 800-445-6991 or (201)909-6361 URL: http://www.prenhall.com • 1985. $125.00. Third edition. Two volumes.

Encyclopedia of Crime and Justice. Available from The Gale Group, 27500 Drake Rd. Farmington Hills, MI 48331-3535. Phone: 800-877-GALE or (248)699-GALE Fax: 800-414-5043 or (248)699-8069 E-mail: galeord@galegroup.com • URL: http://www.galegroup.com • 2001. $425.00. Second edition. Four volumes. Published by Macmillan Reference USA. Contains extensive information on a wide variety of topics pertaining to crime, criminology, social issues, and the courts. (A revision of 1982 edition.)

Encyclopedia of Drugs, Alcohol, and Addictive Behavior. Available from The Gale Group, 27500 Drake Rd. Farmington Hills, MI 48331-3535. Phone: 800-877-GALE or (248)699-GALE Fax: 800-414-5043 or (248)699-8069 E-mail: galeord@galegroup.com • URL: http://www.galegroup.com • 2001. $425.00. Second edition. Four volumes. Published by Macmillan Reference USA. Covers the social, economic, political, and medical aspects of addiction.

Encyclopedia of Emerging Industries. The Gale Group, 27500 Drake Rd. Farmington Hills, MI 48331-3535. Phone: 800-877-GALE or (248)699-GALE Fax: 800-414-5043 or (248)699-8069 E-mail: galeord@galegroup.com • URL: http://www.galegroup.com • 2000. $295.00. Fourth edition. Provides detailed information on 90 ''newly flourishing'' industries. Includes historical background, organizational structure, significant individuals, current conditions, major companies, work force, technology trends, research developments, and other industry facts.

Encyclopedia of Environmental Science. John Mongillo and Linda Zierdt-Warshaw. Oryx Press, 4041 North Central Ave., Suite 700 Phoenix, AZ 85012-3397. Phone: 800-279-6799 or (602)265-2651 Fax: 800-279-4663 or (602)265-6250 E-mail: info@oryxpress.com • URL: http://www.oryxpress.com • 2000. $95.00. Provides information on more than 1,000 topics relating to the environment. Includes graphs, tables, maps, illustrations, and 400 Web site addresses.

Encyclopedia of Environmental Science and Engineering. James R. Pfafflin and Edward N. Ziegler, editors. Gordon and Breach Publishing Group, Two Gateway Center Newark, NJ 07102-0301. Phone: 800-545-8398 or (973)643-7500 Fax: (973)643-7676 E-mail: book.orders@aidcvt.com • URL: http://www.gbhap.com • $1,758.00. Three volumes.

Encyclopedia of Estate Planning. Robert S. Holzman. Boardroom Books, P.O. Box 2614 Greenwich, CT 06836-2614. Phone: (203)625-5900 Fax: (203)861-7443 1995. $59.00. Second revised edition.

Encyclopedia of Food Science, Food Technology, and Nutrition. Robert Macrae and others, editors. Academic Press, Inc., 525 B St., Suite 1900 San Diego, CA 92101-4495. Phone: 800-321-5068 or (619)230-1840 Fax: (619)699-6715 E-mail: ap@acad.com • URL: http://www.academicpress.com • 1993. Eight volumes. $2,414.00.

Encyclopedia of Global Industries. The Gale Group, 27500 Drake Rd. Farmington Hills, MI 48331-3535. Phone: 800-877-GALE or (248)699-GALE Fax: 800-414-5043 or (248)699-8069 E-mail: galeord@galegroup.com • URL: http://www.galegroup.com • 1999. $420.00. Second edition. Provides detailed statistical information on 115 industries. Coverage is international, with country and subject indexes.

Encyclopedia of Governmental Advisory Organizations. The Gale Group, 27500 Drake Rd. Farmington Hills, MI 48331-3535. Phone: 800-877-GALE or (248)699-GALE Fax: 800-414-5043 or (248)699-8069 E-mail: galeord@galegroup.com • URL: http://www.galegroup.com • 2000. $615.00. 15th edition.

Encyclopedia of Health Information Sources. The Gale Group, 27500 Drake Rd. Farmington Hills, MI 48331-3535. Phone: 800-877-GALE or (248)699-GALE Fax: 800-414-5043 or (248)699-8069 E-mail: galeord@galegroup.com • URL: http://www.galegroup.com • 1993. $180.00. Second edition. Both print and nonprint sources of information are listed for 450 health-related topics.

Encyclopedia of Housing. Willem van Vliet, editor. Sage Publications, Inc., 2455 Teller Rd. Thousand Oaks, CA 91320. Phone: (805)499-0721 Fax: (805)499-0871 E-mail: info@sagepub.com • URL: http://www.sagepub.com • 1998. $169.95. Contains 500 entries covering all aspects of housing. Includes index of names and subjects.

Encyclopedia of Human Behavior. Vangipuram S. Ramachandran, editor. Academic Press, Inc., 525 B St., Suite 1900 San Diego, CA 92101-4495. Phone: 800-321-5068 or (619)230-1840 Fax: (619)699-6715 E-mail: ap@acad.com • URL: http://www.academicpress.com • 1994. $685.00. Four volumes. Contains signed articles on aptitude testing, arbitration, career development, consumer psychology, crisis management, decision making, economic behavior, group dynamics, leadership, motivation, negotiation, organizational behavior, planning, problem solving, stress, work efficiency, and other human behavior topics applicable to business situations.

Encyclopedia of Interior Design. Joanna Banham, editor. Fitzroy Dearborn Publishers, 919 N. Michigan Ave., Suite 760 Chicago, IL 60611. Phone: 800-850-8102 or (312)587-0131 Fax: (312)587-1049 E-mail: website@fitzroydearborn.com • URL: http://www.fitzroydearborn.com • 1997. $270.00. Two volumes. Contains more than 500 essays on interior design topics. Includes bibliographies.

Encyclopedia of Legal Information Sources. The Gale Group, 27500 Drake Rd. Farmington Hills, MI 48331-3535. Phone: 800-877-GALE or (248)699-GALE Fax: 800-414-5043 or (248)699-8069 E-mail: galeord@galegroup.com • URL: http://www.galegroup.com • 1992. $180.00. Second edition. Lists more than 23,000 law-related information sources, including print, nonprint, and organizational.

Encyclopedia of Library and Information Science. Allen Kent and others, editors. Marcel Dekker, Inc., 270 Madison Ave. New York, NY 10016. Phone: 800-228-1160 or (212)696-9000 Fax: (212)685-4540 E-mail: bookorders@dekker.com • URL: http://www.dekker.com • 66 volumes. $6,583.50. $99.75 per volume. Dates vary.

Encyclopedia of Major Marketing Campaigns. The Gale Group, 27500 Drake Rd. Farmington Hills, MI 48331-3535. Phone: 800-877-GALE or (248)699-GALE Fax: 800-414-5043 or (248)699-8069 E-mail: galeord@galegroup.com • URL: http://www.galegroup.com • 2000. $265.00. Covers 500 major marketing and advertising campaigns ''of the 20th century.'' Examines historical context, target market, expectations, competition, strategy, development, and outcomes. Includes illustrations.

Encyclopedia of Materials: Science and Technology. K.H.J. Buschow and others, editors. Pergamon Press/Elsevier Science, 655 Ave. of the Americas New York, NY 10010-5107. Phone: 800-437-4636 or (212)633-3730 Fax: (212)633-3680 E-mail: usinfo@elsevier.com • URL: http://www.elsevier.com • 2001. $6,875.00. Eleven volumes. Provides extensive technical information on a wide variety of materials, including metals, ceramics, plastics, optical materials, and building materials. Includes more than 2,000 articles and 5,000 illustrations.

Encyclopedia of Medical Organizations and Agencies. The Gale Group, 27500 Drake Rd. Farmington Hills, MI 48331-3535. Phone: 800-877-GALE or (248)699-GALE Fax: 800-414-5043 or (248)699-8069 E-mail: galeord@galegroup.com • URL: http://www.galegroup.com • 2000. $285.00. 11th edition. Information on over 14,000 public and private organizations in medicine and related fields.

Encyclopedia of Microcomputers. Allen Kent and James G. Williams, editors. Marcel Dekker, Inc., 270 Madison Ave. New York, NY 10016. Phone: 800-228-1160 or (212)696-9000 Fax: (212)685-4540 E-mail: bookorders@dekker.com • URL: http://www.dekker.com • Dates vary. Prices vary. 24 volumes. Contains scholarly articles written by microcomputer experts. Includes bibliographies. Index available, $230.00.

Encyclopedia of Occupational Health and Safety. Available from The Gale Group, 27500 Drake Rd. Farmington Hills, MI 48331-3535. Phone: 800-877-GALE or (248)699-GALE Fax: 800-414-5043 or (248)699-8069 E-mail: galeord@galegroup.com • URL: http://www.galegroup.com • 1999. $495.00. Fourth edition. Four volumes. Published by the International Labor Office (http://www.ilo.org). Covers safety engineering, industrial medicine, ergonomics, hygiene, epidemiology, toxicology, industrial psychology, and related topics. Includes material related to specific chemical, textile, transport, construction, manufacturing, and other industries. Indexed by subject, chemical name, and author, with a ''Directory of Experts.''

Encyclopedia of Occupational Health and Safety 1983. International Labour Office, 1828 L St., N.W., Suite 801 Washington, DC 20036. Phone: (202)653-7652 Fax: (202)653-7687 E-mail: ilopubs@tascol.com • URL: http://www.ilo.org/pubns • 1991. $270.00. Third revised edition. Two volumes.

Encyclopedia of Physical Science and Engineering Information. The Gale Group, 27500 Drake Rd. Farmington Hills, MI 48331-3535. Phone: 800-877-GALE or (248)699-GALE Fax: 800-414-5043 or (248)699-8069 E-mail: galeord@galegroup.com • URL: http://www.galegroup.com • 1996. $160.00. Second edition. Includes print, electronic, and other information sources for a wide range of scientific, technical, and engineering topics.

Encyclopedia of Polymer Science and Engineering. H.F. Mark and others. John Wiley and Sons, Inc., 605 Third Ave. New York, NY 10158-0012. Phone: 800-526-5368 or (212)850-6000 Fax: (212)850-6088 E-mail: info@wiley.com • URL: http://www.wiley.com • 1985. $5,035.00. 19 volumes, volume 22. $295.00 per volume. Second edition.

Encyclopedia of Popular Music. Colin Larkin, editor. Groves Dictionaries, Inc., 345 Park Ave. S., 10th Fl. New York, NY 10010-1707. Phone: 800-221-2123 or (212)689-9200 Fax: (212)696-0052 E-mail: grove@grovereference.com • URL: http://www.grovereference.com • 1998. $500.00. Third edition. Eight volumes. Covers a wide variety of music forms and pop culture. Includes bibliography and index.

Encyclopedia of Small Business. The Gale Group, 27500 Drake Rd. Farmington Hills, MI 48331-3535. Phone: 800-877-GALE or (248)699-GALE Fax: 800-414-5043 or (248)699-8069 E-mail: galeord@galegroup.com • URL: http://www.galegroup.com • 1998. $395.00. Two volumes. Contains about 500 informative entries on a wide variety of topics affecting small business. Arrangement is alphabetical.

Encyclopedia of Smoking and Tobacco. Arlene B. Hirschfelder. Oryx Press, 4041 North Central Ave., Suite 700 Phoenix, AZ 85012-3397. Phone: 800-279-6799 or (602)265-2651 Fax: 800-279-4663 or (602)265-6250 E-mail: info@oryxpress.com • URL: http://www.oryxpress.com • 1999. $65.00. Includes information on the economics of the tobacco industry, health issues, tobacco history, advertising, legal issues, government subsidies, etc. Provides illustrations, charts, and statistical data.

Encyclopedia of Statistical Sciences. Samuel I. Kotz and others, editors. John Wiley and Sons, Inc., 605 Third Ave. New York, NY 10158-0012. Phone: 800-526-5368 or (212)850-6000 Fax: (212)850-6088 E-mail: info@wiley.com • URL: http://www.wiley.com • 1988. $2,395.00. Nine volumes. Supplement available. Price vary for each individual volume.

Encyclopedia of Stock Market Techniques. Chartcraft, Inc., P.O. Box 2046 New Rochelle, NY 10801. Phone: (914)632-0422 Fax: (914)632-0335 1963. $60.00.

Encyclopedia of Technical Market Indicators. Robert W. Colby and Thomas A. Meyers. McGraw-Hill Professional, 1221 Ave. of the Americas New York, NY 10020-1095. Phone: 800-722-4726 or (212)904-2000 Fax: (212)904-2072 E-mail: customer.service@mcgraw-hill.com • URL: http://www.mcgraw-hill.com • 1988. $70.00.

Encyclopedia of Television. Horace Newcomb, editor. Fitzroy Dearborn Publishers, 919 N. Michigan Ave., Suite 760 Chicago, IL 60611. Phone: 800-850-8102 or (312)587-0131 Fax: (312)587-1049 E-mail: website@fitzroydearborn.com • URL: http://www.fitzroydearborn.com • 1997. $300.00. Three volumes. Contains about 1,000 entries on TV performers, programs, organizations, social issues, technical aspects, and historical details.

Encyclopedia of Textiles. French and European Publications, Inc., Rockefeller Center Promenade, 610 Fifth Ave. New York, NY 10020-2497. Phone: 800-322-8755 or (212)581-8810 Fax: 800-678-3633 or (212)265-1094 E-mail: livresny@aol.com • URL: http://www.frencheuropean.com • 1980. $39.95. Third edition.

Encyclopedia of the European Union. Desmond Dinan, editor. Lynne Rienner Publishers, 1800 30th St., Suite 314 Boulder, CO 80301-1026. Phone: (303)444-6684 Fax: (303)444-0824 E-mail: cservice@rienner.com • URL: http://www.rienner.com • 2000. $110.00. Covers ''virtually every aspect'' of the EU. Includes ''maps, glossaries, appendixes, and a comprehensive index.''

Encyclopedia of 20th Century American Humor. Alleen P. Nilsen and Don L. F. Nilsen. Oryx Press, 4041 North Central Ave., Suite 700 Phoenix, AZ 85012-3397. Phone: 800-279-6799 or (602)265-2651 Fax: 800-279-4663 or (602)265-6250 E-mail: info@oryxpress.com • URL: http://www.oryxpress.com • 2000. $67.50. Provides an A-to-Z consideration of American humor in its various forms, from early vaudeville to the Internet. Includes a bibliography, subject index, illustrations, and numerous humorous examples.

Encyclopedia of Urban Planning. Arnold Whittick, editor. Krieger Publishing Co., P.O. Box 9542 Melbourne, FL 32902-9542. Phone: 800-724-0025 or (321)724-9542 Fax: (321)951-3671 E-mail: info@krieger-publishing.com • URL: http://www.krieger-publishing.com • 1980. $79.50.

Encyclopedia of Women's Associations Worldwide. The Gale Group, 27500 Drake Rd. Farmington Hills, MI 48331-3535. Phone: 800-877-GALE or (248)699-GALE Fax: 800-414-5043 or (248)699-8069 E-mail: galeord@galegroup.com • URL: http://www.galegroup.com • 1998. $85.00. Second edition. Provides detailed information for more than 3,400 organizations throughout the world that relate to women and women's issues.

Encyclopedia of Wood. U.S. Dept. of Forestry Staff. Sterling Publishing Co., Inc., 387 Park Ave. S. New York, NY 10016-8810. Phone: 800-367-9692 or (212)532-7160 Fax: (212)213-2495 E-mail: customerservice@sterlingpub.com • URL: http://www.sterlingpub.com • 1989. $24.95. Revised edition.

Encyclopedia of Wood: A Tree by Tree Guide to the World's Most Valuable Resource. Bill Lincoln and others. Facts on File, Inc., 11 Penn Plaza, 15th Fl. New York, NY 10001. Phone: 800-322-8755 or (212)967-8800 Fax: 800-678-3633 or (212)967-8107 E-mail: llittman@factsonfile.com • URL: http://www.factsonfile.com • 1989. $29.95.

Encyclopedia of World Biography. The Gale Group, 27500 Drake Rd. Farmington Hills, MI 48331-3535. Phone: 800-877-GALE or (248)699-GALE Fax: 800-414-5043 or (248)699-8069 E-mail: galeord@galegroup.com • URL: http://www.galegroup.com • 1998. $995.00. Second edition. 17 volumes. Provides biographies of about 7,000 ''internationally renowned'' individuals from all eras and subject fields. Includes illustrations, bibliographies, and index. Formerly *McGraw-Hill Encyclopedia of World Biography* (1973).

Encyclopedic Dictionary of Gears and Gearing. David W. South. McGraw-Hill, 1221 Ave. of the Americas New York, NY 10020. Phone: 800-722-4726 or (212)904-2000 Fax: (212)904-2072 E-mail: customer.servcie@mcgraw-hill.com • URL: http://www.mcgraw-hill.com • 1992. $54.50.

Endpoint Express. United Communications Group (UCG), 11300 Rockville Pike, Suite 1100 Rockville, MD 20852-3030. Phone: 800-287-2223 or (301)287-2700 Fax: (301)816-8945 E-mail: webmaster@ucg.com • URL: http://www.ucg.com • Biweekly. $355.00 per year. Newsletter. Covers bank payment systems, including checks, electronic funds transfer (EFT), point-of-sale (POS), and automated teller machine (ATM) operations. Formerly *Bank Office Bulletin*.

Energetic Materials Research and Testing Center., New Mexico Institute of Mining and Technology, 801 Leroy Place Socorro, NM 87801. Phone: (505)835-5312 Fax: (505)835-5630 E-mail: jcortez@emrtc.nmt.edu • URL: http://www.emrtc.nmt • Research areas include the development of industrial applications for explosives as energy sources.

Energy and Environmental Research Center. University of North Dakota

Energy and Fuels. American Chemical Society, 1155 16th St., N. W. Washington, DC 20036. Phone: 800-333-9511 or (202)872-4600 Fax: (202)872-4615 E-mail: service@acs.org • URL: http://www.pubs.acs.org • Bimonthly. Institutions, $728.00 per year; others, price on application. an interdisciplinary technical journal covering non-nuclear energy sources: petroleum, gas, synthetic fuels, etc.

Energy and Nuclear Sciences International Who's Who. Allyn and Bacon/Longman, 1185 Ave. of the Americas New York, NY 10036. Phone: 800-922-0579 E-mail: the.webmaster@ablongman.com • URL: http://www.ablongman.com • 1990. $310.00. Third edition.

Energy and Problems of a Technical Society. Jack J. Kraushaar and Robert A. Ristinen. John Wiley and Sons, Inc., 605 Third Ave. New York, NY 10158-0012. Phone: 800-225-5945 or (212)850-6000 Fax: (212)850-6088 E-mail: info@wiley.com • URL: http://www.wiley.com • 1993. $58.95. Second edition.

Energy Balances of OECD Countries. Organization for Economic Cooperation and Development. Available from OECD Publications and Information Center, 2001 L St., N. W., Suite 650 Washington, DC 20036-4922. Phone: 800-456-6323 or (202)785-6323 Fax: (202)785-0350 E-mail: washington.contact@oecd.org • URL: http://www.oecd.org • Irregular. $110.00. Presents two-year data on the supply and consumption of solid fuels, oil, gas, and electricity, expressed in oil equivalency terms. Historical tables are also provided. Relates to OECD member countries.

Energy Center.

Energy, Combustion and Environment. Norman Chigier. McGraw-Hill, 1221 Ave. of the Americas New York, NY 10020. Phone: 800-722-4726 or (212)904-2000 Fax: (212)904-2072 E-mail: custom.service@mcgraw-hill.com • URL: http://www.mcgraw-hill.com • 1981. $86.25.

Energy Conservation Digest. Editorial Resources, Inc., P.O. Box 21133 Washington, DC 20009. Phone: (202)783-2929 Semimonthly. $176.00 per year. Newsletter on the conservation of energy resources. Includes legislation, research, new products, job opportunities, calendar of events, and energy economics.

Energy Conservation News. Business Communications Co., Inc., 25 Van Zant St., Suite 13 Norwalk, CT 06855. Phone: (203)853-4266 Fax: (203)853-0348 Monthly. $375.00 per year. Newsletter.

Energy Conversion and Management. Elsevier Science, 655 Ave. of the Americas New York, NY 10010. Phone: 888-437-4636 or (212)989-5800 Fax: (212)633-3680 E-mail: usinfo@elsevier.com • URL: http://www.elsevier.com • 18 times a year. $2,835.00 per year. Presents a scholarly approach to alternative or renewable energy sources. Text in English, French and German.

Energy Daily. King Publishing Group, Inc., 627 National Press Bldg. Washington, DC 20045. Phone: (202)638-4260 Fax: (202)662-9744 Daily. $1,575.00 per year. Newsletter. News on the energy industry and its regulators.

Energy Institute. Pennsylvania State University

Energy Laboratory. Massachusetts Institute of Technology

Energy Magazine. Business Communications Co., Inc., 25 Van Zant St., Suite 13 Norwalk, CT 06855. Phone: (203)853-4266 Fax: (203)853-0348 Five times a year. Institutions, $375.00 per year; others, price on application.

Energy Management. Paul Ocallaghan. McGraw-Hill, 1221 Ave. of the Americas New York, NY 10020. Phone: 800-722-4726 or (212)904-2000 Fax: (212)904-2072 E-mail: customer.service@mcgraw-hill.com • URL: http://www.mcgraw-hill.com • 1993. $55.00.

Energy Management. Prentice Hall, 240 Frisch Court Paramus, NJ 07652-5240. Phone: 800-947-7700 or (201)909-6200 Fax: 800-445-6991 or (201)909-6361 URL: http://www.prenhall.com • 1998. $20.00. (Advanced Electronical Topics Series).

Energy Management and Federal Energy Guidelines. CCH, Inc., 4025 W. Peterson Ave. Chicago, IL 60646-6085. Phone: 800-248-3248 or (773)583-8500 Fax: 800-224-8299 URL: http://www.cch.com • Biweekly. $1,658.00 per year. Seven looseleaf volumes. Periodic supplementation. Reports on petroleum allocation rules, conservation efforts, new technology, and other energy concerns.

Energy Management Handbook. Wayne C. Turner. Prentice Hall, 240 Frisch Court Paramus, NJ 07652-5240. Phone: 800-947-7700 or (201)909-6200 Fax: 800-445-6991 or (201)909-6361 URL: http://www.prenhall.com • 1996. $130.00. Third edition.

Energy Services Marketing Letter: Covering Electric and Gas Utility Marketing Programs., 555 E. City Line Ave., Suite 900 Bala Cynwyd, PA 19004-1111. Phone: (610)667-2160 Fax: (610)667-5593 Monthly. $295.00 per year. Newsletter. Formerly *DSM Letter*.

Energy Sources: Journal of Extraction, Conversion and the Environment. Taylor & Francis, Inc., 325 Chestnut St., 8th Fl. Philadelphia, PA 19106. Phone: 800-821-8312 or (215)625-8900 Fax: (215)625-2940 E-mail: webmaster@taylorandfrancis.com • URL: http://www.tandfdc.com/ • 10 times a year. Individuals, $423.00 per year; institutions, $938.00 per year.

Energy Statistics of OECD Countries. Available from OECD Publications Center, 2001 L St., N.W.,, Suite 650 Washington, DC 20036-4922. Phone: 800-456-6323 or (202)785-6323 Fax: (202)785-0350 E-mail: washington.contact@oecd.org • URL: http://www.oecd.org • Annual. $110.00. Detailed energy supply and consumption data for OECD member countries.

Energy Statistics Yearbook. United Nations Dept. of Economic and Social Affairs. United Nations Publications, Two United Nations Plaza, Rm. DC2-853 New York, NY 10017. Phone: 800-253-9646 or (212)963-8302 Fax: (212)963-3489 Annual. $100.00. Text in English and French.

Energy Systems Handbook. Orjan Isacson and Edward Rideout. McGraw Hill, 1221 Ave. of the Americas New York, NY 10020. Phone: 800-772-4726 or (212)904-2000 Fax: (212)904-2072 E-mail: customer.service@mcgraw-hill.com • URL: http://www.mcgraw-hill.com • 1999. $39.95

Energy Systems Laboratory. Texas A & M University

Energy: The International Journal. Elsevier Science, 655 Ave. of the Americas New York, NY 10010. Phone: 888-437-4636 or (212)989-5800 Fax: (212)633-3680 E-mail: usinfo@elsevier.com • URL: http://www.elsevier.com • Monthly. $1,608.00 per year.

Energy Today. Trends Publishing, Inc., National Press Bldg. Washington, DC 20045. Phone: (202)393-0031 Fax: (202)393-1732 URL: http://www.akran49470aworldnet.att.net • Monthly. $795.00 per year. Newsletter. Provides direct access to U.S. and international policies, plans, programs, projects and events in energy development, research, management and conservation.

Energy User News: Energy Technology Buyers Guide. Cahners Business Information, 1018 W. 9th Ave. King of Prussia, PA 19087. Phone: 800-695-1214 or (610)205-1000 Fax: (610)964-4663 E-mail: corporatecommunications@cahners.com • URL: http://www.cahners.com • Annual. $10.00. List of about 400 manufacturers, manufacturers' representatives, dealers, and distributors of energy management equipment. *Annual Review* and *Forecast* issue.

Energyline. Congressional Information Service, Inc., 4520 East-West Highway Bethesda, MD 20814-3389. Phone: 800-638-8380 or (301)654-1550 Fax: (301)654-4033 E-mail: support@cispubs.com • URL: http://www.cispubs.com • Provides online citations and abstracts to the literature of all forms of energy: petroleum, natural gas, coal, nuclear power, solar energy, etc. Time period is 1971 to 1993 (closed file). Inquire as to online cost and availability.

Engine Manufacturers Association.

Engine Research Center. University of Wisconsin - Madison

Engineered Materials Abstracts. Cambridge Information Group, 7200 Wisconsin Ave., 6th Fl. Bethesda, MD 20814. Phone: 800-843-7751 or (301)961-6700 Fax: (301)961-6720 E-mail: market@csa.com • URL: http://www.csa.com • Monthly. $995.00 per year. Provides citations to the technical and engineering literature of plastic, ceramic, and composite materials.

Engineered Materials Abstracts Îonlinel. Cambridge Scientific Abstracts, 7200 Wisconsin Ave. Bethesda, MD 20814. Phone: 800-843-7751 or (301)961-6700 Fax: (301)961-6720 E-mail: sales@csa.com • URL: http://www.csa.com • Provides online citations to the technical and engineering literature of plastic, ceramic, and composite materials. Time period is 1986 to date, with monthly updates. (Formerly produced by ASM International.) Inquire as to online cost and availability.

Engineered Wood Research Foundation.

Engineering and Industrial Experiment Station, Department of Materials Science and Engineering., University of Florida Gainesville, FL 32611-6400. Phone: (352)846-3301 Fax: (352)392-7219 E-mail: rabba@mse.ufl.edu • URL: http://www.mse.ufl.edu • Research fields include chemical, civil, electrical, industrial, mechanical, and other types of engineering.

Engineering and Mining Journal Annual Buyers' Guide. Intertec Publishing Corp, P.O. Box 12901 Overland Park, KS 66282-2901. Phone: 800-400-5945 or (913)341-1300 Fax: (913)967-1898 E-mail: subs@intertec.com • URL: http://www.intertec.com • Annual. Free to qualified personnel; others, $69.00. List of manufacturers and suppliers of mining equipment; international coverage. Formerly *Engineering and Mining Journal Buying Directory*.

Engineering and Mining Journal (E&MJ). Intertec Publishing Corp., P.O. Box 12901 Overland Park, KS 66682-2901. Phone: 800-400-5945 or (913)341-1300 Fax: (913)967-1898 E-mail: subs@intertec.com • URL: http://www.e-mj.com • Monthly. $69.00 per year.

Engineering Dean's Office., University of California at Berkeley, 308 Mclaughin Hall, No. 1702 Berkeley, CA 94720-1706. Phone: (510)642-7594 Fax: (510)643-8653 E-mail: dma@coe.berkeley.edu • Research fields include civil, electrical, industrial, mechanical, and other types of engineering.

Engineering Design Graphics Journal. American Society for Engineering Education, Engineering Design Graphics Div., c/o Judy A. Birchman, 1419 Knoy Hall, Purdue University W. Lafayette, IN 47907-1419. Phone: (317)494-8206 Fax: (317)494-9267 E-mail: jabirchman@tech.purdue.edu • URL: http://www.tech.purdue.edu • Three times a year. Members, $6.00 per year; non-members, $20.00 per year;institutions, $10.00 per year. Concerned with engineering graphics, computer graphics, geometric modeling, computer-aided drafting, etc.

Engineering Experiment Station., University of Illinois at Urbana-Champaign, College of Engineering, 1101 W. Springfield Urbana, IL 61801. Phone: (217)333-2152 Fax: (217)244-7705 E-mail: rockwood@uiuc.edu/ • URL: http://www.engr.uiuc.edu/ • Research fields include chemical, civil, electrical, industrial, mechanical, and other types of engineering.

Engineering Experiment Station., Purdue University West Lafayette, IN 47907. Phone: (317)494-5340 Fax: (317)494-9321 E-mail: stevens@ecn.purdue.edu • URL: http://www.ecn.purdue.edu • Research fields include chemical, civil, electrical, industrial, mechanical, and other types of engineering.

Engineering Experiment Station. Ohio State University

Engineering for Dairy and Food Products. Arthur W. Farrall. Krieger Publishing Co., P.O. Box 9542 Melbourne, FL 32902-9542. Phone: 800-724-0025 or (321)724-9542 Fax: (321)951-3671 E-mail: info@krieger-publishing.com • URL: http://www.krieger-publishing.com • 1980. $46.50. Revised edition.

Engineering Index Monthly: Abstracting and Indexing Services Covering Sources of the World's Engineering Literature. Engineering Information, Inc., Castle Point on the Hudson Hoboken, NJ 07030. Phone: 800-221-1044 or (201)216-8500 Fax: (201)216-8532 Monthly. $2,300.00 per year. Provides indexing and abstracting of the world's engineering and technical literature.

Engineering Plastics and Composites. William A. Woishnis and others, editors. ASM International, 9639 Kinsman Rd. Materials Park, OH 44073-0002. Phone: 800-336-5152 or (440)338-5151 Fax: (440)338-4634 E-mail: memserv@po.asm-intl.org • URL: http://www.asm-intl.org • 1993. $149.00. Second edition. In four sections: (1) Trade names of plastics, reinforced plastics, and resin composites; (2) Index to materials, with suppliers and other information; (3) Suppliers alphabetically, with trade names; (4) Supplier contact information. (Materials Data Series).

Engineering Systems Research Center. University of California at Berkeley

ENO Transportation Foundation.

ENR Connecting the Industry Worldwide (Engineering News-Record). McGraw-Hill, 1221 Ave. of the Americas New York, NY 10020. Phone: 800-722-4726 or (212)904-2000 Fax: (212)904-2072 E-mail: customer.service@mcgraw-hill.com • URL: http://www.mcgraw.hill.com • Weekly. $74.00 per year.

ENR Top 400 Construction Contractors (Engineering News-Record). McGraw-Hill, Two Penn Plaza New York, NY 10121. Phone: 800-722-4726 or (212)904-2000 Fax: (212)904-6068 E-mail: customer.service@mcgraw-hill.com • URL: http://www.mcgraw-hill.com • Annual. $10.00. Lists 400 United States contractors receiving largest dollar volume of contracts in preceding calendar year.

ENR-Top International Design Firms (Engineering News Record). McGraw-Hill, 1221 Ave of the Americas New York, NY 10020. Phone: 800-722-4726 or (212)904-2000 Fax: (212)904-2072 E-mail: customer.service@mcgraw-hill.com • URL: http://www.mcgraw-hill.com • Annual. $10.00. Lists 200 firms. Includes U. S. firms. Formerly *Engineering News Record-Top International Design Firms*.

Entertainment and Sports Law Bibliography. American Bar Association, 750 N. Lake Shore Dr. Chicago, IL 60611-4497. Phone: 800-287-2221 or (312)988-5000 Fax: (312)988-5528 E-mail: abajournal@abanet.org • URL: http://www.abanet.org • 1986. $40.00.

Entertainment Design: The Art and Technology of Show Business. Theatre Crafts International, 32 W. 18th St. New York, NY 10011-4612. Phone: (212)229-2965 Fax: (212)229-2084 URL: http://www.etecnyuc.net/tci • 11 times a year. $39.95 per year. Contains material on performing arts management, staging, scenery, costuming, etc. Formerly *TCI - Theatre Crafts International*.

Entertainment Industry Economics: A Guide for Financial Analysis. Harold Vogel. Cambridge University Press, 40 W. 20th St. New York, NY 10011. Phone: 800-221-4512 or (212)924-3900 Fax: (212)937-4712 E-mail: info@cup.org • URL: http://www.cup.org • 1998. $39.95. Fourth revised edition.

Entertainment Law. Howard Siegel, editor. New York State Bar Association, One Elk St. Albany, NY 12207. Phone: 800-582-2452 or (518)463-3200 Fax: (518)463-8844 URL: http://www.nysba.org • 1990. $60.00. Contains chapters by various authors on the legal aspects of television, motion pictures, theatre, music, phonograph records, and related topics.

Entertainment Law. Robert Fremlin. West Group, 610 Opperman Dr. Eagan, MN 55123. Phone: 800-328-4880 or (651)687-7000 Fax: 800-213-2323 or (651)687-5827 URL: http://www.westgroup.com • $560.00. Looseleaf service. Includes updates. (Entertainment and Communicat Law Series).

Entertainment Law and Business, 1989-1993: A Guide to the Law and Business Prac Entertainment Industry. Harold Orenstein and David Sinacore-Guinn. LEXIS Publishing, 701 E. Water St. Charlottesville, VA 22902. Phone: 800-446-3410 or (804)972-7600 Fax: 800-643-1280 or (804)972-7686 E-mail: custserv@michie.com • URL: http://www.lexislaw.publishing • $180.00. Two volumes. Looseleaf. Periodic supplementation, $55.00.

Entertainment Marketing Letter. EPM Communications, Inc., 160 Mercer St., 3rd Fl. New York, NY 10012-3212. Phone: (212)941-0099 or (212)941-0099 Fax: (212)941-1622 E-mail: info@epmcom.com • URL: http://www.epmcom.com • 22 times a year. $319.00 per year. Newsletter. Covers the marketing of various entertainment products. Includes television broadcasting, videocassettes, celebrity tours and tie-ins, radio broadcasting, and the music business.

Entertainment, Publishing, and the Arts Handbook. Robert Thorne and John D. Viera, editors. West Group, 610 Opperman Dr. Eagan, MN 55123. Phone: 800-328-4880 or (651)687-7000 Fax: 800-213-2323 or (651)687-5827 URL: http://www.westgroup.com • Annual. $152.00. Presents recent legal cases, issues, developments, and trends.

Entomological Society of America Annals: Devoted to the Interest of Classical Entomology. Entomological Society of America, 9301 Annapolis Rd. Lanham, MD 20706. Phone: (301)731-4535 Fax: (301)731-4538 Bimonthly. Members, $25.00 per year; non-members, $81.00 per year; institutions, $156.00 per year.

Entomology Abstracts. Cambridge Information Group, 7200 Wisconsin Ave., 6th Fl. Bethesda, MD 20814. Phone: 800-843-7751 or (301)961-6700 Fax: (301)961-6720 E-mail: market@csa.com • URL: http://www.csa.com • Monthly. $985.00 per year.

Entrepreneur: The Small Business Authority. Entrepreneur Media, Inc., 2445 McCabe Way Irvine, CA 92614. Phone: 800-421-2300 or (949)261-2325 Fax: (949)261-0234 E-mail: entmag@entrepreneur.com • URL: http://www.entrepreneur.com • Monthly. $19.97 per year. Contains advice for small business owners and prospective owners. Includes numerous franchise advertisements.

Entrepreneur's Annual Franchise 500 Issue. Entrepreneur Media, Inc., 2445 McCabe Way Irvine, CA 92614. Phone: 800-421-2300 or (949)261-2325 Fax: (949)261-0234 E-mail: entmag@entrepreneur.com • URL: http://www.entrepreneur.com • Annual. $4.95. Provides a ranking of 500 "top franchise opportunities," based on a combination of financial strength, growth rate, size, stability, number of years in business, litigation history, and other factors. Includes 17 major business categories, further divided into about 140 very specific groups (22 kinds of fast food, for example).

The Entrepreneur's Guide to Growing Up: Taking Your Small Company to the Next Level. Edna Sheedy. Self-Counsel Press, Inc., 1704 N. State St. Bellingham, WA 98225. Phone: 877-877-6490 or (360)676-4530 Fax: (360)676-4530 E-mail: service@self-counsel.com • URL: http://www.self-counsel.com • 1993. $8.95. Discusses company structure, delegation, management information requirements, and other topics related to company growth. *Business Series*.

Entrepreneurship: Theory and Practice. Baylor University, Hankamer School of Business, BU Box 98006 Waco, TX 76798-8006. Phone: (254)710-4290 Fax: (254)710-2271 E-mail: ray__bagby@baylor.edu • URL: http://www.hsb.baylor.edu/html/dept/bcpr/hsb/genmf.htm • Quarterly. Individuals, $55.00 per year; institutions, $90.00 per year. Formerly *American Journal of Small Business*.

Entrepreneurship.com. Tim Burns. Dearborn Financial Publishing, 155 North Wacker Drive Chicago, IL 60606-1719. Phone: 800-245-2665 or (312)836-4400 Fax: (312)836-9958 URL: http://www.dearborn.com • 2000. $19.95. Provides basic advice and information on the topic of dot.com startups, including business plan creation and financing.

Enviroline. Congressional Information Service, Inc., 4520 East-West Highway Bethesda, MD 20814-3389. Phone: 800-638-8380 or (301)654-1550 Fax: (301)654-4033 E-mail: support@cispubs.com • URL: http://www.cispubs.com • Provides online indexing and abstracting of worldwide environmental and natural resource literature from 1975 to date. Updated monthly. Inquire as to online cost and availability.

Environment. Heldref Publications, 1319 18th St., N.W. Washington, DC 20036-1802. Phone: 800-296-5149 or (202)296-6267 Fax: (202)296-5149 E-mail: orders@allenpress.com • URL: http://www.helderf.org • 10 times a year. Individuals, $39.00 per year; institutions, $79.00 per year.

Environment Abstracts. Congressional Information Service, 4520 East-West Highway, Suite 800 Bethesda, MD 20814-3389. Phone: 800-638-8380 or (301)654-1550 Fax: (301)654-4033 E-mail: cisinfo@lexis-nexis.com • URL: http://www.cispubs.com • Monthly. Price varies. Provides multidisciplinary coverage of the world's environmental literature. Incorporates *Acid Rain Abstracts*.

Environment Abstracts Annual: A Guide to the Key Environmental Literature of the Year. Congressional Information Service, 4520 East-West Highway, Suite 800 Bethesda, MD 20814-3389. Phone: 800-638-8380 or (301)654-1550 Fax: (301)654-4033 E-mail: csinfo@lexis.nexis.com • URL: http://www.cispubs • Annual. $495.00. A yearly cumulation of *Environment Abstracts*.

Environment Abstracts on CD-ROM. Congressional Information Service, Inc., 4520 East-West Highway Bethesda, MD 20814-3389. Phone: 800-638-8380 or (301)654-1550 Fax: (301)654-4033 E-mail: support@cispubs.com • URL: http://www.cispubs.com • Quarterly. $1,295.00 per year. Contains the following CD-ROM databases: *Environment Abstracts, Energy Abstracts*, and *Acid Rain Abstracts*. Length of coverage varies.

Environment Advisor. J.J. Keller & Associates, Inc., P.O. Box 368 Neenah, WI 54957-0368. Phone: 800-558-5011 or (414)722-2848 Fax: (414)727-7516 URL: http://www.jjkeller.com • Monthly. $90.00 per year. Newsletter. Formerly *Hazardous Substances Advisor*.

Environment Reporter. Bureau of National Affairs, Inc., 1231 25th St., N.W. Washington, DC 20037-1197. Phone: 800-372-1033 or (202)452-4200 Fax: (202)452-8092 E-mail: books@bna.com • URL: http://www.bna.com • Weekly. $2,844.00 per year. 18 volumes. Looseleaf. Covers legal aspects of wide variety of environmental concerns.

Environment Reporter. The Bureau of National Affairs, Inc. Trends Publishing, Inc., 1231 25th St., N.W. Washington, DC 20037. Phone: (202)452-4200 Fax: (202)822-8092 Weekly. $2,844.00 per year. Looseleaf. Provides information on the U.S. and international policies, plans, programs, projects, publications and events in environmental and pollution control topics.

Environmental Accounting: Current Issues, Abstracts, and Bibliography. United Nations Publications, Concourse Level, First Ave., 46th St. New York, NY 10017. Phone: 800-553-3210 or (212)963-7680 Fax: (212)963-4910 E-mail: bookstore@un.org • URL: http://www.un.org/publications • 1992. Provides guidelines for environmental disclosure in corporate annual reports.

Environmental Biotechnology Institute.

Environmental Business Journal: Strategic Information for a Changing Industry. Environmental Business Publishing Co., 4452 Park Blvd., Suite 306 San Diego, CA 92116-4039. Phone: 800-446-4325 or (619)295-7685 Fax: (619)295-5743 Monthly. $495.00 per year. Newsletter. Includes both industrial and financial information relating to individual companies and to the environmental industry in general. Covers air pollution, wat es, U. S. Department of Health and Human Services. Provides conference, workshop, and symposium proceedings, as well as extensive reviews of environmental prospects.

Environmental Business Management: An Introduction. Klaus North. International Labour Office, 1828 L St., N.W., Suite 801 Washington, DC 20036. Phone: (202)653-7652 Fax: (202)653-7687 E-mail: ilopubs@tascol.com • URL: http://www.ilo.org/pubns • 1992. $24.75. (Management Development Series, No. 30).

Environmental Career Directory. Visible Ink Press, 27500 Drake Rd. Farmington Hills, MI 48331-3535. Phone: 800-877-GALE or (248)699-GALE Fax: 800-414-5043 or (248)699-8069 E-mail: galeord@galegroup.com • URL: http://www.visibleink.com • 1993. $17.95. Includes career information relating to workers in conservation, recycling, wildlife management, pollution control, and other areas. Provides advice from "insiders," resume suggestions, a directory of companies that may offer entry-level positions, and a directory of career information sources. (Career Advisor Series.)

Environmental Coalition on Nuclear Power., 433 Orlando Ave. State College, PA 16803. Phone: (814)237-3900 Fax: (814)237-3900 Seeks establishment of non-nuclear energy policy.

Environmental Encyclopedia. The Gale Group, 27500 Drake Rd. Farmington Hills, MI 48331-3535. Phone: 800-877-GALE or (248)699-GALE Fax: 800-414-5043 or (248)699-8069 E-mail: galeord@galegroup.com • URL: http://www.galegroup.com • 1998. $235.00. Second edition. Provides over 1,300 articles on all aspects of the environment. Written in non-technical style.

Environmental Engineering. P. Aarne Vesilind and others. Butterworth-Heinemann, 225 Wildwood Ave. Woburn, MA 01081. Phone: 800-366-2665 or (781)904-2500 Fax: 800-466-6520 E-mail: orders@bhusa.com • URL: http://www.bh.com • 1994. $66.95. Third edition.

Environmental Engineering Center., Michigan Technological University, 1400 Townsend Dr. Houghton, MI 49931. Phone: (906)487-2520 Fax: (906)487-2943 E-mail: baillod@mtu.edu • URL: http://www.bigmac.civil.mtu.edu/enveng.html • Applies biotechnological research to waste management and resource recovery.

Environmental Engineering Laboratory. Pennsylvania State University

Environmental Epidemiology and Toxicology. International Society of Occupational Medicine and Toxicology. Princeton Scientific Publishing Co., Inc., P.O. Box 2155, 428 E. Preston St. Princeton, NJ 08543. Phone: (609)683-4750 Fax: (609)683-0838 Quarterly. Individuals, $97.00 per year; institutions, $210.00 per year. Formerly *International Journal of Occupational Medicine, Immunology and Toxicology*.

Environmental Fluid Mechanics Laboratory. Stanford University

Environmental Geology. Edward A. Keller. Prentice Hall, 240 Frisch Court Paramus, NJ 07652-5240. Phone: 800-947-7700 or (201)909-6200 Fax: 800-445-6991 or (201)909-6361 URL: http://www.prenhall.com • 1999. $76.00. Eighth edition.

Environmental Hazards Management Institute.

Environmental Health Perspectives. Available from U. S. Government Printing Office, Washington, DC 20402. Phone: (202)512-1800 Fax: (202)512-2250 E-mail: gpoaccess@gpo.gov • URL: http://www.access.gpo.gov • Monthly. $150.00 per year. Issued by the U.S. Department of Health and Human Services (http://www.dhhs.gov). Contains original research on various aspects of the environment and human health. Includes news of environment-related legislation, regulatory actions, and technological advances.

Environmental Health Perspectives Supplement. Available from U. S. Government Printing Office, Washington, DC 20402. Phone: (202)512-1800 Fax: (202)512-2250 E-mail: gpoaccess@gpo.gov • URL: http://www.access.gpo.gov • Bimonthly. $91.00 per year. Issued by the U.S. Department of Health and Human Services (http://www.dhhs.gov). Provides original, peer-reviewed monographs on environmental health topics. Includes an annual review of the field.

Environmental Health Sciences Research Laboratory. Tulane University

Environmental Law and Management. Available from John Wiley and Sons, Inc., Journals Div., 605 Third Ave. New York, NY 10158-0012. Phone: 800-526-5368 or (212)850-6000 Fax: (212)850-6021 E-mail: info@wiley.com • URL: http://www.wiley.com • Bimonthly. Institutions, $650.00 per year. Provides international coverage of subject matter. Published in England by John Wiley and Sons Ltd. Formerly *Land Management and Environmental Law Report*.

Environmental Law in a Nutshell. Roger W. Findley and Daniel A. Farber. West Publishing Co., College and School Div., 610 Opperman Dr. Eagan, MN 55123. Phone: 800-328-4880 or (651)687-7000 Fax: 800-213-2323 or (651)687-5827 E-mail: legal_ed@westgroup.com • URL: http://www.lawschool.westgroup.com • 1992. $15.50. Fourth edition. (Paralegal Series).

Environmental Law Institute., 1616 P St., N. W., Suite 200 Washington, DC 20036. Phone: (202)939-3800 Fax: (202)939-3868 E-mail: law@eli.org • URL: http://www.eli.org • Conducts research projects relating to environmental regulatory enforcement and reform.

Environmental Law Reporter. Environmental Law Institute, 1616 P St., N. W., Suite 200 Washington, DC 20036. Phone: (202)328-5150 Monthly. $1,045.00 per year. Seven volumes. Looseleaf service.

Environmental Law Reporter Îonlinel. Environmental Law Institute, 1616 P St., N. W., Suite 200 Washington, DC 20036. Phone: (202)939-3800 Fax: (202)939-3868 URL: http://www.eli.org • Provides full text online of *Environmental Law Reporter*, covering administrative materials, news, pending legislation, statutes, bibliography, etc. Time periods vary. Inquire as to online cost and availability.

Environmental Management Association.

Environmental Periodicals Bibliography: A Current Awareness Bibliography Featuring Citations of Scientific and Popular Articles in Serial Publications in the Area of the Environment. Environmental Studies Institute. International Academy at Santa Barbara, 5385 Hollister Ave., No.210 Santa Barbara, CA 93111-2305. Phone: 800-530-2682 or (805)965-0790 Fax: (805)964-0890 E-mail: info@iasb.org • URL: http://www.iasb.org • Monthly. Price varies. An index to current environmental literature.

Environmental Policy Alert. Inside Washington Publishers, Benjamin Franklin Station, P.O. Box 7167 Washington, DC 20044-7167. Phone: 800-424-9068 or (703)416-8500 Fax: (703)416-8543 E-mail: service@iwpnews.com • Biweekly. $645.00 per year. Newsletter on environmental legislation, regulation, and litigation.

Environmental Policy in the 1990s: Reform or Reaction. Norman Vig and Michael Kraft. Congressional Quarterly, Inc., 1414 22nd St., N. W. Washington, DC 20037. Phone: 800-638-1710 or (202)887-8500 Fax: (202)887-6706 E-mail: bookhelp@cq.com • URL: http://www.cq.com • 1996. $43.95 Third edition.

Environmental Politics and Policy. Walter A. Rosenbaum. Congressional Quarterly, Inc., 1414 22nd St., N. W. Washington, DC 20037. Phone: 800-638-1710 or (202)887-8500

Fax: (202)887-6706 E-mail: bookhelp@cq.com • URL: http://www.cq.com • 1998. $31.95. Fourth edition.

Environmental Regulation: State Capitals. Wakeman-Walworth, Inc., P.O. Box 7376 Alexandria, VA 22307-0376. Phone: 800-876-2545 or (703)549-8606 Fax: (703)549-1372 E-mail: newsletters@statecapitals.com • URL: http://www.statecapitals.com • Weekly. $245.00 per year. Newsletter. Formerly *From the State Capitals: Environmental Regulation*.

Environmental Resources Research Institute. Pennsylvania State University

Environmental Science and Technology. Kluwer Academic Publishers, 101 Philip Dr. Norwell, MA 02061. Phone: (781)871-6600 Fax: (781)871-6528 E-mail: kluwer@wkap.nl • URL: http://www.wkap.nl • Irregular. Price varies.

Environmental Toxicology: An International Journal. John Wiley and Sons, Inc. Journals Div., 605 Third Ave. New York, NY 10158-0012. Phone: 800-225-5945 or (212)850-6000 Fax: (212)850-6088 E-mail: info@wiley.com • URL: http://www.wiley.com • Five times a year. Institutions, $545.00 per year. Formerly *Environmental Toxicology and Water Quality*.

Environmental Toxicology Center.

Environmental Viewpoints. The Gale Group, 27500 Drake Rd. Farmington Hills, MI 48331-3535. Phone: 800-877-GALE or (248)699-GALE Fax: 800-414-5043 or (248)699-8069 E-mail: galeord@galegroup.com • URL: http://www.galegroup.com • 1993. $195.00. Three volumes. $65.00 per volume. A compendium of excerpts of about 200 articles on a wide variety of environmental topics, selected from both popular and professional periodicals. Arranged alphabetically by topic, with a subject/keyword index.

EPRI Journal. Electric Power Research Institute, P.O. Box 10412 Palo Alto, CA 94303-0813. Phone: (650)855-2300 Fax: (650)855-2900 E-mail: ddietric@epri.com • URL: http://www.epri.com/epri_journal/index.html • Bimonthly. Free to members; non-members, $29.00 per year.

EQ: The Project Recording and Sound Magazine. United Entertainment Media, Inc., 460 Park Ave. South New York, NY 10016-7315. Phone: (212)378-0400 Fax: (212)378-2160 E-mail: eq@uemedia.com • URL: http://www.eqmag.com • Monthly. $36.00 per year. Provides advice on professional music recording equipment and technique.

The Equal Employer. Y. S. Publications, Inc., P.O. Box 2172 Silver Springs, MD 20902-2172. Phone: (301)649-1231 Biweekly. $245.00 per year. Newsletter on fair employment practices.

Equal Employment Opportunity Compliance Manual: Procedures, Forms, Affirmative Action Programs, Laws, Regulations. Prentice Hall, 240 Frisch Court Paramus, NJ 07652-5240. Phone: 800-947-7700 or (201)909-6200 Fax: 800-445-6991 or (201)909-6361 URL: http://www.prenhall.com • Two looseleaf volumes. Periodic supplementation. Price on application.

Equal Opportunity Law. David P. Twomey. South-Western Publishing Co., 5101 Madison Rd. Cincinnati, OH 45227. Phone: 800-543-0487 or (513)271-8811 Fax: 800-437-8488 E-mail: billhendee@itped.com • URL: http://www.swcollege.com • 1996. $31.50. Third edition.

Equality in the Workplace: An Equal Opportunities Handbook for Trainers. Helen Collins. Blackwell Publishers, 350 Main St., 6th Fl. Malden, MA 02148-5018. Phone: 800-216-2522 or (781)388-8200 Fax: (781)388-8210 E-mail: books@blackwellpub.com • URL: http://www.blackwellpub.com • 1995. $43.95. (Human Resource Management in Action Series).

Equipment Leasing. Matthew Bender and Co., Inc., Two Park Ave. New York, NY 10016. Phone: 800-223-1940 or (212)448-2000 Fax: (212)244-3188 E-mail: international@bender.com • URL: http://www.bender.com • $405.00. Three looseleaf volumes. Periodic supplementation.

Equipment Leasing Association.

Equipment Leasing, Leveraged Leasing. Practising Law Institute, 810 Seventh Ave. New York, NY 10019-5818. Phone: 800-260-4754 or (212)824-5700 Fax: (212)265-4742 E-mail: info@pli.edu • URL: http://www.pli.edu • Two looseleaf volumes. $295.00. Annual revisions. Contains "Practical analyses of the legal, tax, accounting, and financial aspects of equipment leasing." Includes forms, agreements, and checklists.

Equipment Leasing Today. Equipment Leasing Association, 4301 N. Fairfax Ave., Suite 550 Arlington, VA 22203-1608. Phone: (703)527-8655 Fax: (703)527-2649 URL: http://www.elaonline.com/ • 10 times a year. $100.00 per year. Edited for equipment leasing companies. Covers management, funding, marketing, etc.

Equipment Today. Cygnus Publishing, Inc., 1233 Janesville Ave. Fort Atkinson, WI 53538-0460. Phone: 800-547-7377 or (920)563-6388 Fax: (920)563-1707 E-mail: rich.reiff@cygnuspub.com • URL: http://www.cygnuspub.com • Monthly. $65.00 per year. Includes annual *Product* issue Formerly *Equipment Guide News*.

Equities: Investment News of Promising Public Companies. Equities Magazine LLC, 160 Madison Ave., 3rd Fl. New York, NY 10016-5412. Phone: 800-237-8400 or (212)213-1300 Fax: (212)213-5872 Seven times a year. $21.00 per year. Formerly *OTC Review*.

The ERC Closely-Held Corporation Guide. Harvey Frank. Prentice Hall, 240 Frisch Court Paramus, NJ 07652-5240. Phone: 800-947-7700 or (201)909-6200 Fax: 800-445-6991 or (201)909-6361 URL: http://www.prenhall.com • 1983. $59.95. Second edition.

Ergonomics: An International Journal of Research and Practice in Human Factors and Ergonomics. Taylor and Francis, Inc., 325 Chestnut St., 8th Fl. Philadelphia, PA 19106. Phone: 800-821-8312 or (215)625-8900 Fax: (215)625-2940 E-mail: webmasters@taylorandfrancis.com • URL: http://www.tandfdc.com/ • Monthly. Individuals, $1,018.00 per year; institutions, $2,056 per year.

Ergonomics at Work. David A. Osbourne. Books on Demand, 300 N Zeeb Rd. Ann Arbor, MI 48106-1346. Phone: 800-521-0600 or (734)761-4700 Fax: (734)665-5022 E-mail: info@umi.com • URL: http://www.lib.umi.com • 1995. $102.70. Third edition.

The Ergonomics Edge: Improving Safety, Quality, and Productivity. Dan MacLeod. John Wiley and Sons, Inc., 605 Third Ave. New York, NY 10158-0012. Phone: 800-225-5945 or (212)850-6000 Fax: (212)850-6088 E-mail: info@jwiley.com • URL: http://www.wiley.com • 1994. $80.00. (Industrial Health and Safety Series).

ERIC. Educational Resources Information Center, ERIC Processing and Reference Facility, 1100 West St. Laurel, MD 20707. Phone: 800-799-3742 or (301)479-4080 Fax: (301)948-3695 Broad range of educational literature, 1966 to present. Monthly updates. Inquire as to online cost and availability.

ERIC Clearinghouse for Community Colleges. University of California, Los Angeles

ERIC Clearinghouse on Adult, Career and Vocational Education. Ohio State University

ERIC Clearinghouse on Higher Education. George Washington University

ERIC on SilverPlatter. Available from SilverPlatter Information, Inc., 100 River Ridge Rd. Norwood, MA 02062-5026. Phone: 800-343-0064 or (781)769-2599 Fax: (781)769-8763 Quarterly. $700.00 per year. Produced by the Office of Educational Research and Improvement, U. S. Dept. of Education. Provides CD-ROM indexing and abstracting of a wide variety of literature relating to education. Archival discs are available from 1966.

ERISA: The Law and the Code (Employee Retirement Income Security Act). Bureau of National Affairs, Inc., 1231 25th St., N.W. Washington, DC 20037-1197. Phone: 800-372-1033 or (202)452-4200 Fax: (202)452-8092 E-mail: books@bna.com • URL: http://www.bna.com • Irregular. $75.00. The Employee Retirement Income Security Act, as amended, withrelevant provisions of the Internal Revenue Code.

Ernst & Young Almanac and Guide to U. S. Business Cities: 65 Leading Places to Do Business. John Wiley and Sons, Inc., 605 Third Ave. New York, NY 10158-0012. Phone: 800-225-5945 or (212)850-6000 Fax: (212)850-6088 E-mail: info@jwiley.com • URL: http://www.wiley.com • 1994. $16.95. Provides demographic, business, economic, and site selection data for 65 major U. S. cities.

Ernst & Young Tax Guide 2000: The Official IRS Tax Guide and Usable Forms, Plus Easy-to-Use Explanation and Tax Saving Tips from America's Leading Big Six Accounting Firms. Ernst & Young Staff. John Wiley and Sons, Inc., 605 Third Ave. New York, NY 10158-0012. Phone: 800-225-5945 or (212)850-6000 Fax: (212)850-6088 E-mail: info@wiley.com • URL: http://www.wiley.com • Annual. $15.95. (Ernst and Young Tax Guide Series).

Ernst and Young's Oil and Gas Federal Income Taxation. John R. Braden and others. CCH, Inc., 4025 W. Peterson Ave. Chicago, IL 60646-6085. Phone: 800-248-3248 or (773)583-8500 Fax: 800-224-8299 URL: http://www.cch.com • Annual. $92.95. Formerly *Miller's Oil and Gas Federal Income Taxation*.

Ernst & Young's Personal Financial Planning Guide. John Wiley and Sons, Inc., 605 Third Ave. New York, NY 10158-0012. Phone: 800-225-5945 or (212)850-6000 Fax: (212)850-6088 E-mail: info@jwiley.com • URL: http://www.wiley.com • 1999. $19.95. Third edition.

eShopper. Ziff-Davis, 28 E. 28th St. New York, NY 10016-7930. Phone: 800-366-2423 or (212)503-3500 URL: http://www.zdnet.com/ • Bimonthly. $9.97 per year. A consumer magazine providing advice and information for "shopping on the Web."

ESOP Association., 1726 M St., N.W. Suite 501 Washington, DC 20036. Phone: (202)293-2971 Fax: (202)293-7568 E-mail: esop@esopassociation.org • URL: http://www.esopassociation.org • Members are companies with employee stock ownership plans.

ESOP Report (Employee Stock Ownership Plan). ESOP Association, 1726 M St., N.W., Suite 501 Washington, DC 20036. Phone: (202)293-2971 Fax: (202)293-7568 URL: http://www.esopassociation.org • Monthly. Membership. Newsletter.

Essential Business Buyer's Guide, from Cellular Services and Overnight Mail to Internet Access Providers, 401(k) Plans, and Desktop Computers: The Ultimate Guide to Buying Office Equipment, Products, and Services. Sourcebooks, Inc., P.O. Box 372 Naperville, IL 60566. Phone: 800-727-8866 or (630)961-3900 Fax: (630)961-2168 E-mail: custserv@buyerszone.com • URL: http://www.buyerszone.com • 1996. $18.95. Compiled by the staff of *Business Consumer Guide*. Lists recommended brands of office equipment.

The Essential Guide to Bulletin Board Systems. Patrick R. Dewey. Information Today, Inc., 143 Old Marlton Pike Medford, NJ 08055-8750. Phone: 800-300-9868 or (609)654-6266 Fax: (609)654-4309 E-mail: custserv@infotoday.com • URL: http://www.infotoday.com • 1998. $39.50. Provides details on the setup and operation of online bulletin board systems. Covers both hardware and software.

Essentials of Accounting for Governmental and Not-for-Profit Organizations. John H. Engstrom and Leon E. Hay. McGraw-Hill, 1221 Ave of the Americas New York, NY 10020. Phone: 800-722-4726 or (212)904-2000 Fax: (212)904-2072 E-mail: customer.sevice@mcgraw-hill.com • URL: http://www.mcgraw-hill.com • 1998. $53.44. Fifth edition.

Essentials of Cash Management. Peter S. Adam and Wiliam Harrison, editors. Treasury Management Association, 7315 Wisconsin Ave., Suite 600 W. Bethesda, MD 20814. Phone: (301)907-2862 Fax: (301)907-2864 E-mail: communications@tma-net.org • URL: http://www.tma-net.org/treasury • 1998. $95.50. Sixth edition.

Essentials of Federal Income Taxation for Individuals and Business. CCH, Inc., 4025 West Peterson Ave. Chicago, IL 60646-6085. Phone: 800-248-3248 or (773)866-6000 Fax: 800-224-8299 or (773)866-3608 URL: http://www.cch.com • Annual. $59.00. Covers basic tax planning and tax reduction strategies as affected by tax law changes and IRS interpretations. Includes sample filled-in forms.

Essentials of Managerial Finance. J. Fred Weston. Harcourt College Publishers, 301 Commerce St., Suite 3700 Fort Worth, TX 76102. Phone: 800-245-8774 or (817)334-7500 Fax: (817)334-8060 or (800)874 E-mail: wlittle@harbrace.com • URL: http://www.harcourt.com • 1999. $44.50. 12th edition.

Essentials of Media Planning: A Marketing Viewpoint. Arnold M. Barban and others. NTC/Contemporary Publishing, P.O. Box 545 Blacklick, OH 43004. Phone: 800-338-3987 or (614)755-4151 Fax: (614)755-5645 E-mail: ntcpub@mcgraw-hill.com • URL: http://www.ntc-cb.com • 1993. $29.95. Third edition. Practical guide to media analysis. (NTC Business Book Series).

Essentials of Project Management. Dennis Lock. Ashgate Publishing Co., Old Post Rd. Brookfield, VT 05036-9704. Phone: 800-535-9544 or (802)276-3162 Fax: (802)276-3837 E-mail: info@ashgate.com • URL: http://www.ashgate.com • 1996. $26.95. Published by Gower in England.

Essentials of Psychological Testing. Lee J. Cronbach. Addison-Wesley Educational Publishers, Inc., One Jacob Way Reading, MA 01687. Phone: 800-447-2226 or (781)944-3700 Fax: (781)942-1117 URL: http://www.awl.com • 1997. $113.00. Fifth edition.

Essentials of Real Estate Investment. David Sirota. Dearborn, A Kaplan Professional Co., 155 N. Wacker St. Chicago, IL 60606-1719. Phone: 800-621-9621 or (312)836-4400 Fax: (312)836-1021 URL: http://www.dearborn.com • 1997. $45.95. Sixth edition. Tax law revisions.

Estate and Personal Financial Planning. Edward F. Koren. West Group, 610 Opperman Dr. Eagan, MN 55123. Phone: 800-328-4880 or (651)687-7000 Fax: 800-213-2323 or (651)687-5827 URL: http://www.westgroup.com • Monthly. Newsletter. Price on application.

Estate and Retirement Planning Answer Book. William D. Mitchell. Aspen Publshers, 200 Orchard Ridge Dr. Gaithersburg, MD 20878. Phone: 800-638-8437 or (301)417-7500 Fax: (301)417-7550 E-mail: customer.service@aspenpubl.com • URL: http://www.aspenpublishers.com • 1996. $118.00. Second edition. Basic questions and answers by a lawyer.

Estate Plan Book 2000. William S. Moore. American Institute for Economic Research, Division St. Great Barrington, MA 01230. Phone: (413)528-1216 Fax: (413)528-0103 E-mail: info@aier.org • URL: http://www.aier.org • 2000. $10.00. Revision of 1997 edition. Part one: "Basic Estate Planning." Part two: "Reducing Taxes on the Disposition of Your Estate." Part three: "Putting it All Together: Examples of Estate Plans." Provides succinct information on wills, trusts, tax planning, and gifts. (Economic Education Bulletin.)

Estate Planner's Alert. Research Institute of America, Inc., 90 Fifth Ave. New York, NY 10011. Phone: 800-431-9035 or (212)645-4800 Fax: (212)337-4213 Monthly. $140.00 per year. Newsletter. Covers the tax aspects of personal finance, including home ownership, investments, insurance, retirement planning, and charitable giving. Formerly *Estate and Financial Planners Alert*.

Estate Planning. Warren, Gorham and Lamont/RIA Group, 395 Hudson St. New York, NY 10014. Phone: 800-950-1215 or (212)367-6300 Fax: (651)687-5827 E-mail: customer_services@riag.com • URL: http://www.westgroup.com • Bimonthly. $141.50 per year. Semiannual updates.

Estate Planning and Taxation Coordinator. Research Institute of America, Inc., 90 Fifth Ave. New York, NY 10011. Phone: 800-431-9025 or (212)645-4800 Fax: (212)337-4213 Nine looseleaf volumes. $760.00 per year. Biweekly updates. Includes *Estate Planner's Alert* and *Lifetime Planning Alert*.

Estate Planning for Farmers and Ranchers: A Guide to Family Businesses with Agricultural Holdings. Donald H. Kelley and David A. Ludtke. Shepard's, 555 Middle Creek Parkway Colorado Springs, CO 80921. Phone: 800-743-7393 or (719)481-7371 Fax: 800-525-0053 or (719)481-7621 E-mail: customer_service@shepards.com • URL: http://www.shepards.com • 1995. Third edition. Price on application.

Estate Planning: Inheritance Taxes. Prentice Hall, 240 Frisch Court Paramus, NJ 07652-5240. Phone: 800-947-7700 or (201)909-6200 Fax: 800-445-6991 or (201)909-6361 URL: http://www.prenhall.com • Five looseleaf volumes. Periodic supplementation. Price on application.

Estate Planning Primer. Ralph G. Miller. CCH, Inc., 4025 W. Peterson Ave. Chicago, IL 60646-6085. Phone: 800-248-3248 or (773)866-6000 Fax: 800-224-8299 or (773)866-3608 URL: http://www.cch.com • 1999. $99.00. Eighth edition. Written for attorneys and other estate planning professionals. Includes tables, sample tax forms, legal documents, and client letters. letters

Estate Planning Program. Prentice Hall, 240 Frisch Court Paramus, NJ 07652-5240. Phone: 800-947-7700 or (201)909-6200 Fax: 800-445-6991 or (201)909-6361 URL: http://www.prenhall.com • Two looseleaf volumes. Periodic supplementation. Price on application. Includes checklists and forms.

Estate Planning Review. CCH, Inc., 4025 W. Peterson Ave. Chicago, IL 60646-6085. Phone: 800-248-3248 or (773)866-6000 Fax: 800-224-8299 or (773)866-3608 URL: http://www.cch.com • Monthly. $196.00 per year.

Estate Planning Strategies After Estate Tax Reform: Insights and Analysis. CCH, Inc., 4025 West Peterson Ave. Chicago, IL 60646-6085. Phone: 800-248-3248 or (773)866-6000 Fax: 800-224-8299 or (773)866-3608 E-mail: cust_serv@cch.com • URL: http://www.cch.com • 2001. $45.00. Produced by the Estate Planning Department of Schiff, Hardin & Waite. Covers estate planning techniques and opportunities resulting from tax legislation of 2001.

Estate Planning Under the New Law: What You Need to Know. CCH, Inc., 4025 West Peterson Ave. Chicago, IL 60646-6085. Phone: 800-248-3248 or (773)866-6000 Fax: 800-224-8299 or (773)866-3608 E-mail: cust_serv@cch.com • URL: http://www.cch.com • 2001. $7.00. Booklet summarizes significant changes in estate planning brought about by tax legislation of 2001.

Estate Planning: Wills, Trusts and Forms. Research Institute of America, 90 Fifth Ave. New York, NY 10011. Phone: 800-431-9025 or (212)645-4800 Fax: (212)337-4213 Looseleaf service. Includes bimonthly *Report Bulletins* and updates.

Estate Tax Techniques. Matthew Bender & Co., Inc., Two Park Ave. New York, NY 10016. Phone: 800-223-1940 or (212)448-2000 Fax: (212)244-3188 E-mail: international@bender.com • URL: http://www.bender.com • $640.00. Three looseleaf volumes. Periodic supplementation.

Estimating for Home Builders. Jerry Householder. Home Builder Press, 1201 15th St., N. W. Washington, DC 20005-2800. Phone: 800-368-5242 or (202)822-0395 Fax: (202)822-0391 URL: http://www.builderbooks.com • 1998. $30.80. Third edition. Describes the process of developing complete cost estimates-and the shortcut methods-to ensure success in the building business.

Estimating in Building Construction. Frank R. Dagostino. Prentice Hall, 240 Frisch Court Paramus, NJ 07652-5240. Phone: 800-947-7700 or (201)909-6200 Fax: 800-445-6991 or (201)909-6361 URL: http://www.prenhall.com • 1998. $81.00. Fifth edition.

The Ethics of Management. LaRue T. Hosmer. McGraw-Hill Professional, 1221 Ave. of the Americas New York, NY 10020-1095. Phone: 800-722-4726 or (212)904-2000 Fax: (212)904-2072 E-mail: customer.service@mcgraw-hill.com • URL: http://www.mcgraw-hill.com • 1995. $33.50. Third edition.

Ethics Resource Center.

Ethnic Enrollment Data From Institutions of Higher Education. U.S. Dept. of Health and Human Services, Office for Civil Rights, Washington, DC 20201. Phone: (202)619-0671 Annual.

The EU Institutions' Register. Euroconfidentiel S. A., Rue de Rixensart 18 B-1332 Genval, Belgium. Phone: (32)02 653 01 25 Fax: (32)02 653 01 80 E-mail: nigel.hunt@euronet.be • Annual. $130.00. Lists more than 5,000 key personnel in European Union institutions and decentralized agencies. Includes areas of responsibility.

Euroguide Yearbook of the Institutions of the European Union and of the Other European Organiz. Bernan Associates, 4611-F Assembly Dr. Lanham, MD 20706-4391. Phone: 800-274-4447 or (301)459-7666 Fax: 800-865-3450 or (301)459-0056 E-mail: info@bernan.com • URL: http://www.bernan.com • Annual. Free. Published by Editions Delta. Information on public and private institutions in the European Union contributing to European integration.

Euromoney: The Monthly Journal of International Money and Capital Markets. American Educational Systems, 173 W. 81st St. New York, NY 10024. Phone: 800-717-2669 or (212)501-8181 Fax: (212)501-8926 E-mail: gerans@pobox.com • URL: http://www.emwl.com • Monthly. $395.00 per year. Supplement available*Guide to World Equity Markets*.

Euromonitor Directory of Asian Companies. Gale Group, Inc., 27500 Drake Rd. Farmington Hills, MI 48331-3535. Phone: 800-877-GALE or (248)699-GALE Fax: 800-414-5043 or (248)699-8069 E-mail: galeord@gale.com • URL: http://www.gale.com • 1997. $550.00. Provides detailed profiles of 5,000 major companies in Southeast Asia. Countries are China, Hong Kong, India, Indonesia, Korea, Malaysia, Pakistan, Phillippines, Singapore, Sri Lanka, Taiwan, Thailand, and Vietnam.

Euromonitor Journals. Euromonitor International, 122 South Michigan Ave., Suite 1200 Chicago, IL 60603. Phone: 800-577-3876 or (312)922-1115 Fax: (312)922-1157 E-mail: info@euromonitor.com • URL: http://www.euromonitor.com • Contains full-text reports online from *Market Research Europe, Market Research Great Britain, Market Research International*, and *Retail Monitor International*. Time period is 1995 to date, with monthly updates. Inquire as to online cost and availability.

Euromonitor Market Research. Euromonitor International, 122 S. Michigan Ave., Suite 1200 Chicago, IL 60603. Phone: 800-577-3876 or (312)922-1115 Fax: (312)922-1157 E-mail: info@euromonitor.com • URL: http://www.euromonitor.com • Provides the complete text online of Euromonitor market analysis reports. Covers consumer goods market research data for all major countries, with emphasis on specific product categories. Time period is current. Continuous updating. Inquire as to online cost and availability.

Europa: The European Union's Server. European Union 352 4301 35 349E-mail: pressoffice@eurostat.cec.be • URL: http://www.europa.eu.int • Web site provides access to a wide variety of EU information, including statistics (Eurostat), news, policies, publications, key issues, and official exchange rates for the euro. Includes links to the European Central Bank, the European Investment Bank, and other institutions. Fees: Free.

Europa 2000: The American Business Report on Europe. Wolfe Publishing, Inc., South Nashua Station, P.O. Box 7599 Nashua, NH 03060-9883. Phone: 800-882-3876 or (603)888-0338 Fax: (603)888-5816 Monthly. $119.00 per year. Newsletter on consumer and industrial marketing in a unified European Economic Community. Includes classified business opportunity advertisements and a listing by country of forthcoming major trade shows in Europe.

Europa World Yearbook. Taylor and Francis, Inc., 325 Chestnut St. Philadelphic, PA 19106. Phone: (212)625-8900 Fax: (215)625-2940 E-mail: eutopa@taylorandfrancis.com • URL: http://www.europapublications.co.uk • Annual. $815.00. Two volumes. Published by Europa Publications Ltd. Basic source of information on every country and some 1,650 international organizations. Includes detailed directories and surveys for each country.

European Access. European Commission-United Kingdom Offices, EL. Available from Chadwyck-Healey, Inc., 1101 King St., Suite 380 Alexandria, VA 22314-2924. Phone: 800-752-0515 or (703)683-4890 Fax: (703)683-7589 E-mail: mktg@chadwyck.co.uk • URL: http://www.chadwyck.com • Bimonthly. $260.00 per year. Published in England. A journal providing general coverage of developments and trends within the European Community.

European Compendium of Marketing Information. Available from The Gale Group, 27500 Drake Rd. Farmington Hills, MI 48331-3535. Phone: 800-877-GALE or (248)699-GALE Fax: 800-414-5043 or (248)699-8069 E-mail: galeord@galegroup.com • URL: http://www.galegroup.com • 1996. $350.00. Second edition. Volume two. Published by Euromonitor. Provides marketing and production statistics relating to European consumer products and services.

European Direct Marketing Association., 439 Ave. de Tervueren B-1150 Brussels, Belgium. E-mail: edma@skynet.be • A multinational organization. Facilitates contacts and exchange of ideas and techniques among countries and members. Sponsors ''Best of Europe'' contest, with awards for best direct mail campaigns.

European Directory of Retailers and Wholesalers. Available from The Gale Group, 27500 Drake Rd. Farmington Hills, MI 48331-3535. Phone: 800-877-GALE or (248)699-GALE Fax: 800-414-5043 or (248)699-8069 E-mail: galeord@galegroup.com • URL: http://www.galegroup.com • 1997. $790.00. Second edition. Published by Euromonitor. Provides detailed information on more than 4,000 major retail and wholesale businesses in 17 countries of Western Europe. Contains 26 categories, such as supermarkets, superstores, department stores, discount stores, franchise operators, mail order, etc. Includes company, product, and geographic indexes.

European Economy, Series A: Recent Economic Trends. Commission of the European Communities. Bernan Associates, 4611-F Assembly Dr. Lanham, MD 20706-4391. Phone: 800-274-4447 or (301)459-7666 Fax: 800-865-3450 or (301)459-0056 E-mail: info@bernan.com • URL: http://www.bernan.com • Monthly. $65.00 per year. Published by the Commission of the European Communities, Luxembourg.

European Economy, Series B: Business and Consumer Survey Results. Commission of the European Communities. Available from Bernan Associates, 4611-F Assembly Dr. Lanham, MD 20706-4391. Phone: 800-274-4447 or (301)459-7666 Fax: 800-865-3450 or (301)459-0056 E-mail: into@bernan.com • URL: http://www.bernan.com • Monthly. Published by the Commission of the European Communities, Luxembourg. Editions in English, French, German, and Italian.

European Food Marketing Directory. The Gale Group, 27500 Drake Rd. Farmington Hills, MI 48331-3535. Phone: 800-877-GALE or (248)699-GALE Fax: 800-414-5043 or (248)699-8069 E-mail: galeord@galegroup.com • URL: http://www.galegroup.com • 1996. $430.00. Fourth edition. Volume four. Published by Euromonitor. Lists approximately 650 European food distributors and 1,600 food manufacturers. Covers more than 20 countries in all parts of Europe.

European Kompass on Disc. Available from Kompass USA, Inc., 1255 Route 70, Suite 25-S Lakewood, NJ 08701. Phone: 877-566-7277 or (732)730-0340 Fax: (732)730-0342 E-mail: mail@kompass-usa.com • URL: http://www.kompass.com • Annual. $2,070.00. CD-ROM provides information on more than 350,000 companies in Belgium, Denmark, France, Germany, Ireland, Italy, Luxembourg, Netherlands, Norway, Spain, Sweden, and UK. Classification system covers approximately 50,000 products and services.

European Management Journal. Elsevier Science, 655 Ave. of the Americas New York, NY 10010. Phone: 888-437-4636 or (212)989-5800 Fax: (212)633-3680 E-mail: usinfo@elsevier.com • URL: http://www.elsevier.com • Bimonthly. $566.00 per year. Covers a wide variety of topics, including management problems of the European Single Market.

European Marketing Academy., c/o European Institute for Advanced Studies in Management, 13, rue d'Egmont B-1000 32 Brussels, Belgium. E-mail: emac@eiasm.be • URL: http://www.eiasm.be/emac/emachp.html • A multinational organization. Promotes international exchange in the field of marketing.

European Marketing Association., 18 Saint Peters Hill Brixham, Devon, England. A multinational organization. Promotes the marketing profession in Europe.

European Marketing Data and Statistics 2001. Available from The Gale Group, 27500 Drake Rd. Farmington Hills, MI 48331-3535. Phone: 800-877-GALE or (248)699-GALE Fax: 800-414-5043 or (248)699-8069 E-mail: galeord@galegroup.com • URL: http://www.galegroup.com • 2001. $450.00. 36th edition. Published by Euromonitor. Presents essential marketing data, including demographics and consumer expenditure patterns, for 31 European countries.

European Marketing Forecasts 2001. Available from The Gale Group, 27500 Drake Rd. Farmington Hills, MI 48331-3535. Phone: 800-877-GALE or (248)699-GALE Fax: 800-414-5043 or (248)699-8069 E-mail: galeord@galegroup.com • URL: http://www.galegroup.com • 2000. $1,190.00. Third edition. Published by Euromonitor. Contains demographic, economic, and market forecasts for the countries of Europe to the year 2010. Forecasts include market-size data for 15 consumer product sectors (food, clothing, automobiles, consumer electronics, etc.).

European Markets: A Guide to Company and Industry Information Sources. Washington Researchers, 1655 N. Fort Myer Dr., Suite 800 Arlington, VA 22209. Phone: (703)527-4585 Fax: (703)312-2863 E-mail: research@researchers.com • URL: http://www.researchers.com/ • 1996. $335.00. A directory of government offices, ''experts,'' publications, and databases related to European markets and companies. Includes individual chapters on 18 nations of Europe.

European Retail Statistics: 17 Countries. Available from European Business Publications, Inc., P.O. Box 891 Darien, CT 06820-9859. Phone: (203)656-2701 Fax: (203)655-8332 E-mail: centralbank@easynet.co.uk • URL: http://www.easyweb.easynet.co.uk/centralbank • Annual. $375.00. Published in London by Corporate Intelligence Research Publications Ltd. Presents national retail statistics for each of 17 major countries of Europe, including total sales, number of businesses, employment, the food sector, the non-food sector, and demographic data.

European Union Annual Review of Activities. Blackwell Publishers, 350 Main St., 6th Fl. Malden, MA 02148-5018. Phone: 800-216-2522 or (781)388-8200 Fax: (781)388-8210 E-mail: books@blackwellpub.com • URL: http://www.blackwellpub.com • 1998. $15.99.

European Union Encyclopedia and Directory. Taylor and Francis, Inc., 325 Chestnut St. Philadelphic, PA 19106. Phone: (215)625-2940 Fax: (215)625-2940 E-mail: europa@taylorandfrancis.com • URL: http://www.europapublications.co.uk • 1999. $450.00. Second edition. Published by Europa. Provides directory information for major European Union organizations, with detailed descriptions of various groups or concepts in an "Encyclopedia" section. A statistics section contains a wide variety of data related to business, industry, and economics. Formerly *The European Communities Encyclopedia and Directory*.

European Union Office of Press and Public Affairs.

Europe's Major Companies Directory. Available from The Gale Group, 27500 Drake Rd. Farmington Hills, MI 48331-3535. Phone: 800-877-GALE or (248)699-GALE Fax: 800-414-5043 or (248)699-8069 E-mail: galeord@galegroup.com • URL: http://www.galegroup.com • 1997. $590.00. Second edition. Published by Euromonitor. Contains detailed financial and product information for about 6,000 major companies in 16 countries of Western Europe.

Europe's Medium-Sized Companies Directory. Available from The Gale Group, 27500 Drake Rd. Farmington Hills, MI 48331-3535. Phone: 800-877-GALE or (248)699-GALE Fax: 800-414-5043 or (248)699-8069 E-mail: galeord@galegroup.com • URL: http://www.galegroup.com • 1997. $590.00. Published by Euromonitor. Contains detailed financial and product information on about 5,000 medium-sized companies in 16 countries of Western Europe.

Europe's Top Quoted Companies: A Comparative Directory from Seventeen European Stock Exchanges. Available from Hoover's, Inc., 1033 La Posada Drive, Suite 250 Austin, TX 78752. Phone: 800-486-8666 or (512)374-4500 Fax: (512)374-4505 E-mail: orders@hoovers.com • URL: http://www.hoovers.com • Annual. $150.00. Published in the UK by COFISEM. Provides detailed, 5-year financial data on 700 major European companies that are publicly traded. Includes company addresses.

EuroWatch. Worldwide Trade Executives, 2250 Main St., Suite 100 Concord, MA 01742. Phone: (978)287-0301 URL: http://www.wtexec.com • Biweekly. $799.00 per year. Newsletter.

Evaluating Library Staff: A Performance Appraisal System. Patricia Belcastro. American Library Association, 50 E. Huron St. Chicago, IL 60611-2795. Phone: 800-545-2433 or (312)944-6780 Fax: (312)440-9374 E-mail: ala@ala.org • URL: http://www.ala.org • 1998. $35.00. Provides information on an appraisal system applicable to a wide variety of jobs in all types of libraries. Includes guidelines, performance appraisal forms, sample employee profiles, and a "Code of Service."

Evaluating Urban Parks and Recreation. William S. Hendon. Greenwood Publishing Group, Inc., 88 Post Rd., W. Westport, CT 06881-5007. Phone: 800-225-5800 or (203)226-3571 Fax: (203)222-2540 E-mail: bookinfo@greenwood.com • URL: http://www.greenwood.com • 1981. $65.00.

Evaluation Guide to Health and Wellness Programs. The Corporate University, 123 N. Main St. Fairfield, IA 52556. Phone: (515)472-7720 Fax: (515)472-7105 $189.00. Looseleaf service. Semiannual updates, $49.00 each. Provides detailed descriptions and evaluations of more than 200 employee wellness programs that are available nationally. Covers 15 major topics, such as stress management, substance abuse, occupational safety, smoking cessation, blood pressure management, exercise/fitness, diet, and mental health. Programs are available from both profit and non-profit organizations.

Event Planning Service. Entrepreneur Media, Inc., 2445 McCabe Way Irvine, CA 92614. Phone: 800-421-2300 or (949)261-2325 Fax: (949)261-0234 E-mail: entmag@entrepreneur.com • URL: http://www.entrepreneur.com • Looseleaf. $59.50. A practical guide to starting a social or corporate event planning service. Covers profit potential, start-up costs, market size evaluation, pricing, accounting, advertising, promotion, etc. (Start-Up Business Guide No. E1313.)

Every Landlord's Legal Guide. Marcia Stewart. Nolo.com, 950 Parker St. Berkeley, CA 94710. Phone: 800-992-6656 or (510)549-1976 Fax: (510)548-5902 E-mail: cs@nolo.com • URL: http://www.nolo.com • 2000. $44.95. Fourth edition.

Every Manager's Guide to Business Processes: A Glossary of Key Terms and Concepts for Today's Business Leader. Peter G. W. Keen. Harvard Business School Press, 60 Harvard Way Boston, MA 02163. Phone: 800-545-7685 or (617)783-7440 E-mail: custserv@cchbspub.harvard.edu • URL: http://www.hbsp.harvard.edu • 1995. $14.95. Provides definitions of contemporary business terms, such as "outsourcing," "benchmarking," and "groupware."

Every Manager's Guide to Information Technology: A Glossary of Key Terms and Concepts for Today's Business Leader. Peter G. W. Keen. Harvard Business School Press, 60 Harvard Way Boston, MA 02163. Phone: 800-545-7685 or (617)783-7440 E-mail: custserv@cchbspub.harvard.edu • URL: http://www.hbsp.harvard.edu • 1995. $18.95. Second edition. Provides definitions of terms related to computers, data communications, and information network systems. (Harvard Business Economist Reference Series).

Every Tenant's Legal Guide. Janet Portman and Marcia Stewart. Nolo.com, 950 Parker St. Berkeley, CA 94710. Phone: 800-992-6656 or (510)549-1976 Fax: (510)548-5902 E-mail: cs@nolo.com • URL: http://www.nolo.com • 1999. $26.95. Second edition.

Everyone's Money Book: Everything You Need to Know About Investing Wisely, Buying a Home. Jordan E. Goodman. Dearborn, A Kaplan Professional Co., 155 N. Wacker St. Chicago, IL 60606-1719. Phone: 800-621-9621 or (312)836-4400 Fax: (312)836-1021 URL: http://www.dearborn.com • 1998. $26.95. Covers investing, taxes, mortgages, retirement planning, and other personal finance topics. Jordan E. Goodman is a writer for *Money* magazine.

Everything You Need to Know to Start a House Cleaning Service. Mary P. Johnson. Cleaning Consultant Services, Inc., P.O. Box 1273 Seattle, WA 98111-1273. Phone: (206)682-9748 Fax: (206)622-6876 E-mail: wgriffin@seanet.com • URL: http://www.cleaningconsultants.com • 1999. $38.00 Revised edition.

The Evolving Virtual Library: Practical and Philosophical Perspectives. Laverna M. Saunders, editor. Information Today, Inc., 143 Old Marlton Pike Medford, NJ 08055-8750. Phone: 800-300-9868 or (609)654-6266 Fax: (609)654-4309 E-mail: custserv@infotoday.com • URL: http://www.infotoday.com • 1999. $39.50. Second edition. Various authors cover trends in library and school use of the Internet, intranets, extranets, and electronic databases.

eWEEK: Building the .Com Enterprise. Ziff-Davis, 28 E. 28th St. New York, NY 10016-7930. Phone: 800-366-2423 or (212)503-3500 E-mail: lundquist@ziffdavis.com • URL: http://www.zdnet.com/ • Weekly. Controlled circulation (free). Non-qualified: $195.00 per year. Serves as an "information source for companies undertaking e-commerce and Internet-based business initiatives." Formerly *PC Week*.

Excerpta Medica: Biophysics, Bioengineering, and Medical Instrumentation. Elsevier Science, 655 Ave. of the Americas New York, NY 10010. Phone: 888-437-4636 or (212)989-5800 Fax: (212)633-3680 E-mail: usinfo@elsevier.com • URL: http://www.elsevier.com • 16 times a year. $2,207.00 per year. Section 27 of *Excerpta Medica*.

Excerpta Medica: Drug Dependence, Alcohol Abuse, and Alcoholism. Elsevier Science, 655 Ave. of the Americas New York, NY 10010. Phone: 888-437-4636 or (212)989-5800 Fax: (212)633-3680 E-mail: usinfo@elsevier.com • URL: http://www.elsevier.com • Bimonthly. $1,079.00 per year. Section 40 of *Excerpta Medica*.

Excerpta Medica: Environmental Health and Pollution Control. Elsevier Science, 655 Ave. of the Americas New York, NY 10010. Phone: 888-437-4636 or (212)989-5800 Fax: (212)633-3680 E-mail: usinfo-f@elsevier.com • URL: http://www.elsevier.com • 16 times a year. 2,506.00 per year. Section 46 of *Excerpta Medica*. Covers air, water, and land pollution and noise control.

Excerpta Medica: Health Policy, Economics and Management. Elsevier Science, 655 Ave. of the Americas New York, NY 10010. Phone: 888-437-4636 or (212)989-5800 Fax: (212)633-3680 E-mail: usinfo@elsevier.com • URL: http://www.elsevier.com • Bimonthly. $1,327.00 per year. Section 36 of *Excerpta Medica*.

Excerpta Medica: Human Genetics. Elsevier Science, 655 Ave. of the Americas New York, NY 10010. Phone: 888-437-4636 or (212)989-5800 Fax: (212)633-3680 E-mail: usinfo@elsevier.com • URL: http://www.elsevier.com • Semimonthly. $3,196.00 per year. Section 22 of *Excerpta Medica*.

Excerpta Medica: Occupational Health and Industrial Medicine. Elsevier Science, 655 Ave. of the Americas New York, NY 10010. Phone: 888-437-4636 or (212)989-5800 Fax: (212)633-3680 E-mail: usinfo@elsevier.com • URL: http://www.elsevier.com • Monthly. $1,833.00 per year. Section 35 of *Excerpta Medica*.

Exchange and Commissary News. Executive Business Media, Inc., PO Box 1500 Westbury, NY 11590. Phone: (516)334-3030 Fax: (516)334-8958 Monthly. $95.00 per year.

Exchange Rate Determination and Adjustment. Jagdeep S. Bhandari. Greenwood Publishing Group, Inc., 88 Post Rd., W. Westport, CT 06881-5007. Phone: 800-225-5800 or (203)226-3571 Fax: (203)222-2540 E-mail: bookinfo@greenwood.com • URL: http://www.greenwood.com • 1982. $65.00.

Excise Taxes. Prentice Hall, 240 Frisch Court Paramus, NJ 07652-5240. Phone: 800-947-7700 or (201)909-6200 Fax: 800-445-6991 or (201)909-6361 URL: http://www.prenhall.com • Looseleaf. $216.00. Monthly updates. (Information Services Series)

Executive Compensation. Arthur H. Kroll. Prentice Hall, 240 Frisch Court Paramus, NJ 07652-5240. Phone: 800-947-7700 or (201)909-6200 Fax: 800-445-6991 or (201)909-6361 URL: http://www.prenhall.com • Three looseleaf volumes. Periodic supplementation. Price on application. Includes monthly newsletter.

Executive Compensation: A Strategic Guide for the 1990s. Fred Foulkes, editor. Harvard Business School Press, 60 W Harvard Way Boston, MA 02163. Phone: 800-545-7685 or (617)783-7440 E-mail: custserv@cchbspub.harvard.edu • URL: http://www.hbsp.harvard.edu • 1991. $75.00.

Executive Compensation and Taxation Coordinator. Research Institute of America, Inc., 90 Fifth Ave. New York, NY 10011. Phone: 800-431-9025 or (212)645-4800 Fax: (212)337-4213 Three looseleaf volumes. $450.00 per year. Monthly updates.

Executive Compensation Survey Report. Mid Atlantic Employees' Association, PO Box 770 Valley Forge, PA 19482. Phone: (215)666-7330 Fax: (215)666-7866 Annual. $400.00. Looseleaf service.

Executive Education.

Executive Employment Guide. AMACOM, 1601 Broadway, 12th Fl. New York, NY 10019. Phone: 800-262-9699 or (212)586-8100 Fax: (212)903-8168 E-mail: custmserv@amanet.org • URL: http://www.amanet.org • Monthly. $20.00. Concise listing of about 151 firms, such as executive search organizations and employment agencies, that assist executives in locating employment.

Executive Etiquette in the New Workplace. Marjabelle Steward and Marian Faux. St. Martin's Press, 175 Fifth Ave. New York, NY 10010. Phone: 800-221-7945 or (212)674-5151 Fax: 800-672-2054 or (212)529-0594 URL: http://www.stmartins.com • 1995. $14.95.

Executive Excellence: The Newsletter of Personal Development Managerial Effectiveness, and Organizational Productivity. Kenneth M. Shelton, editor. Executive Excellence Publishing, 1344 E.1120 S Provo, UT 84606. Phone: (801)375-4060 Fax: (801)377-5960 E-mail: execexcl@itsnet.com • URL: http://www.eep.com • Monthly. $129.00 per year. Newsletter.

Executive Guide to Specialists in Industrial and Office Real Estate. Society of Industrial and Office Realtors, 700 11th St., N.W., Suite 510 Washington, DC 20001-4511. Phone: (202)737-1150 Fax: (202)737-8796 E-mail: lnasvaderani@mail.sior.com • URL: http://www.sior.com • Annual. $70.00. Approximately 1,800 specialist in industrial real estate.

Executive Manpower Directory. 40 Plus Club of New York, 15 Park Row New York, NY 10038. Phone: (212)233-6086 Monthly.

Executive/Par-3 Golf Course Directory. National Golf Foundation, 1150 S. U.S. Highway 1, Suite 401 Jupiter, FL 33477. Phone: 800-733-6006 or (407)744-6006 Fax: (407)744-6107 E-mail: ngf@ngf.org • URL: http://www.ngf.org • 1998. $99.00. Lists about 1,700 U. S. golf courses of less than regulation size.

Executive Recruiter News. Kennedy Information, LLC, One Kennedy Place, Route 12, S. Fitzwilliam, NH 03447. Phone: 800-531-1026 or (603)585-3101 Fax: (603)585-9555 E-mail: office@kennedypub.com • URL: http://www.kennedyinfo.com • Monthly. $187.00 per year. Newsletter. News and ideas for executive recruiters.

Executive Recruiting Service. Entrepreneur Media, Inc., 2445 McCabe Way Irvine, CA 92614. Phone: 800-421-2300 or (949)261-2325 Fax: (949)261-0234 E-mail: entmag@entrepreneur.com • URL: http://www.entrepreneur.com • Looseleaf. $59.50. A practical guide to starting an executive recruitment service. Covers profit potential, start-up costs, market size evaluation, owner's time required, pricing, accounting, advertising, promotion, etc. (Start-Up Business Guide No. E1228.)

Executive Remuneration. American Banker Newsletter, Thomson Financial Media, One State St. Place New York, NY 10004-1549. Phone: 800-733-4371 or (212)803-8345 Fax: (212)843-9600 URL: http://www.americanbanker.com • Annual.

Executive Search Books. Kennedy Information, LLC, One Kennedy Place, Route 12, S. Fitzwilliam, NH 03447. Phone: 800-531-1026 or (603)585-3101 Fax: (603)585-9555 E-mail: office@kennedypub.com • URL: http://www.kennedyinfo.com • Annual. Free. Contains descriptions of selected books from various publishers on executive recruitment.

Executive Wealth Advisory. National Institute of Business Management, P.O. Box 9266 McLean, VA 22102-0266. Phone: (703)905-8002 Monthly. $96.00 per year. Newsletter.

Executive Women International., 515 S. 700 East, Suite 2E Salt Lake City, UT 84102. Phone: 888-394-1229 or (801)355-2800 Fax: (801)355-2852 E-mail: ewi@executivewomen.org • URL: http://www.executivewomen.org • Members are executive secretaries or administrators.

Executive's Guide to E-Commerce. Martin Deise and Douglas Reagan. John Wiley and Sons, Inc., 605 Third Ave. New York, NY 10158-0012. Phone: 800-225-5945 or (212)850-6000 Fax: (212)850-6088 E-mail: info@

jwiley.com • URL: http://www.wiley.com • 1999. $39.95. Covers the basic principles of doing business successfully by way of the Internet.

Exhibit Builder. Exhibit Builder, Inc., P.O. Box 4144 Woodland Hills, CA 91365. Phone: (818)225-0100 Fax: (818)225-0138 Bimonthly. $25.00 per year. For designers and builders of trade show exhibits.

Exhibit Designers and Producers Association., 5775 Peachtree-Dunwoody Rd., N.E., Suite 500-G Atlanta, GA 30342. Phone: (404)303-7310 Fax: (404)252-0774 E-mail: edpa@asshq.com • URL: http://www.edpa.com • Members are firms that design and build displays for trade shows.

Exhibitor Magazine Buyer's Guide to Trade Show Exhibits. Exhibitor Magazine Group, Inc., 206 S. Broadway, Suite 745 Rochester, MN 55904-6565. Phone: 888-235-6155 or (507)289-6556 Fax: (507)289-5253 E-mail: exhibitornet.com • URL: http://www.exhibitornet.com • Annual. $42.00. Covers manufacturers of trade show exhibit equipment. Formerly *Buyer's Guide to Trade Show Displays*.

Expanded Shale Clay and Slate Institute.

Expanding Services to Meet Community Needs in an Era of Change. American Association of Homes and Services for the Aging, 901 E St., N. W., Suite 500 Washington, DC 20004-2037. Phone: 800-508-9442 or (202)783-2242 Fax: (202)783-2255 E-mail: info@aahsa.org • URL: http://www.aahsa.org • 1996. $30.00. Covers new, innovative models of home health care delivery, intergenerational day care, and senior housing services.

Expanding Technologies, Expanding Careers: Librarianship in Transition. Ellis Mount, editor. Special Libraries Association, 1700 18th St., N. W., 17th Fl. Washington, DC 20009-2514. Phone: (202)234-4700 Fax: 888-411-2856 or (202)234-2442 E-mail: books@sla.org • URL: http://www.sla.org • 1997. $45.00. Contains articles on alternative, non-traditional career paths for librarians, whether as entrepreneurs or employees. All the careers are related to computer-based, information retrieval and technology.

Expansion Management: Growth Strategies for Companies on the Move. Penton Media Inc., Industry Div., 1300 E. Ninth St. Cleveland, OH 44114. Phone: (213)696-7000 Fax: (213)696-0836 E-mail: corpcomm@penton.com • URL: http://www.penton.com • Monthly. Free qualified personnel; others, $40.00 per year. Subject matter is concerned with expansion and relocation of industrial facilities.

Expenditures for Residential Improvements and Repairs. Available from U. S. Government Printing Office, Washington, DC 20402. Phone: (202)512-1800 Fax: (202)512-2250 E-mail: gpoaccess@gpo.gov • URL: http://www.access.gpo.gov • Quarterly. $14.00 per year. Bureau of the Census Construction Report, C50. Provides estimates of spending for housing maintenance, repairs, additions, alterations, and major replacements.

Expert Systems for Business: Concepts and Applications. D. V. Pigford. Course Technology, Inc., One Main St. Cambridge, MA 02142. Phone: 800-648-7450 or (617)225-2595 Fax: (617)621-3078 E-mail: laura-hildebrand@course.com • URL: http://www.course.com • 1995. $42.95. Second edition.

Explorations in Economic History. Academic Press, Inc., Journal Div., 525 B St., Suite 1900 San Diego, CA 92101-4495. Phone: 800-321-5068 or (619)230-1840 Fax: (619)699-6715 E-mail: ap@acad.com • URL: http://www.academicpress.com/ • Quarterly. $360.00 per year.

Explorations in Indexing and Abstracting: Pointing, Virtue, and Power. Brian C. O'Connor. Libraries Unlimited, P.O. Box 6633 Englewood, CO 80155-6633. Phone: 800-237-6124 or (303)770-1220 Fax: (303)220-8843 E-mail: l4-books@lu.com • URL: http://www.lu.com • 1996. $40.00. Presents a philosophy of indexing. (Library and Information Science Text Series).

Exploring Marketing Research. William G. Zikmund. Harcourt Trade Publications, 525 B St., Suite 1900 San Diego, CA 92101-4495. Phone: 800-543-1918 or (619)231-6616 Fax: 800-235-0256 E-mail: apbcs@harcourtbrace.com • URL: http://www.harcourt.com • 1999. $94.50. Seventh edition.

Exploring Windows NT: Tips & Techniques for Microsoft Windows NT Professionals. Z-D Journals, 500 Canal View Blvd. Rochester, NY 14623. Phone: 800-223-8720 or (716)240-7301 Fax: (716)214-2387 E-mail: zdjcr@zd.com • URL: http://www.zdjournals. • Monthly. $99.00 per year. Newsletter on the Windows operating system for networks.

Export America. Available from U. S. Government Printing Office, Washington, DC 20402. Phone: (202)512-1800 Fax: (202)512-2250 E-mail: gpoaccess@gpo.gov • URL: http://www.access.gpo.gov • Monthly. $61.00 per year. Issued by the International Trade Administration, U. S. Department of Commerce (http://www.ita.doc.gov/). Contains articles written to help American exporters penetrate overseas markets. Provides information on opportunities for trade and methods of doing international business. Formerly *Business America*.

Export-Import Financing. Harry M. Vendikian and Gerald Warfield. John Wiley and Sons, Inc., 605 Third Ave. New York, NY 10158-0012. Phone: 800-526-5368 or (212)850-6000 Fax: (212)850-6088 E-mail: info@wiley.com • URL: http://www.wiley.com • 1996. $79.95. Fourth edition.

Export Sales and Marketing Manual. Export Institute, P.O. Box 385883 Minneapolis, MN 55438-5883. Phone: 800-943-3171 or (952)943-1505 Fax: (952)943-1535 E-mail: info@exportinstitute.com • URL: http://www.exportinstitute.com • Looseleaf service. $295.00 Periodic supplementation. Provides detailed information on exporting from the U. S. Includes sections on licenses, markets, pricing, agreements, shipping, payment, and other export topics.

Export Today: The Global Business and Technology Magazine. Trade Communications, Inc., 733 15th St., N.W., Suite 1100 Washington, DC 20005. Phone: (202)737-1060 Fax: (202)783-5966 E-mail: mjohn@interserv.com • URL: http://www.exporttoday.com • Monthly. $49.00 per year. Edited for corporate executives to provide practical information on international business and exporting.

Exporters' Encyclopedia. Dun and Bradstreet Information Services, Dun and Bradstreet Corp., Three Sylvan Way Parsippany, NJ 07054-3896. Phone: 800-526-0651 or (973)455-0900 Fax: (973)254-4063 E-mail: customerservice@dnb.com • URL: http://www.dnb.com • 1995. $495.00. Lease basis.

Exporting from the United States. U.S. Dept. of Commerce. Prima Publishing, 3875 Atherton Rd. Rocklin, CA 95765. Phone: (916)787-7000 Fax: (916)787-7001 URL: http://www.primapublishing.com • 1993. $14.95. Second revised edition.

Exporting with the Internet. Peter J. Robinson and Jonathan Powell. John Wiley and Sons, Inc., 605 Third Ave. New York, NY 10158-0012. Phone: 800-842-3636 or (212)850-6000 Fax: (212)850-6088 E-mail: info@wiley.com • URL: http://www.wiley.com • 1997. $39.95. Explains how the Internet can help with finding overseas buyers and expediting export shipments and payments. (Business Technology Series).

Exposition Service Contractors Association., Dobson/Simmons Associates, 400 S. Houston St., Suite 210 Dallas, TX 75202. Phone: (214)742-9217 Fax: (214)741-2519 E-mail: esca@airmail.net • URL: http://www.esca.org • Members are companies providing supplies and services for trade shows and conventions.

Extending the Librarian's Domain: A Survey of Emerging Occupational Opportunities for Librarians and Information Professionals. Forest W. Horton. Special Libraries Association, 1700 18th St., N. W., 17th Fl. Washington, DC 20009-2514. Phone: (202)234-4700 Fax: 888-411-2856 or (202)234-2442 E-mail: books@sla.org • URL: http://www.sla.org • 1994. $38.00. An examination of non-traditional career possibilities for special librarians. (Occasional Papers: No. 4).

Extraordinary Popular Delusions and the Madness of Crowds. Charles Mackay. Templeton Foundation Press, Five Radonr Corporate Center, Suite 120, 100 Matson Ford Rd. Radnor, PA 19087. Phone: 800-561-3367 or (610)971-2670 Fax: (610)971-2672 E-mail: tfp@templeton.org • URL: http://www.templeton.org/press • 2000. $19.95. A classic work on speculation and crowd psychology, originally published in 1841.

The Extreme Searcher's Guide to Web Search Engines: A Handbook for the Serious Searcher. Randolph Hock. Information Today, Inc., 143 Old Marlton Pike Medford, NJ 08055-8750. Phone: 800-300-9868 or (609)654-6266 Fax: (609)654-4309 E-mail: custserv@infotoday.com • URL: http://www.infotoday.com • 1999. $34.95. Provides detailed information and advice on effective use of the major Internet search engines. (CyberAge Books.)

Eyecare Business: The Magazine for Progressive Dispensing. Boucher Communications, Inc., 1300 Virginia Dr., Suite 400 Fort Washington, PA 19034. Phone: 800-306-6332 or (215)643-8000 Fax: (215)643-8099 URL: http://www.cardinal.com • Monthly. Free to qualified personnel; others, $90.00 per year. Covers the business side of optometry and optical retailing. Each issue features "Frames and Fashion."

F and OS Motor Carrier Annual Report: Results of Operations Class I & II Motor Carriers of Property. American Trucking Associations. Trucking Information Services, Inc., 2200 Mill Rd. Alexandria, VA 22314-4677. Phone: 800-282-5463 or (703)838-1700 Fax: (703)684-5720 E-mail: ata-infocenter@trucking.org • URL: http://www.trucking.org • Annual. $400.00.

F and OS Motor Carrier Quarterly Report. American Trucking Associations. Trucking Information Services, Inc., 2200 Mill Rd. Alexandria, VA 22314-4677. Phone: 800-282-5463 or (703)838-1700 Fax: (703)684-5720 E-mail: ata-infocenter@trucking.org • URL: http://www.trucking.org • Quarterly. $150.00 per number. Includes *Motor Carrier Annual Report*.

F & S Index. The Gale Group, 27500 Drake Rd. Farmington Hills, MI 48331-3535. Phone: 800-877-GALE or (248)699-GALE Fax: 800-414-5043 or (248)699-8069 E-mail: galeord@gale.com • URL: http://www.gale.com • Contains about four million citations to worldwide business, financial, and industrial or consumer product literature appearing from 1972 to date. Weekly updates. Inquire as to online cost and availability.

F & S Index: Europe. The Gale Group, 27500 Drake Rd. Farmington Hills, MI 48331-3535. Phone: 800-877-GALE or (248)699-GALE Fax: 800-414-5043 or (248)699-8069 E-mail: galeord@galegroup.com • URL: http://www.galegroup.com • Monthly. $1,295.00 per year, including quarterly and annual cumulations. Provides annotated citations to marketing, business, financial, and industrial literature. Coverage of European business activity includes trade journals, financial magazines, business newspapers, and special reports. Formerly *Predicasts F & S Index: Europe*.

F & S Index: International. The Gale Group, 27500 Drake Rd. Farmington Hills, MI 48331-3535. Phone: 800-877-GALE or (248)699-GALE Fax: 800-414-5043 or (248)699-8069 E-mail: galeord@galegroup.com • URL: http://www.galegroup.com • Monthly. $1,295.00 per year, including quarterly and annual cumulations. Provides annotated citations to marketing, business, financial, and industrial literature. Coverage of international business activity includes trade journals, financial magazines, business newspapers, and special reports. Areas included are Asia, Latin America, Africa, the Middle East, Oceania, and Canada. Formerly *Predicasts F & S Index: International*.

F & S Index Plus Text. The Gale Group, 27500 Drake Rd. Farmington Hills, MI 48331-3535. Phone: 800-877-GALE or (248)699-GALE Fax: 800-414-5043 or (248)699-8069 E-mail: galeord@gale.com • URL: http://www.gale.com • Monthly. $7,575.00 per year. Provides CD-ROM citations to worldwide business, marketing, and industrial material appearing in a large assortment of trade journals, newspapers, and other publications. Time period is four years.

F & S Index: United States. The Gale Group, 27500 Drake Rd. Farmington Hills, MI 48331-3535. Phone: 800-877-GALE or (248)699-GALE Fax: 800-414-5043 or (248)699-8069 E-mail: galeord@galegroup.com • URL: http://www.galegroup.com • Monthly. $1,295.00 per year, including quarterly and annual cumulations. Provides annotated citations to marketing, business, financial, and industrial literature. Coverage of U. S. business activity includes trade journals, financial magazines, business newspapers, and special reports. Formerly *Predicasts F & S Index: United States*.

F-D-C Reports. FDC Reports, Inc., 5550 Friendship Blvd., Suite One Chevy Chase, MD 20815. Phone: (301)657-9830 Fax: (301)656-3094 E-mail: fdcr@clark.net • URL: http://www.fdcreports.com • An online version of "The Gray Sheet" (medical devices), "The Pink Sheet" (pharmaceuticals), "The Rose Sheet" (cosmetics), "The Blue Sheet" (biomedical), and "The Tan Sheet" (nonprescription). Contains full-text information on legal, technical, corporate, financial, and marketing developments from 1987 to date, with weekly updates. Inquire as to online cost and availability.

F W's Corporate Finance: The Magazine fo the Financing Strategist. Financial World Partners, 1328 Broadway New York, NY 10001. Phone: (212)594-5030 Fax: (212)629-0026 Quarterly. $50.00 per year. Edited for financial executives of U. S. corporations. Covers leveraged buyouts, mergers, insurance, pensions, risk management, and other corporate topics. Includes case studies. Formerly *Corporate Finance*.

FAA Aviation Forecasts. Federal Aviation Administration. Available from U. S. Government Printing Office, Washington, DC 20402. Phone: (202)512-1800 Fax: (202)512-2250 Annual. $15.00.

FAA Aviation News. Federal Aviation Administration. Available from U. S. Government Printing Office, Washington, DC 20402. Phone: (202)512-1800 Fax: (202)512-2250 E-mail: gpoaccess@gpo.gov • URL: http://www.access.gpo.gov • Bimonthly. $28.00. per year. Designed to help airmen become safer pilots. Includes updates on major rule changes and proposals.

FAA Historical Chronology: Civil Aviation and the Federal Government, 1926-1996. Edmund Preston, editor. Available from U. S. Government Printing Office, Washington, DC 20402. Phone: (202)512-1800 Fax: (202)512-2250 E-mail: gpoaccess@gpo.gov • URL: http://www.access.gpo.gov • 1998. $29.00. Third edition. Issued by the Federal Aviation Administration, U. S. Department of Transportation (http://www.dot.gov). Provides a compilation of historical information about the FAA and the earlier Civil Aeronautics Board (CAB). Chronological arrangement.

FAA Statistical Handbook of Aviation. Federal Aviation Administration. Available from U. S. Government Printing Office, Washington, DC 20402. Phone: (202)512-1800 Fax: (202)512-2250 Annual.

Fabric Filter. McIlvaine Co., 2970 Maria Ave. Northbrook, IL 60062-2004. Phone: (847)272-0010 Fax: (847)272-9673 Monthly. $635.00 per year. Newsletter. Subscription includes "Knowledge Network": manual, catalog, video tapes, reprints, and other information sources relating to dry filter products and applications in various industries.

Fabric Science. Arhtur Price and others. Fairchild Books, Seven W. 34th St. New York, NY 10001. Phone: 800-932-4724 or (212)630-3880 Fax: (212)630-3868 URL: http://www.fairchildbooks.com • 1999. $52.00. Looseleaf Service. Includes swatch kit.

The Fabricator. Fabricators and Manufacturers Association International. Croydon Group, Ltd., 833 Featherstone Rd. Rockford, IL 61107-6302. Phone: (815)399-8700 Fax: (815)399-7700 E-mail: info@fmametalfab.org • URL: http://www/.fmametalfab.org • Monthly. $75.00 per year. Covers the manufacture of sheet, coil, tube, pipe, and structural metal shapes.

Fabricators and Manufacturers Association International., 833 Featherstone Rd. Rockford, IL 61107-6302. Phone: (815)399-8700 Fax: (815)399-7279 E-mail: info@fmametal.fab.org • URL: http://www.fmametalfab.org • Members are individuals concerned with metal forming, cutting, and fabricating. Includes a Sheet Metal Division and the Tube and Pipe Fabricators Association.

Facilities and Workplace Design: An Illustrated Guide. Quarterman Lee and others. Engineering and Management Press, 25 Technology Park Norcross, GA 30092-2988. Phone: 800-494-0460 or (770)449-0461 Fax: (770)263-8532 E-mail: cmagee@www.iienet.org • URL: http://www.iienet.org • 1996. $25.00. Written for both new and experienced designers. Features "25 illustrated tasks that can be applied to most projects."(Engineers in Business Series).

Facilities Design and Management. Miller Freeman, Inc., One Penn Plaza New York, NY 10119. Phone: 800-227-4675 or (212)714-1300 Fax: (212)714-1313 URL: http://www.mfi.com • Monthly. $65.00 per year. Edited for planners, designers, and managers of major office facilities. Subject matter includes open plan systems, space allocation, office remodeling, office furniture, and related topics.

Facility Manager. International Association of Auditorium Managers, 4425 W. Airport Freeway, Suite 590 Irving, TX 75062-5835. Phone: (972)255-8020 Fax: (972)255-9582 E-mail: julie.herrick@iaam.org • URL: http://www.iaam.org • Quarterly. Free to members; non-members, $45.00 per year.

Facing Tile Institute., P.O. Box 8880 Canton, OH 44711. Phone: (330)488-1211 Fax: (330)488-0333 Members are manufacturers of glazed and unglazed structural facing tile.

Fact Book on Higher Education, 1989-1990. Charles J. Andersen and others. Pearsono Education and Technology, 201 W. 103rd St. Indianapolis, IN 46290-1097. Phone: 800-858-7674 or (313)581-3500 URL: http://www.mcp.com • 1989. $41.95. Published in conjunction with the American Council on Education. (Ace-Macmillan Higher Education Series).

Factiva. Dow Jones Reuters Business Interactive, LLCPhone: 800-369-7466 or (609)452-1511 Fax: (609)520-5770 E-mail: solutions@factiva.com • URL: http://www.factiva.com • Fee-based Web site provides "global news and business information through Web sites and content integration solutions." Includes Dow Jones and Reuters newswires, The Wall Street Journal, and more than 7,000 other sources of current news, historical articles, market research reports, and investment analysis. Content includes 96 major U. S. newspapers, 900 non-English sources, trade publications, media transcripts, country profiles, news photos, etc.

The Facts About Drug Use: Coping with Drugs and Alcohol in Your Family, at Work, in Your Community. Barry Stimmel, editor. The Haworth Press, Inc., 10 Alice St. Binghamton, NY 13904-1580. Phone: 800-429-6784 or (607)722-5857 Fax: 800-895-0582 or (607)722-1424 E-mail: getinfo@haworthpressinc.com • URL: http://www.haworthpressinc.com • 1992. $14.95. A comprehensive overview of drug dependence, including alcoholism.

Facts About Supermarket Development. Food Marketing Institute, 655 15th St., N.W., No. 700 Washington, DC 20006-5701. Phone: (202)452-8444 Fax: (202)429-4519 E-mail: fmi@fmi.org • URL: http://www.fmi.org • Annual. Members, $20.00; non-members, $40.00.

Facts About the Cities. Allan Carpenter and Carl Provorse. H. W. Wilson Co., 950 University Ave. Bronx, NY 10452. Phone: 800-367-6770 or (718)588-8400 Fax: (718)590-1617 E-mail: custserv@hwwilson.com • URL: http://www.hwwilson.com • 1996. $65.00. Second edition. Contains a wide variety of information on 300 American cities, including cities in Puerto Rico, Guam, and the U. S. Virgin Islands. Data is provided on the workplace, taxes, revenues, cost of living, population, climate, housing, transportation, etc.

Facts and Figures on Government Finance. Tax Foundation, Inc., 1250 H St., N.W., Suite 750 Washington, DC 20005. Phone: (202)783-2760 Fax: (202)942-7675 Annual. $60.00.

Facts-on-File World News Digest With Index. Facts on File, Inc., 11 Penn Plaza, 15th Fl. New York, NY 10001-2006. Phone: 800-322-8755 or (212)967-8800 Fax: (212)967-9196 URL: http://www.factsonfile.com • Weekly. $725.00 per year. Looseleaf service.

Facts-on-File Yearbook. Facts on File, Inc., 11 Penn Plaza, 15th Fl. New York, NY 10001. Phone: 800-322-8755 or (212)967-8800 Fax: 800-678-3633 or (212)967-9196 URL: http://www.factsonfile.com • Annual. $100.00.

Faculty White Pages. The Gale Group, 27500 Drake Rd. Farmington Hills, MI 48331-3535. Phone: 800-877-GALE or (248)699-GALE Fax: 800-414-5043 or (248)699-8069 E-mail: galeord@galegroup.com • URL: http://www.galegroup.com • 1991. $135.00. "Telephone book" classified arrangement of over 537,000 U. S. college faculty members in 41 subject sections. A roster of institutions is included.

Fair Employment Compliance: A Confidential Letter to Management. Management Resources, Inc., P.O. Box 105 Hampton, NH 03842-0105. Semimonthly. $245.00 per year. Newsletter.

Fair Employment Report. Business Publishers, Inc., 8737 Colesville Rd., Suite 1100 Silver Spring, MD 20910-3928. Phone: 800-274-6737 or (301)587-6300 Fax: (301)587-1081 E-mail: bpinews@bpinews.com • URL: http://www.bpinews.com • Biweekly. $327.00 per year. Formerly *Civil Rights Employment Reporter*.

Fair Housing: Discrimination in Real Estate, Community Development and Revitalization. James A. Kushner. Shepard's, 555 Middle Creek Parkway Colorado Springs, CO 80921. Phone: 800-743-7393 or (719)481-7371 Fax: 800-525-0053 or (719)481-7621 E-mail: customer_service@shepards.com • URL: http://www.shepards.com • 1983. $140.00. Second edition. (Individual Rights Series).

Fair, Square, and Legal: Safe Hiring, Managing, and Firing Practices to Keep You and Your Company Out of Court. Donald Weiss. AMACOM, 1601 Broadway, 12th Fl. New York, NY 10019. Phone: 800-262-9699 or (212)586-8100 Fax: (212)903-8168 E-mail: custmserv.@amanet.org • URL: http://www.amanet.org • 1999. $29.95. Third edition. Covers recruiting, interviewing, sexual discrimination, evaluation of employees, disipline, defamation charges, and wrongful discharge.

The Fair Use Privilege in Copyright Law. Bureau of National Affairs, Inc., 1231 25th St., N.W. Washington, DC 20037-1197. Phone: 800-372-1033 or (202)452-4200 Fax: (202)452-8092 E-mail: books@bna.com • URL: http://www.bna.com • 1995. $115.00. Second edition. A comprehensive analysis of fair use.

Fairchild's Dictionary of Fashion. Phyllis B. Tortora. Fairchild Books, Seven W. 34th St. New York, NY 10001. Phone: 800-932-4724 or (212)630-3880 Fax: (212)630-3868 URL: http://www.fairchildbooks.com • 1996. $75.00. Seventh edition.

Fairchild's Dictionary of Textiles. Phyllis B. Tortora, editor. Fairchild Books, Seven W. 34th St. New York, NY 10001. Phone: 800-932-4724 or (212)630-3880 Fax: (212)630-3868 URL: http://www.fairchildbooks.com • 1996. $75.00. Seventh edition.

Fairplay Ports Guide. Available from Fairplay Publications, Inc., 5201 Blue Lagoon Drive, Suite 530 Miami, FL 33126. Phone: (305)262-4070 Fax: (305)262-2006 E-mail: sales@fairplayamericas.com • URL: http://www.lrfairplay.com • Annual. $425.00. Four volumes (CD-ROM is included). Published in the UK by Lloyd's Register-Fairplay Ltd. Provides detailed information about 6,500 worldwide ports and terminals. Includes more than 3,500 port plans and port photographs.

Fairplay: The International Shipping Weekly. Available from Fairplay Publications, Inc., 5201 Blue Lagoon Drive, Suite 530 Miami, FL 33126. Phone: (305)262-4070 Fax: (305)262-2006 E-mail: sales@fairplayamericas.com • URL: http://www.lrfairplay.com • Weekly. $500.00 per year. Published in the UK by Lloyd's Register-Fairplay Ltd. Provides international shipping news, commentary, market reports, reports on shipbuilding activity, advice on operational problems, and other information.

Fairplay World Shipping Directory. Available from Fairplay Publications, Inc., 5201 Blue Lagoon Drive, Suite 530 Miami, FL 33126. Phone: (305)262-4070 Fax: (305)262-2006 E-mail: sales@fairplayamericas.com • URL: http://www.lrfairplay.com • Annual. $360.00. Published in the UK by Lloyd's Register-Fairplay Ltd. Provides information on more than 64,000 companies providing maritime services and products, including 1,600 shipbuilders and data on 55,000 individual ships. Includes shipowners, shipbrokers, engine builders, salvage companies, marine insurance companies, maritime lawyers, consultants, maritime schools, etc. Five indexes cover a total of 170,000 entries.

Families U. S. A. Foundation., 1334 G St., N. W. Washington, DC 20005. Phone: (202)628-3030 Fax: (202)347-2417 E-mail: info@familiesusa.org • URL: http://www.familiesusa.org • Fields of interest are health care and long-term health care, including insurance.

Family Advocate. American Bar Association, Family Law Section, 750 N. Lake Shore Dr. Chicago, IL 60611-4497. Phone: 800-285-2221 or (312)988-5000 Fax: (312)988-5528 E-mail: abajournal@abanet.org • URL: http://www.abanet.org • Quarterly. Members $39.50; non-members, $44.50 per year. Practical advice for attorneys practicing family law.

Family Almanac. National Association of Retail Druggists. Creative Publishing, 1608 S. Dakota Sioux Falls, SD 57105. Phone: 800-423-7158 or (605)336-9434 Fax: (605)338-3501 E-mail: kal1303567@aol.com • Annual. Free at participating pharmacies. Formerly *NARD Almanac and Health Guide*.

Family Court Review. Association of Family and Conciliation Courts. Sage Publications, Inc., 2455 Teller Rd. Thousand Oaks, CA 91320. Phone: (805)499-0721 Fax: (805)499-0871 E-mail: info@sagepub.com • URL: http://www.sagepub.com • Quarterly. $230.00 per year.

Family Economics and Nutrition Review. Available from U. S. Government Printing Office, Washington, DC 20402. Phone: (202)512-1800 Fax: (202)512-2250 E-mail: gpoaccess@gpo.gov • URL: http://www.access.gpo.gov • Quarterly. $19.00 per year. Issued by the Consumer and Food Economics Institute, U. S. Department of Agriculture. Provides articles on consumer expenditures and budgeting for food, clothing, housing, energy, education, etc.

Family Law in a Nutshell. Harry D. Krause. West Publishing Co., College and School Div, 610 Opperman Dr. Eagan, MN 55123. Phone: 800-328-4880 or (651)687-7000 Fax: (651)687-5827 E-mail: legal_ed@westgroup.com • URL: http://www.lawschool.westgroup.com • 1995. $18.00. Third edition. (Paralegal Series).

Family Law Quarterly. American Bar Association, Family Law Section, 750 N. Lake Shore Dr. Chicago, IL 60611-4497. Phone: 800-285-2221 or (312)988-5000 Fax: (312)988-5528 E-mail: abajournal@abanet.org • Quarterly. Free to members; non-members, $49.95 per year.

Family Law Reporter. Bureau of National Affairs, Inc., 1231 25th St., N. W. Washington, DC 20037-1197. Phone: 800-372-1033 or (202)452-4200 Fax: (202)452-8092 E-mail: books@bna.com • URL: http://www.bna.com • Weekly. $709.00 per year. Legal newsletter.

Family Law Tax Guide. CCH, Inc., 4025 W. Peterson Ave. Chicago, IL 60646-6085. Phone: 800-248-3248 or (773)583-8500 Fax: 800-224-8299 URL: http://www.cch.com • Monthly. $567.00 per year. Looseleaf service.

Family Relations: State Capitals. Wakeman-Walworth, Inc., P.O. Box 7376 Alexandria, VA 22307-0376. Phone: 800-876-2545 or (703)549-8606 Fax: (703)549-1372 E-mail: newsletters@statecapitals.com • URL: http://www.statecapitals.com • Weekly. $245.00 per year. Newsletter. Formerly *From the State Capitals: Family Relations*.

Family Tax Guide. Prentice Hall, 240 Frisch Court Paramus, NJ 07652-5240. Phone: 800-947-7700 or (201)909-6200 Fax: (201)909-6361 URL: http://www.prenhall.com • 1985. $44.95.

Family Therapy of Drug Abuse and Addiction. M. Duncan Stanton and Thomas C. Todd. Guilford Publications, Inc., Dept IT, 72 Spring St. New York, NY 10012. Phone: 800-365-7006 or (212)431-9800 Fax: (212)966-6708 E-mail: info@guilford.com • URL: http://www.guilford.com • 1982. $55.00. (Family Therapy Series).

Fancy Food. Talcott Communications Corp., 20 N. Wacker Dr., Suite 1865 Chicago, IL 60606. Phone: (312)849-2220 Fax: (312)849-4994 Monthly. $34.00 per year. Emphasizes new specialty food products and the business management aspects of the specialty food and confection industries. Includes special issues on wine, cheese, candy, "upscale" cookware, and gifts.

FAO Fertilizer Yearbook. United Nations Food and Agriculture Organization. Bernan Associates, 4611-F Assembly Dr. Lanham, MD 20706-4391. Phone: 800-274-4447 or (301)459-7666 Fax: 800-865-3450 or (301)459-0056 E-mail: info@bernan.com • URL: http://www.bernan.com • Annual. $36.00. Text in English, French, and Spanish. Formerly *Annual Fertilizer Review*.

FAO Fishery Series. Food and Agriculture Organization of the United States. Available from Bernan Associates, 4611-F Assembly Dr. Lanham, MD 20706-4391. Phone: 800-274-4447 or (301)459-7666 Fax: 800-865-3450 or (301)459-0056 E-mail: info@bernan.com • URL: http://www.bernan.com • Irregular. Price varies. Text in English, French, and Spanish. Incorporates *Yearbook of Fishery Statistics*.

FAO Quarterly Bulletin of Statistics. Food and Agriculture Organization of the United Nations. Available from UNIPUB, 4611-F Assembly Dr. Lanham, MD 20706-4391. Phone: 800-274-4888 or (301)459-2255 Fax: 800-865-3450 or (301)459-0056 URL: http://www.unesco.org/publications • Quarterly. $20.00 per year. Provides international data on agricultural production, trade, and prices, covering the major commodities of many countries. Text in English, French, and Spanish. Formerly *FAO Monthly Bulletin of Statistics*.

FAO Rice Report. Food and Agriculture Organization of the United Nations, United Nations Plaza New York, NY 10017. Phone: (212)754-6039 Annual.

FAO Yearbook: Trade. Available from Bernan Associates, 4611-F Assembly Dr. Lanham, MD 20706-4391. Phone: 800-274-4447 or (301)459-7666 Fax: 800-865-3450 or (301)459-0056 E-mail: info@bernan.com • URL: http://

www.bernan.com • Annual. Published by the Food and Agriculture Organization of the United Nations (FAO). A compilation of international trade statistics for agricultural, fishery, and forest products. Text in English, French, and Spanish.

The Far East and Australasia 2000. Taylor and Francis, Inc., 325 Chestnut St. Philadelphic, PA 19106. Phone: (215)625-8900 Fax: (215)625-2940 E-mail: europa@taylorandfrancis.com • URL: http://www.europapublications.co.uk • Annual. $480.00. Published by Europa. Includes country statistical surveys of demographics, finance, trade, and agriculture. (Regional Surveys of the World.)

Far Eastern Economic Review. Dow Jones International Marketing Service, 420 Lexington Ave. New York, NY 10170. Phone: 800-568-7625 or (212)808-6615 Fax: (212)808-6652 Weekly. $205.00 per year (air mail). Published in Hong Kong by Review Publishing Co., a Dow Jones subsidiary (GPO Box 160, Hong Kong). Covers Asian business, economics, politics, and international relations. Includes reports on individual countries and companies, business trends, and stock price quotations.

Farm Chemicals. Meister Publishing Co., 37733 Euclid Ave. Willoughby, OH 44094. Phone: 800-572-7740 or (440)942-2000 Fax: (440)942-0662 E-mail: info@meisternet.com • URL: http://www.meisterpro.com • Monthly. $47.00 per year.

Farm Chemicals Handbook. Meister Publishing Co., 37733 Euclid Ave. Willoughby, OH 44094. Phone: 800-572-7740 or (440)942-2000 Fax: (440)942-0662 E-mail: info@meisternet.com • URL: http://www.meisterpro.com • Annual. $92.00. Manufacturers and suppliers of fertilizers, pesticides, and related equipment used in agribusiness.

Farm Equipment. Cygnus Publishing, Inc., 1233 Janesville Ave. Fort Atkinson, WI 53538-0460. Phone: 800-547-7377 or (920)563-6388 Fax: (920)563-1701 E-mail: rich.reiff@cygnuspub.com • URL: http://www.cygnuspub.com • Bimonthly. $48.00 per year. Includes annual*Product* issue.

Farm Equipment Manufacturers Association.

Farm Equipment Wholesalers Association.

Farm Equipment Wholesalers Association Membership Directory. Farm Equipment Wholesalers Association, P.O. Box 1347 Iowa City, IA 52244. Phone: (319)354-5156 Fax: (319)354-5157 E-mail: info@fewa.org • Annual. $50.00. Lists approximately 100 members.

Farm Industry News. Intertec Publishing Co., Agribusiness Div., 7900 International Dr., 3rd Fl. Minneapolis, MN 55425. Phone: 800-400-5945 or (612)851-9329 Fax: (612)851-4601 E-mail: fin@intertec.com • URL: http://www.farmindustrynews.com • 12 times a year. $25.00 per year. Includes new products for farm use.

Farm Journal. Farm Journal, Inc., 1818 Market St., 3rd Fl. Philadelphia, PA 19103-3654. Phone: (215)557-8900 Fax: (215)568-3989 URL: http://www.farmjournal.com • 12 times a year. $18.00 per year. Includes Supplements.

Farm Labor. U.S. Department of Agriculture, Washington, DC 20250. Phone: (202)447-2791 Monthly.

Farm Management. Michael D. Boehlje and Vernon R. Eidman. John Wiley and Sons, Inc., 605 Third Ave. New York, NY 10158-0012. Phone: 800-526-5368 or (212)850-6000 Fax: (212)850-6088 E-mail: info@wiley.com • URL: http://www.wiley.com • 1984. $108.95.

Farm Management. Ronald D. Kay and William M. Edwards. McGraw-Hill Higher Education, 1221 Ave. of the Americas New York, NY 10020. Phone: 800-722-4726 or (212)904-2000 Fax: (212)904-2072 E-mail: customer.service@mcgraw-hill.com • URL: http://www.mcgraw-hill.com • 1999. Fourth edition. Price on application.

Farm Management: Principles, Budgets, Plans. John Herbst and Duane Erickson. Stipes Publishing L.L.C, P.O. Box 526 Champaign, IL 61820. Phone: (217)356-8391 Fax: (217)356-5753 E-mail: stipes@soltec.com • 1996. $25.80. 10th edition.

Farm Mortgage Debt. U.S. Department of Agriculture, Economic Research Service, Washington, DC 20250. Phone: (202)720-2791 Annual.

Farm Power and Machinery Management. Donnell Hunt. Iowa State University Press, 2121 S. State Ave. Ames, IA 50014-8300. Phone: 800-862-6657 or (515)292-0140 Fax: (515)292-3348 E-mail: orders@isupress.edu • URL: http://www.isupress.edu • 1995. $56.95. Ninth edition.

Farmer's Digest. Heartland Communictions Group, Inc., 1003 Central Ave. Fort Dodge, IA 50501. Phone: 800-673-4763 10 times a year. $17.95 per year. Current information on all phases of agriculture.

FASB Accounting Standards. McGraw-Hill Professional, 1221 Ave. of the Americas New York, NY 10020. Phone: 800-722-4726 or (212)904-2000 Fax: (212)904-2072 E-mail: customer.service@mcgraw-hill.com • URL: http://www.mcgraw-hill.com • Annual. Five volumes (prices vary). Includes *Financial Accounting Concepts, General Standards, Industry Standards*, and two volumes of *Original Pronouncements*. An appendix lists titles of American Institute of Certified Public Accountants (AICPA) and Financial Accounting Standards Board (FASB) documents.

FASB Accounting Standards Current Text. Financial Accounting Standards Board, P.O. Box 5116 Norwalk, CT 06856-5116. Phone: (203)847-0700 Fax: (203)849-9714 URL: http://www.fasb.org • Looseleaf.

FASB Accounting Standards Current Text: General Standards. Financial Accounting Standards Board, P.O. Box 5116 Norwalk, CT 06856-5116. Phone: (203)847-0700 Fax: (203)849-9714 URL: http://www.fasb.org • Irregular. Price on application.

FASB Accounting Standards Current Text: Industries Standards. Financial Accounting Standards Board, P.O. Box 5116 Norwalk, CT 06856-5116. Phone: (203)847-0700 Fax: (203)849-9714 URL: http://www.fasb.org • Irregular. Price on application.

FASB Accounting Standards Current Text: Professional Standards. Financial Accounting Standards Board, P.O. Box 5116 Norwalk, CT 06856-5116. Phone: (203)847-0700 Fax: (203)849-9714 URL: http://www.fasb.org • Irregular. Price on application.

FASB Accounting Standards Current Text: Technical Practice Aids. Financial Accounting Standards Board, P.O. Box 5116 Norwalk, CT 06856-5116. Phone: (203)847-0700 Fax: (203)849-9714 URL: http://www.fasb.org • Irregular. Price on application.

FASB Original Pronouncements. Financial Accounting Standards Board, P.O. Box 5116 Norwalk, CT 06856-5116. Phone: (203)847-0700 Fax: (203)849-9714 URL: http://www.fasb.org • Irregular. Price on application.

Fashion Accessories: The Complete Twentieth Century Sourcebook. John Peacock. Macmillan Publishing Co., Inc., W.W. Norton and Co., Inc., 500 Fifth Ave. New York, NY 10110-0017. Phone: 800-223-2584 or (212)354-5500 Fax: (212)869-0856 E-mail: webmaster@wwnorton.com • URL: http://www.wwnorton.com • 2000. $34.95.

Fashion Advertising and Promotion. Jay Diamond and Ellen Diamond. John Wiley and Sons, Inc., 605 Third Ave., 4th Fl. New York, NY 10158-0012. Phone: 800-225-5945 or (212)850-6000 Fax: (212)850-6088 E-mail: info@wiley.com • URL: http://www.wiley.com/compbooks/ • 1995. $10.00 (Fashion Merchandising Series).

Fashion and Merchandising Fads. Frank W. Hoffmann and William G. Bailey. Haworth Press, Inc., 10 Alice St. Binghamton, NY 13904-1580. Phone: 800-429-6784 or (607)722-5857 Fax: 800-895-0582 or (607)722-1424 E-mail: getinfo@haworthpressinc.com • URL: http://www.haworthpressinc.com • 1994. $49.95. Contains descriptions of fashion industry fads or promotions from A to Z (A-2 Flight Jacket to Zipper).

Fashion Association.

Fashion Calendar. Fashion Calendar International, 153 E. 87th St. New York, NY 10128. Phone: (212)289-0420 Fax: (212)289-5917 Bimonthly. $365.00 per year.

Fashion Merchandising: An Introduction. Elaine Stone. McGraw-Hill, 1221 Ave. of the Americas New York, NY 10020. Phone: 800-722-4726 or (212)904-2000 Fax: (212)904-2072 E-mail: customer.service@mcgraw-hill.com • URL: http://www.mcgraw-hill.com • 1989. $45.72. Fifth edition. (Marketing Series).

Fashion Merchandising and Marketing. Marian H. Jernigan and Cynthia R. Easterling. Prentice Hall, 240 Frisch Court Paramus, NJ 07652-5240. Phone: 800-947-7700 or (201)909-6200 Fax: 800-445-6991 or (201)909-6361 URL: http://www.prenhall.com • 1990. $47.20.

Fashion Production Terms. Debbie Ann Gioello and Beverly Berke. Fairchild Books, Seven W.34th St. New York, NY 10001. Phone: 800-932-4724 or (212)630-4000 Fax: (212)630-3868 URL: http://www.fairchildbooks.com • 1979. $50.00. (Language of Fashion Series).

Fashion Showcase Retailer. Fashion Retailer Publishing, P.O. Box 586398 Dallas, TX 75258-6398. Phone: (214)631-6089 Bimonthly. $12.00 per year.

Fast Company: How Smart Business Works. Fast Company Inc., 77 N. Washington St. Boston, MA 02114. Phone: 800-542-6029 or (617)973-0300 Fax: (617)973-0373 E-mail: subscriptions@fastcompany.com • URL: http://www.fastcompany.com • Monthly. $23.95 per year. Covers business management, with emphasis on creativity, leadership, innovation, career advancement, teamwork, the global economy, and the ''new workplace.''

Fast Facts and Figures About Social Security. Available from U. S. Government Printing Office, Washington, DC 20402. Phone: (202)512-1800 Fax: (202)512-2250 E-mail: gpoaccess@gpo.gov • URL: http://www.access.gpo.gov • Annual. $4.50. Issued by the Social Security Administration (http://www.ssa.gov). Provides concise data and charts relating to social security benefits, beneficiaries, disability payments, supplemental security income, and income of the aged.

Fast Food. Available from MarketResearch.com, 641 Ave. of the Americas, Third Floor New York, NY 10011. Phone: 800-298-5699 or (212)807-2629 Fax: (212)807-2716 E-mail: order@marketresearch.com • URL: http://www.marketresearch.com • 1998. $5,000.00. Published by Euromonitor Publications Ltd. Provides consumer market data for the United States, the United Kingdom, Germany, France, and Italy.

Fast Reference Facts. The Gale Group, 27500 Drake Rd. Farmington Hills, MI 48331-3535. Phone: 800-877-GALE or (248)699-GALE Fax: 800-414-5043 or (248)699-8069 E-mail: galeord@gale.com • URL: http://www.gale.com • 1995. $400.00. Contains more than 5,000 CD-ROM entries, providing concise answers to a wide variety of ''everyday'' queries, within 13 broad subject areas (includes business and economics). Sources of questions and answers include public libraries.

Fastener Technology International. Initial Publications, 3869 Darrow Rd., Suite 109 Stow, OH 44224. Phone: (330)686-9544 Fax: (330)686-9563 E-mail: 104251.426@compuserve.com • URL: http://www.fastenertech.com • Bimonthly. $35.00 per year.

Fastener Technology International Buyers' Guide. Initial Publications, Inc., 3869 Darrow Rd. Stow, OH 44224. Phone: (330)686-9544 Fax: (330)686-9563 E-mail: info@fastenertech.com • Annual. $35.00. List of over 2,000 international manufacturers and distributors of fasteners and precision-formed parts.

Faster New Product Development: Getting the Right Product to Market Quickly. Milton D. Rosenau. AMACOM, 1601 Broadway, 12th Fl. New York, NY 10019. Phone: 800-262-9699 or (212)586-8100 Fax: (212)903-8168 E-mail: custmserv@amanet.org • URL: http://www.amanet.org • 1990. $55.00. A guide to new product development for companies of all sizes and kinds.

Fat Pipe: The Business of Marketing Broadband Services. Dagda Mor Media, Inc., 3402 Bonaire Crossing Marietta, GA 30066. Phone: (678)560-4388 Fax: (678)560-4387 E-mail: fatpipe@dagdamor.com • URL: http://www.dagdamor.com • Monthly. Controlled circulation. Edited for those who plan, develop, and market broadband Internet and telecommunications services.

Fats and Oils: Oilseed Crushings. U. S. Bureau of the Census, Washington, DC 20233-0800. Phone: (301)457-4100 Fax: (301)457-3842 URL: http://www.census.gov • Monthly and annual. Provides data on shipments of cottonseed oil and soybean oil: value, quantity, imports, and exports. (Current Industrial Reports, M20J.)

Fats and Oils: Production, Consumption, and Stocks. U. S. Bureau of the Census, Washington, DC 20233-0800. Phone: (301)457-4100 Fax: (301)457-3842 URL: http://www.census.gov • Monthly and annual. Covers the supply and distribution of cottonseed, soybean, and palm oils, and selected inedible products. (Current Industrial Reports, M20K.)

Faulkner and Gray's Medicine and Health. Faulkner & Gray, Healthcare Information Center, 1133 15th St., N.W., Suite 450 Washington, DC 20005. Phone: 800-535-8403 or (202)828-4148 Fax: (202)828-2352 E-mail: orders@faulknergray.com • URL: http://www.faulknergray.com • Weekly. $525.00 per year. Newsletter on socioeconomic developments relating to the health care industry. Formerly *McGraw-Hill's Washington Report on Medicine and Health*.

Faulkner Information Service. Faulkner Information Services, Inc., 114 Cooper Center Pennsauken, NJ 08109-4319. Phone: (856)662-2070 Fax: (856)662-3380 E-mail: faulkner@faulkner.com • URL: http://www.faulkner.com • Looseleaf. Monthly updates. Many titles and volumes, covering virtually all aspects of computer software and hardware. Gives descriptions and technical data for specific products, including producers' names and addresses. Prices and details on request. Formerly (The Auerbach Series).

Faulkner's Enterprise Networking. Faulkner Information Services, Inc., 114 Cooper Center, 7905 Browning Rd. Pennsauken, NJ 08109-4319. Phone: (856)622-2070 Fax: (856)662-3380 Three looseleaf volumes, with monthly updates. $1,275.00 per year. Contains product reports and management articles relating to computer communications and networking. Available on CD-ROM. Quarterly updates. Formerly *Data Communications Reports*.

Faulkner's Local Area Networking. Faulkner Information Services, Inc., 114 Cooper Center, 7905 Browning Rd. Pennsauken, NJ 08109-4319. Phone: (856)662-2070 Fax: (856)662-3380 Looseleaf, with monthly updates. $715.00 per year. Contains product reports and other information relating to PC networking, including security, gateways/bridges, and emerging standards. Formerly *Microcomputer Communications*.

Faulkner's Telecommunications World. Faulkner Information Services, Inc., 114 Cooper Center, 7905 Browning Rd. Pennsauken, NJ 08109-4319. Phone: (856)662-2070 Fax: (856)662-3380 Three looseleaf volumes, with monthly updates. $1,260.00 per year. Contains product reports, technology overviews and management articles relating to all aspects of voice and data communications.

Fax Handbook. Gerald V. Quinn. McGraw-Hill Professional, 1221 Ave. of the Americas New York, NY 10020-1095. Phone: 800-722-4726 or (212)904-2000 Fax: (212)904-2072 E-mail: customer.service@mcgraw-hill.com • URL: http://www.mcgraw-hill.com • 1989. $16.95.

FAX Magazine. Technical Data Publishing Corp., 195A State, Route 33 Hartfield, VA 23071. Phone: (201)770-2633 Quarterly. Price on application.

Fax Modem Sourcebook. Andrew Margolis. John Wiley and Sons, Inc., 605 Third Ave. New York, NY 10158-0012. Phone: 800-225-5945 or (212)850-6000 Fax: (212)850-6088 E-mail: info@wiley.com • URL: http://www.wiley.com • 1995. $85.00. Explains fax modem technology for both the novice and the experienced user. Includes technical programming information and international standards.

Faxon Guide to Electronic Media. Faxon Co., Inc., 15 Southwest Park Westwood, MA 02090. Phone: 800-766-0039 or (617)329-3350 Fax: (617)320-0141 Annual. Free to qualified personnel; others, $12.00. Provides brief descriptions of currently available CD-ROM databases. Formerly *Faxon Guide to CD-ROM*.

Faxon Guide to Serials, Including Annuals, Continuations, GPO Publications, Monographic Series, Newspapers, Periodicals, Proceedings, Transactions, and Yearbooks, and CD-ROM. Faxon Co., Inc., 15 Southwest Park Westwood, MA 02090. Phone: 800-766-0039 or (617)329-3350 Fax: (617)320-0141 Annual. Free to qualified personnel; others, $25.00. Gives prices and frequency, but no addresses.

FaxUSA: A Directory of Facsimile Numbers for Business and Organizations Nationwide. Darren L. Smith, editor. Omnigraphics, Inc., Penobscot Bldg. Detroit, MI 48226. Phone: 800-234-1340 or (313)961-1340 Fax: 800-875-1340 or (313)961-1383 E-mail: info@omnigraphics.com • URL: http://www.omnigraphics.com • Annual. $130.00. Provides more than 111,500 listings, with fax numbers, telephone numbers, and addresses.

FBI Law Enforcement Bulletin. Available from U. S. Government Printing Office, Washington, DC 20402. Phone: (202)512-1800 Fax: (202)512-2250 E-mail: gpoaccess@gpo.gov • URL: http://www.access.gpo.gov • Monthly. $36.00 per year. Issued by Federal Bureau of Investigation, U. S. Department of Justice. Contains articles on a wide variety of law enforcement and crime topics, including computer-related crime.

FCC Record. Available from U. S. Government Printing Office, Washington, DC 20402. Phone: (202)512-1800 Fax: (202)512-2250 E-mail: gpoaccess@gpo.gov • URL: http://www.access.gpo.gov • Biweekly. $535.00 per year. Produced by the Federal Communications Commission (http://www.fcc.gov). An inclusive compilation of decisions, reports, public notices, and other documents of the FCC.

FCC Report: An Exclusive Report on Domestic and International Telecommunications Policy and Regulation. Warren Publishing Inc., 2115 Ward Court, N. W. Washington, DC 20037-1209. Phone: 800-771-9202 or (202)872-9200 Fax: (202)293-3435 E-mail: customerservice@warren-news.com • URL: http://www.telecommunications.com • Semimonthly. $649.00 per year. Newsletter concerned principally with Federal Communications Commission regulations and policy.

FCIB International Bulletin (Finance, Credit and International Business). Finance, Credit and International Business - National Association of Credit Mana. FCIB - NACM, 8840 Columbia Parkway, No.100 Columbia, MD 21045-2158. Phone: (732)283-8606 Fax: (732)283-8613 E-mail: fcib_info@nacm.org • URL: http://www.nacm.org • Monthly. Free.

FCIB/NACM Corp.

FDA Consumer. Available from U. S. Government Printing Office, Washington, DC 20402. Phone: (202)512-1800 Fax: (202)512-2250 E-mail: gpoaccess@gpo.gov • URL: http://www.access.gpo.gov • Bimonthly. $23.00 per year. Issued by the U. S. Food and Drug Administration. Provides consumer information about FDA regulations and product safety.

FDM: Furniture Design and Manufacturing: Serving the Upholstered Furniture Industry. Chartwell Communications, Inc., 380 E. Northwest Highway Des Plaines, IL 60016. Phone: 800-662-7776 or (847)390-6700 Fax: (847)299-7100 URL: http://www.fdmmag.com • Monthly. Free to qualified personnel. Edited for furniture executives, production managers, and designers. Covers the manufacturing of household, office, and institutional furniture, store fixtures, and kitchen and bathroom cabinets.

FDM-The Source-Woodworking Industry Directory. Cahners Business Information, 1350 E. Touhy Ave, Des Plaines, IL 60018-3358. Phone: 800-662-7776 or (847)635-8800 Fax: (847)390-2445 E-mail: corporatecommunications@cahners.com • URL: http://www.cahners.com • Annual. $25.00. A product-classified listing of more than 1,800 suppliers to the furniture and cabinet industries. Includes Canada.

The FED in Print: Economics and Banking Topics. Federal Reserve Bank of Philadelphia, 10 Independence Mall Philadelphia, PA 19106-0066. Phone: (215)574-6540 Fax: (215)574-3847 URL: http://www.phil.frb.org • Semiannual. Free. Business and banking topics.

Federal Administrative Law Judges Conference.

Federal Agency Profiles for Students. The Gale Group, 27500 Drake Rd. Farmington Hills, MI 48331-3535. Phone: 800-877-GALE or (248)699-GALE Fax: 800-414-5043 or (248)699-8069 E-mail: galeord@galegroup.com • URL: http://www.galegroup.com • 1999. $99.00. Provides detailed descriptions of about 200 prominent U.S. government agencies, including major activities, organizational structure, political issues, budget, and history. Includes a glossary, chronology, and index.

Federal Assistance Monitor. Community Development Services. CD Publications, 8204 Fenton St. Silver Spring, MD 20910-2889. Phone: 800-666-6380 or (301)588-6380 Fax: (301)588-6385 E-mail: cdpubs@clark.net • Semimonthly. $279.00 per year. Newsletter. Provides news of federal grant and loan programs for social, economic, and community purposes. Monitors grant announcements, funding, and availability.

Federal Aviation Regulations. Available from U. S. Government Printing Office, Washington, DC 20402. Phone: (202)512-1800 Fax: (202)512-2250 E-mail: gpoaccess@gpo.gov • URL: http://www.access.gpo.gov • Annual. Free. Lists government publications. GPO Subject Bibliography Number 12.

Federal Banking Law Reports. CCH, Inc., 4025 W. Peterson Ave, Chicago, IL 60646-6085. Phone: 800-248-3248 or (773)583-8500 Fax: 800-224-8299 or (773)866-3608 URL: http://www.cch.com • Weekly. $1,402.00 per year. Looseleaf service.

Federal Benefits for Veterans and Dependents (Veterans Administration). U.S. Government Printing Office, Washington, DC 20402. Phone: (202)512-1800 Fax: (202)512-2250 E-mail: gpoaccess@gpo.gov • URL: http://www.access.gpo.gov • Annual. $5.00.

Federal Carriers Reports. CCH, Inc., 4025 W. Peterson Ave. Chicago, IL 60646-6085. Phone: 800-248-3248 Fax: 800-224-8299 or (773)866-3608 URL: http://www.cch.com • Biweekly. $1,372.00 per year. Four looseleaf volumes. Periodic supplementation. Federal rules and regulations for motor carriers, water carriers, and freight forwarders.

Federal Civil Rights Acts. Rodney A. Smolla. West Group, 610 Opperman Dr. Eagan, MN 55123. Phone: 800-328-4880 or (651)687-7000 Fax: 800-213-2323 or (651)687-5827 URL: http://www.westgroup.com • Two looseleaf volumes. $245.00. Covers current legislation relating to a wide range of civil rights issues, including discrimination in employment, housing, property rights, and voting. (Civil Right Series).

Federal Computer Week: The Newspaper for the Government Systems Community. FCW Government Technology Group, 3141 Fairview Park Dr., Suite 777 Falls Church, VA 22042-4507. Phone: (703)876-5100 Fax: (703)876-5126 E-mail: letter@fcw.com • URL: http://www.fcw.com • 41 times a year. $95.00 per year.

Federal Contracts Report. Bureau of National Affairs, Inc., 1231 25th St., N.W. Washington, DC 20037-1197. Phone: 800-372-1033 or (202)452-4200 Fax: (202)452-8092 E-mail: books@bna.com • URL: http://www.bna.com • Weekly. $1,245.00 per year, Two volumes. Looseleaf. Developments affecting federal contracts and grants.

Federal Criminal Investigators Association.

Federal Deposit Insurance Corporation; Annual Report. Federal Deposit Insurance Corp., 550 17th St., N.W. Washington, DC 20429. Phone: (202)393-8400 Annual.

Federal Employee. National Federation of Federal Employees, 1016 16th St. N.W. Washington, DC 20036. Phone: (202)862-4400 Monthly. $15.00 per year.

Federal Employee News Digest. Federal Employee News Digest, Inc., 1850 Centennial Park Dr., Suite 520 Reston, VA 20191. Phone: 800-989-3363 or (703)648-9551 Fax: (703)648-0265 URL: http://www.fedforce.com • Weekly. $59.00 per year. Provides essential information for federal employees.

Federal Employees Almanac. Federal Employees New Digest, Inc., 1850 Centennial Park Dr., Suite 520 Reston, VA 20191. Phone: 800-989-3363 or (703)648-9551 Fax: (703)648-0265 URL: http://www.fedforce.com • Annual. $11.95. Comprehensive guide for federal employees.

Federal Estate and Gift Tax Reports. CCH, Inc., 4025 W. Peterson Ave. Chicago, IL 60646-6085. Phone: 800-248-3248 or (773)583-8500 Fax: 800-224-8299 or (773)866-3608 URL: http://www.cch.com • Weekly. $520.00. Three looseleaf volumes.

Federal Estate and Gift Taxation. Richard B. Stevens and Guy B. Maxfield. Warren, Gorham and Lamont/RIA Group, 395 Hudson St. New York, NY 10014. Phone: 800-950-1215 or (212)367-6300 Fax: (651)687-5827 E-mail: customer_services@riag.com • URL: http://www.westgroup.com • $390.00. Looseleaf service. Semiannual supplementation. Clarification and guidance on estate tax laws.

Federal Estate and Gift Taxes: Code and Regulations, Including Related Income Tax Provisions. CCH, Inc., 4025 W. Peterson Ave. Chicago, IL 60646-6085. Phone: 800-248-3248 or (773)866-6000 Fax: 800-224-8299 or (773)866-3608 URL: http://www.cch.com • Annual. $44.95. Provides full text of estate, gift, and generation-skipping tax provisions of the Internal Revenue Code.

Federal Government Subcontract Forms. Robert J. English. West Group, 610 Opperman Dr. Eagan, MN 55123. Phone: 800-328-4880 or (651)687-7000 Fax: 800-213-2323 or (651)687-5827 URL: http://www.westgroup.com • Three looseleaf volumes. $305.00. Periodic supplementation.

Federal Grants and Contracts Weekly: Funding Opportunities in Research, Training and Services. Aspen Publishers, Inc., 200 Orchard Ridge Dr. Gaithersburg, MD 20878. Phone: 800-638-8437 or (301)417-7500 Fax: (301)695-7931 E-mail: customer.service@aspenpubl.com • URL: http://www.aspenpub.com • Weekly. $394.00 per year.

Federal Human Resources Week. LRP Publications, P.O. Box 980 Horsham, PA 19044-0980. Phone: 800-341-7874 or (215)784-0941 Fax: (215)784-0870 E-mail: custserv@lrp.com • URL: http://www.lrp.com • 48 times a year. $325.00 per year. Newsletter. Covers federal personnel issues, including legislation, benefits, budgets, and downsizing.

Federal Income, Gift and Estate Taxation. Matthew Bender & Co., Inc., Two Park Ave. New York, NY 10016. Phone: 800-223-1940 or (212)448-2000 Fax: (212)244-3188 E-mail: international@bender.com • URL: http://www.bender.com • $1,070.00. Nine looseleaf volumes. Periodic supplementation.

Federal Income Tax Regulations. Prentice Hall, 240 Frisch Court Paramus, NJ 07652. Phone: 800-947-7700 or (201)909-6200 Fax: 800-445-6991 or (201)909-6361 URL: http://www.prenhall.com • 1984. Four volumes. Price on application.

Federal Income Taxation of Corporations and Shareholders. Boris I. Bittker and James S. Eustice. Warren, Gorham and Lamont/RIA Group, 395 Hudson St. New York, NY 10014. Phone: 800-950-1215 or (212)367-6300 Fax: (651)687-5827 E-mail: customer_services@riag.com • URL: http://www.westgroup.com • Looseleaf service. $235.00. Two volumes. Periodic supplementation. Provides details concerning best methods for structuring various corporation transactions. Actual forms used by top tax specialists covering a diverse range of tax situations are shown.

Federal Income Taxation of Corporations Filing Consolidated Returns. Herbert J. Lerner and Richard S. Antes. Matthew Bender & Co., Inc., Two Park Ave. New York, NY 10016. Phone: 800-223-1940 or (212)448-2000 Fax: (212)244-3188 E-mail: international@bender.com • URL: http://www.bender.com • $650.00. Four looseleaf volumes. Periodic supplementation.

Federal Income Taxation of Inventories. Matthew Bender & Co., Inc., Two Park Ave. New York, NY 10016. Phone: 800-223-1940 or (212)448-2000 Fax: (212)244-3188 E-mail: international@bender.com • URL: http://www.bender.com • $710.00. Three looseleaf volumes. Periodic supplementation.

Federal Income Taxation of Life Insurance Companies. Matthew Bender & Co., Inc., Two Park Ave. New York, NY 10016. Phone: 800-223-1940 or (212)448-2000 Fax: (212)244-3188 E-mail: international@bender.com • URL: http://www.bender.com • $630.00. Three looseleaf volumes. Periodic supplementation.

Federal Income Taxes of Decedents, Estates, and Trusts. CCH, Inc., 4025 W. Peterson Ave. Chicago, IL 60646-6085. Phone: 800-248-3248 or (773)866-6000 Fax: 800-224-8299 or (773)866-3608 URL: http://www.cch.com • Annual. $45.00. Provides rules for preparing a decedent's final income tax return. Includes discussions of fiduciary duties, grantor trusts, and bankruptcy estates.

Federal Information Disclosure: Procedures, Forms and the Law. James T. O'Reilly. Shepard's, 555 Middle Creek Parkway Colorado Springs, CO 80921. Phone: 800-743-7393 or (719)481-7371 Fax: 800-525-0053 or (719)481-7621 E-mail: customer_service@shepards.com • URL: http://www.shepards.com • 1977. $200.00. Second edition. Two volumes. Discusses legal aspects of getting information from the government.

Federal Jobs Digest. Breakthrough Publications, Inc., 310 N. Highland Ave. Issining, NY 10562. Phone: 800-824-5000 or (914)762-5111 Fax: (914)762-4818 E-mail: fjdeditor@jobsfed.com • URL: http://www.jobsfed.com • Biweekly. Individuals, $125.00 per year; libraries, $112.50 per year. Lists 15,000 immediate job openings within the federal government in each issue.

Federal Land Use Law: Limitations, Procedures, Remedies. Daniel R. Mandelker and others. West Group, 610 Opperman Dr. Eagan, MN 55123. Phone: 800-328-4880 or (651)687-7000 Fax: 800-213-2323 or (651)687-5827 URL: http://www.westgroup.com • $145.00 per year. Looseleaf service. Annual supplementation.

Federal Manager. Federal Managers' Association, 1641 Prince St. Alexandria, VA 22314-2818. Phone: (703)683-8700 Fax: (703)683-8707 E-mail: fma@ix.netcom.com • URL: http://www.fpmi.com • Quarterly. $24.00 per year. Formerly *Federal Managers Quarterly*.

Federal Managers Association.

The Federal Manager's Handbook: A Guide to Rehabilitating or Removing the Problem Employee. G. Jerry Shaw and William L. Bransford. FPMI Communications, Inc., 707 Fiber St. Huntsville, AL 35801. Phone: (256)539-1850 Fax:

(256)539-0911 E-mail: fpmi@fpmi.com • URL: http://www.fpmi.com • 1997. $24.95. Third revised edition.

Federal Personnel Manual. U.S. Office of Personnel Management. Available from U.S. Government Printing Office, Washington, DC 20402. Phone: (202)512-1800 Fax: (202)512-2250 E-mail: gpoaccess@gpo.gov • URL: http://www.access.gpo.gov • Looseleaf service. Periodic supplementation. Available in parts.

Federal Regional Yellow Book: Who's Who in the Federal Government's Departments, Agencies, Military Installations, and Service Academies Outside of Washington, DC. Leadership Directories, Inc., 104 Fifth Ave., 2nd Fl. New York, NY 10011. Phone: (212)627-4140 Fax: (212)645-0931 E-mail: info@leadershipdirectories.com • URL: http://www.leadershipdirectories.com • Semiannual. $235.00 per year. Lists over 36,000 federal officials and support staff at 8,000 regional offices.

Federal Register. Office of the Federal Register. Available from U.S. Government Printing Office, Washington, DC 20402. Phone: (202)512-1800 Fax: (202)512-2250 E-mail: gpoaccess@gpo.gov • URL: http://www.access.gpo.gov • Daily except Saturday and Sunday. $697.00 per year. Publishes regulations and legal notices issued by federal agencies, including executive orders and presidential proclamations. Issued by the National Archives and Records Administration (http://www.nara.gov).

Federal Regulatory Directory. Congressional Quarterly, Inc., 1414 22nd St., N.W. Washington, DC 20037. Phone: 800-432-2250 or (202)887-8500 Fax: (202)887-6706 E-mail: bookhelp@cq.com • URL: http://www.cq.com • Biennial. $149.95. Published by Congressional Quarterly, Inc. Provides detailed profiles of government agency functions and duties, and describes the laws each agency enforces. Includes extensive directory information.

Federal Research Report: Weekly Report on Federal Grants and Contracts to Research Institutions. Business Publishers, Inc., 8737 Colesville Rd., Suite 1100 Silver Spring, MD 20910-3928. Phone: 800-274-6737 or (301)587-6300 Fax: (301)587-1081 E-mail: bpinews@bpinews.com • URL: http://www.bpinews.com • Weekly. $270.00 per year.

Federal Reserve Bank of Atlanta: Economic Review. Federal Reserve Bank of Atlanta, 104 Marietta St., N.W. Atlanta, GA 30303-2713. Phone: (404)521-8020 URL: http://www.frbatlanta.org • Quarterly. Free.

Federal Reserve Bank of Dallas: Economic Review. Federal Reserve Bank of Dallas, P.O. Box 655906 Dallas, TX 75265-5906. Phone: (214)922-5254 Fax: (214)922-5268 E-mail: kay.champagen@dal.frb.org • URL: http://www.dallasfed.org • Quarterly. Free.

Federal Reserve Bank of Kansas City: Economic Review. Federal Reserve Bank of Kansas City, 925 Grand Blvd. Kansas City, MO 64198-0001. Phone: (816)881-2683 Fax: (816)881-2569 Quarterly.Free.

Federal Reserve Bank of Minneapolis: Quarterly Review. Federal Reserve Bank of Minneapolis, Research Dept., 90 Hennepin Ave Minneapolis, MN 55480-0291. Phone: (612)204-6455 Fax: (612)204-5515 E-mail: err@res.mpls.frb.fed.us • URL: http://www.woodrow.mpls.frb.fed.us • Quarterly. Free.

Federal Reserve Bank of New York: Economic Policy Review. Federal Reserve Bank of New York Public Information Office, 33 Liberty St. New York, NY 10045-0001. Phone: (212)720-6150 Quarterly. Free.

Federal Reserve Bank of Philadelphia: Business Review. Federal Reserve Bank of Philadelphia, Research Dept., P.O. Box 66 Philadelphia, PA 19105-0066. Phone: (215)574-6428 Fax: (215)574-4364 URL: http://www.phil.frb.org • Bimonthly. Free. Contains articles on current topics in economics, finance, and banking. The Bank also maintains a world wide web site at http://www.libertynet.org/~fedrsrv/fedpage.html

Federal Reserve Bank of Richmond: Economic Quarterly. Federal Reserve Bank of Richmond, Research Dept., 701 E. Byrd St. Richmond, VA 23219. Phone: (804)697-8000 Fax: (804)697-8287 E-mail: eg@rich.frb.org • URL: http://www.rich.frb.org • Bimonthly. Free. Formerly *Federal Reserve Bank of Richmond: Economic Review*.

Federal Reserve Bank of Saint Louis: Review. Federal Reserve Bank of Saint Louis, P.O. Box 442 St. Louis, MO 63166. Phone: (314)444-8320 Bimonthly. Free.

Federal Reserve Bank of San Francisco Economic Letter. Federal Reserve Bank of San Francisco. Economic Letter, P.O. Box 7702 San Francisco, CA 94120. Phone: (415)974-3230 Fax: (415)974-3341 URL: http://www.frbsf.org • 38 times a year. Free. Formerly *Federal Reserve Bank of San Francisco: Weekly Letter*.

Federal Reserve Bank of San Francisco: Economic Review. Federal Reserve Bank of San Francisco, P.O. Box 7702 San Francisco, CA 94120. Phone: (415)974-3230 Fax: (415)974-3341 URL: http://www.frbsf.org • Three times a year. Free.

Federal Reserve Board Publications. U.S. Board of Governors of the Federal Reserve System, Washington, DC 20551. Phone: (202)452-3000 URL: http://www.federalreserve.gov • Semiannual. Free.

Federal Reserve Bulletin. U.S. Federal Reserve System, Board of Governors, Publications Services, 20th and Constitution Ave., N.W., Room MS-127 Washington, DC 20551. Phone: (202)452-3244 Fax: (202)728-5886 URL: http://www.federalreserve.gov • Monthly. $25.00 per year. Provides statistics on banking and the economy, including interest rates, money supply, and the Federal Reserve Board indexes of industrial production.

Federal Reserve Regulatory Service. U.S. Federal Reserve System, Board of Governors Publications Services Section, R, 20th and Constitution Ave., N.W. Washington, DC 20551. Phone: (202)452-3244 Fax: (202)728-5886 URL: http://www.federalreserve.gov • Monthly. $200.00 per year. Looseleaf. Includes four handbooks updated monthly: *Consumer and Community Affairs, Monetary Policy and Reserve Requirements Securities, Credit Transactions and Payment Systems*. Irregular supplements.

Federal Reserve System: Purposes and Functions. U.S. Board of Governors of the Federal Reserve System, Washington, DC 20551. Phone: (202)452-3000 URL: http://www.federalreserve.gov • Irregular.

Federal Securities Act of 1933-Treatise and Primary Source Material. A. A. Sommer. Matthew Bender & Co., Inc., Two Park Ave. New York, NY 10016. Phone: 800-223-1940 or (212)448-2000 Fax: (212)244-3188 E-mail: international@bender.com • URL: http://www.bender.com • $660.00. Two looseleaf volumes. Covers application of the Federal Securities Act of 1933 and amendments.

Federal Securities Exchange Act of 1934. Edward N. Gadsby and A. A. Sommer. Matthew Bender & Co., Inc., Two Park Ave. New York, NY 10016. Phone: 800-223-1940 or (212)448-2000 Fax: (212)244-3188 E-mail: international@bender.com • URL: http://www.bender.com • $660.00. Two looseleaf volumes. Periodic supplementation. Covers application of the Federal Securities Exchange Act of 1934 and amendments.

Federal Securities Law Reports. CCH, Inc., Chicago, IL 60646-6085. Phone: 800-248-3248 or (773)583-8500 Fax: 800-224-8299 or (773)866-3608 URL: http://www.cch.com • Weekly. $1,600.00 per year. Looseleaf service. Seven volumes.

Federal Securities Laws: Legislative History, 1933-1982 and the 1987-90 Supplement. Federal Bar Association, Securities Law Committee. Books on Demand, 300 N. Zeeb Rd. Ann Arbor, MI 48106-1346. Phone: 800-521-0600 or (734)761-4700 Fax: (734)665-5022 E-mail: info@umi.com • URL: http://www.lib.umi.com • 1983. $1,150.40. Six volumes.

Federal Staff Directory: With Biographical Information on Executive Staff Personnel. CQ Staff Directories, Inc., 815 Slaters Lane Alexandria, VA 22314. Phone: 800-252-1722 or (703)739-0900 Fax: (703)739-0234 E-mail: staffdir@staffdirectories.com • URL: http://www.staffdirectories.com • Three times a year. $227.00 per year. Single copies, $89.00. Lists 40,000 staff members of federal departments and agencies, with biographies of 2,600 key executives. Includes keyword and name indexes.

Federal Tax Citations. Shepard's, 555 Middle Creek Parkway Colorado Springs, CO 80921. Phone: 800-743-7393 or (719)481-7371 Fax: 800-525-0053 or (719)481-7621 E-mail: customer_service@shepards.com • URL: http://www.shepards.com • 1990. $990.00. 11 volumes. Supplements available.

Federal Tax Coordinator 2D. Research Institute of America, Inc., 90 Fifth Ave. New York, NY 10011. Phone: 800-431-9025 or (212)645-4800 Fax: (212)337-4213 35 looseleaf volumes. $1,375.00 per year. Weekly updates. Includes *Weekly Alert* newsletter and *Internal Revenue Bulletin*. Covers federal income, estate, gift, and excise taxes. Formerly *Federal Tax Coordinator*.

Federal Tax Course. CCH, Inc., 4025 W. Peterson Ave. Chicago, IL 60646-6085. Fax: 800-901-9075 URL: http://www.cch.com • Annual. $136.00. Looseleaf. Summarizes requirements of current federal income tax regulations, revenue codes, laws, and filing requirements.

Federal Tax Course: General Edition. CCH, Inc., 4025 W. Peterson Ave. Chicago, IL 60646-6085. Phone: 800-248-3248 or (773)866-6000 Fax: 800-224-8299 or (773)866-3608 URL: http://www.cch.com • Annual. $123.00. Provides basic reference and training for various forms of federal taxation: individual, business, corporate, partnership, estate, gift, etc. Includes *Federal Taxation Study Manual*.

Federal Tax Forms. CCH, Inc., 4025 W. Peterson Ave. Chicago, IL 60646-6085. Phone: 800-248-3248 or (773)866-6000 Fax: 800-224-8299 or (773)866-3608 URL: http://www.cch.com • Irregular. Looseleaf service. Three volumes. Actual size reproductions of federal income tax forms.

Federal Tax Guide. CCH, Inc., 4025 W. Peterson Ave. Chicago, IL 60646-6085. Phone: 800-248-3248 or (773)583-8500 Fax: 800-224-8299 or (773)866-3608 URL: http://www.cch.com • $850.00 per year. Looseleaf service. Monthly updates. Eight volumes. For everyday business and personal federal income tax questions. Explanation of federal tax system, income tax regulations, check lists, withholding tables, and charts.

Federal Tax Guide: Internal Revenue Code. Prentice Hall, 240 Frisch Court Paramus, NJ 07652-5240. Phone: 800-947-7700 or (201)909-6200 Fax: 800-445-6991 or (201)909-6361 URL: http://www.prenhall.com • Looseleaf. Periodic supplementation. Price on application.

Federal Tax Handbook. Research Institute of America, 90 Fifth Ave. New York, NY 10011. Phone: 800-431-9025 or (212)645-4800 Fax: (212)816-3581 URL: http://www.mcp.com • 2000. $45.00. Revised edition.

Federal Tax Manual. CCH, Inc., 4025 W. Peterson Ave. Chicago, IL 60646-6085. Phone: 800-248-3248 or (773)866-6000 Fax: 800-224-8299 or (773)866-3608 URL: http://www.cch.com • Looseleaf. $175.00 per year. Covers "basic federal tax rules and forms affecting individuals and businesses." Includes a copy of *Annuity, Depreciation, and Withholding Tables*.

Federal Tax Products. Available from U. S. Government Printing Office, Washington, DC 20402. Phone: (202)512-1800 Fax: (202)512-2250 E-mail: gpoaccess@gpo.gov • URL: http://www.access.gpo.gov • Annual. $20.00. CD-ROM issued by the Internal Revenue Service (http://www.irs.treas.gov/forms_pubs/). Provides current tax forms, instructions, and publications. Also includes older tax forms beginning with 1991.

Federal Taxation of Income, Estates and Gifts. Boris I. Bittker. Warren, Gorham and Lamont/RIA Group, 395 Hudson St. New York, NY 10014. Phone: 800-950-1215 or (212)367-6300 Fax: (651)687-5827 E-mail: customer_services@riag.com • URL: http://www.westgroup.com • Looseleaf service. $465.00. Five volumes. Quarterly supplementation. Covers aspects of income taxation of individuals, corporations, partnerships, estates, and gifts. Clear analysis to exact answers to tax questions.

Federal Taxation of Insurance Companies. Dennis P. Van Mieghem and others. Prentice Hall, 240 Frisch Court Paramus, NJ 07652-5240. Phone: 800-947-7700 or (201)909-6200 Fax: 800-445-6991 or (201)909-6361 URL: http://www.prenhall.com • $447.00 per year. Looseleaf service. Biweekly updates.

Federal Taxation of Oil and Gas Transactions. Matthew Bender & Co., Inc., Two Park Ave. New York, NY 10016. Phone: 800-223-1940 or (212)448-2000 Fax: (212)244-3188 E-mail: international@bender.com • URL: http://www.bender.com • $350.00. Two looseleaf volumes. Periodic supplementation.

Federal Taxation of Partnerships and Partners. William S. McKee and others. Warren, Gorham and Lamont/RIA Group, 395 Hudson St. New York, NY 10014. Phone: 800-950-1215 or (212)367-6300 Fax: (651)687-5827 E-mail: customer_services@riag.com • URL: http://www.westgroup.com • Looseleaf. $215.00. Two volumes. Quarterly supplementation. Provides guidance on every aspect of partnership taxation.

Federal Taxation of Trusts, Grantors, and Beneficiaries. John L. Peschel and Edward D. Spurgeon. Warren, Gorham and Lamont/RIA Group, 395 Hudson St. New York, NY 10014. Phone: 800-950-1215 or (212)367-6300 Fax: (651)687-5827 E-mail: customer_services@riag.com • URL: http://www.westgroup.com • Looseleaf. $160.00. Annual supplementation.

Federal Taxation Practice and Procedure. Robert E. Meldman and Richard J. Sideman. CCH, Inc., 4025 W. Peterson Ave. Chicago, IL 60646-6085. Phone: 800-248-3248 or (773)866-6000 Fax: 800-224-8299 or (773)866-3608 URL: http://www.cch.com • 1998. $89.00. Fifth edition. Provides information on the administrative structure of the Internal Revenue Service. Includes discussions of penalties, ethical duties, statute of limitations, litigation, and IRS collection procedures. Contains IRS standardized letters and notices.

Federal Taxes Affecting Real Estate. Matthew Bender & Co., Inc., Two Park Ave. New York, NY 10016. Phone: 800-223-1940 or (212)448-2000 Fax: (212)244-3188 E-mail: international@bender.com • URL: http://www.bender.com • $215.00. Looseleaf service. Periodic supplementation. Explains and illustrates the most important federal tax principles applying to daily real estate transactions.

Federal Taxes Citator. MacMillan Publishing Co., 200 Old Tappan Rd. Old Tappan, NJ 07675. Phone: 800-223-2336 $550.00 per year. Two looseleaf volumes. Monthly supplements.

Federal Taxes: Internal Memoranda of the IRS. Prentice Hall, 240 Frisch Court Paramus, NJ 07652-5240. Phone: 800-947-7700 or (201)909-6200 Fax: 800-445-6991 or (201)909-6361 URL: http://www.prenhall.com • Looseleaf. Periodic supplementation. Price on application.

Federal Times. Army Times Publishing Co., 6883 Commercial Dr. Springfield, VA 22159-0240. Phone: 800-368-5718 or (703)750-8646 Fax: (703)658-8314 URL: http://www.federaltimes.com • Weekly. $52.00 per year.

Federal Trade Commission. Stephanie W. Kanwit. Shepard's, 555 Middle Creek Parkway Colorado Springs, CO 80921. Phone: 800-743-7393 or (719)481-7371 Fax: 800-525-0053 or (719)481-7621 E-mail: customer_service@shepards.com

• URL: http://www.shepards.com • 1979. $190.00. Two volumes. Discussion of regulations and procedures. (Regulatory Manual Series).

Federal Yellow Book: Who's Who in the Federal Departments and Agencies. Leadership Directories, Inc., 104 Fifth Ave., 2nd Fl. New York, NY 10011. Phone: (212)627-4140 Fax: (212)645-0931 E-mail: info@leadershipdirectories.com • URL: http://www.leadershipdirectories.com • Quarterly. $305.00 per year. White House, Executive Office of the President and departments and agencies of the executive branch nationwide, plus 38,000 other personnel.

Federally Employed Women.

Federation of Insurance and Corporate Counsel., c/o Joseph R. Olshan, P.O. Box 111 Walpole, MA 02081. Phone: (508)668-6859 Fax: (508)668-6892 E-mail: jolshan@otw.com • URL: http://www.thefederation.org • Members are insurance lawyers and insurance company executives.

Federation of International Civil Servants' Associations.

Federation of Organizations for Professional Women.

Federation of Societies for Coatings Technology.

Federation of Societies for Coatings Technology: Year Book and Membership Directory. Federation of Societies for Coatings Technology, 492 Norristown Rd. Blue Bell, PA 19422-2350. Phone: (610)940-0777 Fax: (610)940-0292 E-mail: publications@coatingstech.org • URL: http://www.coatingstech.org/products/journal.html • Annual. $150.00. About 7,500 chemists, technicians, and supervisory production personnel in the decorative and protective coatings industry who are members of the 26 constituent societies of the federation. Formerly Federation of Societies for Paint Technology.

Federation of Tax Administrators.

Fedstats. Federal Interagency Council on Statistical Policy-Phone: (202)395-7254 URL: http://www.fedstats.gov • Web site features an efficient search facility for full-text statistics produced by more than 70 federal agencies, including the Census Bureau, the Bureau of Economic Analysis, and the Bureau of Labor Statistics. Boolean searches can be made within one agency or for all agencies combined. Links are offered to international statistical bureaus, including the UN, IMF, OECD, UNESCO, Eurostat, and 20 individual countries. Fees: Free.

FedWorld: A Program of the United States Department of Commerce. National Technical Information ServicePhone: (703)605-6000 Fax: (703)605-6900 E-mail: webmaster@fedworld.gov • URL: http://www.fedworld.gov • Web site offers "a comprehensive central access point for searching, locating, ordering, and acquiring government and business information." Emphasis is on searching the Web pages, databases, and government reports of a wide variety of federal agencies. Fees: Free.

Fee and Expense Policies: Statements of 46 Management Consulting Firms. James H. Kennedy, editor. Kennedy Information, LLC, One Kennedy Place, Route 12, S. Fitzwilliam, NH 03447. Phone: 800-531-1026 or (603)585-3101 Fax: (603)585-9555 E-mail: office@kennedypub.com • URL: http://www.kennedyinfo.com • 1992. $67.00. Presents actual copies of billing and expense policies, including hourly and per diem rates. (Identification of firms has been removed.)

Fee Income Growth Strategies. Siefer Consultants, Inc., P.O. Box 1384 Storm Lake, IA 50588. Phone: (712)732-7340 Fax: (712)732-7906 E-mail: siefer@ncn.net • Monthly. $329.00 per year. Newsletter. Covers operations management for banks and other financial institutions. Formerly *Noninterest Income Growth Strategies*.

Feed Additive Compendium. Miller Publishing Co., P.O. Box 2400 Minnetonka, MN 55343-2524. Phone: (612)931-0211 Fax: (612)938-1832 Annual. $225.00. Eleven supplements. Covers the use of drugs as additives to livestock and poultry feed.

Feed and Feeding Digest. National Grain and Feed Association, 1201 New York Ave., N.W.,, Suite 830 Washington, DC 20005. Phone: (202)289-0873 Fax: (202)289-5388 E-mail: ngfa@ngfa.org • URL: http://www.ngfa.org • Monthly. Membership.

Feed Bulletin. Jacobsen Publishing Co., 300 W. Adams St. Chicago, IL 60606. Phone: (312)726-6600 Fax: (312)726-6654 Daily. $340.00 per year.

Feed Industry Red Book: Reference Book and Buyer's Guide for the Manufacturing Industry. Moffat Publishing, Inc., 317 Main St. Hopkins, MN 55343-9212. E-mail: seedtrade@skypoint.com • Annual. $40.00. List of over 200 firms involved in the large animal and pet food manufacturing and distribution business, including sources of feed ingredients and suppliers of feed materials handling equipment.

Feeds and Feeding. Arthur E. Cullison and Robert S. Lowrey. Prentice Hall, 240 Frisch Court Paramus, NJ 07652-5240. Phone: 800-947-7700 or (201)909-6200 Fax: 800-445-6991 or (201)909-6361 URL: http://www.prenhall.com • 1998. $100.00. Fifth edition.

Feedstuffs: The Weekly Newspaper for Agribusiness. ABC, Inc., P.O. Box 2400 Minnetonka, MN 55343. Phone: (612)931-0211 Fax: (612)938-1832 Weekly. $109.00 per year.

Feminist Economics. International Association for Feminist Economics. Routledge Journals, 29 W. 35th St. New York, NY 10001-2299. Phone: 800-634-7064 or (212)216-7800 Fax: 800-248-4724 or (212)564-7854 E-mail: journals@routledge.com • URL: http://www.routledge.com/routledge/ • Three times a year. Individuals, $50.00 per year; institutions, $150.00 per year. Includes articles on issues relating to the employment and economic opportunities of women.

Feminist Periodicals: A Current Listing of Contents. Women's Studies Librarian, University of Wisconsin System, 430 Memorial Library, 728 State St. Madison, WI 53706. Phone: (608)263-5754 Fax: (608)265-2754 E-mail: wisws1@library.wisc.edu • Quarterly. Individuals, $30.00 per year; institutions, $55.00 per year. Provides reproductions of the tables of contents of over 100 feminist periodicals. Includes *Feminist Collections* and *New Books on Women and Feminism*.

Femme-Lines. Earl Barron Publications, Inc., 226 E. 36th St. New York, NY 10016. Phone: (212)683-6593 Bimonthly. $8.00 per year.

Fertilizer Facts and Figures. Fertilizer Institute, 501 Second St., N.E. Washington, DC 20002. Phone: (202)675-8250 Fax: (202)544-8123 URL: http://www.tfi.org • Annual. Price on application.

Fertilizer Industry Round Table.

The Fertilizer Institute.

FIASCO: Blood in the Water on Wall Street. Frank Partnoy. W. W. Norton & Co., Inc., 500 Fifth Ave. New York, NY 10110. Phone: 800-223-2584 or (212)354-5500 Fax: (212)869-0856 E-mail: webmaster@wwnorton.com • URL: http://www.wwnorton.com • 1997. $25.00. Tells how Wall Street sold risky derivatives to clients who had no understanding of the product.

Fiber and Electro Optics Research Center.

Fiber Optic Communications Handbook. McGraw-Hill Professional, 1221 Ave. of Americas New York, NY 10020-1095. Phone: 800-722-4726 or (212)904-2000 Fax: (212)904-2072 E-mail: customer.service@mcgraw-hill.com • URL: http://www.mcgraw-hill.com • 1990. $89.50. Second edition.

Fiber Optic Systems: An Introduction and Business Overview. Terry Edwards. John Wiley and Sons, Inc., 605 Third Ave. New York, NY 10158-0012. Phone: 800-225-5945 or (212)850-6000 Fax: (212)850-6088 E-mail: info@wiley.com • URL: http://www.wiley.com • 1989. $160.00.

Fiber Optics and Communications. Information Gatekeepers, Inc., 214 Harvard Ave. Boston, MA 02134. Phone: 800-323-1088 or (617)232-3111 Fax: (617)734-8562 E-mail: info@igigroup.com • URL: http://www.igigroup.com • Monthly. $675.00. Emphasis on the use of fiber optics in telecommunications.

Fiber Optics News. Phillips Business Information, Inc., 1201 Seven Locks Rd., Suite 300 Potomac, MD 20854. Phone: 800-777-5006 or (301)340-1520 Fax: (301)309-3847 E-mail: pbi@phillips.com • URL: http://www.phillips.com/marketplaces.htm • Weekly. $697.00 per year. Newsletter.

Fiber Organon: Featuring Manufactured Fibers. Fiber Economics Bureau, Inc., 1150 17th St., N.W. Suite 306 Washington, DC 20036-4603. Phone: (202)467-0916 Fax: (202)467-0917 E-mail: fhorn@afmn.org • Monthly. $300.00 per year. Formerly *Textile Organon*.

Fiber Society.

Fiber Systems International. Available from IOP Publishing, Inc., Public Ledger Building, Suite 1035, 150 South Independence Mall West Philadelphia, PA 19106. Phone: 800-358-4677 or (215)627-0880 Fax: (215)627-0879 E-mail: custserv@ioppublishing.co.uk • URL: http://www.iop.org • Monthly. Controlled circulation. Published in the UK by the Institute of Physics. "Covering the optical communications marketplace within the Americas and Asia." *Fibre Systems Europe* is also available, covering the business and marketing aspects of fiber optics communications in Europe.

Fiberoptic Materials Research Program., 607 Taylor Rd., College of Engineering, P.O. Box 909 Piscataway, NJ 08854-8065. Phone: (732)445-4729 Fax: (908)445-4545 E-mail: sigel@alumnia.rutgers.edu • Research fields include the communications and biomedical applications of fiber optics.

Fiberoptic Product News. Cahners Business Information New Product Information, 301 Gibraltar Dr. Morris Plains, NJ 07950-0650. Phone: (973)292-5100 Fax: (973)292-0783 E-mail: corporatecommunications@cahners.com • URL: http://www.cahners.com • 13 times a year. $119.00 per year. Provides general coverage of the fiber optics industry, for both producers and users.

Fiberoptic Product News Buying Guide. Cahners Business Information, New Product Information, 301 Gibraltar Dr. Morris Plains, NJ 07950. Phone: (973)292-5100 Fax: (973)539-3476 E-mail: corporatecommunications@cahners.com • URL: http://www.cahners.com • Annual. $55.00. Lists over 500 manufacturers and suppliers of fiber optics products, equipment and services.

Fibonacci Applications and Strategies for Traders. Robert Fischer. John Wiley and Sons, Inc., 605 Third Ave. New York, NY 10158-0012. Phone: 800-225-5945 or (212)850-6000 Fax: (212)850-6088 E-mail: info@wiley.com • URL: http://www.wiley.com • 1993. $49.95. Provides a new look at the Elliott Wave Theory and Fibonacci numbers as applied to commodity prices, business cycles, and interest rate movements. (Traders Library).

Fibre Box Association.

Fibre Box Industry Statistical Report. Fibre Box Association, 2850 Golf Rd. Rolling Meadows, IL 60008. Phone: (847)364-9600 Fax: (847)364-9639 Annual.

Fibre Market News. Group Interest Enterprises. G.I.E., Inc., Publishers, 4012 Bridge Ave. Cleveland, OH 44113-3320. Phone: 800-456-0707 or (216)961-4130 Fax: (216)961-0364 URL: http://www.fibremarketnew.com • Bimonthly. $145.00 per year. Newsletter. Serves dealers, brokers and consumers of paper stock and all secondary fibers.

Fibrous Materials Research Center., Drexel University, Dept. of Materials Engineering, 3141 Chestnut St. Philadelphia, PA 19104. Phone: (215)895-1640 Fax: (215)895-6684 E-mail: fko@drexel.edul.edu • URL: http://www.fmac/coe.drexel.edu • Research fields include computer-aided design of nonwoven fabrics and design curves for industrial fibers.

FICC Quarterly. Federation of Insurance and Corporate Counsel, P.O. Box 111 Walpole, MA 02081. Phone: (508)668-6859 Fax: (508)668-6892 Quarterly. $26.00 per year. A journal dealing with the legal aspects of insurance.

Fiduciary Tax Guide. CCH, Inc., 4025 W. Peterson Ave. Chicago, IL 60646-6085. Phone: 800-248-3248 or (773)583-8500 Fax: 800-224-8299 or (773)866-3608 URL: http://www.cch.com • Monthly. $439.00 per year, Includes looseleaf monthly updates. Covers federal income taxation of estates, trusts, and beneficiaries. Provides information on gift and generation- skipping taxation.

Fiduciary Tax Return Guide 1992. Research Institute of America, Inc., 90 Fifth Ave. New York, NY 10011. Phone: 800-431-9025 or (212)645-4800 Fax: (212)337-4213 1992. $10.00.

Field Crop Abstracts: Monthly Abstract Journal on World Annual Cereal, Legume, Root, Oilseed and Fibre Crops. Available from CABI Publishing North America, 10 E. 40th St. New York, NY 10016. Phone: 800-528-4841 or (212)481-7018 Fax: (212)686-7993 E-mail: cabi@cabi.org • URL: http://www.cabi.org • Monthly. $1,465.00 per year. Published in England by CABI Publishing, formerly Commonwealth Agricultural Bureaux. Provides worldwide coverage of the literature.

A Field Guide to Airplanes of North America. M. R. Montgomery. Houghton Mifflin Co., 215 Park Ave., S. New York, NY 10003. Phone: 800-225-3362 or (212)420-5800 Fax: (212)420-5855 URL: http://www.hmco.com • 1992. $12.95. Looseleaf service.

Field Guide to Business Terms: A Glossary of Essential Tools and Concepts for Today's Manager. Alistair D. Williamson, editor. Harvard Business School Press, 60 Harvard Way Boston, MA 02163. Phone: 800-545-7685 or (617)783-7440 E-mail: custserv@cchbspub.harvard.edu • URL: http://www.hbsp.harvard.edu • 1993. $16.95. Defines fundamental terms. (Harvard Business Economist Reference Series).

Field Guide to Marketing: A Glossary of Essential Tools and Concepts for Today's Manager. McGraw-Hill, 1221 Ave. of the Americas New York, NY 10020. Phone: 800-722-4726 or (212)904-2000 Fax: (212)904-2072 E-mail: customer.service@mcgraw-hill.com • URL: http://www.mcgraw.hill.com • 1993. $29.95. Defines fundamental terms.

Field Guide to Negotiation: A Glossary of Essential Tools and Concepts for Today's Manager. Gavin Kennedy. McGraw-Hill, 1221 Ave. of the Americas New York, NY 10020. Phone: 800-722-4726 or (212)904-2000 Fax: (212)904-2072 E-mail: customerservice@mcgraw-hill.com • URL: http://www.mcgraw-hill.com • 1993. $29.95. Defines fundamental terms.

Field Guide to Project Management. David I. Cleland, editor. John Wiley and Sons, Inc., 605 Third Ave. New York, NY 10158-0012. Phone: 800-225-5945 or (212)850-6000 Fax: (212)850-6088 E-mail: info@jwiley.com • URL: http://www.wiley.com • 1998. $39.95. Provides 38 articles by various authors on the major aspects of project management.

Field Guide to Rocks and Minerals. Roger T. Peterson. Houghton Mifflin Co., 215 Park Ave., S. New York, NY 10003. Phone: 800-225-3362 or (212)420-5800 Fax: (212)420-5855 URL: http://www/hmco.com • 1998. $28.00. Sixth edition. Data on where to find rocks and minerals, how to collect them, physical properties and various types. (Peterson Field Guide Series).

Field Guide to Strategy: A Glossary to Essential Tools and Concepts for Today's Manager. McGraw-Hill, 1221 Ave. of the Americas New York, NY 10020. Phone: 800-722-4726 or (212)904-2000 Fax: (212)904-2072 E-mail: customer.service@mcgraw-hill.com • URL: http://

www.mcgraw-hill.com • 1993. $29.95. Defines fundamental terms.

50 Leading Retained Executive Search Firms in North America. Kennedy Information, LLC, One Kennedy Place, Route 12, S. Fitzwilliam, NH 03447. Phone: 800-531-1026 or (603)585-3101 Fax: (603)585-9555 E-mail: office@kennedypub.com • URL: http://www.kennedyinfo.com • Annual. $15.00. Provides profiles of major search firms, including revenue data.

FII Annual Guide to Stocks. Financial Information, Inc., 30 Montgomery St. Jersey City, NJ 07302-0473. Phone: 800-367-3441 or (201)332-5400 Fax: 800-344-3292 Annual. $2,250.00. Monthly supplements. Two volumes. Formerly *Financial Stock Guide Service: Directory of Active Stocks*.

Filing and Records Management. Nathan Krevolin. Prentice Hall, 240 Frisch Court Paramus, NJ 07652. Phone: 800-947-7700 or (201)909-6200 Fax: 800-445-6991 or (201)909-6361 URL: http://www.prenhall.com • 1986. $25.95.

Film and Video Finder. National Information Center for Educational Media. Plexus Publishing, Inc., 143 Old Marlton Pike Medford, NJ 08055-8750. Phone: (609)654-6500 Fax: (609)654-4309 Biennial. $295.00. Contains 92,000 listings of film and video educational, technical and vocational children's programs and literary materials.

Film Finance and Distribution: A Dictionary of Terms. John W. Cones. Silman-James Press, 3624 Shannon Rd. Los Angeles, CA 90027. Phone: (323)661-9922 Fax: (323)661-9933 E-mail: ghfeldman@earthlink.com • 1992. $24.95. Includes commentary on practical approaches to financing and distribution for novice filmmakers.

Film Journal: International. Sunshine Group, 244 W. 49th St., Suite 200 New York, NY 10019. Phone: (212)246-6460 Fax: (212)265-6428 E-mail: jsunshine@sunshineworld.com • URL: http://www.filmjournal.com • Monthly. $65.00 per year. Formerly *Film Journal*.

Film Quarterly. University of California Press, Journals Div., 2000 Center St., Suite 303 Berkeley, CA 94704-1223. Phone: 800-822-6657 or (510)643-7154 Fax: (510)642-9917 E-mail: journals@ucop.edu • URL: http://www.ucpress.edu/journals • Quarterly. Individuals, $26.00 per year; institutions, $70.00 per year.

Film-Video Terms and Concepts: A Focal Handbook. Steven Browne. Butterworth-Heinemann, 225 Wildwood Ave. Woburn, MA 01081. Phone: 800-366-2665 or (781)904-2500 Fax: 800-466-6520 E-mail: orders@bhusa.com • URL: http://www.bh.com • 1992. $31.95. Defines production terms, techniques, and jargon relating to motion pictures, television, and the video industry. (Focal Handbook).

Filmmaker's Dictionary. Ralph S. Singleton and James Conrad. National Book Network, 15200 NBN Way Blur Ridge Summit, PA 17214. Phone: 800-462-6420 or (717)794-3800 Fax: 800-338-4550 URL: http://www.ngnbooks.com • 2000. $22.95. Second edition. Defines technical terms, legal terms, industry jargon, and film slang.

Films and Audiovisual Information. Available from U. S. Government Printing Office, Washington, DC 20402. Phone: (202)512-1800 Fax: (202)512-2250 E-mail: gpoaccess@gpo.gov • URL: http://www.access.gpo.gov • Annual. Free. Issued by the Superintendent of Documents. A list of government publications on motion picture and audiovisual topics. Formerly *Motion Pictures, Films and Audiovisual Information*. (Subject Bibliography No. 73.)

Filmstrip and Slide Set Finder, 1990: A Comprehensive Index to 35mm Educational Filmstrips and Slide Sets. Plexus Publishing, Inc., 143 Old Marlton Pike Medford, NJ 08055-8750. Phone: (609)654-6500 Fax: (609)654-4309 E-mail: patp@plexuspub.com • 1990. $225.00. Three volumes.

Filter Manufacturers Council.

Filters and Filtration Handbook. T. Christopher Dickenson. Elsevier Science, 655 Ave. of the Americas New York, NY 10010. Phone: 888-437-4636 or (212)633-3730 Fax: (212)633-3680 E-mail: usinfo@elsevier.com • URL: http://www.elsevier.com • 1997. $243.00. Fourth edition.

Filtration News. Eagle Publications, Inc., 42400 Grand River Ave., Suite 103 Novi, MI 48375-2572. Phone: 800-783-3491 or (810)347-3490 Fax: (810)347-3492 Bimonthly. Controlled circulation. Emphasis is on new filtration products for industrial use.

Finance and Development. International Monetary Fund, Publication Services, 700 19th St., N.W., Suite 12-607 Washington, DC 20431-0001. Phone: (202)623-7430 Fax: (202)623-7201 URL: http://www.imf.org • Quarterly. Free. Edition available in English, French and Spanish.

Finance Companies. U. S. Federal Reserve System, Board of Governors, Publications Services, MS-127 Washington, DC 20551. Phone: (202)452-3244 Fax: (202)728-5886 URL: http://www.federalreserve.gov • Monthly. $5.00 per year. (Federal Reserve Statistical Release, G.20.)

Finance for the Nonfinancial Manager. Herbert T. Spiro. John Wiley and Sons, Inc., 605 Third Ave. New York, NY 10158-0012. Phone: 800-225-5945 or (212)850-6000 Fax: (212)850-6088 E-mail: info@wiley.com • URL: http://www.wiley.com • 1996. $39.95. Fourth edition.

Financial Accounting Foundation.

Financial Accounting Series. Financial Accounting Standards Board, P.O. Box 5116 Norwalk, CT 06856-5116. Phone: (203)847-0700 Fax: (203)849-9714 URL: http://www.fasb.org • Price on application

Financial Accounting Standards: Explanation and Analysis. CCH, Inc., 4025 W. Peterson Ave. Chicago, IL 60646-6085. Phone: 800-248-3248 or (773)583-8500 Fax: 800-224-8299 or (773)866-3608 URL: http://www.cch.com • Annual.

Financial Analysts Journal. Association for Investment Management and Research, P.O. Box 3668 Charlottesville, VA 22903-0668. Phone: 800-247-8132 or (804)951-5442 Fax: (804)951-5370 E-mail: info@aimr.org • URL: http://www.aimr.org • Bimonthly. $175.00 per year.

Financial and Accounting Guide for Not-for-Profit Organizations, Cumulative Supplement. Malvern J. Gross and others. John Wiley and Sons, Inc., 605 Third Ave. New York, NY 10158-0012. Phone: 800-225-5945 or (212)850-6000 Fax: (212)850-6088 E-mail: info@wiley.com • URL: http://www.wiley.com • 2000. $145.00. Sixth edition. Covers key concepts, financial statement preparation, accounting guidelines, and financial control. Includes tax laws and forms.

Financial and Estate Planning: Analysis, Strategies and Checklists. CCH, Inc., 4025 W. Peterson Ave. Chicago, IL 60646-6085. Phone: 800-248-3248 or (773)583-8500 Fax: 800-224-8299 URL: http://www.cch.com • Looseleaf services. $200.00 per year.

Financial and Operating Results of Department and Specialty Stores. National Retail Federation. John Wiley and Sons, Inc., 605 Third Ave. New York, NY 10158-0012. Phone: 800-225-5945 or (212)850-6000 Fax: (212)850-6088 E-mail: info@wiley.com • URL: http://www.wiley.com • Annual. Members, $80.00; non-members, $100.00.

Financial Counseling and Planning. Association for Financial Counseling and Planning Education, 1787 Neil Ave., C/O Sherman Hanna, Consumer and Textile Science Dept., Ohio State University Columbus, OH 43210-1295. Phone: (614)292-4584 Fax: (614)292-7536 E-mail: hanna.1@osu.edu • URL: http://www.hec.ohio-state.edu • Semiannual. Members, $60. per year; institutions, $100.00 per year; libraries, $60.00 per year. Disseminates scholarly research relating to finacial planning and counseling .

The Financial Elite: Database of Financial Services Companies. Donnelley Marketing, 5711 S. 86th Circle Omaha, NE 68127. Phone: (402)537-7788 Fax: (402)537-7785 URL: http://www.donnelleymarketing.com • Quarterly. Price on application. Formerly compiled by Database America. Provides current information on CD-ROM for 500,000 major U. S. companies offering financial services. Data for each firm includes year started, type of financial service, annual revenues, name of top executive, and number of employees.

Financial Executive. Financial Executives Institute, P.O. Box 1938 Morristown, NJ 07962-1938. Phone: 800-336-0773 or (973)898-4624 Fax: (973)538-6144 URL: http://www.fei.org/ • Bimonthly. $45.00 per year. Published for corporate financial officers and managers.

Financial Executives Institute.

Financial Executives Research Foundation.

Financial Flows and the Developing Countries. World Bank, The Office of the Publisher, 1818 H St., N. W. Washington, DC 20433. Phone: (202)477-1234 Fax: (202)477-6391 E-mail: books@worldbank.org • URL: http://www.worldbank.org • Quarterly. $150.00 per year. Concerned mainly with debt, capital markets, and foreign direct investment. Includes statistical tables.

Financial History: Chronicling the History of America's Capital Markets. Museum of American Financial History, 26 Broadway, Room 200 New York, NY 10004-1763. Phone: (212)908-4695 Fax: (212)908-4601 E-mail: krichard@financialhistory.org • URL: http://www.financialhistory.org • Quarterly. Membership. Contains articles on early stock and bond markets and trading in the U. S., with photographs and other illustrations. Current trading in rare and unusual, obsolete stock and bond certificates is featured. Formerly *Friends or Financial History*.

Financial Institutions. Available from U. S. Government Printing Office, Washington, DC 20402. Phone: (202)512-1800 Fax: (202)512-2250 E-mail: gpoaccess@gpo.gov • URL: http://www.access.gpo.gov • Annual. Free. Lists government publications. Formerly *Banks and Banking*. GPO Subject Bibliography No. 128.

Financial Institutions and Markets. Robert W. Kolb and Ricardo J. Rodriguez. Blackwell Publishers, 350 Main St., 6th Fl. Malden, MA 02148-5018. Phone: 800-216-2522 or (781)388-8200 Fax: (781)388-8210 E-mail: books@blackwellpub.com • URL: http://www.blackwellpub.com • 1996. $77.95. Contains 40 articles (chapters) by various authors on U. S. financial markets and other topics. Includes separate chapters on the International Monetary Fund, inflation, monetary policy, the national debt, bank failures, derivatives, stock prices, initial public offerings, government bonds, pensions, foreign exchange, international markets, and other subjects.

Financial Institutions Center., University of Florida, College of Business Administration, 327 Business Bldg. Gainesville, FL 32611. Phone: (352)392-2610 Studies monetary policy and the regulation of financial institutions.

Financial Institutions, Markets and Money. David S. Kidwell and others. Dryden Press, 6277 Sea Harbor Dr. Orlando, FL 32887. Phone: 800-782-4479 or 800-544-6678 Fax: (817)334-0878 1993. $56.00. Fifth edition.

Financial Management Association International., College of Business Administration, University of South Florida Tampa, FL 33620-5500. Phone: (813)974-2084 Fax: (813)974-3318 E-mail: fma@coba.usf.edu • URL: http://www.fma.org • Members are corporate financial officers and professors of financial management.

Financial Management Association: Membership/Professional Directory. Financial Management Association, University of South Florida, School of Business Tampa, FL 33620-5500. Phone: (813)974-2084 Fax: (813)974-3318 E-mail: fma@coba.usf.edu • URL: http://www.fma.org • Annual. Membership. Lists 4,800 corporate financial officers and professors of financial management.

Financial Management for Pharmacists: A Decision-Making Approach. Norman V. Carroll. Lippincott Williams & Wilkins, 530 Walnut St. Philadelphia, PA 29106-3780. Phone: 800-638-3030 or (215)521-8300 Fax: (215)521-8902 E-mail: custserv@lww.com • URL: http://www.lww.com • 1997. $39.00. Second edition.

Financial Management Handbook. Philip Vale. Ashgate Publishing Co., Old Post Rd. Brookfield, VT 05036. Phone: 800-535-9544 or (802)276-3162 Fax: (802)276-3837 E-mail: info@ashgate.com • URL: http://www.ashgate.com • 1988. $93.95. Third edition.

Financial Management: How to Make a Go of Your Business. Available from U. S. Government Printing Office, Washington, DC 20402. Phone: (202)512-1800 Fax: (202)512-2250 E-mail: gpoaccess@gpo.gov • URL: http://www.accessgpo.gov • 1986. $3.50. Published by U. S. Small Business Administration. (Small Business Management Series, No. 44.)

Financial Management in Agriculture. Peter Barry and others. Interstate Publishers, Inc., P.O. Box 50 Danville, IL 61834-0050. Phone: 800-843-4774 or (217)446-0500 Fax: (217)446-9706 E-mail: info-ipp@ippinc.com • URL: http://www/ippinc.com • 2000. $66.25. Sixth edition.

The Financial Management of Hospitals. Howard J. Berman and others. Health Administration Press, One N. Franklin, Suite 1700 Chicago, IL 60106-3491. Phone: (312)424-2800 Fax: (312)424-0014 URL: http://www.ache.org/hap.html • 1998. $52.00.

Financial Management of Sport-Related Organizations. Terry Haggerty and Garth Paton. Stipes Publishing L.L.C., P.O. Box 526 Champaign, IL 61820. Phone: (217)356-8391 Fax: (217)356-5753 E-mail: stipes@soltec.com • 1984. $4.80. (Sport and Physical Education Management Series).

Financial Management Strategies for Arts Organization. Robert P. Gallo and Frederick J. Turk. Americans for the Arts, One E. 53rd St. New York, NY 10022-4201. Phone: 800-321-4510 or (212)223-2787 Fax: (212)753-1325 E-mail: books@artsusa.org • URL: http://www.artsusa.org • 1984. $16.95.

Financial Management Techniques for Small Business. Art R. DeThomas. PSI Research, P.O. Box 3727 Central Point, OR 97502-0032. Phone: 800-228-2275 or (541)479-9464 Fax: (541)476-1479 E-mail: info@psi-research.com • URL: http://www.psiresearch.com • 1991. $19.95. (Successful Business Library Series).

Financial Management: Theory and Practice. Eugene F. Brigham. Harcourt Trade Publishers, 525 B St., Suite 1900 San Diego, CA 92101-4495. Phone: 800-782-4479 or (619)231-6616 Fax: (817)334-0878 1998. $106.00. Nineth edition.

Financial Managers Society., 230 W. Monroe, Ste. 2205 Chicago, IL 60606. Phone: 800-275-4367 or (312)578-1300 Fax: (312)578-1308 E-mail: lauriek@fmsinc.org • URL: http://www.fmsinc.org • Members are financial managers of financial institutions.

Financial Market Trends. Organization for Economic Cooperation and Development, OECD Washington Center, 2001 L St., N. W., Suite 650 Washington, DC 20036-4922. Phone: 800-456-6323 or (202)785-6323 Fax: (202)785-0350 E-mail: washington.contact@oecd.org • URL: http://www.oecd.org • Three times a year. $100.00 per year. Provides analysis of developments and trends in international and national capital markets. Includes charts and graphs on interest rates, exchange rates, stock market indexes, bank stock indexes, trading volumes, and loans outstanding. Data from OECD countries includes international direct investment, bank profitability, institutional investment, and privatization.

Financial Markets and Institutions. Jeff Madura. South-Western College Publishing Co., 5101 Madison Ave. Cincinnati, OH 45227. Phone: 800-543-0487 or (513)527-1989 Fax: (513)527-6137 URL: http://

www.thomson.com • 2000. $91.95. Fifth edition. (SWC-Economics Series).

Financial Markets, Institutions, and Instruments. New York University, Salomon Center. Blackwell Publishers, 350 Main St., 6th Fl. Malden, MA 02148-5018. Phone: 800-216-2522 or (781)388-8200 Fax: (781)388-8232 E-mail: subscript@blackwellpub.com • URL: http://www.blackwellpub.com • Five times a year. $219.00 per year. Edited to "bridge the gap between the academic and professional finance communities." Special fifth issue each year provides surveys of developments in four areas: money and banking, derivative securities, corporate finance, and fixed-income securities.

Financial Options: From Theory to Practice. Stephen Figlewski. McGraw-Hill Professional, 1221 Ave. of the Americas New York, NY 10020. Phone: 800-722-4726 or (212)904-2000 Fax: (212)904-2072 E-mail: customer.serivce@mcgraw-hill.com • URL: http://www.mcgraw-hill.com • 1992. $29.95. Includes options on financial futures.

Financial Planning and Financial Planning Ideas. Prentice Hall, 240 Frisch Court Paramus, NJ 07652-5240. Phone: 800-947-7700 or (201)909-6200 Fax: 800-445-6991 or (201)909-6361 URL: http://www.prenhall.com • Two looseleaf volumes. Periodic supplementation. Price on application.

Financial Planning Applications. William J. Ruckstuhl. Maple-Vail Book, The Manufacturing Group, P.O. Box 2695 York, PA 17405. Phone: (717)764-5911 Fax: (717)764-4702 URL: http://www.maple-vail.com • 2000. $68.00. 16th edition. Emphasis on annuities and life insurance. (Huebner School Series.)

Financial Planning for Libraries. Ann E. Prentice. Scarecrow Press, 4720 Boston Way Lanham, MD 20706-4310. Phone: 800-462-6420 or (301)459-3366 Fax: 800-338-4550 or (301)459-1705 E-mail: orders@scarecrowpress.com • URL: http://www.scarecrowpress.com • 1996. $39.95. Second edition. Includes examples of budgets for libraries. (Library Administration Series, No. 12).

Financial Planning for Older Clients. James E. Pearman. CCH, Inc., 4025 West Peterson Ave. Chicago, IL 60646-6085. Phone: 800-248-3248 or (773)866-6000 Fax: 800-224-8299 or (773)866-3608 E-mail: cust_serv@cch.com • URL: http://www.cch.com • 2000. $49.00. Covers income sources, social security, Medicare, Medicaid, investment planning, estate planning, and other retirement-related topics. Edited for accountants, attorneys, and other financial advisors.

Financial Planning for the Utterly Confused. Joel Lerner. McGraw-Hill, 1221 Ave. of the Americas New York, NY 10020. Phone: 800-722-4726 or (212)904-2000 Fax: (212)904-2072 E-mail: customer.service@mcgraw-hill.com • URL: http://www.mcgraw-hill.com • 1998. $12.00. Fifth edition. Covers annuities, certificates of deposit, bonds, mutual funds, insurance, home ownership, retirement, social security, wills, etc.

Financial Planning: The Magazine for Financial Service Professionals. Securities Data Publishing, 40 West 57th St. New York, NY 10019. Phone: 800-455-5844 or (212)765-5311 Fax: (212)956-0112 E-mail: sdp@tfn.com • URL: http://www.sdponline.com • Monthly. $79.00 per year. Edited for independent financial planners and insurance agents. Covers retirement planning, estate planning, tax planning, and insurance, including long-term healthcare considerations. Special features include a Retirement Planning Issue, Mutual Fund Performance Survey, and Variable Life and Annuity Survey. (Securities Data Publishing is a unit of Thomson Financial.)

The Financial Post: Canadian's Business Voice. Financial Post Datagroup, 333 King St., E. Toronto, ON, Canada M5A 4N2. Phone: 800-387-9011 Fax: (416)350-6501 E-mail: letters@fpeditor.com • URL: http://www.canoe.ca/fp/home.html • Daily. $234.00 per year. Provides Canadian business, economic, financial, and investment news. Features extensive price quotes from all major Canadian markets: stocks, bonds, mutual funds, commodities, and currencies. Supplement available: *Financial Post 500*. Includes annual supplement.

Financial Post Directory of Directors. Financial Post Datagroup, 333 King St., E. Toronto, ON, Canada M5A 4N2. Phone: 800-387-9011 or (416)350-6116 Fax: (416)350-6501 E-mail: fpdg@fpdata.finpost.com • Annual. $159.95. Provides brief biographical information on 16,000 directors and key officers of Canadian companies who are also Canadian residents.

Financial Post Markets Canadian Demographics: Complete Demographics for Canadian Urban Markets. Financial Post Datagroup, 333 King St., E. Toronto, ON, Canada M5A 4N2. Phone: 800-387-9011 or (416)350-6477 Fax: (416)350-6501 E-mail: fpdg@fppdata.finpost.com • Annual. $145.00 Provides demographic and economic profiles of Canadian urban consumer regions with populations of 10,000 or more. Includes current data and projections for population, retail sales, personal income, and other market characteristics. CD-ROM available. Formerly *Canadian Markets*.

The Financial Post (Web site). National Post Online (Hollinger/CanWest)Phone: (244)383-2300 Fax: (416)383-2443 URL: http://www.nationalpost.com/financialpost/ • Provides a broad range of Canadian business news online, with daily updates. Includes news, opinion, and special reports, as well as "Investing," "Money Rates," "Market Watch," and "Daily Mutual Funds." Allows advanced searching (Boolean operators), with links to various other sites. Fees: Free.

Financial Ratios and Trend Analysis of CCAC Accredited Communities. American Association of Homes and Services for the Aging, 901 E St., N. W., Suite 500 Washington, DC 20004-2037. Phone: 800-508-9442 or (202)783-2242 Fax: (202)783-2255 E-mail: info@aahsa.org • URL: http://www.aahsa.org • 1997. $115.00. A joint project of AAHSA, Ziegler Securities, KPMG Peat Marwick LLP, and the Continuing Care Accreditation Commission (CCAC). Provides analysis of 12 frequently used ratios applied to audited financial statements from 171 accredited retirement communities.

Financial Recordkeeping for Small Stores. Available from U. S. Government Printing Office, Washington, DC 20402. Phone: (202)512-1800 Fax: (202)512-2250 E-mail: gpoaccess@gpo.gov • URL: http://www.accessgpo.gov • 1986. Presents a basic record keeping system for the small retail owner-manager who does not have a trained bookkeeper. Produced by the Office of Business Development, Small Business Administration. (Small Business Management Series, 32.)

Financial Report of the United States Government. Available from U. S. Government Printing Office, Washington, DC 20402. Phone: (202)512-1800 Fax: (202)512-2250 E-mail: gpoaccess@gpo.gov • URL: http://www.access.gpo.gov • Annual. $14.00. Issued by the U. S. Treasury Department (http://www.treas.gov). Presents information about the financial condition and operations of the federal government. Program accounting systems of various government agencies provide data for the report.

Financial Reporting: An Accounting Revolution. William H. Beaver. Prentice Hall, 240 Frisch Court Paramus, NJ 07652-5240. Phone: 800-947-7700 or (201)909-6200 Fax: 800-445-6991 or (201)909-6361 URL: http://www.prenhall.com • 1997. $52.00. Third edition. (Contemporary Topics in Accounting Series).

Financial Sentinel: Your Beacon to the World of Investing. Gulf Atlantic Publishing, Inc., 1947 Lee Rd. Winter Park, FL 32789-1834. Phone: (407)628-5700 Fax: (407)628-0807 Monthly. $29.95 per year. Provides "The only complete listing of all OTC Bulletin Board stocks traded, with all issues listed on the Nasdaq SmallCap Market, the Toronto, and Vancouver Stock Exchanges." Also includes investment advice and recommendations of small capitalization stocks.

Financial Service Online. Faulkner & Gray, Inc., 300 S. Wacker Drive, 18th Floor Chicago, IL 60606. Phone: (312)913-1334 Fax: (312)913-1369 URL: http://www.faulknergray.com • Monthly. $95.00 per year. Covers the operation and management of interactive financial services to consumers in their homes for banking, investments, and bill-paying.

Financial Services Marketing: Finding, Keeping, and Profiting From the Right Customers. American Banker, One State St. Plaza New York, NY 10004. Phone: 800-362-3806 or (212)803-8345 Fax: (212)292-5217 URL: http://www.americanbanker.com • Bimonthly. Price on application. Covers marketing for a variety of financial institutions, including banks, investment companies, securities dealers, and credit unions.

Financial Services Round Table.

Financial Shenanigans: How to Detect Accounting Gimmicks and Fraud in Financial Reports. Howard M. Schilit. McGraw-Hill, 1221 Ave. of the Americas New York, NY 10020. Phone: 800-722-4726 or (212)904-2000 Fax: (212)904-2072 E-mail: customer.service@mcgraw-hill.com • URL: http://www.mcgraw-hill.com • 1993. $22.95. Tells how to interpret the footnotes and fine print in corporate annual and other reports.

Financial Statement Analysis: A Practitioner's Guide. McGraw-Hill, 1221 Ave. of the Americas New York, NY 10020. Phone: 800-722-4726 or (212)904-2000 Fax: (212)904-2072 E-mail: customer.service@mcgraw-hill.com • URL: http://www.mcgraw-hill.com • 1998. $60.00. Sixth edition.

Financial Statement Analysis: The Investor's Self Study Guide to Interpreting and Analyzing. Charles J. Woelfel. McGraw-Hill Professional, 1221 Ave. of the Americas New York, NY 10020. Phone: 800-722-4726 or (212)904-2000 Fax: (212)904-2072 E-mail: customer.service@mcgraw-hill.com • URL: http://www.mcgraw-hill.com • 1993. $22.95. Revised edition.

Financial Statement Analysis: Theory, Application and Interpretation. Leopold A. Bernstein and John J Wild. McGraw-Hill, 1221 Ave. of the Americas New York, NY 10020. Phone: 800-722-4726 or (212)904-2000 Fax: (212)904-2072 E-mail: customer.service@mcgraw-hill.com • URL: http://www.mcgraw-hill.com • 1997. $62.36. Sixth edition.

Financial Statistics of Major Publicly Owned Electric Utilities in the U.S. U.S. Energy Information Administration, U.S. Department of Energy. Available from U.S. Government Printing Office, Washington, DC 20402. Phone: (202)512-1800 Fax: (202)512-2250 E-mail: gpoaccess@gpo.gov • URL: http://www.access.gpo.gov • Annual. $45.00.

Financial Times Currency Forecaster: Consensus Forecasts of the Worldwide Currency and Economic Outlook. Capitol Publications, Inc., 1101 King St., Suite 110 Alexandria, VA 22314. Phone: (703)548-3800 Fax: (703)648-2136 Monthly. $695.00 per year. Newsletter. Provides forecasts of foreign currency exchange rates and economic conditions. Supplement available: *Mid-Month Global Financial Report*.

Financial Times Energy Yearbook: Mining 2000. Available from The Gale Group, 27500 Drake Rd. Farmington Hills, MI 48331-3535. Phone: 800-877-GALE or (248)699-GALE Fax: 800-414-5043 or (248)699-8069 E-mail: galeord@galegroup.com • URL: http://www.galegroup.com • Annual. $320.00. Published by Financial Times Energy. Provides production and financial details for more than 800 major mining companies worldwide. Includes coverage of reserves, operations, properties, and growth rates. Formerly *Financial Times International Yearbook: Mining*.

Financial Times Energy Yearbook: Oil & Gas: 2000. Available from The Gale Group, 27500 Drake Rd. Farmington Hills, MI 48331-3535. Phone: 800-877-GALE or (248)699-GALE Fax: 800-414-5043 or (248)699-8069 E-mail: galeord@galegroup.com • URL: http://www.galegroup.com • Annual. $320.00. Published by Financial Times Energy. Provides production and financial details for more than 800 major oil and gas companies worldwide. Includes coverage of reserves, operations, properties, and growth rates. Formerly *Financial Times Oil & Gas Yearbook*.

Financial Times Global Investors' Digest. Capitol Publications, Inc., 1101 King St., Suite 110 Alexandria, VA 22314. Phone: 800-655-5597 or (703)548-3800 Fax: (703)648-2136 Monthly. $695.00 per year. Newsletter. Contains information, forecasts, data, and analysis relating to international financial markets, including emerging markets. Supplement available *Mid-Month Global Financial Report*. Formerly *Global Investors' Digest*.

Financial Times ÎLondonl. Available from FT Publications, Inc., 14 E. 60th St. New York, NY 10022. Phone: 800-628-8088 or (212)752-4500 Fax: (212)308-2397 E-mail: circulation@ft.com • URL: http://www.ft.com • Daily, except Sunday. $184.00 per year. An international business and financial newspaper, featuring news from London, Paris, Frankfurt, New York, and Tokyo. Includes worldwide stock and bond market data, commodity market data, and monetary/currency exchange information.

Financial Times: Where Information Becomes Intelligence. FT GroupPhone: (212)752-4500 Fax: (212)688-8229 URL: http://www.ft.com • Web site provides extensive data and information relating to international business and finance, with daily updates. Includes Markets Today, Company News, Economic Indicators, Equities, Currencies, Capital Markets, Euro Prices, etc. Fees: Free (registration required).

Financial Times World Insurance Yearbook. Available from The Gale Group, 27500 Drake Rd. Farmington Hills, MI 48331-3535. Phone: 800-877-GALE or (248)699-GALE Fax: 800-414-5043 or (248)699-8069 E-mail: galeord@galegroup.com • URL: http://www.galegroup.com • 1991. $196.00. Published by St. James Press. Provides information on over 1,150 insurance companies in many countries of the world. Includes a summary of recent developments in the insurance industry.

Financial Trader. Miller Freeman, Inc., 600 Harrison St. San Francisco, CA 94107. Phone: 800-227-4675 or (415)905-2200 Fax: (415)905-2233 URL: http://www.mfi.com • 11 times a year. $160.00 per year. Edited for professional traders. Covers fixed income securities, emerging markets, derivatives, options, futures, and equities.

Financial Women International.

Financial Women's Association of New York., 215 Park Ave. S., Suite 1713 New York, NY 10003. Phone: (212)533-2141 Fax: (212)982-3008 E-mail: info@fwa.org • URL: http://www.fwa.org • Members are professional women in finance.

Financial Yellow Book: Who's Who at the Leading U. S. Financial Institutions. Leadership Directories, Inc., 104 Fifth Ave., 2nd Fl. New York, NY 10011. Phone: (212)627-4140 Fax: (212)645-0931 E-mail: info@leadershipdirectories.com • URL: http://www.leadershipdirectories.com • Semiannual. $235.00. Gives the names and titles of over 31,000 key executives in financial institutions. Includes the areas of banking, investment, money management, and insurance. Five indexes are provided: institution, executive name, geographic by state, financial service segment, and parent company.

Financing Graduate School: How to Get Money for Your Master's or Ph.D. Patricia McWade. Peterson's, 202 Carnegie

Center Princeton, NJ 08540. Phone: 800-338-3282 E-mail: info@petersons.com • URL: http://www.petersons.com • 1996. $16.95. Second revised edition. Discusses the practical aspects of various types of financial aid for graduate students. Includes bibliographic and directory information.

Financing the Corporation. Richard A. Booth. West Group, 610 Opperman Dr. Eagan, MN 55123. Phone: 800-328-4880 or (651)687-7000 Fax: 800-213-2323 or (651)687-5827 URL: http://www.westgroup.com • $110.00. Looseleaf service. Periodic supplementation. Covers a wide variety of corporate finance legal topics, from initial capital structure to public sale of securities.

Find It Online: The Complete Guide to Online Research. Alan M. Schlein and others. National Book Network, 15200 NBN Way Blue Ridge Summit, PA 17214. Phone: 800-929-3811 or (717)794-3800 Fax: 800-338-4550 or (717)462-6420 E-mail: brb@brbpub.com • URL: http://www.brbpub.com • 1998. $19.95. Presents the general principles of online searching for information about people, phone numbers, public records, news, business, investments, etc. Covers both free and fee-based sources. (BRB Publications.)

FIND/SVP Market Research Reports. Kalorama Information, 641 Ave. of the Americas, Third Floor New York, NY 10011. Phone: 800-298-5699 or (212)807-2629 Fax: (212)807-2716 E-mail: order@marketresearch.com • URL: http://www.marketresearch.com • Provides online full text of market research reports produced by FIND/SVP, Packaged Facts, Specialists in Business Information and others. Contains market data for a wide variety of industries, products, and services, including market size, forecasts, trends, structure, and opportunities. Inquire as to online cost and availability.

FINDEX. Kalorama Information, 641 Ave. of the Americas, Third Floor New York, NY 10011-2014. Phone: 800-298-5699 or (212)807-2629 Fax: (212)807-2676 E-mail: order@findexonline.com • URL: http://www.findexonline.com • Provides online annotations of market research reports and related publications from about 1,000 publishers. Time period is 1972 to date, with quarterly updates. (Formerly produced by Cambridge Information Group.) Inquire as to online cost and availability.

FINDEX Icd-roml. Available from SilverPlatter Information, Inc., 100 River Ridge Rd. Norwood, MA 02062-5026. Phone: 800-343-0064 or (781)769-2599 Fax: (781)769-8763 Quarterly. $995.00 per year. Produced by Kalorama Information. Formerly produced by Cambridge Scientific Abstracts. Serves as the CD-ROM version of *Findex: The Worldwide Directory of Market Research Reports, Studies, and Surveys*.

Findex: The Worldwide Directory of Market Research Reports, Studies, and Surveys. MarketResearch.com, 641 Ave. of the Americas, Third Floor New York, NY 10011-2014. Phone: 800-298-5699 or (212)807-2629 Fax: (212)807-2676 E-mail: order@marketresearch.com • URL: http://www.marketresearch.com • Annual. $400.00. Provides brief annotations of market research reports and related publications from about 1,000 publishers, arranged by topic. Back of book includes Report Titles by Publisher, Publishers/Distributors Directory, Subject Index, Geography Index, and Company Index. (Formerly published by Cambridge Information Group.)

Finding Business Research on the Web: A Guide to the Web's Most Valuable Sites. MarketResearch.com, 641 Ave. of the Americas, 3rd Fl. New York, NY 10011. Phone: 800-298-5699 or (212)807-2629 Fax: (212)807-2716 E-mail: order@marketresearch.com • URL: http://www.marketresearch.com • Looseleaf. $175.00. Includes detailed rating charts. Contains profiles of the "100 best web sites."

Finding It on the Internet: The Internet Navigator's Guide to Search Tools and Techniques. Paul Gilster. John Wiley and Sons, Inc., 605 Third Ave. New York, NY 10158-0012. Phone: 800-225-5945 or (212)850-6000 Fax: (212)850-6088 E-mail: info@wiley.com • URL: http://www.wiley.com • 1996. $24.95. Second expanded revised edition. A basic guide to efficient use of the World Wide Web, search engines, e-mail, hypertext, and the Internet in general. Includes such programs or systems as Gopher, Archie, Veronica, and Jughead, with emphasis on information searching.

Finding Market Research on the Web: Best Practices of Professional Researchers. Robert I. Berkman. MarketResearch.com, 641 Ave. of the Americas, Third Floor New York, NY 10011. Phone: 800-298-5699 or (212)807-2629 Fax: (212)807-2716 E-mail: order@marketresearch.com • URL: http://www.marketresearch.com • 1999. $235.00. Provides tips and techniques for locating useful market research data through the Internet.

Finding Statistics Online: How to Locate the Elusive Numbers You Need. Paula Berinstein. Information Today, Inc., 143 Old Marlton Pike Medford, NJ 08055-8750. Phone: 800-300-9868 or (609)654-6266 Fax: (609)654-4309 E-mail: custserv@infotoday.com • URL: http://www.infotoday.com • 1998. $29.95. Provides advice on efficient searching when looking for statistical data on the World Wide Web or from commercial online services and database producers. (CyberAge Books.)

FindLaw: Internet Legal Resources. FindLaw, Inc.Phone: (650)322-8430 E-mail: info@findlaw.com • URL: http://www.findlaw.com • Web site provides a wide variety of information and links relating to laws, law schools, professional development, lawyers, the U. S. Supreme Court, consultants (experts), law reviews, legal news, etc. Online searching is provided. Fees: Free.

Fine Homebuilding. Taunton Press, Inc., 63 Main St. Newtown, CT 06470-5506. Phone: 800-888-8286 or (203)426-8171 Fax: (203)270-6751 URL: http://www.taunton.com/ • Bimonthly $36.00. Special interest magazine written by builders for builders - professional and homeowners.

Finishers' Management. Publication Management, Inc., 4350 DiPaolo Center, Dearlove Rd. Glenview, IL 60025. Phone: (847)699-1700 Fax: (847)699-1703 10 times a year. $35.00 per year.

Fire and Casualty Insurance Law Reports. CCH, Inc., 4025 W. Peterson Ave. Chicago, IL 60646-6085. Phone: 800-248-3248 or (773)583-8500 Fax: 800-224-8299 URL: http://www.cch.com • $870.00 per year. Looseleaf service. Semimonthly updates.

Fire and Materials. Available from John Wiley and Sons, Inc., Journals Div., 605 Third Ave. New York, NY 10158-0012. Phone: 800-225-5945 or (212)850-6000 Fax: (212)850-6088 E-mail: info@wiley.com • URL: http://www.wiley.com • Bimonthly. $495.00 per year. Published in England by John Wiley & Sons Ltd. Provides international coverage of subject matter.

Fire, Casualty and Surety Bulletin. The National Underwriter Co., 505 Gest St. Cincinnati, OH 45203-1716. Phone: 800-543-0874 or (513)721-2140 Fax: (513)721-0126 URL: http://www.nauo.com • Monthly. $420.00 per year. Five base volumes. Monthly updates.

Fire Chief: Administration, Training, Operations. Intertec Publishing Corp., 6151 Powers Ferry Rd., N.W. Atlanta, GA 30339-2941. Phone: 800-621-9907 or (770)955-2500 Fax: 800-633-6219 or (770)955-0400 E-mail: subs@intertec.com • URL: http://www.intertec.com • Monthly. $54.00 per year.

Fire Engineering: The Journal of Fire Suppression and Protection. PennWell Corp., Industrial Div., 1421 S. Sheridan Rd. Tulsa, OK 74112. Phone: 800-331-4463 or (918)835-3161 Fax: (918)831-9295 E-mail: webmaster@pennwell.com • URL: http://www.penwell.com • Monthly. $28.50 per year.

Fire International: The Journal of the World's Fire Protection Services. DMG World Media, Queensway House, Two Queensway Redhill, Surrey RH1 1QS 44, England. Phone: 44 1737 768611 Fax: 44 1737 855470 10 times a year. $158.00 per year. Text in English. Summaries in French and German.

Fire Protection Handbook. National Fire Protection Association, P.O. Box 9101 Quincy, MA 02269-9101. Phone: 800-344-3555 or (617)770-3000 Fax: (617)770-0700 E-mail: custserv@nfpa.org • URL: http://www.nfpa.org • Irregular. Members, $112.50; non-members, $125.00.

Fire Technology: An International Journal of Fire Protection Research and Engineering. National Fire Protection Association, One Batterymarch Park Quincy, MA 02269. Phone: 800-344-3555 or (617)770-3000 Fax: (617)770-0700 E-mail: library@nfpa.org • URL: http://www.nfpa.org • Quarterly. $39.50 per year.

First DataBank Blue Book. Hearst Corp., 645 Stewart Ave. Garden City, NY 11530-4709. Phone: (212)969-7568 Fax: (212)969-7564 URL: http://www.hearstcorp.com • Annual. $65.00. List of manufacturers of prescription and over-the-counter drugs, sold in retail drug stores. Formerly *American Druggist Blue Book*.

The First Junk Bond: A Story of Corporate Boom and Bust. Harlan D. Platt. M. E. Sharpe, Inc., 80 Business Park Dr. Armonk, NY 10504. Phone: 800-541-6543 or (914)273-1800 Fax: (914)273-2106 E-mail: mesinfo@usa.net • URL: http://www.mesharpe.com/ • 1994. $76.95. Relates the development and history of Michael Milken's first low-quality bond issue at high interest rates. Includes a chapter, "What Have We Learned?"

First-Line Supervision. American Management Association Extension Institute, P.O. Box 1026 Saranac Lake, NY 12983-9957. Phone: 800-262-9699 or (518)891-1500 Fax: (518)891-0368 Looseleaf. $110.00. Self-study course. Emphasis is on practical explanations, examples, and problem solving. Quizzes and a case study are included.

The First-Time Sales Manager: A Survival Guide. Theodore Tyssen. Self-Counsel Press, Inc., 1704 N. State St. Bellingham, WA 98225. Phone: 877-877-6490 or (360)676-4530 Fax: (360)676-4530 E-mail: service@self-counsel.com • URL: http://www.self-counsel.com • 1994. $8.95. Provides basic information and advice for beginning sales managers. (Business Series).

FirstGov: Your First Click to the U. S. Government. General Services AdministrationPhone: (202)501-0705 E-mail: public.affairs@gsa.gov • URL: http://www.firstgov.gov • Free Web site provides extensive links to federal agencies covering a wide variety of topics, such as agriculture, business, consumer safety, education, the environment, government jobs, grants, health, social security, statistics sources, taxes, technology, travel, and world affairs. Also provides links to federal forms, including IRS tax forms. Searching is offered, both keyword and advanced.

FIS Online: The Preferred Source for Global Business and Financial Information. MergentPhone: 800-342-5647 or (212)413-7601 Fax: (212)413-7777 E-mail: fis@fisonline.com • URL: http://www.fisonline.com • Fee-based Web site provides detailed information on more than 10,000 publicly-owned corporations listed on the New York Stock Exchange, American Stock Exchange, NASDAQ, and U. S. regional exchanges. Searching is offered on eight financial variables and six text fields. Weekly updating. Fees: Rates on application. (Mergent is publisher of Moody's Manuals.)

FISA-Food Industry Suppliers Association.

Fisheries of the United States. Available from U. S. Government Printing Office, Washington, DC 20402. Phone: (202)512-1800 Fax: (202)512-2250 E-mail: gpoaccess@gpo.gov • URL: http://www.access.gpo.gov • Annual. $18.00. Issued by the National Marine Fisheries Service, National Oceanic and Atmospheric Administration, U. S. Department of Commerce.

Fishermen's News. Fishermen's News, Inc., Fishermen's Terminal, West Wall Bldg., Room 110 Seattle, WA 98119. Phone: (206)282-7545 Fax: (206)283-5123 Monthly. $15.00 per year.

Fitch IBCA Ratings Delivery Service. Fitch IBCA, Inc., One State Street Plaza New York, NY 10004. Phone: 800-753-4824 or (212)908-0500 Fax: (212)952-0150 URL: http://www.fitchibca.com • Provides online delivery of Fitch financial ratings in three sectors: "Corporate Finance" (corporate bonds, insurance companies), "Structured Finance" (asset-backed securities), and "U.S. Public Finance" (municipal bonds). Daily updates. Inquire as to online cost and availability.

Fitch Insights. Fitch Investors Service, Inc., One State Street Plaza New York, NY 10004. Phone: 800-753-4824 or (212)908-0500 Fax: (212)480-4435 Biweekly. $1,040.00 per year. Includes bond rating actions and explanation of actions. Provides commentary and Fitch's view of the financial markets.

Fitness Management. Leisure Publications, Inc., 4160 Wilshire Blvd. Los Angeles, CA 90010. Phone: (323)964-4800 Fax: (323)964-4837 E-mail: fitmgt@earthlink.net • URL: http://www.fitnessworld.com • Monthly. $24.00 per year. Published for owners and managers of physical fitness centers, both commercial and corporate.

Fitness Management Products and Services Source Guide. Leisure Publications, Inc., 4160 Wilshire Blvd. Los Angeles, CA 90010. Phone: (323)964-4800 Fax: (323)964-4840 E-mail: fitmgt@earthlink.net • URL: http://www.fitnessworld.com • Annual. $30.00. A directory of fitness equipment manufacturers and suppliers of services. Includes a glossary of terms related to the fitness industry and employee wellness programs.

Fitness Motivation Institute of America Association., 5221 Scotts Valley Dr. Scott Valley, CA 95066. Phone: 800-538-7790 or (408)439-9898 Fax: (408)439-9504 URL: http://www.fmia.com • Seeks to motivate, educate, and evaluate individuals in the area of physical fitness. Members are health and fitness professionals.

Fitzroy Dearborn International Directory of Venture Capital Funds. Jennifer Schellinger, editor. Fitzroy Dearborn Publishers, Inc., 919 N. Michigan Ave., Suite 760 Chicago, IL 60611. Phone: 800-850-8102 or (312)587-0131 Fax: (312)587-1049 E-mail: website@fitzroydearborn.com • URL: http://www.fitzroydearborn.com • 1998. $175.00. Third edition. Provides detailed information on more than 1,000 sources of venture capital, with articles on entrepreneurship.

The 500 Year Delta: What Happens After What Comes Next. Jim Taylor and others. HarperCollins Publishers, 10 E. 53rd St. New York, NY 10022-5299. Phone: 800-242-7737 or (212)207-7000 Fax: 800-822-4090 or (212)207-7145 URL: http://www.harpercollins.com • 1998. $14.00. Provides analysis of major corporate and political trends.

The Five Minute Interview: A New and Powerful Approach to Interviewing. Richard H. Beatty. John Wiley and Sons, Inc., 605 Third Ave. New York, NY 10158-0012. Phone: 800-526-5368 or (212)850-6000 Fax: (212)850-6088 E-mail: info@wiley.com • URL: http://www.wiley.com • 1997. $14.95. Second edition. Advice for job applicants.

Fixed Income Almanac: The Bond Investor's Compendium of Key Market, Product, and Performance Data. Livingston G. Douglas. McGraw-Hill Professional, 1221 Ave. of the Americas New York, NY 10020. Phone: 800-722-4726 or (212)904-2000 Fax: (212)904-2072 E-mail: customer.service@mcgraw-hill.com • URL: http://www.mcgraw-hill.com • 1993. $75.00. Presents 20 years of data in 350 graphs and charts. Covers bond market volatility, yield spreads, high-yield (junk) corporate bonds, default rates, and other items, such as Federal Reserve policy.

Fixed Income Analytics: State-of-the-Art Analysis and Valuation Modeling. Ravi E. Dattatreya, editor. McGraw-Hill

Professional, 1221 Ave. of the Americas New York, NY 10020-1095. Phone: 800-722-4726 or (212)904-2000 Fax: (212)904-2072 E-mail: customer.service@mcgraw-hill.com • URL: http://www.mcgraw-hill.com • 1991. $69.95. Discusses the yield curve, structure and value in corporate bonds, mortgage-backed securities, and other topics.

Fixed-Income Investment: Recent Research. Thomas S. Ho, editor. McGraw-Hill Professional, 1221 Ave. of the Americas New York, NY 10020-1095. Phone: 800-722-4726 or (212)904-2000 Fax: (212)904-2072 E-mail: customer.service@mcgraw-hill.com • URL: http://www.mcgraw-hill.com • 1994. $65.00. Discusses bond portfolio management, the yield curve, bond pricing methods, and related subjects.

Fixed Income Mathematics: Analytical and Statistical Techniques. Frank J. Fabozzi. McGraw-Hill Professional, 1221 Ave. of the Americas New York, NY 10020-1095. Phone: 800-722-4726 or (212)904-2000 Fax: (212)904-2072 E-mail: customer.service@mcgraw-hill.com • URL: http://www.mcgraw-hill.com • 1996. $60.00. Third edition. Covers the basics of fixed income analysis, as well as more advanced techniques used for complex securities.

The Flat Tax. Robert E. Hall and Alvin Rabushka. Hoover Institution Press, Stanford University Stanford, CA 94305-6010. Phone: 800-935-2882 or (650)723-3373 Fax: (650)723-8626 E-mail: digest@hoover.stanford.edu • URL: http://www.hoover.stanford.edu • 1995. $14.95. Second edition. A favorable view of a flat tax as a replacement for the graduated federal income tax.

Flavor and Extract Manufacturers Association of the United States.

Flavour and Fragrance Journal. John Wiley and Sons, Inc., Journals Div., 605 Third Ave. New York, NY 10158-0012. Phone: 800-225-5945 or (212)850-6000 Fax: (212)850-6088 E-mail: info@wiley.com • URL: http://www.wiley.com • Bimonthly. Institutions, $905.00 per year.

Flawless Consulting: A Guide to Getting Your Expertise Used. Peter Block. Jossey-Bass, Inc., Publishers, 350 Sansome St. San Francisco, CA 94104-1342. Phone: 888-378-2537 or (415)433-1740 Fax: (415)433-0499 E-mail: webperson@jbp.com • URL: http://www.josseybass.com • 1999. $39.95. Second edition.

Fleet Owner. Intertec Publishing Corp., P.O. Box 4949 Stamford, CT 06907-0949. Phone: 800-400-5945 or (203)358-9900 Fax: (203)358-5831 E-mail: subs@intertec.com • URL: http://www.fleetowner.com • Monthly. $45.00 per year.

Fleet Owner Specs and Buyers' Directory. Intertec Publishing Corp., P.O. Box 4949 Stamford, CT 06907-0949. Phone: 800-400-5945 or (203)358-9900 Fax: (203)358-5831 E-mail: subs@intertec.com • URL: http://www.fleetowner.com • Annual. $5.00. Lists of manufacturers of equipment and materials used in the operation, management, and maintenance of truck and bus fleets.

Fleet Reserve Association.

Flesh Peddlers and Warm Bodies: The Temporary Help Industry and Its Workers. Robert E. Parker. Rutgers University Press, 100 Joyce Kilmer Ave. Piscataway, NJ 08854-8099. Phone: 800-446-9323 or (732)445-7762 Fax: 888-471-9014 or (732)445-7039 E-mail: bacher@rci.rutgers.edu • URL: http://www.rutgerspress.rutgers.edu • 1994. $40.00. A critical view of temporary work. (Arnold and Caroline Rose Monograph Series of the American Sociological Association).

Fletcher Corporation Forms Annotated, 1980-1990. West Group, 610 Opperman Dr. Eagan, MN 55123. Phone: 800-328-4880 or (651)687-7000 Fax: 800-213-2323 or (651)687-5827 URL: http://www.westgroup.com • $995.00. 12th edition. 21 volumes.

Fletcher Corporation Law Adviser. West Group, 610 Opperman Dr. Eagan, MN 55123. Phone: 800-328-4880 or (651)687-7000 Fax: 800-213-2323 or (651)687-5827 URL: http://www.westgroup.com • Monthly. $250.00 per year. Newsletter.

Flexible Packaging Association.

Flight International. Reed Business Information, Quadrant House, The Quadrant, Brighton Rd. Sutton SM2 5AS Surrey, England. Phone: 44 1816 523500 Fax: 44 1816 528975 E-mail: rbp.subscriptions@rbi.co.uk • URL: http://www.reedbusiness.com • Weekly. $170.00 per year. Technical aerospace coverage.

Flight Mechanics Laboratory.

Flight Research Laboratory. University of Kansas

Flight Safety Foundation.

Floor Covering News. Roel Product Inc., 550 Old Country Rd., Suite 204 Hicksville, NY 11801-4116. Phone: (516)932-7860 URL: http://www.floorcoveringnews.com • Biweekly. $25.00 per year. For retailers, distributors, contractors, and manufacturers.

Floor Covering Weekly. Hearst Business Communications, Inc., FCW Div., 645 Stewart Ave. Garden City, NY 11530-4709. Phone: (516)229-1300 Fax: (516)227-1342 E-mail: smontero@hearst.com • URL: http://www.floorcoveringweekly.com • 32 times a year. $54.00 per year.

Floor Covering Weekly Product Source Guide. Hearst Business Communications, Inc., FCW Div., 645 Stewart Ave. Garden City, NY 11530-4709. Phone: (516)229-3600 Fax: (516)227-1342 URL: http://www.hearstcorp.com • Annual. $29.00. Lists manufacturers and importers of carpeting, rugs, ceramic tile, and other floor coverings. Formerly *Floor Covering Weekly*.

Flooring Buying and Resource Guide. Douglas Publications, Inc., 2807 N. Parham Rd., Suite 200 Richmond, VA 23294. Phone: (804)762-9600 Fax: (804)217-8999 E-mail: amdouglas3@al.com • URL: http://www.douglaspublications.com • Annual. $42.50. Lists of manufacturers, workroom manufacturers' representatives, and distributors of floor and other interior surfacing products and equipment; carpet inspection servicecompanies' and related trade associations in the United States and Canada. Formerly *Flooring Directory and Buying Guide*.

Florafacts. Florafax International, Inc., P.O. Box 45745 Tulsa, OK 74145. Phone: (918)622-8415 Monthly. $15.00 per year.

Florida Agricultural Experiment Station. University of Florida

Florida Citrus Mutual.

Florida Department of Citrus.

Florida Gift Fruit Shippers Association.

Florist. FTD Association, P.O. Box 7051 Downers Grove, IL 60515-7051. Phone: 800-788-9000 or (810)355-9300 Fax: (810)948-6420 Monthly. $39.00 per year.

Florist-Buyers Directory. Florist's Transworld Delivery, 33031 Schoolcraft Livonia, MI 48150. Phone: (770)567-0055 Annual. $6.00. Lists 1,200 suppliers in floral industry.

Florists' Review. Florists' Review Enterprises, 3641 S.W. Plass Ave. Topeka, KS 66611-2588. Phone: (913)266-0888 Fax: (913)266-0333 Monthly. $39.00 per year.

Flour Milling and Baking Research Association Abstracts. Flour Milling and Baking Research Association, Chorleywood Hertsworth WD3 5SH 09, England. Bimonthly. Membership.

Flour Milling Products. U. S. Bureau of the Census, Washington, DC 20233-0800. Phone: (301)457-4100 Fax: (301)457-3842 URL: http://www.census.gov • Monthly and annual. Covers production, mill stocks, exports, and imports of wheat and rye flour. (Current Industrial Reports, M20A.)

Flower Shop. Entrepreneur Media, Inc., 2445 McCabe Way Irvine, CA 92614. Phone: 800-421-2300 or (949)261-2325 Fax: (949)261-0234 E-mail: entmag@entrepreneur.com • URL: http://www.entrepreneura.com • Looseleaf. $59.50. A practical guide to starting a retail flower shop. Covers profit potential, start-up costs, market size evaluation, owner's time required, site selection, lease negotiation, pricing, accounting, advertising, promotion, etc. (Start-Up Business Guide No. E1143.)

Flowers: The Beautiful Magazine About the Business of Flowers. Teleflora, Inc., 11444 W. Olympic Blvd. Los Angeles, CA 90064. Phone: 800-321-2665 or (310)966-3543 Fax: (310)966-3610 Monthly. $38.95 per year.

Fluid Abstracts: Civil Engineering. Elsevier Science, 655 Ave. of the Americas New York, NY 10010. Phone: 888-437-4636 or (212)989-5800 Fax: (212)633-3680 E-mail: usinfo@elsevier.com • URL: http://www.elsevier.com • Monthly. $1,319.00 per year. Annual cumulation. Includes the literature of coastal structures.Published in England by Elsevier Science Publishing Ltd. Formerly *Civil Engineering Hydraulics Abstracts*.

Fluid Abstracts: Process Engineering. Elsevier Science, 655 Ave. of the Americas New York, NY 100010. Phone: 888-437-4636 or (212)989-5800 Fax: (212)633-3680 E-mail: usinfo@elsevier.com • URL: http://www.elsevier.com • Monthly. $1,319.00 per year. Includes annual cumulation. Formerly *Pumps and Other Fluids Machinery: Abstracts*.

Fluid Concepts and Creative Analogies: Computer Models of the Fundamental Mechanisms of Thought. Douglas Hofstadter. Available from Harpercollisn Publishing, 10 E. 53rd St. New York, NY 10022-5299. Phone: 800-242-7737 or (212)207-7000 Fax: (212)207-7703 URL: http://www.hapercollins.com • 1995. $22.00. A readable description of progress in artificial intelligence at the Fluid Analogies Research Group of Indiana University.

Fluid Controls Institute.

Fluid Power Association: Directory and Member Guide. National Fluid Power Association, 3333 N. Mayfair Rd. Milwaukee, WI 53222-3219. Phone: (414)778-3357 Fax: (414)778-3361 Annual. $150.00.

Fluid Power Distributors Association.

Fluid Power Handbook and Directory. Penton Media Inc., 1300 E. Ninth St. Cleveland, OH 44114. Phone: (216)696-7000 Fax: (216)696-0836 E-mail: corpcomm@penton.com • URL: http://www.penton.com • Biennial. $80.00 per year. Over 1,500 manufacturers and 3,000 distributors of fluid power products in the United States and Canada.

Fluid Power Institute.

Fluid Power Laboratory.

Fluid Power Society.

FLUIDEX. Available from Elsevier Science, Inc., Secondary Publishing Division, 655 Ave. of the Americas New York, NY 10010. Phone: (212)633-3850 Fax: (212)633-3990 Produced in the Netherlands by Elsevier Science B.V. Provides indexing and abstracting of the international literature of fluid engineering and technology, 1973 to date, with monthly updates. Also known as *Fluid Engineering Abstracts*. Inquire as to online cost and availability.

Fly-Rights: A Consumer Guide to Air Travel. Available from U. S. Government Printing Office, Washington, DC 20402. Phone: (202)512-1800 Fax: (202)512-2250 E-mail: gpoaccess@gpo.gov • URL: http://www.access.gpo.gov • 1994. $2.00. 10th edition. Issued by the U. S. Department of Transportation. Explains the rights and responsibilities of air travelers.

Flyer. Flyer Media, Inc., P.O. Box 39099 Tacoma, WA 98498-0099. Phone: 800-426-8538 or (253)471-9888 Fax: (253)471-9911 E-mail: comments@flyer-online.com • URL: http://www.flyer-online.com • Biweekly. $29.00 per year. Formerly *General Aviation News and Flyer*

Flying. Hachette Filipacchi Magazines, Inc., 500 W. Putnam Ave. Greenwich, CT 06830. Phone: 800-274-4027 or (203)622-2500 E-mail: flyingmag@aol.com • Monthly. $26.00 per year.

Flying Safety. U.S. Air Force. Available from U.S. Government Printing Office, Washington, DC 20402. Phone: (202)512-1800 Fax: (202)512-2250 E-mail: gpoaccess@gpo.gov • URL: http://www.access.gpo.gov • Monthly. $46.00 per year. Published in the interest of safer flying. Articles cover many fields of flight, aircraft engineering, training and safety measures in the air and on the ground.

FM Data Monthly. Tradeline, Inc., P.O. Box 1568 Orinda, CA 94563. Phone: (510)254-1093 Fax: (510)254-2744 E-mail: fmdm@fmdata.com • Monthly. $248.00 per year. Newsletter. Covers the planning, design, construction, and renovation of of a variety of corporate facilities. Formerly *Facilities Planning News*.

FMA Directory and Buyer's Guide. Floral Marketing Association. Produce Marketing Association, P.O. Box 6036 Newark, DE 19714-6036. Phone: (302)738-7100 Fax: (302)731-2409 Annual. $45.00. Mass-market growers, wholesalers, equipment manufacturers, accessory suppliers, and supermarket retailers handling flowers and foliage plants and related products. Formerly *Floral Marketing Directory and Buyer's Guide*.

FMA's Who's Who in Metal Forming and Fabricating (Fabricator's and ManufacturersAssociation). Fabricators and Manufacturers Association International, 833 Featherstone Rd. Rockford, IL 61107-6302. Phone: (815)399-8700 Fax: (815)484-7700 E-mail: info@fmametalfab.org • URL: http://www.fmametalfab.org • Annual. Free to members; non-members, $200.00. Lists about 2,000 members of the Fabricators and Manufacturers Association (FMA), International; and 1,000 members of the Tube and Pipe Association. Includes five indexes. Formerly *FMA Member Resource Directory*.

FMC (Financial Management): Journal of the Financial Management Association. Financial Management Association International, University of South Florida, College of Business Administration, No. 3331 Tampa, FL 33620-5500. Phone: (813)974-2084 Fax: (813)974-5445 E-mail: fma@coba.usf.edu • URL: http://www.fma.org • Quarterly. Individuals, $80.00 per year; libraries, $100.00 per year. Covers theory and practice of financial planning, international finance, investment banking, and portfolio management. Includes *Financial Practice* and *Education and Contempory Finance Digest*.

FMI Annual Financial Review. Food Marketing Institute, 655 15th St., N.W., No. 700 Washington, DC 20006-5701. Phone: (202)452-8444 Fax: (202)429-4519 E-mail: fmi@fmi.org • URL: http://www.fmi.org • Annual. Members, $30.00; non-members, $75.00. Provides financial data on the supermarket industry.

FMRA News. American Society of Farm Managers and Rural Appraisers, 950 S. Cherry St., Suite 508 Denver, CO 80222-2664. Phone: (303)758-3513 Fax: (303)758-0190 E-mail: asfmra@agri-associations.org • Bimonthly. $24.00.

Focal Encyclopedia of Photography. Leslie Stroebel and Richard D. Zakia, editors. Butterworth-Heinemann, 225 Wildwood Ave. Woburn, MA 01801. Phone: 800-366-2665 or (781)904-2500 Fax: 800-466-6520 E-mail: orders@bhusa.com • URL: http://www.bh.com • 1993. $56.95. Third edition.

Focus Group Directory: International Directory of Focus Group Companies and Services. New York AMA-Green Book, Lakewood Business Park, 4301 32nd St., W., Suite E-11 Bradenton, FL 34210. Phone: 800-792-9202 or (941)752-4498 Fax: 800-879-3751 E-mail: greenbook@nyama.org • URL: http://www.greenbook.org • Annual. $80.00. Contains information on companies offering focus group facilities, including recruiting, moderating, and transcription services.

Focus Group Kit. David L. Morgan and Richard A. Krueger, editors. Sage Publications, Inc., 2455 Teller Rd. Thousand

Oaks, CA 91320. Phone: (805)499-0721 Fax: (805)499-0871 E-mail: info@sagepub.com • URL: http://www.sagepub.com • 1997. $99.95. Six volumes. Various authors cover the basics of focus group research, including planning, developing questions, moderating, and analyzing results.

Focus Groups: A Practical Guide for Applied Research. Richard A. Krueger and Mary Anne Casey. Sage Publications, Inc., 2455 Teller Rd. Thousand Oaks, CA 91320. Phone: (805)499-0721 Fax: (805)499-0871 E-mail: info@sagepub.com • URL: http://www.sagepub.com • 2000. $69.95. Third edition. A step-by-step guide to obtaining useful research data from a focus group.

Focus: On the Center for Research Libraries. Center for Research Libraries, 6050 S. Kenwood Ave. Chicago, IL 60637. Phone: (312)955-4545 Fax: (312)955-4339 Bimonthly. Free. Newsletter. Provides news of Center activites.

Fodor's World Weather Guide. E. A. Pearce and C. G. Smith. Random House, Inc., 201 E. 50th St. New York, NY 10022. Phone: 800-726-0600 or (212)751-2600 Fax: 800-659-2436 or (212)572-8700 URL: http://www.randomhouse.com • 1998. $17.95. Written for travelers. Describes the weather at 2,000 locations in 200 countries. Includes temperature/rainfall charts, climate discomfort factors, a glossary of weather terms, and maps.

Folio: The Magazine for Magazine Management. Intertec Publishing Co., 11 Riverbend Dr., S. Stamford, CT 06907-2524. Phone: 800-795-5445 or (203)358-9900 Fax: (203)358-5824 URL: http://www.intertec.com • 17 times a year. $96.00 per year.

The Folklore of American Holidays. The Gale Group, 27500 Drake Rd. Farmington Hills, MI 48331-3535. Phone: 800-877-GALE or (248)699-GALE Fax: 800-414-5043 or (248)699-8069 E-mail: galeord@galegroup.com • URL: http://www.galegroup.com • 1999. $125.00. Third edition. Festivals, rituals, beliefs, superstitions, etc., arranged according to holiday.

The Folklore of World Holidays. The Gale Group, 27500 Drake Rd. Farmington Hills, MI 48331-3535. Phone: 800-877-GALE or (248)699-GALE Fax: 800-414-5043 or (248)699-8069 E-mail: galeord@galegroup.com • URL: http://www.galegroup.com • 1999. $125.00. Second edition. Contains descriptions of the important holidays in more than 150 countries.

Fontana Corrosion Center., Ohio State University, 477 Watts, 2041 College Rd. Columbus, OH 43210. Phone: (614)688-4128 Fax: (614)292-9857 E-mail: frankel.10@osu.edu • URL: http://www.erbs1.eng.ohio-state.edu/~frankel • Research areas include metal coatings and corrosion of alloys.

Food Additives and Contaminants: Analysis, Surveillance, Evaluation, Control. Taylor and Francis, Inc., 325 Chestnut St., 8th Fl. Philadelphia, PA 19106. Phone: 800-821-8312 or (215)625-8900 Fax: (215)625-2940 E-mail: webmaster@taylorandfrancis.com • URL: http://www.tandfdc.com/ • Eight times a year. $1,598.00 per year.

Food and Beverage Additives. Available from MarketResearch.com, 641 Ave. of the Americas, 3rd Fl. New York, NY 10011. Phone: 800-298-5699 or (212)807-2629 Fax: (212)807-2716 E-mail: order@marketresearch.com • URL: http://www.marketresearch.com • 1998. $3,200.00. Published by the Freedonia Group. Market data with forecasts to 2002 and 2007 on coloring agents, flavors, preservatives, stabilizers, etc.

Food and Beverage Market Place: Suppliers Guide. Grey House Publishing, 185 Millerton Rd. Millerton, NY 12546. Phone: 800-562-2139 or (518)789-8700 Fax: (518)789-0556 E-mail: books@greyhouse.com • URL: http://www.greyhouse.com • 2000. $225.00. Second editon. Contains details on companies providing the food industry with a wide variety of supplies, ingredients, packaging, equipment, machinery, instrumentation, chemicals, etc.

Food and Beverage Newsletter. National Safety Council, Periodicals Dept., 1121 Spring Lake Dr. Itasca, IL 60143-3201. Phone: 800-621-7619 or (630)285-1121 Fax: (630)285-1315 URL: http://www.nsc.org • Bimonthly. Members, $15.00 per year; non-members, $19.00 per year.

Food and Environmental Toxicology Laboratory. University of Florida

Food and Feed Grain Institute. Kansas State University

Food Business Mergers and Acquisitions. Food Institute, P.O. Box 972 Fairlawn, NJ 07410-0972. Phone: (201)791-5570 Fax: (201)791-5222 E-mail: food1@foodinstitute.com • URL: http://www.foodinstitute.com • Annual. $510.00. Gives names, locations, and industry categories of all companies involved in food business mergers during the previous year.

Food Chemical News. Food Chemical News, Inc., 1725 K St., N.W., Suite 506 Washington, DC 20006-1401. Phone: (202)544-1980 Fax: (202)546-3890 Weekly. $1,187.00 per year. Newsletter.

Food Chemicals News Directory. Food Chemical News. CRC Press, Inc., 2000 Corporate Blvd., N.W. Boca Raton, FL 33431. Phone: 800-272-7737 or (561)994-0555 Fax: (561)241-7856 E-mail: orders@crcpress.com • URL: http://www.crcpress.com • Semiannual. $497.00. Over 2,000 subsidiaries belonging to nearly 250 corporate parents plus an additional 3,000 independent processors. Formerly *Herald's 1,500*.

Food Distribution Magazine. Phoenix Media Network, Inc., P.O. Box 811768 Boca Raton, FL 33481-1768. Phone: (561)447-0810 Monthly. $49.00 per year. Edited for marketers and buyers of domestic and imported, specialty or gourmet food products, including ethnic foods, seasonings, and bakery items.

Food Distributors International., 201 Park Washington Court Falls Church, VA 22046. Phone: (703)532-9400 Fax: (703)538-4673 E-mail: staff@fdi.org • URL: http://www.fdi.org • Members are wholesale grocery companies catering to institutions.

Food Engineering Database. Cahners Business Information, 1018 W. 9th Ave. King of Prussia, PA 19406. Phone: 800-695-1214 or (610)205-1000 Fax: (610)964-2915 E-mail: corporatecommunications@cahners.com • URL: http://www.cahners.com • Annual. $325.00. More than 17,000 food and beverage plants with 20 or more employees, food and beverage research and development facilities, and company headquarters. Formerly *Food Engineering Directory of U.S. Food and Beverage Plants*.

Food Engineering International. Cahners Business Information, 1018 W. 9th St. King of Prussia, PA 19406. Phone: 800-695-1214 or (610)205-1000 Fax: (610)964-2915 E-mail: corporatecommunications@cahners.com • URL: http://www.cahners.com • Bimonthly. Price on application. Formerly *Chilton's Food Engineering International*.

Food Equipment Manufacturers Association.

Food Industries Center.

Food Industry Newsletter: All the Food News That Matters. Newsletters, Inc., P.O. Box 342730 Bethesda, MD 20827-2730. Phone: (301)469-8507 Fax: (301)469-7271 E-mail: foodltr@aol.com • 26 times a year. $245.00 per year. Irregular updates. A summary of key industry news for food executives.

Food Law Reports. CCH, Inc., 4025 W. Peterson Ave. Chicago, IL 60646-6085. Phone: 800-248-3248 or (773)583-8500 Fax: 800-224-8299 URL: http://www.cch.com • Weekly. $1,349.00 per year. Six looseleaf volumes. Covers regulation of adulteration, packaging, labeling, and additives. Formerly *Food Drug Cosmetic Law Reports*.

Food Management: Schools, Colleges, Hospitals, Nursing Home Contract Services. Penton Media Inc., 1300 E. Ninth St. Cleveland, OH 44114. Phone: (216)626-7000 Fax: (216)696-0836 E-mail: corpcomm@penton.com • URL: http://www.penton.com • Monthly. Free to qualified personnel; others, $60.00 per year.

Food Manufacturing. Cahners Business Information, New Product Information, 301 Gibraltar Dr. Morris Plains, NJ 07950-0650. Phone: 800-622-7776 or (973)292-5100 Fax: (973)539-3476 E-mail: t.canny@cahners.com • URL: http://www.foodmanufacturing.com • Monthly. $59.75 per year. Edited for food processing operations managers and food engineering managers. Includes end-of-year *Food Products and Equipment Literature Review*. Formerly *Food Products and Equipment*.

Food Marketing Industry Speaks. Food Marketing Institute, 655 15th St., N.W., No. 700 Washington, DC 20006-5701. Phone: (202)452-8444 Fax: (202)429-4529 E-mail: fmi@fmi.org • URL: http://www.fmi.org • Annual. Members, $30.00; non-members, $75.00. Provides data on overall food industry marketing performance, including retail distribution and store operations.

Food Marketing Institute.

Food Master. Cahners Business Information, 1018 W. 9th Ave. King of Prussia, PA 19406. Phone: 800-695-1214 or (610)205-1000 Fax: (610)964-2915 E-mail: corporatecommunications@cahners.com • URL: http://www.cahners.com • Annual. $99.95. Over 5,000 manufacturers and distributors of food machinery and supplies. Formerly *Food Engineering Master*.

Food Processing. Putman Publishing Co., 555 W. Pierce Rd., Suite 301 Itasca, IL 60143-2649. Phone: (630)467-1300 Fax: (630)467-1123 E-mail: jpowers@putnampublishing.com • URL: http://www.foodprocessing.com • Monthly. Free to qualified personnel; others, $98.00 per year. Edited for executive and operating personnel in the food processing industry.

Food Processing Guide and Directory. Putman Publishing Co., 555 W. Pierce Rd., Suite 301 Itasca, IL 60143-2649. Phone: (630)467-1300 Fax: (630)467-1123 URL: http://www.putnampublishing.com • Annual. $75.00. Lists over 5,390 food ingredient and equipment manufacturers.

Food Processing Machinery and Supplies Association.

Food Processing Newsletter. Putman Publishing Co., 555 W. Pierce Rd., Suite 301 Itasca, IL 60143-2649. Phone: (630)467-1300 Fax: (630)467-1123 URL: http://www.putnampublishing.com • Weekly. $100.00 per year. Covers food processing industry news and trends.

Food Processors Institute., 1401 New York Ave., N. W., Suite 400 Washington, DC 20005. Phone: (202)393-0890 or (202)639-5904 Fax: (202)639-5941 E-mail: fpi@nfpa-food.org • URL: http://www.nfpa-food.org • Provides education and training for the food processing industry through schools, seminars, and workshops. Affiliated with the National Food Processors Association.

Food Production/Management: Monthly Publication of the Canning, Glass-Packing Aseptic, and Frozen Food Industry. Arthur Judge, editor. CTI Publications, Inc., Two Oakway Rd. Timonium, MD 21093-4227. Phone: (410)308-2080 Fax: (410)308-2079 E-mail: sales@ctipubs.com • URL: http://www.ctipubs.com • Monthly. $35.00 per year.

Food Research Center. Texas A & M University

Food Research Institute.

Food Review. Available from U. S. Government Printing Office, Washington, DC 20402. Phone: (202)512-1800 Fax: (202)512-2250 E-mail: gpoaccess@gpo.gov • URL: http://www.access.gpo.gov • Three times a year. $13.00 per year. Issued by the U. S. Department of Agriculture. Contains data on domestic and foreign food costs and production. Formerly *National Food Review*.

Food Science and Technology Abstracts. International Food Information Service Publishing, Lane End House, Shinfield Reading RG2 9BB Berks RG2 9BB, England. Phone: 44 118 9883895 Fax: 44 118 9885065 E-mail: ifis@ifis.org • URL: http://www.dimdi.de/ • Monthly. $1,780.00 per year. Provides worldwide coverage of the literature of food technology and food production.

Food Science and Technology Abstracts ÎCD-ROMl. Available from SilverPlatter Information, Inc., 100 River Ridge Rd. Norwood, MA 02062-0543. Phone: 800-343-0064 or (781)769-2599 Fax: (781)769-8763 E-mail: info@silverplatter.com • URL: http://www.silverplatter.com • Quarterly. $3,700 per year. Produced by International Food Information Service (home page is http://www.ifis.org). Provides worldwide coverage on CD-ROM of the literature of food technology and production. Various types of publications are indexed, with abstracts, including about 1,800 periodicals. Time period is 1969 to date.

Food Science and Technology Abstracts Îonlinel. IFIS North American Desk, National Food Laboratory, 6363 Clark Ave. Dublin, CA 94568. Phone: 800-336-3782 or (925)828-1440 Fax: (925)833-8795 URL: http://www.ifis.org • Produced by International Food Information Service. Provides about 500,000 online citations, with abstracts, to the international literature of food science, technology, commodities, engineering, and processing. Approximately 2,000 periodicals are covered. Time period is 1969 to date, with monthly updates. Inquire as to online cost and availability.

Food Technology. Institute of Food Technologists, 221 N. LaSalle St. Chicago, IL 60601. Phone: 800-438-3663 or (312)782-8424 Fax: (312)782-8348 E-mail: info@ift.org • URL: http://www.ift.org • Monthly. Free to members; non-members, $82.00 per year. Articles cover food product development, food ingredients, production, packaging, research, and regulation.

Food Technology Laboratory. University of Puerto Rico

Food Trade News. Best-Met Publishing Co., Inc., 5537 Twin Knolls Rd., Suite 438 Columbia, MD 21045-3240. Phone: (410)730-5013 Fax: (410)740-4680 Monthly. $36.00 per year. Reports on the retail food industry in Pennsylvania, Delaware, southern New Jersey and northern Maryland.

FOODS ADLIBRA. General Mills, Inc., Technical Information Services, Foods Adlibra Publications, 9000 Plymouth Ave. N., Minneapolis, MN 55427. Phone: (612)540-4759 Fax: (612)540-3166 Contains online citations, with abstracts, to the technical and business literature of food processing and packaging. New products and new ingredients are featured. Covers about 250 trade journals and 500 research journals from 1974 to date, with monthly updates. Inquire as to online cost and availability.

Foods Adlibra: Key to the World's Food Literature. Foods Adlibra Publications, 9000 Plymouth Ave., N. Minneapolis, MN 55427. Phone: (612)540-4759 Fax: (612)540-3166 Semimonthly.Provides journal citations and abstracts to the literature of food technology and packaging.

Foods and Nutrition Encyclopedia. Audrey H. Ensminger and others. CRC Press, Inc., 2000 Corporate Blvd., N. W. Boca Raton, FL 33431. Phone: 800-272-7737 or (561)994-0555 Fax: (561)241-7856 E-mail: order@crcpress.com • URL: http://www.crcpress.com • 1993. $382.00. Second edition. Two volumes.

Foodservice and Packaging Institute., 1550 Wilson Blvd., No. 701 Arlington, VA 22209. Phone: (703)527-7505 Fax: (703)527-7512 E-mail: fpi@fpi.org • URL: http://www.fpi.org • Members are manufacturers of one-time-use food containers.

Foodservice Consultants Society International.

Foodservice Consultants Society International: Membership Roster. Foodservice Consultants Society International, 304 W Liberty St., Suite 201 Louisville, KY 40202-3011. Phone: (502)583-3783 Fax: (502)589-3602 E-mail: fcsi@fcsi.org • URL: http://www.fcsi.org • Annual. $450.00. About 950 food service consultants.

Foodservice Equipment and Supplies. Cahners Business Information, 1350 E. Touhy Ave. Des Plaines, IL 60018-3358. Phone: 800-662-7776 or (847)635-8800 Fax: (847)390-2475 E-mail: corporatecommunications@cahners.com • URL: http://www.cahners.com • 13 times a year. $92.90 per year.

Foodservice Equipment and Supplies Product Source Guide. Cahners Business Information, 1350 E. Touhy Ave. Des Plaines, IL 60018-3358. Phone: 800-662-7776 or (847)635-8800 Fax: (847)390-2445 E-mail: corporatecommunications@cahners.com • URL: http://www.cahners.com • Annual. $35.00. Nearly 1,700 manufacturers of food service equipment and supplies. Formerly *Foodservice Equipment Buyer's Guide and Product Directory*.

Foodservice Equipment Distributors Association.

Footwear. U. S. Bureau of the Census, Washington, DC 20233-0800. Phone: (301)457-4100 Fax: (301)457-3842 URL: http://www.census.gov • Quarterly. Covers production and value of shipments of leather and rubber footwear. (Current Industrial Reports, MQ-31A.)

Footwear Distributors and Retailers of America.

Footwear Industries of America.

Footwear Market. Available from MarketResearch.com, 641 Ave. of the Americas, Third Floor New York, NY 10011. Phone: 800-298-5699 or (212)807-2629 Fax: (212)807-2716 E-mail: order@marketresearch.com • URL: http://www.marketresearch.com • 1998. $2,750.00. Published by Packaged Facts. Provides market data on shoes for walking, running, and specific sports.

Footwear News. Fairchild Fashion and Merchandising Group, Seven W. 34th St. New York, NY 10001. Phone: 800-932-4724 or (212)630-4000 Fax: (212)630-4201 E-mail: fneditor@fairchildpub.com • URL: http://www.footwearnews • Weekly. Retailers, $59.00 per year; mannufacturers and others, $72.00 per year.

For Your Information. Western New York Library Resources Council, P.O. Box 400 Buffalo, NY 14225-0400. Phone: (716)633-0705 Fax: (716)633-1736 Bimonthly. Free.

Forbes. Forbes, Inc., 60 Fifth Ave. New York, NY 10011. Phone: 800-888-9896 or (212)620-2200 Fax: (212)620-1857 E-mail: webmaster@forbes.com • URL: http://www.forbes.com/forbes • Biweekly. $59.95 per year. Includes supplements: *Forbes ASAP* and *Forbes FYI*.

Forbes Chief Executive Compensation Survey. Forbes Magazine, 60 Fifth Ave. New York, NY 10011. Phone: 800-888-9698 or (212)620-2200 Fax: (212)206-5174 E-mail: letters@forbesdigital.com • URL: http://www.forbes.com/forbes • Annual. $4.95. List of 800 firms. May issue of *Forbes Magazine*.

Ford's Freighter Travel Guide and Waterways of the world. Ford's Travel Guides, 19448 Londelius St. Northridge, CA 91324. Phone: (818)701-7414 Fax: (818)701-7415 Semiannual. $24.00 per year. Describes freighters with passenger accommodations. Formerly *Ford's Freighter Travel Guide*.

Forecasting and Management of Technology. Alan L. Porter and others. John Wiley and Sons, Inc., 605 Third Ave. New York, NY 10158-0012. Phone: 800-225-5945 or (212)850-6000 Fax: (212)850-6088 E-mail: info@wiley.com • URL: http://www.wiley.com • 1991. $140.00. Includes business aspects of technology. (Engineering and Management Technology Series).

Forecasting Business Trends. American Institute for Economic Research, Division St. Great Barrington, MA 01230-1000. Phone: (413)528-1216 Fax: (413)528-0103 E-mail: info@aier.org • URL: http://www.aier.org • 2000. $6.00. Summarizes methods of economic forecasting, statistical indicators, methods of analyzing business cycles, and use of leading, coincident, and lagging indicators. Includes charts, tables, and a glossary of terms. (Economic Education Bulletin.)

Forecasting Financial Markets. Christian Dunis. John Wiley and Sons, Inc., 605 Third Ave. New York, NY 10158-0012. Phone: 800-225-5945 or (212)850-6000 Fax: (212)850-6088 E-mail: info@wiley.com • URL: http://www.wiley.com • 1996. $110.00. Examines what are said to be the more reliable or ''classic'' theories of continuously recurring price patterns. Practical investment applications are discussed.

Forecasts and Strategies. Phillips Business Information, Inc., 1201 Seven Locks Rd., Suite 300 Potomac, MD 20854. Phone: 800-777-5006 or (301)309-1520 Fax: (301)309-3847 E-mail: pbi@phillips.com • URL: http://www.phillips.com/marketplaces.htm • Monthly. $99.00 per year. Covers inflation, taxes and government controls.

Foreign Agricultural Trade of the United States. Available from U. S. Government Printing Office, Washington, DC 20402. Phone: (202)512-1800 Fax: (202)512-2250 E-mail: gpoaccess@gpo.gov • URL: http://www.access.gpo.gov • Monthly. $50.00 per year. Issued by the Economic Research Service of the U. S. Department of Agriculture. Provides data on U. S. exports and imports of agricultural commodities.

Foreign Consular Offices in the United States. U.S. Department of State. Available from U.S. Government Printing Office, Washington, DC 20402. Phone: (202)512-1800 Fax: (202)512-2250 E-mail: gpoaccess@gpo.gov • URL: http://www.access.gpo.gov • Semiannual. $13.00 per copy.

Foreign Credit Insurance Association.

Foreign Exchange Currency Rates. Dow Jones & Co., Inc., 200 Liberty St. New York, NY 10281. Phone: 800-832-1234 or (212)416-2000 Fax: (212)416-2658 URL: http://www.dowjones.com • Annual. $50.00. Contains a compilation for the year of daily foreign exchange rate tables. These daily tables from *The Wall Street Journal* are also available on a monthly basis at $15.00 per month.

Foreign Exchange Exposure Management: A Portfolio Approach. Niso Abuaf and Stephan Schoess. John Wiley and Sons, Inc., 605 Third Ave., 4th Fl. New York, NY 10158-0012. Phone: (212)850-6000 Fax: (212)850-6088 E-mail: info@wiley.com • URL: http://www.wiley.com • 1994. $99.95.

Foreign Exchange Handbook: Managing Risk and Opportunity in Global Currency Markets. Paul Bishop and Don Dixon. McGraw-Hill, 1221 Ave. of the Americas New York, NY 10020. Phone: 800-722-4726 or (212)904-2000 Fax: (212)904-2072 E-mail: customer.service@mcgraw-hill.com • URL: http://www.mcgraw-hill.com • 1992. $69.95. Discusses factors affecting currency value, currency price forecasting, options trading, futures, credit risk, and related subjects.

Foreign Exchange Letter. Institutional Investor, Newsletters Div., 488 Madison Ave. New York, NY 10022. Phone: (212)224-3300 Fax: (212)224-3353 E-mail: info@iijournals.com • URL: http://www.iijournals.com • Biweekly. $1,595.00 per year. Newsletter. Provides information on foreign exchange rates, trends, and opportunities. Edited for banks, multinational corporations, currency traders, and others concerned with money rates.

Foreign Exchange Rates. U.S. Federal Reserve System, Publications Services, 20th and Constitution Ave., N.W., Room MS-127 Washington, DC 20551. Phone: (202)452-3244 Fax: (202)728-5886 URL: http://www.bog.frb.fed.us • Weekly, $20.00 per year; monthly, $5.00 per year.

Foreign Labor Trends. Available from U. S. Government Printing Office, Washington, DC 20402. Phone: (202)512-1800 Fax: (202)512-2250 E-mail: gpoaccess@gpo.gov • URL: http://www.access.gpo.gov • Irregular (50 to 60 issues per year, each on an individual country). $38.00 per year. Prepared by various American Embassies. Issued by the Bureau of International Labor Affairs, U. S. Department of Labor. Covers labor developments in important foreign countries, including trends in wages, working conditions, labor supply, employment, and unemployment.

Foreign Press Association.

Foreign Representatives in the U. S. Yellow Book: Who's Who in the U. S. Offices of Foreign Corporations, Foreign Nations, the Foreign Press, and Intergovernmental Organizations. Leadership Directories, Inc., 104 Fifth Ave., 2nd Fl. New York, NY 10011. Phone: (212)627-4140 Fax: (212)645-0931 E-mail: info@leadershipdirectories.com • URL: http://www.leadershipdirectories.com • Semiannual. $235.00 per year. Lists executives located in the U. S. for 1,300 foreign companies, 340 foreign banks and other financial institutions, 175 embassies and consulates, and 375 foreign press outlets. Includes five indexes.

Foreign Service Journal. American Foreign Service Association, 2101 E St., N.W. Washington, DC 20037. Phone: 800-627-6247 or (202)338-4045 Fax: (202)338-6820 E-mail: journal@afsa.org • URL: http://www.afsa.org • Monthly. $40.00 per year.

Foreign Tax and Trade Briefs. Matthew Bender & Co., Inc., Two Park Ave. New York, NY 10016. Phone: 800-223-1940 or (212)448-2000 Fax: (212)244-3188 E-mail: international@bender.com • URL: http://www.bender.com • $470.00. Two looseleaf volumes. Periodic supplementation. The latest tax and trade information for over 100 foreign countries.

Foreign Trade by Commodities (Series C). OECD Publications and Information Center, 2001 L St., N.W., Ste. 650 Washington, DC 20036-4922. Phone: 800-456-6323 or (202)785-6323 Fax: (202)785-0350 E-mail: washington.contact@oecd.org • URL: http://www.oecdwash.org • Annual. $625.00. Five volumes. Presents detailed five-year export-import data for specific commodities in OECD member countries.

Foreign Trade of the United States: Including State and Metro Area Export Data. Courtenay M. Slater, and James B. Rice, editors. Bernan Press, 4611-F Assembly Dr. Lanham, MD 20706-4391. Phone: 800-274-4447 or (301)459-7666 Fax: 800-865-3450 or (301)459-0056 E-mail: info@bernan.com • URL: http://www.bernan.com • 1999. $74.00. Provides detailed national, state, and local data relating to U. S. exports and imports.

Forensic Accounting and Financial Fraud. American Management Association Extension Institute, P.O. Box 1026 Saranac Lake, NY 12983-9957. Phone: 800-262-9699 or (518)891-1500 Fax: (518)891-0368 E-mail: amapubs@aol.com • URL: http://www.amanet.org • Looseleaf. $130.00. Self-study course. Emphasis is on practical explanations, examples, and problem solving. Quizzes and a case study are included.

Forest Chemicals Review. Kriedt Enterprises Ltd., 129 S. Cortez St. New Orleans, LA 70119-6118. Phone: (504)482-3914 Fax: (504)482-4205 E-mail: nsreview@aol.com • Bimonthly. $98.00 per year. Formerly *Naval Stores Review*.

Forest Products Abstracts. CABI Publishing North America, 10 E. 40th St., Ste. 3203 New York, NY 10016. Phone: 800-528-4841 or (212)481-7018 Fax: (212)686-7993 E-mail: cabi@cabi.org • URL: http://www.cabi.org • Bimonthly. $1,155.00 per year. Published in England by CABI Publishing. Provides worldwide coverage of forest products literature.

Forest Products and Wood Science: An Introduction. John G. Haygreen and Jim L. Bowyer. Iowa State University Press, 2121 S. State Ave. Ames, IA 50014-8300. Phone: 800-862-6657 or (515)292-0140 Fax: (515)292-0140 E-mail: orders@isupress.edu • URL: http://www.isupress.edu • 1996. $62.95. Third edition.

Forest Products Journal. Forest Products Society, 2801 Marshall Court Madison, WI 53705. Phone: (608)231-1361 Fax: (608)231-2152 URL: http://www.forestprod.org • 10 times a year. $135.00 per year.

Forest Products Society.

Forest Resources Association.

Forestry Abstracts: Compiled from World Literature. Available from CABI Publishing North America, 10 E. 40th St. New York, NY 10016. Phone: 800-528-4841 or (212)481-7018 Fax: (212)686-7993 E-mail: cabi@cabi.org • URL: http://www.cabi.org • Monthly. $1,155 per year. Published in England by CABI Publishing. Provides worldwide coverage of the literature.

Forintek Canada Corporation.

Form: The Voice of the Independent Business Forms Industry. Document Management Industries Association, 433 E. Monroe Ave. Alexandria, VA 22301. Phone: (703)836-6232 Fax: (703)836-2241 E-mail: editors@formag.com • URL: http://www.formag.com • Monthly. Members, $29.00 per year; non-members, $49.00 per year.

Formal Meeting: How to Prepare and Participate. Alice N. Pohl. NTC/Contemporary Publishing, P.O. Box 545 Blacklick, OH 43004. Phone: 800-338-3987 or (614)755-4151 Fax: (614)755-5645 E-mail: ntcpub@mcgraw-hill.com • URL: http://www.ntc-cb.com • 1992. $10.95. (NTC Business Book Series).

Forms and Agreements for Architects, Engineers and Contractors. Albert Dib. West Group, 610 Opperman Dr. Eagan, MN 55123. Phone: 800-328-4880 or (651)687-7000 Fax: 800-213-2323 or (651)687-5827 URL: http://www.westgroup.com • Four looseleaf volumes. $495.00. Periodic supplementation. Covers evaluation of construction documents and alternative clauses. Includes pleadings for litigation and resolving of claims. (Real Property-Zoning Series).

Forms and Agreements on Intellectual Property and International Licensing. Leslie W. Melville. West Group, 610 Opperman Dr. Eagan, MN 55123. Phone: 800-328-4880 or (651)687-7000 Fax: 800-213-2323 or (651)687-5827 URL: http://www.westgroup.com • $375.00. Three looseleaf volumes. Periodic supplementation.

Forms of Business Agreements and Resolutions-Annotated, Tax Tested. Prentice Hall, 240 Frisch Court Paramus, NJ 07652-5240. Phone: 800-947-7700 or (201)909-6200 Fax: 800-445-6991 or (201)909-6361 URL: http://www.prenhall.com • Three looseleaf volumes. Periodic supplementation. Price on application.

Formulary of Cosmetic Preparations. Anthony L. Hunting, editor. Micelle Press, Inc., P.O. Box 1519 Fort Washington, NY 11050-0306. Phone: (516)767-7171 Fax: (516)944-9824 E-mail: info@scholium.com • URL: http://www.scholium.com • 1991. $135.00. Two volumes. Volume one, *Decorative Cosmetics* $60.00; volume two *Creams, Lotions and Milks* $95.00.

Forthcoming Books. R. R. Bowker, 121 Chanlon Rd. New Providence, NJ 07974. Phone: 888-269-5723 or (908)464-6800 Fax: (908)771-7704 E-mail: info@bowker.com • URL: http://www.bowker.com • Bimonthly. $289.00 per year. Supplement to *Books in Print*.

Forthcoming International Scientific and Technical Conferences. Information Today, Inc., 143 Old Marlton Pike Medford, NJ 08055-8750. Phone: 800-300-9868 or (609)654-6266 Fax: (609)654-4309 E-mail: custserv@infotoday.com • URL: http://www.infotoday.com • Quarterly. Members, $164.00 per year; non-members, $204.00 per year.

Fortune Magazine. Time Inc., Business Information Group, Time and Life Bldg., Rockefeller Center, 1271 Ave. of the Americas New York, NY 10020-1393. Phone: 800-621-8000 or (212)522-1212 Fax: (212)522-0970 E-mail: fortune-letters@pathfinder.com • URL: http://www.fortune.com • Biweekly. $59.95 per year. Edited for top executives and upper-level managers.

The Fortune Sellers: The Big Business of Buying and Selling Predictions. William A. Sherden. John Wiley and Sons, Inc., 605 Third Ave. New York, NY 10158-0012. Phone: 800-225-5945 or (212)850-6000 Fax: (212)850-6088 E-mail: info@wiley.com • URL: http://www.wiley.com • 1997. $29.95. The author states that predictions are notoriously unreliable in any field, including the stock market, the economy, and the weather. (Forecasters in all areas don't have to be right; they just have to be interesting.)

40 Largest Management Consulting Firms, U. S. & World. Kennedy Information, LLC, One Kennedy Place, Route 12, S. Fitzwilliam, NH 03447. Phone: 800-531-1026 or (603)585-3101 Fax: (603)585-9555 E-mail: office@kennedypub.com • URL: http://www.kennedyinfo.com • Annual. $15.00. Rankings of consulting firms are by U. S. and world estimated revenues, with tables of staff sizes. Growth trends and market size estimates for the management consulting industry are also provided.

40 Largest Retained Executive Search Firms, U. S. & World. Kennedy Information, LLC, One Kennedy Place, Route 12, S. Fitzwilliam, NH 03447. Phone: 800-531-1026 or (603)585-3101 Fax: (603)585-9555 E-mail: office@kennedypub.com • URL: http://www.kennedyinfo.com • Annual. $15.00. Rankings of search firms are by U. S. and world estimated revenues, with tables of staff sizes. Growth trends and market size estimates for the executive search industry are also provided.

Forum Train Europe. c/o Swiss Federal Railways

Foundation Center.

Foundation Directory. The Foundation Center, 79 Fifth Ave. New York, NY 10003-3076. Phone: 800-424-9836 or (212)620-4230 Fax: (212)807-3677 E-mail: mdn@fdncenter.org • URL: http://www.fdncenter.org • Annual. $215.00. Over 37,700 of the largest foundations in the United States, all having 2,000,000.00 or more assets or awarding $200,000 or more in grants in a recent year.

Foundation for American Communications., 78-85 S. Grand Ave. Pasadena, CA 91105-1602. Phone: (213)851-7372 Fax: (213)851-9186 Conducts Business/News Media Conferences involving business executives and journalists in an effort to improve the participants' understanding of the news media.

Foundation for Cross-Connection Control and Hydraulic Research. University of Southern California

Foundation for Economic Education.

Foundation for the Study of Cycles., 214 Carnegie Center, Suite 204 Princeton, NJ 08540-6237. Phone: (609)987-1401 Fax: (609)987-0726 E-mail: cycles@cycles.org • URL: http://www.cycles.org • Members are individuals interested in economic, financial, natural, and social cycles.

Foundation Fundamentals: A Guide for Grantseekers. The Foundation Center, 79 Fifth Ave. New York, NY 10003-3076. Phone: 800-424-9836 or (212)620-4230 Fax: (212)807-3677 E-mail: mfn@fdncenter.org • URL: http://www.fdncenter.org • 1999. $34.75. Sixth edition.

Foundation Grants Index. The Foundation Center, 79 Fifth Ave. New York, NY 10003-3076. Phone: 800-424-9836 or (212)620-4230 Fax: (212)807-3677 E-mail: mfn@fdncenter.org • URL: http://www.fdncenter.org • Irregular. $165.00 per year. Over 5,000 grants of $10,000 or more. Formerly *Foundation Grants Quarterly*.

Foundation Grants to Individuals. The Foundation Center, 79 Fifth Ave. New York, NY 10003-3076. Phone: 800-424-9836 or (212)620-4230 Fax: (212)807-3677 E-mail: mfn@fdncenter.org • URL: http://www.fdncenter.org • Biennial. $65.00. Over 3,300 foundations that make grants to individuals.

Foundation News and Commentary: Philanthropy and the Nonprofit Sector. Council on Foundations, 1828 L St., N.W., Suite 300 Washington, DC 20036. Phone: 800-771-8187 or (202)466-6512 Fax: (202)785-3926 Bimonthly. $48.00 per year. Formerly *Foundation News*.

The Foundation 1000. The Foundation Center, 79 Fifth Ave. New York, NY 10003-3076. Phone: 800-424-9836 or (212)620-4230 Fax: (212)807-3677 E-mail: mfn@fdncenter.org • URL: http://www.fdncenter.org • Annual. $295.00. Provides detailed descriptions of the 1,000 largest foundations in the U. S., responsible for 64% of all foundation giving. Indexing is by subject, type of support, location, and personnel.

The Foundation Reporter: Comprehensive Profiles and Giving Analyses of America's Major Private Foundations. The Taft Group, 27500 Drake Rd. Farmington Hills, MI 48331-3535. Phone: 800-877-GALE or (248)699-GALE Fax: 800-414-5043 or (248)699-8063 E-mail: galeord@galegroup.com • URL: http://www.taftgroup.com • Annual. $425.00. Provides detailed information on major U. S. foundations. Eight indexes (location, grant type, recipient type, personnel, etc.)

Foundation Trusteeship: Service in the Public Interest. John Nason. The Foundation Center, 79 Fifth Ave. New York, NY 10003-3076. Phone: 800-424-9836 or (212)620-4230 Fax: (212)807-3677 E-mail: mfn@fdncenter.org • URL: http://www.fdncenter.org • 1989. $19.95. Covers the roles and responsibilities of foundation boards.

Foundations of Financial Management. Stanley R. Block and Geoffrey A. Hirt. McGraw-Hill Professional, 1221 Ave. of the Americas New York, NY 10020-1095. Phone: 800-722-4726 or (212)904-2000 Fax: (212)904-2072 E-mail: customer.service@mcgraw-hill.com • URL: http://www.mcgraw-hill.com • 1999. $67.00. Ninth edition (Finance Series).

Foundations of Robotics: Analysis and Control. Tsuneo Yoshikawa. MIT Press, Five Cambridge Center Cambridge, MA 02142-1493. Phone: 800-356-0343 or (617)253-5646 Fax: (617)253-6779 E-mail: mitpress-orders@mit.edu • URL: http://www.mitpress.mit.edu • 1990. $47.50.

Foundry Directory and Register of Forges. Metal Bulletin, Inc., 220 Fifth Ave., 19th Fl. New York, NY 10001-7781. Phone: 800-638-2525 or (212)213-6202 Fax: (212)213-6273 E-mail: sales@metbul.com • URL: http://www.metalbulletin.co.uk • Quarterly. $165.00. Foundries and forges in the United Kingdom and Europe.

Foundry Management and Technology. Penton Media, 1100 Superior Ave. Cleveland, OH 44114-2543. Phone: (216)696-7000 Fax: (216)696-0836 E-mail: corpcomm@penton.com • URL: http://www.penton.com • Monthly. Free to qualified personnel; others, $50.00 per year. Coverage includes nonferrous casting technology and production.

Foundryman's Handbook: Facts, Figures, Formulae. Elsevier Science, 655 Ave. of the Americas New York, NY 10010. Phone: 888-437-4636 or (212)989-5800 Fax: (212)633-3680 E-mail: usinfo@elsevier.com • URL: http://www.elsevier.com • 1986. $119.00. Ninth edition.

401(k) Dimensions. Hearst Business Communications, 645 Stewart Ave. Garden City, NY 11530-4709. Phone: (516)227-1300 Fax: (516)229-3636 URL: http://www.hearstcorp.com • Quarterly. $15.00 per year. Newsletter. Edited for employees of companies offering 401(k) defined contribution retirement plans. Promotes sound investment principles.

401(k) Handbook. Thompson Publishing Group, 1725 K St., N.W., Suite. 200 Washington, DC 20006. Phone: 800-999-2520 or (202)872-4000 Fax: (202)296-1091 Looseleaf. $319.00 per year (includes monthly bulletin and updates). Provides detailed explanations of complex 401(k) rules and regulations.

The 401(k) Plan Handbook. Julie Jason. Prentice Hall, 240 Frisch Court Paramus, NJ 07652-5240. Phone: 800-947-7700 or (201)909-6200 Fax: 800-445-6991 or (201)909-6361 URL: http://www.prenhall.com • 1997. $79.95. Provides technical, legal, administrative, and investment details of 401(k) retirement plans.

FP Corporate Connection. Available from Hoover's, Inc., 1033 La Posada Drive, Suite 250 Austin, TX 78752. Phone: 800-486-8666 or (512)374-4500 Fax: (512)374-4505 E-mail: orders@hoovers.com • URL: http://www.hoovers.com • Annual. $675.00. CD-ROM from the Financial Post DataGroup provides detailed information on Canada's top 4,000 public and private companies. 16,000 executives are listed.

FPDA News. Fluid Power Distributors Association, P.O. Box 1420 Cherry Hill, NJ 08034-0054. Phone: (609)424-8998 Fax: (609)424-9248 Bimonthly. Membership newsletter. Formerly *FPDA Power Planner*.

The Fragile Middle Class: Americans in Debt. Teresa A. Sullivan and others. Yale University Press, 302 Temple St. New Haven, CT 06511. Phone: 800-987-7323 or (203)432-0960 Fax: (203)432-0948 E-mail: yupmkt@yale.edu • URL: http://www.yale.edu/yup/ • 2000. $32.50. Provides an analysis of a 1991 survey of personal bankruptcies in five states of the U. S. Serves as a sequel to the authors' *As We Forgive Our Debtors* (1989), an analysis of 1981 bankruptcies.

Fragrance Foundation.

Fragrance Foundation Reference Guide. Fragrance Foundation, 142 E. 32nd St. New York, NY 10016. Phone: (212)725-2755 Fax: (212)779-9058 E-mail: info@fragrance.org • URL: http://www.fragrance.org • Annual. $85.00. Manufacturers of over 1,100 fragances available in the United States.

Franchise Annual: Complete Handbook and Directory. Info Press Inc., P.O. Box 826 Lewiston, NY 14092-0550. Phone: 888-806-2665 or (716)754-4669 Fax: (905)688-7728 E-mail: infopress@infonews.com • URL: http://www.infonews.com/franchise • Annual. $39.95. Over 4,200 franchises; international coverage.

Franchise Opportunities Guide: A Comprehensive Listing of the World's Leading Franchises. International Franchise Association, 1350 New York Ave., N.W., Suite 900 Washington, DC 20005-4709. Phone: 800-543-1038 or (202)628-8000 Fax: (202)628-0812 E-mail: ifa@franchise.org • URL: http://www.franchise.org • Semiannual. $42.00 per year. More than 600 companies which offer franchises.

Franchise Opportunities Handbook. Available from U. S. Government Printing Office, Washington, DC 20402. Phone: (202)512-1800 Fax: (202)512-2250 E-mail: gpoaccess@gpo.gov • URL: http://www.access.gpo.gov • Annual. Prepared by the U. S. Department of Commerce. Contains descriptions of franchises available in the U. S. and advice for those who are considering investment in a franchise. Government assistance programs from various agencies are outlined.

The Franchise Option: How to Expand Your Business Through Franchising. Kathryn Boe and others. International Franchise Association, 1350 New York Ave., N.W., Suite 900 Washington, DC 20005-4709. Phone: 800-543-1038 or (202)628-8000 Fax: (202)628-0812 E-mail: ifa@franchise.org • URL: http://www.franchise.org • 1987. $24.00. Second edition.

Franchise Times. Restaurant Finance Corp., 2500 Cleveland Ave., N. Roseville, MN 55113-9899. Phone: (651)631-4995 Fax: (651)633-8749 Biweekly. $35.00 per year. Formerly *Continental Franchise Review*.

Franchising and Licensing: Two Ways to Build Your Business. Andrew Sherman. AMACOM, 1601 Broadway, 12th Fl. New York, NY 10019. Phone: 800-262-9699 or (212)586-8100 Fax: (212)903-8168 E-mail: custmserv@amanet.org • URL: http://www.amanet.org • 1999. $45.00. Second edition. Written for the business person who wishes to become a franchiser. Tells how to raise capital, create a prototype, structure franchise agreements, develop operations manuals, market the franchise, and maintain good relations with franchisees.

Franchising: Realities and Remedies. Harold Brown. New York Law Publishing Co., 345 Park Ave., S. New York, NY 10010. Phone: 800-888-8300 or (212)741-8300 Looseleaf service. $90.00.

Franchising World. International Franchise Association, 1350 New York Ave., N.W., Suite 900 Washington, DC 20005-4709. Phone: 800-543-1038 or (202)628-8000 Fax: (202)628-0812 E-mail: ifa@franchise.org • URL: http://www.franchise.org • Bimonthly. $18.00 per year. Formerly *Franchising Opportunities*.

Francis I. Proctor Foundation for Research in Ophthalmology.

Frankfurt Finance. Available from European Business Publications, Inc., P.O. Box 891 Darien, CT 06820-9859. Phone: (203)656-2701 Fax: (203)655-8332 E-mail: centralbank@easynet.co.uk • URL: http://www.easyweb.easynet.co.uk/centralbank • Monthly. $470.00 per year. Newsletter. Published in Germany by Frankfurter Allgemeine Zeitung GmbH Information Services. Presents news of German Bundesbank decisions and the European monetary system, including the European Monetary Union (EMU). Contains charts and tables. Formerly *Old Continent*.

Fraser's Canadian Trade Directory. Fraser's Trade Directories, 777 Bay St. Toronto, ON, Canada M57 1A7. Phone: (416)596-5086 Fax: (416)593-3201 Annual. $200.00. A product classified listing of more than 42,000 Canadian manufacturers and distributors and 14,000 foreign companies having Canadian representation. Includes trade name index.

Fred Goss' What's Working in Direct Marketing. United Communications Group (UCG), 11300 Rockville Pike, Suite 1100 Rockville, MD 20852-3030. Phone: 800-287-2223 or (301)287-2700 Fax: (301)816-8945 E-mail: webmaster@ucg.com • URL: http://www.ucg.com • Biweekly. $242.00 per year. Newsletter. Provides ideas for direct marketing promotions.

Free Magazines for Libraries. Adeline M. Smith. McFarland & Co. Inc., Publishers, P.O. Box 611 Jefferson, NC 28640. Phone: 800-253-2187 or (336)246-4460 Fax: (336)246-5018 E-mail: editorial@mcfarlandpub.com • URL: http://www.mcfarlandpub.com • 1994. $32.50. Fourth edition.

Freedom Forum Media Studies Center., Columbia University, 580 Madison Ave., 42nd Fl. New York, NY 10022. Phone: (212)317-6501 Fax: (212)317-6573 E-mail: b.giles@mediastudies.org • URL: http://www.mediastudies.org • Research fields include mass communication and technological change, including mass media and the public trust.

Freedom of Information Center., University of Missouri, 127 Neff Annex Columbia, MO 65211. Phone: (573)882-4856 Fax: (573)882-9002 E-mail: foiww@showme.missouri.edu • URL: http://www.missouri.edu/~foiwww • Supported by the communications media.

Freedom of Information Clearinghouse., 1600 20th St., N.W. Washington, DC 20009. Phone: (202)588-1000 Fax: (202)588-7790 Promotes citizen access to government-held information.

Freelance Writer's Report. Dana K. Cassell, editor. CNW Publishing, P.O. Box A North Stratford, NH 03590-0167. Phone: 800-351-9278 or (603)922-8338 Fax: (603)922-8339 E-mail: danakenw@moose.ncia.net • Monthly. $39.00 per year. Newsletter. Provides marketing tips and information on new markets for freelance writers. Includes interviews with editors and advice on taxation and legalities.

Freelance Writing. Entrepreneur Media, Inc., 2445 McCabe Way Irvine, CA 92614. Phone: 800-421-2300 or (949)261-2325 Fax: (949)261-0234 E-mail: entmag@entrepreneur.com • URL: http://www.entrepreneur.com 3 • Looseleaf. $59.50. A practical guide to starting a freelance writing service. Covers profit potential, start-up costs, market size evaluation, pricing, accounting, advertising, promotion, etc. (Start-Up Business Guide No. E1258.)

Freight Brokerage. Entrepreneur Media, Inc., 2445 McCabe Way Irvine, CA 92614. Phone: 800-421-2300 or (949)261-2325 Fax: (949)261-0234 E-mail: entmag@entrepreneur.com • URL: http://www.entrepreneur.com • Looseleaf. $59.50. A practical guide to freight transportation brokering. Covers profit potential, start-up costs, market size evaluation, pricing, accounting, advertising, promotion, etc. (Start-Up Business Guide No. E1328.)

Frequent Flyer: For Business People Who Must Travel. OAG Worldwide, 2000 Clearwater Dr. Oak Brook, IL 60523. Phone: 800-323-4000 or (630)574-6000 Fax: (630)574-6222 E-mail: fflyer@oag.com • URL: http://www.oag.com • Monthly. $89.00 per year to individuals. Also known as *OAG Frequent Flyer*. Edited for business travelers. Contains news of frequent flyer programs, airport developments, airline services, and business travel trends. Available only with *OAG Flight Guide*.

Fresh Produce Journal. Lockwood Press, Ltd., 430-438 Market Towers, New Covent Garden Market London SW8 5NN, England. Phone: 44 171 622 6677 Fax: 44 171 720 2047 E-mail: info@fpj.fruitnet.com • URL: http://www.fruitnet.com/fpj/ • Weekly. $148.00 per year. Formerly *Fruit Trades Journal*.

Friends of Libraries Sourcebook. Sandy Dolnick. American Library Association, 50 E. Huron St. Chicago, IL 60611-2795. Phone: 800-545-2433 or (312)944-6780 Fax: (312)440-9374 E-mail: ala@ala.org • URL: http://www.ala.org • 1996. $32.00. Third edition. Provides information and guidance relating to Friends of Libraries support groups.

Friends of the Earth., 1025 Vermont Ave. N.W., Suite 300 Washington, DC 20005. Phone: (202)783-7400 Fax: (202)783-0444 Bimonthly. $25.00 per year. Newsletter on environmental and natural resource issues and public policy.

Friends of the Earth., 1025 Vermont Ave., N.W., Suite. 300 Washington, DC 20005. Phone: (202)783-7400 Fax: (202)783-0444 E-mail: foe@foe.org • URL: http://www.foe.org • Promotes protection of the environment and conservation of natural resources.

Fringe Benefits Tax Guide. CCH, Inc., 4025 W. Peterson Ave. Chicago, IL 60646-6085. Phone: 800-248-3248 or (773)866-6000 Fax: 800-224-8299 or (773)866-3608 URL: http://www.cch.com • Monthly. Looseleaf.

FRM Weekly (Fund Raising Management). Hoke Communications, Inc., 224 Seventh St. Garden City, NY 11530. Phone: 800-229-6700 or (516)746-6700 Fax: (516)294-8141 E-mail: 71410.2423@compuserve.com • Weekly. $115.00 per year.

The Froehlich-Kent Encyclopedia of Telecommunications. Fritz E. Froehlich and Allen Kent, editors. Marcel Dekker, Inc., 270 Madison Ave. New York, NY 10016. Phone: 800-228-1160 or (212)696-9000 Fax: (212)685-4540 E-mail: bookorders@dekker.com • URL: http://www.dekker.com • Dates vary. Five volumes. $975.00. $195.00 per volume. Contains scholarly articles written by telecommunications experts. Includes bibliographies.

From Executive to Entrepreneur: Making the Transition. Gilbert Z. Zoghlin. AMACOM, 1601 Broadway, 12th Fl. New York, NY 10019. Phone: 800-262-9699 or (212)586-8100 Fax: (212)903-8168 E-mail: custmserv@amanet.org • URL: http://www.amanet.org • 1991. $24.95. A self-help guide offering psychological and financial advice to corporate employees who wish to go into business for themselves.

From GATT to the WTO: The Multilateral Trading System in the New Millennium. WTO Secretariat, editor. Available from Kluwer Academic Publishers, 101 Philip Drive, Assinippi Park Norwell, MA 02061. Phone: (781)871-6600 Fax: (781)871-6528 URL: http://www.wkap.nl • 2000. $79.50. Published by the World Trade Organization (http://www.wto.org). A collection of essays on the future of world trade, written on the occasion of the 50th anniversary of the multilateral trading system (GATT/WTO). The authors are described as ''important academics in international trade.''

From Idea to Funded Project: Grant Proposals that Work. Jane C. Belcher and Julia M. Jacobsen. Oryx Press, 4041 N. Central Ave., Ste. 700 Phoenix, AZ 85012-3379. Phone: 800-279-6799 or (602)265-2651 Fax: 800-279-4663 or (602)265-6250 E-mail: info@oryxpress.com • URL: http://www.oryxpress.com • 1992. $26.50. Fourth edition. Formerly *A Process for the Development of Ideas*.

From Kitchen to Market: Selling Your Gourmet Food Specialty. Stephen F. Hall. Dearborn Financial Publishing, 155 North Wacker Drive Chicago, IL 60606-1719. Phone: 800-245-2665 or (312)836-4400 Fax: (312)836-9958 URL: http://www.dearborn.com • 2000. $28.95. Third edition. Covers packaging, labeling, marketing, and distribution of specialty and gourmet food products. Includes charts, graphs, tables, guidelines, checklists, and industry examples.

From Poor Law to Welfare State: A History of Social Welfare in America. Walter I. Trattner. Simon and Schuster Trade, 1230 Ave. of the Americas New York, NY 10020. Phone: 800-223-2336 or (212)698-7000 Fax: 800-943-9831 or (212)698-7007 E-mail: ssonline_feedback@simonsays.com • URL: http://www.simonsays.com • 1998. $16.95. Sixth edition.

From Selling to Managing: Guidelines for the First-Time Sales Manager. Ronald Brown. AMACOM, 1601 Broadway, 12th Fl. New York, NY 10019. Phone: 800-262-9699 or (212)586-8100 Fax: (212)903-8168 E-mail: custmserv@amanet.org • URL: http://www.amanet.org • 1990. $17.95. Revised edition. A practical quide to the transformation of salesperson to sales manager.

From Sundials to Atomic Clocks: Understanding Time and Frequency. James Jespersen. Dover Publications, Inc., 31 E. Second St. Mineola, NY 11501. Phone: 800-223-3130 or (516)294-7000 Fax: (516)742-5049 1999. $12.95. Second revised edition.

Front and Center: The Newsletter of the John W. Hartman Center for Sales, Advertising, and Marketing History. John W. Hartman Center for Sales, Advertising, and Marketing History, Special Collections Library, Duke University Durham, NC 27708-0185. Phone: (919)660-5827 Fax: (919)684-2855 Semiannual. Free.

Front Row Advisor: Business and First Class Air Travel and the Alluring World of Free Upgrades. Diversified Specialties, Inc., 3109 Grand Ave. Coconut Grove, FL 33133-5103. Phone: 800-342-1774 or (305)362-2552 Fax: (305)774-6070 Bimonthly. $145.00 per year. Newsletter. Contains information on opportunities provided by airlines to upgrade coach seats to business class, including frequent flyer upgrades.

Frontline Solutions. Advanstar Communications, Inc., 7500 Old Oak Blvd. Cleveland, OH 44130. Phone: 800-346-0085 or (440)243-8100 Fax: (440)891-2740 E-mail: information@advanstar.com • URL: http://www.advanstar.com • Monthly. $41.00 per year. Provides news and information about the applications and technology of automated data capture systems. Formerly (Automatic I.D. News).

Frontline Solutions Buyer's Guide. Advanstar Communications, Inc., 7500 Old Oak Blvd. Cleveland, OH 44130-3369. Phone: 800-346-0085 or (440)243-8100 Fax: (440)891-2740 E-mail: information@advanstar.com • URL: http://www.advanstar.com • Annual. $34.95. Provides information on manufacturers and suppliers of bar code, magnetic stripe, machine vision, optical character recognition, voice data, smart card, radio frequency, and other automatic identification systems. Formerly (Automatic I.D. News Buyer's Guide).

Frost & Sullivan Market Research Reports. Frost & Sullivan, 2525 Charleston Rd. Mountain View, CA 94043. Phone: (650)961-9000 Fax: (650)961-5042 Contains full text of Frost & Sullivan market research reports on various industries and products. Each report includes a five-year forecast.

Frozen Food Pack Statistics. American Frozen Food Institute, 2000 Corporate Ridge, Suite 1000 McLean, VA 22102. Phone: (703)821-0770 Fax: (703)821-1350 E-mail: affi@pop.dn.net • URL: http://www.affi.com • Annual. Members, $10.00; non-members, $100.00.

Frozen Foods. Available from MarketResearch.com, 641 Ave. of the Americas, Third Floor New York, NY 10011. Phone: 800-298-5699 or (212)807-2629 Fax: (212)807-2716 E-mail: order@marketresearch.com • URL: http://www.marketresearch.com • 1997. $5,000.00. Published by Euromonitor Publications Ltd. Provides consumer market data and forecasts for the United States, the United Kingdom, Germany, France, and Italy. Contains market analyses for many kinds of frozen foods.

Fruit and Tree Nuts Situation and Outlook Report. Available from U. S. Government Printing Office, Washington, DC 20402. Phone: (202)512-1800 Fax: (202)512-2250 E-mail: gpoaccess@gpo.gov • URL: http://www.access.gpo.gov • Three times a year. $13.00 per year. (Economic Research Service, U. S. Department of Agriculture.)

Fruit Juices. Available from MarketResearch.com, 641 Ave. of the Americas, Third Floor New York, NY 10011. Phone: 800-298-5699 or (212)807-2629 Fax: (212)807-2716 E-mail: order@marketresearch.com • URL: http://www.marketresearch.com • 1998. $5,900.00. Published by Euromonitor Publications Ltd. Provides consumer market data and forecasts to 2002 for the United States, the United Kingdom, Germany, France, and Italy. Includes fresh, frozen, bottled, and canned fruit and vegetable juices.

Fruit Research and Extension Center. Pennsylvania State University

Fruit Varieties Journal. American Pomological Society, c/o Dr. Robert M. Crassweller, 103 Tyson Bldg. University Park, PA 16802. Phone: (814)863-6163 Fax: (814)863-6139 E-mail: aps@psu.edu • Quarterly. $30.00 per year. Presents reports and general information on fruit varieties.

FTC Freedom of Information Log (Federal Trade Commission). Washington Regulatory Reporting Associates, P.O. Box 356 Basye, VA 22810. Phone: (202)639-0581 Fax: (202)478-0260 Weekly. $451.00 per year. Newsletter listing Freedom of Information Act requests that have been submitted to the Federal Trade Commission.

Fuel and Energy Abstracts: A Summary of World Literature on All Scientific, Technical, Commercial and Environmental Aspects of Fuel and Energy. Elsevier Science, 655 Ave. of the Americas New York, NY 10010. Phone: 888-437-4636 or (212)989-5800 Fax: (212)633-3680 E-mail: usinfo@elsevier.com • URL: http://www/elsevier.com • Bimonthly. $1,583.00 per year.

Fuel Oil News: Source Book., 2101 S. Arlington Heights Rd., No. 150 Arlington Heights, IL 60005. Phone: (847)427-9512 Fax: (847)427-2097 E-mail: ghradecky@mail.aip.com • URL: http://www.fueloilnews.com • Annual. $28.00. Provides fuel (heating) oil industry data.

Fuel: Science and Technology of Fuel and Energy. Elsevier Science, 655 Ave. of the Americas New York, NY 10010. Phone: 888-437-4636 or (212)989-5800 Fax: (212)633-3680 E-mail: usinfo@elsevier.com • URL: http://www.elsevier.com • 15 times a year. $2,267.00 per year.

Fulbright Scholar Program: Grants for Faculty and Professionals. Council for International Exchange of Scholars, 3007 Tilden St., N.W., Suite 5M Washington, DC 20008-3009. Phone: (202)686-4000 Fax: (202)362-3442 E-mail: ciesnet.cies.org • URL: http://www.cies.org • Annual. Free. Formerly *Fulbright Scholar Program-Faculty Grants, Research and Lecturing Awards*.

Fulfillment Management Association (FMA)., 60 E. 42nd St., Suite 1146 New York, NY 10165. Phone: (212)277-1530 Fax: (212)277-1597 URL: http://www.com/fma • Members includes publishing circulation executives. Includes a Training and Education Committee and a Career Guidance Committee.

Fulltext Sources Online. Information Today, Inc., 143 Old Marlton Pike Medford, NJ 08055-8750. Phone: 800-300-9868 or (609)654-6266 Fax: (609)654-4309 E-mail: custserv@infotoday.com • URL: http://www.infotoday.com • Semiannual. $199.00 per year; $119.50 per issue. Lists more than 8,000 journals, newspapers, magazines, newsletters, and newswires found online in fulltext through DIALOG, LEXIS-NEXIS, Dow Jones, Westlaw, etc. Includes journals that have free Internet archives. (Formerly published by BiblioData.)

The Functions of the Executive. Chester I. Barnard. Harvard University Press, 79 Garden St. Cambridge, MA 02138. Phone: 800-448-2242 or (617)495-2600 Fax: 800-962-4983 or (617)495-5898 E-mail: contacthup@harvard.edu • URL: http://www.hup.harvard.edu • 1971. $18.95.

Fund Action. Institutional Investor, 488 Madison Ave. New York, NY 10022. Phone: (212)224-3300 Fax: (212)224-3353 E-mail: info@iijournals.com • URL: http://www.iijournals.com • Weekly. $2,220.00 per year. Newsletter. Edited for mutual fund executives. Covers competition among funds, aggregate statistics, new products, regulations, service providers, and other subjects of interest to fund managers.

Fund for Constitutional Government., 122 Maryland Ave., N.E., 3rd Fl. Washington, DC 20002. Phone: (202)546-3732 Fax: (202)543-3156 Provides legal and strategic counsel for government ''whistleblowers.''

Fund for Modern Courts.

Fund for Stockowners Rights., P.O. 65563 Washington, DC 20035. Phone: (703)241-3700 Fax: (818)223-8080 Seeks to improve methods of electing corporate boards of directors and encourages the holding of annual meetings for stockholders.

Fund Raising: The Guide to Raising Money from Private Sources. Thomas C. Broce. University of Oklahoma Press, 1005 Asp Ave. Norman, OK 73019-6051. Phone: 800-627-7377 or (405)325-5111 Fax: (405)325-4000 1986. $27.95. Second enlarged revised edition.

Fund Watch: The Official Guide to High-Performance Mutual Funds. Institute for Econometric Research, 2200 S.W. 10th St. Deerfield Beach, FL 33442-8799. Phone: 800-442-0066 or (954)421-1000 Fax: (954)570-8200 URL: http://www.mfmag.com • Monthly. $80.00 per year. A chart service. Each issue provides 10-year charts of ''high-performance'' and widely-held mutual funds.

FundAlarm. Roy WeitzURL: http://www.fundalarm.com • Web site subtitle: ''Know when to hold'em, know when to fold'em, know when to walk away, know when to run.'' Provides lists of underperforming mutual funds (''3-ALARM Funds'') and severely underperforming funds (''Most Alarming 3-ALARM Funds''). Performance is based on various benchmarks. Site also provides mutual fund news, recent manager changes, and basic data for each of about 2,100 funds. Monthly updates. Fees: Free.

Fundamental Accounting Principles. Kermit D. Larson and Paul B. Miller. McGraw-Hill Higher Education, 1221 Ave. of the Americas New York, NY 10020-1095. Phone: 800-722-4726 or (212)904-2000 Fax: (212)904-2072 E-mail: customer.service@mcgraw-hill.com • URL: http://www.mcgraw-hill.com • 1995. $72.00. 14th edition.

Fundamentals of Computer-High Technology Law. James V. Vergari and Virginia V. Shue. American Law Institute-American Bar Association, Committee on Continuing Professional Education, 4025 Chestnut St. Philadelphia, PA 19104-3099. Phone: 800-253-6397 or (215)243-1600 Fax: (215)243-1664 URL: http://www.ali-aba.org • 1991. $29.00.

Fundamentals of Construction Estimating. David Pratt. Delmar Publishing, P.O. Box 15015 Albany, NY 12212-5015. Phone: 800-998-7498 or (518)464-3500 Fax: (518)464-0393 E-mail: cheryl.kean@itped.com • URL: http://www.delmar.com • 1995. $78.95.

Fundamentals of Construction Estimating and Cost Accounting. Keith Collier. Prentice Hall, 240 Frisch Court Paramus, NJ 07652-5240. Phone: 800-947-7700 or (201)909-6200 Fax: 800-445-6991 or (201)909-6361 URL: http://

www.prenhall.com • 2000. Third edition. Price on application.

Fundamentals of Corporate Finance. Stephen Ross and Randy Westerfield. McGraw-Hill, 1221 Ave. of the Americas New York, NY 10020. Phone: 800-722-4726 or (212)904-2000 Fax: (212)904-2072 E-mail: customer.service@mcgraw-hill.com • URL: http://www.mcgraw-hill.com • 1998. $69.25. Fifth edition.

Fundamentals of Employee Benefit Programs. Employee Benefit Research Institute, 2121 K St., N. W., Suite 600 Washington, DC 20037-1986. Phone: (202)659-0670 Fax: (202)775-6312 E-mail: info@ebri.org • URL: http://www.ebri.org • 1996. $49.95. Fifth edition. Provides basic explanation of employee benefit programs in both the private and public sectors, including health insurance, pension plans, retirement planning, social security, and long-term care insurance.

Fundamentals of Engineering Drawing: With an Introduction to Interactive Computer Graphics for Design and Production. Warren J. Luzadder and Jon M. Duff. Prentice Hall, 240 Frisch Court Paramus, NJ 07652-5240. Phone: 800-947-7700 or (201)909-6200 Fax: 800-445-6991 or (201)909-6361 URL: http://www.prenhall.com • 1992. $91.00. 11th edition.

Fundamentals of Finance and Accounting for Nonfinancial Managers. American Management Association Extension Institute, P.O. Box 1026 Saranac Lake, NY 12983-9957. Phone: 800-262-9699 or (518)891-1500 Fax: (518)891-0368 E-mail: amapubs@aol.com • URL: http://www.amanet.org • Looseleaf. $110.00. Self-study course. Emphasis is on practical explanations, examples, and problem solving. Quizzes and a case study are included.

Fundamentals of Financial and Managerial Accounting. Kermit D. Larson and others. McGraw-Hill Higher Education, 1221 Ave. of the Americas New York, NY 10020. Phone: 800-722-4726 or (212)904-2000 Fax: (212)904-2072 E-mail: customer.service@mcgraw-hill.com • URL: http://www.mcgraw-hill.com • 1993. $72.00.

Fundamentals of Financial Management. James C. Van Horne and John M. Wachowicz. Prentice Hall, 240 Frisch Court Paramus, NJ 07652-5240. Phone: 800-947-7700 or (201)909-6200 Fax: 800-445-6991 or (201)909-6361 URL: http://www.prenhall.com • 1997. $80.00. 10th edition.

Fundamentals of Human Resources. American Management Association Extension Institute, P.O. Box 1026 Saranac Lake, NY 12983-9957. Phone: 800-262-9699 or (518)891-1500 Fax: (518)891-0368 URL: http://www.amanet.org • Looseleaf. $110.00. Self-study course on a wide range of personnel topics. Emphasis is on practical explanations, examples, and problem solving. Quizzes and a case study are included.

Fundamentals of Hydraulic Engineering Systems. Ned H. Hwang and R.J. Houghtalen. Prentice Hall, 240 Frisch Court Paramus, NJ 07652-5240. Phone: 800-947-7700 or (201)909-6200 Fax: 800-445-6991 or (201)909-6361 URL: http://www.prenhall.com • 1995. $105.00. Third edition.

Fundamentals of Investing. Lawrence J. Gitman and Michael D. Joehnk. Addison-Wesley Longman, Inc., One Jacob Way Reading, MA 01687. Phone: 800-447-2226 or (781)944-3700 Fax: (781)944-9351 URL: http://www.awl.com • 1998. $98.33. Seventh edition.

Fundamentals of Management. James H. Donnelly. McGraw-Hill, 1221 Ave. of the Americas New York, NY 10020. Phone: 800-722-4726 or (212)904-2000 Fax: (212)904-2072 E-mail: customer.service@mcgraw-hill.com • URL: http://www.mcgraw-hill.com • 1997. 10th edition. Price on application.

Fundamentals of Managerial Economics. James L. and Mark Hirschey Pappas. Dryden Press, 301 Commerce St., Suite 3700 Fort Worth, TX 32887-143. Phone: 800-782-4479 or (817)334-7500 Fax: (817)334-0878 1997. $97.50. Sixth edition.

Fundamentals of Metallurgical Processes. L. Coudurier and others. Franklin Book Co., Inc., 7804 Montgomery Ave. Elkins Park, PA 19027. Phone: (215)635-5252 Fax: (215)635-6155 E-mail: service@franklinbook.com • URL: http://www.franklinbook.com • 1985. $187.00. Second edition. (International Monographs on Materials and Technology Series: Volume 27).

Fundamentals of Municipal Bonds: A Basic, Definitive Text on the Municipal Securities Market. The Bond Market Association, 40 Broad St., 12th Fl. New York, NY 10004-2373. Phone: (212)809-7000 Fax: (212)440-5260 URL: http://www.bondmarkets.com • 1990. $29.95. Fourth revised edition.

Fundamentals of Optical Fibers. John A. Buck. John Wiley and Sons, Inc., 605 Third Ave. New York, NY 10158-0012. Phone: 800-225-5945 or (212)850-6000 Fax: (212)850-6088 E-mail: info@wiley.com • URL: http://www.wiley.com • 1995. $84.95. (Pure and Applied Optics Series).

Fundamentals of Optoelectronics. Clifford R. Pollock. McGraw-Hill Higher Education, 1221 Ave. of the Americas New York, NY 10020. Phone: 800-722-4726 or (212)904-2000 Fax: (212)904-2072 E-mail: customer.service@mcgraw-hill.com • URL: http://www.mcgraw-hill.com • 1994. $77.50.

Fundamentals of Photonics. Bahaa E. Seleh and Malvin C. Teich. John Wiley and Sons, Inc., 605 Third Ave. New York, NY 10158-0012. Phone: 800-225-5945 or (212)850-6000 Fax: (212)850-6088 E-mail: info@wiley.com • URL: http://www.wiley.com • 1991. $105.00. (Pure and Applied Optics Series).

Fundamentals of Private Pensions. Dan McGill and others. University of Pennsylvania Press, 4200 Pine St., 3rd Fl. Philadelphia, PA 19104-4011. Phone: 800-445-9880 or (215)898-6261 Fax: (215)898-0404 1996. $79.95. Seventh revised edition.

Fundamentals of Product Liability Law for Engineers. L. K. Enghagen. Industrial Press, Inc., 200 Madison Ave. New York, NY 10016. Phone: 888-528-7852 or (212)889-6330 Fax: (212)545-8327 E-mail: induspress@aol.com • URL: http://www.industrialpress.com • 1992. $39.95. Covers theories of liability, strategies for protection, defenses, and proving a case. Includes case histories.

Fundamentals of Professional Food Preparation: A Laboratory Text-Workbook. Donald V. Laconi. John Wiley and Sons, Inc., 605 Third Ave. New York, NY 10158-0012. Phone: 800-225-5945 or (212)850-6000 Fax: (212)850-6088 E-mail: info@wiley.com • URL: http://www.wiley.com • 1995. $54.95.

Fundamentals of Project Management. James P. Lewis. AMACOM, 1601 Broadway, 12th Fl. New York, NY 10019. Phone: 800-262-9699 or (212)586-8100 Fax: (212)903-8168 E-mail: custmserv@amanet.org • URL: http://www.amanet.org • 1995. $10.95. (Work Smart Series).

Fundamentals of Real Estate Appraisal. William Ventolo and Martha Williams. Dearborn, A Kaplan Professional Co., 155 N. Wacker St. Chicago, IL 60606-1719. Phone: 800-621-9621 or (312)836-4400 Fax: (312)836-1021 URL: http://www.dearborn.com • 1998. $46.95. Seventh edition. Explanation of real estate appraisal.

Fundamentals of Real Estate Investment. Austin J. Jaffe and C. F. Sirmans. Prentice Hall, 240 Frisch Court Paramus, NJ 07652-5240. Phone: 800-947-7700 or (201)909-6200 Fax: 800-445-6991 or (201)909-6361 URL: http://www.prenhall.com • 1994. $72.00. Third edition.

Fundamentals of Risk and Insurance. Emmett J. Vaughan and Therese J. Vaughan. John Wiley and Sons, Inc., 605 Third Ave. New York, NY 10158-0012. Phone: 800-526-5368 or (212)850-6000 Fax: (212)850-6088 E-mail: info@wiley.com • URL: http://www.wiley.com • 1999. $99.95. Eighth edition.

Fundamentals of Robotics: Analysis and Control. Robert J. Schilling. Prentice Hall, 240 Frisch Court Paramus, NJ 07652-5240. Phone: 800-947-7700 or (201)909-6200 Fax: 800-445-6991 or (201)909-6361 URL: http://www.prenhall.com • 1990. $60.00.

Fundamentals of Selling: Customers for Life. Charles Futrell. McGraw-Hill, 1221 Ave. of the Americas New York, NY 10020. Phone: 800-722-4736 or (212)904-2000 Fax: (212)904-2072 E-mail: customer.service@mcgraw-hill.com • URL: http://www.mcgraw-hill.com • 1998. $67.50. Sixth edition. (Marketing Series).

Fundamentals of Strategic Planning for Healthcare Organizations. Stan Williamson and others. Haworth Press, Inc., 10 Alice St. Binghamton, NY 13904-1580. Phone: 800-429-6784 or (607)722-5857 Fax: 800-895-0582 or (607)722-1424 E-mail: getinfo@haworthpressinc.com • URL: http://www.haworthpressinc.com • 1996. $49.95.

Funding Sources for Community and Economic Development: A Guide to Current Sources for Local Programs and Projects. Oryx Press, 4041 North Central Ave., Suite 700 Phoenix, AZ 85012-3397. Phone: 800-279-6799 or (602)265-2651 Fax: 800-279-4663 or (602)265-6250 E-mail: info@oryxpress.com • URL: http://www.oryxpress.com • 2000. $64.95. Sixth edition. Provides information on 2,600 funding sources. Includes "A Guide to Proposal Planning."

Fundraising: Hands-On Tactics for Nonprofit Groups. L. Peter Edles. McGraw-Hill, 1221 Ave. of the Americas New York, NY 10020. Phone: 800-722-4726 or (212)904-2000 Fax: (212)904-2072 E-mail: customer.service@mcgraw-hill.com • URL: http://www.mcgraw-hill.com • 1992. $32.95. Covers fundamental premises, soliciting major gifts, small gift prospecting, canvassing, telephone appeals, creating publications, direct mail, and other fund-raising topics for nonprofit organizations.

Funeral and Memorial Societies of America., P.O. Box 10 Hinesburg, VT 05461. Phone: 800-765-0107 or (802)482-3437 Fax: (802)482-5246 E-mail: famsa@funerals.org • URL: http://www.funerals.org • Annual. Free. Lists over 150 nonprofit memorial societies which assists members in obtaining simple funeral arrangements at reasonable cost. Includes members of the Memorial Society Association of Canada. Formerly *Continental Association of Funeral and Memorial Societies Directory of Member Societies*.

Funeral and Memorial Societies of America.

Funeral Service Insider. Jean DeSapio, editor. Atcom, Inc., 1541 Morris Ave. Bronx, NY 10457-8702. Phone: (212)873-5900 Fax: (212)799-1728 Weekly. $255.00 per year. News and trends among death-care professionals.

Funworld. International Association of Amusement Parks and Attractions, 1448 Duke St. Alexandria, VA 22314-3403. Phone: (703)836-4800 Fax: (703)836-4801 URL: http://www.iaapa.org • 11 times a year. Members, $22.00 per year; non-members, $40.00 per year. Analysis and statistics of the international amusement park industry. Text in English; sections in French, German, Japanese and Spanish.

Fur Age. Fur Vogue Publishing Co., Inc., Two Main St. Roslyn, NY 11576. Phone: (516)484-0630 Fax: (516)484-8136 E-mail: furage@furs.com • URL: http://www.furs.com • 10 times a year. $100.00 per year. Formerly *Fur Age Weekly*.

Fur Information Council of America.

Fur Rancher. Becker Publishing, PO Box 655 Hopkins, MN 55343. Phone: (952)949-2159 Fax: (952)934-3668 URL: http://www.beckerpublishing.com • Quarterly. $20.00 per year. Covers the farm raising of animals for fur.

Fur World: The Newsmagazine of Fur and Better Outerware. Creative Marketing Plus, Inc., 19 West 21st St. New York, NY 10010. Phone: (212)727-1210 Fax: (212)727-1218 URL: http://www.cmponline.com • Semimonthly. $45.00 per year. Edited for fur retailers, ranchers, pelt dealers, and manufacturers. Provides news and statistics relating to the retail and wholesale fur business.

Furniture/Today: The Weekly Business Newspaper of the Furniture Industry. Cahners Business Newspapers, 7025 Albert Pick Rd., Ste. 200 Greensboro, NC 27409. Phone: (336)605-1033 Fax: (336)605-1143 E-mail: corporatecommunications@cahners.com • URL: http://www.cahners.com • Weekly. $139.97 per year.

Furniture World. Towse Publishing Co., 1333A North Ave. New Rochelle, NY 10804-2807. Phone: (914)235-3095 Fax: (914)235-3278 E-mail: magazinefw@aol.com • URL: http://www.furinfo.com • Monthly. $19.00 per year. Formerly *Furniture World and Furniture Buyer and Decorator*.

Future Banker: The Vision of Leadership in an Electronic Age. American Banker, One State St. Plaza New York, NY 10004. Phone: 800-362-3806 or (212)803-8345 Fax: (212)292-5217 URL: http://www.americanbanker.com • Monthly. $79.00 per year. Covers technology innovation for the banking industry, including online banking.

Future Business Leaders of America-Phi Beta Lambda.

Future-Driven Library Marketing. Darlene E. Weingand. American Library Association, 50 E. Huron St. Chicago, IL 60611-2795. Phone: 800-545-2433 or (312)944-6780 Fax: (312)440-9374 E-mail: ala@ala.org • URL: http://www.ala.org • 1998. $25.00. The author discusses progressive marketing strategies for libraries. An annotated bibliography is included.

Future Libraries: Dreams, Madness, and Reality. Walt Crawford and Michael Gorman. American Library Association, 50 E. Huron St. Chicago, IL 60611-2795. Phone: 800-545-2433 or (312)944-6780 Fax: (312)440-9374 E-mail: ala@ala.org • URL: http://www.ala.org • 1995. $28.00. Discusses the "over-hyped virtual library" and electronic-publishing "fantasies." Presents the argument for the importance of books, physical libraries, and library personnel.

Future Survey: A Monthly Abstract of Books, Articles, and Reports Concerning Trends, Forecasts, and Ideas About the Future. World Future Society, 7910 Woodmont Ave., Suite 450 Bethesda, MD 20814-3032. Phone: 800-989-8274 or (301)656-8274 Fax: (301)951-0394 E-mail: wfsinfo@wfs.org • URL: http://www.wfs.org/ • Monthly. Individuals, $89.00 per year; libraries, $129.00 per year. Includes author and subject indexes.

Future Survey Annual: A Guide to the Recent Literature of Trends, Forecasts, and Policy Proposals. World Future Society, 7910 Woodmont Ave., Suite 450 Bethesda, MD 20814-3032. Phone: 800-989-8274 or (301)656-8274 Fax: (301)951-0394 E-mail: wfsinfo@wfs.org • URL: http://www.wfs.org/wfs • Annual. $35.00.

Future Trends in Telecommunications. R. J. Horrocks and R.W. Scarr. John Wiley and Sons, Inc., 605 Third Ave. New York, NY 10158-0012. Phone: 800-225-5945 or (212)850-6000 Fax: (212)850-6088 E-mail: info@wiley.com • URL: http://www.wiley.com • 1993. $235.00. Includes fiber optics technology, local area networks, and satellite communications. Discusses the future of telecommunications for the consumer and for industry. *Communication and Distributed Systems Series*.

Futures and OTC World: The Futures Portfolio Advisor (Over the Counter). R.R. Wasendorf, editor. Russell R. Wasendorf, P.O. Box 849 Cedar Falls, IA 50613. Phone: (319)268-0441 Fax: (319)277-0880 E-mail: russ-wasendorf@msn.com • URL: http://www.flight2quality.com • Weekly. $435.00 per year. Newsletter. Futures market information. Includes Daily Hotline Information to update advice. Formerly *Futures and Options Factors*.

Futures Guide to Computerized Trading. Futures Magazine, Inc., 250 S. Wacker Dr. Suite 1150 Chicago, IL 60606.

Phone: 800-635-3931 or (312)977-0999 Fax: (312)977-1042 E-mail: futures@aol.com • URL: http://www.futuresmag.com • Annual. $10.00. ''A directory of products and services for the computerized trader.'' Provides information on computer software applications for commodity traders and money managers, including trading methods and technical analysis.

Futures Industry Association.

Futures; The Journal of Forecasting, Planning and Policy. Elsevier Science, 655 Ave. of the Americas New York, NY 10010. Phone: 888-437-4636 or (212)989-5800 Fax: (212)633-3680 E-mail: usinfo@elsevier.com • URL: http://www.elsevier.com • 10 times a year. $764.00 per year.

Futures Magazine SourceBook: The Most Complete List of Exchanges, Companies, Regulators, Organizations, etc., Offering Products and Services to the Futures and Options Industry. Futures Magazine, Inc., 250 S. Wacker Dr. Suite 1150 Chicago, IL 60606. Phone: 800-635-3931 or (312)977-0999 Fax: (312)977-1042 E-mail: futuresm@aol.com • URL: http://www.futuresmag.com • Annual. $19.50. Provides information on commodity futures brokers, trading method services, publications, and other items of interest to futures traders and money managers.

Futures Market Service. Commodity Research Bureau, 30 S. Wacker Dr., Suite 1810 Chicago, IL 60606. Phone: 800-621-5271 or (312)454-1801 Fax: (312)454-0239 E-mail: crbino@ais.net • URL: http://www.krf.com/crb/ • Weekly. $155.00 per year.

Futures Markets. A. G. Malliaris, editor. Edward Elgar Publishing, Inc., 136 West St., Suite 203 Northampton, MA 01060. Phone: 800-390-3149 or (413)584-5551 Fax: (413)584-9933 E-mail: eep.orders@aidcvt.com • URL: http://www.e-elgar.co.uk • 1997. $450.00. Three volumes. Consists of reprints of 70 articles dating from 1959 to 1993, on futures market volatility, speculation, hedging, stock indexes, portfolio insurance, interest rates, and foreign currencies. (International Library of Critical Writings in Financial Economics.)

Futures: News, Analysis, and Strategies for Futures, Options, and Derivatives Traders. Futures Magazine, Inc., 250 S. Wacker Dr., Suite 1150 Chicago, IL 60606. Phone: 800-635-3931 or (312)977-0999 Fax: (312)977-1042 E-mail: jbecker@futuresmag.com • URL: http://www.futuresmag.com • Monthly. $39.00 per year. Edited for institutional money managers and traders, brokers, risk managers, and individual investors or speculators. Includes special feature issues on interest rates, technical indicators, currencies, charts, precious metals, hedge funds, and derivatives. Supplements available.

Futures Online. Oster Communications, Inc.Phone: 800-601-8907 or (319)277-1278 Fax: (319)277-7982 URL: http://www.futuresmag.com • Web site presents updates of *Futures* magazine and links to other futures-related sites. Includes ''Futures Industry News,'' ''Technical Talk,'' ''Today's Hot Markets,'' ''Futures Talk'' (forums), ''Futures Library'' (archives, 1993 to date), and other features. Keyword searching is available. Updating: daily. Fees: Free.

Futures Research Quarterly. World Future Society, 7910 Woodmont Ave., Suite 450 Bethesda, MD 20814. Phone: 800-989-8274 or (301)656-8274 Fax: (301)951-0394 E-mail: wfsinfo@wfs.org • URL: http://www.wfs.org/frq/htm • Quarterly. Members, $70.00 per year; others, $90.00 per year.

Futuretech. Technical Insights, 605 Third Ave. New York, NY 10158-0012. Phone: 800-825-7550 or (212)850-8600 Fax: (212)850-8800 E-mail: insights@wiley.com • URL: http://www.wiley.com/technicalinsights • 18 times a year. $1,600.00 per year. Newsletter on newly emerging technologies and their markets.

The Futurist: A Journal of Forecasts, Trends, and Ideas About the Future. World Future Society, 7910 Woodmont Ave., Suite 450 Bethesda, MD 20814. Phone: 800-989-8274 or (301)656-8274 Fax: (301)951-0394 E-mail: wfsinfo@wfs.org • URL: http://www.wfs.org/ • Bimonthly. Members, $39.00 per year; non-members, $47.00 per year.

FX Manager (Foreign Exchange). American Educational Systems, 173 W. 81st St. New York, NY 10024. Phone: 800-717-2669 or (212)501-8181 Fax: (212)501-8926 E-mail: gerans@pobox.com • URL: http://www.emwl.com • Monthly. $790.00 per year. Foreign exchange forecasts. Formerly *Euromoney Treasury Manager*.

GAAP for Governments: Interpretation and Application of Generally Accepted Accounting Principles for State and Local Governments. John Wiley and Sons, Inc., 605 Third Ave. New York, NY 10158-0012. Phone: 800-225-5945 or (212)850-6000 Fax: (212)850-6088 E-mail: info@jwiley.com • URL: http://www.wiley.com • Annual. $134.00. (Includes CD-ROM.)

Gaining Control of the Corporate Culture. Ralph H. Kilmann and others. Jossey-Bass, Inc., Publishers, 350 Sansome St.,5th Fl. San Francisco, CA 94104. Phone: 888-378-2537 or (415)433-1740 Fax: (415)433-0499 E-mail: webperson@jbp.com • URL: http://www.josseybass.com • 1985. $43.95. (Management Series).

Gaining Word Power. Dorothy Rubin. Allyn and Bacon, Inc., 160 Gould St. Needham Heights, MA 02194-2310. Phone: 800-278-3525 or (781)455-1250 Fax: (781)455-1294 E-mail: ab_webmaster@abacon.com • URL: http://www.abacon.com • 1999. $41.00. Fifth edition. Purpose of book is to help students and others build a ''college-level'' vocabulary, including information-age words.

Gale Biographies. The Gale Group, 27500 Drake Rd. Farmington Hills, MI 48331-3535. Phone: 800-877-GALE or (248)699-GALE Fax: 800-414-5043 or (248)699-8069 E-mail: galeord@gale.com • URL: http://www.gale.com • Provides online biographical profiles (text) of more than 140,000 prominent individuals, past and present, from all fields of activity. Corresponds to various Gale print sources. Quarterly updates. Inquire as to online cost and availability.

Gale Book of Averages. The Gale Group, 27500 Drake Rd. Farmington Hills, MI 48331-3535. Phone: 800-877-GALE or (248)699-GALE Fax: 800-414-5043 or (248)699-8069 E-mail: galeord@galegroup.com • URL: http://www.galegroup.com • 1994. $70.00. Contains 1,100-1,200 statistical averages on a variety of topics, with references to published sources. Subjects include business, labor, consumption, crime, and other areas of contemporary society.

Gale City and Metro Rankings Reporter. The Gale Group, 27500 Drake Rd. Farmington Hills, MI 48331-3535. Phone: 800-877-GALE or (248)699-GALE Fax: 800-414-5043 or (248)699-8069 E-mail: galeord@galegroup.com • URL: http://www.galegroup.com • 1996. $134.00. Second edition. Provides about 3,000 statistical ranking tables covering more than 1,500 U. S. cities and Metropolitan Statistical Areas. Covers economic, demographic, social, governmental, and cultural factors. Sources are private studies and government data.

Gale Country and World Rankings Reporter. The Gale Group, 27500 Drake Rd. Farmington Hills, MI 48331-3535. Phone: 800-877-GALE or (248)699-GALE Fax: 800-414-5043 or (248)699-8069 E-mail: galeord@galegroup.com • URL: http://www.galegroup.com • 1997. $135.00. Second edition. Provides about 3,000 statistical ranking tables and charts covering more than 235 nations. Sources include the United Nations and various government publications.

Gale Database of Publications and Broadcast Media. The Gale Group, 27500 Drake Rd. Farmington Hills, MI 48331-3535. Phone: 800-877-GALE Fax: 800-414-5043 or (248)699-8069 E-mail: galeord@galegroup.com • URL: http://www.galegroup.com • An online directory containing detailed information on over 67,000 periodicals, newspapers, broadcast stations, cable systems, directories, and newsletters. Corresponds to the following print sources: *Gale Directory of Publications and Broadcast Media; Directories in Print; City and State Directories in Print; Newsletters in Print*. Semiannual updates. Inquire as to online cost and availability.

Gale Directory of Databases. The Gale Group, 27500 Drake Rd. Farmington Hills, MI 48331-3535. Phone: 800-877-GALE or (248)699-GALE Fax: 800-414-5043 or (248)699-8069 E-mail: galeord@galegroup.com • URL: http://www.galegroup.com • 2001. $400.00. Two volumes. Volume 1, $270.00; volume 2, $180.00. *Volume 1: Online Databases* and *Volume 2: CD-ROM, Diskette, Magnetic Tape, Handheld, and Batch Access Database Products*.

Gale Directory of Databases Ïonlineİ. The Gale Group, 27500 Drake Rd. Farmington Hills, MI 48331-3535. Phone: 800-877-GALE or (248)699-GALE Fax: 800-414-5043 or (248)699-8069 E-mail: galeord@gale.com • URL: http://www.gale.com • Presents the online version of the printed *Gale Directory of Databases, Volume 1: Online Databases* and *Gale Directory of Databases, Volume 2: CD-ROM, Diskette, Magnetic Tape, Handheld, and Batch Access Database Products*. Semiannual updates. Inquire as to online cost and availability.

Gale Directory of Learning Worldwide: A Guide to Faculty and Institutions of Higher Education, Research, and Culture. The Gale Group, 27500 Drake Rd. Farmington Hills, MI 48331-3535. Phone: 800-877-GALE or (248)699-GALE Fax: 800-414-5043 or (248)699-8069 E-mail: galeord@galegroup.com • URL: http://www.galegroup.com • 2000. $410.00. Two volumes. Describes about 26,000 colleges, universities, research institutes, libraries, museums, scholarly associations, academies, and archives around the world. Arranged by country.

Gale Directory of Publications and Broadcast Media. The Gale Group, 27500 Drake Rd. Farmington Hills, MI 48331-3535. Phone: 800-877-GALE or (248)699-GALE Fax: 800-414-5043 or (248)699-8069 E-mail: galeord@galegroup.com • URL: http://www.galegroup.com • Annual. $650.00. Five volumes. A guide to publications and broadcasting stations in the U. S. and Canada, including newspapers, magazines, journals, radio stations, television stations, and cable systems. Geographic arrangement. Volume three consists of statistical tables, maps, subject indexes, and title index. Formerly *Ayer Directory of Publications*.

The Gale Encyclopedia of Psychology. The Gale Group, 27500 Drake Rd. Farmington Hills, MI 48331-3535. Phone: 800-877-GALE or (248)699-GALE Fax: 800-414-5043 or (248)699-8069 E-mail: galeord@galegroup.com • URL: http://www.galegroup.com • 1998. $130.00. Includes bibliographies arranged by topic and a glossary.

Gale Encyclopedia of U.S. Economic History. The Gale Group, 27500 Drake Rd. Farmington Hills, MI 48331-3535. Phone: 800-877-GALE or (248)699-GALE Fax: 800-414-5043 or (248)699-8069 E-mail: galeordatsgalegroup.com • URL: http://www.galegroup.com • 2000. $205.00. Two volumes. Contains about 1,000 alphabetically arranged entries. Includes industry profiles, biographies, social issue profiles, geographic profiles, and chronological tables.

Gale Environmental Almanac. The Gale Group, 27500 Drake Rd. Farmington Hills, MI 48331-3535. Phone: 800-877-GALE or (248)699-GALE Fax: 800-414-5043 or (248)699-8069 E-mail: galeord@galegroup.com • URL: http://www.galegroup.com • 1994. $110.00. Contains 15 chapters, each on a broad topic related to the environment, such as ''Waste and Recycling.'' Each chapter has a topical overview, charts, statistics, and illustrations. Includes a glossary of environmental terms and a bibliography.

Gale Environmental Sourcebook: A Guide to Organizations, Agencies, and Publications. The Gale Group, 27500 Drake Rd. Farmington Hills, MI 48331-3535. Phone: 800-877-GALE or (248)699-GALE Fax: 800-414-5043 or (248)699-8069 E-mail: galeord@galegroup.com • URL: http://www.galegroup.com • 1993. $95.00. Second edition. A directory of print and non-print information sources on a wide variety of environmental topics.

Gale Five Language Dictionary of Technology: Simultaneous Translations of English, French, Spanish, German, and Italian. The Gale Group, 27500 Drake Rd. Farmington Hills, MI 48331-3535. Phone: 800-877-GALE or (248)699-GALE Fax: 800-414-5043 or (248)699-8069 E-mail: galeord@galegroup.com • URL: http://www.galegroup.com • 1993. $75.00. Contains translations of frequently-used technological words and phrases.

Gale Guide to Internet Databases. The Gale Group, 27500 Drake Rd. Farmington Hills, MI 48331-3535. Phone: 800-877-GALE or (248)699-GALE Fax: 800-414-5043 or (248)699-8069 E-mail: galeord@galegroup.com • URL: http://www.galegroup.com • 1999. $120.00. Sixth edition. Presents critical descriptions and ratings of more than 5,000 useful Internet databases (especially World Wide Web sites). Includes a glossary of Internet terms, a bibliography, and five indexes.

Gale State Rankings Reporter. The Gale Group, 27500 Drake Rd. Farmington Hills, MI 48331-3535. Phone: 800-877-GALE or (248)699-GALE Fax: 800-414-5043 or (248)699-8069 E-mail: galeord@galegroup.com • URL: http://www.galegroup.com • 1996. $110.00. Second edition Provides 3,000 ranked lists of states under 35 subject headings. Sources are newspapers, periodicals, books, research institute publications, and government publications.

GaleNet: Your Information Community. The Gale Group-Phone: 800-877-GALE or (248)699-GALE Fax: 800-414-5043 or (248)699-8069 E-mail: galenet@gale.com • URL: http://www.galenet.com • Web site provides a wide variety of full-text information from Gale databases, Taft, and other sources. Covers associations, biography, business directories, education, the information industry, literature, publishing, and science. Fee-based subscriptions are available for individual databases (free demonstration). Includes Boolean search features and the BRS/Search user interface.

Gale's Guide to Nonprofits: A Gale Ready Reference Handbook. The Gale Group, 27500 Drake Rd. Farmington Hills, MI 48331-3535. Phone: 800-877-GALE or (248)699-GALE Fax: 800-414-5043 or (248)699-8069 E-mail: galeord@galegroup.com • URL: http://www.galegroup.com • 2000. $135.00. Serves to provide a wide variety of information sources of interest to nonprofit organizations, including publications, online databases, and associations. Contains three indexes and a glossary.

Gale's Guide to the Arts: A Gale Ready Reference Handbook. The Gale Group, 27500 Drake Rd. Farmington Hills, MI 48331-3535. Phone: 800-877-GALE or (248)699-GALE Fax: 800-414-5043 or (248)699-8069 E-mail: galeord@galegroup.com • URL: http://www.galegroup.com • 2000. $125.00. Contains descriptions of information sources of interest to nonprofit art groups, including publications, online databases, museums, government agencies, and associations. Three indexes and a glossary are provided.

Gale's Guide to the Media: A Gale Ready Reference Handbook. The Gale Group, 27500 Drake Rd. Farmington Hills, MI 48331-3535. Phone: 800-877-GALE or (248)699-GALE Fax: 800-414-5043 or (248)699-8069 E-mail: galeord@galegroup.com • URL: http://www.galegroup.com • 2000. $125.00. Provides profiles of a wide variety of media-related organizations, publications, broadcasters, agencies, and databases, of interest to nonprofit groups. Contains three indexes and a glossary.

Gam-Anon International Service Office., P.O. Box 570157 Whitestone, NY 11357. Phone: (718)352-1671 Fax: (718)746-2571 Affiliated with Gamblers Anonymous.

GAMA International., 1922 F St., N. W. Washington, DC 20006. Phone: 800-345-2687 or (202)331-6088 Fax: (202)785-5712 E-mail: gamamail@gama.naifa.org • URL:

http://www.gamaweb.com • Members are life insurance agents.

GAMA International Journal. GAMA International, 1922 F St., N. W. Washington, DC 20006-4389. Phone: (202)638-3492 Fax: (202)785-5712 URL: http://www.gamaweb.com • Bimonthly. $30.00 per year. Contains practical articles on the management of life insurance agencies. (GAMA International was formerly General Agents and Managers Association.)

Gamblers Anonymous.

Games, Strategies, and Managers: How Managers Can Use Game Theory to Make Better Business Decisions. John McMillan. Oxford University Press, Inc., 198 Madison Ave. New York, NY 10016-4314. Phone: 800-451-7556 or (212)726-6000 Fax: (212)726-7446 E-mail: custserv@oup-usa.org • URL: http://www.oup-usa.org • 1992. $17.95.

Gaming International Magazine. Boardwalker Magazine, Inc., P.O. Box 7418 Atlantic City, NJ 08404-7418. Phone: (609)345-6848 Quarterly. $28.00 per year.

Garment Manufacturer's Index. Klevens Publications, Inc., 7600 Ave. V Littlerock, CA 93543. Phone: (805)944-4111 Fax: (805)944-1800 Annual. $60.00. A directory of about 8,000 manufacturers and suppliers of products and services used in the making of men's, women's, and children's clothing. Includes fabrics, trimmings, factory equipment, and other supplies.

Gas Abstracts. Institute of Gas Technology, 1700 S. Mount Prospect Rd. Des Plaines, IL 60618-1804. Phone: (847)768-0673 Fax: (847)768-0669 URL: http://www.igt.org • Monthly. $425.00 per year. Abstracts of gas and energy related articles from around the world.

Gas Appliance Manufacturers Association.

Gas Data Book. American Gas Association, 444 N. Capitol St., N.W. Washington, DC 20001-1511. Phone: (202)824-7000 Fax: (202)824-7115 E-mail: amgas@aga.com • URL: http://www.aga.org • Annual.

Gas Digest: The Magazine of Gas Operations. T-P Graphics, 5731 Arboles Dr. Houston, TX 77035. Phone: (713)723-6736 Quarterly. Free. Articles and data relating to operations and management phases of natural gas operations.

Gas Facts: A Statistical Record of the Gas Utility Industry. American Gas Association, Dept. of Statistics, 444 N. Capitol St., N.W., 4th Fl. Washington, DC 20001-1511. Phone: (202)824-7000 Fax: (202)824-7115 E-mail: amgas@aga.com • URL: http://www.aga.org • Annual. Members, $40.00; non-members, $80.00.

Gas Industry Training Directory. American Gas Association, 444 N. Capitol St., N.W. Washington, DC 20001-1511. Phone: (202)824-7000 Fax: (202)824-7115 E-mail: amgas@aga.com • URL: http://www.aga.org • Annual. Free. Lists over 600 programs available from gas transmission and distributions companies, manufacturers of gas-fired equipment, consultants, etc., and from gas associations.

Gas Turbine World. Pequot Publishing, Inc., 250 Pequot Ave. Southport, CT 06490. Phone: (203)259-1112 Fax: (203)255-3313 Bimonthly. $90.00 per year.

Gas Utility and Pipeline Industries: The Executive, Administration, Operations Md Engineering Magazine of Gas Energy Supply, Risk Management, Pipeline Transmission, Utility Distribution. Gas Industries Inc., P.O. Box 558 Park Ridge, IL 60068-0558. Phone: (847)696-2394 Fax: (847)696-3445 Monthly. $20.00 per year. Includes semiannual *AGA News*. Formerly *Gas Industires Magazine*.

Gas Utility Industry Worldwide. Midwest Publishing Co., P.O. Box 50350 Tulsa, OK 74150-0350. Phone: 800-829-2002 or (918)583-2033 Fax: (918)587-9349 E-mail: info@midwestdirectories.com • URL: http://www.pennwell.com • Annual. $115.00. Approximately 8,000 utility companies, contractors, engineering firms, equipment manufacturers, supply companies, underground natural gas storage facilities and regulatory agencies; international coverage.

Gas World International. American Educational Systems, 173 W. 81st St. New York, NY 10024. Phone: 800-717-8935 or (212)501-8181 Fax: (212)501-8926 E-mail: gerans@pobox.com • URL: http://www.emw/.com. • Monthly. $240.00 per year. Formerly *Gas World*.

The Gases and Welding Distributor. Penton Media Inc., 1300 E. Ninth St. Cleveland, OH 44114. Phone: (216)696-7000 Fax: (216)696-0836 E-mail: corpcomm@penton.com • URL: http://www.pennwell.com • Bimonthly. Free to qualified personnel; others, $45.00 Per year. Formerly *Welding Distributor*.

Gasoline and Automotive Service Dealers Association., 9520 Seaview Ave. Brooklyn, NY 11236. Phone: (718)241-1111 Fax: (718)763-6589 Members are owners and operators of automobile service stations and repair shops.

Gates: How Microsoft's Mogul Reinvented an Industry and Made Himself the Richest Man in America. Stephen Manes and Paul Andrews. Simon & Schuster Trade, 1230 Ave. of the Americas New York, NY 10020. Phone: 800-223-2336 or (212)698-7000 Fax: 800-983-9831 or (212)698-7007 E-mail: ssonline_feedback@simonsays.com • URL: http://www.simonsays.com • 1994. $14.00.

GATF World. Graphic Arts Technical Foundation, 200 Deer Run Sewickley, PA 15143-2600. Phone: (412)621-6941 Fax: (412)621-3049 URL: http://www.gaft.org • Bimonthly. $75.00 per year. Technical articles of interest to the graphic communications industry. Incorporates *Graphic Arts Abstracts*.

GDL Alert. Warren, Gorham & Lamont/RIA Group, 395 Hudson St. New York, NY 10014. Phone: 800-950-1215 or (212)367-6300 Fax: (212)367-6718 E-mail: customer_services@riag.com • URL: http://www.riahome.com • Monthly. $110.98 per year. Newsletter. Covers current legal developments of interest to employers. Formerly *Disabilities in the Workplace Alert*.

Gear Dynamics and Gear Noise Research Laboratory.

Gear Technology: The Journal of Gear Manufacturing. Randall Publishing, Inc., 1425 Lunt Ave. Elk Grove Village, IL 60007. Phone: (847)437-6604 Fax: (847)437-6618 E-mail: people@geartechnology.com • URL: http://www.geartechnology.com • Bimonthly. $45.00 per year. Edited for manufacturers, engineers, and designers of gears.

The Geek's Guide to Internet Business Success: The Definitive Business Blueprint for Internet Developers, Programmers, Consultants, Marketers, and Serivce Providers. Bob Schmidt. John Wiley and Sons, Inc., 605 Third Ave. New York, NY 10158-0012. Phone: 800-225-5945 or (212)850-6000 Fax: (212)850-6088 E-mail: info@jwiley.com • URL: http://www.wiley.com • 1997. $22.95. Written for beginning Internet entrepreneurs, especially those with technical expertise but little or no business experience. Covers fee or rate setting, developing new business, product mix, budgeting, partnerships, personnel, and planning. Includes checklists and worksheets.

Gem Identification Made Easy: A Hands-on Guide to More Confident Buying and Selling. Antoinette L. Matlins and Antonio C. Bonanno. Gem Stone Press, Rte. 4 Sunset Farm Offices Woodstock, VT 05091. Phone: 800-962-4544 or (802)457-4000 Fax: (802)457-5032 E-mail: sales@gemstonepress.com • URL: http://www.gemstonepress.com • 1997. $34.95. Second revised edition.

Gem Testing. Basil William Anderson and Alan Jobbins. Butterworth-Heinemann, 225 Wildwood Ave. Woburn, MA 01081. Phone: 800-366-2665 or (781)904-2500 Fax: 800-466-6520 E-mail: orders@bhusa.com • URL: http://www.bh.com • 1990. $34.95. Tenth revised edition.

Gemological Institute of America.

Gems and Gemology. Gemological Institute of America, 5355 Armada Dr. Carlsbad, CA 92008. Phone: 800-421-8161 or (760)603-4200 Fax: (760)603-4595 E-mail: akeller@gia.edu • URL: http://wwwgia.edu • Quarterly. $69.95 per year.

Gemstones of the World. Walter Schumann. Sterling Publishing Co., Inc., 387 Park Ave., S. New York, NY 10016-8810. Phone: 800-367-9692 or (212)532-7160 Fax: (212)213-2495 E-mail: customerservice@sterlingpub.com • URL: http://www.sterlingpub.com • 2000. $24.95. Expanded revised edition.

General Aviation Manufacturers Association.

General Federation of Women's Clubs.

General Information Concerning Patents. Available from U. S. Government Printing Office, Washington, DC 20402. Phone: (202)512-1800 Fax: (202)512-2250 E-mail: gpoaccess@gpo.gov • URL: http://www.access.gpo.gov • 1997. $4.75. Issued by Patent and Trademark Office, U. S. Department of Commerce. Provides basic information on patent applications, fees, searches, specifications, and infringement. Includes "Answers to Questions Frequently Asked."

General Robotics, Automation, Sensing and Perception (GRASP).

General Securities Registered Representative: Self-Study Course. New York Institute of Finance, Two World Trade Center, 17th Fl. New York, NY 10048-0203. Phone: (212)344-2900 Fax: (212)514-8423 Looseleaf. Intended for candidates seeking to become licensed stockbrokers.

General Statistics. Warren Chase and Fred Brown. John Wiley and Sons, Inc., 605 Third Ave. New York, NY 10158-0012. Phone: 800-225-5945 or (212)850-6000 Fax: (212)850-6088 E-mail: info@wiley.com • URL: http://www.wiley.com • 1999. $90.95 Fourth edition.

Generic Line. Washington Business Information, Inc., 300 N. Washington St., Suite 200 Falls Church, VA 22046. Phone: (703)247-3434 Fax: (703)247-3421 Biweekly. $435.00 per year. Newsletter. Covers regulation, legislation, technology, marketing, and other issues affecting companies providing generic pharmaceuticals.

Generic Pharmaceutical Industry Association., 1620 Eye St., N.W., Suite 800 Washington, DC 20006-4005. Phone: (202)833-9070 Fax: (202)833-9612 E-mail: info@gpia.org • URL: http://www.gpia.org • Members are manufacturers, wholesalers, and retailers of generic prescription drugs.

Genetic Engineering and Biotechnology Firms Worldwide Directory. Mega-Type Publishing, 217 Nassau St. Princeton Junction, NJ 08542-4602. Phone: 800-962-7004 or (609)275-6900 Fax: (609)275-8011 E-mail: biotech@megatype.com • Annual. $299.00. About 6,000 firms, including major firms with biotechnology divisions as well as small independent firms.

Genetic Engineering News: The Information Source of the Biotechnology Industry. Mary Ann Liebert, Inc., Two Madison Ave. Larchmont, NY 10538. Phone: (914)834-3100 Fax: (914)834-1388 E-mail: info@liebertpub.com • URL: http://www.genegnews.com • Biweekly. Institutions, $397.00 per year. Newsletter. Business and financial coverage.

Genetic Technology News. Technical Insights, 605 Third Ave. New York, NY 10158-0012. Phone: 800-825-7550 or (212)850-8600 Fax: (212)850-8800 E-mail: insights@wiley.com • URL: http://www.wiley.com/ • 51 times a year. $885.00 per year. Reports on genetic engineering and its uses in the chemical, pharmaceutical, food processing and energy industries as well as in agriculture, animal breeding and medicine. Includes three supplements: *Patent Update, Strategic Partners Reports*, and *Market Forecasts*.

Genetics Abstracts. Cambridge Information Group, 7200 Wisconsin Ave., 6th Fl. Bethesda, MD 20814. Phone: 800-843-7751 or (301)961-6700 Fax: (301)961-6720 E-mail: market@csa.com • URL: http://www.csa.com • Monthly. $1,035.00 per year.

Genetics Society of America., 9650 Rockville Pike Bethesda, MD 20814-3998. Phone: (301)571-1825 Fax: (301)530-7079 E-mail: estraass@genetics.faseb.org • URL: http://www.faseb.org/genetics/ • Members are individuals and organizations with an interest in genetics.

GEOARCHIVE. Geosystems, P.O. Box 40, Didcot Oxon Ox11 9BX, England. Phone: (112)3-581-3913 Citations to literature on geoscience and water. 1974 to present. Monthly updates. Inquire as to online cost and availability.

Geographic Profile of Employment and Unemployment. Available from U. S. Government Printing Office, Washington, DC 20402. Phone: (202)512-1800 Fax: (202)512-2250 E-mail: gpoaccess@gpo.gov • URL: http://www.access.gpo.gov • Annual. Issued by Bureau of Labor Statistics, U. S. Department of Labor. Presents detailed, annual average employment, unemployment, and labor force data for regions, states, and metropolitan areas. Characteristics include sex, age, race, Hispanic origin, marital status, occupation, and type of industry.

Geographic Reference Report: Annual Report of Costs, Wages, salaries, and Human Resource Statistics for the United States and Canada. ERI, 16770 N.E. 79th St., Suite 104 Redmond, WA 98052. Phone: 800-627-3697 or (425)556-0205 Fax: 800-753-4415 E-mail: info@erieri.com • URL: http://www.erieri.com • Annual. $389.00. Provides demographic and other data for each of 298 North American metropolian areas, including local salaries, wage differentials, cost-of-living, housing costs, income taxation, employment, unemployment, population, major employers, crime rates, weather, etc.

Geographical Abstracts: Human and Physical Geography. Elsevier Science, 655 Ave. of the Americas New York, NY 10010. Phone: 888-437-4636 or (212)989-5800 Fax: (212)633-3680 E-mail: usinfo@elsevier.com • URL: http://www.elsevier.com • Monthly. $3,253 per year. *Human Geography* $1,407.00 per year. Annual cumulation. *Physical Geography* $1,846.00 per year. Annual cumulation.

Geophysical Directory. Claudia LaCalli, editor. Geophysical Directory, Inc., P.O. Box 130508 Houston, TX 77219. Phone: 800-929-2462 or (713)529-8789 Fax: (713)529-3646 Annual. $75.00. Worldwide coverage of about 4,500 companies and personnel using and providing supplies and services in petroleum and mineral exploration.

GEOREF. American Geological Institute, 4220 King St. Alexandria, VA 22302-1507. Phone: (703)379-2480 Fax: (703)379-7563 Bibliography and index of geology and geosciences literature, 1785 to present. Inquire as to online cost and availability.

George Washington Journal of International Law and Economics. National Law Center. George Washington University, 2008 G St., N.W. Washington, DC 20052. Phone: (202)676-3847 Fax: (202)676-3876 E-mail: gwjile@gwis2.circ.gwu.edu • Three times a year. $23.00 per year. Articles dealing with a variety of topics within the area of private international comparative law and economics.

Geotechnical/Civil Engineering Materials Research Laboratories. Iowa State University of Science and Technology

Geotechnical Engineering Center., University of Texas at Austin, Dept. of Civil Engineering Austin, TX 78712. Phone: (512)471-4929 Fax: (512)471-6548 E-mail: swright@mail.utexas.edu • Areas of research include offshore complexes.

Geothermal Laboratory.

Geothermal Resources Council., P.O. Box 1350 Davis, CA 95617-1350. Phone: (916)758-2360 Fax: (916)758-2839 E-mail: carth307@concentric.net • URL: http://www.geothermal.org • Encourages research, development, and exploration for worldwide geothermal energy. Includes eight International Groups.

Geothermics: International Journal of Geothermal Research and Its Applications. Elsevier Science, 655 Ave. of the Americas New York, NY 10010. Phone: 888-437-4636 or

(212)989-5800 Fax: (212)633-3680 E-mail: usinfo@elsevier.com • URL: http://www.elsevier.com • Bimonthly. $921.00 per year. Covers theory, exploration, development, and utilization of geothermal energy. Text and summaries in English and French.

Geriatric Care News. Frances Greer, editor. DRS Geriatric Publishing Co., 7435 S.E. 71st St. Mercer Island, WA 98040. Phone: (206)232-9689 Monthly. $89.00 per year. Latest information for health care professionals in the geriatric field. Formerly *Geriatric and Residential Care Newsmonthly*.

Gerontological Society of America.

Get Rich Through Multi-Level Selling: Build Your Own Sales and Distribution Organization. Gini G. Scott. Self-Counsel Press, Inc., 1704 N. State St. Bellingham, WA 98225. Phone: 877-877-6490 or (360)676-4530 Fax: (360)676-4530 E-mail: service@self-counsel.com • URL: http://www.self-counsel.com • 1998. $19.95. Third revised edition. (Business Series).

Getting Ahead at Work: A Proven System for Advancing at Work, Regardless of Your Occupation. Gordon W. Green. Carol Publishing Group, 120 Enterprise Ave. Secaucus, NJ 07094. Phone: 800-447-2665 or (201)866-0490 Fax: 800-866-1966 or (201)866-8159 1989. $9.95. Includes making a good impression in a new job.

Getting Funded: A Complete Guide to Proposal Writing. Mary S. Hall. Portland State University, Continuing Education Press, School of Extended Studies, P.O. Box 1394 Portland, OR 97207-1394. Phone: 800-547-8887 or (503)725-4891 Fax: (503)725-4840 E-mail: scholz@pdx.edu • URL: http://www.extended.pdx.edu/press/ • 1988. $23.95. Third edition. Proposal writing for public and private grants.

Getting It Printed: How to Work with Printers and Graphic Arts Services to Assure Quality, Stay on Schedule, and Control Costs. Mark Beach and Eric Kenly. F and W. Publications, Inc., 1507 Dana Ave. Cincinnati, OH 45207-1005. Phone: 800-289-0963 or (513)531-2690 Fax: 888-590-4082 1998. $32.99. Third edition.

Getting Started in Futures. Todd Lofton. John Wiley and Sons, Inc., 605 Third Ave. New York, NY 10158-0012. Phone: 800-225-5945 or (212)850-6000 Fax: (212)850-6088 E-mail: info@wiley.com • URL: http://www.wiley.com • 1997. $18.95. Third edition. A general introduction to commodity and financial futures trading. Includes case studies and a glossary. (All About Series).

Getting Started in Investment Planning Services. James E. Grant. CCH, Inc., 4025 W. Peterson Ave. Chicago, IL 60646-6085. Phone: 800-248-3248 or (773)866-6000 Fax: 800-224-8299 or (773)866-3608 URL: http://www.cch.com • 1999. $85.00. Second edition. Provides advice and information for lawyers and accountants who are planning to initiate fee-based investment services.

Getting Started in Mutual Funds. Alvin D. Hall. John Wiley and Sons, Inc., 605 Third Ave. New York, NY 10158-0012. Phone: 800-225-5945 or (212)850-6000 Fax: (212)850-6088 E-mail: info@wiley.com • URL: http://www.wiley.com • 1998. $18.95. (Getting Started In. Series).

Getting Started in Real Estate Investing. Michael C. Thomsett and Jean Thomsett. John Wiley and Sons, Inc., 605 Third Ave. New York, NY 10158-0012. Phone: 800-225-5945 or (212)850-6000 Fax: (212)850-6088 E-mail: info@wiley.com • URL: http://www.wiley.com • 1998. $18.95. Second edition. (Getting Started In. Series.)

Getting Started in Stocks, Bonds. Alvin D. Hall. John Wiley and Sons, Inc., 605 Third Ave. New York, NY 10158-0012. Phone: 800-225-5945 or (212)850-6000 Fax: (212)850-6088 E-mail: info@wiley.com • URL: http://www.wiley.com • 1999. $56.85. (Getting Started In. Series).

Getting Your Book Published. Christine S. Smedley and Mitchell Allen. Sage Publications, Inc., 2455 Teller Rd. Thousand Oaks, CA 91320. Phone: (805)499-0721 Fax: (805)499-0871 E-mail: info@sagepub.com • URL: http://www.sagepub.com • 1993. $37.00. A practical guide for academic and professional authors. Covers the initial book prospectus, contract negotiation, production procedures, and marketing. (Survival Skills for Scholars, vol. 10).

Getting Yours; The Complete Guide to Government Money. Matthew Lesko. Viking Penguin, 375 Hudson St. New York, NY 10014-3657. Phone: 800-331-4624 or (212)336-2000 Fax: 800-227-9604 or (212)366-2666 E-mail: customer.service@penguin.co.uk • URL: http://www.penguin.com • 1987. $14.95 Third edition. (Handbook Series).

GFWC Clubwoman. General Federation of Women's Clubs, 1734 N St., N.W. Washington, DC 20036. Phone: (202)347-3168 URL: http://www.gfwc.org • Bimonthly. $6.00 per year.

Giannini Foundation of Agricultural Economics. University of California

Gift and Decorative Accessory Buyers Directory. Geyer-McAllister Publications, Inc., 51 Madison Ave. New York, NY 10010. Phone: (212)689-4411 Annual. Included in subscription to *Gifts and Decorative Accessories*. Manufacturers, importers, jobbers, and manufacturers' representatives of gifts, china and glass, lamps and home accessories, stationery, greeting cards, and related products.

Gift and Stationery Business. Miller Freeman, Inc., One Penn Plaza New York, NY 10119-1198. Phone: 800-950-1314 or (212)714-1300 Fax: (212)714-1313 URL: http://www.mfi.com • Monthly. $45.00 per year. Products and services.

Gift Association of America.

Gift/Specialty Store. Entrepreneur Media, Inc., 2445 McCabe Way Irvine, CA 92614. Phone: 800-421-2300 or (949)261-2325 Fax: (949)261-0234 E-mail: entmag@entrepreneur.com • URL: http://www.entrepreneur.com • Looseleaf. $59.50. A practical guide to starting a gift shop. Covers profit potential, start-up costs, market size evaluation, owner's time required, site selection, lease negotiation, pricing, accounting, advertising, promotion, etc. (Start-Up Business Guide No. E1218.)

Gifts and Decorative Accessories Market. Available from MarketResearch.com, 641 Ave. of the Americas, Third Floor New York, NY 10011. Phone: 800-298-5699 or (212)807-2629 Fax: (212)807-2716 E-mail: order@marketresearch.com • URL: http://www.marketresearch.com • 1998. $1,795.00. Published by Unity Marketing. Market research report covering growth trends and projections.

Gifts and Decorative Accessories: The International Business Magazine of Gifts, Tabletop, Gourmet, Home Accessories, Greeting Card and Social Stationery. Cahners Business Newspapers, 345 Hudson St., 4th Fl. New York, NY 10014-4502. Phone: (212)519-7200 E-mail: corporatecommunications@cahners.com • Monthly. $49.95 per year.

Gifts and Tablewares. Southam Magazine Group, 1450 Don Mills Rd. Don Mills, ON, Canada M3B 2X7. Phone: 800-387-0273 or (416)445-6641 Fax: (416)442-2213 E-mail: hgibson@corporate.southam.ca • Seven times a year. $45.95 per year. Includes annual *Trade Directory*.

Giftware News: The International Magazine for Gifts, China and Glass, Stationery and Home Accessories. Talcott Communications Corp., 20 N. Wacker Dr., Suite 1865 Chicago, IL 60606. Phone: (312)849-2220 Fax: (312)849-4994 E-mail: giftnews@aol.com • URL: http://www.giftwarenews.net • Monthly. $36.00 per year. Includes annual *Directory*.

Gilder Technology Report. George Gilder, editor. Gilder Technology Group, Inc., PO Box 5475 Harlan, IA 51593-4975. Phone: 888-647-7304 E-mail: gtg@gildertech.com • URL: http://www.gildertech.com • Monthly. $295.00 per year. Newsletter. Makes specific recommendations for investing in technology stocks. (A joint publication of Forbes Magazine and the Gilder Technology Group.)

Giving U.S.A: The Annual Compilation of Total Philanthropic Giving Estimates. American Association of Fund-Raising Counsel. AAFRC Trust for Philanthropy, 10293 N. Meridian St., Suite 175 Indianapolis, IN 46290-1130. URL: http://www.aafrc.com • Annual. $49.95.

Giving USA Update. American Association of Fund-Raising Counsel. AAFRC Trust for Philanthropy, 10293 N. Meridian St., Suite 175 Indianapolis, IN 46290-1130. URL: http://www.aafrc.com • Quarterly. $110.00 per year. Legal, economic and social essays on philanthropy.

Glass Association of North America.

Glass Digest Buyers' Guide. Ashlee Publishing Co., Inc., 18 E. 41st St. New York, NY 10017-6222. Phone: (212)376-7722 Fax: (212)376-7723 E-mail: ashleepub@aol.com • URL: http://www.ashlee.com • Annual. $35.00. Included with *Glass Digest*. Formerly *International Glass/Metal Catalog*.

Glass Digest: Trade Magazine Serving the Flat Glass, Architectural Metal an d Allied Products Industry. Ashlee Publishing Co., Inc., 18 E. 41st St. New York, NY 10017-6222. Phone: (212)376-7722 Fax: (212)376-7723 E-mail: ashleepub@aol.com • URL: http://www.ashlee.com • Monthly. $40.00 per year.

Glass Factory Directory of North America and U.S. Industry Factbook. LJV, Inc., P.O. Box 2267 Hempstead, NY 11551-2267. Phone: (516)481-2188 E-mail: manager@glassfactorydir.com • URL: http://www.glassfactorydir.com • Annual. $25.00. Lists over 600 glass factory locations in the U.S., Canada and Mexico.

Glass Industry-Directory. Ashlee Publishing Co., Inc., 18 E. 41st St. New York, NY 10017-6222. Phone: (212)376-7722 Fax: (212)376-7723 E-mail: ashleepub@aol.com • URL: http://www.ashlee.com • Annual. $35.00. Lists of primary and secondary glass manufacturers, suppliers to the glass industry, glass associations and unions, independent research labs, and glass educational institutions. International coverage.

Glass Magazine. National Glass Association, 8200 Greensboro Dr., Suite 302 McLean, VA 22102. Phone: (703)442-4890 Fax: (703)442-0630 E-mail: nga@glass.org • URL: http://www.glass.org • Monthly. $34.95 per year.

Glass Molders, Pottery, Plastics and Allied Workers International Union.

Glass Packaging Institute.

Glass Science. Robert H. Doremus. John Wiley and Sons, Inc., 605 Third Ave. New York, NY 10158-0012. Phone: 800-526-5368 or (212)850-6000 Fax: (212)850-6088 E-mail: info@wiley.com • URL: http://www.wiley.com • 1994. $105.00. Second edition.

Global Appliance Report: A Monthly Digest of International News Affecting the Home Appliance Industry. Association of Home Appliance Manufacturers, 1111 19th St., N.W., Suite 402 Washington, DC 20036. Phone: (202)872-5955 Fax: (202)872-9354 URL: http://www.aham.org • 22 times a year. Members, $300.00 per year; non-members, $500.00 per year.

Global Commodity Markets. The World Bank, Office of the Publisher, 1818 H St., N. W. Washington, DC 20433. Phone: (202)477-1234 Fax: 800-645-7247 or (202)477-6391 E-mail: books@worldbank.org • URL: http://www.worldbank.org • Quarterly. $645.00 per year. Covers international trends in the production, consumption, and trade patterns of primary commodities, including food, metals, minerals, energy, and fertilizers. Includes electronic monthly updates and electronic access to the quarterly.

Global Company Handbook. C I F A R Publications, Inc., P.O. Box 3228 Princeton, NJ 08540-3228. Phone: (609)520-9333 Fax: (609)520-0905 Annual. $495.00. Two volumes. Provides detailed profiles of 7,500 publicly traded companies in 48 countries. Includes global rankings and five years of data.

Global Company News Digest: A Monthly Publication of Corporate News Summaries and Financial Transactions of the Leading 10,000 Companies Worldwide. C I F A R Publications, Inc., P.O. Box 3228 Princeton, NJ 08540-3228. Phone: (609)520-9333 Fax: (609)520-0905 Monthly. $495.00 per year. Subscriptions are available according to region, company characteristics, news topic, or industry. Provides both financial and non-financial news and information.

Global Competitor. Faulkner & Gray, Inc., 11 Penn Plaza, 17th Fl. New York, NY 10001. Phone: 800-535-8403 or (212)967-7000 Fax: (212)967-7155 E-mail: orders@faulknergray.com • URL: http://www.faulknergray.com • Quarterly. $129.00 per year. Edited for executives of multinational corporations.

Global Data Locator. George T. Kurian. Bernan Associates, 4611-F Assembly Dr. Lanham, MD 20706-4391. Phone: 800-274-4447 or (301)459-7666 Fax: 800-865-3450 or (301)459-0056 E-mail: info@bernan.com • URL: http://www.bernan.com • 1997. $89.00. Provides detailed descriptions of international statistical sourcebooks and electronic databases. Covers a wide variety of trade, economic, and demographic topics.

Global Development Finance: Analysis and Summary Tables. World Bank, The Office of the Publisher, 1818 H St., N. W. Washington, DC 20433. Phone: (202)477-1234 Fax: (202)477-6391 E-mail: books@worldbank.org • URL: http://www.worldbank.org • Annual. $40.00. Provides an analysis of debt and equity financial flows to 136 countries that report to the World Bank's Debtor Reporting System. Contains summary statistical tables for 150 countries.

Global Development Finance: Country Tables. World Bank, The Office of the Publisher, 1818 H St., N. W. Washington, DC 20433. Phone: (202)477-1234 Fax: (202)477-6391 E-mail: books@worldbank.org • URL: http://www.worldbank.org • 1998. $300.00 (includes *Analysis and Summary Tables*). Contains detailed statistical tables for 136 countries, covering total external debt, long-term debt ratios, arrears, commitments, disbursements, repayments, etc. Includes "major economic aggregates."

Global Development Finance: External Public Debt of Developing Countries. World Bank, The Office of the Publisher, 1818 H St., N. W. Washington, DC 20433. Phone: (202)477-1234 Fax: (202)477-6391 E-mail: books@worldbank.org • URL: http://www.worldbank.org • Irregular. Prices vary. Includes supplements. Contains detailed data from the International Bank for Reconstruction and Development (World Bank) on the external debt load of over 100 developing countries.

Global Economic Prospects and the Developing Countries, 1999-2000. World Bank, The Office of the Publisher, 1818 H St., N. W. Washington, DC 20433. Phone: (202)477-1234 Fax: (202)477-6391 E-mail: books@worldbank.org • URL: http://www.worldbank.org • 1999. $25.00. Examines the economic connections between industrial and developing countries, with a different theme in each edition.

Global Economic Prospects 2000. The World Bank, Office of the Publisher, 1818 H St., N. W. Washington, DC 20433. Phone: 800-645-7247 or (202)477-1234 Fax: (202)477-6391 E-mail: books@worldbank.org • URL: http://www.worldbank.org • 1999. $25.00. "..offers an in-depth analysis of the economic prospects of developing countries." Emphasis is on the impact of recessions and financial crises. Regional statistical data is included.

Global Equity Selection Strategies. Ross P. Bruner, editor. Fitzroy Dearborn Publishers, Inc., 919 N. Michigan Ave., Suite 760 Chicago, IL 60611. Phone: 800-850-8102 or (312)587-0131 Fax: (312)587-1049 E-mail: website@fitzroydearborn.com • URL: http://www.fitzroydearborn.com • 1999. $65.00. Written by various professionals in the field of international investments.

Contains six major sections covering growth, value, size, price momentum, sector rotation, and country allocation. (Glenlake Business Monographs).

Global Finance. Global Finance Media, Inc., 1001 Ave. of the Americas, 21st Fl. New York, NY 10018. Phone: (212)768-1100 Fax: (212)768-2020 E-mail: mailbox@gfmag.com • URL: http://www.gfmag.com • Monthly. $300.00 per year. Edited for corporate financial executives and money managers responsible for ''cross-border'' financial transactions.

Global Money Management. Institutional Investor, 488 Madison Ave. New York, NY 10022. Phone: (212)224-3300 Fax: (212)224-3353 E-mail: info@iijournals.com • URL: http://www.iijournals.com • Biweekly. $2,330.00 per year. Newsletter. Edited for international pension fund and investment company managers. Includes information on foreign investment opportunities and strategies.

Global Polyurethane Directory and Buyer's Guide. Crain Communications, Inc., 1725 Merriman Rd., Suite 300 Akron, OH 44313-5283. Phone: 800-678-9595 or (330)836-9180 Fax: (216)836-1005 URL: http://www.crain.co.uk • Annual. $30.00. List of over 1,000 rubber product manufacturers and 800 suppliers of equipment, services, and materials; list of trade associations. Formerly Rubber and Plastic News-Rubbicana Directory and Buyer's Guide.

Global Positioning and Navigation News. Phillips Business Information, Inc., 1201 Seven Locks Rd., Suite 300 Potomac, MD 20854. Phone: 800-777-5006 or (301)340-1520 Fax: (301)309-3847 E-mail: pbi@phillips.com • URL: http://www.phillips.com/marketplaces.htm • Biweekly. $597.00. Newsletter. Formerly *Marine Technology News*.

Global Seed Guide: World Reference Source for the Commercial Seed Industry. Ball Publishing, PO Box 9 Batavia, IL 60510. Phone: 800-888-0013 or (630)208-9089 Fax: 800-(888)888-0014 or (603)208-9350 E-mail: info@ballpublishing.com • URL: http://www.ballbookshelf.com • Annual. $40.00. Edited by *Seed Trade News* (http://www.seedtradenews.com). Includes company listings, type of business, type of seed, research centers, industry data, events calendar, and associations.

Global Seed Markets. Theta Reports/PJB Medical Publications, Inc., 1775 Broadway, Suite 511 New York, NY 10019. Phone: (212)262-8230 Fax: (212)262-8234 E-mail: customerservice@thetareports.com • URL: http://www.thetareports.com • 2000. $1,040.00. Market research data. Covers the major seed sectors, including cereal crops, legumes, oilseed crops, fibre crops, and beet crops. Provides analysis of biotechnology developments. (Theta Report No. DS208E.)

Global Stock Guide. C I F A R Publications, Inc., P.O. Box 3228 Princeton, NJ 08540-3228. Phone: (609)520-9333 Fax: (609)520-0905 Monthly. $445.00 per year. Provides financial variables for 10,000 publicly traded companies in 48 countries.

Global Telecommunications: The Technology, Administration, and Policies. Raymond Akwule. Butterworth-Heinemann, 225 Wildwood Ave. Woburn, MA 01081. Phone: 800-366-2665 or (781)904-2500 Fax: 800-466-6520 E-mail: orders@bhusa.com • URL: http://www.bh.com • 1992. $46.95. Provides basic information on networks, satellite systems, socioeconomic impact, tariffs, government regulation, etc.

Globalbase. The Gale Group, 27500 Drake Rd. Farmington Hills, MI 48331-3535. Phone: 800-877-GALE or (248)699-GALE Fax: 800-414-5043 or (248)699-8069 E-mail: galeord@gale.com • URL: http://www.gale.com • Provides more than one million online summaries of business, industrial, and economic news reports from more than 1,000 publications worldwide. Covers a wide range of material appearing in international trade journals, professional magazines, and newspapers. Time period is 1984 to date, with weekly updates. Inquire as to online cost and availability.

The Globe and Mail Online. The Globe and Mail Co., 444 Front St., W. Toronto, ON, Canada M5V 2S9. Phone: 800-268-9128 or (416)585-5250 Fax: (416)585-5249 URL: http://www.globeandmail.ca • Contains full text of more than 1.1 million news stories and articles that have appeared daily in *The Globe and Mail: Canada's National Newspaper*, including ''Report on Business.'' Time span is 1977 to date. Daily updates of the complete newspaper are provided. Inquire as to online cost and availability.

Globe and Mail Report on Business. Globe and Mail Publishing, 444 Front St., W. Toronto, ON, Canada M5V 2S9. Phone: (416)585-5000 Fax: (416)585-5641 URL: http://www.globeandmail.ca • Monthly. Controlled circulation. Provides general coverage of business activity in Canada, with emphasis on the economy, foreign trade, technology, and personal finance.

GLOBEnet: Canada's National Web Site. The Globe and Mail Co.Phone: 800-268-9128 or (416)585-5250 Fax: (416)585-5249 URL: http://www.globeandmail.ca • Web site provides access to selected sections of *The Globe and Mail: Canada's National Newspaper*. Includes current news, national issues, career information, ''Report on Business,'' and other topics. Keyword searching is offered for ''a seven-day archive of the portion of the *Globe and Mail* that we publish online'' (refers to the Web site). Daily updates. Fees: free.

Glossary of Geology. Robert L. Bates and Julia A. Jackson. American Geological Institute, 4220 King St. Alexandria, VA 22302-1502. Phone: (703)379-2480 Fax: (703)379-7563 E-mail: agi@agiweb.org • URL: http://www.aginet.org • 1997. $110.00. Fourth edition.

Glucksman Institute. New York University

Going Freelance: A Guide for Professionals. Robert Laurance. John Wiley and Sons, Inc., 605 Third Ave. New York, NY 10158-0012. Phone: 800-526-5368 or (212)850-6000 Fax: (212)850-6088 E-mail: info@wiley.com • URL: http://www.wiley.com • 1995. $17.95. Third edition. Includes profiles of 150 professions using independent freelancers. Marketing, customer relations, and taxes are discussed.

Going Global: Getting Started in International Trade. American Management Association Extension Institute, P.O. Box 1026 Saranac Lake, NY 12983-9957. Phone: 800-262-9699 or (518)891-1500 Fax: (518)891-0368 Looseleaf. $130.00. Self-study course. Emphasis is on practical explanations, examples, and problem solving. Quizzes and a case study are included.

Going Public and the Public Corporation. Harold S. Bloomenthal. West Group, 610 Opperman Dr. Eagan, MN 55123. Phone: 800-328-4880 or (651)687-7000 Fax: 800-213-2323 or (651)687-5827 URL: http://www.westgroup.com • $495.00 per year. Four looseleaf volumes. Periodic supplementation. Includes legal forms and documents. (Securities Law Series).

Going Public Handbook: Going Public, the Integrated Disclosure System, and Exempt Financing, 1992. Harold S. Bloomenthal. West Group, 610 Opperman Dr. Eagan, MN 55123. Phone: 800-328-4880 or (651)687-7000 Fax: 800-213-2323 or (651)687-5827 URL: http://www.westgroup.com • 1993. $97.50. Covers public financing from initiation of underwriting to closing.

Gold and Liberty. Richard M. Salsman. American Institute for Economic Research, Division St. Great Barrington, MA 01230-1000. Phone: (413)528-1216 Fax: (413)528-0103 E-mail: info@aier.org • URL: http://www.aier.org • 1995. $8.00. Mainly a conservative argument in favor of the gold standard and against central banking, but also contains historical background and 10 unique charts, such as ''Purchasing Power of Gold and of the U. S. Dollar, 1792-1994.'' Includes a 16-page, classified bibliography on the origins of gold as money, the classical gold standard, political issues, gold as an investment, the future of gold, and other topics.

Gold Institute.

Gold Newsletter. James U. Blanchard, editor. Jefferson Financial, Inc., 2400 Jefferson Highway, Suite 600 Jefferson, LA 70121. Phone: 800-877-8847 or (504)837-3033 Fax: (504)837-4885 Monthly. $99.00 per year. Newsletter. Covers news of the international gold market and provides commentary on the price of gold.

Goldsmiths' Kress Library of Economic Literature: A Consolidated Guide to the Microfilm Collection, 1976-1983. Primary Source Media, 12 Lunar Dr. Woodbridge, CT 06525. Phone: 800-444-0799 or (203)397-2600 Fax: (203)397-3892 E-mail: sales@psmedia.com • URL: http://www.psmedia.com • $2,100.00. Seven volumes. Individual volumes, $250.00. An estimated 60,000 titles on 1,500 reels of microfilm (or fiche).

Golf Course Builders Association of America., 920 Airport Rd., Suite 210 Chapel Hill, NC 27514. Phone: (919)942-8922 Fax: (919)942-6955 E-mail: gcbaa@aol.com • URL: http://www.gcbaa.org • Members are golf course builders, designers, and suppliers.

Golf Course Directory. National Golf Foundation, 1150 S., U.S. Highway 1, Suite 401 Jupiter, FL 33477. Phone: 800-733-6006 or (561)744-6006 Fax: (561)744-6107 E-mail: ngf@ngf.org • URL: http://www.ngf.org • 1998. $199.00. Two volumes (Alabama-Montana and Nebraska-Wyoming). Lists about 16,000 public and private golf facilities, with information as to size, number of holes, year opened, and practice ranges.

Golf Course Management. Golf Course Superintendents Association of America, 1421 Research Park Dr. Lawrence, KS 66049-3859. Phone: 800-472-7878 or (785)841-2240 Fax: (785)832-4488 E-mail: infobox@gcsaa.org • Monthly. $48.00 per year. Contains articles on golf course maintenance, equipment, landscaping, renovation, and management.

Golf Course News: The Newspaper for the Golf Course Industry. United Publications, Inc., P.O. Box 997 Yarmouth, ME 04096-1997. Phone: 800-441-6982 or (207)846-0600 Fax: (207)846-0657 Nine times a year. Price on application. Edited for golf course superintendents, managers, architects, and developers.

Golf Course Superintendents Association of America., 1421 Research Park Dr. Lawrence, KS 66049-3859. Phone: 800-472-7878 or (785)841-2240 or (785)832-4430 Fax: (785)832-4488 E-mail: infobox@gcsaa.org • URL: http://www.gcsaa.org • Members are golf course superintendents and others concerned with golf course maintenance and improvement.

Golf Digest: How to Play What to Play, Where to Play. New York Times Co., Magazine Group, P.O. Box 395 Trumbull, CT 06611-0395. Phone: 800-727-4653 or (203)373-7000 Fax: (203)373-7033 Monthly. $27.94 per year. A high circulation consumer magazine for golfers. Editions available in various languages. Supplement available *Golf Digest Woman*.

Golf Index. Ingledue Travel Publications, 444 Burchett St. Glendale, CA 91203. Phone: 800-444-6531 or (818)247-5530 Fax: (818)247-5535 Semiannual. $40.00 per year. Provides directory listings of golf courses and resorts around the world. Contains information on golf travel packages, tour operators, and tournaments.

Golf Magazine. Times Mirror Magazines, Inc., Two Park Ave. New York, NY 10016-5601. Phone: 800-227-2224 or (212)779-5000 Fax: (212)481-8085 URL: http://www.golfonline.com • Monthly. $19.95 per year. Popular consumer magazine for golfers.

Golf Magazine Golf Club Buyers' Guide. Times Mirror Magazines, Inc., Two Park Ave. New York, NY 10016-5601. Phone: 800-227-2224 or (212)779-5000 Fax: (212)779-5522 URL: http://www.golfonline.com • Annual. Price on application. Lists golf club manufacturers, with description of products and prices.

Golf Manufacturers and Distributors Association., P.O. Box 37324 Cincinnati, OH 45222. Phone: (513)631-4400 Members are exhibitors at the Professional Golfers' Association annual trade show. Seeks to improve the ''business habits'' of professional golfers.

Golf Participation in the U. S. Available from MarketResearch.com, 641 Ave. of the Americas, Third Floor New York, NY 10011. Phone: 800-298-5699 or (212)807-2629 Fax: (212)807-2716 E-mail: order@marketresearch.com • URL: http://www.martketresearch.com • 1998. $250.00. Published by the National Golf Foundation. Market research report on consumer attitudes and industry statistics.

Golf Shop Operations. New York Times Co., Magazine Group, P.O. Box 395 Trumbull, CT 06611-0395. Phone: 800-727-4653 or (203)373-7000 Fax: (203)373-7280 E-mail: gso@golf.com • 10 times a year. $72.00 per year. Edited for retailers of golf equipment.

Golf Shop Operations: Buyer's Guide. New York Times Co., Magazine Group, 5520 Park Ave. Trumbull, CT 06611-0395. Phone: 800-727-4653 or (203)373-7000 Fax: (203)371-2505 E-mail: gso@golf.com • Annual. $10.00 Included in subscription. Lists golf equipment and apparel suppliers. Includes suggested retail prices of specific items.

Golf U.S.A.: A Guide to the Best Golf Courses and Resorts. Corey Sandler. NTC/Contemporary Publishing Group, 4255 W. Touhy Ave. Lincolnwood, IL 60712-1975. Phone: 800-323-4900 or (847)679-5500 Fax: 800-998-3103 or (847)679-2494 E-mail: ntcpub@tribune.com • URL: http://www.ntc-cb.com • 2001. $17.95. Second edition. Describes 2,500 public and private golf courses. (Contemporary Books.)

Golfdom. Advanstar Communications, Inc., 201 E. Sandpointe Ave., Sutie 600 Santa Ana, CA 92700-8700. Phone: 800-346-0085 or (714)513-8400 Fax: (714)513-8632 E-mail: infomation@advanstar.com • URL: http://www.advanstar.com • Eight times a year. $25.00 per year. Covers marketing, financing, insurance, human resources, maintenance, environmental factors, and other aspects of golf course management. *Formerly Golf Business*.

Golfweek: America's Golf Newspaper. Turnstile Publishing Co., 7657 Commerce Center Dr. Orlando, FL 32819-8923. Phone: (407)345-5500 Fax: (407)345-9404 URL: http://www.golfweek.com • Weekly. $69.95 per year. Includes biweekly supplement, ''Golfweek's Strictly Business,'' covering business and marketing for the golfing industry.

Golob's Environmental Business. World Information Systems, Harvard Square Station, P.O. Box 535 Cambridge, MA 02238. Phone: 800-666-4430 or (617)491-5100 Fax: (617)492-3312 Weekly. $375.00 per year. Newsletter. Formerly *Hazardous Materials Intelligence Report*.

Gomez. Gomez Advisors, Inc.Phone: (978)287-0095 E-mail: contact@gomez.com • URL: http://www.gomez.com • The Gomez Web site rates e-commerce companies providing products or services to consumers. Numerical scores are specific as to ease of use, customer confidence, resources, costs, etc. More than 30 product categories are covered, including books, music, videos, toys, sporting goods, gifts, travel, prescriptions, health information, online brokers, insurance, banks, and general merchandise. Fees: Free. (GomezPro, a service for e-commerce professionals, is also available.)

Good Fruit Grower. Fruit Commission, 105 S. 18th St., Suite 217 Yakima, WA 98901. Phone: (509)575-2315 Fax: (509)453-4880 E-mail: growing@goodfruit.com • URL: http://www.goodfruit.com • Semimonthly. $30.00 per year.

Good Sam Recreational Vehicle Club.

Goodwill Industries of International.

Gourmet News: The Business Newspaper for the Gourmet Industry. United Publications, Inc., P.O. Box 1056 Yarmouth, ME 04096-1997. Phone: 800-441-6982 or (207)846-0600 Fax: (207)846-0657 Monthly. $55.00 per year. Provides news of the gourmet food industry, including specialty food stores, upscale cookware shops, and gift shops.

Gourmet Retailer. Bill Communications, Business Communications Group, 770 Broadway New York, NY 10003. Phone: 800-266-4712 or (646)654-4500 Fax: (646)654-7212 URL: http://www.billcom.com • Monthly. $24.00 per year. Covers upscale food and housewares, including confectionery items, bakery operations, and coffee.

The Gourmet/Specialty Foods Market. Available from MarketResearch.com, 641 Ave. of the Americas, Third Floor New York, NY 10011. Phone: 800-298-5699 or (212)807-2629 Fax: (212)807-2716 E-mail: order@marketresearch.com • URL: http://www.marketresearch.com • 1998. $2,500.00. Market research data. Published by Packaged Facts. Discusses current trends, with projections to 2002.

Governing: The States and Localities., 1100 Connecticut Ave.,N.W. Suite 1300 Washington, DC 20036. Phone: 800-638-1710 or (202)862-8802 Fax: (202)862-0032 URL: http://www.governing.com • Monthly. $39.95 per year. Edited for state and local government officials. Covers finance, office management, computers, telecommunications, environmental concerns, etc.

Government Accountants Journal. Association of Government Accountants, 2200 Mount Vernon Ave. Arlington, VA 22301-1314. Phone: (703)684-6931 Fax: (703)548-9367 E-mail: jmccumber@agacgfm.org • URL: http://www.agacgfm.org • Quarterly. $60.00 per year.

Government Affairs Yellow Book: Who's Who in Government Affairs. Leadership Directories, Inc., 104 Fifth Ave., 2nd Fl. New York, NY 10011. Phone: (212)627-4140 Fax: (212)645-6931 E-mail: info@leadershipdirectories.com • URL: http://www.leadershipdirectories.com • Semiannual. $235.00 per year. Includes in-house lobbyists of corporations and organizations, Political Action Committees (PACs), congressional liaisons, and independent lobbying firms.

Government Assistance Almanac: The Guide to Federal, Domestic, Financial and Other Programs Covering Grants, Loans, Insurance, Personal Payments and Benefits. J. Robert Dumouchel, editor. Omnigraphics, Inc., Penobscot Bldg. Detroit, MI 48226. Phone: 800-234-1340 or (313)961-1340 Fax: 800-875-1340 or (313)961-1383 E-mail: info@omnigraphics.com • URL: http://www.omnigraphics.com • Annual. $190.00. Describes more than 1,300 federal assistance programs available from about 50 agencies. Includes statistics, a directory of 4,000 field offices, and comprehensive indexing.

Government Auditing Standards. Available from U. S. Government Printing Office, Washington, DC 20402. Phone: (202)512-1800 Fax: (202)512-2250 E-mail: gpoaccess@gpo.gov • URL: http://www.access.gpo.gov • 1994. $6.50. Revised edition. Issued by the U. S. General Accounting Office (http://www.gao.gov). Contains standards for CPA firms to follow in financial and performance audits of federal government agencies and programs. Also known as the ''Yellow Book.''

Government by Judiciary: The Transformation of the Fourteenth Amendment. Raoul Berger. Liberty Fund, Inc., 8335 Allison Pointe Trail, No. 300 Indianapolis, IN 46250-1684. Phone: 800-955-8335 or (317)842-0880 Fax: (317)579-6060 E-mail: webmaster@libertyfund.org • URL: http://www.libertyfund.org • 1997. $19.50. Second revised edition.

Government Computer News: The Newspaper Serving Computer Users Throughout the Federal Government. Cahners Business Information, 8601 Georgia Ave., Suite 300 Silver Spring, MD 20910. Phone: 800-662-7776 or (301)650-2000 Fax: (301)650-2111 E-mail: corporatecommunications@cahners.com • URL: http://www.cahners.com • 32 times a year. Free to qualified personnel.

Government Contract Litigation Reporter: Covers Defense Procurement Fraud Litigation As Well as False Claims Acts (Qui Tam) Litigation. Andrews Publications, 175 Strafford Ave., Bldg. 4, Suite 140 Wayne, PA 19087. Phone: 800-345-1101 or (610)622-0510 Fax: (610)622-0501 URL: http://www.andrewspub.com • Semimonthly. $875.00 per year. Provides reports on defense procurement fraud lawsuits.

Government Contractor. Federal Publications, Inc., 1120 20th St., N.W., Suite 500 S Washington, DC 20036-3483. Phone: 800-922-4330 or (202)337-7000 Fax: (202)659-2233 E-mail: bbolger@fedpub.com • URL: http://www.fedpub.com • Weekly. $1,032.00 per year.

Government Contracts and Subcontract Leads Directory. Government Data Publications, Inc., 1661 McDonald Ave. Brooklyn, NY 11230. Phone: 800-282-8229 or (718)627-0819 Fax: (718)998-5960 Annual. $89.50. Firms which received prime contracts for production of goods or services from federal government agencies during the preceeding twelve months. Formerly *Government Contracts Directory*.

Government Contracts: Law, Administration and Procedure. Matthew Bender & Co., Inc., Two Park Ave. New York, NY 10016. Phone: 800-223-1940 or (212)448-2000 Fax: (212)244-3188 E-mail: international@bender.com • URL: http://www.bender.com • $1,050.00. 17 looseleaf volumes. Periodic supplementation. Coverage of important aspects of government contracts.

Government Contracts Reports. CCH, Inc., 4025 W. Peterson Ave. Chicago, IL 60646-6085. Phone: 800-248-3248 or (773)866-6000 Fax: 800-224-8299 or (773)866-3608 URL: http://www.cch.com • $2,249.00 per year. 10 looseleaf volumes. Weekly updates. Laws and regulations affecting government contracts.

Government Contracts Update: How to Target, Win, and Perform Government Contracts. United Communications Group (UCG), 11300 Rockville Pike, Suite 1100 Rockville, MD 20852-3030. Phone: 800-287-2223 or (301)287-2700 Fax: (301)816-8945 E-mail: webmaster@ucg.com • URL: http://www.ucg.com • Biweekly. $277.00 per year. Newsletter. Formerly *Federal Procurement Update*.

Government Discrimination: Equal Protection Law and Litigation. James A. Kushner. West Group, 610 Opperman Dr. Eagan, MN 55123. Phone: 800-328-4880 or (651)687-7000 Fax: 800-213-2323 or (651)687-5827 URL: http://www.westgroup.com • $140.00 per year. Looseleaf service. Periodic supplementation. Covers discrimination in employment, housing, and other areas by local, state, and federal offices or agencies. (Civil Rights Series).

Government Employee Relations Report. Bureau of National Affairs, Inc., 1231 25th St., N.W. Washington, DC 20037-1197. Phone: 800-372-1033 or (202)452-4200 Fax: (202)452-8092 E-mail: books@bna.com • URL: http://www.bna.com • Weekly. $999.00 per year. Three volumes. Looseleaf. Concerned with labor relations in the public sector.

Government Executive: Federal Government's Business Magazine. National Journal Group, Inc., 1501 M St., N. W., Suite 300 Washington, DC 20005. Phone: 800-424-2921 or (202)739-8400 Fax: (202)739-8511 URL: http://www.nationaljournal.com • Monthly. $48.00 per year. Includes management of computerized information systems in the federal government.

Government Finance Officers Association of the United States and Canada.

Government Finance Officers Center Association Research Center., 180 N. Michigan Ave., Suite 800 Chicago, IL 60601. Phone: (312)977-9700 Fax: (312)977-4806 E-mail: rmiranda@gfoa.org • URL: http://www.gfoa.org • Provides consulting and research services in state and local finance. Designs and produces microcomputer software packages for use in government finance functions.

Government Finance Review. Government Finance Officers Association, 180 N. Michigan Ave., Suite 800 Chicago, IL 60601. Phone: (312)977-9700 Fax: (312)977-4806 Bimonthly. $30.00. per year.

Government Information on the Internet. Greg R. Notess. Bernan Associates, 4611-F Assembly Dr. Lanham, MD 20706-4391. Phone: 800-274-4447 or (301)459-7666 Fax: 800-865-3450 or (301)459-0056 E-mail: info@bernan.com • URL: http://www.bernan.com • Annual. $38.50. directory of publicly-accessible Internet sites maintained by the U. S. Government. Also includes selected foreign government sites, state sites, and non-government sites containing government-provided data.

Government Management Information Sciences., c/o Herschel E. Strickland, P.O. Box 421 Kennesaw, GA 30144-0421. Phone: 800-460-7454 or (770)975-0729 Fax: (770)975-0719 E-mail: gmishdqrs@mindspring.com • URL: http://www.gmis.org • Members are state and local government agencies.

Government Phone Book USA: Your Comprehensive Guide to Federal, State, County, and Local Government Offices in the United States. Omnigraphics, Inc., Penobscot Bldg. Detroit, MI 48226. Phone: 800-234-1340 or (313)961-1340 Fax: 800-875-1340 or (313)961-1383 E-mail: info@omnigraphics.com • URL: http://www.omnigraphics.com • Annual. $230.00. Contains more than 168,500 listings of federal, state, county, and local government offices and personnel, including legislatures. Formerly *Government Directory of Addresses and Phone Numbers*.

Government Prime Contractors Directory. Government Data Publications, Inc., 1155 Connecticut Ave., N.W. Washington, DC 20036. Phone: (718)627-0819 Fax: (718)998-5960 Annual. $15.00. Organizations that received government prime contractors during the previous two years. Formerly *Government Production Prime Contractors*.

Government Primecontracts Monthly. Government Data Publications, Inc., 1155 Connecticut Ave., N.W. Washington, DC 20036. Phone: (718)627-0819 Fax: (718)998-5960 Irregular. $96.00 per year.

Government Product News. Penton Media Inc., 1300 E. Ninth St. Cleveland, OH 44114. Phone: (216)696-7000 Fax: (216)696-0836 E-mail: corpcomm@penton.com • URL: http://www.penton.com • Monthly. Free to qualified personnel; others, $50.00 per year.

Government Publications News. Bernan Associates, 4611-F Assembly Dr. Lanham, MD 20706-4391. Phone: 800-274-4447 or (301)459-7666 Fax: 800-865-3450 or (301)459-0056 E-mail: info@bernan.com • URL: http://www.bernan.com • Monthly. Free. Controlled circulation newsletter providing information on recent publications from the U. S. Government Printing Office and selected international agencies.

Government Research Directory. The Gale Group, 27500 Drake Rd. Farmington Hills, MI 48331-3535. Phone: 800-877-GALE or (248)699-GALE Fax: 800-414-5043 or (248)699-8069 E-mail: galeord@galegroup.com • URL: http://www.galegroup.com • 2000. $530.00 14th edition. Lists more than 4,800 research facilities and programs of the United States and Canadian federal governments.

Government Standard. American Federation of Government Employees, AFL-CIO, 80 F St., N.W. Washington, DC 20001. Phone: (202)639-6419 Fax: (202)639-6441 E-mail: communications@afge.org • URL: http://www.afge.org • Bimonthly. Membership.

Government Technology: Solutions for State and Local Government in the Information Age., 9719 Lincoln Village Dr., No. 500 Sacramento, CA 95827-3303. Phone: (916)363-5000 Fax: (916)363-5197 E-mail: donpears@govtech.net • URL: http://www.govtech.net • Monthly. Free to qualified personnel.

Government Union Review. Public Service Research Foundation, 527 Maple Ave., E., Suite 4 Vienna, VA 22180-4742. Phone: (703)242-3575 Fax: (703)242-3579 E-mail: info@psrf.org • URL: http://www.psrf.org • Quarterly. $20.00 per year. Academic quarterly covering the labor relations field.

Governmental Research Association.

Governors' Staff Directory. National Governor's Association. Publications Fulfillment Service, P.O. Box 421 Annapolis Junction, MD 20701. Phone: (301)498-3738 Semiannual. $9.95 per year. List of more than 1,000 key staff members and their titles in each of the 55 governor's offices.

Gower Handbook of Customer Service. Peter Murley, editor. Ashgate Publishing Co., Old Post Rd. Brookfield, VT 05036-9704. Phone: 800-535-9544 or (802)276-3162 Fax: (802)276-3837 E-mail: info@ashgate.com • URL: http://www.ashgate.com • 1996. $113.95. Consists of 40 articles (chapters) written by various authors. Among the topics covered are benchmarking, customer surveys, focus groups, control groups, employee selection, incentives, training, teamwork, and telephone techniques. Published by Gower in England.

Gower Handbook of Internal Communication. Eileen Scholes, editor. Ashgate Publishing Co., Old Post Rd. Brookfield, VT 05036-9704. Phone: 800-535-9544 or (802)276-3162 Fax: (802)276-3837 E-mail: info@ashgate.com • URL: http://www.ashgate.com • 1997. $113.95. Consists of 38 chapters written by various authors, with case studies. Covers more than 45 communication techniques, ''from team meetings to web sites.'' Published by Gower in England.

Gower Handbook of Management Development. Alan Mumford, editor. Ashgate Publishing Co., Old Post Rd. Brookfield, VT 05036-9704. Phone: 800-535-9544 or (802)276-3162 Fax: (802)276-3837 E-mail: info@ashgate.com • URL: http://www.ashgate.com • 1995. $113.95. Fourth edition. Consists of 28 chapters written by various authors. Published by Gower in England.

Gower Handbook of Project Management. Dennis Lock, editor. Ashgate Publishing Co., Old Post Rd. Brookfield, VT 05036-9704. Phone: 800-535-9544 or (802)276-3162 Fax: (802)276-3837 E-mail: info@ashgate.com • URL: http://www.ashgate.com • 2000. $129.95. Second edition. Consists of 33 chapters written by various authors, with bibliographical references and index. Published by Gower in England.

Gower Handbook of Quality Management. Dennis Lock, editor. Ashgate Publishing Co., Old Post Rd. Brookfield, VT 05036-9704. Phone: 800-535-9544 or (802)276-3162 Fax: (802)276-3837 E-mail: info@ashgate.com • URL: http://www.ashgate.com • 1994. $131.95. Second edition. Consists of 41 chapters written by various authors. Published by Gower in England.

Gower Handbook of Training and Development. John Prior, editor. Ashgate Publishing Co., Old Post Rd. Brookfield, VT 05036-9704. Phone: 800-535-9544 or (802)276-3162 Fax: (802)276-3837 E-mail: info@ashgate.com • URL: http://www.ashgate.com • 1994. $109.95. Second edition. Consists of 40 chapters written by various authors. Includes glossary and index. Published by Gower in England.

GPO Access: Keeping America Informed Electronically. U. S. Government Printing Office Sales Program, Bibliographic Systems BranchPhone: 888-293-6498 or (202)512-1530 Fax: (202)512-1262 E-mail: gpoaccess@gpo.gov • URL: http://www.access.gpo.gov • Web site provides searching of the GPO's Sales Product Catalog (SPC), also known as Publications Reference File (PRF). Covers all ''Government information products currently offered for sale by the Superintendent of Documents.'' There are also specialized search pages for individual databases, such as the *Code of Federal Regulations*, the *Federal Register*, and *Commerce Business Daily*. Updated daily. Fees: Free.

GPO Monthly Catalog. U. S. Government Printing Office, Washington, DC 20402. Phone: (202)512-1530 E-mail: gpoaccess@gpo.gov • URL: http://www.access.gpo.gov •

Contains over 375,000 online citations to U. S. government publications, 1976 to date, with monthly updates. Corresponds to the printed *Monthly Catalog of United States Government Publications*. Inquire as to online cost and availability.

GPO Publications Reference File. U. S. Government Printing Office, Washington, DC 20402. Phone: (202)512-1530 E-mail: gpoaccess@gpo.gov • URL: http://www.access.gpo.gov • An online guide to federal government publications in print (currently for sale), forthcoming, and recently out-of-print. Biweekly updates. Inquire as to online cost and availability.

GQ (Gentleman's Quarterly). Conde Nast Publications, Inc., Four Times Square New York, NY 10036. Phone: (212)582-9090 Fax: (212)286-7093 E-mail: gqmag@aol.com • URL: http://www.gq.com • Monthly. Individuals, $19.97 per year; libraries, $12.50 per year.

GRA Professional Directory of Who's Who in Governmental Research. Governmental Research Association, Inc., Samford University, 402 Samford Hall Birmingham, AL 35229-7017. Phone: (205)726-2482 Fax: (205)726-2900 Annual. $50.00. Lists information on governmental research organization throughout the country.

GRA Reporter. Governmental Research Association, Inc., Samford University, 402 Samford Hall Birmingham, AL 35229-7017. Phone: (205)870-2482 Fax: (205)870-2654 Quarterly. $75.00 per year. Update on GRA-member agencies.

Graduate Aeronautical Laboratories. California Institute of Technology

Graduate Management Admission Council., 1750 Tysons Blvd., No. 1100 McLean, VA 22102-4220. Phone: (703)749-0131 Fax: (703)749-0169 E-mail: gmat@ets.org • URL: http://www.gmat.org • Members are graduate schools of business administration and management.

Graduate Record Examinations Board.

Grain and Feed Weekly Summary and Statistics. U.S. Dept. of Agriculture. Agricultural Marketing Service, Livestock and Seed Div., P.O. Box 96456 Washington, DC 20090-6456. Phone: (202)720-8054 Fax: (202)690-3732 Weekly. $85.00 per year. Formerly *Grain and Feed Market News*.

Grain Elevator and Processing Society.

Grains: Production, Processing, Marketing. Chicago Board of Trade, 141 W. Jackson Blvd., Suite 2210 Chicago, IL 60654-2994. Phone: 800-572-3276 or (312)435-3542 Fax: (312)341-3168 E-mail: bw0050@cbot.com • URL: http://www.cbot.com • 1992. $12.00. Revised edition.

Grant Budgeting and Finance: Getting the Most Out of Your Grant Dollar. Frea E. Sladek and Eugene L. Stein. Perseus Publishing, 11 Cambridge Center Cambridge, MA 02142. Phone: (617)252-5200 Fax: (617)252-5285 E-mail: westview.orders@perseusbooks.com • URL: http://www.perseusbooks.com • 1981. $65.00.

Grants. Oryx Press, 4041 N. Central Ave. at Indian School Rd. Phoenix, AZ 85012-3379. Phone: 800-279-6799 or (602)265-2651 Fax: (602)265-6250 References grants by federal, state, and local governments and other organizations; current file includes grants with deadlines within the next six months. Inquire as to online cost and availability.

Grants for Arts, Culture, and the Humanities. The Foundation Center, 79 Fifth Ave. New York, NY 10003-3076. Phone: 800-424-9836 or (212)620-4230 Fax: (212)807-3677 E-mail: mfn@fdncenter.org • URL: http://www.fdncenter.org • 1997. $75.00. (Grants Guides Series).

Grants for Libraries and Information Services. The Foundation Center, 79 Fifth Ave. New York, NY 10003-3076. Phone: 800-424-9836 or (212)620-4230 Fax: (212)807-3677 E-mail: mfn@fdncenter.org • URL: http://www.fdncenter.org • Annual. $75.00. Foundations and organizations which have awarded grants made the preceding year for public, academic, research, special, and school libraries; for archives and information centers; for consumer information; and for philanthropy information centers.

Grant's Interest Rate Observer. James Grant, editor. Interest Rate Publishing Corp., 30 Wall St. New York, NY 10005-2201. Phone: (212)608-7994 Fax: (212)608-5925 Biweekly. $495.00 per year. Newsletter containing detailed analysis of money-related topics, including interest rate trends, global credit markets, fixed-income investments, bank loan policies, and international money markets.

Grant's Municipal Bond Observer. James Grant, editor. Interest Rate Publishing Corp., 30 Wall St. New York, NY 10005-2201. Phone: (212)608-7994 Fax: (212)608-5925 Biweekly. $650.00 per year. Newsletter. Provides detailed analysis of the municipal bond market.

Grants on Disc. The Gale Group, 27500 Drake Rd. Farmington Hills, MI 48331-3535. Phone: 800-877-8238 or (248)699-GALE Fax: 800-414-5043 or (248)699-8069 E-mail: galeord@gale.com • URL: http://www.gale.com • Quarterly. $695.00 per year. On CD-ROM, provides detailed information on about 410,000 grants. Describes up to 100 of the highest grants awarded by each of 6,000 large foundations and corporations.

Grants Policy Directives. U.S. Dept. of Health, and Human Services. Available from U.S. Government Printing Office, Washington, DC 20402. Phone: (202)512-1800 Fax: (202)512-2250 E-mail: gpoaccess@gpo.gov • URL: http://www.accessgpo.gov • $219.00. Periodic supplementation. Provides guidelines on the fiscal and administrative aspects of grant management to all granting agencies of the Dept. of Health and Human Services.

Grants Register (Graduate Student Financial Aid). St. Martin's Press, 175 Fifth Ave. New York, NY 10010. Phone: 800-221-7945 or (212)674-5151 Fax: 800-672-2054 or (212)529-0594 URL: http://www.stmartins.com • Annual. $120.00. About 2,000 sources in the United Kingdom, Ireland, Australia, Canada and the U.S. and other English-speaking areas which award financial aid for graduate study, research or travel.

Grantsmanship Center Magazine: A Compendium of Resources for Nonprofit Organizations. Grantsmanship Center, P.O. Box 17220 Los Angeles, CA 90017. Phone: 800-421-9512 or (213)482-9860 Fax: (213)482-9863 E-mail: marc@tgci.com • URL: http://www.tgci.com • Irregular. Free to qualified personnel. Contains a variety of concise articles on grant-related topics, such as program planning, proposal writing, fundraising, non-cash gifts, federal project grants, benchmarking, taxation, etc.

Granville Market Letter. Joseph Granville, editor., P.O. Box 413006 Kansas City, MO 64141. Phone: 800-876-5388 46 times a year. $250.00 per year.

Graphic Artists Guild.

Graphic Artists Guild Handbook of Pricing and Ethical Guidelines: Pricing and Ethical Guidelines. Graphic Artists Guild, 90 John St., Suite 403 New York, NY 10038-3202. Phone: (212)791-3400 Fax: (212)791-0333 URL: http://www.gag.org • 2000. 32.95. 10th edition.

Graphic Arts Blue Book. A. F. Lewis and Co. Inc., 345 Hudson St., 4th Fl. New York, NY 10014. Phone: (212)519-7398 Fax: (212)519-7434 E-mail: bluebook@cahners.com • URL: http://www.gabb.com • Auuual. $85.00. Eight regional editions. Printing plants, bookbinders, imagesetters, platemakers, paper merchants, paper manufacturers, printing machine manufacturers and dealers, and others serving the printing industry.

Graphic Arts Monthly. Cahners Business Information, 345 Hudson St. 4th Fl. New York, NY 10014-4502. Phone: 800-662-7776 or (212)519-7200 Fax: (212)519-7434 E-mail: corporatecommunications@cahners.com • URL: http://www.cahners.com • Monthly. $110.00 per year.

Graphic Arts Monthly Sourcebook. Cahners, 345 Hudson St., 4th Fl. New York, NY 10014-4502. Phone: 800-523-9654 or (212)519-7200 Fax: (212)519-7428 E-mail: corporate-communications@cahners.com • URL: http://www.cahners.com • Annual. $50.00. About 1,400 manufacturers and distributors of graphic arts equipment, supplies and services. Also includes list of corporate electronic publishers.

Graphic Arts Technical Foundation.

Graphic Communications International Union.

Graphic Design: U.S.A. Kaye Publishing Corp., 1556 Third Ave., Suite 405 New York, NY 10128-3106. Phone: (212)534-5003 Fax: (212)534-4415 Monthly. $60.00.

Graphic Designer's Production Handbook. Norman Sanders and William Bevington. Hastings House Publishers, Nine Mott Ave., Suite 203 Norwalk, CT 06850. Phone: 800-206-7822 or (203)838-4083 E-mail: hhousebks@aol.com • URL: http://www.upub.com • 1982. $12.95. (Visual Communication Books Series).

Graphically Speaking: An Illustrated Guide to the Working Language of Design and Publishing. Mark Beach. Coast to Coast Books, P.O. Box 633 Manzanita, OR 97130. Phone: (503)368-5584 Fax: (503)368-5929 E-mail: mbeach@pdx.oneworld.com • URL: http://www.gettingprinted.com • 1992. $29.50. Provides practical definitions of 2,800 terms used in printing, graphic design, publishing, and desktop publishing. Over 300 illustrations are included, about 40 in color.

Graphics, Visualization, and Usability Center., Georgia Institute of Technology, Mail Code 0280 Atlanta, GA 30332-0280. Phone: (404)894-4488 Fax: (404)894-0673 E-mail: jarek@cc.gatech.edu • URL: http://www.cc.gatech.edu/gvu/ • Research areas include computer graphics, multimedia, image recognition, interactive graphics systems, animation, and virtual realities.

Graphis Design: International Annual of Design and Illustration. Watson-Guptill Publications, 1695 Oak St. Lakewood, NJ 08701. Phone: 800-451-1741 or (908)363-0338 Fax: (908)363-0338 Annual. $69.00. Text in English, French, and German. Formerly *Graphis Annual*.

Graphis: International Journal of Visual Communication. Graphis Inc., 141 Lexington Ave. New York, NY 10016. Phone: (212)532-9387 Fax: (212)213-3229 URL: http://www.graphis.com/mag/mag • Bimonthly. $90.00 per year. Text in English, French and German.

Gravy Training: Inside the Business of Business Schools. Stuart Crainer and Des Dearlove. Jossey-Bass, Inc., Publishers, 350 Sansome St. San Francisco, CA 94104-9825. Phone: 888-378-2537 or (415)433-1740 Fax: (415)433-0499 E-mail: webperson@jbp.com • URL: http://www.josseybass.com • 1999. $25.00. Provides a critical look at major American business schools.

Great American Trials. The Gale Group, 27500 Drake Rd. Farmington Hills, MI 48331-3535. Phone: 800-877-GALE or (248)699-GALE Fax: 800-414-5C43 or (248)699-8069 E-mail: galeord@galegroup.com • URL: http://www.galegroup.com • 1994. $80.00. Contains discussions and details of momentous American trials from 1637 to 1993.

The Great Game: The Emergence of Wall Street as a World Power, 1653-2000. John S. Gordon. Scribner, 1230 Ave. of the Americas New York, NY 10020. Phone: 800-223-2336 or (212)698-7000 Fax: 800-943-9831 or (212)698-7007 URL: http://www.simonsays.com • 1999. $25.00. Provides a history of U. S. financial markets, featuring such key figures as Alexander Hamilton, Commodore Vanderbilt, J. P. Morgan, Charles Merrill, and Michael Milken.

Great Inflations of the 20th Century: Theories, Policies, and Evidence. Pierre L. Siklos, editor. Edward Elgar Publishing, Inc., 136 West St., Suite 202 Northampton, MA 01060. Phone: 800-390-3149 or (413)584-5551 Fax: (413)584-9933 E-mail: eep.orders@aidcvt.com • URL: http://www.e-elgar.co.uk • 1995. $95.00. Contains reprints of papers on the history and economic analysis of major inflations.

Great Scouts! CyberGuides to Subject Searching on the Web. Margot Williams and others. Independent Publishers Group, 814 N. Franklin St. Chicago, IL 60610. Phone: 800-888-4741 or (312)337-0747 Fax: (312)337-5985 E-mail: ipgbook@mcs.com • URL: http://www.ipgbook.com • 1999. $24.95. Contains descriptions of selected Web sites, arranged by subject. Covers business, investments, computers, travel, the environment, health, social issues, etc. (CyberAge Books.)

The Greatest Direct Mail Sales Letters of All Time: Why They Succeed, How They Are Created, How You Can Create Great Sales Letters, Too. Richard S. Hodgson. Dartnell Corp., 350 Hiatt Dr. Palm Beach, FL 33418. Phone: 800-621-5463 or (561)622-6520 Fax: (561)622-2423 E-mail: custserv@lrp.com • URL: http://www.dartnellcorp.com • 1995. $69.95. Second revised edition. About 100 direct mail sales lettes on a variety of products are reprinted and analyzed.

The Greatest Ever Bank Robbery: The Collapse of the Savings and Loan Industry. Martin Mayer. Pearson Education and Technology, 201 W. 103rd St. Indianapolis, IN 46290-1097. Phone: 800-428-5331 or (317)581-3500 URL: http://www.mcp.com • 1992. $12.95. Reprint edition.

Green Markets. Pike and Fischer, Inc., 1010 Wayne Ave., Suite 1400 Silver Spring, MD 20910-5600. Phone: (301)562-1530 Fax: (301)562-1521 Weekly. $890.00 per year. Newsletter including prices for potash and other agricultural chemicals.

GreenBook: Worldwide Directory of Marketing Research Companies and Services. New York Ama-Green Book, Lakewood Business Park, 4301 32nd St., W., Suite E-11 Bradenton, NY 34210. Phone: 800-972-9202 or (941)752-4498 Fax: 800-879-3751 E-mail: greenbook@nyama.org • URL: http://www.greenbook.org • Annual. $145.00. Contains information in 300 categories on more than 2,500 market research companies, consultants, field services, computer services, survey research companies, etc. Indexed by specialty, industry, company, computer program, and personnel. Formerly (Greenbook Worldwide International Directory of Marketing Research Companies and Services).

Greenhouse Grower. Meister Publishing Co., 37733 Euclid Ave. Willoughby, OH 44094-5992. Phone: 800-572-7740 or (440)942-2000 Fax: (440)942-0662 E-mail: info@meisternet.com • URL: http://www.meisterpro.com • 14 times a year. $37.45 per year. Concerned with all crops grown under glass or plastic.

Greeting Card Association.

The Greeting Card Market. Available from MarketResearch.com, 641 Ave. of the Americas, Third Floor New York, NY 10011. Phone: 800-298-5699 or (212)807-2629 Fax: (212)807-2716 E-mail: order@marketresearch.com • URL: http://www.marketresearch.com • 1998. $2,750.00. Published by Packaged Facts. Provides market data for various kinds of greeting cards, with sales projections to 2002.

Gregg Shorthand Dictionary. John R. Gregg and others. McGraw-Hill, 1221 Ave. of the Americas New York, NY 10020. Phone: 800-722-4726 or (212)904-2000 Fax: (212)904-2072 E-mail: customer.service@mcgraw-hill.com • URL: http://www.mcgraw-hill.com • 1974. $23.56. Second edition. (Diamond Jubilee Series).

Gregg Shorthand for Colleges. L. A. Leslie and others. McGraw-Hill, 1221 Ave. of the Americas New York, NY 10020. Phone: 800-722-4726 or (212)904-2000 Fax: (212)904-2072 E-mail: customer.service@mcgraw-hill.com • URL: http://www.mcgraw-hill.com • Dates vary. Two volumes. Vol. 1, $96.20; Vol. 2, $101.40. (Series 90).

Gregg Shorthand Manual, Simplified. John R. Gregg and others. McGraw-Hill, 1221 Ave. of the Americas New York, NY 10020-1095. Phone: 800-722-4726 or (212)904-2000 Fax: (212)904-2072 E-mail: customer.service@

mcgraw-hill.com • URL: http://www.mcgraw-hill.com • 1955. $23.96. Second edition.

Grey House Directory of Special Issues: A Guide to Business Magazines' Buyer's Guides & Directory Issues. Grey House Publishing, 185 Millerton Rd. Millerton, NY 12546. Phone: 800-562-2139 or (518)789-8700 Fax: (518)789-0556 E-mail: books@greyhouse.com • URL: http://www.greyhouse.com • 2001. $105.00. Provides information on more than 4,000 specialized directories issued by trade journals, arranged according to 90 industry groups.

Grey House Performing Arts Directory. Grey House Publishing, 185 Millerton Rd. Millerton, NY 12546. Phone: 800-562-2139 or (518)789-8700 Fax: (518)789-0556 E-mail: books@greyhouse.com • URL: http://www.greyhouse.com • 2001. $220.00. Contains more than 7,700 entries covering dance, instrumental music, vocal music, theatre, performance series, festivals, performance facilities, and media sources.

Griffin's Modern Grocer. Griffin Publishing Co., Inc., One University Plaza, Suite 200 Hackensack, NJ 07601. Phone: (201)488-1800 Fax: (201)488-7357 Monthly. $45.00 per year. Formerly *Modern Grocer*.

Grits and Grinds. Norton Co., One New Bond St. Worcester, MA 01606. Phone: (508)795-5000 Quarterly. Free.

Grocery Distribution Magazine Directory of Warehouse Equipment, Fixtures, and Services. Trend Publishing, Inc., One E. Erie St., Suite. 401 Chicago, IL 60611. Phone: 800-278-7363 or (312)654-2300 Fax: (312)654-2323 Annual. $7.50. Covers products related to food warehousing, distribution, and storage.

Grocery Headquarters: The Newspaper for the Food Industry. Trend Publishing, Inc., One E. Erie St., Suite 401 Chicago, IL 60611. Phone: 800-278-7363 or (312)654-2300 Fax: (312)654-2323 Monthly. $100.00 per year. Covers the sale and distribution of food products and other items sold in supermarkets and grocery stores. Edited mainly for retailers and wholesalers. Formerly *Grocery Marketing*.

Grocery Manufacturers of America.

Grolier Club.

Grossman on Circulation. Gordon W. Grossman. Intertec Publishing, 11 River Bend Drive South Stamford, CT 06907-0949. Phone: 800-828-1133 or (203)358-4236 Fax: (203)358-5812 URL: http://www.intertec.com • 2000. $99.95. Produced by *Circulation Management* magazine. Covers magazine circulation management and marketing, with emphasis on circulaton incentives, such as free-issue offers, sweepstakes, premiums, ''freemiums,'' and professional courtesy offers. Includes examples of promotions used at 500 consumer and trade publications.

Ground Water. National Ground Water Association. Ground Water Publishing Co., 601 Dempsey Rd. Westerville, OH 43081-8978. Phone: (614)882-8179 Fax: (614)898-7786 Bimonthly. $150.00 per year.

Group Against Smokers' Pollution., P.O. Box 632 College Park, MD 20741-0632. Phone: (301)459-4791 Members are non-smokers seeking to regulate smoking in public places.

Group Practice Journal. American Medical Group Practice Association, 1422 Duke St. Alexandria, VA 22314-3430. Phone: (703)838-0033 Fax: (703)548-1890 E-mail: fhaag@amga.org • URL: http://www.amga.org • 10 times a year. $75.00 per year.

Growth Fund Guide: The Investor's Guide to Dynamic Growth Funds. Growth Fund Research, Inc., P.O. Box 6600 Rapid City, SD 57709. Phone: 800-621-8322 or (605)341-1971 Fax: (605)341-7260 Monthly. $99.00 per year. Newsletter. Covers no-load growth mutual funds.

Growth Stock Outlook. Charles Allmon, editor. Growth Stock Outlook, Inc., 4405 East-West Highway, Suite 305 Bethesda, MD 20814. Phone: (301)654-5205 Semimonthly. $195.00 per year. Newsletter. Provides data on stock earnings, sales, price-earnings ratios, dividends, book values, returns on shareholder equity and institutional holdings. Recommends specific companies for long-term investment. Subscription includes *Junior Growth Stocks, New Issues Digest*, and *Bank Stock Analyst*.

Guerilla Trade Show Selling: New Unconventional Weapons and Tactics to Meet More People, Get More Leads, and Close More Sales. Jay C. Levinson and others. John Wiley and Sons, Inc., 605 Third Ave. New York, NY 10158-0012. Phone: 800-225-5945 or (212)850-6000 Fax: (212)850-6088 E-mail: info@jwiley.com • URL: http://www.wiley.com • 1997. $19.95.

Guide for Authors: Manuscript, Proof, and Illustration. Payne E. Thomas. Charles C. Thomas Publishers, Ltd., P.O. Box 19265 Springfield, IL 62794-9265. Phone: 800-258-8980 or (217)789-8980 Fax: (217)789-9130 E-mail: books@ccthomas.com • URL: http://www.ccthomas.com • 1993. $20.95. Fourth edition.

Guide to ACA Accredited Camps. American Camping Association, 5000 State Rd., 67 N. Martinsville, IN 46151-7902. Phone: 800-428-2267 or (317)342-8456 Fax: (317)342-2065 E-mail: msnider@aca-camps.org • URL: http://www.acacamps.org • Annual. $10.95. Lists over 2,200 summer camps. Included with subscription to *Camping Magazine*. Formerly *Guide to Accredited Camps*.

Guide to American Directories. Bernard Klein. B. Klein Publications, P.O. Box 635 Nyack, NY 10960-0635. Phone: 800-747-1056 or (914)358-6213 Fax: (914)358-1059 E-mail: toddpub@aol.com • URL: http://www.toddpublications.com • Biennial. $95.00. Provides 8,000 listings with descriptions, prices, etc.

Guide to Architecture Schools. Association of Collegiate Schools of Architecture, 1735 New York Ave., N.W. Washington, DC 20006. Phone: (202)785-2324 Fax: (202)628-0448 E-mail: acsanatl@aol.com • URL: http://www.acsa-arch.org • Irregular. $19.95. Descriptions of 120 accredited degree programs and related organizations in architecture. Formerly *Guide to Architecture Schools in North America*.

Guide to Arts Administration Training and Research. Americans for the Arts, One E. 53rd St. New York, NY 10022-4201. Phone: 800-321-4510 or (212)223-2787 Fax: (212)753-1325 E-mail: books@artusa.org • URL: http://www.artsusa.org • Biennial. $12.95. Lists 33 institutions. Formerly *Survey of Arts Administration Training*.

Guide to Banks and Thrifts: A Quarterly Compilation of Financial Institutions Ratings and Analysis. Weiss Ratings, Inc., 4176 Burns Rd. Palm Beach Gardens, FL 33410. Phone: 800-289-9222 or (561)627-3300 Fax: (561)625-6685 URL: http://www.weissratings.com • Quarterly. $438.00 per year. Emphasis is on rating of financial safety and relative risk. Includes annual summary.

A Guide to College Programs in Hospitality and Tourism. Council on Hotel, Restaurant and Institutional Education. John Wiley and Sons, Inc., 605 Third Ave. New York, NY 10158-0012. Phone: 800-225-5945 or (212)850-6000 Fax: (212)850-6088 E-mail: info@wiley.com • URL: http://www.wiley.com • 1995. $29.95. Fifth edition. About 400 secondary and technical institutes, colleges, and universities; international coverage.

Guide to Computer Law. CCH, Inc., 4025 W. Peterson Ave. Chicago, IL 60646-6085. Phone: 800-248-3248 or (773)866-6000 Fax: 800-224-8299 or (773)866-3608 URL: http://www.cch.com • $551.00 per year. Two looseleaf volumes, updated semimonthly.

Guide to Congress; Origins, History and Procedure. Congressional Quarterly, Inc., 1414 22nd St., N.W. Washington, DC 20037. Phone: 800-432-2250 or (202)887-8500 Fax: (202)887-6706 E-mail: bookhelp@cq.com • URL: http://www.cq.com • 1999. $259.00. Fifth edition.

Guide to Dividend Reinvestment Plans. Evergreen Enterprises, P.O. Box 763 Laurel, MD 20725-0763. Phone: (301)549-3939 Quarterly. $142.00 per year. Looseleaf. Provides detailed, current information on the dividend reinvestment programs of over 1,000 publicly traded corporations in the U. S. and Canada.

Guide to Economic Indicators. Norman Frumkin. M. E. Sharpe, Inc., 80 Business Park Dr. Armonk, NY 10504. Phone: 800-541-6543 or (914)273-1800 Fax: (914)273-2106 E-mail: mesinfo@usa.net • URL: http://www.mesharpe.com/ • 2000. $64.95. Third edition. Provides detailed descriptions and sources of 50 economic indicators.

A Guide to Employee Relocation and Relocation Policy Development. Employee Relocation Council, 1720 N St., N. W. Washington, DC 20036. Phone: (202)857-0857 Fax: (202)467-4012 1987. $25.00. Second edition.

Guide to Employment Sources in the Library and Information Professions. American Library Association, Office for Library Personnel Resources, 50 E. Huron St. Chicago, IL 60611-2795. Phone: 800-545-2433 or (312)944-6780 Fax: (312)440-9374 E-mail: ala@ala.org • URL: http://www.ala.org • Annual. Free. Associations and agencies offering library placement services. Formerly *Guide to Library Placement Sources*.

Guide to Energy Efficient Commercial Equipment. Margaret Suozzo and others. American Council for an Energy Efficient Economy, 1001 Connecticut Ave., N. W., Suite 801 Washington, DC 20036. Phone: (202)429-0063 Fax: (202)429-0193 E-mail: ace3pubs@ix.netcom.com • URL: http://www.aceee.org • 1997. $25.00. Provides information on specifying and purchasing energy-saving systems for buildings (heating, air conditioning, lighting, and motors).

Guide to Energy Efficient Office Equipment. Loretta A. Smith and others. American Council for an Energy Efficient Economy, 1001 Connecticut Ave., N.W., Suite 801 Washington, DC 20036. Phone: (202)429-0063 Fax: (202)429-0193 E-mail: ace3pubs@ix.netcom.com • URL: http://www.aceee.org • 1996. $12.00. Second edition. Provides information on selecting, purchasing, and using energy-saving computers, monitors, printers, copiers, and other office devices.

Guide to Equity Mutual Funds: A Quarterly Compilation of Mutual Fund Ratings and Analysis Covering Equity and Balanced Funds. Weiss Ratings, Inc., 4176 Burns Rd. Palm Beach Gardens, FL 33410. Phone: 800-289-9222 or (561)627-3300 Fax: (561)625-6685 URL: http://www.weissratings.com • Quarterly. $438.00 per year. Emphasis is on rating of financial safety and relative risk. Includes annual summary.

Guide to EU Information Sources on the Internet. Euroconfidentiel S. A., Rue de Rixensart 18 B-1332 Genval, Belgium. Phone: (32)02 653 01 25 Fax: (32)02 653 01 80 E-mail: nigel.hunt@euronet.be • Annual. $220.00. Contains descriptions of more than 1,700 Web sites providing information relating to the European Union and European commerce and industry. Includes a quarterly e-mail newsletter with new sites and address changes.

Guide to Everyday Economic Statistics. Gary E. Clayton and Martin G. Giesbrecht. McGraw-Hill, 1221 Ave. of the Americas New York, NY 10020-1095. Phone: 800-722-4726 or (212)904-2000 Fax: (212)904-2072 E-mail: customer.service@mcgraw-hill.com • URL: http://www.mcgraw-hill.com • 1997. $14.38. Fourth edition. Contains clear explanations of the commonly used economic indicators.

Guide to Federal Funding for Education. Education Funding Research Council, 1725 K. St. N.W., Suite 700 Washington, DC 20006. Phone: 800-424-2959 Fax: 800-999-5661 Quarterly. $297.00 per year. Describes approximately 407 federal education programs that award grants and contracts. Includes semimonthly supplement: *Grant Updates*.

Guide to Federal Funding for Governments and Non-Profits. Government Information Services, 1725 K St., N.W., 7th Fl. Washington, DC 20006. Phone: 800-876-0226 or (202)739-9657 Fax: (202)739-9657 Quarterly. $339.00 per year. Contains detailed descriptions of federal grant programs in economic development, housing, transportation, social services, science, etc. Semimonthly supplement available: *Federal Grant Deadline Calendar*.

Guide to Federal Regulation of Derivatives. CCH, Inc., 4025 W. Peterson Ave. Chicago, IL 60646-6085. Phone: 800-248-3248 or (773)866-6000 Fax: 800-224-8299 or (773)866-3608 URL: http://www.cch.com • 1998. $99.00. Explains the complex derivatives regulations of the Securities and Exchange Commission. Covers swap agreements, third-party derivatives, credit derivatives, mutual fund liquidity, and other topics.

Guide to Financial Reporting and Analysis. Eugene E. Comiskey and Charles W. Mulford. John Wiley and Sons, Inc., 605 Third Ave. New York, NY 10158-0012. Phone: 800-225-5945 or (212)850-6000 Fax: (212)850-6088 E-mail: business@jwiley.com • URL: http://www.wiley.com • 2000. $75.00. Provides financial statement examples to illustrate the application of generally accepted accounting principles.

Guide to Franchising. Martin Mendelsohn. Continuum International Publishing Group, Inc., 370 Lexington Ave. New York, NY 10017-6503. Phone: 800-561-7704 or (212)953-5858 Fax: (212)953-5944 URL: http://www.contunuum-books.com • 1999. $32.95. Sixth edition.

A Guide to Hazardous Materials Management: Physical Characteristics, Federal Regulations, and Response Alternatives. Aileen Schumacher. Greenwood Publishing Group Inc., 88 Post Rd., W. Westport, CT 06881-5007. Phone: 800-225-5800 or (203)226-3571 Fax: (203)222-2540 E-mail: bookinfo@greenwood.com • URL: http://www.greenwood.com • 1988. $72.95.

Guide to Health Insurance for People with Medicare. U. S. Health Care Financing Administration, Department of Health and Human Servi, 200 Independence Ave., S. W. Washington, DC 20201. Phone: (202)690-6726 URL: http://www.hcfa.gov • Annual. Free. Contains detailed information on private health insurance as a supplement to Medicare

Guide to HMOs and Health Insurers: A Quarterly Compilation of Health Insurance Company Ratings and Analysis. Weiss Ratings, Inc., 4176 Burns Rd. Palm Beach Gardens, FL 33410. Phone: 800-289-9222 or (561)627-3300 Fax: (561)625-6685 E-mail: wr@weissinc.com • URL: http://www.weissratings.com • Quarterly. $438.00 per year. Emphasis is on rating of financial safety and relative risk. Includes annual summary.

Guide to Life, Health, and Annuity Insurers: A Quarterly Compilation of Insurance Company Ratings and Analysis. Weiss Ratings, Inc., 4176 Burns Rd. Palm Beach Gardens, FL 33410. Phone: 800-289-9222 or (561)627-3300 Fax: (561)625-6685 E-mail: wr@weissinc.com • URL: http://www.weissratings.com • Quarterly. $438.00 per year. Emphasis is on rating of financial safety and relative risk. Includes annual summary.

Guide to Microforms in Print: Author-Title. R. R. Bowker, 121 Chanlon Rd. New Providence, NJ 07974. Phone: 888-269-5372 or (908)464-6800 Fax: (908)771-7704 E-mail: info@bowker.com • URL: http://www.bowker.com • Annual. $475.00. Provides international coverage of authors and titles.

Guide to Microforms in Print: Subject Guide. Available from The Gale Group, 27500 Drake Rd. Farmington Hills, MI 48331-3535. Phone: 800-699-4253 or (248)699-4253 Fax: (249)699-8069 E-mail: galeord@galegroup.com • URL: http://www.galegroup.com • Annual. $450.00. Provides international coverage under 135 subject headings. Published by K. G. Saur.

Guide to Pension and Profit Sharing Plans: Taxation, Selection, and Design. Donald S. Dunkle. Shepard's, 555 Middle

Creek Parkway Colorado Springs, CO 80921. Phone: 800-743-7393 or (719)481-7371 Fax: 800-525-0053 or (719)481-7621 E-mail: customer_service@shepards.com • URL: http://www.shepards.com • 1984. $115.00. (Commercial Law Publications).

Guide to Preparing Financial Statements. John R. Clay and others. Practitioners Publishing Co., 3221 Collinsworth St. Fort Worth, TX 76101. Phone: 800-323-8724 or (817)332-3709 Fax: (817)336-2433 E-mail: linda-lusk@ppctx.com • URL: http://www.ppc.com • 1998. Three looseleaf volumes. Price on application.

Guide to Preparing Nonprofit Financial Statements. Harold L. Monk and others. Practitioners Publishing Co., 3221 Collinsworth St. Fort Worth, TX 76101. Phone: 800-323-8724 or (817)332-3709 Fax: (817)366-2433 E-mail: linda-lusk@ppcty.com • URL: http://www.ppc.com • 1997. $177.00. Two looseleaf volumes.

Guide to Private Fortunes. Available from The Gale Group, 27500 Drake Rd. Farmington Hills, MI 48331-3535. Phone: 800-877-GALE or (248)699-GALE Fax: 800-414-5043 or (248)699-8069 E-mail: galeord@galegroup.com • URL: http://www.galegroup.com • 1994. $255.00. Third edition. Published by The Taft Group. Provides biographical information and philanthropic histories for 1,250 individuals with a net worth of over $25 million or who have demonstrated a pattern of substantial charitable giving. Formerly *Fund Raiser's Guide to Private Fortunes*, and before that, *America's Wealthiest People*.

Guide to Products and Services of Member Companies. International Titanium Association, 350 Interlocken Blvd., Suite 390 Broomfield, CO 80021-3485. Phone: (303)404-2221 Fax: (303)404-9111 E-mail: info@titanium.org • URL: http://www.titanium.org • Annual. Free. Lists about 130 titanium metal industry companies.

Guide to Property and Casualty Insurers: A Quarterly Compilation of Insurance Company Ratings and Analysis. Weiss Ratings, Inc., 4176 Burns Rd. Palm Beach Gardens, FL 33410. Phone: 800-289-9222 or (561)627-3300 Fax: (561)625-6685 E-mail: wr@weissinc.com • URL: http://www.weissratings.com • Quarterly. $438.00 per year. Emphasis is on rating of financial safety and relative risk. Includes annual summary.

Guide to Proposal Writing. Jane C. Geever and Patricia McNeil. The Foundation Center, 79 Fifth Ave. New York, NY 10003-3076. Phone: 800-424-9836 or (212)620-4230 Fax: (212)807-3677 E-mail: mfn@fdncenter.org • URL: http://www.fdncenter.org • 1997. $34.95. Revised edition. An explanation of proposal-writing techniques. Includes interviews with foundation officials and examples of successful grant proposals.

Guide to Record Retention Requirements. CCH, Inc., 4025 W. Peterson Ave. Chicago, IL 60646-6085. Phone: 800-248-3248 or (773)866-6000 Fax: 800-224-8299 or (773)866-3608 URL: http://www.cch.com • Annual. $49.95. Explains federal recordkeeping regulations for individuals and businesses.

Guide to Reference Books. Robert Balay and others. American Library Association, 50 E. Huron St. Chicago, IL 60611-2795. Phone: 800-545-2433 or (312)944-6780 Fax: (312)440-9374 E-mail: ala@ala.org • URL: http://www.ala.org • 1996. $275.00. 11th edition.

Guide to Shipbuilding, Repair, and Maintenance. Available from Informa Publishing Group Ltd., PO Box 1017 Westborough, MA 01581-6017. Phone: 800-493-4080 Fax: (508)231-0856 E-mail: enquiries@informa.com • URL: http://www.informa.com • Annual. $111.00. Published in the UK by Lloyd's List (http://www.lloydslist.com). Provides worldwide coverage of shipbuilding, repair, and maintenance facilities and marine equipment suppliers for the maritime industry. (Included with subscription to *Lloyd's Ship Manager*.)

Guide to Special Issues and Indexes of Periodicals. Miriam Uhlan and Doris B. Katz, editors. Special Libraries Association, 1700 18th St., N. W., 17th Fl. Washington, DC 20009-2514. Phone: (202)234-4700 Fax: 888-411-2856 or (202)234-2442 E-mail: books@sla.org • URL: http://www.sla.org • 1994. $59.00. Fourth edition. A listing, with prices, of the special issues of over 1700 U. S. and Canadian periodicals in business, industry, technology, science, and the arts. Includes a comprehensive subject index.

Guide to Summer Camps and Summer Schools. Porter Sargent Publishers, Inc., 11 Beacon St., Suite 1400 Boston, MA 02108. Phone: (617)523-1670 Fax: (617)523-1021 E-mail: info@portersargent.com • Irregular. $35.00. Over 1,300 summer camping, recreational, pioneering, and academic programs in the United States and Canada, as well as travel programs worldwide.

Guide to the Federal Budget 1998. Stanley E. Collender. Rowman and Littlefield Publishers, Inc., 4720 Boston Way Lanham, MD 20706. Phone: 800-462-6420 or (301)459-3366 Fax: (301)459-2118 E-mail: rogers@univpress.com • URL: http://www.rowmanlittlefield.com • 1997. $56.00. A practical explanation of the federal budget for the most recent fiscal year.

Guide to the Nursing Home Industry. Dorland Healthcare Information, 1500 Walnut St., Suite 1000 Philadelphia, PA 19102. Phone: 800-784-2332 or (215)875-1212 Fax: (215)735-3966 E-mail: info@dorlandhealth.com • URL: http://www.dorlandhealth.com • Annual. $249.00. Analyzes the detailed and operational performance of the U. S. nursing home industry on both national and state levels. Includes detailed statistics and 19 financial performance indicators (aggregate data). Annual CD-ROM version with key word searching is available at $335.00.

Guide to the Project Management Body of Knowledge. Project Management Institute Standards Committee. Project Management Institute, c/o PMI Headquarters Publishing Div., 40 Colonial Square Sylva, NC 28779. Phone: (828)586-3715 Fax: (828)586-4020 E-mail: booked@pmi.org • URL: http://www.pmi.org • 1996. $32.95. Presents the fundamental tenets of project management. Covers the management of integration, scope, time, cost, quality, human resources, communications, risk, and procurement. Includes an extensive glossary.

Guide to the Use of Libraries and Information Sources. Jean K. Gates. McGraw-Hill, 1221 Ave. of the Americas New York, NY 10020. Phone: 800-722-4726 or (212)904-2000 Fax: (212)904-2072 E-mail: customer.service@mcgraw-hill.com • URL: http://www.mcgraw-hill.com • 1994. $32.19. Seventh edition.

Guide to U. S. Government Publications. The Gale Group, 27500 Drake Rd. Farmington Hills, MI 48331-3535. Phone: 800-877-GALE or (248)699-GALE Fax: 800-414-5043 or (248)699-8069 E-mail: galeord@galegroup.com • URL: http://www.galegroup.com • Annual. $360.00. Catalogs "important series, periodicals, and reference tools" published annually by the federal government. Includes references to annual reports of various agencies.

Guidebook to Labor Relations. CCH, Inc., 4025 W. Peterson Ave. Chicago, IL 60646-6085. Phone: 800-248-3248 or (773)866-6000 Fax: 800-224-8299 or (773)866-3608 URL: http://www.cch.com • Annual. $12.00.

Guidebook to Managed Care and Practice Management Terminology. Norman Winegar and L. Michelle Hayter. Haworth Press, Inc., 10 Alice St. Binghamton, NY 13904-1580. Phone: 800-429-6784 or (607)722-5857 Fax: 800-895-0582 or (607)722-1424 E-mail: getinfo@haworthpressinc.com • URL: http://www.haworthpressinc.com • 1998. $39.95. Provides definitions of managed care "terminology, jargon, and concepts."

Guidebook to Pension Planning. CCH, Inc., 4025 W. Peterson Ave. Chicago, IL 60646-6085. Phone: 800-248-3248 or (773)583-8500 Fax: 800-224-8299 URL: http://www.cch.com • Annual.

Guidebook to the Freedom of Information and Privacy Acts. Justin D. Franklin and Robert F. Bouchard, editors. West Group, 610 Opperman Dr. Eagan, MN 55123. Phone: 800-328-4880 or (651)687-7000 Fax: 800-213-2323 or (651)687-5827 URL: http://www.westgroup.com • $120.00 per year. Two looseleaf volumes. Periodic supplementation. Includes procedures for requesting and acquiring business and government data. (Civil Rights Series).

Guidelines for Consumer Protection in the Context of Electronic Commerce. Organization for Economic Cooperation and Development, OECD Washington Center, 2001 L St., N. W., Suite 650 Washington, DC 20036-4922. Phone: 800-456-6323 or (202)785-6323 Fax: (202)785-0350 E-mail: washington.contact@oecd.org • URL: http://www.oecd.org • 2000. $20.00. Provides a guide to effective consumer protection in online business-to-consumer transactions.

Guild of Book Workers.

Guild of Book Workers-Membership List. Guild of Book Workers, 521 Fifth Ave. New York, NY 10175. Phone: (212)292-4444 Annual. $40.00. About 800 amateur and professional workers in the handbook crafts of bookbinding, calligraphy, illuminating, and decorative papermaking.

Guild of Prescription Opticians of America-Guild Reference Directory. Guild of Prescription Opticians of America. Opticians Association of America, 10341 Democracy Lane Fairfax, VA 22030. Phone: 800-443-8997 or (703)691-8355 Fax: (703)691-3929 E-mail: oaa@opticians.org • Annual. $60.00. Lists 250 member firms with a total of 350 retail locations. Formerly *Guild of Prescription Opticians of America-Reference List of Guild Opticians*.

Guns and Ammo. EMAP USA, 6420 Wilshire Blvd. Los Angeles, CA 90048-5515. Phone: 800-800-6848 or (323)782-2000 Fax: (323)782-2467 URL: http://www.emapusa.com • Monthly. $17.94 per year.

Guns Illustrated. DBI Books, Inc., 700 E. State St. Iola, WI 53990. Phone: 800-258-0929 or (715)445-2214 Fax: (715)445-4087 URL: http://www.krause.com • Annual. $20.95. Lists of national and international associations, manufacturers, importers, and distributors of firearms, shooting equipment and services.

Guns Magazine: Finest in the Firearms Field. Publishers Development Corp., 591 Camino de la Reina, Suite 200 San Diego, CA 92108. Phone: 888-732-2299 or (619)297-5350 Fax: (619)297-5353 E-mail: 74673.3624@compuserve.com • Monthly. $19.95 per year. Annual *Supplement* available. Formerly *Guns*.

Guthrie Center for Real Estate Research.

H & R Block Income Tax Guide. Simon & Schuster Trade, 1230 Ave. of the Americas New York, NY 10020. Phone: 800-223-2336 or (212)698-7000 Fax: 800-943-9831 or (212)698-7007 E-mail: ssonline_feedback@simonsays.com • URL: http://www.simonsays.com • 1997. $15.00.

Hack and Band Saw Manufacturers Association of America.

Hair International/Associated Masters Barbers and Beauticians of America.

Hairdressers' Journal International. Reed Business Information, The Quadrant House, The Quadrant, Brighton Rd. Sutton SM2 5AS Surrey, England. Phone: 44 1816 523500 Fax: 44 1816 528975 E-mail: rbp.subscriptions@rbi.co.uk • URL: http://www.reedbusiness.com • Weekly. $112.00 per year.

Halting the Hacker: A Guide to Computer Security. Donald A. Pipkin. Prentice Hall, 240 Frisch Court Paramus, NJ 07652-5240. Phone: 800-947-7700 or (201)909-6200 Fax: 800-445-6991 or (201)909-6361 URL: http://www.prenhall.com • 1996. $44.95.

Handbook for Business Writing. L. Sue Baugh. NTC/Contemporary Publishing, P.O. Box 545 Blacklick, OH 43004. Phone: 800-338-3987 or (614)755-4151 Fax: (614)755-5645 E-mail: ntcpub@mcgraw-hill.com • URL: http://www.ntc-cb.com • 1993. $24.95. Second edition. Covers reports, letters, memos, and proposals. (Handbook for. Series).

Handbook for Focus Group Research. Thomas L. Greenbaum. Sage Publications, Inc., 2455 Teller Rd. Thousand Oaks, CA 91320. Phone: (805)499-0721 Fax: (805)499-0871 E-mail: info@sagepub.com • URL: http://www.sagepub • 1997. $49.95. Second edition. Includes glossary and index.

Handbook for Memo Writing. L. Sue Baugh. NTC/Contemporary Publishing, P.O. Box 545 Blacklick, OH 43004. Phone: 800-338-3987 or (614)755-4151 Fax: (614)755-5645 E-mail: ntcpub@mcgraw-hill.com • URL: http://www.ntc-cb.com • 1995. $32.95. (NTC Business Book Series).

Handbook for Muni Bond Issuers. Joe Mysak. Bloomberg Press, 100 Business Park Dr. Princeton, NJ 08542-0888. Phone: 800-388-2749 or (609)279-4670 Fax: (609)279-7155 E-mail: press@bloomberg.com • URL: http://www.bloomberg.com • 1998. $40.00. Written primarily for the officers and attorneys of municipalities. Provides a practical explanation of the municipal bond market. (Bloomberg Professional Library.)

Handbook for No-Load Fund Investors. Sheldon Jacobs. McGraw-Hill Professional, 1221 Ave. of the Americas New York, NY 10020. Phone: 800-722-4726 or (212)904-2000 Fax: (212)904-2072 E-mail: customer.service@mcgraw-hill.com • URL: http://www.mcgraw-hill.com • 1996. $40.00. 16th edition. Includes data on individual funds.

Handbook for Practical Letter Writing. L. Sue Baugh. NTC/Contemporary Publishing, P.O. Box 545 Blacklick, OH 43004. Phone: 800-338-3987 or (614)755-4151 Fax: (614)755-5645 E-mail: ntcpub@mcgraw-hill.com • URL: http://www.ntc-cb.com • 1993. $29.95.

Handbook for Proofreading. Laura K. Anderson. NTC/Contemporary Publishing, P.O. Box 545 Blacklick, OH 43004. Phone: 800-388-2749 or (609)279-4670 Fax: (614)755-5645 E-mail: ntcpub@mcgraw-hill.com • 1993. $24.95. (NTC Business Book Series).

Handbook for Public Relations Writing. Thomas Bivins. NTC/Contemporary Publishing, P.O. Box 545 Blacklick, OH 43004. Phone: 800-338-3987 or (614)755-4151 Fax: (614)755-5645 E-mail: ntcpub@mcgraw-hill.com • URL: http://www.ntc-cb.com • 1999. $24.95. Third edition. (NTC Business Book Series).

Handbook for Sound Engineers: The New Audio Cyclopedia. Glen M. Ballou, editor. Butterworth-Heineman, 225 Wildwood Ave. Woburn, MA 01801. Phone: 800-366-2665 or (781)904-2500 Fax: 800-446-6520 E-mail: orders@bhusa.com • URL: http://www.bh.com • 1991. $120.00. Second edition. Covers fundamentals of sound, sound-system design, loudspeaker building, sound recording, audio circuits, and computer-generated music.

Handbook for Theatrical Production Managers. Robert S. Telford. Samuel French, Inc., 45 W. 25th St. New York, NY 10010-2751. Phone: (212)206-8990 Fax: (212)206-1429 E-mail: samuelfrench@earthlink.net • URL: http://www.samuelfrench.com • 1983. $8.95.

Handbook of Accounting and Auditing. John C. Burton and others. Warren, Gorham, and Lamont/RIA Group, 395 Hudson St. New York, NY 10014. Phone: 800-950-1215 or (212)367-6300 Fax: (212)367-6718 E-mail: customer_service@riag.com • URL: http://www.riahome.com • Looseleaf service. $160.00. Updated annually.

Handbook of Adhesives. Irving Skeist. Chapman and Hall, 115 Fifth Ave., 4th Fl. New York, NY 10003-1004. Phone: 800-842-3636 or (212)260-1354 Fax: (212)260-1730 E-mail: info@chapall.com • URL: http://www.chapall.com • 1989. $105.00. Third edition.

Handbook of Airline Statistics. National Aeronautics and Space Administration, 600 Independence Ave., S.W. Washington, DC 20546. Phone: (202)358-0000 Biennial.

Handbook of Alternative Investment Strategies. Thomas Schneeweis and Joseph F. Pescatore, editors. Institutional Investor, 488 Madison Ave. New York, NY 10022. Phone: (212)224-3300 Fax: (212)224-3527 E-mail: info@iijournals.com • URL: http://www.iijournals.com • 1999. $95.00. Covers various forms of alternative investment, including hedge funds, managed futures, derivatives, venture capital, and natural resource financing.

Handbook of Artificial Intelligence. Avron Barr and others. Addison-Wesley Longman, Inc., One Jacob Way Reading, MA 01867. Phone: 800-447-2226 or (617)944-3700 Fax: (617)944-9351 URL: http://www.awl.com • 1989. $27.95.

Handbook of Bank Accounting: Understanding and Applying Standards and Regulations. Charles J. Woelfel. McGraw-Hill Professional, 1221 Ave. of the Americas New York, NY 10020. Phone: 800-722-4726 or (212)904-2000 Fax: (212)904-2072 E-mail: customer.service@mcgraw-hill.com • URL: http://www.mcgraw-hill.com • 1992. $65.00. "Written to meet the practical needs of senior- and middle-level bank accountants." Covers managerial accounting, the theory and practice of bank accounting, financial statement analysis, bank examinations, audits, and related topics.

Handbook of Batteries. David Linden. McGraw-Hill, 1221 Ave. of the Americas New York, NY 10020-1095. Phone: 800-722-4726 or (212)904-2000 Fax: (212)904-2072 E-mail: customer.service@mcgraw-hill.com • URL: http://mcgraw-hill.com • 1995. $125.00. Second edition.

Handbook of Budgeting. Robert Rachlin and H. W. Sweeny. John Wiley and Sons, Inc., 605 Third Ave. New York, NY 10158-0012. Phone: 800-225-5945 or (212)850-6000 Fax: (212)850-6088 E-mail: info@wiley.com • URL: http://www.wiley.com • 1998. $160.00. Fourth edition. 2000 Supplement, $60.00.

Handbook of Business Valuation. Thomas L. West and Jeffrey D. Jones. John Wiley and Sons, Inc., 605 Third Ave. New York, NY 10158-0012. Phone: 800-225-5945 or (212)850-6000 Fax: (212)850-6088 E-mail: info@wiley.com • URL: http://www.wiley.com • 1999. $125.00. Second edition. A collection of articles, worksheets, and appraisal techniques.

Handbook of Chemical Engineering Calculations. Nicholas P. Chopey and Tyler G. Hicks, editors. McGraw-Hill, 1221 Ave. of the Americas New York, NY 10020-1095. Phone: 800-722-4726 or (212)904-2000 Fax: (212)904-2072 E-mail: customer.service@mcgraw-hill.com • URL: http://www.mcgraw-hill.com • 1992. $89.95. Second edition.

Handbook of Cost Accounting. Sidney Davidson and Roman L. Weil. Simon and Schuster Trade, 1230 Ave. of the Americas New York, NY 10020. Phone: 800-223-2336 or (212)698-7000 Fax: 800-943-9831 or (212)698-7007 E-mail: ssonline_feedback@simonsays.com • URL: http://www.simonsays.com • 1999. $79.95.

Handbook of Cost Accounting Theory and Techniques. Ahmed Righi-Belkaoui. Greenwood Publishing Group, Inc., 88 Post Rd., W. Westport, CT 06881-5007. Phone: 800-225-5800 or (203)226-3571 Fax: (203)222-2540 E-mail: bookinfo@greenwood.com • URL: http://www.greenwood.com • 1991. $89.50.

Handbook of Derivative Instruments: Investment Research, Analysis, and Portfolio Applications. Atsuo Konishi and Ravi E. Dattatreya, editors. McGraw-Hill Professional, 1221 Ave. of the Americas New York, NY 10020. Phone: 800-722-4726 or (212)904-2000 Fax: (212)904-2072 E-mail: customer.service@mcgraw-hill.com • URL: http://www.mcgraw-hill.com • 1996. $80.00. Second revised edition. Contains 41 chapters by various authors on all aspects of derivative securities, including such esoterica as "Inverse Floaters," "Positive Convexity," "Exotic Options," and "How to Use the Holes in Black-Scholes."

Handbook of Drug and Alcohol Abuse. F. Hofman and others. Oxford University Press, Inc., 198 Madison Ave. New York, NY 10016-4314. Phone: 800-451-7556 or (212)726-6000 Fax: (212)746-6446 E-mail: custserv@oup-usa.org • URL: http://www.oup-usa.org • 1992. $27.95. Third edition.

Handbook of Educational Technology: Practical Guide for Teachers. Fred Percival and others. Nichols Publishing Co., P.O. Box 6036 East Brunswick, NJ 08816-6036. Phone: (732)297-2862 Fax: (732)940-0549 1993. $39.95. Third edition.

Handbook of Employee Benefits: Design, Funding, and Administration. Jerry S. Rosenbloom, editor. McGraw-Hill Higher Education, 1221 Ave. of the Americas New York, NY 10020. Phone: 800-722-4726 or (212)904-2000 Fax: (212)904-2072 E-mail: customer.service@mcgraw-hill.com • URL: http://www.mcgraw-hill.com • 2001. $95.00. Fourth edition.

Handbook of Environmental Health and Safety: Principles and Practices. Herman Koren and Michael S. Bisesi. Lewis Publishers, 2000 Corporate Blvd., N.W. Boca Raton, FL 33431. Phone: 800-272-7737 or (561)994-0555 Fax: 800-374-3401 or (561)998-9114 1995. $199.90 Third edition. Two volumes. Volume one, $99.95; volume two, $99.95.

Handbook of Equipment Leasing: A Deal Maker's Guide. Richard M. Contino. AMACOM, 1601 Broadway, 12th Fl. New York, NY 10019. Phone: 800-262-9699 or (212)586-8100 Fax: (212)903-8168 E-mail: custmserv@amanet.org • URL: http://www.amanet.org • 1996. $65.00. Second edition.

Handbook of Equity Derivatives. Jack C. Francis and others, editors. John Wiley and Sons, Inc., 605 Third Ave. New York, NY 10158-0012. Phone: 800-225-5945 or (212)850-6000 Fax: (212)850-6088 E-mail: info@wiley.com • URL: http://www.wiley.com • 1999. $95.00. Contains 27 chapters by various authors. Covers options (puts and calls), stock index futures, warrants, convertibles, over-the-counter options, swaps, legal issues, taxation, etc. (Financial Engineering Series).

Handbook of Executive Benefits. Towers Perrin. McGraw-Hill Higher Education, 1221 Ave. of the Americas New York, NY 10020-1095. Phone: 800-722-4726 or (212)904-2000 Fax: (212)904-2072 E-mail: customer.service@mcgraw-hill.com • URL: http://www.mcgraw-hill.com • 1995. $75.00.

Handbook of Family Law. Stuart J. Faber. Lega Books, 3699 Wilshire Blvd., Suite 700 Los Angeles, CA 90010-2726. Phone: (213)382-3335 1987. $56.50. Fifth revised edition. Two volumes.

Handbook of Fiber Optics: Theory and Applications. Chai Yeh. Academic Press, Inc., 525 B St., Suite 1900 San Diego, CA 92101-4495. Phone: 800-321-5068 or (619)230-1840 Fax: (619)699-6715 E-mail: ap@acad.com • URL: http://www.academicpress.com • 1990. $116.00.

Handbook of Fixed Income Securities. Frank J. Fabozzi. McGraw-Hill Higher Education, 1221 Ave. of the Americas New York, NY 10020-1095. Phone: 800-722-4726 or (212)904-2000 Fax: (212)904-2072 E-mail: customer.service@mcgraw-hill.com • URL: http://www.mcgraw-hill.com • 2000. $99.95. Sixth edition. Topics include risk measurement, valuation techniques, and portfolio strategy.

Handbook of 401(k) Plan Management. Towers, Perrin, Foster and Crosby Staff. McGraw-Hill Higher Education, 1221 Ave. of the Americas New York, NY 10020-1095. Phone: 800-772-4726 or (212)904-2000 Fax: (212)904-2072 E-mail: customer.service@mcgraw-hill.com • URL: http://www.mcgraw-hill.com • 1992. $70.00. Written for employers and pension plan administrators. In addition to legal details of 401(k) plans, employee stock ownership plans (ESOPs) and basic principles of asset investment are covered. Appendix contains "Sample 401(k) Savings Plan Document."

Handbook of Gem Identification. Richard T. Liddicoat, Jr. Gemological Institute of America, 5355 Armada Dr. Carlsbad, CA 92008. Phone: 800-421-8161 or (760)603-4200 Fax: (760)603-4266 URL: http://www.gia.edu • 1987. $47.50. 12th edition.

The Handbook of Glass Manufacture. Fay V. Tooley, editor. Ashlee Publishing Co., Inc., 18 E. 41st St. New York, NY 10017-6222. Phone: (212)376-7722 Fax: (212)376-7723 E-mail: ashleepub@aol.com • URL: http://www.ashlee.com • 1985. 195.00. Revised edition. Two volumes.

Handbook of Human Factors and Ergonomics. Gavriel Salvendy. John Wiley and Sons, Inc., 605 Third Ave. New York, NY 10158-0012. Phone: 800-225-5945 Fax: (212)850-6088 E-mail: info@wiley.com • URL: http://www.wiley.com • 1997. $225.00. Second edition.

Handbook of Hydraulics. Ernest F. Brater and Horace Williams King. McGraw-Hill, 1221 Ave. of the Americas New York, NY 10020. Phone: 800-722-4726 or (212)904-2000 Fax: (212)904-2072 E-mail: customer.service@mcgraw-hill.com • URL: http://www.mcgraw-hill.com • 1996. $79.95. Seventh edition.

Handbook of Industrial Engineering. Gavriel Salvendy, editor. John Wiley and Sons, Inc., 605 Third Ave. New York, NY 10158-0012. Phone: 800-225-5945 or (212)850-6000 Fax: (212)850-6088 E-mail: info@wiley.com • URL: http://www.wiley.com • 2000. $175.00. Third edition.

Handbook of Industrial Toxicology. E. R. Plunkett, editor. Chemical Publishing Co., Inc., 192 Lexington Ave. New York, NY 10016. Phone: 800-786-3659 or (212)779-0090 Fax: (212)889-1537 E-mail: chempub@aol.com • URL: http://www.chemicalpublishing.com • 1987. $100.00.

Handbook of International Economic Statistics. Available from National Technical Information Service, U. S. Department of Commerce, 5285 Port Royal Rd. Springfield, VA 22161. Phone: 800-553-6847 or (703)487-4600 Fax: (703)321-8547 E-mail: info@ntis.fedworld.gov • URL: http://www.ntis.gov • Annual. $40.00. Prepared by U. S. Central Intelligence Agency. Provides basic statistics for comparing worldwide economic performance, with an emphasis on Europe, including Eastern Europe.

Handbook of International Management. Ingo Walter. John Wiley and Sons, Inc., 605 Third Ave. New York, NY 10158-0012. Phone: 800-526-5368 or (212)850-6000 Fax: (212)850-6088 E-mail: info@wiley.com • URL: http://www.wiley.com • 1988. $180.00.

Handbook of International Trade and Development Statistics. United Nations Publications, United Nations Concourse Level New York, NY 10017. Phone: 800-553-3210 or (212)963-7680 Fax: (212)963-4910 E-mail: bookstore@un.org • URL: http://www.un.org/publications • Annual. $80.00. Text in English and French.

Handbook of Internet Stocks. Mergent, 60 Madison Ave., 6th Fl. New York, NY 10010. Phone: 800-342-5647 or (212)413-7601 Fax: (212)413-7777 E-mail: fis@fisonline.com • URL: http://www.fisonline.com • Annual. $19.95. Contains detailed financial information on more than 200 Internet-related corporations, including e-commerce firms and telecommunications hardware manufacturers. Lists and rankings are provided.

Handbook of Lasers. Marvin J. Weber. CRC Press, Inc., 2000 Corporate Blvd., N. W. Boca Raton, FL 33431. Phone: 800-272-7737 or (561)994-0555 Fax: (561)241-7856 E-mail: order@crcpress.com • URL: http://www.crcpress.com • 1995. $89.95.

Handbook of Machine Vision Engineering. Michael Burke. John Wiley and Sons, Inc., 605 Third Ave., 4th Fl. New York, NY 10158-0012. Phone: 800-225-5945 or (212)850-6000 Fax: (212)850-6088 E-mail: info@wiley.com • URL: http://www.wiley.com/compbooks/ • $159.90. Two volumes. Volume two, $79.95; volume three, $79.95.

Handbook of Management Games and Simulations. Chris Elgood, editor. Ashgate Publishing Co., Old Post Rd. Brookfield, VT 05036. Phone: 800-535-9544 or (802)276-3162 Fax: (802)276-3837 E-mail: info@ashgate.com • URL: http://www.ashgate.com • 1997. $96.95. Sixth edition. Published by Gower in England.

Handbook of Mathematical Economics, 1981-91. Elsevier Science, 655 Ave. of the Americas New York, NY 10010. Phone: 888-437-4636 or (212)989-5800 Fax: (212)633-3680 E-mail: usinfo@elsevier.com • URL: http://www.elsevier.com • 1981. $440.00. Four volumes.

Handbook of Mortgage-Backed Securities. Frank J. Fabozzi, editor. McGraw-Hill Professional, 1221 Ave. of the Americas New York, NY 10020. Phone: 800-722-4726 or (212)904-2000 Fax: (212)904-2072 E-mail: customer.service@mcgraw-hill.com • URL: http://www.mcgraw-hill.com • 1995. $85.00. Fourth edition.

Handbook of Nonprescription Drugs. Tom R. Covington and others, editors. American Pharmaceutical Association, 2215 Constitution Ave., N. W. Washington, DC 20037. Phone: 800-878-0729 or (202)429-7517 Fax: (202)783-2351 E-mail: lly@mail.aphanet.org • URL: http://www.aphanet.org • 2000. $120.00. 12th edition. Contains comprehensive, technical information on over-the-counter drugs.

Handbook of North American Industry: NAFTA and the Economies of its Member Nations. John E. Cremeans, editor. Bernan Press, 4611-F Assembly Dr. Lanham, MD 20706-4391. Phone: 800-274-4447 or (301)459-7666 Fax: 800-865-3450 or (301)459-0056 E-mail: info@bernan.com • URL: http://www.bernan.com • 1999. $89.00. Second edition. Provides detailed industry statistics for the U.S., Canada, and Mexico.

Handbook of Occupational Safety and Health. Louis J. Diberardinis. John Wiley and Sons, Inc, 605 Third Ave. New York, NY 10158-0012. Phone: 800-225-5945 or (212)850-6000 Fax: (212)850-6021 E-mail: info@wiley.com • URL: http://www.wiley.com • 1998. $149.00. Second edition.

Handbook of Organization Studies. Stewart R. Clegg and others, editors. Sage Publications, Inc., 2455 Teller Rd. Thousand Oaks, CA 91320. Phone: (805)499-0721 Fax: (805)499-0871 E-mail: info@sagepub.com • URL: http://www.sagepub.com • 1996. $95.00. Consists of 29 chapters by various authors. Covers "theory, research, and practice in organization studies," including such topics as organizational economics, leadership, decision making, communication, and innovation.

Handbook of Over-the-Counter Drugs. Max Leber and others. Celestial Arts Publishing Co., 999 Harrison St. Berkeley, CA 94710. Phone: 800-841-2665 or (510)559-1600 Fax: (510)559-1637 E-mail: order@tenspeed.com • URL: http://www.tenspeed.com • 1992. $22.95. Provides detailed, consumer information on the ingredients of nonprescription drugs and popular cosmetics.

Handbook of Pest Management in Agriculture. David Pimentel, editor. CRC Press, Inc., 2000 Corporate Blvd., N. W. Boca Raton, FL 33431. Phone: 800-272-7737 or (561)994-0555 E-mail: order@crcprss.com • URL: http://www.crcpress.com • 1990. $975.00. Second edition. Three volumes.

Handbook of Petrochemicals and Processes. G. Margaret Wells. Ashgate Publishing Co., Old Post Rd. Brookfield, VT 05036. Phone: 800-535-9544 or (802)276-3162 Fax: (802)276-3837 E-mail: info@ashgate.com • URL: http://www.ashgate.com • 1991. $122.95. Published by Gower in England.

Handbook of Pressure Sensitive Adhesive Technology. Donatas Satas. Satas and Associates, 99 Shenandoah Rd. Warwickk,

RI 02886. Phone: (410)884-0572 Fax: (410)884-7620 1999. $150.00. Third revised edition.

Handbook of Private Schools: An Annual Descriptive Survey of Independent Education. Porter Sargent Publishers, Inc., 11 Beacon St., Suite 1400 Boston, MA 02108. Phone: (617)523-1670 Fax: (617)523-1021 E-mail: info@portersargent.com • Irregular. $93.00. Lists more than 1,600 elementary and secondary boarding and day schools in the United States.

Handbook of Public Relations. Robert L. Heath, editor. Sage Publications, Inc., 2455 Teller Rd. Thousand Oaks, CA 91320. Phone: (805)499-0721 Fax: (805)499-0871 E-mail: info@sagepub.com • URL: http://www.sagepub.com • 2000. $89.95. Covers best practices, academic research, and theory. Contains articles by various advertising specialists.

Handbook of Recording Engineering. John M. Eargle. Chapman and Hall, 115 Fifth Ave., 4th Fl. New York, NY 10003-1004. Phone: 800-842-3636 or (212)260-1354 Fax: (121)260-1730 E-mail: info@chapall.com • URL: http://www.chapall.com • 1996. $75.00. Third edition.

Handbook of Safety and Health Engineering. Roger L. Bauer and Jeffrey W. Vincoli. Lewis Publishers, 2000 Corporate Blvd., N. W. Boca Raton, FL 33431. Phone: 800-272-7737 or (561)994-0555 Fax: 800-374-3401 or (561)998-9114 1999. $89.95.

Handbook of Services for the Handicapped. Alfred H. Katz and Knute Martin. Greenwood Publishing Group Inc., 88 Post Rd., W. Westport, CT 06881-5007. Phone: 800-225-5800 or (203)226-3571 Fax: (203)222-2540 E-mail: bookinfo@greenwood.com • URL: http://www.greenwood.com • 1982. $65.00.

Handbook of Strategic Planning. Bernard Taylor and Kevin Hawkins, editors. Books on Demand, 300 N. Zeeb Rd. Ann Arbor, MI 48106-1346. Phone: 800-521-0600 or (734)761-4700 Fax: (734)665-5022 E-mail: info@umi.com • URL: http://www.lib.umi.com • 1986. $148.20.

Handbook of the Nations: A Brief Guide to the Economy, Government, Land, Demographics, Communications, and National Defense Establishments of Each of 206 Nations and Other Political Entities. The Gale Group, 27500 Drake Rd. Farmington Hills, MI 48331-3535. Phone: 800-877-GALE or (248)699-GALE Fax: 800-414-5043 or (248)699-8069 E-mail: galeord@galegroup.com • URL: http://www.galegroup.com • 2000. $155.00. 20th edition. Includes maps and tables.

Handbook of Toxic and Hazardous Chemicals and Carcinogens. Marshall Sittig. Noyes Data Corp., 169 Kinderkomack Rd., Ste. 5 Park Ridge, NJ 07676-1338. Phone: (201)505-4965 1992. $249.00. Third edition. Two volumes.

Handbook of Training Evaluation and Measurement Methods. Jack J. Phillips. Gulf Publishing Co., P.O. Box 2608 Houston, TX 77252-2608. Phone: 800-231-6275 or (713)520-4401 Fax: (713)520-4433 E-mail: ezorder@gulfpub.com • URL: http://www.gpcbooks.com • 1997. $55.00. Third edition. (Improving Human Performance Series).

Handbook of Transportation and Marketing in Agriculture. Essex E. Finney, editor. Franklin Book Co., Inc., 7804 Montgomery Ave. Elkins Park, PA 19027. Phone: (215)635-5252 Fax: (215)635-6155 E-mail: service@franklinbook.com • URL: http://www.franklinbook.com • 1981. Vol. 1, $252.00; vol. 2, $282.00. (CRC Agriculture Series).

Handbook of U. S. Labor Statistics: Employment, Earnings, Prices, Productivity, and Other Labor Data. Eva E. Jacobs, editor. Bernan Associates, 4611-F Assembly Drive Lanham, MD 20706-4391. Phone: 800-274-4447 or (301)459-7666 Fax: 800-865-3450 or (301)459-0056 E-mail: info@bernan.com • URL: http://www.bernan.com • 1999. $74.00. Based on *Handbook of Labor Statistics*, formerly issued by the Bureau of Labor Statistics, U. S. Department of Labor. Includes the Bureau's projections of employment in the U. S. by industry and occupation. Provides a wide variety of data on the work force, prices, fringe benefits, and consumer expenditures.

Handbook of World Stock and Commodity Exchanges. Blackwell Publishers, 350 Main St., 6th Fl. Malden, MA 02148-5018. Phone: 800-216-2522 or (781)388-8200 Fax: (781)388-8232 E-mail: books@blackwellpub.com • URL: http://www.blackwellpub.com • Annual. $265.00. Provides detailed information on over 200 stock and commodity exchanges in more than 50 countries.

Handicapped Requirements Handbook. Thompson Publishing Group, 1725 K St., N.W., Suite 200 Washington, DC 20006. Phone: 800-999-2520 or (202)872-4000 Fax: (202)296-1091 $196.00. Looseleaf service. Monthly updates. $35.00 per chapter.

Hands-On Intranets. Vasanthan S. Dasan and others. Prentice Hall, 240 Frisch Court Paramus, NJ 07652-5240. Phone: 800-947-7700 or (201)909-6452 Fax: 800-445-6991 or (201)909-6361 URL: http://www.prenhall.com • 1997. $39.95. A realistic guide to setting up and administering an intranet.

Handweavers Guild of America.

Handwriting Analysts, International.

Hard Drive: Bill Gates and the Making of the Microsoft Empire. James Wallace and Jim Erickson. John Wiley and Sons, Inc., 605 Third Ave. New York, NY 10158-0012. Phone: 800-225-5945 or (212)850-6000 Fax: (212)850-6088 E-mail: info@wiley.com • URL: http://www.wiley.com • 1992. $22.95. A biography of William H. Gates, chief executive of the Microsoft Corporation.

Hard Fibres Association.

Hard Sciences. Cambridge Scientific Abstracts, 7200 Wisconsin Ave., Suite 601 Bethesda, MD 20814. Phone: 800-843-7751 or (301)961-6700 Fax: (301)961-6720 Provides the online version of *Computer and Information Systems Abstracts, Electronics and Communications Abstracts, Health and Safety Science Abstracts, ISMEC: Mechanical Engineering Abstracts (Information Service in Mechanical Engineering)* and *Solid State and Superconductivity Abstracts*. Time period is 1981 to date, with monthly updates. Inquire as to online cost and availability.

Hardware Age. Cahners Business Information, 1018 W. 9th Ave. King of Prussia, PA 19406. Phone: 800-695-1214 or (610)205-1000 Fax: (610)964-4284 E-mail: corporatecommunications@cahners.com • URL: http://www.cahners.com • Monthly. $75.00 per year.

Hardwood Distributors Association.

Hardwood Floors. National Wood Flooring Association. Athletic Business Publications, Inc., 4130 Lien Rd. Madison, WI 53704-3602. Phone: 800-722-8764 or (608)249-0186 Fax: (608)249-1153 E-mail: editors@hardwoodfloorsmag.com • Bimonthly. $36.00 per year. Covers the marketing and installation of hardwood flooring. Published for contractors and retailers.

Hardwood Manufacturers Association., 400 Penn Center Blvd., Suite 530 Pittsburgh, PA 15235. Phone: (412)829-0770 Fax: (412)829-0844 Members are manufacturers of hardwood lumber and hardwood products.

Hardwood Manufacturers Association: Membership Directory. Hardwood Manufacturers Association, 400 Penn Center Blvd., Suite 530 Pittsburgh, PA 15235. Phone: 800-373-9663 or (412)829-0770 Fax: (412)829-0844 Annual. Lists over 100 companies.

Hardwood Plywood and Veneer Association.

Harley Hahn's Internet and Web Yellow Pages. Harley Hahn. Osborne/McGraw-Hill, 2600 10th St. Berkeley, CA 94710. Phone: 800-227-0900 or (510)549-6600 Fax: (510)549-6603 E-mail: customer.service@mcgraw-hill.com • URL: http://www.osborne.com • Annual. $34.95. Lists World Wide Web sites in more than 100 categories.

Harmonized Tariff Schedule of the United States, Annotated, Basic Manual. Available from U.S. Government Printing Office, Washington, DC 20402. Phone: (202)512-1800 Fax: (202)512-2250 E-mail: gpoaccess@gpo.gov • URL: http://www.accessgpo.gov • $67.00, including basic volumes and supplementary service for an indefinite period.

Harper's Bazaar. Hearst Corp., 1700 Broadway New York, NY 10019. Phone: 800-888-3045 or (212)903-5464 Fax: (212)262-7101 E-mail: bazaar@hearst.com • URL: http://www.hearstcorp.com • Monthly. $10.00 per year.

Harris Manufacturers Directory: National Edition. Available from The Gale Group, 27500 Drake Rd. Farmington Hills, MI 48331-3535. Phone: 800-877-GALE or (248)699-GALE Fax: 800-414-5043 or (248)699-8069 E-mail: galeord@galegroup.com • URL: http://www.galegroup.com • 1998. $520.00. Two volumes. Published by Harris InfoSource (http://www.harrisinfo.com). Provides statistical and descriptive information for about 46,000 U.S. industrial firms having 100 or more employees.

Harvard Business Review. Harvard University, Graduate School of Business Administration. Harvard Businss School Publishing, 60 Harvard Way Boston, MA 02163. Phone: 800-545-7685 or (617)783-7440 E-mail: custserv@ccbspub.harvard.edu • URL: http://www.hbsp.harvard.edu • Bimonthly. $95.00 per year.

Harvard Law Review. Harvard Law Review Association, Gannett House Cambridge, MA 02138. Phone: (617)495-4650 Fax: (617)495-2748 URL: http://www.gannett-netserv.law.harvard.edu • Eight times a year. $45.00 per year.

Harvard Legislative Research Bureau., Harvard Law School, 1541 Massachusetts Ave. Cambridge, MA 02138. Phone: (617)495-4400 Fax: (617)495-1110 Concerned with federal and state legislation in all fields.

Harvard Management Communication Letter. Harvard Business School Press, 60 Harvard Way Boston, MA 02163. Phone: 888-500-1016 or (617)783-7440 E-mail: custserv@hbsp.harvard.edu • URL: http://www.hbsp.harvard.edu • Monthly. $79.00 per year. Newsletter. Provides practical advice on both electronic and conventional business communication: e-mail, telephone, cell phones, memos, letters, written reports, speeches, meetings, and visual presentations (slides, flipcharts, easels, etc.). Also covers face-to-face communication, discussion, listening, and negotiation.

Harvard Negotiation Project. Harvard University, Harvard Law School, Pound Hall Room 500 Cambridge, MA 02138. Phone: (617)495-1684 Fax: (617)495-7818 E-mail: info@pon.law.harvard.edu • Seeks to improve the theory and practice of negotiation.

Hat Life Directory: Directory of Men's Hat, Ladie's Hat and Cap Industry., 66 York St. Jersey City, NJ 07302. Phone: (201)434-8322 Fax: (201)434-8277 E-mail: cfuller@dmcreative.com • Annual. $22.00. About 1,000 hat manufacturers, wholesalers, renovators, and importer's of men's headwear, plus trade suppliers. Formerly *Hat Life Yearbook and Directory*.

Hawaii Institute of Tropical Agriculture and Human Resources., University of Hawaii at Manoa Honolulu, HI 96822. Phone: (808)956-8131 Fax: (808)956-9105 E-mail: tadean2@avax.ctahr.hawaii.edu • URL: http://www.ctahr.hawaii.edu • Concerned with the production and marketing of tropical food and ornamental plant products, including pineapples, bananas, coffee, and macadamia nuts.

Hawaii Natural Energy Institute., University of Hawaii at Manoa, 2540 Dole St., Holmes Hall 246 Honolulu, HI 96822. Phone: (808)956-8890 Fax: (808)956-2336 E-mail: hnei@hawaii.edu • URL: http://www.soest.hawaii.edu • Research areas include geothermal, wind, solar, hydroelectric, and other energy sources.

Hazard Prevention. System Safety Society, Inc., 30363 Hicks Rd. Spotsylvania, VA 22553-5525. Phone: (703)444-6520 Quarterly. Free to members; non-members, $45.00 per year.

Hazardous and Toxic Materials: Safe Handling and Disposal. Howard H. Fawcett, editor. John Wiley and Sons, Inc., 605 Third Ave. New York, NY 10158-0012. Phone: 800-526-5368 or (212)850-6000 Fax: (212)850-6088 E-mail: info@wiley.com • URL: http://www.wiley.com • 1988. $139.00. Second edition.

Hazardous Materials Advisory Council., 1110 Vermont Ave., N.W., Suite 301 Washington, DC 20005. Phone: (202)289-4550 Fax: (202)289-4074 E-mail: hmacinfo@hmac.org • URL: http://www.hmac.org • Promotes safe transportation of materials.

Hazardous Materials Dictionary. Ronny J. Coleman. Technomic Publishing Co., Inc., 851 New Holland Ave. Lancaster, PA 17604. Phone: 800-233-9936 or (717)291-5609 Fax: (717)295-4538 E-mail: marketing@techpub.com • URL: http://www.techpub.com • 1994. $79.95. Second revised edition.

Hazardous Materials Newsletter. Hazardous Materials Publishing Co., P.O. Box 204 Barre, VT 05641. Phone: (802)479-2307 E-mail: haznews@aol.com • Bimonthly. $47.00 per year.

Hazardous Materials Transportation. Washington Business Information, Inc., 300 N. Washington St., Suite 200 Falls Church, VA 22246. Phone: (703)247-3434 Fax: (703)247-3421 Biweekly. $797.00 per year. Looseleaf service. Newsletter on the responsibilities of shippers and carriers for the safe transportation of hazardous materials.

Hazardous Substance Management Research Center.

Hazardous Substances Resource Guide. The Gale Group, 27500 Drake Rd. Farmington Hills, MI 48331-3535. Phone: 800-877-GALE or (248)699-GALE Fax: 800-414-5043 or (248)699-8069 E-mail: galeord@galegroup.com • URL: http://www.galegroup.com • 1997. $225.00. Second edition. Provides detailed information on each of about 1,500 hazardous materials, including trade name, health hazard, use, and storage. Information on organizations and a glossary are also included. Written for the lay user.

Hazardous Waste Business. McGraw-Hill, Energy and Business Newsletter, 1221 Ave. of the Americas New York, NY 10020. Phone: 800-722-4726 or (212)904-2000 Fax: (212)904-2072 E-mail: customer.service@mcgraw-hill.com • URL: http://www.mcgraw-hill.com • Biweekly. $695.00 per year. Newsletter on the control and cleanup of hazardous waste from a business viewpoint. Covers regulation, new technology, corporate activities, and industry trends.

Hazardous Waste Consultant. Elsevier Science, 655 Ave. of the Americas New York, NY 10010. Phone: 888-437-4636 or (212)989-5800 Fax: (212)633-3680 E-mail: usinfo@elsevier.com • URL: http://www.elsevier.com • Seven times a year. $798.00 per year. Discusses the technical, regulatory and legal aspects of the hazardous waste industry.

Hazardous Waste Consultant Directory of Commercial Hazardous Waste Management Facilities. Elsevier Science, 655 Ave. of the Americas New York, NY 10010. Phone: 888-437-4636 or (212)989-5800 Fax: (212)633-3680 E-mail: usinfo@elsevier.com • URL: http://www.elsevier.com • Annual. $115.00. List of 170 facilities that process, store, and dispose of hazardous waste materials.

Hazardous Waste Litigation Reporter: The National Journal of Record of Hazardous Waste-Related Litigation. Andrews Publications, 175 Stafford Ave., Bldg. 4, Suite 140 Wayne, PA 19087. Phone: 800-345-1101 or (610)622-0510 Fax: (610)622-0501 URL: http://www.andrewspub.com • Semimonthly. $875.00 per year. Reports on hazardous waste legal cases.

Hazardous Waste Management. McGraw-Hill, 1221 Ave. of the Americas New York, NY 10020. Phone: 800-722-4726 or (212)904-2000 Fax: (212)904-2072 E-mail: customer.service@mcgraw-hill.com • URL: http://www.mcgraw-hill.com • 2000. $85.63. Second edition.

Hazardous Waste Management in Small Businesses: Regulating and Assisting the Small Generator. Robert E. Deyle. Greenwood Publishing Group, Inc., 88 Post Rd., W. Westport, CT 06881-5007. Phone: 800-225-5800 or (203)226-3571 Fax: (203)222-2540 E-mail: bookinfo@greenwood.com • URL: http://www.greenwood.com • 1989. $59.95. Emphasis on legal aspects.

Hazardous Waste News. Business Publishers, Inc., 8737 Colesville Rd., Suite 1100 Silver Spring, MD 20910-3928. Phone: 800-274-6737 or (301)587-6300 Fax: (301)587-1081 E-mail: bpinews@bpinews.com • URL: http://www.bpinews.com • Weekly. $687.00 per year. Newsletter. Incorporates *Lab Waste* and *Hazards Management*. Includes *Nuclear Waste Bulletin*.

The HCEA: A Directory of Health Care Meetings and Conventions. Healthcare Convention and Healthcare Exhibitors Association, 5775 Peachtree-Dunwoody Rd., Suite 500G Atlanta, GA 30342. Phone: (404)252-3663 Fax: (404)252-0774 E-mail: hcea@assnhq.com • Semiannual. Free to members; non-members, $245.00 per year. Lists more than 2,400 health care meetings, most of which have an exhibit program. Formerly *Handbook-A Directory of Health Care Meetings and Conventions*.

Headwear Information Bureau.

Healing the Wounds: Overcoming the Trauma of Layoffs, and Revitalizing Downsized Organizations. David M. Noer. Jossey-Bass, Inc., Publishers, 350 Sansome St. San Francisco, CA 94104. Phone: 888-378-2537 or (415)433-1740 Fax: (415)433-0499 E-mail: webperson@jbp.com • URL: http://www.josseybass.com • 1993. $29.50. (Management Series).

Health Against Wealth: HMOs and the Breakdown of Medical Trust. George Anders. Houghton Mifflin Co., 215 Park Ave., S. New York, NY 10003. Phone: 800-225-3362 or (212)420-5800 Fax: (212)420-5855 URL: http://www.hmco.com • 1996. $15.00. The author, a *Wall Street Journal* reporter, presents the negative side of HMO cost cutting.

Health and Environment in America's Top-Rated Cities: A Statistical Profile. Grey House Publishing, Pocketknife Square Lakeville, CT 06039. Phone: 800-562-2139 or (860)435-0868 Fax: 800-248-0115 or (860)335-0867 E-mail: books@greyhouse.com • URL: http://www.greyhouse.com • Biennial. $195.00. Covers 75 U. S. cities. Includes statistical and other data on a wide variety of topics, such as air quality, water quality, recycling, hospitals, physicians, health care costs, death rates, infant mortality, accidents, and suicides.

The Health and Natural Product Store Market. Available from MarketResearch.com, 641 Ave. of the Americas, 3rd Fl. New York, NY 10011. Phone: 800-298-5699 or (212)807-2629 Fax: (212)807-2716 E-mail: order@marketresearch.com • URL: http://www.marketresearch.com • 1999. $2,750.00. Published by Packaged Facts. Contains market research data.

Health and Safety Science Abstracts. Institute of Safety and Systems Management. Cambridge Information Group, 7200 Wisconsin Ave., 6th Fl. Bethesda, MD 20814. Phone: 800-843-7751 or (301)961-6700 Fax: (301)961-6720 E-mail: market@csa.com • URL: http://www.csa.com • Quarterly. $775.00 per year. Formerly *Safety Science Abstracts Journal*.

Health Care Cost Containment. Karen Davis and others. Johns Hopkins University Press, 2715 N. Charles St. Baltimore, MD 21218. Phone: 800-548-1784 or (410)516-6900 Fax: (410)516-6998 1990. $48.00. (Studies in Health Care Finance and Administrations).

Health Care Costs. DRI/McGraw-Hill, 24 Hartwell Ave. Lexington, MA 02173. Phone: (617)863-5100 Fax: (617)860-6332 Quarterly. Price on application. Cost indexes for hospitals, nursing homes, and home healthcare agencies.

Health Care Economics. Paul J. Feldstein. Delmar Publications, P.O. Box 15015 Albany, NY 12212-5015. Phone: 800-998-7498 or (212)354-6500 Fax: (518)459-3552 E-mail: cheryl.kean@itped.com • URL: http://www.delmar.com • 1998. $80.95. Fifth edition.

Health Care Financing Review. Available from U. S. Government Printing Office, Washington, DC 20402. Phone: (202)512-1800 Fax: (202)512-2250 E-mail: gpoaccess@gpo.gov • URL: http://www.access.gpo.gov • Quarterly. $30.00 per year. Issued by the Health Care Financing Administration, U. S. Department of Health and Human Services. Presents articles by professionals in the areas of health care costs and financing.

Health Care Products and Remedies. Available from MarketResearch.com, 641 Ave. of the Americas, Third Floor New York, NY 10011. Phone: 800-298-5699 or (212)807-2629 Fax: (212)807-2716 E-mail: order@marketresearch.com • URL: http://www.marketresearch.com • 1997. $600.00 each. Consists of market reports published by Simmons Market Research Bureau on each of about 25 health care product categories. Examples are cold remedies, contraceptives, hearing aids, bandages, headache remedies, eyeglasses, contact lenses, and vitamins. Each report covers buying patterns and demographics.

Health Care Resource Management Society., P.O. Box 29253 Cincinnati, OH 45229-0253. Phone: (513)520-1058 or (513)872-6315 Fax: (513)872-6158 E-mail: hcrms@choice.net • URL: http://www.hcrms.com • Members are materials management (purchasing) personnel in hospitals and the healthcare industry. The Society is concerned with hospital costs, distribution, logistics, recycling, and inventory management.

Health Care Strategic Management: The Newsletter for Hospital Strategies. Business Word, Inc., 5350 S. Roslyn St., Suite 400 Englewood, CO 80111-2125. Phone: (303)290-8500 Fax: (303)290-9025 E-mail: sandyc@businessword.com • Monthly. $249.00 per year. Planning, marketing and resource allocation.

Health Care, Technology, and the Competitive Environment. Henry P. Brehm and Ross M. Mullner, editors. Greenwood Publishing Group, Inc., 88 Post Rd., W. Westport, CT 06881-5007. Phone: 800-225-5800 or (203)226-3571 Fax: (203)222-2540 E-mail: bookinfo@greenwood.com • URL: http://www.greenwood.com • 1989. $69.50.

The Health Connection.

Health Data Management. Faulkner & Gray, Inc., 11 Penn Plaza, 17th Fl. New York, NY 10001. Phone: 800-535-8403 or (212)967-7000 Fax: (212)564-7155 E-mail: orders@asfaulknergray.com • URL: http://www.faulkner.gray.com • Monthly. $98.00 per year. Covers the management and automation of clinical data and health care insurance claims. Includes information on claims processors and third-party administrators.

Health Devices Alerts: A Summary of Reported Problems, Hazards, Recalls, and Updates. ECRI (Emergency Care Research Institute), 5200 Butler Pike Plymouth Meeting, PA 19462. Phone: (610)825-6000 Fax: (610)834-1275 Weekly. Newsletter containing reviews of health equipment problems. Includes *Health Devices Alerts Action Items*, *Health Devices Alerts Abstracts*, *Health Devices Alerts FDA Data*, *Health Devices Alerts Implants*, *Health Devices Alerts Hazards Bulletin*.

Health Devices Alerts ÎCD-ROMl. ECRI, 5200 Butler Pike Plymouth Meeting, PA 19462. Phone: (610)825-6000 Fax: (610)834-1275 Weekly. $2,450.00 per year. Provides CD-ROM reports of medical equipment defects, problems, failures, misuses, and recalls.

Health Devices Alerts Îonlinel. ECRI, 5200 Butler Pike Plymouth Meeting, PA 19462. Phone: (610)825-6000 Fax: (610)834-1275 Provides online reports of medical equipment defects, problems, failures, misuses, and recalls. Time period is 1977 to date, with weekly updates. Inquire as to online cost and availability.

Health Devices Sourcebook. ECRI (Emergency Care Research Institute), 5200 Butler Pike Plymouth Meeting, PA 19462. Phone: (610)825-6000 Fax: (610)834-1275 E-mail: ecri@hsic.org • Annual. Lists over 6,000 manufacturers of a wide variety of medical equipment and supplies, including clinical laboratory equipment, testing instruments, surgical instruments, patient care equipment, etc.

Health Facilities Management. American Hospital Association. American Hospital Publishing, Inc., One N. Franklin St., 27th Fl. Chicago, IL 60606-3421. Phone: 800-242-2626 or (312)422-3000 Fax: (312)422-4505 URL: http://www.hfmmagazine.com/hfm-home.html • Monthly. $40.00 per year. Covers building maintenance and engineering for hospitals and nursing homes.

Health Food/Vitamin Store. Entrepreneur Media, Inc., 2445 McCabe Way Irvine, CA 92614. Phone: 800-421-2300 or (949)261-2325 Fax: (949)261-0234 E-mail: entmag@entrepreneur.com • URL: http://www.entrepreneur.com • Looseleaf. $59.50. A practical guide to starting a health food store. Covers profit potential, start-up costs, market size evaluation, owner's time required, site selection, lease negotiation, pricing, accounting, advertising, promotion, etc. (Start-Up Business Guide No. E1296.)

Health Foods: A Source Guide. Gordon Press Publishers, P.O. Box 459 New York, NY 10004. Phone: (212)969-8419 Fax: (718)624-8419 1991. $77.95.

Health Forum. American Hospital Association. American Hospital Publishing, Inc., One N. Franklin St. Chicago, IL 60606-3421. Phone: 800-242-2626 or (312)442-3000 Fax: (312)422-4796 URL: http://www.aha.org • Biweekly. $80.00 per year. Covers the general management of hospitals, nursing homes, and managed care organizations. Formerly *HospitalsHealthNetworks*.

Health Grants and Contracts Weekly: Selected Federal Project Opportunities. Aspen Publishers, Inc., 200 Orchard Ridge Dr. Gaithersburg, MD 20878. Phone: 800-638-8437 or (301)417-7500 Fax: (301)417-7550 E-mail: customer.service@aspenpubl.com • URL: http://www.aspenpub.com • Weekly. $379.00 per year. Lists new health-related federal contracts and grants.

Health Industry Buyers Guide. Spring House, 434 W. Downer Place Aurora, IL 60506. Phone: 800-950-0879 Annual. $195.00. About 4,000 manufacturers of hospital and physician's supplies and equipment. Formerly *Surgical Trade Buyers Guide*.

Health Industry Distributors Association.

Health Industry Manufacturers Association.

Health Industry Representatives Association., 6740 E. Hampden Ave., Suite 306 Denver, CO 80224. Phone: 800-777-4472 or (303)756-8115 Fax: (303)756-5699 URL: http://www.hira.org • Members are manufacturers' representatives working within the health care industry.

Health Industry Today: The Market Letter for Health Care Industry Vendors. Business Word, Inc., 5350 S. Roslyn St., Suite 400 Englewood, CO 80111-2125. Phone: (303)290-8500 Fax: (303)290-9025 E-mail: curthit@buisnessword.com • Monthly. $325.00 per year.

Health Information for International Travel. Available from U. S. Government Printing Office, Washington, DC 20402. Phone: (202)512-1800 Fax: (202)512-2250 E-mail: gpoaccess@gpo.gov • URL: http://www.access.gpo.gov • Annual. Issued by Centers for Disease. Control, U. S. Department of Health and Human Services. Discusses potential health risks of international travel and specifies vaccinations required by different countries.

Health Insurance Association of America., 555 13th St., N.W. Washington, DC 20004. Phone: (202)824-1600 Fax: (202)824-1722 URL: http://www.hiaa.org • Members are commercial health insurers. Includes a Managed Care and Group Insurance Committee, a Disability Insurance Committee, a Medicare Administration Committee, and a Long-Term Care Task Force.

Health Insurance Company Financial Data. The National Underwriter Co., 505 Gest St. Cincinnati, OH 45203-1716. Phone: 800-543-0874 or (513)721-2140 Fax: (513)721-0126 URL: http://www.nuco.com • Annual.

Health Insurance Terminology: A Glossary of Health Insurance Terms. Margaret Lynch, editor. Health Insurance Association of America, 555 13th St., N.W., Suite 600 E. Washington, DC 20004-1109. Phone: 800-509-4422 or (202)824-1840 Fax: (202)824-1800 E-mail: mbell@hiaa.org • URL: http://www.hiaa.org • 1992. $10.00.

Health Insurance Underwriter. National Association of Health Underwriters, 2000 14th St., N., Suite 450 Arlington, VA 22201-2573. Phone: (703)726-0220 Fax: (703)841-7777 11 times a year. Free to members; non-members, $25.00 per year. Includes special feature issues on long-term care insurance, disability insurance, managed health care, and insurance office management.

Health Law Handbook, 1992. Alice G. Gosfield, editor. West Group, 610 Opperman Dr. Eagan, MN 55123. Phone: 800-328-4880 or (651)687-7000 Fax: 800-213-2323 or (651)687-5827 URL: http://www.westgroup.com • 1992. $75.00.

Health Letter. Sidney M. Wolfe, editor. Public Citizen, Inc., 1600 20th St., N. W. Washington, DC 20009. Phone: (202)588-1000 Fax: (202)785-3584 Monthly. $18.00 per year. Newsletter for healthcare consumers.

Health Management and Policy., University of Michigan, 109 S. Observatory St. Ann Arbor, MI 48109-2029. Phone: (734)763-9903 Fax: (734)764-4338 E-mail: weissert@umich.edu • URL: http://www.sph.umich.edu/ • Research fields include health care economics, health insurance, and long-term care.

Health Management Research Center.

Health Management Technology. Nelson Publishing, Inc., 2504 N. Tamiami Trail Nokomis, FL 34275. Phone: (941)966-9521 Fax: (941)966-2590 Monthly. $38.00 per year. Formerly *Computers in Healthcare*.

Health Marketing Quarterly. The Haworth Press, Inc., 10 Alice St. Binghamton, NY 13904-1580. Phone: 800-429-6784 or (607)722-2493 Fax: (607)722-1424 E-mail: getinfo@haworthpressinc.com • URL: http://www.haworthpressinc.com • Quarterly. Individuals, $60.00 per year; institutions, $80.00 per year; libraries, $425.00 per year.

Health News Daily. F-D-C Reports, Inc., 5550 Friendship Blvd., Suite 1 Chevy Chase, MD 20815-7278. Phone: 800-332-2181 or (301)657-9830 Fax: (301)664-7238 URL: http://www.fdcreports.com • Daily. $1,350.00 per year. Newsletter providing broad coverage of the healthcare business, including government policy, regulation, research, finance, and insurance. Contains news of pharmaceuticals, medical devices, biotechnology, and healthcare delivery in general.

Health Policy and Biomedical Research: The Blue Sheet. F-D-C Reports, Inc., 5550 Friendship Blvd., Suite 1 Chevy Chase, MD 20815-7278. Phone: 800-332-2181 or (301)657-9830 Fax: (301)664-7238 URL: http://www.fdcreports.com • 51 Times a year. $619.00 per year. Newsletter. Emphasis is on news of medical research agencies and institutions, especially the National Institutes of Health (NIH).

Health Policy Institute.

Health Products Business Purchasing Guide. Cygnus Business Media, 445 Broad Hollow Rd. Melville, NY 11747. Phone: 800-308-6397 or (631)845-2700 Fax: (631)845-2798 E-mail: rich.reiff@cygnuspub.com • URL: http://www.cygnuspub.com • Annual. $35.00. Listing of manufacturers, importers, exclusive distributors, brokers, and wholesalers of health food products, publishers of health food related books and magazines, and associations interested in the health foods industry. Formerly Health Foods Business Purchasing Guide.

Health Products Business: The Business Publication of the Natural Foods In dustry. Cygnus Business Media, 445 Broad Hollow Rd. Melville, NY 11747. Phone: 800-308-6397 or (631)845-2700 Fax: (631)845-7109 E-mail: rich.reiff@cygnuspub.com • URL: http://www.cygnuspub.com • Monthly. $54.00 per year.

Health Reference Center. The Gale Group, 27500 Drake Rd. Farmington Hills, MI 48331-3535. Phone: 800-877-GALE or (248)699-GALE Fax: 800-414-5043 or (248)699-8069 E-mail: galeord@gale.com • URL: http://www.gale.com • Monthly. Provides CD-ROM citations, abstracts, and selected full-text articles on many health-related subjects. Includes references to medical journals, general periodicals, newsletters, newspapers, pamphlets, and medical reference books.

Health Research Institute., 3538 Torino Way Concord, CA 94518. Phone: (510)676-2320 Fax: (510)676-2342 Conducts applied research in health care financing and delivery of health services, with emphasis on cost containment.

Health Services Research and Development Center.

Health Supplement Retailer. Virgo Publishing, Inc., 3300 N. Central Ave., Suite 2500 Phoenix, AZ 85012. Phone: (480)990-1101 Fax: (480)675-8109 URL: http://www.vpico.com • Monthly. $38.00 per year. Covers all aspects of the vitamin and health supplement market, including new products. Includes an annual buyer's guide, an annual compilation of industry statistics, and annual guides to vitamins and herbs.

Health, United States, 1999: Health and Aging Chartbook. Available from U. S. Government Printing Office, Washington, DC 20402. Phone: (202)512-1800 Fax: (202)512-2250 E-mail: gpoaccess@gpo.gov • URL: http://www.access.gpo.gov • 1999. $37.00. Issued by the National Center for Health Statistics, U. S. Department of Health and Human Services. Contains 34 bar charts in color, with related statistical tables. Provides detailed data on persons over 65 years of age, including population, living arrangements, life expectancy, nursing home residence, poverty, health status, assistive devices, health insurance, and health care expenditures.

Healthcare Business. Healthcare Business Media, Inc., 450 Sansome St., Suite 1100 San Francisco, CA 94111. Phone: (415)956-8242 Fax: ((41)5(956-8333 E-mail: inbox@healthcarebusiness.com • URL: http://www.healthcarebusiness.com • Bimonthly. $28.00 per year. Provides broad coverage of finance, marketing, management, and technology for executives in the health care industry. Includes "Roundtable" discussions of particular health care issues.

Healthcare Career Directory: Nurses and Physicians: A Practical One-Stop Guide to Getting a Job in Public Relations. The Gale Group, 27500 Drake Rd. Farmington Hills, MI 48331-3535. Phone: 800-877-GALE or (248)699-GALE Fax: 800-414-5043 or (248)699-8069 E-mail: galeord@galegroup.com • URL: http://www.galegroup.com • 1993. $17.95. Second edition. Includes information on careers in nursing, family medicine, surgery, and other medical areas. Provides advice from "insiders," resume suggestions, a directory of companies that may offer entry-level positions, and a directory of career information sources. *Career Advisor Series*.

Healthcare Convention and Exhibitors Association., 5775 Peachtree-Dunwoody Rd., Suite 500-G Atlanta, GA 30342. Phone: (404)252-3663 Fax: (404)252-0774 E-mail: hcea@assnhq.com • URL: http://www.hcea.org • Promotes more effective display of health care products at professional conventions.

Healthcare Distributor: The Industry's Multi-Market Information Resource. ELF Publications, 5285 W. Louisiana Ave., Suite 112 Lakewood, CO 80232-5976. Phone: 800-922-8513 or (303)975-0075 Fax: (303)975-0132 Monthly. $30.00 per year. Formerly *Wholesale Drugs Magazine*.

Healthcare Executive. American College of Healthcare Executives, One N. Franklin St., Suite 1700 Chicago, IL 60606-3491. Phone: (312)424-3800 Fax: (312)424-0023 Bimonthly. $60.00 per year. Focuses on critical management issues.

Healthcare Finance for the Non-Financial Manager: Basic Guide to Financial Analysis & Control. Louis Gapenski. McGraw-Hill Professional, 1221 Ave. of the Americas New York, NY 10020. Phone: 800-722-4726 or (212)904-2000 Fax: (212)904-2072 E-mail: customer.service@mcgraw-hill.com • URL: http://www.mcgraw-hill.com • 1994. $47.50.

Healthcare Financial Management. Healthcare Financial Management Association, Two Westbrook Corporate Center, Suite 700 Westchester, IL 60154-5700. Phone: 800-252-4362 or (708)531-9600 Fax: 800-926-9495 or (708)531-0032 E-mail: tarya@hfma.org • URL: http://www.hfma.org • Monthly. $82.00 per year.

Healthcare Financing Management Association.

Healthcare Financing Study Group., 1919 Pennsylvania Ave., N.W., Suite 800 Washington, DC 20006. Phone: (202)887-1400 Fax: (202)466-3215 Concerned with the provision of capital financing for health care institutions.

Healthcare Forum Journal: Leadership Strategies for Healthcare Executives. Healthcare Forum, 425 Market St., 16th Fl. San Francisco, CA 94105. Phone: (415)436-4300 Fax: (415)356-9300 URL: http://www.healthonline.com/thf.htm • Bimonthly. $65.00 per year.

Healthcare Informatics: The Business of Healthcare Information Technology. McGraw-Hill, 1221 Ave. of the Americas New York, NY 10020. Phone: 800-722-4726 or (212)904-2000 Fax: (212)904-2072 E-mail: customer.service@mcgraw-hill.com • URL: http://www.mcgraw-hill.com • Monthly. $40.00 per year. Covers various aspects of information and computer technology for the health care industry.

Healthcare Information and Management Systems Society.

Healthcare Marketing Report. HMR Publication Group, P.O. Box 76002 Atlanta, GA 30358-1002. Phone: (404)457-6105 Fax: (404)457-0049 Monthly. Price on application.

Healthcare PR and Marketing News. Phillips Business Information, Inc., 1201 Seven Locks Rd., Suite 300 Potomac, MD 20854. Phone: 800-777-5006 or (301)340-1520 Fax: (301)424-4297 E-mail: pbi@phillips.com • URL: http://www.phillips.com/pbi.htm • Biweekly. $497.00 per year. Newsletter on public relations and client communications for the healthcare industry.

Healthcare Purchasing News: A Magazine for Hospital Materials Management Central Service, Infection Control Practitioners. McKnight Medical Communications, Two Northfield Plaza, Suite 300 Northfield, IL 60093-1217. Phone: 800-451-7838 or (847)441-3700 Fax: (847)441-3701 E-mail: joan.weiner@medec.com • URL: http://www.medec.com • Monthly. $44.00 per year. Edited for personnel responsible for the purchase of medical, surgical, and hospital equipment and supplies. Features new purchasing techniques and new products. Includes news of the activities of two major purchasing associations, Health Care Material Management Society and International Association of Healthcare Central Service Materiel Management.

Healthplan: The Magazine of Trends, Insights, and Best Practices. American Association of Health Plans, 1129 20th St., N. W., Suite 600 Washington, DC 20036. Phone: (202)778-3200 Fax: (202)331-7487 URL: http://www.aahp.org • Bimonthly. $75.00 per year. Edited for managed care executives.

Healthstar. Medlars Management Section, National Library of Medicine, 8600 Rockville Pike Bethesda, MD 20209. Phone: 800-638-8480 or (301)496-3147 URL: http://www.nlm.nih.gov • Provides indexing and abstracting of non-clinical literature relating to health care delivery, 1975 to date. Monthly updates. Inquire as to online cost and availability.

Healthy Prepared Foods. MarketResearch.com, 641 Ave. of the Americas, Third Floor New York, NY 10011. Phone: 800-298-5699 or (212)807-2629 Fax: (212)807-2716 E-mail: order@marketresearch.com • URL: http://www.marketresearch.com • 1999. $2,750.00. Consumer market data on foods that are low in calories, fat, cholesterol, sodium, and sugar or high in fiber and calcium, with forecasts to 2003.

Heating/Piping/Air Conditioning Engineering: The Magazine of Mechanical Systems Engineering. Penton Media Inc., 1300 E. Ninth St. Cleveland, OH 44114. Phone: (216)696-7000 Fax: (216)696-0836 E-mail: corpcomm@penton.com • URL: http://www.penton.com/hpac • Monthly. Free to qualified personnel; others, $65.00 per year. Covers design, specification, installation, operation, and maintenance for systems in industrial, commercial, and institutional buildings. Formerly Heating, Piping and Air Conditioning.

Heating/Piping/Air Conditioning Info-Dex. Penton Media Inc., 1300 E. Ninth St. Cleveland, OH 44114. Phone: (216)696-7000 Fax: (216)696-0836 E-mail: corpcomm@penton.com • URL: http://www.penton.com • Annual. $30.00. The HVAC/R industry's directory of products, manufacturers, and trade names and a composite of catalog data for mechanical systems engineering professionals.

Heavy Duty Trucking: The Business Magazine of Trucking. Newport Communications, 38 Executive Park, Suite 300 Irvine, CA 92714. Phone: (949)261-1636 Fax: (949)261-2904 E-mail: newport@heavytruck.com • URL: http://www.heavytruck.com • Monthly. $65.00 per year.

Hebrew Immigrant Aid Society.

The Helicopter Annual. Helicopter Association International, 1635 Prince St. Alexandria, VA 22314-2818. Phone: 800-435-4976 or (703)683-4646 Fax: (703)683-4745 E-mail: marilyn.mckinnis@rotor.com • URL: http://www.rotor.com • Annual. Members, $20.00; non-members, $40.00.

Helicopter Association International.

Helicopter News. Phillips Business Information, Inc., 1201 Seven Locks Rd., Ste. 300 Potomac, MD 20854. Phone: 800-777-5006 or (301)340-1520 Fax: (301)309-3847 E-mail: pbi@phillips.com • URL: http://www.phillips.com/pbi.htm • Biweekly. $697.00 per year. Newsletter.

The Helping Relationship: Process and Skills. Lawrence M. Brammer and Ginger A. MacDonald. Allyn and Bacon, Inc., 160 Gould St. Needham Heights, MA 02194-2310. Phone: 800-278-3525 or (781)455-1250 Fax: (781)455-1294 E-mail: ab_webmaster@abacon.com • URL: http://www.abacon.com • 1998. $46.00. Seventh edition.

Herb Farming. Entrepreneur Media, Inc., 2445 McCabe Way Irvine, CA 92614. Phone: 800-421-2300 or (949)261-2325 Fax: (949)261-0234 E-mail: entmag@entrepreneur.com • URL: http://www.entrepreneur.com • Looseleaf. $59.50. A practical guide to the business side of herb farming. Covers profit potential, start-up costs, market size evaluation, owner's time required, pricing, accounting, advertising, promotion, etc. (Start-Up Business Guide No. E1282.)

Herb Quarterly. Long Mountain Press, P.O. Box 689 San Anselmo, CA 94979-0689. Phone: (415)455-9540 Fax: (415)455-9541 E-mail: herquart@aol.com • Quarterly. $24.00 per year. A magazine for herb enthusiasts covering all aspects of herb uses.

Herb Society of America.

Herbal Drugs and Phytopharmaceuticals. Max Wichtl and Norman G. Bisset, editors. CRC Press, Inc., 2000 Corporate Blvd., N. W. Boca Raton, FL 33431. Phone: 800-272-7737 or (561)994-0555 Fax: (561)241-7856 E-mail: orders@crcpress.com • URL: http://www.crcpress.com • 1994. $190.00. Provides a scientific approach to the medicinal use of herbs. (English translation of original German edition.)

The Herbalist. Joseph E. Mayer. Gordon Press Publishers, P.O. Box 459 New York, NY 20004. Phone: (212)969-8419 Fax: (718)624-8419 1992. $79.99. (Alternative Medicine Series).

Herbarist. Herb Society of America, Inc., Vineyard House, Two Independence Court Concord, OH 01742. Phone: (617)371-1486 Annual. $5.00.

Herty Research and Development Center.

Herzfeld's Guide to Closed-End Funds. Thomas J. Herzsfeld. McGraw-Hill, 1221 Ave. of the Americas New York, NY 10020. Phone: 800-722-4726 or (212)904-2000 Fax: (212)904-2072 E-mail: customer.service@mcgraw-hill.com • URL: http://www.mcgraw-hill.com • 1992. $22.95. Provides advice and information on investing in closed-end investment companies.

Herzog's Bankruptcy Forms and Practice. Asa S. Herzog and others. West Group, 610 Opperman Dr. Eagan, MN 55123. Phone: 800-328-4880 or (651)687-7000 Fax: 800-213-2323 or (651)687-5827 URL: http://www.westgroup.com • Two looseleaf volumes. $250.00. Periodic supplementation.

HFN (Home Furnishing Network). Fairchild Publications, Seven W. 34th St. New York, NY 10001. Phone: 800-932-4724 or (212)630-4000 Fax: (212)630-3675 E-mail: hfneditor@fairchildpub.com • URL: http://www.fairchildpub.com • Weekly. Manufacturers, retailers, and agents $65.00 per year; other corporations, $80.00 per year.Formerly *H F D-Home Furnishing Daily*.

High Efficiency Selling: How Superior Salespeople Get That Way. Stephan Schiffman. John Wiley and Sons, Inc., 605 Third Ave. New York, NY 10158-0012. Phone: 800-225-5945 or (212)850-6000 Fax: (212)850-6088 E-mail: info@jwiley.com • URL: http://www.wiley.com • 1997. $19.95.

High Performance Review: Definitive Magazine for Audiophiles and Music Lovers. High Performance Review Publishing, 296 Amherst Dr. Murfreesboro, TN 37128-6233. Phone: (615)893-9788 Fax: (615)893-9717 Quarterly. $15.00 per year.

High-Tech Materials Alert: Advanced Materials-Their Uses and Manufacture. Technical Insights, 605 Third Ave. New York, NY 10158-0012. Phone: 800-825-7550 or (212)850-8600 Fax: (212)850-8800 E-mail: insights@wiley.com • URL: http://www.wiley.com/technicalinsights • Monthly. $695.00 per year. Newsletter on technical developments relating to high-performance materials, including metals and ceramics. Includes market forecasts.

High Technology Fitness Research Institute., 1510 W. Montana St. Chicago, IL 60614. Phone: (773)528-1000 Fax: (773)528-1043 E-mail: bgoldman@worldhalth.net • URL: http://www.worldhealth.net • Research activities include the analysis of health and fitness products and programs on the market.

The High Yield Debt Market: Investment Performance and Economic Impact. Edward I. Altman, editor. McGraw-Hill Professional, 1221 Ave. of the Americas New York, NY 10020. Phone: 800-722-4726 or (212)904-2000 Fax: (212)904-2072 E-mail: customer.service@mcgraw-hill.com • URL: http://www.mcgraw-hill.com • 1990. $55.00.

High Yield Report. Securities Data Publishing, 40 West 57th St. New York, NY 10019. Phone: 800-455-5844 or (212)765-5311 Fax: (212)956-0112 E-mail: sdp@tfn.com • URL: http://www.sdponline.com • Weekly. $995.00 per year. Newsletter covering the junk bond market. (Securities Data Publishing is a unit of Thomson Financial.)

Higher Education and National Affairs. American Council on Education, One Dupont Circle, N.W. Washington, DC 20036-1193. Phone: (202)939-9300 Fax: (202)833-4760 Biweekly. $60.00 per year.

Higher Education in American Society. Phillip G. Altbach and others, editors. Prometheus Books, 59 John Glenn Dr. Amherst, NY 14228-2197. Phone: 800-421-0351 or (716)691-0133 Fax: (716)691-0137 E-mail: pbooks6205@aol.com • URL: http://www.prometheusbooks.com • 1994. $24.95. Third edition. (Frontiers of Education Series).

Highlights and Documents. Tax Analysts, 6830 N. Fairfax Dr. Arlington, VA 22213. Phone: 800-955-3444 or (703)533-4400 Fax: (703)533-4444 E-mail: webmaster@tax.org • URL: http://www.tax.org • Daily. $2,249.00 per year, including monthly indexes. Newsletter. Provides daily coverage of IRS, congressional, judicial, state, and international tax developments. Includes abstracts and citations for "all tax documents released within the previous 24 to 48 hours." Annual compilation available *Highlights and Documents on Microfiche*.

Highway and Traffic Safety and Accident Research, Management, and Issues. Norman Solomon, editor. Transportation Research Board, 2101 Constitution Ave., N. W. Washington, DC 20418. Phone: (202)334-3214 1993. $28.00. (Transportation Research Record Series).

Highway Financing and Construction: State Capitals. Wakeman-Walworth, Inc., P.O. Box 7376 Alexandria, VA 22307-0376. Phone: 800-876-2545 or (703)549-8606 Fax: (703)549-1372 E-mail: newsletters@statecapitals.com • URL: http://www.statecapitals.com • Weekly. $345.00 per year. Newsletter. Formerly *From the State Capitals: Highway Financing and Construction*.

Highway of Dreams: A Critical View Along the Information Superhighway. A. Michael Noll. Lawrence Erlbaum Associates, Inc., 10 Industrial Ave. Mahwah, NJ 07430-2262. Phone: 800-926-6579 or (201)236-9500 Fax: (201)236-0072 E-mail: orders@erlbaum.com • URL: http://www.erlbaum.com • 1996. $49.95. States that such factors as consumer needs and finance are often of more importance to the information industry than technological utopia. Includes such chapter headings as "Historical Perspective," "History Repeats," "Business Considerations," and "The Internet Exposed." (LEA's Telecommunications Series).

Highway Safety Literature., National Highway Traffic Safety Administration, 400 Seventh St., S.W. Washington, DC 20024-2516. Phone: (202)366-4943 Annual. $80.00.

Highway Statistics. Federal Highway Administration, U.S. Department of Transportation. Available from U.S. Government Printing Office, Washington, DC 20402. Phone: (202)512-1800 Fax: (202)512-2250 E-mail: gpoaccess@gpo.gov • URL: http://www.access.gpo.gov • Annual. $26.00.

The Highwaymen: Warriors on the Information Superhighway. Ken Auletta. Harcourt Trade Publications, 525 B St., Ste. 1900 San Diego, CA 92101-4495. Phone: 800-543-1918 or (619)231-6616 Fax: 800-235-0256 URL: http://www.randomhouse.com • 1998. $13.00. Revised expanded edition. Contains critical articles about Ted Turner, Rupert Murdoch, Barry Diller, Michael Eisner, and other key figures in electronic communications, entertainment, and information.

Highways. Good Sam club. Affinity Group, Inc. T L Enterprises, 2575 Vista Del Mar Dr. Ventura, CA 93001. Phone: (805)667-4100 Fax: (805)667-4379 11 times a year. Membership. Five regional editions. Formerly *Good Sam's Hi-Way Herald*.

Hine's Directory of Insurance Adjusters, Investigators, and Appraisers. Hine's, Inc., P.O. Box 143 Geneva, IL 60134-0134. Phone: (630)365-1630 Fax: (630)365-1631 E-mail: hines@hinesdirectories.com • URL: http://www.hinesdirectories.com • Annual. $25.00. Lists selected independent insurance adjusters in the United States and Canada.

Hine's Insurance Counsel. Hine's, Inc., P.O. Box 143 Geneva, IL 60134-0134. Phone: (630)365-1630 Fax: (630)365-1631 E-mail: hines@hinesdirectories.com • URL: http://www.hinesdirectories.com • Annual. $50.00. List of law firms and attorneys in the U. S. and Canada specializing in defense of insurance companies.

The Hiring and Firing Book: A Complete Legal Guide for Employers. Steven M. Sack. Legal Strategies, Inc., 1795 Harvard Ave. Merrick, NY 11566. Phone: 800-327-5113 or (516)377-3940 1996. $149.95. Revised edition. Covers a wide range of legal considerations relative to employment and dismissal. Includes checklists, a glossary, and samples of applications, agreements, contracts, and other documents.

Hiring Right: A Practical Guide. Susan J. Herman. Sage Publications, Inc., 2455 Teller Rd. Thousand Oaks, CA 91320. Phone: (805)499-0721 Fax: (805)499-0871 E-mail: info@sagepub.com • URL: http://www.sagepub.com • 1993. $46.00. A practical manual covering job definition, recruitment, interviewing, testing, and checking of references.

Hiring Winners. Richard J. Pinsker. AMACOM, 1601 Broadway, 12th Fl. New York, NY 10019. Phone: 800-262-9699 or (212)586-8100 Fax: (212)903-8168 E-mail: custmserv@amanet.org • URL: http://www.amanet.org • 1991. $19.95. Presents a practical system for finding and hiring people who will be ideal for a particular company or situation.

Hispanic American Periodicals Index. University of California, Los Angeles, Latin American Studies Center. Latin American Studies Center Publication, P.O. Box 951447 Los Angeles, CA 90095-1447. Phone: (310)825-0810 Fax: (310)206-2634 E-mail: bvalk@ucla.edu • URL: http://www.hapi.gseis.ucla.edu • Annual. $400.00. Indexes about 250 periodicals that regularly include material on Latin America. Supplement available.

The Hispanic Market. Available from MarketResearch.com, 641 Ave. of the Americas, Third Floor New York, NY 10011. Phone: 800-298-5699 or (212)807-2629 Fax: (212)807-2716 E-mail: order@marketresearch.com • URL: http://www.marketresearch.com • 1999. $2,750.00. Published by Packaged Facts. Provides consumer market data and demographics, with projections to 2004.

Hispanic Market Handbook. The Gale Group, 27500 Drake Rd. Farmington Hills, MI 48331-3535. Phone: 800-877-GALE or (248)699-GALE Fax: 800-414-5043 or (248)699-8069 E-mail: galeord@galegroup.com • URL: http://www.galegroup.com • 1995. $85.00. Provides advice on marketing consumer items to Hispanic Americans. Includes case studies and demographic profiles.

Hispanic Media and Market Source. SRDS, 1700 Higgins Rd. Des Plaines, IL 60018. Phone: 800-851-7737 or (847)375-5000 Fax: (847)375-5001 E-mail: ebeer@srds.com • URL: http://www.srds.com • Quarterly. $271.00 per year. Provides detailed information on the following Hispanic advertising media in the U. S.: TV, radio, newspapers, magazines, direct mail, outdoor, and special events. Formerly *Hispanic Media and Markets*.

Historical Statistics of the United States, Colonial Times to 1970: A Statistical Abstract Supplement. U.S. Bureau of the Census. Available from U.S. Government Printing Office, Washington, DC 20402. Phone: (202)512-1800 Fax: (202)512-2250 E-mail: gpoaccess@gpo.gov • URL: http://www.accessgpo.gov • 1975. $79.00. Two volumes.

Historical Tables, Budget of the United States Government. Available from U. S. Government Printing Office, Washington, DC 20402. Phone: (202)512-1800 Fax: (202)512-2250 E-mail: gpoaccess@gpo.gov • URL: http://www.access.gpo.gov • Annual. Issued by the Office of Management and Budget, Executive Office of the President (http://www.whitehouse.gov). Provides statistical data on the federal budget for an extended period of about 60 years in the past to projections of four years in the future. Includes federal debt and federal employment.

The History of Accounting: An Encyclopedia. Michael Chatfield and Richard Vangermeersch, editors. Garland Publishing, Inc., 19 Union Square West, 8th Fl. New York, NY 10003-3382. Phone: 800-627-6273 or (212)414-0650 Fax: (212)414-0659 E-mail: info@garland.com • URL: http://www.garlandpub.com • 1996. $100.00. Contains more than 400 alphabetical entries by various contributors, covering the history of accounting from 750 B.C. to the modern era. Includes a bibliography for each entry and an index. (Reference Library of the Humanities Series, Vol. 1573).

History of Black Business in America: Capitalism, Race, Entrepreneurship. Juliet E. K. Walker. Available from The Gale Group, 27500 Drake Rd. Farmington Hills, MI 48331-3535. Phone: 800-877-GALE or (248)699-GALE Fax: 800-414-5043 or (248)699-8069 E-mail: galeord@galegroup.com • URL: http://www.galegroup.com • 1998. $45.00. Published by Twayne Publishers. Includes profiles of African American business pioneers. (Evolution of Modern Business Series.)

History of Interest Rates. Sidney Homer and Richard Sylla. Rutgers University Press, 100 Joyce Kilmer Ave. Piscataway, NJ 08854-8099. Phone: 800-446-9323 or (732)445-7762 Fax: 888-471-9014 or (732)445-7039 E-mail: ccapps@rci.rutgers.edu • URL: http://www.rutgers.press.rutgers.edu • 1996. $79.00. Third revised edition.

History of Rocketry and Astronautics. American Astronautical Society. Available from Univelt, Inc., P. O. Box 28130 San Diego, CA 92128-0198. Phone: (760)746-4005 Fax: (760)746-3139 E-mail: 76121.1532@compuserve.com • URL: http://www.univelt.staigerland.com • Various volumes and prices. Covers the history of rocketry and astronautics since 1880. Prices vary. (AAS History Series).

History of Work Cooperation in America: Cooperatives, Cooperative Movements, Collectivity, and Communalism From Early America to the Present. John Curl. Homeward Press, P.O. Box 2307 Berkeley, CA 94702. 1980. $8.00.

HMAT (Hot Mix Asphalt Technology). National Asphalt Pavement Association, NAPA Building, 5100 Forbes Blvd. Lanham, MD 20706-4413. Phone: (301)731-4748 Fax: (301)731-4621 Quarterly. Free to qualified personnel. Formerly *HMAT*.

HME News. United Publications, Inc., P.O. Box 997 Yarmouth, ME 04096-1997. Phone: 800-441-6982 or (207)846-0600 Fax: (207)846-0657 Monthly. Controlled circulation. Covers the home medical equipment business for dealers and manufacturers. Provides information on a wide variety of home health care supplies and equipment.

HMO Magazine (Health Maintenance Organization). Group Health Association of America, 1129 20th St., N.W., Suite 600 Washington, DC 20036. Phone: (202)778-3247 Fax: (202)331-7487 Bimonthly. $75.00 per year.

HMO/PPO Directory. Medical Economics Co., Inc., Five Paragon Dr. Montvale, NJ 07645-1742. Phone: 800-442-6657 or (201)358-7500 Fax: (201)573-8999 E-mail: customerservice@medec.com • URL: http://www.medec.com • Annual. $215.00. Provides detailed information on managed care providers in the U. S., chiefly health maintenance organizations (HMOs) and preferred provider organizations (PPOs).

HMO Report and Directory. SMG Marketing Group, Inc., 875 N. Michigan Ave., 31st Fl. Chicago, IL 60611. Phone: 800-678-3026 or (312)642-3026 Fax: (312)642-9729 URL: http://www.smg.com • Annual. $525.00. Contains information relating to over 700 HMOs. Relevant market data is also provided.

Hobby Industry Association of America.

Hobby Shop. Entrepreneur Media, Inc., 2445 McCabe Way Irvine, CA 92614. Phone: 800-421-2300 or (949)261-2325 Fax: (949)261-0234 E-mail: entmag@entrepreneur.com • URL: http://www.entrepreneur.com • Looseleaf. $59.50. A practical guide to starting a hobby shop. Covers profit potential, start-up costs, market size evaluation, owner's time required, site selection, lease negotiation, pricing, accounting, advertising, promotion, etc. (Start-Up Business Guide No. E1132.)

Holiday Institute of Yonkers.

Holidays and Anniversaries of the World. The Gale Group, 27500 Drake Rd. Farmington Hills, MI 48331-3535. Phone: 800-877-GALE or (248)699-GALE Fax: 800-414-5043 or (248)699-8069 E-mail: galeord@galegroup.com • URL: http://www.galegroup.com • 1998. $120.00. Third edition.

Holidays and Festivals Index. Helene Henderson and Barry Puckett, editors. Omnigraphics, Inc., Penobscot Bldg. Detroit, MI 48226. Phone: 800-234-1340 or (313)961-1340 Fax: 800-875-1340 or (313)961-1383 E-mail: info@omnigraphics.com • URL: http://www.omnigraphics.com • 1995. $84.00. Serves as an index to more than 3,000 holidays, festivals, celebrations, and other observances found in 27 standard reference works.

Holidays and Festivals Index. Helene Henderson and Barry Puckett, editors. Omnigraphics, Inc., Penobscot Bldg. Detroit, MI 48226. Phone: 800-234-1340 or (313)961-1340 Fax: 800-875-1340 or (313)961-1383 E-mail: info@omnigraphics.com • URL: http://www.omnigraphics.com • 1994. $48.00. Serves as an index to more than 3,000 holidays, festivals, celebrations, and other observances found in over 20 standard reference works.

Holidays, Festivals, and Celebrations of the World Dictionary: Detailing More Than 2,000 Observances from All 50 States and More Than 100 Nations. Sue Ellen Thompson, editor. Omnigraphics, Inc., Penobscot Bldg. Detroit, MI 48226. Phone: 800-234-1340 or (313)961-1340 Fax: 800-875-1340 or (313)961-1383 E-mail: info@omnigraphics.com • URL: http://www.omnigraphics.com • 1997. $84.00. Second edition.

Hollywood Creative Directory., 3000 W. Olympic Blvd., Suite 2525 Santa Monica, CA 90404. Phone: 800-815-0503 or (310)315-4815 Fax: (310)315-4816 E-mail: hcd@hcdonline.com • URL: http://www.hcdonline.com • Three times a year. $129.95 per year.$54.95 per issue. Lists more than 1,700 motion picture and television development and production companies in the U. S. (mainly California and New York). Includes names of studio and TV network executives.

The Hollywood Reporter., 5055 Wilshire Blvd. Los Angeles, CA 90036-4396. Phone: 800-722-6658 or (213)525-2150 Fax: (213)525-2387 E-mail: subscriptions@hollywoodreporter.com • URL: http://www.hollywoodreporter.com • Daily. $219.00 per year. Covers the latest news in film, TV, cable, multimedia, music, and theatre. Includes box office grosses and entertainment industry financial data.

Home Banking Report. Jupiter Media Metrix, 21 Asor Place New York, NY 10003. Phone: 800-488-4345 or (212)780-6060 Fax: (212)780-6075 E-mail: jupiter@jup.com • URL: http://www.jmm.com • Annual. $695.00. Market research report. Covers banking from home by phone or online, with projections of growth in future years.

Home-Based Newsletter Publishing: A Success Guide for Entrepreneurs. William J. Bond. McGraw-Hill, 1221 Ave. of the Americas New York, NY 10020. Phone: 800-722-4726 or (212)904-2000 Fax: (212)904-2072 E-mail: customer.service@mcgraw-hill.com • URL: http://www.mcgraw-hill.com • 1991. $14.95.

Home Business Bible: Everything You Need to Know to Start and Run Your Home-Based Business. David R. Eyler. John Wiley and Sons, Inc., 605 Third Ave. New York, NY 10158-0012. Phone: 800-225-5945 or (949)850-6000 Fax: (949)850-6088 E-mail: info@wiley.com • URL: http://www.wiley.com • 1994. $60.00. Includes CD-ROM.

Home Business Magazine: The Home-Based Entrepreneur's Magazine. United Marketing and Research Co., Inc., 9061 Five Harbors Drive Huntington Beach, CA 92646. Phone: (714)693-1866 Fax: (714)693-9704 URL: http://www.homebusinessmag.com • Bimonthly. $15.00 per year. Provides practical advice and ideas relating to the operation of a business in the home. Sections include ''Marketing & Sales,'' ''Money Corner'' (financing), ''Businesses & Opportunities,'' and ''Home Office'' (equipment, etc.). Includes an annual directory of more than 250 non-franchised home business opportunities, including start-up costs and information about providers.

Home Care Client Assessment Handbook. Janet E. Jackson and Marianne Neighbors. Aspen Publishers, Inc., 200 Orchard Ridge Dr., Suite 200 Gaithersburg, MD 20878. Phone: 800-638-8437 or (301)417-7500 Fax: (301)417-7550 URL: http://www.aspenpub.com • 1990. $69.00.

Home Care Management: Quality-Based Costing, Pricing, and Productivity. Roey Kirk and Deborah Kranz. Aspen Publishers, Inc., 200 Orchard Ridge Dr. Gaithersburg, MD 20878. Phone: 800-638-8437 or (301)417-7500 Fax: (301)417-7550 E-mail: customer.service@aspenpubl.com • URL: http://www.aspenpub.com • 1988. $66.00.

Home Care Products Market. MarketResearch.com, 641 Ave. of the Americas, Third Floor New York, NY 10011. Phone: 800-298-5699 or (212)807-2629 Fax: (212)807-2716 E-mail: order@marketresearch.com • URL: http://www.marketresearch.com • 2001. $3,250.00. Market data with projections to 2005. Covers a wide variety of products: wheelchairs, crutches, beds, monitoring equipment, etc.

Home Care Services Market. MarketResearch.com, 641 Ave. of the Americas, Third Floor New York, NY 10011. Phone: 800-298-5699 or (212)807-2629 Fax: (212)807-2716 E-mail: order@marketresearch.com • URL: http://www.marketresearch.com • 1999. $3,250.00. Market data with projections. Covers a wide variety of services: primary nursing, respiratory, dialysis, infusion, etc.

Home Entertainment Installation. Entrepreneur Media, Inc., 2445 McCabe Way Irvine, CA 92614. Phone: 800-421-2300 or (949)261-2325 Fax: (949)261-0234 E-mail: entmag@entrepreneur.com • URL: http://www.entrepreneur.com • Looseleaf. $59.50. A practical guide to starting a home entertainment installation service. Covers profit potential, start-up costs, market size evaluation, owner's time required, pricing, accounting, advertising, promotion, etc. (Start-Up Business Guide No. E1349.)

Home Fashions: Buyer's Guide. Fairchild Publications, Seven W.34th St. New York, NY 10001. Phone: 800-932-4724 or (212)630-4000 Fax: (212)630-3868 URL: http://www.fairchildpub.com • Annual. $10.00. Lists manufacturers, importers, and regional sales representatives supplying bed, bath, kitchen, and table linens; window treatments; wall coverings; and fibers and fabrics.

Home Fashions Magazine. Fairchild Fashion and Merchandising Group, Seven W. 34th St. New York, NY 10001. Phone: 800-932-4724 or (212)630-4000 Fax: (212)630-4201 E-mail: hfneditor@fairchildpub • URL: http://www.fairchildpub.com • Monthly. $30.00 per year.

Home Fashions Products Association., 355 Lexington Ave., 17th Fl. New York, NY 10017-6603. Phone: (212)297-2122 Fax: (212)370-9047 Members are manufacturers of curtains and draperies.

Home Health Agencies Report and Directory. SMG Marketing Group, Inc., 875 N. Michigan Ave., Ste. 3100 Chicago, IL 60611. Phone: 800-678-3026 or (312)642-3026 Fax: (312)642-9729 URL: http://www.smg.com • Annual. $575.00. Lists over 13,000 home healthcare agencies and corporations. Includes a market analysis and growth projections.

Home Health Agency Chain Directory. SMG Marketing Group, Inc., 875 N. Michigan Ave., Ste. 3100 Chicago, IL 60611. Phone: 800-678-3026 or (312)642-3026 Fax: (312)642-9729 URL: http://www.smg.com • Annual. $595.00. Lists over 800 corporate home healthcare agencies which own two or more facilities. Includes an analysis of market trends.

Home Health Care Dealer-Provider. Curant Communications, Inc., 4676 Admiralty Way, Suite 202 Marina Del Rey, CA 90292-6603. Phone: (310)306-2200 Fax: (310)306-9548 Bimonthly. Controlled circulation. For home care dealer and home care pharmacies. Formerly *Home Health Care Dealer - Supplier*.

Home Health Care Management. Lazelle E. Benefield. Prentice Hall, 240 Frisch Court Paramus, NJ 07652-5240. Phone: 800-947-7700 or (201)909-6200 Fax: 800-445-6991 or (201)909-6361 URL: http://www.prenhall.com • 1988. $50.00.

Home Health Care Services Quarterly: The Journal of Community Care. Haworth Press, Inc., 10 Alice St. Binghamton, NY 13904-1580. Phone: 800-429-6784 or (607)722-5857 Fax: (607)722-1424 E-mail: getinfo@haworthpressinc.com • URL: http://www.haworthpressinc.com • Quarterly. Individuals, $60.00 per year; institutions $120.00 per year;libraries, $375.00 per year. An academic and practical journal focusing on the marketing and administration of home care.

Home Health Line: The Home Care Industry's National Independent Newsletter., 11300 Rockville Pike, Suite 1100 Rockville, MD 20852-3030. Phone: (301)816-8950 Fax: (301)816-8945 48 times a year. $399.00 per year. Newsletter on legislation and regulations affecting the home health care industry, with an emphasis on federal funding and Medicare programs.

Home Health Products. Stevens Publishing Corp., 5151 Beltline Rd., Suite 10th Fl. Dallas, TX 75240. Phone: (972)687-6700 Fax: (972)687-6769 10 times a year. $99.00 per year. Covers new medical equipment products for the home care industry.

Home Healthcare Nurse. Lippincott Williams and Wilkins, Publishers, 227 E. Washington Square Philadelphia, PA 19106-3780. Phone: 800-777-2295 or (215)238-4200 Fax: (215)238-4277 URL: http://www.lrpub.com • 10 times a year. Individuals, $43.00 per year; institutions, $180.00 per year. For professional nurses in the home health care field.

The Home Improvement Market. Available from MarketResearch.com, 641 Ave. of the Americas, Third Floor New York, NY 10011. Phone: 800-298-5699 or (212)807-2629 Fax: (212)807-2716 E-mail: order@marketresearch.com • URL: http://www.marketresearch.com • 1999. $2,750.00. Market research report published by Packaged Facts. Covers the market for lumber, finishing materials, tools, hardware, etc.

Home Inspection Service. Entrepreneur Media, Inc., 2445 McCabe Way Irvine, CA 92614. Phone: 800-421-2300 or (949)261-2325 Fax: (949)261-0234 E-mail: entmag@entrepreneur.com • URL: http://www.entrepreneur.com • Looseleaf. $59.50. A practical guide to starting a home inspection service. Covers profit potential, start-up costs, market size evaluation, owner's time required, pricing, accounting, advertising, promotion, etc. (Start-Up Business Guide No. E1334.)

Home Lighting and Accessories. Doctorow Communications, Inc., 1011 Clifton Ave., Suite B1 Clifton, NJ 07013-3518. Phone: (973)779-1600 Fax: (973)779-3242 E-mail: info@homelighting.com • URL: http://www.homelighting.com • Monthly. $30.00 per year. Trade magazine of the residential lighting industry for retailers, distributors, designers, architects, specifiers, manufacturers and all lighting professionals.

Home Lighting and Accessories Suppliers Directory. Doctorow Communications, Inc., 1011 Clifton Ave., Suite B1 Clifton, NJ 07013-3518. Phone: (973)779-1600 Fax: (973)779-3242 E-mail: info@homelighting.com • URL: http://www.homelighting.com • Semiannual. $6.00 per issue. Lists suppliers of residential lighting fixtures and accessories.

Home Office Association of America., 133 E. 5th St., Ste. 711 New York, NY 10022. Phone: 800-809-4622 or (212)588-9097 Fax: (212)588-9156 E-mail: hoaa@aol.com • URL: http://www.hoaa.com • A for-profit organization providing advice and information to home office workers and business owners.

Home Office Computing: Building Better Businesses with Technology. Freedom Technology Media Group, 156 W. 56th St., 3rd Fl. New York, NY 10019. Phone: (212)333-7600 Fax: (212)333-4312 URL: http://www.hoc.smalloffice.com • Monthly. $16.97 per year. Office automation for the self-employed and small businesses. Formerly *Family and Home Office Computing*.

Home Office Connections: A Monthly Journal of News, Ideas, Opportunities, and Savings for Those Who Work at Home. Home Office Association of America, Inc., 909 Third Ave., Suite 990 New York, NY 10022. Phone: 800-809-4622 E-mail: info@hoaa.com • URL: http://www.hoaa.com • Monthly. $49.00 per year. Newsletter. Includes membership in the Home Office Association of America.

Home Office Design: Everything You Need to Know about Planning, Organizing, and Furnishing Your Work Space. Neal Zimmerman. John Wiley and Sons, Inc., 605 Third Ave. New York, NY 10158-0012. Phone: 800-225-5945 or (212)850-6000 Fax: (212)850-6088 E-mail: info@jwiley.com • URL: http://www.wiley.com • 1996. $19.95. Covers furniture, seating, workstations, filing, storage, task lighting, etc.

Home Recording Rights Coalition., 1341 G St., N.W., Suite 200 Washington, DC 20005-3105. Phone: 800-282-8273 or (202)628-9212 Fax: (202)628-9227 URL: http://www.hrrc.work.org • Opposes efforts to restrict or tax audiovideo recording by consumers.

Home Sewing Association.

HomeCare Magazine Buyers' Guide. Intertec Publishing Corp., 23815 Stuart Ranch Rd. Malibu, CA 90265. Phone: 800-400-5945 or (310)317-4522 Fax: (310)317-9644 E-mail: subs@intertec.com • URL: http://www.intertec.com • Annual. $25.00. Lists about 800 manufacturers and distributors of home health care and rehabilitation products. Includes key personnel and trade names. Formerly *Homecare Product Directory and Buyers' Guide*.

Homecare News. National Association for Home Care, 228 Seventh St., S.E. Washington, DC 20003-4306. Phone: (202)547-7424 Fax: (202)547-3540 E-mail: webmaster@nahc.org • URL: http://www.nahc.org • Quarterly. $20.00 per year.

Homecare: The Business Magazine of the Home Health Industry. Intertec Publishing, P.O. Box 8987 Malibu, CA 90265-8987. Phone: 800-543-4116 or (310)317-4522 Fax: (310)317-9644 E-mail: subs@intertec.com • URL: http://www.homecaremag.com • Monthly. $65.00 per year. Edited for dealers and suppliers of home medical equipment, including pharmacies and chain stores. Includes information on new products.

Homemade Money: How to Select, Start, Manage, Market and Multiply the Profits of a Business at Home. Barbara Brabec. F and W Publications, Inc., 1507 Dana Ave. Cincinnati, OH 45207-1005. Phone: 800-289-0963 or (513)531-2690 Fax: 888-590-4082 1997. $21.99. Fifth revised edition. Covers sales, advertising, publicity, pricing, financing, legal issues, and other topics relating to businesses operated from home.

HomeOffice: The Homebased Office Authority. Entrepreneur Media, Inc., 2445 McCabe Way Irvine, CA 92614. Phone: 800-421-2300 or (949)261-2325 Fax: (949)261-0234 E-mail: entmag@entrepreneur.com • URL: http://www.entrepreneur.com • Bimonthly. $11.97 per year. Contains advice for operating a business in the home.

Homeowner or Tenant? How to Make a Wise Choice. Lawrence S. Pratt. American Institute for Economic Research, Division St. Great Barrington, MA 01230-1000. Phone: (413)528-1216 Fax: (413)528-0103 E-mail: info@aier.org • URL: http://www.aier.org • 1997. $6.00. Provides detailed information for making rent or buy decisions. Includes ''Mortgage Arithmetic,'' ''Hints for Buyers, Sellers, and Renters,'' worksheets, mortgage loan interest tables, and other data. (Economic Education Bulletin.)

The Honest Herbal: A Sensible Guide to the Use of Herbs and Related Remedies. Varro E. Tyler. The Haworth Press, Inc., 10 Alice St. Binghamton, NY 13904-1580. Phone: 800-429-6784 or (607)722-5857 Fax: 800-895-0582 or (607)722-1424 E-mail: getinfo@haworthpressinc.com • URL: http://www.haworthpressinc.com • 1993. $49.95. Third edition.

Honey Bee Research Unit.

Honey Production, Annual Summary. U.S. Department of Agriculture, Washington, DC 20250. Phone: (202)720-2791 Annual.

Hong Kong Business: The Portable Encyclopedia for Doing Business with Hong Kong. World Trade Press, 1450 Grant Ave., Suite 204 Novato, CA 94945-3142. Phone: 800-833-8586 or (415)454-9934 Fax: (415)453-7980 E-mail: worldpress@aol.com • URL: http://www.worldtradepress.com • 1994. $24.95. Covers economic data, import/export possibilities, basic tax and trade laws, travel information, and other useful facts for doing business with Hong Kong. (Country Business Guides Series).

Hong Kong Week. Dow Jones & Co., 200 Liberty St. New York, NY 10281. Phone: 800-832-1234 or (212)416-2000 Fax: (212)416-2658 Weekly. $260.00 per year (air mail). A guide to investing in Hong Kong and China. Provides stock prices, market analysis, and commentary. Edited and published in Hong Kong by the *Asian Wall Street Journal*.

Hoover's Company Capsules on CD-ROM. Hoover's, Inc., 1033 La Posada Dr., Suite 250 Austin, TX 78752. Phone: 800-486-8666 or (512)374-4500 Fax: (512)374-4501 E-mail: orders@hoovers.com • URL: http://www.hoovers.com • Quarterly. $349.95 per year (single-user). Provides the CD-ROM version of *Hoover's Handbook of American Business, Hoover's Handbook of Emerging Companies, Hoover's Handbook of World Business, Hoover's Guide to Computer Companies, Hoover's Guide to Media Companies, Hoover's Handbook of Private Companies,* and various regional guides. Includes more than 11,000 profiles of companies.

Hoover's Handbook of American Business: Profiles of Major U. S. Companies. Hoover's, Inc., 1033 La Posada Dr., Suite 250 Austin, TX 78752. Phone: 800-486-8666 or (512)374-4500 Fax: (512)374-4501 E-mail: orders@hoovers.com • URL: http://www.hoovers.com • $149.95. 10th revised edition. Two volumes. Provides detailed profiles of more than 700 large public and private companies, including history, executives, brand names, key competitors, and up to 10 years of financial data. Includes indexes by industry, location, executive name, company name, and brand name.

Hoover's Handbook of Emerging Companies: Profiles of America's Most Exciting Growth Enterprises. Hoover's, Inc., 1033 La Posada Dr., Suite 250 Austin, TX 78752. Phone: 800-486-8666 or (512)374-4500 Fax: (512)374-4501 E-mail: orders@hoovers.com • URL: http://www.hoovers.com • 2000. $89.95. Contains detailed profiles of 300 rapidly growing corporations. Includes indexes by industry, location, executive name, company name, and brand name.

Hoover's Handbook of Private Companies: Profiles of Major U. S. Private Enterprises. Hoover's, Inc., 1033 La Posada Dr., Suite 250 Austin, TX 78752. Phone: 800-486-8666 or (512)374-4500 Fax: (512)374-4501 E-mail: orders@

hoovers.com • URL: http://www.hoovers.com • Annual. $139.95. Contains profiles of 800 private companies and organizations. Includes indexes by industry, location, executive name, and product.

Hoover's Handbook of World Business: Profiles of Major European, Asian, Latin American, and Canadian Companies. Hoover's, Inc., 1033 La Posada Dr., Suite 250 Austin, TX 78752. Phone: 800-486-8666 or (512)374-4500 Fax: (512)374-4501 E-mail: orders@hoovers.com • URL: http://www.hoovers.com • Annual. $99.95. Contains detailed profiles of more than 300 large foreign companies. Includes indexes by industry, location, executive name, company name, and brand name.

Hoover's Masterlist of Major U. S. Companies. Hoover's, Inc., 1033 La Posada Dr., Suite 250 Austin, TX 78752. Phone: 800-486-8666 or (512)374-4500 Fax: (512)374-4501 E-mail: orders@hoovers.com • URL: http://www.hoovers.com • Biennial. $99.95. Provides brief information, including annual sales, number of employees, and chief executive, for about 5,100 U. S. companies, both public and private.

Hoover's Online. Hoover's, Inc.Phone: 800-486-8666 or (512)374-4500 Fax: (512)374-4501 URL: http://www.hoovers.com • Web site provides stock quotes, lists of companies, and a variety of business information at no charge. In-depth company profiles are available at $29.95 per month.

Horizons. Indiana University School of Business. JAI Press Inc., P.O. Box 811 Stamford, CT 06904-0811. Phone: (203)323-9606 Fax: (203)357-8446 E-mail: order@jaipress.com • URL: http://www.jaipress.com • Bimonthly. Individuals, $105.00 per year; institutions, $225.00 per year. Presents articles on issues of interest to business executives.

Horseman and Fair World: Devoted to the Trotting and Pacing Horse. Horseman Publishing Co., Inc., Insite Communications, P.O. Box 8480 Lexington, KY 40533-8480. Phone: (859)276-4026 Fax: (859)277-8100 URL: http://www.harnessracing.com/hfw/ • Weekly. $80.00 per year.

Horticultural Abstracts: Compiled from World Literature on Temperate and Tropical Fruits, Vegetables, Ornaments, Plantation Crops. Available from CABI Publishing North America, 10 E. 40th St. New York, NY 10016. Phone: 800-528-4841 or (212)481-7018 Fax: (212)686-7993 E-mail: cabi@cabi.org • URL: http://www.cabi.org • Monthly. $1,605.00 per year. Published in England by CABI Publishing. Provides worldwide coverage of the literature of fruits, vegetables, flowers, plants, and all aspects of gardens and gardening.

Horticulture: The Art of American Gardening. PRIMEDIA Consumer Magazines and Internet Group, 98 N. Washington St. Boston, MA 02114. Phone: 800-234-2415 E-mail: feedback@hortmag.com • URL: http://www.hortmag.com • 10 times a year. $28.00 per year.

The Hosiery Association.

Hosiery News. Hosiery Association, 3623 Latrobe Dr., Suite 130 Charlotte, NC 28211-2117. Phone: (704)365-0913 Fax: (704)362-2056 Monthly. Membership. Hosiery-related news including new offerings for retail, industry changes, legislative updates of hosiery-impacting laws, foreign trade and statistical information.

Hosiery Statistics. Hosiery Association, 3623 Latrobe Dr., Suite 130 Charlotte, NC 28211-2117. Phone: (704)365-0913 Fax: (704)362-2056 Annual. $50.00.

Hospital Cost Management. Prentice Hall, 240 Frisch Court Paramus, NJ 07652-5240. Phone: 800-947-7700 or (201)909-6452 Fax: 800-445-6991 URL: http://www.prenhall.com • Looseleaf. Periodic supplementation. Price on application.

Hospital Finance Almanac. Healthcare Financial Management Association, Two Westbrook Corporate Center, Suite 700 Westchester, IL 60154-5700. Phone: 800-252-4362 or (708)531-9600 Fax: 800-926-9495 or (708)531-0032 E-mail: tarya@hfma.org • URL: http://www.hfma.com • Annual. $350.00. Provides five-year data relating to the financial and operating performance of the U. S. hospital industry. A consolidation of the former *Financial Report of the Hospital Industry* and *Performance Report of the Hospital Industry*.

Hospital Home Health: The Monthly Updates for Executives and Health Care Professionals. American Health Consultants, Inc., 3525 Piedmont Rd. N.E., Bldg.6, Suite 400 Atlanta, GA 30305-5278. Phone: 800-688-2421 or (404)262-7436 Fax: (404)262-7837 E-mail: custserv@ahcpub.com • URL: http://www.ahcpub.com • Monthly. $399.00 per year. Newsletter for hospital-based home health agencies.

Hospital Pharmacist Report. Medical Economics Co., Inc., Five Paragon Dr. Montvale, NJ 07645-1742. Phone: 800-232-7379 or (201)358-7200 Fax: (201)573-8999 E-mail: customerservice@medec.com • URL: http://www.medec.com • Monthly. $39.00 per year. Covers both business and clinical topics for hospital pharmacists.

Hospital Revenue Report. United Communications Group, 11300 Rockville Pike, Suite 1100 Rockville, MD 20852-3030. Phone: (301)816-8950 Fax: (301)816-8945 E-mail: cdonoghue@ucg.com • URL: http://www.ucg.com • 25 times a year. $379.00 per year. Newsletter. Advises hospitals on how to cut costs, increase patient revenue, and maximize Medicare income. Incorporates *Health Care Marketer*.

Hospitality Financial and Technology Professionals., 11709 Boulder Lane, Suite 110 Austin, TX 78726. Phone: 800-646-4387 or (512)249-5333 Fax: (512)249-1533 E-mail: hftp@hftp.org • URL: http://www.hitecshow • Members are accounting and finance officers in the hotel, motel, casino, club, and other areas of the hospitality industry.

Hospitality Industry Managerial Accounting. Raymond S. Schmidgall. Educational Institute of the American Hotel & Motel Association, P.O. Box 1240 East Lansing, MI 48826-1240. Phone: 800-344-4381 or (517)372-8800 Fax: (517)372-5141 E-mail: info@ei-ahma.org • URL: http://www.ei.ahma.org • 1997. Fourth edition. Price on application. A reference to improve decision-making.

Hospitality Sales and Marketing Association International.

Hospitality Technology: Infosystems for Foodservice and Lodging. Edgell Communications, Inc., 10 W. Hanover Ave., Suite 107 Randolph, NJ 07869-4214. Phone: (973)895-3300 Fax: (973)895-7711 E-mail: edgell@edgellmail.com • URL: http://www.edgellcommunications.com • Monthly. $36.00 per year. Covers information technology, computer communications, and software for foodservice and lodging enterprises.

Hotel and Motel Management. Advanstar Communications, Inc., 201 E. Sandpointe Ave., Suite 600 Santa Ana, CA 92700-8700. Phone: 800-346-0085 or (714)513-8400 Fax: (714)513-8632 E-mail: Information@advanstar.com • URL: http://www.advanstar.com • 21 times a year. $45.00 per year.

Hotel and Restaurant Business. Donald E. Lundberg. John Wiley and Sons, Inc., 605 Third Ave. New York, NY 10158-0012. Phone: 800-225-5945 or (212)850-6000 Fax: (212)850-6088 E-mail: info@wiley.com • URL: http://www.wiley.com • 1994. $54.95. Sixth edition. (Hospitality, Travel and Tourism Series).

Hotel and Travel Index: The World Wide Hotel Directory. Cahners Travel Group, 500 Plaza Dr. Secaucus, NJ 07094-3626. Phone: 800-662-7776 or (201)902-2000 Fax: (201)902-1914 E-mail: corporatecommunications@cahners.com • URL: http://www.cahners.com • Quarterly. $130.00 per year. Contains concise information on more than 45,000 hotels in the U. S. and around the world. Includes 400 maps showing location of hotels and airports.

Hotel Business. ICD Publications, 45 Research Way, Suite 106 East Setauket, NY 11733-6401. Phone: (631)246-9300 Fax: (631)246-9496 E-mail: info@hotelbusiness.com • URL: http://www.hotelbusiness.com • Semimonthly. $100.00 per year. Covers management, technology, design, business trends, new products, finance, and other topics for the hotel-motel industry.

Hotel Development. Urban Land Institute, 1025 Thomas Jefferson St., N. W., Suite 500 W. Washington, DC 20007-5201. Phone: 800-321-5011 or (202)624-7000 Fax: (202)624-7140 E-mail: bookstore@uli.org • URL: http://www.uli.org • 1996. $59.95. Provides practical information on developing, acquiring, and renovating hotels in urban areas. Covers market analysis, financing, construction, and management. Includes case studies.

Hotels. International Hotel Association. Cahners Business Information, 1350 E. Touhy Ave. Des Plaines, IL 60018-5080. Phone: 800-662-7776 or (847)635-8800 Fax: (847)635-6856 E-mail: corporatecommunications@cahners.com • URL: http://www.cahners.com • Monthly. Free to qualified personnel; others, $75.00 per year.

Hourly Precipitation Data. U.S. National Climatic Data Center, National Oceanic and Atmospheric Administration, U.S. Dept. of Commerce, Federal Bldg., Room 120, 151 Patton Ave. Ashville, NC 28801-5001. Phone: (704)271-4476 E-mail: orders@ncdc.noaa.gov • URL: http://www.ncdc.noaa.gov • Monthly. Published separately for 41 states.

House Painting. Entrepreneur Media, Inc., 2445 McCabe Way Irvine, CA 92614. Phone: 800-421-2300 or (949)261-2325 Fax: (949)261-0234 E-mail: entmag@entrepreneur.com • URL: http://www.entrepreneur.com • Looseleaf. $59.50. A practical guide to starting a house painting business. Covers profit potential, start-up costs, market size evaluation, owner's time required, pricing, accounting, advertising, promotion, etc. (Start-Up Business Guide No. E1249.)

Household and Personal Products Industry - Buyers Guide. Rodman Publications, P.O. Box 555 Ramsey, NJ 07446. Phone: (201)825-2552 Fax: (201)825-0553 E-mail: rpubl@aol.com • URL: http://www.happi.com • Annual. $12.00. Lists of suppliers to manufacturers of cosmetics, toiletries, soaps, detergents, and related household and personal products.

Household and Personal Products Industry Contract Packaging and Private Label Directory. Rodman Publications, P.O. Box 555 Ramsey, NJ 07446. Phone: (201)825-2552 Fax: (201)825-0553 E-mail: rpubl@aol.com • URL: http://www.happi.com • Annual. $12.00. Provides information on about 450 companies offering private label or contract packaged household and personal care products, such as detergents, cosmetics, polishes, insecticides, and various aerosol items.

Household and Personal Products Industry: The Magazine for the Detergent, Soap, Cosmetic and Toiletry, Wax, Polish and Aerosol Industries. Rodman Publications, 17 S. Franklin Parkway Ramsey, NJ 07446. Phone: (201)825-2552 Fax: (201)825-0553 E-mail: rpubl@aol.com • URL: http://www.happi.com • Monthly. $48.00 per year. Covers marketing, packaging, production, technical innovations, private label developments, and aerosol packaging for soap, detergents, cosmetics, insecticides, and a variety of other household products.

Household Cleaning Agents. Available from MarketResearch.com, 641 Ave. of the Americas, Third Floor New York, NY 10011. Phone: 800-298-5699 or (212)807-2629 Fax: (212)807-2716 E-mail: order@marketresearch.com • URL: http://www.marketresearch.com • 1998. $5,900.00. Published by Euromonitor Publications Ltd. Provides consumer market data and forecasts to 2002 for the United States, the United Kingdom, Germany, France, and Italy. Covers dishwashing detergents, floor cleaning products, scourers, polishes, bleaching products, etc.

Household Spending: Who Spends How Much On What. Hoai Tran. New Strategist Publications, Inc., 120 W. State St., 4th Fl. Ithaca, NY 14851. Phone: 800-848-0842 or (607)273-0913 Fax: (607)277-5009 E-mail: demographics@newstrategist.com • URL: http://www.newstrategist.com • 1999. $94.95. Fifth edition. Gives facts about the buying habits of U. S. consumers according to income, age, household type, and household size. Includes spending data for about 1,000 products and services.

Housewares Retail Directory. American Business Directories, P.O. Box 27347 Omaha, NE 68127. Phone: 800-555-6124 or (402)593-4600 Fax: (402)331-5481 E-mail: internet@infousa.com • URL: http://www.abii.com • Annual. Price on application. A listing of about 3,103 retailers. Compiled from telephone company yellow pages.

Housing Affairs Letter: The Weekly Washington Report on Housing. Community Services Development, Inc. C D Publications, 8204 Fenton St. Silver Springs, MD 20910. Phone: (301)588-6380 Fax: (301)588-0519 E-mail: hal@cdpublications.com • Weekly. $409.00 per year.

Housing Affairs Letter: Weekly Washington Report on Housing. Community Development Services, Inc. CD Publications, 8204 Fenton St. Silver Spring, MD 20910-2889. Phone: 800-666-6380 or (301)588-6380 Fax: (301)588-6385 E-mail: cdpubs@clark.net • Weekly. $409.00 per year. Newsletter. Covers mortgage activity news, including forecasts of mortgage rates.

Housing and Urban Development Trends: Annual Summary. U.S. Department of Housing and Urban Development, 451 Seventh St., S.W. Washington, DC 20410. Phone: (202)708-0980 Annual.

Housing Discrimination: Law and Litigation. Robert G. Schwemm. West Group, 610 Opperman Dr. Eagan, MN 55123. Phone: 800-328-4880 or (651)687-7000 Fax: 800-213-2323 or (651)687-5827 URL: http://www.westgroup.com • Looseleaf. $130.00. Periodic supplementation. Covers provisions of the Fair Housing Act and related topics. (Civil Rights Series).

Housing Market Report: Forecasting Home Sales and Construction Trends Since 1976. Community Development Services, Inc., CD Publications, 8204 Fenton St. Silver Springs, MD 20910-2889. Phone: (301)588-6380 Fax: (301)588-6385 E-mail: cdpubs@clark.net • Semimonthly. $347.00 per year. Real estate outlook for U.S. housing markets.

Housing Starts. U.S. Bureau of the Census. Available from U.S. Government Printing Office, Washington, DC 20402. Phone: (202)512-1800 Fax: (202)512-2250 E-mail: gpoaccess@gpo.gov • URL: http://www.access.gpo.gov • Monthly. $39.00 per year. Construction Reports: C-20.

Housing Statistics of the United States. Patrick A. Simmons, editor. Bernan Press, 4611-F Assembly Dr. Lanham, MD 20706-4391. Phone: 800-274-4447 or (301)459-7666 Fax: 800-865-3450 or (301)459-0056 E-mail: info@bernan.com • URL: http://www.bernan.com • 2000. $74.00. Third edition. (Bernan Press U.S. Data Book Series).

Housing the Elderly Report. Community Development Services, Inc. CD Publications, 8204 Fenton St. Silver Spring, MD 20910-2889. Phone: 800-666-6380 or (301)588-6380 Fax: (301)588-0519 E-mail: her@cdpublications.com • Monthly. $197.00 per year. Newsletter. Edited for retirement communities, apartment projects, and nursing homes. Covers news relative to business and property management issues.

How Advertising Works: The Role of Research. John P. Jones, editor. Sage Publications, Inc., 2455 Teller Rd. Thousand Oaks, CA 91320. Phone: (805)499-0721 Fax: (805)499-0871 E-mail: info@sagepub.com • URL: http://www.sagepub.com • 1998. $74.00. Includes sections entitled "Research Before the Advertising Runs" and "Research After the Advertising Has Run."

How Consumers Pick a Hotel: Strategic Segmentation and Target Marketing. Dennis J. Cahill. The Haworth Press, Inc., 10 Alice St. Binghamton, NY 13904-1580. Phone: 800-429-6784 or (607)722-5857 Fax: 800-895-0582 or (607)722-1424 E-mail: getinfo@haworthpressinc.com • URL: http://www.haworthpressinc.com • 1997. $39.95.

How Our Laws Are Made. Available from U. S. Government Printing Office, Washington, DC 20402. Phone: (202)512-1800 Fax: (202)512-2250 E-mail: gpoaccess@gpo.gov • URL: http://www.access.gpo.gov • 2000. $3.75. 22nd edition. Issued by U. S. House of Representatives.

How Products Are Made. The Gale Group, 27500 Drake Rd. Farmington Hills, MI 48331-3535. Phone: 800-877-GALE or (248)699-GALE Fax: 800-414-5043 or (248)699-8069 E-mail: galeord@galegroup.com • URL: http://www.galegroup.com • Dates vary. Three volumes. $99.00 per volume. Provides easy-to-read, step-by-step descriptions of how approximately 100 different products are manufactured. Items are of all kinds, both mechanical and non-mechanical.

How to Avoid Financial Fraud. C. Edgar Murray. American Institute for Economic Research, Division St. Great Barrington, MA 01230-1000. Phone: (413)528-1216 Fax: (413)528-0103 E-mail: info@aier.org • URL: http://www.aier.org • 1999. $3.00. Provides concise discussions of fraud victims, perpetrators, and sales tactics. Also includes practical advice on "Selecting a Financial Planner" and "Selecting a Broker." Contains a directory of state securities regulators and a glossary defining various fraudulant financial schemes. (Economic Education Bulletin.)

How to Avoid Liability: The Information Professionals' Guide to Negligence and Warrant Risks. T. R. Halvorson. Burwell Enterprises, Inc., 5619 Plumtree Dr. Dallas, TX 75252. Phone: (281)537-9051 Fax: (281)537-8332 E-mail: burwellinfo@burwellinc.com • URL: http://www.burwellinc.com • 1998. $24.50. Second edition. Provides legal advice, cases, and decisions relating to information brokers and others in the information business.

How To Be a Manager: A Practical Guide to Tips and Techniques. Robert W. Gallant. Lewis Publishers, 2000 Corporate Blvd., N.W. Boca Raton, FL 33431. Phone: 800-272-7737 or (561)994-0555 Fax: 800-374-3401 or (561)998-9114 1991. $49.95. A concise handbook of principles, techniques, and methods of problem solving. Covers negotiation, discipline, management ethics, training, and other subjects.

How to Be an Effective Sales Manager. American Management Association Extension Institute, P.O. Box 1026 Saranac Lake, NY 12983-9957. Phone: 800-262-9699 or (518)891-1500 Fax: (518)891-0368 Looseleaf. $130.00. Self-study course. Emphasis is on practical explanations, examples, and problem solving. Quizzes and a case study are included.

How to Be the Life of the Podium: Openers, Closers and Everything in Between to Keep Them Listening. Sylvia Simmons. AMACOM, 1601 Broadway, 12th Fl. New York, NY 10019. Phone: 800-262-9699 or (212)586-8100 Fax: (212)903-8168 E-mail: custmserv@amanet.org • URL: http://www.amanet.org • 1992. $15.95. A collection of 1,000 quips, quotes, analogies, stories, proverbs, and one-liners.

How to Become a Successful Consultant in Your Own Field. Hubert Bermont. Prima Publishing, 3875 Atherton Rd. Rocklin, CA 95765. Phone: (916)787-7000 Fax: (916)787-7001 URL: http://www.primapublishing.com • 1991. $21.95. Third enlarged revised edition.

How to Build Wealth with Tax-Sheltered Investments. Kerry Anne Lynch. American Institute for Economic Research, Division St. Great Barrington, MA 01230-1000. Phone: (413)528-1216 Fax: (413)528-0103 E-mail: info@aier.org • URL: http://www.aier.org • 2000. $6.00. Provides practical information on conservative tax shelters, including defined-contribution pension plans, individual retirement accounts, Keogh plans, U. S. savings bonds, municipal bonds, and various kinds of annuities: deferred, variable-rate, immediate, and foreign-currency. (Economic Education Bulletin.)

How to Buy a House, Condo, or Co-op. Jean C. Thomsett. Consumers Union of the United States, Inc., 101 Truman Ave. Yonkers, NY 10703-1057. Phone: 800-234-1645 or (914)378-2000 Fax: (914)378-2900 URL: http://www.consumerreports.org • 1996. $84.75. Fifth edition.

How to Buy and Understand Refracting Telescopes. Jordan Levenson. Levenson Press, P.O. Box 19606 Los Angeles, CA 90019. 1991. $43.50. Third edition.

How to Buy Stocks. Louis Engel and Henry L. Hecht. Little Brown and Co., Inc., 1271 Ave. of the Americas New York, NY 10020. Phone: 800-343-9204 or (212)522-8700 Fax: 800-286-9741 or (202)522-2067 E-mail: cust.service@littlebrown.com • 1994. $16.00. Eighth edition.

How to Charter a Commercial Bank. Douglas V. Austin and others. CCH, Inc., 4025 West Peterson Ave. Chicago, IL 60646-6085. Phone: 800-248-3248 or (773)866-6000 Fax: 800-224-8299 or (773)866-3608 URL: http://www.cch.com • 1999. $350.00. Provides detailed information on how to start a commercial bank, including both technical and practical requirements.

How to Choose and Use Temporary Services. Bill Lewis and Nancy H. Molloy. Books on Demand, 200 N. Zeeb Rd. Ann Arbor, MI 48106-1346. Phone: 800-521-0600 or (734)761-4700 Fax: (734)665-5022 E-mail: info@umi.com • URL: http://www.lib.umi.com • 1991. $80.60. Tells what to expect from temporary services and their workers.

How to Conduct Training Seminars: A Complete Reference Guide for Training Managers. Lawrence S. Munson. McGraw-Hill, 1221 Ave. of the Americas New York, NY 10020. Phone: 800-722-4726 or (212)904-2000 Fax: (212)904-2072 E-mail: customer.service@mcgraw-hill.com • URL: http://www.mcgraw-hill.com • 1992. $34.95. Second edition.

How to Cover the Gaps in Medicare: Health Insurance and Long-Term Care Options for the Retired. Robert A. Gilmour. American Institute for Economic Research, Division St. Great Barrington, MA 01230-1000. Phone: (413)528-1216 Fax: (413)528-0103 E-mail: info@aier.org • URL: http://www.aier.org • 2000. $5.00. 12th revised edition. Four parts: "The Medicare Quandry," "How to Protect Yourself Against the Medigap," "Long-Term Care Options", and "End-of-Life Decisions" (living wills). Includes discussions of long-term care insurance, retirement communities, and HMO Medicare insurance, (Economic Education Bulletin Series, No. 10).

How to Cut Your Company's Health Care Costs. George Halvorson. Prentice Hall, 240 Frisch Court Paramus, NJ 07652-5240. Phone: 800-947-7700 or (201)909-6200 Fax: 800-445-6991 or (201)909-6361 URL: http://www.prenhall.com • 1987. $27.50.

How to Design and Install Management Incentive Compensation Plans: A Practical Guide to Installing Performance Bonus Plans. Dale Arahood. Dale Arahood and Associates, 213 Wesley St.,Suite 203 Wheaton, IL 60187-5135. Phone: (603)653-5443 Fax: (603)653-5462 E-mail: compub98@aol.com • URL: http://www.memebers.aol.com/compub98 • 1996. $129.00. Revised edition. "This book focuses on how pay should be determined rather than how much should be paid."

How to Develop a Personnel Policy Manual. Joseph Lawson. AMACOM, 1601 Broadway, 12th Fl. New York, NY 10019. Phone: 800-262-9699 or (212)586-8100 Fax: (212)903-8168 E-mail: custmserv@amanet.org • URL: http://www.amanet.org • 1998. $75.00. Sixth edition.

How to Develop an Employee Handbook. Joseph W. Lawson. AMACOM, 1601 Broadway, 12th Fl. New York, NY 10019. Phone: 800-262-9699 or (212)586-8100 Fax: (212)903-8168 E-mail: custmserv@amanet.org • URL: http://www.amanet.org • 1997. $75.00. Second edition. Includes sample handbooks, personnel policy statements, and forms.

How to Develop and Promote Successful Seminars and Workshops: A Definitive Guide to Creating and Marketing Seminars, Workshops, Classes, and Conferences. Howard L. Shenson. John Wiley and Sons, Inc., 605 Third Ave. New York, NY 10158-0012. Phone: 800-225-5945 or (212)850-6000 Fax: (212)850-6088 E-mail: info@wiley.com • URL: http://www.wiley.com • 1990. $99.50.

How to Develop Multilevel Marketing Sales. Entrepreneur Media, Inc., 2445 McCabe Way Irvine, CA 92614. Phone: 800-421-2300 or (949)261-2325 Fax: (949)261-0234 E-mail: entmag@entrepreneur.com • URL: http://www.entrepreneur.com • Looseleaf. $59.50. A practical guide to starting a multilevel marketing business. Covers profit potential, start-up costs, owner's time required, pricing, accounting, advertising, market size evaluation, promotion, etc. (Start-Up Business Guide No. E1222.)

How to Develop Successful Sales Promotions. American Management Association Extension Institute, P.O. Box 1026 Saranac Lake, NY 12983-9957. Phone: 800-262-9699 or (518)891-1500 Fax: (518)891-0368 Looseleaf. $130.00. Self-study course. Emphasis is on practical explanations, examples, and problem solving. Quizzes and a case study are included.

How to Do a Performance Appraisal: A Guide for Managers and Professionals. William S. Swan. John Wiley and Sons, Inc., 605 Third Ave. New York, NY 10158-0012. Phone: 800-225-5945 or (212)850-6000 Fax: (212)850-6088 E-mail: info@wiley.com • URL: http://www.wiley.com • 1991. $29.95. Contains advice on face-to-face discussions and offers guidelines on legal aspects.

How to Evaluate a New Product. American Management Association Extension Institute, P.O. Box 1026 Saranac Lake, NY 12983-9957. Phone: 800-262-9699 or (518)891-1500 Fax: (518)891-0368 Looseleaf. $130.00. Self-study course. Emphasis is on practical explanations, examples, and problem solving. Quizzes are included.

How to Find Chemical Information: A Guide for Practicing Chemists, Educators, and Students. Robert E. Maizell. John Wiley and Sons, Inc., 605 Third Ave. New York, NY 10158-0012. Phone: 800-526-5368 or (212)850-6000 Fax: (212)850-6088 E-mail: info@wiley.com • URL: http://www.wiley.com • 1998. $69.95. Third edition.

How to Find Information About AIDS. Jeffrey T. Huber, editor. Haworth Press, Inc., 10 Alice St. Binghamton, NY 13904-1580. Phone: 800-429-6784 or (607)722-5857 Fax: 800-895-0582 or (607)722-1424 E-mail: getinfo@haworthpressinc.com • URL: http://www.haworthpressinc.com • 1992. $49.95. Second edition. Includes print, electronic, and organizational sources of information. Local and national hotlines are listed.

How To Find Information About Companies: The Corporate Intelligence Source Book. Washington Researchers, 1655 N. Fort Myer Dr., Suite 800 Arlington, VA 22209. Phone: (703)527-4585 Fax: (703)312-2863 E-mail: research@researchers.com • URL: http://www.researchers.com/pub • Annual. $885.00. In three parts. $395.00 per volume. In part one, over 9,000 sources of corporate intelligence, including federal, state and local repositories of company filings, individual industry experts, published sources, databases, CD-Rom products, and corporate research services. Parts two and three provide guidelines for company research.

How to Find Information About Private Companies. Washington Researchers, 1655 N. Fort Myer Dr., Suite 800 Arlington, VA 22209. Phone: (703)527-4585 Fax: (703)312-2863 E-mail: researchers@researchers.com • URL: http://www.researchers.com/pub • Irregular. $145.00. Organizations, publications, and individuals that collect information on private companies.

How to Find Market Research Online. Robert I. Berkman. MarketResearch.com, 641 Ave. of the Americas, Third Floor New York, NY 10011. Phone: 800-298-5699 or (212)807-2629 Fax: (212)807-2716 E-mail: order@marketresearch.com • URL: http://www.marketresearch.com • Looseleaf. $182.50, including updates for one year. Analyzes and compares the online products of 80 market research publishers. Describes popular Internet search engines and provides information on useful World Wide Web sites.

How to Find Out About Financial Aid: 1998-2000. Gail A. Schlachter. Reference Service Press, 5000 Windplay Dr., Suite 4 El Dorado Hills, CA 95762. Phone: (916)939-9620 Fax: (916)939-9626 E-mail: findaid@aol.com • URL: http://www.rspfunding.com • 2001. $37.50. Annotated bibliography of student aid directories. Author, title, subject, and geographical indexes.

How to Form a Nonprofit Corporation. Anthony Mancuso. Nolo.com, 950 Parker St. Berkeley, CA 94710. Phone: 800-992-6656 or (510)549-1976 Fax: (510)548-5902 E-mail: cs@nolo.com • URL: http://www.nolo.com • 1997. $39.95. Fourth edition.

How to Form Your Own Corporation Without a Lawyer for Under $75.00. Ted Nicholas and Sean P. Melvin. Dearborn Financial Publishing, 155 North Wacker Drive Chicago, IL 60606-1719. Phone: 800-245-2665 or (312)836-4400 Fax: (312)836-9958 URL: http://www.dearborn.com • 1999. $19.95. 26th edition.

How to Get Happily Published: Complete and Candid Guide. Judith Appelbaum. HarperCollins Publishers, 10 E. 53rd St. New York, NY 10022-5299. Phone: 800-242-7737 or (212)207-7000 Fax: 800-822-4090 or (212)207-7145 URL: http://www.harpercollins.com • 1998. $14.00. Fifth edition. Provides advice for writers on dealing with book and magazine publishers.

How to Get Results from Interviewing: A Practical Guide for Operating Management. James M. Black. Krieger Publishing Co., P.O. Box 9542 Melbourne, FL 32902-9542. Phone: 800-724-0025 or (321)724-9542 Fax: (321)951-3671 E-mail: info@krieger-publishing.com • URL: http://www.krieger-publishing.com • 1982. $22.00. Reprint of 1970 edition.

How to Get the Most Out of Trade Shows. Steve Miller. NTC/Contemporary Publishing, P.O. Box 545 Blacklick, OH 43004. Phone: 800-338-3987 or (614)755-4151 Fax: (614)755-5645 E-mail: ntcpub@mcgraw-hill.com • URL: http://www.ntc-cb.com • 1999. $29.95. Third revised edition. (NTC Business Book Series).

How to Incorporate: A Handbook for Entrepreneurs and Professionals. Michael Diamond. John Wiley and Sons, Inc., 605 Third Ave. New York, NY 10158-0012. Phone: 800-225-5945 or (212)850-6000 Fax: (212)850-6088 E-mail: info@wiley.com • URL: http://www.wiley.com • 1996. $49.95. Third edition.

How to Interview Effectively. American Management Association Extension Institute, P.O. Box 1026 Saranac Lake, NY 12983-9957. Phone: 800-262-9699 or (518)891-1500 Fax: (518)891-0368 URL: http://www.amanet.org • Looseleaf. $110.00. Self-study course on employment, performance, evaluation, disciplinary, and exit interviewing. Emphasis is on practical explanations, examples, and problem solving. Quizzes and a case study are included.

How to Invest in Real Estate Using Free Money. Laurie Blum. John Wiley and Sons, Inc., 605 Third Ave. New York, NY 10158-0012. Phone: 800-225-5945 or (212)850-6000 Fax: (212)850-6068 E-mail: info@wiley.com • URL: http://www.wiley.com • 1991. $89.95.

How to Invest in Your First Works of Art: A Guide for the New Collector. John Carlin. Yarrow Press, 101 Monterey Ave. Pelham, NY 10803. Phone: (914)738-3884 1990. $11.95.

How to Invest Wisely. Lawrence S. Pratt. American Institute for Economic Research, Division St. Great Barrington, MA 01230-1000. Phone: (413)528-1216 Fax: (413)528-0103 E-mail: info@aier.org • URL: http://www.aier.org • 1998. $9.00. Presents a conservative policy of investing, with emphasis on dividend-paying common stocks. Gold and other inflation hedges are compared. Includes a reprint of *Toward an Optimal Stock Selection Strategy* (1997). (Economic Education Bulletin.)

How to Lie with Statistics. Darrell Huff. W. W. Norton and Co., Inc., 500 Fifth Ave. New York, NY 10110. Phone: 800-223-2584 or (212)354-5500 Fax: (212)869-0856 E-mail: webmaster@wwnorton.com • URL: http://www.norton.com • 1993. $8.95.

How to Make Big Money in Multilevel Marketing. Dave Roller. Prentice Hall, 240 Frisch Court Paramus, NJ 07652-5240. Phone: 800-947-7700 or (201)909-6200 Fax: 800-445-6991 or (201)909-6361 URL: http://www.prenhall.com • 1989. $14.95.

How to Make It Big as a Consultant. William A. Cohen. AMACOM, 1601 Broadway, 12th Fl. New York, NY 10019. Phone: 800-262-9699 or (212)586-8100 Fax: (212)903-8168 E-mail: custmserv@amanet.org • URL: http://www.amanet.org • 2001. $17.95. Third edition. Step-by-step instructions for finding clients, writing proposals, pricing services, etc.

How to Make it Big in the Seminar Business. Paul Karasik. McGraw-Hill, 1221 Ave. of the Americas New York, NY 10020. Phone: 800-722-4726 or (212)904-2000 Fax: (212)904-2072 E-mail: customer.service@mcgraw-hill.com • URL: http://www.mcgraw-hill.com • 1995. $15.95. Covers the organizing and marketing of seminars or workshops, including fee determination, promotion, scheduling, and evaluation.

How to Make Money in Cake Decorating: Owning and Operating a Successful Business in Your Home. Del Carnes. Deco-Press Publishing Co., 5660 Olde Wadsworth Blvd. Arvada, CO 80002. Phone: (303)424-0100 Fax: (303)360-9348 1987. $10.99 Revised edition. (How to Profit Series: volume one).

How to Make Tax-Saving Gifts. William S. Moore. American Institute for Economic Research, Division St. Great Barrington, MA 01230. Phone: (413)528-1216 Fax: (413)528-0103 E-mail: info@aier.org • URL: http://www.aier.org • 1999. $3.00. Provides practical advice on the tax consequences of gifts, including gifts for college tuition expenses, gifts of real estate, charitable gifts, and the use of life insurance trusts. (Economic Education Bulletin.)

How to Make the Right Leasing Decisions. American Management Association Extension Institute, P.O. Box 1026 Saranac Lake, NY 12983-9957. Phone: 800-262-9699 or (518)891-1500 Fax: (518)891-0368 Looseleaf. $110.00. Self-study course. Emphasis is on practical explanations, examples, and problem solving. Quizzes and a case study are included.

How to Manage a Successful Catering Business. Manfred Ketterer. John Wiley and Sons, Inc., 605 Third Ave. New York, NY 10158-0012. Phone: 800-225-5945 or (212)850-6000 Fax: (212)850-6068 E-mail: info@wiley.com • URL: http://www.wiley.com • 1990. $54.95. Second edition.

How to Manage Conflict in the Organization. American Management Association Extension Institute, P.O. Box 1026 Saranac Lake, NY 12983-9957. Phone: 800-262-9699 or (518)891-1500 Fax: (518)891-0368 Looseleaf. $110.00. Self-study course. Emphasis is on practical explanations, examples, and problem solving. Quizzes and a case study are included.

How to Manage Corporate Cash. American Management Association Extension Institute, P.O. Box 1026 Saranac Lake, NY 12983-9957. Phone: 800-262-9699 or (518)891-1500 Fax: (518)891-0368 Looseleaf. $110.00. Self-study course. Emphasis is on practical explanations, examples, and problem solving. Quizzes and a case study are included.

How to Manage Corporate Cash Effectively. Joseph E. Finnerty. AMACOM, 1601 Broadway, 12th Fl. New York, NY 10019. Phone: 800-262-9699 or (212)586-8100 Fax: (212)903-8168 E-mail: custmserv@amanet.org • URL: http://www.amanet.org • 1991. $59.95. A practical approach to cash flow problems.

How to Manage Training: A Guide to Administration, Design and Delivery. Carolyn Nilson. AMACOM, 1601 Broadway, 12th Fl. New York, NY 10019. Phone: 800-262-9699 or (212)586-8100 Fax: (212)903-8168 E-mail: custmserv.amanet.org • URL: http://www.amanet.org • 1991. $69.95. Looseleaf service. Presents ideas and techniques for cost-effective training.

How to Manage Your Law Office. Matthew Bender & Co., Inc., Two Park Ave. New York, NY 10016. Phone: 800-223-1940 or (212)448-2000 Fax: (212)244-3188 E-mail: international@bender.com • URL: http://www.bender.com • $210.00 Two looseleaf volumes. Periodic supplementation.

How to Obtain Government Contracts. Entrepreneur Media, Inc., 2445 McCabe Way Irvine, CA 92614. Phone: 800-421-2300 or (949)261-2325 Fax: (949)261-0234 E-mail: entmag@entrepreneur.com • URL: http://www.entrepreneur.com • Looseleaf. $59.50. A practical guide to acquiring and negotiating government contracts. (Start-Up Business Guide No. E1227.)

How to Organize a Babysitting Cooperative and Get Some Free Time Away From the Kids. Carole T. Meyers. Carousel Press, P.O. Box 6038 Berkeley, CA 94706-0038. Phone: 800-788-3123 or (510)527-5849 Fax: (510)528-3444 E-mail: carous4659@aol.com • URL: http://www.carousel-press.com • 1976. $6.95.

How to Plan and Manage Warehouse Operations. American Management Association Extension Institute, P.O. Box 1026 Saranac Lake, NY 12983-9957. Phone: 800-262-9699 or (518)891-1500 Fax: (518)891-0368 Looseleaf. $130.00. Self-study course. Emphasis is on practical explanations, examples, and problem solving. Quizzes and a case study are included.

How to Plan for a Secure Retirement. Elias Zuckerman and others. Consumer Reports Books, 101 Truman Ave. Yonkers, NY 10703. Phone: 800-500-9760 or (914)378-2000 Fax: (914)378-2925 URL: http://www.consumerreports.org • 2000. $29.95. Covers pension plans, health insurance, estate planning, retirement communities, and related topics. (Consumer Reports Money Guide.)

How to Plan Your Retirement Years. Kerry A. Lynch, editor. American Institute for Economic Research, Division St. Great Barrington, MA 01230-1000. Phone: (413)528-1216 Fax: (413)528-0103 E-mail: info@aier.org • URL: http://www.aier.org • 1996. $6.00. Provides concise, conservative advice on retirement planning, savings, pensions, IRAs, Keogh plans, annuities, and making effective use of social security. (Economic Education Bulletin.)

How to Practice Before the New IRS. Robert S. Schriebman. CCH, Inc., 4025 W. Peterson Ave. Chicago, IL 60646-6085. Phone: 800-248-3248 or (773)866-6000 Fax: 800-224-8299 or (773)866-3608 URL: http://www.cch.com • 1999. $115.00. Reflects changes made by the IRS Restructuring and Reform Act of 1998. Covers audits, appeals, tax court basics, refunds, penalties, etc., for tax professionals.

How to Prepare an Initial Public Offering. Practising Law Institute, 810 Seventh Ave. New York, NY 10019-5818. Phone: 800-260-4754 or (212)824-5700 Fax: (212)265-4742 E-mail: info@pli.edu • URL: http://www.pli.edu • 1997. $129.00. (Corporate Law and Practice Course Handbook Series).

How to Produce Creative Advertising: Traditional Techniques and Computer Applications. Thomas Bivins and Ann Keding. NTC/Contemporary Publishing, P.O. Box 545 Blacklick, OH 43004. Phone: 800-338-3987 or (614)755-4151 Fax: (614)755-5645 E-mail: ntcpub@mcgraw-hill.com • URL: http://www.ntc-cb.com • 1993. $37.95. Covers copywriting, advertising design, and the use of desktop publishing techniques in advertising. (NTC Business Book Series).

How to Produce Creative Publications: Traditional Techniques and Computer Applications. Thomas Bivins and William E. Ryan. NTC/Contemporary Publishing, P.O. Box 545 Blacklick, OH 43004. Phone: 800-338-3987 or (614)755-4151 Fax: (614)755-5645 E-mail: ntcpub@mcgraw-hill.com • URL: http://www.ntc-cb.com • 1994. $32.95. A practical guide to the writing, designing, and production of magazines, annual reports, brochures, and newsletters by traditional methods and by desktop publishing.

How to Promote, Publicize, and Advertise Your Growing Business: Getting the Word Out Without Spending a Fortune. Kim Baker and Sunny Baker. John Wiley and Sons, Inc., 605 Third Ave. New York, NY 10158-0012. Phone: 800-225-5945 or (212)850-6000 Fax: (212)850-6088 E-mail: info@wiley.com • URL: http://www.wiley.com • 1992. $107.50.

How to Read a Financial Report: Wringing Cash Flow and Other Vital Signs Out of the Numbers. John A. Tracy. John Wiley and Sons, Inc., 605 Third Ave. New York, NY 10158-0012. Phone: 800-526-5368 or (212)850-6000 Fax: (212)850-6088 E-mail: info@wiley.com • URL: http://www.wiley.com • 1999. $29.95. Fifth edition.

How to Recruit and Select Successful Salesmen. Ashgate Publishing Co., Old Post Rd. Brookfield, VT 05036. Phone: 800-535-9544 or (802)276-3162 Fax: (802)276-3837 E-mail: info@ashgate.com • URL: http://www.ashgate.com • 1983. $78.95. Revised edition. Published by Gower in England.

How to Register Copyrights and Protect Them. Robert B. Chickering and Susan Hartman. Available from Gale Group, 27500 Drake Rd. Farmington Hills, MI 48331-3535. Phone: 800-877-4253 or (248)699-4253 Fax: 800-414-5043 E-mail: galeord@galegroup.com • URL: http://www.galegroup.com • 1981. $12.95.

How to Research, Write, and Package Administrative Manuals. Leo R. Lunine. AMACOM, 1601 Broadway, 12th Fl. New York, NY 10019. Phone: 800-262-9699 or (212)586-8100 Fax: (212)903-8168 E-mail: custmserv@amanet.org • URL: http://www.amanet.org • 1985. $75.00.

How to Run a Small Business. Jacob K. Lasser. McGraw-Hill, 1221 Ave. of the Americas New York, NY 10020. Phone: 800-722-4726 or (212)904-2000 Fax: (212)904-2072 E-mail: customer.service@mcgraw-hill.com • URL: http://www.mcgraw-hill.com • 1993. $27.95. Seventh edition.

How to Run Better Business Meetings: A Reference Guide for Managers. McGraw-Hill, 1221 Ave. of the Americas New York, NY 10020. Phone: 800-722-4726 or (212)904-2000 Fax: (212)904-2072 E-mail: customer.service@mcgraw-hill.com • URL: http://www.mcgraw-hill.com • 1987. Price on application. Compiled by the 3M Meeting Management Team. Covers the planning, formatting, and executing of various kinds of business meetings. Charts, checklists, diagrams, and case studies are included.

How to Save Time and Taxes in Handling Estates. Matthew Bender & Co., Inc., Two Park Ave. New York, NY 10016. Phone: 800-223-1940 or (212)448-2000 Fax: (212)244-3188 E-mail: international@bender.com • URL: http://www.bender.com • $235.00. Looseleaf servie. Periodic supplementation. (How to Save Time and Taxes Series).

How to Save Time and Taxes Preparing Fiduciary Income Tax Returns: Federal and State. Matthew Bender & Co., Inc., Two Park Ave. New York, NY 10016. Phone: 800-223-1940 or (212)448-2000 Fax: (212)244-3188 E-mail: international@bender.com • URL: http://www.bender.com • $230.00. Looseleaf service. Periodic supplementation. (How to Save Time and Taxes Series).

How to Save Time and Taxes Preparing the Federal Partnership Return. Matthew Bender & Co., Inc., Two Park Ave. New York, NY 10016. Phone: 800-223-1940 or (212)448-2000 Fax: (212)244-3188 E-mail: international@bender.com • URL: http://www.bender.com • Looseleaf. Price on application. Periodic supplementation. (How to Save Time and Taxes Series).

How to Sell Your Business for More Money. Gary Schine. Consultants Press, PO Box 599 Waterville, ME 04903. Phone: 800-274-3476 or (207)873-0493 Fax: (207)873-5999 E-mail: vigue@mint.net • 1991. $29.95.

How to Sell Your Home for Top Dollar. Michael C. Thomsett. McGraw-Hill Professional, 1221 Ave. of the Americas New York, NY 10020. Phone: 800-722-4726 or (212)904-2000 Fax: (212)904-2072 E-mail: customer.service@mcgraw-hill.com • URL: http://www.mcgraw-hill.com • 1989. $13.00. (One Hour Guides Series).

How to Set Up a Qualified Pension Plan Practice. American Management Association Extension Institute, P.O. Box 1026 Saranac Lake, NY 12983-9957. Phone: 800-262-9699 or (518)891-1500 Fax: (518)891-0368 URL: http://www.amanet.org • Looseleaf. $130.00. Self-study course. Emphasis is on practical explanations, examples, and problem solving. Quizzes and a case study are included. Covers pension plan consulting and administration for small and medium-sized companies.

How to Start and Operate a Mail Order Business. Julian L. Simon. McGraw-Hill, 1221 Ave of the Americas New York, NY 10020. Phone: 800-722-4726 or (212)904-2000 Fax: (212)904-2072 E-mail: customer.service@mcgraw-hill.com • URL: http://www.mcgraw-hill.com • 1991. $42.95. Fifth edition.

How to Start Your Own School. Robert Love. Jameson Books, Inc., P.O. Box 738 Ottawa, IL 61350. Phone: 800-426-1357 or (815)434-7905 Fax: (815)434-7907 E-mail: 72557.3635@compuserve.com • 1973. $1.95.

How to Succeed as an Independent Consultant. Herman Holtz. John Wiley and Sons, Inc., 605 Third Ave. New York, NY 10158-0012. Phone: 800-225-5945 or (212)850-6000 Fax: (212)850-6088 E-mail: info@wiley.com • URL: http://www.wiley.com • 1993. $34.95. Third edition. Covers a wide variety of marketing, financial, professional, and ethical issues for consultants. Includes bibliographic and organizational information.

How to Take the Fog Out of Business Writing. Robert Gunning and Richard A. Kallan. Dartnell Corp., 350 Hiatt Dr. Palm Beach, FL 33418. Phone: 800-621-5463 or (561)622-6520 Fax: (561)622-2423 E-mail: custserv@lrp.com • URL: http://www.dartnellcorp.com • 1994. $12.95. Includes "The 10 Principles of Clear Statement."

How to Use Credit Wisely. American Institute for Economic Research, Division St. Great Barrington, MA 01230-1000. Phone: (413)528-1216 Fax: (413)528-0103 E-mail: info@aier.org • URL: http://www.aier.org • 1996. $6.00. Provides succinct coverage of various consumer debt topics, including credit cards, credit scoring systems, credit history, credit reports, and bankruptcy. Relevant federal legislation is briefly described, including the Fair Credit Reporting Act (FCRA) and the Fair Credit Billing Act (FCBA). (Economic Education Bulletin.)

How to Use Math as a Business Tool. American Management Association Extension Institute, P.O. Box 1026 Saranac Lake, NY 12983-9957. Phone: 800-262-9699 or (518)891-1500 Fax: (518)891-0368 Looseleaf. $89.95. Self-study course. Emphasis is on practical explanations, examples, and problem solving. Quizzes are included.

How to Win Arguments; More Often Than Not. William A. Rusher. University Press of America, 4720 Boston Way

Lanham, MD 20706. Phone: 800-462-6420 or (301)459-3366 Fax: (301)459-2118 URL: http://www.univpress.com • 1985. $17.75.

How to Win the Job You Really Want. Janice Weinberg. Henry Holt and Co.,LLC, 115 W. 18th St., 5th Fl. New York, NY 10011. Phone: (212)886-9200 Fax: (212)633-0748 E-mail: info@hholt.com • URL: http://www.henryholt.com • 1995. $11.95. Second edition.

How to Write a Business Plan. American Management Association Extension Institute, P.O. Box 1026 Saranac Lake, NY 12983-9957. Phone: 800-262-9699 or (518)891-1500 Fax: (518)891-0368 Looseleaf. $130.00. Self-study course. Emphasis is on practical explanations, examples, and problem solving. Quizzes and a case study are included.

How to Write a Marketing Plan. American Management Association Extension Institute, P.O. Box 1026 Saranac Lake, NY 12983-9957. Phone: 800-262-9699 or (518)891-1500 Fax: (518)891-0368 Looseleaf. $130.00. Self-study course. Emphasis is on practical explanations, examples, and problem solving. Quizzes and a case study are included.

How to Write a Patent Application. Practising Law Institute, 810 Seventh Ave. New York, NY 10019-5818. Phone: 800-260-4754 or (212)824-5700 Fax: (212)265-4742 E-mail: info@pli.edu • URL: http://www.pli.edu • Looseleaf. $195.00. Annual revisions. Edited for ''both novice and experienced patent attorneys.'' Includes consideration of specific kinds of patent applications, such as design, electrical, software, chemical, and biotechnological. Checklists, sample forms, and case citations are provided.

How to Write a Successful Marketing Plan: A Disciplined and Comprehensive Approach. Roman G. Hiebing. Prentice Hall, 240 Frisch Court Paramus, NJ 07652-5240. Phone: 800-947-7700 or (201)909-6200 Fax: 800-445-6991 or (201)909-6361 URL: http://www.prenhall.com • 1999. $79.95. Second edition. The four main sections cover marketing background, the marketing plan, plan execution, and evaluation. Includes worksheets and formats.

How to Write and Present Technical Information. Charles H. Sides. Oryx Press, 4041 N. Central Ave., 700 Phoenix, AZ 85012-3379. Phone: 800-279-6799 or (602)265-2651 Fax: 800-279-4663 or (602)265-6250 E-mail: info@oryxpress.com • URL: http://www.oryxpress.com • 1998. $24.95. Third edition.

How to Write Better Resumes. Gary Grappo and Adele Lewis. Barron's Educational Series, Inc., 250 Wireless Blvd. Hauppauge, NY 11788. Phone: 800-645-3476 or (516)434-3311 Fax: (516)434-3723 E-mail: barrons@barronseduc.com • URL: http://www.barronseduc.com • 1998. $11.95. Fifth edition.

How to Write Proposals that Produce. Joel P. Bowman and Bernadine P. Branchaw. Oryx Press, 4041 N. Central Ave., Ste. 700 Phoenix, AZ 85012-3379. Phone: 800-279-6799 or (602)265-2651 Fax: 800-279-4663 or (602)265-6250 E-mail: info@oryxpress.com • URL: http://www.oryxpress.com • 1992. $23.50. An extensive guide to effective proposal writing for both nonprofit organizations and businesses. Covers writing style, intended audience, format, use of graphs, charts, and tables, documentation, evaluation, oral presentation, and related topics.

How to Write Successful Promotional Copy. American Management Association Extension Institute, P.O. Box 1026 Saranac Lake, NY 12983-9957. Phone: 800-262-9699 or (518)891-1500 Fax: (518)891-0368 Looseleaf. $98.00. Self-study course. Emphasis is on practical explanations, examples, and problem solving. Quizzes are included.

How to Write Usable User Documentation. Edmond H. Weiss. Oryx Press, 4041 N. Central Ave., Ste. 700 Phoenix, AZ 85012-3379. Phone: 800-279-6799 or (602)265-2651 Fax: 800-279-4663 or (602)265-6250 E-mail: info@oryxpress.com • URL: http://www.oryxpress.com • 1991. $24.95. Second edition. Shows how to explain a product, system, or procedure. Includes a glossary and a list of books and periodicals.

Howe Laboratory of Ophthalmology. Harvard University, Massachusetts Eye and Ear Infirmary, 243 Charles St. Boston, MA 02114. Phone: (617)573-3963 Fax: (617)573-4290 URL: http://www.howelaboratory.harvard.edu • A research unit of Harvard Medical School.

HPAC Techlit Selector (Heating, Piping, Air Conditioning). Penton Media, Inc., 1300 E. Ninth St. Cleveland, OH 44114. Phone: (216)696-7000 Fax: (216)696-0836 E-mail: corpcomm@penton.com • URL: http://www.penton.com • Semiannual. Free to qualified personnel. Manufacturers' catalogs and technical literature.

HR Briefing (Human Resources). Bureau of Business Practice, Inc., 24 Rope Ferry Rd. Waterford, CT 06386. Phone: 800-243-0876 or (860)442-4365 Fax: (860)437-3555 E-mail: rebecca_armitage@prenhall.com • URL: http://www.bbpnews.com • Semimonthly. $195.00 per year. Newsletter. Formerly *Personnel Manager's Letter*.

HR Focus: The Hands-On Tool for Human Resources Professionals. American Management Association, 1601 Broadway New York, NY 10019-7420. Phone: 800-313-8650 or (212)586-8100 Fax: (212)903-8168 E-mail: amapubs@aol.com • URL: http://www.amanet.org • Monthly. $99.00 per year. Newsletter. Covers ''all aspects of HR management,'' including corporate culture, the impact of technology, recruiting strategies, and training. Formerly *Personnel*.

HR Magazine (Human Resources): Strategies and Solutions for Human Resource Professionals. Society for Human Resource Management, 1800 Duke St. Alexandria, VA 22314-3499. Phone: (703)548-3440 Fax: (703)535-6490 E-mail: shrm@shrm.org • URL: http://www.shrm.org • Monthly. Free to members; non-members, $125.00 per year. Formerly *Personnel Administrator*.

HR Words You Gotta Know! Essential Human Resources, Terms, Laws, Acronyms and Abbreviations for Everyone in Business. William R. Tracey, editor. AMACOM, 1601 Broadway, 12th Fl. New York, NY 10019. Phone: 800-262-9699 or (212)586-8100 Fax: (212)903-8168 E-mail: custmserv@amanet.org • URL: http://www.amanet.org • 1994. $17.95. Explains important human relations management terms.

Hubert H. Humphrey Institute of Public Affairs., University of Minnesota, 300 Hubert Center, 301 19th Ave., S. Minneapolis, MN 55455. Phone: (612)625-0669 Fax: (612)625-6351 E-mail: jbrandl@hhh.umn.edu • URL: http://www.hhh.umn.edu • Studies strategic management in both the private and the public sectors.

Hudson Institute.

Hudson's Subscription Newsletter Directory. Newsletter Clearinghouse, P.O. Box 311 Rhinebeck, NY 12572. Phone: 800-572-3451 or (914)876-2081 Fax: (914)876-2561 Annual. $189.00. About 4,800 newsletters available by subscription.

Huenefeld Report: For Managers and Planners in Modest-Sized Book Publishing Houses. John Huenefeld. Huenefeld Co., Inc., P.O. Box 665 Bedford, MA 01730-0665. Phone: (781)275-1070 Biweekly. $88.00 per year.

The Hulbert Financial Digest. Hulbert Financial Digest, Inc., 5051 B Backlick Rd. Annandale, VA 22003-6045. Phone: 888-485-2378 E-mail: hfd@hulbertdigest.com • URL: http://www.hulbertdigest.com • Monthly. $135.00 per year. Trial subscriptions available. Rates the performance of investment advisory newsletters and services. Includes a stock market sentiment index based on bullish, bearish, or neutral opinions of advisors. Subscription includes *HFD's Thirteen-Year Longer Term Performance Report* and *HFD's Financial Newsletter Directory*.

Human Behavior at Work. O. Jeff Harris and Sandra Hartman. West Publishing Co., College and School Div., 610 Opperman Dr. Eagan, MN 55123. Phone: 800-328-4880 or (651)687-7000 Fax: 800-213-2323 or (651)687-5827 E-mail: legal_ed@westgroup.com • URL: http://www.lawschool.westgroup.com • 1991. $55.50.

Human Communication: An Interpersonal Introduction. Thomas Steinfatt. Pearson Education and Technology, 201 W. 103rd St. Indianapolis, IN 46290-1097. Phone: 800-858-7674 or (317)581-3500 URL: http://www.mcp.com • 1977. Price on application.

Human Communication Research. International Communication Association. Oxford University Press, Journals, 2001 Evans Rd. Cary, NC 27513. Phone: 800-252-7523 Fax: (919)677-1714 Quarterly. Individuals, $74.00 per year; institutions, $243.00 per year. A scholarly journal of interpersonal communication.

Human Factors and Aviation Medicine. Flight Safety Foundation, 601 Madison St., Suite 300 Alexandria, VA 22314-1756. Phone: (703)739-6700 Fax: (703)739-6708 E-mail: fsf@radix.net • Bimonthly. Members, $120.00 per year; non-members, $240.00 per year.

Human Factors and Ergonomics in Manufacturing. Available from John Wiley and Sons, Inc., Journals Div., 605 Third Ave. New York, NY 10158-0012. Phone: 800-225-5945 or (212)850-6000 Fax: (212)850-6088 E-mail: info@wiley.com • URL: http://www.wiley.com • Quarterly. Institutions, $545.00 per year. Published in England by John Wiley and Sons Ltd. Formerly *International Journal of Human Factors in Manufacturing*.

Human Factors and Ergonomics Society.

Human Factors Design Handbook. Wesley E. Woodson and others. McGraw-Hill, 1221 Ave. of the Americas New York, NY 10020. Phone: 800-722-4726 or (212)904-2000 Fax: (212)904-2072 E-mail: customer.service@mcgraw-hill.com • 1991. $150.00. Second edition.

Human Factors/Ergonomics Laboratory. Kansas State University

The Human Marketplace: An Examination of Private Employment Agencies. Tomas Martinez. Transaction Publishers, 35 Berrue Circle Piscataway, NJ 08854-8042. Phone: 888-999-6778 or (732)445-2280 Fax: (732)445-3138 E-mail: trans@transactionpub.com • URL: http://www.transactionpub.com • 1995. $34.95.

Human Power, Biochemechanics, and Robotics Laboratory., Cornell University, Dept. of Theoretical and Applied Mechanics, 306 Kimball Hall Ithaca, NY 14853. Phone: (607)255-7108 Fax: (607)255-2011 E-mail: ruina@cornell.edu • URL: http://www.tam.cornell.edu/~ruina • Conducts research relating to human muscle-powered machines, such as bicycles and rowers.

Human Relations. Andrew J. Dubrin. Prentice Hall, 240 Frisch Court Paramus, NJ 07652-5240. Phone: 800-947-7700 or (201)909-6200 Fax: 800-445-6991 or (201)909-6361 URL: http://www.prenhall.com • 1996. $55.00. Sixth edition.

Human Relations: Towards the Integration of Social Sciences. Tavistock Institute of Human Relations. Sage Publications, Inc., 2455 Teller Rd. Thousand Oaks, CA 91320. Phone: (805)499-0721 Fax: (805)499-0871 E-mail: info@sagepub.com • URL: http://www.sagepub.com • Monthly. Individuals, $92.00 per year; institutions, $677.00 per year.

Human Resource Executive. LRP Publications, Inc., P.O. Box 980 Horsham, PA 19044-0980. Phone: 800-341-7874 or (215)784-0941 Fax: (215)784-0870 E-mail: custserv@lrp.com • URL: http://www.hrexecutive.com • Monthly. $89.95 per year. Edited for directors of corporate human resource departments. Special issues emphasize training, benefits, retirement planning, recruitment, outplacement, workers' compensation, legal pitfalls, and oes emphasize training, benefits, retirement planning, recruitment, outplacement, workers' compensation, legal pitfalls, and other personnel topics.

The Human Resource Executive's Market Resource. LRP Publications, P.O. Box 980 Horsham, PA 19044-0980. Phone: 800-341-7874 or (215)784-0941 Fax: (215)784-9639 E-mail: custserv@lrp.com • Annual. $25.00. A directory of services and products of use to personnel departments. Includes 20 categories, such as training, outplacement, health benefits, recognition awards, testing, workers' compensation, temporary staffing, recruitment, and human resources software.

Human Resource Management. John Wiley and Sons, Inc., Journals Div., 605 Third Ave. New York, NY 10158-0012. Phone: 800-526-5368 or (212)850-6418 Fax: (212)850-6088 E-mail: info@wiley.com • URL: http://www.wiley.com • Quarterly. Institutions, $390.00 per year.

Human Resource Management. George T. Milkovich and John W. Boudreau. McGraw-Hill, 1221 Ave. of the Americas New York, NY 10020. Phone: 800-722-4726 or (212)904-2000 Fax: (212)904-2072 E-mail: customer.service@mcgraw-hill.com • URL: http://www.mcgraw-hill.com • 1999. $63.25. Ninth edition.

Human Resource Management: A Strategic and Global Perspective. John B. Miner and Donald P. Crane. Addison-Wesley Educational Publications, Inc., One Jacob Way Reading, MA 01867. Phone: 800-447-2226 or (781)944-3700 Fax: (781)942-1117 URL: http://www.awl.com • 1997. Price on application.

Human Resource Management: An Economic Approach. David Lewin and Daniel J. Mitchell. South-Western Publishing Co., 5101 Madison Rd. Cincinnati, OH 45227. Phone: 800-543-0487 or (513)271-8811 Fax: 800-437-8488 E-mail: billhendee@itped.com • URL: http://www.swcollege.com • 1989. $57.25. Second edition.

Human Resource Management for Golf Course Superintendents. Robert A. Milligan and Thomas R. Maloney. Ann Arbor Press, Inc., P.O. Box 310 Chelsea, MI 48118. Phone: 800-858-5299 or (313)475-8787 Fax: (313)475-8852 E-mail: aap310@aol.com • 1996. $34.95. Covers various personnel topics as related to golf course management, including organizational structure, recruitment, employee selection, training, motivation, and discipline.

Human Resource Management in Libraries: Theory and Practice. Richard Rubin. Neal-Schuman Publishers, Inc., 100 Varick St. New York, NY 10013. Phone: (212)925-8650 Fax: 800-584-2414 or (212)219-8916 E-mail: info@neal-schuman.com • URL: http://www.neal-schuman.com • 1991. $55.00. Covers such topics as performance rating, pay equity, and collective bargaining.

Human Resource Manager's Legal Reporter. Business and Legal Reports, Inc., P.O. Box 6001 Old Saybrook, CT 06475-6001. Phone: 800-727-5257 or (203)318-0000 Fax: (203)245-2559 Monthly. $95.00 per year. Reports and advises on the practical aspects of EEO and human resource compliance. Formerly *Manager's Legal Reporter*.

Human Resource Planning. Human Resource Planning Society, 317 Madison Ave., Suite 1509 New York, NY 10017-5200. Phone: (212)490-6387 Fax: (212)682-6851 E-mail: info@hrps.org • URL: http://www.hrps.org • Quarterly. $90.00 per year.

Human Resource Planning Society., 317 Madison Ave., Suite 1509 New York, NY 10017. Phone: (212)490-6387 Fax: (212)682-6851 Members are corporate human resource planning professionals and others concerned with employee recruitment, development, and utilization.

Human Resource Skills for the Project Manager: The Human Aspects of Project Management, Volume Two. Vijay K. Verma. Project Management Institute, c/o PMI Headquarters Publishing Div., 40 Colonial Square Sylva, NC 28779. Phone: (828)586-3715 Fax: (828)586-4020 E-mail: booked@pmi.org • URL: http://www.pmi.org • 1996. $32.95. (Human Aspects of Project Management Series).

Human Resources Abstracts: An International Information Service. Sage Publications, Inc., 2455 Teller Rd. Thousand Oaks, CA 91320. Phone: (805)499-0721 Fax: (805)499-0871 E-mail: info@sagepub.com • URL: http://

www.sagepub.com • Quarterly. Individuals, $150.00 per year; institutions, $610.00 per year.

Human Resources and Personnel Management. William B. Werther and Keith Davis. McGraw-Hill, 1221 Ave. of the Americas New York, NY 10020. Phone: 800-722-4726 or (212)904-2000 Fax: (212)904-2072 E-mail: customer.serivce@mcgraw-hill.com • URL: http://www.mcgraw-hill.com • 1995. $82.50. Fifth edition.

Human Resources Glossary: A Complete Desk Reference for HR Executives, Managers and Practitioners. William R. Tracey. Saint Lucie Press, 2000 Corporate Blvd., N. W. Boca Raton, FL 33431-7372. Phone: 800-272-7737 or (561)274-9906 Fax: 800-374-3401 E-mail: information@slpress.com • URL: http://www.slpress.com • 1997. $69.95. Second edition. (First edition published in 1991 by Amacom.)

Human Resources Institute. University of Alabama

Human Resources Management and Development Handbook. William R. Tracey, editor. AMACOM, 1601 Broadway, 12th Fl. New York, NY 10019. Phone: 800-262-9699 or (212)586-8100 Fax: (212)903-8168 E-mail: custmserv@amanet.org • URL: http://www.amanet.org • 1993. $99.00. Second edition.

Human Resources Management Whole. CCH, Inc., 4025 W. Peterson Ave. Chicago, IL 60646-6085. Phone: 800-835-5224 or (773)866-6000 Fax: 800-224-8299 URL: http://www.cch.com • Nine looseleaf volumes. $1,572 per year. Includes monthly updates. Components are *Ideas and Trends Newsletter, Employment Relations, Compensation, Equal Employment Opportunity, Personnel Practices/ Communications* and *OSHA Compliance*. Components are available separately.

Human Resources Report. Bureau of National Affairs, Inc., 1231 25th St., N.W. Washington, DC 20037-1197. Phone: 800-372-1033 or (202)452-4200 Fax: (202)452-8092 E-mail: books@bna.com • URL: http://www.bna.com • Weekly. $875.00 per year. Newsletter. Formerly *BNA'S Employee Relations Weekly*.

Human Resources Research Organization.

Human Resources Yearbook. Prentice Hall, 240 Frisch Court Paramus, NJ 07652-5240. Phone: 800-947-7700 or (201)909-6200 Fax: 800-445-6991 or (201)909-6361 URL: http://www.prenhall.com • Annual. $75.00.

Human Rights Organizations and Periodicals Directory. Meiklejohn Civil Liberties Institute, P.O. Box 673 Berkeley, CA 94701-0673. Phone: 888-848-0599 or (510)848-0599 Fax: (510)848-6008 E-mail: mcli@igc.org • Biennial. Individuals, $70.00 per year; libraries and institutions, $76.00 per year. Over 1,100 United States organiations and periodicals dedicated to improving human rights.

The Human Side of Enterprise. Douglas McGregor. McGraw-Hill, 1221 Ave. of the Americas New York, NY 10020-1095. Phone: 800-722-4726 or (212)904-2000 Fax: (212)904-2072 E-mail: customer.service@mcgraw-hill.com • URL: http://www.mcgraw-hill.com • 1985. $40.00.

The Human Side of Intranets: Content, Style, and Politics. Thom Dupper. Saint Lucie Press, 2000 Corporate Blvd., N. W. Boca Raton, FL 33431-7372. Phone: 800-272-7737 or (561)274-9906 Fax: 800-374-3401 or (561)274-9927 E-mail: information@slpress.com • URL: http://www.slpress.com • 1997. $54.95. A nontechnical, general discussion of corporate intranets.

Humanities Index. H.W. Wilson Co., 950 University Ave. Bronx, NY 10452. Phone: 800-367-6770 or (718)588-8400 Fax: (718)590-1617 E-mail: custserv@hwwilson.com • URL: http://www.hwwilson.com • Quarterly. Annual cumulation. Service basis.

Huntsman Center for Global Competition and Innovation., University of Pennsylvania, 3620 Locust Walk, Suite 1400 Philadelphia, PA 19104. Phone: (215)898-2104 Fax: (215)573-2129 E-mail: dayg@wharton.upenn.edu • URL: http://www.fourps.wharton.upenn.edu/ • Conducts research related to international business.

Hydraulic Engineering. Michael A. Ports, editor. American Society of Civil Engineers, 1801 Alexander Graham Bell Dr. Reston, VA 20191-4400. Phone: 800-548-2723 or (703)295-6300 Fax: (703)295-6222 E-mail: marketing@asce.org • URL: http://www.asce.org • 1988. $117.00

Hydraulic Institute.

Hydraulic Tool Manufacturers Association.

Hydraulics and Pneumatics: The Magazine of Fluid Power and Motion Control Systems. Penton Media Inc., 1300 E. Ninth St. Cleveland, OH 44114. Phone: (216)696-7000 Fax: (216)696-0836 E-mail: corpcomm@penton.com • URL: http://www.penton.com • Monthly. Free to qualified personnel; others, $55.00 per year.

Hydro Review: A Magazine Covering the North American Hydroelectric Industry. HCI Publications, 410 Archibald St. Kansas City, MO 64111-3046. Phone: (816)931-1311 Fax: (816)931-2015 E-mail: hci@aol.com • URL: http://www.hydroreview.com • Eight times a year. $65.00 per year. Covers hydroelectric power generation in North America. Supplement available *Industry Directory*.

Hydro Review Worldwide Industry Directory. HCI Publications, 410 Archibald St. Kansas City, MO 64111. Phone: (816)931-1311 Fax: (816)931-2015 E-mail: info@hcipub.com • Annual. $20.00. Lists more than 250 manufacturers and suppliers of products and services to the hydroelectric industry worldwide. Formerly *Hydro Review-Industry Directory*.

Hydrocarbon Processing. Gulf Publishing Co., P.O. Box 2608 Houston, TX 77252-2608. Phone: 800-231-6275 or (713)529-4301 Fax: (713)520-4433 E-mail: ezorder@gulfpub.com • URL: http://www.gpcbooks.com • Monthly. Free to qualified personnel; others, $28.00 per year. International edition available.

Hypertension. American Heart Association. Available from Williams and Wilkins, 351 W. Camden St. Baltimore, MD 21201-2436. Phone: 800-527-5597 or (410)528-4000 Fax: (410)528-4312 URL: http://www.hypertensionaha.org • Individuals, $226.00 per year; institutions, $608.00 per year.

Hypertension Research Center. Indiana University-Purdue University at Indianapolis

I B C's Money Fund Report. IBC Financial Data, Inc., P.O. 9104 Ashland, MA 01721-9104. Phone: 800-343-5413 or (508)881-2800 Fax: (508)881-0982 URL: http://www.ibcdata.com • Weekly. $975.00 per year. Looseleaf. Contains detailed information on about 1,000 U. S. money market funds, including portfolios and yields. Formerly *Money Fund Report*.

I Love Pasta. National Pasta AssociationPhone: (703)841-0818 Fax: (703)528-6507 E-mail: npa@ilovepasta.org • URL: http://www.ilovepasta.org • Web site provides a wide variety of information about pasta and the pasta industry. Includes 250 pasta recipes, pasta FAQs, and nutritional data. Industry statistics can be displayed, including data on imports, production, and per capita use in various countries. Extensive durum wheat data is provided.

A I S E Steel Technology. Association of Iron and Steel Engineers, Three Gateway Center, Suite 1900 Pittsburgh, PA 15222. Phone: (412)281-6323 Fax: (412)281-4657 E-mail: subscriptions@aise.org • URL: http://www.aise.org • Monthly. $58.00 per year. Formerly (Iron and Steel Engineer).

IAA World News. International Advertising Association, 521 Fifth Ave., Room 1807 New York, NY 10175-0003. Phone: (212)557-1133 Fax: (212)983-0455 E-mail: webmaster@iaaglobal.org • Quarterly. $80.00 per year. Formerly *International Advertiser*.

IAFE Directory. International Association of Fairs and Expositions, P.O. Box 985 Springfield, MO 65801. Phone: 800-516-0313 or (417)862-5771 Fax: (417)862-0156 E-mail: iaf@iafenet.org • URL: http://www.iafenet.org • Annual. Free to members; non-members, $85.00. Lists more than 1,300 member agricultural fairs in the United States and Canada. Formerly *International Association of Fairs and Expositions Directory*.

IAS: Interpretation and Application of International Accounting Standards. John Wiley and Sons, Inc., 605 Third Ave. New York, NY 10158-0012. Phone: 800-225-5945 or (212)850-6000 Fax: (212)850-6088 E-mail: info@jwiley.com • URL: http://www.wiley.com • Annual. $65.00. (Also available on CD-ROM.)

Iberia Research Station. Louisiana State University

IBM Journal of Research and Development. International Business Machines Corp., P.O. Box 218 Yorktown Heights, NY 10598. Phone: (914)945-3836 URL: http://www.research.ibm.com • Bimonthly. $180.00 per year.

IC Master (Integrated circuits). Hearst Business Communications, UTP Div., 645 Stewart Ave. Garden City, NY 11530-4709. Phone: (516)227-1300 Fax: (516)227-1453 E-mail: gamsler@hearst.com • URL: http://www.icmaster.com • Annual. $195.00. Semiannual supplements. List of over 1,500 manufacturers and distributors of integrated circuits.

The ICAO Journal. International Civil Aviation Organization c/o Document Sales Unit, 999 University St. Montreal PQ, QC, Canada H3C 5H7. Phone: (514)954-8022 Fax: (514)954-6769 E-mail: sales_unit@icao.org • URL: http://www.sales_unit@icao.orgm • Ten times a year. $25.00 per year. Editions in English, French and Spanish.

The Ice Cream Market. MarketResearch.com, 641 Ave. of the Americas, Third Floor New York, NY 10011. Phone: 800-298-5699 or (212)807-2629 Fax: (212)807-2716 E-mail: order@marketresearch.com • URL: http://www.marketresearch.com • 2000. $2,500.00. Market data and forecasts to 2004 on ice cream and related products (ice milk, frozen yogurt, etc.).

Ice Cream Reporter: The Newsletter for Ice Cream Executives. MarketResearch.com, 641 Ave. of the Americas, 3rd Floor New York, NY 10011. Phone: 800-298-5699 or (212)807-2629 Fax: (212)807-2716 E-mail: order@marketresearch.com • URL: http://www.marketresearch.com • Monthly. $395.00 per year. Covers new products, mergers, research, packaging, etc.

Ice Cream Store. Entrepreneur Media, Inc., 2445 McCabe Way Irvine, CA 92614. Phone: 800-421-2300 or (949)261-2325 Fax: (949)261-0234 E-mail: entmag@entrepreneur.com • URL: http://www.entrepreneur.com • Looseleaf. $59.50. A practical guide to starting an ice cream shop. Covers profit potential, start-up costs, market size evaluation, owner's time required, site selection, lease negotiation, pricing, accounting, advertising, promotion, etc. (Start-Up Business Guide No. E1187.)

ICMA Newsletter. International City/County Management Association, 777 N. Capitol St., N. E., Suite 500 Washington, DC 20002-4201. Phone: 800-745-8780 or (202)289-4262 Fax: (202)962-3500 E-mail: dbrooks@icma.org • URL: http://www.icma.org • Biweekly. $175.00 per year. Covers news of developments in local government, professional municipal management, and federal regulation applied to municipalities.

ICS Cleaning Specialists Annual Trade Directory and Buying Guide. Business News Publishing Co., II, L.L.C, 22801 Ventura Blvd.,, Ste. 115 Woodland Hills, CA 91364-1222. Phone: 800-835-4398 or (818)224-8035 Fax: (818)224-8042 E-mail: ics@bnp.com • URL: http://www.icsmag.com • Annual. $25.00. Lists about 6,000 manufacturers and distributors of floor covering installation and cleaning equipment. Formerly *Installation and Cleaning Specialists Trade Directory and Buying Guides*.

ICTA Travel Management Text Series. Institute of Certified Travel Agents, 148 Linden St. Wellesley, MA 02181. Phone: 800-542-4282 or (617)237-0280 Four volumes. Volume one, *Business Management for Travel Agents*; volume two, *Personnel Management for Travel Agents*; volume three, *Marketing for Travel Agents*; volume four, *Domestic Leisure and International Tourism*.

ID Systems Buyers Guide. Helmers Publishing, Inc., P.O. Box 874 Peterborough, NH 03458-0874. Phone: (603)924-9631 Fax: (603)924-7408 E-mail: editors@idsystems.com • URL: http://www.idsystems.com • Annual. Price on application. Provides information on over 750 companies manufacturing automatic identification equipment, including scanners, data collection terminals, and bar code systems.

ID Systems: Integrating Data Capture Across the Supply Chain. Helmers Publishing, Inc., P.O. Box 874 Peterborough, NH 03458-0874. Phone: (603)924-9631 Fax: (603)924-7408 E-mail: editors@idsystems.com • URL: http://www.idsystems.com • Monthly. $55.00 per year. Covers trends in automatic identification technology and management.

ID-The Voice of Foodservice Distribution. Bill Communications, Inc., 770 Broadway New York, NY 10003-9595. Phone: 800-266-4712 or (646)654-5400 Fax: (646)654-7212 URL: http://www.billcom.com • 14 times a year. $105.00 per year. For foodservice distribution executives and sales representatives. Formerly *Institutional Distribution*.

ID World: The Magazine of Personal Identification and Biometrics. Faulkner & Gray, Inc., 300 S. Wacker Drive, 18th Floor Chicago, IL 60606. Phone: (312)913-1334 Fax: (312)913-1369 URL: http://www.faulknergray.com • Bimonthly. Controlled circulation. Covers personal identification systems, including smart cards and finger prints. Includes articles on legal, regulatory, and privacy issues.

Idaho Agricultural Experiment Station. University of Idaho

Idea Source Guide; A Monthly Report to Executives in Advertising, Merchandising and Sales Promotion. Bramlee, Inc., c/o Fred Davis, P.O. Box 366 Devon, PA 19333. Monthly. $150.00 per year. Lists new premiums and novelty products.

IDEA, The Health and Fitness Source., 6190 Cornerstone Court E., Suite 204 San Diego, CA 92121. Phone: 800-999-4332 or (619)535-8979 Fax: (619)535-8234 E-mail: member@ideafit.com • URL: http://www.ideafit.com • An educational network and forum for fitness instructors, personal trainers, exercise club owners, and others.

Ideas Unlimited: For Editors. Omniprints, Inc., 9700 Philadelphia Court Lanham, MD 20706-4405. Phone: (301)731-5202 Fax: (301)731-5203 Monthly. $195.00 per year. Contains fillers for company newsletters: articles, cartoons, jokes, seasonal items, etc.

IDH: National Buying Guide and Directory of Interior Furnishings, Allied Products and Services. E.W. Williams Publications Co., 2125 Center Ave., Suite 305 Fort Lee, NJ 07024. Phone: (201)532-9290 Fax: (201)779-8345 Semiannual. $20.00 per year. Over 5,000 manufacturers and distributors of furniture, accessories, floor coverings, fabrics, wallcoverings, etc., and services relatedto these products. Formerly *Interior Decorator's Handbook*.

IEE Solutions. Institute of Industrial Engineers, 25 Technology Park/Atlanta Norcross, GA 30092. Phone: 800-494-0460 or (770)449-0460 Fax: (770)263-8532 Monthly. Free to members; non-members, $49.00 per year. Features articles on material handling, computers, quality control, production and inventory control, engineering economics, worker motivation, management strategies, and factory automation. Formerly *Industrial Engineers*.

IEEE Communications Magazine. Institute of Electrical and Electronics Engineers, Three Park Ave., 17th Fl. New York, NY 10016-5997. Phone: 800-678-4333 or (212)419-7900 Fax: (212)752-4929 E-mail: customer.service@ieee.org • URL: http://www.ieee.org • Monthly. $190.00 per year.

IEEE Computer Graphics and Applications. Insityte of Electrical and Electronics Engineers, Inc., Three Park Ave., 17th Fl. New York, NY 10017. Phone: 800-678-4333 E-mail: customerservice@ieee.org • URL: http://www.computer.org:80/pubs/cg&a/cg&a.htm • Bimonthly. Free to members; non-members, $485.00 per year.

IEEE Computer Society., 1730 Massachusetts Ave., N. W. Washington, DC 20036. Phone: (202)371-0101 Fax: (202)728-9614 E-mail: csinfo@computer.org • URL: http://www.computer.org • A society of the Institute of Electrical and Electronics Engineers. Said to be the world's largest organization of computer professionals. Some of the specific committees are: Computer Communications; Computer Graphics; Computers in Education; Design Automation; Office Automation; Personal Computing; Robotics; Security and Privacy; Software Engineering.

IEEE Consumer Electronics Society., c/o IEEE Corporate Office, 445 Hoes Lane Piscataway, NJ 08855-1331. Phone: (212)419-7900 Fax: (212)419-7570 URL: http://www.ieee.org • Affiliated with the Institute of Electrical and Electronics Engineers. Concerned with design and manufacture.

IEEE Electron Devices Society., c/o IEEE Corporate Office, Three Park Ave., 17th Fl. New York, NY 10016-5997. Phone: (212)419-7900 URL: http://www.ieee.org • A society of the Institute of Electrical and Electronics Engineers.

IEEE Engineering in Medicine and Biology Magazine. Institute of Electrical and Electronics Engineers, Inc., Three Park Ave., 17th Fl. New York, NY 10016-5997. Phone: 800-678-4333 or (212)419-7900 Fax: (212)752-4929 E-mail: customer.service@ieee.org • URL: http://www.ieee.org • Bimonthly. $176.00 per year. Published for biomedical engineers.

IEEE Industry Applications Magazine. Institute of Electrical and Electronics Engineers, Three Park Ave., 17th Fl. New York, NY 10016-5997. Phone: 800-678-4333 or (212)419-7900 Fax: (212)752-4929 E-mail: customer.service@ieee.org • URL: http://www.ieee.org • Bimonthly. $190.00 per year. Covers new industrial applications of power conversion, drives, lighting, and control. Emphasis is on the petroleum, chemical, rubber, plastics, textile, and mining industries.

IEEE Lasers and Electro-Optics Society., Institute of Electrical and Electronics Engineers, P.O. Box 1331 Piscataway, NJ 08855-1331. Phone: (732)981-0060 Fax: (732)981-1721 E-mail: g.walters@ieee.org • URL: http://www.ieee.org/leos • A society of the Institute of Electrical and Electronics Engineers. Fields of interest include lasers, fiber optics, optoelectronics, and photonics.

IEEE Membership Directory. Institute of Electrical and Electronics Engineers, Inc., Three Park Ave., 17th Fl. New York, NY 10016-5997. Phone: 800-678-4333 or (212)419-7900 Fax: (212)752-4929 E-mail: customer.service@ieee.org • URL: http://www.ieee.org • Annual. $190.00.

IEEE Micro. Institute of Electrical and Electronics Engineers, Inc., Three Park Ave., 17th Fl. New York, NY 10017. Phone: 800-678-4333 E-mail: customerservice@ieee.org • Bimonthly. Free to members; non members, $455.00 per year.

IEEE Multimedia Magazine. Institute of Electrical and Electronic Engineers, Three Park Ave., 17th Fl. New York, NY 10017-5997. Phone: 800-678-4333 or (212)419-7900 Fax: (212)752-4929 E-mail: customerservice@ieee.org • URL: http://www.ieee.org • Quarterly. Free to members; non-members, $390.00 per year. Provides a wide variety of technical information relating to multimedia systems and applications. Articles cover research, advanced applications, working systems, and theory.

IEEE Proceedings-Circuits, Devices and Systems. Institute of Electrical and Electronics Engineers, Inc., Three Park Ave., 17th Fl. New York, NY 10016-5997. Phone: 800-678-4333 or (212)419-7900 Fax: (212)752-4929 E-mail: customer.service@ieee.org • URL: http://www.ieee.org • Monthly. $720.00 per year.

IEEE Publications Bulletin. Institute of Electrical and Electronics Engineers, Three Park Ave., 17th Fl. New York, NY 10017. Phone: 800-678-4333 or (212)419-7900 Fax: (212)752-4929 E-mail: customer.service@ieee.org • URL: http://www.ieee.org • Quarterly. Free. Provides information on all IEEE journals, proceedings, and other publications.

IEEE Software. Insutitute of Electrical and Electronic Engineers, Inc., Three Park Ave., 17th Fl. New York, NY 10017. Phone: 800-678-4333 E-mail: customerservice@ieee.org • URL: http://www.computer.org:80/pubs/software/software.htm • Bimonthly. Free to members; non-members, $495.00 per year. Covers software engineering, technology, and development. Affiliated with the Institute of Electrical and Electronics Engineers.

IEEE Solid State Circuits Council., c/o IEEE Corporate Office, Three Park Ave., 17th Fl. New York, NY 10016-5997. Phone: (212)419-7900 URL: http://www.ieee.org • A council of the Institute of Electrical and Electronics Engineers.

IEEE Spectrum. Institute of Electrical and Electronics Engineers, Inc., Three Park Ave., 17th Fl. New York, NY 10016-5997. Phone: 800-678-4333 or (212)419-7900 Fax: (212)752-4929 E-mail: customer.service@ieee.org • URL: http://www.ieee.org • Monthly. $195.00 per year. Supplement available *The Institute*.

IEEE Transactions on Communications. Institute of Electrical and Electronics Engineers, Inc., Three Park Ave., 17th Fl. New York, NY 10016-5997. Phone: 800-678-4333 or (212)419-7900 Fax: (212)752-4929 E-mail: customer.service@ieee.org • URL: http://www.ieee.org • Monthly. Individuals, $150.00 per year; institutions, $215.00 per year.

IEEE Transactions on Visualization and Computer Graphics. Institute of Electrical and Electronics Engineers, Three Park Ave., 17th Fl. New York, NY 10016-5997. Phone: 800-678-4333 or (212)419-7900 Fax: (212)752-4929 E-mail: customer.service@ieee.org • URL: http://www.ieee.org • Quarterly. $490.00 per year. Topics include computer vision, computer graphics, image processing, signal processing, computer-aided design, animation, and virtual reality.

IEG Sponsorship Sourcebook. International Events Group, Inc., 640 N. LaSalle Dr., Suite 600 Chicago, IL 60610. Phone: (312)944-1727 Fax: (312)944-1897 E-mail: ieg@sponsorship.com • URL: http://www.sponsorship.com • Annual. $199.00. Provides information on about 3,000 festivals, celebrations, and sports events that are available for commercial sponsorship. Information is also given on public relations firms, sports marketing companies, fireworks suppliers, and other companies providing services for special events. Formerly *IEG Directory of Sponsorship Marketing*.

IEG's Sponsorship Report: The International Newsletter of Event Sponsorship and Lifestyle Marketing. International Events Group, Inc., 640 N. LaSalle, Suite 600 Chicago, IL 60610. Phone: (312)944-1727 Fax: (312)944-1897 E-mail: ieg@sponsorship.com • URL: http://www.sponsorship.com • Biweekly. $415.00 per year. Newsletter reporting on corporate sponsorship of special events: sports, music, festivals, and the arts. Edited for event producers, directors, and marketing personnel.

I.E.S. Lighting Handbook. Illuminating Engineering Society, 120 Wall St., 17th Fl. New York, NY 10005-4001. Phone: (212)248-5000 Fax: (212)248-5017 Quadrennial. $389.00.

If Your Strategy is So Terrific, How Come It Doesn't Work? William S. Birnbaum. Books on Demand, 300 Zeeb Rd. Ann Arbor, MI 48106-1346. Phone: 800-521-0600 or (734)761-4700 Fax: (734)665-5022 E-mail: info@umi.com • URL: http://www.lib.umi.com • 1990. $77.50. Introduces the strategic matrix for business analysis and planning.

IFAP Newsletter. International Federation of Agricultural Producers, 21 rue Chaptal 75009 45 2 Paris, France. Bimonthly. Price on application.

I.I.I. Data Base Search. Insurance Information Institute, 110 William St. New York, NY 10038. Phone: (212)669-9200 Fax: (212)267-9591 URL: http://www.iii.org • Provides online citations and abstracts of insurance-related literature in magazines, newspapers, trade journals, and books. Emphasis is on property and casualty insurance issues, including highway safety, product safety, and environmental liability. Inquire as to online cost and availability.

I'll Get Back to You: 156 Ways to Get People to Return Your Calls and Other Helpful Sales Tips. Robert L. Shook and Eric Yaverbaum. McGraw-Hill, 1221 Ave. of the Americas New York, NY 10020. Phone: 800-722-4726 or (212)904-2000 Fax: (212)904-2072 E-mail: customer.service@mcgraw-hill.com • URL: http://www.mcgraw-hill.com • 1996. $9.95. Presents advice from business executives, celebrities, and others on how to make telephone calls seem important.

Illuminating Engineering Society of North America., 120 Wall St., 17th Fl. New York, NY 10005-4001. Phone: (212)248-5000 Fax: (212)248-5017 E-mail: bbay@iesna.org • URL: http://www.iesna.org • Members are lighting engineers, designers, architects, and manufacturers.

Illustrated Dictionary of Building Materials and Techniques: An Invaluable Sourcebook to the Tools, Terms, Materials, and Techniques Used by Building Professionals. Paul Bianchina. John Wiley and Sons, Inc., 605 Third Ave. New York, NY 10158-0012. Phone: 800-225-5945 or (212)850-6000 Fax: (212)850-6088 E-mail: info@wiley.com • URL: http://www.wiley.com • 1993. $49.95. Contains 4,000 definitions of building and building materials terms, with 500 illustrations. Includes materials grades, measurements, and specifications.

Illustrated Dictionary of Cargo Handling. Peter Brodie. Available from Informa Publishing Group Ltd., PO Box 1017 Westborough, MA 01581-6017. Phone: 800-493-4080 Fax: (508)231-0856 E-mail: enquiries@informa.com • URL: http://www.informa.com • 1996. $100.00. Second edition. Published in the UK by Lloyd's List (http://www.lloydslist.com). Provides definitions of about 600 terms relating to ''the vessels and equipment used in modern cargo handling and shipping,'' including containerization.

Illustrated Dictionary of Historic Architecture. Cyril M. Harris, editor. Dover Publications, Inc., 31 E. Second St. Mineola, NY 11501. Phone: 800-223-3130 or (516)294-7000 Fax: (516)742-5049 1983. $16.95.

Illustrated Dictionary of Jewelry. Harold Newman. W. W. Norton & Co., Inc., 500 Fifth Ave. New York, NY 10110-0017. Phone: 800-223-2588 or (212)354-5500 Fax: 800-233-2588 or (212)869-0856 E-mail: webmaster@wwnorton.com • URL: http://www.wwnorton.com • 1994. $29.95.

Illustrated Dictionary of Microcomputers. Michael Hordeski. McGraw Hill Professional, 1221 Ave. of the Americas New York, NY 10020. Phone: 800-722-4726 or (212)904-2000 Fax: (212)904-2072 E-mail: customer.service@mcgraw-hill.com • URL: http://www.mcgraw-hill.com • 1990. $19.95. Third edition.

Image Science Research Group., Worcester Polytechnic Institute, Computer Science Department, 100 Institute Rd. Worcester, MA 01609. Phone: (508)831-5671 Fax: (508)831-5776 E-mail: isrg@cs.wpi.edu • URL: http://www.cs.wpi.edu/research/ • Areas of research include image processing, computer graphics, and computational vision.

IMAGE Society., P.O. Box 6221 Chandler, AZ 85246-6221. Phone: (602)839-8709 E-mail: image@asu.edu • URL: http://www.public.asu.edu/~image • Promotes the technical advancement and application of real-time visual simulation. Special Interest Groups include Computer Image Generation, Virtual Reality Ancillary Technologies, and Virtual Reality in Education and Training.

IMAGES. IMAGE Society, P.O. Box 6221 Chandler, AZ 85246-6221. Phone: (602)839-8709 E-mail: image@acvax.inre.asu.edu • Semiannual. $25.00 per year. Provides news of virtual reality developments and the IMAGE Society.

Images of Organization. Gareth Morgan. Sage Publications, Inc., 2455 Teller Rd. Thousand Oaks, CA 91320. Phone: (805)499-0721 Fax: (805)499-0871 E-mail: info@sagepub.com • URL: http://www.sagepub.com • 1996. $59.95. Second edition. Includes bibliography and index.

Imaginative Events: A Sourcebook of Innovative Simulations, Exercises, Puzzles, and Games. Ken Jones. McGraw-Hill, 1221 Ave. of the Americas New York, NY 10020. Phone: 800-722-4726 or (212)904-2000 Fax: (212)904-2072 E-mail: customer.service@mcgraw-hill.com • URL: http://www.mcgraw-hill.com • 1992. $110.00. Two volumes. (Training Series).

Imaging Abstracts. Royal Photographic Society of Great Britain, Imaging Science and Technology Grou. Elsevier Science, 655 Ave. of the Americas New York, NY 10010. Phone: 888-437-4636 or (212)989-5800 Fax: (212)633-3680 E-mail: usinfo@elsevier.com • URL: http://www.elsevier.com • Bimonthly. $792.00 per year. Formerly *Photographic Abstracts*.

Imaging and Computer Vision Center-Computer Vision Center for Vertebrate Brain Mapping., Drexel University, 32nd and Market Sts., Room 110-7 Philadelphia, PA 19104. Phone: (215)895-2279 Fax: (215)895-4987 URL: http://www.drexel.icvc.com • Fields of research include computer vision, robot vision, and expert systems.

Imaging and Document Solutions. Miller Freeman, Inc., 600 Harrison St. San Francisco, CA 94107. Phone: 800-227-4675 or (415)905-2200 Fax: (415)905-2232 Monthly. $17.95 per year. Emphasis is on descriptions of new imaging products, including CD-ROM items. Formerly *Imaging Magazines*.

Imaging Business: The Voice of the Document Imaging Channel. Phillips Business Information, Inc., 1201 Seven Locks Rd., Suite 300 Potomac, MD 20854. Phone: 800-777-5006 or (301)340-1520 Fax: (301)309-3847 E-mail: pbi@phillips.com • URL: http://www.phillips.com/pbi.htm • Monthly. Free to qualified personnel. Edited for resellers of document imaging equipment.

Imaging KM: Creating and Managing the Knowledge-Based Enterprise (Knowledge Management). Knowledge Asset Media, 18 Bayview Landing Camden, ME 04843. Phone: (207)236-8524 Fax: (207)236-6452 E-mail: publisher@kmworld.com • URL: http://www.kmworld.com • 10 times a year. Free to qualified personnel; others, $48.00 per year. Covers automated and networked document image handling.

Imaging Systems Laboratory., Carnegie Mellon University, Robotics Institute, 5000 Forbes Ave. Pittsburgh, PA 15213. Phone: (412)268-3824 Fax: (412)683-3763 E-mail: rht@cs.cmu.edu • Fields of research include computer vision and document interpretation.

Imaginization: The Art of Creative Management. Gareth Morgan. Sage Publications, Inc., 2455 Teller Rd. Thousand Oaks, CA 91320. Phone: (805)499-0721 Fax: (805)499-0871 E-mail: info@sagepub.com • URL: http://www.sagepub.com • 1993. $45.00.

IMF Survey. International Monetary Fund, Publication Services, 700 19th St., N.W., Suite 12-607 Washington, DC 20431-0001. Phone: (202)623-7430 Fax: (202)623-7201 URL: http://www.imf.org • 23 times a year. $79.00 per year. Newsletter. Covers IMF activities in international finance, trade, commodities, and foreign exchange. Editions in English, French, and Spanish.

IMM Abstracts and Index: A Survey of World Literature on the Economic Geology and Mining of All Minerals (Except Coal), Mineral Processing, and Nonferrous Extraction Metallurgy. Institution of Mining and Metallurgy, 44 Portland Place London W1N 4BR W1N 4BR, England. Bimonthly. Members, $142.00 per year; non-members, $215.00 per year. Provides international coverage of the literature of mining and nonferrous metallurgy. Includes mineral economics, tunnelling, and rock mechanics.

Immigration Fundamentals: A Guide to Law and Practice. Practising Law Institute, 810 Seventh Ave. New York, NY 10019-5818. Phone: 800-260-4754 or (212)824-5700 Fax: (212)265-4742 E-mail: info@pli.edu • URL: http://www.pli.edu • Looseleaf. $110.00. Semiannual revisions. Includes the legal aspects of employment-based immigration, family-sponsored immigration, nonimmigrants, refugees, deportation, naturalization, and citizenship. (Basic Practice Skills Series).

Immigration History Research Center. University of Minnesota

Immigration Law and Business. Austin T. Fragomen and others. West Group, 610 Opperman Dr. Eagan, MN 55123. Phone: 800-328-4880 or (651)687-7000 Fax: 800-213-2323 or (651)687-5827 URL: http://www.westgroup.com • Three looseleaf volumes. $345.00. Periodic supplementation. Covers labor certification, temporary workers, applications, petitions, etc.

Immigration Law and Crimes. National Lawyers Guild. West Group, 610 Opperman Dr. Eagan, MN 55123. Phone: 800-328-4880 or (651)687-7000 Fax: 800-213-2323 or (651)687-5827 URL: http://www.westgroup.com • Looseleaf. $140.00. Periodic supplementation. Covers legal representation of the foreign-born criminal defendant.

Immigration Law and Defense. National Lawyers Guild. West Group, 610 Opperman Dr. Eagan, MN 55123. Phone: 800-328-4880 or (651)687-7000 Fax: 800-213-2323 or (651)687-5827 URL: http://www.westgroup.com • Two looseleaf volumes. $235.00. Periodic supplementation. Covers legal defense of immigrants and aliens.

Immigration Law and Procedure. Matthew Bender & Co., Inc., Two Park Ave. New York, NY 10016. Phone: 800-223-1940 or (212)488-2000 Fax: (212)244-3188 E-mail: international@bender.com • URL: http://www.bender.com • $1,600.00. 20 looseleaf volumes. Periodic supplementation.

Immigration Law Report. West Group, 610 Opperman Dr. Eagan, MN 55123. Phone: 800-328-4880 or (651)687-7000 Fax: 800-213-2323 or (651)687-5827 URL: http://www.westgroup.com • 24 times a year. $310.00 per year. Newsletter.

Immigration Procedures Handbook; A How-To Guide for Legal and Business Professionals. Austin T. Fragomen and others. West Group, 610 Opperman Dr. Eagan, MN 55123. Phone: 800-328-4880 or (651)687-7000 Fax: 800-213-2323 or (651)687-5827 URL: http://www.westgroup.com • 1993. $155.00. How to bring foreign nationals to the U. S. on a temporary or permanent basis.

Impact Beverage Trends in America. M. Shanken Communications, Inc., 387 Park Ave. S. New York, NY 10016. Phone: (212)684-4424 Fax: (212)684-5424 Annual. $695.00. Detailed compilations of data for various segments of the liquor, beer, and soft drink industries.

Impact of Advertising Law on Business and Public Policy. Ross D. Petty. Greenwood Publishing Group, Inc., 88 Post Rd., W., Westport, CT 06881. Phone: 800-225-5800 or (203)226-3571 Fax: (203)222-1502 E-mail: bookinfo@greenwood.com • URL: http://www.greenwood.com • 1992. $55.00. Analyzes cases under the Federal Trade Commission and Lanham Acts.

Impact: U.S. News and Research for the Wine, Spirits, and Beer Industries. M. Shanken Communications, Inc., 387 Park Ave., S. New York, NY 10016. Phone: (212)684-4424 Fax: (212)684-5424 Biweekly. $375.00 per year. Newsletter covering the marketing, economic, and financial aspects of alcoholic beverages.

Implement and Tractor Product File. Intertec Publishing, 6151 Powers Ferry Rd., N.W., Suite 200 Atlanta, GA 30339. Phone: 800-621-9907 or (770)995-2500 Fax: (770)955-0400 E-mail: subs@intertec.com • URL: http://www.intertec.com • Annual. $25.00.

Implement and Tractor: The Business Magazine of the Farm and Industrial Equipment Industry. Freiburg Publishing Co., Inc., P.O. Box 7 Cedar Falls, IA 50613. Phone: (319)277-3599 Fax: (319)277-3783 URL: http://www.ag-implement.com • Seven times a year. $25.00 per year. Includes annuals *Product File* and *Red Book*.

Import and Export. Entrepreneur Media, Inc., 2445 McCabe Way Irvine, CA 92614. Phone: 800-421-2300 or (949)261-2325 Fax: (949)261-0234 E-mail: entmag@entrepreneur.com • URL: http://www.entrepreneur.com • Looseleaf. $59.50. A practical guide to starting an import/export business. Covers profit potential, start-up costs, market size evaluation, owner's time required, pricing, accounting, advertising promotion, etc. (Start-Up Business Guide No. E1092.)

Importcar: The Complete Import Service Magazine. Babcox Publications, Inc., 11 S. Forge St. Akron, OH 44304-1810. Phone: (330)535-6117 Fax: (330)535-0874 Monthly. $64.00 per year. Includes *Automotive Aftermarket Training Guide*. Formerly *Importcar and Truck*.

Importers Manual U. S. A.: The Single Source Reference for Importing to the United States. Edward G. Hinkelman. World Trade Press, 1450 Grant Ave., Suite 204 Novato, CA 94945-3142. Phone: 800-833-8586 or (415)898-1124 Fax: (415)898-2080 E-mail: worldpress@aol.com • URL: http://www.worldtradepress.com • 1997. $87.00. Second edition. Published by World Trade Press. Covers U. S. customs regulations, letters of credit, contracts, shipping, insurance, and other items relating to importing. Includes 60 essays on practical aspects of importing.

Importing into the United States. Available from U. S. Government Printing Office, Washington, DC 20402. Phone: (202)512-1800 Fax: (202)512-2250 E-mail: gpoaccess@gpo.gov • URL: http://www.access.gpo.gov • 1998. $10.50. Issued by the U. S. Customs Service, Department of the Treasury. Formerly *Exporting to the United States*. Explains customs organization, entry of goods, invoices, assessment of duty, marking requirements, and other subjects.

Imports and Exports of Fishery Products. National Marine Fisheries Service. U.S. Department of Commerce, Washington, DC 20235. Phone: (301)713-2239 Annual.

Improving Access to Bank Information for Tax Purposes. Organization for Economic Cooperation and Development, OECD Washington Center, 2001 L St., N. W., Suite 650 Washington, DC 20036-4922. Phone: 800-456-6323 or (202)785-6323 Fax: (202)785-0350 E-mail: washington.contact@oecd.org • URL: http://www.oecd.org • 2000. $66.00. Discusses ways to improve the international exchange of bank account information for tax determinations.

Improving Online Public Access Catalogs. Martha M. Yee and Sara S. Layne. American Library Association, 50 E. Huron St. Chicago, IL 60611-2795. Phone: 800-545-2433 or (312)944-6780 Fax: (312)440-9374 E-mail: ala@ala.org • URL: http://www.ala.org • 1998. $48.00. A practical guide to developing user-friendly online catalogs (OPACs).

Improving Poor People: The Welfare State, the "Underclass," and Urban Schools as History. Michael B. Katz. California Princeton Fulfillment Services, 1445 Lower Ferry Rd. Ewing, NJ 08618. Phone: 800-777-4726 or (609)883-1759 E-mail: donnaw@cpfs.pupress.princeton.edu • 1995. $35.00.

Improving Public Productivity: Concepts and Practice. Ellen D. Rosen. Sage Publications, Inc., 2455 Teller Rd. Thousand Oaks, CA 91320. Phone: (805)499-0721 Fax: (805)499-0871 E-mail: info@sagepub.com • URL: http://www.sagepub.com • 1993. $52.00. A discussion of strategies for improving service quality and client satisfaction in public agencies at the local, state, and national level. Methods for measuring public sector productivity are included.

Improving Writing Skills: Memos, Letters, Reports, and Proposals. Arthur A. Berger. Sage Publications, Inc., 2455 Teller Rd. Thousand Oaks, CA 91320. Phone: (805)499-0721 Fax: (805)499-0871 E-mail: info@sagepub.com • URL: http://www.sagepub.com • 1993. $37.00. Emphasis is on the business correspondence required of university professors and other academic personnel. (Survival Skills for Scholars, vol. 9).

In Business: The Magazine for Environmental Entrepreneuring. J G Press, Inc., 419 State Ave. Emmaus, PA 18049. Phone: (610)967-4135 E-mail: biocycle@jgpress.com • URL: http://www.jgpress.com • Bimonthly. $33.00 per year. Magazine for environmental entrepreneuring.

In Command! A Series of Messages About Getting the Most From Your Word Processor. Economics Press, Inc., 12 Daniel Road Fairfield, NJ 07006. Phone: 800-526-2554 or (973)227-1224 Fax: (973)227-9742 E-mail: info@epinc.com • URL: http://www.epinc.com • Weekly. $146.00 per year. Quantity prices available. A newsletter for word processing operators.

In-Plant Graphics. North American Publishing Co., 401 N. Broad St. Philadelphia, PA 19108-9988. Phone: 800-627-2689 or (215)238-5300 Fax: (215)238-5457 E-mail: editor.ipg@napco.com • URL: http://www.napco.com • Monthly. $79.00 per year. Formerly *In-Plant Reproductions*.

In-Plant Printer Buyer's Guide. Innes Publishing Co., P.O. Box 7280 Libertyville, IL 60048-7280. Phone: 800-247-3306 or (847)816-7900 Fax: (847)247-8855 Annual. $10.00. Manufacturers of equipment for the in-plant and grahic arts industry. Formerly *In-Plant Printer and Electronic Publisher Buyer's Guide*.

In-Plant Printer: The In-Plant Management Magazine. Innes Publishing Co., P.O. Box 7280 Libertyville, IL 60048-7280. Phone: 800-247-3306 or (847)816-7900 Fax: (847)247-8855 Bimonthly. $75.00 per year. Formerly *In-Plant Printer and Electronic Publisher*.

Incentive: Managing and Marketing Through Motivation. Bill Communications, Inc., 770 Broadway New York, NY 10003-9595. Phone: 800-266-4712 or (646)654-4500 Fax: (646)654-7212 URL: http://www.billcom.com • Monthly. $55.00 per year.

Incentive Manufacturers Representatives Association.

Incentive-Merchandise and Travel Directory. Bill Communications, Inc., 770 Broadway New York, NY 10003-9595. Phone: 800-266-4712 or (646)654-5400 Fax: (646)654-7212 E-mail: info@bpi.com • URL: http://www.billcom.com • Annual. $5.00. A special issue of *Incentive* magazine.

Incentive-State of the Industry and Annual Facts Review. Bill Communications, Inc., 770 Broadway New York, NY 10003-9595. Phone: 800-266-4712 or (646)654-5400 Fax: (646)654-7212 E-mail: info@bpi.com • URL: http://www.billcom.com • Annual. $5.00. A special issue of *Incentive* magazine.

Income and Fees of Accountants in Public Practice. National Society of Accountants, 1010 N. Fairfax St. Alexandria, VA 22314-1574. Phone: 800-966-6679 or (703)549-6400 Fax: (703)594-2984 E-mail: nsa@wizard.net • URL: http://www.nspa.org/ • Triennial. Members, $35.00; non-members, $50.00.

Income Fund Outlook. Institute for Econometric Research, 2200 S.W. 10th St. Deerfield Beach, FL 33442-8799. Phone: 800-442-0066 or (954)421-1000 Fax: (954)570-8200 Monthly. $100.00 per year. Newsletter. Contains tabular data on money market funds, certificates of deposit, bond funds, and tax-free bond funds. Includes specific recommendations, fund news, and commentary on interest rates.

Income of the Population 55 and Older. Available from U. S. Government Printing Office, Washington, DC 20402. Phone: (202)512-1800 Fax: (202)512-2250 E-mail: gpoaccess@gpo.gov • URL: http://www.access.gpo.gov • Biennial. $19.00. Issued by the Social Security Administration (http://www.ssa.gov). Covers major sources and amounts of income for the 55 and older population in the U. S., "with special emphasis on some aspects of the income of the population 65 and older."

Income Opportunities: The Original Small Business - Home Office Magazine. Natcom, Inc., 2448 E. 81st St., 5300 City-Plex Tower Tulsa, OK 74137-4207. Phone: 800-554-1999 or (918)491-6100 Fax: (918)491-9424 URL: http://www.incomeps.com/ • Monthly. $31.95 per year.

Income Tax Regulations. CCH, Inc., 4025 W. Peterson Ave. Chicago, IL 60646-6085. Phone: 800-248-3248 or (773)866-6000 Fax: 800-224-8299 or (773)866-3608 URL: http://www.cch.com • Annual. $95.00. Six volumes. Contains full text of official Internal Revenue Code regulations (approximately 11,000 pages).

Income Taxation: Accounting Methods and Periods. George Bauernfeind. Shepard's, 555 Middle Creek Parkway Colorado Springs, CO 80921. Phone: 800-743-7393 or (719)481-7371 Fax: 800-525-0053 or (719)481-7621 E-mail: customer_service@shepards.com • URL: http://www.shepards.com • 1983. $235.00. Two volumes. (Tax and Estate Planning Series).

Income Taxation of Foreign Related Transactions. Matthew Bender and Co., Inc., Two Park Ave. New York, NY 10016. Phone: 800-223-1940 or (212)448-2000 Fax: (212)244-3188 E-mail: international@bender.com • URL: http://www.bender.com • Six looseleaf volumes. Annual supplements available. Price on application. All aspects of U.S. taxation of Americans doing business abroad and foreigners investing in the U.S.

Income Taxation of Natural Resources. Research Institute of America, Inc., 90 Fifth Ave. New York, NY 10011. Phone: 800-431-9025 or (212)645-4800 Fax: (212)337-4213 2000. $99.00. Revised edition.

Incorporate Your Business: The National Corporation Kit. Daniel Sitarz. Nova Publishing Co., 1103 W. College St. Carbondale, IL 62901. Phone: 800-748-1175 or (618)457-3521 Fax: (618)457-2541 E-mail: dansitarz@earthlink.net • URL: http://www.novapublishing.com • 1996. $29.95. Second revised edition. Includes basic forms and instructions for incorporating a small business in any state. Forms are also available on IBM or MAC diskettes. (Small Business Library Series).

Inc.-The Inc. 500. Inc. Publishing Corp., 38 Commerical Wharf Boston, MA 02110. Phone: 800-234-0999 or (617)248-8000 Fax: (617)248-8090 E-mail: editors@inc.com • URL: http://www.inc.com • Annual. $3.50. Information on each of the 500 fastest-growing privately held companies in the U. S. Based on percentage increase in sales over the five year period prior to compilation of current year's list.

Inc.: The Magazine for Growing Companies. Goldhirsh Group, Inc., 38 Commercial Wharf Boston, MA 02110. Phone: 800-234-0999 or (617)248-8000 Fax: (617)248-8090 URL: http://www.inc.com • 18 times a year. $19.00 per year. Edited for small office and office-in-the-home businesses with from one to 25 employees. Covers management, office technology, and lifestyle. Incorporates *Self-Employed Professional*.

Incorporating in Îstatel Without a Lawyer. W. Dean Brown. Consumer Publishing, Inc., 12320 Oakley Downs Rd., Suite

102 Knoxville, TN 37922. Phone: 800-677-2462 or (423)671-4858 Fax: (423)671-4854 E-mail: mail@consumercorp.com • URL: http://www.consumercorp.com • Annual. $24.95. Available in separate editions for each of 32 states and the District of Columbia. Includes specific instructions for creating a simple corporation in a particular state, with legal forms and sample stock certificates.

Incorporating Your Business: The Complete Guide That Tells All You Should Know About Establishing and Operating a Small Corporation. Professional Report Editors and John Kirk. NTC/Contemporary Publishing, P.O. Box 545 Blacklick, OH 43004. Phone: 800-338-3987 or (614)755-4151 Fax: (614)755-5645 E-mail: ntcpub@mcgraw-hill.com • URL: http://www.ntc-cb.com • 1986. $14.95.

Incorporation Kit. Entrepreneur Media, Inc., 2445 McCabe Way Irvine, CA 92614. Phone: 800-421-2300 or (949)261-2325 Fax: (949)261-0234 E-mail: entmag@entrepreneur.com • URL: http://www.entrepreneur.com • Looseleaf. $59.50. A practical guide to incorporating a small business. Includes sample forms and information on how to construct bylaws and articles of incorporation. (Start-Up Business Guide No. E7100.)

INDA: Association of the Nonwoven Fabrics Industry.

Independent Agent. Independent Insurance Agents of North America, Inc. MSI, 127 S. Peyton St. Alexandria, VA 22314. Phone: (703)683-4422 Fax: (703)683-7556 E-mail: magazine@iiaa.org • URL: http://www.iiaa.iix.com • Monthly. $24.00 per year.

Independent Battery Manufacturers Association., 100 Larchwood Dr. Largo, FL 34640. Phone: (727)586-1408 Manufacturers of lead-acid storage batteries.

Independent Cash Register Dealers Association.

Independent Community Bankers of America.

Independent Electrical Contractors.

Independent Energy: The Power Industry's Business Magazine. PennWell Corp., Industrial Div., 1421 S. Sheridan Rd. Tulsa, OK 74112. Phone: 800-331-4463 or (918)831-9421 Fax: (918)831-9295 E-mail: webmaster@pennwell.com • URL: http://www.pennwell.com • 10 times a year. $127.00 per year. Covers non-utility electric power plants (cogeneration) and other alternative sources of electric energy.

Independent Insurance Agents of America.

Independent Medical Distributors Association., 5800 Foxridge Dr., No. 115 Mission, KS 66202-2333. Phone: (913)262-4510 Fax: (913)262-0174 URL: http://www.imda.org • Members are distributors of high technology health care products.

Independent Petroleum Association of America.

Independent Power Report: An Exclusive Biweekly Covering the Cogeneration and Small Power Market. McGraw-Hill, Energy and Business Newsletter, 1221 Ave. of the Americas New York, NY 10020-1095. Phone: 800-722-4726 or (212)904-2000 Fax: (212)904-2072 E-mail: customer.service@mcgraw-hill.com • URL: http://www.mcgraw-hill.com • Biweekly. $815.00 per year. Newsletter. Covers industry trends, new projects, new contracts, rate changes, and regulations, with emphasis on the Federal Energy Regulatory Commission (FERC). Formerly *Cogeneration Report*.

Independent Publisher: Leading the World of Book Selling in New Directions. Jenkins Group, Inc., 121 E. Front St., 4th Fl. Traverse City, MI 49684. Phone: 800-706-4636 or (616)933-0445 Fax: (616)933-0919 E-mail: subscribe@bookpublishing.com • URL: http://www.bookpublishing.com • Bimonthly. $34.00 per year. Covers business, finance, production, marketing, and other management topics for small publishers, including college presses. Emphasis is on book publishing.

Independent School. National Association of Independent Schools, 1620 L St., N.W., Suite 1100 Washington, DC 20036-5605. Phone: (202)973-9700 Fax: (202)973-9790 Three times a year. $17.50 per year. An open forum for exchange of information about elementary and secondary education in general, and independent education in particular

Independent Sector.

Index and Directory of Industry Standards. Information Handling Services, P.O. Box 1154 Englewood, CO 80150. Phone: 800-841-7179 or (303)397-7956 Fax: (303)799-4085 Annual. Seven volumes. Price varies. Covers approximately 20,000 international and 35,000 U.S. industrial standards as well as 362 industrial organizations.

Index Medicus. National Library of Medicine. Available from U. S. Government Printing Office, Washington, DC 20402. Phone: (202)512-1800 Fax: (202)512-2250 E-mail: gpoaccess@gpo.gov • URL: http://www.access.gpo.gov • Monthly. $522.00 per year. Bibliographic listing of references to current articles from approximately 3,000 of the world's biomedical journals.

Index of Economic Articles in Journals and Collective Volumes. American Economic Association, 2014 Broadway, Suite 305 Nashville, TN 37203-2418. Phone: (615)322-2595 Fax: (615)343-7590 URL: http://www.vanderbilt.edu/aea • Irregular. $160.00.

Index of Majors. The College Board Publications, 45 Columbus Ave. New York, NY 10023-6992. Phone: 800-323-7155 or (212)713-8000 Fax: (212)713-8143 Annual. $17.95.

Index of Patents Issued from the United States Patent and Trademark Office, Part One: List of Patentees. Available from U. S. Government Printing Office, Washington, DC 20402. Phone: (202)512-1800 Fax: (202)512-2250 E-mail: gpoaccess@gpo.gov • URL: http://www.access.gpo.gov • Annual. Lists patentees and reissue patentees for each year.

Index of Patents Issued from the United States Patent and Trademark Office, Part Two: Index to Subjects of Invention. Available from U. S. Government Printing Office, Washington, DC 20402. Phone: (202)512-1800 Fax: (202)512-2250 E-mail: gpoaccess@gpo.gov • URL: http://www.access.gpo.gov • Annual. A subject index to patents issued each year, arranged by class and subclass numbers. Includes a list of patent and tradmark depository libraries.

Index of Trademarks Issued from the United States Patent and Trademark Office. Available from U. S. Government Printing Office, Washington, DC 20402. Phone: (202)512-1800 Fax: (202)512-2250 E-mail: gpoaccess@gpo.gov • URL: http://www.access.gpo.gov • Annual. Arranged alphabetically by name of registrant. The caption title is ''List of Trademark Registrants.''

Index to Anthologies on Postsecondary Education, 1960-1978. Richard H. Quay, compiler. Greenwood Publishing Group, Inc., 88 Post Rd., W. Westport, CT 06881-5007. Phone: 800-225-5800 or (203)226-3571 Fax: (203)222-2540 E-mail: bookinfo@greenwood.com • URL: http://www.greenwood.com • 1980. $55.00.

Index to AV Producers and Distributors (Educational Audiovisual Materials). National Information Center for Educational Media. c/o Plexus Publishing, Inc., 143 Old Marlton Pike Medford, NJ 08055-8750. Phone: (609)654-6500 Fax: (609)654-4309 Biennial. $89.00. A directory listing about 23,300 producers and distributors of all types of audiovisual educational materials.

Index to Current Urban Documents. Greenwood Publishing Group, Inc., Subscription Publications, 88 Post Rd., W. Westport, CT 06881-5007. Phone: 800-225-5800 or (203)226-3571 Fax: (203)222-2540 E-mail: bookinfo@greenwood.com • URL: http://www.greenwood.com • Quarterly. $425.00 per year. Annual cumulation.

Index to Federal Tax Articles. Warren, Gorham and Lamont/RIA Group, 395 Hudson St. New York, NY 10014. Phone: 800-950-1215 or (212)367-6300 Fax: (212)924-0460 URL: http://www.wgl.com • $695.00 per year. Looseleaf service. Seven volumes. Quarterly supplementation. Bibliographic listing of every significant article on federal income, estate and gift taxation since 1913. Lists over 36,000 articles.

Index to Foreign Legal Periodicals. American Association of Law Libraries. University of California Press, Journals Div., 2000 Certer St. Suite 303 Berkeley, CA 94704-1223. Phone: (510)643-7154 Fax: (510)642-9917 E-mail: journals@ucop.edu • URL: http://www.ucpress.edu/journals • Quarterly. $630.00 per year. Annual cumulation.

Index to Health Information. Congressional Information Service, Inc., 4520 East-West Highway, Suite 800 Bethesda, MD 20814-3389. Phone: 800-638-8380 or (301)654-1550 Fax: (301)654-4033 E-mail: info@cispubs.com • URL: http://www.cispubs • Quarterly. $945.00 per year, including two-volume annual cumulation. Provides index and abstracts covering the medical and health field in general, with emphasis on statistical sources and government documents. Service with microfiche source documents, $4,995.00 per year.

Index to Legal Citations and Abbreviations. Donald Raistrick. Bowker-Saur, 121 Chanlon Rd. New Providence, NJ 07974. Phone: 800-521-8110 or (908)464-6800 Fax: (908)771-8784 1993. $100.00. Second edition. Explains about 25,000 legal abbreviations and acronyms used in the U. S., U. K., and Europe.

Index to Legal Periodicals and Books. H. W. Wilson Co., 950 University Ave. Bronx, NY 10452. Phone: 800-367-6770 or (718)588-8400 Fax: (718)590-1617 E-mail: custserv@hwwilson.com • URL: http://www.hwwilson.com • Monthly. Quarterly and annual cumulations. $270.00 per year. CD-ROM version available at $1,495.00 per year.

Index to Legal Periodicals and Books (Online). H. W. Wilson Co., 950 University Ave. Bronx, NY 10452. Phone: 800-367-6770 or (718)588-8400 Fax: (718)590-1617 E-mail: hwwmsg@info.hwwilson.com • URL: http://www.hwwilson.com • Broad coverage of law journals and books 1981 to date. Monthly updates. Inquire as to online cost and availability.

Index to Marquis Who's Who Publications. Marquis Who's Who, 121 Chanlon Rd. New Providence, NJ 07974. Phone: 800-521-8110 or (908)464-6800 Fax: (908)665-6688 E-mail: info@marquiswhoswha.com • URL: http://www.marquiswhoswho.com • Annual. $115.00. A combined index to current editions of most Marquis Who's Who publications. Contains over 320,000 entries.

Index to Periodical Articles Related to Law. Glanville Publishers, Inc., 75 Main St. Dobbs Ferry, NY 10522. Phone: (914)693-8100 Fax: (914)693-0402 E-mail: glanville@oceanalaw.com • URL: http://www.oceanalaw • Quarterly. $95.00 per year. Selected from journals not included in the *Index to Legal Periodicals, Current Law Index, Index to Foreign Legal Periodicals, Legal Resolve Index or Legaltrac*.

Index to Proceedings of the Economic and Social Council. United Nations Publications, United Nations Concourse Level, First Ave., 46th St. New York, NY 10017. Phone: 800-553-3210 or (212)963-7680 Fax: (212)963-4910 E-mail: bookstore@un.org • URL: http://www.un.org/publications • Irregular.

Index Veterinarius: Comprehensive Monthly and Author Index to the World's Veterinary Literature. Availabe in Print and on the Internet. Available from CABI Publishing North America, 10 E. 40th St. New York, NY 10016. Phone: 800-528-4841 Fax: (212)686-7993 E-mail: cabi@cabi.org • URL: http://www.cabi.org • Monthly. $1,450.00 per year. Published in England by CABI Publishing. Provides worldwide coverage of the literature.

The Indexer. American Society of Indexers, 11250 Roger Bacon Dr., Suite 8 Reston, VA 20190-5202. Phone: (703)234-4147 Fax: (703)735-4390 E-mail: info@asindexing.org • URL: http://www.asindexing.org • Semiannual. $40.00 per year. Devoted specifically to all aspects of indexing.

The Indexer Locater. American Society of Indexers, Inc., 11250 Roger Bacon Dr., Suite 8 Reston, VA 20190-5202. Phone: (703)234-4147 Fax: (703)735-4390 E-mail: info@asindexing.org • URL: http://www.asindexing.org • Annual. Members, $10.00; non-members, $15.00. Lists over 200 free-lance indexers in the U. S. and their subject specialties. Formerly *Register of Indexers*.

Indexing and Abstracting in Theory and Practice. F. Wilfrid Lancaster. University of Illinois, Graduate School of Library and Information Science,, 501 E. Daniel St. Champaign, IL 61820. Phone: (217)333-1359 Fax: (217)244-7329 E-mail: puboff@alexia.lis.uiuc.edu • URL: http://www.edfu.lis.uiuc.edu • 1998. $47.50. Second revised edition. Includes indexing and abstracting exercises.

Indexing for Maximum Investment Results. Albert S. Neuberg. Fitzroy Dearborn Publishers, 919 N. Michigan Ave., Suite 760 Chicago, IL 60611. Phone: 800-850-8102 or (312)587-0131 Fax: (312)587-1049 E-mail: website@fitzroydearborn.com • URL: http://www.fitzroydearborn.com • 1998. $65.00. Covers the Standard & Poor's 500 and other indexing strategies for both individual and institutional investors.

Indexing from A to Z. Hans H. Wellisch. H. W. Wilson Co., 950 University Ave. Bronx, NY 10452. Phone: 800-367-6770 or (718)588-8400 Fax: (718)590-1617 E-mail: custserv@hwwilson.com • URL: http://www.hwwilson.com • 1996. $40.00. Second enlarged revised edition. A practical guide to the indexing of books, periodicals, and non-print materials. Covers such technical topics as exhaustivity, specificity, thesauri, and keywords, and such mundane topics as contracts and fees.

Indexing: The State of Our Knowledge and the State of Our Ignorance. Bella H. Weinberg, editor. Information Today, Inc., 143 Old Marlton Pike Medford, NJ 08055-8750. Phone: 800-300-9868 or (609)654-6266 Fax: (609)654-4309 E-mail: custserv@infotoday.com • URL: http://www.infotoday.com • 1989. $30.00. Ten papers presented at the 1988 annual meeting of the American Society of Indexers.

Indicators of Industrial Activity. OECD Publications and Information Center, 2001 L St., N.W., Ste. 650 Washington, DC 20036-4922. Phone: 800-456-6323 or (202)785-6323 Fax: (202)785-0350 E-mail: washington.contact@oecd.org • URL: http://www.oecdwash.org • Quarterly. $114.00 per year. Information on production, deliveries, orders, prices and employment for 17 industrial sectors in selected OECD member countries.

Individual Income Tax Returns. U.S. Department of the Treasury, Internal Revenue Service. Available from U.S. Government Printing Office, Washington, DC 20402. Phone: (202)512-1800 Fax: (202)512-2250 E-mail: gpoaccess@gpo.gov • URL: http://www.accessgpo.gov • Annual. $17.00.

Individual Investor. Individual Investor Group, 125 Broad St. New York, NY 10004. Phone: 800-888-4741 or (212)742-0747 E-mail: letters@individualinvestor.com • Monthly. $22.95 per year. Emphasis is on stocks selling for less than ten dollars a share. Includes a ''Guide to Insider Transactions'' and ''New Issue Alert.''

The Individual Investor Revolution: Unlock the Secrets of Wall Street and Invest Like a Pro. Charles B. Carlson. McGraw-Hill, 1221 Ave. of the Americas New York, NY 10020-1095. Phone: 800-722-4726 or (212)904-2000 Fax: (212)904-2072 E-mail: customer.service@mcgraw-hill.com • URL: http://www.mcgraw-hill.com • 1998. $21.95. Emphasizes the growing importance of the individual investor, especially with regard to online trading (e-trading). Includes the author's favorite websites for investors and traders.

Individual Retirement Account Answer Book. Donald R. Levy and Steven G. Lockwood. Panel Publishers, 1185 Ave. of the Americas New York, NY 10036. Phone: 800-638-8437 or (212)597-0200 Fax: 800-901-9075 or (212)597-0334 E-mail: customer.service@aspenpubl.com • URL: http://

www.panelpublishers.com • 1999. $136.00. Sixth edition. Periodic supplementation available. Questions and answers include information about contributions, distributions, rollovers, Roth IRAs, SIMPLE IRAs (Savings Incentive Match Plans for Employees), Education IRAs, and SEPs (Simplified Employee Pension plans). Chapters are provided on retirement planning, estate planning, and tax planning.

Individual Retirement Plans Guide. CCH, Inc., 4025 W. Peterson Ave. Chicago, IL 60646-6085. Phone: 800-248-3248 or (773)583-8500 Fax: 800-224-8299 URL: http://www.cch.com • $230.00 per year. Looseleaf service. Monthly updates. Covers IRA plans (Individual Retirement Accounts), SEP plans (Simplified Employee Pensions), and Keogh plans (self-employed retirement accounts).

Individual Tax Return Guide, 1992. Research Institute of America, Inc., 90 Fifth Ave. New York, NY 10011. Phone: 800-431-9025 or (212)645-4800 Fax: (212)337-4213 1993. $10.00. Revised edition.

Individual Taxation. James W. Pratt and William N. Kulsrud. McGraw-Hill Higher Education, 1221 Ave. of the Americas New York, NY 10020-1095. Phone: 800-722-4726 or (212)904-2000 Fax: (212)904-2072 E-mail: customer.service@mcgraw-hill.com • URL: http://www.mcgraw-hill.com • 1996. $69.95. Tenth edition. Focuses on the federal income tax.

Individual Taxes: Worldwide Summaries. Pricewaterhouse-Coopers. John Wiley and Sons, Inc., 605 Third Ave. New York, NY 10158-0012. Phone: 800-225-5945 or (212)850-6000 Fax: (212)850-6088 E-mail: info@jwiley.com • URL: http://www.wiley.com • 1999. $95.00. Summarizes the personal tax regulations of more than 125 countries. Provides information useful for international tax planning and foreign investments.

Individuals' Filled-In Tax Return Forms. CCH, Inc., 4025 W. Peterson Ave. Chicago, IL 60646-6085. Phone: 800-248-3248 or (773)583-8500 Fax: 800-224-8299 URL: http://www.cch.com • 1999. $29.50. Revised edition.

Industrial and Engineering Chemistry Research. American Chemical Society, 1155 16th St., N.W. Washington, DC 20036. Phone: 800-333-9511 or (202)872-4600 Fax: (202)872-4615 E-mail: services@acs.org • URL: http://www.pub.acs.org • Monthly. Institutions, $1,343 per year; others, price on application. Available on line . Fromerly *Industrial and Engineering Chemistry Product Research and Development*.

Industrial and Labor Relations Review. Cornell University, New York State School of Industrial and Labor Relations, Ithaca, NY 14853-3901. Phone: (607)255-2732 Fax: (607)255-8016 E-mail: blk5cornell.edu • URL: http://www.ilr.cornell.edu • Quarterly. Individuals, $26.00 per year; institutions, $43.00 per year; students, $13.00 per year.

Industrial and Organizational Psychology: From Fundamentals to Practice. Paul E. Spector. John Wiley and Sons, Inc., 605 Third Ave. New York, NY 10158-0012. Phone: 800-225-5945 or (212)850-6000 Fax: (212)850-6088 E-mail: info@wiley.com • URL: http://www.wiley.com • 1999. $83.95. Second edition.

Industrial Association of Juvenile Apparel Manufacturers.

Industrial Coatings: Properties, Applications, Quality, and Environmental Compliance. ASM International, 9639 Kinsman Rd. Materials Park, OH 44073-0002. Phone: 800-336-5152 or (440)338-5151 Fax: (440)338-4634 E-mail: custserv@po.asm-intl.org • URL: http://www.asm-intl.org • 1992. $90.00.

Industrial Color Technology. Ruth M. Johnston and Max Saltzman, editors. American Chemical Society, 1155 16th St., N.W. Washington, DC 20036. Phone: 800-333-9511 or (202)872-4600 Fax: (202)872-4615 E-mail: service@acs.org • URL: http://www.pubs.acs.org • 1972. $21.95. (Advances in Chemistry Series: No. 107).

Industrial Color Testing: Fundamentals and Techniques. Hans G. Volz. John Wiley and Sons, Inc., 605 Third Ave. New York, NY 10158-0012. Phone: 800-225-5945 or (212)850-0662 E-mail: info@jwiley.com • URL: http://www.wiley.com • 1995. $195.00.

Industrial Commodity Statistics Yearbook. United Nations Dept. of Economic and Social Affairs. United Nations Publications, United Nations Concourse Level, First Ave., 46th St. New York, NY 10017. Phone: 800-553-3210 or (212)963-7680 Fax: (212)963-4910 E-mail: bookstore@un.org • URL: http://www.org/publications • Annual.

Industrial Compressor Distributors Association.

Industrial Computing. ISA Services, Inc., PO Box 12277 Research Triangle Park, NC 27709. Phone: (919)549-8411 Fax: (919)549-8288 E-mail: info@isa.org • URL: http://www.isa.org • Monthly. $50.00 per year. Published by the Instrument Society of America. Edited for engineering managers and systems integrators. Subject matter includes industrial software, programmable controllers, artificial intelligence systems, and industrial computer networking systems.

Industrial Controls. Available from MarketResearch.com, 641 Ave. of the Americas, 3rd Fl. New York, NY 10011. Phone: 800-298-5699 or (212)807-2629 Fax: (212)807-2716 E-mail: order@marketresearch.com • URL: http://www.marketresearch.com • 1998. $3,400.00. Published by the Freedonia Group. Market data with forecasts to 2002 and 2006. Includes computerized controls and conventional controls.

Industrial Designers Society of America., 1142 E.Walker Rd., Suite E Great Falls, VA 22066. Phone: (703)759-0100 Fax: (703)759-7679 E-mail: idsa@erols.com • URL: http://www.idsa.org • A professional society of industrial designers.

Industrial Diamond Association.

Industrial Diamond Review. De Beers Industrial Diamond Div., Charters, Sunninghill Ascot Berks SL5 9PX 44, England. Bimonthly. Free to qualified personnel. Incorporating *Industrial Diamond Abstracts*.

Industrial Distribution Association.

Industrial Distribution: For Industrial Distributors and Their Sales Personnel. Cahners Business Information, 275 Washington St. Newton, MA 02158-1630. Phone: 800-662-7776 or (617)964-3030 Fax: (617)558-4677 E-mail: corporatecommunications@cahners.com • URL: http://www.cahners.com • Monthly. $97.90 per year.

Industrial Engineering Terminology. Institute of Industrial Engineering Staff. McGraw-Hill, 1221 Ave. of the Americas New York, NY 10020. Phone: 800-722-4726 or (212)904-2000 Fax: (212)904-2072 E-mail: customer.service@mcgraw-hill.com • URL: http://www.mcgraw-hill.com • 1992. $80.95. Revised edition.

Industrial Equipment News. Thomas Publishing Co., Five Penn Plaza, 250 W. 34th St. New York, NY 10001. Phone: 800-699-9822 or (212)695-0500 Fax: (212)629-1585 URL: http://www.thomaspublishing.com • Monthly. $95.00 per year. Free. What's new in equipment, parts and materials.

Industrial Fabric Products Review. Industrial Fabrics Association International, 1801 W. Country Rd., B Roseville, MN 55113-4061. Phone: 800-225-4324 or (651)222-2508 Fax: (651)631-9334 E-mail: generalinfo@ifai.com • Monthly. $47.00 per year. Includes *Buyers Guide*.

Industrial Fabric Products Review Buyer's Guide: The Encyclopedia of Industrial Fabrics. Industrial Fabrics Association International, 1801 W. Country Rd., B W. Roseville, MN 55113-4061. Phone: 800-225-4324 or (651)222-2508 Fax: (651)631-9334 E-mail: generalinfo@ifai.com • URL: http://www.ifai.com • Annual. $20.00. Includes manufacturers of fabrics, fibers, and end products. Included with subscriptions to *Industrial Fabric Products Review*.

Industrial Fabrics Association International., 1801 Country Rd B W. Roseville, MN 55113-4061. Phone: 800-225-4324 or (651)222-2508 Fax: (651)631-9334 E-mail: generalinfo@ifai.com • URL: http://www.ifai.com • Members include nonwoven industrial fabric producers.

Industrial Fabrics Association International Membership Directory. Industrial Fabrics Association International, 1801 W. Country Rd., B W. Roseville, MN 55113-4061. Phone: 800-225-4324 or (651)222-2508 Fax: (651)631-9334 E-mail: generalinfo@ifai.com • URL: http://www.ifai.com • Annual. Free to members; non-members, $40.00.

Industrial Fasteners Institute.

Industrial Heating Equipment Association.

Industrial Hydraulics. John H. Pippenger and Tyler G. Hicks. McGraw-Hill, 1221 Ave. of the Americas New York, NY 10020. Phone: 800-722-4726 or (212)904-2000 Fax: (212)904-2072 E-mail: customer.service@mcgraw-hill.com • URL: http://www.mcgraw-hill.com • 1979. $102.50. Third edition.

Industrial Hygiene News. Rimbach Publishing, Inc., 8650 Babcock Blvd. Pittsburgh, PA 15237. Phone: 800-245-3182 or (412)364-5366 Fax: (412)369-9721 E-mail: rimbach@sgi.net • URL: http://www.rimbach.com • Seven times a year. Free to qualified personnel.

Industrial Hygiene News Buyer's Guide. Rimbach Publishing, Inc., 8650 Babcock Blvd. Pittsburgh, PA 15237. Phone: 800-245-3182 or (412)364-5366 Fax: (412)369-9720 E-mail: rimbach@sgi.net • URL: http://www.rimbach.com • Annual. $50.00. Lists about 1,000 manufacturers and suppliers of products, equipment, and services to the occupational health, industrial hygiene, and high-tech safety industry.

Industrial Laser Buyers Guide. PennWell Corp., Advanced Technology Div., 98 Spit Brook Rd. Nashua, NH 03062-5737. Phone: 800-331-4463 or (603)891-0123 Fax: (603)891-0539 E-mail: webmaster@penwell.com • URL: http://www.pennwell.com • Annual. $85.00. Lists industrial laser suppliers by category and geographic location. (Included with subscription to *Industrial Laser Solutions*.)

Industrial Laser Solutions. PennWell Corp., Advanced Technology Div., 98 Spit Brook Rd. Nashua, NH 03062-5737. Phone: 800-331-4463 or (603)891-0123 Fax: (603)891-0539 E-mail: webmaster@pennwell.com • URL: http://www.pennwell.com • Monthly. $250.00 per year. Covers industrial laser technology, especially machine tool applications. (Subscription includes annual *Industrial Laser Buyers Guide*.)

Industrial Launderer. Institute of Industrial Launderers, 1300 N. 17th St., Suite 750 Arlington, VA 22209. Phone: (703)247-2600 Fax: (703)841-4750 Monthly. $100.00 per year.

Industrial Literature Review: Presents Catalogs and Brochures to Buyers and Specifiers in the United States Industrial Marketplace. Thomas Publishing Co., Five Penn Plaza New York, NY 10001. Phone: 800-699-9822 or (212)695-0500 Fax: (212)629-1585 URL: http://www.thomaspublishing.com • Quarterly. Controlled circulation. Describes new catalogs and other new industrial literature.

Industrial Location: Principles and Policies. J.W. Harrington and Barney Warf. Routledge, 29 W. 35th St. New York, NY 10001-2299. Phone: 800-634-7064 or (212)244-3336 Fax: 800-248-4724 or (212)564-7854 E-mail: info@routledge.com • URL: http://www.routledge-ny.com • 1995. $85.00. Second revised edition.

Industrial Maintenance and Plant Operation. Cahners Business Information, 1018 W. 9th Ave. King of Prussia, PA 19406. Phone: 800-695-1214 or (610)205-1000 Fax: (610)964-2915 E-mail: corporatecommunications@cahners.com • URL: http://www.cahners.com • Monthly. $39.00 per year.

Industrial Marketing Management: The International Journal of Marketing for Industrial and High Tech Firms. Elsevier Science, 655 Ave. of the Americas New York, NY 10010. Phone: 888-437-4636 or (212)989-5800 Fax: (212)633-3680 E-mail: usinfo@elsevier.com • URL: http://www.elsevier.com • Eight times a year. $669.00 per year.

Industrial Marketing Strategy. Frederick E. Webster. John Wiley and Sons, Inc., 605 Third Ave. New York, NY 10158-0012. Phone: 800-225-5945 or (212)850-6000 Fax: (212)850-6088 E-mail: info@wiley.com • URL: http://www.wiley.com • 1991. $114.95. Third edition. (Marketing Management Series).

Industrial Mathematics Society., P.O. Box 159 Roseville, MI 48066. Phone: (810)771-0403 Areas of interest include applied mathematics, computers, statistics, and operations analysis.

Industrial Paint and Powder Buyer's Guide. Cahners Business Information, 2000 Cleanwater Dr. Oak Brook, IL 60523-8809. Phone: 800-662-7776 or (630)320-7000 E-mail: corporatecommunications@cahners.com • URL: http://www.cahners.com • Annual. Free to qualified personnel; others, $15.00. List of about 2,000 manufacturers of finishing and formulating products. Formerly *Industrial Finishing Buyer's Guide*.

Industrial Paint and Powder: Coatings Manufacturing and Application. Cahners Business Information, 2000 Clearwater Dr. Oak Brook, IL 60523. Phone: (630)462-2310 Fax: (630)462-2225 E-mail: emcallum@cahners.com • URL: http://www.cahners.com • Monthly. $72.90 per year. Supplement available, *Annual Buyer's Guide*. Formerly *Industrial Finishing*.

Industrial Pollution Prevention Handbook. Harry M. Freeman. McGraw-Hill, 1221 Ave. of the Americas New York, NY 10020. Phone: 800-722-4726 or (212)904-2000 Fax: (212)904-2072 E-mail: customer.service@mcgraw-hill.com • URL: http://www.mcgraw-hill.com • 1992. $115.00.

Industrial Pumps and Pumping Equipment. Available from MarketResearch.com, 641 Ave. of the Americas, Third Floor New York, NY 10011. Phone: 800-298-5699 or (212)807-2629 Fax: (212)807-2716 E-mail: order@marketresearch.com • URL: http://www.marketresearch.com • 1997. $1,195.00. Market research report published by Specialists in Business Information. Covers centrifugal, rotary, turbine, reciprocating, and other types of pumps. Presents market data relative to sales growth, shipments, exports, imports, and end-use. Includes company profiles.

Industrial Purchasing Agent. Publications for Industry, 21 Russell Woods Rd. Great Neck, NY 11021. Phone: (516)487-0990 Fax: (516)487-0809 Monthly. $25.00 per year. New product releases.

Industrial Relations: A Journal of Economy and Society. University of California at Berkeley Institute of Industrial Relations. Blackwell Publishers, 350 Main St., 6th Fl. Malden, MA 02148-5018. Phone: 800-216-2522 or (781)388-8200 Fax: (781)388-8232 E-mail: subscript@blackwellpub.com • URL: http://www.blackwellpub.com • Quarterly. $99.00 per year.

Industrial Relations Research Association.

Industrial Relations Research Institute.

Industrial Relations Section., Princeton University, Firestone Library Pinceton, NJ 08544. Phone: (609)258-4040 Fax: (609)258-2907 URL: http://www.irs.princeton.edu/ • Fields of research include labor supply, manpower training, unemployment, and equal employment opportunity.

Industrial Relations Section. Massachusetts Institute of Technology

Industrial Research Institute.

Industrial Research Institute for Pacific Nations., California State Polytechnic University, Pomona, School of Business Administration, 3801 W. Temple Ave., Bldg. 66, Room 217 Pomona, CA 91768. Phone: (909)869-2399 Fax:

(909)869-6799 URL: http://www.hkjinacsu.edu • Conducts research on the Pacific nations marketplace.

Industrial Safety and Health Management. C. Ray Asfahl. Prentice Hall, 240 Frisch Court Paramus, NJ 07652-5240. Phone: 800-947-7700 or (201)909-6200 Fax: 800-445-6991 or (201)909-6361 URL: http://www.prenhall.com • 1998. $92.00. Fourth edition.

Industrial Safety and Hygiene News: News of Safety, Health and Hygiene, Environmental, Fire, Security and Emergency Protection Equipment. Business News Publishing Co., 755 W. Big Beaver Rd., Suite 1000 Troy, MI 48084. Phone: 800-837-7370 or (248)362-3700 Fax: (248)362-0317 URL: http://www.ishn.com • Monthly. Free to qualified personnel; others, $120.00 per year.

Industrial Truck Association.

Industries in Transition; A Newsletter Written for Growth Directed Management and Business Planners. Business Communications Co., Inc., 25 Van Zant St., Suite 13 Norwalk, CT 06855. Phone: (203)853-4266 Fax: (203)853-0348 Monthly. $375.00 per year. Newsletter. Formerly *Growth Industry News*.

Industry and Product Classification Manual (SIC Basis). Available from National Technical Information Service, U. S. Department of Commerce, Technology Administration, 5285 Port Royal Rd. Springfield, VA 22161. Phone: 800-553-6847 or (703)487-4600 Fax: (703)321-8547 E-mail: info@ntis.fedworld.gov • URL: http://www.ntis.gov • 1992. Issued by U. S. Bureau of the Census. Contains extended Standard Industrial Classification (SIC) numbers used by the Census Bureau to allow a more detailed classification of industry, services, and agriculture.

Industry Coalition on Technolgy Transfer., 1400 L St., N.W., 8th Fl. Washington, DC 20005-3502. Phone: (202)371-5994 Fax: (202)371-5950 Members are computer industry associations concerned with federal regulations on technology transfer in the computer industry.

Industry Insider. Thomson Financial Securities Data, Two Gateway Center Newark, NJ 07102. Phone: 888-989-8373 or (973)622-3100 Fax: (973)622-1421 URL: http://www.securitiesdata.com • Contains full-text online industry research reports from more than 200 leading trade associations, covering 50 specific industries. Reports include extensive statistics and market research data. Inquire as to online cost and availability.

Industry Norms and Key Business Ratios. Desk Top Edition. Dun and Bradstreet Corp., Business Information Services, One Diamond Hill Rd. Murray Hill, NJ 07974. Phone: 800-223-0141 or (201)665-5330 Fax: (908)665-5418 URL: http://www.dnb.com • Annual. Five volumes. $475.00 per volume. $1,890.00 per set. Covers over 800 kinds of businesses, arranged by Standard Industrial Classification number. More detailed editions covering longer periods of time are also available.

The Industry Standard: The Newsmagazine of the Internet Economy. International Data Group, Inc., 315 Pacific Ave. San Francisco, CA 94111-1701. Phone: (415)733-5400 Fax: (415)733-5401 E-mail: info@thestandard.com • URL: http://www.thestandard.com • Weekly. $76.00 per year. Presents news and trends affecting the Internet and intranet industries.

Industry Week: The Industry Management Magazine. Penton Media, Inc., 1300 E. Ninth St. Cleveland, OH 44114. Phone: (216)696-7000 Fax: (216)696-0836 E-mail: corpcomm@penton.com • URL: http://www.penton.com • 18 times a year. Free to qualified personnel; others, $65.00 per year. Edited for industrial and business managers. Covers organizational and technological developments affecting industrial management.

Industry's Future: Changing Patterns of Industrial Research. Herbert I. Fusfeld. American Chemical Society, 1155 16th St., N. W. Washington, DC 20036. Phone: 800-333-9511 or (202)872-4600 Fax: (202)872-4615 E-mail: service@acs.org • URL: http://www.pubs.acs.org • 1994. $45.00.

Industry's Guide to ISO 9000. Adedeji B. Badiru. John Wiley and Sons, Inc., 605 Third Ave. New York, NY 10158-0012. Phone: 800-225-5945 or (212)850-6000 Fax: (212)850-6088 E-mail: info@wiley.com • URL: http://www.wiley.com • 1995. $99.00. (Engineering and Technology Management Series).

Infant and Juvenile Manufacturers Association.

Inflation, Exchange Rates, and the World Economy: Lectures on International Monetary Economics. W. M. Corden. University of Chicago Press, 5801 S. Ellis Ave., 4th Fl. Chicago, IL 60637. Phone: 800-621-2736 or (773)702-7700 Fax: (773)702-9756 E-mail: marketing@press.uchicago.edu • URL: http://www.press.uchicago.edu • 1986. $22.50. Third edition. (Studies in Business and Society Series).

The Influence of Disney Entertainment Parks on Architecture and Development. Stephen J. Rebori. Sage Publications, Inc., 2455 Teller Rd. Thousand Oaks, CA 91320. Phone: (805)499-0721 Fax: (805)499-0871 E-mail: info@sagepub.com • URL: http://www.sagepub.com • 1995. $10.00. (CPL-Bibliographies Series, vol. 321).

INFO. Tulsa City-County Library, Business & Technology Dept., 400 Civic Center Tulsa, OK 74103-3830. Phone: (918)596-7988 Fax: (918)596-7895 E-mail: kcurtis@tulsalibrary.org • URL: http://www.tulsalibrary.org • Bimonthly. Free. Newsletter listing selected new books in business, economics, and technology.

Info Franchise Newsletter. Info Franchise News Inc., P.O. Box 826 Lewiston, NY 14092. Phone: (716)754-4669 Fax: (905)688-7728 E-mail: infopress@infonews.com • URL: http://www.infonews.com/franchise • Monthly. $120.00 per year. Newsletter. New franchisors, litigation, legislation, trends, forecasts, etc.

Info Rich-Info Poor: Access and Exchange in the Global Information Society. Trevor Haywood. Bowker-Saur, 121 Chanlon Rd. New Providence, NJ 07974. Phone: 800-521-8110 or (908)464-6800 Fax: (908)771-8784 1995. $60.00. Published by K. G. Saur.

InfoAlert: Your Expert Guide to Online Business Information. Economics Press, Inc., 12 Daniel Rd. Fairfield, NJ 07004-2565. Phone: 800-526-2554 or (973)227-1224 Fax: (973)227-9742 E-mail: edit@epinc.com • URL: http://www.epinc.com • Monthly. $129.00 per year. Newsletter. Provides information on recommended World Wide Web sites in various business, marketing, industrial, and financial areas.

Infogate. Infogate, Inc.Phone: (858)348-3000 Fax: (858)348-3100 URL: http://www.infogate.com • Web site provides current news and information on seven ''channels'': News, Fun, Sports, Info, Finance, Shop, and Travel. Among the content partners are Business Wire, CBS MarketWatch, CNN, Morningstar, Standard & Poor's, and Thomson Investors Network. Fees: Free, but downloading of Infogate software is required (includes personalized news feature). Updating is continuous. Formerly Pointcast Network.

The Infomation Management Journal. Association of Records Managers and Administrators, 4200 Somerset Dr., Suite 215 Prairie Village, KS 66208. Phone: 800-442-2762 or (913)341-3808 URL: http://www.arma.org • Quarterly. Free to members; non-members, $60.00 per year; institutions and libraries, $53.00 per year. Formerly (Records management Quarterly).

Infopreneurs: Turning Data into Dollars. H. Skip Weitzen. John Wiley and Sons, Inc., 605 Third Ave. New York, NY 10158-0012. Phone: 800-526-5368 or (949)850-6000 Fax: (949)850-6088 E-mail: info@wiley.com • URL: http://www.wiley.com • 1988. $27.95. Infopreneurs are entrepreneurs who market information. A how-to-do-it manual.

Inform: International News on Fats, Oils, and Related Materials. American Oil Chemists Society, 1608 Broadmoor Dr. Champaign, IL 61821-5930. Phone: (217)359-2344 Fax: (217)351-8091 URL: http://www.aocs.org • Monthly. $115.00 per year. Covers a wide range of technical and business topics relating to the processing and utilization of edible oils, essential oils, and oilseeds.

Inform: The Magazine of Information and Image Management. Association for Information and Image Management, 1100 Wayne Ave., Suite 1100 Silver Spring, MD 20910-5603. Phone: 800-477-2446 or (301)587-8202 Fax: (301)587-2711 E-mail: aiim@aiim.org • URL: http://www.aiim.org • Monthly. $85.00 per year. Covers technologies, applications, and trends.

The Information Advisor: Tips and Techniques for Smart Information Users. MarketResearch.com, 641 Ave. of the Americas, Third Floor New York, NY 10011. Phone: 800-298-5699 or (212)807-2629 Fax: (212)807-2716 E-mail: order@marketresearch.com • URL: http://www.marketresearch.com • Monthly. $149.00 per year. Newsletter. Evaluates and discusses online, CD-ROM, and published sources of business, financial, and market research information.

Information and Image Management: The State of the Industry. Association for Information and Image Management, 1100 Wayne Ave., Suite 1100 Silver Spring, MD 20910-5603. Phone: 800-477-2446 or (301)587-8202 Fax: (301)587-2711 E-mail: aiim@aiim.org • URL: http://www.aiim.org • Annual. $130.00. Market data with five-year forecasts. Covers electronic imaging, micrographics supplies and equipment, software, and records management services.

Information and Management; International Journal of Information Systems Applications. Elsevier Science, 655 Ave. of the Americas New York, NY 10010. Phone: 888-437-4636 or (212)989-5800 Fax: (212)633-3680 E-mail: usinfo@elsevier.com • URL: http://www.elsevier.com • Bimonthly. $382.00 per year.

Information Bank Abstracts. New York Times Index Dept., 1133 Ave. of the Americas New York, NY 10036. Phone: (212)221-3471 Fax: (212)221-5052 URL: http://www.nytimes.com • Provides indexing and abstracting of current affairs, primarily from the final late edition of *The New York Times* and the Eastern edition of *The Wall Street Journal*. Time period is 1969 to present, with daily updates. Inquire as to online cost and availability.

Information Broker. Helen P. Burwell, editor. Burwell Enterprises, Inc., 5619 Plumtree Dr. Dallas, TX 75252. Phone: (281)537-9051 Fax: (281)537-8332 E-mail: burwellinfo@burwellinc.com • URL: http://www.burwellinc.com • Bimonthly. $40.00 per year. Newsletter provides advice and news for those in the fee-based information business.

Information Broker. Entrepreneur Media, Inc., 2445 McCabe Way Irvine, CA 92614. Phone: 800-421-2300 or (949)261-2325 Fax: (949)261-0234 E-mail: entmag@entrepreneur.com • URL: http://www.entrepreneur.com • Looseleaf. $59.50. A practical guide to starting an information retrieval business. Covers profit potential, start-up costs, market size evaluation, pricing, accounting, advertising, promotion, etc. (Start-Up Business Guide No. E1237.)

Information Brokering: A How-To-Do-It Manual for Librarians. Florence M. Mason and Chris Dobson. Neal-Schuman Publishers, Inc., 100 Varick St. New York, NY 10013. Phone: (212)925-8650 Fax: 800-584-2414 or (212)219-8916 E-mail: info@neal-schuman.com • URL: http://www.neal-schuman.com • 1998. $45.00. A practical guide to business plans, location, costs, fees, billing, marketing, accounting, taxes, and legal issues. Covers information brokering as a small business enterprise.

Information Broker's Handbook. Sue Rugge and Alfred Glossbrenner. McGraw-Hill, 1221 Ave. of the Americas New York, NY 10020. Phone: 800-722-4726 or (212)904-2000 Fax: (212)904-2072 E-mail: customer.service@mcgraw-hill.com • URL: http://www.mcgraw-hill.com • 1997. $49.95. Third edition. Covers a wide range of topics relating to the information business and specifically to information brokering as a career. Includes a diskette with sample forms, contracts, letters, and reports. (Windcrest Books.)

The Information Catalog. MarketResearch.com, 641 Ave. of the Americas, Third Floor New York, NY 10011. Phone: 800-298-5699 or (212)807-2629 Fax: (212)807-2642 E-mail: order@marketresearch.com • URL: http://www.marketresearch.com • Quarterly. Free. Mainly a catalog of market research reports from various publishers, but also includes business and marketing reference sources. Includes keyword title index. Formerly *The Information Catalog: Marketing Intelligence Studies, Competitor Reports, Business and Marketing Sources*.

Information Executive: A Monthly Publication for DPMA and the Information Systems Profession. AITP-Association of Information Technology Professional, 315 S. Northwest Highway, Suite 200 Park Ridge, IL 60068-4278. Phone: 800-224-9371 Fax: (847)825-1693 Monthly. $45.00 per year. Articles reporting developmental and technical aspects of EDP services, supplies, equipment, accessories and related contemporary trends and issues. Formerly *Inside DPMA*.

Information, Finance, and Services USA. The Gale Group, 27500 Drake Rd. Farmington Hills, MI 48331-3535. Phone: 800-877-GALE or (248)699-GALE Fax: 800-414-5043 or (248)699-8069 E-mail: galeord@galegroup.com • URL: http://www.galegroup.com • 2001. $240.00. Replaces *Service Industries USA* and *Finance, Insurance, and Real Estate USA*. Presents statistics and projections relating to economic activity in a wide variety of non-manufacturing areas.

Information for Sale: How to Start and Operate Your Own Data Research Service. John H. Everett and Elizabeth P. Crowe. McGraw-Hill Professional, 1221 Ave. of the Americas New York, NY 10020. Phone: 800-722-4726 or (212)904-2000 Fax: (212)904-2072 E-mail: customer.service@mcgraw-hill.com • URL: http://www.mcgraw-hill.com • 1988. $15.95. Second edition. A revision of *The Information Broker's Handbook*.

The Information Freeway Report: Free Business and Government Information Via Modem. Washington Researchers Ltd., 1655 N. Fort Myer Dr., Suite 800 Arlington, VA 22209. Phone: (703)312-2863 Fax: (703)527-4585 E-mail: research@researchers.com • URL: http://www.researchers.com • Monthly. $160.00 per year. Newsletter. Provides news of business and government databases that are available free of charge through the Internet or directly. Emphasis is on federal government databases and electronic bulletin boards (Fedworld).

Information Graphics-A Comprehensive Illustrated Reference: Visual Tools for Analyzing, Managing, and Communicating. Robert L. Harris. Management Graphics, 795 Hammond St., Suite 2306 Atlanta, GA 30328-5568. Phone: (404)256-2414 Fax: (404)256-1931 E-mail: mgmtgraph@aol.com • 1996. $60.00. Provides more than 850 alphabetical entries and about 4,000 illustrations. Covers the practical application of charts, graphs, maps, diagrams, and tables.

Information Hotline. Science Associates International, Inc., Six Hastings Rd. Marlboro, NJ 07746-1313. Phone: 800-721-1080 Fax: (908)536-7673 10 times a year. Individuals and corporations, $150.00 per year; non-profit organizations, $135.00 per year. Newsletter.

Information Imagineering: Meeting at the Interface. Milton T. Wolf and others, editors. American Library Association, 50 E. Huron St. Chicago, IL 60611-2795. Phone: 800-545-2433 or (312)944-6780 Fax: (312)440-9374 E-mail: ala@ala.org • URL: http://www.ala.org • 1997. $36.00. A collection of articles on the effect of information technology on libraries, museums, and other institutions.

Information Industry Directory. The Gale Group, 27500 Drake Rd. Farmington Hills, MI 48331-3535. Phone: 800-877-GALE or (248)699-GALE Fax: 800-414-5043 or (248)699-8069 E-mail: galeord@galegroup.com • URL: http://www.galegroup.com • 2000. $635.00. 22nd edition. Two volumes. Lists nearly 4,600 producers and vendors of electronic information and related services. Subject, geographic, and master indexes are provided.

Information Management for the Intelligent Organization: The Art of Scanning the Environment. Chun Wei Choo. Information Today, Inc., 143 Old Marlton Pike Medford, NJ 08055-8750. Phone: 800-300-9868 or (609)654-6266 Fax: (609)654-4309 E-mail: custserv@infotoday.com • URL: http://www.infotoday.com • 1998. $39.50. Second edition. Published on behalf of the American Society for Information Science (ASIS). Covers the general principles of acquiring, creating, organizing, and using information within organizations.

Information Management Report: An International Newsletter for Information Professionals and Librarians. R. R. Bowker, 121 Chanlon Rd. New Providence, NJ 07974. Phone: 888-269-5372 or (908)464-6800 Fax: (908)771-7704 E-mail: info@bowker.com • URL: http://www.bowker.com • Monthly. $470.00 per year. Incorporates *Outlook on Research Libraries*.

Information Marketplace Directory. SIMBA Information, P.O. Box 4234 Stamford, CT 06907-0234. Phone: 800-307-2529 or (203)358-4100 Fax: (203)358-5824 E-mail: info@simbanet.com • URL: http://www.simbanet.com • 1996. $295.00. Second edition. Lists computer-based information processing and multimedia companies, including those engaged in animation, audio, video, and interactive video.

Information Outlook: The Monthly Magazine of the Special Libraries Association. Special Libraries Association, 1700 18th St., N. W., 17th Fl. Washington, DC 20009-2514. Phone: (202)234-4700 Fax: 888-411-2856 or (202)234-2442 E-mail: books@sla.org • URL: http://www.sla.org • Monthly. $65.00 per year. Topics include information technology, the Internet, copyright, research techniques, library management, and professional development. Replaces *Special Libraries* and *SpeciaList*.

Information Please Business Almanac. Information Please LLC, 31 Saint James Ave., 6th Fl. Boston, MA 02116-4101. Phone: (617)832-0300 Fax: (617)956-3696 E-mail: info@infoplease.com • URL: http://www.infoplease.com • Annual. $21.95.

Information Processing and Management: An International Journal. Elsevier Science, 655 Ave. of the Americas New York, NY 10010. Phone: 888-437-4636 or (212)989-5800 Fax: (212)633-3680 E-mail: usinfo@elsevier.com • URL: http://www.elsevier.com • Bimonthly. $981.00 per year. Text in English, French, German and Italian.

The Information Report. Washington Researchers Ltd., 1655 N. Fort Myer Dr., Suite 800 Arlington, VA 22209. Phone: (703)312-2863 Fax: (703)527-4585 E-mail: research@researchers.com • URL: http://www.researchers.com • Monthly. $160.00 per year. Newsletter listing private and government sources of information, mainly on business or economics

Information Retrieval and Library Automation. Lomond Publications, Inc., P.O. Box 88 Mount Airy, MD 21771. Phone: (301)694-0123 Fax: (301)694-5151 E-mail: lomondpubs@prodigy.net • URL: http://www.lomondpubs.com • Monthly. $75.00 per year. Summarizes research events and literature worldwide.

Information Science Abstracts. Information Today, Inc., 143 Old Marlton Pike Medford, NJ 08055-8750. Phone: 800-300-9868 or (609)654-6266 Fax: (609)654-4309 E-mail: custserv@infotoday.com • URL: http://www.infotoday.com • Quarterly. $1,095.00 per year. Presents CD-ROM abstracts of worldwide information science and library science literature from 1966 to date.

Information Science Abstracts. American Society for Information Science. Information Today, Inc., 143 Marlton Pike Medford, NJ 08055-8750. Phone: 800-300-9868 or (609)654-6266 Fax: (609)654-4309 E-mail: custservl@infotoday.com • URL: http://www.infotoday.com • 11 times a year. $685.00 per year.

Information Science Abstracts Ionlinel. Information Today, Inc., 143 Old Marlton Pike Medford, NJ 08055-8750. Phone: 800-300-9868 or (609)654-6266 Fax: (609)654-4309 E-mail: custserv@infotoday.com • URL: http://www.infotoday.com • Provides indexing and abstracting of the international literature of information science, including library science, from 1966 to date. Monthly updates. Inquire as to online cost and availability.

Information Science: An Integrated View. Anthony Debons and others. Pearson Education and Technology, 201 W. 103rd St. Indianapolis, IN 46290-1097. Phone: 800-858-7674 or (317)581-3500 URL: http://www.mcp.com • 1988. $35.00. History, theory, and methodology. (Professional Librarian Series).

Information Sciences Institute., University of Southern California, 4676 Admiralty Way, Suite 1001 Marina del Rey, CA 90292. Phone: (310)822-1511 Fax: (310)823-6714 URL: http://www.isi.edu • Research fields include online information and computer science, with emphasis on the World Wide Web.

Information Sciences; An International Journal. Elsevier Science, 655 Ave. of the Americas New York, NY 10010. Phone: 888-437-4636 or (212)989-5800 Fax: (212)633-3680 E-mail: usinfo@elsevier.com • URL: http://www.elsevier.com • 36 times a year. $2,917.00 per year. Three sections, A: Informatics and Computer Science, B: Intelligent Systems, C: Applications.

Information Services and Use: An International Journal. I O S Press, 5795-G Burke Centre Parkway Burke, VA 22015-0558. Phone: (703)323-5554 Fax: (703)323-3368 E-mail: market@iospress.nl • URL: http://www.isopress.nl • Quarterly. Individiuals, $100.00 per year; institutions, $257.00 per year.

The Information Society: An International Journal. Taylor & Francis, Inc., 325 Chestnut St., 8th Fl. Philadelphia, PA 19106. Phone: 800-821-8312 or (215)625-8900 Fax: (215)625-2940 E-mail: webmaster@taylorandfrancis.com • URL: http://www.tandfdc.com/ • Quarterly. Individuals, $89.00 per year; institutions, $194.00 per year.

Information Sources in Advertising History. Richard W. Pollay, editor. Greenwood Publishing Group, Inc., 88 Post Rd., W. Westport, CT 06881-5007. Phone: 800-225-5800 or (203)226-3571 Fax: (203)222-2540 E-mail: bookinfo@greenwood.com • URL: http://www.greenwood.com • 1979. $65.00.

Information Sources in Chemistry. Fy Hon Rowland and Peter Rhodes, editors. Bowker-Saur, 121 Chanlon Rd. New Providence, NJ 07974. Phone: 800-521-8110 or (908)464-6800 Fax: (908)771-8784 2000. $100.00. Fifth edition. Evaluates information sources on a wide range of chemical topics. (Guides to Information Sources Series).

Information Sources in Finance and Banking. R. G. Lester, editor. Bowker-Saur, 121 Chanlon Rd. New Providence, NJ 07974. Phone: (908)464-6800 Fax: (908)771-8784 1995. $125.00. Published by K. G. Saur. International coverage.

Information Sources in Music. Lewis Foreman, editor. Bowker-Saur, 121 Chanlon Rd. New Providence, NJ 07974. Phone: 800-521-8110 or (908)464-6800 Fax: (908)771-8784 2001. $100.00. Evaluates information sources on a wide range of music topics, including copyright, music publishing, reprographics, and the use of computers in music publishing. (Guides to Information Sources Series).

Information Sources in Patents. Peter Auger, editor. Bowker-Saur, 121 Chanlon Rd. New Providence, NJ 07974. Phone: 800-521-8110 or (908)464-6800 Fax: (908)771-8784 1992. $75.00. Published by K. G. Saur. International coverage. (Guides to Information Sources Series).

Information Sources in Sports and Leisure. Michele Shoebridge, editor. Bowker-Saur, 121 Chanlon Rd. New Providence, NJ 07974. Phone: 800-521-8110 or (908)464-6800 Fax: (908)771-8784 1992. $95.00. (Guides to Information Sources Series).

Information Sources in the Life Sciences. H. V. Wyatt, editor. Bowker-Saur, 121 Chanlon Rd. New Providence, NJ 07974. Phone: 800-521-8110 or (908)464-6800 Fax: (908)771-8784 1997. $95.00. Fourth edition. Includes an evaluation of biotechnology information sources. (Guides to Information Sources Series).

Information Sources: The Annual Directory of the Information Industry Association. Software and Information Industry Association, 1730 M St., N.W., Suite 700 Washington, DC 20036-4510. Phone: (202)452-1600 Fax: (202)223-8756 URL: http://www.siia.net • Annual. Members, $75.00; non-members, $125.00.

Information Standards Quarterly: News About Library, Information Sciences, and Publishing Standards. National Information Standards Organization (NISO), 4733 Bethesda Ave., Suite 300 Bethesda, MD 20814-5248. Phone: (301)654-2512 Fax: (301)654-1721 E-mail: nisohq@niso.org • URL: http://www.niso.org • Quarterly. $80.00 per year. Newsletter. Reports on activities of the National Information Standards Organization.

Information Strategy: The Executive's Journal. Auerbach Publications, 535 Fifth Ave., Suite 806 New York, NY 10017. Phone: 800-272-7737 or (212)286-1010 Fax: (212)297-9176 E-mail: orders@crcpress.com • URL: http://www.auerbach-publications.com • Quarterly. $195.00 per year.

Information Systems Audit and Control Association.

Information Systems Concepts for Management. Henry C. Lucas. McGraw-Hill, 1221 Ave. of the Americas New York, NY 10020-1095. Phone: 800-722-4726 or (212)904-2000 Fax: (212)904-2072 E-mail: customer.service@mcgraw-hill.com • URL: http://www.mcgraw-hill.com • 1994. $25.00. Fifth edition.

Information Systems; Data Bases: Their Creation, Management and Utilization. Elsevier Science, 655 Ave. of the Americas New York, NY 10010. Phone: 888-437-4636 or (212)989-5800 Fax: (212)633-3680 E-mail: usinfo@elsevier.com • URL: http://www.elsevier.com • Eight times a year. $1,194.00 per year.

Information Systems Laboratory., Stanford University Stanford, CA 94305-9510. Phone: (650)723-4539 Fax: (650)723-8473 E-mail: char@isl.stanford.edu • URL: http://www-isl.stanford.edu • Research fields include speech coding and recognition.

Information Systems Management. Auerbach Publications, 535 Fifth Ave., Suite 806 New York, NY 10017. Phone: (212)286-1010 Fax: (212)297-9716 E-mail: orders@crcpress.com • URL: http://www.auerbach-publications.com • Quarterly. $175.00 per year. Formerly *Journal of Information Systems Management*.

Information Systems Security. Auerbach Publications, 535 Fifth Ave., Suite 806 New York, NY 10017. Phone: (212)286-1010 Fax: (212)297-9176 E-mail: orders@crcpress.com • URL: http://www.auerbach-publications.com • Quarterly. $175.00 per year. Formerly *Journal of Information Systems Security*.

Information Systems Spending: An Analysis of Trends and Strategies. Computer Economics, Inc., 5841 Edison Place Carlsbad, CA 92008. Phone: 800-326-8100 or (760)438-8100 Fax: (760)431-1126 E-mail: custserv@compecon.com • URL: http://www.computereconomics.com • Annual. $1,595.00. Three volumes. Based on ''in-depth surveys of public and private companies amd government organizations.'' Provides detailed data on management information systems spending, budgeting, and benchmarks. Includes charts, graphs, and analysis.

Information Technology Association of America., c/o ITAA, 1616 N. Fort Myer Dr., Suite 1300 Arlington, VA 22209-9998. Phone: (703)522-5055 Fax: (703)525-2279 Members are computer software and services companies. Maintains an Information Systems Integration Services Section.

Information Technology Industry Council.

Information Technology Outlook. OECD Publications and Information Center, 2001 L St., N.W., Ste. 650 Washington, DC 20036-4922. Phone: 800-456-6323 or (202)785-6323 Fax: (202)785-0350 E-mail: washington.contact@oecd.org • URL: http://www.oecdwash.org • Biennial. $72.00. A review of recent developments in international markets for computer hardware, software, and services. Also examines current legal provisions for information systems security and privacy in OECD countries.

Information Times. Software and Information Industry Association, 1730 M St., N.W., Suite 700 Washington, DC 20036-4510. Phone: (202)452-1600 Fax: (202)223-8756 URL: http://www.siia.net • Monthly. Membership. Formerly *Friday Memo*.

Information Today, Inc. Anne Leach, editor. American Society of Indexers, 11250 Roger Bacon Dr., Suite 8 Reston, VA 20190-5202. Phone: (703)234-4147 Fax: (703)735-4390 E-mail: info@asindexing.org • URL: http://www.asindexing.org • 1998. $20.00. Second edition.

Information Today: The Newspaper for Users and Producers of Electronic Information Services. Information Today, Inc., 143 Old Marlton Pike Medford, NJ 08055-8750. Phone: 800-300-9868 or (609)654-6266 Fax: (609)654-4309 E-mail: custserv@infotoday.com • URL: http://www.infotoday.com • 11 times a year. $57.95 per year.

Information Week: For Business and Technology Managers. CMP Publications, Inc., 600 Community Dr. Manhasset, NY 11030. Phone: 800-577-5356 or (516)562-5000 Fax: (516)733-6916 E-mail: bevans@cmp.com • URL: http://www.informationweek.com • Weekly. $149.00 per year. The magazine for information systems management.

Information World Review: The Information Community Newspaper. Information Today, Inc., 143 Old Marlton Pike Medford, NJ 08055-8750. Phone: 800-300-9868 or (609)654-6266 Fax: (609)654-4309 E-mail: custserv@infotoday.com • URL: http://www.infotoday.com • Monthly. $92.00 per year. International coverage. Includes columns in French, German, and Dutch.

InfoTech Trends. Data Analysis GroupPhone: (707)894-9100 Fax: (707)486-5618 E-mail: support@infotechtrends.com • URL: http://www.infotechtrends.com • Web site provides both free and fee-based market research data on the information technology industry, including computers, peripherals, telecommunications, the Internet, software, CD-ROM/DVD, e-commerce, and workstations. Fees: Free for current (most recent year) data; more extensive information has various fee structures. Formerly *Computer Industry Forecasts*.

InfoWorld: Defining Technology for Business. InfoWorld Publishing, 155 Bovet Rd., Suite 800 San Mateo, CA 94402. Phone: 800-227-8365 or (650)572-7341 Fax: (650)312-0584 URL: http://www.infoworld.com • Weekly. $160.00 per year. For personal computing professionals.

Infrastructure Industries USA. The Gale Group, 27500 Drake Rd. Farmington Hills, MI 48331-3535. Phone: 800-877-GALE or (248)699-GALE Fax: 800-414-5043 or (248)699-8069 E-mail: galeord@galegroup.com • URL: http://www.galegroup.com • 2001. $240.00. Replaces *Agriculture, Forestry, Fishing, Mining, and Construction USA* and *Transportation and Public Utilities USA*. Presents statistics and projections relating to economic activity in a wide variety of natural resource and construction industries.

Inheritor's Handbook: A Definitive Guide for Beneficiaries. Dan Rottenberg. Bloomberg Press, 100 Business Park Dr. Princeton, NJ 08542-0888. Phone: 800-388-2749 or (609)279-4670 Fax: (609)279-7155 E-mail: press@bloomberg.net • URL: http://www.bloomberg.com • 1998. $23.95. Covers both financial and emotional issues faced by beneficiaries. (Bloomberg Personal Bookshelf Series.)

INIS Newsletter. International Atomic Energy Agency, Division of Publications, P.O. Box 100 W-1400 Vienna, Austria. Phone: 43 1 2600 22841 Fax: 43 1 2600 29882 E-mail: inis.centreservies.unit@iaea.org • URL: http://www.iaea.org/inis.inis.htm • Irregular. Free. Newsletter of the International Nuclear Information System (INIS).

Initial Public Offerings: All You Need to Know About Taking a Company Public. David Sutton and M. William Benedetto. McGraw-Hill Professional, 1221 Ave. of the Americas New York, NY 10020. Phone: 800-722-4726 or (212)904-2000 Fax: (212)904-2072 E-mail: customer.service@mcgraw-hill.com • URL: http://www.mcgraw-hill.com • 1990. $24.95. (Entrepreneur's Guide Series).

Inland Marine Underwriters Association.

Inland River Guide. Waterways Journal, Inc., 319 N. Fourth St.,, 650 Security Bldg. Saint Louis, MO 63102. Phone: (314)241-7354 Fax: (314)241-4207 E-mail: waterwayj@socket.net • URL: http://www.web-net.com/irl/watjrn.html • Annual. $60.00. Covers domestic barge and towing industry.

Innovation and Entrepreneurship: Practice and Principles. Peter F. Drucker. HarperInformation, 10 E. 53rd St. New York, NY 10022-5299. Phone: 800-242-7737 or (212)207-7000 Fax: 800-822-4090 or (212)207-7145 URL: http://www.harpercollins.com • 1986. $14.50.

Innovation: Leadership Strategies for the Competitive Edge. Thomas D. Kuczmarski. NTC/Contemporary Publishing, P.O. Box 545 Blacklick, OH 43004. Phone: 800-388-3987 or (614)755-4151 Fax: (614)755-5645 E-mail: ntcpub@mcgraw-hill.com • URL: http://www.ntc-cb.com • 1995. $37.95. (NTC Business Book Series).

Innovations in Education and Training International. Association for Educational and Training Technology, Routledge Journals, 29 W. 35th St. New York, NY 10001-2299. Phone: (212)216-7800 Fax: (212)564-7854 Quarterly. Individuals, $62.00 per year; libraries and other institutions, $190.00 per year. Provides up-to-date coverage of educational and training technologies. Formerly *Educational and Training Technology International*.

Innovative Publisher: Publishing Strategies for New Markets. Emmelle Publishing Co., Inc., 370 Seventh Ave., Suite 905 New York, NY 10001. Phone: (212)714-1881 Fax: (212)714-1488 Biweekly. $69.00 per year. Provides articles and news on electronic publishing (CD-ROM or online) and desktop publishing.

The Innovator's Dilemma: When New Technologies Cause Great Firms to Fail. Clayton M. Christensen. Harvard Business School Press, 60 Harvard Way Boston, MA 02163. Phone: 800-545-7685 or (617)783-7440 E-mail: custserv@cchbspub.harvard.edu • URL: http://www.hbsp.harvard.edu • 1997. $27.50. Discusses management myths relating to innovation, change, and research and development. (Mangement of Innovation and Change Series).

Inquiry: The Journal of Health Care Organization, Provision, and Financing. Finger Lakes Blue Cross and Blue Shield Association, P.O. Box 25399 Rochester, NY 14625. Phone: (716)264-9122 Fax: (716)264-9122 URL: http://www.inquiryjournal.org • Quarterly. Individuals, $50.00 per year; institutions, $70.00 per year.

Insect Control Guide. Meister Publishing Co., 37733 Euclid Ave. Willoughby, OH 44094. Phone: 800-572-7740 or (440)942-2000 Fax: (440)942-0662 E-mail: info@meisternet.com • URL: http://www.meisterpro.com • Semiannual. $59.00. Includes trade names and usage information. Formerly *Insecticide Product Guide*.

Inside Cellular: An Operating Manual for Dealers, Carriers, and Investors. Kim A. Mayyasi. Brick House Publishing Co., P.O. Box 266 Amherst, NH 03031. Phone: 800-446-8642 or (603)672-5112 Fax: (603)673-6250 $95.00. Looseleaf.

Inside Chips Ventures: The Global Report with Executive Perspective. HTE Research, Inc., 119 N. Commercial St., Suite 480 Bellingham, WA 98225-4437. Phone: (360)676-2260 Fax: (360)676-2265 E-mail: sibs@hte-sibs.com • URL: http://www.hte-sibs.com/sibs.htm • 12 times a year. $595.00 per year. Tracks the activities of semiconductor firms worldwide. Formerly *Semiconductor Industry and Business Survey Newsletter*.

Inside Flyer. Frequent Flyer Services, 4715 Town Center Drive, Suite C Colorado Springs, CO 80916-4702. Phone: (719)597-8899 Fax: (719)597-6855 URL: http://www.insideflyer.com • Monthly. $75.00 per year. Newsletter. Provides information relating to frequent flyer awards and air travel.

Inside Microsoft Word: Tips and Techniques for Microsoft Windows. Z-D Journals, 500 Can View Blvd. Rochester, NY 14623. Phone: 800-223-8720 or (716)240-7301 Fax: (716)214-2387 E-mail: zdjcr@zd.com • URL: http://www.zdjournals.com • Monthly. $49.00 per year. Newsletter on word processing with Microsoft Word for Windows. Covers applications and problem-solving.

Inside Negotiations. EFR Corp, P.O. Box 15236 Colorado Spring, FL 80935-5236. Monthly. $98.00 per year. Newsletter. Labor negotiations.

Inside R and D: A Weekly Report on Technical Innovation. Technical Insights, 605 Third Ave. New York, NY 10158-0012. Phone: 800-825-7550 or (212)850-8600 Fax: (212)850-8800 E-mail: insights@wiley.com • URL: http://www.wiley.com/technicalinsights • Weekly. $840.00 per year. Concentrates on new and significant developments. Formerly *Technolog Transfer Week*.

Inside Retailing. Lebhar-Friedman Inc., 425 Park Ave. New York, NY 10022-3556. Phone: 800-766-6999 or (212)756-5000 Fax: (212)756-5120 E-mail: info@lf.com • URL: http://www.lf.com • Biweekly. $229.00 per year. Newsletter.

Inside the Financial Futures Markets. Mark Powers and Mark Castelino. John Wiley and Sons, Inc., 605 Third Ave. New York, NY 10158-0012. Phone: 800-225-5945 or (212)850-6000 Fax: (212)850-6088 E-mail: info@wiley.com • URL: http://www.wiley.com • 1991. $55.00. Third edition.

Inside the Juror: The Psychology of Juror Decision Making. Reid Hastie, editor. Cambridge University Press, 40 W. 20th St. New York, NY 10011. Phone: 800-221-4512 or (212)924-3900 Fax: (212)937-4712 E-mail: info@cup.org • URL: http://www.cup.org • 1994. $22.95. (Judgement and Decision Making Series).

Inside Wordperfect for Windows. Z-D Journals, 500 Canal View Blvd. Rochester, NY 14623. Phone: 800-223-8720 or (716)240-7301 Fax: (716)214-2387 E-mail: zdjcr@zd.com • URL: http://www.zdjournals.com • Monthly. $59.00 per year. Newsletter on word processing with Wordperfect software. Includes tips and techniques for both beginners and experts.

Insider Trading: Regulation: Enforcement and Prevention. Donald C. Langevoort. West Group, 610 Opperman Dr. Eagan, MN 55123. Phone: 800-328-4880 or (651)687-7000 Fax: 800-213-2323 or (651)687-5827 URL: http://www.westgroup.com • $145.00. Looseleaf service. (Securities Law Series).

The Insiders: America's Most Knowledgeable Investors. Institute for Econometric Research, 2200 S.W. 10th St. Deerfield Beach, FL 33442-8799. Phone: 800-442-0066 or (954)421-1000 Fax: (954)570-8200 Semimonthly. $100.00 per year. Newsletter.

An Insider's Guide to Home Health Care. Tova Navarra and Margaret Ferrer. SLACK, Inc., 6900 Grove Rd. Thorofare, NJ 08086-9447. Phone: 800-257-8290 or (609)848-1000 Fax: (609)853-5991 E-mail: orders@slackinc.com • URL: http://www.slackinc.org • 1996. $28.00. Covers "unexpected situations, cultural differences, and potential comflicts" for professionals in the home health care field. Emphasizes teamwork for optimal care management.

Insider's Guide to the Top Ten Business Schools. Tom Fischgrund, editor. Little, Brown and Co., Time and Life Bldg., 1271 Ave. of the Americas New York, NY 10020. Phone: 800-343-9204 or (212)522-8700 Fax: 800-286-9741 or (212)522-2067 E-mail: cust.service@littlebrown.com • URL: http://www.littlebrown.com • 1990. $10.95. Fourth edition.

InSite 2. Intelligence Data/Thomson FinancialPhone: 800-654-0393 or (617)856-1890 Fax: (617)737-3182 E-mail: intelligence.data@tfn.com • URL: http://www.insite2.gale.com/ • Fee-based Web site consolidates information in a "Base Pack" consisting of Business In-Site, Market InSite, and Company InSite. Optional databases are Consumer InSite, Health and Wellness InSite, Newsletter InSite, and Computer InSite. Includes fulltext content from more than 2,500 trade publications, journals, newsletters, newspapers, analyst reports, and other sources. Continuous updating. Formerly produced by The Gale Group.

Insolvency Law & Practice. Tolley Publishing Co. Ltd., Tolley House, Two Addiscombe Rd., Croyden CR9 5AF Surrey, England. Phone: 44 181 6869141 Fax: 44 181 6863155 URL: http://www.tolley.co.uk • Bimonthly. $250.00 per year. United Kingdom emphasis.

INSPEC. Institute of Electrical and Electronics Engineers (IEEE), 445 Hoes Lane Piscataway, NJ 08855. Phone: 800-678-4333 or (732)562-3998 Fax: (732)981-1721 E-mail: iel@ieee.org • URL: http://www.ieee.org • Provides indexing and abstracting of the worldwide literature of electrical engineering, electronics, physics, computer technology, information technology, and industrial controls. Time period is 1970 to date, with weekly updates. Inquire as to online cost and availability. (INSPEC is Information Services for the Physics and Engineering Communities.)

Installation and Cleaning Specialist. Specialist Publications, Inc., 22801 Ventura Blvd., Suite 115 Woodland Hills, CA 91364-1222. Phone: (818)224-8035 Fax: (818)224-8042 URL: http://www.icsmag.com • Monthly. $38.00 per year. Written for floor covering installers and cleaners.

Installment Credit Survey Report. American Bankers Association, 1120 Connecticut Ave., N.W. Washington, DC 20036-3971. Phone: 800-338-0626 or (202)663-5000 Fax: (202)663-7543 URL: http://www.aba.org • Annual. Members, $225.00; non-members, $325.00. Information covers installment loans. Formerly*Installment Credit Report*.

Instant Computer Arbitration Search. LRP Publications, 747 Dresher Rd. Horsham, PA 19044. Phone: (215)784-0941 Fax: (215)784-9639 Provides citations to U. S. labor arbitration cases and a detailed directory of about 2,500 public and private labor arbitrators. Weekly updates. Cases date from 1970. Inquire as to online cost and availability.

Instant Print/Copy Shop. Entrepreneur Media, Inc., 2445 McCabe Way Irvine, CA 92614. Phone: 800-421-2300 or (949)261-2325 Fax: (949)261-0234 E-mail: entmag@entrepreneur.com • URL: http://www.entrepreneur.com • Looseleaf. $59.50. A practical guide to starting a quick printing and copying business. Covers profit potential, start-up costs, market size evaluation, owner's time required, site selection, lease negotiation, pricing, accounting, advertising, promotion, etc. (Start-Up Business Guide No. E1298.)

Instant Sign Store. Entrepreneur Media, Inc., 2445 McCabe Way Irvine, CA 92614. Phone: 800-421-2300 or (949)261-2325 Fax: (949)261-0234 E-mail: entmag@entrepreneur.com • URL: http://www.entrepreneur.com • Looseleaf. $59.50. A practical guide to starting an instant sign store. Covers profit potential, start-up costs, market size evaluation, owner's time required, site selection, lease negotiation, pricing, accounting, advertising, promotion, etc. (Start-Up Business Guide No. E1336.)

Institute for Advanced Safety Studies.

Institute for Alternative Futures., 100 N. Pitt St., Suite 235 Alexandria, VA 22314. Phone: (703)684-5880 Fax: (703)684-0640 E-mail: futurist@altfutures.com • URL: http://www.altfutures.com • Conducts studies in the future of communications, health care, bioengineering, the legal system, etc.

Institute for Case Development and Research., Simmons College, Graduate School of Management, 409 Commonwealth Ave. Boston, MA 02215. Phone: (617)521-3800 Fax: (617)521-3880 E-mail: jennifer.bruce@simmons.edu • Studies issues and problems confronting women in management.

Institute for Communications Research.

Institute for Defense Analyses.

Institute for Econometric Research.

Institute for Economic Analysis.

Institute for Economic Research. University of Washington

Institute for Environmental Negotiation., University of Virginia, Campbell Hall Charlottesville, VA 22903. Phone: (804)924-1970 Fax: (804)924-0231 E-mail: rcc3f@virginia.edu • URL: http://www.virginia/edu/~evening/ien.html • Research activities are related to the resolution of environmental disputes through negotiation, mediation, and consensus building.

Institute for Environmental Research. Kansas State University

Institute for Fisheries Research.

Institute for Fluitronics Education., P.O. Box 106 Elm Grove, WI 53122-0160. Phone: (414)782-0410 Fax: (414)786-0410 Concerned with microcomputer control of fluid power.

Institute for Food Law and Regulations., Michigan State University, 165C National Food Safety and Toxicology Bldg. East Lansing, MI 48224. Phone: 888-579-3663 or (517)355-8295 Fax: (517)432-1492 E-mail: vhegarty@pilot.msu.edu • URL: http://www.msu.edu • Conducts research on the food industry, including processing, packaging, marketing, and new products.

Institute for Health, Health Care Policy, and Aging Research., Rutgers University, 30 College Ave. New Brunswick, NJ 08903. Phone: (732)932-8413 Fax: (732)982-6872 E-mail: caboyer@rci.rutgers.edu • URL: http://www.ihhcpar.rutgers.edu/ • Areas of study include HMO use by older adults.

Institute for Health Policy Research., Health Science Center, J. Hillis Miller Health Center, University of Florida, P.O. Box 100177 Gainesville, FL 32610-0177. Phone: (352)395-8039 Fax: (352)395-8047 E-mail: admin@hpe.ufl.edu • URL: http://www.hpe.ufl.edu • Research areas include health economics, financing, and long-term care considerations.

Institute for Health Services Research and Policy Studies.

Institute for Information Science and Technology., George Washington University, 801 22nd St., N. W., 6th Fl. Washington, DC 20052. Phone: (202)994-6208 Fax: (202)994-0227 E-mail: helgert@seas.gwu.edu • Research areas include computer graphics and image processing.

Institute for Information Storage Technology.

Institute for International Economics., 11 Dupont Circle, N. W., Suite 620 Washington, DC 20036. Phone: (202)328-9000 Fax: (202)328-5432 URL: http://

www.iie.com • Research fields include a wide range of international economic issues, including foreign exchange rates.

Institute for Mathematics and Its Applications., University of Minnesota, 514 Vincent Hall, 206 Church St., S. E. Minneapolis, MN 55455-0436. Phone: (612)624-6066 Fax: (612)626-7370 E-mail: staff@ima.umn.edu • URL: http://www.ima.umn.edu • Research areas include various topics connected with industrial and applied mathematics.

Institute for Metal Forming. Lehigh University

Institute for Professionsals in Taxation., 3350 Peachtree Rd., N.E., Suite 280 Atlanta, GA 30326. Phone: (404)240-2300 Fax: (404)240-2315 E-mail: ipt@ipt.org • URL: http://www.ipt.org • Promotes education in the area of property taxation.

Institute for Public Policy and Business Research. University of Kansas Survey Research Center

Institute for Pure and Applied Physical Sciences., University of California, San Diego, 9500 Gilman Dr. La Jolla, CA 92093-0360. Phone: (858)534-3560 Fax: (858)534-7649 E-mail: mbmaple@uscd.edu • Areas of study include superconductivity.

Institute for Quantitative Research in Finance., Church Street Station, P.O. Box 6194 New York, NY 10249-6194. Phone: (212)744-6825 Fax: (212)517-2259 E-mail: daleberman@compuserve • Financial research areas include quantitative methods, securities analysis, and the financial structure of industries. Also known as the ''Q Group.''

Institute for Real Estate Studies.

Institute for Retired Professionals.

Institute for Social Research.

Institute for Studies in the Arts., Arizona State University, College of Fine Arts, P.O. Box 873302 Tempe, AZ 85287-3302. Phone: (602)965-9438 Fax: (602)965-0961 E-mail: loveless@asu.edu • URL: http://www.researchnet.vprc.asu.edu/isa • Research areas include the fine arts aspects of interactive media.

Institute for Survey Research., Temple University Center for Public Policy, 1601 N. Broad St. Philadelphia, PA 19122. Phone: 800-827-5477 or (215)204-8355 Fax: (215)204-3797 E-mail: lenlo@temss2.isr.temple.edu • URL: http://www.temple.edu/isr • Conducts methodological studies in various aspects of survey research.

Institute for Systems Research., University of Maryland, A. V. Williams Bldg., No. 115 College Park, MD 20742-3311. Phone: (301)405-6602 Fax: (301)314-9220 E-mail: isr@isr.umd.edu • URL: http://www.isr.umd.edu/ • A National Science Foundation Engineering Research Center. Areas of research include communication systems, manufacturing systems, chemical process systems, artificial intelligence, and systems integration.

Institute for Tax Administration. Academy for International Training

Institute for Telecommunications Studies.

Institute for the Future.

Institute for the Management of Information Systems.

Institute for the Study of Business Markets., Pennsylvania State University, 402 Business Administration Bldg. University Park, PA 16802-3004. Phone: (814)863-2782 Fax: (814)863-0413 E-mail: isbm@psu.edu • URL: http://www.smeal.psu.edu/isbm/ • Research areas include international distribution channels.

Institute of Advanced Manufacturing Sciences, Inc., 1111 Edison Dr. Cincinnati, OH 45216. Phone: (513)948-2000 Fax: (513)948-2109 E-mail: conley@iams.org • URL: http://www.iams.org • Fields of research include quality improvement, computer-aided design, artificial intelligence, and employee training.

Institute of Atmospheric Physics. University of Arizona

Institute of Aviation Research Laboratory. University of Illinois

Institute of Business and Economic Research., University of California at Berkeley, School of Business, F502 Haas Berkeley, CA 94720-1922. Phone: (510)642-1922 Fax: (510)642-5018 E-mail: barde@uclink4.berkeley.edu • URL: http://www.haas.berkeley.edu/groups/iber • Research fields are business administration, economics, finance, real estate, and international development.

Institute of Certified Financial Planners., 3801 E. Florida Ave., Ste. 708 Denver, CO 80210-2571. Phone: 800-322-4237 or (303)759-4900 Fax: (303)759-0749 Members are Certified Financial Planners or are enrolled in programs accredited by the International Board of Standards and Practices for Certified Financial Planners.

Institute of Certified Travel Agents.

Institute of Collective Bargaining and Group Relations.

Institute of Cultural Affairs.

Institute of Electrical and Electronics Engineers.

Institute of Electrical and Electronics Engineers; Aerospace and Electronic Systems Society.

Institute of Electrical and Electronics Engineers; Consumer Electronics Society.

Institute of Electrical and Electronics Engineers; Control Systems Society.

Institute of Electrical and Electronics Engineers-Engineering in Medicine and Biology Society., Three Park Ave., 17th Fl. New York, NY 10017-2394. Phone: (212)419-7900 Fax: (212)752-4929 URL: http://www.ieee.org • Members are engineers, technicians, physicians, manufacturers, and others with an interest in medical instrumentation.

Institute of Electrical and Electronics Engineers; Engineering in Medicine and Biology Society.

Institute of Electrical and Electronics Engineers; Nuclear and Plasma Sciences Society.

Institute of Financial Education., 55 W. Monroe St., Suite 2800 Chicago, IL 60603. Phone: 800-946-0488 or (312)364-0100 Fax: (312)364-0190 E-mail: ifego@theinstitute.com • URL: http://www.theinstitute.com • Provides courses in banking, lending, personal finance, and mortgages for personnel of banks and savings institutions.

Institute of Food Science., Cornell University, 114 Stocking Hall Ithaca, NY 14853. Phone: (607)255-7915 Fax: (607)254-4868 E-mail: mrm1@cornell.edu • URL: http://www.nysaes.cornell.edu/cifs/ • Research areas include the chemistry and processing of food commodities, food processing engineering, food packaging, and nutrition.

Institute of Food Technologists., 221 N. LaSalle St., Suite 300 Chicago, IL 60601. Phone: (312)782-8424 Fax: (312)782-8348 E-mail: info@ift.org • URL: http://www.ift.org • A professional society of food scientists active in government, academia, and industry.

Institute of Gas Technology.

Institute of Human Nutrition. Columbia University

Institute of Hydraulic Research. University of Iowa

Institute of Industrial Engineers.

Institute of Industrial Relations.

Institute of Industrial Relations. University of California, Los Angeles

Institute of Internal Auditors.

Institute of International Education., 809 United Nations Plaza New York, NY 10017-3580. Phone: (212)984-5200 Fax: (212)984-5452 E-mail: info@iie.org • URL: http://www.iie.org • Promotes international educational exchange programs. Administers scholarships, fellowships, and other grants provided by over 120 sponsors.

Institute of Judicial Administration.

Institute of Labor and Industrial Relations.

Institute of Labor and Industrial Relations. University of Illinois at Urbana-Champaign

Institute of Makers of Explosives., 1120 19th St., N. W., Suite 310 Washington, DC 20036. Phone: (202)429-9280 Fax: (202)293-2420 E-mail: info@ime.org • URL: http://www.ime.org • Members are manufacturers of commercial explosives.

Institute of Management Accountants.

Institute of Management Consultants., 1200 19th St., N.W., Suite 300 Washington, DC 20036-2422. Phone: 800-221-2557 or (202)857-5334 Fax: (202)857-5337 E-mail: office@imcusa.org • URL: http://www.imcusa.org • Provides professional services and certification to management consultants. One of the two divisions of the Council of Consulting Organizations.

Institute of Management, Innovation and Organization., University of California, Berkeley, F402 Haas School of Business Berkeley, CA 94720-1930. Phone: (510)642-4041 Fax: (510)273-1072 E-mail: teece@haas.berkeley.edu • URL: http://www.haasberkeley.edu/~imio • Research areas include a wide range of business management functions.

Institute of Marine Engineers., 76 Mark Lane London EC3R 7JN, England. Phone: 44 207 3822600 Fax: 44 207 3822670 E-mail: mic@imare.org.uk • URL: http://www.imare.org.uk • An international organization of marine engineers, offshore engineers, and naval architects.

Institute of Mathematical Statistics.

Institute of Mathematical Statistics Bulletin. Institute of Mathematical Statistics, Business Office, 3401 Investment Blvd., Suite 7 Hayward, CA 94545-3819. Phone: (510)783-8141 Fax: (510)783-4131 E-mail: ims@imstat.org • URL: http://www.jstor.org • Bimonthly. $50.00 per year.

Institute of Noise Control Engineering.

Institute of Nuclear Materials Management.

Institute of Nuclear Power Operations., 700 Galleria Parkway Atlanta, GA 30339-5957. Phone: (770)644-8000 Fax: (770)644-8549 An organization of electric utilities operating nuclear power plants.

Institute of Optics.

Institute of Packaging Professionals.

Institute of Paper Science and Technology. Abstract Bulletin. Institute of Paper Science and Technology, 500 10th St., N.W. Atlanta, GA 30318. Phone: (404)894-5726 Fax: (404)894-9596 E-mail: info.support@ipst.edu • Monthly. Worldwide coverage of the scientific and technical literature of interest to the pulp and paper industry.

Institute of Paper Science and Technology Graphic Arts Bulletin. Institute of Paper Science and Technology, 500 10th St., N.W. Atlanta, GA 30318. Phone: (404)894-5726 Fax: (404)894-9596 E-mail: info.support@ipst.edu • URL: http://www.ipst.edu/isd/gabipst.html • Monthly. $400.00 per volume. Formerly *Graphic Arts Literature Abstracts*.

Institute of Personality and Social Research. University of California at Berkeley

Institute of Public Administration.

Institute of Real Estate Management.

Institute of Scrap Recycling Industries.

Institute of Shortening and Edible Oils.

Institute of State and Regional Affairs., Pennsylvania State University at Harrisburg, 777 W. Harrisburg Pike Middletown, PA 17057-4898. Phone: (717)948-6178 Fax: (717)948-6306 E-mail: xvc@psu.edu • URL: http://www.psdc.hbg.psu.edu/isra • Conducts research in environmental, general, and socioeconomic planning. Zoning is included.

Institute of Tax Consultants.

Institute of Textile Technology.

Institute of Transportation Engineers., 525 School St., S.W., Suite 410 Washington, DC 20024-2797. Phone: (202)554-8050 Fax: (202)863-5486 URL: http://www.ite.org • Members are professionals in surface transportation, mass transit, and traffic engineering.

Institute of Transportation Studies. University of California at Berkeley

Institute of Urban and Regional Development., University of California at Berkeley, 316 Wurster Hall Berkeley, CA 94720-1870. Phone: (510)642-4874 Fax: (510)643-9576 E-mail: iurd@uclink.berkeley.edu • URL: http://www.ced.berkeley.edu/iurd • Research topics include the effects of changing economic trends in urban areas.

Institute on Federal Taxation, New York University. Proceedings, 1942-1953. William S. Hein and Co., Inc., 1285 Main St. Buffalo, NY 14209-1987. Phone: 800-828-7571 or (716)882-2600 Fax: (716)883-8100 E-mail: mail@wshein.com • URL: http://www.wshein.com • $4,750.00. 51 volume set.

Institute on Planning, Zoning and Eminent Domain, Southwestern Legal Foundation:Proceedings, 1971-1994. William S. Hein & Co., Inc., 1285 Main St. Buffalo, NY 14209-1987. Phone: 800-828-7571 or (716)882-2600 Fax: (716)883-8100 E-mail: mail@wshein.com • URL: http://www.wshein.com • 1971. $2,887.00. 24 volumes.

Institutional and Service Textile Distributors Association., 1609 Connecticut Ave. Washington, DC 20009. Phone: (202)986-0105 Fax: (202)986-0448 Members are wholesalers of textile products to hospitals, hotels, airlines, etc.

Institutional Buyers of Bank and Thrift Stocks: A Targeted Directory. Investment Data Corp., 6935 Wisconsin Ave., Suite 208 Chevy Chase, MD 20815. Phone: (301)657-4271 Fax: (301)215-7104 Annual. $645.00. Provides detailed profiles of about 600 institutional buyers of bank and savings and loan stocks. Includes names of financial analysts and portfolio managers.

Institutional Buyers of Energy Stocks: A Targeted Directory. Investment Data Corp., 6935 Wisconsin Ave., Suite 208 Chevy Chase, MD 20815. Phone: (301)657-4271 Fax: (301)215-7104 Annual. $645.00. Provides detailed profiles 555 institutional buyers of petroleum-related and other energy stocks. Includes names of financial analysts and portfolio managers.

Institutional Buyers of Foreign Stocks: A Targeted Directory. Investment Data Corp., 6935 Wisconsin Ave., Suite 208 Chevy Chase, MD 20815. Phone: (301)657-4271 Fax: (301)215-7104 Annual. $595.00. Provides detailed profiles of institutional buyers of international stocks. Includes names of financial analysts and portfolio managers.

Institutional Buyers of REIT Securities: A Targeted Directory. Investment Data Corp., 6935 Wisconsin Ave., Suite 208 Chevy Chase, MD 20815. Phone: (301)657-4271 Fax: (301)215-7104 Semiannual. $995.00 per year. Provides detailed profiles of about 500 institutional buyers of REIT securities. Includes names of financial analysts and portfolio managers.

Institutional Buyers of Small-Cap Stocks: A Targeted Directory. Investment Data Corp., 6935 Wisconsin Ave., Suite 208 Chevy Chase, MD 20815. Phone: (301)657-4271 Fax: (301)215-7104 Annual. $295.00. Provides detailed profiles of more than 837 institutional buyers of small capitalization stocks. Includes names of financial analysts and portfolio managers.

Institutional Investor International Edition: The Magazine for International Finance and Investment. Institutional Investor, 488 Madison Ave. New York, NY 10022. Phone: (212)224-3300 Fax: (212)224-3527 E-mail: info@iijournals.com • URL: http://www.iijournals.com • Monthly. $415.00 per year. Covers the international aspects of professional investing and finance. Emphasis is on Europe, the Far East, and Latin America.

Institutional Investor: The Magazine for Finance and Investment. Institutional Investor, 488 Madison Ave. New York, NY 10022. Phone: (212)224-3300 Fax: (212)224-3527 E-mail: info@iijournals.com • URL: http://www.iijournals.com • Monthly. $475.00 per year. Edited for portfolio managers and other investment professionals. Special feature issues include ''Country Credit Ratings,'' ''Fixed Income Trading Ranking,'' ''All-America Research Team,'' and ''Global Banking Ranking.''

Institutional Research Office. University of the Pacific

Instructional Media Development Center. University of Wisconsin - Madison

Instructional Technology Center.

Instrument Society of America: Aerospace Division.
Instrument Society of America: Automatic Control Systems Division.
Instrument Society of America: Electro-Optics Division.
Instrument Society of America: Food and Pharmaceutical Division.
Instrument Society of America (ISA)., P.O. Box 12277 Research Triangle Park, NC 27709. Phone: (919)549-8411 Fax: (919)549-8288 E-mail: info@isa.org • URL: http://www.isa.org • Members are engineers and others concerned with industrial instrumentation, systems, computers, and automation.
Instrumentalist: A Magazine for School and College Band and Orchestra Directors, Professional Instrumentalist, Teacher-Training Specialists in Instrumental Music Education and Instrumental Teachers. Instrumentalist Co., 200 Northfield Rd. Northfield, IL 60093-3390. Phone: (847)446-5000 Fax: (847)446-6263 Monthly. $22.00 per year. Professional journal for school band and orchestra directors and teachers of instruments in those ensembles.
Instrumentation and Automation News: Instruments, Controls, Manufacturing Software, Electronics and Mechanical Components. Cahners Business Information, 1018 W. 9th Ave. King of Prussia, PA 19406. Phone: 800-695-1214 or (610)205-1000 Fax: (610)964-2915 E-mail: corporatecommunications@cahners.com • URL: http://www.cahners.com • Monthly. Price on application.
Instrumentation and Control Laboratory. Princeton University
Insulation Contractors Association of America.
Insulation Outlook: Business Solutions for Expanding or Relocating Companies. National Insulation Association, 99 Canal Center Palza, Suite 222 Alevandria, VA 22314. Phone: (703)683-6480 Fax: (703)549-4838 $45.00 per year. Covers site selection and related topics.
Insurance Advocate. Emanuel Levy, editor. Shea-Haarmann, P.O. Box 9001 Mount Vernon, NY 10552-9001. Phone: (914)699-2020 Fax: (914)664-1503 E-mail: insuranceadvocate@cinn.com • URL: http://www.cinn.com/iadvocate/ • Weekly. $59.00 per year. News and features on all aspects of insurance business for industry professionals.
Insurance Almanac: Who, What, When and Where in Insurance. Underwriter Printing and Publishing Co., 50 E. Palisade Ave. Englewood, NJ 07631. Phone: 800-526-4700 or (201)569-8808 Fax: (201)569-8817 Annual. $145.00. Lists insurance agencies and brokerage firms; U.S. and Canadian insurance companies, adjusters, appraisers, auditors, investigators, insurance officials and insurance organizations.
Insurance and Employee Benefits Literature. Special Libraries Association, Insurance and Employee Benefits Div., c/o Business Manager, I E B Literature, 201 E. 12th St., PH6 New York, NY 10003. Phone: (212)234-4700 Fax: (212)423-9166 E-mail: saporito@brainlink.com • Bimonthly. $15.00 per year.
Insurance and Technology. Miller Freeman, One Penn Plaza New York, NY 10119-1198. Phone: (212)714-1300 Fax: (212)219-3959 E-mail: kburger@mfi.com • URL: http://www.mfi.com • Monthly. $65.00 per year. Covers information technology and systems management as applied to the operation of life, health, casualty, and property insurance companies.
Insurance Bar Directory. The Bar List Publishing Co., P.O. Box 948 Northbrook, IL 60065. Phone: 800-726-1007 or (847)498-0100 Fax: (847)498-6695 E-mail: info@barlist.com • Annual. $80.00. Lists law firms that handle defense in insurance litigation.
Insurance Day. Available from Informa Publishing Group Ltd., PO Box 1017 Westborough, MA 01581-6017. Phone: 800-493-4080 Fax: (508)231-0856 E-mail: enquiries@informa.com • URL: http://www.informa.com • Three times a week. $440.00 per year. Published in the UK by Lloyd's List (http://www.lloydslist.com). A newspaper providing international coverage of property/casualty/liability insurance, reinsurance, and risk, with an emphasis on marine insurance.
Insurance Finance and Investment. Institutional Investor, 488 Madison Ave. New York, NY 10022. Phone: (212)224-3300 Fax: (212)224-3353 E-mail: info@iijournals.com • URL: http://www.iijournals.com • Biweekly. $1,885.00 per year. Newsletter. Edited for insurance company investment managers.
The Insurance Forum: For the Unfettered Exchange of Ideas About Insurance. Joseph M. Belth, editor. Insurance Forum, Inc., P.O. Box 245 Ellettsville, IN 47429. Phone: (812)876-6502 Monthly. $90.00 per year. Newsletter. Provides analysis of the insurance business, including occasional special issues showing the ratings of about 1,600 life-health insurance companies, as determined by four major rating services: Duff & Phelps Credit Rating Co., Moody's Investors Service, Standard & Poor's Corp., and Weiss Research, Inc.
An Insurance Guide for Seniors. Insurance Forum, Inc., P.O. Box 245 Ellettsville, IN 47429-0245. Phone: (812)876-6502 1997. $15.00. Provides concise advice and information on Medicare, Medicare supplement insurance, HMOs, long-term care insurance, automobile insurance, life insurance, annuities, and pensions. An appendix lists "Financially Strong Insurance Companies." (*The Insurance Forum*, vol. 24, no. 4.)
Insurance Handbook for the Medical Offices. Marilyn T. Fordney. Harcourt Health Sciences Group, 11830 Westline Industrial Dr. Saint Louis, MO 63146. Phone: (314)872-8370 Fax: 800-535-9935 URL: http://www.harcourt-international.com • 1999. $43.95. Sixth edition.
Insurance Information Institute.
Insurance Institute for Highway Safety., 1005 N. Glebe Rd. Arlington, VA 22201-4751. Phone: (703)247-1500 Fax: (703)247-1678 E-mail: iihs@hwysafety.org • URL: http://www.hwysafety.org • Studies highway safety, including seat belt use, air bags, property damage, vehicle recalls, and the role of alcohol and drugs.
Insurance Institute for Highway Safety, Status Report. Insurance Institute for Highway Safety, 1005 N. Glebe Rd. Arlington, VA 22201. Phone: (703)247-1500 Monthly. Free.
Insurance Law Review. Pat Magarick. West Group, 610 Opperman Dr. Eagan, MN 55123. Phone: 800-328-4880 or (651)687-7000 Fax: 800-213-2323 or (651)687-5827 URL: http://www.westgroup.com • 1990. $125.00. Provides review of legal topics within the casualty insurance area, including professional liability, product liability, and environmental issues.
Insurance Market Place: The Agents and Brokers Guide to Non-Standard and Specialty Lines, Aviation, Marine and International Insurance. Rough Notes Co., Inc., 11690 Technology Dr. Carmel, IN 46032-5600. Phone: 800-428-4384 or (317)582-1600 Fax: (317)816-1000 E-mail: rnc@in.net • URL: http://www.insurancemarket.com • Annual. $12.95. Lists specialty, excess, and surplus insurance lines.
Insurance Marketing: The Ins and Outs of Recruiting and Retaining More Agents. Agent Media Corp., 1255 Cleveland St., Suite 300 Clearwater, FL 33755-4910. Phone: (727)446-1100 Fax: (727)446-1166 Bimonthly. Controlled circulation. Provides practical advice for insurance companies on how to hire and keep sales personnel.
Insurance Networking: Strategies and Solutions for Electronic Commerce. Faulkner & Gray, Inc., 300 S. Wacker Dr., 18th Fl. Chicago, IL 60606. Phone: 800-535-8403 or (312)913-1334 Fax: (312)913-1959 E-mail: order@faulknergray.com • URL: http://www.indm.faulknergray.com • 10 times a year. $63.95 per year. Covers information technology for the insurance industry, with emphasis on computer communications and the Internet.
Insurance of Accounts Handbook: A Practical Guide to the FDIC Regulations. Institute of Financial Education, 55 W. Monroe St., Suite 2800 Chicago, IL 60603-5014. Phone: 800-946-0488 or (312)364-0100 Fax: (312)364-0190 E-mail: ystoffregen@bai.org • URL: http://www.theinstitute.com • 1993. $25.00. Second edition. A guide for bankers to the regulations of the Federal Deposit Insurance Corporation.
Insurance Periodicals Index. Specials Libraries Association, Insurance and Employees Benefits Div. CCH/NILS Publishing Co., P.O. Box 2507 Chatsworth, CA 91313. Phone: 800-423-5910 or (818)998-8830 Fax: (818)718-8482 Annual. $250.00. Compiled by the Insurance and Employee Benefits Div., Special Libraries Association. A yearly index of over 15,000 articles from about 35 insurance periodicals. Arrangement is by subject, with an index to authors.
Insurance Regulation: State Capitals. Wakeman-Walworth, Inc., P.O. Box 7376 Alexandria, VA 22307-0376. Phone: (703)549-8606 or 800-876-2545 Fax: (703)549-1372 E-mail: newsletters@statecapitals.com • URL: http://www.statecapitals.com • Weekly. $245.00 per year. Formerly *From the State Capitals: Insurance Regulation*.
Insurance Services Office.
Insurance Smart: How to Buy the Right Insurance at the Right Price. Jeffrey P. O'Donnell. John Wiley and Sons, Inc., 605 Third Ave. New York, NY 10158-0012. Phone: 800-225-5945 or (212)850-6000 Fax: (212)850-6088 E-mail: info@wiley.com • URL: http://www.wiley.com • 1991. $12.95. Advice for insurance buyers on automobile, homeowner, business, farm, health, and life coverage.
Insurance Statistics Yearbook. OECD Publications and Information Center, 2001 L St., N.W., Ste. 650 Washington, DC 20036-4922. Phone: 800-456-6323 or (202)785-6323 Fax: (202)785-0350 E-mail: washington.contact@oecd.org • URL: http://www.oecdwash.org • Annual. $75.00. Presents detailed statistics on insurance premiums collected in OECD countries, by type of insurance.
Insurance Words and Their Meanings: A Dictionary of Insurance Terms. Diana Kowatch. The Rough Notes Co., Inc., 11690 Techonology Dr. Carmel, IN 46032. Phone: 800-428-4384 or (317)582-1600 Fax: (317)816-1003 E-mail: rnc@in.net • URL: http://www.roughnotes.com • 1998. $38.50. 16th revised edition.
InsuranceWeek. I.W. Publications, Inc., 1001 Fourth Ave., Plaza, Suite 3320 Seattle, WA 98154. Phone: (206)624-6965 Fax: (206)624-5021 Weekly. $30.00 per year.
Insuring Your Business: What You Need to Know to Get the Best Insurance Coverage for Your Business. Sean Mooney. Insurance Information Institute, 110 William St. New York, NY 10038. Phone: 800-331-9146 or (212)669-9200 Fax: (212)732-1916 E-mail: info@iii.org • URL: http://www.iii.org • 1992. $22.50.
InsWeb. InsWeb Corp.Phone: (650)372-2129 E-mail: info@insweb.com • URL: http://www.insweb.com • Web site offers a wide variety of advice and information on automobile, life, health, and "other" insurance. Includes glossaries of insurance terms, Standard & Poor's ratings of individual insurance companies, and "Financial Needs Estimators." Searching is available. Fees: Free.
INTECH: The International Journal of Instrumentation and Control. ISA Services, Inc., P.O. Box 12277 Research Triangle Park, NC 27709. Phone: (919)549-8411 Fax: (919)549-8288 E-mail: info@isa.org • URL: http://www.isa.org • Monthly. $85.00 per year.
Integrated Circuits International: An International Bulletin for Suppliers and Users of Integrated Circuits. Elsevier Science, 655 Ave. of the Americas New York, NY 10010. Phone: 888-437-4636 or (212)989-5800 Fax: (212)633-3680 E-mail: usinfo@elsevier.com • URL: http://www.elsevier.com • Monthly. $541.00 per year. For suppliers and users of integrated circuits.
Integrated Media Systems Center., University of Southern California, 3740 McClintock Ave., Suite 131 Los Angeles, CA 90089-2561. Phone: (213)740-0877 Fax: (213)740-8931 E-mail: nikias@imsc.usc.edu • URL: http://www.imsc.usc.edu • Media areas for research include education, mass communication, and entertainment.
Integrated Plant Protection Center. Oregon State University
Intellectual Property and Antitrust Law. William C. Holmes. West Group, 610 Opperman Dr. Eagan, MN 55123. Phone: 800-328-4880 or (651)687-7000 Fax: 800-213-2323 or (651)687-5827 URL: http://www.westgroup.com • Looseleaf. $145.00. Periodic supplementation. Includes patent, trademark, and copyright practices.
Intellectual Property in the International Marketplace. Melvi Simensky and others. John Wiley and Sons, Inc., 605 Third Ave. New York, NY 10158-0012. Phone: 800-225-5945 or (212)850-6000 Fax: (212)850-6088 E-mail: info@jwiley.com • URL: http://www.wiley.com • 1999. $250.00. Two volumes. Volume one: *Valuation, Protection, and Electronic Commerce*. Volume two: *Exploitation and Country-by-Country Profiles*. Includes contributions from lawyers and consultants in various countries.
Intellectual Property Infringement Damages: A Litigation Support Handbook. Russell L. Parr. John Wiley and Sons, Inc., 605 Third Ave. New York, NY 10158-0012. Phone: 800-225-5945 or (212)850-6000 Fax: (212)850-6088 E-mail: info@wiley.comm • URL: http://www.wiley.com • 1999. $145.00. Annual supplement, $60.00. Describes how to calculate damages for patent, trademark, and copyright infringement. (Intellectual Property Series).
Intellectual Property Law Review. W. Bryan Forney, editor. West Group, 610 Opperman Dr. Eagan, MN 55123. Phone: 800-328-4880 or (651)687-7000 Fax: 800-213-2323 or (651)687-5827 URL: http://www.westgroup.com • 1992. $115.00. Patent, trademark, and copyright practices.
Intellectual Property Newsletter. LLP Professional Publishing, 69-77 Paul St. London EC2A 4LQ, England. Monthly. $460.00 per year.
Intellectual Property Owners., 1255 23rd St., N.W., Suite 200 Washington, DC 20037. Phone: (202)466-2396 Fax: (202)466-2893 E-mail: info@ipo.org • URL: http://www.ipo.org • Seeks to strengthen patent, trademark, and copyright laws.
Intellectual Property Today. Omega Communications, 1935 S. Plum Grove Rd., Suite 158 Palantine, IL 60067. Phone: (847)705-7194 Fax: (847)705-7112 Monthly. $48.00 per year. Covers legal developments in copyright, patents, trademarks, and licensing. Emphasizes the effect of new technology on intellectual property. Formerly *Law Works*.
Intelligence Data. Thomson FinancialPhone: 800-654-0393 or (212)806-8023 Fax: (212)806-8004 URL: http://www.intelligencedata.com • Fee-based Web site provides a wide variety of information relating to competitive intelligence, strategic planning, business development, mergers, acquisitions, sales, and marketing. "Intelliscope" feature offers searching of other Thomson units, such as Investext, MarkIntel, InSite 2, and Industry Insider. Weekly updating.
Intelligence Digest: A Review of World Affairs; International Political, Economic and Strategic Intelligence. Intelligence International, Ltd., The Stoneyhill Centre Brimpsfield Gloucester Glos GL40 8LF, England. Phone: 01452 864764 Fax: 01452 864848 46 times a year. $227.00 per year. Provides political, strategic and economic information. Gives warnings on political trends and current affairs.
Intelligence Essentials for Everyone. Available from U. S. Government Printing Office, Washington, DC 20402. Phone: (202)512-1800 Fax: (202)512-2250 E-mail: gpoaccess@gpo.gov • URL: http://www.access.gpo.gov • 1999. $6.50. Issued by the Joint Military Intelligence College, Defense Intelligence Agency, U. S. Department of Defense (http://www.dia.mil/). Written for "businesses worldwide." Ex-

plains how to collect, process, analyze, and manage business intelligence information.

Intelligent Computer Systems Research Institute.

Intelligent Investor: The National Bestseller on Value Investing for Over 35 Years. Benjamin Graham. HarperInformation, 10 E. 53rd St. New York, NY 10022-5299. Phone: 800-242-7737 or (212)207-7000 Fax: 800-822-4090 or (212)207-7145 URL: http://www.harpercollins.com • 2000. $30.00. Fifth edition.

Intelligent Systems Report (ISR). Lionheart Publishing, Inc., 2555 Cumberland Parkway, Suite 299 Atlanta, GA 30339. Phone: (770)431-0967 Fax: (770)432-6969 E-mail: lpi@lionhrtpub.com • URL: http://www.lionrtpub.com • Monthly. $299.00 per year. Newsletter. Formed by merger of*Neural Network News*and *AI Week*.

Inter-American Development Bank., 1300 New York Ave., N. W. Washington, DC 20577. Phone: (202)623-1000 Fax: (202)623-3096 E-mail: webmaster@iadb.org • URL: http://www.iadb.org • Members are 27 Western Hemisphere countries and 17 other countries. Promotes economic development and investment in Latin America. Makes long-term, low-interest loans to less-developed Latin American countries.

Inter-American Tropical Tuna Commission.

Inter-American Tropical Tuna Commission Annual Report. William H. Bayliff, editor., c/o Scripps Institution of Oceanography, 8604 La Jolla Shores Dr. La Jolla, CA 92037-1508. Phone: (619)546-7100 Fax: (619)546-7133 E-mail: wbaylife@lattc.ucsd.edu • Annual. Price varies. Summary of scientific research carried on during the year. Includes financial statements. Text in English and Spanish.

Inter-American Tropical Tuna Commission Bulletin. Inter-American Tropical Tuna Commission, c/o Scripps Institution of Oceanography, 8604 La Jolla Shores Dr. La Jolla, CA 92037-1508. Phone: (619)546-7100 Fax: (619)546-7133 E-mail: wbaylife@lattc.ucsd.edu • Irregular. Price varies. Description of results of scientific studies. Text in English and Spanish.

Inter-Arts Center., San Francisco State University, School of Creative Arts, 1600 Holloway Ave. San Francisco, CA 94132. Phone: (415)338-1478 Fax: (415)338-6159 E-mail: jimdavis@sfsu.edu • URL: http://www.sfsu.edu/~iac • Research areas include multimedia, computerized experimental arts processes, and digital sound.

Inter-NOT: Online & Internet Statistics Reality Check. Bruce Kushnick. New Networks Institute, 26 Broadway, Suite 400 New York, NY 10004. E-mail: internot@interport.net • URL: http://www.newnetworks.com • Annual. $495.00. Compares, analyzes, and criticizes statistics issued by Nielsen Media, Forrester Research, FIND/SVP, Yankelovich Partners and many others relating to online and Internet activities. For example, estimates of the number of Internet users have ranged from about 40 million down to six million. Topics include ''Adjusting for the Puffery'' and ''The Most Plausible Statistics.''

Inter-NOT: The Terrible Twos-Online Industry's Learning Curve. Bruce Kushnick. New Networks Institute, 26 Broadway, Suite 400 New York, NY 10004. E-mail: internot@interport.net • URL: http://www.newnetworks.com • 1996. $495.00. Second edition. A market research report discussing the growing pains of the online industry, especially with regard to the Internet. The importance of market segmentation and customer service is emphasized.

Inter-University Consortium for Political and Social Research. University of Michigan

Interactive Advertising Source. SRDS, 1700 Higgins Rd. Des Plaines, IL 60018. Phone: 800-851-7737 or (847)375-5000 Fax: (847)375-5001 E-mail: prome@srds.com • URL: http://www.srds.com • Quarterly. $561.00 per year. Provides descriptive profiles, rates, audience, personnel, etc., for producers of various forms of interactive or multimedia advertising: online/Internet, CD-ROM, interactive TV, interactive cable, interactive telephone, interactive kiosk, and others. Includes online supplement *SRDS' URlink*.

Interactive Computer Animation. Nadia M. Thalmann and Daniel Thalmann, editors. Prentice Hall, 240 Frisch Court Paramus, NJ 07652-5240. Phone: 800-947-7700 or (201)909-6200 Fax: 800-445-6991 or (201)909-6361 URL: http://www.prenhall.com • 1996. $55.00. Contains 11 chapters by various authors. Includes such items as ''Warp Generation and Transition Control in Image Morphing'' and ''Sculpting, Clothing and Hairdressing Our Virtual Humans.''

Interactive Computer Systems: Videotex and Multimedia. Antone F. Alber. Perseus Publishing, 11 Cambridge Center Cambridge, MA 02142. Phone: (617)252-5200 Fax: (617)252-5285 E-mail: westview.order@perseusbooks.com • URL: http://www.perseusbooks.com • 1993. $79.50.

InterActive Consumers. MarketResearch.com, 641 Ave. of the Americas, 3rd Fl. New York, NY 10011. Phone: 800-298-5699 or (212)807-2629 Fax: (212)807-2716 E-mail: order@marketresearch.com • URL: http://www.marketresearch.com • Monthly. $395.00 per year. Newsletter. Covers the emerging markets for digital content, products, and services. Includes market information on telecommuting, online services, the Internet, online investing, and other areas of electronic commerce.

Interactive Content: Consumer Media Strategies Monthly. Jupiter Media Metrix, 21 Astor Place New York, NY 10003. Phone: 800-488-4345 or (212)780-6060 Fax: (212)780-6075 E-mail: jupiter@jup.com • URL: http://www.jmm.com • Monthly. $675.00 per year; with online edition, $775.00 per year. Newsletter. Covers the broad field of providing content (information, news, entertainment) for the Internet/World Wide Web.

The Interactive Corporation: Using Interactive Media and Intranets to Enhance Business Performance. Roger Fetterman. Reference Information Publishing, 201 E. 50th St. New York, NY 10022. Phone: 800-726-0600 or (212)751-2600 Fax: 800-659-2436 or (212)572-8700 URL: http://www.randomhouse.com • 1997. $30.00. Presents corporate case studies of successful ''networked interactive media in business processes.''

Interactive Digital Software Association., 1775 Eye St., N.W., Ste. 420 Washington, DC 20005. E-mail: info@idsa.com • URL: http://www.e3expo.com • Members are interactive entertainment software publishers concerned with rating systems, software piracy, government relations, and other industry issues.

An Interactive Guide to Multimedia. Que Education and Training, 201 W. 103rd St. Indianapolis, IN 46290-1094. Phone: 800-428-5331 or 800-858-7674 Fax: 800-882-8253 URL: http://www.mcp.com/que • 1996. $85.00, including CD-ROM. Explains multimedia production and application, including graphics, text, video, sound, editing, etc.

Interactive Home: Consumer Technology Monthly. Jupiter Media Metrix, 627 Broadway, 2nd Fl. New York, NY 10003. Phone: 800-488-4345 or (212)780-6060 Fax: (212)780-6075 E-mail: jupiter@jup.com • URL: http://www.jmm.com • Monthly. $625.00 per year. Newsletter on devices to bring the Internet into the average American home. Covers TV set-top boxes, game devices, telephones with display screens, handheld computer communication devices, the usual PCs, etc.

Interactive Marketing and P R News: News and Practical Advice on Using Interactive Advertising and Marketing to Sell Your Products. Phillips Business Information, Inc., 1201 Seven Locks Rd., Suite 300 Potomac, MD 20854. Phone: 800-777-5006 or (301)340-1520 Fax: (301)309-3847 E-mail: pbi@phillips.com • URL: http://www.phillips.com/pbi.htm • Biweekly. $495.00 per year. Newsletter. Provides information and guidance on merchandising via CD-ROM (''multimedia catalogs''), the Internet, and interactive TV. Topics include ''cybermoney'', addresses for e-mail marketing, ''virtual malls,'' and other interactive subjects. Formerly *Interactive Marketing News*.

Interactive Marketing: The Future Present. Edward Forrest and Richard Mizerski, editors. NTC/Contemporary Publishing, P.O. Box 545 Blacklick, OH 43004. Phone: 800-338-6987 or (614)755-4151 Fax: (614)755-5645 E-mail: ntcpub@mcgraw-hill.com • URL: http://www.ntc-cb.com • 1995. $47.95. Contains articles on the collection and analysis of interactive marketing data, database management, interactive media, marketing research strategies, and related topics.(NTC Business Book Series).

Interactive Multimedia Association Membership Directory. Interactive Multimedia Association, 48 Maryland Ave., Suite 202 Annapolis, MD 21401-8011. Phone: (410)626-1380 Fax: (410)263-0590 E-mail: info@ima.org • URL: http://www.ima.org • Annual. $60.00. Includes membership listing and a *Buyer's Guide*.

Interactive Music Handbook. Jodi Summers, editor. Carronade Group, 2355 Francisco St., No. 6 San Francisco, CA 94123. Phone: (415)474-3500 Fax: (415)474-3809 E-mail: fort@liquidnau.com • URL: http://www.carronade.com • 1996. $24.95. Covers interactive or enhanced music CD-ROMs and online music for producers, audio technicians, and musicians. Includes case studies and interviews.

Interactive Television Buyer's Guide and Directory. Chilton Co., 600 S. Cherry St., Suite 400 Denver, CO 80222. Phone: 800-695-1214 or (303)393-7449 Fax: (303)329-3453 URL: http://www.chilton.net • Annual. Price on application. (A special issue of the periodical *Convergence*.)

Interactive Television: Profiles and Analysis. Arlen Communications, Inc., 7315 Wisconsin Ave., Suite 600-E Bethesda, MD 20814. Phone: (301)656-7940 Annual. $2,295.00. Provides current information on interactive-TV applications and technical developments. Includes forecasts.

Interactive Update. Alexander and Associates, 38 E. 29th St., 10th Fl. New York, NY 10016. Phone: (212)684-2333 Fax: (212)684-0291 Semimonthly. $395.00 per year. Newsletter on the interactive entertainment industry.

Interactive Week: The Internet's Newspaper. Ziff Davis Media, Inc., 28 E. 28th St. New York, NY 10016. Phone: (212)503-3500 Fax: (212)503-5680 E-mail: iweekinfo@zd.com • URL: http://www.zd.com • Weekly. $99.00 per year. Covers news and trends relating to Internet commerce, computer communications, and telecommunications.

Interactivity: Tools and Techniques for Interactive Media Developers. Miller Freeman, Inc., 411 Borel Ave., Suite 100 San Mateo, CA 94402. Phone: (415)358-9500 Fax: (415)655-4560 E-mail: mfibooks@mfi.com • URL: http://www.mfi.com • Monthly. $59.95 per year. Edited for professional interactive media developers. Includes a special issue on computer animation.

Interbike Directory. Miller Freeman, Inc., 502 W. Cordova Rd. Santa Fe, NM 87501. Phone: 800-486-2701 or (505)988-7224 Fax: (505)988-5099 Annual. $75.00. Provides information on approximately 1,850 worldwide manufacturers and distributors of bicycles, parts, and accessories.

Interbrand Choice, Strategy and Bilateral Market Power. Michael E. Porter. Harvard University Press, 79 Garden St. Cambridge, MA 02138. Phone: 800-448-2242 or (617)495-2600 Fax: 800-962-4983 or (617)495-5898 E-mail: contacthup@harvard.edu • URL: http://www.hup.harvard.edu • 1976. $16.50. (Economic Studies No. 146).

Interest Rate Risk Measurement and Management. Sanjay K. Nawalkha and Donald R. Chambers, editors. Institutional Investor, Inc., 488 Madison Ave. New York, NY 10022. Phone: (212)224-3185 Fax: (212)224-3527 E-mail: info@iijournals.com • URL: http://www.iijournals.com • 1999. $95.00. Provides interest rate risk models for fixed-income derivatives and for investments by various kinds of financial institutions.

Interest Rate Service. World Reports Ltd., 280 Madison Ave., Suite 1209 New York, NY 10016-0802. Phone: (212)679-0095 Fax: (212)679-1094 10 times a year. $950.00 per year.

Interface Culture: How New Technology Transforms the Way We Create and Communicate. Steven Johnson. HarperCollins Publishers, 10 E. 53rd St. New York, NY 10022-5299. Phone: 800-242-7737 or (212)207-7000 Fax: 800-822-4090 or (212)207-7145 URL: http://www.harpercollins.com • 1997. $24.00. A discussion of how computer interfaces and online technology (''cyberspace'') affect society in general.

Intergovernmental Relations. Available from U. S. Government Printing Office, Washington, DC 20402. Phone: (202)512-1800 Fax: (202)512-2250 E-mail: gpoaccess@gpo.gov • URL: http://www.access.gpo.gov • Annual. Free. Lists government publications. (Subject Bibliography 211.)

Interior Design. Cahners Business Information, Interior Design Group, 345 Hudson St. 4th Fl. New York, NY 10014-4502. Phone: 800-662-7776 or (212)519-7200 Fax: (212)463-7424 E-mail: corporatecommunications@cahners.com • URL: http://www.cahners.com • Monthly. $46.71 per year. For the professional designed, provides information on trends and new products. Includes annual-*Buyers' Guide* and *Interior Design Market*

Interior Design Buyers Guide. Cahners Business Information, Interior Design Group, 345 Hudson St., 4th Fl. New York, NY 10014. Phone: 800-662-7776 or (212)519-7200 Fax: (212)463-7424 E-mail: corporatecommunications@cahners.com • URL: http://www.cahners.com • Annual. Included with subscription to *Interior Design*

Interior Design Laboratory.

Interior Designer. Entrepreneur Media, Inc., 2445 McCabe Way Irvine, CA 92614. Phone: 800-421-2300 or (949)261-2325 Fax: (949)261-0234 E-mail: entmag@entrepreneur.com • URL: http://www.entrepreneur.com • Looseleaf. $59.50. A practical guide to starting an interior design and decoration business. Covers profit potential, start-up costs, market size evaluation, owner's time required, pricing, accounting, advertising, promotion, etc. (Start-Up Business Guide No. E1314.)

Interiors and Sources. L. C. Clark Publishing Co., Inc., 450 Skokie Blvd., Suite 507 Northbrook, IL 60062. Phone: (407)627-3393 Fax: (407)627-3447 Bimonthly. $18.00 per year. Promotes professionalism for interior designers and design firms. Includes special features on office systems, work stations, and office furniture.

Interiors and Sources: Directory and Buyer's Guide. L. C. Clark Publishing Co., Inc., 450 Skokie Blvd., Suite 507 Northbrook, IL 60062. Phone: (407)627-3393 Fax: (407)498-9299 Annual. $10.00. Lists sources of surface materials, furniture, lighting, etc., for interior designers.

Interiors: For the Contract Design Professional. BPI Communications, Inc., 770 Broadway New York, NY 10003-9595. Phone: 800-344-7119 or (646)654-5500 Fax: (646)654-5834 E-mail: info@bpi.com • URL: http://www.bpicomm.com • Monthly. $42.00 per year.

Interline Adventures. Grand Adventures Tour and Travel Publishing Corp., 211 E. Seventh St., Suite 1000 Austin, TX 78701. Phone: (512)391-2000 E-mail: kendra@perx.com • URL: http://www.perx.com • Bimonthly. $18.95 per year. Contains information on air travel for airline personnel. Formerly *Airfair and Airfare Interline*.

Internal Auditing Alert. Warren, Gorham and Lamont/RIA Group, 395 Hudson St. New York, NY 10014. Phone: 800-950-1215 or (212)367-6300 Fax: (212)367-6718 E-mail: customer_service@riag.com • URL: http://www.riahome.com • Monthly. $180.00 per year. Newsletter. Focuses on the means of monitoring and controlling the accounting system used by any enterprise or organization. Gives hints, ideas and suggestions for administering operations and improving the usefulness of the internal audit function.

Internal Auditing Manual. Warren, Gorham & Lamont/RIA Group, 395 Hudson St. New York, NY 10014. Phone: 800-950-1215 or (212)367-6300 Fax: (212)367-6718 E-mail: customer_services@riag.com • URL: http://www.riahome.com • Quarterly. $195.00 per year.

Internal Auditor. Institute of Internal Auditors, Inc., 249 Maitland Ave. Altamonte Springs, FL 32701-4201. Phone: (407)830-7600 Fax: (407)830-4832 E-mail: custserv@theiia.org • URL: http://www.theiia.org • Bimonthly. $60.00 per year.

Internal Auditor's Handbook. Paul E. Heeschen and others. Institute of Internal Auditors, Inc., P.O. Box 371 Annapolis, MD 20701-0371. Phone: (407)830-7600 Fax: (407)831-5171 E-mail: custserv@theiia.org • URL: http://www.theiia.org • 1984. $43.75.

Internal Revenue Bulletin. Available from U. S. Government Printing Office, Washington, DC 20402. Phone: (202)512-1800 Fax: (202)512-2250 E-mail: gpoaccess@gpo.gov • URL: http://www.access.gpo.gov • Weekly. $230.00 per year. Issued by the Internal Revenue Service. Contains IRS rulings, Treasury Decisions, Executive Orders, tax legislation, and court decisions. (Semiannual *Cumulative Bulletins* are sold separately.)

Internal Revenue Code: All the Income, Estate, Gift, Employment, and Excise Procedure and Administrative Provisions. Research Institute of America, Inc., 90 Fifth Ave New York, NY 10011. Phone: 800-431-9025 or (212)645-4800 Fax: (212)337-4213 Semiannual $35.50 per edition.

Internal Revenue Code: Income, Estate, Gift, Employment, and Excise Taxes. CCH, Inc., 4025 W. Peterson Ave. Chicago, IL 60646-6085. Phone: 800-248-3248 or (773)866-6000 Fax: 800-224-8299 or (773)866-3608 URL: http://www.cch.com • Annual. $69.00. Two volumes. Provides full text of the Internal Revenue Code (5,000 pages), including procedural and administrative provisions.

Internal Revenue Cumulative Bulletin. Available from U. S. Government Printing Office, Washington, DC 20402. Phone: (202)512-1800 Fax: (202)512-2250 E-mail: gpoaccess@gpo.gov • URL: http://www.access.gpo.gov • Semiannual. Issued by the Internal Revenue Service. Cumulates all items of a "permanent nature" appearing in the weekly *Internal Revenue Bulletin*.

Internal Revenue Manual: Administration. CCH, Inc., 4025 W. Peterson Ave. Chicago, IL 60646-6085. Phone: 800-248-3248 or (773)583-8500 Fax: 800-224-8299 URL: http://www.cch.com • Six looseleaf volumes. Reproduces IRS tax administration provisions and procedures.

Internal Revenue Manual: Audit and Administration. CCH, Inc., 4025 W. Peterson Ave. Chicago, IL 60646-6085. Phone: 800-248-3248 or (773)866-6000 Fax: 800-224-8299 or (773)866-3608 URL: http://www.cch.com • Irregular $1,156.00. Reproduces IRS audit provisions and procedures.

Internal Revenue Service Data Book. Available from U. S. Government Printing Office, Washington, DC 20402. Phone: (202)512-1800 Fax: (202)512-2250 E-mail: gpoaccess@gpo.gov • URL: http://www.access.gpo.gov • Annual. $3.50. "Contains statistical tables and organizational information previously included in the Internal Revenue Service annual report." (Internal Revenue Service Publication, 55B.)

International ABC Aerospace Directory. Janes's Information Group, Dept. DSM, Ste. 300 Alexandria, VA 22314. Phone: 800-824-0768 or (703)683-3700 Fax: 800-836-0297 E-mail: info@janes.com • 1998. $500.00. 28,000 aviation aerospace manufacturers, airlines, associations, government agencies, etc. Formerly *Interavia ABC Aerospace Directory*.

International Abstracts in Operations Research. International Federation of Operational Research Societies. Elsevier Science, 655 Ave. of the Americas New York, NY 10010. Phone: 888-437-4636 or (212)989-5800 Fax: (212)633-3680 E-mail: usinfo@elsevier.com • URL: http://www.elsevier.com • Bimonthly. $589.00 per year.

International Acronyms, Initialisms, and Abbreviations Dictionary. The Gale Group, 27500 Drake Rd. Farmington Hills, MI 48331-3535. Phone: 800-877-GALE or (248)699-GALE Fax: 800-414-5043 or (248)699-8069 E-mail: galeord@galegroup.com • URL: http://www.galegroup.com • 2000. $465.00. Fifth edition. Two volumes. Contains over 210,000 English and non-English entries used internationally and in specific countries.

International Advertising Association.

International Advertising Association.

International Advertising Association Membership Directory. International Advertising Association, 521 Fifth Ave., Suite 1807 New York, NY 10175-0003. Phone: (212)557-1133 Fax: (212)983-0455 E-mail: webmaster@iaaglobal.org • Annual. Membership. Over 3,600 advertisers, advertising agencies, media, and other firms involved in advertising.

International Advertising: Realities and Myths. John P. Jones, editor. Sage Publications, Inc., 2455 Teller Rd. Thousand Oaks, CA 91320. Phone: (805)499-0721 Fax: (805)499-0871 E-mail: info@sagepub.com • URL: http://www.sagepub.com • 1999. $76.00. Includes articles by advertising professionals in 10 different countries.

International Aerospace Abstracts. American Institute of Aeronautics and Astronautics, Inc., 1801 Alexander Bell Dr., Suite 500 Reston, VA 20191-4344. Phone: 800-639-2422 or (703)264-7500 Fax: (703)264-7551 E-mail: custserv@aiaa.org • URL: http://www.aiaa.org/publications • Monthly. $1,625.00 per year.

International Agreement on Jute and Jute Products. United Nations Publications, United Nations Concourse Level, First Ave., 46th St. New York, NY 10017. Phone: 800-553-3210 or (212)963-7680 Fax: (212)963-4910 E-mail: bookstore@un.org • URL: http://www.un.org/publications • 1992. Second revised edition. An international trade agreement.

International Agreement on Olive Oil and Table Olives. United Nations Publications, United Nations Concourse Level, First Ave., 46th St. New York, NY 10017. Phone: 800-553-3210 or (212)963-7680 Fax: (212)963-4910 E-mail: bookstore@un.org • URL: http://www.un.org/publications • 1986. Trade agreements.

International Agricultural Club.

International Air Transport Association.

International Airline Passengers Association.

The International Alliance, An Association of Executive and Professional Women., P.O. Box 1119 Baltimore, MD 21203-1119. Phone: (410)472-4221 Fax: (410)472-2920 E-mail: info@t-i-a.com • URL: http://www.t-i-a.com • Facilitates communication (networking) among women executives.

International Amusement Industry Buyers Guide. Amusement Business, PO Box 24970 Nashville, TN 37202. Phone: 800-999-3322 or (615)321-4250 Fax: (615)327-1575 E-mail: info@amusementbusiness.com • URL: http://www.amusementbusiness.com • Annual. $60.00. Manufacturers, importers and suppliers of all types of rides, games and merchandise as well as food and drink equipment and supplies. Formerly *Amusement Industry Buyers Guide*.

International and Comparative Law Quarterly. British Institute of International and Comparative Law, Charles Clore House, 17 Russell Square London WC1B 5DR, England. Quarterly. $190.00 per year. Includes *Quarterly Newsletter*.

International Animated Film Society, ASIFA-Hollywood., 725 S. Victory Blvd. Burbank, CA 91502. Phone: (818)842-8330 Fax: (818)842-5645 E-mail: info@asita.hollywood.org • URL: http://www.home.earthlink.net/~asifa • Members are professional animation artists, fans, and students. Promotes advancements in the art of animation.

International Association for Feminist Economics., c/o Jean Schackleford, Dept. of Economics, Bucknell University Lewisburg, PA 17837. Phone: (570)524-3441 Fax: (570)524-3451 E-mail: jshackle@bucknell.edu • Members are economists having a feminist viewpoint. Promotes greater economic opportunities for women.

International Association for Financial Planning., 5775 Glenridge Dr. N.E., Suite B-300 Atlanta, GA 30328-5364. Phone: 800-322-4237 or (404)845-0011 Fax: (404)845-3660 E-mail: membership@fpanet.org • URL: http://www.iafp.org • Members are individuals involved in some aspect of financial planning.

International Association for Insurance Law in the United States., P.O. Box 9001 Mount Vernon, NY 10552. Phone: (914)699-2020 Fax: (914)699-2025 Members are attorneys and others concerned with the international aspects of insurance law.

International Association for Research in Income and Wealth.

International Association of Administrative Professionals.

International Association of Agricultural Economists.

International Association of Amusement Parks and Attractions.

International Association of Amusement Parks and Attractions International Directory and Buyers Guide. International Association of Amusement Parks and Attractions, 1448 Duke St. Alexandria, VA 22314-3403. Phone: (703)836-4800 Fax: (703)836-4801 URL: http://www.iaapa.org • Annual. $83.00. Over 1,800 member amusement parks, attractions and industry suppliers.

International Association of Assembly Managers., 4425 W. Airport Freeway, Suite 590 Irving, TX 75062. Phone: 800-935-4226 or (972)255-8020 Fax: (972)255-9582 E-mail: iaam.info@iaam.org • URL: http://www.iaam.org • Members are auditorium, theater, exhibit hall, and other facility managers.

International Association of Assessing Officers.

International Association of Assessing Officers: Membership Directory. International Association of Assessing Officers, 130 E. Randolph St., Suite 850 Chicago, IL 60601-6217. Phone: (312)819-6100 Fax: (312)819-6149 E-mail: webmaster@iaao.org • URL: http://www.iaao.org • Annual. $400.00. Lists about 8,500 state and local officials concerned with valuation of property tax.

International Association of Association Management Companies.

International Association of Business Communicators.

International Association of Chiefs of Police (IACP)., 515 N. Washington St. Alexandria, VA 22314. Phone: 800-843-4227 or (703)836-6767 Fax: (703)836-4543 URL: http://www.theiacp.org • The IACP Law Enforcement Information Management Section is concerned with law enforcement management information systems, including data processing, telecommunications, and automated systems.

International Association of Clothing Designers and Executives.

International Association of Clothing Designers Convention Yearbook. International Association of Clothing Designers, 475 Park Ave., S., 17th Fl. New York, NY 10016-6901. Phone: (212)685-6602 Annual. Price on application.

International Association of Commercial Collectors., 4040 W. 70th St. Minneapolis, MN 55435. Phone: (612)925-0760 Fax: (612)926-1624 E-mail: smitht@collector.com • URL: http://www.commercialcollector.com • Collection agencies specializing in the recovery of commercial accounts receivable.

International Association of Conference Translators.

International Association of Convention and Visitor Bureaus.

International Association of Counseling Services.

International Association of Defense Counsel.

International Association of Drilling Contractors., P.O. Box 4287 Houston, TX 77210-4287. Phone: (281)578-7171 Fax: (281)578-0589 E-mail: info@iadc.org • URL: http://www.iadc.org • Includes an Offshore Committee.

International Association of Electrical Inspectors.

International Association of Exposition Management.

International Association of Fairs and Expositions.

International Association of Financial Crimes., 385 Bel Marin Keys Blvd., Ste. H Novato, CA 94949-5636. Phone: (415)897-8800 Fax: (415)898-0798 Members are officials who investigate criminal violations of credit card laws.

International Association of Financial Crimes Investigators: Membership Directory. International Association of Financial Crimes Investigators, 385 Bel Marin Keys Blvd., Suite H Novato, CA 94949-5636. Phone: (415)897-8800 Fax: (415)898-0798 Annual. Membership. About 3,500 firms and individuals engaged in investigation of fraudulent use of credit cards. Formerly *International Association of Credit Card Investigators-Membership Directory*. Formerly International Association of Credit Card Investigators.

International Association of Fire Chiefs.

International Association of Fire Fighters.

International Association of Food Industry Supliers Reporter. International Association on Food Industry Suppliers, 1451 Dolley Madison Blvd. McLean, VA 22101-3850. Phone: (703)761-2600 Fax: (703)761-4334 E-mail: info@iafis.org • Monthly. Free.

International Association of Food Industry Suppliers.

International Association of Healthcare Central Service Materiel Management., 213 W. Institute Place, Suite 307 Chicago, IL 60610. Phone: 800-962-8274 or (312)440-0078 Fax: (312)440-9474 E-mail: mailbox@iahcsmm.com • URL: http://www.iahcsmm.com • Members are professional personnel responsible for management and distribution of supplies from a central service material management (purchasing) department of a hospital.

International Association of Hydraulic Engineering and Research.

International Association of Industrial Accident Boards and Commissions., 1201 Wakarusa Dr. Lawrence, KS 66049. Phone: (785)840-9103 Fax: (785)840-9107 E-mail: workcomp@iaiabc.org • URL: http://www.iaiabc.org • Members are government agencies, insurance companies, lawyers, unions, self-insurers, and others with an interest in industrial safety and the administration of workers' compensation laws.

International Association of Jewish Vocational Services.

International Association of Machinists and Aerospace Workers.

International Association of Meteorology and Atmospheric Sciences.

International Association of Personnel in Employment Security.

International Association of Plastic Distributors.

International Association of Ports and Harbors.

International Association of Printing House Craftsmen.

International Association of Professional Bureaucrats., c/o Dr. James H. Boren, One Plaza S., Suite 129 Tahlequah, OK 74464. Phone: (918)456-1357 Fax: (918)458-0124 E-mail: mumbles@www.jimboren.com • URL: http://www.jimboren.com • Motto of Association: "When in doubt, mumble."

International Association of Refrigerated Warehouses.

International Association of Technological University Libraries.

International Association of Theoretical and Applied Limnology.

International Auction Records: Engravings, Drawings, Watercolors, Paintings, Sculpture. Archer Fields, Inc., 155 Sixth

Ave. New York, NY 10013. Phone: 800-338-2665 or (212)627-1999 Fax: (212)627-9484 1993. $179.00. Back volumes available for most years.

International Authors and Writers Who's Who. Available from Taylor & Francis, Inc., 325 Chestnus St., 8th Fl. Philadelphia, PA 19106. Phone: 800-821-8312 or (215)625-8900 Fax: (215)625-2940 E-mail: webmaster@taylorandfrancis.com • URL: http://www.tandfdc.com/ • Biennial. $155.00. About 8,000 authors, writers, and poets, primarily American and British but including writers from nearly 40 countries in the English-speaking world. Published by Melrose Press Ltd.

International Bank Credit Analyst. BCA Publications Ltd., 1002 Sherbrooke St., W., 16th Fl. Montreal, PQ, Canada H3A 3L6. Phone: (514)499-9706 Fax: (514)499-9709 Monthly. $795.00 per year. "A monthly forecast and analysis of currency movements, interest rates, and stock market developments in the principal countries, based on a continuous appraisal of money and credit trends worldwide." Includes many charts and graphs providing international coverage of money, credit, and securities.

International Banking. Peter K. Oppenheim. American Bankers Association, 1120 Connecticut Ave., N. W. Washington, DC 20036-3971. Phone: 800-338-0626 or (212)663-5000 Fax: (202)663-7543 URL: http://www.aba.org • 1991. $51.00. Sixth edition. Covers letters of credit, money transfers, collections, and other aspects of global banking.

International Bar Association.

International Bearing Interchange (IBI Guide). Interchange, Inc., P.O. Box 16244 Saint Louis Park, MN 55416. Phone: 800-669-6208 or (612)929-6669 Biennial. $195.00. Two volumes. Cross-references for ball bearing, straight and curved roller bearings, tappered cones and cups, pillow blocks and flange units; from the latest back to 1918.

International Bee Research Association.

International Bibliography of Studies on Alcohol. Sarah S. Jordy, compiler. Rutgers Center of Alcohol Studies Publications, Rutgers State University of New Jersey, 607 Alison Rd. Pisataway, NJ 08854-8001. Phone: (732)445-2190 Fax: (732)445-5944 E-mail: chrouse@rci.rutgers.edu • URL: http://www.rci.rutgers.edu • 1966-1974. $250.00. Three volumes. Volume one, *References*, 1901-1950; volume two, *Indexes*. 1901-1980; volume three, *References* and *Indexes*, 1951-1960.

International Bibliography of the Social Sciences: Economics. British Library of Political and Economic Science. Routledge, 29 W. 35th St. New York, NY 10001-2291. Phone: 800-634-7064 or (212)216-7800 Fax: 800-248-4724 or (212)564-7854 E-mail: info@routledge.com • URL: http://www.routledge-ny.com • Annual. $230.00.

International Black Writers.

International Booksellers Federation.

International Bottled Water Association.

International Brands and Their Companies. The Gale Group, 27500 Drake Rd. Farmington Hills, MI 48331-3535. Phone: 800-877-GALE or (248)699-GALE Fax: 800-414-5043 or (248)699-8069 E-mail: galeord@galegroup.com • URL: http://www.galegroup.com • 1998. $295.00. Fifth edition. Contains about 84,000 worldwide (non-U. S.) entries for trade names, trademarks, and brand names of consumer-oriented products and their manufacturers, importers, distributors, or marketers. Formerly *International Trade Names Dictionary*.

International Bridge, Tunnel and Turnpike Association.

International Broadcast Engineer. DMG World Media., Queensway House, Two Queensway Redhill RH1 1QS Surrey, England. Phone: (44-)1737-855485 Fax: (44-)1737-855470 URL: http://www.dmg.co.uk • Eight times a year. $180.00 per year.

International Bureau of Fiscal Documentation.

International Bureau of Weights and Measures., Pavillon de Breteuil F-92312 Sevres Cedex, France. Phone: 33 1 45077070 Fax: 33 1 45342021 E-mail: info@bipm.fr • URL: http://www.bipm.fr • Works for the establishment of international weights and measures standards, including international time standards.

International Business. M. Woods, editor. Chapman and Hall, 115 Fifth Ave., 4th Fl. New York, NY 10003-1004. Phone: 800-842-3636 or (212)260-1354 Fax: (212)260-1730 E-mail: info@chapall.com • URL: http://www.chapall.com • 1995. Price on application.

International Business and Multinational Enterprises. Stefan H. Robock and Kenneth Simmonds. McGraw-Hill Higher Education, 1221 Ave. of the Americas New York, NY 10020. Phone: 800-722-4726 or (212)904-2000 Fax: (212)904-2072 E-mail: customer.service@mcgraw-hill • URL: http://www.mcgraw-hill.com • 1988. $68.50. Fourth edition.

International Business Finance: A Bibliography of Selected Business and Academic Sources. Raj Aggarwal. Greenwood Publishing Group, Inc., 88 Post Rd., W. Westport, CT 06881-5007. Phone: 800-225-5800 or (203)226-3571 Fax: (203)222-2540 E-mail: bookinfo@greenwood.com • URL: http://www.greenwood.com • 1984. $65.00.

International Business Handbook. Vishnu H. Kirpalani, editor. Haworth Press, Inc., 10 Alice St. Binghamton, NY 13904-1580. Phone: 800-429-6784 or (607)722-5857 Fax: (607)722-1424 E-mail: getinfo@haworthpressinc.com • URL: http://www.haworthpressinc.com • 1990. $89.95. (International Business Series, No. 1).

International Business Information: How to Find It, How to Use It. Ruth Pagell and Michael Halperin. Oryx Press, 4041 N. Central Ave., Ste. 700 Phoenix, AZ 85012-3379. Phone: 800-279-6799 or (602)265-2651 Fax: 800-279-4663 or (602)265-6250 E-mail: info@oryxpress.com • URL: http://www.oryxpress.com • 1997. $84.50. Second revised edition.

International Business Information on the Web: Searcher Magazine's Guide to Sites and Strategies for Global Business Research. Sheri R. Lanza and Barbara Quint. Information Today, Inc., 143 Old Marlton Pike Medford, NJ 08055-8750. Phone: 800-300-9868 or (609)654-6266 Fax: (609)654-4309 E-mail: custserv@infotoday.com • URL: http://www.infotoday.com • 2001. $29.95. (CyberAge Books.)

International Business Institute.

International Business Planning: Law and Taxation (United States). William P. Streng and Jeswald W. Salacuse. Mathew Bender & Co., Inc., Two Park Ave. New York, NY 10016. Phone: 800-223-1940 or (212)448-2000 Fax: (212)244-3188 E-mail: international@bender.com • URL: http://www.bender.com • $1,200.00. Six looseleaf volumes. Periodic supplementation. Formerly *Federal Taxes*.

International Capital Markets and Securities Regulation. Harold S. Bloomenthal. West Group, 610 Opperman Dr. Eagan, MN 55123. Phone: 800-328-4880 or (651)687-7000 Fax: 800-213-2323 or (651)687-5827 URL: http://www.westgroup.com • Six looseleaf volumes. $795.00. Periodic supplementation. Securities regulation in industrialized nations. (Securities Law Series).

International Cast Polymer Association.

International Center for Law in Development.

International Center for the Disabled.

International Centre for Settlement of Investment Disputes - Annual Report. International Centre for Settlement of Investment Disputes, 1818 H St., N.W. Washington, DC 20433. Phone: (202)458-1535 Fax: (202)522-2027 Annual. Free. Editions available in French and Spanish.

International Ceramic Association.

International Chemical Workers Union.

International City/County Management Association., 777 N. Capitol St., N. E., Suite 500 Washington, DC 20002-4201. Phone: (202)289-4262 Fax: (202)962-3500 URL: http://www.icma.org • Members are administrators and assistant administrators of cities, counties, and regions. Formerly known as the International City Managers' Association (ICMA).

International Civil Aviation Organization Digests of Statistics. International Civil Aviation Organization c/o Document Sales Unit, 999 University St. Montreal PQ, QC, Canada H3C 5H7. Phone: (514)954-8022 Fax: (514)954-6769 E-mail: sales_unit@icao.org • URL: http://www.sales_unit@icao.org • Irregular. $54.00. Contains financial data and traffic data for international airports. Text in English, French, Russian and Spanish.

International Co-operative Alliance.

International Coatings and Formulation Institute.

International Coffee Organization.

International Communications Agency Network.

International Communications Association.

International Communications Industries Association., 11242 Waples Mill Rd., Suite 200 Fairfax, VA 22030-6079. Phone: 800-659-7469 or (703)273-2700 Fax: (703)278-8082 E-mail: icia@icia.org • Members are manufacturers and suppliers of audio-visual, video, and computer graphics equipment and materials.

International Company Data. Mergent FIS, Inc., 60 Madison Ave., Sixth Floor New York, NY 10010. Phone: 800-342-5647 or (212)413-7670 Fax: (212)413-7777 E-mail: fis@fisonline.com • URL: http://www.fisonline.com • Monthly. Price on application. CD-ROM provides detailed financial statement information for more than 11,000 public corporations in 100 foreign countries. Formerly *Moody's International Company Data*.

The International Competitive Power Industry Directory. PennWell Corp., 1421 S. Sheridan Rd. Tulsa, OK 74112-6619. Phone: 800-331-4463 or (918)835-3161 Fax: (918)831-9295 E-mail: webmaster@penwell.com • URL: http://www.pennwell.com • Annual. $75.00. Lists suppliers of services, products, and equipment for the hydro, geothermal, solar, and wind power industries.

International Confederation of Art Dealers.

International Conference of Building Officials.

International Conference of Building Officials - Membership Directory. International Conference of Building Officials, 5360 Workman Mill Rd. Whittier, CA 90601-2298. Phone: 800-336-1963 or (562)699-6031 Fax: (562)692-3853 URL: http://www.icbo.org • Annual. Price on application.

International Conference of Building Officials. Uniform Building Code. International Conference of Building Officials, 5360 Workman Mill Rd. Whittier, CA 90601-2298. Phone: 800-336-1963 or (562)669-0541 Fax: (562)699-9721 URL: http://www.icbo.org • Members, $144.55; non-members, $180.70.

International Congress Calendar. Union of International Associations, 40 Rue Washington Brussels 1050, Belgium. Phone: 32 2 6401 808 Fax: 32 2 6460 525 Quarterly. $375.00 per year. Over 7,000 international meetings scheduled up to 12 to 15 months.

International Contact Lens Clinic. Elsevier Science, 655 Ave. of the Americas New York, NY 10010. Phone: 888-437-4636 or (212)989-5800 Fax: (212)633-3680 E-mail: usinfo@elsevier.com • URL: http://www.elsevier.com • Bimonthly. $272.00 per year.

International Copper Association.

International Copyright Information Center.

International Council for Computer Communication.

International Council for Small Business.

International Council of Aircraft Owner and Pilot Associations.

International Council of Shopping Centers.

International Council of Societies of Industrial Design.

International Counterpurchase Contracts. United Nations Publications, United Nations Concourse Level, First Ave., 46th St. New York, NY 10017. Phone: 800-553-3210 or (212)963-7680 Fax: (212)963-3489 E-mail: bookstore@un.org • URL: http://www.un.org/publications • 1990. Trade agreements.

International Country Risk Guide. The P R S Group, P.O. Box 248 Syracuse, NY 13057-0248. Phone: (315)431-0511 Fax: (315)431-0200 E-mail: custserv@prsgroup.com • URL: http://www.prsgroup.com • Monthly. $3,595.00 per year. Each issue provides detailed analysis of a group of countries, covering financial risks, political trends, and economic developments. More than 130 countries are covered during the course of a year, with specific business risk point ratings assigned.

International Credit Association.

International Currency Review. World Reports Ltd., 280 Madison Ave., Suite 1209 New York, NY 10016. Phone: (212)679-0095 Fax: (212)679-1094 Quarterly. $475.00 per year.

International Customer Service Association., 401 N. Michigan Ave. Chicago, IL 60611-4267. Phone: 800-360-4272 or (312)321-6800 Fax: (312)245-1084 E-mail: icsa@sba.com • URL: http://www.icsa.com • Members are customer service professionals in business and government.

International Customs Tariffs Bureau.

International Data Corp. (IDC)., Five Speen St. Framingham, MA 01701. Phone: (508)935-4389 Fax: (508)935-4789 URL: http://www.idcresearch.com • Private research firm specializing in market research related to computers, multimedia, and telecommunications.

International Defense Electronic Systems Handbook. Intertec Publishing, 6151 Powers Ferry Rd., N.W. Atlanta, GA 30339. Phone: 800-621-9907 or (770)955-2500 Fax: (770)955-0400 E-mail: subs@intertec.com • URL: http://www.intertec.com • Annual. $195.00. Includes information concerning federal budget for electronic military equipment. Gives descriptions of equipment.

International Desalination Association., P.O. Box 387 Topsfield, MA 01983. Phone: (978)887-0410 Fax: (978)887-0411 E-mail: idalpab@ix.netcom.com • URL: http://www.ida.bm • Members are users and suppliers of desalination equipment.

International Development Association., The World Bank, 1818 H St., N.W., Room E1227 Washington, DC 20433. Phone: (202)477-1234 Fax: (202)477-6391 URL: http://www.worldbank.org • Promotes the economic development of poor countries.

International Development Research Council.

International Dictionary of Accounting Acronyms. Thomas W. Morris, editor. Fitzroy Dearborn Publishers, 919 N. Michigan Ave., Suite 760 Chicago, IL 60611. Phone: 800-850-8102 or (312)587-0131 Fax: (312)587-1049 E-mail: website@fitzroydearborn.com • URL: http://www.fitzroydearborn.com • 1999. $45.00. Defines 2,000 acronyms used in worldwide accounting and finance.

International Dictionary of Architects and Architecture. Randall Van Vynckt. St. James Press, 27500 Drake Rd. Farmington Hills, MI 48331-3535. Phone: 800-877-GALE or (248)699-GALE Fax: 800-414-5043 or (248)699-8063 E-mail: galeord@galegroup.com • URL: http://www.galegroup.com • 1993. $260.00. Two volumes. Volume one: *Architects*. Volume two: *Architecture*.

International Dictionary of Film and Filmmakers. St. James Press, 27500 Drake Rd. Farmington Hills, MI 48232. Phone: 800-877-GALE or (248)699-GALE Fax: 800-414-5043 or (248)699-8063 E-mail: galeord@galegroup.com • URL: http://www.galegroup.com • 1996. $510.00. Second edition. Five volumes. Vol. 1:*Films*. Vol. 2: *Directors*. Vol. 3: *Actors and Actresses*. Vol. 4: *Writers and Production Artists*. Vol. 5: *Title Index*

International Digital Imaging Association.

International Direct Investment Statistics Yearbook. OECD Publications and Information Center, 2001 L St., N.W., Ste. 650 Washington, DC 20036-4922. Phone: (202)785-6323 Fax: (202)785-0350 E-mail: washington.contact@oecd.org

• URL: http://www.oecdwash.org • Annual. $79.00. Provides direct investment inflow and outflow data for OECD countries.

International Directory of Agricultural Engineering Institutions. Food and Agriculture Organization of the United Nations. Available from Bernan Associates, 4711-F Assembly Dr. Lanham, MD 20706-4391. Phone: 800-274-4447 or (301)459-7666 Fax: 800-865-3450 or (301)459-0056 E-mail: info@bernan.com • URL: http://www.bernan.com • 1995. Free for institutions and development agencies.

International Directory of Arts. Available from The Gale Group, 27500 Drake Rd. Farmingtono Hills, MI 48331-3535. Phone: 800-699-4253 or (248)699-4253 Fax: (248)699-8069 E-mail: galeord@galegroup.com • URL: http://www.galegroup.com • Biennial. $295.00. Three volumes. A guide to 150,000 art sources and markets in 175 countries. Includes artists, collectors, dealers, galleries, museums, art schools, auctioneers, restorers, publishers, libraries, and associations. Published by K. G. Saur.

International Directory of Book Collectors. Oak Knoll Press, 310 Delaware St. New Castle, DE 19720. Phone: 800-996-2556 or (302)328-7232 Fax: (302)328-7274 E-mail: oakknoll@oakknoll.com • URL: http://www.oakknoll.com • Irregular. $50.00. Over 1,500 listings. Published in England by Trigon Press.

International Directory of Company Histories. St. James Press, 27500 Drake Rd. Farmington Hills, MI 48331-3535. Phone: 800-877-GALE or (248)699-GALE Fax: 800-414-5043 or (248)699-8063 E-mail: galeord@galegroup.com • URL: http://www.galegroup.com • 1989-2000. 33 volumes. Prices vary. Provides detailed histories of about 2,200 major corporations. Cumulative indexing is provided for company names, personal names, and industries.

International Directory of Consumer Brands and Their Owners. Available from The Gale Group, 27500 Drake Rd. Farmington Hills, MI 48331-3535. Phone: 800-877-GALE or (248)699-GALE Fax: 800-414-5043 or (248)699-8069 E-mail: galeord@galegroup.com • URL: http://www.galegroup.com • 1997. $450.00. Published by Euromonitor. Contains detailed information on more than 38,000 consumer product brands and their companies in 62 countries of the world, excluding Europe.

International Directory of Corporate Art Collections. ARTnews, P.O. Box 1608 Largo, FL 34649. Phone: 800-227-7585 or (813)581-7328 Fax: (813)585-6398 E-mail: the-iaa@ix.netcom.com • Biennial. $109.95. Contains information on about 1,300 corporate art collections maintained or sponsored in the U. S., Canada, Europe, and Japan.

International Directory of Little Magazines and Small Presses. Dustbooks, P.O. Box 100 Paradise, CA 95967. Phone: 800-477-6110 or (530)877-6110 Fax: (530)877-0222 URL: http://www.dustbooks.com • Annual. $40.00. Over 6,000 small, independent magazines, presses, and papers.

International Directory of Public Refrigerated Warehouses and Distribution Centers. International Association of Refrigerated Warehouses, 7315 Wisconsin Ave., Suite 1200 N Bethesda, MD 20814. Phone: (301)652-5674 Fax: (301)652-7269 Annual. Free to qualified personnel; others, $150.00 per year. Lists locations/services of 1,000 public refrigerated warehouses in 30 countries.

International Directory of the Nonwoven Fabrics Industry. INDA Association of the Nonwoven Fabrics Industry, P.O. Box 1288 Cary, NC 27511. Phone: (919)233-1210 Fax: (919)233-1282 Biennial. Members, $135.00 per year; non-members, $195.00 per year. Lists about 3,000 manufacturers of nonwoven fabrics and suppliers of raw material and equipment.

International District Energy Association.

International Door Association., P.O. Box 117 West Milton, OH 45383-0117. Phone: (937)698-4186 Members are manufacturers, dealers, and installers of overhead garage door systems.

International Drug Report. International Narcotic Enforcement Officers Association, 112 State St., Suite 1200 Albany, NY 12207. Phone: (518)463-6232 Quarterly. $35.00 per year. Text in English, French and Spanish.

International Dyer. World Textile Publications Ltd., Perkins House, One Longlands St., c/o Keith Higgenbottom, Bradford West Yorkshire BD1 2TP, England. E-mail: info@worldtextile.com • URL: http://www.worldtextile.com • Monthly. $120.00 per year.

International Economic Insights. Institute for International Economics, 11 Dupont Circle, N. W., Suite 620 Washington, DC 20036-1207. Phone: (202)328-9000 Fax: (202)328-5432 E-mail: orders@iie.com • URL: http://www.iie.com • Bimonthly. $60.00 per year.

International Economic Review. University of Pennsylvania, Dept. of Economics. Blackwell Publishers, Inc., 350 Main St. Malden, MA 02148. Phone: 800-835-6770 or (781)388-8200 Fax: (781)388-8232 E-mail: books@blackwellpub.com • URL: http://www.blackwellpub.com • Quarterly. $192.00 per year.

International Economics. McGraw-Hill, 1221 Ave. of the Americas New York, NY 10020. Phone: 800-722-4726 or (212)904-2000 Fax: (212)904-2072 E-mail: customer.service@mcgraw-hill.com • URL: http://www.mcgraw-hill.com • 2000. $66.25. Fourth edition.

International Economics. Peter H. Lindert and Thomas A. Pugel. McGraw-Hill, 1221 Ave. of the Americas New York, NY 10020. Phone: 800-722-4726 or (212)904-2000 Fax: (212)904-2072 E-mail: customer.service@mcgraw-hill.com • URL: http://www.mcgraw-hill.com • 1999. $84.69. 11th edition.

International Employment Hotline. Cantrell Corp., 1088 Middle River Rd. Standardsville, VA 22973-2301. Phone: (703)620-1972 Monthly. $39.00 per year. Newsletter. Lists current overseas job openings by country and employer. Gives job titles and job descriptions as well as candidate qualificaitons.

International Encyclopedia of Business and Management. Malcolm Warner, editor. Routledge, Inc., 29 W. 35th St. New York, NY 10001-2291. Phone: 800-634-7064 or (212)216-7800 Fax: 800-248-4724 or (212)564-7854 E-mail: info@routledge-ny.com • URL: http://www.routledge-ny.com • 1996. $1,319.95. Six volumes. Contains more than 500 articles on global management issues. Includes extensive bibliographies, cross references, and an index of key words and phrases.

International Encyclopedia of Futures and Options. Michael R. Ryder, editor. Fitzroy Dearborn Publishers, 919 N. Michigan Ave., Suite 760 Chicago, IL 60611. Phone: 800-850-8102 or (312)587-0131 Fax: (312)587-1049 E-mail: website@fitzroydearborn.com • URL: http://www.fitzroydearborn.com • 2000. $275.00. Two volumes. Covers terminology, concepts, events, individuals, and markets.

International Encyclopedia of Public Policy and Administration. Jay M. Shafritz, editor. HarperCollins Publishers, 10 E. 53rd St. New York, NY 10022-5299. Phone: 800-242-7737 or (212)207-7000 Fax: 800-822-4090 URL: http://www.harpercollins.com • 1997. $550.00. Four volumes. Covers 20 major areas, such as public administration, government budgeting, industrial policy, nonprofit management, organizational theory, public finance, labor relations, and taxation. Includes a brief bibliography for each major entry and a comprehensive index.

International Encyclopedia of the Stock Market. Michael Sheimo and Andreas Loizou, editors. Fitzroy Dearborn Publishers, 919 N. Michigan Ave., Suite 760 Chicago, IL 60611. Phone: 800-850-8102 or (312)587-0131 Fax: (312)587-1049 E-mail: website@fitzroydearborn.com • URL: http://www.fitzroydearborn.com • 1999. $275.00. Two volumes. Covers the terminology of stock exchanges around the world. Individual country entries provide details of stock exchange conditions, practices, regulation, and brokers.

International Energy Agency.

International Energy Agency. Energy Prices and Taxes. OECD Publications and Information Center, 2001 L St., N.W., Suite 650 Washington, DC 20036-4922. Phone: (202)785-6323 Fax: (202)785-0350 E-mail: washington.contact@oecd.org • URL: http://www.oecdwash.org • Quarterly. $350.00 per year. Compiled by the International Energy Agency. Provides data on prices and taxation of petroleum products, natural gas, coal, and electricity. Diskette edition, $800.00. (Published in Paris).

International Energy Annual. Available from U. S. Government Printing Office, Washington, DC 20402. Phone: (202)512-1800 Fax: (202)512-2250 E-mail: gpoaccess@gpo.gov • URL: http://www.access.gpo.gov • Annual. $34.00. Issued by the Energy Information Administration, U. S. Department of Energy. Provides production, consumption, import, and export data for primary energy commodities in more than 200 countries and areas. In addition to petroleum products and alcohol, renewable energy sources are covered (hydroelectric, geothermal, solar, and wind).

International Executive Service Corps.

International Fabricare Institute.

International Federation for Information and Documentation.

International Federation for Information Processing.

International Federation of Beekeepers' Associations.

International Federation of Business and Professional Women.

International Federation of Freight Forwarders Associations.

International Federation of Press Cutting Agencies.

International Fertilizer Development Center., P.O. Box 2040 Muscle Shoals, AL 35662. Phone: (205)381-6600 Fax: (205)381-7408 E-mail: general@ifdc.org • URL: http://www.ifdc.org • Conducts research relating to all aspects of fertilizer production, marketing, and use. Supported by the United Nations, the World Bank, and other international agencies.

International Fiber Journal. International Media Group, Inc., 1515 Mockingbird Lane, Suite 210 Charlotte, NC 28209-4628. Phone: (704)565-5175 Fax: (704)565-5177 E-mail: ifj@bluenet.com • URL: http://www.ifj.com • Bimonthly. $30.00 per year. Covers manmade fiber technology and manufacturing.

International Fiber Optics Yellow Pages. Information Gatekeepers, Inc., 214 Harvard Ave. Boston, MA 02134. Phone: 800-323-1088 or (617)232-3111 Fax: (617)734-8562 E-mail: info@igigroup.com • URL: http://www.igigroup.com • Annual. $89.95. Includes manufacturers of fiber optics products. Provides a glossary and a discussion of current uses of fiber optics. Formerly *Fiber Optics Yellow Pages*.

International Film Guide. Silman-James Press, 3624 Shannon Rd. Los Angeles, CA 90027. Phone: (323)661-9922 Fax: (323)661-4442 Annual. $24.95. Film production companies, distributors, organizations and government agencies. Also includes film festivals, non-theatrical distributors in the U.S., sources of films for collectors, film archives, services for the industry and film schools.

International Film, Television, and Video Acronyms. Matthew Stevens, editor. Greenwood Publishing Group, Inc., 88 Post Rd., W. Westport, CT 06881-5007. Phone: 800-225-5800 or (203)226-3571 Fax: (203)222-2540 E-mail: bookinfo@greenwood.com • URL: http://www.greenwood.com • 1993. $85.00. A guide to 3,400 acronyms and 1,400 technical terms.

International Finance Section. Princeton University

International Financial Law Review. American Educational Systems, 173 W. 81st St. New York, NY 10024. Phone: 800-717-2669 or (212)501-8181 Fax: (212)501-8926 E-mail: gerans@pobox.com • URL: http://www.emwl.com • Monthly. $695.00 per year.

International Financial Statistics. International Monetary Fund, Publications Services, 700 19th St., N.W., Suite 12-607 Washington, DC 20431-0001. Phone: (202)623-7430 Fax: (202)623-7201 URL: http://www.imf.org • Monthly. Individuals, $246.00 per year; libraries, $123.00 per year. Includes a wide variety of current data for individual countries in Europe and elsewhere. Annual issue available. Editions available in French and Spanish.

International Fire Marshals Association.

International Fire Service Training Association.

International Food Additives Council., 5775 Peachtree-Dunwoody Rd., Suite 500-G Atlanta, GA 30342. Phone: (404)252-3663 Fax: (404)252-0774 E-mail: ifac@assnhq.com • Manufacturers of additives.

International Food Service Executive's Association.

International Foodservice Editorial Council.

International Foodservice Manufacturers Association.

International Foodservice Manufacturers Association: Membership Directory. International Foodservice Manufacturers Association, Two Prudential Plaza, 180 N. Stetson, Suite 4400 Chicago, IL 60601. Phone: (312)540-4400 Fax: (312)540-4401 E-mail: ifma@ifmaworld.com • URL: http://www.ifmaworld.com • Annual. Membership. Manufacturers of processed foods equipment and supplies for schools, hospitals, hotels, restaurants, and institutions and related services in the foodservice industry.

International Foundation for Art Research, Inc., 500 Fifth Ave., Suite 1234 New York, NY 10110. Phone: (212)391-6234 Fax: (212)391-8794 E-mail: kferg@ifar.org • URL: http://www.ifar.org • Research fields are art theft and the authenticity of art objects. Maintains an information archive on stolen art and operates an authentication service.

International Foundation for Telemetering.

International Foundation of Employee Benefit Plans.

The International Foundations Directory. Taylor and Francis, Inc., 325 Chestnut St. Philadelphic, PA 19106. Phone: 800-877-GALE or (248)699-GALE Fax: 800-414-5043 or (248)699-8069 E-mail: galeord@galegroup.com • URL: http://www.galegroup.com • 1998. $210.00. Eighth edition. Published by Europa. A directory of international foundations, trusts, and other nonprofit organizations.

International Franchise Association.

International Freighting Weekly: Sea, Air, Rail, Road. Emap-Business International Ltd., Meed House, 21 John St. London WC1N 2BP, England. Phone: 44 20 7513 1122 Fax: 44 20 7513 0630 Weekly. Members, $165.00 per year; non-members, $325.00 per year.

International Gaming and Wagering Business. Gem Communications, 888 Seventh Ave., 24th Fl. New York, NY 10106-0001. Phone: 800-223-9638 Fax: (212)636-2961 Monthly. $60.00 per year.

International Gaming Resource Guide. Gem Communications, 888 Seventh Ave., 24th Fl. New York, NY 10106-0001. Phone: 800-223-9638 or (212)363-2960 Fax: (212)636-2961 Annual. $50.00. Includes gambling establishments, race tracks, racing commissions, etc. Formery International Gaming and Wagering Business Directory.

International Grains Council. World Grain Statistics. International Grains Council, One Canada Square Canary Wharf E14 5AE, England. Phone: 44 20 7513 1122 Fax: 44 20 7513 0630 Annual. $125.00. Text in English, French, Russian and Spanish. Formerly *International Wheat Council. World Grain Statistics*.

International Guide to Foreign Currency Management. Gary Shoup, editor. Fitzroy Dearborn Publishers, 919 N. Michigan Ave., Suite 760 Chicago, IL 60611. Phone: 800-850-8102 or (312)587-0131 Fax: (312)587-1049 E-mail: website@fitzroydearborn.com • URL: http://

www.fitzroydearborn.com • 1998. $65.00. Written for corporate financial managers. Covers the market for currencies, price forecasting, exposure of various kinds, and risk management.

International Guide to Securities Market Indices. Henry Shilling, editor. Fitzroy Dearborn Publishers, 919 N. Michigan Ave., Suite 760 Chicago, IL 60611. Phone: 800-850-8102 or (312)587-0131 Fax: (312)587-1049 E-mail: website@fitzroydearborn.com • URL: http://www.fitzroydearborn.com • 1996. $140.00. Describes 400 stock market, bond market, and other financial price indexes maintained in various countries of the world (300 of the indexes are described in detail, including graphs and 10-year data).

International Hand Protection Association.

International Handbook of Convertible Securities. Thomas C. Noddings and others. AMACOM, 1601 Broadway, 12th Fl. New York, NY 10019. Phone: 800-262-9699 or (212)586-8100 Fax: (212)903-8168 E-mail: custmserv@amanet.org • URL: http://www.amanet.org • 1998. $75.00. Includes new structures for convertible securities and advanced hedging strategies.

International Handbook on Mental Health Policy. Donna R. Kemp, editor. Greenwood Publishing Group, Inc., 88 Post Rd., W. Westport, CT 06881-5007. Phone: 800-225-5800 or (203)226-3571 Fax: (203)222-2540 E-mail: bookinfo@greenwood.com • URL: http://www.greenwood.com • 1993. $125.00. Provides information on critical mental health issues in 20 countries.

International Hardware Distributors Association.

International Health and Temperance Association.

International Health, Racquet and Sportsclub Association., 263 Summer St. Boston, MA 02210. Phone: 800-228-4772 or (617)951-0055 Fax: (617)951-0056 E-mail: info@ihrsa.org • URL: http://www.ihrsa.org • Members are for-profit health clubs, sports clubs, and gyms.

International Home Furnishings Representatives Association.

International Hotel Trends: A Statistical Summary. PKF Consulting, 425 California St., Suite 1650 San Francisco, CA 94104. Phone: 800-633-4931 or (415)421-5378 Fax: (205)995-1588 URL: http://www.pkf.com • Annual. $125.00. Provides detailed financial analysis of hotel operations around the world. (PKF is Pannell Kerr Forster.)

International Ice Cream Association.

International Income Taxation: Code and Regulations, Selected Sections. CCH, Inc., 4025 W. Peterson Ave. Chicago, IL 60646-6085. Phone: 800-248-3248 or (773)866-6000 Fax: 800-224-8299 or (773)866-3608 URL: http://www.cch.com • Annual. $66.95. Covers U. S. taxation of foreign entities and U. S. taxation of domestic entities having foreign income.

International Information Management Congress.

The International Information Report: The International Industry Dossier. Washington Researchers Ltd., 1655 N. Fort Myer Dr., Suite 800 Arlington, VA 22209. Phone: (703)312-2863 Fax: (703)527-4585 E-mail: research@researchers.com • URL: http://www.researchers.com • Monthly. $160.00 per year.

International Institute for Lath and Plaster.

International Institute of Communications. Wescott House, 3rd Fl.

International Institute of Municipal Clerks.

International Institute of Synthetic Rubber Producers.

International Instrumentation and Controls Buyers Guide. Keller International Publishing, LLC, 150 Great Neck Rd. Great Neck, NY 11021. Phone: (516)829-9210 Fax: (516)829-5414 E-mail: kellpub@world.att.net • Annual. Controlled circulation. Lists over 310 suppliers of precision instrument products and services.

International Intellectual Property Alliance., 1747 Pennsylvania Ave., N.W., Suite 825 Washington, DC 20006. Phone: (202)833-4198 Fax: (202)872-0546 E-mail: smimet@iipa.com • URL: http://www.iipa.com • Promotes global protection of intellectual property.

International Intellectual Property Association.

International Interactive Communications Society., 4840 McKnight Rd., Suite A Pittsburgh, PA 15237. Phone: (412)734-1928 Fax: (412)369-3507 E-mail: worldhq@iics.org • URL: http://www.iics.org • Members are interactive media professionals concerned with intetractive arts and technologies.

International Interior Design Association.

International Intertrade Index: New Foreign Products Marketing Techniques. John E. Felber., P.O. Box 636 Newark, NJ 07101. Phone: (908)686-2382 Fax: (201)622-1740 Monthly. $45.00 per year. Lists new foreign products being offered to U.S. firms. Supplement available *Foreign Trade Fairs New Products*.

International Journal for Vitamin and Nutrition Research. Hogrefe & Huber Publishers, P.O. 2487 Kirkland, WA 98083. Phone: 800-228-3749 or (425)820-1500 Fax: (425)823-8324 URL: http://www.hhpub.com/journals • Quarterly. $198.00 per year.

International Journal of Adhesion and Adhesives. Elsevier Science, 655 Ave. of the Americas New York, NY 10010. Phone: 888-437-4636 or (212)989-5800 Fax: (212)633-3680 E-mail: usinfo@elsevier.com • URL: http://www.elsevier.com • Six times a year. $797.00 per year. Published in England.

International Journal of Advertising: The Quarterly Review of Marketing Communications. Advertising Association. NTC Publications, Ltd., Farm Rd., Henley-on-Thames Oxen RG9 1EJ, England. Phone: 44 1491 411000 Fax: 44 1491 571188 Quarterly. Price on application.

International Journal of Applied Radiation and Isotopes. Elsevier Science, 655 Ave. of the Americas New York, NY 10010. Phone: 888-437-4636 or (212)989-5800 Fax: (212)633-3680 E-mail: usinfo-f@elsevier.com • URL: http://www.elsevier.com • Monthly. $465.00 per year.

International Journal of Bank Marketing. MCB University Press Ltd., 60-62 Toller Lane Bradford West Yorkshire BD8 9B, England. Fax: 44 1274 785200 E-mail: editorial@mcb.co.uk • URL: http://www.mcb.co.uk • Seven times a year. $10,899.00 per year.

International Journal of Climatology. Royal Meteorological Society. Available from John Wiley and Sons, Inc., Journals Div., 605 Third Ave. New York, NY 10158-0012. Phone: 800-225-5945 or (212)850-6000 Fax: (212)850-6088 E-mail: info@wiley.com • URL: http://www.wiley.com • 15 time a year. Institutions, $1,730.00 per year. Published in England by John Wiley and Sons Ltd.

International Journal of Communication Systems. Available from John Wiley and Sons, Inc., Journals Div., 605 Third Ave. New York, NY 10158-0012. Phone: 800-225-5945 or (212)850-6000 Fax: (212)850-6088 E-mail: info@wiley.com • URL: http://www.wiley.com • Bimonthly. Institutions, $995.00 per year. Published in England by John Wiley and Sons Ltd. Formerly *International Journal of Digital and Analog Communication Systems*.

International Journal of Electronic Commerce. M. E. Sharpe, Inc., 80 Business Park Dr. Armonk, NY 10504. Phone: 800-541-6563 or (914)273-1800 Fax: (914)273-2106 E-mail: mesinfo@usa.net • URL: http://www.mesharpe.com • Quarterly. Individuals, $64.00 per year. Institutions, $286.00 per year. A scholarly journal published to advance the understanding and practice of electronic commerce.

International Journal of Energy Research. Available from John Wiley and Sons, Inc., Journals Div., 605 Third Ave. New York, NY 10158-0012. Phone: 800-225-5945 or (212)850-6000 Fax: (212)850-6088 E-mail: info@wiley.com • URL: http://www.wiley.com • 15 times a year. Institutions, $2,735.00 per year. Published in England by John Wiley & Sons Ltd.

International Journal of Health Planning and Management. Available from John Wiley and Sons, Inc., Journals Div., 605 Third Ave. New York, NY 10158-0012. Phone: 800-526-5368 or (212)850-6000 Fax: (212)850-6088 E-mail: info@wiley.com • URL: http://www.wiley.com • Quarterly. Institutions, $980.00 per year. Published in England by John Wiley and Sons Ltd.

International Journal of Hospitality and Tourism Administration: A Multinationaland Cross-Cultural Journal of Applied Research. Haworth Press, Inc., 10 Alice St. Binghamton, NY 13904-1580. Phone: 800-429-6784 or (607)722-5857 Fax: 800-895-0582 or (607)722-1424 E-mail: getinfo@haworthpressinc.com • URL: http://www.haworthpressinc.com • Quarterly. Individuals, $36.00 per year; institutions, $48.00 per year; libraries, $85.00 per year. An academic journal with articles relating to lodging, food service, travel, tourism, and the hospitality/leisure industries in general. Formerly *Journal of International Hospitality, Leisure, and Tourism Management*.

International Journal of Intelligent Systems. John Wiley and Sons, Inc., Journals Div., 605 Third Ave. New York, NY 10158-0012. Phone: 800-225-5945 or (212)850-6000 Fax: (212)850-6088 E-mail: info@wiley.com • URL: http://www.wiley.com • Monthly. Institutions, $1,549.00 per year.

International Journal of Machine Tools and Manufacture: Design, Research and Application. Elsevier Science, 655 Ave. of the Americas New York, NY 10010. Phone: 888-437-4636 or (212)989-5800 Fax: (212)633-3680 E-mail: usinfo@elsevier.com • URL: http://www.elsevier.com • Monthly. $2,273 per year.

International Journal of Mechanical Sciences. Elsevier Science, 655 Ave. of the Americas New York, NY 10010. Phone: 888-437-4636 or (212)989-5800 Fax: (212)633-3680 E-mail: usinfo@sevier.com • URL: http://www.elsevier.com • Monthly. $2,197.00 per year.

International Journal of Powder Metallurgy. American Powder Metallurgy Institute. APMI International, 105 College Rd., E. Princeton, NJ 08540-6692. Phone: (609)452-7700 Fax: (609)987-8523 E-mail: apmi@mpif.org • URL: http://www.mpif.org • Eight times a year. Institutions, $175.00 per year. Formerly *PM Technology Newsletter*.

International Journal of Refrigeration. Elsevier Science, 655 Ave. of the Americas New York, NY 10010. Phone: 888-437-4636 or (212)989-5800 Fax: (212)633-3680 E-mail: usinfo@elsevier.com • URL: http://www.elsevier.com • Eight times a year. $803.00 per year. Text in English or French.

International Journal of Rehabilitation and Health. Plenum Publishing Corp., 223 Spring St. New York, NY 10013. Phone: 800-221-9369 or (212)620-8000 Fax: (212)463-0742 E-mail: info@plenum.com • URL: http://www.plenum.com • Quarterly. $239.50 per year.

International Journal of Robotics Research. Sage Publications, Inc., 2455 Teller Rd. Thousand Oaks, CA 91320. Phone: (805)499-0721 Fax: (805)499-0871 E-mail: info@sagepub.com • URL: http://www.sagepub.com • Monthly. Individuals, $130.00 per year; institutions, $810.00 per year.

International Journal: The News and Views Paper for the Hobbyist. Levine Publications, P.O. Box 9090 Trenton, NJ 08650. Quarterly. $52.50.

International Labour Review. International Labour Office. ILO Publications Center, 49 Sheridan Ave. Albany, NY 12210. Phone: (518)436-9686 Fax: (518)436-7433 URL: http://www.ilo.org • Bimonthly. $64.00. Editions in English, French and Spanish.

International Law Association.

International Law Institute., 1615 New Hampshire Ave., N.W., Suite 100 Washington, DC 20009. Phone: (202)483-3036 Fax: (202)483-3029 E-mail: training@ili.org • URL: http://www.ili.org • Research in foreign trade law and in other areas of international law is done in cooperation with Georgetown University.

International Lawyer. American Bar Association. International Law and Practice Section, 740 15th St., N.W. Washington, DC 20005. Phone: 800-285-2221 or (312)988-5730 Fax: (312)988-6081 URL: http://www.lexis-nexis.com/incc • Quarterly. Free to members; non-members, $35.00 per year.

International Lead Zinc Research Organization.

International League of Electrical Associations.

International Legal Books in Print. Bowker-Saur, Windsor Court E., Grinstead House E. W. Sussex RH19 1HH 4, England. Irregular. $375.00. Two volumes. Covers English-language law books published or distributed within the United Kingdom, Europe, and current or former British Commonwealth countries.

International Legal Materials. American Society of International Law, 2223 Massachusetts Ave., N.W. Washington, DC 20008-2864. Phone: (202)939-6000 Fax: (202)797-7133 URL: http://www.asil.org • Bimonthly. $190.00 per year.

International Licensing Industry Merchandisers' Association., 350 Fifth Ave., Suite 2309 New York, NY 10118. Phone: (212)244-1944 Fax: (212)563-6552 E-mail: info@licensing.org • URL: http://www.licensing.org • Promotes the legal protection of licensed properties.

International Literary Market Place: The Directory of the International Book Publishing Industry. R. R. Bowker, 121 Chanlon Rd. New Providence, NJ 07974. Phone: 888-269-5372 or (908)464-6800 Fax: (908)771-7704 E-mail: info@bowker.com • URL: http://www.bowker.com • Annual. $189.95. More than 10,370 publishers in over 180 countries outside the U.S.and Canada and about 1,150 trade and professional organizations related to publishing abroad.

International Magnesium Association.

International Magnesium Association-Buyers Guide. International Magnesium Association, 1303 Vincent Place, No. 1 McLean, VA 22101-3615. Phone: (703)442-8888 Fax: (703)821-1824 Biennial. $40.00 per year.

International Mail Manual. Available from U. S. Government Printing Office, Washington, DC 20402. Phone: (202)512-1800 Fax: (202)512-2250 E-mail: gpoaccess@gpo.gov • URL: http://www.access.gpo.gov • Semiannual. $36.00 per year. Issued by U. S. Postal Service. Contains rates, regulations, classes of mail, special services, etc., for mail sent from the U. S. to foreign countries.

International Maintenance Institute.

International Management Council of the YMCA.

International Market Alert. International Reports, Inc., 11300 Rockville Pike, Suite 1100 Rockville, MD 20852-3035. Daily. Prices varies. Newsletter. Covers activities of central banks, foreign exchange markets, and New York bond and money markets. Gives specific hedging advice for major currencies. Available online.

International Marketing. Philip R. Cateora and John Graham. McGraw-Hill, 1221 Ave. of the Americas New York, NY 10020. Phone: 800-722-4726 or (212)904-2000 Fax: (212)904-2072 E-mail: customer.service@mcgraw-hill.com • URL: http://www.mcgraw-hill.com • 1998. $84.38. 10th edition.

International Marketing Data and Statistics 2001. Available from The Gale Group, 27500 Drake Rd. Farmington Hills, MI 48331-3535. Phone: 800-877-GALE or (248)699-GALE Fax: 800-414-5043 or (248)699-8069 E-mail: galeord@galegroup.com • URL: http://www.galegroup.com • 2001. $450.00. 25th edition. Published by Euromonitor. Contains statistics on population, economic factors, energy, consumer expenditures, prices, and other items affecting marketing in 158 countries of the world.

International Marketing Forecasts 2001. Available from The Gale Group, 27500 Drake Rd. Farmington Hills, MI 48331-3535. Phone: 800-877-GALE or (248)699-GALE Fax: 800-414-5043 or (248)699-8069 E-mail: galeord@galegroup.com • URL: http://www.galegroup.com • 2000. $1,090.00. Third edition. Published by Euromonitor. Contains demographic, economic, and market forecasts to the year 2010 for major, non-European countries, including the U. S. and Canada. Forecasts include market-size data for 15 consumer product sectors, such as food, clothing, and automobiles.

International Masonry Institute.

International Mass Retail Association.

International Materials Review. ASM International, Materials Information, 9639 Kinsman Rd. Materials Park, OH 44073-0002. Phone: 800-336-5152 or (440)338-5151 Fax: (440)338-8091 E-mail: memserv@po.asm-intl.org • URL: http://www.asm.intl.org • Bimonthly. Members, $305.00 per year; non-members, $734.00 per year. Provides technical and research coverage of metals, alloys, and advanced materials. Formerly *International Metals Review*.

International Media Guide: Business Professional Publications: Asia Pacific/Middle East/Africa. International Media Guides, Inc., 114 Perimeter Rd. Nashua, NH 03063-1325. Phone: 800-964-6334 or (603)882-9576 Fax: (603)595-0437 E-mail: info@internationalmedia.com • URL: http://www.internationalmedia.com • Annual. $285.00. Provides information on 3,000 trade journals "from Africa to the Pacific Rim," including advertising rates and circulation data.

International Media Guide: Business Professional Publications: Europe. International Media Guides, Inc., 114 Perimeter Rd. Nashua, NH 03063-1325. Phone: 800-964-6334 or (603)882-9576 Fax: (603)595-0437 E-mail: info@internationalmedia.com • URL: http://www.internationalmedia.com • Annual. $285.00. Describes 6,000 trade journals from Eastern and Western Europe, with advertising rates and circulation data.

International Media Guide: Business/Professional Publications: The Americas. International Media Guides, Inc., 114 Perimeter Rd. Nashua, NH 03063-1325. Phone: 800-964-6334 or (603)882-9576 Fax: (603)595-0437 E-mail: info@internationalmedia.com • URL: http://www.internationalmedia.com • Annual. $285.00. Describes trade journals from North, South, and Central America, with advertising rates and circulation data.

International Media Guide: Consumer Magazines Worldwide. International Media Guides, Inc., 114 Perimeter Rd. Nashua, NH 03063-1325. Phone: 800-964-6334 or (603)882-9576 Fax: (603)595-0437 E-mail: info@internationalmedia.com • URL: http://www.internationalmedia.com • Annual. $285.00. Contains descriptions of 4,500 consumer magazines in 24 subject categories in 200 countries, including U. S. Provides details of advertising rates and circulation.

International Media Guide: Newspapers Worldwide. International Media Guides, Inc., 114 Perimeter Rd. Nashua, NH 03063-1325. Phone: 800-964-6334 or (603)882-9576 Fax: (603)595-0437 E-mail: info@internationalmedia.com • URL: http://www.internationalmedia.com • Annual. $285.00. Provides advertising rates, circulation, and other details relating to newspapers in major cities of the world (covers 200 countries, including U. S.).

International Merger and Acquisition Professionals., 3232 Cobb Parkway, Suite 437 Atlanta, GA 30339. Phone: (770)319-7797 Fax: (770)319-9838 E-mail: imap@mindspring.com • URL: http://www.imap.com • Mainly concerned with medium-sized businesses having annual sales of less than 50 million dollars.

International Microwave Power Institute.

International Migration of the Highly Qualified: A Bibliographic and Conceptual Itinerary. Anne Marie Gaillard and Jacques Gaillard. Center for Migration Studies, 209 Flagg Place Staten Island, NY 10304. Phone: (718)351-8800 Fax: (718)667-4598 E-mail: sales@cmsny.org • URL: http://www.cmsny.org • 1998. Price on application. Includes more than 1,800 references from 1954 to 1995 on the migration patterns of skilled or highly qualified workers. (CMS Bibliographies and Documentation Series).

International Migration Review: A Quarterly Studying Sociological, Demographic, Economic, Historical, and Legislative Aspects of Human Migration Movements and Ethnic Group Relations. Center for Migration Studies, 209 Flagg Place Staten Island, NY 10304-1122. Phone: (718)351-8800 Fax: (718)667-4598 E-mail: sales@cmsny.org • URL: http://www.cmsny.org/imr3.htm • Quarterly. Individuals, $39.50 per year; institutions, $80.00 per year.

International Military Community Executives Association.

International Mobile Air Conditioning Association., P.O. Box 9000 Fort Worth, TX 76147-2000. Phone: (817)732-4600 or (817)732-6348 Fax: (817)732-9610 E-mail: info@imaca.org • URL: http://www.imaca.org • Serves the automotive, boat, and aircraft air conditioning industries.

International Monetary Fund.

International Monetary Fund: A Selected Bibliography. Anne C. Salda. Transaction Publishers, 35 Berrue Circle Piscataway, NJ 08854-8042. Phone: 888-999-6778 or (732)445-2280 Fax: (732)445-3138 E-mail: trans@transactionpub.com • URL: http://www.transactionpub.com • 1992. $64.95.

International Monetary Fund. Annual Report on Exhange Arrangements and Exchange Restrictions. International Monetary Fund Publications Services, 700 19th St., N.W., Suite 12-607 Washington, DC 20431-0001. Phone: (202)623-7000 Fax: (202)623-7201 URL: http://www.imf.org • Annual. Individuals, $95.00; libraries, $47.50.

International Monetary Fund Staff Papers. International Monetary Fund, Publication Services, 700 19th St., N.W., Suite 12-607 Washington, DC 20431-0001. Phone: (202)623-7430 Fax: (202)623-7201 URL: http://www.imf.org • Quarterly. Individuals, $56.00 per year; students, $28.00 per year. Contains studies by IMF staff members on balance of payments, foreign exchange, fiscal policy, and related topics.

The International Money Market: An Assessment of Forecasting Techniques and Market Efficiency. Richard M. Levich. JAI Press, Inc., P.O. Box 811 Stamford, CT 06904-0811. Phone: (203)323-9606 Fax: (203)357-8446 E-mail: order@jaipress.com • URL: http://www.jaipress.com • 1979. $78.50. (Contemporary Studies in Economic and Financial Analysis Series, Vol. 22).

International Motion Picture Almanac: Reference Tool of the Film Industry. Quigley Publishing Co., Inc., 6639 La Jolla Blvd. La Jolla, CA 92037. Phone: 800-231-8239 or (858)459-1159 Fax: (858)459-1590 E-mail: quigleypub@aol.com • URL: http://www.members.aol.com/quigleypub/qp.html • Annual. $100.00. Reference covering the motion picture industry.

International Municipal Lawyers Association.

International Narcotic Enforcement Officers Association.

International New Product Newsletter. INPN, Inc., P.O. Box 1146 Marblehead, MA 01945-5146. Phone: (617)639-2623 Monthly. $175.00 per year. Includes licensing opportunities.

International Newspaper Financial Executives.

International Newspaper Marketing Association.

International Numismatic Society Authentication Bureau.

International Oceanographic Foundation.

International Oil News. William F. Bland Co., P.O. Box 16666 Chapel Hill, NC 27516-6666. Phone: (919)490-0700 Fax: (919)490-3002 E-mail: crs@petrochemical-news.com • URL: http://www.petrochemical-news.com • Weekly. $579.00 per year. Reports news of prime interest to top executives in the international oil industry.

International Organization for Standardization., One, rue de Varembe CH-1211 Geneva 20, Switzerland. E-mail: central@iso.ch • URL: http://www.iso.ch/ • Members are national standards organizations. Develops and publishes international standards, including ISO 9000 quality management standards.

International Personnel Management Association.

International Petroleum Encyclopedia. PennWell Publishing, P.O. Box 1260 Tulsa, OK 74101. Phone: (918)835-3161 Fax: (918)831-9497 E-mail: info@midwestdirectories.com • URL: http://www.pennwell.com • Annual. $95.00. A worldwide petroleum directory. Features statistics and a complete atlas of the international petroleum market.

International Petroleum Monthly. Available from U. S. Government Printing Office, Washington, DC 20402. Phone: (202)512-1800 Fax: (202)512-2250 E-mail: gpoaccess@gpo.gov • URL: http://www.access.gpo.gov • Monthly. $70.00 per year. Issued by Energy Information Administration, U. S. Department of Energy. Contains data on worldwide petroleum production, consumption, imports, exports, and available stocks.

International Pharmaceutical Abstracts ÎCD-ROMl. American Society of Health-System Pharmacists, 7272 Wisconsin Ave. Bethesda, MD 20814. Phone: (301)657-3000 Fax: (301)657-1251 Quarterly. $1,795.00 per year. Contains CD-ROM indexing and abstracting of international pharmaceutical literature from 1970 to date.

International Pharmaceutical Abstracts: Key to the World's Literature of Pharmacy. American Society of Health-System Pharmacists, 7272 Wisconsin Ave. Bethesda, MD 20814. Phone: (301)657-3000 Fax: (301)657-1641 Semimonthly. Members, $142.95 per year; non-members, $552.50 per year.

International Pharmaceutical Abstracts Îonlinel. American Society of Health-System Pharmacists, 7272 Wisconsin Ave. Bethesda, MD 20814. Phone: (301)657-3000 Fax: (301)657-1257 Provides online indexing and abstracting of the world's pharmaceutical literature from 1970 to date. Monthly updates. Inquire as to online cost and availability.

International Physical Fitness Association., 415 W. Court St. Flint, MI 48503. Phone: (810)239-2166 Fax: (810)239-9390 Members are physical fitness centers of all types.

International Plastics Selector. Data Business Publishing, Post Office Box 6510 Englewood, CO 80155-6510. Phone: 800-447-4666 or (303)799-0381 Fax: (303)799-4082 Semiannual. CD-ROM index version (technical data only), $695.00 per year or $495.00 per disc. CD-ROM image version (technical data and specification sheet images), $1,295.00 per year or $995.00 per disc. Provides detailed information on the properties of 20,000 types of plastic, both current and obsolete. Time period is 1977 to date. Includes trade names and supplier names and addresses.

International Platform Association.

International Police Review. Jane's Information Group, Inc., Dept. DSM, Ste. 300 Alexandria, VA 22314. Phone: 800-824-0768 or (703)683-3700 E-mail: info@janes.com • URL: http://www.janes.com • Bimonthy. Institutions, $215.00 per year. Covers "every aspect" of policing and security throughout the world, including organized crime, money laundering, drugs, illegal immigration, forensic science, and police technology.

International Prepress Association.

International Press Journal: International Press News and Views., Drawer G Kenmore, NY 14217. Quarterly. $20.00 per year.

International Private Label Directory. E. W. Williams Publications Co., 2125 Center Ave., Suite 305 Fort Lee, NJ 07024-5859. Phone: (201)592-7007 Fax: (201)592-7171 Annual. $75.00. Provides information on over 2,000 suppliers of a wide variety of private label and generic products: food, over-the-counter health products, personal care items, and general merchandise. Formerly *Private Label Directory*.

International Public Relations: How to Establish Your Company's Product, Service, and Image in Foreign Markets. Joyce Wouters. Books on Demand, 300 N. Zeeb Rd. Ann Arbor, MI 48106-1346. Phone: 800-521-0600 or (734)761-4700 Fax: (734)665-5022 E-mail: info@umi.com • URL: http://www.lib.umi.com • 1991. $99.20.

International Pulp and Paper Directory. Miller Freeman Books, 6600 Silacci Way Gilroy, CA 95020. Phone: 800-848-5594 or (408)848-5296 Fax: (408)848-5784 E-mail: mfi@rushorder.com • URL: http://www.books.mfi.com • Biennial. $317.00.

International Radio and Television Society Foundation.

International Radio and Television Society: Foundation-Roster Yearbook. International Radio and Television Society, Inc., 420 Lexington Ave., Room 1714 New York, NY 10170-0002. Phone: (212)867-6650 Fax: (212)867-6653 Annual. Membership. A directory of approximately 1,600 members (persons involved professionally with radio or television).

International Radio and Television Society Newsletter. International Radio and Television Society, 420 Lexington Ave., No. 1714 New York, NY 10170-0002. Phone: (212)867-6650 Fax: (212)867-6653 Quarterly.

International Railway Journal: The First International Railway and Rapid Transit Journal. Simmons-Boardman Publishing Corp., 345 Hudson St. New York, NY 10014-4502. Phone: (212)620-7200 Fax: (212)633-1165 Monthly. $72.00 per year. Formerly *International Railway Journal and Rapid Transit Review*. Text in English; summaries in French, German and Spanish.

International Reciprocal Trade Association., 175 W. Jackson, Blvd., Suite 625 Chicago, IL 60604. Phone: (312)461-0236 Fax: (312)461-0474 E-mail: admin1@irta.net • URL: http://www.irta.net • Promotes commercial barter industry.

International Recording Media Association., 182 Nassau St., Suite 204 Princeton, NJ 08542. Phone: (609)279-1700 Fax: (609)279-1999 E-mail: info@recordingmedia.org • URL: http://www.recordingmedia.org • Members are manufacturers and distributors of audiotape, videotape, and associated equipment.

International Rehabilitation Review. Rehabilitation International, 25 E. 31st St., 4th Fl. New York, NY 10010. Phone: (212)420-1500 Fax: (212)505-0871 Three times a year. $30.00 per year.

International Reprographic Association.

International Research Centers Directory. The Gale Group, 27500 Drake Rd. Farmington Hills, MI 48331-3535. Phone: 800-877-GALE or (248)699-GALE Fax: 800-414-5043 or (248)699-8069 E-mail: galeord@galegroup.com • URL: http://www.galegroup.com • 2000. $515.00. 14th edition. Describes over 8,200 research centers in all countries of the world other than the U. S.

International Review for Business Education., 3550 Anderson St. Madison, WI 53704-2599. Phone: (608)837-7518 Fax: (608)834-1301 E-mail: gkantin@madison.tec.wi.us • URL: http://www.bminet.com/siec • Semiannual. $36.00 per year. Text in English, French, German, Italian, and Spanish.

International Review of Applied Economics. Carfax Publishing Co., 875-81 Massachusetts Ave. Cambridge, MA 02139. E-mail: enquiries@carfax.co.uk • URL: http://www.carfax.co.uk • Three times a year. Individuals, $148.00 per year; institutions, $512.00 per year.

International Review of Industrial and Organizational Psychology. Available from John Wiley and Sons, Inc., Journals Div., 605 Third Ave. New York, NY 10158-0012. Phone: 800-526-5368 or (212)850-6000 Fax:

(212)850-6088 E-mail: info@wiley.com • URL: http://www.wiley.com • Annual. $155.00. Published in England by John Wiley and Sons Ltd.

International Road Federation., 1010 Massachusetts Ave., N.W., Suite 410 Washington, DC 20001. Phone: (202)371-5544 Fax: (202)371-5565 E-mail: info@irfnet.org • A federation of associations promoting highway improvement.

International Sanitary Supply Association.

International Satellite Directory: A Complete Guide to the Satellite Communications Industry. Design Publishers, Inc., 800 Siesta Way Sonoma, CA 95476-4413. Phone: (707)939-9306 Fax: (707)939-9235 E-mail: design@satnews.com • URL: http://www.satnews.com • Annual. $275.00. Lists satellite operators, common carriers, earth stations, manufacturers, associations, etc.

International Save the Pun Foundation.

International Saw and Knife Association.

International Security Management Association., 66 Charles St., Suite 280 Boston, MA 02114. Phone: (319)381-4008 Fax: (319)381-4283 E-mail: isma3@aol.com • URL: http://www.ismanet.com • Members are executives of security service companies and executives of security operations at large corporations.

International Sign Association.

International Silk Association-U.S.A.

International Society for Business Education-United States Chapter.

International Society for Community Development Newsletter., c/o Glen Leet, 54 Riverside Dr. New York, NY 10024. Phone: (212)362-7958 Fax: (212)877-7464 Semiannual. Membership.

International Society for Labor Law and Social Security.

International Society for Performance Improvement.

International Society for Pharmaceutical Engineering.

International Society for Technology in Education.

International Society for the Performing Arts.

International Society of Beverage Technologists., 8120 S. Suncoast Blvd. HomoSassa, FL 34446. Phone: (352)382-2008 Fax: (352)382-2018 E-mail: isbt@bevetch.org • URL: http://www.bevtech.org • Members are professionals engaged in the technical areas of soft drink production.

International Society of Certified Employee Beneift Plan Specialists., P.O. Box 209 Brookfield, WI 53008-0209. Phone: (414)786-8771 Fax: (414)786-8650 E-mail: iscebs@ifebp.org • URL: http://www.ifebp.org/ishmpage.html • Affiliated with International Foundation of Employee Benefit Plans.

International Society of Explosives Engineers.

International Society of Weighing and Measurement.

International Society of Weighing and Measurement Membership Directory and Product Guide. International Society of Weighing and Measurement, 10 Kimball St., W. Winder, GA 30680. Phone: (770)868-5300 Fax: (770)868-5301 E-mail: staff@iswm.org • URL: http://www.iswm.org • Annual. Free to members; non-members, $50.00.

International Special Events Society., 9202 N. Meridian St., Suite 200 Indianapolis, IN 46260. Phone: 800-688-4737 or (317)571-5601 Fax: (317)571-5603 E-mail: info@ises.com • URL: http://www.ises.com • Members are meeting planners, caterers, florists, and others involved in the conducting of special events. Promotes the art and science of special event planning and production.

International Standard Industrial Classification of All Economic Activities. United Nations Publications, United Nations Concourse Level, First Ave., 46th St. New York, NY 10017. Phone: 800-553-3210 or (212)963-7680 Fax: (212)953-4910 E-mail: bookstore@un.org • URL: http://www.un.org/publications • 1992. Third revised edition.

International Standards Desk Reference: Your Passport to World Markets. Amy Zuckerman. AMACOM, 1601 Broadway, 12th Fl. New York, NY 10019. Phone: 800-262-9699 or (212)586-8100 Fax: (212)903-8168 E-mail: custmserv@amanet.org • URL: http://www.amanet.org • 1996. $35.00. Provides information on standards important in export-import trade, such as ISO 9000.

International Statistical Institute.

International Survey Library Association., University of Connecticut, 341 Mansfield Rd., U-164 Storrs Mansfield, CT 06269. Phone: (860)486-4440 Fax: (860)486-2123 Members are colleges, research organizations, and corporations. Holdings include basic data from over 10,000 public opinion surveys conducted since 1936.

International Survey of Business Expectations. Dun & Bradstreet Corp., Economic Analysis Dept., Three Sylvan Way Parsippany, NJ 07054-3896. Phone: 800-526-0651 or (973)455-0900 Fax: (973)254-4063 E-mail: customerservice@dnb.com • URL: http://www.dnb.com • Quarterly. $40.00 per year. A survey of international business executives regarding their quarterly expectations for sales, profits, prices, inventories, employment, and new orders. Results are given for each of 14 major foreign countries and the U. S.

International Tape/Disc Directory. Billboard, 1515 Broadway, 39th Fl. New York, NY 10036. Phone: 800-344-7119 or (212)764-7300 Fax: (212)382-6090 URL: http://www.billboard.com • Annual. $75.00. Tape/Audio/Video professional equipment manufacturers, audio/video duplicators; pre-recorded tape, tape service and supply companies; video music producers, production facilities, and video program suppliers. Primarily U.S. and Canadian coverage, with some international listings.

International Tax Agreements. United Nations Publications, United Nations Concourse Level, First Ave., 46th St. New York, NY 10017. Phone: 800-553-3210 or (212)963-7680 Fax: (212)963-4910 E-mail: bookstore@un.org • URL: http://www.un.org/publications • Irregular. Price varies. Looseleaf.

International Tax Institute., 345 Park Ave. New York, NY 10154. Phone: (212)872-6729 Fax: (212)872-3311 Mainly concerned with U. S. taxation of foreign income.

International Tax Journal. Panel Publishers, 1185 Ave. of the Americas New York, NY 10036. Phone: 800-447-1717 or (212)597-0200 Fax: 800-901-9075 or (212)597-0334 E-mail: customer.service@aspenpubl.com • URL: http://www.panelpublisher.com • Quarterly. $195.00 per year. Articles, columns and tax notes pertaining to the international tax market.

International Tax Planners Alert. Research Institute of America, Inc., 90 Fifth Ave. New York, NY 10011. Phone: 800-431-9025 or (212)645-4800 Fax: (212)337-4213 Monthly. $150.00 per year. Newsletter.

International Tax Planning Manual-Corporations. CCH, Inc., 4025 W. Peterson Ave. Chicago, IL 60646-6085. Phone: 800-248-3248 or (773)866-6000 Fax: 800-224-8299 or (773)866-3608 URL: http://www.cch.com • Eight times a year. Price on application. Two looseleaf volumes. Periodic supplementation. Tax strategies for doing business in 38 major countries. Formerly *International Tax Planning Manual*.

International Tax Program., Harvard University, Pound Hall, Room 400 Cambridge, MA 02138. Phone: (617)495-4406 Fax: (617)495-0423 URL: http://www.law.harvard.edu/programs/itp • Studies the worldwide problems of taxation, including tax law and tax administration.

International Tax Report: Maximizing Tax Opportunities Worldwide. I B C Donoghue Organization, P.O. Box 9104 Ashland, MA 01721-9104. Phone: 800-343-5413 or (508)881-2800 Fax: (508)881-0982 URL: http://www.monitorpress.co.uk • Monthly. $1,110.00 per year.

International Taxicab and Livery Association.

International Telecommunications Satellite Organization.

International Teleconferencing Association., P.O. Box 906 Syosset, NY 11791-0079. Phone: (516)941-2020 Fax: (516)941-2015 E-mail: staff@itca.org • URL: http://www.itca.org • Members are vendors and users of teleconferencing equipment. Special Interest Groups include Telecommuting.

International Television and Video Almanac: Reference Tool of the Television and Home Video Industries. Quigley Publishing Co., Inc., 9 Railroad Hwy Larchmont, NY 10538-3004. Phone: 800-231-8239 or (914)834-2348 Fax: (914)834-2194 E-mail: quigleypub@aol.com • URL: http://www.members.aol.com/quigleypub/intl.html • Annual. $119.00.

International Television Association., 9202 N. Meridian St., Suite 200 Indianapois, IN 46260-1810. Phone: 888-879-4882 or (317)816-6269 Fax: 800-801-8926 E-mail: chris@itva.org • URL: http://www.itva.org • Concerned with non-broadcast industrial television recording for business training and corporate communications.

International Television Association-Membership Directory. International Television Association, 9202 N. Meridian St., Suite 200 Indianapolis, IN 46260-1834. Phone: (317)816-6269 Fax: (317)571-5603 E-mail: itvahq@worldnet.att.net • URL: http://www.itva.org • Annual. Membership.

International Telework Association Council., 204 E St., N. E. Washington, DC 20002. Phone: (202)547-6157 Fax: (202)546-3289 URL: http://www.telecommute.org • Members are individuals and organizations promoting the benefits of telecommuting and the ''virtual office.''

International Textile Bulletin: Dyeing-Printing-Finishing Edition. ITS Publishing, International Textile Service, Kesslerstrasse 9, 8952 Schlieren, Switzerland. Phone: 41 1 7384800 Fax: 41 1 7384832 E-mail: circulation-management@its-publishing.com • URL: http://www.its-publishing.com • Quarterly. $170.00 per year. Editions in Chinese, English, French, German, Italian and Spanish.

International Textile Bulletin: Nonwovens and Industrial Textiles Edition. ITS Publishing, International Textile Service, Kesslerstrasse 9, CH-8952 Schlieren, Switzerland. Phone: 41 1 7384800 Fax: 41 1 7384832 E-mail: circulation-management@itis-publishing.com • URL: http://www.its-publishing.com • Quarterly. $170.00 per year. Editions in Chinese, English, French, German, Italian and Spanish.

International Textile Bulletin: Yarn and Fabric Forming Edition. ITS Publishing, International Textile Service, Kesslerstrasse 9, CH-8952 Schlieren, Switzerland. Phone: 41 1 7384800 Fax: 41 1 7384832 E-mail: circulation-management@itis-publishing.com • URL: http://www.its-publishing.com • Quarterly. $170.00 per year. Editions in Chinese, English, French, German, Italian and Spanish.

International Textile Center. Texas Tech University

International Textile Machinery Shipment Statistics. International Textile Manufacturers Federation, Am Schanrengraben 29, Postfach 8039 Zurich, Switzerland. Phone: (41-)1-2017080 Fax: (41-)1-2017134 Annual. 250 Swiss francs. Formerly *International Cotton Industry Statistics*.

International Textiles: Information and Inspiration. Textile Institute. Benjamin Dent and Co., Ltd., P.O. Box 1897 Lawrence, KS 66044-8897. 10 times a year. $445.00 per year. Text in English, French and German; supplement in Japanese.

International Theatre Equipment Association.

International Theatre Studies Center.

The International Ticketing Association., 250 W. 57th St., Suite 722 New York, NY 10107. Phone: (212)264-0600 Fax: (212)581-0885 E-mail: info@intix.org • URL: http://www.itea.com • Members are box office managers, theater marketing managers, and other entertainment management personnel.

International Tin Council. Quarterly Statistical Bulletin. International Tin Council, One Oxendon St. London SW1Y 4EQ, England. Quarterly. $100.00 per year. Includes eight monthly statistical summaries.

International Tire and Rubber Association.

International Titanium Association., 350 Interlocken Blvd., Suite 390 Broomfield, CO 80021-3485. Phone: (303)404-2221 Fax: (303)404-9111 E-mail: info@titanium.org • URL: http://www.titanium.org • Members are producers, fabricators, and users of titanium and titanium alloys.

International Titanium Association Buyers Guide. International Titanium Association, 350 Interlocken Blvd., Suite 390 Broomfield, CO 80021-3485. Phone: (303)404-2221 Fax: (303)404-9111 E-mail: info@titanium.org • URL: http://www.titanium.org • Annual. Members, $5.00; non-members, $20.00.

International Trade Alert. American Association of Exporters and Importers, 51 W. 42nd St., 7th Fl. New York, NY 10017-5404. Phone: (212)944-2606 Fax: (212)382-2606 Weekly. Membership.

International Trade and Investment Letter: Trends in U.S Policies, Trade Finance and Trading Operations. International Business Affairs Corp., 4938 Hampden Lane Bethesda, MD 20814-2914. Phone: (301)907-8647 Monthly. $240.00 per year. Newsletter.

International Trade Council., 3114 Circle Hill Rd. Alexandria, VA 22305-1606. Phone: (703)548-1234 Fax: (703)548-6126 E-mail: wisdom@itctrade.com • Promotes free trade for agricultural products.

International Trade Reporter Export Reference Manual. Bureau of National Affairs, Inc., 1231 25th St., N.W. Washington, DC 20037-1197. Phone: 800-372-1033 or (202)452-4200 Fax: (202)452-8092 E-mail: books@bna.com • URL: http://www.bna.com • Weekly. $874.00 per year. Looseleaf. Formerly *Export Shipping Manual*.

International Trade Statistics Yearbook. United Nations Statistical Office. United Nations Publications, United Nations Concourse Level, First Ave., 46th St. New York, NY 10017. Phone: 800-553-3210 or (212)963-7680 Fax: (212)963-4910 E-mail: bookstore@un.org • URL: http://www.un.org/publications • Annual. $135.00. Two volumes.

International Trademark Association., 1133 Ave. of the Americas New York, NY 10036. Phone: (212)768-9887 Fax: (212)768-7796 URL: http://www.inta.org • Members are trademark owners, lawyers, designers, and others concerned with the proper use of trademarks and trade names.

International Tradeshow Directory: The Annual Statistical Directory of U.S. and Canadian Tradeshows and Public Shows. Tradeshow Week, 5700 Wilshire Blvd., Suite 120 Los Angeles, CA 90036-5804. Phone: 800-375-4212 or (323)965-5300 Fax: (323)665-5300 E-mail: dgudea@tsweek • URL: http://www.tradesweek.com • Annual. $450.00. Provides detailed information for more than 9,000 U. S. and Canadian trade shows of 5,000 square feet or more scheduled for the next four years.

International Training in Communication.

International Travel and Tourism. Donald E. Lundberg. John Wiley and Sons, Inc., 605 Third Ave. New York, NY 10158-0012. Phone: 800-225-5945 or (212)850-6000 Fax: (212)850-6088 E-mail: info@wiley.com • URL: http://www.wiley.com • 1993. $59.50. Second edition. Provides an overview of the international travel business.

International Union United Mine Workers of America.

International Venture Capital Institute.

International Vital Records Handbook. Thomas J. Kemp. Genealogical Publishing Co., Inc., 1001 N. Calvert St. Baltimore, MD 21202-3827. Phone: 800-296-6687 or (410)837-8271

Fax: (410)752-8492 E-mail: orders@genealogical.com • URL: http://www.genealogical.com • Triennial. $29.95. Provides procedures and copies of forms for obtaining birth, marriage, divorce, and death records from 67 countries and territories in North America, the British Isles and other English-speaking countries and Europe.

International Warehouse Logistics Association.

International Warehouse Logistics Association Membership Directory and Resource Guide. International Warehouse Logistics Association, 1300 W. Higgins Rd., Suite 111 Park Ridge, IL 60068-5764. Phone: (847)292-1891 Fax: (847)292-1896 URL: http://www.warehouselogistics.com • Annual. Free to members, manufacturers, and distributors. Detailed listing of 700 public merchandise warehousing firms located throughout the U.S., Canada, Mexico, Costa Rica, Dominacan Republic, Panama, Venezuela, and Russia. Formerly *American Warehouse Association and Canadian Association of Warehousing and Distribution Services Membership Directory and Resource Guide*.

International Wealth Success Newsletter: The Monthly Newsletter of Worldwide Wealth Opportunities. Tyler G. Hicks, editor. International Wealth Success, Inc., 24 Canterbury Rd. Rockville Center, NY 11570. Phone: 800-323-0548 or (516)766-5850 Fax: (516)766-5619 Monthly. $24.00 per year. Newsletter. Provides information on a variety of small business topics, including financing, mail order, foreign opportunities, licensing, and franchises.

International Who's Who. The Gale Group, 27500 Drake Rd. Farmington Hills, MI 48331-3535. Phone: 800-877-GALE or (248)699-GALE Fax: 800-414-5043 or (248)699-8069 E-mail: galeord@galegroup.com • URL: http://www.galegroup.com • Annual. $365.00. Provides up-to-date biographical information on important individuals in international affairs, government, diplomacy, the liberal professions, and all branches of the arts and sports. Published by Europa.

International Who's Who of Women. Available from Taylor and Francis, Inc., 325 Chestnut St. Philadelphia, PA 19106. Phone: 800-821-8312 or (215)625-2940 Fax: (215)625-2940 E-mail: webmaster@taylorandfrancis.com • URL: http://www.tandfdc.com • 1997. $390.00. Second edition. Published by Europa. Contains biographical profiles of more than 5,000 eminent women from all countries.

International Women's Writing Guild.

Internet Alliance., P.O. Box 65782 Washington, DC 20035-5782. Phone: (202)955-8091 Fax: (202)955-8081 E-mail: ia@internetalliance.org • URL: http://www.internetalliance.org • Members are companies associated with the online and Internet industry. Promotes the Internet as "the global mass market medium of the 21st century." Concerned with government regulation, public policy, industry advocacy, consumer education, and media relations. Formerly Interactive Services Association.

Internet and Electronic Commerce Strategies: Using Technology to Improve Your Bottom Line. Computer Economics, Inc., 5841 Edison Place Carlsbad, CA 92008. Phone: 800-326-8100 or (760)438-8100 Fax: (760)431-1126 E-mail: custserv@compecon.com • URL: http://www.computereconomics.com • Monthly. $387.00 per year. Newsletter on management strategies for making money from the Internet. Compares online marketing with traditional marketing.

Internet and Personal Computing Abstracts. Information Today, Inc., 143 Old Marlton Pike Medford, NJ 08055-8750. Phone: 800-300-9868 or (609)654-6266 Fax: (609)654-4309 E-mail: custserv@infotoday.com • URL: http://www.infotoday.com • Contains abstracts covering a wide variety of personal and business microcomputer literature appearing in more than 100 journals and popular magazines. Time period is 1981 to date, with monthly updates. Formerly *Microcomputer Index*. Inquire as to online cost and availability.

The Internet Blue Pages: The Guide to Federal Government Web Sites. Information Today, Inc., 143 Old Marlton Pike Medford, NJ 08055-8750. Phone: 800-300-9868 or (609)654-6266 Fax: (609)654-4309 E-mail: custserv@infotoday.com • URL: http://www.infotoday.com • Annual. $34.95. Provides information on more than 900 Web sites used by various agencies of the federal government. Includes indexes to agencies and topics. Links to all Web sites listed are available at http://www.fedweb.com. (CyberAge Books.)

Internet Book: Everything You Need to Know About Computer Networking and How the Internet Works. Douglas Comer. Simon and Schuster Trade, 1230 Ave. of the Americas New York, NY 10020. Phone: 800-223-2336 or (212)698-7000 Fax: 800-943-9831 or (212)698-7007 E-mail: ssonline_feedback@simonsays.com • URL: http://www.simonsays.com • 1997. $32.50. Second edition.

The Internet Bubble: Inside the Overvalued World of High-Tech Stocks, and What You Should Know to Avoid the Coming Catastrophe. Tony Perkins and Michael C. Perkins. HarperCollins Publishers, Inc., 10 E. 53rd St. New York, NY 10022-5299. Phone: 800-242-7737 or (212)207-7000 Fax: 800-822-4090 or (212)207-7145 URL: http://www.harpercollins.com • 1999. $27.00. The authors predict a shakeout in e-commerce stocks and other Internet-related investments. (HarperBusiness.)

Internet Business Handbook. Daniel Dern. Prentice Hall, 240 Frisch Court Paramus, NJ 07652-5240. Phone: 800-947-7700 or (201)909-6200 Fax: 800-445-6991 or (201)909-6361 URL: http://www.prenhall.com • 1997. $29.95.

Internet Business Intelligence: How to Build a Big Company System on a Small Company Budget. David Vine. Information Today, Inc., 143 Old Marlton Pike Medford, NJ 08055-8750. Phone: 800-300-9868 or (609)654-6266 Fax: (609)654-4309 E-mail: custserv@infotoday.com • URL: http://www.infotoday.com • 2000. $29.95. Covers the obtaining of valuable business intelligence data through use of the Internet.

Internet Business Journal: Commercial Opportunities in the Networking Age. Strangelove Internet Enterprises, Inc., 208-A Somerset St., E. Ottawa, ON, Canada K1N 6V2. Phone: (613)565-0982 Fax: (613)569-4433 Monthly. $149.00 per year. $75.00 per year to individuals and nonprofit libraries. Emphasis is on commercial opportunities presented by the Internet.

Internet Business Report: Software, Tools and Platforms. Jupiter Media Metrix, 627 Broadway, 2nd Fl. New York, NY 10003. Phone: 800-488-4345 or (212)780-6060 Fax: (212)780-6075 E-mail: jupiter@jup.com • URL: http://www.jmm.com • Semimonthly. $695.00 per year; with electronic software, $795.00 per year. Newsletter. Covers Internet advertising, fee collection, and attempts in general to make the Internet/World Wide Web profitable. Includes news of how businesses are using the Internet for sales promotion and public relations.

The Internet Compendium: Guide to Resources by Subject: Subject Guides to Health and Science Resources. Joseph Jones and others, editors. Neal-Schuman Publishers, Inc., 100 Varick St. New York, NY 10013. Phone: (212)925-8650 Fax: 800-584-2414 E-mail: info@neal-schuman.com • URL: http://www.neal-schuman.com • 1995. $82.50. Editors are with the University of Michigan Internet Clearinghouse. Provides direct location access to "thousands" of Internet addresses, in a detailed subject arrangement, with critical analysis of content. Contains information databases, text archives, library catalogs, bulletin boards, newsletters, forums, etc. Includes topics in medicine, agriculture, biology, chemistry, mathematics, physics, engineering, computers, and science in general.

The Internet Compendium: Guide to Resources by Subject: Subject Guides to Social Sciences, Business, and Law Resources. Joseph James and others, editors. Neal-Schuman Publishers, Inc., 100 Varick St. New York, NY 10013. Phone: (212)925-8650 Fax: 800-584-2414 or (212)219-8916 E-mail: info@neal-schuman.com • URL: http://www.neal-schuman.comp • 1995. $82.50. Editors are with the University of Michigan Internet Clearinghouse. Provides direct location access to "thousands" of Internet addresses, in a detailed subject arrangement, with critical analysis of content. Contains information databases, text archives, library catalogs, bulletin boards, newsletters, forums, etc. Includes topics in economics, finance, taxation, history, population, civil rights law, law careers, women's studies, and so forth.

The Internet Compendium: Guide to Resources by Subject: Subject Guides to the Humanities. Louis Rosenfeld and others, editors. Neal-Schuman Publishers, Inc., 100 Varick St. New York, NY 10013. Phone: (212)925-8650 Fax: 800-584-2414 or (212)219-8916 E-mail: info@neal-schuman.com • URL: http://www.neal-schuman.com • 1995. $82.50. Editors are with the University of Michigan Internet Clearinghouse. Provides direct location access to "thousands" of Internet addresses, in a detailed subject arrangement, with critical analysis of content. Contains information databases, text archives, library catalogs, bulletin boards, newsletters, forums, etc. Includes topics in literature, art, religion, philosophy, music, education, library science, games, magic, and the humanities in general.

Internet Connection: Your Guide to Government Resources. Glasser Legalworks, 150 Clove Rd. Little Falls, NJ 07424. Phone: 800-308-1700 or (973)890-0008 Fax: (973)890-0042 E-mail: legalwks@aol.com • URL: http://www.legalwks.com • 10 times a year. $89.00 per year. Newsletter (print) devoted to finding free or low-cost U. S. Government information on the Internet. Provides detailed descriptions of government Web sites.

Internet for Everyone: A Guide for Users and Providers. Richard Wiggins. McGraw-Hill, 1221 Ave. of the Americas New York, NY 10020. Phone: 800-722-4726 or (212)904-2000 Fax: (212)904-2072 E-mail: customer.service@mcgraw-hill.com • URL: http://www.mcgraw-hill.com • 1994. $29.95.

Internet Industry Directory. Internet Industry Magazine, 101 W. 23rd St., Ste. 2286 New York, NY 10011. Phone: (212)977-3800 Fax: (212)977-4545 E-mail: andrea@internetindustry.com • URL: http://www.internetindustry.com • Semiannual. Price on application. Lists products and services for Internet service providers. Includes Internet-related articles and interviews.

The Internet Initiative: Libraries Providing Internet Services and How They Plan, Pay, and Manage. Edward J. Valauskas and others. American Library Association, 50 E. Huron St. Chicago, IL 60611-2795. Phone: 800-545-2433 or (312)944-6780 Fax: (312)440-9374 E-mail: ala@ala.org • URL: http://www.ala.org • 1995. $27.00. Provides 18 reports on Internet services in various kinds of libraries.

Internet Insider. Ruffin Prevost. Osborne/McGraw-Hill, 2600 10th St. Berkeley, CA 94710. Phone: 800-227-0900 or (510)549-6600 Fax: (510)549-6603 E-mail: customer.service@mcgraw-hill.com • URL: http://www.osborne.com • 1995. $14.95. A colorful presentation. (Internet Series).

Internet Marketing and Technology Report: Advising Marketing, Sales, and Corporate Executives on Online Opportunities. Computer Economics, Inc., 5841 Edison Place Carlsbad, CA 92008. Phone: 800-326-8100 or (760)438-8100 Fax: (760)431-1126 E-mail: custserv@compecon.com • URL: http://www.computereconomics.com • Monthly. $387.00 per year. Newsletter. Covers strategic marketing, sales, advertising, public relations, and corporate communications, all in relation to the Internet. Includes information on "cutting-edge technology" for the Internet.

Internet Marketing Report: News and Advice to Help Companies Harness the Power of the Internet to Achieve Business Objectives. Progressive Business Publications, 370 Technology Dr. Malvern, PA 19355-1315. Phone: 800-220-5000 or (610)695-8600 Fax: (610)647-8089 E-mail: editor@pbp.com • URL: http://www.pbp.com • Semimonthly. $299.00 per year. Newsletter. Covers Internet marketing strategy, site traffic, success stories, technology, cost control, and other Web site advertising and marketing topics.

Internet Payments Report. Jupiter Media Metrix, 21 Astor Place New York, NY 10003. Phone: 800-488-4345 or (212)780-6060 Fax: (212)780-6075 E-mail: jupiter@jup.com • URL: http://www.jmm.com • Annual. $1,095.00. Market research report. Provides data, comment, and forecasts on the collection of electronic payments ("e-money") for goods and services offered through the Internet.

Internet-Plus Directory of Express Library Services: Research and Document Delivery for Hire. American Library Association, 50 E. Huron St. Chicago, IL 60611-2795. Phone: 800-545-2433 or (312)944-6780 Fax: (312)440-9374 E-mail: ala@ala.org • URL: http://www.ala.org • 1997. $49.50. Covers fee-based services of various U. S., Canadian, and international libraries. Paid services include online searches, faxed documents, and specialized professional research. Price ranges are quoted. (A joint production of FISCAL, the ALA/ACRL Discussion Group of Fee-Based Information Service Centers in Academic Libraries, and FYI, the Professional Research and Rapid Information Delivery Service of the County of Los Angeles Public Library.) Formerly *FISCAL Directory of Fee-Based Information Services in Libraries*.

Internet Power Tools. John Ross. Alfred A. Knopf, Inc., 201 E. 50th St. New York, NY 10022. Phone: 800-726-0600 or (212)751-2600 Fax: (212)572-2593 1995. $40.00.

Internet Publishing Magazine. North American Publishing Co., 401 North Broad St. Philadelphia, PA 19108. Phone: (215)238-5300 Fax: (215)238-5457 URL: http://www.ipubmag.com • Eight times a year. Controlled circulation. Edited for print publishers, online-only publishers, web designers, advertising agencies, and others concerned with the publishing of content through the Web.

Internet Reference Services Quarterly: A Journal of Innovative Information Practice, Technologies, and Resources. Haworth Press, Inc., 10 Alice St. Binghamton, NY 13904-1580. Phone: 800-429-6784 or (607)722-5857 Fax: 800-895-0582 or (607)722-1424 E-mail: getinfo@haworthpressinc.com • URL: http://www.haworthpressinc.com • Quarterly. Individuals, $36.00 per year; libraries and other institutions, $48.00 per year. Covers both theoretical research and practical applications.

Internet Research Guide: A Concise, Friendly, and Practical Handbook for Anyone Researching in the Wide World of Cyberspace. Timothy K. Maloy. Allworth Press, 10 E. 23rd St., Suite 210 New York, NY 10010. Phone: 800-491-2808 or (212)777-8395 Fax: (212)777-8261 E-mail: jbarager@allworth.com • URL: http://www.allworth.com • 1999. $18.95. Revised edition. Provides "hype-free" advice on practical use of the World Wide Web.

Internet Resources: A Subject Guide. Available from American Library Association, 50 E. Huron St. Chicago, IL 60611-2795. Phone: 800-545-2433 or (312)944-6780 Fax: (312)280-3255 E-mail: ala@ala.org • URL: http://www.ala.org • 1995. $18.00. Published by Association of College and Research Libraries. Provides updated versions of Internet subject directories appearing originally in *College and Research Libraries News*.

Internet Resources and Services for International Business: A Global Guide. Lewis-Guodo Liu. Oryx Press, 4041 N. Central Ave., Suite 700 Phoenix, AZ 85012-3397. Phone: 800-279-6799 or (602)265-2651 Fax: 800-279-4663 or

(602)265-6250 E-mail: info@oryxpress.com • URL: http://www.oryxpress.com • 1998. $49.95. Describes more than 2,500 business-related Web sites from 176 countries. Includes five major categories: general information, economics, business and trade, business travel, and contacts. Indexed by Web site name, country, and subject.

Internet Retailer: Merchandising in an Age of Virtual Stores. Faulkner & Gray, Inc., 300 S. Wacker Dr., 18th Fl. Chicago, IL 60606. Phone: 800-535-8403 or (312)913-1334 Fax: (312)913-1959 E-mail: order@faulknergray.com • URL: http://www.faulknergray.com • Bimonthly. $82.95. Covers the selling of retail merchandise through the Internet.

Internet Search Advantage: Professional's Guide to Internet Searching. Z-D Journals, 500 Canal View Blvd. Rochester, NY 14623. Phone: 800-223-8720 or (716)240-7301 Fax: (716)214-2387 E-mail: zdjcr@zd.com • URL: http://www.zdjournals.com • Monthly. $199.00 per year. Newsletter. Covers Internet research, utilities, agents, configurations, subject searches, search theory, etc. Emphasis is on the efficient use of various kinds of search engines. Includes E-mail alert service.

Internet Society., 11150 Sunset Hills Rd., Suite 100 Reston, VA 20190-5321. Phone: (703)326-9880 Fax: (703)326-9881 E-mail: membership@isoc.org • URL: http://www.isoc.org • Members are technical personnel, corporations, business people, students, and others with an interest in Internet applications and technology.

Internet Telephony Magazine: The Authority on Voice, Video, Fax, and Data Convergence. Technology Marketing Corp., One Technology Plaza Norwalk, CT 06854. Phone: 800-243-6002 or (203)852-6800 Fax: (203)853-2845 E-mail: cahenderson@tmcnet.com • URL: http://www.internettelephonymag.com • Monthly. $29.00 per year. Covers the business and technology of telephone and other communications service via the Internet.

Internet Tools of the Profession. Special Libraries Association-Phone: (202)234-4700 Fax: (202)265-9317 E-mail: hope@tiac.net • URL: http://www.sla.org/pubs/itotp • Web site is designed to update the printed *Internet Tools of the Profession*. Provides links to a wide range of useful databases in business, finance, industry, information technology, insurance, law, library management, telecommunications, and other subject areas. Fees: Free.

Internet Tools of the Profession: A Guide for Information Professionals. Hope N. Tillman, editor. Special Libraries Association, 1700 18th St., N. W., 17th Fl. Washington, DC 20009-2514. Phone: (202)234-4700 Fax: 888-411-2856 or (202)234-2442 E-mail: books@sla.org • URL: http://www.sla.org • 1997. $49.00. Second edition. Consists of 14 sections by various authors or compilers. After two introductory articles on searching the Internet, there are 12 annotated lists of useful Web sites, covering the SLA, business and finance, chemistry, education, food and agriculture, information technology, insurance and employee benefits, law, library management, metals and materials, pharmaceuticals, and telecommunications. An index is provided.

The Internet Troubleshooter: Help for the Logged-On and Lost. Nancy R. John and Edward J. Valauskas. American Library Association, 50 E. Huron St. Chicago, IL 60611-2795. Phone: 800-545-2433 or (312)944-6780 Fax: (312)440-9374 E-mail: ala@ala.org • URL: http://www.ala.org • 1994. $27.00. A basic question-and-answer guide to the Internet. Includes illustrations and a glossary.

Internet World: The Voice of E-Business and Internet Technology. Internet World Media, 250 Park Ave., S., 10th Fl. New York, NY 10003. Phone: 800-632-5537 or (212)547-1800 Fax: (212)547-1830 E-mail: info@iw.com • URL: http://www.iw.com • Semimonthly. Edited for "Internet professionals." Includes industry news, new products, e-business news, and technical developments. (Formerly *WebWeek*.)

Internet.com: The E-Business and Internet Technology Network. Internet.com Corp.Phone: (212)547-7900 Fax: (212)953-1733 E-mail: info@internet.com • URL: http://www.internet.com • Web site provides a wide variety of information relating to Internet commerce, search engines, news, Web design, servers, browsers, Java, service providers, advertising, marketing, etc. Online searching is offered. Fees: Free. (Formerly produced by Mecklermedia Corp.)

Internetweek: The Newspaper for the Communications Industry. CMP Publications, Inc., 600 Community Dr. Manhasset, NY 11030. Phone: 800-577-5356 or (516)562-5000 Fax: (516)733-6916 URL: http://www.internetwk.com • 48 times a year. $175.00 per year. Edited for professionals involved with the Internet, intranets, and extranets. Formerly *Communications Week*.

The Internship Bible. Random House, Inc., 201 E. 50th St. New York, NY 10022. Phone: 800-726-0600 or (212)751-2600 Fax: 800-659-2436 or (212)572-8700 URL: http://www.randomhouse.com • Annual. $25.00. Compiled by the staff of the Princeton Review. Lists internships in various fields.

Interoperability. Miller Freeman, Inc., 600 Harrison St. San Francisco, CA 94107. Phone: (415)905-2200 Fax: (415)905-2232 E-mail: mfibooks@mfi.com • URL: http://www.mfi.com • Quarterly. Price on application. Covers the operation of wide-area networks, including UNIX systems.

Interracial Council for Business Opportunity., 550 Fifth Ave., Suite 2202 New York, NY 10118-2202. Phone: (212)779-4360 Fax: (212)779-4365 Provides technical and financial assistance to minority business people.

Interservice. American Logistics Association, 1133 15th St., N.W., Suite 600 Washington, DC 20005. Phone: (202)466-2520 Fax: (202)296-4419 Quarterly. $20.00 per year. Official Journal of the American Logistics Association.

Interstate Natural Gas Association of America.

Interstate Producers Livestock Association.

Interstate Tax Insights. Interstate Tax Corp., 193 East Ave. Norwalk, CT 06855-1109. Phone: (203)854-0704 Fax: (203)853-9510 Monthly. $195.00 per year. Formerly *Interstate Tax Report*.

Interviewing Principles and Practices. Charles J. Stewart and William B. Cash. Brown and Benchmark, 25 Kessel Court Madison, WI 53711. Phone: 800-338-5578 or (608)273-0040 Fax: 800-346-2377 E-mail: customer.service@mcgraw-hill.com • URL: http://www.mhhe.com • 1997. $40.00. Eighth edition.

Intimate Apparel Manufacturers Association.

Intimate Fashion News. MacKay Publishing Corp., 307 Fifth Ave., 16th Fl. New York, NY 10016-6517. Phone: (212)679-6677 Fax: (212)679-6374 Semimonthly. $30.00 per year. Provides essential information on the intimate apparel industry. Includes *Fashion Merchandiser*.

Intranet and Networking Strategies Report: Advising IT Decision Makers on Best Practices and Current Trends. Computer Economics, Inc., 5841 Edison Place Carlsbad, CA 92008. Phone: 800-326-8100 or (760)438-8100 Fax: (760)431-1126 E-mail: custserv@compecon.com • URL: http://www.computereconomics.com • Monthly. $395.00 per year. Newsletter. Edited for information technology managers. Covers news and trends relating to a variety of corporate computer network and management information systems topics. Emphasis is on costs.

Intranet News. Publications Resource Group, P.O. Box 765 North Adams, MA 01247. Phone: (413)664-6185 Fax: (413)664-9343 Monthly. $545.00 per year. Newsletter. Covers intranet applications, products, services, and company implementation.

IntraNet Professional: IntraNet Applications and Knowledge Management for Libraries and Information Professionals. Information Today, Inc., 143 Old Marlton Pike Medford, NJ 08055-8750. Phone: 800-300-9868 or (609)654-6266 Fax: (609)654-4309 E-mail: custserv@infotoday.com • URL: http://www.infotoday.com • Bimonthly. $79.95 per year. Newsletter on the use of Internet technology for local library networks.

Intranets: What's the Bottom Line? Randy J. Hinrichs. Prentice Hall, 240 Frisch Court Paramus, NJ 07652-5240. Phone: 800-947-7700 or (201)909-6452 Fax: 800-445-6991 or (201)909-6361 URL: http://www.prenhall.com • 1997. $29.95. Explains the practical value of intranets for business communication.

Introducing Computers: Concepts, Systems, and Applications with Getting Started Set, 1990-1991. Robert H. Blissmer. John Wiley and Sons, Inc., 605 Third Ave. New York, NY 10158-0012. Phone: 800-225-5945 or (212)850-6000 Fax: (212)850-6088 E-mail: info@wiley.com • URL: http://www.wiley.com • 1995. $20.95.

Introducing Windows 95: The Next Generation of Microsoft Windows. Microsoft Press, One Microsoft Way Redmond, WA 98052-6399. Phone: 800-677-7377 or (425)882-0800 Fax: (425)936-7329 URL: http://www.microsoft.com • 1995. $12.95. An introductory description of features. (Professional Editions Series).

Introduction to Advertising and Promotion: An Integrated Marketing Communications Perspective. George E. Belch and Michael A. Belch. McGraw-Hill Higher Education, 1221 Ave. of the Americas New York, NY 10020. Phone: 800-722-4726 or (212)904-2000 Fax: (212)904-2072 E-mail: customer.service@mcgraw-hill.com • URL: http://www.mcgraw-hill.com • 1994. $69.94. Third edition.

Introduction to Agricultural Marketing. Robert E. Branson and Douglas G. Norvell. McGraw-Hill, 1221 Ave. of the Americas New York, NY 10020. Phone: 800-722-4726 or (212)904-2000 Fax: (212)904-2072 E-mail: customer.service@mcgraw-hill.com • URL: http://www.mcgraw-hill.com • 1983. $43.74.

Introduction to Automation for Librarians. William Saffady. American Library Association, 50 E. Huron St. Chicago, IL 60611-2795. Phone: 800-545-2433 or (312)944-6780 Fax: (312)440-9374 E-mail: ala@ala.org • URL: http://www.ala.org • 1999. $60.00. Fourth edition. Provides basic information on electronic technology (computers, telecommunications) and library applications of technology.

Introduction to Biotechnology: Demystifying the Concepts. David B. Bourgaize. Addison-Wesley Longman, Inc., One Jacob Way Reading, MA 94002. Phone: 800-447-2226 or (781)944-3700 Fax: (781)944-9351 URL: http://www.thomson.com/wadsworth • 1999. $63.00.

Introduction to Ceramics. W. David Kingery and others. John Wiley and Sons, Inc., 605 Third Ave. New York, NY 10158-0012. Phone: 800-526-5368 or (212)850-6000 Fax: (212)850-6088 E-mail: info@wiley.com • URL: http://www.wiley.com • 1976. $175.00. Second edition. (Science and Technology of Materials Series).

An Introduction to Clay Colloid Chemistry: For Clay Technologists, Geologists and Soil Scientists. H. Van Olphen. Krieger Publishing Co., P.O. Box 9542 Melbourne, FL 32902-9542. Phone: 800-724-0025 or (321)724-9542 Fax: (321)951-3671 E-mail: info@krieger-publishing.com • URL: http://www.krieger-publishing.com • 1991. $69.50. Second edition.

Introduction to Computer Theory. Daniel I. Cohen. John Wiley and Sons, Inc., 605 Third Ave. New York, NY 10158-0012. Phone: 800-225-5945 or (212)850-6000 Fax: (212)850-6088 E-mail: info@wiley.com • URL: http://www.wiley.com • 1996. $92.95. Second edition.

Introduction to Ecological Economics. Robert Costanza and others. Saint Lucie Press, 2000 Corporate Blvd., N. W. Boca Raton, FL 33431-7372. Phone: 800-272-7737 or (561)274-9906 Fax: 800-374-3401 E-mail: information@slpress.com • URL: http://www.slpress.com • 1997. $54.95. Advocates environmental policy changes on local, regional, national, and international levels.

Introduction to Financial Management. Lawrence D. Schall. McGraw-Hill, 1221 Ave. of the Americas New York, NY 10020. Phone: 800-722-4726 or (212)904-2000 Fax: (212)904-2072 E-mail: customer.service@mcgraw-hill.com • URL: http://www.mcgraw-hill.com • 1990. $83.75. Sixth edition.

Introduction to Forest Science. Raymond A. Young. John Wiley and Sons, Inc., 605 Third Ave. New York, NY 10158-0012. Phone: 800-225-5945 or (212)850-6000 Fax: (212)850-6088 E-mail: info@wiley.com • URL: http://www.wiley.com • 1990. $106.95. Second edition.

Introduction to Futures and Options Markets. John C. Hull. Prentice Hall, 240 Frisch Court Paramus, NJ 07652-5240. Phone: 800-947-7700 or (201)909-6200 Fax: 800-445-6991 or (201)909-6361 URL: http://www.prenhall.com • 1997. $94.00. Third edition.

Introduction to Glass Science and Technology. J. E. Shelby. American Chemical Society, 1155 16th St., N. W. Washington, DC 20036. Phone: 800-333-9511 or (202)872-4600 Fax: (202)872-4615 E-mail: service@acs.org • URL: http://www.pubs.acs.org • 1997. $40.00. Covers the basics of glass manufacture, including the physical, optical, electrical, chemical, and mechanical properties of glass. (RCS Paperback Series).

Introduction to Hospital Accounting. L. Vann Seawell. Healthcare Financial Management Educational Foundation, Two Westbrook Corporate Center, Suite 700 Westchester, IL 60154. Phone: 800-252-4362 or (708)531-9600 E-mail: tarya@hfma.org • URL: http://www.hfma.org • 1992. $45.00. Third edition.

Introduction to Industrial-Organization Psychology. Ronald E. Riggio, editor. Addison-Wesley Educational Publications, Inc., One Jacob Way Reading, MA 01867. Phone: 800-447-2226 or (781)944-3700 Fax: (781)942-1117 URL: http://www.awl.com • 1999. $80.00. Third edition. Price on application.

Introduction to Information Systems. James A. O'Brien. McGraw-Hill, 1221 Ave. of the Americas New York, NY 10020. Phone: 800-722-4726 or (212)904-2000 Fax: (212)904-2072 E-mail: customer.service@mcgraw-hill.com • URL: http://www.mcgraw-hill.com • 1999. $63.25. Ninth edition.

Introduction to Insect Pest Management. Robert L. Metcalf and William H. Luckmann. John Wiley and Sons, Inc., 605 Third Ave. New York, NY 10158-0012. Phone: 800-225-5945 or (212)850-6000 Fax: (212)850-6088 E-mail: info@wiley.com • URL: http://www.wiley.com • 1994. $125.00. Third edition. (Environmental Science and Technology Series).

Introduction to Law and the Legal System. Harold J. Grilliot. Houghton Mifflin Co., 215 Park Ave., S. New York, NY 10003. Phone: 800-225-3362 or (212)420-5800 Fax: (212)420-5855 URL: http://www.hmco.com • 1995. $69.56. Sixth edition. Six volumes.

Introduction to Librarianship. Jean K. Gates. Neal-Schuman Publishers, Inc., 100 Varick St. New York, NY 10013. Phone: (212)925-8650 Fax: 800-584-2414 E-mail: info@neal-schuman.com • URL: http://www.neal-schuman.com • 1990. $38.50. Third edition.

An Introduction to Linear Programming and Game Theory. Paul R. Thie. John Wiley and Sons, Inc., 605 Third Ave. New York, NY 10158-0012. Phone: 800-225-5945 or (212)850-6000 Fax: (212)850-6088 E-mail: info@wiley.com • URL: http://www.wiley.com • 1988. $102.95. Second edition.

Introduction to Mass Communications. Phillip H. Agee. Addison-Wesley Educational Publications, Inc., One Jacob Way Reading, MA 01871. Phone: 800-447-2226 or (781)944-3700 Fax: (781)942-1117 URL: http://www.awl.com • 2000. 13th edition. Price on application.

Introduction to Object-Oriented Programming with Java. C. Thomas Wu. McGraw-Hill, 1221 Ave. of the Americas New York, NY 10020. Phone: 800-722-4726 or (212)904-2000 Fax: (212)904-2072 E-mail: customer.service@mcgraw-hill.com • URL: http://www.mcgraw-hill.com • 2001. Second edition. Price on application.

Introduction to Option-Adjusted Spread Analysis. Tom Windas. Bloomberg Press, 100 Business Park Dr. Princeton, NJ 08542-0888. Phone: 800-388-2749 or (609)279-4670 Fax: (609)279-7155 E-mail: press@bloomberg.net • URL: http://www.bloomberg.com • 1996. $40.00. Discusses the limitations of traditional, yield-based, risk and return analysis of bonds. (Bloomberg Professional Library.)

Introduction to Practical Linear Programming. David J. Pannell. John Wiley and Sons, Inc., 605 Third Ave. New York, NY 10158-0012. Phone: 800-225-5945 or (212)850-6000 Fax: (212)850-6088 E-mail: info@wiley.com • URL: http://www.wiley.com • 1996. $84.95. Explains how to apply linear programming to real-world situations in various areas, such as agriculture, manufacturing, finance, and advertising. Includes an IBM PC diskette containing ''user-friendly'' software.

Introduction to Reference Work. William A. Katz. McGraw-Hill, 1221 Ave. of the Americas New York, NY 10020. Phone: 800-722-4726 or (212)904-2000 Fax: (212)904-2072 E-mail: customer.service@mcgraw-hill.com • URL: http://www.mcgraw-hill.com • 1996. $92.19. Seventh edition. Two volumes. Volume one, $48.13; volume two, $44.06.

Introduction to Security. Robert J. Fishcher and Gion Green. Butterworth-Heinemann, 225 Wildwood Ave. Woburn, MA 01081. Phone: 800-366-2665 or (781)904-2500 Fax: 800-466-6520 E-mail: orders@bhusa.com • URL: http://www.bh.com • 1998. $39.95. Sixth edition.

Introduction to Serial Management. Marcia Tuttle. JAI Press, Inc., P.O. Box 811 Stamford, CT 06904-0811. Phone: (203)323-9606 Fax: (203)357-8446 E-mail: order@jaipress.com • URL: http://www.jaipress.com • 1978. $78.50. (Foundations in Library and Information Science Series, Vol. 11).

Introduction to the Counseling Profession. Dave Capuzzi and Douglas Gross. Allyn and Bacon, Inc., 160 Gould St. Needham Heights, MA 02194-2310. Phone: 800-278-3525 or (781)455-1250 Fax: (781)455-1294 E-mail: ab_webmaster@abacon.com • URL: http://www.abacon.com • 2000. $73.00. Third edition.

An Introduction to the Law of Contract. Patrick S. Atiyah. Oxford University Press, Inc., 198 Madison Ave. New York, NY 10016-4314. Phone: 800-451-7556 or (212)726-6000 Fax: (212)726-6446 E-mail: custserv@oup.usa.org • URL: http://www.oup-press.org • 1995. $80.00. Fifth edition. (Claredon Law Series).

An Introduction to the Mathematics of Financial Derivatives. Salih N. Neftci. Academic Press, Inc., 525 B St., Suite 1900 San Diego, CA 92101-4495. Phone: 800-321-5068 or (619)230-1840 Fax: (619)699-6715 E-mail: ap@acad.com • URL: http://www.academicpress.com • 2000. $59.95. Second edition. Covers the mathematical models underlying the pricing of derivatives. Includes explanations of basic financial calculus for students, derivatives traders, risk managers, and others concerned with derivatives.

Introduction to the Study of Bibliography. H. Horne. Gordon Press Publishers, P.O. Box 459 New York, NY 10004. Phone: (212)969-8419 Fax: (718)624-8419 1976. $59.95.

An Introduction to the Theory and Practice of Econometrics. George G. Judge and others. John Wiley and Sons, Inc., 650 Third Ave. New York, NY 10158-0012. Phone: 800-526-5368 or (212)850-6000 Fax: (212)850-6088 E-mail: info@wiley.com • URL: http://www.wiley.com • 1988. $108.95. Second edition.

Introduction to the Use of Computers in Libraries: A Textbook for the Non-Technical Student. Harold C. Ogg. Information Today, Inc., 143 Old Marlton Pike Medford, NJ 08055-8750. Phone: 800-300-9868 or (609)654-6266 Fax: (609)654-4309 E-mail: custserv@infotoday.com • URL: http://www.infotoday.com • 1997. $42.50. Provides basic information on computer programs for libraries, including spreadsheets, database applications, desktop publishing, automated circulation systems, and public access online catalogs.

Introductory CD-ROM Searching: The Key to Effective Ondisc Searching. Joseph Meloche. Haworth Press, Inc., 10 Alice St. Binghamton, NY 13904-1580. Phone: 800-429-6784 or (607)722-5857 Fax: 800-895-0582 or (607)722-1424 E-mail: getinfo@haworthpressinc.com • URL: http://www.haworthpressinc.com • 1994. $49.95. Covers basic search strategies, with specific suggestions for Dialog OnDisc, Silverplatter, Wilsondisc, UMI, and others.

Inventing and Patenting Sourcebook. The Gale Group, 27500 Drake Rd. Farmington Hills, MI 48331-3535. Phone: 800-877-GALE or (248)699-GALE Fax: 800-414-5043 or (248)699-8069 E-mail: galeord@galegroup.com • URL: http://www.galegroup.com • 1992. $95.00. Second edition. A general guide for inventors. Contains how-to-do-it text, information sources, and sample forms.

Inventors Desktop Companion: A Guide to Successfully Marketing and Protecting Your Ideas. Richard C. Levy. Visible Ink Press, 27500 Drake Rd. Farmington Hills, MI 48331. Phone: 800-776-6265 or (248)699-GALE Fax: 800-414-5043 or (248)699-8069 E-mail: galeord@galegroup.com • URL: http://www.galegroup.com • 1998. $24.95. Second edition. Explains how to patent, trademark, or copyright an idea. Includes a listing of 2,000 associations and services for inventors.

Inventors Workshop International Education Foundation.

Inventory Control and Management. C. D. Waters. John Wiley and Sons, Inc., 605 Third Ave. New York, NY 10158-0012. Phone: 800-225-5945 or (212)850-6000 Fax: (212)850-6088 E-mail: info@wiley.com • URL: http://www.wiley.com • 1992. $129.95.

Inventory of Electrtic Utility Power Plants in the United States. Energy Information Administration, U.S. Department of Energy. Available from U.S. Government Printing Office, Washington, DC 20402. Phone: (202)512-1800 Fax: (202)512-2250 E-mail: gpoaccess@gpo.gov • URL: http://www.access.gpo.gov • Annual. $33.00.

InvesTech Market Analyst: Technical and Monetary Investment Analysis. InvesTech Research, 2472 Birch Glen Whitefish, MT 59937-3349. Phone: 800-955-8500 or (406)862-7777 Fax: (406)862-7707 URL: http://www.investech.com • Every three weeks. $190.00 per year. Newsletter. Provides interpretation of monetary statistics and Federal Reserve actions, especially as related to technical analysis of stock market price trends.

InvesTech Mutual Fund Advisor: Professional Portfolio Allocation. InvesTech Research, 2472 Birch Glen Whitefish, MT 59937-3349. Phone: 800-955-8500 or (406)862-7777 Fax: (406)862-7707 URL: http://www.investech.com • Every three weeks. $190.00 per year. Newsletter. Contains model portfolio for mutual fund investing.

InvesText. Thomson Financial Securities Data, Two Gateway Center Newark, NJ 07102. Phone: 888-989-8373 or (973)622-3100 Fax: (973)622-1421 URL: http://www.investext.com • Provides full text online of investment research reports from more than 300 sources, including leading brokers and investment bankers. Reports are available on approximately 50,000 U. S. and international corporations. Separate industry reports cover 54 industries. Time span is 1982 to date, with daily updates. Inquire as to online cost and availability.

InvesText ÎCD-ROMl. Thomson Financial Securities Data, Two Gateway Center Newark, NJ 07102. Phone: 888-989-8373 or (973)622-3100 Fax: (973)622-1421 URL: http://www.investext.com • Monthly. $5,000.00 per year. Contains full text on CD-ROM of investment research reports from about 250 sources, including leading brokers and investment bankers. Reports are available on both U. S. and international publicly traded corporations. Separate industry reports cover more than 50 industries. Time span is 1982 to date.

Investigative Reporters and Editors., School of Journalism, 138 Neff Annex Columbia, MO 65211. Phone: (573)882-2042 Fax: (573)882-5431 E-mail: info@ire.org • URL: http://www.ire.org • Provides educational services to those engaged in investigative journalism.

Investing and Selling in Latin America. Judith Evans and others. Morning Light Publishing Co., 6836 Glenwood Overland Park, KS 66204. Phone: (913)677-4116 E-mail: 102673-1532@compuserve.com • 1995. $60.00. Consists of one chapter for each of 12 Latin American countries. Covers a wide variety of legal, economic, and practical information relating to doing business in the region.

Investing During Retirement: The Vanguard Guide to Managing Your Retirement Assets. Vanguard Group. McGraw-Hill Professional, 1221 Ave. of the Americas New York, NY 10020. Phone: 800-722-4726 or (212)904-2000 Fax: (212)904-2072 E-mail: customer.service@mcgraw-hill.com • URL: http://www.mcgraw-hill.com • 1996. $17.95. A basic, general guide to investing after retirement. Covers pension plans, basic principles of investing, types of mutual funds, asset allocation, retirement income planning, social security, estate planning, and contingencies. Includes glossary and worksheets for net worth, budget, and income.

Investing in Call Options; An Alternative to Common Stock and Real Estate. James A. Willson. Greenwood Publishing Group, Inc., 88 Post Rd., W. Westport, CT 06881-5007. Phone: 800-225-5800 or (203)226-3571 Fax: (203)222-2540 E-mail: bookinfo@greenwood.com • URL: http://www.greenwood.com • 1982. $59.95.

Investing in Education: Analysis of the 1999 World Education Indicators. Organization for Economic Cooperation and Development, OECD Washington Center, 2001 L St., N. W., Suite 650 Washington, DC 20036-4922. Phone: 800-456-6323 or (202)785-6323 Fax: (202)785-0350 E-mail: washington.contact@oecd.org • URL: http://www.oecd.org • 2000. $31.00. Compares educational performance data in various countries of the world, including the U. S., other OECD countries, and selected non-OECD nations.

Investing in IPOs: New Paths to Profit with Initial Public Offerings. Tom Taulli. Bloomberg Press, PO Box 888 Princeton, NJ 08542-0888. Phone: 800-388-2749 or (609)279-4670 Fax: 800-458-6515 or (609)279-7155 E-mail: info@bloomberg.com • URL: http://www.bloomberg.com • 1999. $24.95. Explains how individual investors can invest profitably in new stock offerings. (Bloomberg Personal Bookshelf.)

Investing in Latin America: Best Stocks, Best Funds. Michael Molinski. Bloomberg Press, PO Box 888 Princeton, NJ 08542-0888. Phone: 800-388-2749 or (609)279-4670 Fax: 800-458-6515 or (609)279-7155 E-mail: info@bloomberg.com • URL: http://www.bloomberg.com • 1999. $24.95. Provides Latin American stock and mutual fund recommendations for individual investors. (Bloomberg Personal Bookshelf.)

Investing in REITs: Real Estate Investment Trusts. Ralph L. Block. Bloomberg Press, 100 Business Park Dr. Princeton, NJ 08542-0888. Phone: 800-388-2749 or (609)279-4670 Fax: (609)279-7155 E-mail: press@bloomberg.net • URL: http://www.bloomberg.com • 1998. $21.95. A basic guide to real estate investment trusts. (Bloomberg Personal Bookshelf.)

Investing in Small-Cap Stocks. Christopher Graja and Elizabeth Ungar. Bloomberg Press, 100 Business Park Dr. Princeton, NJ 08542-0888. Phone: 800-388-2749 or (609)279-4670 Fax: (609)279-7155 E-mail: press@bloomberg.com • URL: http://www.bloomberg.com • 1999. $26.95. Second expanded revised edition. Provides a practical strategy for investing in small-capitalization stocks. (Bloomberg Personal Bookshelf Series.)

Investing in the Over-the-Counter Markets: Stocks, Bonds, IPOs. Alvin D. Hall. John Wiley and Sons, Inc., 605 Third Ave. New York, NY 10158-0012. Phone: 800-225-5945 or (212)850-6000 Fax: (212)850-6088 E-mail: info@jwiley.com • URL: http://www.wiley.com • 1995. $29.95. Provides advice and information on investing in ''unlisted'' or NASDAQ (National Association of Securities Dealers Automated Quotation System) stocks, bonds, and initial public offerings (IPOs).

Investing, Licensing, and Trading. Economist Intelligence Unit, 111 W. 57th St. New York, NY 10019. Phone: 800-938-4685 or (212)554-0600 Fax: (212)586-1181 URL: http://www.eiu.com • Semiannual. $345.00 per year for each country. Key laws, rules, and licensing provisions are explained for each of 60 countries. Information is provided on political conditions, markets, price policies, foreign exchange practices, labor, and export-import.

Investment Advisor. Dow Jones Financial Publishing Corp., 170 Ave. at the Common Shrewsbury, NJ 07002. Phone: (732)389-8700 Fax: (732)389-6065 URL: http://www.djfpc.com • Monthly. $79.00 per year. Edited for professional investment advisors, financial planners, stock brokers, bankers, and others concerned with the management of assets.

Investment Banking Handbook. J. Peter Williamson. John Wiley and Sons, Inc., 605 Third Ave. New York, NY 10158-0012. Phone: 800-225-5945 or (212)850-6000 Fax: (212)850-6088 E-mail: info@wiley.com • URL: http://www.wiley.com • 1988. $175.00. (Professional Banking and Finance Series).

Investment Companies Yearbook. Securities Data Publishing, 40 West 57th St. New York, NY 10019. Phone: 800-455-5844 or (212)765-5311 Fax: (212)956-0112 E-mail: sdp@tfn.com • URL: http://www.sdponline.com • Annual. $310.00. Provides an ''entire history of recent events in the mutual funds industry,'' with emphasis on changes during the past year. About 100 pages are devoted to general information and advice for fund investors. Includes 600 full-page profiles of popular mutual funds, with brief descriptions of 10,000 others, plus 7,000 variable annuities and 500 closed-end funds. Contains a glossary of technical terms, a Web site index, and an overall book index. Also known as *Wiesenberger Investment Companies Yearbook*. (Securities Data Publishing is a unit of Thomson Financial.)

Investment Company Institute., 1401 H St., N. W., 12th Fl. Washington, DC 20005-2148. Phone: (202)326-5800 Fax: (202)326-8309 E-mail: info@ici.com • URL: http://www.ici.com • Members are investment companies offering mutual funds (open-end) and closed-end funds. Includes a Closed-End Investment Company Division.

Investment Council of American Directory of Member Firms. Investment Counsel Association of America, 1050 17th St., N.W., Suite 725 Washington, DC 20036-5503. Phone: (202)293-4222 Fax: (202)293-4223 E-mail: icaa@icaa.org • URL: http://www.icaa.org • Annual. Free.

Investment Counsel Association of America.

Investment Dealers' Digest. Securities Data Publishing, 40 West 57th St. New York, NY 10019. Phone: 800-455-5844 or (212)765-5311 Fax: (212)956-0112 E-mail: sdp@tfn.com • URL: http://www.sdponline.com • Weekly. $750.00 per year. Covers financial news, trends, new products, people, private placements, new issues of securities, and other aspects of the investment business. Includes feature stories. (Securities Data Publishing is a unit of Thomson Financial.)

Investment Guide. American Investment Services, P.O. Box 1000 Great Barrington, MA 01230-1000. Phone: (413)528-1216 Fax: (413)528-0103 Monthly. $49.00 per year. Newsletter. Emphasis is on blue-chip stocks with high dividend yields.

Investment Limited Partnerships. Robert J. Haft and Peter M. Fass. West Group, 610 Opperman Dr. Eagan, MN 55123. Phone: 800-328-4880 or (651)687-7000 Fax: 800-213-2323 or (651)687-5827 URL: http://www.westgroup.com • Six looseleaf volumes. $795.00. Periodic supplementation. Provides extensive coverage of both the tax and securities law aspects of tax motivated investments. (Securities Law Series).

Investment Limited Partnerships Handbook. Robert J. Haft and Peter M. Fass. West Group, 610 Opperman Dr. Eagan, MN 55123. Phone: 800-328-4880 or (651)687-7000 Fax: 800-213-2323 or (651)687-5827 URL: http://www.westgroup.com • 1992. $97.50.

Investment Management Weekly. Securities Data Publishing, 40 West 57th St. New York, NY 10019. Phone: 800-455-5844 or (212)765-5311 Fax: (212)956-0112 E-mail: sdp@tfn.com • URL: http://www.sdponline.com • Weekly. $1,370.00 per year. Newsletter. Edited for money managers and other investment professionals. Covers personnel news, investment strategies, and industry trends. (Securities Data Publishing is a unit of Thomson Financial.)

Investment News: The Weekly Newspaper for Financial Advisers. Crain Communications, Inc., 1400 Woodbridge Ave. Detroit, MI 48207-3187. Phone: (313)446-6000 Fax: (313)446-0383 URL: http://www.investmentnews.com • Weekly. $38.00 per year. Edited for both personal and institutional investment advisers, planners, and managers.

Investment Reporter. MPL Communication, Inc., 133 Richmond St., W., Suite 700 Toronto, ON, Canada M5H 3M8. Phone: (416)869-1177 Fax: (416)869-0456 Weekly. $279.00 per year. Newsletter. Monthly supplement, *Investment Planning Guide*. Recommendations for Canadian investments. Formerly *Personal Wealth Reporter*.

Investment Statistics Locator. Linda H. Bentley and Jennifer J. Kiesl, editors. Oryx Press, 4041 N. Central Ave., Ste. 700 Phoenix, AZ 85012-3397. Phone: 800-279-6799 or (602)265-2651 Fax: 800-279-4663 or (602)265-6250 E-mail: info@oryxpress.com • URL: http://www.oryxpress.com • 1994. $69.95. Expanded revised edition. Provides detailed subject indexing of more than 50 of the most-used sources of financial and investment data. Includes an annotated bibliography.

Investments: An Introduction to Analysis and Management. Frederick Amling. Pearson Custom Publishing, 75 Arlington St., Ste. 300 Boston, MA 02116. Phone: 800-428-4466 or (617)848-6300 Fax: 800-445-6991 or (617)848-6333 E-mail: pcp@pearsoncustom.com • URL: http://www.pearsoncustom.com • 1999. Seventh edition.

Investments: Analysis and Management. Charles P. Jones. John Wiley and Sons, Inc., 605 Third Ave. New York, NY 10158-0012. Phone: 800-526-5368 or (212)850-6000 Fax: (212)850-6088 E-mail: info@wiley.com • URL: http://www.wiley.com • 1997. $102.95. Sixth edition.

Investor Relations Business. Securities Data Publishing, 40 West 57th St. New York, NY 10019. Phone: 800-455-5844 or (212)765-5311 Fax: (212)956-0112 E-mail: sdp@tfn.com • URL: http://www.sdponline.com • Semimonthly. $435.00 per year. Covers the issues affecting stockholder relations, corporate public relations, and institutional investor relations. (Securities Data Publishing is a unit of Thomson Financial.)

Investor Responsibility Research Center, Inc., 1350 Connecticut Ave., N. W., Suite 700 Washington, DC 20036. Phone: (202)833-0700 Fax: (202)833-3555 E-mail: sfenn@irrc.org • URL: http://www.irrc.org • Studies developments of interest to institutional investors.

Investor's Business Daily. Investor's Business Daily, Inc., 12655 Beatrice St. Los Angeles, CA 90066. Phone: 800-831-2525 or (310)448-6000 Fax: (310)577-7301 URL: http://www.ibd.ensemble.com • Daily. $169.00 per year. Newspaper.

Investor's Digest. Institute for Econometric Research, 2200 S.W. 10th St. Deerfield Beach, FL 33442-8799. Phone: 800-442-0066 or (954)421-1000 Fax: (954)570-8200 Monthly. $60.00 per year. Newsletter. Contains digests of investment advice from a wide variety of advisory services.

Investor's Guide to Closed-End Funds. Thomas J. Herzfeld Advisors, Inc., P.O. Box 161465 Miami, FL 33116. Phone: (305)271-1900 Fax: (305)270-7040 Monthly. $475.00 per year. Looseleaf. Provides detailed information on closed-end investment funds, including charts and recommendations.

Investor's Guide to Economic Indicators. Charles R. Nelson. John Wiley and Sons, Inc., 605 Third Ave. New York, NY 10158-0012. Phone: 800-526-5368 or (212)850-6000 Fax: (212)850-6088 E-mail: info@wiley.com • URL: http://www.wiley.com • 1989. $17.95.

Investors Intelligence. Michael Burke, editor. Chartcraft, Inc., P.O. Box 2046 New Rochelle, NY 10801. Phone: (914)632-0422 Fax: (914)632-0335 Biweekly. $184.00 per year. Monitors about 130 investment advisory services and prints summaries of advice from about half of them in each issue. Provides numerical index of bearish sentiment among services.

Investors Manual. National Association of Investors Corporation, P.O. Box 220 Royal Oak, MI 48068. Phone: (810)583-6242 Fax: (810)583-4880 URL: http://www.better-investing.org • Irregular. Price on application. Provides stock study tools and procedures for do-it-yourself equity investors.

The Invisible Web: Uncovering Information Sources Search Engines Can't See. Chris Sherman and Gary Price. Information Today, Inc., 143 Old Marlton Pike Medford, NJ 08055-8750. Phone: 800-300-9868 or (609)654-6266 Fax: (609)654-4309 E-mail: custserv@infotoday.com • URL: http://www.infotoday.com • 2001. $29.95. A guide to Web sites from universities, libraries, associations, government agencies, and other sources that are inadequately covered by conventional search engines (see also http://www.invisible-web.net). (CyberAge Books.)

An Invitation to Fly: Basics for the Private Pilot. Dennis Glaeser. Wadsworth Publishing, 10 Davis Dr. Belmont, CA 94002. Phone: 800-354-9706 or (650)595-2350 Fax: (650)637-9955 URL: http://www.thomson.com/wadsworth • 1998. $69.95. Sixth edition. Prepares beginning pilots for FAA written test. (Aviation Series).

Involvement and Participation Association., 42 Colebrooke Row London N1 8AF, England. Phone: 44 171 3548040 Fax: 44 171 3548041 Promotes employee participation in the workplace.

IOMA's Report on Defined Contribution Plan Investing. Institute for Management and Administration, Inc., 29 W. 35th St., 5th Fl. New York, NY 10001-2299. Phone: (212)244-0360 Fax: (212)564-0465 E-mail: subserve@ioma.com • URL: http://www.ioma.com • Semimonthly. $1,156.90 per year. Newsletter. Edited for 401(k) and other defined contribution retirement plan managers, sponsors, and service providers. Reports on such items as investment manager performance, guaranteed investment contract (GIC) yields, and asset allocation trends.

IOMA's Report on Managing 401(k) Plans. Institute for Management and Administration, 29 W. 35th St., 5th Fl. New York, NY 10001-2299. Phone: (212)244-0360 Fax: (212)564-0465 E-mail: subserve@ioma.com • URL: http://www.ioma.com • Monthly. $275.95 per year. Newsletter for retirement plan managers.

IPA Magazine. Involvement and Participation Association, 42 Colebrooke Row London N1 8AF, England. Quarterly. $60.00 per year. Formerly *Involvement of Participation and Industrial Participation*

IPO Reporter. Securities Data Publishing, 40 West 57th St. New York, NY 10019. Phone: 800-455-5844 or (212)765-5311 Fax: (212)956-0112 E-mail: sdp@tfn.com • URL: http://www.sdponline.com • Weekly. $1,295.00 per year. Newsletter. Provides detailed information on new and upcoming initial public offerings. Includes aftermarket data and market trend analysis. (Securities Data Publishing is a unit of Thomson Financial.)

IPOfn. IPO Financial NetworkPhone: (973)379-5100 Fax: (973)379-1696 E-mail: info@ipofinancial.com • URL: http://www.ipofinancial.com • Web site provides free information on initial public offerings: "Pricing Recap" (price performance), "Calendar Update" (weekly listing of new offerings), "Company Roster" (Web sites), "Stock Brokers" (IPO dealers), and "Brokerage Firms" (underwriters). Fees: Basic data is free. Extensive analysis and recommendations are available through fee-based telephone, fax, and database services. Daily updates.

Ira B. McGladrey Institute of Accounting Research.

IRA Basics. Institute of Financial Education, 55 W. Monroe St., Suite 2800 Chicago, IL 60603-5014. Phone: 800-946-0488 or (312)364-0100 Fax: (312)364-0190 E-mail: ystoffregen@bai.org • URL: http://www.theinstitute.com • 1997. $34.95. Seventh edition. A guide for bank personnel.

IRA Reporter (Individual Retirement Account). Universal Pensions, Inc., P.O. Box 979 Brainerd, MN 56401-9965. Phone: 800-346-3860 or (218)829-4781 Fax: (218)829-2106 Monthly. $115.00 per year. Newsletter. Edited for financial planners. Provides information on the rules and regulations of individual retirement accounts (IRAs).

The IRE Journal. Investigative Reporters and Editors, Inc., P.O. Box 838, School of Journalism, University of Missouri Columbia, MO 65211. Phone: (314)882-2042 Fax: (314)882-5431 Bimonthly. $25.00 per year. Contains practical information relating to investigative journalism.

Iron and Steel Society.

IRRA-Membership Directory. Industrial Relations Research Association, Social Science Bldg. 4233, University of Wisconsin Madison, WI 53706. Phone: (608)262-2762 Fax: (608)265-4591 Quadrennial. $25.00. About 4,200 business people, union leaders, government officials, lawyers, arbitrators, academics, consultants, and others interested in labor relations.

IRRA Newsletter. Industrial Relations Research Association, 4233 Social Science Bldg., University of Wisconsin Madison, WI 53706. Phone: (608)262-2762 Fax: (608)265-4591 Quarterly. $75.00 per year. Membership.

Irrational Exuberance. Robert J. Shiller. Princeton University Press, 41 William St. Princeton, NJ 08540. Phone: 800-777-4726 or (609)258-4900 Fax: (609)258-1335 E-mail: orders@cpfs.pupress.princeton.edu • URL: http://www.pup.princeton.edu • 2000. $27.95. States that below-average stock market returns occur in the years following very high price-earnings ratios and very low dividend yields. 1901, 1929, 1966, and 2000 are cited as portentous years.

Irrigation and Drainage Abstracts. Available from CABI Publishing North America, 10 E. 40th St. New York, NY 10016. Phone: 800-528-4841 or (212)481-7018 Fax: (212)686-7993 E-mail: cabi@cabi.org • URL: http://www/cabi.org • Quarterly. $545.00 per year. Published in England by CABI Publishing. Provides worldwide coverage of the literature.

Irrigation Association.

Irrigation Association Membership-Directory and Industry Buyers' Guide. Irrigation Association, 8260 Willow Oaks Corporate Dr., Ste. 120 Fairfax, VA 22031-4513. Phone: (703)573-3551 Fax: (703)573-1913 URL: http://www.irrigation.org • Annual. Free to members; non-members, $25.00. Includes manufacturing, distribution, contracting, consultation, research and educational information.

IRS Publications. CCH, Inc., 4025 W. Peterson Ave. Chicago, IL 60646-6085. Phone: 800-248-3248 or (773)866-6000 Fax: 800-224-8299 or (773)866-3608 URL: http://www.cch.com • Irregular. Three looseleaf volumes. Periodic supplementation. Photographic reproductions of current Internal Revenue Service tax publications intended for public use.

IRS Tax Collection Procedures. CCH, Inc., 4025 W. Peterson Ave. Chicago, IL 60646-6085. Phone: 800-248-3248 or (773)866-6000 Fax: 800-224-8299 or (773)866-3608 URL: http://www.cch.com • Looseleaf. $189.00. Supplementation available. Covers IRS collection personnel, payment arrangements, penalties, abatements, summons, liens, etc.

Irwin Business and Investment Almanac, 1996. Summer N. Levine and Caroline Levine. McGraw-Hill Professional, 1221 Ave. of The Americas New York, NY 10020. Phone: 800-722-4726 or (212)904-2000 Fax: (212)904-2072 E-mail: customer.service@mcgraw-hill.com • URL: http://www.mcgraw-hill.com • 1995. $75.00. A review of last year's business activity. Covers a wide variety of business and economic data: stock market statistics, industrial information, commodity futures information, art market trends, comparative living costs for U. S. metropolitan areas, foreign stock market data, etc. Formerly *Business One Irwin Business and Investment Almanac*.

Irwin Handbook of Telecommunications. James H. Green. McGraw-Hill Professional, 1221 Ave. of the Americas New York, NY 10020. Phone: 800-722-4726 or (212)904-2000 Fax: (212)904-2072 E-mail: customer.service@mcgraw-hill.com • URL: http://www.mcgraw-hill.com • 2000. $95.00. Fourth dition. Formerly *Dow Jones-Irwin Handbook of Telecommunications*.

Irwin International Almanac: Business and Investments. McGraw-Hill Professional, 1221 Ave. of the Americas New York, NY 10020. Phone: 800-722-4726 or (212)904-2000 Fax: (212)904-2072 E-mail: customer.service@mcgraw-hill.com • URL: http://www.mcgraw-hill.com • 1994. $95.00. Second edition. Covers trends in global business and summarizes trading in major foreign securities markets.

Is It Too Late to Run Away and Join the Circus? Finding the Life You Really Want. Marti Smye. Simon and Schuster Trade, 1230 Ave. of teh Americas New York, NY 10020. Phone: 800-223-2336 or (212)698-7000 Fax: (212)698-7007 URL: http://www.simonsays.com • 1998. $14.95. Provides philosophical and inspirational advice on leaving corporate life and becoming self-employed as a consultant or whatever. Central theme is dealing with major changes in life style and career objectives. (Macmillan Business Book.)

ISA Directory of Instrumentation. Instrument Society of America, P.O. Box 12277 Research Triangle Park, NC 27709. Phone: (919)549-8411 Fax: (919)549-8288 E-mail: info@isa.org • URL: http://www.isa.org/directory • Annual. $100.00. Over 2,400 manufacturers of control and instrumentation equipment, over 1,000 manufacturers' representatives, and several hundred service companies; coverage includes Canada.

ISA Transactions. Instrument Society of America, United States. Elsevier Science, 655 Ave. of the Americas New York, NY 10010. Phone: 888-437-4636 or (212)633-3730 Fax: (212)633-3680 E-mail: usinfo@elsevier.com • URL: http://www.elsevier.com • Quarterly. $348.00 per year.

ISEA: The Safety Equipment Association.

ISO 9000: Achieving Compliance and Certification. Maureen A. Dalfonso. John Wiley and Sons, Inc., 605 Third Ave. New York, NY 10158-0012. Phone: 800-225-5945 or (212)850-6000 Fax: (212)850-6088 E-mail: info@wiley.com • URL: http://www.wiley.com • 1996. $155.00.

ISO 9000 and ISO 14000 News (International Organization for Standardization). Available from American National Standards Institute, 11 W. 42nd St., 13th Fl. New York, NY 10036. Phone: (212)642-4900 Fax: (212)398-0023 URL: http://www.ansi.org • Bimonthly. Price on application. Newsletter on quality standards. Published by the International Organization for Standardization (ISO). Text in English. Formerly *ISO 9000 News*.

ISO 9000 and the Service Sector. James L. Lamprecht. American Society for Quality, P.O. Box 3005 Milwaukee, WI 53202-3005. Phone: 800-248-1946 or (414)272-8575 Fax: (414)272-1734 E-mail: asq@asq.org • URL: http://www.asqc.org • 1994. $38.00. A review of the ISO 9000 quality standards as they relate to service organizations. Includes examples of applications.

ISO 9000 Auditor's Companion. Kent A. Keeney and Joseph J. Tsiakals. American Society for Quality, P.O. Box 3005 Milwaukee, WI 53202-3005. Phone: 800-248-1946 or (414)272-8575 Fax: (414)272-1734 E-mail: mhagen@asq.org • URL: http://www.asq.org • 1994. $30.00. Designed to help companies prepare for ISO 9000 quality management audits.

ISO 9000 Book: A Global Competitor's Guide to Compliance and Certification. John T. Rabbitt and Peter Bergh. AMACOM, 1601 Broadway, 12th Fl. New York, NY 10019. Phone: 800-262-9699 or (212)586-8100 Fax: (212)903-8168 E-mail: custmserv@amanet.org • URL: http://www.amanet.org • 1994. $26.95. Second edition.

ISO 9000 Handbook. Robert W. Peach, editor. McGraw-Hill Professional, 1221 Ave. of the Americas New York, NY 10020. Phone: 800-722-4726 or (212)904-2000 Fax: (212)904-2072 E-mail: customer.service@mcgraw-hill.com • URL: http://www.mcgraw-hill.com • 1996. $80.00. Third edition. Includes detailed information for the ISO 9000 registration process.

ISO 9000 Made Easy: A Cost-Saving Guide to Documentation and Registration. Amy Zuckerman. AMACOM, 1601 Broadway, 12th Fl. New York, NY 10019. Phone: 800-262-9699 or (212)586-8100 Fax: (212)903-8168 E-mail: custmserv@amanet.org • URL: http://www.amanet.org • 1994. $75.00.

Isotopes for Medicine and the Life Sciences. S. James Adelstein and Frederick J. Manning, editors. National Academy Press, 2101 Constitution Ave., N. W., HA 384 Washington, DC 20418. Phone: 800-624-6242 or (202)334-3180 Fax: (202)334-2793 URL: http://www.nap.edu • 1995. $30.00. Includes bibliographical references and a glossary.

Israel Diamond and Precious Stones. International Diamond Publications, Ltd., 54 Bezalel St. 52131 972 Ramat Gon, Israel. Phone: 972 3 7512165 Fax: 972 3 5752201 Bimonthly. $78.00 per year. Text in English. Formerly *Israel Diamonds*.

ISSA Today. International Sanitary Supply Association, Inc., 7373 N. Lincoln Ave. Lincolnwood, IL 60712-1799. Phone: 800-225-4772 or (847)982-0800 Fax: (847)982-1012 E-mail: info@issa.com • URL: http://www.issa.com • Monthly. $75.00 per year.

ISWM News. International Society of Weighing and Measurement, 10 Kimball St., W. Winder, GA 30680. Phone: (770)868-5300 Fax: (770)868-5301 E-mail: staff@iswm.org • URL: http://www.iswm.org • Quarterly.

IT Cost Management Strategies: The Planning Assistant for IT Directors. Computer Economics, Inc., 5841 Edison Place Carlsbad, CA 92008-6519. Phone: 800-326-8100 or (760)438-8100 Fax: (760)431-1126 E-mail: custserv@compecon.com • URL: http://www.computereconomics.com • Monthly. $495.00 per year. Newsletter for information technology professionals. Covers data processing costs, budgeting, financial management, and related topics.

It was a Very Good Year: Extraordinary Moments in Stock Market History. Martin S. Fridson. John Wiley and Sons, Inc., 605 Third Ave. New York, NY 10158-0012. Phone: 800-225-5945 or (212)850-6000 Fax: (212)850-6088 E-mail: info@wiley.com • URL: http://www.wiley.com • 1997. $29.95. Provides details on what happened during each of the ten best years for the stock market since 1900.

Italian American Librarians Caucus.

Italian Trade Commission., 499 Park Ave. New York, NY 10022. Phone: (212)980-1500 Fax: (212)758-1050 E-mail: newyork@italtrade.com • URL: http://www.italtrade.com • Promotes the use of Italian ceramic tile in the U. S.

ITE Journal. Institute of Transportation Engineers, 525 School St., S.W., Suite 410 Washington, DC 20024. Phone: (202)554-8050 Fax: (202)863-5486 URL: http://www.ite.org/ • Monthly. $60.00 per year. Formerly *Transportation Engineering*.

Item Processing Report. Phillips Business Information, Inc., 1201 Seven Locks Rd., Suite 300 Potomac, MD 20854. Phone: 800-777-5006 or (301)340-1520 Fax: (301)309-3847 E-mail: pbi@phillips.com • URL: http://www.phillips.com/pbi.htm • Biweekly. $695.00 per year. Newsletter for banks on check processing, document imaging, and optical character recognition.

ITS-The Association of Imaging Technology and Sound., 527 Maple Ave., E., Suite 204 Vienna, VA 22180. Phone: (703)319-0800 Fax: (703)319-1120 URL: http://www.itsnet.org • Members are individuals interested in various aspects of prerecorded videotape production. Acts as a source of general information about videotape.

ITVA News. International Television Association, 9202 N. Meridian St., Suite 200 Indianapolis, IN 46260-1834. Phone: (317)816-6269 Fax: (317)571-5603 E-mail: itvahq@worldnet.att.net • URL: http://www.itva.org • Bimonthly. Membership newsletter. Formerly *International Television News*.

IVCI Directory of Business Incubators in United States and Canada. Baxter Associates, Inc. International Venture Capital Institute, Inc., P.O. Box 1333 Stamford, CT 06904. Phone: (203)323-3143 Fax: (203)838-5714 $49.95. Lists approximately 700 start-up services (office space, accounting, legal, financial advice, research, etc.). Formerly *IVCI Directory of Business Incubators and University Research and Science Parks*.

Izaak Walton League of America., IWLA Conservation Center, 707 Conversation Lane Gaithersburg, MD 20878. Phone: 800-453-5463 or (301)548-0150 Fax: (301)548-0146 E-mail: general@iwla.org • URL: http://www.iwla.org • Sponsors the Acid Rain Project, an environmental protection program.

J. K. Lasser's Your Income Tax, 2001. J. K. Lasser Tax Institute Staff. John Wiley and Sons, Inc., 605 Third Ave. New York, NY 10158-0012. Phone: 800-526-5368 or (212)850-6000 Fax: (212)850-6088 E-mail: info@wiley.com • URL: http://www.wiley.com • 2000. $15.95.

Jake Bernstein's New Guide to Investing in Metals. Jacob Bernstein. John Wiley and Sons, Inc., 605 Third Ave. New York, NY 10158-0012. Phone: 800-526-5368 or (212)850-6000 Fax: (212)850-6088 E-mail: info@wiley.com • URL: http://www.wiley.com • 1991. $34.95. Covers bullion, coins, futures, options, mining stocks, and precious metal mutual funds. Includes the history of metals as an investment.

JAMA: The Journal of the American Medical Association. American Medical Association, 515 N. State St. Chicago, IL 60610. Phone: 800-262-2350 or (312)464-5000 Fax: (312)464-4814 E-mail: amaa@ama-assn.org • URL: http://www.ama-assn.org • 48 times a year. Two volumes. Individuals, $145.00 per year; institutions, $245.00 per year.

James Martin Productivity Series, Volume Seven. Digital Consulting Associates, 204 Andover St. Andover, MA 01810-5697. Phone: (508)470-3870 1989. $50.00. Covers intelligent desktop workstations, expert systems (artificial intelligence), computer-aided software engineering (CASE), advanced development methodologies, and other high technology computer topics.

Jane's Air Traffic Control. Jane's Information Group, 1340 Braddock Place, Dept. DSM, Ste. 300 Alexandria, VA 22314. Phone: 800-824-0768 or (703)683-3700 E-mail: info@janes.con • URL: http://www.janes.com • Annual. $350.00; CD-Rom edition, $650.00. International coverage of equipment and supplies for both civil and military airports. Formerly *Jane's Airport and ATC Equipment*.

Jane's Airport Review: The Global Airport Business Magazine. Jane's Information Group, Inc., Dept. DSM, Ste. 300 Alexandria, VA 22314. Phone: 800-824-0768 or (703)683-3700 E-mail: info@janes.com • URL: http://www.janes.com • 10 times a year. $170.00 per year. CD-Rom edition, $1,075.00 per year. Edited for airport managers. Covers all aspects of airport operations.

Jane's All the World's Aircraft. Jane's Information Group, Inc., Dept. DSM, Ste. 300 Alexandria, VA 22314. Phone: 800-824-0768 or (703)683-3700 Fax: 800-836-0297 E-mail: info@janes.com • URL: http://www.janes.com • Annual. $300.00; CD-Rom edition, $425.00.

Jane's Avionics., 1340 Braddock Place, Suite 300 Alexandria, VA 22314-1657. Phone: 800-824-0768 or (703)683-3700 Fax: 800-836-0297 E-mail: info@janes.com • URL: http://www.janes.com • Annual. $350.00. Civil/military airborne equipment. International coverage.

Jane's Fighting Ships. Jane's Information Group, Inc., Dept. DSM, Ste. 300 Alexandria, VA 22314. Phone: 800-824-0768 or (703)683-3700 Fax: 800-836-0297 E-mail: info@janes.com • URL: http://www.janes.com • Annual. $405.00; CD-Rom edition, $650.00 Navies of the world and ship details, weapons fits and specifications.

Jane's Police and Security Equipment: The Complete Source on Worldwide Law Enforcement Equipment. Jane's Information Group, 1340 Braddock Place, Dept. DSM, Ste. 300 Alexandria, VA 22314. Phone: 800-824-0768 or (703)683-3700 Fax: 800-836-0297 E-mail: info@janes.com • URL: http://www.janes.com • Annual. $350.00. Provides information on sources of more than 2,000 items of law enforcement equipment. Covers traffic control, riot control, communications, personal protection, surveillance, and other equipment categories. Includes detailed product descriptions.

Jane's Road Traffic Management. Jane's Information Group, Inc., Dept. DSM, Ste. 300 Alexandria, VA 22314. Phone: 800-824-0768 or (703)683-3700 E-mail: info@janes.com • URL: http://www.janes.com • Annual. $375.00. A directory of traffic control equipment and services. Includes detailed product descriptions.

Jane's Urban Transport Systems. Jane's Information Group, Inc., Dept. DSM, Ste. 300 Alexandria, VA 22314. Phone: 800-824-0678 or (703)683-3700 Fax: 800-836-0297 E-mail: info@janes.com • URL: http://www.janes.com • Annual. $352.00; CD-Rom edition, $650.00. Operating bus, metro, light rail, tram, ferry, and trolley bus transport systems. Includes manufacturers of equipment for urban systems.

Jane's World Airlines. Jane's Information Group, 1340 Braddock Place, Dept. DSM, Ste. 300 Alexandria, VA 22314. Phone: 800-824-0768 or (703)683-3700 Fax: 800-836-0297 E-mail: info@janes.com • URL: http://www.janes.com • $892.00. Looseleaf. Quarterly updates. CD-Rom edition, $1,475.00. Provides detailed financial and operating data for 500 airlines throughout the world.

Jane's World Railways. Jane's Information Group, 1340 Braddock Place, Dept. DSM, Suite 300 Alexandria, VA 22314. Phone: 800-824-0768 or (703)683-3700 Fax: 800-836-0297 E-mail: info@janes.com • URL: http://www.janes.com • Annual. $390.00. Monthy updates. Lists nearly 1,400 railway industry manufacturers, 400 railway systems, and 200 rapid transit systems throughout 115 countries.

Janitorial Service. Entrepreneur Media, Inc., 2445 McCabe Way Irvine, CA 92614. Phone: 800-421-2300 or (949)261-2325 Fax: (949)261-0234 E-mail: entmag@entrepreneur.com • URL: http://www.entrepreneur.com • Looseleaf. $59.50. A practical guide to starting a janitorial service business. Covers profit potential, start-up costs, market size evaluation, owner's time required, site selection, lease negotiation, pricing, accounting, advertising, promotion, etc. (Start-Up Business Guide No. E1034.)

Japan Business: The Portable Encyclopedia for Doing Business with Japan. Christine Genzberger and others. World Trade Press, 1450 Grant Ave., Suite 204 Novato, CA 94945-3142. Phone: 800-833-8586 or (415)898-1124 Fax: (415)898-1080 E-mail: worldpress@aol.com • URL: http://www.worldtradepress.com • 1944. $24.95. (Country Business Guide Series).

Japan Camera Trade News: Monthly Information on Photographic Products, Optical Instruments and Accessories. K. Eda, editor. Genyosha Publications, Inc., 8-7 Shibuya 2-chome, Shibuya-ku Tokyo 150-0002, Japan. E-mail: zj8k-ed@asahi.net.or.jp • Monthly. $75.00 per year. Information on the photographic industry worldwide. Text in English.

Japan Company Handbook. Available from Hoover's, Inc., 1033 La Posada Drive, Suite 250 Austin, TX 78752. Phone: 800-486-8666 or (512)374-4500 Fax: (512)374-4505 E-mail: orders@hoovers.com • URL: http://www.hoovers.com • Quarterly. $444.00 per year. Two volumes (current quarterly two-volume edition available at $120.00). Published by Toyo Keizai, Japan. Text in English. Contains profiles of 2,500 Japanese companies. First volume covers larger publicly-held companies; second volume provides information on smaller publicly-held firms.

Japan Economic Almanac: An Annual In-Depth Report on the State of the Japanese Economy. Nihon Keizai Shimbun America, Inc. Japan Economic Almanac, P.O. Box 15 Leonia, NJ 07605. Phone: (201)224-9480 Fax: (201)585-2343 Annual. $59.50. Lists of Japanese government agencies, and professional and trade organizations. Text in English.

Japan Economic Institute of America., 1000 Connecticut Ave., N. W., Suite 211 Washington, DC 20036. Phone: (202)296-5633 Fax: (202)296-8333 E-mail: jei@jei.org • URL: http://www.jei@.org • Provides current information on U. S.-Japan economic and trade relations. Funded by the Japanese Foreign Ministry.

Japan Economic Newswire Plus. Kyodo News International, Inc., 50 Rockefeller Plaza, Room 803 New York, NY 10020. Phone: 800-536-3510 or (212)397-3723 Fax: (212)397-3721 Provides full text in English of news items relating to business, economics, industry, trade, and finance in Japan and the Pacific Rim countries. Time period is 1982 to date, with daily updates. Inquire as to online cost and availability.

Japan External Trade Organization., 1221 Ave. of the Americas New York, NY 10020. Phone: (212)997-0400 Fax: (212)997-0464 URL: http://www.jetro.org • Encourages American companies to export goods to Japan. Makes information available on Japanese marketing and distribution systems.

The Japan Times: Weekly International Edition. JTUSA, Inc., 3655 Torrance Blvd., 2nd Fl. Torrance, CA 90503. Phone: (310)540-6862 Fax: (310)540-3462 Weekly. $140.00 per year. Provides news and commentary on Japan's economy, trade policies, and Japanese life in general. Regular features include "Business Briefs," "Market Reports," "Lifestyle," and "Issue Analysis." Supplement available *The Japan Times Weekly*. Text in English.

Japan Trade Directory 2000-2001. Available from The Gale Group, 27500 Drake Rd. Farmington Hills, MI 48331-3535. Phone: 800-877-GALE or (248)699-GALE Fax: 800-414-5043 or (248)699-8069 E-mail: galeord@galegroup.com • URL: http://www.galegroup.com • 2000. $350.00. 18th edition. Published by the Japan External

Trade Organization (JETRO). Provides information on about 2,800 Japanese companies currently active in exporting or importing.

Japan 250,000 CD-ROM. Available from Dun & Bradstreet, Inc., One Diamond Hill Rd. Murray Hill, NJ 07974-1218. Phone: 800-234-3867 or (908)665-5000 Fax: (908)665-5803 URL: http://www.dnb.com • Annual. Price on application. Produced by Tokyo Shoko Research, Ltd. CD-ROM contains basic information on 250,000 Japanese companies.

Japanese Affiliated Companies In the U.S. and Canada. Available from The Gale Group, 27500 Drake Rd. Farmington Hills, MI 48331-3535. Phone: 800-877-GALE or (248)699-GALE Fax: 800-414-5043 or (248)699-8069 E-mail: galeord@galegroup.com • URL: http://www.galegroup.com • 1994. $190.00. Published by the Japan External Trade Organization (JETRO). Lists approximately 10,000 affiliates of Japanese companies operating in the U. S. and Canada. Provides North American and Japanese addresses. Six indexes.

Japanese Automobile Industry: An Annotated Bibliography. Sheu-Yueh J. Chao, compiler. Greenwood Publishing Group, Inc., 88 Post Rd., W. Westport, CT 06881-5007. Phone: 800-225-5800 or (203)226-3571 Fax: (203)222-2540 E-mail: bookinfo@greenwood.com • URL: http://www.greenwood.com • 1994. $75.00. Describes about 600 books, articles, papers, and documents written in English. Emphasis is on material published since 1980. (Bibliographies and Indexes in Economics and Economic History Series, No. 157).

Japanese Company Factfinder: Teikoku Databank. Teikoku Databank America, Inc., 747 Third Ave., 25th Floor New York, NY 10017. Phone: (212)421-9805 Fax: (212)421-9806 E-mail: office@teikoku.com • URL: http://www.teikoku.com • Quarterly. $1,920.00 per year to academic and public libraries. $3,200 per year to businesses. CD-ROM provides detailed financial and descriptive information on more than 186,000 Japanese companies doing business overseas.

JASA (Journal of the American Statistical Association). American Statistical Association, 1429 Duke St. Alexandria, VA 22314-3415. Phone: (703)684-1221 Fax: (703)684-2036 E-mail: asainfo@amstat.org • URL: http://www.amstat.org • Quarterly. Members, $39.00 per year; non-members, $310.00 per year. Formerly *Amercan Statistical Association Journal*

Java Cookbook: Solutions and Examples for Java Developers. Ian Darwin. O'Reilly & Associates, Inc., 101 Morris St. Sebastopol, CA 95472-9902. Phone: 800-998-9938 or (707)829-0515 Fax: (707)829-0104 E-mail: order@oreilly.com • URL: http://www.oreilly.com • 2001. $44.95. Presents a "comprehensive collection of problems, solutions, and practical examples" for Java developers.

Java Developer's Journal. Sys-Con Publications, 39 E. Central Ave. Pearl River, NY 10965. Phone: (914)735-1900 Fax: (914)735-3922 E-mail: subscribe@sys-con.com • URL: http://www.sys-con.com • Monthly. $49.00 per year. Provides technical information for Java professionals.

Java FAQs. Clifford J. Berg. Prentice Hall, 240 Frisch Court Paramus, NJ 07652-5240. Phone: 800-947-7700 or (201)909-6200 Fax: 800-445-6991 or (201)909-6361 URL: http://www.prenhall.com • 2001. $26.95.

Java for Students 1.2. Doug Bell and Mike Parr. Prentice Hall, 240 Frisch Court Paramus, NJ 07652-5240. Phone: 800-947-7700 or (201)909-6200 Fax: 800-445-6991 or (201)909-6361 URL: http://www.prenhall.com • 1998. $62.00. A basic introduction to Java.

Java Primer. David Forster. Addison-Wesley Longman, Inc., One Jacob Way Reading, MA 01867. Phone: 800-447-2226 or (781)944-3700 Fax: (781)944-9351 URL: http://www.awl.com • 1999. $10.01.

Java Pro. Fawcette Technical Publications, 209 Hamilton Ave. Palo Alto, CA 94301-2500. Phone: 800-848-5523 or (650)833-7100 Fax: (650)833-0230 E-mail: pspyksma@fawcette.com • URL: http://www.fawcette.com • Monthly. $35.00 per year. Contains technical articles for Java developers.

Java Report: The Independent Source for Java Development. Sigs Publications, Inc., 71 W. 23rd St., 3rd Fl. New York, NY 10010-4102. Phone: (212)242-7447 Fax: (212)242-7574 E-mail: subscriptions@sigs.com • URL: http://www.sigs.com • Monthly. $329.00 per year. Covers Java programming and development for software professionals.

Java Tutorial: Object-Oriented Programming for the Internet. Mary Campione and Kathy Walrath. Addison-Wesley Longman, Inc., One Jacob Way Reading, MA 01867. Phone: 800-447-2226 or (781)944-3700 Fax: (781)944-9351 URL: http://www.awl.com • 1996. $41.95. Third edition. Presents a self-guided tour of the Java programming language. CD-ROM included. (Java Tutorial Services).

Jax Fax Travel Marketing Magazine: The Official Leisure Travel Booking Magazine. Jet Airtransport Exchange, Inc., 48 Wellington Rd. Milford, CT. Phone: (203)301-0255 Fax: (203)301-0250 E-mail: dcjaxfax@aol.com-email • URL: http://www.jaxfax.com • Monthly. $15.00 per year. Trade magazine for travel agents.

JCT:Journal of Coatings Technology. Federation of Societies for Coatings Technology, 492 Norristown Rd. Blue Bell, PA 19422-2350. Phone: (610)940-0777 Fax: (610)940-0292 E-mail: subscriptions@coatingstech.org • URL: http://www.coatingstech.org/products/journal.html • Monthly. $120.00 per year.

Jerome Lawrence and Robert E. Lee Theatre Research Institute.

Jet and Propjet: Corporate Directory. AvCom International, P.O. Box 2398 Wichita, KS 67201. Phone: (316)262-1493 Fax: (312)262-5333 E-mail: avdata@wichita.fn.net • Annual. $21.95. Owners of business jet and turboprop aircraft. Formerly *Propjet*.

Jet Cargo News: For Air Shipping Decision Makers. Hagall Publishing Co., P.O. Box 920952 Houston, TX 77292-0952. Phone: (713)681-4760 Fax: (713)682-3871 Monthly. $30.00 per year. Covers development of air cargo related technologies, containerization, regulation and documentation, market opportunities, routing, rates, trends and interviews with transportation industry executives worldwide.

Jet Propulsion Laboratory.

Jewelers Board of Trade., 95 Jefferson Blvd. Warwick, RI 02888-1046. Phone: (401)467-0055 Fax: (401)467-1199 URL: http://www.jewelersboard.com • A credit reporting and collection organization for the jewelry business.

Jewelers' Circular Keystone. Cahners Business Information, 1018 W. 9th Ave. King of Prussia, PA 19406. Phone: 800-695-1214 or (610)205-1000 Fax: (610)964-2915 E-mail: corporatecommunications@cahners.com • URL: http://www.cahners.com • Monthly. $90.00 per year.

Jewelers' Circular/Keystone-Jewelers' Directory. Cahners Business Information, 1018 W. 9th Ave. King of Prussia, PA 19406. Phone: 800-695-1214 or (610)205-1000 Fax: (610)964-2915 E-mail: corporatecommunications@cahners.com • URL: http://www.cahners.com • Annual. $33.95. About 8,500 manufacturers, importers and wholesale jewelers providing merchandise and supplies to the jewelry retailing industry; and related trade organizations. Included with subscription to *Jewelers' Circular Keystone*.

Jewelers' Dictionary. Donald S. McNeil, editor. Jewelers' Circular/Keystone, 201 King of Prussia Rd. Radnor, PA 19089-0230. Phone: 800-866-0206 or (610)964-4480 Fax: (610)694-4481 1979. $39.95. Third edition.

Jewelers of America.

Jewelers Security Alliance of the U.S.

Jewelers Vigilance Committee.

Jewelry and Gems: The Buying Guide-How to Buy Diamonds, Pearls, Precious and Other Popular Gems with Confidence and Knowledge. Antoinette L. Matlins and Antonio C. Bonanno. GemStone Press, P.O. Box 237 Woodstock, VT 05091. Phone: 800-962-4544 or (802)457-4000 Fax: (802)457-5032 E-mail: sales@gemstonepress.com • URL: http://www.gemstonepress.com • 1998. $24.95. Fourth revised edition.

Jewelry Information Center.

Job & Career Books. Kennedy Information, LLC, One Kennedy Place, Route 12, S. Fitzwilliam, NH 03447. Phone: 800-531-1026 or (603)585-3101 Fax: (603)585-9555 E-mail: office@kennedypub.com • URL: http://www.intertec.com • Annual. Free. Contains descriptions of selected books from various publishers on job searching and choice of career.

Job Hunter's Sourcebook: Where to Find Employment Leads and Other Job Search Resources. The Gale Group, 27500 Drake Rd. Farmington Hills, MI 48331-3535. Phone: 800-877-GALE or (248)699-GALE Fax: 800-414-5043 or (248)699-8069 E-mail: galeord@galegroup.com • URL: http://www.galegroup.com • 1999. $99.00. Fourth edition. Covers 179 professions and occupations.

Job Safety and Health Quarterly. Available from U. S. Government Printing Office, Washington, DC 20402. Phone: (202)512-1800 Fax: (202)512-2250 E-mail: gpoaccess@gpo.gov • URL: http://www.access.gpo.gov • Quarterly. $17.00 per year. Issued by the Occupational Safety and Health Administration (OSHA), U. S. Department of Labor. Contains articles on employee safety and health, with information on current OSHA activities.

Job Search: The Total System. Kenneth Dawson and Sheryl N. Dawson. John Wiley and Sons, Inc., 605 Third Ave. New York, NY 10158-0012. Phone: 800-526-5368 or (212)850-6000 Fax: (212)850-6088 E-mail: info@wiley.com • URL: http://www.wiley.com • 1996. $15.95. Second edition.

Job Seeker's Guide to Private and Public Companies. The Gale Group, 27500 Drake Rd. Farmington Hills, MI 48331-3535. Phone: 800-877-GALE or (248)699-GALE Fax: 800-414-5043 or (248)699-8069 E-mail: galeord@galegroup.com • URL: http://www.galegroup.com • 1995. $365.00. Third edition. Four regional volumes: *The West, The Midwest, The Northeast,* and *The South*. Covers about 15,000 companies, providing information on personnel department contacts, corporate officials, company benefits, application procedures, etc. Regional volumes are available separately at $99.00.

John Liner Letter. Standard Publishing Corp., 155 Federal St. Boston, MA 02110. Phone: 800-682-5759 or (617)457-0600 Fax: (617)457-0608 E-mail: stnd@earthlink.net • URL: http://www.standard-pub.com • Monthly. $178.00 per year. Newsletter for users of business insurance.

John W. Hartman Center for Sales, Advertising, and Marketing History., Special Collections Library, Duke University, P.O. Box 90185 Durham, NC 27708-0185. Phone: (919)660-5827 Fax: (919)660-5934 E-mail: hartman-center@duke.edu • URL: http://www.scriptorium.lib.duke.edu/hartman/ • Concerned with the study of the roles of sales, advertising, and marketing in society.

Joining of Composite Matrix Materials. Mel M. Schwartz. ASM International, 9639 Kinsman Rd. Materials Park, OH 44073-0002. Phone: 800-336-5152 or (440)338-5151 Fax: (440)338-4634 E-mail: custserv@po.asm-intl.org • URL: http://www.asm.intl.org • 1994. $59.00.

Joint Committee of the States to Study Alcoholic Beverage Laws.

Joint Electron Device Engineering Council.

Joint Industry Board of the Electrical Industry., 158-11 Harry Van Arsdale, Jr. Ave. Flushing, NY 11365. Phone: (718)591-2000 Fax: (718)380-7741 Concerned with labor-management relations of electrical contractors.

Joint Institute for Advancement of Flight Sciences., George Washington University, NASA Langley Research Center, Mail Stop 269 Hampton, VA 23681-2199. Phone: (757)864-1982 Fax: (757)864-5894 E-mail: jiafs@seas.gwu.edu • URL: http://www.seas.gwu.edu/seas/jiafs • Conducts research in aeronautics, astronautics, and acoustics (flight-produced noise).

JOM: Journal of Metals. Minerals, Metals, and Materials Society, 184 Thornhill Rd. Warrendale, PA 15086. Phone: 800-759-4867 or (724)776-9080 Fax: (724)776-3770 E-mail: csc@tms.org • URL: http://www.tms.org • Monthly. Individuals. $79.00 per year; institutions, $154.00 per year. A scholarly journal covering all phases of metals and metallurgy.

Jones Dictionary of Cable Television Terminology: Including Related Computer and Satellite Definitions. Glenn R. Jones. Jones Twenty-First Century Ltd., 9697 E Mineral Ave. Englewood, CO 80112. Phone: (303)792-3111 1996. $14.95.

Journal of Finacial Services Professionals. American Society of CLU and Ch F C, 270 S. Bryn Mawr Ave. Bryn Mawr, PA 19010-2195. Phone: 888-243-2258 or (610)526-2500 Fax: (610)527-4010 Bimonthly. $38.00 per year. Provides information on life insurance and financial planning, including estate planning, retirement, tax planning, trusts, business insurance, long-term care insurance, disability insurance, and employee benefits. Formerly (American Society of CLU and Ch F C Journal)

The Journal of Academic Librarianship: Articles, Features, and Book Reviews for the Academic Librarian Professional. Jai Press, Inc., P.O. Box 811 Stamford, CT 06904-0811. Phone: (203)323-9606 Fax: (203)357-8446 E-mail: order@jaipress.com • URL: http://www.jaipress.com • Bimonthly. $208.00 per year.

Journal of Accountancy. American Institute of Certified Public Accountants, 1211 Ave. of the Americas New York, NY 10036-8775. Phone: 800-862-4272 or (212)596-6200 Fax: (212)596-6213 E-mail: journal@aicpa.org • URL: http://www.aicpa.org/pubs • Monthly. $59.00 per year.

Journal of Accounting, Auditing and Finance. New York University Vincent C. Ross Institute of Accounting Research. Greenwood Publishing Group Inc., Subscription Publications, P.O. Box 5007 Westport, CT 06881-5007. Phone: 800-225-5800 or (203)226-3571 Fax: (203)222-2540 E-mail: bookinfo@greenwood.com • URL: http://www.greenwood.com • Quarterly. $135.00 per year.

Journal of Accounting Research. Institute of Professional Accounting, University of Chicago, Graduate School of Business, 1101 E. 58th St. Chicago, IL 60637. Phone: (773)702-7460 Fax: (773)834-4585 E-mail: jar@gsb.uchicago.edu • URL: http://www.gsbwww.uchicago.ed • Semiannual. Students, $80.00 per year; others, $90.00 per year. Includes annual supplement. Accepts for review unpublished research in the fields of empirical and experimental accounting.

Journal of Adhesion. Gordon and Breach Publishing Group, Two Gateway Center Newark, NJ 07102-0301. Phone: 800-545-8398 or (973)643-7500 Fax: (973)643-7676 E-mail: book.orders@aidcvt.com • URL: http://www.gbhap.com • 16 times a year. Four volumes. Academic institutions, $3,954.00 per year; corporations, $6,510.00 per year.

Journal of Advanced Materials. Society for the Advancement of Material and Process Engineering, P.O. Box 2459 Covina, CA 91722. Phone: (626)331-0616 Fax: (626)332-8929 Quarterly. Members $20.00 per year; non-members, $60.00 per year. Contains technical and research articles. Formerly *SAMPE Quarterly*.

Journal of Advertising Research. Advertising Research Foundation, 641 Lexington Ave., 11th Fl. New York, NY 10022. Phone: (212)751-5656 Fax: (212)319-5265 URL: http://www.arfsite.org/publish.html • Bimonthly. $100.00 per year.

Journal of Aging and Social Policy: A Journal Devoted to Aging and Social Policy. Haworth Press, Inc., 10 Alice St. Binghamton, NY 13904-1580. Phone: 800-429-6784 or (607)722-5857 Fax: 800-895-0582 or (607)722-1424 E-mail: getinfo@haworthpressinc.com • URL: http://www.haworthpressinc.com • Quarterly. Individuals, $60.00 per year; institutions, $120.00 per year; libraries, $275.00 per year.

Journal of Agricultural and Food Information. Haworth Press, Inc., 10 Alice St. Binghamton, NY 13904-1580. Phone: 800-429-6784 or (607)722-5857 Fax: 800-895-0582 or (607)722-1424 E-mail: getinfo@haworthpressinc.com • URL: http://www.haworthpressinc.com • Quarterly. Individuals, $45.00 per year; libraries and other institutions, $85.00 per year. A journal for librarians and others concerned with the acquisition of information on food and agriculture.

Journal of Aircraft: Devoted to Aeronautical Science and Technology. American Institute of Aeronautics and Astronautics, Inc., 1801 Alexander Bell Dr., Suite 500 Reston, VA 20191-4344. Phone: 800-639-2422 or (703)264-7500 Fax: (703)264-7551 E-mail: custserv@aiaa.org • URL: http://www.aiaa.org/publications/ • Bimonthly. Members, $50.00 per year; non-members, $175.00 per year; institutions, $350.00 per year.

Journal of Alcohol and Drug Education. American Alcohol and Drug Information Foundation, P.O. Box 10212 Lansing, MI 48901-0212. Phone: (517)484-2636 Fax: (517)484-0444 E-mail: dcorbin@coe.uomaha.edu • URL: http://www.uomaha.edu/~TLDhealthed.jade.html • Three times a year. Free to members; non-members, $45.00 per year.

Journal of Alternative Investments. Institutional Investor, 488 Madison Ave. New York, NY 10022. Phone: (212)224-3300 Fax: (212)224-3527 E-mail: info@iijournals.com • URL: http://www.iijournals.com • Quarterly. $380.00 per year. Covers such items as hedge funds, private equity financing, funds of funds, real estate investment trusts, natural resource investments, foreign exchange, and emerging markets.

Journal of Animal Science. American Society of Animal Science, 1111 N. Dunlap Ave. Savoy, IL 68174. Phone: (217)356-3182 Fax: (217)398-4119 E-mail: johne@assochq.org • URL: http://www.asas.uiuc.edu • Monthly. $250.00 per year.

Journal of Apicultural Research. International Bee Research Association, 18 North Rd. Cardiff CF1 3DY Wales, Wales. E-mail: ibra@cardiff.ac.uk • Quarterly. $170.00 per year. Primary research

Journal of Applied Behavioral Science. Sage Publications, Inc., 2455 Teller Rd. Thousand Oaks, CA 91320. Phone: (805)499-0721 Fax: (805)499-0871 E-mail: info@sagepub.com • URL: http://www.sagepub.com • Individuals, $75.00 per year; institutions, $350.00 per year.

Journal of Applied Communication Research. National Communication Association, 5105 Backlick Rd., Bldg. E Annandale, VA 22003. Phone: (703)750-0533 Fax: (703)914-9471 Quarterly. $110.00 per year.

Journal of Applied Econometrics. John Wiley and Sons, Inc., Journals Div., 605 Third Ave. New York, NY 10158-0012. Phone: 800-526-5368 or (212)850-6000 Fax: (212)850-6088 E-mail: info@wiley.com • URL: http://www.wiley.com • Bimonthly. Institutions, $870.00 per year.

Journal of Applied Mechanics. American Society of Mechanical Engineers, 22 Law Dr. Fairfield, NJ 07007-2900. Phone: 800-843-2763 or (973)882-1167 Fax: (973)882-1717 E-mail: infocentral@asme.org • URL: http://www.asme.org • Quarterly. Members, $40.00 per year; non-members, $250.00 per year. Series E of the *Transactions of the ASME*.

Journal of Applied Meteorology. American Meteorological Society, 45 Beacon St. Boston, MA 02108-3693. Phone: (617)227-2425 Fax: (617)742-8718 E-mail: amspubs@ametsoc.org • URL: http://www.ametsoc.org • Monthly. $335.00 per year.

Journal of Applied Polymer Science. John Wiley and Sons, Inc., Journals Div., 605 Third Ave. New York, NY 10158-0012. Phone: 800-526-5368 or (212)850-6000 Fax: (212)850-6088 E-mail: info@wiley.com • URL: http://www.wiley.com • 56 times a year. Institutions, $11,570.00 per year.

Journal of Aquatic Food Product Technology: An International Journal Devoted to Foods from Marine and Inland Waters of the World. Haworth Press, Inc., 10 Alice St. Binghamton, NY 13904-1580. Phone: 800-429-6784 or (607)722-5857 Fax: 800-895-0582 or (607)722-1424 E-mail: getinfo@haworthpressinc.com • URL: http://www.haworthpressinc.com • Quarterly. Individuals, $60.00 per year; institutions, $95.00 per year; libraries, $225.00 per year.

Journal of Architectural Education. Association of Collegiate Schools of Architecture. MIT Press, Five Cambridge Center Cambridge, MA 02142. Phone: 800-353-0343 or (617)253-2889 Fax: (617)253-1545 E-mail: journals-orders@mit.edu • URL: http://www.mitpress.mit.edu • Quarterly. Individuals, $50.00 per year; institutions, $175.00 per year. Articles on architectural education, theory and practice.

Journal of Arts Management, Law, and Society. Helen Dwight Reid Educational Foundation. Helderf Publications, 1319 18th St., N.W. Washington, DC 20036-1802. Phone: (202)296-6267 Fax: (202)296-5149 URL: http://www.helderf.org • Quarterly. Individuals, $50.00 per year; institutions, $100.00 per year. Addresses current and ongoing issues in arts policy, management, low and governance from a range of philosophical and national perspectives encompassing diverse disciplinary viewpoints. Formerly *Journal of Arts Management and Law*.

Journal of Asia-Pacific Business. Haworth Press, Inc., 10 Alice St. Binghamton, NY 13904-1580. Phone: 800-429-6784 or (607)722-5857 Fax: 800-895-0582 or (607)722-1424 E-mail: getinfo@haworthpressinc.com • URL: http://www.haworthpressinc.com • Quarterly. Individuals, $60.00 per year; institutions, $100.00 per year; libraries, $125.00 per year. An academic and practical journal concerned with marketing, finance, and other aspects of doing business in Asia.

Journal of Asian Business. Southeast Asia Business Program. University of Michigan, 914 Hill St. Ann Arbor, MI 48109-1234. Phone: (734)998-7276 Fax: (734)936-1721 E-mail: jab@umich.edu • Quarterly. Individuals, $25.00 per year; institutions, $40.00 per year. An international academic journal covering business in all parts of Asia.

Journal of Astronautical Sciences. American Astronautical Society, 6352 Rolling Mill Place, Suite 102 Springfield, VA 22152-2354. Phone: (703)866-0020 Fax: (703)866-3526 E-mail: aas@astronautical.org • URL: http://www.astronautical.org • Quarterly.Institutions, $155.00 per year.

Journal of Bank Cost and Management Accounting. Association for Management Information in Financial Services, 7950 E. LaJunta Rd. Scottsdale, AZ 85255-2798. Fax: (480)515-2101 E-mail: ami@amifs.org • URL: http://www.amifs.org • Three times a year. $100.00 per year.

Journal of Banking and Financial Services. Warren, Gorham and Lamont, Inc., 31 Saint James Ave. Boston, MA 02116-4101. Phone: 800-950-1215 or (617)423-2020 Fax: (617)337-4280 E-mail: customer_services@riag.com • URL: http://www.riahome.com • Bimonthly. $115.00. per year. Enables bankers to obtain a more generalized view of the industry. Contains articles for bankers, by bankers and top consultants in the field. Formerly*Bankers' Magazine*.

Journal of Bankruptcy Law and Practice. Warren, Gorham & Lamont/RIA Group, 395 Hudson St. New York, NY 10014. Phone: 800-950-1215 or (212)367-6300 Fax: (212)337-4280 E-mail: customer_services@riag.com • URL: http://www.riahome.com • Bimonthly. $228.00 per year. Provides guidance in bankruptcy law practice, including analysis of recent developments in case law.

Journal of Behavioral Health Services and Research. Association of Behaviorial Healthcare Management. Sage Publications, Inc., 2455 Teller Rd. Thousand Oaks, CA 91320. Phone: (805)499-0721 Fax: (805)499-0871 E-mail: info@sagepub.com • URL: http://www.sagepub.com • Quarterly. Individuals, $63.00 per year; institutions, $233.00 per year. Pertains to the financing and organization of behavioral health services. Formerly *Journal of Mental Health Administration*.

Journal of Biotechnology. Elsevier Science, 655 Ave. of the Americas New York, NY 10010. Phone: 888-437-4636 or (212)989-5800 Fax: (212)633-3680 E-mail: usinfo@elsevier.com • URL: http://www.elsevier.com • 25 times a year. $2,758.00 per year. Text and summaries in English.

Journal of Broadcasting and Electronic Media. Broadcast Education Association, 1771 N St., N.W. Washington, DC 20036. Phone: (202)429-5354 Fax: (202)775-2981 E-mail: jfletche@uga.cc.uga.edu • URL: http://www.beaweb.org • Quarterly. $86.50 per year. Scholarly articles about developments, trends and research.

The Journal of Business. University of Chicago Press, Journals Div., P.O. Box 37005 Chicago, IL 60637. Phone: 800-621-2736 or (773)753-3347 Fax: (312)753-0811 E-mail: subscriptions@journals.uchicago.edu • URL: http://www.journals.uchicago.edu • Quarterly. Individuals, $27.00 per year; institutions, $65.00 per year; students, $17.00 per year.

Journal of Business and Economic Statistics. American Statistical Association, 1429 Duke St. Alexandria, VA 22314-3415. Phone: (703)684-1221 Fax: (703)684-2036 E-mail: asainfo@amstat.org • URL: http://www.amstat.org • Quarterly. Libraries, $90.00 per year. Emphasis is on statistical measurement and applications for business and economics.

Journal of Business and Finance Librarianship. Haworth Press, Inc., 10 Alice St. Binghamton, NY 13904-1580. Phone: 800-429-6784 or (607)722-5857 Fax: 800-895-0582 or (607)722-1424 E-mail: getinfo@haworthpressinc.com • URL: http://www.haworthpressinc.com • Quarterly. Individuals, $40.00 per year; institutions, $85.00 per year; libraries, $85.00 per year.

Journal of Business and Psychology. Business Psychology Research Institute. Kluwer Plenum Academic Publishers, 233 Spring St., 5th Fl. New York, NY 10013-1578. Phone: 800-221-9369 or (212)620-8000 Fax: (212)463-0742 E-mail: info@plenum.com • URL: http://www.plenum.com • Quarterly. Institutions, $556.80 per year.

Journal of Business and Technical Communication. Sage Publications, Inc., 2455 Teller Rd. Thousand Oaks, CA 91320. Phone: (805)499-0721 Fax: (805)499-0871 E-mail: info@sagepub.com • URL: http://www.sagepub.com • Individuals, $65.00 per year; institutions, $340.00 per year.

Journal of Business Communication. Association for Business Communication, Baruch College, c/o Dr. Robert J. Myers, Dept. of Speech Communication, 17 Lexington Ave. New York, NY 10010. Phone: (212)387-1620 Fax: (212)387-1655 E-mail: abcrjm@compuserve.com • URL: http://www.theabc.org • Individuals, $65.00 per year; Insititutions, $150.00 per year. Includes *Association for Business Communiation Bulletin*.

Journal of Business Ethics. Kluwer Academic Publishers, 101 Philip Dr. Norwell, MA 02061. Phone: (781)871-6000 Fax: (781)871-6528 E-mail: kluwer@wkap.nl • URL: http://www.wkap.nl • 20 times a year. Institutions, $1,202.40 per year.

Journal of Business Forecasting Methods and Systems. Graceway Publishing Co., P.O. Box 670159 Flushing, NY 11367-0159. Phone: 800-440-0499 or (516)504-7576 Fax: (516)498-2029 E-mail: ibf@ibf.org • URL: http://www.ibf.org • Quarterly. $70.00 per year. Includes articles on forecasting methods and provides actual business and economic forecasts.

Journal of Business Research. Elsevier Science, 655 Ave. of the Americas New York, NY 10010. Phone: 888-437-4636 or (212)989-5800 Fax: (212)633-3680 E-mail: usinfo@elsevier.com • URL: http://www.elsevier.com • Nine times a year. $1,128.00 per year. Covers theoretical and empirical advances in marketing, finance, international business, risk management, and other business topics.

Journal of Business Strategy. Faulkner and Gray, Inc., 11 Penn Plaza, 17th Fl. New York, NY 10001. Phone: 800-535-8403 or (212)967-7000 Fax: (212)967-7155 E-mail: orders@faulknergray.com • URL: http://www.faulknergray.com • Bimonthly. $84.00 per year. Devoted to the theory and practice of strategy, planning, implementation and competitive analysis. Covers every aspect of business from advertising to systems design. Incorporates*Journal of European Business*.

Journal of Business-to-Business Marketing: Innovations in Basic and Applied Research for Industrial Marketing. Haworth Press, Inc., 10 Alice St. Binghamton, NY 13904-1580. Phone: 800-429-6784 or (607)722-5857 Fax: 800-895-0582 or (607)722-1424 E-mail: getinfo@haworthpressinc.com • URL: http://www.haworthpressinc.com • Quarterly. Individuals, $60.00 per year; institutions, $95.00 per year; libraries, $175.00 per year.

Journal of Business Venturing. Elsevier Science, 655 Ave. of the Americas New York, NY 10010. Phone: 888-437-4636 or (212)989-5800 Fax: (212)633-3680 E-mail: usinfo@elsevier.com • URL: http://www.elsevier.com • Bimonthly. $545.00 per year.

Journal of Career Planning and Employment: The International Magazine of Placement and Recruitment. National Association of Colleges and Employers, 62 Highland Ave. Bethlehem, PA 18017. Phone: 800-544-5272 or (610)868-1421 Fax: (610)868-0208 Quarterly. Free to members; non-members, $72.00 per year. Includes *Spotlight* newsletter. Formerly *Journal of College Placement*.

Journal of Chemical and Engineering Data. American Chemical Society, 1155 16th St., N.W. Washington, DC 20036. Phone: 800-333-9511 or (202)872-4600 Fax: (202)872-4615 E-mail: service@acs.org • URL: http://www.pubs.acs.org • Bimonthly. Institutions, $659.00 per year; others, price on application.

Journal of Chemical Information and Computer Sciences. American Chemical Society, 1155 16th St., N.W. Washington, DC 20036. Phone: 800-333-9511 or (202)872-4600 Fax: (202)872-4615 E-mail: service@acs.org • URL: http://www.pubs.acs.org • Bimonthly. Institutions, $454.00 per year; others, price on application.

Journal of Chemical Technology and Biotechnology. John Wiley and Sons, Inc. Journals Div., 605 Third Ave. New York, NY 10158-0012. Phone: (212)526-5368 Fax: (212)850-6088 E-mail: info@wiley.com • URL: http://www.wiley.com • Monthly. Institutions, $1,275.00 per year.

Journal of Clinical Laboratory Analysis. John Wiley and Sons, Inc., Journals Div., 605 Third Ave. New York, NY 10158-0012. Phone: 800-526-5368 or (212)850-6000 Fax: (212)850-6088 E-mail: info@wiley.com • URL: http://

www.wiley.com • Bimonthly. Institutions, $935.00 per year. Original articles on newly developing assays.

Journal of Clinical Ultrasound. John Wiley and Sons, Inc., Journals Div., 605 Third Ave. New York, NY 10158-0012. Phone: 800-526-5368 or (212)850-6000 Fax: (212)850-6088 E-mail: info@wiley.com • URL: http://www.wiley.com • Nine times a year. Institutions, $680.00 per year. Devoted exclusively to the clinical application of ultrasound in medicine.

Journal of Compensation and Benefits. Warren, Gorham & Lamont/RIA Group, 395 Hudson St. New York, NY 10014. Phone: 800-950-1215 or (212)367-6300 Fax: (212)337-4280 E-mail: customer_services@riag.com • URL: http://www.riahome.com • Bimonthly. $170.00 per year. Working advisor for benefits administrators, company specialists and consultants.

Journal of Computer Documentation. Special Interest Group for Documentation, Association for Computing Machinery, 1515 Broadway, 17th Fl. New York, NY 10036. Phone: (212)869-7440 Fax: (212)869-0481 Quarterly. Members, $24.00 per year; non-members, $44.00 per year.

Journal of Consumer Affairs. American Council on Consumer Interests, University of Wisconsin Press Journal Div., 2537 Daniel St. Columbia, MO 53718-6772. Phone: (608)224-3880 Fax: (608)224-3883 E-mail: acci@showme.missouri.edu • URL: http://www.wisc.edu/ • Semiannual. Individuals, $80.00 per year; institutions, $205.00 per year. Includes *Consumer News and Reviews, Advancing the Consumer Interest* and *Consumer Interest Annual.*

Journal of Consumer Research; An Interdisciplinary Quarterly. University of Chicago Press, Journals Div., P.O. Box 37005 Chicago, IL 60637. Phone: 800-621-2736 or (773)753-3347 Fax: (773)753-0811 E-mail: subscriptions@journals.uchicago.edu • URL: http://www.journals.uchicago.edu • Quarterly. Members, $45.00 per year; institutions, $99.00 per year; students, $25.00. Covers various aspects of consumer behavior.

Journal of Convention and Exhibition Management. Haworth Press, Inc., 10 Alice St. Binghamton, NY 13904-1580. Phone: 800-429-6784 or (607)722-5857 Fax: 800-895-0582 or (607)722-1424 E-mail: getinfo@haworthpressinc.com • URL: http://www.haworthpressinc.com • Quarterly. Individuals $50.00 per year; institutions, $85.00 per year; libraries, $95.00 per year.

Journal of Corporate Accounting and Finance. John Wiley and Sons, Inc., Subscription Dept., 605 Third Ave. New York, NY 10158-0012. Phone: 800-825-7550 or (212)850-6000 Fax: (212)850-6021 E-mail: info@wiley.com • URL: http://www.wiley.com • Bimonthly. $263.00 per year. Topics include government regulation, corporate taxation, financial risk, business valuation, and strategic planning.

Journal of Corporate Taxation. Warren, Gorham, and Lamont/RIA Group, 395 Hudson St. New York, NY 10014. Phone: 800-950-1215 or (212)367-6300 Fax: (212)367-6718 E-mail: customer_service@riag.com • URL: http://www.riahome.com • Looseleaf service. $195.00 per year. Quarterly updates. Analysis and guidance for practitioners. Provides ongoing coverage of currently proposed tax reform bills.

Journal of Cost Management. Warren, Gorham and Lamont/RIA Group, 395 Hudson St. New York, NY 10014. Phone: 800-950-1215 or (212)367-6300 Fax: (212)367-6718 E-mail: customer_service@riag.com • URL: http://www.riahome.com • Bimonthly. $123.98 per year. Includes articles on business budgeting.

Journal of Counseling and Development. American Counseling Association, 5999 Stevenson Ave. Alexandria, VA 22304-3300. Phone: 800-347-6647 or (703)823-9800 Fax: (703)823-0252 URL: http://www.counseling.org • Bimonthly. Individuals, $60.00 per year; institutions, $128.00 per year. Contains authoritative in-depth articles on professional and scientific issues. Formerly *Personnel and Guidance Journal.*

Journal of Counseling Psychology. American Psychological Association, 750 First St., N.E. Washington, DC 20002-4242. Phone: 800-374-2721 or (202)336-5500 Fax: (202)336-5568 URL: http://www.apa.org/journals • Quarterly. Members, $38.00 per year; non-members, $76.00 per year; institutions, $164.00 per year.

Journal of Court Reporting. National Court Reporters Association, 8224 Old Courthouse Rd. Vienna, VA 22182-3808. Phone: 800-272-6272 or (703)556-6272 Fax: (703)556-6291 E-mail: msic@ncrahq.org • URL: http://www.verbatimreporters.com • 10 times a year. $49.00 per year. News and features about court reporting, reporter technology. Computer-aided transcription, real time translation captioning for the hearing- impaired, etc. Formerly *National Shorthand Reporter.*

Journal of Creative Behavior. Creative Education Foundation, Inc., 1050 Union Rd. Buffalo, NY 14224. Phone: (716)675-3181 Fax: (716)675-3209 E-mail: cefhq@cef-cpsi.org • URL: http://www.cef-cpsi.org • Quarterly. Individuals, $70.00 per year; institutions, $85.00 per year.

Journal of Current Laser Abstracts. PennWell Corp., Advanced Technology Div., 98 Spit Brook Rd. Nashua, NH 03062-5737. Phone: 800-331-4463 or (603)891-0123 Fax: (603)891-0539 E-mail: webmaster@pennwell.com • URL: http://www.pennwell.com • Monthly. $495.00 per year. Covers the world's literature of lasers: industrial, medical, and military. Subscription includes annual subject and author index.

Journal of Dairy Research. Cambridge University Press, Journals Dept., 40 W. 20th St. New York, NY 10011. Phone: 800-221-4512 or (212)924-3900 Fax: (212)691-3239 E-mail: info@cup.org • URL: http://www.cup.org • Quarterly. $395.00 per year.

Journal of Dairy Science. American Dairy Science Association, 1111 N. Dunlap Ave. Savoy, IL 61874. Phone: (217)356-3182 Fax: (217)398-4119 E-mail: jeanr@assochq.org • URL: http://www.adsa.uiuc.edu/ • Monthly. $250.00 per year. Provides primary scientific research on all aspects of dairy foods and dairy cattle production and management.

Journal of Derivatives. Institutional Investor, 488 Madison Ave. New York, NY 10022. Phone: (212)224-3300 Fax: (212)224-3527 E-mail: info@iijournals.com • URL: http://www.iijournals.com • Quarterly. $280.00 per year. Covers the structure and management of financial derivatives. Includes graphs, equations, and detailed analyses.

Journal of Developing Areas. Western Illinois University, Morgan Hall 232 Macomb, IL 61455. Phone: (309)298-1108 Fax: (309)298-2585 E-mail: se-schisler@wiu.edu • URL: http://www.wiu.edu/ • Quarterly. Individuals, $29.00 per year; institutions, $39.00 per year.

The Journal of Development Economics. Elsevier Science, 655 Ave. of the Americas New York, NY 10010. Phone: 888-437-4636 or (212)989-5800 Fax: (212)633-3680 E-mail: usinfo@elsevier.com • URL: http://www.elsevier.com • Bimonthly. $1,223.00 per year.

The Journal of Development Studies. ISBS, 5804 N.E. Hassalo St. Portland, OR 97213-3644. Phone: 800-944-6190 Fax: (503)280-8832 E-mail: journals@frankcass.com • URL: http://www.frankcass.com • Bimonthy. Individuals, $75.00 per year; institutions, $320.00 per year.

Journal of Divorce and Remarriage: Research and Clinical Studies in Family Theory, Family Law, Family Meditation and Family Therapy. Haworth Press, Inc., 10 Alice St. Binghamton, NY 13904-1580. Phone: 800-429-2394 or (607)722-5857 Fax: 800-895-0582 or (607)722-1424 E-mail: getinfo@haworthpressinc.com • URL: http://www.haworthpressinc.com • Quarterly. Individuals, $60.00 per year; institutions, $140.00 per year; libraries, $400.00 per year. Two volumes.

Journal of Documentation: Devoted to the Recording, Organization and Dissemination of Specialized Knowledge. Information Today, Inc., 143 Old Marlton Pike Medford, NJ 08055-8750. Phone: 800-300-9868 or (609)654-6266 Fax: (609)654-4309 E-mail: custserv@infotoday.com • URL: http://www.infotoday.com • Five times a year. Members, $200.00 per year; non-members, $252.00 per year. Scholarly journal covering information science since 1945.

Journal of Drug Education. Baywood Publishing Co., Inc., P.O. Box 337 Amityville, NY 11701. Phone: 800-638-7819 or (631)691-1270 Fax: (631)691-1770 E-mail: baywood@baywood.com • URL: http://www.baywood.com • Quarterly. $175.50 per year.

Journal of Drug Issues. Florida State University, School of Criminology and Criminal Justice, P.O. Box 66696 Tallahassee, FL 32313-6696. Phone: (850)664-7368 Fax: (850)644-9614 Quarterly. Individuals, $80.00 per year; institutions, $105.00 per year.

Journal of East-West Business. Haworth Press, Inc., 10 Alice St. Binghamton, NY 13904-1580. Phone: 800-429-6784 or (607)722-5857 Fax: 800-895-0582 or (607)722-1424 E-mail: getinfo@haworthpressinc.com • URL: http://www.haworthpressinc.com • Quarterly. Individuals, $60.00 per year; institutions, $120.00 per year; libraries, $174.00 per year. An academic and practical journal focusing on business in the developing regions of Asia and Eastern Europe.

Journal of Econometrics. Elsevier Science, 655 Ave. of the Americas New York, NY 10010. Phone: 888-437-4636 or (212)989-5800 Fax: (212)633-3680 E-mail: usinfo@elsevier.com • URL: http://www.elsevier.com • Monthly. $2,020.00 per year.

Journal of Economic History. Economic History Association. Cambridge University Press, Journals Dept., 40 W. 20th St. New York, NY 10011. Phone: 800-221-4512 or (212)924-3900 Fax: (212)937-4712 E-mail: info@cup.org • URL: http://www.cup.org • Quarterly. $115.00 per year.

Journal of Economic Literature. American Economic Association, 2014 Broadway, Suite 305 Nashville, TN 37203. Phone: (615)322-2595 Fax: (615)343-7590 URL: http://www.vanderbilt.edu/aea • Quarterly. $135.00 per year. Includes *American Economic Review* and *Journal of Economic Perspectives.*

Journal of Economics and Business. Temple University, School of Business Administration. Elsevier Science, 655 Ave. of the Americas New York, NY 10010. Phone: 888-437-4636 or (212)989-5800 Fax: (212)633-3680 E-mail: usinfo@elsevier.com • URL: http://www.elsevier.com • Bimonthly. $418.00 per year. Professional and academic research primarily in economics, finance and related business disciplines.

Journal of Economics and Management Strategy. MIT Press, Five Cambridge Center Cambridge, MA 02142-1493. Phone: 800-356-0343 or (617)253-2864 Fax: (617)253-1545 E-mail: journals-orders@mit.edu • URL: http://www.mitpress.mit.edu • Quarterly. Individuals, $45.00 per year; institutions, $135.00 per year. Covers "theoretical and empirical industrial organization, applied game theory, and management strategy."

Journal of Education for Business. Helen Dwight Reid Educational Foundation. Heldref Publications, 1319 18th St., N.W. Washington, DC 20036-1802. Phone: 800-296-5149 or (202)296-6267 Fax: (202)296-5149 E-mail: jeb@heldref.org • URL: http://www.helderf.org • Bimonthly. Individuals, $38.00 per year; institutions, $64.00 per year. Features basic and applied research-based articles on business fundamentals, career education, consumer economics, distributive education, management, and trends in communications, information systems, and knowledge systems in business.

Journal of Elastomers and Plastics. Technomic Publishing Co., Inc., 851 New Holland Ave. Lancaster, PA 17604. Phone: 800-223-9936 or (717)291-5609 Fax: (717)295-4538 E-mail: marketing@techpub.com • URL: http://www.techpub.com • Quarterly. $340.00 per year.

Journal of Electronic Defense. Association of Old Crows. Horizon-House Publications, Inc., 685 Canton St. Norwood, MA 02062. Phone: (781)769-9750 Fax: (781)762-9230 E-mail: mjw@mjw.com • URL: http://www.jedefense.com • Monthly. Free to members; non-members, $120.00 per year.

Journal of Employment Counseling. National Employment Counsel Association. American Counseling Association, 5999 Stevenson Ave. Alexandria, VA 22304-3300. Phone: 800-347-6647 Fax: (703)823-0252 URL: http://www.counseling.org • Quarterly. Institutions, $38.00 Per year.

Journal of Environmental Sciences. Chinese Academy of Sciences, Environmental Science Council. IOS Press, Inc., P.O. Box 10558 Burke, VA 22009-0558. Phone: (703)323-5554 Fax: (703)250-4705 E-mail: market@iospress.nl • URL: http://www.iospress.nl • Quarterly. $100.00 per year.

Journal of Ethnic and Multicultural Marketing. Haworth Press, Inc., 10 Alice St. Binghamton, NY 13904-1580. Phone: 800-429-6784 or (607)722-5857 Fax: 800-895-0582 or (607)722-1424 E-mail: getinfo@haworthpressinc.com • URL: http://www.haworthpressinc.com • Quarterly. Price on application.

Journal of Euromarketing. Haworth Press, Inc., 10 Alice St. Binghamton, NY 13904-1580. Phone: 800-429-6784 or (607)722-5857 Fax: 800-895-0582 or (607)722-1424 E-mail: getinfo@haworthpressinc.com • URL: http://www.haworthpressinc.com • Quarterly. Individuals, $50.00 per year; institutions, $85.00 per year; libraries, $275.00 per year.

Journal of Explosives Engineering. International Society of Explosives Engineers, 29100 Aurora Rd. Cleveland, OH 44139-1800. Phone: (216)349-4004 Fax: (216)349-3788 Bimonthly. $35.00 per year.

Journal of Finance. American Finance Association. Blackwell Publishers, 350 Main St., 6th Fl. Malden, MA 02148-5018. Phone: 800-216-2522 or (781)388-8200 Fax: (781)338-8232 E-mail: subscript@blackwellpub.com • URL: http://www.blackwellpub.com • Bimonthly. $190.00 per year.

Journal of Financial and Quantitative Analysis. University of Washington, School of Business Administration, 115 Lewis Hall Seattle, WA 98195. Fax: (206)616-1894 URL: http://www.weber.uwashington.edu/ • Quarterly. Individuals, $45.00 per year; libraries, $95.00 per year; students, $25.00 per year.

Journal of Financial Economics. Elsevier Science, 655 Ave. of the Americas New York, NY 10010. Phone: 888-437-4636 or (212)989-5800 Fax: (212)633-3680 E-mail: usinfo@elsevier.com • URL: http://www.elsevier.com • Monthly. $1,429.00 per year.

Journal of Financial Planning. Financial Planning Association, 3801 E. Florida Ave., Suite 708 Denver, CO 80210-2571. Phone: (303)759-4900 Fax: (303)759-0749 E-mail: journal@fpanet.org • URL: http://www.journalfp.net • 12 times a year. Free to members; non-members, $90.00 per year. Edited for professional financial and investment planners.

Journal of Financial Planning Today. New Directions Publications, Inc., P. O. Box 6888 Lake Worth, FL 33460-6888. Phone: (321)434-0100 Fax: (321)641-4801 Quarterly. $100.00 per year. Formerly *Financial Planning Today.*

Journal of Financial Statement Analysis. Institutional Investor, 488 Madison Ave. New York, NY 10022. Phone: (212)224-3300 Fax: (212)224-3527 E-mail: info@iijournals.com • URL: http://www.iijournals.com • Quarterly. $280.00 per year. Covers the practical analysis and interpretation of corporate financial reports.

Journal of Fixed Income. Institutional Investor, 488 Madison Ave. New York, NY 10022. Phone: (212)224-3300 Fax: (212)224-3527 E-mail: info@iijournals.com • URL: http://www.iijournals.com • Quarterly. $325.00 per year. Covers a wide range of fixed-income investments for institutions, including bonds, interest-rate options, high-yield securities, and mortgages.

Journal of Fluid Control: Applications and Research on Fluid Control, Hydraulics and Pneumatics, Instrumentation, and Fluidics. David H. Tarumoto, editor. Delbridge Publishing Co., P.O. Box 2694 Saratoga, CA 95070-0694. Phone: (408)446-3131 Quarterly. $145.00 per volume.

Journal of Food Products Marketing: Innovations in Food Advertising, Food Promotion, Food Publicity, Food Sales Promotion. Haworth Press, Inc., 10 Alice St. Binghamton, NY 13904-1580. Phone: 800-429-6784 or (607)722-5857 Fax: 800-895-0582 or (607)722-1424 E-mail: getinfo@haworthpressinc.com • URL: http://www.haworthpressinc.com • Quarterly. Individuals, $60.00 per year; institutions, $95.00 per year; libraries, $175.00 per year.

Journal of Food Science. Institute of Food Technologists, 221 N. LaSalle St. Chicago, IL 60601. Phone: 800-438-3663 or (312)782-8424 E-mail: info@ift.org • URL: http://www.ift.org • Bimonthly. Members, $20.00 per year; non-members, $100.00 per year. A peer-reviewed research journal.

Journal of Forecasting. Available from John Wiley and Sons, Inc., Journals Div., 605 Third Ave. New York, NY 10158-0012. Phone: 800-526-5368 or (212)850-6000 Fax: (212)850-6088 E-mail: info@wiley.com • URL: http://www.wiley.com • Seven times a year. Institutions, $760.00 per year. A centralized focus on recent development in the art and science of forecasting International coverage. Published in England by John Wiley and Sons Ltd.

The Journal of Futures Markets. John Wiley and Sons, Inc., Journals Div., 605 Third Ave. New York, NY 10158-0012. Phone: 800-526-5368 or (212)850-6000 Fax: (212)850-6088 E-mail: info@wiley.com • URL: http://www.wiley.com • Eight times a year. $1,140.00 per year.

Journal of Global Marketing. Haworth Press, Inc., 10 Alice St. Binghamton, NY 13904-1580. Phone: 800-429-6784 or (607)722-5857 Fax: 800-895-0582 or (607)722-1424 E-mail: getinfo@haworthpressinc.com • URL: http://www.haworthpressinc.com • Quarterly. Individuals, $60.00 per year; institutions, $90.00 per year; libraries, $300.00 per year.

Journal of Government Information: An International Review of Policy, Issues an d Resources. Elsevier Science, 655 Ave. of the Americas New York, NY 10010. Phone: 888-437-4636 or (212)989-5800 Fax: (212)633-3680 E-mail: usinfo@elsevier.com • URL: http://www.elsevier.com • Bimonthly. $570.00 per year.

Journal of Healthcare Information Management. Healthcare Information and Management Systems Society. Jossey-Bass Inc., Publishers, 350 Sansome St. San Francisco, CA 94104. Phone: 888-378-2537 or (415)433-1740 Fax: (415)433-0499 E-mail: webperson@jbp.com • URL: http://www.josseybass.com • Quarterly. Institutions, $114.00 per year.

Journal of Healthcare Management. Foundation of the American College of Healthcare Executives. Health Administration Press, One N. Franklin, Suite 1700 Chicago, IL 60606-3491. Phone: (312)424-2800 Fax: (312)424-0014 URL: http://www.ache.org • Quarterly. $65.00 per year. Information on the latest trends, developments and innovations in the industry. Formerly (Hospital and Health Services Administration).

Journal of Heat Transfer. American Society of Mechanical Engineers, 22 Law Dr. Fairfield, NJ 00707-2900. Phone: 800-843-2763 or (973)882-1167 Fax: (973)882-1717 E-mail: infocentral@asme.org • URL: http://www.asme.org • Quarterly. Members, $40.00 per year; non-members, $250.00 per year.

Journal of Herbs, Spices and Medicinal Plants. Haworth Press, Inc., 10 Alice St. Binghamton, NY 13904-1580. Phone: 800-429-6784 or (607)722-5857 Fax: 800-895-0582 or (607)722-1424 E-mail: getinfo@haworthpressinc.com • URL: http://www.haworthpressinc.com • Quarterly. Individuals, $45.00 per year; institutions, $65.00 per year; libraries, $175.00 per year. An academic and practical journal on production, marketing, and other aspects of herbs and spices.

Journal of Higher Education. Ohio State University Press, 1070 Carmack Rd. Columbus, OH 43210. Phone: (614)292-6930 Fax: (614)292-2065 E-mail: mcgrothers.1@osu.edu • URL: http://www.sbs.ohio-state.edu • Bimonthly. Individuals, $42.00 per year; institutions, $90.00 per year. Issues important to faculty administrators and program managers in higher education.

Journal of Hospital Marketing. Haworth Press, Inc., 10 Alice St. Binghamton, NY 13904-1580. Phone: 800-429-6784 or (607)722-5857 Fax: 800-895-0582 or (607)722-1424 E-mail: getinfo@haworthpressinc.com • URL: http://www.haworthpressinc.com • Semiannual. Individuals, $45.00 per year; institutions, $85.00 per year; libraries, $275.00 per year.

Journal of Hospitality and Leisure Marketing: The International Forum for Research, Theory and Practice. Haworth Press, Inc., 10 Alice St. Binghamton, NY 13904-1580. Phone: 800-429-6784 or (607)722-5857 Fax: 800-895-0582 or (607)722-1424 E-mail: getinfo@haworthpressinc.com • URL: http://www.haworthpressinc.com • Quarterly. Individuals, $60.00 per year; institutions, $95.00 per year; libraries, $175.00 per year. An academic and practical journal covering various aspects of hotel, restaurant, and recreational marketing.

Journal of Housing and Community Development. National Association of Housing and Redevelopment Officials (NAHRO), 630 Eye St., N.W. Washington, DC 20001-3736. Phone: (202)289-3500 Fax: (202)429-8181 E-mail: nahro@nahro.org • URL: http://www.nahro.org • Bimonthly. $24.00 per year. Formerly *Journal of Housing*.

Journal of Housing Economics. Academic Press, Inc., Journal Div., 525 B St., Suite 1900 San Diego, CA 92101-4495. Phone: 800-321-5068 or (619)230-1840 Fax: (619)699-6715 E-mail: ap@acad.com • URL: http://www.academicpress.com • Quarterly. $245.00 per year.

Journal of Housing for the Elderly. Haworth Press, Inc., 10 Alice St. Binghamton, NY 13904-1580. Phone: 800-429-6784 or (607)722-5857 Fax: 800-895-0582 or (607)722-1424 E-mail: getinfo@haworthpressinc.com • URL: http://www.haworthpressinc.com • Semiannual. Individuals, $60.00 per year; institutions, $150.00 per year; libraries, $275.00 per year. Covers a wide variety of topics related to retirement communities and housing conditions for the elderly.

Journal of Human Resources: Education, Manpower and Welfare Economics. University of Wisconson at Madison, Industrial Relations Research Institute. University of Wisconsin Press, 2537 Daniels St. Madison, WI 53718-6772. Phone: (608)224-3880 Fax: (608)224-3833 E-mail: bajohnso@facstaff.wisc.edu • URL: http://www.ssc.wisc.edu/jhr • Quarterly. Individuals, $54.00 per year; institutions, $124.00 per year. Articles on manpower, health and welfare policies as they relate to the labor market and to economic and social development.

Journal of Hydraulic Research. International Association for Hydraulic Research, Rotterdamseweg 185 2629 HD Delft, Netherlands. Phone: 31 15 285 8557 E-mail: iahr@iahr.nl • URL: http://www.iahr.nl • Bimonthly. $340.00 per year. Text in English; summaries in English and French.

The Journal of Imaging Science and Technology. Society for Imaging Science and Technolgy, 7003 Kilworth Lane Springfield, VA 22151. Phone: (703)642-9090 Fax: (703)642-9094 E-mail: info@imaging.org • URL: http://www.imaging.org/ • Bimonthly. $135.00 per year. Formerly *Journal of Imaging Technology*.

Journal of Industrial Ecology. Yale University, School of Forestry and Environmental Studies. MIT Press, Five Cambridge Center Cambridge, MA 02142-1493. Phone: 800-356-0343 or (617)253-2864 Fax: (617)253-1545 E-mail: journals-orders@mit.edu • URL: http://www.mitpress.mit.edu • Quarterly. Individuals, $40.00 per year; institutions, $115.00 per year; students and retired persons, $30.00 per year. Contains multidisciplinary articles on the relationships between industrial activity and the environment.

Journal of Industrial Textiles. Technomic Publishing Co., Inc., 851 New Holland Ave. Lancaster, PA 17604. Phone: 800-233-9936 or (717)291-5609 Fax: (717)295-4538 E-mail: marketing@techpub.com • URL: http://www.techpub.com • Quarterly. $370.00 per year for print or electronic edition; $425.00 per year for print and electronic editions. Formerly *Journal of Coated Fabrics*.

Journal of Information Science: Principles and Practice. Institute of Information Scientists. Elsivier Science, 655 Ave. of the Americas New York, NY 10010. Phone: 888-437-4636 or (212)989-5800 Fax: (212)633-3680 E-mail: usinfo@elsevier.com • URL: http://www.elsevier.com • Bimonthly. $310.00 per year.

Journal of Insurance Regulation. National Association of Insurance Commissioners, 120 W. 12th St., Suite 1100 Kansas City, MO 64105-1925. Phone: (816)374-7529 Fax: (816)471-7004 URL: http://www.naic.com • Quarterly. $65.00 per year.

Journal of Interactive Marketing. Direct Marketing Educational Foundation. John Wiley and Sons, Inc., Journals Div., 605 Third Ave. New York, NY 10158-0012. Phone: 800-526-5368 or (212)850-6000 Fax: (212)850-6088 E-mail: info@wiley.com • URL: http://www.wiley.com • Quarterly. Institutions, $550.00 per year. Exchange of ideas in the field of direct marketing. Formerly *Journal of Direct Marketing*.

Journal of International Consumer Marketing. Haworth Press, Inc., 10 Alice St. Binghamton, NY 13904-1580. Phone: 800-429-6784 or (607)722-5857 Fax: 800-895-0582 or (607)722-1424 E-mail: getinfo@haworthpressinc.com • URL: http://www.haworthpressinc.com • Quarterly. Individuals, $60.00 per year; institutions, $90.00 per year; libraries, $300.00 per year.

Journal of International Food and Agribusiness Marketing. Haworth Press, Inc., 10 Alice St. Binghamton, NY 13904-1580. Phone: 800-429-6784 or (607)722-5857 Fax: 800-895-0582 or (607)722-1424 E-mail: getinfo@haworthpressinc.com • URL: http://www.haworthpressinc.com • Quarterly. Individuals, $60.00 per year; institutions, $75.00 per year; libraries, $175.00 per year.

Journal of International Marketing. American Marketing Association, 311 S. Wacker Dr., Suite 5800 Chicago, IL 60606-5819. Phone: 800-262-1150 or (312)542-9000 Fax: (312)542-9001 E-mail: info@ama.org • URL: http://www.ama.org/pubs/ • Members $45.00; non-members, $80.00 per year institutions, $150.00 per year.

Journal of International Taxation. Warren, Gorham & Lamont/RIA Group, 395 Hudson St. New York, NY 10014. Phone: 800-950-1215 or (212)367-6300 Fax: (212)924-0460 URL: http://www.wgl.com • Looseleaf service. $290.00 per year. Monthly updates. Edited for tax accountants and tax lawyers.

The Journal of International Trade and Economic Development. Routledge Journals, 29 W. 35th St. New York, NY 10001-2299. Phone: 800-634-7064 or (212)216-7800 Fax: 800-248-4724 or (212)564-7854 E-mail: journals@routledge.com • URL: http://www.routledge.com/routledge/ • Quarterly. Individuals, $68.00 per year; institutions, $445.00 per year. Emphasizes the effect of trade on the economies of developing nations.

Journal of Internet Cataloging: The International Quarterly of Digital Organization, Classification, and Access. Haworth Press, Inc., 10 Alice St. Binghamton, NY 13904-1580. Phone: 800-429-6784 or (607)722-5857 Fax: 800-895-0582 or (607)722-1424 E-mail: getinfo@haworthpressinc.com • URL: http://www.haworthpressinc.com • Quarterly. Individuals, $40.00 per year; libraries and other institutions, $85.00 per year.

Journal of Internet Law. Aspen Law and Business, 1185 Ave. of the Americas New York, NY 10036. Phone: 800-447-1717 or (212)597-0200 Fax: 800-901-9075 or (212)597-0334 E-mail: customer.service@aspenpubl.com • URL: http://www.aspenpub.com • Monthly. $295.00 per year. Covers such Internet and e-commerce topics as domain name disputes, copyright protection, Uniform Commercial Code issues, international law, privacy regulation, electronic records, digital signatures, liability, and security.

Journal of Investing. Institutional Investor, 488 Madison Ave. New York, NY 10022. Phone: (212)224-3300 Fax: (212)224-3527 E-mail: info@iijournals.com • URL: http://www.iijournals.com • Quarterly. $310.00 per year. Edited for professional investors. Topics include equities, fixed-income securities, derivatives, asset allocation, and other institutional investment subjects.

Journal of Lending and Credit Risk Management. Robert Morris Associates, One Liberty Place, Suite 2300, 1650 Market St. Philadelphia, PA 19103-7398. Phone: 800-677-7621 or (215)446-4000 Fax: (215)446-4100 E-mail: info@rmahq.org • URL: http://www.rmahq.org • 10 times a year. Members, $35.00 per year; non-members, $85.00 per year. Formerly *Journal of Commercial Bank Lending*.

Journal of Library Administration. Haworth Press, Inc., 10 Alice St. Binghamton, NY 13904-1580. Phone: 800-429-6784 or (607)722-2493 Fax: 800-895-0582 or (607)722-1424 E-mail: getinfo@haworthpressinc.com • URL: http://www.haworthpressinc.com • Quarterly. Individuals, $45.00 per year; libraries and other institutions, $125.00 per year. Two volumes. Supplement available *Monographic*. Demonstrates the application of theory to everyday problems faced by library administrators.

Journal of Low Temperature Physics. Plenum Publishing Corp., 233 Spring St. New York, NY 10013-1578. Phone: 800-221-9369 or (212)620-8000 Fax: (212)463-0742 E-mail: info@plenum.com • URL: http://www.plenum.com • Semimonthly. $1,350.00 per year. Covers the science of cryogenics.

Journal of Management Education. Organizational Behavior Teaching Society. Sage Publications, Inc., 2455 Teller Rd. Thousand Oaks, CA 91320. Phone: (805)499-0721 Fax: (805)499-0871 E-mail: info@sagepub.com • URL: http://www.sagepub.com • Quarterly. Individuals, $65.00 per year; institutions, $270.00 per year. A scholarly journal dealing with the teaching and training of business students and managers.

Journal of Management Information Systems. M. E. Sharpe, Inc., 80 Business Park Dr. Armonk, NY 10504. Phone: 800-541-6543 or (914)273-1800 Fax: (914)273-2106 E-mail: mesinfo@usa.net • URL: http://www.mesharpe.com • Quarterly. Individuals, $75.00 per year; institutions, $380.00 per year. Includes analysis, case studies, and current research.

Journal of Maritime Law and Commerce. Jefferson Law Book Co., 2100 Huntingdon Ave. Baltimore, MD 21211. Phone: (410)727-7300 Fax: (410)783-2448 E-mail: jefflawl@juno.com • URL: http://www.jmlc.org • Quarterly. $150.00 per year.

Journal of Marketing. American Marketing Association, 311 S. Wacker Dr., Suite 5800 Chicago, IL 60606-5819. Phone:

800-262-1150 or (312)542-9000 Fax: (312)542-9001 E-mail: info@ama.org • URL: http://www.ama.org/pubs • Quarterly. Members, $45.00; per year; non-members, $80.00 per year; institutions, $200.00 per year. Covers both marketing theory and marketing practice.

Journal of Marketing Channels: Distribution Systems, Strategy, and Management. Haworth Press, Inc., 10 Alice St. Binghamton, NY 13904-1580. Phone: 800-429-6784 or (607)722-5857 Fax: 800-895-0582 or (607)722-1424 E-mail: getinfo@haworthpressinc.com • URL: http://www.haworthpressinc.com • Quarterly. Individuals, $60.00 per year; institutions, $75.00 per year; libraries, 175.00 per year. Subject matter has to do with the management of product distribution systems.

Journal of Marketing for Higher Education. Haworth Press, Inc., 10 Alice St. Binghamton, NY 13904-1580. Phone: 800-429-6784 or (607)722-5857 Fax: 800-895-0582 or (607)722-1424 E-mail: getinfo@haworthpressinc.com • URL: http://www.haworthpressinc.com • Quarterly. Individuals, $60.00 per year; institutions, $120.00 per year; libraries, $225.00 per year.

Journal of Marketing Research. American Marketing Association, 311 S. Wacker Dr., Suite 5800 Chicago, IL 60606-5819. Phone: 800-262-1150 or (312)542-9000 Fax: (312)542-9001 E-mail: info@ama.org • URL: http://www.ama.org/ • Quarterly. Members, $45.00 per year; non-members, $80.00 per year; institutions, $200.00 per year. Provides analysis of marketing research theory and practice.

Journal of Materials Research. Materials Research Society, 506 Keystone Rd. Warrendale, PA 15086-7573. Phone: (724)779-3003 Fax: (724)779-8313 E-mail: info@mrs.org • URL: http://www.mrs.org • Monthly. Members, $80.00 per year; non-members, $750.00 per year. Covers the preparation, properties, and processing of advanced materials.

Journal of Mechanical Design. American Society of Mechanical Engineers, 22 Law Dr. Fairfield, NJ 07007-2900. Phone: 800-843-2763 or (973)882-1167 Fax: (973)882-1717 E-mail: infocentral@asme.org • URL: http://www.asme.org • Quarterly. Members, $40.00 per year; non-members, $215.00 per year. Formerly *Journal of Mechanisms, Transmissions and Automation in Design*.

Journal of Medical Practice Management. Williams and Wilkins, 351 W. Camden St. Baltimore, MD 21201-2436. Phone: 800-527-5597 or (410)528-4000 Fax: (410)528-4422 E-mail: custserv@wilkins.com • URL: http://www.wwilkins.com • Bimonthly. Individuals, $159.00 per year; institutions, $199.00 per year.

Journal of Mental Health Counseling. American Counseling Association, 5999 Stevenson Ave. Alexandria, VA 22304-3300. Phone: 800-347-6647 or (703)823-9800 Fax: (703)823-0252 URL: http://www.counseling.org • Quarterly.$131.00 per year. The official journal of the American Mental Health Counselors Association.

Journal of Microwave Power and Electromagnetic Energy. International Microwave Power Institute, 10210 Leatherleaf Court Manassas, VA 22111-4245. Phone: (703)257-1415 Quarterly. $195.00 per year. Formerly *Journal of Microwave Power*.

Journal of Money, Credit and Banking. Paul D. Evans, editor. Ohio State University Press, 1070 Carmack Rd. Columbus, OH 43210. Phone: (614)292-6930 Fax: (614)292-2065 E-mail: mcgrothers.1@osu.edu • URL: http://www.ohiostatepress.org • Quarterly. Individuals $48.00 per year; institutions, $135.00 per year. Reports major findings in the study of financial markets, monetary and fiscal policy credit markets, money and banking, portfolio management and related subjects.

Journal of Nonprofit and Public Sector Marketing. Haworth Press, Inc., 10 Alice St. Binghamton, NY 13904-1580. Phone: 800-429-6784 or (607)722-5857 Fax: 800-895-0582 or (607)722-1424 E-mail: getinfo@haworthpressinc.com • URL: http://www.haworthpressinc.com • Quarterly. Individuals, $60.00 per year; institutions, $120.00 per year; libraries, $225.00 per year. Subject matter has to do with the promotion or marketing of the services of nonprofit organizations and governmental agencies.

Journal of Nuclear Materials Management. Institute of Nuclear Materials Management, Inc., 60 Revere Dr., Suite 500 Northbrook, IL 60062-1563. Phone: (847)480-9573 Fax: (847)480-9282 Quarterly. $100.00 per year. Summaries in England Japanese.

Journal of Nutrition. American Institute of Nutrition, 9650 Rockville Pike Bethesda, MD 20814. Phone: (301)530-7050 Fax: (301)571-1892 E-mail: jnutri@uiuc.edu • URL: http://www.faseb.org • Monthly. Individuals, $105.00 per year; institutions, $295.00 per year; students, $30.00 per year.

Journal of Nutrition Education. Society for Nutrition Education. Decker, Inc., P.O. Box 620 Hamilton, ON, Canada L8N 3K 7. Phone: 800-568-7281 or (905)522-7017 Fax: (905)522-7839 E-mail: info@bcdecker.com • URL: http://www.bcdecker.com • Bimonthly. Individuals, $129.00 per year; institutions, $170.00 per year.

Journal of Nutritional Science and Vitaminology. Japanese Society of Nutrition and Food Science. Center for Academic Pulbications, 2-4 16 Yoyoi, Bunkyo-ku Tokyo 113 0032, Japan. E-mail: capj@crisscross.com • Bimonthly. $145.00 per year.

Journal of Occupational and Organizational Psychology. British Psychological Society, St. Andrews House, 48 Princess Rd. E. Leicester LE1 7DR, England. Phone: 44 116 254 9568 Fax: 44 116 247 0787 E-mail: journals@bpsorg.uk • URL: http://www.journals.eecs.qub.ac.uk • Quarterly. $230.00 per year. Formerly *Journal of Occupational Psychology*.

Journal of Organizational Behavior Management. Haworth Press, Inc., 10 Alice St. Binghamton, NY 13904-1580. Phone: 800-429-6784 or (607)722-5857 Fax: 800-895-0582 or (607)722-1424 E-mail: getinfo@haworthpressinc.com • URL: http://www.haworthpressinc.com • Semiannual. Individuals, $50.00 per year; institutions, $160.00 per year; libraries, $325.00 per year.

Journal of Pension Planning and Compliance. Panel Publishers, 1185 Ave. of the Americas New York, NY 10036. Phone: 800-447-1717 or (212)597-0200 Fax: 800-901-9075 or (212)597-0334 E-mail: customer.service@aspenpubl.com • URL: http://www.panelpublisher.com • Quarterly. $195.00 per year. Technical articles and regular columns on major issues confronting the pension community.

Journal of Petroleum Technology. Society of Petroleum Engineers, Inc., P.O.Box 833836 Richardson, TX 75083-3836. Phone: (972)952-9393 Fax: (972)952-9435 Monthly. Free to members; non-members, $45.00 per year. Covers oil and gas exploration, drilling and production, engineering management, resevoir engineering, geothermal energy sources and emerging technologies. Also includes society news, programs, events and activities. Supplement available *SPE Computer Applications*.

Journal of Pharmaceutical Marketing and Management. Haworth Press, Inc., 10 Alice St. Binghamton, NY 13904-1580. Phone: 800-429-6784 or (607)722-5857 Fax: 800-895-0582 or (607)722-1424 E-mail: getinfo@haworthpressinc.com • URL: http://www.haworthpressinc.com • Quarterly. Individuals, $60.00 per year; institutions, $90.00 per year; libraries, $275.00 per year.

Journal of Planning Literature. Ohio State University, Dept. of City and Regional Planning. Sage Publications, Inc., 2455 Teller Rd. Thousand Oaks, CA 91320. Phone: (805)499-0721 Fax: (805)499-0871 E-mail: info@sagepub.com • URL: http://www.sagepub.com • Quarterly. Individuals, $75.00 per year; institutions, $525.00 per year. Provides reviews and abstracts of city and regional planning lierature.

Journal of Portfolio Management: The Journal for Investment Professionals. Institutional Investor, 488 Madison Ave. New York, NY 10022. Phone: (212)224-3300 Fax: (212)224-3527 E-mail: info@iijournals.com • URL: http://www.iijournals.com • Quarterly. $370.00 per year. Edited for professional portfolio managers. Contains articles on investment practice, theory, and models.

Journal of Practical Estate Planning. CCH, Inc., 4025 W. Peterson Ave. Chicago, IL 60646-6085. Phone: 800-248-3248 or (773)866-6000 Fax: 800-224-8299 or (773)866-3608 URL: http://www.cch.com • Bimonthly. $195.00 per year. Edited for attorneys and other estate planning professionals.

Journal of Private Equity: Strategies and Techniques for Venture Investing. Institutional Investor, 488 Madison Ave. New York, NY 10022. Phone: (212)224-3300 Fax: (212)224-3527 E-mail: info@iijournals.com • URL: http://www.iijournals.com • Quarterly. $355.00 per year. Includes venture capital case histories, financial applications, foreign opportunities, industry analysis, management methods, etc.

Journal of Private Portfolio Management. Institutional Investor, 488 Madison Ave. New York, NY 10022. Phone: (212)224-3300 Fax: (212)224-3527 E-mail: info@iijournals.com • URL: http://www.iijournals.com • Quarterly. $280.00 per year. Edited for managers of wealthy individuals' investment portfolios.

Journal of Product Innovation Management: An International Publication of the Product Development and Management Association. Product Development and Management Association. Elsevier Science, 655 Ave. of the Americas New York, NY 10010. Phone: 888-437-4636 or (212)989-5800 Fax: (212)633-3680 E-mail: usinfo@elsevier.com • URL: http://www.elsevier.com • Bimonthly. $425.00 per year. Covers new product planning and development.

Journal of Project Finance. Institutional Investor, 488 Madison Ave. New York, NY 10022. Phone: (212)224-3300 Fax: (212)224-3527 E-mail: info@iijournals.com • URL: http://www.iijournals.com • Quarterly. $290.00 per year. Covers the financing of large-scale construction projects, such as power plants and convention centers.

Journal of Promotion Management: Innovations in Planning and Applied Research for Advertising, Sales Promotion, Personal Selling, Public Relations, and Re-Seller Support. Haworth Press, Inc., 10 Alice St. Binghamton, NY 13904-1580. Phone: 800-429-6784 or (607)722-5857 Fax: 800-895-0582 or (607)722-1424 E-mail: getinfo@haworthpressinc.com • URL: http://www.haworthpressinc.com • Semiannual. Individuals, $40.00 per year; institutions, $65.00 per year; libraries, $95.00 per year.

Journal of Property Management. Institute of Real Estate Management, 430 N. Michigan Ave. Chicago, IL 60611-9025. Phone: 800-837-0706 or (312)329-6058 Fax: (312)661-0217 E-mail: mevans@irem.org • URL: http://www.irem.org • Bimonthly. $43.95 per year.

Journal of Public Policy and Marketing. American Marketing Association, 311 S. Wacker Dr., Suite 5800 Chicago, IL 60606-5819. Phone: 800-262-1150 or (312)542-9000 Fax: (312)542-9001 E-mail: info@ama.com • URL: http://www.ama.org • Semiannual. Members, $50.00 per year; non-members, $70.00 per year; institutions, $100.00 per year. Devoted to the social and cultural impact of marketing activities.

Journal of Quality Technology. American Society for Quality, P.O. Box 3005 Milwaukee, WI 53201-3005. Phone: 800-248-1946 or (414)272-8575 Fax: (414)272-1734 E-mail: mhagen@asq.org • URL: http://www.asq.org • Quarterly. $30.00 per year.

Journal of Range Management: Covering the Study, Management, and Use of Rangeland Ecosystems and Range Resources. Society for Range Management, 1839 York St. Denver, CO 80206-1213. Phone: (303)355-7070 E-mail: srmden@ix.netcom.com • Bimonthly. $95.00 per year., with *Rangelands*, $140.00 per year. Technical articles oriented towards research in range science and management.

Journal of Real Estate Taxation. Warren, Gorham and Lamont/RIA Group, 395 Hudson St. New York, NY 10014. Phone: 800-950-1215 or (212)367-6300 Fax: (212)367-6718 E-mail: customer_service@riag.com • URL: http://www.riahome.com • Looseleaf service. $195.00 per year. Quarterly updates. Continuing coverage of the latest tax developments.

Journal of Relationship Marketing: Innovations for Service, Quality and Value. Haworth Press, Inc., 10 Alice St. Binghamton, NY 13904-1580. Phone: 800-429-6784 or (607)722-5857 Fax: 800-895-0582 or (607)722-1424 E-mail: getinfo@haworthpressinc.com • URL: http://www.haworthpressinc.com • Quarterly. Individuals, $50.00 per year; institutions, $75.00 per year; libraries, $200.00 per year.

Journal of Research in Pharmaceutical Economics. Haworth Press, Inc., 10 Alice St. Binghamton, NY 13904-1580. Phone: 800-429-6784 or (607)722-5857 Fax: 800-895-0582 or (607)722-1424 E-mail: getinfo@haworthpressinc.com • URL: http://www.haworthpressinc.com • Quarterly. Individuals, $60.00 per year; institutions, $120.00 per year; libraries, $275.00 per year.

Journal of Research of the National Institute of Standards and Technology. Available from U. S. Government Printing Office, Washington, DC 20402. Phone: (202)512-1800 Fax: (202)512-2250 E-mail: gpoaccess@gpo.gov • URL: http://www.access.gpo.gov • Bimonthly. $31.00 per year. Formerly *Journal of Research of the National Bureau of Standards*.

Journal of Restaurant and Foodservice Marketing. Haworth Press, Inc., 10 Alice St. Binghamton, NY 13904-1580. Phone: 800-429-6784 or (607)722-5857 Fax: 800-895-0582 or (607)722-1424 E-mail: getinfo@haworthpressinc.com • URL: http://www.haworthpressinc.com • Quarterly. Individuals, $50.00 per year; institutions, $60.00 per year; libraries, $75.00 per year.

Journal of Retailing. New York University, Stern School of Business. JAI Press, Inc., P.O. Box 811 Stamford, CT 06904-0811. Phone: (203)323-9606 Fax: (203)357-8446 E-mail: order@jaipress.com • URL: http://www.jaipress.com • Quarterly. $287.00 per year.

Journal of Retirement Planning. CCH, Inc., 4025 W. Peterson Ave. Chicago, IL 60646-6085. Phone: 800-248-3248 or (773)866-6000 Fax: 800-224-8299 or (773)866-3608 URL: http://www.cch.com • Bimonthly. $169.00 per year. Emphasis is on retirement and estate planning advice provided by lawyers and accountants as part of their practices.

Journal of Risk and Insurance. American Risk and Insurance Association, PO Box 3028 Malvern, PA 19355-0278. Phone: (610)640-1997 Fax: (610)725-1007 E-mail: aria@cpcuiia.org • URL: http://www.aria.org • Quarterly. $90.00 per year.

Journal of Risk Finance: The Convergence of Financial Products and Insurance. Institutional Investor, 488 Madison Ave. New York, NY 10022. Phone: (212)224-3185 Fax: (212)224-3527 E-mail: info@iijournals.com • URL: http://www.iijournals.com • Quarterly. $395.00 per year. Covers the field of customized risk management, including securitization, insurance, hedging, derivatives, and credit arbitrage.

Journal of Robotic Systems. John Wiley and Sons, Inc., Journals Div., 605 Third Ave. New York, NY 10158-0012. Phone: 800-225-5945 or (212)850-6000 Fax: (212)850-6088 E-mail: info@wiley.com • URL: http://www.wiley.com • Monthly. $1,920.00 per year. An international journal presenting high-level, scholarly discussions and case studies on automation, taskware design and implementation of robot systems. Text in English and Japanese; summaries in English and Japanese.

Journal of Safety Research. National Safety Council. Elsevier Science, 655 Ave. of the Americas New York, NY 10010. Phone: 888-437-4636 or (212)989-5800 Fax: (212)633-3680 E-mail: usinfo@elsevier.com • URL: http://www.elsevier.com • Quarterly. $564.00 per year.

Journal of Ship Research. Society of Naval Architects and Marine Engineers, 601 Pavonia Ave. Jersey City, NJ 07306-2907. Phone: (201)798-4800 Fax: (201)798-4975 E-mail: jhorowitz@sname.org • URL: http://www.sname.org • Quarterly. Individuals, $25.00 per year; institutions, $98.00 per year.

Journal of Small Business Management. West Virginia University Bureau of Business Research, P.O. Box 6025 Morgantown, WV 26506-6025. Phone: (304)293-7534 E-mail: jsbm@wvu.edu • URL: http://www.wvu.edu • Quarterly. Individuals, $65.00 per year; institutions, $110.00 per year. Articles and features on small business and entrepreneurship.

Journal of Social Welfare and Family Law. Routledge Journals, 29 W. 35th St. New York, NY 10001-2299. Phone: 800-634-7064 or (212)216-7800 Fax: (212)564-7854 E-mail: journals@routledge.com • URL: http://www.routledge.com/routledge/ • Quarterly. Individuals, $83.00 per year; institutions, $324.00 per year.

Journal of Software Maintenance and Evolution Research and Practice. Available from John Wiley and Sons, Inc., Journals Div., 605 Third Ave. New York, NY 10158-0012. Phone: 800-526-5368 or (212)850-6000 Fax: (212)850-6088 E-mail: info@wiley.com • URL: http://www.wiley.com • Bimonthly. Institutions, $1,145.00 per year. Published in England by John Wiley and Sons Ltd. Provides international coverage of subject matter.

Journal of Spacecraft and Rockets: Devoted to Astronautical Science and Technology. American Institute of Aeronautics and Astronautics, Inc., 1801 Alexander Bell Dr., Suite 500 Reston, VA 20191-4344. Phone: 800-639-2422 or (703)264-7500 Fax: (703)264-7551 E-mail: custserv@aiaa.org • URL: http://www.aiaa.org/publication • Bimonthly. Members, $45.00 per year; non-members, $165.00 per year; institutions, $330.00 per year.

Journal of Studies on Alcohol. Rutgers Center of Alcohol Studies. Alcohol Research Documentation, Inc., c/o Charles Rouse, Business Administration, 607 Allison Rd. Piscataway, NJ 08854-8001. Phone: (732)445-2190 Fax: (732)445-3500 Bimonthly. Individuals, $140.00 per year; institutions, $175.00 per year.

Journal of Supply Chain Management: A Global Review of Purchasing and Supply. National Association of Purchasing Management, PO Box 22160 Tempe, AZ 85285-9781. Phone: 800-888-6276 or (480)752-6276 Fax: (480)752-2299 URL: http://www.napm.org • Quarterly. $59.00 per year. Formerly *International Journal of Purchasing and Materials Management*.

Journal of Sustainable Agriculture: Innovations for the Long-Term and Lasting Maintenance and Enhancement of Agricultural Resources, Production and Environmental Quality. Haworth Press, Inc., 10 Alice St. Binghamton, NY 13904-1580. Phone: 800-429-6784 or (607)722-5857 Fax: 800-895-0582 or (607)722-1424 E-mail: getinfo@haworthpressinc.com • URL: http://www.haworthpressinc.com • Quarterly. Individuals, $50.00 per year; institutions, $75.00 per year; libraries, $185.00 per year. Two volumes. An academic and practical journal concerned with resource depletion and environmental misuse.

Journal of Sustainable Forestry. Haworth Press, Inc., 10 Alice St. Binghamton, NY 13904-1580. Phone: 800-429-6784 or (607)722-5857 Fax: 800-895-0582 or (607)722-1424 E-mail: getinfo@haworthpressinc.com • Quarterly. Individuals, $65.00 per year; institutions, $95.00 per year; libraries, $135.00 per year. Two volumes. An academic and practical journal. Topics include forest management, forest economics, and wood science.

Journal of Systems Integration: An International Journal. Kluwer Academic Publishers, 101 Philip Dr. Norwell, MA 02061. Phone: (781)871-6000 Fax: (781)871-6528 E-mail: kluwer@wkap.nl • URL: http://www.wkap.nl • Quarterly. $354.00 per year. Presents papers on systems integration research and applications. Online edition available.

Journal of Systems Management. Association for Systems Management, P.O. Box 38370 Cleveland, OH 44138. Phone: (216)243-6900 URL: http://www.singlesrc.com/asmp5.htm • Monthly. $60.00 per year.

Journal of Tax Practice and Procedure. CCH, Inc., 4025 W. Peterson Ave. Chicago, IL 60646-6085. Phone: 800-248-3248 or (773)866-6000 Fax: 800-224-8299 or (773)866-3608 URL: http://www.cch.com • Bimonthly. $195.00 per year. Covers the representation of taxpayers before the IRS, "from initial contact through litigation."

The Journal of Taxation: A National Journal of Current Developments, Analysis and Commentary for Tax Professionals. Warren, Gorham & Lamont/RIA Group, 395 Hudson St. New York, NY 10014. Phone: 800-950-1215 or (212)367-6300 Fax: (212)337-4280 E-mail: customer_services@riag.com • URL: http://www.riahome.com • Monthly. $215.00 per year. Analysis of current tax developments for tax specialists.

Journal of Taxation of Financial Products. CCH, Inc., 4025 West Peterson Ave. Chicago, IL 60646-6085. Phone: 800-248-3248 or (773)866-6000 Fax: 800-224-8299 or (773)866-3608 URL: http://www.cch.com • Bimonthly. $249.00 per year.

Journal of Teaching in International Business. Haworth Press, Inc., 10 Alice St. Binghamton, NY 13904-1580. Phone: 800-429-6784 or (607)722-5857 Fax: 800-895-0582 or (607)722-1424 E-mail: getinfo@haworthpressinc.com • URL: http://www.haworthpressinc.com • Quarterly. Individuals, $50.00 per year; institutions, $75.00 per year; libraries, $185.00 per year.

Journal of Technical Writing and Communication. Baywood Publishing Co., Inc., P.O. Box 337 Amityville, NY 11701. Phone: 800-638-7819 or (631)691-1270 Fax: (631)691-1770 E-mail: baywood@baywood.com • URL: http://www.literary.com/baywood • Quarterly. $170.00 per year.

Journal of Technology Transfer. Technology Transfer Society. Kluwer Academic Publishers, 101 Philip Dr. Norwell, MA 02061. Phone: (781)871-6600 Fax: (781)871-6528 E-mail: kluwe@wkap.nl • URL: http://www.wkap.nl • Three times a year. $292.50 per year. Topics include technology transfer ventures, models, mechanisms, and case studies.

Journal of the American Society for Information Science. John Wiley and Sons, Inc., Journals Div., 605 Third Ave. New York, NY 10158-0012. Phone: 800-526-5368 or (212)850-6000 Fax: (212)850-6088 E-mail: info@wiley.com • URL: http://www.wiley.com • Bimonthly. $456.00 per year.

Journal of the Asia Pacific Economy. Routledge Journals, 29 W. 35th St. New York, NY 10001-2299. Phone: 800-634-7064 or (212)216-7800 Fax: (212)564-7854 E-mail: journals@routledge.com • URL: http://www.routledge.com/routledge/ • Three times a year. Individuals, $64.00 per year; institutions, $292.00 per year. Covers economic, political, social, cultural, and historical factors affecting Asian commerce and trade.

Journal of the Atmospheric Sciences. American Meteorological Society, 45 Beacon St. Boston, MA 02108-3693. Phone: (617)227-2425 Fax: (617)742-8718 E-mail: amspubs@ametsoc.org/ams • URL: http://www.ametsoc.org/ams • Semimonthly. $495.00 per year.

Journal of the Coin Laundry and Drycleaning Industry. Coin Laundry Association, 1315 Butterfield Rd., Suite 212 Downers Grove, IL 60515. Phone: (630)963-5547 Fax: (630)963-5864 E-mail: info@coinlaundry.org • URL: http://www.coinlaundry.org • Monthly. $24.00 per year. Edited for owners and operators of coinoperated laundries.

Journal of Thermal Enevelope and Building Science. Technomic Publishing Co., Inc., 851 New Holland Ave. Lancaster, PA 17604. Phone: 800-233-9936 or (717)291-5609 Fax: (717)295-4538 E-mail: marketing@techpub.com • URL: http://www.techpub.com • Quarterly. $465.00 per year. Formerly *Journal of Thermal Insulation and Building Envelopes*.

Journal of Traffic Safety Education. California Association for Safety Education, 5151 State University Dr. Los Angeles, CA 90032. Phone: (213)343-4622 Quarterly. $8.00 per year.

Journal of Transnational Management Development: The Official Publication of the International Management Development Association. International Management Development Association. Haworth Press, Inc., 10 Alice St. Binghamton, NY 13904-1580. Phone: 800-429-6784 or (607)722-5857 Fax: 800-895-0582 or (607)722-1424 E-mail: getinfo@haworthpressinc.com • URL: http://www.haworthpressinc.com • Quarterly. Individuals, $50.00 per year; institutions, $80.00 per year; libraries, $225.00 per year.

Journal of Transport Economics and Policy. University of Bath, Claverton Down Bath BA2 7AY, England. Phone: 44 1225 826302 Fax: 44 1225 826767 E-mail: mnskam@bath.ac.uk • Three times a year. Individuals, $54.00 per year; institutions, $120.00 per year; students, $20.00 per year. Text in English, French, German and Spanish.

Journal of Travel and Tourism Marketing. Haworth Press, Inc., 10 Alice St. Binghamton, NY 13904-1580. Phone: 800-429-6784 or (607)722-5857 Fax: 800-895-0582 or (607)722-1424 E-mail: getinfo@haworthpressinc.com • URL: http://www.haworthpressinc.com • Quarterly. Individuals, $45.00 per year; institutions, $95.00 per year; libraries, $175.00 per year.

Journal of Travel Research. University of Colorado, Business Research Div. Sage Publications, Inc., 2455 Teller Rd. Thousand Oaks, CA 91320. Phone: (805)499-0721 Fax: (805)499-0871 E-mail: info@sagepub.com • Quarterly. Individuals, $150.00 per year; institutions, $195.00 per year. Includes *Travel Research Bookshelf* which abstracts current literature in the field.

Journal of Tree Fruit Production. Haworth Press, Inc., 10 Alice St. Binghamton, NY 13904-1580. Phone: 800-429-6784 or (607)722-5857 Fax: 800-895-0582 or (607)722-1424 E-mail: getinfo@haworthpressinc.com • URL: http://www.haworthpressinc.com • Semiannual. Individuals, $45.00 per year; institutions, $75.00 per year; libraries, $85.00 per year. A research journal for tree fruit growers.

Journal of Tribology. American Society of Mechanical Engineers, 22 Law Dr. Fairfield, NJ 00007-2900. Phone: 800-843-2763 or (973)882-1167 Fax: (973)882-1717 E-mail: infocentral@asme.org • URL: http://www.asme.org • Quarterly. Members, $40.00 per year; non-members, $255.00 per year. Details lubrication and lubricants.

Journal of Turbomachinery. American Society of Mechanical Engineers, 22 Law Dr. Fairfield, NJ 07007-2900. Phone: 800-843-2763 or (973)882-1167 Fax: (973)882-1717 E-mail: infocentral@asme.org • URL: http://www.asme.org • Quarterly. Members, $40.00 per year; non-members, $215.00 per year. Series A of the *Transactions of the ASME*. Formerly *Journal of Gas Turbines*.

Journal of Turfgrass Management: Developments in Basic and Applied Turfgrass Research. Haworth Press, Inc., 10 Alice St. Binghamton, NY 13904-1580. Phone: 800-429-6784 or (607)722-5857 Fax: 800-895-0582 or (607)722-1424 E-mail: getinfo@haworthpressinc.com • URL: http://www.haworthpressinc.com • Quarterly. Individuals, $45.00 per year; institutions, $65.00 per year; libraries, $75.00 per year. An applied research journal.

Journal of Vegetable Crop Production. Haworth Press, Inc., 10 Alice St. Binghamton, NY 13904-1580. Phone: 800-429-6784 or (607)722-5857 Fax: 800-895-0582 or (607)722-1424 E-mail: getinfo@haworthpressinc.com • URL: http://www.haworthpressinc.com • Semiannual. Individuals, $50.00 per year; institutions, $85.00 per year; libraries, $125.00 per year. Covers the production and marketing of vegetables.

The Journal of Visualization and Computer Animation. Available from John Wiley and Sons, Inc., Journals Div., 605 Third Ave. New York, NY 10158-0012. Phone: 800-526-5368 or (212)850-6000 Fax: (212)850-6088 E-mail: info@wiley.com • URL: http://www.wiley.com • Quarterly. Institutions, $760.00 per year. Research papers on the technological developments (both hardware and software) that will make animation tools more accessible to end-users. International coverage. Published in England by John Wiley and Sons Ltd.

Journal of Workers Compensation. John Liner Organization. Standard Publishing Corp., 155 Federal St. Boston, MA 02110. Phone: 800-682-5759 or (617)457-0600 Fax: (617)457-0608 E-mail: stnd@earthlink.net • URL: http://www.standard-pub.com • Quarterly. $130.00 per year. Compensation topics include legal considerations, cost control, worker coverage, appropriate medical treatment, and managed care.

Journal of World Business. Columbia University, Trustees of Columbia University. JAI Press, Inc., P.O. Box 811 Stamford, CT 06904-0811. Phone: (203)323-9606 Fax: (203)357-8446 E-mail: order@jaipress.com • URL: http://www.jaipress.com • Quarterly. $258.00 per year.

Journal of World Trade. Kluwer Law International, 675 Massachusetts Ave. Cambridge, MA 02139. Phone: (617)354-0140 Fax: (617)654-8595 E-mail: kluwer@wkap.nl • URL: http://www.wkap.nl • Bimonthly. $609.60 per year. Includes online edition. Formerly *Journal of World Trade Law*.

Journal Suisse d'Horlogerie et de Bijouterie Internationale. Editions Scriptar S.A., 25 Chemin du Creux-de-Corsy CH-1093 41 La Conversion-Lausanne, Switzerland. Phone: 41 21 7960096 Fax: 41 21 7914084 E-mail: info@jsh.ch • URL: http://www.jsh.ch • Six times a year. $95.00. Text in English, French and German. Formery J S H- Journal Suisse d'Horlogerie e+ de Bijouterie Internationale.

Journalism and Mass Communication Directory. Association for Education in Journalism and Mass Communication, 234 Outlet Pointe Blvd., Suite A Columbia, SC 29210-5667. Phone: (803)798-0271 Fax: (803)772-3509 Annual $25.00. Schools and departments of journalism and mass communication.

Journalism and Mass Communication Quarterly: Devoted to Research and Commentary in Journalism and Mass Communication. Association for Education in Journalism and Mass Communication, 234 Outlet Pointe Blvd., Suite A Columbia, SC 29210-5667. Phone: (803)798-0271 Fax: (803)772-3509 Quarterly. Individuals, $50.00 per year; institutions, $70.00 per year. Formerly *Journalism Quarterly*.

Journalist's Road to Success: Career and Scholarship Guide. Dow Jones Newspaper Fund, Inc., P.O. Box 300 Princeton, NJ 08543-0300. Phone: 800-369-3863 or (609)452-2820 Fax: (609)520-5804 E-mail: newsfund@wsj.dowjones.com • URL: http://www.dowjones.com/newsfund • Annual. Price on application. Lists more than 400 colleges and universities offering journalism/mass communications; general journalism career information; section of minority scholarships and special training programs; section on fellowships for continuing education. Formerly *Journalism Career and Scholarship Guide*.

Judges' Journal. American Bar Association, Judicial Administration Div., 750 N. Lake Shore Dr. Chicago, IL

60611-4497. Phone: 800-285-2221 or (312)988-5000 Fax: (312)988-5528 E-mail: abajournal@abanet.org • URL: http://www.abanet.org. • Quarterly. Free to members; non-members, $25.00 per year. Focuses on the court.

Judgment in Managerial Decision Making. May H. Bazerman. John Wiley and Sons, Inc., 605 Third Ave. New York, NY 10158-0012. Phone: 800-526-5368 or (212)850-6000 Fax: (212)850-6088 E-mail: info@wiley.com • URL: http://www.wiley.com • 1997. $40.95. Fourth edition.

Judicature. American Judicature Society, 180 N. Michigan Ave., Suite 600 Chicago, IL 60601-7401. Phone: (312)558-6900 URL: http://www.ajs.org • Bimonthly. $66.00 per year.

Judicial Staff Directory: With Biographical Information on Judges and Key Court Staff. CQ Staff Directories, Inc., 815 Slaters Lane Alexandria, VA 22314. Phone: 800-252-1722 or (703)739-0900 Fax: (703)739-0234 E-mail: staffdir@staffdirectories.com • URL: http://www.staffdirectories.com • Annual. $89.00 per no. Lists 16,000 federal court personnel, including 1,300 federal judges and their staffs, with biographies of judges and key executives. Includes maps of court jurisdictions.

Judicial Yellow Book: Who's Who in Federal and State Courts. Leadership Directories, Inc., 104 Fifth Ave., 2nd Fl. New York, NY 10011. Phone: (212)627-4140 Fax: (212)645-0931 E-mail: info@leadershipdirectories.com • URL: http://www.leadershipdirectories.com • Semiannual. $235.00 per year. Lists more than 3,200 judges and staffs in various federal courts and 1,200 judges and staffs in state courts. Includes biographical profiles of judges.

Jumbo Rate News. Bauer Financial Newsletters, Inc., Drawer 145510 Coral Gables, FL 33114-5510. Phone: 800-388-6686 or (305)445-9500 Fax: 800-230-9569 or (305)445-6775 URL: http://jumboratenews.com • Weekly. $445.00 per year. Newsletter. Lists more than 1,100 of the highest interest rates available for ''jumbo'' certificates of deposit ($100,000 or more).

Junk Bonds: How High Yield Securities Restructured Corporate America. Glenn Yago. Oxford University Press, Inc., 198 Madison Ave. New York, NY 10016-4314. Phone: 800-451-7556 or (212)726-6000 Fax: (212)726-6446 E-mail: custserv@oup-usa.org • URL: http://www.oup-press.org • 1990. $25.00.

Juran's Quality Control Handbook. Joseph M. Juran and Blandfor Godfrey, editors. McGraw-Hill, 1221 Ave. of the Americas New York, NY 10020. Phone: 800-722-4726 or (212)904-2000 Fax: (212)904-2072 E-mail: customer.service@mcgraw-hill.com • URL: http://www.mcgraw-hill.com • 1999. $150.00. Fifth edition.

Jury Manual: A Guide for Prospective Jurors. William R. Pabst. Metro Publishing, P. O. Box 270776 Houston, TX 77277. Phone: (713)666-7841 1985. $19.95.

Just in Case; A Passenger's Guide to Airplane Safety and Survival. Daniel A. Johnson. Perseus Publishing, 11 Cambridge Center Cambridge, MA 02142. Phone: (617)252-5200 Fax: (617)252-5285 E-mail: westview.orders@perseusbooks.com • URL: http://www.perseusbooks.com • 1984. $19.95.

Jute and Jute Fabrics-Bangladesh. Bangladesh Jute Research Institute, Sher-e-Banglanagar Dhaka 7, Bangladesh. Monthly. $5.00 per year. Text in English.

Jute Carpet Backing Council and Burlap and Jute Association.

Juvenile Merchandising - Directory and Buyers Guide. E.W. Williams Publications Co., 2125 Center Ave., Suite 305 Fort Lee, NJ 07024. Phone: (201)532-9290 Fax: (201)779-8345 Annual. $15.00. Manufacturers, suppliers, and distributors of products for juveniles, including furniture, bedding, pre-school toys, etc.; trade associations.

Kagan Media Index. Paul Kagan Associates, Inc., 126 Clock Tower Place Carmel, CA 93923. Phone: (831)624-1536 Fax: (831)625-3225 E-mail: info@kagan.com • Monthly. $675.00 per year. Provides electronic and entertainment media industry statistics. Includes television, radio, motion pictures, and home video.

Kane's Beverage Week: The Newsletter of Beverage Marketing. Whitaker Newsletters, Inc., P.O. Box 192 Fanwood, NJ 07023. Phone: (908)889-6336 Fax: (908)889-6339 Weekly. $449.00 per year. Newsletter. Covers news relating to the alcoholic beverage industries, including social, health, and legal issues.

Kansas Agricultural Experiment Station - Performance Test Program. Kansas State University

Kansas Farmer. Farm Progress Cos., 191 S. Gary Ave. Carol Stream, IL 60188. Phone: (630)690-5600 Fax: (630)462-2869 15 times a year. $19.95 per year.

Katharine Gibbs Handbook of Business English. Pearson Education and Technology, 201 W. 103rd St. Indianapolis, IN 46290-1097. Phone: 800-858-7674 or (317)581-3500 URL: http://www.mcp.com • 1987. $5.95.

Kauai Agricultural Station. University of Hawaii at Manoa

Keeping Customers for Life. Joan K. Cannie and Donald Caplin. AMACOM, 1601 Broadway, 12th Fl. New York, NY 10019. Phone: 800-262-9699 or (212)586-8100 Fax: (212)903-8168 E-mail: custmserv@amanet.org • URL: http://www.amanet.org • 1990. $14.95. A guide to keeping customers satisfied by providing quality service.

Keeping Customers Happy: Strategies for Success. Jacqueline Dunckel. Self-Counsel Press, Inc., 1704 N. State St. Bellingham, WA 98225. Phone: 877-877-6490 or (360)676-4530 Fax: (360)676-4530 E-mail: service@self-counsel.com • URL: http://www.self-counsel.com • 1994. $9.95. Third edition.

Keeping the Books: Basic Recordkeeping and Accounting for the Successful Small Business. Linda Pinson. Dearborn Financial Publishing, 155 North Wacker Drive Chicago, IL 60606-1719. Phone: 800-245-2665 or (312)836-4400 Fax: (312)836-9958 URL: http://www.dearborn.com • 2000. $22.95. Fifth edition. Covers bookkeeping systems, financial statements, and IRS tax record requirements. Includes illustrations, worksheets, and forms.

Keesing's Record of World Events. Keesing's Worldwide,LLC, P.O. Box 5590 Washington, DC 20016-1190. Phone: (301)718-8770 Fax: (301)718-8494 E-mail: info@kessings.com • URL: http://www.kessings.com • Monthly. $357.00 per year.

Kelly's Directory. Reed Business Information, Windsor Court, East Grinstead House, East Grinstead W. Sussex RH19 1XA, England. Phone: 01342 326972 Fax: 01342 335747 URL: http://www.kellys.co.uk • Annual. $400.00. Lists approximately 77,000 manufacturers and merchants. Formerly *Kelly's Business Directory*.

Kennedy's Directory of Executive Temporary Placement Firms. Kennedy Information, LLC, One Kennedy Place, Route 12, S. Fitzwilliam, NH 03447. Phone: 800-531-1026 or (603)585-3101 Fax: (603)585-9555 E-mail: office@kennedypub.com • URL: http://www.intertec.com • 1995. $24.95. Eighth revised edition. Provides information on about 225 executive search firms that have temporary placement as a specialty.

Kennedy's Pocket Guide to Working with Executive Recruiters. James H. Kennedy, editor. Kennedy Information, LLC, One Kennedy Place, Route 12, S. Fitzwilliam, NH 03447. Phone: 800-531-1026 or (603)585-3101 Fax: (603)585-9555 E-mail: office@kennedypub.com • URL: http://www.kennedy.com • 1996. $9.95. Second revised editon. Consists of 30 chapters written by various experts. Includes a glossary: ''Lexicon of Executive Recruiting.''

Key Abstracts: Advanced Materials. Available from INSPEC, Inc., 379 Thornall St. Edison, NJ 08337-2225. Phone: (732)321-5575 Fax: (732)321-5702 E-mail: inspec@iee.org • URL: http://www.iee.org • Monthly. $240.00 per year. Provides international coverage of journal and proceedings literature, including publications on ceramics and composite materials. Published in England by the Institution of Electrical Engineers (IEE).

Key Abstracts: Artificial Intelligence. Available from INSPEC, Inc., 379 Thornall St. Edison, NJ 08337. Phone: (732)321-5575 Fax: (732)321-5702 E-mail: inspec@iee.org • URL: http://www.iee.org • Monthly. $240.00 per year. Provides international coverage of journal and proceedings literature, including material on expert systems and knowledge engineering. Published in England by the Institution of Electrical Engineers (IEE).

Key Abstracts: Business Automation. Available from INSPEC, Inc., 379 Thornall St. Edison, NJ 08337. Phone: (732)321-5575 Fax: (732)321-5702 E-mail: inspec@iee.org • URL: http://www.iee.org • Monthly. $240.00 per year. Provides international coverage of journal and proceedings literature. Published in England by the Institution of Electrical Engineers (IEE).

Key Abstracts: Computer Communications and Storage. Available from INSPEC, Inc., 379 Thornall St. Edison, NJ 08337. Phone: (732)321-5575 Fax: (732)321-5702 E-mail: inspec@iee.org • URL: http://www.iee.org • Monthly. $240.00 per year. Provides international coverage of journal and proceedings literature, including material on optical disks and networks. Published in England by the Institution of Electrical Engineers (IEE).

Key Abstracts: Computing in Electronics and Power. Available from INSPEC, Inc., 379 Thornall St. Edison, NJ 08357-2225. Phone: (732)321-5575 Fax: (732)321-5702 E-mail: inspec@iee.org • URL: http://www.iee.org • Monthly. $240.00 per year. Provides international coverage of journal and proceedings literature. Published in England by the Institution of Electrical Engineers (IEE).

Key Abstracts: Electronic Circuits. INSPEC, Inc., 379 Thornall St. Edison, NJ 08857-2225. Phone: (732)321-5575 Fax: (732)321-5702 Monthly. $240.00 per year. Provides international coverage of journal and proceedings literature. Published in England by the Institution of Electrical Engineers (IEE).

Key Abstracts: Electronic Instrumentation. Available from INSPEC, Inc., 379 Thornall St. Edison, NJ 08857-2225. Phone: (732)321-5575 Fax: (732)321-5702 E-mail: inspec@iee.org • URL: http://www.iee.org • Monthly. $240.00 per year. Provides international coverage of journal and proceedings literature. Published in England by the Institution of Electrical Engineers (IEE).

Key Abstracts: Factory Automation. Available from INSPEC, Inc., 379 Thornall St. Edison, NJ 08857-2225. Phone: (732)321-5572 Fax: (732)321-5702 E-mail: inspec@iee.org • URL: http://www.iee.org • Monthly. $240.00 per year. Provides international coverage of journal and proceedings literature, including publications on CAD/CAM, materials handling, robotics, and factory management. Published in England by the Institution of Electrical Engineers (IEE).

Key Abstracts: High Temperature Superconductors. Available from INSPEC, Inc., 379 Thornall St. Edison, NJ 08857-2225. Phone: (732)321-5575 Fax: (732)321-5702 E-mail: inspec@iee.org • URL: http://www.iee.org • Monthly. $240.00 per year. Provides international coverage of journal and proceedings literature. Published in England by the Institution of Electrical Engineers (IEE).

Key Abstracts: Machine Vision. Available from INSPEC, Inc., 379 Thornall St. Edison, NJ 08857-2225. Phone: (732)321-5575 Fax: (732)321-5702 E-mail: inspec@iee.org • URL: http://www.iee.org • Monthly. $240.00 per year. Provides international coverage of journal and proceedings literature on optical noncontact sensing. Published in England by the Institution of Electrical Engineers (IEE).

Key Abstracts: Microwave Technology. Available from INSPEC, Inc., 379 Thornall St. Edison, NJ 08857-2225. Phone: (732)321-5575 Fax: (732)321-5702 E-mail: inspec@iee.org • URL: http://www.iee.org • Monthly. $240.00 per year. Provides international coverage of journal and proceedings literature. Published in England by the Institution of Electrical Engineers (IEE).

Key Abstracts: Optoelectronics. Available from INSPEC, Inc., 379 Thornall St. Edison, NJ 08857-2225. Phone: (732)321-5575 Fax: (732)321-5702 E-mail: inspec@iee.org • URL: http://www.iee.erg • Monthly. $240.00 per year. Provides international coverage of journal and proceedings literature relating to fiber optics, lasers, and optoelectronics in general. Published in England by the Institution of Electrical Engineers (IEE).

Key Abstracts: Power Systems and Applications. Available from INSPEC, Inc., 379 Thornall St. Edison, NJ 08857-2225. Phone: (732)321-5575 Fax: (732)321-5702 E-mail: inspec@iee.org • URL: http://www.iee.org • Monthly. $240.00 per year. Provides international coverage of journal and proceedings literature, including publications on electric power apparatus and machines. Published in England by the Institution of Electrical Engineers (IEE).

Key Abstracts: Robotics and Control. Available from INSPEC, Inc., 379 Thornall St. Edison, NJ 08857-2225. Phone: (732)321-5575 Fax: (732)321-5702 E-mail: inspec@iee.org • URL: http://www.iee.org • Monthly. $240.00 per year. Provides international coverage of journal and proceedings literature. Published in England by the Institution of Electrical Engineers (IEE).

Key Abstracts: Semiconductor Devices. Available from INSPEC, Inc., 379 Thornall St. Edison, NJ 08857-2225. Phone: (732)321-5575 Fax: (732)321-5702 E-mail: inspec@iee.org • URL: http://www.iee.org • Monthly. $240.00 per year. Provides international coverage of journal and proceedings literature. Published in England by the Institution of Electrical Engineers (IEE).

Key Abstracts: Software Engineering. Available from INSPEC, Inc., 379 Thornall St. Edison, NJ 08857-2225. Phone: (732)321-5575 Fax: (732)321-5702 E-mail: inspec@iee.org • URL: http://www.iee.org • Monthly. $240.00 per year. Provides international coverage of journal and proceedings literature. Published in England by the Institution of Electrical Engineers (IEE).

Key Abstracts: Telecommunications. Available from INSPEC, Inc., 379 Thornall St. Edison, NJ 08857-2225. Phone: (732)321-5575 Fax: (732)321-5702 E-mail: inspec@iee.org • URL: http://www.iee.org • Monthly. $240.00 per year. Provides international coverage of journal and proceedings literature. Published in England by the Institution of Electrical Engineers (IEE).

Key European Executive Search Firms and Their U. S. Links. Kennedy Information, LLC, One Kennedy Place, Route 12, S. Fitzwilliam, NH 03447. Phone: 800-531-1026 or (603)585-3101 Fax: (603)585-9555 E-mail: office@kennedypub.com • URL: http://www.kennedyinfo.com • 1995. Price on application. Includes 440 search offices in Europe and the U. S.

Key Note Market Report: Home Shopping. Jupiter Media Metrix, 21 Astor Place New York, NY 10003. Phone: 800-488-4345 or (212)780-6060 Fax: (212)780-6075 E-mail: jupiter@jup.com • URL: http://www.jmm.com • Irregular. $365.00. Market research report. Covers ''interactive retailing,'' mainly through the Internet and television, with predictions of future trends. Formerly *Key Note Report: Home Shopping*.

Key Women in Retained Executive Search. Kennedy Information, LLC, One Kennedy Place, Route 12, S. Fitzwilliam, NH 03447. Phone: 800-531-1026 or (603)585-3101 Fax: (603)585-9555 E-mail: office@kennedypub.com • URL: http://www.kennedyinfo.com • 1994. Price on application. Lists about 600 women executives in 300 search firms in North America. Arranged by name of firm, with an index to names of individuals.

Keyboard: Making Music with Technology. United Entertainment Media, Inc., 460 Park Ave. South New York, NY

10016-7315. Phone: (212)378-0400 Fax: (212)378-2160 E-mail: keyboard@uemedia.com • URL: http://www.keyboardmag.com • Monthly. $36.00 per year. Emphasis is on recording systems, keyboard technique, and computer-assisted music (MIDI) systems.

Keynotes. Associated Locksmiths of America, Inc., 3003 Live Oak St. Dallas, TX 75204. Phone: (214)827-1701 Fax: (214)827-1810 Monthly. Membership.

Keystone Center., 1628 Saints John Rd. Keystone, CO 80435-7998. Phone: (970)513-5800 Fax: (970)262-0152 URL: http://www.keystone.org • Research areas include product liability.

Keystone Coal Industry Manual. Intertec Publishing Corp., 29 N. Wacker Dr. Chicago, IL 60606-3298. Phone: 800-400-5945 or (913)341-1300 Fax: (913)967-1898 E-mail: subs@intertec.com • URL: http://www.intertec.com • Annual. $275.00.

The Keywords. American Society of Indexers, 11250 Roger Bacon Dr., Suite 8 Reston, VA 20190-5602. Phone: (703)234-4149 Fax: (703)735-4390 E-mail: info@asindexing.org • URL: http://www.asindexing.org • Six times a year. Free to members; non-members, $40.00 per year. Formerly *American Society of Indexes Newsletter*.

KidTrends Newsletter. Available from MarketResearch.com, 641 Ave. of the Americas, Third Floor New York, NY 10011. Phone: 800-298-5699 or (212)807-2629 Fax: (212)807-2716 E-mail: order@marketresearch.com • URL: http://www.marketresearch.com • Monthly. $199.00 per year. Published by Children's Market Research, Inc. Market data newsletter.

KidTrends Report: Trends, Buying Patterns, and Lifestyles. Available from MarketResearch.com, 641 Ave. of the Americas, Third Floor New York, NY 10011. Phone: 800-298-5699 or (212)807-2629 Fax: (212)807-2716 E-mail: order@marketresearch.com • URL: http://www.marketresearch.com • 1998. $2595.00 Market research report published by Children's Market Research, Inc. Covers computer software, video games, music, books, electronic equipment, and toys for children and pre-teens.

Kika de la Garza Subtropical Agricultural Research Center.

Kimball Letter. Kimball Associates, 4640 Rummel Rd. St. Cloud, FL 34771-9696. Phone: (407)892-8555 Biweekly. $60.00 per year. Provides information on large trader positions in commodity futures.

Kiplinger Agriculture Letter. Kiplinger Washington Editors, Inc., 1729 H St., N.W. Washington, DC 20006. Phone: 800-544-1055 or (202)887-6400 Fax: (202)778-8976 URL: http://www.kiplinger.com • Biweekly. $56.00 per year. Newsletter.

Kiplinger Tax Letter. Kiplinger Washington Editors, Inc., 1729 H St., N.W. Washington, DC 20006. Phone: 800-544-1055 or (202)887-6400 Fax: (202)223-8990 E-mail: feedback@kiplinger.com • URL: http://www.kiplinger.com/newsletter/tax.html • Biweekly. $59.00 per year.

Kiplinger Washington Letter. Kiplinger Washington Editors, Inc., 1729 H St., N.W. Washington, DC 20006. Phone: (202)887-6400 Fax: (202)331-1206 E-mail: letterresponse@kiplinger.com • URL: http://www.kiplinger.com • Weekly. $76.00 per year.

Kiplinger's Personal Finance Magazine. Kiplinger Washington Editors, Inc., 1729 H St., N.W. Washington, DC 20006. Phone: (202)887-6400 Fax: (202)331-1206 E-mail: magazine@kiplinger.com • URL: http://www.kiplinger.com/ • Monthly. $23.95 per year. Formerly *Changing Times*.

Kiplinger's Retirement Report. Kiplinger Washington Editors, Inc., 1729 H St., N. W. Washington, DC 20006. Phone: 800-544-1055 or (202)887-6400 Fax: (202)331-1206 E-mail: feedback@kiplinger.com • URL: http://www.kiplinger.com/ • Bimonthly. $29.95 per year. Newsletter on various aspects of retirement, including finances, health, and leisure.

Kirk-Othmer Encyclopedia of Chemical Technology. John Wiley and Sons, Inc., 605 Third Ave. New York, NY 10158-0012. Phone: 800-526-5368 or (212)850-6000 Fax: (212)850-6088 E-mail: info@wiley.com • URL: http://www.wiley.com • 1991-97. $7,350.00, prepaid. 21 volumes. Fourth edition. Four volumes are scheduled to be published each year, with individual volumes available at $350.00.

Kiss Your Stockbroker Goodbye: A Guide to Independent Investing. John G. Wells. St. Martin's Press, 175 Fifth Ave. New York, NY 10010. Phone: 800-221-7945 or (212)674-5151 Fax: 800-672-2054 or (212)529-0594 URL: http://www.stmartins.com • 1997. $25.95. The author believes that the small investor is throwing money away by using full-commission brokers when discount brokers and many sources of information are easily available. Contains separate chapters on stocks, bonds, mutual funds, asset allocation, financial planners, and related topics. Wells is a securities analyst (CFA) and portfolio manager.

Kitchen and Bath Business. Miller Freeman, Inc., One Penn Plaza New York, NY 10119. Phone: 800-227-4675 or (212)714-1300 Fax: (212)279-3960 E-mail: mfibooks@mfi.com • URL: http://www.mfi.com • Monthly. $70.00 per year.

Kitchen and Bath Business Buyers' Guide. Miller Freeman, Inc., One Penn Plaza New York, NY 10119. Phone: (212)714-1300 Fax: (212)279-3955 E-mail: mfibooks@mfi.com • URL: http://www.kitchen-bath.com • Annual. $7.00. Guide to kitchen and bath products, supplies and services. Formerly *Kitchen and Bath Business and Buyers' Guide/Almanac*.

Kitchen Cabinet Manufacturers Association.

Kitchen Cabinet Manufacturers Association Income and Expense Study. Kitchen Cabinet Manufacturers Association, 1899 Preston White Dr. Reston, VA 22091-4326. Phone: (703)264-1690 Fax: (703)620-6530 Annual. Membership. Formerly National Kitchen Cabinet Association.

Kitchen Cabinets and Countertops. Available from MarketResearch.com, 641 Ave. of the Americas, Third Floor New York, NY 10011. Phone: 800-298-5699 or (212)807-2629 Fax: (212)807-2716 E-mail: order@marketresearch.com • URL: http://www.marketresearch.com • 1999. $2,250.00. Market research report published by Specialists in Business Information. Covers both custom and stock cabinets. Presents market data relative to demographics, sales growth, shipments, exports, imports, price trends, and end-use. Includes company profiles.

Kleppner's Advertising Procedure. Prentice Hall, 240 Frisch Court Paramus, NJ 07652-5240. Phone: 800-947-7700 or (201)909-6200 Fax: 800-445-6991 or (201)909-6361 URL: http://www.prenhall.com • 1995. $230.00. 13th edition. (Prentice Hall College Title Series).

KMWorld Buyer's Guide. Knowledge Asset Media, 18 Bayview Landing Camden, ME 04843. Phone: (207)236-8524 Fax: (207)236-6452 E-mail: publisher@kmworld.com • URL: http://www.kmworld.com • Semiannual. Controlled circulation as part of *KMWorld*. Contains corporate and product profiles related to various aspects of knowledge management and information systems. (Knowledge Asset Media is a an affiliate of Information Today, Inc.)

KMWorld: Creating and Managing the Knowledge-Based Enterprise. Knowledge Asset Media, 18 Bayview Landing Camden, ME 04843. Phone: (207)236-8524 Fax: (207)236-6452 E-mail: publisher@kmworld.com • URL: http://www.kmworld.com • Monthly. Controlled circulation. Provides articles on knowledge management, including business intelligence, multimedia content management, document management, e-business, and intellectual property. Emphasis is on business-to-business information technology. (Knowledge Asset Media is a an affiliate of Information Today, Inc.)

Knight Center for Specialized Journalism., University of Maryland, 290 University College College Park, MD 20742-1645. Phone: (301)985-7279 Fax: (301)985-7840 E-mail: knight@umail.umd.edu • URL: http://www.inform.umd.edu/knight • Research area is media coverage of complex subjects, such as economics, law, science, and medicine.

Knit Fabric Production. U.S. Bureau of the Census, Washington, DC 20233-0800. Phone: (301)457-4100 Fax: (301)457-3842 URL: http://www.census.gov • Annual. (Current Industrial Reports MA-22K.)

Knitwear Division - American Apparel Manufacturers Association.

Knowledge Exchange Business Encyclopedia: Your Complete Business Advisor. Lorraine Spurge, editor. Knowledge Exchange LLC, 16350 Ventura Blvd., Suite 364 Encino, CA 91436. Phone: (818)705-3740 Fax: (818)708-8764 E-mail: kex@kex.com • URL: http://www.kex.com • 1997. $45.00. Provides definitions of business terms and financial expressions, profiles of leading industries, tables of economic statistics, biographies of business leaders, and other business information. Includes "A Chronology of Business from 3000 B.C. Through 1995." Contains illustrations and three indexes.

Knowledge Management. CurtCo Freedom Group, 29160 Heathercliff Rd., Suite 200 Malibu, CA 90265. Phone: (310)589-3100 Fax: (310)589-3131 URL: http://www.kmmag.com • Monthly. Controlled circulation. Covers applications of information technology and knowledge management strategy.

Knowledge Management for the Information Professional. T. Kanti Srikantaiah and Michael Koenig, editors. Information Today, Inc., 143 Old Marlton Pike Medford, NJ 08055-8750. Phone: 800-300-9868 or (609)654-6266 Fax: (609)654-4309 E-mail: custserv@infotoday.com • URL: http://www.infotoday.com • 2000. $44.50. Contains articles by 26 contributors on the concept of "knowledge management."

Koldfax. Air-Conditioning and Refrigeration Institute, 4301 Fairfax Dr., Suite 425 Arlington, VA 22203-1627. Phone: (703)524-8800 Fax: (703)528-3816 E-mail: ari@ari.org • URL: http://www.ari.com • Monthly. Membership. Newsletter.

Kompass CD-ROM Editions. Available from Kompass USA, Inc., 1255 Route 70, Suite 25-S Lakewood, NJ 08701. Phone: 877-566-7277 or (732)730-0340 Fax: (732)730-0342 E-mail: mail@kompass-usa.com • URL: http://www.kompass.com • Annual. Prices vary. CD-ROM versions of Kompass international trade directories are available for each of 30 major countries and eight world regions. Searching is provided for 50,000 product/service items and many company details.

Kompass International Trade Directories. Available from MarketResearch.com, 641 Ave. of the Americas, 3rd Fl. New York, NY 10011. Phone: 800-298-5699 or (212)807-2629 Fax: (212)807-2716 E-mail: order@marketresearch.com • URL: http://www.marketresereach.com • Annual. Prices and volumes vary. Kompass directories are published internationally for each of more than 70 countries, from Algeria to Yugoslavia. The Kompass classification system covers 50,000 individual product and service categories. Most directories include a tradename index and company profiles.

Kompass USA. Kompass USA, Inc., 1255 Route 70, Suite 25-S Lakewood, NJ 08701. Phone: 877-566-7277 or (732)730-0340 Fax: (732)730-0342 E-mail: mail@kompass-usa.com • URL: http://www.kompass.com • Annual. $375.00. Four volumes. Includes information on about 125,000 U.S. companies. Classification system covers approximately 50,000 products and services. Product and tradename indexes are provided.

Korea Trade Promotion Center., 460 Park Ave., Room 402 New York, NY 10022. Phone: 800-568-7248 or (212)826-0900 Fax: (212)888-4930 Provides information about Korean products and promotes trade between the U. S. and Korea.

Kosher Directory :Directory of Kosher Products and Services. Union of Orthodox Jewish Congregations of America, Kashruth Div., 11 Broadway, 13th Fl. New York, NY 10004-1303. Phone: (212)563-4000 Fax: (212)564-9058 Annual. $10.00. Over 10,000 consumer, institutional and industrial products and services produced under the rabbinical supervision of the Union.

Kovels' Antiques and Collectibles. Ralph and Terry Kovel. Crown Publishers Group, Inc., 201 E. 50th St. New York, NY 10022. Phone: 800-726-0600 or (212)751-2600 Fax: (301)857-9460 URL: http://www.randomhouse.com/ • Annual. $19.95.

Kurata Thermodynamics Laboratory., University of Kansas, Dept. of Chemical and Petroleum Engineering Lawrence, KS 66045. Phone: (913)864-3860 Fax: (913)864-4967 E-mail: cshowat@ukans.edu • URL: http://www.engr.ukans.edu/~ktl • Investigates the behavior of various materials over a wide range of temperatures.

L D & A: Lighting Equipment and Accessories Directory. Illuminating Engineering Society, 120 Wall St., 17th Fl. New York, NY 10005-4001. Phone: (212)248-5000 Fax: (212)248-5017 E-mail: iesna@iesna.org • URL: http://www.iesna.org • Annual. $10.00. Lists over 800 manufacturers of lighting fixtures, controls, components, mounting devices, maintenance equipment, etc.

Label Printing Industries of America.

Labels. Available from MarketResearch.com, 641 Ave. of the Americas, Third Floor New York, NY 10011. Phone: 800-298-5699 or (212)807-2629 Fax: (212)807-2716 E-mail: order@marketresearch.com • URL: http://www.marketresearch.com • 1998. $3,300.00. Market research report published by the Freedonia Group. Covers types of label materials, methods of application, printing technology, and end-use markets. Includes company profiles and forecasts to the year 2002.

Labor and Employment Law. Labor and Employment Law Section. American Bar Association, 750 N. Lake Shore Dr. Chicago, IL 60611-4497. Phone: 800-285-2221 or (312)988-5000 Fax: (312)988-5528 E-mail: abajournal@abanet.org • URL: http://www.abanet.org • Quarterly. Membership.

Labor and Employment Law Newsletter. Matthew Bender & Co., Inc., Two Park Ave. New York, NY 10016. Phone: 800-223-1940 or (212)448-2000 Fax: (212)244-3188 E-mail: international@bender.com • URL: http://www.bender.com • Irregular. $275.00 per year. Newsletter.

Labor and Employment Law: Text and Cases. David P. Twomey. South-Western Publishing Co., 5101 Madison Rd. Cincinnati, OH 45227. Phone: 800-543-0487 or (513)271-8811 Fax: 800-437-8488 E-mail: billhendee@itped.com • URL: http://www.swcollege.com • 1993. $73.75. Ninth edition.

Labor Arbitration: An Annotated Bibliography, 1991-1996. Charles J. Coleman and others, editors. Cornell Universtiy Press, Cornell University Press, P.O. Box 250 Ithaca, NY 14851. Phone: 800-666-2211 or (607)277-2338 Fax: 800-688-2877 or (607)277-6292 E-mail: orderbook@cupserv.org • URL: http://www.cornellpress.cornell.edu • 1997. $25.00. (ILR Bibliography Series, No. 18).

Labor Arbitration Awards. CCH, Inc., 4025 W. Peterson Ave. Chicago, IL 60646-6085. Phone: 800-248-3248 or (773)866-6000 Fax: 800-224-8299 or (773)866-3608 URL: http://www.cch.com • Weekly. $1,099.00 per year. Looseleaf service.

Labor Arbitration Reports. Bureau of National Affairs, Inc., 1231 25th St., N.W. Washington, DC 20037-1197. Phone: 800-372-1033 or (202)452-4200 Fax: (202)452-8092 E-mail: books@bna.com • Weekly. $797 per year. Looseleaf.

Labor Division Newsletter. National Safety Council, Periodicals Dept., 1121 Spring Lake Dr. Itasca, IL 60143-3201. Phone: 800-621-7619 or (630)285-1121 Fax: (630)285-1315 URL: http://www.nsc.org • Monthly. $19.00 per year.

Labor Law: Annual Institute. Theodore W. Kheel and others. Matthew Bender & Co., Inc., Two Park Ave. New York, NY 10016. Phone: 800-223-1940 or (212)440-2000 Fax: (212)244-3188 E-mail: international@bender.com • URL: http://www.bender.com • $650.00. Eleven looseleaf volumes. Quarterly updates. Covers all aspects of labor relations.

Labor Law Developments: Annual Institute. Matthew Bender & Co., Inc., Two Park Ave. New York, NY 10016. Phone: 800-223-1940 or (212)448-2000 Fax: (212)244-3188 E-mail: international@bender.com • URL: http://www.bender.com • Annual. Price on application. Annual collection of papers presented at the SWLF Labor Law Institute, by practitioners, labor law professors and NRLB members.

Labor Law Journal: To Promote Sound Thinking on Labor Law Problems. CCH, Inc., 4025 W. Peterson Ave. Chicago, IL 60646-6085. Phone: 800-248-3248 or (773)866-6000 Fax: 800-224-8299 or (773)866-3608 URL: http://www.cch.com • Monthly. $169.00 per year.

Labor Law Reports. CCH, Inc., 4025 W. Peterson Ave. Chicago, IL 60646-6085. Phone: 800-248-3248 or (773)866-6000 Fax: 800-224-8299 or (773)866-3608 URL: http://www.cch.com • 16 looseleaf volumes. $2,151.00 per year, including weekly updates. Covers laborrelations, wages and hours, state labor laws, and employment practices. Supplement available *Guide to Fair Employment Practices*.

Labor-Management Relations. Daniel Q. Mills. McGraw-Hill, 1221 Ave. of the Americas New York, NY 10020. Phone: 800-722-4726 or (212)904-2000 Fax: (212)904-2072 E-mail: customer.service@mcgraw-hill.com • URL: http://www.mcgraw-hill.com • 1993. $83.75. Fifth edition. (Management Series).

Labor-Management Relations: Strikes, Lockouts, and Boycotts. Douglas E. Ray and Emery W. Bartle. West Group, 610 Opperman Dr. Eagan, MN 55123. Phone: 800-328-4880 or (651)687-7000 Fax: 800-213-2323 or (651)687-5827 URL: http://www.westgroup.com • Looseleaf. $110.00. Covers legal issues involved in labor-management confrontations. Includes recent decisions of the National Labor Relations Board (NLRB).

Labor Policy Association.

Labor Relations. Arthur A. Sloan and Fred Witney. Prentice Hall, 240 Frisch Court Paramus, NJ 07652-5240. Phone: 800-947-7700 or (201)909-6200 Fax: 800-445-6991 or (201)909-6361 URL: http://www.prenhall.com • 1996. $91.00. Ninth edition. Emphasizes collective bargaining and arbitration.

Labor Relations Bulletin. Bureau of Business Practice, Inc., 24 Rope Ferry Rd. Waterford, CT 06386. Phone: 800-243-0876 or (860)442-4365 Fax: (860)437-3555 E-mail: rebecca_armitage@prenhall.com • URL: http://www.bbpnews.com • Monthly. $99.84 per year. Labor arbitration case analysis. Formerly *Discipline and Grievances*.

Labor Relations: Development, Structure, Process. John A. Fossum. McGraw-Hill Professional, 1221 Ave. of the Americas New York, NY 10020. Phone: 800-722-4726 or (212)904-2000 Fax: (212)904-2072 E-mail: customer.service@mcgraw-hill.com • URL: http://www.mcgraw-hill.com • 1999. Seventh edition. Price on application.

Labor Relations Reporter. Bureau of National Affairs, Inc., 1231 25th St., N.W. Washington, DC 2003-1197. Phone: 800-372-1033 or (202)452-4200 Fax: (202)452-8092 E-mail: books@bna.com • URL: http://www.bna.com • Biweekly. $4,118.00 per year. Six volumes. Looseleaf. Legal service.

Labor Research Association.

Labor Trends. Business Research Publishing, Inc., 65 Bleecker St., 5th Fl. New York, NY 10012-2450. Phone: (212)673-4700 Fax: (212)475-1790 Weekly. $259.00 per year. Provides labor relations/personnel news.

Labor Unions. Gary M. Fink. Greenwood Publishing Group, Inc., 88 Post Rd. W. Westport, CT 06881. Phone: 800-225-5800 or (203)226-3571 Fax: (203)222-1502 1977. $50.95. Encyclopedia of trade union history. Essays on more than 200 unions. (Encyclopedia of American Institutions Series).

Laboratories Medical Directory. InfoUSA, P.O. Box 27347 Omaha, NE 68127. Phone: 800-555-6124 or (402)593-4600 Fax: (402)331-5481 E-mail: internet@infousa.com • Annual. Price on application. Lists over 8,234 laboratories. Compiled from telephone company yellow pages.

Laboratory Equipment. Cahners Business Information, New Product Information, 301 Gibraltar Dr. Morris Plains, NJ 07950-0650. Phone: 800-662-7776 or (973)292-5100 Fax: (973)539-3476 E-mail: corporatecommunications@cahners.com • URL: http://www.cahners.com • 13 times a year. $65.95 per year.

Laboratory for Computer Science., Massachusetts Institute of Technology, 545 Technology Square, Bldg. NE43 Cambridge, MA 02139. Phone: (617)253-5851 Fax: (617)258-8682 E-mail: mld@hq.lcs.mit.edu • URL: http://www.lcs.mit.edu/ • Research is in four areas: Intelligent Systems; Parallel Systems; Systems, Languages, and Networks; and Theory. Emphasis is on the application of online computing.

Laboratory for Electromagnetic and Electronic Systems., Massachusetts Institute of Technology, 77 Massachusetts Ave., Bldg. 10, Room 172 Cambridge, MA 02139. Phone: (617)253-4631 Fax: (617)258-6774 E-mail: jgk@mit.edu • URL: http://power.mit.edu/index.html • Research areas include heat transfer and cryogenics.

Laboratory for Information and Decision Systems., Massachusetts Institute of Technology, Bldg. 35, Room 308 Cambridge, MA 02139-4307. Phone: (617)253-2141 Fax: (617)253-3578 E-mail: chan@mit.edu • URL: http://www.justice.mit.edu • Research areas include data communication networks and fiber optic networks.

Laboratory for Manufacturing and Productivity.

Laboratory for Nuclear Science.

Laboratory for Pest Control Application Technology., Ohio State University, Ohio Agricultural Research and Development Center Wooster, OH 44691. Phone: (330)263-3726 Fax: (330)263-3686 E-mail: hall.1@osu.edu • URL: http://www.oardc.ohio-state.edu/lpcat/ • Conducts pest control research in cooperation with the U. S. Department of Agriculture.

Laboratory of Electronics., Rockefeller University, 1230 York Ave. New York, NY 10021. Phone: (212)327-8613 Fax: (212)327-7613 E-mail: ros@rockvax.rockefeller.edu • Studies the application of computer engineering and electronics to biomedicine.

Labordoc. International Labour Office, 1828 L St., N.W., Suite 801 Washington, DC 20006. Phone: (202)653-7652 Fax: (202)653-6187 Indexing of labor literature and the publications of the International Labour Organization, 1965 to present. Monthly updates. Inquire as to online cost and availability.

Labour Force Statistics, 1977/1997: 1998 Edition. Organization for Economic Cooperation and Development. Available from OECD Publications and Information Center, 2001 L St., N. W., Suite 650 Washington, DC 20036-4922. Phone: 800-456-6323 or (202)785-6323 Fax: (202)785-0350 E-mail: washington.contact@oecd.org • URL: http://www.oecd.org • 1999. $98.00. Provides 21 years of data for OECD member countries on population, employment, unemployment, civilian labor force, armed forces, and other labor factors.

Ladies Professional Golf Association., 100 International Golf Dr. Daytona Beach, FL 32124-1092. Phone: (904)274-6200 Fax: (904)274-1099 URL: http://www.lpga.com • Divisions are Teaching and Tournamemt.

Laffirmations: 1001 Ways to Add Humor to Your Life and Work. Joel Goodman. Health Communications, Inc., 3201 S. W. 15th St. Deerfield Beach, FL 33442-8157. Phone: 800-851-9100 or (954)360-0909 Fax: (954)360-0034 URL: http://www.hcibooks.com • 1995. $8.95. The author is director of the Humor Project, a private company promoting humor in the corporate workplace.

Lagniappe Letter: Biweekly Report of Issues Affecting Business in Latin America. Latin American Information Services, Inc., 159 W. 53rd St., 28th Fl. New York, NY 10019. Phone: (212)765-5520 Fax: (212)765-2927 URL: http://www.lais.com • Biweekly. $675.00 per year. Newsletter on key trade, economic, business, financial, and political developments in Central and Latin America. Includes *Lagniappe Quarterly Monitor*.

Lakewood Report on Positive Employee Practices. Lakewood Publications, Inc., 50 S. Ninth St. Minneapolis, MN 55402. Phone: 800-328-4329 or (612)333-0471 Fax: (612)333-6526 URL: http://www.lakewoodpub.com • Monthly. $128.00 per year. Newsletter. Provides news for quality improvement managers. Includes columns entitled "Eye on Quality" and "Quality Movement News." Formerly *Total Quality*.

Laminate Flooring. Available from MarketResearch.com, 641 Ave. of the Americas, Third Floor New York, NY 10011. Phone: 800-298-5699 or (212)807-2629 Fax: (212)807-2716 E-mail: order@marketresearch.com • URL: http://www.marketresearch.com • 1997. $495.00. Market research report published by Specialists in Business Information. Presents laminate flooring market data relative to demographics, sales growth, shipments, exports, imports, price trends, and end-use. Includes company profiles.

Lamme Power Systems Laboratory. Ohio State University

LAMP (Literature Analysis of Microcomputer Publications). Soft Images, 200 Route 17 Mahwah, NJ 07430. Phone: (201)529-1440 Bimonthly. $89.95 per year. Annual cumulation.

Land Economics: A Quarterly Journal Devoted to the Study of Economic and Social Institutions. University of Wisconsin at Madison, Land Tenure Center. University of Wisconsin Press, Journals Div., 2537 Daniels St. Madison, WI 53718-6772. Phone: (608)224-3880 Fax: (608)224-3883 URL: http://www.wisc.edu/ • Quarterly. Individuals, $47.00 per year; institutions, $127.00 per year.

Land Use and Environment Law Review, 1984. West Group, 610 Opperman Dr. Eagan, MN 55123. Phone: 800-328-4880 or (651)687-7000 Fax: 800-213-2323 or (651)687-5827 URL: http://www.westgroup.com • Dates vary. $215.00. Five volumes.

Land Use Digest. Urban Land Institute, 1025 Thomas Jefferson St., N. W., Suite 500 W. Washington, DC 20004-5201. Phone: 800-321-5011 or (202)624-7000 Fax: (202)624-7140 E-mail: bookstore@uli.org • URL: http://www.uli.org • Monthly. Membership.

Land Use Law and Zoning Digest. American Planning Association, 122 S. Michigan Ave., Suite 1600 Chicago, IL 60603-6107. Phone: (312)431-9100 Fax: (312)431-9985 URL: http://www.planning.org • Monthly. $275.00 per year. Covers judicial decisions and state laws affecting zoning and land use. Edited for city planners and lawyers. Monthly supplement available *Zoning News*.

Land Use Law Report. Business Publishers, Inc., 8737 Colesville Rd., Suite 1100 Silver Spring, MD 20910-3928. Phone: 800-274-6737 or (301)587-6300 Fax: (301)587-1081 E-mail: bpinews@bpinews.com • URL: http://www.bpinews.com • Biweekly. $367.00 per year. Provides current reports on planning issues affecting urban, suburban, agricultural and natural resources land jurisdictions. Formerly *Land Use Planning Report*.

Landscape Architecture. American Society of Landscape Architects, 636 Eye St., N.W. Washington, DC 20001-3736. Phone: (202)216-2320 Fax: (202)898-1115 E-mail: scahill@asla.org • URL: http://www.asla.org • Monthly. $49.00 per year.

Landscape Architecture: An Illustrated History in Timelines, Site Plans, and Biography. William A. Mann. John Wiley and Sons, Inc., 605 Third Ave. New York, NY 10158-0012. Phone: 800-225-5945 or (212)850-6000 Fax: (212)850-6088 E-mail: info@wiley.com • URL: http://www.wiley.com • 1993. $64.95. Includes illustrations of notable site plans and biographies of people important to landscape architecture history.

Landscape Architecture Foundation.

Landscape Architecture News Digest. American Society of Landscape Architects, 636 Eye St., N.W. Washington, DC 20001-3736. Phone: (202)216-2320 Fax: (202)898-1115 E-mail: scahill@asla.org • URL: http://www.asla.org • 10 times a year. Free to members; non-members, $32.00 per year.

Landscape Journal: Design, Planning, and Management of the Land. Council of Education in Landscape Architecture. University of Wisconsin Press, Journal Div., 2537 Daniels St. Madison, WI 53718-6772. Phone: (608)224-3880 Fax: (608)224-3883 URL: http://www.wisc.edu/ • Semiannual. Individuals, $34.00 per year; institutions, $92.00 per year.

Landscape Maintenance News. Landscape Information Services, P.O. Box 2694 Casper, WY 82602. Phone: (307)265-7801 Monthly. $48.00 per year. Newsletter for landscape service companies.

Landscape Management: Commercial Magazine for Lawn, Landscape and Grounds Managers. Advanstar Communications, Inc., One Park Ave., 2nd Fl. New York, NY 10016-5802. Phone: 800-346-0085 or (212)951-6600 Fax: (212)951-6623 E-mail: information@advanstar.com • URL: http://www.advanstar.com • Monthly. $41.00 per year.

Landscape Planning: Environmental Applications. William M. Marsh. John Wiley and Sons, Inc., 605 Third Ave. New York, NY 10158-0012. Phone: 800-526-5368 or (212)850-6000 Fax: (212)850-6088 E-mail: info@wiley.com • URL: http://www.wiley.com • 1997. $58.95. Third edition. A handbook on environmental problems associated with landscape design, land planning, and land use. Includes techniques for obtaining data.

The Language of Banking: Terms and Phrases Used in the Financial Industry. Michael G. Hales. McFarland & Co., Inc., Publishers, P.O. Box 611 Jefferson, NC 28640. Phone: 800-253-2187 or (336)246-4460 Fax: (336)246-5018 E-mail: editorial@mcfarlandpub.com • URL: http://www.mcfarlandpub.com • 1994. $32.50. Provides detailed explanations of about 1,200 banking and finance terms.

Language of Real Estate. John Reilly. Dearborn, A Kaplan Professional Co., 155 N. Wacker St. Chicago, IL 60606-1719. Phone: 800-921-9621 or (312)836-4400 Fax: (312)836-1021 URL: http://www.dearborn.com • 2000. Fith edition. Price on application. Encyclopedia of real estate terms.

Language Translation Service. Entrepreneur Media, Inc., 2445 McCabe Way Irvine, CA 92614. Phone: 800-421-2300 or (949)261-2325 Fax: (949)261-0234 E-mail: entmag@entrepreneur.com • URL: http://www.entrepreneur.com • Looseleaf. $59.50. A practical guide to starting a language translation service. Covers profit potential, start-up costs, market size evaluation, pricing, accounting, advertising, promotion, etc. (Start-Up Business Guide No. E1353.)

Lapidary Journal. PRIMEDIA Special Interest Publications, P.O. Box 1790 Peoria, IL 61656. Phone: 800-521-2885 or (309)682-6626 Fax: (203)682-7394 E-mail: ljmagazine@aol.com • URL: http://www.lapidaryjournal.com • Monthly. $30.00

Laptop Buyer's Guide and Handbook. Bedford Communications, Inc., 150 Fifth Ave. New York, NY 10011. Phone: 888-270-7652 or (212)807-8220 Fax: (212)807-1098 URL: http://www.bedfordmags.com • Monthly. $18.00 per year. Contains informative articles and critical reviews of laptop, notebook, subnotebook, and handheld computers. Includes portable peripheral equipment, such as printers and scanners. Directory information includes company profiles (major manufacturers), product comparison charts, street price guide, list of manufacturers, and list of dealers.

Large Animal Practice: Covering Health and Nutrition. Fancy Publications, Inc., 2401 Beverly Blvd. Los Angeles, CA 90057-0900. Bimonthly. $40.00 per year. Services the large animal veterinary (food animal) field.

Larousse Encyclopedia of Wine. Christopher Foulkes, editor. Larousse Kingfisher Chambers, Inc., 95 Madison Ave. New York, NY 10016. Phone: 800-497-1657 or (212)686-1060 Fax: (212)686-1082 1994. $40.00. Provides information on major wine producers of the world, with emphasis on French vineyards. Includes statistics and a glossary.

Laser Biomedical Research Center., Massachusetts Institute of Technology, 77 Massachusetts Ave. Cambridge, MA 02139. Phone: (617)253-7700 Fax: (617)253-4513 E-mail: msfeld@mit.edu • URL: http://www.web.mit.edu/spectroscopy/www/staff/msfeld.html • Concerned with the medical use of lasers.

Laser Focus World Buyers' Guide. PennWell Corp., Advanced Technology Div., 98 Spit Brook Rd. Nashua, NH 03062-5737. Phone: 800-331-4463 or (603)891-0123 Fax: (603)891-0539 E-mail: webmaster@pennwell.com • URL: http://www.pennwell.com • Annual. $125.00. Lists more than 2,000 suppliers of optoelectronic and laser products and services.

Laser Focus World: The World of Optoelectronics. PennWell Corp., Advanced Technology Div., 98 Spit Brook Rd. Nashua, NH 03062-5737. Phone: 800-331-4463 or (603)891-0123 Fax: (603)891-0574 E-mail: webmaster@pennwell.com • URL: http://www.pennwell.com • Monthly. $156.00 per year. Covers business and technical aspects of electro-optics, including lasers and fiberoptics. Includes *Buyer's Guide*.

Laser Institute of America.

Laserlog Reporter: CD Reporter. Phonlog Publishing, P.O. Box 85007 San Diego, CA 92138. Phone: (619)457-5920 Fax: (619)457-1320 Biweekly. $228.00 per year. Looseleaf. Contains detailed listings of currently available compact disc music recordings, both popular and classical.

Lasers. Joseph H. Eberly and Peter W. Milonni. John Wiley and Sons, Inc., 605 Third Ave. New York, NY 10158-0012. Phone: 800-526-5368 or (212)850-6000 Fax: (212)850-6088 E-mail: info@wiley.com • URL: http://www.wiley.com • 1988. $125.00.

Lasers in Surgery and Medicine. John Wiley and Sons, Inc., Journals Div., 605 Third Ave. New York, NY 10158-0012. Phone: 800-526-5368 or (212)850-6000 Fax: (212)850-6088 E-mail: info@wiley.com • URL: http://www.wiley.com • 11 times a year. $1,090.00 per year. Original articles in laser surgery and medicine.

The Last Word. American Consulting Engineers Council, 1015 15th St., N.W. Washington, DC 20005-2670. Phone: (202)347-7474 Fax: (202)898-0068 Weekly. $149.00 per year.

Lateral Thinking: Creativity Step by Step. Edward de Bono. HarperTrade, 10 E. 53rd St. New York, NY 10022. Phone: 800-242-7737 or (212)207-7000 Fax: (212)207-7145 URL: http://www.harpercollins.com • 1990. $15.00.

Latin America: A Directory and Sourcebook. Available from The Gale Group, 27500 Drake Rd. Farmington Hills, MI 48331-3535. Phone: 800-877-GALE or (248)699-GALE Fax: 800-414-5043 or (248)699-8069 E-mail: galeord@galegroup.com • URL: http://www.galegroup.com • 1999. $590.00. Second edition. Published by Euromonitor. Describes major companies in Latin America. Sourcebook section provides marketing and business information sources.

Latin America and the Caribbean in the World Economy. United Nations Publications, Two United Nations Plaza, Room DC2-853 New York, NY 10017. Phone: 800-253-9646 or (212)963-8302 Fax: (212)963-3489 E-mail: publications@un.org • URL: http://www.un.org/publications • 1999. $25.00. Discusses trade policy, trade activity, regional integration, and environmental protection issues.

Latin America in Graphs: Demographic and Economic Trends. Inter-American Development Bank, 1300 New York Ave., N. W. Washington, DC 20577. Phone: (202)623-1000 Fax: (202)623-3531 E-mail: webmaster@.iadb.org • URL: http://www.iadb.org • 1994. $12.50.

Latin American Advertising, Marketing, and Media Data. Available from The Gale Group, 27500 Drake Rd. Farmington Hills, MI 48331-3535. Phone: 800-877-GALE or (248)699-GALE Fax: 800-414-5043 or (248)699-8069 E-mail: galeord@galegroup.com • URL: http://www.galegroup.com • 1995. $470.00. Published by Euromonitor. Provides country profiles, demographics, economic indicators, advertising data, and media data. Also lists advertising agencies, newspaper publishers, magazine publishers, and market research companies.

Latin American and Caribbean Center., Florida International University, University Park, DM 353 Miami, FL 33199. Phone: (305)348-2894 Fax: (305)348-3593 E-mail: lacc@fiu.edu • URL: http://www.lacc.fiu.edu • Research fields include economic development and trade.

Latin American Business Review: Journal of the Business Association of Latin American Studies. Haworth Press, Inc., 10 Alice St. Binghamton, NY 13904-1580. Phone: 800-429-6784 or (607)722-5857 Fax: 800-895-0582 or (607)722-1424 E-mail: getinfo@haworthpressinc.com • URL: http://www.haworthpressinc.com • Quarterly. Individuals, $50.00 per year; institutions, $75.00 per year; libraries, $95.00 per year.

Latin American Center, University of California, Los Angeles.

Latin American Market Planning Report. Available from MarketResearch.com, 641 Ave. of the Americas, Third Floor New York, NY 10011. Phone: 800-298-5699 or (212)807-2629 Fax: (212)807-2716 E-mail: order@marketresearch.com • URL: http://www.marketresearch.com • 2000. $750.00.Market research report published by Strategy Research Corporation. Provides results of U. S. Hispanic Market Study covering demographics, product usage, media usage, public opinion issues, and other items.

Latin American Studies, Volume I: Multidisciplinary. National Information Services Corp., Wyman Towers, Suite Six, 3100 Saint Paul St. Baltimore, MD 21218. Phone: (410)243-0797 Fax: (410)243-0982 Semiannual. Provides more than 700,000 CD-ROM citations to scholarly literature on a wide variety of Latin American topics, including agriculture, business, demography, economics, government, and politics. Producers are the University of Texas, the University of California, and the Library of Congress.

Latin American Studies, Volume II: Current Affairs and Law. National Information Services Corp., Wyman Towers, Suite Six, 3100 Saint Paul St. Baltimore, MD 21218. Phone: (410)243-0797 Fax: (410)243-0982 Semiannual. Contains a wide variety of information on CD-ROM, from various producers, relating to Latin American business, current events, and legislation. Includes periodical citations and abstracts in *INFO-SOUTH*; the full-text newsletters, *Chronicle of Latin American Economic Affairs, Central America Update*, and *SourceMex*; and other databases. Time periods are typically 1986, 1988, or 1990 to date.

Latin America's Economy: Diversity, Trends, and Conflicts. Eliana Cardoso and Ann Helwege. MIT Press, Five Cambridge Center Cambridge, MA 02142-1493. Phone: 800-356-0343 or (617)253-5646 Fax: (617)253-6779 E-mail: mitpress-order@mit.edu • URL: http://www.mitpress.mit.edu • 1995. $22.00.

Latin Finance. Latin American Financial Publications, Inc., 2121 Ponce de Leon Blvd., Suite 1020 Coral Gables, FL 33134. Phone: (305)448-6593 Fax: (305)448-0718 Monthly. $215.00 per year. Covers finance, investment, venture capital, and banking in Latin America.

Latin Fund Management. Securities Data Publishing, 40 West 57th St. New York, NY 10019. Phone: 800-455-5844 or (212)765-5311 Fax: (212)956-0112 E-mail: sdp@tfn.com • URL: http://www.sdponline.com • Monthly. $495.00 per year. Newsletter (also available online at www.latinfund.net). Provides news and analysis of Latin American mutual funds, pension funds, and annuities. (Securities Data Publishing is a unit of Thomson Financial.)

Latin Trade: Your Business Source for Latin America. Freedom Publications, Inc., 200 S Biscayne Blvd., Suite 1150 Miami, FL 33131. Phone: 800-783-4903 or (305)358-8373 Fax: (305)358-9166 E-mail: lattrade@aol.com • URL: http://www.latintrade.com • Monthly. $36.00 per year. English and Spanish editions. Covers various aspects of Latin American business and trade, including economic indicators, export-import, finance, commodity news, company profiles, and political developments. Formerly *U.S.-Latin Trade*.

Laundromat. Entrepreneur Media, Inc., 2445 McCabe Way Irvine, CA 92614. Phone: 800-421-2300 or (949)261-2325 Fax: (949)261-0234 E-mail: entmag@entrepreneur.com • URL: http://www.entrepreneur.com • Looseleaf. $59.50. A practical guide to starting a coin-operated, self-service laundry business. Covers profit potential, start-up costs, market size evaluation, owner's time required, site selection, lease negotiation, pricing, accounting, advertising, promotion, etc. (Start-Up Business Guide No. E1162.)

Law and Banking: Applications. Craig W. Smith. American Bankers Association, 1120 Connecticut Ave., N. W. Washington, DC 20036-3971. Phone: 800-338-0626 or (212)663-5000 Fax: (202)663-7543 URL: http://www.aba.org • 1996. $60.00. Covers laws pertaining to collections, secured transactions, letters of credit, check processing, collateral, fraud, and default.

Law and Banking Principles. James C. Conboy. American Bankers Association, 1120 Connecticut Ave., N. W. Washington, DC 20036-3971. Phone: 800-338-0626 or (212)663-5000 Fax: (202)663-7543 URL: http://www.aba.org • 1996. $60.00. Sixth edition. Discusses legal issues facing the banking industry.

Law and Contemporary Problems. Duke University, School of Law, P.O. Box 90364 Durham, NC 27708-0364. Phone: (919)613-7101 Fax: (919)613-7231 E-mail: tom@faculty.law.duke.edu • URL: http://www.law.duke.edu/ • Quarterly. $48.00 per year.

Law and Economics Center., University of Miami, Business School, P.O. Box 248000 Coral Gables, FL 33124. Phone: (305)284-6174 Fax: (305)662-9159 Research areas include product liability law.

Law and Economics Center., George Mason University, School of Law, 3401 N. Fairfax Dr. Arlington, VA 22201-4498. Phone: (703)993-8040 Fax: (703)993-8088 URL: http://www.gmu.edu.departments/law/lec.html • Research fields include product liability law.

Law and Legal Information Directory. The Gale Group, 27500 Drake Rd. Farmington Hills, MI 48331-3535. Phone: 800-877-GALE or (248)699-GALE Fax: 800-414-5043 or (248)699-8069 E-mail: galeord@galegroup.com • URL: http://www.galegroup.com • 2000. $405.00. 11th edition. Two volumes. Contains a wide range of sources of legal information, such as associations, law schools, courts, federal agencies, referral services, libraries, publishers, and research centers. There is a separate chapter for each of 23 types of information source or service.

Law and Order Magazine Police Equipment Buyer's Guide. Hendon, Inc., 1000 Skokie Blvd. Wilmette, IL 60091. Phone: 800-843-9764 or (708)256-8555 Fax: (708)256-8574 E-mail: info@hendonpub.com • URL: http://www.lawandordermag.com • Annual. $15.00. Lists manufacturers, dealers, and distributors of equipment and services for police departments.

Law and Order Magazine: The Magazine for Police Management. Hendon Publishing Co., 1000 Skokie Blvd., Suite 500 Wilmette, IL 60091. Phone: 800-843-9764 or (847)256-8555 Fax: (847)256-8574 E-mail: info@hendonpub.com • URL: http://www.lawandordermag.com • Monthly. $22.00 per year. Edited for law enforcement officials. Includes special issues on communications, technology, weapons, and uniforms and equipment.

Law and Practice of International Finance. Philip Wood. West Group, 610 Opperman Dr. Eagan, MN 55123. Phone: 800-328-4880 or (651)687-7000 Fax: 800-213-2323 or (651)687-5827 URL: http://www.westgroup.com • Two looseleaf volumes. $250.00. Periodic supplementation.

Law Books in Print: Law Books in English Published Throughout the World. Glanville Publishers, Inc., 75 Main St. Dobbs Ferry, NY 10522. Phone: (914)693-8100 Fax: (914)693-0402 E-mail: glanville@oceanalaw • URL: http://www.oceanalaw.com • Triennial. $750.00. Supplement available, *Law Books Publisher*.

Law Books 1876-1981; Books and Serials on Law and its Related Subjects. R. R. Bowker, 121 Chanlon Rd. New Providence, NJ 07974. Phone: 888-269-5372 or (908)464-6800 Fax: (908)771-7704 E-mail: info@bowker.com • URL: http://www.bowker.com • Looseleaf service. $695.00. Three volumes. Annual supplementation. Lists publishers and producers of over 55,000 legal reference publications, periodicals, software, audio cassette titles and video cassettes.

Law Books Published. Glanville Publishers, Inc., 75 Main St. Dobbs Ferry, NY 10522. Phone: (914)693-8100 Fax: (914)693-0402 E-mail: glanville@oceanalaw.com • URL: http://www.oceanalaw.com • Two times a year. $160.00 per year. Supplement to *Law Books in Print*.

Law Dictionary for Non-Lawyers. Daniel Oran. West Publishing Co., College and School Div., 610 Opperman Dr. Eagan, MN 55123. Phone: 800-328-4880 or (651)687-7000 Fax: 800-213-2323 or (651)687-5827 E-mail: legal_ed@westgroup.com • URL: http://www.lawschool.westgroup.com • 1999. $31.95. Fourth edition.

Law Enforcement Product News. General Communications, Inc., 100 Garfield St., 3rd. Fl. Denver, CO 80206-5550. Phone: 800-291-3911 or (303)322-6400 Fax: (303)322-0627 E-mail: mlg@great.net • URL: http://www.law-enforcement.com • Bimonthly. Free. Covers new products and equipment for police departments and other law enforcement and correctional agencies.

Law Enforcement Technology. Cygnus Business Media, 445 Broad Hollow Rd. Melville, NY 11747. Phone: 800-308-6397 or (631)845-2700 Fax: (631)845-2798 E-mail: rich.reiff@cygnuspub.com • URL: http://www.cygnuspub.com • Monthly. $60.00 per year. Covers new products and technologies for police professionals. Includes special issues on weapons, uniforms, communications equipment, computers (hardware-software), vehicles, and enforcement of drug laws.

Law Enforcement Technology Directory. Cygnus Business Media, 445 Broad Hollow Rd. Melville, NY 11747. Phone: 800-308-6397 or (631)845-2700 Fax: (631)845-2736 E-mail: rich.reiff@cygnusplub.com • URL: http://www.cygnuspub.com • Annual. $60.00 per year. $6.00 per issue; a directory of products, equipment, services, and technology for police professionals. Includes weapons, uniforms, communications equipment, and software.

Law Firm Governance: Journal of Practice Managment, Development, and Technology. Aspen Law and Business, 1185 Ave. of the Americas New York, NY 10036. Phone: 800-447-1717 or (212)597-0200 Fax: 800-901-9075 or (212)597-0334 URL: http://www.aspenpub.com • Quarterly. $196.00 per year. Covers project management, strategic planning, compensation systems, advertising, etc. Regular columns include ''Best Practices,'' ''Technology Trends,'' and ''Professional Development.'' Formerly *Law Governance Review*.

Law Firms Yellow Book: Who's Who in the Management of the Leading U. S. Law Firms. Leadership Directories, Inc., 104 Fifth Ave., 2nd Fl. New York, NY 10011. Phone: (212)627-4140 Fax: (212)645-0931 E-mail: info@leadershipdirectories.com • URL: http://www.leadershipdirectories.com • Semiannual. $235.00 per year. Provides detailed information on more than 800 major U. S. law firms. Includes domestic offices, foreign offices, subsidiaries, and affiliates. There are seven indexes: geographic, subject specialty, management, administrative, law school attended, personnel, and law firm.

Law for Business. John E. Adamson. South-Western Publishing Co., 5101 Madison Rd. Cincinnati, OH 45227. Phone: 800-543-0487 or (513)271-8811 Fax: 800-437-8488 E-mail: billhendee@itped.com • URL: http://www.swcollege.com • 1992. $49.95. 14th edition. (LA-Business Law Series).

The Law in (Plain English) for Small Businesses. Leonard D. DuBoff. Allworth Press, Ten E. 23rd St., Ste. 210 New York, NY 10010. Phone: 800-491-2808 or (212)777-8395 Fax: (212)777-8261 E-mail: jbarager@allworth.com • URL: http://www.allworth.com • 1998. $19.95. Third revised edition. Discusses and explains legal issues relating to the organization, financing, and operation of a small business.

Law of Associations: An Operating Legal Manual for Executives and Counsel. George D. Webster, editor. Matthew Bender & Co., Inc., Two Park Ave. New York, NY 10016. Phone: 800-223-1940 or (212)448-2000 E-mail: international@bender.com • URL: http://www.bender.com • $255.00. Looseleaf service. Periodic supplementation. Coverage of all legal and tax aspects of non-profit associations.

Law of Corporate Officers and Directors: Indemnification and Insurance. Joseph W. Bishop, Jr. West Group, 610 Opperman Dr. Eagan, MN 55123. Phone: 800-328-4880 or (651)687-7000 Fax: 800-213-2323 or (651)687-5827 URL: http://www.westgroup.com • 1990. $130.00. Practical guidance for developing corporate policy, drafting agreements and litigation.

Law of Corporate Officers and Directors: Rights, Duties, and Liabilities. Edward Brodsky and M. Patricia Adamski. West Group, 610 Opperman Dr. Eagan, MN 55123. Phone: 800-328-4880 or (651)687-7000 Fax: 800-213-2323 or (651)687-5827 URL: http://www.westgroup.com • 1990. $130.00. Defines accountability for making policy.

Law of Distressed Real Estate: Foreclosure, Workouts, and Procedures. Baxter Dunaway. West Group, 610 Opperman Dr. Eagan, MN 55123. Phone: 800-328-4880 or (651)687-7000 Fax: 800-213-2323 or (651)687-5827 URL: http://www.westgroup.com • Four looseleaf volumes. $495.00. Periodic supplementation. (Real Property-ZoningSeries).

The Law of Electronic Funds Transfer. Matthew Bender and Co., Inc., Two Park Ave. New York, NY 10016. Phone: 800-223-1940 or (212)448-2000 E-mail: international@bender.com • URL: http://www.bender.com • Looseleaf service. Price on application. Periodic supplementation.

Law of Federal Estate and Gift Taxation, 1978-1990. David T. Link and Larry D. Soderquist. West Group, 610 Opperman Dr. Eagan, MN 55123. Phone: 800-328-4880 or (651)687-7000 Fax: 800-213-2323 or (651)687-5827 URL: http://www.westgroup.com • $100.00. Revised edition.

The Law of Fund-Raising. Bruce R. Hopkins. John Wiley and Sons, Inc., 605 Third Ave. New York, NY 10158-0012. Phone: 800-526-5368 or (212)850-6000 Fax: (212)850-6088 E-mail: info@wiley.com • URL: http://www.wiley.com • 1995. $160.00. Second edition. Annual supplements available. Covers all aspects of state and federal nonprofit fund-raising law. Includes summaries of the relevant laws and regulations of each state. *Nonprofit Law, Finance and Management Series*.

The Law of Fund-Raising: 1999 Cumulative Supplement. Bruce R. Hopkins. John Wiley and Sons, Inc., 605 Third Ave. New York, NY 10158-0012. Phone: 800-526-5368 or (212)850-6000 Fax: (212)850-6088 E-mail: info@wiley.com • URL: http://www.wiley.com • 1998. $65.00. *Nonprofit Law, Finance and Management Series*.

The Law of Liability Insurance. Matthew Bender & Co., Inc., New York, NY 10016. Phone: 800-223-1940 or (212)448-2000 Fax: (212)244-3188 E-mail: international@bender.com • URL: http://www.bender.com • $1,230.00. Five looseleaf volumes. Periodic supplementation. Explains the terms and phases essential for a general understanding of liability insurance, and discusses injuries to both persons and property.

Law of Professional and Amateur Sports. Gary A. Uberstine. West Group, 610 Opperman Dr. Eagan, MN 55123. Phone: 800-328-4880 or (651)687-7000 Fax: 800-213-2323 or (651)687-5827 URL: http://www.westgroup.com • $230.00 per year. Two looseleaf volumes. Periodic supplementation. Covers agent-player agreements, collective bargaining, negotiation of player contracts, taxation, and other topics. (Entertainment and Communication Law Series).

Law of Tax-Exempt Organizations. Bruce R. Hopkins. John Wiley and Sons, Inc., 605 Third Ave. New York, NY 10158-0012. Phone: 800-225-5945 or (212)850-6000 Fax: (212)850-6088 E-mail: info@wiley.com • URL: http://www.wiley.com • 1998. $165.00. Seventh edition.(Nonprofit Law, Finance and Management Series).

Law of the Sea: A Select Bibliography. United Nations Publications, Two United Nations Plaza, Room DC2-853 New York, NY 10017. Phone: 800-253-9646 or (212)963-8302 Fax: (212)963-3489 E-mail: publications@un.org • URL: http://www.un.org/publications • Annual. $17.00. Includes 23 subject categories.

Law of the Sea Bulletin. United Nations Publications, United Nations Concourse Level, First Ave., 46th St. New York, NY 10017. Phone: 800-533-3210 or (212)963-7680 Fax: (212)963-4910 E-mail: bookstore@un.org • URL: http://www.un.org/publications • Three times per year. $15.00 per issue. $40.00 per year.

Law of the Super Searchers: The Online Secrets of Top Legal Researchers. T. R. Halvorson and Reva Basch. Information Today, Inc., 143 Old Marlton Pike Medford, NJ 08055-8750. Phone: 800-300-9868 or (609)654-6266 Fax: (609)654-4309 E-mail: custserv@infotoday.com • URL: http://www.infotoday.com • 1999. $24.95. Eight law researchers explain how to find useful legal information online. (CyberAge Books.)

Law of the Workplace: Rights of Employers and Employees. James Hunt and Patricia Strongin. Bureau of National Affairs, Inc., 1231 25th St., N.W. Washington, DC 20037-1197. Phone: 800-372-1033 or (202)452-4200 Fax: (202)452-8092 E-mail: books@bna.com • URL: http://www.bna.com • 1994. $45.00. Third edition. Wages, hours, working conditions, benefits, and so forth.

Law of Transnational Business Transactions. Ved P. Nanda. West Group, 610 Opperman Dr. Eagan, MN 55123. Phone: 800-328-4880 or (651)687-7000 Fax: 800-213-2323 or (651)687-5827 URL: http://www.westgroup.com • $375 per year. Three looseleaf volumes. Periodic supplementation. (International Business and Law Series).

Law Office Automation and Technology. Matthew Bender & Co., Inc., Two Park Ave. New York, NY 10016. Phone: 800-223-1940 or (212)448-2000 Fax: (212)244-3188 E-mail: international@bender.com • URL: http://www.bender.com • $180.00. Looseleaf. Periodic supplementation.

Law Office Economics and Management. West Group, 610 Opperman Dr. Eagan, MN 55123. Phone: 800-328-4880 or (651)687-7000 Fax: 800-213-2323 or (651)687-5827 URL: http://www.westgroup.com • Quarterly. $150.00 per year.

Law Office Economics and Management Manual, 1970-1990. Paul S. Hoffman, editor. West Group, 610 Opperman Dr. Eagan, MN 55123. Phone: 800-328-4880 or (651)687-7000 Fax: 800-213-2323 or (651)687-5827 URL: http://www.westgroup.com • $200.00. Two volumes. Collection of articles by experts exploring the management and financial issues facing law firms.

Lawmaking and the Legislative Process: Committees, Connections, and Compromises. Tommy Neal. Oryx Press, 4041 N. Central Ave., Ste. 700 Phoenix, AZ 85012-3397. Phone: 800-279-6799 or (602)265-2651 Fax: 800-279-4663 or (602)265-6250 E-mail: info@oryxpress.com • URL: http://www.oryxpress.com • 1996. $26.50. Explains how bills are enacted into laws through the state legislative process. Provides step-by-step examples, using fictitious bills.

Lawn and Garden Market. Available from MarketResearch.com, 641 Ave. of the Americas, Third Floor New York, NY 10011. Phone: 800-298-5699 or (212)807-2629 Fax: (212)807-2716 E-mail: order@marketresearch.com • URL: http://www.marketresearch.com • 1999. $2,850.00. Published by Packaged Facts. Provides market data on garden equipment, fertilizers and other substances, and professional lawn care services.

Lawn and Landscape. Group Interest Enterprises. G.I.E., Media Inc., 4012 Bridge Ave. Cleveland, OH 44113-3320. Phone: 800-456-0707 or (216)961-4130 Fax: (216)961-0364 E-mail: pmorales@gie.net • URL: http://www.lawnandlandscape.com/ • Monthly. $30.00 per year. Supplement available. Formerly *Lawn and Landscape Maintenance*.

Lawn Care Service. Entrepreneur Media, Inc., 2445 McCabe Way Irvine, CA 92614. Phone: 800-421-2300 or (949)261-2325 Fax: (949)261-0234 E-mail: entmag@entrepreneur.com • URL: http://www.entrepreneur.com • Looseleaf. $59.50. A practical guide to starting a lawn care business. Covers profit potential, start-up costs, market size evaluation, owner's time required, pricing, accounting, advertising, promotion, etc. (Start-Up Business Guide No. E1198.)

Lawn Institute., 1509 N.E. Johnson Ferry Rd., Suite 190 Marietta, GA 30062-8122. Phone: (404)977-5492 Fax: (404)977-8205 Members are producers of lawn seed and lawn care products.

The Laws of Innkeepers: For Hotels, Motels, Restaurants, and Clubs. J. E. H. Sherry. Cornell University Press, Sage House, 512 E. State St. Ithaca, NY 14851. Phone: 800-666-2211 or (607)257-2338 Fax: 800-688-2877 E-mail: orderbook@cupserv.org • URL: http://www.cornellpress.cornell.edu • 1993. $45.00. Third edition.

Lawyer-Pilots Bar Association.

The Lawyer's Almanac; An Encyclopedia of Information about Law, Lawyers, and the Profession. Harcourt Trade, 525 B St., Suite 1900 San Diego, CA 92101-4495. Phone: 800-831-7799 or (619)699-6707 Fax: 800-876-0186 E-mail: wlittle@harbrace.com • URL: http://www.harcourt.com • 1985. $60.00.

Lawyers' List. CCH, Inc., 8706 Commerce Dr., Suite 4 Easton, MD 21601. Phone: 800-824-9911 or (410)820-4474 Fax: (410)820-4474 Annual. $75.00. About 2,500 lawyers engaged in general, corporate, trial, patent, trademark, copyright practices in the United States.

Lawyer's Register International by Specialties and Fields of Law Including a Directory of Corporate Counsel. Lawyer's Register Publishing Co., 4555 Renaissance Parkway, No. 101 Cleveland, OH 44128-5767. Phone: 800-477-6345 or (216)591-1492 Fax: (216)591-0265 URL: http://www.sportsref.com • Annual. $329.00. Three volumes. Referral source for law firms.

LC MARC: Books. U. S. Library of Congress, Cataloging Distribution Service Washington, DC 20541-4912. Phone: 800-255-3666 or (202)707-6100 Fax: (202)707-1334 Contains online bibliographic records for over five million books cataloged by the Library of Congress since 1968. Updating is weekly or monthly. Inquire as to online cost and availability. (MARC is machine readable cataloging.)

LD & A: (Lighting Design and Application). Illuminating Engineering Society, 120 Wall St., 17th Fl. New York, NY 10005-4001. Phone: (212)248-5000 Fax: (212)248-5017 Monthly. $39.00 per year. Information on current events, products, projects and people in the lighting industry.

LDB Interior Textiles. E.W. Williams Publications Co., 2125 Center Ave., Suite 305 Fort Lee, NJ 07024. Phone: (201)532-9290 Fax: (201)779-8345 E-mail: lbd342@aol.com • Monthly. $66.00 per year. Supplement available *Linens, Domestics and Baths-Interior Textile Annual Buyer's Guide*. Formerly *Interior Textiles*.

LDB Interior Textiles Buyer's Guide. E.W. Williams Publications Co., 2125 Center Ave., Suite 305 Fort Lee, NJ 07024. Phone: (201)532-9290 Fax: (201)779-8345 E-mail: lbd342@aol.com • Annual. $40.00. Includes over 2,000 manufacturers, distributors, and importers of curtains, draperies, hard window treatments, bedspreads, pillows, etc. Formerly *LDB Interior Textiles Directory*.

Lead and Zinc Statistics. International Lead and Zinc Study Group, Two King St. London SW1Y 6QP, England. E-mail: catherine_baumber@ilzsg.org • Monthly. $370.00 per year. Supplement available *Advance Data Service*. Text in English and French.

Lead Industries Association.

The Leader of the Future: New Essays by World-Class Leaders and Thinkers. Jossey-Bass, Inc., Publishers, 350 Sansome St. San Francisco, CA 94104-1342. Phone: 888-378-2537 or (650)433-1740 Fax: (650)433-0499 E-mail: webperson@jbp.com • URL: http://www.josseybass.com • 1996. $25.00. Contains 32 articles on leadership by ''executives, consultants, and commentators.'' (Management Series).

Leader to Leader. Peter F. Drucker Foundation for Nonprofit Management. Jossey-Bass Publishers, 350 Sansome St. San Francisco, CA 94104-9825. Phone: 888-378-2537 or (415)433-1740 Fax: (415)433-0499 E-mail: webperson@jbp.com • URL: http://www.josseybass.com • Quarterly. Individuals, $149.00 per year; institutions, $149.00 per year. Contains articles on ''management, leadership, and strategy'' written by ''leading executives, thinkers, and consultants.'' Covers both business and nonprofit issues.

Leaders, Fools, and Imposters: Essays on the Psychology of Leadership. Manfred F. R. Kets de Vries. Jossey-Bass, Inc., Publishers, 350 Sansome St. San Francisco, CA 94104. Phone: 888-378-2537 or 888-378-2537 or (415)433-1740 Fax: (415)433-0499 E-mail: webperson@jbp.com • URL: http://www.josseybass.com • 1993. $30.95. (Management Series).

Leadership Conference on Civil Rights.

Leadership Library on CD-ROM: Who's Who in the Leadership of the United States. Leadership Directories, Inc., 104 Fifth Ave. New York, NY 10011. Phone: (212)627-4140 Fax: (212)645-0931 E-mail: info@leadershipdirectories.com • URL: http://www.leadershipdirectories.com • Quarterly. $2,641.00 per year, including access to Internet version (weekly updates). Contains all 14 *Yellow Book* personnel directories on CD-ROM, providing contact and brief biographical information for about 400,000 individuals. Covers business, government, financial institutions, news media, law firms, associations, foreign representatives, and nonprofit organizations. Includes photographs.

Leadership Skills for Managers. American Management Association Extension Institute, P.O. Box 1026 Saranac Lake, NY 12983-9957. Phone: 800-262-9699 or (518)891-1500 Fax: (518)891-0368 Looseleaf. $110.00. Self-study course. Emphasis is on practical explanations, examples, and problem solving. Quizzes and a case study are included.

Leadership Strategies: The Tools to Help You Lead Effectively. Georgetown Publishing House, 1101 30th St., N. W., Suite 130 Washington, DC 20007. Phone: 800-915-0022 or (202)337-8096 Fax: (202)337-1512 E-mail: cs@gphinc.com • URL: http://www.gphinc.com • Monthly. $99.00 per year. Newsletter. Includes concise articles on change management, delegation of authority, team building, conflict resolution, and other leadership topics.

Leadership: Theory and Practice. Peter G. Northouse. Sage Publications, Inc., 2455 Teller Rd. Thousand Oaks, CA 91320. Phone: (805)499-0721 Fax: (805)499-0871 E-mail: info@sagepub.com • URL: http://www.sagepub.com • 1997. $48.00. Considers the strengths and criticisms of specific leadership approaches, such as trait, style, situational, transformational, psychodynamic, path-goal, and others.

Leading Economic Indicators and Related Composite Indexes. Conference Board, Inc., 845 Third Ave. New York, NY 10022-6679. Phone: (212)759-0900 Fax: (212)980-7014 E-mail: lei@conference-board.org • URL: http://www.tcb-indicators.org • Monthly. $24.00 per year. Shows monthly changes in the composite indexes of leading, coincident, and lagging economic indicators, formerly computed by the U. S. Department of Commerce. Tables present monthly data for up to 10 years, with a one-page line chart covering 18 years. (The Conference Board News.)

Leadscan: A Review of Recent Technical Literature on the Uses of lead and its Products. Clive Larson,ed. C and C Associates, Glebe House, 12 Parkside Green Meanwood,Leeds LS6 4NY 44, England. Quarterly. $110.00 per year. Provides technical articles and abstracts of recent technical and market related literature on lead and its uses.

League of Advertising Agencies.

League of American Theatres and Producers., 226 W. 47th St. New York, NY 10036. Phone: (212)764-1122 or (212)703-0200 Fax: (212)719-4389 E-mail: league@broadway.org • URL: http://www.broadway.org • Members are legitimate theater producers and owners and operators of legitimate theaters.

League of Women Voters Education Fund., 1730 M St., N. W., Suite 1000 Washington, DC 20036. Phone: (202)429-1965 Fax: (202)429-0854 E-mail: lwv@lwv.orgc • URL: http://www.lwv.org • Research fields include federal deficit issues.

Lean Manufacturing Advisor: Techniques and Technologies Supporting Lean Manufacturing and TPM. Productivity, Inc, 541 N.E., 20th Ave., Suite 108 Portland, OR 97232-2862. Phone: (503)294-6868 or (503)235-0909 Fax: (503)846-6883 E-mail: cmarchwi@productivityinc.com • URL: http://www.productivityinc.com • Monthly. $167.00 per year. Formerly *Lean Marketing Advisor*.

The Leap: A Memoir of Love and Madness in the Internet Gold Rush. Tom Ashbrook. Houghton Mifflin Co., 215 Park Ave. S. New York, NY 10003. Phone: 800-225-3362 or (212)420-5800 Fax: (212)420-5855 URL: http://www.hmco.com • 2000. $25.00. The author relates his personal and family tribulations while attempting to obtain financing for an eventually successful e-business startup, HomePortfolio.com.

Learn to Earn: An Introduction to the Basics of Investing and Business. Peter Lynch and John Rothchild. Simon & Schuster Trade, 1230 Ave. of the Americas New York, NY 10020. Phone: 800-223-2336 or (212)698-7000 Fax: 800-943-9831 or (212)698-7007 E-mail: ssonline_feedback@simonsays.com • URL: http://www.simonsays.com • 1996. $13.00.

Learned Publishing: ALPSP Bulletin. Association of Learned and Professional Society Publishers, South House, The Street, Clapham, Worthing West Sussex BN13 3UU, England. Phone: 44 1903 871686 Fax: 44 1903 871457 E-mail: alpsp@morris-assocs.demon.co.uk • URL: http://www.alpsp.org.uk • Quarterly. Free to members; non-members, $295.00 per year. Articles and news of interest to publishers of academic and learned society material.

Learning and Motivation. Academic Press, Inc. Journal Div., 525 B St., Suite 1900 San Diego, CA 92101-4495. Phone: 800-321-5068 or (619)230-1840 Fax: 800-336-7377 or (619)699-6715 E-mail: ap@acad.com • URL: http://www.academicpress.com/ • Quarterly. $425.00 per year.

Learning Java. Pat Niemeyer and Jonathan Knudsen. O'Reilly & Associates, Inc., 101 Morris St. Sebastopol, CA 95472-9902. Phone: 800-998-9938 or (707)829-0515 Fax: (707)829-0104 E-mail: order@oreilly.com • URL: http://www.oreilly.com • 2000. $34.95, including CD-ROM. Covers the essentials for programmers beginning to use Java.

Learning Web Design: A Beginner's Guide to HTML, Graphics, and Beyond. Jennifer Niederst. O'Reilly & Associates, Inc., 101 Morris St. Sebastopol, CA 95472-9902. Phone: 800-998-9938 or (707)829-0515 Fax: (707)829-0104 E-mail: order@oreilly.com • URL: http://www.oreilly.com • 2001. $34.95. Written for beginners who have no previous knowledge of how Web design works.

Lease or Buy? Principles for Sound Corporate Decision Making. James S. Schallheim. Harvard Business School Press, 60 Harvard Way Boston, MA 02163. Phone: 800-545-7685 or (617)783-7440 E-mail: custserv@cchbspub.harvard.edu • URL: http://www.hpsp.harvard.edu • 1994. $35.00. Discusses leasing arrangements, tax implications, accounting problems, net present value, and internal rate of return analysis. (Financial Management Association Survey and Synthesis Series).

Leasing Sourcebook: The Directory of the U. S. Capital Equipment Leasing Industry. Bibliotechnology Systems and Publishing Co., P.O. Box 657 Lincoln, MA 01773. Phone: (617)259-0524 Fax: (617)259-9861 E-mail: barbara_low@hotmail.com • URL: http://www.leasingsourcebook.com • Irregular. $135.00. Lists more than 5,200 capital equipment leasing companies.

Least Developed Countries. United Nations Publications, United Nations Concourse Level, First Ave., 46th St. New York, NY 10017. Phone: 800-533-3210 or (212)963-7680 Fax: (212)963-4910 E-mail: bookstore@un.org • URL: http://www.un.org/publications • Annual. $45.00 Report on least developed countries compiled by the United Nations Conference on Trade and Development (UNCTAD). Contains basic data.

Leather Industries of America.

Leather Industries Research Laboratory.

Leather Industry Statistics. Leather Industries of America, 1000 Thomas Jefferson St., N.W. Washington, DC 20007. Phone: (202)342-8086 Fax: (202)342-9063 Annual. Free to members; non-members, $25.00. Provides detailed analysis of domestic and foreign trade.

Leather Manufacturer. Shoe Trades Publishing Co., P.O. Box 198 Cambridge, MA 02140. Phone: (781)648-8160 Fax: (781)646-9832 E-mail: info@shoetrades.com • Monthly. $52.00 per year. Edited for hide processors, tanners and leather finishers in the U.S. and Canada.

Leather Manufacturer Directory. Shoe Trades Publishing Co., P.O. Box 198 Cambridge, MA 02140. Phone: (781)648-8160 Fax: (781)646-9832 E-mail: info@shoetrades.com • Annual. $55.00. Lists hide processors, tanners and leather finishers in the U.S. and Canada.

Ledger Quarterly: A Financial Review for Community Association Practitioners. Community Associations Institute, 225 Reinekers Lane, Suite 300 Alexandria, VA 22314. Phone: (703)548-8600 Fax: (703)836-6907 URL: http://www.caionline.org • Quarterly. Members, $40.00 per year; non-members, $67.00 per year. Newsletter. Provides current information on issues affecting the finances of condominium, cooperative, homeowner, apartment, and other community housing associations.

Legal Aspects of AIDS. Donald H. Hermann and William P. Schurgin. West Group, 610 Opperman Dr. Eagan, MN 55123. Phone: 800-328-4880 or (651)687-7000 Fax: 800-213-2323 or (651)687-5827 URL: http://www.westgroup.com • $130.00 per year. Looseleaf Service. Periodic supplementation. Includes issue employment discrimination, housing discrimination, and insurance. This work also "traces the historical progression of the disease and its spread." (Civil Rights Series).

Legal Assistant's Handbook. Thomas W. Brunner and others. Bureau of National Affairs, Inc., 1231 25th St., N.W. Washington, DC 20037-1197. Phone: 800-372-1033 or (202)452-4200 Fax: (202)452-8092 E-mail: books@bna.com • URL: http://www.bna.com • 1988. $44.00. Second edition.

Legal Checklists, 1965-1991. Benjamin Becker and others. West Group, 610 Opperman Dr. Eagan, MN 55123. Phone: 800-328-4880 or (651)687-7000 Fax: 800-213-2323 or (651)687-5827 URL: http://www.westgroup.com • 1989. $240.00. Two volumes.

Legal Guide to Independent Contractor Status. Robert W. Wood. Panel Publishers, 1185 Ave. of the Americas, 37th Fl. New York, NY 10036. Phone: 800-447-1717 or (212)597-0200 Fax: (212)597-0334 l999. $165.00. Third edition. A guide to the legal and tax-related differences between employers and independent contractors. Includes examples of both "safe" and "troublesome" independent contractor designations. Penalties and fines are discussed.

Legal Information Alert: What's New in Legal Publications, Databases, and Research Techniques. Donna T. Heroy, editor. Alert Publications, Inc., 401 W. Fullerton Parkway, Suite 1403E Chicago, IL 60614-3857. Phone: (773)525-7594 Fax: (773)525-7015 E-mail: alertpub@compuserve.com • URL: http://www.alertpub.com • 10 times per year. $169.00 per year. Newsletter for law librarians and legal information specialists.

Legal Information: How to Find It, How to Use It. Kent Olson. Oryx Press, 4041 North Central Ave., Suite 700 Phoenix, AZ 85012-3397. Phone: 800-279-6799 or (602)265-2651 Fax: 800-279-4663 or (602)265-6250 E-mail: info@oryxpress.com • URL: http://www.oryxpress.com • 1998. $59.95. Recommends sources for various kinds of legal information.

Legal-Legislative Reporter News Bulletin. International Foundation of Employee Benefit Plans, Inc., P.O. Box 69 Brookfield, WI 53008-0069. Phone: 888-334-3327 or (252)786-6700 Fax: (262)786-5960 E-mail: pr@ifebp.org • URL: http://www.ifebp.org • Monthly. $190.00 per year. Review of legislative developments, court cases, arbitration awards and administrative decisions of importance.

Legal Liability Problems in Cyberspace: Craters in the Information Highway. T. R. Halvorson. Burwell Enterprises, Inc., 5619 Plumtree Dr. Dallas, TX 75252. Phone: (281)537-9051 Fax: (281)537-8332 E-mail: burwellinfo@burwellinc.com • URL: http://www.burwellinc.com • 1998. $24.50. Covers the legal risks and liabilities involved in doing online research as a paid professional. Includes a table of cases.

Legal Looseleafs in Print. Arlene L. Eis, editor. Infosources Publishing, 140 Norma Rd. Teaneck, NJ 07666. Phone: (201)836-7072 Fax: (201)836-7072 E-mail: aeis@carroll.com • Annual. $106.00. Lists over 3,800 titles by more than 300 publishers.

Legal Malpractice: Liability, Prevention, Litigation, Insurance. Ronald E. Mallen and Jeffrey M. Smith. West Publishing Co., College and School Div., 610 Opperman Dr. Eagan, MN 55123. Phone: 800-328-4880 or (651)687-7000 Fax: 800-213-2323 or (651)687-5827 E-mail: legal_ed@westgroup.com • URL: http://www.lawschool.westgroup.com • 1995. Fourth edition. Three volumes. Price on application. Periodic supplementation.

Legal Reference Services Quarterly. Haworth Press, Inc., 10 Alice St. Binghamton, NY 13904-1580. Phone: 800-429-6784 or (607)722-5857 Fax: 800-895-0582 or (607)722-1424 E-mail: getinfo@haworthpressinc.com • URL: http://www.haworth.pressinc.com • Quarterly. Individuals, $60.00 per year; institutions and libraries, $135.00 per year.

Legal Resource Index. The Gale Group, 27500 Drake Rd. Farmington Hills, MI 48331-3535. Phone: 800-877-GALE or (248)699-GALE Fax: 800-414-5043 E-mail: galeord@gale.com • URL: http://www.gale.com • Broad coverage of law literature appearing in legal, business, and other periodicals, 1980 to date. Monthly updates. Inquire as to online cost and availability.

Legal Thesaurus. William C. Burton, editor. Pearson Education and Technology, 201 W. 103rd St. Indianapolis, IN 46290-1097. Phone: 800-858-7674 or (317)581-3500 URL: http://www.mcp.com • 1992. $27.00. Second edition.

Legal Times. American Lawyer Media, L.P., 345 Park Ave., S. New York, NY 10010-1707. Phone: 800-888-8300 or (212)545-6170 Fax: (212)696-1848 E-mail: catalog@amlaw.com • URL: http://www.americanlawyermedia.com • Weekly. Individuals, $249.00 per year; institutions, $635.00 per year.

LegalTrac. The Gale Group, 27500 Drake Rd. Farmington Hills, MI 48331-3535. Phone: 800-877-GALE or (248)699-GALE Fax: 800-414-5043 or (248)699-8069 E-mail: galeord@gale.com • URL: http://www.gale.com • Monthly. $5,000.00 per year. Price includes workstation. Provides CD-ROM indexing of periodical literature relating to legal matters from 1980 to date. Corresponds to online *Legal Resource Index*.

Legislative Process. Abner J. Mikva. Aspen Publishers, Inc., 200 Orchard Ridge Dr. Gaithersburg, MD 20878. Phone: 800-234-1660 or (301)417-7500 Fax: (301)695-7931 E-mail: customerservice@aspenpubl.com • URL: http://www.aspenpubl.com • 1995. $62.00.

Legislative Reference Services and Sources. Kathleen Low. Haworth Press, Inc., 10 Alice St. Binghamton, NY 13904-1580. Phone: 800-429-6784 or (607)722-5857 Fax: 800-895-0582 or (607)722-1424 E-mail: getinfo@haworthpressinc.com • URL: http://www.haworthpressinc.com • 1994. $39.95. Describes more than 100 reference sources that are frequently consulted in providing information to legislators and their staffs. Includes a discussion of online services used for legislative reference.

Leisure, Recreation, and Tourism Abstracts. Available from CABI Publishing North America, 10 E. 40th St. New York, NY 10016. Phone: 800-528-4841 or (212)481-7018 Fax: (212)686-7993 E-mail: cabi@cabi.org • URL: http://www.cabi.org • Quarterly. $470.00 per year. Published in England by CABI Publishing. Provides coverage of the worldwide literature of travel, recreation, sports, and the hospitality industry. Emphasis is on research.

Lender Liability Law Report. Warren, Gorham & Lamont/RIA Group, 395 Hudson St. New York, NY 10014. Phone: 800-950-1215 or (212)367-6300 Fax: (212)924-0460 E-mail: customer_services@riag.com • URL: http://www.wgl.com • Monthly. $183.00 per year. Newsletter on cases and legislation affecting lenders.

Leonard Davis Institute of Health Economics., University of Pennsylvania, 3641 Locust Walk Philadelphia, PA 19104-6218. Phone: (215)898-1655 Fax: (215)898-0229 E-mail: levyj@wharton.upenn.edu • URL: http://

www.upenn.edu/ldi/ • Research fields include health care management and cost-quality trade-offs.

Leonard's Annual Price Index of Art Auctions. Auction Index, Inc., P.O. Box 650190 Newton, MA 02465-0190. Phone: (617)964-2867 Fax: (617)969-9912 Annual. $245.00. List 19 major auction houses.

LES Nouvelles. Licensing Executives Society, c/o Jack Stuart Ott, 1444 W. 10th St., Suite 403 Cleveland, OH 44113-1221. Phone: (216)241-3940 Fax: (216)566-9267 Quarterly. Free to members; libraries, $35.00 per year. Concerned with licensing agreements, patents, and trademarks.

Lesko's Info-PowerIII: Over 45,000 Free and Low Cost Sources of Information. Visible Ink Press, 27500 Drake Rd. Farmington Hills, MI 48331-3535. Phone: 800-877-GALE or (248)699-GALE Fax: 800-414-5043 or (248)699-8069 E-mail: galeord@galegroup.com • URL: http://www.visibleink.com • 1996. $29.95. Third edition.

Lesly's Handbook of Public Relations and Communications. Philip Lesly. NTC/Contemporary Publishing, P.O. Box 545 Blacklick, OH 43004. Phone: 800-338-3987 or (614)755-4151 Fax: (614)755-5645 E-mail: ntcpub@mcgraw-hill.com • 1997. $100.00. Fifth edition.

Lessons to be Learned Just in Time. James J. Cammarano. Engineering and Management Press, 25 Technology Park Norcross, GA 30092-2988. Phone: 800-494-0460 or (770)449-0461 Fax: (770)263-8532 E-mail: cmagee@www.iienet.org • URL: http://www.iienet.org • 1997. $34.95. Discusses the background, theory, and practical application of just-in-time (JIT) inventory control in manufacturing.

Letters of Credit Report: Bank Guaranties and Acceptance. Aspen Law and Business, 1185 Ave. of the Americas New York, NY 10036. Phone: 800-901-9075 or (212)597-0200 Fax: (212)597-0338 E-mail: customer.service@aspenpubl.com • URL: http://www.aspenpub.com • Bimonthly. $299.00 per year. Newsletter. Covers letters of credit, bank acceptances, and bank guarantees.

The Levy Institute Forecast. Bard College, Jerome Levy Economics Institute, Forecasting Center, 69 S. Moger Ave. Mount Kisko, NY 10549. Phone: 888-244-8617 Fax: (914)666-0725 12 times a year. $295.00 per year. Looseleaf service. Includes quarterly supplement. Formerly *Industry Forecast*.

Lexique General; A General Lexicon of Terms-United Nations as Well as General-Used by Translators, Interpreters, etc. United Nations Publications, United Nations Concourse Level, First Ave., 46th St. New York, NY 10017. Phone: 800-533-3210 or (212)963-7680 Fax: (212)963-4910 E-mail: bookstore@un.org • URL: http://www.un.org/publications • 1991. Fourth edition.

LEXIS. LEXIS-NEXIS, Post Office Box 933 Dayton, OH 45401-0933. Phone: 800-227-4908 or (937)865-6800 Fax: (937)865-6909 URL: http://www.lexis-nexis.com • The various LEXIS databases provide full text and indexing for a wide variety of legal cases, statutes, orders, and opinions.

LEXIS Banking Library. LEXIS-NEXIS, Post Office Box 933 Dayton, OH 45401-0933. Phone: 800-227-4908 or (937)865-6800 Fax: (937)865-6909 Provides legal decisions and regulatory material relating to the banking industry, as well as full text of banking journals. Time period varies. Inquire as to online cost and availability.

LEXIS Environmental Law Library. LEXIS-NEXIS, Post Office Box 933 Dayton, OH 45401-0933. Phone: 800-227-4908 or (937)865-6800 Fax: (937)865-6909 Provides legal decisions and regulatory material relating to the environment, as well as full text of *Environmental Law Reporter* and other legal publications dealing with the environment. Time period varies. Inquire as to online cost and availability.

LEXIS Financial Information Service. LEXIS-NEXIS, Post Office Box 933 Dayton, OH 45401-0933. Phone: 800-227-4908 or (937)865-6800 Fax: (937)865-6909 Includes many business and financial files, including the full text of *SEC News Digest*, *Zacks Earnings Forecaster*, SEC filings, and brokerage house research reports. Various time spans and updating frequencies. Inquire as to online cost and availability.

Lexis.com Research System. Lexis-Nexis GroupPhone: 800-227-9597 or (937)865-6800 Fax: (937)865-6909 E-mail: webmaster@prod.lexis-nexis.com • URL: http://www.lexis.com • Fee-based Web site offers extensive searching of a wide variety of legal sources. Additional features include Daily Opinion Service, lexis.com Bookstore, Career Center, CLE Center, Law Schools, and Practice Pages (''Pages specific to areas of specialty'').

The Liberator: Male Call. Men's Defense Association, 17854 Lyons St. Forest Lake, MN 55025. Phone: (612)464-7663 E-mail: rdoyle@mensdefense.org • URL: http://www.mensdefense.org • Monthly. $24.00 per year. Newsletter supporting men's rights in family law. Formerly *Legal Beagle*.

Librarian-Author: A Practical Guide on How to Get Published. Betty Carol Sellen, editor. Neal-Schuman Publishers, Inc., 100 Varick St. New York, NY 10013. Phone: (212)925-8650 Fax: 800-584-2414 E-mail: info@neal-schuman.com • URL: http://www.neal-schuman.com • 1985. $38.50.

Librarian's Companion: A Handbook of Thousands of Facts on Libraries, Librarians, Books, Newspapers, Publishers, Booksellers. Vladimir F. Wertsman. Greenwood Publishing Group, Inc., 88 Post Rd., W. Westport, CT 06881-5007. Phone: 800-225-5800 or (203)226-3571 Fax: (203)222-2540 E-mail: bookinfo@greenwood.com • URL: http://www.greenwood.com • 1996. $67.95. Second edition. Provides international statistics on libraries and publishing. Includes directory and biographical information.

Librarians on the Internet: Impact on Reference Services. Robin Kinder, editor. Haworth Press, Inc., 10 Alice St. Binghamton, NY 13904-1580. Phone: 800-429-6784 or (607)722-5857 Fax: 800-895-0582 or (607)722-1424 E-mail: getinfo@haworthpressinc.com • URL: http://www.haworthpressinc.com • 1994. $69.95. Contains discussions by various authors on library use of the Internet. (Reference Librarian Series, Nos. 41&42).

The Librarians' Thesaurus: A Concise Guide to Library and Information Terms. Mary E. Soper and others. American Library Association, 50 E. Huron St. Chicago, IL 60611-2795. Phone: 800-545-2433 or (312)944-6780 Fax: (312)440-9374 E-mail: ala@ala.org • URL: http://www.ala.org • 1990. $25.00.

Librarian's Yellow Pages: Publications, Products, and Services for Libraries and Information Centers. Garance, Inc., P.O. Box 179 Larchmont, NY 10538. Phone: 800-235-9723 or (914)834-7070 Fax: (914)833-3053 E-mail: info@librariansyellowpages.com • URL: http://www.librariansyellowpages.com • Irregular. Free to librains; others, $15.00. A classified compilation of advertisements. for library items from more than 1,000 U. S. and Canadian companies. Major sections cover audio, automation, books, CD-ROMs, periodicals, and video. Subject and company indexes are included.

Librarianship and Information Work Worldwide. Available from The Gale Group, 27500 Drake Rd. Farmington Hills, MI 48331-3535. Phone: 800-877-GALE or (248)699-GALE Fax: 800-414-5043 or (248)699-8069 E-mail: galeord@galegroup.com • URL: http://www.galegroup.com • Annual. $189.00. Published by K. G. Saur. International coverage.

Libraries and Copyright: A Guide to Copyright Law in the Nineties. Laura N. Gasaway and Sarah K. Wiant. Special Libraries Association, 1700 18th St., N. W., 17th Fl. Washington, DC 20009-2514. Phone: (202)234-4700 Fax: 888-411-2856 or (202)234-2442 E-mail: books@sla.org • URL: http://www.sla.org • 1994. $59.00. Provides practical explanations of copyright law. Includes an extensive bibliography.

Libraries and the Future: Essays on the Library in the Twenty-First Century. F. W. Lancaster, editor. Haworth Press, Inc., 10 Alice St. Binghamton, NY 13904-1580. Phone: 800-429-6784 or (607)722-5857 Fax: 800-895-0582 or (607)722-1424 E-mail: getinfo@haworthpressinc.com • URL: http://www.haworthpressinc.com • 1993. $49.95. Emphasis is on information services in libraries of the future. (Original Book Series).

Library Administration and Management Association.

The Library Administrator's Automation Handbook. Richard Boss. Information Today, Inc., 143 Old Marlton Pike Medford, NJ 08055-8750. Phone: 800-300-9868 or (609)654-6266 Fax: (609)654-4309 E-mail: custserv@infotoday.com • URL: http://www.infotoday.com • 1997. $39.50. Covers the library administrator's role in the planning, selection, and implementation of hardware and software for automated library systems.

Library Administrator's Digest. BCPL Friends, 320 York Rd. Towson, MD 21204. Phone: (410)887-4622 Fax: (410)887-6103 10 times a year. $39.00 per year. Newsletter.

Library and Information Technology Association., 50 E. Huron St. Chicago, IL 60611. Phone: 800-545-2433 or (312)280-4270 Fax: (312)280-3257 E-mail: lita@ala.org • URL: http://www.lita.org • The Library and Information Technology Association is a Division of the American Library Association.

Library Binding Institute.

The Library Bookseller; Books Wanted by College and University Libraries. Danna D'Esopo Jackson, editor, P.O. Box 1818 Bloomington, IN 47402-1818. Phone: (812)332-4440 Fax: (812)332-2999 E-mail: betweenl@bluemarble.net • Monthly. $50.00 per year.

Library Computing. Sage Publications, Inc., 2455 Teller Rd. Thousand Oaks, CA 91320. Phone: (805)499-0721 Fax: (805)499-0871 E-mail: info@sagepub.com • URL: http://www.sagepub.com • Quarterly. Individuals, $65.00 per year; institutions, $255.00 per year. Formerly *Library Software Review*.

Library Displays Handbook. Mark Schaeffer. H. W. Wilson Co., 950 University Ave. Bronx, NY 10452. Phone: 800-367-6770 or (718)588-8400 Fax: (718)590-1617 E-mail: custserv@hwwilson.com • URL: http://www.hwwilson.com • 1991. $42.00. Provides detailed instructions for signs, posters, wall displays, bulletin boards, and exhibits.

Library Forms Illustrated Handbook. Elizabeth Futas. Neal-Schuman Publishers, Inc., 100 Varick St. New York, NY 10013. Phone: (212)925-8650 Fax: 800-584-2414 E-mail: info@neal-schuman.com • URL: http://www.neal-schuman.com • Looseleaf service $125.00 per year. Contains forms for acquisition, cataloging, circulation, reference, online searching, interlibrary loan, bibliographic instruction, personnel, administration, budgets, software control, hardware control, statistics, and special collections.

Library Hotline. Cahners Business Information, Broadcasting & Cable's International Group, 245 W. 17th St. New York, NY 10011-5300. Phone: 800-662-7776 or (212)645-0067 Fax: (212)463-6734 E-mail: corporatecommunications@cahners.com • URL: http://www.cahners.com • 50 times a year. $95.00 per year. News and developments affecting libraries and librarians.

Library Journal. Cahners Business Information, Broadcasting and Cable's International Group, 245 W. 17th St. New York, NY 10011-5300. Phone: 800-622-7776 or (212)645-0067 Fax: (212)463-6734 E-mail: corporatecommunications@cahners.com • URL: http://www.cahners.com • 20 times a year. $109.00 per year.

Library Journal: Reference Íyear\: Print, CD-ROM, Online. Cahners Business Information, 245 W. 17th St. New York, NY 10011-5300. Phone: 800-662-7776 or (212)645-0067 Fax: (212)463-6734 E-mail: corporatecommunications@cahners.com • URL: http://www.cahners.com • Annual. Issued in November as supplement to *Library Journal*. Lists new and updated reference material, including general and trade print titles, directories, annuals, CD-ROM titles, and online sources. Includes material from more than 150 publishers, arranged by company name, with an index by subject. Addresses include e-mail and World Wide Web information, where available.

Library Journal Sourcebook: The Reference for Library Products and Services. Cahners Business Information, Bowker Magazine Group, 245 W. 17th St. New York, NY 10011-5300. Phone: 800-662-7776 or (212)645-0067 Fax: (212)337-7066 URL: http://www.libraryjournal.com • Annual. $5.75. Includes ''Directory of Products and Services'' (alphabetical by product) and ''Directory of Suppliers'' (alphabetical by company). Formerly *Library Journal Buyers' Guide*.

Library Literature and Information Science: An Index to Library and Information Science Publications. H. W. Wilson Co., 950 University Ave. Bronx, NY 10452. Phone: 800-367-6770 or (718)588-8400 Fax: (718)590-1617 E-mail: custserv@hwwilson.com • URL: http://www.hwwilson.com • Bimonthly. Annual cumulation. Service basis. Formerly *Library Literature*.

Library Literature Online. H. W. Wilson Co., 950 University Ave. Bronx, NY 10452. Phone: 800-367-6770 or (718)588-8400 Fax: (718)590-1617 Contains online indexing of a wide variety of library and information science literature from 1984 to date, with updating quarterly. Inquire as to online cost and availability.

Library Management Without Bias. Ching-Chih Chen. JAI Press, Inc., P.O. Box 811 Stamford, CT 06904-0811. Phone: (203)323-9606 Fax: (203)357-8446 E-mail: order@jaipress.com • URL: http://www.jaipress.com • 1981. $78.50. (Foundations in Library and Information Science).

Library Manager's Deskbook: 102 Expert Solutions to 101 Common Dilemmas. Paula P. Carson and others. American Library Association, 50 E. Huron St. Chicago, IL 60611-2795. Phone: 800-545-2433 or (312)944-6780 Fax: (312)440-9374 E-mail: ala@ala.org • URL: http://www.ala.org • 1995. $32.00. ''..focuses on issues relevant to today's administrators and supervisors in all types and sizes of libraries.''

Library Manager's Guide to Automation. Richard Boss. Pearson Education and Technology, 201 W. 103rd St. Indianapolis, IN 46290-1097. Phone: 800-858-7674 or (317)581-3500 URL: http://www.mcp.com • 1990. $45.00. Third edition. (Professional Librarian Series).

Library of Investment Banking. Robert L. Kuhn, editor. McGraw-Hill Professional, 1221 Ave. of the Americas New York, NY 10020. Phone: 800-722-4276 or (212)904-2000 Fax: (212)904-2072 E-mail: customer.service@mcgraw-hill.com • URL: http://www.mcgraw-hill.com • 1990. $475.00. Seven volumes: 1. Investing and Risk Management; 2. Capital Raising and Financial Structure; 3. Corporate and Municipal Securities; 4. Mergers, Acquisitions, and Leveraged Buyouts; 5. Mortgage and Asset Securitization; 6. International Finance and Investing; 7. Index.

Library Personnel Administration. Lowell A. Martin. Scarecrow Press, Inc., 4720 Boston Way Lanham, MD 20706-4310. Phone: 800-462-6420 or (301)459-3366 Fax: 800-338-4550 or (301)459-1705 E-mail: orders@scarecrowpress.com • URL: http://www.scarecrowpress.com • 1994. $31.00. (Library Administration Series, No. 11).

Library Personnel News. Office for Library Personnel Resources. American Library Association, 50 E. Huron St. Chicago, IL 60611-2795. Phone: 800-545-2433 or (312)944-6780 Fax: (312)440-9374 E-mail: ala@ala.org •

URL: http://www.ala.org • Six times a year. $20.00 per year. Newsletter covering personnel trends and issues.

The Library Quarterly: A Journal of Investigation and Discussion in the Field of Library Science. University of Chicago Graduate Library School. University of Chicago Press, Journals Div., P.O. Box 37005 Chicago, IL 60637. Phone: 800-621-2736 or (773)753-3347 Fax: (773)753-0811 E-mail: subscriptions@journals.uchicago.edu • URL: http://www.journals.uchicago.edu • Quarterly. Individuals, $36.00 per year; institutions, $76.00 per year.

Library Research Center. University of Illinois at Urbana-Champaign

Library Resource Guide: A Catalog of Services and Suppliers for the Library Community. R. R. Bowker, 121 Chanlon Rd. New Providence, NJ 07974. Phone: 888-269-5372 or (908)464-6800 Fax: (908)771-7704 E-mail: info@bowker.com • URL: http://www.bowker.com • Irregular. Free to qualified personnel. An advertising directory listing several hundred manufacturers or distributors of library supplies, services, and equipment in such areas as audiovisual, automation, bar codes, binding, furniture, microfilm, shelving, and storage. Some book dealers, document delivery services, online services, and publishers are also included.

Library Space Planning: A How-To-Do-It Manual for Assessing, Allocating and Recognizing Collections, Resources, and Physical Facilities. Ruth A. Fraley and Carol Lee Anderson. Neal-Schuman Publishers, Inc., 100 Varick St. New York, NY 10013. Phone: (212)925-8650 Fax: 800-584-2414 E-mail: info@neal-schuman.com • URL: http://www.neal-schuman.com • 1990. $45.00. Second edition.

Library Systems Newsletter. Library Technology Reports. American Library Association, 50 E. Huron St. Chicago, IL 60611-2795. Phone: 800-545-2433 or (312)944-6780 Fax: (312)440-9374 E-mail: ala@ala.org • URL: http://www.ala.org • Monthly. $55.00 per year. Articles and news briefs covering all aspects of library automation.

Library Technology Reports: Evaluative Information on Library Systems, Equipment and Supplies. American Library Association, 50 E. Huron St. Chicago, IL 60611-2795. Phone: 800-545-2433 or (312)944-6780 Fax: (312)440-9374 E-mail: ala@ala.org • URL: http://www.ala.org • Bimonthly. $225.00 per year.

Library Trends. University of Illinois at Urbana-Champaign, Graduate School of Library and Information Science, Publications Office. University of Illinois Press, 501 E. Daniel St. Champaign, IL 61820-6211. Phone: (217)333-1359 Fax: (217)244-7329 E-mail: puboff@alexia.lis.uiuc.edu • URL: http://www.edfu.lis.uiuc.edu • Quarterly. Individuals, $60.00 per year; institutions; $85.00 per year.

License to Steal: The Secret World of Wall Street and the Systematic Plundering of the American Investor. Anonymous and Timothy Harper. HarperCollins Publishers, Inc., 10 E. 53rd St. New York, NY 10022-5299. Phone: 800-242-7737 or (212)207-7000 Fax: 800-822-4090 or (212)207-7145 URL: http://www.harpercollins.com • 1999. $26.00. A former stockbroker explains how brokers use persuavive and sometimes shady techniques to keep effective control of customers' accounts, regardless of losses. (HarperBusiness.)

Licensed Operating Reactors; Status Summary Report. Nuclear Regulatory Commission. Available from U. S. Government Printing Office, Washington, DC 20402. Phone: (202)512-1800 Fax: (202)512-2250 E-mail: gpoaccess@gpo.gov • URL: http://www.access.gpo.gov • Annual. Provides data on the operation of nuclear units.

The Licensing Book. Adventure Publishing, 1501 Broadway, Suite 500 New York, NY 10036-5503. Phone: (212)575-4510 Fax: (212)575-4521 Monthly. $36.00 per year. Contains articles about licensed product merchandising.

Licensing Executives Society.

Licensing Executives Society Membership Directory. Licensing Executives Society International, 1800 Diagonal Rd., Suite 280 Alexandria, VA 22314-2840. Phone: (703)836-3106 Fax: (703)836-3107 E-mail: info@les.org • URL: http://www.les.org • Annual. Membership.

Licensing Law and Business Report. West Group, 610 Opperman Dr. Eagan, MN 55123. Phone: 800-328-4880 or (651)687-7000 Fax: 800-213-2323 or (651)687-5827 URL: http://www.westgroup.com • Bimonthly. $323.00 per year. Newsletter.

Licensing Law Handbook. West Group, 610 Opperman Dr. Eagan, MN 55123. Phone: 800-328-4880 or (651)687-7000 Fax: 800-213-2323 or (651)687-5827 URL: http://www.westgroup.com • Annual. $175.00.

The Licensing Letter. EPM Communications, Inc., 160 Mercer St., 3rd Fl. New York, NY 10012-3212. Phone: 888-852-9467 or (212)941-0099 Fax: (212)941-1622 E-mail: info@epmcom.com • URL: http://www.epmcom.com • Monthly. $447.00 per year. Newsletter. Covers all aspects of licensed merchandising (compensation of a person or an organization for being associated with a product or service).

Lieber on Pensions. William M. Lieber. Aspen Law and Business, 1185 Ave. of the Americas New York, NY 10036. Phone: 800-444-1717 or (212)597-0200 Fax: 800-901-9075 or (212)597-0338 E-mail: customer.service@aspenpubl.com • URL: http://www.aspenpub.com • 1991. $595.00. Five volumes. Looseleaf periodic supplementation available. Organizes, describes, and analyzes ERISA and IRS pension rules. Topical arrangement.

Life After Stress. Martin Shaffer. Perseus Publishing, 11 Cambridge Center Cambridge, MA 02142. Phone: (617)252-5200 Fax: (617)252-5285 E-mail: westview.orders@perseusbooks.com • URL: http://www.perseusbooks.com • 1982. $15.95.

Life and Health Insurance Law. William F. Meyer. West Group, 610 Opperman Dr. Eagan, MN 55123. Phone: 800-328-4880 or (651)687-7000 Fax: 800-213-2323 or (651)687-5827 URL: http://www.westgroup.com • 1972. $125.00. Covers the legal aspects of life, health, and accident insurance.

Life Communicators Association.

Life, Health, and Accident Insurance Law Reports. CCH, Inc., 4025 W. Peterson Ave. Chicago, IL 60646-6085. Phone: 800-248-3248 or (773)583-8500 Fax: 800-224-8299 URL: http://www.cch.com • $835.00 per year. Looseleaf service. Monthly updates.

Life in Medicine: Business and Lifestyle Issues for New Physicians. Dynamic Graphics, Inc., 6000 N. Forest Park Dr. Peoria, IL 61614-3592. Phone: 800-255-8800 or (309)688-2300 Fax: (309)698-8515 Bimonthly. $42.00 per year. Covers practice management and financial topics for new physicians.

Life Insurance and Annuities from the Buyer's Point of View. American Institute for Economic Research, Division St. Great Barrington, MA 01230-1000. Phone: (413)528-1216 Fax: (413)528-0103 E-mail: info@aier.org • URL: http://www.aier.org • Annual. $10.00.

Life Insurance Answer Book: For Qualified Plans and Estate Planning. Gary S. Lesser and Lawrence C. Starr, editors. Panel Publishers, 1185 Ave. of the Americas New York, NY 10036. Phone: 800-447-1717 or (212)597-0200 Fax: 800-901-9075 or (212)597-0334 E-mail: customer.service@aspenpubl.com • URL: http://www.panelpublishers.com • 1998. $118.00. Second edition. Four parts by various authors cover life insurance in general, qualified plans, fiduciary responsibility, and estate planning. Includes sample documents, worksheets, and information in Q&A form.

Life Insurance Fact Book. American Council of Life Insurance, 1001 Pennsylvania Ave., N. W. Washington, DC 20004-2599. Phone: (202)624-2000 Biennial. $37.50 per year; with diskette, $55.00 per year.

Life Insurance in Estate Planning. James C. Munch, Jr. Aspen Books, 2961 W. California Ave., Suite E Salt Lake City, UT 84104. Phone: 800-748-4850 or (801)974-0414 Fax: 800-286-9741 or (801)886-1603 E-mail: prawlins@aspenbook.com • 1981. $80.00. Includes current supplement.

Life Office Management Association.

Lifestyle Market Analyst. SRDS, 1700 Higgins Rd. Des Plaines, IL 60018. Phone: 800-851-7737 or (847)375-5000 Fax: (847)375-5001 E-mail: jlevy@srds.com • URL: http://www.srds.com • Annual. $391.00. Published in conjunction with NDL (National Demographics & Lifestyles). Provides extensive lifestyle data on interests, activities, and hobbies within specific geographic and demographic markets.

The Lifetime Book of Money Management. Grace W. Weinstein. Visible Ink Press, 27500 Drake Rd. Farmington Hills, MI 48331-3535. Phone: 800-877-GALE or (248)699-GALE Fax: 800-414-5043 or (248)699-8069 E-mail: galeord@galegroup.com • URL: http://www.visibleink.com • 1993. $15.95. Third edition. Gives popularly-written advice on investments, life and health insurance, owning a home, credit, retirement, estate planning, and other personal finance topics.

Lifetime Encyclopedia of Letters. Harold E. Meyer. Prentice Hall, 240 Frisch Court Paramus, NJ 07652-5240. Phone: 800-947-7700 or (201)909-6200 Fax: 800-445-6991 or (201)909-6361 URL: http://www.prenhall.com • 1999. $35.00. Third revised expanded edition. Contains about 800 model letters and 400 alternative opening and closing sentences. Model letters are for sales, collection, complaints, apology, congratulations, fund raising, resignation, termination, etc.

Lifting and Transportation International. Specialized Carriers and Rigging Association. Douglas Publications, Inc., 2807 N. Parham Rd., Suite 200 Richmond, VA 23294. Phone: (804)762-9600 Fax: (804)217-8999 URL: http://www.douglaspublications.com/ • Nine times a year.$65.00 per year. Covers specialized trucking, including oversized loads, cranes, hauling steel, heavy rigging, etc. Serves as the official publication of the Specialized Carriers and Rigging Association.

Light Metal Age. Fellom Publishing Co., 170 S. Spruce Ave., Suite 120 South San Francisco, CA 94080. Phone: (415)588-8832 Fax: (415)588-0901 Bimonthly. $40.00 per year. Edited for production and engineering executives of the aluminum industry and other nonferrous light metal industries.

Lighting Design: An Introductory Guide for Professionals. Carl Gardner and Barry Hannaford. Ashgate Publishing Co., Old Post Rd. Brookfield, VT 05036. Phone: (802)276-3162 Fax: (802)276-3837 E-mail: info@ashgate.com • URL: http://www.ashgate.com • 1993. $96.95. Includes project case studies and product/effect examples. Emphasis is on commercial interior and exterior lighting. Published by Design Council Books.

Lightwave Buyers Guide. PennWell Corp., Advanced Technology Div., 98 Spit Brook Rd. Nashua, NH 03062-5737. Phone: 800-331-4463 or (603)891-0123 Fax: (603)891-0587 E-mail: webmaster@pennwell.com • URL: http://www.pennwell.com • Annual. $68.00. Lists manufacturers and distributors of fiberoptic systems and components.

Lightwave: Fiber Optics Technology and Applications Worldwide. PennWell Corp., Advaned Technology Div., 98 Spit Brook Rd. Nashua, NH 03062-5737. Phone: 800-331-4463 or (603)891-0123 Fax: (603)891-0587 E-mail: webmaster@pennwell.com • URL: http://www.pennwell.com • Monthly. $79.00 per year.

Lilly Digest. Eli Lilly and Co., Lilly Corporate Center Indianapolis, IN 46285. Phone: (317)276-3641 Fax: (317)276-5985 Annual. $30.00. Includes drug store financial data.

Lilly Hospital Pharmacy Survey. Eli Lilly and Co., Lilly Corporate Center Indianapolis, IN 46285. Phone: (317)276-3641 Fax: (317)276-5985 Annual. $30.00. Includes financial data for drug stores located in hospitals.

Limited Partnership Investment Review. Limited Partnership Investment Review, Inc., 55 Morris Ave. Springfield, NJ 07081. Phone: (201)467-8700 Fax: (201)467-0368 Monthly. $197.00 per year. Newsletter. Formerly *Tax Shelter Investment Review*

The Limits of Liberty: Between Anarchy and Leviathan. James M. Buchanan. University of Chicago Press, 5801 S. Ellis Ave., 4th Fl. Chicago, IL 60637. Phone: 800-621-2736 or (773)702-7700 Fax: (773)702-9756 E-mail: marketing@press.uchicago.edu • URL: http://www.press.chicago.edu • 2000. $20.00. (Collected Works of James M. Buchanan: Vol. 7).

Limousine Service. Entrepreneur Media, Inc., 2445 McCabe Way Irvine, CA 92614. Phone: 800-421-2300 or (949)261-2325 Fax: (949)261-0234 E-mail: entmag@entrepreneur.com • URL: http://www.entrepreneur.com • Looseleaf. $59.50. A practical guide to starting a limousine service. Covers profit potential, start-up costs, market size evaluation, owner's time required, site selection, lease negotiation, pricing, accounting, advertising, promotion, etc. (Start-Up Business Guide No. E1224.)

LIMRA International.

Lincoln Laboratory., Massachusetts Institute of Technology, 244 Wood St. Lexington, MA 02173. Phone: (781)863-5500 Fax: (781)862-9057 URL: http://www.ll.mit.edu • Multidisciplinary off-campus research unit. Research fields include solid state devices.

Lindcove Research and Extension Center. University of California

Lindey on Entertainment, Publishing and the Arts: Agreements and the Law. Alexander Lindey, editor. West Group, 610 Opperman Dr. Eagan, MN 55123. Phone: 800-328-4880 or (651)687-7000 Fax: 800-213-2323 or (651)687-5827 URL: http://www.westgroup.com • $673.00 per year. Looseleaf service. Periodic supplementation. Provides basic forms, applicable law, and guidance. (Entertainment and Communication Law Series).

Lingerie Shop. Entrepreneur Media, Inc., 2445 McCabe Way Irvine, CA 92614. Phone: 800-421-2300 or (949)261-2325 Fax: (949)261-0234 E-mail: entmag@entrepreneur.com • URL: http://www.entrepreneur.com • Looseleaf. $59.50. A practical guide to starting a lingerie store. Covers profit potential, start-up costs, market size evaluation, owner's time required, site selection, lease negotiation, pricing, accounting, advertising, promotion, etc. (Start-Up Business Guide No. E1152.)

Link-Up: The Newsmagazine for Users of Online Services, CD-Rom, and the Internet. Information Today, Inc., 143 Old Marlton Pike Medford, NJ 08055-8750. Phone: 800-300-9868 or (609)654-6266 Fax: (609)654-4309 E-mail: custserv@infotoday.com • URL: http://www.infotoday.com • Bimonthly. $29.95 per year.

Linn's Stamp News. Amos Press, Inc., P.O. Box 29 Sidney, OH 45365. Phone: 800-253-4555 or (937)498-2111 Fax: (937)498-0812 E-mail: cweditor@amospress • Weekly. $39.00 per year.

Lipper Mutual Fund Performance Analysis. Lipper Analytical Services, Inc., 47 Maple St., Suite 101 Summit, NJ 07901-2571. Phone: (908)273-2772 Weekly. Available to institutional clients only. (For detailed summaries of Lipper data on about 6,000 funds, see "Lipper Mutual Funds Quarterly" in *Barron's*, usually in the second week of January, April, July, and October.)

Liquid Filtration. McIlvaine Co., 2970 Maria Ave. Northbrook, IL 60062-2024. Phone: (847)272-0010 Fax: (847)272-9673

Monthly. $635.00 per year. Newsletter. Subscription includes "Knowledge Network": manual, catalog, video tapes, reprints, and other information sources relating to the filtration of liquids.

Liquor Control Law Reports: Federal and All States. CCH, Inc., 4025 W. Peterson Ave. Chicago, IL 60646-6085. Phone: 800-248-3248 or (773)866-6000 Fax: 800-224-8299 or (773)866-3608 URL: http://www.cch.com • $3,338.00 per year. Nine looseleaf volumes. Biweekly updates. Federal and state regulation and taxation of alcoholic beverages.

Liquor Store. Entrepreneur Media, Inc., 2445 McCabe Way Irvine, CA 92614. Phone: 800-421-2300 or (949)261-2325 Fax: (949)261-0234 E-mail: entmag@entrepreneur.com • URL: http://www.entrepreneur.com • Looseleaf. $59.50. A practical guide to starting a liquor store. Covers profit potential, start-up costs, market size evaluation, owner's time required, site selection, lease negotiation, pricing, accounting, advertising, promotion, etc. (Start-Up Business Guide No. E1024.)

LISA: Library and Information Science Abstracts. Bowker-Saur, 121 Chanlon Rd. New Providence, NJ 07974. Phone: 800-521-8110 or (908)464-6800 Fax: (908)464-3553 E-mail: custserv@bowker-saur.co.uk • URL: http://www.reed-elsevier.com • Monthly. $800.00 per year. Annual cumulation.

LISA Online: Library and Information Science Abstracts. Bowker-Saur, Reed Reference Publishing, 121 Chanlon Rd. New Providence, NJ 07974. Phone: 800-521-8110 or (908)464-6800 Fax: (908)665-6688 Provides abstracting and indexing of the world's library and information science literature from 1969 to the present. Covers a wide variety of topics in over 550 journals from 60 countries, with biweekly updates. Inquire as to online cost and availability.

LISA Plus: Library and Information Science Abstracts. Bowker-Saur, Reed Reference Publishing, 121 Chanlon Rd. New Providence, NJ 07974. Phone: 800-521-8110 or (908)464-6800 Fax: (908)665-6688 Quarterly. $1,450.00 per year. Provides CD-ROM abstracting and indexing of the world's library and information science literature. Covers a wide variety of topics.

List of Certificated Pilot Schools. Federal Aviation Administration. Available from U. S. Government Printing Office, Washington, DC 20402. Phone: (202)512-1800 Fax: (202)512-2250 E-mail: gpoaccess@gpo.gov • URL: http://www.access.gpo.gov • Annual.

List of Shipowners, Managers, and Managing Agents. Available from Fairplay Publications, Inc., 5201 Blue Lagoon Drive, Suite 530 Miami, FL 33126. Phone: (305)262-4070 Fax: (305)262-2006 E-mail: sales@fairplayamericas.com • URL: http://www.lrfairplay.com • Annual. $270.00, including 10 updates per year. Published in the UK by Lloyd's Register-Fairplay Ltd. Lists 40,000 shipowners, managers, and agents worldwide. Cross-referenced with *Lloyd's Register of Ships*.

List of Worthwhile Life and Health Insurance Books. American Council of Life Insurance, 1001 Pennsylvania Ave., N. W. Washington, DC 20004-2599. Phone: (202)624-2000 Annual. Free. Books in print on life and health insurance and closely related subjects.

Literary Market Place: The Directory of the American Book Publishing Industry. R. R. Bowker, 121 Chanlon Rd. New Providence, NJ 07974. Phone: 888-269-5372 or (908)464-6800 Fax: (908)771-7704 E-mail: info@bowker.com • URL: http://www.bowker.com • Annual. $199.95. Two volumes. Over 16,000 firms or organizations offering services related to the publishing industry.

Literature of the Nonprofit Sector: A Bibliography with Abstracts. The Foundation Center, 79 Fifth Ave. New York, NY 10003-3076. Phone: 800-424-9836 or (212)620-4230 Fax: (212)807-3677 E-mail: mfn@fdncenter.org • URL: http://www.fdncenter.org • Dates vary. Six volumes. $45.00 per volume. Covers the literature of philanthropy, foundations, nonprofit organizations, fund-raising, and federal aid.

Literature Review. Water Environment Federation, 601 Wythe St. Alexandria, VA 22314-1994. Phone: 800-666-0206 or (703)684-2400 Fax: (703)684-2492 URL: http://www.wef.org • Annual. Price on application.

Little Black Book of Budgets and Forecasts. Michael C. Thomsett. AMACOM, 1601 Broadway, 12th Fl. New York, NY 10019. Phone: 800-262-9699 or (212)586-8100 Fax: (212)903-8168 E-mail: custmserv@amanet.org • URL: http://www.amanet.org • 1988. $14.95. A concise guide to business budgeting and forecasting. (Little Black Book Series).

Little Black Book of Business Etiquette. Michael C. Thomsett. AMACOM, 1601 Broadway, 12th Fl. New York, NY 10019. Phone: 800-262-9699 or (212)586-8100 Fax: (212)903-8168 E-mail: custmserv@amanet.org • URL: http://www.amanet.org • 1991. $14.95. Covers company politics, chain of command, business lunches, dress codes, etc. (Little Black Book Series).

Little Black Book of Business Letters. Michael C. Thomsett. AMACOM, 1601 Broadway, 12th Fl. New York, NY 10019. Phone: 800-262-9699 or (212)586-8100 Fax: (212)903-8168 E-mail: custmserv@amanet.org • URL: http://www.amanet.org • 1988. $14.95. Includes examples of various kinds of business correspondence. (Little Black Book Series).

Little Black Book of Business Meetings. Michael C. Thomsett. AMACOM, 1601 Broadway, 12th Fl. New York, NY 10019. Phone: 800-262-9699 or (212)586-8100 Fax: (212)903-8168 E-mail: custmserv@amanet.org • URL: http://www.amanet.org • 1989. $14.95. How to run a business meeting. (Little Black Book Series).

Little Black Book of Business Reports. Michael C. Thomsett. AMACOM, 1601 Broadway, 12th Fl. New York, NY 10019. Phone: 800-262-9699 or (212)586-8100 Fax: (212)903-8168 E-mail: custmserv@amanet.org • URL: http://www.amanet.org • 1988. $14.95. How to write effective business reports. (Little Black Book Series).

Little Black Book of Business Statistics. Michael C. Thomsett. AMACOM, 1601 Broadway, 12th Fl. New York, NY 10019. Phone: 800-262-9699 or (212)586-8100 Fax: (212)903-8168 E-mail: custmserv@amanet.org • URL: http://www.amanet.org • 1990. $14.95. A practical guide to the effective use and interpretation of statistics by business managers. (Little Black Book Series).

Little Black Book of Project Management. Michael C. Thomsett. AMACOM, 1601 Broadway, 12th Fl. New York, NY 10019. Phone: 800-262-9699 or (212)586-8100 Fax: (212)903-8168 E-mail: custmserv@amanet.org • URL: http://www.amanet.org • 1990. $14.95. Gives practical advice on the day-to-day management of new projects, including budgeting and scheduling. (Little Black Book Series).

Livestock Market Digest. Livestock Market Digest, Inc., P.O. Box 7458 Albuquerque, NM 87194. Phone: (816)531-2235 Weekly. $20.00 per year.

Livestock Marketing Association.

Livestock, Meat, Wool, Market News. U.S. Department of Agriculture, Washington, DC 20250. Phone: (202)720-2791 Weekly.

Livestock Production Science. Elsevier Science, 655 Ave. of the Americas New York, NY 10010. Phone: 888-437-4636 or (212)989-5800 Fax: (212)633-3680 E-mail: usinfo@elsevier.com • URL: http://www.elsevier.com • Monthly. $1,288.00.

Livestock Weekly. Southwest Publishing, Inc., P.O. Box 3306 San Angelo, TX 76902. Phone: (915)949-4611 Fax: (915)949-4614 Weekly. $25.00 per year.

Living Logos: How U. S. Corporations Revitalize Their Trademarks. David E. Carter, editor. Art Direction Book Co., 456 Glenbrook Rd. Stamford, CT 06906-1800. Phone: (203)353-1441 Fax: (203)353-1371 1993. $22.95. Traces the history and evolution of 70 famous U. S. company logos.

Lloyd's Cruise International. Available from Informa Publishing Group Ltd., PO Box 1017 Westborough, MA 01581-6017. Phone: 800-493-4080 Fax: (508)231-0856 E-mail: enquiries@informa.com • URL: http://www.informa.com • Bimonthly. $198.00 per year. Published in the UK by Lloyd's List (http://www.lloydslist.com). Edited for management professionals in the cruise ship industry. Covers industry trends, technical/equipment developments, regulatory issues, new cruise ships, ship management, cruise marketing, and related topics.

Lloyd's List. Available from Informa Publishing Group Ltd., PO Box 1017 Westborough, MA 01581-6017. Phone: 800-493-4080 Fax: (508)231-0856 E-mail: enquiries@informa.com • URL: http://www.informa.com • Daily. $1,665.00 per year. Published in the UK by Lloyd's List (http://www.lloydslist.com). Marine industry newspaper. Covers a wide variety of maritime topics, including global news, business/insurance, regulation, shipping markets, financial markets, shipping movements, freight logistics, and marine technology. (Also available weekly at $385.00 per year.)

Lloyd's List Marine Equipment Buyers' Guide. Available from Informa Publishing Group Ltd., PO Box 1017 Westborough, MA 01581-6017. Phone: 800-493-4080 Fax: (508)231-0856 E-mail: enquiries@informa.com • URL: http://www.informa.com • Annual. $270.00. Published in the UK by Lloyd's List (http://www.lloydslist.com). Lists more than 6,000 companies worldwide supplying over 2,000 types of marine products and services, including offshore equipment.

Lloyd's Maritime and Commercial Law Quarterly. Available from Informa Publishing Group Ltd., PO Box 1017 Westborough, MA 01581-6017. Phone: 800-493-4080 Fax: (508)231-0856 E-mail: enquiries@informa.com • URL: http://www.informa.com • Quarterly. $245.00 per year. Published in the UK by Lloyd's List (http://www.lloydslist.com). Provides international coverage of relevant cases, decisions, and developments.

Lloyd's Maritime Atlas of World Ports and Shipping Places. Available from Informa Publishing Group Ltd., PO Box 1017 Westborough, MA 01581-6017. Phone: 800-493-4080 Fax: (508)231-0856 E-mail: enquiries@informa.com • URL: http://www.informa.com • Annual. $119.00. Published in the UK by Lloyd's List (http://www.lloydslist.com). Contains more than 70 pages of world, ocean, regional, and port maps in color. Provides additional information for the planning of world shipping routes, including data on distances, port facilities, recurring weather hazards at sea, international load line zones, and sailing times.

Lloyd's Maritime Directory. Available from Informa Publishing Group Ltd., PO Box 1017 Westborough, MA 01581-6017. Phone: 800-493-4080 Fax: (508)231-0856 E-mail: enquiries@informa.com • URL: http://www.informa.com • Annual. $468.00. Two volumes. Published in the UK by Lloyd's List (http://www.lloydslist.com). Lists more than 5,500 shipowners, container companies, salvage firms, towing services, shipbuilders, ship repairers, marine engine builders, ship management services, maritime lawyers, consultants, etc.

Lloyd's Maritime Law, North American Edition: Incorporating Court Case Digest, Maritime Personal Injury Report, and Arbitration Awards Digest. Available from Informa Publishing Group Ltd., PO Box 1017 Westborough, MA 01581-6017. Phone: 800-493-4080 Fax: (508)231-0856 E-mail: enquiries@informa.com • URL: http://www.informa.com • Biweekly. $630.00 per year. Newsletter. Published in the UK by Lloyd's List (http://www.lloydslist.com). Provides "in-depth analysis of developments in U. S. maritimne law and maritime trends."

Lloyd's Port Management. Available from Informa Publishing Group Ltd., PO Box 1017 Westborough, MA 01581-6017. Phone: 800-493-4080 Fax: (508)231-0856 E-mail: enquiries@informa.com • URL: http://www.informa.com • Quarterly. $135.00 per year. Published in the UK by Lloyd's List (http://www.lloydslist.com). Covers port management issues for port operators and users.

Lloyd's Register of Ships. Available from Fairplay Publications, Inc., 5201 Blue Lagoon Drive, Suite 530 Miami, FL 33126. Phone: (305)262-4070 Fax: (305)262-2006 E-mail: sales@fairplayamericas.com • URL: http://www.lrfairplay.com • Annual. $982.00. Three volumes and 10 cumulative supplements. Published in the UK by Lloyd's Register-Fairplay Ltd. Provides detailed information on more than 80,000 seagoing merchant ships of the world. Includes name, former names if any, date when built, owner, registration, tonnage, cargo capabilities, mechanical details, and other ship data.

Lloyd's Ship Manager. Available from Informa Publishing Group Ltd., PO Box 1017 Westborough, MA 01581-6017. Phone: 800-493-4080 Fax: (508)231-0856 E-mail: enquiries@informa.com • URL: http://www.informa.com • Monthly. $251.00 per year, including annual supplementary guides and directories. Published in the UK by Lloyd's List (http://www.lloydslist.com). Covers all management, technical, and operational aspects of ocean-going shipping.

Lloyd's Shipping Economist. Available from Informa Publishing Group Ltd., PO Box 1017 Westborough, MA 01581-6017. Phone: 800-493-4080 Fax: (508)231-0856 E-mail: enquiries@informa.com • URL: http://www.informa.com • Monthly. $1,446.00 per year. Published in the UK by Lloyd's List (http://www.lloydslist.com). Provides current analysis of world shipping markets, including coverage of the economics and costs of various kinds of ship operations. Statistical data and financial/legal directory listings are included.

Local Area Networks. David A. Stamper. Prentice Hall, 240 Frisch Court Paramus, NJ 07652-5240. Phone: 800-947-7700 or (201)909-6200 Fax: 800-445-6991 URL: http://www.prenhall.com • 2000. $69.33. Third edition.

Local Area Networks: A Client/Server Approach. James E. Goldman. John Wiley and Sons, Inc., 605 Third Ave. New York, NY 10158-0012. Phone: 800-225-5945 or (212)850-6000 Fax: (212)850-6088 E-mail: info@wiley.com • URL: http://www.wiley.com • 1996. $86.95. A business-oriented guide to local area networks and client server architecture. Covers technology, installation, and management, including a glossary of LAN terms.

Local Area Networks in Information Management. Harry M. Kibrige. Greenwood Publishing Group, Inc., 88 Post Rd., W. Westport, CT 06881-5007. Phone: 800-225-5800 or (203)226-3571 Fax: (203)222-2540 E-mail: bookinfo@greenwood.com • URL: http://www.greenwood.com • 1989. $55.00. (New Directions in Information Management Series).

Local Area Networks: Newsletter Covering Worldwide Technology Trends, Applications and Markets. Information Gatekeepers, Inc., 214 Harvard Ave. Boston, MA 02134. Phone: 800-323-1088 or (617)232-3111 Fax: (617)734-8562 E-mail: info@igigroup.com • URL: http://www.igigroup.com • Monthly. $695.00 per year. Cover new developments, new products, and marketing.

Local Climatological Data. U.S. National Climatic Data Center, National Oceanic and Atmospheric Administration, U. S. Dept. of Commerce, Federal Bldg., Room 120, 151 Patton Ave. Asheville, NC 28801-5001. Phone: (704)271-4476 Fax: (704)271-4246 E-mail: orders@ncdc.noaa.gov • URL: http://www.ncdc.noaa.gov • Monthly.

Local Government Law. Chester J. Antieau. Matthew Bender & Co., Inc., Two Park Ave. New York, NY 10016. Phone: 800-223-1940 or (212)448-2000 Fax: (212)244-3188 E-mail: international@bender.com • URL: http://

www.bender.com • $1,070.00. Seven looseleaf volumes. Periodic supplementation. States the principle of law for all types of local governments, and backs those principles with case citations from all jurisdictions. Examines the laws and their impact in three primary cases.

Locksmith Ledger International. Locksmith Publishing Corp., 850 Busse Highway Park Ridge, IL 60068-5980. Phone: (847)692-5940 Fax: (847)692-4604 E-mail: lledger@simon.net.com • URL: http://www.simon-net.com • Monthly. $38.00 per year. Includes *Directory* issue. Formerly *Locksmith Ledger*.

Locksmith Ledger-International Directory. Locksmith Publishing Corp., 850 Busse Highway Park Ridge, IL 60068-5980. Phone: (847)692-5440 Fax: (847)692-4604 E-mail: lledger@simon.net.com • Annual. $28.00 per year. Formerly *Locksmith Ledger-Security Guide and Directory*.

Lockwood-Post's Directory of the Pulp, Paper and Allied Trades. Miller Freeman, Inc., 600 Harrison St. San Francisco, CA 94107. Phone: (415)905-2200 Fax: (415)905-2232 E-mail: mfibooks@mfi.com • URL: http://www.mfi.com • Annual. $277.00. Formerly *Lockwood's Directory of the Paper and Allied Trades*.

Lodging. American Hotel and Motel Association, 1201 New York Ave., N. W., Suite 600 Washington, DC 20005-3931. Phone: (202)289-3100 Fax: (202)289-3129 E-mail: info@ahma.com • URL: http://www.ahma.com • Monthly. $49.00 per year. Editorial sections include news, finance, technology, foodservice, new products, human resources, marketing, design, and renovation.

The Lodging and Food Service Industry. Gerald W. Lattin and others. Educational Institute of the American Hotel & Motel Association, P.O. Box 1240 East Lansing, MI 48826-1240. Phone: 800-344-4381 or (517)372-8800 Fax: (517)372-5141 E-mail: info@ei-ahma.org • URL: http://www.eiahma.org • 1998. $60.95. Fourth revised edition. General survey of the hospitality industry.

Lodging Hospitality: Management Magazine for Hotels, Motels and Resorts. Penton Media Inc., 1300 E. Ninth St. Cleveland, OH 44114. Phone: (216)696-7000 Fax: (216)696-0836 E-mail: corpcomm@penton.com • URL: http://www.penton.com • Monthly. $65.00 per year. Covers a wide variety of topics relating to hotels, motels, and resorts, including management, marketing, finance, operations, and technology.

Lodging, Restaurant and Tourism Index. Distance Learning Service, Consumer and Faamily Sciences Library. Purdue University, 1002 Stone Hall West Lafayette, IN 47907-1002. Phone: (765)494-2914 Fax: (765)496-2484 URL: http://www.cea.purdue.edu/ • Quarterly. $225.00 per year. Provides subject indexing to 52 periodicals related to the hospitality industry. Annual bound cumulations are available. Formerly *Lodging and Restaurant Index*.

The Logic of Organizations. Bengt Abrahamsson. Sage Publications, Inc., 2455 Teller Rd. Thousand Oaks, CA 91320. Phone: (805)499-0721 Fax: (805)499-0871 E-mail: info@sagepub.com • URL: http://www.sagepub.com • 1993. $42.00. Consists of two major sections: ''The Emergence of Bureaucracy.'' and ''Administration Theory.''

Logistics Management and Distribution Report: For Buyers of Logistics, Transportation Services, Logistic Technology and Related Equipment. Cahners Publishing Co., 275 Washington St. Newton, MA 02158-1630. Phone: 800-662-7776 or (617)964-3030 Fax: (617)558-4327 E-mail: corporatecommunications@cahners.com • URL: http://www.cahners.com • Monthly. $92.90 per year. Includes *International Shipping* and *Warehousing and Distribution*. Formerly *Logistics Management*.

Logo Power: How to Create Effective Company Logos. William Haig and Laurel Harper. John Wiley & Sons, Inc., 605 Third Ave., 4th Fl. New York, NY 10158-0012. Phone: 800-225-5945 or (212)850-6000 Fax: (212)850-6088 E-mail: info@wiley.com • URL: http://www.wiley.com • 1997. $39.95. Explains how to plan, develop, evaluate, and implement a company logo system.

London Currency Report. World Reports Ltd., 280 Madison Ave., Suite 1209 New York, NY 10016-0802. Phone: (212)679-0095 Fax: (212)679-1094 10 times a year. $950.00 per year. Formerly *Gold and Silver Survey*.

Long Range Planning. Strategic Planning Society. Elsevier Science, 655 Ave. of the Americas New York, NY 10010. Phone: 888-437-4636 or (212)989-5800 Fax: (212)633-3680 E-mail: usinfo@elsevier.com • URL: http://www.elsevier.com • Bimonthly. $1,104.00 per year.

Long Term Care Administration; The Management of Institutional and Non-Institutional Components of the Continuum of Care. Ben Abramovice. The Haworth Press, Inc., 10 Alice St. Binghamton, NY 13904-1580. Phone: 800-429-6784 or (607)722-5857 Fax: 800-895-0582 or (607)722-1424 E-mail: getinfo@haworthpressinc.com • URL: http://www.haworthpressinc.com • 1987. $39.95. Explores the multidisciplinary nature of long-term care. (Marketing and Health Services Administration, No. 1)

Long-Term Care: An Annotated Bibliography. Theodore H. Koff. Greenwood Publishing Group, Inc., 88 Post Rd., W. Westport, CT 06881. Phone: 800-225-5800 or (203)226-3571 Fax: (203)222-1502 E-mail: bookinfo@greenwood.com • URL: http://www.greenwood.com • 1995. $59.95.

Long-Term Care and Its Alternatives. Charles B. Inlander. People's Medical Society, 462 Walnut St. Allentown, PA 18102. Phone: 800-624-8773 or (610)770-1670 Fax: (610)770-0607 1996. $16.95. Provides practical advice on the financing of long-term health care. The author is a consumer advocate and president of the People's Medical Society.

Long-Term Care Campaign., P.O. Box 27394 Washington, DC 20038. Phone: (202)434-3744 or (202)434-3829 Fax: (202)434-6403 E-mail: info@ltccampaign.org • URL: http://www.ltccampaign.org • Promotes legislation that would provide social insurance for long-term health care.

The Long-Term Care Market. MarketResearch.com, 641 Ave. of the Americas, Third Floor New York, NY 10011. Phone: 800-298-5699 or (212)807-2629 Fax: (212)807-2716 E-mail: order@marketresearch.com • URL: http://www.marketresearch.com • 1999. $3,250.00. Market data with forecasts to the year 2005. Emphasis is on the over-85 age group. Covers health insurance, the nursing home industry, pharmaceuticals, healthcare supplies, etc.

Look Before You Leap: Market Research Made Easy-How to Find Out What You Really Need to Know to Make Your Business Grow. Don Doman and others. Self-Counsel Press, Inc., 1704 N. State St. Bellingham, WA 98225. Phone: 877-877-6490 or (360)676-4530 Fax: (360)676-4549 E-mail: service@self-counsel.com • URL: http://www.self-counsel.com • 1993. $14.95.

Looking Fit. Virgo Publishing, Inc., 3300 N. Central Ave., Suite 2500 Phoenix, AZ 85012. Phone: (480)990-1101 Fax: (480)675-8109 E-mail: lookfit@vpico.com • URL: http://www.lookingfit.com • 14 times a year. $40.00 per year. Covers the business and marketing side of health clubs, aerobic studios, and tanning salons.

Looking Fit Buyers Guide. Virgo Publishing, Inc., 3300 N. Central Ave., Suite 2500 Phoenix, AZ 85012. Phone: (480)990-1101 Fax: (480)675-8109 E-mail: lookfit@vpico.com • Annual. $4.00. Lists suppliers of products and equipment for health clubs, aerobic studios, and tanning salons.

Looking for Gold: The Modern Prospector's Handbook. Bradford Angier. Stackpole Books, Inc., 5067 Ritter Rd. Mechanicsburg, PA 17055. Phone: 800-732-3669 or (717)769-0411 Fax: (717)796-0412 E-mail: sales@stackpolebooks.com • URL: http://www.stackpolebooks.com • 1995. $16.95.

Looking Good in Print: A Guide to Basic Design for Desktop Publishing. Roger C. Parker. Ventana Communications Group, Inc., P.O. Box 13964 Research Park, NC 27709-3964. Phone: 800-777-7955 or (919)544-9404 Fax: (919)942-9472 E-mail: contact@vmedia.com • URL: http://www.vmedia.com • 1999. $29.99. Tenth edition. Covers newsletters, advertisements, brochures, manuals, and correspondence.

Lookout. National Boating Federation, P.O. Box 4111 Annapolis, MD 21403. Phone: (410)280-1911 Fax: (410)280-1911 E-mail: wmmitch@execpc.com • URL: http://www.outdoorsource.com/nbf • Bimonthly. Membership.

Los Alamos National Laboratory.

Louis Rukeyser's Mutual Funds. Louis Rukeyser's Wall Street Club, 1750 Old Meadow Rd., Suite 300 McLean, VA 22102-4304. Phone: 800-892-9702 or (703)394-4920 E-mail: lrwsc@rukfsa.com • URL: http://www.rukeyser.com • Monthly. $79.00 per year. Newsletter. Provides conservative advice on mutual fund investing.

Louis Rukeyser's Wall Street., 1750 Old Meadow Rd., Suite 300 Mclean, VA 22102-4304. Phone: 800-892-9702 or (703)394-4920 E-mail: c@rukfsa.com • URL: http://www.rukeyser.com • Monthly. $79.00 per year. Newsletter. Gives recommendations for personal investing.

Lovejoy's College Guide. Pearson Education and Technology, 201 W. 103rd St. Indianapolis, IN 46290-1094. Phone: 800-858-7674 or (317)581-3520 URL: http://www.mcp.com • Semiannual. $45.00. 2,500 American colleges, universities, and technical institutes and selected foreign colleges accredited by U.S. regional accrediting associations.

Low Priced Stock Survey. Horizon Publishing Co., LLC, 7412 Calumet Ave., Suite 200 Hammond, IN 46324-2692. Phone: (219)852-3200 Fax: (219)931-6487 Monthly. $129.00 per year.

Low Rate and No Fee List. Bankcard Holders of America, 333 Maple Ave., E., No. 2005 Vienna, VA 22180-4717. Phone: (703)389-5445 Fax: (703)481-6037 Quarterly. $4.00 per copy. Lists about 50 banks offering relatively low interest rates and/or no annual fee for credit card accounts. Formerly *Low Interest Rate*.

Lowe Institute of Political Economy., Claremont McKenna College, 850 Columbia Ave. Claremont, CA 91711. Phone: (909)621-8012 Fax: (909)607-8008 E-mail: lowe@mckenna.edu • URL: http://www.lowe.research.mckenna.edu • Research topics include NAFTA.

Lower Coastal Plain Research Station/Cunningham Research Station.

LP-GAS. Advanstar Communications, Inc., 201 E. Sandpointe Ave., Suite 600 Santa Ana, CA 92700. Phone: 800-346-0085 or (714)513-8400 Fax: (714)513-8632 E-mail: information@advanstar.com • URL: http://www.advanstar.com • Monthly. $30.00 per year. Covers the production, storage, utilization, and marketing of liquefied petroleum gas (propane). Gas appliances are included. Includes annual supplement.

Lubrication Engineering. Society of Tribiologists and Lubrication Engineers, 840 Busse Highway Park Ridge, IL 60068-2376. Phone: (847)825-5536 Fax: (847)825-1456 E-mail: stle@interaccess.com • URL: http://www.stle.org • Monthly. $70.00 per year.

Ludwig Von Mises Institute for Austrian Economics.

Luggage and Leather Goods Manufacturers of America.

Lumber Co-Operator. Northeastern Retail Lumber Association, 585 N. Greenbush Rd. Rensselaer, NY 12144-9453. Phone: 800-292-6752 or (518)286-1010 Fax: (518)286-1755 E-mail: amy@nrla.org • URL: http://www.nrla.org • Bimonthly. Members, $35.00 per year; non-members, $40.00 per year.

Lumber Production and Mill Stocks. U.S. Bureau of the Census, Washington, DC 20233-0800. Phone: (301)457-4100 Fax: (301)457-3842 URL: http://www.census.gov • Annual. (Current Industrial Reports MA-24T).

Lumbermens Red Book: Reference Book of the Lumbermens Credit Association. Lumbermens Credit Association, 20 Wacker St., Suite 1800 Chicago, IL 60606-2905. Phone: (312)553-0943 Fax: (312)553-2149 E-mail: lumbermenscredit@compuserve.com • URL: http://www.lumbermenscredit.com • Semiannual $2,057.00 per year. Weekly supplements. Lists United States firms in the lumber and woodworking industries, with credit ratings.

Lundberg Letter. Tele-Drop, Inc., P.O. Box 6002 Camarillo, CA 93011-6002. Phone: (805)383-2400 Fax: (805)383-2424 Semimonthly. $950.00 per year. Petroleum newsletter.

Lynch Municipal Bond Advisory. James F. Lynch., ed. Lynch Municipal Bond Advisory,Inc., 2840 Broadway, No. 201 New York, NY 10025. Phone: (212)663-5552 Fax: (212)663-5552 Monthly. $250.00 per year. Newsletter covering events and trends in the municipal bond market.

Machinability Laboratory. Pennsylvania State University

Machine Design: Magazine of Applied Technology for Design Engineering. Penton Media, Inc., 1300 E. Ninth St. Cleveland, OH 44114. Phone: (216)696-7000 Fax: (216)696-0836 E-mail: corpcomm@penton.com • URL: http://www.penton.com • 23 times a year. Free to qualified personnel; others, $105.00 per year. Includes *Machine Design Reference Issues* and *Penton Executive Network*.

Machine Shop Operations and Setups. Orville D. Lascoe and others. American Technical Publishers, Inc., 1155 W. 175th St. Homewood, IL 60430. Phone: 800-323-3471 or (708)957-1100 Fax: (708)957-1137 E-mail: service@americantech.org • URL: http://www.americantech.org • 1973. $25.96. Fourth edition.

Machine Shop Practice. K. H. Meltrecht. Industrial Press, Inc., 200 Madison Ave. New York, NY 10016. Phone: 888-528-7852 or (212)889-6330 Fax: (212)545-8327 E-mail: induspress@aol.com • URL: http://www.industrialpress.com • 1981. $41.90. Second edition. Two volumes. Vol. one, $20.95; vol. two, $20.95.

The Machine That Changed the World. James P. Womack and others. Available from Gale Group, 27500 Drake Rd. Farmington Hills, MI 48331-3535. Phone: 800-877-4253 or (248)699-4253 Fax: 800-414-5043 E-mail: galeord@galegroup.com • URL: http://www.galegroup.com • 1990. $24.95. Based on a five-year study of the future of the automobile industry by the International Motor Vehicle Program at Massachusetts Institute of Technology.

Machine Tool Practices. Richard R. Kibbe. Prentice Hall, 240 Frisch Court Paramus, NJ 07652-5240. Phone: 800-947-7700 or (201)909-6200 Fax: 800-445-6991 or (201)909-6361 URL: http://www.prenhall.com • 1998. $90.67. Sixth edition.

Machine Vision and Robotics Industry Directory. Society of Manufacturing Engineers, P.O. Box 930 Dearborn, MI 48121-0930. Phone: 800-733-4763 or (313)271-1500 Fax: (313)271-2861 URL: http://www.sme.org • Biennial. $25.00. Provides information on suppliers of machine vision systems, services, and equipment. Formerly *Machine Vision Industry Directory*.

Machine Vision Association of the Society of Manufacturing Engineers., P.O. Box 930 Dearborn, MI 48121-0930. Phone: (313)271-1500 Fax: (313)271-2861 URL: http://www.sme.org/mva • Members are professional engineers, managers, and students. Promotes the effective use of machine vision (optical sensing of actual scenes for use in machine control).

Machinery Buyers Guide: The Annual Directory of Engineering and Products Services. Findlay Publications Ltd., Franks Lane, Franks Hall, Horton Kirby Dartfield, Kent DA4 9LL, England. Annual. $200.00. About 6,000 firms offering machine tool, engineering products, machinery, industrial equipment and services worldwide.

Machinery Dealers National Association.

Machinery's Handbook. E. Oberg and others. Industrial Press, Inc., 200 Madison Ave. New York, NY 10016. Phone: 888-528-7852 or (212)889-6330 Fax: (212)545-8327 E-mail: induspress@aol.com • URL: http://www.industrialpress.com • 2000. $99.95. 26th edition. Reference book for the mechanical engineer, draftsman, toolmaker, and machinist.

Machining of Composite Materials No. 2: Proceedings of ASM 1993 Materials Congress, Materials Week' 93, October 17-21, 1993. Held in Pittsburgh, PA. T. S. Srivatsan and others, editors. Books on Demand, 300 N. Zeeb Rd. Ann Arbor, MI 48106-1346. Phone: 800-521-0060 or (734)761-4700 Fax: (734)665-5022 E-mail: info@umi.com • URL: http://www.lib.umi.com • 1994. $58.00.

Macmillan Encyclopedia of Energy. Available from The Gale Group, 27500 Drake Rd. Farmington Hills, MI 48331-3535. Phone: 800-877-GALE or (248)699-GALE Fax: 800-414-5043 or (248)699-8069 E-mail: galeord@galegroup.com • URL: http://www.galegroup.com • 2001. $350.00. Three volumes. Published by Macmillan Reference USA. Covers the business, technology, and history of a wide variety of energy sources.

Macmillan Encyclopedia of the Environment. Stephen R. Kellert, editor. Pearson Education and Technology, Indianapolis, IN 46290-1097. Phone: 800-858-7674 or (317)581-3500 Fax: (317)581-5670 URL: http://www.mcp.com • 1997. $300.00. Six volumes.

Macmillan Encyclopedia of Transportation. Available from The Gale Group, 27500 Drake Rd. Farmington Hills, MI 48331-3535. Phone: 800-877-GALE or (248)699-GALE Fax: 800-414-5043 or (248)699-8069 E-mail: galeord@galegroup.com • URL: http://www.galegroup.com • 2000. $375.00. Six volumes. Published by Macmillan Reference USA. Covers the business, technology, and history of transportation on land, on water, in the air, and in space. Includes definitions, cross-references, and 200 color illustrations.

Macmillan Encyclopedia of Weather. Available from The Gale Group, 27500 Drake Rd. Farmington Hills, MI 48331-3535. Phone: 800-877-GALE or (248)699-GALE Fax: 800-414-5043 or (248)699-8069 E-mail: galeord@galegroup.com • URL: http://www.galegroup.com • 2001. $125.00. Published by Macmillan Reference USA. Contains 150 entries covering the basics of weather and weather forecasting. Includes illustrations in color.

Macrae's Blue Book: Serving the Original Equipment Market. MacRae's Blue Book, Inc., 210 E. 39th St. New York, NY 10016. Phone: 800-622-7237 or (212)673-4700 Fax: (212)475-1790 URL: http://www.d-net.com/macraes • Annual. $170.00. Two volumes. Lists about 50,000 manufacturers of a wide variety of industrial equipment and supplies.

Macroeconomics and Company Planning. Continuing Professional Education Div. American Institute of Certified Public Accountants, 1211 Ave. of the Americas New York, NY 10036-8775. Phone: 800-862-4272 or (212)596-6200 Fax: (212)596-6213 E-mail: journal@aicpa.org • URL: http://www.aicpa.org/pubs • Looseleaf. Self-study course.

Macworld. Mac Publishing, L.L.C., 301 Howard St. San Francisco, CA 94105. Phone: 800-217-7874 or (415)243-0505 Fax: (415)442-0766 E-mail: letters@macworld.com • URL: http://www.macworld.com • Monthly. $30.00 per year. For Macintosh personal computer users.

Made to Measure. Halper Publishing Co., 600 Central Ave., Suite 295 Highland Park, IL 60035. Phone: (847)433-1114 Fax: (847)433-6602 Semiannual. Controlled circulation.

Mademoiselle. Conde Nast Publications, Inc.,, Four Times Square New York, NY 10034. Phone: 800-289-9330 or (212)582-9090 Fax: (212)880-8289 URL: http://www.madesmoiselle.com • Monthly. $16.00 per year.

Magazine and Bookseller: The Retailer's Guide to Magazines and Paperbacks. North American Publishing Co., 401 N. Broad St. Philadelphia, PA 19108-9988. Phone: 800-627-2689 or (215)238-5300 Fax: (215)238-5457 E-mail: jcancio@napco.com • URL: http://www.magazinebookseller.com • Bimonthly. Free to qualified personnel; others, $59.00 per year.

The Magazine Antiques. Brant Publications, Inc., 575 Broadway, 5th Fl. New York, NY 10012. Phone: 800-925-9271 or (212)941-2800 Fax: (212)941-2870 Monthly. Individuals, $39.95 per year; libraries, $34.95 per year. Emphasizes antique furniture, but also covers paintings, architecture, glass and textiles. Formerly *Antiques*.

Magazine Index. The Gale Group, 27500 Drake Rd. Farmington Hills, MI 48331-3535. Phone: 800-877-GALE or (248)699-GALE Fax: 800-414-5043 or (248)699-8069 E-mail: galeord@gale.com • URL: http://www.gale.com • General magazine indexing (popular literature), 1973 to present. Daily updates. Inquire as to online cost and availability.

Magazine Index Plus. The Gale Group, 27500 Drake Rd. Farmington Hills, MI 48331-3535. Phone: 800-877-GALE or (248)699-GALE Fax: 800-414-5043 or (248)699-8069 E-mail: galeord@gale.com • URL: http://www.gale.com • Monthly. $4,000.00 per year (includes InfoTrac workstation). Provides full text on CD-ROM for about 100 popular, general interest magazines and indexing for 300 others. Includes special indexing of reviews and product evaluations. Time period is 1980 to date.

Magazine of Masonry Construction Buyers' Guide. The Aberdeen Group, 426 S. Westgate St. Addison, IL 60101-4546. Phone: 800-837-0870 or (630)543-0870 Fax: (630)543-3112 E-mail: aberdeen@wocnet.com • URL: http://www.wocnet.com • Annual. $3.00. Lists manufacturers or suppliers of products and services related to masonry construction.

Magazine Publishers of America., 919 Third Ave., 22nd Fl. New York, NY 10022. Phone: (212)872-3700 Fax: (212)888-4217 E-mail: infocenter@magazine.org • URL: http://www.magazine.org • Members are publishers of consumer and other periodicals.

Magazines Careers Directory: A Practical One-Stop Guide to Getting a Job in Publc Relations. Visible Ink Press, 27500 Drake Rd. Farmington Hills, MI 48331. Phone: 800-776-6265 or (248)699-GALE Fax: 800-414-5043 or (248)699-8069 E-mail: galeord@galegroup.com • URL: http://www.galegroup.com • 1993. $17.95. Fifth edition. Includes information on magazine publishing careers in art, editing, sales, and business management. Provides advice from "insiders," resume suggestions, a directory of companies that may offer entry-level positions, and a directory of career information sources. *Career Advisor Series*.

Magazines for Libraries: For the General Reader and School, Junior College, University and Public Libraries. Bill Katz and Linda Steinberg Katz. R. R. Bowker, 121 Chanlon Rd. New Providence, NJ 07974. Phone: 888-269-5372 or (908)464-6800 Fax: (908)771-7704 E-mail: info@bowker.com • URL: http://www.bowker.com • 2000. $185.00. 10th edition. About 7,300 periodicals listed.

Magill's Cinema Annual. The Gale Group, 27500 Drake Rd. Farmington Hills, MI 48331-3535. Phone: 800-877-GALE or (248)699-GALE Fax: 800-414-5043 or (248)699-8069 E-mail: galeord@galegroup.com • URL: http://www.galegroup.com • Annual. $115.00. Provides reviews and facts for new films released each year in the United States. Typically covers about 300 movies, with nine indexes to title, director, screenwriter, actor, music, etc. Includes awards, obituaries, and "up-and- coming" performers of the year.

Mail Advertising Service Association International.

Mail Order Association of America.

Mail Order Business. Entrepreneur Media, Inc., 2445 McCabe Way Irvine, CA 92614. Phone: 800-421-2300 or (949)261-2325 Fax: (949)261-0234 E-mail: entmag@entrepreneur.com • URL: http://www.entrepreneur.com • Looseleaf. $59.50. A practical guide to starting a mail order business. Covers profit potential, start-up costs, pricing, market size evaluation, accounting, advertising, promotion, etc. (Start-Up Business Guide No. E1015.)

Mail Order Business Directory. B. Klein Publications, P.O. Box 6578 Delray Beach, FL 33482. Phone: (407)496-3316 Fax: (407)496-5546 Annual. $85.00. Provides 12,000 listings of mail order and catalog houses in the U.S.; international coverage.

Mail Service Pharmacy Market. MarketResearch.com, 641 Ave. of the Americas, Third Floor New York, NY 10011. Phone: 800-298-5699 or (212)807-2629 Fax: (212)807-2716 E-mail: order@marketresearch.com • URL: http://www.marketresearch.com • 1999. $3,250.00. Provides detailed market data, with forecasts to the year 2003.

Mailing Services. Entrepreneur Media, Inc., 2445 McCabe Way Irvine, CA 92614. Phone: 800-421-2300 or (949)261-2325 Fax: (949)261-0234 E-mail: entmag@entrepreneur.com • URL: http://www.entrepreneur.com • Looseleaf. $59.50. A practical guide to starting a mailing services business. Covers profit potential, start-up costs, market size evaluation, owner's time required, site selection, pricing, accounting, advertising, promotion, etc. (Start-Up Business Guide No. E1354.)

Main Economic Indicators. OECD Publication and Information Center, 2001 L St., N.W., Suite 650 Washington, DC 20036-4910. Phone: 800-456-6323 or (202)785-6323 Fax: (202)785-0350 E-mail: washington.contact@oecd.org • URL: http://www.oecdwash.org • Monthly. $450.00 per year. "The essential source of timely statistics for OECD member countries." Includes a wide variety of business, economic, and industrial data for the 29 OECD nations.

Main Economic Indicators: Historical Statistics. OECD Publications and Information Center, 2001 L St., N.W., Ste. 650 Washington, DC 20036-4922. Phone: (202)785-6323 Fax: (202)785-0350 E-mail: washington.contact@oecd.org • URL: http://www.oecdwash.org • Annual. $50.00.

Main Science and Technology Indicators. OECD Publications and Information Center, 2001 L St., N.W., Ste. 650 Washington, DC 20036-4922. Phone: (202)785-6323 Fax: (202)785-0350 E-mail: washington.contact@oecd.org • URL: http://www.oecdwash.org • Semiannual. $75.00 per year. Provides latest available data on research and development expenditures in OECD countries.

Maine Lobstermen's Association.

Mainly Marketing: The Schoonmaker Report to Technical Managements. Warren K. Schoonmaker, editor. Schoonmaker Associates, Drawer 973 Coram, NY 11727. Phone: (516)473-8741 Monthly. $200.00 per year. Report to technical managements focusing on methods of marketing high technology.

Maintenance Engineering Handbook. Lindley R. Higgins. McGraw-Hill, 1221 Ave. of the Americas New York, NY 10020. Phone: 800-722-4726 or (212)904-2000 Fax: (212)904-2072 E-mail: customer.service@mcgraw-hill.com • URL: http://www.mcgraw-hill.com • 1994. $125.00. Fifth edition. Contains about 60 chapters by various authors in 12 major sections covering all elements of industrial and plant maintenance.

Maintenance Supplies. Cygnus Publishing Co., 1233 Janesville Ave. Fort Atkinson, WI 53538. Phone: 800-547-7377 or (920)563-6388 Fax: (920)563-1707 E-mail: rich.reiff@cygnuspub.com • URL: http://www.cygnuspub.com • Monthly. $60.00 per year. Geared to distributors of sanitary supplies, maintenance equipment, etc.

Maintenance Supplies Buyers' Guide. Cygnus Business Media, 445 Broad Hollow Rd., Suite 21 Melville, NY 11747. Phone: 800-308-6397 or (631)845-2700 Fax: (631)845-2798 Annual. $15.00. Approximately 1,000 manufacturers and associations for commercial, industrial, and institutional janitorial supplies; international coverage. Formerly *Maintenance Supplies Annual*.

Maize Abstracts. Available from CABI Publishing North America, 10 E. 40th St. New York, NY 10016. Phone: 800-528-4841 or (212)481-7018 Fax: (212)686-7993 E-mail: cabi@cabi.org • URL: http://www.cabi.org • Bimonthly. $795.00 per year. Published in England by CABI Publishing. Provides worldwide coverage of the literature.

Major Chemical and Petrochemical Companies of Europe. Kluwer Law International, 675 Massachusetts Ave. Cambridge, MA 02139. Phone: (617)354-0140 Fax: (617)354-8595 E-mail: kluwer@wkap.nl • URL: http://www.wkap.nl • Annual. $315.00. Published by Graham & Whiteside Ltd., London. Includes financial, personnel, and product information for chemical companies in Western Europe.

Major Chemical and Petrochemical Companies of the World. Available from The Gale Group, 27500 Drake Rd. Farmington Hills, MI 48331-3535. Phone: 800-877-GALE or (248)699-GALE Fax: 800-414-5043 or (248)699-8069 E-mail: galeord@galegroup.com • URL: http://www.galegroup.com • 2001. $855.00. Third edition. Two volumes. Published by Graham & Whiteside. Contains profiles of more than 7,000 important chemical and petrochemical companies in various countries. Subject areas include general chemicals, specialty chemicals, agricultural chemicals, petrochemicals, industrial gases, and fertilizers.

Major Companies of Europe. Available from The Gale Group, 27500 Drake Rd. Farmington Hills, MI 48331-3535. Phone: 800-877-GALE or (248)699-GALE Fax: 800-414-5043 or (248)699-8069 E-mail: galeord@galegroup.com • URL: http://www.galegroup.com • Annual. $1,780.00. Six volumes ($360.00 per volume). Published by Graham & Whiteside. Regional volumes provide detailed information on a total of more than 24,000 of Europe's largest companies: 1. Austria, Belgium, Cyprus, Denmark, Ireland, Finland. 2. France. 3. Germany. 4. Greece, Italy, Liechtenstein, Luxembourg, The Netherlands, Norway. 5. Portugal, Spain, Sweden, Switzerland. 6. United Kingdom.

Major Companies of Latin America and the Caribbean 2001. Available from The Gale Group, 27500 Drake Rd. Farmington Hills, MI 48331-3535. Phone: 800-877-GALE or (248)699-GALE Fax: 800-414-5043 or (248)699-8069 E-mail: galeord@galegroup.com • URL: http://www.galegroup.com • 2001. $795.00. Sixth edition. Published by Graham & Whiteside, London. Contains detailed information on 7,500 major companies in Central and South America. Includes manufacturers, exporters, importers, service companies, and financial institutions.

Major Companies of South West Asia 2001. Available from The Gale Group, 27500 Drake Rd. Farmington Hills, MI 48331-3535. Phone: 800-877-GALE or (248)699-GALE Fax: 800-414-5043 or (248)699-8069 E-mail: galeord@galegroup.com • URL: http://www.galegroup.com • 2001. $550.00. Fifth edition. Published by Graham and Whiteside. Provides information on 3,600 leading businesses in India and 2,500 in Turkey, Pakistan, Iran, and other countries of the region.

Major Companies of the Arab World 2001. Available from The Gale Group, 27500 Drake Rd. Farmington Hills, MI 48331-3535. Phone: 800-877-GALE or (248)699-GALE Fax: 800-414-5043 or (248)699-8069 E-mail: galeord@galegroup.com • URL: http://www.galegroup.com • 1999. $890.00. 23rd edition. Contains basic information on 8,000 companies. Published by Graham & Whiteside, London.

Major Companies of the Far East and Australasia 2001. Available from The Gale Group, 27500 Drake Rd. Farmington Hills, MI 48331-3535. Phone: 800-877-GALE or (248)699-GALE Fax: 800-414-5043 or (248)699-8069 E-mail: galeord@galegroup.com • URL: http://www.galegroup.com • 2001. $1,475.00. 17th edition. Three volumes. Published in London by Graham & Whiteside, Provides information on about 13,000 major companies. Volume one ($575.00): *South East Asia*. Volume two

($575.00): *East Asia.* Volume three *Australia, New Zealand, and Papua New Guinea.*($390.00).

Major Employers of Europe 2000/2001. Available from The Gale Group, 27500 Drake Rd. Farmington Hills, MI 48331-3535. Phone: 800-877-GALE or (248)699-GALE Fax: 800-414-5043 or (248)699-8069 E-mail: galeord@galegroup.com • URL: http://www.galegroup.com • Annual. $270.00. Published by Graham & Whiteside. Provides concise information on the top 10,000 companies in Europe, according to number of employees. Firms are indexed by country and by business activity.

Major Energy Companies of the World. Available from The Gale Group, 27500 Drake Rd. Farmington Hills, MI 48331-3535. Phone: 800-877-GALE or (248)699-GALE Fax: 800-414-5043 or (248)699-8069 E-mail: galeord@galegroup.com • URL: http://www.galegroup.com • 2001. $855.00. Fourth edition. Published by Graham & Whiteside. Contains detailed information on more than 3,300 important energy companies in various countries. Industries include electricity generation, coal, natural gas, nuclear energy, petroleum, fuel distribution, and equipment for energy production.

Major Financial Institutions of Europe. European Business Publications, Inc., P.O. Box 891 Darien, CT 06820. Phone: (203)658-2701 Fax: (203)655-8332 Annual. $495.00. Contains profiles of over 7,000 financial institutions in Europe such as banks, investment companies, and insurance companies. Formerly *Major Financial Institutions of Continental Europe.*

Major Financial Institutions of the World. Available from The Gale Group, 27500 Drake Rd. Farmington Hills, MI 48331-3535. Phone: 800-877-GALE or (248)699-GALE Fax: 800-414-5043 or (248)699-8069 E-mail: galeord@galegroup.com • URL: http://www.galegroup.com • 2001. $855.00. Fourth edition. Two volumes. Published by Graham & Whiteside. Contains detailed information on more than 7,500 important financial institutions in various countries. Includes banks, investment companies, and insurance companies.

Major Food and Drink Companies of the World. Available from The Gale Group, 27500 Drake Rd. Farmington Hills, MI 48331-3535. Phone: 800-877-GALE or (248)699-GALE Fax: 800-414-5043 or (248)699-8069 E-mail: galeord@galegroup.com • URL: http://www.galegroup.com • 2001. $855.00. Fourth edition. Two volumes. Published by Graham & Whiteside. Contains profiles and trade names for more than 9,000 important food and beverage companies in various countries. In addition to foods, includes both alcoholic and nonalcoholic drink products.

Major Home Appliance Industry Fact Book: A Comprehensive Reference on the United States Major Home Appliance Industry. Association of Home Appliance Manufacturers, 1111 19th St., N.W., Suite 402 Washington, DC 20036. Phone: (202)872-5955 Fax: (202)872-9354 URL: http://www.aham.org • Biennial. $35.00. Includes statistical data on manufacturing, industry shipments, distribution, and ownership.

Major Household Appliances. U.S. Bureau of the Census, Washington, DC 20233-0800. Phone: (301)457-4100 Fax: (301)457-3842 URL: http://www.census.gov • Annual. (Current Industrial Reports MA-36F.)

Major Information Technology Companies of the World. Available from The Gale Group, 27500 Drake Rd. Farmington Hills, MI 48331-3535. Phone: 800-877-GALE or (248)699-GALE Fax: 800-414-5043 or (248)699-8069 E-mail: galeord@galegroup.com • URL: http://www.galegroup.com • 2001. $885.00. Third edition. Published by Graham & Whiteside. Contains profiles of more than 2,600 leading information technology companies in various countries.

Major Legislation of the Congress. Available from U. S. Government Printing Office, Washington, DC 20402. Phone: (202)512-1800 Fax: (202)512-2250 E-mail: gpoaccess@gpo.gov • URL: http://www.access.gpo.gov • Irregular. Issued by the Legislative Reference Service, Library of Congress. Usually consists of five or six issues per session of Congress. Provides summaries of topical congressional concerns and major legislation introduced in response to those concerns.

Major Market Share Companies: Asia Pacific. Available from The Gale Group, 27500 Drake Rd. Farmington Hills, MI 48331-3535. Phone: 800-877-GALE or (248)699-GALE Fax: 800-414-5043 or (248)699-8069 E-mail: galeord@galegroup.com • URL: http://www.galegroup.com • 2000. $900.00. Published by Euromonitor (http://www.euromonitor.com). Provides consumer market share data and rankings for multinational and regional companies. Covers leading firms in Japan, China, Australia, South Korea, Indonesia, Malaysia, Philippines, and Thailand.

Major Market Share Companies: Europe. Available from The Gale Group, 27500 Drake Rd. Farmington Hills, MI 48331-3535. Phone: 800-877-GALE or (248)699-GALE Fax: 800-414-5043 or (248)699-8069 E-mail: galeord@galegroup.com • URL: http://www.galegroup.com • 2000. $900.00. Published by Euromonitor (http://www.euromonitor.com). Provides consumer market share data and rankings for multinational and regional companies. Covers leading firms in 14 European countries.

Major Market Share Companies: The Americas. Available from The Gale Group, 27500 Drake Rd. Farmington Hills, MI 48331-3535. Phone: 800-877-GALE or (248)699-GALE Fax: 800-414-5043 or (248)699-8069 E-mail: galeord@galegroup.com • URL: http://www.galegroup.com • 2000. $900.00. Published by Euromonitor (http://www.euromonitor.com). Provides consumer market share data and rankings for multinational and regional companies. Covers leading firms in the U.S., Canada, Mexico, Brazil, Argentina, Venezuela, and Chile.

Major Marketing Campaigns Annual. The Gale Group, 27500 Drake Rd. Farmington Hills, MI 48331-3535. Phone: 800-877-GALE or (248)699-GALE Fax: 800-414-5043 or (248)699-8069 E-mail: galeord@galegroup.com • URL: http://www.galegroup.com • Annual. $140.00. Describes in detail "100 major marketing initiatives of the previous calendar year." Includes illustrations.

Major Non-Hospital Clinical Laboratories. SMG Marketing Group, Inc., 875 N. Michigan Ave., Ste. 3100 Chicago, IL 60611. Phone: 800-678-3026 or (312)642-3026 Fax: (312)642-9729 URL: http://www.smg.com • Annual. $525.00.

Major Performance Rankings. Available from The Gale Group, 27500 Drake Rd. Farmington Hills, MI 48331-3535. Phone: 800-877-GALE or (248)699-GALE Fax: 800-414-5043 or (248)699-8069 E-mail: galeord@galegroup.com • URL: http://www.galegroup.com • 2001. $1,100.00. Published by Euromonitor. Ranks 2,500 leading consumer product companies worldwide by various kinds of business and financial data, such as sales, profit, and market share. Includes international, regional, and country rankings.

Major Pharmaceutical Companies of the World. Available from The Gale Group, 27500 Drake Rd. Farmington Hills, MI 48331-3535. Phone: 800-877-GALE or (248)699-GALE Fax: 800-414-5043 or (248)699-8069 E-mail: galeord@galegroup.com • URL: http://www.galegroup.com • 2001. $885.00. Third edition. Published by Graham & Whiteside. Contains detailed information and trade names for more than 2,500 important pharmaceutical companies in various countries.

Major Telecommunications Companies of the World. Available from The Gale Group, 27500 Drake Rd. Farmington Hills, MI 48331-3535. Phone: 800-877-GALE or (248)699-GALE Fax: 800-414-5043 or (248)699-8069 E-mail: galeord@galegroup.com • URL: http://www.galegroup.com • 2001. $855.00. Fourth edition. Published by Graham & Whiteside. Contains detailed information and trade names for more than 4,000 important telecommunications companies in various countries.

Major 20th-Century Writers: A Selection of Sketches from Contemporary Authors. The Gale Group, 27500 Drake Rd. Farmington Hills, MI 48331-3535. Phone: 800-877-GALE or (248)699-GALE Fax: 800-414-5043 or (248)699-8069 E-mail: galeord@galegroup.com • URL: http://www.galegroup.com • 1999. $314.00. Second edition. Five volumes. Includes important nonfiction writers and journalists.

Making Money with the Telephone: The Complete Handbook of Telephone Marketing. M. T. Brown. Future Shop, 915 W. Morrison, No. 76 Santa Maria, CA 93454. Phone: (805)925-2150 1977. $12.95.

Making Money with Vending Machines. Billy Mason. Kelso Manufacturing Co., 3676 Highway 1, S. Greenville, MS 38701. Phone: (662)332-7926 E-mail: kelso@tecinfo.com • 1995. $7.00.

Making Telecommuting Happen: A Guide for Telemangers and Telecommuters. Jack M. Nilles. John Wiley and Sons, Inc., 605 Third Ave. New York, NY 10158-0012. Phone: 800-225-5945 or (212)850-6000 Fax: (212)850-6088 E-mail: info@wiley.com • URL: http://www.wiley.com • 1994. $25.95. Includes tips for working productively in a home environment while maintaining good relationships with workers in the corporate office.

Malcolm Wiener Center for Social Policy., Harvard University, John F. Kennedy School of Government, 79 John F. Kennedy Cambridge, MA 02138. Phone: (617)495-1461 Fax: (617)496-9053 E-mail: juliewilson@harvard.edu • URL: http://www.ksg.harvard.edu/socpol • Does multidisciplinary research on health care access and financing.

Mallinckrodt Institute of Radiology - Hyperthermia Service., Washington University in Saint Louis, Radiation Oncology Center, 4939 Children's Place, Suite 5500 St. Louis, MO 63110. Phone: (314)362-8503 Fax: (314)362-8521 E-mail: moros@castor.wustl.edu • URL: http://www.mir.wustl.edu/ • Maintains laboratories for research pertaining to various kinds of radiological equipment.

Malt Advocate. Malt Advocate, Inc., 3416 Oak Hill Rd. Emmaus, PA 18049. Phone: (610)967-1083 Fax: (610)965-2995 E-mail: maltman999@aol.com • URL: http://www.whiskeypages.com • Quarterly. $16.00 per year. Provides information for consumers of upscale whiskey and beer.

Managed Account Reports: The Clearing House for Commodity Money Management. Managed Account Reports, Inc., 220 Fifth Ave., 19th Fl. New York, NY 10001. Phone: (212)213-6202 Fax: (212)213-1870 Monthly. $425.00 per year. Newsletter. Reviews the performance and other characteristics of commodity trading advisors and their commodity futures funds or managed accounts. Includes tables and graphs.

Managed Care: A Guide for Physicians. Stezzi Communications, Inc., 301 Oxford Valley Rd., Suite 301 Yardley, PA 19067. Phone: (215)321-6663 Fax: (215)321-6670 E-mail: stezzicomm@aol.com • URL: http://www.managedcaremag.com • Monthly. $78.00 per year. Edited for physicians and managed care administrators. Includes advice on careers and the business aspects of managed care.

The Managed Care Contracting Handbook: Planning and Negotiating the Managed Care Relationship. Maria K. Todd. Available from McGraw Hill Higher Education, 1333 Burr Ridge Parkway Burr Ridge, IL 60521. URL: http://www.mhhe.com • 1996. $65.00. Copublished by McGraw-Hill Healthcare Education Group and the Healthcare Financial Management Association. Covers managed care planning, proposals, strategy, negotiation, and contract law. Written for healthcare providers.

Managed Care Handbook: How to Prepare Your Medical Practice for the Managed Care Revolution. James Lyle and Hoyt Torras. Practice Management Information Corp., 4727 Wilshire Blvd., Suite 300 Los Angeles, CA 90010. Phone: 800-633-4215 or (323)954-0224 Fax: (323)954-0253 E-mail: pmiceditor@lainet.com • URL: http://www.medicalbookstore.com • 1994. $49.95. Second edition. A management guide for physicians in private practice.

Managed Care Interface: Today's Experts Tomorrow's Health Care. Medicom International, Inc., 66 Palmer Ave., Suite 49 Bronxville, NY 10708. Phone: (914)337-7878 Fax: (914)337-5023 URL: http://www.medicomint.com • Monthly. $80.00 per year. Provides news and information on all aspects of the managed health care industry.

Managed Care Marketing. Engel Publishing Partners, 820 Bear Tavern Rd. West Trenton, NJ 08628. Phone: (609)530-0044 Fax: (609)530-0207 Quarterly. $24.00 per year. Edited for executives of managed health care companies and organizations.

Managed Care Outlook: The Insider's Business Briefing on Managed Health Care. Aspen Publishers, Inc., 200 Orchard Ridge Dr. Gaithersburg, MD 20878. Phone: 800-638-8437 or (301)417-7500 Fax: (301)695-7931 E-mail: customer.service@aspenpubl.com • URL: http://www.aspenpubl.com • 50 times a year. $499.00 per year. Newsletter relating to health maintenance organizations (HMOs), preferred provider organizations (PPOs), and other managed care systems.

Managed Care: The Vision and the Strategy. American Association of Homes and Services for the Aging, 901 E. St., N. W., Suite 500 Washington, DC 20004. Phone: 800-508-9442 or (202)783-2242 Fax: (202)783-2255 E-mail: info@aahsa.org • URL: http://www.aahsa.org • 1996. $30.00. A report on an AAHSA national managed care summit. Topics include delivery models, regulatory conflicts, costs, finances, consumer choice, and related subjects.

Managed Healthcare News: The Managed Care Industry's News Authority. Quadrant HealthCom, Inc., 26 Main St. Chatham, NJ 07928-2402. Phone: (973)701-8900 Fax: (973)701-8894 URL: http://www.managedhealthcarenews.com • Monthly. $75.00 per year. Presents new developments and trends for medical directors, pharmacists, administrators, and others concerned with managed care.

Managed Healthcare: The News Magazine for Managers of Healthcare Costs and Quality. Advanstar Healthcare Croup. Advanstar Communications, Inc., 201 E. Sandpointe Ave., Suite 600 Santa Ana, CA 92700-8700. Phone: 800-346-0085 or (714)513-8400 Fax: (714)513-8632 E-mail: information@advanstar.com • URL: http://www.advanstar.com • Monthly. $64.00 per year. Edited for managers of HMOs and other managed care organizations. Covers outcomes, quality assurance, technology, long term care, and trends in the health care industry.

The Managed Medicare and Medicaid Market. MarketResearch.com, 641 Ave. of the Americas, Third Floor New York, NY 10011. Phone: 800-298-5699 or (212)807-2629 Fax: (212)807-2716 E-mail: order@marketresearch.com • URL: http://www.marketresearch.com • 1997. $1,250.00. Market research report on medicare HMOs. Includes analysis of legal issues and the impact of managed care on older consumers. Providers such as Kaiser Permanente, Humana, and U. S. Healthcare are profiled.

Management. John Schermerhorn. John Wiley and Sons, Inc., 605 Third Ave. New York, NY 10158-0012. Phone: 800-225-5945 or (212)850-6000 Fax: (212)850-6088 E-mail: info@wiley.com • URL: http://www.wiley.com • 1998. $97.95. Sixth edition.

Management Accounting. Don R. Hansen. South-Western College Publishing, 5101 Madison Rd. Cincinnati, OH 45227. Phone: 800-543-0487 or (513)527-1989 Fax: (513)527-6137 URL: http://www.thomson.com • 1999. $98.95. Fifth edition. (SWC-Accounting).

Management Accounting for Healthcare Organizations. Bruce R. Neumann and Keith E. Boles. Teach'em, 160 E. Illinois St. Chicago, IL 60611. Phone: 800-225-3775 or (312)467-0580 Fax: (312)467-9271 E-mail: bb@bonus-books.com • URL: http://www.bonus-books.com • 1998. $65.00. Fifth revised edition.

Management Advisory Services Guideline Series. American Institute of Certified Public Accountants, 1211 Ave. of the Americas New York, NY 10036-8775. Phone: 800-862-4272 or (212)596-6200 Fax: (212)596-6213 E-mail: journal@aicpa.org • URL: http://www.aicpa.org/pubs • Irregular. Price varies.

Management and Leadership Resources for Non-Profits. Available from Applied Research and Development Institute, 1805 S. Bellaire St., Suite 219 Denver, CO 80222. Phone: (303)691-6076 Fax: (303)691-6077 Annual. $3.50. Compiled by the Applied Research and Development Institute and published as a special issue of *The Journal of Philanthropy*. Lists and describes over 800 books, periodicals, and other publications in 14 categories (general management, finance, marketing, development, etc.). Includes a directory of publishers. No indexes.

Management Communication Quarterly: An International Journal. Sage Publications, Inc., 2455 Teller Rd. Thousand Oaks, CA 91320. Phone: (805)499-0721 Fax: (805)499-0871 E-mail: info@sagepub.com • URL: http://www.sagepub.com • Quarterly. Individuals, $65.00; institutions, $310.00 per year. A scholarly journal on managerial and organizational communication effectiveness.

Management: Concepts, Practice, and Skills. Premeaux Mondy. South-Western College Publishing, 5101 Madison Rd. Cincinnati, OH 45227. Phone: 800-543-0487 or (513)527-1989 Fax: (513)527-6137 URL: http://www.thomson.com • 1999. $39.95. Eighth edition. (SWC-General Business Series).

Management Consultant Books. Kennedy Information, LLC, One Kennedy Place, Route 12, S. Fitzwilliam, NH 03447. Phone: 800-531-1026 or (603)585-3101 Fax: (603)585-9555 E-mail: office@kennedypub.com • URL: http://www.kennedy.com • Annual. Free. Contains descriptions of selected books from various publishers on management consulting.

Management Contents. The Gale Group, 27500 Drake Rd. Farmington Hills, MI 48331-3535. Phone: 800-877-GALE or (248)699-GALE Fax: 800-414-5043 or (248)699-8069 E-mail: galeord@gale.com • URL: http://www.gale.com • Covers a wide range of management, financial, marketing, personnel, and administrative topics. About 150 leading business journals are indexed and abstracted from 1974 to date, with monthly updating. Inquire as to online cost and availability.

Management Control in Nonprofit Organizations. Robert N. Anthony and David W. Young. McGraw-Hill, 1221 Ave. of the Americas New York, NY 10020. Phone: 800-722-4726 or (212)904-2000 Fax: (212)904-2072 E-mail: customer.service@mcgraw-hill.com • URL: http://www.mcgraw-hill.com • 1998. $89.06. Sixth edition.

Management Control in Nonprofit Organizations. Robert N. Anthony and David W. Young. McGraw-Hill Higher Education, 1221 Ave. of the Americas New York, NY 10020. Phone: 800-722-4726 or (212)904-2000 Fax: (212)904-2072 E-mail: customer.service@mcgraw-hill.com • URL: http://www.mcgraw-hill.com • 1998. $89.06. Sixth edition.

Management Education and Development: An Annotated Resource Book. Theodore T. Herbert and Edward Yost. Greenwood Publishing Group, Inc., 88 Post Rd., W. Westport, CT 06881-5007. Phone: 800-225-5800 or (203)226-3571 Fax: (203)222-2540 E-mail: bookinfo@greenwood.com • URL: http://www.greenwood.com • 1978. $59.95.

Management for Strategic Business Ideas. Society of Management Accountants of Canada, 120 King St. W., Ste. 850 Hamilton, ON, Canada L8P 4V2. Phone: (905)525-4100 Fax: (905)525-4533 E-mail: dfidler@managementmag.com • URL: http://www.managementmag.com • 10 times a year. $60.00 per year. Text in English and French.

A Management Guide to Leveraged Buyouts. Edward K. Crawford. John Wiley and Sons, Inc., 605 Third Ave. New York, NY 10158-0012. Phone: 800-225-5945 or (212)850-6000 Fax: (212)850-6088 E-mail: info@wiley.com • URL: http://www.wiley.com • 1987. $110.00. (Professional Banking and Finance Series).

Management Information Systems. Raymond McLeod and George Schell. Prentice Hall, 240 Frisch Court Paramus, NJ 07652-5240. Phone: 800-947-7700 or (201)909-6452 Fax: 800-445-6991 or (201)909-6361 URL: http://www.prenhall.com • 2000. $89.33. Sixth edition.

Management Information Systems: Managing Information. Fritz J. Erickson and James A. O'Brien. McGraw-Hill Higher Education, 1221 Ave. of the Americas New York, NY 10020-1095. Phone: 800-722-4726 or (212)904-2000 Fax: (212)904-2072 E-mail: customer.service@mcgraw-hill.com • URL: http://www.mcgraw-hill.com • 1996. $72.25. Third edition.

Management Information Systems Research Center. University of Minnesota

Management Information Systems: The Manager's View. Robert A. Schultheis. McGraw-Hill Higher Education, 1221 Ave. of the Americas New York, NY 10020-1095. Phone: 800-722-4726 or (212)904-2000 Fax: (212)904-2072 E-mail: customer.service@mcgraw-hill.com • URL: http://www.mcgraw-hill.com • 1997. $62.00. Fourth edition.

Management Information Systems: With Application Cases and Internet Primer. James A. O'Brien and others. McGraw-Hill Higher Education, 1221 Ave. of the Americas New York, NY 10020-1095. Phone: 800-722-4726 or (212)904-2000 Fax: (212)904-2072 E-mail: customer.service@mcgraw-hill.com • URL: http://www.mcgraw-hill.com • 1996. $85.00. Third edition. Includes CD-ROM.

Management International Review: Journal of International Business. Betriebswirtschaftlicher Verlag Dr. Th. Gabler Gmbh, Abraham-Lincoln-Str. 46 65189 49 6 Wiesbaden, Germany. Phone: 49 611 7878129 Fax: 49 611 7878423 Quarterly.

Management of a Public Library. Harold R. Jenkins. JAI Press, Inc., P.O. Box 811 Stamford, CT 06904-0811. Phone: (203)323-9606 Fax: (203)357-8446 E-mail: order@jaipress.com • URL: http://www.jaipress.com • 1980 $78.50. (Foundations in Library and Information Science Series, Vol. 87).

Management of a Sales Force. William J. Stanton and others. McGraw-Hill, 1221 Ave. of the Americas New York, NY 10020. Phone: 800-722-4726 or (212)904-2000 Fax: (212)904-2072 E-mail: customer.service@mcgraw-hill.com • URL: http://www.mcgraw-hill.com • 1998. $85.00. 10th edition.

Management of Hazardous Materials and Wastes: Treatment, Minimization, and Environmental Impacts. Shyamal K. Majumdar and others, editors. Pennsylvania Academy of Science, Department of Biology, Lafayette College Easton, PA 18042. Phone: (610)330-5464 Fax: (610)330-5705 1989. $45.00.

Management of Healthcare Organizations. Kerry D. Carson and others. Brooks/Cole Publishing Co., 511 Forest Lodge Rd. Pacific Grove, CA 93950. Phone: 800-345-9706 or (831)373-0728 Fax: (831)375-6414 E-mail: info@brookscole.com • URL: http://www.brookscole.com • Price on application. (SWC-Management Series).

Management of Hotel and Motel Security. Harvey Burstein. Marcel Dekker, Inc., 270 Madison Ave. New York, NY 10016. Phone: 800-228-1160 or (212)696-9000 Fax: (212)685-4540 1980. $110.00. (Occupational Safety and Health Series).

The Management of Nonprofit Organizations. Sharon M. Oster, editor. Ashgate Publishing Co., Old Post Rd. Brookfield, VT 05036. Phone: (802)276-3162 Fax: (802)276-3837 E-mail: info@ashgate.com • URL: http://www.ashgate.com • 1994. $235.95. Published by Dartmouth Publisher.

Management of People in Hotels and Restaurants. Donald E. Lundberg and James P. Armatas. Brown and Benchmark, 25 Kessel Court Madison, WI 53711. Phone: 800-338-5578 or (608)273-0040 Fax: 800-346-2377 E-mail: customer.service@mcgraw-hill.com • URL: http://www.mhhe.com • 1992. $36.50. Fifth edition.

Management of Quality Assurance. Madhav N. Sinha and Walter O. Willborn. John Wiley and Sons, Inc., 605 Third Ave. New York, NY 10158-0012. Phone: 800-526-5368 or (212)850-6000 Fax: (212)850-6088 E-mail: info@wiley.com • URL: http://www.wiley.com • 1985. $99.95.

Management of Retail Buying. R. Patrick Cash and others. John Wiley and Sons, Inc., 605 Third Ave. New York, NY 10158-0012. Phone: 800-225-5945 or (212)850-6000 Fax: (212)850-6088 E-mail: info@wiley.com • URL: http://www.wiley.com • 1995. $110.00. Third edition.

Management OHS and E. Stevens Publishing Corp., 5151 Beltline Rd., Suite 1010 Dallas, TX 75240. Phone: (972)687-6700 Fax: (972)687-6769 Monthly. Free to qualified personnel; others, $150.00 per year. Includes news, interviews, feature articles, legal developments, and reviews of literature. Includes *Buyer's Guide*.

Management Review. American Management Association, 1601 Broadway New York, NY 10019-7420. Phone: 800-313-8650 or (212)586-8100 Fax: (212)903-8168 E-mail: amapubs@aol.com • URL: http://www.amanet.org • Membership.

Management Science. Institute for Operations Research and the Management Sciences, 901 Elkridge Landing Rd., Suite 400 Linthicum, MD 21090-2909. Phone: 800-446-3676 or (410)850-0300 Fax: (410)684-2963 URL: http://www.informs.org • Monthly. Individuals, $143.00 per year; institutions, $327.00 per year. Provides an interchange of information between management and management scientists in industry, academia, the military and government.

Management: Skills and Application. Leslie W. Rue and Lloyd L. Byars. McGraw-Hill, 1221 Ave. of the Americas New York, NY 10020. Phone: 800-722-4726 or (212)904-2000 Fax: (212)904-2072 E-mail: customer.service@mcgraw-hill.com • URL: http://www.mcgraw-hill.com • 1999. $59.65. Ninth edition. An introductory text covering the principles of successful management. Arranged according to the following "Skills:" Planning, Organizing, Staffing, Directing, and Controlling. Includes a glossary of key terms and three indexes. (Irwin Professional Publishing.)

Management: Skills and Application. Leslie W. Rue. McGraw-Hill Higher Education, 1221 Ave. of the Americas New York, NY 10020-1095. Phone: 800-722-4726 or (212)904-2000 Fax: (212)904-2072 E-mail: customer.service@mcgraw-hill.com • URL: http://www.mcgraw-hill.com • 1996. $39.95. Eighth edition.

Management Strategies for Libraries: A Basic Reader. Beverly Lynch, editor. Neal-Schuman Publishers, Inc., 100 Varick St. New York, NY 10013. Phone: (212)925-8650 Fax: 800-584-2414 E-mail: info@neal-schuman.com • URL: http://www.neal-schuman.com • 1985. $55.00.

Management: Theory, Process, and Practice. Richard M. Hodgetts. harcourt Trade Publishers, 525 B St., Suite 1900 San Deigo, CA 92101-4495. Phone: 800-782-4479 or (619)231-6616 Fax: 800-334-0878 1989. Fifth edition. Price on application.

Management Update. Harvard Business School Publishing, 60 Harvard Way Boston, MA 02163. Phone: 800-545-7685 or (617)783-7440 E-mail: muopinion@hbsp.harvard.edu • URL: http://www.hbsp.harvard.edu • Monthly. $99.00 per year. Newsletter. Covers "ideas, trends, and solutions" for middle management.

Managerial Accounting. Harold M. Sollenberger and Arnold Schneider. South-Western Publishing Co., 5101 Madison Rd. Cincinnati, OH 45227. Phone: 800-543-0487 or (513)271-8811 Fax: 800-437-8488 E-mail: billhendee@itped.com • URL: http://www.swcollege.com • 1996. $80.95. Ninth edition. (SWC-Accounting).

Managerial and Decision Economics: The International Journal of Research and Progress in Management Economics. Available from John Wiley and Sons, Inc., Journals Div., 605 Third Ave. New York, NY 10158-0012. Phone: 800-526-5368 or (212)850-6000 Fax: (212)850-6088 E-mail: info@wiley.com • URL: http://www.wiley.com • Eight times a year. $905.00 per year. Deals with economic problems in the field of managerial and decision economics. International coverage. Published in England by John Wiley and Sons Ltd.

Managerial Economics. Mark Hirschey. Harcourt Trade Publications, 525 B St., Suite 1900 San Diego, CA 92101-4495. Phone: 800-543-1918 or (619)231-6616 Fax: 800-235-0256 E-mail: apbcs@harcourtbrace.com • URL: http://www.harcourt.com. • 1995. $31.25. Eighth edition.

Managerial Economics. James R. McGuigan. South-Western Publishing Co., 5101 Madison Rd. Cincinnati, OH 45227. Phone: 800-354-9706 or (513)271-8811 E-mail: billhendee@itped.com • URL: http://www.swcollege.com • 1998. $90.95. Eighth edition. (HT-Mangerial Economics Series).

Managerial Economics: Analysis, Problems, Cases. Dale Truett and Lila Truett. South-Western College Publishing, 5101 Madison Rd. Cincinnati, OH 45227. Phone: 800-543-0487 or (513)527-1989 URL: http://www.thomson.com • 1995. $75.25. Fifth edition. (Principles of Economics Series).

Managerial Economics and Business Strategy. Michael R. Baye. McGraw-Hill Professional, 1221 Ave. of the Americas New York, NY 10020. Phone: 800-722-4726 or (212)904-2000 Fax: (212)904-2072 E-mail: customer.service@mcgraw-hill.com • URL: http://www.mcgraw-hill.com • 2000. Third edition. Price on application.

Managerial Economics: Applied Microeconomics for Decision Making. Charles S. Maurice and Christopher R. Thomas. McGraw-Hill Higher Education, 1221 Ave. of the Americas New York, NY 10020-1095. Phone: 800-722-4726 or (212)904-2000 Fax: (212)904-2072 E-mail: customer.service@mcgraw-hill.com • URL: http://www.mcgraw-hill.com • 1994. $69.75. Fifth edition.

The Managerial Woman. Margaret Henning and Anne Jardim. Pocket Books, 1230 Ave. of the Americas New York, NY 10020. Phone: 800-223-2348 or (212)698-7000 Fax: 800-943-9831 1983. $5.99.

The Manager's Book of Quotations. Lewis D. Eigen and Jonathan P. Siegel. AMACOM, 1601 Broadway, 12th Fl. New York, NY 10019. Phone: 800-262-9699 or (212)586-8100 Fax: (212)903-8168 E-mail: custmserv@amanet.org • URL: http://www.amanet.org • 1991. $21.95. Reprint edition. Provides 5,000 modern and traditional quotations arranged by topics useful to business people for speeches and writing.

Manager's Guide to Financial Statement Analysis. Stephen F. Jablonsky and Noah P. Barsky. John Wiley and Sons, Inc., 605 Third Ave. New York, NY 10158-0012. Phone: 800-225-5945 or (212)850-6000 Fax: (212)850-6088 E-mail: info@wiley.com • URL: http://www.wiley.com • 1998. $67.95. The two main sections are "Financial Statements and Business Strategy'' and ''Market Valuation and Business Strategy.''

Manager's Intelligence Report: Insider's Fast Track to Better Management. Lawrence Ragan Communications, Inc., 316 N. Michigan Ave., Suite 300 Chicago, IL 60601. Phone: 800-878-5331 or (312)960-4100 Fax: (312)960-4106 E-mail: cservice@ragan.com • URL: http://www.ragan.com • Monthly. $129.00 per year. Newsletter on various aspects of management, including strategy, employee morale, and time management.

Manager's Negotiating Answer Book. George Fuller. DIANE Publishing Co., 330 Pusey Ave., Ste. 3 Collingdale, PA 19023. Phone: (610)461-6200 Fax: (610)461-6130 E-mail: dianepubs@erol.com • URL: http://www.dianepublishing.com • 1999. $40.00.

Manager's Tool Kit: Practical Tips for Tackling 100 On-the-Job Problems. Cy Charney. AMACOM, 1601 Broadway, 12th Fl. New York, NY 10019. Phone: 800-262-9699 or (212)586-8100 Fax: (212)903-8168 E-mail: custmserv@amanet.org • URL: http://www.amanet.org • 1995. $17.95.

Managing a Public Relations Firm for Growth and Profit. A. C. Croft. The Haworth Press, Inc., 10 Alice St. Binghamton, NY 13904-1580. Phone: 800-429-6784 or (607)722-5857 Fax: 800-895-0582 or (607)722-1424 E-mail: getinfo@haworthpressinc.com • URL: http://www.haworthpressinc.com • 1995. $39.95.

Managing and Operating a Closely-Held Corporation. Michael Diamond. John Wiley and Sons, Inc., 605 Third Ave. New York, NY 10158-0012. Phone: 800-526-5368 or (212)850-6000 Fax: (212)850-6088 E-mail: info@wiley.com • URL: http://www.wiley.com • 1991. $135.00.

Managing Automation. Thomas Publishing Co., Five Penn Plaza, 250 W. 34th St. New York, NY 10001. Phone: 800-699-9822 or (212)695-0500 Fax: (212)629-1564 URL: http://www.thomaspublishing.com • Monthly. Free to qualified personnel. Coverage includes software for manufacturing, systems planning, integration in process industry automation, computer integrated manufacturing (CIM), computer networks for manufacturing, management problems, industry news, and new products.

Managing Business Ethics: Straight Talk About How to Do It Right. Linda K. Trevino and Katherine A. Nelson. John Wiley and Sons, Inc., 605 Third Ave. New York, NY 10158-0012. Phone: 800-225-5945 or (212)850-6000 Fax: (212)850-6088 E-mail: info@wiley.com • URL: http://www.wiley.com • 1999. $49.95. Second edition. Includes ''Ethics and the Individual,'' ''Ethics and the Manager,'' and ''Ethics and the Organization.''

Managing Casinos: A Guide for Entrepreneurs, Management Personnel, and Aspiring Managers. Ruben Martinez. Barricade Books, Inc., 150 Fifth Ave., Suite 700 New York, NY 10011. Phone: 800-592-6657 or (212)627-7000 Fax: (212)627-7028 URL: http://www.barricadebooks.com • 1995. $75.00. Covers such topics as the installation of profitable games, providing credit to players, casino business math, and understanding odds.

Managing Contingent Workers: How to Reap the Benefits and Reduce the Risk. Stanley Nollen and Helen Axel. AMACOM, 1601 Broadway, 12th Fl. New York, NY 10019. Phone: 800-262-9699 or (212)586-8100 Fax: (212)903-8168 E-mail: custmserv@amanet.org • URL: http://www.amanet.org • 1995. $55.00.

Managing Credit and Collections to Improve Cash Flow. American Management Association Extension Institute, P.O. Box 1026 Saranac Lake, NY 12983-9957. Phone: 800-262-9699 or (518)891-1500 Fax: (518)891-0368 Looseleaf. $130.00. Self-study course. Emphasis is on practical explanations, examples, and problem solving. Quizzes and a case study are included.

Managing Expert Systems. Efraim Tuban and Jay Liebowitz. Idea Group Publishing, 1331 E. Chocolate Ave. Hershey, PA 17033-1117. Phone: 800-345-8845 or (717)533-8845 Fax: (717)533-8661 E-mail: jtravers@idea-group.com • URL: http://www.idea-group.com • 1992. $53.50.

Managing Factory Maintenance. Joel Levitt. Industrial Press, Inc., 200 Madison Ave. New York, NY 10016. Phone: 888-528-7852 or (212)889-6330 Fax: (212)545-8327 E-mail: induspress@aol.com • URL: http://www.industrialpress.com • 1996. $39.95.

Managing Financial Risk with Forwards, Futures, Options, and Swaps. American Management Association Extension Institute, P.O. Box 1026 Saranac Lake, NY 12983-9957. Phone: 800-262-9699 or (518)891-1500 Fax: (518)891-0368 Looseleaf. $130.00. Self-study course. Emphasis is on practical explanations, examples, and problem solving. Quizzes and a case study are included.

Managing Front Office Operations. Michael L. Kasavana and Richard M. Brooks. Educational Institute of the American Hotel & Motel Association, P.O. Box 1240 East Lansing, MI 48826-1240. Phone: 800-344-4381 or (517)372-8800 Fax: (517)372-5141 E-mail: info@el-ahma.org • URL: http://www.ei.ahma.org • 1998. $66.95. Fifth revised edition. Covers all aspects of the front office. Includes computer appliations throughout all phases of the guest cycle.

Managing Globally: A Complete Guide to Competing Worldwide. Carl A. Nelson. McGraw-Hill Professional, 1221 Ave. of the Americas New York, NY 10020. Phone: 800-722-4726 or (212)904-2000 Fax: (212)904-2072 E-mail: customer.service@mcgraw-hill.com • URL: http://www.mcgraw-hill.com • 1993. $65.00. Emphasis is on global strategic management and tactics.

Managing High-Technology Programs and Projects. Russell D. Archibald. John Wiley and Sons, Inc., 605 Third Ave. New York, NY 10158-0012. Phone: 800-225-5945 or (212)850-6000 Fax: (212)850-6088 E-mail: info@wiley.com • URL: http://www.wiley.com • 1992. $107.50. Second edition. Written for senior executives, professional project managers, engineers, and information systems managers.

Managing Housing Letter. Community Development Services, Inc. CD Publications, 8204 Fenton St. Silver Spring, MD 20910-2889. Phone: 800-666-6380 or (301)588-6380 Fax: (301)588-6385 E-mail: mhl@cdpublications.com • Monthly. $225.00 per year. Newsletter for housing professionals. Provides property management advice and news relating to private and publicly-funded rental housing.

Managing Human Resource Issues: Confronting Challenges. William J. Heisler and others. Jossey-Bass, 350 Sansome St. San Francisco, CA 94104. Phone: 800-378-2537 or (415)433-1740 Fax: (415)433-0499 E-mail: webperson@jbp.com • URL: http://www.josseybass.com • 1999. $32.95.

Managing Human Resources. Arthur W. Sherman and George Bohlander. Thomson Learning, 7625 Empire Dr. Florence, KY 41042. Phone: 800-347-7707 or (606)525-6620 Fax: (606)525-0978 URL: http://www.thomsonlearning.com • 2000. $50.50. 12th edition. (SWC-Management Series).

Managing Information Systems and Technologies; A Basic Guide for Design, Selection, Evaluation and Use. Edwin M. Cortez and Edward J. Kazlauskas. Neal-Schuman Publishers, Inc., 100 Varick St. New York, NY 10013. Phone: (212)925-8650 Fax: 800-584-2414 E-mail: info@neal-schuman.com • URL: http://www.neal-schuman.com • 1985. $45.00.

Managing More Effectively: A Professional Approach to Get the Best Out of People. Madhurendra K. Varma. Sage Publications, Inc., 2455 Teller Rd. Thousand Oaks, CA 91320. Phone: (805)499-0721 Fax: (805)499-0871 E-mail: info@sagepub.com • URL: http://www.sagepub.com • 1997. $28.00. Focuses on the daily and practical application of management principles.

Managing Nonprofit Organizations in the 20th Century. James P. Gelatt. Oryx Press, 4041 N. Central Ave., Ste. 700 Phoenix, AZ 85012-3379. Phone: 800-279-6799 or (602)265-2651 Fax: 800-279-4663 or (602)265-6250 E-mail: info@oryxpress.com • URL: http://www.orypress.com • 1992. $29.95. The author ''emphasizes successful ideas and working solutions.'' Includes charts and tables.

Managing Online Reference Services. Ethel Auster, editor. Neal-Schuman Publishers, Inc., 100 Varick St. New York, NY 10013. Phone: (212)925-8650 Fax: 800-584-2414 E-mail: info@neal-schuman.com • URL: http://www.neal-schuman.com • 1986. $45.00. Articles and bibliographies.

Managing People in Today's Law Firm: The Human Resources Approach to Surviving Change. Ellen Weisbord and others. Greenwood Publishing Group, Inc., 88 Post Rd., W. Westport, CT 06881-5007. Phone: 800-225-5800 or (203)226-3571 Fax: (203)222-2540 E-mail: bookinfo@greenwood.com • URL: http://www.greenwood.com • 1995. $62.95.

Managing Public-Access Computers: A How-To-Do-It Manual for Librarians. Donald A. Barclay. Neal-Schuman Publishers, Inc., 100 Varick St. New York, NY 10013. Phone: (212)925-8650 Fax: 800-584-2414 or (212)219-8916 E-mail: info@neal-schuman.com • URL: http://www.neal-schuman.com • 2000. $59.95. Part one covers hardware, software, and other components. Part two discusses computers users. Part three is about systems management, library policy, and legal issues.

Managing Purchasing: Making the Supply Team Work. John W. Kamauff and Kenneth H. Killen. McGraw-Hill Professional, 1221 Ave. of the Americas New York, NY 10020-1095. Phone: 800-722-4726 or (212)904-2000 Fax: (212)904-2072 E-mail: customer.service@mcgraw-hill.com • URL: http://www.mcgraw-hill.com • 1995. $45.00. (NAPM Professional Development Series: Vol. 2).

Managing Quality in America's Most Admired Companies. Jay W. Spechler. Engineering and Management Press, 25 Technology Park Norcross, GA 30092-2988. Phone: 800-494-0460 or (770)449-0461 Fax: (770)263-8532 E-mail: cmagee@www.iienet.org • URL: http://www.iienet.org • 1993. $49.95. Part one provides ''Guidelines for Implementing Quality Management,'' including detailed information on the Malcolm Baldridge National Quality Award. Part two contains 30 ''Case Studies of Quality Management in Leading Companies.''

Managing Sales Professionals: The Reality of Profitability. Joseph P. Vaccaro. The Haworth Press, Inc., 10 Alice St. Binghamton, NY 13904-1580. Phone: 800-429-6784 or (607)722-5857 Fax: 800-895-0582 or (607)722-1424 E-mail: getinfo@haworthpressinc.com • URL: http://www.haworthpressinc.com • 1995. $49.95.

Managing Software Development Projects: Formula for Success. Neal Whitten. John Wiley and Sons, Inc., 605 Third Ave. New York, NY 10158-0012. Phone: 800-225-5945 or (212)850-6000 Fax: (212)850-6088 E-mail: info@wiley.com • URL: http://www.wiley.com • 1995. $54.99. Second edition.

Managing Stress: Subjectivity and Power in the Workplace. Tim Newton. Sage Publications, Inc., 2455 Teller Rd. Thousand Oaks, CA 91320. Phone: (805)499-0721 Fax: (805)499-0871 E-mail: info@sagepub.com • URL: http://www.sagepub.com • 1995. $69.95.

Managing the Corporate Intranet. Mitra Miller and others. John Wiley and Sons, Inc., 605 Third Ave. New York, NY 10158-0012. Phone: 800-225-5945 or (212)850-6000 Fax: (212)850-6088 E-mail: info@wiley.com • URL: http://www.wiley.com • 1998. $39.99. Written for intranet managers and administrators. Includes checklists.

Managing the Law Library 1999: Forging Effective Relationships in Today's Law Office. Practising Law Institute, 810 Seventh Ave. New York, NY 10019-5818. Phone: 800-260-4754 or (212)824-5700 Fax: (212)265-4742 E-mail: info@pli.edu • URL: http://www.pli.edu • 1999. $99.00. Produced to provide background material for PLI seminars on the role of libraries and librarians in law firms.

Managing the Non-Profit Organization: Practices and Principles. Peter F. Drucker. HarperInformation, 10 E. 53rd St. New York, NY 10022-5299. Phone: 800-242-7737 or (212)207-7000 Fax: 800-822-4090 or (212)207-7145 URL: http://www.harpercollins.com • 1992. $23.00. General advice on strategy, leadership, marketing, and human relations for the non-profit manager.

Managing the Office Building. Mark Ingerbretsen, editor. Institute of Real Estate Management, 430 N. Michigan Ave. Chicago, IL 60611-9025. Phone: 800-837-0706 or (312)329-6000 Fax: (312)329-6000 1985. $62.95. Revised edition.

Managing the Project Team: The Human Aspects of Project Management, Volume Three. Vijay K. Verma. Project Management Institute, c/o PMI Headquarters Publishing Div., 40 Colonial Square Sylva, NC 28779. Phone: (828)586-3715 Fax: (828)586-4020 E-mail: booked@pmi.org • URL: http://www.pmi.org • 1997. $32.95. (Human Aspects of Project Management Series).

Managing the Publishing Process: An Annotated Bibliography. Bruce W. Speck. Greenwood Publishing Group, Inc., 88 Post Rd., W. Westport, CT 06881-5007. Phone: 800-225-5800 or (203)226-3571 Fax: (203)222-2540 E-mail: bookinfo@greenwood.com • URL: http://www.greenwood.com • 1995. $75.00. (Bibliographies and Indexes in Mass Media and Communications Series, No. 9).

Managing the Small to Mid-Sized Company: Concepts and Cases. James C. Collins and William C. Lazier. McGraw-Hill Higher Education, 1221 Ave. of the Americas New York, NY 10020-1095. Phone: 800-722-4726 or (212)904-2000 Fax: (212)904-2072 E-mail: customer.service@mcgraw-hill.com • URL: http://www.mcgraw-hill.com • 1994. $68.95.

Managing the World's Forests: Looking for Balance Between Conservation and Development. Narendra P. Sharma. Kendall-Hunt Publishing Co., 4050 Westmark Dr. Dubuque, IA 52002. Phone: 800-228-0810 or (319)589-1046 Fax: 800-772-9165 E-mail: rburlage@kendalhunt.com • URL: http://www.kendallhunt.com • 1992. $35.95. A study by The World Bank.

Managing to Communicate: Using Telecommunications for Increased Business Efficiency. M. P. Clark. John Wiley and Sons, Inc., 605 Third Ave. New York, NY 10158. Phone: 800-225-5945 or (212)850-6000 Fax: (212)850-6088 E-mail: info@wiley.com • URL: http://www.wiley.co. • 1994. $79.95.

Managing Worker's Compensation: A Guide to Injury Reduction and Effective Claim Management. Keith Wertz and C. Bradley Layton. Lewis Publishers, 2000 Corporate Blvd., N. W. Boca Raton, FL 33431. Phone: 800-272-7737 or (561)994-0555 Fax: 800-374-3401 or (561)998-9114 E-mail: orders@crcpress.com • URL: http://www.crcpress.com • Date not set. $59.95. (Occupation Safety and Health Guide Series).

Managing Workplace Stress. Susan Cartwright and Cary L. Cooper. Sage Publications, Inc., 2455 Teller Rd. Thousand Oaks, CA 91320. Phone: (805)499-0721 Fax: (805)499-0871 E-mail: info@sagepub.com • URL: http://www.sagepub.com • 1996. $34.00. Includes references and indexes. *Advanced Topics in Organizational Behavior, vol. 1*.

Managing World Economic Change: International Political Economy. Prentice Hall, 240 Frisch Court Paramus, NJ 07652-5240. Phone: 800-947-7700 or (201)909-6200 Fax: 800-445-6991 or (201)909-6361 URL: http://

www.prenhall.com • 2000. Third edition. Price on application.

Mandel Center for Nonprofit Organizations. Case Western Reserve University, 10900 Euclid Ave. Cleveland, OH 44106-7167. Phone: (216)368-2275 Fax: (216)368-8592 E-mail: jps@po.cwru.eduu • URL: http://www.cwru.edu/mandelcenter • Engages in research relating to the management of nonprofit organizations.

Manpower Education Institute.

Mansfield Stock Chart Service. R.W. Mansfield Co., Inc., 2973 Kennedy Blvd. Jersey City, NJ 07306. Phone: 877-626-7353 or (201)795-0630 Fax: (201)795-5476 Weekly. Price varies. Covers New York Stock Exchange, American Stock Exchange, OTC exchange, international stocks and industry groups. Partial subscriptions available.

Manual for Managing the Law Office. Prentice Hall, 240 Frisch Court Paramus, NJ 07652-5240. Phone: 800-947-7700 or (201)909-6200 Fax: 800-445-6991 or (201)909-6361 URL: http://www.prenhall.com • Looseleaf service. Price on application. (Information Services Series).

Manual for Writers of Term Papers, Theses, and Dissertations. Kate L. Turabian. University of Chicago Press, 5801 S. Ellis Ave., 4th Fl. Chicago, IL 60637. Phone: 800-621-2736 or (773)702-7700 Fax: (773)702-9756 URL: http://www.press.chicago.edu • 1996. $27.50. Sixth edition. (Chicago Guides to Writing, Editing and Publishing Series).

A Manual of Bibliography. Walter T. Rogers. Gordon Press Publishers, P.O. Box 459 New York, NY 10004. Phone: (212)969-8419 Fax: (718)624-8419 1977. $75.00.

Manual of Classification. U.S. Patent Office. Available from U.S. Government Printing Office, Washington, DC 20402. Phone: (202)512-1800 Fax: (202)512-2250 E-mail: accessgpo@gpo.gov • URL: http://www.accessgpo.gov • $177.00. Two volumes. Index and revised looseleaf pages for an indefinite period. Lists patent classes and subclasses.

Manual of Corporate Forms for Securities Practice. Arnold S. Jacobs. West Group, 610 Opperman Dr. Eagan, MN 55123. Phone: 800-328-4880 or (651)687-7000 Fax: 800-213-2323 or (651)687-5827 URL: http://www.westgroup.com • $395.00. Three looseleaf volumes. Periodic supplementation. (Securitie Laws Series).

Manual of Credit and Commercial Laws. National Association of Credit Management. John Wiley and Sons, Inc., 605 Third Ave. New York, NY 10158-0012. Phone: 800-225-5945 or (212)850-6000 Fax: (212)850-6088 E-mail: info@jwiley.com • URL: http://www.wiley.com • Annual. $125.00. Formerly *Credit Manual of Commercial Laws*.

Manual of Credit and Commercial Laws. National Association of Credit Management, 8840 Columbia 100 Parkway Columbia, MD 21045. Phone: (410)740-5560 Fax: (410)740-5574 E-mail: info@nacm.org • URL: http://www.nacm.org • Annual. Free to members; non-members, $125.00. Formerly *Credit Manual of Commercial Laws*.

Manual of Mineralogy: With Minerals and Rock Exercises in Crystallography Mineralogy and Hand Speciman Petrology. Cornelius Klein and Cornelius Hurlburt. John Wiley and Sons, Inc., 605 Third Ave. New York, NY 10158-0012. Phone: 800-225-5945 or (212)850-6000 Fax: (212)850-6088 E-mail: info@wiley.com • URL: http://www.wiley.com • 1998. $102.95. Revised edition.

Manual of Oil and Gas Terms: Annotated. Matthew Bender & Co., Inc., Two Park Ave. New York, NY 10016. Phone: 800-223-1940 or (212)448-2000 Fax: (212)244-3188 E-mail: international@bender.com • URL: http://www.bender.com • 1983. 10th edition. Periodic supplementation. Price on application. Defines technical, legal, and tax terms relating to the oil and gas industry

Manual of Patent Examining Procedure. U.S. Patent Office. Available from U.S. Government Printing Office, Washington, DC 20402. Phone: (202)512-1800 Fax: (202)512-2250 E-mail: accessgpo@gpo.gov • URL: http://www.accessgpo.gov • Looseleaf. $248.00. Periodic supplementation included. Information on the practices and procedures relative to the prosecution of patent applications before the Patent and Trademark Office.

Manual of Remote Working. Kevin Curran and Geoff Williams. Ashgate Publishing Co., Old Post Rd. Brookfield, VT 05036-9704. Phone: 800-535-9544 or (802)276-3162 Fax: (802)276-3837 1997. $113.95. A British approach to telecommuting or "remote working." Among the chapters are "Planning a Remote Working Operation," "Human Resources," "Communication Systems," and "Project Management." Includes bibliographical references, glossary, and index. Published by Gower in England.

Manual on Employment Discrimination Law and Civil Rights Action in the Federal Courts. Charles R. Richey. West Group, 610 Opperman Dr. Eagan, MN 55123. Phone: 800-328-4880 or (651)687-7000 Fax: 800-213-2323 or (651)687-5827 URL: http://www.westgroup.com • $100.00. Looseleaf service. Periodic supplementation.

Manufactured Fiber Fact Book. American Fiber Manufactures Association, Inc., 1150 17th St., N.W., Suite 310 Washington, DC 20036. Phone: (202)296-6508 Biennial $5.00. Provides information an production, characteristies, uses physical properties and history of manufactured fibers.

Manufactured Fiber Handbook. Fiber Economics Bureau, Inc., 1150 17th St., N.W. Suite 306 Washington, DC 20036-4603. Phone: (202)467-0916 Fax: (202)467-0917 Looseleaf. Periodic supplementation. Contains extensive production, export, inventory, and other statistics. Formerly *Man-Made Fiber Producers' Handbook*.

Manufactured Home Merchandiser Manufactured Home Producers Guide. RLD Group, Inc., 203 N. Wabash St., Suite 800 Chicago, IL 60601-2476. Phone: (312)236-3528 E-mail: mhmerch@meritech.net • Annual. $10.00. Lists about 163 manufacturers of mobil homes, modular homes and other types of manufactured housing. Includes trade associations. Formerly *Mobile/Manufactured Home Merchandiser Manufactured Home Producers Guide*.

Manufactured Homes; Making Sense of a Housing Opportunity. Thomas E. Nutt-Powell. Greenwood Publishing Group, Inc., 88 Post Rd., W. Westport, CT 06881. Phone: 800-225-5800 or (203)226-3571 Fax: (203)222-1502 E-mail: bookinfo@greenwood.com • URL: http://www.greenwood.com • 1982. $62.95.

Manufactured Housing Institute.

Manufacturers' Agents for Food Service Industry., 2402 Mount Vernon Rd., Suite 110 Dunwood, GA 30338. Phone: (770)698-8994 Fax: (770)698-8043 E-mail: info@mafsi.org • URL: http://www.mafsi.org • Members are independent manufacturers' representatives who sell food service equipment and supplies.

Manufacturers' Agents National Association.

Manufacturers' Agents National Association - Directory of Manufacturers' Sales Agencies. Manufacturers' Agents National Association, P.O. Box 3467 Laguna Hills, CA 92654-3467. Phone: 877-626-2776 or (949)859-4040 Fax: (949)855-2973 E-mail: mana@manaonline.org • URL: http://www.manaonline.org • Annual. $129.00. Lists over 6,500 independent agents and firms. Price includes one year subscription to *Agency Sales Magazines*. Formerly *Manufacturers' Agents National Association-Directory of Members*.

Manufacturers Alliance/MAPI Inc.

Manufacturers' Shipments, Inventories, and Orders. Available from U. S. Government Printing Office, Washington, DC 20402. Phone: (202)512-1800 Fax: (202)512-2250 E-mail: gpoaccess@gpo.gov • URL: http://www.access.gpo.gov • Monthly. $70.00 per year. Issued by Bureau of the Census, U. S. Department of Commerce. Includes monthly *Advance Report on Durable Goods*. Provides data on production, value, shipments, and consumption for a wide variety of manufactured products. (Current Industrial Reports, M3-1.)

Manufacturers Standardization Society of the Valve and Fittings Industry., 127 Park St., N. E. Vienna, VA 22180. Phone: (703)281-6613 Fax: (703)281-6671 E-mail: info@mss-hq.com • URL: http://www.mss-hq.com • Members are valve and fitting companies. Publishes standards and specifications.

Manufacturers' Tax Alert. CCH, Inc., 4025 West Peterson Ave. Chicago, IL 60646-6085. Phone: 800-248-3248 or (773)866-6000 Fax: 800-224-8299 or (773)866-3608 E-mail: cust_serv@cch.com • URL: http://www.cch.com • Monthly. $297.00 per year. Newsletter. Covers the major tax issues affecting manufacturing companies. Includes current developments in various kind of federal, state, and international taxes: sales, use, franchise, property, and corporate income.

Manufacturing and Distribution USA. The Gale Group, 27500 Drake Rd. Farmington Hills, MI 48331-3535. Phone: 800-877-GALE or (248)699-GALE Fax: 800-414-5043 or (248)699-8069 E-mail: galeord@galegroup.com • URL: http://www.galegroup.com • 2000. $375.00. Three volumes. Replaces *Manufacturing USA* and *Wholesale and Retail Trade USA*. Presents statistics and projections relating to economic activity in more than 500 business classifications.

Manufacturing Computer Solutions. Hitchcock Publishing, 2000 Clearwater Dr. Oak Brook, IL 60523. Phone: (630)665-1000 Fax: (630)462-2225 E-mail: bpalmer@chilton.net • URL: http://www.manufacturingsystems.com • Monthly. Free to qualified personnel; others; $75.00 per year. Edited for managers of factory automation, emphasizing the integration of systems in manufacturing. Subjects include materials handling, CAD/CAM, specialized software for manufacturing, programmable controllers, machine vision, and automatic identification systems. Formerly *Manufacturing Systems*.

Manufacturing Computer Solutions: The Management Magazine of Integrated Manufacturing. Findlay Publications Ltd., Hadlow House, Nine High St., Green St. Green Orpington, Kent BR6 6BG, England. Monthly. Formed by the merger of *Engineering Computers* and *Manufacturing Systems*.

Manufacturing Confectioner. Manufacturing Confectioner Publishing Co., 175 Rock Rd. Glen Rock, NJ 07452. Phone: (201)652-2655 Fax: (201)652-3419 Monthly. $35.00 per year. Buying guide available *Purchasing Executives' Number*.

Manufacturing Engineering. Society of Manufacturing Engineers, One SME Dr. Dearborn, MI 48121-0930. Phone: 800-733-4763 or (313)271-1500 Fax: (313)271-2861 URL: http://www.sme.org • Monthly. $60.00 per year.

Manufacturing Jewelers and Suppliers of America.

Manufacturing Jewelers Buyers' Guide. Manufacturing Jewelers and Suppliers of America, 45 Royal Little Dr. Providence, RI 02904. Phone: 800-444-6572 or (401)274-3840 Fax: (401)274-0265 Biennial. $25.00. Lists manufacturers and suppliers and has cross-reference by products listed.

Manufacturing Processes Reference Guide. R. H. Todd and others, editors. Industrial Press, Inc., 200 Madison Ave. New York, NY 10016. Phone: 888-528-7852 or (212)889-6330 Fax: (212)545-8327 E-mail: induspress@aol.com • URL: http://www.industrialpress.com • 1994. $44.95. Describes 130 manufacturing processes used in industry.

Manufacturing Profiles. Available from U. S. Government Printing Office, Washington, DC 20402. Phone: (202)512-1800 Fax: (202)512-2250 E-mail: gpoaccess@gpo.gov • URL: http://www.access.gpo.gov • Annual. Issued by the U. S. Census Bureau. A printed consolidation of the entire *Current Industrial Report* series, presenting "all the data compiled." Contains statistics on production, shipments, inventories, consumption, exports, imports, and orders for a wide variety of manufactured products. (See also Census Bureau home page, http://www.census.gov/.)

Manufacturing Systems: Buyers Guide. Cahners Business Information, 1018 W. 9th Ave. King of Prussia, PA 19406. Phone: 800-695-1214 or (610)205-1000 Fax: (610)964-4745 E-mail: corporatecommunications@cahners.com • URL: http://www.cahners.com • Annual. Price on application. Contains information on companies manufacturing or supplying materials handling systems, CAD/CAM systems, specialized software for manufacturing, programmable controllers, machine vision systems, and automatic identification systems.

Manufacturing Worldwide: Industry Analyses, Statistics, Products, Leading Companies and Countries. The Gale Group, 27500 Drake Rd. Farmington Hills, MI 48331-3535. Phone: 800-877-GALE or (248)699-GALE Fax: 800-414-5043 or (248)699-8069 E-mail: galeord@galegroup.com • URL: http://www.galegroup.com • 1999. $220.00. Third edition. A guide to worldwide economic activity in 500 product lines within 140 countries. Includes 37 detailed industry profiles. Name, address, phone, fax, employment, and ranking are shown for major companies worldwide in each industry sector.

Map Librarianship: An Introduction. Libraries Unlimited, Inc., P.O. Box 6633 Englewood, CO 80155-6633. Phone: 800-237-6124 or (303)770-1220 Fax: (303)220-8843 E-mail: lu-books@lu.com • URL: http://www.lu.com • 1998. $68.50. Third edition.

Maps on File. Facts on File, ll Penn Plaza, 15th Fl. New York, NY 10001. Phone: 800-322-8755 or (212)967-8800 Fax: 800-678-3633 or (212)967-8107 E-mail: llitman@factsonfile.com • URL: http://www.factsonfile.com • Annual. $195.00. Update, $45.00. 300 country and other maps in looseleaf binder.

Marble Institute of America.

Marconi's International Register: Linking Buyers and Sellers Worldwide Through Fax and Business Listings. Telegraphic Cable and Radio Registrations, Inc., P.O. Box 14 Larchmont, NY 10538-0014. Phone: (914)632-1392 E-mail: marconis99@aol.com • Annual. $150.00. Lists more than 45,000 firms throughout the world in all lines of business. In four sections.

Marina Dock Age. Preston Publications, Inc., 6600 W. Touhy Ave. Niles, IL 60714. Phone: (847)967-2900 Fax: (847)647-1155 URL: http://www.boatdealer.marina.info.com • Bimonthly. $24.00 per year. Published for owners and managers of marinas and boatyards.

Marine Claims Handbook. N. Geoffry Hudson and Jeffrey Allen. Available from Informa Publishing Group Ltd., PO Box 1017 Westborough, MA 01581-6017. Phone: 800-493-4080 Fax: (508)231-0856 E-mail: enquiries@informa.com • URL: http://www.informa.com • 1996. $60.00. Fifth edition. Published in the UK by Lloyd's List (http://www.lloydslist.com). Covers the basic principles of marine insurance claims, including "correct procedural steps" and documentation.

Marine Digest. Newman-Burrows Publishing, 1710 S. Norman St. Seattle, WA 98144-2819. Phone: (206)709-1840 Fax: (206)324-8939 Monthly. $28.00 per year. Formerly *Marine Digest*.

Marine Encyclopaedic Dictionary. Eric Sullivan. Available from Informa Publishing Group Ltd., PO Box 1017 Westborough, MA 01581-6017. Phone: 800-493-4080 Fax: (508)231-0856 E-mail: enquiries@informa.com • URL: http://www.informa.com • 1996. $110.00. Fifth edition. Published in the UK by Lloyd's List (http://www.lloydslist.com). Provides more than 20,000 marine-related definitions, including 2,000 technical terms. Covers all operational aspects of the shipping business: shipbroking, chartering, insurance, freight forwarding, maritime law, etc.

Marine Engineers Review: Journal of the Institute of Marine Engineers. Available from Information Today, Inc., 143 Old Marlton Pike Medford, NJ 08055-8750. Phone: 800-300-9868 or (609)654-6266 Fax: (609)654-4309 E-mail: custserv@infotoday.com • URL: http://www.infotoday.com • Monthly. $140.00 per year. Published in London by the Institute of Marine Engineers. Covers marine engineering, offshore industries, and ocean shipping. Supplement available *Directory of Marine Diesel Engines*.

Marine Life Research Group. University of California, San Diego

Marine Log. Simmons-Boardman Publishing Corp., 345 Hudson St. New York, NY 10014-4502. Phone: (212)620-7200 Fax: (212)633-1165 URL: http://www.marinelog.com • Monthly. $35.00 per year. Formerly *Marine Engineering-Log*.

Marine Management Holdings: Transactions. Available from Information Today, Inc., 143 Old Marlton Pike Medford, NJ 08055-8750. Phone: 800-300-9868 or (609)654-6266 Fax: (609)654-4309 E-mail: custserv@infotoday.com • URL: http://www.infotoday.com • Bimonthly. $220.00 per year. Published in London by Marine Management Holdings Ltd. Contains technical and regulatory material on a wide variety of marine and offshore topics. Formerly *Institute of Marine Engineers: Transactions*.

Marine Policy; The International Journal on the Organization, Management and Regulation of the Multiple Use of Ocean Space. Elsevier Science, 655 Ave. of the Americas New York, NY 10010. Phone: 888-437-4636 or (212)989-5800 Fax: (212)633-3680 E-mail: usinfo@elsevier.com • URL: http://www.elsevier.com • Bimonthly. $723.00 per year.

Marine Pollution Bulletin: The International Journal for Marine Environmentalists, Scientists, Engineers, Administrators, Politicians, and Lawyers. Elsevier Science, 655 Ave. of the Americas New York, NY 10010. Phone: 888-437-4636 or (212)989-5800 Fax: (212)633-3680 E-mail: usinfo@elsevier.com • URL: http://www.elsevier.com • Semimonthly. $942.00 per year.

Marine Technology and SNAME News. Society of Naval Architects and Marine Engineers, 601 Pavonia Ave. Jersey City, NJ 07306-2907. Phone: (201)798-4800 Fax: (201)798-4975 E-mail: jhorowitz@sname.org • URL: http://www.sname.org • Bimonthly. Individuals, $25.00 per year; institutions, $98.00 per year. Formerly *Marine Technology*.

Marine Technology Society.

Maritime Guide. Available from Fairplay Publications, Inc., 5201 Blue Lagoon Drive, Suite 530 Miami, FL 33126. Phone: (305)262-4070 Fax: (305)262-2006 E-mail: sales@fairplayamericas.com • URL: http://www.lrfairplay.com • Annual. $232.00. Published in the UK by Lloyd's Register-Fairplay Ltd. Serves as a worldwide directory of maritime services, equipment, builders, and manufacturers. Provides information on dry docks, ports, harbours, pontoons, docking installations, shipbuilders, marine engine builders, boilermakers, etc. Includes world maps and a gazetteer.

Maritime Law Association of the U.S.

Maritime Reporter and Engineering News. Maritime Activity Reports, Inc., 118 E. 25th St. New York, NY 10010. Phone: (212)477-6700 Monthly. $44.00 per year.

Maritime Transport. Organization for Economic Cooperation and Development, 2001 L St., N.W., Ste. 650 Washington, DC 20036-4922. Phone: 800-456-6323 or (202)785-6323 Fax: (202)785-0350 E-mail: washington.contact@oecd.org • URL: http://www.oecd.org • Annual. $36.00. Review of the maritime transport industry for OECD member countries. Includes statistical information.

Mark Skousen's Forecasts & Strategies. Phillips Business Information, Inc., 1201 Seven Locks Rd., Suite 300 Potomac, MD 20854. Phone: 800-777-5006 or (301)340-1520 Fax: (301)309-3847 E-mail: pbi@phillips.com • URL: http://www.phillips.com/pbi.com • Monthly. $99.00 per year. Newsletter.

Market Absorption of Apartments. U.S. Bureau of the Census. Available from U.S. Government Printing Office, Washington, DC 20402. Phone: (202)512-1800 Fax: (202)512-2250 E-mail: gpoaccess@gpo.gov • URL: http://www.access.gpo.gov • Quarterly and annual. $16.00 per year. Current Housing Report H-130.

Market: Asia Pacific. Available from MarketResearch.com, 641 Ave. of the Americas, Third Floor New York, NY 10011. Phone: 800-298-5699 or (212)807-2629 Fax: (212)807-2716 E-mail: order@marketeresearch.com • URL: http://www.marketresearch.com • Monthly. $397.00 per year. Newsletter. Published by Market Newsletters. Provides market trends and demographic data for countries of the Asia Pacific region.

Market Efficiency: Stock Market Behavior in Theory and Practice. Andrew W. Lo, editor. Edward Elgar Publishing, Inc., 136 West St., Suite 202 Northampton, MA 01060. Phone: 800-390-3149 or (413)584-5551 Fax: (413)584-9933 E-mail: eep.orders @aidcvt.com • URL: http://www.e-elgar.co.uk • 1997. $430.00. Two volumes. Consists of reprints of 49 articles dating from 1937 to 1993, in five sections: "Theoretical Foundations," "The Random Walk Hypothesis," "Variance Bounds Tests," "Overreaction and Underreaction," and "Anomalies." (International Library of Critical Writings in Financial Economics Series: No. 3).

The Market for Consumer Products in Southeast Asia. MarketResearch.com, 641 Ave. of the Americas, Third Floor New York, NY 10011. Phone: 800-298-5699 or (212)807-2629 Fax: (212)807-2716 E-mail: order@marketresearch.com • URL: http://www.marketresaerch.com • 1997. $2,500.00. Market research report. Covers Asian consumer markets for food, cosmetics, pharmaceuticals, medical devices, and building materials. Market projections are provided to the year 2001.

The Market for Craft and Specialty Beer. MarketResearch.com, 641 Ave. of the Americas, Third Floor New York, NY 10011. Phone: 800-298-5699 or (212)807-2629 Fax: (212)807-2716 E-mail: order@marketresearch.com • URL: http://www.marketresearch.com • 1997. $595.00. Market research report with projections to the year 2001. Includes brewing company profiles.

The Market for Generic Drugs. MarketResearch.com, 641 Ave. of the Americas, Third Floor New York, NY 10011. Phone: 800-298-5699 or (212)807-2629 Fax: (212)807-2716 E-mail: order@marketresearch.com • URL: http://www.marketresearch.com • 2000. $3,000.00. Market research data. Includes a discussion of current trends in the use of generic prescription drugs to reduce healthcare costs, with forcasts to 2004.

Market for Healthy Snacks. MarketResearch.com, 641 Ave. of the Americas, Third Floor New York, NY 10011. Phone: 800-298-5699 or (212)807-2629 Fax: (212)807-2716 E-mail: order@marketresearch.com • URL: http://www.marketresearch.com • 1996. $1,250.00. Provides market data on granola bars, dried fruit, trail mix, rice cakes, etc.

The Market for Ice Cream and Other Frozen Desserts. MarketResearch.com, 641 Ave. of the Americas, Third Floor New York, NY 10011. Phone: 800-298-5699 or (212)807-2629 Fax: (212)807-2716 E-mail: order@marketresearch.com • URL: http://www.marketresearch.com • 2000. $2,500.00. Provides market data and discusses the impact on the ice cream industry of new technology and the Nutrition Labeling and Education Act. Includes sales projections to 2004.

The Market for Interactive Television. MarketResearch.com, 641 Ave. of the Americas, Third Floor New York, NY 10011. Phone: 800-298-5699 or (212)807-2629 Fax: (212)807-2716 E-mail: order@marketresearch.com • URL: http://www.markerresearch.com • 2000. $995.00. Market research data.

The Market for Ophthalmic Pharmaceuticals. MarketResearch.com, 641 Ave. of the Americas, Third Floor New York, NY 10011. Phone: 800-298-5699 or (212)807-2629 Fax: (212)807-2716 E-mail: order@marketresearch.com • URL: http://www.marketresearch.com • 1997. $2,500.00. Market research report. Covers topical and internal drugs for eye disorders, with market estimates. Includes pharmaceutical company profiles.

The Market for Pasta. MarketResearch.com, 641 Ave. of the Americas, Third Floor New York, NY 10011. Phone: 800-298-5699 or (212)807-2629 Fax: (212)807-2716 E-mail: order@marketresearch.com • URL: http://www.marketresearch.com • 2000. $2,250.00. Provides market data on various kinds of pasta, with sales forecasts to 2004.

The Market for Physical Fitness and Exercise Equipment. MarketResearch.com, 641 Ave. of the Americas, Third Floor New York, NY 10011. Phone: 800-298-5699 or (212)807-2629 Fax: (212)807-2716 E-mail: order@marketresearch.com • URL: http://www.marketresearch.com • 1999. $3,250.00. Provides consumer and institutional market data, with forecasts to the year 2003.

The Market for Rx-to-OTC Switched Drugs. MarketResearch.com, 641 Ave. of the Americas, Third Floor New York, NY 10011. Phone: 800-298-5699 or (212)807-2629 Fax: (212)807-2716 E-mail: order@marketresearch.com • URL: http://www.marketresearch.com • 2000. $3,250.00. Market research report. Covers the market for over-the-counter drugs that were formerly available only by prescription. Includes profiles of relevant pharmaceutical companies.

The Market for Salted Snacks. MarketResearch.com, 641 Ave. of the Americas, Third Floor New York, NY 10011. Phone: 800-298-5699 or (212)807-2629 Fax: (212)807-2716 E-mail: order@marketresearch.com • URL: http://www.marketresearch.com • 2000. $2,750.00. Market research report. Covers potato chips, corn chips, popcorn, nuts, pretzels, and other salted snacks. Market projections are provided to the year 2004.

The Market for Stress Management Products and Services. Available from MarketResearch.com, 641 Ave. of the Americas, Third Floor New York, NY 10011. Phone: 800-298-5699 or (212)807-2629 Fax: (212)807-2716 E-mail: order@marketresearch.com • URL: http://www.marketresearch.com • 1996. $1,195.00. Market research report published by Marketdata Enterprises. Covers anti-anxiety drugs, stress management clinics, biofeedback centers, devices, seminars, workshops, spas, institutes, etc. Includes market size projections to the year 2000.

The Market for Sweet Baked Goods. MarketResearch.com, 641 Ave. of the Americas, Third Floor New York, NY 10011. Phone: 800-298-5699 or (212)807-2629 Fax: (212)807-2716 E-mail: order@marketresearch.com • URL: http://www.marketresearch.com • 2000. $2,750.00. Market research data. Covers both fresh and frozen, bakery products.

The Market for Value-Added Fresh Produce. MarketResearch.com, 641 Ave. of the Americas, Third Floor New York, NY 10011. Phone: 800-298-5699 or (212)807-2629 Fax: (212)807-2716 E-mail: order@marketresearch.com • URL: http://www.marketresearch.com • 1999. $2,750.00. Market research report. Covers packaged salad mixes, bulk salad mixes, pre-cut fruits, and pre-cut vegetables. Market projections are provided to the year 2003.

Market Logic. Norman Fosback, editor. Institute for Econometric Research, 2200 S.W. 10th St. Deerfield Beach, FL 33442-8799. Phone: 800-442-0066 or (954)421-1000 Fax: (954)570-8200 Semimonthly. $200.00 per year. Newsletter. Forecasts of market prices.

Market Research Europe. Available from MarketResearch.com, 641 Ave. of the Americas, 3rd Fl. New York, NY 10011. Phone: 800-298-5699 or (212)807-2629 Fax: (212)807-2716 E-mail: order@marketresearch.com • URL: http://www.marketresearch.com • Monthly. $1,050.00 per year. Published by Euromonitor Publications. Newsletter on consumer spending in Europe.

Market Research Handbook. Statistics Canada, Publications Div., Ottawa, ON, Canada K1A OT6. Phone: 800-267-6677 or (613)951-7277 Fax: 800-899-9734 or (613)951-1582 URL: http://www.statcan.ca • Annual. $132.00. Contains a wide variety of demographic and other data relevant to Canadian markets.

Market Research International. Euromonitor International, 122 S. Mchigan Ave., Suite 1200 Chicago, IL 60603. Phone: 800-577-3876 or (312)922-1115 Fax: (312)922-1157 E-mail: info@euromonitor.com • URL: http://www.euromonitor.com/mri.html • Monthly. $1,130.00 per year. Emphasis is on international consumer market research. Includes International Market Review, Global Market Trends and Developments, USA Market Report, Japan Market Report, Emerging Markets, and Market Focus (concise country reports).

Market Research Toolbox: A Concise Guide for Beginners. Edward F. McQuarrie. Sage Publications, Inc., 2455 Teller Rd. Thousand Oaks, CA 91320. Phone: (805)499-0721 Fax: (805)499-0871 E-mail: info@sagepub.com • URL: http://www.sagepub.com • 1996. $46.00.

Market Share Reporter: An Annual Compilation of Reported Market Share Data on Companies, Products, and Services. The Gale Group, 27500 Drake Rd. Farmington Hills, MI 48331-3535. Phone: 800-877-GALE Fax: 800-414-5043 or (248)699-8069 E-mail: galeord@galegroup.com • URL: http://www.galegroup.com • Annual. $265.00. Contains summaries of market share reports. Actual data is given, with many charts and graphs. List more than 2,000 entries.

***Market Share Reporter (MSR) Îonline*l**. The Gale Group, 27500 Drake Rd. Farmington Hills, MI 48331-3535. Phone: 800-877-GALE or (248)699-GALE Fax: 800-414-5043 or (248)699-8069 E-mail: galeord@gale.com • URL: http://www.gale.com • Provides online market share data for individual companies, products, and services, covering all industries. Sources include various publications, trade journals, associations, government agencies, corporate reports, investment research reports, etc. Time period is 1991 to date, with annual updates. Inquire as to online cost and availability.

Market Share Tracker. Available from The Gale Group, 27500 Drake Rd. Farmington Hills, MI 48331-3535. Phone: 800-877-GALE or (248)699-GALE Fax: 800-414-5043 or (248)699-8069 E-mail: galeord@galegroup.com • URL: http://www.galegroup.com • 2000. $1,000.00. Published by Euromonitor (http://www.euromonitor.com). Provides consumer market share data for leading companies in 30 major countries.

Market Structure of Sports. Gerald W. Scully. University of Chicago Press, 5801 Ellis Ave., 4th Fl. Chicago, IL 60637. Phone: 800-621-2736 or (773)702-7700 Fax: (773)702-9756 E-mail: marketing@press.uchicago.edu • URL: http://www.press.chicago.edu • 1995. $39.95.

The Marketer: Official Voice of Petroleum Marketers in Oklahoma. Oklahoma Petroleum Marketers Association, 5115 N. Western Ave. Oklahoma City, OK 73118. Phone: (405)842-6625 Fax: (405)842-9564 Quarterly. $12.00 per year.

Marketer's Guide to E-Commerce: Everything You Need to Know to Successfully Sell, Promote, and Market Your Business, Product, or Service Online. Arthur Bell and Vincent Leger. NTC/Contemporary Publishing Group, 4255 W. Touhy Ave. Lincolnwood, IL 60712-1975. Phone:

800-323-4900 or (847)679-5500 Fax: 800-998-3103 or (847)679-2494 E-mail: ntcpub@tribune.com • URL: http://www.ntc-cb.com • 2001. $39.95. Covers website marketing strategies, including guidelines and examples. (NTC Business Books.)

Marketer's Guide to Media. BPI Communications, Inc., 770 Broadway New York, NY 10003-9595. Phone: 800-344-7119 or (646)654-5500 Fax: (646)654-5834 E-mail: info@bpi.com • URL: http://www.bpicomm.com • Quarterly. $105.00. Presents cost, circulation, and audience statistics for various mass media segments, including television, radio, magazines, newspapers, telephone yellow pages, and cinema. Formerly *Mediaweek's Guide to Media*.

Marketing. Eric Berkowitz. McGraw-Hill, 1221 Ave. of the Americas New York, NY 10020. Phone: 800-722-4726 or (212)904-4509 Fax: (212)904-2072 E-mail: customer.service@mcgraw-hill.com • URL: http://www.mcgraw-hill.com • 1999. $65.25. Sixth edition.

Marketing. Damico Zikmund. Thomson Learning, 7625 Empire Dr. Florence, KY 41042. Phone: 800-347-7707 or (606)525-6620 URL: http://www.thomson.com • 2000. $65.00 Seventh edition. (SWC-General Business Series).

Marketing: A How-To-Do-It Manual for Librarians. Suzanne Walters. Neal-Schuman Publishers, Inc., 100 Varick St. New York, NY 10013. Phone: (212)925-8650 Fax: 800-584-2414 E-mail: info@neal-schuman.com • URL: http://www.neal-schuman.com • 1992. $45.00. Includes a sample library marketing plan with worksheets. Covers market research, strategies, tactics, and evaluation. (How-to-Do-It Series).

Marketing and Advertising Reference Service (MARS). The Gale Group, 27500 Drake Rd. Farmington Hills, MI 48331-3535. Phone: 800-877-GALE or (248)699-GALE Fax: 800-414-5043 or (248)699-8069 E-mail: galeord@gale.com • URL: http://www.gale.com • Provides abstracts of literature relating to consumer marketing and advertising, including all forms of advertising media. Time period is 1984 to date. Daily updates. Inquire as to online cost and availability.

Marketing: Contemporary Concepts and Practices. William F. Schoell. Allyn and Bacon, Inc., 160 Gould St. Needham Heights, MA 02194-2310. Phone: 800-278-3525 or (781)455-1250 Fax: 800-445-6991 or (781)455-1294 E-mail: ab_webmaster@abacon.com • URL: http://www.abacon.com • 1995. $87.00. Sixth edition.

Marketing for CPAs, Accountants, and Tax Professionals. William J. Winston. Haworth Press, Inc., 10 Alice St. Binghamton, NY 13904-1580. Phone: 800-429-6784 or (607)722-5857 Fax: 800-895-0582 or (607)722-1424 E-mail: getinfo@haworthpressinc.com • URL: http://www.haworthpressinc.com • 1995. $49.95.

Marketing for Lawyers. Leader Publications, 345 Park Ave. S. New York, NY 10010. Phone: 800-888-8300 or (212)545-6170 Fax: (212)696-1848 E-mail: circ@amlaw.com • URL: http://www.americanlawyer.com • Monthly. $138.00 per year. Newsletter. Provides advice for law firms on attracting new clients and providing good service to present clients.

Marketing for Non-profit Organizations. David L. Rados. Greenwood Publishing Group, Inc., 88 Post Rd., W. Westport, CT 06881-5007. Phone: 800-225-5800 or (203)226-3571 Fax: (203)222-2540 E-mail: bookinfo@greenwood.com • URL: http://www.greenwood.com • 1996. $59.95. Second edition.

Marketing for Nonmarketers: Principles and Tactics That Everyone in Bu siness Must Know. Houston G. Elamand and Norton Paley. Books on Demand, 300 N. Zeeb Rd. Ann Arbor, MI 48106-1346. Phone: 800-521-0600 or (734)761-4700 Fax: (734)665-5022 E-mail: info@umi.com • URL: http://www.lib.umi.com • 1992. $78.50. Second edition.

Marketing Health Care into the Twenty-First Century: The Changing Dynamic. Alan K. Vitberg. Haworth Press, Inc., 10 Alice St. Binghamton, NY 13904-1580. Phone: 800-429-6784 or (607)722-5857 Fax: 800-895-0582 or (607)722-1424 E-mail: getinfo@haworthpressinc.com • URL: http://www.haworthpressinc.com • 1996. $39.95.

Marketing Health Services. American Marketing Association, 311 S. Wacker Dr., Suite 5800 Chicago, IL 60606-5819. Phone: 800-262-1150 or (312)542-9000 Fax: (312)542-9001 E-mail: info@ama.org • URL: http://www.ama.org • Quarterly. Members, $45.00 per year; non-members, $70.00 per year; institutions, $90.00 per year. Formerly*Journal of Health Care Marketing*.

Marketing in the Third World. Denise M. Johnson and Erdener Kaynak, editors. Haworth Press, Inc., 10 Alice St. Binghamton, NY 13904-1580. Phone: 800-429-6784 or (607)722-5857 Fax: 800-895-0582 or (607)722-1424 E-mail: getinfo@haworthpressinc.com • URL: http://www.haworthpressinc.com • 1996. $29.95. Various authors discuss marketing, advertising, government regulations, and other topics relating to business promotion in developing countries. (Also published in the *Journal of Global Marketing*, vol. 9.)

Marketing in Travel and Tourism. Victor Middleton. Butterworth-Heinemann, 225 Wildwood Ave. Woburn, MA 01081. Phone: 800-366-2665 or (781)904-2500 Fax: 800-466-6520 E-mail: orders@bhusa.com • URL: http://www.bh.com • 2000. $37.95. Third edition. Explains, with examples, the application of marketing concepts and principles to the travel industry.

Marketing Information Revolution. Robert C. Blattberg, editor. McGraw-Hill, 1221 Ave. of the Americas New York, NY 10020. Phone: 800-722-4726 or (212)904-2000 Fax: (212)904-2072 E-mail: customer.service@mcgraw-hill.com • URL: http://www.mcgraw-hill.com • 1993. $39.95. Third edition. Includes a wide variety of sources for specific kinds of marketing.

Marketing Know-How: Your Guide to the Best Marketing Tools and Sources. Intertec Publishing, 11 Riverbend Dr., S. Stamford, CT 06907-2524. Phone: 800-828-1133 or (203)358-4236 Fax: (203)358-5812 E-mail: subs@intertec.com • URL: http://www.intertec.com • 1996. $49.95. Describes more than 700 public and private sources of consumer marketing data. Also discusses market trends and provides information on such marketing techniques as cluster analysis, focus groups, and geodemographic analysis.

Marketing Magazine. Maclean Hunter Business Publications, 777 Bay St. Toronto, ON, Canada M5W 1A7. Phone: (416)596-5000 Fax: (416)596-5553 URL: http://www.mhbizlink.com • Weekly. $60.00 per year. "Canada's national weekly publication dedicated to the businesses of marketing, advertising, and media." Includes annual Marketing Awards, quarterly Digital Marketing (emerging technology), Promo Marketing, and PR Quarterly (special issues on public relations).

Marketing Management for the Hospitality Industry: A Strategic Approach. Allen Z. Reich. John Wiley and Sons, Inc., 605 Third Ave. New York, NY 10158-0012. Phone: 800-225-5945 or (212)850-6000 Fax: (212)850-6088 E-mail: info@wiley.com • URL: http://www.wiley.com • 1997. $59.95.

Marketing Management: Knowledge and Skills. J. Paul Peter. McGraw-Hill Professional, 1221 Ave. of the Americas New York, NY 10020-1095. Phone: 800-722-4726 or (212)904-2000 Fax: (212)904-2072 E-mail: customer.service@mcgraw-hill.com • URL: http://www.mcgraw-hill.com • 2000. $85.63. Sixth edition.

Marketing Management: Shaping the Profession of Marketing. American Marketing Association, 311 S. Wacker Dr., Suite 5800 Chicago, IL 60606-5819. Phone: 800-262-1150 or (312)542-9000 Fax: (312)542-9001 E-mail: info@ama.org • URL: http://www.ama.org • Quarterly. Members, $45.00 per year; non-members, $70.00 per year; institutions, $90.00 per year. Covers trends in the management of marketing, sales, and distribution.

Marketing Management: Text and Cases. Douglas J. Dalrymple and Leonard J. Parsons. John Wiley and Sons, Inc., 605 Third Ave. New York, NY 10158-0012. Phone: 800-225-5945 or (212)850-6000 Fax: (212)850-6088 E-mail: info@wiley.com • URL: http://www.wiley.com • 1994. $92.95. Sixth edition.

Marketing Manager's Handbook. Sidney J. Levy and others. Prentice Hall, 240 Frisch Court Paramus, NJ 07652-5240. Phone: 800-947-7700 or (201)909-6200 Fax: 800-445-6991 or (201)909-6361 URL: http://www.prenhall.com • 2000. Price on application. Contains 71 chapters by various authors on a wide variety of marketing topics, including market segmentation, market research, international marketing, industrial marketing, survey methods, customer service, advertising, pricing, planning, strategy, and ethics.

Marketing News: Reporting on Marketing and Its Association. American Marketing Association, 311 S. Wacker Dr., Suite 5800 Chicago, IL 60606-5819. Phone: 800-262-1150 or (312)542-9000 Fax: (312)542-9001 E-mail: info@ama.org • URL: http://www.ama.org/pubs • Biweekly. Free to members; non-members, $100.00 per year; institutions, $130.00 per year.

Marketing on the Internet: Multimedia Strategies for the World Wide Web. Jill Ellsworth and Matthew Ellsworth. John Wiley and Sons, Inc., 605 Third Ave. New York, NY 10158-0012. Phone: 800-225-5945 or (212)850-6000 Fax: (212)850-6088 E-mail: info@wiley.com • URL: http://www.wiley.com • 1996. $29.99. Second revised expanded edition.

Marketing Planning. William Cohen. John Wiley and Sons, Inc., 605 Third Ave. New York, NY 10158-0012. Phone: 800-225-5945 or (212)850-6000 Fax: (212)850-6088 E-mail: info@wiley.com • URL: http://www.wiley.com • 1997. Second edition. Price on application.

Marketing Planning Guide. Robert E. Stevens and others. Haworth Press, Inc., 10 Alice St. Binghamton, NY 13904-1580. Phone: 800-429-6784 or (607)722-5857 Fax: 800-895-0582 or (607)722-1424 E-mail: getinfo@haworthpressinc.com • URL: http://www.haworthpressinc.com • 1997. $49.95. Second edition. Covers market segmentation, product positioning, and other marketing planning topics.

Marketing Plans: How to Prepare Them, How to Use Them. Malcolm H. McDonald. Butterworth-Heinemann, 225 Wildwood Ave. Woburn, MA 01801. Phone: 800-366-2665 or (781)904-2500 Fax: 800-466-6520 E-mail: orders@bhusa.com • URL: http://www.bh.com • 1999. $44.95. Fourth edition. (Professional Development Series).

Marketing Power: Your Guide to Successful Research. American Demographics, Inc., P.O. Box 4949 Stamford, CT 06907. Phone: 800-828-1133 E-mail: editors@demographics.com • URL: http://www.marketingtools.com • Quarterly. Issued as a supplement to *American Demographics* and *Marketing Tools*. Describes a wide variety of current market research material issued by various publishers and available from American Demographics, Inc.

Marketing: Principles and Perspectives. William O. Bearden. McGraw-Hill, 1221 Ave. of the Americas New York, NY 10020-1095. Phone: 800-722-4726 or (212)904-2000 Fax: (212)904-2072 E-mail: customer.service@mcgraw-hill.com • URL: http://www.mcgraw-hill.com • 1994. $68.95. Second edition. (Marketing Series).

The Marketing Pulse: The Exclusive Insight Provider to the Entertainment, Marketing, Advertising and Media Industries. Unlimited Positive Communications, Inc., Seven Innis Ave. New Paltz, NY 12561. Phone: (914)255-2222 Fax: (914)255-2231 E-mail: gdnem1@ix.netcom • Monthly. $300.00 per year. Newsletter concerned with advertising media forecasts and analyses. Emphasis is on TV and radio.

The Marketing Report: The Best Time-Saving Information Source for Marketing Execcutives. Progressive Business Publications, 370 Technology Dr. Malvern, PA 19355-1315. Phone: 800-220-5000 or (610)695-8600 Fax: (610)647-8089 E-mail: editor@pbp.com • URL: http://www.pbp.com • Semimonthly. $264.00 per year. Newsletter. Covers marketing ideas, problem solving, and new product development. Includes case histories.

Marketing Research. Al Burns and Ronald Bush. John Wiley & Sons, Inc., 605 3rd Ave., 4th Fl. New York, NY 10158-0012. Phone: 800-225-5945 or (212)850-6000 Fax: (212)850-6088 URL: http://www.prenhall.com • 2000. Seventh edition. Price on application.

Marketing Research. David A. Aaker and others. John Wiley and Sons, Inc., 605 Third Ave. New York, NY 10158-0012. Phone: 800-225-5945 or (212)850-6000 Fax: (212)850-6088 E-mail: info@wiley.com • URL: http://www.wiley.com • 2000. Seventh edition. Price on application. Covers data collection methods, data analysis, advanced data analysis, and applications of market research.

Marketing Research: A Magazine of Management and Applications. American Marketing Association, 311 S. Wacker Dr., Suite 5800 Chicago, IL 60606-5819. Phone: 800-262-1150 or (312)542-9000 Fax: (312)542-9001 E-mail: info@ama.org • URL: http://www.ama.org • Quarterly. Members, $45.00 per year; non-members, $70.00 per year; institutions,$120.00 per year.

Marketing Research: An Applied Approach. Thomas C. Kinnear and James R. Taylor. McGraw-Hill, 1221 Ave. of the Americas New York, NY 10020-1095. Phone: 800-722-4726 or (212)904-2000 Fax: (212)904-2072 E-mail: customer.service@mcgraw-hill.com • URL: http://www.mcgraw-hill.com • 1995. $80.50. Fifth edition. Includes CD-ROM.

Marketing Research Association.

Marketing Research Guide. Robert E. Stevens and others. Haworth Press, Inc., 10 Alice St. Binghamton, NY 13904-1580. Phone: 800-429-6784 or (607)722-5857 Fax: 800-895-0582 or (607)722-1424 E-mail: getinfo@haworthpressinc.com • URL: http://www.haworthpressinc.com • 1997. $79.95. A practical guide to the preparation of a market research report, including worksheets, sample proposals, questionnaires, and an example of a final report.

Marketing Research in a Marketing Environment. William R. Dillion and others. McGraw-Hill Higher Education, 1221 Ave. of the Americas New York, NY 10020-1095. Phone: 800-722-4726 or (212)904-2000 Fax: (212)904-2072 E-mail: customer.service@mcgraw-hill.com • URL: http://www.mcgraw-hill.com • 1993. $67.50. Third edition.

Marketing Research Process. Len T. Wright and Margaret Crimp. Prentice Hall, 240 Frisch Court Paramus, NJ 07652-5240. Phone: 800-947-7700 or (201)909-6200 Fax: 800-445-6991 or (201)909-6361 URL: http://www.prenhall.com • 2000. Fifth edition. Price on application.

Marketing Research Project Manual. Glen R. Jarboe. South-Western Publishing Co., 5101 Madison Rd. Cuncinnati, OH 45227. Phone: 800-354-9706 or (513)271-8811 E-mail: billhendee@itped.com • URL: http://www.swcollege.com • 1998. $27.95. Fourth edition. Covers the methodology of market research surveys.(SWC-Marketing Series).

Marketing Research That Pays Off: Case Histories of Marketing Research Leading to Success in the Marketplace. Larry Percy, editor. Haworth Press, Inc., 10 Alice St. Binghamton, NY 13904-1580. Phone: 800-429-6784 or (607)722-5857 Fax: 800-895-0582 or (607)722-1424 E-mail: getinfo@haworthpressinc.com • URL: http://www.haworthpressinc.com • 1997. $49.95.

Marketing Science Institute.

Marketing Strategies for the Mature Market. George P. Moschis. Greenwood Publishing Group, Inc., 88 Post Rd.,

W. Westport, CT 06881-5007. Phone: 800-225-5800 or (203)226-3571 Fax: (203)222-2540 E-mail: bookinfo@greenwood.com • URL: http://www.greenwood.com • 1994. $59.95.

Marketing Strategy. Orville C. Walker and others. McGraw Hill, 1221 Ave of the Americas New York, NY 10020-1095. Phone: 800-722-4726 or (212)904-2000 Fax: (212)904-2072 E-mail: customer.service@mcgraw-hill.com • URL: http://www.mcgraw-hill.com • 1998. $61.56. Third edition.

Marketing Strategy: Relationships, Offerings, Timing, and Resource Allocations. Devanathan Sudharshan. Prentice Hall, 240 Frisch Court Paramus, NJ 07652-5240. Phone: 800-947-7700 or (201)909-6200 Fax: 800-445-6991 or (201)909-6361 URL: http://www.prenhall.com • 1995. $98.00.

Marketing the Arts: Praeger Series in Public and Nonprofit Sector Marketing. Michael P. Mokwa and others. Greenwood Publishing Group Inc., 88 Post Rd., W. Westport, CT 06881-5007. Phone: 800-225-5800 or (203)226-3571 Fax: (203)222-2540 E-mail: bookinfo@greenwood.com • URL: http://www.greenwood.com • 1980. $59.95. (Praeger Special Studies Series).

Marketing Times. Sales and Marketing Executives International, Statler Office Tower, Suite 458 Cleveland, OH 44115. Phone: (216)771-6650 Fax: (216)771-6652 Quarterly. Membership.

Marketing to Older Consumers: A Handbook of Information for Strategy Development. George P. Moschis. Greenwood Publishing Group, Inc., 88 Post Rd., W. Westport, CT 06881-5007. Phone: 800-225-5800 or (203)226-3571 Fax: (203)222-2540 E-mail: bookinfo@greenwood.com • URL: http://www.greenwood.com • 1992. $69.50.

Marketing to the Affluent. Thomas J. Stanley. McGraw-Hill Professional, 1221 Ave. of the Americas New York, NY 10020-1095. Phone: 800-722-4726 or (212)904-2000 Fax: (212)904-2072 E-mail: customer.service@mcgraw-hill.com • URL: http://www.mcgraw-hill.com • 1988. $55.00. Discusses demographics, psychographics, and buying habits.

Marketing to the Emerging Minorities. EPM Communications, Inc., 160 Mercer St., 3rd. Fl. New York, NY 10012-3212. Phone: 888-852-9467 or (212)941-0099 Fax: (212)941-1622 E-mail: info@epmcom.com • URL: http://www.epmcom.com • Monthly. $295.00 per year. Newsletter on market research relating to African American, Asian American, and U. S. Hispanic populations.

Marketing Today. Gordon Oliver. Harcourt College Publishers, 301 Commerce St., Ste. 3700, City Center Tower Two Houston, TX 76102. Phone: 800-245-8744 or (817)334-7500 Fax: 800-445-6991 or (817)334-7844 URL: http://www.prenhall.com • 1994. $30.25. Third edition.

Marketing Today's Fashion. Carol Mueller. Prentice Hall, 240 Frisch Court Paramus, NJ 07652-5240. Phone: 800-947-7700 or (201)909-6200 Fax: 800-445-6991 or (201)909-6361 URL: http://www.prenhall.com • 1994. $85.00. Third edition.

Marketing Without Advertising. Michael Phillips and Salli Rasberry. Nolo.com, 950 Parker St. Berkeley, CA 94710. Phone: 800-992-6656 or (510)549-1976 Fax: (510)548-5902 E-mail: cs@nolo.com • URL: http://www.nolo.com • 1996. $19.00. Second revised edition. How to market a small business economically.

MarketingClick Network: American Demographics. Intertec Publishing, a Primedia Co.Phone: (212)745-0100 Fax: (212)745-0121 URL: http://www.marketingtools.com • Web site provides full-text articles from *American Demographics*, *Marketing Tools*, and *Forecast*, with keyword searching. The *Marketing Tools Directory* can also be searched online, listing suppliers of products, information, and services for advertising, market research, and marketing. Fees: Free.

Markets of the United States for Business Planners: Historical and Current Profiles of 183 U. S. Urban Economies by Major Section and Industry, with Maps, Graphics, and Commentary. Thomas F. Conroy, editor. Omnigraphics, Inc., Penobscot Bldg. Detroit, MI 48226. Phone: 800-234-1340 or (313)961-1340 Fax: 800-875-1340 or (313)961-1383 E-mail: info@omnigraphics.com • URL: http://www.omnigraphics.com • 1995. $240.00. Second edition. Two volumes. Based on statistics from the Personal Income and Earnings Database of the Bureau of Economic Analysis, U. S. Dept. of Commerce. Provides extensive personal income data for all urban market areas of the U. S.

Marketscore. CB Richard Ellis, 353 Sacramento St., Suite 1900 San Francisco, CA 94111. Phone: 800-992-7257 or (415)986-7255 URL: http://www.realestateindex.com • Quarterly. Price on application. Newsletter. Provides proprietary forecasts of commercial real estate performance in metropolitan areas.

Marking Industry Magazine. Marking Devices Publishing, Inc., 136 W. Vallette St., Suite 6 Elmhurst, IL 60126-4377. Phone: 888-627-6564 or (630)832-5200 Fax: (630)832-5206 E-mail: markingdev@aol.com • Monthly. $44.00 per year. Includes annual buyer's guide *Marking Products and Equipment*.

Marking Products and Equipment Buyer's Guide. Marking Devices Publishing Co., Inc., 136 W. Vallete St., Suite 6 Elmhurst, IL 60126-4377. Phone: 888-627-5464 or (630)852-5200 Fax: (630)832-5206 E-mail: markingdev@aol.com • Annual. $30.00. Included in subscription to *Marking Industry Magazine*.

MarkIntel. Thomson Financial Securities Data, Two Gateway Center Newark, NJ 07102. Phone: 888-989-8373 or (973)622-3100 Fax: (973)622-1421 URL: http://www.tfsd.com • Provides the current full text online of more than 45,000 market research reports covering 54 industries, from 43 leading research firms worldwide. Reports include extensive forecasts and market analysis. Inquire as to online cost and availability.

Marquis Who's Who Online. Marquis Who's Who, Reed Reference Publishing, 121 Chanlon Rd. New Providence, NJ 07974. Phone: 800-521-8110 or (908)464-6800 Fax: (908)665-6688 Contains information on over 825,000 prominent individuals, present and past. Semiannual updates. Inquire as to online cost and availability.

Martin E. Segal Theatre Center.

Martindale-Hubbell Bar Register of Preeminent Lawyers. Martindale-Hubbell, 121 Chanlon Rd. New Providence, NJ 07974. Phone: 800-526-4902 or (908)464-6800 Fax: (908)771-7792 E-mail: info@martindale.com • URL: http://www.martindale.com • Annual. $195.00. Lists over 10,000 ''outstanding members of the bar'' in general practice and in 28 specific fields. Covers the U. S. and Canada.

Martindale-Hubbell Dispute Resolution Directory. Martindale-Hubbell, 121 Chanlon Rd. New Providence, NJ 07974. Phone: 800-526-4902 or (908)464-6800 Fax: (908)464-3553 E-mail: info@martindale.com • URL: http://www.martindale.com • Annual. Produced in cooperation with the American Arbitration Association. Over 45,000 judges, attorneys, law firms, and other neutral experts that specialize in dispute resolution and arbitration.

Martindale-Hubbell Law Directory. Martindale-Hubbell, 121 Chanlon Rd. New Providence, NJ 07974. Phone: 800-526-4902 or (908)464-6800 Fax: (908)771-7792 E-mail: info@martindale.com • URL: http://www.martindale.com • Annual. $695.00. 25 volumes. Lists 800,000 lawyers in the U. S., Canada, and 150 other countries, with an index to areas of specialization. Three of the 25 volumes provide the *Martindale-Hubbell Law Digest*, summarizing the statutary laws of the U. S. (state and federal), Canada, and 61 other countries.

Martindale-Hubbell Law Directory on CD-ROM. Martindale-Hubbell, Reed Reference Publishing, 121 Chanlon Rd. New Providence, NJ 07974. Phone: 800-521-8110 or (908)464-6800 Fax: (908)665-6688 Quarterly. $995.00 per year. Provides CD-ROM information on over 900,000 lawyers. International coverage.

Mason Contractors Association of America.

Masonry. Mason Contractors Association of America, 1910 S. Highland Ave., Suite 101 Lombard, IL 60148. Phone: (630)705-4200 Fax: (630)705-4209 Bimonthly. $20.00 per year.

Masonry Design West. Pleasanton Publishing Co., 6284 Wade Court Pleasanton, CA 95688. Phone: (415)846-5623 Fax: (415)846-1753 Bimonthly. Price on application.

Mason's Manual of Legislative Procedure. American Society of Legislative Clerks and Secretaries. National Conference of State Legislatures, 1560 Broadway, Suite 700 Denver, CO 80202-5140. Phone: (303)830-2200 Fax: (303)863-8003 E-mail: name.name@ncsl.org • URL: http://www.ncsl.org • 1989. $40.00. Revised edition. Contains parliamentary law and rules, rules of debate, rules governing motions, how to conduct business, etc.

Mass Communications Research Center.

The Mass Media and the School Newspaper. De Witt C. Reddick. West Publishing Co., College and School Div., 610 Opperman Eagan, MN 55123. Phone: 800-328-4880 or (651)687-7000 Fax: 800-213-2323 E-mail: legal_ed@westgroup.com • URL: http://www.lawschool.westgroup.com • 1986. $24.75. Second edition. (Mass Communication Series).

Mass Media Law and Regulation. William E. Francois. Waveland Press, Inc., P.O. Box 400 Prospect Heights, IL 60070. Phone: (847)634-0081 Fax: (847)634-9501 E-mail: info@waveland.com • 1994. $45.95. Sixth revised edition.

Mass Storage News: Opportunities and Trends in Data Storage and Retrieval. Corry Publishing, Inc., 2840 W. 21st St. Erie, PA 16506-9945. Phone: (814)838-0025 Fax: (814)835-0441 E-mail: edm@corrypub.com • URL: http://www.corrypub.com • Biweekly. $597.00 per year. Newsletter. Provides descriptions of products and systems using optical storage. Formerly *Optical Memory News*.

Mass Transit. Cygnus Publishing Co., 1233 Janesville Ave. Fort Atkinson, WI 11747. Phone: 800-547-7377 or (920)563-6388 Fax: (920)563-1707 E-mail: rich.reiff@cygnuspub.com • URL: http://www.cygnuspub.com • Bimonthly. 48.00 per year.

Mass Transit: Consultants. Cygnus Publishing Co., 1233 Janesville Ave. Fort Atkinson, WI 53538. Phone: 800-547-7377 or (920)563-6388 Fax: (920)563-1707 E-mail: rich.reiff@cygnuspub.com • URL: http://www.cygnuspub.com • Annual. $40.00. Listings for over 300 urban transportation architects, designers, engineers, planners, consultants and other specialists serving the urban transportation industry.

Mass Transit: Supplier's Guide. Mass Transit, 1233 Janesville Ave. Fort Atkinson, WI 53538. Phone: (920)563-6388 Fax: (920)563-1702 E-mail: pbowers@airportbiz.com • Seven times a year. $48.00. Directory of over 800 manufacturers and distributors serving the urban transportation industry.

Master Brewer's Association of America. Communications. Master Brewer's Association of America, 2421 N. Mayfair Rd., Suite 310 Wauwatosa, WI 53226-1407. Phone: (414)774-8558 Bimonthly. $60.00 per year. Included with membership.

Master Brewers Association of the Americas.

Master Franchising: Selecting, Negotiating, and Operating a Master Franchise. Carl E. Zwisler. CCH, Inc., 4025 W. Peterson Ave. Chicago, IL 60646-6085. Phone: 800-248-3248 or (773)866-6000 Fax: 800-224-8299 or (773)866-3608 URL: http://www.cch.com • 1999. $80.00. Written for franchisees, franchisers, and professional advisors. Emphasis is on international franchise transactions.

MasterCard International., 2000 Purchase St. Purchase, NY 10577. Phone: (914)249-2000 Fax: (914)249-5510 Members are banks and financial institutions issuing the MasterCard credit card. MasterCard International is the licensor.

Mastering Competitive Debate. Dana Hensley and Diana Carlin. Clark Publishing, Inc., P.O. Box 19240 Topeka, KS 66619-0240. Phone: 800-845-1916 or (785)862-0218 Fax: (785)862-8224 E-mail: custservice@clarkpub.com • URL: http://www.clarkpub.com • 1999. $38.00. Fith edition.

Mastering Management Education: Innovations in Teaching Effectiveness. Charles M. Vance, editor. Sage Publications, Inc., 2455 Teller Rd. Thousand Oaks, CA 91320. Phone: (805)499-0721 Fax: (805)499-0871 E-mail: info@sagepub.com • URL: http://www.sagepub.com • 1993. $52.00. A collection of articles from the *Journal of Management Education*. Chapters cover lecture and discussion methods, case-study teaching, group-learning skills, and other business education topics.

Mastering Online Investing: How to Use the Internet to Become a More Successful Investor. Michael C. Thomsett. Dearborn Financial Publishing, 155 North Wacker Drive Chicago, IL 60606-1719. Phone: 800-245-2665 or (312)836-4400 Fax: (312)836-9958 URL: http://www.dearborn.com • 2001. $19.95. Emphasis is on the Internet as an information source for intelligent investing, avoiding ''speculation and fads.''

Mastering Real Estate Mathematics. Ralph Tamper. Dearborn, Kaplan Professional Co., 155 N. Wacker St. Chicago, IL 60606-1719. Phone: 800-621-9621 or (312)836-4400 Fax: (312)836-1021 URL: http://www.dearborn.com • 1995. $26.95. Sixth edition. Step-by-step workbook written to help sharpen real estate math skills.

Material Handling Equipment Distributors Association.

Material Handling Industry.

Material Handling Management: Educating Industry on Product Handling, Flow Strategies, and Automation Technology. Penton Media Inc., 1300 E. Ninth St. Cleveland, OH 44114. Phone: (216)696-7000 Fax: (216)696-0836 E-mail: corpcomm@penton.com • URL: http://www.penton.com • 13 times a year. Free to qualified personnel; other, $50.00 per year. Formerly *Material Handling Engineering*.

Materials Business File. Cambridge Scientific Abstracts, 7200 Wisconsin Ave. Bethesda, MD 20814. Phone: 800-843-7751 or (301)961-6700 Fax: (301)961-6720 E-mail: sales@csa.com • URL: http://www.csa.com • Provides online abstracts and citations to worldwide materials literature, covering the business and industrial aspects of metals, plastics, ceramics, and composites. Corresponds to *Steels Alert, Nonferrous Metals Alert,* and *Polymers/Ceramics/Composites Alert*. Time period is 1985 to date, with monthly updates. (Formerly produced by ASM International.) Inquire as to online cost and availability.

Materials Evaluation. American Society for Nondestructive Testing, P.O. Box 28518 Columbus, OH 43228-0158. Phone: (614)274-6003 Fax: (614)274-6899 Monthly. $105.00 per year. Provides up-to-date information about NDT applications and technical articles addressing nondestructive testing applications.

Materials for Occupational Education: An Annotated Source Guide. Patricia Glass Schuman, editor'. Neal-Schuman Publishers, Inc., 100 Varick St. New York, NY 10013. Phone: (212)925-8650 Fax: 800-584-2414 or (212)219-8916 E-mail: info@neal-schuman.com • URL: http://www.neal-schuman.com • 1983. $39.95. Second edition. (Neal-Schuman Sourcebook Series).

Materials Handbook. George S. Brady and others. McGraw-Hill, 1221 Ave. of the Americas New York, NY 10020. Phone: 800-722-4726 or (212)904-2000 Fax: (212)904-2072 E-mail: customer.service@mcgraw-hill.com • URL: http://www.mcgraw-hill.com • 1996. $99.00. 14th edition.

Materials Handling and Management Society.

Materials of Construction. Ronald C. Smith. McGraw-Hill, 1221 Ave. of the Americas New York, NY 10020-1095. Phone: 800-262-4726 or (212)904-2000 Fax:

(212)904-2072 E-mail: customer.service@mcgraw-hill.com • URL: http://www.mcgraw-hill.com • 1987. $53.85. Fourth edition.

Materials Performance: Articles on Corrosion Science and Engineering Solutions for Corrosion Problems. National Association of Corrosion Engineers. NACE International, P.O. Box 218340 Houston, TX 77218. Phone: (281)228-6200 Fax: (281)228-6300 E-mail: pubs@mail.nace.org • URL: http://www.nace.org • Monthly. $100.00 per year. Covers the protection and performance of materials in corrosive environments. Includes information on new materials and industrial coatings.

Materials Processing Center., Massachusetts Institute of Technology, 77 Massachusetts Ave., Room 12-007 Cambridge, MA 02139-4307. Phone: (617)253-5179 Fax: (617)258-6900 E-mail: fmpage@.mit.edu • URL: http://www.web.mit.edu/mpc/www/ • Conducts processing, engineering, and economic research in ferrous and nonferrous metals, ceramics, polymers, photonic materials, superconductors, welding, composite materials, and other materials.

Materials Properties Handbook: Titanium Alloys. E.W. Collings and others, editors. ASM International, 9639 Kinsman Rd. Materials Park, OH 44073-0002. Phone: 800-336-5152 or (440)338-5151 Fax: (440)338-4634 E-mail: custserv@po.asm-intl.org • URL: http://www.asm-intl.org • 1994. $290.00. Covers titanium alloy applications, fabrication, properties, specifications, effects of processing, corrosion, etc.

Materials Research Center. Lehigh University

Materials Research Centres: A World Directory of Organizations and Programmes in Materials Science. Allyn and Bacon/Longman, 1185 Ave. of the American New York, NY 10036. Phone: 800-922-0579 E-mail: the.webmaster@ablongman.com • URL: http://www.ablongman.com • 1991. $475.00. Fourth edition. Profiles of research centers in 75 countries. Materials include plastics, metals, fibers, etc.

Materials Research Society., 506 Keystone Dr. Warrendale, PA 15086-7537. Phone: (724)779-3003 Fax: (724)779-8313 E-mail: info@mrs.org • URL: http://www.mrs.org • Members are individuals concerned with multidisciplinary research in the technology of advanced materials.

Materials Science and Technology: A Comprehensive Treatment. R. W. Cahn and others, editors. John Wiley and Sons, Inc., 605 Third Ave. New York, NY 10158-0012. Phone: 800-225-5945 or (212)850-6000 Fax: (212)850-6088 E-mail: info@wiley.com • URL: http://www.wiley.com • 1997. $7,349.00. 18 volumes. Each volume covers a particular area of high-performance materials technology.

Materials Science Center. University of Wisconsin - Madison

Materials Science Citation Index. Institute for Scientific Information, 3501 Market St. Philadelphia, PA 19104. Phone: 800-336-4474 or (215)386-0100 Fax: (215)386-2911 Bimonthly. Contains current, CD-ROM citations and abstracts, providing international coverage of materials science journals.

Mathematical Finance: An International Journal of Mathematics, Statistics, and Financial Economics. Blackwell Publishers, 350 Main St., 6th Fl. Malden, MA 02148-5018. Phone: 800-216-2522 or (781)388-8200 Fax: (781)388-8210 E-mail: subscript@blackwellpub.com • URL: http://www.blackwellpub.com • Quarterly. $342.00 per year. Covers the use of sophisticated mathematical tools in financial research and practice.

Mathematics and Computer Education. George M. Miller, editor. MATYC Journal, Inc., P.O. Box 158 Old Bethpage, NY 11084. Phone: (516)822-5475 URL: http://www.nsiweb.com • Three times a year. Individuals, $29.00 per year; institutions, $70.00 per year. Articles for high school and college teachers.

Mathematics for Economic Analysis. Knut Sydsaeter and Peter J. Hammond. Prentice Hall, 240 Frisch Court Paramus, NJ 07652-5240. Phone: 800-947-7700 or (201)909-6200 Fax: 800-445-6991 or (201)909-6361 URL: http://www.prenhall.com • 1994. $57.80.

Mathematics with Applications in Management and Economics. Gordon D. Prichett and John C. Saber. McGRaw-Hill Higher Education, 1221 Ave. of the Americas New York, NY 10020-1095. Phone: 800-722-4726 or (212)904-2000 Fax: (212)904-2072 E-mail: customer.service@mcgraw-hill.com • URL: http://www.mcgraw-hill.com • 1993. $72.75. Seventh revised edition.

MathSci. American Mathematical Society, Post Office Box 6248 Providence, RI 02940-6248. Phone: 800-321-4267 or (401)455-4000 Fax: (401)455-4004 Provides online citations, with abstracts, to the literature of mathematics, statistics, and computer science. Time period is 1940 to date, with monthly updates. Inquire as to online cost and availability.

MathSci Disc. American Mathematical Society, P.O. Box 6248 Providence, RI 02940-6248. Phone: 800-321-4267 or (401)455-4000 Fax: (401)455-4004 Semiannual. Price on application. Provides CD-ROM citations, with abstracts, to the literature of mathematics, statistics, and computer science, 1940 to date.

Matrimonial Strategist. American Lawyer Media, L.P., 645 Park Ave., S. New York, NY 10010-1707. Phone: 800-888-8300 or (212)545-6170 Fax: (212)696-1848 E-mail: catalog@amlaw.com • URL: http://www.americanlawyermedia.com • Monthly. $175.00 per year. Newsletter on legal strategy and matrimonial law.

Mature Outlook.

Maximizing Employee Productivity: A Manager's Guide. Robert E. Sibson. AMACOM, 1601 Broadway, 12th Fl. New York, NY 10019-7406. Phone: 800-262-9699 or (212)586-8100 Fax: (212)903-8168 E-mail: custmserv@amanet.org • URL: http://www.amanet.org • 1994. $22.95.

Maxium PC (Personal Computer). Imagine Media, Inc., 150 N. Hill Dr. Brisbane, CA 94005. Phone: 800-706-9500 or (415)468-4684 Fax: (415)468-4686 Quarterly. $12.00 per year. Provides articles and reviews relating to multimedia hardware and software. Each issue includes a CD-ROM sampler (emphasis is on games). Formed by the merger of *Home PC* and *Boot*.

Maynard's Industrial Engineering Handbook. Kjell B. Zandin. McGraw-Hill, 1221 Ave. of the Americas New York, NY 10020-1095. Phone: 800-722-4726 or (212)904-2000 Fax: (212)904-2072 E-mail: customer.service@mcgraw-hill.com • URL: http://www.mcgraw-hill.com • 2000. $150.00. Fifth edition.

Mayo Biomedical Imaging Resource., Mayo Clinic, 200 First St., S. W. Rochester, MN 55902. Phone: (507)284-4937 Fax: (507)284-1632 E-mail: rar@mayo.edu • URL: http://www.mayo.edu/bir • Develops three-dimensional medical imaging systems and software.

Mayo Clinic Diet Manual: A Handbook of Nutrition Practices. Jennifer K. Nelson and others. Harcourt Health Sciences, P.O. Box 620075 Orlando, FL 32887. Phone: 800-426-4545 or (407)345-2000 URL: http://www.harcourt.com • 1994. $75.00. Seventh edition.

Mayors of America's Principal Cities. United States Conference of Mayors, 1620 Eye St., N.W. Washington, DC 20006. Phone: (202)293-7330 Fax: (202)293-2352 Semiannual. About 1,000 mayors of cities with populations of 30,000 or more.

MBA Mortgage Banking Performance Report. Mortgage Bankers Association of America, c/o Janice Stango, 1125 15th St., N.W. Washington, DC 20005. Phone: 800-793-6222 or (202)861-6500 Fax: (202)785-2967 E-mail: info@mbaa.org • URL: http://www.mbaa.org • Quarterly. $400.00 per year, including annual summary. Annual summary only is $175.00. Contains the following kinds of data for mortgage banking companies: balance sheet, income statement, operating ratios, performance ratios.

MBA National Delinquency Survey. Mortgage Bankers Association of America, c/o Janice Stango, 1125 15th St., N.W. Washington, DC 20005. Phone: 800-793-6222 or (202)861-6500 Fax: (202)785-2967 E-mail: info@mbaa.org • URL: http://www.mbaa.org • Quarterly. $30.00 per year. Provides delinquency and foreclosure data for single-family mortgage loans.

MBAA Technical Quarterly. Master Brewers Association of the Americas., 2421 N. Mayfair Rd., Suite 310 Madison, WI 53226-1407. Phone: (414)774-8558 Quarterly. $100.00 per year. Includes membership.

MBEMAG. Minority Business Entrepreneur MagazinePhone: (310)540-9398 Fax: (310)792-8263 E-mail: webmaster@mbemag.com • URL: http://www.mbemag.com • Web site's main feature is the ''MBE Business Resources Directory.'' This provides complete mailing addresses, phone, fax, and Web site addresses (URL) for more than 40 organizations and government agencies having information or assistance for ethnic minority and women business owners. Some other links are ''Current Events,'' ''Calendar of Events,'' and ''Business Opportunities.'' Updating is bimonthly. Fees: Free.

MBI: The National Report on Minority, Women-Owned, and Disadvantaged Businesses. Community Development Services, Inc. CD Publications, 8204 Fenton St. Silver Spring, MD 20910-2889. Phone: 800-666-6380 or (301)588-6380 Fax: (301)588-0519 E-mail: cdpubs@clark.net • Semimonthly. $372.00 per year. Newsletter. Provides news of affirmative action, government contracts, minority business employment, and education/training for minorities in business. Formerly *Minorities in Business*.

MC: Technology Marketing Intelligence. BPI Communications, Inc., 770 Broadway New York, NY 10003-9595. Phone: 800-344-7119 or (646)654-5500 Fax: (646)654-5834 E-mail: info@bpi.com • URL: http://www.bpicomm.com • Monthly. $47.00 per year. Edited for marketing executives in high technology industries. Covers both advertising and marketing.

McCarthy's Desk Encyclopedia of Intellectual Property. J. Thomas McCarthy. BNA Books, Bureau of National Affairs, Inc., 1231 25th St., N.W. Washington, DC 20037. Phone: (202)372-1033 or (202)833-7470 Fax: (202)833-7490 E-mail: books@bna.com • URL: http://www.bna.com/bnabooks • 1995. $75.00.Second edition. Defines legal terms relating to patents, trademarks, copyrights, trade secrets, entertainment, and the computer industry.

McCutcheon's: Emulsifiers and Detergents. Publishing Co., McCutcheon's Div., 175 Rock Rd. Glen Rock, NJ 07452. Phone: (201)652-2655 Fax: (201)652-3419 E-mail: themc@gomc.com • Annual. $180.00. Two volumes. $275.00 per volume. North American volume contains detailed information on surface active agents produced in North America. Company names, addresses and telephone numbers are included. International volume contains detailed information on surface active agents produced in Europe and Asia or in any country outside North America. Company names, addresses and telephone numbers are included.

McCutcheon's Functional Materials: North American Edition. Publishing Co., McCutcheon Div., 175 Rock Rd. Glen Rock, NJ 07452. Phone: (201)652-2655 Fax: (201)652-3419 E-mail: themc@gomc.com • Annual. $170.00. Two volumes. North American edition contains detailed information on surfactant-related products produced in North America. Examples are enzymes, lubricants, waxes, and corrosion inhibitors. Company names, addresses and telephone numbers are included. International edition contains detailed information on surfactant-related products produced in Europe and Asia. Examples are enzymes, lubricants, waxes, and corrosion inhibitors. Company names, addresses, and telephone numbers are included.

McFadden American Financial Directory. Thomson Financial Publishing, 4709 W. Golf Rd. Skokie, IL 60076-1253. Phone: 800-321-3373 or (847)676-9600 Fax: (847)933-8101 E-mail: customerservice@tfp.com • URL: http://www.tfp.com • Semiannual. $415.00 per year. Five volumes. Contains information on more than 23,000 banks, savings institutions, and credit unions in the U. S., Canada, and Mexico. Includes names of officers for key departments, financial statistics, hours of operation, branch information, and other data.

McGill Centre for Intelligent Machines.

McGill's Life Insurance. Edward E. Graves, editor. The American College, 270 S. Bryn Mawr Ave. Bryn Mawr, PA 19010-2196. Phone: 800-421-0654 or (610)526-1000 Fax: (610)526-1310 URL: http://www.amercoll.edu • 1998. $71.00. Second edition. Contains chapters by various authors on diverse kinds of life insurance, as well as annuities, disability insurance, long-term care insurance, risk management, reinsurance, and other insurance topics. Originally by Dan M. McGill.

McGraw-Hill Encyclopedia of Science & Technology. McGraw-Hill, 1221 Ave. of the Americas New York, NY 10020. Phone: 800-722-4726 or (212)904-2000 Fax: (212)904-2072 E-mail: customer.service@mcgraw-hill.com • URL: http://www.mcgraw-hill.com • 1997. $1,995.00. Eighth edition. 20 volumes.

McGraw-Hill Guide to Starting Your Own Business: A Step-By-Step Blueprint for the First-Time Entrepreneur. Stephen C. Harper. McGraw-Hill, 1221 Ave. of the Americas New York, NY 10020. Phone: 800-722-4726 or (212)904-2000 Fax: (212)904-2072 E-mail: customer.service@mcgraw-hill.com • URL: http://www.mcgraw-hill.com • 1992. $12.95. Places emphasis on the construction of an effective, realistic business plan.

McGraw-Hill Handbook of Business Letters. Roy W. Poe. McGraw-Hill, 1221 Ave. of the Americas New York, NY 10020. Phone: 800-722-4726 or (212)904-2000 Fax: (212)904-2072 E-mail: customer.service@mcgraw-hill.com • URL: http://www.mcgraw-hill.com • 1993. $59.50. Third edition. Contains about 200 model business letters in 13 categories. Writing style, organization, objective, and underlying psychology are discussed for each example.

McGraw-Hill Machining and Metalworking Handbook. Ronald A. Walsh. McGraw-Hill, 1221 Ave. of the Americas New York, NY 10020. Phone: 800-722-4726 or (212)904-2000 Fax: (212)904-2072 E-mail: customer.service@mcgraw-hill.com • URL: http://www.mcgraw-hill.com • 1998. $99.95. Second edition. Coverage includes machinery, machining techniques, machine tools, machine design, parts, fastening, and plating.

McGraw-Hill Pocket Guide to Business Finance: 201 Decision- Making Tools for Managers. Joel G. Siegel and others. McGraw-Hill, 1221 Ave. of the Americas New York, NY 10020. Phone: 800-722-4726 or (212)904-2000 Fax: (212)904-2072 E-mail: customer.service@mcgraw-hill.com • URL: http://www.mcgraw-hill.com • 1992. $14.95. Includes ratios, formulas, models, guidelines, instructions, strategies, and rules of thumb.

McGraw-Hill Yearbook of Science and Technology. McGraw-Hill, Engineering and Science Group, 11 W. 19th St. New York, NY 10011. Phone: 800-722-4726 or (212)337-5904 Fax: (212)337-5999 E-mail: customer.service@mcgraw-hill.com • URL: http://www.mcgraw-hill.com • Annual. $125.00.

McGraw-Hill's Biotechnology Newswatch. McGraw-Hill Chemical Engineering Div., 1221 Ave. of the Americas New York, NY 10020. Phone: 800-722-4726 or (212)904-2000 Fax: (212)904-2072 E-mail: customer.service@mcgraw-hill.com • URL: http://

www.mcgraw-hill.com • Semimonthly. $825.00 per year. Newsletter.

McKnight's Long Term Care News. McKnight Medical Communications, Inc., Two Northfield Plaza Northfield, IL 60093. Phone: 800-451-7838 or (847)441-3700 Fax: (847)441-3701 URL: http://www.medec.com • Monthly. $44.95 per year. Edited for retirement housing directors and nursing home administrators.

McKnight's Long-Term Care News Industry Guide. McKnight Medical Communications Co., Two Northfield Plaza, Suite 200 Northfield, IL 60093. Phone: 800-451-7838 or (847)441-3700 Fax: (847)441-3701 E-mail: joan.weiner@medec.com • URL: http://www.medec.com • Annual. $49.95. Lists suppliers of goods and services for retirement homes and nursing homes.

McQuillan Municipal Law Report: A Monthly Review for Lawyers, Administrators and Officials. West Group, 610 Opperman Dr. Eagan, MN 55123. Phone: 800-328-4880 or (651)687-7000 Fax: 800-213-2323 or (651)687-5827 URL: http://www.westgroup.com • Monthly. $277.00 per year. Newsletter. Summary of recent court decisions affecting municipalities.

Means Construction Cost Indexes. R.S. Means Co., Inc., 100 Construction Plaza Kingston, MA 02364-0800. Phone: 800-334-3509 or (781)422-5000 Fax: 800-632-6732 E-mail: meanscustserv@rsmeans.com • URL: http://www.rsmeans.com • Quarterly. $198.00 per year.

Means Facilities Construction Cost Data. R.S. Means Co., Inc., 100 Construction Plaza Kingston, MA 02364-0800. Phone: 800-334-3509 or (781)422-5000 Fax: 800-632-6732 E-mail: meanscustserv@rsmeans.com • URL: http://www.rsmeans.com • Annual. Price on application. Provides costs for use in building estimating.

Means Interior Cost Data. R.S. Means Co., Inc., 100 Construction Plaza Kingston, MA 02364-0800. Phone: 800-334-3509 or (781)422-5000 Fax: 800-632-6732 E-mail: meanscustserv@rsmeans.com • URL: http://www.rsmeans.com • Annual. $79.95.

Means Labor Rates for the Construction Industry. R. S. Means Co., Inc., 100 Construction Plz. Kingston, MA 02364-0800. Phone: 800-334-3509 or (781)422-5000 Fax: 800-632-6732 E-mail: meanscustserv@rsmeans.com • URL: http://www.rsmeans.com • Annual. $174.95. Formerly *Labor Rates for the Construction Industry*.

Means Repair and Remodeling Cost Data. R.S. Means Co., Inc., 100 Construction Plaza Kingston, MA 02364-0800. Phone: 800-334-3509 or (781)422-5000 Fax: 800-632-6732 E-mail: meanscustserv@rsmeans.com • URL: http://www.rsmeans.com • Annual. $79.95.

Means Residential Cost Data. R.S. Means Co., Inc., 100 Construction Plaza Kingston, MA 02364-0800. Phone: 800-334-3509 or (781)422-5000 Fax: 800-632-6732 E-mail: meanscustserv@rsmeans.com • URL: http://www.rsmeans.com • Annual. $72.95.

Measurement and Control. Measurements and Data Corp., 100 Wallace Ave., Ste. 100 Sarasota, FL 34237-6041. Phone: (941)366-1153 10 times a year. $22.00 per year. Supplement available: *M & C: Measurement and Control News*.

Measurement and Evaluation in Counseling and Development. Association for Measurement and Evaluation in Counseling and Development. American Counseling Association, 5999 Stevenson Ave. Alexandria, VA 22304-3300. Phone: 800-347-6647 or (703)823-9800 Fax: (703)823-0252 URL: http://www.counsuling.org • Quarterly. $50.00 per year.

Meat and Poultry Inspection Directory. U.S. Department of Agriculture. Available from U.S. Government Printing Office, Washington, DC 20402. Phone: (202)512-1800 Fax: (202)512-2250 E-mail: gpoaccess@gpo.gov • URL: http://www.access.gpo.gov • Semiannual. $42.00 per year.

Meat and Poultry Inspection Regulations. U.S. Department of Agriculture. Available from U.S. Government Printing Office, Washington, DC 20402. Phone: (202)512-1800 Fax: (202)512-2250 E-mail: gpoaccess@gpo.gov • URL: http://www.access.gpo.gov • Looseleaf. $297.00. Monthly updates included. Regulations for slaughter and processing of livestock and poultry as well as for certain voluntary services and humane slaughter.

Meat and Poultry: The Business Journal of the Meat and Poultry Industry. Sosland Publishing Co., 4800 Main St., Suite 100 Kansas City, MO 64112-2513. Phone: (816)756-1000 Fax: (816)756-0494 E-mail: meatandpoultry@sosland.com • Monthly. $42.00 per year.

Meat Balances in OECD Countries. Organization for Economic Cooperation and Development, Available from OECD Publications and Information Center, 2001 L St., N. W., Suite 650 Washington, DC 20036-4922. Phone: 800-456-6323 or (202)785-6323 Fax: (202)785-0350 E-mail: washington.contact@oecd.org • URL: http://www.oecd.org • Irregular. Price varies. Presents data for seven years on meat production, trade, and consumption. Covers various categories of meat in OECD member countries.

Meat Industry Suppliers Association.

Meat Processing. Watt Publishing Co., 122 S. Wesley Ave. Mount Morris, IL 60154-1497. Phone: (815)734-4171 Fax: (815)734-4201 URL: http://www.wattnet.com • Monthly. Free to qualified personnel; others, $72.00 per year.

Meat Processing-Buyer's Guide. Watt Publishing Co., 122 S. Wesley Ave. Mount Morris, IL 61054-1497. Phone: (815)734-4171 Fax: (815)734-4201 URL: http://www.wattnet.com • Annual. $8.00. In-depth statistical review of the meat, poultry, and seafood industries with easy-to-read graphs and tables; governmental phonebook; listing of meat associations, list of suppliers to the industry; list of equipment, services, and supplies, list of meat processors and their respective products.

Mechanical and Nuclear Engineering Research Laboratories. Kansas State University

Mechanical Engineering. American Society of Mechanical Engineers, 22 Law Dr. Fairfield, NJ 07007-2900. Phone: 800-843-2763 or (973)882-1167 Fax: (973)882-1717 E-mail: inforcentral@asme.org • URL: http://www.asme.org • Monthly. $100.00 per year.

Mechanical Engineering Abstracts. Cambridge Information Group, 7200 Wisconsin Ave., 6th Fl. Bethesda, MD 20814. Phone: 800-843-7751 or (301)961-6700 Fax: (301)961-6720 E-mail: market@csa.com • URL: http://www.csa.com • Bimonthly. $975.00 per year. Formerly *ISMEC - Mechanical Engineering Abstracts*.

Mechanical Engineering Department. Stevens Institute of Technology

Mechanical Engineering Design. Charles R. Mischke. McGraw-Hill, 1221 Ave. of the Americas New York, NY 10020-1095. Phone: 800-722-4726 or (212)904-2000 Fax: (212)904-2072 E-mail: customer.service@mcgraw-hill.com • URL: http://www.mcgraw-hill.com • 2000. $85.00. Sixth edition. (Mechanical Engineering Series).

Mechanical Engineers' Handbook. Myer P. Kutz, editor. John Wiley and Sons, Inc., 605 Third Ave. New York, NY 10158-0012. Phone: 800-526-5368 or (212)850-6000 Fax: (212)850-6088 E-mail: info@wiley.com • URL: http://www.wiley.com • 1998. $250.00. Second edition.

Mechanical Engineer's Reference Book. E. H. Smith, editor. Society of Automotive Engineers, Inc., 400 Commonwealth Dr. Warrendale, PA 15096-0001. Phone: 800-832-6732 or (724)776-4841 Fax: (724)776-5960 E-mail: sae@sae.org • URL: http://www.sae.org • 1994. $135.00. 12th edition. Covers mechanical engineering principles, computer integrated engineering systems, design standards, materials, power transmission, and many other engineering topics. (Authored Royalty Series).

Mechanical Power Transmission Association.

Mechanism and Machine Theory. Elsevier Science, 655 Ave. of the Americas New York, NY 10010. Phone: 888-437-4636 or (212)989-5800 Fax: (212)633-3680 E-mail: usinfo@elsevier.com • URL: http://www.elsevier.com • Eight times a year $2,106.00 per year.

Med Ad News. Engel Publishing Partners, 820 Bear Tavern Rd. West Trenton, NJ 08628. Phone: (609)530-0044 Fax: (609)530-1274 URL: http://www.engelpub.com • Monthly. $150.00 per year. Covers the field of pharmaceutical advertising and marketing.

Media and Methods: Educational Products, Technologies and Programs for Schools and Universities. American Society of Educators, 1429 Walnut St. Philadelphia, PA 19102. Phone: 800-555-5657 or (215)563-6005 Fax: (215)587-9706 E-mail: michelesok@aol.com • URL: http://www.media-methods.com • Five times a year. $33.50 per year.

Media and the Law. SIMBA Information, P.O. Box 4234 Stamford, CT 06907-0234. Phone: 800-307-2529 or (203)358-4100 Fax: (203)358-5824 E-mail: info@simbanet.com • URL: http://www.simbanet.com • Semimonthly. $327.00 per year. Newsletter.

Media for Business. Robert H. Amend and Michael A. Schrader. Butterworth-Heinemann, 225 Wildwood Ave Newton, MA 01801. Phone: 800-366-2665 or (781)904-2500 Fax: 800-466-6520 E-mail: orders@bhusa.com • URL: http://www.bh.com • 1991. $44.95.

Media Industry Newsletter. Phillips Business Information, Inc., 1201 Seven Locks Rd., Suite 300 Potomac, MD 20854. Phone: 800-777-5006 or (301)340-1520 Fax: (301)309-3847 E-mail: pbi@phillips.com • URL: http://www.phillips.com/pbi.htm • Weekly. $595.00 per year. News of advertising, broadcasting, and publishing. Reports on the number of advertising pages in major magazines.

Media Laboratory., Massachusetts Institute of Technology, 20 Ames St., Room E-15 Cambridge, MA 02139. Phone: (617)253-0338 Fax: (617)258-6264 E-mail: casr@media.mit.edu • URL: http://www.media.mit.edu • Research areas include electronic publishing, spatial imaging, human-machine interface, computer vision, and advanced television.

Media Market Guide. Media Market Resources, 322 E. 50th St. New York, NY 10022. Phone: 800-242-9618 or (212)832-7170 Fax: (212)826-3169 E-mail: info@mediamarket.com • URL: http://www.mediamarket.com • Quarterly. $675.00 per year. Presents circulation and cost data for television, radio, magazines, newspapers and outdoor markets.

Media Math: Basic Techniques for Media Evaluation. Robert W. Hall. NTC/Contemporary Publishing, P.O. Box 545 Blacklick, OH 43004. Phone: 800-338-3987 or (614)755-4151 Fax: (614)755-5645 E-mail: ntcpub@mcgraw-hill.com • URL: http://www.ntc-cb.com • 1994. $19.95. Second edition. (NTC Business Book Series).

Media Mergers and Acquisitions. Paul Kagan Associates, Inc., 126 Clock Tower Place Carmel, CA 93923. Phone: (831)624-1536 Fax: (831)625-3225 E-mail: info@kagan.com • Monthly. $695.00 per year. Newsletter on media merger activity. Covers broadcasting, motion pictures, advertising, and publishing.

The Media Monopoly. Ben H. Bagdikian. Beacon Press, 25 Beacon St. Boston, MA 02108-2892. Phone: (617)742-2110 Fax: (617)723-3097 E-mail: emiller@beacon.org • URL: http://www.beacon.org • 1997. $17.50. Fifth edition.

Media Rating Council., 200 W. 57th St., Suite 204 New York, NY 10019. Phone: (212)765-0200 Fax: (212)765-1868 Purpose is to set standards for audience measurement services, such as A. C. Nielsen, Arbitron, and Statistical Research.

Media Sports Business. Paul Kagan Associates, Inc., 126 Clock Tower Place Carmel, CA 93923. Phone: (831)624-1536 Fax: (831)625-3225 E-mail: info@kagan.com • Monthly. $645.00. Newsletter. Primary subject is broadcasting of sports events by national and regional cable and pay television systems.

Media Systems Society. Joseph Turow. Addison-Wesley Longman, Inc., One Jacob Way Reading, MA 01867. Phone: 800-447-2226 or (617)944-3700 Fax: (617)944-9351 URL: http://www.awl.com • 1997. $67.50. Second edition. Provides commentary on the role of U.S. mass media in a global economy.

MediaFinder CD-ROM: Oxbridge Directories of Print Media and Catalogs. Oxbridge Communications, Inc., 150 Fifth Ave., Suite 302 New York, NY 10011. Phone: 800-955-0231 or (212)741-0231 Fax: (212)633-2938 E-mail: info@oxbridge.com • URL: http://www.mediafinder.com • Quarterly. $1,695.00 per year. CD-ROM includes about 100,000 listings from *Standard Periodical Directory, National Directory of Catalogs, National Directory of British Mail Order Catalogs, National Directory of German Mail Order Catalogs, Oxbridge Directory of Newsletters, National Directory of Mailing Lists, College Media Directory*, and *National Directory of Magazines*.

Mediaweek: Incorporating Marketing and Media Decisions. BPI Communications, Inc., 770 Broadway New York, NY 10003-9595. Phone: 800-344-7119 or (646)654-5500 Fax: (646)654-5834 E-mail: info@bpi.com • URL: http://www.bpicomm.com • 47 times a year. $145.00 per year. Published for advertising media buyers and managers.

Medical and Health Care Books and Serials in Print: An Index to Literature in Health Sciences. R. R. Bowker, 121 Chanlon Rd. New Providence, NJ 07974. Phone: 888-269-5372 or (908)464-6800 Fax: (908)771-7704 E-mail: info@bowker.com • URL: http://www.bowker.com • Annual. $265.95. Two volumes.

Medical and Health Information Directory. The Gale Group, 27500 Drake Rd. Farmington Hills, MI 48331-3535. Phone: 800-877-GALE or (248)699-GALE Fax: 800-414-5043 or (248)699-8069 E-mail: galeord@galegroup.com • URL: http://www.galegroup.com • 1999. $630.00. Three volumes. 12th edition. Vol. one covers medical organizations, agencies, and institutions; vol. two includes bibliographic, library, and database information; vol. three is a guide to services available for various medical and health problems.

Medical and Healthcare Marketplace Guide. Dorland Healthcare Information, 1500 Walnut St., Suite 1000 Philadelphia, PA 19102. Phone: 800-784-2332 or (215)875-1212 Fax: (215)735-3966 E-mail: info@dorlandhealth.com • URL: http://www.dorlandhealth.com • Annual. $690.00. Two volumes. Provides market survey summaries for about 500 specific product and service categories (volume one: "Research Reports"). Contains profiles of nearly 6,000 pharmaceutical, medical product, and healthcare service companies (volume two: "Company Profiles").

Medical Benefits. Panel Publishers, 1185 Ave. of the Americas New York, NY 10036. Phone: 800-447-1717 or (212)597-0200 Fax: 800-901-9075 or (212)597-0334 E-mail: customer.service@aspenpubl.com • URL: http://www.panelpublisher.com • Semimonthly. $216.00 per year. Newsletter. Provides summaries of periodical articles.

Medical Care, Medical Costs: The Search for a Health Insurance Policy. Rashi Fein. Replica Books, P.O. Box 734 Sommerville, NJ 08876-0734. Phone: 800-775-1800 or (408)260-3056 Fax: (908)722-7420 E-mail: btinfo@baker_taylor.com • URL: http://www.replicabooks.com • 1999. $26.95.

Medical Claims Processing. Entrepreneur Media, Inc., 2445 McCabe Way Irvine, CA 92614. Phone: 800-421-2300 or (949)261-2325 Fax: (949)261-0234 E-mail: entmag@entrepreneur.com • URL: http://www.entrepreneur.com • Looseleaf. $59.50. A practical guide to starting a medical claims processing service. Covers profit potential, start-up costs, market size evaluation, owner's time required, site selection, pricing, accounting, advertising, promotion, etc. (Start-Up Business Guide No. E1345.)

Medical Design Technology. Cahners Business Information, 301 Gibraltar Dr. Morris Plains, NJ 07950-0650. Phone: (973)292-5100 Fax: (973)539-3476 E-mail: corporatecommunications@cahners.com • URL: http://www.cahners.com • Monthly. $70.00 per year. Edited for medical technology personnel. Includes new product introductions and applications.

Medical Device and Diagnostic Industry. Canon Communications LLC, 11444 W. Olympic Blvd., Ste. 900 Los Angeles, CA 90064-1549. Phone: (310)445-4200 Fax: (310)445-4299 E-mail: feedback@devicelink.com • URL: http://www.devicelink.com • Monthly. Free to qualified personnel; others, $125.00 per year.

Medical Device Register. Medical Economics, Five Paragon Dr. Montvale, NJ 07645-1742. Phone: 800-222-3045 or (201)358-7200 Fax: (201)572-8999 E-mail: customerservice@medec.com • URL: http://www.medec.com • Annual. $325.00. Lists more than 12,000 suppliers of a wide variety of medical devices and clinical laboratory products.

Medical Device Technology. Advanstar Communications, Inc., One Park Ave., 2nd Fl. New York, NY 10016-5802. Phone: 800-346-0085 or (212)951-6600 Fax: (212)951-6623 E-mail: information@advanstar.com • URL: http://www.advanstar.com • Ten times a year. Free to qualified personnel; others, $180.00 per year.

Medical Devices, Diagnostics, and Instrumentation: The Gray Sheet Reports. F-D-C Reports, Inc., 5550 Friendship Blvd., Suite 1 Chevy Chase, MD 20815-7278. Phone: 800-332-2181 or (301)657-9830 Fax: (301)664-7238 URL: http://www.fdcreports.com • Weekly. $955.00 per year. Newsletter. Provides industry and financial news, including a medical sector stock index. Monitors regulatory developments at the Center for Devices and Radiological Health of the U. S. Food and Drug Administration.

Medical Economics. Medical Economics Co., Inc., Five Paragon Dr. Montvale, NJ 07645-1742. Phone: 800-232-7379 or (201)358-7200 Fax: (201)573-8999 E-mail: customerservice@medec.com • URL: http://www.medec.com • 25 times a year. $109.00 per year. Covers the financial, economic, insurance, administrative, and other non-clinical aspects of private medical practice. Provides investment and estate planning advice.

Medical Economics General Surgery-Orthopedic Surgery. Medical Economics Co., Inc., Five Paragon Dr. Montvale, NJ 07645-1742. Phone: 800-232-7379 or (201)358-7200 Fax: (201)573-8999 E-mail: customerservice@medec.com • URL: http://www.medec.com • Monthly. $65.00 per year. Provides information and advice on practice management (non-clinical) for surgeons. Formerly *Medical Economics for Surgeons*.

Medical Electronics. Measurements & Data Corp., 100 Wallace Ave., Ste. 100 Sarasota, FL 34237-6041. Phone: (941)366-6041 Bimonthly. $22.00 per year. Includes information on new medical electronic products, technology, industry news, and medical safety.

Medical Electronics and Equipment News. Reilly Publishing Co., 16 E. Schaumberg Rd. Schaumberg, IL 60194-3536. Phone: (847)882-6336 Fax: (847)519-0166 E-mail: rcgroup@flash.net • Bimonthly. Free to qualified personnel; others, $50.00 per year. Provides medical electronics industry news and new product information.

Medical Electronics Laboratory., University of Wisconsin, 1300 University Ave. Madison, WI 53706. Phone: (608)262-1326 Fax: (608)262-2327 E-mail: yee@physiology.wisc.edu • Develops electronic instrumentation for medical and biological research.

Medical Group Management Association., 104 Inverness Terrace E. Englewood, CO 80112-5306. Phone: 888-608-5601 or (303)799-1111 Fax: (303)643-4439 URL: http://www.mgma.com • Members are medical group managers.

Medical Group Management Association Directory. Medical Group Management Association, 104 Inverness Terrace E. Englewood, CO 80112-5306. Phone: 888-608-5601 or (303)799-1111 Fax: (303)397-1824 E-mail: beh@mgma.com • URL: http://www.mgma.com • Annual. More than 16,000 individual members and 6,000 member groups representing over 130,000 physicians.

Medical Group Management Journal. Medical Group Management Association, 104 Inverness Terrace E. Englewood, CO 80112-5306. Phone: 888-608-5601 or (303)759-1111 Fax: (303)397-1824 E-mail: beh@mgma.com • URL: http://www.mgma.com • Bimonthly. $68.00 per year.

Medical Instrumentation Laboratory., University of Wisconsin-Madison, 1415 Engineering Dr. Madison, WI 53706. Phone: (608)263-1574 Fax: (608)265-9239 E-mail: webster@engr.wisc.edu • URL: http://www.engr.wisc.edu/bme/faculty/websterjohn.html • Research subjects include medical electrodes, medical amplifiers, bioimpedance techniques, and miniature tactile pressure sensors.

Medical Laser Report. PennWell Corp., Advanced Technology Div., 98 Spit Brook Rd. Nashua, NH 03062-5737. Phone: 800-331-4463 or (603)891-0123 Fax: (603)891-0574 E-mail: webmaster@pennwell.com • URL: http://www.pennwell.com • Monthly. $345.00 per year. Newsletter. Covers the business and financial side of the medical laser industry, along with news of technological developments and clinical applications. Supplement available *Buyers' Guide*. Formerly *Medical Laser Industrial Report*.

Medical Malpractice. Thomas A. Moore and Daniel Kramer, editors. Practising Law Institute, 810 Seventh Ave. New York, NY 10019-5818. Phone: 800-260-4754 or (212)824-7500 Fax: (212)265-4742 E-mail: info@pli.edu • URL: http://www.pli.edu • 1990. $25.00. Sixth edition. Legal handbook.

Medical Marketing and Media. CPS Communications, Inc., 7200 W. Camino Real, Suite 215 Boca Raton, FL 33433. Phone: (407)368-9301 Fax: (407)368-7870 E-mail: mmm@cpsnet.com • URL: http://www.cpsnet.com • Monthly. Individuals, $75.00 per year; institutions, $100.00 per person. Contains articles on marketing, direct marketing, advertising media, and sales personnel for the healthcare and pharmaceutical industries.

Medical Product Manufacturing News. Canon Communications LLC, 11444 W. Olympic Blvd., Ste. 900 Los Angeles, CA 90064-1549. Phone: (310)445-4200 Fax: (310)445-4299 E-mail: feedback@devicelink.com • URL: http://www.devicelink.com • 10 times a year. Free to qualified personnel; others, $125.00 per year. Directed at manufacturers of medical devices and medical electronic equipment. Covers industry news, service news, and new products.

Medical Product Manufacturing News Buyers Guide. Canon Communications LLC, 11444 W. Olympic Blvd., Suite 900 Los Angeles, CA 90064. Phone: (310)445-4200 Fax: (310)445-3799 E-mail: mpmn@cancom.com • URL: http://www.cancom.com • Annual. Controlled circulation. A directory of over 3,000 medical device and medical electronic equipment. Formerly *Medical Product Manufacturing News-Buyer's Guide and Designer's Sourcebook*.

Medical Product Sales. Health Industry Distribution Association. Douglas Publications, Inc., 2807 N. Parham Rd., Suite 200 Richmond, VA 23294. Phone: (804)762-9600 Fax: (804)217-8999 E-mail: wernmps@aol.com • URL: http://www.douglaspublications.com • Monthly. $49.95 per year.

Medical Reference Services Quarterly. Haworth Press, Inc., 10 Alice St. Binghamton, NY 13904-1580. Phone: 800-429-6784 or (607)722-5857 Fax: 800-895-0582 or (607)722-1424 E-mail: getinfo@haworthpressinc.com • URL: http://www.haworthpressinc.com • Quarterly. Individuals, $50.00 per year; libraries and other institutions, $175.00 per year. An academic and practical journal for medical reference librarians.

Medical Research Centres: A World Directory of Organizations and Programmes. Allyn and Bacon/Longman, 1185 Ave. of the Americas New York, NY 10036. Phone: 800-922-0579 E-mail: the.webmaster@ablongman.com • URL: http://www.ablongman.com • Irregular. $535.00. Two volumes. Contains profiles of about 7,000 medical research facilities around the world. Includes medical, dental, nursing, pharmaceutical, psychiatric, and surgical research centers.

Medical Technology and Society: An Interdisciplinary Perspective. Joseph Bronzino and Vincent Smith. MIT Press, Five Cambridge Center Cambridge, MA 02142-1493. Phone: 800-356-0343 or (617)253-5646 Fax: (617)253-6779 E-mail: mitpress-orders@mit.edu • URL: http://www.mitpress.mit.edu • 1990. $50.00.

Medical Technology Stock Letter. Piedmont Venture Group, P.O. Box 40460 Berkeley, CA 94704. Phone: (510)843-1857 Fax: (510)843-0901 E-mail: mtsl@bioinvest.com • URL: http://www.bioinvest.com • Semimonthly. $320.00 per year. Newsletter. Provides health care industry investment recommendations, including information on initial public offerings.

Medical Tribune: World News of Medicine and Its Practice. Press Corps, Inc., 444 Park Ave., S., Rm. 503 New York, NY 10016-7321. Phone: (212)686-9080 Fax: (212)686-5310 URL: http://www.medtrib.com • Biweekly. Free to qualified personnel; others, $95.00 per year. Includes *Family Physicians, Internist and Cardiologist* and *Obstetetrician and Gynecologist*.

Medical Utilization Management. Faulkner & Gray, Healthcare Information Center, 11 Penn Plaza, 17th Fl. New York, NY 10001. Phone: 800-535-5403 or (212)967-7000 Fax: (212)967-7155 E-mail: orders@faulknergray.com • URL: http://www.faulknergray.com • Biweekly. $395.00 per year. Newsletter. Formerly *Medical Utilization Review*.

Medicare and Coordinated Care Plans. Available from Consumer Information Center, Department 59 Pueblo, CO 81009. Free. Published by the U. S. Department of Health and Human Services. Contains detailed information on services to Medicare beneficiaries from health maintenance organizations (HMOs). (Publication No. 509-X.)

Medicare and Medicaid Claims and Procedures. Harvey L. McCormick. West Publishing Co., College and School Div., 610 Opperman Dr. Eagan, MN 55123. Phone: 800-328-4880 or (651)687-7000 Fax: 800-213-2323 or (651)687-5827 E-mail: legal_ed@westgroup.com • URL: http://www.lawschool.westgroup.com • 1986. Two volumes. Price on application. Periodic supplementation.

Medicare Compliance Alert. United Communications Group, 11300 Rockville Pike, Suite 1100 Rockville, MD 20852-3030. Phone: (301)816-8950 Fax: (301)816-8945 E-mail: cdonoghue@ucg.com • URL: http://www.ucg.com • Biweekly. $370.00 per year. Newsletter. Supplement available, *Civil Money Penalties Reporter*. Newsletter. Provides news of changes in Medicare regulations and legislation. Advises physicians on Medicare rules relating to physician investments, joint ventures, limited partnerships, and patient referrals.

Medicare Compliance Alert. United Communications Group, 11300 Rockville Pike, Suite 1100 Rockville, MD 20852-3030. Phone: (301)816-8950 Fax: (301)816-8945 E-mail: cdonoghue@ucg.com • URL: http://www.ucg.com • Biweekly. $370.00 per year. Newsletter. Explains Medicare Part B reimbursement program and rules for healthcare providers. Gives advice and strategies for physicians.

Medicare: Employer Health Plans. Available from Consumer Information Center, Department 59 Pueblo, CO 81009. Free. Published by the U. S. Department of Health and Human Services. Explains the special rules that apply to Medicare beneficiaries who have employer group health plan coverage. (Publication No. 520-Y.)

Medicare Explained. CCH, Inc., 4025 W. Peterson Ave. Chicago, IL 60646-6085. Phone: 800-248-3248 or (773)583-8500 Fax: 800-224-8299 URL: http://www.cch.com • Annual. $30.00.

Medicare Made Easy: Everything You Need to Know to Make Medicare Work for You. Charles B. Inlander and Michael A. Danio. Fine Communications, Two Lincoln Square, 66 W. 66th St., 2nd Fl. New York, NY 10023. Phone: (212)595-3500 Fax: (212)595-3779 E-mail: scott@mjfbooks.com • 1999. $19.98. Revised edition. Provides basic information on Medicare claims processing and the manner in which Medicare relates to other health insurance. The author is a consumer advocate and president of the People's Medical Society.

Medicare Supplement Price Survey. Weiss Ratings, Inc., 4176 Burns Rd. Palm Beach Gardens, FL 33410-4606. Phone: 800-289-9222 or (561)627-3300 Fax: (561)625-6685 E-mail: wr@weissinc.com • URL: http://www.martinweiss.com • Continuous revision. Price on application. Available for individual geographic areas to provide detailed price information for various types of Medicare supplement health insurance policies issued by specific insurance companies.

Medicare: The Official U. S. Government Site for Medicare Information. Health Care Financing Administration (HCFA)Phone: (410)786-3151 URL: http://www.medicare.gov • Web site provides extensive information on Medicare health plans, publications, fraud, nursing homes, top 20 questions and answers, etc. Includes access to the National Nursing Home Database, providing summary compliance information on "every Medicare and Medicaid certified nursing home in the country." Online searching is offered. Fees: Free.

Mediphotonics Laboratory.

Medline. Medlars Management Section, National Library of Medicine, 8600 Rockville Pike Bethesda, MD 20894. Phone: 800-638-8480 or (301)496-1131 Fax: (301)480-3537 URL: http://www.nlm.nih.gov • Provides indexing and abstracting of worldwide medical literature, 1966 to date. Weekly updates. Inquire as to online cost and availability.

Meeting and Conference Executives. MCEA, 554 Strawberry Hill Rd Centerville, MA 02632-3037. Phone: (617)859-0022 Fax: (617)267-9214 E-mail: joanmather@aol.com • Monthly. $99.00 per year. Newsletter. Formerly *Meeting Planners Alert*.

The Meeting Professional. Meeting Professionals International, 4455 LBJ Freeway, Suite 1200 Dallas, TX 75244-5903. Phone: (972)702-3000 Fax: (214)712-7770 Monthly. $50.00 per year. Published for professionals in the meeting and convention industry. Contains news, features, and how-to's for domestic and international meetings management. Formerly *Meeting Manager*.

Meeting Professionals International., 4455 LBJ Freeway, Suite 1200 Dallas, TX 75244-5903. Phone: (972)702-3000 Fax: (972)702-3070 URL: http://www.mpiweb.org • Members are fee-based meeting planners, meeting consultants, and providers of meeting services.

Megatrends Two Thousand: Ten New Directions for the 1990's. John Naisbitt and Patricia Aburdene. Avon Books, 1350 Ave. of the Americas, 2nd Fl. New York, NY 10016. Phone: (212)261-6788 Fax: (570)941-1599 URL: http://www.avonbooks.com • 1991. $6.99. Social forecasting to the year 2000 and into the 21st century.

Mental Health Abstracts. IFI/Plenum Data Corp., 3202 Kirkwood Hwy., Ste. 203 Wilmington, DE 19808. Phone: 800-331-4955 or (302)998-0478 Fax: (302)998-0733 URL: http://www.ifiplenum.com • Provides indexing and abstracting of mental health and mental illness literature appearing in more than 1,200 journals and other sources from 1969 to date. Monthly updates. Inquire as to online cost and availability.

Mental Health Report. Business Publishers, Inc., 8737 Colesville Rd., Suite 1100 Silver Spring, MD 20910-3928. Phone: 800-274-6437 or (301)587-6300 Fax: (301)587-1081

E-mail: bpinews@bpinews.com • URL: http://www.bpinews.com • Biweekly. $396.00 per year.

Mental Measurements Yearbook. University of Nebraska-Lincoln Buros Institute of Mental Measurements, 135 Bancroft Lincoln, NE 68588-0348. Phone: 800-755-1105 or (402)472-6203 Fax: (402)472-6207 E-mail: bimm@unlinfol.unl.edu • URL: http://www.unl.edu/ • Biennial. Price varies.

Mental Sciences Institute. University of Texas Houston Health Science Center

Merchandise and Operating Results of Department and Specialty Stores. National Retail Federation. John Wiley and Sons, Inc., Financial Executives Div., 605 Third Ave. New York, NY 10158-0012. Phone: 800-225-5945 or (212)850-6000 Fax: (212)850-6088 E-mail: info@wiley.com • URL: http://www.wiley.com • Annual. Members, $80.00; non-members, $100.00.

Merck Veterinary Manual: A Handbook of Diagnosis and Therapy for the Veterinarian. Merck Publishing Group, P.O. Box 2000 Rahway, NJ 07065. Phone: (732)594-4600 Fax: (732)388-9778 1998. $32.00. 8th edidion.

Mergent Company Data. Mergent FIS, Inc., 60 Madison Ave., Sixth Floor New York, NY 10010. Phone: 800-342-5647 or (212)413-7670 Fax: (212)413-7777 E-mail: fis@fisonline.com • URL: http://www.fisonline.com • Monthly. Price on application. CD-ROM provides detailed financial statement information for more than 10,000 New York Stock Exchange, American Stock Exchange, and NASDAQ corporations. Includes balance sheets, income statements, dividend history, annual price ranges, stock splits, Moody's debt ratings, etc. Formerly *Moody's Company Data*.

Merger Yearbook. Securities Data Publishing, 40 West 57th St. New York, NY 10019. Phone: 800-455-5844 or (212)765-5311 Fax: (212)956-0112 E-mail: sdp@tfn.com • URL: http://www.sdponline.com • Annual. $595.00. Provides detailed information on mergers and acquisitions announced or completed during the year. Includes many charts. (Securities Data Publishing is a unit of Thomson Financial.)

Mergers, Acquisitions, and Corporate Restructurings. Patrick A. Gaughan. John Wiley and Sons, Inc., 605 Third Ave. New York, NY 10158-0012. Phone: 800-225-5945 or (212)850-6000 Fax: (212)850-6088 E-mail: info@jwiley.com • URL: http://www.wiley.com • 1999. $75.00. Second edition. Covers mergers, acquisitions, divestitures, internal reorganizations, joint ventures, leveraged buyouts, bankruptcy workouts, and recapitalizations.

Mergers and Acquisitions Handbook. Milton L. Rock and Martin Sikora. McGraw-Hill, 1221 Ave. of the Americas New York, NY 10020. Phone: 800-722-4726 or (212)904-2000 Fax: (212)904-2072 E-mail: customer.service@mcgraw-hill.com • URL: http://www.mcgraw-hill.com • 1994. $84.95. Second edition. The first and last word on successful mergers and acquisitions, from putting together an m&a team and targeting acquistion candidates to merging managements and benefits plans-and every step in between.

Mergers & Acquisitions Report. Securities Data Publishing, 40 West 57th St. New York, NY 10019. Phone: 800-455-5844 or (212)765-5311 Fax: (212)956-0112 E-mail: sdp@tfn.com • URL: http://www.sdponline.com • Weekly. $1,295.00 per year. Newsletter. Covers pending and ongoing mergers, acquisitions, restructurings, and bankruptcies. (Securities Data Publishing is a unit of Thomson Financial.)

Mergers & Acquisitions: The Dealmaker's Journal. Securities Data Publishing, 40 West 57th St. New York, NY 10019. Phone: 800-455-5844 or (212)765-5311 Fax: (212)956-0112 E-mail: sdp@tfn.com • URL: http://www.sdponline.com • Bimonthly. $475.00 per year. Provides articles on various aspects of M & A, including valuation, pricing, taxes, and strategy. Current M & A deals are listed and described. (Securities Data Publishing is a unit of Thomson Financial.)

Mergerstat Quarterly Reports. Houlihan Lokey Howard & Zukin, 1930 Century Park West Los Angeles, CA 90099-5098. Phone: 800-455-8871 or (310)553-8871 Fax: 800-554-4515 or (310)553-2173 URL: http://www.mergerstat.com • Quarterly. $100.00 per year. Newsletter. Provides details and analysis of recent corporate merger activity. Includes "Top deals year-to-date" and rankings of financial and legal advisors.

Mergerstat Review. Mergerstat, 1933 Pontius Ave. Los Angeles, CA 90025. Phone: 800-455-8871 or (310)966-9492 Fax: (310)966-9462 E-mail: info@mergerstat.com • URL: http://www.mergerstat.com • Annual. $299.00. Provides analysis of merger and acquisition activity and trends during the year. Contains statistical, industry, and geographical data, including a 25-year historical review.

Mergerstat Transaction Roster. Mergerstat, 1933 Pontius Ave. Los Angeles, CA 90025. Phone: (310)966-9492 Fax: (310)966-9462 E-mail: info@mergerstat.com • URL: http://www.mergerstat.com • Annual. $299.00. A directory of all U. S. companies that were involved in merger and acquisition activity during the year covered. Includes details of each transaction.

METADEX. Cambridge Scientific Abstracts, 7200 Wisconsin Ave. Bethesda, MD 20814. Phone: 800-843-7751 or (301)961-6700 Fax: (301)961-6720 E-mail: sales@csa.com • URL: http://www.csa.com • Covers the worldwide literature of metals, metallurgy, and materials science, 1966 to date. Includes detailed alloys indexing from 1974. Biweekly updating. Inquire as to online cost and availability. (Formerly produced by ASM International.)

METADEX Materials Collection: Metals-Polymers-Ceramics. Cambridge Scientific Abstracts, 7200 Wisconsin Ave. Bethesda, MD 20814. Phone: 800-843-7751 or (301)961-6700 Fax: (301)961-6720 E-mail: sales@csa.com • URL: http://www.csa.com • Quarterly. $6,950.00 per year. Provides CD-ROM citations to the worldwide literature of materials science and metallurgy. Corresponds to *Metals Abstracts, Alloys Index, Steels Alert, Nonferrous Alert, Polymers/Ceramics/Composites Alert*, and *Engineered Materials Abstracts*. (Formerly produced by ASM International.)

Metal Bulletin. Metal Bulletin, Inc., 220 Fifth Ave., 19th Fl. New York, NY 10001-7781. Phone: 800-638-2525 or (212)213-6202 Fax: (212)213-1870 E-mail: sales@metbul.com • URL: http://www.metalbulletin.co.uk • Semiweekly. $1,378 per year. Provides news of international trends, prices, and market conditions for both steel and non-ferrous metal industries. (Published in England.)

Metal Bulletin Monthly. Metal Bulletin, Inc., 220 Fifth Ave., 19th Fl. New York, NY 10001-7781. Phone: 800-638-2525 or (212)213-6202 Fax: (212)213-1870 E-mail: sales@metbul.com • URL: http://www.metalbulletin.co.uk • Monthly. Price on application. Edited for international metal industry business executives and senior technical personnel. Covers business, economic, and technical developments. (Published in England.)

Metal Casting Laboratory.

Metal Center News. Hitchcock Publishing, 2000 Clearwater Dr. Oak Brook, IL 60523. Phone: (630)462-2285 Fax: (630)462-2862 E-mail: bhiggins@cahners.com • URL: http://www.cahners.com • 13 times a year. $89.00 per year.

Metal Finishing: Devoted Exclusively to Metallic Surface Treatments. Elsevier Science, 655 Ave. of the Americas New York, NY 10010. Phone: 888-437-4636 or (212)989-5800 Fax: (212)633-3680 E-mail: usinfo@elsevier.com • URL: http://www.elsevier.com • Monthly. $64.00 per year. Includes annual *Metal Finishing Guidebook and Directory*.

Metal Finishing Guidebook and Directory. Elsevier Science, 655 Ave of the Americas New York, NY 10010. Phone: 888-437-4636 or (212)989-5800 Fax: (212)633-3680 E-mail: usinfo@elsevier.com • URL: http://www.elsevier.com • Annual. Price on application. Included with subscription to *Metal Finishing*. Lists manufacturers and suppliers to the industry.

Metal Finishing Suppliers' Association.

Metal Powder Industries Federation.

Metal Powder Report. Elsevier Science, Inc., 655 Ave. of the Americas New York, NY 10010. Phone: 888-437-4636 or (212)989-5800 Fax: (212)633-3680 E-mail: usinfo@elsevier.com • URL: http://www.elsevier.com • 11 times a year. $373.00. per year. Technical articles, company reports, up-to-date news and book reviews cover powder metallurgy worldwide

Metal Statistics. Cahners Business Information, 350 Hudson St., 4th Fl. New York, NY 10014. Phone: 800-662-7776 or (212)519-7700 E-mail: corporatecommunications@cahners.com • URL: http://www.cahners.com • Annual. $250.00. Provides statistical data on a wide variety of metals, metal products, ores, alloys, and scrap metal. Includes data on prices, production, consumption, shipments, imports, and exports.

Metalforming Digest. Cambridge Information Group, 7200 Wisconsin Ave., 6th Fl. Bethesda, MD 20814. Phone: (301)961-6700 Fax: (301)961-6720 E-mail: market@csa.com • URL: http://www.csa.com • Monthly. Provides abstracts of the international literature of metal forming, including powder metallurgy, stamping, extrusion, forging, etc.

Metallurgia, The Journal of Metals Technology, Metal Forming and Thermal Processing. British Forging Industry Association. DMG World Media, Queensway House, Two Queensway Redhill, Surrey RH1 1QS, England. Phone: 44 1737 855485 Fax: 44 1737 855470 URL: http://www.dmg.co.uk • Monthly. $275.00 per year.

Metallurgical and Materials Transactions A: Physical Metallurgy and Materials Sc. ASM International, Materials Park, OH 44073-0002. Phone: 800-336-5152 or (216)338-5151 Fax: (216)338-4634 E-mail: custserv@po.asm-intl.org • URL: http://www.asm-intl.org • Monthly. Members, $75.00 per year; non-members, $1,361.00 per year; students, $35.00 per year. Formerly *Metallurgical Transactions APhysical Metallurgy and Materials Science*.

Metallurgical and Materials Transactions B: Process Metallurgy. ASM International, Materials Information, 9639 Kinsman Rd. Materials Park, OH 44073-0002. Phone: 800-336-5152 or (440)338-5151 Fax: (440)338-4634 E-mail: cust.serv@po.asm-intl.org • URL: http://www.asm-intl.org • Nine times a year. Members, $58.00 per year; non-members, $978.00 per year; students, $26.00 per year. Formerly *Metallurgical Transactions B: Process Metallurgy*.

Metals Abstracts. Cambridge Information Group, 7200 Wisconsin Ave., 6th Fl. Bethesda, MD 20814. Phone: 800-843-7751 or (301)961-6700 Fax: (301)961-6720 E-mail: market@csa.com • URL: http://www.csa.com • Monthly. $2,305.00 per year.

Metals Week. McGraw-Hill Commodity Services Group, 1221 Ave. of the Americas New York, NY 10020. Phone: 800-722-4726 or (212)904-2000 Fax: (212)904-2072 E-mail: customer.service@mcgraw-hill.com • URL: http://www.mcgraw-hill.com • Weekly. $770.00 per year.

Metalworking Digest. Cahners Business Information, New Product Information, 301 Gibraltar Dr. Morris Plains, NJ 07950-0650. Phone: 800-662-7776 or (973)292-5100 Fax: (973)539-3476 E-mail: corporatecommunications@cahners.com • URL: http://www.cahners.com • Monthly. $36.90. Includes *Metalworking Digest Literature Review*.

Meteorological and Geoastrophysical Abstracts. American Meteorological Society, C/O Inforanics, Inc., 550 Newton Rd. Littleton, MA 01460. Phone: (508)486-8976 Fax: (508)487-0027 E-mail: mga@infor.com • URL: http://www.mganet.org • Monthly. $1.120.00 per year.

Metric Reporter. American National Metric Council, 4330 East-West Highway, Suite 401 Bethesda, MD 20814. Phone: (301)718-6508 Fax: (301)656-0989 E-mail: anmcmetric@aol.com • Bimonthly. Membership. Updates and developments in the progress of voluntary implementation of the metric system of measurement.

Metric Today. U.S. Metric Association, Inc., 10245 Andasol Ave. Northridge, CA 91325-1504. Phone: (818)368-5606 Fax: (818)368-7443 Bimonthly. Individuals, $30.00 per year; institutions, $150.00 per year. Formerly *USMA Newsletter*.

Metro. Bobit Publishing Co., 21061 S. Western Ave. Torrance, CA 90501. Phone: (310)533-2400 Fax: (310)533-2500 E-mail: peggyn@bobit.com • URL: http://www.transit-center.com • Bimonthly. $40.00 per year. Subject matter is the management of public transportation-systems. Includes *Factbook*.

Metropolitan Home: Style for Our Generation. Hachette Filipacchi Magazines, Inc., 1633 Broadway New York, NY 10019. Phone: 800-274-4027 or (212)767-6000 Fax: (212)333-2283 Bimonthly. $17.94 per year.

Metropolitan Life Insurance Co. Statistical Bulletin SB. Metropolitan Life Insurance Co., One Madison Ave., Area 2-D New York, NY 10010. Phone: (212)578-5014 Fax: (212)685-7987 URL: http://www.statbull.com • Quarterly. Individuals, $50.00 per year. Covers a wide range of social, economic and demographic health concerns.

Mexico Business: The Portable Encyclopedia for Doing Business with Mexico. World Trade Press, 1450 Grant Ave., Suite 204 Novato, CA 94945-3142. Phone: 800-833-8586 or (415)898-1124 Fax: (415)898-1124 E-mail: worldpress@aol.com • URL: http://www.worldtradepress.com • 1994. $24.95. Covers economic data, import/export possibilities, basic tax and trade laws, travel information, and other useful facts for doing business with Mexico. Includes a special section on NAFTA. (Country Business Guides-Series).

Mexico Company Handbook: Data on Major Listed Companies. Available from Hoovers, Inc., 1033 La Posada Dr., Suite 250 Austin, TX 78752. Phone: 800-486-8666 or (512)374-4500 Fax: (512)374-4501 E-mail: orders@hoovers.com • URL: http://www.hoovers.com • Annual. $29.95. Published by IMF Editora. Contains profiles of publicly traded companies in Mexico. Includes information on local stock exchanges and the nation's economic situation.

MH/RV Builders News: The Magazine for Builders of Manufactured-Mobile-Modular-Marine Homes and Recreational Vehicles. Patrick Finn, editor. Dan Kamrow and Associates, Inc., P.O. Box 72367 Roselle, IL 60172. Phone: (747)891-8872 Bimonthly. $20.00 per year.

Michie on Banks on Banking. LEXIS Publishing, 701 E. Water St. Charlottesville, VA 22902. Phone: 800-446-3410 or (804)972-7600 Fax: 800-643-1280 or (804)972-7686 E-mail: custserv@michie.com • URL: http://www.lexislaw.publishing • 13 volumes. Price on application.

Michigan Agricultural Experiment Station. Michigan State University

Michigan Health and Social Security Research Institute., 8000 E. Jefferson Ave. Detroit, MI 48214-2699. Phone: (313)926-5563 Fax: (313)824-7220 Studies the health and social security problems of trade union members.

Michigan Institute for Environmental and Health Sciences.

Michigan Memorial-Phoenix Project., University of Michigan, Phoenix Memorial Laboratory, Ford Nuclear Reactor, 2301 Bonisteel Blvd. Ann Arbor, MI 48109-2100. Phone: (734)764-6200 Fax: (734)936-1571 E-mail: jcl@umich.edu • URL: http://www.umich.edu/~mmpp • Conducts research in peaceful uses of nuclear energy.

Microbanker Software Buyer's Guide. Microbanker, Inc., P.O. Box 708 Lake George, NY 12845-0708. Phone: (518)745-7071 Fax: (518)745-7009 E-mail: webmaster@

microbanker.com • URL: http://www.microbanker.com • Annual. $245.00 per year. Includes suppliers of over 1,550 financial application programs for microcomputers.

Microcomputer Abstracts. Information Today, Inc., 143 Old Marlton Pike Medford, NJ 08055-8750. Phone: 800-300-9868 or (609)654-6266 Fax: (609)654-4309 E-mail: custserv@infotoday.com • URL: http://www.infotoday.com • Quarterly. $225.00 per year. Provides abstracts covering a wide variety of personal and business microcomputer literature. Formerly *Microcomputer Index*.

Microcomputer Engineering. Gene H. Miller. Prentice Hall, 240 Frisch Court Paramus, NJ 07652-5240. Phone: 800-947-7700 or (201)909-6200 Fax: 800-445-6991 or (201)909-6361 URL: http://www.prenhall.com • 1998. $100.00. Second edition.

Microcomputer Investors Association., 902 Anderson Dr. Fredericksburg, VA 22405. Phone: (703)371-5474 Members are professional investors who make use of microcomputers for portfolio management.

Microcomputer Software Guide Online. R. R. Bowker, 121 Chanlon Rd. New Providence, NJ 07974. Phone: 800-521-8110 or (908)464-6800 Fax: (908)665-6688 Provides information on more than 30,000 microcomputer software applications from more than 4,000 producers. Corresponds to printed *Software Encyclopedia*, but with monthly updates. Inquire as to online cost and availability.

Microelectronics Laboratory.

Microform and Imaging Review. R. R. Bowker, 121 Chanlon Rd. New Providence, NJ 07974. Phone: 888-269-5372 or (908)464-6800 Fax: (908)771-7704 E-mail: info@bowker.com • URL: http://www.bowker.com • Quarterly. $165.00 per year. Evaluates scholarly micropublications for libraries. Includes articles on microform management.

Microform Market Place: An International Directory of Micropublishing. Available from Reed Reference Publishing, 121 Chanlon Rd. New Providence, NJ 07974. Phone: 800-521-8110 or (908)464-6800 Fax: (908)665-6688 E-mail: info@bowker.com • URL: http://www.bowker.com • Biennial. $75.00. Published by K. G. Saur. International coverage. Lists microform publishers by name, by subject area of specialization, and by country.

Micrographics and Hybrid Imaging Systems Newsletter: Monthly Report for Busines Excutives Who Use of Market Microfilm Services and Hybrid Imaging Services and Equipment. Microfilm Publishing. Inc., P.O. Box 950 Larchmont, NY 10538-0950. Phone: (914)834-3044 Fax: (914)834-3993 E-mail: mngreenshtl@aol.com • URL: http://www.micrographicsnews.com • Monthly. $168.30 per year. A report for business executives who use or market microfilm services and equipment. Formerly *Micrographics Newsletter*.

Microkelvin Laboratory., Cornell University, Clark Hall, H Corridor Ithaca, NY 14853. Phone: (607)255-6059 Fax: (607)255-6428 Focuses on electronic behavior changes in metals, insulators, and semiconductors at ultra-low temperatures.

MicroLeads Vendor Directory on Disk (Personal Computer Industry). Chromatic Communications Enterprises, Inc., P.O. Box 30127 Walnut Creek, CA 94598-9878. Phone: 800-782-3475 or (510)945-1602 Fax: (707)746-0542 Annual. $495.00. Includes computer hardware manufacturers, software producers, book-periodical publishers, and franchised or company-owned chains of personal computer equipment retailers, support services and accessory manufacturers. Formerly *MicroLeads U.S. Vender Directory*.

Microprocessor Report: The Insiders' Guide to Microprocessor Hardware. Micro Design Resources, 298 S. Sunnyvale Ave., Suite 101 Sunnyvale, CA 94086-6245. Phone: 800-527-0288 or (408)328-3900 Fax: (408)737-2242 E-mail: cs@mdr.cahners.com • URL: http://www.mdronline.com • 17 times a year. $695.00 per year. Newsletter. Covers the technical aspects of microprocessors from Intel, IBM, Cyrix, Motorola, and others.

Micropublishers' Trade List Annual. Chadwyck-Healey, Inc., 1101 King St., Suite 380 Alexandria, VA 22314-2924. Phone: 800-752-0515 or (703)683-4890 Fax: (703)683-7589 E-mail: marketing@chadwyck.com • Annual. $375.00. About 250 publishers of microfilm and microfiche and their catalogs. Worldwide coverage.

Micropublishing News: The Newsmonthly for Electronic Designers and Publishers. Cygnus Business Media, 445 Broad Hollow Rd. Melville, NY 11747. Phone: 800-308-6397 or (631)845-2700 Fax: (631)845-2798 E-mail: rich.reiff@cygnuspub.com • URL: http://www.cygnuspub.com • Monthly. Free to qualified personnel. Price on application. Edited for business and professional users of electronic publishing products and services. Topics covered include document imaging, CD-ROM publishing, digital video, and multimedia services. Available in four regional editions.

Microsoft Secrets: How the World's Most Powerful Software Company Creates Technology, Shapes Markets, and Manages People. Michael A. Cusumano and Richard W. Selby. Free Press, 1230 Ave. of the Americas New York, NY 10020. Phone: 800-223-2348 or (212)698-7000 Fax: 800-445-6991 or (212)698-7007 URL: http://www.thefreepress.com • 1995. $29.50. Describes the internal workings of the Microsoft Corporation, including marketing, technical innovation, and human relations.

Microwave and Optical Technology Letters. John Wiley and Sons, Inc., Journals Div., 605 Third Ave. New York, NY 10158-0012. Phone: 800-526-5368 or (212)850-6000 Fax: (212)850-6088 E-mail: info@wiley.com • URL: http://www.wiley.com • 24 times a year. $1,540.00 per year.

Microwave Device and Physical Electronics Laboratory. University of Utah

Microwave Journal. Horizon House Publications, Inc., 685 Canton St. Norwood, MA 02060. Phone: (781)769-9750 Fax: (781)769-5037 E-mail: mjw@mwjournal.com • URL: http://www.mwjournal.com • Monthly. $110.00 per year. International coverage.

Microwaves and RF Directory. Penton Media Inc., 611 Route 46 W. Hasbrouck Heights, NJ 07604. Phone: 800-526-6052 or (201)393-6060 Fax: (201)393-0204 E-mail: info@buyused.com • URL: http://www.penton.com • Annual. $125.00. About 2,000 manufacturers of high frequency equipment components. International coverage. Formerly *Microwaves and RF Product Data Directory*.

Mid-Am Antique Appraisers Association.

Middle-East/Africa Kompass on Disc. Available from Kompass USA, Inc., 1255 Route 70, Suite 25-S Lakewood, NJ 08701. Phone: 877-566-7277 or (732)730-0340 Fax: (732)730-0342 E-mail: mail@kompass-usa.com • URL: http://www.kompass.com • Annual. $1,540.00. CD-ROM provides information on more than 150,000 companies in Algeria, Bahrain, Cyprus, Egypt, Lebanon, Mauritania, Morocco, Oman, Saudi Arabia, South Africa, Tunisia, and United Arab Emirates. Classification system covers approximately 50,000 products and services.

Middle East Librarians' Association.

Midwest Research Institute.

Migration World: A Bimonthly Magazine Focusing on the Newest Immigrant and Refuee Groups; Policy and Legislation; Resources. Center for Migration Studies, 209 Flagg Place Staten Island, NY 10304-1199. Phone: (718)351-8800 Fax: (718)667-4598 E-mail: sales@cmsny.org • URL: http://www.cmsny.org • Five times a year. Individuals, $31.00 per year; institutions, $50.00 per year.

Milan Experiment Station. University of Tennessee, Knoxville

The Milbank Quarterly. Milbank Memorial Fund. Blackwell Publishers, 350 Main St., 6th Fl. Malden, MA 02148-5018. Phone: 800-216-2522 Fax: (781)388-8210 E-mail: subscript@blackwell.com • URL: http://www/blackwellpub.com • Quarterly. $101.00 per year. Formerly*Health and Society*.

Military Grocer. Downey Communications, Inc., 4800 Montgomery Lane, Suite 710 Bethesda, MD 20814-5341. Phone: (301)718-7600 Fax: (301)718-7604 E-mail: exchange@downey-date.com • Bimonthly. $40.00 per year. Edited for managers and employees of supermarkets on military bases. (These are supermarkets administered by the Defense Commissary Agency.)

Military Market: Magazine for the Military Retail System. Army Times Publishing Co., 6883 Commercial Dr. Springfield, VA 22159-0240. Phone: 800-368-5718 or (703)750-8676 Fax: (703)658-8314 URL: http://www.armytimes.com • Monthly. $79.00 per year. Aimed at officials who buy for and operate military base stores. *Buyers Guide* and *Almanac and Directory* available, $10.00 each.

Military Prime Contract Awards and Subcontract Payments. U.S. Department of Defense, Office of the Secretary, The Pentagon Washington, DC 20301. Phone: (703)545-6700 Annual.

Military Retailing Directory. Military Retailing Publisher, 270 Ross Ave. Melbourbe Beach, FL 32951. Phone: (407)952-9171 Semiannual. $95.00 per year. Edited for use by military commissaries in making purchasing decisions. Lists sources of goods and sevices, with official military department and retail order numbers.

Milk Industry Foundation.

Millennium Intelligence: Understanding and Conducting Competitive Intelligence in the Digital Age. Jerry Miller, editor. Information Today, Inc., 143 Old Marlton Pike Medford, NJ 08055-8750. Phone: 800-300-9868 or (609)654-6266 Fax: (609)654-4309 E-mail: custserv@infotoday.com • URL: http://www.infotoday.com • 1999. $29.95. Contains essays by various authors on competitive intelligence information sources, legal aspects, intelligence skills, corporate security, and other topics. (CyberAge Books.)

Miller GAAP Guide: A Comprehensive Restatement of All Current Promulgated Generally Accepted Accounting Principles. Harcourt Brace Professional Publishing, 525 B St., Suite 1900 San Diego, CA 92101-4495. Phone: 800-543-1918 or (619)699-6716 Fax: 800-876-0186 E-mail: wlittle@harbrace.com • URL: http://www.harcourt.com • Annual. $69.00. Monthly updates. Includes all current Financial Accounting Standards Board (FASB) statements, interpretations, and technical bulletins.

Miller GAAS Guide: A Comprehensive Restatement of Generally Accepted Auditing Standards for Auditing, Attestation, Compilation and Review and the Code of Professional Conduct. Larry P. Bailey. Harcourt Brace Professional Publishing, 525 B St., Suite 1900 San Diego, CA 92101-4495. Phone: 800-543-1918 or (619)699-6716 Fax: 800-876-0186 URL: http://www.harcourt.com • Annual. $69.00. Monthly updates. Includes industry audit guides and a model audit program.

Miller Governmental GAAP Guide: A Comprehensive Interpretation of All Current Promulgated Governmental Generally Accepted Accounting Principles for State and Local and Local Governments. Larry P. Bailey. Harcourt Brace Professional Publishing, 525 B St., Suite 1900 San Diego, CA 92101-4495. Phone: 800-543-1918 or (619)699-6716 Fax: 800-876-0186 Annual. $79.00. Includes reporting standards for hospitals, colleges, and other non-profit organizations. Provides a model comprehensive annual financial report.

Miller's Antiques Price Guide. Judith Miller, compiler and editor. Antique Collectors' Club, 91 Market St., Suite 52, Industrial Park Wappingers Falls, NY 12590. Phone: 800-225-5231 or (914)297-0003 Fax: (914)297-0068 E-mail: info@antiquecc.com • URL: http://www.antiquecc.com • Annual. $35.00.

Milling and Baking News. Sosland Publishing Co., 4800 Main, Suite 100 Kansas City, MO 64112-2513. Phone: (816)756-1000 Fax: (816)756-0494 E-mail: mbn@sosland.com • Weekly. $122.00 per year. News magazine for the breadstuffs industry.

Mind-Machine Interaction Research Center.

Mineral Commodity Summaries. Available from U. S. Government Printing Office, Washington, DC 20402. Phone: (202)512-1800 Fax: (202)512-2250 E-mail: gpoaccess@gpo.gov • URL: http://www.access.gpo.gov • Annual. Published by the U. S. Geological Survey, Department of the Interior (http://www.usgs.gov). Contains detailed, five-year data for about 90 nonfuel minerals. Covers a wide range of statistics, including production, imports, exports, consumption, reserves, prices, tariff information, and industry employment. (Two pages are devoted to each mineral.)

Mineral Industry Research Laboratory. University of Alaska Fairbanks

Mineralogical Abstracts: A Quarterly Journal of Abstracts in English, Covering the World Literature of Mineralogy and Related Subjects. Mineralogical Society, 41 Queen's Gate London SW7 5HR, England. Phone: 44 207 5847516 Fax: 44 207 8238021 E-mail: adrian@minersoc.demon.co.uk • URL: http://www.minersoc.org • Quarterly. $350.00 per year.

Mineralogical Society of America.

Minerals, Metals and Materials Society., 184 Thorn Hill Dr. Warrendale, PA 15086-7528. Phone: 800-759-4867 or (724)776-9000 Fax: (724)776-3770 E-mail: tmsgeneral@tms.org • URL: http://www.tms.org • Members are metallurgists, metallurgical engineers, and materials scientists. Divisions include Light Metals and Electronic, Magnetic, and Photonic Materials.

Minerals Yearbook. Available from U.S. Government Printing Office, Washington, DC 20402. Phone: (202)512-1800 Fax: (202)512-2250 E-mail: gpoaccess@gpo.gov • URL: http://www.access.gpo.gov • Annual. Three volumes.

Mines Magazine. Colorado School of Mines Alumni Association, Inc., P.O. Box 1410 Golden, CO 80402. Phone: (303)273-3291 Fax: (303)273-3583 E-mail: cwarren@mines.edu • Seven times a year. Free to members; other, $30.00 per year.

Mining and Metallurgical Society of America.

Mining Engineering. Society for Mining, Metallurgy and Exploration, P.O. Box 625002 Littleton, CO 80162-5002. Phone: (303)973-9550 Fax: (303)973-3845 Monthly. $125.00 per year. Includes *Who's Who in Mining Engineering*.

Mining Machinery and Equipment. U.S. Bureau of the Census, Washington, DC 20233-0800. Phone: (301)457-4100 Fax: (301)457-3842 URL: http://www.census.gov • Annual. (Current Industrial Reports MA35F.)

The Mining Record. Howell International Enterprises, P.O. Box 37510 Denver, CO 80237. Phone: (303)663-7820 Fax: (303)663-7823 E-mail: don@miningrecord.com • Weekly. $45.00 per year.

Mining Voice. National Mining Association, 1130 17th St., N. W. Washington, DC 20036. Phone: (202)463-2625 Fax: (202)833-9636 E-mail: rlawson@nma.org • URL: http://www.nma.org • Bimonthly. $36.00 per year. Covers U. S. mining issues and trends, with emphasis on coal. Formerly *Coal Voice*.

Mining Week. National Mining Association, 1130 17th St., N. W. Washington, DC 20036. Phone: (202)463-2625 Fax: (202)833-9636 E-mail: rlawson@nma.org • URL: http://www.nma.org • Weekly. Free to members; non-members, $100.00 per year. Newsletter. Covers legislative, business, research, and other developments of interest to the mining industry.

Minorities in Media., P.O. Box 9198 Petersburg, VA 23806. Phone: (804)524-5924 Members are minority media professionals.

Minority Business Entrepreneur., 3528 Torrance Blvd., Suite 101 Torrance, CA 90503-4803. Phone: (310)540-9398 Fax: (310)792-8263 E-mail: mbewbe@ix.netcom.com • URL: http://www.mbemag.com • Bimonthly. $16.00 per year. Reports on issues ''critical to the growth and development of minority and women-owned firms.'' Provides information on relevant legislation and profiles successful women and minority entrepreneurs.

MIS Quarterly (Management Information Systems). University of Minnesota School of Management. MIS Research Center, University of Minnesota, Carlson School of Management, 321 19th Ave., S. Minneapolis, MN 55455. Phone: (952)624-2035 Fax: (952)624-2056 E-mail: misq@csom.umn.edu • URL: http://www.misq.org • Quarterly. $80.00 per year.

Mix Magazine: Professional Recording, Sound, and Music Production. Intertec Publishing Corp., 6400 Hollis St., Suite 12 Emeryville, CA 94608. Phone: 800-888-5139 or (510)653-3307 Fax: (510)653-5142 E-mail: subs@intertec.com • URL: http://www.intertec.com • Monthly. $34.95 per year.

MixPlus: Music and Audio Resources for the U. S. and Canada. Intertec Publishing Corp., 6400 Hollis St., Suite 12 Emeryville, CA 94608. Phone: 800-888-5139 or (510)653-3307 Fax: (510)653-5142 E-mail: subs@intertec.com • URL: http://www.intertec.com • Annual. $14.95 for each regional edition (East, West, Central). A professional directory for the recording and music businesses, listing concert promoters, rehearsal halls, consultants, record labels, recording studios, tape and disc mastering services, legal services, facility designers, music education programs, and other music and audio services.

MLA Handbook for Writers of Research Papers. Joseph Gibaldi. Modern Language Association of America, 10 Astor Place New York, NY 10003. Phone: (212)475-9500 Fax: (212)477-9863 E-mail: info@mla.org • URL: http://www.mla.org • 1999. $14.75. Fifth edition.

MLO (Medical Laboratory Observer). Medical Economics Publishing Co., Inc., Five Paragon Dr. Montvale, NJ 07645-1742. Phone: 800-232-7379 or (201)358-7200 Fax: (201)573-8999 E-mail: customer-service@medec.com • URL: http://www.medec.com • Monthly. $70.00 per year. Covers management, regulatory, and technical topics for clinical laboratory administrators.

MLS (Marketing Library Services). Information Today, Inc., 143 Old Marlton Pike Medford, NJ 08055-8750. Phone: 800-300-9868 or (609)654-6266 Fax: (609)654-4309 E-mail: custserv@infotoday.com • URL: http://www.infotoday.com • Eight times a year. $69.95 per year. Newsletter. Provides advice on public relations, publicity, promotion of new services, and other library marketing topics.

Mobile Computing and Communication. EMAP USA, 110 Fifth Ave. New York, NY 10011. Phone: 800-777-0555 Fax: (323)782-2467 URL: http://www.mobilecomputing.com • Monthly. $11.97 per year. Covers cellular phones, notebook computers, and other portable electronic items. New products are featured. Formerly *Mobile Office*.

Mobile Industrial Caterers' Association.

Mobility. Employee Relocation Council, 1720 N St., N.W. Washington, DC 20036. Phone: (202)857-0857 Fax: (202)467-4012 12 times a year. $48.00 per year. Covers various aspects of the moving of corporate employees.

Model Business Corporation Act Annotated. American Bar Association Business Law Staff. Prentice Hall, 240 Frisch Court Paramus, NJ 07652-5240. Phone: 800-947-7700 or (201)909-6200 Fax: 800-445-6991 or (201)909-6361 URL: http://www.prenhall.com • 1985. Third edition. Four volumes. Price on application.

The Modem Reference: The Complete Guide to PC Communications. Michael A. Banks. Information Today, Inc., 143 Old Marlton Pike Medford, NJ 08055-8750. Phone: 800-300-9868 or (609)654-6266 Fax: (609)654-4309 E-mail: custserv@infotoday.com • URL: http://www.infotoday.com • 2000. $29.95. Fourth edition. Covers personal computer data communications technology, including fax transmissions, computer networks, modems, and the Internet. Popularly written.

Moderating Focus Groups: A Practical Guide for Group Facilitation. Thomas L. Greenbaum. Sage Publications, Inc., 2455 Teller Rd. Thousand Oaks, CA 91320. Phone: (805)499-0721 Fax: (805)499-0871 E-mail: info@sagepub.com • URL: http://www.sagepub.com • 2000. $70.00. Covers participant recruitment, characteristics of successful moderators, moderating fundamentals, and related topics.

Modern Accident Investigation and Analysis: An Executive Guide to Accident Investigation. Ted S. Ferry. John Wiley and Sons, Inc., 605 Third Ave. New York, NY 10158-0012. Phone: 800-526-5368 or (212)850-6000 Fax: (212)850-6088 E-mail: info@wiley.com • URL: http://www.wiley.com • 1988. $140.00. Second edition.

Modern Auditing. William C. Boynton and Walter G. Kell. John Wiley and Sons, Inc., 605 Third Ave. New York, NY 10158-0012. Phone: 800-526-5368 or (212)850-6000 Fax: (212)850-6088 E-mail: info@wiley.com • URL: http://www.wiley.com • 2000. Seventh edition. Price on application.

Modern Aviation Electronics. Albert D. Helfrick. Prentice Hall, 240 Frisch Court Paramus, NJ 07652-5240. Phone: 800-947-7700 or (201)909-6200 Fax: 800-445-6991 or (201)909-6361 URL: http://www.prenhall.com • 1994. $67.60. Second edition.

Modern Brewery Age. Business Journals, Inc., P.O. Box 5550 Norwalk, CT 06856. Phone: 800-521-0227 or (203)853-6015 Fax: (203)852-8175 Bimonthly. $85.00 per year. Annual supplement available *Blue Book*.

Modern Brewery Age Blue Book. Business Journals, Inc., P.O. Box 5550 Norwalk, CT 06856. Phone: 800-521-0227 or (203)853-6015 Fax: (203)852-8175 Annual. $265.00. Over 3,000 breweries, beer wholesalers, importers, trade associations, regulatory agencies, and suppliers to malt beverage industry; international coverage. Supplement to *Modern Brewery Age*.

Modern Bulk Transporter. Intertec Publishing Corp., 9800 Metcalf Ave. Overland Park, KS 66212-2286. Phone: 800-400-5945 or (913)341-1300 Fax: (913)967-1898 E-mail: subs@intertec.com • URL: http://www.intertec.com • Monthly. Price on application.

Modern Bulk Transporter Buyers Guide. Tunnell Publications, Inc., 4200 S. Shepherd Dr., Suite 200 Houston, TX 77098. Phone: 800-441-0294 or (713)523-8124 Fax: (713)523-8384 Annual. Controlled circulation. Suppliers of products or services for companies operating tank trucks.

Modern Business Law. Thomas W. Dunfee and others. McGraw-Hill, 1221 Ave. of the Americas New York, NY 10020. Phone: 800-722-4726 or (212)904-2000 Fax: (212)940-2072 E-mail: customer.service@mcgraw-hill.com • URL: http://www.mcgraw-hill.com • 1995. $90.94. Third edition.

Modern Carpentry: Building Construction Details in Easy-To-Understand Form. Willis H. Wagner and Howard S. Smith. Goodheart-Willcox Publishers, 18604 W. Creek Dr. Tinley Park, IL 60477-6243. Phone: 800-323-0440 or (708)687-5000 Fax: 888-409-3900 or (708)687-0315 E-mail: custerv@goodheartwillcox.com • URL: http://www.goodheartwillcox.com • 2000. $49.28.

Modern Casting. American Foundrymen's Society, Inc., 505 State St. Des Plaines, IL 60016-8399. Phone: 800-537-4237 or (847)824-0181 Fax: (847)824-7848 E-mail: gendel@afsinc.com • Monthly. $50.00 per year.

Modern Casting-Buyer's Reference Issue. American Foundrymen's Society, Inc., 505 State St. Des Plaines, IL 60016-8399. Phone: 800-537-4237 or (847)824-0181 Fax: (847)824-7848 E-mail: gendel@afsinc.com • Annual. $25.00. About 1,700 manufacturers, suppliers, and distributors of foundry and metal casting equipment and products. Formerly *Modern Castings - Buyer's Guide*.

Modern Dictionary of Electronics. Rudolf F. Graf. Butterworth-Heineman, 225 Wildwood Ave Newton, MA 01801. Phone: 800-366-2665 or (781)904-2500 Fax: 800-446-6520 E-mail: orders@bhusa.com • URL: http://www.bh.com • 1999. $59.95. Seventh edition.

Modern Economics. Jan S. Hogendorn. Prentice Hall, 240 Frisch Court Paramus, NJ 07652-5240. Phone: 800-947-7700 or (201)909-6200 Fax: 800-445-6991 or (201)909-6361 URL: http://www.prenhall.com • 1994. $75.00.

Modern Estate Planning. Ernest D. Fiore and M. Friedlich. Matthew Bender & Co., Inc., Two Park Ave. New York, NY 10016. Phone: 800-223-1940 or (212)448-2000 Fax: (212)244-3188 E-mail: international@bender.com • URL: http://www.bender.com • $1,210.00. Seven looseleaf volumes. Updates, $875.00.

Modern Fashion Drawing. Dora Shackell and W. Stuart Masters. Gordon Press Publishers, P.O. Box 459 New York, NY 10004. Phone: (212)969-8419 Fax: (718)624-8419 1978. $250.00. Reprint of the 1934 edition.

Modern Guns: Identification and Values. Russell C. Quertermous and Steven C. Quertermous. Collector Books, 5801 Kentucky Dam Rd. Paducah, KY 42003. Phone: 800-626-5420 or (270)898-6211 Fax: (270)898-8890 2000. $14.95. 13th edition.

Modern Healthcare: The Newsmagazine for Adminstrators and Managers in Hospitals and Other Healthcare Institutions. Crain Communications, Inc., 740 N. Rush St. Chicago, IL 60611-2590. Phone: 800-678-9595 or (312)649-5200 Fax: (312)280-3183 URL: http://www.modernhealthcare.com/ • Weekly. $135.00 per year; students, $63.00 per year.

Modern Intellectual Property. Michael A. Epstein. Aspen Law and Business, 1185 Ave. of the Americas New York, NY 10036. Phone: 800-638-8437 or (212)597-0200 Fax: 800-901-9075 or (212)597-0338 E-mail: customer.service@aspenpubl.com • URL: http://www.aspenpub.com • 1995. Third edition. Price on application.

Modern International Economics. Wilfred Ethier. W. W. Norton & Co., Inc., 500 Fifth Ave. New York, NY 10110. Phone: 800-223-2584 or (212)354-5500 Fax: (212)869-0856 E-mail: webmaster@wwnorton.com • URL: http://www.norton.com • 1995. $91.00. Third edition.

Modern Jeweler. Cygnus Business Media, 445 Broad Hollow Rd. Melville, NY 11747. Phone: 800-308-6397 or (631)845-2700 Fax: (631)845-2798 E-mail: rich.reiff@cygnuspub.com • URL: http://www.cygnuspub.com • Monthly. $60.00 per year. Edited for retail jewelers. Covers the merchandising of jewelry, gems, and watches. Supersedes in part *Modern Jeweler*.

Modern Law of Marine Insurance. D. Rhidian Thomas, editor. Available from Informa Publishing Group Ltd., PO Box 1017 Westborough, MA 01581-6017. Phone: 800-493-4080 Fax: (508)231-0856 E-mail: enquiries@informa.com • URL: http://www.informa.com • 1996. $160.00. Published in the UK by Lloyd's List (http://www.lloydslist.com). Contains contributions from both academics and practitioners on contracts, clauses, perils, proof, losses, seaworthiness, causation, insurance brokers, etc.

Modern Machine Shop. Gardner Publications, Inc., 6915 Valley Ave. Cincinnati, OH 45244-3029. Phone: 800-950-8020 or (513)527-8800 Fax: (513)527-8801 URL: http://www.mmsonline.com • Monthly. $50.00 per year.

Modern Machine Shop Material Working Technology Guide. Gardner Publications, Inc., 6915 Valley Ave. Cincinnati, OH 45244-3029. Phone: 800-950-8020 or (513)527-8800 Fax: (513)527-8801 URL: http://www.mmsonline.com • Annual. $15.00. Lists products and services for the metalworking industry. Formerly *Modern Machine Shop CNC and Software Guide*.

Modern Materials Handling. Cahners Publishing Co., Inc., 275 Washington St. Newton, MA 02458-1630. Phone: 800-662-7776 or (617)964-3030 Fax: (617)558-4327 E-mail: corporatecommunications@cahners.com • URL: http://www.cahners.com • 14 times a year. $92.90 per year. For managers and engineers who buy or specify equipment used to move, store, control and protect products throughout the manufacturing and warehousing cycles. Includes *Casebook Directory* and *Planning Guide*. Also includes *ADC News and Solutions*.

Modern Materials Handling Casebook Directory. Cahners Business Information, 275 Washington St. Newton, MA 02458-1630. Phone: 800-662-7776 or (617)964-3030 Fax: (617)558-4402 E-mail: corporatecommunications@cahners.com • URL: http://www.cahners.com • Annual. $25.00. Lists about 2,300 manufacturers of equipment and supplies in the materials handling industry. Supplement to *Modern Materials Handling*.

Modern Maturity. American Association of Retired Persons, 601 E. St., N.W. Washington, DC 20049. Phone: (202)434-2277 Fax: (202)434-6881 URL: http://www.aarp.org/mmaturity/ • Bimonthly. Membership.

Modern Metals. Trend Publishing, Inc., One E. Erie St., Suite 401 Chicago, IL 60611. Phone: 800-278-7363 or (312)654-2300 Fax: (312)654-2323 Monthly. $95.00 per year. Covers management and production for plants that fabricate and finish metals of various kinds.

Modern Methods for Quality Control and Improvement. Harrison M. Wadsworth and others. John Wiley and Sons, Inc., 605 Third Ave. New York, NY 10158-0012. Phone: 800-526-5368 or (212)850-6000 Fax: (212)850-6088 E-mail: info@wiley.com • URL: http://www.wiley.com • 1986. $99.95.

Modern Organizations: Administrative Theory in Contemporary Society. Ali Farazmand. Greenwood Publishing Group, Inc., 88 Post Rd., W. Westport, CT 06881-5007. Phone: 800-225-5800 or (203)226-3571 Fax: (203)222-2540 E-mail: bookinfo@greenwood.com • URL: http://www.greenwood.com • 1994. $59.95.

Modern Paint and Coatings. Chemical Week Associates, 110 Williams St., 11th Fl. New York, NY 10038. Phone: 800-308-6397 or (212)621-4900 Fax: (212)621-4949 E-mail: webmaster@chemweek.com • URL: http://www.chemweek.com • Monthly. $52.00 per year.

Modern Parliamentary Procedure. Ray E. Keesey. American Psychological Association, 750 First St., N. E. Washington, DC 20002-4242. Phone: 800-374-2721 or (202)336-5500 Fax: (202)336-5530 URL: http://www.apa.org/books • 1994. $24.95. Revised edition. A modernization and simplification of traditional, complex rules of procedure. Written for associations, clubs, community groups, and other deliberative bodies.

Modern Patent Law Precedent: Dictionary of Key Terms and Concepts. Irwin M. Alsenberg. Glasser Legalworks, 150 Clove Rd. Little Falls, NJ 07424. Phone: 800-308-1700 or (973)890-0008 Fax: (973)890-0042 E-mail: legalwks@aol.com • URL: http://www.legalwks.com • 1997. $175.00. Third edition. Dictionary covers ''3,000 relevant cases in which words and phrases are interpreted by decision-makers.'' Sources include the U. S. Code, patent examiners, terms of art, and general legal concepts relating to patent practice.

Modern Physician: Essential Business News for the Executive Physician. Crain Communications, Inc., 740 Rush St. Chicago, IL 60611-2590. Phone: 800-678-9595 or (312)649-5200 Fax: (312)649-5393 E-mail: moderndoc@mindspring.com • URL: http://www.modernphysician.com • Monthly. $39.50. Edited for physicians responsible for business decisions at hospitals, clinics, HMOs, and other health groups. Includes special issues on managed care, practice management, legal issues, and finance.

Modern Plastics Encyclopedia. McGraw-Hill, 1221 Ave. of the Americas New York, NY 10020. Phone: 800-722-4726 or (212)904-2000 Fax: (212)904-2072 E-mail: customer.service@mcgraw-hill.com • URL: http://www.mcgraw-hill.com • Annual. $125.00. List of about 5,000 suppliers of over 350 types of products and services to the plastic industry in the U.S. and Canada. Included with subscription to *Modern Plastics*.

Modern Portfolio Theory and Investment Analysis. Edwin J. Elton and Martin J. Gruber. John Wiley and Sons, Inc., 605 Third Ave. New York, NY 10158-0012. Phone: 800-526-5368 or (212)850-6000 Fax: (212)850-6088 E-mail: info@wiley.com • URL: http://www.wiley.com • 1995. $52.95. Fifth edition. The authors' central concern is that of mixing assets to achieve maximum overall return consonant with an acceptable level of risk. (Portfolio Management Series).

Modern Real Estate. Charles H. Wurtzebach and Mike E. Miles. John Wiley and Sons, Inc., 605 Third Ave. New York, NY 10158-0012. Phone: 800-526-5368 or (212)850-6000 Fax: (212)850-6088 E-mail: info@wiley.com • URL: http://www.wiley.com • 1994. $92.95. Fifth edition.

Modern Real Estate and Mortgage Forms: Basic Forms and Agreements. Alvin L. Arnold. Warren, Gorham and Lamont/RIA Group, 395 Hudson St. New York, NY 10014. Phone: 800-950-1215 or (212)367-6300 Fax: (212)367-6718 E-mail: customer_service@riag.com • URL: http://www.riahome.com • Looseleaf. $130.00. Annual supplementation. Over 1,000 pages of forms.

Modern Real Estate Practice. Fillmore W. Galaty and others. Dearborn, Kaplan Professional Co., 155 N. Wacker St. Chicago, IL 60606-1719. Phone: 800-921-9621 or (312)836-4400 Fax: (312)836-1021 URL: http://www.dearborn.com • 1997. $44.95. 15th edition. Provides essential up-to-date information to students preparing for a state licensing exam.

Modern Recording Techniques. David M. Huber and Robert Runstein. Butterworth-Heinemann, 225 Wildwood Ave. Woburn, MA 01801. Phone: 800-366-2665 or (781)904-2500 Fax: 800-466-6520 E-mail: orders@bhusa.com • URL: http://www.bh.com • 1995. $29.95. Fourth edition.

Modern Refrigeration and Air Conditioning. Andrew D. Althouse and others. Goodheart-Willcox Publishers, 18604 W. Creek Dr. Tinley Park, IL 60477-6243. Phone: 800-323-0440 or (708)687-5000 Fax: 888-409-3900 or (708)687-0315 E-mail: custerv@goodheartwillcox.com • URL: http://www.goodheartwillcox.com • 1996. $55.96.

Modern Retailing: Theory and Practice. Joseph B. Mason and others. McGraw-Hill Higher Education, 1221 Ave. of the Americas New York, NY 10020-1095. Phone: 800-722-4726 or (212)904-2000 Fax: (212)904-2072 E-mail: customer.service@mcgraw-hill.com • URL: http://www.mcgraw-hill.com • 1992. $69.95. Sixth edition.

Modern Salon Magazine. Vance Publishing Corp., 400 Knightsbridge Parkway Lincolnshire, IL 60069-1414. Phone: 800-621-2845 or (847)634-2600 Fax: (847)634-4379 URL: http://www.vancepublishing.com • Monthly. $20.00 per year.

Modern Tire Dealer: Covering Tire Sales and Car Service. Bill Communications, Inc., P.O. Box 3599 Akron, OH 44309-3599. Phone: 800-266-4712 or (330)867-4401 Fax: (330)867-0019 URL: http://www.billcom.com • Monthly. $60.00 per year. Serves independent tire dealers. Cover automotive service and dealership management topics.

Modern Tire Dealer: Facts/Directory. Bill Communications, Inc., 770 Broadway New York, NY 10003-9595. Phone: 800-266-4712 or (646)654-4500 Fax: (646)654-7212 URL: http://www.billcom.com • Annual. $30.00. Directories of tire and car service suppliers, tire shop jobbers, and national state associations.

Modern Workers Compensation. West Group, 610 Opperman Dr. Eagan, MN 55123. Phone: 800-328-4880 or (651)687-7000 Fax: 800-213-2323 or (651)687-5827 URL: http://www.westgroup.com • $395.00. Three looseleaf volumes. Periodic supplementation. Provides detailed coverage of workers' compensation law and procedure, including medical benefits, rehabilitation benefits, compensation costs, noncompensable injuries, etc.

Molasses Market News. U.S. Dept. of Agriculture, Agricultural Marketing Service, Washington, DC 20250. Phone: (202)720-8999 Weekly. Provides the market news on molasses and its imports and exports.

Molding Systems. Society of Manufacturing Engineers, One SME Dr. Dearborn, MI 48128. Phone: (313)271-1500 Fax: (313)271-2861 E-mail: destjam@sme.org • URL: http://www.sme.org • Monthly. $100.00. Formerly *Plastics World*.

Molecular Biology Institute.

Molluscan Shellfish Institute.

Monell Chemical Senses Center., 3500 Market St. Philadelphia, PA 19104-3308. Phone: (215)898-8878 Fax: (215)898-2084 E-mail: beauchamp@monell.org • URL: http://www.monell.org • Does multidisciplinary research relating to taste and smell (the chemical senses), including investigation of the sensory qualities of food.

The Monell Connection: From the Monell Chemical Senses Center, a Nonprofit Scientific Institute Devoted to Research on Taste and Smell. Monell Chemical Senses Center, 3500 Market St. Philadelphia, PA 19104. Phone: (215)898-6666 Three times a year. Free. Newsletter. Includes brief summaries of selected papers describing ongoing work of Monell scientists.

Monetary Policy and Reserve Requirements Handbook. U.S. Federal Reserve System. Board of Governors Publications Services, Room MS-1, 20th and Constitution Ave., N.W. Washington, DC 20551. Phone: (202)752-3244 Fax: (202)728-5886 URL: http://http://www.federalreserve.gov • Annual. $75.00.

Money. Time Inc., Time & Life Bldg., Rockefeller Center, 1271 Ave. of the Americas New York, NY 10020-1393. Phone: 800-633-9970 or (212)522-1212 Fax: (212)522-1796 URL: http://www.money.com • Monthly. $39.95 per year. Covers all aspects of family finance; investments, careers, shopping, taxes, insurance, consumerism, etc.

Money, Banking, and Financial Markets. Lloyd Thomas. McGraw-Hill, 1221 Ave. of the Americas New York, NY 10020. Phone: 800-722-4726 or (212)904-2000 Fax: (212)904-2072 E-mail: customer.service@mcgraw-hill.com • URL: http://www.mcgraw-hill.com • 1996. $82.50.

Money, Banking, and the Economy. Thomas Mayer and others. W. W. Norton & Co., Inc., 500 Fifth Ave. New York, NY 10110. Phone: 800-223-2584 or (212)354-5500 Fax: (212)869-0856 E-mail: webmaster@wwnorton.com • URL: http://www.norton.com • 1996. $85.50. Sixth edition.

Money, Banking and the Economy. Thomas Mayer and others. W. W. Norton & Co., Inc., 500 Fifth Ave. New York, NY 10110-0017. Phone: 800-223-2584 or (212)354-5500 Fax: (212)869-0856 E-mail: webmaster@wworton.com • URL: http://www.wwnorton.com • 1996. $85.50. Sixth edition.

Money Income in the United States. Available from U. S. Government Printing Office, Washington, DC 20402. Phone: (202)512-1800 Fax: (202)512-2250 E-mail: gpoaccess@gpo.gov • URL: http://www.access.gpo.gov • Annual. $19.00. Issued by the U. S. Bureau of the Census. Presents data on consumer income in current and constant dollars, both totals and averages (means, medians, distributions). Includes figures for a wide variety of demographic and occupational characteristics. (Current Population Reports, P60-209.)

Money Income Tax Handbook. Mary L. Sprouse, editor. Little, Brown & Co., 1271 Ave. of the Americas New York, NY 10020. Phone: 800-343-9204 or (212)522-8700 Fax: 800-286-9471 or (212)522-2067 E-mail: cust.service@littlebrown.com • 1995. $13.99. (Title refers to *Money* magazine.)

Money: Its Origins, Development, Debasement, and Prospects. John H. Wood. American Institute for Economic Research, Division St. Great Barrington, MA 01230. Phone: (413)528-1216 Fax: (413)528-0103 E-mail: info@aier.org • URL: http://www.aier.org • 1999. $10.00. A politically conservative view of monetary history, the gold standard, banking systems, and inflation. Includes a list of references. (Economic Education Bulletin.)

Money Madness: Strange Manias and Extraordinary Schemes On and Off Wall Street. John M. Waggoner. McGraw-Hill Professional, 1221 Ave. of the Americas New York, NY 10020-1095. Phone: 800-722-4726 or (212)904-2000 Fax: (212)904-2072 E-mail: customer.service@mcgraw-hill.com • URL: http://www.mcgraw-hill.com • 1990. $26.00.

Money Management Letter: Bi-Weekly Newsletter Covering the Pensions and Money Maagement Industry. Institutional Investor, 488 Madison Ave. New York, NY 10022. Phone: (212)224-3300 Fax: (212)224-3527 E-mail: info@iijournals.com • URL: http://www.iijournals.com • Bi-weekly. $2,550.00 per year. Newsletter. Edited for pension fund investment managers.

Money Management Strategies for Futures Traders. Nauzer J. Balsara. John Wiley and Sons, Inc., 605 Third Ave. New York, NY 10158-0012. Phone: 800-526-5368 or (212)850-6000 Fax: (212)850-6088 E-mail: info@wiley.com • URL: http://www.wiley.com • 1992. $69.95. How to limit risk and avoid catastrophic losses. (Financial Editions Series).

Money Market Directory of Pension Funds and Their Investment Managers. Money Market Directories, Inc., P.O. Box 1608 Charlottesville, VA 22902. Phone: 800-446-2810 or (804)977-1450 Fax: (804)979-9962 URL: http://www.mmdaccess.com • Annual. $995.00. Institutional funds and managers.

Money of the Mind: Borrowing and Lending in America from the Civil War to Michael Milken. James Grant. Farrar, Straus, and Giroux, LLC, 19 Union Square W. New York, NY 10003. Phone: 800-788-6262 or (212)741-6900 Fax: (212)633-9385 1992. $16.00. A critical anlysis by the editor of *Grant's Interest Rate Observer*.

Money Reporter: The Insider's Letter for Investors Whose Interest is More Interest. MPL Communication, Inc., 133 Richmond St., W., Suite 700 Toronto, ON, Canada M5H 3M8. Phone: (416)869-1177 Fax: (416)869-0456 Biweekly. $197.00 per year. Newsletter. Supplement available, *Monthly Key Investment*.Canadian interest-bearing deposits and investments.

Money Stock Liquid Assets, and Debt Measures, in Billions of Dollars. U.S. Federal Reserve System. U.S. Board of Governors, Publications Service,, Room MS-127 Washington, DC 20551. Phone: (202)452-3244 Fax: (202)728-5886 URL: http://www.federalreserve.gov • Weekly. $35.00 per year.

Money: Who Has How Much and Why. Andrew Hacker. Available from Simon & Schuster Trade, 1230 Ave. of the Americas New York, NY 10020. Phone: 800-223-2336 or (212)698-7000 Fax: 800-445-6991 or (212)698-7007 URL: http://www.simonandschuster.com • 1998. $13.00. Published by Scribner's Reference. A discourse on the distribution of wealth in America, with emphasis on the gap between rich and poor.

The Moneyletter. IBC-Donoghue, Inc., P.O. Box 9104 Ashland, MA 01721-9104. Phone: 800-343-5413 or (508)881-2800 Fax: (508)881-0982 URL: http://www.ibcdata.com • Semimonthly. $109.00 per year. Newsletter giving specific advice on interest rates, trends, money market funds, bond funds, and equity mutual funds. Formerly *Donoghue's Moneyletter*.

Moneyletter's Mutual Funds Almanac. Agora, Inc., 1217 St. Paul St. Baltimore, MD 21202. Phone: 800-433-1528 or (410)223-2510 Fax: (410)223-2559 E-mail: 75127.1411@compuserve.com • Annual. $39.95. Lists more than 3,000 open and closed-end funds. Formerly *IBC/Donaghue's Mutual Funds Almanac*.

Moneypaper., 1010 Mamaroneck Ave. Mamaroneck, NY 10543. Phone: 800-388-9993 or (914)381-5400 Fax: (914)381-7206 Monthly. $81.00 per year. Newsletter. Provides general investment advice, including summaries from other investment advisory services. Emphasis is on company-sponsored dividend reinvestment plans. Subscription includes annual directory: *The Moneypaper's Guide to Dividend Reinvestment Plans*.

Moneypaper's Guide to Dividend Reinvestment Plans. Moneypaper, 1010 Mamaroneck Ave. Mamaroneck, NY 10543. Phone: 800-388-9993 or (914)381-5400 Fax: (914)381-7206 URL: http://www.moneypaper.com • Annual. $9.00. Provides details on about 900 corporate dividend reinvestment plans that permit optional cash investments.

Moneytalk. Moneytalk, Inc., 334 Highlark Dr. Larksville, PA 18704. Phone: (717)287-6498 Monthly. $22.00 per year. Newsletter for consumers on how to save money through the use of manufacturers' coupons and refund offers.

Monitor: An Analytical Review of Current Events in the Online and Electronic Publishing Industry. Information Today, Inc., 143 Old Marlton Pike Medford, NJ 08055-8750. Phone: 800-300-9868 or (609)654-6266 Fax: (609)654-4309 E-mail: custserv@infotoday.com • URL: http://www.infotoday.com • Monthly. $290.00 per year. Newsletter. Covers the international industry.

Monopolies in America: Empire Builders and Their Enemies from Jay Gould to Bill Gates. Charles R. Geisst. Oxford University Press, Inc., 198 Madison Ave. New York, NY 10016-4314. Phone: 800-451-7556 or (212)726-6000 Fax: (212)726-6446 E-mail: custserv@oup-usa.org • URL: http://www.oup-usa.org • 2000. $30.00. Provides a panoramic, historical view of U. S. trusts, monopolies, and antitrust activities.

Montana Farmer. Western Farmer-Stockman Magazines, P.O. Box 2160 Spokane, WA 99210-1615. Phone: (509)459-5361 Fax: (509)459-5102 Monthly. $15.00. per year.

Montana Wool Laboratory. Montana State University-Bozeman

Monthly Bibliography. United Nations Publications, United Nations Concourse Level, First Ave., 46th St. New York, NY 10017. Phone: 800-533-3210 or (212)963-7680 Fax: (212)963-4910 E-mail: bookstore@un.org • URL: http://www.un.org/publications • Monthly. $125.00 per year. Text in English and French.

Monthly Bulletin of Statistics. United Nations Publications, United Nations Concourse Level, First Ave., 46th St. New York, NY 10017. Phone: 800-553-3210 or (212)963-7680 Fax: (212)963-4910 E-mail: bookstore@un.org • URL: http://www.un.org/publications • Monthly. $295.00 per year. Provides current data for about 200 countries on a wide variety of economic, industrial, and demographic subjects. Compiled by United Nations Statistical Office.

Monthly Business Failures. Dun & Bradstreet, Economic Analysis Dept., Three Sylvan Way Parsippany, NJ 07054-3896. Phone: 800-526-0651 or (973)455-0900 Fax: (973)254-4063 E-mail: customerservice@@dnb.com • URL: http://www.dnb.com • Monthly. $30.00 per year. Provides number of failures and liabilities in over 100 lines of business.

Monthly Catalog of United States Government Publications. U. S. Government Printing Office, Washington, DC 20402. Phone: (202)512-1800 Fax: (202)512-2250 E-mail: gpoaccess@gpo.gov • URL: http://www.access.gpo.gov • Monthly. $52.00 per year. Modified in 1996. Print edition now consists of very brief entries, indexed only by key words in titles.

Monthly Catalog of United States Government Publications ÎCD-ROMl. U. S. Government Printing Office, Washington, DC 20402. Phone: (202)512-1800 Fax: (202)512-2250 E-mail: gpoaccess@gpo.gov • URL: http://www.access.gpo.gov • Monthly. $199.00 per year. Entries contain complete bibliographic information formerly appearing in the print edition of the *Monthly Catalog*. Each issue is cumulative, with author, title, and subject indexes. The January issue includes the *Periodicals Supplement*.

Monthly Climatic Data for the World. U.S. National Climatic Data Center, National Oceanic and Atmospheric Administration, U.S. Dept. of Commerce, Federal Bldg., Room 120, 151 Patton Ave. Asheville, NC 28801-5001. Phone: (704)271-4476 Fax: (704)271-4246 E-mail: orders@ncdc.noaa.gov • URL: http://www.ncdc.noaa.gov • Monthly.

Monthly Commodity Price Bulletin. United Nations Publications, United Nations Concourse Level, First Ave., 46th St. New York, NY 10017. Phone: 800-553-3210 or (212)963-7680 Fax: (212)963-4910 E-mail: bookstore@un.org • URL: http://www.un.org/publications • Monthly. $125.00 per year. Provides monthly average prices for the previous 12 months for a wide variety of commodities traded internationally.

Monthly Digest of Tax Articles. Newkirk Products Inc., 15 Corporate Place Albany, NY 12203. Phone: (518)862-3200 Monthly. $60.00 per year.

Monthly Energy Review. Available from U. S. Government Printing Office, Washington, DC 20402. Phone: (202)512-1800 Fax: (202)512-2250 E-mail: gpoaccess@gpo.gov • URL: http://www.access.gpo.gov • Monthly. $98.00 per year. Issued by the Energy Information Administration, Office of Energy Markets and End Use, U. S. Department of Energy. Contains current and historical statistics on U. S. production, storage, imports, and consumption of petroleum, natural gas, and coal.

Monthly Labor Review. Available from U. S. Government Printing Office, Washington, DC 20402. Phone: (202)512-1800 Fax: (202)512-2250 E-mail: gpoaccess@gpo.gov • URL: http://www.access.gpo.gov • Monthly. $43.00 per year. Issued by the Bureau of Labor Statistics, U. S. Department of Labor. Contains data on the labor force, wages, work stoppages, price indexes, productivity, economic growth, and occupational injuries and illnesses.

Monthly Payment Direct Reduction Loan Schedules. Financial Publishing Co., 3975 William Richardson Dr. South Bend, IN 46628. Phone: 800-247-3214 or (219)243-6040 Fax: (219)243-6060 URL: http://www.finacial-publishing.com • $75.00. 13th edition.

Monthly Price Review. Urner Barry Publications Inc., P.O. Box 389 Toms River, NJ 08754. Phone: 800-932-0617 or (732)240-5330 Fax: (732)341-0891 E-mail: mail@urnerbarry.com • URL: http://www.urnerbarry.com • Monthly. $131.00 per year. Annual summary.

Monthly Product Announcement. U. S. Bureau of the Census, Customer Services, Washington, DC 20233-0800. Phone: (301)457-4100 Fax: (301)457-4714 URL: http://www.census.gov • Monthly. Lists Census Bureau publications and products that became available during the previous month.

Monthly Statement of the Public Debt of the United States. U. S. Dept. of the Treasury, Public Debt Bureau. Available from U. S. Government Printing Office, Washington, DC 20402. Phone: (202)512-1800 Fax: (202)512-2250 E-mail: gpoaccess@gpo.gov • URL: http://www.access.gpo.gov • Monthly. $29.00 per year.

Monthly Statistical Bulletin. Cigar Association of America, 1100 17th St., N.W., Suite 504 Washington, DC 20036. Phone: (202)223-8204 Fax: (202)833-0379 Monthly. Membership.

Monthly Statistical Release: Beer. U. S. Bureau of Alcohol, Tobacco, and Firearms, Treasury Department Washington, DC 20226. Phone: (202)927-8500 URL: http://www.atf.treas.gov • Monthly.

Monthly Statistical Release: Distilled Spirits. U. S. Bureau of Alcohol, Tobacco, and Firearms, Treasury Department Washington, DC 20226. Phone: (202)927-8500 URL: http://www.atf.treas.gov • Monthly.

Monthly Statistical Release: Tobacco Products. U.S. Bureau of Alcohol, Tobacco, and Firearms, Washington, DC 20226. Phone: (202)927-8500 URL: http://www.atf.treas.gov • Monthly.

Monthly Statistical Release: Wines. U.S. Bureau of Alcohol, Tobacco, and Firearms, Washington, DC 20226. Phone: (202)927-8500 URL: http://www.atf.treas.gov • Monthly.

Monthly Statistics of Foreign Trade (Series A). OECD Publications and Information Center, 2001 L St., N.W., Ste. 650 Washington, DC 20036-4922. Phone: (202)785-6323 Fax: (202)785-0350 E-mail: washington.contact@oecd.org • URL: http://www.oecdwash.org • Monthly. $190.00 per year. Shows value of exports and imports in OECD member countries, including volume-of-trade indicators. Formerly *OECD Statistics of Foreign Trade (Series A)*.

Monthly Treasury Statement of Receipts and Outlays of the United States Government. Available from U. S. Government Printing Office, Washington, DC 20402. Phone: (202)512-1800 Fax: (202)512-2250 E-mail: gpoaccess@gpo.gov • URL: http://www.access.gpo.gov • Monthly. $40.00 per year. Issued by the Financial Management Service, U. S. Treasury Department.

Monthly Truck Tonnage Report. American Trucking Associations. Trucking Information Services, Inc., 2200 Mill Rd. Alexandria, VA 22314-4677. Phone: 800-282-5463 or (703)838-1700 Fax: (703)684-5720 E-mail: ata-infocenter@trucking.org • URL: http://www.trucking.org • Monthly. $50.00 per year.

Monthly Vital Statistics Report. U. S. Department of Health and Human Services, Data Dissemination Branch, Public Health Service, National Center for Health Statistics Hyattsville, MD 20782. Phone: (301)458-4636 E-mail: nchsquery@nchioa.em.cdc.gov • URL: http://www.cdc.gov/nchswww • Monthly. Provides data on births, deaths, cause of death, marriage, and divorce.

Monthly Weather Review. American Meteorological Society, 45 Beacon St. Boston, MA 02108-3693. Phone: (617)227-2425 Fax: (617)742-8718 E-mail: amspubs@ametsoc.org • URL: http://www.amet.org • Monthly. $445.00 per year.

Moody's Bank and Finance Manual. Moody's Investor Service, 99 Church St. New York, NY 10007-2701. Phone: 800-342-5647 or (212)553-0300 Fax: (212)553-4700 E-mail: fis@moodys.com/fis • URL: http://www.moodys.com • Annual. $995.00 per year. Four volumes. Includes biweekly supplements in *Moody's Bank and Finance News Report*.

Moody's Bond Record and Annual Bond Record Service. Information Services, 60 Madison Ave., 6th Fl. New York, NY 10010. Phone: 800-342-5647 or (212)413-7601 Fax: (212)413-7777 E-mail: fis@moodys.com • URL: http://www.moodys.com • Monthly. $425.00 per year. Formerly *Moody's Bond Record*.

Moody's Bond Survey. Financial Information Services, 60 Madison Ave., 6th Fl. New York, NY 10010. Phone: 800-342-5647 or (212)413-7601 Fax: (212)413-7777 E-mail: fis@moodys.com • URL: http://www.moodys.com • Weekly. $1,350.00 per year. Newsletter.

Moody's Corporate News: International. Moody's Investors Service, Inc., 99 Church St. New York, NY 10007-0300. Phone: 800-342-5647 or (212)553-0300 Fax: (212)553-4063 Provides financial and other business news relating to over 5,000 corporations in 100 countries, excluding the U. S. Time period is 1983 to date, with weekly updates. Inquire as to online cost and availability.

Moody's Dividend Record and Annual Dividend Record. Information Services, 60 Madison Ave., 6th Fl. New York, NY 10010. Phone: 800-342-5647 or (212)413-7601 Fax: (212)413-7777 E-mail: fis@moodys.com • URL: http://www.moodys.com • Semiweekly. $775.00 per year. Includes annual and cumulative supplement. Formerly *Moody's Dividend Record*.

Moody's Handbook of Common Stocks. Financial Information Services, 60 Madison Ave., 6th Fl. New York, NY 10010. Phone: 800-342-5647 or (212)413-7601 Fax: (212)413-7777 E-mail: fis@moodys.com • URL: http://www.moodys.com • Annual. $275.00 per year.

Moody's Handbook of Dividend Achievers. Mergent, 60 Madison Ave., 6th Fl. New York, NY 10010. Phone: 800-342-5647 or (212)413-7601 Fax: (212)413-7777 E-mail: fis@fisonline.com • URL: http://www.fisonline.com • Annual. $29.95. Compiled by Moody's Investors Service. Provides information on about 330 companies that have increased cash dividends for the past 10 consecutive years or more.

Moody's Handbook of NASDAQ Stocks (National Association of Securities Dealers Automated Quotations). Financial Information Services, 60 Madison Ave., 6th Fl. New York, NY 10010. Phone: 800-342-5647 or (212)413-7601 Fax: (212)413-7777 E-mail: fis@moodys.com • URL: http://www.moodys.com • Quarterly. $375.00 per year. Formerly *Moody's Handbook of O-T-C Stocks*.

Moody's International Manual. Financial Information Services, 60 Madison Ave., 6th Fl. New York, NY 10010. Phone: 800-342-5647 or (212)413-7601 Fax: (212)413-7777 E-mail: fis@moodys.com • URL: http://www.moodys.com • Annual. $3,175.00 per year. Includes weekly *News Reports*. Financial and other information about 3,000 publicly-owned corporations in 95 countries.

Moody's Manuals. Bank and Finance Manual, Industrial Manual, Municipal and Government Manual, OTC Industrial Manual, Public Utility Manual, Transportation Manual. Financial Information Services, 60 Madison Ave., 6th Fl. New York, NY 10010. Phone: 800-342-5647 or (212)413-7601 Fax: (212)413-7777 E-mail: fis@moodys.com • URL: http://www.moodys.com • Annual. Looseleaf supplements. Prices on application.

Moody's Municipal and Government Manual. Financial Information Services, 60 Madison Ave., 6th Fl. New York, NY 10010. Phone: 800-342-5647 or (212)413-7601 Fax: (212)413-7777 E-mail: fis@moodys.com • URL: http://www.moodys.com • Annual. $2,495.00 per year. Updated biweekly in *News Reports*.

Moody's OTC Industrial Manual. Financial Information Services, 60 Madison Ave., 6th Fl. New York, NY 10010. Phone: 800-342-5647 or (212)413-7601 Fax: (212)413-7777 E-mail: fis@moodys.com • URL: http://www.moodys.com • Annual, $1,675.00 per year. Includes biweekly *Moody's OTC Industrial News Report*.

Moody's OTC Unlisted Manual (Over the Counter). Financial Information Services, 60 Madison Ave., 6th Fl. New York, NY 10010. Phone: 800-342-5647 or (212)413-7601 Fax: (212)413-7777 E-mail: fis@moodys.com • URL: http://www.moodys.com • Annual, $1,550.00 per year. Includes supplement *Moody's OTC Unlisted News Report*.

Moody's Public Utility Manual. Financial Information Services, 60 Madison Ave., 6th Fl. New York, NY 10010. Phone: 800-342-5647 or (212)413-7601 Fax: (212)413-7777 E-mail: fis@moodys.com • URL: http://www.moodys.com • Annual. $1,595.00. Two volumes. Supplemented twice weekly by *Moody's Public Utility News Reports*. Contains financial and other information concerning publicly-held utility companies (electric, gas, telephone, water).

The Moral Foundations of Professional Ethics. Alan H. Goldman. Rowman and Littlefield Publishing Inc., 4720 Boston Way Lanham, MD 20706. Phone: 800-462-6420 or (301)459-3366 Fax: (301)459-2118 E-mail: rogers@univpress.com • URL: http://www.rowmanlittlefield.com • 1980. $25.50. (Philosophy and Society Series).

Morbidity and Mortality Weekly Report. Available from U. S. Government Printing Office, Washington, DC 20402. Phone: (202)512-1800 Fax: (202)512-2250 E-mail: gpoaccess@gpo.gov • URL: http://www.access.gpo.gov • Weekly. $255.00 per year (priority mail). Issued by the Center for Disease Control (Atlanta), U. S. Department of Health and Human Services. Provides analysis and statistics on the occurrence of disease and death from all causes in the U. S.

More Internet Troubleshooter: New Help for the Logged-On and Lost. Nancy R. John and Edward J. Valauskas. American Library Association, 50 E. Huron St. Chicago, IL 60611-2795. Phone: 800-545-2433 or (312)944-6780 Fax: (312)440-9374 E-mail: ala@ala.org • URL: http://www.ala.org • 1998. $36.00. A question-and-answer sequel to *Internet Troubleshooter: Help for the Logged-On and Lost*

Morin Center for Banking and Financial Law., Boston University, School of Law, 765 Commonwealth Ave. Boston, MA 02215. Phone: (617)353-3023 Fax: (617)353-2444 E-mail: banklaw@bu.edu • URL: http://www.web.bu.edu/law • Research fields include banking law, regulation of depository institutions, and deposit insurance.

Morningstar American Depositary Receipts. Morningstar, Inc., 225 W. Wacker Dr. Chicago, IL 60606. Phone: 800-735-0700 or (312)696-6000 Fax: (312)696-6001 E-mail: productsupport@morningstar.com • URL: http://www.morningstar.com • Biweekly. $195.00 per year. Looseleaf. Provides detailed profiles of 700 foreign companies having shares traded in the U. S. through American Depositary Receipts (ADRs).

Morningstar Closed-End Fund 250. Morningstar Staff. McGraw-Hill Professional, 1221 Ave. of the Americas New York, NY 10020-1095. Phone: 800-722-4726 or (212)904-2000 Fax: (212)904-2072 E-mail: customer.service@mcgraw-hill.com • URL: http://www.mcgraw-hill.com • 1996. $35.00. Provides detailed information on 50 actively traded closed-end investment companies. Past data is included for up to 12 years, depending on life of the fund.

Morningstar Fund Investor. Morningstar, Inc., 225 W. Wacker Dr. Chicago, IL 60606. Phone: 800-735-0700 or (312)696-6000 Fax: (312)696-6001 E-mail: productsupport@morningstar.com • URL: http://www.morningstar.com • Monthly. $79.00 per year. Newsletter. Provides tables of statistical data and star ratings for leading mutual funds (''The Morningstar 500''). News of funds and financial planning advice for investors is also included.

Morningstar Mutual Funds. Morningstar, Inc., 225 W. Wacker Dr. Chicago, IL 60606. Phone: 800-735-0700 or (312)696-6000 Fax: (312)696-6001 E-mail: productsupport@morningstar.com • URL: http://www.morningstar.com • Biweekly. $495.00 per year. Looseleaf. Contains detailed information and risk-adjusted ratings on over 1,240 load and no-load, equity and fixed-income mutual funds. Annual returns are provided for up to 12 years for each fund.

Morningstar No-Load Funds. Morningstar, Inc., 225 W. Wacker Dr. Chicago, IL 60606. Phone: 800-735-0700 or (312)696-6000 Fax: (312)696-6001 E-mail: productsupport@morningstar.com • URL: http://www.morningstar.com • Monthly. $145.00 per year. Looseleaf. Provides detailed information and risk-adjusted ratings on about 600 no-load and low-load mutual funds. Includes up to eight years of quarterly returns and 12 years of annual returns for each fund.

Morningstar Stock Investor. Morningstar, Inc., 225 W. Wacker Dr. Chicago, IL 60606. Phone: 800-735-0700 or (312)696-6000 Fax: (312)696-6001 E-mail: productsupport@morningstar.com • URL: http://www.morningstar.com • Monthly. $89.00 per year. Newsletter. Provides detailed information on the financial fundamentals of 450 selected, undervalued stocks. Estimated future worth of each stock is given, according to an ''Intrinsic Value Measure.''

Morningstar Variable Annuity Performance Report. Morningstar, Inc., 225 W. Wacker Dr. Chicago, IL 60606. Phone: 800-735-0700 or (312)696-6000 Fax: (312)696-6001 E-mail: productsupport@morningstar.com • URL: http://www.morningstar.com • Monthly. $125.00 per year. Provides detailed statistics and ratings for more than 2,000 variable annuities and variable-life products.

Morningstar.com: Your First Second Opinion. Morningstar, Inc.Phone: 800-735-0700 or (312)696-6000 Fax: (312)696-6001 E-mail: productsupport@morningstar.com • URL: http://www.morningstar.com • Web site provides a broad selection of information and advice on both mutual funds and individual stocks, including financial news and articles on investment fundamentals. Basic service is free, with ''Premium Membership'' available at $49.00 per year. Annual fee provides personal portfolio analysis, screening tools, and more extensive profiles of funds and stocks.

Mortgage & Asset-Based Desk Reference: U. S. Buyside and Sellside Profiles. Capital Access International, 430 Mountain Ave. Murray Hill, NJ 07974. Phone: 800-866-5987 or (908)771-0800 Fax: (908)771-0330 E-mail: info@capital-access.com • URL: http://www.capital-access.com • Annual. $395.00. Provides ''detailed buyside and sellside profiles and contacts'' for the mortgage and asset-based securities market.

Mortgage and Real Estate Executives Report. Warren, Gorham and Lamont/RIA Group, 395 Hudson St. New York, NY 10014. Phone: 800-950-1215 or (212)367-6300 Fax: (212)367-6718 E-mail: customer_service@riag.com • URL: http://www.riahome.com • Semimonthly. $159.75 per year. Newsletter. Source of ideas and new updates. Covers the latest opportunities and developments.

Mortgage-Backed Securities: Developments and Trends in the Secondary Mortgage Market. Kenneth G. Lore. West Group, 610 Opperman Dr. Eagan, MN 55123. Phone: 800-328-4880 or (651)687-7000 Fax: 800-213-2323 or (651)687-5827 URL: http://www.westgroup.com • Annual. $196.00.

Mortgage-Backed Securities Letter. Securities Data Publishing, 40 West 57th St. New York, NY 10019. Phone: 800-455-5844 or (212)765-5311 Fax: (212)956-0112 E-mail: sdp@tfn.com • URL: http://www.sdponline.com • Weekly. $1,595.00 per year. Newsletter. Provides news and analysis of the mortgage-backed securities market, including performance reports. (Securities Data Publishing is a unit of Thomson Financial.)

Mortgage Bankers Association of America.

Mortgage Banking. Mortgage Bankers Association of America, c/o Janice Stango, 1125 15th St., N.W. Washington, DC 20005. Phone: 800-793-6222 or (202)861-6500 Fax: (202)785-2967 E-mail: info@mbaa.org • URL: http://www.mbaa.org • Monthly. $45.00 per year.

Mortgage Insurance Companies of America.

Mortgage Loan Disclosure Handbook: A Step-by-Step Guide with Forms. West Group, 610 Opperman Dr. Eagan, MN 55123. Phone: 800-328-4880 or (651)687-7000 Fax: 800-213-2323 or (651)687-5827 URL: http://www.westgroup.com • Annual. $210.00. Covers disclosure requirements that lenders must meet under federal laws and regulations. Discusses the Truth-in-Lending Act, RESPA (Real Estate Settlement Procedures Act), the Equal Credit Opportunity Act, and the Fair Credit Reporting Act.

Morton Collectanea. University of Miami Dept. of Biology

The Mosaic Navigator TM: The Essential Guide to the Internet Interface. Paul Gilster. John Wiley and Sons, Inc., 605 Third Ave. New York, NY 10158-0012. Phone: 800-225-5945 or (212)850-6000 Fax: (212)850-6088 E-mail: info@wiley.com • URL: http://www.wiley.com • 1995. $16.95. Explains how to use the Mosaic graphical user interface.

Mosby's GenRx: The Complete Reference for Generic and Brand Drugs. Harcourt Health Sciences, P.O. Box 620075 Orlando, FL 32887. Phone: 800-426-4545 or (407)345-2000 URL: http://www.harcourt.com • 1998. $72.95. Provides detailed information on a wide variety of generic and brand name prescription drugs. Includes color identification pictures, prescribing data, and price comparisons. Formerly *Physicians GenRx*.

Mosby's GenRx Ìyearl. CME, Inc., 2801 McGaw Ave. Irvine, CA 92614-5835. Phone: 800-447-4474 or (949)250-1008 Fax: (949)250-0445 E-mail: infostore@cmeinc.com • URL: http://www.cmeinc.com • Annual. $99.00. CD-ROM contains detailed monographs for more than 2,200 generic and brand name prescription drugs. Includes color pill images and customizable patient education handouts.

Mote Marine Laboratory.

The Mother of All Windows 98 Books. Woody Leonhard and Barry Simon. Addison-Wesley Longman, Inc., One Jacob Way Reading, MA 01867. Phone: 800-447-2226 or (781)944-3700 Fax: (781)944-9338 URL: http://www.awl.com • 1999. $39.95.

Motion and Time Study: Design and Management of Work. Ralph M. Barnes. John Wiley and Sons, Inc., 605 Third Ave. New York, NY 10158-0012. Phone: 800-526-5368 or (212)850-6000 Fax: (212)850-6088 E-mail: info@wiley.com • URL: http://www.wiley.com • 1980. $103.95. Seventh edition.

Motion Picture Association of America.

The Motion Picture Guide Annual. Available from R. R. Bowker, 121 Chanlon Rd. New Providence, NJ 07974. Phone: 888-269-5372 or (908)464-6800 Fax: (908)665-6688 E-mail: info@bowker.com • URL: http://www.bowker.com • Annual. $162.00. Published by CineBooks (http://www.cinebooks.com). Provides detailed information on every domestic and foreign film released theatrically in the U. S. during the year covered. Includes annual Academy Award listings and film industry obituaries. Yearly volumes are available for older movies, beginning with the 1987 edition for films of 1986.

Motion Picture TV and Theatre Directory: For Services and Products. MPE Publications, Inc., P.O.Box 276 Tarrytown, NY 10591. Phone: (212)245-0969 Fax: (212)245-0974 Semiannual. $15.20. Companies providing products and services to the motion picture and television industries.

Motivation and Emotion. Plenum Publishing Corp., 233 Spring St. New York, NY 10013-1578. Phone: 800-221-9369 or (212)620-8000 Fax: (212)463-0742 E-mail: info@plenum.com • URL: http://www.plenum.com • Quarterly. $385.00 per year.

The Motivational Manager: Strategies to Increase Morale and Productivity in the Workplace. Lawence Ragan Communications, Inc., 316 N. Michigan Ave., Suite 300 Chicago, IL 60601. Phone: 800-878-5331 or (312)960-4100 Fax: (312)960-4106 E-mail: cservice@ragan.com • URL: http://www.ragan.com • Monthly. $119.00 per year. Newsletter. Emphasis is on participative management.

Motor Age: For the Professional Automotive Import and Domestic Service Industry. Cahners Business Information, 1018 W. 9th Ave. King of Prussia, PA 19406. Phone: 800-695-1214 or (610)205-1000 Fax: (610)964-4745 E-mail: corporatecommunications@cahners.com • URL: http://www.cahners.com • Monthly. $49.00 per year. Published for independent automotive repair shops and gasoline service stations.

Motor and Equipment Manufacturers Association.

Motor Carrier Permit and Tax Bulletin. J.J. Keller and Associates, Inc., P.O Box 368 Neenah, WI 54957-0368. Phone: 800-327-6868 or (920)722-2848 Fax: (920)727-7526 URL: http://www.jjkeller.com • Monthly. $125.00 per year. Formerly *Trucking Permit and Tax Bulletin*.

MOTOR: Covering the World of Automotive Service. Hearst Business Publishing, 645 Stewart Ave. Garden City, NY 11530-4709. Phone: (516)227-1300 Fax: (516)227-1405 E-mail: jlypen@motor.com • URL: http://www.motor.com • Monthly. $48.00 per year. Edited for professional automobile and light-truck mechanics. Includes industry news and market trends.

Motor Ship Directory of Shipowners and Shipbuilders. Reed Business Information, 121 Chanlon Rd. New Providence, NJ 07974. Phone: (908)464-6800 Fax: (908)665-6688 URL: http://www.reedbusiness.com • Annual. $120.00. Formerly *Directory of Shipowners, Shipbuilders and Marine Engineers*.

Motor Trend. EMAP USA, 6420 Wilshire Blvd. Los Angeles, CA 90048-5515. Phone: 800-800-6848 or (323)782-2000 Fax: (323)782-2477 URL: http://www.emapusa.com • Monthly.$17.94. per year.

Motor Vehicle Regulation: State Capitals. Wakeman-Walworth, Inc., P.O. Box 7376 Alexandria, VA 22307-0376. Phone: 800-876-2545 or (703)549-8606 Fax: (703)549-1372 E-mail: newsletters@statecapitals.com • URL: http://www.statecapitals.com • Weekly. $245.00 per year. Formerly *From the State Capitals: Motor Vehicle Regulation*.

Motorcycle Industry Council.

Motorcycle Product News. Athletic Business Publications, Inc., 4130 Lien Rd. Madison, WI 53404-3602. Phone: 800-722-8764 or (608)249-0186 Fax: (608)249-1153 E-mail: editors@mpnmag.com • Monthly. $50.00 per year. Edited for wholesalers and retailers of motorcycles and supplies.

Motorcycle Product News Trade Directory. Intertec Publishing Corp., 9800 Metcalf Ave. Overland Park, KS 66212-2286. Phone: 800-400-5945 or (913)341-1300 Fax: (913)967-1898 E-mail: subs@intertec.com • URL: http://www.intertec.com • Annual. $25.00. Provides information on approximately 1,300 companies related to the motorcycle business.

Motorcycle Shopper: The Source for Motorcycles, Parts, Accessories, Sidecars, Tools, Clubs, Events, and More. Payne Corp., 1353 Herndon Ave. Deltona, FL 32725-9046. Phone: 800-982-4599 or (407)860-1989 Fax: (407)574-1014 E-mail: mshopper@iag.net • URL: http://www.shopper.eurografix.com • Monthly. $19.95 per year. Contains consumer advertisements for buying, selling, and trading motorcycles and parts.

Motorcyclist. EMAP USA, 6420 Wilshire Blvd. Los Angeles, CA 90048-5515. Phone: (323)782-2000 Fax: (323)782-2467 URL: http://www.emapusa.com • Monthly. $11.97 per year.

Mount Vernon Research and Extension Unit. Washington State University

Movie Money: Understanding Hollywood's Creative Accounting Practices. Bill Daniels and others. Silman-James Press, 3624 Shannon Rd. Los Angeles, CA 90027. Phone: 800-729-6423 or (323)661-9922 Fax: (323)661-9933 E-mail: silmanjamespress@earthlink.net • 1998. $19.95. Explains the numerous amd mysterious accounting methods used by the film industry to arrive at gross and net profit figures. The authors also discuss profit participation, audits, claims, and negotiating.

Moving and Relocation Sourcebook and Directory: Reference Guide to the 100 Largest Metropolitan Areas in the United States. Kay Gill, editor. Omnigraphics, Inc., Penobscot Bldg. Detroit, MI 48226. Phone: 800-234-1340 or (313)961-1340 Fax: 800-875-1340 or (313)961-1383 E-mail: info@omnigraphics.com • URL: http://www.omnigraphics.com • 1998. $185.00. Second edition. Provides extensive statistical and other descriptive data for the 100 largest metropolitan areas in the U. S. Includes maps and a discussion of factors to be considered when relocating.

Moving and Reorganizing a Library. Marianna Wells and Rosemary Young. Ashgate Publishing Co., Old Post Rd. Brookfield, VT 05036-9704. Phone: 800-535-9544 or (802)276-3162 Fax: (802)276-3837 E-mail: info@ashgate.com • URL: http://www.ashgate.com • 1997. $74.95. ''This book provides detailed guidance on how to plan, design, prepare, and implement the move of a small or medium sized library from the time of the project's inception to its completion.'' Includes a case study and checklists. Published by Gower in England.

Moving Beyond Gridlock: Traffic and Development. Robert T. Dunphy. Urban Land Institute, 1025 Thomas Jefferson St., N. W., Suite 500 W. Washington, DC 20007-5201. Phone: 800-321-5011 or (202)624-7000 Fax: (202)624-7140 E-mail: bookstore@uli.org • URL: http://www.uli.org • 1996. $45.95. Describes how various regions have dealt with traffic growth. Includes case studies from seven cities.

Moving Power and Money: The Politics of Census Taking. Barbara E. Bryant and William Dunn. New Strategist Publications, Inc., 120 W. State St., 4th Fl. Ithaca, NY 14851. Phone: 800-848-0842 or (607)273-0913 Fax: (607)277-5009 E-mail: demographics@newstrategist.com • URL: http://www.newstrategist.com • 1995. $24.95. Barbara Everitt Bryant was Director of the U. S. Census Bureau from 1989 to 1993. She provides a plan for reducing the costs of census taking, improving accuracy, and overcoming public resistance to the census.

Moving Toward More Effective Public Internet Access: The 1998 National Survey of Public Library Outlet Internet Connectivity. Available from U. S. Government Printing Office, Washington, DC 20402. Phone: (202)512-1800 Fax: (202)512-2250 E-mail: gpoaccess@gpo.gov • URL: http://www.access.gpo.gov • 1999. $16.00. Issued by the National Commission on Libraries and Information Science.

MPC Corporation., 5000 Forbes Ave. Pittsburgh, PA 15213. Phone: (412)268-2091 Fax: (412)268-5841 E-mail: te9b@andrew.cmu.edu • Research fields include mass rapid transit for metropolitan areas. Affiliated with Carnegie Mellon University and the University of Pittsburgh.

MPT Review; Specializing in Modern Portfolio Theory. Navellier and Associates, Inc., One E. Liberty St. Reno, NV 89501-2110. Phone: 800-454-1395 or (775)785-2300 Fax: (775)785-2321 E-mail: info@navellier.com • URL: http://www.mptreview.com • Monthly. $275.00 per year. Newsletter. Provides specific stock selection and model portfolio advice (conservative, moderately aggressive, and aggressive) based on quantitative analysis and modern portfolio theory.

MRA Blue Book Research Services Directory. Marketing Research Association, 1344 Silas Deane Highway, Suite 306 Rocky Hill, CT 06067-0230. Phone: (860)257-4008 Fax: (860)257-3990 E-mail: bluebook@mra-net.org • URL: http://www.bluebook.org • Annual. $169.95. Lists more than 1,200 international marketing research companies and survey services. Formerly *Directory of Research Services*

Provided by Members of the Marketing Research Association.

MS. Liberty Media for Women, L.L.C., 20 Exchange Place, 22nd Fl. New York, NY 10005. Phone: 800-234-4486 or (212)509-2092 Fax: (212)509-2407 E-mail: info@ms.magazine.com • URL: http://www.msmagazine.com • Bimonthly. $35.00 per year.

MSDN Magazine (Microsoft Systems for Developers)., P.O. Box 56621 Boulder, CO 80322-6621. Phone: 800-666-1084 Fax: (303)661-1181 E-mail: msdnmag@neodata.com • URL: http://www.msdn.microsoft.com • Monthly. $84.95 per year. Produced for professional software developers using Windows, MS-DOS, Visual Basic, and other Microsoft Corporation products. Incorporates *Microsoft Systems Journal*.

MTM Association for Standards and Research.

Multi-Housing Laundry Association.

Multi-Housing News (MHN). Miller Freeman, Inc., One Penn Plaza New York, NY 10119. Phone: (212)714-1300 Fax: (212)714-1313 E-mail: mfibooks@mfi.com • URL: http://www.mfi.com • Six times a year. $30.00 per year. Individuals and firms primarily engaged in the development, construction, planning and management of multi-housing.

Multi-State Sales Tax Guide. CCH, Inc., 4025 W. Peterson Ave. Chicago, IL 60646-6085. Phone: 800-248-3248 or (773)583-8500 Fax: 800-224-8299 URL: http://www.cch.com • $1,160.00 per year. Looseleaf service. Nine volumes. Periodic supplementation. Formerly *All State Sales Tax Reports*.

Multichannel News. Cahners Business Information, 245 W. 17th St. New York, NY 10011-5300. Phone: 800-622-7776 or (212)645-0067 Fax: (212)463-6406 E-mail: corporatecommunications@cahners.com • URL: http://www.cahners.com • Weekly. $119.00 per year. Covers the business, programming, marketing, and technology concerns of cable television operators and their suppliers.

Multimedia and CD-ROM Directory: The Global Source of Information for the Multimedia and CD-ROM Industries. Available from Omnigraphics, Inc., Penobscot Bldg. Detroit, MI 48226. Phone: 800-234-1340 or (313)961-1340 Fax: 800-875-1340 or (313)961-1383 E-mail: info@omnigraphics.com • URL: http://www.omnigraphics.com • Annual. $390.00. Two volumes: vol. 1, *New Media Companies* ($195.00); vol. 2, *New Media Titles* ($195.00). Published in London by Macmillan Reference Ltd. Volume one consists of statistics (''Facts and Figures''), articles on multimedia publishing, market profiles (countries), interviews, company directory, bibliography, and indexes. Volume two describes more than 19,000 CD-ROM titles, with publisher directory, indexes, and glossary. Formerly *CD-ROM Directory*.

Multimedia and the Web from A to Z. Patrick M. Dillon and David C. Leonard. Oryx Press, 4041 N. Central Ave., Suite 700 Phoenix, AZ 85012-3397. Phone: 800-279-6799 or (602)265-2651 Fax: 800-279-4663 or (602)265-6250 E-mail: info@oryxpress.com • URL: http://www.oryxpress.com • 1998. $39.95. Second enlarged revised edition. Defines more than 1,500 terms relating to software and hardware in the areas of computing, online technology, telecommunications, audio, video, motion pictures, CD-ROM, and the Internet. Includes acronyms and an annotated bibliography. Formerly *Multimedia Technology from A to Z* (1994).

Multimedia Communications Laboratory., Boston University, PHO 445, Eight Saint Mary's St. Boston, MA 02215. Phone: (617)353-8042 Fax: (617)353-6440 E-mail: mcl@spiderman.bu.edu • URL: http://www.hulk.bu.edu • Research areas include interactive multimedia applications.

Multimedia Schools: A Practical Journal of Multimedia, CD-Rom, Online and Internet in K-12. Information Today, Inc., 143 Old Marlton Pike Medford, NJ 08055-8750. Phone: 800-300-9868 or (609)654-6266 Fax: (609)654-4309 E-mail: custserv@infotoday.com • URL: http://www.infotoday.com • Five times a year. $39.95 per year. Edited for school librarians, media center directors, computer coordinators, and others concerned with educational multimedia. Coverage includes the use of CD-ROM sources, the Internet, online services, and library technology.

Multimedia Schools: A Practical Journal of Multimedia, CD-ROM, Online, and Internet in K-12. Information Today, Inc., 143 Old Marlton Pike Medford, NJ 08055-8750. Phone: 800-300-9868 or (609)654-6266 Fax: (609)654-4309 E-mail: custserv@infotoday.com • URL: http://www.infotoday.com • Bimonthly. $39.95 per year. Provides purchasing recommendations and technical advice relating to the use of high-tech multimedia products in schools.

Multimedia Telecommunications Association., 2500 Wilson Blvd., Suite 300 Arlington, VA 22201-3834. Phone: 800-799-6682 or (703)907-7472 Fax: (703)907-7478 E-mail: info@mmta.org • URL: http://www.mmta.org • Members are manufacturers and suppliers of interconnect telephone equipment.

Multimedia Title Publishing: Review, Trends, and Forecast. SIMBA Information, P.O. Box 4234 Stamford, CT 06907-0234. Phone: 800-307-2529 or (203)358-4100 Fax: (203)358-5824 E-mail: info@simbanet.com • URL: http://www.simbanet.com • Annual. $895.00. Provides industry statistics and market research data. Covers both business and consumer multimedia items, with emphasis on CD-ROM publishing.

Multimedia Week. Phillips Business Information, Inc., 1201 Seven Locks Rd., Suite 300 Potomac, MD 20854. Phone: 800-777-5006 or (301)340-1520 Fax: (301)309-3847 E-mail: pbi@phillips.com • URL: http://www.phillips.com/pbi.htm • 50 times a year. $697.00 per year. Newsletter. Covers industry news and trends in multimedia hardware and software.

Multinational Financial Management. Alan C. Shapiro. Prentice Hall, 240 Frisch Court Paramus, NJ 07652-5240. Phone: 800-947-7700 or (201)909-6200 Fax: 800-445-6991 or (201)909-6361 URL: http://www.prenhall.com • 1999. $74.67. Sixth edition.

Multinational Monitor. Essential Information, P. O. Box 19405 Washington, DC 20036. Phone: (202)387-8034 Fax: (202)234-5176 E-mail: monitor@essential.org • URL: http://www.essential.org/ • Monthly. Individuals, $25.00 per year; non-profit organizations, $30.00 per year; corporations, $40.00 per year. Track the activities of multinational corporations and their effects on the Third World, labor and the environment.

Multinational P R Report. Pigafetta Press, P.O. Box 39244 Washington, DC 20016. Phone: (202)244-2580 Fax: (202)244-2581 Monthly. $85.00 per year. International public relations newsletter.

Municipal and Industrial Water and Pollution Control. Zanny Publications Ltd., 11966 Woodbine Ave. Gormley Ontario LOH 1G0, ON, Canada LOH 1G0. Phone: (905)887-5048 Fax: (905)887-0764 Bimonthly. $65.00 per year. Formerly *Water and Pollution Control*.

Municipal Bonds: The Comprehensive Review of Municipal Securities and Public Finance. Robert Lamb and Stephen Rappaport. McGraw-Hill, 1221 Ave. of the Americas New York, NY 10020. Phone: 800-722-4726 or (212)904-2000 Fax: (212)904-2072 E-mail: customer.service@mcgraw-hill.com • URL: http://www.mcgraw-hill.com • 1987. $34.95.

Municipal Finance Journal. Panel Publishers, 1185 Ave. of the Americas New York, NY 10036. Phone: 800-447-1717 or (212)597-0200 Fax: 800-901-9075 or (212)597-0334 E-mail: customer.service@aspenpubl.com • URL: http://www.panelpublisher.com • Quarterly. $260.00 per year. Recent tax and legal trends affecting both large and small state municipalities.

Municipal Issuer's Registry. The Bond Buyer's Municipal Marketplace, 1216 Richmond Lane Wilmette, IL 60091. Phone: 800-362-4364 or (847)920-1928 Fax: (847)920-1929 URL: http://www.munimarketplace.com • Annual. $235.00. Provides contact information relating to 6,000 issuers of municipal debt, including individuals responsible for municipal bond assignments.

Municipal Management Series. International City/County Management Association, 777 Capitol St., N.E., Suite 500 Washington, DC 20002-4201. Phone: 800-745-8780 or (202)289-4262 Fax: (202)962-3500 E-mail: dbrooks@icma.org • URL: http://www.icma.org • 14 volumes. Various dates, 1968 to 1988. Finance, planning, training, public relations, and other subjects.

Municipal Technical Advisory Service Library., University of Tennessee, Knoxville, Conference Center Bldg.,, Suite 120 Knoxville, TN 37996-4105. Phone: (423)974-0411 Fax: (423)974-0423 E-mail: rschwartz@utk.edu • URL: http://www.mtas.utk.edu • Research areas include municipal finance, police administration, and public works.

Municipal Year Book. International City/County Management Association, 777 Capitol St., N.E., Suite 500 Washington, DC 20002-4201. Phone: 800-745-8780 or (202)289-4262 Fax: (202)962-3500 E-mail: dbrooks@icma.org • URL: http://www.icma.org • Annual. $84.95. An authoritative resume of activities and statistical data of American cities.

Municipal Yellow Book: Who's Who in the Leading City and County Governments and Local Authorities. Leadership Directories, Inc., 104 Fifth Ave., 2nd Fl. New York, NY 10011. Phone: (212)627-4140 Fax: (212)645-0931 E-mail: info@leadershipdirectories.com • URL: http://www.leadershipdirectories.com • Semiannual. $235.00 per year. Lists approximately 32,000 key personnel in city and county departments, agencies, subdivisions, and branches.

MuniStatements. American Banker Newsletter, Thomson Financial Services Co., One State St. Place New York, NY 10004-1549. Phone: 800-753-4371 or (212)803-8345 Fax: (212)843-9600 E-mail: glicke@tfn.com • URL: http://www.americanbanker.com • Microfiche. Monthly shipments of Official Statements of municipal bond offerings. Back files available. Price on application.

Murphy's Will Clauses: Annotations and Forms with Tax Effects. Matthew Bender & Co., Inc., Two Park Ave. New York, NY 10016. Phone: 800-223-1940 or (212)448-2000 Fax: (212)244-3188 E-mail: international@bender.com • URL: http://www.bender.com • $928.00. Four looseleaf volumes. Periodic supplementation. Over 1,400 framed will clauses.

Mushroom Journal. Mushroom Growers' Association, Two Saint Paul's St. Stamford, Lincs PE9 2BE, England. Phone: 44 178 0766888 Monthly. Membership.

Mushroom News. American Mushroom Institute, One Massachusetts Ave., N.W., Suite 800 Washington, DC 20001-1401. Phone: (202)842-4344 Fax: (202)408-7763 Monthly. $275.00. Includes *News Flash*.

Music Address Book: How to Reach Anyone Who's Anyone in the Music Business. Michael Levine. HarperCollins Publishers, 10 E. 53rd St. New York, NY 10022-5299. Phone: 800-242-7737 or (212)207-7000 Fax: 800-822-4090 or (212)207-7145 URL: http://www.harpercollins.com • 1994. $16.00. Second editon.

Music and Sound Retailer. Testa Communications, 25 Willowdale Ave. Port Washington, NY 11050. Phone: (516)767-2500 Fax: (516)767-9335 URL: http://www.msretailer.com • Monthly. $18.00 per year. Provides news and advice on the retailing of a wide range of music and sound products, including musical instruments, electronic keyboards, sound amplification systems, music software, and recording equipment.

Music Distributors Association.

Music Inc. Maher Publications, Inc., 102 N. Haven Rd. Elmhurst, IL 60126. Phone: 800-535-7496 or (630)941-2030 Fax: (630)941-3210 11 times a year. $16.00. per year. Music and sound retailing. Formerly *Up Beat Monthly*.

Music Index: A Subject-Author Guide to Over 300 Current International Periodicals. Harmonie Park Press, 23630 Pinewood Warren, MI 48091-4759. Phone: 800-422-4880 or (810)755-3080 Fax: (810)755-4213 E-mail: hpp@wwnet.com • URL: http://www.harmoniepress.com • Quarterly. $1,850.00 per year. Annual cummulation. Supplement available: *Music Index Subject Heading List*. Guide to current periodicals. Entries are in language of country issuing the index.

Music Industry Conference.

Music Journal. Incorporated Society of Musicians, 10 Stratford Place London W1N 9AE, England. Phone: 44 20 46294413 Fax: 44 20 74081538 E-mail: membership@ism.org • Monthly. $50.00 per year.

Music Library Association Notes. Music Library Association, P.O. Box 487 Canton, MA 02021-0487. Phone: (781)828-8450 URL: http://www.musiclibraryassoc.org • Quarterly. Individuals, $70.00 per year; institutions, $80.00 per year. Indexes record reviews (classical).

Music Reference Services Quarterly. Haworth Press, Inc., 10 Alice St. Binghamton, NY 13904-1580. Phone: 800-429-6784 or (607)722-5857 Fax: 800-895-0582 or (607)722-1424 E-mail: getinfo@haworthpressinc.com • URL: http://www.haworthpressinc.com • Quarterly. Individuals, $40.00 per year; libraries and other institutions, $75.00 per year. An academic journal for music librarians.

Music Technology Buyer's Guide. United Entertainment Media, Inc., 460 Park Ave. South New York, NY 10016-7315. Phone: (212)378-0400 Fax: (212)378-2160 URL: http://www.musicgearonline.com • $7.95. Annual. Lists more than 4,000 hardware and software music production products from 350 manufacturers. Includes synthesizers, MIDI hardware and software, mixers, microphones, music notation software, etc. Produced by the editorial staffs of *Keyboard* and *EQ* magazines.

Music Trades. Music Trades Corp., c/o Paul Majeski, P.O. Box 432 Englewood, NJ 07631. Phone: (201)871-1965 Monthly. $14.00 per year. Includes *Purchaser's Guide to the Music Industries*.

Musical America International Directory of the Performing Arts. Commonwealth Business Media, 10 Lake Dr. Hightstown, NJ 08520-5397. Phone: 800-221-5488 or (609)371-7700 Fax: (609)371-7879 URL: http://www.primediainfo.com • Annual. $105.00. Covers United States and Canada.

Musical Merchandise Review. Larkin Publications, Inc., 50 Brook Rd. Needham, MA 02494. Phone: (781)453-9310 Fax: (781)453-9389 URL: http://www.mmrmagazine.com • Monthly. $24.00 per year. Edited for musical instrument dealers selling pianos, organs, band/orchestra instruments, electronic keyboards, guitars, music amplifiers, microphones, sheet music, and other musical merchandise.

Musical Merchandise Review: Directory of Musical Instrument Dealers. Larkin Publications, Inc., 50 Brook Rd. Needham, MA 02494. Phone: (781)453-9310 Fax: (781)453-9389 URL: http://www.mmrmagazine.com • Annual. $125.00. Lists retailers of musical instruments and supplies.

Musical Merchandise Review: Music Industry Directory. Larkin Publications, Inc., 50 Brook Rd. Needham, MA 02494. Phone: (781)453-9310 Fax: (781)453-9389 URL: http://www.mmrmagazine.com • Annual. $25.00. Lists about 1,500 manufacturers and distributors of musical instruments and supplies. Includes indexes to products and trade names.

Mutual Atomic Energy Liability Underwriters., 330 N. Wabash, Suite 2600 Chicago, IL 60611. Phone: (312)467-0003

Fax: (312)467-0774 Members are mutual casualty insurance companies writing nuclear energy liability policies.

Mutual Fund Advisor: The Top Performing Mutual Funds. Mutual Fund Advisor, Inc., One Sarasota Tower, Suite 602, Two N. Tamiami Trail Sarasota, FL 34236. Phone: (813)954-5500 Fax: (813)364-8447 Monthly. $75.00 per year. Newsletter.

Mutual Fund Buyer's Guide. Institute for Econometric Research, 2200 S.W. 10th St. Deerfield Beach, FL 33442-8799. Phone: 800-442-0066 or (954)421-1000 Fax: (954)570-8200 Monthly. $80.00 per year. Each issue provides tabular data for about 1,500 mutual funds. Includes performance figures for various time periods from one month to 10 years. Up-market and down-market ratings are also given.

Mutual Fund Buyer's Guide: Performance Ratings, Five Year Projections, Safety Ratings, Sales. Norman G. Fosback. McGraw-Hill Professional, 1221 Ave. of the Americas New York, NY 10020-1095. Phone: 800-722-4726 or (212)904-2000 Fax: (212)904-2072 E-mail: customer.service@mcgraw-hill.com • URL: http://www.mcgraw-hill.com • 1994. $17.95.

Mutual Fund Education Alliance (The Association of No-Load Funds).

Mutual Fund Fact Book: Industry Trends and Statistics. Investment Company Institute, 1401 H St. N.W., Suite 1200 Washington, DC 20005-2148. Phone: (202)326-5800 Fax: (202)326-5985 E-mail: info@ici.com • URL: http://www.ici.com • 1997. $25.00. 37th edition. Industry trends and statistics.

Mutual Fund Forecaster: Profit and Projections and Risk Ratings for Traders and Investors. Institute for Econometric Research, 2200 S.W. 10th St. Deerfield Beach, FL 33442-8799. Phone: 800-442-0066 or (954)421-1000 Fax: (954)570-8200 Monthly. $100.00 per year. Newsletter. Contains buy recommendations, profit projections, risk ratings, and past performance data for individual mutual funds and closed-end funds.

Mutual Fund Investing. Jay Schabacker, editor. Phillips Publishing, Inc., 1201 Seven Locks Rd., Suite 300 Potomac, MD 20854. Phone: 800-777-5006 or (301)340-2100 Fax: (301)424-4297 E-mail: pbi@phillips.com • URL: http://www.phillips.com/pbi.htm • Monthly. $127.00 per year. Newsletter.

Mutual Fund Letter. Investment Information Services, Inc., 10 S. Riverside Plaza, Room 1520 Chicago, IL 60606-3802. Phone: 800-362-6941 or (312)649-6940 Fax: (312)649-5537 Monthly. $125.00 per year. Newsletter. Provides mutual fund recommendations.

Mutual Fund Market News. Securities Data Publishing, 40 West 57th St. New York, NY 10019. Phone: 800-455-5844 or (212)765-5311 Fax: (212)956-0112 E-mail: sdp@tfn.com • URL: http://www.sdponline.com • Weekly. $1,425 per year. Newsletter (also available online at www.mfmarketnews.com). Edited for executives concerned with mutual fund administration and management. Covers marketing, distribution, new funds, mergers, regulations, legal issues, pricing, Internet use, and related topics. (Securities Data Publishing is a unit of Thomson Financial.)

Mutual Fund Profiles. Standard & Poor's, 55 Water St. New York, NY 10041. Phone: 800-221-5277 or (212)438-2000 Fax: (212)438-0040 E-mail: questions@standardandpoors.com • URL: http://www.standardandpoors.com • Quarterly. $158.00 per year. Produced jointly with Lipper Analytical Services. Provides detailed information on approximately 800 of the largest stock funds and taxable bond funds. In addition, contains concise data on about 2,400 smaller funds and municipal bond funds.

Mutual Fund Strategies. Progressive Investing, Inc., P.O. Box 446 Burlington, VT 05402. Phone: (802)658-3515 Monthly. $127.00 per year. Newsletter.

Mutual Fund Trends. Growth Fund Research, Inc., P.O. Box 6600 Rapid City, SD 57709. Phone: 800-621-8322 or (605)341-1971 Fax: (605)341-7260 Monthly. $139.00 per year. Newsletter. Includes charts of mutual funds.

Mutual Funds Interactive. Brill Editorial Services, Inc.Phone: 877-442-7455 URL: http://www.brill.com • Web site provides specific information on individual funds in addition to general advice on mutual fund investing and 401(k) plans. Searching is provided, including links to moderated newsgroups and a chat page. Fees: Free.

Mutual Funds Magazine: Your Monthly Guide to America's Best Investments. Institute for Econometric Research, 2200 S.W. 10th St. Deerfield Beach, FL 33442-8799. Phone: 800-442-0066 or (954)421-1000 Fax: (954)570-8200 URL: http://www.mfmag.com • Monthly. $19.94 per year. Popular magazine for mutual fund investors. Regular features include "Platinum Funds: The Investor's Guide to America's Most Popular Funds" (full-page evaluations), "Hot Funds," "Funding Retirement," and book reviews.

Mutual Funds Update. Securities Data Publishing, 40 West 57th St. New York, NY 10019. Phone: 800-455-5844 or (212)765-5311 Fax: (212)956-0112 E-mail: sdp@tfn.com • URL: http://www.sdponline.com • Monthly. $325.00 per year. Provides recent performance information and statistics for approximately 10,000 mutual funds, as compiled from the CDA/Wiesenberger database. Includes commentary and analysis relating to the mutual fund industry. Information is provided on new funds, name changes, mergers, and liquidations. (Securities Data Publishing is a unit of Thomson Financial.)

Mutual Funds: Your Key to Sound Financial Planning. Lyle Allen. Morrow/Avon, 1350 Ave. of the Americas, 2nd Fl. New York, NY 10019. Phone: 800-223-0690 or (212)261-6800 Fax: (212)261-6895 URL: http://www.avonbooks.com • 1994. $10.00.

My Little Salesman Heavy Equipment Catalog; New and Used Equipment Guide. MSL, Inc., P.O. Box 70208 Eugene, OR 97401. Phone: (541)341-4650 Fax: (541)342-3307 Monthly. $18.00 per year.

My Little Salesman Truck Catalog. MSL, Inc., P.O. Box 70208 Eugene, OR 97401. Phone: (541)341-4650 Fax: (541)342-3307 Monthly. $18.00 per year. Products serving the trucking industry. Central and Western editions.

NABE News. National Association for Business Economics, 1233 20th St., N.W., Suite 505 Washington, DC 20036-2304. Phone: (202)463-6223 Fax: (202)463-6239 E-mail: nabe@nabe.com • URL: http://www.nabe.com • Bimonthly. $95.00 per year. Membership newsletter. Contains feature articles, news of local chapters and roundtables, reviews of seminars and meetings, personal notes and advertisements of interest to the business economist.

NACAC Bulletin. National Association for College Admission Counseling, 1631 Prince St. Alexandria, VA 22314-2818. Phone: (703)836-2222 Fax: (703)836-8015 URL: http://www.nacac.com • 10 times a year. Members, $30.00 per year; non-members, $40.00 per year. Provides news of counseling and admission trends, tools and strategies in admission counseling to 4,500 member association.

NACE International: The Corrosion Society., P.O. Box 218340 Houston, TX 77218-8340. Phone: (281)228-6223 Fax: (281)228-6300 E-mail: msd@mail.nace.org • URL: http://www.nace.org • Members are engineers, scientists, and technicians concerned with corrosion control and prevention.

NACE National Directory: Who's Who in Career Planning, Placement, and Recruitment. National Association of Colleges and Employers, 62 Highland Ave. Bethlehem, PA 18017. Phone: 800-544-5272 or (610)868-1421 Fax: (610)868-0208 Annual. Members, $32.95; non-members, $47.95. Lists over 2,200 college placement offices and about 2,000 companies interested in recruiting college graduates. Gives names of placement and recruitment personnel. Formerly *CPC National Dierctory*.

NACE Salary Survey: A Study of Beginning Salary Offers. National Association of Colleges and Employers, 62 Highland Ave. Bethlehem, PA 18017. Phone: 800-544-5272 or (610)868-1421 Fax: (610)868-0208 Four times a year. Free to members; non-members, $220.00 per year. Formerly *PC Salary Survey*. Formerly College Placement Council, Inc.

NACHA: The Electronic Payments Association.

NACORE International.

NADA Appraisal Guides. National Automobile Dealers Association, 8400 Westpark Dr., 10th Fl. McLean, VA 22102. Phone: (703)821-7000 Fax: (703)821-7075 Prices and frequencies vary. Guides to prices of used cars, old used cars, motorcycles, mobile homes, recreational vehicles, and mopeds.

NADA Marine Appraisal Guide. National Automobile Dealers Association. N.A.D.A. Appraisal Guides, P.O. Box 7800 Costa Mesa, CA 92628-7800. Phone: 800-966-6232 or (714)556-8511 Fax: (714)556-8715 Three times a year. $100.00 per year. Formerly *NADA Small Boat Appraisal Guide*.

NADA'S Automotive Executive. National Automobile Dealers Association, 8400 Westpark Dr., 10th Fl. McLean, VA 22102. Phone: (703)821-7000 Fax: (703)821-7234 Monthly. $24.00 per year.

NAEDA Equipment Dealer. North American Equipment Dealers Association, 1195 Smizer Mill Rd. Fenton, MO 63026-3480. Phone: (636)349-5000 URL: http://www.naeda.com • Monthly. $40.00 per year. Covers power equipment for farm, outdoor, and industrial use. Formerly *Farm and Power Equipment Dealer*.

NAEDA Equipment Dealer Buyer's Guide. North American Equipment Dealers Association, 1195 Smizer Mill Rd. Fenton, MO 63026-3480. Phone: (636)349-5000 E-mail: naeda@naeda.com • URL: http://www.naeda.com • Annual. $28.00. List of manufacturers and suppliers of agricultural, lawn and garden, and light industrial machinery.

NAFA Annual Reference Book. National Association of Fleet Administrators, 100 Wood Ave. Suite 310 Iselin, NJ 08830-2716. Phone: (732)494-8100 Fax: (732)494-6789 E-mail: jsyp@nafa.org • Annual. $45.00. Automobile manufacturers' sales and leasing representatives throughout the country.

NAFSA/Association of International Educators., 1307 New York Ave., N.W., 8th Fl. Washington, DC 20005. Phone: (202)737-3699 Fax: (202)737-3657 E-mail: inbox@nafsa.org • URL: http://www.nafsa.org • Members are individuals, organizations, and institutions involved with international educational interchange, including foreign student advisors, overseas educational advisers, foreign student admission officers, and U. S. students abroad.

NAFSA Newsletter. National Association for Foreign Student Affairs, Association of International E, 1307 New York Ave., N.W., 8th Fl. Washington, DC 20005-4704. Phone: (202)462-4811 Fax: (202)667-3419 Six times a year. Membership. Reports on international educational exchange. Formerly *National Association for Foreign Student Affairs*.

NAFTA: The North American Free Trade Agreement, A Guide to Customs Procedures. Available from U. S. Government Printing Office, Washington, DC 20402. Phone: (202)512-1800 Fax: (202)512-2250 E-mail: gpoaccess@gpo.gov • URL: http://www.access.gpo.gov • 1994. $7.00. Revised edition. Issued by the Customs Service, U. S. Treasury Department. Provides a summary of NAFTA customs requirements and benefits. (Customs Publication No. 571.)

NAFTA Watch. CCH Canadian Ltd., Six Garamond Court North York, ON, Canada M3C 1Z5. Phone: 800-268-4522 or (416)441-0086 Fax: (416)444-9011 Semimonthly. $350.00 per year. Looseleaf. Legal and business service covering the North American Free Trade Agreement.

NAFTA Works for America: Administration Update on the North American Free Trade Agreement, 1993-1998. Available from U. S. Government Printing Office, Washington, DC 20402. Phone: (202)512-1800 Fax: (202)512-2250 E-mail: gpoaccess@gpo.gov • URL: http://www.access.gpo.gov • 1999. $7.00. Cover title: *Bridging into the 21st Century*. Issued by the Office of the U. S. Trade Representative, Executive Office of the President (http://www.ustr.gov). Summarizes the accomplishment of NAFTA over its first five years.

NAHB Research Center.

NAHRO Directory of Local Agencies and Resource Guide., 630 Eye St., N.W. Washington, DC 20001-3736. Phone: (202)289-3500 E-mail: nahro@nahro.org • URL: http://www.nahro.org • Triennial. Members, $85.00; non-members, $100.00. Formerly *Directory of Local Agencies: Housing, Community Development, Redevelopment*.

NAIC News. National Association of Insurance Commissioners, 120 W. 12th St., Suite 1100 Kansas City, MO 64105-1925. Phone: (816)374-7259 Fax: (816)471-7004 URL: http://www.naic.com • Monthly. $200.00 per year. Newsletter covering insurance legislation and regulation.

NAMIC Magazine. National Association of Mutual Insurance Cos., P.O. Box 68700 Indianapolis, IN 46268. Phone: (317)875-5250 Fax: (317)879-8408 Bimonthly. $18.00 per year. Formerly *Mutual Insurance Bulletin*.

NAPEX Trade Price Reporter. National Partnership Exchange, Inc., P.O. Box 578 Tampa, FL 33601. Phone: 800-356-2739 or (813)222-0555 Quarterly. $160.00 per year. Provides high, low, and last-trade prices (resale prices) for about 500 limited partnerships, including many that have invested primarily in real estate.

Narcotic Drugs: Estimated World Requirements. International Narcotics Control Board. United Nations Publications, United Nations Concourse Level, First Ave., 46th St. New York, NY 10017. Phone: 800-553-3210 or (212)963-7680 Fax: (212)963-4910 E-mail: bookstore@un.org • URL: http://www.un.org/publications • Annual. $38.00. Includes production and utilization data relating to legal narcotics. Text in French, English and Spanish.

Narcotics and Drug Abuse A to Z. Croner Publications, Inc., 10951 Sorrento Valley Rd., Suite 1-D San Diego, CA 92121-1613. Phone: 800-441-4033 or (619)546-1894 Fax: (619)546-1855 Three volumes. Price on application. Lists treatment centers.

NARDA Independent Retailer. North American Retail Dealers Association, 10 E. 22nd St., Suite 310 Lombard, IL 60148-6191. Phone: (630)953-8950 Fax: (630)953-8957 E-mail: nardanews@aol.com • Monthly. $78.00. Formerly *NARDA News*.

NARDA's Cost of Doing Business Survey. North American Retail Dealers Association, 10 E. 22nd St., Suite 310 Lombard, IL 60148-6191. Phone: (630)953-8950 Fax: (630)953-8957 E-mail: nardahq@aol.com • Annual. $250.00.

NASD Manual. National Association of Securities Dealers, Inc. Available from CCH, Inc., 4025 W. Peterson Ave. Chicago, IL 60646-6085. Phone: 800-835-5224 or (773)866-6000 Fax: 800-224-8299 URL: http://www.cch.com • Quarterly. $430.00 per year.

Nasdaq Fact Book and Company Directory. National Association of Security Dealers, Inc. Corporate Communications, 1735 K St., N.W. Washington, DC 20006-1500. Phone: (202)728-6900 Fax: (202)728-8882 Annual. $20.00. Contains statistical data relating to the Nasdaq Stock Market. Also provides corporate address, phone, symbol, stock price, and trading volume information for more than 5,000 securities traded through the National Association of Securities Dealers Automated Quotation System (Nasdaq), including Small-Cap Issues. Includes indexing by Standard Industrial Classification (SIC) number.

NASPA., 7044 S. 13th St. Milwaukee, WI 53154. Phone: (414)768-8000 Fax: (414)768-8001 E-mail: sherer@naspa.com • URL: http://www.naspa.net • Members are systems programmers, communications analysts, database administrators, and other technical management personnel.

National Academy of Arbitrators.

National Academy of Opticianry.

National Academy of Recording Arts and Sciences.

National Academy of Television Arts and Sciences.

National Accounts of OECD Countries. OECD Publications and Information Center, 2001 L St., N.W., Ste. 650 Washington, DC 20036-4910. Phone: (202)785-6323 Fax: (202)785-0350 E-mail: washington.contact@oecd.org • URL: http://www.oecdwash.org • Annual. Two volumes. Price varies.

National Accounts Statistics: Main Aggregates and Detailed Tables. United Nations Publications, United Nations Concourse Level, First Ave., 46th St. New York, NY 10017. Phone: 800-553-3210 or (212)963-7680 Fax: (212)963-4910 E-mail: bookstore@un.org • URL: http://www.un.org/publications • Annual. $160.00.

National Advertising Review Board.

National Aeronautic Association of the U.S.A.

National Agri-Marketing Association., 11020 King St., Suite 205 Overland Park, KS 66210. Phone: (913)491-6500 Fax: (913)491-6502 E-mail: agrimktg@nama.org • URL: http://www.nama.org • Agricultural advertisers and marketers.

National Air Carrier Association., 1730 M St., N.W., Suite 806 Washington, DC 20036. Phone: (202)833-8200 Fax: (202)659-9479 Charter airlines.

National Air Transportation Association.

National Air Transportation Association Official Membership Directory. National Air Transportation Association, 4226 King St. Alexandria, VA 22302. Phone: 800-808-6282 or (703)845-9000 Fax: (703)845-8176 Annual. $95.00. List more than 1,000 regular, associate, and affiate members; regular members include airport service organizations, air taxi operators, and commuter airlines.

National Alcohol Beverage Control Association.

National Alliance of Senior Citizens., 1700 18th St.,N.W., Suite 401 Washington, DC 20009. Phone: (202)986-0117 Fax: (202)986-2974 Members are individuals concerned with the needs of older Americans. Includes a Consumerism Advisory Council.

National Antique and Art Dealers Association of America.

National Antique and Art Dealers Association of America Membership Directory. National Antique and Art Dealers Association of America, 202 E. 57th St. New York, NY 10022. Phone: (212)826-9707 Fax: (212)832-9493 Annual. $5.00. Provides a list of 46 members and their areas of specialization in the decorative arts.

National Apartment Association.

National Appliance Parts Suppliers Association.

National Appliance Service Association.

National Architectural Accrediting Board.

National Asphalt Pavement Association.

National Association for Business Economics.

National Association for Business Economists: Membership Directory. National Association for Business Economists, 1233 20th St., N.W., Suite 505 Washington, DC 20036-2304. Phone: (202)463-6223 Fax: (202)463-6239 E-mail: nabe@nabe.com • URL: http://www.nabe.com • Annual. Membership.

National Association for College Admission Counseling.

National Association for Community Leadership., 200 S. Meridian St., Suite 250 Indianapolis, IN 46225. Phone: (317)637-7408 Fax: (317)637-7413 E-mail: commlead@indy.net • Affiliated with American Chamber of Commerce Executives.

National Association for Court Management.

National Association for Creative Children and Adults.

National Association for Equal Opportunity in Higher Education.

National Association for Female Executives.

National Association for Home Care., 228 Seventh St., S.E. Washington, DC 20003. Phone: (202)547-7424 Fax: (202)547-3540 E-mail: clc@nahc.org • URL: http://www.nahc.org • Promotes high standards of patient care in home care services. Members are home health care providers.

National Association for Industry-Education Cooperation.

National Association for Medical Equipment Services., 625 Slaters Lane, Suite 200 Alexandria, VA 22314-1171. Phone: (703)836-6263 Fax: (703)836-6730 E-mail: info@names.org • URL: http://www.names.org • Members are durable medical equipment and oxygen suppliers, mainly for home health care. Has Legislative Affairs Committee that is concerned with Medicare/Medicaid benefits.

National Association for Public Health Statistics and Information Systems., 1220 19th St., N. W., Ste. 802 Washington, DC 20036. Phone: (202)463-8851 Fax: (202)463-4870 E-mail: tme.nq@naphsis.org • URL: http://www.naphsis.org • Members are officials of state and local health agencies.

National Association for the Advancement of Colored People.

National Association for the Self-Employed., P.O. Box 612067 Dallas, TX 75261-2067. Phone: 800-232-6273 Fax: 800-551-4446 URL: http://www.nase.org • Members are very small businesses and the self-employed. Acts as an advocacy group at the state and federal levels.

National Association for the Specialty Food Trade., 120 Wall St., 27th Fl. New York, NY 10005-4001. Phone: (212)482-6440 Fax: (212)482-6459 URL: http://www.fancyfoodshows.com • Members are manufacturers, processors, importers, retailers, and brokers of specialty and gourmet food items.

National Association for Women in Education: Member Directory. NAWE: Advancing Women in Higher Education, 1325 18th St., N.W.,, Suite 210 Washington, DC 20036-6511. Phone: (202)659-9330 Fax: (202)457-0946 E-mail: nawe@clark.net • URL: http://www.nawe.org • Membership. 2,000 American and foreign members.

National Association Insurance and Financial Advisors.

National Association of Agricultural Journalists.

National Association of Aluminum Distributors.

National Association of Attorneys General.

National Association of Band Instrument Manufacturers.

National Association of Beverage Retailers.

National Association of Black Owned Broadcasters.

National Association of Boards of Pharmacy.

National Association of Broadcasters.

National Association of Business Travel Agents., 3699 Wilshire Blvd.,, Ste. 700 Los Angeles, CA 90010-2726. Phone: (213)382-3335 Fax: (213)480-7712 E-mail: sjfaber@earthlink.net • Members specialize in corporate and business travel services.

National Association of Catalog Showroom Merchandisers.

National Association of Chain Drug Stores.

National Association of Chain Drug Stores - Communications Directory. National Association of Chain Drug Stores, 413 N. Lee St. Alexandria, VA 22313. Phone: (703)549-3001 Fax: (703)836-4869 E-mail: homepage_info@nacds.org • URL: http://www.nacds.org • Annual. Membership. About 150 chain drug retailers and their 31,000 individual pharmacies; 900 supplier companies; state boards of pharmacy, pharmaceutical and retail associations, colleges of pharmacy; drug trade associations.

National Association of Chemical Distributors.

National Association of College Auxiliary Services.

National Association of College Stores.

National Association of Concessionaires.

National Association of Consumer Credit Administrators.

National Association of Container Distributors.

National Association of Convenience Stores., 1605 King St. Alexandria, VA 22314-2792. Phone: (703)684-3600 Fax: (703)836-4564 E-mail: nacs@cstorecentral.com • URL: http://www.cstorecentral.com • Members are small retail stores that sell a variety of food and nonfood items and that usually have extended hours of opening.

National Association of Corporate Directors.

National Association of Corporate Treasurers., 11250 Roger Bacon Dr., Suite 8 Reston, VA 20190. Phone: (703)318-4227 Fax: (703)435-4390 E-mail: nact@nact.org • URL: http://www.nact.org • Members are corporate financial executives.

National Association of Counties.

National Association of County Administrators.

National Association of County Park and Recreation Officials.

National Association of County Planners.

National Association of County Treasurers and Finance Officers.

National Association of Credit Management.

National Association of Criminal Defense Lawyers.

National Association of Decorative Fabric Distributors.

National Association of Desktop Publishers. Journal. National Association of Desktop Publishers. Desktop Publishing Institute, 462 Old Boston St. Topsfield, MA 01983-1232. Phone: 800-847-4113 or (978)887-7900 Fax: (978)887-6117 E-mail: nadtp@aol.com • Monthly. Free to members; non-members, $48.00 per year. Covers desktop, electronic, and multimedia publishing.

National Association of Display Industries.

National Association of Elevator Contractors.

National Association of Enrolled Federal Tax Accountants.

National Association of Environmental Professionals.

National Association of Export Companies.

National Association of Fashion and Accessory Designers.

National Association of Federal Credit Unions.

National Association of Flight Instructors.

National Association of Flour Distributors.

National Association of Fruits, Flavors and Syrups., P.O. Box 545 Matawan, NJ 07747. Phone: (732)583-8272 Fax: (732)583-0798 E-mail: naffs@naffs.org • URL: http://www.naffs.org • Manufacturers of fruit and syrup toppings, flavors and stabilizers for the food industry.

National Association of Government Employees.

National Association of Health Underwriters., 200 N. 14th St., Ste. 450 Arlington, VA 22201. Phone: (703)276-0220 Fax: (703)841-7797 URL: http://www.nahu.org • Members are engaged in the sale of health and disability insurance.

National Association of Home-Based Businesses.

National Association of Home Builders of the United States.

National Association of Housing and Redevelopment Officials.

National Association of Independent Insurers.

National Association of Independent Schools.

National Association of Industrial and Office Properties., 2201 Cooperative Way Herndon, VA 20171. Phone: 800-666-6780 or (703)904-7100 Fax: (703)904-7942 E-mail: naiop@naiop.org • URL: http://www.naiop.org • Members are owners and developers of business, industrial, office, and retail properties.

National Association of Institutional Linen Management.

National Association of Institutional Linen Management Survey. National Association of Institutional Laundry Management, 2130 Lexington Rd., Suite H Richmond, KY 40475. Phone: 800-669-0863 or (606)624-0177 URL: http://www.nailm.com • Biennial. $100.00. Lists managers of in-house laundries for institutions, hotels, schools, etc.

National Association of Insurance Brokers.

National Association of Insurance Commissioners., 2301 McGee St., Ste. 800 Kansas City, MO 64108-2604. Phone: (816)842-3600 URL: http://www.naic.org • Members are state officials involved in the regulation of insurance companies.

National Association of Insurance Women International.

National Association of Investment Companies.

National Association of Investors Corporation.

National Association of Manufacturers.

National Association of Margarine Manufacturers.

National Association of Marine Services.

National Association of Metal Finishers., 112 J Elden St. Herndon, VA 20170. Phone: (703)709-8299 Fax: (703)709-1036 E-mail: namf@erols.com • URL: http://www.namf.org • Members are management personnel of metal and plastic finishing companies. Finishing includes plating, coating, polishing, rustproofing, and other processes.

National Association of Minority Women in Business.

National Association of Music Merchants.

National Association of Mutual Insurance Companies.

National Association of Off-Track Betting.

National Association of Older Worker Employment Services., 409 Third St., S.W., Suite 200 Washington, DC 20024. Phone: (202)479-1200 Fax: (202)479-0735 URL: http://www.ncoa.org • Seeks to improve employment opportunities for older workers.

National Association of Optometrists and Opticians.

National Association of Parliamentarians.

National Association of Personal Financial Advisors., 355 W. Dundee Rd., Suite 107 Buffalo Grove, IL 60089-3500. Phone: 800-366-2732 or (847)537-7722 Fax: (847)537-7740 E-mail: turfe@napfa.org • URL: http://www.napfa.org • Members are full-time financial planners who are compensated on a fee-only basis.

National Association of Personnel Services., 3133 Mount Vernon Ave. Alexandria, VA 22305. Phone: (703)684-0180 or (703)684-0181 Fax: (703)684-0071 E-mail: info@napsweb.org • URL: http://www.napsweb.org • Members are private employment agencies.

National Association of Pharmaceutical Manufacturers.

National Association of Photo Equipment Technicians.

National Association of Pizza Operators., P.O. Box 1347 New Albany, IN 47151-1347. Phone: (812)949-0909 Fax: (812)941-9711 URL: http://www.pizzatoday.com • Members are pizza establishment operators, food suppliers, and equipment manufacturers.

National Association of Plumbing-Heating-Cooling Contractors.

National Association of Power Engineers.

National Association of Printers and Lithographers.

National Association of Printing Ink Manufacturers.

National Association of Private Enterprise., 7819 Shelburne Circle Spring, TX 77379-4687. Phone: 800-223-6273 or (512)863-2699 Fax: (512)868-8037 E-mail: info@nape.org • URL: http://www.nape.org • Members are people involved in small businesses.

National Association of Produce Market Managers.

National Association of Professional Insurance Agents., 400 N. Washington St. Alexandria, VA 22314. Phone: (703)836-9340 Fax: (703)836-1279 E-mail: piaweb@pianet.org • URL: http://www.pianet.com • Members are independent agents in various fields of insurance.

National Association of Professional Organizers., 1033 La Posada Drive, Suite 220 Austin, TX 78752. Phone: (512)454-8626 Fax: (512)454-3036 E-mail: napo@assnmgmt.com • URL: http://www.napo.net • Members are concerned with time management, productivity, and the efficient organization of documents and activities.

National Association of Psychiatric Health Systems.

National Association of Purchasing Management.

National Association of Railroad Passengers.

National Association of Railway Business Women.

National Association of Real Estate Appraisers.

National Association of Real Estate Brokers.

National Association of Real Estate Investment Trusts.

National Association of Realtors.

National Association of Recording Merchandisers.

National Association of Regulatory Utility Commissioners.

National Association of Retired Federal Employees.
National Association of Rocketry., P.O. Box 177 Altoona, WI 54720. Phone: 800-262-4872 or (715)832-1946 Fax: (715)832-6432 E-mail: nar-hq@nar.org • URL: http://www.nar.org • Model rockets.
National Association of RV Parks and Campgrounds.
National Association of Securities Dealers.
National Association of Service Managers.
National Association of Small Business Investment Companies.
National Association of Sporting Goods Wholesalers.
National Association of State Aviation Officials.
National Association of State Boards of Accountancy.
National Association of State Budget Officers.
National Association of State Charity Officials., c/o Richard C. Allen, Office of Attorney General, One Ashburton Place Boston, MA 02108. Phone: (617)727-2200 Fax: (617)727-2920 Members are state officials responsible for the administration of charitable solicitation laws.
National Association of State Departments of Agriculture.
National Association of State Development Agencies.
National Association of State Directors of Veterans Affairs.
National Association of State Mental Health Program Directors.
National Association of State Procurement Officials., c/o Association Management Resources, 167 W. Main St., Suite 600 Lexington, KY 40507. Phone: (606)231-1877 or (606)231-1963 Fax: (606)231-1928 E-mail: croberts@amrinc.net • URL: http://www.naspo.org • Purchasing officials of the states and territories.
National Association of State Supervisors of Trade and Industrial Education.
National Association of Student Financial Aid Administrators., 1129 20th St., N.W. Ste 400 Washington, DC 20036-5020. Phone: (202)785-0453 Fax: (202)785-1487 E-mail: ask@nasfaa.org • URL: http://www.nsfaa.org • Serves as a national forum for matters related to student aid.
National Association of Swine Records.
National Association of Tax Practitioners., 720 Association Dr. Appleton, WI 54914. Phone: (920)749-1040 Fax: (920)749-1062 URL: http://www.natptax.com • Promotes high professional standards for tax practitioners.
National Association of Television Program Executives.
National Association of the Physically Handicapped.
National Association of the Remodeling Industry.
National Association of Theatre Owners.
National Association of Towns and Townships., 444 N. Capitol St., N.W. Suite 208 Washington, DC 20001. Phone: (202)624-3550 Fax: (202)625-3554 Provides technical and other assistance to officials of small communities.
National Association of Uniform Manufacturers and Distributors.
National Association of Video Distributors., 700 Frederica St., Suite 205 Owensboro, KY 42301. Phone: (502)926-6002 Fax: (502)685-6080 Members are wholesalers of home video software, both tapes and discs.
National Association of Waterfront Employers.
National Association of Wheat Growers.
National Association of Wholesaler-Distributors.
National Association of Women Artists.
National Association of Women Business Owners.
National Association of Women Business Owners., 1100 Wayne Ave., Suite 830 Silver Spring, MD 20910-5603. Phone: (301)608-2590 Fax: (301)608-2596 E-mail: nawbohq@aol.com • URL: http://www.nfwbo.org • Provides research reports and statistical studies relating to various aspects of women-owned business enterprises. Affiliated with the National Association of Women Business Owners.
National Association of Women In Construction.
National Association of Women Lawyers.
National Association of Women Lawyers. President's Newsletter. National Association of Women Lawyers, 750 N. Lake Shore Dr. Chicago, IL 60611. Phone: (312)988-6186 Quarterly.
National Auctioneers Association.
NAtional Auto Auction Association.
National Automatic Merchandising Association.
National Automatic Merchandising Association-Directory of Members. National Automatic Merchandising Association, 20 N. Wacker Dr., Suite 3500 Chicago, IL 60606. Phone: 888-337-8363 or (312)346-0370 Fax: (312)704-4140 URL: http://www.vending.org • Annual. $150.00. Lists 2,300 vending and food service management firms, along with vending machine manufacturers and distributors and producers of other equipment and food items.
National Automobile Dealers Association.
National Aviation Club.
National Bankers Association., 1513 P St., N.W. Washington, DC 20005. Phone: (202)588-5432 Fax: (202)588-5443 Minority bankers.
National Beauty Culturists' League.
National Beer Wholesalers' Association.
National Beverage Packaging Association., c/o Gary Lile, No. 1 Busch Place, OSC-2N St. Louis, MO 63118. Phone: (314)577-2443 Fax: (314)577-2972 E-mail: gary.lileoanheuser-busch.com • Members are concerned with the packaging of soft drinks, beer, and juices.
National Bicycle Dealers Association., 777 W. 19th St., Ste. 0 Costa Mesa, CA 92627. Phone: (949)722-6909 Fax: (949)722-1747 E-mail: bikeshops@aol.com • URL: http://www.nbda.com • Members are independent bicycle retailers.
National Board of Trial Advocacy: Directory of Board Members and Certified Diplomates. National Board of Trial Advocacy, 18 Tremont St., Suite 403 Boston, MA 021308. Phone: (617)720-2032 Fax: (617)720-2038 E-mail: rhugus@world.std.com • URL: http://www.nbtanet.org • Biennial. Free. More than 2,400 trial lawyers board certified in civil and criminal trial advocacy; members of the board.
National Bond Summary. National Quotation Bureau, Inc., 150 Commerce Rd. Cedar Grove, NJ 07009-1208. Phone: (201)239-6100 Fax: (201)239-0080 Monthly. $420.00 per year. Semiannual cumulations. Includes price quotes for both active and inactive issues.
National Building Cost Manual. Craftsman Book Co., 6058 Corte del Cedro Carlsbad, CA 92009. Phone: 800-829-8123 or (760)438-7828 Fax: (760)438-0398 E-mail: jacobs@costbook.com • URL: http://www.craftsman-books.com • Annual. $20.00.
National Building Granite Quarries Association.
National Bulk Vendors Association.
National Bureau of Economic Research, Inc.
National Burglar and Fire Alarm Association.
National Burglar and Fire Alarm Association Members Services Directory. National Burglar and Fire Alarm Association, 8300 Colesville Rd., Suite 750 Silver Spring, MD 20910-6225. Phone: (301)907-3202 Fax: (301)907-7897 E-mail: staff@alarm.org • URL: http://www.alarm.org • Annual. Membership. Names and addresses of about 4,000 alarm security companies. Formerly *National Burglar and Fire Alarm Association-Directory of Members.*
National Business Aviation Association.
National Business Education Association.
National Business Education Yearbook. National Business Education Association, 1914 Association Dr. Reston, VA 20191-1596. Phone: (703)860-8300 Fax: (703)620-4483 E-mail: nbea@nbea.org • URL: http://www.nbea.org/nbea.html • Annual. $15.00.
National Business Employment Weekly. Dow Jones and Co., Inc., P.O. Box 300 Princeton, NJ 08543-0300. Phone: 800-568-7625 or (212)416-2000 Fax: (609)520-5840 Weekly. $199.00 per year. In addition to employment advertisements reprinted from various editions of the *Wall Street Journal*, contains substantial articles on how to find a job.
National Business Incubation Association., 20 E. Circle Dr., Suite 190 Athens, OH 45701. Phone: (740)593-4331 Fax: (740)593-1996 E-mail: info@nbia.org • URL: http://www.nbia.org • Members are business assistance professionals concerned with business startups, entrepreneurship, and effective small business management.
National Business Woman. National Federation of Business and Professional Women's Clubs, Inc., 2012 Massachusetts Ave. N.W. Washington, DC 20036. Phone: (202)293-1100 Fax: (202)861-0298 Quarterly. $10.00 per year. Focuses on the activities and interests of working women.
National Cable Television Association.
National Cable Television Institute.
National Candy Brokers Association., 710 East Ogden Ave., Suite 600 Naperville, IL 60563-8603. Phone: (630)369-2406 Fax: (630)369-2488 E-mail: ncba@b-online.com • URL: http://www.candynet.com • Members are manufacturers' and importers' brokers specializing in the marketing of candy and related products.
National Career Development Association.
National Catalog Managers Association.
National Cattlemen's Beef Association.
National Center for Computer Crime Data., 1222 17th Ave., Suite B Santa Cruz, CA 95062. Phone: (408)475-4457 Fax: (408)475-5336 E-mail: nudnic@ix.netcom.com • Conducts research, compiles statistics, provides case studies and other information.
National Center for Disablity Services., 201 I.U. Willets Rd. Albertson, NY 11507. Phone: (516)747-5400 Fax: (516)746-3298 URL: http://www.ncds.org • Seeks to improve employment opportunities for persons with disabilities.
National Center for Employee Ownership.
National Center for Freedom of Information Studies., Loyola University of Chicago, 820 N. Michigan Ave. Chicago, IL 60611. Phone: (312)915-6549 Fax: (312)915-6520 Legal emphasis.
National Center for Health Statistics: Monitoring the Nation's Health. National Center for Health Statistics, Centers for Disease Control and PreventioPhone: (301)458-4636 E-mail: nchsquery@cdc.gov • URL: http://www.cdc.gov/nchswww • Web site provides detailed data on diseases, vital statistics, and health care in the U. S. Includes a search facility and links to many other health-related Web sites. "Fastats A to Z" offers quick data on hundreds of topics from Accidents to Work-Loss Days, with links to Comprehensive Data and related sources. Frequent updates. Fees: Free.
National Center for Housing Management.
National Center for Manufacturing Sciences., 3025 Boardwalk Ann Arbor, MI 48108. Phone: (734)995-0300 Fax: (734)995-4004 E-mail: johnd@ncms.org • URL: http://www.ncms.org • Research areas include process technology and control, machine mechanics, sensors, testing methods, and quality assurance.
National Center for Nonprofit Boards., 1828 L St., N. W., Suite 900 Washington, DC 20036. Phone: 800-883-6262 or (202)452-6262 Fax: (202)452-6299 E-mail: ncnb@ncnb.org • URL: http://www.ncnb.org • Seeks to improve the effectiveness of nonprofit boards of trustees.
National Center for Policy Analysis., 12655 N. Central Expressway, Suite 720 Dallas, TX 75243-1739. Phone: (972)386-6272 Fax: (972)386-0924 E-mail: jgoodman@ncpa.public-policy.org • URL: http://www.ncpa.org • Includes studies on medicare.
National Center for State Courts.
National Certified Pipe Welding Bureau.
National Charities Information Bureau., 19 Union Square, W., 6th Fl. New York, NY 10003-3395. Phone: (212)929-6300 Fax: (212)463-7083 E-mail: ncib@bway.net • URL: http://www.give.org • Sets accountability standards and provides information for nonprofit organizations that solicit contributions from the public.
National Cheese Institute.
National Chicken Council.
National Child Labor Committee.
National Child Safety Council.
National Civic League National Headquarters.
National Civic Review. National Civic League, Inc. Jossey-Bass Inc., Publishers, 350 Sansome St. San Francisco, CA 94104. Phone: 888-378-2537 or (415)433-1740 Fax: (415)433-0499 E-mail: webperson@jbp.com • URL: http://www.josseybass.com • Quarterly. Institutions, $83.00 per year. Presents civic strategies for improving local government operations and community life.
National Clay Pipe Institute.
National Club Association.
National Coffee Association of the U.S.A.
National Committee for an Effective Congress.
National Committee for Clinical Laboratory Studies., 940 W. Valley Rd., Suite 1400 Wayne, PA 19087-1898. Phone: (610)688-0100 Fax: (610)688-0700 E-mail: exoffice@nccls.org • URL: http://www.nccls.org • Promotes the development of national standards for clinical laboratory testing.
National Committee for Responsive Philanthropy., 2001 S St., N.W., Suite 620 Washington, DC 20009. Phone: (202)387-9177 Fax: (202)332-5084 E-mail: info@ncrp.org • URL: http://www.ncrp.org • Promotes charitable giving to new organizations working for social change or controversial issues.
National Committee on Uniform Traffic Laws and Ordinances.
National Committee to Preserve Social Security and Medicare., 10 G St., N.E., Ste. 600 Washington, DC 20002. Phone: 800-966-1935 or (202)216-0420 Fax: (202)216-0451 Members are individuals concerned with Medicare and social security programs.
National Community Development Association.
National Compensation Survey. Available from U. S. Government Printing Office, Washington, DC 20402. Phone: (202)512-1800 Fax: (202)512-2250 E-mail: gpoaccess@gpo.gov • URL: http://www.access.gpo.gov • Irregular. $300.00 per year. Consists of bulletins reporting on earnings for jobs in clerical, professional, technical, and other fields in 70 major metropolitan areas. Formerly *Occupational Compensation Survey.*
National Concrete Masonry Association.
National Confectioners Association of the U.S.
National Confectionery Sales Association.
National Conference of Bankruptcy Judges.
National Conference of Commissioners on Uniform State Laws.
National Conference of Local Environmental Health Administrators.
National Conference of Standards Laboratories.
National Conference of State Legislatures.
National Conference of State Liquor Administrators.
National Conference of State Social Security Administrators. Social Security Div.
National Conference on Citizenship.
National Conference on Fluid Power.
National Conference on Weights and Measures.
National Construction Estimator. Martin Kiley and William Moselle. Craftsman Book Co., 6058 Corte del Cedro Carlsbad, CA 92009. Phone: 800-829-8123 or (760)438-7828 Fax: (760)438-0398 URL: http://www.craftsman-book.com • Annual. $47.50.
National Constructors Association.
National Consumer Law Center.
National Consumers League., 1701 K. St. N.W., No. 1200 Washington, DC 20006. Phone: (202)835-3323 Fax:

(202)835-0747 E-mail: ncl@nclnet.org • URL: http://www.fraud.org/ • Promotes consumer affairs.

National Contract Management Association.

National Cooperative Business Association.

National Corn Growers Association.

National Corrugated Steel Pipe Association.

National Cosmetology Association.

National Cotton Council of America.

National Cottonseed Products Association.

National Council for Prescription Drug Programs., 4201 N. 24th St., Suite 365 Phoenix, AZ 85016-6268. Phone: (602)957-9105 Fax: (602)955-0749 E-mail: ncpdp@ncpdp.org • URL: http://www.ncpdp.org • Concerned with standardization of third party prescription drug programs.

National Council for Public-Private Partnerships., 1010 Massachusetts Ave., N.W., Suite 350 Washington, DC 20001-5400. Phone: (202)467-6800 Fax: (202)467-6312 E-mail: ncppp@ncppp.org • URL: http://www.ncppp.org • Promotes private ownership of public services.

National Council for Research on Women.

National Council of Administrative Women in Education.

National Council of Agricultural Employers.

National Council of Chain Restaurants.

National Council of Commercial Plant Breeders.

National Council of Higher Education Loan Programs., 1100 Connecticut Ave. N.W., 12th Fl. Washington, DC 20036. Phone: (202)822-2106 Fax: (202)822-2142 Attempts to coordinate federal, state, and private functions in the student loan program.

National Council of Juvenile and Family Court Judges.

National Council of Senior Citizens.

National Council of Women of the United States.

National Council on Alcoholism and Drug Dependence.

National Council on Compensation Insurance., 750 Park of Commerce Dr. Boca Raton, FL 33487. Phone: 800-622-4123 URL: http://www.5ncci.com/ncciweb/ • Members are insurance companies.

National Council on Crime and Delinquency.

National Council on Economic Education.

National Council on Problem Gambling.

National Council on Public Polls., 1375 Kings Highway East, Suite 300 Fairfield, CT 06430. Phone: 800-239-0909 Fax: (203)331-1750 Members are public opinion polling organizations.

National Court Reporters Association.

National Credit Union Administration Rules and Regulations. Available from U. S. Government Printing Office, Washington, DC 20402. Phone: (202)512-1800 Fax: (202)512-2250 E-mail: gpoaccess@gpo.gov • URL: http://www.access.gpo.gov • Looseleaf. $130.00 for basic manual, including updates for an indeterminate period. Incorporates all amendments and revisions.

National Credit Union Management Association., c/o J.K. Anchors, 4989 Rebel Trial, N.W. Atlanta, GA 30327. Phone: (404)255-6828 Fax: (404)851-1752 URL: http://www.nacuso.org • Members are large credit unions.

National Customs Brokers and Forwarders Association of America.

National Customs Brokers and Forwarders Association of America: Membership Directory. National Customs Brokers and Forwarders Association of America, Inc., 1200 18th St., N.W., Suite 901 Washington, DC 20036. Phone: (202)466-0222 Fax: (202)466-0226 E-mail: staff@ncbfaa.org • URL: http://www.ncbfaa.org • Annual. $25.00. Lists about 600 customs brokers, international air cargo agents, and freight forwarders in the U.S.

National Dairy Council.

National Defense. National Defense Industrial Association, 2111 Wilson Blvd., Suite 400 Arlington, VA 22201-3001. Phone: (703)522-1820 Fax: (703)522-1885 URL: http://www.ndia.org • 10 times a year. $35.00 per year.

National Defense Industrial Association., 2111 Wilson Blvd., No. 400 Arlington, VA 22201-3061. Phone: (703)522-1820 or (703)247-2589 Fax: (703)522-1885 E-mail: info@india.org • URL: http://www.adpa.org • Concerned with industrial preparedness for national defense.

National Defense Transportation Association.

National Development Council., 51 E. 42nd St., Suite 300 New York, NY 10017. Phone: (212)682-1106 Fax: (212)573-6118 Provides technical and financial assistance to minority business people.

The National Dipper: The Magazine for Ice Cream Retailers. U. S. Exposition Corp., 1841 Hicks Rd., Suite C Rolling Meadows, IL 60008-1215. Phone: (847)202-4770 Fax: (847)202-4791 Bimonthly. $55.00 per year. Edited for ice cream store owners and managers. Includes industry news, new product information, statistics, and feature articles.

National Dipper Yellow Pages. U. S. Exposition Corp., 1841 Hicks Rd., Suite C Rolling Meadows, IL 60008-1215. Phone: (847)202-4770 Fax: (847)202-4791 Annual. $10.00. Special directory issue of *The National Dipper*. Lists products and services for the ice cream retail industry.

The National Directory of Catalogs. Oxbridge Communications, 150 Fifth Ave., Suite 302 New York, NY 10011. Phone: 800-955-0231 or (212)741-0231 Fax: 800-414-5043 or (212)633-2938 E-mail: info@mediafinder.com • URL: http://www.mediafinder.com • Annual. $595.00. Describes over 7,000 catalogs within 78 subject areas. Includes CD-ROM.

National Directory of Community Newspapers. American Newspaper Representatives, Inc., 1700 W. Big Beaver Rd., Suite 200 Troy, MI 48084-3543. Phone: 800-550-7557 Fax: (248)643-0606 Annual. $105.00. Supersedes *National Directory of Weekly Newspapers*.

National Directory of Corporate Distress Specialists: A Comprehensive Guide to Firms and Professionals Providing Services in Bankruptcies, Workouts, Turnarounds, and Distressed Investments. Joel W. Lustig, editor. Lustig Data Research, Inc., 653 Arbuckle Ave. Woodmere, NY 11598-2701. Phone: (516)295-4165 Fax: (516)295-4165 E-mail: jlustig@aol.com • Annual. $245.00. Provides information on 1,400 specialist firms in 17 subject areas-attorneys, accountants, financial advisors, investors, valuation consultants, turnaround managers, liquidators, etc. Nine indexes are included.

National Directory of Corporate Giving: A Guide to Corporate Giving Programs and Corporate Foundations. The Foundation Center, 79 Fifth Ave. New York, NY 10003-3076. Phone: 800-424-9836 or (212)620-4230 Fax: (212)807-3677 E-mail: mfn@fdncenter.org • URL: http://www.fdncenter.org • Biennial. $225.00. Provides information on 2,895 corporations that maintain philanthropic programs (direct giving programs or company-sponsored foundations).

National Directory of Corporate Public Affairs. Columbia Books, Inc., 1212 New York Ave., N. W., Suite 330 Washington, DC 20005. Phone: 888-265-0600 or (202)898-0662 Fax: (202)898-0775 E-mail: info@columbiabooks.com • URL: http://www.columbiabooks.com • Annual. $109.00. Lists about 2,000 corporations that have foundations or other public affairs activities.

National Directory of Drug Abuse and Alcoholism Treatment Programs. Substance Abuse and Mental Health Services Administration, Office of Applied Studies, 5600 Fishers Lane, Room 16-105 Rockville, MD 20857. Phone: 800-729-6686 or (301)443-0525 Fax: (301)443-9847 E-mail: directory@smdi.com • URL: http://www.findtreatment.samhsa.gov • Annual. Free. Lists 10,000 federal, state, local, and privately funded agencies administering or providing drug abuse and alcoholism treatment services.

National Directory of HMOs. Group Health Association of America, 1129 20th St., N. W., Suite 600 Washington, DC 20036. Phone: (202)778-3247 Fax: (202)331-7487 Annual. $125.00. Includes names of key personnel and benefit options.

National Directory of Internships. National Society for Experiential Education, 1703 N. Beauregard St., Suite 400 Alexandria, VA 22311. Phone: (703)933-0017 Fax: (703)933-1053 Biennial. $33.95. Lists many internships in 85 corporate, nonprofit, and government areas.

National Directory of Investment Newsletters. GPS Co., P.O. Box 372 Yardley, PA 19067. Phone: (215)493-6783 Biennial. $49.95. Describes about 800 investment newsletters, and their publishers.

National Directory of Law Enforcement Administrators and Correctional Institutions. National Public Safety Information Bureau, P.O. Box 365 Stevens Point, WI 54481. Phone: 800-618-0730 or (715)345-2772 Fax: (715)345-7288 E-mail: info@safetysource.com • URL: http://www.safetysource.com • Annual. $99.00. Lists a wide variety of law enforcement administrators and institutions, including city police departments, sheriffs, prosecutors, state agencies, federal agencies, correctional institutions, college campus police departments, airport police, and harbor police.

National Directory of Mailing Lists 1997. Oxbridge Communications, Inc., 150 Fifth Ave., Suite 302 New York, NY 10011-4311. Phone: 800-955-0231 or (212)741-0231 Fax: (212)633-2938 E-mail: info@oxbridge.com • URL: http://www.mediafinder.com • Annual. $695.00. Describes over 15,000 mailing lists in about 200 categories. Includes CD-ROM.

National Directory of Minority-Owned Business Firms. Available from The Gale Group, 27500 Drake Rd. Farmington Hills, MI 48331-3535. Phone: 800-877-GALE or (248)699-GALE Fax: 800-414-5043 or (248)699-8069 E-mail: galeord@galegroup.com • URL: http://www.galegroup.com • 2001. $285.00. 11th edition. Published by Business Research Services. Includes more than 47,000 minority-owned businesses.

National Directory of Nonprofit Organizations 2002. Available from The Gale Group, 27500 Drake Rd. Farmington Hills, MI 48331-3535. Phone: 800-877-GALE or (248)699-GALE Fax: 800-414-5043 or (248)699-8069 E-mail: galeord@galegroup.com • URL: http://www.galegroup.com • 2001. $535.00. 13th edition. Two volumes. Volume one, $370.00; volume two, $240.00. Contains over 250,000 listings of nonprofit organizations, indexed by 260 areas of activity. Indicates income range and IRS tax filing status for each organization.

National Directory of Personnel Service Firms. National Association of Personnel Services, 3133 Mount Vernon Ave. Alexandria, VA 22305-2540. Phone: (703)684-0180 Fax: (703)684-0071 Annual. $15.95. Lists over 1,100 member private (for-profit) employment firms. Formerly *ACCESS*.

National Directory of Women-Owned Business Firms. The Gale Group, 27500 Drake Rd. Farmington Hills, MI 48331-3535. Phone: 800-877-GALE or (248)699-GALE Fax: 800-414-5043 or (248)699-8069 E-mail: galeord@galegroup.com • URL: http://www.galegroup.com • 2000. $285.00. 11th edition. Published by Business Research Services. Includes more than 28,000 businesses owned by women.

National E-Mail and Fax Directory. The Gale Group, 27500 Drake Rd. Farmington Hills, MI 48331-3535. Phone: 800-877-GALE or (248)699-GALE Fax: 800-414-5043 or (248)699-8069 E-mail: galeord@galegroup.com • URL: http://www.galegroup.com • Annual. $150.00. Provides fax numbers, telephone numbers, and addresses for U. S. companies, organizations, government agencies, and libraries. Includes alphabetic listings and subject listings.

National Economic Development and Law Center.

National Education Association.

National Electrical Contractors Association.

National Electrical Manufacturers Association.

National Electronic Distributors Association.

National Electronics Service Dealers Association.

National Elevator Industry.

National Elevator Industry, Inc. Newsletter. National Elevator Industry, Inc., 400 Frank W. Burr Blvd. Teanek, NJ 07666. Phone: (201)928-2828 Fax: (201)928-4200 Quarterly. Price on application.

National Employee Benefits Institute.

National Employee Services and Recreation Association.

National Employee Services and Recreation Association Membership Directory. National Employee Services and Recreation Association, 2211 York Rd., Suite 207 Oak Brook, IL 60523-2371. Phone: (630)368-1280 Fax: (630)368-1286 E-mail: nesrahq@nesra.org • URL: http://www.nesra.org • Annual. Membership. Lists more than 4,500 personnel managers, recreation directors and certified administrators in employee recreation, fitness and services. Formerly *National Employee Services and Recreation Association Membership Directory*.

National Energy Journal. c/o J. P. Dunlavey. National Wood Stove and Fireplace Journal, Inc., 7873 E. Via Costa Scottsdale, AZ 85258-2822. Monthly. $21.00 per year.

The National Estimator. Society of Cost Estimating and Analysis, 101 S. Whiting St., Suite 201 Alexandria, VA 22304. Phone: (703)751-8069 Fax: (703)461-7328 Semiannual. $30.00 per year. Covers government contract estimating.

National Faculty Directory. Available from The Gale Group, 27500 Drake Rd. Farmington Hills, MI 48331-3535. Phone: 800-877-GALE or (248)699-GALE Fax: 800-414-5043 or (248)699-8069 E-mail: galeord@galegroup.com • URL: http://www.galegroup.com • 2001. $770.00. 32nd edition. Four volumes. 2001 supplement, $325.00. Complied by CMG Information Services.

National Family Business Council., 1640 W. Kennedy Rd. Lake Forest, IL 60045. Phone: (847)295-1040 Fax: (847)295-1898 E-mail: lmsnfbc@email.msn.com • Seeks to ensure the survival of family-owned businesses.

National Farmers Organization.

National Farmers Union.

National Fastener Distributors Association.

National Federation of Abstracting and Information Services.

National Federation of Federal Employees.

National Federation of Independent Business., 53 Century Blvd., Suite 300 Nashville, TN 37214. Phone: 800-634-2669 or (615)872-5800 Fax: (615)872-5353 URL: http://www.nfibonline.com • Members are independent business and professional people.

National Federation of Independent Unions.

National Federation of Nonprofits.

National Federation of Press Women.

National Fenestration Rating Council., 1300 Spring St., Suite 500 Silver Spring, MD 20910. Phone: (301)589-6372 Fax: (301)588-0854 E-mail: nfrcusa@aol.com • URL: http://www.nfrc.org • Conducts insulation efficiency testing of doors and windows. Encourages informed purchase by consumers of windows, doors, and skylights.

National Fire Protection Association.

National Fire Protection Association. National Fire Codes. National Fire Protection Association, One Batterymarch Park Quincy, MA 02269. Phone: 800-344-3555 or (617)770-3000 Fax: (617)770-0700 E-mail: library@nfpa.org • URL: http://www.nfpa.org • Annual. Members, $610.00; non-members, $675.00. Includes supplement. Lists over 270 codes.

National Fisherman. Diversified Business Communications, P.O. Box 7238 Rockland, ME 04112-7438. Phone: (207)842-5608 Fax: (207)842-5609 Monthly. $22.95 per year. American fishing industry and boat building trade.

National Five Digit Zip Code and Post Office Directory. U.S. Postal Service, National Customer Support Center, United

States Postal Service, 6060 Primacy Parkway, Suite 101 Memphis, TN 38188-0001. Phone: 800-238-3150 Fax: (901)767-8853 Annual. Two volumes. Formerly *National Zip Code and Post Office Directory-*.

National Fluid Power Association., 3333 N. Mayfair Rd. Milwaukee, WI 53222-3219. Phone: (414)778-3344 Fax: (414)778-3361 E-mail: nfpa@nfpa.com • URL: http://www.nfpa.com • Manufacturers.

National Fluid Power Association Reporter. National Fluid Power Association, 3333 N. Mayfair Rd. Milwaukee, WI 53222-3219. Phone: (414)778-3344 Fax: (414)778-3361 E-mail: nfpa@nfpa.com • URL: http://www.nfpa.com • Bimonthly. $50.00 per year. Newsletter.

National Food Distributors Association.

National Food Processors Association.

National Food Processors Association Research Foundation., 1350 Eye St., N.W., Suite 300 Washington, DC 20005. Phone: (202)639-5958 Fax: (202)639-5991 E-mail: rappleb@nfpa-food.org • URL: http://www.nfpa-food.org • Conducts research on food processing engineering, chemistry, microbiology, sanitation, preservation aspects, and public health factors.

National Food Service Association.

National Foreign Trade Council.

National Forensic League.

National Foundation for Consumer Credit.

National Foundation for Unemployment Compensation and Workers Compensation.

National Foundation Manufactured Home Owners.

National Foundation of Funeral Service.

National Frozen Food Association.

National Frozen Food Association Directory. National Frozen Food Association, Inc., 4755 Linglestown Rd., Suite 300 Harrisburg, PA 17112. Phone: (717)657-8601 Fax: (717)657-9862 E-mail: info@nffa.org • URL: http://www.nffa.org • Annual. $195.00. Lists products, services and personnel.

National Frozen Food Dessert and Fast Food Association.

National Funeral Directors and Morticians Association.

National Funeral Directors Association.

National Futures Association.

National Futures Association Manual. National Futures Association, 200 W. Madison St., Suite 1600 Chicago, IL 60606. Phone: (312)781-1300 Fax: (312)781-1467 E-mail: publicaffairs@nfa.futures.org • URL: http://www.nfa.futures.org • Quarterly. Looseleaf. Price on application. Rules and regulations concerning commodity futures trading.

National Glass Association.

National Golf Course Owners Association., 1470 Ben Sawyer Blvd., Suite 18 Mount Pleasant, SC 29464-4535. Phone: 800-933-4262 or (843)881-9956 Fax: (843)881-9958 E-mail: info@ngcoa.com • URL: http://www.ngcoa.com • Members are owners and operators of private golf courses.

National Golf Foundation., 1150 S. U. S. Highway One, Suite 401 Jupiter, FL 33477. Phone: (561)744-6006 Fax: (561)744-6107 URL: http://www.ngf.org • Research areas include golf consumers, golf course operations, and other aspects of the golf industry.

National Governors' Association.

National Grain and Feed Association.

National Grain and Feed Association Directory., 1201 New York Ave., N.W.,, Suite 830 Washington, DC 20005. Phone: (202)289-0873 Fax: (202)289-5388 E-mail: ngfa@ngfa.org • URL: http://www.ngfa.org • Annual. Price on application.

National Grain Trade Council.

National Grange.

National Grants Management Association.

National Grocers Association.

National Ground Water Association.

National Ground Water Association - Membership Directory. National Ground Water Association, 601 Dempsey Rd. Westerville, OH 43081. Phone: 800-551-7379 or (614)898-7791 Fax: (614)898-7786 E-mail: ngwa@ngwa.org • URL: http://www.ngwa.org • Triennial. Membership.

National Guide to Funding for Libraries and Information Services. The Foundation Center, 79 Fifth Ave. New York, NY 10003-3076. Phone: 800-424-9836 or (212)620-4230 Fax: (212)807-3677 E-mail: mfn@fdncenter.org • URL: http://www.fdncenter.org • 1997. $95.00. Contains detailed information on about 600 foundations and corporate direct giving programs providing funding to libraries. Includes indexing by type of support, subject field, location, and key personnel.

National Hardwood Lumber Association., P.O. Box 34518 Memphis, TN 38184-0518. Phone: (901)377-1818 Fax: (901)382-6419 URL: http://www.natlhardwood.org • Members are hardwood lumber and veneer manufacturers and distributors. Users of hardwood products are also members.

National Hardwood Lumber Association Membership Directory. National Hardwood Lumber Association, P.O. Box 34518 Memphis, TN 38184-0518. Phone: 800-933-0318 or (901)377-1818 Fax: (901)382-6419 E-mail: nhla@natlhardwood.org • URL: http://www.natlhardwood.org • Annual. $85.00. Members are hardwood lumber and veneer manufacturers, distributors, and users.

National Hardwood Magazine. Miller Publishing Co., P.O. Box 34908 Memphis, TN 38184-0908. Phone: (901)372-8280 Fax: (901)373-9058 Monthly. $45.00 per year.

National Hay Association.

National Health Club Association., 12596 W. Bayaud Ave., Suite 160 Denver, CO 80228. Phone: 800-765-6422 or (303)753-6422 Fax: (303)986-6813 Members are fitness centers, health clubs, spas, etc.

National Health Directory. Aspen Publishers, Inc., 200 Orchard Ridge Dr. Gaithersburg, MD 20878. Phone: 800-638-8437 or (301)417-7500 Fax: (301)417-7550 E-mail: customer.service@aspenpubl.com • URL: http://www.aspenpub.com • 1997. $95.00. Lists about 10,000 federal and state public health care officials.

National Hog Farmer. Intertec Publishing Co., Agribusiness Div., 7900 International Dr., 3rd Fl. Minneapolis, MN 55425. Phone: 800-400-5945 or (612)851-9329 Fax: (612)851-4601 E-mail: subs@intertec.com • URL: http://www.intertec.com • Monthly. $35.00 per year.

National Home Center News: News and Analysis for the Home Improvement, Building, Material Industry. Lebhar-Friedman, Inc., 425 Park Ave. New York, NY 10022. Phone: 800-766-6999 or (212)756-5000 Fax: (212)756-5176 E-mail: info@lf.com • URL: http://www.homecenternews.com/ • 22 times a year. $99.00 per year. Includes special feature issues on hardware and tools, building materials, millwork, electrical supplies, lighting, and kitchens.

National Home Furnishings Association.

National Homeowners Association.

National Honey Packers and Dealers Association.

National Housewares Manufacturers Association., 6400 Shafer Court, Suite 650 Rosemont, IL 60018. Phone: 800-843-6462 or (847)292-4200 Fax: (847)292-4211 URL: http://www.housewares.org • Members are manufacturers of housewares and small appliances.

National Housing Conference.

National Human Resource Association.

National Hydropower Association., One Massachusetts Ave., N.W., Ste. 850 Washington, DC 20001. Phone: (202)682-1700 Fax: (202)682-9478 E-mail: info@hydro.org • URL: http://www.hydro.org • Members are utilities, developers, manufacturers, organizations, bankers, architects, and others with an active interest in hydropower. Promotes the development of hydroelectric energy.

National Ice Cream and Yogurt Retailers Association.

National Immigration Forum.

National Independent Automobile Dealers Association.

National Independent Bank Equipment and Systems Association.

National Industrial Glove Distributors Association.

National Industrial Security Program Operating Manual. U.S. Department of Defense. Available from U.S. Government Printing Office, Washington, DC 20402. Phone: (202)512-1800 Fax: (202)512-2250 E-mail: gpoaccess@gpo.gov • URL: http://www.accessgpo.gov • 1995. $14.00.

National Industrial Transportation League.

National Information Standards Organization., 4733 Bethesda Ave., Suite 300 Bethesda, MD 20814-5248. Phone: (301)654-2512 Fax: (301)654-1721 E-mail: nisohq@niso.org • URL: http://www.niso.org • Develops and promotes technical standards for the information industry and libraries, including the Z39.50 protocol for Internet database searching.

National Institute for Automotive Service Excellence., 13505 Dulles Technology Dr., Suite 2 Herndon, VA 20171-3421. Phone: 877-273-8324 or (703)713-3800 Fax: (703)713-0727 URL: http://www.asecert.org • A public interest organization which promotes high standards in automotive service and repair. Encourages effective training programs for automobile mechanics/technicians.

National Institute for Fitness and Sport.

National Institute for Work and Learning., Academy for Educational Development, 1875 Connecticut Ave., N.W. Washington, DC 20009. Phone: (202)884-8187 Fax: (202)884-8422 E-mail: ichaner@aed.org • URL: http://www.niwl.org • Research areas include adult education, training, unemployment insurance, and career development.

National Institute of Ceramic Engineers.

National Institute of Credit.

National Institute of Government Purchasing.

National Institute of Hypertension Studies-Institute of Hypertension School of Research.

National Institute of Management Counsellors.

National Institute of Oilseed Products.

National Institute of Senior Housing., c/o National Council on the Aging, 409 Third St. S.W., 2nd Fl. Washington, DC 20024. Phone: (202)479-6654 Fax: (202)479-0735 E-mail: info@ncoa.org • URL: http://www.ncoa.org • Members are organizations and individuals concerned with the housing needs of older persons. Provides information on the development and management of housing suitable for the elderly.

National Institute on Community-Based Long-Term Care., c/o National Council on the Aging, 409 Third St., S.W., Suite 200 Washington, DC 20024. Phone: (202)479-1200 Fax: (202)479-0735 E-mail: info@ncoa.org • URL: http://www.ncoa.org • Affiliated with the National Council on the Aging. Seeks to promote and develop a comprehensive long-term health care system.

National Insulation Association.

National Insurance Association.

National Insurance Law Review. CCH/NILS Publishing Co., P.O. Box 2507 Chatsworth, CA 91313. Phone: 800-423-5910 or (818)998-8830 Fax: (818)718-8482 Quarterly. $95.00 per year. Contains insurance-related articles from major law reviews.

National Interfaith Coalition on Aging.

National Interstate Council of State Boards of Cosmetology.

National Investor Relations Institute.

National Jeweler. Miller Freeman, Inc., One Penn Plaza New York, NY 10119-1198. Phone: (212)714-1300 Fax: (212)714-1313 E-mail: mfibooks@mfi.com • URL: http://www.mfi.com • 24 times a year. $100.00 per year. For jewelry retailers.

National Journal: The Weekly on Politics and Government. National Journal Group, Inc., 1501 M St. N.W., Suite 300 Washington, DC 20005. Phone: 800-424-2921 or (202)739-8400 Fax: (202)739-8580 E-mail: trials@njdc.com • URL: http://www.nationaljournal.com • Semiweekly. $1,197.00 per year. Includes semiannual supplement *Capital Source*. A non-partisan weekly magazine on politics and government.

National Kitchen and Bath Association.

National Knitwear and Sportswear Association.

National Law Journal: The Weekly Newspaper for the Profession. American Lawyer Media, L.P., 345 Park Ave., S. New York, NY 10010-1707. Phone: 800-888-8300 or (212)779-9200 E-mail: catalog@amlaw.com • URL: http://www.americanlawyermedia.com • Weekly. $158.00 per year. News and analysis of the latest developments in the law and the law profession.

National Lawyers Guild.

National League of Cities.

National Legal Aid and Defender Association.

National Library of Medicine (NLM). National Institutes of Health (NIH)Phone: 888-346-3656 or (301)496-1131 Fax: (301)480-3537 E-mail: access@nlm.nih.gov • URL: http://www.nlm.nih.gov • NLM Web site offers free access through MEDLINE (''PubMed'') to about nine million references to articles appearing in some 3,800 biomedical journals, with abstracts. Search interfaces range from ''simple keywords to advanced Boolean expressions.'' The NLM site offers many links to other sources of biomedical and technical information (the National Center for Biotechnology Information, for example). Fees: Free.

National Licensed Beverage Association-Members Directory. National Licensed Beverage Association, 20 S. Quaker Lane Suite 230 Alexandria, VA 22314. Phone: 800-441-9894 or (703)751-9730 Fax: (703)751-9748 E-mail: nlba-mail@nlba.org • URL: http://www.nlba.org • Annual. $40.00.

National Locksmith. National Publishing Co., 1533 Burgundy Parkway Streamwood, IL 60107. Phone: (708)837-2044 Monthly. $41.00.

National Lubricating Grease Institute.

National Luggage Dealers Association.

National Lumber and Building Materials Dealers Association.

National Management Association.

National Marine Manufacturers Association.

National Marine Representatives Association.

National Marine Representatives Association-Directory. National Marine Representatives Association, P.O. Box 360 Gurnee, IL 60031. Phone: (847)662-3167 Fax: (847)336-7126 Annual. Membership. Approximately 400 independent representatives selling pleasure craft and other small boats, motors, and marine accessories.

National Materials Advisory Board.

National Meat Canners Association.

National Mental Health Association.

National Mining Association.

National Minority Supplier Development Council.

National Mortgage News. Faulkner and Gray, 11 Penn Plaza, 17th Fl. New York, NY 10001. Phone: 800-535-8403 or (212)967-7000 Fax: (212)967-7155 E-mail: orders@faulknergray.com • URL: http://www.faulknergray.com • Weekly. $198.00 per year. Newsletter.

National Motor Freight Traffic Association.

National Newspaper Association.

National Newspaper Index. The Gale Group, 27500 Drake Rd. Farmington Hills, MI 48331-3535. Phone: 800-877-GALE or (248)699-GALE Fax: 800-414-5043 or (248)699-8069 E-mail: galeord@gale.com • URL: http://www.gale.com • Citations to news items in five major newspapers, 1970 to present. Weekly updates. Inquire as to online cost and availability.

National Newspaper Index CD-ROM. The Gale Group, 27500 Drake Rd. Farmington Hills, MI 48331-3535. Phone: 800-877-GALE or (248)699-GALE Fax: 800-414-5043 or (248)669-8069 E-mail: galeord@gale • URL: http://www.gale.com • Monthly. Provides comprehensive CD-ROM indexing of all material appearing in the late edition of the *New York Times*, the final edition of the *Washington Post*, the national edition of the *Christian Science Monitor*, the home edition of the *Los Angeles Times*, and the *Wall Street Journal*. Time period is four years. Also available online.

National Newspaper Publishers Association.

National Notary. National Notary Association, P.O. Box 2024 Chatsworth, CA 91313-2402. Phone: 800-876-6827 or (818)739-4000 Fax: (818)700-0920 E-mail: nna@nationalnotary.org • URL: http://www.nationalnotary.org • Bimonthly. $34.00 per year.

National Notary Association.

National Nutritional Foods Association.

National Ocean Industries Association.

National Oilseed Processors Association.

National Onion Association.

National Opinion Research Center.

National Optometric Association.

National Organization for Men., 11 Park Place, Ste. 1100 New York, NY 10007. Phone: (212)686-6253 or (212)766-4030 Fax: (212)791-3056 URL: http://www.tnom.com • Encourages rational and objective state and national divorce laws.

National Organization for Women.

National Packing News. Jack W. Soward, P.O. Box 1349 Murphys, CA 95247-1349. Phone: (209)728-1455 Fax: (209)728-3277 Monthly. $25.00 per year. Newsletter for food processing executives. Covers production, marketing, new products, new processing plants, research news, news of personnel, etc. Formerly *Eastern Packing News* and *Western Packing News*.

National Paint and Coatings Association.

National Paper Trade Association.

National Paperbox Association.

National Paperbox Association Membership Directory. National Paperbox Association, 801 N. Fairfax St., Sui0te 211 Alexandria, VA 22314-1757. Phone: (703)684-2212 Fax: (703)683-6920 E-mail: boxmaker@paperbox.org • URL: http://www.paperbox.org • Annual. $125.00.

National Park Hospitality Association.

National Parking Association.

National Parliamentarian. National Association of Parliamentarians, 213 S. Main St. Independence, MO 64050-3808. Phone: 888-627-2929 or (816)833-3892 Fax: (816)833-3893 E-mail: ffgpooa@prodigy.com • URL: http://www.parlimentarians.org • Quarterly. $20.00 per year. Articles and questions with answers on parliamentary procedure.

National Partnership for Women and Families., 1875 Connecticut Ave., N. W., Suite 710 Washington, DC 20009. Phone: (202)986-2600 Fax: (202)986-2539 E-mail: info@nationalpartnership.org • URL: http://www.nationalpartnership.org • Includes a Counseling on Employment Discrimination Committee. Offers telephone referral services.

National Pasta Association.

National Pasta Association FYI Newsletter. National Pasta Association, 2101 Wilson Blvd., No. 920 Arlington, VA 22201. Phone: (703)841-0818 Fax: (703)528-6507 E-mail: npa@ilovepasta.org • URL: http://www.ilovepasta.org • Weekly. Membership.

National Peach Council.

National Pecan Shellers Association.

National Pest Control Association.

National Petrochemical and Refiners Association.

National Petroleum Council.

National Pharmaceutical Association., 107 Kilmayne Dr., Ste. C Cary, NC 27511. Phone: 800-944-6742 or (919)831-5368 Fax: (919)469-5870 A professional society of African-American pharmacists and pharmacy students.

National Pharmaceutical Council., 1894 Preston White Dr. Reston, VA 20191. Phone: (703)620-6390 Fax: (703)476-0904 URL: http://www.npcnow.org • Members are drug manufacturers producing prescription medication.

National Plumbing Code Handbook. R. Dodge Woodson. McGraw-Hill, 1221 Ave of the Americas New York, NY 10020-1095. Phone: 800-722-4726 or (212)904-2000 Fax: (212)904-2072 E-mail: customer.service@mcgraw-hill.com • URL: http://www.mcgraw-hill.com • 1997. $49.95. Second revised edition.

National Policy Association.

National Pork Producers Council.

National Ports and Waterways Institute.

National Potato Council.

National Prepared Food Association.

National Press Club.

National Press Photographers Association.

National Private Truck Council.

National Productivity Review: The Journal of Productivity Management. John Wiley and Sons, Inc., Journals Div., 605 Third Ave. New York, NY 10158-0012. Phone: 800-526-5368 Fax: (212)850-6088 E-mail: info@wiley.com • URL: http://www.wiley.com • Quarterly. Institutions, $345.00 per year.

National Propane Gas Association.

National Property Management Association.

The National Provisioner: Serving Meat, Poultry, and Seafood Processors. Stagnito Communications, Inc., 1935 Shermer Rd., Suite 100 Northwood, IL 60062. Phone: (847)205-5660 Fax: (847)205-5680 E-mail: info@stagnito.com • URL: http://www.stagnito.com • Monthly. Free to qualified personnel; others, $65.00 per year. Annual *Buyer's Guide* available. Meat, poultry and seafood newsletter.

National Public Accountant. National Society of Accountants, 1010 N. Fairfax St. Alexandria, VA 22314-1574. Phone: 800-966-6679 or (703)549-6400 Fax: (703)549-2984 E-mail: nsa@wizard.net • URL: http://www.nspa.org/ • Monthly. Free to members; non-members, $18.00 per year. For accounting and tax practitioners.

National Ready Mixed Concrete Association.

National Real Estate Index. CB Richard Ellis, 353 Sacramento St., Suite 1900 San Francisco, CA 94111. Phone: 800-992-7257 or (415)986-7255 URL: http://www.realestateindex.com • Price and frequency on application. Provides reports on commercial real estate prices, rents, capitalization rates, and trends in more than 65 metropolitan areas. Time span is 12 years. Includes urban office buildings, suburban offices, warehouses, retail properties, and apartments.

National Real Estate Investor. Intertec Publishing Corp., 6151 Powers Ferry Rd., N.W., Suite 200 Atlanta, GA 30339-2941. Phone: 800-400-5945 or (770)955-2500 E-mail: subs@intertec.com • URL: http://www.intertec.com • Monthly. $85.00 per year. Includes annual *Directory*. Market surveys by city.

National Real Estate Investor Sourcebook. Intertec Publishing Corp., 6151 Powers Ferry Rd., N.W., Suite 200 Atlanta, GA 30339. Phone: 800-400-5945 or (770)955-2500 Fax: 800-400-5945 or (770)618-0476 E-mail: subs@intertec.com • URL: http://www.nreionline.com • Annual. $79.95. List about 7,000 companies and individuals in eighteen real estate fields. Formerly *National Real Estate Investor Directory*.

National Records Management Council.

National Recreation and Park Association.

National Recreation and Park Association., 22377 Belmont Ridge Rd. Ashburn, VA 20148-4501. Phone: 800-626-6772 or (703)858-0784 Fax: (703)858-0794 E-mail: info@nrpa.org • Monthly. Individuals, $28.00 per year; libraries, $35.00 per year. *Buyer's Guide* available.

National Referral Roster: The Nation's Directory of Residential Real Estate Firms. Stamats Communications, Inc., 615 5th St., S.E. Cedar Rapids, IA 54206-1888. Phone: 800-553-8878 or (319)364-6167 Fax: (319)365-5421 E-mail: infoequest@stamats.com • URL: http://www.stamats.com • Annual. $50.00. Formerly *National Roster of Realtors*.

National Registration Center for Study Abroad., P.O. Box 1393 Milwaukee, WI 53201. Phone: (414)278-7410 Fax: (414)271-8884 E-mail: info@nrcsa.com • URL: http://www.nrcsa.com • Members are foreign universities, foreign language institutions, and other institutions or organizations offering foreign study programs designed for North Americans.

National Regulatory Research Institute.

National Rehabilitation Information Center.

National Renderers Association.

National Research Council.

National Restaurant Association.

National Restaurant Association Educational Foundation.

National Retail Federation.

National Retail Hardware Association.

National Retail Hardware Association Management Report: Cost of Doing Business Survey. National Retail Hardware Association, 5822 W. 74th St. Indianapolis, IN 46278. Phone: 800-772-4424 or (317)290-0338 Fax: (317)328-4354 E-mail: nrha@lquest.net • URL: http://www.nrha.org • Annual. Members, $49.00; non-members, $98.00.

National Rifle Association of America.

National Roofing Contractors Association.

National Rural Electric Cooperative Association.

National Rural Housing Coalition.

National Safe Workplace Institute/safeplaces.com.

National Safety Council.

National Sales Tax Rate Directory. Vertex Systems, Inc., 1041 Old Cassatt Rd. Berwyn, PA 19312-1151. Phone: (610)640-4200 Looseleaf, with monthly updates. $585.00 Per year. Provides state, county, city, and special sales tax rates for all states.

National Sash and Door Jobbers Association., 10047 Robert Trent Jones Parkway New Port Richey, FL 34655-4649. Phone: 800-786-7274 or (727)372-3665 Fax: (727)372-2879 E-mail: info@nsdja.com • URL: http://www.nsdja.com • Members are wholesale distributors of door and window products.

National Scholastic Press Association. University of Minnesota

National School Boards Association.

National School Supply and Equipment Association.

National Selected Morticians.

National Shellfisheries Association.

National Shoe Retailers Association.

National Shooting Sports Foundation.

National Small Business United.

National Society for Experiential Education., 1703 N. Beauregard St. Alexandria, VA 22311-1717. Phone: (919)787-3263 Fax: (919)787-3381 E-mail: info@nsee.org • URL: http://www.nsee.org • Members include representatives of internship programs.

National Society for the Study of Education Yearbook. National Society for the Study of Education. University of Chicago Press, Journals Div., P.O. Box 37005 Chicago, IL 60637. Phone: 800-621-2736 or (773)753-3347 Fax: (773)702-0248 E-mail: subscriptions@journals.uchicago.edu • URL: http://www.journals.uchicago.edu • Annual. Membership. Two volumes per year.

National Society of Fund Raising Executives.

National Society of Public Accountants.

National Society of Public Accountants - Yearbook. National Society of Accountants, 1010 N. Fairfax St. Alexandria, VA 22314-1574. Phone: 800-966-6679 or (703)549-6400 Fax: (703)549-2984 E-mail: nsa@wizard.net • URL: http://www.nspa.org • Annual. Free to members, government agencies and libraries; not available to others

National Soft Drink Association.

National Soil Dynamics Laboratory-U.S. Dept. of Agriculture Agricultural Research Service.

National Solid Waste Management Association.

National Solid Waste Management Association Directory of Professional Services. National Solid Wastes Management Association, 4301 Connecticut Ave., N.W., Suite 300 Washington, DC 20008. Phone: 800-424-2869 or (202)244-4700 Fax: (202)966-4868 Annual. Lists waste management consulting firms.

National Spa and Pool Institute., 2111 Eisenhower Ave. Alexandria, VA 22314. Phone: (703)838-0083 Fax: (703)549-0493 E-mail: memberserviceinfo@nspi.org • URL: http://www.nspi.org • Members include a wide variety of business firms and individuals involved in some way with health spas, swimming pools, or hot tubs.

National Speakers Association.

National Sporting Goods Association.

National Sports Law Institute., Marquette University Law School, P.O. Box 1881 Milwaukee, WI 53201-1881. Phone: (414)288-5815 Fax: (414)288-5818 E-mail: anderson@vms.csd.mu.edu • URL: http://www.marquette.edu/law/sports/sports.htm • Promotes ethical practices in amateur and professional sports activities.

National Sportscasters and Sportswriters Association., P.O. Box 559 Salisbury, NC 28144. Phone: (704)633-4275 Fax: (704)633-4275 Members are sportswriters and radio/TV sportscasters.

National Stock Summary. National Quotation Bureau, Inc., 150 Commerce Rd. Cedar Grove, NJ 07009-1208. Phone: (201)239-6100 Fax: (201)239-0080 Monthly. $480.00 per year. Semiannual cumulations. Includes price quotes for both active and inactive issues, with transfer agents, market makers (brokers), and other information. (The National Quotation Bureau also provides daily and weekly stock price services.)

National Stone Association.

National Student Employment Association.

National Survey of State Laws. The Gale Group, 27500 Drake Rd. Farmington Hills, MI 48331-3535. Phone: 800-877-GALE or (248)699-GALE Fax: 800-414-5043 or (248)699-8069 E-mail: galeord@galegroup.com • URL: http://www.galegroup.com • 1999. $85.00. Third edition. Provides concise state-by-state comparisons of current state laws on a wide variety of topics. Includes references to specific codes or statutes.

National Tank Truck Carrier Directory. National Tank Truck Carriers, Inc., 2200 Mill Rd. Alexandria, VA 22314-4677. Phone: (703)838-1960 Fax: (703)684-5753 Annual. Members, $54.00; non-members, $80.00. For-hire tank truck carriers.

National Tank Truck Carriers.

National Tax Association.

National Tax Association Proceedings of the Annual Conference. National Tax Association, 725 15th St., N.W., Suite 600 Washington, DC 20005-2109. Phone: (202)737-3325 Fax: (202)737-7308 Annual. Members, $85.00; individuals, $70.00; libraries, $90.00.

National Tax Journal. National Tax Association - Tax Institute of America, 725 15th St., N.W., Suite No. 600 Washington, DC 20005-2109. Phone: (202)737-3325 Fax: (202)737-7308 Quarterly. Members, $85.00 per year; membership libraries, $100.00 per year; membership corporations, $130.00 per year. Topics of current interest in the field of taxation and public finance in the U.S. and foreign countries.

National Taxpayers Union.

National Technical Services Association.

National Telephone Cooperative Association., 4121 Wilson Blvd., 10th Fl. Arlington, VA 22203. Phone: (703)351-2000 E-mail: frs@ntca.com • Members are telephone cooperatives and statewide associations.

National Tile Roofing Manufacturers Association., P.O. Box 40337 Eugene, OR 97404-0049. Phone: (541)689-0366 Fax: (541)689-5530 E-mail: rolson@ntrma.org • URL: http://www.ntrma.org • Members are producers of clay and concrete tile roofing.

National Tooling and Machining Association.

National Tour Association.

National Trade and Professional Associations of the United States. Columbia Books, Inc., 1212 New York Ave., N.W., Suite 330 Washington, DC 20005. Phone: 888-265-0600 or (202)898-0662 Fax: (202)898-0775 E-mail: info@columbiabooks.com • URL: http://www.columbiabooks.com • Annual. $99.00. Provides key facts on approximately 7,500 trade associations, labor and professional organizations. Formerly *National Trade and Professional Association of the United States and Labor Unions*.

National Trade Data Bank: The Export Connection. U. S. Department of Commerce, Economics and Statistics Administration, Office of Business Analysis Washington, DC 20230. Phone: (202)482-1986 Fax: (202)482-2164 Monthly. $575.00 per year. Provides over 150,000 trade-related data series on CD-ROM. Includes full text of many government publications. Specific data is included on national income, labor, price indexes, foreign exchange, technical standards, and international markets. Website address is http://www.stat-usa.gov/

National Treasury Employees Union.

National Truck Equipment Association.

National Truck Equipment Association Membership Roster and Product Directory. National Truck Equipment Association, 37400 Hills Tech Dr. Farmington Hills, MI 48331-3414. Phone: 800-441-6832 or (248)489-7090 Fax: (248)489-8950 E-mail: info@tea.com • URL: http://www.ntea.com • Annual. $50.00. Provides company information and products for over 850 of the nation's commercial truck body and equipment manufacturers and distributors.

National Turkey Federation.

National Underwriter. The National Underwriter Co., 505 Gest St. Cincinnati, OH 45202-1716. Phone: 800-543-0874 or (513)721-2140 Fax: (513)721-0126 URL: http://www.nuco.com • Weekly. Two editions: *Life* or *Health*. $83.00 per year, each edition.

National Underwriter, Property and Casualty Edition. The National Underwriter Co., 505 Gest St. Cincinnati, OH 45203-1716. Phone: 800-543-0874 or (513)721-2140 Fax: (513)721-0126 URL: http://www.nuco.com • Weekly. $88.00 per year.

National Urban League.

National Venture Capital Association., 1655 N. Fort Myer Dr., Suite 850 Arlington, VA 22209. Phone: (703)524-2549 Fax: (703)524-3940 URL: http://www.nvca.org • Members are providers of venture capital.

National Water Conditions. U.S. Geological Survey, 12201 Sunrise Valley Dr. Reston, VA 20192. Phone: (703)648-4000 URL: http://www.usgs.gov/major-sites.html • Monthly. Free.

National Water Resources Association.

National Waterways Conference.

National Welding Supply Association.

National Wellness Institute, Inc.

National Wholesale Druggists' Association.

National Wildlife Federation.

National Women's Economic Alliance Foundation., 1001 D St., No. 1000 Washington, DC 20003-1830. Phone: (202)863-8689 Promotes dialogue between executive level women and men.

National Women's Law Center., 11 Dupont Circle, N.W., Suite 800 Washington, DC 20036. Phone: (202)588-5180 Fax: (202)588-5185 E-mail: nwlcinfo@aol.com • Seeks protection and advancement of women's legal rights. Includes employment issues among areas of interest.

National Wool Marketing Corporation.

National Writers Association.

National Writers Association.

National Youth Employment Coalition.

Nation's Cities Weekly. National League of Cities, 1301 Pennsylvania Ave., N.W. Washington, DC 20004-1763. Phone: (202)626-3000 Fax: (202)626-3043 E-mail: pa@nlc.org • URL: http://www.nlc.org • Weekly. $96.00 per year. Topics covered by special issues include city budgets, surface transportation, water supply, economic development, finances, telecommunications, and computers.

Nations of the World: A Political, Economic, and Business Handbook. Grey House Publishing, 185 Millerton Rd. Millerton, NY 12546. Phone: 800-562-2139 or (518)789-8700 Fax: (518)789-0556 E-mail: books@greyhouse.com • URL: http://www.greyhouse.com • 2000. $135.00. Includes descriptive data on economic characteristics, population, gross domestic product (GDP), banking, inflation, agriculture, tourism, and other factors. Covers "all the nations of the world."

Nation's Restaurant News: The Newspaper of the Food Service Industry. Lebhar-Friedman, Inc., 425 Park Ave. New York, NY 10022. Phone: 800-766-6999 or (212)756-5000 Fax: (212)756-5250 E-mail: info@lf.com • URL: http://www.nrn.com • 50 times a year. $39.95 per year.

Nationwide Directory of Gift, Housewares and Home Textiles Buyers. Salesman's Guide, 2807 N. Parham Rd., Ste. 200 Richmond, VA 23294. Phone: 800-223-1719 or (804)762-4455 Fax: (804)935-0271 E-mail: eblank@douglaspublications.com • URL: http://www.salesmansguide.com • Annual. $195.00.

Nationwide Directory of Major Mass Market Merchandisers. Salesman's Guide, 2807 N. Parham Rd., Ste. 200 Richmond, VA 23294. Phone: 800-223-1797 or (804)762-4455 Fax: (804)935-0271 E-mail: eblank@douglaspublications.com • URL: http://www.salesmanguide.com • Annual. $179.95. Lists buyers of clothing for major retailers. (Does not include the metropolitan New York City area.)

Nationwide Directory of Men's and Boys' Wear Buyers. Salesman's Guide, 2807 N. Parham Ave., Ste. 200 Richmond, VA 23294. Phone: 800-223-1797 or (804)762-4455 Fax: (804)935-0271 E-mail: eblank@douglaspublications.com • URL: http://www.salesmansguide.com • Annual. $229.00. About 6,000 retail stores selling men's and boys' clothing, sportswear, furnishings, and accessories; coverage does not include New York metropolitan area.

Nationwide Directory of Sporting Goods Buyers. Salesman's Guide, 2807 N. Parham Rd., Ste. 200 Richmond, VA 23294. Phone: 800-223-1797 or (804)762-4455 Fax: (804)935-0271 E-mail: eblank@douglaspublications.com • URL: http://www.salesmansguide.com • Annual. $209.00. About 9,000 retail stores selling athletic and recreational equipment, footwear, apparel.

Nationwide Directory of Women's and Children's Wear Buyers. Salesman's Guide, 2807 N. Parham Rd., Ste. 200 Richmond, VA 23294. Phone: 800-223-1797 or (804)762-4455 Fax: (804)935-0271 E-mail: eblank@douglaspublications.com • URL: http://www.salesmansguide.com • Annual. $229.00. About 7,200 retail stores selling women's dresses, coats, sportswear, intimate apparel, and women's accessories, infants' to teens wear, and accessories; coverage does not include New York metropolitan area.

NATO News. National Association of Theatre Owners, 4605 Lankershim Blvd., No. 340 North Hollywood, CA 91602. Phone: (818)506-1778 Fax: (818)506-0269 Monthly. $65.00 per year. Newsletter. Highlights industry trends and activities. Formerly *NATO News and Views*.

NATPE International-Programmer's Guide. National Association of Television Program Executives, 2425 Olympic Blvd., Suite 600E Santa Monica, CA 90404. Phone: (310)453-4440 Fax: (310)453-5258 URL: http://www.natpe.org/ • Annual. $75.00 per copy. Lists production and distribution companies with titles of TV series or shows that each company provides. Includes categorized indexes of programs. Formerly *NATPE Programmer's Guide*.

NATPE: Pocket Guides Reps Groups Distributors. National Association of Television Program Executives, 2425 Olympic Blvd., Suite 600E Santa Monica, CA 90404. Phone: (310)453-4440 Fax: (310)453-5258 URL: http://www.natpe.org/ • Semiannual. Price on application. Includes station representatives, group owners (with stations owned), and program distributors.

Natural Dyes and Home Dyeing. Rita J. Adrosko. Dover Publications, Inc., 31 E. Second St. Mineola, NY 11501. Phone: 800-223-3130 or (516)294-7000 Fax: (516)742-5049 1971. $5.95.

Natural Energy Services Association.

Natural Food Associates., 8345 Walnut Hill Lane, Suite 225 Dallas, TX 75231-4205. Members are professionals and consumers interested in natural foods and organic farming.

Natural Gas Monthly. Energy Information Administration. Available from U.S. Government Printing Office, Washington, DC 20402. Phone: (202)512-1800 Fax: (202)512-2250 E-mail: gpoaccess@gpo.gov • URL: http://www.access.gpo.gov • Monthly. $89.00 per year. Annual cumulation. State and national data on production, storage, imports, exports and consumption of natural gas.

Natural Gas: The Monthly Journal for Producers, Marketers, Pipeline, Distributors and End Users. John Wiley and Sons, Inc., Journals Div., 605 Third Ave. New York, NY 10158-0012. Phone: 800-526-5368 Fax: (212)850-6088 E-mail: info@wiley.com • URL: http://www.wiley.com • Monthly. Institution, $649.00 per year. Newsletter. Covers business, economic, regulatory, and high-technology news relating to the natural gas industry.

Natural Resources Defense Council., 40 W. 20th St. New York, NY 10011. Phone: (212)727-2700 Fax: (212)727-1773 E-mail: nrdcinfo@nrdc.org • URL: http://www.nrdc.org • Studies the use of the judicial system to enforce environmental protection laws.

The Natural Resources Journal. University of New Mexico School of Law, 1117 Stanford, N.E. Albuquerque, NM 87131-1431. Phone: (505)277-4820 Fax: (505)277-4165 Quarterly. $40.00 per year.

Nature and Resources: International News about Research on Environment, Resources, and Conservation of Nature. Parthenon Publishing Group, P.O. Box 1564 Pearl River, NY 10564. Phone: (914)735-9363 Fax: (914)735-1385 Quarterly. $92.00 per year.

The Nature of Recreation: A Handbook in Honor of Frederick Law Olmsted. Richard S. Wurman and others. MIT Press, Five Cambridge Center Cambridge, MA 02142-1493. Phone: 800-356-0343 or (617)253-5646 Fax: (617)253-6779 E-mail: journals-orders@mit.edu • URL: http://www.mitpress.mit.edu • 1972. $12.95.

NAUMD News. National Association of Uniform Manufacturers and Distributors, 1156 Ave. of the Americas New York, NY 10036. Phone: (212)869-0670 Fax: (212)575-2847 Three times a year. Price on application.

Naval Affairs: In the Interest of the Enlisted Active Duty Reserve, and Retired Personnel of the U.S. Navy, Marine Corps and Coast Guard. Fleet Reserve Association, 125 N. West St. Alexandria, VA 22314-2754. Phone: (703)683-1400 Fax: (703)549-6610 E-mail: news-fra@fra.org • URL: http://www.fra.org • Free to members; non-members, $7.00 per year.

Naval Aviation News. Chief of Naval Operations Bureau of Aeronautics. Available from U.S. Government Printing Office, Washington, DC 20402. Phone: (202)512-1800 Fax: (202)512-2250 E-mail: gpoaccess@gpo.gov • URL: http://www.access.gpo.gov • Bimonthly. $16.00 per year. Articles on all phases on Navy and Marine activity.

Naval Engineers Journal. American Society of Naval Engineers, Inc., 1452 Duke St. Alexandria, VA 22314. Phone: (703)836-6727 Fax: (703)836-7491 E-mail: asnehq@navalengineers.org • URL: http://www.navalengineers.org • Bimonthly. $100 per year.

Naval Historical Foundation.

Naval Research Logistics: An International Journal. John Wiley and Sons, Inc., Journals Div., 605 Third Ave. New York, NY 10158-0012. Phone: 800-526-5368 or (212)850-6645 Fax: (212)850-6088 E-mail: info@wiley.com • URL: http://www.wiley.com • Eight times a year. $945.00 per year.

Naval Review: Annual Review of World Seapower. U.S. Naval Institute. Naval Institute Press, 291 Wood Rd. Annapolis, MD 21402. Phone: 800-223-8764 or (410)268-6110 Fax: (410)295-1084 E-mail: customer@usni.org • URL: http://www.usni.org • Annual. Price on application. Covers the previous year's events. May issue of *U.S. Naval Institute Proceedings*.

Navy Club of the United States of America.

Navy League of the United States.

Navy Supply Corps Newsletter. Available from U. S. Government Printing Office, Washington, DC 20402. Phone: (202)512-1800 Fax: (202)512-2250 E-mail: gpoaccess@gpo.gov • URL: http://www.access.gpo.gov • Bimonthly. $20.00 per year. Newsletter issued by U. S. Navy Supply Systems Command. Provides news of Navy supplies and stores activities.

Navy Times: Marine Corps, Navy, Coast Guard. Army Times Publishing Co., 6883 Commercial Dr. Springfield, VA 22159-0240. Phone: 800-368-5718 or (703)750-8646 Fax: (703)750-8607 URL: http://www.armytimes.com • Weekly. $52.00 per year. In two editions: Domestic and International.

NAWE: Advancing Women in Higher Education.

NCBA Membership Roster. National Candy Brokers Association, 710 East Ogden Ave., Suite 600 Naperville, IL 60563-8603. Phone: (630)369-2406 Fax: (630)369-2488 E-mail: ncba@b-online.com • URL: http://www.candynet.com • Annual. $25.00. Lists broker, manufacturer, and distributor members of the National Candy Brokers Association.

NCJRS: National Criminal Justice Reference Service. U.S. Department of Justice, P.O. Box 6000 Rockville, MD 20849-6000. Phone: 800-851-3420 or (301)251-5500 Fax: (301)251-5212 References print and non-print information on law enforcement and criminal justice, 1972 to present. Monthly updates. Inquire as to online cost and availability.

The NCO Guide. Robert L. Rush. Stackpole Books, Inc., 5067 Ritter Rd. Mechanicsburg, PA 17055. Phone: 800-732-3669 or (717)769-0411 Fax: (717)796-0412 E-mail: sales@stackpolebooks.com • URL: http://www.stackpolebooks.com • 1999. $18.95. edition.

NDA Pipeline(New Drug Approval). F-D-C Reports, Inc., 5550 Friendship Blvd., Suite 1 Chevy Chase, MD 20815-7278. Phone: 800-332-2181 or (301)657-9830 Fax: (301)664-7238 URL: http://www.fdcreports.com • Annual. $965.00. Provides information on U. S. drugs in the development stage and products receiving new drug approval (NDA) from the Food and Drug Administration. Listings are company-by-company and by generic name, with orphan drug designations. Includes an industry directory.

NDT and E International; The Independent Journal of Non-Destructive Testing. Elsevier Science, 655 Ave. of the

Americas New York, NY 10010. Phone: 888-437-4636 or (212)989-5800 Fax: (212)633-3680 E-mail: usinfo@elsevier.comp • URL: http://www.elsevier.com • Eight times a year. $596.00 per year. Formerly *NDT International*.

Nebraska Farmer. Nebraska Farmer Co. Farm Progress Cos., 191 S. Gary Ave. Carol Stream, IL 60188. Phone: (630)690-5600 Fax: (630)462-2869 15 times a year. $19.95 per year.

Negotiating and Influencing Skills: The Art of Creating and Claiming Value. Brad McRae. Sage Publications, Inc., 2455 Teller Rd. Thousand Oaks, CA 91320. Phone: (805)499-0721 Fax: (805)499-0871 E-mail: info@sagepub.com • URL: http://www.sagepub.com • 1997. $42.00. Presents a practical approach to various circumstances, based on the Harvard Project on Negotiation. Chapters include "Dealing with Difficult People and Difficult Situations." Contains a bibliography and glossary of terms.

Negotiating for Business Results. Judith E. Fisher. McGraw-Hill Professional, 1221 Ave. of the Americas New York, NY 10020-1095. Phone: 800-722-4726 or (212)904-2000 Fax: (212)904-2072 E-mail: customer.service@mcgraw-hill.com • URL: http://www.mcgraw-hill.com • 1993. $10.95. (Business Skills Express Series).

Negotiating to Settlement in Divorce. Sanford N. Katz, editor. Aspen Law and Business, 1185 Ave. of the Americas New York, NY 10036. Phone: 800-444-1717 or (212)597-0200 Fax: 800-901-9075 or (212)597-0338 E-mail: customer.service@aspenpubl.com • URL: http://www.aspenpub.com • 1987. $75.00. Looseleaf service.

Negotiation. Roy J. Lewicki and others. McGraw-Hill Higher Education, 1221 Ave. of the Americas New York, NY 10020-1095. Phone: 800-722-4726 or (212)904-2000 Fax: (212)904-2072 E-mail: customer.service@mcgraw-hill.com • URL: http://www.mcgraw-hill.com • 1994. $51.95. Second edition.

Negotiation Basics: Concepts, Skills, and Exercises. Ralph A. Johnson. Sage Publications, Inc., 2455 Teller Rd. Thousand Oaks, CA 91320. Phone: (805)499-0721 Fax: (805)499-0871 E-mail: info@sagepub.com • URL: http://www.sagepub.com • 1993. $42.00. Topics include goal building, the role of information, cost-benefit decision making, strategy, and creating a positive negotiating climate.

Negotiation Journal: On the Process of Dispute Settlement. Program on Negotiation. Plenum Publishing Corp., 233 Spring St. New York, NY 10013-1578. Phone: 800-221-9369 or (212)620-8000 Fax: (212)463-0742 E-mail: info@plenum.com • URL: http://www.plenum.com • Quarterly. $330.00 per year.

Negotiation: Strategies for Mutual Gain - The Basic Seminar of the Harvard Program on Negotiation. Lavina Hall, editor. Sage Publications, Inc., 2455 Teller Rd. Thousand Oaks, CA 91320. Phone: (805)499-0721 Fax: (805)499-0871 E-mail: info@sagepub.com • URL: http://www.sagepub.com • 1992. $48.00. Fourteen contributors provide practical advice on the art of negotiation.

Neighborhood Cleaners Association International., 252 West 29th St., 2nd Fl. New York, NY 10001-5201. Phone: (212)967-3002 Fax: (212)967-2242 Members are dry cleaning establishments.

Nelson's Directory of Institutional Real Estate. Wiesenberger/Thomson Financial, 1455 Research Blvd. Rockville, MD 20850. Phone: 888-371-4575 or (301)545-4000 Fax: (301)545-6400 E-mail: wiespubs@tfn.com • URL: http://www.wiesenberger.com • Annual. $335.00. Includes real estate investment managers, service firms, consultants, real estate investment trusts (REITs), and various institutional investors in real estate.

Nelson's Directory of Investment Managers. Wiesenberger/Thomson Financial, 1455 Research Blvd. Rockville, MD 20850. Phone: 888-371-4575 or (301)545-4000 Fax: (301)545-6400 E-mail: wiespubs@tfn.com • URL: http://www.wiesenberger.com • Annual. $545.00. Three volumes. Provides information on 2,600 investment management firms, both U.S. and foreign.

Nelson's Directory of Investment Research. Wiesenberger/Thomson Financial, 1455 Research Blvd. Rockville, MD 20850. Phone: 888-371-4575 or (301)545-4000 Fax: (301)545-6400 E-mail: wiespubs@tfn.com • URL: http://www.wiesenberger.com • Annual. $590.00. Three volumes. Provides information on 10,000 investment research analysts at more than 800 firms. Indexes include company name, industry, and name of person.

Nelson's Directory of Pension Fund Consultants. Wiesenberger/Thomson Financial, 1455 Research Blvd. Rockville, MD 20850. Phone: 888-371-4575 or (301)545-4000 Fax: (301)545-6400 E-mail: wiespubs@tfn.com • URL: http://www.wiesenberger.com • Annual. $350.00. Covers the pension plan sponsor industry. More than 325 worldwide consulting firms are described.

Nelson's Directory of Plan Sponsors. Wiesenberger/Thomson Financial, 1455 Research Blvd. Rockville, MD 20850. Phone: 888-371-4575 or (301)545-4000 Fax: (301)545-6400 E-mail: wiespubs@tfn.com • URL: http://www.wiesenberger.com • Annual. $545.00. Three volumes. Available in two versions, alphabetic or geographic. Covers pension plan sponsors and pension funds, including more than 11,000 corporate funds, 4,000 endowment or foundation funds, 1,300 multi-employer funds, 1,000 hospital funds, and 900 public employee funds. Includes information on asset allocation and investment style. Eight indexes.

NERAC, Inc.

Net Curriculum: An Educator's Guide to Using the Internet. Linda Joseph. Information Today, Inc., 143 Old Marlton Pike Medford, NJ 08055-8750. Phone: 800-300-9868 or (609)654-6266 Fax: (609)654-4309 E-mail: custserv@infotoday.com • URL: http://www.infotoday.com • 1999. $29.95. Covers various educational aspects of the Internet. Written for K-12 teachers, librarians, and media specialists by a columnist for *Multimedia Schools*. (CyberAge Books.)

Net Income: Cut Costs, Boost Profits, and Enhance Operations Online. Wally Bock and Jeff Senne. John Wiley and Sons, Inc., 605 Third Ave. New York, NY 10158-0012. Phone: 800-225-5945 or (212)850-6000 Fax: (212)850-6088 E-mail: info@wiley.com • URL: http://www.wiley.com • 1997. $29.95. "Net Income" in this case is hoped-for Internet income. Promotes the use of the Internet, intranet, and extranet to improve business operations or start new businesses. The authors take a nontechnical, business strategy approach.

The Net: The Ultimate Guide to the Internet. Imagine Publishing, Inc., 150 North Hill Dr. Brisbane, CA 94005. Phone: 800-706-9500 or (415)468-4869 Fax: (415)656-2486 E-mail: editor@bootnet.com • URL: http://www.bootnet.com • Monthly. $24.95 per year. Consumer magazine for users of the Internet. Features reviews and ratings of Internet software, sites (destinations), and publications. Includes articles on basic procedures for beginners.

net.people: The Personalities and Passions Behind the Web Sites. Eric C. Steinert and Thomas E. Bleier. Information Today, Inc., 143 Old Marlton Pike Medford, NJ 08055-8750. Phone: 800-300-9868 or (609)654-6266 Fax: (609)654-4309 E-mail: custserv@infotoday.com • URL: http://www.infotoday.com • 2000. $19.95. Presents the personal stories of 36 Web "entrepreneurs and visionaries." (CyberAge Books.)

NetResearch: Finding Information Online. Daniel J. Barrett. Thomson Learning, 7625 Empire Dr. Florence, KY 41042. Phone: 800-347-7707 or (606)525-6620 Fax: (606)525-0978 URL: http://www.thomsonlearning.com • 1997. $24.95. A guide to "power searching" on the Internet, with emphasis on the intricacies of search engines.

NetSavvy: Building Information Literacy in the Classroom. Ian Jukes and others. Phi Delta Kappa International, 408 North Union St. Bloomington, IN 47405. Phone: 800-766-1156 or (812)339-1156 Fax: (812)339-0018 E-mail: headquarters@pdkintl.org • URL: http://www.pdkintl.org • 2000. $27.95. Second edition. Provides practical advice on the teaching of computer, Internet, and technological literacy. Includes sample lesson plans and grade-level objectives.

Network Buyers Guide. Miller Freeman, 600 Harrison St. San Francisco, CA 94107. Phone: (415)905-2200 Fax: (415)905-2232 E-mail: mfibooks@mfi.com • URL: http://www.mfi.com • Annual. $5.00. Lists suppliers of products for local and wide area computer networks. Formerly *LAN Buyers Guide Issue*.

Network Computing: Computing in a Network Environment. CMP Publications, Inc., 600 Community Dr. Manhasset, NY 11030. Phone: 800-577-5356 or (516)562-5000 Fax: (516)733-6916 URL: http://www.cmpnet.com • Semimonthly. $95.00 per year

Network: Strategies and Solutions for the Network Professional. Miller Freeman, 600 Harrison St. San Francisco, CA 94107. Phone: 800-227-4675 or (415)905-2200 Fax: (415)905-2232 URL: http://www.mfi.com • Monthly. $29.95 per year. Covers network products and peripherals for computer professionals. Includes annual network managers salary survey and annual directory issue. Formerly *LAN: The Network Solutions Magazine*.

Network World: The Newsweekly of Enterprise Network Computing. Network World Inc., 118 Turnpike Rd. Southborough, MA 01772. Phone: 800-622-1108 or (508)460-3333 Fax: (508)460-6438 URL: http://www.nwfusion • Weekly. $129.00 per year. Includes special feature issues on enterprise Internets, network operating systems, network management, high-speed modems, LAN management systems, and Internet access providers.

Networking Windows for Workgroups. Barry Nance. John Wiley and Sons, Inc., 605 Third Ave. New York, NY 10158-0012. Phone: 800-225-5945 or (212)850-6000 Fax: (212)850-6088 E-mail: info@wiley.com • URL: http://www.wiley.com • 1993. $22.95. Designed for small businesses or small groups. Covers the installation and troubleshooting of local area networks using Microsoft's Windows for Workgroups.

Networking with the Affluent and Their Advisers. Thomas J. Stanley. McGraw-Hill Professional, 1221 Ave. of the Americas New York, NY 10020. Phone: 800-722-4726 or (212)904-2000 Fax: (212)904-2072 E-mail: customer.service@mcgraw-hill.com • URL: http://www.mcgraw-hill.com • 1993. $17.95. Discusses specific methods of prospecting for wealthy clients, with examples.

Never Call Your Broker on Monday: And 300 Other Financial Lessons You Can't Afford Not to Know. Nancy Dunnan. HarperCollins Publishers, 10 E. 53rd St. New York, NY 10022-5299. Phone: 800-242-7737 or (212)207-7000 Fax: 800-822-4090 or (212)207-7145 URL: http://www.harpercollins.com • 1996. $8.50. Presents a wide range of personal finance advice, covering investments, insurance, wills, credit, real estate, etc.

New and Breaking Technologies in the Pharmaceutical and Medical Device Industries. Theta Reports/PJB Medical Publications, Inc., 1775 Broadway, Suite 511 New York, NY 10019. Phone: (212)262-8230 Fax: (212)262-8234 E-mail: customerservice@thetareports.com • URL: http://www.thetareports.com • 1999. $1,695.00. Market research data. Includes forecasts of medical technology and drug developments to 2005-2010.

New and Breaking Technologies in the Pharmaceutical and Medical Device Industries. Theta Reports/PJB Medical Publications, Inc., 1775 Broadway, Suite 511 New York, NY 10019. Phone: (212)262-8230 Fax: (212)262-8234 E-mail: customerservice@thetareports.com • URL: http://www.thetareports.com • 1999. $1,695.00. Contains market research predictions of medical technology trends over the next 5 to 10 years (2004-2009), including developments in biotechnology, genetic engineering, medical device technology, therapeutic vaccines, non-invasive diagnostics, and minimally-invasive surgery. (Theta Report No. 931.)

A New Archetype for Competitive Intelligence. John J. McGonagle and Carolyn M. Vella. Greenwood Publishing Group, Inc., 88 Post Rd., W. Westport, CT 06881-5007. Phone: 800-225-5800 or (203)226-3571 Fax: (203)222-2540 E-mail: bookinfo@greenwood.com • URL: http://www.greenwood.com • 1996. $59.95. Covers competitive intelligence, strategic intelligence, market intelligence, defensive intelligence, and cyber-intelligence. Includes an overview of sources and techniques for data gathering. A bibliography, glossary, and index are provided.

New Business Incorporations. Dun & Bradstreet, Economic Analysis Dept., Three Sylvan Way Parisppany, NJ 07054-3896. Phone: 800-526-0651 or (973)455-0900 Fax: (973)254-4063 E-mail: customerservice@dnb.com • URL: http://www.dnb.com • Monthly. $25.00 per year. Gives the number of new business incorporations in each of the 50 states. Includes commentary.

New Century Family Money Book: Your Comprehensive Guide to a Lifetime of Financial Security. Jonathan D. Pond. Dell Publishing Co., Inc., 1540 Broadway New York, NY 10036-4094. Phone: 800-223-6834 or (212)354-6500 Fax: (212)492-9698 1995. $19.95.

New Choices: Living Even Better After Fifty. Reader's Digest Association, Inc., 260 Madison Ave. New York, NY 10016. Phone: 800-388-6111 or (212)696-2303 Fax: (212)696-5031 E-mail: newchoices@readersdigest.com • URL: http://www.newchoices.com • 10 times a year. $18.97 per year. Formerly *New Choices for Retirement Living*.

The New Commonsense Guide to Mutual Funds. Mary Rowland. Bloomberg Press, 100 Business Park Dr. Princeton, NJ 08542-0888. Phone: 800-388-2749 or (609)279-4670 Fax: (609)279-7155 E-mail: press@bloomberg.com • URL: http://www.bloomberg.com • 1998. $15.95. Revised edition. Includes "Do's and Don'ts" for mutual fund investors. (Bloomberg Personal Bookshelf Series).

New Competitor Intelligence: The Complete Resource for Finding, Analyzing, and Using Information About Your Competitors. Leonard M. Fuld. John Wiley and Sons, Inc., 605 Third Ave. New York, NY 10158-0012. Phone: 800-225-5945 or (212)850-6000 Fax: (212)850-6088 E-mail: info@wiley.com • URL: http://www.wiley.com • 1994. $80.50. Second edition. Topics include data sources, strategy, analysis of competition, and how to establish a competitive intelligence system.

The New Complete Job Search. Richard H. Beatty. John Wiley and Sons, Inc., 605 Third Ave. New York, NY 10158-0012. Phone: 800-225-5945 or (212)850-6000 Fax: (212)850-6088 E-mail: info@wiley.com • URL: http://www.wiley.com • 1992. $12.95. Tells how to conduct an effective job hunting campaign. Resumes, making contacts, interviews, and decision-making are discussed.

The New Direct Marketing: How to Implement a Profit-Driven Database Marketing Strategy. Spepard, Davis, Associates Staff. McGraw-Hill Professional, 1221 Ave. of the Americas New York, NY 10020-1095. Phone: 800-722-4726 or (212)904-2000 Fax: (212)904-2072 E-mail: customer.service@mcgraw-hill.com • URL: http://www.mcgraw-hill.com • 1998. $114.95. Third edition. Discusses the construction, analysis, practical use, and evaluation of direct marketing databases containing primary and/or secondary data.

New Directions for Higher Education. Jossey-Bass, 350 Sansome St. San Francisco, CA 94104-1342. Phone: 888-378-2337 or (415)433-1740 Fax: (415)433-0499 URL: http://www.josseybass.com • Quarterly. Institutions, $114.00 per year. Sample issue free to librarians.

New Encyclopedia of Real Estate Forms. Jerome S. Gross. Prentice Hall, 240 Frisch Court Paramus, NJ 07652-5240. Phone: 800-947-7700 or (201)909-6200 Fax: 800-445-6991 or (201)909-6361 URL: http://www.prenhall.com • 1983. $59.95.

New England Journal of Medicine. Massachusetts Medical Society, Publishing Div., 860 Winter St. Waltham, MA 02451-1411. Phone: 800-843-6356 URL: http://www.nejm.org • Weekly. Individuals, $135.00 per year; institutions, $349.00 per year. The offical journal of the Massachusetts Medical Society.

New Equipment Digest Market. Penton Media Inc., 1300 E. Ninth St. Cleveland, OH 44114. Phone: (216)696-7000 Fax: (216)696-0836 E-mail: corpcomm@penton.com • URL: http://www.penton.com • Monthly. Free to qualified personnel; others, $55.00 per year. Formerly *Material Handling Engineering*.

New Equipment Reporter: New Products Industrial News. De Roche Publications, 12 Del Italia Irvine, CA 92714-5355. Monthly. Controlled circulation.

The New Face of Credit Risk Management: Balancing Growth and Credit Quality in an Integrated Risk Management Environment. Charles B. Wendel. Robert Morris Associates, One Liberty Place, 1650 Market St., Suite 2300 Philadelphia, PA 19103. Phone: 800-677-7621 or (215)446-4000 Fax: (215)446-4100 E-mail: info@rmahq.org • URL: http://www.rmahq.org • 1999. $65.00. Contains ''In-depth interviews with senior credit officers from five major financial institutions.'' Coverage includes modeling, scoring, and other technology related to the management of credit risk.

New Federal Graduated Withholding Tax Tables. CCH, Inc., 4025 W. Peterson Ave. Chicago, IL 60646-6085. Phone: 800-248-3248 or (773)866-6000 Fax: 800-224-8299 or (773)866-3608 URL: http://www.cch.com • Annual.

The New Finance: The Case Against Efficient Markets. Robert A. Haugen. Prentice Hall, 240 Frisch Court Paramus, NJ 07652-5240. Phone: 800-947-7700 or (201)909-6452 Fax: 800-445-6991 or (201)909-6361 URL: http://www.prenhall.com • 1999. $26.20. Second edition.

New-Format Digital Television. Available from MarketResearch.com, 641 Ave. of the Americas, 3rd Fl. New York, NY 10011. Phone: 800-298-5699 or (212)807-2629 Fax: (212)807-2716 E-mail: order@marketresearch.com • URL: http://www.marketresearch.com • 1999. $3,995.00. Market research data. Published by Fuji- Keizai USA. Covers the developing U. S. market for digital TV.

The New Guide to Identity: How to Create and Sustain Change Through Managing Identity. Wally Olins. Ashgate Publishing Co., Old Post Rd. Brookfield, VT 05036-9704. Phone: 800-535-9544 or (802)276-3162 Fax: (802)276-3837 1996. $22.95. A guide to corporate identity through the effective use of industrial design and graphics. Includes color illustrations.

New Hacker's Dictionary. Eric S. Raymond. MIT Press, Five Cambridge Center Cambridge, MA 02142. Phone: 800-356-0343 or (617)253-5646 Fax: (617)253-6779 E-mail: mitpress-orders@.edu • URL: http://www.mitpress.mit.edu • 1996. $39.00. Third edition. Includes three classifications of hacker communication: slang, jargon, and ''techspeak.''

New Horizons. Employee Involvement Association, 525 S.W. Fifth St., Suite A Des Moines, IA 50309. Phone: (515)282-8192 Fax: (515)282-9117 E-mail: eia@assoc-mgmt.com • URL: http://www.eia.com • Quarterly. Membership. Newsletter.

A New Housing Policy for America: Recapturing the American Dream. David C. Schwartz and others. Temple University Press, 1601 N. Broad St., University Services Bldg., Room 305 Philadelphia, PA 19122-6099. Phone: 800-447-1656 or (215)204-8787 Fax: (215)204-4719 E-mail: tempress@astro.ocis.temple.edu • URL: http://www.temple.edu/tempress • 1988. $24.95.

The New Internet Business Book. Jill H. Ellsworth and Matthew V. Ellsworth. John Wiley and Sons, Inc., 605 Third Ave. New York, NY 10158-0012. Phone: 800-225-5945 or (212)850-6000 Fax: (212)850-6088 E-mail: info@wiley.com • URL: http://www.wiley.com • 1996. $24.95. Second edition. A basic guide to internet business opportunities and market research.

New Introduction to Bibliography. Philip Gaskell. Oak Knoll Press, 310 Delaware St. Newcastle, DE 19720. Phone: 800-996-2556 or (302)328-7232 Fax: (302)328-7274 E-mail: oakknoll@oakknoll.com • URL: http://www.oakknoll.com • 1996. $29.95.

New Issues: The Investor's Guide to Initial Public Offerings. Norman G. Fosback. Institute for Econometric Research, 2200 S.W. 10th St. Fort Lauderdale, FL 33442-8799. Phone: 800-442-0066 or (954)421-1000 Fax: (954)570-8200 Monthly. $200.00 per year. Newsletter. Includes ''Penny Stock Calendar''.

The New Library Scene. Library Binding Institute, 5241 Lincoln Dr., Apt. 321 Edina, MN 55436-2703. E-mail: sallymoyter@lbinders.org • URL: http://www.lbibinders.org • Quarterly. $24.00 per year.

New Media Market Place and New Media Titles. Waterlow New Media Information, 6-14 Underwood St. New York, NY 10010. Phone: 800-221-2123 or (212)689-9200 Fax: (212)689-9711 E-mail: grove@grovereference.com • URL: http://www.grovereference.com • 1996. $155.00. Provides a wide variety of information on multimedia industries, including CD-ROM publishing, digital video, interactive TV, portable information products, and video CD. Includes industry review articles, interviews, market data, profiles of 2,000 multimedia companies, product directories, and a bibliography.

New Mexico Agricultural Experiment Station. New Mexico State University

New Mexico Engineering Research Institute. University of New Mexico

New Office: Designs for Corporations, People, and Technology. Karin Tetlow. PBC International, One School St. Glen Cove, NY 11542. Phone: 800-527-2826 or (516)676-2727 Fax: (516)676-2738 1997. $47.50. Includes 200 color pictures by leading international photographers.

New One-Family Houses Sold. Available from U. S. Government Printing Office, Washington, DC 20402. Phone: (202)512-1800 Fax: (202)512-2250 E-mail: gpoaccess@gpo.gov • URL: http://www.access.gpo.gov • Monthly. $45.00 per year. Bureau of the Census Construction Report, C25. Provides data on new, privately-owned, one-family homes sold during the month and for sale at the end of the month.

New Ophthalmology: Treatments and Technologies. Theta Reports/PJB Medical Publications, Inc., 1775 Broadway, Suite 511 New York, NY 10019. Phone: (212)262-8230 Fax: (212)262-8234 E-mail: customerservice@thetareports.com • URL: http://www.thetareports.com • 2000. $1,695. Provides market research data relating to eye surgery, including LASIK, cataract surgery, and associated technology. (Theta Report No. 911.)

The New Palgrave Dictionary of Money and Finance. Peter Newman and others, editors. Groves Dictionaries, 345 Park Ave. S., 10th Fl. New York, NY 10010. Phone: 800-221-2123 or (212)689-9200 Fax: (212)689-9711 E-mail: grove@grovereference.com • URL: http://www.grovereference.com • 1998. $550.00. Three volumes. Consists of signed essays on over 1,000 financial topics, each with a bibliography. Covers a wide variety of financial, monetary, and investment areas. A detailed subject index is provided.

New Plant Report. Conway Data Inc., 35 Technology Parkway, Suite 150 Norcross, GA 30092-9990. Phone: (770)446-6996 Fax: (770)263-8825 URL: http://www.sitenet.com • Monthly. $1,800.00 per year. Provides geographical listings of annoucements of corporate facility location plans and facility expansions. International coverage.

New Product Announcements Plus. The Gale Group, 27500 Drake Rd. Farmington Hills, MI 48331-3535. Phone: 800-877-GALE or 800-699-GALE Fax: 800-414-5043 or (248)699-8069 E-mail: galeord@gale.com • URL: http://www.gale.com • Contains the full text of new product and corporate activity press releases, with special emphasis on high technology and emerging industries. Covers 1985 to date. Weekly updates. Inquire as to online cost and availability.

New Product Development and Marketing: A Practical Guide. Italo S. Servi. Greenwood Publishing Group, Inc., 88 Post Rd., W. Westport, CT 06881-5007. Phone: 800-225-5800 or (203)226-3571 Fax: (203)222-2540 E-mail: bookinfo@greenwood.com • URL: http://www.greenwood.com • 1990. $55.00. Looseleaf. A practical guide to the creation, testing, and marketing of a new product.

New Product Development Checklists: From Mission to Market. George Gruenwald. NTC/Contemporary Publishing, P.O. Box 545 Blacklick, OH 43004. Phone: 800-338-3987 or (614)755-4151 Fax: (614)755-5645 E-mail: ntcpub@mcgraw-hill.com • URL: http://www.ntc-cb.com • 1994. $22.95. (NTC Business Book Series).

New Products Management. Merle C. Crawford. McGraw-Hill Higher Education, 1221 Ave. of the Americas New York, NY 10020-1095. Phone: 800-722-4726 or (212)904-2000 Fax: (212)904-2072 E-mail: customer.service@mcgraw-hill.com • URL: http://www.mcgraw-hill.com • 1996. $86.25. Fifth edition.

The New Publicity Kit. Jeanette Smith. John Wiley and Sons, Inc., 605 Third Ave. New York, NY 10158-0012. Phone: 800-225-5945 or (212)850-6000 Fax: (212)850-6088 E-mail: info@wiley.com • URL: http://www.wiley.com • 1995. $19.95 multi-media campaigns, and other forms of publicity.

New Research Centers. The Gale Group, 27500 Drake Rd. Farmington Hills, MI 48331-3535. Phone: 800-877-GALE or (248)699-GALE Fax: 800-414-5043 or (248)699-8069 E-mail: galeord@galegroup.com • URL: http://www.galegroup.com • 2000. $395.00. A supplement to *Research Centers Directory*.

New Riders' Official World Wide Web Yellow Pages. Pearson Education and Technology, 201 W. 103rd St. Indianapolis, IN 46290. Phone: 800-428-5331 or (317)581-3500 Fax: (317)581-4670 URL: http://www.mcp.com • 1997. $34.99. A broadly classified listing of Web sites, with brief descriptions of sites and a subject index to narrower topics. Includes a guide to using the Internet and a separate, alphabetical listing of more than 1,500 college and university Web sites, both U. S. and foreign. Includes CD-ROM.

The New Science of Technical Analysis. Thomas R. DeMark. John Wiley and Sons, Inc., 605 Third Ave. New York, NY 10158-0012. Phone: 800-225-5945 or (212)850-6000 Fax: (212)850-6088 E-mail: info@wiley.com • URL: http://www.wiley.com • 1994. $59.95. (Wiley Finance Editions Series).

New Steel: Mini and Integrated Mill Management and Technologies. Cahners Business Information, 2000 Clearwater Dr. Oak Brook, IL 60523-8809. Phone: 800-695-1214 or (630)320-7000 Fax: (630)462-2862 E-mail: corporatecommunications@cahners.com • URL: http://www.cahners.com • Monthly. $89.00 per year. Covers the primary metals industry, both ferrous and nonferrous. Includes technical, marketing, and product development articles. Formerly *Iron Age*.

New Technical Books: A Selective List With Descriptive Annotations. New York Public Library Science and Technology Research Center, Fifth Ave. and 42nd St., Room 120 New York, NY 10018. Phone: (212)930-0920 Fax: (212)869-7824 Bimonthly. $30.00 per year.

The New Technical Trader: Boost Your Profit by Plugging into the Latest Indicators. Tushar S. Chande and Stanley Kroll. John Wiley and Sons, Inc., 605 Third Ave. New York, NY 10158-0012. Phone: 800-225-5945 or (212)850-6000 Fax: (212)850-6088 E-mail: info@wiley.com • URL: http://www.wiley.com • 1994. $64.95. (Finance Edition Series).

New Technologies and the Employment of Disabled Persons. H. Allan Hunt and Monroe Berkowitz, editors. International Labour Office, 1828 L St., N.W., Suite 801 Washington, DC 20036. Phone: (202)653-7652 Fax: (202)653-7687 E-mail: ilopubs@tascol.com • URL: http://www.ilo.org/pubns • 1992. $18.00. Discusses the development and use of new technologies to create job opportunities for the disabled in various countries.

New Uses for Obsolete Buildings. Urban Land Institute, 1025 Thomas Jefferson St., N. W., Suite 500 W. Washington, DC 20007-5201. Phone: 800-321-5011 or (202)624-7000 Fax: (202)624-7140 E-mail: bookstore@uli.org • URL: http://www.uli.org • 1996. $64.95. Covers various aspects of redevelopment: zoning, building codes, environment, economics, financing, and marketing. Includes eight case studies and 75 descriptions of completed ''adaptive use projects.''

New Uses of Sulfur-II. Douglas Bourne, editor. American Chemical Society, 1155 16th St., N.W. Washington, DC 20036. Phone: 800-333-9511 or (202)872-4600 Fax: (202)872-4615 E-mail: seervice@acs.org • URL: http://www.pubs.acs.org • 1978. $32.95. (Advances in Chemistry Series: No. 165).

New Venture Creation: Entrepreneurship for the 21st Century. Jeffrey A. Timmons and others. McGraw-Hill Professional, 2120 Ave. of the Americas New York, NY 10020-1095. Phone: 800-722-4726 or (212)904-2000 Fax: (212)904-2072 E-mail: customer.service@mcgraw-hill.com • URL: http://www.mcgraw-hill.com • 1998. Fifth edition. Price on application.

New Woman. Rodale Press, Inc., 733 Third Ave. New York, NY 10017. Phone: 800-627-2557 or (212)745-0100 URL: http://www.newwomanonline.co.uk • Monthly. $27.60 per year.

The New Working Woman's Guide to Retirement Planning. Martha P. Patterson. University of Pennsylvania Press, 4200 Pine St. Philadelphia, PA 19104-4011. Phone: 800-445-9880 or (215)898-6261 Fax: (215)898-0404 E-mail: custserv@pobox.upenn.edu • URL: http://www.upenn.edu/press • 1999. $17.50. Second edition. Provides retirement advice for employed women, including information on various kinds of IRAs, cash balance and other pension plans, 401(k) plans, and social security. Four case studies are provided to illustrate retirement planning at specific life and career stages.

New York Botanical Garden Illustrated Encyclopedia of Horticulture. Thomas H. Everett. Garland Publishing, Inc., 19 Union Square West, 8th Fl. New York, NY 10003-3382. Phone: 800-627-6273 or (212)414-0650 Fax: (212)414-0659 E-mail: info@garland.com • URL: http://www.garlandpub.com • 1980. $1,070.00. Ten volumes.

New York Genealogical and Biographical Society.

New York Mercantile Exchange.

New York No-Fault Arbitration Reports. American Arbitration Association, 335 Madison Ave. New York, NY 10017-5905. Phone: 800-778-7879 or (212)484-4000 Fax: (212)541-4841 URL: http://www.adr.org • Monthly. $90.00 per year. Looseleaf. Clear and concise summaries of cases dealing with important issues in the field. Back issues available.

New York Public Library Book of Chronologies. Bruce Wetterau. Pearson Education and Technology, 201 W. 103rd. St. Indianapolis, IN 46290-1097. Phone: 800-858-7674 or (317)581-3500 URL: http://www.mcp.com • 1994. $16.00.

The New York Public Library Writer's Guide to Style and Usage. Andrea Sutcliffe, editor. HarperCollins Publishers, 10 E. 53rd St. New York, NY 10022-5299. Phone:

800-242-7737 or (212)207-7000 Fax: 800-822-4090 or (212)207-7145 URL: http://www.harpercollins.com • 1994. $40.00

New York Society of Security Analysts.

New York State Agricultural Experiment Station. Cornell University

New York Stock Exchange.

New York Stock Exchange Fact Book. Available from Hoover's, Inc., 1033 La Posada Dr., Suite 250 Austin, TX 78752. Phone: 800-486-8666 or (512)374-4500 Fax: (512)374-4501 E-mail: orders@hoovers.com • URL: http://www.hoovers.com • Annual. $9.95. Published by the New York Stock Exchange, Inc. Contains statistical data relating to the New York Stock Exchange. Includes information on new listings and name changes.

New York Stock Exchange Guide. CCH, Inc., 4025 W. Peterson Ave. Chicago, IL 60646-6085. Phone: 800-835-5224 or (773)866-6000 Fax: 800-224-8299 or (773)866-3608 URL: http://www.cch.com • Monthly. $634.00 per year.

The New York Times. New York Times Co., 229 W. 43rd St. New York, NY 10036. Phone: 800-631-2580 or (212)556-1234 Fax: (212)556-4603 URL: http://www.nytimes.com • Daily. $374.40 per year. Supplements available: *New York Times Book Review*, *New York Times Magazine*, *Sophisticated Traveler* and *Fashions of the Times*.

The New York Times Biographical File. New York Times Online Services, 520 Speedwell Ave Morris Plains, NY 07950. Phone: (973)829-0036 Fax: (973)829-0999 Makes available online the full text of more than 15,000 biographies that have appeared in *The New York Times* from 1980 to the present. Updating is weekly. Inquire as to online cost and availability.

The New York Times Biographical Service. UMI, 300 N. Zeeb Rd. Ann Arbor, MI 48106-1346. Phone: 800-521-0600 or (313)761-4700 Fax: 800-864-0019 URL: http://www.umi.com • Monthly. Price on application.

New York Times Book Review. New York Times Co., 229 W. 43rd St. New York, NY 10036. Phone: 800-631-2580 or (212)556-1234 Fax: (212)556-4603 URL: http://www.nytimes.com/books • Weekly. $54.60 per year. Supplement to *New York Times*.

The New York Times Manual of Style and Usage. Allan M. Siegal and William G. Connolly, editors. Times Books, 201 E. 50th St. New York, NY 10022. Phone: 800-726-0600 or (212)751-2600 Fax: (212)572-8797 URL: http://www.randomhouse.com • 1999. $30.00. A revised and expanded version of the 1976 manual edited by Lewis Jordan.

The New York Times Ondisc. New York Times Online Services, 520 Speedwell Ave. Morris Plains, NJ 07950. Phone: (973)829-0036 Fax: (973)829-0999 URL: http://www.nytimes.com • Monthly. $2,650.00 per year. CD-ROM discs contain the full text of *The New York Times*, final edition. Inquire as to time period covered and availability of backfiles.

New York University Annual Institute on Federal Taxation. Melvin Cornfield. Matthew Bender & Co., Inc., Two Park Ave. New York, NY 10016. Phone: 800-223-1940 or (212)448-2000 Fax: (212)244-3188 E-mail: international@bender.com • URL: http://www.bender.com • Annual. Looseleaf service. Price on application. (New York University School of Continuing Education Series).

The New Yorker Book of Business Cartoons from the New Yorker. Robert Mankoff, editor. Bloomberg Press, 100 Business Park Dr. Princeton, NJ 08542-0888. Phone: 800-388-2749 or (609)279-4670 Fax: (609)279-7155 E-mail: press@bloomberg.com • URL: http://www.bloomberg.com • 1998. $21.95. Contains reprints of 110 cartoons relating to business and finance. Artists are Charles Addams, George Booth, Roz Chast, William Hamilton, Edward Sorel, and other *New Yorker* cartoonists.

Newcomen Society of the United States.

NewMedia: The Magazine for Creators of the Digital Future. HyperMedia Communications, Inc., 901 Mariner's Island Blvd., Suite 365 San Mateo, CA 94404. Phone: 800-253-6641 or (650)573-5170 Fax: (650)573-7446 E-mail: edit@newmedia.com • URL: http://www.newmedia.com • Monthly. $29.95 per year. Edited for multimedia professionals, with emphasis on digital video and Internet graphics, including animation. Contains reviews of new products. Formerly *NewMedia Age*.

News for Family Farmers and Rural Americans. Farmers Educational and Cooperative Union of America, 400 Virginia Ave., S.W., Suite 710 Washington, DC 20024. Phone: (202)554-1600 Fax: (202)554-1654 Monthly. $10.00 per year. Formerly *National Farmers Union Washington Newsletter*.

News from OECD. Available from OECD Publications and Information Center, 2001 L St., N.W.., Suite 650 Washington, DC 20036-4922. Phone: 800-456-6323 or (202)785-6323 Fax: (202)785-0350 E-mail: washington.contact@oecd.org • URL: http://www.oecd.org • Monthly. Free. Lists OECD's calender of activities.

News Media Yellow Book: Who's Who Among Reporters, Writers, Editors, and Producers in the Leading National News Media. Leadership Directories, Inc., 104 Fifth Ave., 2nd Fl. New York, NY 10011. Phone: (212)627-4140 Fax: (212)645-6931 E-mail: info@leadershipdirectories.com • URL: http://www.leadershipdirectories.com • Quarterly. $305.00 per year. Lists the staffs of major newspapers and news magazines, TV and radio networks, news services and bureaus, and feature syndicates. Includes syndicated columnists and programs. Seven specialized indexes are provided.

News Photographer: Dedicated to the Service and Advancement of News Photography. National Press Photographers Association, Inc., 3200 Croasdaile Dr., Suite 306 Durham, NC 27705. Phone: (919)383-7246 Fax: (919)383-7261 E-mail: nppa@mindspring.org • URL: http://www.nppa.org • Monthly. $38.00 per year.

Newsbank. Newsbank, Inc., 58 Pine St. New Canaan, CT 06840-5426. Phone: (203)966-1100 Fax: (203)966-6254 Monthly. Price varies. Quarterly and annual cumulations. Index to articles of current interest from over 500 U.S. newspapers. Full text available on microfiche

Newsbreak. Leather Industries of America, 1000 Thomas Jefferson St., N.W. Washington, DC 20007. Phone: (202)342-8086 Fax: (202)342-9063 Free to members and other qualified personnel. Reports on issues and events in the luggage industry.

NewsInc.: The Business of the Newspapers Business. The Cole Group, P.O. Box 3426 Daly City, CA 94015-0426. Phone: (650)994-2100 Fax: (650)994-2108 E-mail: info@colegroup.com • URL: http://www.colegroup.com/newsinc/ • Biweekly. $425.00 per year. Newsletter. Reports on trends in mass media, especially with regard to newspaper publishing. Articles on cable TV and other competitive media are included.

Newsletter Database. The Gale Group, 27500 Drake Rd. Farmington Hills, MI 48331-3535. Phone: 800-877-GALE or (248)699-GALE Fax: 800-414-5043 or (248)699-8069 E-mail: galeord@gale.com • URL: http://www.gale.com • Contains the full text of about 600 U. S. and international newsletters covering a wide range of business and industrial topics. Time period is 1988 to date, with daily updates. Inquire as to online cost and availability.

Newsletter on Newsletters: Reporting on the Newsletter World: Editing, Graphics, Management, Promotion, Newsletter Reviews, and Surveys., 89 Valley St. East Providence, RI 02914. Phone: (401)431-2381 Fax: (401)435-3328 E-mail: bradinal@aol.com • Bimonthly. $196.00 per year.

Newsletter Publishers Association.

Newsletter Publishing. Entrepreneur Media, Inc., 2392 Morse Ave. Irvine, CA 92714. Phone: 800-421-2300 or (949)261-2325 Fax: (949)851-9088 E-mail: entmag@entrepreneurmag.com • URL: http://www.entrepreneurmag.com • Looseleaf. $59.50. A practical guide to starting a newsletter. Covers profit potential, start-up costs, market size evaluation, pricing, accounting, advertising, promotion, etc. (Start-Up Business Guide No. E1067.)

Newsletters in Print. The Gale Group, 27500 Drake Rd. Farmington Hills, MI 48331-3535. Phone: 800-877-GALE or (248)699-GALE Fax: 800-414-5043 or (248)699-8069 E-mail: galeord@galegroup.com • URL: http://www.galegroup.com • 2000. $285.00. 14th edition. Details 11,500 sources of information on a wide range of topics.

Newsline: Research News from the U. S. Travel Data Center. Travel Industry Association of America, 1100 New York Ave., N. W., Suite 450 Washington, DC 20005-3934. Phone: (202)408-8422 Fax: (202)408-1255 E-mail: membership@tia.org • URL: http://www.tia.org • Monthly. $55.00 per year. Newsletter. Covers trends in the U. S. travel industry.

Newsmakers. The Gale Group, 27500 Drake Rd. Farmington Hills, MI 48331-3535. Phone: 800-877-GALE or (248)699-GALE Fax: 800-414-5043 E-mail: galeord@galegroup.com • URL: http://www.galegroup.com • Annual. $145.00. Three softbound issues and one hardbound annual. Biographical information on individuals currently in the news. Includes photographs. Formerly *Contemporary Newsmakers*.

Newspaper Abstracts Ondisc. Bell & Howell Information and Learning, 300 North Zeeb Rd. Ann Arbor, MI 48103. Phone: 800-521-0600 or (734)761-4700 Fax: 800-864-0019 URL: http://www.umi.com • Monthly. $2,950.00 per year (covers 1989 to date; archival discs are available for 1985-88). Provides cover-to-cover CD-ROM indexing and abstracting of 19 major newspapers, including the *New York Times, Wall Street Journal, Washington Post, Chicago Tribune,* and *Los Angeles Times*.

Newspaper Advertising Source. SRDS, 1700 Higgins Rd. Des Plaines, IL 60018. Phone: 800-851-7737 or (847)375-5000 Fax: (847)375-5001 E-mail: srobe@srds.com • URL: http://www.srds.com • Monthly. $662.00 per year. Lists newspapers geographically, with detailed information on advertising rates, special features, personnel, circulation, etc. Includes a section on college newspapers. Also provides consumer market data for population, households, income, and retail sales. Formerly *Newspaper Rates and Data*.

Newspaper and Periodical Abstracts. Bell & Howell Information and Learning, 300 North Zeeb Rd. Ann Arbor, MI 48103. Phone: 800-521-0600 or (734)761-4700 Fax: 800-864-0019 URL: http://www.umi.com • Provides online coverage (citations and abstracts) of 25 major newspapers, 1,600 perodicals, and 70 TV programs. Covers business, economics, current affairs, health, fitness, sports, education, technology, government, consumer affairs, psychology, the arts, and the social sciences. Time period is 1986 to date, with daily updates. Inquire as to online cost and availability.

Newspaper Association of America: Newspaper Advertising Planbook. Newspaper Association of America, 1921 Gallows Rd., Suite 600 Vienna, VA 22182-3900. Phone: (703)902-1600 Fax: (703)917-0636 URL: http://www.naa.org • Annual. Price on application. Formerly *Newspaper Advertising Bureau. Newspaper Advertising Planbook*.

Newspaper Designer's Handbook. Timothy Harrower. McGraw-Hill Higher Education, 1221 Ave. of the Americas New York, NY 10020-1095. Phone: 800-722-4726 or (212)904-2000 Fax: (212)904-2072 E-mail: customer.service@mcgraw-hill.com • URL: http://www.mcgraw-hill.com • 1997. $28.25. Fourth edition.

Newspaper Financial Executives Journal. International Newspaper Financial Executives, 21525 Ridgetop Circle, Suite 200 Sterling, VA 20166-6510. Phone: (703)648-1160 Fax: (703)476-5961 10 times a year. $100.00. Provides financially related information to newspaper executives.

The Newspaper Guild.

Nexis.com. Lexis-Nexis GroupPhone: 800-227-4908 or (937)865-6800 Fax: (937)865-6909 E-mail: webmaster@prod.lexis-nexis.com • URL: http://www.nexis.com • Fee-based Web site offers searching of about 2.8 billion documents in some 30,000 news, business, and legal information sources. Features include a subject directory covering 1,200 topics in 34 categories and a Company Dossier containing information on more than 500,000 public and private companies. Boolean searching is offered.

NFAIS Yearbook of the Information Industry. Arthur W. Elias, editor. Information Today, Inc., 143 Old Marlton Pike Medford, NJ 08055-8750. Phone: 800-300-9868 or (609)654-6266 Fax: (609)654-4309 E-mail: custserv@infotoday.com • URL: http://www.infotoday.com • 1993. $40.00. Compiled by the National Federation of Abstracting and Information Services (NFAIS). Summarizes and analyzes the impacts of each year's events on information, abstracting, and indexing activities.

NFDA Directory of Members and Resource Guide. NFDA Publications, Inc., 13625 Bishops Dr. Brookfield, WI 53005-6600. Phone: 800-228-6332 or (262)541-2500 Fax: (262)541-1909 E-mail: nfda@nfda.org • URL: http://www.nfda.org • Annual. $75.00. 20,000 members of state funeral director associations affiliated with the National Funeral Directors Association. Formerly *National Funeral Directors Association-Membership Listing and Resources*.

NFPA Buyer's Guide. National Fire Protection Association, One Batterymarch Park Quincy, MA 02269. Phone: 800-344-3555 or (617)770-3000 Fax: (617)770-0700 E-mail: library@nfpa.org • URL: http://www.nfpa.org • Annual. $12.00. Listing of fire protection equipment manufacturers. Formerly *Fire Protection Reference Directory*.

NFPA Journal. National Fire Protection Association, One Batterymarch Park Quincy, MA 02269. Phone: 800-344-3555 or (617)770-3000 Fax: (617)770-0700 E-mail: library@nfpa.org • URL: http://www.nfpa.org • Bimonthly. Membership. Incorporates *Fire Journal* and *Fire Command*.

NHLA Newsletter. National Hardwood Lumber Association, P. O. Box 34518 Memphis, TN 38184-0518. Phone: 800-933-0318 or (901)377-1818 Fax: (901)382-6419 E-mail: nhla@natlhardwood.org • URL: http://www.natlhardwood.org • Monthly. Membership. Newsletter on hardwood products, industry trends, and legislation.

Nichols Cyclopedia of Legal Forms: Annotated; 1925-1990. West Group, P.O. Box 64526 Eagan, MN 55123. Phone: 800-328-9352 or (651)687-7000 Fax: 800-213-2323 or (651)687-5664 URL: http://www.westgroup.com • 31 volumes. $1,320.00. Periodic supplementation. Provides personal and business forms and alternative provisions for more than 250 subjects.

Nielsen Report on Television. Nielsen Media Research, 299 Park Ave. New York, NY 10171. Phone: (212)708-7500 Annual. $25.00. General statistics on television programming, plus ranking of the year's most popular shows. Pamphlet.

Nielsen Station Index. Nielsen Media Research, 299 Park Ave. New York, NY 10171. Phone: (212)708-7500 Fax: (212)708-7795 E-mail: info@nielsenmedia.com • URL: http://www.nielsenmedia.com • Measures local television station audiences in about 220 U. S. geographic areas. Includes current and some historical data. Inquire as to online cost and availability.

Nielsen Television Index. Nielsen Media Research, 299 Park Ave. New York, NY 10171. Phone: (212)708-7500 Fax: (212)708-7795 E-mail: info@nielsenmedia.com • URL: http://www.nielsenmedia.com • Measures national television program audiences by sampling approximately 4,000 U. S. households. Time period is 1970 to date, with weekly updates.

Nightclub & Bar Magazine: The Magazine for Nightclub and Bar Management. Oxford Publishing, 307 W. Jackson Ave. Oxford, MS 38655. Phone: 800-247-3881 or (662)236-5510 Fax: (662)236-5541 E-mail: ncb@nightclub.com • URL: http://www.nightclub.com • Monthly. $25.00 per year. Provides news and business advice for owners and managers of bars, nightclubs, and themed restaurants. Includes special issues on seasonal drinks, bar technology, beer trends, appetizers, food service, etc.

The Nikkei Weekly: Japan's Leading Business Newspaper. Nikkei America, Inc., 1325 Ave. of the Americas, Suite 2500 New York, NY 10019. Phone: (212)261-6200 Fax: (212)261-6208 URL: http://www.nikkei.co.jp/enews • Weekly. $108.00 per year. A newspaper in English "dedicated to all aspects of Japanese business and its influence on people, markets and political trends around the world." Includes English versions of articles appearing in leading Japanese business newspapers, such as *Nihon Keizai Shimbun, Nikkei Marketing Journal*, and *Nikkei Financial Daily*.

The Nilson Report. HSN Consultants, Inc., 2218 Main St. Santa Monica, CA 90405. Phone: (310)586-2425 Fax: (310)396-0615 Semimonthly. $695.00 per year. Newsletter. Provides market and other data on the credit card industry.

NIMBYS and LULUs (Not-in-My-Back-Yard and Locally-Unwanted-Land-Uses). Jan Horah and Heather Scott. Sage Publications, Inc., 2455 Teller Rd. Thousand Oaks, CA 91320. Phone: (805)499-0721 Fax: (805)499-0871 E-mail: info@sagepub.com • URL: http://www.sagepub.com • 1993. $10.00.

Nimmer on Copyright. Melville B. Nimmer. Matthew Bender & Co., Inc., Two Park Ave. New York, NY 10016. Phone: 800-223-1940 or (212)448-2000 Fax: (212)244-3188 E-mail: international@bender.com • URL: http://www.bender.com • $1,116.00. Six looseleaf volumes. Periodic supplementation. Analytical and practical guide on the law of literary, musical, and artistic proprerty.

9-1-1 Magazine: Public Safety Communications and Response. Official Publications, Inc., 18201 Weston Place Tustin, CA 92780. Phone: 800-231-8911 or (714)544-7776 Fax: (714)838-9233 URL: http://www.9-1-1magazine.com • Bimonthly. $31.95 per year. Covers technical information and applications for public safety communications personnel.

The 9 to 5 Guide to Combating Sexual Harassment: Candid Advice from 9 to 5, the National Association of Working Women. Ellen Bravo and Ellen Cassedy. John Wiley and Sons, Inc., 605 Third Ave. New York, NY 10158-0012. Phone: 800-225-5945 or (212)850-6000 Fax: (212)850-6088 E-mail: info@wiley.com • URL: http://www.wiley.com • 1992. $12.95.

Nine to Five: National Association of Working Women., 231 W. Wisconsin Ave., Suite 900 Milwaukee, WI 53203. Phone: 800-522-0925 or (414)274-0925 Fax: (414)272-2870 E-mail: naww9to5@execpc.com • Members are women office workers. Strives for the improvement of office working conditions for women and the elimination of sex and race discrimination.

Nine to Five Newsletter. National Association of Working Women, 238 W. Wisconsin Ave., Suite 900 Milwaukee, WI 53203. Phone: (414)274-0925 Fax: (414)272-2870 Five times a year. Free to members; individuals, $25.00 per year. A newsletter dealing with the rights and concerns of women office workers.

Ninety-Nines, International Organization of Women Pilots., 501 Third St., N.W., 2nd Fl. Washington, DC. E-mail: lgildersleeve@cwa-union.org • URL: http://www.newsguild.org • Licensed women pilots.

NIOSHTIC: National Institute for Occupational Safety and Health Technical Information Center Database. National Institute for Occupational Safety and Health, Technical Information Bra, 4676 Columbia Parkway Cincinnati, OH 45226. Phone: 800-356-4674 or (513)533-8359 Fax: (513)533-8347 Provides citations and abstracts of technical literature in the areas of industrial safety, industrial hygiene, and toxicology. Covers 1890 to date, but mostly 1973 to date. Monthly updates. (Database is also known as *Occupational Safety and Health*.) Inquire as to online cost and availability.

NLADA Directory of Legal Aid and Defender Offices in the United States and Territories. National Legal Aid and Defender Association, 1625 K St., N.W., Suite 800 Washington, DC 20006. Phone: (202)452-0620 Fax: (202)872-1031 E-mail: info@nlada.org • URL: http://www.nlada.org • Biennial. $70.00. Geographical list of approximately 3,600 legal aid and defender offices and their branches. Formerly *NLADA Directory Legal Aid and Defender Offices in the United States*.

NLGI Spokesman. National Lubricating Grease Institute, 4635 Wyandotte St. Kansas City, MO 64112. Phone: (816)931-9480 Fax: (816)753-5026 Monthly. $24.00 per year. Information about the lubricating grease industry.

NMA. National Mining AssociationPhone: (202)463-2625 Fax: (202)463-6152 URL: http://www.nma.org • Web site provides information on the U. S. coal and mineral industries. Includes "Salient Statistics of the Mining Industry," showing a wide variety of annual data (six years) for coal and non-fuel minerals. Publications of the National Mining Association are described and links are provided to other sites. (National Mining Association formerly known as National Coal Association.) Fees: Free.

No-Fault and Uninsured Motorist Auto Insurance. Matthew Bender & Co., Inc., Two Park Ave. New York, NY 10016. Phone: 800-223-1940 or (212)448-2000 Fax: (212)244-3188 E-mail: international@bender.com • URL: http://www.bender.com • $880.00. Four looseleaf volumes. Periodic supplementation. For both plaintiff's and defendant's counsel.

The No-Load Fund Investor., P.O. Box 318 Irvington-on-Hudson, NY 10533. Phone: 800-252-2042 or (914)693-7420 Monthly. $139.00 per year without *Handbook*; *Handbook* included, $159.00 per year. Latest performance statistics for no-loads, specific fund recommendations, market forecasts, and timely fund news.

No-Regrets Remodeling: Creating a Comfortable, Healthy Home That Saves Energy. Available from American Council for an Energy-Efficient Economy, 2124 Kittredge St., No. 95 Berkeley, CA 94704. Phone: (510)524-5405 1997. $19.95. Edited by *Home Energy* magazine. Serves as a home remodeling guide to efficient heating, cooling, ventilation, water heating, insulation, lighting, and windows.

Noise Control Association.

Noise Control Engineering Journal. Institute of Noise Control Engineering, Department of Mechanical Engineering, Auburn University Auburn, AL 36849-5341. Phone: (205)844-3306 Fax: (205)844-3407 Bimonthly. $70.00 per year.

Noise Regulation Report: The Nation's Only Noise Control Publication. Business Publishers, Inc., 8737 Colesville Rd., Suite 1100 Silver Spring, MD 20910-3928. Phone: 800-274-6737 or (301)587-6300 Fax: (301)587-1081 E-mail: bpinews@bpinews.com • URL: http://www.bpinews.com • Monthly. $487.00 per year. Newsletter. Covers federal and state rules and regulations for the control of excessive noise.

Non-Ferrous Founders Society., 1480 Renaissnace Dr., Ste. 310 Park Ridge, IL 60068. Phone: (847)299-0950 Fax: (847)299-3598 E-mail: staff@nffs.org • URL: http://www.nffs.org • Members are manufacturers of brass, bronze, aluminum and other nonferrous castings.

Non-Ferrous Metal Data Yearbook. American Bureau of Metal Statistics, 400 N. Main St., Suite Six Manahawkin, NJ 08050. Phone: (609)597-3375 Fax: (609)597-6625 E-mail: info@abms.com • URL: http://www.abms.com • Annual. $395.00. Provides about 200 statistical tables covering many nonferrous metals. Includes production, consumption, inventories, exports, imports, and other data.

Non-Ferrous Metals Producers Committee., c/o Kenneth Button, Economic Consulting Service, 2030 M. St., N.W., Suite 800 Washington, DC 20036. Phone: (202)466-7720 Fax: (202)466-2710 Members are copper, lead, and zinc producers. Promotes the copper, lead, and zinc mining and metal industries.

Non-Foods Merchandising: For Sales and Disbribution of Non-Foods. Cardinal Business Media, Inc., 200 Connecticut Ave., Suite 5-D Norwalk, CT 06854. Phone: (203)838-9100 Fax: (203)838-2550 Monthly. Free to qualified personnel; others, $85.00 per year. Trade publication for supermarket merchandisers and retailers across the nation.

The Non-Profit Handbook: Books, Periodicals, Software, Internet Sites, and Other Essential Resources for Non-Profit Leaders. Chronicle of Higher Education, Inc., 1255 23rd St., N.W., Suite 700 Washington, DC 20037. Phone: 800-728-2819 or (202)466-1032 Fax: (202)659-2236 E-mail: editor@chronicle.com • URL: http://www.chronicle.com • Annual. $5.00. A special issue of *Chronicle of Philanthropy*. Contains annotations of books, periodicals, and other material from various sources, relating to Advocacy, Boards, Communications and Marketing, Financial Management, Fund Raising, General Information, Managing, Philanthropic Tradition, Technology, and Volunteers. Includes index to titles.

Non-Profit Legal and Tax Letter. Organization Management Inc., 4289 Ellzey Dr. Ashburn, VA 20148-5026. Phone: (703)729-7052 Fax: (703)729-7053 18 times a year. $235.00 per year. Newsletter. Covers fund raising, taxation, management, postal regulations, and other topics for nonprofit organizations.

Non-Store Marketing Report. Maxwell Sroge Publishing, Inc., 522 Forest Ave. Evanston, IL 60202-3005. Phone: (847)866-1890 Fax: (847)866-1899 Biweekly. $275.00 per year. Newsletter covering mail order, telephone selling, and direct selling.

Nonferrous Castings. U. S. Bureau of the Census, Washington, DC 20233-0800. Phone: (301)457-4100 Fax: (301)457-3842 URL: http://www.census.gov • Annual. (Current Industrial Reports MA-33E.)

Nonferrous Metals Alert. Cambridge Information Group, 7200 Wisconsin Ave., 6th Fl. Bethesda, MD 20814. Phone: 800-843-7751 or (301)961-6700 Fax: (301)961-6720 E-mail: market@csa.com • URL: http://www.csa.com • Monthly. $340.00 per year. Provides citations to the business and industrial literature of nonferrous metals. (Materials Business Information Series).

Nonprescription Pharmaceuticals and Nutritionals: The Tan Sheet. F-D-C Reports, Inc., 5550 Friendship Blvd., Suite 1 Chevy Chase, MD 20815-7278. Phone: 800-332-2181 or (301)657-9830 Fax: (301)664-7238 URL: http://www.fdcreports.com • Weekly. $860.00 per year. Newsletter covering over-the-counter drugs and vitamin supplements. Emphasis is on regulatory activities of the U. S. Food and Drug Administration (FDA).

Nonprofit Almanac: A Publication Independent Sector. Virginia A. Hodgkinson and others. Jossey-Bass, Inc., Publishers, 350 Sansome St. San Francisco, CA 94104. Phone: 888-378-2537 or (415)433-1740 Fax: (415)433-0499 E-mail: webperson@jbp.com • URL: http://www.josseybass.com • 1996. $25.95. Provides trends and statistics for nonprofit wages, finances, employment, and giving patterns. Includes a glossary.

Nonprofit Counsel. John Wiley and Sons, Inc., Journals Div., 605 Third Ave. New York, NY 10158-0012. Phone: 800-526-5368 or (212)850-6000 Fax: (212)850-6088 E-mail: info@wiley.com • URL: http://www.wiley.com • Monthly. Institutions, $275.00 per year. Newsletter.

The Nonprofit Entrepreneur: Creating Ventures to Earn Income. Edward Skloot, editor. The Foundation Center, 79 Fifth Ave. New York, NY 10003-3076. Phone: 800-424-9836 or (212)620-4230 Fax: (212)807-3677 E-mail: mfn@fdncenter.org • URL: http://www.fdncenter.org • 1988. $19.95. Advice on earning income through fees and service charges.

Nonprofit Management and Leadership. Jossey-Bass, Inc., Publishers, 350 Sansome St. San Francisco, CA 94104-1342. Phone: 888-378-2537 or (415)433-1740 Fax: (415)433-0499 E-mail: webperson@jbp.com • URL: http://www.josseybass.com • Quarterly. Individuals, $56.00 per year; institutions, $125.00 per year. Sample issue free to librarians.

Nonprofit Management Handbook: Operating Policies and Procedures. Tracy D. Connors. John Wiley and Sons, Inc., 605 Third Ave. New York, NY 10158-0012. Phone: 800-225-5945 or (212)850-6000 Fax: (212)850-6088 E-mail: info@wiley.com • URL: http://www.wiley.com • 1999. $65.00. Second edition. Includes sample forms.

Nonprofit Sector Yellow Book: Who's Who in the Management of the Leading Foundations, Universities, Museums, and Other Nonprofit Organizations. Leadership Directories, Inc., 104 Fifth Ave. New York, NY 10011. Phone: (212)627-4140 Fax: (212)645-0931 E-mail: info@leadershipdirectories.com • URL: http://www.leadershipdirectories.com • Semiannual. $235.00 per year. Covers management personnel and board members of about 1,000 prominent, nonprofit organizations: foundations, colleges, museums, performing arts groups, medical institutions, libraries, private preparatory schools, and charitable service organizations.

Nonprofit Times. NPT Publishing Group, 240 Cedar Knolls Rd., Suite 318 Cedar Knolls, NJ 07927. Phone: (973)734-1700 Fax: (973)734-1777 URL: http://www.nptimes.com • 18 times a year. $59.00 per year. Edited for executives of nonprofit organizations. Covers fund raising, personnel, management, and technology topics. Includes an annual nonprofit salary survey.

Nonprofit World: The National Bi-Monthly Nonprofit Leadership and Management Journal. Society for Nonprofit Organizations, 6314 Odana Rd., Suite 1 Madison, WI 53719. Phone: (608)274-9777 Fax: (608)274-9978 E-mail: snpo@danenet.wicip.org • URL: http://www.uwex.edu/danenet/snpo • Bimonthly. $79.00 per year. Includes *National Directory of Service and Product Providers to Nonprofit Organizations* and *Resource Center Catalog*.

Nonwoven Disposables. Theta Reports/PJB Medical Publications, Inc., 1775 Broadway, Suite 511 New York, NY 10019. Phone: (212)262-8230 Fax: (212)262-8234 E-mail: customerservice@thetareports.com • URL: http://www.thetareports.com • 1999. $1,495.00. Provides market research data, including sales projections. Covers hospital disposable items, such as surgical drapes, masks, head covers, patient gowns, and incontinence products. (Theta Report No. 922.)

Nonwovens Industry: The International Magazine for the Nonwoven Fabrics and Disposable Soft Goods Industry. Rodman Publications, 17 S. Franklin Parkway Ramsey, NJ 07446. Phone: (201)825-2552 Fax: (201)825-0553 E-mail: rpubl@aol.com • URL: http://www.happi.com • Monthly. $48.00 per year.

North American Advertising Agency Network.

North American Agricultural Marketing Officials.

North American Apples Varieties, Rootstocks, Outlook. R.F. Carlson and others. Michigan State University Press, 1405 S. Harrison Rd., Suite 25 East Lansing, MI 48823-5202. Phone: (517)355-9543 Fax: (517)432-2611 E-mail: mspos@msu.edu • URL: http://www.web.msu.edu/press • 1970. $15.00.

North American Association of Food Equipment Manufacturers.

North American Building Material Distribution Association.

North American Building Material Distribution Association-Membership. North American Building Material Distribution Association, 401 N. Michigan Ave. Chicago, IL 60611-4274. Phone: 888-747-7862 or (312)321-6845 Fax: (312)644-0310 E-mail: nbmda@sba.com • URL: http://www.nbmda.org • Annual. $895.00, About 200 wholesale distributors of building products who are members, and 150 manufacturers in that field who are associate members and over 600 of their locations. Formerly *National Building Material Distributors Association Membership and Product Directory*.

North American Die Casting Association.

North American Equipment Dealers Association.

North American Export Grain Association.

North American Fax Directory. Dial-A-Fax Directories Corp., 930 Fox Pavilion Jenkintown, PA 19046. Phone: (215)887-5700 Fax: (215)887-7076 E-mail: berylwolk@aol.com • Annual. $289.00. Approximately 209,000 companies that possess facsimile machines. Formerly *Dial-A-Fax Directory*.

North American Free Trade Agreement Between the Government of the United States of America, the Government of Canada, and the Government of the United Mexican States. Available from U. S. Government Printing Office, Washington, DC 20402. Phone: (202)512-1800 Fax: (202)512-2250 E-mail: gpoaccess@gpo.gov • URL: http://www.access.gpo.gov • 1993. $40.00. Two volumes. Cover title: ''The NAFTA.'' Issued by the Office of the United States Trade Representative, Executive Office of the President. Contains full legal text of the trade agreement, including objectives and definitions.

North American Free Trade Agreement: Opportunities for U. S. Industries, NAFTA Industry Sector Reports. Available from U. S. Government Printing Office, Washington, DC 20402. Phone: (202)512-1800 Fax: (202)512-2250 E-mail: gpoaccess@gpo.gov • URL: http://www.access.gpo.gov • 1993. Issued by the International Trade Administration, U. S. Department of Commerce. Contains NAFTA Industry Sector Reports showing statistical data on exports from 36 U. S. manufacturing sectors to Mexico, Canada, and other parts of the world.

North American Grain and Milling Annual. Sosland Publishing Co., 4800 Main St., Suite 100 Kansas City, MO 64112-2513. Phone: (816)756-1000 Fax: (816)756-0494 E-mail: worldgrain@sosland.com • Annual. $95.00. Features listings of the major grain facilities in the U.S. and Canada. Provides an annual overview of the U.S. grain industry and a complete reference to equipment and service suppliers. Formerly *Milling Directory Buyer's Guide*.

North American Industry Classification System (NAICS). Available from Bernan Press, 4611-F Assembly Dr. Lanham, MD 20706-4391. Phone: 800-274-4447 or (301)459-7666 Fax: 800-865-3450 or (301)459-0056 E-mail: info@bernan.com • URL: http://www.bernan.com • 1998. $32.50. Issued by the Executive Office of the President, Office of Management and Budget (OMB). The 1997 NAICS six-digit classification scheme replaces the 1987 Standard Industrial Classification (SIC) four-digit system. Detailed information on NAICS is available at http://www.census.gov/epcd/www/naics.html.

North American Insulation Manufacturers Association.

North American Interactive Television Markets. Available from MarketResearch.com, 641 Ave. of the Americas, 3rd Fl. New York, NY 10011. Phone: 800-298-5699 or (212)807-2629 Fax: (212)807-2716 E-mail: order@marketresearch.com • URL: http://www.marketresearch.com • 1999. $3,450.00. Published by Frost & Sullivan. Contains market research data on growth, end-user trends, and market strategies. Company profiles are included.

North American Meat Processors Association.

North American Millers' Association.

North American Retail Dealers Association.

North American Scrap Metals Directory. G.I.E. Media, Inc., 4012 Bridge Ave. Cleveland, OH 44113. Phone: (216)961-4130 Fax: (216)961-0364 URL: http://www.recyclingtoday.com • Annual. $85.00. Lists more than 9,000 scrap metal processors, brokers, and dealers.

North American Securities Administrators Association., 10 G St., N.E., Ste. 710 Washington, DC 20002. Phone: (202)737-0900 Fax: (202)783-3571 E-mail: info@nasaa.org • Members are state officials who administer ''blue sky'' securities laws.

North American Simulation and Gaming Association., P.O. Box 78636 Indianapolis, IN 46278. Phone: 888-432-4263 or (317)387-1424 Fax: (317)387-1921 E-mail: info@nasaga.org • URL: http://www.nasaga.org • Members are professionals interested in the use of games and simulations for problem solving and decision-making in all types of organizations.

North American Wholesale Lumber Association - Distribution Directory. North American Wholesale Lumber Association, 3601 W. Algonquin Rd., No. 400 Rolling Meadows, IL 60008-3108. Phone: 800-527-8258 or (847)870-7470 Fax: (847)870-0201 E-mail: nawla@lumber.org • URL: http://www.lumber.org • Annual. $50.00. Over 600 wholesalers and manufacturers of lumber and related forest products.

Northeast Research and Extension Center. University of Arkansas

The Northern Miner: Devoted to the Mineral Resources Industry of Canada. Southam Magazine Group, 1450 Don Mills Rd. Don Mills, ON, Canada M3B 2X7. Phone: 800-387-0273 or (416)445-6641 Fax: (416)442-2175 Weekly. $87.00 per year.

Northern Nut Growers Association.

Northwest Farm Managers Association.

Northwestern University-Media Management Center., 1007 Church St., No. 312 Evanston, IL 60201-5912. Phone: (847)491-4900 Fax: (847)491-5619 E-mail: nmc@nwu.edu • URL: http://www.nmc-nwu.org • Research areas are related to various business aspects of the newspaper industry: management, marketing, personnel, planning, accounting, and finance. A joint activity of the J. L. Kellogg Graduate School of Management and the Medill School of Journalism.

Norton Bankruptcy Law Adviser. William L. Norton, Jr. West Group, 620 Opperman Dr. Eadanield, MN 55123. Phone: 800-328-4880 or (651)687-8000 Fax: 800-213-2323 or (651)847-7302 URL: http://www.westgroup.com • Monthly. $310.00 per year. Newsletter.

Not-for-Profit GAAP: Interpretation and Application of Generally Accepted Accounting Principles for Not-for-Profit Organizations. John Wiley and Sons, Inc., 605 Third Ave. New York, NY 10158-0012. Phone: 800-225-5945 or (212)850-6000 Fax: (212)850-6088 E-mail: info@jwiley.com • URL: http://www.wiley.com • Annual. $65.00. (Also available on CD-ROM.)

Notable Corporate Chronologies. The Gale Group, 27500 Drake Rd. Farmington Hills, MI 48331-3535. Phone: 800-877-GALE or (248)699-GALE Fax: 800-414-5043 or (248)699-8069 E-mail: galeord@galegroup.com • URL: http://www.galegroup.com • 1998. $390.00. Second edition. Two volumes. Contains about 1,150 chronological profiles of major corporations, showing events that were important in each company's development. Volume four is a *Master Index*.

Notary Bulletin. National Notary Association, P.O. Box 2402 Chatsworth, CA 91313-2402. Phone: 800-876-6827 or (818)739-4000 Fax: (818)700-0920 E-mail: nna@nationalnotary.org • URL: http://www.nationalnotary.org • Bimonthly. $34.00 per year. Formerly *State Notary Bulletin*.

Notary Public Practices and Glossary. National Notary Association, P.O. Box 2402 Chatsworth, CA 91313-2402. Phone: 800-876-6827 or (818)739-4000 Fax: (818)700-0920 E-mail: nna@nationalnotary.org • URL: http://www.nationalnotary.org • 1998. $22.00.

Novel and Short Story Writer's Market: 2000 Places to Sell Your Fiction. F & W Publications, Inc., 1507 Dana Ave. Cincinnati, OH 45207-1005. Phone: 800-289-0963 or (513)531-2690 Fax: 888-590-4082 Annual. $22.99. List of more than 2,000 literary magazines, general periodicals, small presses, book publishers, and authors' agents; contests awards; and writers' organizations.

NOW Legal Defense and Education Fund.

NSF International.

NSFRE News. National Society of Fund Raising Executives, 1101 King St., Suite 700 Alexandria, VA 22314. Phone: (703)684-0410 Fax: (703)684-0540 6 times a year. Free to members; non-members, $25.00 per year. Information on events, people and issues in the fundraising profession.

NSGA Retail Focus. National Sporting Goods Association, 1699 Wall St. Mt. Prospect, IL 60056-5780. Phone: 800-815-5422 or (847)296-6742 Fax: (847)391-9827 E-mail: nsga1699@aol.com • URL: http://www.nsga.org • Bimonthy. Free to members; non-members, $50.00 per year. Covers news and marketing trends for sporting goods retailers. Formerly *NSGA Sports Retailer*.

NSPA Washington Reporter. National Society of Accountants, 1010 N. Fairfax St. Alexandria, VA 22314-1574. Phone: 800-966-6679 or (703)549-6400 Fax: (703)549-2984 E-mail: nsa@wizard.net • URL: http://www.nspa.org • Monthly. Membership.

NTC's Business Writer's Handbook. Arthur H. Bell. NTC/Contemporary Publishing, P.O. Box 545 Blacklick, OH 43004. Phone: 800-338-3987 or (614)755-4151 Fax: (614)755-5645 E-mail: ntcpub@mcgraw-hill.com • URL: http://www.ntc-cb.com • 1995. $35.00. (NTC Business Book Series).

NTC's Dictionary of Tricky Words: With Complete Examples of Correct Usage. Deborah K. Williams. NTC/Contemporary Publishing, P.O. Box 545 Blacklick, OH 43004. Phone: 800-338-3987 or (614)755-4151 Fax: (614)755-5645 E-mail: ntcpub@mcgraw-hill.com • URL: http://www.ntc-cb.com • 1996. $19.95. Focuses on words that commonly cause confusion in everyday usage (can & may, shall & will, infer & imply, disinterested & uninterested, and so forth).

NTC's Mass Media Dictionary. R. Terry Ellmore. NTC/Contemporary Publishing, P.O. Box 545 Blacklick, OH 43004. Phone: 800-338-3987 or (614)755-4151 Fax: (614)755-5645 E-mail: ntcpub@mcgraw-hill.com • URL: http://www.ntc-cb.com • 1993. $24.95. Covers television, radio, newspapers, magazines, film, graphic arts, books, billboards, public relations, and advertising. Terms are related to production, research, audience measurement, audio-video engineering, printing, publishing, and other areas.

NTIS Alerts: Agriculture & Food. National Technical Information Service, U. S. Department of Commerce, Technology Administration, 5285 Port Royal Rd. Springfield, VA 22161. Phone: 800-553-6847 or (703)487-4600 Fax: (703)321-8547 E-mail: info@ntis.fedworld.gov • URL: http://www.ntis.gov • Semimonthly. $195.00 per year. Provides descriptions of government-sponsored research reports and software, with ordering information. Covers agricultural economics, horticulture, fisheries, veterinary medicine, food technology, and related subjects. Formerly *Abstract Newsletter*.

NTIS Alerts: Biomedical Technology & Human Factors Engineering. National Technical Information Service, U. S. Department of Commerce, Technology Administration, 5285 Port Royal Rd. Springfield, VA 22161. Phone: 800-553-6847 or (703)487-4600 Fax: (703)321-8547 E-mail: info@ntis.fedworld.gov • URL: http://www.ntis.gov • Semimonthly. $210.00 per year. Provides descriptions of government-sponsored research reports and software, with ordering information. Covers biotechnology, ergonomics, bionics, artificial intelligence, prosthetics, and related subjects. Formerly *Abstract Newsletter*.

NTIS Alerts: Building Industry Technology. National Technical Information Service, U. S. Department of Commerce, Technology Administration, 5285 Port Royal Rd. Springfield, VA 22161. Phone: 800-553-6847 or (703)487-4600 Fax: (703)321-8547 E-mail: info@ntis.fedworld.gov • URL: http://www.ntis.gov • Semimonthly. $210.00 per year. Provides descriptions of government-sponsored research reports and software, with ordering information. Covers architecture, construction management, building materials, maintenance, furnishings, and related subjects. Formerly *Abstract Newsletter*.

NTIS Alerts: Business & Economics. National Technical Information Service

NTIS Alerts: Communication. National Technical Information Service, U. S. Department of Commerce, Technology Administration, 5285 Port Royal Rd. Springfield, VA 22161. Phone: 800-553-6847 or (703)487-4600 Fax: (703)321-8547 E-mail: info@ntis.fedworld.gov • URL: http://www.ntis.gov • Semimonthly. $210.00 per year. . Provides descriptions of government-sponsored research reports and software, with ordering information. Covers common carriers, satellites, radio/TV equipment, telecommunication regulations, and related subjects.

NTIS Alerts: Computers, Control & Information Theory. National Technical Information Service, U. S. Department of Commerce, Technology Administration, 5285 Port Royal Rd. Springfield, VA 22161. Phone: 800-553-6847 or (703)487-4600 Fax: (703)321-8547 E-mail: info@ntis.fedworld.gov • URL: http://www.ntis.gov • Semimonthly. $235.00 per year. Provides descriptions of government-sponsored research reports and software, with ordering information. Covers computer hardware, software, control systems, pattern recognition, image processing, and related subjects. Formerly *Abstract Newsletter*.

NTIS Alerts: Electrotechnology. National Technical Information Service, U. S. Department of Commerce, Technology Administration, 5285 Port Royal Rd. Springfield, VA 22161. Phone: 800-553-6847 or (703)487-4600 Fax: (703)321-8547 E-mail: info@ntis.fedworld.gov • URL: http://www.ntis.gov • Semimonthly. $210.00 per year. Provides descriptions of government-sponsored research reports and software, with ordering information. Covers electronic components, semiconductors, antennas, circuits, optoelectronic devices, and related subjects. Formerly *Abstract Newsletter*.

NTIS Alerts: Energy. National Technical Information Service, U. S. Department of Commerce, Technology Administration, 5285 Port Royal Rd. Springfield, VA 22161. Phone: 800-553-6847 or (703)487-4600 Fax: (703)321-8547 E-mail: info@ntis.fedworld.gov • URL: http://www.ntis.gov • Semimonthly. $245.00 per year. Provides descriptions of government-sponsored research reports and software, with ordering information. Covers electric power, batteries, fuels, geothermal energy, heating/cooling systems, nuclear technology, solar energy, energy policy, and related subjects. Formerly *Abstract Newsletter*.

NTIS Alerts: Environmental Pollution & Control. National Technical Information Service, U. S. Department of Commerce, Technology Administration, 5285 Port Royal Rd. Springfield, VA 22161. Phone: 800-553-6847 or (703)487-4600 Fax: (703)321-8547 E-mail: info@ntis.fedworld.gov • URL: http://www.ntis.gov • Semimonthly. $245.00 per year. Provides descriptions of government-sponsored research reports and software, with ordering information. Covers the following categories of environmental pollution: air, water, solid wastes, radiation, pesticides, and noise. Formerly *Abstract Newsletter*.

NTIS Alerts: Government Inventions for Licensing. National Technical Information Service, U. S. Department of Commerce, Technology Administration, 5285 Port Royal Rd. Springfield, VA 22161. Phone: 800-553-6847 or (703)487-4600 Fax: (703)321-8547 E-mail: info@ntis.fedworld.gov • URL: http://www.ntis.gov • Semimonthly. $270.00 per year. Identifies new inventions available from various government agencies. Covers a wide variety of industrial and technical areas. Formerly *Abstract Newsletter*.

NTIS Alerts: Health Care. National Technical Information Service, U. S. Department of Commerce, Technology Administration, 5285 Port Royal Rd. Springfield, VA 22161. Phone: 800-553-6847 or (703)487-4600 Fax: (703)321-8547 E-mail: info@ntis.fedworld.gov • URL: http://www.ntis.gov • Semimonthly. $210.00 per year. Provides descriptions of government-sponsored research reports and software, with ordering information. Covers a wide variety of health care topics, including quality assurance, delivery organization, economics (costs), technology, and legislation. Formerly *Abstract Newsletter*.

NTIS Alerts: Manufacturing Technology. National Technical Information Service, U. S. Department of Commerce, Technology Administration, 5285 Port Royal Rd. Springfield, VA 22161. Phone: 800-553-6847 or (703)487-4600 Fax: (703)321-8547 E-mail: info@ntis.fedworld.gov • URL: http://www.ntis.gov • Semimonthly. $265.00 per year. Provides descriptions of government-sponsored research reports and software, with ordering information. Covers computer-aided design and manufacturing (CAD/CAM), engineering materials, quality control, machine tools, robots, lasers, productivity, and related subjects. Formerly *Abstract Newsletter*.

NTIS Alerts: Materials Sciences. National Technical Information Service, U. S. Department of Commerce, Technology Administration, 5285 Port Royal Rd. Springfield, VA 22161. Phone: 800-553-6847 or (703)487-4600 Fax: (703)321-8547 E-mail: info@ntis.fedworld.gov • URL: http://www.ntis.gov • Semimonthly. $220.00 per year. Provides descriptions of government-sponsored research reports and software, with ordering information. Covers ceramics, glass, coatings, composite materials, alloys, plastics, wood, paper, adhesives, fibers, lubricants, and related subjects. Formerly *Abstract Newsletter*.

NTIS Alerts: Ocean Sciences and Technology. National Technical Information Service, U. S. Department of Commerce, Technology Administration, 5285 Port Royal Rd. Springfield, VA 22161. Phone: 800-553-6847 or (703)487-4600 Fax: (703)321-8547 E-mail: info@ntis.fedworld.gov • URL: http://www.ntis.gov • Semimonthly. $210.00 per year. Provides descriptions of government-sponsored research reports and software, with ordering information. Formerly *Abstract Newsletter*.

NTIS Alerts: Transportation. National Technical Information Service, U. S. Department of Commerce, Technology Administration, 5285 Port Royal Rd. Springfield, VA 22161. Phone: 800-553-6847 or (703)487-4600 Fax: (703)321-8547 E-mail: info@ntis.fedworld.gov • URL: http://www.ntis.gov • Semimonthly. $210.00 per year. Provides descriptions of government-sponsored research reports and software, with ordering information. Covers air, marine, highway, inland waterway, pipeline, and railroad transportation. Formerly *Abstract Newsletter*.

NTIS Bibliographic Data Base. National Technical Information Service, 5285 Port Royal Rd. Springfield, VA 22161. Phone: 800-553-6847 or (703)487-6515 Fax: (703)487-4134 Contains citations and abstracts to unrestricted reports of government-sponsored research, 1964 to date. Covers a wide range of technical, engineering, business, and social science topics. Monthly updates. Inquire as to online cost and availability.

NTIS on SilverPlatter. Available from SilverPlatter Information, Inc., 100 River Ridge Rd. Norwood, MA 02062-5026. Phone: 800-343-0064 or (781)769-2599 Fax: (781)769-8763 Quarterly. $2,850.00 per year. Produced by the National Technical Information Service. Provides a CD-ROM guide to over 500,000 government reports on a wide variety of technical, industrial, and business topics.

Nuclear Energy Institute., 1776 Eye St., N.W., Suite 400 Washington, DC 20006. Phone: (202)739-8000 Fax: (202)785-4019 E-mail: webmaster@nei.org • URL: http://www.nei.org • Consists mainly of industrial firms engaged in the development of nuclear energy for constructive purposes.

Nuclear Engineering International. Wilmington Publishers Ltd., Wilmington House, Church Hill, Wilmington Dartford, Kent DA2 7EF, England. E-mail: energy@wilmington.co.uk • Monthly. $341.00 per year. Text in English; summaries in French and German.

Nuclear Fuel. McGraw-Hill, 1221 Ave. of the Americas New York, NY 10020-1095. Phone: 800-722-4726 or (212)904-2000 Fax: (212)904-2072 E-mail: customer.service@mcgraw-hill.com • URL: http://www.mcgraw-hill.com • Biweekly. $1,035.00 per year. Newsletter.

Nuclear Information and Records Management Association., 210 Fifth Ave. New York, NY 10010. Phone: (603)432-6476 Fax: (603)432-3024 URL: http://www.nirma.org • Concerned with the maintenance of nuclear industry corporate records.

Nuclear Information and Resource Service., 1424 16th St., N.W., No. 404 Washington, DC 20036. Phone: (202)328-0002 Fax: (202)462-2183 E-mail: nirsnet@nirs.org • URL: http://www.nirs.org • Promotes alternatives to nuclear power.

Nuclear News. American Nuclear Society, 555 N. Kensington Ave. La Grange Park, IL 60525. Phone: 800-682-6397 or (708)352-6611 Fax: (708)352-0499 URL: http://www.ans.org/pubs/magazines • Monthly. $224.00 per year. Includes *Nuclear News Buyers Guide and 3 Special Issues*.

Nuclear News Buyers Guide. American Nuclear Society, 555 N. Kensington Ave. La Grange Park, IL 60525. Phone: 800-682-6397 or (708)352-6611 Fax: (708)352-6464 URL: http://www.ans.org/pubs/magazines • Annual. $77.00. Lists approximately 1,600 manufacturers and suppliers of nuclear components. Included with subscription to *Nuclear News*.

Nuclear News-World List of Nuclear Power Plants. American Nuclear Society, 555 N. Kensington Ave. La Grange Park, IL 60525. Phone: 800-682-6397 or (708)352-6611 Fax: (708)352-6464 E-mail: nucleus@ans.org • URL: http://www.ans.org/pubs/magazines • Annual. $19.00 per copy. List of over 100 U. S. and foreign nuclear power plants that are in operation, under construction, or on order.

Nuclear Plant Journal. Newal K. Agnihotri, editor. EQES, Inc., 799 Roosevelt Rd., Bldg. 6, Suite 208 Glen Ellyn, IL 60137-5925. Phone: (630)858-6161 Fax: (630)858-8787 Bimonthly. $120.00 per year.

Nuclear Power. Available from U. S. Government Printing Office, Washington, DC 20402. Phone: (202)512-1800 Fax: (202)512-2250 E-mail: gpoaccess@gpo.gov • URL: http://www.access.gpo.gov • Annual. Free. Lists government publications. GPO Subject Bibliography Number 200.

Nuclear Science and Engineering: Research and Development Related to Peaceful Utilization of Nuclear Energy. American Nuclear Society, 555 N. Kensington Ave. La Grange Park, IL 60525. Phone: 800-682-6397 or (708)352-6611 Fax: (708)352-0499 URL: http://www.ans.org.pubs/magazines • Three volumes per year. $585.00 per year.

Nuclear Standards News. American Nuclear Society, 555 N. Kensington Ave. La Grange Park, IL 60525. Phone: 800-682-6397 or (708)352-6611 Fax: (708)352-0499 URL: http://www.ans.org.pubs/magazines • Monthly. $295.00 per year.

Nuclear Suppliers Association.

Nuclear Technology: Applications for Nuclear Science, Nuclear Engineering and Related Arts. American Nuclear Society, 555 N. Kensington Ave. La Grange Park, IL 60525. Phone: 800-682-6397 or (708)352-6611 Fax: (708)352-0499 URL: http://www.ans.org.pubs/magazines • Monthly. $595.00 per year.

Nuclear Waste News: Generation, Packaging, Transportation, Processing, Disposal. Business Publishers, Inc., 8737 Colesville Rd., Suite 1100 Silver Spring, MD 20910-3928. Phone: 800-274-6737 or (301)587-6300 Fax: (301)587-1081 E-mail: bpinews@bpinews.com • URL: http://www.bpinews.com • Weekly. $867.00. per year. Newsletter.

Nucleonics Week. McGraw-Hill, Energy & Business Newsletters, 1221 Ave. of the Americas New York, NY 10020-1095. Phone: 800-722-4726 or (212)512-2000 Fax: (212)512-2072 E-mail: customer.service@mcgraw-hill.com • URL: http://www.mcgraw-hill.com • Weekly. $1,395.00 per year. Newsletter.

The Numbers You Need. The Gale Group, 27500 Drake Rd. Farmington Hills, MI 48331-3535. Phone: 800-877-GALE or (248)699-GALE Fax: 800-414-5043 or (248)699-8069 E-mail: galeord@galegroup.com • URL: http://www.galegroup.com • 1993. $55.00. Contains mathematical equations, formulas, charts, and graphs, including many that are related to business or finance. Explanations, step-by-step directions, and examples of use are provided.

Numismatic News. Krause Publications, Inc., 700 E. State St. Iola, WI 54990. Phone: 800-258-0929 or (715)445-2214 Fax: (715)445-4087 E-mail: info@krause.com • URL: http://www.krause.com/ • Weekly. $32.00 per year.

Numismatics International.

Nursery Business Retailer. Brantwood Publications, 3023 Eastland Blvd., Suite 103 Clearwater, FL 34621-4106. Bimonthly. Price on application.

Nursery Stock and Supply Locator. American Association of Nurserymen, 1250 Eye St., N.W., Suite 500 Washington, DC 20005. Phone: (202)789-2900 Fax: (202)789-1893 Annual. $3.00.

Nursing Economics: Business Perspectives for Nurses. Jannetti Publications, Inc., P.O. Box 56 Pitman, NJ 08071-0056. Phone: (856)256-2300 Fax: (856)589-7463 E-mail: nejrnl@aol.com • URL: http://www.cinahl.com • Bimonthly. Individuals, $45.00 per year; institutions, $60.00 per year.

Nursing Home Report and Directory. SMG Marketing Group, Inc., 875 N. Michigan Ave., Ste. 3100 Chicago, IL 60611. Phone: 800-678-3026 or (312)642-3026 Fax: (312)642-9729 URL: http://www.smg.com • Annual. $525.00. Lists almost 4,000 nursing homes with 50 beds or more.

Nursing Homes: Long Term Care Management. Medquest Communications, LLC, 629 Euclid Ave., Ste. 1200 Cleveland, OH 44114-3003. Phone: (216)522-9700 Fax: (216)522-9707 Monthly. $95.00 per year. Covers business, finance, and management topics for nursing home directors and administrators.

Nursing Management. Springhouse Corp., 1111 Bethlehem Trpk. Springhouse, PA 19477-0903. Phone: 800-950-0879 or (215)646-8700 Fax: (215)643-4153 URL: http://www.springnet.com • Monthly. Individuals, $38.00 per year; institutions, $60.00 per year. Non-clinical subject matter.

Nutrition Abstracts and Reviews, Series A: Human and Experimental. Available from CABI Publishing North America, 10 E. 40th St. New York, NY 10016. Phone: 800-528-4841 or (212)481-7018 Fax: (212)686-7993 E-mail: cabi@cabi.org • URL: http://www.cabi.org • Monthly. $1,385.00 per year. Published in England by CABI Publishing. Provides worldwide coverage of the literature.

Nutrition Abstracts and Reviews, Series B: Livestock Feeds and Feeding. Available from CABI Publishing North America, 10 E. 40th St. New York, NY 10016. Phone: 800-528-4841 or (212)481-7018 Fax: (212)686-7993 E-mail: cabi@cabi.org • URL: http://www.cabi.org • Monthly. $930.00 per year. Published in England by CABI Publishing. Provides worldwide coverage of the literature.

Nutrition Reviews. International Life Science Institute, 1126 16th St., N.W., No. 110 Washington, DC 20036-4810. E-mail: nutrition.reviews@hnrc.tufts.edu • URL: http://www.ilsi.org • Monthly. Individuals, $97.50 per year; institutions, $160.00 per year.

Nutrition Today. Williams and Wilkins, 351 W. Camden St. Baltimore, MD 21201-2436. Phone: 800-527-5597 or (410)528-4000 Fax: (410)528-4422 E-mail: cvalton@wilkins.com • URL: http://www.wwilkins.com • Bimonthly. Individuals, $67.00 per year; institutions, $146.00 per year.

Nutshell. Northern Nut Growers Association, 654 Beinhower Rd. Etters, PA 17319-9774. Phone: (717)938-6090 Fax: (717)938-6090 Four times a year. Membership.

NWDA Operating Survey. National Wholesale Druggists' Association, 1821 Michael Faraday Dr., Suite 400 Reston, VA 20190. Phone: (703)787-0000 Fax: (703)787-6930 Annual. Members, $30.00; non-members, $295.00. A 48-page report of financial and operating ratios for the wholesale drug industry.

OAG Air Cargo Guide. OAG Worldwide, 2000 Clearwater Dr. Oakbrook, IL 60521. Phone: 800-323-4000 or (630)574-6000 Fax: (630)574-6091 URL: http://www.oag.com • Monthly. $239.00 per year. Shows current domestic and international air freight schedules. Diskette edition, $449.00 per year.

OAG Business Travel Planner: North America. Cahners Travel Group, 500 Plaza Dr. Secaucus, NJ 07094-3626. Phone: 800-662-7776 or (201)902-2000 Fax: (201)902-1914 E-mail: corporatecommunications@cahners.com • URL: http://www.cahners.com • Quarterly. $149.00 per year. Arranged according to more than 14,700 destinations in the U. S., Canada, Mexico, and the Caribbean. Lists more than 32,000 hotels, with AAA ratings where available. Provides information on airports, ground transportation, coming events, and climate.

OAG Desktop Flight Guide, North American Edition. OAG Worldwide, 2000 Clearwater Dr. Oak Brook, IL 60521. Phone: 800-323-4000 or (630)574-6000 Fax: (630)574-6091 URL: http://www.oag.com • Biweekly. $285.00 per year. Provides detailed airline travel schedules for the U. S., Canada, Mexico, and the Caribbean. Includes aircraft seat charts and airport diagrams. Formerly *Official Airline Guide, North American Edition*.

OAG Electronic Edition Travel Service. Official Airline Guides, Inc., 2000 Clearwater Dr. Oak Brook, IL 60521. Phone: 800-323-4000 or (630)574-6000 Fax: (630)574-6699 Current airline flight schedules and fare information. Inquire as to online cost and availability.

OAG Flight Guide. OAG Worldwide, 2000 Clearwater Dr. Oak Brook, IL 60521. Phone: 800-323-4000 or (630)574-6000 Fax: (630)574-6091 URL: http://www.oag.com • Monthly. $399.00 per year. Provides detailed airline schedules for international travel (travel within North America not included).

OAG Pocket Flight Guide. OAG Worldwide, 2000 Clearwater Dr. Oak Brook, IL 60521. Phone: 800-323-4000 or (630)574-6000 Fax: (630)574-6091 URL: http://www.oag.com • Monthly. $96.00 per year. Regional editions available for international areas.

OAG Travel Planner: Asia Pacific. Cahners Travel Group, 500 Plaza Dr. Secaucus, NJ 07094-3626. Phone: 800-662-7776 or (201)902-2000 Fax: (201)902-1914 E-mail: corporate-communications@cahners.com • URL: http://

www.cahners.com • Quarterly. $130.00 per year. Arranged according to more than 5,000 destinations throughout Asia and the Pacific. Lists about 5,000 hotels, with information on airports, ground transportation, coming events, and climate.

OAG Travel Planner: Europe. Cahners Travel Group, 500 Plaza Dr. Secaucus, NJ 07094-3626. Phone: 800-662-7776 or (201)902-2000 Fax: (201)902-1914 E-mail: corporatecommunications@cahners.com • URL: http://www.cahners.com • Quarterly. $130.00 per year. Arranged according to more than 13,850 destinations in Europe. Lists more than 14,700 hotels, with information on airports, ground transportation, coming events, and climate.

Oak Ridge Associated Universities., P.O. Box 117 Oak Ridge, TN 37831-0117. Phone: (423)576-3000 Fax: (423)576-3643 E-mail: townsenr@orau.org • URL: http://www.orau.gov • Consortium of 87 universities operating under direct contract with the U. S. Department of Energy. Purpose is to further nuclear energy education and research.

Oak Ridge National Laboratory.

OB/GYN Reference Guide. Access Publishing Co., 1301 W. Park Ave. Ocean, NJ 07712. Phone: 800-458-0990 or (732)493-8811 Fax: (732)493-9713 E-mail: access@accesspub.com • URL: http://www.accesspub.com • Annual. Price on application. Includes directory information for obstetrical/gynecological equipment, supplies, pharmaceuticals, services, organizations, and publications.

Occupational Earnings and Wage Trends in Metropolitan Areas. U.S. Bureau of Labor Statistics, Washington, DC 20212. Phone: (202)606-5900 Three times a year.

Occupational Hazards: Magazine of Health and Environment. Penton Media Inc., 1300 E. Ninth St. Cleveland, OH 44114. Phone: (216)696-7000 Fax: (216)696-0836 E-mail: corpcomm@penton.com • URL: http://www.penton.com • Monthly. $50.00 per year. Industrial safety and security management.

Occupational Health and Safety Letter...Towards Productivity and Peace of Mind. Business Publishers, Inc., 8737 Colesville Rd., Suite 1100 Silver Spring, MD 20910-3928. Phone: 800-274-6737 or (301)587-6300 Fax: (301)587-1081 E-mail: bpinews@bpinews.com • URL: http://www.bpinews.com • Biweekly. $317.00 per year.

Occupational Injuries and Illnesses by Industry. Bureau of Labor Statistics, U.S. Department of Labor. Available from U.S. Government Printing Office, Washington, DC 20402. Phone: (202)512-1800 Fax: (202)512-2250 E-mail: gpoaccess@gpo.gov • URL: http://www.access.gpo.gov • Annual.

Occupational Outlook Handbook. Bureau of Labor Statistics, U.S. Department of Labor. Available from U.S. Government Printing Office, Washington, DC 20402. Phone: (202)512-1800 Fax: (202)512-2250 E-mail: gpoaccess@gpo.gov • URL: http://www.access.gpo.gov • Biennial. $53.00. Issued as one of the Bureau's *Bulletin* series and kept up to date by *Occupational Outlook Quarterly*.

Occupational Outlook Quarterly. U.S. Department of Labor. Available from U.S. Government Printing Office, Washington, DC 20402. Phone: (202)512-1800 Fax: (202)512-2250 E-mail: gpoaccess@gpo.gov • URL: http://www.accessgpo.gov • Quarterly. $9.50 per year.

Occupational Projections and Training Data. Available from U. S. Government Printing Office, Washington, DC 20402. Phone: (202)512-1800 Fax: (202)512-2250 E-mail: gpoaccess@gpo.gov • URL: http://www.access.gpo.gov • Biennial. $7.00. Issued by Bureau of Labor Statistics, U. S. Department of Labor. Contains projections of employment change and job openings over the next 15 years for about 500 specific occupations. Also includes the number of associate, bachelor's, master's, doctoral, and professional degrees awarded in a recent year for about 900 specific fields of study.

Occupational Safety and Health Administration (OSHA): Regulations, Documents, and Technical Information. Available from U. S. Government Printing Office, Washington, DC 20402. Phone: (202)512-1800 Fax: (202)512-2250 E-mail: gpoaccess@gpo.gov • URL: http://www.access.gpo.gov • Quarterly. $46.00 per year. CD-ROM contains all OSHA regulations and standards currently in force, with selected documents and technical information.

Occupational Safety and Health Law. Mark A. Rothstein. West Publishing Co., College and School Div., 610 Opperman Dr. Eagan, MN 55123. Phone: 800-328-4880 or (651)687-7000 Fax: 800-213-2323 or (651)687-5827 E-mail: billhendee@itped.com • URL: http://www.lawschool.westgroup.com • 1990. Third edition. Price on application. Periodic supplementation. Discusses requirements of the Occupational Safety and Health Act (OSHA). (Handbook Series).

Occupational Safety and Health Management. Thomas Anton. McGraw-Hill, 1221 Ave. of the Americas New York, NY 10020. Phone: 800-722-4726 or (212)904-2000 Fax: (212)904-2072 E-mail: customer.service@mcgraw-hill.com • URL: http://www.mcgraw-hill.com • 1989. $88.44. Second edition.

Occupational Safety and Health Standards for General Industry. CCH, Inc., 4025 W. Peterson Ave. Chicago, IL 60646-6085. Phone: 800-248-3248 Fax: 800-224-8299 or (773)866-3608 URL: http://www.cch.com • Annual. $42.95.

Occupational Therapy in Health Care: A Journal of Contemporary Practice. Haworth Press, Inc., 10 Alice St. Binghamton, NY 13904-1580. Phone: 800-429-6784 or (607)722-5857 Fax: 800-895-0582 or (607)722-1424 E-mail: getinfo@haworthpressinc.com • URL: http://www.haworthpressinc.com • Quarterly. Individuals, $50.00 per year; institutions, $75.00 per year; libraries, $150.00 per year.

Occupational Therapy in Mental Health: A Journal of Psychosocial Practice and Research. Haworth Press, Inc., 10 Alice St. Binghamton, NY 13904-1580. Phone: 800-429-6784 or (607)722-5857 Fax: 800-895-0582 or (607)722-1424 E-mail: getinfo@haworthpressinc.com • URL: http://www.haworthpressinc.com • Quarterly. Individuals, $50.00 per year; institutions, $120.00 per year; libraries, $250.00 per year.

Ocean Development and International Law; The Journal of Marine Affairs. Taylor & Francis, Inc., 325 Chestnut St., 8th Fl. Philadelphia, PA 19106. Phone: 800-821-8312 or (215)625-8900 Fax: (215)625-2940 E-mail: webmaster@taylorandfrancis.com • URL: http://www.tandfdc.com/ • Quarterly. Individuals, $191.00 per year; institutions, $385.00 per year.

Ocean Engineering: An International Journal of Research and Development. Elsevier Science, 655 Ave. of the Americas New York, NY 10010. Phone: 888-437-4636 or (212)989-5800 Fax: (212)633-3680 E-mail: usinfo@elsevier.com • URL: http://www.elsevier.com • 12 times a year. $1,798.00 per year.

Ocean Navigator: Marine Navigation and Ocean Voyaging. Navigator Publishing LLC, P.O. Box 569 Portland, ME 04112-0569. Phone: (207)772-2466 Fax: (207)772-2879 E-mail: subscriptions@oceannavigator.com • Eight times a year. $26.00 per year.

Ocean Oil Weekly Report: News, Analysis, and Market Trends of the Worldwide Offshore Oil and Gas Industry. PennWell Corp., Petroleum Div., 1700 W. Loop S., Suite 1000 Houston, TX 77027. Phone: 800-736-6935 or (713)621-9720 Fax: (713)963-6296 E-mail: webmaster@pennwell.com • URL: http://www.pennwell.com • Weekly. $495.00 per year. Newsletter with emphasis on the Gulf of Mexico offshore oil industry. Includes statistics.

Oceanic Abstracts. Cambridge Information Group, 7200 Wisconsin Ave., 6th Fl. Bethesda, MD 20814. Phone: 800-843-7751 or (301)961-6700 Fax: (301)961-6720 E-mail: market@csa.com • URL: http://www.csa.com • Bimonthly. $1,045.00 per year. Covers oceanography, marine biology, ocean shipping, and a wide range of other marine-related subject areas.

Oceanic Abstracts (Online). Cambridge Scientific Abstracts, 7200 Wisconsin Ave., 6th Fl. Bethesda, MD 20814. Phone: 800-843-7751 or (301)961-6700 Fax: (301)961-6720 Oceanographic and other marine-related technical literature, 1981 to present.Monthly updates. Inquire as to online cost and availability.

OCLC Online Union Catalog. OCLC, Inc., 6565 Frantz Rd. Dublin, OH 43017. Phone: 800-848-5878 or (614)764-6000 Fax: (614)764-6096 Online cooperative library cataloging service. Daily updates. Inquire as to online cost and availability.

Ocular Surgery News. Slack, Inc., 6900 Grove Rd. Thorofare, NJ 08086-9447. Phone: 800-257-8290 or (609)848-1000 Fax: (609)853-5991 URL: http://www.slackinc.com • Biweekly. Individuals, $295.00 per year; institutions, $315.00 per year. Formerly *IOL & Ocular Surgery News*.

O'Dwyer's Directory of Corporate Communications. J. R. O'Dwyer Co., Inc., 271 Madison Ave. New York, NY 10016. Phone: (212)679-2471 Fax: (212)683-2750 Annual. $130.00. Public relations departments of major corporations.

O'Dwyer's Directory of Public Relations Firms. J. R. O'Dwyer Co., Inc., 271 Madison Ave. New York, NY 10016. Phone: (212)679-2471 Fax: (212)683-2750 Annual. $120.00. Over 2,200 public relations firms; international coverage.

OE Reports (Optical Engineering). International Society for Optical Engineering, P.O. Box 10 Bellingham, WA 98227-0010. Phone: (360)676-3290 Fax: (360)647-1440 Monthly. $25.00 per year. News and articles on optical and optoelectronic applied science and engineering. Formerly *Optical Engineering Reports*.

OECD Agricultural Outlook. Organization for Economic Cooperation and Development, OECD Washington Center, 2001 L St., N. W., Suite 650 Washington, DC 20036-4922. Phone: 800-456-6323 or (202)785-6323 Fax: (202)785-0350 E-mail: washington.contact@oecd.org • URL: http://www.oecd.org • Annual. $31.00. Provides a five-year outlook for agricultural markets in various countries of the world, including the U. S., other OECD countries, and selected non-OECD nations.

OECD Catalogue of Publications. Organization for Economic Cooperation and Development. Available from OECD Publications and Information Center, 2001 L St., N.W.,, Suite 650 Washington, DC 20036-4922. Phone: 800-456-6323 or (202)785-6323 Fax: (202)785-0350 E-mail: washington.contact@oecd.org • URL: http://www.oecd.org • Annual. Free. Supplements available.

OECD Economic Outlook. OECD Publications and Information Center, 2001 L St., NW, Ste. 650 Washington, DC 20036-4922. Phone: (202)785-6323 Fax: (202)785-0350 E-mail: washington.contact@oecd.org • URL: http://www.oecdwash.org • Semiannual. $95.00 per year. Contains a wide range of economic and monetary data relating to the member countries of the Organization for Economic Cooperation and Development. Includes about 100 statistical tables and graphs, with 24-month forecasts for each of the OECD countries. Provides extensive review and analysis of recent economic trends.

OECD Economic Survey of the United States. OECD Publications and Information Center, 2001 L St., N.W., Ste. 650 Washington, DC 20036-4922. Phone: (202)785-6323 Fax: (202)785-0350 E-mail: washington.contact@oecd.org • URL: http://www.oecdwash.org • Annual. $30.00.

OECD Economic Surveys. OECD Publications and Information Center, 2001 L St., N.W., Ste. 650 Washington, DC 20036-4922. Phone: (202)785-6323 Fax: (202)785-0350 E-mail: washington.contact@oecd.org • URL: http://www.oecdwash.org • Annual. $30.00 each. These are separate, yearly reviews for each of the economies of the industrialized nations that comprise the OECD. Each edition includes forecasts, analyses, and detailed statistical tables for the country being surveyed. (The combined series, one annual volume for each nation, is available at $485.00.)

OECD Information Technology Outlook 2000: ICTs, E-Commerce and the Information Economy. Organization for Economic Cooperation and Development, OECD Washington Center, 2001 L St., N. W., Suite 650 Washington, DC 20036-4922. Phone: 800-456-6323 or (202)785-6323 Fax: (202)785-0350 E-mail: washington.contact@oecd.org • URL: http://www.oecd.org • 2000. $72.00. Provides data on information and communications technology (ICT) and electronic commerce in 11 OECD nations (includes U. S.). Coverage includes network infrastructure, electronic payment systems, financial transaction technologies, intelligent agents, global navigation systems, and portable flat panel display technologies.

OECD Iron and Steel Industry. Organization for Economic Cooperation and Development. Available from OECD Publications and Information Center, 2001 L St., N.W.,, Suite 650 Washington, DC 20036-4922. Phone: 800-456-6323 or (202)785-6323 Fax: (202)785-0350 E-mail: washington.contact@oecd.org • URL: http://www.oecd.org • Annual. Price varies. Data for orders, production, manpower, imports, exports, consumption, prices and investment in the iron and steel industry in OECD member countries. Text in English and French.

OECD Main Economic Indicators. Organization for Economic Cooperation and Development, 2 rue Andre-Pascal, Cedex 16 75775 Paris, France. Phone: 331 45 248002 Fax: 331 45 241391 International statistics provided by OECD, 1960 to date. Monthly updates. Inquire as to online cost and availability.

OECD Nuclear Energy Data. Organization for Economic Cooperation and Development. Available from OECD Publications and Information Center, 2001 L St., N. W., Suite 650 Washington, DC 20036-4922. Phone: 800-456-6323 or (202)785-6323 Fax: (202)785-0350 E-mail: washington.contact@oecd.org • URL: http://www.oecd.org • Annual. $32.00. Produced by the OECD Nuclear Energy Agency. Provides a yearly compilation of basic statistics on electricity generation and nuclear power in OECD member countries. Text in English and French.

OECD Observer. Available from OECD Publications and Information Center, 2001 L St., N.W.,, Suite 650 Washington, DC 20036-4922. Phone: 800-456-6323 or (202)785-6323 Fax: (202)785-0350 E-mail: washington.contact@oecd.org • URL: http://www.oecd.org • Bimonthly. Price on application.

OECD Oil and Gas Information. Available from OECD Publications and Information Center, 2001 L St., N.W.,, Suite 650 Washington, DC 20036-4922. Phone: 800-456-6323 or (202)785-6323 Fax: (202)785-0350 E-mail: washington.contact@oecd.org • URL: http://www.oecd.org • Annual. Price varies. Data on oil and gas balances, supplies, consumption by end use sector and trade of OECD countries. Text in English and French.

OECD Quarterly National Accounts Bulletin. OECD Publications and Information Center, 2001 L St., N.W.,, Ste. 650 Washington, DC 20036-4910. Phone: 800-456-6323 or (202)785-6323 Fax: (202)785-0350 E-mail: sales@oecd.org • URL: http://www.oecd.org • Quarterly. $120.00 per year. National accounts data of OECD countries.

OECD Steel Market and Outlook. Organization for Economic Cooperation and Development. OECD Publications and Information Center, 2001 L St., N.W.,, Ste. 650 Washington, DC 20036-4910. Phone: 800-456-6323 or (202)785-6323

Fax: (202)785-0350 E-mail: sales@oecd.org • URL: http://www.oecd.org • Annual. Price varies.

Of Counsel: The Monthly Legal Practice Report. Aspen Law and Business, 1185 Ave. of the Americas New York, NY 10036. Phone: 800-638-8437 or (212)597-0200 Fax: (212)597-0338 E-mail: customer.service@aspenpubl.com • URL: http://www.aspenpub.com • Monthly. $426.00 per year. Newsletter on the management, marketing, personnel, and compensation of law firms.

Off-Course Golf Retail Stores Directory. National Golf Foundation, 1150 S., U.S. Highway 1, Suite 401 Jupiter, FL 33477. Phone: 800-733-6006 or (561)744-6006 Fax: (561)744-6107 E-mail: ngf@ngf.org • URL: http://www.ngf.org • 1998. $99.00. Lists about 2,000 retail stores selling golf equipment, but not located on a golf course.

Office Dealer: Updating the Office Industry's Products. Quality Publishing, Inc., P.O. Box 1028 Mount Airy, NC 27030. Phone: (336)783-0000 Fax: (336)783-0045 Six times a year. $36.00 per year. Supplies information on new products for dealers in office automation equipment and systems. Formerly *Office Systems Dealer*.

Office Equipment Adviser: The Essential What-to-Buy and How-to-Buy Resource for Offices with One to 100 People. What to Buy for Business, Inc., 370 Technology Dr. Malvern, PA 19355. Phone: 800-626-4330 E-mail: orders@betterbuys.com • URL: http://www.betterbuys.com • 1995. $24.95. Third revised edition.

Office for Sponsored Research.

Office Interior Design Guide: An Introduction for Facility and Design. Julie K. Rayfield. John Wiley and Sons, Inc., 605 Third Ave. New York, NY 10158-0012. Phone: 800-225-5945 or (212)850-6000 Fax: (212)850-6088 E-mail: info@wiley.com • URL: http://www.wiley.com • 1997. $59.95

Office of Climatology. Arizona State University

Office of Government Programs. Louisiana State University

Office of Manpower Studies. Purdue University

Office of Personnel Management Operating Manuals. Available from U. S. Government Printing Office, Washington, DC 20402. Phone: (202)512-1800 Fax: (202)512-2250 E-mail: gpoaccess@gpo.gov • URL: http://www.access.gpo.gov • Four looseleaf manuals at various prices ($25.00 to $190.00). Price of each manual includes updates for an indeterminate period. Manuals provides details of the federal wage system, the federal wage system "Nonappropriated Fund", personnel recordkeeping, personnel actions, qualification standards, and data reporting.

Office of Real Estate Research.

Office of Research Services.

Office of Sponsored Programs.

Office of Sponsored Research.

Office of the Texas State Chemist. Texas A & M University

Office Planners and Users Group., P.O. Box 11182 Philadelphia, PA 19136. Phone: (215)335-9400 Members include office designers, space planners, and architects.

Office Planning and Design Desk Reference: A Guide for Architects and Design Professionals. James Rappoport and others, editors. John Wiley and Sons, Inc., 605 Third Ave. New York, NY 10158-0012. Phone: 800-526-5368 or (212)850-6000 Fax: (212)850-6088 E-mail: info@wiley.com • URL: http://www.wiley.com • 1991. $120.00. Covers the planning and designing of new or retrofitted office space.

Office Procedures and Technology for Colleges. Patsy J. Fulton. South-Western Publishing Co., 5101 Madison Rd. Cincinnati, OH 45227. Phone: 800-543-0487 or (513)271-8811 Fax: 800-437-8488 E-mail: billhendee@itped.com • URL: http://www.swcollege.com • 1998. $39.95. 11th edition. (KF-Office Education Series).

Office Products Analyst: A Monthly Report Devoted to the Analysis of Office Products. Industry Analysts, Inc., 50 Chestnut St. Rochester, NY 14604. Phone: (716)232-5320 Fax: (716)458-3950 E-mail: theopa001@aol.com • URL: http://www.industryanalysts.com • Monthly. $195.00 per year. Newsletter. Includes user ratings of office automation equipment.

Office Professional's Quick Reference Handbook. Sheryl Lindsell-Roberts. Pearson Education and Technology, 201 W. 103rd St. Indianapolis, IN 46290-1097. Phone: 800-858-7674 or (317)581-3500 Fax: (317)581-4678 URL: http://www.mcp.com • 1995. $9.00. Fifth revised edition.

Office Relocation Magazine. ORM Group, 354 W. Lancaster Ave., c/o J. Barthelmess Haverford, PA 19041. Phone: (610)649-6565 Fax: (610)642-8020 Bimonthly. $39.00 per year. Provides articles on the relocation of office facilities.

Office Systems. Quality Publishing, Inc, 252 N. Main St., Suite 200 Mount Airy, NC 27030. Phone: (336)783-0000 Fax: (336)783-0045 URL: http://www.os.od.com • Monthly. Price on application. Special feature issue topics include document imaging, document management, office supplies, and office equipment. Incorporates *Managing Office Technology*.

Office Systems Research Association., Morehead State University, Dept. of Information Systems Morehead, KY 40351-1689. Phone: (606)783-2724 Fax: (606)783-5025 E-mail: dikizzier@moreheadst.edu • URL: http://www.osra.org • Research areas include the analysis, design, and administration of office systems.

Office World News. BUS Publications, 366 Ramtown Greenville Rd. Howell, NJ 07731-2789. Phone: (732)785-8300 Fax: (732)785-1347 E-mail: ownews@worldnet.att.net • URL: http://www.officeworldnews.com • Monthly. $50.00 per year. Formerly *Office Products News*.

OfficePro. Stratton Publishing and Marketing Inc., 5501 Backlick Rd., Suite 240 Springfield, VA 22206. Phone: (703)914-9200 Fax: (703)914-6777 Nine times a year. $25.00 per year. Provides statistics and other information about secretaries and office trends. Formerly *Secretary*.

Official ABMS Directory of Board Certified Medical Specialists. Marquis Who's Who, 121 Chanlon Rd. New Providence, NJ 07974. Phone: 800-521-8110 or (908)464-6800 Fax: (908)665-6688 E-mail: info@marquiswhoswho.com • URL: http://www.marquiswhoswho.com • Annual. $525.00. Four volumes. Published in conjunction with the American Board of Medical Specialties. Includes information on more than 565,000 specialists. Volumes are arranged by medical specialty and then geographically, with an overall index to physicians' names. Formerly *Directory of Medical Specialists*.

The Official America Online Internet Guide. David Peal. Ventana Communications Group, Inc., P.O. 13964 Research Triangle Park, NC 27709-3964. Phone: 800-743-5369 or (919)544-9404 Fax: (919)942-9472 E-mail: contact@media.com • URL: http://www.vmedia.com • 1999. $24.95. Provides a detailed explanation of the various features of versio of America Online, including electronic mail procedures and "Using the Internet."

Official Board Markets: "The Yellow Sheet". Mark Arzoumanian. Advanstar Communications, Inc., One Park Ave., 2nd Fl. New York, NY 10016-5802. Phone: 800-346-0085 or (212)951-6000 Fax: (212)951-6693 E-mail: information@advanstar.com • URL: http://www.advanstar.com • Weekly. $150.00 per year. Covers the corrugated container, folding carton, rigid box and waste paper industries.

Official Container Directory. Advanstar Communications, Inc., One Park Ave., 2nd Fl. New York, NY 10016-5802. Phone: 800-346-0085 or (212)951-6600 Fax: (212)951-6693 E-mail: information@advanstar.com • URL: http://www.advanstar.com • Semiannual. $75.00. About 3,000 manufacturers of corrugated and solid fiber containers, folding cartons, rigid boxes, fiber cans and tubes, and fiber drums. Includes a buying guide.

Official Cruise Guide. Cahners Travel Group, 500 Plaza Dr. Secaucus, NJ 07094-3626. Phone: 800-323-4000 or (201)902-2000 Fax: (201)902-1914 E-mail: corporatecommunications@cahners.com • URL: http://www.cahners.com • Annual. $85.00. Provides detailed information on more than 375 cruise ships and 150 cruise lines worldwide. Includes color coded deck plans, booking information, and fare schedules.

Official Directory of Industrial and Commercial Traffic Executives. Commonwealth Business Media, 10 Lake Dr. Hightstown, NJ 08520-5397. Phone: 800-221-5488 or (609)371-7700 Fax: (609)371-7879 E-mail: pcoleman@primediainfo.com • URL: http://www.primediainfo.com • Annual. $395.00. About 16,000 U.S. and Canadian commercial firms with full-time or part-time traffic/transportation departments, and 28,000 traffic executives.

Official Gazette of the United States Patent and Trademark Office: Patents. Available from U. S. Government Printing Office, Washington, DC 20402. Phone: (202)512-1800 Fax: (202)512-2250 E-mail: gpoaccess@gpo.gov • URL: http://www.access.gpo.gov • Weekly. $1,425.00 per year. ($1,700.00 per year by first class mail.) Contains the Patents, Patent Office Notices, and Designs issued each week (http://www.uspto.gov). Annual indexes are sold separately.

Official Gazette of the United States Patent and Trademark Office: Trademarks. Available from U. S. Government Printing Office, Washington, DC 20402. Phone: (202)512-1800 Fax: (202)512-2250 E-mail: gpoaccess@gpo.gov • URL: http://www.access.gpo.gov • Weekly. $980.00 per year by first class mail. Contains Trademarks, Trademark Notices, Marks Published for Opposition, Trademark Registrations Issued, and Index of Registrants (http://www.uspto.gov).

Official Guide for GMAT Review (Graduate Management Admission Test). Graduate Management Admissions Council. Educational Testing Service, Princeton, NJ 08541-0001. Phone: 800-759-0190 or (609)951-1236 Fax: 800-286-9471 URL: http://www.warnerbooks.com • Biennial. $11.95. Provides sample tests, answers, and explanations for the Graduate Management Admission Test (GMAT).

Official Hotel Guide. Cahners Travel Group, 500 Plaza Dr. Secaucus, NJ 07096. Phone: 800-662-7776 or (201)902-2000 Fax: (201)319-1797 E-mail: corporatecommunications@cahners.com • URL: http://www.cahners.com • Annual. $229.00. Three volumes. Contains detailed descriptions of about 30,000 hotels and resorts worldwide, graded by a 10-level classification system. Includes more than 350 maps.

Official Industrial Equipment Guide. North American Equipment Dealers Association, 1195 Smizer Mill Rd. Fenton, MO 63026-3480. Phone: (636)349-5000 E-mail: naeda@naeda.com • URL: http://www.naeda.com • Semiannual. Price varies.

Official International Toy Center Directory.

Official Motor Shippers Guide. Official Motor Freight Guide, Inc., 1700 W. Cortland St. Chicago, IL 60622-1150. Phone: 800-621-4650 or (773)278-2454 Fax: (773)489-0482 $60.50 per year. 17 regional editions. Includes one update. Formerly *Offical Shippers Guide*.

Official Railway Guide. Freight Service Edition. Commonwealth Business Media, Inc., 10 Lake Dr. Hightstown, NJ 08520-5397. Phone: 800-221-5488 or (609)371-7700 Fax: (609)317-7879 E-mail: aschumann@cbizmedia.com • URL: http://www.cbizmedia.com • Bimonthly. $234.00 per year.

Official Summary of Security Transactions and Holdings. U. S. Securities and Exchange Commission. Available from U. S. Government Printing Office, Washington, DC 20402. Phone: (202)512-1800 Fax: (202)512-2250 E-mail: gpoaccess@gpo.gov • URL: http://www.access.gpo.gov • Monthly. $166.00 per year. Lists buying or selling of each publicly held corporation's stock by its officers, directors, or other insiders.

Offshore: Incorporating The Oilman. PennWell Corp., Industrial Div., 1421 S. Sheridan Rd Tulsa, OK 74112. Phone: 800-331-4463 or (918)831-9421 Fax: (918)831-9295 E-mail: webmaster@pennwell.com • URL: http://www.pennwell.com • Monthly. $75.00 per year.

Offshore Marine Service Association., 990 N. Corporate Dr., Suite 210 Harahan, LA 70123. Phone: (504)734-7622 Fax: (504)734-7134 Members are owners and operators of vessels servicing offshore oil installations.

Ohio Aerospace Institute., 22800 Cedar Point Rd. Cleveland, OH 44142. Phone: (440)962-3000 Fax: (440)962-3120 E-mail: michaelsalkind@oai.org • URL: http://www.oai.org • Aerospace-related research, education, and technology transfers.

Ohio Agricultural Research and Development Center. Ohio State University

Oil and Gas Investor. Hart Publications, Inc., 4545 Post Oak Place, Suite 210 Houston, TX 77027. Phone: (713)993-9320 Fax: (713)840-8585 E-mail: hartinfo@phillips.com • URL: http://www.hartpub.com • Monthly. $195.00 per year.

Oil and Gas Journal. PennWell Corp., Industrial Div., 1421 S. Sheridan Rd. Tulsa, OK 74112. Phone: 800-331-4463 or (918)831-9421 Fax: (918)831-9295 E-mail: webmaster@pennwell.com • URL: http://www.ogjonline.com • Weekly. $84.00 per year.

The Oil and Natural Gas Producing Industry in Your State. Independent Petroleum Association of America. Petroleum Independent Publishers, Inc., Petroleum Independent Publishers, Inc., 1101 16th St., N.W. Washington, DC 20036. Phone: 800-433-2851 or (202)857-4774 Fax: (202)857-4799 Annual. $75.00. Statistical issue of *Petroleum Independent*.

Oil Daily: Daily Newspaper of the Petroleum Industry. Energy Intelligence Group, 575 Broadway, 4th Fl. New York, NY 10012-3230. Phone: (212)941-5500 Fax: (212)941-5509 E-mail: bkruzel@energyintel.com • URL: http://www.energytel.com • Daily. $1,145.00 per year. Newspaper for the petroleum industry.

Oil/Energy Statistics Bulletin: And Canadian Oil Reports. Oil Statistics Co., Inc., P.O. Box 189 Whitman, MA 02382. Phone: (781)447-6407 Fax: (781)447-3977 E-mail: oilstats@compuserve.com • Biweekly. $185.00 per year.

Oil Express: Inside Report on Trends in Petroleum Marketing Without the Influ nce of Advertising. Aspen Publishers, Inc., 200 Orchard Ridge Dr. Gaithersburg, MD 20878. Phone: 800-638-8437 or (301)417-7500 Fax: (301)695-7931 E-mail: customer.service@aspenpubl.com • URL: http://www.aspenpubl.com • Weekly. $337.00 per year. Newsletter. Provides news of trends in petroleum marketing and convenience store operations. Includes *U. S. Oil Week's Price Monitor* (petroleum product prices) and *C-Store Digest* (news concerning convenience stores operated by the major oil companies) and *Fuel Oil Update*. Formerly (U.S. Oil Week).

Oil Express: Inside Report on Trends in Petroleum Marketing without the Influence of Advertising. United Communications Group, 11300 Rockville Pike, Suite 1100 Rockville, MD 20852-3030. Phone: (301)816-8950 Fax: (301)816-8945 E-mail: cdonoghue@ucg.com • URL: http://www.ucg.com • Weekly. $337.00 per year. Newsletter for petroleum marketers.

Oil, Gas and Energy Quarterly. Matthew Bender & Shepard, Two Park Ave. New York, NY 10016. Phone: 800-223-1940 or (212)448-2000 Fax: (212)244-3188 E-mail: international@bender.com • URL: http://www.bender.com • Quarterly. $165.00 per year. Formerly *Oil and Gas Tax Quarterly*.

Oil, Gas and Petrochem Equipment. PennWell Corp., Industrial Div., 1421 S. Sheridan Rd. Tulsa, OK 74112. Phone: 800-331-4463 or (918)831-9421 Fax: (918)831-9295 E-mail: webmaster@pennwell.com • URL: http://www.pennwell.com • Monthly. $35.00 per year.

Oil Price Information Service. United Comunications Group, 11300 Rockville Pike, Suite 1100 Rockville, MD 20852-3030. Phone: (301)816-8950 Fax: (301)816-8945 URL: http://www.ucg.com • Weekly. $545.00 per year. Regional editions available at $150.00 per year. Quotes wholesale terminal prices for various petroleum products.

Oilheating. Industry Publications, Inc., 3621 Hill Rd. Parsippany, NJ 07054. Phone: (973)331-9545 Fax: (973)331-9537 E-mail: fooh@aol.com • 12 times a year. $30.00 per year. Formerly *Fueloil and Oil Heat with Air Conditioning*

The Oilman Weekly Newsletter. PennWell Corp., Petroleum Div., 1700 W. Loop St., Ste. 1000 Houston, TX 77027. Phone: 800-331-4463 or (713)621-9720 Fax: (713)499-6310 E-mail: webmaster@pennwell.com • URL: http://www.pennwell.com • Weekly. $1360.00 per year. Newsletter. Provides news of developments concerning the North Sea and European oil and gas businesses. Each issue contains four pages of statistical data.

Older Americans Information Directory. Laura Mars, editor. Grey House Publishing, Inc., Pocketknife Square Lakeville, CT 06039. Phone: 800-562-2149 or (860)435-0686 Fax: 800-248-0115 or (860)435-3004 E-mail: books@greyhouse.com • URL: http://www.greyhouse.com • 1998. $160.00. First edition. Provides information on about 5,000 organizations and agencies concerned with the needs of older people in the U. S.

Older Americans Information Directory. Group Grey House Publshing, Inc., Pocket Knife Square Lakeville, CT 06039. Phone: 800-562-2139 or 800-435-0868 Fax: (860)435-3004 E-mail: books@greyhouse/com • URL: http://www.greyhouse.com • 2000. $190.00. Second edition. Presents articles (text) and sources of information on a wide variety of aging and retirement topics. Includes an index to personal names, organizations, and subjects.

Older Americans Report. Business Publishers, Inc., 8737 Colesville Rd., Suite 1100, ‘ Silver Spring, MD 20910-3928. Phone: 800-274-6737 or (301)587-6300 Fax: (301)587-1081 E-mail: bpinews@bpinews.com • URL: http://www.bpinews.com • Weekly. $432.00 per year. Newsletter on health, economic, and social services for the aging, including social security, medicare, pensions, housing, nursing homes, and programs under the Older Americans Act. Edited for service providers.

Olsson Center for Applied Ethics. University of Virginia

OMB Watcher (Office of Management and Budget). O M B Watch, 1742 Connecticut Ave., N.W. Washington, DC 20009. Phone: (202)234-8494 Fax: (202)234-8584 Bimonthly. Individuals, $35.00 per year. Monitors operations of the federal Office of Management and Budget.

Omni Gazetteer of the United States of America: A Guide to 1,500,000 Place Names in the United States and Territories. Frank R. Abate, editor. Omnigraphics, Inc., Penobscot Bldg. Detroit, MI 48226. Phone: 800-234-1340 or (313)961-1340 Fax: 800-875-1340 or (313)961-1383 E-mail: info@omnigraphics.com • URL: http://www.omnigraphics.com • 1991. $3,025.00. 11 volumes. Comprehensive listing of cities, towns, suburbs, villages, boroughs, structures, facilities, locales, historic places, and named geographic features. Population is shown where applicable. Individual regional volumes are available at $275.00.

On Becoming a Counselor: A Basic Guide for Non-Professional Counselors. Eugene Kennedy and Sara Charles. Crossroad Publishing Co., 481 Eighth Ave., Suite 1550 New York, NY 10001. Phone: 800-395-0690 or (212)868-1801 Fax: (212)868-2171 E-mail: sales@crossroadpublishing.com • 1989. $19.95.

On the Mhove. Material Handling Institute, 8720 Red Oak Blvd., Suite 201 Charlotte, NC 28217-3992. Phone: 800-345-1815 or (704)676-1190 Fax: (704)676-1199 E-mail: hmcelroy@mhia.org • URL: http://www.mhia.org • Quarterly. Free. Formerly *MHI News*.

On Wall Street. Securities Data Publishing, 40 West 57th St. New York, NY 10019. Phone: 800-455-5844 or (212)765-5311 Fax: (212)956-0112 E-mail: sdp@tfn.com • URL: http://www.sdponline.com • Monthly. $96.00 per year. Edited for securities dealers. Includes articles on financial planning, retirement planning, variable annuities, and money management, with special coverage of 401(k) plans and IRAs. (Securities Data Publishing is a unit of Thomson Financial.)

One-Hour Photo Processing Lab. Entrepreneur Media, Inc., 2445 McCabe Way Irvine, CA 92614. Phone: 800-421-2300 or (949)261-2325 Fax: (949)261-0234 E-mail: entmag@entrepreneur.com • URL: http://www.entrepreneur.com • Looseleaf. $59.50. A practical guide to starting a film developing and printing business. Covers profit potential, start-up costs, market size evaluation, owner's time required, site selection, lease negotiation, pricing, accounting, advertising, promotion, etc. (Start-Up Business Guide No. E1209.)

One Hundred Highest Yields Among Federally-Insured Banks and Savings Institutions. Advertising News Service, Inc., P.O. Box 88888 North Palm Beach, FL 33408-8888. Phone: (407)627-7330 Fax: (407)627-7335 Weekly. $124.00 per year. Newsletter.

100 Leading Management Consulting Firms in U. S. Kennedy Information, LLC, One Kennedy Place, Route 12, S. Fitzwilliam, NH 03447. Phone: 800-531-1026 or (603)585-3101 Fax: (603)585-9555 E-mail: office@kennedypub.com • URL: http://www.kennedyinfo.com • Annual. $15.00. Includes company profiles and revenue data. These are ''best firms in the business'' as selected by Kennedy Publications.

175 High-Impact Cover Letters. Richard H. Beatty. John Wiley and Sons, Inc., 605 Third Ave. New York, NY 10158-0012. Phone: 800-225-5945 or (212)850-6000 Fax: (212)850-6088 E-mail: info@wiley.com • URL: http://www.wiley.com • 1996. $10.95. Second edition. Provides samples of cover letters for resumes.

100 Years of Wall Street. Charles R. Geisst. McGraw-Hill, 1221 Ave. of the Americas New York, NY 10020. Phone: 800-722-4726 or (212)904-2000 Fax: (212)904-2072 E-mail: customer.service@mcgraw-hill.com • URL: http://www.mcgraw-hill.com • 1999. $29.95. A popularly written, illustrated history of the American stock market. About 200 photographs, charts, cartoons, and reproductions of stock certificates are included.

The One-Minute Manager: Putting the One-Minute Manager to Work. Kenneth Blanchard. Berkley Publishing Group, 375 Hudson St. New York, NY 10014. Phone: 800-631-8571 or (212)366-2000 Fax: (212)213-6706 E-mail: online@penguinputnam.com • URL: http://www.penguinputnam.com • 1993. $21.90. Two volumes.

The One-Person Library: A Newsletter for Librarians and Management. Information Bridges International, Inc., 447 Harris Rd. Cleveland, OH 44143-2537. Phone: (216)486-7443 Fax: (216)486-8810 E-mail: jsiess@ibi-opl.com • URL: http://www.ibi-opl.com • Monthly. $85.00 per year. Newsletter for librarians working alone or with minimal assistance. Contains reports on library literature, management advice, case studies, book reviews, and general information.

1040 Preparation. Sidney Kess and Ben Eisenberg. CCH, Inc., 4025 W. Peterson Ave. Chicago, IL 60646-6085. Phone: 800-248-3248 or (773)866-6000 Fax: 800-224-8299 or (773)866-3608 URL: http://www.cch.com • 2001. $62.00. How to prepare individual federal income tax returns.

1997 NAICS and 1987 SIC Correspondence Tables. U. S. Census BureauPhone: (301)457-4100 Fax: (301)457-1296 E-mail: naics@census.gov • URL: http://www.census.gov/epcd/www/naicstab.htm • Web site provides detailed tables for converting four-digit Standard Industrial Classification (SIC) numbers to the six-digit North American Industrial Classification System (NAICS) or vice versa: ''1987 SIC Matched to 1997 NAICS'' or ''1997 NAICS Matched to 1987 SIC.'' Fees: Free.

One Up on Wall Street: How to Use What You Already Know to Make Money in the Market. Peter Lynch and John Rothchild. Viking Penguin, 375 Hudson St. New York, NY 10014-3657. Phone: 800-331-4624 or (212)336-2000 Fax: 800-227-9604 or (212)366-2666 E-mail: customer.service@penguin.co.uk • URL: http://www.penguin.com • 1990. $14.95.

Onion Newsletter. National Onion Association, 822 Seventh St., Suite 510 Greeley, CO 80631. Phone: (970)353-5895 Fax: (970)353-5897 E-mail: wminiger@weldnet.com • URL: http://www.onions-usa.org • Monthly. Free to members.

Online Advertising Report. Jupiter Media Metrix, 21 Astor Place New York, NY 10003. Phone: 800-488-4345 or (212)780-6060 Fax: (212)780-6075 E-mail: jupiter@jup.com • URL: http://www.jmm.com • Annual. $750.00. Market research report. Provides five-year forecasts of Internet advertising and subscription revenue. Contains analysis of online advertising trends and practices, with company profiles.

Online and CD Notes. Available from Information Today, Inc., 143 Old Marlton Pike Medford, NJ 08055-8750. Phone: 800-300-9868 or (609)654-6266 Fax: (609)654-4309 E-mail: custserv@infotoday.com • URL: http://www.infotoday.com • 10 times a year. Members $80.00 per year; non-members, $140.00 per year. Published in London by Aslib: The Association for Information Management. Contains news and reviews of the online information industry. Formerly *Online and CD-ROM Notes*.

Online Banking. MarketResearch.com, 641 Ave. of the Americas, Third Floor New York, NY 10011. Phone: 800-298-5699 or (212)807-2629 Fax: (212)807-2716 E-mail: order@marketresearch.com • URL: http://www.marketresearch.com • 2000. $3,450.00. Market research report. Includes demographics relating to the users and nonusers of online banking services. Provides market forecasts.

Online Competitive Intelligence: Increase Your Profits Using Cyber-Intelligence. Helen P. Burwell. Facts on Demand Press, 4653 South Lakeshore Drive, Suite No. 3 Tempe, AZ 85285. Phone: 800-929-3811 or (602)838-8909 Fax: 800-929-4981 or (602)838-8324 E-mail: brb@brbpub.com • URL: http://www.brbpub.com • 1999. $25.95. Covers the selection and use of online sources for competitive intelligence. Includes descriptions of many Internet Web sites, classified by subject.

Online Deskbook: Online Magazine's Essential Desk Reference for Online and Internet Searchers. Mary E. Bates. Information Today, Inc., 143 Old Marlton Pike Melton, NJ 08055-8750. Phone: 800-300-9868 or (609)654-6266 Fax: (609)654-4309 E-mail: custserv@infotoday.com • URL: http://www.infotoday.com • 1996. $29.95. Covers the World Wide Web, as well as America Online, CompuServe, Dialog, Lexis-Nexis, and all other major online services. (Pemberton Press Books.)

Online Information Review: The International Journal of Digital Information Research and Use. Information Today, Inc., 143 Old Marlton Pike Medford, NJ 08055-8750. Phone: 800-300-9868 or (609)654-6266 Fax: (609)654-4309 E-mail: custserv@infotoday.com • URL: http://www.infotoday.com • Bimonthly. $154.00 per year. Provides peer-reviewed research papers and online information industry news. Formerly *Online and CD-ROM Review*.

Online Investor: Personal Investing for the Digital Age. Stock Trends, Inc., PO Box 344 Mt. Morris, IL 61054-0344. Phone: 800-770-3070 URL: http://www.onlineinvestor.com/ • Monthly. $24.95 per year. Provides advice and Web site reviews for online traders.

Online Libraries and Microcomputers. Information Intelligence, Inc., P.O. 31098 Phoenix, AZ 85046. Phone: (602)996-2283 E-mail: order@infointelligence.com • URL: http://www.infointelligence.com/www/iii-info • Monthly. Individuals $43.75 per year; libraries. $62.50 per year. Newsletter. Covers library automation and electronic information (online, CD-ROM). Reviews or describes new computer hardware and software for library use.

Online Marketing Handbook: How to Promote, Advertise and Sell, Your Products and Services on the Internet. Daniel S. Janal. John Wiley and Sons, Inc., 605 Third Ave. New York, NY 10158-0012. Phone: 800-225-5945 or (212)850-6000 Fax: (212)850-6088 E-mail: info@wiley.com • URL: http://www.wiley.com • 1998. $29.95. Revised edition. Provides step-by-step instructions for utilizing online publicity, advertising, and sales promotion. Contains chapters on interactive marketing, online crisis communication, and Web home page promotion, with numerous examples and checklists.

Online Marketplace. Jupiter Media Metrix, 21 Astor Place New York, NY 10003. Phone: 800-488-4345 or (212)780-6060 Fax: (212)780-6075 E-mail: jupiter@jup.com • URL: http://www.jmm.com • Monthly. $695.00 per year. Newsletter on the collection of electronic payments (''e-money'') for goods and services offered through the Internet. Covers trends in retailing, banking, travel, and other areas.

Online Newsletter. Information Intelligence, Inc., P.O. 31098 Phoenix, AZ 85046. Phone: (602)996-2283 E-mail: order@infointelligence.com • URL: http://www.infointelligence.com • 10 times a year. Individuals, $43.75 per year; libraries, $62.50 per year; students, $25.00 per year. Covers the online and CD-ROM information industries, including news of mergers, acquisitions, personnel, meetings, new products, and new technology.

The Online 100: Online Magazine's Field Guide to the 100 Most Important Online Databases. Mick O'Leary. Information Today, Inc., 143 Old Marlton Pike Medford, NJ 08055-8750. Phone: 800-300-9868 or (609)654-6266 Fax: (609)654-4309 E-mail: custserv@infotoday.com • URL: http://www.infotoday.com • 1996. $22.95. Provides detailed descriptions of 100 ''important and useful'' online databases in various subject areas.

Online Retrieval: A Dialogue of Theory and Practice. Geraldene Walker and Joseph Janes. Libraries Unlimited, PO Box 6633 Englewood, CO 80155-6633. Phone: 800-237-6124 or (303)770-1220 Fax: (303)220-8843 E-mail: lu-books@lu.com • URL: http://www.lu.com • 1999. $55.00. Second edition. Edited by Carol Tenopir. Covers a wide variety of online information topics, with emphasis on bibliographic databases. (Database Searching Series.)

Online: The Leading Magazine for Information Professionals. Online, Inc., 462 Danbury Rd. Wilton, CT 06897-2126. Phone: 800-248-8466 or (203)761-1466 Fax: (203)761-1444 E-mail: info@onlineinc.com • URL: http://www.onlineinc.com/onlinemag • Bimonthly. $110.00 per year. General coverage of the online information industry.

The Only Investment Guide You'll Ever Need. Andrew Tobias. Harcourt Brace and Co., 525 B St., Suite 1900 San Diego, CA 92101-4495. Phone: 800-543-1918 or (619)699-6707 Fax: 800-876-0186 URL: http://www.harcourt.com • 1999. $14.00. Expanded revised edition. An entertaining, optimistic look at investing, written for the ''average'' investor. Provides generally conservative advice, favoring no-load, low-expense index funds.

The Only Job-Hunting Guide You'll Ever Need: The Most Comprehensive Guide for Job Hunters and Career Switchers. Kathryn Petras and Ross Petras. Simon & Schuster Trade, 1230 Ave. of the Americas New York, NY 10020. Phone: 800-223-2336 or (212)698-7000 Fax: 800-445-6991 or (212)698-7007 E-mail: sson-line_feedback@simonsays.com • URL: http://www.simonsays.com • 1995. $15.00. Revised edition.

The Only Sales Promotion Techniques You'll Ever Need: Proven Tactics and Expert Insights. Tamara Block, editor. Dartnell Corp., 350 Hiatt Dr. Palm Beach, FL 33418. Phone: 800-621-5463 or (561)622-6520 Fax: (561)622-2423 E-mail: custserv@lrp.com • URL: http://www.dartnellcorp.com • 1996. $39.95. Covers sampling, sweepstakes, co-op advertising, event marketing, database management, and other topics.

OPAC Directory: A Guide to Internet-Accessible Online Public Access Catalogs. Information Today, Inc., 143 Old Marlton Pike Medford, NJ 08055-8750. Phone: 800-300-9868 or (609)654-6266 Fax: (609)654-4309 E-mail: custserv@infotoday.com • URL: http://www.infotoday.com • Annual. $70.00. Provides the Internet addresses of more than 1,400 online public access catalogs, U. S. and foreign. Includes information on library size, subject strengths, and search characteristics.

OPD Chemical Buyers Directory. Schnell Publishing Co., Inc., Two Rector St., 26th Fl. New York, NY 10006-1819. Phone: (212)791-4200 Fax: (212)791-4313 URL: http://www.chemexpo.com • Annual. $129.00. Included in subscription to *Chemical Marketing Reporter*. About 1,500 suppliers of chemical process materials and more than 300 companies which transport and store chemicals in the U.S.

Open Systems Products Directory. UniForum, 10440 Shaker Dr., Suite 203 Columbia, MD 21046. Phone: 800-255-5620 or (410)596-8803 Fax: (301)596-8803 E-mail: pubs@uniforum.org • URL: http://www.uniform.org • Annual. $50.00. A guide to Unix and open systems products from about 2,100 vendors. Lists software, hardware, systems, tools, peripherals, services, and publications.

Opening New Doors: Alternative Careers for Librarians. Ellis Mount, editor. Special Libraries Association, 1700 18th St., N. W., 17th Fl. Washington, DC 20009-2514. Phone: (202)234-4700 Fax: 888-411-2856 or (202)234-2442 E-mail: books@sla.org • URL: http://www.sla.org • 1992. $39.00. Information professionals in careers outside the library field discuss the nature of their work, qualifications, rewards, finding a job, etc.

Operating During Strikes: Company Experience, NLRB Policies, and Governmental Regulations. Charles R. Perry and others. Univ. of Pennsylvania, Center for Human Resources, The Wharton School, 205 Avon Rd. Haverford, PA 19041. Fax: (610)642-1576 1982. $20.00. (Labor Relations and Public Policy Series No. 23).

Operating Results of Independent Supermarkets. Food Marketing Institute, 655 15th St., N.W., No.700 Washington, DC 20005-5701. Phone: (202)452-8444 Fax: (202)429-4519 E-mail: fmi@fmi.org • URL: http://www.fmi.org • Annual. Members, $30.00; non-members, $75.00. Includes data on gross margins, inventory turnover, expenses, etc.

Operational Cash Flow Management and Control. Morris A. Nunes. Prentice Hall, 240 Frisch Court Paramus, NJ 07652-5240. Phone: 800-947-7700 or (201)909-6200 Fax: 800-445-6991 or (201)909-6361 URL: http://www.prenhall.com • 1982. $34.95.

Operational Research Society Journal. Groves Dictionaries, Inc., 345 Park Ave. S., 10th Fl. New York, NY 10010. Phone: 800-221-2123 or (212)689-9200 Fax: (212)689-9711 E-mail: grove@grovereference.com • URL: http://www.grovereference.com • Monthly. $846.00 per year. Covers various applications of operations research, including forecasting, inventory, logistics, project management, and scheduling. Includes technical approaches (simulation, mathematical programming, expert systems, etc.).

Operations Alert. America's Community Bankers, 900 19th St., N.W., Suite 400 Washington, DC 20006-2105. Phone: (202)857-3100 Fax: (202)296-8716 URL: http://www.acbankers.org • Biweekly. Free to members; non-members, $200.00 per year. Newsletter reporting on regulatory and new product developments that affect community banking operations.

Operations and Management, Guide/Safety Manual. Helicopter Association International, 1635 Prince St. Alexandria, VA 22314-2818. Phone: 800-435-4976 or (703)683-4646 Fax: (703)683-4745 E-mail: rotor@rotor.com • URL: http://www.rotor.com • Annual.

Operations Management. Institutional Investor, 488 Madison Ave. New York, NY 10022. Phone: (212)224-3300 Fax: (212)224-3353 E-mail: info@iijournals.com • URL: http://www.iijournals.com • Weekly. $2,105.00 per year. Newsletter. Edited for managers of securities clearance and settlement at financial institutions. Covers new products, technology, legalities, management practices, and other topics related to securities processing.

Operations Management Education and Research Foundation., P.O. Box 661 Rockford, MI 49341. Phone: (616)732-5543 Research focuses on office operations, environment, and physical structures, including furniture fixtures.

Operations Research. Institute for Operations Research and the Management Sciences, 901 Elkridge Landing Rd., Suite 400 Linthicum, MD 21090-2909. Phone: 800-343-0062 or (410)850-0300 Fax: (410)684-2963 URL: http://www.informs.org • Bimonthly. Individuals, $109.00 per year; institutions, $227.00 per year.

Operations Research Letters. Elsevier Science, 655 Ave. of the Americas New York, NY 10010. Phone: 888-437-4636 or (212)989-5800 Fax: (212)633-3680 E-mail: usinfo@elsevier.com • URL: http://www.elsevier.com • 10 times a year. $472.00 per year.

Operations Review. Food Marketing Institute, 655 15th St., N.W., No.700 Washington, DC 20006-5701. Phone: (202)452-8444 Fax: (202)429-4519 E-mail: fmi@fmi.org • URL: http://www.fmi.org • Quarterly. $50.00 per year. Includes operating ratios for food retailing companies.

Operative Plasterers and Cement Masons International Association of U.S. and Canada.

Ophthalmic Research Institute.

Ophthalmology. American Academy of Opthalmology. Elsevier Science Inc., 655 Ave. of the Americas New York, NY 10010. Phone: 888-437-4636 or (212)989-5800 Fax: (212)633-3680 E-mail: usinfo@elsevier.com • URL: http://www.elsevier.com • Monthly. $342.00 per year.

Ophthalmology Times: All the Clinical News in Sight. Advanstar Communications, Inc., One Park Ave., 2nd Fl. New York, NY 10016-5802. Phone: 800-346-0085 or (212)951-6600 Fax: (212)951-6693 E-mail: information@advanstar.com • URL: http://www.advanstar.com • Semimonthly. $190.00 per year.

Opportunities for Study in Hand Bookbinding and Calligraphy. Guild of Book Workers, Inc., 521 Fifth Ave. New York, NY 10175. Phone: (212)292-4444 Free. About 150 teachers, schools, and centers offering hand bookbinding and calligraphic services; international coverage.

Opportunities in Airline Careers. Adrian A. Paradis. NTC/Contemporary Publishing, P.O. Box 545 Blacklick, OH 43004. Phone: 800-338-3987 or (614)755-4151 Fax: (614)755-5645 E-mail: ntcpub@mcgraw-hill.com • URL: http://www.ntc-cb.com • 1989. $14.95. Covers the full scope of careers with commercial airlines. (Opportunities in. Series).

Opportunities in Government Careers. Neale J. Baxter. NTC/Contemporary Publishing Group, 4255 W. Touhy Ave. Lincolnwood, IL 60712-1975. Phone: 800-323-4900 or (847)679-5500 Fax: 800-998-3103 or (847)679-2494 E-mail: ntcpub@tribune.com • URL: http://www.ntc-cb.com • 2001. $15.95. Edited for students and job seekers. Includes education requirements and salary data. (VGM Career Books.)

Opportunities in Interactive TV Applications & Services: An Analysis of Market Interest & Price Sensitivity. Available from MarketResearch.com, 641 Ave. of the Americas, Third Floor New York, NY 10011. Phone: 800-298-5699 or (212)807-2629 Fax: (212)807-2642 E-mail: order@marketresearch.com • URL: http://www.marketresearch.com • 2001. $1,395. Published by TechTrends, Inc. Market research data. Includes an analysis of how much consumers are willing to pay per month for each application.

Opportunities in Journalism Careers. Donald L. Ferguson and Jim Patten. NTC/Contemporary Publishing Group, 4255 W. Touhy Ave. Lincolnwood, IL 60712-1975. Phone: 800-323-4900 or (847)679-5500 Fax: 800-998-3103 or (847)679-2494 E-mail: ntcpub@tribune.com • URL: http://www.ntc-cb.com • 2001. $15.95. Edited for students and job seekers. Includes education requirements and salary data. (VGM Career Books.)

Opportunities in Visual Arts Careers. Mark Salmon. NTC/Contemporary Publishing Group, 4255 W. Touhy Ave. Lincolnwood, IL 60712-1975. Phone: 800-323-4900 or (847)679-5500 Fax: 800-998-3103 or (847)679-2494 E-mail: ntcpub@tribune.com • URL: http://www.ntc-cb.com • 2001. $15.95. Edited for students and job seekers. Includes education requirements and salary data. (VGM Career Books.)

Opportunities Industrialization Centers of America., 1415 N. Broad St. Philadelphia, PA 19122. Phone: (215)236-4500 Fax: (215)236-7480 E-mail: oica@aol.com • URL: http://www.oicafamerica.org • Provides services for the hard core unemployed and under-employed.

Optical Discs in Libraries: Uses and Trends. Ching-chih Chen. Information Today, Inc., 143 Old Marlton Pike Medford, NJ 08055-8750. Phone: 800-300-9868 or (609)654-6266 Fax: (609)654-4309 E-mail: custserv@infotoday.com • URL: http://www.infotoday.com • 1991. $79.50. Includes summaries of over 250 use studies.

Optical Engineering. International Society of Optical Engineering, PO Box 10 Bellingham, WA 98227-0010. Phone: (360)676-3290 Fax: (360)647-1445 E-mail: journals@spie.org • URL: http://www.spie.org/web/journals/oehome.html • Monthly. Free to members; non-members and institutions, $340.00 per year. Technical papers and letters.

Optical Fiber Technology: Materials, Devices, and Systems. Academic Press, Inc., Journal Div., 525 B St., Suite 1900 San Diego, CA 92101-4495. Phone: 800-321-5068 or (619)230-1840 Fax: (619)699-6715 E-mail: ap@acad.com • URL: http://academicpress.com • Quarterly. $230.00 per year.

Optical Fibre Sensor Technology. Ken Grattan and Beverley Meggitt. Chapman and Hall, 115 Fifth Ave., 4th Fl. New York, NY 10003-1004. Phone: 800-842-3636 or (212)260-1354 Fax: (212)260-1730 E-mail: info@chapall.com • URL: http://www.chaphall.com • 1999. Price on application.

Optical Industry Association.

Optical Laboratories Association.

Optical Publishing Industry Assessment. Julie B. Schwerin and Theodore A. Pine, editors. InfoTech, Inc., P.O. Box 1563 Norwich, VT 05055-1563. Phone: (802)649-8700 Fax: (802)649-8877 E-mail: info@infotechresearch.com • URL: http://www.infotechresearch.com • 1998. $1,295.00. Ninth edition. Provides market research data and forecasts to 2005 for DVD-ROM, ''Hybrid ROM/Online Media,'' and other segments of the interactive entertainment, digital information, and consumer electronics industries. Covers both software (content) and hardware. Includes Video-CD, DVD- Video, CD-Audio, DVD-Audio, DVD-ROM, PC-Desktop, TV Set-Top, CD-R, CD-RW, DVD-R and DVD-RAM.

Optical Sciences Center.

Optical Society of America.

Optical Society of America Journal. Optical Society of America, Inc., 2010 Massachusetts Ave., N.W. Washington, DC 20036-1023. Phone: 800-762-6960 or (202)223-8130 Fax: (202)223-1096 E-mail: info@osa.org • URL: http://www.osa.org • Monthly. Part A, $1,075.00 per year; Part B, $1,075.00 per year

Opticians Association of America.

Optics. Miles V. Klein and Thomas Furtak. John Wiley and Sons, Inc., 605 Third Ave. New York, NY 10158-0012. Phone: 800-225-5945 or (212)850-6000 Fax: (212)850-6088 E-mail: info@wiley.com • URL: http://www.wiley.com • 1988. $106.95. Second edition. (Manchester Physics Series).

Optics and Laser Technology. Elsevier Science, 655 Ave. of the Americas New York, NY 10010. Phone: 888-437-4636 or (212)989-5800 Fax: (212)633-3680 E-mail: usinfo@elsevier.com • URL: http://www.elsevier.com • Eight times a year. $981.00 per year.

Optics and Photonics News. Optical Society of America, Inc., 2010 Massachusetts Ave., N.W. Washington, DC 20036-1023. Phone: 800-762-6960 or (202)223-8130 Fax: (202)223-1096 E-mail: info@osa.org • URL: http://www.osa.org • Monthly. $99.00 per year.

Option Advisor. Investment Research Institute, Inc., 1259 Kemper Meadow Dr., Suite 100 Cincinnati, OH 45240. Phone: 800-872-6600 or (513)589-3800 Fax: (513)589-3810 URL: http://www.optionadvisor.com • Monthly. $200.00 per year. Newsletter. Provides specific advice and recommendations for trading in stock option contracts (puts and calls).

Options., 225 S. 15th St., Suite 1635 Philadelphia, PA 19102-3916. Phone: (215)735-2202 Fax: (215)735-8097 E-mail: lmwendell@opticscareers.org • URL: http://www.optionscareers.org • Helps men and women of all ages and backgrounds in career planning and job hunting techniques.

Options: Essential Concepts and Trading Strategies. Options Institute Staff. McGraw-Hill, 1221 Ave. of the Americas New York, NY 10020. Phone: 800-722-4726 or (212)904-2000 Fax: (212)904-2072 E-mail: customer.service@mcgraw-hill.com • URL: http://www.mcgraw-hill.com • 1999. $55.00. Third edition.

Options, Futures, and Other Derivatives. John C. Hull. Prentice Hall, 240 Frisch Court Paramus, NJ 07652-5240. Phone: 800-947-7700 or (201)909-6200 Fax: 800-445-6991 or (201)909-6361 URL: http://www.prenhall.com • 1999. $94.00. Fourth edition.

Options: The International Guide to Valuation and Trading Strategies. Gordon Gemmill. McGraw-Hill, 1221 Ave. of the Americas New York, NY 10020. Phone: 800-722-4726 or (212)904-2000 Fax: (212)904-2072 E-mail: customer.service@mcgraw-hill.com • URL: http://www.mcgraw-hill.com • 1993. $37.95. Covers valuation techniques for American, European, and Asian options. Trading strategies are discussed for options on currencies, stock indexes, interest rates, and commodities.

The Options Workbook: Proven Strategies from a Market Wizard. Anthony J. Saliba. Dearborn Financial Publishing, 155 North Wacker Drive Chicago, IL 60606-1719. Phone: 800-245-2665 or (312)836-4400 Fax: (312)836-9958 URL: http://www.dearborn.com • 2001. $40.00. Emphasis is on computerized trading on the Chicago Board Options Exchange. Includes information on specific trading strategies.

Optoelectronic Computing Systems Center., University of Colorado at Boulder, Campus Box 525 Boulder, CO 80309. Phone: (303)492-7967 Fax: (303)492-3674 E-mail: jneff@colorado.edu • URL: http://www.ocs.colorado.edu • Explores the advantages of optics over electronics for information processing.

Optoelectronic Devices. Safa Kasap. Addison Wesley Longman, Inc., One Jacob Way Reading, MA 01867. Phone: 800-447-2226 or (718)944-3700 Fax: (718)944-9351 E-mail: webmaster@aol.com • URL: http://www.awl.com • 2000. $87.00.

Optoelectronics: An Introduction. John Wilson. Prentice Hall, 240 Frisch Court Paramus, NJ 07652-5240. Phone: 800-947-7700 or (201)909-6200 Fax: 800-445-6991 or (201)909-6361 URL: http://www.prenhall.com • 1998. $86.00.

Optometric Management: The Business and Marketing Magazine for Optometry. Boucher Communications, Inc., 1300 Virginia Dr., Suite 400 Fort Washington, PA 19034-3221. Phone: 800-306-6332 or (215)643-8000 Fax: (215)643-8099 Monthly. $48.00 per year. Provides information and advice for optometrists on practice management and marketing.

Optometry and Vision Science-Geographical Directory, American Academy of Optometry. American Academy of Optometry, 6110 Executive Blvd., Suite 506 North Bethesda, MD 20852. Phone: 800-222-3790 or (301)984-1441 Fax: (301)984-4737 E-mail: aaoptom@aol.com • URL: http://www.aaopt.org • Biennial. $25.00. List of 3,400 members; international coverage.

Optometry: Journal of the American Optometric Society. American Optometric Association, 243 N. Lindbergh Blvd. St. Louis, MO 63141. Phone: (314)991-4100 Fax: (314)991-4101 E-mail: almiller@theaoa.org • URL: http://www.aoanet.org • Monthly. Free to members; non-members, $90.00 per year. Formerly (American Optometric Association Journal).

Oregon Wheat. Oregon Wheat Growers League, P.O. Box 1365 Pendleton, OR 97801-9289. Phone: (541)276-7330 Fax: (541)276-1723 Monthly. Free to members; non-members, $15.00 per year. Deals with planting, weeds, and disease warnings, storage and marketing of wheat and barley. Specifically for Oregon growers.

Organisation for Economic Co-Operation and Development.

Organization Charts: Structures of More Than 200 Businesses and Non-Profit Organizations. The Gale Group, 27500 Drake Rd. Farmington Hills, MI 48331-3535. Phone: 800-877-GALE or (248)699-GALE Fax: 800-414-5043 or (248)699-8069 E-mail: galeord@galegroup.com • URL: http://www.galegroup.com • 1999. $165.00. Third edition. Includes an introductory discussion of the history and use of such charts.

Organization for the Enforcement of Child Support., 1712 Deer Park Rd. Finksburg, MD 21048. Phone: (410)876-1826 Fax: (410)876-1826 Promotes more effective child support laws.

Organization for the Promotion and Advancement of Small Telecommunications Companies., 21 Dupont Circle, N.W. Washington, DC 20036. Phone: (202)659-5990 Fax: (202)659-4619 E-mail: jnr@opastco.org • URL: http://www.opastco.org • Members are small telephone companies serving rural areas.

The Organization of Industry. George J. Stigler. University of Chicago Press, 5801 Ellis Ave., 4th Fl. Chicago, IL 60637. Phone: 800-621-2736 or (773)702-7700 Fax: (773)702-9756 E-mail: marketing@press.uchicago.edu • URL: http://www.press.uchicago.edu • 1983. $14.95.

Organizational Dynamics: A Quarterly Review of Organizational Behavior for Management Executives. American Management Association, 1601 Broadway New York, NY 10019-7420. Phone: 800-313-8650 or (212)586-8100 Fax: (212)903-8168 E-mail: amapubs@aol.com • URL: http://www.amanet.org • Quarterly. $74.00 per year. Covers the application of behavioral sciences to business management.

Organizational Structure of Libraries. Lowell A. Martin. Scarecrow Press, Inc., 4720 Boston Way Lanham, MD 20706. Phone: 800-462-6420 or (301)459-3366 Fax: 800-338-4550 or (301)459-1705 E-mail: orders@scarecrowpress.com • URL: http://www.scarecrowpress.com • 1996. $39.50.

Organizing Corporate and Other Business Enterprises. Matthew Bender & Co., Inc., Two Park Ave. New York, NY 10016. Phone: 800-223-1940 or (212)448-2000 E-mail: international@bender.com • URL: http://www.bender.com • $240.00. Looseleaf service. Periodic supplementation. A guide to and tax factors to be considered in selecting a form of business organization for the attorney advising proposed or existing small businesses.

Organizing Projects for Success: The Human Aspects of Project Management, Volume One. Vijay K. Verma. Project Management Institute, c/o PMI Headquarters Publishing Div., 40 Colonial Square Sylva, NC 28779. Phone: (828)586-3715 Fax: (828)586-4020 E-mail: booked@pmi.org • URL: http://www.pmi.org • 1995. $32.95. (Human Aspects of Project Management Series).

Oriental Rug Importers Association.

Oriental Rug Review. Oriental Rug Auction Review, Inc., P.O. Box 709 Meredith, NH 03253. Phone: (603)744-9191 Fax: (603)744-6933 Bimonthly. $48.00 per year.

Orion Audio Blue Book. Orion Research Corp., 14555 N. Scottsdale Rd., Suite 330 Scottsdale, AZ 85254-3457. Phone: 800-844-0759 Fax: 800-375-1315 E-mail: orion@bluebook.com • URL: http://www.netzone.com/orion • Annual. $179.00. Quotes retail and wholesale prices of used audio equipment. Original list prices and years of manufacture are also shown.

Orion Camera Blue Book. Orion Research Corp., 14555 N. Scottsdale Rd., Suite 330 Scottsdale, AZ 85254-3457. Phone: 800-844-0759 Fax: 800-375-1315 E-mail: orion@bluebook.com • URL: http://www.netzone.com/orion • Annual. $144.00. Published by Orion Research Corporation. Quotes retail and wholesale prices of used cameras and equipment. Original list prices and years of manufacture are also shown.

Orion Car Stereo Blue Book. Orion Research Corp., 14555 N. Scottsdale Rd., Suite 330 Scottsdale, AZ 85254-3457. Phone: 800-844-0759 Fax: 800-375-1315 E-mail: orion@bluebook.com • URL: http://www.netzone.com/orion • Annual. $144.00. Quotes retail and wholesale prices of used stereo sound equipment for automobiles. Original list prices and years of manufacture are also shown.

Orion Computer Blue Book. Orion Research Corp., 14555 N. Scottsdale Rd., Suite 330 Scottsdale, AZ 85254-3457. Phone: 800-844-0759 Fax: 800-375-1315 E-mail: orion@bluebook.com • URL: http://www.netzone.com/orion • Quarterly. $516.00 per year. $129.00 per issue. Quotes retail and wholesale prices of used computers and equipment. Original list prices and years of manufacture are also shown.

Orion Copier Blue Book. Orion Research Corp., 14555 N. Scottsdale Rd., Suite 330 Scottsdale, AZ 85254-3457. Phone: 800-844-0759 Fax: 800-375-1315 E-mail: orion@bluebook.com • URL: http://www.netzone.com/orion • Annual. $39.00. Quotes retail and wholesale prices of used office equipment. Original list prices and years of manufacture are also shown. Formerly *Orion Office Equipment Blue Book*.

Orion Guitars and Musical Instruments Blue Book. Orion Research Corp., 14555 N. Scottsdale Rd., Suite 330 Scottsdale, AZ 85254-3457. Phone: 800-844-0759 Fax: 800-375-1315 E-mail: orion@bluebook.com • URL: http://www.netzone.com/orion • Annual. $179.00. List of manufacturers of guitars and musical instruments. Original list prices and years of manufacture are also shown. Formerly *Orion Professional Sound and Musical Instruments*.

Orion Video and Television Blue Book. Orion Research Corp., 14555 N. Scottsdale Rd., Suite 330 Scottsdale, AZ 85254-3457. Phone: 800-844-0759 Fax: 800-375-1315 E-mail: orion@bluebook.com • URL: http://www.netzone.com/orion • Annual. $144.00. Quotes retail and wholesale prices of used video and TV equipment. Original list prices and years of manufacture are also shown.

ORTECH Corporation.

OSA/SPIE/OSJ Membership Directory. Optical Society of America, Inc., 2010 Massachusetts Ave., N.W. Washington, DC 20036-1023. Phone: 800-762-6960 or (202)223-8130 Fax: (202)223-1096 E-mail: info@osa.org • URL: http://www.osa.org • Annual. List of over 20,000 persons interested in any branch of optics. Formerly *Optical Society of America-Membership Directory*. Includes coverage of the Optical Society of America, the Optical Society of Japan, and the International Society for Optical Engineering.

OSH-ROM: Occupational Safety and Health Information on CD-ROM. Available from SilverPlatter Information, Inc., 100 River Ridge Rd. Norwood, MA 02062-5026. Phone: 800-343-0064 or (781)769-2599 Fax: (781)769-8763 E-mail: info@silverplatter.com • URL: http://www.silverplatter.com • Price and frequency on application. Produced in Geneva by the International Occupational Safety and Health Information Centre, International Labour Organization (http://www.ilo.org). Provides about two million citations and abstracts to the worldwide literature of industrial safety, industrial hygiene, hazardous materials, and accident prevention. Material is included from journals, technical reports, books, government publications, and other sources. Time span varies.

OSHA Required Safety Training for Supervisors. Occupational Safety and Health Administration. Business and Legal Reports, Inc., P.O. Box 6001 Old Saybrook, CT 06475-6001. Phone: 800-727-5257 or (203)318-0000 Fax: (203)245-2559 Monthly. $99.00 per year. Newsletter. Formerly *Safetyworks for Supervisors*.

Our National Parks and the Search for Sustainability. Bob R. O'Brien. University of Texas Press, PO Box 7819 Austin, TX 78713-7819. Phone: 800-252-3206 or (512)471-4034 Fax: (512)320-0668 E-mail: utpress@utpress.ppb.uteuas.edu • URL: http://www.utexas.edu/utpress • 1999. $40.00. Sustainability is defined as "a balance that allows as many people as possible to visit a park that is kept in as natural a state as possible."

Out-of-Home Advertising Source. SRDS, 1700 Higgins Rd. Des Plaines, IL 60018. Phone: 800-851-7737 or (847)375-5000 Fax: (847)375-5001 E-mail: srobe@srds.com • URL: http://www.srds.com • Annual. $299.00. Provides detailed information on non-traditional or "out-of-home" advertising media: outdoor, aerial, airport, mass transit, bus benches, school, hotel, in-flight, in-store, theater, stadium, taxi, truck-stop, kiosk, shopping malls, and others.

Outdoor Advertising Association of America.

Outdoor Advertising of America/Marketing Div.

Outdoor Amusement Business Association.

Outdoor Power Equipment Institute., 341 S. Patrick St. Alexandria, VA 22314. Phone: (703)549-7600 Fax: (703)549-7604 Members are manufacturers of lawn mowers, garden tractors, snow throwers, leaf vacuums, power trimmers, etc.

Outlook for Travel and Tourism. Travel Industry Association of America, 1100 New York Ave., N.W., Suite 240 Washington, DC 20005-3934. Phone: (202)408-8422 Fax: (202)408-1255 E-mail: rmcclur@tia.org • URL: http://www.tia.org • Annual. Members, $100.00; non-members, $175.00. Contains forecasts of the performance of the U. S. travel industry, including air travel, business travel, recreation (attractions), and accomodations.

Outlook for United States Agricultural Trade. Available from U. S. Government Printing Office, Washington, DC 20402. Phone: (202)512-1800 Fax: (202)512-2250 E-mail: gpoaccess@gpo.gov • URL: http://www.access.gpo.gov • Quarterly. $10.00 per year. Issued by the Economic Research Service, U. S. Department of Agriculture. (Situation and Outlook Reports.)

Outspokin'. National Bicycle Dealers Association, 2240 University Dr., No. 130 Newport Beach, CA 92660-3319. Phone: (714)722-6909 Fax: (714)722-6975 Monthly. $100.00 per year. Association membership newsletter for bicycle retailers.

Outstanding Investor Digest: Perspectives and Activities of the Nation's Most Successful Money Managers. Outstanding Investor Digest, Inc., 14 E. Fourth St., Ste. 501 New York, NY 10012. Phone: (212)777-3330 $395.00 for 10 issues. Newsletter. Each issue features interviews with leading money managers.

Over-the-Counter Derivatives Products: A Guide to Legal Risk Management and Documentation. Robert M. McLaughlin. McGraw-Hill Professional, 1221 Ave. of the Americas New York, NY 10020. Phone: 800-722-4726 or (212)904-2000 Fax: (212)904-2072 E-mail: customer.service@mcgraw-hill.com • URL: http://www.mcgraw-hill.com • 1998. $75.00.

Over-the-Counter Securities Markets. Julian G. Buckley and Leo M. Loll. Prentice Hall, 240 Frisch Court Paramus, NJ 07652-5240. Phone: 800-947-7700 or (201)909-6200 Fax: 800-445-6991 or (201)909-6361 URL: http://www.prenhall.com • 1986. $33.95. Third edition.

Overeducation in the U.S. Labor Market. Russell W. Rumberger. Greenwood Publishing Group, Inc., 88 Post Rd., W. Westport, CT 06881-5007. Phone: 800-225-5800 or (203)226-3571 Fax: (203)222-2540 E-mail: bookinfo@greenwood.com • URL: http://www.greenwood.com • 1981. $57.95.

Overseas Automotive Council Membership Roster. Overseas Automotive Council, P.O. Box 13966 Research Triangle Park, NC 27709-3966. Phone: (919)406-8810 Fax: (919)549-4824 E-mail: aac@mema.org • URL: http://www.oac-intl.org • Annual. $50.00 per year. Lists over 700 U.S. and overseas members. Newsletter.

Overseas Development Council.

Overseas Writers.

Oxbridge Directory of Newsletters. Oxbridge Communications, Inc., 150 Fifth Ave., Suite 302 New York, NY 10011-4311. Phone: 800-955-0231 or (212)741-0231 Fax: (212)633-2938 E-mail: info@mediafinder.com • URL: http://www.mediafinder.com • Annual. $705.00. Lists approximately 20,000 newsletters in the United States and Canada.

Oxfam America.

Oxford Companion to Wine. Jancis Robinson, editor. Oxford University Press, Inc., 198 Madison Ave. New York, NY 10016. Phone: 800-451-7556 or (212)726-6000 Fax: (212)726-6446 E-mail: custserv@oup-usa.org • URL: http://www.oup-usa.org • 1999. $65.00. Second edition. Contains approximately 3,000 entries explaining the making of wine, varieties of wine, and characteristics of vineyards.

Oxford English Dictionary. J. A. Simpson and Edmund S. Weiner. Oxford University Press, Inc., 198 Madison Ave. New York, NY 10016-4314. Phone: 800-451-7556 or (212)726-6000 Fax: (212)746-6446 E-mail: custserv@oup-usa.org • URL: http://www.oup-usa.org • 1989. $3,000.00. Second edition. 20 volumes.

Oxford Guide to Library Research. Thomas Mann. Oxford University Press, Inc., 198 Madison Ave. New York, NY 10016-4314. Phone: 800-451-7556 or (212)726-6000 Fax: (212)726-6446 E-mail: custserv@oup-usa.org • URL: http://www.oup-usa.org • 1998. $35.00. Covers print sources, electronic sources, and "nine research methods."

Oxford Tobacco Research Station. North Carolina Department of Agriculture

P-O-P Design (Point-of-Purchase): Products and News for High-Volume Pro ducers and Designers of Displays, Signs and Fixtures. Hoyt Publishing Co., 7400 Skokie Blvd. Skokie, IL 60077-3339. Phone: (847)675-7400 Fax: (847)675-7494 E-mail: getinfo@hoytpub.com • Bimonthly. $59.00 per year.

Pacific Boating Almanac. ProStar Publications, Inc., 13468 Beach Ave. Marine Del Rey, CA 90292. Phone: (310)557-9575 Fax: (310)577-9272 E-mail: prostarpub@earthlink.net • Annual. $24.95 per volume. Three volumes.

Volume one, *Pacific Northwest*; volume two, *Northern California and the Delta*; volume three *Southern California and Mexico*. Lists over 3,000 marine facilities serving recreational boating.

Pacific Coast Oyster Growers Association.

Pacific Coast Paper Box Manufacturers' Association.

Pacific International Center for High Technology Research., 2800 Woodlawn Dr., Suite 180 Honolulu, HI 96822-1843. Phone: (808)539-3900 Fax: (808)539-3892 E-mail: keithm@htdc.org • URL: http://www.pichtr.htdc.org • Desalination is included as a field of research.

Pacific Salmon Commission.

Package Printing: For Printers and Converters of Labels, Flexible Packaging and Folding Cartons. North American Publishing Co., 401 N. Broad St. Philadelphia, PA 19108-9988. Phone: 800-627-2689 or (215)238-5300 Fax: (215)238-5457 E-mail: dbrennan@napco.com • URL: http://www.napco.com • Monthly. Free to qualified personnel; others, $59.00 per year. Formerly Package Printing and Converting.

Packaging Digest. Cahners Business Information, 2000 Clearwater Dr. Oak Brooks, IL 60523. Phone: 800-662-7776 or (630)320-7000 Fax: (630)320-7457 E-mail: corporatecommunications@cahners.com • URL: http://www.cahners.com • 13 times a year. $92.90 per year.

Packaging Digest Machinery/Materials Guide. Cahners Business Information, 1350 E. Touhy Ave. Des Plaines, IL 60018-3358. Phone: 800-662-7776 or (847)635-8800 Fax: (847)390-2460 E-mail: corporatecommunications.com • URL: http://www.cahners.com • Annual. $46.00. List of more than 3,100 manufacturers of machinery and materials for the packaging industry, and about 260 contract packagers.

Packaging Machinery Manufacturers Institute.

Packaging Technology and Science. Available from John Wiley and Sons, Inc., Journals Div., 605 Third Ave. New York, NY 10158-0012. Phone: 800-526-5368 or (212)850-6000 Fax: (212)850-6088 E-mail: info@wiley.com • URL: http://www.wiley.com • Bimonthly. $995.00 per year. Provides international coverage of subject matter. Published in England by John Wiley & Sons Ltd.

The Packer: Devoted to the Interest of Commericial Growers, Packers, Shippers, Receivers and Retailers of Fruits, Vegetables and Other Products. Vance Publishing Corp., Produce Div., 10901 W. 84th Terrace Lenexa, KS 66214-0695. Phone: 800-255-5113 or (913)438-8700 Fax: (913)438-0695 E-mail: ltimm@vancepublishing.com • URL: http://www.vancepublishing.com • Weekly. $65.00 per year. Supplments available, *Brand Directory* and *Fresh Trends*, *Packer's Produce Availiability and Merchandising Guide* and *Produce Services Sourcebooks*.

Packer Produce Availability and Merchandising Guide. Vance Publishing Corp., 10901 W. 84th Terrace Lenexa, KS 66214-1631. Phone: 800-255-5113 or (913)438-8700 Fax: (913)438-0657 E-mail: news@thepacker.com • URL: http://www.packer.com • Annual. $35.00. A buyer's directory giving sources of fresh fruits and vegetables. Shippers are listed by location for each commodity.

The Page. Z-D Journals, 500 Canal View Blvd. Rochester, NY 14623. Phone: 800-223-8720 or (716)240-7301 Fax: (716)214-2387 E-mail: zdjcr@zd.com • URL: http://www.zdjournals.com • 10 times a year. $59.00 per year. Newsletter on the use of MacIntosh computers for desktop publishing.

Paint and Coatings Industry. Business News Publishing Co., 755 W. Big Beaver Rd., Suite 1000 Troy, MI 48084. Phone: 800-837-7370 or (248)362-3700 Fax: (248)362-0317 URL: http://www/bnp.com • Monthly. $55.00 per year. Includes annual *Raw Material* and *Equipment Directory and Buyers Guide*.

Paint and Decorating Retailer. Paint and Decorating Retailers Association, 403 Axminster Dr. Fenton, MO 63026-2941. Phone: 800-737-0107 or (314)326-2636 Fax: (314)326-1823 E-mail: info@pdra.org • URL: http://www.pdra.org • Monthly. $45.00 per year. Formerly *Decorating Retailer*.

Paint and Decorating Retailer's Directory of the Wallcoverings Industry: The Gold Book. Paint and Decorating Retailers Association, 403 Axminster Dr. Fenton, MO 63026-2941. Phone: 800-737-0107 or (314)326-2636 Fax: (314)326-1823 E-mail: info@pdra.org • URL: http://www.pdra.org • Annual. $25.00. Formerly *Decorating Retailer's Directory of the Wallcovering Industry*.

Paint Handbook. Guy E. Weismantel, editor. McGraw-Hill, 1221 Ave of the Americas New York, NY 10020-1095. Phone: 800-722-4726 or (212)904-2000 Fax: (212)904-2072 E-mail: customer.service@mcgraw-hill.com • URL: http://www.mcgraw-hill.com • 1981. $89.95.

Paint Red Book. PTN Publishing Co., 445 Broad Hollow Rd. Melville, NY 11747. Phone: (516)845-2700 Fax: (516)845-7109 Annual. $53.00. Lists manufacturers of paint, varnish, lacquer, and specialized coatings. Suppliers of raw materials, chemicals, and equipment are included.

Paint, Varnish, and Lacquer. U. S. Bureau of the Census, Washington, DC 20233-0800. Phone: (301)457-4100 Fax: (301)457-3842 URL: http://www.census.gov. • Quarterly and annual. Provides data on shipments: value, quantity, imports, and exports. Includes paint, varnish, lacquer, product finishes, and special purpose coatings. (Current Industrial Reports, MQ-28F.)

Painting and Decorating Contractors of America.

PAIS International. Public Affairs Information Service, Inc., 521 W. 43rd St. New York, NY 10036. Phone: 800-288-7247 or (212)736-6629 Fax: (212)643-2848 E-mail: inquiries@pais.org • URL: http://www.pais.org • Corresponds to the former printed publications, *PAIS Bulletin* (1976-90) and *PAIS Foreign Language Index* (1972-90), and to the current *PAIS International in Print* (1991 to date). Covers economic, political, and sociological material appearing in periodicals, books, government documents, and other publications. Updating is monthly. Inquire as to online cost and availability.

PAIS International in Print. Public Affairs Information Service, Inc., 521 W. 43rd St., 5th Fl. New York, NY 10036-4396. Phone: 800-288-7247 or (212)736-6629 Fax: (212)643-2848 E-mail: inquiries@pais.org • URL: http://www.pais.org • Monthly. $650.00 per year; cumulations three times a year. Provides topical citations to the worldwide literature of public affairs, economics, demographics, sociology, and trade. Text in English; indexed materials in English, French, German, Italian, Portuguese and Spanish.

PAIS on CD-ROM. Public Affairs Information Service, Inc., 521 West 43rd St. New York, NY 10036. Phone: 800-288-7247 or (212)736-6629 Fax: (212)643-2848 E-mail: inquiries@pais.org • URL: http://www.pais.org • Quarterly. $1,995.00 per year. Provides a CD-ROM version of the online service, *PAIS International*. Contains over 400,000 citations to the literature of contemporary social, political, and economic issues.

Palm Beach Illustrated: The Best of Boca Raton to Vero Beach. Palm Beach Media Group, 1000 N. Dixie Highway West Palm Beach, FL 33401. Phone: (407)659-0210 Fax: (407)659-1736 E-mail: pbillus@aol.com • URL: http://www.pbol.com • 10 times a year. $30.00 per year. Includes *Palm Beach Social Observer*. Formerly *Illustrated*.

Panel World. Hatton-Brown Publishers, Inc., 225 Hanrick St. Montgomery, AL 36104. Phone: 800-669-5613 or (334)834-1170 Fax: (334)834-4525 E-mail: mail@hattonbrown.com • URL: http://www.hattonbrown.com • Bimonthly. $28.00. Formerly *Plywood and Panel World*.

Panel World Directory and Buyers' Guide. Hatton-Brown Publisher, Inc., 225 Hanrick St. Montgomery, AL 36104. Phone: 800-669-5613 or (334)834-1170 Fax: (334)834-4525 E-mail: mail@hattonbrown.com • URL: http://www.hattonbrown.com • Annual. $10.00. Included with subscription to *Paper, Film and Foil Converter*. Supersedes *Plywood and Panel World Directory and Buyer's Guide*.

Paper Age. Global Publications, 77 Waldron Ave. GlenRock, NJ 07452-2830. Phone: (201)666-2262 Fax: (201)666-9046 Monthly. $20.00 per year.

Paper Basics: Forestry, Manufacture, Selection, Purchasing, Mathematics and Metrics, Recycling. David Saltman. Krieger Publishing Co., P.O. Box 9542 Melbourne, FL 32902-9542. Phone: 800-724-0025 or (321)724-9542 Fax: (321)951-3671 E-mail: info@krieger-publishing.com • URL: http://www.krieger-publishing.com • 1991. $29.50. Reprint of 1978 edition.

Paper, Film and Foil Converter. Intertec Publishing Corp., 29 N. Wacker Dr. Chicago, IL 60606-3298. Phone: 800-400-5945 or (312)726-2802 Fax: (312)726-0241 E-mail: subs@intertec.com • URL: http://www.intertec.com • Monthly. $62.50 per year.

Paper Industry Management Association.

Paper Money. Society of Paper Money Collectors, Inc., P.O. Box 1085 Florissant, MO 63031-0085. Bimonthly. $20.00 per year.

Paper Money of the United States: A Complete Guide with Valuations. Arthur L. Friedberg and others. Coin and Currency Institute, Inc., P.O. Box 1057 Clifton, NJ 07014. Phone: 800-421-1866 or (973)471-4441 Fax: (973)471-1062 E-mail: coincurin@aol.com • URL: http://www.coin-currency.com • 1998. $35.00. 15th revised edition.

Paper Shipping Sack Manufacturers Association.

Paperboard Packaging Council.

Paperboard Packaging Worldwide. Advanstar Communications, Inc., 7500 Old Oak Blvd. Cleveland, OH 44130. Phone: 800-346-0085 or (440)243-8100 Fax: (440)891-2740 E-mail: infromation@advanstar.com • URL: http://www.advanstar.com • Monthly. $39.00 per year.

PaperChem Database. Information Services Div., Institute of Paper Science and Technology, 500 Tenth St., N.W. Atlanta, GA 30318. Phone: (404)894-5700 Fax: (404)894-4778 Worldwide coverage of the scientific and technical paper industry chemical literature, including patents, 1967 to present. Weekly updates. Inquire as to online cost and availability.

Parcel Shippers Association.

Parking Publications for Planners. Dennis Jenks. Sage Publications, Inc., 2455 Teller Rd. Thousand Oaks, CA 91320. Phone: (805)499-0721 Fax: (805)499-0871 E-mail: info@sagepub.com • URL: http://www.sagepub.com • 1993. $10.00.

Parking: The Magazine of the Parking Industry. National Parking Association, 1112 16th St., N.W., Suite 300 Washington, DC 20036. Phone: (202)296-4336 Fax: (202)331-8523 10 times a year. $95.00 per year. Includes *Product and Services Directory*.

Parks and Recreation Buyers' Guide. National Recreation and Park Association, 22377 Belmont Ridge Rd. Ashburn, VA 20148-4501. Phone: 800-626-6772 or (703)858-0784 Fax: (703)858-0794 Annual. Price upon application. List of 800 companies supplying products and services to private and governmental park and recreation agencies.

Parks Directory of the United States: A Guide to 4,700 National and State Parks, Recreation Areas, Historic Sites, Battlefields, Monuments, Forests, Preserves, Memorials, Seashores...and Other Designated Recreation Areas in the United State. Darren L. Smith, editor. Omnigraphics, Inc., Penobscot Bldg. Detroit, MI 48226. Phone: 800-234-1340 or (313)961-1340 Fax: 800-875-1340 or (313)961-1383 E-mail: info@omnigraphics.com • URL: http://www.omnigraphics.com • Biennial. $145.00. Consists of three sections: National Parks, State Parks, and Park-Related Organizations and Agencies. Includes an alphabetical index and a park classification index.

Parliamentary Journal. American Institute of Parliamentarians, P.O. Box 2173 Wilmington, DE 19899-2173. Phone: (302)762-1811 Fax: (302)762-2170 Quarterly. $20.00 per year.

Parliamentary Law and Practice for Nonprofit Organizations. Howard L. Oleck and Cami Green. American Law Institute-American Bar Association, Committee on Continuing Professional Education, 4025 Chestnut St. Philadelphia, PA 19104-3099. Phone: 800-253-6397 or (215)243-1600 Fax: (215)243-1664 URL: http://www.ali.org • 1991. $20.00. Second edition. Covers meeting procedures, motions, debate, voting, nominations, elections, committees, duties of officers, rights of members, and other topics.

Participative Management: An Analysis of Its Affect on Productivity. Michael H. Swearingen. Garland Publishing, Inc., 19 Union Square West, 8th Fl. New York, NY 10003-3382. Phone: 800-627-6273 or (212)414-0650 Fax: (212)414-0659 E-mail: info@garland.com • URL: http://www.garlandpub.com • 1997. $35.00. (Garland Studies on Industrial Productivity).

Participative Management in Academic Libraries. Maurice P. Marchant. Greenwood Publishing Group, Inc., 88 Post Rd., W. Westport, CT 06881-5007. Phone: 800-225-5800 or (203)226-3571 Fax: (203)222-2540 E-mail: bookinfo@greenwood.com • URL: http://www.greenwood.com • 1977. $45.00. (Contributions in Librarianship and Information Science Series, No. 16).

Partnership Book: How You and a Friend Can Legally Start Your Own Business. Denis Clifford and Ralph Warner. Nolo.com, 950 Parker St. Berkeley, CA 94710. Phone: 800-992-6656 or (510)549-1976 Fax: (510)548-5902 E-mail: cs@nolo.com • URL: http://www.nolo.com • 2000. Sixth edition. Price on application.

Partnerships and LLCs: Tax Practice and Analysis. Thomas G. Manolakas. CCH, Inc., 4025 West Peterson Ave. Chicago, IL 60646-6085. Phone: 800-248-3248 or (773)866-6000 Fax: 800-224-8299 or (773)866-3608 E-mail: cust_serv@cch.com • URL: http://www.cch.com • 2001. $99.00. Covers the taxation of partnerships and limited liability companies.

Passenger Transport. American Public Transit Association, 1201 New York Ave., N.W., Suite 400 Washington, DC 20005. Phone: (202)898-4119 Fax: (202)898-4095 URL: http://www.apta.com • Weekly. $65.00 per year. Covers current events and trends in mass transportation.

Passive Solar Industries Council.

Passport Newsletter. Remy Publishing Co., 401 N. Franklin St., 3rd Fl. Chicago, IL 60610. Phone: (312)464-0300 Fax: (312)464-0166 Monthly. $89.00 per year. Formerly *Passport*.

Pasta Industry Directory. National Pasta Association, 2101 Wilson Blvd., Suite 920 Arlington, VA 22201. Phone: (703)841-0818 Fax: (703)528-6507 E-mail: npa@ilovepasta.org • URL: http://www.ilovepasta.org • Annual. $50.00. Lists pasta manufacturers and industry suppliers in various categories. (A special issue of *Pasta Journal*.)

Pasta Journal. National Pasta Association, 2101 Wilson Blvd., Suite 920 Arlington, VA 22201-3008. Phone: (703)841-0818 Fax: (703)528-6507 E-mail: npa@ilovepasta.org • URL: http://www.ilovepasta.org • Bimonthly. $35.00 per year.

Patent and Trademark Office Society Journal. Patent and Trademark Office Society, P.O. Box 2600 Arlington, VA 22202. E-mail: societypto@aol.com • URL: http://www.jptos.org • Individuals, $40.00 per year; associates $47.00 per year; students, $26.00 per year.

Patent, Copyright, and Trademark: A Desk Reference to Intellectual Property Law. Stephen Elias. Nolo.com, 950 Parker

St. Berkeley, CA 94710. Phone: 800-992-6656 or (510)549-1976 Fax: (510)548-5902 E-mail: cs@nolo.com • URL: http://www.nolo.com • 1999. $24.95. Third revised edition. Contains practical explanations of the legalities of patents, copyrights, trademarks, and trade secrets. Includes examples of relevant legal forms. A 1985 version was called *Nolo's Intellectual Property Law Dictionary.* (Nolo Press Self-Help Law Series).

Patent It Yourself. David R. Pressman. Nolo.com, 950 Parker St. Berkeley, CA 94710. Phone: 800-992-6656 or (510)549-1976 Fax: (510)548-5902 E-mail: cs@nolo.com • URL: http://www.nolo.com • 2000. Eighth edition. Price on application.

Patent Law Annual, Southwestern Legal Foundation: Proceedings, lst-26th, l963-1988. William S. Hein and Co., Inc., 10368 W. Centennial Rd. Littleton, CO 80127. Phone: 800-457-1956 or (303)979-5657 Fax: (303)978-1457 1963. $1,300.00 per set. Latest problem-solving information.

Patent Law Basics. Peter D. Rosenberg. West Group, 610 Opperman Dr. Eagan, MN 55123. Phone: 800-328-4880 or (651)687-7000 Fax: 800-213-2323 or (651)687-5827 URL: http://www.westgroup.com • $125.00. Looseleaf service. Periodic supplement. Overs Patent and Trademark Office applications, patent ownership, rights, protection, infringement, litigation, and other fundamentals of patent law.

Patent Law Handbook. West Group, 610 Opperman Dr. Eagan, MN 55123. Phone: 800-328-4880 or (651)687-7000 Fax: 800-213-2323 or (651)687-5827 URL: http://www.westgroup.com • Annual. $167.00.

Patent, Trademark, and Copyright Laws, 2000. Jeffrey Samuels. BNA Books, Bureau of National Affairs, Inc., 1231 25th St., N. W. Washington, DC 20037. Phone: 800-372-1033 or (202)833-7470 Fax: (202)833-7490 E-mail: books@bna.com • URL: http://www.bna.com/bnabooks • $95.00. Date not set. Contains text of "all pertinent intellectual property legislation to date."

Patents. Matthew Bender & Co., Inc., Two Park Ave. New York, NY 10016. Phone: 800-223-1940 or (212)448-2000 Fax: (212)244-3188 E-mail: international@bender.com • URL: http://www.bender.com • 1,735.00. 13 looseleaf volumes. Periodic supplementation. An analysis of patent law in the U. S. Includes bibliography and glossary.

Patents, Trademarks and Related Rights: National and International Protection. Stephen Ladas. Harvard University Press, 79 Garden St. Cambridge, MA 02138. Phone: 800-448-2242 or (617)495-2600 Fax: 800-962-4983 or (617)495-4898 E-mail: contacthup@harvard.edu • URL: http://www.hup.harvard.edu • 1975. $197.00. Three volumes.

Patient Management. Cahners Business Information, New Product Information, 301 Gibraltar Dr. Morris Plains, NJ 07950-0650. Phone: 800-662-7776 or (973)292-5100 Fax: (973)539-3476 E-mail: corporatecommunications@cahners.com • URL: http://www.cahners.com • Nine times a year. $24.00 per year. Formerly *Medical Care Products.*

Patterson's American Education. Educational Directories, Inc., P.O. Box 199 Mount Prospect, IL 60056-0199. Phone: (847)459-0605 Fax: (847)459-0608 Annual. Individuals, $87.00; Schools and libraries, $75.00 schools in the U. S. Includes enrollment, grades offered, and name of principal. Geographical arrangement, with indexing by name of school and type of school.

Patterson's Schools Classified. Educational Directories, Inc., P.O. Box 199 Mount Prospect, IL 60056-0199. Phone: (847)459-0605 Fax: (847)459-0608 Annual. $15.00. Lists more than 7,000 accredited colleges, universities, junior colleges, and vocational schools. Includes brief descriptions. Classified arrangement, with index to name of school. Included in *Patterson's American Education.*

Patty's Industrial Hygiene and Toxicology. George D. Clayton and Florence E. Clayton, editors. John Wiley and Sons, Inc., 605 Third Ave. New York, NY 10158-0012. Phone: 800-225-5945 or (212)850-6000 Fax: (212)850-6088 E-mail: info@wiley.com • URL: http://www.wiley.com • 2000. $2,195.00. Three volumes in 10 parts. Provides broad coverage of environmental factors and stresses affecting the health of workers. Contains detailed information on the effects of specific substances.

Paytech. American Payroll Association, 711 Navarro St., Suite 100 San Antonio, TX 78205. Phone: (210)226-4600 Fax: (210)226-4027 URL: http://www.americanpayroll.org • Bimonthly. Membership. Covers the details and technology of payroll administration.

PC Letter: The Insider's Guide to the Personal Computer Industry. David Coursey, editor. Stewart Alsop, 155 Bovet Rd., Suite 800 San Mateo, CA 94402-3115. Phone: 800-432-2478 or (415)592-8880 Fax: (415)312-0547 22 times a year. $495.00 per year. Newsletter. Includes reviews of new PC hardware and software.

PC Magazine: The Independent Guide to Personal Computing and the Internet. Ziff-Davis Publishing Co., 28 E. 28th St. New York, NY 10016. Phone: 800-451-1032 or (212)503-5100 URL: http://www.pcmag.com • Biweekly. $49.97 per year.

PC Management: A How-To-Do-It Manual for Librarians. Michael Schuyler and Jake Hoffman. Neal-Schuman Publishers, Inc., 100 Varick St. New York, NY 10013. Phone: (212)925-8650 Fax: 800-584-2414 E-mail: info@neal-schuman.com • URL: http://www.neal-schuman.com • 1990. $45.00. Covers the use of personal computers for library routines. Includes evaluations of software. (How-to-Do-It Series).

PC Publishing and Presentations: Desktop Publishing. International Desktop Communications, Ltd., 342 Madison Ave., Suite 622 New York, NY 10173-0002. Phone: (212)768-7666 Fax: (212)768-0288 Monthly. $36.00 per year. Formerly *PC Publishing.*

PC World: The No. 1 Source for Definitive How-to-Buy, How-to-Use Advice on Personal Computing Systems and Software. PC World Communications, Inc., 501 Second St. San Francisco, CA 94107. Phone: 800-234-3498 or (415)243-0500 Fax: (415)442-1891 E-mail: letters@pcworld.com • URL: http://www.pcworld.com • Monthly. $29.90 per year.

PCS Systems and Technology: Personal Communications Services Technology of the Digital Wireless Age. Cahners Business Information, 301 Gibraltar Dr. Morris Plains, NJ 07950-0650. Phone: 800-662-7776 Fax: (973)539-3476 E-mail: corporatecommunications@cahners.com • URL: http://www.cahners.com • Nine times a year. Price on application. Covers network management and other technical topics.

PDR Family Guide to Nutrition and Health: The Facts to Remember...The Claims to Forget. Medical Economics Co., Inc., Five Paragon Dr. Montvale, NJ 07645-1742. Phone: 800-442-6657 or (201)358-7200 Fax: (201)573-8999 E-mail: customerservice@medec.com • URL: http://www.medec.com • 1995. $25.95. Provides advice on diet, vitamins, minerals, fat, salt, cholesterol, and other topics related to nutrition.

PDR for Herbal Medicines. Medical Economics Co., Inc., Five Paragon Dr. Montvale, NJ 07645-1742. Phone: 800-442-6657 or (201)358-7500 Fax: (201)573-8999 E-mail: customerservice@medec.com • URL: http://www.medec.com • 1999. $59.95. Published in cooperation with PhytoPharm, U. S. Institute for Phytopharmaceuticals, Inc. Provdies detailed information on more than 600 herbal remedies, including scientific names, common names, indications, usage, adverse reactions, drug interaactions, and literature citations.

PDR Guide to Drug Interactions, Side Effects, Indications. American Medical Association. Medical Economics Co., Inc., Five Paragon Dr. Montvale, NJ 07645-1742. Phone: 800-232-7379 or (201)358-7200 Fax: (201)573-8999 E-mail: customerservice@medec.com • URL: http://www.medec.com • Annual. $48.95. Includes a list of prescription drugs by "precise clinical situation."

PE Update. Project Equality, 6301 Rockhill Rd., Suite 315 Kansas City, MO 64131. Phone: (816)361-9222 Fax: (816)361-8997 E-mail: kirkp@projectequality.org • URL: http://wwwprojectequality.org • Quarterly. Membership. Formerly *Project Equality Update.*

Peace Corps Times. U. S. Peace Corps, 1111 20th St., N. W. Washington, DC 20526. Phone: 800-424-8580 or (202)692-2000 Fax: (202)692-2231 URL: http://www.peacecorps.gov • Quarterly. Presents news of the programs and activities of the Peace Corps.

Peaceworkers.

Peach-Times. National Peach Council, 12 Nicklaus Lane, Suite 101 Columbia, SC 29229. Phone: (803)778-7101 Quarterly. Membership.

Peanut and Tree Nut Processors Association.

The Peanut Farmer: For Commercial Growers of Peanuts and Related Agribusiness. SpecComm International, Inc., 3000 Highwoods Blvd., Suite 300 Raleigh, NC 27604-1029. Phone: (919)872-5040 Fax: (919)872-6531 E-mail: spec_circ@juno.com • URL: http://www.peanutfarmer.com • Seven times a year. $15.00 per year.

Peanut Journal and Nut World. Virginia-Carolina Peanut Association. Peanut Journal Publishing Co., 2921 N. Radcliffe Lane Chesapeake, VA 23321-4551. Monthly. $8.00 per year.

Peanut Science. American Peanut Research and Education Association, c/o Dr. J. Ronald Sholar, 376 Ag Hall, Oklahoma State University Stillwater, OK 74078. Phone: (405)744-9634 Fax: (405)744-0354 E-mail: hts@ncsu.edu • URL: http://www.agr.okstate.edu • Semiannual. $40.00 per issue.

Pecan South. Texas Pecan Growers Association, Inc., P.O. Drawer CC College Station, TX 77841. Phone: (409)846-3285 Fax: (409)846-1752 Monthly. $18.00 per year.

Penguin Dictionary of Architecture and Landscape Architecture. Nicolas Pevsner and others. Viking Penguin, 375 Hudson St. New York, NY 10014-3657. Phone: 800-331-4624 or (212)336-2000 Fax: 800-227-9604 or (212)366-2666 URL: http://www.penguin.com • 2000. $16.95. Fifth edition.

Peninsular Agricultural Research Station. University of Wisconsin - Madison

Penny Fortune Newsletter. James M. Fortune, editor., 1837 S. Navajo Colorado Springs, CO 80906. Phone: (719)576-9200 Fax: (719)576-3036 Monthly. $79.00 per year. Reports on special situations and low- priced stocks. Includes charts and graphs.

Pension and Employee Benefits: Code-ERISA-Regulations. CCH, Inc., 4025 W. Peterson Ave. Chicago, IL 60646-6085. Phone: 800-248-3248 or (773)866-6000 Fax: 800-224-8299 or (773)866-3608 URL: http://www.cch.com • Three volumes. Looseleaf.

Pension and Profit Sharing Plans. Matthew Bender & Co., Inc., Two Park Ave. New York, NY 10016. Phone: 800-223-1940 or (212)448-2000 Fax: (212)244-3188 E-mail: international@bender.com • URL: http://www.bender.com • Six looseleaf volumes. Periodic supplementation. Price on application. Full treatment of pension and profit sharing plans, including forms and legal analysis.

Pension and Profit Sharing Plans for Small or Medium Size Businesses. Panel Publishers, Inc., 1185 Ave. of the Americas New York, NY 10036. Phone: 800-447-1717 or (212)597-0200 Fax: 800-901-9075 or (212)597-0334 E-mail: customer.service@aspenpubl.com • URL: http://www.panelpublisher.com • Monthly. $191.50 per year. Newsletter. Topics of interest and concern to professionals who serve small and medium size pension and profit sharing plans.

Pension Facts. American Council of Life Insurance, 1001 Pennsylvania Ave., N. W. Washington, DC 20004. Phone: (202)624-2000 Biennial. Free.

Pension Fund Investment Management: A Handbook for Sponsors and Their Advisors. Fran K. Fabozzi. McGraw-Hill Professional, 1221 Ave. of the Americas New York, NY 10020. Phone: 800-722-4726 or (212)904-2000 Fax: (212)904-2072 E-mail: customer.service@mcgraw-hill.com • URL: http://www.mcgraw-hill.com • 1990. $65.00.

Pension Fund Litigation Reporter. Andrews Publications, 175 Strafford Ave., Bldg 4, Suite 140 Wayne, PA 19087. Phone: 800-345-1101 or (610)622-0510 Fax: (610)622-0501 URL: http://www.andrewspub.com • Monthly. $750.00 per year. Contains reports on legal cases involving pension fund fiduciaries (trustees).

Pension Plan Guide. CCH, Inc., 4025 W. Peterson Ave. Chicago, IL 60646-6085. Phone: 800-248-3248 or (773)866-6000 Fax: 800-224-8299 or (773)866-3608 URL: http://www.cch.com • Weekly. $1,129.00 per year. Newsletter. Formerly *Pension Plan Guide Summary.*

Pension Planning: Pensions, Profit Sharing, and Other Deferred Compensation Plans. Everett T. Allen and others. McGraw-Hill Higher Education, 1221 Ave. of the Americas New York, NY 10020. Phone: 800-722-4726 or (212)904-2000 Fax: (212)904-2072 E-mail: customer.service@mcgraw-hill.com • URL: http://www.mcgraw-hill.com • 1992. $69.75. Seventh edition.

Pension Research Council., University of Pennsylvania, 304 CPC, 3641 Locust Walk Philadelphia, PA 19104-6218. Phone: (215)898-7620 Fax: (215)898-0310 E-mail: mitchelo@wharton.upenn.edu • URL: http://www.prc.wharton.upenn.edu/prc/prc.html • Research areas include various types of private sector and public employee pension plans.

Pensions and Investments 1000 Largest Retirement Funds. Crain Communications, Inc., 740 N. Rush St. Chicago, IL 60611-2590. Phone: (312)649-5200 Fax: (312)649-5360 E-mail: jmurphy@crain.com • URL: http://www.pionline.com • Annual. $50.00. List of the largest retirement plans in terms of total assets. Formerly *Pensions and Investments Top 100 Retirement Funds.*

Pensions and Investments: The Newspaper of Corporate and Institutional Investing. Crain Communications, Inc., 1400 Woodbridge Ave. Detroit, MI 48207-3187. Phone: 800-678-9595 or (313)446-6000 Fax: (313)446-0383 URL: http://www.pionline.com • Biweekly. $215.00 per year. Formerly *Pensions and Investment Age.*

People and Productivity. Robert A. Sutemeister. McGraw-Hill, 1221 Ave of the Americas New York, NY 10020. Phone: 800-722-4726 or (212)904-2000 Fax: (212)904-2072 E-mail: customer.service@mcgraw-hill.com • URL: http://www.mcgraw-hill.com • 1976. $24.95. Third edition. (Management Series).

People at Work. Professional Training Associates, Inc., 210 Commerce Blvd. Round Rock, TX 78664-2189. Phone: 800-822-7824 or (512)255-6006 Fax: (512)255-7532 Monthly. $89.00 per year. Newsletter on common personnel problems of supervisors and office managers. Formerly *Practical Supervision.*

People's Medical Society., 462 Walnut St. Allentown, PA 18102. Phone: 800-624-8773 or (610)770-1670 Fax: (610)770-0607 E-mail: madl@peoplesmed.org • URL: http://www.peoplesmed.org • A consumer affairs society concerned with the cost, quality, and management of the American health care system.

People's Republic of China Year Book. International Publications Service, 1900 Frost Rd., Suite 101 Bristol, PA 17057. Phone: 800-821-8312 or (215)785-5800 Annual. $146.00.

Published by China Year Book Publishing House. Serves as the official yearbook of the People's Republic of China. Covers developments in various aspects of life in China, including the economy, industry, transportation, telecommunications, agriculture, technology, demographics, the legal system, health, and foreign relations. Includes many statistical tables and photographs. Text in Chinese.

Perelman's Pocket Cyclopedia of Cigars. Perelman, Pioneer and Co., 5757 Wilshire Blvd., Suite 540 Los Angeles, CA 90036. Phone: 888-766-5308 or (323)965-4900 Fax: (323)965-4919 E-mail: perelmanco@aol.com • Annual. $12.95. Contains profiles of more than 1,000 brands of cigars marketed in the U. S.

The Perfect Interview: How to Get the Job You Really Want. John D. Drake. AMACOM, 1601 Broadway, 12th Fl. New York, NY 10019. Phone: 800-262-9699 or (212)586-8100 Fax: (212)903-8168 E-mail: custmserv@amanet.org • URL: http://www.amanet.org • 1996. $17.95. Second edition. Contains advice for jobseekers on how to control an interview and deal with difficult questions. Includes examples of both successful and unsuccessful interviews.

The Perfect Sales Piece: A Complete Do-It-Yourself Guide to Creating Brochures, Catalogs, Fliers, and Pamphlets. Robert W. Bly. John Wiley and Sons, Inc., 605 Third Ave. New York, NY 10158-0012. Phone: 800-225-5945 or (212)850-6000 Fax: (212)850-6088 E-mail: info@wiley.com • URL: http://www.wiley.com • 1994. $49.95. A guide to the use of various forms of printed literature for direct selling, sales promotion, and marketing. (Small Business Editions Series).

Performance Analysis and Appraisal: A How-To-Do-It Manual for Librarians. Robert D. Stueart and Maureen Sullivan. Neal-Schuman Publishers, Inc., 100 Varick St. New York, NY 10013. Phone: (212)925-8650 Fax: 800-584-2414 E-mail: info@neal-schuman.com • URL: http://www.neal-schuman.com • 1991. $49.95. (How-to-Do-It Series).

Performance Management in Government: Contemporary Illustrations. OECD Publications and Information Center, 2001 L St., N. W., Suite 650 Washington, DC 20036-4922. Phone: (202)785-6323 Fax: (202)785-0350 E-mail: washcont@oecd.org • URL: http://www.oecd.org • 1996.

Performing Arts: A Guide to the Reference Literature. Linda K. Simons. Libraries Unlimited, Inc., P.O. Box 6633 Englewood, CO 80155-6633. Phone: 800-237-6124 or (303)770-1220 Fax: (303)220-8843 E-mail: lu-books@lu.com • URL: http://www.lu.com • 1994. $42.00. (Reference Sources in Humanities Series).

Performing Arts Forum. International Society of Performing Arts Administrators, 2920 Fuller Ave., N.E., Suite 205 Grand Rapids, MI 49505-3458. Phone: (616)364-3000 Fax: (616)364-9010 10 times a year. Free to members; non-members, $25.00 per year. Newsletter for performing arts managers, promoters, and talent representatives.

Perfumer and Flavorist. Allured Publishing Corp., 362 S. Schmale Rd. Carol Stream, IL 60188-2787. Phone: (630)653-2155 Fax: (630)653-2192 E-mail: allured@allured.com • URL: http://www.allured.com • Bimonthly. $135.00 per year. Provides information on the art and technology of flavors and fragrances, including essential oils, aroma chemicals, and spices.

Periodical Title Abbreviations. The Gale Group, 27500 Drake Rd. Farmington Hills, MI 48331-3535. Phone: 800-877-GALE or (248)699-GALE Fax: 800-414-5043 or (248)699-8069 E-mail: galeord@galegroup.com • URL: http://www.galegroup.com • 2000. $735.00. 13th edition. Two volumes. $245.00 per volume Vol. 1 *By Abbreviation*; vol. 2 *By Title*. Lists more than 145,000 different abbreviations.

Personal and Business Bartering. James Stout. McGraw-Hill Professional, 1221 Ave. of the Americas New York, NY 10020. Phone: 800-722-4726 or (212)904-2000 Fax: (212)904-2072 E-mail: customer.service@mcgraw-hill.com • URL: http://www.mcgraw-hill.com • 1985. $14.95.

Personal Communications Industry Association., 500 Montgomery St., No. 700 Alexandria, VA 22314. Phone: 800-759-0300 or (703)739-0300 Fax: (703)836-1608 URL: http://www.pcia.com • Promotes development of industry standards for mobile telephone systems. Also concerned with the advertising and marketing of mobile telephones.

Personal Finance. Robert Rosefsky. John Wiley and Sons, Inc., 605 Third Ave. New York, NY 10158-0012. Phone: 800-526-5368 or (212)850-6000 Fax: (212)850-6088 E-mail: info@wiley.com • URL: http://www.wiley.com • 1998. $95.95. Seventh edition.

Personal Finance. Kephart Communications, Inc., 1750 Old Meadow Rd., 3rd Fl. Mclean, VA 22102-4304. Phone: (703)548-2400 Fax: (703)683-6974 Biweekly. $118.00 per year. Investment advisory newsletter.

Personal Finance. Jack R. Kapoor and others. McGraw-Hill, 1221 Ave. of the Americas New York, NY 10020. Phone: 800-722-4726 or (212)904-2000 Fax: (212)904-2072 E-mail: customer.service@mcgraw-hill.com • URL: http://www.mcgraw-hill.com • 2000. $82.50 Sixth edition.

Personal Financial Planning. G. Victor Hallman. McGraw-Hill, 1221 Ave. of the Americas New York, NY 10020. Phone: 800-722-4726 or (212)904-2000 Fax: (212)904-2072 E-mail: customer.service@mcgraw-hill.com • URL: http://www.mcgraw-hill.com • 2000. $42.95. Sixth edition.

Personal Financial Planning: Strategies for Professional Advisors. Warren, Gorham & Lamont/RIA Group, 395 Hudson St. New York, NY 10014. Phone: 800-950-1215 or (212)367-6300 Fax: (212)337-4280 E-mail: customer_services@riag.com • URL: http://www.riahome.com • Bimonthly. $145.00 per year.

Personal Financial Planning: The Advisor's Guide. Rolf Auster. CCH, Inc., 4025 W. Peterson Ave. Chicago, IL 60646-6085. Phone: 800-248-3248 or (773)866-6000 Fax: 800-224-8299 or (773)866-3608 URL: http://www.cch.com • 1998. $55.95. Third edition. Covers personal taxes, investments, credit, mortgages, insurance, pensions, social security, estate planning, etc.

Personal Financial Planning: With Forms and Checklists. Jonathan Pond. Warren, Gorham & Lamont/RIA Group, 395 Hudson St. New York, NY 10014. Phone: 800-950-1215 or (212)367-6300 Fax: (212)337-4280 E-mail: customer_services@riag.com • URL: http://www.riahome.com • $165.00. Biennial supplementation. Designed for professional financial planners, accountants, attorneys, insurance marketers, brokers, and bankers.

Personal Health Reporter. The Gale Group, 27500 Drake Rd. Farmington Hills, MI 48331-3535. Phone: 800-877-GALE or (248)699-GALE Fax: 800-414-5043 or (248)699-8069 E-mail: galeord@galegroup.com • URL: http://www.galegroup.com • 1992. $105.00. Two volumes. Volume one, $105.00; volume two, $105.00. Presents a collection of professional and popular articles on 150 topics relating to physical and mental health conditions and treatments.

Personal Selling: A Relationship Approach. Ronald B. Marks. Prentice Hall, 240 Frisch Court Paramus, NJ 07652-5240. Phone: 800-947-7700 or (201)909-6200 Fax: 800-445-6991 or (201)909-6361 URL: http://www.prenhall.com • 1996. $92.00. Sixth edition. Covers buying behavior, prospecting, presentation, objections, closing, selling as a career, and related topics. Includes a glossary.

Personal Strategies for Managing Stress. American Management Association Extension Institute, P.O. Box 1026 Saranac Lake, NY 12983-9957. Phone: 800-262-9699 or (518)891-1500 Fax: (518)891-0368 Looseleaf. $110.00. Self-study course. Emphasis is on practical explanations, examples, and problem solving. Quizzes and a case study are included.

Personnel Administration in Libraries. Sheila Creth and Frederick Duda, editors. Neal-Schuman Publishers, Inc., 100 Varick St. New York, NY 10013. Phone: (212)925-8650 Fax: 800-584-2414 E-mail: info@neal-schuman.com • URL: http://www.neal-schuman.com • 1989. $55.00. Second edition.

Personnel Management Abstracts., 704 Island Lake Rd. Chelsea, MI 48118. Phone: (313)475-1979 Quarterly. $190.00 per year. Includes annual cumulation.

Personnel Management: Communications. Prentice Hall, 240 Frisch Court Paramus, NJ 07652-5240. Phone: 800-947-7700 or (201)909-6200 Fax: 800-445-6991 or (201)909-6361 URL: http://www.prenhall.com • Looseleaf. Periodic supplementation. Price on application. Includes how to write effectively and how to prepare employee publications.

Personnel Management: Compensation. Prentice Hall, 240 Frisch Ct. Paramus, NJ 07652-5240. Phone: 800-947-7700 or (201)909-6452 Fax: 800-445-6991 URL: http://www.prenhall.com • Looseleaf. Periodic supplementation. Price on application.

Personnel Management: Labor Relations Guide. Prentice Hall, 240 Frisch Court Paramus, NJ 07652-5240. Phone: 800-947-7700 or (201)909-6200 Fax: 800-445-6991 or (201)909-6361 URL: http://www.prenhall.com • Three looseleaf volumes. Periodic supplementation. Price on application.

Personnel Management: Policies and Practices. Prentice Hall, 240 Frisch Court Paramus, NJ 07652-5240. Phone: 800-947-7700 or (201)909-6200 Fax: 800-445-6991 or (201)909-6361 URL: http://www.prenhall.com • Looseleaf. Periodic supplementation. Price on application.

Personnel Psychology. Personnel Psychology, Inc., 745 Haskins Rd., Suite D Bowling Green, OH 43402-1600. Phone: (419)352-1562 Fax: (419)352-2645 URL: http://www.wcnet.org • Quarterly. $65.00 per year. Publishes research articles and book reviews.

Perspective. Catalyst, Inc., 120 Wall St. New York, NY 10005. Phone: (212)514-7600 Fax: (212)514-8470 E-mail: info@catalystwomen.org • URL: http://www.catalystwomen.org • Monthly. $60.00 per year. Newsletter. Covers leadership, mentoring, work/family programs, success stories, and other topics for women in the corporate world.

Perspectives on Radio and Television: Telecommunication in the United States. F. Leslie Smith and others. Lawrence Erlbaum Associates, 10 Industrial Ave. Mahwah, NJ 07430-2226. Phone: 800-926-6579 or (201)236-9500 Fax: (201)236-0072 1998. Fourth edition. Price on application. (Communication Series).

Persuasive Business Speaking. Elayne Snyder. AMACOM, 1601 Broadway, 12th Fl. New York, NY 10019. Phone: 800-262-9699 or (212)586-8100 Fax: (212)903-8168 E-mail: custmserv@amanet.org • URL: http://www.amanet.org • 1990. $17.95. Includes ready-to-use openers, sample speeches, anecdotes, and quotes.

Pest Control. Advanstar Communications, Inc., 7500 Old Oak Blvd. Cleveland, OH 44130. Phone: 800-346-0085 or (440)243-8100 Fax: (440)891-2740 E-mail: information@advanstar.com • URL: http://www.advanstar.com • Monthly. $39.00 per year.

Pest Control Technology. G. I. E., Inc., Publishers, 4012 Bridge Ave. Cleveland, OH 44113-3320. Phone: (216)961-4130 Fax: (216)961-0364 URL: http://www.pctonline.com/ • Monthly. $32.00 per year. Provides technical and business management information for pest control personnel.

Pesticide Biochemistry and Physiology: An International Journal. Academic Press, Inc. Journal Div., 525 B St., Suite 1900 San Diego, CA 92101-4495. Phone: 800-321-5068 or (619)230-1840 Fax: (619)699-6715 E-mail: ap@acad.com • URL: http://www.academicpress.com/ • Nine times a year. $820.00 per year.

Pesticide Litigation Manual. John M. Johnson and George W. Ware. West Group, 610 Opperman Dr. Eagan, MN 55123. Phone: 800-328-4880 or (651)687-7000 Fax: 800-213-2323 or (651)687-5827 URL: http://www.westgroup.com • Annual. $193.00. Discusses liability and other legal issues related to the manufacture and use of pesticides. Includes a guide to FIFRA (Federal Insecticide, Fungicide, and Rodenticide Act).

PestWeb: The Pest Control Industry Website. Van Waters & Rogers, Inc.Phone: 800-888-4897 or (425)889-3941 E-mail: webmaster@pestweb.com • URL: http://www.pestweb.com • Web site provides a wide variety of information on pest control products, manufacturers, associations, news, and education. Includes "Insects and Other Organisms," featuring details on 27 different kinds of pests, from ants to wasps. Online searching is offered. Fees: Free.

Pet Age: The Magazine for the Professional Retailer. Karen Long MacLeod, editor. H.H. Backer Associates, Inc., 200 S. Michigan Ave., Suite 840 Chicago, IL 60604-2404. Phone: (312)663-4040 Fax: (312)663-5676 Monthly. $25.00 per year.

Pet Dealer Purchasing Guide. Cygnus Business Media, 445 Broad Hollow Rd. Melville, NY 11747. Phone: 800-308-6397 or (631)845-2700 Fax: (631)845-2798 E-mail: rich.reiff@cygnuspub.com • URL: http://www.cygnuspub.com • Annual. $35.00. Lists of manufacturers and importers of pet supplies; distributors and wholesalers of pet supples; wholesalers, breeders, and importers of pets (livestock); trade associations; publishers of pet books, records, and educational and training materials; pet care schools.

Pet Food Institute.

Pet Industry Distributors Association.

Pet Industry Joint Advisory Council.

Pet Product News. Fancy Publications, Inc., P.O. Box 6050 Mission Viejo, CA 92690-6050. Phone: 800-365-4421 or (949)855-8822 Fax: (949)855-3045 E-mail: ppn@fancypubs.com • URL: http://www.petchannel.com/petindustry/ppn • Free to qualified personnel; others, $118.00 per year. Supplement available *Pet Product News Buyer's Guide*.

Pet Shop. Entrepreneur Media, Inc., 2445 McCabe Way Irvine, CA 92614. Phone: 800-421-2300 or (949)261-2325 Fax: (949)851-9088 E-mail: entmag@entrepreneurmag.com • URL: http://www.entrepreneurmag.com • Looseleaf. $59.50. A practical guide to starting a pet store. Covers profit potential, start-up costs, market size evaluation, owner's time required, site selection, lease negotiation, pricing, accounting, advertising, promotion, etc. (Start-Up Business Guide No. E1007.)

Pet Supplies Market. Available from MarketResearch.com, 641 Ave. of the Americas, Third Floor New York, NY 10011. Phone: 800-298-5699 or (212)807-2629 Fax: (212)807-2716 E-mail: order@marketresearch.com • URL: http://www.marketresearch.com • 1999. $2,750.00. Published by Packaged Facts. Provides market data with projections to 2001 on products for dogs, cats, fish, birds, and other pets.

Peterson's College Money Handbook: The Only Complete Guide to Scholarships, College Costs, and Financial Aid at U. S. Colleges. Peterson's Magazine Group, 202 Carnegie Center Princeton, NJ 08540. Phone: 800-338-3282 E-mail: info@petersons.com • URL: http://www.petersons.com • Annual. $26.95. Provides information on more than 1,600 scholarships, loans, and financial aid programs.

Peterson's Computer Science and Electrical Engineering Programs. Peterson's, 202 Carnegie Center Princeton, NJ 08540. Phone: 800-338-3282 E-mail: info@petersons.com • URL: http://www.petersons.com • 1996. $24.95. A guide to 900 accredited graduate degree programs related to computers or electrical engineering at colleges and universities in the U. S. and Canada.

Peterson's Graduate and Professional Programs: Business, Education, Health, Information Studies, Law, and Social Work. Peterson's Magazine Group, 202 Carnegie Center Princeton, NJ 08540. Phone: 800-338-3282 E-mail: info@petersons.com • URL: http://www.petersons.com • Annual. $27.95. Provides details of graduate and professional programs in business, law, information, and other fields at colleges and universities. Formerly *Peterson's Guide to Graduate Programs in Business, Education, Health, Information Studies, Law and Social Work.*

Peterson's Graduate and Professional Programs: Engineering and Applied Sciences. Peterson's, 202 Carnegie Center Princeton, NJ 08540. Phone: 800-338-3282 E-mail: info@petersons.com • URL: http://www.petersons.com • Annual. $37.95. Provides details of more than 3,400 graduate and professional programs in engineering and related fields at colleges and universities. Formerly *Peterson's Guide to Graduate Programs in Engineering and Professional Sciences.*

Peterson's Guide to Colleges for Careers in Computing: The Only Combined Career and College Guide for Future Computer Professionals. Peterson's, Princeton Pike Dr. Lawrenceville, NJ 08648. Phone: 800-338-3282 or (609)896-1800 E-mail: info@petersons.com • URL: http://www.petersons.com • 1996. $14.95. Describes career possibilities in various fields related to computers.

Peterson's Guide to Distance Learning. Peterson's, 202 Carnegie Center Princeton, NJ 08540. Phone: 800-338-3282 E-mail: info@petersons.com • URL: http://www.petersons.com • 1996. $24.95. Provides detailed information on accredited college and university programs available through television, radio, computer, videocassette, and audiocassette resources. Covers 700 U. S. and Canadian institutions. Formerly *The Electronic University.*

Peterson's Guide to Four-Year Colleges. Peterson's, 202 Carnegie Center Princeton, NJ 08540. Phone: 800-338-3282 E-mail: info@petersons.com • URL: http://www.petersons.com • Annual. $19.95. Provides information on more than 2,000 accredited degree-granting colleges and universities in the U. S. and Canada.

Peterson's Guide to Graduate and Professional Programs: An Overview. Peterson's, Princeton Pike Dr. Lawrenceville, NJ 08648. Phone: 800-338-3282 or (609)896-1800 E-mail: info@petersons.com • URL: http://www.petersons.com • Annual. $27.95. Six volumes provide details of more than 31,000 graduate programs at 1,600 colleges and universities: 1. An Overview; 2. Humanities, Arts, and Social Sciences; 3. MBA; 4. Visual and Performing Arts; 5. Engineering and Applied Sciences; 6. Business, Education, Health, Information Studies, Law, and Social Work. (Volumes are available individually.)

Peterson's Guide to MBA Programs: The Most Comprehensive Guide to U. S., Canadian, and International Business Schools. Peterson's, Princeton Pike Dr. Lawrencevile, NJ 08648. Phone: 800-338-3282 or (609)896-1800 E-mail: info@petersons.com • URL: http://www.petersons.com • 1996. $21.95. Provides detailed information on about 850 graduate programs in business at 700 colleges and universities in the U. S., Canada, and other countries.

Peterson's Guide to Two-Year Colleges. Peterson's, Princeton Pike Dr. Princeton, NJ 08648. Phone: 800-338-3282 or (609)896-1800 E-mail: info@patersons.com • URL: http://www.petersons.com • Annual. $19.95. Provides information on more than 1,500 U. S. academic institutions granting associate degrees.

Peterson's Internships: More Than 40,000 Opportunities to Get an Edge in Today's Competitive Job Market. Peterson's, Princeton Pike Dr. Lawrenceville, NJ 08648. Phone: 800-338-3282 or (609)896-1800 E-mail: info@petersons.com • URL: http://www.petersons.com • Annual. $24.95. Lists about 40,000 career-oriented internships in a wide variety of fields, including business.

Peterson's Job Opportunities for Business Majors. Peterson's, Princeton Pike Dr. Lawrenceville, NJ 08648. Phone: 800-338-3282 or (609)896-1800 E-mail: info@petersons.com • URL: http://www.petersons.com • Annual. $21.95. Provides career information for the 2,000 largest U. S. employers in various industries.

Peterson's Private Secondary Schools. Peterson's, 202 Carnegie Center Princeton, NJ 08640. Phone: 800-338-3282 E-mail: info@petersons.com • URL: http://www.petersons.com • Annual. $29.95. Provides information on more than 1,400 accredited private secondary schools in the U. S. Formerly *Peterson's Guide to Private Secondary Schools.*

Peterson's Professional Degree Programs in the Visual and Performing Arts. Peterson's, 202 Carnegie Center Princeton, NJ 08640. Phone: 800-338-3282 E-mail: info@petersons.com • URL: http://www.petersons.com • Annual. $24.95. A directory of more than 900 degree programs in art, music, theater, and dance at 600 colleges and professional schools.

Peterson's Register of Higher Education. Peterson's, Princeton Pike Dr. Lawrenceville, NJ 08648. Phone: 800-338-3282 or (609)896-1800 E-mail: info@petersons.com • URL: http://www.petersons.com • Annual. $49.95. Provides concise information on 3,700 colleges and other postsecondary educational institutions in the U. S.

Peterson's Scholarships, Grants, and Prizes: Your Complete Guide to College Aid from Private Sources. Peterson's, 202 Carnegie Center Princeton, NJ 08640. Phone: 800-338-3282 E-mail: info@petersons.com • URL: http://www.petersons.com • 1998. $26.95. Second edition.

Peterson's Study Abroad: A Guide to Semester and Year Abroad Academic Programs. Peterson's, 202 Carnegie Center Princeton, NJ 08640. Phone: 800-338-3282 E-mail: info@petersons.com • URL: http://www.petersons.com • Annual. $26.95. Describes about 1,300 academic programs available to U. S. students at 350 United States and foreign institutions.

Peterson's Vocational and Technical Schools and Programs. Peterson's, 202 Carnegie Center Princeton, NJ 08640. Phone: 800-338-3282 or (609)896-1800 E-mail: info@petersons.com • URL: http://www.petersons.com • Annual. $34.95. Provides information on vocational schools in the eastern part of the U. S. Covers more than 370 career fields.

Petfood Industry. Watt Publishing Co., 122 S. Wesley Ave. Mount Morris, IL 61054-1497. Phone: (815)734-4171 Fax: (815)734-4201 URL: http://www.wattnet.com • Bimonthly. $36.00 per year.

PetroChemical News: A Weekly News Service in English Devoted to the Worldwide Petrochemical Industry. William F. Bland Co., P.O. Box 16666 Chapel Hill, NC 27516-6666. Phone: (919)490-0700 Fax: (919)490-3002 Weekly. $739.00 per year. Report of current and significant news about the petrochemical business worldwide.

Petrochemicals: The Rise of an Industry. Peter H. Spitz. John Wiley and Sons, Inc., 605 Third Ave. New York, NY 10158-0012. Phone: 800-526-5368 or (212)850-6000 Fax: (212)850-6088 E-mail: info@wiley.com • URL: http://www.wiley.com • 1988. $125.00.

Petroleum Abstracts. University of Tulsa, Information Services Div., 600 S. College Ave. Tulsa, OK 74104-3189. Phone: 800-247-8678 or (918)631-2297 Fax: (918)599-9361 E-mail: question@tured.pa.utulsa.edu • URL: http://www.pa.utulsa.edu/ • 50 times a year. Service basis. Worldwide literature related to petroleum exploration and production.

Petroleum/Energy Business News Index. API Encompass, One Castel Point Ter Hoboken, NJ 07030-5906. Phone: (212)366-4040 Fax: (212)366-4298 E-mail: info@apiencompass.org • URL: http://www.api.org • Monthly. Members, $475.00 per year; non-members, $950.00 per year.

Petroleum Engineer International Drilling and Production Yearbook. Hart Publications, Inc., 4545 Post Oak Place, Suite 210 Houston, TX 77027. Phone: (713)993-9320 Fax: (713)840-8585 E-mail: hartinfo@phillips.com • URL: http://www.hartpub.com • Annual. $10.00.

Petroleum Engineer International: The Worldwide Magazine of Drilling, Production,and Reservoir Technology. Hart Publications, Inc., 4545 Post Oak Place, Suite 210 Houston, TX 77027. Phone: (713)993-9320 Fax: (713)840-8585 E-mail: hartinfo@phillips.com • URL: http://www.hartpub.com • Monthly. $99.00 per year. Edited for "decision makers" in petroleum exploration and production. Emphasis is on technology.

Petroleum Equipment Directory. Petroleum Equipment Institute, P.O. Box 2380 Tulsa, OK 74101. Phone: (918)494-9696 Fax: (918)491-9895 E-mail: info@pei.org • URL: http://www.pei.org • Annual. $100.00. Listing of over 1,600 member manufacturers, distributors and installers of petroleum marketing equipment worldwide.

Petroleum Equipment Institute.

Petroleum Equipment Suppliers Association.

Petroleum Marketers Association of America.

Petroleum Marketing Monthly. Available from U. S. Government Printing Office, Washington, DC 20402. Phone: (202)512-1800 Fax: (202)512-2250 E-mail: gpoaccess@gpo.gov • URL: http://www.access.gpo.gov • Monthly. $116.00 per year. Current information and statistics relating to a wide variety of petroleum products. (Office of Oil and Gas, Energy Information Administration, U. S. Department of Energy.)

Petroleum Newsletter. National Safety Council, Periodicals Dept., 1121 Spring Lake Dr. Itasca, IL 60143-3201. Phone: 800-621-7619 or (630)285-1121 Fax: (630)285-1315 URL: http://www.nsc.org • Bimonthly. Members, $15.00 per year; non-members, $19.00 per year.

Petroleum Statement, Annual Energy Report. Energy Information Administration. U.S. Department of Energy, Washington, DC 20585. Phone: (202)586-4940 Annual.

Petroleum Supply Annual. Available from U. S. Government Printing Office, Washington, DC 20402. Phone: (202)512-1800 Fax: (202)512-2250 E-mail: gpoaccess@gpo.gov • URL: http://www.access.gpo.gov • Annual. $78.00. Two volumes. Produced by the Energy Information Administration, U. S. Department of Energy. Contains worldwide data on the petroleum industry and petroleum products.

Petroleum Supply Monthly. Available from U. S. Government Printing Office, Washington, DC 20402. Phone: (202)512-1800 Fax: (202)512-2250 E-mail: gpoaccess@gpo.gov • URL: http://www.access.gpo.gov • Monthly. $100.00 per year. Produced by the Energy Information Administration, U. S. Department of Energy. Provides worldwide statistics on a wide variety of petroleum products. Covers production, supplies, exports and imports, transportation, refinery operations, and other aspects of the petroleum industry.

Petroprocess Directory. Atlantic Communications, 1635 W. Alabama St. Houston, TX 77006-4196. Phone: (713)529-1616 Fax: (713)523-7804 E-mail: ac@oilonline.com • URL: http://www.oilonline.com/atcom.html • Annual. $69.00. Provides information on petrochemical companies and their products. Includes 24 industry categories.

Pets Supplies Marketing. Fancy Publications, Two Burroughs Irvine, CA 92618-2804. Phone: 800-365-4221 or (949)855-8822 Fax: (949)855-3045 Quarterly. $250.00 per year.

PGA Tour Tournament Association., 13000 Sawgrass Village Circle, No. 36 Ponte Vedra Beach, FL 32082. Phone: (904)285-4222 Fax: (904)273-5726 E-mail: pgatourta@aol.com • URL: http://www.pgatta.org • Members are sponsors of major professional golf tournaments. Committees include Finance, Marketing, and Media Relations.

Pharma Business: The International Magazine of Pharmaceutical Business and Marketing. Engel Publishing Partners, 820 Bear Tavern Rd. West Trenton, NJ 08628. Phone: (609)530-0044 Fax: (609)530-1274 URL: http://www.engelpub.com • Eight times a year. $185.00 per year. Circulated mainly in European countries. Coverage includes worldwide industry news, new drug products, regulations, and research developments.

Pharma Marketletter. Marketletter Publications Ltd., 54-55 Wilton Rd. London SW1V 1DE, England. E-mail: pharmaletter@marketletter.com • URL: http://www.marketletter.com • Weekly. $700.00 per year. Newsletter. Formerly *Marketletter.*

Pharmaceutical Engineering. International Society for Pharmaceutical Engineering, Inc., 3816 W. Linebaugh Ave., Suite 412 Tampa, FL 33624-4702. Phone: (813)960-2105 Fax: (813)264-2816 E-mail: ispehq@ispe.org • URL: http://www.ispe.org • Bimonthly. $60.00 per year. Feature articles provide practical application and specification information on the design, construction, supervision and maintenance of process equipment, plant systems, instrumentation and pharmaceutical facilities.

Pharmaceutical Executive: For Global Business and Marketing Leaders. Advanstar Communications, Inc., 7500 Old Oak Blvd. Cleveland, OH 44130-3369. Phone: 800-346-0085 or (440)243-8100 Fax: (440)826-2833 E-mail: information@advanstar.com • URL: http://www.advanstar.com • Monthly. $64.00 per year.

Pharmaceutical Litigation Reporter: The National Journal of Record of Pharmaceutical Litigation. Andrews Publications, 175 Strafford Ave., Bldg. 4, Suite 140 Wayne, PA 19087. Phone: 800-345-1101 or (610)622-0510 Fax: (610)622-0501 URL: http://www.andrewspub.com • Monthly. $775.00 per year. Reports on a wide variety of legal cases involving the pharmaceutical and medical device industries. Includes product liability lawsuits.

Pharmaceutical Marketers Directory. CPS Communications, Inc., Directories Div., 7200 W. Camino Real, Suite 215 Boca Raton, FL 33433. Phone: (561)368-9301 Fax: (561)368-7870 E-mail: pmd@cpsnet.com • URL: http://www.cpsnet.com • Annual. $175.00. About 15,000 personnel of pharmaceutical, medical products and equipment, and biotechnology companies; advertising agencies with clients in the medical field; health care publications; alternative media and medical industry suppliers.

Pharmaceutical Marketing and Management Research Program.

Pharmaceutical Marketing in the 21st Century. Mickey C. Smith, editor. Haworth Press, Inc., 10 Alice St. Binghamton, NY 13904-1580. Phone: 800-429-6784 or (607)722-5857 Fax: 800-895-0582 or (607)722-1424 E-mail: getinfo@haworthpressinc.com • URL: http://www.haworthpressinc.com • 1996. $49.95. Various authors discuss the marketing, pricing, distribution, and retailing of prescription drugs. (Pharmaceutical Marketing and Management Series, Vol. 10, Nos. 2,3&4).

Pharmaceutical News Index. Bell & Howell Information and Learning, 300 N. Zeeb Rd. Ann Arbor, MI 48103. Phone: 800-521-0600 or (734)761-4700 Fax: 800-864-0019 URL: http://www.umi.com • Indexes major pharmaceutical industry newsletters, 1974 to present. Weekly updates. Inquire as to online cost and availability.

Pharmaceutical Processing. Cahners Business Information, New Product Information, 301 Gibraltar Dr. Morris Plains, NJ 07950. Phone: 800-622-7776 or (973)292-5100 Fax: (973)539-3476 E-mail: corporatecommunications@cahners.com • URL: http://www.cahners.com • Monthly. $69.95 per year. Formerly *Pharmaceutical and Cosmetic Equipment.*

Pharmaceutical Processing Annual Buyers Guide. Cahners Business Information, 301 Gibraltar Dr. Morris Plains, NJ 07950-0650. Phone: 800-662-7776 or (973)292-5100 Fax: (973)539-3476 URL: http://www.cahners.com • Annual. Price on application. Lists makers and distributors of supplies and equipment for the pharmaceutical manufacturing industry.

Pharmaceutical Representative. McKnight Medical Communications, Two Northfield Plaza, Suite 300 Northfield, IL 60093-1219. Phone: 800-451-7838 or (847)441-3700 Fax: (847)441-3701 E-mail: pr@medec.com • URL: http://www.medec.com • Monthly. $35.95 per year. Edited for drug company salespeople and sales managers.

Pharmaceutical Research and Manufacturers Association.

Pharmaceutical Research Manufacturers Association Annual Fact Book. Pharmaceutical Research and Manufacturers Association, 1100 15th St., N.W., Suite 900 Washington, DC 20005. Phone: (202)835-3400 Fax: (202)835-3429 URL: http://www.phrma.org • Annual.

Pharmaceutical Technology. Advanstar Communications, Inc., 7500 Old Oak Blvd. Cleveland, OH 44130-3369. Phone: 800-346-0085 or (440)243-8100 Fax: (440)826-2833 E-mail: information@advanstar.com • URL: http://www.advanstar.com • Monthly. $64.00 per year. Practical hands on information about the manufacture of pharmaceutical products, focusing on applied technology.

Pharmacological and Chemical Synonyms: A Collection of Names of Drugs, Pesticides, and Other Compounds Drawn from the Medical Literature of the World. E. E. Marler. Elsevier Science, 655 Ave. of the Americas New York, NY 100010. Phone: 888-437-4636 or (212)989-5800 Fax: (212)633-3680 E-mail: usinfo@elsevier.com • URL: http://www.elsevier.com • 1994. $292.00. Tenth edition.

Pharmacology Research Laboratory.

Pharmacopeia of Herbs. CME, Inc., 2801 McGaw Ave. Irvine, CA 92614-5835. Phone: 800-447-4474 or (949)250-1008 Fax: (949)250-0445 E-mail: infostore@cmeinc.com • URL: http://www.cmeinc.com • $149.00. Frequently updated CD-ROM provides searchable data on a wide variety of herbal medicines, vitamins, and amino acids. Includes information on clinical studies, contraindications, side-effects, phytoactivity, and 534 therapeutic use categories. Contains a 1,000 word glossary.

Pharmacopeial Forum. United States Pharmacopeial Convention, Inc., 12601 Twinbrook Parkway Rockville, MD 20852. Phone: 800-227-8772 or (301)881-0666 Fax: (301)816-8299 E-mail: jac@usp.org • URL: http://www.usp.org • Bimonthly. $310.00 per year.

Pharmacy Times: Practical Information for Today's Pharmacists. Romaine Pierson Publishing Co., 1065 Old Country Rd., Suite 213 Westbury, NY 11590-5628. Phone: (516)997-0377 Fax: (516)997-0344 URL: http://www.pharmacytimes.com • Monthly. $43.00 per year. Edited for pharmacists. Covers store management, new products, regulations, home health care products, managed care issues, etc.

Phelon's Discount/Jobbing Trade. Phelon, Sheldon and Marsar, Inc., 1364 Georgetowne Circle Sarasota, FL 34232-2048. Phone: 800-234-8804 or (941)921-6450 Annual. $175.00. Up-to-date information on the discount and mass merchandising chains, clubs, outlets, stores and warehouses throughout the United States. Also wholesalers, jobbers and distributors of all kinds of goods.

Phelon's Women's Apparel and Accessory Shops. Kenneth W. Phelon, Jr., editor. Phelon, Sheldon and Marsar, Inc., 1364 Georgetowne Circle Sarasota, FL 34232-2048. Phone: 800-234-8804 or (941)921-6450 Biennial. $175.00. Lists ladies boutiques from popular to higher priced clothing and accessories throughout the U.S. Formerly *Phelon's Women's Apparel Shops*.

Philanthropic Digest. Philanthropic Digest, Inc., P.O. Box 325 Clinton, NY 13323-0325. Phone: (315)853-5207 Fax: (315)853-5647 Monthly. $79.50 per year. Reports on current grants given to non-profit organizations by foundations, corporations and individuals.

Philanthropy and Voluntarism: An Annotated Bibliography. Daphne N. Layton. The Foundation Center, 79 Fifth Ave. New York, NY 10003-3076. Phone: 800-424-9836 or (212)620-4230 Fax: (212)807-3577 E-mail: mfn@fdncenter.org • URL: http://www.fdncenter.org • 1987. $18.50.

Philatelic Foundation.

Phillips World Satellite Almanac. Phillips Business Information, Inc., 1201 Seven Locks Rd., Ste. 300 Potomac, MD 20854. Phone: 800-777-5006 or (301)340-2100 Fax: (301)340-0542 E-mail: pbi@phillips.com • URL: http://www.phillips.com • Annual. $267.00. All commercial satellite systems and operators (operational and planned), booking contracts, PTT decision makers, and transportation brokers. Incorporates *Satellite Systems Handbook* and *World Satellite Annual*.

PHL Bulletin (Packaging, Handling, Logistics). National Institute of Packaging, Handling, and Logistics Engineers, 6902 Lyle St. Lanham, MD 20706-3454. Phone: (301)459-9105 Fax: (301)459-4925 Monthly. $50.00 per year.

Phonefacts. United States Telephone Association, 1401 H St., N. W., Suite 600 Washington, DC 20005. Phone: (202)326-7300 Fax: (202)326-7333 Annual. Members, $5.00; non-members, $10.00. Presents basic statistics on the independent telephone industry in the U. S.

Phonolog Reporter: All-in-One Reporter. i2 Technologies, P.O. Box 85007 San Diego, CA 92121. Phone: (858)457-5920 Fax: (858)457-1320 Weekly. $486.00 per year. Looseleaf. Contains over one million listings of recorded music (compact discs, cassette tapes, and phonograph records). Includes both popular and classical releases. Popular music is classified by title, artist, and album; classical performances are accessible by title, artist, and composer.

Photo Marketing. Photo Marketing Association International, 3000 Picture Place Jackson, MI 49201. Phone: (517)788-8100 Fax: (517)788-8371 E-mail: gpageau@pmai.org • URL: http://www.pmai.org • Monthly. Membership.

Photo Marketing Association International.

Photographer's Market: 2000 Places to Sell Your Photographs. F & W Publications, Inc., 1507 Dana Ave. Cincinnati, OH 45207-1005. Phone: 800-289-0963 or (513)531-2690 Fax: 888-590-4082 Annual. $23.99. Lists 2,000 companies and publications that purchase original photographs.

Photographic and Imaging Manufacturers Association.

Photographic Evidence. Charles C. Scott. West Publishing Co., College and School Div., 610 Opperman Dr. Eagan, MN 55123. Phone: 800-328-4880 or (651)687-7000 Fax: 800-213-2323 or (651)687-5827 E-mail: legal-ed@westgroup.com • URL: http://www.lawschool.westgroup.com • Second edition. Three volumes. Price on application. Includes current supplement. Supplement edition available. Photography from a technical-legal standpoint.

Photographic Society of America.

Photography in Focus. Mark Jacobs and Ken Kokrda. NTC/Contemporary Publishing, P.O. Box 545 Blacklick, OH 43004. Phone: 800-338-3987 or (614)755-4151 Fax: (614)755-5645 E-mail: ntcpub@mcgraw-hill.com • URL: http://www.ntc-cb.com • 1996. $27.95. Fifth revised edition.

Photoimaging Manufacturers and Distributors Association.

Photonic Devices and Systems. R. G. Hunsperger. Marcel Dekker, Inc., 270 Madison Ave. New York, NY 10016. Phone: 800-228-1160 or (212)696-9000 Fax: (212)685-4540 E-mail: bookorders@dekker.com • URL: http://www.dekker.com • 1994. $165.00. (Optical Engineering Series: Vol. 45).

Photonics Directory. Laurin Publishing Co., Inc., P.O. Box 4949 Pittsfield, MA 01202-4949. Phone: 800-553-0051 or (413)499-0514 Fax: (413)442-3180 E-mail: photonics@laurin.com • URL: http://www.phononicsdirectory.com • Annual. $138.00. Four volumes. Volume one is a corporate guide; volume two is a buyer's guide; volume three is a designer's handbook; volume four is a dictionary. Formerly *Photonics Industry and System Purchasing Directory*.

Photonics Research Laboratory.

Photonics Spectra. Laurin Publishing Co., Inc., P.O. Box 4949 Pittsfield, MA 01202-4949. Phone: 800-553-0051 or (413)499-0514 Fax: (413)442-3180 E-mail: photonics@laurin.com • URL: http://www.photonicsdirectory.com • Monthly. $112.00 per year.

Physical Fitness Center. Entrepreneur Media, Inc., 2445 McCabe Way Irvine, CA 92614. Phone: 800-421-2300 or (949)261-2325 Fax: (949)851-9088 E-mail: entmag@entrepreneur.com • URL: http://www.entrepreneur.com • Looseleaf. $59.50. A practical guide to starting a physical fitness center. Covers profit potential, start-up costs, market size evaluation, owner's time required, site selection, lease negotiation, pricing, accounting, advertising, promotion, etc. (Start-Up Business Guide No. E1172.)

Physical Science Laboratory. New Mexico State University

Physician Insurers Association of America., 2275 Research Blvd., Suite 250 Rockville, MD 20878. Phone: (301)947-9000 Fax: (301)947-9090 URL: http://www.thepiaa.org • Members are cooperative physicians' professional liability insurers affiliated with state medical societies.

Physician Insurers Association of America: Membership Directory. Physician Insurers Association of America, 2275 Research Blvd., Suite 250 Rockville, MD 20850. Phone: (301)947-9000 Fax: (301)947-9090 Annual. Lists 60 cooperative physicians' professional liability insurers affiliated with state medical societies. Formerly *Physician-Owned Medical-Society-Created Professional Liability Insurance Companies*.

Physicians & Computers. Moorhead Publications Inc., 810 S. Waukegan Rd., Suite 200 Lake Forest, IL 60045-2672. Phone: (847)615-8333 Fax: (847)615-8345 Monthly. $40.00 per year. Includes material on computer diagnostics, online research, medical and non-medical software, computer equipment, and practice management.

Physicians' Desk Reference. Medical Economics Co., Inc., Five Paragon Dr. Montvale, NJ 07645-1742. Phone: 800-232-7379 or (201)358-7200 Fax: (201)573-8999 E-mail: customerservice@medec.com • URL: http://www.medec.com • Annual. $82.95. Generally known as "PDR". Provides detailed descriptions, effects, and adverse reactions for about 4,000 prescription drugs. Includes data on more than 250 drug manufacturers, with brand name and generic name indexes and drug identification photographs. Discontinued drugs are also listed.

Physicians' Desk Reference for Nonprescription Drugs and Dietary Supplements. Medical Economics Co., Inc., Five Paragon Dr. Montvale, NJ 07645-1742. Phone: 800-232-7379 or (201)358-7200 Fax: (201)573-8999 E-mail: customerservice@medec.com • URL: http://www.medec.com • Annual. $82.95. Contains detailed descriptions of "commonly used" over-the-counter drug products. Includes drug identification photographs. Indexing is by product category, product name, manufacturer, and active ingredient. Formerly *Physicians' Desk Reference for Nonprescription Drugs*.

Physicians' Desk Reference for Ophthalmology. Medical Economics Publishing Co., Inc., Five Paragon Dr. Montvale, NJ 07645-1742. Phone: 800-232-7379 or (201)358-7200 Fax: (201)573-8999 E-mail: customerservice@medec.com • URL: http://www.medec.com • Irregular. $49.95. Provides detailed descriptions of ophthalmological instrumentation, equipment, supplies, lenses, and prescription drugs. Indexed by manufacturer, product name, product category, active drug ingredient, and instrumentation. Editorial discussion is included.

Physicians' Desk Reference Library on CD-ROM. Medical Economics, Five Paragon Drive Montvale, NJ 07645. Phone: 800-222-3045 or (201)358-7657 Fax: (201)358-2662 Three times a year. $595.00 per year. Contains the CD-ROM equivalent of *Physicians' Desk Reference (PDR), Physicians' Desk Reference for Nonprescription Drugs, Physicians' Desk Reference for Opthalmology*, and other PDR publications.

Physicians Financial News. McGraw-Hill, 1221 Ave. of the Americas New York, NY 10020. Phone: 800-722-4726 or (212)904-2000 Fax: (212)904-2072 E-mail: customer.service@mcgraw-hill.com • URL: http://www.mcgraw-hill.com • Monthly. $105.00 per year.

Physician's Marketing and Management. American Health Consultants, Inc., 3525 Piedmont Rd., N.E., Bldg.6, Suite 400 Atlanta, GA 30305-5278. Phone: 800-688-2421 or (404)262-7436 Fax: (404)262-7837 E-mail: custserv@ahcpub.com • URL: http://www.ahcpub.com • Monthly. Individuals, $299.00 per year; institutions, $323.00 per year. Formerly*Physician's Marketing*.

*The Physics and Chemistry of Color: ÏThe Fifteen Causes of Color*l. Kurt Nassau. John Wiley and Sons, Inc., 605 Third Ave. New York, NY 10158-0012. Phone: 800-526-5368 or (212)850-6000 Fax: (212)850-6088 E-mail: info@wiley.com • URL: http://www.wiley.com • 1983. $170.00. (Pure and Applied Optics Series).

Physics Research Center and Vitreous State Laboratory. Catholic University of America

PIA Financial Ratio Studies. Printing Industries of America, Inc., 100 Daingerfield Rd. Alexandria, VA 23314-2888. Phone: 800-742-2666 or (703)519-8100 Fax: (703)548-3227 Annual. Members, $650.00 set or $100.00 per volume; non-members, $995.00 set or $1,155.00 per volume. 14 volumes.

PICA Bulletin: News and Analysis for the Personal Communication Industry. Personal Communications Industry Association, 500 Montgomery St., Suite 700 Alexandria, VA 22314. Phone: (703)739-0300 Fax: (703)836-1608 URL: http://www.pica.com • Weekly. $550.00 per year.

Pictorial Price Guide to American Antiques: 2000-2001. Dorothy Hammond. Viking Penguin, 375 Hudson St. New York, NY 10014-3657. Phone: 800-331-4624 or (212)336-2000 Fax: (212)366-2666 URL: http://www.penguin.com • 1999. $19.95. 21st edition.

Picture Framing Magazine. Hobby Publications, Inc., P.O. 429 Manalapan, NJ 07726. Phone: (732)446-4900 Fax: (732)446-5488 E-mail: webmaster@hyper-tek.com • URL: http://www.pictureframe.com/ • Monthly. $20.00 per year. Published for retailers, wholesalers, and manufacturers of picture frames.

Pilots International Association.

PIMA Directory. Paper Industry Management Association, 1699 Wall St., No. 212 Mount Prospect, IL 60056-5782. Phone: (847)956-0250 Fax: (847)956-0520 URL: http://www.pima-online.org • Annual. $140.00. Manufacturers and distributors of chemicals, equipment, supplies, and services used in the manufacture of paper. Formerly *PIMA Catalog*.

Pimsleur's Checklists of Basic American Legal Publications. American Association of Law Libraries. Fred B. Rothman and Co., 10368 W. Centennial Rd. Littleton, CO 80127. Phone: 800-457-1986 or (303)979-5657 Fax: (303)978-1457 Irregular. Price varies. Looseleaf service.

Pine Chemicals Association.

Pineapple Growers Association of Hawaii., 1116 Whitmore Ave. Wahiawa, HI 96786. Phone: (808)877-3855 Fax: (808)871-0953 Promotes the sale of pineapple products.

Pipe Line and Gas Industry: Crude Oil and Products Pipelines, Gas Transmission and Gas Distribution. Gulf Publishing Co., P.O. Box 2608 Houston, TX 77252-2608. Phone:

800-231-6275 or (713)529-4301 Fax: (713)520-4433 E-mail: ezorder@gulfpub.com • URL: http://www.gpcbooks.com • Monthly. Free to qualified personnel; others, $29.00 per year. International edition available.

Pipe Line Contractors Association.

Pipeline and Gas Journal Buyer's Guide. Oildom Publishing Co. of Texas, Inc., 14115 Briarhills Pkwy., No. 208 Houston, TX 77077. Phone: (281)558-6930 Fax: (281)558-7029 Annual. $75.00. Supplies and services. Lists over 700 companies supplying products and services used in construction and operation of cross-country pipeline and gas distribution systems.

Pipeline and Gas Journal: Energy Construction, Transportation and Distribution. Oildom Publishing of Texas, Inc., P.O. Box 219368 Houston, TX 77218-9368. Phone: (281)558-6930 Fax: (281)558-7029 E-mail: ginfo@undergroundinfo.com • Monthly. $33.00 per year. Covers engineering and operating methods on cross-country pipelines that transport crude oil products and natural gas. Includes *Energy Management Report*. Incorporates *Pipeline*.

Piping Guide: A Compact Reference for the Design and Drafting of Piping Systems. David R. Sherwood and Dennis J. Whistance. SYNTEC, Inc., 2702 Church Creek Lane Edgewater, MD 21037-1214. 1991. $89.00. Second edition.

PIRA. Technical Centre for the Paper and Board, Printing and Packaging Industries, Randalls Rd. Leatherhead, Surrey KT22 7RU, England. Phone: (137)2-802058 Fax: (137)2-802239 URL: http://www.pira.co.uk • Citations and abstracts pertaining to bookbinding and other pulp, paper, and packaging industries, 1975 to present. Weekly updates. Inquire as to online cost and availability.

Pit and Quarry. Advanstar Communications, Inc., 201 E. Sandpoint Ave., Suite 600 Santa Ana, CA 92700. Phone: 800-346-0085 or (714)513-8400 Fax: (714)513-8632 E-mail: information@advanstar.com • URL: http://www.advanstar.com • Monthly. $49.00 per year. Covers crushed stone, sand and gravel, etc.

Pit and Quarry Buyers' Guide. Advanstar Communications, Inc., 7500 Old Oak Blvd. Cleveland, OH 44130-3369. Phone: 800-346-0085 or (440)243-8100 Fax: (440)826-2833 E-mail: information@advanstar.com • URL: http://www.advanstar.com • Annual. $25.00. Lists approximately 1,000 manufacturers and other suppliers of equipment products and services to the nonmetallic mining and quarrying industry. Absorbed: *Ready-Mix-Reference Manual*.

Pizza Today. National Association of Pizza Operators, PO Box 1347 New Albany, IN 47151-1347. Phone: (812)949-0909 Fax: (812)941-9711 URL: http://www.pizzatoday.com • Monthly. $30.00 per year. Covers both practical business topics and food topics for pizza establishments.

Pizzeria. Entrepreneur Media, Inc., 2445 McCabe Way Irvine, CA 92614. Phone: 800-421-2300 or (949)261-2325 Fax: (949)261-0234 E-mail: entmag@entrepreneur.com • URL: http://www.entrepreneur.com • Looseleaf. $59.50. A practical guide to starting a pizza shop. Covers profit potential, start-up costs, market size evaluation, owner's time required, site selection, lease negotiation, pricing, accounting, advertising, promotion, etc. (Start-Up Business Guide No. E1006.)

Placemaking: The Art and Practice of Building Communities. Lynda H. Schneekloth and Robert G. Shibley. John Wiley and Sons, Inc., 605 Third Ave. New York, NY 10158-0012. Phone: 800-225-5945 or (212)850-6000 Fax: (212)850-6088 E-mail: info@wiley.com • URL: http://www.wiley.com • 1995. $59.95.

Places, Towns, and Townships, 1998. Deirdre A. Gaquin and Richard W. Dodge, editors. Bernan Press, 4611-F Assembly Dr. Lanham, MD 20706-4391. Phone: 800-274-4447 or (301)459-7666 Fax: 800-865-3450 or (301)459-0056 E-mail: info@bernan.com • URL: http://www.bernan.com • 1997. $89.00. Second edition. Presents demographic and economic statistics from the U. S. Census Bureau and other government sources for places, cities, towns, villages, census designated places, and minor civil divisions. Contains more than 60 data categories.

Plan Sponsor. Asset International, Inc., 125 Greenwich Ave. Greenwich, CT 06830. Phone: (203)629-5014 Fax: (203)629-5024 Monthly. $150.00 per year. Edited for professional pension plan managers and executives. Defined contribution plans are emphasized.

Plane and Pilot. Werner Publishing Corp., 12121 Wilshire Blvd., No. 1200 Los Angeles, CA 90025-1175. Monthly. $16.95 per year.

Planning. American Planning Association, 122 S. Michigan Ave., Suite 1600 Chicago, IL 60603-6107. Phone: (312)431-9100 Fax: (312)431-9985 URL: http://www.planning.org • Monthly. Free to members; non-members, $60.00 per year.

Planning and Zoning News. Planning and Zoning Center, Inc., 715 N. Cedar St. Lansing, MI 48906-5206. Phone: (517)886-0555 Fax: (517)886-0564 E-mail: freebury@pzcenter.com • URL: http://www.pzcenter.com • Monthly. $175.00 per year. Newsletter on planning and zoning issues in the United States.

Planning Cash Flow. American Management Association Extension Institute, P.O. Box 1026 Saranac Lake, NY 12983-9957. Phone: 800-262-9699 or (518)891-1500 Fax: (518)891-0368 Looseleaf. $110.00. Self-study course. Emphasis is on practical explanations, examples, and problem solving. Quizzes and a case study are included.

Planning for Water Source Protection. Philip M. Kappen. Sage Publications, Inc., 2455 Teller Rd. Thousand Oaks, CA 91320. Phone: (805)499-0721 Fax: (805)499-0871 E-mail: info@sagepub.com • URL: http://www.sagepub.com • 1993. $10.00.

Planning for Your Retirement: IRA and Keogh Plans. CCH, Inc., 4025 W. Peterson Ave. Chicago, IL 60646-6085. Phone: 800-248-3248 or (773)866-3608 Fax: 800-224-8299 or (773)866-3608 URL: http://www.cch.com • Annual.

Planning Resource Directory. American Bankers Association, 1120 Connecticut Ave., N.W. Washington, DC 20036-3971. Phone: 800-338-0626 or (202)663-5000 Fax: (202)663-7543 URL: http://www.aba.org • Annual. $45.00. Describes consulting firms and other organizations that assist banks in strategic planning.

Planning Tax-Exempt Organizations. Shepard's, 555 Middle Creek Parkway Colorado Springs, CO 80921. Phone: 800-743-7393 or (719)481-7371 Fax: 800-525-0053 or (719)481-7621 E-mail: customer_service@shepards.com • URL: http://www.shepards.com • 1983. $210.00. Two volumes. How to form a nonprofit organization. (Tax and Estate Planning Series).

Plant Biotechnology Institute. National Research Council of Canada

Plant Engineering. Cahners Business Information, 2000 Clearwater Dr. Oak Brook, IL 60523. Phone: 800-662-7776 or (630)320-7000 E-mail: corporatecommunications@cahners.com • URL: http://www.cahners.com • 13 times a year. $135.90. per year. Includes *Plant Engineering Product Supplier Guide*.

Plant Layout and Materials Handling. James M. Apple. Krieger Publishing Co., P.O. Box 9542 Melbourne, FL 32902-9542. Phone: 800-724-0025 or (321)724-9542 Fax: (321)951-3671 E-mail: info@krieger-publishing.com • URL: http://www.krieger-publishing.com • 1991. $59.50. Reprint edition.

Plant Science Bulletin. Botanical Society of America, Inc., Ohio State University, Dept. of Genetics, 1735 Neil Ave. Columbus, OH 43210. Phone: (314)977-3903 Fax: (314)977-3658 E-mail: leverich@sluvca.slu.edu • Quarterly. Membership.

Plant Services. Putman Media, 555 W. Pierce Rd., Suite 301 Itasca, IL 60143-2649. Phone: (630)467-1300 Fax: (630)467-1123 URL: http://www.putnampublishing.com • Monthly. $95.00 per year.

Plants, Sites, and Parks. Cahners Business Information, 245 W. 17th St. New York, NY 10011-5360. Phone: (212)645-0067 E-mail: corporatecommunications@cahners.com • URL: http://www.cahners.com • Bimonthly. $30.00 per year. Covers economic development, site location, industrial parks, and industrial development programs.

Plastics Engineering. Society of Plastics Engineers, Inc., P.O. Box 403 Brookfield, CT 06804-0403. Phone: (203)775-0471 Fax: (203)775-8490 Monthly. $110.00 per year.

Plastics Extrusion Technology Handbook. Sidney Levy and others. Industrial Press, Inc., 200 Madison Ave. New York, NY 10016. Phone: 888-528-7852 or (212)889-6330 Fax: (212)545-8327 E-mail: induspress@aol.com • URL: http://www.industrialpress.com • 1989. $44.95. Second edition.

Plastics Institute of America.

Plastics News: Crain's International Newspaper for the Plastics Industry. Crain Communications, Inc., 740 N. Rush St. Chicago, IL 60611-2590. Phone: 800-678-9595 or (312)649-5200 URL: http://www.plasticsnews.com • Weekly. $62.00 per year.

Plastics Pipe Institute.

Plastics Processing Technology. Edward A. Muccio. ASM International, 9639 Kinsman Rd. Materials Park, OH 44073-0002. Phone: 800-336-5152 or (440)338-5151 Fax: (440)338-4634 E-mail: custserv@po.asm-intl.org • URL: http://www.asm-intl.org • 1994. $87.00. Contains basic terminology and information on plastics for engineers, managers, technicians, purchasing agents, and students. Written to serve as a primer on plastics technology and processing.

Plastics Recognized Component Directory. Underwriters Laboratories, Inc., 333 Pfingsten Rd. Northbrook, IL 60062-2096. Phone: (847)272-8800 Fax: (847)272-0472 E-mail: northbrook@ul.com • Annual. $46.00. Lists electrical component manufacturers authorized to use UL label. Formerly *Recognized Component Directory*.

Plastics Technology Manufacturing Handbook and Buyers' Guide. Bill Communications, Inc, 770 Broadway New York, NY 10003. Phone: 800-266-4712 or (646)654-4500 Fax: (646)654-7212 URL: http://www.billcom.com • Annual. Over 4,000 manufacturers of plastics processing equipment and materials. Included in subscription to *Plastics Technology*.

Plastics Technology: The Only Magazine for Plastics Processors. Bill Communications, Inc., 770 Broadway New York, NY 10003-9595. Phone: 800-266-4712 or (646)654-4500 Fax: (646)654-7212 E-mail: dmarone@plasticstechnology.com • URL: http://www.billcom.com • 13 times a year. $89.00 per year.

Plastics Week: The Global Newsletter. McGraw-Hill Chemicals and Plastics Information Services, 1221 Ave. of the Americas New York, NY 10020. Phone: 800-722-4726 or (212)904-2000 Fax: (212)904-2072 E-mail: customer.service@mcgraw-hill.com • URL: http://www.mcgraw-hill.com • Weekly. $530.00 per year. Newsletter. Covers international trends in plastics production, technology, research, and legislation.

Plating and Surface Finishing: Electroplating, Finishing of Metals, Organic Finishing. American Electroplaters and Surface Finishers Society, 12644 Research Parkway Orlando, FL 32826-3298. Phone: 800-334-2052 or (407)281-6441 Fax: (407)281-6446 E-mail: editors@aesf.org • URL: http://www.aesf.org • Monthly. Members, $16.00 per year; non-members, $60.00 per year.

Platinum Metals Review. Johnson, Matthey PLC, 40-42 Hatton Garden London EC1N 8EE, England. Phone: 44 171 2698000 Fax: 44 171 2698389 E-mail: jmpmr@matthey.com • URL: http://www.matthey.com/ • Quarterly. Free. Text in English and Japanese.

Platt's Energy Prices. Data Products Division, 24 Hartwell Ave. Lexington, MA 02173. Phone: 800-933-3374 or (781)863-5100 Fax: (781)860-6332 URL: http://www.dri.mcgraw-hill.com • Contains daily high and low prices for crude oil and petroleum products, including gasoline, fuel oil, and liquefied petroleum gas (LPG). Coverage is international from 1983 to present, with daily updates. Inquire as to online cost and availability.

Platt's Oil Marketing Bulletin. McGraw-Hill, 1221 Ave. of the Americas New York, NY 10020. Phone: 800-722-4726 or (212)904-2000 Fax: (212)904-2072 E-mail: customer.service@mcgraw-hill.com • URL: http://www.mcgraw-hill.com • Weekly. $427.00 per year. Newsletter. Marketing information service.

Platt's Oilgram News. McGraw-Hill, Commodity Services Group, 1221 Ave. of the Americas New York, NY 10020. Phone: 800-722-4726 or (212)904-2000 Fax: (212)904-2072 E-mail: customer.service@mcgraw-hill.com • URL: http://www.mcgraw-hill.com • Daily. $1,347.00 per year. Covers oil industry in general.

Platt's Oilgram Price Report: an International Daily Oil-Gas Price and Marketing Letter. McGraw-Hill, 1221 Ave. of the Americas New York, NY 10020. Phone: 800-722-4726 or (212)904-2000 Fax: (212)904-2072 E-mail: customer.service@mcgraw-hill.com • URL: http://www.mcgraw-hill.com • Daily. $1,517.00 per year. Prices and marketing intelligence for petroleum products. Includes weekly statistical summaries. Worldwide coverage.

Playthings Buyers Guide. Geyer-McAllister Publications, Inc., 51 Madison Ave. New York, NY 10010-1603. Phone: (212)689-4411 Fax: (212)683-7929 Annual. Included in subscription to *Playthings*. Lists of toy manufacturers and their suppliers, designers and inventors, manufacturers' representatives, licensor, importers. Formerly *Playthings. Who Makes It*.

Playthings: For Today's Merchandiser of Toys, Hobbies and Crafts. Frank Reysen, editor. Cahners Business Newspapers, 7025 Albert Pick Rd. Greensboro, NC 27409. Phone: 800-662-7776 or (336)605-0121 Fax: (336)605-1143 E-mail: corporatecommunications@cahners.com • URL: http://www.cahners.com • Monthly. $32.00 per year. Covers the major toy and hobby categories, industry news and news products.

Pleasure Boats. Available from MarketResearch.com, 641 Ave. of the Americas, Third Floor New York, NY 10011. Phone: 800-298-5699 or (212)807-2629 Fax: (212)807-2716 E-mail: order@marketresearch.com • URL: http://www.marketresearch.com • 1997. $1,495.00. Market research report published by Specialists in Business Information. Covers inboard, outboard, sterndrive, sail, inflatable, personal watercraft, and canoes.

PlugIn Datamation: Profit and Value from Information Technology. Earth Web, Inc., Datamation, 250 Summer St. Boston, MA 02210. Phone: 800-662-7776 or (617)303-7906 Fax: (617)345-5486 E-mail: info@earthweb.com • URL: http://www.datamation. • Monthly. Price on application. Technical, semi-technical and general news covering EDP topics.

Plumbers Handbook. Howard C. Massey. Craftsman Book Co., 6058 Corte del Cedro Carlsbad, CA 92009. Phone: 800-829-8123 or (760)438-7828 Fax: (760)438-0398 E-mail: jacobs@costbook.com • URL: http://www.craftsman-book.com • 1998. $32.00. Third Revised edition.

Plumbing and Drainage Institute.

Plumbing Engineer. American Society of Plumbing Engineers. TMB Publishing, 1884 Techny Court Northbrook, IL 60062. Phone: (847)564-1127 Fax: (847)564-1264 Monthly. $50.00 per year.

Plumbing Fixtures. U. S. Bureau of the Census, Washington, DC 20233-0800. Phone: (301)457-4100 Fax: (301)457-3842 URL: http://www.census.gov • Quarterly and annual. Provides data on shipments: value, quantity, imports, and exports. Includes both metal and plastic fixtures. (Current Industrial Reports, MQ-34E.)

Plunkett's Biotech and Genetics Industry Almanac. Plunkett Research, Ltd., P. O. Drawer 541737 Houston, TX 77254-1737. Phone: (713)932-0000 Fax: (713)932-7080 E-mail: info@plunkettresearch.com • URL: http://www.plunkettresearch.com • Annual. $199.99. Provides detailed profiles of 400 leading biotech corporations. Includes information on current trends and research in the field of biotechnology/genetics.

Plunkett's Companion to the Almanac of American Employers: Mid-Size Firms. Plunkett Research, Ltd., P. O. Drawer 541737 Houston, TX 77254-1737. Phone: (713)932-0000 Fax: (713)932-7080 E-mail: info@plunkettresearch.com • URL: http://www.plunkettresearch.com • Annual. $149.99. Provides job-seekers with detailed information about fast-growing, medium-size corporations. Includes diskette.

Plunkett's E-Commerce and Internet Business Almanac. Plunkett Research, Ltd., P. O. Drawer 541737 Houston, TX 77254-1737. Phone: (713)932-0000 Fax: (713)932-7080 E-mail: info@plunkettresearch.com • URL: http://www.plunkettresearch.com • Annual. $199.99. Contains detailed profiles of 250 large companies engaged in various areas of Internet commerce, including e-business Web sites, communications equipment manufacturers, and Internet service providers. Includes CD-ROM.

Plunkett's Employers' Internet Sites with Careers Information. Plunkett Research, Ltd., P. O. Drawer 541737 Houston, TX 77254-1737. Phone: (713)932-0000 Fax: (713)932-7080 E-mail: info@plunkettresearch.com • URL: http://www.plunkettresearch.com • Annual. $149.99. Includes diskette.

Plunkett's Energy Industry Almanac: Complete Profiles on the Energy Industry 500 Companies. Plunkett Research Ltd., P. O. Drawer 541737 Houston, TX 77254-1737. Phone: (713)932-0000 Fax: (713)932-7080 E-mail: info@plunkettresearch.com • URL: http://www.plunkettresearch.com • Annual. $149.99. Includes major oil companies, utilities, pipelines, alternative energy companies, etc. Provides information on industry trends.

Plunkett's Engineering and Research Industry Almanac. Plunkett Research, Ltd., P. O. Drawer 541737 Houston, TX 77254-1737. Phone: (713)932-0000 Fax: (713)932-7080 E-mail: info@plunkettresearch.com • URL: http://www.plunkettresearch.com • Annual. $179.99. Contains detailed profiles of major engineering and technology corporations. Includes CD-ROM.

Plunkett's Entertainment and Media Industry Almanac. Available from Plunkett Research, Ltd., P.O. Drawer 541737 Houston, TX 77254-1737. Phone: (713)932-0000 Fax: (713)932-7080 E-mail: info@plunkettresearch.com • URL: http://www.plunkettresearch.com • Biennial. $149.99. Provides profiles of leading firms in online information, films, radio, television, cable, multimedia, magazines, and book publishing. Includes World Wide Web sites, where available, plus information on careers and industry trends.

Plunkett's Financial Services Industry Almanac: The Leading Firms in Investments, Banking, and Financial Information. Available from Plunkett Research, Ltd., P.O. Drawer 541737 Houston, TX 77254-1737. Phone: 800-486-8666 or (409)765-8530 Fax: (409)765-8571 E-mail: info@plunkettresearch.com • URL: http://www.plunkettresearch.com • Annual. $245.00. Discusses important trends in various sectors of the financial industry. Five hundred major banking, credit card, investment, and financial services companies are profiled.

Plunkett's Health Care Industry Almanac: The Only Complete Guide to the Fastest-Changing Industry in America. Available from Plunkett Research, Ltd., P.O. Drawer 541737 Houston, TX 77254-1737. Phone: 800-486-8666 or (713)932-0000 Fax: (713)932-7080 E-mail: customersupport@plunkettresearch.com • URL: http://www.plunkettresearch.com • Biennial. $179.99. Includes detailed profiles of 500 large companies providing health care products or services, with indexes by products, services, and location. Provides statistical and trend information for the health insurance industry, HMOs, hospital utilization, Medicare, medical technology, and national health expenditures.

Plunkett's InfoTech Industry Almanac: Complete Profiles on the InfoTech 500-the Leading Firms in the Movement and Management of Voice, Data, and Video. Available from Plunkett Research, Ltd., P.O. Drawer 541737 Houston, TX 77254-1734. Phone: 800-486-8666 or (713)932-0000 Fax: (713)932-7080 E-mail: customersupport@plunkettresearch.com • URL: http://www.plunkettresearch.com • Annual. $149.99. Five hundred major information companies are profiled, with corporate culture aspects. Discusses major trends in various sectors of the computer and information industry, including data on careers and job growth. Includes several indexes.

Plunkett's On-Line Trading, Finance, and Investment Web Sites Almanac. Plunkett Research, Ltd., P. O. Drawer 541737 Houston, TX 77254-1737. Phone: (713)932-0000 Fax: (713)932-7080 E-mail: info@plunkettresearch.com • URL: http://www.plunkettresearch.com • Annual. $149.99. Provides profiles and usefulness rankings of financial Web sites. Sites are rated from 1 to 5 for specific uses. Includes diskette.

Plunkett's Retail Industry Almanac: Complete Profiles on the Retail 500-The Leading Firms in Retail Stores, Services, Catalogs, and On-Line Sales. Available from Plunkett Research, Ltd., P.O. Drawer 541737 Houston, TX 77254-1737. Phone: 800-486-8666 or (713)932-0000 Fax: (713)932-7080 E-mail: customersupport@plunkettresearch.com • URL: http://www.plunkettresearch.com • Annual. $179.99. Provides detailed profiles of 500 major U. S. retailers. Industry trends are discussed.

Plunkett's Telecommunications Industry Almanac. Plunkett Research, Ltd., P. O. Drawer 541737 Houston, TX 77254-1737. Phone: (713)932-0000 Fax: (713)932-7080 E-mail: info@plunkettresearch.com • URL: http://www.plunkettresearch.com • Annual. $179.99. Provides detailed profiles of major telecommunications industry corporations. Includes CD-ROM.

PMI Book of Project Management Forms. Project Management Institute, c/o PMI Headquarters Publishing Div., 40 Colonial Square Sylva, NC 28779. Phone: (828)586-3715 Fax: (828)586-4020 E-mail: booked@pmi.org • URL: http://www.pmi.org • 1997. $49.95. Contains more than 100 sample forms for use in project management. Includes checklists, reports, charts, agreements, schedules, requisitions, order forms, and other documents.

PMMI: Official Packaging Machinery Directory. Packaging Machinery Manufacturers Institute, 4350 Fairfax Dr., Suite 600 Arlington, VA 22203-1619. Phone: (703)243-8555 Fax: (703)243-8556 E-mail: pmmi@pmmi.org • URL: http://www.packnet.com • Biennial. $25.00 per year.

Pocket List of Railroad Officials. PRIMEDIA Information Group Inc., 10 Lake Dr. Hightstown, NJ 08520-5397. Phone: 800-221-5488 or (609)371-7700 Fax: (609)371-7879 URL: http://www.primediainfo.com • Quarterly. $198.00 per year. Guide to over 30,000 officials in the freight railroad, rail transit and rail supply industries. Includes *Buyers' Guide*.

Pocket Station Listing Guide. National Association of Television Program Executives, 2425 Olympic Blvd., Suite 550E Santa Monica, CA 90404. Phone: (310)453-4440 Fax: (310)453-5258 URL: http://www.natpe.org/ • Quarterly. $15.00 per copy. Pocket-sized directory of all TV stations in the U. S. and Canada, and Latin America. Geographic arrangement. Includes major personnel.

Podiatry Management. Kane Communications, Inc., 7000 Terminal Square, Suite 210 Upper Darby, PA 19082. Phone: (610)734-2420 Fax: (610)734-2423 Nine times a year. $30.00 per year. Non-clinical subject matter.

Point-of-Purchase Advertising International.

Police: Buyer's Guide. Bobit Publications, 21061 S. Western Ave. Torrance, CA 90501. Phone: (310)533-2400 Fax: (310)533-2504 URL: http://www.policemag.com • Annual. $3.00. Lists suppliers of products and services for police departments.

Police Chief: Buyer's Guide. International Association of Chiefs of Police, 515 N. Washington St. Alexandria, VA 22314-2340. Phone: 800-843-4227 or (703)243-6500 Fax: (703)836-4543 Annual. $3.00. Contains a list of suppliers of equipment and services for police departments.

Police Chief: Professional Voice of Law Enforcement. International Association of Chiefs of Police, 515 N. Washington St., Suite 200 Alexandria, VA 22314-2340. Phone: 800-843-4227 or (703)243-6500 Fax: (703)836-4543 Monthly. $25.00 per year. Subject matter includes information on law enforcement technology and new products.

Police Executive Research Forum., 1120 Connecticut Ave., N. W., Suite 930 Washington, DC 20036. Phone: 877-576-5423 or (202)466-7820 Fax: (202)466-7826 E-mail: perf@policeforum.org • URL: http://www.policeforum.org • Research areas include police operational and administrative procedures. Provides consulting services to local governments.

Police Markets of North America and the European Union: Jane's Special Report. Jane's Information Group, 1340 Braddock Place, Dept. DSM, Ste. 300 Alexandria, VA 22314. Phone: 800-824-0768 or (703)683-3700 Fax: 800-836-0297 E-mail: info@janes.com • URL: http://www.janes.com • 1997. $695.00. Provides detailed market research data relative to the police and security industry. Covers a wide range of equipment and vehicle markets geographically for U. S. states, Canadian provinces, and countries. (Law Enforcement-Related Special Report Series).

Police Misconduct and Civil Rights Law Report. National Lawyers Guild Civil Liberties Committee. West Group, 610 Opperman Dr. Eagan, MN 55123. Phone: 800-328-4880 or (651)687-7000 Fax: 800-213-2323 or (651)687-5827 Bimonthly. $194.00 per year. Newsletter.

Police Science and Technology Review. Jane's Information Group, 1340 Braddock Place, Dept. DSM, Ste. 300 Alexandria, VA 22314. Phone: 800-824-0768 or (703)683-3700 E-mail: info@janes.com • URL: http://www.janes.com • Quarterly. $90.00 per year. Includes detailed information on technology relating to surveillance, forensics, and fingerprints.

Police: The Law Officer's Magazine. Bobit Publications, 21061 S. Western Ave. Torrance, CA 90501. Phone: (310)533-2400 Fax: (310)533-2500 URL: http://www.policemag.com • Monthly. $38.95 per year. Edited for law enforcement professionals. Includes information on new technology and equipment.

Policy Statistics Service. The National Underwriter Co.

Political Risk Letter. Available from MarketResearch.com, 641 Ave. of the Americas, Third Floor New York, NY 10011. Phone: 800-298-5699 or (212)807-2629 Fax: (212)807-2716 E-mail: order@marketreseach.com • URL: http://www.marketresearch.com • Monthly. $435.00 per year. Newsletter published by Political Risk Services. Contains forecasts of the political risks of doisg business in each of 100 countries.

Political Risk Yearbook. The P R S Group, P.O. Box 248 East Syracuse, NY 13057-0248. Phone: (315)431-0511 Fax: (315)431-0200 E-mail: custserv@prsgroup.com • URL: http://www.prsgroup.com • Annual. $1,200.00. Eight regional volumes. Each volume covers a separate region of the world and assesses economic and political conditions as they relate to the risk of doing business.

Politics of Taxation: Revenue Without Representation. Susan B. Hansen. Greenwood Publishing Group, Inc, 88 Post Rd., W. Westport, CT 06881-5007. Phone: 800-225-5800 or (203)226-3571 Fax: (203)222-2540 E-mail: bookinfo@greenwood.com • URL: http://www.greenwood.com • 1983. $55.00.

Polk Financial Institutions Directory. Thomson Financial Publishing, 4709 W. Golf Rd. Skokie, IL 60076-1253. Phone: 800-321-3373 or (847)676-9600 Fax: (847)933-8101 E-mail: customerservice@tfp.com • URL: http://www.tfp.com • Semiannual. $330.00 per semiannual volume. Provides detailed information on "virtually every bank, savings and loan, and major credit union in North America, including banks and branches in Canada, Mexico, the Caribbean, and Central America." Supersedes *Polk's Bank Directory*.

Polk World Bank Directory. Thomson Financial Publishing, 4709 W. Golf Rd. Skokie, IL 60076-1253. Phone: 800-321-3373 or (847)676-9600 Fax: (847)933-8101 E-mail: customerservice@tfp.com • URL: http://www.tfp.com • Annual. $330.00. Contains detailed listings of banks around the world, including the top 1,000 U. S. banks. Includes performance ratios for the three most recent fiscal years (return on assets, return on equity, etc.).

Polk World Banking Profiles: 2,000 Major Banks of the World. Thomson Financial Publishing, 4709 W. Golf Rd. Skokie, IL 60076-1253. Phone: 800-321-3373 or (847)676-9600 Fax: (847)933-8101 E-mail: customerservice@tfp.com • URL: http://www.tfp.com • Annual. $319.00. Provides extensive, three-year financial data for 2,000 U. S. and foreign banks. Includes analysis of 12 financial ratios and credit ratings from five leading bank rating agencies.

Polling Report: An Independent Survey of Trends Affecting Elections, Government, and Business. Polling Report, Inc., P.O. Box 42580 Washington, DC 20015-0580. Phone: (202)237-2000 Fax: (202)237-2001 E-mail: editor@pollingreport.com • URL: http://www.pollingreport.com • Biweekly. Students and teachers, $78.00 per year; others, $195.00 per year. Newsletter. Reports on the results of a wide variety of public opinion polls.

Pollution Abstracts. Cambridge Information Group, 7200 Wisconsin Ave., 6th Fl. Bethesda, MD 20814. Phone: 800-843-7751 or (301)961-6700 Fax: (301)961-6720 E-mail: market@csa.com • URL: http://www.csa.com • Monthly. $895.00 per year; with index, $985.00 per year.

Pollution Abstracts Íonlinel. Cambridge Scientific Abstracts, 7200 Wisconsin Ave., 6th Fl. Bethesda, MD 20814. Phone: 800-843-7751 or (301)961-6700 Fax: (301)961-6720 Provides indexing and abstracting of international, environmentally related literature, 1970 to date. Monthly updates. Inquire as to online cost and availability.

Pollution: Causes, Effects, and Control. R. M. Harrison, editor. American Chemical Society, 1155 16th St., N. W. Washington, DC 20036. Phone: 800-333-9511 or (202)872-4600 Fax: (202)872-4615 E-mail: service@acs.org • URL: http://www.pubs.acs.org • 1996. $71.00. Third edition. Published by The Royal Society of Chemistry. A basic introduction to pollution of air, water, and land. Includes discussions of pollution control technologies.

Pollution Engineering: Magazine of Environmental Control. Cahners Business Information, 1350 E. Touhy Ave. Des Plains, IL 60068-3358. Phone: 800-662-7776 or (847)635-8800 Fax: (847)390-2636 E-mail: corporatecommunications@cahners.com • URL: http://www.cahners.com • 13 times a year. $85.90 per year. Includes *Product-Service Locater*.

Pollution Engineering-Product/Service Locator. Cahners Business Information, 2000 Clearwater Dr. Oak Brook, IL 60523-8809. Phone: 800-662-7776 or (630)320-7000 E-mail: corporatecommunications@cahners.com • URL: http://www.cahners.com • Annual. $24.95. Supplement to

Pollution Engineering. Formerly *Pollution Engineering Locator*.

Pollution Equipment News Buyer's Guide. Rimbach Publishing, Inc., 8650 Babcock Blvd. Pittsburgh, PA 15237. Phone: 800-245-3182 or (412)364-5366 Fax: (412)369-9720 E-mail: rimbach@sgi.net • URL: http://www.rimbach.com • Annual. $100.00. Over 3,000 manufacturers of pollution control equipment and products.

Polymer Engineering and Science. Society of Plastics Engineers, Inc., P.O. Box 403 Brookfield, CT 06804-0403. Phone: (203)775-0471 Fax: (203)775-8490 Monthly. $220.00 per year. Includes six special issues.

Polymer Processing: Principles and Design. Donald G. Baird and Dimitria I. Collias. John Wiley and Sons, Inc., 605 Third Ave., 4th Fl. New York, NY 10158-0012. Phone: 800-225-5945 or (212)850-6000 Fax: (212)850-6088 E-mail: info@wiley.com • URL: http://www.wiley.com/compbooks/ • 1998. $94.95. A practical guide to thermoplastics.

Polymer Research Center. University of Cincinnati

Polymer Research Laboratory. University of Michigan

Polymers/Ceramics/Composites Alert. Cambridge Information Group, 7200 Wisconsin Ave., 6th Fl. Bethesda, MD 20814. Phone: 800-843-7751 or (301)961-6700 Fax: (301)961-6720 E-mail: market@csa.com • URL: http://www.csa.com • Monthly. $340.00 per year. Provides citations to the business and industrial literature of plastic, ceramic, and composite materials. (Materials Business Information Series).

Pool and Spa News Directory. Leisure Publications, 4160 Wilshire Blvd. Los Angeles, CA 90010. Phone: (323)964-4800 Fax: (323)964-4838 E-mail: psn@poolspanews.com • URL: http://www.poolspanews.com • Annual. $49.50. List of 1,500 manufacturers and distributors of pool, spa, and hot water equipment and supplies. Formerly *Pool and Spa News Source Book* .

Pool and Spa News: The National Trade Magazine for the Swimming Poool & Spa Industry. Leisure Publications, 4160 Wilshire Blvd. Los Angeles, CA 90010. Phone: (323)964-4800 Fax: (323)964-4838 E-mail: psn@poolspanews.com • URL: http://www.poolspanews.com • Semimonthly. $19.97 per year.

Popcorn Institute., 401 N. Michigan Ave. Chicago, IL 60611-4267. Phone: (312)644-6610 Fax: (312)527-6658 URL: http://www.popcorn.org • Members are popcorn companies.

Poptronics. Gernsback Publications, Inc., 500 Bi-County Blvd. Farmingdale, NY 11735. Phone: (516)293-3000 Fax: (516)293-3115 URL: http://www.gernsback.com • Monthly. $19.99 per year. Incorporates *Electronics Now*.

Population Abstract of the U. S. The Gale Group, 27500 Drake Rd. Farmington Hills, MI 48331-3535. Phone: 800-877-GALE or (248)699-GALE Fax: 800-414-5043 or (248)699-8069 E-mail: galeord@galegroup.com • URL: http://www.galegroup.com • 2000. $185.00. Historical emphasis. Includes a "breakdown of urban and rural population from the earliest census to the present."

Population Action International.

Population and Development Review. Population Council, One Dag Hammarskjold Plaza New York, NY 10017. Phone: (212)339-0500 Fax: (212)755-6052 E-mail: pubinfo@popcouncil.org • URL: http://www.popcouncil.org/pdr • Quarterly. $36.00 per year. *Supplements* available. Text in English, summaries in English, French and Spanish.

Population and Vital Statistics Report. United Nations Publications, United Nations Concourse Level, First Ave., 46th St. New York, NY 10017. Phone: 800-553-3210 or (212)963-7680 Fax: (212)963-4910 E-mail: bookstore@un.org • URL: http://www.un.org/publications • Quarterly. $40.00 per year. Contains worldwide demographic statistics.

Population Association of America.

Population Bulletin. Population Reference Bureau, Inc., 1875 Connecticut Ave., N.W., Suite 520 Washington, DC 20009. Phone: (202)483-1100 Fax: (202)328-3937 E-mail: popref@prb.org • URL: http://www.prb.org • Quarterly. $7.00 per issue.

Population Council.

Population of States and Counties of the United States: 1790-1990. Available from National Technical Information Service, 5285 Port Royal Rd. Springfield, VA 22161. Phone: 800-553-6847 or (703)487-4600 Fax: (703)321-8547 E-mail: info@ntis.fedworld.gov • URL: http://www.ntis.gov • 1996. $35.00. Issued by the U. S. Census Bureau (http://www.census.gov). Provides data on the number of inhabitants of the U. S., states, territories, and counties according to 21 decennial censuses from 1790 to 1990. Includes descriptions of county origins and lists prior county names, where applicable.

Population Projections of the United States by Age, Sex, Race, and Hispanic Origin: 1995 to 2050. Available from U. S. Government Printing Office, Washington, DC 20402. Phone: (202)512-1800 Fax: (202)512-2250 E-mail: gpoaccess@gpo.gov • URL: http://www.access.gpo.gov • 1996. $8.50. Issued by the U. S. Bureau of the Census (http://www.census.gov). Contains charts and tables. Appendixes include detailed data on fertility rates by age, life expectancy, immigration, and armed forces population. (Current Population Reports, P25-1130.)

Population Reference Bureau.

Population Research Center. University of Chicago

Populations Studies Center. University of Michigan

Port Engineering. Per Bruun. Gulf Publishing Co., P.O. Box 2608 Houston, TX 77252-2608. Phone: 800-231-6275 or (713)520-4301 Fax: (713)520-4433 E-mail: ezorder@gulfpub.com • URL: http://www.gpcbooks.com • 1989. Fourth edition. Two volumes. Vol. 1, $195.00; Volume 2, $195.00.

Port Planning and Development. Ernst G. Frankel. John Wiley and Sons, Inc., 605 Third Ave. New York, NY 10158-0012. Phone: 800-225-5945 or (212)850-6000 Fax: (212)850-6088 E-mail: info@wiley.com • URL: http://www.wiley.com • 1987. $200.00.

Portable Power Equipment Manufacturers Association.

Portable Power Tools. Time-Life, Inc., 2000 Duke St. Alexandria, VA 22314. Phone: 800-621-7026 or (703)838-7000 Fax: (703)684-5224 1992. $14.95. Contains popular descriptions of power tools for woodworking. (Art of Woodworking Series).

Portfolio Management Formulas: Mathematical Trading Methods for the Futures, Options, and Stock Markets. Ralph Vince. John Wiley and Sons, Inc., 605 Third Ave. New York, NY 10158-0012. Phone: 800-526-5368 or (212)850-6000 Fax: (212)850-6088 E-mail: info@wiley.com • URL: http://www.wiley.com • 1990. $85.00. Discusses optimization of trading systems by exploiting the rules of probability and making use of the principles of modern portfolio management theory. Computer programs are included.

Portfolio Selection: Efficient Diversification of Investments. Harry M. Markowitz. Blackwell Publishers, 350 Main St., 6th Fl. Malden, MA 02148-5018. Phone: 800-216-2522 or (781)388-8200 Fax: (781)388-8210 E-mail: books@blackwellpub.com • URL: http://www.blackwellpub.com • 1991. $52.95. Second edition. A standard work on diversification of investments for institutions. Provides a mathematical approach.

Portland Cement Association.

Ports of the World. Available from Informa Publishing Group Ltd., PO Box 1017 Westborough, MA 01581-6017. Phone: 800-493-4080 Fax: (508)231-0856 E-mail: enquiries@informa.com • URL: http://www.informa.com • Annual. $399.00. Published in the UK by Lloyd's List (http://www.lloydslist.com). Provides detailed information on more than 2,600 ports worldwide.

Position Descriptions in Special Libraries. Del Sweeney and Karin Zilla, editors. Special Libraries Association, 1700 18th St., N. W., 17th Fl. Washington, DC 20009-2514. Phone: (202)234-4700 Fax: 888-411-2856 or (202)234-2442 E-mail: books@sla.org • URL: http://www.sla.org • 1996. $41.00. Third revised edition. Provides 87 descriptions of library and information management positions.

Positive Leadership: Improving Performance Through Value-Centered Management. Lawence Ragan Communications, Inc., 316 N. Michigan Ave. Chicago, IL 60601. Phone: 800-878-5331 or (312)960-4100 Fax: (312)960-4106 E-mail: cservice@ragan.com • URL: http://www.ragan.com • Monthly. $119.00 per year. Newsletter. Emphasis is on employee motivation, family issues, ethics, and community relations.

Postal Bulletin. Available from U. S. Government Printing Office, Washington, DC 20402. Phone: (202)512-1800 Fax: (202)512-2250 E-mail: gpoaccess@gpo.gov • URL: http://www.access.gpo.gov • Biweekly. $140.00 per year. Issued by the United States Postal Service. Contains orders, instructions, and information relating to U. S. mail service.

Postal Service. Available from U. S. Government Printing Office, Washington, DC 20402. Phone: (202)512-1800 Fax: (202)512-2250 E-mail: gpoaccess@gpo.gov • URL: http://www.access.gpo.gov • Annual. Free. Issued by the Superintendent of Documents. A list of government publications on mail services and the post office. (Subject Bibliography No. 169.)

Postal World. United Communications Group, 11300 Rockville Pike, Suite 1100 Rockville, MD 20852-3030. Phone: (301)816-8950 Fax: (301)816-8945 E-mail: cdonoghue@ucg.com • URL: http://www.ucg.com • Biweekly. $349.00 per year. Newsletter for mail users.

Potash and Phosphate Institute.

Potato Abstracts. Available from CABI Publishing North America, 10 E. 40th St. New York, NY 10016. Phone: 800-528-4841 or (212)481-7018 Fax: (212)686-7993 E-mail: cabi@cabi.org • URL: http://www.cabi.org • Bimonthly. $435.00 per year. Published in England by CABI Publishing. Provides worldwide coverage of the literature.

Potato Association of America.

Potato Grower of Idaho. Potato Growers of Idaho, Inc. Harris Publishing, Inc., 520 Park Ave. Idaho Falls, ID 83402. Phone: (208)524-7000 Fax: (208)522-5241 E-mail: gary@potatogrower.com • URL: http://www.potatogrower.com • Monthly. $15.95 per year.

Potentials: Ideas and Products that Motivate. Lakewood Publications, Inc., 50 S. Ninth St. Minneapolis, MN 55402. Phone: 800-328-4329 or (612)333-0471 Fax: (612)333-6526 E-mail: mkaeter@potentialsmag.com • URL: http://www.lakewoodpub.com • 10 times a year. $24.00 per year. Covers incentives, premiums, awards, and gifts as related to promotional activities. Formerly *Potentials in Marketing*.

Potter's Dictionary of Materials and Techniques. Frank Hamer and Janet Hamer. University of Pennsylvania Press, 4200 Pine St. Philadelphia, PA 19104-4011. Phone: 800-445-9880 or (215)898-6261 Fax: (215)898-0404 1997. $49.95. Fourth edition.

Poultry Abstracts. Available from CABI Publishing North America, 10 E. 40th St. New York, NY 10016. Phone: 800-528-4841 or (212)481-7018 Fax: (212)686-7993 E-mail: cabi@cabi.org • URL: http://www.cabi.org • Monthly. $615.00 per year. Published in England by CABI Publishing. Provides worldwide coverage of the literature.

Poultry and Egg Marketing: The Bi-Monthly News Magazine of the Poultry Marketing Industry. Poultry and Egg News, P.O. Box 1338 Gainesville, GA 30503. Phone: (770)536-2476 Fax: (770)532-4894 Six times a year. Free to qualified personnel; others, $12.00 per year. Processing and marketing of eggs and poultry products.

Poultry Digest. Watt Publishing Co., 122 S. Wesley Ave. Mount Morris, IL 61054-1497. Phone: (815)734-4171 Fax: (815)734-4201 URL: http://www.wattnet.com • Bimonthly. Free to qualified personnel, others, $28.00 per year.

Poultry Science. M. E. Ensminger. Interstate Publishers, Inc., P.O. Box 50 Danville, IL 61834-0050. Phone: 800-843-4774 or (217)446-0500 Fax: (217)446-9706 E-mail: info-ipp@ippinc.com • URL: http://www.ippinc.com • 1992. $69.95. Third edition.

Poultry Science. Poultry Science Association, Inc., 1111 N. Dunlap Ave. Savoy, IL 61874. Phone: (217)356-3182 Fax: (217)398-4119 E-mail: psa@assochq.org • URL: http://www.psa.uiuc.edu • Monthly. $180.00 per year.

Poultry Science Association.

Poultry Times. Poultry and Egg News, P.O. Box 1338 Gainesville, GA 30503. Phone: (770)536-2476 Fax: (770)532-4894 Biweekly. $9.00 per year. Directed to grow-out operations for the egg and poultry business.

Powder Coating Institute.

Powder Metallurgy. IOM Communications Ltd., One Carlton House Terrace London SW1Y 5DB, England. E-mail: pm@materials.org.uk • URL: http://www.materials.org • Quarterly. Members $233.25 per year; non-members, $495.00 per year.

Powell Monetary Analyst. Larson M. Powell, editor. Reserve Research Ltd., P.O. Box 4135 Portland, ME 04101. Phone: (207)774-4971 Biweekly. $285.00 per year. Newsletters. Information on precious metals, coins and currencies.

Power. McGraw-Hill, 1221 Ave. of the Americas New York, NY 10020. Phone: 800-722-4726 or (212)904-2000 Fax: (212)904-2072 E-mail: customer.service@mcgraw-hill.com • URL: http://www.mcgraw-hill.com • Monthly. Free to qualified personnel; others, $55.00 per year.

Power and Communication Contractors Association.

Power Engineering International. PennWell Corp., Industrial Div., 1421 S. Sheridan Rd Tulsa, OK 74112. Phone: 800-331-4463 or (918)831-9421 Fax: (918)831-9295 E-mail: webmaster@pennwell.com • URL: http://www.pennwell.com • 10 times a year. $168.00 per year.

Power Equipment Trade. Hatton-Brown Publishers, Inc., 225 Hanrick St. Montgomery, AL 36104. Phone: (334)834-1170 Fax: (334)834-4525 E-mail: mail@hattonbrown.com • URL: http://www.hattonbrown.com • 10 times a year. $40.00 per year. Formerly *Chain Saw Age and Power Equipment Trade*.

Power Generation. Pasha Publishing, 1600 Wilson Blvd. Arlington, VA 22209. Phone: 800-424-2908 or (703)528-1244 Fax: (703)528-1253 Weekly. $790.00 per year. Newsletter. Formerly *Coals and Synfuels Technology*.

Power Media "Selects". Broadcast Interview Source, 2233 Wisconsin Ave., N. W., Suite 301 Washington, DC 20007-4104. Phone: 800-932-7266 or (202)333-4904 Fax: (202)342-5411 E-mail: editor@yearbook.com • URL: http://www.yearbooknews.com • Annual. $166.50. A directory of approximately 3,000 important newswire services, syndicates, national newspapers, magazines, radio and TV talk shows, etc.

Power - Motion Technology Representatives Association.

The Power of Gold: The History of an Obsession. Peter L. Bernstein. John Wiley and Sons, Inc., 605 Third Ave. New York, NY 10158-0012. Phone: 800-225-5945 or (212)850-6000 Fax: (212)850-6088 E-mail: info@wiley.com • URL: http://www.wiley.com • 2000. $27.95. Covers the economic and financial history of gold from ancient times to the present.

Power Pitches: How to Produce Winning Presentations Using Charts, Slides, Video, and Multimedia. Alan L. Brown. McGraw-Hill Professional, 1221 Ave. of the Americas New York, NY 10020. Phone: 800-722-4726 or (212)904-2000 Fax: (212)904-2072 E-mail: customer.service@

mcgraw-hill.com • URL: http://www.mcgraw-hill.com • 1997. $39.95. Includes "Ten Rules of Power Pitching."

Power Plant Engineers Guide. Frank Graham and Charles Buffinghon. Pearson Education and Technology, 201 W. 103rd St. Indianapolis, IN 46290-1097. Phone: 800-858-7674 or (317)581-3500 URL: http://www.mcp.com • 1984. $32.50. Third edition.

Power Pricing: How Managing Price Transforms the Bottom Line. Robert J. Dolan and Hermann Simon. Free Press, 1230 Ave. of the Americas New York, NY 10020. Phone: 800-223-2348 or (212)698-7000 Fax: 800-445-6991 or (212)698-7007 URL: http://www.thefreepress.com • 1997. $40.00. Among topics included are pricing strategy, price customization, international pricing, nonlinear pricing, product-line pricing, and price bundling.

Power Resumes. Ronald Tepper. John Wiley and Sons, Inc., 605 Third Ave. New York, NY 10158-0012. Phone: 800-225-5945 or (212)850-6000 Fax: (212)850-6088 E-mail: info@wiley.com • URL: http://www.wiley.com • 1998. $14.95. Third edition. Offers 71 techniques for more effective resumes.

Power System Operation. Robert H. Miller. McGraw-Hill, 1221 Ave. of the Americas New York, NY 10020. Phone: 800-722-4726 or (212)904-2000 Fax: (212)904-2072 E-mail: customer.service@mcgraw-hill.com • URL: http://www.mcgraw-hill.com • 1994. $60.00. Third edition.

Power Tool Institute., 1300 Sumner Ave. Cleveland, OH 44115-2851. Phone: (216)241-7333 Fax: (216)241-0105 E-mail: pti@taol.com • URL: http://www.taol.com/pti • Members are manufacturers of various kinds of portable and stationary power tools.

Power Transmission Distributors Association.

PPI Detailed Report. Bureau of Labor Statistics, U.S. Department of Labor. Available from U.S. Government Printing Office, Washington, DC 20402. Phone: (202)512-1800 Fax: (202)512-2250 E-mail: gpoaccess@gpo.gov • URL: http://www.access.gpo.gov • Monthly. $55.00 per year. Formerly *Producer Price Indexes*.

PR News Casebook. The Gale Group, 27500 Drake Rd. Farmington Hills, MI 48331-3535. Phone: 800-877-GALE or (248)699-GALE Fax: 800-414-5043 or (248)699-8069 E-mail: galeord@galegroup.com • URL: http://www.galegroup.com • 1993. $99.00. A collection of about 1,000 case studies covering major public relations campaigns and events, taken from the pages of *PR News*. Covers such issues as boycotts, new products, anniversaries, plant closings, downsizing, and stockholder relations.

The Practical Accountant: Accounting and Taxes in Everyday Practice. Faulkner and Gray, Inc., 11 Penn Plaza, 17th Fl. New York, NY 10001. Phone: 800-535-8403 or (212)967-7000 Fax: (212)967-7155 E-mail: orders@faulknergray.com • URL: http://www.faulknergray.com • Monthly. $60.00 per year. Covers tax planning, financial planning, practice management, client relationships, and related topics.

Practical Baking. William J. Sultan. John Wiley and Sons, Inc., 605 Third Ave. New York, NY 10158-0012. Phone: 800-225-5945 Fax: (973)302-2300 E-mail: info@wiley.com • URL: http://www.wiley.com • 1990. $55.95. Fifth edition.

Practical Business Statistics with StatPad. Andrew F. Siegel. McGraw-Hill Higher Education, 1221 Ave. of the Americas New York, NY 10020. Phone: 800-722-4726 or (212)904-2000 Fax: (212)904-2072 E-mail: customer.service@mcgraw-hill.com • URL: http://www.mcgraw-hill.com • 1999. $87.81. Fourth edition. Includes CD-Rom.

Practical Guide to Credit and Collection. George O. Bancroft. AMACOM, 1601 Broadway, 12th Fl. New York, NY 10019. Phone: 800-262-9699 or (212)586-8100 Fax: (212)903-8168 E-mail: custmserv@amanet.org • URL: http://www.amanet.org • 1989. $29.95.

Practical Guide to Foreign Direct Investment in the European Union. Euroconfidentiel S. A., Rue de Rixensart 18 B-1332 Genval, Belgium. Phone: (32)02 653 01 25 Fax: (32)02 653 01 80 E-mail: nigel.hunt@euronet.be • Annual. $260.00. Provides coverage of national and EU business incentives. In addition to 70 charts and tables, includes EU country profiles of taxation, labor costs, and employment regulations.

Practical Guide to Handling IRS Income Tax Audits. Ralph L. Guyette. Prentice Hall, 240 Frisch Court Paramus, NJ 07652-5240. Phone: 800-947-7700 or (201)909-6200 Fax: 800-445-6991 or (201)909-6361 URL: http://www.prenhall.com • 1986. $39.95.

Practical Guide to Tax Issues in Employment. Julia K. Brazelton. CCH, Inc., 4025 W. Peterson Ave. Chicago, IL 60646-6085. Phone: 800-248-3248 or (773)866-6000 Fax: 800-224-8299 or (773)866-3608 URL: http://www.cch.com • 1999. $95.00. Covers income taxation as related to labor law and tax law, including settlements and awards. Written for tax professionals.

Practical Guide to U. S. Taxation of International Transactions. Robert E. Meldman and Michael S. Schadewald. CCH, Inc., 4025 W. Peterson Ave. Chicago, IL 60646-6085. Phone: 800-248-3248 or (773)866-6000 Fax: 800-224-8299 or (773)866-3608 URL: http://www.cch.com • 2000. $99.00. Third edition. Contains three parts: Basic Principles, U. S. Taxation of Foreign Income, and U. S. Taxation of Foreign Persons.

The Practical Lawyer. Committee on Continuing Professional Education. American Law Institute-American Bar Association, 4025 Chestnut St. Philadelphia, PA 19104-3099. Phone: 800-253-6397 or (215)243-1600 Fax: (215)243-1664 URL: http://www.ali-aba.org • Eight times a year. $40.00 per year.

The Practical Real Estate Lawyer. American Law Institute-American Bar Association, Committee on Continuing Profess, 4025 Chestnut St. Philadelphia, PA 19104-3099. Phone: 800-253-6397 or (215)243-1600 Fax: (215)243-1664 URL: http://www.ali-aba.org • Bimonthly. $37.00 per year. Frequently includes legal forms for use in real estate practice.

Practical Sign Shop Operations. Bob Fitzgerald. ST Publications, Inc., 407 Gilbert Ave. Cincinnati, OH 45202-2285. Phone: 800-925-1110 or (513)421-2050 Fax: (513)421-5144 E-mail: books@stpubs.com • URL: http://www.stpubs.com • 1992. $19.95. Seventh revised edition.

Practical Solar Energy Technology. Martin L. Greenwald and Thomas K. McHugh. Prentice Hall, 240 Frisch Court Paramus, NJ 07652-5240. Phone: 800-947-7700 or (201)909-6200 Fax: 800-445-6991 or (201)909-6361 URL: http://www.prenhall.com • 1985. $45.00.

The Practical Tax Lawyer. American Law Institute-American Bar Association, 4025 Chestnut St. Philadelphia, PA 19104-3099. Phone: 800-253-6397 or (215)243-1604 Fax: (215)243-1664 URL: http://www.ali-aba.org • Quarterly. Members, $27.50 per year; non-members, $35.00 per year.

Practical Tax Strategies. Warren, Gorham & Lamont/RIA Group, 395 Hudson St. New York, NY 10014. Phone: 800-950-1216 or (212)367-6300 Fax: (212)337-4280 E-mail: customer_services@riag.com • URL: http://www.riahome.com • Monthly. $125.00 per year. Provides advice and information on tax planning for tax accountants, attorneys, and advisers.

Practical Upholstery: And the Cutting of Slip Covers. Frederick Palmer. Madison Books, Inc., USA, 4720 Boston Way Lanham, MD 20706. Phone: 800-462-6420 or (301)459-3366 1982. $11.95.

The Practice of Local Government Planning. Frank S. So and Judith Getzels. International City/County Management Association, 777 N. Capitol St., N.E., Suite 500 Washington, DC 20002-4201. Phone: (202)289-4262 Fax: (202)962-3500 2000. Third edition. Price on application. (Municipal Management Series).

Practicing Financial Planning: A Complete Guide for Professionals. Sid Mittra. Mittra and Associates, 445 Livernois Rd., No. 327 Rochester, MI 48307. Phone: (248)650-3839 Fax: (248)650-3657 1993. $29.95. Approved for continuing education of financial planners by the International Board of Standards and Practices for Certified Financial Planners. Covers planning strategies, funds allocation, insurance considerations, risk management, ethics, and other topics.

Practising Law Institute.

Practitioner's Guide to GAAS. John Wiley and Sons, Inc., 605 Third Ave. New York, NY 10158-0012. Phone: 800-225-5945 or (212)850-6000 Fax: (212)850-6088 E-mail: info@jwiley.com • URL: http://www.wiley.com • Annual. $131.00. Covers GAAS: Generally Accepted Auditing Standards, promulgated by the American Institute of Certified Public Accountants. (Includes CD-ROM.)

Pratt's Guide to Venture Capital Sources. Securities Data Publishing, 40 West 57th St. New York, NY 10019. Phone: 800-455-5844 or (212)765-5311 Fax: (212)956-0112 E-mail: sdp@tfn.com • URL: http://www.sdponline.com • Annual. $575.00. Describes about 1,400 venture capital firms, including key personnel, capital under management, and recent investments. Company, personnel, and industry indexes are provided. (Securities Data Publishing is a unit of Thomson Financial.)

Precious Stones and Gems. Edwin M. Streeter. Gordon Press Publishers, P.O. Box 459 New York, NY 10004. Phone: (212)969-8419 Fax: (718)624-8419 1977. $79.95.

Precision Metalforming Association.

The Predator's Ball: The Inside Story of Drexel Burnham and the Rise of the Junk Bond Raiders. Connie Bruck. Viking Penguin, 375 Hudson St. New York, NY 10014-3657. Phone: 800-331-4624 or (212)366-2000 Fax: 800-227-9604 or (212)366-2666 E-mail: customer.service@penguin.co.uk • URL: http://www.penguin.com • 1989. $14.95.

Predictability of Corporate Failure. R. A. I. Van Frederikslust. Kluwer Academic Publishers, 101 Philip Dr. Norwell, MA 02061. Phone: (781)871-6600 Fax: (781)871-6528 E-mail: kluwer@wkap.nl • URL: http://www.wkap.nl • 1978. $77.50.

Predicting Successful Hospital Mergers and Acquisitions: A Financial and Analytical Marketing Tool. David P. Angrisani and Robert L. Goldman. Haworth Press, Inc., 10 Alice St. Binghamton, NY 13904-1580. Phone: 800-429-6784 or (607)722-5857 Fax: 800-895-0582 or (607)722-1424 E-mail: getinfo@haworthpressinc.com • URL: http://www.haworthpressinc.com • 1997. $49.95.

Predicting the Future: An Introduction to the Theory of Forecasting. Nicholas Rescher. State University of New York Press, State University Plaza Albany, NY 12246-0001. Phone: 800-666-2211 or (518)472-5000 Fax: (518)472-5038 E-mail: info@sunypress.edu • URL: http://www.sunypress.edu • 1997. $65.50. Provides a general theory of prediction, including the principles and methodology of forecasting. Includes "The Evaluation of Predictions and Predictors."

Predictions: Specific Investment Forecasts and Recommendations from the World's Top Financial Experts. Lee Euler, editor. Agora, Inc., 105 W. Monument Baltimore, MD 21201. Phone: (410)223-2500 Fax: (410)223-2696 Monthly. $78.00 per year. Newsletter.

A Preface to Marketing Management. J. Paul Peter and James H. Donnelly. McGraw-Hill Higher Education, 1221 Ave. of the Americas New York, NY 10020. Phone: 800-722-4726 or (212)904-2000 Fax: (212)904-2072 E-mail: customer.service@mcgraw-hill.com • URL: http://www.mcgraw-hill.com • 1997. $37.50. Seventh edition. (Marketing Series).

Prentice Hall Directory of Online Business Information. Christopher Engholm and Scott Grimes. Prentice Hall, 240 Frisch Court Paramus, NJ 07652-5240. Phone: 800-947-7700 or (201)909-6200 Fax: 800-445-6991 or (201)909-6361 URL: http://www.prenhall.com • Annual. $34.95. Contains reviews of about 1,000 World Wide Web sites related to business. Sites are rated according to content, speed, and other factors.

Prepared Foods. Cahners Business Information, 2000 Clearwater Dr. Oak Brook, IL 60523. Phone: 800-662-7776 or (630)320-7000 E-mail: corporatecommunications@cahners.com • URL: http://www.cahners.com • Monthly. $99.90 per year. Edited for food manufacturing management, marketing, and operations personnel.

Prepared Foods Food Industry Sourcebook. Cahners Business Information, 1350 E. Touhy Ave. Des Plaines, IL 60018-3358. Phone: 800-662-7776 or (847)635-8800 Fax: (847)390-2445 E-mail: corporatecommunications@cahners.com • URL: http://www.cahners.com • Annual. $35.00. Provides information on more than 3,000 manufacturers and suppliers of products, ingredients, supplies, and equipment for the food processing industry.

Preparing a Successful Business Plan: How to Plan to Succeed and Secure Financial Banking. Matthew Record. Trans-Atlantic Publications, Inc., 311 Bainbridge St. Philadelphia, PA 19147. Phone: (215)925-5083 Fax: (215)925-1912 2000. $19.95. Thirdd edition. (Business and Management Series).

Preparing for the Twenty-First Century. Paul Kennedy. Villard Books, 201 E. 50th St. New York, NY 10022. Phone: 800-726-0600 or (212)751-2600 Fax: 800-659-2436 or (212)572-8700 URL: http://www.randomhouse.com • 1993. $15.00. A somber view of the future.

Preparing Loan Proposals. John C. Wisdom. John Wiley and Sons, Inc., 605 Third Ave. New York, NY 10158-0012. Phone: 800-225-5945 or (212)850-6000 Fax: (212)850-6088 E-mail: info@wiley.com • URL: http://www.wiley.com • 1997. $150.00. Second editon. 1998 Supplement, $55.00.

Prepress Bulletin. Bessie Halfacre, editor. International Prepress Association, 552 W. 167th St. South Holland, IL 60473. Phone: (708)596-5110 Fax: (708)596-5112 E-mail: bessiepa@earthlink.net • Bimonthly. $15.00 per year. Provides management and technical information on the graphic arts prepress industry.

Prescription Pharmaceuticals and Biotechnology: The Pink Sheet. F-D-C Reports, Inc., 5550 Friendship Blvd., Suite 1 Chevy Chase, MD 20815-7278. Phone: 800-332-2181 or (301)657-9830 Fax: (301)664-7238 URL: http://www.fdcreports.com • Weekly. $1,170 per year. Newsletter covering business and regulatory developments affecting the pharmaceutical and biotechnology industries. Provides information on generic drug approvals and includes a drug sector stock index.

Presentations: Technology and Techniques for Effective Communication. Lakewood Publications, Inc., Lakewood Bldg., 50 S. Ninth St. Minneapolis, MN 55402. Phone: 800-328-4329 or (612)333-0471 Fax: (612)333-6526 E-mail: tsimons@presentations.com • URL: http://www.presentations.com • Monthly. $50.00 per year. Covers the use of presentation hardware and software, including audiovisual equipment and computerized display systems. Includes an annual *"Buyers Guide to Presentation Products."*

Presenting Performances: A Handbook for Sponsors. Thomas Wolf. Americans for the Arts, One E. 53rd St. New York, NY 10022-4201. Phone: 800-321-4510 or (212)223-2787 Fax: (212)753-1325 E-mail: books@artsusa.org • URL: http://www.artsusa.org • 1991. $16.95. Revised edition.

Preservation Microfilming: A Guide for Librarians and Archivists. Nancy E. Gwinn. Books on Demand, 300 N. Zeeb Rd. Ann Arbor, MI 48106-1346. Phone: 800-521-0600 or (734)761-4700 Fax: (734)665-5022 E-mail: info@umi.com • URL: http://www.lib.umi.com • 1995. $73.80. Second edition. Covers all aspects of planning and managing a microfilming operation.

The Presidency: The Magazine for Higher Education Leaders. American Council on Education, One Dupont Circle, N.W. Washington, DC 20036-1193. Phone: (202)939-9300 Fax: (202)833-4760 Three times a year. Members, $27.00 per year; non-members, $30.00 per year. Formerly *Educational Record*.

Presidential Studies Quarterly. Center for the Study of the Presidency, 1020 19th St., N.W., Suite 250 Washington, DC 20036. Phone: (202)872-9800 Fax: (202)872-9811 E-mail: center@thepresidency.org • URL: http://www.thepresidency.org • Quarterly. Individuals, $120.00 per year; institutions, $195.00 per year.

Preventing Bank Crises: Lessons from Recent Global Bank Failures. Gerard Caprio and others, editors. The World Bank, Office of the Publisher, 1818 H St., N. W. Washington, DC 20433. Phone: 800-645-7247 or (202)477-1234 Fax: (202)477-6391 E-mail: books@worldbank.org • URL: http://www.worldbank.org • 1998. $40.00. Examines worldwide problems with bank regulation, bank infrastructure, public accountability, and political influence.

Prevention; The Magazine for Better Health. Rodale Press, Inc., 33 E. Minor St. Emmaus, PA 18098-0099. Phone: 800-813-8070 or (610)967-5171 Fax: (610)967-8963 E-mail: customer_service@rodale.com • URL: http://www.prevention.com • Monthly $21.97. per year.

Preventive Care Sourcebook. Aspen Publishers, Inc., 200 Orchard Ridge Dr. Gaithersburg, MD 20878. Phone: 800-638-8437 or (301)417-7500 Fax: (301)417-7550 E-mail: customer.service@aspenpubl.com • URL: http://www.aspenpub.com • Annual. $89.00. Lists sources of programs and materials on preventive care, community health, and employee wellness.

Prices and Earnings Around the Globe. Union Bank of Switzerland, 299 Park Ave. New York, NY 10171-0034. Phone: (212)821-3000 Fax: (212)821-3285 URL: http://www.ubs.com • Irregular. Free. Published in Zurich. Compares prices and purchasing power in 48 major cities of the world. Wages and hours are also compared. Text in English, French, German, and Italian.

Prices of Agricultural Products and Selected Inputs in Europe and North America. Economic Commission for Europe. United Nations Publications, Two United Nations Plaza, Rm. DC2-853 New York, NY 10017. Phone: 800-253-9646 or (212)963-8302 Fax: (212)963-3489 Annual.

Pricing and Capacity Determination in International Air Transport. Peter P. C. Haanappel. Kluwer Law International, 675 Massachusetts Ave. Cambridge, MA 02139. Phone: (617)354-0140 Fax: (617)354-8595 E-mail: kluwer@wkap.nl • URL: http://www.wkap.nl • 1984. $66.00.

A Primer for New Corporate Lawyers: What Business Lawyers Do. Clifford R. Ennico. West Group, 610 Opperman Dr. Eagan, MN 55123. Phone: 800-328-4880 or (651)687-7000 Fax: 800-213-2323 or (651)687-5827 URL: http://www.westgroup.com • 1990. $39.95. Covers client relations, client counseling, negotiation, managing business transactions, and other topics.

Primer of Labor Relations. Linda G. Kahn. BNA Books, Bureau of National Affairs, Inc., 1231 25th St., N.W. Washington, DC 20037. Phone: 800-372-1033 or (202)833-7470 Fax: (202)833-7490 E-mail: books@bna.com • URL: http://www.bna.com/bnabooks • 1994. $45.00. 25th edition.

A Primer on Organizational Behavior. James L. Bowditch and Anthony F. Buono. John Wiley and Sons, Inc., 605 Third Ave. New York, NY 10158-0012. Phone: 800-225-5945 or (212)850-6000 Fax: (212)850-6088 E-mail: info@wiley.com • URL: http://www.wiley.com • 1996. $48.95. Fourth edition. Price on application. Includes a discussion of participative management. Emphasis is on research and the theory of organizations. (Wiley Management Series).

Princeton Forrestal Center., Princeton University, 105 College Rd., E. Princeton, NJ 08540. Phone: (609)452-7720 Fax: (609)452-7485 E-mail: picus@picusassociates.com • Designed to create an interdependent mix of academia and business enterprise.

Principal International Businesses: The World Marketing Directory. Dun and Bradstreet Information Services, Dun and Bradstreet Corp, Three Sylvan Way Parsippany, NJ 07054-3896. Phone: 800-526-0521 or (973)455-0900 Fax: (973)254-4063 E-mail: customerservice@dnb.com • URL: http://www.dnb.com • Annual. $5000. Provides information about 50,000 major businesses located in over 140 countries. Geographic arrangement with company name and product indexes.

Principles and Practices of TQM. Thomas J. Cartin. American Society for Quality, P.O. Box 3005 Milwaukee, WI 53201-3005. Phone: 800-248-1946 or (414)272-8575 Fax: (414)272-1734 E-mail: mhagen@asq.org • URL: http://www.asq.org • 1993. $28.00.

Principles and Trends in Business Education. Louis C. Nanassy. Pearson Education and Technology, 201 W. 103rd St. Indianapolis, IN 46290-1097. Phone: 800-858-7674 or (317)581-3500 URL: http://www.mcp.com • 1977. Price on application.

Principles of Association Management. Henry Ernstthal and Bob Jones. American Society of Association Executives, 1575 Eye St., N. W. Washington, DC 20005-1168. Phone: (202)626-2723 Fax: (202)371-8825 E-mail: asea@aseanet.org • URL: http://www.asaenet.org • 1996. $43.95. Third edition.

Principles of Auditing. O. Ray Whittington and Kurt Pany. McGraw-Hill Higher Education, 1221 Ave. of the Americas New York, NY 10020. Phone: 800-722-4726 or (212)904-2000 Fax: (212)904-2072 E-mail: customer.service@mcgraw-hill.com • URL: http://www.mcgraw-hill.com • 2000. $90.31. 13th edition.

Principles of Banking. American Bankers Association, 1120 Connecticut Ave., N. W. Washington, DC 20036-3971. Phone: 800-338-0626 or (202)663-5000 Fax: (202)663-7543 URL: http://www.aba.org • 1998. Price on application.

Principles of Communications Satellites. Gary D. Gordon and Walter L. Morgan. John Wiley and Sons, Inc., 605 Third Ave. New York, NY 10158-0012. Phone: 800-225-5945 or (212)850-6000 Fax: (212)850-6088 E-mail: info@wiley.com • URL: http://www.wiley.com • 1993. $99.00.

Principles of Corporate Governance: Analysis and Recommendations. Mike Greenwald, editor. American Law Institute-American Bar Association, 4025 Chestnut St. Philadelphia, PA 19104-3099. Phone: 800-253-6397 or (215)243-1600 Fax: (215)243-1664 URL: http://www.ali.org • 1994. $135.00. Two volumes. An examination of the duties and responsibilities of directors and officers of business corporations. Seven parts cover (1) definitions, (2) objectives and conduct, (3) corporate structure and oversight committees, (4) business judgment, (5) fair dealing, (6) tender offers, and (7) legal remedies.

Principles of Economics. Richard G. Lipsey and K. Alec Chrystal. Oxford University Press, Inc., 198 Madison Ave. New York, NY 10016-4314. Phone: 800-445-9714 or (212)726-6000 Fax: (212)726-6440 E-mail: custserv@oup-usa.org • URL: http://www.oup-usa.org • 1999. Ninth edition. Price on application.

Principles of Health and Hygiene in the Workplace. Timothy J. Key and Michael A. Mueller. Lewis Publishers, 2000 Corporate Blvd., N. W. Boca Raton, FL 33431. Phone: 800-272-7737 or (561)994-0555 Fax: 800-374-3401 or (561)998-9114 E-mail: orders@crcpress.com • URL: http://www.crcpress.com • Date not set. $69.95.

Principles of Highway Engineering and Traffic Analysis. Fred L. Mannering and Walter P. Kilareski. John Wiley and Sons, Inc., 605 Third Ave. New York, NY 10158-0012. Phone: 800-526-5368 or (212)850-6000 Fax: (212)850-6088 E-mail: info@wiley.com • URL: http://www.wiley.com • 1997. $64.95. Second edition.

Principles of Inventory and Materials Management. Richard J. Tersine. Prentice Hall, 240 Frisch Court Paramus, NJ 07652-5240. Phone: 800-947-7700 or (201)909-6200 Fax: 800-445-6991 or (201)909-6361 URL: http://www.prenhall.com • 1993. $60.80. Fourth edition. Includes material on just-in-time inventory systems.

Principles of Macroeconomics. Gerry F. Welch. Harcourt Brace College Publishers, 301 Commerce St., Suite 3700 Fort Worth, TX 76102. Phone: 800-245-8774 or (817)334-7500 Fax: 800-874-6418 or (817)334-8060 E-mail: wlittle@harbrace.com • URL: http://www.harcourt.com • 1998. $25.00.

Principles of Money, Banking and Financial Markets. Lawrence S. Ritter, editor. Addison Wesley Educational Publications, Inc., One Jacob Way Reading, MA 08167. Phone: 800-447-2226 or (781)944-3700 Fax: (781)944-9351 URL: http://www.awl.com • 1999. $26.00 10th edition.

Principles of Operation Management. Barry Render. Thomson Learning, 7625 Empire Dr. Florence, KY 41042. Phone: 800-347-7707 or (606)525-6620 Fax: (606)525-0978 URL: http://www.thomsonlearning.com • 2000. $35.00. Sixth edition. (SWC-Management Series).

Principles of Project Management: Collected Handbooks from the Project Management Institute. John R. Adams and others. Project Management Institute, c/o PMI Headquarters Publishing Div., 40 Colonial Square Sylva, NC 28779. Phone: (828)586-3715 Fax: (828)586-4020 E-mail: booked@pmi.org • URL: http://www.pmi.org • 1997. $59.95. Consists of reprints of eight "handbooks" by various authors, previously published by the Project Management Institute. Includes such topics as contract administration, conflict management, team building, and coping with stress.

Print: America's Graphic Design Magazine. RC Publications, Inc., 104 Fifth Ave., 19th Fl. New York, NY 10011. Phone: (212)463-0600 Fax: (212)989-9891 Bimonthly. $53.00 per year. Emphasizes creative trends.

Print Media Production Source. SRDS, 1700 Higgins Rd. Des Plaines, IL 60018. Phone: 800-851-7737 or (847)375-5000 Fax: (847)375-5001 E-mail: lalbr@srds.com • URL: http://www.srds.com • Quarterly. $401.00 per year. Contains details of printing and mechanical production requirements for advertising in specific trade journals, consumer magazines, and newspapers. Formerly *Print Media Production Data*.

Printimage International.

Printing Impressions. North American Publishing Co., 401 N. Broad St. Philadelphia, PA 19108-9988. Phone: 800-627-2689 or (215)238-5300 Fax: (215)238-5457 E-mail: dbrennan@napco.com • URL: http://www.napco.com • Monthly. Free to qualified personnel; others, $90.00 per year. Annual buyer's guide *Master Specifier*.

Printing Industries of America.

Prisoners in State and Federal Institutions. Bureau of Justice Statistics, U.S. Department of Justice. Available from U.S. Government Printing Office, Washington, DC 20402. Phone: (202)512-1800 Fax: (202)512-2250 E-mail: gpoaccess@gpo.gov • URL: http://www.accessgpo.gov • Annual.

Private Asset Management. Institutional Investor, 488 Madison Ave. New York, NY 10022. Phone: (212)224-3300 Fax: (212)224-3353 E-mail: info@iijournals.com • URL: http://www.iijournals.com • Biweekly. $2,105.00 per year. Newsletter. Edited for managers investing the private assets of wealthy ("high-net-worth") individuals. Includes marketing, taxation, regulation, and fee topics.

Private Carrier. National Private Truck Council, Private Carrier Conference, 66 Canal Center Plaza, Suite 600 Alexandria, VA 22314-1649. Phone: (703)683-1300 Fax: (703)683-1217 E-mail: nptcpfmi@aol.com • URL: http://www.nptc.org • Monthly. Free to qualified personnel.

Private Independent Schools: The Bunting and Lyon Blue Book. Bunting and Lyon, Inc., 238 N. Main St. Wallingford, CT 06492. Phone: (203)269-3333 Fax: (203)269-5697 E-mail: bandblubk@aol.com • URL: http://www.buntingandlyon.com • Annual. $100.00. Over 1,200 elementary and secondary schools and summer programs in the United States and abroad.

Private Investigator. Entrepreneur Media, Inc., 2445 McCabe Way Irvine, CA 92614. Phone: 800-421-2300 or (949)261-2325 Fax: (949)261-0234 E-mail: entmag@entrepreneur.com • URL: http://www.entrepreneur.com • Looseleaf. $59.50. A practical guide to starting a private investigation agency. Covers profit potential, start-up costs, market size evaluation, pricing, accounting, advertising, promotion, etc. (Start-Up Business Guide No. E1320.)

Private Investments Abroad: Problems and Solutions in International Business. Southwestern Legal Foundation, International and Comparative Law Center. Matthew Bender & Co., Inc., Two Park Ave. New York, NY 10016. Phone: 800-223-1940 or (212)448-2000 Fax: (212)244-3188 E-mail: international@bender.com • URL: http://www.bender.com • Annual. $153.00. Symposium on worthwhile investment opportunities abroad and explains the best methods of transacting international business by integrating professional knowledge from the fields of law, economics and business management.

Private Label International: The Magazine for Store Labels (Own Brands) and Generics. E. W. Williams Publications Co., 2125 Center Ave., Suite 305 Fort Lee, NJ 07024-5859. Phone: (201)592-7007 Fax: (201)592-7171 Semiannual. $20.00 per year. Edited for large chain store buyers and for manufacturers of private label products. Text in English; summaries in French and German.

Private Label Manufacturers Association., 369 Lexington Ave. New York, NY 10017. Phone: (212)972-3131 Fax: (212)983-1382 URL: http://www.plma.com • Members are manufacturers, wholesalers, and retailers of private brand products. Seeks to promote the private label industry.

Private Label News. Stagnito Communcitions, Inc., 1935 Shermar Rd., Suite 100 Norhtbrok, IL 60062. Phone: (847)205-5660 Fax: (847)205-5680 E-mail: info@stagnito.com • URL: http://www.plnews.com • Eight times a year. $75.00 per year. Covers new private label product developments for chain stores. Formerly *Private Label Product News*.

Private Label: The Magazine for House Brands and Generics. E. W. Williams Publications Co., 2125 Center Ave., Suite 305 Fort Lee, NJ 07024-5859. Phone: (201)592-7007 Fax: (201)592-7171 Bimonthly. $36.00 per year. Edited for buyers of private label, controlled packer, and generic-labeled products. Concentrates on food, health and beauty aids, and general merchandise.

Private Pensions in OECD Countries: The United States. OECD Publications and Information Center, 2001 L St., N.W., Suite 650 Washington, DC 20036-4922. Phone: (202)785-6323 Fax: (202)785-0350 E-mail: washington.contact@oecd.org • URL: http://www.oecdwash.org • 1993. $22.00. Provides data relating to the characteristics of private pension arrangements in the U. S.

Private Power Executive. Pequot Publishing, Inc., 250 Pequot Ave. Southport, CT 06490-1112. Phone: (203)259-1812 Fax: (203)255-3313 Bimonthly. $90.00 per year. Covers private power (non-utility) enterprises, including cogeneration projects and industrial self-generation.

Private Practice. Congress of County Medical Societies (CCMS) Publishing Co., P.O. Box 1485 Shawnee, OK 74802-1485. Monthly. $18.00 per year.

Private Sector Council., 1101 16th St., N.W., Suite 300 Washington, DC 20036. Phone: (202)822-3910 Fax: (202)822-0638 URL: http://www.privatesectorcouncil.org

• Members are officers of large corporations who seek to facilitate reduction of the federal deficit.

PRO. Cygnus Publishing, Inc., Johnson Hill Press, Inc., 1233 Janesville Ave. Fort Atkinson, WI 53538-0460. Phone: 800-547-7377 or (920)563-6388 Fax: (920)563-1704 E-mail: rich.reiff@cygnuspub.com • URL: http://www.cygnuspub.com • Seven times a year. $48.00 per year. For owners and operators of lawn maintenance service firms. Includes annual *Product* issue.

Pro Sound News: The International News Magazine for the Professional Recording and Sound Production Industry. United Entertainment Media, Inc., 460 Park Ave. South New York, NY 10016-7315. Phone: (212)378-0400 Fax: (212)378-2160 E-mail: pro@uemedia.com • URL: http://www.prosoundnews.com • Monthly. $30.00 per year. Provides industry news for recording studios, audio contractors, sound engineers, and sound reinforcement specialists.

Probable Tomorrows: How Science and Technology Will Transform Our Lives in the Next Twenty Years. Marvin J. Cetron and Owen L. Davies. St. Martin's Press, 175 Fifth Ave. New York, NY 10010. Phone: 800-221-7945 or (212)674-5151 Fax: 800-672-2054 or (212)529-0594 URL: http://www.stmartins.com • 1997. $24.95. Predicts the developments in technological products, services, and "everyday conveniences" by the year 2017. Covers such items as personal computers, artificial intelligence, telecommunications, highspeed railroads, and healthcare.

Problem Loan Strategies; A Decision Process for Commercial Bankers. John E. McKinley and others. Robert Morris Associates, One Liberty Place, Suite 2300, 1650 Market St. Philadelphia, PA 19103-7398. Phone: 800-677-7621 or (215)446-4000 Fax: (215)446-4100 E-mail: kbeans@rmahq.org • URL: http://www.rmahq.org • 1998. $53.00. Revised edition.

Procedures for the Automated Office. Sharon Burton and others. Prentice Hall, 240 Frisch Court Paramus, NJ 07652-5240. Phone: 800-947-7700 or (201)909-6200 Fax: 800-445-6991 or (201)909-6361 URL: http://www.prenhall.com • 2000. $46.67. Fifth edition.

Process Engineering Suppliers Guide. Information Handling Services, P.O. Box 1154 Englewood, CO 80150. Phone: 800-841-7179 or (303)790-0600 Fax: (303)790-4097 Semiannual. Price on application. Manufacturers and suppliers of materials, components and equipment for process engineering in the United Kingdom; includes foreign firms represented in the United Kingdom. Formerly *Process Engineering Index*.

Process Equipment Manufacturers Association.

Process Quality Control. Ellis R. Ott. McGraw-Hill, 1221 Ave. of the Americas New York, NY 10020. Phone: 800-722-4726 or (212)904-2000 Fax: (212)904-2072 E-mail: customer.service@mcgraw-hill.com • URL: http://www.mcgraw-hill.com • 2000. $74.95. Third edition.

Processed Apples Institute.

Processing. Putman Media, 555 W. Pierce Rd., Suite 301 Itasca, IL 60143-2649. Phone: (630)467-1300 Fax: (630)467-1123 URL: http://www.putmanpublishing.com • 14 times a year. $54.00 per year. Emphasis is on descriptions of new products for all areas of industrial processing, including valves, controls, filters, pumps, compressors, fluidics, and instrumentation.

Produce Marketing Association.

Produce Merchandising: The Packer's Retailing and Merchandising Magazine. Vance Publishing Corp., Produce Div., 10901 W. 84th Terrace Lenexa, KS 66214-1631. Phone: 800-255-5113 or (913)438-8700 Fax: (913)438-0695 E-mail: ltimm@vancepublishing.com • URL: http://www.vancepublishing.com • Monthly. $35.00 per year. Provides information and advice on the retail marketing and promotion of fresh fruits and vegetalbe.

Produce News. Zim-Mer Trade Publications, Inc., 2185 Lemoine Ave. Fort Lee, NJ 07024. Phone: (201)592-9100 Fax: (201)592-0809 Weekly. $35.00 per year.

Producers Guild of America.

Producer's Masterguide: The International Production Manual for Motion Pictures, Television, Commercials, Cable and Videotape Industries in the United States, Canada, the United Kingdom, Bermuda, the Caribbean Islands, Mexico, South America., 60 E. Eighth St., 34th Fl. New York, NY 10003-6514. Phone: (212)777-4002 Fax: (212)777-4101 URL: http://www.producers.masterguide.com • Annual. $125.00. A standard reference guide of the professional film, television, commercial and video tape industry throughout the U.S. and Canada. More than 30,000 listings.

Product Design and Development. Cahners Business Information, 1018 W. 9th Ave. King of Prussia, PA 19406. Phone: 800-695-1214 or (610)205-1000 Fax: (610)964-4947 E-mail: corporatecommunications@cahners.com • URL: http://www.cahners.com • Monthly. $60.00 per year. Edited for design engineers. Emphasis is on materials, components, and processes.

Product Distribution Law Guide. CCH, Inc., 4025 West Peterson Ave. Chicago, IL 60646-6085. Phone: 800-248-3248 or (773)866-6000 Fax: 800-224-8299 or (773)866-3608 URL: http://www.cch.com • Looseleaf. $199.00. Annual updates available. Covers the legal aspects of various methods of product distribution, including franchising.

The Product Liability Alliance., c/o National Association of Wholesaler-Distributors, 1725 K St., N. W., Suite 300 Washington, DC 20006. Phone: (202)872-0885 Fax: (202)296-5940 E-mail: naw@nawd.org • URL: http://www.nawd.org • Promotes reform of federal product liability laws.

Product Liability Law and Strategy Newsletter. Leader Publications, Inc., 345 Park Ave., S. New York, NY 10010. Phone: (212)779-9200 Fax: (212)696-1848 Monthly. $185.00 per year. Formerly *Product Liability Newsletter*.

Product Liability Prevention and Defense., 111 Park Place Falls Church, VA 22046-4513. Phone: (703)538-1797 Fax: (703)241-5603 E-mail: plpdhq@aol.com • Purpose is to achieve more efficient product liability legal defense for machinery manufacturers.

Product Safety Letter. Washington Business Information, Inc., 300 N. Washington St., Suite 200 Falls Church, VA 22046. Phone: (703)247-3423 Fax: (703)247-3421 Weekly. $967.00 per year. Newsletter on product safety regulation and legislation. *Supplement* available.

Product Safety News. National Safety Council, 1121 Spring Lake Dr. Itasca, IL 60143. Phone: (630)285-1121 Fax: (630)775-2310 Monthly. Members, $21.00 per year; non-members, $25.00 per year.

Production. Gardner Publications, Inc., 6915 Valley Ave. Cincinnati, OH 45244-4090. Phone: 800-950-8020 or (513)527-8800 Fax: (513)527-8801 Monthly. $48.00 per year. Covers the latest manufacturing management issues. Discusses the strategic and financial implications of various tecnologies as they impact factory management, quality and competitiveness.

Production and Inventory Control Handbook. James H. Greene. McGraw-Hill, 1221 Ave. of the Americas New York, NY 10020. Phone: 800-722-4726 or (212)904-2000 Fax: (212)904-2072 E-mail: customer.service@mcgraw-hill.com • URL: http://www.mcgraw-hill.com • 1997. $95.00. Third edition.

Production and Inventory Management Journal. APICS: The Educational Society for Resource Management, 5301 Shawnee Rd. Alexandria, VA 22312-2317. Phone: 800-444-2742 or (703)354-8851 Fax: (703)354-8106 URL: http://www.apics.org • Quarterly. Members, $64.00 per year; non-members, $80.00 per year.

Production and Operations Management. Production and Operations Management Society, c/o Dr. Sushil K. Gupta, Florida International University, PC-543 Miami, FL 33199. Phone: (305)348-1413 Fax: (305)348-1908 E-mail: poms@fiu.edu • URL: http://www.poms.org • Quarterly. Individuals, $60.00 per year; institutions, $90.00 per year.

Production and Operations Management: An Applied Modern Approach. Joseph S. Martinich. John Wiley and Sons, Inc., 605 Third Ave. New York, NY 10158-0012. Phone: 800-225-5945 or (212)850-6000 Fax: (212)850-6088 E-mail: info@wiley.com • URL: http://www.wiley.com • 1996. $105.95. Covers capacity planning, facility location, process design, inventory planning, personnel scheduling, etc.

Production and Operations Management Society. c/o Sushil Gupta, Florida International University, College of Engineering, EAS 2460, 10555 W. Flagler St. Miami, FL 33174. Phone: (305)348-1413 Fax: (305)348-6890 E-mail: poms@fiu.edu • URL: http://www.poms.org • Members are professionals and educators in fields related to operations management and production.

Production and Operations Management: Total Quality and Responsiveness. Hamid Noori and Russell Radford. McGraw-Hill, 1221 Ave. of the Americas New York, NY 10020. Phone: 800-722-4726 or (212)904-2000 Fax: (212)904-2072 E-mail: customer.service@mcgraw-hill.com • URL: http://www.mcgraw-hill.com • 1994. $70.25.

Products Finishing. Gardner Publications, Inc., 6915 Valley Ave Cincinnati, OH 45244-3029. Phone: 800-950-8020 or (513)527-8800 Fax: (513)527-8801 Monthly. $40.00 per year.

Products Finishing Directory. Gardner Publications, Inc., 6915 Valley Ave. Cincinnati, OH 45244-3029. Phone: 800-950-8020 or (513)527-8800 Fax: (513)527-8801 Annual. $15.00. Lists manufacturers and suppliers of equipment and processes which finish metal, plastics and composites.

Professional Agent. National Association of Professional Insurance Agents, 400 N. Washington St. Alexandria, VA 22314. Phone: (703)836-9340 Fax: (703)836-1279 URL: http://www.pianet.com • Monthly. Members, $12.00 per year; non-members, $24.00 per year. Provides sales and marketing advice for independent agents in various fields of insurance, including life, health, property, and casualty.

Professional and Occupational Licensing Directory. The Gale Group, 27500 Drake Rd. Farmington Hills, MI 48331-3535. Phone: 800-877-GALE or (248)699-GALE Fax: 800-414-5043 or (248)699-8069 E-mail: galeord@galegroup.com • URL: http://www.galegroup.com • 1996. $120.00. Second edition. Provides detailed national and state information on the requirements for obtaining a license in each of about 500 occupations. Information needed to contact the appropriate licensing agency or organization is included in each case.

Professional Arts Management Institute.

Professional Audiovideo Retailers Association., 10 E. 22nd St., Suite 310 Lombard, IL 60148. Phone: (630)268-1500 Fax: (630)953-8957 E-mail: parahdq@aol.com • URL: http://www.paralink.org • Members are retailers of high quality equipment.

Professional Builder. Cahners Business Information, 1350 E. Touhy Ave. Des Plaines, IL 60018-3358. Phone: 800-662-7776 or (847)635-8800 Fax: (847)635-9950 E-mail: corporatecommunications@.cahners.com • URL: http://www.cahners.com • Monthly. $99.90 per year. Provides price and market forecasts on industrial products, components and materials. Office products, business systems and transportation. Includes supplement *Luxury Homes*. Formerly *Professional Builder and Remodeler*.

Professional Careers Sourcebook. The Gale Group, 27500 Drake Rd. Farmington Hills, MI 48331-3535. Phone: 800-877-GALE or (248)699-GALE Fax: 800-414-5043 or (248)699-8069 E-mail: galeord@galegroup.com • URL: http://www.galegroup.com • 1999. $105.00. Sixth edition. Includes information sources for 122 professions or occupations.

Professional Carwashing and Detailing. National Trade Publications, Inc., 13 Century Hill Dr. Latham, NY 12110-2113. Phone: (518)783-1281 Fax: (518)783-1386 URL: http://www.carwash.com • Monthly. $49.00 per year. Edited for owners, operators, and managers of automatic carwashes, custom hand carwash facilities, detail shops, and coin-operated, self-service carwashes.

Professional Construction Estimators Association of America., P.O. Box 11626 Charlotte, NC 28220-1626. Phone: (704)522-6376 Fax: (704)522-7013 E-mail: pcea@pcea.com • URL: http://www.pcea.org • Members are building and construction cost estimators.

Professional Convention Management Association.

Professional Corporations and Associations. Berrien C. Eaton. Matthew Bender & Co., Inc., Two Park Ave. New York, NY 10016. Phone: 800-223-1940 or (212)448-2000 Fax: (212)244-3188 E-mail: international@bender.com • URL: http://www.bender.com • $1,140.00. Six looseleaf volumes. Periodic supplementation. Detailed information on forming, operating and changing a professional corporation or association.

The Professional Cosmetologist. John Dalton. West Publishing Co., College and School Div., 610 Opperman Dr. Eagan, MN 55123. Phone: 800-328-4880 or (651)687-7000 Fax: 800-213-2323 or (651)687-5827 E-mail: legal-ed@westgroup.com • URL: http://www.lawschool.westgroup.com • 1992. $42.50. Fourth edition.

Professional Counselor Magazine: Serving the Mental Health and Addictions Fields. Health Communications, Inc., 3201 S. W. 15th St. Deerfield Beach, FL 33442-8190. Phone: 800-851-9100 or (305)360-0909 Fax: (305)360-0034 URL: http://www.hcibooks.com • Bimonthly. $26.00 per year. Covers both clinical and societal aspects of substance abuse.

Professional Freelance Writers Directory. The National Writers Association, 3140 S. Peoria St., No. 295 Aurora, CO 80014-3155. Phone: (303)841-0246 Fax: (303)751-8593 E-mail: sandywrter@aol.com • URL: http://www.nationalwriters.com • Annual. $15.00. About 200 professional members selected from the club's membership on the basis of significant articles or books, or production of plays or movies.

Professional Golfers' Association of America.

Professional Lawn Care Association of America., 1000 Johnson Ferry Rd., Suite C-135 Marietta, GA 30068. Phone: 800-458-3466 or (770)977-5222 Fax: (770)578-6071 E-mail: plcaa@plcaa.org • URL: http://www.plcaa.org • Members are active in the business of treating lawns with chemicals.

Professional Liability: An Economic Analysis. Roger Bowles and Philip Jones. Pearson Education and Technology, 201 W. 103rd St. Indianapolis, IN 46290-1097. Phone: 800-858-7674 or (317)581-3500 URL: http://www.mcp.com • 1989. $14.00. (David Hume Papers, No. 11).

Professional Liability Reporter: Recent Decisions of National Significance. Shepard's, 555 Middle Creek Pkwy. Colorado Springs, CO 80921. Phone: 800-743-7393 or (719)481-7371 Fax: (719)481-7621 E-mail: customer_service@shepards.com • URL: http://www.shepards.com • Monthly. $305.00 per year.

Professional Management of Housekeeping Operations. Robert J. Martin and Tom Jones. John Wiley and Sons, Inc., 605 Third Ave. New York, NY 10158-0012. Phone: 800-526-5368 or (212)850-6000 Fax: (212)850-6088 E-mail: info@wiley.com • URL: http://www.wiley.com • 1998. $59.95. Third edition. For hotels and motels.

The Professional Manager. Institute of Industrial Engineers, 25 Technology Park/Atlanta Norcross, GA 30092. Phone: 800-494-0460 or (770)449-0460 Fax: (770)263-8532 Bimonthly. Free to members; non-members, $40.00 per year. Features articles on the latest problem-solving techniques and trends available to industrial managers. Formerly *Industrial Management*.

Professional Negligence Law Reporter. Association of Trial Lawyers of America, 1050 31st St., N. W. Washington, DC 20007-4499. Phone: 800-424-2725 or (202)965-3500 Fax: (202)965-0030 URL: http://www.atlanet.org/ • Monthly. Members $95.00 per year; non-members, $155.00 per year. Legal newsletter focusing on the liability of health care personnel, accountants, lawyers, engineers, insurance brokers, and real estate agents.

Professional Numismatists Guild.

Professional Photographer. Professional Photographers of America. PPA Publications and Events, Inc., 57 Forsyth St., N.W., Suite 1600 Atlanta, GA 30303-2206. Phone: 800-742-7468 or (404)522-8600 Fax: (404)614-6405 Monthly. $27.00 per year.

Professional Photographers of America.

Professional Pilot-FBO Directory. Queensmith Communications Corp., 3014 Colvin St. Alexandria, VA 22314. Phone: (703)370-0606 Fax: (703)370-7082 E-mail: editorial@propilotmag.com • Annual. $8.00. Includes information for about 1,500 airports and fixed-base operators.

Professional Pilot Magazine. Queensmith Communications Corp., 3014 Colvin St. Alexandria, VA 22314. Phone: (703)370-0606 Fax: (703)370-7082 E-mail: editorial@propilotmag.com • URL: http://www./propilot.com • Monthly. $36.00 per year. Edited for career pilots in all areas of aviation: airline, corporate, charter, and military. Includes flying technique, avionics, navigation, accident analysis, career planning, corporate profiles, and business aviation news.

Professional Practice for Interior Design. Christine M. Piotrowski. John Wiley and Sons, Inc., 605 Third Ave. New York, NY 10158-0012. Phone: 800-842-3636 or (212)850-6000 Fax: (212)850-6088 E-mail: info@wiley.com • URL: http://www.wiley.com • 1994. $64.95. Second edition. (interior Design Series).

Professional Reactor Operator Society.

Professional Resumes for Tax and Accounting Occupations. David H. Noble. CCH, Inc., 4025 W. Peterson Ave. Chicago, IL 60646-6085. Phone: 800-248-3248 or (773)866-6000 Fax: 800-224-8299 or (773)866-3608 URL: http://www.cch.com • 1999. $49.95. Written for accounting, tax, law, and finance professionals. In addition to advice, provides 335 sample resumes and 22 cover letters.

Professional Safety. American Society of Safety Engineers, 1800 E. Oakton St. Des Plaines, IL 60018-2187. Phone: (708)692-4121 Fax: (708)296-3769 URL: http://www.usaor.net/who/who.htm • Monthly. $60.00 per year. Emphasis is on research and technology in the field of accident prevention.

Professional Secretary's Encyclopedic Dictionary. Prentice Hall, 240 Frisch Court Paramus, NJ 07652-5240. Phone: 800-947-7700 or (201)909-6200 Fax: 800-445-6991 or (201)909-6361 URL: http://www.prenhall.com • 1994. $29.95. Fifth edition.

Professional Services Management Association.

Professional's Guide to Successful Management: The Eight Essentials for Running Your Firm, Practice, or Partnership. Carol A. O'Connor. McGraw-Hill, 1221 Ave. of the Americas New York, NY 10020. Phone: 800-722-4726 or (212)904-2000 Fax: (212)904-2072 E-mail: customer.service@mcgraw-hill.com • URL: http://www.mcgraw-hill.com • 1994. Price on application.

The Profile of Franchising: A Statistical Profile of the 1996 Uniform Franchise Offering Circular Data. International Franchise Association, 1350 New York Ave., N. W., Suite 900 Washington, DC 20005-4709. Phone: 800-543-1038 or (202)628-8000 Fax: (202)628-0812 E-mail: ifa@franchise.org • URL: http://www.franchise.org • 1998. $175.00. Based on data from 1,156 franchise systems. Includes information on 30 characteristics of franchises.

Profiles in Business and Management: An International Directory of Scholars and Their Research ĨCD-ROMĪ. Harvard Business School Publishing, 60 Harvard Way Boston, MA 02163. Phone: 800-545-7685 or (617)495-6700 Fax: (617)495-6985 URL: http://www.hbsp.harvard.edu • Annual. $595.00 per year. Fully searchable CD-ROM version of two-volume printed directory. Contains bibliographic and biographical information for over 5600 business and management experts active in 21 subject areas. Formerly *International Directory of Business and Management Scholars*.

Profiles in Business and Management: An International Directory of Scholars and Their Research Version 2.0. Claudia Bruce, editor. Harvard Business School Press, Soldiers Field Boston, MA 02163. Phone: 800-545-7685 or (617)783-7440 E-mail: custserv@cchbspub.harvard.edu • URL: http://www.hbsp.harvard.edu • 1996. $495.00. Two volumes. Provides backgrounds, publications, and current research projects of more than 5,600 business and management experts.

Profiles of American Labor Unions. The Gale Group, 27500 Drake Rd. Farmington Hills, MI 48331-3535. Phone: 800-877-GALE or (248)699-GALE Fax: 800-414-5043 or (248)699-8069 E-mail: galeord@gale.com • URL: http://www.gale.com • 1998. $305.00. Second edition. Provides detailed information on more than 280 national labor unions. Includes descriptions of about 800 bargaining agreements and biographies of more than 170 union officials. Local unions are also listed. Four indexes. Formerly *American Directory of Organized Labor* (1992).

Profiles of Success. International Health, Racquet, and Sportsclub Association, 263 Summer St. Boston, MA 02210. Phone: 800-228-4772 or (617)951-0055 Fax: (617)951-0056 Annual. Members, $125.00; non-members, $500.00. Provides detailed financial statistics for commercial health clubs, sports clubs, and gyms.

Profiles of U. S. Hospitals. Dorland Healthcare Information, 1500 Walnut St., Suite 1000 Philadelphia, PA 19102. Phone: 800-784-2332 or (215)875-1212 Fax: (215)735-3966 E-mail: info@dorlandhealth.com • URL: http://www.dorlandhealth.com • Annual. $299.00. Contains profiles of more than 6,000 community, teaching, children's, specialty, psychiatric, and rehabilitation hospitals. Emphasis is on 50 key financial and performance measures. Annual CD-ROM version with key word searching is available at $395.00.

Profit Investor Portfolio: The International Magazine of Money and Style. Profit Publications, Inc., 69-730 Highway 111, Suite 102 Rancho Mirage, CA 92270-9822. Phone: (619)202-1545 Fax: (619)202-1544 URL: http://www.profitinc.com • Bimonthly. $29.95 per year. A glossy consumer magazine featuring specific investment recommendations and articles on upscale travel and shopping.

Profit Sharing. Profit Sharing-401(K) Council of America, 10 S. Riverside Plaza, Suite 1610 Chicago, IL 60606-3802. Phone: (312)441-8550 Fax: (312)441-8559 Bimonthly. Membership.

Profit Sharing: Does It Make a Difference? The Productivity and Stability Effects of Profit Sharing Plans. Douglas L. Kruse. W. E. Upjohn Institute for Employment Research, 300 S. Westnedge Ave. Kalamazoo, MI 49007-5541. Phone: (616)343-5541 Fax: (616)343-7310 E-mail: publications@we.upjohninst.org • URL: http://www.upjohninst.org • 1993. $27.00.

Profit Sharing/401(K) Council of America., 10 S. Riverside Plaza, No. 1610 Chicago, IL 60606. Phone: (312)441-8550 Fax: (312)441-8559 E-mail: psca@psca.org • URL: http://www.psca.org • Members are business firms with profit sharing and/or 401(K) plans. Affiliated with the Profit Sharing/401(K) Education Foundation at the same address.

Profit Sharing/401(K) Education Foundation.

Profitable Investing. Richard E. Band, editor. Phillips Business Information, Inc., 1201 Seven Locks Rd., Ste. 300 Potomac, MD 20854. Phone: 800-777-5006 or (301)340-2100 Fax: (301)340-0542 E-mail: pbi@phillips.com • URL: http://www.phillips.com • Monthly. $149.00 per year. Newsletter.

Profitable Restaurant Management. Kenneth L. Solomon and Norman Katz. Prentice Hall, 240 Frisch Court Paramus, NJ 07652-5240. Phone: 800-947-7700 or (201)909-6200 Fax: 800-445-6991 or (201)909-6361 URL: http://www.prenhall.com • 1981. $60.00. Second edition.

Profiting from Real Estate Rehab. Sandra M. Brassfield. John Wiley and Sons, Inc., 605 Third Ave. New York, NY 10158-0012. Phone: 800-225-5945 or (212)850-6000 Fax: (212)850-6088 E-mail: info@wiley.com • URL: http://www.wiley.com • 1992. $39.95. How to fix up old houses and sell them at a profit.

Program: Electronic Library and Information Systems. Available from Information Today, Inc., 143 Old Marlton Pike Medford, NJ 08055-8750. Phone: 800-300-9868 or (609)654-6266 Fax: (609)654-4309 E-mail: custserv@infotoday.com • URL: http://www.infotoday.com • Quarterly. Members, $175.00 per year; non-members, $214.00 per year. Published in London by Aslib: The Association for Information Management. Discusses computer applications for libraries.

Program on International Studies in Planning., Cornell University, 200 W. Sibley Hall Ithaca, NY 14853. Phone: (607)255-2186 Fax: (607)255-6681 E-mail: bdl5@cornell.edu • URL: http://www.inet.crp.cornell.edu/organizations/isp/default.htm • Research activities are related to international urban and regional planning, with emphasis on developing areas.

Progreso. Vision, Inc., 2655 Lejeune Rd., Suite 610 Miami, FL 33134. Phone: (305)567-9095 Fax: (305)567-9094 Monthly. $64.00 per year. Covers developments in Latin America affecting business and trade. Text in Spanish.

Progress Center: University of Florida Research and Technology Park., P.O. Box 10 Alachua, FL 32615. Phone: (904)462-4040 Fax: (904)462-3932 E-mail: sburgess@hawley-realply.com • Designed to transfer new technologies from the laboratory to the marketplace.

Progress in Aerospace Sciences: An International Journal. Elsevier Science, 655 Ave. of the Americas New York, NY 10010. Phone: 888-437-4636 or (212)989-5800 Fax: (212)633-3680 E-mail: usinfo@elsevier.com • URL: http://www.elsevier.com • Bimonthly. $1,257.00 per year. Text in English, French and German.

Progress in Low Temperature Physics. D. F. Brewer, editor. Elsevier Science, 655 Ave. of the Americas New York, NY 10010. Phone: 888-437-4636 or (212)989-5800 Fax: (212)633-3680 E-mail: usinfo@elsevier.com • URL: http://www.elsevier.com • 1996. $244.00. Volume 14.

Progress in Materials Science: An International Review Journal. Elsevier Science, 655 Ave. of the Americas New York, NY 10010. Phone: 888-437-4636 or (212)989-5800 Fax: (212)633-3680 E-mail: usinfo@elsevier.com • URL: http://www.elsevier.com • Bimonthly. $992.00 per year.

Progress in Oceanography. Elsevier Science, 655 Ave. of the Americas New York, NY 10010. Phone: 888-437-4636 or (212)989-5800 Fax: (212)633-3680 E-mail: usinfo@elsevier.com • URL: http://www.elsevier.com • 16 times a year. $1,962.00 per year.

Progress in Planning. Donald R. Diamond and J.B. McLoughlin, editors. Elsevier Science, 655 Ave. of the Americas New York, NY 10010. Phone: 888-437-4636 or (212)989-5800 Fax: (212)633-3680 E-mail: usinfo@elsevier.com • URL: http://www.elsevier.com • Eight times a year. $619.00 per year.

Progressive Farmer. Progressive Farmer, Inc., 2100 Lakeshore Dr. Birmingham, AL 35209. Phone: (205)877-6419 Fax: (205)877-6750 E-mail: jodie@progressivefarmer.com • URL: http://www.pathfinder.com/pf • 18 times a year. $18.00 per year. 17 regional editions. Includes supplement *Rural Sportsman*.

Progressive Grocer Annual Report of the Grocery Industry. Bill Communications, Inc., 770 Broadway New York, NY 10003-9595. Phone: 800-266-4712 or (646)654-4500 Fax: (646)654-7212 URL: http://www.billcom.com • Annual. $15.00.

Progressive Grocer: The Magazine of Supermarketing. Bill Communications, Inc., 770 Broadway New York, NY 10003-9595. Phone: 800-266-4712 or (646)654-4500 Fax: (646)654-7212 URL: http://www.billcom.com • Monthly. $99.00 per year.

Progressive Railroading. Trade Press Publishing Corp., 2100 W. Florist Ave. Milwaukee, WI 53209-3799. Phone: 800-727-7995 or (414)228-7701 Fax: (414)228-1134 URL: http://www.tradepress.com • Monthly. Free to qualified personnel; others, $50.00 per year. Provides feature articles, news, new product information, etc. Relative to the railroad and rail transit industry.

Project Finance: The Magazine for Global Development. Institutional Investor Journals, 488 Madison Ave. New York, NY 10022. Phone: (212)224-3300 Fax: (212)224-3527 E-mail: info@iijournals.com • URL: http://www.iijournals.com • Monthly. $635.00 per year. Provides articles on the financing of the infrastructure (transportation, utilities, communications, the environment, etc). Coverage is international. Supplements available *World Export Credit Guide* and *Project Finance Book of Lists*. Formed by the merger of *Infrastructure Finance* and *Project and Trade Finance*.

Project Finance: The Monthly Analysis of Export, Import and Project Finance. Institutional Investor, 488 Madison Ave. New York, NY 10022. Phone: (212)224-3300 Fax: (212)224-3527 E-mail: info@iijournals.com • URL: http://www.iijournals.com • Monthly. $635.00 per year. An analysis of the techniques and practice used in international trade and project finance. Supplements available *World Export Credit Guides* and *Project Finance Book of Lists*. Formed by the merger of *Infrastructure Finance* and *Project and Trade Finance*.

Project Management. Dennis Lock. John Wiley and Sons, Inc., 605 Third Ave. New York, NY 10158-0012. Phone: 800-225-5945 or (212)850-6000 Fax: (212)850-6088 E-mail: info@wiley.com • URL: http://www.wiley.com • 1996. $69.95. Sixth edition.

Project Management: A Managerial Approach. Jack R. Meredith and Samuel J. Mantel. John Wiley and Sons, Inc., 605 Third Ave. New York, NY 10158-0012. Phone: 800-526-5368 or (212)850-6000 Fax: (212)850-6088 E-mail: info@wiley.com • URL: http://www.wiley.com • 1995. $95.95. Third edition. (Productions-Operations Management Series).

Project Management: A Systems Approach to Planning, Scheduling, and Controlling. Harold Kerzner. John Wiley & Sons, Inc., 605 Third Ave., 4th Fl. New York, NY 10158-0012. Phone: 800-225-5945 or (212)850-6000 Fax: (212)850-6088 E-mail: info@wiley.com • URL: http://www.wiley.com • 1994. $65.00. Sixth edition. Includes chapters on time management, risk management, quality management, and program evaluation and review techniques (PERT). (Business Technology Series).

Project Management Casebook. David I. Cleland and others, editors. Project Management Institute, Four Campus Blvd. Newtown Square, PA 19073-3299. Phone: (610)356-4600 Fax: (610)356-4647 E-mail: booked@pmi.org • URL: http://www.pmi.org • 1998. $69.95. Provides 50 case studies in various areas of project management.

Project Management: How to Plan and Manage Successful Projects. Joan Knutson and Ira Bitz. AMACOM, 1601

Broadway, 12th Fl. New York, NY 10019. Phone: 800-262-9699 or (212)586-8100 Fax: (212)903-8168 E-mail: custmserv@amanet.org • URL: http://www.amanet.org • 1991. $55.00. Covers both technical and organizational skills.

Project Management Institute.

Project Management Journal. Project Management Institute, Project Management Institute, Publishing Div., c/o Linda V. Gillman, 40 Colonial Square Sylva, NC 28779. Phone: (828)586-3715 Fax: (828)586-4664 E-mail: booked@pmi.org • URL: http://www.pmi.org • Quarterly. $100.00 per year. Contains technical articles dealing with the interests of the field of project management.

Project Management Salary Survey. Project Management Institute, Project Management Institute, Publishing Div., c/o Linda V. Gillman, 40 Colonial Square Sylva, NC 28779. Phone: (828)586-3715 Fax: (828)586-4664 E-mail: booked@pmi.org • URL: http://www.pmi.org • Annual. $129.00. Gives compensation data for key project management positions in North America, according to job title, level of responsibility, number of employees supervised, and various other factors. Includes data on retirement plans and benefits.

Project Management: Strategic Design and Implementation. David I. Cleland. McGraw-Hill, 1221 Ave. of the Americas New York, NY 10020-1095. Phone: 800-262-4726 or (212)904-2000 Fax: (212)904-2072 1998. $64.95. Third edition.

Project Management with CPM, Pert and Precedence Diagramming. Joseph J. Moder and others. Blitz Publishing Co., 1600 N. High Point Rd. Middleton, WI 53562-3635. Phone: 800-434-5595 or (608)836-7550 Fax: (608)831-5598 E-mail: wcdries@hotmail.com • URL: http://www.badgerbooks.com • 1995. $40.00. Third edition.

Promax International., 2029 Century Park E., Suite 555 Los Angeles, CA 90067-3283. Phone: (310)788-7600 Fax: (310)788-7616 URL: http://www.promax.org • Members are advertising and public relations personnel in the radio and television broadcasting industries.

PROMO Magazine's SourceBook: The Only Guide to the $70 Billion Promotion Industry. Intertec Publishing, 11 River Bend Dr., S. Stamford, CT 06907-0949. Phone: 800-543-4116 or (203)358-9900 Fax: (203)358-5835 E-mail: subs@intertec.com • URL: http://www.intertec.com • Annual. $49.95. Lists service and supply companies for the promotion industry. Includes annual salary survey and award winning campaigns.

The PROMO 100 Promotion Agency Ranking. Intertec Publishing Co., 11 River Bend Dr., S. Stamford, CT 06907-0225. Phone: 800-795-5445 or (203)358-9900 Fax: (203)358-5834 URL: http://www.promomagazine.com • Annual. $9.95. Provides information on 100 leading product promotion agencies.

PROMO: Promotion Marketing Worldwide. Simba Information Inc., P.O. Box 4234 Stamford, CT 06907-0234. Phone: 800-307-2529 or (203)358-4100 Fax: (203)358-5824 E-mail: info@simbanet.com • URL: http://www.promomagazine.com • Monthly. $65.00 per year. Edited for companies and agencies that utilize couponing, point-of-purchase advertising, special events, games, contests, premiums, product samples, and other unique promotional items.

Promotional Marketing. Entrepreneur, Inc., 2392 Morse Ave. Irvine, CA 92714. Phone: 800-421-2300 or (949)261-2325 Fax: (949)851-9088 E-mail: entmag@entrepreneurmag.com • URL: http://www.entrepreneurmag.com • Looseleaf. $59.50. A practical guide to sales promotion and marketing for small businesses. (Start-Up Business Guide No. E1111.)

Promotional Products Association International.

Prompt. Pasadena IBM User Group, 2303 Glen Canyon Rd. Altadena, CA 91001-3539. Phone: (818)791-1600 Fax: (818)791-1600 E-mail: 71333.130@compuserve.com • Monthly. Membership. Helps users of IBM compatibles understand their system.

PROMT: Predicasts Overview of Markets and Technology. The Gale Group, 27500 Drake Rd. Farmington Hills, MI 48331-3535. Phone: 800-877-GALE or (248)699-GALE Fax: 800-414-5043 or (248)699-8069 E-mail: galeord@gale.com • URL: http://www.gale.com • Companies, products, applied technologies and markets. U.S. and international literature coverage, 1972 to date. Inquire as to online cost and availability. Provides abstracts from more than 1,600 publications. Weekly updates.

Proofs: Buyers' Guide and United States Manufacturers' Directory. Dental Economics Div. PennWell Corp., Industrial Div., 1421 S. Sheridan Rd. Tulsa, OK 74112. Phone: 800-331-4463 or (918)835-3161 Fax: (918)831-9295 E-mail: webmaster@pennwell.com • URL: http://www.pennwell.com • Annual. $40.00. List of over 600 manufacturers of dental products and equipment; coverage includes foreign listings.

Proofs: The Magazine of Dental Sales. PennWell Corp., Industrial Div., 1421 S. Sheridan Rd. Tulsa, OK 74112. Phone: 800-331-4463 or (918)835-3161 Fax: (918)831-9295 E-mail: webmaster@pennwell.com • URL: http://www.pennwell.com • 10 times a year. $35.00 per year.

Properties. Properties Magazine, Inc., P.O. Box 112127 Cleveland, OH 44111-8127. Phone: (216)251-0035 Monthly. $15.00 per year. News and features of interest to income property owners managers and related industries in Northeastern Ohio.

Property and Casualty Insurance: Year in Review. CCH, Inc., 4025 W. Peterson Ave. Chicago, IL 60646-6085. Phone: 800-248-3248 or (773)866-6000 Fax: 800-224-8299 or (773)866-3608 URL: http://www.cch.com • Annual. $75.00. Summarizes the year's significant legal and regulatory developments.

Property and Liability Insurance. Solomon S. Huebner and others. Prentice Hall, 240 Frisch Court Paramus, NJ 07652-5240. Phone: 800-947-7700 or (201)909-6200 Fax: 800-445-6991 or (201)909-6361 URL: http://www.prenhall.com • 1995. $96.00.

Property-Casualty Insurance Facts. Insurance Information Institute, 110 William St., 24th Fl. New York, NY 10038. Phone: 800-331-9146 or (212)669-9200 Fax: (212)732-1916 E-mail: info@iii.org • URL: http://www.iii.org • Annual. $22.50. Formerly *Insurance Facts*.

Property Management Association.

Property Tax Alert. CCH, Inc., 4025 West Peterson Ave. Chicago, IL 60646-6085. Phone: 800-248-3248 or (773)866-6000 Fax: 800-224-8299 or (773)866-3608 URL: http://www.cch.com • Monthly. $197.00 per year. Newsletter. Covers trends in real estate valuation, assessment, and taxation.

Property Tax Manual. Vertex Systems, Inc., 1041 Old Cassatt Rd. Berwyn, PA 19312. Phone: (610)640-4200 Annual. $1,060.00. Four regions. $265.00 per region. Monthly updates, $808.00 per year. Lists tax rates, assessment ratios, assessors, filing requirements, depreciation schedules, etc.

Proposal Development: How to Respond and Win the Bid. Bud Porter-Roth. PSI Research, P.O. Box 3727 Central Point, OR 97502-0032. Phone: 800-228-2275 or (541)479-9464 Fax: (541)476-1479 E-mail: info@psi-research.com • URL: http://www.psiresearch.com • 1998. $21.95. Third revised edition. A step-by-step guide to the practical details of preparing, printing, and submitting business proposals of various kinds. (Successful Business Library Series).

Proposal Planning and Writing. Lynn E. Miner and others. Oryx Press, 4041 N. Central Ave., Ste. 700 Scottsdale, AZ 85012-3379. Phone: 800-279-6799 or (602)265-2651 Fax: 800-279-4663 or (602)265-6250 E-mail: info@oryxpress.com • URL: http://www.oryxpress.com • 1998. $34.50. Second edition. Discusses the steps necessary to locate and obtain funding from the federal government, foundations, and corporations.

Proposal Preparation. Rodney D. Stewart and Ann L. Stewart. John Wiley and Sons, Inc., 605 Third Ave. New York, NY 10158-0012. Phone: 800-526-5368 or (212)850-6000 Fax: (212)850-6088 E-mail: info@wiley.com • URL: http://www.wiley.com • 1992. $125.00. Second edition. Covers proposals of various kinds.

ProQuest Direct. Bell & Howell Information and Learning-Phone: 800-521-0600 or (313)761-4700 Fax: (313)973-9145 URL: http://www.umi.com/proquest • Fee-based Web site providing Internet access to more than 3,000 periodicals, newspapers, and other publications. Many items are available full-text, with daily updates. Includes extensive corporate and financial information from Disclosure, Inc. Fees: Apply.

ProSales Buyer's Guide. Hanley-Wood, LLC., One Thomas Circle, Suite 600 Washington, DC 20005. Phone: 888-269-8410 or (202)452-0800 Fax: (202)785-1974 URL: http://www.hanleywood.com • Annual. $5.00. A directory of equipment for professional builders.

ProSales: For Dealers and Distributors Serving the Professional Contractor. Hanley-Wood, LLC., One Thomas Circle, Suite 600 Washington, DC 20005. Phone: 888-269-8410 or (202)452-0800 Fax: (202)785-1974 URL: http://www.hanleywood.com • Monthly. $36.00 per year. Includes special feature issues on selling, credit, financing, and the marketing of power tools.

Prospector's Choice: The Electronic Product Profiling 10,000 Corporate and Foundation Grantmakers. The Gale Group, 27500 Drake Rd. Farmington Hills, MI 48331-3535. Phone: 800-877-GALE or (248)699-GALE Fax: 800-414-5043 or (248)699-8069 E-mail: galeord@gal.com • URL: http://www.gale.com • Annual. $849.00. Provides detailed CD-ROM information on foundations and corporate philanthropies. Also known as *Corporate and Foundation Givers on Disk*.

Prosperity and Depression: A Theoretical Analysis of Cyclical Movements. Gottfried Haberler. Harvard University Press, 79 Garden St. Cambridge, MA 02138. Phone: 800-448-2242 or (617)495-2600 Fax: 800-962-4983 or (617)495-4898 E-mail: contacthup@harvard.edu • URL: http://www.hup.harvard.edu • 1964. $35.00. Fourth edition. (Economic Studies No. 105).

Protecting Stream Corridors. Lee Nellis. Sage Publications, Inc., 2455 Teller Rd. Thousand Oaks, CA 91320. Phone: (805)499-0721 Fax: (805)499-0871 E-mail: info@sagepub.com • URL: http://www.sagepub.com • 1993. $10.00.

Protecting Trade Secrets, Patents, Copyrights, and Trademarks. Robert C. Dorr and Christopher H. Munch. Panel Publishers, 1185 Ave. of the Americas, 37th Fl. New York, NY 10036. Phone: 800-447-1717 or (212)597-0200 Fax: (212)597-0334 Looseleaf service. $165.00.

Protecting Your Practice. Katherine Vessenes. Bloomberg Press, 100 Business Park Dr. Princeton, NJ 08542-0888. Phone: 800-388-2749 or (609)279-4670 Fax: (609)279-7155 E-mail: press@bloomberg.net • URL: http://www.bloomberg.com • 1997. $50.00. Discusses legal compliance issues for financial planners. (Bloomberg Professional Library.)

Protocol (Corporate Meetings, Entertainment, and Special Events). Protocol Directory, Inc., 101 W. 12th St., Suite PHH New York, NY 10011. Phone: (212)633-6934 Fax: (212)633-6934 E-mail: protoefg@aol.com • Annual. $48.00. Provides information on about 4,000 suppliers of products and services for special events, shows (entertainment), and business meetings. Geographic arrangement.

Provider: For Long Term Care Professionals. American Health Care Association, 1201 L St., N. W. Washington, DC 20005. Phone: (202)842-4444 Fax: (202)842-3860 URL: http://www.ahca.org • Monthly. $48.00 per year. Edited for medical directors, administrators, owners, and others concerned with extended care facilities and nursing homes. Covers business management, legal issues, financing, reimbursement, care planning, ethics, human resources, etc.

Provider: LTC Buyers' Guide. American Health Care Association, 1201 L St., N. W. Washington, DC 20005-4046. Phone: (202)898-4444 Fax: (202)842-3860 URL: http://www.ahca.org • Annual. $10.00. Lists several hundred manufacturers and suppliers of products and services for long term care (LTC) facilities.

Provincial Outlook. Conference Board of Canada, 255 Smyth Rd., Suite 100 Ottawa, ON, Canada K1H 8M7. Phone: (613)526-3280 Fax: (613)526-4857 E-mail: pubsales@conferenceboard.ca • URL: http://www.conferenceboard.ca • Quarterly. Free to members; non-members, $3,000.00 per year. Contains detailed forecasts of economic conditions in each of the Canadian provinces.

The Prudent Speculator. Al Frank Asset Management, Inc., P.O. Box 1438 Laguna Beach, CA 92652. Phone: (714)497-7657 Fax: (714)797-7658 Monthly. $175.00 per year. Newsletter. Presents a fundamental approach to stock selection and buying strategies for long-term capital gains appreciation.

The Prudent Speculator: Al Frank on Investing. Al Frank. McGraw-Hill Professional, 1221 Ave. of the Americas New York, NY 10020. Phone: 800-722-4726 or (212)904-2000 Fax: (212)904-2072 E-mail: customer.service@mcgraw-hill.com • URL: http://www.mcgraw-hill.com • 1989. $30.00. How to be a sensible investor or speculator. Includes advice on the use of margin accounts and stock market timing.

Psychiatric Services. American Psychiatric Association. American Psychiatric Press, Inc., Journals Div., 1400 K St., N.W., Suite 1101 Washington, DC 20005. Phone: 800-368-5777 or (202)682-6070 Fax: (202)682-6189 E-mail: psjournal@psych.org • URL: http://www.psychservices.psychiatryonline.org/ • Monthly. Individuals, $51.00 per year; Institutions, $85.00 per year. Formerly *Hospital and Community Psychiatry*.

Psychological Abstracts. American Psychological Association, 750 First St., N. E. Washington, DC 20002-4242. Phone: 800-374-2721 or (202)336-5500 Fax: (202)336-5568 URL: http://www.apa.org/journals • Monthly. Members, $799.00 per year; individuals and institutions, $1,075.00 per year. Covers the international literature of psychology and the behavioral sciences. Includes journals, technical reports, dissertations, and other sources.

Psychological Symptoms. Frank J. Bruno. John Wiley and Sons, Inc., 605 Third Ave. New York, NY 10158-0012. Phone: 800-225-5945 or (212)850-6000 Fax: (212)850-6088 E-mail: info@wiley.com • URL: http://www.wiley.com • 1994. $24.95. Explains the meaning of common mental symptoms, what may cause them, and how to deal with them.

Psychological Testing. Anne Anastasi. Prentice Hall, 240 Frisch Court Paramus, NJ 07652-5240. Phone: 800-947-7700 or (201)909-6200 Fax: 800-445-6991 or (201)909-6361 URL: http://www.prenhall.com • 1996. $89.00. Seventh edition.

Psychology and Marketing. John Wiley and Sons, Inc., Journals Div., 605 Third Ave. New York, NY 10158-0012. Phone: 800-526-5368 or (212)850-6000 Fax: (212)850-6088 E-mail: info@wiley.com • URL: http://www.wiley.com • Eight times a year. $780.00 per year. Spots the latest social, economic, and cultural trends that affect marketing decisions.

Psychology for Leaders: Using Motivation, Conflict, and Power to Manage More Effectively. Dean Tjosvold and Mary Tjosvold. John Wiley and Sons, Inc., 605 Third Ave. New York, NY 10158-0012. Phone: 800-225-5945 or (212)850-6000 Fax: (212)850-6088 E-mail: info@

wiley.com • URL: http://www.wiley.com • 1995. $32.95. (Portable MBS Series).

Psychology in Industrial Organizations. Norman R. Maier and Gertrude Verser. Houghton Mifflin Co., 215 Park Ave., S. New York, NY 10003. Phone: 800-225-3362 or (212)420-5800 Fax: (212)420-5855 URL: http://www.hmco.com • 1982. $79.96. Fifth edition. Five volumes.

The Psychology of Decision Making: People in Organizations. Lee R. Beach. Sage Publications, Inc., 2455 Teller Rd. Thousand Oaks, CA 91320. Phone: (805)499-0721 Fax: (805)499-0871 E-mail: info@sagepub.com • URL: http://www.sagepub.com • 1997. $30.00. Includes references and index. (Foundations for Organizational Science).

Psychology Today. Sussex Publishers Inc., 49 E. 21st St., 11th Fl. New York, NY 10010. Phone: 800-234-8361 or (212)260-7210 Fax: (212)260-7445 Bimonthly. $18.00 per year.

Psychotropic Substances. United Nations Publications, Two United Nations Plaza, Rm. DC2-853 New York, NY 10017. Phone: 800-253-9646 or (212)963-8302 Fax: (212)963-3489 Annual. $42.00.

PsycINFO. American Psychological Association, 750 First St., N. E. Washington, DC 20002-4242. Phone: 800-374-2722 or (202)336-5650 Fax: (202)336-5568 URL: http://www.apa.org/psycinfo • Provides indexing and abstracting of the worldwide literature of psychology and the behavioral sciences. Time period is 1967 to date, with monthly updates. Inquire as to online cost and availability.

PT Design Motion Systems Handbook (Power Transmission). Penton Media Inc., 1300 E. Ninth St. Cleveland, OH 44114. Phone: (216)696-7000 Fax: (216)696-0836 E-mail: corpcomm@penton.com • URL: http://www.penton.com • Annual. $30.00. Formerly *Power Transmission Design Handbook.*

PTC Research Foundation. Franklin Pierce Law Center

Public Accounting Report. Strafford Publications, Inc., Specialized Information Services, 590 Dutch Valley Rd., N.E. Atlanta, GA 30324-0729. Phone: 800-926-7926 or (404)881-1141 Fax: (404)881-0074 E-mail: custserv@straffordpub.com • URL: http://www.straffordpubs.com • 23 times a year. $297.00 per year. Newsletter. Presents news and trends affecting the accounting profession.

Public Administration and Development: An International Journal of Training, Research and Practice. Available from John Wiley and Sons, Inc., Journals Div., 605 Third Ave. New York, NY 10158-0012. Phone: 800-526-5368 or (212)850-6000 Fax: (212)850-6088 E-mail: info@wiley.com • URL: http://www.wiley.com • Five times a year. $760.00 per year. Focuses on administrative practice at the local, regional and national levels. International coverage. Published in England by John Wiley and Sons Ltd.

Public Administration and Public Affairs. Nicholas L. Henry. Prentice Hall, 240 Frisch Court Paramus, NJ 07652-5240. Phone: 800-947-7700 or (201)909-6200 Fax: 800-445-6991 or (201)909-6361 URL: http://www.prenhall.com • 2000. $53.33. Eighth edition.

Public Administration: Design and Problem Solving. Jong S. Jun. Chatelaine Press, 6454 Honey Tree Court Burke, VA 22015. Phone: 800-249-9527 or (703)569-2062 Fax: (703)569-9610 E-mail: arlene@chatpress.com • URL: http://www.chatpress.com • 1986. $41.95.

Public Administration Review. American Society for Public Administration, 1120 G St., N.W., Suite 700 Washington, DC 20005. Phone: (202)393-7878 Fax: (202)638-4952 URL: http://www.nd.org. • Bimonthly. $80.00 per year.

Public Administration Service.

Public Affairs Report. Institute of Govermental Studies, University of California, Berkeley, 109 Moses Hall Berkeley, CA 94720-2370. Phone: (510)642-6723 Fax: (510)642-3020 E-mail: jlubenow@uclink2.berkeley.edu • URL: http://www.garnet.berkeley.edu:80/~igs/ • Bimonthly. Free.

Public Assistance and Welfare Trends: State Capitals. Wakeman-Walworth, Inc., P.O. Box 7376 Alexandria, VA 22307-0376. Phone: 800-876-2545 or (703)549-8606 Fax: (703)549-1372 E-mail: newsletters@statecapitals.com • URL: http://www.statecapitals.com • Weekly. $245.00 per year. Newsletter. Formerly *From the State Capitals: Public Assistance and Welfare Trends.*

Public Citizen., 1600 20th St., N.W. Washington, DC 20009. Phone: (202)588-1000 Fax: (202)588-7798 E-mail: pcmail@citizen.org • URL: http://www.citizen.org • Founded by Ralph Nader. Promotes citizen advocacy of consumer rights.

Public Citizen's Critical Mass Energy Project., 215 Pennsylvania Ave., S.E. Washington, DC 20003. Phone: (202)546-4996 Fax: (202)547-7392 E-mail: cmep@citizens.org • URL: http://www.citizens.org/cmep • Maintains national network of anti-nuclear groups.

Public Corporate New Issues. Thomson Financial Securities Data, Two Gateway Center Newark, NJ 07102. Phone: (973)622-3100 Fax: (973)622-1421 URL: http://www.tfsd.com • Provides detailed online information relating to initial public stock offerings (new issues) from 1970 to date. Updating is daily. Inquire as to online cost and availability. Inquire as to online cost and availability.

Public Employment. Bureau of the Census, U.S. Department of Commerce. Available from U.S. Government Printing Office, Washington, DC 20402. Phone: (202)512-1800 Fax: (202)512-2250 Annual.

Public Finance Review. Sage Publications, Inc., 2455 Teller Rd. Thousand Oaks, CA 91320. Phone: (805)499-0721 Fax: (805)499-0871 E-mail: info@sagepub.com • URL: http://www.sagepub.com • Quarterly. Individuals, $85.00 per year, institutions, $450.00 per year. Formerly *Public Finance Quarterly.*

Public Interest Profiles, 1998-1999. Available from Congressional Quarterly, Inc., 1414 22nd St., N.W. Washington, DC 20037. Phone: 800-638-1710 or (202)887-8500 Fax: 800-380-3810 E-mail: bookhelp@cq.com • URL: http://www.cq.com • 1996. $175.00. Published by Foundation for Public Affairs. Provides detailed information on more than 250 influential public interest and public policy organizations (lobbyists) in the U.S. Includes e-mail addresses and Web sites where available.

Public Law Education Institute.

Public Library Association; Technology Committee., c/o American Library Association, 50 E. Huron St. Chicago, IL 60611. Phone: 800-545-2433 or (312)280-5752 Fax: (312)280-5029 E-mail: pla@pla.org • URL: http://www.pla.org • The Public Library Association is a Division of the American Library Association.

Public Library Catalog: Guide to Reference Books and Adult Nonfiction. Juliette Yaakov, editor. H. W. Wilson Co., 950 University Ave. Bronx, NY 10452. Phone: 800-367-6770 or (718)588-8400 Fax: (718)590-1617 E-mail: custserv@hwwilson.com • URL: http://www.hwwilson.com • Quinquennial. $230.00. Contains annotations for 8,000 of the ''best'' reference and other nonfiction books in English. Covers a wide range of topics, including many that are related to business, economics, finance, or industry. (Standard Catalog Series).

Public Library Quarterly. The Haworth Press, Inc., 10 Alice St. Binghamton, NY 13904-1580. Phone: 800-429-6784 or (607)722-5857 Fax: 800-895-0582 or (607)722-1424 E-mail: getinfo@haworthpressinc.com • URL: http://www.haworthpressinc.com • Quarterly. Individuals, $40.00 per year; institutions, $140.00 per year; libraries, $140.00 per year.

Public Management: Devoted to the Conduct of Local Government. International City-County Management Association, 777 N. Capital, N.E., Suite 500 Washington, DC 20002-4201. Phone: 800-745-8780 or (202)289-4262 Fax: (202)962-3500 E-mail: bpayne@icma.org • URL: http://www.icma.org • Monthly. $34.00 per year.

The Public Manager: The Journal for Practitioners. Bureaucrat, Inc., 12007 Titian Way Potomac, MD 20854. Phone: (301)279-9445 Fax: (301)251-5872 URL: http://www.feiaa.org/ • Quarterly. Individuals, $30.00 per year; institutions, $55.00 per year. Formerly *Bureaucrat.*

Public Opinion: Politics, Communication and Social Process. Carroll J. Glyn and others. HarperCollins Publishers, 10 E. 53rd St. New York, NY 10022-5299. Phone: 800-242-7737 or (212)207-7000 Fax: 800-822-4090 or (212)207-7145 URL: http://www.harpercollins.com • 1998. $75.00.

Public Opinion Polls and Survey Research: A Selected Annotated Bibliography of U.S. Guides and Studies from the 1980s. Graham R. Waldon. Garland Publishing, Inc., 19 Union Square West, 8th Fl. New York, NY 10003-3382. Phone: 800-627-6273 or (212)414-0650 Fax: (212)414-0659 E-mail: info@garland.com • URL: http://www.garlandpub.com • 1990. $15.00. (Public Affairs and Administration Series, Vol. 24).

Public Opinion Quarterly. American Association for Public Opinion Research. University of Chicago Press, Journals Div., P.O. Box 37005 Chicago, IL 60637. Phone: 800-621-2736 or (773)753-3347 Fax: (773)753-0811 E-mail: subscriptions@.journals.uchicago.edu • URL: http://www.journals.uchicago.edu/ • Quarterly.. Individuals, $25.00 per year; institutions, $66.00 per year; students, $20.00 per year.

Public Personnel Administration: Policies and Procedures for Personnel. Prentice Hall, 240 Frisch Court Paramus, NJ 07652-5240. Phone: 800-947-7700 or (201)909-6200 Fax: 800-445-6991 or (201)909-6361 URL: http://www.prenhall.com • Looseleaf service. Price on application.

Public Personnel Management. International Personnel Management Association, 1617 Duke St. Alexandria, VA 22314. Phone: (703)549-7100 Fax: (703)684-0948 E-mail: publications@ipma-hr.org • URL: http://www.ipma-hr.org • Quarterly. $50.00 per year.

Public Policies for Environmental Protection. Paul R. Portney, editor. Johns Hopkins University Press, 2715 N. Charles St. Baltimore, MD 21218-4319. Phone: 800-537-5487 or (410)516-6900 Fax: (410)516-6998 E-mail: info@rff.org • URL: http://www.press.jhu.edu • 2000. Second edition. Price on application. A discussion of issues, progress, and problems in the regulation of air pollution, water pollution, hazardous wastes, and toxic substances. Economic factors are emphasized.

Public Policy and College Management: Title III of the Higher Education Act. Edward P. Saint John. Greenwood Publishing Group, Inc., 88 Post Rd., W. Westport, CT 06881-5007. Phone: 800-225-5800 or (203)226-3571 Fax: (203)222-2540 E-mail: bookinfo@greenwood.com • URL: http://www.greenwood.com • 1981. $55.00.

Public Power. American Public Power Association, 2301 M St., N.W. Washington, DC 20037-1484. Phone: (202)467-2900 Fax: (202)467-2910 Bimonthly. $50.00 per year.

Public Power Annual Directory and Statistical Reprot. American Public Power Association, 2301 M St., N.W. Washington, DC 20037-1484. Phone: (202)467-2900 Fax: (202)467-2910 Annual. $90.00. List of more than 2,000 local publicly owned electric utilities in United States and possessions. Formerly (Public Power Directory of Local Publicly Owned Electric Utilities).

Public Power Weekly. American Public Power Association, 2301 M St., N.W. Washington, DC 20037-1484. Phone: (202)467-2900 Fax: (202)467-2910 Weekly. $400.00 per year. Newsletter.

Public Pulse: Roper's Authoritative Report on What Americans are Thinking, D oing, and Buying. Roper Starch Worldwide, 205 E. 42nd St. New York, NY 10017. Phone: (212)599-0700 Fax: (212)687-7008 Monthly. $297.00. Newsletter. Contains news of surveys of American attitudes, values, and behavior. Each issue includes a research supplement giving ''complete facts and figures behind each survey question.''

Public Relations News. Phillips Business Information, Inc., 1201 Seven Locks Rd., Suite 300 Potomac, MD 20854. Phone: 800-777-5006 or (301)340-2100 Fax: (301)340-0542 E-mail: pbi@phillips.com • URL: http://www.phillips.com • Weekly. $347.00 per year. Newsletter on public relations for business, government, and nonprofit organizations.

Public Relations Practices: Managerial Case Studies and Problems. Allen H. Center. Prentice Hall, 240 Frisch Court Paramus, NJ 07652-5240. Phone: 800-947-7700 or (201)909-6200 Fax: 800-445-6991 or (201)909-6361 URL: http://www.prenhall.com • 2000. $46.67. Sixth edition.

Public Relations Quarterly., P.O. Box 311 Rhinebeck, NY 12572. Phone: (914)876-2081 Fax: (914)876-2561 E-mail: hphudson@aol.com • URL: http://www.wwmedia.com/prq/prq.html • Quarterly. $49.00 per year. Opinion articles and case studies on the theory and practice of public relations for and by leading practitioners and academicians.

Public Relations Review: Journal of Research and Comment. JAI Press, P.O. Box 811 Stamford, CT 06904-0811. Phone: (203)323-9606 Fax: (203)357-8446 E-mail: order@jaipress.com • URL: http://www.jaipress.com • Quarterly. Individuals, $125.00 per year; institutions, $296.00 per year. Includes annual *Bibliography.*

Public Relations Society of America.

Public Relations Strategist: Issues and Trends That Affect Management. Public Relations Society of America, 33 Irving Place, 3rd Fl. New York, NY 10003-2376. Phone: (212)995-2230 Fax: (212)995-0757 E-mail: hq@prsa.org • URL: http://www.prssa.org • Quarterly. $48.00 per year. Provides public relations advice for corporate and government executives.

Public Relations Tactics-Register The Blue Book. Public Relations Society of America, 33 Irving Place, 3rd Fl. New York, NY 10003-2376. Phone: (212)995-2230 Fax: (212)995-0757 E-mail: hq@prsa.org • URL: http://www.prssa.org • Annual. $100.00. About 17,000 public relations practioners in business, government, education, etc. who are members. Formerly *Public Relations Journal-Register.*

Public Relations Writer's Handbook. Merry Aronson and Donald E. Spetner. Jossey-Bass, Inc., Publishers, 350 Sansome St. San Francisco, CA 94104. Phone: 888-378-2537 or (415)433-1740 Fax: (415)433-0499 E-mail: webperson@jbp.com • URL: http://www.josseybass.com • 1998. $20.95.

Public Risk. Public Risk Management Association, 1815 N. Fort Meyer Dr., Suite 1020 Arlington, VA 22209-1805. Phone: (703)528-7701 Fax: (703)528-7966 E-mail: info@primacentral.org • URL: http://www.primacentral.org • 10 times a year. $125.00 per year. Covers risk management for state and local governments, including various kinds of liabilities.

Public Risk Management Association., 1815 N. Fort Meyer Dr., Ste. 1020 Arlington, VA 22209-1805. Phone: (703)528-7701 Fax: (703)528-7966 E-mail: info@primacentral.org • URL: http://www.primacentral.org • Members are state and local government officials concerned with risk management and public liabilities.

Public Roads: A Journal of Highway Research and Development. Available from U.S. Government Printing Office, Washington, DC 20402. Phone: (202)512-1800 Fax: (202)512-2250 E-mail: gpoaccess@gpo.gov • URL: http://www.accessgpo.gov • Bimonthly. $18.00 per year.

Public Speaking. Thomas Farrell and Maureen M. Farrell. McGraw-Hill Higher Education, 1221 Ave. of the Americas New York, NY 10020. Phone: 800-722-4726 or (212)904-2000 Fax: (212)904-2072 E-mail: customer.service@mcgraw-hill.com • URL: http://www.mcgraw-hill.com • 1996. $24.95. Third edition.

Public Utilities Fortnightly. Public Utilities Reports, Inc., 8229 Boone Blvd., Suite 401 Vienna, VA 22182. Phone: 800-368-5001 or (703)847-7720 Fax: (703)917-6964 E-mail: pur_info@pur.com • URL: http://www.pur.com • 22 times a year. $129.00 per year. Management magazine for utility executives in electric, gas, telecommunications and water industries.

Public Utility Research Center. University of Florida

Public Welfare. American Public Welfare Association, c/o Publication Services, 810 First St., N.E., Suite 500 Washington, DC 20002-4267. Phone: (202)682-0100 Fax: (202)289-6555 URL: http://www.apwa.org • Quarterly. $35.00 per year.

Public Welfare Directory. American Public Welfare Association, 810 First St., N.E., Suite 500 Washington, DC 20002-4267. Phone: (202)682-0100 Fax: (202)289-6555 URL: http://www.apwa.org • Annual. Members, $75.00; non-members, $80.00. Federal, state, territorial, county, and major municipal human service agencies.

Public Works: City, County and State. Public Works Journal Corp., 200 S. Broad St. Ridgewood, NJ 07451. Phone: 800-524-2364 or (201)445-5800 Fax: (201)445-5170 E-mail: jkircher@pwmag.com • URL: http://www.pwmag.com • 13 times a year. $60.00 per year. Includes *Public Works Manual*.

Public Works Manual. Public Works Journal Corp., 200 S. Broad St. Ridgewood, NJ 07451. Phone: 800-524-2364 or (201)445-5800 Fax: (201)445-5170 E-mail: jkircher@pwmag.com • URL: http://www.pwmag.com • Annual. $45.00. Includes about 3,500 manufacturers and distributors of materials and equipment used in heavy construction. Special issue of (Public Works).

Public Works News. Reynolds Publishing Co., Inc., P.O. Box 578 Glen Echo, MD 20812-0578. Phone: (301)229-2930 Weekly. $520.00 per year.

Publications of the National Institute of Standards and Technology. U.S. Government Printing Office, Washington, DC 20402. Phone: (202)512-1800 Fax: (202)512-2250 E-mail: gpoaccess@gpo.gov • URL: http://www.accessgpo.gov • Annual. Keyword and author indexes.

The Publicity Handbook: How to Maximize Publicity for Products, Services, and Organizations. David Yale. NTC/Contemporary Publishing, P.O. Box 545 Blacklick, OH 43004. Phone: 800-338-3987 or (614)755-4151 Fax: (614)755-5645 E-mail: ntcpub@mcgraw-hill.com • URL: http://www.ntc-cb.com • 1994. $19.95. (NTC Business Books Series).

Publicly Traded Corporations: Governance, Operation, and Regulation. John H. Matheson. West Group, 610 Opperman Dr. Eagan, MN 55123. Phone: 800-328-4880 or (651)687-7000 Fax: 800-213-2323 or (651)687-5827 URL: http://www.westgroup.com • 1993. $130.00. Covers a wide range of corporate legal problems and issues, including shareholder communications and "tender offers and change of control transactions." (Corporate Law Series).

Publish: The Magazine for Electronic Publishing Professionals. International Data Group, 501 Second St., Suite 310 San Francisco, CA 94107. Phone: 800-656-7995 or (415)243-0600 Fax: (415)442-1891 E-mail: mnaman@publish.com • URL: http://www.publish.com/ • Monthly. $39.90 per year. Edited for electronic publishing professionals. Covers new technologies and new products.

Publishers' Auxiliary. National Newspaper Association, 1010 N. Glebe Rd., Suite 450 Arlington, VA 22209-4749. Phone: 800-829-4662 or (703)907-7900 E-mail: pubaux@nna.org • Biweekly. $85.00 per year.

Publishers' Catalogues Home Page. Northern Lights Internet Solutions Ltd.Phone: (306)931-0020 Fax: (306)931-7667 E-mail: info@lights.com • URL: http://www.lights.com/publisher • Provides links to the Web home pages of about 1,700 U. S. publishers (including about 80 University presses) and publishers in 48 foreign countries. "International/Multinational Publishers" are included, such as the International Monetary Fund, the World Bank, and the World Trade Organization. Publishers are arranged in convenient alphabetical lists. Searching is offered. Fees: Free.

Publishers Directory: A Guide to New and Established Private and Special-Interest, Avant-Garde and Alternative, Organizational Association, Government and Institution Presses. The Gale Group, 27500 Drake Rd. Farmington Hills, MI 48331-3535. Phone: 800-877-GALE or (248)699-GALE Fax: 800-414-5043 or (248)699-8069 E-mail: galeord@galegroup.com • URL: http://www.galegroup.com • 2000. $400.00. 23rd edition. Contains detailed information on more than 20,000 U.S. and Canadian publishers as well as small, independent presses.

Publishers, Distributors, and Wholesalers of the United States: A Directory of Publishers, Distributors, Associations, Wholesalers, Software Producers and Manufactureres Listing Editorial and Ordering Addresses, and and ISBN Publisher Prefi. R. R. Bowker, 121 Chanlon Rd. New Providence, NJ 07974. Phone: 888-269-5372 or (908)464-6800 Fax: (908)771-7704 E-mail: info@bowker.com • URL: http://www.bowker.com • Annual. $229.00. Two volumes. Lists more than 101,000 publishers, book distributors, and wholesalers. Includes museum and association imprints, inactive publishers, and publishers' fields of activity.

Publishers Information Bureau.

Publishers' International ISBN Directory. Available from The Gale Group, 27500 Drake Rd. Farmington Hills, MI 48331-3535. Phone: 800-699-4253 or (248)699-4253 Fax: (248)699-8069 E-mail: galeord@galegroup.com • URL: http://www.galegroup.com • Annual. $425.00. Three volumes. Compiled by the International ISBN Agency and published by K. G. Saur. Provides names and addresses of over 426,000 publishers in the United States and 210 other countries. Three sections: alphabetical, geographic, and ISBN number. Formerly *International ISBN Publishers' Directory*. Published by K. G. Saur.

Publishers' Trade List Annual: A Buying and Reference Guide to Books and Related Products. R. R. Bowker, 121 Chanlon Rd. New Providence, NJ 07974. Phone: 888-269-5372 or (908)464-6800 Fax: (908)771-7704 E-mail: info@bowker.com • URL: http://www.bowker.com • Annual. $315.00. Three volumes. About 1,000 publishers in the United States, with their catalogs.

Publishers Weekly: The International News Magazine of Book Publishing. Cahners Business Information, Broadcasting and Cables International Group, 245 W. 17th St. New York, NY 10011-5300. Phone: 800-662-7776 or (212)645-0067 Fax: (212)463-6631 E-mail: corporatecommunications@cahners.com • URL: http://www.cahners.com • Weekly. $189.00 per year. The international news magazine of book publishing.

PubList.com: The Internet Directory of Publications. Bowes & Associates, Inc.Phone: (781)792-0999 Fax: (781)792-0988 E-mail: info@publist.com • URL: http://www.publist.com • "The premier online global resource for information about print and electronic publications." Provides online searching for information on more than 150,000 magazines, journals, newsletters, e-journals, and monographs. Database entries generally include title, publisher, format, address, editor, circulation, subject, and International Standard Serial Number (ISSN). Fees: Free.

Pulp and Paper. Miller Freeman, Inc., 600 Harrison St. San Francisco, CA 94107. Phone: (415)905-2200 Fax: (415)905-2232 E-mail: mfibooks@mfi.com • URL: http://www.mfi.com • Monthly. $135.00 per year.

Pulp and Paper Buyer's Guide. Miller Freeman, Inc., 600 Harrison St. San Francisco, CA 94107. Phone: (415)905-2200 Fax: (415)905-2232 E-mail: mfibooks@mfi.com • URL: http://www.mfi.com • Annual. $155.00. Supplies and equipment.

Pulp and Paper Canada. Pulp and Paper Technical Association of Canada. Southam Magazine Group, One Holiday St., East Tower, Ste. 705 Pointe-Claire, QC, Canada PQ H9R 5N3. Phone: (514)630-5955 Fax: (514)630-5980 Monthly. $73.00 per year.

The Pulp and Paper Industry in the OECD Member Countries. Organization for Economic Cooperation and Development. Available from OECD Publications and Information Center, 2001 L St., N. W., Suite. 650 Washington, DC 20036-4922. Phone: 800-456-6323 or (202)785-6323 Fax: (202)785-0350 E-mail: washington.contact@oecd.org • URL: http://www.oecd.org • Annual. $31.00. Presents annual data on production, consumption, capacity, utilization, and foreign trade. Covers 33 pulp and paper products in OECD countries. Text in English and French.

Pulp and Paper International. Miller Freeman, Inc., 600 Harrison St. San Francisco, CA 94107. Phone: (415)905-2200 Fax: (415)905-2232 E-mail: mfibooks@mfi.com • URL: http://www.mfi.com • Monthly. Free to qualified personnel; others, $130.00 per year.

Pulp and Paper Laboratory. North Carolina State University

Pulp and Paper Week. Miller Freeman, Inc., 600 Harrison St. San Francisco, CA 94107. Phone: (415)905-2200 Fax: (415)905-2232 E-mail: mfibooks@mfi.com • URL: http://www.mfi.com • 48 times a year. $737.00 per year. Newsletter.

Pump Application Desk Book. Paul N. Garay. Prentice Hall, 240 Frisch Court Paramus, NJ 07652-5240. Phone: 800-947-7700 or (201)909-6200 Fax: 800-445-6991 or (201)909-6361 URL: http://www.prenhall.com • 1996. $82.00. Third edition.

Pumps and Compressors. U. S. Bureau of the Census, Washington, DC 20233-0800. Phone: (301)457-4100 Fax: (301)457-3842 URL: http://www.census.gov • Annual. Provides data on value of manufacturers' shipments, quantity, exports, imports, etc. (Current Industrial Reports, MA-35P.)

Puns Corps. c/o Robert L. Birch.

Purchasers Guide to the Music Industries. Music Trades Corp., c/o Paul Majeski, P.O. Box 432 Englewood, NJ 07631. Phone: (201)871-1965 Annual. Available only with subscription to *Music Trades*.

Purchasing and Materials Management. Michiel R. Leenders and Harold E. Fearon. McGraw-Hill Professional, 1221 Ave. of the Americas New York, NY 10020. Phone: 800-722-4726 or (212)904-2000 Fax: (212)904-2072 E-mail: customer.service@mcgraw-hill.com • URL: http://www.mcgraw-hill.com • 1996. $71.75. 11th edition.

Purchasing and Supply Management. P. J. Baily. Chapman and Hall, 115 Fifth Ave., 4th Fl. New York, NY 10003-1004. Phone: 800-842-3636 or (212)260-1354 Fax: (212)260-1730 E-mail: info@chapall.com • URL: http://www.chapall.com • 1987. $34.95. Fifth edition.

Purchasing/CPI Chemicals Yellow Pages. Cahners Publishing Co., 275 Washington St. Newton, MA 02158-1630. Phone: 800-662-7776 or (617)964-3030 Fax: (617)558-4700 E-mail: marketaccess@cahners.com • URL: http://www.com • Annual. $85.00. Manufacturers and distributors of 10,000 chemicals and raw materials, containers and packaging, transportation services and storage facilities; includes environmental servicer companies. Formerly *CPI Purchasing-Chemicals Directory*.

Purchasing: The Magazine of Total Supply Chain Management. Cahners Business Information, 275 Washington St. Newton, MA 02458-1630. Phone: 800-662-7776 or (617)946-3030 Fax: (617)558-4327 E-mail: corporatecommunications@cahners.com • URL: http://www.cahners.com • 19 times a year. $99.90 per year.

Purchasing Today: For the Purchasing and Supply Professional. National Association of Purchasing Management, PO Box 22160 Tempe, AZ 85285-9781. Phone: 800-888-6276 or (480)752-6276 Fax: (480)752-7890 URL: http://www.napm.org • Monthly. $24.00 per year to libraries. Includes special issues on logistics, transportation, cost management, and supply chain management.

Putting Total Quality Management to Work: What TQM Means, How to Use It, and How to Sustain It Over the Long Run. Marshall Sashkin and Kenneth J. Kiser. Berrett-Koehler Publications, Inc., 450 Sansome St., Suite 1200 San Francisco, CA 94111-3320. Phone: 800-929-2929 or (415)288-0260 Fax: (415)362-2512 E-mail: bkpub@bkpubl.com • URL: http://www.bkconnection.com • 1993. $19.95. Includes control charts, flow charts, scatter diagrams, and criteria for the Baldridge Quality Award.

PVC Furniture Manufacturing. Entrepreneur Media, Inc., 2445 McCabe Way Irvine, CA 92614. Phone: 800-421-2300 or (949)261-2325 Fax: (949)261-0234 E-mail: entmag@entrepreneur.com • URL: http://www.entrepreneur.com • Looseleaf. $59.50. A practical guide to starting a business for the manufacture of plastic furniture. Covers profit potential, start-up costs, market size evaluation, owner's time required, site selection, lease negotiation, pricing, accounting, advertising, promotion, etc. (Start-Up Business Guide No. E1262.)

QSR: The Magazine of Quick Service Restaurant Success. Journalistic, Inc., 4905 Pine Cone Drive, Suite Two Durham, NC 27707. Phone: (919)489-1916 Fax: (919)489-4767 URL: http://www.qsrmagazine.com • Nine times a year. $32.00 per year. Provides news and management advice for quick-service restaurants, including franchisors and franchisees.

Quadrilingual Economics Dictionary: English/American, French, German, Dutch. Frits J. de Jong and others, editors. Kluwer Academic Publishers, 101 Philip Dr. Norwell, MA 02061. Phone: (781)871-6600 Fax: (781)871-6528 E-mail: kluwer@wkap.com • URL: http://www.wkap.com • 1981. $234.00.

Quality and Reliability Engineering International. Available from John Wiley and Sons, Inc., Journals Div., 605 Third Ave. New York, NY 10158-0012. Phone: 800-526-5368 or (212)850-6000 Fax: (212)850-6088 E-mail: info@wiley.com • URL: http://www.wiley.com • Bimonthly. $1,145.00 per year. Designed to bridge the gap between existing theoretical methods and scientific research on the one hand, and current industrial practices on the other. Published in England by John Wiley and Sons Ltd.

Quality Bakers of America Cooperative Laboratory.

Quality-Buyers Guide for; QA/QC Equipment. Cahners Business Information, 2000 Clearwater Dr. Oak Brook, IL 60523. Phone: 800-662-7776 or (630)320-7000 Fax: (630)320-7150 E-mail: corporatecommunications@cahners.com • URL: http://www.cahners.com • Annual. $15.00. List of manufacturers and distributors of quality control equipment for measurement, inspection, data analysis evaluation and destructive and nondestructive testing; also lists testing laboratories, consultants, software and training organizations. Formerly *Quality Buyers Guide for Test, Inspection, Measurement and Evaluation*.

Quality Control. Dale H. Besterfield. Prentice Hall, 240 Frisch Court Paramus, NJ 07652-5240. Phone: 800-947-7700 or (201)909-6200 Fax: 800-445-6991 or (201)909-6361 URL: http://www.prenhall.com • 2000. $78.67. Sixth edition. Covers basic quality control concepts and procedures, including statistical process control (SPC). Includes disk.

Quality Management. Bureau of Business Practice, Inc., 24 Rope Ferry Rd. Waterford, CT 06386. Phone: 800-243-0876 or (860)442-4365 Fax: (860)437-3555 E-mail: rebecca_armitage@prenhall.com • URL: http://www.bbpnews.com • Semimonthly. $167.00 per year. Newsletter. Covers news of quality management issues and trends. Formerly *Quality Assurance Bulletin*.

Quality Management Journal. American Society for Quality, P.O. Box 3005 Milwaukee, WI 53201-3005. Phone: 800-248-1946 or (414)272-8575 Fax: (414)272-1734 URL: http://www.asq.org • Quarterly. Members, $50.00 per year; non-members, $60.00 per year. Emphasizes research in quality control and management.

Quality Manager's Complete Guide to ISO 9000. Richard B. Clements. Prentice Hall, 240 Frisch Ct. Paramus, NJ 07652-5240. Phone: 800-947-7700 or (201)909-6452 Fax: 800-445-6991 URL: http://www.prenhall.com • 1996. $39.95. Third edition.

Quality Manager's Complete Guide to ISO 9000: 2000 Edition. Richard B. Clements. Prentice Hall, 240 Frisch Ct. Paramus, NJ 07652-5240. Phone: 800-947-7700 or (201)909-6452 Fax: 800-445-6991 URL: http://www.prenhall.com • 2000. $39.95. Supplement to *Quality Manager's Complete Guide to ISO 9000* (third edition).

Quality Movement: What Total Quality Management is All About. Helga Drummond. Nichols Publishing Co., P.O. Box 6036 East Brunswick, NJ 08816-6036. Phone: (732)297-2862 Fax: (732)940-0549 1992. $14.95.

Quality of Cotton Report. Agricultural Marketing Service. U.S. Department of Agriculture, Washington, DC 20250. Phone: (202)720-2791 Weekly.

Quality Planning and Analysis. Joseph M. Juran. McGraw-Hill, 1221 Ave. of the Americas New York, NY 10020-1095. Phone: 800-722-4726 or (212)904-2000 Fax: (212)904-2072 E-mail: customer.service@mcgraw-hill.com • URL: http://www.mcgraw-hill.com • 1993. $90.63. Third edition.

Quality Progress. American Society for Quality, P.O. Box 3005 Milwaukee, WI 53201-3005. Phone: 800-248-1946 or (414)272-8575 Fax: (414)272-1734 URL: http://www.asq.org • Monthly. $50.00 per year. Covers developments in quality improvement throughout the world.

Quality Progress: QA/QC Services Directory. American Society for Quality, P.O. Box 3005 Milwaukee, WI 53201-3005. Phone: 800-248-1946 or (414)272-8575 Fax: (414)272-1734 E-mail: asq@asq.org • URL: http://www.asq.org • Annual. $12.00. Provides information on companies offering services related to quality management, such as consulting, inspection, auditing, calibrating, and training.

Quality Progress: Quality Assurance and Quality Control Software Directory. American Society for Quality, P.O. Box 3005 Milwaukee, WI 53201-3005. Phone: 800-248-1946 or (414)272-8575 Fax: (414)272-1734 E-mail: asq@asq.org • URL: http://www.asq.org • Annual. Price on application. Covers computer software application packages related to quality management. Includes information about software companies and descriptions of programs offered. Formerly *Quality Progress Directory of Software for Quality Assurance and Quality Contol*.

Quantitative Finance. Available from IOP Publishing, Inc., Public Ledger Building, Suite 1035, 150 South Independence Mall West Philadelphia, PA 19106. Phone: 800-358-4677 or (215)627-0880 Fax: (215)627-0879 E-mail: info@ioppubusa.com • URL: http://www.iop.org/journals/quant • Bimonthly. $199.00 per year. Published in the UK by the Institute of Physics. A technical journal on the use of quantitative tools and applications in financial analysis and financial engineering. Covers such topics as portfolio theory, derivatives, asset allocation, return on assets, risk management, price volatility, financial econometrics, market anomalies, and trading systems.

Quantitative Methods for Business Decisions:with cases. Lawrence L. Lapin. Wadsworth Publishing Co., 10 Davis Dr. Belmont, CA 94002. Phone: 800-354-9706 or (650)595-2350 Fax: (650)637-9955 URL: http://www.wadsworth.com • 1995. $75.95. Sixth edition.

Quantum PC Report for CPAs. Quantum Professional Publishing, Seven Fourth St., Suite 4 Petaluma, CA 94952. Phone: 800-325-8858 or (707)763-3500 Fax: (707)763-5800 E-mail: info@quantum.org • URL: http://www.quantum.org • Monthly. $235.00 per year. Newsletter on personal computer software and hardware for the accounting profession.

Quarry Management: The Monthly Journal for the Quarrying, Asphalt, Concrete and Recycling Industries. Institute of Quarrying. QMJ Publishing Ltd., Seven Regent St. Nottingham NG1 5BS, England. Phone: 44 115 9411315 Fax: 44 115 9484035 E-mail: mail@qmj.co.uk • URL: http://www.qmj.co.uk • Monthly. $60.00 per year.

Quarterly Analysis of Failures. Dun & Bradstreet, Economic Analysis Dept., The Sylvan Way Parisppany, NJ 07054-3896. Phone: 800-526-0651 or (973)455-0900 Fax: (973)254-4063 E-mail: customerservice@dnb.com • URL: http://www.dnb.com • Quarterly. $20.00.

Quarterly Coal Report. Energy Information Administration, U.S. Department of Energy. Available from U.S. Government Printing Office, Washington, DC 20402. Phone: (202)512-1800 Fax: (202)512-2250 E-mail: gpoaccess@gpo.gov • URL: http://www.accessgpo.gov • Quarterly. $30.00 per year. Annual summary.

Quarterly Financial Report for Manufacturing, Mining, and Trade Corporations. U.S. Federal Trade Commission and U.S. Securities and Exchange Commission. Available from U.S. Government Printing Office, Washington, DC 20402. Phone: (202)512-1800 Fax: (202)512-2250 E-mail: gpoaccess@gpo.gov • URL: http://www.accessgpo.gov • Quarterly. $39.00 per year.

Quarterly Journal of Business and Economics. University of Nebraska at Lincoln, College of Business Administration, CBA Bldg. Lincoln, NE 68588-0407. Phone: (402)472-3309 Fax: (402)472-9777 E-mail: myoung1@unl.edu • URL: http://www.cba.unl.edu • Quarterly. Individuals, $16.00 per year; institutions, $30.00 per year.

Quarterly Journal of Economics. Harvard University, Dept. of Economics. MIT Press, Five Cambridge Center Cambridge, MA 02142-1493. Phone: 800-356-0343 or (617)253-2864 Fax: (617)253-1545 E-mail: journals-orders@mit.edu • URL: http://www.mitpress.mit.edu • Quarterly. Individuals, $40.00 per year; Instutions, $148.00 per year.

Quarterly Labour Force Statistics. Organization for Economic Cooperation and Development. Available from OECD Publications and Information Center, 2001 L St., N. W., Suite 650 Washington, DC 20036-4922. Phone: 800-456-6323 or (202)785-6323 Fax: (202)785-0350 E-mail: washington.contact@oecd.org • URL: http://www.oecd.org • Quarterly. $60.00 per year. Provides current data for OECD member countries on population, employment, unemployment, civilian labor force, armed forces, and other labor factors.

Quarterly Market Report. CB Richard Ellis, 353 Sacramento St., Suite 1900 San Francisco, CA 94111. Phone: 800-992-7257 or (415)986-7255 URL: http://www.realestateindex.com • Quarterly. Price on application. Newsletter. Reviews current prices, rents, capitalization rates, and occupancy trends for commercial real estate.

Quarterly Mining Review. National Mining Association, 1130 17th St., N. W. Washington, DC 20036-4677. Phone: (202)463-2625 Fax: (202)463-6152 E-mail: rlawson@nma.org • URL: http://www.nma.org • Quarterly. $300.00 per year. Contains detailed data on production, shipments, consumption, stockpiles, and trade for coal and various minerals. (Publisher formerly National Coal Association.)

Quarterly Operating Data of 68 Telephone Carriers. Federal Communications Commission, 1919 M St., N.W. Washington, DC 20554. Phone: (202)418-0200 Quarterly.

Quarterly Pension Investment Report. Employee Benefit Research Institute, 2121 K St., N. W., Suite 600 Washington, DC 20037-1986. Phone: (202)659-0670 Fax: (202)775-6312 E-mail: info@ebri.org • URL: http://www.ebri.org • Quarterly. $1,500.00 per year. $400.00 per year to nonprofit organizations. Provides aggregate financial asset data for U. S. private and public pension systems. Statistics are given for both defined contribution and defined benefit plans, including investment mixes (stocks, bonds, cash, other). Contains historical data for private trust, life insurance, and state and local government funds.

Quarterly Report on Money Fund Performance. IBC-Donoghue, Inc., P.O. 9104 Ashland, MA 01721-9104. Phone: 800-343-5413 or (508)881-2800 Fax: (508)881-0982 URL: http://www.ibcdata.com • Quarterly. $525.00 per year. Provides expense ratio and yield data for about 1,000 money market funds in the U. S.

The Quarterly Review of Economics and Finance. University of Illinois at Urbana-Champaign, Bureau of Economics and Business Res. Available from JAI Press, Inc., P.O. Box 811 Stamford, CT 06904-0811. Phone: (203)323-9606 Fax: (203)357-8446 E-mail: order@jaipress.com • URL: http://www.jaipress.com • Five times a year. $349.00 per year. Includes annual supplement. Formerly *Quarterly Review of Economics and Business*.

Quebec Dairy Herd Analyses Service.

The Questers., 210 S. Quince St. Philadelphia, PA 19107. Phone: (215)923-5183 For the study and appreciation of antiques.

Questions and Answers on Real Estate. Robert W. Semenow. Prentice Hall, 240 Frisch Court Paramus, NJ 07652-5240. Phone: 800-947-7700 or (201)909-6200 Fax: 800-445-6991 or (201)909-6361 URL: http://www.prenhall.com • 1993. $24.95. Tenth edition.

Quick Caller Area Air Cargo Directories. Fourth Seacoast Publishing Co., Inc., P.O. Box 145 St. Clair Shores, MI 48080. Phone: (810)779-5570 Fax: (908)771-8736 E-mail: quickcal@ix.netcom.com • Annual. $16.00 for each regional edition. Six regionals. Reference source for the air cargo industry.

Quick Frozen Foods Annual Directory of Frozen Food Processors and Buyers' Guide. Saul Beck Publications, 271 Madison Ave. New York, NY 10016. Phone: (212)557-8600 Fax: (212)986-9868 Annual. $130.00. Lists 10,500 frozen food processors; suppliers of freezing and food processing machinery, equipment, and supplies; broker locaters, refrigerated warehouses, truck and rail freight lines, and packaging systems handling frozen food.

Quick Frozen Foods International. E.W. Williams Publications Co., 2125 Center Ave., Suite 305 Fort Lee, NJ 07024. Phone: (201)532-9290 Fax: (201)779-8345 Quarterly. $38.00 per year. Text in English, summaries in French and German.

Quick Printing: The Information Source for Commercial Copyshops and Printshops. Cygnus Business Media, 445 Broad Hollow Rd. Melville, NY 11747. Phone: 800-308-6397 or (631)845-2700 Fax: (631)845-2798 E-mail: rich.reiff@cygnuspub.com • URL: http://www.cygnuspub.com • Monthly. $48.00 per year.

Quill and Scroll. International Honorary Society for High School Journalists. Quill and Scroll Society, School of Journalism and Mass Communication, University of Iowa Iowa City, IA 52242. Phone: (319)335-5795 Fax: (319)335-5210 URL: http://www.uiowa.edu/ • Quarterly. $13.00 per year. Devoted exclusively to the field of high school publications.

Quill and Scroll Society. School of Journalism. University of Iowa

Quill: The Magazine for Journalists. Society of Professional Journalists, P.O. Box 77 Greencastle, IN 46135-0077. Phone: (765)653-3333 Fax: (765)653-4631 E-mail: spj@spjhq.org • URL: http://www.spj.org • Monthly. $29.00 per year. A magazine for journalists.

The Quintessential Searcher: The Wit and Wisdom of Barbara Quint. Marylaine Block, editor. Information Today, Inc., 143 Old Marlton Pike Medford, NJ 08055-8750. Phone: 800-300-9868 or (609)654-6266 Fax: (609)654-4309 E-mail: custserv@infotoday.com • URL: http://www.infotoday.com • 2001. $19.95. Presents the sayings of Barbara Quint, editor of *Searcher* magazine, who is often critical of the online information industry. (CyberAge Books.)

R and D Contracts Monthly (Research and Development): A Continuously Up-dated Sales nd R and D Tool For All Research Organizations and Manufacturers. Government Data Publications, Inc., 1155 Connecticut Ave., N.W. Washington, DC 20036. Phone: (718)627-0819 Fax: (718)998-5960 Monthly. $96.00 per year. Lists recently awarded government contracts. Annual *Directory* available.

R and I Blue Book (Recognition and Identification). Engravers Journal, Inc., P.O. Box 318 Brighton, MI 48116. Phone: (810)229-5725 Fax: (810)229-8320 Price on application. Annual. Over 200 manufacturers and suppliers of trophies, plaques, engraving and marking equipment and supplies to the recognition and identification (R&I) industry. Formerly *Awards Specialist Directory*.

R E Magazine (Rural Electrification). National Rural Electric Cooperative Association, 4301 Wilson Blvd. Arlington, VA 22203-1860. Phone: (703)907-5500 E-mail: nreca@nreca.org • Monthly. Free to members; non-members, $50.00 per year. News and information about the rural electric utility industry. Formerly *Rural Electrification*.

The R V D A Membership Directory. Recreation Vehicle Dealers Association of North America, 3930 University Dr., No. 100 Fairfax, VA 22030-2515. Phone: (703)591-7130 Fax: (703)591-0734 E-mail: rvdanat@aol.com • Annual. Members, $20.00; non-members, $100.00. Over 900 retail sales firms. Formerly *Recreation Vehicle Dealers Association Membership Directory*.

Radio Advertising Bureau.

Radio Advertising Source. SRDS, 1700 Higgins Rd. Des Plaines, IL 60018. Phone: 800-851-7737 or (847)375-5000 Fax: (847)375-5001 E-mail: rcoop@srds.com • URL: http://www.srds.com • Quarterly. $490.00 per year. Contains detailed information on U. S. radio stations, networks, and corporate owners, with maps of market areas. Includes key personnel.

Radio Advertising: The Authoritative Guide. Pete Schulberg. NTC/Contemporary Publishing, P.O. Box 545 Blacklick, OH 43004. Phone: 800-388-3987 or (614)755-4151 Fax: (614)755-5645 E-mail: ntcpub@mcgraw-hill.com • URL: http://www.ntc-cb.com • 1994. $29.95. Second edition. (NTC Business Book Series).

Radio & Records. Radio & Records, Inc., 10100 Santa Monica Blvd. Los Angeles, CA 90067. Phone: (310)553-4330 Fax: (310)203-8450 Weekly. $299.00 per year. Provides news and information relating to the record industry and to regional and national radio broadcasting. Special features cover specific types of programming, such as "classic rock," "adult alternative," "oldies," "country," and "news/talk." Radio station business and management topics are included.

Radio and Television Commercial. Albert C. Book and others. NTC/Contemporary Publishing, P.O. Box 545 Blacklick, OH 43004. Phone: 800-338-3987 or (614)755-4151 Fax: (614)755-5645 E-mail: ntcpub@mcgraw-hill.com • URL: http://www.ntc-cb.com • 1995. $19.95. Third revised edition. How to guide showing how to create effective radio and television advertisements. (NTC Business Book Series).

Radio Business Report. RBR, 6208-B Old Franconia Rd. Alexandria, VA 22310. Phone: (703)719-9500 Fax: (703)719-7910 URL: http://www.rbr.com • Weekly. $220.00 per year. Covers radio advertising, FCC regulations, audience ratings, market research, station management, business conditions, and related topics.

Radio Co-op Directory. Radio Advertising Bureau, 1320 Greenway Dr., Ste. 500 Irving, TX 75038. Phone: 800-232-3131 or (972)753-6786 Fax: (972)753-6727 E-mail: bbarr@rab.com • URL: http://www.rab.com • Annual. $199.00.

Lists over 5,000 manufacturers providing cooperative allowances for radio advertising.

Radio Facts. Radio Advertising Bureau, 261 Madison Ave., 23rd Fl. New York, NY 10016. Phone: 800-232-3131 or (212)681-7200 Fax: (212)681-7223 URL: http://www.rab.com • Annual. $50.00.

Radio Financial Report. National Association of Broadcasters, 1771 N St., N. W. Washington, DC 20036-2891. Phone: 800-368-5644 or (202)429-5373 Fax: (202)775-3515 1993. $225.00.

Radio World. IMAS Publishing, 5827 Columbia Pike, Suite 310 Falls Church, VA 22041. Phone: 800-336-3045 or (703)998-7600 Fax: (703)820-3310 E-mail: adsales@imaspub.com • URL: http://www.imaspub.com • Biweekly. $59.00 per year. Emphasis is on radio broadcast engineering and equipment. Text in English, Portuguese and Spanish.

Radioisotope Laboratory. Texas A&M University

Radiological Society of North America., 820 Jorie Blvd. Oak Brook, IL 60523-2251. Phone: (630)571-2670 Fax: (630)571-7837 URL: http://www.rsna.org • Members are radiologists and scientists. Includes a Technical Exhibits Committee and a Scientific Exhibits Committee.

Radiology and Imaging Letter. Lippincott Williams and Wilkins Publishers, 227 E. Washington Square Philadelphia, PA 19106-3780. Phone: 800-777-2295 or (215)238-4200 Fax: (215)238-4227 URL: http://www.1rpub.com • 22 times a year. Individuals, $363.00 per year; institutions, $425.00 per year. Edited for radiologists, technicians, hospital administrators, and medical equipment manufacturers. Provides imformation on advances in medical imaging technology

Radiology Business Management Association., 1550 S. Coast Highway, Suite 201 Laguna Beach, CA 92651. Phone: 888-224-7262 Fax: (949)376-2246 URL: http://www.rbma.org • Members include vendors of X-ray equipment, services, and supplies.

Radiology Reference Guide. Access Publishing Co., 1301 W. Park Ave. Ocean, NJ 07712. Phone: 800-458-0990 or (732)493-8811 Fax: (732)493-9713 E-mail: access@accesspub.com • URL: http://www.accesspub.com • Annual. Price on application. Includes directory information for radiological equipment, supplies, services, organizations, and publications.

Ragan's Annual Report Review. Lawence Ragan Communications, Inc., 316 N. Michigan Ave. Chicago, IL 60601. Phone: 800-878-5331 or (312)960-4100 Fax: (312)960-4106 E-mail: cservice@ragan.com • URL: http://www.ragan.com • Monthly. $287.00 per year. Newsletter on business trends and tactics as reflected in corporate annual reports. Formerly *Corporate Annual Report*.

Ragan's Journal of Business Intelligence. Lawence Ragan Communications, Inc., 316 N. Michigan Ave., Suite 300 Chicago, IL 60601. Phone: 800-878-5331 or (312)960-4100 Fax: (312)960-4106 E-mail: cservice@ragan.com • URL: http://www.ragan.com • Bimonthly. $199.00 per year. Includes articles on competitive intelligence, knowledge management, legalities, ethics, and counterintelligence.

Railroad Facts. Association of American Railroads, American Railroads Bldg., 50 F St., N.W. Washington, DC 20001. Phone: (202)639-2100 Fax: (202)639-2156 URL: http://www.aar.org • Annual.

Railway Age. Simmons-Boardman Publishing Corp., 345 Hudson St. New York, NY 10014-4502. Phone: (212)620-7200 Fax: (212)633-1165 Monthly. $50.00 per year.

Railway Directory: A Railway Gazette Yearbook. Reed Business Information, Quadrant House, The Quadrant, Brighton Rd. Sutton SM2 5AS Surrey, England. Phone: 44 1816 523500 Fax: 44 1816 528975 URL: http://www.railgaz.co.uk • Annual. $255.00. Lists approximately 14,000 senior personnel from railroads worldwide and over 1,800 manufacturers, suppliers and consultants in the railroad industry.

Railway Engineering-Maintenance Suppliers Association.

Railway Progress Institute.

Railway Supply Association.

Railway Systems Suppliers, Inc.

Railway Track and Structures. Simmons-Boardman Publishing Corp., 345 Hudson St. New York, NY 10014-4502. Phone: (212)620-7200 Fax: (212)633-1165 Monthly. Qualified railroad personnel, $14.00 per year; others, $30.00 per year.

Raise More Money for Your Nonprofit Organization: A Guide to Evaluating and Improving Your Fundraising. Anne L. New. The Foundation Center, 79 Fifth Ave. New York, NY 10003-3076. Phone: 800-424-9836 or (212)620-4230 Fax: (212)807-3677 E-mail: mfn@fdncenter.org • URL: http://www.fdncenter.org • 1991. $14.95.

Raising Money for Academic and Research Libraries: A How-To- Do-It Manual for Librarians. Barbara I. Dewey, editor. Neal-Schuman Publishers, Inc., 100 Varick St. New York, NY 10013. Phone: (212)925-8650 Fax: 800-584-2414 E-mail: info@neal-schuman.com • URL: http://www.neal-schuman.com • 1991. $45.00. (How-to-Do-It Series).

RAND.

Random Lengths: The Weekly Report on North American Forest Products Markets. Random Lengths Publications, Inc., P.O. Box 867 Eugene, OR 97440-0867. Phone: (541)686-9925 Fax: 800-874-7979 E-mail: rlmail@randomlengths.com • URL: http://www.randomlengths.com • Weekly. $249.50 per year. Newsletter. Information covering the wood products industry. Supplement available *Random Lengths Midweek Market Report*.

A Random Walk Down Wall Street: Including a Life-Cycle Guide to Personal Investing. Burton G. Malkiel. W. W. Norton & Co., Inc., 500 Fifth Ave. New York, NY 10110-0017. Phone: 800-223-2584 or (212)354-5500 Fax: (212)869-0856 E-mail: webmaster@wwnorton.com • URL: http://www.norton.com • 1999. $29.95. Seventh edition.

Ranking the Banks. American Banker, One State St. Plaza New York, NY 10004. Phone: 800-362-3806 or (212)803-8345 Fax: (212)292-5217 URL: http://www.americanbanker.com • Annual. Price on application. Ranks domestic and foreign banks by 75 financial parameters.

RAPRA Abstracts. RAPRA Technology Ltd., Shawbury Shrewsbury SY4 4NR Shrops, England. Phone: 44 1939 250383 or 44 1939 251118 E-mail: ruth@rapra.net • URL: http://www.rapra.net • Monthly. $2,465.00 per year. Up-to-date survey of current international information relevant to the rubber, plastics and associated industries.

Rare Earth Bulletin. Multi-Science Publishing Co. Ltd., P.O. Box 176 Avenel, NJ 07001. Bimonthly. $212.00 per year.

Rare Earth Research Conference. c/o Professor Larry Thomson

Rare Fruit Council International.

RateGram: A Compendium of the Nation's Highest Federally Insured Rates. Bradshaw Group Ltd., P.O. Box 264 Roslyn, NY 11576-0264. Phone: (415)479-3815 Biweekly. Individuals, $395.00 per year; libraries, $195.00 per year. Newsletter. Quotes highest interest rates available, with safety ratings, according to a survey of about 10,000 federally insured banks and savings institutions. Covers a wide variety of rates, although most space is devoted to insured certificates of deposit. Also covers foreign exchange rates, foreign interest rates, and foreign government long term bond yields.

Ratings Guide to Life, Health and Annuity Insurers. Weiss Ratings, Inc., 4176 Burns Rd. Palm Beach, FL 33410-4606. Phone: 800-289-9222 or (561)627-3300 Fax: (561)625-6685 E-mail: wr@weissinc.com • URL: http://www.weissratings.com • Quarterly. $438.00 per year. Rates life insurance companies for overall safety and financial stability. Formerly *Weiss Ratings' Guide to Life, Health and Annuity Insurers*.

Rauch Guide to the U. S. Ink Industry. Impact Marketing Consultants, P.O. Box 1226 Manchester Center, VT 05255. Phone: (802)362-2325 Fax: (802)362-3693 E-mail: impactmkt@compuserve.com • URL: http://www.impactmarket.com • $389.00. Looseleaf. 250 leading ink manufacturers with over $1 million in annual sales; and lists of activities, organizations, and sources of information in the ink industry. Formerly *Kline Guide to the U.S. Ink Industry*.

Rauch Guide to the U.S. Paint Industry. Carl Verbanic and Donald Dykes. Impact Marketing Consultants, P.O. Box 1226 Manchester Center, VT 05255. Phone: (802)362-2325 Fax: (802)362-3693 E-mail: impactmkt@compuserve.com • URL: http://www.impactmarket.com • $389.00. Looseleaf. Includes market data in addition to directory information. Formerly *Kline Guide to the Paint Industry*.

Ray W. Herrick Laboratories.

RCR (Radio Communications Report): The Newspaper for the Wireless Communications Industry. RCR Publications/Crain Communications, 777 East Speer Blvd. Denver, CO 80203. Phone: (303)733-2500 Fax: (303)733-2244 URL: http://www.rcrnews.com • Weekly. $39.00 per year. Covers news of the wireless communications industry, including business and financial developments.

Readers' Guide Abstracts Online. H. W. Wilson Co., 950 University Ave. Bronx, NY 10452. Phone: 800-367-6770 or (718)588-8400 Fax: (718)590-1617 URL: http://www.hwwilson.com • Indexes and abstracts general interest periodicals, 1983 to date. Weekly updates. Inquire as to online cost and availability.

Readers' Guide to Periodical Literature. H. W. Wilson Co., 950 University Ave. Bronx, NY 10452. Phone: 800-367-6770 or (718)588-8400 Fax: (718)590-1617 E-mail: custserv@hwwilson.com • URL: http://www.hwwilson.com • Monthly. $220.00 per year. CD-ROM edition, $1,495 per year, including annual cumulation. Indexes about 250 periodicals of general interest.

Real Estate. Larry E. Wofford and Terrance M. Clauretie. John Wiley and Sons, Inc., 605 Third Ave. New York, NY 10158-0012. Phone: 800-526-5368 or (212)850-6000 Fax: (212)850-6088 E-mail: business@wiley.com • URL: http://www.wiley.com • 1992. $81.95. Third edition.

Real Estate. Jerome Dasso. Prentice Hall, 240 Frisch Ct. Paramus, NJ 07652-5240. Phone: 800-947-7700 or (201)909-6452 Fax: 800-445-6991 URL: http://www.prenhall.com • 2000. $86.67. 13th edition.

Real Estate Appraisal. Jack P. Friedman and others. Prentice Hall, 240 Frisch Ct. Paramus, NJ 07652-5240. Phone: 800-947-7700 or (201)909-6452 Fax: 800-445-6991 URL: http://www.prenhall.com • 1999. $25.00.

Real Estate Appraisal Bibliography, 1973-1980. Appraisal Institute, 875 N. Michigan Ave., Suite 2400 Chicago, IL 60611-1980. Phone: (312)335-4100 Fax: (312)335-4400 1981. $12.50. Several thousand articles published in major perodicals between 1973 and 1980.

Real Estate Brokerage. John E. Cyr and others. Dearborn , A Kaplan Professional Co., 155 N. Wacker St. Chicago, IL 60606-1719. Phone: 800-621-9621 or (312)836-4400 Fax: (312)836-1021 URL: http://www.dearborn.com • 1995. $37.95. Fourth edition. Covers the industry standard on opening and operation a real brokerage office.

Real Estate Dictionary. Michael C. Thomsett. McFarland and Co., Inc., Publishers, P.O Box 611 Jefferson, NC 28640. Phone: 800-253-2187 or (336)246-4460 Fax: (336)246-5018 E-mail: editorial@mcfarlandpub.com • URL: http://www.mcfarlandpub.com • 1988. $38.50.

Real Estate Economics: Journal of the American Real Estate and Urban Economics Association. MIT Press, Five Cambridge Center Cambridge, MA 02142-1493. Phone: 800-356-0343 or (617)253-2864 Fax: (617)253-1545 E-mail: journals-orders@mit.edu • URL: http://www.mitpress.mit.edu • Quarterly. Institutions, $165.00 per year.

Real Estate Finance. Institutional Investor, 488 Madison Ave. New York, NY 10022. Phone: (212)224-3300 Fax: (212)224-3527 E-mail: info@iijournals.com • URL: http://www.iijournals.com • Quarterly. $225.00 per year. Covers real estate for professional investors. Provides information on complex financing, legalities, and industry trends.

Real Estate Finance and Investment. Institutional Investor, 488 Madison Ave. New York, NY 10022. Phone: (212)224-3300 Fax: (212)224-3353 E-mail: info@iijournals.com • URL: http://www.iijournals.com • Weekly. $2,105.00 per year. Newsletter for professional investors in commercial real estate. Includes information on financing, restructuring, strategy, and regulation.

Real Estate Finance and Investment Manual. Jack Cummings. Prentice Hall, 240 Frisch Court Paramus, NJ 07652-5240. Phone: 800-947-7700 or (201)909-6200 Fax: 800-445-6991 or (201)909-6361 URL: http://www.prenhall.com • 1997. $34.95. Second edition.

Real Estate Finance and Investments. William B. Brueggeman and Jeffrey Fisher. McGraw-Hill, 1221 Ave. of the Americas New York, NY 10020. Phone: 800-722-4726 or (212)904-2000 Fax: (212)904-2072 E-mail: customer.service@mcgraw-hill.com • URL: http://www.mcgraw-hill.com • 1996. $68.25. 10th edition. Covers mortgage loans, financing, risk analysis, income properties, land development, real estate investment trusts, and related topics.

Real Estate Forum. Real Estate Media, Inc., 111 Eighth Ave., Suite 1511 New York, NY 10011-5201. Phone: (212)929-6900 Fax: (212)929-7124 E-mail: jschein@remediainc.com • URL: http://www.reforum.com • Monthly. $55.00 per year. Emphasis on corporate and industrial real estate.

Real Estate Handbook. Financial Publishing Co., 3975 William Richardson Dr. South Bend, IN 46628. Phone: 800-433-0900 Fax: (219)243-6060 E-mail: dhickey@carletonic.com • URL: http://www.carletonic.com • 1999. $20.00. Third revised edition.

Real Estate Index. National Association of Realtors, 430 N. Michigan Ave. Chicago, IL 60611. Phone: 800-874-6500 or (312)329-8292 Fax: (312)329-5962 E-mail: narpubs@realtor.com • URL: http://www.realtor.com • 1987. $169.00 Two volumes. Vol. one, $99.00; vol. two, $99.00. Supplement available, 1988. $49.50.

Real Estate Investing Letter. Orm Publishing Co., Inc., P.O. Box 105 Hampton, NH 03842-0105. Monthly. $96.00 per year.

Real Estate Investment Trusts Handbook: 1997. Peter M. Fass and others. West Group, 610 Opperman Dr. Eagan, MN 55123. Phone: 800-328-4880 or (651)687-7000 Fax: 800-213-2323 or (651)687-5827 URL: http://www.westgroup.com • 1998. $92.00. Covers the legal and tax aspects of REITs. (Securities Law Series).

Real Estate Investor's Answer Book. Jack Cummings. McGraw-Hill, 1221 Ave. of the Americas New York, NY 10020-1095. Phone: 800-262-4726 or (212)904-2000 Fax: (212)904-2072 1994. $17.95. Answers key questions relating to both residential and commercial real estate investments.

Real Estate Issues. The Counselors of Real Estate, 430 N. Michigan Ave. Chicago, IL 60611. Phone: (312)329-8427 Fax: (312)329-8881 E-mail: cre@interaccess.com • URL: http://www.cre.org • Semiannual. $48.00 per year.

Real Estate Law Journal. Warren, Gorham and Lamont/RIA Group, 395 Hudson St. New York, NY 10014. Phone: 800-950-1215 or (212)367-6300 Fax: (212)924-0460 URL: http://www.wgl.com • Quarterly. $141.50 per year. Continuing practical concerns of real estate law professionals. Covers timely issues.

Real Estate Law Report. Warren, Gorham and Lamont/RIA Group, 395 Hudson St. New York, NY 10014. Phone: 800-950-1215 or (212)367-6300 Fax: (212)924-0460 URL: http://www.wgl.com • Monthly. $123.75 per year. Provides complete, up-to-the-minute coverage of major developments in the field.

Real Estate Marketing and Sales. Paddy Amyett. Prentice Hall, 240 Frisch Ct. Paramus, NJ 07652-5240. Phone: 800-947-7700 or (201)909-6452 Fax: 800-445-6991 URL: http://www.prenhall.com • 2000. $33.33.

Real Estate New York., 111 Eighth Ave. New York, NY 10011-5201. Phone: (212)929-6900 Fax: (212)929-7124 E-mail: jonathan.schein@scheinpublications.com • URL: http://www.reforum.com • Ten times a year. $35.00 per year. Formerly *Better Bulidings*.

Real Estate Research Center. University of Florida

Real Estate Review. Warren, Gorham, and Lamont/RIA Group, 395 Hudson St. New York, NY 10014. Phone: 800-950-1215 or (212)367-6300 Fax: (212)367-6718 E-mail: customer_service@riag.com • URL: http://www.riahome.com • Quarterly. $104.48 per year. Gives inside information on the latest ideas in real estate. Provides advice from the leaders of the real estate field.

Real Estate Tax Digest. Matthew Bender & Shepard, Two Park Ave. New York, NY 10016. Phone: 800-223-1940 or (212)448-2000 Fax: (212)244-3188 E-mail: international@bender.com • URL: http://www.bender.com • Monthly. $295.00 per year. Newsletter.

Real Estate Tax Ideas. Warren, Gorham & Lamont/RIA Group, 395 Hudson St. New York, NY 10014. Phone: 800-950-1215 or (212)367-6300 Fax: (212)337-4280 E-mail: customer_services@riag.com • URL: http://www.wgl.com • Monthly. $150.00 per year. Newsletter. Analysis of the current marketplace and regulatory agencies and new opportunities in real estate. Continuing coverage of recent and proposed tax developments.

Real Estate Taxation: A Practitioner's Guide. David F. Windish. CCH, Inc., 4025 W. Peterson Ave. Chicago, IL 60646-6085. Phone: 800-248-3248 or (773)866-6000 Fax: 800-224-8299 or (773)866-3608 URL: http://www.cch.com • 1998. $125.00. Second edition. Serves as a guide to the federal tax consequences of real estate ownership and operation. Covers mortgages, rental agreements, interest, landlord income, forms of ownership, and other tax-oriented topics.

Real Estate Transactions, Tax Planning and Consequences. Mark L. Levine. West Publishing Co., College and School Div., 610 Opperman Dr. Eagan, MN 55123. Phone: 800-328-4880 or (651)687-7000 Fax: 800-213-2323 or (651)687-5827 E-mail: legal-ed@westgroup.com • URL: http://www.lawschool.westgroup.com • 1997. Periodic supplementation.

Realtor Magazine. National Association of Realtors, 430 N. Michigan Ave. Chicago, IL 60611. Phone: 800-874-6500 or (312)329-8292 Fax: (312)329-5962 E-mail: narpubs@realtor.org • URL: http://www.realtor.com • Monthly. Free to members; non-members, $54.00 per year. Provides industry news and trends for realtors. Special features include Annual Compensation Survey, Annual Technology Survey, Annual All Stars, and The Year in Real Estate.

Realty and Building. Realty and Building, Inc., 11 E. Hubbard St., Suite 300 Chicago, IL 60611-3536. Phone: 800-843-3266 or (312)467-1888 Fax: (312)467-0225 Biweekly. $48.00 per year.

Realty Stock Review: Market Analysis of Securities of REITS and Real Estate Companies., P.O. Box 7 Tranquility, NJ 07879-0007. Phone: (908)850-1155 Semimonthly. $325.00 per year.

ReCareering Newsletter: An Idea and Resource Guide to Second Career and Relocation Planning. Publications Plus, Inc., 434 Ridge Rd. Wilimette, IL 60091-2471. Phone: (708)735-1981 Fax: (708)735-0046 Monthly. $59.00 per year. Edited for "downsized managers, early retirees, and others in career transition after leaving traditional employment." Offers advice on second careers, franchises, starting a business, finances, education, training, skills assessment, and other matters of interest to the newly unemployed.

Recent Advances and Issues in Computers. Martin K. Gay. Oryx Press, 4041 North Central Ave., Suite 700 Phoenix, AZ 85012-3397. Phone: 800-279-6799 or (602)265-2651 Fax: 800-279-4663 or (602)265-6250 E-mail: info@oryxpress.com • URL: http://www.oryxpress.com • 2000. $44.95. Includes recent developments in computer science, computer engineering, and commercial software applications. (Oryx Frontiers of Science Series.)

Recent Advances and Issues in Environmental Science. John R. Callahan. Oryx Press, 4041 North Central Ave., Suite 700 Phoenix, AZ 85012-3397. Phone: 800-279-6799 or (602)265-2651 Fax: 800-279-4663 or (602)265-6250 E-mail: info@oryxpress.com • URL: http://www.oryxpress.com • 2000. $44.95. Includes environmental economic problems, such as saving jobs vs. protecting the environment. (Oryx Frontiers of Science Series.)

Recent Advances in Cryogenic Engineering. J. P. Kelley and J. Goodman, editors. American Society of Mechanical Engineers, 22 Law Dr. Fairfield, NJ 07007-2900. Phone: 800-843-2763 or (973)882-1167 Fax: (973)882-1717 E-mail: infocentral@asme.org • URL: http://www.asme.org • 1993. $30.00.

Reciprocity, U. S. Trade Policy, and the GATT Regime. Carolyn Rhodes. Cornell University Press, Sage House, 512 E. State St. Ithaca, NY 14851. Phone: 800-666-2211 or (607)277-2338 Fax: 800-688-2877 E-mail: orderbook@cupserv.org • URL: http://www.cornellpress.cornell.edu • 1993. $37.50.

Recommendations on the Transport of Dangerous Goods. United Nations Publications, United Nations Concourse Level, First Ave., 46th St. New York, NY 10017. Phone: 800-553-3210 or (212)963-7680 Fax: (212)963-4910 E-mail: bookstore@un.org • URL: http://www.un.org/publications • 1999. $120.00. 11th edition. Covers regulations imposed by various governments and international organizations.

Recommended Bank and Thrift Report. Bauer Communications, Inc., Penthouse One, Gables International Plaza, 2655 LeJeune Rd. Coral Gables, FL 33134. Phone: 800-388-6686 or (305)445-9500 Fax: 800-230-9569 or (305)445-6775 URL: http://www.bauerfinancial.com • Quarterly. $585.00 per year. Newsletter provides information on "safe, financially sound" commercial banks, savings banks, and savings and loan institutions. Various factors are considered, including tangible capital ratios and total risk-based capital ratios. (Six regional editions are also available at $150.00 per edition per year.)

Record Retailing Directory. BPI Communications, 770 Broadway, Sixth Floor New York, NY 10003. Phone: (646)654-4697 Fax: (646)654-4799 URL: http://www.billboard.com • Annual. $169.00. Lists record (music CD-ROMs) dealers, both independent and chain-owned.

Recording Industry Association of America.

Recording Industry Sourcebook. Intertec Publishing, 9800 Metcalf Ave. Overland Park, KS 66212-2216. Phone: 800-233-3359 or (913)341-1300 Fax: (913)967-1898 E-mail: subs@intertec.com • URL: http://www.intertec.com • Annual. $79.95. Provides more than 12,000 listings in 57 categories of record/tape/compact disc labels, producers, distributors, managers, equipment suppliers, and others.

Records Management: A Practical Guide. Susan Z. Diamond. AMACOM, 1601 Broadway, 12th Fl. New York, NY 10019. Phone: 800-262-9699 or (212)586-8100 Fax: (212)903-8168 E-mail: custmserv@amanet.org • URL: http://www.amanet.org • 1995. $29.95. Third edition. A guide to on-site and off- site storage of business documents, including a discussion of filing systems.

Recreation Vehicle Dealers Association of North America.

Recreation Vehicle Industry Association.

Recruiter's Research Blue Book: A How-To Guide for Researchers, Search Consultants, Corporate Recruiters, Small Business Owners, Venture Capitalists, and Line Executives. Andrea A. Jupina. Kennedy Information, One Kennedy Place, Route 12 South Fitzwilliam, NH 03447. Phone: 800-531-0007 or (603)585-3101 Fax: (603)585-6401 E-mail: bookstore@kennedyinfo.com • URL: http://www.kennedyinfo.com • 2000. $179.00. Second edition. Provides detailed coverage of the role that research plays in executive recruiting. Includes such practical items as "Telephone Interview Guide," "Legal Issues in Executive Search," and "How to Create an Execuive Search Library." Covers both person-to-person research and research using printed and online business information sources. Includes an extensive directory of recommended sources. Formerly *Handbook of Executive Search Research*.

Recruiting, Interviewing, Selecting, and Orienting New Employees. Diane Arthur. AMACOM, 1601 Broadway, 12th Fl. New York, NY 10019. Phone: 800-262-9699 or (212)586-8100 Fax: (212)903-8168 E-mail: custmserv@amanet.org • URL: http://www.amanet.org • 1998. $59.95. Third edition. A practical guide to the basics of hiring, including legal considerations and sample forms.

Recruiting Library Staff: A How-To-Do-It Manual for Librarians. Kathleen Low. Neal-Schuman Publishers, Inc., 100 Varick St. New York, NY 10013. Phone: (212)925-8650 Fax: 800-584-2414 or (212)219-8916 E-mail: info@neal-schuman.com • URL: http://www.neal-schuman.com • 2000. $45.00. Includes position description forms, sample announcements, and checklists. Discusses job fairs and other career events.

Recruiting Trends: The Monthly Newsletter for the Recruiting Executive. Kennedy Information LLC, One Kennedy Place, Route 12, S. Fitzwilliam, NH 03447. Phone: 800-531-1026 or (603)585-3101 Fax: (603)585-9555 E-mail: officer@kennedyinfo.com • URL: http://www.kennedyinfo.com • Monthly. $155.00 per year.

Recycling Sourcebook. The Gale Group, 27500 Drake Rd. Farmington Hills, MI 48331-3535. Phone: 800-877-GALE or (248)699-GALE Fax: 800-414-5043 or (248)699-8069 E-mail: galeord@galegroup.com • URL: http://www.galegroup.com • 1992. $90.00. Provides information on organizations, agencies, recycling companies, and publications. Recycling methods and approaches are described, with case studies. (Environmental Library Series).

Recycling Today. Group Interest Enterprises. G.I.E., Media Inc., 4012 Bridge Ave. Cleveland, OH 44113-3320. Phone: 800-456-0707 or (216)961-4130 Fax: (216)961-0364 E-mail: pmoralew@gie.net • URL: http://www.recyclingtoday.com/ • Monthly. $30.00 per year. Serves the recycling industry in all areas.

The Red Book. Medical Economics Co., Inc., Five Paragon Dr. Montvale, NJ 07645-1742. Phone: 800-232-7379 or (201)358-7200 Fax: (201)358-7522 E-mail: customer_service@medec.com • URL: http://www.medec.com • Annual. $57.95 for basic volume or $99.00 per year with monthly updates. Provides product information and prices for more than 100,000 prescription and nonprescription drugs and other items sold by pharmacies. Also known as *Drug Topics Red Book*.

The Red Herring: The Business of Technology. Herring Communications, Inc., 1550 Bryant St., Suite 450 San Francisco, CA 94103. Phone: 800-627-4931 or (415)865-2277 Fax: (415)865-2280 E-mail: info@redherring.com • URL: http://www.redherring.com • Monthly. $49.00 per year. Contains ars on investing in high technology, especially within the computer, communications, and information industries. Initial public offerings (IPOs) are emphasized. Includes technology stock listings and the Red Herring "Tech 250" stock index.

Reducing Inflation: Motivation and Strategy. Christina D. Romer and David H. Romer, editors. University of Chicago Press, 5801 Ellis Ave., 4th Fl. Chicago, IL 60637. Phone: 800-621-2736 or (773)702-7700 Fax: (773)702-9756 E-mail: marketing@press.uchicago.edu • URL: http://www.press.uchicago.edu • 1997. $58.00. Consists of 10 essays and comments by various economists on strategies for controlling inflation. *National Bureau of Economic Research Project Reports*.

Reengineering Management: The Mandate for New Leadership. James Champy. DIANE Publishing Co., 330 Pusey Ave. Collingdale, PA 19023. Phone: (610)461-6200 Fax: (610)461-6130 E-mail: dianepub@erols.com • URL: http://www.dianepublishing.com • 1998. $25.00.

Reengineering Revolution: A Handbook. Michael Hammer and Steven Stanton. HarperInformation, 10 E. 53rd St. New York, NY 10022-5299. Phone: 800-242-7737 or (212)207-7000 Fax: 800-822-4090 or (212)207-7145 URL: http://www/harpercollins.com • 1995. $16.00.

Reengineering the Bank: A Blueprint for Survival and Success. Paul H. Allen. McGraw-Hill Professional, 1221 Ave. of the Americas New York, NY 10020. Phone: 800-722-4726 or (212)904-2000 Fax: (212)904-2072 E-mail: customer.service@mcgraw-hill.com • URL: http://www.mcgraw-hill.com • 1994. $40.00.

Reengineering the Corporation: A Manifesto for Business Revolution. Michael Hammer and James Champy. HarperCollins Publishers, Inc., 10 E. 53rd St. New York, NY 10022-5299. Phone: 800-242-7737 or (212)207-7000 Fax: 800-822-4090 or (212)207-7145 URL: http://www.harpercollins.com • 1999. $16.00. Revised edition.

Reference and User Services Association of the American Library Association: Machine Assisted Reference Section.

Reference and User Services Quarterly. American Library Association, 50 E. Huron St. Chicago, IL 60611-2795. Phone: 800-545-2433 or (312)944-6780 Fax: (312)440-9374 E-mail: rusa@ala.org • URL: http://www.ala.org • Quarterly. $50.00 per year. Official publication of the Reference and User Services Association (RUSA), a division of the American Library Association. In addition to articles, includes reviews of databases, reference books, and library professional material. Formerly *RQ*.

Reference Book for World Traders. Croner Publications, Inc., 10951 Sorrento Valley Rd., Suite 1-D San Diego, CA 92121-1613. Phone: 800-441-4033 or (619)546-1894 Fax: (619)546-1955 URL: http://www.sdic.net/croner • $170.00. Three volumes. A looseleaf handbook covering information required for planning and executing exports and imports to and from all foreign countries; kept up to date by an amendment service.

Reference Book of Corporate Managements. Dun and Bradstreet Information Services, Dun and Bradstreet Corp., Three Sylvan Way Parsippany, NJ 07054-3896. Phone: 800-526-0651 or (973)455-0900 Fax: (973)254-4063 E-mail: customerservice@dnb.com • URL: http://www.dnb.com • Annual. Libraries, $650.00 per year; others, $795.00 per year. Lease basis. Management executives at over 12,000 leading United States companies.

Reference Books Bulletin: A Compilation of Evaluations. Mary Ellen Quinn, editor. American Library Association, 50 E. Huron St. Chicago, IL 60611. Phone: 800-545-2433 or (312)944-6780 Fax: (312)440-9374 E-mail: ala@ala.org • URL: http://www.ala.org • Annual. $28.50. Contains reference book reviews that appeared during the year in *Booklist*.

Reference Librarian. Haworth Press, Inc., 10 Alice St. Binghamton, NY 13904-1580. Phone: 800-429-6784 or (607)722-5857 Fax: 800-895-0582 or (607)722-1424 E-mail: getinfo@haworthpressinc.com • URL: http://www.haworthpressinc.com • Semiannual. Individuals, $60.00 per year; libraries and other institutions, $225.00 per year. Two volumes.

Reference Source. Sosland Publishing Co., 4800 Main St., Suite 100 Kansas City, MO 64112-2513. Phone: (816)756-1000 Fax: (816)756-0494 E-mail: bakesnack@sosland.com • Annual. $45.00 per year. A statistical reference manual and specification guide for wholesale baking. Formerly *Bakers Digest*.

Reference Sources for Small and Medium-sized Libraries. Scott E. Kennedy, editor. American Library Association, 50 E. Huron St. Chicago, IL 60611-2795. Phone: 800-545-2433 or (312)944-6780 Fax: (312)440-9374 E-mail: ala@ala.org • URL: http://www.ala.org • 1999. $60.00. Sixth edition. Includes alternative (electronic) formats for reference works.

Refining and Gas Processing Industry Worldwide. PennWell Publishing Co., 1700 W. Loop St., Ste. 1000 Houston, TX 77027. Phone: 800-736-6935 or (713)621-9720 Fax: (713)499-6310 E-mail: info@midwestdirectories.com • URL: http://www.pennwell.com • Annual. $165.00. International coverage. Formerly *Refining and Gas Processing*.

Reform of Health Care Systems: A Review of Seventeen OECD Countries. OECD Publications and Information Center, 2001 L St., N.W., Ste. 650 Washington, DC 20036-4922. Phone: (202)785-6323 Fax: (202)785-0350 E-mail: washington.contact@oecd.org • 1994. An extensive review of attempts by major countries to control health care costs.

Reforming the Bank Regulatory Structure. Andrew S. Carron. Brookings Institution Press, 1775 Massachusetts Ave., N.W. Washington, DC 20036-2188. Phone: 800-275-1447 or (202)797-6258 Fax: (202)797-6004 E-mail: bibooks@brook.edu • URL: http://www.brookings.edu • 1985. $8.95.

Refractories. U. S. Bureau of the Census, Washington, DC 20233-0800. Phone: (301)457-4100 Fax: (301)457-3842 URL: http://www.census.gov • Annual. Provides data on value of manufacturers' shipments, quantity, exports, imports, etc. (Current Industrial Reports, MA-32C.)

Refractories Institute.

Refrigerating Engineers and Technicians Association.

Refrigeration. John W. Yopp Publications, Inc., P.O. Box 1147 Beaufort, SC 29901. Phone: 800-849-9677 E-mail: jcronley@jwyopp.com • URL: http://www.jwyopp.com • Monthly. $30.00 per year.

Refrigeration, Air Conditioning, and Warm Air Heating Equipment. U. S. Bureau of the Census, Washington, DC 20233-0800. Phone: (301)457-4100 Fax: (301)457-3842 URL: http://www.census.gov • Annual. Provides data on quantity and value of shipments by manufacturers. Formerly *Air Conditioning and Refrigeration Equipment*. (Current Industrial Reports, MA-35M.)

Refrigeration and Air Conditioning. A.R. Trott and T. Welch. Butterworth-Heinemann, 225 Wildwood Ave. Woburn, MA 01801. Phone: 800-366-2665 or (781)904-2500 Fax: 800-446-6520 E-mail: orders@bhusa.com • URL: http://www.bh.com • 2000. $59.95. Third edition.

Refundable Bundle., Centuck Station, P.O. Box 140 Yonkers, NY 10710. Phone: (914)472-2227 Bimonthly. $10.00 per year. Newsletter for grocery shoppers. Each issue provides details of new coupon and refund offers.

Regency International Directory of Private Investigators, Private Detectives, Security Guards, and Security Equipment Suppliers. Available from Thomas Publications, P.O. Box 33244 Austin, TX 78764. Annual. $60.00. Over 5,000 detective agencies, firms specializing in security. bailiffs, and trade protection societies; worldwide coverage. Published in England by Regency International Directory.

Regional Airline Association., 1200 19th St., N.W., Suite 300 Washington, DC 20036-2422. Phone: (202)857-1170 Fax: (202)429-5113 E-mail: raa@dc.sba.com • URL: http://www.raa.org • Scheduled commuter air carriers.

Regional Developement Services. East Carolina University

Regional Directory of Minority-and Women-Owned Business Firms. Business Research Services, Inc., 4201 Connecticut Ave., N.W., Suite 610 Washington, DC 20008. Phone: 800-845-8420 or (202)364-6947 Fax: (202)686-3228 E-mail: brspubs@sba8.com • Annual. Three volumes. $175.00 per volume. Regional editions are Eastern, Central,and Western.

Regional Economic Development Center. University of Memphis

Regional Economic Development: Theories amd Strategies for Developing Countries. Marguerite N. Abd El-Shahid. Sage Publications, Inc., 2455 Teller Rd. Thousand Oaks, CA 91320. Phone: (805)499-0721 Fax: (805)499-0871 E-mail: info@sagepub.com • URL: http://www.sagepub.com • 1994. $10.00.

Regional Official Guides: Tractors and Farm Equipment. North American Equipment Dealers Association, 1195 Smizer Mill Rd. Fenton, MO 63026-3480. Phone: (636)349-5000 E-mail: naeda@naeda.com • URL: http://www.naeda.com • Quarterly. Membership.

Regional Science Association International.

Regions Statistical Yearbook. Bernan Associates, 4611-F Assembly Dr. Lanham, MD 20706-4391. Phone: 800-274-4888 or (301)459-7666 Fax: 800-865-3450 or (301)459-0056 E-mail: info@bernan.com. • URL: http://www.bernan.com • Annual. $45.00. Published by the Commission of European Communities. Provides data on the social and economic situation in specific European areas. Includes population, employment, migration, industry, living standards, etc.

Register of International Shipowning Groups. Available from Fairplay Publications, Inc., 5201 Blue Lagoon Drive, Suite 530 Miami, FL 33126. Phone: (305)262-4070 Fax: (305)262-2006 E-mail: sales@fairplayamericas.com • URL: http://www.lrfairplay.com • Three times a year. $697.00 per year. Published in the UK by Lloyd's Register-Fairplay Ltd. ''Provides intelligence on shipowners and managers, their subsidiary and associate companies, and owners' representatives.'' Includes detailed information on individual ships.

Register of Officers [United States Coast Guard]. U.S. Coast Guard, Washington, DC 20593. Phone: (202)267-2229 Annual.

Registered Representative. Intertec Publishing Corp., 18818 Teller Ave.,, Ste. 280 Irvin, CA 92715. Phone: (949)851-2220 Fax: (949)851-1636 E-mail: webmaster@rrmag.com • URL: http://www.rrmag.com • Monthly. $48.00 per year.

Regulation of the Commodities Futures and Options Markets. Bob McKinney. Shepard's, 555 Middle Creek Parkway Colorado Springs, CO 80921. Phone: 800-743-7393 or (719)481-7371 Fax: 800-525-0053 or (719)481-7621 E-mail: customer_service@shepards.com • URL: http://www.shepards.com • 1995. Second revised edition. Price on application.

Regulatory Policy and Practices: Regulating Better and Regulating Less. Fred Thompson. Greenwood Publishing Group, Inc., 88 Post Rd., W. Westport, CT 06881-5007. Phone: 800-225-5800 or (203)226-3571 Fax: (203)222-2540 E-mail: bookinfo@greenwood.com • URL: http://www.greenwood.com • 1982. $55.00.

Rehabilitation International; Vocational Commission.

Rehabilitation Program. University of Arizona

Reinforced Concrete Fundamentals. Phil M. Ferguson and others. John Wiley and Sons, Inc., 605 Third Ave. New York, NY 10158-0012. Phone: 800-526-5368 or (212)850-6000 Fax: (212)850-6088 E-mail: info@wiley.com • URL: http://www.wiley.com • 1988. $117.95. Fifth edition.

Relative Dividend Yield: Common Stock Investing for Income and Appreciation. Anthony E. Spare and Paul Ciotti. John Wiley and Sons, Inc., 605 Third Ave. New York, NY 10158-0012. Phone: 800-225-5945 or (212)850-6000 Fax: (212)850-6088 E-mail: info@wiley.com • URL: http://www.wiley.com • 1999. $59.95. Second edition. (Frontiers in Finance Series).

Release 1.0: Esther Dyson's Monthly Report. EDventure Holdings, Computer Publications Div., 104 Fifth Ave., 20th Fl. New York, NY 10011-6987. Phone: (212)924-8800 Fax: (212)924-0240 E-mail: trista@edventure.com • URL: http://www.edventure.com/releasel/ • 15 times a year. $695.00 per year. Newsletter.

Releasing an Independent Record: How to Successfully Start and Run Your Own Record Label in the 1990s. Gary Hustwit. Rockpress Publishing, P.O. Box 99090 San Diego, CA 92169-2535. Phone: (619)234-9400 Fax: (619)234-9479 1998. $26.95. Sixth edition.

Reliable Financial Reporting and Internal Control: A Global Implementation Guide. Dmitris N. Chorafas. John Wiley and Sons, Inc., 605 Third Ave. New York, NY 10158-0012. Phone: 800-225-5945 or (212)850-6000 Fax: (212)850-6088 E-mail: business@jwiley.com • URL: http://www.wiley.com • 2000. $65.00. Discusses financial reporting and control as related to doing business internationally.

Religious Conference Management Association.

Relocation Journal and Real Estate News. Mobility Services International, 124 High St. Newburyport, MA 01950. Phone: (978)463-0348 E-mail: diane@msimobility.com • URL: http://www.relojournal.com • Monthly. Free. Magazine for real estate, building, financing and investing. Formed by the merger of *Real Estate News* and *Relocation Journal*.

Remarks: Trademark News for Business. International Trademark Association, 1133 Sixth Ave. New York, NY 10036-6710. Phone: (212)768-9887 Fax: (212)768-7796 Quarterly. Newsletter.

Remodeling: Excellence in Professional Remodeling. Hanley-Wood, LLC., One Thomas Circle, Suite 600 Washington, DC 20005-5811. Phone: 888-269-8410 or (202)452-0800 Fax: (202)785-1974 URL: http://www.hanley-wood.com • Monthly. $44.95 per year. Covers new products, construction, management, and marketing for remodelers.

Remodeling Product Guide. Hanley-Wood, LLC., One Thomas Circle, Suite 600 Washington, DC 20005-5811. Phone: 888-269-8410 or (202)452-0800 Fax: (202)785-1974 URL: http://www.hanleywood.com/publications/ • Annual. $10.00. A directory of products and services for the home remodeling industry. Formerly *Remodeling-Guide to Manufacturers*.

Renewable Energy: An International Journal. Elsevier Science, 655 Ave. of the Americas New York, NY 10010. Phone: 888-437-4636 or (212)989-5800 Fax: (212)633-3680 E-mail: usinfo@elsevier.com • URL: http://www.elsevier.com • Monthly. $1,505.00 per year. Incorporates *Solar and Wind Technology*.

Renewable Energy News Digest. Sun Words, 14 S. Church St. Schenectady, NY 12305. Phone: (518)372-1799 Monthly. $60.00 per year. Newsletter. Covers geothermal, solar, wind, cogenerated, and other energy sources.

Renewable Energy: Power for a Sustainable Future. Godfrey Boyle, editor. Available from Taylor & Francis, 325 Chestnut St., 8th Fl. Philadelphia, PA 19106. Phone: 800-821-8312 or (215)625-8900 Fax: (215)625-2940 E-mail: webmaster@taylorandfrancis.com • URL: http://www.tandfdc.com/ • 1996. $39.95. Published by Open University Press. Contains ten chapters, each on a particular renewable energy source, including solar, biomass, hydropower, wind, and geothermal.

Renewable Natural Resources Foundation.

Rensselaer Polytechnic Institute., Rensselaer Technology Park, 100 Jordan Rd. Troy, NY 12180. Phone: (518)283-7102 Fax: (518)283-0695 E-mail: wachom@rpi.edu • URL: http://www.rpi.edu/dept/rtp • Serves as a conduit for research interactions between Rensselaer Polytechnic Institute and private companies.

Rental Equipment Register. Intertec Publishing Corp., 23815 Stuart Ranch Rd. Malibu, CA 90265. Phone: 800-400-5945 or (310)317-4522 Fax: (310)317-9644 E-mail: subs@intertec.com • URL: http://www.rermag.com • Monthly. $75.00 per year.

Rental Equipment Register Buyer's Guide. Intertec Publishing Corp., 23815 Stuart Ranch Rd. Malibu, CA 90265. Phone: 800-400-5945 or (310)317-4522 Fax: (310)317-9644 E-mail: subs@intertec.com • URL: http://www.intertec.com • Annual. $39.95. Formerly *Rental Equipment Register Product Directory and Buyer's Guide*.

Rental Management. American Rental Association, 1900 19th St. Moline, IL 61265. Phone: (309)764-2475 Fax: (309)764-1533 URL: http://www.ararental.org • Monthly. Free to qualified personnel.

Rental Product News. Cygnus Publishing, Inc., 1233 Janesville Ave. Fort Atkinson, WI 53538-0460. Phone: 800-547-7377 or (920)563-6388 Fax: (920)563-1707 E-mail: rich.reiff@cygnuspub.com • URL: http://www.cygnuspub.com • Bimonthly. $48.00 per year. Includes annual *Product* issue.

Rep-Letter. Manufacturers' Agents National Association, P.O. Box 3467 Laguna Hills, CA 92654-3467. Phone: (949)859-4040 Fax: (949)855-2973 E-mail: mana@manaonline.org • URL: http://www.manaonline.org • Monthly. $37.50. A bound-in monthly feature of *Agency Sales Magazine*.

Report. Louis G. Robinson and Associates, Robinett/Kent, 1723 Jackson St. Santa Clara, CA 95050. Phone: (408)723-7311 Monthly. $295.00 per year. Newsletter. Articles cover the artificial intelligence field. Formerly *Artificial Intelligence Report*.

Report of the International Narcotics Control Board on Its Work. United Nations Publications, United Nations Concourse Level, First Ave., 46th St. New York, NY 10017. Phone: 800-553-3210 or (212)963-7680 Fax: (212)963-4910 E-mail: bookstore@un.org • URL: http://www.un.org/publications • Annual. $20.00.

Report on Corporate Library Spending. Primary Research, 68 W. 38th St., No. 202 New York, NY 10018. Phone: (212)769-1579 Fax: (212)397-5056 E-mail: primarydat@aol.com • 1995. $75.00. Provides market research data on corporate library expenditures for books, periodicals, and online/CD-ROM sources.

Report on Electronic Commerce: Online Business, Financial and Consumer Strategies and Trends. Telecommunications Reports International, Inc., 1333 H St., N. W., Suite 100 Washington, DC 20005. Phone: 800-822-6338 or (202)312-6060 Fax: (202)842-3023 E-mail: customerservice@tr.com • URL: http://www.tr.com • 23 times a year. $745.00 per year. Newsletter. Includes *Daily Multimedia News Service*. Incorporates *Interactive Services Report*.

Report on Healthcare Information Management: A Strategic Guide to Technology and Data Integration. Aspen Publishers, Inc., 200 Orchard Ridge Dr. Gaithersburg, MD 20878. Phone: 800-638-8437 or (301)417-7500 Fax: (301)695-7931 E-mail: customer.service@aspenpubl.com • URL: http://www.aspenpubl.com • Monthly. $358.00 per year. Newsletter. Covers management information sytems for hospitals and physicians' groups.

Report on the American Workforce. Available from U. S. Government Printing Office, Washington, DC 20402. Phone: (202)512-1800 Fax: (202)512-2250 E-mail: gpoaccess@gpo.gov • URL: http://www.access.gpo.gov • Annual. $15.00. Issued by the U. S. Department of Labor (http://www.dol.gov). Appendix contains tabular statistics, including employment, unemployment, price indexes, consumer expenditures, employee benefits (retirement, insurance, vacation, etc.), wages, productivity, hours of work, and occupational injuries. Annual figures are shown for up to 50 years.

Report Writing for Business. Raymond V. Lesikar and John Pettit. McGraw-Hill Professional, 1221 Ave. of the Americas

New York, NY 10020. Phone: 800-722-4726 or (212)904-2000 Fax: (212)904-2072 E-mail: customer service@mcgraw-hill.com • URL: http://www.mcgraw-hill.com • 1998. $64.38. 10th edition.

Reporters Committee for Freedom of the Press., 1815 N. Fort Meyer Dr., Ste. 900 Arlington, VA 22209. Phone: (703)807-2100 Fax: (703)807-2109 E-mail: rcfp@rcfp.org • URL: http://www.rcfp.org/rcfp • Concerned with protecting freedom of information rights for the working press.

Research Alert: A Bi-Weekly Report of Consumer Marketing Studies. EPM Communications, Inc., 160 Mercer St., 3rd Fl. New York, NY 10012-3212. Phone: 888-852-9467 or (212)941-0099 Fax: (212)941-1622 E-mail: info@epmcom.com • URL: http://www.epmcom.com • Semimonthly. $369.00 per year. Newsletter. Provides descriptions (abstracts) of new, consumer market research reports from private, government, and academic sources. Includes sample charts and tables.

Research Alert Yearbook: Vital Facts on Consumer Behavior and Attitudes. EPM Communications, Inc., 160 Mercer St., 3rd Fl. New York, NY 10012-3212. Phone: 888-852-9467 or (212)941-0099 Fax: (212)941-1622 E-mail: info@epmcom.com • URL: http://www.epmcom.com • Annual. $295.00. Provides summaries of consumer market research from the newsletters *Research Alert, Youth Markets Alert, and Minority Markets Alert*. Includes tables, charts, graphs, and textual summaries for 41 subject categories. Sources include reports, studies, polls, and focus groups.

Research: All a Broker Needs to Succeed. Research Holdings, Ltd., 2201 Third St. San Francisco, CA 94107. Phone: (415)621-0220 Fax: (415)621-0735 E-mail: info@researchmagazine.com • URL: http://www.researchmagazine.com • Monthly. $35.00 per year. Provides advice and information for full-service stockbrokers.

Research and Development Associates for Military Food and Packaging Systems.

Research and Development: The Voice of the Research and Development Community. Cahners Business Information, 2000 Clearwater Dr. Oak Brook, IL 60523. Phone: 800-662-7776 or (630)320-7000 Fax: (630)720-7160 E-mail: corporatecommunications@cahners.com • URL: http://www.cahners.com • 13 times a year. $81.90 per year.

Research and Engineering Council of the Graphic Arts Industry.

Research and Investigation in Adult Education: Annual Register. American Association for Adult and Continuing Education, 1200 19th St., N.W., Suite 300 Washington, DC 20036. Phone: (202)429-5131 Fax: (202)223-4579 URL: http://www.albany.edu/aaace • Annual.

Research Centers and Services Directories. The Gale Group, 27500 Drake Rd. Farmington Hills, MI 48331-3535. Phone: 800-877-GALE or (248)699-GALE Fax: 800-414-5043 or (248)699-8069 E-mail: galeord@gale.com • URL: http://www.gale.com • Contains profiles of about 30,000 research centers, organizations, laboratories, and agencies in 147 countries. Corresponds to the printed *Research Centers Directory, International Research Centers Directory, Government Research Directory*, and *Research Services Directory*. Updating is semiannual. Inquire as to online cost and availability.

Research Centers Directory. The Gale Group, 27500 Drake Rd. Farmington Hills, MI 48331-3535. Phone: 800-877-GALE or (248)699-GALE Fax: 800-414-5043 or (248)699-8069 E-mail: galeord@galegroup.com • URL: http://www.galegroup.com • Annual. $575.00. Two volumes. Lists more than 14,200 centers.

Research Corporation Technologies., 101 N. Wilmot Rd., Suite 600 Tucson, AZ 85711-3335. Phone: (520)748-4400 Fax: (520)748-0025 URL: http://www.rctech.com • Mainly concerned with the commercialization of technology from colleges, universities, medical research centers, and other nonprofit organizations.

Research Foundation of AIMR (Association for Investment Management and Research)., P.O. Box 3668 Charlottesville, VA 22903. Phone: (804)951-5390 Fax: (804)951-5370 E-mail: info@aimr.com • URL: http://www.aimr.org/aimr/knowledge/research • Affiliated with Financial Analysts Federation.

Research in Accounting Regulation. JAI Press, Inc., P.O. Box 811 Stamford, CT 06904-0811. Phone: (203)323-9606 Fax: (203)357-8446 E-mail: order@jaipress.com • URL: http://www.jaipress.com • Irregular. $78.50.

Research in Corporate Social Performance and Policy. JAI Press, Inc., P.O. Box 811 Stamford, CT 06904-0811. Phone: (203)323-9606 Fax: (203)357-8446 E-mail: order@jaipress.com • URL: http://www.jaipress.com • Irregular. $78.50.

Research in Domestic and International Agribusiness Management. JAI Press, Inc., P.O. Box 811 Stamford, CT 06904-0811. Phone: (203)323-9606 Fax: (203)357-8446 E-mail: order@jaipress.com • URL: http://www.jaipress.com • Irregular. $73.25.

Research in Experimental Economics. JAI Press, Inc., P.O. Box 811 Stamford, CT 06904-0811. Phone: (203)323-9606 Fax: (203)357-8446 E-mail: order@jaipress.com • URL: http://www.jaipress.com • Irregular.$78.50. Supplement available *An Experiment in Non-Cooperative Oligopoly*.

Research in Governmental and Nonprofit Accounting. JAI Press, Inc., P.O. Box 811 Stamford, CT 06904-0811. Phone: (203)323-9606 Fax: (203)357-8446 E-mail: order@jaipress.com • URL: http://www.jaipress.com • Irregular.$78.50.

Research in International Business and Finance. JAI Press, Inc., P.O. Box 811 Stamford, CT 06904-0811. Phone: (203)323-9606 Fax: (203)357-8446 E-mail: order@jaipress.com • URL: http://www.jaipress.com • Irregular.$78.50.

Research in Law and Economics: A Research Annual. Richard O. Zerbe. JAI Press, Inc., P.O. Box 811 Stamford, CT 06904-0811. Phone: (203)323-9606 Fax: (203)357-8446 E-mail: order@jaipress.com • URL: http://www.jaipress.com • Irregular.$78.50. Supplement available:*Economics of Nonproprietary Organizations*.

Research in Marketing: An Annual Compilation of Research. Jagdish N. Sheth, editor. JAI Press, Inc., P.O. Box 811 STamford, CT 06904-0811. Phone: (203)323-9606 Fax: (203)357-8446 E-mail: jai@jaipress.com • URL: http://www.jaipress.com • Annual. Institutions, $78.50. Supplement available *Choice Models for Buyer Behavior*.

Research in Personnel and Human Resources Management. Gerald D. Ferris, editor. JAI Press, Inc., P.O. Box 811 Stamford, CT 06904-0811. Phone: (203)323-9606 Fax: (203)357-8446 E-mail: order@jaipress.com • URL: http://www.jaipress.com • Irregular. $78.50.

Research in Philosophy and Technology. Society for Philosophy and Technology. JAI Press, Inc., P.O. Box 811 Stamford, CT 06904-0811. Phone: (203)323-9606 Fax: (203)357-8446 E-mail: order@jaipress.com • URL: http://www.jaipress.com • Irregular. $78.50. Supplement available.

Research in Population Economics. JAI Press, Inc., P.O. Box 811 Stamford, CT 06904-0811. Phone: (203)323-9606 Fax: (203)357-8446 E-mail: order@jaipress.com • URL: http://www.jaipress.com • Irregular. $90.25.

Research in Transportation Economics. JAI Press, Inc., P.O. Box 811 Stamford, CT 06904-0811. Phone: (203)323-9606 Fax: (203)357-8446 E-mail: order@jaipress.com • URL: http://www.jaipress.com • Irregular. $78.50.

Research Institute on Addictions.

Research Laboratory of Electronics. Massachusetts Institute of Technology

Research Libraries Group.

Research on Technological Innovation, Management and Policy. Richard S. Rosenbloom, editor. JAI Press, Inc., P.O. Box 811 Stamford, CT 06904-0811. Phone: (203)323-9606 Fax: (203)357-8446 E-mail: order@jaipress.com • URL: http://www.jaipress.com • Irregular. $73.25.

Research on Transport Economics. OECD Publications and Information Center, 2001 L St., N.W.,, Ste. 650 Washington, DC 20036-4910. Phone: (202)785-6323 Fax: (202)785-0350 E-mail: sales@oecd.org • URL: http://www.oecd.org • Annual. $98.00.

Research Program in Takeovers and Corporate Restructuring. University of California, Los Angeles

Research Reports. American Institute for Economic Research, Division St. Great Barrington, MA 01230-1000. Phone: (413)528-1216 Fax: (413)528-0103 E-mail: info@aier.org • URL: http://www.aier.org • Semimonthly. $59.00 per year. Newsletter. Alternate issues include charts of "Primary Leading Indicators," "Primary Roughly Coincident Indicators," and "Primary Lagging Indicators," as issued by The Conference Board (formerly provided by the U. S. Department of Commerce).

Research Services Directory: Commercial & Corporate Research Centers. Grey House Publishing, Pocket Knife Square Lakeville, CT 06039. Phone: 800-562-2139 or (860)435-0868 Fax: 800-248-0115 or (860)435-3004 E-mail: books@greyhouse.com • URL: http://www.greyhouse.com • 1999. $395.00. Seventh edition. Lists more than 6,200 independent commercial research centers and laboratories offering contract or fee-based services. Includes corporate research departments, market research companies, and information brokers.

Research Strategies: A Journal of Library Concepts and Instruction. JAI Press, Inc., P.O. Box 811 Stamford, CT 06904-0811. Phone: (203)323-9606 Fax: (203)357-8446 E-mail: order@jaipress.com • URL: http://www.jaipress.com • Quarterly. $135.00 per year. Edited for librarians involved in bibliographic or library instruction.

Research-Technology Management. Industrial Research Institute, Inc., 1550 M St., N. W., Suite 1100 Washington, DC 20005-1712. Phone: (202)296-8811 Fax: (202)776-0756 URL: http://www.iriinc.org • Bimonthly. $150.00 per year. Covers both theoretical and practical aspects of the management of industrial research and development.

Research Triangle Institute., P.O. Box 12194 Research Triangle Park, NC 27709-2194. Phone: (919)541-6000 Fax: (919)541-7004 E-mail: listen@rti.org • URL: http://www.rti.org • Affiliated with the University of North Carolina, North Carolina State University, and Duke University.

Reserves of Crude Oil, Natural Gas Liquids and Natural Gas in the United States and Canada and United States Productive Capacity. American Gas Association, 444 N. Capitol St., N.W., 4th Fl. Washington, DC 20001-1511. Phone: (202)824-7000 Fax: (202)824-7115 E-mail: amgas@aga.com • URL: http://www.aga.org • Annual. Price on application.

Resident and Staff Physician. Romaine Pierson Publishers, Inc., 1065 Old Country Rd., Suite 213 Westbury, NY 11090-5628. Phone: (516)883-6350 Fax: (516)883-6609 Monthly. $62.00 per year.

Residential Mortgage Lending: From Application to Servicing. Institute of Financial Education, 55 W. Monroe St., Suite 2800 Chicago, IL 60603-5014. Phone: 800-946-0488 or (312)364-0100 Fax: (312)364-0190 E-mail: ystoffregen@bai.org • URL: http://www.theinstitute.com • 1998. $64.95. Fifth edition. A guide for bankers.

Resilient Floor Covering Institute., 401 E. Jefferson St., Ste. 102 Rockville, MD 20805-2617. Phone: (301)340-8580 Fax: (301)340-7283 Members include manufacturers of solid vinyl tile and vinyl composition tile.

Resistance Welder Manufacturers' Association.

Resort Development Handbook. Dean Schwanke and others. Urban Land Institute, 1025 Thomas Jefferson St., N. W., Suite 500 W. Washington, DC 20007-5201. Phone: 800-321-5011 or (202)624-7000 Fax: (202)624-7140 E-mail: bookstore@uli.org • URL: http://www.uli.org • 1997. $89.95. Covers a wide range of resort settings and amenities, with details of development, market analysis, financing, design, and operations. Includes color photographs and case studies. (ULI Development Handbook Series).

Resort Management and Operations: The Resort Resource. Finan Publishing Co., Inc., 107 West Pacific Ave. St. Louis, MO 63119. Phone: (314)961-6644 Fax: (314)961-4809 URL: http://www.finan.com • Quarterly. $21.95 per year. Edited for hospitality professionals at both large and small resort facilities.

Resorts and Parks Purchasing Guide. Klevens Publications, Inc., 7600 Ave. V Littlerock, CA 93543. Phone: (805)944-4111 Fax: (805)944-1800 E-mail: klevenspub@aol.com • URL: http://www.garmentindex.com • Annual. $60.00. Lists suppliers of products and services for resorts and parks, including national parks, amusement parks, dude ranches, golf resorts, ski areas, and national monument areas.

Resource: An Association Magazine for Life Insurance Management. LOMA, 2300 Windy Ridge Parkway, Suite 600 Atlanta, GA 30339-8443. Phone: (770)984-3718 Fax: (770)984-6417 URL: http://www.loma.org • Monthly. $36.00 per year. Covers management topics for life insurance home and field office personnel. (LOMA was formerly Life Office Management Association.)

Resource and Energy Economics: A Journal Devoted to the Interdisciplinary Studies in the Allocation of Natural Resources. Elsevier Science, 655 Ave. of the Americas New York, NY 10010. Phone: 888-437-4636 or (212)989-5800 Fax: (212)633-3680 E-mail: usinfo@elsevier.com • URL: http://www.elsevier.com • Quarterly. $478.00 per year. Text in English.

Resource Center Catalog. Society for Nonprofit Organizations, 6314 Odana Rd., Suite 1 Madison, WI 53719. Phone: (608)274-9777 Fax: (608)274-9978 E-mail: snpo@danenet.wicip.org • URL: http://www.uwex.edu/danenet/snpo • Included in subscription to *Non-profit World*.

Resources. Resources for the Future, Inc., 1616 P St., N.W. Washington, DC 20036. Phone: (202)328-5000 Fax: (202)939-3460 E-mail: info@rff.org • URL: http://www.rff.org • Quarterly. Free. Includes feature articles about environmental and natural resources issues as well as organizational news about books, research programs and related activities.

Resources, Conservation and Recycling. Elsevier Science, 655 Ave. of the Americas New York, NY 10010. Phone: 888-473-4636 or (212)989-5800 Fax: (212)633-3680 E-mail: usinfo@elsevier.com • URL: http://www.elsevier.com • Monthly. $1,269.00 per year.

Resources for the Future: An International Annotated Bibliography. Alan J. Mayne. Greenwood Publishing Group, Inc., 88 Post Rd., W. Westport, CT 06881-5007. Phone: 800-225-5800 or (203)226-3571 Fax: (203)222-2540 E-mail: bookinfo@greenwood.com • URL: http://www.greenwood.com • 1993. $79.50. (Bibliographies and Indexes in Economics and Economic History Series, No 13).

Resources in Education. Educational Resources Information Center. Available from U.S. Government Printing Office, Washington, DC 20402. Phone: (202)512-1800 Fax: (202)512-2250 E-mail: gpoaccess@gpo.gov • URL: http://www.access.gpo.gov • Monthly. $102.00 per year. Reports on educational research.

Resources Policy; The International Journal on the Economics, Planning and Use of Non-Renewable Resources. Elsevier Science, 655 Ave. of the Americas New York, NY 10010. Phone: 888-437-4636 or (212)989-5800 Fax: (212)633-3680 E-mail: usinfo@elsevier.com • URL: http:/ /www.elsevier.com • Quarterly. $647.00 per year.

Responsibilities of Corporate Officers and Directors Under Federal Securities Law. CCH, Inc., 4025 W. Peterson Ave. Chicago, IL 60646-6085. Phone: 800-248-3248 or (773)866-6000 Fax: 800-224-8299 or (773)866-3608 URL: http://www.cch.com • Annual. $55.00. Includes discussions of indemnification, ''D & O'' insurance, corporate governance, and insider liability.

Responsibilities of Corporate Officers and Directors Under Federal Securities Laws. CCH, Inc., 4025 W. Peterson Ave. Chicago, IL 60646-6085. Phone: 800-248-3248 or (773)866-6000 Fax: 800-224-8299 or (773)866-3608 URL: http://www.cch.com • 2000. $65.00.

Responsibilities of Insurance Agents and Brokers. Matthew Bender & Co., Inc., Two Park Ave. New York, NY 10016. Phone: 800-223-1940 or (212)448-2000 Fax: (212)244-3188 E-mail: international@bender.com • URL: http://www.bender.com • $750.00. Four looseleaf volumes. Semiannual updates, $520.00. Covers legal responsibilities of agents and federal tax consequences of insurance arrangements.

Responsible Computing. National Center for Computer Crime Data, 1222 17th Ave., Suite B Santa Cruz, CA 95062. Phone: (408)475-4457 Fax: (408)475-5336 E-mail: nudnic@ix.netcom.com • Semiannual. $54.00 per year. Newsletter.

Responsive Regulation: Transcending the Deregulation Debate. Ian Ayres and John Braithwaite. Oxford University Press, Inc., 198 Madison Ave. New York, NY 10016-4314. Phone: 800-451-7556 or (212)726-6000 Fax: (212)726-6446 E-mail: custserv@oup-usa.org • URL: http://www.oup-usa.org • 1992. $70.00. (Oxford Socio-Legal Studies).

Restatement of the Law. American Law Institute, 4025 Chestnut St. Philadelphia, PA 19104-3099. Phone: 800-253-6397 or (215)243-1600 Fax: (215)243-1664 URL: http://www.ali-aba.org • Multivolume set. Periodic supplementation. Price varies. Statements of the common law-an overview, clarification, and simplification of American law.

Restaurant Business. Bill Communications, Inc., 770 Broadway New York, NY 10003-9595. Phone: 800-266-4712 or (646)654-4500 Fax: (646)654-7390 URL: http://www.billcom.com • 24 times a year. $110.00 per year.

Restaurant Hospitality. Penton Media Inc., 1300 E. Ninth St. Cleveland, OH 44114. Phone: (216)696-7000 Fax: (216)696-0836 E-mail: corpcomm@penton.com • URL: http://www.penton.com • Monthly. Free to qualified personnel; others, $65.00 per year.

Restaurant Industry Operations Report. National Restaurant Association, 1200 17th St., N.W. Washington, DC 20036-3097. Phone: (202)331-5900 Fax: (202)331-2429 E-mail: info@dineout.org • URL: http://www.restaurant.org • Annual. Members, $44.95 per year; non-members, $89.95 per year.

Restaurant Start-Up. Entrepreneur Media, Inc., 2445 McCabe Way Irvine, CA 92694. Phone: 800-421-2300 or (949)261-2325 Fax: (949)261-0234 E-mail: entmag@entrepreneur.com • URL: http://www.entrepreneur.com • Looseleaf. $59.50. A practical guide to starting a restaurant. Covers profit potential, start-up costs, market size evaluation, owner's time required, site selection, lease negotiation, pricing, accounting, advertising, promotion, etc. (Start-Up Business Guide No. E1279.)

Restaurant Start-Up Guide: A 12-Month Plan for Successfully Starting a Restaurant. Peter Rainsford and David H. Bangs. Dearborn Financial Publishing, 155 North Wacker Drive Chicago, IL 60606-1719. Phone: 800-245-2665 or (312)836-4400 Fax: (312)836-9958 URL: http://www.dearborn.com • 2000. $22.95. Second edition. Emphasizes the importance of advance planning for restaurant startups.

Restaurants and Institutions. Cahners Business Information, 1350 E. Touhy Ave. Des Plaines, IL 60018-3358. Phone: 800-662-7776 or (847)635-8800 Fax: (847)390-2080 E-mail: corporatecommunications@cahners.com • URL: http://www.cahners.com • Semimonthly. $136.90 per year. Features news, new products, recipes, menu concepts and merchandising ideas from the most successful foodservice operations around the U.S.

The Resume Kit. Richard H. Beatty. John Wiley and Sons, Inc., 605 Third Ave. New York, NY 10158-0012. Phone: 800-526-5368 or (212)850-6000 Fax: (212)850-6088 E-mail: info@wiley.com • URL: http://www.wiley.com • 2000. $12.95. Fourth edition. Includes information on the linear resume, a form said to be favored by outplacement firms.

Resume Writing: A Comprehensive How-To-Do-It Guide. Burdette Bostwick. John Wiley and Sons, Inc., 605 Third Ave. New York, NY 10158-0012. Phone: 800-526-5368 or (212)850-6000 Fax: (212)850-6088 E-mail: info@wiley.com • URL: http://www.wiley.com • 1990. $14.95. Fourth edition.

Resume Writing and Career Counseling. Entrepreneur Media, Inc., 2445 McCabe Way Irvine, CA 92614. Phone: 800-421-2300 or (949)261-2325 Fax: (949)261-0234 E-mail: entmag@entrepreneur.com • URL: http://www.entrepreneur.com • Looseleaf. $59.50. A practical guide to starting a resume writing and career counseling service. Covers profit potential, start-up costs, market size evaluation, owner's time required, site selection, pricing, accounting, advertising, promotion, etc. (Start-Up Business Guide No. E1260.)

Resumes for Banking and Financial Careers, With Sample Cover Letters. NTC/Contemporary Publishing Group, 4255 W. Touhy Ave. Lincolnwood, IL 60712-1975. Phone: 800-323-4900 or (847)679-5500 Fax: 800-998-3103 or (847)679-2494 E-mail: ntcpub@tribune.com • URL: http://www.ntc-cb.com • 2001. $10.95. Second edition. Contains 100 sample resumes and 20 cover letters. (VGM Professional Resumes Series.)

Resumes That Get Jobs. Pearson Education and Technology, 201 W. 103rd St. Indianapolis, IN 46290-1097. Phone: 800-858-7674 or (317)581-3500 URL: http://www.simonsays.com • 1998. $16.00. Includes CD-ROM.

Retail Ad World. Visual Reference Publications, Inc., 302 Fifth Ave. New York, NY 10001. Phone: 800-251-4545 or (212)279-7000 Fax: (212)279-7014 E-mail: visualreference@visualreference.com • URL: http://www.visualreference.com • Semimonthly. $399.00 per year. Weekly report on outstanding advertising by department stores, specialty stores and shopping centers with reprints of current advertising. Formerly *Retail Rd Week*.

Retail Broker-Dealer Directory. Securities Data Publishing, 40 West 57th St. New York, NY 10019. Phone: 800-455-5844 or (212)765-5311 Fax: (212)956-0112 E-mail: sdp@tfn.com • URL: http://www.sdponline.com • Annual. $385.00. Provides detailed information on more than 1,300 retail stockbrokers, including key personnel, revenue, capital, and assets under management. (Securities Data Publishing is a unit of Thomson Financial.)

Retail Confectioners International.

Retail Florist Business. Peter B. Pfahl and P. Blair Pfahl. Interstate Publishers, P.O. Box 50 Danville, IL 61834-0050. Phone: 800-843-4774 or (217)446-0500 Fax: (217)446-9706 E-mail: info-ipp@ippinc.com • URL: http://www.ippinc.com • 1994. $48.75. Fifth edition.

The Retail Management Letter. Management Facts Co., Colony Farm Center, Rupp 48153 Plymouth, MI 48170-3304. Phone: (313)459-1080 Monthly. $167.00 per year.

Retail Merchandiser. Bill Communications, Communications Group, 770 Broadway New York, NY 10003. Phone: 800-266-4712 or (646)654-4500 Fax: (646)654-7212 URL: http://www.billcom.com • Monthly. $55.00 per year. Mass merchandising retail industry. Formerly *Discount Merchandiser*.

Retail Monitor International. Euromonitor International, 122 S.Michigan Ave., Suite 1200 Chicago, IL 60603. Phone: 800-577-3876 or (312)922-1115 Fax: (312)922-1157 E-mail: info@euromonitor.com • URL: http://www.euromonitor.com • Monthly. $1,050.00 per year. Covers many aspects of international retailing, with emphasis on market research data. Includes profiles of leading retail groups, country profiles, retail news, trends, consumer credit information, and ''Retail Factfile'' (statistics).

Retail Pharmacy News. McMahon Publishing Group, 545 W. 45th St., 8th Fl. New York, NY 10036. Phone: (212)957-5300 Fax: (212)957-7230 E-mail: dbron@mcmahonmed.com • Monthly. $70.00 per year. Featues include product news for pharmacists and financial news for chain store executives.

The Retail Revolution: Market Transformation, Investment, and Labor in the Modern Department Store. Barry Bluestone and others. Greenwood Publishing Group, Inc., 88 Post Rd., W. Westport, CT 06881-5007. Phone: 800-225-5800 or (203)266-3571 Fax: (203)222-2540 E-mail: bookinfo@greenwood.com • URL: http://www.greenwood.com • 1980. $52.95.

Retail Store Planning and Design Manual. Michael J. Lopez. John Wiley and Sons, Inc., 605 Third Ave. New York, NY 10158-0012. Phone: 800-225-5945 or (212)850-6000 Fax: (212)850-6088 E-mail: info@wiley.com • URL: http://www.wiley.com • 1995. $190.00. Second edition. (NRF Publishing Program Series).

Retail Tobacco Dealers of America.

Retail Trade International. The Gale Group, 27500 Drake Rd. Farmington Hills, MI 48331-3535. Phone: 800-877-GALE or (248)699-GALE Fax: 800-414-5043 or (248)699-8069 E-mail: galeord@galegroup.com • URL: http://www.gale.com • 2000. $1,990.00. Second edition. Six volumes. Presents comprehensive data on retail trends in 51 countries. Includes textual analysis and profiles of major retailers. Covers Europe, Asia, the Middle East, Africa and the Americas.

Retail, Wholesale and Department Store Union.

Retailer's Bakery Association.

Retailing Managment. Michael Levy. McGraw-Hill Professional, 1221 Ave. of the Americas New York, NY 10020. Phone: 800-722-4726 or (212)904-2000 Fax: (212)904-2072 E-mail: customer.service@mcgraw-hill.com • URL: http://www.mcgraw-hill.com • 2000. $65.50. Fourth edition.

Retailing Today. Robert Kahn and Associates, 3684 Happy Valley Rd. Lafayette, CA 94549-3040. Phone: (510)254-4434 Fax: (510)284-5612 Monthly. $70.00 per year. Newsletter. Written for retail chief executive officers and other top retail management.

Rethinking Organization: New Directions in Organization Theory and Analysis. Michael Reed and Michael Hughes. Sage Publications, Inc., 2455 Teller Rd. Thousand Oaks, CA 91320. Phone: (805)499-0721 Fax: (805)499-0871 E-mail: info@sagepub.com • URL: http://www.sagepub.com • 1992. $62.00.

Rethinking Rental Housing. John I. Gilderbloom and Richard P. Applebaum. Temple University Press, 1601 N. Broad St., University Services Bldg., Room 305 Philadelphia, PA 19122-6099. Phone: 800-447-1656 or (215)204-8787 Fax: (215)204-4719 E-mail: tempress@astro.ocis.temple.edu • URL: http://www.temple.edu/tempress • 1987. $44.95. Emphasis on social and political factors.

The Retired Officer. Retired Officers' Association, 201 N. Washington St. Alexandria, VA 22314-2539. Phone: 800-245-8762 or (703)838-8115 Fax: (703)838-8179 E-mail: dale@troa.org • URL: http://www.troa.org • Monthly. $20.00 per year.

The Retired Officers Association.

Retirement Benefits Tax Guide. CCH, Inc., 4025 W. Peterson Ave. Chicago, IL 60646-6085. Phone: 800-248-3248 or (773)866-6000 Fax: 800-224-8299 or (773)866-3608 URL: http://www.cch.com • Looseleaf. $199.00. Supplementation available.

Retirement Communities in Florida: A Consumer's Guide and Directory to Service-Oriented Facilities. Mary L. Brooks. Pineapple Press, Inc., P.O. 3899 Sarasota, FL 34230-3899. Phone: 800-746-3275 or (941)359-0886 Fax: (941)351-9988 E-mail: info@pineapplepress.com • URL: http://www.pineapplepress.com • 1993. $12.95.

Retirement Community Business. Great River Publishing, Inc., 2026 Exeter Rd., Suite 2 Germantown, TN 38138. Phone: (901)624-5911 Fax: (901)624-5910 Quarterly. $15.00 per year. Contains articles on management, marketing, legal concerns, development, construction, and other business-related topics.

Retirement Housing Business Report. C D Publications, 8204 Fenton St. Silver Spring, MD 20910. Phone: (301)588-6380 Fax: (301)588-6385 E-mail: cdpubs@clark.net • Monthly. $149.00 per year. Newsletter. Contains practical information on designing, developing, financing, managing, and marketing residential facilities for the elderly.

Retirement Letter: The Money Newsletter for Mature People. Peter A. Dickinson, editor. Phillips Inc., Consumer Publishing, 7811 Montrose Rd. Potomac, MD 20854. Phone: 800-784-0870 or (301)340-2100 Fax: (301)424-0245 E-mail: pbi@phillips.com • URL: http://www.phillips.com • Monthly. $49.00 per year.

Retirement Life. National Association of Retired Federal Employees, 606 N. Washington St. Alexandria, VA 24314-1943. Phone: (703)838-7760 Fax: (703)838-7781 URL: http://www.narfe.com • Monthly. Free to members; non-members, $25.00 per year.

Retirement Planning Guide. Sidney Kess and Barbara Weltman. CCH, Inc., 4025 W. Peterson Ave. Chicago, IL 60646-6085. Phone: 800-248-3248 or (773)866-6000 Fax: 800-224-8299 or (773)866-3608 URL: http://www.cch.com • 1999. $49.00. Presents an overview for attorneys, accountants, and other professionals of the various concepts involved in retirement planning. Includes checklists, tables, forms, and study questions.

Retirement Plans Bulletin: Practical Explanations for the IRA and Retirement Plan Professional. Universal Pensions, Inc., P.O. Box 979 Brainerd, MN 56401-9965. Phone: 800-346-3860 or (218)829-4781 Fax: (218)829-2106 Monthly. $99.00 per year. Newsletter. Provides information on the rules and regulations governing qualified (tax-deferred) retirement plans.

Retirement Research Foundation.

Retirement Security: Understanding and Planning Your Financial Future. David M. Walker. John Wiley and Sons, Inc., 605 Third Ave. New York, NY 10158-0012. Phone: 800-225-5945 or (212)850-6000 Fax: (212)850-6088 E-mail: info@wiley.com • URL: http://www.wiley.com • 1996. $29.95. Topics include investments, social security, Medicare, health insurance, and employer retirement plans.

Reuse/Recycle. Technomic Publishing Co., Inc., 851 New Holland Ave. Lancaster, PA 17604. Phone: 800-223-9936 or (717)291-5609 Fax: (717)295-4538 E-mail: marketing@techpub.com • URL: http://www.techpub.com • Monthly. $260.00 per year. Newsletter.

Revenue Statistics. OECD Publications and Information Center, 2001 L St., N.W., Ste. 650 Washington, DC 20036-4922. Phone: (202)785-6323 Fax: (202)785-0350 E-mail: washington.contact@oecd.org • URL: http://www.oecdwash.org • Annual. $65.00. Presents data on government revenues in OECD countries, classified by type of tax and level of government. Text in English and French.

Reverse Acronyms, Initialisms, and Abbreviations Dictionary. The Gale Group, 27500 Drake Rd. Farmington Hills, MI 48331-3535. Phone: 800-877-GALE or (248)699-GALE Fax: 800-414-5043 or (248)699-8069 E-mail: galeord@

galegroup.com • URL: http://www.galegroup.com • 1998. $375.00. In three parts.

Review of Agricultural Entomology: Consisting of Abstracts of Reviews of Current Literature on Applied Entomology Throughout the World. Available from CABI Publishing North America, 10 E. 40th St. New York, NY 10016. Phone: 800-528-4841 or (212)481-7018 Fax: (212)686-7993 E-mail: cabi@cabi.org • URL: http://www.cabi.org • Monthly. $1220.00 per year. Published in England by CABI Publishing. Provides worldwide coverage of the literature. (Formerly *Review of Applied Entomology, Series A: Agricultural*.)

The Review of Economics and Statistics. Harvard University, Economics Dept. MIT Press, Five Cambridge Center Cambridge, MA 02142. Phone: 800-356-0343 or (617)253-2864 Fax: (617)253-6779 E-mail: mitpress-orders@mit.edu • URL: http://www.mitpress.mit.edu • Quarterly. Individuals, $48.00 per year; institutions, $190.00 per year; students and retired persons, $25.00 per year.

Review of Financial Economics. University of New Orleans,Lake Front, College of Business Administration, Busine. JAI Press Inc., P.O. Box 811 Stamford, CT 06904-0811. Phone: (203)323-9606 Fax: (203)357-8446 E-mail: order@jaipress.com • Three times a year. $266.00 per year. Formerly *Review of Business and Economic Research*.

Review of Income and Wealth. International Association for Research in Income and Wealth, New York University, Dept. of Economics, 269 Mercer St., Room 700 New York, NY 10003. Phone: (212)998-8917 Fax: (212)366-5067 E-mail: wolffe@fasecon.econ.nyu.edu • URL: http://www.econ.nyu.edu • Quarterly. $110.00 per year.

Review of International Political Economy. Routledge Journals, 29 W. 35th St. New York, NY 10001-2299. Phone: 800-634-7064 or (212)216-7800 Fax: 800-248-4724 or (212)564-7854 E-mail: journals@routledge.com • URL: http://www.thomson.com/routledge/ • Quarterly. Individuals, $72.00 per year; institutions, $275.00 per year. Includes articles on international trade, finance, production, and consumption.

Review of Maritime Transport. United Nations Conference on Trade and Development. United Nations Publications, United Nations Concourse Level, First Ave., 46th St. New York, NY 10017. Phone: 800-553-3210 or (212)963-7680 Fax: (212)963-4910 E-mail: bookstore@un.org • URL: http://www.un.org/publications • Annual. $55.00.

Review of Medical and Veterinary Entomology. Available from CABI Publishing North America, 10 E. 40th St. New York, NY 10016. Phone: 800-528-4841 or (212)481-7018 Fax: (212)686-7993 E-mail: cabi@cabi.org • URL: http://www.cabi.org • Monthly. $710.00 per year. Provides worldwide coverage of the literature. Formerly *Review of Applied Entomology, Series B: Medical and Veterinary*.

Review of Scientific Instruments. American Institute of Physics, One Physics Ellipse College Park, MD 20740-3843. Phone: (301)209-3100 Fax: (301)209-0843 E-mail: rsi@anl.gov • URL: http://www.aip.org/journals/rsi/rsi.html • Monthly. $1,125.00 per year.

The Review of Securities and Commodities Regulations: An Analysis of Current Laws, Regulations Affecting the Securities and Futures Industries. Standard and Poor's, 55 Water St. New York, NY 10041. Phone: 800-221-5277 or (212)438-2000 Fax: (212)438-0040 E-mail: questions@standardandpoors.com • URL: http://www.standardandpoors.com • 22 times a year. $350.00 per year.

Review of Social Economy. Association for Social Economics. Routledge Journals, 29 W. 35th St. New York, NY 10001-2299. Phone: 800-634-7064 or (212)216-7800 Fax: 800-248-4724 or (212)564-7854 E-mail: journals@routledge.com • URL: http://www.routledge.com/routledge/ • Quarterly. Individuals, $65.00 per year; institutions, $177.00 per year. Subject matter is concerned with the relationships between social values and economics. Includes articles on income distribution, poverty, labor, and class.

Revising Your Resume. Nancy Schuman and William Lewis. John Wiley and Sons, Inc., 605 Third Ave. New York, NY 10158-0012. Phone: 800-526-5368 or (212)850-6000 Fax: (212)850-6088 E-mail: info@wiley.com • URL: http://www.wiley.com • 1986. $12.95. How to emphasize positive factors.

Revocable Trusts. George M. Turner. Shepard's, 555 Middle Creek Parkway Colorado Springs, CO 80921. Phone: 800-743-7393 or (719)481-7371 Fax: 800-525-0053 or (719)481-7621 E-mail: customer_service@sheprds.com • URL: http://www.shepards.com • 1995. Third edition. Price on application.

Rhythms of Academic Life: Personal Accounts of Careers in Academia. Peter J. Frost and M. Susan Taylor, editors. Sage Publications, Inc., 2455 Teller Rd. Thousand Oaks, CA 91320. Phone: (805)499-0721 Fax: (805)499-0871 E-mail: info@sagepub.com • URL: http://www.sagepub.com • 1996. $62.00. Contains articles by various authors on college teaching, research, publishing, tenure, and related topics. Contributions are described as ''sometimes poignant and often humorous.'' (Foundations for Organizational Science and Series).

RIA Federal Income Tax Regulations. Research Institute of America, Inc., 90 Fifth Ave. New York, NY 10011. Phone: 800-431-9025 or (212)645-4800 Fax: (212)337-4213 Annual. Contains the official U. S. Treasury Department interpretation of federal income tax law. Three volumes cover final and temporary regulations and one volume covers proposed regulations.

RIA Federal Tax Handbook. Research Institute of America, Inc., 90 Fifth Ave. New York, NY 10011. Phone: 800-431-9025 or (212)645-4800 Fax: (212)337-4213 Annual. $45.00. Formerly *Master Federal Tax Manual*.

RIC News (Rare-Earth Information Center). Rare-Earth Information Center, Institute for Physical Research and Technology, Iowa State University, 112 Wilhelm Hall Ames, IA 50011-3020. Phone: (515)294-2272 Fax: (512)294-3709 E-mail: ric@ameslab.gov • URL: http://www.ameslab.gov/ • Quarterly. Free. Containing items of current interest concerning the science and technology of the rare earth.

Rice Abstracts. Available from CABI Publishing North America, 10 E. 40th St. New York, NY 10016. Phone: 800-528-4841 or (212)481-7018 Fax: (212)686-7993 E-mail: cabi@cabi.org • URL: http://www.cabi.org • Quarterly. $485.00 per year. Published in England by CABI Publishing. Provides worldwide coverage of the literature.

Rice Farming. Vance Publishing Corp., 400 Knightsbridge Parkway Lincolnshire, IL 60069-1414. Phone: 800-621-2845 or (847)634-2600 Fax: (847)634-4379 URL: http://www.vancepublishing.com • Six times a year. $30.00 per year.

Rice Journal: For Commerical Growers of Rice and Related Agribusiness. SpecComm International, Inc., 3000 Highwoods Blvd., Ste. 300 Raleigh, NC 27625-1029. Phone: (919)872-5040 Fax: (919)872-6531 E-mail: editor@ricejournal.com • URL: http://www.ricejournal.com • Six times a year. $15.00 per year.

Rice Millers' Association.

Rice: Origin, History, Technology, and Production. C. Wayne Smith and Robert Dilday, editors. John Wiley and Sons, Inc., 605 Third Ave. New York, NY 10158-0012. Phone: 800-225-5945 or (212)850-6000 Fax: (212)850-6088 E-mail: info@wiley.com • URL: http://www.wiley.com • 2001. $195.00. (Wiley Series in Crop Science.)

Richard C. Young's Intelligence Report. Phillips Publishing International, Inc., 7811 Montrose Rd. Potomac, MD 20854. Phone: 800-784-0870 or (301)340-2100 Fax: (301)424-0245 E-mail: pbi@phillips.com • URL: http://www.phillips.com/marketplaces.htm • Monthly. $99.00 per year. Newsletter. Provides conservative advice for investing in stocks, fixed-income securities, and mutual funds.

Rights and Liabilities of Publishers, Broadcasters, and Reporters. Slade R. Metcalf and Robin Bierstedt. Shepard's, 555 Middle Creek Parkway Colorado Springs, CO 80921. Phone: 800-743-7393 or (719)481-7371 Fax: 800-525-0053 or (719)481-7621 E-mail: customer_service@shepards.com • URL: http://www.shepards.com • 1982. $200.00. Two volumes. A legal manual for the media.

Rise and Fall of the Cigarette: A Social and Cultural History of Smoking in the U. S. Allan Brandt. Basic Books, 10 E. 53rd St. New York, NY 10022-5299. Phone: 800-386-5656 or (212)207-7600 Fax: (212)207-7703 E-mail: westview.order@perseusbooks.com • URL: http://www.perseusbooksgroup.com • 1997. $25.00.

Risk and Insurance. LRP Publications, P.O. Box 980 Horsham, PA 19044-0980. Phone: 800-341-7874 or (215)784-0910 Fax: (215)784-0870 E-mail: custserve@lrp.com • URL: http://www.riskandinsurance.com • Monthly. Price on application. Topics include risk management, workers' compensation, reinsurance, employee benefits, and managed care.

Risk and Insurance Management Society.

Risk Management. Risk and Insurance Management Society. Risk Management Society Publishing, Inc., 655 Third Ave., 2nd Fl. New York, NY 10017-5637. Phone: (212)286-9364 Fax: (212)922-0716 URL: http://www.rims.org/rmmag.html • Monthly. $54.00 per year.

Road and Track. Hachette Filipacchi Magazines, Inc., 1499 Monrovia Ave. Newport Beach, CA 92663. Phone: 800-274-4027 or (949)720-5300 Fax: (949)631-2757 E-mail: rtletters@aol.com • URL: http://www.roadandtrack.com • Monthly. $21.94 per year.

Road Construction and Safety. Available from U. S. Government Printing Office, Washington, DC 20402. Phone: (202)512-1800 Fax: (202)512-2250 E-mail: gpoaccess@gpo.gov • URL: http://www.access.gpo.gov • Annual. Free. Issued by the Superintendent of Documents. A list of government publications on highway construction and traffic safety. Formerly *Highway Construction, Safety and Traffic*. (Subject Bibliography No. 3.)

The Road Information Program., 1726 M St., N.W., Ste. 401 Washington, DC 20036-4521. Phone: (202)466-6706 Fax: (202)785-4722 E-mail: trip@trip.org • URL: http://www.tripnet.org • Public relations for the highway construction industry.

Road Maintenance and Rehabilitation: Funding and Allocation Strategies. OECD Publications and Information Center, 2001 L St., N. W., Ste. 650 Washington, DC 20036-4922. Phone: (202)785-6323 Fax: (202)785-0350 E-mail: washcont@oecd.org • URL: http://www.oecd.org • 1995. Discusses the allocation of public funds for highway maintenance.

Roads and Bridges. Scranton Gillette Communications, Inc., 380 E. Northwest Highway Des Plaines, IL 60016-2282. Phone: (847)391-1000 Fax: (847)390-0408 URL: http://www.sgcpubs.com/roadsbridges • Monthly. $35.00 per year. Provides information on the planning/design, administration/management, engineering and contract execution for the road and bridge industry.

Robb Report: The Magazine for the Luxury Lifestyle. Robb Report, Inc., One Acton Place Acton, MA 01720. Phone: 800-229-7622 or (978)795-3000 Fax: (978)795-3266 Monthly. $65.00 per year. Consumer magazine featuring advertisements for expensive items-antique automobiles, boats, airplanes, large houses, etc.

Robert Morris Associates- Association of Lending and Credit Risk Professionals.

Roberts' Dictionary of Industrial Relations. Books on Demand, 300 N. Zeeb Rd. Ann Arbor, MI 48106-1346. Phone: 800-521-0600 or (734)761-4700 Fax: (734)665-5022 E-mail: info@umi.com • URL: http://www.lib.umi.cam • 1993. $85.00. Fourth edition.

Robert's Rules of Order. Henry M. Roberts and William J. Evans, editors. HarperCollins Publishers, 10 E. 53rd St. New York, NY 10022-5299. Phone: 800-242-7737 or (212)207-7000 Fax: 800-822-4090 or (212)207-7145 URL: http://www.harpercollins.com • 2000. $17.00. 10th edition.

Robot Technology and Applications. Ulrich Rembold, editor. Marcel Dekker, Inc., 270 Madison Ave. New York, NY 10016. Phone: 800-228-1160 or (212)696-9000 Fax: (212)685-4540 E-mail: bookorders@dekker.com • URL: http://www.dekker.com • 1990. $230.00. (Manufacturing Engineering Material Processing Series).

Robot Vision Laboratory.

Robotic Industries Association., P.O. Box 3724 Ann Arbor, MI 48106. Phone: (734)994-6088 Fax: (734)994-3338 E-mail: ria@robotics.org • URL: http://www.robotics.org • Members are manufacturers and others concerned with the development and utilization of robot technology.

Robotics and Automation Laboratory.

Robotics and Computer-Integrated Manufacturing: An International Journal. Elsevier Science, 655 Ave. of the Americas New York, NY 10010. Phone: 888-437-4636 or (212)989-5800 Fax: (212)633-3680 E-mail: usinfo@elsevier.com • URL: http://www.elsevier.com • Bimonthly. $900.00 per year.

Robotics Institute.

Robotics International of the Society of Manufacturing Engineers., P.O. Box 930 Dearborn, MI 48121-0930. Phone: (313)271-1500 Fax: (313)271-2861 URL: http://www.sme.org/ri • Affiliated with the Society of Manufacturing Engineers.

Robotics Research Center.

Robots and Manufacturing: Recent Trends in Research, Education, and Applications. American Society of Mechanical Engineers, 22 Law Dr. Fairfield, NJ 07007-2900. Phone: 800-843-2763 or (973)882-1167 Fax: (973)882-1717 E-mail: infocentral@asme.org • URL: http://www.asme.org • Biennial. $189.00.

Rock Mechanics and Explosives Research Center.

Rock Products: Industry's Recognized Authority. Intertec Publishing Corp., P.O. Box 12901 Overland Park, KS 66282-2901. Phone: 800-400-5945 or (913)341-1300 Fax: (913)967-1898 E-mail: subs@intertec.com • URL: http://www.rockproducts • Monthly. Price on application.

Rocket Propulsion Elements: An Introduction to the Engineering of Rockets. George P. Sutton. John Wiley and Sons, Inc., 605 Third Ave. New York, NY 10158-0012. Phone: 800-526-5368 or (212)850-6000 Fax: (212)850-6088 E-mail: info@wiley.com • URL: http://www.wiley.com • 2000. $89.95. Seventh edition.

Rocks and Minerals: Mineralogy, Geology, Lapidary. Helen Dwight Reid Educational Foundation. Helderf Publications, 1319 18th St., N.W. Washington, DC 20036-1802. Phone: 800-365-9753 or (202)296-6267 Fax: (202)296-5149 E-mail: rm@helderf.org • URL: http://www.helderf.org • Bimonthly. Individuals, $38.00. per year; institutions, $74.00 per year.

Rocky Mountain Coal Mining Institute.

Rodney L. White Center for Financial Research., University of Pennsylvania, 3254 Steinberg Hall-Dietrich Hall Philadelphia, PA 19104. Phone: (215)898-7616 Fax: (215)573-8084 E-mail: rlwtcr@finance.wharton.upenn.edu • URL: http://www.finance.wharton.upenn.edu/~rlwctr • Research areas include financial management, money markets, real estate finance, and international finance.

Roget's International Thesaurus. Robert L. Chapman, editor. HarperCollins Publishers, 10 E. 53rd St. New York, NY 10022-5299. Phone: 800-242-7737 or (212)207-7000 Fax: 800-822-4090 or (212)207-7145 URL: http://www.harpercollins.com • 1992. $19.95. Fifth edition.

The Rome, Maastricht, and Amsterdam Treaties: Comparative Texts. Euroconfidentiel S. A., Rue de Rixensart 18 B-1332 Genval, Belgium. Phone: (32)02 653 01 25 Fax: (32)02 653 01 80 E-mail: nigel.hunt@euronet.be • 1999. $42.00. Includes a comprehensive keyword index.

Roof Framing. Marshall Gross. Craftsman Book Co., 6058 Corte del Cedro Carlsbad, CA 92009. Phone: 800-829-8123 or (760)438-7828 Fax: (760)438-0398 E-mail: jacobs@costbook.com • URL: http://www.craftsman-book.com • 1989. $22.00. Revised edition. (Home Craftsman Books).

Ross Reports Television and Film Casting, Production Scripts. BPI Communications, Inc., 770 Broadway New York, NY 10003-9595. Phone: 800-344-7119 or (646)654-5500 Fax: (646)654-5834 E-mail: info@bpi.com • URL: http://www.bpicomm.com • Monthly. $50.00. per year. Directory, production and casting guide, designed for actors and writers. Formerly *Ross Reports Television*.

Roster of Clubs. International Training in Communication, 2519 Woodland Dr. Anaheim, CA 92801. Phone: (714)995-3600 Fax: (714)995-6974 Annual. Price on application.

Rotor and Wing International: Serving the Worldwide Helicopter Industry. Phillips Business Information, Inc., 1201 Seven Locks Rd., Suite 300 Potomac, MD 20854. Phone: 800-777-5006 or (301)340-2100 Fax: (301)340-0542 E-mail: pbi@phillips.com • URL: http://www.phillips • Monthly. Free to qualified personnel; others, $49.00 per year. Includes supplement *World Helicopter Resources*.

Rough Notes: Property, Casualty, Surety. The Rough Notes Co., Inc., 11690 Technology Dr. Carmel, IN 46032. Phone: 800-428-4384 or (317)582-1600 Fax: (317)816-1003 E-mail: rnc@in.net • URL: http://www.roughnotes.com/ • Monthly. $27.50 per year.

RSI (Roofing, Siding, Insulation). Advanstar Communications, Inc., 7500 Old Oak Blvd. Cleveland, OH 44130-3369. Phone: 800-346-0085 or (440)243-8100 Fax: (440)891-2740 E-mail: information@advanstar.com • URL: http://www.advanstar.com • Monthly. $39.00 per year.

RTCA.

R3: Ratios, Ratings, and Reference. Anne L. Buchanan, editor. Available from American Library Association, 50 E. Huron St. Chicago, IL 60611-2795. Phone: 800-545-2433 or (312)944-6780 Fax: (312)280-3255 E-mail: ala@ala.org • URL: http://www.ala.org • 1996. $20.00. Published by the Reference and User Services Association. Contains basic information on the construction and uses of financial ratios, with extensive listings of ratio data sources. (RUSA Occasional Papers, No. 20.)

Rubber and Plastics News: The Rubber Industry's International Newspaper. Crain Communications, Inc., 1725 Merriman Rd., Suite 300 Akron, OH 44313-5283. Phone: 800-678-9595 or (330)836-9180 Fax: (330)836-1005 URL: http://www.rubbernews.com • Biweekly. $74.00 per year. Written for rubber product manufacturers.

Rubber Chemistry and Technology. American Chemical Society, Rubber Div., University of Akron Akron, OH 44309-0499. Phone: 800-333-9511 or (216)972-7814 Fax: (216)972-5269 E-mail: service@acs.org • URL: http://www.chemcenter.org • Five times a year. $95.00 per year.

Rubber Manufacturers Association.

Rubber Red Book: Directory of the Rubber Industry. Intertec Publishing, 6151 Powers Ferry Rd., N.W., Suite 200 Atlanta, GA 30339-2941. Phone: 800-621-9907 or (770)955-2500 Fax: (770)955-0476 E-mail: subs@intertec.com • URL: http://www.intertec.com • Annual. $89.95. Lists manufacturers and suppliers of rubber goods in U.S., Puerto Rico and Canada.

Rubber Statistical Bulletin. International Rubber Study Group, 115 Heron House, 115 Wembley Hill Rd., 1st Fl., Flat 109 Wembley, Middlesex HA9 8DA, England. Phone: (44-)20-8903-7727 Fax: (44-)20-8903-2848 E-mail: irsg@compuserve.com • URL: http://www.rubberstudy.com • Monthly. Members, $346.00 per year; non-members, $327.00 per year.

Rubber Technology. Maurice Morton. Chapman and Hall, 115 Fifth Ave., 4th Fl. New York, NY 10003-1004. Phone: 800-842-3636 or (212)260-1354 Fax: (212)260-1730 E-mail: info@chapall.com • URL: http://www.chapall.com • 1987. $62.95. Third edition.

Rubber World. Lippincott and Peto, Inc., 1867 W. Market St. Akron, OH 44313. Phone: (216)864-2122 Fax: (216)864-5298 URL: http://www.rubberworld.com/ • 16 times a year. $29.00 per year.

Rubber World Blue Book of Materials, Compounding Ingredients and Machinery for Rubber. Don R. Smith, editor. Lippincott and Peto, Inc., P.O. Box 5451 Akron, OH 44313-0486. Phone: (216)864-2122 Fax: (216)864-5298 URL: http://www.rubberworld.com/ • Annual. $111.00.

Rundt's World Business Intelligence. S. J. Rundt and Associates, Inc., 130 E. 63rd St. New York, NY 10021-7334. Phone: (212)838-0141 Fax: (212)973-3073 E-mail: info@rundtsintelligence.com • URL: http://www.rundtsintelligence.com • Weekly. $695.00 per year. Formerly *Rundt's Weekly Intelligence*.

Running an Effective Sales Office. Patrick Forsythe. John Wiley and Sons, Inc., 605 Third Ave. New York, NY 10158-0012. Phone: 800-225-5945 or (212)850-6000 Fax: (212)850-6088 E-mail: info@wiley.com • URL: http://www.wiley.com • 1998. $35.95.

Runzheimer Reports on Relocation. Runzheimer International, Runzheimer Park Rochester, WI 53167. Phone: 800-942-9949 or (414)767-2200 Fax: (414)767-2276 URL: http://www.runzheimer.com • Monthly. $295.00 per year. Newsletter.

Runzheimer Reports on Travel Management. Runzheimer International, Runzheimer Park Rochester, WI 53167. Phone: 800-942-9949 or (414)767-2200 Fax: (414)767-2276 URL: http://www.runzheimer.com • Monthly. $354.00 per year. Newsletter on the control of business travel costs.

Rupp's Insurance and Risk Management Glossary. Richard V. Rupp. Available from CCH, Inc., 4025 W. Peterson Ave. Chicago, IL 60646-6085. Phone: 800-248-3248 or (773)866-6000 Fax: 800-224-8299 or (773)866-3608 URL: http://www.cch.com • 1996. $35.00. Second edition. Published by NILS Publishing Co. Provides definitions of 6,400 insurance words and phrases. Includes a guide to acronyms and abbreviations.

Rural Cooperatives. Available from U. S. Government Printing Office, Washington, DC 20402. Phone: (202)512-1800 Fax: (202)512-2250 E-mail: gpoaccess@gpo.gov • URL: http://www.access.gpo.gov • Bimonthly. $15.00 per year. Issued by the U. S. Department of Agriculture. Contains articles on cooperatives in rural America. Formerly *Farmer Cooperatives*.

RUSA Update. American Library Association, 50 E. Huron St. Chicago, IL 60611-2795. Phone: 800-545-2433 or (312)944-6780 Fax: (312)440-9374 E-mail: rusa@ala.org • URL: http://www.ala.org • Quarterly. Free to members; non-members, $20.00 per year. Serves as news letter for the Reference and User Services Association, a division of the American Library Association. Includes activities of the Business Reference and Services Section (BRASS). Formerly *RASD Update*.

Russell's Official National Motor Coach Guide: Official Publications of Bus Lines for the United States and Canada. Russell's Guides, Inc., P.O. Box 278 Cedar Rapids, IA 52406. Phone: (319)364-6138 Fax: (319)364-4853 Monthly. $100.35 per year. Publications of bus lines for the U.S., Canada, and Mexico.

Russian Ultrasonics. Multi-Science Publishing Co. Ltd., P.O. Box 176 Avenel, NJ 07001. E-mail: sciencem@hotmail.com • URL: http://www.futurenet.co.uk/ads/multisience • Bimonthly. $303.00 per year.

Rutgers Accounting Web (RAW). Rutgers University Accounting Research CenterPhone: (201)648-5172 Fax: (201)648-1233 URL: http://www.rutgers.edu/accounting • RAW Web site provides extensive links to sources of national and international accounting information, such as the Big Six accounting firms, the Financial Accounting Standards Board (FASB), SEC filings (EDGAR), journals, publishers, software, the International Accounting Network, and "Internet's largest list of accounting firms in USA." Searching is offered. Fees: Free.

Rutgers Agricultural Research and Extension Center. Rutgers University

RV Business (Recreational Vehicle). Affinity Group Inc.,T L Enterprises, 2575 Vista Del Mar Dr. Ventura, CA 93001-3920. Phone: 800-766-1674 or (805)667-4100 Fax: (805)667-4454 URL: http://www.rv.net • Monthly. $48.00 per year. Includes annual *Directory*. News about the entire recreational vehicle industry in the U.S.

RV Buyer's Guide (Recreational Vehicle). Affinity Group, Inc.,T L Enterprises, 2575 Vista Del Mar Dr. Ventura, CA 93001-3920. Phone: 800-234-3450 or (805)667-4100 Fax: (805)667-4454 URL: http://www.rv.net • Annual. $7.95.

RxList: The Internet Drug Index. Neil SandowPhone: (707)746-8754 E-mail: info@rxlist.com • URL: http://www.rxlist.com • Web site features detailed information (cost, usage, dosage, side effects, etc.) from Mosby, Inc. for about 300 major pharmaceutical products, representing two thirds of prescriptions filled in the U. S. (3,700 other products are listed). The "Top 200" drugs are ranked by number of prescriptions filled. Keyword searching is provided. Fees: Free.

S & P's Insurance Book. Standard & Poor's Ratings Group, Insurance Rating Services, 55 Water St. New York, NY 10041. Phone: 800-221-5277 or (212)438-2000 Fax: (212)438-0040 E-mail: questions@standardandpoors.com • URL: http://www.standardandpoors.com • Quarterly. Price on application. Contains detailed financial analyses and ratings of various kinds of insurance companies.

S & P's Insurance Digest: Life Insurance Edition. Standard & Poor's Ratings Group, Insurance Rating Services, 55 Water St. New York, NY 10041. Phone: 800-221-5277 or (212)438-2000 Fax: (212)438-0040 E-mail: questions@standardandpoors.com • URL: http://www.standardandpoors.com • Quarterly. Contains concise financial analyses and ratings of life insurance companies.

S & P's Insurance Digest: Property-Casualty and Reinsurance Edition. Standard & Poor's Ratings Group, Insurance Rating Services, 55 Water St. New York, NY 10041. Phone: 800-221-5277 or (212)438-2000 Fax: (212)438-0040 E-mail: questions@standardandpoors.com • URL: http://www.standardandpoors.com • Quarterly. Contains concise financial analyses and ratings of property-casualty insurance companies.

S & P's Municipal Bond Book, with Notes, Commercial Paper, & IRBs. Standard & Poor's, 55 Water St. New York, NY 10041. Phone: 800-221-5277 or (212)438-2000 Fax: (212)438-0040 E-mail: questions@standardandpoors.com. • URL: http://www.standardandpoors.com • Bimonthly. $965.00 per year. Includes ratings and statistical information for about 20,000 municipal bonds, notes, commercial paper issues, and industrial revenue bonds (IRBs). The creditworthiness ("Rationales") of 200 selected municipalities and other issuers is discussed. Securities "under surveillance" by S & P are listed.

A S B P E Editor's Notes. American Society of Business Press Editors, 107 W. Ogden Ave. La Grange, IL 60525-2022. Phone: (708)352-6950 Fax: (708)352-3780 E-mail: 71114.34@compuserve.com • URL: http://www.asbpe.org • Bimonthly. Membership. Newsletter. Formerly (American Society of Business Press Editors).

S. Klein Directory of Computer Suppliers: Hardware, Software, Systems and Services. Technology and Business Communications, Inc., P.O. Box 915 Sudbury, MA 01776. Phone: (508)443-4671 1987. $73.00.

S. S. Huebner Foundation., University of Pennsylvania, Vance Hall, Room 430 Philadelphia, PA 19104-6301. Phone: (215)898-9631 Fax: (215)573-2218 E-mail: cummins@wharton.upenn.edu • URL: http://www.rider.wharton.upenn.edu/~sshuebne/ • Awards grants for research in various areas of insurance.

SAE Handbook. Society of Automotive Engineers, 400 Commonwealth Dr. Warrendale, PA 15096-0001. Phone: 800-832-6732 or (724)776-4841 Fax: (724)776-5960 E-mail: sae@sae.org • URL: http://www.sae.org • Annual. $425.00. Three volumes. Contains standards, recommended practices and information reports on ground vehicle design, manufacturing, testing and performance.

SAE International.

SAEGIS Internet Search. Thomson & ThomsonPhone: 800-692-8833 or (617)479-1600 Fax: (617)786-8273 E-mail: support@thomson-thomson.com • URL: http://www.thomson-thomson.com • Fee-based Web site provides extensive, common law screening of the World Wide Web for trademarks. Searches are performed offline, with final report delivered to user's "SAEGIS Inbox." Context of trademark within each relevant Web site is indicated, and links are provided.

Safe Deposit Bulletin. New York State Safe Deposit Association c/o Paul Sanchez, P.O. Box 5074 New York, NY 10185. Phone: (212)484-2260 Quarterly. Membership

The Safe Money Report. Weiss Ratings, Inc., 4176 Burns Rd. Palm Beach Gardens, FL 33410-4606. Phone: 800-289-9222 or (561)627-3300 Fax: (561)625-6685 E-mail: clara@weissinc.com • URL: http://www.martinweiss.com • Monthly. $148.00 per year. Newsletter. Provides financial advice and current safety ratings of various banks, savings and loan companies, insurance companies, and securities dealers.

Safe Trip Abroad. Available from U. S. Government Printing Office, Washington, DC 20402. Phone: (202)512-1800 Fax: (202)512-2250 E-mail: gpoaccess@gpo.gov • URL: http://www.access.gpo.gov • 1996. $1.25. Issued by the Bureau of Consular Affairs, U. S. State Department (http://www.state.gov). Provides practical advice for international travel.

Safety. Alton, L. ThyGerson. Jones and Bartlett Publishing, Inc, 40 Tall Pine Dr. Sudbury, MA 01776-2256. Phone: 800-832-0034 or (978)443-5000 Fax: (978)443-8000 E-mail: info@jbpub.com • URL: http://www.jbpub.com • 1992. $33.75. Second edition.

Safety and Health at Work. International Labour Office, 1828 L St., N.W., Suite 801 Washington, DC 20036. Phone: (202)653-7652 Fax: (202)653-7687 E-mail: ilopubs@tascol.com • URL: http://www.ilo.org • Bimonthly. $240.00 per year. Formerly *Occupational Safety and Health Abstracts*.

Safety and Health Safety Equipment Buyers' Guide. National Safety Council, Periodicals Dept., 1121 Spring Lake Dr. Itasca, IL 60143-3201. Phone: 800-621-7619 or (630)285-1121 Fax: (630)285-1315 E-mail: safety-health.org • URL: http://www.nsc.org • Annual. $5.00.

Safety and Health: The International Safety Health and Environment Magazine. National Safety Council, Periodicals Dept., 1121 Spring Lake Dr. Itasca, IL 60143-3201. Phone: 800-621-7619 or (630)285-1121 Fax: (630)285-1315 URL: http://www.nsc.org • Monthly. Members, $80.00 per year; non-members, $91.00 per year. Formerly *National Safety and Health News*.

Sage Family Studies Abstracts. Sage Publications, Inc., 2455 Teller Rd. Thousand Oaks, CA 91320. Phone: (805)499-0721 Fax: (805)499-0871 E-mail: info@sagepub.com • URL: http://www.sagepub.com • Quarterly. Individuals, $125.00 per year; institutions, $575.00 per year.

Sage Public Administration Abstracts. Sage Publications, Inc., 2455 Teller Rd. Thousand Oaks, CA 91320. Phone: (805)499-0721 Fax: (805)499-0871 E-mail: info@sagepub.com • URL: http://www.sagepub.com • Quarterly. Individuals, $150.00 per year; institutions, $575.00 per year.

Sage Series in Written Communication: An International Survey of Research and Theory. Sage Publications, Inc., 2455 Teller Rd. Thousand Oaks, CA 91320. Phone: (805)499-0721 Fax: (805)499-0871 E-mail: info@sagepub.com • URL: http://www.sagepub.com • Irregular. $22.95.

Sage Urban Studies Abstracts. Sage Publications, Inc., 2455 Teller Rd. Thousand Oaks, CA 91320. Phone: (805)499-0721 Fax: (805)499-0871 E-mail: info@sagepub.com • URL: http://www.sagepub.com • Quarterly. Individuals, $150.00 per year; institutions, $560.00 per year.

Sailboat Buyers Guide. Commonwealth Business Media, 84 State St., Suite 9C Boston, MA 02159-1630. Phone: 800-362-8433 or (617)720-8600 Fax: (617)723-0911 E-mail: sailads@primediasi.com • URL: http://www.sailbuyersguide.com • Annual. $5.95. Over 2,000 Sailboat and equipment manufacturers. Formerly *Sailboat and Equipment and Shipbuilding*.

St. James Encyclopedia of Mortgage and Real Estate Finance. James Newell, editor. St. James Press, 27500 Drake Rd. Farmington Hills, MI 48331-3535. Phone: 800-877-GALE or (248)699-GALE Fax: 800-414-5043 or (248)699-8063 E-mail: galeord@galegroup.com • URL: http://www.galegroup.com • 1991. $55.00. Defines over 1,000 terms related to the buying, selling, and financing of real estate. Includes charts and graphs.

St. James World Directory of Futures and Options. St. James Press, 27500 Drake Rd. Farmington Hills, MI 48331-3535. Phone: 800-877-GALE or (248)699-GALE Fax: 800-414-5043 or (248)699-8063 E-mail: galeord@galegroup.com • URL: http://www.galegroup.com • 1991. $95.00. Contains information on approximately 50 commodity futures exchanges located in various countries. Over 350 futures and options trading contracts are described.

Salaries of Scientists, Engineers, and Technicians: A Summary of Salary Surveys. Commission on Professionals in Science and Technology. CPST Publications, 1333 H St., N.W. Washington, DC 20005-4707. Phone: (202)223-6995 Fax: (202)223-6444 Irregular. $100.00. A summary of salary surveys.

Sales and Marketing Executives.

Sales and Marketing Management. Bill Communications, Inc., 770 Broadway New York, NY 10003. Phone: 800-266-4712 or (646)654-4500 Fax: (646)654-7212 E-mail: info@bpi.com • URL: http://www.billcom.com • Monthly. $48.00 per year.

Sales and Marketing Management Survey of Buying Power. Bill Communications, Inc., 770 Broadway New York, NY 10003-9595. Phone: 800-266-4712 or (646)654-4500 Fax: (646)654-7212 E-mail: info@bpi.com • URL: http://www.billcom.com • Annual. $150.00.

Sales & Marketing Report: Practical Ideas for Successful Selling. Lawence Ragan Communications, Inc., 316 N. Michigan Ave. Chicago, IL 60601. Phone: 800-878-5331 or (312)960-4100 Fax: (312)960-4106 E-mail: cservice@ragan.com • URL: http://www.ragan.com • Monthly. $119.00 per year. Newsletter. Emphasis is on sales training, staff morale, and marketing productivity.

Sales and Sales Management. Butterworth-Heinemann, 225 Wildwood Ave. Woburn, MA 01801. Phone: 800-366-2665 or (781)904-2500 Fax: 800-446-6520 E-mail: orders@bhusa.com • URL: http://www.bh.com • 1998. $34.95.

Sales and Use Tax Alert. CCH, Inc., 4025 West Peterson Ave. Chicago, IL 60646-6085. Phone: 800-248-3248 or (773)866-6000 Fax: 800-224-8299 or (773)866-3608 URL: http://www.cch.com • Monthly. $197.00 per year. Newsletter. Provides nationwide coverage of new developments in sales tax laws and regulations.

Sales and Use Taxation of E-Commerce: State Tax Administrators' Current Thinking, with CCH Commentary. CCH, Inc., 4025 West Peterson Ave. Chicago, IL 60646-6085. Phone: 800-248-3248 or (773)866-6000 Fax: 800-224-8299 or (773)866-3608 E-mail: cust_serv@cch.com • URL: http://www.cch.com • 2000. $129.00. Provides advice and information on the impact of state sales taxes on e-commerce activity.

Sales Association of the Chemical Industry., 66 Morris Ave., Suite 2-A Springfield, NJ 07081. Phone: (973)379-1100 Fax: (973)379-6507 Members are chemical sales personnel, including sales managers and executives.

Sales Compensation Handbook. John K. Moynahan, editor. AMACOM, 1601 Broadway, 12th Fl. New York, NY 10019. Phone: 800-262-9699 or (212)586-8100 Fax: (212)903-8168 E-mail: custmserv@amanet.org • URL: http://www.amanet.org • 1998. $75.00. Second edition. Topics include salespeople compensation plans based on salary, commission, bonuses, and contests.

Sales Forecasting. American Management Association Extension Institute, P.O. Box 1026 Saranac Lake, NY 12983-9957. Phone: 800-262-9699 or (518)891-1500 Fax: (518)891-0368 Looseleaf. $110.00. Self-study course. Emphasis is on practical explanations, examples, and problem solving. Quizzes and a case study are included.

Sales Management. William C. Moncrief and Shannon Shipp. Addison-Wesley Longman, Inc., One Jacob Way Reading, MA 01867. Phone: 800-447-2226 or (781)944-3700 Fax: (781)944-9351 URL: http://www.awl.com • 1997. $98.00. Includes chapters on personal selling, organization, training, motivation, compensation, evaluation, sales forecasting, and strategy. A glossary and case histories are provided.

Sales Management: Concepts and Cases. Douglas J. Dalyrmple and William J. Cron. John Wiley and Sons, Inc., 605 Third Ave. New York, NY 10158-0012. Phone: 800-526-5368 or (212)850-6000 Fax: (212)850-6088 E-mail: info@wiley.com • URL: http://www.wiley.com • 1997. $95.95 Sixth edition.

Sales Manager's Desk Book. Gene Garofalo. Prentice Hall, 240 Frisch Court Paramus, NJ 07652-5240. Phone: 800-947-7700 or (201)909-6200 Fax: 800-445-6991 or (201)909-6361 URL: http://www.prenhall.com • 1996. $69.95. Second edition. A handbook covering many aspects of selling and sales management. Includes information on telemarketing, communications technology, voice mail, and teleconferencing.

Sales Manager's Handbook. John P. Steinbrink. Dartnell Corp., 350 Hiatt Dr. Palm Beach, FL 33418. Phone: 800-621-5463 or (561)622-6520 Fax: (561)622-2423 E-mail: custserv@lrp.com • URL: http://www.dartnellcorp.com • 1989. $93.50. 14th edition.

Sales Manager's Model Letter Desk Book. Hal Fahner and Morris E. Miller. Prentice Hall, 240 Frisch Court Paramus, NJ 07652-5240. Phone: 800-947-7700 or (201)909-6200 Fax: 800-445-6991 or (201)909-6361 URL: http://www.prenhall.com • 1988. $32.95. Second edition.

Sales Manager's Portable Answer Book. Gene Garofalo. Prentice Hall, 240 Frisch Court Paramus, NJ 07652-5240. Phone: 800-947-7700 or (201)909-6200 Fax: 800-445-6991 or (201)909-6361 URL: http://www.prenhall.com • 1997. $59.95. Contains succinct information and advice on demonstrations, proposals, closing the sale, leadership, expenses, forecasting ("Crystal Balls, Tea Leaves, Palm Reading: Forecasting Sales"), compensation, sales meetings, trade shows, training, regional office management, and various other subjects.

Sales Negotiation Skills That Sell. Robert E. Kellar. AMACOM, 1601 Broadway, 12th Fl. New York, NY 10019. Phone: 800-262-9699 or (212)586-8100 Fax: (212)903-8168 E-mail: custmserv@amanet.org • URL: http://www.amanet.org • 1996. $17.95. Covers negotiating objectives, risk assessment, planning, strategy, tactics, and face-to-face skills.

Sales Promotion. Robert C. Blattberg. Prentice Hall, 240 Frisch Court Paramus, NJ 07652-5240. Phone: 800-947-7700 or (201)909-6200 Fax: 800-445-6991 or (201)909-6361 URL: http://www.prenhall.com • 1995. $23.60.

Sales Promotion Handbook. Tamara Brezen and William Robinson. Dartnell Corp., 350 Hiatt Dr. Palm Beach, FL 33418. Phone: 800-621-5463 or (561)622-6520 Fax: (561)622-2423 E-mail: custserv@lrp.com • URL: http://www.dartnellcorp.com • 1994. $69.95. Eighth edition. Covers licensing, tie-ins, legal aspects, event marketing, database marketing, and other topics.

Sales Prospector. Prospector Research Services, Inc, P.O. Box 185 Lake Bluff, IL 60044-0185. Monthly. $495.00 per year. In 14 United States regional editions. Reports on expansions and relocations of manufacturing firms, distribution centers, and transportation terminals in new existing buildings.

Sales Representative Law Guide. CCH, Inc., 4025 W. Peterson Ave. Chicago, IL 60646-6085. Phone: 800-248-3248 or (773)866-6000 Fax: 800-224-8299 or (773)866-3608 URL: http://www.cch.com • Looseleaf. $149.00 per year (updated annually). Covers state laws on independent sales representation. Includes checklists and forms.

Sales Tax Rate Directory. Vertex Systems, Inc., 1041 Old Cassatt Rd. Berwyn, PA 19312. Phone: (610)640-4200 Annual. $670.00. Monthly updates. U.S. and Canadian sales/use tax rates in standardized format.

Salk Institute for Biological Studies.

Salomon Center. New York University

Salt Institute.

Sam Advanced Management Journal. Society for the Advancement of Management. Texas A & M University - Corpus Christi, College of Business, 6300 Ocean Dr., FC 111 Corpus Christi, TX 78412. Phone: (361)825-6045 Fax: (361)825-2725 E-mail: moustafa@falcon.tamucc.edu • URL: http://www.enterprise.tamucc.edu/ • Quarterly. $49.00. Provides information on leading business topics for practicing managers.

SAMA Group of Associations.

Samir Husni's Guide to New Consumer Magazines. Oxbridge Communications, Inc., 150 Fifth Ave., Suite 302 New York, NY 10011. Phone: 800-955-0231 or (212)741-0231 Fax: (212)633-2938 E-mail: info@mediafinder.com • URL: http://www.mediafinder.com • Annual. $95.00. A directory of more than 500 consumer magazines that began publication during the previous year. Includes names of key personnel.

SAMPE Journal. Society for the Advancement of Material and Process Engineering, P.O. Box 2459 Covina, CA 91722. Phone: (626)331-0616 Fax: (626)332-8929 Bimonthly. $65.00 per year. Provides technical information.

Samuel Zell and Robert Lurie Real Estate Center at Wharton.

Sandhills Research Station. North Carolina Dept. of Agriculture

Sandwich Shop/Deli. Entrepreneur Media, Inc., 2445 McCabe Way Irvine, CA 92614. Phone: 800-421-2300 or (949)261-2325 Fax: (949)261-0234 E-mail: entmag@entrepreneur.com • URL: http://www.entrepreneur.com • Looseleaf. $59.50. A practical guide to starting a sandwich shop and delicatessen. Covers profit potential, start-up costs, market size evaluation, owner's time required, site selection, lease negotiation, pricing, accounting, advertising, promotion, etc. (Start-Up Business Guide No. E1156.)

Sanitary Maintenance Buyers' Guide. Trade Press Publishing Corp., 2100 W. Florist Ave. Milwaukee, WI 53209-3799. Phone: 800-727-7995 or (414)228-7701 Fax: (414)228-1134 URL: http://www.tradepress.com • Annual. $20.00.

Sanitary Maintenance: The Journal of the Sanitary Supply Industry. Trade Press Publishing Corp., 2100 W. Florist Ave. Milwaukee, WI 53209-3799. Phone: 800-727-7995 or (414)228-7701 Fax: (414)228-1134 URL: http://www.tradepress.com • Monthly. $55.00 per year.

Satellite-Based Cellular Communications. Bruno Pattan. McGraw-Hill, 1221 Ave. of the Americas New York, NY 10020. Phone: 800-722-4726 or (212)904-2000 Fax: (212)904-2072 E-mail: customer.service@mcgraw-hill.com • URL: http://www.mcgraw-hill.com • 1997. $69.00. (Telecommunications Series).

Satellite Broadcasting: The Politics and Implications of the New Media. Ralph M. Negrine, editor. Routledge, 29 W. 35th St. New York, NY 10001-2299. Phone: 800-634-7064 or (212)244-3366 Fax: 800-248-4724 or (212)564-7854 E-mail: info@routledge.com • URL: http://www.thomson.com/routledge • 1988. $65.00. Second edition.

Satellite Communications. Intertec Publishing Corp., P.O. Box 12901 Overland Park, KS 66282-2901. Phone: 800-400-5945 or (913)341-1300 Fax: (913)967-1898 E-mail: subs@intertec.com • URL: http://www.intertec.com • Monthly. $42.00 per year.

Satellite Communications - Satellite Industry Directory. Phillips Business Information, Inc., 1201 Seven Locks Rd., Suite 300 Potomac, MD 20854-2958. Phone: 800-777-5006 or (301)340-1520 Fax: (301)340-0542 E-mail: pbi@phillips.com • URL: http://www.phillips.com • Annual. $275.00. Provides information on about 2,000 providers of equipment and services for the satellite communications industry.

Satellite Communications: The First Quarter Century of Service. David W. Rees. John Wiley and Sons, Inc., 605 Third Ave. New York, NY 10158-0012. Phone: 800-526-5368 or (212)850-6000 Fax: (212)850-6088 E-mail: info@wiley.com • URL: http://www.wiley.com • 1990. $123.00. A survey of the history of communications satellites, emphasizing business applications.

Satellite News: The Monthly Newsletter Covering Management, Marketing Technology, and Regulation. Phillips Business Information, Inc., 1201 Seven Locks Rd., Suite 300 Potomac, MD 20854. Phone: 800-777-5006 or (301)340-1520 Fax: (301)340-0542 E-mail: pbi@phillips.com • URL: http://www.phillips.com/pbi.htm • 50 times a year. $997.00 per year.

Satellite Week: The Authoritative News Service for Satellite Communications and Allied Fields. Warren Publishing Inc., 2115 Ward Court, N. W. Washington, DC 20037-1209. Phone: 800-771-9202 or (202)872-9200 Fax: (202)293-3435 E-mail: customerservice@warren-news.com • URL: http://www.telecommunications.com • Weekly. $964.00 per year. Newsletter. Covers satellite broadcasting, telecommunications, and the industrialization of space.

SAVE International., 60 Revere Dr., Suite 500 Northbrook, IL 60062. Phone: (847)480-1730 Fax: (847)480-9282 E-mail: value@value-eng.com • Members are value engineers and value analysts. Purpose is to achieve the necessary function of a product or service at the lowest cost, consistent with quality requirements.

The Savings and Loan Crisis: An Annotated Bibliography. Pat L. Talley, compiler. Greenwood Publishing Group, Inc., 88 Post Rd., W. Westport, CT 06881-5007. Phone: 800-225-5800 or (203)226-3571 Fax: (203)222-2540 E-mail: bookinfo@greenwood.com • URL: http://www.greenwood.com • 1993. $65.00. Includes 360 scholarly and popular titles (books and research papers). (Bibliographies and Indexes in Economic History, No. 14).

Sawyer's Success Tactics for Information Businesses. Deborah C. Sawyer. Burwell Enterprises, Inc., 5619 Plumtree Dr. Dallas, TX 75252. Phone: (281)537-9051 Fax:

(281)537-8332 E-mail: burwellinfo@burwellinc.com • URL: http://www.burwellinc.com • 1998. $24.50. Covers such items as pricing, costs, and service for information brokers and others in the fee-based information business.

Sawyer's Survival Guide for Information Brokers. Deborah C. Sawyer. Burwell Enterprises, Inc., 5619 Plumtree Dr. Dallas, TX 75252-4928. Phone: (281)537-9051 Fax: (281)537-8332 E-mail: burwellinfo@burwellinc.com • URL: http://www.burwellinc.com • 1995. $39.50. Provides practical advice for information entrepreneurs.

Sax's Dangerous Properties of Industrial Materials. Richard J. Lewis. John Wiley and Sons, Inc., 605 Third Ave. New York, NY 10158-0012. Phone: 800-225-5945 or (212)850-6000 Fax: (212)850-6088 E-mail: info@jwiley.com • URL: http://www.wiley.com • 1999. $545.00. 10th edition. Three volumes. Provides detailed information on the chemical, physical, and toxicity characteristics of more than 22,000 industrial materials. Hazard ratings and safety profiles are specified.

SBA Loan Guide. Entrepreneur Meida, Inc., 2445 McCabe Way Irvine, CA 92614. Phone: 800-421-2300 or (949)261-2325 Fax: (949)261-0234 E-mail: entmag@entrepreneur.com • URL: http://www.entrepreneur.com • Looseleaf. $59.50. A practical guide to obtaining loans through the Small Business Administration. (Start-Up Business Guide No. E1315.)

SBBI Monthly Market Reports. Ibbotson Associates, 225 N. Michigan Ave., Suite 700 Chicago, IL 60601-7676. Phone: 800-758-3557 or (312)616-1620 Fax: (312)616-0404 Monthly. $995.00 per year. These reports provide current updating of stocks, bonds, bills, and inflation (SBBI) data. Each issue contains the most recent month's investment returns and index values for various kinds of securities, as well as monthly statistics for the past year. Analysis is included.

SBBI Quarterly Market Reports. Ibbotson Associates, 225 N. Michigan Ave., Suite 700 Chicago, IL 60601-7676. Phone: 800-758-3557 or (312)616-1620 Fax: (312)616-0404 Quarterly. $495.00 per year. Each quarterly volume contains detailed updates to stocks, bonds, bills, and inflation (SBBI) data. Includes total and sector returns for the broad stock market, small company stocks, intermediate and long-term government bonds, long-term corporate bonds, and U. S. Treasury Bills. Analyses, tables, graphs, and market consensus forecasts are provided.

SBIC Directory and Handbook of Small Business Finance. International Wealth Success, Inc., P.O. Box 186 Merrick, NY 11566. Phone: 800-323-0548 or (516)766-5850 Fax: (516)766-5919 Annual. $15.00 per year. Includes small business investment companies.

Scale Manufacturers Association.

Scandinavian Kompass on Disc. Available from Kompass USA, Inc., 1255 Route 70, Suite 25-S Lakewood, NJ 08701. Phone: 877-566-7277 or (732)730-0340 Fax: (732)730-0342 E-mail: mail@kompass-usa.com • URL: http://www.kompass.com • Annual. $1,950.00. CD-ROM provides information on more than 66,000 companies in Denmark, Finland, Norway, and Sweden. Classification system covers approximately 50,000 products and services.

Schaum's Outline of Unix. Harley Hahn. McGraw-Hill, 1221 Ave. of the Americas New York, NY 10020. Phone: 800-722-4726 or (212)904-2000 Fax: (212)904-2072 E-mail: customer.service@mcgraw-hill.com • URL: http://www.mcgraw-hill.com • 1995. $7.38. (Schaum's Outline Series).

Schiffli Embroidery Manufacturers Promotion Fund.

The Scholarship Book: The Complete Guide to Private Scholarships, Grants, and Loans for Undergraduates. Daniel J. Cassidy. Prentice Hall, 240 Frisch Court Paramus, NJ 07652-5240. Phone: 800-947-7700 or (201)909-6200 Fax: 800-445-6991 or (201)909-6361 URL: http://www.prenhall.com • 2000. $35.95. Sixth edition.

Scholarships, Fellowships, and Loans. The Gale Group, 27500 Drake Rd. Farmington Hills, MI 48331-3535. Phone: 800-877-GALE or (248)699-GALE Fax: 800-414-5043 or (248)699-8069 E-mail: galeord@galegroup.com • URL: http://www.galegroup.com • 1999. $190.00. 17th edition. Describes more than 3,700 scholarships, fellowships, loans, and other educational funding sources available to U. S. and Canadian undergraduate and graduate students.

Scholastic Journalism. Earl E. English and others. Iowa State University Press, 2121 S. State Ave. Ames, IA 50014-8300. Phone: 800-862-6657 or (515)292-0140 Fax: (515)292-3348 E-mail: orders@isupress.edu • URL: http://www.isupress.edu • 1996. $32.95. Ninth edition.

School Administrator's Complete Letter Book. Gerald Tomlinson. Prentice Hall, 240 Frisch Court Paramus, NJ 07652-5240. Phone: 800-947-7700 or (201)909-6200 Fax: 800-445-6991 or (201)909-6361 URL: http://www.prenhall.com • 1984. $37.95.

School Bus Fleet. Bobit Publishing Corp., 21061 S. Western Ave. Torrance, CA 90501. Phone: (310)533-2400 Fax: (310)533-2500 E-mail: peggyn@bobit.com • URL: http://www.schoolbusfleet.com • Bimonthly. $25.00 per year. Includes *Factbook*.

School Business Affairs. Association of School Business Officials. ASBO International, 11401 N. Shore Dr. Reston, VA 20190-4200. Phone: (703)478-0405 Fax: (703)478-0205 URL: http://www.asbointl.org • Monthly. Free to members; non-members, $68.00 per year.

School Enrollment, Social and Economic Characteristics of Students. Available from U. S. Government Printing Office, Washington, DC 20402. Phone: (202)512-1800 Fax: (202)512-2250 E-mail: gpoaccess@gpo.gov • URL: http://www.access.gpo.gov • Annual. Issued by the U. S. Bureau of the Census. Presents detailed tabulations of data on school enrollment of the civilian noninstitutional population three years old and over. Covers nursery school, kindergarten, elementary school, high school, college, and graduate school. Information is provided on age, race, sex, family income, marital status, employment, and other characteristics.

School Foodservice Who's Who Directory. Information Central Inc., P.O. Box 3900 Prescott, AZ 86302. Phone: (520)778-1513 Fax: (520)778-1513 E-mail: awoodman@oldwest.net • Triennial. $675.00. Two volumes. Gives food service details for approximately 5,800 large school districts. Serves as a marketing information source for food and equipment suppliers.

School Law News: The Independent Biweekly News Service on Legal Developments in Education. Aspen Publishers, Inc., 200 Orchard Ridge Dr. Gaithersburg, MD 20878. Phone: 800-638-8437 or (301)417-7500 Fax: (301)695-7931 E-mail: customer.service@aspenpubl.com • URL: http://www.aspenpubl.com • Biweekly. $305.00 per year.

School Library Journal: The Magazine of Children, Young Adults and School Librarians. Cahners Business Information, Printing and Publishing Div., 245 W. 17th St. New York, NY 10011-5300. Phone: 800-662-7776 or (212)645-0067 Fax: (212)463-6689 E-mail: corporatecommunications@cahners.com • URL: http://www.cahners.com • Monthly. $97.50 per year. Supplement available *Sourcebook*

School of Architecture-Building Research Council. University of Illinois at Urbana-Champaign

School Planning and Management. Peter Li, Inc., P.O. Box 49699 Dayton, OH 45449-0699. Phone: (937)847-5900 Fax: (937)847-5910 Monthly. $48.00 per year. Formerly *School and College*.

Schwann Inside: Jazz and Classical. Schwann Publications, 1280 Santa Anita Court Woodland, CA 95776. Phone: 800-792-9447 or (530)669-5077 Fax: 800-999-1794 or (530)669-5184 E-mail: schwann@valley-media.com • URL: http://www.schwann.com • Monthly. $55.95 per year. Provides reviews and listings of new classical and jazz recordings. Includes ''Billboard Charts'' of top selling jazz, contemporary jazz, classical, classical crossover, classical midline, and classical budget albums.

Schwann Opus: The Classical Music Resource. Schwann Publications, 1280 Santa Anita Court Woodland, CA 95776. Phone: 800-792-9447 or (530)669-5077 Fax: 800-999-1794 or (530)669-5184 E-mail: schwann@valley-media.com • URL: http://www.schwann.com • Annual. $27.45 per year. Lists classical music recordings by composer. Covers compact discs, minidiscs, and cassette tapes. Includes an extensive, alphabetical list of recording labels and distributors, with addresses and telephone numbers (many listings also include fax numbers and Internet addresses).

Schwann Spectrum: The Guide to Rock, Jazz, World...and Beyond. Schwann Publications, 1280 Santa Anita Court Woodland, CA 95776. Phone: 800-792-9447 or (530)669-5077 Fax: 800-999-1794 or (530)669-5184 E-mail: schwann@valley-media.com • URL: http://www.schwann.com • Annual. $27.45 per year. Lists rock, jazz, country, folk, soundtrack, international, new age, religious, and other disc and tape popular recordings by performer. Includes an extensive, alphabetical list of recording labels and distributors, with addresses and telephone numbers (some listings also include fax numbers and Internet addresses).

Science and Practice of Welding. A. C. Davies. Cambridge University Press, 40 W. 20th St. New York, NY 10022. Phone: 800-221-4512 or (212)924-3900 Fax: (212)937-4712 E-mail: info@cup.org • URL: http://www.cup.org • 1993. 10th edition. Two volumes. Vol. 1, *Welding Science and Technology, $29.95; volume two, The Practice of Welding*, $39.95.

Science and Technology Almanac. Oryx Press, 4041 North Central Ave., Suite 700 Phoenix, AZ 85012-3397. Phone: 800-279-6799 or (602)265-2651 Fax: 800-279-4663 or (602)265-6250 E-mail: info@oryxpress.com • URL: http://www.oryxpress.com • Annual. $65.00. Covers technological news, research, and statistics.

Science and Technology Desk Reference: Answers to Frequently Asked and Difficult to Answer Reference Questions in Science and Technology. Carnegie Library of Pittsburgh, Science and Technology Department Staff, editors. The Gale Group, 27500 Drake Rd. Farmington Hills, MI 48331-3535. Phone: 800-877-GALE or (248)699-GALE Fax: 800-414-5043 or (248)699-8069 E-mail: galeord@galegroup.com • URL: http://www.galegroup.com • 1997. $70.00. Second edition. *The Handy Science Answer Book*. Covers a wide variety of subject areas, including biology, astronomy, chemistry, geology, the environment, and health.

Science and Technology Libraries. Haworth Press, Inc., 10 Alice St. Binghamton, NY 13904-1580. Phone: 800-429-6784 or (607)722-5857 Fax: 800-895-0582 or (607)722-1424 E-mail: getinfo@haworthpressinc.com • URL: http://www.haworthpressinc.com • Quarterly. Individuals, $45.00 per year; institutions, $160.00 per year; libraries, $160.00 per year.

Science Citation Index. Institute for Scientific Information, 3501 Market St. Philadelphia, PA 19104. Phone: 800-386-4474 or (215)386-0100 Fax: (215)386-2911 URL: http://www.isinet.com • Bimonthly. $15,020.00 per year. Annual cumulation. Includes *Source Index*, *Citation Index*, *Permuterm Subject Index*, and *Corporate Index*.

Science Citation Index: Compact Disc Edition. Institute for Scientific Information, 3501 Market St. Philadelphia, PA 19104. Phone: 800-336-4474 or (215)386-0100 Fax: (215)386-2911 Quarterly. Provides CD-ROM indexing of the world's scientific and technical literature. Corresponds to online *Scisearch* and printed *Science Citation Index*.

Science Park Development Corporation., P.O. Box 35 New Haven, CT 06511. Phone: (203)786-5018 Fax: (203)786-5001 E-mail: dennis.lyndon@sciencepark.org • URL: http://www.sciencepark.org • Affiliated with Yale University.

Scientific Meetings. Scientific Meetings Publications, 5214 Soledad Mountain Rd. San Diego, CA 92138. Phone: (858)270-2910 Fax: (858)270-2910 E-mail: scimeeting@access.net • Quarterly. $85.00 per year. Provides information on forthcoming scientific, technical, medical, health, engineering and management meetings held throughout the world.

The Scientist: The Newspaper for the Life Science Professionals. Information Science Institute, 3600 Market St., Suite 450 Philadelphia, PA 19104-2645. Phone: 800-523-1850 or (215)386-9601 Fax: (215)387-7542 E-mail: info@the-scientist.com • URL: http://www.the-scientist.com • Semimonthly. Individuals, $29.00 per year; institutions, $58.00 per year. Contains news for scientific, research, and technical personnel.

Scisearch. Institute for Scientific Information, 3501 Market St. Philadelphia, PA 19104. Phone: 800-523-1850 or (215)386-0100 Fax: (215)386-2911 URL: http://www.isinet.com • Broad, multidisciplinary index to the literature of science and technology, 1974 to present. Inquire as to online cost and availability. Coverage of literature is worldwide, with weekly updates.

The Scope of Faculty Collective Bargaining: An Analysis of Faculty Union Agreements at Four-Year Institutions of Higher Education. Ronald L. Johnstone, editor. Greenwood Publishing Group, Inc., 88 Post Rd., W. Westport, CT 06881-5007. Phone: 800-225-5800 or (203)226-3571 Fax: (203)222-2540 E-mail: bookinfo@greenwood.com • URL: http://www.greenwood.com • 1981. $52.95.(Contributions to the Study of Education Series, No. 2).

Score Association.

Scott Stamp Monthly: With Catalogue Update. Scott Publishing Co., 911 Vandemark Rd. Sidney, OH 45365. Phone: (513)498-0802 Fax: (513)498-0807 URL: http://www.scottonline.com • Monthly. $17.95 per year.

Scrap. Institute of Scrap Recycling Industries, 1325 G St., N.W., Suite 1000 Washington, DC 20005. Phone: (202)737-1770 Fax: (202)626-0900 URL: http://www.scrap.org • Bimonthly. Free to members; non-members, $32.95 per year. Formerly *Scrap Processing and Recycling*.

Scripps Institution of Oceanography, Center for Coastal Studies. University of California, San Diego

Scripta Materialia. Acta Metallurgica, Inc. Elsevier Science, 655 Ave. of the Americas New York, NY 10010. Phone: 888-437-4636 or (212)989-5800 Fax: (212)633-3680 E-mail: usinfo@elsevier.com • URL: http://www.elsevier.com • Semimonthly. $1,188.00 per year.

Scriptwriters Market. Scriptwriters-Filmmakers Publishing Co., 3681 Berry Dr. Studio City, CA 91604. Phone: (818)726-3726 Fax: (818)505-5062 Annual. $39.95. 450 literary agents, 375 film producers, over 3,000 actors and actresses, 325 directors, and 275 television producers.

Sea Power. Navy League of the United States, 2300 Wilson Blvd. Arlington, VA 22201-3308. Phone: (703)528-1775 Fax: (703)243-8251 E-mail: mail@navyleague.org • URL: http://www.navyleague.org • Monthly. Free to members; non-members $25.00 per year. Includes annual *Almanac of Seapower*.

Sea Technology Buyers Guide/Directory. Compass Publications, Inc., 1117 N. 19th St., Suite 1000 Arlington, VA 22209. Phone: (703)524-3136 Fax: (703)841-0852 E-mail: oceanbiz@seatechnology.com • Annual. $25.50. Manufacturing, service, research and development, engineering, construction, drilling, equipment lease and rental firms, and testing organizations providing goods and services to the oceanographic, offshore, marine sciences, and undersea defense industries. Formerly *Sea Technology Handbook/Directory*.

Sea Technology: For Design Engineering and Application of Equipment and Services for the Marine Environment.

Compass Publications, Inc., 1117 N. 19th St., Suite 1000 Arlington, VA 22209. Phone: (703)524-3136 Fax: (703)841-0852 E-mail: oceanbiz@seatechnology.com • Monthly. $35.00 per year.

The Seafood Business Annual Buyer's Guide. Diversified Business Communications, P.O. Box 7438 Portland, ME 04112-7438. Phone: (207)842-5600 Fax: (207)842-5603 E-mail: bspringer@divcom.com • Annual. Price on application. Lists about 1,300 North American fish and shellfish suppliers, distributors, importers and exporters and suppliers of related services and equipment. Formerly *Seafood Buyer's Sourcebook*.

The Seafood Market. MarketResearch.com, 641 Ave. of the Americas, Third Floor New York, NY 10011. Phone: 800-298-5699 or (212)807-2629 Fax: (212)807-2716 E-mail: order@marketresearch.com • URL: http://www.marketresearch.com • 1997. $595.00. Market research report. Covers fresh, frozen, and canned seafood. Market projections are provided to the year 2001.

Seafood Price-Current. Urner Barry Publications, Inc., P.O. Box 389 Toms River, NJ 08754. Phone: 800-932-0617 or (732)240-5330 Fax: (732)341-0891 E-mail: mail@urnerbarry.com • URL: http://www.seafoodnet.com • Semiweekly. $295.00 per year.

Sealed Insulating Glass Manufacturers Association.

Search Engine Watch: You Want Answers? Internet.com Corp.Phone: (212)547-7900 Fax: (212)953-1733 URL: http://www.searchenginewatch.com • Web site offers information on various aspects of search engines, including new developments, indexing systems, technology, ratings and reviews of major operators, specialty services, tutorials, news, history, "Search Engine EKGs," "Facts and Fun," etc. Online searching is provided. Fees: Free. Formerly *A Webmaster's Guide to Search Engines*.

Search Master Tax Library. Matthew Bender & Co., Inc., 1275 Broadway Albany, NY 12204-2694. Phone: 800-223-5297 or (518)487-3000 Fax: (518)487-3584 Monthly. $1,200.00 per year. Provides current CD-ROM full text of *Bender's Federal Tax Service, Bender's Master Federal Tax Handbook*, and the current full text of Bender's state tax services for California, Florida, Illinois, New Jersey, New York, Ohio, Pennsylvania, and Texas.

Searcher: The Magazine for Database Professionals. Information Today, Inc., 143 Old Marlton Pike Medford, NJ 08055-8750. Phone: 800-300-9868 or (609)654-6266 Fax: (609)654-4309 E-mail: custserv@infotoday.com • URL: http://www.infotoday.com • 10 times per year. $64.95 per year. Covers a wide range of topics relating to online and CD-ROM database searching.

SEC Accounting Rules, with Financial Reporting Releases, Codification of Financial Reporting Policies, Accounting and Auditing Enforcement Releases, and Staff Accounting Bulletins. CCH, Inc., 4025 W. Peterson Ave. Chicago, IL 60646-6085. Phone: 800-248-3248 or (773)866-6000 Fax: 800-224-8299 or (773)866-3608 URL: http://www.cch.com • Looseleaf. $448.00.

SEC Filing Companies. Disclosure Inc., 5161 River Rd. Bethesda, MD 20816. Phone: (301)951-1300 Semiannual. Free. A list of all public companies that file reports with the U.S. Securities and Exchange Commission.

SEC Financial Reporting: Annual Reports to Shareholders, Form 10-K, and Quarterly Financial Reporting. Matthew Bender & Co., Inc., Two Park Ave. New York, NY 10016. Phone: 800-223-1940 or (212)448-2000 Fax: (212)244-3188 E-mail: international@bender.com • URL: http://www.bender.com • $215.00. Looseleaf service. Periodic supplementation. Coverage of aspects of financial reporting and disclosure under Regulations S-X and S-K, with step-by-step procedures for preparing information for Form 10-K and annual shareholders reports.

SEC Handbook: Rules and Forms for Financial Statements and Related Disclosures. CCH, Inc., 4025 W. Peterson Ave. Chicago, IL 60646-6085. Phone: 800-248-3248 or (773)866-6000 Fax: 800-224-8299 or (773)866-3608 URL: http://www.cch.com • Annual. $54.00. Contains full text of rules and requirements set by the Securities and Exchange Commisssion for preparation of corporate financial statements.

SEC News Digest. U.S. Securities and Exchange Commission, Public Reference Room, 450 Fifth St., N.W., MISC-11 Washington, DC 20549. Phone: (202)272-7460 Fax: (202)272-7050 URL: http://www.sec.gov/ • Daily.

SEC Online. Disclosure, Inc., 5161 River Rd. Bethesda, MD 20816. Phone: 800-945-3647 or (301)951-1300 Fax: (301)657-1962 URL: http://www.disclosure.com • Provides complete text online of reports filed by over 5,000 public corporations with the U. S. Securities and Exchange Commission. Includes 10-K (official annual reports), 10-Q (quarterly), proxy statements, annual reports for stockholders, and other documents. Covers 1987 to date, with updates two or three times a week. Inquire as to online cost and availability.

SEC Online on SilverPlatter. Available from SilverPlatter Information, Inc., 100 River Ridge Drive Norwood, MA 02062-5026. Phone: 800-343-0064 or (781)769-2599 Fax: (781)769-8763 Quarterly. $3,950.00 per year to nonprofit organizations; $6,950.00 per year to businesses. Produced by Disclosure, Inc. Provides complete text on CD-ROM of documents filed with the Securities and Exchange Commission by over 5,000 publicly held corporations, including 10K forms (annual), 10Q forms (quarterly), and proxies. Also includes annual reports to stockholders.

SEC Today (Securities Exchange Commission). Washington Service Bureau, Inc., 655 15th St., N.W. Washington, DC 20005. Phone: 800-828-5354 or (202)508-0600 Fax: (202)659-3655 URL: http://www.wsb.com/sectoday • Daily. $760.00 per year. Newsletter. Includes the official *SEC News Digest* from the Securities and Exchange Commission and reports on public company filing activity.

Secondary Mortgage Market: Strategies for Surviving and Thriving in Today's Challenging Markets. McGraw-Hill Professional, 1221 Ave. of the Americas New York, NY 10020. Phone: 800-722-4726 or (212)904-2000 Fax: (212)904-2072 E-mail: customer.service@mcgraw-hill.com • URL: http://www.mcgraw-hill.com • 1992. $70.00. Revised edition.

Secretarial/Word Processing Service. Entrepreneur Media, Inc., 2445 McCabe Way Irvine, CA 92614. Phone: 800-421-2300 or (949)261-2325 Fax: (949)261-0234 E-mail: entmag@entrepreneur.com • URL: http://www.entrepreneur.com • Looseleaf. $59.50. A practical guide to starting a secretarial and word processing business. Covers profit potential, start-up costs, market size evaluation, owner's time required, site selection, pricing, accounting, advertising, promotion, etc. (Start-Up Business Guide No. E1136.)

Secrets of a Top Headhunter: How to Get the High-Paying Job You've Always Wanted. Lester Korn. Simon & Schuster Trade, 1230 Ave. of the Americas New York, NY 10020. Phone: 800-223-2336 or (212)698-7000 Fax: 800-943-9831 or (212)698-7007 E-mail: ssonline_feedback@simonsays.com • URL: http://www.simonsays.com • 1988. $17.45.

Secrets of Closing Sales. Charles B. Roth. Prentice Hall, 240 Frisch Court Paramus, NJ 07652-5240. Phone: 800-947-7700 or (201)909-6452 Fax: 800-445-6991 or (201)909-6361 URL: http://www.prenhall.com • 1993. $16.95. Sixth edition.

Secrets of the Street: The Dark Side of Making Money. Gene Marcial. McGraw-Hill, 1221 Ave. of the Americas New York, NY 10020. Phone: 800-722-4726 or (212)904-2000 Fax: (212)904-2072 E-mail: customer.service@mcgraw-hill.com • URL: http://www.mcgraw-hill.com • 1996. $10.95. Explains how the small, individual investor can be taken advantage of by Wall Street professionals.

Secrets of the Super Net Searchers: The Reflections, Revelations and Hard-Won Wisdom of 35 of the World's Top Internet Researchers. Reva Basch. Information Today, Inc., 143 Old Marlton Pike Medford, NJ 08055-8750. Phone: 800-300-9868 or (609)654-6266 Fax: (609)654-4309 E-mail: custserv@infotoday.com • URL: http://www.infotoday.com • 1996. $29.95. Tells how to find "cyber-gems" among the "cyber-junk." (Cyber Age Books.)

Secrets of the Super Searchers: The Accumulated Wisdom of 23 of the World's Top Online Searchers. Reva Basch. Information Today, Inc., 143 Old Marlton Pike Medford, NJ 08055-8750. Phone: 800-300-9868 or (609)654-6266 Fax: (609)654-4309 E-mail: custserv@infotoday.com • URL: http://www.infotoday.com • 1993. $39.95. Contains interviews with experienced online searchers, covering such topics as pre-search interviewing, search strategy, full-text considerations, search limiting, and client relations.

Section for Psychiatric and Substance Abuse Services.

Section for Women in Public Administration.

Secured Lender. Commercial Finance Association, 225 W. 34th St.,, Room 1815 New York, NY 10122-0008. Phone: (212)594-3480 Bimonthly. Members, $24.00 per year; non-members, $48.00 per year.

Securities and Federal Corporate Law Report. West Group, 610 Opperman Dr. Eagan, MN 55123. Phone: 800-328-4880 or (651)687-7000 Fax: 800-213-2323 or (651)687-5827 URL: http://www.westgroup.com • 11 times a year. $308.00 per year. Newsletter.

Securities Arbitration Commentator: Covering Significant Issues and Events in Securities/Commodities Arbitration. Richard P. Ryder, P.O. Box 112 Maplewood, NJ 07040. Phone: (973)761-5880 Fax: (973)761-1504 Monthly. $348.00 per year. Newsletter. Edited for attorneys and other professionals concerned with securities arbitration.

Securities, Commodities, and Banking: Year in Review. CCH, Inc., 4025 W. Peterson Ave. Chicago, IL 60646-6085. Phone: 800-248-3248 or (773)866-6000 Fax: 800-224-8299 or (773)866-3608 URL: http://www.cch.com • Annual. $55.00. Summarizes the year's significant legal and regulatory developments.

Securities Counseling for New and Developing Companies. Stuart R. Cohn. West Group, 610 Opperman Dr. Eagan, MN 55123. Phone: 800-328-4880 or (651)687-7000 Fax: 800-213-2323 or (651)687-5827 URL: http://www.westgroup.com • 1993. $130.00. Covers securities planning for new businesses, with an emphasis on the avoidance of legal violations and civil liabilities. (Corporate Law Series).

Securities Crimes. Marvin Pickholz. West Group, 610 Opperman Dr. Eagan, MN 55123. Phone: 800-328-4880 or (651)687-7000 Fax: 800-213-2323 or (651)687-5827 URL: http://www.westgroup.com • $145.00. Looseleaf service. Periodic supplementation. Analyzes the enfo of federal securities laws from the viewpoint of the defendant. Discusses Securities and Exchange Commission (SEC) investigations and federal sentencing guidelines.

Securities Industry Association.

Securities Industry News. American Banker, One State St. Plaza New York, NY 10004. Phone: 800-362-3806 or (212)803-8345 Fax: (212)292-5217 URL: http://www.americanbanker.com • Weekly. $275.00 per year. Covers securities dealing and processing, including regulatory compliance, shareholder services, human resources, transaction clearing, and technology.

Securities Industry Yearbook. Securities Industry Association, 120 Broadway, 35th Fl. New York, NY 10271. Phone: (212)608-1500 Fax: (212)608-1604 Annual. Members, $85.00; non-members, $125.00. Information about securities industry firms and capital markets.

Securities Law Compliance: A Guide for Brokers, Dealers, and Investors. Allan H. Pessin. McGraw-Hill Professional, 1221 Ave. of the Americas New York, NY 10020. Phone: 800-722-4726 or (212)904-2000 Fax: (212)904-2072 E-mail: customer.service@mcgraw-hill.com • URL: http://www.mcgraw-hill.com • 1989. $70.00.

Securities Law Handbook. Harold S. Bloomenthal. West Group, 610 Opperman Dr. Eagan, MN 55123. Phone: 800-328-4880 or (651)687-7000 Fax: 800-213-2323 or (651)687-5827 URL: http://www.westgroup.com • Annual. $206.00.

Securities Law Review. West Group, 610 Opperman Dr. Eagan, MN 55123. Phone: 800-328-4880 or (651)687-7000 Fax: 800-213-2323 or (651)687-5827 URL: http://www.westgroup.com • Annual. $189.00. Current thinking in securities law.

Securities Litigation and Regulation Reporter: The National Journal of Record ofCommodities Litigation. Andrews Publications, 175 Strafford Ave., Bldg. 4, Suite 140 Wayne, PA 19087. Phone: 800-345-1101 or (610)622-0510 Fax: (610)622-0501 Semimonthly. $1,294.00 per year. Provides reports on litigation involving the rules and decisions of the Commodity Futures Trading Commission. Formerly *Securities and Commodities Litigation Reporter*.

Securities Markets. Kenneth D. Garbade. McGraw-Hill, 1221 Ave of the Americas New York, NY 10020-1095. Phone: 800-722-4726 or (212)904-2000 Fax: (212)904-2072 E-mail: customer.service@mcgraw-hill.com • URL: http://www.mcgraw-hill.com • 1982. $66.25. (Finance Series).

Securities: Public and Private Offerings. William W. Prifti. West Group, 610 Opperman Dr. Eagan, MN 55123. Phone: 800-328-4880 or (651)687-7000 Fax: 800-213-2323 or (651)687-5827 URL: http://www.westgroup.com • $250.00. Two looseleaf volumes. Periodic supplementation. How to issue securities. (Securities Law Series).

Securities Regulation. Louis Loss and Joel Seligman. Little, Brown and Co., Time and Life Bldg., 1271 Ave. of the Americas New York, NY 10020. Phone: 800-343-9204 or (212)522-8700 Fax: 800-286-9741 E-mail: cust.service@littlebrown.com • URL: http://www.littlebrown.com • 1988. $240.00. Third edition. Three volumes. Includes 1969 supplement. Covers the fundamentals of government regulation of securities.

Securities Regulation and Law Report. Bureau of National Affairs, 1231 25th St., N.W. Washington, DC 20037-1197. Phone: 800-372-1033 or (202)452-4200 Fax: (202)452-8092 E-mail: books@bna.com • URL: http://www.bna.com • Weekly. $1,294.00 per year. Two volumes. Looseleaf.

Securities Regulation Law Journal. Warren, Gorham and Lamont/RIA Group, 395 Hudson St. New York, NY 10014. Phone: 800-950-1215 or (212)367-6300 Fax: (212)924-0460 URL: http://www.wgl.com • Quarterly. $224.00 per year. Provides analysis and in-depth advice including regulations, SEC pronouncements, legislation and litigation. Shows how to comply with all the regulations affecting issuance and sale of securities and their transfer and trading.

Securities Week. McGraw-Hill, 1221 Ave. of the Americas New York, NY 10020-1095. Phone: 800-722-4726 or (212)904-2000 Fax: (212)904-2072 E-mail: customer.service@mcgraw-hill.com • URL: http://www.mcgraw-hill.com • Weekly. $1,325.00 per year.

Security Analysis. S. Cottle. McGraw-Hill, 1221 Ave of the Americas New York, NY 10020. Phone: 800-722-4726 or (212)904-2000 Fax: (212)904-2072 E-mail: customer.service@mcgraw-hill.com • URL: http://www.mcgraw-hill.com • 1988. $59.95. Fifth edition.

Security Analysis and Portfolio Management. Donald E. Fischer and Ronald L. Jordan. Prentice Hall, 240 Frisch Court Paramus, NJ 07652-5240. Phone: 800-947-7700 or (201)909-6200 Fax: 800-445-6991 or (201)909-6361 URL: http://www.prenhall.com • 1995. $87.00. Sixth edition.

Security Applications in Industry and Institutions. Lawrence J. Fennelly, editor. Butterworth-Heinemann, 225 Wildwood Ave. Woburn, MA 01081. Phone: 800-366-2665 or (781)904-2500 Fax: 800-466-6520 E-mail: orders@bhusa.com • URL: http://www.bh.com • 1992. $46.95. Contains 19 chapters written by various security professionals in the U. S. Covers bank security, hotel security, shoplifting, college campus crime prevention, security in office buildings, hospitals, museums, libraries, etc.

Security Distributing and Marketing. Cahners Business Information, 1350 E. Touhy Ave. Des Plaines, IL 60018-3358. Phone: 800-662-7776 or (847)635-8800 Fax: (847)635-9950 E-mail: corporatecommunications@cahners.com • URL: http://www.cahners.com • 13 times a year. $82.00 per year. Covers applications, merchandising, new technology and management.

Security Distributing and Marketing-Security Products and Services Locater. Cahners Business Information, 1350 E. Touhy Ave. Des Plaines, IL 60018-3358. Phone: 800-662-7776 or (847)635-8800 Fax: (847)390-2445 E-mail: corporatecommunications@cahners.com • URL: http://www.cahners.com • Annual. $50.00. Formerly *SDM: Security Distributing and Marketing-Security Products and Services Directory*.

Security Hardwear Distributors Association.

Security Letter., 166 E. 96th St. New York, NY 10128. Phone: (212)348-1553 Fax: (212)534-2957 22 times a year. $187.00 per year. News and insight on protection of assets from loss. Includes stock market and other data on the security industry.

Security Management. American Society for Industrial Security, 1625 Prince St. Alexandria, VA 22314-2818. Phone: (703)519-6200 Fax: (703)518-1518 E-mail: sharowitz@asisonline.org • URL: http://www.securitymanagement.com • Monthly. Free to members; non-members, $48.00 per year. Articles cover the protection of corporate assets, including personnel property and information security.

Security Options Strategy. Albert I. Bookbinder. Programmed Press, 599 Arnold Rd. West Hempstead, NY 11552. Phone: (516)599-6527 1976. $15.00.

Security Owner's Stock Guide. Standard and Poor's, 55 Water St. New York, NY 10041. Phone: 800-221-5277 or (212)438-2000 Fax: (212)438-0040 E-mail: questions@standardandpoors.com • URL: http://www.standardandpoors.com • Monthly. $125.00 per year.

Security: Product Service Suppliers Guide. Cahners Business Information, 1350 E. Touhy Ave. Des Plains, IL 60018-3358. Phone: 800-662-7776 or (847)635-8800 Fax: (847)390-2690 E-mail: corporatecomunications@cahners.com • URL: http://www.cahners.com • Annual. $50.00 Includes computer and information protection products. Formerly *Security - World Product Directory*.

Security Systems Administration. Cygnus Business Media, 445 Broad Hollow Rd. Melville, NY 11747. Phone: 800-308-6397 or (631)845-2700 Fax: (631)845-2798 E-mail: rich.reiff@cygnuspub.com • URL: http://www.cygnuspub.com • Monthly. $10.00 per year.

Security: The Magazine for Buyers of Security Products, Systems and Service. Cahners Business Information, 1350 E. Touhy Ave. Des Plaines, IL 60018-3358. Phone: 800-662-7776 or (847)635-6880 Fax: (847)299-8622 E-mail: corporatecommunications@cahners.com • URL: http://www.cahners.com • Monthly. $82.90 per year.

Security Traders Association.

Seed Abstracts. Available from CABI Publishing North America, 10 E. 40th St. New York, NY 10016. Phone: 800-528-4841 or (212)481-7018 Fax: (212)686-7993 E-mail: cabi@cabi.org • URL: http://www.cabi.org • Monthly. $540.00 per year. Published in England by CABI Publishing. Provides worldwide coverage of the literature.

The Seed Technologist Newsletter. Society of Commercial Seed Technologists, c/o Andy Evans, Ohio State University, 202 Kottman Hall, 2021 Coffey Rd. Columbus, OH 43210. Phone: (614)292-8242 URL: http://www.zianet.com/aosa/index.html • Three times a year. $35.00 per year. Includes annual *Proceedings*.

Seed Trade News. Z M A G Publishing, Inc., 317 Main St., No. A Hopkins, MN 55343-9212. Phone: (612)448-5402 Fax: (612)448-6935 E-mail: seedtrade@skypoint.com • Monthly. $30.00 per year. Includes *International Seed Directory*.

Seed World. Scranton Gillette Communications, Inc., 380 E. Northwest Highway, Ste. 200 Des Plaines, IL 60016-2282. Phone: (847)391-1000 Fax: (847)390-0408 E-mail: seedworld@aol.com • URL: http://www.sgcpubs.com • Monthly. $30.00 per year. Provides information on the seed industry for buyers and sellers. Supplement available *Seed Trade Buyer's Guide*.

SEI Center for Advanced Studies in Management., University of Pennsylvania, 1400 Steinberg Hall-Dietrich, 3620 Locust Walk Philadelphia, PA 19104-6371. Phone: (215)898-2349 Fax: (215)898-1703 E-mail: seicenter@wharton.upenn.edu • URL: http://www.marketing.wharton.upenn.edu/seicenter • Conducts interdisciplinary management studies.

Selected Characteristics of Occupations Defined in the Revised Dictionary of Occupational Titles. Available from U. S. Government Printing Office, Washington, DC 20402. Phone: (202)512-1800 Fax: (202)512-2250 E-mail: gpoaccess@gpo.gov • URL: http://www.access.gpo.gov • 1993. Provides data on training time, physical demands, and environmental conditions for various occupations. (Employment and Training Administration, U. S. Department of Labor.)

Selected Instruments and Related Products. U.S. Bureau of the Census, Washington, DC 20233-0800. Phone: (301)457-4100 Fax: (301)457-3842 URL: http://www.census.gov • Annual. (Current Industrial Reports, MA-38B.)

Selected Interest Rates. U.S. Federal Reserve System, Board of Governors, Publications Services, 20th and Constitution Ave., N.W. Room MS-127 Washington, DC 20551. Phone: (202)452-3244 Fax: (202)728-5886 URL: http://www.federalreserve.gov • Weekly release, $20.00 per year; monthly release, $5.00 per year.

Self. Conde Nast Publications, Inc., Four Times Square, 5th Fl. New York, NY 10036. Phone: 800-289-9330 or (212)582-9090 Fax: (212)286-8110 Monthly. $16.00 per year. Written for business women.

Self-Employed America. National Association for the Self-Employed, 2121 Precinct Rd. Hurst, TX 76054. Phone: 800-232-6273 or (817)428-4243 Fax: (817)428-4210 Controlled circulation. Provides articles on marketing, management, motivation, accounting, taxes, and other topics for businesses having fewer than 15 employees.

Selling by Phone: How to Reach and Sell to Customers. Linda Richardson. McGraw-Hill, 1221 Ave. of the Americas New York, NY 10020. Phone: 800-722-4726 or (212)904-2000 Fax: (212)904-2072 E-mail: customer.service@mcgraw-hill.com • URL: http://www.mcgraw-hill.com • 1995. $14.95.

Selling Through Independent Reps. Harold J. Novick. AMACOM, 1601 Broadway, 12th Fl. New York, NY 10019. Phone: 800-262-9699 or (212)586-8100 Fax: (212)903-8168 E-mail: custmserv@amanet.org • URL: http://www.amanet.org • 1999. $75.00. Third edition. Tells how to make good use of independent sales representatives.

Selling Through Negotiation: The Handbook of Sales Negotiation. Homer B. Smith. Marketing Education Associates, 4004 Rosemary St. Chevy Chase, MO 20185. Phone: (301)656-5550 Fax: (301)982-7086 E-mail: homsmith@erols.com • 1988. $14.95.

Selling to Kids: News and Practical Advice on Successfully Marketing to Children. Available from MarketResearch.com, 641 Ave. of the Americas, Third Floor New York, NY 10011. Phone: 800-298-5699 or (212)807-2629 Fax: (212)807-2716 E-mail: order@marketresearch.com • URL: http://www.marketresearch.com • Biweekly. $495.00 per year. Newsletter. Published by Phillips Business Information.

Selling to Seniors: The Monthly Report on Marketing. Community Development Services, Inc. CD Publications, 8204 Fenton St. Silver Spring, MD 20910-2889. Phone: 800-666-6380 or (301)588-6380 Fax: (301)588-0519 E-mail: cdpubs@clark.net • Monthly. $225.00 per year. Newsletter on effective ways to reach the ''over 50'' market.

Selling to the Affluent: The Professional's Guide to Closing the Sales That Count. Thomas Stanley. McGraw-Hill Professional, 1221 Ave. of the Americas New York, NY 10020. Phone: 800-722-4726 or (212)904-2000 Fax: (212)904-2072 E-mail: customer.service@mcgraw-hill.com • URL: http://www.mcgraw-hill.com • 1990. $55.00.

Selling Today: Building Quality Partnerships. Gerald L. Manning and Barry L. Reece. Prentice Hall, 240 Frisch Court Paramus, NJ 07652-5240. Phone: 800-947-7700 or (201)909-6200 Fax: 800-445-6991 or (201)909-6361 URL: http://www.prenhall.com • 2000. $84.00. Eighth edition.

Sell's Products and Services Directory. Miller Freeman Information Services, Riverbank House, Angel Lane Tonbridge TN9 1SE, England. Phone: 44 173 2362666 Fax: 44 173 2767301 URL: http://www.mffplc.com • Annual. $175.00. Approximately 60,000 firms in United Kingdom and Ireland. Formerly *Sell's Directory*.

SEMA News. Specialty Equipment Marketing Association, P.O. Box 4910 Diamond Bar, CA 91765-0910. Phone: (909)860-2961 Fax: (909)860-1709 E-mail: julie@sema.org • URL: http://www.sema.org • Monthly. 24.95 per year.

Semiconductor Device Laboratory.

Semiconductor Industry Association., 181 Metro Dr. San Jose, CA 95110-1344. Phone: (408)436-6600 Fax: (408)246-6646 URL: http://www.semichips.org • Members are producers of semiconductors and semiconductor products.

Semiconductor International. Cahners Business Information, Global Electronics Group, 1350 E Touhy Ave. Des Plaines, IL 60018-3358. Phone: 800-662-7776 or (847)635-8800 Fax: (847)390-2770 E-mail: corporatecommunications@cahners.com • URL: http://www.cahners.com • Monthly. $99.90 per year. Devoted to processing, assembly and testing techniques.

Semiconductor International Product Data Source. Cahners Business Information, 1350 E. Touhy Ave. Des Plaines, IL 60018-3358. Phone: 800-662-7776 or (847)635-8800 Fax: (847)390-2770 E-mail: corporatecommunications@cahners.com • URL: http://www.cahners.com • Annual. $50.00. Products relating to the manufacture of semiconductors. Included in subscription to *Semiconductor International*. Formerly *Semiconductor International Technical Products Reference Source*.

Semiconductor Research Laboratory.

Semiconductors, Printed Circuit Boards, and Other Electronic Components. U. S. Bureau of the Census, Washington, DC 20233-0800. Phone: (301)457-4100 Fax: (301)457-3842 URL: http://www.census.gov • Annual. Provides data on shipments: value, quantity, imports, and exports. (Current Industrial Reports, MA-36Q.)

Seminar Promoting. Entrepreneur Media, Inc., 2445 McCabe Way Irvine, CA 92614. Phone: 800-421-2300 or (949)261-2325 Fax: (949)261-0234 E-mail: entmag@entrepreneur.com • URL: http://www.entrepreneur.com • Looseleaf. $59.50. A practical guide to starting a seminar promotion business. Covers profit potential, start-up costs, market size evaluation, owner's time required, site selection, pricing, accounting, advertising, promotion, etc. (Start-Up Business Guide No. E1071.)

Seminars in Ultrasound, CT, and MR (Computerized Tomography and Magnetic Resonance. Harcourt Health Sciences, 11830 Westline Industrial Dr. Saint Louis, MO 63146. Phone: 800-545-2522 or (314)872-8370 E-mail: wbsbcs@harcourt.com • URL: http://www.wbsaunders.com • Bimonthly. $169.00 per year.

Senate Manual. U.S. Government Printing Office, Washington, DC 20402. Phone: (202)512-1800 Fax: (202)512-2250 E-mail: gpoaccess@gpo.gov • URL: http://www.accessgpo.gov • Biennial. $57.00.

Senior Day Care Center. Entrepreneur Media, Inc., 2445 McCabe Way Irvine, CA 92614. Phone: 800-421-2300 or (949)261-2325 Fax: (949)261-0234 E-mail: entmag@entrepreneur.com • URL: http://www.entrepreneur.com • Looseleaf. $59.50. A practical guide to starting a day care center for older adults (supervised environment for frail individuals). Covers profit potential, start-up costs, market size evaluation, owner's time required, site selection, lease negotiation, pricing, accounting, advertising, promotion, etc. (Start-Up Business Guide No. E1335.)

Sensible Sound., 403 Darwin Dr. Snyder, NY 14226-4804. Phone: (716)833-0930 Fax: (716)833-0929 E-mail: sensisound@aol.com • Bimonthly. $29.00 per year. High fidelity equipment review.

Sensor Technology: A Monthly Intgelligence Service. Technical Insights, 605 Third Ave. New York, NY 10158-0012. Phone: 800-825-7550 or (212)850-8600 Fax: (212)850-8800 E-mail: insights@wiley.com • URL: http://www.wiley.com/technicalinsights • Monthly. $685.00 per year. Newsletter on technological developments relating to industrial sensors and process control.

Sensors Buyers Guide. Advanstar Communications, One Phoenix Lane, Suite 401 Peterborough, NH 03458. E-mail: info@sensormag.com • URL: http://www.sensorsmag.com • Annual. Price on application. Provides information on over 1,400 manufacturers of high technology sensors.

Sensors: The Journal of Applied Sensing Technology. Advanstar Communications, One Phoenix Lane, Suite 401 Peterborough, NH 03458. E-mail: info@sensormag.com • URL: http://www.sensorsmag.com • Monthly. $62.00 per year. Edited for design, production, and manufacturing engineers involved with sensing systems. Emphasis is on emerging technology.

Serials Directory: An International Reference Book. EBSCO Industries, Inc., EBSCO Industries, Inc., Title Information Dept., 5724 Highway 280 E Birmingham, AL 35242. Phone: 800-633-6088 or (205)991-6600 Fax: (205)995-1582 Annual. $339.00. Five volumes. Include cumulative updates. Over 155,000 current and ceased periodicals and serials worldwide.

Serials Directory: EBSCO CD-ROM. Ebsco Publishing, 10 Estes St. Ipswitch, MA 01938. Phone: 800-653-2726 or (978)356-6500 Fax: (978)356-6565 Quarterly. $525.00 per year. The CD-ROM version of Ebsco's *The Serials Directory: An International Reference Book*.

Serials for Libraries; An Annotated Guide to Continuations, Annuals, Yearbooks, Almanacs, Transactions, Proceedings, Directories, Services. Diane Sciattara. Neal-Schuman Publishers, Inc., 100 Varick St. New York, NY 10013. Phone: (212)925-8650 Fax: 800-584-2414 or (212)219-8916 E-mail: info@neal-schuman.com • URL: http://www.neal-schuman.com • 1985. $85.00. Second edition.

Serials in Microform. UMI, 300 N. Zeeb Rd. Ann Arbor, MI 48106-1346. Phone: 800-521-0600 or (313)761-4700 Fax: 800-864-0019 URL: http://www.umi.com • Annual. Free to libraries.

Serials Librarian: The International Quarterly Journal of Serials Management. Haworth Press, Inc., 10 Alice St. Binghamton, NY 13904-1580. Phone: 800-429-6784 or (607)722-5857 Fax: 800-895-0582 or (607)722-1424

E-mail: getnfo@haworthpressinc.com • URL: http://www.haworthpressinc.com • Quarterly. Individuals, $45.00 per year; institutions, $180.00 per year; libraries, $180.00 per year. Supplement available: *Serials Librarian*.

Serials Review. JAI Press, P.O. Box 811 Stamford, CT 06904-0811. Phone: (203)323-9606 Fax: (203)357-8446 E-mail: order@jaipress.com • URL: http://www.jaipress.com • Quarterly. $224.00 per year.

Service Management: Strategy and Leadership in Service Business. Richard Normann. John Wiley and Sons, Inc., 605 Third Ave. New York, NY 10158-0012. Phone: 800-526-5368 or (212)850-6000 Fax: (212)850-6088 E-mail: info@wiley.com • URL: http://www.wiley.com • 1991. $115.00. Second edition. Discusses the characteristics of successful service management.

Service Quality Handbook. Eberhard E. Scheuing and William F. Christopher, editors. AMACOM, 1601 Broadway, 12th Fl. New York, NY 10019. Phone: 800-262-9699 or (212)586-8100 Fax: (212)903-8168 E-mail: custmserv@amanet.org • URL: http://www.amanet.org • 1993. $75.00. Contains articles by various authors on the management of service to customers.

Service Reporter: The Magazine That Works for Contractors and In-Plant Engineers. Palmer Publishing Co., 651 W. Washington St., Suite 300 Chicago, IL 60661. Phone: (312)993-0929 Fax: (312)993-0960 Monthly. $12.00 per year.

Services Marketing Quarterly. Haworth Press, Inc., 10 Alice St. Binghamton, NY 13904-1580. Phone: 800-429-6784 or (607)722-5857 Fax: 800-895-0582 or (607)722-1424 E-mail: getinfo@haworthpressinc.com • URL: http://www.haworthpressinc.com • Semiannual. Two volumes. Individuals, $60.00 per year; institutions, $90.00 per year; libraries, $275.00 per year. Supplies "how to" marketing tools for specific sectors of the expanding service sector of the economy. Formerly *Journal of Professional Services Marketing*.

Services: Statistics on International Transactions. Organization for Economic Cooperation and Development. Available from OECD Publications and Information Center, 2001 L St., N. W., Suite 650 Washington, DC 20036-4922. Phone: 800-456-6323 or (202)785-6323 Fax: (202)785-0350 E-mail: washington.contact@oecd.org • URL: http://www.oecd.org • Annual. $71.00. Presents a compilation and assessment of data on OECD member countries' international trade in services. Covers four major categories for 20 years: travel, transportation, government services, and other services.

Services: Statistics on Value Added and Employment. Organization for Economic Cooperation and Development, OECD Washington Center, 2001 L St., N. W., Suite 650 Washington, DC 20036-4922. Phone: 800-456-6323 or (202)785-6323 Fax: (202)785-0350 E-mail: washington.contact@oecd.org • URL: http://www.oecd.org • Annual. $67.00. Provides 10-year data on service industry employment and output (value added) for all OECD countries. Covers such industries as telecommunications, business services, and information technology services.

Setting National Priorities: Budget Choices for the Next Century. Robert D. Reischauer and Henry J. Aaron, editors. Brookings Institution Press, 1775 Massachusetts Ave., N. W. Washington, DC 20036-2188. Phone: 800-275-1447 or (202)797-6258 Fax: (202)797-6004 E-mail: bibooks@brook.edu • URL: http://www.brookings.edu • 1996. $42.95. Contains discussions of the federal budget, economic policy, and government spending policy.

Sex-Based Employment Discrimination. Susan M. Omilian. West Group, 610 Opperman Dr. Eagan, MN 55123. Phone: 800-328-4880 or (651)687-7000 Fax: 800-213-2323 or (651)687-5827 URL: http://www.westgroup.com • 1990. $130.00. Covers the legal aspects of all areas of sexual discrimination, including compensation issues, harassment, sexual orientation, and pregnancy.

Sexual Harassment: A Selected, Annotated Bibliography. Lynda J. Hartel and Helena M. VonVille. Greenwood Publishing Group, Inc., 88 Post Rd., W. Westport, CT 06881-5007. Phone: 800-225-5800 or (203)226-3571 Fax: (203)222-1502 E-mail: bookinfo@greenwood.com • URL: http://www.greenwood.com • 1995. $62.95. Includes articles and books on workplace sexual harassment. (Bibliographies and Indexes in Women's Studies, No. 23.)

Sexual Harassment Awareness Training: 60 Practical Activities for Trainers. Andrea P. Baridon and David R. Eyler. McGraw-Hill, 1221 Ave. of the Americas New York, NY 10020. Phone: 800-722-4726 or (212)904-2000 Fax: (212)904-2072 E-mail: customer.service@mcgraw-hill.com • URL: http://www.mcgraw-hill.com • 1996. $21.95. Discusses the kinds of sexual harassment, judging workplace behavior, application of the "reasonable person standard," employer liability, and related issues.

Sexual Harassment in Employment Law. Barbara Lindemann and David D. Kadue. BNA Books, Bureau of National Affairs, Inc., 1231 25th St., N.W. Washington, DC 20037. Phone: 800-372-1033 or (202)833-7470 Fax: (202)833-7490 E-mail: books@bna.com • URL: http://www.bna.com/bnabooks • 1992. $165.00. Includes 1999 *Supplement*.

Sexual Harassment in the Workplace: A Guide to the Law and A Research Overview for Employers and Employees. Titus Aaron and Judith A. Isaksen. McFarland & Co., Inc., Publishers, P.O. Box 611 Jefferson, NC 28640. Phone: 800-253-2187 or (336)246-4460 Fax: (336)246-5018 E-mail: editorial@mcfarlandpub.com • URL: http://www.mcfarlandpub.com • 1993. $32.50.

Sexual Harassment in the Workplace: Designing and Implementing a Successful Policy, Conducting the Investigation, Protecting the Rights of the Parties. Practising Law Institute, 810 Seventh Ave. New York, NY 10019-5818. Phone: 800-260-4754 or (212)824-7500 Fax: (212)265-4742 E-mail: info@pli.edu • URL: http://www.pli.edu • 1992. $70.00. (Litigation and Administrative Practice Series).

Sexual Harassment in the Workplace: How to Prevent, Investigate, and Resolve Problems in Your Organization. Ellen J. Wagner. AMACOM, 1601 Broadway, 12th Fl. New York, NY 10019. Phone: 800-262-9699 or (212)586-8100 Fax: (212)903-8168 E-mail: custmserv@amanet.org • URL: http://www.amanet.org • 1992. $17.95.

Sexual Harassment in the Workplace: Perspectives, Frontiers, and Response Strategies. Margaret S. Stockdale, editor. Sage Publications, Inc., 2455 Teller Rd. Thousand Oaks, CA 91320. Phone: (805)499-0721 Fax: (805)499-0871 E-mail: info@sagepub.com • URL: http://www.sagepub.com • 1996. $55.00. Contains articles by various authors. (Women and Work Series, vol. 5).

Sexual Harassment: Investigator's Manual. Susan L. Webb. Pacific Resource Development Group, Inc., 145 N. W. 85th St., Suite 104 Seattle, WA 98117-3148. Phone: (206)782-7015 1996. $189.95. Revised edition. Looseleaf. Contains information relating to successfully investigating and resolving sexual harassment complaints in both private companies and public organizations.

Sexual Harassment on the Job: What It Is and How to Stop It. William Petrocelli and Barbara K. Repa. Nolo.com, 950 Parker St. Berkeley, CA 94710. Phone: 800-992-6656 or (510)549-1976 Fax: (510)548-5902 E-mail: cs@nolo.com • URL: http://www.nolo.com • 1999. $18.95. Fourth edition.

Sexual Orientation in the Workplace: Gays, Lesbians, Bisexuals and Heterosexuals Working Together. Amy J. Zuckerman and George F. Simons. Sage Publications, Inc., 2455 Teller Rd. Thousand Oaks, CA 91320. Phone: (805)499-0721 Fax: (805)499-0871 E-mail: info@sagepub.com • URL: http://www.sagepub.com • 1996. $18.95. A workbook containing "a variety of simple tools and exercises" to provide skills for "working realistically and effectively with diverse colleagues."

Seybold Report on Publishing Systems. Seybold Publications, 428 E. Baltimore Ave. Media, PA 19063. Phone: 800-325-3830 or (610)565-2480 Fax: (610)565-1858 Semimonthly. $365.00 per year. Newsletter.

SFNOW Times. National Organization for Women, San Francisco Chapter, 3543 18th St., Suite 27 San Francisco, CA 94110-1687. Phone: (415)861-8880 Monthly. $4.50.

The Shape of Things to Come: Seven Imperatives for Winning in the New World of Business. Richard W. Oliver. McGraw-Hill, 1221 Ave. of the Americas New York, NY 10020. Phone: 800-722-4726 or (212)904-2000 Fax: (212)904-2072 E-mail: customer.service@mcgraw-hill.com • URL: http://www.mcgraw-hill.com • 1998. $24.95. Contains predictions relating to the influence of information technology on 21st century business. (Business Week Books.)

Shaping the Corporate Image: An Analytical Guide for Executive Decision Makers. Marion G. Sobol and others. Greenwood Publishing Group, Inc., 88 Post Rd., W. Westport, CT 06881-5007. Phone: 800-225-5800 or (203)226-3571 Fax: (203)222-2540 E-mail: bookinfo@greenwood.com • URL: http://www.greenwood.com • 1992. $49.95.

Sharing the Burden: Strategies for Public and Private Long-Term Care Insurance. Joshua M. Wiener and others. Brookings Institution Press, 1775 Massachusetts Ave., N. W. Washington, DC 20036-2188. Phone: 800-275-1447 or (202)797-6258 Fax: (202)797-6004 E-mail: bibooks@brook.edu • URL: http://www.brookings.edu • 1994. $42.95.

Sheep and Goat Science. M. E. Ensminger and Ronald B. Parker. Interstate Publishers, P.O. Box 50 Danville, IL 61834-0050. Phone: 800-843-4774 or (217)446-0500 Fax: (217)446-9706 E-mail: info-ipp@ippinc.com • URL: http://www.ippinc.com • 1998. $81.25. Fifth edition.

Sheep Breeder and Sheepman. Mead Livestock Services, P.O. Box 796 Columbia, MO 65205. Phone: (314)442-8257 Monthly. $18.00 per year.

Sheet Metal and Air Conditioning Contractors' National Association.

Sheet Metal Cutting: Collected Articles and Technical Papers. Amy Nickel, editor. Croyden Group, Ltd./FMA, 833 Featherstone Rd. Rockford, IL 61107-6302. Phone: (815)399-8700 Fax: (815)484-7700 E-mail: info@fmametalfab.org • URL: http://www.fmametalfab.com • 1994. $33.00.

Sheet Metal Industry Promotion Plan.

Sheldon's Major Stores and Chains. Phelon Sheldon and Marsar, Inc., 1364 Georgetowne Circle Sarasota, FL 34232-2048. Phone: 800-234-8804 or (941)921-6450 Annual. $175.00. Lists department stores and chains in, women's specialty and chains, home furnishing chains and resident buying offices in the U.S. and Canada. Formerly *Sheldon's Retail Stores*.

Sheppard's Bookdealers in Europe: A Directory of Dealers in Secondhand and Antiquarian Books on the Continent of Europe. Richard Joseph Publishers, Ltd., Unit Two, Monks Walk Farnham Surrey GU9 28HT, England. Phone: 1252 734347 Fax: 1252 734307 E-mail: rjoe01@aol.com • URL: http://www.members.aol.com/rjoe01/sheppards.htm • Biennial. $54.00. 1,746 dealers in antiquarian and secondhand books in 24 European countries.

Sheppard's Bookdealers in North America. Richard Joseph Publishers, Ltd., Unit Two, Monks Walk Farnham Surrey GU9 28HT, England. Phone: 1252 734347 Fax: 1252 734307 E-mail: rjoe01@aol.com • URL: http://www.members.aol.com/rjoe01/sheppards.htm • Biennial. $54.00. Over 3,364 dealers in antiquarian and secondhand books in the U.S. and Canada.

Ship Management. Malcolm Willingale and others. Available from Informa Publishing Group Ltd., PO Box 1017 Westborough, MA 01581-6017. Phone: 800-493-4080 Fax: (508)231-0856 E-mail: enquiries@informa.com • URL: http://www.informa.com • 1998. $105.00. Third edition. Published in the UK by Lloyd's List (http://www.lloydslist.com). Covers recruitment of personnel, training, quality control, liability, safety, responsibilities of ship managers, and other topics.

Shipbuilders Council of America.

Shipcare. Available from Informa Publishing Group Ltd., PO Box 1017 Westborough, MA 01581-6017. Phone: 800-493-4080 Fax: (508)231-0856 E-mail: enquiries@informa.com • URL: http://www.informa.com • Quarterly. $188.00 per year. Published in the UK by Lloyd's List (http://www.lloydslist.com). Edited for the global ship repair, conversion, and maintenance industry. Provides news, market information, and technical analysis, including contract and pricing data.

Shipping Digest: For Export and Transportation Executives. Geyer-McAllister Publications, Inc., 51 Madison Ave. New York, NY 10010. Phone: (212)689-4411 Fax: (212)683-7929 Weekly. $57.00 per year.

Ships and Aircraft of the United States Fleet. James C. Fahey, editor. Naval Institute Press, Beach Hall, 291 Wood Rd. Annapolis, MD 21402-5034. Phone: 800-223-8764 or (410)268-6110 Fax: (410)295-1084 E-mail: customer@usni.org • URL: http://www.nip.org • Dates vary. $63.90. Two volumes.

Shoe Factory Buyer's Guide: Directory of Suppliers to the Shoe Manufacturing Industry. Shoe Trades Publishing Co., P.O. Box 198 Cambridge, MA 02140. Phone: (781)648-8160 Fax: (781)646-9832 E-mail: info@shoetrades.com • Annual. $59.00. Lists over 750 suppliers and their representatives to the North American footwear industry.

Shoe Stats. Footwear Industries of America, 1420 K St., N.W., Suite 600 Washington, DC 20005. Phone: 800-688-7653 or (202)789-1420 Fax: (202)789-4058 URL: http://www.fia.org • Annual. Free to members; non-members, $350.00; libraries, $225.00. Includes *Statistical Reporter*.

The SHOOT Directory for Commercial Production and Postproduction. BPI Communications, 1515 Broadway New York, NY 10036. Phone: 800-278-8477 or (212)764-7300 Fax: (212)536-5321 E-mail: shoot@shootonline.com • URL: http://www.shootonline.com • Annual. $79.00. Lists production companies, advertising agencies, and sources of professional television, motion picture, and audio equipment.

SHOOT: The Leading Newsweekly for Commercial Production and Postproduction. BPI Communications, 770 Broadway New York, NY 10003. Phone: (212)764-7300 Fax: (212)536-5321 E-mail: info@bpi.com • URL: http://www.bpicomm.com • Weekly. $115.00 per year. Covers animation, music, sound design, computer graphics, visual effects, cinematography, and other aspects of television and motion picture production, with emphasis on TV commercials.

Shooting Industry. Publishers Development Corp., 591 Camino de la Reina, Suite 200 San Diego, CA 92108. Phone: 888-732-2299 or (619)297-5350 Fax: (619)297-5353 E-mail: 74673.3624@compuserve.com • Monthly. $25.00 per year.

Shooting Industry-Buyers Guide. Publishers' Development Corp., 591 Camino de la Reina, Suite 200 San Diego, CA 92108. Phone: 888-752-2299 or (619)297-5350 Fax: (619)297-8520 E-mail: 74673.3624@compuserve.com • Annual. $15.00. Manufacturers, wholesalers, and importers of guns and related equipment and supplies.

Shop Talk. Paul Allen. International Mobile Air Conditioning Association, 2100 N. Highway 360, Suite 1300 Grand Prairie, TX 75050. Phone: (214)988-6081 Monthly. Free to members; non-members, $50.00 per year. News and features relating to motor vehicle air conditioning and installed accessory industry.

A Shopper's Guide to Long-Term Care Insurance. DIANE Publishing Co., 330 Pusey Ave., Suite 3 Collingdale, PA 19023. Phone: (610)461-6200 Fax: (610)461-6130 E-mail: dianepub@erols.com • URL: http://www.dianepublishing.com • 1995. $15.00. Revised edition. Provides impartial, consumer-oriented information and advice on long-term care insurance policies. Includes worksheets.

Shopping Center and Store Leases. Emanuel B. Halper. New York Law Publishing Co., 345 Park Ave., S. New York, NY 10010. Phone: 800-888-8300 or (212)741-8300 URL: http://www.ljx.com • Looseleaf service. $140.00. Two volumes.

Shopping Center Development Handbook. Michael D. Beyard and W. Paul O'Mara. Urban Land Institute, 1025 Thomas Jefferson St., N. W., Suite 500 W. Washington, DC 20007-5201. Phone: 800-321-5011 or (202)624-7000 Fax: (202)624-7140 E-mail: bookstore@uli.org • URL: http://www.uli.org • 1998. $89.95. Third edition. (Development Handbook Series).

Shopping Center Directory. National Research Bureau, Inc., 200 W. Jackson Blvd., No. 2700 Chicago, IL 60606-6910. Phone: (312)541-0100 Fax: (312)541-1492 URL: http://www.nrbonline.com • Annual. $655.00. Consists of four regional volumes. Individual volumes, $335.00 each. Provides detailed information on about 37,000 U. S. shopping centers. Includes *Top Contracts*.

Shopping Center World. Intertec Publishing Corp., 6151 Powers Ferry Rd., N.W., Suite 200 Atlanta, GA 30339-2941. Phone: 800-400-5945 or (770)955-2500 Fax: (913)967-1898 E-mail: subs@intertec.com • URL: http://www.intertec.com • Monthly. $74.00 per year. Provides coverage of all phases of the shopping center industry. Includes annual *Directory*. Includes supplement *Outlet Retailer*.

Shopping for a Better World: A Quick and Easy Guide to Socially Responsible Supermarket Shopping. Council on Economic Priorities, 30 Irving Place New York, NY 10003. Phone: 800-729-4237 Fax: (212)420-0988 Annual. $14.00. Rates 186 major corporations according to 10 social criteria: advancement of minorities, advancement of women, environmental concerns, South African investments, charity, community outreach, nuclear power, animal testing, military contracts, and social disclosure. Includes American, Japanese and British firms.

Short Course on Computer Viruses. Frederick B. Cohen. John Wiley and Sons, Inc., 605 Third Ave. New York, NY 10158-0012. Phone: 800-225-5945 or (212)850-6000 Fax: (212)850-6088 E-mail: info@wiley.com • URL: http://www.wiley.com • 1994. $44.95. Second edition.

A Short History of Financial Euphoria. John Kenneth Galbraith. Viking Penguin, 375 Hudson St. New York, NY 10014-3657. Phone: 800-331-4624 or (212)366-2000 Fax: 800-227-9604 or (212)366-2920 E-mail: customer.service@penguin.co.uk • URL: http://www.penguin.com • 1994. $10.95. An analysis of speculative euphoria and subsequent crashes, from the Holland tulip mania in 1637 to the 1987 unpleasantness in the U. S. stock market.

A Short History of the Future. W. Warren Wagar. University of Chicago Press, 5801 Ellis Ave., 4th Fl. Chicago, IL 60637. Phone: 800-621-2736 or (773)702-7700 Fax: (773)702-9756 E-mail: marketing@press.uchicago.edu • URL: http://www.press.uchicago.edu • 1989. $29.95.

Short-Term Economic Indicators: Transition Economies. OECD Publications and Information Center, 2001 L St., N.W., Ste. 650 Washington, DC 20036-4922. Phone: (202)785-6323 Fax: (202)785-0350 E-mail: washington-contact@oecd.org • URL: http://www.oecdwash.org • Quarterly. Presents annual, quarterly, and monthly economic indicators for the developing countries of Eastern Europe and the New Independent States.

Short-Term Energy Outlook: Quarterly Projections. Available from U. S. Government Printing Office, Washington, DC 20402. Phone: (202)512-1800 Fax: (202)512-2250 E-mail: gpoaccess@gpo.gov • URL: http://www.access.gpo.gov • Semiannual. $10.00 per year. Issued by Energy Information Administration, U. S. Department of Energy. Contains forecasts of U. S. energy supply, demand, and prices.

Show and Sell: 133 Business Building Ways to Promote Your Trade Show Exhibit. Margit B. Weisgal. AMACOM, 1601 Broadway, 12th Fl. New York, NY 10019. Phone: 800-262-9699 or (212)586-8100 Fax: (212)903-8168 E-mail: custmserv@amanet.org • URL: http://www.amanet.org • 1996. $55.00. Contains information and advice on pre-show advertising and promotion, booth management, literature distribution, customer dialogue, ''damage control,'' follow-up, evaluation, and other exhibit topics. Includes bibliography, checklists, worksheets, and index.

Show Business Law: Motion Pictures, Television, Videos. Peter Muller. Greenwood Publishing Group, Inc., 88 Post Rd., W. Westport, CT 06881-5007. Phone: 800-225-5800 or (203)226-3571 Fax: (203)222-2540 E-mail: bookinfo@greenwood.com • URL: http://www.greenwood.com • 1990. $59.95.

Shutterbug. Patch Communications, 5211 S. Washington Ave. Titusville, FL 32780. Phone: (321)268-5010 Fax: (321)267-1894 E-mail: editorial@shutterbug.net • URL: http://www.shutterbug.net • Monthly. $17.95 per year. Articles about new equipment, test reports on film accessories, how-to articles, etc. Annual *Buying Guide* available.

Shuttle, Spindle, and Dyepot. Handweavers Guild of America, Two Executive Concourse, Suite 201 Duluth, GA 30136. Phone: (612)646-0802 Fax: (612)646-0806 E-mail: http://www.weavespindye.org/ • Quarterly. $25.00 per year.

SI: Special Issues. Trip Wyckoff, editor. Hoover's, Inc., 1033 La Posada Dr., Suite 250 Austin, TX 78752. Phone: 800-486-8666 or (512)374-4500 Fax: (512)374-4501 E-mail: orders@hoovers.com • URL: http://www.hoovers.com • Bimonthly. $149.95 per year. Newsletter. Serves as a supplement to *Directory of Business Periodical Special Issues*. Provides current information on trade journal special issues and editorial calendars.

SIA Status Report and Industry Directory. Semiconductor Industry Association, 181 Metro Dr., Suite 450 San Jose, CA 95110-1346. Phone: (408)436-6600 Fax: (408)436-6646 E-mail: siaweb@attglobal.net • URL: http://www.semichips.org • Annual. Members, $105.00; non-members, $150.00. Provides information on key semiconductor issues. Formerly *Semiconductor Industry Association Yearbook/Directory*.

SIE Guide to Investment Publications: The Only Directory of Investment Advisory Publications for Investors. George H. Wein, editor. Select Information Exchange, 244 W. 54th St. New York, NY 10019. Phone: 800-743-9346 or (212)247-7123 Fax: (212)247-7326 Annual. Free. Provides descriptions and prices of about 100 financial newsletters covering stocks, bonds, mutual funds, commodity futures, options, gold, and foreign investments. Offers subscription services, including short trials of any 20 investment newsletters for a total of $11.95. Formerly *SIE Market Letter Directory*.

Signs of the Times: The National Journal of Signs and Advertising Displays. ST Publications, Inc., 407 Gilbert Ave. Cincinnati, OH 45202-2285. Phone: 800-925-1110 or (513)421-2050 Fax: (513)421-5144 E-mail: books@stpubs.com • URL: http://www.st.com • 13 times a year. $36.00 per year. For designers and manufacturers of all types of signs. Features how-to-tips. Includes *Sign Erection, Maintenance Directory* and annual *Buyer's Guide*.

Silicon Alley Reporter. Rising Tide Studios, 101 East 15th St., 3rd Fl. New York, NY 10003. Phone: (212)475-8000 Fax: (212)475-9955 E-mail: info@siliconalleyreporter.com • URL: http://www.siliconalleyreporter.com • Monthly. $29.95 per year. Covers the latest trends in e-commerce, multimedia, and the Internet.

Silicon Snake Oil: Second Thoughts on the Information Highway. Clifford Stoll. Doubleday, 1540 Broadway New York, NY 10036-4094. Phone: 800-223-6834 or (212)354-6500 Fax: (212)492-9700 URL: http://www.doubledaybookclub.com • 1996. $14.00. The author discusses the extravagant claims being made for online networks and multimedia.

Silver Institute.

Silver Users Association.

Silversmithing and Art Metal for Schools, Tradesmen, Craftsmen. Murray Bovin. Bovin Publishing, 68-36 108th St. Forest Hills, NY 11375. Phone: (718)268-2292 1977. $22.95. Revised edition.

The SIMBA Report on Directory Publishing. SIMBA Information, P.O. Box 4234 Stamford, CT 06907-0234. Phone: 800-307-2529 or (203)358-4100 Fax: (203)358-5824 E-mail: info@simbanet.com • URL: http://www.simbanet.com • Monthly. $59.00 per year. Newsletter.

Simmons Study of Media and Markets. Simmons Market Research Bureau, 530 5th Ave. New York, NY 10036. Phone: (212)373-8900 Fax: (212)373-8918 URL: http://www.smrb.com • Market and media survey data relating to the American consumer. Inquire as to online cost and availability.

Simplified Small Business Accounting. Daniel Sitarz. National Book Network, 15200 NBN Way Blur Ridge Summit, PA 17214. Phone: 800-462-6420 or (717)794-3800 Fax: 800-338-4550 URL: http://www.nbnbooks.com • 1998. $19.95. Second edition. Includes basic forms and instructions for small business accounting and bookkeeping. (Small Business Library Series).

Simulation & Gaming: An International Journal of Theory, Design and Research. Sage Publications, Inc., 2455 Teller Rd. Thousand Oaks, CA 91320. Phone: (805)499-0721 Fax: (805)499-0871 E-mail: info@sagepub.com • URL: http://www.sagepub.com • Quarterly. Individuals, $75.00 per year; institutions, $355.00 per year.

Singapore Business: The Portable Encyclopedia for Doing Business with Singapore. World Trade Press, 1450 Grant Ave., Suite 204 Novato, CA 94945-3142. Phone: 800-833-8586 or (415)898-1124 Fax: (415)898-1124 E-mail: worldpress@aol.com • URL: http://www.worldtradepress.com • 1994. $24.95. Covers economic data, import/export possibilities, basic tax and trade laws, travel information, and other useful facts for doing business with Singapore. (Country Business Guides Series).

Site Selection. Conway Data, Inc., 35 Technology Parkway, Suite 150 Norcross, GA 30092-9990. Phone: (770)446-6996 Fax: (770)263-8825 URL: http://www.sitenet.com • Bimonthly. Six volumes, $20.00 per volume. $85.00 per set. Each of the six issues per year is a separate directory: *Geo-Corporate* (facility planners), *Geo-Economic* (area development officials), *Geo-Labor* (labor force data), *Geo-Life* (quality of life information), *GeoPolitical* (government agencies), and *Geo-Sites* (industrial/office parks). Formerly *Site Selection and Industrial Development*.

16 Million Businesses Phone Directory. Info USA., 5711 South 86th Circle Omaha, NE 68127. Phone: 800-634-1949 or (402)593-4500 Fax: (402)331-8561 Annual. $29.95. Provides more than 16 million yellow pages telephone directory listings on CD-ROM for all ZIP Code areas of the U. S.

Skipmaster: Collection Reference Manual. Skipmaster, Inc., P.O. Box 69 Eureka, MO 63025. Phone: (314)274-7200 Fax: (314)285-9044 Annual. Price on application. Lists sources of information useful for debt collecting and skip tracing, such as city clerks and tax assesors.

Sky and Telescope: The Essential Magazine of Astronomy. Leif J. Robinson, editor. Sky Publishing Co., 49 Bay State Rd. Cambridge, MA 02138. Phone: 800-253-0245 or (617)864-7360 Fax: (617)864-6117 E-mail: postmaster@skypub.com • URL: http://www.skypub.com • Monthly. $39.95 per year. Reports astronomy and space science for amateurs and professionals. Many ''how to'' features.

SLA Salary Survey. Special Libraries Association, 1700 18th St., N. W. Washington, DC 20009-2514. Phone: (202)234-4700 Fax: (202)234-2442 E-mail: books@sla.org • URL: http://www.sla.org • Annual. Members, $36.00; non-members, $45.00. Provides data on salaries for special librarians in the U. S. and Canada, according to location, job title, industry, budget, and years of experience.

SLIG Buyers' Guide: Starting, Lighting, Ignition, Generating Systems. Independent Battery Manufacturers Association, 100 Larchwood Dr. Largo, FL 34640. Phone: 800-237-6126 or (727)586-1408 Fax: (727)586-1400 E-mail: thebatteryman@juno.com • Biennial. $25.00 per year. Over 1,900 manufacturers and rebuilders of heavy-duty storage batteries.

Sloan Management Review. Sloan Management Review Association. Massachusetts Institute of Technology, Sloan School of Management, 77 Massachusetts Ave. Cambridge, MA 02139. Phone: (617)253-7170 Fax: (617)258-9739 E-mail: smr@mit.edu • URL: http://www.web.mit.edu • Quarterly. $89.00 per year.

Sludge Newsletter: The Newsletter on Municipal Wastewater and Biosolids. Business Publishers, Inc., 8737 Colesville Rd., Suite 1100 Silver Spring, MD 20910-3928. Phone: 800-274-6737 or (301)587-6300 Fax: (301)587-1081 E-mail: bpinews@bpinews.com • URL: http://www.bpinews.com • Biweekly. $409.00 per year. per year. Monitors sludge management developments in Washington and around the country.

Small Business Administration. Annual Report. U.S. Government Printing Office, Washington, DC 20402. Phone: (202)512-1800 Fax: (202)512-2250 E-mail: gpoaccess@gpo.gov • URL: http://www.accessgpo.gov • Annual. Two volumes.

Small Business Advisory. Financial News Associates, 1940 Biltmore St., N. W. Washington, DC 20009. Phone: 800-433-8004 or (202)347-2147 Monthly. $120.00 per year. Newsletter.

Small Business Development Center.

Small Business Incorporation Kit. Robert L. Davidson. John Wiley and Sons, Inc., 605 Third Ave. New York, NY 10158-0012. Phone: 800-225-5945 or (212)850-6000 Fax: (212)850-6088 E-mail: info@wiley.com • URL: http://www.wiley.com • 1992. $16.95.

Small Business Legal Smarts. Deborah L. Jacobs. Bloomberg Press, 100 Business Park Dr. Princeton, NJ 08542-0888. Phone: 800-388-2749 or (609)279-4670 Fax: (609)279-7155 E-mail: press@bloomberg.net • URL: http://www.bloomberg.com • 1998. $16.95. Discusses common legal problems encountered by small business owners. (Small Business Series Personal Bookshelf.)

Small Business Management. Justin Longenecker and others. South-Western Publishing Co., 5101 Madison Rd. Cincinnati, OH 45227. Phone: 800-543-0487 or (513)271-8811 Fax: 800-437-8488 E-mail: billhendee@itped.com • URL: http://www.swcollege.com • 1996. $62.95. 10th edition. (GG-Small Business Management Series).

Small Business Management Fundamentals. Daniel Steinhoff and John Burgess. McGraw-Hill, 1221 Ave. of the Americas New York, NY 10020. Phone: 800-722-4726 or (212)904-2000 Fax: (212)904-2072 E-mail: customer.service@mcgraw-hill.com • URL: http://www.mcgraw-hill.com • 1993. $62.50. Sixth edition.

Small Business Opportunities. Harris Publications, Inc., 1115 Broadway New York, NY 10010. Phone: (212)807-7100 Fax: (212)627-4678 Bimonthly. $9.97.

Small Business Retirement Savings Advisor. U. S. Department of Labor, Pension and Welfare Benefits Administration- Phone: (202)219-8921 URL: http://www.dol.gov/elaws/pwbaplan.htm • Web site provides "answers to a variety of commonly asked questions about retirement saving options for small business employers." Includes a comparison chart and detailed descriptions of various plans: 401(k), SEP-IRA, SIMPLE-IRA, Payroll Deduction IRA, Keogh Profit-Sharing, Keogh Money Purchase, and Defined Benefit. Searching is offered. Fees: Free.

Small Business Sourcebook. The Gale Group, 27500 Drake Rd. Farmington Hills, MI 48331-3535. Phone: 800-877-GALE or (248)699-GALE Fax: 800-414-5043 or (248)699-8069 E-mail: galeord@galegroup.com • URL: http://www.galegroup.com • 2000. $335.00. 14th edtion. Two volumes. Information sources for about 100 kinds of small businesses.

Small Business Survival Guide: How to Manage Your Cash, Profits and Taxes. Robert E. Fleury. Sourcebooks, Inc., P. O. Box 372 Naperville, IL 60566. Phone: 800-727-8866 or (630)961-3900 Fax: (630)961-2168 E-mail: custserv@buyerszone.com • URL: http://www.buyerszone.com • 1995. $17.95. Third revised edition.

Small Business Tax News. Inside Mortgage Finance Publications, P.O. Box 42387 Washington, DC 20015. Phone: (301)951-1240 Fax: (301)656-1709 URL: http://www.imfpubs.com • Monthly. $175.00 per year. Newsletter. Formerly *Small Business Tax Control*.

Small Business Tax Review. A/N Group, Inc., P.O. Box 895 Melville, NY 11747-0895. Phone: (516)549-4090 E-mail: angroup@pb.net • URL: http://www.smbiz.com • Monthly. $84.00 per year. Newsletter. Contains articles on Federal taxes and other issues affecting businesses.

Small Fruits Review. Haworth Press, Inc., 10 Alice St. Binghamton, NY 13904-1580. Phone: 800-429-6784 or (607)722-5857 Fax: 800-895-0582 or (607)722-1424 E-mail: getinfo@haworthpressinc.com • URL: http://www.haworthpressinc.com • Quarterly. Individuals, $36.00 per year; institutions, $48.00 per year; libraries, $125.00 per year. An academic and practical journal focusing on the marketing of grapes, berries, and other small fruit. Formerly *Journal of Small Fruits and Viticulture*.

Small Law Firm Economic Survey. Altman Weil Publications, Inc., Two Campus Blvd. Newtown Square, PA 19073. Phone: 888-782-7297 or (610)359-9900 Fax: (610)359-0467 E-mail: info@altmanweil.com • URL: http://www.altmanweil.com • Annual. $295.00. Provides aggregate data (benchmarks) on the economics, finances, billing, and staffing of law offices in the U. S. having "less than 12 lawyers."

Small Libraries: A Handbook for Successful Management. Sally G. Reed. McFarland and Co., Inc., Publishers, P. O. Box 611 Jefferson, NC 28640. Phone: 800-253-2187 or (336)246-4460 Fax: (336)246-5018 E-mail: editorial@macfarlandpub.com • URL: http://www.mcfarlandpub.com • 1991. $28.50. Covers personnel (including volunteers), buildings, collections, service policies, community politics, and other topics.

Small Theatre Handbook: A Guide to Management and Production. Joann Green. Harvard Common Press, 535 Albany St. Boston, MA 02118. Phone: 888-657-3755 or (617)423-5803 Fax: (617)695-9794 E-mail: orders.@harvardcommonpress.com • URL: http://www.harvardcommonpress.com • 1981. $9.95.

Small Time Operator: How to Start Your Own Small Business, Keep Your Books, Pay Your Taxes, and Stay Out of Trouble. Bernard Kamoroff. Bell Springs Publishing, 106 State St. Willits, CA 95490. Phone: 800-515-8050 or (707)459-6372 Fax: (707)459-8614 E-mail: bellsprings@saber.net • 1997. $16.95. Sixth edition. Concise, practical advice. Includes bookkeeping forms.

Small Towns Institute.

Smart Business for the New Economy. Ziff-Davis, 28 E. 28th St. New York, NY 10016-7930. Phone: 800-366-2423 or (212)503-3500 URL: http://www.zdnet.com/ • Monthly. $12.00 per year. Provides practical advice for doing business in an economy dominated by technology and electronic commerce.

Smart Choices: A Practical Guide to Making Better Decisions. John S. Hammond and others. Harvard Business School Press, 60 Harvard Way Boston, MA 02163. Phone: 888-500-1016 or (617)783-7440 E-mail: custserv@hbsp.harvard.edu • URL: http://www.hbsp.harvard.edu • 1998. $22.50. Provides a systematic approach to effective decision-making. Eight fundamentals of decision-analysis are described, involving problems, objectives, alternatives, consequences, tradeoffs, uncertainty, risks, and choices.

Smart Hiring: The Complete Guide for Recruiting Employees. Robert W. Wendover. Leadership Resources, Inc., 15200 E.Girard Ave., Suite 2300 Aurora, CO 80014-5039. 1989. $17.95.

Smart Questions to Ask Your Financial Advisers. Lynn Brenner. Bloomberg Press, 100 Business Park Dr. Princeton, NJ 08542-0888. Phone: 800-388-2749 or (609)279-4670 Fax: (609)279-7155 E-mail: press@bloomberg.net • URL: http://www.bloomberg.com • 1997. $19.95. Provides practical advice on how to deal with financial planners, stockbrokers, insurance agents, and lawyers. Some of the areas covered are investments, estate planning, tax planning, house buying, prenuptial agreements, divorce arrangements, loss of a job, and retirement. (Bloomberg Personal Bookshelf Series Library.)

Smart TV: For Selective and Interactive Viewers. Videomaker, Inc., P.O. 4591 Chico, CA 95927. Phone: (916)891-8410 Fax: (916)891-8443 E-mail: customer@smarttvmag.com • URL: http://www.smarttvmag.com • Bimonthly. $14.97 per year. Consumer magazine covering WebTV, PC/TV appliances, DVD players, "Smart TV," advanced VCRs, and other topics relating to interactive television, the Internet, and multimedia.

Smarter Insurance Solutions. Janet Bamford. Bloomberg Press, 100 Business Park Dr. Princeton, NJ 08542-0888. Phone: 800-388-2749 or (609)279-4670 Fax: (609)279-7155 E-mail: press@bloomberg.net • URL: http://www.bloomberg.com • 1996. $19.95. Provides practical advice to consumers, with separate chapters on the following kinds of insurance: automobile, homeowners, health, disability, and life. (Bloomberg Personal Bookshelf Series)

SmartMoney: The Wall Street Journal Magazine of Personal Business. Hearst Corp., 1755 Broadway, 2nd Fl. New York, NY 10019. Phone: 800-444-4204 or (201)767-4100 Fax: (201)767-7337 E-mail: letters@smartmoney.com • URL: http://www.smartmoney.com • Monthly. $24.00 per year. Includes *Stock Trader's Almanac*.

Smithells Metals Reference Book. Colin J. Smithells. Butterworth-Heinemann, 225 Wildwood Ave. Woburn, MA 01801. Phone: 800-366-2665 or (781)904-2500 Fax: 800-466-6520 E-mail: orders@bhusa.com • URL: http://www.bh.com • 1998. $125.00. Seventh edition. (Engineering Materials Selector Series).

Smokeshop. Lockwood Publications, 130 W. 42nd St., Suite 1050 New York, NY 10036. Phone: (212)594-4120 Fax: (212)714-0514 E-mail: ssmagazine@aol.com • URL: http://www.gosmokeshop.com • Bimonthly. $32.00 per year.

Smoking and Politics: Policy Making and the Federal Bureaucracy. A. Lee Fritschler and James M. Hoepler. Prentice Hall, 240 Frisch Court Paramus, NJ 07652-5240. Phone: 800-947-7700 or (201)909-6200 Fax: 800-445-6991 or (201)909-6361 URL: http://www.prenhall.com • 1995. $33.00. Fifth edition.

Smoking: The Health Consequences of Tobacco Use. Cecilia M. Schmitz and Richard A. Gray. Pierian Press, P.O. Box 1808 Ann Arbor, MI 48106. Phone: 800-678-2435 or (734)434-5530 Fax: (734)434-6409 E-mail: pubinfo@pierianpress.com • URL: http://www.pierianpress.com • 1995. $30.00. (Science and Social Responsibility Series).

SMPTE Journal. Society of Motion Picture and Television Engineers, 595 W. Hartsdale Ave. White Plains, NY 10607-1824. Phone: (914)761-1100 Fax: (914)761-3115 Monthly. $125.00 per year.

Snack Food and Wholesale Bakery: The Magazine That Defines the Snack Food Industry. Stagnito Publishing Co., 1935 Shermer Rd., Ste. 100 Northbrook, IL 60062-5354. Phone: (847)205-5660 Fax: (847)205-5680 E-mail: info@stagnito.com • URL: http://www.stagnito.com • Monthly. Free to qualified personnel; others, $65.00 per year. Provides news and information for producers of pretzels, potato chips, cookies, crackers, nuts, and other snack foods. Includes *Annual Buyers Guide* and *State of Industry Report*.

Snack Food Association.

Snack Food Buyer's Guide. Stagnito Publishing Co., 1935 Shermer Rd., Suite 100 Northbrook, IL 60062-5354. Phone: (847)205-5660 Fax: (847)205-5680 E-mail: info@stagnito.com • URL: http://www.stagnito.com • Annual. $55.00. Lists approximately 900 companies that provide supplies and services to the snack food industry.

Snips. Business News Publishing Co., 755 W. Big Beaver Rd. Troy, MI 48084-4903. Phone: 800-837-7370 or (248)362-3700 Fax: (248)362-6317 Monthly. $12.00 per year. Provides information for heating, air conditioning, sheet metal and ventilating contractors, wholesalers, manufacturers representatives and manufacturers.

Snowdon's Official International Protocols: The Definitive Guide to Business and Social Customs of the World. Sondra Snowdon. McGraw-Hill Professional, 1221 Ave. of the Americas New York, NY 10020. Phone: 800-722-4726 or (212)904-2000 Fax: (212)904-2072 E-mail: customer.service@mcgraw-hill.com • URL: http://www.mcgraw-hill.com • 1996. $75.00. Discusses the protocols of 60 nations: social customs, business climate, personal characteristics, relevant history, and politics.

Soap and Cosmetics. Cygnus Business Media, 445 Broad Hollow Rd. Melville, NY 11747. Phone: 800-308-6397 or (631)845-2700 Fax: (631)845-2798 E-mail: rich.reiff@cygnuspub.com • URL: http://www.cygnuspub.com • Monthly. $60.00 per year. Formerly *Soap, Cosmetics, Chemical Specialities*.

Soap and Detergent Association.

Soap/Cosmetics/Chemical Specialties Blue Book. Cygnus Business Media, 445 Broad Hollow Rd. Melville, NY 11747. Phone: 800-308-6397 or (631)845-2700 Fax: (631)845-2736 E-mail: rich.reiff@cygnuspub.com • URL: http://www.cygnuspub.com • Annual. $15.00. Sources of raw materials, equipment and services for the soap, cosmetic and chemical specialities. Formerly Soap/Cosetics/Chemical Special.

Social and Behavioral Aspects of Female Alcoholism: An Annotated Bibliography. H. Paul Chalfant and Brent S. Roper, compliers. Greenwood Publishing Group, Inc., 88 Post Rd., W. Westport, CT 06881-5007. Phone: 800-225-5800 or (203)226-3571 Fax: (203)222-2540 E-mail: bookinfo@greenwood.com • URL: http://www.greenwood.com • 1980. $55.00.

Social Effects of Inflation. Marvin E. Wolfgang and Richard D. Lambert, editors. American Academy of Political and Social Science, 3937 Chestnut St. Philadelphia, PA 19104. Phone: (215)573-8212 1981. $28.00. (Annuals of the American Academy of Political and Social Science Series: No. 456).

Social Indicators of Development. John Hopkins University Press, 2715 N. Charles St. Baltimore, MD 21218-4319. Phone: 800-537-5487 or (410)516-6900 Fax: (410)516-6998 E-mail: bkinfo@chaos.press.jhu.edu • URL: http://www.muse.jhu.edu/ • 1996. $26.95. Provides social and economic statistics for over 170 countries. Includes population, labor force, income, poverty level, natural resources, medical care, education, the environment, and expenditures on living essentials. Covers a 30-year period. (World Bank Series).

Social Insurance and Economic Security. George E. Rejda. Prentice Hall, 240 Frisch Court Paramus, NJ 07652-5240. Phone: 800-947-7700 or (201)909-6200 Fax: 800-445-6991 or (201)909-6361 URL: http://www.prenhall.com • 1998. $92.00. Sixth edition.

Social Science Source. EBSCO Publishing, 10 Estes St. Ipswitch, MA 01938. Phone: 800-653-2726 or (978)356-6500 Fax: (978)356-6565 E-mail: ep@epnet.com • URL: http://www.epnet.com • Monthly. $1,495.00 per year. Provides CD-ROM citations and abstracts to social science articles in more than 600 periodicals, with full text from 125 periodicals. Covers economics, political science, public policy, international relations, psychology, and other topics. Time period is most recent five years.

Social Sciences Citation Index. Institute for Scientific Information, 3501 Market St. Philadelphia, PA 19104. Phone: 800-386-4474 or (215)386-0100 Fax: (215)386-2911 URL: http://www.isinet.com • Three times a year. $6,900 per year. Annual cumulation. Includes *Source Index*, *Citation Index*, *Permuterm Subject Index*, and *Corporate Index*.

Social Sciences Citation Index: Compact Disc Edition. Institute for Scientific Information, 3501 Market St. Philadelphia, PA 19104. Phone: 800-523-1850 or (215)386-0100 Fax: (215)386-2911 Quarterly. Provides CD-ROM indexing of the world's social sciences literature, including economics, business, finance, management, communications, demographics, information and library science, political science, sociology, etc. Corresponds to online *Social Scisearch* and printed *Social Sciences Citation Index*.

Social Sciences Citation Index: Compact Disc Edition with Abstracts. Institute for Scientific Information, 3501 Market St. Philadelphia, PA 19104. Phone: 800-523-1850 or (215)386-0100 Fax: (215)386-6362 Quarterly. Provides CD-ROM indexing and abstracting of "significant articles" from 1,400 social science journals worldwide, with additional selections from 3,200 other journals, 1986 to date. Includes economics, business, finance, management, communications, demographics, information and library science, political science, sociology, and many other subjects.

Social Sciences Index. H. W. Wilson Co., 950 University Ave. Bronx, NY 10452. Phone: 800-367-6770 or (718)588-8400 Fax: (718)590-1617 E-mail: custserv@hwwilson.com • URL: http://www.hwwilson.com • Quarterly, with annual cumulation. Service basis for print edition; CD-ROM edition, $1,495 per year. Indexes more than 400 periodicals covering economics, environmental policy, government, insurance, labor, health care policy, plannning, public administration, public welfare, urban studies, women's issues, criminology, and related topics.

Social Scisearch. Institute for Scientific Information, 3501 Market Street Philadelphia, PA 19104. Phone: 800-523-1850 or (215)386-0100 Fax: (215)386-2911 URL: http://www.isinet.com • Broad, multidisciplinary index to the literature of the social sciences, 1972 to present. Weekly updates. Worldwide coverage. Inquire as to online cost and availability.

Social Security Benefits, Including Medicare. CCH, Inc., 4025 W. Peterson Ave. Chicago, IL 60646-6085. Phone: 800-248-3248 or (773)866-6000 Fax: 800-224-8299 or (773)866-3608 URL: http://www.cch.com • Annual.

Social Security Bulletin. Social Security Administration. Available from U.S. Government Printing Office, Washington, DC 20402. Phone: (202)512-1800 Fax: (202)512-2250 E-mail: gpoaccess@gpo.gov • URL: http://

www.access.gpo.gov • Quarterly. $23.00 per year. Annual statistical supplement.

Social Security Claims and Procedures. Harvey L. McCormick. West Publishing Co., College and School Div., 610 Opperman Dr. Eagan, MN 55123. Phone: 800-328-4880 or (651)687-7000 Fax: 800-213-2323 or (651)687-5827 E-mail: legal_ed@westgroup.com • URL: http://www.westgroup.com • 1991. Two volumes. Fourth edition. Price on application. Periodic supplementation.

Social Security Explained. CCH, Inc., 4025 W. Peterson Ave. Chicago, IL 60646-6085. Phone: 800-248-3248 or (773)866-6000 Fax: 800-224-8299 or (773)866-3608 URL: http://www.cch.com • Annual. $32.00.

Social Security Handbook. Available from U. S. Government Printing Office, Washington, DC 20402. Phone: (202)512-1800 Fax: (202)512-2250 E-mail: gpoaccess@gpo.gov • URL: http://www.access.gpo.gov • Annual. $45.00. Issued by the Social Security Administration (http://www.ssa.gov). Provides detailed information about social security programs, including Medicare, with brief descriptions of related programs administered by agencies other than the Social Security Administration.

Social Security Manual. The National Underwriter Co., 505 Gest St. Cincinnati, OH 45203-1716. Phone: 800-543-0874 or (513)721-2140 Fax: (513)721-0126 URL: http://www.nuco.com • Annual. $17.50.

Social Security, Medicare, and Pensions: Get the Most Out of Your Retirement and Medical Benefits. Joseph Matthews and Dorothy M. Berman. Nolo.com, 950 Parker St. Berkeley, CA 94710. Phone: 800-992-6656 or (510)549-1976 Fax: 800-645-0895 or (510)548-5902 E-mail: cs@nolo.com • URL: http://www.nolo.com • 1999. $21.95. Seventh edition. In addition to the basic topics, includes practical information on Supplemental Security Income (SSI), disability benefits, veterans benefits, 401(k) plans, Medicare HMOs, medigap insurance, Medicaid, and how to appeal decisions.

Social Security Online: The Official Web Site of the Social Security Administration. U. S. Social Security AdministrationPhone: 800-772-1213 or (410)965-7700 URL: http://www.ssa.gov • Web site provides a wide variety of online information relating to social security and Medicare. Topics include benefits, disability, employer wage reporting, personal earnings statements, statistics, government financing, social security law, and public welfare reform legislation.

Social Security Practice Guide. Matthew Bender & Co., Inc., Two Park Ave. New York, NY 10016. Phone: 800-223-1940 or (212)448-2000 Fax: (212)244-3188 E-mail: international@bender.com • URL: http://www.bender.com • $870.00. Five looseleaf volumes. Periodic supplementation. Complete, practical guide on all substantive and procedural aspects of social security practice. Prepared under the supervision of the National Organization of Social Security Claimants' Representatives (NOSSCR).

Social Security Programs Throughout the World. Available from U. S. Government Printing Office, Washington, DC 20402. Phone: (202)512-1800 Fax: (202)512-2250 E-mail: gpoaccess@gpo.gov • URL: http://www.access.gpo.gov • Annual. $43.00. Issued by the Social Security Administration (http://www.ssa.gov). Presents basic information on more than 170 social security systems around the world.

Social Statistics of the United States. Mark S. Littman, editor. Bernan Press, 4611-F Assembly Dr. Lanham, MD 20706-4391. Phone: 800-274-4447 or (301)459-7666 Fax: 800-865-3450 or (301)459-0056 E-mail: info@bernan.com • URL: http://www.bernan.com • 2000. $65.00. Includes statistical data on population growth, labor force, occupations, environmental trends, leisure time use, income, poverty, taxes, and other economic or demographic topics.

Social Welfare Research Institute. Boston College

Society for Advancement of Management.

Society for Computer Simulation International.

Society for Economic Botany.

Society for Foodservice Management.

Society for Health Strategy and Market Development-Directory of Membership and Services. Society for Healthcare Strategy and Market Development. American Hospital Association, One N. Franklin St., 31st Fl. Chicago, IL 60606. Phone: 800-242-2626 or (312)422-3000 Fax: (312)422-4505 Annual. Membership. Formerly *American Society for Health Care Marketing and Public Relations-Membership Directory*.

Society for Healthcare Strategy and Market Development-Directory of Membership and Service. Society for Healthcare Strategy and Market Development. American Hospital Association, One N. Franklin, 31st Fl. Chicago, IL 60606. Phone: (312)280-6155 Fax: (312)422-4577 E-mail: stratsoc@aha.org • Annual. Membership.

Society for Historians of American Foreign Relations Newsletter. Society for Historians of American Foreign Relations, c/o Tennessee Technological University, Dept. of History Cookeville, TN 38505. Phone: (931)372-3332 Fax: (931)372-6142 Quarterly.

Society for Human Resource Management.

Society for Imaging Science and Technology.

Society for Industrial and Applied Mathematics.

Society for Information Management.

Society for International Development.

Society for International Numismatics.

Society for Mining, Metallurgy, and Exploration.

Society for Nonprofit Organizations.

Society for Range Management.

Society for Technical Communication.

Society for the Advancement of Material and Process Engineering.

Society for the Eradication of Television., P.O. Box 10491 Oakland, CA 94610. Phone: (510)763-8712 Encourages the removal of television sets from homes.

Society for the History of Technology.

Society for the Investigation of Recurring Events.

Society of Actuaries.

Society of Actuaries Yearbook. Society of Actuaries, 475 N. Martingale Rd., Suite 800 Schaumburg, IL 60173-2226. Phone: (847)706-3500 Fax: (847)706-3599 E-mail: bhaynes@soa.org • URL: http://www.soa.org • Annual. $25.00. Includes alphabetical list of actuaries.

Society of American Business Editors and Writers.

Society of American Florists.

Society of American Graphic Artists.

Society of American Registered Architects.

Society of Broadcast Engineers.

Society of Cable Telecommunications Engineers.

Society of Certified Credit Executives.

Society of Commercial Seed Technologists.

Society of Competitive Intelligence Professionals., 1700 Diagonal Rd., Suite 600 Alexandria, VA 22314. Phone: (703)739-0696 Fax: (703)739-2524 E-mail: info@scip.org • URL: http://www.scip.org • Members are professionals involved in competitor intelligence and analysis.

Society of Consumer Affairs Professionals in Business., 801 N. Fairfax St., Suite 404 Alexandria, VA 22314. Phone: (703)519-3700 Fax: (703)549-4886 E-mail: socap@socap.com • URL: http://www.socap.org • Members are managers of consumer affairs departments of business firms.

Society of Corporate Meeting Professionals., 2965 Flowers Rd. S., Ste. 105 Atlanta, GA 30341. Phone: (770)457-9212 Fax: (770)458-3314 E-mail: assnhq@mindspring.com • URL: http://www.scmp.org • Members are company and corporate meeting planners.

Society of Cosmetic Chemists.

Society of Cost Estimating and Analysis., 101 S. Whiting St., Suite 201 Alexandria, VA 22304. Phone: (703)751-8069 Fax: (703)461-7328 E-mail: scea@erols.com • URL: http://www.scea.com • Members are engaged in government contract estimating and pricing.

Society of Craft Designers.

Society of Economic Geologists.

Society of Experimental Test Pilots.

Society of Federal Linguists.

Society of Financial Service Professionals.

Society of Fire Protection Engineers.

Society of Flavor Chemists.

Society of Government Meeting Professionals., Six Clouser Rd. Mechanicsburg, PA 17055-9735. Members are individuals involved in the planning of government meetings.

Society of Illustrators.

Society of Incentive and Travel Executives., 21 W. 38th St., 10th Fl. New York, NY 10018. Phone: (212)575-0910 Fax: (212)575-1838 E-mail: hq@site-intl.org • URL: http://www.site-intl.org • Members include both users and suppliers of incentive travel.

Society of Independent Gasoline Marketers of America.

Society of Indexers.

Society of Industrial and Office Realtors.

Society of Leather Technologists and Chemists Journal. Society of Leather Technologies and Chemists, 38 Roseholme Rd. Abington, Northampton NN1 4TQ, England. Phone: 44 1604 639306 Fax: 44 1604 635932 E-mail: graham@sltc.org • URL: http://www.sltc.org • Bimonthly. $65.00 per year. Scientific, technical, historical and commercial papers on leather and allied industries.

Society of Manufacturing Engineers.

Society of Medical-Dental Management Consultants.

Society of Medical-Dental Management Consultants: Membership Directory. Society of Medical-Dental Management Consultants, 3646 E. Ray Rd., B16-45 Phoenix, AZ 85044. Phone: 800-826-2264 Fax: (602)759-3530 E-mail: chuck@smdmc.org • URL: http://www.smdmc.org • Annual. Free. About 100 consultants in business and financial aspects of the management of medical and dental practices.

Society of Motion Picture and Television Engineers.

Society of Motion Picture and Television Engineers Directory for Members. Society of Motion Picture and Television Engineers, 595 W. Hartsdale Ave. White Plains, NY 10607. Phone: (914)761-1100 Fax: (914)761-3115 E-mail: smpte@smpte.org • URL: http://www.smpte.org • Annual. Membership.

Society of Naval Architects and Marine Engineers.

Society of Paper Money Collectors.

Society of Petroleum Engineers.

Society of Philatelists and Numismatists.

Society of Plastics Engineers.

Society of Professional Investigators.

Society of Professional Journalists.

Society of Publication Designers.

Society of Recreation Executives., P. O. Box 520 Gonzalez, FL 35260-0520. Phone: (850)944-7992 Fax: (850)944-0018 E-mail: nrvockws@spyder.net • Members are corporate executives employed in the recreation and leisure industries.

Society of Research Administrators.

Society of Research Administrators Journal. Society of Research Administrators, Inc., 1200 19th St., N.W., Suite 300 Washington, DC 20036-2401. Phone: (202)857-1141 Fax: (202)223-4579 Quarterly. Members, $35.00 per year; non-members, $45.00 per year.

Society of the Plastics Industry.

Society of Tribologists and Lubrication Engineers.

Society of Vacuum Coaters.

Society of Wine Educators.

Society of Women Engineers.

Sociological Abstracts. Cambridge Information Group, 7200 Wisconsin Ave., 6th Fl. Bethesda, MD 20814. Phone: 800-843-7751 or (301)961-6700 Fax: (301)961-6720 URL: http://www.csa.com • Bimonthly. $635.00 per year. A compendium of non-evaluative abstracts covering the field of sociology and related disciplines. Includes an annual *Index*.

Sock Shop. Entrepreneur Media, Inc., 2445 McCabe Way Irvine, CA 92614. Phone: 800-421-2300 or (949)261-2325 Fax: (949)261-0234 E-mail: entmag@entrepreneur.com • URL: http://www.entrepreneur.com • Looseleaf. $59.50. A practical guide to starting a store that sells stockings of various kinds. Covers profit potential, start-up costs, market size evaluation, owner's time required, site selection, lease negotiation, pricing, accounting, advertising, etc. (Start-Up Business Guide No. E1340.)

Soft Drink Letter. Whitaker Newsletter, Inc., 313 South Ave. Fanwood, NJ 07023. Phone: (908)889-6336 Fax: (908)889-6339 Biweekly. $299.00 per year. For owners and managers of bottling operations. Covers soft drinks, juices. Formerly *Leisure Beverage Insider Newsletter*.

SoftBase: Reviews, Companies, and Products. Information Sources, Inc., Post Office Box 8120 Berkeley, CA 94707. Phone: (510)525-6220 Fax: (510)525-1568 Describes and reviews business software packages. Inquire as to online cost and availability.

Soft.Letter: Trends and Strategies in Software Publishing. Mercury Group,Inc, 17 Main St. Watertown, MA 02172-4491. Phone: (617)924-3944 Fax: (617)924-7288 E-mail: jtarter@softletter.com • URL: http://www.softletter.com • Semimonthly. $395.00 per year. Newsletter on the software industry, including new technology and financial aspects.

Software and Information Industry Association., 1730 M St., N. W., Suite 700 Washington, DC 20036-4510. Phone: (202)452-1600 Fax: (202)223-8756 URL: http://www.siia.net • A trade association for the software and digital content industry. Divisions are Content, Education, Enterprise, Financial Information Services, Global, and Internet. Includes an Online Content Committee. Formerly Software Publishers Association.

Software Digest: The Independent Comparative Ratings Report for PC and LAN Software. National Software Testing Laboratories, Inc., Plymouth Corporate Center, 625 W. Ridge Pike, No. 6D Conshohocken, PA 19428-1180. Phone: 800-257-9402 or (610)941-9600 Fax: (610)941-9950 12 times a year. $450.00 per year. Critical evaluations of personal computer software.

Software Economics Letter: Maximizing Your Return on Corporate Software. Computer Economics, Inc., 5841 Edison Place Carlsbad, CA 92008-6519. Phone: 800-326-8100 or (760)438-8100 Fax: (760)431-1126 E-mail: custserv@compecon.com • URL: http://www.computereconomics.com • Monthly. $395.00 per year. Newsletter for information systems managers. Contains data on business software trends, vendor licensing policies, and other corporate software management issues.

The Software Encyclopedia: A Guide for Personal, Professional, and Business Users. R. R. Bowker, 121 Chanlon Rd. New Providence, NJ 07974. Phone: 888-269-5372 or (908)464-6800 Fax: (908)771-7704 E-mail: info@bowker.com • URL: http://www.bowker.com • Annual. $255.00. Two volumes. Volume one lists software programs by title and producer. Volume two provides information on programs according to application and operating system. Includes prices and requirements for hardware and memory.

Software Engineering. Ian Sommerville. Addison Wesley Longman, Inc., One Jacob Way Reading, MA. Phone: 800-447-2226 or (781)944-3700 Fax: (781)944-9351 URL: http://www.awl.com • 2000. $80.00. Sixth edition. (International Computer Science Series).

Software Law Journal. Center for Computer Law, P.O. Box 3549 Manhattan Beach, CA 90266. Phone: (301)544-7372 Quarterly. $97.50 per year.

Software Magazine. Wiesner Publishing, Inc., 40 Steen St. Framingham, MA 01701. Phone: (508)875-9555 Fax:

(508)875-3365 URL: http://www.softwaremaqazine.com • Monthly. $42.00 per year.

Software Reviews and Audits Handbook. Charles P. Hollocker. John Wiley and Sons, Inc., 605 Third Ave. New York, NY 10158-0012. Phone: 800-526-5368 or (212)850-6000 Fax: (212)850-6088 E-mail: info@wiley.com • URL: http://www.wiley.com • 1990. $79.99. Includes document samples, forms, and checklists. (Industrial Software Engineering Practice Series).

Software Store. Entrepreneur Media, Inc., 2445 McCabe Way Irvine, CA 92614. Phone: 800-421-2300 or (949)261-2325 Fax: (949)261-0234 E-mail: entmag@entrepreneur.com • URL: http://www.entrepreneur.com • Looseleaf. $59.50. A practical guide to opening a computer software retail establishment. Covers profit potential, start-up costs, market size evaluation, owner's time required, site selection, lease negotiation, pricing, accounting, advertising, promotion, etc. (Start-Up Business Guide No. E1261.)

SoHo Central. Home Office Association of America, Inc.Phone: 800-809-4622 Fax: 800-315-4622 E-mail: info@hoaa.com • URL: http://www.hoaa.com • Web site provides extensive lists of "Home Office Internet Resources" (links), including Business, Government, Continuing Education, Legal, Employment, Telecommunications, and Publishing. Includes an online newsletter. Fees: Free. (Membership in the Home Office Association of America is $49.00 per year.)

SOHO Journal (Small Office Home Office). National Association for the Cottage Industry, P.O. Box 14850 Chicago, IL 60614. Phone: (312)472-8116 Members, $25.00 per year; libraries, $35.00 per year. Newsletter on business in the-home. Formerly *Mind Your Own Business at Home*.

Soil Science: An Interdisciplinary Approach to Soils Research. Williams and Wilkins Co., 351 W. Camden St. Baltimore, MD 21202-2436. Phone: 800-527-5597 or (410)528-4000 Fax: (410)528-4422 E-mail: custserv@wilkins.com • URL: http://www.wwilkins.com • Monthly. Individuals, $131.00 per year; institutions, $236.00 per year.

Soil Testing Laboratory. University of Massachusetts at Amherst

Solar Energy. Available from U. S. Government Printing Office, Washington, DC 20402. Phone: (202)512-1800 Fax: (202)512-2250 E-mail: gpoaccess@gpo.gov • URL: http://www.access.gpo.gov • Annual. Free. Lists government publications. GPO Subject Bibliography Number 9.

Solar Energy and Energy Conversion Laboratory.

Solar Energy Center.

Solar Energy Industries Association.

Solar Energy: International for Scientists, Engineers and Technologists in SolarEnergy and Its Application. International Solar Energy Society. Elsevier Science, 655 Ave. of the Americas New York, NY 10010. Phone: 888-437-4636 or (212)989-5800 Fax: (212)633-3680 E-mail: usinfo@elsevier.com • URL: http://www.elsevier.com • 18 times a year. $1,889.00 per year.

The Solar Home: How to Design and Build a House You Heat with the Sun. Mark Freeman. Stackpole Books, Inc., 5067 Ritter Rd. Mechanicsburg, PA 17055. Phone: 800-732-3669 or (717)796-0411 Fax: (717)796-0412 E-mail: sales@stackpolebooks.com • URL: http://www.stackpolebooks.com • 1994. $14.95.

Solartherm., 1315 Apple Ave. Silver Spring, MD 20910. Phone: (301)587-8686 Fax: (301)587-8688 Members are scientists engaged in the development of low-cost solar energy systems.

Soldiers. Available from U. S. Government Printing Office, Washington, DC 20402. Phone: (202)512-1800 Fax: (202)512-2250 E-mail: gpoaccess@gpo.gov • URL: http://www.access.gpo.gov • Monthly. $28.00 per year. Provides information on the policies, plans, operations, and technical developments of the U.S. Department of the Army (http://www.army.mil).

SOLE-The International Society of Logistics., 8100 Professional Place, Suite 211 Hyattsville, MD 20785. Phone: (301)459-8446 Fax: (301)459-1522 Concerned with designing, supplying, and maintaining resources to support objectives, plans, and operations.

Solid State and Superconductivity Abstracts. Cambridge Information Group, 7200 Wisconsin Ave., 6th Fl. Bethesda, MD 20814. Phone: 800-843-7751 or (301)961-6700 Fax: (301)961-6720 E-mail: market@csa.com • URL: http://www.csa.com • Bimonthly. $1,045.00 per year. Formerly *Solid State Abstracts Journal*.

Solid-State Device and Materials Research Laboratory.

Solid State Electronic Devices. Prentice Hall, 240 Frisch Court Paramus, NJ 07652-5240. Phone: 800-947-7700 or (201)909-6200 Fax: 800-445-6991 or (201)909-6361 URL: http://www.prenhall.com • 2000. Fifth edition. Price on application.

Solid State Electronics. George Rutkowski. Glencoe/McGraw-Hill, 8787 Orion Place Columbus, OH 43240-4027. URL: http://www.glencoe.com • Date not set. $104.25. Fourth edition.

Solid State Technology. PennWell Corp., Advanced Technology Div., 98 Spit Brook Rd. Nashua, NH 03062-5737. Phone: 800-331-4463 or (603)891-0123 Fax: (603)891-0539 E-mail: webmaster@pennwell.com • URL: http://www.pennwell.com • Monthly. $185.00 per year. Covers the technical and business aspects of semiconductor and integrated circuit production. Includes *Buyers Guide*.

Solid State Technology Resource Guide. PennWell Corp., Advanced Technology Div., 98 Spit Brook Rd. Nashua, NH 03062-5737. Phone: 800-331-4463 or (603)891-0123 Fax: (603)891-0539 E-mail: webmaster@pennwell.com • URL: http://www.pennwell.com • 1998. $99.00. Lists suppliers of products and services related to the production and testing of solid state devices.

Solid Waste Association of North America., P.O. Box 7219 Silver Spring, MD 20907. Phone: 800-467-9262 or (301)585-2898 Fax: (301)589-7068 E-mail: info@swana.org • URL: http://www.swana.org • Members are officials from both public agencies and private companies. Attempts to improve waste management services to the public and industry.

Solid Waste Handbook: A Practical Guide. William D. Robinson, editor. John Wiley and Sons, Inc., 605 Third Ave. New York, NY 10158-0012. Phone: 800-526-5368 or (212)850-6000 Fax: (212)850-6088 E-mail: info@wiley.com • URL: http://www.wiley.com • 1986. $225.00.

Solid Waste Report: Resource Recovery-Recycling-Collection-Disposal. Business Publishers, Inc., 8737 Colesville Rd., Suite 1100 Silver Spring, MD 20910-3928. Phone: 800-274-6737 or (301)587-6300 Fax: (301)587-1081 E-mail: bpinews@bpinews.com • URL: http://www.bpinews.com • Weekly. $627.00 per year. Newsletter. Covers regulation, business news, technology, and international events relating to solid waste management.

The SOLO Librarian's Sourcebook. Judith A. Siess. Information Today, Inc., 143 Old Marlton Pike Medford, NJ 08055-8750. Phone: 800-300-9868 or (609)654-6266 Fax: (609)654-4309 E-mail: custserv@infotoday.com • URL: http://www.infotoday.com • 1997. $39.50. Covers management and other aspects of one-librarian libraries.

Some Aspects of Bibliography. J. Ferguson. Gordon Press Publishers, P.O. Box 459 New York, NY 10004. Phone: (212)969-8419 Fax: (718)624-8419 1976. $59.95.

Sound and Communications. Testa Communications, Inc., 25 Willowdale Ave. Port Washington, NY 11050. Phone: (516)767-2500 Fax: (516)767-9335 Monthly. $15.00 per year. A business, news and technical journal for contractors, consultants, engineers and system managers who design, install and purchase sound and communications equipment.

Sound and Communications: The Blue Book. Testa Communications, 25 Willowdale Ave. Port Washington, NY 11050. Phone: (516)767-2500 Fax: (516)767-9335 Annual. $15.00. Approximately 1,000 suppliers of sound and communications equipment; including audio/video products in the United States and Canada.

Sound and Recording: An Introduction. Francis Rumsey. Butterworth-Heinemann, 225 Wildwood Ave. Woburn, MA 01801. Phone: 800-366-2665 or (781)904-2500 Fax: 800-466-6520 E-mail: orders@bhusa.com • URL: http://www.bh.com • 1997. $39.95. Third edition. Covers the theory and principles of sound recording and reproduction, with chapters on amplifiers, microphones, mixers, and other components.

Sound and Vibration Buyer's Guide. Acoustical Publications, Inc., P.O. Box 40416 Bay Village, OH 44140. Phone: (440)835-0101 Fax: (440)835-9303 E-mail: sv@mindspring.com • Annual. Free to qualified personnel. Lists of manufacturers of products for noise and vibration control, dynamic measurements instrumentation, and dynamic testing equipment.

Sound and Vibration (S/V). Acoustical Publications, Inc., P.O. Box 40416 Bay Village, OH 44140. Phone: (440)835-0101 Fax: (440)835-9303 E-mail: sv@mindspring.com • Monthly. Free to qualified personnel; others, $60.00 per year.

Sound Check: The Basics of Sound and Sound Systems. Tony Moscal. Hal Leonard Corp., 7777 W. Bluemound Rd. Milwaukee, WI 53213. Phone: 800-524-4425 or (414)774-3630 Fax: (414)774-3259 E-mail: halinfo@halleonard.com • URL: http://www.halleonard.com • 1994. $14.95. Explains the fundamentals of sound and related electronics.

Source Book of Health Insurance Data, 1997-1998. Health Insurance Association of America, 555 13th St., N.W., No. 600 E. Washington, DC 20004-1109. Phone: 800-509-4422 or (202)824-1840 Fax: (202)824-1800 E-mail: mbell@hiaa.org • URL: http://www.hiaa.org • 1998. $35.00. Data on health insurance, medical care costs, morbidity and health manpower in the U. S.

Sourcebook America. The Gale Group, 27500 Drake Rd. Farmington Hills, MI 48331-3535. Phone: 800-877-GALE or (248)699-GALE Fax: 800-414-5043 or (248)699-8069 E-mail: galeord@gale.com • URL: http://www.gale.com • Annual. $995.00. Produced by CACI Marketing Systems. A combination on CD-ROM of *The Sourcebook of ZIP Code Demographics* and *The Sourcebook of County Demographics*. Provides detailed population and socio-economic data (about 75 items) for each of 3,141 U. S. counties and approximately 30,000 ZIP codes, plus states, metropolitan areas, and media market areas. Includes forecasts to the year 2004.

The Sourcebook of County Demographics. Available from The Gale Group, 27500 Drake Rd. Farmington Hills, MI 48331-3535. Phone: 800-877-GALE or (248)699-GALE Fax: 800-414-5043 or (248)699-8069 E-mail: galeord@galegroup.com • URL: http://www.galegroup.com • 1999. $395.00. 13th edition. Published by CACI. Marketing Systems. Contains demographic and socio-economic data (70 characteristics) for each U. S. county. Formerly *Sourcebook of Demographics and Buying Power for Every County in the USA*.

Sourcebook of Criminal Justice Statistics. Available from U. S. Government Printing Office, Washington, DC 20402. Phone: (202)512-1800 Fax: (202)512-2250 E-mail: gpoaccess@gpo.gov • URL: http://www.access.gpo.gov • Annual. $56.00. Issued by the Bureau of Justice Statistics, U. S. Department of Justice (http://www.usdoj.gov/bjs). Contains both crime data and corrections statistics.

The Sourcebook of ZIP Code Demographics. Available from The Gale Group, 27500 Drake Rd. Farmington Hills, MI 48331-3535. Phone: 800-877-GALE or (248)699-GALE Fax: 800-414-5043 or (248)699-8069 E-mail: galeord@galegroup.com • URL: http://www.galegroup.com • 2000. $495.00. 15th edition. Published by CACI Marketing Systems. Presents detailed statistical profiles of every ZIP code in America, based on the 1990 census. Each profile contains data on more than 70 variables.

Sourcebook of Zip Code Demographics. CACI Marketing Systems, 1100 N. Glebe Rd., Suite 200 Arlington, VA 22201-4714. Phone: 800-292-2224 or (703)841-2924 Fax: (703)243-6272 E-mail: msgw@caci.com • URL: http://www.demographics.caci.com • 2000. $495.00. 15th revised edition. Published by CACI, Inc. Provides data on 75 demographic and socio-economic characteristics for each ZIP code in the U. S.

Sourcebooks America CD-ROM. CACI Marketing Systems, 1100 N. Glebe Rd., Suite 200 Arlington, VA 22201-4714. Phone: 800-292-2224 or (703)841-7800 Fax: (703)243-6272 Annual. $1,250.00. Provides the CD-ROM version of *The Sourcebook of ZIP Code Demographics: Census Edition* and *The Sourcebook of County Demographics: Census Edition*.

SourceMex. Latin America Data Base, Latin American Institute, University of New Mexico, 801 Yale Blvd., N. E. Albuquerque, NM 87131-1016. Phone: 800-472-0888 or (505)277-6839 Fax: (505)277-5989 An online newsletter covering economic conditions in Mexico, including foreign trade, public finances, foreign debt, agriculture, and the oil industry. Time period is 1990 to date, with weekly updates. Inquire as to online cost and availability.

Sources of Supply/Buyers Guide. William O. Dannhausen Corp., Drawer 795 Park Ridge, IL 60068. Phone: (847)823-3145 Fax: (847)696-3445 E-mail: wmdann@compuserve.com • URL: http://www.dannhqusen.com • Annual. $90.00. About 2,200 mills and converters, 2,700 merchants and 500 manufacturers' representatives in paper, films, foils, and allied lines.

Southern Christian Leadership Conference.

Southern Lumberman. Greysmith Publishing, Inc., P.O. Box 681629 Franklin, TN 37067. Phone: (615)791-1961 Fax: (615)790-6188 13 times a year. $23.00 per year. A magazine for the sawmill industry.

Southern Pulp and Paper. Ernest H. Abernathy Publishing Co., Six Piedmont Center, N.E., Suite 300 Atlanta, GA 30305-1515. Phone: (404)881-6442 Monthly. $18.00 per year.

Southwest Research Institute.

Souvenir and Novelty Trade Association.

Soya and Oilseed Bluebook. Soyatech, Inc., 7 Pleasant St. Bar Harbour, ME 04609. Phone: 800-424-7692 or (207)288-4969 Fax: (207)288-5264 E-mail: data@soyatech.comm • URL: http://www.soyatech.com • Annual. $70.00. Includes quarterly *Bluebook Update*. Formerly *Soya Bluebook Plus*.

Soyabean Abstracts. Available from CABI Publishing North America, 10 E. 40th St. New York, NY 10016. Phone: 800-528-4841 or (212)481-7018 Fax: (212)686-7993 E-mail: cabi@cabi.org • URL: http://www.cabi.org • Bimonthly. $425.00 per year. Published in England by CABI Publishing. Provides worldwide coverage of the literature.

Soybean Digest. American Soybean Association. Intertec Publishing Corp., Agribusiness Div., 7900 International Dr., Suite 300 Minneapolis, MN 55425. Phone: (612)851-9329 Fax: (612)351-4601 E-mail: sbd@intertec.com • URL: http://www.intertec.com • 11 times a year. $25.00 per year. Provides high acreage farmers who grow soy beans in rotation with other crops timely production, marketing and management information.

Space Business News. Phillips Business Information, Inc., 1201 Seven Locks Rd., Suite 300 Potomac, MD 20854. Phone: 800-777-5006 or (301)340-1520 Fax: (301)340-0542 E-mail: pbi@phillips.com • URL: http://www.phillips.com • Biweekly. $797.00 per year. Newsletter. Covers business applications in space, including remote sensing and satellites.

Space Institute. University of Tennessee

Space Planning in the Special Library. Roberta Freifeld and Caryl Masyr. Special Libraries Association, 1700 18th St., N. W., 17th Fl. Washington, DC 20009-2514. Phone: (202)234-4700 Fax: 888-411-2856 or (202)265-9317 E-mail: books@sla.org • URL: http://www.sla.org • 1991. $23.00. Provides practical advice for planners of new libraries, renovations, and relocations.

Space, Telecommunications, and Radioscience Laboratory. Stanford University

Space Times. American Astronautical Society, 6352 Rolling Mill Place, Suite 102 Springfield, VA 22152-2354. Phone: (703)866-0020 Fax: (703)866-3526 E-mail: aas@astronautical.org • URL: http://www.astronautical.org • Bimonthly. Institutions, $80.00 per year. Covers current developments in astronautics.

Special Events Magazine. Intertec Publishing Corp., 23815 Stuart Ranch Rd. Malibu, CA 90265-8987. Phone: 800-400-5945 or (310)317-4522 Fax: (310)317-9644 E-mail: subs@intertec.com • URL: http://www.specialevents.com • Monthly. $39.00 per year. Edited for professionals concerned with parties, meetings, galas, and special events of all kinds and sizes. Provides practical ideas for the planning of special events. Formerly *Special Events*.

Special Interest Autos. Watering Inc., Special Interest Publications, P.O. Box 904 Bennington, VT 05201. Phone: (802)442-3101 Fax: (802)447-1561 E-mail: hmnmail@hemmings.com • URL: http://www.hemmings.com • Bimonthly. $19.95 per year.

Special Interest Group for Computer Personnel Research., c/o Association for Computing Machinery, 1515 Broadway, 17th Fl. New York, NY 10036. Phone: (212)869-7440 Fax: (212)302-5826 E-mail: acmhelp@acm.org • URL: http://www.acm.org/sigcpr • Concerned with the selection, training, and evaluation of computer personnel.

Special Interest Group for Computer Science Education., c/o Association for Computing Machinery, 1515 Broadway New York, NY 10036-5701. Phone: (212)869-7440 Fax: (212)302-5826 E-mail: sigs@acm.org • URL: http://www.acm.org • Concerned with education relating to computer science and technology on various levels, ranging from secondary school to graduate degree programs.

Special Interest Group for Computer Uses in Education., c/o Association for Computing Machinery, 1515 Broadway New York, NY 10036-5701. Phone: (212)869-7440 Fax: (212)302-5826 E-mail: sigs@acm.org • URL: http://www.acm.org • Concerned with the use of the computer as a teaching device.

Special Interest Group for Design Automation.

Special Interest Group for Systems Documentation., Association for Computing Machinery, 1515 Broadway New York, NY 10036. Phone: (212)626-7440 Fax: (212)302-5826 E-mail: sigs@acm.org • URL: http://www.acm.org • Members are individuals who write user manuals and other documentation for computer software applications and computer hardware.

Special Interest Group on Applied Computing., Association for Computing Machinery, 1515 Broadway New York, NY 10036-5701. Phone: (212)869-7440 Fax: (212)302-5826 E-mail: sigs@acm.org • URL: http://www.acm.org/sigapp • Concerned with "innovative applications, technology transfer, experimental computing, strategic research, and the management of computing." Publishes a semiannual newsletter, *Applied Computing Review*.

Special Interest Group on Artificial Intelligence.

Special Interest Group on Biomedical Computing., Association for Computing Machinery, 1515 Broadway New York, NY 10036. Phone: (212)869-7440 Fax: (212)302-5826 E-mail: sigs@acm.org • URL: http://www.acm.org/sigbio • Concerned with medical informatics, molecular databases, medical multimedia, and computerization in general as related to the health and biological sciences.

Special Interest Group on Computer Graphics and Interactive Techniques., Association for Computing Machinery, 1515 Broadway New York, NY 10036. Phone: (212)869-7440 Fax: (212)302-5826 E-mail: sigs@acm.org • URL: http://www.acm.org/siggraph • Concerned with research, technology, and applications for the technical, academic, business, and art communities. Publishes the quarterly newsletter *Computer Graphics*.

Special Interest Group on Computers and Society.

Special Interest Group on Computers and the Physically Handicapped., c/o Association for Computing Machinery, 1515 Broadway, 17th Fl. New York, NY 10036. Phone: (212)869-7440 Fax: (212)302-5826 E-mail: acmhelp@acm.org • URL: http://www.acm.org/sigcaph • Members are physically disabled computer professionals.

Special Interest Group on Data Communication., Association for Computing Machinery, 1515 Broadway New York, NY 10036. Phone: (212)869-7440 Fax: (212)302-5826 E-mail: sigs@acm.org • URL: http://www.acm.org/sigcomm • Focuses on network architecture, protocols, and distributed systems. Publishes a quarterly newsletter *Computer Communication Review*.

Special Interest Group on Design Automation., Association for Computing Machinery, 1515 Broadway New York, NY 10036. Phone: (212)869-7440 Fax: (212)302-5826 E-mail: sigs@acm.org • URL: http://www.acm.org/sigda • Concerned with computer-aided design systems and software. Publishes the semiannual *SIGDA Newsletter*.

Special Interest Group on Electronic Sound Technology., Association for Computing Machinery, 1515 Broadway New York, NY 10036. Phone: (212)869-7440 Fax: (212)302-5826 E-mail: sigs@acm.org • URL: http://www.acm.org/sigsound • Concerned with software, algorithms, hardware, and applications relating to digitally generated audio.

Special Interest Group on Hypertext, Hypermedia, and Web., Association for Computing Machinery, 1515 Broadway New York, NY 10036. Phone: (212)869-7440 Fax: (212)302-5826 E-mail: sigs@acm.org • URL: http://www.acm.org/sigweb • Concerned with the design, use, and evaluation of hypertext and hypermedia systems. Provides a multi-disciplinary forum for the promotion, dissemination, and exchange of ideas relating to research technologies and applications. Publishes the *SIGWEB Newsletter* three times a year.

Special Interest Group on Information Retrieval.

Special Interest Group on Management Information Systems., Association for Computing Machinery, 1515 Broadway New York, NY 10036. Phone: (212)869-7440 Fax: (212)302-5826 E-mail: sigs@acm.org • URL: http://www.acm.org/sigmis • Concerned with research, development, and innovation in business information technology. Publishes the *Database Quarterly*.

Special Interest Group on Management of Data., Association for Computing Machinery, 1515 Broadway New York, NY 10036. Phone: (212)869-7440 Fax: (212)302-5826 E-mail: sigs@acm.org • URL: http://www.acm.org/sigmod • Concerned with database management systems. Publishes the quarterly newsletter *SIGMOD Record*.

Special Interest Group on Multimedia., Association for Computing Machinery, 1515 Broadway New York, NY 10036. Phone: (212)869-7440 Fax: (212)302-5826 E-mail: sigs@acm.org • URL: http://www.acm.org/sigmm • Concerned with multimedia computing, communication, storage, and applications.

Special Interest Group on Operating Systems.

Special Interest Group on Programming Languages.

Special Interest Group on Security, Audit, and Control.

Special Interest Group on Software Engineering., Association for Computing Machinery, 1515 Broadway New York, NY 10036. Phone: (212)869-7440 Fax: (212)302-5826 E-mail: sigs@acm.org • URL: http://www.acm.org/sigsoft • Concerned with all aspects of software development and maintenance. Publishes *Software Engineering Notes*, a bimonthly newsletter.

Special Interest Group on Supporting Group Work., Association for Computing, 1515 Broadway, 17th Fl. New York, NY 10036. Phone: (212)869-7440 Fax: (212)302-5826 E-mail: rivkin@acm.org • URL: http://www.acm.org/siggroup/ • Concerned with office automation and computer communications.

Special Interest Group Profiles for Students. The Gale Group, 27500 Drake Rd. Farmington Hills, MI 48331-3535. Phone: 800-877-GALE or (248)699-GALE Fax: 800-414-5043 or (248)699-8069 E-mail: galeord@galegroup.com • URL: http://www.galegroup.com • 1999. $99.00. Provides detailed descriptions for about 200 lobbies, political action committees, civic action groups, and political parties. Includes a glossary, chronology, and index.

Special Libraries: A Guide for Management. Cathy A. Porter and Elin B. Christianson. Special Libraries Association, 1700 18th St., N. W., 17th Fl. Washington, DC 20009-2514. Phone: (202)234-4700 Fax: 888-411-2856 or (202)265-9317 E-mail: books@sla.org • URL: http://www.sla.org • 1997. $42.00. Fourth edition. Provides basic information for the managers of business and other organizations on starting, staffing, and maintaining a special library.

Special Libraries and Information Centers: An Introductory Text. Ellis Mount and Renee Massoud. Special Libraries Association, 1700 18th St., N. W., 17th Fl. Washington, DC 20009-2514. Phone: (202)234-4700 Fax: 888-411-2856 or (202)265-9317 E-mail: books@sla.org • URL: http://www.sla.org • 1999. $49.00. Fourth edition. Includes descriptions of 13 outstanding libraries and information centers.

Special Libraries Association.

Special Libraries Association; Information Technology Division.

Special Situations Newsletter: In-depth Survey of Under-Valued Stocks. Charles Howard Kaplan, 26 Broadway, Suite 200 New York, NY 10004-1703. Phone: 800-756-1811 or (201)418-4411 Fax: (201)418-5085 Monthly. $75.00 per year. Newsletter. Principal content is "This Month's Recommendation," a detailed analysis of one special situation stock.

Special Statistical Report on Profit, Production and Sales Trends in the Men's and Boy's Tailored Clothing Industry. Clothing Manufacturers Association of the U.S.A., 730 Broadway, 9th Fl. New York, NY 10003-9511. Phone: (212)519-0823 Fax: (212)529-1739 1983. $15.00

Specialty Advertising. Entrepreneur Media, Inc., 2445 McCabe Way Irvine, CA 92614. Phone: 800-421-2300 or (949)261-2325 Fax: (949)261-0234 E-mail: entmag@entrepreneur.com • URL: http://www.entrepreneur.com • Looseleaf. $59.50. A practical guide to starting a business dealing in advertising specialties. Covers profit potential, market size evaluation, start-up costs, pricing, accounting, advertising, promotion, etc. (Start-Up Business Guide No. E1292.)

Specialty Baker's Voice. Specialty Bakery Owners of America, 1568 Ralph Ave. Brooklyn, NY 11236-3129. Phone: (212)227-7754 Monthly. $25.00 per year.

Specialty Food Industry Directory. Phoenix Media Network, Inc., P.O. Box 811768 Boca Raton, FL 33481-1768. Phone: (561)447-0810 Annual. Included in subscription to Food Distribution Magazine. Lists manufacturers and suppliers of specialty foods, and services and equipment for the specialty food industry. Featured food products include legumes, sauces, spices, upscale cheese, specialty beverages, snack foods, baked goods, ethnic foods, and specialty meats.

Specialty Occupational Outlook: Professions. The Gale Group, 27500 Drake Rd. Farmington Hills, MI 48331-3535. Phone: 800-877-GALE or (248)699-GALE Fax: 800-414-5043 or (248)699-8069 E-mail: galeord@galegroup.com • URL: http://www.galegroup.com • 1995. $70.00. Provides information on 150 professional occupations.

Specialty Occupational Outlook: Trade and Technical. The Gale Group, 27500 Drake Rd. Farmington Hills, MI 48331-3535. Phone: 800-877-GALE or (248)699-GALE Fax: 800-414-5043 or (248)699-8069 E-mail: galeord@galegroup.com • URL: http://www.galegroup.com • 1996. $70.00. Provides information on 150 "high-interest" careers that do not require a bachelor's degree.

Specialty Tools and Fasteners Distributors Association.

Spectra. American Gem Society, 5901 W. Third St. Los Angeles, CA 90036. Phone: (213)936-4367 Fax: (213)936-9629 Monthly. Membership. Newsletter.

Spectra. National Communication Association, 5105 E. Backlick Rd., Bldg. E Annandale, VA 22003. Phone: (703)750-0533 Fax: (703)914-9471 Monthly. $45.00 per year.

Spectrum: Journal of State Government. Council of State Governments, P.O. Box 11910 Lexington, KY 40578-1910. Phone: 800-800-1910 or (606)244-8000 Fax: (606)244-8001 E-mail: psantos@csg.org • URL: http://www.csg.org • Quarterly. $49.99 per year. Formerly *Journal of State Government*.

Speech Index: An Index to Collections of World Famous Orations and Speeches for Various Occasions, 1966-1980. Scarecrow Press, Inc., 4720 Boston Way Lanham, MD 20706-4310. Phone: 800-462-6420 or (301)459-3366 Fax: 800-338-4550 or (301)459-1705 E-mail: orders@scarecrowpress.com • URL: http://www.scarecrowpress.com • 1982. $80.00. Fourth edition.

Speech Synthesis and Recognition. J.N. Holmes. Chapman and Hall, 115th Fifth Ave., 4th Fl. New York, NY 10003-1004. Phone: 800-842-3636 or (212)260-1354 Fax: (212)260-1730 E-mail: info@chapall.com • URL: http://www.thomson.com.chapall • 1987. $56.95.

SPI Composites Institute., 1801 K St., N.W., Suite 600K Washington, DC 20006-1301. E-mail: ci@socplas.org • URL: http://www.socplas.org/businessunits/index/ci.html • A division of the Society of the Plastics Industry. Members are molders and fabricators of reinforced plastics.

Spices and Seasonings. Available from MarketResearch.com, 641 Ave. of the Americas, Third Floor New York, NY 10011. Phone: 800-298-5699 or (212)807-2629 Fax: (212)807-2716 E-mail: order@marketresearch.com • URL: http://www.marketresearch.com • 1999. $2,250.00. Market research data. Published by Specialists in Business Information. Covers salt, pepper, garlic, salt substitutes, seasoning mixes, etc.

Spices: Flavor Chemistry and Antioxidant Properties. Sara J. Risch and Chi-Tang Ho, editors. American Chemical Society, Available from Oxford University Press, Inc., 198 Madison Ave. New York, NY 10016-4314. Phone: 800-445-9714 or (212)726-6000 Fax: (212)726-6446 E-mail: egt.@oup • URL: http://www.oup-usa.org • 1997. $105.00. A review of spice chemistry "from both practical and historical perspectives." Covers antioxidant properties of specific spices and potential health benefits. (ACS Symposium Series, No. 660.)

Spices: Their Botanical Origin, Their Chemical Composition, Their Commercial Use, Including Seeds, Herbs, and Leaves. Joseph K. Jank. Gordon Press Publishers, P.O. Box 459 New York, NY 10004. Phone: (212)969-8419 Fax: (718)624-8419 1980. $49.95.

SPIE-The International Society for Optical Engineering.

Spilled Milk: A Special Collection from The Journal of Commercial Bank Lending on Loans that Went Sour. Robert Morris Associates, One Liberty Place, Suite 2300, 1650 Market St. Philadelphia, PA 19103-7398. Phone: 800-677-7621 or (215)446-4000 Fax: (215)446-4100

E-mail: info@rmahq.org • URL: http://www.rmahq.org • 1985. $33.50. Two volumes.

Sportbil. International Sport Summit, 6550 Rock Spring Dr., Suite 500 Bethesda, MD 20817-1126. Fax: (301)493-0536 Annual. Price on application. A yearly review of the business of sport.

Sporting Arms and Ammunition Manufacturers Institute.

Sporting Goods Business: The National Newsmagazine of the Sporting Goods Industry. Miller Freeman, Inc., One Penn Plaza New York, NY 10119. Phone: (212)714-1300 Fax: (212)714-1313 E-mail: mfibooks@mfi.com • URL: http://www.mfi.com • Monthly. $65.00 per year. The national news magazine of the sporting goods industry.

Sporting Goods Dealer: The Voice of Team Dealers Since 1899. Shore-Varrone, Inc., 6255 Barfield Rd., N.E., Suite 200 Atlanta, GA 30328-4300. Phone: 800-241-9034 or (404)252-8831 Fax: (404)252-4436 Quarterly. $38.00 per year.

Sporting Goods Manufacturers Association.

Sporting Goods Store. Entrepreneur Media, Inc., 2445 McCabe Way Irvine, CA 92614. Phone: 800-421-2300 or (949)261-2325 Fax: (949)261-0234 E-mail: entmag@entrepreneur.com • URL: http://www.entrepreneur.com • Looseleaf. $59.50. A practical guide to starting a retail sporting goods business. Covers profit potential, start-up costs, market size evaluation, owner's time required, site selection, lease negotiation, pricing, accounting, advertising, promotion, etc. (Start-Up Business Guide No. E1286.)

Sports and Entertainment Litigation Reporter: National Journal of Record Covering Crititcal Issues in Entertainment Law Field. Andrews Publications, 175 Strafford Ave., Bldg. 4, Suite 140 Wayne, PA 19087. Phone: 800-345-1101 or (610)622-0510 Fax: (610)622-0501 URL: http://www.andrewspub.com • Monthly. $775.00 per year. Provides reports on lawsuits involving films, TV, cable broadcasting, stage productions, radio, and other areas of the entertainment business.Formerly *Entertainment Litigation Reporter*.

Sports, Convention, and Entertainment Facilities. David C. Petersen. Urban Land Institute, 1025 Thomas Jefferson St., N. W., Suite 500 W. Washington, DC 20007-5201. Phone: 800-321-5011 or (202)624-7000 Fax: (202)624-7140 E-mail: bookstore@uli.org • URL: http://www.uli.org • 1996. $59.95. Provides advice and information on developing, financing, and operating amphitheaters, arenas, convention centers, and stadiums. Includes case studies of 70 projects.

Sports Foundation., 1699 Wall St. Mount Prospect, IL 60056-5780. Phone: (847)439-4000 Fax: (847)439-0111 Seeks to stimulate interest in the development of new recreational activities and facilities through the promotion of sports and the sporting goods industry.

Sports Industry News: Management and Finance, Regulation and Litigation, Media and Marketing. Game Point Publishing, P. O. Box 946 Camden, ME 04843. Weekly. $244.00 per year. Newsletter. Covers ticket promotions, TV rights, player contracts, concessions, endorsements, etc.

Sports Market Place. Franklin Covey Co., Sports Div., 7520 N. 16th St., Suite 402 Phoenix, AZ 85020. Phone: (602)943-4882 Fax: (602)943-4544 E-mail: fqsports@sprintmail.com • Annual. $199.00. Includes a wide variety of professional sports teams, marketing services, organizations, broadcasting services, syndicators, manufacturers, trade shows, and publications.

Sports Trend. Shore-Varrone, Inc., 6225 Barfield Rd., N.E., Suite 200 Atlanta, GA 30328-4300. Phone: 800-241-9034 or (404)252-8831 Fax: (404)252-4436 E-mail: ddrevik@svi-atl.com • Monthly. $75.00 per year. Formerly *Sports Merchandiser*.

Sportstyle. Fairchild Merchandising Group, Seven W. 34th St. New York, NY 10001. Phone: 800-932-4724 or (212)630-4000 Fax: (212)630-4879 URL: http://www.fairchildpub.com • Monthly. $35.00 per year.

The Spotlight. Cordite Fidelity, Inc., 300 Independence Ave., S.E. Washington, DC 20003. Phone: (202)544-1793 Weekly. $59.00 per year.

Spray Equipment Directory. American Business Directories, P.O. Box 27347 Omaha, NE 68127. Phone: 800-555-6124 or (402)593-4600 Fax: (402)331-5481 E-mail: internet@infousa.com • URL: http://www.abii.com • Annual. Price on application.

Spray Technology and Marketing: The Magazine of Spray Pressure Packaging. Industry Publications, Inc., 3621 Hill Rd. Parsippany, NJ 07054. Phone: (973)331-9545 Fax: (973)331-9547 E-mail: spraytec@aol.com • URL: http://www.members.spraytec.com • Monthly. $30.00 per year. Formerly *Aerosol Age*.

SRC Green Book of 35-Year Charts., 101 Prescott St. Wellesley Hills, MA 02481-7258. Phone: 888-223-7412 or (617)235-0900 Fax: (617)235-8834 Annual. $119.00. Chart book presents statistical information on the stocks of 400 leading companies over a 35-year period. Each full page chart is in semi-log format to avoid visual distortion. Also includes charts of 12 leading market averages or indexes and 39 major industry groups.

SRI International., 333 Ravenswood Ave. Menlo Park, CA 94025-3493. Phone: (650)859-2000 Fax: (650)326-5512 E-mail: inquiryline@sri.com • URL: http://www.sri.com • Private research firm specializing in market research in high technology areas.

Sri Lanka Journal of Tea Science. Tea Research Institute of Sri Lanka, Saint Coombs Talawakelle, Sri Lanka. Phone: 052 8385 Fax: 052 8311 Semiannual. $20.00 per year. Text in English. Formerly *Tea Quarterly*.

SSA Publications on CD-ROM. Available from U. S. Government Printing Office, Washington, DC 20402. Phone: (202)512-1800 Fax: (202)512-2250 E-mail: gpoaccess@gpo.gov • URL: http://www.access.gpo.gov • Monthly. $238.00 per year. Provides updated text of three Social Security Administration publications: *Program Operations Manual; Social Security Handbook; Social Security Rulings*.

Staff Directories on CD-ROM. CQ Staff Directories, Inc., 815 Slaters Lane Alexandria, VA 22314. Phone: 800-252-1722 or (703)739-0900 Fax: (703)739-2964 E-mail: staffdir@staffdirectories.com • URL: http://www.staffdirectories.com • Three times a year. $495.00 per year. Provides the contents on CD-ROM of *Congressional Staff Directory, Federal Staff Directory*, and *Judicial Staff Directory*. Includes photographs and maps.

Stained Glass Association of America.

Stainless Steels, 87: Proceedings of Conference, University of York, 14-16 September, 87. Available from Ashgate Publishing Co., Old Post Rd. Brookfield, VT 05036. Phone: (802)276-3162 Fax: (802)276-3837 E-mail: info@ashgate.com • URL: http://www.ashgate.com • 1988. $94.50. Published by Inst Material.

Stamp Collector. Krause Publications, Inc., 700 State St. Iola, WI 54990. Phone: 800-258-0929 or (715)445-2214 Fax: (715)445-4087 E-mail: info@krause.com • URL: http://www.krause.com/ • Biweekly. $31.98 per year. Newspaper.

Stamp Exchangers Annual Directory. Levine Publications, P.O. Box 9090 Trenton, NJ 08650. Annual. $18.00. Lists over 500 people worldwide who are interested in exchanging stamps, coins, and other collectibles with Americans.

Stamps: The Weekly Magazine of Philately. American Publishing Co. of New York, 85 Canisteo St. Hornell, NY 14843. Phone: (607)324-2212 Fax: (607)324-1753 Weekly. $23.50 per year.

Standard and Poor's Bond Guide. Standard and Poor's, 55 Water St. New York, NY 10041. Phone: 800-221-5277 or (212)438-2000 Fax: (212)438-0040 E-mail: questions@standardandpoors.com • URL: http://www.standardandpoors.com • Monthly. $239.00 per year.

Standard & Poor's Corporate Descriptions. Standard & Poor's Corp., 55 Water St. New York, NY 10041. Phone: 800-221-5277 or (212)438-7280 Provides current, detailed financial and other information on approximately 12,000 publicly held U. S. and foreign corporations. Corresponds to the printed *Standard & Poor's Corporation Records*. Updating is twice a month. Inquire as to online cost and availability.

Standard and Poor's Corporate Registered Bond Interest Record. Standard and Poor's, 55 Water St. New York, NY 10041. Phone: 800-221-5277 or (212)438-2000 Fax: (212)438-0040 E-mail: questions@standardandpoors.com • URL: http://www.standardandpoors.com • Annual. $2,600.00 per year. Weekly updates.

Standard & Poor's Corporations. Available from Dialog OnDisc, 11000 Regency Parkway, Suite 10 Cary, NC 27511. Phone: 800-334-2564 or (919)462-8600 Fax: (919)468-9890 E-mail: ondisc@dialog.com • URL: http://products.dialog.com/products/ondisc/ • Monthly. Price on application. Produced by Standard & Poor's. Contains three CD-ROM files: Executives, Private Companies, and Public Companies, providing detailed information on more than 70,000 business executives, 55,000 private companies, and 12,000 publicly-traded corporations.

Standard and Poor's Daily News Online. Standard and Poor's Corp., 5 Water St. New York, NY 10041. Phone: 800-221-5277 or (212)438-7280 Full text of business news and other information, 1984 to present. Inquire as to online cost and availability.

Standard and Poor's Daily Stock Price Records. Standard and Poor's, 55 Water St. New York, NY 10041. Phone: 800-221-5277 or (212)438-2000 Fax: (212)438-0040 E-mail: questions@standardandpoors.com • URL: http://www.standardandpoors.com • Quarterly. New York Stock Exchange, $420.00 per year; American Stock Exchange, $441.00 per year; NASDAQ, $530.00 per year.

Standard and Poor's Directory of Bond Agents. Standard and Poor's, 55 Water St. New York, NY 10041. Phone: 800-221-5277 or (212)438-2000 Fax: (212)438-0040 E-mail: questions@standardandpoors.com • URL: http://www.standardandpoors.com • Bimonthly. $1,075.00 per year.

Standard and Poor's Dividend Record. Standard and Poor's, 55 Water St. New York, NY 10041. Phone: 800-221-5277 or (212)438-2000 Fax: (212)438-0040 E-mail: questions@standardandpoors.com • URL: http://www.standardandpoors.com • Daily. $825.00 per year.

Standard & Poor's 500 Guide. McGraw-Hill, 1221 Ave. of the Americas New York, NY 10020. Phone: 800-722-4726 or (212)904-2000 Fax: (212)904-2072 E-mail: customer.service@mcgraw-hill.com • URL: http://www.mcgraw-hill.com • Annual. $24.95. Contains detailed profiles of the companies included in Standard & Poor's 500 Index of stock prices. Includes income and balance sheet data for up to 10 years, with growth and stability rankings for 500 major corporations.

Standard & Poor's Industry Surveys. Standard & Poor's, 55 Water St. New York, NY 10041. Phone: 800-221-5277 or (212)438-2000 Fax: (212)438-0040 E-mail: questions@standardandpoors.com • URL: http://www.standardandpoors.com • Semiannual. $1,800.00. Two looseleaf volumes. Includes monthly supplements. Provides detailed, individual surveys of 52 major industry groups. Each survey is revised on a semiannual basis. Also includes "Monthly Investment Review" (industry group investment analysis) and monthly "Trends & Projections" (economic analysis).

Standard & Poor's MidCap 400 Guide. McGraw-Hill, 1221 Ave. of the Americas New York, NY 10020. Phone: 800-722-4726 or (904)512-2000 Fax: (212)904-2072 E-mail: customer.service@mcgraw-hill.com • URL: http://www.mcgraw-hill.com • Annual. $24.95. Contains detailed profiles of the companies included in Standard & Poor's MidCap 400 Index of stock prices. Includes income and balance sheet data for up to 10 years, with growth and stability rankings for 400 midsized corporations.

Standard and Poor's Ratings Handbook. Standard & Poor's, 55 Water St. New York, NY 10041. Phone: 800-221-5277 or (212)438-2000 Fax: (212)438-0040 E-mail: questions@standardandpoors.com • URL: http://www.standardandpoors.com • Monthly. $275.00 per year. Newsletter. Provides news and analysis of international credit markets, including information on new bond issues. Formerly *Credit Week International Ratings*.

Standard & Poor's Register: Biographical. Standard & Poor's Corp., 55 Water St. New York, NY 10041. Phone: 800-221-5277 or (212)438-7280 Contains brief biographies of approximately 70,000 business executives and directors. Corresponds to the biographical volume of *Standard & Poor's Register of Corporations, Directors, and Executives*. Updated twice a year. Inquire as to online cost and availability.

Standard & Poor's Register: Corporate. Standard & Poor's Corp., 55 Water St. New York, NY 10041. Phone: 800-221-5277 or (212)438-7280 Contains brief descriptions, with names of key executives, of about 55,000 public and private U. S. companies. Corresponds to the corporate volume of *Standard & Poor's Register of Corporations, Directors, and Executives*. Updated quarterly. Inquire as to online cost and availability.

Standard and Poor's Register of Corporations, Directors and Executives. Standard and Poor's, 55 Water St. New York, NY 10041. Phone: 800-221-5277 or (212)438-2000 Fax: (212)438-0040 E-mail: questions@standardandpoors.com • URL: http://www.standardandpoors.com • Annual. $675.00. Periodic supplementation. Over 55,000 public and privately held corporations in the U.S. Three volumes. Three supplements.

Standard and Poor's Security Dealers of North America. Standard & Poor's, 55 Water St. New York, NY 10041. Phone: 800-221-5277 or (212)438-2000 Fax: (212)438-0040 E-mail: questions@standardandpoors.com • URL: http://www.standardandpoors.com • Semiannual. $480.00 per year; with *Supplements* every six weeks, $590.00 per year. Geographical listing of over 12,000 stock, bond, and commodity dealers.

Standard and Poor's Semiweekly Called Bond Record. Standard & Poor's, 55 Water St. New York, NY 10041. Phone: 800-221-5277 or (212)438-2000 Fax: (212)438-0040 E-mail: questions@standardandpoors.com • URL: http://www.standardandpoors.com • Semiweekly. $1,175.00 per year.

Standard & Poor's SmallCap 600 Guide. McGraw-Hill, 1221 Ave. of the Americas New York, NY 10020. Phone: 800-722-4726 or (212)904-2000 Fax: (212)904-2072 E-mail: customer.service@mcgraw-hill.com • URL: http://www.mcgraw-hill.com • Annual. $24.95. Contains detailed profiles of the companies included in Standard & Poor's SmallCap 600 Index of stock prices. Includes income and balance sheet data for up to 10 years, with growth and stability rankings for 600 small capitalization corporations.

Standard & Poor's Statistical Service. Current Statistics. Standard & Poor's, 55 Water St. New York, NY 10041. Phone: 800-221-5277 or (212)438-2000 Fax: (212)438-0040 E-mail: questions@standardandpoors.com • URL: http://www.standardandpoors.com • Monthly. $688.00 per year. Includes 10 *Basic Statistics* sections, *Current Statistics Supplements* and *Annual Security Price Index Record*.

Standard & Poor's Stock Reports: American Stock Exchange. Standard & Poor's, 55 Water St. New York, NY 10041.

Phone: 800-221-5277 or (212)438-2000 Fax: (212)438-0040 E-mail: questions@standardandpoors.com • URL: http://www.standardandpoors.com • Irregular. $1,035.00 per year. Looseleaf service. Provides two pages of financial details and other information for each corporation listed on the American Stock Exchange.

Standard & Poor's Stock Reports: NASDAQ and Regional Exchanges. Standard & Poor's, 55 Water St. New York, NY 10041. Phone: 800-221-5277 or (212)438-2000 Fax: (212)438-0040 E-mail: questions@standardandpoors.com • URL: http://www.standardandpoors.com • Irregular. $1,100.00 per year. Looseleaf service. Provides two pages of financial details and other information for each corporation included.

Standard & Poor's Stock Reports: New York Stock Exchange. Standard & Poor's, 55 Water St. New York, NY 10041. Phone: 800-221-5277 or (212)438-2000 Fax: (212)438-0040 E-mail: questions@standardandpoors.com • URL: http://www.standardandpoors.com • Irregular. $1,295.00 per year. Looseleaf service. Provides two pages of financial details and other information for each corporation with stock listed on the N. Y. Stock Exchange.

Standard Business Forms for the Entrepreneur. Entrepreneur Media, Inc., 2445 McCabe Way Irvine, CA 92614. Phone: 800-421-2300 or (949)261-2325 Fax: (949)261-0234 E-mail: entmag@entrepreneur.com • URL: http://www.entrepreneur.com • Looseleaf. $59.50. A practical collection of forms useful to entrepreneurial small businesses. (Start-Up Business Guide No. E1319.)

Standard Directory of Advertisers: Business Classifications Edition. National Register Publishing, 121 Chanlon Rd. New Providence, NJ 07974. Phone: 800-521-8110 or (908)464-6800 Fax: (908)790-5405 E-mail: info@reedref.com • URL: http://www.reedref.com • Annual $659.00; with supplements, $759.00. Arranged by product or service. Provides information on the advertising programs of over 20,000 companies, including advertising/marketing personnel and the names of advertising agencies used.

Standard Directory of Advertisers: Geographic Edition. National Register Publishing, 121 Chanlon Rd. New Providence, NJ 07974. Phone: 800-521-8110 or (908)464-6800 Fax: (908)771-7704 E-mail: info@reedref.com • URL: http://www.reedref.com • Annual $659.00; with supplements, $759.00. Arranged geographically by state. Provides information on the advertising programs of over 10,000 companies, including advertising/marketing personnel and the names of advertising agencies used. Includes *Advertiser/Agency* supplement.

Standard Directory of Advertising Agencies: The Agency Red Book. National Register Publishing, 121 Chanlon Rd. New Providence, NJ 07974. Phone: 800-521-8110 or (908)464-6800 Fax: (908)771-7704 E-mail: info@reedref.com • URL: http://www.reedref.com • Semiannual $659.00. With supplements, $829.00. information on nearly 10,000 Provides advertising agencies and branch offices. Includes annual billings by media and names of clients. Includes *Advertiser/Agency* supplement.

Standard Directory of International Advertisers and Agencies: The International Red Book. R. R. Bowker, 121 Chanlon Rd. New Providence, NJ 07974. Phone: 888-269-5372 or (908)464-6800 Fax: (908)771-7704 E-mail: info@bowker.com • URL: http://www.bowker.com • Annual. $569.00. Includes about 8,000 foreign companies and their advertising agencies. Geographic, company name, personal name, and trade name indexes are provided.

Standard Handbook for Civil Engineers. Frederick S. Merritt and others. McGraw-Hill, 1221 Ave. of the Americas New York, NY 10020. Phone: 800-722-4726 or (212)904-2000 Fax: (212)904-2072 E-mail: customer.service@mcgraw-hill.com • URL: http://www.mcgraw-hill.com • 1995. $150.00. Fourth edition.

Standard Handbook for Electrical Engineers. Douglas G. Fink and Wayne Beaty, editors. McGraw-Hill, 1221 Ave. of the Americas New York, NY 10020. Phone: 800-722-4726 or (212)904-2000 Fax: (212)904-2072 E-mail: customer.service@mcgraw-hill.com • URL: http://www.mcgraw-hill.com • 1999. $150.00. 14th edtion.

Standard Handbook of Hazardous Waste Treatment and Disposal. Harry M. Freeman, editor. McGraw-Hill, 1221 Ave. of the Americas New York, NY 10020. Phone: 800-722-4726 or (212)904-2000 Fax: (212)904-2072 E-mail: customer.service@mcgraw-hill.com • URL: http://www.mcgraw-hill.com • 1997. $140.00. Second expanded revised edition.

Standard Handbook of Plant Engineering. Robert C. Rosaler. McGraw-Hill, 1221 Ave. of the Americas New York, NY 10020. Phone: 800-722-4726 or (212)904-2000 Fax: (212)904-2072 E-mail: customer.service@mcgraw-hill.com • URL: http://www.mcgraw-hill.com • 1991. $125.00. Second edition.

Standard Handbook of Power Plant Engineering. Thomas C. Elliott. McGraw-Hill, 1221 Ave. of the Americas New York, NY 10020. Phone: 800-722-4726 or (212)904-2000 Fax: (212)904-2072 E-mail: customer.service@mcgraw-hill.com • URL: http://www.mcgraw-hill.com • 1997. $115.00. Second edition.

Standard Handbook of Structural Details for Building Construction. Morton Newman. McGraw-Hill, 1221 Ave. of the Americas New York, NY 10020. Phone: 800-722-4726 or (212)904-2000 Fax: (212)904-2072 E-mail: customer.service@mcgraw-hill.com • URL: http://www.mcgraw-hill.com • 1993. $99.95. Second edition.

Standard Highway Signs, as Specified in the Manual on Uniform Traffic Control Devices. Available from U. S. Government Printing Office, Washington, DC 20402. Phone: (202)512-1800 Fax: (202)512-2250 E-mail: gpoaccess@gpo.gov • URL: http://www.access.gpo.gov • Looseleaf. $70.00. Issued by the U. S. Department of Transportation (http://www.dot.gov). Includes basic manual, with updates for an indeterminate period. Contains illustrations of typical standard signs approved for use on streets and highways, and provides information on dimensions and placement of symbols.

Standard Industrial Classification Manual. U.S. Department of Commerce, Bureau of the Census. Available from U.S. Government Printing Office, Washington, DC 20402. Phone: (202)512-1800 Fax: (202)512-2250 E-mail: gpoaccess@gpo.gov • URL: http://www.accessgpo.gov • 1987. $36.00.

Standard Occupational Classification Manual. Available from Bernan Associates, 4611-F Assembly Drive Lanham, MD 20706-4391. Phone: 800-274-4888 or (301)459-2255 Fax: 800-865-3450 or (301)459-0056 E-mail: order@bernan.com • URL: http://www.bernan.com • 2000. $38.00. Replaces the *Dictionary of Occupational Titles*. Produced by the federal Office of Management and Budget, Executive Office of the President. "Occupations are classified based on the work performed, and on the required skills, education, training, and credentials for each one." Six-digit codes contain elements for 23 Major Groups, 96 Minor Groups, 451 Broad Occupations, and 820 Detailed Occupations. Designed to reflect the occupational structure currently existing in the U. S.

The Standard Periodical Directory 2001. Available from The Gale Group, 27500 Drake Rd. Farmington Hills, MI 48331-3535. Phone: 800-877-GALE or (248)699-GALE Fax: 800-414-5043 or (248)699-8069 E-mail: galeord@galegroup.com • URL: http://www.galegroup.com • 2000. $1,095.00. 24rd edition. Published by Oxbridge Communications. Covers 75,000 periodicals published in the United States and Canada arranged into more than 250 major subjects.

Standard Textbook of Cosmetology: A Practical Course on the Scientific Fundamentals of Beauty Culture for Students and Practicing Cosmetologists. Constance V. Kibbe. Milady Publishing Co., P.O. Box 15015 Albany, NY 12212-5015. Phone: 800-347-7707 or (518)464-3500 Fax: (518)464-0357 1992. $51.95. Ninth edition. (Standard Texts of Cosmetology).

Standards Action. American National Standards Institute, 11 W. 42nd St. New York, NY 10036. Phone: (212)642-4900 Fax: (212)302-1286 URL: http://www.ansi.org • Biweekly. Membership. Includes *ANSI Reporter*.

Standards Activities of Organizations in the United States. Available from U. S. Government Printing Office, Washington, DC 20402. Phone: (202)512-1800 Fax: (202)512-2250 E-mail: gpoaccess@gpo.gov • URL: http://www.access.gpo.gov • 1996. $70.00. Prepared by the Office of Standards Code and Information, National Institute of Standards and Technology, U. S. Dept. of Commerce. Describes the activities of over 750 U. S. organizations that develop and publish standards. Formerly *Directory of United States Standardization Activities*.

Standards Engineering. Standards Engineering Society, 13340 S.W. 96th Ave. Miami, FL 33176. Phone: (305)971-4798 Fax: (305)971-4799 E-mail: hgz1ggy@worldnet.att.net • URL: http://www.ses-standards.org • Bimonthly. $45.00 per year.

Standards Engineering Society.

Stanford Integrated Manufacturing Association., Stanford University, Bldg. 02-530 Stanford, CA 94305-3036. Phone: (650)723-9038 Fax: (650)723-5034 E-mail: susan.hansen@stanford.edu • URL: http://www.sima.stanford.edu/ • Consists of four research centers: Center for Automation and Manufacturing Science, Center for Design Research, Center for Materials Formability and Processing Science, and Center for Teaching and Research in Integrated Manufacturing Systems. Research fields include automation, robotics, intelligent systems, computer vision, design in manufacturing, materials science, composite materials, and ceramics.

Stanford Research Park., Stanford University, 2770 Sand Hill Rd. Menlo Park, CA 94025. Phone: (650)926-0211 Fax: (650)926-2000 Links research resources of Stanford University with private enterprise.

Stanger Report: A Guide to Partnership Investing. Robert A. Stanger and Co., 1129 Broad St., 2nd Fl. Shrewsbury, NJ 07702-4314. Phone: (908)389-3600 Fax: (908)544-0779 Monthly. $447.00 per year. Newsletter providing analysis of limited partnership investments.

Star Service: The Critical Guide to Hotels and Cruise Ships. Cahners Travel Group, 500 Plaza Dr. Secaucus, NJ 07096. Phone: 800-662-7776 or (201)902-2000 Fax: (201)319-1797 E-mail: corporatecommunications@cahners.com • URL: http://www.cahners.com • $249.00. Looseleaf. Quarterly supplements. Provides "honest and unbiased descriptions of accommodations, facilities, amenities, ambience, appearance, and service" for more than 10,000 hotels worldwide and 150 cruise ships. Ship information includes history, passenger profiles, crew profiles, and other data.

Start and Run a Profitable Catering Business: From Thyme to Timing: Your Step-by-Step Business Plan. George Erdosh. Self-Counsel Press, Inc., 1704 N. State St. Bellingham, WA 98225. Phone: 877-877-6490 or (360)676-4530 Fax: (360)676-4530 E-mail: service@self-counsel.com • URL: http://www.self-counsel.com • 1994. $14.95. Provides information on contracts, equipment, licenses, staff, planning, organizing catered events, and other aspects of catering.

Start and Run a Profitable Craft Business: A Step-by-Step Business Plan. William G. Hynes. Self-Counsel Press, Inc., 1704 N. State St. Bellingham, WA 98225. Phone: 877-877-6490 or (360)676-4530 Fax: (360)676-4530 E-mail: service@self-counsel.com • URL: http://www.self-counsel.com • 1996. $14.95. Sixth edition.

Start Right in E-Business: A Step-by-Step Guide to Successful E-Business Implementation. Bennet P. Lientz and Kathryn P. Rea. Academic Press, 525 B St., Suite 1900 San Diego, CA 92101. Phone: 800-321-5068 or (619)699-6719 Fax: 800-336-7377 or (619)699-6380 E-mail: ap@acad.com • URL: http://www.academicpress.com • 2000. $44.95.

Start, Run, and Profit From Your Own Home-Based Business. Gregory Kishel and Patricia Kishel. John Wiley & Sons, Inc., 605 Third Ave. New York, NY 10158-0012. Phone: 800-526-5368 or (212)850-6000 Fax: (212)850-6088 E-mail: info@wiley.com • URL: http://www.wiley.com • 1991. $37.95.

Start-Up Business Guides. Entrepreneur Media, Inc., 2445 McCabe Way Irvine, CA 92614. Phone: 800-421-2300 or (949)261-2325 Fax: (949)261-0234 E-mail: entmag@entrepreneur.com • URL: http://www.entrepreneur.com • Looseleaf. $59.50 each. Practical guides to starting a wide variety of small businesses.

Starting and Running a Nonprofit Organization. Joan Hummel. University of Minnesota Press, 111 Third Ave., S. Suite 290 Minneapolis, MN 55401-2520. Phone: 800-621-2736 or (612)627-1970 Fax: (612)627-1980 E-mail: ump@staff.tc.umn.edu • 1996. $14.95. Second revised edition.

Starting on a Shoestring: Building a Business Without a Bankroll. Arnold S. Goldstein. John Wiley and Sons, Inc., 605 Third Ave. New York, NY 10158-0012. Phone: 800-526-5368 or (212)850-6000 Fax: (212)850-6088 E-mail: info@wiley.com • URL: http://www.wiley.com • 1995. $29.95. Third edition. Includes chapters on venture capital and Small Business Administration (SBA) loans.

Startup: An Entrepreneur's Guide to Launching and Managing a New Business. William J. Stolze. Rock Beach Press, 1255 University Press Rochester, NY 14607. Phone: (360)805-0699 Fax: (360)805-0695 1989. $24.95.

State and Local Communications Report. Telecommunications Reports International, Inc., 1333 H St., N.W., Suite 100 Washington, DC 20005. Phone: 800-822-6338 or (202)312-6060 Fax: (202)842-3023 E-mail: customerservice@tr.com. • URL: http://www.tr.com • Biweekly. $645.00 per year. Newsletter. Formerly *Telecommunications Week*.

State and Metropolitan Area Data Book. Available from U. S. Government Printing Office, Washington, DC 20402. Phone: (202)512-1800 Fax: (202)512-2250 E-mail: gpoaccess@gpo.gov • URL: http://www.access.gpo.gov • 1998. $31.00. Issued by the U. S. Bureau of the Census. Presents a wide variety of statistical data for U. S. regions, states, counties, metropolitan areas, and central cities, with ranking tables. Time period is 1970 to 1990.

State and Regional Associations of the United States. Columbia Books, Inc., 1212 New York Ave., N. W., Suite 330 Washington, DC 20005. Phone: 888-265-0600 or (202)898-0662 Fax: (202)898-0775 E-mail: info@columbiabooks.com • URL: http://www.comlubiabooks.com • Annual. $79.00. Provides information on over 7,500 state and regional business associations, professional societies, and labor unions

State Budget Actions. Corina Eckl and Arturo Perez. National Conference of State Legislatures, 1560 Broadway, Suite 700 Denver, CO 80202-5140. Phone: (303)830-2200 Fax: (303)863-8003 E-mail: name.name@ncsl.org • URL: http://www.ncsl.org • 1997. $35.00. Presents yearly summaries of state spending priorities and fiscal climates. Includes end-of-year general fund balances and other information on state funds.

State Budget and Tax News. State Policy Research, Inc., P.O. Box 5968 Hilton Head, SC 29938. Phone: (803)686-5110 Fax: (803)686-5132 Semimonthly. $245.00 per year. Newsletter. Covers fiscal activities in the 50 states.

State Capitals. Wakeman-Walworth, Inc., P.O. Box 7376 Alexandria, VA 22307-0376. Phone: 800-876-2545 or (703)549-8606 Fax: (703)549-1372 E-mail: newsletters@

statecapitals.com • URL: http://www.statecapitals.com • Irregular. Prices may vary. A group of 39 newsletters, with each publication having its own subtitle and topic of relevance to state government.

State Court Caseload Statistics. National Center for State Courts, 300 Newport Ave. Williamsburg, VA 23187-8798. Phone: (757)259-1838 Fax: (757)259-1520 Annual. Price on application.

State Government Affairs Council.

State Government News: The Monthly Magazine Covering All Facets of State Government. Council of State Governments, P.O. Box 11910 Lexington, KY 40578-1910. Phone: 800-800-1910 or (606)244-8000 Fax: (606)244-8001 E-mail: psantos@csg.org • URL: http://www.csg.org/sgn/index.html • Monthly. $39.00 per year.

State Government Research Checklist. Council of State Governments, P.O. Box 11910 Lexington, KY 40578-1910. Phone: 800-800-1910 or (606)244-8000 Fax: (606)244-8001 E-mail: psantos@csg.org • URL: http://www.csg.org • Bimonthly. $24.99 per year. Lists reports by state legislative research agencies, study committees, commissions, and independent organizations.

State Income Tax Alert. CCH, Inc., 4025 West Peterson Ave. Chicago, IL 60646-6085. Phone: 800-248-3248 or (773)866-6000 Fax: 800-224-8299 or (773)866-3608 URL: http://www.cch.com • Semimonthly. $247.00 per year. Newsletter. Provides nationwide coverage of latest state income tax laws, regulations, and court decisions.

State Legislative Report. National Conference of State Legislatures, 1560 Broadway, Suite 700 Denver, CO 80202-5140. Phone: (303)830-2200 Fax: (303)863-8003 E-mail: name@name.ncsl.org • URL: http://www.ncsl.org • 12 to 16 times per year. $15.00 per issue. Discusses significant state legislation.

State Legislators' Occupations: 1994, A Survey. National Conference of State Legislatures, 1560 Broadway, Suite 700 Denver, CO 80202. Phone: (303)830-2200 Fax: (303)863-8003 E-mail: name.name@ncsl.org • URL: http://www.ncsl.org • 1994. $20.00. Presents survey results concerning the occupations of more than 7,000 state legislators. (Members of state legislatures usually combine government service with other occupations.)

State Legislatures. National Conference of State Legislatures, 1560 Broadway, Suite 700 Denver, CO 80202-5140. Phone: (303)830-2200 Fax: (303)863-8003 E-mail: name.name@ncsl.org • URL: http://www.ncsl.org • Monthly. $49.00 per year. Newsletter. Covers state legislative issues and politics.

The State of Food and Agriculture. Available from Bernan Associates, 4611-F Assembly Dr. Lanham, MD 20706-4391. Phone: 800-274-4447 or (301)459-7666 Fax: 800-865-3450 or (301)459-0056 E-mail: info@bernan.com • URL: http://www.bernan.com • Annual. Published by the Food and Agriculture Organization of the United Nations (FAO). A yearly review of world and regional agricultural and food activities. Includes tables and graphs. Text in English.

State Policy Reports. State Policy Research, Inc., P.O. Box 5968 Hilton Head, SC 29938. Phone: (803)686-5110 Fax: (803)686-5132 Semimonthly. $445.00 per year. Newsletter. Information about tax and budget activities in all states.

State Profiles: The Population and Economy of Each U. S. State. Courtenay Slater and Martha Davis, editors. Bernan Press, 4611-F Assembly Dr. Lanham, MD 20706-4391. Phone: 800-274-4447 or (301)459-7666 Fax: 800-865-3450 or (301)459-0056 E-mail: info@bernan.com • URL: http://www.bernan.com • 1999. $74.00. Presents charts, tables, and text in an eight-page profile for each state. Covers population, labor force, income, poverty, employment, wages, industry, trade, housing, education, health, taxes, and government finances.

State Reference Publications: A Bibliographic Guide to State Blue Books, Legislative Manuals and Other General Reference Sources. Government Research Service, P.O. Box 2067 Topeka, KS 66601-2067. Phone: 800-346-6898 or (785)232-7720 Fax: (785)232-1615 Biennial. $70.00. State government directories, blue books, legislative manuals, statistical abstracts, judicial direcories, local government directories, and other general publications; state capitols.

State Tax Actions. Judy Zelio. National Conference of State Legislatures, 1560 Broadway, Suite 700 Denver, CO 80202. Phone: (303)830-2200 Fax: (303)863-8003 E-mail: books@ncsl.org • URL: http://www.ncsl.org • Annual. $35.00. Summarizes yearly tax changes by type and by state.

State Tax Handbook. CCH, Inc., 4025 W. Peterson Ave. Chicago, IL 60646-6085. Phone: 800-248-3248 or (773)866-6000 Fax: 800-224-8299 or (773)866-3608 URL: http://www.cch.com • Annual. $41.95. Summarizes rates, deductions, exemptions, and reporting requirements for the 45 income tax states, the District of Columbia, and major cities.

State Tax Notes. Tax Analysts, 6830 N. Fairfax Dr. Arlington, VA 22213. Phone: 800-955-3444 or (703)533-4400 Fax: (703)533-4444 E-mail: webmaster@tax.org • URL: http://www.tax.org • Weekly. $949.00 per year, including annual CD-ROM. Newsletter. Covers tax developments in all states. Provides state tax document summaries and citations.

State Tax Review. CCH, Inc., 4025 W. Peterson Ave. Chicago, IL 60646-6085. Phone: 800-248-3248 or (773)866-6000 Fax: 800-224-8299 or (773)866-3608 URL: http://www.cch.com • Weekly. $129.00. per year.

State Yellow Book: Who's Who in the Executive and Legislative Branches of the 50 Governments. Leadership Directories, Inc., 104 Fifth Ave., 2nd Fl. New York, NY 10011. Phone: (212)627-4140 Fax: (212)645-6931 E-mail: info@leadershipdirectories.com • URL: http://www.leadershipdirectories.com • Quarterly. $305.00 per year. Lists more than 37,000 elected and administrative officials by state, District of Columbia, and U. S. Territory. Includes state profiles, with historical and statistical data. County population and per capita income is also included.

Statements of Financial Accounting Standards: Original Pronouncements. John Wiley and Sons, Inc., 605 Third Ave. New York, NY 10158-0012. Phone: 800-225-5945 or (212)850-6000 Fax: (212)850-6088 E-mail: info@wiley.com • URL: http://www.wiley.com • 1996. Price on application.

The Statesman's Yearbook: Statistical and Historical Annual of the States of the World. Stockton Press Direct Marketing, 49 W. 24th St. New York, NY 10010. Phone: 800-221-2123 or (212)627-5757 Fax: (212)627-9256 Annual. $65.00.

Station Representatives Association., 16 W. 77th St., No. 9-E New York, NY 10024-5126. Phone: (212)362-8868 Fax: (212)362-4999 E-mail: srajerry@aol.com • Members are sales representatives concerned with the sale of radio and television "spot" advertising.

Statistical Abstract of Latin America. University of California, Los Angeles, P.O. Box 951447 Los Angeles, CA 90095-1447. Phone: (310)825-6634 Fax: (310)206-6859 E-mail: lacpubs@isop.ucla.edu • URL: http://www.lib.berkeley.edu • Annual. $325.00. Two volumes.

Statistical Abstract of the United States. Available from U. S. Government Printing Office, Washington, DC 20402. Phone: (202)512-1800 Fax: (202)512-2250 E-mail: gpoaccess@gpo.gov • URL: http://www.access.gpo.gov • Annual. $51.00. Issued by the U. S. Bureau of the Census.

Statistical Abstract of the United States on CD-ROM. Hoover's, Inc., 1033 La Posada Drive, Suite 250 Austin, TX 78752. Phone: 800-486-8666 or (512)374-4500 Fax: (512)374-4501 E-mail: orders@hoovers.com • URL: http://www.hoovers.com • Annual. $49.95. Provides all statistics from official print version, plus expanded historical data, greater detail, and keyword searching features.

Statistical Abstract of the World. The Gale Group, 27500 Drake Rd. Farmington Hills, MI 48331-3535. Phone: 800-877-GALE or (248)699-GALE Fax: 800-414-5043 or (248)699-8069 E-mail: galeord@galegroup.com • URL: http://www.galegroup.com • 1997. $80.00. Third edition. Provides data on a wide variety of economic, social, and political topics for about 200 countries. Arranged by country.

Statistical Annual: Grains, Options on Agricultural Futures. Chicago Board of Trade, Education and Marketing Services Dept., 141 W. Jackson Blvd., Suite 2210 Chicago, IL 60604-2994. Phone: 800-572-3276 or (312)435-3542 Fax: (312)341-3168 E-mail: bw0050@cbot.com • URL: http://www.cbot.com • Annual. Includes historical data on Wheat Futures, Options on Wheat Futures, Corn Futures, Options on Corn Futures, Oats Futures, Soybean Futures, Options on Soybean Futures, Soybean Oil Futures, Soybean Meal Futures.

Statistical Annual: Interest Rates, Metals, Stock Indices, Options on Financial Futures, Options on Metals Futures. Chicago Board of Trade, Education and Marketing Services Dept., 141 W. Jackson Blvd., Suite 2210 Chicago, IL 60604-2994. Phone: 800-572-3276 or (312)435-3542 Fax: (312)341-3027 E-mail: bw0050@cbot.com • URL: http://www.cbot.com • Annual. Includes historical data on GNMA CDR Futures, Cash-Settled GNMA Futures, U. S. Treasury Bond Futures, U. S. Treasury Note Futures, Options on Treasury Note Futures, NASDAQ-100 Futures, Major Market Index Futures, Major Market Index MAXI Futures, Municipal Bond Index Futures, 1,000-Ounce Silver Futures, Options on Silver Futures, and Kilo Gold Futures.

Statistical Bulletin of the International Office of Cocoa, Chocolate and Sugar Confectionary. International Office of Cocoa, Chocolate and Sugar Confectionary, Ave. de Cortenbergh 172 B-1040 Brussels, Belgium. Phone: (322)-7351072 Fax: (322)-7363623 Annual.

Statistical Forecasts of the United States. The Gale Group, 27500 Drake Rd. Farmington Hills, MI 48331-3535. Phone: 800-877-GALE or (248)699-GALE Fax: 800-414-5043 or (248)699-8069 E-mail: galeord@galegroup.com • URL: http://www.galegroup.com • 1995. $99.00. Second edition. Provides both long-term and short-term statistical forecasts relating to basic items in the U. S.: population, employment, labor, crime, education, and health care. Data in the form of charts, graphs, and tables has been taken from a wide variety of government and private sources. Includes a subject index and an "Index of Forecast by Year."

Statistical Handbook of Working America. The Gale Group, 27500 Drake Rd. Farmington Hills, MI 48331-3535. Phone: 800-877-GALE or (248)699-GALE Fax: 800-414-5043 or (248)699-8069 E-mail: galeord@galegroup.com • URL: http://www.galegroup.com • 1997. $125.00. Second edition. Provides statistics, rankings, and forecasts relating to a wide variety of careers, occupations, and working conditions.

Statistical Handbook on Aging Americans. Renee Schick, editor. Oryx Press, 4041 N. Central Ave., Ste. 700 Phoenix, AZ 85012-3397. Phone: 800-279-6799 or (602)265-2651 Fax: 800-279-4663 or (602)265-6250 E-mail: info@oryxpress.com • URL: http://www.oryxpress.com • 1994. $65.00. Second edition. Provides data on demographics, social characteristics, health, employment, economic conditions, income, pensions, and social security. Includes bibliographic information and a glossary. (Statistical Handbook Series).

Statistical Handbook on Consumption and Wealth in the United States. Chandrika Kaul and Valerie Tomaselli-Moschovitis. Oryx Press, 4041 North Central Ave., Suite 700 Phoenix, AZ 85012-3397. Phone: 800-279-6799 or (602)265-2651 Fax: 800-279-4663 or (602)265-6250 E-mail: info@oryxpress.com • URL: http://www.oryxpress.com • 1999. $65.00. Provides more than 400 graphs, tables, and charts dealing with basic income levels, income inequalities, spending patterns, taxation, subsidies, etc. (Statistical Handbook Series).

Statistical Handbook on Poverty in the Developing World. Chandrika Kaul. Oryx Press, 4041 North Central Ave., Suite 700 Phoenix, AZ 85012-3397. Phone: 800-279-6799 or (602)265-2651 Fax: 800-279-4663 or (602)265-6250 E-mail: info@oryxpress.com • URL: http://www.oryxpress.com • 1999. $65.00. Provides international coverage, including special sections on women and children, and on selected cities. (Statistical Handbook Series).

Statistical Handbook on Technology. Paula Berinstein, editor. Oryx Press, 4041 North Central Ave., Suite 700 Phoenix, AZ 85012-3397. Phone: 800-279-6799 or (602)265-2651 Fax: 800-279-4663 or (602)265-6250 E-mail: info@oryxpress.com • URL: http://www.oryxpress.com • 1999. $65.00. Provides statistical data on such items as the Internet, online services, computer technology, recycling, patents, prescription drug sales, telecommunications, and aerospace. Includes charts, tables, and graphs. Edited for the general reader. (Statistical Handbook Series).

Statistical Handbook on the American Family. Bruce A. Chadwick and Tim B. Heaton, editors. Oryx Press, 4041 N. Central Ave., Ste. 700 Phoenix, AZ 85012-3379. Phone: 800-279-6799 or (602)265-2651 Fax: 800-279-4663 or (602)265-6250 E-mail: info@oryxpress.com • URL: http://www.oryxpress.com • 1998. $65.00. Includes data on education, health, politics, employment, expenditures, social characteristics, the elderly, and women in the labor force. Historical statistics on marriage, birth, and divorce are shown from 1900 on. A list of sources and a subject index are provided. (Statistical Handbook Series).

Statistical Handbook on U. S. Hispanics. Frank L. Schick and Renee Schick, editors. Oryx Press, 4041 N. Central Ave., 700 Phoenix, AZ 85012-3379. Phone: 800-279-6799 or (602)265-2651 Fax: 800-279-4663 or (602)265-6250 E-mail: info@oryxpress.com • URL: http://oryxpress.com • 1991. $65.00. Includes data on demographics, employment, income, assets, etc. (Statistical Handbook Series).

Statistical Handbook on Women in America. Cynthia M. Taeuber, editor. Oryx Press, 4041 N. Central Ave., Ste. 700 Phoenix, AZ 85012-3379. Phone: 800-279-6799 or (602)265-2651 Fax: 800-279-4663 or (602)265-6250 E-mail: info@oryxpress.com • URL: http://www.oryxpress.com • 1996. $65.00. Includes data on demographics, employment, earnings, economic status, educational status, marriage, divorce, household units, health, and other topics. (Statistical Handbook Series).

Statistical Indicators for Asia and the Pacific. United Nations Publications, United Nations Concourse Level New York, NY 10017. Phone: 800-553-3210 or (212)963-7680 Fax: (212)963-4910 E-mail: bookstore@un.org • URL: http://www.un.org/publications • Quarterly. $80.00 per year. Provides data on economic and demographic trends in the region. Text in English.

Statistical Information on the Financial Services Industry. American Bankers Association, 1120 Connecticut Ave., N. W. Washington, DC 20036-3971. Phone: 800-338-0626 or (202)663-5000 Fax: (202)663-7543 E-mail: reflib@aba.com • URL: http://www.aba.com • Annual. Members, $150.00; non-members, $275.00. Presents a wide variety of data relating to banking and financial services, including consumer economics, personal finance, credit, government loans, capital markets, and international banking.

Statistical Masterfile. Congressional Information Service, 4520 East-West Highway, Suite 800 Bethesda, MD 20814-3389. Phone: 800-638-8380 or (301)654-1550 Fax: (301)657-3203 Quarterly. Price varies. Provides CD-ROM versions of *American Statistics Index, Index to International Statistics,* and *Statistical Reference Index*. Contains indexing and abstracting of a wide variety of published statistics sources, both governmental and private.

A Statistical Portrait of the United States: Social Conditions and Trends. Mark S. Littman, editor. Bernan Press, 4611-F Assembly Dr. Lanham, MD 20706-4391. Phone: 800-274-4447 or (301)459-7666 Fax: 800-865-3450 or (301)459-0056 E-mail: info@bernan.com • URL: http://www.bernan.com • 1998. $89.00. Covers "social, economic, and environmental trends in the United States over the past 25 years." Includes statistical tables, graphs, and analysis relating to such topics as population, income, poverty, wealth, labor, housing, education, healthcare, air/water quality, and government.

Statistical Quality Control. Eugene L. Grant and Richard S. Leavenworth. McGraw-Hill, 1221 Ave of the Americas New York, NY 10020. Phone: 800-722-4726 or (212)904-2000 Fax: (212)904-2072 E-mail: customer.service@mcgraw-hill.com • URL: http://www.mcgraw-hill.com • 1996. $103.44. Seventh edition.

Statistical Record of Black America. The Gale Group, 27500 Drake Rd. Farmington Hills, MI 48331-3535. Phone: 800-877-GALE or (248)699-GALE Fax: 800-414-5043 or (248)699-8069 E-mail: galeord@galegroup.com • URL: http://www.galegroup.com • 1996. $115.00. Fourth edition. Contains more than 1,000 statistical graphs, tables, and lists arranged in 16 broad subject chapters. Covers population, housing, business, income, education, etc. Includes an extensive bibliography and a detailed subject index.

Statistical Record of Older Americans. The Gale Group, 27500 Drake Rd. Farmington Hills, MI 48331-3535. Phone: 800-877-GALE Fax: 800-414-5043 or (248)699-8069 E-mail: galeord@galegroup.com • URL: http://www.galegroup.com • 1996. $109.00. Second edition. Includes income and pension data.

Statistical Record of the Environment. The Gale Group, 27500 Drake Rd. Farmington Hills, MI 48331-3535. Phone: 800-877-GALE or (248)699-GALE Fax: 800-414-5043 or (248)699-8069 E-mail: galeord@galegroup.com • URL: http://www.galegroup.com • 1996. $120.00. Third edition. Provides over 875 charts, tables, and graphs of major environmental statistics, arranged by subject. Covers population growth, hazardous waste, nuclear energy, acid rain, pesticides, and other subjects related to the environment. A keyword index is included.

Statistical Record of Women Worldwide. The Gale Group, 27500 Drake Rd. Farmington Hills, MI 48331-3535. Phone: 800-877-GALE or (248)699-GALE Fax: 800-414-5043 or (248)699-8069 E-mail: galeord@galegroup.com • URL: http://www.galegroup.com • 1996. $125.00. Second edition. Includes employment data and other economic statistics relating to women in the U. S. and internationally.

Statistical Reference Index: A Selective Guide to American Statistical Publications from Sources Other than the United States Government. Congressional Information Service, Inc., 4520 East-West Highway, Suite 800 Bethesda, MD 20814-3389. Phone: 800-638-8380 or (301)654-1550 Fax: (301)654-4033 E-mail: cisinfo@lexis-nexis.com • URL: http://www.cispubs.com • Monthly. Quarterly and annual cumulations. Price varies. Service basis.

Statistical Reports. National Alcoholic Beverage Control Association, 4216 King St., W. Alexandria, VA 22302. Phone: (703)578-4200 Fax: (703)820-3551 Monthly. Price on application. Includes quarterly and annual cumulations.

Statistical Techniques in Business and Economics. Robert D. Mason and Douglas A. Lind. McGraw-Hill, 1221 Ave. of the Americas New York, NY 10020. Phone: 800-722-4726 or (212)904-2000 Fax: (212)904-2072 E-mail: customer.service@mcgraw-hill.com • URL: http://www.mcgraw-hill.com • 1998. 10th edition. Price on application.

Statistical Theory and Method Abstracts. International Statistical Institute, Postbus 950 2270 Voorburg, Netherlands. E-mail: isi@cbs.nl • URL: http://www.cbs.nl/isi • Quarterly. Members, $85.00 per year; non-members, $170.00 per year. Worldwide coverage of published papers on mathematical statistics and probability.

Statistical Yearbook. United Nations Publications, United Nations Concourse Level, First Ave., 46th St. New York, NY 10017. Phone: 800-553-3210 or (212)963-7680 Fax: (212)963-4910 E-mail: bookstore@un.org • URL: http://www.un.org/publications • Annual. $125.00. Contains statistics for about 200 countries on a wide variety of economic, industrial, and demographic topics. Compiled by United Nations Statistical Office.

Statistical Yearbook for Asia and the Pacific. United Nations Publications, United Nations Concourse Level, First Ave., 46th St. New York, NY 10017. Phone: 800-553-3210 or (212)963-7680 Fax: (212)963-4910 E-mail: bookstore@un.org • URL: http://www.un.org/publications • Annual. $90.00. Includes 56 countries of the region. Contains data on national accounts, trade, industry, banking, wages, consumption, population, and other economic and demographic subjects. Text in English and French.

Statistical Yearbook for Latin America and the Caribbean. Available from United Nations Publications, United Nations Concourse Level, First Ave., 46th St. New York, NY 10017. Phone: 800-553-3210 or (212)963-7680 Fax: (212)963-4910 E-mail: bookstore@un.org • URL: http://www.un.org/publications • Annual. $79.00. Issued by the Economic Commission for Latin America and the Caribbean. Includes a wide variety of economic, industrial, and trade data for Latin American nations. Text in English and Spanish.

Statistical YearBook of the Electric Utility Industry. Edison Electric Institute, 701 Pennsylvania Ave., N.W. Washington, DC 20004-2696. Phone: 800-334-5453 or (202)508-5000 Fax: 800-525-5562 or (202)508-5360 URL: http://www.eei.org • Annual. $225.00.

Statistics Canada., Ottawa, ON, Canada K1A OT6. Phone: 800-267-6677 or (613)951-7277 Fax: 800-899-9734 or (613)951-1582 URL: http://www.statcan.ca • Issues compilations of census data and other facts relating to Canadian business, finance, industry, economics, and society in general. Statistics Canada is the country's national statistical agency, required to collect data according to the Statistics Act.

Statistics Canada! Statistics CanadaPhone: 800-267-6677 or (613)951-7277 Fax: 800-899-9734 or (613)951-1582 URL: http://www.statcan.ca • Web site in English and French provides basic statistical information relating to economic and social conditions in Canada: "The Land," "The People," "The Economy," "The State." Includes daily news, latest indicators, products and services, and links to other sites. Keyword searching is provided. Fees: Free.

Statistics for Management. Richard Levin and David S. Rubin. Prentice Hall, 240 Frisch Court Paramus, NJ 07652-5240. Phone: 800-947-7700 or (201)909-6200 Fax: 800-445-6991 or (201)909-6361 URL: http://www.prenhall.com • 1997. $99.00. Seventh edition.

Statistics for the Environment: Statistical Aspects of Health and the Environment. Vic Barnett and K. Feridun Turkman, editors. John Wiley and Sons, Inc., 605 Third Ave. New York, NY 10158-0012. Phone: 800-225-5945 or (212)850-6000 Fax: (212)850-6088 E-mail: info@wiley.com • URL: http://www.wiley.com • 1999. $180.00. Contains articles on the statistical analysis and interpretation of environmental monitoring and sampling data. Areas covered include meteorology, pollution of the environment, and forest resources.

Statistics of Income Bulletin. Available from U.S. Government Printing Office, Washington, DC 20402. Phone: (202)512-1800 Fax: (202)512-2250 E-mail: gpoaccess@gpo.gov • URL: http://www.access.gpo.gov • Quarterly. $35.00 per year. Current data compiled from tax returns relating to income, assets, and expenses of individuals and businesses. (U. S. Internal Revenue Service.)

Statistics of Income: Corporation Income Tax Returns. U.S. Internal Revenue Service. Available from U.S. Government Printing Office, Washington, DC 20402. Phone: (202)512-1800 Fax: (202)512-2250 E-mail: gpoaccess@gpo.gov • URL: http://www.access.gpo.gov • Annual. $26.00.

Statistics of Paper, Paperboard and Wood Pulp. American Forest and Paper Association, 1111 19th St., N.W. Washington, DC 20036. Phone: (202)463-2700 Fax: (202)463-2785 Annual. $395.00. Formerly *Statistics of Paper and Paperboard*.

Statistics of World Trade in Steel. United Nations Economic Commission for Europe. Available from United Nations Publications, United Nations Concourse Level, First Ave., 46th St. New York, NY 10017. Phone: 800-553-3210 or (212)963-7680 Fax: (212)963-4910 E-mail: bookstores@un.org • URL: http://www.un.org/publications • Annual. $90.00

Statistics on Alcohol, Drug, and Tobacco Use: A Selection of Statistical Charts, Graphs and Tables about Alcohol, Drug and Tobacco Use from a Variety of Published Sources with Explanatory Comments. The Gale Group, 27500 Drake Rd. Farmington Hills, MI 48331-3535. Phone: 800-877-GALE or (248)699-GALE Fax: 800-414-5043 or (248)699-8069 E-mail: galeord@galegroup.com • URL: http://www.galegroup.com • 1995. $65.00. Includes graphs, charts, and tables arranged within subject chapters. Citations to data sources are provided.

Statistics on Crime, Justice, and Punishment. The Gale Group, 27500 Drake Rd. Farmington Hills, MI 48331-3535. Phone: 800-877-GALE or (248)699-GALE Fax: 800-414-5043 or (248)699-8069 E-mail: galeord@galegroup.com • URL: http://www.galegroup.com • 1996. $65.00. Volume three. Includes graphs, charts, and tables arranged within subject chapters. Citations to data sources are provided.

Statistics on Weapons and Violence: A Selection of Statistical Charts, Graphs and Tables about Weapons and Violence from a Variety of Published Sources with Explanatory Comments. The Gale Group, 27500 Drake Rd. Farmington Hills, MI 48331-3535. Phone: 800-877-GALE or (248)699-GALE Fax: 800-414-5043 or (248)699-8069 E-mail: galeord@galegroup.com • URL: http://www.galegroup.com • 1995. $65.00. Includes graphs, charts, and tables arranged within subject chapters. Citations to data sources are provided. (Statistics for Students Series).

Statistics Sources: A Subject Guide to Data on Industrial, Business, Social, Educational, Financial and Other Topics for the U. S. and Selected Foreign Countries. The Gale Group, 27500 Drake Rd. Farmington Hills, MI 48331-3535. Phone: 800-877-GALE or (248)699-GALE Fax: 800-414-5043 or (248)699-8069 E-mail: galeord@galegroup.com • URL: http://www.galegroup.com • 2000. $475.00. 25th edition. Two volumes. Lists sources of statistical information for more than 20,000 topics.

Statistics Summaries. American Frozen Food Institute, 2000 Corporate Ridge, Suite 1000 McLean, VA 22102. Phone: (703)821-0770 Fax: (703)821-1350 E-mail: affi@pop.dn.net • URL: http://www.affi.com • Membership.

Staying Wealthy: Strategies for Protecting Your Assets. Brian H. Breuel. Bloomberg Press, 100 Business Park Dr. Princeton, NJ 08542-0888. Phone: 800-388-2749 or (609)279-4670 Fax: (609)279-7155 E-mail: press@bloomberg.net • URL: http://www.bloomberg.com • 1998. $21.95. Presents ideas for estate planning and personal wealth preservation. Includes case studies. (Bloomberg Personal Bookshelf Series).

Steam Electric Market Analysis. National Mining Association, 1130 17th St., N. W. Washington, DC 20036-4677. Phone: (202)463-2625 Fax: (202)463-6152 E-mail: rlawson@nma.org • URL: http://www.nma.org • Monthly. $300.00 per year. Covers 400 major electric power plants, with detailed data on coal consumption and stockpiles. Shows percent of power generated by fuel type. (Publisher formerly National Coal Association.)

Steel Door Institute., 30200 Detroit Rd. Cleveland, OH 44145. Phone: (440)899-0010 Fax: (440)892-1404 URL: http://www.steeldoor.org • Members are manufacturers of all-metal doors and frames.

Steel Founders' Society of America.

Steel Mill Products. U.S. Bureau of the Census, Washington, DC 20233-0800. Phone: (301)457-4100 Fax: (301)457-3842 URL: http://www.census.gov • Annual. (Current Industrial Reports MA-33B).

Steel Service Center Institute.

Steel Shipping Container Institute.

Steel Times International. DMG World Media, Queensway House, Two Queensway Redhill, Surrey RH1 1QS, England. Phone: 44 1737 855485 Fax: 44 1737 855470 URL: http://www.dmg.co.uk • Bimonthly. $252.00 per year. Includes *Iron and Steel Directory*.

Steels Alert. Cambridge Information Group, 7200 Wisconsin Ave., 6th Fl. Bethesda, MD 20814. Phone: 800-843-7751 or (301)961-6700 Fax: (301)961-6720 E-mail: market@csa.com • URL: http://www.csa.com • Monthly. $340.00 per year. Provides citations to the business and industrial literature of iron and steel. (Materials Business Information Series).

Step-By-Step Electronic Design: The How-To Newsletter for Electronic Designers. Dynamic Graphics, Inc., 6000 Forest Park Dr. Peoria, IL 61614-3592. Phone: 800-255-8800 or (309)688-2300 Fax: (309)688-8515 E-mail: sxsgl@aol.com • Monthly. $48.00 per year;with*Step-by-Step Graphics*,$90.00 per year.

Step-By-Step Graphics: The How-To Reference Magazine for Visual Communicators. Dynamic Graphics, Inc., 6000 N. Forest Park Dr. Peoria, IL 61614-3592. Phone: 800-255-8800 or (309)688-2300 Fax: (309)698-8515 E-mail: sxsgl@aol.com • Bimonthly. $42.00 per year; with *Step-by-Step Electronic Design*, $90.00 per year.

Stereo Review's Sound & Vision: Home Theater- Audio-Video- MultimediaMovies- Music. Hachette Filipacchi Magazines, Inc., 1633 Broadway New York, NY 10019. Phone: 800-274-4027 or (212)767-6000 Fax: (212)767-5600 E-mail: soundandvision@hfmmag.com • URL: http://www.soundandvisionmag.com • 10 times a year. $24.00 per year. Popular magazine providing explanatory articles and critical reviews of equipment and media (CD-ROM, DVD, videocassettes, etc.). Supplement available *Stero Review's Sound and Vision Buyers Guide*. Replaces *Stereo Review* and *Video Magazine*.

Stereophile: For the High Fidelity Stereo Perfectionist. EMAP USA, 6420 Wilshire Blvd. Los Angeles, CA 90048-5515. Phone: 800-800-4681 or (323)782-2000 Fax: (323)782-2865 E-mail: jatkinson@stereophile.com • URL: http://www.emapusa.com • Monthly. $24.94 per year. Review of high-end audio products.

Stock Index Futures: Buying and Selling the Market Averages. Charles Sutcliffe. Thomson Learning, 7625 Empire Dr. Florence, KY 41042. Phone: 800-347-7707 or (606)525-6620 Fax: (606)252-0978 E-mail: info@chapall.com • URL: http://www.chapall.com • 1998. $37.95. Third edition.

Stock Index Options: How to Use and Profit from Indexed Options in Volatile and Uncertain Markets. Scot G. Barenblat and Donald T. Mesler. McGraw-Hill Professional, 1221 Ave. of the Americas New York, NY 10020. Phone: 800-722-4726 or (212)904-2000 Fax: (212)904-2072 E-mail: customer.service@mcgraw-hill.com • URL: http://www.mcgraw-hill.com • 1991. $29.95. Revised editon.

The Stock Market Barometer: A Study of Its Forecast Value Based on Charles H. Dow's Theory of the Price Movement, with an Analysis of the Market and Its History Since 1897. William P. Hamilton. Omnigraphics, Inc., Penobscot

Bldg. Detroit, MI 48226. Phone: 800-234-1340 or (313)961-1340 Fax: 800-875-1340 or (313)961-1383 E-mail: info@omnigraphics.com • URL: http://www.omnigraphics.com • 1990. $45.00. Reprint of 1922 edition.

Stock Market Crashes and Speculative Manias. Eugene N. White, editor. Edward Elgar Publishing, Inc., 136 West St., Suite 202 Northampton, MA 01060. Phone: 800-390-3149 or (413)584-5551 Fax: (413)584-9933 E-mail: eep.orders@aidcvt.com • URL: http://www.e-elgar.co.uk • 1996. $230.00. Contains reprints of 23 articles dating from 1905 to 1994. (International Library of Macroeconomic and Financial History Series: No. 13).

Stock Market Trading Systems. Gerald Appel and Fred Hitschler. Traders Press, Inc., P.O. Box 6206 Greenville, SC 29606. Phone: 800-927-8222 or (803)298-0222 Fax: (803)864-0221 E-mail: tradersprs@aol.com • URL: http://www.traderspress.com • 1990. $45.00. Reprint of 1980 edition.

Stock Market Values and Yields for 1997. Research Institute of America, 90 Fifth Ave. New York, NY 10011. Phone: 800-431-9025 or (212)645-4800 Fax: (212)337-4713 URL: http://www.prenhall.com • 1997. $20.00. Revised edition. Gives year-end prices and dividends for tax purposes.

Stock Values and Dividends for Tax Purposes. CCH, Inc., 4025 W. Peterson Ave. Chicago, IL 60646-6085. Phone: 800-248-3248 or (773)866-6000 Fax: 800-224-8299 or (773)866-3608 Annual. Gives year-end prices and dividends for tax purposes.

Stockman's Handbook. R. M. Ensminger. Interstate Publishers, Inc., P.O. Box 50 Danville, IL 61834-0050. Phone: 800-843-4774 or (217)446-0500 Fax: (217)446-9706 E-mail: info-ipp@ippinc.com • URL: http://www.ippinc.com • 1992. $91.25. Seventh edition.

Stocks, Bonds, Bills, and Inflation Yearbook. Ibbotson Associates, 225 N. Michigan Ave., Suite 700 Chicago, IL 60601-7676. Phone: 800-758-3557 or (312)616-1620 Fax: (312)616-0404 Annual. $92.00. Provides detailed data from 1926 to the present on inflation and the returns from various kinds of financial investments, such as small-cap stocks and long-term government bonds.

Stocks for the Long Run: A Guide to Selecting Markets for Long-Term Growth. Jeremy J. Siegel. McGraw-Hill, 1221 Ave. of the Americas New York, NY 10020. Phone: 800-722-4726 or (212)904-2000 Fax: (212)904-2072 E-mail: customer.service@mcgraw-hill.com • URL: http://www.mcgraw-hill.com • 1998. $29.95. Second expanded edition. A favorable view of a buy-and-hold strategy for stock market investors. *Business Week Books*.

Stores. National Retail Federation. N R F Enterprises, Inc., Financial Executives Div., 325 Seventh St., N.W., Suite 1000 Washington, DC 20004-2802. Phone: 800-673-4692 or (202)626-8101 Fax: (202)626-8191 URL: http://www.stores.com • Monthly. $49.00 per year.

Storm Data. U.S. National Climatic Data Center, National Oceanic and Atmospheric Administration, U.S. Dept of Commerce, Federal Bldg., Room 120, 151 Patton Ave. Asheville, NC 28801-5001. Phone: (704)271-4476 E-mail: orders@ncdc.noaa.gov • URL: http://www.ncdc.noaa.gov • Monthly.

Straight Talk About Mutual Funds. Dian Vujovich. McGraw-Hill, 1221 Ave. of the Americas New York, NY 10020. Phone: 800-722-4726 or (212)904-2000 Fax: (212)904-2072 E-mail: customer.service@mcgraw-hill.com • URL: http://www.mcgraw-hill.com • 1996. $12.95. Second revised edition. The author provides basic advice and information for both beginning and experienced investors in mutual funds. (Straight Talk Series).

Strategic Finance. Institute of Management Accountants, Ten Paragon Dr. Montvale, NJ 07645-1760. Phone: 800-638-4427 or (201)573-9000 Fax: (201)573-8185 E-mail: info@strategicfinancemag.com • URL: http://www.imanet.org • Monthly. $140.00 per year; non-profit institutions, $70.00 per year. Provides articles on corporate finance, cost control, cash flow, budgeting, corporate taxes, and other financial management topics.

Strategic Health Care Marketing. Health Care Communications, P.O. Box 594 Rye, NY 10580. Phone: (914)967-6741 Fax: (914)967-3054 E-mail: healthcomm@aol.com • URL: http://www.strategichealthcare.com • Monthly. $269.00 per year. Newsletter.

Strategic Hotel Motel Marketing. Christopher W. L. Hart and David Troy. Educational Institute of the American Hotel & Motel Association, P.O. Box 1240 East Lansing, MI 48826-1240. Phone: 800-344-4381 or (517)372-8800 Fax: (517)372-5141 E-mail: info@ei-ahma.org • URL: http://www.ei.ahma.org • 1998. $59.95. Third edition. Price on application.

Strategic Leadership Forum.

Strategic Leadership Forum Membership Directory. Strategic Leadership Forum, 435 N. Michigan Ave. Chicago, IL 60611-4067. Phone: 800-873-5995 or (312)644-0829 Fax: (312)644-8557 URL: http://www.slfnet.org • Annual. About 4,000 strategic management executives, consultants and academics. Membership.

Strategic Management. David Hunger and Thomas L. Wheelen. Prentice Hall, 240 Frisch Court Paramus, NJ 07652-5240. Phone: 800-947-7700 or (201)909-6200 Fax: 800-445-6991 or (201)909-6361 URL: http://www.prenhall.com • 1999. $51.00. Seventh edition.

Strategic Management for Academic Libraries: A Handbook. Robert M. Hayes. Greenwood Publishing Group, Inc., 88 Post Rd., W. Westport, CT 06881-5007. Phone: 800-225-5800 or (203)226-3571 Fax: (203)222-1502 E-mail: bookinfo@greenwood.com • URL: http://www.greenwood.com • 1993. $65.00. (Library Management Collection).

Strategic Management for Bankers. Richard W. Sapp and Roger W. Smith. Strategic Leadership Forum, 435 N. Michigan Ave., Suite 1717 Chicago, IL 60611-4067. Phone: 800-873-5995 or (312)644-0829 Fax: (312)644-8557 URL: http://www.slfnet.org • 1984. $23.00.

Strategic Management for Public Libraries: A Handbook. Robert M. Hayes and Virginia A. Walter. Greenwood Publishing Group, Inc., 88 Post Rd., W. Westport, CT 06881-5007. Phone: 800-225-5800 or (203)226-3571 Fax: (203)222-2540 E-mail: bookinfo@greenwood.com • URL: http://www.greenwood.com • 1996. $65.00. (Library Management Collection).

Strategic Management for Today's Libraries. Marilyn G. Mason. American Library Association, 50 E. Huron St. Chicago, IL 60611-2795. Phone: 800-545-2433 or (312)944-6780 Fax: (312)440-9374 E-mail: ala@ala.org • URL: http://www.ala.org • 1999. $35.00.

Strategic Management: Formulation, Implementation, and Control. John A. Pearce and Richard B. Robinson. McGraw-Hill Higher Education, 1221 Ave. of the Americas New York, NY 10020. Phone: 800-722-4726 or (212)904-2000 Fax: (212)904-2072 E-mail: customer.service@mcgraw-hill.com • URL: http://www.mcgraw-hill.com • 1996. $72.75. Sixth edition.

Strategic Management in Non-Profit Organizations: An Administrator's Handbook. Robert D. Hay. Greenwood Publishing Group, Inc., 88 Post Rd., W. Westport, CT 06881-5007. Phone: 800-225-5800 or (203)226-3571 Fax: (203)222-2540 E-mail: bookinfo@greenwood.com • URL: http://www.greenwood.com • 1990. $75.00.

Strategic Management Journal. Available from John Wiley and Sons, Inc., Journals Div., 605 Third Ave. New York, NY 10158-0012. Phone: 800-526-5368 or (212)850-6000 Fax: (212)850-6088 E-mail: info@wiley.com • URL: http://www.wiley.com • Monthly. Insitutions, $145.00 per year. Original refereed material concerned with all aspects of strategic management. Devoted to the development and improvement of both theory and practice. Provides international coverage. Published in England by John Wiley and Sons Ltd.

Strategic Market Management. David A. Aaker. John Wiley and Sons, Inc., 605 Third Ave. New York, NY 10158-0012. Phone: 800-225-5945 or (212)850-6000 Fax: (212)850-6088 E-mail: info@wiley.com • URL: http://www.wiley.com • 1998. $79.00. Fifth edition.

Strategic Marketing. David W. Cravens. McGraw-Hill Professional, 1221 Ave. of the Americas New York, NY 10020. Phone: 800-722-4726 or (212)904-2000 Fax: (212)904-2072 E-mail: customer.service@mcgraw-hill.com • URL: http://www.mcgraw-hill.com • 2000. Sixth edition. Price on application.

Strategic Marketing Problems: Cases and Comments. Roger A. Kerin and Robert A. Peterson. Prentice Hall, 240 Frisch Ct. Paramus, NJ 07652-5240. Phone: 800-947-7700 or (201)909-6452 Fax: 800-445-6991 URL: http://www.prenhall.com • 2000. $91.33. Ninth edition.

Strategic Planning: A How-To-Do-It Manual for Librarians. M. E. Jacob. Neal-Schuman Publishers, Inc., 100 Varick St. New York, NY 10013. Phone: (212)925-8650 Fax: 800-584-2414 E-mail: info@neal-schuman.com • URL: http://www.neal-schuman.com • 1990. $45.00. (How-to-Do-It Series).

Strategic Planning: A Practical Guide. Peter Rea and Harold Kerzner. John Wiley and Sons, Inc., 605 Third Ave. New York, NY 10158-0012. Phone: 800-842-3636 or (212)850-6000 Fax: (212)850-6088 E-mail: info@wiley.com • URL: http://www.wiley.com • 1997. $69.95. Covers strategic planning for manufacturing firms, small businesses, and large corporations. (Industrial Engineering Series).

Strategic Planning Institute., P.O. Box 447 Newton Center, MA 02459-0004. Phone: (617)491-9200 Fax: (617)491-1634 Conducts research in business information and strategy.

Strategic Planning Plus: An Organizational Guide. Roger Kaufman. Sage Publications, Inc., 2455 Teller Rd. Thousand Oaks, CA 91320. Phone: (805)499-0721 Fax: (805)499-0871 E-mail: info@sagepub.com • URL: http://www.sagepub • 1992. $48.00.

Strategic Sales Management. Bureau of Business Practice, Inc., 24 Rope Ferry Rd. Waterford, CT 06386. Phone: 800-243-0876 or (860)442-4365 Fax: (860)437-3555 E-mail: rebecca_armitage@prenhall.com • URL: http://www.bbpnews.com • Semimonthly. $187.80 per year. Newsletter. Provides advice and information for sales managers. Formerly *Sales Managers' Bulletin*.

Strategic Supply Management: A Blueprint for Revitalizing the Manufacturer-Supplier Partnership. Keki R. Bhote. AMACOM, 1601 Broadway, 12th Fl. New York, NY 10019. Phone: 800-262-9699 or (212)586-8100 Fax: (212)903-8168 E-mail: custmserv@amanet.org • URL: http://www.amanet.org • 1989. $65.00. How to reduce the expense of supply management and improve quality, delivery time, and inventory control.

Strategic Trading in the Foreign Exchange Markets. Gary Klopfenstein. Fitzroy Dearborn Publishers, 919 N. Michigan Ave., Suite 760 Chicago, IL 60611. Phone: 800-850-8102 or (312)587-0131 Fax: (312)587-1049 E-mail: website@fitzroydearborn.com • URL: http://www.fitzroydearborn.com • 1999. $65.00. Describes the tactics of successful foreign exchange traders.

Strategy and Business. Booz-Allen & Hamilton, 101 Park Ave. New York, NY 10178. Phone: 888-557-5550 or (212)551-6154 E-mail: editorial@mcb.co.uk • URL: http://www.mcb.co.uk • Quarterly. $38.00 per year.

Stratis Health.

Stress and Burnout in Library Service. Janette S. Caputo. Oryx Press, 4041 N. Central Ave., Ste. 700 Phoenix, AZ 85012-3379. Phone: 800-279-6799 or (602)265-2651 Fax: 800-279-4663 or (602)265-6250 E-mail: info@oryxpress.com • URL: http://www.oryxpress.com • 1991. $24.95. Discusses symptoms of stress in library staff members and ways of dealing with stress. Includes self-help checklists and a list of references for further information.

Stress and Well-Being at Work: Assessments and Interventions for Occupational Mental Health. James C. Quick and others, editors. American Psychological Association, 750 First St., N. E. Washington, DC 20002-4242. Phone: 800-374-2721 or (202)336-5500 Fax: (202)336-5530 URL: http://www.apa.org/books • 1992. $19.95.

Stress Management for Wellness. Walt Schafer. Harcourt Brace College Publishers, 301 Commerce St., Suite 3700 Fort Worth, TX 76102-4137. Phone: 800-245-8774 or (817)334-7500 Fax: (817)334-8060 E-mail: wlittle@harbrace.com • URL: http://www.harcourt.com • 1995. $48.00. Third edition.

Stress Medicine. Available from John Wiley and Sons, Inc., Journals Div., 605 Third Ave. New York, NY 10158-0012. Phone: 800-526-5368 or (212)850-6000 Fax: (212)850-6088 E-mail: info@wiley.com • URL: http://www.wiley.com • Five times a year. Institutions, $870.00 per year. A forum for discussion of all aspects of stress which affect the individual in both health and disease. Provides international coverage.

Stress Solution: An Action Plan to Manage the Stress in Your Life. Lyle H. Miller and others. Pocket Books, 1230 Ave. of the Americas New York, NY 10020. Phone: 800-223-2336 or (212)698-7000 Fax: 800-943-9831 1993. $6.99.

Strike! Jeremy Brecher. South End Press, Seven Brookline St., No. 1 Cambridge, MA 02139-4146. Phone: 800-533-8478 or (617)547-4002 Fax: (617)547-1333 1997. $40.00. Fourth revised edition. (Classics Series, volume one).

Structural Clay Products. W.E. Brownell. Springer-Verlag New York, Inc., 175 Fifth Ave. New York, NY 10010. Phone: 800-777-4643 or (212)460-1500 Fax: (212)473-6272 E-mail: orders@springer.ny.com • URL: http://www.springer.ny.com • 1977. $91.95. (Applied Mineralogy Series: Vol. 9).

Structural Materials in Nuclear Power Systems. J.T. Roberts, editor. Perseus Publishing, 11 Cambridge Center Cambridge, MA 02142. Phone: (617)252-5200 Fax: (617)252-5285 E-mail: westview.orders@perseusbooks.com • URL: http://www.perseusbooks.com • 1981. $89.50. (Modern Perspectives in Energy Series).

Structures and Composites Laboratory. Stanford University

Structuring Commercial Loan Agreements. Rodger Tighe. Warren, Gorham & Lamont/RIA Group, 395 Hudson St. New York, NY 10014. Phone: 800-950-1215 or (212)367-6300 Fax: (212)367-6718 E-mail: customer_services@riag.com • URL: http://www.riahome.com • Looseleaf. $115.00. Biennial supplementation. An aid to structuring commercial loan agreements.

Student Aid News: The Independent Biweekly News Service on Student Financial Assistance Programs. Aspen Publishers, Inc., 200 Orchard Ridge Dr. Gaithersburg, MD 20878. Phone: 800-638-8437 or (301)417-7500 Fax: (301)695-7931 E-mail: customer.service@aspenpubl.com • URL: http://www.aspenpubl.com • Biweekly. $297.00 per year. Newsletter on federal student aid programs.

The Student Guide: Financial Aid. U.S. Dept. of Education, Federal Student Aid Information Center, P.O. Box 84 Washington, DC 20044-0084. Phone: 800-322-3213 URL: http://www.ed.gov/prog-info/sfa/studentguide • Annual. Describes financial aid for college and vocational school students. Available online.

Studies in American Humor. American Human Studies Association, c/o Joseph Alvarez, Central Piedmont Community College, P.O. Box 35009 Charlotte, NC 28235-5009.

Phone: (704)330-4097 Fax: (704)330-5930 E-mail: joe_alvarez@cpcc.cc.nc.us • Annual. Membership.

Studio Business Book: A Guide to Professional Recording Studio Business and Management. Jim Mandell. Intertec Publishing Corp., 6400 Hollis St., Suite 10 Emeryville, CA 94608. Phone: 800-888-5139 or (510)653-3307 Fax: (510)653-5142 E-mail: subs@intertec.com • URL: http://www.intertec.com • 1995. $34.95. Second expanded edition. Includes information on business plans, studio equipment, financing, expenses, rate setting, and personnel.

Studio for Creative Inquiry., Carnegie Mellon University, College of Fine Arts Pittsburgh, PA 15213-3890. Phone: (412)268-3454 Fax: (412)268-2829 E-mail: mmbm@andrew.cmu.edu/ • URL: http://www.cmu.edu/studio/ • Research areas include artificial intelligence, virtual reality, hypermedia, multimedia, and telecommunications, in relation to the arts.

Studio Photography and Design. Cygnus Business Media, 445 Broad Hollow Rd. Melville, NY 11747. Phone: 800-308-6397 or (631)845-2700 Fax: (631)845-2798 E-mail: rich.reiff@cygnuspub.com • URL: http://www.cygnuspub.com • Monthly. $60.00 per year. Incorporates *Comercial Image*.

Study Abroad: Scholarships and Higher Education Courses Worldwide. Available from Bernan Associates, 4611-F Assembly Dr. Lanham, MD 20706. Phone: 800-274-4447 or (301)459-7666 Fax: 800-865-3450 or (301)459-0056 E-mail: info@bernan.com • URL: http://www.bernan.com • Biennial. Provides information on a wide variety of scholarships, fellowships, and educational exchange programs in over 100 countries. Text in English, French, and Spanish. Published by the United Nations Educational, Scientific, and Cultural Organization (UNESCO).

Study Abroad: The Experience of American Undergraduates. Jerry S. Carlson and others. Greenwood Publishing Group, Inc., 88 Post Rd., W. Westport, CT 06881-5007. Phone: 800-225-5800 or (203)226-3571 Fax: (203)222-2540 E-mail: bookinfo@greenwood.com • URL: http://www.greenwood.com • 1990. $62.95. (Contributions to the Study of Education Series, No 37).

Study on the Operation and Effects of the North American Free Trade Agreement. Available from U. S. Government Printing Office, Washington, DC 20402. Phone: (202)512-1800 Fax: (202)512-2250 E-mail: gpoaccess@gpo.gov • URL: http://www.access.gpo.gov • 1997. $17.00. Produced by the Executive Office of the President (http://www.whitehouse.gov). Presents a generally favorable view of the effects of NAFTA on the U. S. and Mexican economies.

Studying Your Workforce: Applied Research Methods and Tools for the Training and Development Practitioner. Alan Clardy. Sage Publications, Inc., 2455 Teller Rd. Thousand Oaks, CA 91320. Phone: (805)499-0721 Fax: (805)499-0871 E-mail: info@sagepub.com • URL: http://www.sagepub.com • 1997. $45.00. Describes how to apply specific research methods to common training problems. Emphasis is on data collection methods: testing, observation, surveys, and interviews. Topics include performance problems and assessment.

Style: Toward Clarity and Grace. Joseph M. Williams. University of Chicago Press, 5801 Ellis Ave., 4th Fl. Chicago, IL 60637. Phone: 800-621-2736 or (773)702-7700 Fax: (773)702-9756 E-mail: marketing@press.uchicago.edu • URL: http://www.press.uchicago.edu • 1990. $17.95. (Chicago Guides to Writing, Editing and Publishing Series).

Subchapter S Manual. P. L. Faber and Martin E. Holbrook. Prentice Hall, 240 Frisch Court Paramus, NJ 07652-5240. Phone: 800-947-7700 or (201)909-6200 Fax: 800-445-6991 or (201)909-6361 URL: http://www.prenhall.com • Annual. Price on application.

The Subcontractor. American Subcontractors Association, 1004 Duke St. Alexandria, VA 22314-3588. Phone: (703)684-3450 Fax: (703)836-3482 E-mail: asaoffice-hq@aol.com • URL: http://www.asaonline.com • Monthly. $40.00 per year.

Subject Bibliography: Art and Artists. Available from U. S. Government Printing Office, Washington, DC 20402. Phone: (202)512-1800 Fax: (202)512-2250 E-mail: gpoaccess@gpo.gov • URL: http://www.access.gpo.gov • Annual. Free. Lists books, pamphlets, periodicals, and other government publications on art-related topics. (Subject Bibliography No. SB-107.)

Subject Bibliography Index: A Guide to U. S. Government Information. Available from U. S. Government Printing Office, Washington, DC 20402. Phone: (202)512-1800 Fax: (202)512-2250 E-mail: gpoaccess@gpo.gov • URL: http://www.access.gpo.gov • Annual. Free. Issued by the Superintendent of Documents. Lists currently available subject bibliographies by title and by topic. Each *Subject Bibliography* describes government books, periodicals, posters, pamphlets, and subscription services available for sale from the Government Printing Office.

Subject Collections: A Guide to Special Book Collections and Subject Emphasis in Libraries. Lee Ash and William G. Miller, editors. R. R. Bowker, 121 Chanlon Rd. New Providence, NJ 07974. Phone: 888-269-5372 or (908)464-6800 Fax: (908)771-7704 E-mail: info@bowker.com • URL: http://www.bowker.com • Irregular. $275.00. Two volumes. A guide to special book collections and subject emphases as reported by university, college, public and special libraries in th United States and Canada.

Subject Directory of Special Libraries and Information Centers. The Gale Group, 27500 Drake Rd. Farmington Hills, MI 48331-3535. Phone: 800-877-GALE or (248)699-GALE Fax: 800-414-5043 or (248)699-8069 E-mail: galeord@galegroup.com • URL: http://www.galegroup.com • Annual. $845.00. Three volumes, available separately: volume one, *Business, Government, and Law Libraries*, $595.00; volume two, *Computer, Engineering, and Law Libraries*, $595.00; volume three, *Health Sciences Libraries*, $340.00. Altogether, 14,000 entries from the *Directory of Special Libraries and Information Centers* are arranged in 14 subject chapters.

Subject Encyclopedias: User's Guide, Review Citations, and Keyword Index. Allan N. Mirwis. Oryx Press, 4041 North Central Ave., Suite 700 Phoenix, AZ 85012-3397. Phone: 800-279-6799 or (602)265-2651 Fax: 800-279-4663 or (602)265-6250 E-mail: info@oryxpress.com • URL: http://www.oryxpress.com • 1999. $135.00. Two volumes. Volume one describes 1,000 subject encyclopedias; volume two provides a keyword index to articles appearing in 100 selected encyclopedias.

Subject Guide to Books in Print. R. R. Bowker, 121 Chanlon Rd. New Providence, NJ 07974. Phone: 888-269-5372 or (908)464-6800 Fax: (908)771-7704 E-mail: info@bowker.com • URL: http://www.bowker.com • Annual. $339.00. Seven volumes.

Subject Indexing: An Introductory Guide. Trudi Bellardo. Special Libraries Association, 1700 18th St, N. W., 17th Fl. Washington, DC 20009-2514. Phone: (202)234-4700 Fax: 888-411-2856 or (202)265-9317 E-mail: books@sla.org • URL: http://www.sla.org • 1991. $85.00. A self-study guide to creating subject indices for a variety of materials and formats.

Submersible Wastewater Pump Association.

Substance Abuse: A Comprehensive Textbook. Joyce H. Lowinson and others. Lippincott Williams & Wilkins, 530 Walnut St. Philadelphia, PA 19106-3780. Phone: 800-638-3030 or (215)521-8300 Fax: (215)521-8902 E-mail: custserv@lwws.com • URL: http://www.lww.com • 1997. $155.00. Third edition. Covers the medical, psychological, socioeconomic, and public health aspects of drug and alcohol abuse.

Success: For the Innovative Entrepreneur. Success Holdings LLC, 150 Fayetteville St. Mall, Suite 1110 Raleigh, NC 27601. Phone: 800-234-7324 or (919)807-1100 Fax: (919)807-1200 E-mail: info@successmagazine.com • URL: http://www.successmagazine.com • Monthly. $19.97 per year. Provides information to help individuals advance in business.

Successful Advertising Research Methods. Jack B. Haskins and Alice Gagnard-Kendrick. NTC/Contemporary Publishing, P.O. Box 545 Blacklick, OH 43004. Phone: 800-338-3987 or (614)755-4151 Fax: (614)755-5645 E-mail: ntcpub@mcgraw-hill.com • URL: http://www.ntc-cb.com • 1994. $49.95. (NTC Business Book Series).

The Successful Benefits Communicator. Lawence Ragan Communications, Inc., 316 N. Michigan Ave. Chicago, IL 60601. Phone: 800-878-5331 or (312)960-4100 Fax: (312)960-4106 E-mail: cservice@ragan.com • URL: http://www.ragan.com • Monthly. $117.00 per year. Newsletter on techniques for providing useful information to employees about benefits. Formerly *Techniques for the Benefits Communicator*.

Successful Business Plan: Secrets and Strategies. Rhonda M. Abrams. Rhonda, Inc., 555 Bryant St., No. 180 Los Altos Hills, CA 94022. Phone: (650)941-0776 Fax: (650)941-0885 E-mail: rhonda@rhondaonline.com • URL: http://www.rhondaonline.com • 1999. $27.95. Third edition. (Successful Business Library Series).

Successful Catering. William Reynolds and Michael Roman. John Wiley & Sons, Inc., 605 Third Ave., 4th Fl. New York, NY 10158-0012. Phone: 800-225-5945 or (212)850-6000 Fax: (212)850-6088 E-mail: info@wiley.com • URL: http://www.wiley.com • 1991. $59.95. Third edition.

Successful Cold Call Selling. Lee Boyan. AMACOM, 1601 Broadway, 12th Fl. New York, NY 10019. Phone: 800-262-9699 or (212)586-8100 Fax: (212)903-8168 E-mail: custmserv@amanet.org • URL: http://www.amanet.org • 1989. $16.95. Second edition.

Successful Dealer. Kona Communications, Inc., 707 Lake Cook Rd., Suite 300 Deerfield, IL 60015. Phone: (847)498-3180 Fax: (847)498-3197 Bimonthly. $50.00 per year. For truck and heavy duty equipment dealers.

The Successful Exhibitor's Handbook: Trade Show Techniques for Beginners and Pros. Barry Siskind. Self-Counsel Press, Inc., 1704 N. State St. Bellingham, WA 98225. Phone: 877-877-6490 or (360)676-4530 Fax: (360)676-4530 E-mail: service@self-counsel.com • URL: http://www.self-counsel.com • 1996. $14.95. Third edition.

Successful International Marketing: How to Gain the Global Advantage. American Management Association Extension Institute, P.O. Box 1026 Saranac Lake, NY 12983-9957. Phone: 800-262-9699 or (518)891-1500 Fax: (518)891-0368 Looseleaf. $130.00. Self-study course. Emphasis is on practical explanations, examples, and problem solving. Quizzes and a case study are included.

Successful Meetings: The Authority on Meetings and Incentive Travel Management. Bill Communications, Inc., 770 Broadway New York, NY 10003-9595. Phone: 800-266-4712 or (646)654-5400 Fax: (646)654-7212 URL: http://www.billcom.com • Monthly. $65.00 per year.

Successful Negotiating. American Management Association Extension Institute, P.O. Box 1026 Saranac Lake, NY 12983-9957. Phone: 800-262-9699 or (518)891-1500 Fax: (518)891-0368 Looseleaf. $110.00. Self-study course. Emphasis is on practical explanations, examples, and problem solving. Quizzes and a case study are included.

Successful Project Management. American Management Association Extension Institute, P.O. Box 1026 Saranac Lake, NY 12983-9957. Phone: 800-262-9699 or (518)891-1500 Fax: (518)891-0368 Looseleaf. $130.00. Self-study course. Emphasis is on practical explanations, examples, and problem solving. Quizzes and a case study are included.

Successful Small Business Management: It's Your Business...Mind It! David Siegel and Harold L. Goldman. Books on Demand, 300 N. Zeeb Rd. Ann Arbor, MI 48106-1346. Phone: 800-521-0600 or (734)761-4700 Fax: (734)665-5022 E-mail: info@umi.com • URL: http://www.lib.umi.com • $111.60. Reprint edition.

Successful Telemarketing: Opportunities and Techniques for Increasing Sales and Profits. Bob Stone and John Wyman. NTC/Contemporary Publishing, P.O. Box 545 Blacklick, OH 43004. Phone: 800-323-4900 or (847)679-5500 Fax: (847)679-2494 E-mail: ntcpub@tribune.com • URL: http://www.ntc-contemporary.com • 1993. $29.95. Second edition. Includes case histories and examples of effective telemarketing.

Sugar and Sweetener Situation and Outlook. Available from U. S. Government Printing Office, Washington, DC 20402. Phone: (202)512-1800 Fax: (202)512-2250 E-mail: gpoaccess@gpo.gov • URL: http://www.access.gpo.gov • Three times per year. $11.00 per year. Issued by Economic Research Service, U. S. Department of Agriculture. Provides current statistical information on supply, demand, and prices.

Sugar Association.

Sugar Bulletin. American Sugar Cane League of the U.S.A., Drawer 938 Thibodaux, LA 70302-0938. Phone: (504)448-3707 Fax: (504)448-3722 Semimonthly. Free to members; non-members, $15.00 per year.

Sugar Journal: Covering the World's Sugar Industry. Kriedt Enterprises Ltd., 129 S. Cortez St. New Orleans, LA 70119-6118. Phone: (504)482-3914 Fax: (504)482-4205 Monthly. $36.00 per year. A monthly technical publication designed to inform sugar beet and cane farms, factories, and refineries throughout the world about the latest developments in the sugar industry.

The Sugar Producer: Representing the Sugar Beet Industry in the United States. Harris Publishing, Inc., 520 Park Ave. Idaho Falls, ID 83402. Phone: (208)524-7000 Fax: (208)522-5241 Seven times a year. $10.95 per year. Supplies sugar beet growers with information to assist them in production of quality sugar beet crops.

Sugar y Azucar. Ruspam Communications, Inc., 452 Hudson Terrace Englewood, NJ 07632. Phone: (201)871-9200 Fax: (201)871-9639 Monthly. $75.00 per year. Text in English and Spanish

Sugar y Azucar Yearbook. Ruspam Communications, Inc., 452 Hudson Terrace Englewood, NJ 07632. Phone: (201)871-9200 Fax: (201)871-9639 Annual. $55.00. List of over 1,700 cane sugar mills and refineries-international coverage.

Suggested State Legislation. Council of State Governments, P.O. Box 11910 Lexington, KY 40578-1910. Phone: 800-800-1910 or (606)244-8000 Fax: (606)244-8001 E-mail: psantos@csg.org • URL: http://www.csg.org • Annual. $59.00. A source of legislative ideas and drafting assistance for state government officials.

Sulphur: Covers All Aspects of World Sulphur and Sulphuric Acid Industry. British Sulphur Publishing, 31 Mount Pleasant London WC1X 0AD, England. E-mail: smoore@cruint.tcom.co.uk • URL: http://www.cru.co.uk • Bimonthly. $520.00 per year.

Sulphur Institute.

Summary of Health Information for International Travel. U. S. Department of Health and Human Services, Centers for Disease Control, 1600 Clifton Rd., N. E. Atlanta, GA 30333. Phone: (404)639-3286 Fax: (404)639-3889 URL: http://www.cdc.gov • Biweekly. Formerly *Weekly Summary of Health Information for International Travel*.

Summary of International Travel to the United States. International Trade Administration, Tourism Industries. U.S. Dept. of Commerce, Washington, DC 20230. Phone: (202)482-3809 Fax: (202)482-2877 URL: http://www.tinet.ita.doc.gov • Monthly. Quarterly and annual versions available. Provides statistics on air travel to the

U.S. from each of 90 countries. Formerly *Summary and Analysis of International Travel to the United States*.

Summary of Labor Arbitration Awards. American Arbitration Association, Inc., 335 Madison Ave. New York, NY 10017. Phone: 800-778-7879 or (212)716-5800 Fax: (212)716-5905 URL: http://www.aaa.org • Monthly. $120.00 per year.

Summary of Sanitation Inspections of International Cruise Ships. U. S. Public Health Service, Centers for Disease Control and Prevention (CDC), Vessel Sanitation Program, 4770 Buford Highway, N. E., Mailstop F-16 Atlanta, GA 30341-3724. Phone: (770)488-7333 Fax: 888-232-6789 URL: http://www2.cdc.gov/nceh/vsp/vspmain.asp • Biweekly. Apply. "All passenger cruise ships arriving at U. S. ports are subject to unannounced inspection..to achieve levels of sanitation that will minimize the potential for gastrointestinal disease outbreaks on these ships." Individual ships are listed, with sanitation rating and date of inspection. (CDC Document No. 510051.)

Summers on Oil and Gas. West Publishing Co., College and School Div., 610 Opperman Dr. Eagan, MN 55123. Phone: 800-328-4880 or (651)687-7000 Fax: 800-213-2323 or (651)687-5827 E-mail: legal-ed@westgroup.com • URL: http://www.lawschool.westgroup.com • Price on application. Periodic supplementation. Legal aspects of the petroleum industry.

Sump and Sewage Pump Manufacturers Association.

The Suncare Products Market. Available from MarketResearch.com, 641 Ave. of the Americas, 3rd Fl. New York, NY 10011. Phone: 800-298-5699 or (212)807-2629 Fax: (212)807-2716 E-mail: order@marketresearch.com • URL: http://www.marketresearch.com • 1996. $1,230.00. Published by Packaged Facts. Provides market data on sun screen lotions, after-sun products, and sunless tanning cosmetics, with sales projections.

Sunkist Growers.

Super Searchers Cover the World: The Online Secrets of International Business Researchers. Mary E. Bates and Reva Basch. Information Today, Inc., 143 Old Marlton Pike Medford, NJ 08055-8750. Phone: 800-300-9868 or (609)654-6266 Fax: (609)654-4309 E-mail: custserv@infotoday.com • URL: http://www.infotoday.com • 2001. $24.95. Presents interviews with 15 experts in the area of online searching for international business information. (CyberAge Books.)

Super Searchers Do Business: The Online Secrets of Top Business Researchers. Mary E.Bates and Reva Basch. Information Today, Inc., 143 Old Marlton Pike Medford, NJ 08055-8750. Phone: 800-300-9868 or (609)654-6266 Fax: (609)654-4309 E-mail: custserv@infotoday.com • URL: http://www.infotoday.com • 1999. $24.95. Presents the results of interviews with "11 leading researchers who use the Internet and online services to find critical business information." (CyberAge Books.)

Super Searchers Go to the Source: The Interviewing and Hands-On Information Strategies of Top Primary Researchers - Online, On the Phone, and In Person. Risa Sacks and Reva Basch. Information Today, Inc., 143 Old Marlton Pike Medford, NJ 08055-8750. Phone: 800-300-9868 or (609)654-6266 Fax: (609)654-4309 E-mail: custserv@infotoday.com • URL: http://www.infotoday.com • 2001. $24.95. Explains how information-search experts use various print, electronic, and live sources for competitive intelligence and other purposes. (CyberAge Books.)

Super Searchers in the News: The Online Secrets of Journalists and News Researchers. Paula J. Hane and Reva Basch. Information Today, Inc., 143 Old Marlton Pike Medford, NJ 08055-8750. Phone: 800-300-9868 or (609)654-6266 Fax: (609)654-4309 E-mail: custserv@infotoday.com • URL: http://www.infotoday.com • 2000. $24.95. Contains online searching advice from 10 professional news researchers and fact checkers. (CyberAge Books.)

Super Searchers on Health and Medicine: The Online Secrets of Top Health and Medical Researchers. Susan M. Detwiler and Reva Basch. Information Today, Inc., 143 Old Marlton Pike Medford, NJ 08055-8750. Phone: 800-300-9868 or (609)654-6266 Fax: (609)654-4309 E-mail: custserv@infotoday.com • URL: http://www.infotoday.com • 2000. $24.95. Provides the results of interviews with 10 experts in online searching for medical research data and healthcare information. Discusses both traditional sources and Web sites. (CyberAge Books.)

Super Searchers on Mergers & Acquisitions: The Online Secrets of Top Corporate Researchers and M & A Pros. Jan Tudor and Reva Basch. Information Today, Inc., 143 Old Marlton Pike Medford, NJ 08055-8750. Phone: 800-300-9868 or (609)654-6266 Fax: (609)654-4309 E-mail: custserv@infotoday.com • URL: http://www.infotoday.com • 2001. $24.95. Presents the results of interviews with 13 "top M & A information pros." Covers the finding, evaluating, and delivering of relevant data on companies and industries. (CyberAge Books.)

Super Searchers on Wall Street: Top Investment Professionals Share Their Online Research Secrets. Amelia Kassel and Reva Basch. Information Today, Inc., 143 Old Marlton Pike Medford, NJ 08055-8750. Phone: 800-300-9868 or (609)654-6266 Fax: (609)654-4309 E-mail: custserv@infotoday.com • URL: http://www.infotoday.com • 2000. $24.95. Gives the results of interviews with "10 leading financial industry research experts." Explains how online information is used by stock brokers, investment bankers, and individual investors. Includes relevant Web sites and other sources. (CyberAge Books.)

Superconductivity. Charles P. Poole and others. Academic Press, Inc., 525 B St., Suite 1900 San Diego, CA 92101-4495. Phone: 800-321-5068 or (619)230-1840 Fax: (619)699-6715 E-mail: ap@acad.com • URL: http://www.academicpress.com • 1995. $65.00.

Superconductivity: An Annotated Bibliography with Abstracts. A. Bisarsh, editor. Nova Science Publishers, Inc., 227 Main St., Ste. 100 Huntington, NY 11743-6682. Phone: (631)424-6682 Fax: (631)424-4666 E-mail: novascil@aol.com • URL: http://www.nexusworld.com • 1998. $115.00.

Superconductivity Flash Report. Alan R. Lind, 111 E. Wacker Dr. Chicago, IL 60601. Phone: (312)565-1200 Semimonthly. $295.00 per year. Newsletter.

Superconductivity: The Next Revolution? Gianfranco Vidali. Cambridge University Press, 40 W. 20th St. New York, NY 10011. Phone: 800-221-4512 or (212)924-3900 Fax: (212)937-4712 E-mail: info@cup.org • URL: http://www.cup.org • 1993. $21.95.

Superconductor and Cyroelectronics. WestTech, P.O. Box 411506 San Francisco, CA 94141-1506. Phone: 800-446-7778 or (415)837-0891 Fax: (415)837-0327 E-mail: abitterman@aol.com • URL: http://www.superconductorweek.com • Quarterly. $22.00 per year.

Superconductor Week. WestTech, 5478 Wilshire Blvd., Suite 205 Los Angeles, CA 90036. Phone: (323)937-1211 Fax: (323)937-1030 URL: http://www.superconductorweek.com • Weekly. $397.00 per year. Newsletter. Covers applications of superconductivity and cryogenics, including new markets and products.

Supermarket Business. Bill Communications, Inc., 770 Broadway New York, NY 10003-9595. Phone: 800-266-4712 or (646)654-4500 Fax: (646)654-7212 URL: http://www.billcom.com • Monthly. $85.00 per year.

Supermarket News: The Industry's Weekly Newspaper. Fairchild Publications, Seven W. 34th St. New York, NY 10001. Phone: 800-932-4724 or (212)630-4000 Fax: (212)630-4760 E-mail: snedit@fairchildpub.com • URL: http://www.supermarketnews.com • Weekly. Individuals, $68.00 per year; instututions, $44.50 per year; corporations, $89.00 per year.

Superstudy of Sports Participation. Available from MarketResearch.com, 641 Ave. of the Americas, Third Floor New York, NY 10011. Phone: 800-298-5699 or (212)807-2629 Fax: (212)807-2716 E-mail: order@marketresearch.com • URL: http://www.marketresearch.com • 1999. $650.00. Three volumes. Published by American Sports Data, Inc. Provides market research data on 102 sports and activities. Vol. 1: *Physical Fitness Activities*. Vol. 2: *Recreational Sports*. Vol. 3: *Outdoor Activities*. (Volumes are available separately at $275.00.)

Supertrader's Almanac-Reference Manual: Reference Guide and Analytical Techniques for Investors. Market Movements, Inc., 5212 E. 69th St. Tulsa, OK 74136-3402. Phone: 800-878-7442 or (918)493-2897 Fax: (918)493-3892 E-mail: taucher@supertraderalmanac.com • URL: http://www.supertraderalmanac.com • 1991. $55.00. Explains technical methods for the trading of commodity futures, and includes data on seasonality, cycles, trends, contract characteristics, highs and lows, etc.

Supervision in the Hospitality Industry. Raphael R. Kavanaugh and Jack D. Ninemeier. Educational Institute of the American Hotel & Motel Association, P.O. Box 1240 East Lansing, MI 48826-1240. Phone: 800-344-4381 or (517)353-5500 Fax: (517)353-5527 E-mail: info@ei-ahma.org • URL: http://www.ei.ahma.org • 1998. $59.95. Third edition. Principles of communication, motivation, recruiting, training, etc.

Supplement Industry Executive. Vitamin Retailer Magazine, Inc., A-2 Brier Hill Court East Brunswick, NJ 08816. Phone: (732)432-9600 Fax: (732)432-9288 Bimonthly. $25.00 per year. Edited for manufacturers of vitamins and other dietary supplements. Covers marketing, new products, industry trends, regulations, manufacturing procedures, and related topics. Includes a directory of suppliers to the industry.

Suppliers of Advanced Composite Materials Association., 1600 Wilson Blvd., Suite 901 Arlington, VA 22209. Phone: (703)841-1556 Fax: (703)841-1559 E-mail: staff@sacma.org • URL: http://www.sacma.org • Members are manufacturers and suppliers of fiber-reinforced advanced composite finished products.

Supplier's Source Directory. Intertec Publishing Corp., 9800 Metcalf Ave. Overland Park, KS 66212-2286. Phone: 800-400-5945 or (913)341-1300 Fax: (913)967-1898 E-mail: subs@intertec.com • URL: http://www.intertec.com • Annual. $10.00. Lists companies that furnish services and equipment for new car dealers. Formerly *Auto Age Buyer's Guide*.

Supply, Distribution Manufacturing and Service: Supply and Service Companies and Equipment Manufacturers. Midwest Publishing Co., P.O. Box 50350 Tulsa, OK 74150-0350. Phone: 800-829-2002 or (918)583-2033 Fax: (918)587-9349 Annual. $115.00. 8,000 oil well supply stores, service companies, and equipment manufacturers. Formerly *Directory of Oil Well Supply Companies*.

Sure-Hire Resumes. Robbie M. Kaplan. Impact Publications, 9104 Manassas Dr., Suite N Manassas, VA 20111-5211. Phone: (703)361-7300 Fax: (703)335-9486 E-mail: impactp@impactpublicctions.com • URL: http://www.impactpublications.com • 1998. $14.95. Includes sample cover letters and 25 sample resumes.

Surface Coatings: Science and Technology. Swaraj Paul. John Wiley and Sons, Inc., 605 Third Ave. New York, NY 10158-0012. Phone: 800-526-5368 or (212)850-6000 Fax: (212)850-6088 E-mail: info@wiley.com • URL: http://www.wiley.com • 1996. $225.00. Second edition.

Surface Finishing Technology. ASM International, 9639 Kinsman Rd. Materials Park, OH 44073-0002. Phone: 800-336-5152 or (440)338-5151 Fax: (440)338-4634 E-mail: custserv@po.asm-intl.org • URL: http://www.asm-intl.org • Monthly. Members, $130.00 per year; non-members, $160.00 per year. Provides abstracts of the international literature of metallic and nonmetallic industrial coating and finishing. Formerly *Cleaning-Finishing-Coating Digest*.

Surface Treatment Technology Abstracts. Finishing Publications Ltd., 105 Whitney Dr., Stevenage Herts SG1 4BL 44, England. Phone: (441)438-745115 Fax: (441)438-364536 E-mail: finpubs@compuserve.com • URL: http://www.finpus.demon.co.uk • Bimonthly. $880.00 per year. Includes *Printed Circuits* and *Electronics Coating Abstracts*.

Surgeons' Desk Reference for Minimally Invasive Surgery Products. Medical Economics Co., Inc., Five Paragon Dr. Montvale, NJ 07645-1742. Phone: 800-232-7379 or (201)358-7200 Fax: (201)358-7522 E-mail: customer_service@medec.com • URL: http://www.medec.com • Annual. $125.00. A directory of products for laparoscopic surgery. Includes commentary.

Surgical Products. Cahners Business Information, 301 Gibraltar Dr. Morris Plains, NJ 07950-0650. Phone: 800-662-7776 or (973)292-5100 Fax: (973)539-3476 E-mail: corporatecommunications@cahners.com • URL: http://www.cahners.com • 10 times a year. $24.00 per year. Covers new Technology and products for surgeons and operation rooms.

Surplus Record: Index of Available Capital Equipment. Surplus Record, Inc., 20 N. Wacker Dr. Chicago, IL 60606. Phone: (312)372-9077 Fax: (312)372-6537 E-mail: surplus@surplusrecord.com • URL: http://www.surplusrecord.com • Monthly. $33.00 per year. Lists over 46,000 items of used and surplus machine tools, chemical processing and electrical equipment.

Survey and Analysis of Employee Relocation Policies and Costs. Runzheimer International, Runzheimer Park Rochester, WI 53167. Phone: 800-942-9949 or (414)767-2200 Fax: (414)767-2276 URL: http://www.runzheimer.com • Annual. Based on surveys of relocation administrators.

Survey of Advanced Technology. Computer Economics, Inc., 5841 Edison Place Carlsbad, CA 92008-6519. Phone: 800-326-8100 or (760)438-8100 Fax: (760)431-1126 E-mail: custserv@compecon.com • URL: http://www.computereconomics.com • Annual. $795.00. Surveys the corporate use (or neglect) of advanced computer technology. Topics include major technology trends and emerging technologies.

Survey of Black Newspapers in America. Mercer House Press, Clover Leaf Farm, Old Route Nine, R.F.D. 1 Biddeford, ME 04005. Phone: (207)282-7116 1980. $6.00. (Mass Communication and Journalism Series).

Survey of Business Travelers. Travel Industry Association of America, 1100 New York Ave., N. W., Suite 240 Washington, DC 20005-3934. Phone: (202)408-8422 Fax: (202)408-1255 E-mail: rmcclur@tia.org • URL: http://www.tia.org • Biennial. Members, $100.00 per year; non-members, $175.00 per year.

Survey of Corporate Contributions. Conference Board, Inc., 845 Third Ave. New York, NY 10022-6679. Phone: (212)759-0900 Fax: (212)980-7014 E-mail: lei@conference-board.org • URL: http://www.tcb-indicators.org • Annual.

Survey of Current Business. Available from U. S. Government Printing Office, Washington, DC 20402. Phone: (202)512-1800 Fax: (202)512-2250 E-mail: gpoaccess@gpo.gov • URL: http://www.access.gpo.gov • Monthly. $49.00 per year. Issued by Bureau of Economic Analysis, U. S. Department of Commerce. Presents a wide variety of business and economic data.

Survey of Industrials. Financial Post Datagroup, 333 King St., E. Toronto, ON, Canada M5A 4N2. Phone: 800-387-9011 or (416)350-6477 Fax: (416)350-6501 E-mail: fpdg@fpdata.finpost.com • Annual. $119.95 Contains detailed information on more than 2,200 publicly owned Canadian manufacturing, retailing, and service corporations. Includes the ''Financial Post 500,'' a ranking of the largest Canadian companies.

Survey of Industry Activity. Equipment Leasing Association of America, 4301 N. Fairfax Ave., Suite 550 Arlington, VA 22203-1608. Phone: (703)527-8655 Fax: (703)527-2649 E-mail: ela@elamail.com • URL: http://www.elaonline.com/ • Annual. $395.00. Provides financial and statistical data on the equipment leasing industry.

Survey of Law Firm Economics: A Management and Planning Tool. Altman Weil Publications, Inc., Two Campus Blvd. Newtown Square, PA 19073. Phone: 888-782-7297 or (610)359-9900 Fax: (610)359-0467 E-mail: info@altmanweil.com • URL: http://www.altmanweil.com • Annual. $595.00. Provides aggregate economic statistics and financial data (benchmarks) relating to the legal profession in the U. S. Includes income, expenses, hourly rates, billable hours, compensation, staffing, data by states, and trends. Most information is arranged by region, firm size, years of experience, and other factors.

Survey of Mortgage Lending Activity. U.S. Department of Housing and Urban Development, 451 Seventh St., S.W. Washington, DC 20410. Phone: (202)708-0980 Monthly.

Survey of Salaries. American Assembly of Collegiate Schools of Business, 605 Old Ballas Rd., Suite 220 Saint Louis, MO 63141. Phone: (314)872-8481 Fax: (314)872-8495 URL: http://www.aacsb.edu • Annual. $20.00, Reports aggregate salary data of business school administrators and faculty.

Survey Research. Survey Research Laboratory, University of Illinois, 909 W. Oregon St., Suite 300 Urbana, IL 61801. Phone: (217)333-4273 Fax: (217)244-4408 E-mail: survey@srl.uic.edu • URL: http://www.srl.uic.edu • Three times a year. Individuals, $10.00 per year; institutions, $50.00-$500.00 per year. Includes information on current research and descriptions of recent methodological publications on survey research.

Survey Research Center., University of California at Berkeley, 2538 Channing Way Berkeley, CA 94720-5100. Phone: (510)642-6578 Fax: (510)643-8292 E-mail: hbrady@bravo.berkeley.edu • URL: http://www.grad.berkeley.edu:4229/ • Research areas include the utilization and development of survey methods.

Survey Research Handbook: Guidelines and Strategies for Conducting a Survey. Pamela L. Alreck and Robert B. Settle. McGraw-Hill Higher Education, 1221 Ave. of the Americas New York, NY 10020. Phone: 800-722-4726 or (212)904-2000 Fax: (212)904-2072 E-mail: customer.service@mcgraw-hill.com • URL: http://www.mcgraw-hill.com • 1994. $50.00. Second edition. Consists of four major parts: 1. Planning and Designing the Survey, 2. Developing Survey Instruments, 3. Collecting and Processing Data, 4. Interpreting and Reporting Results. Includes a glossary and index. (Marketing Series).

Survey Research Laboratory., University of Illinois at Chicago, 410 S. Peoria St. Chicago, IL 60607. Phone: (312)996-5300 Fax: (312)996-3358 E-mail: info@srl.uic.edu • URL: http://www.srl.uic.edu • Research areas include survey methodology and sampling techniques.

Surveying and Land Information Systems: Devoted to the Advancement of the Sciences of Surveying and Mapping. American Congress on Surveying and Mapping, 5410 Grosvenor Lane, Suite 100 Bethesda, MD 20814. Phone: (301)493-0200 Fax: (301)493-8245 E-mail: infoacsm@mindspring.com • URL: http://www.survmap.org • Quarterly. Free to members; non-members, $90.00 per year. Formerly *Surveying and Mapping*.

Surviving Your Dissertation: A Comprehensive Guide to Content and Process. Kjell E. Rudestam and Rae R. Newton. Sage Publications, Inc., 2455 Teller Rd. Thousand Oaks, CA 91320. Phone: (805)499-0721 Fax: (805)499-0871 E-mail: info@sagepub.com • URL: http://www.sagepub.com • 2000. Price on application. Provides general advice on how to successfully complete a dissertation or thesis.

Sustainability Perspectives for Resources and Business. Orie L. Loucks and others. Saint Lucie Press, 2000 Corporate Blvd., N. W. Boca Raton, FL 33431-7372. Phone: 800-272-7737 or (561)274-9906 Fax: 800-374-3401 or (561)274-9927 E-mail: information@slpress.com • URL: http://www.slpress.com • 1999. $44.95. Discusses the business and economic aspects of environmental protection.

Swap and Derivative Financing: The Global Reference to Products Pricing Applications and Markets. Satyajit Das. McGraw-Hill Professional, 1221 Ave. of the Americas New York, NY 10020-1095. Phone: 800-722-4726 or (212)904-2000 Fax: (212)904-2072 E-mail: customer.service@mcgraw-hill.com • URL: http://www.mcgraw-hill.com • 1993. $95.00. Second revised edition.

Swap Literacy. Elizabeth Ungar. Bloomberg Press, 100 Business Park Dr. Princeton, NJ 08542-0888. Phone: 800-388-2749 or (609)279-4670 Fax: (609)279-7155 E-mail: press@bloomberg.net • URL: http://www.bloomberg.com • 1996. $40.00. Written for corporate finance officers. Provides basic information on arbitrage, hedging, and speculation, involving interest rate, currency, and other types of financial swaps. (Bloomberg Professional Library.)

Swaps and Financial Engineering: A Self-Study Guide to Mastering and Applying Swaps and Financial Engineering. Coopers and Lybrand Staff. McGraw-Hill Professional, 1221 Ave. of the Americas New York, NY 10020. Phone: 800-722-4726 or (212)904-2000 Fax: (212)904-2072 E-mail: customer.servicemcgraw-hill.com • URL: http://www.mcgraw-hill.com • 1994. $55.00.

SWE. Anne Perusek, editor. Society of Women Engineers, 120 Wall St., 11th Fl. New York, NY 10005-3902. Phone: (212)705-7855 Fax: (212)319-0947 Bimonthly. Members, $10.00 per year; non-members, $20.00 per year. Covers technical articles, continuing development, career guidance and recruitment and product advertising. Formerly *U.S. Woman Engineer*.

Sweaty Palms: The Neglected Art of Being Interviewed. H. Anthony Medley. Ten Speed Press, 999 Harrison St. Berkeley, CA 94707. Phone: 800-841-2665 or (510)559-1600 Fax: (510)524-1052 E-mail: order@tenspeed.com • URL: http://www.tenspeed.com • 1991. $8.95. Revised edition.

Sweetener Users Association., 3231 Valley Lane Falls Church, VA 22044. Phone: (703)532-2683 Fax: (703)532-9361 Members are industrial users of sweeteners and companies in the sweetener industry.

Swimming Pool-Spa Age. Intertec Publishing Corp., 6151 Powers Ferry Rd., N.W., Suite 200 Atlanta, GA 30339. Phone: 800-400-5945 or (770)955-2500 Fax: (770)955-0400 E-mail: subs@intertec.com • URL: http://www.intertec.com • Monthly. $48.00 per year. Includes annual *Data and Reference Directory*. Formerly *Swimming Pool Age and Swimming Pool Merchandiser*.

Swimming Pool/Spa Age-Product Directory. Intertec Publishing Corp., 6151 Powers Ferry Rd., N.W., Suite 200 Atlanta, GA 30339. Phone: 800-400-5945 or (770)955-2500 Fax: (770)955-0400 E-mail: subs@intertec.com • URL: http://www.intertec.com • Annual. $44.95. About 2,000 manufacturers of swimming pool and spa equipment. Formerly *Swimming Pool and Spa Age-Data and Reference Annual*.

Switchboard. Switchboard, Inc.Phone: (508)898-1000 Fax: (508)898-1755 E-mail: webmaster@switchboard.com • URL: http://www.switchboard.com • Web site provides telephone numbers and street addresses for more than 100 million business locations and residences in the U. S. Broad industry categories are available. Fees: Free.

SYNERJY: A Directory of Renewable Energy. Synerjy, P.O. Box 1854, Cathedral Station New York, NY 10025. Phone: (212)865-9595 E-mail: synerjy@worldnet.att.net • Semiannual. Individuals, $30.00 per year; others, $62.00 per year. Includes organizations, publishers, and other resources. Lists articles, patents, government publications, research groups and facilities.

Synthetic Organic Chemical Manufacturers Association., 1850 M St., N.W., Suite 700 Washington, DC 20036. Phone: (202)721-4100 Fax: (202)296-8120 URL: http://www.socma.com • Members are manufacturers of synthetic organic chemicals, many of which are made from petroleum or natural gas.

Synthetic Organic Chemicals: United States Production and Sales. International Trade Commission. Available from U.S. Government Printing Office, Washington, DC 20402. Phone: (202)512-1800 Fax: (202)512-2250 E-mail: gpoaccess@gpo.gov • URL: http://www.accessgpo.gov • Annual.

SysAdmin: The Journal for Unix System Administrators. Miller Freeman, Inc., 55 Hawthorne St., Suite 600 San Francisco, CA 94105. Phone: (415)808-3900 Fax: (415)808-3995 E-mail: mfibooks@mfi.com • URL: http://www.mfi.com • Monthly. $39.00 per year. Provides technical information for managers of Unix systems.

System Administrator's Guide to Windows NT Server 5. Robin Burke. Simon And Schuster Trade, 1230 Ave. of the Americas New York, NY 10020. Phone: 800-223-2348 or (212)698-7000 Fax: 800-943-9831 or (212)698-7007 E-mail: ssonline_feedback@simonsays.com • URL: http://www.simonsays.com • 1999. $49.99.

System Integration. Jeffrey O. Grady. CRC Press, Inc., 2000 Corporate Blvd., N. W. Boca Raton, FL 33431-7372. Phone: 800-272-7737 or (561)994-0555 E-mail: orders@crcpress.com • URL: http://www.crcpress.com • 1994. $99.95. (Systems Engineering Series).

System Integration with Corba. Thomas Mowbray and Ron Zahavi. John Wiley and Sons, Inc., 605 Third Ave. New York, NY 10158-0012. Phone: 800-225-5945 or (212)850-6000 Fax: (212)850-6088 E-mail: info@wiley.com • URL: http://www.wiley.com • 1996. $49.95. Corba is ''common object request broker architecture.''

Systems Analysis and Design. Kenneth E. Kendall and Julie E. Kendall. Prentice Hall, 240 Frisch Court Paramus, NJ 07652-5240. Phone: 800-947-7700 or (201)909-6200 Fax: 800-445-6991 URL: http://www.prenhall.com • 1998. $90.67. Fourth edition.

Systems and Decision Making: A Management Science Approach. Hans G. Daellenbach. John Wiley and Sons, Inc., 605 Third Ave. New York, NY 10158-0012. Phone: 800-225-5945 or (212)850-6000 Fax: (212)850-6088 E-mail: info@wiley.com • URL: http://www.wiley.com • 1994. $118.95.

Systems Approach to Computer-Integrated Design and Manufacturing. Nanua Singh. John Wiley and Sons, Inc., 605 Third Ave. New York, NY 10158-0012. Phone: 800-225-5945 or (212)850-6000 Fax: (212)850-6088 E-mail: info@wiley.com • URL: http://www.wiley.com • 1995. $99.95.

Systems Engineering: Concepts and Applications. Andrew P. Sage. John Wiley and Sons, Inc., 605 Third Ave. New York, NY 10158-0012. Phone: 800-526-5368 or (212)850-6000 Fax: (212)850-6088 E-mail: info@wiley.com • URL: http://www.wiley.com • 1992. $84.95. Discusses practical engineering techniques for use in given situations. (Systems Engineering Series).

Systems User. Caulfield Publishing Ltd, 308 E. Van Buren St. Janesville, WI 53545-4047. Monthly. $62.00 per year.

T H E Journal (Technological Horizons in Education). Ed Warnshius Ltd., 150 El Camino Real, Suite 112 Tustin, CA 92680-3670. Phone: (714)730-4011 Fax: (714)730-3739 E-mail: cedwards@thejournal.com • URL: http://www.thejournal.com • 11 times a year. $29.00 per year. For educators of all levels.

Tablebase. Responsive Database Services, Inc., 23611 Chagrin Blvd., Suite 320 Beachwood, OH 44122. Phone: 800-313-2212 or (216)292-9620 Fax: (216)292-9621 E-mail: customer_service@rdsinc.com • URL: http://www.rdsinc.com • Provides online numerical tabular data from a wide variety of business, organization, and government sources, including 900 trade journals. Includes industry and individual company statistics relating to products, market share, sales forecasts, production, exports, market trends, etc. Time span is 1997 to date. Weekly updates. Inquire as to online cost and availability. (Also available in a CD-ROM version.)

Tables of Redemption Values for United States Savings Bonds, Series EE. Available from U. S. Government Printing Office, Washington, DC 20402. Phone: (202)512-1800 Fax: (202)512-2250 E-mail: gpoaccess@gpo.gov • URL: http://www.access.gpo.gov • Semiannual. $5.00 per year. Issued by the Public Debt Bureau, U. S. Treasury Department.

Tables of Redemption Values for United States Series E Savings Bonds and Saving Notes. Available from U. S. Government Printing Office, Washington, DC 20402. Phone: (202)512-1800 Fax: (202)512-2250 E-mail: gpoaccess@gpo.gov • URL: http://www.access.gpo.gov • Semiannual. $5.00 per year. Issued by the Public Debt Bureau, U. S. Treasury Department.

The Tabletop Market. Available from MarketResearch.com, 641 Ave. of the Americas, Third Floor New York, NY 10011. Phone: 800-298-5699 or (212)807-2629 Fax: (212)807-2716 E-mail: order@marketresearch.com • URL: http://www.marketresearch.com • 2000. $2,750.00. Published by Packaged Facts. Provides market data on dinnerware, glassware, and flatware, with projections to 2002.

Taft Monthly Portfolio. Taft Group, 27500 Drake Rd. Farmington Hills, MI 48331-3535. Phone: 800-877-GALE or (248)699-GALE Fax: 800-414-5043 or (248)699-8069 E-mail: galeord@gale.com • URL: http://www.taftgroup.com • Monthly. $75.00 per year. New ideas and proven techniques used by universitites, hospitals and a wide range of other nonprofit organizations to raise philanthropic gifts. Formerly *FRI Monthly Portfolio*.

Tag and Label Manufacturers Institute.

Taga Newsletter. Technical Association of the Graphic Arts, P.O. Box 9887 Rochester, NY 14623. Phone: (716)475-7470 Fax: (716)475-2250 Quarterly. Membership.

Taiwan Business: The Portable Encyclopedia for Doing Business with Taiwan. World Trade Press, 1450 Grant Ave., Suite 204 Novato, CA 94945-3142. Phone: 800-833-8586 or (415)898-1124 Fax: (415)898-1080 E-mail: worldpress@aol.com • URL: http://www.worldtradepress.com • 1994. $24.95. Covers economic data, import/export possibilities, basic tax and trade laws, travel information, and other useful facts for doing business with Taiwan. (Country Business Guides).

The Take-Charge Assistant. American Management Association, 1601 Broadway New York, NY 10019-7420. Phone: 800-262-9699 or (212)586-8100 Fax: (212)903-8168 E-mail: amapubs@aol.com • URL: http://www.amanet.org • Monthly. $75.00 per year. Newsletter. Provides advice on personal and professional skills for office assistants.

Taking Rights Seriously. Ronald Dworkin. Harvard University Press, 79 Garden St. Cambridge, MA 02138. Phone: 800-448-2242 or (617)495-2600 Fax: 800-962-4983 or (617)495-4898 E-mail: contacthup@harvard.edu • URL: http://www.hup.harvard.edu • 1977. $40.50.

Taking the Mystery Out of TQM: A Practical Guide to Total Quality Management. Peter Capezio and Debra Morehouse. Career Press, Inc., P.O. Box 687 Franklin Lakes, NJ 07417-1322. Phone: 800-227-3371 or (201)848-0310 Fax: (201)848-1727 E-mail: careerprs@aol.com • URL: http://www.careerpress.com • 1995. $16.99. Second edition. A step-by-step guide for managers, executives, and entrepreneurs.

Tanker Market Quarterly. Available from Informa Publishing Group Ltd., PO Box 1017 Westborough, MA 01581-6017. Phone: 800-493-4080 Fax: (508)231-0856 E-mail: enquiries@informa.com • URL: http://www.informa.com • Quarterly. $495.00 per year. Published in the UK by Lloyd's List (http://www.lloydslist.com). Provides supply and demand information ''required to make accurate market decisions.'' Includes detailed graphs and analytical commentary.

Tanker Operations: A Handbook for the Ship's Officer. G. S. Marton. Cornell Maritime Press, Inc., P.O. Box 456 Centreville, MD 21617. Phone: 800-638-7641 or (410)758-1075 Fax: (410)758-6849 E-mail: cornell@crosslink.net • 2000. $45.00. Fourth edition.

The Tanker Register. Clarkson Research Studies, Ltd., 12 Camomile St. London EC3A 7BP, England. Phone: 44 171 3343131 Fax: 44 171 5220330 Annual. $290.00. Details more than 3,300 tankers and combined carriers throughout the world having deadweight tonnage exceeding 10,000, and their owners and managers.

TAPPI.

TAPPI Journal. Technical Association of the Pulp and Paper Industry, Inc., P.O. Box 105113 Atlanta, GA 30348. Phone: (770)446-1400 Fax: (770)446-6947 E-mail: dmeadows@tappi.org • URL: http://www.tappi.org • Monthly. Membership.

Tapping the Government Grapevine: The User-Friendly Guide to U. S. Government Information Sources. Judith S. Robinson. Oryx Press, 4041 N. Central Ave., 700 Phoenix, AZ 85012-3397. Phone: 800-279-6799 or (602)265-2651 Fax: 800-279-4663 or (602)265-6250 E-mail: info@oryxpress.com • URL: http://oryxpress.com • 1998. $45.50. Third edition. Includes source information on statistics, regulations, patents, technology, nonprint items, bibliographies, and indexes. A special chapter by Karen Smith covers ''Foreign and International Documents.''

Target Marketing: The Leading Magazine for Integrated Database Marketing. North American Publishing Co., 401 N. Broad St. Philadelphia, PA 19108-9988. Phone: 800-627-2689 or (215)238-5300 Fax: (215)238-5457 E-mail: dbrennan@napco.com • URL: http://www.napco.com • Monthly. $65.00 per year. Dedicated to direct marketing excellence. Formerly *Zip Target Marketing*.

Targeting Teens Newsletter. Available from MarketResearch.com, 641 Ave. of the Americas, Third Floor New York, NY 10011. Phone: 800-298-5699 or (212)807-2629 Fax: (212)807-2716 E-mail: order@maeketresearch.com • URL: http://www.marketresearch.com • Monthly. $199.00 per year. Published by Children's Market Research, Inc. Provides current data and information for marketing to the 12 to 18 age group.

Tax Administrators News. Federation of Tax Administrators, 444 N. Capitol St., N.W., Suite 348 Washington, DC 20001. Phone: (202)624-5890 Fax: (202)624-7888 URL: http://www.taxadmin.org • Monthly. $35.00 per year.

Tax-Advantaged Securities. Robert J. Haft and Peter M. Fass, editors. West Group, 610 Opperman Dr. Eagan, MN 55123. Phone: 800-328-4880 or (651)687-7000 Fax: 800-213-2323 or (651)687-5827 URL: http://www.westgroup.com • 10 times a year. $280.00 per year. Newsletter. Formerly *Investment Limited Partnerships Law Report*.

The Tax Adviser: A Magazine of Tax Planning, Trends and Techniques. American Institute of Certified Public Accountants, 1211 Ave. of the Americas New York, NY 10036-8775. Phone: 800-862-4272 or (212)596-6200 Fax: (212)596-6213 E-mail: journal@aicpa.org • URL: http://www.aicpa.org/pubs • Monthly. Members, $71.00 per year; non-members, $98.00 per year. Newsletter.

Tax Analysts., 6830 N. Fairfax Dr. Arlington, VA 22213. Phone: 800-955-3444 or (703)533-4400 Fax: (703)533-4444 E-mail: webmaster@tax.org • URL: http://www.tax.org • An advocacy group reviewing U. S. and foreign income tax developments. Includes a Tax Policy Advisory Board.

Tax Analysts ÎWeb sitel. Tax AnalystsPhone: 800-955-3444 or (703)533-4400 Fax: (703)533-4444 URL: http://www.tax.org • The three main sections of Tax Analysts home page are ''Tax News'' (Today's Tax News, Feature of the Week, Tax Snapshots, Tax Calendar); ''Products & Services'' (Product Catalog, Press Releases); and ''Public Interest'' (Discussion Groups, Tax Clinic, Tax History Project). Fees: Free for coverage of current tax events; fee-based for comprehensive information. Daily updating.

Tax Avoidance Digest. Agora, Inc., 105 W. Monument Baltimore, MD 21201. Phone: (410)223-2500 Fax: (410)223-2696 Monthly. $71.00 per year. Includes digests of tax advice from other publications.

The Tax Directory. Tax Analysts, 6830 N. Fairfax Dr. Arlington, VA 22213. Phone: 800-955-3444 or (703)533-4400 Fax: (703)533-4444 E-mail: webmaster@tax.org • URL: http://www.tax.org • Annual. $299.00. ($399.00 with quarterly CD-ROM updates.) Four volumes: *Government Officials Worldwide* (lists 15,000 state, federal, and international tax officials, with basic corporate and individual income tax rates for 100 countries); *Private Sector Professionals Worldwide* (lists 25,000 U.S. and foreign tax practitioners: accountants, lawyers, enrolled agents, and actuarial firms); *Corporate Tax Managers Worldwide* (lists 10,000 tax managers employed by U.S. and foreign companies).

The Tax Directory ÎCD-ROMl. Tax Analysts, 6830 North Fairfax Drive Arlington, VA 22213. Phone: 800-955-3444 or (703)533-4600 Fax: (703)533-4444 E-mail: taxdir@tax.org • URL: http://www.tax.org • Quarterly. Provides *The Tax Directory* listings on CD-ROM, covering federal, state, and international tax officials, tax practitioners, and corporate tax executives.

Tax Examples. John C. Wisdom. West Group, 610 Opperman Dr. Eagan, MN 55123. Phone: 800-328-4880 or (651)687-7000 Fax: 800-213-2323 or (651)687-5827 URL: http://www.westgroup.com • 1993. $125.00. Presents yearly examples, with forms, of a wide variety of tax problems and issues. Subjects include taxable income, deductions, alternative minimum tax, dependents, gift taxes, partnerships, and other problem areas. Includesaccounting method considerations. (Tax Series).

The Tax Executive. Tax Executives Institute, 1200 G St., N.W., No. 300 Washington, DC 20005-3814. Phone: (202)638-5601 Fax: (202)638-5607 Bimonthly. $115.00 per year. Professional journal for corporate tax executives.

Tax Executives Institute.

Tax Foundation.

Tax Guide for Small Business. U.S. Department of the Treasury, Internal Revenue Service. Available from U.S. Government Printing Office, Washington, DC 20402. Phone: (202)512-1800 Fax: (202)512-2250 E-mail: gpoaccess@gpo.gov • URL: http://www.accessgpo.gov • Annual. $5.00.

Tax Law Review. New York University, School of Law. Warren, Gorham and Lamont/RIA Group, 395 Hudson St. New York, NY 10014. Phone: 800-950-1215 or (212)367-6300 Fax: (212)367-6718 E-mail: customer_service@riag.com • URL: http://www.riahome.com • Quarterly. $149.00 per year.

Tax Legislation 2001: Highlights. CCH, Inc., 4025 West Peterson Ave. Chicago, IL 60646-6085. Phone: 800-248-3248 or (773)866-6000 Fax: 800-224-8299 or (773)866-3608 E-mail: cust_serv@cch.com • URL: http://www.cch.com • 2001. $7.00. Booklet summarizes significant changes in U. S. tax law resulting from the legislation of 2001.

Tax Legislation 2001: Law, Explanation, and Analysis. CCH, Inc., 4025 West Peterson Ave. Chicago, IL 60646-6085. Phone: 800-248-3248 or (773)866-6000 Fax: 800-224-8299 or (773)866-3608 E-mail: cust_serv@cch.com • URL: http://www.cch.com • 2001. $42.50. Provides explanation and interpretation of federal tax legislation enacted in 2001.

Tax Management Compensation Planning Journal. Bureau of National Affairs, Inc., 1231 25th St., N.W. Washington, DC 20037-1197. Phone: 800-371-1033 or (202)452-4200 Fax: (202)452-8092 E-mail: books@bna.com • URL: http://www.bna.com • Monthly. $426.00 per year. Formerly *Compensation Planning Journal*.

Tax Management International Forum. Bureau of National Affairs, Inc., 1231 25th St., N.W. Washington, DC 20037-1197. Phone: 800-372-1033 or (202)452-4200 Fax: (202)452-8092 E-mail: books@bna.com • URL: http://www.bna.com • Quarterly. $370.00 per year.

Tax Management International Journal: A Monthly Professional Review of Current International Tax Developments. Bureau of National Affairs, Inc., 1231 25th St., N.W. Washington, DC 20037-1197. Phone: 800-372-1033 or (202)452-4200 Fax: (202)452-8092 E-mail: books@bna.com • URL: http://www.bna.com • Monthly. $426.00 per year.

Tax Management Weekly Report. Tax Management Inc., 1231 25th St., N.W. Washington, DC 20037. Phone: 800-223-7270 or (202)785-7191 Fax: (202)785-7195 URL: http://www.bnatax.com • Weekly. 1,073.00 per year. Newsletter.

Tax Notes International. Tax Analysts, 6830 N. Fairfax Dr. Arlington, VA 22213. Phone: 800-955-3444 or (703)533-4400 Fax: (703)533-4444 E-mail: webmaster@tax.org • URL: http://www.tax.org • Weekly. $949.00 per year. Newsletter. Provides ''news and in-depth reports on a variety of international tax topics.'' Summarizes tax statutes, regulations, rulings, court decisions, and treaties from various countries of the world.

Tax Notes: The Weekly Tax Service. Tax Analysts, 6830 N. Fairfax Dr. Arlington, VA 22213. Phone: 800-955-3444 or (703)533-4400 Fax: (703)533-4444 E-mail: webmaster@tax.org • URL: http://www.tax.org • Weekly. $1,699.00 per year. Includes an *Annual* and 1985-1996 compliations on CD-ROM. Newsletter. Covers ''tax news from all federal sources,'' including congressional committees, tax courts, and the Internal Revenue Service. Each issue contains ''summaries of every document that pertains to federal tax law,'' with citations. Commentary is provided.

Tax Penalties and Interest Handbook. Howard Davidoff and David A. Minars. LEXIS Publishing, 701 E. Water St. Charlottesville, VA 22902. Phone: 800-446-3410 or (804)972-7600 Fax: 800-643-1280 or (804)972-7686 E-mail: custserv@michie.com • URL: http://www.lexislawpublishing • $80.00. Looseleaf. Annual supplements.

Tax Planning and Compliance for Tax-Exempt Organizations: Forms, Checklists, Procedures. Jody Blazek. John Wiley and Sons, Inc., 605 Third Ave. New York, NY 10158-0012. Phone: 800-225-5945 or (212)850-6000 Fax: (212)850-6088 E-mail: info@wiley.com • URL: http://www.wiley.com • 1999. $135.00. Third edition. Annual supplements available. (Wiley Nonprofit, Law, Finance, and Management Series).

Tax Planning for Corporations and Shareholders: Forms. Matthew Bender & Co., Inc., Two Park Ave. New York, NY 10016. Phone: 800-223-1940 or (212)448-2000 Fax: (212)244-3188 E-mail: international@bender.com • URL: http://www.bender.com • $200.00. Looseleaf service. Periodic supplementation.

Tax Planning for Dispositions of Business Interests. Theodore Ness and William Indoe. Warren, Gorham & Lamont/RIA Group, 395 Hudson St. New York, NY 10014. Phone: 800-950-1215 or (212)367-6300 Fax: (212)337-4280 E-mail: customer_services@riag.com • URL: http://www.riahome.com • $145.00. Biennial supplementation.

Tax Planning for Highly Compensated Individuals. Robert E. Madden. Warren, Gorham & Lamont/RIA Group, 395 Hudson St. New York, NY 10014. Phone: 800-950-1215 or (212)367-6300 Fax: (212)337-4280 E-mail: customer_services@riag.com • URL: http://www.riahome.com • Looseleaf service. $160.00. Biennial supplementation.

Tax Planning for Individuals and Small Businesses. Sidney Kess. CCH, Inc., 4025 West Peterson Ave. Chicago, IL 60646-6085. Phone: 800-248-3248 or (773)866-6000 Fax: 800-224-8299 or (773)866-3608 E-mail: cust_serv@cch.com • URL: http://www.cch.com • 2000. $49.00. Includes illustrations, charts, and sample client letters. Edited primarily for accountants and lawyers.

Tax Policy and the Economy. MIT Press, Five Cambridge Center Cambridge, MA 02142-1493. Phone: 800-356-0343 or (617)253-5646 Fax: (617)253-6779 E-mail: mitpress-orders@mit.edu • URL: http://www.mitpress.mit.edu • Annual. $30.00. Reviews ''issues in the current tax debate.'' Produced by the National Bureau of Economic Research. (Tax Policy and the Economy Series).

Tax Practice. Tax Analysts, 6830 N. Fairfax Dr. Arlington, VA 22213. Phone: 800-955-3444 or (703)533-4400 Fax: (703)533-4444 E-mail: webmaster@tax.org • URL: http://www.tax.org • Weekly. $199.00 per year. Newsletter. Covers news affecting tax practitioners and litigators, with emphasis on federal court decisions, rules and regulations, and tax petitions. Provides a guide to Internal Revenue Service audit issues.

Tax Preparation Service. Entrepreneur Media, Inc., 2445 McCabe Way Irvine, CA 92614. Phone: 800-421-2300 or (949)261-2325 Fax: (949)261-0234 E-mail: entmag@entrepreneur.com • URL: http://www.entrepreneur.com • Looseleaf. $59.50. A practical guide to starting a business for the preparation of income tax returns. Covers profit potential, start-up costs, market size evaluation, owner's time required, site selection, lease negotiation, pricing, accounting, advertising, promotion, etc. (Start-Up Business Guide No. E2332.)

The Tax Reform Act of 1986 and Its Impact on the Real Estate Industry. Marilyn Hankel. Sage Publications, Inc., 2455 Teller Rd. Thousand Oaks, CA 91320. Phone: (805)499-0721 Fax: (805)499-0871 E-mail: info@sagepub.com • URL: http://www.sagepub.com • 1993. $10.00.

Tax Strategies for the Self-Employed. CCH, Inc., 4025 W. Peterson Ave. Chicago, IL 60646-6085. Phone: 800-248-3248 or (773)866-6000 Fax: 800-224-8299 or (773)866-3608 URL: http://www.cch.com • Annual. $89.00 Covers tax-deferred retirement plans.

Tax Strategies for the Self-Employed. CCH, Inc., 4025 West Peterson Ave. Chicago, IL 60646-6085. Phone: 800-248-3248 or (773)866-6000 Fax: 800-224-8299 or (773)866-3608 E-mail: cust_serv@cch.com • URL: http://www.cch.com • 2001. $89.00. Covers accounting methods, start-up expenses, transportation deductions, depreciation, pension deductions, tax penalties, and other topics related to tax planning for the self-employed.

Tax Year in Review. CCH, Inc., 4025 W. Peterson Ave. Chicago, IL 60646-6085. Phone: 800-248-3248 or (773)866-6000 Fax: 800-224-8299 or (773)866-3608 URL: http://www.cch.com • Annual. Covers the year's ''major new legislative and regulatory changes.''

Taxation and Revenue Policies: State Capitals. Wakeman-Walworth, Inc., P.O. Box 7376 Alexandria, VA 22307-0376. Phone: 800-876-2545 or (703)549-8606 Fax: (703)549-1372 E-mail: newsletters@statecapitals.com • URL: http://www.statecapitals.com • Weekly. $345.00 per year. Formerly *From the State Capitals: Taxation and Revenue Policies*.

Taxation for Accountants. Warren, Gorham & Lamont/RIA Group, 395 Hudson St. New York, NY 10014. Phone: 800-950-1215 or (212)367-6300 Fax: (212)337-4280 E-mail: customer_services@riag.com • URL: http://

www.riahome.com • Monthly. $125.00. per year. Emphasis is on current tax developments as they affect accountants and their clients. Includes advice on tax software and computers.

Taxation for Lawyers. Warren, Gorham & Lamont/RIA Group, 395 Hudson St. New York, NY 10014. Phone: 800-950-1215 or (212)367-6300 Fax: (212)924-0460 URL: http://www.wgl.com • Bimonthly. $114.98 per year. Edited for attorneys who are not tax specialists. Emphasis is on tax planning, estates, trusts, partnerships, and taxation of real estate.

Taxation of Financially Distressed Businesses. David B. Newman. West Group, 610 Opperman Dr. Eagan, MN 55123. Phone: 800-328-4880 or (651)687-7000 Fax: 800-213-2323 or (651)687-5827 URL: http://www.westgroup.com • 1993. $120.00. Covers bankruptcy, foreclosure, abandonment, legal reporting requirements, and other tax-related subjects. (Tax Series).

Taxation of Real Estate Transactions. Sanford M. Guerin. Shepard's, 555 Middle Creek Parkway Colorado Springs, CO 80921. Phone: 800-743-7393 or (719)481-7371 Fax: 800-525-0053 or (719)481-7621 E-mail: customer_service@shepards.com • URL: http://www.shepards.com • 1988. $195.00. Second edition. Two volumes. Covers deferred payment sales, non-taxable exchanges, wraparound financing, defaults, foreclosures, and repossessions. Formerly *Taxation of Real Estate Dispositions*.

Taxation of Securities Transactions. Matthew Bender & Co., Inc., 1275 Broadway Albany, NY 12204-2694. Phone: 800-833-9844 or (518)487-3000 Fax: (518)487-3584 E-mail: customer.support@bender.com • URL: http://www.bender.com • $260.00. Looseleaf service.Periodic supplementation. Covers taxation of a wide variety of securities transactions, including those involving stocks, bonds, options, short sales, new issues, mutual funds, dividend distributions, foreign securities, and annuities.

Taxation of the Closely Held Corporation. Theodore Ness and Eugene L. Vogel. Warren, Gorham and Lamont/RIA Group, 395 Hudson St. New York, NY 10014. Phone: 800-950-1215 or (212)367-6300 Fax: (212)367-6718 E-mail: customer_service@riag.com • URL: http://www.riahome.com • Looseleaf service. $160.00 per year. Periodic supplementation.

Taxes on Parade. CCH, Inc., 4025 W. Peterson Ave. Chicago, IL 60646-6085. Phone: 800-248-3248 or (773)866-6000 Fax: 800-224-8299 or (773)866-3608 URL: http://www.cch.com • Weekly. $113.00 per year. Newsletter.

Taxes-Property: State Capitals. Wakeman-Walworth, Inc., P.O. Box 7376 Alexandria, VA 22307-0376. Phone: 800-876-2545 or (703)549-8606 Fax: (703)549-1372 E-mail: newsletters@statecapitals.com • URL: http://www.statecapitals.com • Weekly. $345.00 per year. Formerly *From the State Capitals: Taxes-Property*.

Taxes: The Tax Magazine. CCH, Inc., 4025 W. Peterson Ave. Chicago, IL 60646-6085. Phone: 800-248-3248 or (773)866-6000 Fax: 800-224-8299 or (773)866-3608 URL: http://www.cch.com • Monthly. $195.00. per year. Mainly for accountants and lawyers.

Taxi and Livery Management. International Taxicab and Livery Association, 3849 Farragut Ave. Kensington, MD 20895-2004. Phone: (301)946-5701 Fax: (301)946-4641 E-mail: itla@itla-info.org • URL: http://www.taxinetwork.com • Quarterly. $16.00 per year.

Taxicab and Transportation Service Directory. American Business Directories, P.O. Box 27347 Omaha, NE 68127. Phone: 800-555-6124 or (402)593-4600 Fax: (402)331-5481 E-mail: internet@infousa.com • URL: http://www.abii.com • Annual. Price on application. Provides a geographical list for over 7,788 taxicab companies. Compiled from telephone company yellow pages. Formerly *Taxicab Directory*.

TAXNET. Carswell/Thomas Professional PublishingPhone: 800-387-5164 or (416)609-3800 Fax: (416)298-5082 URL: http://www.carswell.com/taxnet.htm • Fee-based Web site provides complete coverage of Canadian tax law and regulation, including income tax, provincial taxes, accounting, and payrolls. Daily updates. Base price varies according to product.

TCA-The Information Technology and Telecommunications Association.

Tea and Coffee Trade Journal. Lockwood Trade Journal Co., Inc., 130 W. 42nd St., Suite 1050 New York, NY 10036-7802. Phone: (212)391-2060 Fax: (212)827-0945 E-mail: teacof@aol.com • Monthly. $30.00 per year. Current trends in coffee roasting and tea packing industry.

Tea Council of the United States of America., 420 Lexington Ave., Suite 825 New York, NY 10170. Phone: (212)986-6998 Fax: (212)697-8658 Membership is international. Includes Tea Association of the U.S.A.

Teach Yourself Advanced Java in 21 Days. Scott Williams., 201 W. 103rd St. Indianapolis, IN 46290-1097. Phone: 800-428-5331 or (317)581-3500 Fax: (317)581-4670 URL: http://macmillan.com • Date not set. $35.00.

Teach Yourself Copywriting. J. Jonathan Gabay. NTC/Contemporary Publishing Group, 4255 W. Touhy Ave. Lincolnwood, IL 60712-1975. Phone: 800-323-4900 or (847)679-5500 Fax: 800-998-3103 or (847)679-2494 E-mail: ntcpub@tribune.com • URL: http://www.ntc-cb.com • 2001. $14.95. Second edition. Includes material on copywriting for e-commerce websites.

Teach Yourself Desktop Publishing. Christopher Lumgair. NTC/Contemporary Publishing Group, 4255 W. Touhy Ave. Lincolnwood, IL 60712-1975. Phone: 800-323-4900 or (847)679-5500 Fax: 800-998-3103 or (847)679-2494 E-mail: ntcpub@tribune.com • URL: http://www.ntc-cb.com • 2001. $10.95. Describes current desktop publishing software and techniques.

Teach Yourself Java. Chris Wright. NTC/Contemporary Publishing Group, 4255 W. Touhy Ave. Lincolnwood, IL 60712-1975. Phone: 800-323-4900 or (847)679-5500 Fax: 800-998-3103 or (847)679-2494 E-mail: ntcpub@tribune.com • URL: http://www.ntc-cb.com • 2001. $12.95. Second edition. Covers the basics of designing websites and interactive pages.

Teaching Business Studies. David Needham and others. McGraw-Hill, 1221 Ave. of the Americas New York, NY 10020. Phone: 800-722-4726 or (212)904-2000 Fax: (212)904-2072 E-mail: customer.service@mcgraw-hill.com • URL: http://www.mcgraw-hill.com • 1992. $15.99.

Team Leader. Dartnell Corp., 350 Hiatt Dr. Palm Beach, FL 33418. Phone: 800-621-5463 or (561)622-6520 Fax: (561)622-2423 E-mail: custserv@lrp.com • URL: http://www.dartnellcorp.com • Biweekly. $76.70 per year. Newsletter. Includes coverage of self-directed work groups.

Teambuilding and Total Quality: A Guidebook to TQM Success. Gene Milas. Engineering and Management Press, 25 Technology Park Norcross, GA 30092-2988. Phone: 800-494-0460 or (770)449-0461 Fax: (770)263-8532 E-mail: cmagee@www.iienet.org • URL: http://www.iienet.org • 1997. $29.95. A practical, how-to-do-it guide to total quality management in industry. The importance of employee involvement is stressed.

Teamwork: Your Personal Guide to Working Successfully with People. Dartnell Corp., 350 Hiatt Dr. Palm Beach, FL 33418. Phone: 800-621-5463 or (561)622-6520 Fax: (561)622-2423 E-mail: custserv@lrp.com • URL: http://www.dartnellcorp.com • Biweekly. $76.70 per year. Provides advice for employees on human relations, motivation, and team spirit.

Technical Analysis Explained: The Successful Investor's Guide to Spotting Investment Trends and Turning Points. Martin J. Pring. McGraw-Hill, 1221 Ave. of the Americas New York, NY 10020. Phone: 800-722-4726 or (212)904-2000 Fax: (212)904-2072 E-mail: customer.service@mcgraw-hill.com • URL: http://www.mcgraw-hill.com • 1991. $49.95. Third edition.

Technical Analysis from A to Z: Covers Every Trading Tool from the Absolute Breadth Index to Zig Zag. Steven B. Achelis. McGraw-Hill Professional, 1221 Ave. of the Americas New York, NY 10020. Phone: 800-722-4726 or (212)904-2000 Fax: (212)904-2072 E-mail: customer.service@mcgraw-hill.com • URL: http://www.mcgraw-hill.com • 2000. $39.95. Second edition. Provides definitions and explanations of more than 100 technical indicators used in attempts to predict stock and commodity price trends. Includes a general introduction to technical analysis.

Technical Analysis of Stock Trends. Robert D. Edwards and John Magee. AMACOM, 1601 Broadway, 12th Fl. New York, NY 10019. Phone: 800-262-9699 or (212)586-8100 Fax: (212)903-8168 E-mail: custmserv@amanet.org • URL: http://www.amanet.org • 1998. $79.85. 7th revised edition. Standard manual of technical analysis.

Technical Analysis of Stocks & Commodities: The Trader's Magazine. Technical Analysis, Inc., 4757 California Ave., S.W. Seattle, WA 98116-4499. Phone: 800-832-4642 or (206)938-0570 Fax: (206)938-1307 E-mail: mail@traders.com • URL: http://www.traders.com • 13 times a year. $49.95 per year. Covers use of personal computers for stock trading, price movement analysis by means of charts, and other technical trading methods.

Technical and Educational Center of the Graphic Arts and Imaging.

Technical Association of the Graphic Arts.

Technical Communication. Society for Technical Communication, 901 N. Stuart St., Suite 904 Arlington, VA 22203-1822. Phone: (703)522-4114 URL: http://www.stc.va.org • Quarterly. $60.00 per year. Production of technical literature.

Technical Education and Training Abstracts. Carfax Publishing Co., 875-81 Massachusetts Ave. Cambridge, MA 02139. E-mail: enquiries@carfax.co.uk • URL: http://www.carfax.co.uk • Quarterly. Individuals, $238.00 per year; institutions, $754.00 per year. Published in England. Formerly *Technical Education Abstracts*.

Technical Education News. Glencoe-McGraw Hill, 8787 Orion Place Columbus, OH 43240-4027. Phone: (614)430-4000 or 800-848-1567 Fax: (614)860-1877 E-mail: customer.service@mcgraw-hill.com • URL: http://www.mcgraw-hill.com • Semiannual. Free to qualified personnel.

Technical Report Writing Today. Daniel Riordan. Houghton Mifflin Co., 215 Park Ave., S. New York, NY 10003. Phone: 800-225-3362 or (212)420-5800 Fax: (212)420-5855 URL: http://www.hmco.com • 1995. $46.36. Sixth edition. Six volumes.

Technical Services Quarterly: New Trends in Computers, Automation, and Advanced Technologies in the Technical Operation of Libraries and Information Centers. Haworth Press, Inc., 10 Alice St. Binghamton, NY 13904-1580. Phone: 800-429-6784 or (607)722-5857 Fax: 800-895-0582 or (607)722-1424 E-mail: getinfo@haworthpressinc.com • URL: http://www.haworthpressinc.com • Quarterly. Individuals, $45.00 per year; institutions, $225.00 per year; libraries, $225.00 per year.

Technical Trends: The Indicator Accuracy Service., P.O. Box 792 Wilton, CT 06897. Phone: 800-736-0229 or (203)762-0229 Fax: (203)761-1504 URL: http://www.capecod.net/techtrends • 40 times a year. $147.00 per year. Technical investment newsletter.

Technical Writing. John M. Lannon. Addison-Wesley Educational Publications, Inc., One Jacob Way Reading, MA 01867. Phone: 800-447-2226 or (781)944-3700 Fax: (781)942-1117 URL: http://www.awl.com • 2000. Eighth edition. Price on application.

Techniques. Association for Career and Technical Education, 1410 King St. Alexandria, VA 22314. Phone: 800-826-9972 or (703)683-3111 Fax: (703)683-7424 URL: http://www.acteonline.org • Eight times a year. Free to members; non-members, $39.00 per year. Formerly *Vocational Educational Journal*

Techniques of Financial Analysis: A Modern Approach. Erich A. Helfert. McGraw-Hill Higher Education, 1221 Ave. of the Americas New York, NY 10020-1095. Phone: 800-722-4726 or (212)904-2000 Fax: (212)904-2072 E-mail: customer.serivce@mcgraw-hill.com • URL: http://www.mcgraw-hill.com • 1996. $32.00. Ninth edition.

Technological Forecasting and Social Change. Elsevier Science, 655 Ave. of the Americas New York, NY 10010. Phone: 888-437-4636 or (212)989-5800 Fax: (212)633-3680 E-mail: usinfo@elsevier.com • URL: http://www.elsevier.com • Nine times a year. $688.00 per year. Three volumes.

Technology and Learning: The Leading Magazine of Electronic Education. Miller Freeman, Inc., 600 Harrison St. San Francisco, CA 94107. Phone: (415)905-2200 Fax: (415)905-2232 E-mail: mfibooks@mfi.com • URL: http://www.techlearning.com • Eight times a year. $29.95 per year. Covers all levels of computer/electronic education-elementary to college. Formerly *Classroom Computer Learning*.

Technology and Teaching. Les Lloyd, editor. Information Today, Inc., 143 Old Marlton Pike Medford, NJ 08055-8750. Phone: 800-300-9868 or (609)654-6266 Fax: (609)654-4309 E-mail: custserv@infotoday.com • URL: http://www.infotoday.com • 1997. $42.50. Contains multimedia computer application case studies relating to college level curricula and teaching.

Technology Based Learning and Research., Arizona State University, College of Education, Community Service Center Tempe, AZ 85287-0908. Phone: (480)965-4960 Fax: (480)946-1423 E-mail: bitter@asu.edu • URL: http://tblr.ed.asu.edu/projects.html • Research activities are related to computer literacy.

Technology Business: The Magazine of Strategies for Innovation, Management, and Marketing. Technology Business LLC, 1483 Chain Bridge Rd., Suite 202 McLean, VA 22101. Phone: (703)848-0500 Fax: (703)448-0270 URL: http://www.techbusiness.com • Bimonthly. Price on application. Edited for executives and managers of high technology firms.

Technology Forecasts and Technology Surveys. Technology Forecasts, 205 S. Beverly Dr.,, Suite 208 Beverly Hills, CA 90212. Phone: (310)273-3486 Fax: (310)858-8272 Monthly. $170.00 per year. Newsletter. Information on major breakthroughs in advanced technologies along with forecasts of effects on future applications and markets.

Technology in Society: An International Journal. Elsevier Science, 655 Ave. of the Americas New York, NY 10010. Phone: 888-437-4636 or (212)989-5800 Fax: (212)633-3680 E-mail: usinfo@elsevier.com • URL: http://www.elsevier.com • Quarterly. $804.00 per year.

Technology Investing. Michael Murphy, editor. Phillips Publishing International, Inc., 7811 Montrose Rd. Potomac, MD 20854. Phone: 800-784-0870 or (301)340-2100 Fax: (301)424-0245 E-mail: pbi@phillips.com • URL: http://www.phillips.com • Monthly. $195.00 per year. Newsletter. Provides specific recommendations for investing in high technology companies.

Technology Media Source. SRDS, 1700 Higgins Rd. Des Plaines, IL 60018. Phone: 800-851-7737 or (847)375-5000 Fax: (847)375-5001 E-mail: lalbr@srds.com • URL: http://www.srds.com • Annual. $291.00. Contains detailed information on business publications, consumer magazines, and direct mail lists that may be of interest to ''technology marketers.'' Emphasis is on aviation and telecommunications.

Technology Review: MITs National Magazine of Technology and Policy. Massachusetts Institute of Technology, W59-200 Cambridge, MA 02139. Phone: (617)253-8250 E-mail: trcomments@mit.edu • URL: http://www.mit.edu/ • Six times a year. $19.95 per year. Examines current technological issues facing society.

Technology Transfer Highlights. Argonne National Laboratory, Industrial Technology Development Center, 9700 S. Cass Ave., Bldg. 201 Argonne, IL 60439. Phone: (630)252-6393 Fax: (630)252-5230 E-mail: mmhanley@anl.gov • URL: http://www.anl.gov/ITD/hilead.html • Quarterly. Free. Newsletter on the transfer of federal technology.

Technology Transfer Society., 230 E. Ohio St., Suite 400 Chicago, IL 60611. Phone: (312)644-0828 Fax: (312)644-8557 E-mail: bbecker@bostrom.com • Members are individuals and institutions involved in the process of technology transfer and utilization.

TechTrends: For Leaders in Education and Training. Association for Educational Communications and Technology, 1800 N. Stonelake Dr., Suite 2 Bloomington, IN 47404-1517. Phone: (812)335-7675 Fax: (812)335-7675 URL: http://www.aect.org • Bimonthly. $40.00 per year.

Teenage Economic Power. Available from MarketResearch.com, 641 Ave. of the Americas, 3rd Fl. New York, NY 10011. Phone: 800-298-5699 or (212)807-2629 Fax: (212)807-2716 E-mail: order@marketresearch.com • URL: http://www.marketresearch.com • 1998. $1,200.00. Published by Rand Youth Poll. Provides consumer market data on the 13-year to 19-year age group. Gives results of an extensive survey of teenage attitudes toward shopping and spending.

Telco Business Report: Executive Briefings on the Bell Operating Companies and Independent Telcos. Capitol Publications Inc., Telecom Publishing Group, 1101 King St., Ste. 444 Alexandria, VA 22314. Phone: (703)548-3800 Fax: (703)739-6490 URL: http://www.telecommunications.com • Biweekly. $759.00 per year. Newsletter. Covers long-distance markets, emerging technologies, strategies of Bell operating companies, and other telephone business topics.

Tele.com: Business and Technology for Public Network Service Providers. CMP Publications, Inc., 600 Community Dr. Manhasset, NY 11030. Phone: 800-577-5356 or (516)562-5000 Fax: (516)733-6916 URL: http://www.teledotcom.com • 14 times a year. $125.00 per year. Edited for executives and managers at both traditional telephone companies and wireless communications companies. Also provides news and information for Internet services providers and cable TV operators.

Telecom Business: Opportunities for Network Service Providers, Resellers, and Suppliers in the Competitive Telecom Industry. MultiMedia Publishing Corp., 3535 Briarpark, Suite 200 Houston, TX 77042-5234. Phone: (713)974-5252 Fax: (713)974-5459 E-mail: info@telecombusiness.com • URL: http://www.telecombusiness.com • Monthly. $56.95 per year. Provides business and technical information for telecommunications executives in various fields.

Telecom Lingo Guide. Warren Communication News, 2115 Ward Court, N. W. Washington, DC 20037-1209. Phone: 800-771-9202 or (202)872-9200 Fax: (202)293-3435 E-mail: customerservice@warren-news.com • URL: http://www.telecommunications.com • 1996. $60.00. Eighth edition. Defines more than 1,000 words, phrases, and acronyms frequently used in the telecommunications industry.

Telecom Made Easy: Money-Saving, Profit-Building Solutions for Home Businesses, Telecommuters, and Small Organizations. June Langhoff. Aegis Publishing Group Ltd., 796 Aquidneck Ave. Newport, RI 02842. Phone: 800-828-6961 or (401)849-4200 Fax: (401)849-4231 E-mail: aegis@aegisbooks.com • URL: http://www.aegisbooks.com • 2000. $19.95. Fouth edition.

Telecom Strategies. Thomson Financial Securities Data, Two Gateway Center Newark, NJ 07102. Phone: 888-989-8373 or (973)622-3100 Fax: (973)622-1421 E-mail: tfsd.cs@tfn.com • URL: http://www.tfsd.com • Monthly. $2,995.00 per year. CD-ROM contains full text of investment analysts' reports on companies operating in the following fields: telecommunications, broadcasting, and cable communications.

Telecommunication Transmission Handbook. Roger L. Freeman. John Wiley and Sons, Inc., 605 Third Ave. New York, NY 10158-0012. Phone: 800-526-5368 or (212)850-6000 Fax: (212)850-6088 E-mail: info@wiley.com • URL: http://www.wiley.com • 1998. $185.00. Fourth edition.

Telecommunications. Horizon-House Pubications, Inc., 685 Canton St. Norwood, MA 02060. Phone: (781)769-9750 Fax: (781)762-9230 E-mail: tcs@telecom-mag.com • URL: http://www.telecomms-mag.com • Monthly. Free to qualified personnel; others, $75.00 per year. International coverage.

Telecommunications. Warren Hioki. Prentice Hall, 240 Frisch Court Paramus, NJ 07652-5240. Phone: 800-947-7700 or (201)909-6200 Fax: 800-445-6991 or (201)909-6361 URL: http://www.prenhall.com • 2000. $95.00. Fourth edition.

Telecommunications and Signal Processing Research Center. University of Texas at Austin

Telecommunications and Telephone Association., P.O. 2387 Arlington, VA 22202. Phone: (202)628-5696 or (202)521-1089 Fax: (202)521-1007 Represents consumer interests in the areas of telephone communications, service, and equipment.

Telecommunications Directory. The Gale Group, 27500 Drake Rd. Farmington Hills, MI 48331-3535. Phone: 800-877-GALE or (248)699-GALE Fax: 800-414-5043 or (248)699-8069 E-mail: galeord@galegroup.com • URL: http://www.galegroup.com • 2000. $595.00. 12th edition. National and international voice, data, facsimile, and video communications services. Formerly *Telecommunications Systems and Services Directory*.

Telecommunications Engineer's Reference Book. Fraidoon Mazda, editor. Butterworth-Heinemann, 225 Wildwood Ave. Woburn, MA 01801. Phone: 800-366-2665 or (781)904-2500 Fax: 800-466-6520 E-mail: orders@bhusa.com • URL: http://www.bh.com • 1998. $150.00.

Telecommunications Industry Association.

Telecommunications Policy. Elsevier Science, 655 Ave. of the Americas New York, NY 10010. Phone: 888-437-4636 or (212)989-5800 Fax: (212)633-3680 E-mail: usinfo@elsevier.com • URL: http://www.elsevier.com • 11 times a year. $883.00 per year.

Telecommunications Regulation: Cable, Broadcasting, Satellite, and the Internet. Matthew Bender & Co., Inc., 1275 Broadway Albany, NY 12204-2694. Phone: 800-833-9844 or (518)487-3000 Fax: (518)487-3584 E-mail: customer.support@bender.com • URL: http://www.bender.com • Looseleaf. $700.00. Four volumes. Semiannual updates. Covers local, state, and federal regulation, with emphasis on the Telecommunications Act of 1996. Includes regulation of television, telephone, cable, satellite, computer communication, and online services. Formerly *Cable Television Law*.

Telecommunications Reports. Telecommunications Reports International, Inc., 1333 H St., N.W., Suite 100 Washington, DC 20005. Phone: 800-822-6338 or (202)842-6060 Fax: (202)842-3023 E-mail: customerservice@tr.com • URL: http://www.tr.com • Weekly. Institutions, $1,695.00 per year. Includes *TR Daily*. Regulatory newsletter.

Telecommunicator. Association of Telemessaging Services International, Inc., 1200 19th St. N.W. Washington, DC 20036-2412. Phone: (202)429-5151 URL: http://www.206.69.69.91.109/icenter • Biweekly. Membership. Formerly *Telephone Secretary*.

Telecommute! Go to Work Without Leaving Home. Lisa Shaw. John Wiley and Sons, Inc., 605 Third Ave. New York, NY 10158-0012. Phone: 800-225-5945 or (212)850-6000 Fax: (212)850-6088 E-mail: info@wiley.com • URL: http://www.wiley.com • 1996. $14.95. Includes ''Are You Right for Telecommuting?'' and ''How to Negotiate with Your Boss.''

Telecommuters, the Workforce of the Twenty-First Century: An Annotated Bibliography. Teri R. Switzer. Scarecrow Press, Inc., 4720 Boston Way Lanham, MD 20706-4310. Phone: 800-462-6420 or (301)459-3366 Fax: 800-388-4550 or (301)459-1705 E-mail: orders@scarecrowpress.com • URL: http://www.scarecrowpress.com • 1996. $34.00. Covers material published since 1970.

Telecommuting: A Manager's Guide to Flexible Work Arrangements. Joel Kugelmass. Jossey-Bass, Inc., Publishers, 350 Sansome St., 5th Fl. San Francisco, CA 94104. Phone: 888-378-2537 or (415)433-1740 Fax: (415)433-0499 E-mail: webperson@jbp.com • URL: http://www.josseybass.com • 1995. $25.00. Part one is ''Understanding Flexible Work'' and part two is ''Implementing Flexible Work.'' Includes bibliography and index.

Telecommuting, Teleworking, and Alternative Officing. Gil Gordon AssociatesPhone: (732)329-2266 Fax: (732)329-2703 URL: http://www.gilgordon.com • Web site includes ''About Telecommuting'' (questions and answers), ''Worldwide Resources'' (news groups, publications, conferences), and ''Technology'' (virtual office, intranets, groupware). Other features include monthly updates and an extensive list of telecommuting/telework related books. Fees: Free.

Teleconference Magazine: The Magazine on Interactive Mulitmedia. Advanstar Communications, Inc., 201 E. Sandpointe Ave., Suite 600 Santa Ana, CA 92707. Phone: 800-854-3112 or (714)513-8600 Fax: (714)513-8632 E-mail: information@advanstar.com • URL: http://www.advanstar.com • Monthly. $60.00 per. year. Provides articles on new technology and the practical use of teleconferencing in business communications.

Teleconnect. Miller Freeman, Inc., 12 W. 21st St. New York, NY 10010. Phone: (212)691-8215 Fax: (212)691-1191 E-mail: mfibooks@mfi.com • URL: http://www.teleconnect.com • Monthly. Free to qualified personnel.

Telecons. Applied Business Telecommunications, P.O. Box 5106 San Ramon, CA 94583. Phone: (510)606-5150 Fax: (510)606-9410 Bimonthly. $30.00 per year. Topics include teleconferencing, videoconferencing, distance learning, telemedicine, and telecommuting.

Telehealth Buyer's Guide. Miller Freeman, 600 Harrison St. San Francisco, CA 94107. Phone: (415)905-2200 Fax: (415)905-2232 URL: http://www.telehealthmag.com • Annual. $10.00. Lists sources of telecommunications and information technology products and services for the health care industry.

Telehealth Magazine. Miller Freeman, 600 Harrison St. San Francisco, CA 94107. Phone: (415)905-2200 Fax: (415)905-2232 URL: http://www.telehealthmag.com • Bimonthly. $50.00 per year. Covers Internet, wireless, and other telecommunications technologies for health care professionals.

The Telemarketer. Actel Marketing, 163 Third Ave., Suite 303 New York, NY 10003. Phone: (212)674-2545 Semimonthly. $285.00 per year. Newsletter.

Telematics and Informatics: An International Journal. Elsevier Science, 655 Ave. of the Americas New York, NY 10010. Phone: 888-437-4636 or (212)989-5800 Fax: (212)633-3680 E-mail: usinfo-f@elsevier.com • URL: http://www.elsevier.com • Quarterly. $713.00 per year.

Telephone Answering Service. Entrepreneur Media, Inc., 2445 McCave Way Irvine, CA 92614. Phone: 800-421-2300 or (949)261-2325 Fax: (949)851-9088 E-mail: entmag@entrepreneurmag.com • URL: http://www.entrepreneurmag.com • Looseleaf. $59.50. A practical guide to starting a telephone answering service. Covers profit potential, start-up costs, market size evaluation, owner's time required, pricing, accounting, advertising, promotion, etc. (Start-Up Business Guide No. E1148).

The Telephone Industry Directory. Phillips Publishing International, Inc., 7811 Montrose Rd. Potomac, MD 20854. Phone: 800-784-0870 or (301)340-2100 Fax: (301)424-0245 E-mail: pbi@phillips.com • URL: http://www.phillips.com • Annual. $249.00. Lists telecommunications carriers, equipment manufacturers, distributors, agencies, and organizations.

Telephone Management Strategist. Buyers Laboratory, Inc., 108 John St.Ave. Hackensack, NJ 07601. Phone: (201)489-6439 Fax: (201)489-9365 E-mail: ctd@buyerslaboratory.com • URL: http://www.buyers-lab.com • Monthly. $125.00 per year. Newsletter. Information on business telecommunications.

Telephone Selling Report: Providing Proven Sales Ideas You Can Use. Art Sobczak, editor. Business By Phone, Inc., 13254 Stevens Rd. Omaha, NE 68137-1728. Phone: (402)895-9399 Fax: (402)896-3353 URL: http://www.businessbyphone.com • Monthly. $109.00 per year. Newsletter. How-to newsletter providing proven ideas, tips, and techniques for telephone prospecting and selling.

Telephony: For Today's Competing Network Market. Intertec Publishing Corp., 330 N. Wabash Ave. Chicago, IL 60611. Phone: 800-400-5945 or (312)595-1080 Fax: (312)595-0295 URL: http://www.internettelephony.com • 51 times per year. $114.00 per year.

Teleselling: A Self-Teaching Guide. James D. Porterfield. John Wiley and Sons, Inc., 605 Third Ave. New York, NY 10158-0012. Phone: 800-225-5945 or (212)850-6000 Fax: (212)850-6088 E-mail: info@wiley.com • URL: http://www.wiley.com • 1996. $19.95. Second revised edition. Provides practical information and advice on selling by telephone, including strategy, prospecting, script development, and performance evaluation.

Teleselling Techniques That Close the Sale. Flyn L. Penoyer. AMACOM, 1601 Broadway, 12th Fl. New York, NY 10019. Phone: 800-262-9699 or (212)586-8100 Fax: (212)903-8168 E-mail: custmserv@amanet.org • URL: http://www.amanet.org • 1997. $19.95.

TeleTrends. International Telework Association Council, 204 E St., N. E. Washington, DC 20002. Phone: (202)547-6157 URL: http://www.telecommute.org • Quarterly. Price on application.

Television and Cable Factbook. Warren Publishing Inc., 2115 Ward Court, N.W. Washington, DC 20037-1209. Phone: 800-771-9202 or (202)872-9200 Fax: (202)293-3435 E-mail: customerservice@warren-news.com • URL: http://www.warrenpub.com • Annual. $495.00. Three volumes. Commercial and noncommercial television stations and networks.

Television Broadcast. United Entertainment Media, Inc., 460 Park Ave. South New York, NY 10016-7315. Phone: (212)378-0400 Fax: (212)378-2160 E-mail: tvbcast@uemedia.com • URL: http://www.tvbroadcast.com • Monthly. $40.00 per year. Contains articles on management, production, and technology for TV stations.

Television Bureau of Advertising.

Television Digest with Consumer Electronics. Warren Communication News, 2115 Ward Court, N. W. Washington, DC 20037-1209. Phone: 800-771-9202 or (202)872-9200 Fax: (202)293-3435 E-mail: customerservice@warren-news.com • URL: http://www.telecommunications.com • Weekly. $944.00 per year. Newsletter featuring new consumer entertainment products utilizing electronics. Also covers the television broadcasting and cable TV industries, with corporate and industry news.

Television Financial Report. National Association of Broadcasters, 1771 N St., N. W. Washington, DC 20036-2891. Phone: 800-368-5644 or (202)429-5300 Fax: (202)429-5343 Annual. Members, $100.00; non-members, $300.00. Provides data on the revenues, expenses, and profit margins of TV stations.

Television International Magazine. Television International Publications, Ltd., P.O. Box 2430 Hollywood, CA 90028. Phone: (213)462-1099 E-mail: tui@smartgo.com • URL: http://www.tuimagazine.com • Bimonthly. $42.00 per year.

Television Production Handbook. Herbert Zettl. Wadsworth Publishing Co., 10 Davis Dr. Belmont, CA 94002. Phone: 800-354-9706 or (650)595-2350 Fax: (650)637-9955 URL: http://www.wadsworth.com • 1996. $64.95. Sixth edition. (Radio/TV/Film Series).

Television Quarterly. National Academy of Television Arts and Sciences, c/o Ed Eberung, 111 W. 57th St., Suite 1020 New York, NY 10019. Phone: (212)586-8424 Fax: (212)246-8129 URL: http://www.emmys.org • Quarterly. $30.00 per year.

Temporary Help Service. Entrepreneur Media, Inc., 2445 McCabe Way Irvine, CA 92614. Phone: 800-421-2300 or (949)261-2325 Fax: (949)261-0234 E-mail: entmag@entrepreneur.com • URL: http://www.entrepreneur.com • Looseleaf. $59.50. A practical guide to starting an employment agency for temporary workers. Covers profit potential, start-up costs, market size evaluation, owner's time required, site selection, lease negotiation, pricing, accounting, advertising, promotion, etc. (Start-Up Business Guide No. E1189.)

Tenants' Rights. Myron Moskovitz and Ralph Warner. Nolo.com, 950 Parker St. Berkeley, CA 94710. Phone: 800-992-6656 or (510)549-1976 Fax: (510)548-5902 E-mail: cs@nolo.com • URL: http://www.nolo.com • 1999. $21.95. 14th edition.

Tennessee Agricultural Experiment Station. University of Tennessee, Knoxville

Tennis Buyer's Guide Buying Directory. Golf Digest/Tennis, Inc., P.O. Box 0395 Trumbull, CT 06611-0395. Phone: 800-451-2386 or (203)373-7000 Fax: (203)371-2505 Annual $5.00. Lists more than 200 manufacturers of tennis rackets, apparel, shoes, equipment, and accessories.

Tennis Industry. Miller Publishing Group, 801 Seventh Ave. New York, NY 10019. Phone: (212)636-2700 Fax: (212)636-2710 URL: http://www.tennisindustry.com • 11 times a year. $22.00 per year. Edited for retailers serving the "serious tennis enthusiast." Provides news of apparel, rackets, equipment, and court construction.

Tenting Directory. Woodall Publishing Co., 13975 W. Polo Trail Dr. Lake Forest, IL 60045-5000. Phone: 800-323-9076 or (847)362-6700 Fax: (847)362-8776 E-mail: emd@woodallpub.com • URL: http://www.woodall's.com • Annual. $12.95. Campgrounds in the United States and Canada that have tent sites and tent rentals.

TESS: (The Educational Software Selector). Educational Products Information Exchange. EPIE Institute, 103-3 W. Montauk Highway Hampton Bays, NY 11946-4006. Phone: 888-776-7730 or (516)728-9100 Fax: (516)728-9228 E-mail: epieinst@aol.com • URL: http://www.epie.org • Semiannual. $79.95 per year. Lists over 900 suppliers of educational software for Mackintosh, Apple II, MS-DOS and Windows compatible computers and videodisc players. Formerly *The Latest and Best of TESS: The Educational Software Selector.*

Test and Measurement World Annual Buyer's Guide. Cahners Business Information, Global Electronics Div., 275 Washington Ave. Newton, MA 02158-1630. Phone: 800-662-7776 or (617)964-3030 Fax: (617)558-4470 E-mail: corporatecommunications@cahner.com • URL: http://www.cahners.com • Annual. Free to qualified personnel; others, $32.95. List of over 1,500 suppliers of test, measurement, inspection, and monitoring products and services.

Test and Measurement World: The Magazine for Quality in Electronics. Cahners Business Information, Global Electronics Div., 275 Washington Ave. Newton, MA 02158-1630. Phone: 800-662-7776 or (617)964-3030 Fax: (617)558-4470 E-mail: corporatecommunications@cahner.com • URL: http://www.cahners.com • 15 times a year. $77.90 per year.

Test Critques. Pro-Ed, 8700 Shoal Creek Blvd. Austin, TX 78757-6897. Phone: 800-897-3202 or (512)451-3246 Fax: (248)699-8069 E-mail: info@proedinc.com • URL: http://www.proedinc.com • 1998. 11 volumes. Prices vary. Presents detailed evaluations of the validity of tests in psychology, education, and business. Published by ProEd, Inc.

Tests: A Comprehensive Reference for Assessments in Psychology, Education and Business. Available from The Gale Group, 27500 Drake Rd. Farmington Hills, MI 48331-3535. Phone: 800-877-GALE or (248)699-GALE Fax: 800-414-5043 or (248)699-8069 E-mail: galeord@galegroup.com • URL: http://www.galegroup.com • 1997. $99.00. Fourth edition. List nearly 500 publishers for over 3,000 tests. Published by Pro-Ed Inc.

Tests in Print. Linda L. Murphy and others. University of Nebraska-Lincoln Buros Institute of Mental Measurements, 135 Bancroft Lincoln, NE 68588-0484. Phone: 800-755-1105 or (402)472-6203 Fax: (402)472-6207 E-mail: bimm@unlinfol.unl.edu • URL: http://www.unl.edu/buros • Quinquennial. Price varies. Two volumes. Lists over 4,000 testing instruments.

Texas Agricultural Experiment Station at Sonora. Texas A & M University

Texas Agricultural Market Research Center. Texas A & M University

Texas Longhorn Breeders Association of America.

Texas Transportation Institute., Texas A & M University System College Station, TX 77843-3135. Phone: (979)845-8552 Fax: (979)845-9356 E-mail: h.hrichardson@tamu.edu • URL: http://tti.tamu.edu • Concerned with all forms and modes of transportation. Research areas include transportation economics, highway construction, traffic safety, public transportation, and highway engineering.

Texas Transportation Institute, Systems Planning Division. Texas A & M University

Textbook of Soil Chemical Analysis. P.R. Hesse. Chemical Publishing Co., Inc., 192 Lexington Ave. New York, NY 10016. Phone: 800-786-3659 or (212)779-0090 Fax: (212)889-1537 E-mail: chempub@aol.com • URL: http://www.chemicalpublishing.com • 1972. $85.00.

Textile Bag and Packing Association.

Textile Business Outlook. Statistikon Corp., P.O. Box 246 East Norwich, NY 11732. Phone: (516)922-0882 Fax: (516)624-3145 Quarterly. $985.00 per year. Analyzes current business, marketing, and financial conditions for the worldwide textile industry (fibers and fabrics). Includes statistical forecasts.

Textile Care Allied Trades Association.

Textile Chemist and Colorist. American Association of Textile Chemists and Colorists, P.O. Box 12215 Research Triangle Park, NC 27709-2215. Phone: (919)549-8141 Fax: (919)549-8933 URL: http://www.aatcc.org • Monthly. Free to members; non-members, $60.00 per year. Annual *Buyer's Guide* available.

Textile Distributors Association.

Textile Fibers and By-Products Association.

Textile Hi-Lights. American Textile Manufacturers Institute, Inc., 1130 Connecticut Ave., N.W., Suite. 1200 Washington, DC 20036-3954. Phone: (202)862-0500 Fax: (202)862-0570 URL: http://www.atmi.org • Quarterly. $125.00 per year. Monthly supplements.

Textile Horizons: Providing Essential Reading for All Present and Future Decision Makers in Textiles and Fashion Worldwide. Textile Institute. Benjamin Dent and Co. Ltd., P.O. Box 1897 Lawrence, KS 66044-8897. Bimonthly. $180.00 per year.

Textile Institute., Saint James Bldgs., 4th Fl., Oxford St. Manchester M1 6FQ, England. Phone: 44 161 2371188 Fax: 44 161 2361991 E-mail: tiihq@textileinst.org.uk • URL: http://www.texi.org • Members in 100 countries involved with textile industry management, marketing, science, and technology.

Textile Processors, Service Trades, Health Care, Professional and Technical Employees International Union.

Textile Research Journal. Textile Research Institute, 601 Prospect Ave. Princeton, NJ 08540. Phone: (609)924-3150 Fax: (609)683-7836 Monthly. $265.00 per year.

Textile Technology Digest. Institute of Textile Technology, 2551 Ivy Rd. Charlottesville, VA 22903-4614. Phone: (804)296-5511 Fax: (804)977-5400 Monthly. $535.00 per year. Provides indexing and abstracting of a wide variety of textile technology literature.

Textile Technology Digest ÎCD-ROMl. Textile Information Center, Institute of Textile Technology, 2551 Ivy Rd. Charlottesville, VA 22903-4614. Phone: (804)296-5511 Fax: (804)296-2957 Quarterly. $1,700.00 per year. Provides CD-ROM indexing and abstracting of worldwide journals and monographs in various areas of textile technology, production, and management. Covers 1978 to date.

Textile Technology Digest Îonlinel. Textile Information Center, Institute of Textile Technology, 2551 Ivy Rd. Charlottesville, VA 22903-4614. Phone: (804)296-5511 Fax: (804)977-5400 Contains indexing and abstracting of more than 300 worldwide journals and monographs in various areas of textile technology, production, and management. Time period is 1978 to date, with monthly updating. Inquire as to online cost and availability.

Textile Terms and Definitions. J.E. McIntyre and Paul N. Daniels, editors. Available from State Mutual Book and Periodical Service Ltd., Trade Order Dept., 521 Fifth Ave., 17th Fl. New York, NY 10175. Phone: (718)261-1704 Fax: (516)537-0412 1995. $110.00. 10th edition. Published by the Textile Insitute (UK). Includes more than 1,000 definitions of textile processes, fiber types, and end products. Illustrated.

Textile World. Intertec Publishing Corp., Textile Publications, 6151 Powers Ferry Rd., N.W., Suite 200 Atlanta, GA 30339. Phone: 800-400-5945 or (770)955-2500 E-mail: subs@intertec.com • URL: http://www.textileworld.com • Monthly. Price on application.

Textiles and Materials., Philadelphia University, Schoolhouse Lane and Henry Ave. Philadelphia, PA 19144. Phone: (215)951-2751 Fax: (215)951-2651 E-mail: brooksteind@philaau.edu • URL: http://www.philaau.edu • Many research areas, including industrial and nonwoven textiles.

Textiles Information Treatment Users' Service (TITUS). Institut Textile de France, 280 av. Aristide-Briand-BP141 92223 Bagneuv Cedex, France. Phone: (01-)46641540 Citations and abstracts of the worldwide literature on textiles, 1968 to present. Monthly updates. Inquire as to online cost and availability.

Theatre Design and Technology. U. S. Institute for Theatre Technology, 3001 Springcrest Drive Louisville, KY 40241. Phone: (502)426-1211 Fax: (502)423-7467 URL: http://www.usitt.org • Quarterly. $48.00 per year. Covers developments in theatre lighting, sound, scenic design, costuming, and safety.

Theatre Journal. Association for Theatre in Higher Education. Johns Hopkins University Press, Journals Publishing Div., 2715 N. Charles St. Baltimore, MD 21218. Phone: 800-548-1784 or (410)516-6900 Fax: (410)516-6968 Quarterly. Individuals $31.00 per year; institutions, $80.00 per year. Contains material on theatre history, theatre news, and reviews of books and plays.

Theatre Management and Production in America: Commercial, Stock, Resident, College, Community and Presenting Organizations. Stephen Langley. Quite Specific Media Group, Ltd., 260 Fifth Ave. New York, NY 10001. Phone: (212)725-5377 Fax: (212)725-8506 E-mail: info@quitespecifimedia.com • URL: http://wwwquitespecificmedia.com • 1990. $37.50. Revised edition.

Theatrical Index. Theatrical Index Ltd., 888 Eighth Ave., 16th Fl. New York, NY 10019. Phone: (212)586-6343 Weekly. $300.00 per year. (Lower rates available for biweekly or monthly service.) Lists pre-production theatrical presentations that are seeking investors.

The Theory and Practice of Econometrics. George G. Judge and others. John Wiley and Sons, Inc., 605 Third Ave. New York, NY 10158-0012. Phone: 800-526-5368 or (212)850-6000 Fax: (212)850-6088 E-mail: info@wiley.com • URL: http://www.wiley.com • 1985. $111.95. Second edition. (Probability and Mathematical Statistics Series).

Theory of Corporate Finance. Michael J. Brennan, editor. Edward Elgar Publishing, Inc., 136 West St., Suite 202 Northampton, MA 01060. Phone: 800-390-3149 or (413)584-5551 Fax: (413)584-9933 E-mail: eep.orders@aidcvt.com • URL: http://www.e-elgar.co.uk • 1996. $440.00. Two volumes. Consists of reprints of 46 articles dating from 1976 to 1994. (International Library of Critical Writings in Financial Economics Series: volume one).

Thermophysical Properties Research Laboratory., 2595 Yeager Rd. West Lafayette, IN 47906. Phone: (765)463-1581 Fax: (765)463-5235 E-mail: rtaylor@tprl.com • URL: http://www.tprl.com • Studies the thermophysical properties of materials from cryogenic to very high temperatures.

TheStreet.com: Your Insider's Look at Wall Street. TheStreet.com, Inc.Phone: 800-562-9571 or (212)321-5000 Fax: (212)321-5016 URL: http://www.thestreet.com • Web site offers "Free Sections" and "Premium Sections" ($9.95 per month). Both sections offer iconoclastic advice and comment on the stock market, but premium service displays a more comprehensive selection of news and analysis. There are many by-lined articles. "Search the Site" is included.

Third World Handbook. Available from Fitzroy Dearborn Publications, Inc., 919 Michigan Ave., Suite 760 Chicago, IL 60611. Phone: 800-850-8102 or (312)587-0131 Fax: (312)587-1049 E-mail: fitzroy@aol.com • URL: http://www.fitzroydearborn.com • 1994. $45.00. Second revised edition. Published by Cassell Publications. Discusses background, organizations, and movements within each country and region. Includes maps and photographs.

33 Metalproducing: For Primary Producers of Steel, Aluminum, and Copper-Base Alloys. Penton Media, Inc., 1100 Superior Ave. Cleveland, OH 44114-2543. Phone: (216)696-7000 Fax: (216)696-0836 E-mail: corpcomm@penton.com • URL: http://www.penton.com • Monthly. $65.00 per year. Covers metal production technology and methods and industry news. Includes a bimonthly *Nonferrous Supplement*.

This Business of Art. Lee E. Caplin. Prentice Hall, 240 Frisch Court Paramus, NJ 07652-5240. Phone: 800-947-7700 or (201)909-6200 Fax: 800-445-6991 or (201)909-6361 URL: http://www.prenhall.com • 1997. $24.95. Third edition.

Thomas A. Roe Institute for Economic Policy Studies., Heritage Foundation, 214 Massachusetts Ave., N. E. Washington, DC 20002. Phone: (202)546-4400 Fax: (202)546-5421 E-mail: angela.antonelli@heritage.org • URL: http://www.heritage.org • Concerned with the financing of Medicare.

Thomas Cook Overseas Timetable: Railway, Road and Shipping Services Outside Europe. Thomas Cook Publishing Co., P.O. Box 227 Thorpe Wood, Peterborough PE5 GPU, England. Phone: 44 1733 503571 Fax: 44 1733 503596 Bimonthly. $100.00. per year. International railroad passenger schedules. Text in English; summaries in French, German, Italian and Spanish.

Thomas Food and Beverage Market Place. Grey House Publishing, 185 Millerton Rd. Millerton, NY 12546. Phone: 800-562-2139 or (518)789-8700 Fax: (518)789-0556 E-mail: books@greyhouse.com • URL: http://www.greyhouse.com • Annual. $295.00. Three volumes. Contains more than 40,000 entries covering food companies, beverages, food equipment, warehouse companies, food brokers, wholesalers, importers, and exporters. Formerly *Thomas Food Industry Register*.

Thomas Register of American Manufacturers and Thomas Register Catalog File. Thomas Publishing Co., Inc., Five Penn Plaza, 250 W. 34th St. New York, NY 10001. Phone: 800-699-9822 or (212)695-0500 Fax: (212)290-7365 URL: http://www.thomaspublishing.com • Annual. $149.00. 34 volumes. A three-part system offering information on a wide variety of industrial equipment and supplies.

Thomas Register Online. Thomas Publishing Co., Inc., Five Penn Plaza New York, NY 10001. Phone: (212)695-0500 Fax: (212)290-7362 URL: http://www.thomasregister.com • Provides concise information on approximately 194,000 U. S. companies, mainly manufacturers, with over 50,000 product classifications. Indexes over 115,000 trade names. Information is updated semiannually. Inquire as to online cost and availability.

Thomson Bank Directory. Thomson Financial Publishing, 4709 W. Golf Rd. Skokie, IL 60076-1253. Phone: 800-321-3373 or (847)676-9600 Fax: (847)933-8101 E-mail: support@bankinfo.com • URL: http://www.tfp.com • Semiannual. $395.00 per year. Four volumes. Provides detailed information on head offices and branches of banks in the United States and foreign countries.

Thomson Credit Union Directory. Thomson Financial Publishing, 4709 W. Golf Rd. Skokie, IL 60076-1253. Phone: 800-321-3373 or (847)676-9600 Fax: (847)933-8101 E-mail: customerservice@tfp.com • URL: http://www.tfp.com • Semiannual. $145.00 per year. Provides information on all U. S. credit unions, including branch offices. Includes national statistics and ranking of 300 top credit unions.

Thomson Derivatives and Risk Management Directory. Thomson Learning, 7625 Empire Dr. Florence, KY 41042. Phone: 800-347-7707 or (859)525-6620 Fax: (859)647-5963 E-mail: findit@kiofk.thomson.com • 1998. $297.00. Lists "over 9,000 contacts at more than 4,000 institutions."

Thomson Investors Network. Thomson FinancialPhone: (212)807-3800 URL: http://thomsoninvest.net • Web site provides detailed data on insider trading, institutional portfolios, and "First Call" earnings estimates. Includes a stock screening (filtering) application, a search facility, and price quotes on stocks, bonds, and mutual funds. Continuous updating. Fees: $34.95 per year for general service. First Call earnings service is $19.95 per month or $199.00 per year.

Thomson National Directory of Mortgage Brokers. Thomson Financial Publishing, 4709 W. Golf Rd. Skokie, IL 60076-1253. Phone: 800-321-3373 or (847)676-9600 Fax: (847)933-8101 E-mail: customerservice@tfp.com • URL: http://www.tfp.com • Semiannual. $295.00 per year. Provides detailed information on 11,000 mortgage brokers in the U. S.

Thomson Real Time Quotes: Real Fast...Real Free...Real Quotes...Real Time. Thomson FinancialPhone: (212)807-3800 URL: http://www.thomsonfn.com/ • Web site provides continuous updating of prices for stocks, bonds, mutual funds, and options. Includes headline business news and market analysis. Fees: Free.

Thomson Savings Directory. Thomson Financial Publishing, 4709 W. Golf Rd. Skokie, IL 60076-1253. Phone: 800-321-3373 or (847)676-9600 Fax: (847)933-8101 E-mail: customerservice@tfp.com • URL: http://www.tfp.com • Semiannual. $169.00 per year. Contains information on nearly 2,000 U.S. savings institutions.

The Thorndike Encyclopedia of Banking and Financial Tables. David Thorndike. Warren, Gorham and Lamont/RIA Group, 395 Hudson St. New York, NY 10014. Phone: 800-950-1215 or (212)367-6300 Fax: (212)367-6718 E-mail: customer_service@riag.com • URL: http://www.righome.com • 1991. $79.00.

303 Software Programs to Use in Your Library: Descriptions, Evaluations, and Practical Advice. Patrick R. Dewey. American Library Association, 50 E. Huron St. Chicago, IL 60611-2795. Phone: 800-545-2433 or (312)944-6780 Fax: (312)440-9374 E-mail: editionsmarketing@alo.org • URL: http://www.ala.org • 1997. $36.00. Contains profiles of a wide variety of software (21 categories) that may be useful in libraries. Includes prices, company addresses, glossary, bibliography, and an index.

3D Design. Miller Freeman, Inc., 600 Harrison St. San Francisco, CA 94107. Phone: 800-227-4675 or (415)905-2200 Fax: (415)905-2232 URL: http://www.mfi.com • Monthly. $50.00 per year. Edited for computer graphics and multimedia professionals. Special features include "Animation Mania" and "Interactive 3D."

Thriving as a Broker in the 21st Century. Thomas J. Dorsey. Bloomberg Press, PO Box 888 Princeton, NJ 08542-0888. Phone: 800-388-2749 or (609)279-4670 Fax: 800-458-6515 or (609)279-7155 E-mail: info@bloomberg.com • URL: http://www.bloomberg.com • 1999. $39.95. Provides advice for stockbrokers operating in today's rapidly changing financial environment.

Thunderbird International Business Review. Thunderbird American Graduate School of International Management. John Wiley and Sons, Inc., Journals Div., 605 Third Ave. New York, NY 10158-0012. Phone: 800-225-5945 or (212)850-6000 Fax: (212)850-6088 E-mail: info@wiley.com • URL: http://www.wiley.com • Bimonthly. Institutions, $320.00 per year. Formerly *International Executive*.

TIA-MMTA Directory and Desk Reference. Telecommunications Industry Association Multimedia Telecommunications Associatio, 2500 Wilson Blvd., Suite 300 Arlington, VA 22201-3834. Phone: (703)907-7472 Fax: (703)907-7478 E-mail: info@mmta.org • URL: http://www.mmta.org • Annual. $199.00. Lists manufacturers and suppliers of interconnect telephone equipment. Formerly *Multimedia Telecommunications Sourcebook*.

Ticker: Tools for the Investment Professional. Individual Investor Group, Inc., 125 Broad St., 14th Fl. New York, NY 10004. Phone: 800-888-4741 or (212)742-0747 E-mail: letters@individualinvestor.com • URL: http://www.iionline.com • Bimonthly. Price on application. A trade journal for stockbrokers.

Tight Money Timing: The Impact of Interest Rates and the Federal Reserve on the Stock Market. Wilfred R. George. Greenwood Publishing Group, Inc., 88 Post Rd., W. Westport, CT 06881-5007. Phone: 800-225-5800 or (203)226-3571 Fax: (203)222-2540 E-mail: bookinfo@greenwood.com • URL: http://www.greenwood.com • 1982. $55.00.

Tile and Decorative Surfaces: Directory and Purchasing Guide. Tile and Stone, Inc., 18 E. 41st St., 20th Fl. New York, NY 10017-6222. Phone: (212)376-7722 Fax: (212)376-7723 E-mail: ashleepub@aol.com • URL: http://www.infotile.com • Annual. $12.00. List of over 2,000 manufacturers and distributors of the products and tile setting materials.

Tile and Decorative Surfaces: The Voice of America's Tile Market. Tile and Stone, Inc., 18 E. 41st St., 20th Fl. New York, NY 10017-6222. Phone: (212)376-7722 Fax: (212)376-7723 E-mail: ashleepub@aol.com • URL: http://www.infotile.com • Monthly. $50.00 per year.

Tile Design and Installation. Business News Publishing Co., 755 W. Big Beaver Rd., Suite 1000 Troy, MI 48084. Phone: 800-837-7370 or (248)362-3700 Fax: ((24)8)362-0317 E-mail: ashleepub@aol.com • URL: http://www.bnp.com • Quarterly. $55.00 per year. Formerly *Tile World*.

Timber Bulletin. Economic Commission for Europe. United Nations Publications, United Nations Concourse Level, First Ave., 46th St. New York, NY 10017. Phone: 800-553-3210 or (212)963-7680 Fax: (212)963-4910 E-mail: bookstore@un.org • URL: http://www.un.org/publications • Irregular. Price on application. Contains international statistics on forest products, including price, production, and foreign trade data.

Timber Construction Manual. American Institute of Timber Construction Staff. John Wiley and Sons, Inc., 605 Third Ave. New York, NY 10158-0012. Phone: 800-526-5368 or (212)850-6008 Fax: (212)850-6088 E-mail: info@wiley.com • URL: http://www.wiley.com • 1994. $130.00. Fourth edition.

Timber Harvesting. Hatton Brown Publishers, Inc., 225 Hanrick St. Montgomery, AL 36104. Phone: 800-669-5613 or (334)834-1170 Fax: (334)834-4525 E-mail: mail@hattonbrown.com • URL: http://www.hattonbrown.com • 10 times a year. $40.00 per year.

Timber Harvesting Loggers' Resource Guide. Hatton Brown Publishers, Inc., 225 Hanrick St. Montgomery, AL 36104. Phone: 800-669-5613 or (334)834-1170 Fax: (334)834-4525 E-mail: mail@hattonbrown.com • URL: http://www.hattonbrown.com • Annual. $10.00. List of industrial timber corporations; manufacturers and distributors of equipment used in harvesting and handling timber. Formerly *Timber Harvesting-Wood and Woodlands Directory*.

Timing Financial Advisory Service. William Jaeger, 3219 W. Mescal Phoenix, AZ 85029. Phone: (602)942-3111 Fax: (602)789-7883 Biweekly. $144.00 per year. Newsletter. Follows the financial markets with emphasis on futures. Also includes weather and its effect on agricultural commodities. Formerly*Timing Commodity and Financial Advisory Service*.

Tin. J. W. Price and R. Smith. Springer-Verlag New York, Inc., 175 Fifth Ave. New York, NY 10010. Phone: 800-777-4643 or (212)460-1500 Fax: (212)473-6272 E-mail: orders@springer.ny.com • URL: http://www.springer.ny.com • 1978. $117.95. (Handbook of Analytical Chemistry Series: Vol. 4, Part 3, Section A,Y).

Tin International. Tin Magazines Ltd., Kingston Lane Uxbridge, Middlesex UB8 3PJ, England. Monthly. $215.00 per year. News and analysis for the international tin industry.

Tin: Its Production and Marketing. William Robertson. Greenwood Publishing Group, Inc., 88 Post Rd., W. Westport, CT 06881-5007. Phone: 800-225-5800 or (203)226-3571 Fax: (203)222-2540 E-mail: bookinfo@greenwood.com • URL: http://www.greenwood.com • 1982. $55.00. (Contributions in Economics and Economic History Series, No. 51).

Tips and Traps for Saving on All Your Real Estate Taxes. Robert Irwin and Norman Lane. McGraw-Hill, 1221 Ave. of the Americas New York, NY 10020. Phone: 800-722-4726 or (212)904-2000 Fax: (212)904-2072 E-mail: customer.service@mcgraw-hill.com • URL: http://www.mcgraw-hill.com • 1992. $12.95.

Tips and Traps When Buying a Franchise. Mary E. Tomzack. Source Book Publications, 1814 Franklin St., Suite 820 Oakland, CA 94612. Phone: (510)839-5471 Fax: (510)547-3245 1999. $19.95. Second edition. Provides specific cautionary advice and information for prospective franchisees.

Tips and Traps When Mortgage Hunting. Robert Irwin. McGraw-Hill, 1221 Ave. of the Americas New York, NY 10020. Phone: 800-722-4726 or (212)904-2000 Fax: (212)904-2072 E-mail: customer.service@mcgraw-hill.com • URL: http://www.mcgraw-hill.com • 1995. $12.95. Second revised edition. Contains practical advice for home buyers and small real estate investors.

Tire and Rim Association.

Tire and Rim Association Year Book. Tire and Rim Association, Inc., Crown Pointe, 175 Montrose Ave., W., No. 150 Copley, OH 44321. Phone: (216)666-8121 Annual. $50.00.

Tire Association of North America., 11921 Freedom Dr., Suite 550 Reston, VA 20190-5608. Phone: 800-876-8372 or (703)736-8082 Fax: (703)904-4339 E-mail: members@tana.net • URL: http://www.tana.net • Members are tire dealers and retreaders.

Tire Business. Crain Communications, Inc., 1725 Merriman Rd., Suite 300 Akron, OH 44313-5283. Phone: 800-678-9595 or (330)836-9180 Fax: (330)836-1005 URL: http://www.tirebusiness.com • Biweekly. $62.00 per year. Edited for independent tire retailers and wholesalers.

Tire Industry Safety Council.

Tire Review: The Authority on Tire Dealer Profitability. Babcox Publications, Inc., 11 S. Forge St. Akron, OH 44304-1810. Phone: (216)535-6117 Fax: (216)535-0874 Monthly. $64.00. Includes*LiftGuide, Custom Wheel and Tire Style Guide, Sourcebook and Directory and NTDRA Show*.

Titanium: A Statistical Review. International Titanium Association, 350 Interlocken Blvd., Suite 390 Broomfield, CO 80021-3485. Phone: (303)404-2221 Fax: (303)404-9111 E-mail: info@titanium.org • URL: http://www.titanium.org • Annual. Free to members; non-members, $100.00.

Titanium: A Technical Guide. Matthew J. Donachie, editor. ASM International, 9639 Kinsman Rd. Materials Park, OH 44073-0002. Phone: 800-336-5152 or (440)338-5151 Fax: (440)338-4634 E-mail: custserv@po.asm-intl.org • URL: http://www.asm-intl.org • 2000. Second edition. Provides coverage of all major, technical aspects of titanium and titanium alloys. Price on application.

Titanium Newsletter. International Titanium Association, 350 Interlocken Blvd., Suite 390 Broomfield, CO 80021-3485. Phone: (303)404-2221 Fax: (303)404-9111 E-mail: info@titanium.org • URL: http://www.titanium.org • Quarterly. $42.00 per year. Formerly Titanium Development Association.

Titanium Technology: Present Status and Future Trends. F. H. Froes and others. International Titanium Association, 350 Interlocken Blvd., Suite 390 Broomfield, CO 80021-3485. Phone: (303)404-2221 Fax: (303)404-9111 E-mail: info@titanium.org • URL: http://www.titanium.org • 1985. $19.95.

Title Insurance and Real Estate Securities Terminology. Real Estate Publishing Co., P.O. Box 41177 Sacramento, CA 95841. Phone: (530)677-3864 1980. $6.95.

Title News. American Land Title Association, 1828 L St., N.W. Washington, DC 20036. Phone: 800-787-2582 or (202)296-3671 Fax: (202)223-5843 E-mail: service@alta.org • URL: http://www.alta.org • Bimonthly. $48.00 per year.

Tlargi Rubber Technology Foundation. University of Southern California

TMA Guide to Tobacco Taxes: Summaries of Key Provisions of Tobacco Tax Laws, All Tobacco Products, All States. Tobacco Merchant's Association of the United States, Inc., 231 Clarksville Rd., Suite 6 Princeton, NJ 08543-8019. Phone: (609)275-4900 Fax: (609)275-8379 Looseleaf service. Members, $495.00 per year; non-members, $895.00 per year. Quarterly updates.

TMA Membership Directory. Treasury Management Association, 7315 Wisconsin Ave., Suite 600 W. Bethesda, MD 20814. Phone: (301)907-2862 Fax: (301)907-2864 E-mail:

communications@tma-net.org • URL: http://www.tma-net.org/treasury • Annual. Membership. Formerly *NCCMA Membership Directory*.

TMA News. Treasury Management Association, 7315 Wisconsin Ave., Suite 600 W. Bethesda, MD 20814. Phone: (301)907-2862 Fax: (301)907-2864 E-mail: communications@tma-net.org • URL: http://www.tma-net.org/ • Monthly. Membership.

The Toastmaster: For Better Listening, Thinking, Speaking. Suzanne Frey, editor. Toastmasters International, P.O. Box 9052 Mission Viejo, CA 92690. Phone: (714)858-8255 Fax: (714)858-1207 URL: http://www.toastmasters.org • Monthly. Membership. Provides information and ''how-to'' articles on communication and leadership.

Toastmasters International.

Toastmasters International Club Directory. Toastmasters International, P.O. Box 9052 Mission Viejo, CA 92690. Phone: (714)858-8255 Fax: (714)858-1207 URL: http://www.toastmasters.org • Annual. Price on application. Lists toastmasters clubs across the world.

Tobacco Abstracts: World Literature on Nicotiana. Tobacco Literature Service, 2314 D.H. Hill Library, North Carolina State University Raleigh, NC 27695-8009. Phone: (919)515-2836 E-mail: cbridges@cals1.cals.ncsu.edu • Bimonthly. $39.50 per year.

Tobacco and Health Research Institute. University of Kentucky

Tobacco Associates.

Tobacco Association of the U.S.

Tobacco Barometer: Cigars, Cigarettes. Tobacco Merchants Association of the United States, Inc., 231 Clarksville Rd., Suite 6 Princeton, NJ 08543-8019. Phone: (609)275-4900 Fax: (609)275-8379 Monthly. Free. Guide to manufactured production, taxable removals, and tax-exempt removals for cigarettes, large cigars, little cigars, chewing tobacco, snuff, and pipe tobacco.

Tobacco-Cigarette News. International Press Cutting Service, P.O. Box 121 Allahabad 211 001, Uttar Pradesh, India. Phone: (91-)532-622392 Weekly. $75.00 per year. Text in English. Formerly *Tobacco News*.

Tobacco Industry Litigation Reporter: The National Journal of Record of Litigation Affecting the Tobacco Industry. Andrews Publications, 175 Strafford Ave., Bldg. 4, Suite 140 Wayne, PA 19087. Phone: 800-345-1101 or (610)622-0510 Fax: (610)622-0501 URL: http://www.andrewspub.com • Monthly. $725.00 per year. Reports on major lawsuits brought against tobacco companies.

Tobacco International. Lockwood Trade Journal Co., Inc., 130 W. 42nd St. New York, NY 10036-7802. Phone: (212)391-2060 Fax: (212)827-0945 E-mail: lockmin@aol.com • Weekly. $32.00 per year.

Tobacco International Buyers' Guide and Directory. Lockwood Trade Journal Co., Inc., 130 W 42nd St., Suite 1050 New York, NY 10036-7802. Phone: (212)391-2060 Fax: (212)827-0945 E-mail: locmin@aol.com • Annual. $40.00. Formerly*Tobacco Internatonal Directory and Buyers' Guide*.

Tobacco Market Review. U.S. Department of Agriculture, Agricultural Marketing Service, Washington, DC 20250. Phone: (202)720-2791 Annual.

Tobacco Merchants Association.

Tobacco Reporter: Devoted to All Segments of the International Tobacco Trade Processing, Trading, Manufacturing. SpecComm International, Inc., 3000 Highwoods Blvd., Suite 300 Raleigh, NC 27604-1029. Phone: (919)872-5040 Fax: (919)872-6531 E-mail: tobacco_reporter@juno.com • URL: http://www.tobaccoreporter.com • Monthly. $36.00 per year. Two supplements. Formerly *TR: Tobacco Reporter*.

Tobacco Retailers Almanac. Retail Tobacco Dealers of America, 107 E. Baltimore St. Baltimore, MD 21202-1604. Phone: (301)547-6996 Fax: (301)727-7533 Annual. Price on application.

Tobacco Science Yearbook. Lockwood Trade Journal Co., Inc., 130 W. 42nd St., Suite 1050 New York, NY 10036-7802. Phone: (212)391-2060 Fax: (212)827-0945 E-mail: lockmin@aol.com • Annual. $26.00.

Tobacco Situation and Outlook. Available from U. S. Government Printing Office, Washington, DC 20402. Phone: (202)512-1800 Fax: (202)512-2250 E-mail: gpoaccess@gpo.gov • URL: http://www.access.gpo.gov • Three times per year. $11.00 per year. Issued by the Economic Research Service of the U. S. Department of Agriculture. Provides current statistical information on supply, demand, and prices.

Tobacconists' Association of America.

Today's Chemist at Work. American Chemical Society, 1155 16th St., N. W. Washington, DC 20036. Phone: 800-333-9511 or (202)872-4600 Fax: (202)872-4615 E-mail: service@acs.org • URL: http://www.pubs.acs.org • Monthly. Institutions, $160.00 per year; others, price on application. Provide pracrtical information for chemists on day-to-day operations. Product coverage includes chemicals, equipment, apparatus, instruments, and supplies.

Today's Facility Manager: The Magazine of Facilities-Interior Planning Team. Group C Communications, Inc., P.O. Box 2060 Red Bank, NJ 07701. Phone: 800-524-0337 or (908)758-6634 Fax: (908)758-6634 E-mail: jcarzon@group.com • Monthly. $30.00 per year. Covers office design, furnishings, and furniture, including open plan systems. Formerly *Business Interiors*.

Today's Insurance Woman. National Association of Insurance Women, P.O. Box 4410 Tulsa, OK 74159. Phone: (918)744-5195 Fax: (918)743-1968 URL: http://www.naiw.org • Quarterly. $15.00 per year. Provides advice on professional and personal development for women in the insurance business.

Today's Video: Equipment, Setup, and Production. Peter Utz. Prentice Hall, 240 Frisch Court Paramus, NJ 07652-5240. Phone: 800-947-7700 or (201)909-6200 Fax: 800-445-6991 or (201)909-6361 URL: http://www.prenhall.com • 1998. $89.00. Third edition.

Toiletries, Fragrances, and Skin Care: The Rose Sheet. F-D-C Reports, Inc., 5550 Friendship Blvd., Suite 1 Chevy Chase, MD 20815-7278. Phone: 800-332-2181 or (301)657-9830 Fax: (301)664-7238 URL: http://www.fdcreports.com • Weekly. $710.00 per year. Newsletter. Provides industry news, regulatory news, market data, and a ''Weekly Trademark Review'' for the cosmetics industry.

Tollways. International Bridge, Tunnel and Turnpike Association, 2120 L St., N.W. Suite 305 Washington, DC 20037. Phone: (202)659-4620 Fax: (202)659-0500 E-mail: 102234.1271@compuserve.com • Monthly. Membership. Newsletter.

Tools and Techniques of Financial Planning. Stephan Leimberg and others. The National Underwriter Co., 505 Gest St. Cincinnati, OH 45203-1716. Phone: 800-543-0874 or (513)721-2140 Fax: (513)721-0126 URL: http://www.nuco.com • 1993. $37.50. Fourth revised edition.

Top Contacts: Major Owners, Leasing Agents, and Managers. National Research Bureau, 200 W. Jackson Blvd., No. 2700 Chicago, IL 60606-6910. Phone: (312)541-0100 Fax: (312)541-1492 URL: http://www.nrbonline.com • Annual. $305.00. Contains information on more than 1,300 owners, agents, and managers, each with control of three or more shopping centers.

Top Executive Compensation. Conference Board, Inc., 845 Third Ave., 3rd. Fl. New York, NY 10022-6679. Phone: (212)759-0900 Fax: (212)980-7014 E-mail: info@conference-board.org • URL: http://www.conference-board.org • Annual. Members $30.00; non-members $120.00. Provides data on compensation of highest paid executives in major corporations.

The Top 500 Design Firms Sourcebook. McGraw-Hill, 1221 Ave. of the Americas New York, NY 10020-1095. Phone: 800-722-4726 or (212)904-2000 Fax: (212)904-2072 E-mail: customer.service@mcgraw-hill.com • URL: http://www/mcgraw-hill.com • Annual. $25.00. Lists 500 leading architectural, engineering and speciality design firms selected on basis of annual billings. Formerly *ENR Directory of Design Firms*.

The Top 5,000 European Companies 2000/2001. Available from The Gale Group, 27500 Drake Rd. Farmington Hills, MI 48331-3535. Phone: 800-877-GALE or (248)699-GALE Fax: 800-414-5043 or (248)699-8069 E-mail: galeord@galegroup.com • URL: http://www.galegroup.com • 2001. $630.00. Second edition. Published by Graham & Whiteside. In addition to about 5,000 manufacturing and service companies, includes the 500 largest banks in Europe and the 100 largest insurance companies.

The Top 5,000 Global Companies 2000/2001. Available from The Gale Group, 27500 Drake Rd. Farmington Hills, MI 48331-3535. Phone: 800-877-GALE or (248)699-GALE Fax: 800-414-5043 or (248)699-8069 E-mail: galeord@galegroup.com • URL: http://www.galegroup.com • Published by Graham & Whiteside. Includes about 5,000 manufacturing and service companies worldwide, plus the world's 500 largest banks and 100 largest insurance companies.

Topical Reference Books: Authoritative Evaluations of Recommended Resources in Specialized Subject Areas. R. R. Bowker, 121 Chanlon Rd. New Providence, NJ 07974. Phone: 888-269-5372 or (908)464-6800 Fax: (908)771-7704 E-mail: info@bowker.com • URL: http://www.bowker.com • 1991. $109.00. Ranks 2,000 reference books (''Core Titles,'' ''New and Noteworthy,'' ''Supplementary''). (Buying Guide Series).

Topicator: Classified Guide to Articles in the Advertising/Communications/Marketing Periodical Press., P.O. Box 757 Terrebonne, OR 97760-0757. Phone: (956)581-4197 Bimonthly. $110.00 per year. An index of major articles appearing in 20 leading magazines in the advertising, communications, and marketing fields.

Total Business Budgeting: A Step-by-Step Guide with Forms. Robert Rachlin. John Wiley and Sons, Inc., 605 Third Ave. New York, NY 10158-0012. Phone: 800-225-5945 or (212)850-6000 Fax: (212)850-6088 E-mail: info@jwiley.com • URL: http://www.wiley.com • 1999. $69.95. Second edition.

The Total Business Plan: How to Write, Rewrite, and Revise. Patrick D. O'Hara. John Wiley and Sons, Inc., 605 Third Ave. New York, NY 10158-0012. Phone: 800-225-5945 or (212)850-6000 Fax: (212)850-6088 E-mail: info@wiley.com • URL: http://www.wiley.com • 1994. $49.95. Second edition. Covers concept, strategy, research, writing, revising, and presentation. Includes a disk.

Total Business Planning: A Step-by-Step Guide with Forms. James E. Burton and W. Blan McBride. John Wiley and Sons, Inc., 605 Third Ave. New York, NY 10158-0012. Phone: 800-526-5368 or (212)850-6000 Fax: (212)850-6088 E-mail: info@wiley.com • URL: http://www.wiley.com • 1999. $29.95. Second edition. How to construct and activate an internal business plan, whether short-term or long-term. Includes CD-ROM.

Total Customer Service-The Ultimate Weapon: A Six Point Plan for Giving Your Business the Competitive Edge in the 1990's. William H. Davidow and Bro Uttal. Harper Trade, 10 E. 53rd St. New York, NY 10022-5299. Phone: 800-242-7737 or (212)207-7000 Fax: 800-822-4090 or (212)207-7145 URL: http://www.harpercollins.com • 1990. $13.00.

The Total Package: The Secret History and Hidden Meanings of Boxes, Bottles, Cans, and Other Persuasive Containers. Thomas Hine. Little, Brown and Co., Time and Life Bldg., 1271 Ave. of the Americas New York, NY 10020. Phone: 800-759-0190 or (212)522-8700 Fax: 800-286-9741 or (212)522-2067 E-mail: cust.service@littlebrown.com • URL: http://www.littlebrown.com • 1997. $14.95. A popularly written history of packaging.

Total Quality Management Handbook. John L. Hradesky. McGraw-Hill, 1221 Ave. of the Americas New York, NY 10020. Phone: 800-722-4726 or (212)904-2000 Fax: (212)904-2072 E-mail: customer.service@mcgraw-hill.com • URL: http://www.mcgraw-hill.com • 1994. $74.50.

Total Quality Management in Action. Gopal K. Kanji. Chapman and Hall, 115 Fifth Ave., 4th Fl. New York, NY 10003-1004. Phone: 800-842-3636 or (212)260-1354 Fax: (212)260-1730 E-mail: info@chapall.com • URL: http://www.chapall.com • 1996. $129.95.

Total Telemarketing: Complete Guide to Increasing Sales and Profits. Robert J. McHatton. John Wiley and Sons, Inc., 605 Third Ave. New York, NY 10158-0012. Phone: 800-526-5368 or (212)850-6000 Fax: (212)850-6088 E-mail: info@wiley.com • URL: http://www.wiley.com • 1988. $49.95.

The Touche Ross Personal Financial Planning and Investment Workbook. John R. Connell and others. Prentice Hall, 240 Frisch Court Paramus, NJ 07652-5240. Phone: 800-947-7700 or (201)909-6200 Fax: 800-445-6991 or (201)909-6361 URL: http://www.prenhall.com • 1989. $39.95. Third edition.

Tough-Minded Leadership. Joe D. Batten. AMACOM, 1601 Broadway, 12th Fl. New York, NY 10019. Phone: 800-262-9699 or (212)586-8100 Fax: (212)903-8168 E-mail: custmserv@amanet.org • URL: http://www.amanet.org • 1989. $15.95.

Tourism Planning. David Marcouiller. Sage Publications, Inc., 2455 Teller Rd. Thousand Oaks, CA 91320. Phone: (805)499-0721 Fax: (805)449-0871 E-mail: info@sagepub.com • URL: http://www.sagepub.com • 1995. $10.00. (CPL Bibliographies Series).

Tourism Policy and International Tourism in OECD Member Countries. Available from OECD Publications and Information Center, 2001 L St., N.W.,, Suite 700 Washington, DC 20036-4922. Phone: 800-456-6323 or (202)785-6323 Fax: (202)785-0350 E-mail: washington.contact@oecd.org • URL: http://www.oecd.org • Annual. $50.00. Reviews developments in the international tourism industry in OECD member countries. Includes statistical information.

Tourism: Principles, Practices, Philosophies. Robert W. McIntosh and others. John Wiley and Sons, Inc., 605 Third Ave. New York, NY 10158-0012. Phone: 800-526-5368 or (212)850-6000 Fax: (212)850-6088 E-mail: info@wiley.com • URL: http://www.wiley.com • 1999. $64.95. Eighth edition. General review of the travel industry.

Tourist Attractions and Parks Magazine Buyers Guide. Kane Communications, Inc., 7000 Terminal Square, Suite 210 Upper Darby, PA 19082. Phone: (610)734-2420 Fax: (610)734-2423 E-mail: tapmag.com • URL: http://www.tapmag.com • Annual. $10.00. Lists companies making products or services for leisure facilities.

Toward an Optimal Stock Selection Strategy. Lawrence S. Pratt. American Institute for Economic Research, Division St. Great Barrington, MA 01230-1000. Phone: (413)528-1216 Fax: (413)528-0103 E-mail: info@aier.org • URL: http://www.aier.org • 1997. $6.00. Second edition. Discusses the strategy of buying only the stocks in the Dow Jones Industrial Average that have the highest-yielding dividends. Includes detailed charts and tables. (Economic Education Bulletin.)

Towards a Sustainable Energy Future. Organization for Economic Cooperation and Development, OECD Washington Center, 2001 L St., N. W., Suite 650 Washington, DC 20036-4922. Phone: 800-456-6323 or (202)785-6323 Fax: (202)785-0350 E-mail: washington.contact@oecd.org • URL: http://www.oecd.org • 2001. $100.00. Prepared by the International Energy Agency (IEA). Describes various policies for promoting sustainable energy, especially. Prepared by the International Energy Agency (IEA). Describes various policies for promoting sustainable energy, especially as related to economic development. Discusses "growing concerns about climate change and energy-supply security."

Towards Electronic Journals: Realities for Scientists, Librarians, and Publishers. Carol Tenopir and Donald W. King. Special Libraries Association, 1700 18th St., N. W., 17th Fl. Washington, DC 20009-2514. Phone: (202)234-4700 Fax: (202)234-2442 E-mail: books@sla.org • URL: http://www.sla.org • 2000. $59.00. Discusses journals in electronic form vs. traditional (paper) scholarly journals, including the impact of subscription prices.

Towards Electronic Publishing: Realities for Scientists, Librarians, and Publishers. Carol Tenopir and Donald W. King. Special Libraries Association, 1700 18th St., N. W., 17th Fl. Washington, DC 20009-2514. Phone: (202)234-4700 Fax: 888-411-2856 or (202)234-2442 E-mail: books@sla.org • URL: http://www.sla.org • 2000. $59.00. Discusses 40-year developments, trends, and price escalation in the academic journal publishing system.

Town and Country. Hearst Corp., 1700 Broadway New York, NY 10019-5970. Phone: 800-289-8696 or (212)903-5000 Fax: (212)765-8308 E-mail: town&country@hearst.com • URL: http://www.hearstmagsb2b.com • Monthly. $24.00 per year.

Township Atlas of the United States. The Gale Group, 27500 Drake Rd. Farmington Hills, MI 48331-3535. Phone: 800-877-GALE or (248)699-GALE Fax: 800-414-5043 or (248)699-8069 E-mail: galeord@galegroup.com • URL: http://www.galegroup.com • 2000. $85.00. Fourth edition. Covers the 48 contiguous states. Includes state maps, county maps, townships, subdivisions, and indexes.

Toxic Chemicals Laboratory. Cornell University

Toxic Substances Controls Guide. Mary D. Worobec and Cheryl Hogue. Bureau of National Affairs, Inc., 1231 25th St., N. W. Washington, DC 20037-1197. Phone: 800-372-1033 or (202)452-4200 Fax: (202)452-8092 E-mail: books@bna.com • URL: http://www.bna.com • 1992. 45.00. Second edition. Emphasis on legal aspects.

Toxline. National Library of Medicine, 8600 Rockville Pike Bethesda, MD 20894. Phone: 800-638-8480 or (301)496-6531 Fax: (301)480-3537 Abstracting service covering human and animal toxicity studies, 1965 to present (older studies available in *Toxback* file). Monthly updates. Inquire as to online cost and availability.

Toy Manufacturers of America.

TPG Briefing on Local Exchange Statistics. Warren Communication News, 2115 Ward Court, N. W. Washington, DC 20037-1209. Phone: 800-771-9202 or (202)872-9200 Fax: (202)293-3435 E-mail: customerservice@warren-news.com • URL: http://www.telecommunications.com • Annual. $325.00. Contains statistics on local telephone companies: revenues, expenses, debt, income, advertising, access lines, network usage, etc. Provides "Current Information on Major Competitors."

TQM: Leadership for the Quality Transformation. Richard S. Johnson. American Society for Quality, P.O. Box 3005 Milwaukee, WI 53201-3005. Phone: 800-248-1946 or (414)272-8575 Fax: (414)272-1734 E-mail: asa@asq.org • URL: http://www.asq.org • 1993. $37.95. Covers leadership styles and the creation of a quality environment. *Johnson TQM Series: volume one*.

TQM: Management Processes for Quality Operations. Richard S. Johnson. American Society for Quality, P.O. Box 3005 Milwaukee, WI 53201-3005. Phone: 800-248-1946 or (414)272-8575 Fax: (414)272-1734 E-mail: asq@asq.org • URL: http://www.asq.org • 1993. $45.00. Topics include management systems, planning, hiring, performance management, procedure manuals, and time managment. ASQC Total Quality Control Management Series: volume. 12.

TQM: Quality Training Practices. Richard S. Johnson. American Society for Quality, P.O. Box 3005 Milwaukee, WI 53201-3005. Phone: 800-248-1946 or (414)272-8575 Fax: (414)272-1734 E-mail: asq.asq.org • URL: http://www.asq.org • 1993. $45.00. An industrial quality training manual, with samples of checklists, charts, surveys, comparisons, and questionnaires. (Johnson TQM Series: volume 4.)

Trade-a-Plane., 6666 Van Winkle Dr. Falls Church, VA 22044-1010. Phone: (615)484-5137 Fax: (615)484-5137 36 times a year. $98.00 per year. Subject matter is aircraft for sale or trade.

Trade & Culture: How to Make it in the World Market. Key Communications Corp., 5617 Warwick Place Chevy Chase, MD 20815-5503. Phone: (301)426-2906 Fax: (301)444-7837 Quarterly. $29.95 per year. Edited for businesses actively involved in exporting or importing.

Trade and Development Report and Overview. Available from United Nations Publications, United Nations Concourse Level, First Ave., 46th St. New York, NY 10017. Phone: 800-553-3210 or (212)963-7680 Fax: (212)963-4910 E-mail: bookstore@un.org • URL: http://www.un.org/publications • Annual. $45.00. Yearly overview of trends in international trade, including an analysis of the economic and trade situation in developing countries. Published by the United Nations Conference on Trade and Development (UNCTAD).

Trade and Employment in Developing Countries. Anne O. Krueger, editor. University of Chicago Press, 5801 S. Ellis Ave., 4th Fl. Chicago, IL 60637. Phone: 800-621-2736 or (773)702-7700 Fax: (773)702-9756 E-mail: marketing@press.uchicago.edu • URL: http://www.press.uchicago.edu • Three volumes. Vol. 1, 1980, $66.00; Vol. 2, 1982, $35.00; Vol. 3, 1983, $16.00. (National Bureau of Economic Research Project Report Series).

Trade & Industry Index. The Gale Group, 27500 Drake Rd. Farmington Hills, MI 48331-3535. Phone: 800-877-GALE or (248)699-GALE Fax: 800-414-5043 or (248)699-8069 E-mail: galeord@gale.com • URL: http://www.gale.com • Provides indexing of business periodicals, January 1981 to date. Daily updates. (Full text articles from some periodicals are available online, 1983 to date, in the companion database, *Trade & Industry ASAP*.) Inquire as to online cost and availability.

Trade Associations amd Professional Bodies of the Continental European Union. Available from The Gale Group, 27500 Drake Rd. Farmington Hills, MI 48331-3535. Phone: 800-877-GALE or (248)699-GALE Fax: 800-414-5043 or (248)699-8069 E-mail: galeord@galegroup.com • URL: http://www.galegroup.com • 2000. $280.00. Published by Graham & Whiteside. Provides detailed information on more than 3,600 business and professional organizations in Europe.

Trade Book Publishing: Review, Forecast, and Segment Analysis. SIMBA Information, P.O. Box 4234 Stamford, CT 06907-0234. Phone: 800-307-2529 or (203)328-4100 Fax: (203)358-5824 E-mail: info@simbanet.com • URL: http://www.simbanet.com • 1999. $1,495.00. Reviews current conditions in the book publishing industry, including analysis of market segments, retailing aspects, and profiles of major publishers.

Trade Channel. Trade Channel Organization, Stolbergstraat 14 2012 EP Haarlem, Netherlands. Phone: 31 23 5319022 Fax: 31 23 5317974 E-mail: tco_nl@compuserve.com • URL: http://www.tradechannel.com • Monthly. $88.00 per year. Features export "offers" and import "wants." Worldwide coverage. Technical products and consumer products. Each edition $88.00 per year. Formerly *Export Channel*.

Trade Dimensions' Directory of Convenience Stores. Trade Dimensions, 45 Danbury Rd. Wilton, CT 06897-4445. Phone: (203)563-3000 Fax: (203)563-3131 E-mail: info@tradedimensions.com • URL: http://www.tradedimensions.com • Annual. $245.00. Provides information on over 1,300 convenience store chains having four or more convenience stores. Formerly *Directory of Convenience Stores*.

Trade Dimensions' Market Scope. Trade Dimensions, 45 Danbury Rd. Wilton, CT 06897-4445. Phone: (203)563-3000 Fax: (203)563-3131 E-mail: info@tradedimensions.com • URL: http://www.tradedimensions.com • Annual. $325.00. Statistics of grocery distribution for 249 metropolitan areas. Formerly *Progressive Grocer's market Scope*.

Trade Dimensions' Marketing Guidebook. Trade Dimensions, 45 Danbury Rd. Wilton, CT 06897-4445. Phone: (203)563-3000 Fax: (203)563-3131 E-mail: info@tradedimensions.com • URL: http://www.tradedimensions.com • Annual. $340.00. Over 850 major chain and independent food retailers and wholesalers in the United States and Canada; also includes food brokers, rack jobbers, candy and tobacco distributors, and magazine distributors. Formerly *Progressive Grocer's Marketing Guidebook*.

Trade Directories of the World. Croner Publications, Inc., 10951 Sorrento Valley Rd., Suite 1-D San Diego, CA 92121-1613. Phone: 800-441-4033 or (619)546-1894 Fax: (619)546-1955 E-mail: paul@croner.com • URL: http://www.sdic.net/croner • Annual. 100.00.Looseleaf. Monthly supplements. Lists over 3,300 publications.

Trade Directory of Mexico. Mexican Foreign Trade Bank, c/o Walker's Research, 1650 Borel Place, Suite 130 San Mateo, CA 94402. Phone: 800-258-5737 Fax: (650)341-2351 URL: http://www.hoovers.com • Annual. $100.00. Provides information on more than 4,200 Mexican companies involved in foreign trade. Lists forwarding agencies, customs brokers, consulting groups, transportation companies, and other trade-related Mexican organizations.

Trade Policy Review - Japan. Bernan Press, 4611-F Assembly Dr. Lanham, MD 20706-4391. Phone: 800-274-4447 or (301)459-7666 Fax: 800-865-3450 or (301)459-0056 E-mail: info@bernan.com • URL: http://www.bernan.com • 1998. $50.00. Co-published by Bernan Press and the World Trade Organization. Available in English, French, or Spanish versions. Provides WTO analysis of Japan's overall economic environment, trade policy objectives, and "policy developments affecting trade and investment."

Trade Policy Reviews. Bernan Press, 4611-F Assembly Dr. Lanham, MD 20706-4391. Phone: 800-274-4447 or (301)459-7666 Fax: 800-865-3450 or (301)459-0056 E-mail: info@bernan.com • URL: http://www.bernan.com • Annual. Price varies for each country's review (31 are available). Each review describes "trade policies, practices, and macroeconomic situations." Prepared by the Trade Policy Review Board of the World Trade Organization.

Trade Secret Protection in an Information Age. Gale R. Peterson. Glasser Legalworks, 150 Clove Rd. Little Falls, NJ 07424. Phone: 800-308-1700 or (973)890-0008 Fax: (973)890-0042 E-mail: legalwks@aol.com • URL: http://www.legalwks.com • Looseleaf. $149.00, including sample forms on disk. Periodic supplementation available. Covers trade secret law relating to computer software, online databases, and multimedia products. Explanations are based on more than 1,000 legal cases. Sample forms on disk include work-for-hire examples and covenants not to compete.

Trade Show Central: The Internet's Leading Trade Show Information Resource! Trade Show CentralPhone: (781)235-8095 Fax: (781)416-4500 URL: http://www.tscentral.com • Web site provides information on "more than 30,000 Trade Shows, Conferences, and Seminars, 5,000 service providers, and 5,000 venues and facilities around the world." Searching is offered by trade show name, industry category, date, and location. Results may be sorted by event name, city, country, or date. Includes a "Career Center" for trade show personnel. Continuous updating. Fees: Free.

Trade Show Exhibitors Association., 5501 Backlick Rd., Suite 105 Springfield, VA 22151. Phone: (703)941-3725 Fax: (703)941-8275 E-mail: tsea@tsea.org • Promotes the use of trade shows for marketing products and services.

Trade Show Exhibitors Association Membership Directory and Product/Service Guide. Trade Show Exhibitors Association, 5501 Backlick Rd., Suite 105 Springfield, VA 22151. Phone: (703)941-3725 Fax: (703)941-8275 E-mail: tsea@tsea.org • Annual. 55.00. Provides listings and details for approximately 2,300 exhibit professionals. Formerly *International Exhibitors Association-Membership Directory and Product/Service Guide*.

Trade Shows Worldwide: An International Directory of Events, Facilities and Suppliers. The Gale Group, 27500 Drake Rd. Farmington Hills, MI 48331-3535. Phone: 800-877-GALE or (248)699-GALE Fax: 800-414-5043 or (248)699-8069 E-mail: galeord@galegroup.com • URL: http://www.galegroup.com • 2000. $299.00. 16th edition. Provides detailed information from over 75 countries on more than 8,400 trade shows and exhibitions. Separate sections are provided for trade shows/exhibitions, for sponsors/organizers, and for services, facilities, and information sources. Indexing is by date, location, subject, name, and keyword.

Trade Union. International Confederation of Free Trade Unions, Bd. Emil Jacqmain 155, Bte. One 1210 Brussels, Belgium. Monthly. Formerly *Free Labour World*.

Trade Unions of the World. John C. Turbine & Associates, 1825 E. Faunsdale Dr. Sandy, UT 84092-3817. Phone: (801)572-0999 2000. $99.00. Fifth edition. Trade union federations and affiliated unions.

Trademark Alert. Thomson & Thomson, 500 Victory Rd. North Quincy, MA 02171-1545. Phone: 800-692-8833 or (617)479-1600 Fax: (617)786-8273 E-mail: support@thomson-thomson.com • URL: http://www.thomson-thomson.com • Weekly. $1,075.00 per year. Contains information on new trademark applications filed with the U. S. Patent and Trademark Office. Arranged by International Class and indexed by significant word or character.

Trademark Law Handbook. United States Trademark Association. West Group, 610 Opperman Dr. Eagan, MN 55123. Phone: 800-328-4880 or (651)687-7000 Fax: 800-213-2323 or (651)687-5827 URL: http://www.westgroup.com • Annual. $65.00.

Trademark Manual of Examining Procedure. Available from U. S. Government Printing Office, Washington, DC 20402. Phone: (202)512-1800 Fax: (202)512-2250 E-mail: gpoaccess@gpo.gov • URL: http://www.access.gpo.gov • $51.00 for basic manual and semiannual changes for an indeterminate period. Covers "practices and procedures" relating to the processing of applications to register trademarks in the U. S. Patent and Trademark Office.

Trademark Protection and Practice. Jerome Gilson. Matthew Bender & Co., Inc., Two Park Ave. New York, NY 10016. Phone: 800-223-1940 or (212)448-2000 Fax: (212)244-3188 E-mail: international@bender.com • URL: http://www.bender.com • $1,160.00. 11 looseleaf volumes. Periodic supplementation. Covers U. S. trademark practice.

Trademark Register of the United States. Trademark Register, 2100 National Press Bldg. Washington, DC 20045-1000. Phone: (202)662-1233 Fax: (202)347-4408 E-mail: info@trademarkreg.com • URL: http://www.trademarkregister.com • Annual. $435.00. Lists all trademarks currently registered and renewed trademarks in the U.S. Patent and Trademark Office.

Trademark Reporter. International Trademark Association, 1133 Sixth Ave. New York, NY 10036-6710. Phone: (212)768-9887 Fax: (212)768-7796 Bimonthly. Membership. Contains articles on trademark developments, trademark law, and the use of trademarks.

TRADEMARKSCAN: International Register. Thomson & Thomson, 500 Victory Rd. North Quincy, MA 02171-3145. Phone: 800-692-8833 or (617)479-1600 Fax: (617)786-8273 URL: http://www.thomson-thomson.com • Supplies current information on more than 400,000 trademarks registered with the World Intellectual Property Organization. Updates are monthly. Inquire as to online cost and availability. (TRADEMARKSCAN also maintains extensive databases for individual countries: Canada, U. K., Germany, Italy, France, and others.)

TRADEMARKSCAN: U. S. Federal. Thomson & Thomson, 500 Victory Rd. North Quincy, MA 02171-3145. Phone: 800-692-8833 or (617)479-1600 Fax: (617)786-8273 URL: http://www.thomson-thomson.com • Provides information on more than two million trademarks registered and pending at the U. S. Patent and Trademark Office. Time period is 1884 to date for active trademarks, with updates twice a week. Graphic images are shown for approximately 40% of the records. Inquire as to online cost and availability.

TRADEMARKSCAN: U. S. Federal ÎCD-ROMl. Thomson & Thomson, 500 Victory Rd. North Quincy, MA 02171-1545. Phone: 800-692-8833 or (617)479-1600 Fax: (617)786-8273 Monthly. $7,500.00 per year. Contains information on CD-ROM for more than two million trademarks from the U. S. Patent and Trademark Office. For active trademarks, time period is 1884 to date. Graphic images are shown for many of the records.

TRADEMARKSCAN: U. S. State. Thomson & Thomson, 500 Victory Rd. North Quincy, MA 02171-3145. Phone: 800-692-8833 or (617)479-1600 Fax: (617)786-8273 URL: http://www.thomson-thomson.com • Contains information on more than 970,000 trademarks registered with the Office of the Secretary of State in all 50 states and in Puerto Rico. Time period is 1900 to date for active trademarks, with weekly updates. Inquire as to online cost and availability.

TRADEMARKSCAN: U. S. State ÎCD-ROMl. Thomson & Thomson, 500 Victory Rd. North Quincy, MA 02171-1545. Phone: 800-692-8833 or (617)479-1600 Fax: (617)786-8273 Monthly. $3,500.00 per year. Provides information on CD-ROM for more than one million trademarks registered with the Office of the Secretary of State in all 50 states and in Puerto Rico. For active trademarks, time period is 1900 to date.

Trader Vic: Methods of a Wall Street Master. Victor Sperandeo. John Wiley and Sons, Inc., 605 Third Ave. New York, NY 10158-0012. Phone: 800-526-5367 or (212)850-6000 Fax: (212)850-6088 E-mail: info@wiley.com • URL: http://www.wiley.com • 1993. $19.95.

Traders Magazine. Securities Data Publishing, 40 West 57th St. New York, NY 10019. Phone: 800-455-5844 or (212)765-5311 Fax: (212)956-0112 E-mail: sdp@tfn.com • URL: http://www.sdponline.com • Monthly. $60.00 per year. Edited for institutional buy side and sell side equity traders. Covers industry news, market trends, regulatory developments, and personnel news. Serves as the official publication of the Security Traders Association. (Securities Data Publishing is a unit of Thomson Financial.)

TradeShow and Convention Guide. BPI Communications, Amusement Business Div., P.O. Box 24970 Nashville, TN 37202. Phone: 800-407-6874 or (615)321-4250 Fax: (615)327-1575 E-mail: info@amusementbusiness.com • URL: http://www.amusementbusiness.com • Annual. $115.00. Dates and data for convention and trade shows for the next five years; local companies that supply services such as photograpy, exhibit design etc.; halls and hotels catering to conventions and shows.

Tradeshow and Exhibit Manager. Goldstein and Associates, 1150 Yale St., Suite 12 Santa Monica, CA 90403-4738. Phone: (310)828-1309 Fax: (310)829-1169 Bimonthly. $80.00 per year. Edited for exhibit, tradeshow, and exposition managers. Covers design trends, site selection, shipping problems, industry news, etc. Supplement available *Tradeshow Directory*.

Tradeshow and Exhibit Manager Buyer's Guide. Goldstein and Associates, 1150 Yale St., Suite 12 Santa Monica, CA 90403. Phone: (310)828-1309 Fax: (310)829-1169 Annual. $10.00. Lists about 1,000 suppliers providing products and services for exhibits and tradeshows.

Tradeshow Week: Since 1971, the Only Weekly Source of News and Statistics on the Tradeshow Industry. Tradeshow Week, Inc., 5700 Wilshire Blvd., Suite 120 Los Angeles, CA 90036-5804. Phone: 800-375-4212 or (323)965-5335 Fax: (323)965-5336 E-mail: dgudea@tsweek.com • URL: http://www.tradesweek.com • 49 times a year. $389.00 per year. Edited for corporate and association trade show and exhibit managers. Includes show calendars and labor rates.

Trading and Investing in Bond Options: Risk Management, Arbitrage, and Value Investing. Anthony M. Wong. John Wiley and Sons, Inc., 605 Third Ave. New York, NY 10158-0012. Phone: 800-526-5368 or (212)850-6000 Fax: (212)850-6088 E-mail: info@wiley.com • URL: http://www.wiley.com • 1991. $55.00. Covers dealing, trading, and investing in U. S. government bond futures options (puts and calls).

Trading Cycles. R.E. Andrews, editor. Andrews Publications, Inc., 156 Shadow Creek Lane Paso Robles, CA 93446-1922. Phone: (408)778-2925 Monthly. $97.99 per year. Technical investment newsletter. Formerly *Andrews Trading Cycles*.

Trading Financial Futures: Markets, Methods, Strategies, and Tactics. John W. Labuszewski and John E. Nyhoff. John Wiley and Sons, Inc., 605 Third Ave. New York, NY 10158-0012. Phone: 800-526-5368 or (212)850-6000 Fax: (212)850-6088 E-mail: info@wiley.com • URL: http://www.wiley.com • 1997. $49.95. Second edition. (Wiley Finance Editions Series).

Trading for a Living: Psychology, Trading Tactics, Money Management. Alexander Elder. John Wiley and Sons, Inc., 605 Third Ave. New York, NY 10158-0012. Phone: 800-225-5945 or (212)850-6000 Fax: (212)850-6088 E-mail: info@wiley.com • URL: http://www.wiley.com • 1993. $59.95. Covers technical and chart methods of trading in commodity and financial futures, options, and stocks. Includes Elliott Wave Theory, oscillators, moving averages, point-and- figure, and other technical approaches. (Finance Editions Series).

Trading Options on Futures: Markets, Methods, Strategies, and Tactics. John W. Labuszewski and John E. Nyhoff. John Wiley and Sons, Inc., 605 Third Ave. New York, NY 10158-0012. Phone: 800-526-5368 or (212)850-6000 Fax: (212)850-6088 E-mail: info@wiley.com • URL: http://www.wiley.com • 1996. $39.95. Second edition.

Trading to Win: The Psychology of Mastering the Markets. Ari Kiev. John Wiley and Sons, Inc., 605 Third Ave. New York, NY 10158-0012. Phone: 800-225-5945 or (212)850-6000 Fax: (212)850-6088 E-mail: info@wiley.com • URL: http://www.wiley.com • 1998. $34.95. A mental health guide for stock, bond, and commodity traders. Tells how to keep speculative emotions in check, overcome self-doubt, and focus on a winning strategy. (Trading Advantage Series).

Traffic Engineering and Control. Printerhall Ltd., 29 Newman St. London W1P 3PE, England. Phone: 44 171 6363956 Fax: 44 171 4367016 Monthly. $120.00 per year. Provides authoritative articles on planning, engineering and management of highways for safe and efficient operation.

Traffic Safety: The Magazine for Traffic Safety Professionals. National Safety Council, Periodicals Dept., 1121 Spring Lake Dr. Itasca, IL 60143-3201. Phone: 800-621-7619 or (630)285-1121 Fax: (630)285-1315 URL: http://www.nsc.org • Bimonthly. Members, $33.00 per year; non-members, $44.00 per year.

Traffic World: The Weekly Newsmagazine of Transportation and Distribution. Journal of Commerce, Inc., 1230 National Press Bldg. Washington, DC 20045. Phone: (202)737-1101 Fax: (202)661-3383 URL: http://www.trafficworld.com • Weekly. $174.00 per year.

Trailer Body Builders Buyers Guide. Tunnell Publications, Inc., 4200 S. Shepherd Dr., Suite 200 Houston, TX 77098. Phone: 800-441-0294 or (713)523-8124 Fax: (713)523-8384 Annual. Controlled circulation. List of 8,000 products used by original equipment manufacturers of truck trailers and truck bodies.

Trailer Life Campground and RV Services Directory. Good Sam Club. Affinity Group Inc.,T L Enterprises, 2575 Vista Del Mar Dr. Ventura, CA 93001-3920. Phone: 800-766-1674 or (805)667-4100 Fax: (805)667-4419 URL: http://www.tl.com/ssl • Annual. Members, $9.95;non-members, $10.95. Describes and rates over 25,000 RV campgrounds, service centers and tourist attractions. Formerly *Good Sam Club's Recreational Vehicle Owners Directory*.

Trailer Life: RVing At Its Best. Good Sam Club. Affinity Group Inc., T L Enterprises, 2575 Vista Del Mar Dr. Ventura, CA 93001. Phone: 800-766-1674 or (805)667-4100 Fax: (805)667-4213 URL: http://www.trailerlife.com • Monthly. $22.00 per year.

Training and Development. American Society for Training and Development, P.O. Box 1443 Alexandria, VA 22313. Phone: 800-628-2873 or (703)683-8100 Fax: (703)683-9203 URL: http://www.astd.org/ • Monthly. Free to members; non-members, $85.00 per year.

Training and Development Handbook: A Guide to Human Resource Development. Robert L. Craig. McGraw-Hill, 1221 Ave. of the Americas New York, NY 10020. Phone: 800-722-4726 or (212)904-2000 Fax: (212)904-2072 E-mail: customer.service@mcgraw-hill.com • URL: http://www.mcgraw-hill.com • 1996. $89.50. Fourth edition.

Training and Development Organizations Directory. The Gale Group, 27500 Drake Rd. Farmington Hills, MI 48331-3535. Phone: 800-877-GALE or (248)699-GALE Fax: 800-414-5043 or (248)699-8069 E-mail: galeord@galegroup.com • URL: http://www.galegroup.com • 1994. $385.00. Sixth edition.

Training and Development Yearbook. Carolyn Nilson. Prentice Hall, 240 Frisch Court Paramus, NJ 07652-5240. Phone: 800-947-7700 or (201)909-6200 Fax: 800-445-6991 or (201)909-6361 URL: http://www.prenhall.com • Annual. $79.95. Includes reprints of journal articles on employee training and development.

Training for Non-Trainers: A Do-It-Yourself Guide for Managers. Carolyn Nilson. AMACOM, 1601 Broadway, 12th Fl. New York, NY 10019. Phone: 800-262-9699 or (212)586-8100 Fax: (212)903-8168 E-mail: custmserv.amanet.org • URL: http://www.amanet.org • 1990. $16.95.

Training: The Magazine of Covering the Human Side of Business. Lakewood Publications, Inc., Lakewood Bldg., 50 S. Ninth St. Minneapolis, MN 55402. Phone: 800-328-4329 or (612)333-0471 Fax: (612)333-6526 E-mail: jgordon@trainingmag.com • URL: http://www.lakewood.com • Monthly. $78.00 per year.

Trains; The Magazine of Railroading. Kalmbach Publishing Co., P.O. Box 1612 Waukesha, WI 53187-1612. Phone: 800-558-1544 or (262)796-8776 Fax: (262)796-1615 E-mail: webmaster@kalmbach.com • URL: http://www.kalmbach.com • Monthly. $39.95 per year.

Transdex Index. UMI, 300 N. Zeeb Rd. Ann Arbor, MI 48106-1346. Phone: 800-864-0019 or (313)761-4700 Fax: 800-864-0019 URL: http://www.umi.com • Monthly. Price on application.

Transit Fact Book. American Public Transit Association, 1201 New York Ave., N.W., Suite 400 Washington, DC 20036. Phone: (202)898-4119 Fax: (202)898-4095 URL: http://www.apta.com/press/thisweek.htm • Annual.

Transitions Abroad: The Guide to Learning, Living, and Working Overseas. Transitions Abroad Publishing, Inc., 18 Hulst Rd. Amherst, MA 01004-1300. Phone: (413)256-3414 Fax: (413)256-0373 E-mail: editor@transitionabroad.com • URL: http://www.transitionabroad.com • Bimonthly. $28.00 per year, including annual directory of information sources. Provides practical information and advice on foreign education and employment. Supplement available *Overseas Travel Planner*.

Translating and the Computer. Available from Information Today, Inc., 143 Old Marlton Pike Medford, NJ 08055-8750. Phone: 800-300-9868 or (609)654-6266 Fax: (609)654-4309 E-mail: custserv@infotoday.com • URL: http://www.infotoday.com • Annual. $49.00. Published in London by Aslib: The Association for Information Management. Includes papers from the annual International Conference on Translating and the Computer.

Transnational Accounting. Dieter Ordelheide and others, editors. Groves Dictionaries, 345 Park Ave. S., 10th Fl. New York, NY 10010-1707. Phone: 800-221-2123 or (212)689-9200 Fax: (212)689-9711 E-mail: grove@grovereference.com • URL: http://www.grovereference.com • 2000. $650.00. Three volumes. Published by Macmillan (UK). Provides detailed descriptions of financial accounting principles and practices in 14 major countries (10 European, plus the U. S., Canada, Australia, and Japan). Includes tables, exhibits, index, and a glossary of 244 accounting terms in eight languages.

Transnational Bank Behavior and the International Debt Crisis. United Nations Publications, United Nations Concourse Level, First Ave., 46th St. New York, NY 10017. Phone: 800-553-3210 or (212)963-7680 Fax: (212)963-4910 E-mail: bookstore@un.org • URL: http://www.un.org/publications • 1990.

Transnational Corporations. United Nations Conference on Trade and Development. United Nations Publications, United Nations Concourse Level, First Ave., 46th St. New York, NY 10017. Phone: 800-553-3210 or (212)963-7608 Fax: (212)963-4910 E-mail: bookstore@un.org • URL: http://www.un.org/publications • Three times a year. $45.00 per year. Reports on both governmental and non-governmental aspects of multinational corporations. Issued by the United Nations Centre on Transnational Corporations (UNCTC). Formerly *CTC Reporter*.

Transport Topics: National Newspaper of the Trucking Industry. American Trucking Associations, 2200 Mill Rd. Alexandria, VA 22314-4677. Phone: 800-282-5463 or (703)838-1700 Fax: (703)684-5720 E-mail: ata-infocenter@trucking.org • URL: http://www.truckline.com • Weekly. $79.00 per year.

Transport 2000 and Intermodal World. BuenaVentura Publishing Co., 870 Market St., No. 954 San Francisco, CA 94102. Phone: (415)892-0818 Bimonthly. $15.00 per year.

Transportation. Time-Life, Inc., 2000 Duke St. Alexandria, VA 22314. Phone: 800-621-7026 or (703)838-7000 Fax: (703)684-5224 1999. $16.95. Revised edition. (Understanding Computers Series.)

Transportation: An International Journal Devoted to the Improvement of Transportation Planning and Practice. Kluwer Academic Publishers, 101 Philip Dr. Norwell, MA 02061. Phone: (781)871-6600 Fax: (781)871-6528 E-mail: kluwer@wkap.nl • URL: http://www.wkap.nl • Quarterly. $370.00 per year.

Transportation and Distribution. Penton Media Inc., 1300 E. Ninth St. Cleveland, OH 44114. Phone: (216)696-7000 Fax: (216)696-0836 E-mail: corpcomm@penton.com • URL: http://www.penton.com • Monthly. Free to qualified personnel; others, $50.00 per year. Essential information on transportation and distribution practices in domestic and international trade.

Transportation Builder. American Road and Transportation Builders Association. Heartland Custom Publishers Group, 1003 Central Ave. Fort Dodge, IA 50501. Phone: 800-247-2000 or (515)955-1600 Fax: 800-247-2000 Monthly. $50.00 per year.

Transportation Center.

Transportation Clubs International.

Transportation, Elevator and Grain Merchants Association.

Transportation Engineering and Planning. C. S. Papacostas and Panos D. Prevedouros. Prentice Hall, 240 Frisch Court Paramus, NJ 07652-5240. Phone: 800-947-7700 or (201)909-6200 Fax: 800-445-6991 or (201)909-6361 URL: http://www.prenhall.com • 2000. $105.00. Third edition.

Transportation Institute.

Transportation Journal. American Society of Transportation and Logistics, Inc., 229 Peachtree St., No. 401 Atlanta, GA 30303. Phone: (570)748-8515 URL: http://www.astl.org • Quarterly. $55.00 per year.

Transportation Planning Handbook. John D. Edwards. Institute of Transportation Engineers Staff, 525 School St., S.W., Ste. 410 Washington, DC 20024-2797. Phone: (202)554-8050 Fax: (202)863-5486 E-mail: jwet2@ite.org • URL: http://www.ite.org • 1999. $110.00. Second edition.

Transportation Program. Princeton University Operations Research and Financial

Transportation Quarterly. Eno Transportation Foundation, 1634 Eye St., N.W., Suite 500 Washington, DC 20006-4003. Phone: (202)879-4700 Fax: (202)879-4719 Quarterly. $55.00 per year. To qualify a written request must be submitted.

Transportation Research Center. University of Florida

Transportation Research Information Services (TRIS). Transportation Research Board, Highway Research Information, 2101 Constitution Ave. N.W. Washington, DC 20418. Phone: (202)334-2990 Fax: (202)334-2527 Monthly. Price on application. Formerly *Highway Research Abstracts*.

Transportation Research Institute., University of Michigan, 2901 Baxter Rd. Ann Arbor, MI 48109-2150. Phone: (734)764-6504 Fax: (734)936-1081 E-mail: umtri@umich.edu • URL: http://www.umtri.umich.edu • Research areas include highway safety, transportation systems, and shipbuilding.

Transportation Review Part E: Logistics and Transportation Review. University of British Columbia Centre for Transportation Studies. Available from Elsevier Science Inc., PO Box 945 New York, NY 10159-0545. Phone: 888-633-3730 or (212)989-5800 Fax: (212)633-3680 E-mail: usinfo.f@elsevier.com • URL: http://www.elsevier.com • Bimonthly. $735.00 per year.

Transportation Science., P.O. Box 64794 Baltimore, MD 21264-4794. URL: http://www.informs.org • Quarterly. $69.00 per year.

Transportation Statistics Annual Report. Available from U. S. Government Printing Office, Washington, DC 20402. Phone: (202)512-1800 Fax: (202)512-2250 E-mail: gpoaccess@gpo.gov • URL: http://www.accessgpo.gov • Annual. $21.00. Issued by Bureau of Transportation Statistics, U. S. Department of Transportation. Provides data on operating revenues, expenses, employees, passenger miles (where applicable), and other factors for airlines, automobiles, buses, local transit, pipelines, railroads, ships, and trucks.

Transportation Statistics Annual Report. Available from U. S. Government Printing Office, Washington, DC 20402. Phone: (202)512-1800 Fax: (202)512-2250 E-mail: gpoaccess@gpo.gov • URL: http://www.access.gpo.gov • Annual. $21.00. Issued by the U. S. Bureau of Transportation Statistics, Transportation Department (http://www.bts.gov). Summarizes national data for various forms of transportation, including airlines, railroads, and motor vehicles. Information on the use of roads and highways is included.

Transportation Systems Institute., University of Central Florida, Dept. of Civil Engineering, 400 Central Florida Blvd. Orlando, FL 32816-2450. Phone: (407)823-2156 Fax: (407)823-3315 E-mail: haldeek@pegasus.cc.ucf.edu • Research areas include mass transportation systems.

Transportation Telephone Tickler. Journal of Commerce, Inc., Two World Trade Center, 27th Fl. New York, NY 10048-0203. Phone: 800-222-0356 or (212)837-7000 Fax: (212)837-7130 E-mail: editor@mail.joc.com • URL: http://www.joc.com • Annual. $99.95. Four volumes. National edition. Directory of freight services and facilities in all U.S. and Canadian ports. Eleven regional editions are also available. $15.00 per volume.

Travel Agency. Entrepreneur Media, Inc., 2445 McCabe Way Irvine, CA 92614. Phone: 800-421-2300 or (949)261-2325 Fax: (949)261-0234 E-mail: entmag@entrepreneur.com • URL: http://www.entrepreneur.com • Looseleaf. $59.50. A practical guide to starting a travel agency. Covers profit potential, start-up costs, market size evaluation, owner's time required, site selection, lease negotiation, pricing, accounting, advertising, promotion, etc. (Start-Up Business Guide No. E1154.)

Travel Agent: The National Newsweekly Magazine of the Travel Industry. Advanstar Communications Inc., One Park Ave. New York, NY 10016-5802. Phone: 800-346-0085 or (212)951-6600 Fax: (212)951-6793 E-mail: information@advanstar.com • URL: http://www.advanstar.com • 54 times a year. 250.00 per. year.

Travel and Leisure. American Express Publishing Corp., 1120 Ave. of the Americas New York, NY 10036. Phone: (212)382-5600 Fax: (212)768-1568 URL: http://www.amexpub.com/ • Monthly. $39.00 per year. In three regional editions and one demographic edition.

Travel and Tourism. Available from U. S. Government Printing Office, Washington, DC 20402. Phone: (202)512-1800 Fax: (202)512-2250 E-mail: gpoaccess@gpo.gov • URL: http://www.access.gpo.gov • Annual. Free. Issued by the Superintendent of Documents. A list of government publications on the travel industry and tourism. Formerly *Mass Transit, Travel and Tourism*. (Subject Bibliography No. 302.)

Travel and Tourism Research Association., P.O. Box 2133 Boise, ID 83701-2133. Phone: (208)429-9511 Fax: (208)429-9512 E-mail: ttr@uswest.net • URL: http://www.ttra.com • Members are travel directors, airline officials, hotels, government agencies, and others interested in the travel field.

Travel Holiday. Hachette Filipacchi Magazines, Inc., 1633 Broadway, 43rd Fl. New York, NY 10019. Phone: 800-274-4027 or (212)767-6000 Fax: (212)767-5111 URL: http://www.travelholiday.com • 10 times a year. $17.94 per year.

Travel Industry Association of America., Research Dept., 1100 New York Ave., N.W., No. 450 Washington, DC 20005. Phone: (202)408-8422 Fax: (202)408-1255 E-mail: scook@tia.org • URL: http://www.tia.org • Conducts economic, statistical, and market research relating to the U. S. travel industry. Affiliated with the Travel Industry Association of America.

Travel Industry Association of America.

Travel Industry Personnel Directory. Fairchild Books, Seven W. 34th St. New York, NY 10001. Phone: 800-932-4724 or (212)630-3880 Fax: (212)887-1946 URL: http://www.fairchildbooks.com • Annual. $25.00. Air and steamship lines, tour operators, bus lines, hotel representatives, foreign and domestic railroads, foreign and domestic tourist information offices, travel trade associations, etc. Includes names of personnel

Travel Management Daily. Cahners Travel Group, 500 Plaza Dr. Secaucus, NJ 07094-3626. Phone: 800-662-7776 or (201)902-2000 Fax: (201)902-1914 E-mail: corporatecommunications@cahners.com • URL: http://www.cahners.com • Daily. $797.00 per year. Newsletter for travel industry professionals.

Travel Manager's Executive Briefing. American Business Publishing, 1913 Atlantic Ave., Suite F4 Manasquan, NJ 08736. Phone: (732)292-1100 Fax: (732)292-1111 E-mail: info@themcic.com • URL: http://www.themcic.com • Semimonthly. $437.00 per year. Newsletter on travel expense cost control. Formerly *Travel Expense Management*.

Travel Smart: Pay Less, Enjoy More. Communications House, Inc., 40 Beechdale Rd. Dobbs Ferry, NY 10522-9989. Phone: 800-327-3633 or (914)693-8300 Monthly. $44.00 per year. Newsletter. Provides information and recommendations for travelers. Emphasis is on travel value and opportunities for bargains.

Travel Trade News Edition: The Business Paper of the Travel Industry. Travel Trade Publications, 15 W. 44th St., 6th Fl. New York, NY 10036. Phone: (212)730-6600 Fax: (212)730-7137 E-mail: travelcat@aol.com • URL: http://www.traveltrade.com • Weekly. $10.00 per year. Formerly *Travel Trade*.

Travel Weekly. Cahners Travel Group, 500 Plaza Dr. Secaucus, NJ 07096. Phone: 800-662-7776 or (201)902-2000 Fax: (201)902-1967 E-mail: corporatecommunications@cahners.com • URL: http://www.cahners.com • Weekly. $220.00 per year. Includes cruise guides, a weekly "Business Travel Update," and special issues devoted to particular destinations and areas. Edited mainly for travel agents and tour operators.

Travelware. Business Journals, Inc., P.O. Box 5550 Norwalk, CT 06856. Phone: 800-521-0227 or (203)853-6015 Fax: (203)852-8175 Seven times a year. $32.00. Formerly *Luggage and Travelware*.

Travelware Resources Directory. Business Journals, Inc., P.O. Box 5550 Norwalk, CT 06856. Phone: 800-521-0227 or (203)853-6015 Fax: (203)852-8175 Annual. $20.00. Manufacturers of trunks, luggage, brief cases, and personal leather goods are listed. Formerly *Luggage and Travelware Directory*.

Travelware Suppliers Directory. Business Journals, Inc., P.O. Box 5550 Norwalk, CT 06856. Phone: 800-521-0227 or (203)853-6015 Fax: (203)852-8175 Annual. $20.00. Lists 500 manufacturers and importers of components to the luggage and leather goods industry.

Treasury and Risk Management. CFO Publishing Corp., 253 Summer St. Boston, MA 02210. Phone: 800-877-5416 or (617)345-9700 Fax: (617)951-4090 E-mail: mailehulihan@cfopub.com • URL: http://www.cfonet.com • 10 times a year. $64.00 per year. Covers risk management tools and techniques. Incorporates *Corporate Risk Management*.

Treasury Bulletin. Available from U. S. Government Printing Office, Washington, DC 20402. Phone: (202)512-1800 Fax: (202)512-2250 E-mail: gpoaccess@gpo.gov • URL: http://www.access.gpo.gov • Quarterly. $39.00 per year. Issued by the Financial Management Service, U. S. Treasury Department. Provides data on the federal budget, government securities and yields, the national debt, and the financing of the federal government in general.

Treasury Manager's Report: Strategic Information for the Financial Executive. Phillips Business Information, Inc., 1201 Seven Locks Rd., Suite 300 Potomac, MD 20854. Phone: 800-777-5006 or (301)340-2100 Fax: (301)309-3847 E-mail: pbi@phillips.com • URL: http://www.phillips.com/pbi.htm • Biweekly. $595.00. Newsletter reporting on legal developments affecting the operations of banks, savings institutions, and other financial service organizations. Formerly *Financial Services Law Report*.

The Treatment of Mental Illness in an Evolving Health Care System. Available from MarketResearch.com, 641 Ave. of the Americas, Third Floor New York, NY 10011. Phone: 800-298-5699 or (212)807-2629 Fax: (212)807-2716 E-mail: order@marketresearch.com • URL: http://www.marketresearch.com • 1997. $995.00. Market research report published by Theta Corporation. Provides market data on drugs and therapy used for treatment of mood, anxiety, and psychotic disorders. Includes pharmaceutical company profiles and forecasts to the year 2001.

Tree Fruit Research and Education Center. West Virginia University

Tree Planters' Notes. Available from U. S. Government Printing Office, Washington, DC 20402. Phone: (202)512-1800 Fax: (202)512-2250 E-mail: gpoaccess@gpo.gov • URL: http://www.access.gpo.gov • Quarterly. $10.00 per year. Issued by the Forest Service, U. S. Department of Agriculture. Covers reforestation and related forestry issues.

Trends and Developments in Business Administration Programs. Donald L. Joyal. Greenwood Publishing Group, Inc., 88 Post Rd., W. Westport, CT 06881-5007. Phone: 800-225-5800 or (203)226-3571 Fax: (203)222-2540 E-mail: bookinfo@greenwood.com • URL: http://www.greenwood.com • 1982. $35.00.

Trends in International Migration. Organization for Economic Cooperation and Development, OECD Washington Center, 2001 L St., N. W., Suite 650 Washington, DC 20036-4922. Phone: 800-456-6323 or (202)785-6323 Fax: (202)785-0350 E-mail: washington.contact@oecd.org • URL: http://www.oecd.org • Annual. $59.00. Contains detailed data on population migration flows, channels of immigration, and migrant nationalities. Includes demographic analysis.

Trends in Mutual Fund Activity. Investment Company Institute, 1401 H St., N. W., Suite 1200 Washington, DC 20005-2148. Phone: (202)326-5800 Fax: (202)326-5806 E-mail: info@ici.com • URL: http://www.ici.com • Monthly. $225.00 per year. Contains statistical tables showing fund industry sales, redemptions, assets, cash, and other data.

Trends in the Hotel Industry: U. S. Edition. PKF Consulting, 425 California St., Suite 1650 San Francisco, CA 94104. Phone: 800-633-4931 or (415)421-5378 URL: http://www.pkf.com • Annual. $225.00. Provides detailed financial analysis of hotel operations in the U. S. (PKF is Pannell Kerr Forster.)

The Trends Journal: The Authority on Trends Management. Gerald Celente, editor. Trends Research Institute, P.O. Box 660 Rhinebeck, NY 12572-0660. Phone: (914)876-6700 Fax: (914)758-5252 E-mail: gcelente@trendsresearch.com • URL: http://www.trendsresearch.com • Quarterly. $185.00 per year. Newsletter. Provides forecasts on a wide variety of economic, social, and political topics. Includes "Hot Trends to Watch."

Trends 2000: How to Prepare For and Profit From the Changes of the 21st Century. Gerald Celente. Little, Brown and Co., Time and Life Bldg., 1271 AVe. of the Americas New York, NY 10020. Phone: 800-343-9204 or (212)522-8700 Fax: 800-286-9741 or (212)522-2067 E-mail: cust.service@littlebrown.com • URL: http://www.littlebrown.com • 1998. $14.99. Emphasis is on economic, social, and political trends.

TRI/Princeton.

Trial. Association of Trial Lawyers of America, 1050 31st St., N.W. Washington, DC 20007-4499. Phone: 800-424-2725 or (202)965-3500 Fax: (202)965-0030 URL: http://www.atlanet.org/ • Monthly. $79.00 per year.

Trial Lawyer's Guide. West Group, 610 Opperman Dr. Eagan, MN 55123. Phone: 800-328-4880 or (651)687-7000 Fax: 800-213-2323 or (651)687-5827 URL: http://www.westgroup.com • Quarterly. $100.00 per year.

Trial Lawyers Quarterly. New York State Trial Lawyers Association, 132 Nassau St.,, Suite 200 New York, NY 10038. Phone: (212)349-5890 Fax: (212)608-2310 Quarterly. $50.00 per year.

Triangle. Florida Citrus Mutual, P.O. Box 89 Lakeland, FL 33802. Phone: (941)682-1111 Fax: (941)682-1074 Weekly. Membership.

Tribology International; The Practice and Technology of Lubrication, Wear Prevention and Friction Control. Elsevier Science, 655 Ave. of the Americas New York, NY 10010. Phone: 888-437-4636 or (212)989-5800 Fax: (212)633-3680 E-mail: usinfo@elsevier.com • URL: http://www.elsevier.com • Bimonthly. $1,253. 00 per year.

TRIS: Transportation Research Information Service. National Research Council, 2101 Constitution Ave., N. W. Washington, DC 20418. Phone: (202)334-3250 Fax: (202)334-3459 Contains abstracts and citations to a wide range of transportation literature, 1968 to present, with monthly updates. Includes references to the literature of air transportation, highways, ships and shipping, railroads, trucking, and urban mass transportation. Formerly *TRIS-ON-LINE*. Inquire as to online cost and availability.

Tropical Research and Education Center.

The Trouble with Computers: Usefulness, Useability, and Productivity. Thomas K. Landauer. MIT Press, Five Cambridge Center Cambridge, MA 02142-1493. Phone: 800-356-0343 or (617)253-5646 Fax: (617)253-6779 E-mail: mitpress-orders@mit.edu • URL: http://www.mitpress.mit.edu • 1995. $30.00. A critical view of computers and how they are being used.

Troubled and Problematic Bank and Thrift Report. Bauer Communications, Inc., Penthouse One, Gables International Plaza, 2655 LeJeune Rd. Coral Gables, FL 33134. Phone: 800-388-6686 or (305)445-9500 Fax: 800-230-9569 or (305)445-6775 URL: http://www.bauerfinancial.com • Quarterly. $225.00 per year. Newsletter provides information on seriously undercapitalized (''Troubled'') banks and savings institutions, as defined by a federal Prompt Corrective Action Rule. ''Problematic'' banks and thrifts are those meeting regulatory capital levels, but showing negative trends.

Truck Trailer Manufacturers Association.

Truck Trailer Manufacturers Association Membership Directory. Truck Trailer Manufacturers Association, 1020 Princess St. Alexandria, VA 22314. Phone: (703)549-3010 Fax: (703)549-3014 Annual. $135.00. About 100 trucks and tank trailer manufacturers and 120 suppliers to the industry.

Truck Trailers. U. S. Bureau of the Census, Washington, DC 20233-0800. Phone: (301)457-4100 Fax: (301)457-3842 URL: http://www.census.gov • Monthly and annual. Provides data on shipments of truck trailers and truck trailer vans: value, quantity, imports, and exports. (Current Industrial Reports, M37L.)

Trucksource: Sources of Trucking Industry Information. American Trucking Associations, Inc., 2200 Mill Rd. Alexandria, VA 22314-4677. Phone: 800-282-5463 or (703)838-1700 Fax: (703)519-5972 URL: http://www.trucking.org • Annual. $55.00. Lists various kinds of hard copy and electronic information sources on the subject of trucking.

Trust Administration and Taxation. Matthew Bender & Co., Inc., Two Park Ave. New York, NY 10016. Phone: 800-223-1940 or (212)448-2000 Fax: (212)244-3188 E-mail: international@bender.com • URL: http://www.bender.com • $830.00. Four looseleaf volumes. Periodic supplementation. Text on establishment, administration, and taxation of trusts.

Trust Department Administration and Operations. Matthew Bender & Co., Inc., Two Park Ave. New York, NY 10016. Phone: 800-223-1940 or (212)448-2000 Fax: (212)244-3188 E-mail: international@bender.com • URL: http://www.bender.com • $305.00. Two looseleaf volumes. Periodic supplementation. A procedural manual, training guide and idea source.

Trust Letter. American Bankers Association, Trust and Private Banking Center, 1120 Connecticut Ave., N. W. Washington, DC 20036-3971. Phone: 800-338-0626 or (202)663-5000 Fax: (202)663-7543 URL: http://www.aba.org • Members $140.00 per year, non-members, $210.00 per year. Current information on national legislation and regulation that impacts the trust and investment businesses.

Trust Management Update. American Bankers Association, 1120 Connecticut Ave., N.W. Washington, DC 20036-3971. Phone: 800-338-0626 or (202)663-5000 Fax: (202)663-7543 URL: http://www.aba.org • Bimonthly. $95.00 per year.

Trustee: The Magazine for Hospital Governing Boards. American Hospital Association. American Hospital Publishing, Inc., One N. Franklin St., 27th Fl. Chicago, IL 60606-3421. Phone: 800-242-2626 or (312)422-3000 Fax: (312)422-4505 URL: http://www.trusteemag.com/trustee-home.html • 10 times a year. $35.00 per year. Emphasis is on community health care.

Trusts and Estates. Intertec Publishing Corp., 6151 Powers Ferry Rd., N.W., Suite 200 Atlanta, GA 30339. Phone: 800-400-5945 or (770)955-2500 Fax: (770)955-0400 E-mail: subs@intertec.com • URL: http://www.trustsandestates.com • Monthly. $129.00 per year. Includes annual *Directory*.

Trusts and Estates - Directory of Trust Institutions. Intertec Publishing Corp., 6151 Powers Ferry Rd., N.W., Suite 200 Atlanta, GA 30339. Phone: 800-400-5945 or (770)955-2500 Fax: (770)955-0400 URL: http://www.trustsandestates.com • Annual. $79.95. Lists approximately 5,000 trust departments in U.S. and Canadian banks.

Truth in Lending Manual. Warren, Gorham & Lamont/RIA Group, 395 Hudson St. New York, NY 10014. Phone: 800-950-1215 or (212)367-6300 Fax: (212)337-4280 E-mail: customer_services@riag.com • URL: http://www.riahome.com • 1991. $175.00. Semiannual updates.

TRW Business Credit Profiles. TRW Inc., Business Credit Services Division, 505 City Parkway West Orange, CA 92668. Phone: 800-344-0603 or (714)385-7700 Fax: (714)938-2561 Provides credit history (trade payments, payment trends, payment totals, payment history, etc.) for public and private U. S. companies. Key facts and banking information are also given. Updates are weekly. Inquire as to online cost and availability.

Try Us: National Minority Business Directory. Try Us Resources, Inc., 2105 Central Ave., N.E. Minneapolis, MN 55418. Phone: 800-627-4347 or (612)781-6819 Fax: (612)781-0109 E-mail: tryusdir@mr.net • Annual. $69.00. Over 7,000 minority-owned companies, capable of supplying their goods and services on national or regional levels.

Try Us Resources.

Tubular Rivet and Machine Institute.

Tulane Maritime Law Journal. Tulane University, School of Law, John Giffen Weinmann Hall, 6329 Freret St. New Orleans, LA 70118. Phone: (504)865-5959 Fax: (504)865-8878 E-mail: lbecnel@law.tulane.edu • URL: http://www.law.tulane.edu/journals • Semiannual. $28.00 per year. Formerly *Maritime Lawyer*.

Tulsa (Petroleum Abstracts). Information Services, 600 S. College, Harwell 101 Tulsa, OK 74104. Phone: 800-247-8678 or (918)631-2297 Fax: (918)599-9361 Worldwide literature in the petroleum and natural gas areas, 1965 to present. Inquire as to online cost and availability. Includes petroleum exploration patents. Updated weekly. Over 600,000 entries.

Tuned In: Radio World's Management Magazine. IMAS Publishing, 5827 Columbia Pike, Suite 310 Falls Church, VA 22041. Phone: 800-336-3045 or (703)998-7600 Fax: (703)820-3310 E-mail: adsales@imaspub.com • URL: http://www.imaspub.com • Monthly. Price on application. Edited for radio broadcasting managers and producers, with an emphasis on marketing.

Turkey World. Watt Publishing, 122 S. Wesley Ave. Mount Morris, IL 61054-1497. Phone: (815)734-4171 Fax: (815)734-4201 URL: http://www.wattnet.com • Bimonthly. $28.00 per year.

Turning Your Human Resources Department into a Profit Center. Michael W. Mercer. AMACOM, 1601 Broadway, 12th Fl. New York, NY 10019. Phone: 800-262-9699 or (212)586-8100 Fax: (212)903-8168 E-mail: custmserv@amanet.org • URL: http://www.amanet.org • 1989. $59.95. Concerned with costs, employee efficiency, and productivity.

TV and Cable Source. SRDS, 1700 Higgins Rd. Des Plaines, IL 60018. Phone: 800-851-7737 or (847)375-5000 Fax: (847)375-5001 E-mail: srobe@srds.com • URL: http://www.srds.com • Quarterly. $464.00 per year. Provides detailed information on U. S. television stations, cable systems, networks, and group owners, with maps and market data. Includes key personnel.

TV Guide. News America Publications, Inc., P.O. Box 500 Radnor, PA 19088-0925. Phone: 800-866-1400 or (610)293-8500 Fax: (610)688-6216 URL: http://www.tvguide.com • Weekly. $52.00 per year.

TV Technology. IMAS Publishing Group, 5827 Columbia Pike, Suite 310 Falls Church, VA 22041. Phone: 800-336-3045 or (703)998-7600 Fax: (703)998-2966 E-mail: adsales@imaspub.com • URL: http://www.imaspub.com • Biweekly. $125.00 per year. International coverage available.

Twentieth-Century American City. Jon C. Teaford. Johns Hopkins University Press, 2715 N. Charles St. Baltimore, MD 21218. Phone: 800-548-1784 or (410)516-6900 Fax: (410)516-6998 1993. $38.95. Second edition. (American Moment Series).

21.C: Scanning the Future: A Magazine of Culture, Technology, and Science. International Publishers Distributors, P.O. Box 200029, Riverfront Plaza Station Newark, NJ 07102-0301. Phone: 800-545-8398 or (973)643-7500 Fax: (973)643-7676 URL: http://www.21c.com • Quarterly. $24.00 per year. Contains multidisciplinary articles relating to the 21st century.

The 22 Immutable Laws of Branding: How to Build a Product or Service Into a World-Class Brand. Al Ries and Laura Ries. HarperInformation, 10 E. 53rd St. New York, NY 10022-5299. Phone: 800-242-7737 or (212)207-7000 Fax: 800-822-4090 or (212)207-7145 URL: http://www.harpercollins.com • 1999. $23.00. Provides advice on attaining positive brand recognition.

TWICE: This Week in Consumer Electronics. Cahners Business Information, Broadcasting and Cable's International Group, 245 W. 17th St. New York, NY 10011-5300. Phone: 800-662-7776 or (212)645-0067 Fax: (212)337-7066 E-mail: corporatecommunications@cahners.com • URL: http://www.cahners.com • 29 times a year. Free to qualified personnel; others, $99.90 per year. Contains marketing and manufacturing news relating to a wide variety of consumer electronic products, including video, audio, telephone, and home office equipment.

Twin Plant News: The Magazine of the Maquiladora Industries. Nibbe, Hernandez and Associates, Inc., 4110 Rio Bravo Dr., No. 108 El Paso, TX 79902. Phone: (915)532-1567 Fax: (915)544-7556 Monthly. $85.00 per year. Focuses on Mexican labor laws, taxes, economics, industrial trends, and culture. Industries featured include electronic components, plastics, automotive supplies, metals, communications, and packaging.

Type Directors Club.

U. S. Almanac of International Trade. Bernan Press, 4611-F Assembly Dr. Lanham, MD 20706-4391. Phone: 800-274-4447 or (301)459-7666 Fax: 800-865-3450 or (301)459-0056 E-mail: info@bernan.com • URL: http://www.bernan.com • 2000. $225.00. Fifth edition. Provides directory information on individuals and organizations concerned with foreign trade. Contains four sections dealing with: U. S. government, foreign governments, international organizations, and trade-related groups. Formerly *Washington Almanac of International Trade and Business*.

U. S. Banker. Faulkner & Gray, Inc., 11 Penn Plaza, 17th Fl. New York, NY 10001. Phone: 800-535-8403 or (212)967-7000 Fax: (212)967-7155 E-mail: orders@faulknergray.com • URL: http://www.faulknergray.com • Monthly. $52.00 per year. Covers a wide variety of current banking topics.

U. S. Business Advisor. Small Business AdministrationPhone: (202)205-6600 Fax: (202)205-7064 URL: http://www.business.gov • Web site provides ''a one-stop electronic link to all the information and services government provides for the business community.'' Covers about 60 federal agencies that exist to assist or regulate business. Detailed information is provided on financial assistance, workplace issues, taxes, regulations, international trade, and other business topics. Searching is offered. Fees: Free.

U. S. Census Bureau: The Official Statistics. U. S. Bureau of the CensusPhone: (301)763-4100 Fax: (301)763-4794 URL: http://www.census.gov • Web site is ''Your Source for Social, Demographic, and Economic Information.'' Contains ''Current U. S. Population Count,'' ''Current Economic Indicators,'' and a wide variety of data under ''Other Official Statistics.'' Keyword searching is provided. Fees: Free.

U. S. Cheese Market. Available from MarketResearch.com, 641 Ave. of the Americas, Third Floor New York, NY 10011. Phone: 800-298-5699 or (212)807-2629 Fax: (212)807-2716 E-mail: order@marketresearch.com • URL: http://www.marketresearch.com • 1999. $2,750.00. Market research data published by Packaged Facts. Includes projections to 2003.

The U. S. College Market. Available from MarketResearch.com, 641 Ave. of the Americas, Third Floor New York, NY 10011. Phone: 800-298-5699 or (212)807-2629 Fax: (212)807-2642 E-mail: order@marketresearch.com • URL: http://www.marketresearch.com • 2001. $2,799.00. Published by Packaged Facts. Market research report on college students as consumers.

U. S. Commercial and Residential Cleaning Services Industry. Available from MarketResearch.com, 641 Ave. of the Americas, Third Floor New York, NY 10011. Phone: 800-298-5699 or (212)807-2629 Fax: (212)807-2716 E-mail: order@marketresearch.com • URL: http://www.marketresearch.com • 1999. $1,395.00. Market research report published by Marketdata Enterprises. Covers commercial contract cleaning services and residential services. Provides actual industry and market statistics for 1987 to 1996, estimates for 1997-98, and forecasts to the year 2003.

U. S. Copyrights. Available from DIALOG, 11000 Regency Pkwy., Ste. 400 Cary, NC 27511. Phone: 800-334-2564 or (919)462-8600 Fax: (919)468-9890 URL: http://www.dialog.com • Provides access to registration details for all active copyright registrations on file at the U. S. Copyright Office since 1978. Contains information on initial registration, renewal, assignments, and ownership status. Weekly updates. Inquire as to online cost and availability.

U. S. Credit Bureaus and Collection Agencies: An Industry Analysis. Available from MarketResearch.com, 641 Ave. of the Americas, 3rd Fl. New York, NY 10011. Phone: 800-298-5699 or (212)807-2629 Fax: (212)807-2716 E-mail: order@marketresearch.com • URL: http://www.marketresearch.com • 1999. $1,395.00. Market research report published by Marketdata Enterprises. Includes forecasts of industry growth to the year 2002 and provides profiles of Dun & Bradstreet, Equifax, Experion, and Trans-Union.

U. S. Exports of Merchandise on CD-ROM. U. S. Bureau of the Census, Foreign Trade Div.,, Washington, DC 20233-0800. Phone: (301)457-4100 Fax: (301)457-3842 Monthly. $1,200 per year. Provides export data in the most extensive detail available, including product, quantity, value, shipping weight, country of destination, customs district of exportation, etc.

U. S. Floor Coverings Industry. Available from MarketResearch.com, 641 Ave. of the Americas, Third Floor New York, NY 10011. Phone: 800-298-5699 or (212)807-2629 Fax: (212)807-2716 E-mail: order@marketresearch.com • URL: http://www.marketresearch.com • 1999. $1,795.00. Market research report published by Specialists in Business Information. Covers carpets, hardwood flooring, and tile. Presents market data relative to demographics, sales growth, shipments, exports, imports, price trends, and end-use. Includes company profiles.

U. S. FullText. MicroPatent, 250 Dodge Ave. East Haven, CT 06512-3358. Phone: 800-648-6787 or (203)466-5055 Fax: (203)466-5054 E-mail: info@micropat.com • URL: http://www.micropat.com • Monthly. Contains complete text on CD-ROM of all patents issued by the U. S. Patent and Trademark Office. Archival discs are available from 1975.

U. S. Glass, Metal, and Glazing. Key Communications, Inc., P.O. Box 569 Garrisonville, VA 22463. Phone: (540)720-5584 Fax: (540)720-5687 E-mail: usglass@aol.com • URL: http://www.usglassmag.com • Monthly. $39.00 per year. Edited for glass fabricators, glaziers, distributors, and retailers. Special feature issues are devoted to architectural glass, mirror glass, windows, storefronts, hardware, machinery, sealants, and adhesives. Regular topics include automobile glass and fenestration (window design and placement).

U. S. Glass, Metal, and Glazing: Buyers Guide. Key Communications, Inc., P.O. Box 569 Garrisonville, VA 22463. Phone: (540)720-5584 Fax: (540)720-5687 E-mail: bg@aol.com • URL: http://www.usglass.com • Annual. $20.00. A directory of supplies and equipment for the glass fabrication and installation industry.

U. S. Government Books: Publications for Sale by the Government Printing Office. U. S. Government Printing Office, Washington, DC 20402. Phone: (202)512-1800 Fax: (202)512-2250 E-mail: gpoaccess@gpo.gov • URL: http://www.accessgpo.gov • Quarterly. Free. Describes best selling government documents and "new titles that reflect today's news and consumer issues."

U. S. Government Information Catalog of New and Popular Titles. U. S. Government Printing Office, Washington, DC 20402. Phone: (202)512-1800 Fax: (202)512-2250 E-mail: gpoaccess@gpo.gov • URL: http://www.access.gpo.gov • Irregular. Free. Includes recently issued and popular publications, periodicals, and electronic products.

U. S. Government Information for Business. U. S. Government Printing Office, Washington, DC 20402. Phone: (202)512-1800 Fax: (202)512-2250 E-mail: gpoaccess@gpo.gov • URL: http://www.access.gpo.gov • Annual. Free. A selected list of currently available publications, periodicals, and electronic products on business, trade, labor, federal regulations, economics, and other topics. Also known as *Business Catalog*.

U. S. Government Periodicals Index. Congressional Information Service, Inc., 4520 East-West Highway, Suite 800 Bethesda, MD 20814-3389. Phone: 800-638-8380 or (301)654-1550 Fax: (301)654-4033 E-mail: info@cispubs.com • URL: http://www.cispubs • Quarterly. $995.00 per year. Annual cumulation. An index to approximately 180 periodicals issued by various agencies of the federal government.

U. S. Government Periodicals Index (CD-ROM). Congressional Information Service, Inc., 4520 East-West Highway, Suite 800 Bethesda, MD 20814-3389. Phone: 800-638-8380 or (301)654-1550 Fax: (301)654-4033 Quarterly. $795.00 per year. Provides indexing on CD-ROM to about 180 federal government periodicals.

U. S. Herbal Supplement Market. Available from MarketResearch.com, 641 Ave. of the Americas, Third Floor New York, NY 10011. Phone: 800-298-5699 or (212)807-2629 Fax: (212)807-2716 E-mail: order@marketresearch.com • URL: http://www.marketresearch.com • 1999. $2,750.00. Market research data published by Packaged Facts. Includes forecasts to 2003.

U. S. Home Theater Market. Available from MarketResearch.com, 641 Ave. of the Americas, 3rd Fl. New York, NY 10011. Phone: 800-298-5699 or (212)807-2629 Fax: (212)807-2716 E-mail: order@marketresearch.com • URL: http://www.marketresearch.com • 1997. $2,,500.00. Market research report published by Packaged Facts. Covers big-screen TV, high definition TV, audio equipment, and video sources. Market projections are provided to the year 2001.

U. S. Housing Markets. Hanley-Wood, Inc, 42000 Koppernick Rd., Suite 40 Canton, MI 48187-2409. Phone: 800-755-6269 or (734)416-1122 Fax: (313)416-3374 E-mail: info@housingusa.com • URL: http://www.housingusa.com • Monthly. $345.00 per year. Includes eight interim reports. Provides data on residential building permits, apartment building completions, rental vacancy rates, sales of existing homes, average home prices, housing affordability, etc. All major U. S. cities and areas are covered.

U. S. Imports of Merchandise (CD-ROM). U. S. Bureau of the Census, Foreign Trade Division, Washington, DC 20233-0800. Phone: (301)457-4100 Fax: (301)457-3842 Monthly. $1,200 per year. Provides import data in the most extensive detail available, including product, quantity, value, shipping weight, country of origin, customs district of entry, rate provision, etc.

U. S. Industry and Trade Outlook: The McGraw-Hill Companies and the U.S. Department of Commerce/International Trade Administration. Datapso Research Corp., 600 Delran Pkwy. Delran, NJ 08075. Phone: 800-328-2776 or (609)764-0100 Annual. $69.95. Produced by the International Trade Administration, U. S. Department of Commerce, in a "public-private" partnership with DRI/McGraw-Hill and Standard & Poor's. Provides basic data, outlook for the current year, and "Long-Term Prospects" (five-year projections) for a wide variety of products and services. Includes high technology industries. Formerly *U. S. Industrial Outlook*.

U. S. Industry Profiles: The Leading 100. The Gale Group, 27500 Drake Rd. Farmington Hills, MI 48331-3535. Phone: 800-877-GALE or (248)699-GALE Fax: 800-414-5043 or (248)699-8069 E-mail: galeord@galegroup.com • URL: http://www.galegroup.com • 1998. $120.00. Second edition. Contains detailed profiles, with statistics, of 100 industries in the areas of manufacturing, construction, transportation, wholesale trade, retail trade, and entertainment.

U. S. Insurance: Life, Accident, and Health. Sheshunoff Information Services, Inc., 505 Barton Springs Rd., Suite 1200 Austin, TX 78704. Phone: 800-505-8333 or (512)472-2244 Fax: (512)476-1251 URL: http://www.sheshunoff.com • Monthly. Price on application. CD-ROM provides detailed, current information on the financial characteristics of more than 2,300 life, accident, and health insurance companies.

U. S. Insurance: Property and Casualty. Sheshunoff Information Services, Inc., 505 Barton Springs Rd., Suite 1200 Austin, TX 78704. Phone: 800-505-8333 or (512)472-2244 Fax: (512)476-1251 URL: http://www.sheshunoff.com • Monthly. Price on application. CD-ROM provides detailed, current financial information on more than 3,200 property and casualty insurance companies.

The U. S. Market for Assisted-Living Facilities. MarketResearch.com, 641 Ave. of the Americas, Third Floor New York, NY 10011. Phone: 800-298-5699 or (212)807-2629 Fax: (212)807-2716 E-mail: order@marketresearch.com • URL: http://www.marketresearch.com • 1997. $1,125.00. Market research report. Includes market demographics and estimates of future revenues. Facility operators such as Emeritus, Manor Care, and Marriott Senior Living are profiled.

The U. S. Market for Catalog Shopping. Available from MarketResearch.com, 641 Ave. of the Americas, Third Floor New York, NY 10011. Phone: 800-298-5699 or (212)807-2629 Fax: (212)807-2716 E-mail: order@marketresearch.com • URL: http://www.marketresearch.com • 1997. $2,250.00. Market research report published by Packaged Facts. Includes analysis of catalog shopping market by age, ethnic groups, and income.

The U. S. Market for Funeral and Cremation Services. Available from MarketResearch.com, 641 Ave. of the Americas, Third Floor New York, NY 10011. Phone: 800-298-5699 or (212)807-2629 Fax: (212)807-2716 E-mail: order@marketresearch.com • URL: http://www.marketresearch.com • 1997. $2,350.00. Market research report published by Packaged Facts. Includes information on multinational funeral service chains.

The U. S. Market for Home Medical Tests. Available from MarketResearch.com, 641 Ave. of the Americas, Third Floor New York, NY 10011. Phone: 800-298-5699 or (212)807-2629 Fax: (212)807-2716 E-mail: order@marketresearch.com • URL: http://www.marketresearch.com • 1997. $2,350.00. Market research report published by Packaged Facts. Covers the market for diagnostic products used in the home and the effect of regulation.

The U. S. Market for Plastic Payment Cards. Available from MarketResearch.com, 641 Ave. of the Americas, Third Floor New York, NY 10011. Phone: 800-298-5699 or (212)807-2629 Fax: (212)807-2716 E-mail: order@marketresearch.com • URL: http://www.marketresearch.com • 1998. $2,500.00. Market research report published by Packaged Facts. Covers credit cards, charge cards, debit cards, and smart cards. Provides profiles of Visa, Mastercard, American Express, Discover, Diners Club, and others.

The U. S. Market for Vitamins, Supplements, and Minerals. Available from MarketResearch.com, 641 Ave. of the Americas, 3rd Fl. New York, NY 10011. Phone: 800-298-5699 or (212)807-2629 Fax: (212)807-2716 E-mail: order@marketresearch.com • URL: http://www.marketresearch.com • 2000. $2,750.00. Market research report published by Packaged Facts. Includes company profiles and sales forecasts to the year 2003.

U. S. Market Trends and Forecasts. The Gale Group, 27500 Drake Rd. Farmington Hills, MI 48331-3535. Phone: 800-877-GALE or (248)699-GALE Fax: 800-414-5043 or (248)699-8069 E-mail: galeord@galegroup.com • URL: http://www.galegroup.com • 2000. $315.00. Second edition. Provides graphic representation of market statistics by means of pie charts and tables for each of 30 major industries and 400 market segments. Includes market forecasts and historical overviews.

U. S. Master Accounting Guide. CCH, Inc., 4025 W. Peterson Ave. Chicago, IL 60646-6085. Phone: 800-248-3248 or (773)866-6000 Fax: 800-224-8299 or (773)866-3608 URL: http://www.cch.com • Annual. $65.95. Summarizes key accounting, business, and financial information from various sources. Includes digests, tables, charts, formulas, ratios, examples, and explanatory text.

U. S. Master Auditing Guide. CCH, Inc., 4025 West Peterson Ave. Chicago, IL 60646-6085. Phone: 800-248-3248 or (773)866-6000 Fax: 800-224-8299 or (773)866-3608 E-mail: cust_serv@cch.com • URL: http://www.cch.com • Annual. $65.00. Covers such topics as auditing standards, audit management, compliance, consulting, governmental audits, forensic auditing, and fraud. Includes checklists, charts, graphs, and sample reports.

U. S. Master Compensation Tax Guide. CCH, Inc., 4025 W. Peterson Ave. Chicago, IL 60646-6085. Phone: 800-248-3248 or (773)866-6000 Fax: 800-224-8299 or (773)866-3608 URL: http://www.cch.com • Annual. $54.95. Provides concise coverage of taxes on salaries, bonuses, fringe benefits, other current compensation, and deferred compensation (qualified and nonqualified).

U. S. Master Depreciation Guide. CCH, Inc., 4025 W. Peterson Ave. Chicago, IL 60646-6085. Phone: 800-248-3248 or (773)866-6000 Fax: 800-224-8299 or (773)866-3608 URL: http://www.cch.com • Annual. $49.00. Contains explanations of ADR (asset depreciation range), ACRS (accelerated cost recovery system), and MACRS (modified accelerated cost recovery system). Includes the historical background of depreciation.

U. S. Master Employee Benefits Guide. CCH, Inc., 4025 W. Peterson Ave. Chicago, IL 60646-6085. Phone: 800-248-3248 or (773)866-6000 Fax: 800-224-8299 or (773)866-3608 URL: http://www.cch.com • Annual. $49.00. Explains federal tax and labor laws relating to health care benefits, disability benefits, workers' compensation, employee assistance plans, etc.

U. S. Master Estate and Gift Tax Guide. CCH, Inc., 4025 West Peterson Ave. Chicago, IL 60646-6085. Phone: 800-248-3248 or (773)866-6000 Fax: 800-224-8299 or (773)866-3608 E-mail: cust_serv@cch.com • URL: http://www.cch.com • Annual. $49.00. Covers federal estate and gift taxes, including generation-skipping transfer tax plans. Includes tax tables and sample filled-in tax return forms.

U. S. Master Excise Tax Guide. CCH, Inc., 4025 W. Peterson Ave. Chicago, IL 60646-6085. Phone: 800-248-3248 or (773)866-6000 Fax: 800-224-8299 or (773)866-3608 URL: http://www.cch.com • Annual. $49.00. Provides detailed explanations of significant excise tax regulations, rulings, and court decisions.

U. S. Master GAAP Guide. CCH, Inc., 4025 W. Peterson Ave. Chicago, IL 60646-6085. Phone: 800-248-3248 or (773)866-6000 Fax: 800-224-8299 or (773)866-3608 URL: http://www.cch.com • Annual. $69.00. Covers the generally accepted accounting principles (GAAP) contained in the professional pronouncements of the Accounting Principles Board (APB) or the Financial Accounting Standards Board (FASB). Includes general discussions, flow charts, and detailed examples. Arranged by topic.

U. S. Master Multistate Corporate Tax Guide. CCH, Inc., 4025 West Peterson Ave. Chicago, IL 60646-6085. Phone: 800-248-3248 or (773)866-6000 Fax: 800-224-8299 or (773)866-3608 E-mail: cust_serv@cch.com • URL: http://www.cch.com • Annual. $67.00. Provides corporate income tax information for 47 states, New York City, and the District of Columbia.

U. S. Master Payroll Guide. CCH, Inc., 4025 W. Peterson Ave. Chicago, IL 60646-6085. Phone: 800-248-3248 or (773)866-6000 Fax: 800-224-8299 or (773)866-3608 URL: http://www.cch.com • Annual. $75.00. Covers the basics of payroll management, including employer obligations, recordkeeping, taxation, unemployment insurance, processing of new employees, and government penalties.

U. S. Master Pension Guide. CCH, Inc., 4025 W. Peterson Ave. Chicago, IL 60646-6085. Phone: 800-248-3248 or (773)866-6000 Fax: 800-224-8299 or (773)866-3608 URL: http://www.cch.com • Annual. $49.00. Explains IRS rules and regulations applying to 401(k) plans, 403(k) plans, ESOPs (employee stock ownership plans), IRAs, SEPs (simplified employee pension plans), Keogh plans, and nonqualified plans.

U. S. Master Property Tax Guide. CCH, Inc., 4025 West Peterson Ave. Chicago, IL 60646-6085. Phone: 800-248-3248 or (773)866-6000 Fax: 800-224-8299 or (773)866-3608 E-mail: cust_serv@cch.com • URL: http://www.cch.com • Annual. $67.00. Provides state-by-state coverage of "key property tax issues and concepts,'' including exemptions, assessments, taxpayer remedies, and property tax calendars.

U. S. Master Sales and Use Tax Guide. CCH, Inc., 4025 W. Peterson Ave. Chicago, IL 60646-6085. Phone: 800-248-3248 or (773)866-6000 Fax: 800-224-8299 or (773)866-3608 URL: http://www.cch.com • Annual. $65.00. Contains concise information on sales and use taxes in all states and the District of Columbia.

U. S. Master Tax Guide. CCH, Inc., 4025 W. Peterson Ave. Chicago, IL 60646-6085. Phone: 800-248-3248 or (773)866-6000 Fax: 800-224-8299 or (773)866-3608 URL: http://www.cch.com • Annual. $46.00. Provides concise information on personal and business income tax, with cross-references to the Internal Revenue Code and Income Tax Regulations.

U. S. Master Tax Guide on CD-ROM. CCH, Inc., 4025 West Peterson Ave. Chicago, IL 60646-6085. Phone: 800-248-3248 or (773)866-6000 Fax: 800-224-8299 or (773)866-3608 URL: http://www.cch.com • Annual. $97.95. CD-ROM version of the printed *U. S. Master Tax Guide*. Includes search commands, link commands, and on-screen prompts.

U. S. Master Tax Guide Plus: Federal CD. CCH, Inc., 4025 West Peterson Ave. Chicago, IL 60646-6085. Phone: 800-248-3248 or (773)866-6000 Fax: 800-224-8299 or (773)866-3608 URL: http://www.cch.com • Monthly. $199.00 per year. Includes *U. S. Master Tax Guide* on CD-ROM, plus the IRS Code, IRS Regulations, tax court opinions, tax cases, and other source material.

U. S. Patents Fulltext. Available from DIALOG, 11000 Regency Parkway, Ste. 400 Cary, NC 27511. Phone: 800-334-2564 or (919)462-8600 Fax: (919)468-9890 URL: http://www.dialog.com • Contains complete text of patents issued by the U. S. Patent and Trademark Office since 1971. Weekly updates. Inquire as to online cost and availability.

U. S. Pharmacist. Jobson Publishing LLC, 100 Ave. of the Americas New York, NY 10013-1678. Phone: 800-747-1652 or (212)274-7000 Fax: (212)431-0500 E-mail: uspharmacist@jobson.com • URL: http://www.uspharmacist.com • Monthly. $30.00 per year. Covers a wide variety of topics for independent, chain store, hospital, and other pharmacists.

U. S. Securities and Exchange Commission.Phone: 800-732-0330 or (202)942-7040 Fax: (202)942-9634 E-mail: webmaster@sec.gov • URL: http://www.sec.gov • SEC Web site offers free access through EDGAR to text of official corporate filings, such as annual reports (10-K), quarterly reports (10-Q), and proxies. (EDGAR is ''Electronic Data Gathering, Analysis, and Retrieval System.'') An example is given of how to obtain executive compensation data from proxies. Text of the daily *SEC News Digest* is offered, as are links to other government sites, non-government market regulators, and U. S. stock exchanges. Search facilities are extensive. Fees: Free.

U. S. Supreme Court Bulletin. CCH, Inc., 4025 W. Peterson Ave. Chicago, IL 60646-6085. Phone: 800-248-3248 or (773)866-6000 Fax: 800-224-8299 or (773)866-3608 URL: http://www.cch.com • Monthly and on each decision day while the Court is in session.

U. S. Survey of Business Expectations. Dun & Bradstreet Corp., Economic Analysis Dept., Three Sylvan Way Parsippany, NJ 07054-3896. Phone: 800-526-0651 or (973)455-0900 Fax: (973)254-4063 E-mail: customersevice@dnb.com • URL: http://www.dnb.com • Quarterly. 40.00 per year. A survey of 3,000 U. S. business executives as to their expectations for next quarter's sales, profits, prices, inventories, employment, exports, and new orders.

The U. S. Tweens Market. Available from MarketResearch.com, 641 Ave. of the Americas, Third Floor New York, NY 10011. Phone: 800-298-5699 or (212)807-2629 Fax: (212)807-2642 E-mail: order@marketresearch.com • URL: http://www.marketresearch.com • 2001. $2,750.00. Published by Packaged Facts. Market research report on American consumers aged 8 to 14.

UCLA Film and Television Archive-Research and Study Center., University of California, Los Angeles, 405 Hilgard Ave., 45 Powell Library Los Angeles, CA 90095-1517. Phone: (310)206-5388 Fax: (310)206-5392 E-mail: arsc@ucla.edu • URL: http://www.cinema.ucla.edu/ • Research areas include animation.

Uker's International Tea and Coffee Directory and Buyers' Guide. Lockwood Trade Journal Co., Inc., 130 W. 42nd St., Suite 1050 New York, NY 10036-7802. Phone: (212)391-2060 Fax: (212)827-0945 E-mail: teacof@aol.com • Annual. $40.00. Lists firms which export and import tea and coffee.

ULI Market Profiles: North America. Urban Land Institute, 1025 Thomas Jefferson St., N. W., Suite 500 W. Washington, DC 20007-5201. Phone: 800-321-5011 or (202)624-7000 Fax: (202)624-7140 E-mail: bookstore@uli.org • URL: http://www.uli.org • Annual. Members, $249.95; non-members, $299.95. Provides real estate marketing data for residential, retail, office, and industrial sectors. Covers 76 U. S. metropolitan areas and 13 major foreign metropolitan areas.

Ulrich's International Periodicals Directory. R. R. Bowker, 121 Chanlon Rd. New Providence, NJ 07974. Phone: 888-269-5372 or (908)464-6800 Fax: (908)771-7704 E-mail: info@bowker.com • URL: http://www.bowker.com • Annual. $595.00. Five volumes. Over 165,000 current periodicals published worldwide; 7,000 newspapers published in the United States. Approximately 10,000 periodicals that have ceased or suspended publication. Includes *Ulrich's Update*. Incorporates information from *Irregular Serials and Annuals*.

Ulrich's International Periodicals Directory Online. Bowker Electronic Publishing, 121 Chanlon Rd. New Providence, NJ 07974. Phone: 800-521-8110 or (908)464-6800 Fax: (908)665-3528 Includes over 250,000 periodicals currently published worldwide and publications discontinued. Corresponds to *Ulrich's International Periodcals Directory, Irregular Serials and Annuals, Bowker International Serials Database Update,* and *Sources of Serials*. Inquire as to online cost and availability.

Ulrich's on Disc: The Complete International Serials Database on Compact Laser Disc. Bowker Electronic Publishing, 121 Chanlon Rd. New Providence, NJ 07974. Phone: 800-323-3288 or (908)464-6800 Fax: (908)665-6688 Quarterly. $850.00 per year. The CD-ROM version of *Ulrich's International Periodicals Directory* and *Magazines for Libraries*.

Ulrichsweb.com. R. R. BowkerPhone: 888-269-5372 or (908)464-6800 Fax: (908)464-3553 E-mail: info@bowker.com • URL: http://www.ulrichsweb.com • Web site provides fee-based access to about 250,000 serials records from the *Ulrich's International Periodicals Directory* database. Includes periodical evaluations from *Library Journal* and *Magazines for Libraries*. Monthly updates.

Ultimate Guide to Raising Money for Growing Companies. Michael C. Thomsett. McGraw-Hill Professional, 1221 Ave. of the Americas New York, NY 10020. Phone: 800-722-4726 or (212)904-2000 Fax: (212)904-2072 E-mail: customer.service@mcgraw-hill.com • URL: http://www.mcgraw-hill.com • 1990. $45.00. Discusses the preparation of a practical business plan, how to manage cash flow, and debt vs. equity decisions.

Ultrasonic Imaging, An International Journal. Dynamedia, Inc., Two Fulham Court Silver Spring, MD 20902. Phone: 800-468-4680 or (301)649-3447 Fax: (301)649-3447 Quarterly. $182.00 per year.

Ultrasonic Industry Association.

Ultrasonics: The World's Leading Journal Covering the Science and Technology of Ultrasound. Elsevier Science, 655 Ave. of the Americas New York, NY 10010. Phone: 888-437-4636 or (212)989-5800 Fax: (212)633-3680 E-mail: usinfo@elsevier.com • URL: http://www.elsevier.com • 10 times a year. $1,198.00 per year. Text in English.

Ultrasound in Medicine and Biology. Elsevier Science, 655 Ave. of the Americas New York, NY 10010. Phone: 888-437-4636 or (212)989-5800 Fax: (212)633-3680 E-mail: usinfo@elsevier.com • URL: http://www.elsevier.com • Monthly. $1,041.00 per year.

UN Chronicle. United Nations Pulications, Sales and Marketing Section, Roon DC2-0853 New York, NY 10017. Phone: 800-253-9646 or (212)963-8302 Fax: (212)963-3489 E-mail: publications@un.org • URL: http://www.un.org/publications • 11 times a year. $20.00 per year. Editions in English, French and Spanish.

The Unabashed Librarian: The ''How I Run My Library Good'' Letter. Maurice J. Freedman, PO Box 325 Mt. Kisco, NY 10549. Phone: (914)674-3617 Fax: (914)244-0941 E-mail: editor@unabashedlibrarian.com • URL: http://www.unabashedlibrarian.com • Quarterly. $57.50 per year. Newsletter. Provides practical library management ideas and library humor.

Unabridged Dictionary of Occupational and Environmental Safety and Health with CD-ROM. Jeffrey W. Vincoli and Kathryn L. Bazan. Lewis Publishers, 2000 Corporate Blvd., N. W. Boca Raton, FL 33431. Phone: 800-272-7737 or (561)994-0555 Fax: 800-374-3401 or (561)998-9114 1999. $89.95.

Unbridled Power: Inside the Secret Culture of the IRS. Shelley L. Davis. HarperCollins Publishers, 10 E. 53rd St. New York, NY 10022-5299. Phone: 800-242-7737 or (212)207-7000 Fax: 800-822-4090 or (212)207-7065 URL: http://www.harpercollins.com • 1997. $25.00. A highly critical view of the Internal Revenue Service by its former historian.

UNCTAD Commodity Yearbook. United Nations Conference on Trade and Development. United Nations Publications, United Nations Concourse Level, First Ave., 46th St. New York, NY 10017. Phone: 800-253-9646 or (212)963-7608 Fax: (212)963-3489 E-mail: bookstore@un.org • URL: http://www.un.org/publications • Annual.

Underground Guide to Telecommuting: Slightly Askew Advice on Leaving the Rat Race Behind. Woody Leonhard. Addison-Wesley Longman, Inc., One Jacob Way Reading, MA 01867. Phone: 800-447-2226 or (781)944-3700 Fax: (781)944-9351 URL: http://www.awl.com • 1995. $24.95. Provides advice on hardware, software, telecommunications, zoning, taxes, mail, and other topics for telecommuters.

Understanding and Managing Financial Information: The Non-Financial Manager's Guide. Michael M. Coltman. Self-Counsel Press, Inc., 1704 N. State St. Bellingham, WA 98225. Phone: 877-877-6490 or (360)676-4530 Fax: (360)676-4530 E-mail: service@self-counsel.com • URL: http://www.self-counsel.com • 1993. $9.95. (Business Series).

Understanding Business. William G. Nickels and others. McGraw-Hill Professional, 1221 Ave. of the Americas New York, NY 10020. Phone: 800-722-4726 or (212)904-2000 Fax: (212)904-2072 E-mail: customer.service@mcgraw-hill.com • URL: http://www.mcgraw-hill.com • 2001. $56.25. Sixth edition.

Understanding Business Statistics. John E. Hanke and Arthur G. Reitsch. McGraw-Hill Higher Education, 1221 Ave. of the Americas New York, NY 10020. Phone: 800-722-4726 or (212)904-2000 Fax: (212)904-2072 E-mail: customer.service@mcgraw-hill.com • URL: http://www.mcgraw-hill.com • 1993. $71.25. Second edition.

Understanding Corporate Bonds. Harold Kerzner. McGraw-Hill Professional, 1221 Ave. of the Americas New York, NY 10020. Phone: 800-722-4726 or (212)904-2000 Fax: (212)904-2072 E-mail: customer.service@mcgraw-hill.com • URL: http://www.mcgraw-hill.com • 1990. $24.95. A general introduction to investing in corporate bonds. Includes a discussion of high-risk (junk) bonds.

Understanding Economics Today. Gary M. Walton and Frank C. Wykoff. McGraw-Hill Professional, 1221 Ave. of the Americas New York, NY 10020-1095. Phone: 800-722-4726 or (212)904-2000 Fax: (212)904-2072 E-mail: customer.service@mcgraw-hill.com • URL: http://www.mcgraw-hill.com • 2001. Seventh edition. Price on application.

Understanding Financial Derivatives: How to Protect Your Investments. Donald Strassheim. McGraw-Hill Professional, 1221 Ave. of the Americas New York, NY 10020-1095. Phone: 800-722-4726 or (212)904-2000 Fax: (212)904-2072 E-mail: customer.service@mcgraw-hill.com • URL: http://www.mcgraw-hill.com • 1996. $40.00. Covers three basic risk management instruments: options, futures, and swaps. Includes advice on equity index options, financial futures contracts, and over-the-counter derivatives markets.

Understanding Financial Statements. Adlyn M. Fraser and Aileen Orminston. Prentice Hall, 240 Frisch Court Paramus, NJ 07652-5240. Phone: 800-947-7700 or (201)909-6200 Fax: 800-445-6991 or (201)909-6361 URL: http://www.prenhall.com • 2000. Sixth edition. Price on application. Emphasis is on the evaluation and interpretation of financial statements.

Understanding Object-Oriented Programming with Java. Timothy Budd. Addison-Wesley Longman, Inc., One Jacob Way Reading, MA 01867. Phone: 800-447-2226 or (781)944-3700 Fax: (781)944-9351 URL: http://www.awl.com • 1999. $63.00. Second edition.

Understanding the Census: A Guide for Marketers, Planners, Grant Writers, and Other Data Users. Michael R. Lavin. Epoch Books, Inc., 22 Byron Ave. Kenmore, NY 14223. Phone: (716)837-4341 1996. $49.95. Contains basic explanations of U. S. Census ''concepts, methods, terminology, and data sources.'' Includes practical advice for locating and using Census data.

Understanding Toxicology: Chemicals, Their Benefits and Uses. H. Bruno Schiefer and others. CRC Press, Inc., 2000 Corporate Blvd., N. W. Boca Raton, FL 33431-7372. Phone: 800-272-7737 or (561)994-0555 Fax: (561)241-7856 E-mail: orders@crcpress.com • URL: http://www.crcpress.com • 1997. $34.95. Provides a basic introduction to chemical interactions and toxicology for the general reader.

UNDOC: Current Index (United Nations Documents). United Nations Publications, United Nations Concourse Level, Sales and Marketing Section, Room DC2-0853 New York, NY 10017. Phone: 800-553-3210 or (212)963-7680 Fax: (212)963-4810 E-mail: bookstore@un.org • URL: http://www.un.org/publications • Quarterly. $150.00. Annual cumulation on microfiche. Text in English.

Unemployment and Inflation: Institutional and Structuralist Views: A Reader in Labor Economics. Michael J. Piore, editor. M. E. Sharpe, Inc., 80 Business Park Dr. Armonk, NY 10504. Phone: 800-541-6563 or (914)273-1800 Fax: (914)273-2106 E-mail: mesinfo@usa.net • URL: http://www.mesharpe.com/ • 1980. $32.95.

Unemployment Insurance Claims Weekly Report. U.S. Department of Labor, Employment and Training Administration, Washington, DC 20210. Phone: (202)219-6050 Weekly.

UNESCO Statistical Yearbook. Bernan Press, 4611-F Assembly Dr. Lanham, MD 20706-4391. Phone: 800-274-4447 or (301)459-7666 Fax: 800-865-3450 or (301)459-0056 E-mail: info@bernan.com • URL: http://www.bernan.com • Annual. $95.00. Co-published by Bernan Press and the United Nations Educational, Scientific, and Cultural Organization (http://www.unesco.org). Presents statistical data from more than 200 countries on education, technology, research, broadcasting, cinema, book publishing, newspapers, libraries, museums, and population. Includes charts, maps, and graphs.

Unified Abrasives Manufacturers Association - Bonoded Division.

Uniform and Textile Service Association.

Uniform Code Council., 7887 Washington Village Dr., Ste. 300 Dayton, OH 45459-8605. Phone: (937)435-3870 Fax: (937)435-7317 E-mail: info@uc-council.org • URL: http://www.uc-council.org • Concerned with developing a universal product coding system to assign a unique identification number to every product sold in the United States.

Uniform Commercial Code. James White and Robert S. Summers. West Publishing Co., College and School Div., 610 Opperman Dr. Eagan, MN 55123. Phone: 800-328-4880 or (651)687-7000 Fax: 800-213-2323 or (651)687-5827 E-mail: legal-ed@westgroup.com • URL: http://www.lawschool.westgroup.com • 1995. Fourth edition. Four volumes. Price on application. (Practitioner Treatise Series).

Uniform Commercial Code Bulletin. West Group, 610 Opperman Dr. Eagan, MN 55123. Phone: 800-328-4880 or (651)687-7000 Fax: 800-213-2323 or (651)687-5827 URL: http://www.westgroup.com • Monthly. $200.00 per year. Newsletter. Includes case summaries of recent UCC decisions.

Uniform Commercial Code in a Nutshell. Bradford Stone. West Publishing Co., 610 Opperman Dr. Eagan, MN 55123. Phone: 800-328-4880 or (651)687-7000 Fax: 800-213-2323 or (651)687-5827 URL: http://www.westgroup.com • 1995. $23.50. Fourth edition. (Nutshell Series).

Uniform Crime Reports for the United States. Federal Bureau of Investigation, U.S. Department of Justice. Available from U.S. Government Printing Office, Washington, DC 20402. Phone: (202)512-1800 Fax: (202)512-2250 E-mail: gpoaccess@gpo.gov • URL: http://www.accessgpo.gov • Annual. Price varies.

Uniform System of Accounts for the Lodging Industry. Timothy J. Eaton, editor. Educational Institute of the American Hotel & Motel Association, P.O. Box 1240 East Lansing, MI 48826-1240. Phone: 800-344-4381 or (517)372-8800 Fax: (517)372-5141 E-mail: info@el-ahma.org • URL: http://www.ei.ahma.org • 1998. Tenth edition. Price on application.

Union Labor Report. Bureau of National Affairs, Inc., 1231 25th St., N.W. Washington, DC 20037-1197. Phone: 800-372-1033 or (202)452-4200 Fax: (202)452-8092 E-mail: books@bna.com • URL: http://www.bna.com • Biweekly. $848.00 per year.

Union of Needletrades, Industrial and Textile Employees.

Union of Orthodox Jewish Congregations of America.

Unipro Foodservice.

Unique Homes: The National Magazine of Luxury Real Estate. Unique Homes, Inc., 801 Second Ave., No. 11 New York, NY 10017-4706. Phone: (212)599-3377 Eight times a year. $30.97 per year. Homes for sale.

Unique 3-in-1 Research and Development Directory. Government Data Publications, Inc., 1155 Connecticut Ave., N.W. Brooklyn, NY 11230. Phone: (718)627-0819 Fax: (718)998-5960 Annual. $15.00. Government contractors in the research and development fields. Included with subscription to *R and D Contracts Monthly.* Formerly *Research and Development Directory.*

United Abrasives Manufacturers Association - Coated Division.

United Brotherhood of Carpenters and Joiners of America.

United Dairy Industry Association.

United Food and Commercial Workers International Union.

United Fresh Fruit and Vegetable Association.

United Furniture Workers Insurance Fund.

United Infants' and Children's Wear Association.

United Kingdom National Committee of International Association on Water Quality.

United Knitwear Manufacturers League.

The United Nations and Drug Abuse Control. United Nations Publications, United Nations Concourse Level, First Ave., 46th St. New York, NY 10017. Phone: 800-253-9646 or (212)963-7608 Fax: (212)963-4910 E-mail: bookstore@un.org • URL: http://www.un.org/publications • 1992. An overview of international drug control efforts.

United Nations Association of the United States of America.

United Nations Disarmament Yearbook. United Nations Publications, Two United Nations Plaza, Rm. DC2-853 New York, NY 10017. Phone: 800-253-9646 or (212)963-8302 Fax: (212)963-3489 E-mail: bookstore@un.org • URL: http://www.un.org/publications • Annual. $55.00.

United Press International.

United Products Formulators and Distributors Association.

U.S. Apple Association.

United States Association of Former Members of Congress.

United States Association of Independent Gymnastic Clubs., 235 Pinehurst Rd. Wilmington, DE 19803. Phone: (302)656-3706 Fax: (302)656-8929 Members include gym clubs and manufacturers of gymnastic equipment.

The U.S. Beer Market: Impact Databank Review and Forecast. M. Shanken Communications, Inc., 387 Park Ave. S. New York, NY 10016. Phone: (212)684-4424 Fax: (212)684-5424 Annual. $845.00. Includes industry commentary and statistics.

United States Beet Sugar Association.

United States Budget in Brief. U.S. Office of Management and Budget, Executive Office of the President. Available from U.S. Government Printing Office, Washington, DC 20402. Phone: (202)512-1800 Fax: (202)512-2250 E-mail: gpoaccess@gpo.gov • URL: http://www.accessgpo.gov • Annual.

United States Business History, 1602-1988: A Chronology. Richard B. Robinson. Greenwood Publishing Group, Inc., 88 Post Rd. W. Westport, CT 06881-5007. Phone: 800-225-5800 or (203)226-3571 Fax: (203)222-2540 E-mail: bookinfo@greenwood.com • URL: http://www.greenwood.com • 1990. $75.00.

United States Census of Agriculture. U.S. Bureau of the Census, Washington, DC 20233-0800. Phone: (301)457-4100 Fax: (301)457-3842 URL: http://www.census.gov • Quinquennial. Results presented in reports, tape, CD-ROM, and Diskette files.

United States Census of Construction Industries. U.S. Bureau of the Census, Washington, DC 20233-0800. Phone: (202)512-1800 Fax: (202)512-2250 URL: http://www.census.gov • Quinquennial. Results presented in reports, tape, and CD-ROM files.

United States Census of Governments. Bureau of the Census, U.S. Department of Commerce. Available from U.S. Government Printing Office, Washington, DC 20402. Phone: (202)512-1800 Fax: (202)512-2250 E-mail: gpoaccess@gpo.gov • URL: http://www.accessgpo.gov • Quinquennial.

United States Census of Manufactures. U.S. Bureau of the Census, Washington, DC 20233-0800. Phone: (301)457-4100 Fax: (301)457-3842 URL: http://www.census.gov • Quinquennial. Results presented in reports, tape, CD-ROM, and Diskette files.

United States Census of Mineral Industries. Bureau of the Census, U.S. Department of Commerce. Available from U.S. Government Printing Office, Washington, DC 20402. Phone: (202)512-1800 Fax: (202)512-2250 E-mail: gpoaccess@gpo.gov • URL: http://www.accessgpo.gov • Quinquennial.

United States Census of Population. Bureau of the Census, U.S. Department of Commerce. Available from U.S. Government Printing Office, Washington, DC 20402. Phone: (202)512-1800 Fax: (202)512-2250 E-mail: gpoaccess@gpo.gov • URL: http://www.accessgpo.gov • Quinquennial.

United States Census of Retail Trade. U.S. Bureau of the Census, Washington, DC 20233-0800. Phone: (301)457-4100 Fax: (301)457-3842 URL: http://www.census.gov • Quinquennial.

United States Census of Service Industries. U.S. Bureau of the Census, Washington, DC 20233-0800. Phone: (301)457-4100 Fax: (301)457-3842 URL: http://www.census.gov • Quinquennial. Various reports available.

United States Census of Transportation. Bureau of the Census, U.S. Department of Commerce. Available from U.S. Government Printing Office, Washington, DC 20402. Phone: (202)512-1800 Fax: (202)512-2250 E-mail: gpoaccess@gpo.gov • URL: http://www.accessgpo.gov • Quinquennial.

United States Census of Wholesale Trade. Bureau of the Census, U.S. Department of Commerce. Available from U.S. Government Printing Office, Washington, DC 20402. Phone: (202)512-1800 Fax: (202)512-2250 E-mail: gpoaccess@gpo.gov • URL: http://www.accessgpo.gov • Quinquennial.

United States Coast Guard Auxiliary.

United States Coast Guard Chief Petty Officer Association.

United States Coast Guard Marine Safety Council Proceedings. U.S. Coast Guard, Washington, DC 20593. Phone: (202)267-2229 Bimonthly.

United States Code. U.S. Congress. Available from U.S. Government Printing Office, Washington, DC 20402. Phone: (202)512-1800 Fax: (202)512-2250 E-mail: gpoaccess@gpo.gov • URL: http://www.accessgpo.gov • Continual supplements. Price varies. Permanent and general public law of the United States from 1789 to the codification date.

United States Code Annotated: Crimes and Criminal Procedures. West Publishing Co., College and School Div., 610 Opperman Dr. Eagan, MN 55123. Phone: 800-328-4880 or (612)687-7000 Fax: (810)213-2323 or (612)687-5827 E-mail: legal-ed@westgroup.com • URL: http://www.lawschool.westpub.com • 15 volumes. Price on application. Arranged in parallel fashion to *United States Code.* Gives abstracts of relevant federal and state court decisions pertaining to each section of the code. Supplemented by annual pocket parts.

United States Code Service: Lawyers Edition. West Group, 610 Opperman Dr. Eagan, MN 55123. Phone: 800-328-4880 or (651)687-7000 Fax: 800-213-2323 or (651)687-5827 URL: http://www.westgroup.com • 1991. $2,000.00. 184 volumes. All federal laws of a general and permanent nature arranged in accordance with the section numbering of the *United States Code* and the supplements thereto. Each code is annotated. Annual pocket supplements.

U.S. Committee on Irrigation and Drainage.

United States Conference of Mayors., 1620 Eye St., N. W. Washington, DC 20006. Phone: (202)293-7330 Fax: (202)293-2352 E-mail: info@usmayors.org • URL: http://www.usmayors.org • Promotes improved municipal government, with emphasis on federal cooperation.

United States Council for International Business.

U.S. Custom House Guide. Commonwealth Business Media, 10 Lake Dr. Hightstown, NJ 08520. Phone: 800-221-5488 or (609)371-7700 Fax: (609)371-7879 URL: http://www.primediainfo.com • Annual. $475.00. Quarterly supplements. List of ports having custom facilities, customs officials, port authorities, chambers of commerce, embassies and consulates, foreign trade zones, and other organizations; related trade services.

U.S. Department of Agricultural Research Service Fort Keogh Livestock and Range Research Laboratory. Montana Agricultural Experiment Station

United States Department of State Indexes of Living Costs Abroad, Quarters Allowances, and Hardship Differentials. Available from U. S. Government Printing Office, Washington, DC 20402. Phone: (202)512-1800 Fax: (202)512-2250 E-mail: gpoaccess@gpo.gov • URL: http://www.access.gpo.gov • Quarterly. $10.00 per year. Provides data on the difference in living costs between Washington, DC and each of 160 foreign cities.

The U.S. Distilled Spirits Market: Impact Databank Market Review and Forecast. M. Shanken Communications, Inc., 387 Park Ave. S. New York, NY 10016. Phone: (212)684-4424 Fax: (212)684-5424 Annual. $845.00. Includes industry commentary and statistics.

United States Distribution Journal-Source Book. Bill Communications, 770 Broadway New York, NY 10003. Phone: (646)654-4500 Fax: (646)654-7212 URL: http://www.billcom.com • Annual. $95.00. Formerly *United States Distribution Journal Buyers Guide.*

United States Durum Growers Association.

U.S. Energy Association.

U.S. Energy Association; Research and Development Committee.

United States Equal Employment Opportunity Commission Annual Report: Job Patterns for Minorities and Women in Private Industry. U.S. Equal Employment Opportunity Commission, Washington, DC 20507. Phone: (202)663-4900 Annual.

United States Export Administration Regulations. Available from U. S. Government Printing Office, Washington, DC 20402. Phone: (202)512-1800 Fax: (202)512-2250 E-mail: gpoaccess@gpo.gov • URL: http://www.access.gpo.gov • $116.00. Looseleaf. Includes basic manual and supplementary bulletins for one year. Issued by the Bureau of Export Administration, U. S. Department of Commerce (http://www.doc.gov). Consists of export licensing rules and regulations.

United States Golf Association (USGA)., P.O. Box 708 Far Hills, NJ 07931. Phone: (908)234-2300 Fax: (908)234-9687 E-mail: usga@usga.org • URL: http://www.usga.org • Members are established golf courses and clubs. Serves as governing body for golf in the U. S. and provides rules and regulations.

United States Government Annual Report, Fiscal Year. Available from U. S. Government Printing Office, Washington, DC 20402. Phone: (202)512-1800 Fax: (202)512-2250 E-mail: gpoaccess@gpo.gov • URL: http://www.access.gpo.gov • Annual. $5.00. Issued by the Financial Management Service, U. S. Treasury Department (http://www.fms.treas.gov). Contains the official report on the receipts and outlays of the federal government. Presents budgetary results at the summary level.

United States Government Manual. National Archives and Records Administration. Available from U.S. Government Printing Office, Washington, DC 20402. Phone: (202)512-1800 Fax: (202)512-2250 E-mail: gpoaccess@gpo.gov • URL: http://www.accessgpo.gov • Annual. $46.00.

United States Government Printing Office Style Manual. U. S. Government Printing Office, Washington, DC 20402. Phone: (202)512-1800 Fax: (202)512-2250 E-mail: gpoaccess@gpo.gov • URL: http://www.access.gpo.gov • 2000. $41.00. 29th edition. Supersedes the 1984 edition (28th). Designed to achieve uniformity in the style and form of government printing.

United States Government Purchasing and Sales Directory. U.S. Small Business Administration. Available from U.S. Government Printing Office, Washington, DC 20402. Phone: (202)512-1800 Fax: (202)512-2250 E-mail: gpoaccess@gpo.gov • URL: http://www.accessgpo.gov • 1994.

U.S. Government Subscriptions. U. S. Government Printing Office, Washington, DC 20402. Phone: (202)512-1800 Fax: (202)512-2250 E-mail: gpoaccess@gpo.gov • URL: http://www.access.gpo.gov • Quarterly. Free. Includes agency and subject indexes.

U.S. Grains Council.

U.S. Hide, Skin and Leather Association.

United States Immigration Laws, General Information. U.S. Immigration and Naturalization Service. Available from U.S. Government Printing Office, Washington, DC 20402. Phone: (202)512-1800 Fax: (202)512-2250 E-mail: gpoaccess@gpo.gov • URL: http://www.accessgpo.gov • Irregular.

United States Import-Export Publications Co. New Media Productions, P.O. Box 428 Bellflower, CA 90707-0428. Phone: (212)683-2426 Monthly. $48.00 per year.

United States Institute for Theatre Technology., 6443 Ridings Rd. Syracuse, NY 13206-1111. Phone: 800-938-7488 or (315)463-6463 Fax: (315)463-6525 E-mail: info@office.usitt.com • URL: http://www.usitt.com • Members include acousticians, architects, costumers, educators, engineers, lighting designers, and others.

United States International Air Travel Statistics. U. S. Department of Transportation, Center for Transportation Information, Kendall Square Cambridge, MA 02142. Phone: (617)494-2450 Fax: (617)494-2497 Provides detailed statistics on air passenger travel between the U. S. and foreign countries for both scheduled and charter flights. Time period is 1975 to date, with monthly updates. Inquire as to online cost and availability.

United States Law Week: A National Survey of Current Law. Bureau of National Affairs, Inc., 1231 25th St., N.W. Washington, DC 20037-1197. Phone: 800-372-1033 or (202)452-4200 Fax: (202)452-8092 E-mail: books@bna.com • URL: http://www.bna.com • Weekly. $989.00 per year. Covers U.S. Supreme Court proceedings and gives full text of decisions. Also provides detailed reports on important legislative and regulatory actions.

U.S. Mayor. United States Conference of Mayors, 1620 Eye St., N.W. Washington, DC 20006. Phone: (202)293-7330 Fax: (202)297-2352 Biweekly. $35.00 per year. Formerly*Mayor.*

U.S. Metric Association.

United States-Mexico Chamber of Commerce., 1300 Pennsylvania Ave., Ste. 270 Washington, DC 20004-3021. Phone: (202)371-8680 Fax: (202)371-8686 E-mail: news-hq@susmcoc.org • Works to promote trade and investment between the U. S. and Mexico.

United States National Credit Union Administration NCUA Quarterly. National Credit Union Administration

United States Naval Institute.

United States Pharmacopeia.

United States Pharmacopeia National Formulary. United States Pharmacopeial Convention, 12601 Twinbrook Parkway Rockville, MD 20852. Phone: 800-227-8772 or (301)881-0666 Fax: (301)816-8148 E-mail: jac@usp.org • URL: http://www.usp.org • Quinquennial. $450.00. Includes annual: *Supplement.*

United States Postal Service: Make Your Mark. U. S. Postal ServicePhone: (202)268-2000 E-mail: webmaster@email.usps.gov • URL: http://www.usps.gov • Web site contains detailed information on U. S. mail services and post offices, including ZIP codes, postage rates, stamps, addressing, Express Mail tracking, and consumer postal information in general. Links are provided to the State Department for passport procedures and to the IRS for tax forms.

U.S. Postal Service Revenue and Cost Analysis Report. U.S. Postal Service, Rates and Classification Dept., 475 L'Enfant Plaza W., SW., Rm. 5300 Washington, DC 20260-1300. Phone: (202)268-2000 Annual.

United States Professional Tennis Association., 3535 Briarpark Dr., Ste. 1 Houston, TX 77042. Phone: 800-877-8248 or (713)978-7782 Fax: (713)978-7780 E-mail: uspta@uspta.org • URL: http://www.uspta.org • Members are professional tennis instructors and college coaches

United States Rail News. Business Publishers, Inc., 8737 Colesville Rd., Suite 1100 Silver Spring, MD 20910-3928. Phone: 800-274-6737 or (301)587-6300 Fax: (301)587-1081 E-mail: bpinews@bpinews.com • URL: http://www.bpinews.com • Biweekly. $499.00. Newsletter. Reports developments in all aspects of the rail transportation industry.

U.S. Real Estate Register. Barry, Inc., P.O. Box 551 Wilmington, MA 01887-0551. Phone: 800-752-1269 or (978)658-0441 Fax: (978)657-8691 E-mail: info@usrealestateregister.com • URL: http://www.usrealestateregister.com • Annual. $87.50. Formerly *Industrial Real Estate Managers Directory.*

United States Securities and Exchange Commission Annual Report. U.S. Government Printing Office, Washington, DC 20402. Phone: (202)512-1800 Fax: (202)512-2250 E-mail: gpoaccess@gpo.gov • URL: http://www.accessgpo.gov • Annual. The Commission maintains a Web site at http://www.sec.gov

The U.S. Skincare Market. Available from MarketResearch.com, 641 Ave. of the Americas, 3rd Fl. New York, NY 10011. Phone: 800-298-5699 or (212)807-2629 Fax: (212)807-2716 E-mail: order@marketresearch.com • URL: http://www.marketresearch.com • 1999. $2,750.00. Published by Packaged Facts. Provides market data on skincare products such as moisturizers, cleansers, and toners, with sales projections to 2003.

United States Statutes at Large. U.S. Office of the Federal Register. Available from U.S. Government Printing Office, Washington, DC 20402. Phone: (202)512-1800 Fax: (202)512-2250 E-mail: gpoaccess@gpo.gov • URL: http://www.accessgpo.gov • Annual. Price varies. Congressional acts and presidential proclamations issued during the Congressional session. For all laws in force at a specific date, refer to *United States Code.*

United States Telephone Association., 1401 H St., N. W., Suite 600 Washington, DC 20005-2164. Phone: (202)326-7300 Fax: (202)326-7333 URL: http://www.usta.org • An association of independent telephone companies.

United States Tennis Association., 70 W. Red Oak Lane White Plains, NY 10604. Phone: (914)696-7000 Fax: (914)696-7167 URL: http://www.usta.com • Members are individuals, institutions, and groups interested in the promotion of tennis as a recreational and healthful sport.

United States Timber Production, Trade, Consumption, And Price Statistics. Forest Service. U.S. Department of Agriculture, Washington, DC 20250. Phone: (202)205-2791 Annual.

United States Tuna Foundation.

United States Waterborne Exports and General Imports. U.S. Bureau of the Census, Washington, DC 20233-0800. Phone: (301)457-4100 Fax: (301)457-3842 URL: http://www.census.gov • Quarterly and annual.

U.S. Wheat Associates.

The U.S. Wine Market: Impact Databank Review and Forecast. M. Shanken Communications, Inc., 387 Park Ave. S. New York, NY 10016. Phone: (212)684-4424 Fax: (212)684-5424 Annual. $845.00. Includes industry commentary and statistics.

United Way Annual Report. United Way of America, 701 N. Fairfax St. Alexandria, VA 22314. Phone: (703)836-7100 Fax: (703)683-7840 Annual. Price on application.

United Way of America.

United Weighers Association.

Units Available for Purchase. American Partnership Board, Inc., 10 S. Riverside Plaza, Suite 1100 Chicago, IL 60606-3708. Phone: 800-272-6273 or (312)332-4100 Fax: (312)332-3171 Weekly. $99.00 per year. Lists limited partnership units being offered for purchase, with current offering price, original price, most recent distribution (annualized), most recent general partner valuation where available, and brief description.

Universal Cooperatives.

Universal Healthcare Almanac: A Complete Guide for the Healthcare Professional - Facts, Figures, Analysis. Silver & Cherner, Ltd., 10221 N. 32nd St., Suite D Phoenix, AZ 85028-3849. Phone: (602)996-2220 Fax: (602)996-2330 E-mail: uhaeditor@aol.com • Looseleaf service. $195.00 per year. Quarterly updates. Includes a wide variety of health care statistics: national expenditures, hospital data, health insurance, health professionals, vital statistics, demographics, etc. Years of coverage vary, with long range forecasts provided in some cases.

University Aviation Association.

University Business: Solutions for Today's Higher Education. University Business, LLC, 135 Madison Ave. New York, NY 10016. E-mail: subs@universitybusiness.com • URL: http://www.universitybusiness.com • Bimonthly. $49.00 per year. Edited for college administrators, including managers of business services, finance, computing, and telecommunications. Includes information on relevant technological advances.

University Continuing Education Association.

University of Miami Law Center's Philip E. Heckerling Institute on Estate Planning. John T. Graubatz. Matthew Bender & Co., Inc., Two Park Ave. New York, NY 10016. Phone: 800-223-1940 or (212)448-2000 Fax: (212)244-3188 E-mail: international@bender.com • URL: http://www.bender.com • Annual. Looseleaf service. Price on application. Review of estate, gift, generation-skipping transfer and income tax developments.

University Professors for Academic Order.

University Science and Engineering Libraries. Ellis Mount. Greenwood Publishing Group, Inc., 88 Post Rd., W. Westport, CT 06881-5007. Phone: 800-225-5800 or (203)226-3571 Fax: (203)222-2540 E-mail: bookinfo@greenwood.com • URL: http://www.greenwood.com • 1985. $59.95. Second edition. (Contributions in Librarianship and Information Science Series, No 49).

UNIX and Windows 2000 Integration Toolkit: A Complete Guide for System Administrators and Developers. Rawn Shah. John Wiley and Sons, Inc., 605 Third Ave. New York, NY 10158-0012. Phone: 800-225-5945 or (212)850-6000 Fax: (212)850-6088 E-mail: info@jwiley.com • URL: http://www.wiley.com • 2000. $49.99. Includes CD-ROM.

UNIX and Windows 2000: Interoperability Guide. Alan Roberts. Prentice Hall, 240 Frisch Ct. Paramus, NJ 07652-5240. Phone: 800-947-7700 or (201)909-6452 Fax: 800-445-6991 or (201)909-6361 URL: http://www.prenhall.com • 2000. $44.99.

UNIX Dictionary of Commands, Terms, and Acronyms. John Levine and Margaret L. Young. McGraw-Hill, 1221 Ave. of the Americas New York, NY 10020. Phone: 800-722-4726 or (212)904-2000 Fax: (212)904-2072 E-mail: customer.service@mcgraw-hill.com • URL: http://www.mcgraw-hill.com • 1996. $39.50.

Unix Secrets. James Armstrong. IDG Books Worldwide, 7260 Shadeland Station, Suite 100 Indianapolis, IN 46256. Phone: 800-762-2974 or (317)596-5200 Fax: (317)596-5299 E-mail: siteemail@idgbooks.com • URL: http://www.idgbooks.com • 1999. $49.99. Second edition.

UNIX System Administration Handbook. Evi Nemeth. Prentice Hall, 240 Frisch Court Paramus, NJ 07652-5240. Phone: 800-947-7700 or (201)909-6200 Fax: 800-445-6991 or (201)909-6361 URL: http://www.prenhall.com • 1995. $74.00. Second edition. Includes CD-Rom.

UNIX Unbounded: A Beginning Approach. Amir Afzal. Prentice Hall, 240 Frisch Court Paramus, NJ 07652-5240. Phone: 800-947-7700 or (201)909-6200 Fax: 800-445-6991 or (201)909-6361 URL: http://www.prenhall.com • 1999. $85.00. Third edition.

Unofficial Business Traveler's Pocket Guide: 249 Tips Even the Best Business Travelers May Not Know. Christopher J. McGinnis. McGraw-Hill, 1221 Ave. of the Americas New York, NY 10020. Phone: 800-722-4726 or (212)904-2000 Fax: (212)904-2072 E-mail: customer.service@mcgraw-hill.com • URL: http://www.mcgraw-hill.com • 1998. $10.95. Arranged by subject categories, such as airports, frequent traveler programs, eating, and staying well.

Up Against the Corporate Wall: Cases in Business and Society. S. Prakash Sethi and Paul Steidlmeier. Prentice Hall, 240 Frisch Court Paramus, NJ 07652-5240. Phone: 800-947-7700 or (201)909-6200 Fax: 800-445-6991 or (201)909-6361 URL: http://www.prenhall.com • 1996. $57.00. Sixth edition.

Upgrade. Software and Information Industry Association, 1730 M St., N. W., Suite 700 Washington, DC 20036-4510. Phone: (202)452-1600 Fax: (202)223-8756 URL: http://www.siia.net • Monthly. $75.00 per year. Covers news and trends relating to the software, information, and Internet industries. Formerly *SPA News* from Software Publisers Association.

Upholstered Furniture Action Council.

Upholstering Methods. Fred W. Zimmerman. Goodheart - Willcox Publishers, 18604 W. Creek Dr. Tinley Park, IL 60477-6243. Phone: 800-323-0440 or (708)687-5068 Fax: 888-409-3900 E-mail: custserv@goodheartwillcox.com • URL: http://www.goodheartwillcox.com • 1992. $26.60.

Upjohn Center for Clinical Pharmacology. University of Michigan

Upside: People, Technology, Capital. Upside Publishing Co., 731 Market St., No. 2 San Francisco, CA 94103-2002. Phone: (650)377-0950 Fax: (650)377-1961 E-mail: feedback@upside.com • URL: http://www.upsidetoday.com • Monthly. $29.95 per year. Covers the business, investment, and entrepreneurial aspects of high technology.

Urban Affairs Review. Sage Publications, Inc., 2455 Teller Rd. Thousand Oaks, CA 91320. Phone: (805)499-0721 Fax: (805)499-0871 E-mail: info@sagepub.com • URL: http://www.sagepub.com • Bimonthly. Individuals, $80.00 per year; institutions, $410.00 per year. Formerly *Urban Affairs Quarterly.*

Urban Institute., 2100 M St., N. W. Washington, DC 20037. Phone: (202)833-7200 Fax: (202)728-0232 E-mail: paffairs@ui.urban.org • URL: http://www.urban.org • Research activities include the study of urban economic affairs, development, housing, productivity, and municipal finance.

Urban Land Institute., 1025 Thomas Jefferson Ave. N.W., Suite 500W Washington, DC 20004. Phone: (202)624-7000 Fax: (202)624-7140 E-mail: rlevitt@uli.org • URL: http://www.uli.org • Studies urban land planning and the growth and development of urbanized areas, including central city problems, industrial development, community development, residential development, taxation, shopping centers, and the effects of development on the environment.

Urban Land: News and Trends in Land Development. Urban Land Institute, 1025 Thomas Jefferson St., N. W., Suite 500 W. Washington, DC 20007-5201. Phone: 800-321-5011 or (202)624-7000 Fax: (202)624-7140 E-mail: bookstore@uli.org • URL: http://www.uli.org • Monthly. Membership.

Urban Parks and Open Space. Gayle L. Berens and others. Urban Land Institute, 1025 Thomas Jefferson St., N. W., Suite 500 W. Washington, DC 20007-5201. Phone: 800-321-5011 or (202)624-7000 Fax: (202)624-7140 E-mail: bookstore@uli.org • URL: http://www.uli.org • 1997. Price on application. Covers financing, design, management, and public-private partnerships relative to the development of open space for new urban parks. Includes color illustrations and the history of urban parks.

Urban Revitalization: Policies and Practices. Fritz W. Wagner and others. Sage Publications, Inc., 2455 Teller Rd. Thousand Oaks, CA 91320. Phone: (805)499-0721 Fax: (805)499-0871 E-mail: info@sagepub.com • URL: http://www.sagepub.com • 1995. $48.00.

Urban Transport News: Management, Funding, Ridership, Technology. Business Publishers, Inc., 8737 Colesville Rd., Suite 1100 Silver Spring, MD 20910-3928. Phone: 800-274-6737 or (301)587-6300 Fax: (301)587-1081 E-mail: bpinews@bpinews.com • URL: http://www.bpinews.com • Biweekly. $407.00 per year. Provides current news from Capitol Hill, the White House, the Dept. of Transportation, as well as transit operations and industries across the country.

Urethanes Technology. Crain Communications, Inc., 1725 Merriman Rd., Suite 300 Akron, OH 44313. Phone: 800-678-9595 or (330)836-9180 Fax: (330)836-1005 E-mail: urethanes@crain.demon.co.uk • URL: http://www.crain.co.uk • Bimonthly. $175.00 per year. Covers the international polyurethane industry.

USA Group., P.O. Box 7039 Indianapolis, IN 46207. Phone: 800-824-7044 or (317)849-6510 Fax: (317)951-5072 USA Funds is a nonprofit corporation guaranteeing low-cost loans from about 10,000 lenders. Approximately 1,000 colleges participate.

U.S.A. Oil Industry Directory. PennWell Corp., Petroleum Div., 1700 W. Loop S., Suite 100 Houston, TX 77027. Phone: 800-331-4463 or (713)621-9720 Fax: (713)499-6310 E-mail: webmaster@pennwell.com • URL: http://www.pennwell.com • Annual. $125.00.

USA Today Weather Book. Jack Williams. Random House, Inc., 201 East 50th St. New York, NY 10022. Phone: 800-726-0600 or (212)751-2600 Fax: 800-659-2436 or (212)572-8700 URL: http://www.randomhouse.com • 1997. $20.00. Contains a state-by-state guide to U. S. climate, with color illustrations. Author (weather editor of *USA Today*) includes discussions of weather patterns and computerized forecasting.

USAN and the USP Dictionary of Drug Names. United States Pharmacopeial Convention, 12601 Twinbrook Parkway Rockville, MD 20852. Phone: 800-227-8772 or (301)881-0666 Fax: (301)816-8299 E-mail: jac@usp.org • URL: http://www.usp.org • Annual. $105.00. Adopted names, brand names, compendial and other generic names, CAS Registry Numbers, molecular weights, and other information.

USAPat: Facsimile Images of United States Patents. U. S. Patent and Trademark Office, Office of Electronic Information Products, Crystal Park 3, Suite 441 Washington, DC 20231. Phone: (703)306-2600 Fax: (703)306-2737 E-mail: oeip@uspto.gov • URL: http://www.uspto.gov • Weekly (3 or 4 discs per week). $2,400.00 per year. Allows computer laser printing of original patent documents, including drawings. Calendar-year backfiles available from 1994. (Not a search system; documents are retrieved by patent number only.)

USDA. United States Department of AgriculturePhone: (202)720-2791 E-mail: agsec@usda.gov • URL: http://www.usda.gov • The USDA home page has six sections: News and Information; What's New; About USDA; Agencies; Opportunities; Search and Help. Keyword searching is offered from the USDA home page and from various individual agency home pages. Agencies are the Economic Research Service, Agricultural Marketing Service, National Agricultural Statistics Service, National Agricultural Library, and about 12 others. Updating varies. Fees: Free.

Used Boat Price Guide. BUC International Corp., 1314 N.E. 17th Court Fort Lauderdale, FL 33305. Phone: 800-327-6929 or (954)565-6715 Fax: (954)561-3095 Semiannual. Three volumes. Formerly *Older Boat Price Guide*.

Used Book Store. Entrepreneur Media, Inc., 2445 McCabe Way Irvine, CA 92614. Phone: 800-421-2300 or (949)261-2325 Fax: (949)261-0234 E-mail: entmag@entrepreneur.com • URL: http://www.entrepreneur.com • Looseleaf. $59.50. A practical guide to starting a used book store. Covers profit potential, start-up costs, market size evaluation, owner's time required, site selection, lease negotiation, pricing, accounting, advertising, promotion, etc. (Start-Up Business Guide No. E1117.)

Used Car Dealer. National Independent Automobile Dealers Association, 2521 Brown Blvd., Suite 100 Arlington, TX 76006-5203. Phone: (817)640-3838 Fax: (817)649-2377 Monthly. Members, $36.00 per year; non-members, $120.00 per year.

Used-Car Rental Agency. Entrepreneur Media, Inc., 2445 McCabe Way Irvine, CA 92614. Phone: 800-421-2300 or (949)261-2325 Fax: (949)261-0234 E-mail: entmag@entrepreneur.com • URL: http://www.entrepreneur.com • Looseleaf. $59.50. A practical guide to starting a used-car rental business. Covers profit potential, start-up costs, market size evaluation, owner's time required, site selection, lease negotiation pricing, accounting, advertising, promotion, etc. (Start-Up Business Guide No. E1108.)

Used Car Sales. Entrepreneur Media, Inc., 2445 McCabe Way Irvine, CA 92614. Phone: 800-421-2300 or (949)261-2325 Fax: (949)261-0234 E-mail: entmag@entrepreneur.com • URL: http://www.entrepreneur.com • Looseleaf. $59.50. A practical guide to getting started in the business of selling used cars. Covers profit potential, start-up costs, market size evaluation, owner's time required, site selection, lease negotiation, pricing, accounting, advertising, etc. (Start-Up Business Guide No. E2330.)

Used Equipment Directory. Penton Media Inc., 611 Route 46 W. Hasbrouck Heights, NJ 07604-0823. Phone: (201)393-6060 Fax: (201)393-0204 E-mail: fvetter@penton.com • URL: http://www.penton.com • Monthly. $30.00 per year. Lists of 800 dealers, in used metalworking, electrical power, process, and material handling equipment, machine tools, etc.

Usenix Association., 2560 Ninth St., Suite 215 Berkeley, CA 94710. Phone: (510)528-8649 Fax: (510)548-5738 E-mail: office@usenix.org • URL: http://www.usenix.org • Members are professional and technical users of UNIX computer operating systems.

Using Bar Code: Why It's Taking Over. David J. Collins and Nancy N. Whipple. Data Capture Press, P.O. Box 1625 Duxbury, MA 02331. Phone: 800-733-7592 or (508)746-5120 Fax: (508)746-7193 E-mail: datacapture@compuserve.com • URL: http://www.datacaptureinstitute.com • 1994. $34.95. Second edition.

Using Computers: Gateway to Information. Gary B. Shelley and T. Cashman. South-Western Publishing Co., 5101 Madison Rd. Cincinnati, OH 45227. Phone: 800-543-0487 or (513)271-8811 Fax: 800-437-8488 E-mail: billhendee@itped.com • URL: http://www.swcollege.com • 1995. $44.65. Second edition.

Using Desktop Publishing to Create Newsletters, Library Guides, and Web Pages: A How-To-Do-It Manual for Librarians. John Maxymuk. Neal-Schuman Publishers, Inc., 100 Varick St. New York, NY 10013. Phone: (212)925-8650 Fax: 800-584-2414 or (212)219-8916 E-mail: info@neal-schuman.com • URL: http://www.neal-schuman.com • 1997. $55.00. Includes more than 90 illustrations.

Using Econometrics: A Practical Guide. A. H. Studenmund. Addison-Wesley Longman, Inc., One Jacob Way Reading, MA 01867. Phone: 800-447-2226 or (781)944-3700 Fax: (781)944-9351 URL: http://www.awl.com • 2001. Fourth edition. Price on application.

Using Government Documents: A How-To-Do-It Manual for School Librarians. Melody S. Kelly. Neal-Schuman Publishers, Inc., 100 Varick St. New York, NY 10013. Phone: (212)925-8650 Fax: 800-584-2414 E-mail: info@neal-schuman.com • URL: http://www.neal-schuman.com • 1992. $27.50. (How-to-Do-It Series).

Using Government Information Sources, Print and Electronic. Jean L. Sears and Marilyn K. Moody. Oryx Press, 4041 N. Central Ave., Ste. 700 Phoenix, AZ 85012-3397. Phone: 800-279-6799 or (602)265-2651 Fax: 800-279-4663 or (602)265-6250 E-mail: info@oryxpress.com • URL: http://www.oryxpress.com • 1994. $115.00. Second edition. Contains detailed information in four sections on subject searches, agency searches, statistical searches, and special techniques for searching. Appendixes give selected agency and publisher addresses, telephone numbers, and computer communications numbers.

Using Technical Analysis: A Step-by-Step Guide to Understanding and Applying Stock Market. Clifford Pistolese, editor. McGraw-Hill Professional, 1221 Ave. of the Americas New York, NY 10020. Phone: 800-722-4726 or (212)904-2000 Fax: (212)904-2072 E-mail: customer.service@mcgraw-hill.com • URL: http://www.mcgraw-hill.com • 1994. $24.95. Revised edition.

Using Technology to Increase Student Learning. Linda E. Reksten. Phi Delta Kappa International, 408 North Union St. Bloomington, IN 47405. Phone: 800-766-1156 or (812)339-1156 Fax: (812)339-0018 E-mail: headquarters@pdkintl.org • URL: http://www.pdkintl.org • 2000. $34.95. Emphasis is on the use of computer technology in schools.

Using Windows for Library Administration. Kenneth E. Marks and Steven P. Nielson. Information Today, Inc., 143 Old Marlton Pike Medford, NJ 08055-8750. Phone: 800-300-9868 or (609)654-6266 Fax: (609)654-4309 E-mail: custserv@infotoday.com • URL: http://www.infotoday.com • 1997. $34.95. Contains details on the use of Microsoft Windows software applications for library management: spreadsheets, desktop publishing, project planning, forms, etc.

Utilities Industry Litigation Reporter: National Coverage of the Many Types of Litigation Stemming From the Transmission and Distribution of Energy By Publicly and Privately Owned Utilities. Andrews Publications, 175 Strafford Ave., Bldg. 4, Suite 140 Wayne, PA 19087. Phone: 800-345-1101 or (610)622-0510 Fax: (610)622-0501 URL: http://www.andrewspub.com • Monthly. $775.00 per year. Reports on legal cases involving the generation or distribution of energy.

Utility Automation. PennWell Corp., Industrial Div., 1421 S. Sheridan Rd. Tulsa, OK 74112. Phone: 800-331-4643 or (918)831-9421 Fax: (918)831-9295 E-mail: webmaster@pennwell.com • URL: http://www.pennwell.com • Seven times a year. $48.00 per year. Covers new information technologies for electric utilities, including automated meter reading, distribution management systems, and customer information systems.

Utility Automation Buying Guide. Pennwell Publishing Co., 1421 S. Sheridan Rd. Tulsa, OK 74112-6619. Phone: 800-331-4643 or (918)831-9421 Fax: (918)831-9295 E-mail: webmaster@pennwell.com • URL: http://www.pennwell.com • Annual. Price on application. A directory of information technology products and services for electric utility companies.

Utility Business. Intertec Publishing Corp., P.O. Box 12901 Overland Park, KS 66282-2901. Phone: 800-400-5945 or (913)341-1300 Fax: (913)967-1898 E-mail: subs@intertec.com • URL: http://www.utilitybusiness.com • Monthly. Controlled circulation. Edited for executives in various public utilities: electric, telephone, gas, and water. Covers a wide range of business issues affecting utilities.

Utility Communicators International.

Vacation Study Abroad. Institute of International Education, P.O. Box 371 Annapolis, MD 20701-0371. Phone: 800-445-0443 or (301)617-7804 Fax: (301)953-2838 E-mail: iiebooks@iie.org • URL: http://www.iie.org/ • Annual. $36.95. Lists approximately 2,200 college-level and adult education summer courses sponsored by U. S. and foreign schools.

Vacuum Cleaner Manufacturers Association.

Valuating Information Intangibles: Measuring the Bottom Line Contribution of Librarians and Information Professionals. Frank H. Portugal. Special Libraries Association, 1700 18th St., N. W., 17th Fl. Washington, DC 20009-2514. Phone: (202)234-4700 Fax: (202)234-2442 E-mail: books@sla.org • URL: http://www.sla.org • 2000. $79.00. Focuses on the importance of the intangible aspects of appraising information resources and services.

Valuation: Measuring and Managing the Value of Companies. Tom Copeland and others. John Wiley and Sons, Inc., 605 Third Ave. New York, NY 10158-0012. Phone: 800-526-5368 or (212)850-6000 Fax: (212)850-6088 E-mail: info@wiley.com • URL: http://www.wiley.com • 2000. $75.00. Second editon. A practical guide to economic value analysis for bankers, accountants, financial analysts, and others concerned with company valuation. (Frontiers in Finance Series).

Valuation Strategies in Divorce. Robert D. Feder. John Wiley and Sons, Inc., 605 Third Ave. New York, NY 10158-0012. Phone: 800-225-5945 or (212)850-6000 Fax: (212)850-6088 E-mail: info@wiley.com • URL: http://www.wiley.com • 1997. Fourth edition. Two volumes. Price on application. Explains the basic principles of asset valuation in divorce cases. Discusses financial statements, tax returns, retirement benefits, real estate, and personal property.

Value Line Convertible Data Base. Value Line Publishing, Inc., 220 East 42nd St. New York, NY 10017. Phone: (212)907-1550 Fax: (212)907-1922 Provides online data for about 600 convertible bonds and other convertible securities: price, yield, premium, issue size, liquidity, and maturity. Information is current, with weekly updates. Inquire as to online cost and availability.

The Value Line Investment Survey. Value Line Publishing, Inc., 220 E. 42nd St. New York, NY 10017. Phone: 800-223-0818 or (212)907-1500 Fax: (212)818-9474 E-mail: vloptions@valucline.com • URL: http://www.valueline.com • Weekly. $570.00 per year. Provides detailed information and ratings for 1,700 stocks actively-traded in the U. S.

Value Line Mutual Fund Survey. Value Line Publishing, Inc., 220 E. 42nd St. New York, NY 10017-5891. Phone: 800-223-0818 or (212)907-1500 Fax: (212)818-9474 E-mail: vloptions@valueline.com • URL: http://www.valueline.com • Biweekly. $295.00 per year. Looseleaf. Provides ratings and detailed performance information for 2,300 equity and fixed income funds.

Value Line Options: the All-in-One Service for Listed Options. Value Line, Inc., 220 E. 42nd St. New York, NY 10017-5891. Phone: 800-223-0818 or (212)907-1500 Fax: (212)818-9747 E-mail: vloptions@valueline.com • URL: http://www.valueline.com • Weekly. $445.00 per year. Formerly *Value Line Option and Convertible Survey*.

The Value of a Dollar. Grey House Publishing, Inc., Pocket Knife Square Lakeville, CT 06039. Phone: 800-562-2139 or (860)435-0868 Fax: 800-248-0115 or (860)435-3004 E-mail: books@greyhouse.com • URL: http://www.greyhouse.com • 1999. $125.00.

The Value of a Dollar: Millennium Edition, 1860-1999. Grey House Publishing, 185 Millerton Rd. Millerton, NY 12546. Phone: 800-562-2139 or (518)789-8700 Fax: (518)789-0556 E-mail: books@greyhouse.com • URL: http://www.greyhouse.com • 1999. $135.00. Second edition. Shows the actual prices of thousands of items available to consumers from the Civil War era to recent years. Includes selected data on consumer expenditures, investments, income, and jobs. (Universal Reference Publications.)

Value of New Construction Put in Place. U.S. Bureau of the Census. Available from U.S. Government Printing Office, Washington, DC 20402. Phone: (202)512-1800 Fax: (202)512-2250 E-mail: gpoaccess@gpo.gov • URL: http://www.access.gpo.gov • Monthly. $42.00 per year.

Value Retail News: The Journal of Outlet and Off-Price Retail and Development. Off-Price Specialists, Inc. Value Retail News, 29399 U.S. Highway 19 N., Suite 370 Clearwater,

FL 33773-2138. Phone: (727)536-4047 Fax: (727)536-4389 Monthly. Members $99.00 per year; non-members, $144.00 per year. Provides news of the off-price and outlet store industry. Emphasis is on real estate for outlet store centers.

Valuing a Business: Analysis and Appraisal of Closely Held Companies. Shannon P. Pratt and others. McGraw-Hill, 1221 Ave. of the Americas New York, NY 10020-1095. Phone: 800-722-4726 or (212)904-2000 Fax: (212)904-2072 E-mail: customer.service@mcgraw-hill.com • URL: http://www.mcgraw-hill.com • 2000. $95.00. Fourth edition. Includes information on how to appraise partial interests and how to write a valuation report.

Valuing Professional Practices: A Practitioner's Guide. Robert Reilly and Robert Schweihs. CCH, Inc., 4025 W. Peterson Ave. Chicago, IL 60646-6085. Phone: 800-248-3248 or (773)866-6000 Fax: 800-224-8299 or (773)866-3608 URL: http://www.cch.com • 1997. $99.00. Provides a basic introduction to estimating the dollar value of practices in various professional fields.

Valve Manufacturers Association of America.

Van Dean Manual. Milady Staff Editors. Milady Publishing Co., P.O. Box 15015 Albany, NY 12212-5015. Phone: 800-347-7707 or (518)464-3500 Fax: (518)464-0357 1990. $36.95. Revised edition.

Vanguard Retirement Investing Guide: Charting Your Course to a Secure Retirement. Vanguard Group. McGraw-Hill Professional, 1221 Ave. of the Americas New York, NY 10020. Phone: 800-722-4726 or (212)904-2000 Fax: (212)904-2072 E-mail: customer.service@mcgraw-hill.com • URL: http://www.mcgraw-hill.com • 1995. $24.95. Second edition. Covers saving and investing for future retirement. Topics include goal setting, investment fundamentals, mutual funds, asset allocation, defined contribution retirement savings plans, social security, and retirement savings strategies. Includes glossary and worksheet for retirement saving.

Vanity Fair. Conde Nast Publications, Inc.,, Four Times Square New York, NY 10034. Phone: 800-289-9330 or (212)582-9090 Fax: (212)880-8289 URL: http://www.vf.com • Monthly. $20.00 per year.

Vapor Trail's Boating News and International Yachting and Cruiser and Manufacturers Report. Gemini Productions, Ltd., 8962 Bainford Dr. Huntington Beach, CA 92646. Phone: (714)833-8003 Monthly. $24.00 per year.

Variety International Film Guide. Peter Cowie, editor. Silman-James Press, 3624 Shannon Rd. Los Angeles, CA 90027. Phone: 800-729-6423 or (323)661-9922 Fax: (323)661-9933 E-mail: silmanjamespress@earthlink.net • Annual. $23.95. Covers the ''who, what, where, and when of the international film scene.'' Includes information from 70 countries on film festivals, top-grossing films, awards, schools, etc.

Variety: The International Entertainment Weekly. Cahners Business Information, Broadcasting and Cable's International Group, 245 W. 17th St. New York, NY 10011-5300. Phone: 800-662-7776 or (212)645-0067 Fax: (212)337-6975 E-mail: corporatecommunications@cahners.com • URL: http://www.cahners.com • Weekly. $219.00 per year. Contains national and international news of show business, with emphasis on motion pictures and television.

Vegetable Growing: Traditional Methods. Arthur Billitt. State Mutual Book and Periodical Service, Ltd., 521 Fifth Ave., 17th Fl. New York, NY 10175. Phone: (718)261-1704 Fax: (516)537-0412 1988. $55.00. Third edition.

Vegetables and Specialties Situation and Outlook. Available from U. S. Government Printing Office, Washington, DC 20402. Phone: (202)512-1800 Fax: (202)512-2250 E-mail: gpoaccess@gpo.gov • URL: http://www.access.gpo.gov • Three times a year. $15.00 per year. Issued by the Economic Research Service of the U. S. Department of Agriculture. Provides current statistical information on supply, demand, and prices.

Vehicle Leasing. Entrepreneur Media, Inc., 2445 McCabe Way Irvine, CA 92614. Phone: 800-421-2300 or (949)261-2325 Fax: (949)261-0234 E-mail: entmag@entrepreneur.com • URL: http://www.entrepreneur.com • Looseleaf. $59.50. A practical guide to starting an automobile leasing business. Covers profit potential, start-up costs, market size evaluation, owner's time required, site selection, lease negotiation, pricing, accounting, advertising, promotion, etc. (Start-Up Business Guide No. E2329.)

Vending Machines. U. S. Bureau of the Census, Washington, DC 20233-0800. Phone: (301)457-4100 Fax: (301)457-3842 URL: http://www.census.gov • Annual. Provides data on value of manufacturers' shipments, quantity, exports, imports, etc. (Current Industrial Reports, MA-35U.)

Vending Times Buyers Guide and Directory. Vending Times Inc., 1375 Broadway, 6th Fl. New York, NY 10018-7001. Phone: (212)302-4700 Fax: (212)221-3311 E-mail: vendtime@idt.net • URL: http://www.vending.org/ • Annual. $35.00. Formerly *Vending Times International Buyers Guide and Directory*.

Vending Times Census of the Industry. Vending Times, Inc., 1375 Broadway, 6th Fl. New York, NY 10018-7001. Phone: (212)302-4700 Fax: (212)221-3311 E-mail: vendtime@idt.net • URL: http://www.vending.org/ • Annual. $25.00.

Vending Times: Vending-Feeding-Coffee Service-Music and Games. Vending Times, Inc., 1375 Broadway, 6th Fl. New York, NY 10018-7001. Phone: (212)302-4700 Fax: (212)221-3311 URL: http://www.vending.org/ • Monthly. $35.00 per year. Incorporates *V-T Music and Games*.

Venezuela Company Handbook: Data on Major Listed Companies. Hoovers, Inc., 1033 La Posada Dr., Suite 100 Austin, TX 78752. Phone: 800-486-8666 or (512)374-4500 Fax: (512)374-4501 E-mail: orders@hoovers.com • URL: http://www.hoovers.com • Annual. $29.95. Published by IMF Editora. Contains profiles of publicly traded companies in Venezuela. Includes information on local stock exchanges and the nation's economic situation. Text in English.

Venezuelan American Association of the United States., 30 Vesey St., Rm. 2015 New York, NY 10007. Phone: (212)233-7776 Fax: (212)233-7779 E-mail: andean@nyct.ent • Faciltates trade and investment between the U. S. and Venezuela.

Venture Capital: An Authoritative Guide for Investors, Entrepreneurs, and Managers. Douglas A. Lindgren. McGraw-Hill Professional, 1221 Ave. of the Americas New York, NY 10020. Phone: 800-722-4726 or (212)904-2000 Fax: (212)904-2072 E-mail: customer.service@mcgraw-hill.com • URL: http://www.mcgraw-hill.com • 1998. $65.00.

Venture Capital Directory (Small Business Administation). Forum Publishing Co., 383 E. Main St. Centerport, NY 11721. Phone: (516)754-5000 Fax: (516)754-0630 E-mail: forum23@juno.com • Annual. $12.95. Over 500 members of the Small Business Administration and the Small Business Investment. Companies that provide funding for small and minority businesses.

Venture Capital Journal. Securities Data Publishing, 40 West 57th St. New York, NY 10019. Phone: 800-455-5844 or (212)765-5311 Fax: (212)956-0112 E-mail: sdp@tfn.com • URL: http://www.sdponline.com • Monthly. $1,165.00 per year. Provides information and analysis concerning the venture capital and private equity markets. (Securities Data Publishing is a unit of Thomson Financial.)

Venture Capital Report Guide to Venture Capital in Europe. Pitman Publishing, 128 Long Acre London WC2E 9AN, England. 1991. $125.00. Provides information on more than 500 European venture capital firms. Lists current investments.

Vertex National Sales Tax Manuals. Vertex Systems, Inc., 1041 Old Cassatt Rd. Berwyn, PA 19312. Phone: (610)640-4200 Six looseleaf regional volumes, $1,122.00 Monthly updates. $750.00 Price on application. Volumes include state by state charts of taxable goods and services, guides to exemptions, reporting requirements, a directory of taxing authorities, and other state and local sales tax information.

Vertical File Index: Guide to Pamphlets and References to Current Topics. H.W. Wilson Co., 950 University Ave. Bronx, NY 10452. Phone: 800-367-6770 or (718)588-8400 Fax: (718)590-1617 E-mail: custserv@hwwilson.com • URL: http://www.hwwilson.com • 11 times a year. $50.00 per year. A subject and title index to selected pamphlet material.

Vertiflite. American Helicopter Society, Inc., 217 N. Washington St. Alexandria, VA 22314. Phone: (703)684-6777 Fax: (703)739-9279 URL: http://www.vtol.org/journal • Bimonthly. $60.00 per year.

Vertiflite-American Helicopter Society Membership Directory. American Helicopter Society, Inc., 217 N. Washington St. Alexandria, VA 22314. Phone: (703)684-6777 Fax: (703)739-9279 URL: http://www.vtol.org/journal • Annual. $45.00. Lists over 6,000 individuals and 150 companies concerned with vertical take off and landing craft.

Veterans of Foreign Wars of the United States.

Veterinary Economics: Business Solutions for Practicing Veterinarians. Veterinary Medicine Publishing Group, 15333 W. 95th St. Lenexa, KS 66219. Phone: 800-255-6864 or (913)492-4300 Fax: (913)492-4157 URL: http://www.vetmetpub.com • Monthly. $42.00 per year. Provides business management and financial articles for veterinarians.

VFW Magazine. Veterans of Foreign Wars of the United States, 406 W. 34th St. Kansas City, MO 64111. Phone: (816)756-3390 Fax: (816)968-1169 E-mail: communications@vva.org • URL: http://www.vva.org • 11 times a year. Free to members; non-members,$10.00 per year. Events and general features.

Via Satellite. Phillips Business Information, Inc., 1201 Seven Locks Rd., Ste. 300 Potomac, MD 20854. Phone: 800-777-5006 or (301)340-2100 Fax: (301)309-3847 E-mail: pbi@phillips.com • URL: http://www.phillips.com/pbi.com • Monthly. $49.00 per year. Covers the communications satellite industry.

Vickers Directory of Institutional Investors. Vickers Stock Research Corp., 226 New York Ave. Huntington, NY 11743. Phone: 800-645-5043 or (516)423-7710 Fax: (516)423-7715 E-mail: vickers2@ix.com • Semiannual. $195.00 per year. Detailed alphabetical listing of more than 4,000 U. S., Canadian, and foreign institutional investors. Includes insurance companies, banks, endowment funds, and investment companies. Formerly *Directory of Institutional Investors*.

Vickers On-Line. Vickers Stock Research Corp., 226 New York Ave. Huntington, NY 11743. Phone: 800-645-5043 or (516)423-7710 Fax: (516)423-7715 Provides detailed online information relating to insider trading and the securities holdings of institutional investors. Daily updates. Inquire as to online cost and availability.

Vickers Weekly Insider Report. Vickers Stock Research Corp., 226 New York Ave. Huntington, NY 11743. Phone: 800-645-5043 or (516)423-7710 Fax: (516)423-7715 E-mail: vickers2@ix.com • Weekly. $176.00 per year. Newsletter. Provides information on the trading activities of corporate officers and directors in their own companies' securities.

Video Investor. Paul Kagan Associates, Inc., 126 Clock Tower Place Carmel, CA 93923. Phone: (831)624-1536 Fax: (831)625-3225 E-mail: info@kagan.com • Monthly. $695.00 per year. Newsletter on the pre-recorded videocassette industry. Includes statistics and forecasts. Formerly *VCR Letter*.

Video Recorder Dealers Directory. American Business Directories, P.O. Box 27347 Omaha, NE 68127. Phone: 800-555-6124 or (402)593-4600 Fax: (402)331-5481 E-mail: internet@infousa.com • Annual. Price on application. Lists over 1,106 dealers. Compiled from U.S. yellow pages.

Video Software Dealers Association., 16530 Ventura Blvd., Suite 400 Encino, CA 91436. Phone: (818)385-1500 Fax: (818)385-0567 E-mail: vsdaoffice@usda.org • URL: http://www.vsda.org • Members are retailers and wholesalers of videocassettes and videodiscs.

The Video Source Book. The Gale Group, 27500 Drake Rd. Farmington Hills, MI 48331-3535. Phone: 800-877-GALE or (248)699-GALE Fax: 800-414-5043 or (248)699-8069 E-mail: galeord@galegroup.com • URL: http://www.galegroup.com • 2000. $345.00. 26th edition. Two volumes. Describes 160,000 video programs currently available on tape and disc. Includes Subject Category Index, Videodisc Index, Captioned Index (for hearing impaired), and Credits Index (actors, directors, etc.).

Video Store: News, Research, Trends, Analysis. Advanstar Communications, Inc., 201 E. Sandpointe Ave., Suite 600 Santa Ana, CA 92707. Phone: (714)513-8600 Fax: (714)513-8632 E-mail: information@advanstar.com • URL: http://www.advanstar.com • Monthly. $85.00 per year.

Video Systems: Equipment Buyer's Guide. Intertec Publishing Corp., P.O. Box 12901 Overland Park, KS 66282-2901. Phone: 800-400-5945 or (913)341-1300 Fax: (913)967-1898 E-mail: subs@intertec.com • URL: http://www.intertec.com • Annual. $10.00. Lists approximately 1,000 manufacturers and suppliers of professional video equipment.

Video Systems: Guide to Production Services. Intertec Publishing Corp., P.O. Box 12901 Overland Park, KS 66282-2901. Phone: 800-400-5945 or (913)341-1300 Fax: (913)967-1898 URL: http://www.intertec.com • Annual. $10.00. Lists of about 1,000 firms offering services to videotape production companies.

Video Systems: The Magazine for Video Professionals. Intertec Publishing Corp., P.O. Box 12901 Overland Park, KS 66282-2901. Phone: 800-400-5945 or (913)341-1300 Fax: (913)967-1898 E-mail: subs@intertec.com • URL: http://www.videosystems.com • Monthly. Price on application.

Video Technology News. Phillips Business Information, Inc., 1201 Seven Locks Rd., Suite 300 Potomac, MD 20854. Phone: 800-777-5006 or (301)340-2100 Fax: (301)309-3847 E-mail: pbi@phillips.com • URL: http://www.phillips.com/pbi.htm • Biweekly. $697.00 per year. Newsletter. Covers developments relating to the introduction of high definition television technology and broadcasting. Formerly *H D T V Report*.

Video Week: Devoted to the Business of Program Sales and Distribution for Videocassettes, Disc, Pay TV and Allied News Media. Warren Publishing Inc., 2115 Ward Court, N. W. Washington, DC 20037-1209. Phone: 800-771-9202 or (202)872-9200 Fax: (202)293-3435 E-mail: customerservice@warren-news.com • URL: http://www.warrenpub.com • Weekly. $907.00 per year. Newsletter. Covers video industry news and corporate developments.

Videocassette Rental Store. Entrepreneur Media, Inc., 2445 McCabe Way Irvine, CA 92614. Phone: 800-421-2300 or (949)261-2325 Fax: (949)261-0234 E-mail: entmag@entrepreneur.com • URL: http://www.entrepreneur.com • Looseleaf. $59.50. A practical guide to starting a videocassette rental store. Covers profit potential, start-up costs, market size evaluation, owner's time required, site selection, lease negotiation, pricing, accounting, advertising, promotion, etc. (Start-Up Business Guide No. E1192.)

Videography. United Entertainment Media, Inc., 460 Park Ave. South New York, NY 10016-7315. Phone: (212)378-0400 Fax: (212)378-2160 E-mail: videography@uemedia.com • URL: http://www.vidy.com • Monthly. $30.00 per year. Edited for the professional video production industry. Covers trends in technique and technology.

Videolog. Trade Service Corp., P.O. Box 85007 San Diego, CA 92186-9982. Phone: (619)457-5920 Fax: (619)457-1320 Weekly. $252.00 per year. Looseleaf. Contains over 30,000 descriptive listings of videocassettes and videodiscs arranged by title, director, and "Stars." Titles are grouped also by genre (15 sections).

Viking Systems International.

Vinyl Sheet and Floor Tile. Available from MarketResearch.com, 641 Ave. of the Americas, 3rd Fl. New York, NY 10011. Phone: 800-298-5699 or (212)807-2629 Fax: (212)807-2716 E-mail: order@marketresearch.com • URL: http://www.marketresearch.com • 1997. $495.00. Market research report published by Specialists in Business Information. Presents vinyl flooring market data relative to demographics, sales growth, shipments, exports, imports, price trends, and end-use. Includes company profiles.

Virtual City: *The City Magazine of Cyberspace. Virtual Communications, Inc., 888 Seventh Ave. New York, NY 10106-0001. Phone: (212)593-1593 Fax: (212)223-0674 E-mail: virtcity@aol.com • URL: http://www.cirtnow.com • Quarterly. $11.80 per year. Covers new developments in World Wide Web sites, access, software, and hardware.

Virtual Office Survival Handbook: What Telecommuters and Entrepreneurs Need to Succeed in Today's Nontraditional Workplace. Alice Bredin. John Wiley and Sons, Inc., 605 Third Ave. New York, NY 10158-0012. Phone: 800-225-5945 or (212)850-6000 Fax: (212)850-6088 E-mail: info@jwiley.com • URL: http://www.wiley.com • 1996. $34.95. Presents broad coverage of telecommuting considerations, including workplace customizing and the evaluation of electronic office equipment. Coping with distractions and psychological issues are discussed.

Virtual Realism. Michael Heim. Oxford University Press, Inc., 198 Madison Ave. New York, NY 10016-4314. Phone: 800-451-7556 or (212)726-6000 Fax: (212)726-6446 E-mail: custserv@oup-usa.org • URL: http://www.oup-usa.org • 1998. $26.00. Discusses computer simulation and human/computer interaction.

Virtual Reality Annual International Symposium. IEEE Computer Society, 10662 Los Vacqueros Circle Los Alamitos, CA 90720-1264. Phone: 800-272-6657 or (714)821-8380 Fax: (714)821-4010 E-mail: csinfo@computer.org • URL: http://www.computer.org • Annual. $70.00.

Virtual Reality: Computers Mimic the Physical World. Sean M. Grady. Facts on File, Inc., 11 Penn Plaza, 15th Fl. New York, NY 10001-2006. Phone: 800-322-8755 or (212)967-8800 Fax: (212)967-9196 E-mail: lharris@factsonfile.com • URL: http://www.factsonfile.com • 1998. $19.95. (Facts on File Science Sourcebooks Series.)

Vision: La Revista Latinoamericana. Vision, Inc., 2655 Lejune Rd., Suite 610 Miami, FL 33134. Phone: (305)567-9095 Fax: (305)567-9094 Semimonthly. $72.00 per year. Text in Spanish. A popular newsmagazine covering Latin American politics, economics, business, and culture.

Vision Research Center in Ophthalmology.

The Visual Display of Quantitative Information. Edward R. Tufte. Graphics Press, P.O. Box 430 Cheshire, CT 06410. Phone: 800-822-2454 or (203)272-9187 Fax: (203)272-8600 1992. $40.00. A classic work on the graphic display of numerical data, including many illustrations. The two parts are "Graphical Practice," and "Theory of Data Graphics."

Visual Sciences Center.

Vital and Health Statistics. Available from U. S. Government Printing Office, Washington, DC 20402. Phone: (202)512-1800 Fax: (202)512-2250 E-mail: gpoaccess@gpo.gov • URL: http://www.access.gpo.gov • Annual. Free. Lists government publications. (GPO Subject Bibliography Number 121).

Vital Speeches of the Day. City News Publishing Co., Inc., P.O. Box 1247 Mount Pleasant, SC 29465-1247. Phone: (843)881-8733 Fax: (843)843-4007 E-mail: vitalspeeches@awod.com • Bimonthly. $45.00 per year.

Vital Statistics of the United States. Public Health Service, U.S. Dept. of Health and Human Services. Available from U.S. Government Printing Office, Washington, DC 20402. Phone: (202)512-1800 Fax: (202)512-2250 E-mail: gpoaccess@gpo.gov • URL: http://www.access.gpo.gov • Annual. Two volumes.

Vital Statistics of the United States: Life Tables. Available from U. S. Government Printing Office, Washington, DC 20402. Phone: (202)512-1800 Fax: (202)512-2250 E-mail: gpoaccess@gpo.gov • URL: http://www.access.gpo.gov • Annual. $2.25. Produced by the National Center for Health Statistics, Public Health Service, U. S. Department of Health and Human Services. Provides detailed data on expectation of life by age, race, and sex. Historical data is shown annually from the year 1900. (Vital Statistics, volume 2, section 6.)

Vitamin Book. Consumer Guide editors. Simon and Schuster Trade, 1230 Ave. of the Americas New York, NY 10020. Phone: 800-223-2336 or (212)698-7000 Fax: 800-943-9831 or (212)698-7007 E-mail: ssonline_feedback@simonsays.com • URL: http://www.simonsays.com • 1979. $5.95.

Vitamin Retailer. Vitamin Retailer Magazine, Inc., A-2 Brier Hill Court East Brunswick, NJ 08816. Phone: (732)432-9600 Fax: (732)432-9288 Monthly. $45.00 per year. Edited for retailers of vitamins, herbal remedies, minerals, antioxidants, essential fatty acids, and other food supplements.

Vitamins and Hormones: Advances in Research and Applications. Academic Press, 525 B St., Suite 1900 San Diego, CA 92101. Phone: 800-321-5068 or (619)230-1840 Fax: (619)699-6715 E-mail: ap@acad.com • URL: http://www.academicpress.com • Irregular. Price on applications.

VITIS: Viticulture and Enology Abstracts. Bundesanstalt fuer Zuechtungsforschungan an Kulturpflanzen Institut fuer Rebenzu, 76833 Siebeldiingen-Pflaz, Germany. Phone: 49 634 5410 Fax: 49 6345 919050 E-mail: doku-vitis@geilweilerhof.suew.shuttle.de • Quarterly. $65.00 per year. Provides abstracts of journal and other literature relating to wine technology and the cultivation of grapes.

VM & SD (Visual Merchandising and Store Design). International Authority on Visual Merchandising and Store Design. S T Publications, Inc., 407 Gilbert Ave. Cincinnati, OH 45202. Phone: 800-925-1110 or (513)421-2050 Fax: (513)421-5144 E-mail: cwinters@stpubs.com • URL: http://www.visualstore.com • Monthly. $39.00 per year. Ideas for retailers on store design and display. Includes *Buyers' Guide*. Formerly *Visual Merchandising*.

Vocational and Rehabilitation Research Institute., 3304 33rd St., N.W. Calgary, AB, Canada T2L 2A6. Phone: (403)284-1121 Fax: (403)289-6427 E-mail: vrri@cadvision.com • URL: http://www.vrri.org • Associated with University of Calgary.

Vocational Careers Sourcebook. The Gale Group, 27500 Drake Rd. Farmington Hills, MI 48331-3535. Phone: 800-877-GALE or (248)699-GALE Fax: 800-414-5043 or (248)699-8069 E-mail: galeord@galegroup.com • URL: http://www.galegroup.com • 1999. $110.00. Fourth edition. A companion volume to *Professional Careers Sourcebook*. Includes information sources for 1345 occupations that typically do not require a four-year college degree. Compiled in cooperation with InfoPLACE of the Cuyahoga County Public Library, Ohio.

Vocational Evaluation and Work Adjustment Association.

Vocational Training News: The Independent Weekly Report on Employment, Training, and Vocational Education. Aspen Publishers, Inc., 200 Orchard Ridge Dr. Gaithersburg, MD 20878. Phone: 800-638-8437 or (301)417-7500 Fax: (301)695-7931 E-mail: customer.service@aspenpubl.com • URL: http://www.aspenpub.com • Weekly. $319.00 per year. Newsletter. Emphasis is on federal job training and vocational education programs. Formerly *Manpower and Vocational Education Weekly*.

Vogue. Conde Nast Publications, Inc., Four Times Square New York, NY 10034. Phone: 800-289-9330 or (212)582-9090 Fax: (212)286-6921 URL: http://www.vogue.com • Monthly. $28.00 per year.

Volunteers in Technical Assistance.

W. E. Upjohn Institute for Employment Research., 300 S. Westnedge Ave. Kalamazoo, MI 49007-4686. Phone: (616)343-5541 Fax: (616)343-3308 E-mail: eberts@we.upjohninst.org • URL: http://www.upjohninst.org • Research fields include unemployment, unemployment insurance, worker's compensation, labor productivity, profit sharing, the labor market, economic development, earnings, training, and other areas related to employment.

W. W. Hansen Experimental Physics Laboratory., Stanford University, 445 Via Palou St. Stanford, CA 94305-4085. Phone: (650)723-0280 Fax: (650)725-8311 Conducts large-scale cryogenic research.

WACA News. Western Agricultural Chemicals Association, 3835 N. Freeway Blvd., Suite 140 Sacramento, CA 95834. Phone: (916)446-9222 Fax: (916)565-0113 Quarterly. Free.

WaferNews Confidential. PennWell Corp., Advanced Technology Div., 98 Spit Brook Rd. Nashua, NH 03062-5737. Phone: 800-331-4463 or (603)891-0123 Fax: (603)891-0574 E-mail: webmaster@pennwell.com • URL: http://www.pennwell.com • Semimonthly. $350.00 per year. Newsletter. Covers developments and trends in the semiconductor equipment industry.

Wageweb: Salary Survey Data On-Line. HRPDI: Human Resources Programs Development and ImprovementPhone: (609)254-5893 Fax: (856)232-6989 E-mail: salaries@wageweb.com • URL: http://www.wageweb.com • Web site provides salary information for more than 170 benchmark positions, including (for example) 29 information management jobs. Data shows average minimum, median, and average maximum compensation for each position, based on salary surveys. Fees: Free for national salary data; $169.00 per year for more detailed information (geographic, organization size, specific industries).

Waland Window Trends. Cygnus Business Media, 445 Broad Hollow Rd. Melville, NY 11747. Phone: 800-308-6397 or (631)845-2700 Fax: (631)845-2798 E-mail: rich.reiff@cygnuspub.com • URL: http://www.cygnuspub.com • Monthly $36.00 per year. Edited for retailers of interior decoration products, with an emphasis on wallcoverings. Formerly *Wallcoverings, Windows and Interior Fashion*.

Walden's ABC Guide and Paper Production Yearbook. Walden-Mott Corp, 225 N. Franklin Turnpike Ramsey, NJ 07446-1600. Phone: 888-292-5336 or (201)818-8630 Fax: (201)818-8720 E-mail: walden@walden-mott.com • Annual. $145.00. Detailed listings on about 7,662 paper manufacturers, converters and distributors in North America.

Walker's Building Estimator's Reference Book. Scott Siddens, editor. Frank R. Walker Co., 1989 University Lane Lisle, IL 60532. Phone: 800-458-3737 or (630)971-8989 Fax: (630)971-0586 E-mail: frw60532@aol.com • URL: http://www.frankrwalker.com • 1999 $69.95. 26th revised edition.

Walker's Manual of Unlisted Stocks. Harry K. Eisenberg, editor. Walker's Manual, LLC, 3650 Mount Diablo Blvd., Suite 240 Lafayette, CA 94549. Phone: 800-932-2922 or (925)283-9993 Fax: (925)283-9513 E-mail: info@walkersmanual.com • URL: http://www.walkersmanual.com • Annual. $85.00. Provides information on 500 over-the-counter stocks,including many "penny stocks" trading at less than $5.00 per share.

The Wall Paper: The Only Monthly Journal Serving the Wallcovering Trade Exclusively. G & W McNamara Publishing, Inc., 4215 White Bear Parkway, Suite 100 Saint Paul, MN 55110-7635. Phone: (651)293-1544 Fax: (651)293-4308 URL: http://www.gwmcnamara.com • Monthly. $25.00 per year. News, events, trends, marketing, and merchandising covering the wallcovering industry.

Wall Street: A History. Charles R. Geisst. Oxford University Press, 198 Madison Ave. New York, NY 10016-4314. Phone: 800-451-7556 or (212)726-6000 Fax: (212)726-6446 E-mail: custserv@oup-usa.org • URL: http://www.oup-usa.org • 1997. $35.00. Presents the history of the U. S. stock market according to four distinct eras: 1790 to the Civil War, the Civil War to 1929, 1929 to 1954, and from 1954 to recent years.

Wall Street and Technology: For Senior-Level Executives in Technology and Information Management in Securities and Invesment Firms. Miller Freeman, Inc., One Penn Plaza New York, NY 10119. Phone: (212)714-1300 Fax: (212)714-1313 E-mail: mfibooks@mfi.com • URL: http://www.mfi.com • Monthly. $99.00 per year. Includes material on the use of computers in technical investment strategies. Formerly *Wall Computer Review*.

Wall Street Digest. Wall Street Digest, Inc., Two N. Tamiami Trail,, Suite 602 Sarasota, FL 34236. Phone: (941)954-5500 Fax: (941)364-8447 E-mail: editor@wallstreetdigest.com • URL: http://www.wallstreetdigest • Monthly. $150.00 per year. Digest of investment advice from leading financial advisors.

The Wall Street Journal. Dow Jones & Co., Inc., 200 Liberty St. New York, NY 10281. Phone: 800-832-1234 or (212)416-2000 Fax: (212)416-2658 E-mail: wsj.service@cor.dowjones.com • URL: http://www.wsj.com • Daily. $175.00 per year. Covers news and trends relating to business, industry, finance, the economy, and international commerce. Provides extensive price and other data for the securities, commodity, options, futures, foreign exchange, and money markets.

Wall Street Journal/Europe. Dow Jones & Co., Inc., 200 Liberty St. New York, NY 10281. Phone: 800-832-1234 or (212)416-2000 Fax: (212)416-2658 URL: http://www.dowjones.com • Daily. $700.00 per year (air mail). Published in Europe. Text in English.

Wall Street Journal Guide to Planning Your Financial Future: The Easy-to-Read Guide to Lifetime Planning for Retirement. Kenneth M. Morris. Simon & Schuster Trade, 1230 Ave. of the Americas New York, NY 10020. Phone: 800-223-2336 or (212)698-7000 Fax: 800-943-9831 or (212)698-7007 E-mail: ssonline_feedback@simonsays.com • URL: http://wwwsimonsays.com • 1998. $14.95. Revised edition. (Wall Street Journal Guides Series).

Wall Street Journal Interactive Edition. Dow Jones & Co., Inc.Phone: 800-369-2834 or (212)416-2000 Fax: (212)416-2658 E-mail: inquiries@interactive.wsj.com • URL: http://www.wsj.com • Fee-based Web site providing online searching of worldwide information from the *The Wall Street Journal*. Includes "Company Snapshots," "The Journal's Greatest Hits," "Index to Market Data," "14-Day Searchable Archive," "Journal Links," etc. Financial price quotes are available. Fees: $49.00 per year; $29.00 per year to print subscribers.

Wall Street Letter: Newsweekly for Investment Banking and Brokerage Community. Institutional Investor, 488 Madison Ave. New York, NY 10022. Phone: (212)224-3300 Fax: (212)224-3353 E-mail: info@iijournals.com • URL: http://www.iijournals.com • Weekly. $2,665.00 per year. Newsletter for stock brokers and companies providing services for stock brokers. Emphasis is on regulatory matters.

Wall Street Thesaurus. Paul Sarnoff. Astor-Honor, Inc., 16 E. 40th St., 3rd Fl. New York, NY 10016. Phone: (212)840-8800 Fax: (212)840-7246 1963. $19.95.

Wall Street Transcript: A Professional Publication for the Business and Financial Community. Wall Street Transcript Corp., 100 Wall St. New York, NY 10005-4301. Phone: (212)952-7400 Fax: (212)668-9842 E-mail: transcrit@twst.com • URL: http://www.twst.com • Weekly. $1,890.00. per year. Provides reprints of investment research reports.

Wall Street Words: The Basics and Beyond. Richard J. Maturi. McGraw-Hill Professional, 16 E. 40th St., 3rd Fl. New York, NY 10016. Phone: 800-722-4726 or (212)904-2000 Fax: (212)904-2072 E-mail: customer.service@mcgraw-hill.com • URL: http://www.mcgraw-hill.com • 1991. $14.95. (Investor's Quick Reference Series).

Wallcoverings Association.

Want's Federal-State Court Directory. Want Publishing Co., 420 Lexington Ave., Suite 300, Graybar Bldg.-Grand Central New York, NY 10170-0399. Phone: (212)687-3774 Fax: (212)687-3779 E-mail: rwant@publishing.com • URL: http://www.wantpublishing.com • Annual. $35.00. All federal court judges and clerks of court, and United States attorneys and magistrates, judges; state supreme court justices and State court administrators; Supreme Court Chief Justices of Canada and other nations.

Ward's Auto World., 300 Town Center, Suite 2750 Southfield, MI 48075-1212. Phone: (248)357-0800 Fax: (248)357-0810 E-mail: mike_arnholt@intertec.com • URL: http://www.wardsauto.com • Monthly. Free to members; non-members, $55.00 per year. In-depth news and analysis of the automotive industry.

Ward's AutoInfoBank. Ward's Communications, Inc., 3000 Town Center, Suite 2750 Southfield, MI 48075. Phone: (248)357-0800 Fax: (248)357-0810 Provides weekly, monthly, quarterly, and annual statistical data drom 1965 to date for U. S. and imported cars and trucks. Covers production, shipments, sales, inventories, optional equipment, etc. Updating varies by series. Inquire as to online cost and availability.

Ward's Automotive Reports. Ward's Communications, 300 Town Center, Suite 2750 Southfield, MI 48075-1212. Phone: (248)357-0800 Fax: (248)357-0810 E-mail: mike_arnholt@intertec.com • URL: http://www.wardsauto.com • Weekly. $1,195.00. per year. Vital statistical information on production, sales and inventory. Exclusive news of critical interest to the automotive industry. *Ward's Automotive Yearbook* included with subscription.

Ward's Automotive Yearbook. Ward's Communications, Inc., 300 Town Center, Suite 2750 Southfield, MI 48075-1212. Phone: (248)357-0800 Fax: (248)357-0810 E-mail: mike_arnholt@intertec.com • URL: http://www.wardsauto.com • Annual. $385.00. Comprehensive statistical information on automotive production, sales, truck data and suppliers. Included with subscription to *Ward's Automotive Reports*.

Ward's Business Directory of U. S. Private and Public Companies. The Gale Group, 27500 Drake Rd. Farmington Hills, MI 48331-3535. Phone: 800-877-GALE or (248)699-GALE Fax: 800-414-5043 or (248)699-8069 E-mail: galeord@galegroup.com • URL: http://www.galegroup.com • 2000. $2,590.00. Eight volumes. *Ward's* contains basic information on about 120,000 business firms, of which 90 percent are private companies. Includes mid-year *Supplement*. Volumes available individually. Prices vary.

Ward's Private Company Profiles: Excerpts and Articles on 150 Privately Held U. S. Companies. The Gale Group, 27500 Drake Rd. Farmington Hills, MI 48331-3535. Phone: 800-877-GALE or (248)699-GALE Fax: 800-414-5043 or (248)699-8069 E-mail: galeord@galegroup.com • URL: http://www.galegroup.com • 1994. $139.00. Fourth edition. A collection of detailed information on 150 private companies.

Warehouse Management Handbook. James A. Tompkins. McGraw-Hill, 1221 Ave. of the Americas New York, NY 10020. Phone: 800-722-4726 or (212)904-2000 Fax: (212)904-2072 E-mail: customer.service@mcgraw-hill.com • URL: http://www.mcgraw-hill.com • 1997. $89.95. Second edition. Covers site selection, order fulfillment, inventory control systems, storage space determination, equipment maintenance programs, and other warehousing topics.

Warehouse Management's Guide to Public Warehousing. Cahners Business Information, 1018 W. 9th Ave. King of Prussia, PA 19406. Phone: 800-695-1214 or (610)205-1000 Fax: (610)964-2915 E-mail: corporatecommunications@cahners.com • URL: http://www.cahners.net • Annual. $55.00. List of general merchandise,contract and refrigerated warehouses. Formerly *Distribution Guide to Public Warehousing*.

Warehousing Distribution Directory. Commonwealth Business Media, 10 Lake Dr. Hightstown, NJ 08520-5397. Phone: 800-221-5488 or (609)371-7700 Fax: (609)371-7879 E-mail: pcoleman@primediainfo.com • URL: http://www.primediainfo.com • Semiannual. $63.00. Lists about 800 warehousing and consolidation companies and firms offering trucking, trailer on flatcar, container on flatcar, and piggyback carriers services.

Warman's Antiques and Collectibles Price Guide. Krause Publications, Inc., 700 E. State St. Iolaor, WI 54990-0230. Phone: 800-258-0929 or (715)445-2214 Fax: (715)445-4087 E-mail: info@krause.com • URL: http://www.krause.com/ • Annual. $16.95. Manufacturer profiles, key events, current status, collector's clubs, museums, resources available for Americana and collectibles.

WARN Act: A Manager's Compliance Guide to Workforce Reductions. Joseph A. Brislin. BNA Plus Books, Bureau of National Affairs, Inc., 1231 25th St., N.W. Washington, DC 20037. Phone: 800-372-1033 or (202)833-7470 Fax: (202)833-7490 E-mail: books@bna.com • URL: http://www.bna.com • 1990. $195.00.

Warren's Cable Regulation Monitor: The Authoritative Weekly News Service Covering Federal, State, and Local Cable Activities and Trends. Warren Publishing Inc., 2115 Ward Court, N. W. Washington, DC 20037-1209. Phone: 800-771-9202 or (202)872-9200 Fax: (202)293-3435 E-mail: customerservice@warren-news.com • URL: http://www.warrenpub.com • Weekly. $594.00 per year. Newsletter. Emphasis is on Federal Communications Commission regulations affecting cable television systems. Covers rate increases made by local systems and cable subscriber complaints filed with the FCC.

Warren's Forms of Agreements. Matthew Bender & Co., Inc., Two Park Ave. New York, NY 10016. Phone: 800-223-1940 or (212)448-2000 Fax: (212)244-3188 E-mail: international@bender.com • URL: http://www.bender.com • $940.00. Seven looseleaf volumes. Periodic supplementation. A compact source of forms that business transaction lawyers are most frequently asked to document.

Washington Agricultural Record., Georgetown Station, P.O. Box 25001 Washington, DC 20007. Phone: (202)333-8190 Fax: (202)337-3809 Weekly. $65.00 per year. Newsletter.

Washington Drug Letter. Washington Business Information, Inc., 300 N. Washington St., Suite 200 Falls Church, VA 22246. Phone: (703)247-3434 Fax: (703)247-3421 Daily. $867.00 per year. Newsletter on legislative and regulatory concerns.

Washington Information Directory. Congressional Quarterly, Inc., 1414 22nd St., N.W. Washington, DC 20037. Phone: 800-432-2250 or (202)887-8500 Fax: (202)887-6706 E-mail: books.help@cq.com • URL: http://www.cq.com • Annual. $119.00. Published by Congressional Quarterly, Inc. Lists names, addresses, phone numbers, fax numbers, and some Internet addresses for Congress, federal agencies, and nonprofit organizations in Washington, DC. Includes brief descriptions of each group and a subject index.

Washington International Arts Letter. Allied Business Consultants, Inc. Allied Business Consultants, Inc., 317 Fairchild St. Iowa City, IA 55245-2115. Quarterly. 124.00 per year.

Washington International Business Report: An Analytical Review and Outlook on Major Government Developments Impacting International Trade and Investment. International Business-Government Counsellors, Inc., 818 Connecticut Ave., N.W., 12th Fl. Washington, DC 20006-2702. Phone: (202)872-8181 Fax: (202)872-8696 E-mail: arobbins@ibgc.com • URL: http://www.ibgc.com • Monthly. $288.00 per year. Newsletter.

Washington Representatives: Lobbyists, Foreign Agents, Consultants, Legal Advisors, Public Affairs, and Government Relations. Columbia Books, Inc., 1212 New York Ave., N.W., Suite 330 Washington, DC 20005. Phone: 888-265-0600 or (202)898-0662 Fax: (202)898-0775 E-mail: info@columbiabooks.com • URL: http://www.columbiabooks.com • Annual. $109.00. Over 14,000 individuals and law or public relations firms registered as lobbyists, foreign agents, or otherwise acting as representatives in Washington, DC, for companies, associations, labor unions, and special interest groups; legislative affairs personnel of federal government agencies and departments and the White House.

Washington Ĭyearl. Columbia Books, Inc., 1825 Connecticut Ave., N. W., Suite 625 Washington, DC 20009. Phone: 800-265-0600 or (202)464-1662 Fax: (202)464-1775 E-mail: info@columbiabooks.com • URL: http://www.columbiabooks.com • Annual. $129.00. Provides information on about 5,000 Washington, DC key businesses, government offices, non-profit organizations, and cultural institutions, with the names of about 25,000 principal executives. Includes Washington media, law offices, foundations, labor unions, international organizations, clubs, etc.

Waste Age. Environmental Industry Association. Intertec Publishing Corp., 6151 Powers Ferry Rd., N.W. Atlanta, GA 30339-2941. Phone: 800-621-9007 or (770)955-2500 Fax: (770)955-0400 E-mail: subs@intertec.com • URL: http://www.wasteage.com • Monthly. Price on application.

Waste Age Buyers' Guide. Intertec Publishing Corp., 6151 Powers Ferry Rd., N.W., Suite 200 Atlanta, GA 30339. Phone: 800-400-5945 or (770)955-2500 Fax: (770)955-0400 E-mail: subs@intertec.com • URL: http://www.wasteage.com • Annual. $39.95. Manufacturers of equipment and supplies for the waste management industry.

Waste Age Specification Guide. Intertec Publishing Corp., 6151 Powers Ferry Rd., N.W., Suite 200 Atlanta, GA 30339. Phone: 800-621-9907 or (770)955-2500 Fax: (770)955-0400 E-mail: subs@intertec.com • URL: http://www.wasteage.com • Annual. $49.95. Lists manufacturers of refuse handling machinery and equipment in North America and Europe. Includes specifications and photographs of trucks and heavy equipment.

Waste Management: Industrial-Radioactive-Hazardous. Elsevier Science, 655 Ave. of the Americas New York, NY 10010. Phone: 888-437-4636 or (212)989-5800 Fax: (212)633-3680 E-mail: usinfo@elsevier.com • URL: http://www.elsevier.com • Eight times a year. $1,350.00 per year. Formerly *Nuclear and Chemical Waste Management*.

Waste Management Research and Education Institute., University of Tennessee, Knoxville, 600 Henley St., Suite 311 Knoxville, TN 37996-4134. Phone: (865)674-4251 Fax: (865)974-1838 E-mail: kdavis17@utk.edu • URL: http://www.eerc.ra.utk.edu/wmrei • Research fields include chemical, nuclear, and solid waste management, especially waste policy and environmental biotechnology studies.

Waste Treatment and Disposal. Paul T. Williams. John Wiley and Sons, Inc., 605 Third Ave. New York, NY 10158-0012. Phone: 800-225-5945 or (212)850-6000 Fax: (212)850-6088 E-mail: info@wiley.com • URL: http://www.wiley.com • 1998. $165.00.

Waste Treatment Technology News. Business Communications Co., Inc., 25 Van Zant St., Suite 13 Norwalk, CT 06855. Phone: (203)853-4266 Fax: (203)853-0348 Monthly. $395.00 per year. Newsletter.

Watch and Clock Review. Golden Bell Press Inc., 2403 Champa St. Denver, CO 80205. Phone: (303)296-1600 Fax: (303)295-2159 10 times a year. $19.50 per year. Formerly *American Horologist and Jeweler*.

Watch Officer's Guide: A Handbook for All Deck Watch Offices. James Stavridis. Naval Institute Press, U.S. Naval Institute, Beach Hall, 291 Wood Rd. Annapolis, MD 21402. Phone: 800-223-8764 or (410)268-6110 Fax: (410)295-1084 E-mail: customer@usni.org • URL: http://www.nip.org • 1999. $19.95. 14th edition.

The Watch Repairer's Manual. Henry B. Fried. American Watchmakers Institute, 701 Enterprise Dr. Harrison, OH 45030. Phone: (513)367-9800 Fax: (513)367-1414 $35.00. Fourth revised edition.

Watchmakers of Switzerland Information Center.

Water, Air and Soil Pollution: An International Journal of Environmental Pollution. Kluwer Academic Publishers, 101 Philip Dr. Norwell, MA 02061. Phone: (781)871-6600 Fax: (781)871-6528 E-mail: kluwer@wkap.nl • URL: http://www.wkap.nl • 32 times a year. $2,813.00 per year. Includes online edition.

Water and Wastes Digest. Scranton Gillette Communications, Inc., 380 E. Northwest Highway Des Plaines, IL 60016-2282. Phone: (847)391-1000 Fax: (847)390-0408 URL: http://www.sgcpubs.com • 10 times a year. Free to qualified personnel; others, $40.00 per year. Exclusively designed to serve engineers, consultants, superintendents, managers and operators who are involved in water supply, waste water treatment and control.

Water and Wastewater Equipment Manufacturers Association.

Water Desalination Report. Maria C. Smith, P. O. Box 10 Tracey's Landing, MD 20779. Phone: (301)261-5010 Fax: (301)261-5010 Weekly. $325.00 per year. Newsletter.

Water Encyclopedia. Frits Von Der Leeden and others, editors. Lewis Publishers, 2000 Corporate Blvd., N.W. Boca Raton, FL 33431. Phone: 800-272-7737 or (561)994-0555 Fax: 800-374-3401 or (561)998-9114 E-mail: orders@crdpress.com • 1990. $179.00. Second edition. Covers a wide variety of topics relating to water. (Geraghty and Miller Ground Water Series).

Water Engineering and Management. Scranton Gillette Communications, Inc., 380 E. Northwest Highway Des Plaines, IL 60016-2282. Phone: (847)391-1000 Fax: (847)390-0408 URL: http://www.sgcpubs.com • Monthly. $40.00 per year.

Water Environment Federation.

Water Environment Research. Water Environment Federation, 601 Wythe St. Alexandria, VA 22314-1994. Phone: 800-666-0206 or (703)684-2400 Fax: (703)684-2492 E-mail: kroy@wef.org • URL: http://www.wef.org • Bimonthly. Members, $158.00 per year; non-members, $404.00 per year. Formerly *Water Pollution Control Federation. Research Journal*.

Water Operation and Maintenance Bulletin., Denver Federal Center, Bldg. 67 Denver, CO 80225. Phone: (303)234-3217 Quarterly.

Water Quality Association.

Water Quality Management for Pond Fish Culture. Claude E. Boyd. Elsevier Science, 655 Ave. of the Americas New York, NY 10010. Phone: 888-437-4636 or (212)989-5800 Fax: (212)633-3680 E-mail: usinfo@elsevier.com • URL: http://www.elsevier.com • 1982. $162.00. (Developments in Aquaculture and Fisheries Science Series: volume nine).

Water Research. International Association on Water Quality. Elsevier Science, 655 Ave. of the Americas New York, NY 10010. Phone: 888-437-4636 or (212)989-5800 Fax: (212)633-3680 E-mail: usinfo@elsevier.com • URL: http://www.elsevier.com • 18 times a year. $3,721.00 per year.

Water Resources Center. University of Illinois, Urbana-Chapaign

Water Resources: Distribution, Use and Management. John R. Mather. John Wiley and Sons, Inc., 605 Third Ave. New York, NY 10158-0012. Phone: 800-526-5368 or (212)850-6000 Fax: (212)850-6088 E-mail: info@wiley.com • URL: http://www.wiley.com • 1983. $150.00. (Environmental Science and Technology Series).

Water Science and Technology. International Association on Water Quality. Elsevier Science, 655 Ave. of the Americas New York, NY 10010. Phone: 888-437-4636 or (212)989-5800 Fax: (212)633-3680 E-mail: usinfo@elsevier.com • URL: http://www.elsevier.com • 24 times a year. $3,514.00 per year.

Water Systems Council.

Water Well Journal. Ground Water Publishing Co., 601 Dempsey Rd. Westerville, OH 43081-8978. Phone: (614)882-8179 Fax: (614)898-7786 Monthly. $39.00 per year.

Waterfront Revitalization. Eric J. Fournier. Sage Publications, Inc., 2455 Teller Rd. Thousand Oaks, CA 91320. Phone: (805)499-0721 Fax: (805)449-0871 E-mail: info@sagepub.com • URL: http://www.sagepub.com • 1994. $10.00. (CPL Bibliographies Series, No. 310).

Waterway Guide: The Yachtman's Bible. Intertec Publishing Corp., 6151 Powers Ferry Rd., N.W., Suite 200 Atlanta, GA 30339. Phone: (770)955-2500 URL: http://www.intertec.com • Annual. $33.95 per edition. Three regional editions: Northern, and Middle Atlantic, Southern. Provides detailed information concerning marinas on inland and coastal waterways.

Waterways Journal: Devoted to the Marine Profession and Commercial Interest of All Inland Waterways. Waterways Journal, Inc., 319 N. Fourth St., 650 Security Bldg. Saint Louis, MO 63102. Phone: (314)241-7354 Fax: (314)241-4207 E-mail: waterwayj@socket.net • URL: http://www.web-net.com/ • Weekly. $32.00 per year. Weekly business journal serving nation's inland marine industry. Supplement available *Annual Review Number*.

Wealth in a Decade: Brett Matchtig's Proven System for Creating Wealth, Living Off Your Investments and Attaining a Financially Secure Life. Brett Machtig and Ryan D. Behrends. McGraw-Hill Professional, 1221 Ave. of the Americas New York, NY 10020. Phone: 800-722-4726 or (212)904-2000 Fax: (212)904-2072 E-mail: customer.service@mcgraw-hill.com • URL: http://www.mcgraw-hill.com • 1996. $24.95. The authors advocate systematic saving, prudent investing, and no credit card debt. Advice is given on constructing a diversified investment portfolio.

Wealth Ranking Annual. Mark W. Scott. The Taft Group, 27500 Drake Rd. Farmington Hills, MI 48331-3535. Phone: 800-877-GALE or (248)699-GALE Fax: 800-414-5043 or (248)699-8063 E-mail: galeord@galegroup.com • URL: http://www.taftgroup.com • 1997. $95.00. Contains reprints of wealth rankings and compensation lists appearing in periodicals and newspapers. Includes about 600 lists naming more than 6,000 individuals.

The Weather Almanac: A Reference Guide to Weather, Climate, and Air Quality in the United States and Its Key Cities, Comprising Statistics, Principles, and Terminology. The Gale Group, 27500 Drake Rd. Farmington Hills, MI 48331-3535. Phone: 800-877-GALE or (248)699-GALE Fax: 800-414-5043 or (248)699-8069 E-mail: galeord@galegroup.com • URL: http://www.galegroup.com • 1999. $145.00. Ninth edition. Weather reports for 108 major U.S. cities and a climatic overview of the country.

Weather America: A Thirty-Year Summary of Statistical Data and Weather Trends. Grey House Publishing, 185 Millerton Rd. Millerton, NY 12546. Phone: 800-562-2139 or (518)789-8700 Fax: (518)789-0556 E-mail: books@greyhouse.com • URL: http://www.greyhouse.com • 2000. $175.00. Second edition. Contains detailed climatological data for 4,000 national and cooperative weather stations in the U. S. Organized by state, with an index to cities. (Universal Reference Publications.)

Weather and Climate Report. Nautilus Press, Inc., 1201 National Press Bldg. Washington, DC 20045. Phone: (202)347-6643 Monthly. $95.00 per year.

Weather Modification Association.

Weather of U.S. Cities. The Gale Group, 27500 Drake Rd. Farmington Hills, MI 48331-3535. Phone: 800-877-GALE or (248)699-GALE Fax: 800-414-5043 or (248)699-8069 E-mail: galeord@galegroup.com • URL: http://www.galegroup.com • 1996. $225.00. Fifth edition.

Weatherwise: The Magazine About the Weather. Helen Dwight Reid Educational Foundation. Heldref Publications, 1319 18th St., N.W. Washington, DC 20036-1802. Phone: 800-296-5149 or (202)296-6267 Fax: (202)296-5149 E-mail: ww@helderf.org • URL: http://www.helderf.org • Bimonthly. Individuals, $29.00 per year; institutions, $62.00 per year. Popular magazine devoted to weather.

Web Commerce: Building a Digital Business. Kate Maddox and Dana Blankenhorn. John Wiley and Sons, Inc., 605 Third Ave. New York, NY 10158-0012. Phone: 800-225-5945 or (212)850-6000 Fax: (212)850-6088 E-mail: info@jwiley.com • URL: http://www.wiley.com • 1998. $29.95. Provides advice on doing business or providing services through the Internet.

Web Feet: The Internet Traveler's Desk Reference. RockHill Communications, 14 Rock Hill Rd. Bala Cynwyd, PA 19004. Phone: 888-762-5445 or (610)667-2040 Fax: (610)667-2291 E-mail: info@rockhillpress.com • URL: http://www.rockhillpress.com • Monthly. $165.00 per year. Looseleaf. Serves as a subject guide to the ''best'' Web sites.

Web Finance: Covering the Electronic Evolution of Finance. Securities Data PublishingPhone: (212)765-5311 or 800-455-5844 Fax: (212)321-2336 E-mail: webfinance@tfn.com • URL: http://www.webfinance.net • Bi-weekly print and daily web-site publication of financial services on the Web, including financial links, archives, brokerage stocks, deal financing, and other financial and investment news and information.

Web Marketing Update: Quick, Actionable, Internet Intelligence for Marketing Executives. Computer Economics, Inc., 5841 Edison Place Carlsbad, CA 92008. Phone: 800-326-8100 or (760)438-8100 Fax: (760)431-1126 E-mail: info@compecon.com • URL: http://www.computereconomics.com • Monthly. $347.00 per year. Newsletter on various aspects of promoting or selling products and services through an Internet Web site: technology, advertising, strategy, customer base, cost projections, search engines, etc.

The Web of Inclusion: Building an Organization for Everyone. Sally Helgesen. Doubleday, 1540 Broadway New York, NY 10036-4094. Phone: 800-223-6834 or (212)354-6500 Fax: (212)492-9700 URL: http://www.doubledaybookclub.com • 1995. $25.95.

Web Site Source Book: A Guide to Major U. S. Businesses, Organizations, Agencies, Institutions, and Other Information Resources on the World Wide Web. Omnigraphics, Inc., Penobscot Bldg. Detroit, MI 48226. Phone: 800-234-1340 or (313)961-1340 Fax: 800-875-1340 or (313)961-1383 E-mail: info@omnigraphics.com • URL: http://www.omnigraphics.com • Annual. $110.00. About 40,000 Web sites are arranged alphabetically by business or organization and by 1,350 subject categories. Surface mail addresses, phone numbers, fax numbers, and e-mail addresses are included.

Web Style Guide: Basic Design Principles for Creating Web Sites. Patrick J. Lynch and Sarah Horton. Yale University Press, 302 Temple St. New Haven, CT 06520-9040. Phone: 800-987-7323 or (203)432-0948 Fax: (203)432-8487 E-mail: yupmkt@yale.edu • URL: http://www.yale.edu/yup • 1999. $35.00. Covers design of content, interface, page layout, graphics, and multimedia aspects.

Web Techniques: Solutions for Internet and World Wide Web Developers. Miller Freeman, Inc., 600 Harrison St. San Francisco, CA 94107. Phone: (415)905-2200 Fax: (415)905-2233 E-mail: mfloyd@web-techniques.com • URL: http://www.mfi.com • Monthly. $34.95 per year. A technical magazine edited for Internet and World Wide Web professionals.

Web Visions: An Inside Look at Successful Business Strategies on the Net. Eugene Marlow. John Wiley and Sons, Inc., 605 Third Ave. New York, NY 10158-0012. Phone: 800-842-3636 or (212)850-6000 Fax: (212)850-6088 E-mail: info@wiley.com • URL: http://www.wiley.com • 1996. $30.95. The author explains the techniques that have been used by various corporations for success on the World Wide Web.

The Webb Report: A Newsletter on Sexual Harassment. Susan L. Webb, editor. Pacific Resource Development Group, Inc., 145 N. W. 85th St., Suite 104 Seattle, WA 98117-3148. Phone: (206)782-7015 Monthly. $96.00 per year. Contains news and information on sexual harassment issues and court cases. Provides guidelines for supervisors and employees as to what constitutes harassment.

WebFinance. Securities Data Publishing, 40 West 57th St. New York, NY 10019. Phone: 800-455-5844 or (212)765-5311 Fax: (212)956-0112 E-mail: sdp@tfn.com • URL: http://www.sdponline.com • Semimonthly. $995.00 per year. Newsletter (also available online at www.webfinance.net). Covers the Internet-based provision of online financial services by banks, online brokers, mutual funds, and insurance companies. Provides news stories, analysis, and descriptions of useful resources. (Securities Data Publishing is a unit of Thomson Financial.)

Weekly Alert. Research Institute of America, Inc., 90 Fifth Ave. New York, NY 10011. Phone: 800-431-9025 or (212)645-4800 Fax: (212)337-4213 Weekly. Newsletter. $175.00 per year. Federal tax trends and new legislation.

Weekly Business Failures. Dun & Bradstreet, Economic Analysis Dept., Three Sylvan Way Parsippany, NJ 07054-3896. Phone: 800-526-0651 or (973)455-0900 Fax: (973)254-4063 E-mail: customerservice@dnb.com • URL: http://www.dnb.com • Weekly. $450.00 per year.

Weekly Cotton Trade Report. New York Cotton Exchange, Four World Trade Center New York, NY 10048. Phone: (212)938-7909 Weekly. $100.00 per year.

Weekly Digest. American Institute of Food Distribution, 28-12 Broadway Fair Lawn, NJ 07410. Phone: (201)791-5570 Fax: (201)791-5222 Weekly. $495.00. (Includes *Report on Food Markets*, *Food Distribution Digest* and *Washington Food Report*).

Weekly Insiders Dairy and Egg Letter. Urner Barry Publications, Inc., P.O. Box 389 Toms River, NJ 08754. Phone: 800-932-0617 or (732)240-5330 Fax: (732)341-0891 E-mail: mail@urnerbarry.com • URL: http://www.unerbarry.com • Weekly. $173.00 per year.

Weekly of Business Aviation. Aviation Week Newsletter. McGraw-Hill, 1221 Ave. of the Americas New York, NY 10020. Phone: 800-722-4726 or (212)904-2000 Fax: (212)904-2072 E-mail: customer.service@mcgraw-hill.com • URL: http://www.mcgraw-hill.com • Weekly. $540.00 per year.

Weekly Petroleum Status Report. Energy Information Administration. Available from U.S. Government Printing Office, Washington, DC 20402. Phone: (202)512-1800 Fax: (202)512-2250 E-mail: gpoaccess@gpo.gov • URL: http://www.accessgpo.gov • Weekly. $85.00 per year. Current statistics in the context of both historical information and selected prices and forecasts.

Weekly Pharmacy Reports: The Green Sheet. F-D-C Reports, Inc., 5550 Friendship Blvd., Suite 1 Chevy Chase, MD 20815-7278. Phone: 800-332-2181 or (301)657-9830 Fax: (301)664-7238 URL: http://www.fdcreports.com • Weekly. $82.00 per year. Newsletter for retailers and wholesalers of pharmaceutical products. Includes pricing developments and new drug announcements.

Weekly Statistical Summary. National Mining Association, 1130 17th St., N. W. Washington, DC 20036-4677. Phone: (202)463-2625 Fax: (202)463-6152 E-mail: rlawson@nma.org • URL: http://www.nma.org • Weekly. $100.00 per year. A detailed report on coal production and consumption.

Weekly Summary of the National Labor Relations Board Cases. Available from U. S. Government Printing Office, Washington, DC 20402. Phone: (202)512-1800 Fax: (202)512-2250 E-mail: gpoaccess@gpo.gov • URL: http://www.access.gpo.gov • Weekly. $174.00 per year. Issued by the Division of Information, National Labor Relations Board.

Weekly Weather and Crop Bulletin. Available from U.S. Department of Agriculture, Agricultural Weather Facility, Washington, DC 20250. Phone: (202)720-2791 Weekly.

WEFA Industrial Monitor. John Wiley and Sons, Inc., 605 Third Ave. New York, NY 10158-0012. Phone: 800-225-5945 or (212)850-6000 Fax: (212)850-6088 E-mail: info@wiley.com • URL: http://www.wiley.com • Annual. $65.00. Prepared by industry analysts at WEFA, an economic forecasting and consulting firm (originally Wharton Econometric Forecasting Associates). Contains discussions of the outlook for major U. S. industries, with many 10-year forecasts (WEFA Web site is http://www.wefa.com).

Weighing and Measurement. Key Markets Publishing Co., P.O. Box 270 Roscoe, IL 61073-0270. Phone: (815)636-7739 Fax: (815)636-7741 Bimonthly. $30.00 per year. Provides information relating to industrial weighing methods.

Weight Loss and Diet Control Market. Available from MarketResearch.com, 641 Ave. of the Americas, Third Floor New York, NY 10011. Phone: 800-298-5699 or (212)807-2629 Fax: (212)807-2716 E-mail: order@marketresearch.com • URL: http://www.marketresearch.com • 1999. $1,695.00. Market research report published by Marketdata Enterprises. Covers commercial diet programs, medical plans, nonprescription appetite suppressants low-calorie foods, artifical sweeteners, health clubs, and diet books. Includes forecasts to the year 2003.

Welcome to the Foundation Center. The Foundation CenterPhone: (212)620-4230 Fax: (212)691-1828 E-mail: mfn@fdncenter.org • URL: http://www.fdncenter.org • Web site provides a wide variety of information about foundations, grants, and philanthropy, with links to philanthropic organizations. ''Grantmaker Information'' link furnishes descriptions of available funding. Fees: Free.

Weldasearch. The Welding Institute, Abington Hall, Abington Cambridge CB1 6AL, England. Phone: (122)3-891162 Fax: (122)3-892588 Contains abstracts of international welding literature, 1967 to date. Inquire as to online cost and availability.

Welding and Fabricating Data Book. Penton Media Inc., 1300 E. Ninth St. Cleveland, OH 44114. Phone: (216)696-7000 Fax: (216)696-0836 E-mail: corpcomm@penton.com • URL: http://www.penton.com • Biennial. $30.00. List of over 1,500 manufacturers and suppliers of products and equipment for the welding and fabricating industry.

Welding and Metal Fabrication. DMG World Media, Queensway House, Two Queensway Redhill Surrey RH1 1QS,

England. Phone: 44 1737 768611 Fax: 44 1737 855470 URL: http://www.dmg.co.uk • 10 times a year. $293.00 per year.

Welding Design and Fabrication. Penton Media Inc., 1300 E. Ninth St. Cleveland, OH 44114. Phone: (216)696-7000 Fax: (216)696-0836 E-mail: corpcomm@penton.com • URL: http://www.penton.com • Monthly. Free to qualified personnel; others, $70.00 per year.

The Welding Encyclopedia. Ted B. Jefferson and Don Jefferson, editors. Jefferson Publications, Inc., P.O. Box 1123 Libertyville, IL 60047. Phone: (708)438-4114 1988. $27.50. 18th edition.

Welding in the World. International Institute of Welding. Elsevier Science, 655 Ave. of the Americas New York, NY 10010. Phone: 888-437-4636 or (212)989-5800 Fax: (212)633-3680 E-mail: usinfo@elsevier.com • URL: http://www.elsevier.com • Semiannual. $449.00 per year. Text in English and French.

Welding Journal. American Welding Society, 550 N.W. LeJeune Rd. Miami, FL 33126. Phone: 800-443-9353 or (305)443-9353 Fax: (305)443-7559 E-mail: info@aws.org • URL: http://www.aws.org • Monthly. Membership.

Welding Research Abroad. Welding Research Council, Three Park Ave., 27th Fl. New York, NY 10016-5902. Phone: (212)705-7956 10 times a year. $1,100.00. Includes *Progress Reports, WRC Bulletins, WRC News* and *Welding Journal*.

Welding Research Council.

Welding Research Council Yearbook. Welding Research Council, Three Park Ave., 27th Fl. New York, NY 10016-5902. Phone: (212)705-7956 Annual. Membership.

Welding Technology. Gower A. Kennedy. Pearson Education and Technology, 201 W. 103rd St. Indianapolis, IN 46290-1097. Phone: 800-858-7674 or (317)581-3500 URL: http://www.mcp.com • 1982. $52.94.

Welfare: The Political Economy of Welfare Reform in the United States. Martin Anderson. Hoover Institution Press, Stanford University Stanford, CA 94305-6010. Phone: 800-935-2882 or (650)723-3373 Fax: (650)723-8626 E-mail: digest@hoover.stanford.edu • URL: http://www.hoover.stanford.edu • 1978. $6.78. (Publication Series, No. 181).

Wellness Center., 145 W. 28th St., Room 9R New York, NY 10001. Phone: (212)465-8062 Members include business firms and organizations with wellness centers for employees.

Western Crop Protection Association.

Western Fruit Grower: The Business Magazines of the Western Produce Industry. Meister Publishing Co., 37733 Euclid Ave. Willoughby, OH 44094. Phone: 800-572-7740 or (440)942-2000 Fax: (440)942-0662 E-mail: info@meisternet.com • URL: http://www.meisterpro.com • Monthly. $15.95 per year. Covers the commercial fruit industry in 13 western states.

Western Grower and Shipper: The Business Magazine of the Western Product Industry. Western Growers Association. Western Grower and Shipper Publishing Co., P.O. Box 2130 Newport Beach, CA 92658. Phone: (949)863-1000 Fax: (949)863-9028 Monthly. $18.00 per year.

Western Growers Association-Membership Directory. Western Growers Association, P.O. Box 2130 Newport Beach, CA 92658. Phone: (949)863-1000 Fax: (949)863-9028 E-mail: flower@wga.com • Annual. Membership.

Western Management Science Institute. University of California, Los Angeles

Western States Advertising Agencies Association.

West's Business Law: Text and Cases, Legal, Ethical, Regulatory and International Environment. Kenneth Clarkson. South-Western College Publishing, 5101 Madison Dr. Cincinnati, OH 45227. Phone: 800-543-0487 or (513)527-1989 Fax: (513)527-6137 URL: http://www.thomson.com • 2000. $109.95. Eighth edition.

West's Encyclopedia of American Law. Available from The Gale Group, 27500 Drake Rd. Farmington Hills, MI 48331-3535. Phone: 800-877-GALE or (248)699-GALE Fax: 800-414-5043 or (248)699-8069 E-mail: galeord@galegroup.com • URL: http://www.galegroup.com • 1997. $995.00. Second edition. 12 volumes. Published by West Group. Covers a wide variety of legal topics for the general reader. Formerly *Guide to American Law: Everyone's Legal Encyclopedia* (1985).

West's Legal Forms. West Publishing Co., College and School Div., 610 Opperman Dr. Eagan, MN 55123. Phone: 800-328-4880 or (651)687-7000 Fax: 800-213-2323 or (651)687-5827 E-mail: legal-ed@westgroup.com • URL: http://www.lawschool.westgroup.com • Second edition. Multivolume set. Price on application. Periodic supplementation.

West's Textbook of Cosmetology. Jerry J. Ahern. West Publishing Co., College and School Div., 610 Opperman Dr. Eagen, MN 55123. Phone: 800-328-4880 or (612)687-7000 Fax: 800-213-2323 or (612)687-5827 E-mail: legal_ed@westgroup.com • URL: http://www.lawschool.westpub.com • 1986. $37.00. Second edition.

WFDSA Directory of Members (World Federation of Direct Selling Association). World Federation of Direct Selling Associations, 1666 K St., N.W., Ste. 1010 Washington, DC 20006-2808. Phone: (202)293-5760 Fax: (202)463-4569 E-mail: info@dsa.org • URL: http://www.org • Annual. Price on application.

What America's Small Companies Pay Their Sales Forces and How They Make It Pay Off. Christen P. Heide. Dartnell Corp., 4660 N. Ravenswood Ave. Chicago, IL 60640-4595. Phone: 800-621-5463 or (773)561-4000 Fax: (773)561-3801 URL: http://www.dartnellcorp.com • 1997. $29.95. Provides advice on attracting, motivating, and retaining productive sales personnel. Includes sales position descriptions and "latest sales compensation figures for companies under $5 million in sales."

What Color is Your Parachute? 2001: A Practical Manual for Job Hunters and Career Changers. Richard N. Bolles. Ten Speed Press, 999 Harrison St. Berkeley, CA 94707. Phone: 800-841-2665 or (510)559-1600 Fax: (510)524-1052 E-mail: order@tenspeed.com • URL: http://www.tenspeed.com • 2000. $24.95. Revised edition. Features non-traditional job searching methods.

What Corporate and General Practitioners Should Know About Intellectual Property Litigation. Raphael V. Lupo and Donna M. Tanguay. American Law Institute-American Bar Association, Committee on Continuing Professional Education, 4025 Chestnut St. Philadelphia, PA 19104-3099. Phone: 800-253-6397 or (215)243-1600 Fax: (215)243-1664 URL: http://www.ali-aba.org • 1991. $34.00. A lawyer's guide to patents, trademarks, copyrights, and trade secrets.

What the IRS Doesn't Want You to Know: A CPA Reveals the Tricks of the Trade. Martin Kaplan and Naomi Weiss. Villard Books, 201 E. 50th St. New York, NY 10022. Phone: 800-726-0600 or (212)751-2600 Fax: 800-659-2436 URL: http://www.randomhouse.com • 1999. $15.95. Sixth edition. Explains how to legally pay as little income tax as possible.

What Will Be: How the New World of Information Will Change Our Lives. Michael L. Dertouzos. HarperSan Francisco, 353 Sacramento St., Suite 500 San Francisco, CA 94111. Phone: 800-242-7737 or (415)477-4400 Fax: 800-822-4090 or (415)477-4444 URL: http://www.harpercollins.com • 1997. $25.00. A discussion of the "information market place" of the future, including telecommuting, virtual reality, and computer recognition of speech. The author is director of the MIT Laboratory for Computer Science.

What Will the Next Recession Mean to You? C. Edgar Murray, editor. American Institute for Economic Research, Division St. Great Barrington, MA 01230-1000. Phone: (413)528-1216 Fax: (413)528-0103 E-mail: info@aier.org • URL: http://www.aier.org • 2001. $6.00. Revised edition. Provides historical background of U.S. recessions and gives conservative advice on "Coping with a Recession." (Economic Education Bulletin Series).

What Works on Wall Street: A Guide to the Best-Performing Investment Strategies of All Time. James P. O'Shaughnessy. McGraw-Hill, 1221 Ave. of the Americas New York, NY 10020. Phone: 800-722-4726 or (212)904-2000 Fax: (212)904-2072 E-mail: customer.service@mcgraw-hill.com • URL: http://www.mcgraw-hill.com • 1998. $22.95. Second revised edition. Examines investment strategies over a 43-year period and concludes that large capitalization, high-dividend-yield stocks produce the best results.

What You Need to Know About Mutual Funds. Kenneth M. Lefkowitz. American Institute for Economic Research, Division St. Great Barrington, MA 01230-1000. Phone: (413)528-1216 Fax: (413)528-0103 E-mail: info@aier.org • URL: http://www.aier.org • 1996. $6.00. Provides conservative advice on investing in mutual funds, unit investment trusts, closed-end investment companies, and other funds. Includes a glossary and lists of recommended information sources.

What Your Car Really Costs: How to Keep a Financially Safe Driving Record. American Institute for Economic Research, Division St. Great Barrington, MA 01230. Phone: (413)528-1216 Fax: (413)528-0103 E-mail: info@aier.org • URL: http://www.aier.org • 1999. $6.00. Contains "Should You Buy or Lease?," "Should You Buy New or Used?," "Dealer Trade-in or Private Sale?," "Lemon Laws," and other car buying information. Includes rankings of specific models for resale value, 1992 to 1998. (Economic Education Bulletin.)

What's New in Advertising and Marketing. Special Libraries Association, Advertising and Marketing Div., c/o John Patton Suffolk Cooperative Library System, 627 N. Sunrise Service Rd. Bellport, NY 11713. Phone: (516)286-1600 Fax: (516)286-1647 Quarterly. Non-profit organizations, $20.00 per year; corporations, $30.00 per year. Lists and briefly describes a wide variety of free or inexpensive material relating to advertising, marketing, and media.

Wheat, Barley, and Triticale Abstracts. Available from CABI Publishing North America, 10 E. 40th St. New York, NY 10016. Phone: 800-528-4841 or (212)481-7018 Fax: (212)686-7993 E-mail: cabi@cabi.org • URL: http://www.cabi.org • Bimonthly. $895.00 per year. Published in England by CABI Publishing. Provides worldwide coverage of the literature of wheat, barley, and rye.

Wheat Facts. National Association of Wheat Growers, 415 Second St., N.E., Suite 300 Washington, DC 20002. Phone: (202)547-7800 Fax: (202)546-2638 E-mail: nawgl@aol.com • URL: http://www.wheatworld.org • Annual. Price on application.

Wheat Life. Washington Association of Wheat Growers, 109 E. First St. Ritzville, WA 99169-2394. Phone: (509)659-0610 11 times a year. $12.00 per year. Covers research, marketing information, and legislative and regulatory news pertinent to the wheat and barley industries of the Pacific Northwest.

When Talk Works: Profiles of Mediators. Deborah M. Kolb. Jossey-Bass, Inc., Publishers, 350 Sansome St. San Francisco, CA 94104. Phone: 888-378-2537 or (415)433-1740 Fax: (415)433-0499 E-mail: webperson@jbp.com • URL: http://www.josseybass.com • 1997. $25.95. Provides interview-based profiles of expert mediators in labor, business, education, family matters, community relations, foreign affairs, and other fields. (Management Series).

When Technology Fails. The Gale Group, 27500 Drake Rd. Farmington Hills, MI 48331-3535. Phone: 800-877-GALE or (248)699-GALE Fax: 800-414-5043 or (248)699-8069 E-mail: galeord@galegroup.com • URL: http://www.galegroup.com • 1994. $80.00. The stories of about 100 important technological disasters, accidents, and failures in the 20th century, caused by faults in design, construction, planning, and testing. Arranged in broad subject categories, with a keyword index.

When Work Doesn't Work Anymore: Women, Work, and Identity. Elizabeth P. McKenna. Doubleday, 1540 Broadway New York, NY 10036-4094. Phone: 800-223-6834 or (212)354-6500 Fax: (212)492-9700 URL: http://www.doubledaybookclub.com • 1997. $12.95. A popularly written discussion of the conflict between corporate culture and the traditional, family roles of women.

When You Lose Your Job: Laid Off, Fired, Early Retired, Relocated, Demoted. Cliff Hakim. Berrett-Koehler Publishers, Inc., 450 Sansome St., Suite 1200 San Francisco, CA 94111-3320. Phone: 800-929-2929 or (415)288-0260 Fax: (415)362-2512 E-mail: bkpub@aol.com • URL: http://www.bkconnection.com/ • 1993. $14.95. A guide to overcoming job loss. Covers emotional responses, as well as practical matters such as networking, resumes, and preparing for interviews.

Where the Suckers Moon: The Life and Death of an Advertising Campaign. Randall Rothenberg. Random House, Inc., 201 E. 50th St. New York, NY 10022. Phone: 800-726-0600 or (212)751-2600 Fax: 800-659-2436 or (212)572-8700 URL: http://www.randomhouse.com/ • 1995. $16.00. Presents the story of an advertising agency's failed automobile campaign.

Where to Buy Hardwood Plywood and Veneer. Hardwood Plywood Manufacturers Association, P.O. 2789 Reston, VA 20195-0789. Phone: (703)435-2900 Fax: (703)435-2537 E-mail: hpva@hpva.org • URL: http://www.hpva.org • Annual. $20.00. Lists about 190 member manufacturers, prefinishers, and suppliers of hardwood veneer and plywood.

Where to Go When the Bank Says No: Alternatives to Financing Your Business. David R. Evanson. Bloomberg Press, 100 Business Park Dr. Princeton, NJ 08542-0888. Phone: 800-388-2749 or (609)279-4670 Fax: (609)279-7155 E-mail: press@bloomberg.com • URL: http://www.bloomberg.com • 1998. $24.95. Emphasis is on obtaining business financing in the $250,000 to $15,000,000 range. Business plans are discussed. (Bloomberg Small Business Series).

Where to Write for Vital Records: Births, Deaths, Marriages, and Divorces. Available from U. S. Government Printing Office, Washington, DC 20402. Phone: (202)512-1800 Fax: (202)512-2250 E-mail: gpoaccess@gpo.gov • URL: http://www.access.gpo.gov • 1999. $3.00. Issued by the National Center for Health Statistics, U. S. Department of Health and Human Services. Arranged by state. Provides addresses, telephone numbers, and cost of copies for various kinds of vital records or certificates. (DHHS Publication No. PHS 93-1142.)

Whirly-Girls (International Women Helicopter Pilots).

White-Collar Crime Reporter: Information and Analyses Concerning White-Collar Practice. Andrews Publications, 175 Strafford Ave., Bldg 4, Suite 140 Wayne, PA 19087. Phone: 800-345-1101 or (610)622-0510 Fax: (610)622-0501 URL: http://www.andrewspub.com • 10 times a year. $550.00 per year. Newsletter. Provides information on trends in white collar crime.

Whittington's Dictionary of Plastics. Society of Plastics Engineers. Available from Technomic Publishing Co., P.O. Box 3535 Lancaster, PA 17604. Phone: 800-233-9936 or (717)291-5609 Fax: (717)295-4538 E-mail: marketing@techpub.com • URL: http://www.techpub.com • 1993. $99.95. Third expanded revised edition.

Who Audits America: A Directory of Publicly Held Corporations and the Accounting Firms Who Audit Them. Data Financial Press, P.O. Box 668 Menlo Park, CA 94026. Phone: (415)321-4553 Semiannual. $125.00. 8,500 publicly held corporations that report to the Securities and Exchange Commission, and their accounting firms.

Who Cares for Them? Workers in the Home Care Industry. Penny H. Feldman and others. Greenwood Publishing Group, Inc., 88 Post Rd., W. Westport, CT 06881-5007. Phone: 800-225-5800 or (203)226-3571 Fax: (203)222-2540 E-mail: bookinfo@greenwood.com • URL: http://www.greenwood.com • 1990. $55.00. (Contributions to the Study of Aging Series, No.16).

Who Knows Who: Networking Through Corporate Boards. Who Know Who Publishing, 568A 62nd St. Oakland, CA 94609-1245. Phone: (510)654-3543 1994. $150.00. Fifth edition. Shows the connections between the board members of major U. S. corporations and major foundations and non-profit organizations.

Who Owns Whom. Dun and Bradstreet Information Services, Dun and Bradstreet Corp., Three Sylvan Way Parsippany, NJ 07054-3896. Phone: 800-526-0521 or (973)455-0900 Fax: (973)254-4063 E-mail: customerservice@dnb.com • URL: http://www.dnb.com • Annual. Four editions: Australasia and Far East; Continental, Europe, two volumes; North America; United Kingdom, two volumes. Prices vary.

Who Owns Whom: Australasia & Asia, Middle East and Africa. Dun & Bradstreet Information Services, Three Sylvan Way Parsippany, NJ 07054-3896. Phone: 800-526-0651 or (973)455-0900 Fax: (973)254-4063 E-mail: customerservice@dnb.com • URL: http://www.dnb.com • Annual. $500.00. Two volumes. Published in England by Dun & Bradstreet Ltd. Provides information on 5,500 parent companies and their foreign and domestic subsidiaries. Parent companies are located in Singapore, Hong Kong, Japan, the Philippines, South Korea, Taiwan, Thailand, New Guinea, Malaysia, Indonesia, New Zealand, and Australia. Formerly *Who Owns Whom: Australasia and Far East*.

Who Writes What in Life and Health Insurance. The National Underwriter Co., 505 Gest St. Cincinnati, OH 45203-1716. Phone: 800-543-0874 or (513)721-2140 Fax: (513)721-0126 URL: http://www.nuco.com • Annual. $9.95.

Wholesale Commodity Report. Financial Times, 14 E. 60th St. New York, NY 10022. Phone: (212)752-4500 Weekly. $144.00 to $165.00 per year depending on postal rates.

Wholesale Florists and Florist Suppliers of America.

Wholesale Florists and Florist Suppliers of America-Membership Directory. Wholesale Florists and Florist Suppliers of America, Old Solomons Island Rd., Suite 302 Annapolis, MD 21401. Phone: 888-289-3372 or (410)576-5001 Fax: (410)573-0400 E-mail: jwanka@wffsa.org • Annual. $100.00. 1,275 listings.

Wholesale Nursery Growers of America.

The Wholesaler. TMB Publishing, Inc., 1838 Techny Court Northbrook, IL 60062. Phone: (847)564-1127 Fax: (847)564-1264 E-mail: tmbpub@eartlink.net • Monthly. $75.00 per year. Edited for wholesalers and distributors of plumbing, piping, heating, and air conditioning equipment.

The Wholesaler "Wholesaling 100". TMB Publishing, Inc., 1838 Techny Court Northbrook, IL 60062. Phone: (847)564-1127 Fax: (847)564-1264 E-mail: tmbpubs@earthlink.net • Annual. $25.00. Provides information on the 100 leading wholesalers of plumbing, piping, heating, and air conditioning equipment.

Who's Mailing What!: The Monthly Newsletter Analysis and Record of the Direct Mareting Archive. North American Publishing Co., 401 N. Broad St. Philadelphia, PA 19108-9988. Phone: 800-627-2689 or (215)238-5300 Fax: (215)238-5457 E-mail: dbrennan@napco.com • URL: http://www.napco.com • Monthly. $295.00 per year. Newsletter and listing of promotional mailings. Photocopies of mailings are available to subscribers.

Who's Wealthy in America: A Directory of the 109,100 Richest People in the United States. The Taft Group, 27500 Drake Rd. Farmington Hills, MI 48331-3535. Phone: 800-347-4253 or (248)699-4253 Fax: (248)699-8097 Annual. $445.00. Two volumes. Includes Company Name Index (indicates insider stock holdings), Geographic Index, Political Contribution Index, and Alma Mater Index.

Who's Who Among African Americans. The Gale Group, 27500 Drake Rd. Farmington Hills, MI 48331-3535. Phone: 800-877-GALE or (248)699-GALE Fax: 800-414-5043 or (248)699-8069 E-mail: galeord@galegroup.com • URL: http://www.galegroup.com • 2000. $175.00. 13th edition. Includes many business leaders.

Who's Who: An Annual Biographical Dictionary. St. Martin's Press, Inc., 175 Fifth Ave. New York, NY 10010. Phone: 800-221-7945 or (212)674-5151 Fax: (212)529-0594 URL: http://www.stmartins.com • Annual. $110.00. Over 29,000 prominent individuals worldwide, but with emphasis on the United Kingdom.

Who's Who and What's What in Packaging. Institute of Packaging Professionals, 481 Carlisle Dr. Herndon, VA 20170-4823. Phone: 800-432-4085 or (703)318-8970 Fax: (703)381-4961 E-mail: iopp@pkgmatters.com • URL: http://www.packinfo-world.orgiopp • Annual. Price on application.

Who's Who in America. Marquis Who's Who, 121 Chanlon Rd. New Providence, NJ 07974. Phone: 800-521-8110 or (908)464-6800 Fax: (908)665-6688 E-mail: info@marquiswhoswho.com • URL: http://www.marquiswhoswho.com • Annual. Libraries, $575.00. Three volumes. Contains over 105,000 concise biographies, with a Geographic/Professional Index.

Who's Who in American Art. Available from Reed Elsevier, 121 Chanlon Rd. New Providence, NJ 07974. Phone: 800-521-8110 or (908)464-6800 Fax: (908)665-6688 E-mail: marquiswhoswho.com • URL: http://www.bowker.com • Biennial. $210.00. Lists about 11,800 people active in visual arts. Published by Marquis Who's Who.

Who's Who in American Education. Marquis Who's Who, 121 Chanlon Rd. New Providence, NJ 07974. Phone: 800-521-8110 or (908)464-6800 Fax: (908)665-6688 E-mail: info@marquiswhoswho.com • URL: http://www.marquiswhoswho.com • Biennial. $159.95. Contains over 27,000 concise biographies of teachers, administrators, and other individuals involved in all levels of American education.

Who's Who in American Law. Marquis Who's Who, 121 Chanlon Rd. New Providence, NJ 07974. Phone: 800-521-8110 or (908)464-6800 Fax: (908)665-6688 E-mail: info@marquiswhoswho.com • URL: http://www.marquiswhoswho.com • Biennial. $285.00. Contains over 22,000 concise biographies of American lawyers, judges, and others in the legal field.

Who's Who in American Politics. Marquis Who's Who, 121 Chanlon Rd. New Providence, NJ 07974. Phone: 800-521-8110 or (908)464-6800 Fax: (908)665-6688 E-mail: info@marquiswhoswho.com • URL: http://www.marquiswhoswho.com • Biennial. $275.00. Two volumes. Contains about 27,000 biographical sketches of local, state, and national elected or appointed individuals.

Who's Who in Art. Available from The Gale Group, 27500 Drake Rd. Farmington Hills, MI 48331-3535. Phone: 800-877-4253 or (248)699-4253 Fax: 800-414-5043 or (248)699-8069 E-mail: galeord@galegroup.com • URL: http://www.galegroup.com • 2000. $135.00. 29th edition. Contains about 3,000 brief biographies of artists, designers, curators, critics, and other art-related individuals. International coverage, with British emphasis. Published by Art Trade Press.

Who's Who in Art Materials. National Art Materials Trade Association, 10115 Kincey Ave., Suite 260 Huntersville, NC 28078. Phone: (704)948-5554 Fax: (704)948-5658 Annual. Free to members; non-members, $110.00 per year. Lists retailers and manufacturers of artists' supplies.

Who's Who in Association Management. American Society of Association Executives, 1575 Eye St., N.W. Washington, DC 20005-1168. Phone: (202)626-2723 Fax: (202)371-8825 E-mail: asea@aseanet.org • URL: http://www.asaenet.org • Annual. $160.00. Lists paid executives who are members of the association and suppliers of products and services to the association.

Who's Who in Canadian Business. Who's Who Publications, 777 Bay St., 5th Fl. Toronto, ON, Canada M57 1A7. Phone: (416)596-5156 Fax: (416)596-5235 Annual. $179.95. Contains brief biographies of 5,000 individuals prominent in Canadian business.

Who's Who in Engineering. American Association of Engineering Societies, 1111 19th St., N.W., Suite 403 Washington, DC 20036-3690. Phone: 888-400-2237 or (202)296-2237 Fax: (202)296-1151 E-mail: aaes@access.digex.net • URL: http://www.aaes.org/ewc • Triennial. Members, $149.00; non-members, $242.00. Lists about 15,000 engineers who have received professional recognition for outstanding achievement.

Who's Who in Equipment Leasing. Equipment Leasing Association, 4301 N. Fairfax Ave., Suite 550 Arlington, VA 22203-1608. Phone: (703)527-8655 Fax: (703)527-2649 E-mail: ela@elamail.com • URL: http://www.elaonline.com • Annual. $350.00. Provides information on about 750 commercial equipment leasing companies.

Who's Who in Finance and Industry. Marquis Who's Who, 121 Chanlon Rd. New Providence, NJ 07974. Phone: 800-521-8110 or (908)464-6800 Fax: (908)665-6688 E-mail: info@marquiswhoswho.com • URL: http://www.marquiswhoswho.com • Biennial. $295.00. Provides over 22,400 concise biographies of business leaders in all fields.

Who's Who in Insurance. Underwriter Printing and Publishing Co., 50 E. Palisade Ave. Englewood, NJ 07631. Phone: 800-526-4700 or (201)569-8808 Fax: (201)569-8817 Annual. $130.00. Contains over 5,000 biographies of insurance officials, leading agents and brokers, and high-ranking company officials.

Who's Who in Interior Design. Baron's Who's Who, 11 Petria Irvine, CA 92606. Phone: (949)497-8615 Fax: (949)786-8918 E-mail: info@baronswhoswho.com • URL: http://www.baronswhoswho.com • Annual. $280.00. Contains biographical data for over 3,500 interior designers worldwide.

Who's Who in International Banking. Bowker-Saur, 121 Chanlon Rd. New Providence, NJ 07974. Phone: 800-521-8110 or (908)464-6800 Fax: (908)771-8784 Irregular. $400.00. Contains biographical sketches of about 4,000 bankers. Worldwide coverage.

Who's Who in Professional Imaging. Professional Photographers of America, Inc., 22 Peachtree St., N.E., Suite 2200 Atlanta, GA 30303. Phone: 800-786-6277 or (404)522-8600 Fax: (404)614-6405 E-mail: info@ppa-world.org • URL: http://www.ppa-world.org • Annual. $110.00. Lists over 18,000 members. Formerly *Buyers Guide to Qualified Photographers*.

Who's Who in Risk Management. Underwriter Printing and Publishing Co., 50 E. Palisade Ave. Englewood, NJ 07631. Phone: 800-526-4700 or (201)569-8808 Fax: (201)569-8817 Annual. $75.00. Contains specialized biographies of insurance buyers for large business and industrial firms throughout the U.S.

Who's Who in Science and Engineering. Marquis Who's Who, 121 Chanlon Rd. New Providence, NJ 07974. Phone: 800-521-8110 or (908)464-6800 Fax: (908)665-6688 E-mail: info@marquiswhoswho.com • URL: http://www.marquiswhoswho.com • Biennial. $269.00. Provides concise biographical information on 26,000 prominent engineers and scientists. International coverage, with geographical and professional indexes.

Who's Who in Special Libraries. Special Libraries Association, 1700 18th St, N. W., 17th Fl. Washington, DC 20009-2514. Phone: (202)234-4700 Fax: 888-411-2856 or (202)265-9317 E-mail: books@sla.org • URL: http://www.sla.org • Annual. Free to members; non-members, $45.00. About 14,000 librarians of libraries and special collections having a specific subject focus.

Who's Who in Technology [Online]. The Gale Group, 27500 Drake Rd. Farmington Hills, MI 48331-3535. Phone: 800-877-GALE or (248)669-GALE Fax: 800-414-5043 or (248)699-8069 E-mail: galeord@gale.com • URL: http://www.gale.com • Provides online biographical profiles of over 25,000 American scientists, engineers, and others in technology-related occupations. Inquire as to online cost and availability.

Who's Who in the Dental Laboratory Industry. National Association of Dental Laboratories, 8201 Greensboro Dr., Suite 300 McLean, VA 22102. Phone: 800-950-1150 or (703)610-9035 Fax: (703)610-9005 E-mail: nadl@nadl.org • URL: http://www.nadl.org • Annual. $55.00. About 3,300 dental laboratories; 12,000 certified dental technicians, manufacturers, and schools of dental technology.

Who's Who in the Egg and Poultry Industries. Watt Publishing Co., 122 S. Wesley Ave. Mount Morris, IL 61054-1497. Phone: (815)734-4171 Fax: (815)734-4201 URL: http://www.wattnet.com • Annual. $100.00. Producers, processors, and distributors of poultry meat and eggs in the United States; manufacturers of supplies and equipment for the poultry industry; breeders and hatcheries; refrigerated public warehouses;. food chain buyers of poultry meat and eggs; related government agencies; poultry associations.

Who's Who in the Securities Industry. Securities Industry Association. Economist Publishing Co., 11 E. Hubbard St., Suite 3A Chicago, IL 60611-3536. Phone: 800-843-3266 or (312)467-1888 Fax: (312)467-0225 Annual. Price on application about 1,000 investment bankers.

Who's Who in the Snack Food Industry. Snack Food Association, 1711 King St., Suite 1 Alexandria, VA 22314. Phone: 800-628-1334 or (703)836-4500 Fax: (703)836-8262 E-mail: sfa@sfa.org • URL: http://www.snax.com • Annual. $150.00. A directory of snack food manufacturers and suppliers to the industry.

Who's Who in the Southern Furniture Industry. American Furniture Manufacturers Association, P.O. Box HP-7 High Point, NC 27261. Phone: (336)884-5000 Fax: (336)884-5303 Annual. $50.00. Lists about 400 manufacturers of furniture and their suppliers.

Who's Who in the Wall and Ceiling Industry. Association of the Wall and Ceiling Industries International, 803 W. Broad St., Suite 600 Falls Church, VA 22046. Phone: (703)534-8307 Fax: (703)534-8307 Annual. Price on application. Contractors, manufacturers, suppliers, unions, organizations, and periodicals affiliated with the industry.

Who's Who in the World. Marquis Who's Who, 121 Chanlon Rd. New Providence, NJ 07974. Phone: 800-521-8110 or (908)464-6800 Fax: (908)665-6688 E-mail: info@marquiswhoswho.com • URL: http://www.marquiswhoswho.com • Annual. $379.95. Provides biographical profiles of about 40,000 prominent individuals. International coverage.

Who's Who in World Petrochemicals and Plastics. Available from Reed Business Information, 3730 Kirby Dr., Suite 1030 Houston, TX 77098. Phone: (713)525-2600 Fax: (713)525-2659 Annual. $175.00. Names, addresses, telephone numbers, and company affiliations of individuals active in the petrochemical business. Formerly *Who's Who in World Petrochemicals*.

Who's Who-Masa's Buyers' Guide to Blue Ribbon Mailing Service. Mail Advertising Service Association International, 1421 Prince St., Suite 200 Alexandria, VA 22314-2806. Phone: 800-333-6272 or (703)836-9200 Fax: (703)548-8204 Annual. Free. Member firms that provide printing, addressing, inserting, sorting, and other mailing services, and mailing list brokers.

Who's Who of American Women. Marquis Who's Who, 121 Chanlon Rd. New Providence, NJ 07974. Phone: 800-521-8110 or (908)464-6800 Fax: (908)665-6688 E-mail: info@marquiswhoswho.com • URL: http://www.marquiswhoswho.com • Biennial. $259.00. Provides over 27,000 biographical profiles of important women, including individuals prominent in business, finance, and industry.

Who's Who of European Business: and Industry. Triumph Books, 1436 W. Randolph St. Chicago, IL 60607. Phone: 800-335-5323 or (312)939-3330 Fax: (312)733-3107 E-mail: triumphbooks@aol.com • Irregular. $295.00. Lists over 9,500 business executives from 36 countries in Eastern and Western Europe. Two volumes.

Who's Who: The CTFA Membership Directory (Cosmetics Industry). Cosmetic, Toiletry, and Fragrance Association, 1101 17th St., N. W., Suite 300 Washington, DC 20036-4702. Phone: (202)331-1770 Fax: (202)331-1969 E-mail: membership@ctfa.org • URL: http://www.ctfa.org • Annual. $100.00. Lists about 1,000 member companies, with key personnel, products, and services.

Why Entrepreneurs Fail: Avoid the 20 Fatal Pitfalls of Running Your Own Business. James W. Halloran. McGraw-Hill Professional, 1221 Ave. of the Americas New York, NY 10020. Phone: 800-722-4726 or (212)904-2000 Fax: (212)904-2072 E-mail: customer.service@mcgraw-hill.com • URL: http://www.mcgraw-hill.com • 1991. $14.95.

Why Leaders Can't Lead: The Unconscious Conspiracy Continues. Warren Bennis. Jossey-Bass, Inc., Publishers, 350 Sansome St. San Francisco, CA 94104. Phone: 888-378-2537 or (415)433-1740 Fax: (415)433-0499 E-mail: webperson@jbp.com • URL: http://www.josseybass.com • 1997. $30.00. (Management Series).

Why This Horse Won't Drink: How to Win and Keep Employee Commitment. Ken Matejka. AMACOM, 1601 Broadway, 12th Fl. New York, NY 10019. Phone: 800-262-9699 or (212)586-8100 Fax: (212)903-8168 E-mail: custmserv@amanet.org • URL: http://www.amanet.org • 1990. $22.95. How to set up programs to build trust and change behavior.

Wiley Encyclopedia of Electrical and Electronics Engineering. John G. Webster, editor. John Wiley and Sons, Inc., 605 Third Ave. New York, NY 10158-0012. Phone: 800-225-5945 or (212)850-6000 Fax: (212)850-6088 E-mail: info@wiley.com • URL: http://www.wiley.com • 1999. $6,495.00. 24 volumes. Contains about 1,400 articles, each with bibliography. Arrangement is according to 64 categories.

Wiley Encyclopedia of Energy and the Environment. Frederick John Francis. John Wiley and Sons, Inc., 605 Third Ave. New York, NY 10158-0012. Phone: 800-225-5945 or (212)850-6000 Fax: (212)850-6088 E-mail: info@wiley.com • URL: http://www.wiley.com • 1999. $1,500.00. Four volumes. Second edition. Covers a wide variety of energy and environmental topics, including legal and policy issues.

Wiley Encyclopedia of Packaging Technology. Aaron Brody and Kenneth Marsh, editors. John Wiley and Sons, Inc., 605 Third Ave. New York, NY 10158-0012. Phone: 800-225-5945 or (212)850-6000 Fax: (212)850-6088 E-mail: info@wiley.com • URL: http://www.wiley.com • 1997. $190.00. Second edition.

Willings Press Guide. Hollis Directories Ltd., Harlequin House, Seven High St. Teddington, Middlesex TW11 8EL, England. E-mail: orders@hollis-pr.co.uk • Annual. $325.00. Two volumes. Over 30,000 periodicals and newspapers, plus some annuals and directories published in the United Kingdom and Ireland, with listings for major publications in Europe, the Americas, Australasia, Africa, the Far East and the Middle East; also includes 3,000 services to publishers in the United Kingdom.

Williston on Contracts. Richard A. Lord. West Group, 610 Opperman Dr. Eagan, MN 55123. Phone: 800-328-4880 or (651)687-7000 Fax: 800-213-2323 or (651)687-5827 URL: http://www.westgroup.com • 1990. $507.00. 28 volumes. Encyclopedic coverage of contract law.

Wilson Business Abstracts Online. H. W. Wilson Co., 950 University Ave. Bronx, NY 10452. Phone: 800-367-6770 or (718)588-8400 Fax: (718)590-1617 E-mail: hwwmsg@info.hwwilson.com • URL: http://ww.hwwilson.com • Indexes and abstracts 600 major business periodicals, plus the *Wall Street Journal* and the business section of the *New York Times*. Indexing is from 1982, abstracting from 1990, with the two newspapers included from 1993. Updated weekly. Inquire as to online cost and availability. (*Business Periodicals Index* without abstracts is also available online.)

Wilson Publishers Directory Online. H. W. Wilson Co., 950 University Ave. Bronx, NY 10452. Phone: 800-367-6770 or (718)588-8400 Fax: (718)590-1617 Provides names and addresses of more than 34,000 English-language book publishers and distributors appearing in *Cumulative Book Index* and other H. W. Wilson databases. Updated three times a week. Inquire as to online cost and availability.

Wilson Social Sciences Abstracts Online. H. W. Wilson Co., 950 University Ave. Bronx, NY 10452. Phone: 800-367-6770 or (718)588-8400 Fax: (718)590-1617 E-mail: hwwmsg@info.hwwilson.com • URL: http://www.hwwilson.com • Provides online abstracting and indexing of more than 415 periodicals covering area studies, community health, public administration, public welfare, urban studies, and many other social science topics. Time period is 1994 to date for abstracts and 1983 to date for indexing, with updates monthly. Inquire as to online cost and availability.

WILSONDISC: Applied Science and Technology Abstracts. H. W. Wilson Co., 950 University Ave. Bronx, NY 10452. Phone: 800-367-6770 or (718)588-8400 Fax: 800-590-1617 Monthly. $1,495.00 per year, including unlimited access to the online version of *Applied Science and Technology Abstracts* through WILSONLINE. Provides CD-ROM indexing and abstracting of 400 prominent scientific, technical, engineering, and industrial periodicals. Indexing coverage is provided from 1983 to date and abstracting from 1993 to date.

WILSONDISC: Art Index. H. W. Wilson Co., 950 University Ave. Bronx, NY 10452. Phone: 800-367-6770 or (718)588-8400 Fax: 800-590-1617 Monthly. $1,495.00 per year. Provides CD-ROM indexing of art-related literature from 1982 to date. Price includes online service.

WILSONDISC: Biography Index. H. W. Wilson Co., 950 University Ave. Bronx, NY 10452. Phone: 800-367-6770 or (718)588-8400 Fax: 800-590-1617 Quarterly. $1,095.00 per year, including unlimited online access to *Biography Index* through WILSONLINE. Provides CD-ROM indexing of biographical information appearing in books, critical studies, fiction, periodicals, obituaries, and other printed sources. Time period is 1984 to date. Corresponds to the printed and online *Biography Index*.

WILSONDISC: Biological and Agricultural Index. H. W. Wilson Co., 950 University Ave. Bronx, NY 10452. Phone: 800-367-6770 or (718)588-8400 Fax: 800-590-1617 Monthly. $1,495.00 per year, including unlimited online access to *Biological and Agricultural Index* through WILSONLINE. Provides CD-ROM indexing of over 250 periodicals covering agriculture, agricultural chemicals, biochemistry, biotechnology, entomology, horticulture, and related topics.

WILSONDISC: Business Periodicals Index. H. W. Wilson Co., 950 University Ave. Bronx, NY 10452. Phone: 800-367-6770 or (718)588-8400 Fax: 800-590-1617 Monthly. $1,495.00 per year. Provides CD-ROM indexing of business periodicals from 1982 to date. Price includes online service.

WILSONDISC: Education Index. H. W. Wilson Co., 950 University Ave. Bronx, NY 10452. Phone: 800-367-6770 or (718)588-8400 Fax: 800-590-1617 Monthly. $1,295.00 per year. Provides CD-ROM indexing of education-related literature from 1983 to date. Price includes online service.

WILSONDISC: Index to Legal Periodicals and Books. H. W. Wilson Co., 950 University Ave. Bronx, NY 10452. Phone: 800-367-6770 or (718)588-8400 Fax: 800-590-1617 Monthly. Including unlimited online access to *Index to Legal Periodicals* through WILSONLINE. Contains CD-ROM indexing of more than 800 English language legal periodicals from 1981 to date and 2,500 books.

WILSONDISC: Library Literature and Information Science Index. H. W. Wilson Co., 950 University Ave. Bronx, NY 10452. Phone: 800-367-6770 or (718)588-8400 Fax: 800-590-1617 Quarterly. Including unlimited access to the online version of *Library Literature*. Provides CD-ROM indexing of about 300 periodicals, covering a wide range of topics having to do with libraries, library management, and the information industry.

WILSONDISC: Readers' Guide to Periodical Literature. H. W. Wilson Co., 950 University Ave. Bronx, NY 10452. Phone: 800-367-6770 or (718)588-8400 Fax: 800-590-1617 Monthly. $1,095.00 per year, including unlimited online access to *Readers' Guide to Periodical Literature* through WILSONLINE. Provides CD-ROM indexing of about 250 general interest periodicals. Covers 1983 to date. (*Readers' Guide Abstracts* also available on CD-ROM at $1,995 per year.)

WILSONDISC: Wilson Business Abstracts. H. W. Wilson Co., 950 University Ave. Bronx, NY 10452. Phone: 800-367-6770 or (718)588-8400 Fax: 800-590-1617 E-mail: hwwmsg@info.hwwilson.com • URL: http://www.hwwilson.com • Monthly. $2,495.00 per year, including unlimited online access to *Wilson Business Abstracts* through WILSONLINE. Provides CD-ROM "cover-to-cover" abstracting and indexing of over 600 prominent business periodicals. Indexing is from 1982, abstracting from 1990. (*Business Periodicals Index* without abstracts is available on CD-ROM at $1,495 per year.)

WILSONDISC: Wilson Social Sciences Abstracts. H. W. Wilson Co., 950 University Ave. Bronx, NY 10452. Phone: 800-367-6770 or (718)588-8400 Fax: 800-590-1617 E-mail: hwwmsg@info.hwwilson.com • URL: http://www.hwwilson.com • Monthly. Including unlimited online access to *Social Sciences Index* through WILSONLINE. Provides CD-ROM indexing from 1983 and abstracting from 1994 of more than 400 periodicals covering economics, area studies, community health, public administration, public welfare, urban studies, and many other topics related to the social sciences.

WilsonWeb Periodicals Databases. H. W. WilsonPhone: 800-367-6770 or (718)588-8400 Fax: 800-590-1617 or (718)992-8003 E-mail: custserv@hwwilson.com • URL: http://www.hwwilson.com/ • Web sites provide fee-based access to *Wilson Business Full Text, Applied Science & Technology Full Text, Biological & Agricultural Index, Library Literature & Information Science Full Text*, and *Readers' Guide Full Text, Mega Edition*. Daily updates.

WIMA Bulletin. Writing Instrument Manufacturers Association, 236 Route 38 W., Suite 100 Moorestown, NJ 08057. Phone: (609)231-8500 Fax: (609)231-4664 E-mail: wima@ahint.com • 50 times a year. Price on application.

WIMA Directory. Writing Instrument Manufacturers Association, 263 Route 38 W., Suite 100 Moorestown, NJ 08057. Phone: (609)231-8500 Fax: (609)231-4664 E-mail: wima@ahint.com • Biennial. $50.00. Lists manufacturers, suppliers and products of the writing industry.

WIN. Gambling Times, Inc., 16140 Valerio St., Suite B Van Nuys, CA 91406-2916. Phone: (818)781-9355 Fax: (818)781-3125 URL: http://www.gamblingtimes.com • Monthly. $44.00 per year. Formerly *Gambling Times*.

WIN News: All the News that is Fit to Print By, For and About Women. Women's International Network, 187 Grant St. Lexington, MA 02173-2140. Phone: (781)862-9431 Fax: (781)862-9431 E-mail: winnews@igc.org • URL: http://www.feminist.com/win.htm • Quarterly. Individuals $35.00 per year; institutions, $48.00 per year. World-wide communication system by, for and about women of all backgrounds, beliefs, nationalities and age-groups.

Win-Win Negotiating: Turning Conflict into Agreement. Fred E. Jandt. John Wiley and Sons, Inc., 605 Third Ave. New York, NY 10158-0012. Phone: 800-526-5368 or (212)850-6000 Fax: (212)850-6088 E-mail: info@wiley.com • URL: http://www.wiley.com • 1987. $19.95. (Sound Business Cassette Books).

The Winchester Handbook. George Madis. Art and Reference House, 2543 W. Five Mile Parkway Dallas, TX 75233. Phone: (214)330-7168 1981. $24.95.

Window and Door Manufactures Association., 1400 E Touhy Ave., No. 470 Des Plaines, IL 60018. Phone: 800-223-2301 or (847)299-5200 Fax: (847)299-1286 URL: http://www.nwwda.org • Members are manufacturers of wooden door and window products.

Window Covering Manufacturers Association., 355 Lexington Ave., 17th Fl. New York, NY 10017. Phone: (212)661-4261 Fax: (212)370-9047 E-mail: assocmgmt@aol.com • Members are manufacturers of venetian blinds, vertical blinds, and pleated shades.

Window Fashions. G & W McNamara Publishing, Inc., 4215 White Bear Parkway, Suite 100 St. Paul, MN 55110-7635. Phone: (651)293-1544 Fax: (651)653-4308 E-mail: bcarlson@gwmcnamara.com • URL: http://www.gwmcnamara.com • Monthly. $39.00 per year. Published for designers and retailers of draperies, blinds, and shades.

Window Fashions Magazine. G & W McNamara Publishing, Inc., 4215 White Bear Parkway, Suite 100 St. Paul, MN 55110. Phone: (651)293-1544 Fax: (651)293-4308 E-mail: bcarlson@gwmcnamara.com • URL: http://www.gwmcnamara.com • Monthly. $39.00 per year. A directory of suppliers, manufacturers, and fabricators of vertical blinds, soft shades, curtains, draperies, and other window treatment items. Appears as a regular feature of *Window Fashions Magazine* and covers a different product category each month.

Window Treatments. Karla J. Nielson. John Wiley and Sons, Inc., 605 Third Ave. New York, NY 10158-0012. Phone: 800-225-5945 or (212)850-6000 Fax: (212)850-6088 E-mail: info@wiley.com • URL: http://www.wiley.com • 1989. $75.00.

Window Washing Service. Entrepreneur Media, Inc., 2445 McCabe Way Irvine, CA 92614. Phone: 800-421-2300 or (949)261-2325 Fax: (949)261-0234 E-mail: entmag@entrepreneur.com • URL: http://www.entrepreneur.com • Looseleaf. $59.50. A practical guide to starting a window cleaning business. Covers profit potential, start-up costs, market size evaluation, owner's time required, pricing, accounting, advertising, promotion, etc. (Start-Up Business Guide No. E1012.)

Windows. Available from MarketResearch.com, 641 Ave. of the Americas, Third Floor New York, NY 10011. Phone: 800-298-5699 or (212)807-2629 Fax: (212)807-2716 E-mail: order@marketresearch.com • URL: http://www.marketresearch.com • 1999. $2,250.00. Market research report published by Specialists in Business Information. Covers metal, wood, and vinyl windows. Presents market data relative to demographics, sales growth, shipments, exports, imports, price trends, and end-use. Includes company profiles.

Windows Developer's Journal. Miller Freeman, Inc., 55 Hawthorne St. San Francisco, CA 94105. Phone: 800-365-1425 or (415)808-3900 Fax: (415)808-3995 E-mail: wdsub@mfi.com • URL: http://www.wdj.com • Monthly. $34.99 per year. Edited for advanced programming developers working under DOS and Windows. Formerly *Windows-DOS Developer's Journal*.

Windows Internet Tour Guide: Cruising the Internet the Easy Way. Michael Fraase and Phil James. Ventana Communications Group, Inc., P.O. Box 13964 Research Park, NC 27709-3964. Phone: 800-777-7955 or (919)544-9404 Fax: (919)942-9472 E-mail: contact@media.com • URL: http://www.vmedia.com • 1995. $29.95. Second edition., An introduction to the Internet via Windows software.

Windows ME Annoyances. David Karp. O'Reilly & Associates, Inc., 101 Morris St. Sebastopol, CA 95472-9902. Phone: 800-998-9938 or (707)829-0515 Fax: (707)829-0104 E-mail: order@oreilly.com • URL: http://www.oreilly.com • 2001. $29.95. A critical but helpful view of Windows Millennium Edition.

Windows Millennium Edition: The Complete Reference. John R. Levine and Margaret L. Young. Osborne-McGraw, 2600 Tenth St. Berkeley, CA 94710. Phone: 800-227-0900 or (510)549-6600 Fax: (510)549-6603 URL: http://www.osborne.com • 2000. $39.99. Includes CD-ROM.

Windows Millennium: The Missing Manual - The Book That Should Have Been in the Box. David Pogue. O'Reilly & Associates, Inc., 101 Morris St. Sebastopol, CA 95472-9902. Phone: 800-998-9938 or (707)829-0515 Fax: (707)829-0104 E-mail: order@oreilly.com • URL: http://www.oreilly.com • 2000. $19.95. Popularly written explanation of Windows ME features. (Pogue Press.)

Windows 98 Bible. Fred Davis and Kip Crosby. Available from Addison-Wesley Longman, Inc., One Jacob Way Reading, MA 01867. Phone: 800-447-2226 or (781)944-3700 Fax: (781)944-9351 URL: http://www.awl.com • 1998. $34.95. Published by Peachpit Press (http://www.peachpit.com).

Windows 98 for Dummies. IDG Books Worldwide, 7260 Shadeland Station, Suite 100 Indianapolis, IN 46256. Phone: 800-762-2974 or (317)596-5200 Fax: (317)596-5299 E-mail: siteemail@idgbooks.com • URL: http://www.idgbooks.com • 1999. $19.99.

Windows 98 in a Nutshell. Tim O'Reilly and Troy Mott. O'Reilly & Associates, Inc., 101 Morris St. Sebastopol, CA 95472. Phone: 800-998-9938 or (707)829-0515 Fax: (707)829-0104 E-mail: nuts@ora.com • URL: http://www.oreilly.com • 1999. $24.95. (Nutshell Handbooks.)

Windows 98 Unleashed. Paul McFedries. Pearson Education and Technology, 201 W.103rd St. Indianapolis, IN 46290-1097. Phone: 800-858-7674 or (317)581-3500 Fax: (317)581-4670 URL: http://www.mcp.com • 1998. $34.99.

Windows 98: Visual Quick-Start Guide. Steve Sagman. Available from Addison-Wesley Longman, Inc., One Jacob Way Reading, MA 01867. Phone: 800-447-2226 or (781)944-3700 Fax: (781)944-9351 URL: http://www.awl.com • 1998. Price on application. Published by Peachpit Press (http://www.peachpit.com).

Windows 95 for Busy People. Ron Mansfield. Osborne/McGraw-Hill, 2600 Tenth St. Berkeley, CA 94710. Phone: 800-227-0900 or (510)549-6600 Fax: (510)549-6603 E-mail: customer.service@mcgraw-hill.com • URL: http://www.osborne.com • 1997. $24.99. Second edition. A basic guide to Windows, featuring many illustrations.

Windows 95 is Driving Me Crazy! A Practical Guide to Windows 95 Headaches, Hassles, Bugs, Potholes, and Installation Problems. Kay Y. Nelson. Peachpit Press, 1249 Eighth St. Berkeley, CA 94710. Phone: 800-283-9444 or (510)524-2178 Fax: (510)524-2221 URL: http://www.peachpit.com • 1996. $24.95. Includes many illustrations.

Windows 95: The Complete Reference. John Levine and Margaret L. Young. Osborne/McGraw-Hill, 2600 Tenth St. Berkeley, CA 94710. Phone: 800-227-0900 or (510)549-6600 Fax: (510)549-6603 E-mail: customer.service@mcgraw-hill.com • URL: http://www.osborne.com • 1997. $39.99. Provides detailed coverage of the various Windows attributes.

Windows 97 Professional Reference. Joe Casad. Pearson Education and Technology, 201 W. 103rd St. Indianapolis, IN 46290. Phone: 800-428-5331 or (317)581-3500 Fax: (317)581-4670 URL: http://www.mcp.com • 1999. $59.99.

Windows NT Administration and Security. Richard O. Hudson. Prentice Hall, 240 Frisch Ct. Paramus, NJ 07652-5240. Phone: 800-947-7700 or (201)909-6452 Fax: 800-445-6991 URL: http://www.prenhall.com • 2001. $79.00.

Windows NT Administrators Handbook. Mark Graham and Becky Campbell. Simon and Schuster Trade, 1230 Ave. of the Americas New York, NY 10020. Phone: 800-223-2348 or (212)698-7000 Fax: 800-943-9831 or (212)698-7007 E-mail: ssonline_feedback@simonsays.com • URL: http://www.simonsays.com • 1997. $24.99.

Windows NT Server Concise. Jerry Dixon and J. Scott Reeves. Pearson Education and Technology, 201 W. 103rd St. Indianapolis, IN 46290. Phone: 800-428-5331 or (317)581-3500 Fax: (317)581-4670 URL: http://www.mcp.com • Date not set. $19.99.

Windows NT System Administration. Pearson Education and Technology, 201 W. 103rd St. Indianapolis, IN 46290. Phone: 800-428-5331 or (317)581-3500 Fax: (317)581-4670 URL: http://www.mcp.com • 1999. Price on application.

Windows NT Systems: The Magazine for Windows NT Systems Management and Administration. Miller Freeman, 411 Borel Ave., Suite 100 San Mateo, CA 94402. Phone: 800-227-4675 or (415)358-9500 Fax: (415)358-9739 E-mail: nbaran@mfi.com • URL: http://www.ntsystems.com • Monthly. $39.95 per year. Provides articles on Windows NT administration, communications, and performance.

Windows 2000 Commands Pocket Reference. Aeleen Frisch. O'Reilly & Associates, Inc., 101 Morris St. Sebastopol, CA 95472-9902. Phone: 800-998-9938 or (707)829-0515 Fax: (707)829-0104 E-mail: order@oreilly.com • URL: http://www.oreilly.com • 2001. $9.95.

Windows 2000 Magazine. Duke Communications International, 221 E. 29th St. Loveland, CO 80538. Phone: 800-621-1544 or (970)663-4700 Fax: (970)663-3285 E-mail: subs@winntmag.com • URL: http://www.winntmag.com • Monthly. $39.95 per year. Edited for information systems personnel developing business applications for Windows NT software.

Windows 2000 Performance Guide: Help for Windows 2000 Administrators. Mark Friedman. O'Reilly & Associates, Inc., 101 Morris St. Sebastopol, CA 95472-9902. Phone: 800-998-9938 or (707)829-0515 Fax: (707)829-0104 E-mail: order@oreilly.com • URL: http://www.oreilly.com • 2001. $39.95.

Windows 2000 Professional Reference. Karanjit Siyan. Pearson Education and Technology, 201 W. 103rd St. Indianapolis, IN 46290-1097. Phone: 800-858-7674 or (317)581-3500 Fax: (317)581-4675 URL: http://www.mcp.com • 2000. $75.00. Third edition.

Windows 2000 Quick Fixes. Jim Boyce. O'Reilly & Associates, Inc., 101 Morris St. Sebastopol, CA 95472-9902. Phone: 800-998-9938 or (707)829-0515 Fax: (707)829-0104 E-mail: order@oreilly.com • URL: http://www.oreilly.com • 2000. $29.95. Covers troubleshooting for Windows 2000, both Professional Edition and Server Edition.

Windows 2000 System Administration Handbook. David Watts and others. Prentice Hall, 240 Frisch Ct. Paramus, NJ 07652-5240. Phone: 800-947-7700 or (201)909-6452 Fax: 800-445-6991 URL: http://www.prenhall.com • 2000. $59.99.

Wine and Spirits Guild of America. c/o James Newberry

Wine and Spirits Wholesalers of America.

Wine Business Monthly and Grower and Seller News. Smart-Wired Inc., 867 W. Napa St. Sonoma, CA 94576. Phone: (707)939-0822 Fax: (707)939-0833 E-mail: winebiz@aol.com • URL: http://www.smartwine.com • Monthly. $69.00 per year; students, $24.00 per year. Edited for executives in the North American wine making industry. Covers marketing, finance, export-import, management, new technology, etc.

Wine Enthusiast., Eight Saw Mill River Rd. Hawthorne, NY 10532. Phone: 800-829-5901 or (914)345-8463 Fax: (914)345-3028 E-mail: winenthmag@aol.com • URL: http://www.wineenthusiast.com • 13 times a year. $32.95 per year. Covers domestic and world wine. Formerly *Wine Times*.

Wine Institute.

Wine: Nutritional and Therapeutic Benefits. Thomas R. Watkins, editor. American Chemical Society Publications, 1155 16th St., N. W. Washington, DC 20036. Phone: 800-333-9511 or (202)872-4600 Fax: (202)872-4615 E-mail: service@acs.org • URL: http://www.chemcenter.org • 1997. $95.95. A review of wine chemistry, agronomic practice at vineyards, and the potential health benefits of wine drinking. (ACS Symposium Series, No. 661.)

Wine Price File. Wine Appreciation Guild, 360 Swift Ave. San Francisco, CA 94080. Phone: 800-231-9463 or (650)866-3020 Fax: (650)866-3513 E-mail: info@wineappreciation.com • URL: http://www.wineappreciation.com • Annual. $45.00. Lists prices of more than 90,000 ''good to great'' wines for collectors, wholesalers, retailers, and appraisers.

The Wine Spectator. M. Shanken Communications, Inc., 387 Park Ave. S. New York, NY 10016. Phone: (212)684-4424 Fax: (212)684-5424 URL: http://www.winespectator.com • 20 times a year. $40.00 per year. Wine ratings.

Winemaking Basics. Cornelius S. Ough. Haworth Press, Inc., 10 Alice St. Binghamton, NY 13904-1580. Phone: 800-429-6784 or (607)722-5857 Fax: 800-895-0582 or (607)722-1424 E-mail: getinfo@haworthpressinc.com • URL: http://www.haworthpressinc.com • 1992. $59.95. Covers all practical aspects of commercial winemaking from harvesting grapes to bottling and storage.

Winery Technology and Operations: A Handbook for Small Wineries. Yair Margalit. Wine Appreciation Guild, 360 Swift Ave. San Francisco, CA 94080. Phone: 800-231-9463 or (650)866-3020 Fax: (650)866-3513 E-mail: info@wineappreciation.com • URL: http://www.wineappreciation.com • 1990. $29.95. Covers a wide variety of topics from grape harvest to wine bottling, including aging and quality control.

Wines and Vines: Directory of the Wine Industry in North America. Hiaring Co., 1800 Lincoln Ave. San Rafael, CA 94901-1298. Phone: (415)453-9700 Fax: (415)453-2517 E-mail: geninfo@winesandvines.com • Annual. $65.00. List of wineries and wine bottlers in the United States, Canada, and Mexico; also lists industry suppliers.

Wines and Vines: The Authoritative Voice of the Grape and Wine Industry. Hiaring Co., 1800 Lincoln Ave. San Rafael, CA 94901-1298. Phone: (415)453-9700 Fax: (415)453-2517 E-mail: geninfo@winesandvines.com • Monthly. $32.50 per year.

Winning is the Only Thing: Sports in America Since 1945. Randy Roberts and James Olson. Johns Hopkins University Press, 2715 N. Charles St. Baltimore, MD 21218. Phone: 800-548-1784 or (410)516-6667 Fax: (410)516-6968 1989. $38.95.

Winning Numbers: How to Use Business Facts and Figures to Make Your Point and Get Ahead. Michael C. Thomsett. AMACOM, 1601 Broadway, 12th Fl. New York, NY 10019. Phone: 800-262-9699 or (212)586-8100 Fax: (212)903-8168 E-mail: custmserv@amanet.org • URL: http://www.amanet.org • 1990. $22.95. A short course in financial communication, or finance for the nonfinancial manager.

The Winning Portfolio: Choosing Your 10 Best Mutual Funds. Paul B. Farrell. Bloomberg Press, PO Box 888 Princeton, NJ 08542-0888. Phone: 800-388-2749 or (609)279-4670 Fax: 800-458-6515 or (609)279-7155 E-mail: info@bloomberg.com • URL: http://www.bloomberg.com • 1999. $15.95. Tells how to select 10 from among the 10,000 mutual funds that are available. (Bloomberg Personal Bookshelf.)

Wire and Cable Technology International Buyers' Guide. Initial Publications, Inc., 3869 Darrow Rd. Stow, OH 44224. Phone: (216)686-9544 Fax: (216)686-9563 Annual. $35.00. About 2,000 companies listed by product categories. Formerly *Wire Technology International Buyers' Guide*.

Wire Association International.

Wire Industry: International Monthly Journal. Publex International Ltd., 110 Station Rd. E. Oxted, Surrey RH8 0QA, England. Phone: 44 1883 717755 Fax: 44 1883 714554 Monthly. $151.00 per year. News, information and technical articles on manufacture of wire, wire products and cable. International coverage.

Wire Industry Suppliers Association.

Wire: International Technical Journal for the Wire and Cable Industries and All Areas of Wire Processing. Meisenbach GMBH, Hainstrausse 18 96047 Bamberg, Germany. Bimonthly. $70.00 per year. (English edition of *Draht-Welt*.)

Wire Journal International. Wire Association International. Wire Journal, Inc., 1570 Boston Rd. Guilford, CT 06437. Phone: (203)453-2777 Fax: (203)453-8384 Monthly. $75.00 per year.

Wire Journal International Reference Guide. Wire Association International. Wire Journal, Inc., 1570 Boston Rd. Guilford, CT 06437. Phone: (203)453-2777 Fax: (203)453-8384 Annual. Free to members; non-members, $125.00. Manufacturers and suppliers of steel and nonferrous rods, strip, wire, wire products, electrical wire and cable, fiber optics, and machinery and equipment to the industry.

Wire Reinforcement Institute.

Wirebound Box Manufacturers Association.

Wired. Wired Ventures Ltd., 520 Third St., 4th Fl. San Francisco, CA 94107-1815. Phone: 800-769-4733 or (415)276-5000 Fax: (415)276-5100 E-mail: editor@wired.com • URL: http://www.wired.com/ • Monthly. $24.00 per year. Edited for creators and managers in various areas of electronic information and entertainment, including multimedia, the Internet, and video. Often considered to be the primary publication of the ''digital generation.''

Wired for the Future: Developing Your Library Technology Plan. Diane Mayo and others. American Library Association, 50 E. Huron St. Chicago, IL 60611-2795. Phone: 800-545-2433 or (312)944-6780 Fax: (312)440-9374 E-mail: ala@ala.org • URL: http://www.ala.org • 1998. $38.00. Describes various technologies and applications available to libraries.

Wired Neighborhood. Stephen Doheny-Farina. Yale University Press, 302 Temple St. New Haven, CT 06511. Phone: 800-987-7323 or (203)432-0960 Fax: (203)432-0948 E-mail: yupmkt@yale.edu • URL: http://www.yale.edu/yup/ • 1996. $32.00. The author examines both the hazards and the advantages of ''making the computer the center of our public and private lives,'' as exemplified by the Internet and telecommuting.

Wired News. Wired Digital, Inc.Phone: (415)276-8400 Fax: (415)276-8499 E-mail: newsfeedback@wired.com • URL: http://www.wired.com • Provides summaries and full-text of ''Top Stories'' relating to the Internet, computers, multimedia, telecommunications, and the electronic information industry in general. These news stories are placed in the broad categories of Politics, Business, Culture, and Technology. Affiliated with *Wired* magazine. Fees: Free.

Wireless Business and Technology: Products and Systems for the Mobile Communicattions Marketplace. Phillips Business Information, Inc., 1201 Seven Locks Rd., Suite 300 Potomac, MD 20854. Phone: 800-722-5006 or (301)340-2100 Fax: (301)309-3847 E-mail: pbi@phillips.com • URL: http://www.phillips.com/pbi.htm • Monthly. Free to qualified personnel. Trade journal for mobile radio and telephone dealers. Incorporates *Wireless Product News*.

Wireless Data Networks. Warren Publishing Inc., 2115 Ward Court, N. W. Washington, DC 20037-1209. Phone: 800-771-9202 or (202)872-9200 Fax: (202)293-3435 E-mail: customerservice@warren-news.com • URL: http://www.warrenpub.com • 1998. $1,995.00. Fourth edition. Presents market research information relating to cellular data networks, paging networks, packet radio networks, satellite systems, and other areas of wireless communication. Contains ''summaries of recent developments and trends in wireless markets.''

Wireless Data News. Phillips Business Information, Inc., 1201 Seven Locks Rd., Ste. 300 Potomac, MD 20854. Phone: 800-777-5006 or (301)340-2100 Fax: (301)309-3848 E-mail: pbi@phillips.com • URL: http://www.phillips.com/pbi.htm • 25 times a year. $797.00 per year. Newsletter. Covers the wireless data communications industry, including wireless LANs.

Wireless Dealers Association., 9746 Tappanbeck Dr. Houston, TX 77055. Phone: 800-624-6918 Fax: 800-820-2284 E-mail: mail@wirelessindustry.com • URL: http://www.wirelessindustry.com • Members are individuals working within the cellular mobile telephone industry.

Wireless Industry Directory. Phillips Business Information, Inc., 1201 Seven Locks Rd., Suite 300 Potomac, MD 20854. Phone: 800-777-5006 or (301)340-2100 Fax: (301)309-3847 E-mail: pbi@phillips.com • URL: http://www.phillips.com/marketplace.htm • Annual. $249.00. Lists over 4,000 radio common carriers offering mobile telephone services. Formerly *Cellular Mobile Communications Directory*.

Wireless Integration: Solutions for Enterprise Decision Makers. PennWell Corp., Advanced Technology Div., 98 Spit Brook Rd. Nashua, NH 03062. Phone: (603)891-0123 Fax: (603)891-0574 E-mail: webmaster@pennwell.com • URL: http://www.pennwell.com • Bimonthly. $48.00 per year. Edited for networking and communications managers. Special issues cover the wireless office, wireless intranet/ Internet, mobile wireless, telemetry, and buyer's guide directory information.

Wireless Review: Intelligence for Competitive Providers. Intertec Publishing Corp., P.O. Box 12901 Overland Park, KS 66282-2901. Phone: 800-400-5945 or (913)341-1300 Fax: (913)967-1898 E-mail: subs@intertec.com • URL: http://www.wirelessreview.com • Semimonthly. $48.00 per year. Covers business and technology developments for wireless service providers. Includes special issues on a wide variety of wireless topics. Formed by merger of *Cellular Business* and *Wireless World*.

Wireless Week. Cahners Business Information, 8878 Barrons Blvd. Highlands Ranch, CO 80126. Phone: 800-695-1214 or (303)470-4000 Fax: (303)399-2034 URL: http://www.cahners.com • 51 times a year. $59.00 per year. Covers news of cellular telephones, mobile radios, communications satellites, microwave transmission, and the wireless industry in general.

Wisconsin Agricultural Experiment Station. University of Wisconsin - Madison

Wisconsin Center for Film and Theater Research., University of Wisconsin-Madison, 816 State St. Madison, WI 53706. Phone: (608)264-6466 Fax: (608)264-6472 E-mail: tbalio@facstaff.wisc.edu • URL: http://www.shsw.wisc.edu/archives/wcftr • Studies the performing arts in America, including theater, cinema, radio, and television.

Wisconsin Cheese Makers' Association.

Wise Giving Guide. National Charities Information Bureau, Inc., 19 Union Square, W. New York, NY 10003-3995. Phone: (212)929-6300 Fax: (212)463-7083 Quarterly. Single copy free; individuals, $25.00 per year. Evaluates 400 national charities against a set of standards concerning management, government and budget.

The Witch Doctor of Wall Street: A Noted Financial Expert Guides You Through Today's Voodoo Economics. Robert H. Parks. Prometheus Books, 59 John Glenn Dr. Amherst, NY 14228-2197. Phone: 800-421-0351 or (716)691-0133 Fax: (716)691-0137 E-mail: pbooks6205@aol.com • URL: http://wwwprometheusbooks.com • 1996. $25.95. The author, a professor of finance at Pace University, discusses ''Practice and Malpractice'' in relation to the following: business forecasting, economic theory, interest rates, monetary policy, the stock market, and corporate finance. Includes ''A Short Primer on Derivatives,'' as an appendix.

The Witch Doctors: Making Sense of the Management Gurus. John Micklethwait and Adrian Wooldridge. Crown Publishing Group, Inc., 299 Park Ave. New York, NY 10171. Phone: 800-726-0600 or (212)751-2600 Fax: 800-659-2436 or (212)572-2165 URL: http://www.randomhouse.com • 1996. $25.00. A critical, iconoclastic, and practical view of consultants, business school professors, and modern management theory, written by two members of the editorial staff of *The Economist*.

Women and Careers: Issues, Pressures, and Challenges. Carol W. Konek and Sally L. Kitch, editors. Sage Publications, Inc., 2455 Teller Rd. Thousand Oaks, CA 91320. Phone: (805)499-0721 Fax: (805)499-0871 E-mail: info@sagepub.com • URL: http://www.sagepub.com • 1993. $49.95. Based on a major survey assessing women's experiences in the workplace.

Women and Philanthropy., 1015 18th St., N.W., Suite 202 Washington, DC 20036. Phone: (202)887-9660 Fax: (202)861-5483 URL: http://www.womenphil.org • Purpose is to increase the amount of money given to programs benefiting women.

Women and Sexual Harassment: A Guide to the Legal Protections of Title VII and the Hostile Environment Claim. Anja A. Chan. Haworth Press, Inc., 10 Alice St. Binghamton, NY 13904-1580. Phone: 800-429-6784 or (607)722-5857 Fax: 800-895-0582 or (607)722-1424 E-mail: Getinfo@haworthpressinc.com • URL: http://www.haworthpressinc.com • 1994. $29.95. Emphasis is on hostile environment claims under Title VII of the Civil Rights Act of 1964. Discusses employer liability, the statute of limitations, remedies, discovery and evidence, and related claims. Includes a research guide and lists of primary and secondary sources.

Women and the Law. Carol H. Lefcourt, editor. West Group, 610 Opperman Dr. Eagan, MN 55123. Phone: 800-328-4880 or (651)687-7000 Fax: 800-213-2323 or (651)687-5827 URL: http://www.westgroup.com • $140.00. Looseleaf service. Periodic supplementation. Covers such topics as employment discrimination, pay equity (comparable worth), sexual harassment in the workplace, property rights, and child custody issues. (Civil Rights Series).

Women and Work: Exploring Race, Ethnicity, and Class. Elizabeth Higginbotham and Mary Romero, editors. Sage Publications, Inc., 2455 Teller Rd. Thousand Oaks, CA 91320. Phone: (805)499-0721 Fax: (805)499-0871 E-mail: info@sagepub.com • URL: http://www.sagepub.com • 1997. $55.00. Contains articles by various authors, including material on the historical and economic background of women in the workplace. (Women and Work, vol. 6.)

Women as Managers: Strategies for Success. Economics Press, Inc., 12 Daniel Rd. Fairfield, NJ 07004-2565. Phone: 800-526-2554 or (973)227-1224 Fax: (973)227-9742 E-mail: edit@epinc.com • URL: http://www.epinc.com • Biweekly. $69.00 per year. Newsletter. Covers management skills and techniques leading to higher career levels. Discusses problems women face on the job.

Women Breaking Through: Overcoming the Final 10 Obstacles at Work. Deborah J. Swiss. Peterson's, 202 Carnegie Center Princeton, NJ 08640. Phone: 800-338-3282 E-mail: info@petersons.com • URL: http://www.petersons.com • 1996. $24.95. Discusses specific strategies for women to use to advance beyond the middle management level. Based on a survey of 300 women ''on the leading edge of change.''

Women Employed Institute., 22 W. Monroe St., Suite 1400 Chicago, IL 60603-2505. Phone: (312)782-3902 Fax: (312)782-5249 E-mail: info@womenemployed.org • URL: http://www.womenemployed.org • Research areas include the economic status of working women, sexual harassment in the workplace, equal employment opportunity, and career development.

Women Entrepreneurs: Moving Beyond the Glass Ceiling. Dorothy P. Moore and E. Holly Buttner. Sage Publications, Inc., 2455 Teller Rd. Thousand Oaks, CA 91320. Phone: (805)499-0721 Fax: (805)499-0871 E-mail: info@sagepub.com • URL: http://www.sagepub.com • 1997. $46.00. Contains profiles of ''129 successful female entrepreneurs who previously worked in corporate environments.''

Women Executives in Public Relations.

Women in American Music; A Bibliography of Music and Literature. Adrienne Fried Block and Carol Neuls-Bates, editors. Greenwood Publishing Group, Inc., 88 Post Rd., W. Westport, CT 06881-5007. Phone: 800-225-5800 or (203)226-3571 Fax: (203)222-2540 E-mail: bookinfo@greenwood.com • URL: http://www.greenwood.com • 1979. $59.95.

Women in Cable and Telecommunications.

Women in Management: Trends, Issues, and Challenges in Managerial Diversity. Ellen A. Fagenson, editor. Sage Publications, Inc., 2455 Teller Rd. Thousand Oaks, CA 91320. Phone: (805)499-0721 Fax: (805)499-0871 E-mail: info@sagepub.com • URL: http://www.sagepub.com • 1993. $55.00. Includes material from 22 contributors on topics related to the experiences of women managers. (Women and Work Series, Vol. 4).

Women in the World of Work: Statistical Analysis and Projections to the Year 2000. Shirley Nuss and others. International Labour Office, 1828 L St., N.W., Suite 801 Washington, DC 20036. Phone: (202)653-7652 Fax: (202)653-7687 E-mail: ilopubs@tascol.com • URL: http://www.ilo.org • 1989. $18.00. (Women, Work, and Development Series, No. 18).

Women Lawyers Journal. National Association of Women Lawyers, 750 N. Lake Shore Dr. Chicago, IL 60611-4479. Phone: (312)988-6186 Quarterly. $16.00 per year.

Women, Men, the Family and HIV/AIDS: A Sociological Perspective on the Epidemic in America. Carole A. Campbell. Cambridge University Press, 40 West 20th St. New York, NY 10011. Phone: 800-221-4512 or (212)924-3900 Fax: (212)691-3239 E-mail: info@cup.org • URL: http://www.cup.org • 1999. $49.95.

Women of the Street: Making It on Wall Street-the World's Toughest Business. Sue Herera. John Wiley and Sons, Inc., 605 Third Ave. New York, NY 10158-0012. Phone: 800-225-5945 or (212)850-6000 Fax: (212)850-6088 E-mail: info@wiley.com • URL: http://www.wiley.com • 1997. $24.95. The author is a CNBC business television anchorperson.

Women Studies Abstracts. Transaction Publishers, 35 Berrue Circle Piscataway, NJ 08854-8042. Phone: 888-999-6778 or (732)445-2280 Fax: (732)445-3138 E-mail: trans@transactionpub.com • URL: http://www.transactionpub.com • Quarterly. Individuals, $102.00 per year; institutions, $216.00 per year.

Women Today. M and O Communications, 120 E. 34th St., 7th Fl. New York, NY 10016. Phone: (202)628-6999 Biweekly. $40.00 per year.

Women Who Embezzle or Defraud: A Study of Convicted Felons. Dorothy Zietz. Greenwood Publishing Group, Inc., 88 Post Rd., W. Westport, CT 06881-5007. Phone: 800-225-5800 or (203)226-3571 Fax: (203)222-2540 E-mail: bookinfo@greenwood.com • URL: http://www.greenwood.com • 1981. $45.00.

Women's Accessories Store. Entrepreneur Media, Inc., 2445 McCabe Way Irvine, CA 92614. Phone: 800-421-2300 or (949)261-2325 Fax: (949)261-0234 E-mail: entmag@entrepreneur.com • URL: http://www.entrepreneur.com • Looseleaf. $59.50. A practical guide to starting a women's clothing accessories shop. Covers profit potential, start-up costs, market size evaluation, owner's time required, site selection, lease negotiation, pricing, accounting, advertising, promotion, etc. (Start-Up Business Guide No. E1333.)

The Women's Advocate. National Center on Women and Family Law, 799 Broadway, Suite 402 New York, NY 10003. Phone: (212)674-8200 Fax: (212)533-5104 Irregular. Price on application. Manuals supporting women's rights in family law.

Women's Apparel Shop. Entrepreneur Media, Inc., 2445 McCabe Way Irvine, CA 92614. Phone: 800-421-2300 or (949)261-2325 Fax: (949)261-0234 E-mail: entmag@entrepreneur.com • URL: http://www.entrepreneur.com • Looseleaf. $59.50. A practical guide to starting a women's clothing store. Covers profit potential, start-up costs, market size evaluation, owner's time required, site selection, lease negotiation, pricing, accounting, advertising, promotion, etc. (Start-Up Business Guide No. E1107.)

Women's Army Corps Veterans Association.

Women's Business Exclusive: For Women Entrepreneurs., 3528 Torrance Blvd., Suite 101 Torrance, CA 90503. Phone: (310)540-9398 Fax: (310)792-8263 E-mail: mbewbe@ix.netcom.com • URL: http://www.mbemag.com • Bimonthly. $39.00 per year. Newsletter. Reports news and information relating to financing, business procurement initiatives, technical assistance, and policy research. Provides advice on marketing, negotiating, and other management topics.

Women's Council of Realtors.

Women's Information Directory. The Gale Group, 27500 Drake Rd. Farmington Hills, MI 48331-3535. Phone: 800-877-GALE or (248)699-GALE Fax: 800-414-5043 or (248)699-8069 E-mail: galeord@galegroup.com • URL: http://www.galegroup.com • 1992. $75.00. A guide to approximately 6,000 organizations, agencies, institutions, programs, and publications concerned with women in the United States. Includes subject and title indexes.

Women's Law Project., 125 S. Ninth St., Suite 401 Philadelphia, PA 19107. Phone: (215)928-9801 Fax: (215)928-9848 URL: http://www.women'slawproject.org • Offers telephone counseling and referral services relating to women's legal rights in employment and other areas.

Women's National Book Association.

Women's Rights Law Reporter. Rutgers University School of Law, 123 Washington St. Newark, NJ 07102. Phone: (973)353-5320 URL: http://www.info.rutgers.edu • Three times a year. Individuals $20.00 per year; institutions, $40.00 per year; students, $15.00 per year. Provides analysis and commentary on legal issues affecting women, including gender-based discrimination.

Women's Studies International Forum: A Multidisciplinary Journal for the Rapid Publication of Research Communications and Review Articles in Women's Studies. Elsevier Science, 655 Ave. of the Americas New York, NY 10010. Phone: 888-437-4636 or (212)989-5800 Fax: (212)633-3680 E-mail: usinfo-f@elsevier.com • URL: http://www.elsevier.com • Bimonthly. $479.00 per year.

Women's Studies Quarterly: The First U.S. Journal Devoted to Teaching about Women. Feminist Press, CUNY Graduate Center, 365 Fifth Ave. New York, NY 10016. Phone: (212)650-8890 Fax: (212)650-8893 URL: http://www.feministpress.org • Four times a year. Individuals, $30.00 per year; institutions, $40.00 per year. Provides coverage of issues and events in women's studies and feminist education, including in-depth articles on research about women and current projects to transform traditional curricula. Includes two double thematic issues.

Women's Undergarments. Available from MarketResearch.com, 641 Ave. of the Americas, Third Floor New York, NY 10011. Phone: 800-298-5699 or (212)807-2629 Fax: (212)807-2716 E-mail: order@marketresearch.com • URL: http://www.marketresearch.com • 1997. $995.00. Published by Specialists in Business Information, Inc. Provides market data with forecasts of sales to the year 2005 for various kinds of women's underwear.

Wood and Paper Science., North Carolina State University, P.O. Box 8005 Raleigh, NC 27695. Phone: (919)515-5807 Fax: (919)515-6302 E-mail: mikekocurek@ncsu.edu • URL: http://www.cfr.ncsu.edu/wps/ • Studies the mechanical and engineering properties of wood, wood finishing, wood anatomy, wood chemistry, etc.

Wood and Wood Products: Furniture, Cabinets, Woodworking and Allied Products Management and Operations. Vance Publishing Corp., 400 Knightsbridge Parkway Lincolnshire, IL 60069-1414. Phone: 800-621-2845 or (847)634-2600 Fax: (847)634-4379 URL: http://www.vancepublishing.com • 13 times a year. $50.00 per year.

Wood Component Manufacturers Association., 1000 Johnson Ferry Rd., Suite A-130 Marietta, GA 30068. Phone: (770)565-6660 URL: http://www.woodcomponents.org • Members are manufacturers of prefabricated hardwood parts for the furniture industry.

Wood Digest. Cygnus Publishing, Inc., 1233 Janesville Ave. Fort Atkinson, WI 53538-0460. Phone: 800-547-7377 or (920)563-6388 Fax: (920)536-1707 E-mail: rich.reiff@cygnuspub.com • URL: http://www.cygnuspub.com • Monthly. $60.00 per year. Formerly *Furniture Wood Digest.*

Wood Digest Showcase. Cygnus Publishing, Inc., Johnson Hill Press, Inc., 1233 Janesville Ave. Fort Atkinson, WI 53538-0460. Phone: 800-547-7377 or (920)563-6388 Fax: (920)563-1707 E-mail: rich.rieff@cyhnuspub.com • URL: http://www.cygnuspub.com • Annual. Controlled circulation. Formerly *Furniture Wood/Digest-Showcase.*

Wood Flooring. Available from MarketResearch.com, 641 Ave. of the Americas, Third Floor New York, NY 10011. Phone: 800-298-5699 or (212)807-2629 Fax: (212)807-2716 E-mail: order@marketresearch.com • URL: http://www.marketresearch.com • 1999. $2,250.00. Market research report published by Specialists in Business Information. Presents hardwood flooring market data relative to demographics, sales growth, shipments, exports, imports, price trends, and end-use. Includes company profiles.

Wood Machinery Manufacturers of America.

Wood Products Manufacturers Association.

Wood Research Laboratory.

Wood Technology-Equipment Catalog and Buyers' Guide. Miller Freeman, Inc., 600 Harrison St. San Francisco, CA 94107. Phone: (415)905-2200 Fax: (415)905-2232 E-mail: mfibooks@mfi.com • URL: http://www.books.mfi.com • Annual. $55.00. Formerly *Forest Industries-Lumber Review and Buyers' Guide.*

Wood Technology: Logging, Pulpwood, Forestry, Lumber, Panels. Miller Freeman, Inc., 600 Harrison St. San Francisco, CA 94107. Phone: (415)905-2200 Fax: (415)905-2232 E-mail: mfibooks@mfi.com • URL: http://www.mfi.com • Eight times a year. $120.00 per year. Formerly *Forest Industries.*

Woodturner's Bible. Percy Blandford. McGraw-Hill Professional, 1221 Ave. of the Americas New York, NY 10020. Phone: 800-722-4726 or (212)904-2000 Fax: (212)904-2072 E-mail: customer.service@mcgraw-hill.com • URL: http://www.mcgraw-hill.com • 1990. $26.95. Third edition.

Woodworking Factbook: Basic Information on Wood for Wood Carvers, Home Woodshop Craftsmen, Tradesmen and Instructors. Donald G. Coleman. Robert Speller and Sons Publishers, Inc., P.O. Box 411 New York, NY 10159. Phone: (212)473-0333 1996. $22.50.

Woodworking for Industry: Technology and Practice. John L. Feirer and Gilbert R. Hutchings. Glencoe/McGraw-Hill, 8787 Orion Place Columbus, OH 43240-4027. Phone: 800-848-1567 or (614)430-4000 Fax: (614)860-1877 E-mail: customer.service@mcgraw-hill.com • URL: http://www.mcgraw-hill.com • 1979. $23.72.

Wool Record. World Textile Publications Ltd., Perkins House, One Longlands St., c/o Keith Higgenbottom, Bradford West Yorkshire BDI 2TP, England. E-mail: 104470.3070@compuserve.com • URL: http://www./worldtextile.com • Monthly. $120.00 per year.

Wool Research Organization of New Zealand, Inc., Private Bag 4749 Christchurch 2052 643 3, New Zealand. Irregular. Individuals, $75.00 per year; institutions, $115.00 per year.

The Wool Sack. Mid-States Wool Growers Cooperative, 9449 Basil Western Rd. Canal Winchester, OH 43110-9728. Semiannual. Free. Information on lamb production and the wool industry.

Woolmark Company.

The Word Processor Book. Peter McWilliams. Putnam Publishing Group, 375 Hudson St. New York, NY 10014. Phone: 800-631-8571 or (212)366-2000 Fax: (212)366-2643 E-mail: online@penguinputnam.com • URL: http://www.penguinputnam.com • 1997. $14.95.

Words and Phrases Legally Defined. John B. Saunders, Editor. LEXIS Publishing, 701 E. Water St. Charlottesville, VA 22902. Phone: 800-446-3410 or (804)972-7600 Fax: 800-643-1280 or (804)972-7686 E-mail: custserv@michie.com • URL: http://www.lexislaw.publishing • 1990. $520.00. Third edition. Four volumes. Definitions taken from court cases.

Words into Type. M. Skillen and R. Gay. Prentice Hall, 240 Frisch Court Paramus, NJ 07652-5240. Phone: 800-947-7700 or (201)909-6200 Fax: 800-445-6991 or (201)909-6361 URL: http://www.prenhall.com • 1974. $39.95. Third edition.

Words That Mean Business: Three Thousand Terms for Access to Business Information. Warner-Eddison Associates. Neal-Schuman Publishers, Inc., 100 Varick St. New York, NY 10013. Phone: (212)925-8650 Fax: 800-584-2414 E-mail: info@neal-schuman.com • URL: http://www.neal-schuman.com • 1981. $60.00.

Work and Health: Strategies for Maintaining a Vital Workforce. Panel Publishers, 1185 Ave. of the Americas, 37th Fl. New York, NY 10036. Phone: 800-447-1717 or (212)597-0200 Fax: 800-901-9075 or (212)597-0334 E-mail: customer.service@aspenpubl.com • URL: http://www.panelpublishers.com • 1989. $79.00.

Work and Occupations: An International Sociological Journal. Sage Publications, Inc., 2455 Teller Rd. Thousand Oaks, CA 91320. Phone: (805)499-0721 Fax: (805)499-0871 E-mail: info@sagepub.com • URL: http://www.sagepub.com • Quarterly. Individuals, $70.00 per year; institutions, $310.00 per year.

Work Simplification: An Analyst's Handbook. Pierre Theriault. Engineering and Management Press, 25 Technology Park Norcross, GA 30092-2988. Phone: 800-494-0460 or (770)449-0461 Fax: (770)263-8532 E-mail: cmagee@www.iienet.org • URL: http://www.iienet.org • 1996. $25.00. A basic guide to work simplification as an industrial management technique.

Work Study. MCB University Press Ltd., 60-62 Toller Lane, Bradford West Yorkshire BD8 9BY, England. Fax: 44 1274 785200 E-mail: editorial@mcb.co.uk • URL: http://www.mcb.co.uk • Seven times a year. $3,199.00 per year. Provides information on management services and industrial engineering.

Work, Study, Travel Abroad; 1994-1995: The Whole World Handbook. Council on International Educational Exchange Staff. St. Martin's Press, 175 Fifth Ave. New York, NY 10010. Phone: 800-221-7945 or (212)674-5151 Fax: 800-672-2054 or (212)529-0594 URL: http://www.stmartins.com • 1994. $13.95. 12th edition. Lists more than 1,000 employment, travel, and educational opportunities for the U. S. student abroad.

Worker Self-Management in Industry: The West European Experience. G. David Garson, editor. Greenwood Publishing Group, Inc., 88 Post Rd., W. Westport, CT 06881-5007. Phone: 800-225-5800 or (203)226-3571 Fax: (203)222-2540 E-mail: bookinfo@greenwood.com • URL: http://www.greenwood.com • 1977. $48.95. (Praeger Special Studies).

Workers' Compensation Law Bulletin. Quinlan Publishing Co., Inc., 23 Drydock Ave., 2nd Fl. Boston, MA 02210-2387. Phone: 800-229-2084 or (617)542-0048 Fax: (617)345-9646 Monthly, $79.00 per year; semimonthly, $129.00 per year.

Workers' Compensation Monitor. LRP Publications, P.O. Box 980 Horsham, PA 19044-0980. Phone: 800-341-7874 or (215)784-0941 Fax: (215)784-9639 E-mail: custserv@lrp.com • URL: http://www.lrp.com • Monthly. $175.00 per year. Newsletter. Covers workers' compensation legislation, regulations, and publications. Formerly *John Burton's Workers' Compensation.*

Workforce: The Business Magazine for Leaders in Human Resources. ACC Communications, Inc., C/O Vanessa Tosti, P.O. Box 2440C Costa Mesa, CA 92626. Phone: (714)751-1883 Fax: (714)751-4106 E-mail: tostiv@workforcemag.com • URL: http://www.workforceonline • Monthly. $59.00 per year. Edited for human resources managers. Covers employee benefits, compensation, relocation, recruitment, training, personnel legalities, and related subjects. Supplements include bimonthly "New Product News" and semiannual "Recruitment/Staffing Sourcebook." Formerly *Personnel Journal.*

Working Americans, 1880-1999, Volume One: The Working Class. Grey House Publishing, 185 Millerton Rd. Millerton, NY 12546. Phone: 800-562-2139 or (518)789-8700 Fax: (518)789-0556 E-mail: books@greyhouse.com • URL: http://www.greyhouse.com • 2000. $135.00. Provides detailed information on the lifestyles and economic life of working class families in the 12 decades from 1880 to 1999. Includes such items as selected consumer prices, income, family finances, budgets, life at home, jobs, and working conditions. (Universal Reference Publications.)

Working Americans, 1880-1999, Volume Two: The Middle Class. Grey House Publishing, 185 Millerton Rd. Millerton, NY 12546. Phone: 800-562-2139 or (518)789-8700 Fax: (518)789-0556 E-mail: books@greyhouse.com • URL: http://www.greyhouse.com • 2000. $135.00. Furnishes details of the social and economic lives of middle class Americans during the years 1880 to 1999. Describes such items as selected consumer prices, income, family finances, budgets, life at home, jobs, and working conditions. (Universal Reference Publications.)

Working from Home: Everything You Need to Know About Living and Working Under the Same Roof. Paul Edwards and Sarah Edwards. Putnam Publishing Group, 375 Hudson St. New York, NY 10014. Phone: 800-631-8571 or (212)366-2000 Fax: (212)366-2643 E-mail: online@penguinputnam.com • URL: http://www.penguinputnam.com • 1999. $18.95. Fifth revised expanded edition.

Working Mother. MacDonald Communications Corp., 135 W. 50th St., 16th Fl. New York, NY 10020. Phone: 800-234-9675 or (212)445-6100 Fax: (212)586-7420 URL: http://www.workingmother.com • 10 times a year. $12.97 per year.

Working Options. Association of Part-Time Professionals, 2727 S. Hayes St. Arlington, VA 22202-2417. Phone: (703)734-7975 Fax: (703)734-7405 Bimonthly. Members in the Washington Metropolitan Area, $45.00 per year; other members, $20.00 per year. Formerly *The Part-Time Professional.*

Working Press of the Nation. R. R. Bowker, 121 Chanlon Rd. New Providence, NJ 07974. Phone: 888-269-5372 or (908)464-6800 Fax: (908)771-7704 E-mail: info@bowker.com • URL: http://www.bowker.com • Annual. $450.00. Three volumes: (1) *Newspaper Directory*; (2) *Magazine and Internal Publications Directory*; (3) *Radio and Television Directory*. Includes names of editors and other personnel. Individual volumes, $249.00.

Working with Faculty to Design Undergraduate Information Literacy Programs: A How-To-Do-It Manual for Librarians. Rosemary M. Young and Stephana Harmony. Neal-Schuman Publishers, Inc., 100 Varick St. New York, NY 10013. Phone: 800-584-2414 or (212)925-8650 Fax: (212)219-8916 E-mail: info@neal-schuman.com • URL: http://www.neal-schuman.com • 1999. $45.00. Includes sample forms, surveys, evaluations, and assignments for credit courses or single sessions.

Working with Tax-Sheltered Annuities. CCH, Inc., 4025 W. Peterson Ave. Chicago, IL 60646-6085. Phone: 800-835-5224 or (773)866-6000 Fax: 800-224-8299 or (773)866-3608 URL: http://www.cch.com • 1997. $69.00. Emphasis is on legal aspects of tax-deferred annuities.

Working Woman. MacDonald Communications Corp., 135 W. 50th St., 16th Fl. New York, NY 10020. Phone: 800-234-9675 or (212)445-6100 Fax: (212)586-7420 URL: http://www.workingwoman.com • 10 times a year. $15.00 per year. Focuses on solutions of business problems.

Workplace Sexual Harassment. Anne Levy. Simon and Schuster Trade, 1230 Ave. of the Americas New York, NY 10020. Phone: 800-223-2348 or (212)698-7000 Fax: 800-943-9831 or (212)698-7007 E-mail: sson-line_feedback@simonsays.com • URL: http://www.simonsays.com • 1996. $41.00. A management guide to confronting and preventing sexual harassment in organizations. Includes case studies and training materials.

Workplace Substance Abuse Advisor. LRP Publications, P.O. Box 980 Horsham, PA 19044-0980. Phone: 800-341-7874 or (215)784-0941 Fax: (215)784-9639 E-mail: custserve@lrp.com • URL: http://www.lrp.com • Biweekly. $377.00 per year. Newsletter. Covers federal and local laws relating to alcohol and drug use and testing. Provides information on employee assistance plans. Formerly *National Report on Substance Abuse.*

Workshops: Designing and Facilitating Experiential Learning. Jeff E. Brooks-Harris and Susan R. Stock-Ward. Sage Publications, Inc., 2455 Teller Rd. Thousand Oaks, CA 91320. Phone: (805)499-0721 Fax: (805)499-0871 E-mail: info@sagepub.com • URL: http://www.sagepub.com • 1999. $55.00. Presents a practical approach to designing, running, and evaluating workshops in business, adult education, and other areas. Includes references.

Worksite Wellness: A New and Practical Approach to Reducing Health Care Cost. David W. Jensen. Prentice Hall, 240 Frisch Court Paramus, NJ 07652-5240. Phone:

800-947-7700 or (201)909-6200 Fax: 800-445-6991 or (201)909-6361 URL: http://www.prenhall.com • 1987. $25.00.

World Agricultural Economics and Rural Sociology Abstracts: Abstracts of World Literature. Available from CABI Publishing, 10 E. 40th St. New York, NY 10016. Phone: 800-528-4841 or (212)481-7018 Fax: (212)686-7993 E-mail: cabi@cabi.org • URL: http://www.cabi.org • Monthly. $1095.00 per year. Published in England by CABI Publishing. Provides worldwide coverage of the literature.

World Agricultural Supply and Demand Estimates. Available from U. S. Government Printing Office, Washington, DC 20402. Phone: (202)512-1800 Fax: (202)512-2250 E-mail: gpoaccess@gpo.gov • URL: http://www.access.gpo.gov • Monthly. $38.00 per year. Issued by the Economics and Statistics Service and the Foreign Agricultural Service of the U. S. Department of Agriculture. Consists mainly of statistical data and tables.

World Agrochemical Markets. Theta Reports/PJB Medical Publications, Inc., 1775 Broadway, Suite 511 New York, NY 10019. Phone: (212)262-8230 Fax: (212)262-8234 E-mail: customerservice@thetareports.com • URL: http://www.thetareports.com • 2000. $1,040.00. Market research data. Covers the demand for crop protection products in 11 countries having major markets and 20 countries having minor markets. (Theta Report No. DS196E.)

World Air Transport Statistics. International Air Transport Association, P.O. Box 113 Montreal, QC, Canada PQ H4Z 1M1. Phone: (514)874-0202 Fax: (514)874-9632 E-mail: sales@iata.org • URL: http://www.iata.org.charts • Annual. $180.00.

World Airline News. Phillips Business Information, Inc., 1201 Seven Locks Rd., Suite 300 Potomac, MD 20854. Phone: 800-777-5006 or (301)340-2100 Fax: (301)309-3847 E-mail: pbi@phillips.com • URL: http://www.phillips.com/marketplaces.htm • Weekly. $697.00 per year. Newsletter. Covers the international airline industry.

World Almanac and Book of Facts. World Almanac Education Group, Inc., One International Blvd., Suite 630 Mahwah, NJ 07945-0017. Phone: (201)529-6900 Fax: (201)529-6901 E-mail: info@wacgroup.com • Annual. $10.95.

The World Almanac Dictionary of Dates. Laurence Urdang, editor. Allyn and Bacon/Longman, 1185 Ave. of the Americas New York, NY 10036. Phone: 800-922-0579 E-mail: the.webmaster@ablongman.com • URL: http://www.ablonglman.com • 1982. $31.95.

World Animal Health Markets. Theta Reports/PJB Medical Publications, Inc., 1775 Broadway, Suite 511 New York, NY 10019. Phone: (212)262-8230 Fax: (212)262-8234 E-mail: customerservice@thetareports.com • URL: http://www.thetareports.com • 2000. $830.00. Market research data. Covers the market for animal health products in 15 major countries, including the U.S. (Theta Report No. SR198E.)

World Antique Dealers Association.

World Association for Public Opinion Research., University of North Carolina, School of Journalism and Mass, Communication, Howell Hall, No. CB-3365 Chapel Hill, NC 27599-3365. Phone: (919)962-6396 Fax: (919)962-4079 E-mail: wapor@unc.edu • URL: http://www.wapor.org • Members are opinion survey research experts, both academic and commercial. Promotes the use of objective, scientific, public opinion methodology and research. International emphasis.

World Association of Alcohol Beverage Industries.

World Aviation Directory. McGraw-Hill Aviation Week Group, 1200 G St., N.W., Ste. 922 Washington, DC 20005. Phone: 800-722-4726 or (202)383-2484 Fax: (202)383-2446 E-mail: avweek@mgh.com • URL: http://www.aviationnow.com • Semiannual. $225.00 per year. Two volumes. Lists aviation, aerospace, and missile manufacturers. Includes *World Aviation Directory Buyer's Guide*.

World Bank., 1818 H St., N. W. Washington, DC 20433. Phone: (202)477-1234 Fax: (202)477-6391 URL: http://www.worldbank.org • Comprises the International Bank for Reconstruction and Development and the International Development Association, with over 130 member countries.

The World Bank and the Poorest Countries: Support for Development in the 1990s. World Bank, The Office of the Publisher, 1818 H St., N. W. Washington, DC 20433. Phone: (202)477-1234 Fax: (202)477-6391 E-mail: books@worldbank.org • URL: http://www.worldbank.org • 1994. $22.00. Describes progress in poverty reduction, economic management, and environmental protection in the 70 poorest countries of the world.

World Bank Atlas. The World Bank, Office of the Publisher, 1818 H St., N. W. Washington, DC 20433. Phone: (202)477-1234 Fax: 800-645-7247 or (202)477-6391 E-mail: books@worldbank.org • URL: http://www.worldbank.org • Annual. Price on application. Contains "color maps, charts, and graphs representing the main social, economic, and environmental indicators for 209 countries and territories" (publisher).

World Banking Abstracts: The International Journal of the Financial Services Industry. Basil Blackwell, Inc., Three Cambridge Center Cambridge, MA 02142. Phone: 800-216-2522 or (617)225-0430 Fax: (617)225-0412 Bimonthly. $866.00 per year. Provides worldwide coverage of articles appearing in over 400 financial publications.

World Book of IABC Communicators. International Association of Business Communicators, One Hallidie Plaza, Suite 600 San Francisco, CA 94102. Phone: (415)544-4700 Fax: (415)544-4747 E-mail: service_centre@iabc.com • URL: http://www.iabc.com • Annual. Membership. About 13,000 association members involved with organizational, corporate, and public relations and other communications fields. Formerly *Directory of Business and Organizational Communicators*.

World Business Directory. The Gale Group, 27500 Drake Rd. Farmington Hills, MI 48331-3535. Phone: 800-877-GALE or (248)699-GALE Fax: 800-414-5043 or (248)699-8069 E-mail: galeord@galegroup.com • URL: http://www.galegroup.com • 2000. $615.00. Four volumes. Ninth edition. Covers about 140,000 companies in 180 countries.

World Business Directory 2001. World Trade Centers Association. Available from The Gale Group, 27500 Drake Rd. Farmington Hills, MI 48331-3535. Phone: 800-877-GALE or (248)699-GALE Fax: 800-414-5043 or (248)699-8069 E-mail: galeord@galegroup.com • URL: http://www.galegroup.com • 2000. $615.00. Ninth edition. Four volumes. Addresses and contact information for 300 world trade centers and affiliate organizations worldwide.

World Business Rankings Annual. The Gale Group, 27500 Drake Rd. Farmington Hills, MI 48331-3535. Phone: 800-877-GALE or (248)699-GALE Fax: 800-414-5043 or (248)699-8069 E-mail: galeord@galegroup.com • URL: http://www.galegroup.com • 1998. $189.00. Provides 2,500 ranked lists of international companies, compiled from a variety of published sources. Each list shows the "top ten" in a particular category. Keyword indexing, a country index, and citations are provided.

World Cartography. United Nations, Department of Economic and Social Affairs. United Nations Publications, United Nations Concourse Level, First Ave., 46th St. New York, NY 10017. Phone: 800-553-3210 or (212)963-7680 Fax: (212)963-3489 E-mail: bookstore@un.org • URL: http://www.un.org/publications • Various volumes. Price on application.

World Ceramics Abstracts. British Ceramic Research Ltd. Ceram Research, Queens Rd., Penkull Stoke-on-Trent, Staffs. ST4 7LQ, England. E-mail: info@ceram.co.uk • URL: http://www.ceram.co.uk • Monthly. $710.00 per year. Formerly *British Ceramic Abstracts*.

World Chamber of Commerce Directory., P.O. Box 1029 Loveland, CO 80539. Phone: (970)663-3231 Fax: (970)663-6187 E-mail: worldchamberdirectory@compuserve.com • Annual. $35.00.

World Class Quality: Using Design of Experiments to Make It Happen. Keki R. Bhote. AMACOM, 1601 Broadway, 12th Fl. New York, NY 10019. Phone: 800-262-9699 or (212)586-8100 Fax: (212)903-8168 E-mail: custmserv@amanet.org • URL: http://www.amanet.org • 1999. $34.95. Second revised expanded edition. An explanation of seven Shainin techniques for quality control. Exercises and case studies are included.

World Coffee and Tea. GCI Publishing Co., Inc., P.O. Box 1110 Olney, MD 20830-1110. Phone: (301)984-7333 Fax: (301)984-7340 Monthly. $24.00.

World Coffee and Tea OCS Buyer's Guide. GCI Publishing Co., Inc., P.O. Box 1110 Olney, MD 20830-1110. Phone: (301)984-7333 Fax: (301)984-7340 Annual. $5.00. Directory of manufacturers and suppliers of equipment and products for the office coffee service industry. Formerly *World Coffee and Tea-Office Coffee Service Red Book Directory*.

World Cogeneration: A Power Source for Partnering in the 90's. Dick Flanagan, Two Penn Plaza, Suite 1500 New York, NY 10121. Phone: (212)432-7300 Five times a year. $36.00 per year. Edited for managers and executives of independent and cogeneration electric power plants. Provides analysis of industry trends.

World Computer Graphics Association.

World Consumer Income and Expenditure Patterns. Available from The Gale Group, 27500 Drake Rd. Farmington Hills, MI 48331-3535. Phone: 800-877-GALE or (248)699-GALE Fax: 800-414-5043 or (248)699-8069 E-mail: galeord@galegroup.com • URL: http://www.galegroup.com • 2001. $990.00. Second edition. Two volumes. Published by Euromonitor. Provides data for 52 countries on consumer income, earning power, spending patterns, and savings. Expenditures are detailed for 75 product or service categories.

World Consumer Income and Expenditure Patterns. Available from The Gale Group, 27500 Drake Rd. Farmington Hills, MI 48331-3535. Phone: 800-877-GALE or (248)699-GALE Fax: 800-414-5043 or (248)699-8069 E-mail: galeord@galegroup.com • URL: http://www.galegroup.com • 2001. $650.00. Published by Euromonitor (http://www.euromonitor.com). Provides data on consumer income, earning power, and expenditures for 52 countries around the world.

World Consumer Markets. The Gale Group, 27500 Drake Rd. Farmington Hills, MI 48331-3535. Phone: 800-877-GALE or (248)699-4253 Fax: 800-414-5043 or (248)699-8069 E-mail: galeord@gale.com • URL: http://www.gale.com • Annual. $2,500.00. Pblished by Euromonitor. Provides five- year historical data, current data, and forecasts, on CD-ROM for 330 consumer products in 55 countries. Market data is presented in a standardized format for each country.

World Contact and Intraocular Lenses and Ophthalmic Devices Markets. Available from MarketResearch.com, 641 Ave. of the Americas, Third Floor New York, NY 10011. Phone: 800-298-5699 or (212)807-2629 Fax: (212)807-2716 E-mail: order@marketresearch.com • URL: http://www.marketresearch.com • 1996. $995.00. Published by Theta Corporation. Provides market data on soft contact lenses, hard lenses, and lens care products, with forecasts to 2000.

World Cosmetics and Toiletries Directory. Available from The Gale Group, 27500 Drake Rd. Farmington Hills, MI 48331-3535. Phone: 800-877-GALE or (248)699-GALE Fax: 800-414-5043 or (248)699-8069 E-mail: galeord@galegroup.com • URL: http://www.galegroup.com • 2001. $1,90.00. Second edition. Three volumes. Published by Euromonitor. Provides detailed descriptions of the world's cosmetics and toiletries companies. Includes consumers market research data.

World Cost of Living Survey. The Gale Group, 27500 Drake Rd. Farmington Hills, MI 48331-3535. Phone: 800-877-GALE or (248)699-GALE Fax: 800-414-5043 or (248)699-8069 E-mail: galeord@galegroup.com • URL: http://www.galegroup.com • 1999. $255.00. Second edition. Arranged by country and then by city within each country. Provides cost of living data for many products and services. Includes indexes and an annotated bibliography.

World Council of Credit Unions.

World Currrency Yearbook. International Currency Analysis, Inc., 7595 Baymeadows Circle, W., Suite 2714 Jacksonville, FL 32256-1864. Phone: (718)531-3685 Annual. $250.00. Directory of more than 110 central banks worldwide.

World Database of Business Information Sources on CD-ROM. The Gale Group, 27500 Drake Rd. Farmington Hills, MI 48331-3535. Phone: 800-877-GALE or (248)699-4253 Fax: 800-414-5043 or (248)699-8069 E-mail: galeord@gale.com • URL: http://www.gale.com • Annual. Produced by Euromonitor. Presents Euromonitor's entire information source database on CD-ROM. Contains a worldwide total of about 35,000 publications, organizations, libraries, trade fairs, and online databases.

World Database of Consumer Brands and Their Owners on CD-ROM. The Gale Group, 27500 Drake Rd. Farmington Hills, MI 48331-3535. Phone: 800-877-GALE or (248)669-GALE Fax: 800-414-5043 or (248)699-8069 E-mail: galeord@gale.com • URL: http://www.gale.com • Annual. $3,190.00. Produced by Euromonitor. Provides detailed information on CD-ROM for about 10,000 companies and 80,000 brands around the world. Covers 1,000 product sectors.

World Development. Elsevier Science, 655 Ave. of the Americas New York, NY 10010. Phone: 888-437-4636 or (212)989-5800 Fax: (212)633-3680 E-mail: usinfo@elsevier.com • URL: http://www.elsevier.com • Monthly. $1,548.00 per year.

World Development Indicators. World Bank, The Office of the Publisher, 1818 H St., N. W. Washington, DC 20433. Phone: (202)477-1234 Fax: (202)477-6391 E-mail: books@worldbank.org • URL: http://www.worldbank.org • Annual. $60.00. Provides data and information on the people, economy, environment, and markets of 148 countries. Emphasis is on statistics relating to major development issues.

World Development Report. The World Bank, Office of the Publisher, 1818 H St., N. W. Washington, DC 20433. Phone: 800-645-7247 or (202)477-1234 Fax: (202)477-6391 E-mail: books@worldbank.org • URL: http://www.worldbank.org • Annual. $50.00. Covers history, conditions, and trends relating to economic globalization and localization. Includes selected data from *World Development Indicators* for 132 countries or economies. Key indicators are provided for 78 additional countries or economies.

World Development Report ÎCD-ROMl. The World Bank, Office of the Publisher, 1818 H St., N. W. Washington, DC 20433. Phone: 800-645-7247 or (202)477-1234 Fax: (202)477-6391 E-mail: books@worldbank.org • URL: http://www.worldbank.org • Annual. Single-user, $375.00. Network version, $750.00. CD-ROM includes the current edition of *World Development Report* and 21 previous editions.

World Directory of Business Information Libraries. Available from The Gale Group, 27500 Drake Rd. Farmington Hills, MI 48331-3535. Phone: 800-877-GALE or (248)699-GALE Fax: 800-414-5043 or (248)699-8069

E-mail: galeord@galegroup.com • URL: http://www.galegroup.com • 2000. $590.00. Fourth edition. Published by Euromonitor. Provides detailed information on 2,000 major business libraries in 145 countries. Emphasis is on collections relevant to consumer goods and services markets.

World Directory of Business Information Web Sites. Available from The Gale Group, 27500 Drake Rd. Farmington Hills, MI 48331-3535. Phone: 800-877-GALE or (248)699-GALE Fax: 800-414-5043 or (248)699-8069 E-mail: galeord@galegroup.com • URL: http://www.galegroup.com • 2001. $650.00. Fourth edition. Published by Euromonitor. Provides detailed descriptions of a wide variety of business-related Web sites. More than 1,500 sites are included from around the world. Covers statistics sources, market research, company information, rankings, surveys, economic data, etc.

World Directory of Marketing Information Sources. Available from The Gale Group, 27500 Drake Rd. Farmington Hills, MI 48331-3535. Phone: 800-877-GALE or (248)699-GALE Fax: 800-414-5043 or (248)699-8069 E-mail: galeord@galegroup.com • URL: http://www.galegroup.com • 2001. $590.00. Third edition. Published by Euromonitor. Provides details on more than 6,000 sources of marketing information, including publications, libraries, associations, market research companies, online databases, and governmental organizations. Coverage is worldwide.

World Directory of Non-Official Statistical Sources. Gale Group, Inc., 27500 Drake Rd. Farmington Hills, MI 48331-3535. Phone: 800-877-GALE or (248)699-GALE Fax: 800-414-5043 or (248)699-8069 E-mail: galeord@gale.com • URL: http://www.gale.com • 2001. $590.00. Provides detailed descriptions of more than 4,000 regularly published, non-governmental statistics sources. Includes surveys, studies, market research reports, trade journals, databank compilations, and other print sources. Coverage is international, with four indexes.

World Directory of Pesticide Control Organizations. Springler-Verlag New York, Inc., PO Box 2485 Secaucus, NJ 07096-2485. Phone: 800-777-4643 Fax: (201)348-4505 E-mail: sales@rsc.org • 1996. $85.00. Third edition. Published by The Royal Society of Chemistry. Provides detailed information on organizations and authorities concerned with the use and control of pesticides in 180 countries.

World Directory of Trade and Business Associations. Available from The Gale Group, 27500 Drake Rd. Farmington Hills, MI 48331-3535. Phone: 800-877-GALE or (248)699-GALE Fax: 800-414-5043 or (248)699-8069 E-mail: galeord@galegroup.com • URL: http://www.galegroup.com • 2000. $595.00. Third edition. Published by Euromonitor. Provides detailed information on approximately 5,000 trade associations in various countries of the world. Includes subject and geographic indexes.

World Drinks Marketing Directory. Available from The Gale Group, 27500 Drake Rd. Farmington Hills, MI 48331-3535. Phone: 800-877-GALE or (248)699-GALE Fax: 800-414-5043 or (248)699-8069 E-mail: galeord@galegroup.com • URL: http://www.galegroup.com • 2001. $1,090.00. Second edition. Published by Euromonitor. Provides detailed infromation on the leading beverage companies of the world, including specifi brand data.

World Drug Report. United Nations Publications, Two United Nations Plaza, Room DC2-853 New York, NY 10017. Phone: 800-253-9646 or (212)963-8302 Fax: (212)963-3489 E-mail: publications@un.org • URL: http://www.un.org/publications • Annual. $25.00. Issued by the United Nations Office for Drug Control and Crime Prevention. Includes maps, graphs, charts, and tables.

World Economic and Social Survey: Trends and Policies in the World Economy. United Nations Publications, Two United Nations Plaza, Room DC2-853 New York, NY 10017. Phone: 800-253-9646 or (212)963-8302 Fax: (212)963-3489 E-mail: publications@un.org • URL: http://www.un.org/publications • Annual. $55.00. Includes discussion and ''an extensive statistical annex of economic, trade, and financial indicators, incorporating current data and forecasts.''

The World Economic Factbook. Available from The Gale Group, 27500 Drake Rd. Farmington Hills, MI 48331-3535. Phone: 800-877-GALE or (248)699-GALE Fax: 800-414-5043 or (248)699-8069 E-mail: galeord@galegroup.com • URL: http://www.galegroup.com • 2000. $450.00. Seventh edition. Published by Euromonitor. Presents key economic facts and figures for each of 200 countries, including details of chief industries, export-import trade, currency, political risk, household expenditures, and the economic situation in general.

World Economic Outlook: A Survey by the Staff of the International Monetary Fund. International Monetary Fund, Publications Services, 700 19th St., N.W., Suite 12-607 Washington, DC 20431-0001. Phone: (202)623-7000 Fax: (202)623-7201 URL: http://www.imf.org • Semiannual. $62.00 per year. Presents international statistics combined with forecasts and analyses of the world economy. Editions available in Arabic, English, French and Spanish.

World Economic Prospects: A Planner's Guide to International Market Conditions. Available from The Gale Group, 27500 Drake Rd. Farmington Hills, MI 48331-3535. Phone: 800-877-GALE or (248)699-GALE Fax: 800-414-5043 or (248)699-8069 E-mail: galeord@galegroup.com • URL: http://www.galegroup.com • 2000. $450.00. Second edition. Published by Euromonitor. Ranks 78 countries by specific economic characteristics, such as gross domestic product (GDP) per capita and short term growth prospects. Discusses the economic situation, prospects, and market potential of each of the countries.

World Economic Situation and Prospects. United Nations Publications, Two United Nations Plaza, Room DC2-853 New York, NY 10017. Phone: 800-253-9646 or (212)963-8302 Fax: (212)963-3489 E-mail: publications@un.org • URL: http://www.un.org/publications • Annual. $15.00. Serves as a supplement and update to the UN *World Economic and Social Survey*.

The World Economy: A Millennial Perspective. Angus Maddison. Organization for Economic Cooperation and Development, OECD Washington Center, 2001 L St., N. W., Suite 650 Washington, DC 20036-4922. Phone: 800-456-6323 or (202)785-6323 Fax: (202)785-0350 E-mail: washington.contact@oecd.org • URL: http://www.oecd.org • 2001. $63.00. ''...covers the development of the entire world economy over the past 2000 years,'' including data on world population and gross domestic product (GDP) since the year 1000, and exports since 1820. Focuses primarily on the disparity in economic performance among nations over the very long term. More than 200 statistical tables and figures are provided (detailed information available at http://www.theworldeconomy.org).

World Encyclopedia of Library and Information Services. Robert Wedgeworth, editor. American Library Association, 50 E. Huron St. Chicago, IL 60611-2795. Phone: 800-545-2433 or (312)944-6780 Fax: (312)440-9374 E-mail: ala@ala.org • URL: http://www.ala.org • 1993. $200.00. Third edition. Contains about 340 articles from various contributors.

World Energy and Nuclear Directory. Allyn and Bacon/ Longman, 1185 Ave. of the Americas New York, NY 10036. Phone: 800-922-0579 E-mail: the.webmaster@ablongman.com • URL: http://www.ablongman.com • 1996. Fifth edition. Price on application. Lists 5,000 public and private, international research and development organizations functioning in a wide variety of areas related to energy.

World Energy Outlook. OECD Publications and Information Center, 2001 L St., N.W., Ste. 650 Washington, DC 20036-4922. Phone: 800-456-6323 or (202)785-6323 Fax: (202)785-0350 E-mail: washington.contact@oecd.org • URL: http://www.oecdwash.org • Annual. $150.00. Provides detailed, 15-year projections by the International Energy Agency (IEA) for world energy supply and demand.

World Environment Report: News and Information on International Resource Management. Business Publishers, Inc., 8737 Colesville Rd., Suite 1100 Silver Spring, MD 20910-3928. Phone: 800-274-6737 or (301)587-6300 Fax: (301)587-1081 E-mail: bpinews@bpinews.com • URL: http://www.bpinews.com • Biweekly. $494.00 per year. Newsletter on international developments having to do with the environment, energy, pollution control, waste management, and toxic substances.

World Environmental Business Handbook. Available from The Gale Group, 27500 Drake Rd. Farmington Hills, MI 48331-3535. Phone: 800-877-GALE or (248)699-GALE Fax: 800-414-5043 or (248)699-8069 E-mail: galeord@galegroup.com • URL: http://www.galegroup.com • 1993. $190.00. Second edition. Published by Euromonitor. An overview of environmental business activities, trends, issues, and problems throughout the world.

World Factbook. U.S. National Technical Information Service, 5285 Port Royal Rd. Springfield, VA 22161. Phone: 800-553-6847 or (703)605-6060 Fax: (703)605-6880 E-mail: orders@ntis.fedworld.gov • URL: http://www.ntis.gov • Annual. $83.00. Prepared by the Central Intelligence Agency. For all countries of the world, provides current economic, demographic, geographic, communications, government, defense force, and illicit drug trade information (where applicable).

World Fleet Statistics. Available from Fairplay Publications, Inc., 5201 Blue Lagoon Drive, Suite 530 Miami, FL 33126. Phone: (305)262-4070 Fax: (305)262-2006 E-mail: sales@fairplayamericas.com • URL: http://www.lrfairplay.com • Annual. $142.00. Published in the UK by Lloyd's Register-Fairplay Ltd. Provides data on the ''world fleet of propelled seagoing merchant ships of 100 gross tonnage and above.'' Includes five-year summaries.

World Food Logistics Organization., 7315 Wisconsin Ave., Suite 1200 N Bethesda, MD 20814. Phone: (301)652-5674 Fax: (301)652-7269 E-mail: email@iarw.org • URL: http://www.iarw.org • Concerned with food storage. Affiliated with the International Association of Refrigerated Warehouses and the University of Maryland.

World Food Marketing Directory. Available from The Gale Group, 27500 Drake Rd. Farmington Hills, MI 48331-3535. Phone: 800-877-GALE or (248)699-GALE Fax: 800-414-5043 or (248)699-8063 E-mail: galeord@galegroup.com • URL: http://www.galegroup.com • 2001. $1,090.00. Second edition. Three volumes. Published by Euromonitor. Provides detailed information on the major food companies of the world, including specific brand data.

World Future Society., 7910 Woodmont Ave., Suite 450 Bethesda, MD 20814. Phone: 800-989-8274 or (301)656-8274 Fax: (301)951-0394 E-mail: info@wfs.org • URL: http://www.wfs.org • Members are individuals concerned with forecasts and ideas about the future.

World Futures Studies Federation., c/o WFSF Secretariat Office, Main Administration Bldg., 2nd Fl., University of Saint La Salle Bacolod City 6100, Philippines. Phone: 63 34 4353857 Fax: 63 34 4353857 E-mail: secretariat@worldfutures.org • Members are institutions and individuals involved with study of the future.

World Futures Studies Federation Membership Directory. World Future Studies Federation, c/o Ceasar Villanueva, Secretary General, University of Saint LaSalle, P.O. Box 249 6100 Bacowd City NEG OCC, Australia. Phone: 63 34 435857 Fax: 63 34 435857 E-mail: secretariat@worldfutures.org • Annual. $50.00. Lists over 700 member individuals and 60 institutions with an interest in the study of the world's future. Formerly *World Future Studies-Newsletter Membership Directory*.

World Guide to Abbreviations of Organizations. Available from The Gale Group, 27500 Drake Rd. Farmington Hills, MI 48331-3535. Phone: 800-877-GALE or (248)699-GALE Fax: 800-414-5043 or (248)699-8069 E-mail: galeord@galegroup.com • URL: http://www.galegroup.com • 1987. $125.00. 11th edition. Published by Chapman and Hall.

World Guide to Libraries. Available from The Gale Group, 27500 Drake Rd. Farmington Hills, MI 48331-3535. Phone: 800-699-4253 or (248)699-4253 Fax: (248)699-8069 E-mail: galeord@galegroup.com • URL: http://www.galegroup.com • Biennial. $450.00. Two volumes. Provides information on more than 44,000 academic, government, and public libraries in 196 countries. Published by K. G. Saur.

World Guide to Special Libraries. Available from The Gale Group, 27500 Drake Rd. Farmington Hills, MI 48331-3535. Phone: 800-877-GALE or (248)699-GALE Fax: 800-414-5043 or (248)699-8069 E-mail: galeord@galegroup.com • URL: http://www.galegroup.com • 2001. $400.00. Fifth edition. Two volumes. Published by K. G. Saur. Classifies more than 37,000 libraries in 183 countries under 750 subject headings.

World Highways. International Road Federation, 2600 Virginia Ave., N.W., Suite 208 Washington, DC 20037. Phone: (202)338-4641 Fax: (202)338-8104 Eight times a year. $165.00 per year. Text in English, French, German and Spanish.

The World in 2020: Power, Culture, and Prosperity. Hamish McRae. Harvard Business School Press, 60 Harvard Way Boston, MA 02163. Phone: 800-545-7685 or (617)783-7440 E-mail: custserv@cchbspub.harvard.edu • URL: http://www.hpsp.harvard.edu • 1995. $24.95. States that the best predictor of economic success will be a nation's creativity and social responsibility.

World Interactive Television and Video Transmission Overview. Primary Research, 68 W. 38th St., No. 202 New York, NY 10018. Phone: (212)769-1579 Fax: (212)397-5056 E-mail: primarydat@aol.com • 1994. Contains market research data. Price on application.

World Investment Report. United Nations Publications, Two United Nations Plaza, Room DC2-853 New York, NY 10017. Phone: 800-253-9646 or (212)963-8302 Fax: (212)963-3489 E-mail: publications@un.org • URL: http://www.un.org/publications • Annual. $49.00. Concerned with foreign direct investment, economic development, regional trends, transnational corporations, and globalization.

World Labour Report. International Labour Office, 1828 L St., N.W., Suite 801 Washington, DC 20036. Phone: (202)653-7652 Fax: (202)653-7687 E-mail: ilopubs@tascol.com • URL: http://www.ilo.org/pubns • Irregular. Price varies. Volume eight. International coverage. Reviews significant recent events and labor policy developments in the following areas: employment, human rights, labor relations, and working conditions.

World Leisure and Recreation: Official Publication of the World Leisure and Recreation Association. World Leisure and Recreation Association, WLRA Secretariat, Site 81 C Compo Okanagan Falls BC V0H 1R0, People's Republic of China. Phone: (250)497-6578 Fax: (250)497-6578 E-mail: secretariat@worldleisure.com • Bimonthly. Libraries $80.00 per year. Formerly *World Leisure Review*.

World Market Share Reporter: A Compilation of Reported World Market Share Data and Rankngs on Companies, Products, and Services. The Gale Group, 27500 Drake Rd. Farmington Hills, MI 48331-3535. Phone: 800-877-GALE or (248)699-GALE Fax: 800-414-5043 or (248)699-8069 E-mail: galeord@galegroup.com • URL: http://www.galegroup.com • 1999. $330.00. Fourth edition. Provides market share data for companies, products, and industries in countries or regions other than North America and Mexico.

World Marketing Data and Statistics on CD-ROM. The Gale Group, 27500 Drake Rd. Farmington Hills, MI 48331-3535. Phone: 800-877-GALE or (248)699-GALE Fax: 800-414-5043 or (248)699-8069 E-mail: galeord@gale.com • URL: http://www.gale.com • Annual. $1,750.00. Published by Euromonitor. Provides demographic, marketing, socioeconomic, and political data on CD-ROM for each of 209 countries.

World Marketing Forecasts on CD-ROM. The Gale Group, 27500 Drake Rd. Farmington Hills, MI 48331-3535. Phone: 800-877-GALE or (248)699-4253 Fax: 800-414-5043 or (248)699-8069 E-mail: galeord@gale.com • URL: http://www.gale.com • Annual. $2,500.00. Produced by Euromonitor. Provides detailed forecast data for the years to 2012 on CD-ROM for 54 countries in all parts of the world. Covers a wide range of social, demographic, economic, and market factors. Includes specific forecasts for many kinds of consumer products.

World Meetings: Outside United States and Canada. Available from Gale Group, 27500 Drake Rd. Farmington Hills, MI 48331-3535. Phone: 800-877-4253 or (248)699-4253 Fax: 800-414-5043 E-mail: galeord@galegroup.com • URL: http://www.galegroup.com • Quarterly. $195.00 per year

World Meetings: United States and Canada. Available from Gale Group, 27500 Drake Rd. Farmington Hills, MI 48331-3535. Phone: 800-877-4253 or (248)699-4253 Fax: 800-414-5043 E-mail: galeord@galegroup.com • URL: http://www.galegroup.com • Quarterly. $195.00 per year.

World Metal Statistics. World Bureau of Metal Statistics, 27a High St. Ware SG12 9BA Herts, England. E-mail: 100010.2037@compuserve.com • Monthly. $1,930.00 per year.

World Meteorological Organization.

World Migration Report. United Nations Publications, Two United Nations Plaza, Room DC2-853 New York, NY 10017. Phone: 800-253-9646 or (212)963-8302 Fax: (212)963-3489 E-mail: publications@un.org • URL: http://www.un.org/publications • Annual. $39.00. Analyzes major trends in world migration, including individual country profiles.

World Non-Agricultural Pesticide Markets. Theta Reports/PJB Medical Publications, Inc., 1775 Broadway, Suite 511 New York, NY 10019. Phone: (212)262-8230 Fax: (212)262-8234 E-mail: customerservice@thetareports.com • URL: http://www.thetareports.com • 2000. $1,670.00. Market research data. Includes home/garden pesticides, herbicides, professional pest-control products, and turf pesticides. (Theta Report No. DS191E.)

World of Computer Science. The Gale Group, 27500 Drake Rd. Farmington Hills, MI 48331-3535. Phone: 800-877-GALE or (248)699-GALE Fax: 800-414-5043 or (248)699-8069 E-mail: galeord@galegroup.com • URL: http://www.galegroup.com • 2001. $150.00. Alphabetical arrangement. Contains 650 entries covering discoveries, theories, concepts, issues, ethics, and people in the broad area of computer science and technology.

World of Criminal Justice. The Gale Group, 27500 Drake Rd. Farmington Hills, MI 48331-3535. Phone: 800-877-GALE or (248)699-GALE Fax: 800-414-5043 or (248)699-8069 E-mail: galeord@galegroup.com • URL: http://www.galegroup.com • 2001. $150.00. Two volumes. Contains both topical and biographical entries relating to the criminal justice system and criminology.

World of Invention: History's Most Significant Inventions and the People Beh ind Them. The Gale Group, 27500 Drake Rd. Farmington Hills, MI 48331-3535. Phone: 800-877-GALE or (248)699-GALE Fax: 800-414-5043 or (248)699-8069 E-mail: galeord@galegroup.com • URL: http://www.galegroup.com • 1999. $105.00. Second edition.

The World of Learning. Available from The Gale Group, 27500 Drake Rd. Farmington Hills, MI 48331-3535. Phone: 800-877-GALE or (248)699-GALE Fax: 800-414-5043 or (248)699-8069 E-mail: galeord@galegroup.com • URL: http://www.galegroup.com • $712.50. 50th edition. Covers about 26,000 colleges, libraries, museums, learned societies, academies, and research institutions throughout the world. Published by Europa Publications.

World of Winners: A Current and Historical Perspective on Awards and Their Winners. The Gale Group, 27500 Drake Rd. Farmington Hills, MI 48331-3535. Phone: 800-877-GALE or (248)699-GALE Fax: 800-414-5043 or (248)699-8069 E-mail: galeord@galegroup.com • URL: http://www.galegroup.com • 1991. $80.00 Second edition. Lists 100,000 recipients of 2,500 awards, honors, and prizes in 12 subject categories. Indexed by organization, recipient, and award. Covers all years for each award.

World Oil. Gulf Publishing Co., P.O. Box 2608 Houston, TX 77252-2608. Phone: 800-231-6275 or (713)529-4301 Fax: (713)520-4433 E-mail: ezorder@gulfpub.com • URL: http://www.gpcbooks.com • Monthly. Free to qualified personnel; others, $34.00 per year. Covers worldwide oil and gas exploration, drilling and production.

World Oil Tanker Trends. Jacobs and Partners Ltd., 18 Mansell St. London E1 8AA, England. Phone: 44 171 4592100 Fax: 44 171 4592199 Semiannual. $520.00 per year.

World Online Markets. Jupiter Media Metrix, 21 Astor Place New York, NY 10003. Phone: 800-488-4345 or (212)780-6060 Fax: (212)780-6075 E-mail: jupiter@jup.com • URL: http://www.jmm.com • Annual. $1,895.00. Market research report. Provides broad coverage of worldwide Internet and online information business activities, including country-by-country data. Includes company profiles and five-year forecasts or trend projections.

World Opinion Update. Survey Research Consultants International, Inc. Hastings Publications, 156 Bulkley St. Williamstown, MA 01267. Phone: (413)458-4414 Fax: (413)458-4414 E-mail: update@interport.net • URL: http://www.worldopinionupdate.com • Monthly. Individuals, $90.00 per year; educational libraries, $80.00 per year. Newsletter giving tabular results of recent public opinion polls around the world.

World Patent Information: International Journal for Patent Documentation, Clasification and Statistics. Commission of the European Communities. Elsevier Science, 655 Ave. of the Americas New York, NY 10010. Phone: 888-437-4636 or (212)989-5800 Fax: (212)633-3680 E-mail: usinfo@elsevier.com • URL: http://www.elsevier.com • Quarterly. $538.00 per year.

World Population Chart. United Nations Publications, United Nations Concourse Level, First Ave., 46th St. New York, NY 10017. Phone: 800-553-3210 or (212)963-7680 Fax: (212)963-3489 E-mail: bookstore@un.org • URL: http://www.un.org/publications • 1998. $5.95. Shows population, birth rate, death rate, etc., for all countries of the world, with forecasts to the year 2015 and to the year 2050.

World Population Data Sheet. Population Reference Bureau, Inc., 1875 Connecticut Ave., N.W., Suite 520 Washington, DC 20009. Phone: (202)483-1100 Fax: (202)328-3937 E-mail: popref@prb.org • URL: http://www.prb.org • Annual. $3.50

World Population Projections to 2150. United Nations Publications, Two United Nations Plaza, Room DC2-853 New York, NY 10017. Phone: 800-253-9646 or (212)963-8302 Fax: (212)963-3489 E-mail: publications@un.org • URL: http://www.un.org/publications • 1998. $15.00. Presents very long-range population projections for eight major areas of the world: Africa, Asia, China, Europe, India, Latin America, North America, and Oceania.

World Population Society.

World Press Review: News and Views from Around the World. Stanley Foundation, 700 Broadway, 3rd Fl. New York, NY 10003-9536. Phone: (212)982-8880 Fax: (212)982-6968 Monthly. $26.97 per year. International news and information on a wide variety of subjects that do not appear in other American publications.

World Pumps. Elsevier Science, 655 Ave. of the Americas New York, NY 10010. Phone: 888-437-4636 or (212)989-5800 Fax: (212)633-3680 E-mail: usinfo@elsevier.com • URL: http://www.elsevier.com • Monthly. $248.00 per year. Text in English, French and German.

World Radio TV Handbook. BPI Communications, Inc., 770 Broadway New York, NY 10003-9595. Phone: 800-344-7119 or (646)654-5500 Fax: (646)654-5834 E-mail: info@bpi.com • URL: http://www.bpicomm.com • Annual. $19.95. 25,000 radio and television stations worldwide.

World Retail Data and Statistics 1999/2000. Available from The Gale Group, 27500 Drake Rd. Farmington Hills, MI 48331-3535. Phone: 800-877-GALE or (248)699-GALE Fax: 800-414-5043 or (248)699-8069 E-mail: galeord@galegroup.com • URL: http://www.galegroup.com • 2000. $1,190.00. Fourth edition. Published by Euromonitor. Provides detailed retail industry statistics for 51 countries.

World Retail Directory and Sourcebook 1999. Available from The Gale Group, 27500 Drake Rd. Farmington Hills, MI 48331-3535. Phone: 800-877-GALE or (248)699-GALE Fax: 800-414-5043 or (248)699-8069 E-mail: galeord@galegroup.com • URL: http://www.galegroup.com • 1999. $590.00. Fourth edition. Published by Euromonitor. Provides information on more than 2,600 retailers around the world, with detailed profiles of the top 70. Information sources, conferences, trade fairs, and special libraries are also listed.

World Robotics: Statistics, Market Analysis, Forecasts, Case Studies, and Profitability of Robot Investment. United Nations Publications, Two United Nations Plaza, Room DC2-853 New York, NY 10017. Phone: 800-253-9646 or (212)963-8302 Fax: (212)963-3489 E-mail: publications@un.org • URL: http://www.un.org/publications • Annual. $120.00. Presents international data on industrial robots and service robots. Statistical tables allow uniform comparison of numbers for 20 countries, broken down by type of application, type of robot, and other variables.

World Semiconductor Trade Statistics. SIA (Semiconductor Industry Association), 181 Metro Dr., Suite 450 San Jose, CA 95110-1346. Phone: (408)436-6600 Fax: (408)436-6646 E-mail: semichips@semichips.org • URL: http://www.semichips.org • Monthly. $2,200 per year. Provides data on all world semiconductor markets including industry forecasts.

World Shipbuilding Statistics. Available from Fairplay Publications, Inc., 5201 Blue Lagoon Drive, Suite 530 Miami, FL 33126. Phone: (305)262-4070 Fax: (305)262-2006 E-mail: sales@fairplayamericas.com • URL: http://www.lrfairplay.com • Quarterly. $142.00 per year. Published in the UK by Lloyd's Register-Fairplay Ltd. Contains detailed, current data on shipbuilding orders placed and completions.

World Statistics Pocketbook. United Nations Publications, Two United Nations Plaza, Room DC2-853 New York, NY 10017. Phone: 800-253-9646 or (212)963-8302 Fax: (212)963-3489 E-mail: publications@un.org • URL: http://www.un.org/publications • Annual. $10.00. Presents basic economic, social, and environmental indicators for about 200 countries and areas. Covers more than 50 items relating to population, economic activity, labor force, agriculture, industry, energy, trade, transportation, communication, education, tourism, and the environment. Statistical sources are noted.

World Statistics Pocketbook. United Nations Publications, United Nations Concourse Level, First Ave., 46st St. New York, NY 10017. Phone: 800-553-3210 or (212)963-7680 Fax: (212)963-3489 Annual $10.00.

World Surface Coatings Abstracts. Paint Research Association, Eight Waldgreave Rd. Teddington, Middlesex TW11 8LD 4, England. E-mail: coatings@pra.org.uk • URL: http://www.pra.org.uk • 13 times a year. Members, $1,260.00 per year; non-members, $1,980.00 per year.

World Surface Coatings Abstracts ÎOnlineI. Paint Research Association of Great Britain, Waldegrave Rd. Teddington, Middlesex TW11 8LD 4, England. Phone: 181 6144800 Indexing and abstracting of the literature of paint and surface coatings, 1976 to present. Monthly updates. Inquire as to online cost and availability.

World Technology: Patent Licensing Gazette. Techni Research Associates, Inc., P.O. Box T Willow Grove, PA 19090-0922. Phone: (215)887-5980 Fax: (215)576-7924 Bimonthly. $165.00 per year. Lists items available for license or acquisition.

World Textile Abstracts. Elsevier Science, 655 Ave. of the Americas New York, NY 10010. Phone: 888-437-4637 or (212)989-5800 Fax: (212)633-3680 E-mail: usinfo@elsevier.com • URL: http://www.elsevier.com • Monthly. $1,309.00 per year. Digests of articles published in the world's textile literature. Includes subscription to *World Textile Digest*.

World Textiles. Elsevier Science, Inc., 655 Ave. of the Americas New York, NY 10010. Phone: (212)633-3730 Fax: (212)633-3680 URL: http://www.elsevier.com • Provides abstracting and indexing from 1970 of worldwide textile literature (periodicals, books, pamphlets, and reports). Includes U. S., European, and British patent information. Updating is monthly. Inquire as to online cost and availability.

World Tobacco. DMG World Media., Queensway House, Two Queensway Redhill, Surrey RH1 1QS, England. Phone: (44-)1737-855485 Fax: (44-)1737-855470 URL: http://www.dmg.co.uk • Six times a year. $230.00 per year.

World Trade Annual. United Nations Statistical Office. Walker and Co., 435 Hudson St. New York, NY 10014-3941. Phone: (212)727-8300 Fax: (212)727-0984 Annual. Prices vary.

World Trade Atlas CD-ROM. Global Trade Information Services, Inc., 2218 Devine St. Columbia, SC 29205. Phone: 800-982-4847 or (803)765-1860 Fax: (803)799-5589 E-mail: trade@gtis.com • URL: http://www.gtis.com • Monthly. $4,920.00 per year. ($3,650.00 per year with quarterly updates.) Provides government statistics on trade between the U. S. and each of more than 200 countries. Includes import-export data, trade balances, product information, market share, price data, etc. Time period is the most recent three years.

World Trade Centers Association., One World Trade Center, Suite 7701 New York, NY 10048. Phone: (212)435-7168 Fax: (212)435-2810 URL: http://www.wtca.org • Members are associated with centers devoted to the increase of international trade.

World Trade Database. Statistics Canada, International Trade Division, Ottawa, ON, Canada K1A OT6. Phone: 800-267-6677 or (613)951-7277 Fax: 800-899-9734 or (613)951-1582 URL: http://www.statcan.ca • Annual. $3,500.00. CD-ROM provides 13 years of export-import data for 600 commodities traded by the 160 member countries of the United Nations.

World Trade: For the Executive with Global Vision. World Trade Magazine, 27130A Paseo Espada, Suite 1427 San Juan Capistrano, CA 92675. Phone: (949)234-1700 Fax: (929)234-1701 URL: http://www.worldtrademag.com • Monthly. $36.00 per year. Edited for senior management of U. S. companies engaged in international business and trade.

World Trade Organization. Centre William Rappard

World Trade Organization Annual Report. Available from Bernan Associates, 4611-F Assembly Drive Lanham, MD

20706-4391. Phone: 800-274-4447 or (301)459-2255 Fax: 800-865-3450 or (301)459-0056 E-mail: info@bernan.com • URL: http://www.bernan.com • Annual. $80.00. Two volumes ($40.00 per volume). Published by the World Trade Organization. Volume one: *Annual Report*. Volume two: *International Trade Statistics*.

World Trade Organization Dispute Settlement Decisions: Bernan's Annotated Reporter. Bernan Press, 4611-F Assembly Dr. Lanham, MD 20706-4391. Phone: 800-274-4447 or (301)459-7666 Fax: 800-865-3450 or (301)459-0056 E-mail: info@bernan.com • URL: http://www.bernan.com • Dates vary. $75.00 per volume. Contains all World Trade Organization Panel Reports and Appellate Decisions since the establishment of the WTO in 1995. Includes such cases as "The Importation, Sale, and Distribution of Bananas."

World Trade Organization Trade Policy Review. Bernan Press, 4611-F Assembly Dr. Lanham, MD 20706-4391. Phone: 800-274-4447 or (301)459-7666 Fax: 800-865-3450 or (301)459-0056 E-mail: info@bernan.com • URL: http://www.bernan.com • Annual. $95.00. CD-ROM provides detailed trade information for each of 40 countries. Includes search capabilities, hypertext links, charts, tables, and graphs.

World Trademark Law and Practice. Matthew Bender & Co., Inc., Two Park Ave. New York, NY 10016. Phone: 800-223-1940 or (212)448-2000 Fax: (212)244-3188 E-mail: international@bender.com • URL: http://www.bender.com • $720.00. Four looseleaf volumes. Periodic Supplementation. A guide to international trademark practice with detailed coverage of 35 major jurisdictions and summary coverage for over 100.

World Wastes: The Independent Voice of the Industry. Intertec Publishing Corp., 6151 Powers Ferry Rd., N.W. Atlanta, GA 30339. Phone: 800-400-5945 or (770)955-2500 Fax: (770)955-0400 E-mail: subs@intertec.com • URL: http://www.worldwastes.com • Monthly. $52.00 per year. Includes annual catalog. Formerly *Management of World Wastes: The Independent Voice of the Industry*.

World WeatherDisc. WeatherDisc Associates,Inc., 4584 N. E. 89th Seattle, WA 98115. Phone: (206)524-4314 Fax: (206)433-1162 Annual. $195.00. Provides climatological and meteorological data on CD-ROM from as far back as the 18th century to recent months and years. Coverage is international, including weather observations from over 5,700 airports around the world and about 1,900 U. S. weather stations.

World Who is Who and Does What in Environment and Conservation. Nicholas Polunin, editor. St. Martin's Press, 175 Fifth Ave. New York, NY 10010. Phone: 800-221-7945 or (212)674-5151 Fax: 800-672-2054 or (212)529-0594 URL: http://www.stmartins.com • 1997. $75.00. Provides biographies of 1,300 individuals considered to be leaders in environmental and conservation areas.

World Wide Pet Supply Association.

World Wide Web Troubleshooter: Help for the Ensnared and Entangled. Nancy R. John and Edward J. Valauskas. American Library Association, 50 E. Huron St. Chicago, IL 60611-2795. Phone: 800-545-2433 or (312)944-6780 Fax: (312)440-9374 E-mail: ala@ala.org • URL: http://www.ala.org • 1998. $36.00. Covers all aspects of the WWW in question-and-answer format.

Worldmark Encyclopedia of National Economies. The Gale Group, 27500 Drake Rd. Farmington Hills, MI 48331-3535. Phone: 800-877-GALE or (248)699-GALE Fax: 800-414-5043 or (248)699-8069 E-mail: galeord@galegroup.com • URL: http://www.galegroup.com • 2002. $295.00. Four volumes. Covers both the current and historical development of the economies of 200 foreign nations. Includes analysis and statistics.

Worldmark Yearbook. The Gale Group, 27500 Drake Rd. Farmington Hills, MI 48331-3535. Phone: 800-877-GALE or (248)699-GALE Fax: 800-414-5043 or (248)699-8069 E-mail: galeord@galegroup.com • URL: http://www.galegroup.com • Annual. $305.00. Three volumes. Covers economic, social, and political events in about 230 countries. Includes statistical data, directories, and a bibliography.

World's Greatest Brands: An International Review by Interbrand. John Wiley and Sons, Inc., 605 Third Ave. New York, NY 10158-0012. Phone: 800-225-5945 or (212)850-6000 Fax: (212)850-6088 E-mail: info@wiley.com • URL: http://www.wiley.com • 1992. $49.95. Compiled by Interbrand. Provides details on 330 of the most successful international brand names and trademarks. Includes color illustrations.

The World's Largest Market: A Business Guide to Europe 1992. Robert Williams and others. AMACOM, 1601 Broadway, 12th Fl. New York, NY 10019. Phone: 800-262-9699 or (212)586-8100 Fax: (212)903-8168 E-mail: custmserv@amanet.org • URL: http://www.amanet.org • 1991. $19.95. Reprint edition. Provides information on agencies, organizations programs, and regulations relevant to the forthcoming 1992 unified European Community.

The World's Major Multinationals. Available from The Gale Group, 27500 Drake Rd. Farmington Hills, MI 48331-3535. Phone: 800-877-GALE or (248)699-GALE Fax: 800-414-5043 or (248)699-8069 E-mail: galeord@galegroup.com • URL: http://www.galegroup.com • 2000. $1,100.00. Published by Euromonitor (http://www.euromonitor.com). Provides profiles of leading companies around the world selling branded products to consumers. Includes detailed financial data for each firm.

Worldtariff Guidebook on Customs Tariff Schedules of Import Duties. Worldtariff Division, Morse Agri-Energy Associates, 220 Montgomery St., Suite 432 San Francisco, CA 94104. Phone: 800-556-9334 or (415)391-7501 Fax: (415)391-7537 Looseleaf. Over 60 volumes. Prices vary. Consists generally of volumes for individual countries and volumes for broad classes of products, such as clothing. (Country volumes are typically $500.00 each.)

Worldwide Branch Locations of Multinational Companies. The Gale Group, 27500 Drake Rd. Farmington Hills, MI 48331-3535. Phone: 800-877-GALE or (248)699-GALE Fax: 800-414-5043 or (248)699-8069 E-mail: galeord@galegroup.com • URL: http://www.galegroup.com • 1993. $200.00. A guide to subsidiaries, sales offices, manufacturing facilities, and other corporate units operating outside the headquarters country. Includes over 500 leading multinational companies and their 20,000 branch locations.

Worldwide Government Directory 2001. Available from The Gale Group, 27500 Drake Rd. Farmington Hills, MI 48331-3535. Phone: 800-877-GALE or (248)699-GALE Fax: 800-414-5043 or (248)699-8069 E-mail: galeord@galegroup.com • URL: http://www.galegroup.com • 2001. $394.00. 19th edition. Published by Keesings Worldwide. Lists more than 32,000 key officials in the governments of over 199 countries.

Worldwide Offshore Petroleum Directory. PennWell Corp., Petroleum Div., 1700 W. Loop S., Suite 1000 Houston, TX 77027. Phone: 800-736-6935 or (713)621-9720 Fax: (713)499-6310 E-mail: webmaster@pennwell.com • URL: http://www.penwell.com • Annual. $165.00. Lists about 3,500 companies with 13,000 personnel.

Worldwide Petrochemical Directory. PennWell Corp., Petroleum Div., 1700 W. Loop S., Suite 1000 Houston, TX 77027. Phone: 800-736-6935 or (713)621-9720 Fax: (713)499-6310 E-mail: webmaster@pennwell.com • URL: http://www.petroleumdirectories.com • Annual. $165.00. Do more than 3,400 petrochemical plants; separate section on new construction; worldwide coverage. Formerly *Refining and Petrochemical Technology Yearbook*.

Worldwide Pipelines and Contractors Directory. PennWell Corp., Petroleum Div., 1700 W. Loop S., Ste. 1000 Houston, TX 77027. Phone: 800-736-6935 or (713)621-9720 Fax: (713)499-6310 E-mail: webmaster@pennwell.com • URL: http://www.pennwell.com • Annual. $145.00. More than 4,000 companies, subsidiaries, branch offices, and engineering-construction services worldwide active in natural gas, crude oil, and products pipeline.

Worldwide Refining and Gas Processing Directory. PennWell Corp., Petroleum Div., 1700 W. Loop S., Ste. 1000 Houston, TX 77027. Phone: 800-736-6935 or (713)621-9720 Fax: (713)499-6310 E-mail: webmaster@pennwell.com • URL: http://www.petroleumdirectories.com • Annual. $165.00. Lists over 1,000 crude oil refineries, 1,300 gas processing plants and over 600 engineering and construction firms which build and service these plants; worldwide coverage.

Worldwide Trade Secrets Law. Terrence F. MacLaren, editor. West Group, 610 Opperman Dr. Eagan, MN 55123. Phone: 800-328-4880 or (651)687-7000 Fax: 800-213-2323 or (651)687-5827 URL: http://www.westgroup.com • $425.00. Looseleaf service. Periodic supplementation.

Worst Pills Best Pills News. Public Citizen, 1600 20th St., N. W. Washington, DC 20009. Phone: (202)588-1000 Monthly. $16.00 per year. Newsletter. Provides pharmaceutical news and information for consumers, with an emphasis on harmful drug interactions.

Worth: Financial Intelligence. Worth Media, 575 Lexington Ave. New York, NY 10022. Phone: 800-777-1851 or (212)223-3100 Fax: (212)223-1598 E-mail: info@worth.com • URL: http://www.worth.com • 10 times a year. $18.00 per year. Contains articles for affluent consumers on personal financial management, including investments, estate planning, and taxes.

WRC Progress Reports. Welding Research Council, Three Park Ave., 27th Fl. New York, NY 10016-5902. Phone: (212)705-7956 Bimonthly. $1,100 per year. Includes *Welding Research Abroad; WRC Bulletins, WRC News* and *Welding Journal*.

The Writer. Writer, Inc., 120 Boylston St. Boston, MA 02116. Phone: (617)423-3157 Fax: (617)423-2168 E-mail: writer@userl.channell.com • URL: http://www.channell.com/thewriter • Monthly. $29.00 per year. Freelance writers.

Writers' and Artists' Yearbook: A Directory for Writers, Artists, Playwrights, Writers for Film, Radio and Television, Photographers and Composers. MidPoint Trade Books, 1263 Southwest Blvd. Kansas City, KS 66103. Phone: (913)362-7400 Fax: (913)362-7401 Annual. $20.00. A worldwide guide to markets for various kinds of writing and artwork. Formerly*International Writers' and Artists' Yearbook*.

Writer's Digest. F and W Publications, 1507 Dana Ave. Cincinnati, OH 45207-1005. Phone: 800-289-0963 or (513)531-2690 Fax: 888-590-4082 Monthly. $27.00 per year.

The Writers Directory 2001. Available from The Gale Group, 27500 Drake Rd. Farmington Hills, MI 48331-3535. Phone: 800-877-GALE or (248)699-GALE Fax: 800-414-5043 or (248)699-8063 E-mail: galeord@galegroup.com • URL: http://www.galegroup.com • 2000. $165.00. 15th edition. Lists more than 17,500 authors from English-Speaking countries. Includes classification by writing category.

Writer's Guide to Book Editors, Publishers, and Literary Agents, 2000-2001: Who They Are, What They Want, and How to Win Them Over. Jeff Herman. Prima Publishing, 3875 Atherton Rd. Rocklin, CA 95765. Phone: (916)787-7000 Fax: (916)787-7001 URL: http://www.primapublishing.com • Annual. $27.95; with CD-ROM, $49.95. Directory for authors includes information on publishers' response times and pay rates.

The Writer's Handbook. Writer, Inc., 120 Boylston St. Boston, MA 02116. Phone: (617)423-3157 Fax: (617)423-2168 E-mail: writer@userl.channell.com • URL: http://www.channell.com/thewriter • Annual. $32.95. List of 3,000 markets for writer's work.

Writer's Handbook for Editing and Revision. Rick Wilber. NTC/Contemporary Publishing, P.O. Box 545 Blacklick, OH 43004. Phone: 800-338-3987 or (614)755-4151 Fax: (614)755-5645 E-mail: ntcpub@mcgraw-hill.com • URL: http://www.ntc-cb.com • 1996. $19.95. Discusses rewrites and before-and-after drafts.

Writer's Market: 8000 Editors Who Buy What You Write. F & W Publications, Inc., 1507 Dana Ave. Cincinnati, OH 45207-1005. Phone: 800-289-0963 or (513)531-2690 Fax: 888-590-4082 Annual. $27.99. More than 4,000 buyers of books, articles, short stories, plays, gags, verses, fillers, and other original written material. Includes book and periodical publishers, greeting card publishers, play producers and publishers, audiovisual material producers, syndicates, and contests, and awards. Formerly *Writer's Market: Where and How to Sell What You Write*.

Writing and Designing Manuals: Operator's Manuals, Service Manuals, Manuals for International Markets. Gretchen H. Schoff and Patricia A. Robinson. Lewis Publishers, 2000 Corporate Blvd., N. W. Boca Raton, FL 33431. Phone: 800-272-7737 or (407)994-0555 Fax: (407)998-9114 1991. $54.95. Includes planning, organization, format, visuals, writing strategies, and other topics.

Writing and Editing School News: A Basic Project Text in Scholastic Journalism. William Harwood. Clark Publishing, Inc., P.O. Box 19240 Topeka, KS 66619-0240. Phone: 800-845-1916 or (785)862-0218 Fax: (785)862-8224 E-mail: custservice@clarkpub.com • URL: http://www.clarkpub.com • 1996. $33.33. Fourth revised edition.

Writing Business Letters and Reports. Carmella E. Mansfield and Margaret Hilton Bahniuk. Pearson Education and Technology, 201 W. 103rd St. Indianapolis, IN 46290-1097. Phone: 800-858-7674 or (317)581-3500 Fax: (317)581-4670 URL: http://www.mcp.com • 1981. $24.61.

Writing Effective Business Plans. Entrepreneur Media, Inc., 2445 McCabe Way Irvine, CA 92614. Phone: 800-421-2300 or (949)261-2325 Fax: (949)261-0234 E-mail: entmag@entrepreneur.com • URL: http://www.entrepreneur.com • Looseleaf. $49.50. A step-by-step guide. Includes a sample business plan.

Writing Instrument Manufacturers Association.

Writing That Works: How to Write Effective E-Mails, Letters, Resumes, Presentations, Plans, Reports and Other Business Communications. Kenneth Roman. HarperCollins Publishers, Inc., 10 E. 53rd St. New York, NY 10022-5299. Phone: 800-242-7737 or (212)207-7000 Fax: 800-822-4090 or (212)207-7145 URL: http://www.harpercollins.com • 2000. $13.00. Enlarged revised edition.

Writing That Works: The Business Communications Report. Writing That Works, 7481 Huntsman Blvd., Suite 720 Springfield, VA 22153-1648. Phone: (703)643-2200 Fax: (703)643-2329 E-mail: concepts@writingthatworks.com • Monthly. $119.00 per year.

Written Communication: A Quarterly Journal of Research, Theory, and Application. Sage Publications, Inc., 2455 Teller Rd. Thousand Oaks, CA 91320. Phone: (805)499-0721 Fax: (805)499-0871 E-mail: info@sagepub.com • URL: http://www.sagepub.com • Quarterly. Individuals, $70.00 per year; institutions, $320.00 per year.

WTO Annual Report World Trade Organization. Available from Bernan Associates, 4611-F Assembly Dr. Lanham, MD 20706-4391. Phone: 800-274-4447 or (301)459-7666 Fax: 800-274-4447 or (301)459-0056 E-mail: info@bernan.com • URL: http://www.bernan.com • Annual. Review of activities. Published in Switzerland by GATT. Editions in English, French and Spanish. Formerly *GATT Activities*.

WTO Focus. World Trade Organization, Publications Service, Centre William Rappard, 154 Rue de Lausanne 1211 Geneva 10, Switzerland. Phone: (41)22 739 52 08 Fax: (41)22 739 57 92 E-mail: publications@wto.org • URL: http://

www.wto.org • Newsletter. Free. 10 times a year. Text in English. Provides current news about activities relating to the World Trade Organization (WTO) and the General Agreement on Tariffs and Trade (GATT). Formerly *GATT Focus*.

WWD (Women's Wear Daily): The Retailer's Daily Newspaper. Fairchild Publications, Seven W. 34th St. New York, NY 10001. Phone: 800-289-0273 or (212)630-4000 Fax: (212)630-4201 E-mail: wwedit@fairchildpub.com • URL: http://www.wwd.com • Daily. Institutions, $75.00 per year; corporations $195.00 per year.

X-Change. Virgo Publishing, Inc., 3300 N. Central Ave., Suite 2500 Phoenix, AZ 85012. Phone: (480)990-1101 Fax: (480)675-8109 E-mail: xchngmag@vpico.com • URL: http://www.x-changemag.com • 18 times per year. $70.00 per year. Edited for local telecommunications exchange services, both wireline and wireless.

Yale Daily News Guide to Internships. Simon & Schuster Trade, 1230 Ave. of the Americas New York, NY 10020. Phone: 800-223-2336 or (212)698-7000 Fax: 800-943-9831 or (212)698-7007 E-mail: ssonline_feedback@simonsays.com • URL: http://www.simonsays.com • Annual. $25.00. Compiled by the staff of the Yale Daily News. Lists internships in various fields.

Yale Law Journal. Yale Journal Co., Inc., P.O. Box 208215 New Haven, CT 06520-8215. Phone: (203)432-1666 Fax: (203)432-7482 URL: http://www.yale.edu/ • Eight times a year. $40.00 per year.

Yard and Garden. Cygnus Publishing, Inc., Johnson Hill Press, Inc., 1233 Janesville Ave. Fort Atkinson, WI 53538. Phone: 800-547-7377 or (920)563-6388 Fax: (920)563-1707 E-mail: rich.reiff@cygnuspub.com • URL: http://www.cygnuspub.com • Seven times a year. $48.00. Includes retailers and distributors of lawn and garden power equipment, lawn and plant care products, patio furniture, etc. Arranged by type of product. Includes a *Product* issue.

Year Book of Labour Statistics. International Labour Office, 1828 L St., N.W., Suite 801 Washington, DC 20036. Phone: (202)653-7652 Fax: (202)653-7687 E-mail: ilopubs@tascol.com • URL: http://www.ilo.org • Annual. $168.00. Presents a wide range of labor and price data for most countries of the world. Supplement available *Sources and Methods. Labour Statistics*.

Yearbook. Association of Government Accountants, 2200 Mount Vernon Ave. Arlington, VA 22301-1314. Phone: (703)684-6931 Fax: (703)548-9367 E-mail: jmccumber@agacgfm.org • URL: http://www.agacgfm.org • Annual.

Yearbook of Agriculture. U.S. Department of Agriculture. Available from U.S. Government Printing Office, Washington, DC 20402. Phone: (202)512-1800 Fax: (202)512-2250 E-mail: gpoaccess@gpo.gov • URL: http://www.access.gpo.gov • Annual.

Yearbook of Forest Products. Food and Agriculture Organization of the United Nations. Available from Bernan Associates, 4611-F Assembly Dr. Lanham, MD 20706-4391. Phone: 800-274-4888 or (301)459-7666 Fax: 800-865-3450 or (301)459-0056 E-mail: info@bernan.com • URL: http://www.bernan.com • Annual. Test in English, French, and Spanish.

Yearbook of International Organizations. Available from The Gale Group, 27500 Drake Rd. Farmington Hills, MI 48331-3535. Phone: 800-699-4253 or (248)699-4253 Fax: (248)699-8069 E-mail: galeord@galegroup.com • URL: http://www.galegroup.com • Annual. $1,300.00. Four volumes: (1) *Organization Descriptions and Index* (32,000 organizations in 225 countries); (2) *International Organization Participation* (geographic arrangement); (3) *Global Action Networks* (a subject directory with 4,300 categories); (4) *Internationa Organization Bibliography and Resources*. Published by K. G. Saur.

Yearbook of International Organizations PLUS. R. R. Bowker, 121 Chanlon Rd. New Providence, NJ 07974. Phone: 800-521-8110 or (908)464-6800 Fax: (908)665-6688 Annual. $1,500.00. Compiled by the Union of International Organizations, Brussels. Includes the *Yearbook of International Organizations* and *Who's Who in International Organizations*.

Yearbook of Procurement Articles. Federal Publications, Inc., 1120 20th St., N.W. Suite 500 S Washington, DC 20036-3483. Phone: 800-922-4330 or (202)337-7000 E-mail: bbolger@fedpub.com • URL: http://www.fedpub.com • Annual.

Yearbook of the International Law Commission. Available from United Nations Publications, United Nations Concourse Level, First Ave., 46th St. New York, NY 10017. Phone: 800-553-3210 or (212)963-7680 Fax: (212)963-3489 E-mail: bookstore@un.org • URL: http://www.un.org/publications • Annual. $90.00. Two volumes. Volume one, $35.00; volume two, $55.00.

Yellow Pages and Directory Report: The Newsletter for the Yellow Page and Directory Publishing Industry. SIMBA Information, P.O. Box 4234 Stamford, CT 06907-0234. Phone: 800-307-2529 or (203)358-4100 Fax: (203)358-5824 E-mail: info@simbanet.com • URL: http://www.simbanet.com • 22 times a year. $579.00 per year. Newsletter. Covers the yellow pages publishing industry, including electronic directory publishing, directory advertising, and special interest directories.

Yes, You Can Achieve Financial Independence. James E. Stowers and others. Stowers Innovations, Inc., 4500 Main St. Kansas City, MO 64111. Phone: 800-234-3445 or (816)753-8887 Fax: (816)753-7787 URL: http://www.stowersinternational.com • 2000. $34.00.

You and Your 401(k): How to Manage Your 401(k) for Maximum Returns. Julie Jason. Simon & Schuster Trade, 1230 Ave. of the Americas New York, NY 10020. Phone: 800-223-2336 or (212)698-7000 Fax: 800-943-9831 or (212)698-7007 E-mail: ssonline_feedback@simonsays.com • URL: http://www.simonsays.com • 1996. $10.00. Presents popularly written advice and information concerning the key features of 401(k) plans and how to choose appropriate investments. Includes a glossary and sample forms. The author is an investment consultant.

Young Presidents' Organization.

Your Dream Home: A Comprehensive Guide to Buying a House, Condo, or Co-op. Marguerite Smith. Available from Little, Brown & Co., Time and Life Bldg., 1271 Ave of the Americas New York, NY 10020. Phone: 800-343-9204 or (212)522-8700 Fax: 800-759-0190 or (212)522-2067 E-mail: cust.service@littlebrown.com • URL: http://www.littlebrown.com • 1997. $10.99. Published by Warner Books.

Your Federal Income Tax. U.S. Department of the Treasury, Internal Revenue Service. Available from U.S. Government Printing Office, Washington, DC 20402. Phone: (202)512-1800 Fax: (202)512-2250 E-mail: gpoaccess@gpo.gov • URL: http://www.accessgpo.gov • Annual. $22.00. Layman's guide to income tax preparation.

Your Life Insurance Options. Alan Lavine. John Wiley and Sons, Inc., 605 Third Ave. New York, NY 10158-0012. Phone: 800-225-5945 or (212)850-6000 Fax: (212)850-6088 E-mail: info@wiley.com • URL: http://www.wiley.com • 1993. $12.95. Tells how to buy life insurance, including the selection of a company and agent. Describes term life, whole life, variable life, universal life, and annuities. Includes a glossary of insurance terms and jargon. (ICFP Personal Wealth Building Guide Series).

Your Medicare Handbook. Available from U. S. Government Printing Office, Washington, DC 20402. Phone: (202)512-1800 Fax: (202)512-2250 E-mail: gpoaccess@gpo.gov • URL: http://www.access.gpo.gov • Annual. Issued by the Health Care Financing Administration, U. S. Department of Health and Human Services. Provides information on Medicare hospital insurance and medical insurance, including benefits, options, and rights. Discusses the functions of Medigap insurance, managed care plans, peer review organizations, and Medicare insurance carriers. Formerly *Medicare Handbook*.

Your Money. Consumers Digest, Inc., 8001 N. Lincoln Ave., 6th Fl. Skokie, IL 60077-3657. Phone: 800-777-0025 or (847)763-9200 Fax: (847)763-0200 URL: http://www.consumersdigest.com • Bimonthly. $25.97 per year. Provides information and advice on personal finance and investments.

Your Telephone Personality. Economics Press, Inc., 12 Daniel Rd. Fairfield, NJ 07006. Phone: 800-526-2554 or (973)227-1224 Fax: (973)227-9742 E-mail: edit@epinc.com • URL: http://www.epinc.com • Biweekly. $33.00 per year. Telephone skills for office employees.

Youth for Understanding International Exchange., 3501 Newark St., N. W. Washington, DC 20016. Phone: 800-833-6243 or (202)966-6808 Fax: (202)895-1104 E-mail: pio@yfu.org • URL: http://www.youth.forunderstanding.org • Provides educational opportunities for young people and adults through international student exchange. Administers study abroad scholarship programs in cooperation with other governments, the U. S. Senate, the U. S. Information Agency, and various educational organizations.

Youth Markets Alert. EPM Communications, Inc., 160 Mercer St., 3rd Fl. New York, NY 10012-3212. Phone: 888-852-9467 or (212)941-0099 Fax: (212)941-1622 E-mail: info@epmcom.com • URL: http://www.epmcom.com • Monthly. $295.00 per year. Newsletter on youth market research. Covers age groups from elementary school to college years.

Zacks Analyst Directory: Listed by Broker. Zacks Investment Research, 155 N. Wacker Dr. Chicago, IL 60606. Phone: 800-786-4377 or (312)630-9880 Fax: (312)630-9898 Quarterly. $395.00 per year. Lists stockbroker investment analysts and gives the names of major U. S. corporations covered by those analysts.

Zacks Analyst Directory: Listed by Company. Zacks Investment Research, 155 N. Wacker Dr. Chicago, IL 60606. Phone: 800-786-4377 or (312)630-9880 Fax: (312)630-9898 Quarterly. $395.00 per year. Lists major U. S. corporations and gives the names of stockbroker investment analysts covering those companies.

Zacks Analyst Watch. Zacks Investment Research, 155 N. Wacker Dr. Chicago, IL 60606. Phone: 800-786-4377 or (312)630-9880 Fax: (312)630-9898 Biweekly. $250.00 per year. Provides the results of research by stockbroker investment analysts on major U. S. corporations.

Zacks Earnings Estimates. Zacks Investment Research, 155 N. Wacker Drive Chicago, IL 60606. Phone: 800-399-6659 or (312)630-9880 Fax: (312)630-9898 E-mail: support@zacks.com • URL: http://www.zacks.com • Provides online earnings projections for about 6,000 U. S. corporations, based on investment analysts' reports. Data is mainly from 200 major brokerage firms. Time span varies according to online provider, with daily or weekly updates. Inquire as to online cost and availability.

Zacks Earnings Forecaster. Zacks Investment Research, 155 N. Wacker Dr. Chicago, IL 60606. Phone: 800-786-4377 or (312)630-9880 Fax: (312)630-9898 Biweekly. $495.00 per year. (Also available monthly at $375.00 per year.) Provides estimates by stockbroker investment analysts of earnings per share of individual U. S. companies.

Zacks EPS Calendar. Zacks Investment Research, 155 N. Wacker Dr. Chicago, IL 60606. Phone: 800-786-4377 or (312)630-9880 Fax: (312)630-9898 Biweekly. $1,250.00 per year. (Also available monthly at $895.00 per year.) Lists anticipated reporting dates of earnings per share for major U. S. corporations.

Zacks Profit Guide. Zacks Investment Research, 155 N. Wacker Dr. Chicago, IL 60606. Phone: 800-786-4377 or (312)630-9880 Fax: (312)630-9898 Quarterly. $375.00 per year. Provides analysis of total return and stock price performance of major U. S. companies.

Zero Population Growth-Seattle Chapter.

Zincscan: A Review of Recent Technical Literature On the Use of Zinc and Its Products. C & C Associates, 12 Parkside Green Meanwood Leeds LS6 4NY, England. Quarterly. $125.00. per year. Provides technical articles and abstracts of recent technical and market related literature on zinc. Formerly *Zinc Abstracts*.

Zip Code Mapbook of Metropolitan Areas. CACI Marketing Systems, 1100 N. Glebe Rd., Suite 200 Arlington, VA 22201-4714. Phone: 800-292-2224 or (703)841-2924 Fax: (703)243-6272 E-mail: msgw@caci.com • URL: http://www.demographics.caci.com • 1992. $195.00. Second edition. Contains Zip Code two-color maps of 326 metropolitan areas. Includes summary statistical profiles of each area: population characteristics, employment, housing, and income.

Zoning and Planning Deskbook. Douglas W. Kmiec. West Group, 610 Opperman Dr. Eagan, MN 55123. Phone: 800-328-4880 or (651)687-7000 Fax: 800-213-2323 or (651)687-5827 URL: http://www.westgroup.com • $145.00. Looseleaf service. Periodic supplementation. Emphasis is on legal issues.

Zoning and Planning Law Handbook. West Group, 610 Opperman Dr. Eagan, MN 55123. Phone: 800-328-4880 or (651)687-7000 Fax: 800-213-2323 or (651)687-5827 URL: http://www.westgroup.com • 1996. Price on application. (Real Property-Zoning Series).

Zoning and Planning Law Report. West Group, 610 Opperman Dr. Eagan, MN 55123. Phone: 800-328-4880 or (651)687-7000 Fax: 800-213-2323 or (651)687-5827 URL: http://www.westgroup.com • 11 times a year. $283.00 per year. Newsletter.

Zoning Bulletin. Quinlan Publishing Co., Inc., 23 Drydock St., 2nd Fl. Boston, MA 02210-2387. Phone: 800-229-2084 or (617)542-0048 Fax: (617)345-9646 Semimonthly. $89.00 per year. Newsletter dealing with zoning legal issues.

Zoning News. American Planning Association, 122 S. Michigan Ave., Suite 1600 Chicago, IL 60603-6107. Phone: (312)431-9100 Fax: (312)431-9985 URL: http://www.planning.org • Monthly. $55.00 per year. Newsletter on local community zoning.

The ZPG Reporter. Zero Population Growth, Inc., 1400 16th St., N.W., Suite 320 Washington, DC 20036. Phone: 800-767-1956 or (202)332-2200 Fax: (202)332-2302 E-mail: zpg@igc.apc.org • URL: http://www.zpg.org • Bimonthly. $25.00 per year. Special reports on global issues and domestic issues as they relate to over population and its social, environmental and economic consequences. 20180